Essential English Dictionary

COLLINS PUBLISHERS

THE UNIVERSITY OF BIRMINGHAM

Collins
London and Glasgow

Collins ELT
8 Grafton Street
London W1X 3LA

First published 1988

10 9 8 7 6 5 4 3 2

ISBN 0 00 370261 8 Paperback
ISBN 0 00 375022 1 Cased

Computer typeset by C R Barber & Partners
Wrotham, England.

Printed and bound in Great Britain by
William Collins Sons & Co Ltd, Glasgow

輸入　日本総代理店
株式会社　秀文インターナショナル
東京都豊島区駒込4－12－7

NOTE Entered words that we have reason to believe constitute trademarks have been designated as such. However, neither the presence nor absence of such designation should be regarded as affecting the legal status of any trademark.

Contents

EDITORIAL TEAM

EDITOR IN CHIEF
John Sinclair

MANAGING EDITOR
Patrick Hanks

EDITOR
Gwyneth Fox

SENIOR COMPILERS
Sheila Dignen
Ramesh Krishnamurthy

EXTRA COLUMN
Stephen Bullon
Rosamund Moon

COMPILERS
Deborah Kirby
Helen Liebeck
Elizabeth Manning
John Todd

COMPUTER OFFICER
Tim Lane

PRONUNCIATION REVISION
Martin Hewings
Tim Lane

CLERICAL STAFF
Sue Smith
Debbie Morris

COLLINS PUBLISHERS
Annette Capel
Lorna Heaslip
Douglas Williamson

Illustrated by **Jerry Collins**

We would also like to thank all the people who worked on the *Collins COBUILD English Language Dictionary,* whose original work provided the impetus for this book.

Preface

Collins COBUILD Essential English Dictionary is the second *COBUILD* dictionary. The first one, *Collins COBUILD English Language Dictionary,* was published in 1987 and offers learners a great deal of new information which they can use to help them learn the language. However, it was clear from the start that a smaller dictionary was also needed for everyday use. The *Essential* is that dictionary.

The *Essential* keeps all the main features of the original *COBUILD* dictionary, but it concentrates them into a smaller space. Also, we have added some new features that are designed to make the dictionary both more useful and more enjoyable to use.

The most important feature about *COBUILD* is that it is a completely new description of the English of today. The information in the entries comes from a study of about twenty million words of text. It is reliable and up-to-date, and has been made possible by using the latest computer techniques.

Because of this method of work, the examples given in the dictionary are from actual texts, and show the word or phrase as it has been used in these texts. The examples are not meant to show just the meaning of the word. The explanation does that. The examples are there to show you how to use it.

COBUILD is already famous for the way in which it sets out the explanations. They are in sentences, and the actual way they are written can help you use the words.

Here is the entry for **inside:**

inside /ɪnsaɪd/, **insides. 1** Something or someone that is **inside** a place, container, or object is surrounded by its sides. EG *Two minutes later we were inside the taxi... You left your lighter inside... It is a fruit with a seed inside.* ▸ used as an adjective. EG *The door had no inside bolt.* — PREP OR ADV; ▸ ADJ CLASSIF : ATTRIB

2 The **inside** of something is the part or area that its sides surround or contain. EG *The inside of my mouth was dry... ...the inside of the castle.* — N COUNT

3 You can also say that someone is **inside** when they are in prison. — ADV, Informal

4 On a wide road, the **inside** lanes are the ones which are closest to the edge of the road. — ADJ CLASSIF : ATTRIB

5 Inside information is obtained from someone who is involved in a situation and therefore knows a lot about it. — ADJ CLASSIF : ATTRIB

6 If you are **inside** an organization, you belong to it. EG *Nobody inside the company will be surprised.* — PREP

7 If you say that someone has a feeling **inside** them, you mean that they have not expressed this feeling. EG *His true feelings keep surging up inside him... I always felt inside that I wanted to write.* — PREP OR ADV

8 If something such as a piece of clothing is **inside out**, the inside part has been turned so that it faces outwards. — PHRASE

9 Your **insides** are your internal organs, especially your stomach. EG *What we all need is a bit of food in our insides.* — N PLURAL : USU+POSS, Informal

Notice that paragraph 1 starts 'Something or someone . . . ', while paragraph 2 has only 'something' and paragraph 3 has only 'someone'. This means that the kind of meaning in paragraph 2 applies to things, and not to people; and in paragraph 3 people, not things, are sent to prison.

In paragraph 4, this meaning of **inside** applies only to traffic lanes on a main road. Paragraph 5 is about a kind of information, and so on. As you can see, you can learn a lot by reading the explanations carefully.

A special feature of *COBUILD* is the extra column of information about the grammar and usage. There is a lot of very useful information in this column, and it is worthwhile making sure you understand the simple terms that are used: V = verb, ADJ = adjective, and so on. If you are not sure of any of the words or abbreviations in the Extra Column, you can look them up in their alphabetical place in the dictionary. So you will find ATTRIB on page 45 and ADJ PRED on page 12. Each one is in a box to make it easier to find. A list of everything used in the Extra Column is given on page vii.

You will also find helpful labels such as *Informal* and *American* in the Extra Column. These give you more information about the word and tell you when you can use it.

The Extra Column can also help you to find the meaning you want in a long entry. For example if you read 'The doctors had worked without a break', and you do not know the meaning of **break,** you can at least tell that it is a noun. So you can run your finger down the **break** entry, past the verbs until you find the nouns, starting at the end of paragraph 6, with the meaning you want in paragraph 10. You thus only need to read the noun meanings.

All the headwords are written in a phonetic transcription which shows you how to pronounce a word. A key to the symbols is given on page ix – they are all symbols of the International Phonetics Association. We have added some information on what happens to a word in connected speech, because many words can vary in pronunciation. This information is in tiny numbers above vowel letters, and you can ignore it if you want to say just one word out loud.

These are all features of the original dictionary. The *Essential* has some new features, which we hope will make the dictionary easier and more interesting to use. For example, the illustrations have been specially drawn for this book, to help where an object is not easy to describe, but is easy to recognize.

The grammar notes have been written specially for use by students. In addition to the short explanations, we have taken a whole page for each of seventeen major points of grammar. The list is on page viii, and the page-long entries are as near as possible to their alphabetical places. In these entries we have gathered together a lot of information and examples about the main categories of English grammar.

We have also added over 400 language activities, called *Checkpoints.* You will find one at the bottom of the right-hand column on each left-hand page. They are puzzles or points for discussion, and all the information you need is somewhere on the two pages that will be open around the *Checkpoint.* A key to these activities is given on pages 945-948.

These activities can be used to make you think a bit about words and to extend your vocabulary range. They can also be used during a class lesson, and should help to make the dictionary a regular tool for language learning. I hope that you, the user, will enjoy these activities. They won't interfere with using the dictionary in the normal way, but they should add some interest to your learning of English.

On pages 938-944 we have included a list of the words that we have found useful in explaining the meanings and uses of English. Teachers may also find this list useful as the basis of a syllabus, to develop students' dictionary skills. The language we have used has been kept as simple as possible but we have avoided the restrictions and awkwardness of a fixed defining vocabulary. In this book only about 2000 words have been used ten times or more, and there are only a total of 3000 different forms in the Wordlist.

These new features are part of *COBUILD's* general policy of trying out new ways to present information about the English Language. I would be glad to hear what things you find easy or difficult, useful or useless. I have had a lot of valuable criticism from users of the first *COBUILD* dictionary, and some of the points made have already been used to improve this new one.

John Sinclair
Editor in Chief

A Guide to the Use of the Dictionary

1 Finding words

1.1 Main entries

The order of entries is alphabetical, with no notice being taken of capital letters, hyphens, or spaces between words. So the order of words in a small section of 'B' is:

backbiting
backbone
back-breaking
backdate
backdoor
backer
backfire
backgammon
background

1.2 Phrasal verbs

Phrasal verbs are put in paragraphs immediately after the simple verb. So you will find **close down** and **close in** at the end of the entry for **close** and before the entry for **close-cropped,** so that the dictionary headword list reads:

close
  close down
  close in
closed

1.3 Phrases

Phrases are fixed combinations of words which have their own special meanings, so that you cannot normally guess the meaning from the individual words.

Phrases are printed in bold type in the entry for the most important word in the phrase. When the phrase is close in meaning to another meaning of the word, the phrase will be found in the same paragraph as that meaning, but will be introduced by a •. For example:

If a part of your body is **bare**, it is not covered by any clothing. • If someone does something **with their bare hands**, they do it without using any weapons or tools.

Other phrases are put in separate paragraphs or sometimes a number of phrases are put in one paragraph. For example:

12 Back is also used in these phrases. **12.1** If you are wearing something **back to front**, you are wearing it incorrectly, with the back of it on the front of your body. **12.2** If you do something **behind** someone's **back**, you do it without them knowing about it. PHRASES

1.4 Cross-references

If you cannot find the explanation of a phrase, expression, or compound at the word you have looked up, you will often find a note telling you which entry has the explanation. For example, at the entry for **bag**, **bag 6** reads:

6 a **bag of bones**: see **bone**.

Similarly, **face 9.14** reads:

9.14 at face value: see **value**.

At the end of **cover up 2** you will find:

• See also **cover-up**.

1.5 Words which are defined together

The dictionary tells you how to use all the important members of a word family, such as adjectives, adverbs, and nouns. Where the meaning of the words is similar, the meaning is only given for the headword. The other words in the family are printed at the end of a paragraph dealing with that meaning. Each word of this kind is introduced by a ◇, to show that you have a word with a new word class but with very little change of meaning.

The different endings that can be added to form the new words are all explained in alphabetical order in the text of the dictionary. So there are entries for **-ly**, **-ness**, **-ation**, and so on.

Even though these words are not defined separately, they always have grammatical information in the Extra Column and an example in the main text to show how they have been used.

eager /iːgə/. If you are **eager** to do something, you want to do it very much. EG *The majority were eager to express their opinions... ...people eager for a quick cure.* ◇ **eagerly**. EG *They began to talk eagerly.* ◇ **eagerness**. EG *...my eagerness to learn... ...an eagerness for total freedom.* ADJ QUALIT: OFT+to-INF OR for ◇ ADV ◇ N UNCOUNT

Words which belong to the same family but which have differences in meaning are treated as separate headwords and will be found in their correct alphabetical place. So there are different entries for words such as **hopeful** and **hopefully,** and **sure** and **surely.**

There is sometimes very little difference in meaning between words with different grammatical functions. When this is the case, one word is defined, and the other is treated in the same paragraph, preceded by a ▸. For example:

When you **amble,** you walk slowly and in a relaxed manner. EG *I ambled home through the village.* V:USU+A
▸ used as a noun. EG *He slowed down to his usual steady amble.* ▸ N SING

2 Forms and spelling

The spelling for each form of word is given in bold letters at the beginning of an entry. For example:

earthquake /ɜːθkweɪk/, **earthquakes**.

echo /ɛkəʊ/, **echoes, echoing, echoed**.

easy /iːzi¹/, **easier, easiest**.

light /laɪt/, **lights, lighting, lighted, lit** /lɪt/; **lighter, lightest**.

If there is anything unusual about the use of the forms, this is explained in a note immediately after they are given. for example:

burst /bɜːst/, **bursts, bursting**. The form **burst** is used in the present tense and is the past tense and past participle of the verb.

If the word is spelled differently in American English, this is explained in a note immediately after the forms, for example:

fuel /fjʊəl/, **fuels, fuelling, fuelled**; also spelled **fueling, fueled** in American English.

3 Pronunciation

The pronunciation is normally given after the first form of the word. For example:

key /kiː/, **keys**.

But if the word is pronounced in different ways, this is explained after all the forms. For example:

bow, bows, bowing, bowed; pronounced /baʊ/ for paragraphs 1 to 4 and for the phrasal verbs, and /bəʊ/ for paragraphs 5, 6 and 7.

When the pronunciation of one of the forms is very different from the first form given, then its pronunciation is also given immediately after it. For example:

give /gɪv/, **gives, giving, gave** /geɪv/, **given**.

For further information about pronunciation and a key to symbols used see pages viii-ix.

4 Explanations

Words are explained in simple English, easy to understand, and with a lot of information about their uses. If you read the explanations carefully, you should be able to use the word yourself in good, natural English.

5 Examples

The dictionary contains a large number of examples, showing how the words have been used by English writers and speakers. The examples have been chosen to show the most typical grammatical patterns in which the words are used, and also to show the situations in which you are most likely to find each word used. Examples are printed in italic type after the explanation of meaning. For example:

1 When you **leave** a place, you go away from it. EG *They left the house to go for a walk after tea.*

6 Grammar

All the words that are explained in the dictionary have grammatical information given about them in the Extra Column. Explanations of the labels used in the Extra Column are in the main dictionary text, in alphabetical order but inside a box, to show that we are talking about the language used in the dictionary. For example:

> **COMPAR** stands for **comparative**
> Adjectives which have the label COMPAR in the Extra Column are in the comparative form. A few adverbs are also labelled COMPAR.
> See the entry headed ADJECTIVES for more information.

Here is a list of the grammatical labels used in the Extra Column, all of which have special entries in the dictionary text:

A	MODAL	QUANTIF
ADJ	N	QUOTE
ADJ AFTER N	N COLL	RECIP
ADJ CLASSIF	N COUNT	REPORT
ADJ COLOUR	N ING	SUBMOD
ADJ PRED	N MASS	SUFFIX
ADJ QUALIT	N MOD	SUPERL
ADV	N PART	SUPP
ADV SEN	N PLURAL	USU
ADV AFTER VB	N PROPER	V
ADV BRD NEG	N SING	V+A
ATTRIB	N UNCOUNT	V+C
AUX	NEG	V+O
BROAD NEG	O	V+O+A
C	ORDINAL	V+O+C
COMPAR	POSS	V+O+O
CONJ	PREDET	V−ERG
CONT	PREFIX	V−PASS
DET	PREP	V−REFL
DET POSS	PRON	V−SPEECH
EXCLAM	PRON INDEF	VB
IMPER	PRON POSS	VOCATIVE
INF	PRON REFL	WH
-ING	PRON REL	

The following punctuation marks are used in the Extra Column.

, A comma comes between basic word classes if more than two are mentioned – for example V+O, V+O+O, or V+O+A. Commas also come between pieces of extra information that follow a basic word class. For example, ADJ PRED+*to*−INF, REPORT, OR *for*.

: A colon comes after a basic word class and introduces extra information about the way the word works. For example, ADJ CLASSIF: ATTRIB.

/ Sometimes, the Extra Column tells you what preposition is likely to come after a particular verb, adjective, or noun. If more than one preposition is likely, they are separated by a slash. For example, V+*for*/*of*.

\+ A plus sign introduces information about whether a verb has an object (V+O), a complement (V+C), a quote structure (V+QUOTE), and so on. Plus signs are also used with other word classes to introduce the sort of words or structures that typically occur with the word being explained. For example, N COUNT+POSS.

7 Style and Usage

In addition to the grammar codes, the Extra Column also has information about how and when you should use a word. It tells you, for example, whether a word is formal or informal, whether it is British or American, or whether it is used mainly in technical or literary writing. For example:

ignominious /ɪgnə⁶mɪniəs/. **Ignominious** behaviour is considered shameful or morally unacceptable. — ADJ QUALIT Formal

inferno /ɪnfɜːnəʊ/, **infernos**. You can refer to a very large, dangerous fire as an **inferno**. — N COUNT Literary

The explanations for many words tell you the situations in which you would be likely to use the word or hear it used. So, if a word is used mainly by someone who is angry or worried or frightened, then the explanation says so. For example, in the entry for **help**, you find:

10 You shout **'Help!'** when you are in danger, in order to attract someone's attention.

There is a lot of information of this kind in the explanations in this dictionary. It is there in order to help you to use the right language for each particular situation.

8 Study Pages

As well as having grammar explanations in the main dictionary text, more detailed information is given on Study Pages, where the main grammatical categories, such as adjectives, phrasal verbs, and pronouns, are dealt with. Here is a list of the topics covered in the Study Pages:

ADJECTIVES	NUMBER
ADJUNCTS	PHRASAL VERBS
ADVERBS	PHRASES
COMPLEMENTS	PRONOUNS
CONJUNCTIONS	QUANTIFIERS
CONVENTIONS	SEMI-MODALS
DETERMINERS	SUBMODIFIERS
MODAL VERBS	VERBS
NOUNS	

The verbs BE and HAVE are also explained on full pages, rather than in the main text.

There are also special entries for AGE, DATE, MEASUREMENT, MONEY, and TIME, where examples are given of the different ways in which these can be expressed.

Pronunciation

In this dictionary a guide is given to the pronunciation of English words using the International Phonetic Alphabet. The accent represented is Received Pronunciation, or RP for short, which is an accent used by many speakers of Southern British English. There are several other accents of English, but RP is perhaps the most widely used as a norm for teaching purposes.

Two kinds of information are needed if a word is to be appropriately pronounced. We need to know about each of the sounds that make up the word, and we need to know about stress. In each of the pronunciations shown in this dictionary, at least one vowel symbol is in heavier type and underlined. Sometimes more than one vowel is in heavier type and underlined:

result /rɪzʌlt/

disappointing /dɪsəpɔɪntɪŋ/

Heavy type and underlining give important information both about stress and the sounds that make up a word.

When a word is spoken in isolation, stress falls on all the syllables that contain vowels that are in heavier type and underlined. When two syllables are marked in this way, the second syllable has primary stress while the first has secondary stress; if only one is marked, it has primary stress. A word spoken in isolation is called the citation form.

When a word is used in context, either or both of the stresses found in the citation form may be absent. The one-stress or two-stress patterns of English speech are associated not with individual words but with the information units that a speaker constructs:

The result was disappointing
/ðə rɪzʌlt wəz dɪsəpɔɪntɪŋ/

A disappointing result
/ə dɪsəpɔɪntɪŋ rɪzʌlt/

Very disappointing indeed
/vɛri¹ dɪsəpɔɪntɪŋ ɪndiːd/

Because stress patterns are associated with linguistic units larger than the word, a dictionary cannot state in advance which of the stresses present in a citation form will be absent when a word is used in context.

Vowels that are in heavier type and underlined are called protected vowels. This means that, irrespective of whether a vowel is stressed or unstressed in a particular context, there is very little variation in the way a speaker pronounces it. Unprotected vowels, conversely, which are always unstressed, may show considerable variation in the way they are pronounced.

In this dictionary, the range of possible variation is shown by the tiny superscript numbers printed just above and to the right of the vowel symbol. In the word /s**ɪ**ti^{1}/ (*city*), for example, the protected vowel is always pronounced /ɪ/, irrespective of whether it is stressed or not. Conversely, the key at the foot of this page shows that the pronunciation of the unprotected vowel may be made in the range between /i:/ and /ɪ/. In the word /j**u:**slɪ^{2}s/ (*useless*) the protected vowel is always pronounced /u:/, irrespective of whether it is stressed or not, while the pronunciation of the unprotected vowel may be made in the range between /ɪ/ and /ɛ/.

Some unprotected vowels are pronounced in only one way. For example, the second vowel in /h**ɔ:**lma:k/ (*hallmark*) is stressed neither in its citation form nor when the word is used in context, but there is still very little variation in the way it is pronounced.

Some sounds, both vowels and consonants, are heard only in rather slow and careful speech. /j**u:**ʒʊəl/ (*usual*) and /k**ɒ**ləmnɪst/ (*columnist*) are often heard as /ju:ʒəl/ and /kɒləmɪst/. In such cases, the superscript ^{0} indicates that the sound in question is often omitted:

usual /j**u:**ʒʊ^{0}əl/
columnist /k**ɒ**ləmn^{0}ɪst/

All superscripts and the variations they stand for are given in the key below.

Pronunciation Key

Vowels

ɑ:	heart, start, calm.
æ	act, mass, lap.
aɪ	dive, cry, mind.
aɪə	fire, tyre, buyer.
aʊ	out, down, loud.
aʊə	flour, tower, sour.
ɛ	met, lend, pen.
eɪ	say, main, weight.
ɛə	fair, care, wear.
ɪ	fit, win, list.
i:	feed, me, beat.
ɪə	near, beard, clear.
ɒ	lot, lost, spot.
əʊ	note, phone, coat.
ɔ:	more, cord, claw.
ɔɪ	boy, coin, joint.
ʊ	could, stood, hood.
u:	you, use, choose.
ʊə	sure, pure, cure.
ɜ:	Turn, third, word.
ʌ	but, fund, must.
ə	the weak vowel in butter, about, forgotten.

Consonants

b	bed	t	talk
d	done	v	van
f	fit	w	win
g	good	x	loch
h	hat	z	zoo
j	yellow	ʃ	ship
k	king	ʒ	measure
l	lip	ŋ	sing
m	mat	tʃ	cheap
n	nine	θ	thin
p	pay	ð	then
r	run	dʒ	joy
s	soon		

Superscripts

ə^{0} (ə ⇔ 0)	ɪ^{0} (ɪ ⇔ 0)
ə^{1} (ə ⇔ ɪ)	ɪ^{1} (ɪ ⇔ ə)
ə^{2} (ə ⇔ ɛ)	ɪ^{2} (ɪ ⇔ ɛ)
ə^{3} (ə ⇔ æ)	ɪ^{3} (ɪ ⇔ eɪ)
ə^{4} (ə ⇔ ʊ)	ɪ^{5} (ɪ ⇔ aɪ)
ə^{5} (ə ⇔ ɜ:)	i^{1} (ɪ ⇔ i:)
ə^{6} (ə ⇔ əʊ)	ɛ^{1} (ɛ ⇔ ɪ)
ə^{7} (ə ⇔ ɒ)	u^{4} (u: ⇔ ʊ)
ə^{8} (ə ⇔ ɔ:)	m^{1} (m ⇔ n)
ə^{9} (ə ⇔ ʌ)	ŋ^{1} (ŋ ⇔ n)

^{0} after a consonant symbol indicates probable omission; k^{0}, t^{0}, h^{0}, etc

Corpus Acknowledgements

We wish to thank the following, who have kindly given permission for the use of copyright material in the the Birmingham Collection of English Texts.

Associated Business Programmes Ltd for: *The Next 200 Years* by Herman Kahn with William Brown and Leon Martel first published in Great Britain by Associated Business Programmes Ltd 1977 © Hudson Institute 1976. David Attenborough and William Collins Sons & Co Ltd for: *Life on Earth* by David Attenborough first published by William Collins Sons & Co Ltd 1979 © David Attenborough Productions LTD 1979. James Baldwin for: *The Fire Next Time* by James Baldwin Published in Great Britain by Michael Joseph Ltd 1963 © James Baldwin 1963. B T Batsford Ltd for: *Witchcraft in England* by Christina Hole first published by B T Batsford Ltd 1945 © Christina Hole 1945. Michael Billington for: 'Lust at First Sight' by Michael Billington in the *Illustrated London News* July 1981 and 'Truffaut's Tolerance' by Michael Billington in the *Illustrated London News* August 1981. Birmingham International Council For Overseas Students' Aid for: BICOSA Information Leaflets 1981. Basil Blackwell Publishers Ltd for: *Breaking the Mould? The Birth and Prospects of the Social Democratic Party* by Ian Bradley first Published by Martin Robertson & Co Ltd 1981 © Ian Bradley 1981. *Seeing Green (The Politics of Ecology Explained)* by Jonathon Porritt first published by Basil Blackwell Publisher Ltd 1984 © Jonathon Porritt 1984. Blond & Briggs Ltd for: *Small is Beautiful* by E F Schumacher first published in Great Britain by Blond & Briggs Ltd 1973 © E F Schumacher 1973. The Bodley Head Ltd for: *The Americans (Letters from America 1969-1979)* by Alistair Cooke first published by Bodley Head Ltd 1979 © Alistair Cooke 1979. *Baby and Child Care* by Dr Benjamin Spock published in Great Britain by The Bodley Head Ltd 1955 © Benjamin Spock MD 1945, 1946, 1957, 1968, 1976, 1979. *What's Wrong With The Modern World?* by Michael Shanks first published by The Bodley Head Ltd 1978 © Michael Shanks 1978. *Future Shock* by Alvin Toffler first published in Great Britain by The Bodley Head Ltd 1970 © Alvin Toffler 1970. *Zen and the Art of Motorcycle Maintenance* by Robert M Pirsig first published in Great Britain by The Bodley Head Ltd 1974 © Robert M Pirsig 1974. *Marnie* by Winston Graham first published by the Bodley Head Ltd 1961 © Winston Graham 1961. *You Can Get There From Here* by Shirley MacLaine first published in Great Britain by The Bodley Head Ltd 1975 © Shirley MacLaine 1975. *It's An Odd Thing, But ...* by Paul Jennings first published by Max Reinhardt Ltd 1971 © Paul Jennings 1971. *King of the Castle (Choice and Responsibility in the Modern World)* by Gai Eaton first published by the Bodley Head Ltd 1977 © Gai Eaton 1977. *Revolutionaries in Modern Britain* by Peter Shipley first published by The Bodley Head Ltd 1976 © Peter Shipley 1976. *The Prerogative of the Harlot (Press Barons and Power)* by Hugh Cudlipp first published by The Bodley Head Ltd 1980 © Hugh Cudlipp 1980. *But What About The Children (A Working Parents' Guide to Child Care)* by Judith Hann first published by The Bodley Head Ltd 1976 © Judith Hann 1976. *Learning to Read* by Margaret Meek first published by The Bodley Head Ltd 1982 © Margaret Meek 1982. Bolt & Watson for: *Two is Lonely* by Lynne Reid Banks first published by Chatto & Windus 1974 © Lynne Reid Banks 1974. The British and Foreign Bible Society with William Collins Sons & Co Ltd for: *Good News Bible (with Deuterocanonical Books/Apocrypha)* first published by The British and Foreign Bible Society with William Collins Sons & Co Ltd 1979 © American Bible Society: Old Testament 1976, Deuterocanonical Books/Apocrypha 1979, New Testament 1966, 1971, 1976, © Maps, British and Foreign Bible Society 1976, 1979. The British Council for: *How to Live in Britain (The British Council's Guide for Overseas Students and Visitors)* first published by The British Council 1952 © The British Council 1984. Mrs R Bronowski for: *The Ascent of Man* by J Bronowski published by Book Club Associates by arrangement with The British Broadcasting Corporation 1977 © J Bronowski 1973. Alison Busby for: *The Death of Trees* by Nigel Dudley first published by Pluto Press Ltd 1985 © Nigel Dudley 1985. Tony Buzan for: *Make The Most of your Mind by* Tony Buzan first published by Colt Books Ltd 1977 © Tony Buzan 1977. Campbell Thomson & McLaughlin Ltd for: *Ring of Bright Water* by Gavin Maxwell first published by Longmans Green & Co 1960, published in Penguin Books Ltd 1976 © The Estate of Gavin Maxwell 1960. Jonathan Cape Ltd for: *Manwatching (A Field Guide to Human Behaviour)* by Desmond Morris first published in Great Britain by Jonathan Cape Ltd 1977 © Text, Desmond Morris 1977 © Compilation, Elsevier Publishing Projects SA, Lausanne, and Jonathan Cape Ltd, London 1977. *Tracks* by Robyn Davidson first published by Jonathan Cape Ltd 1980 © Robyn Davidson 1980. *In the Name of Love* by Jill Tweedie first published by Jonathan Cape Ltd 1979 © Jill Tweedie 1979. *The Use of Lateral Thinking* by Edward de Bono first published by Jonathan Cape 1967 © Edward de Bono 1967. *Trout Fishing in America* by Richard Brautigan first published in Great Britain by Jonathan Cape Ltd 1970 © Richard Brautigan 1967. *The Pendulum Years: Britain and the Sixties* by Bernard Levin first published by Jonathan Cape Ltd 1970 © Bernard Levin 1970. *The Summer Before The Dark* by Doris Lessing first published in Great Britain by Jonathan Cape Ltd 1973 © Doris Lessing 1973. *The Boston Strangler* by Gerold Frank first published in Great Britain by Jonathan Cape Ltd 1967 © Gerold Frank 1966. *I'm OK - You're OK* by Thomas A Harris MD first published in Great Britain as The Book of Choice by Jonathan Cape Ltd 1970 © Thomas A Harris MD, 1967, 1968, 1969. *The Vivisector* by Patrick White first published by Jonathan Cape Ltd 1970 © Patrick White 1970. *The Future of Socialism* by Anthony Crosland first published by Jonathan Cape Ltd 1956 © C A R Crosland 1963. *Funeral in Berlin* by Len Deighton first published by Jonathan Cape Ltd 1964 © Len Deighton 1964. Chatto & Windus Ltd for: *A Postillion Struck by Lightning* by Dirk Bogarde first published by Chatto & Windus Ltd 1977 © Dirk Bogarde 1977. *Nuns and Soldiers* by Iris Murdoch published by Chatto & Windus Ltd 1980 © Iris Murdoch 1980. *Wounded Knee (An Indian History of the American West)* by Dee Brown published by Chatto & Windus Ltd 1978 © Dee Brown 1970. *The Virgin in the Garden* by A S Byatt published by Chatto & Windus Ltd 1978 © A S Byatt 1978. *A Story Like The Wind* by Laurens van der Post published by Clarke Irwin & Co Ltd in association with The Hogarth Press Ltd 1972 © Laurens van der Post 1972. *Brave New World* by Aldous Huxley published by Chatto & Windus Ltd 1932 © Aldous Huxley and Mrs Laura Huxley 1932, 1960. *The Reivers* By William Faulkner first published by Chatto & Windus Ltd 1962 © William Faulkner 1962. *Cider With Rosie* by Laurie Lee published by The Hogarth Press 1959 © Laurie Lee 1959 *The Tenants* by Bernard Malamud first published in Great Britain by Chatto & Windus Ltd 1972 © Bernard Malamud 1971. *Kinflicks* by Lisa Alther first published in Great Britain by Chatto & Windus Ltd 1976 © Lisa Alther 1975. William Collins Sons & Co Ltd for: *The Companion Guide to London* by David Piper published by William Collins Sons & Co Ltd 1964 © David Piper 1964. *The Bedside Guardian 29* edited by W L Webb published by William Collins & Sons Ltd 1980 © Guardian Newspapers Ltd 1980. *Bear Island* by Alistair MacLean first published by William Collins Sons Co Ltd 1971 © Alistair MacLean 1971. *Inequality in Britain: Freedom, Welfare and the State* By Frank Field first published by Fontana Paperbacks 1981 © Frank Field 1981. *Social Mobility* by Anthony Heath first published by Fontana Paperbacks 1981©Anthony Heath 1981. *Yours Faithfully* by Gerald Priestland first published by Fount Paperbacks 1979 © British Broadcasting Corporation 1977, 1978. *Power Without Responsibility: The Press and Broadcasting in Britain* by James Curran and Jean Seaton first published by Fontana Paperbacks 1981 © James Curran and Jean Seaton 1981. *The Times Cookery Book* by Katie Stewart first published by William Collins Sons & Co Ltd 1972 © Times Newspapers Ltd. *Friends from the Forest* by Joy Adamson by Collins and Harvill Press 1981 © Elsa Limited 1981. *The Media Mob* by Barry Fantoni and George Melly first published by William Collins Sons & Co Ltd 1980 © Text, George Melly 1980 © Illustrations, Barry Fantoni 1980. *Shalom (a collection of Australian and Jewish Stories)* compiled by Nancy Keesing first published by William Collins Publishers Pty Ltd 1978© William Collins Sons &Co Ltd 1978. *The Bedside Guardian 31* edited by W L Webb first published by William Collins Sons & Co Ltd 1982 © Guardian Newspapers Ltd 1982. *The Bedside Guardian 32* edited by W L Webb first published by William Collins Sons & Co Ltd 1983 © Guardian Newspapers Ltd 1983. *Design for the Real World* by Victor Papanek first published in Great Britain by Thames & Hudson Ltd 1972 © Victor Papanek 1971. *Food For Free* by Richard Mabey first published by William Collins Sons & Co Ltd 1972 © Richard Mabey 1972. *Unended Quest* by Karl Popper (first published as Autobiography of Karl Popper in The Philosophy of Karl Popper in The Library of Philosophers edited by Paul Arthur Schlipp by the Open Court Publishing Co 1974) published by Fontana Paperbacks 1976 © The Library of Living Philosophers Inc 1974 © Karl R Popper 1976. *My Mother My Self* by Nancy Friday first published in Great Britain by Fontana Paperbacks 1979 © Nancy Friday 1977. *The Captain's Diary* by Bob Willis first published by Willow Books/William Collins Sons & Co Ltd 1984 © Bob Willis and Alan Lee 1984 © New Zealand Scorecards, Bill Frindall 1984. *The Bodywork Book by Esme Newton-Dunn* first published in Great Britain by Willow Books/William Collins Sons & Co Ltd 1982 © TVS Ltd/Esme Newton-Dunn 1982. *Collins' Encyclopaedia of Fishing in The British Isles* edited by Michael Prichard first published by William Collins Sons & Co Ltd 1976 © William Collins Sons & Co Ltd 1976. *The AAA Runner's Guide* edited by Heather Thomas first published by William Collins Sons & Co Ltd 1983 © Sackville Design Group Ltd 1983. *Heroes and Contemporaries* by David Gower with Derek Hodgson first published by William Collins Sons & Co Ltd 1983 © David Gower Promotions Ltd 1983. *The Berlin Memorandum* by Adam Hall first published by William Collins Sons & Co Ltd 1965 © Jonquil Trevor 1965. *Arlott on Cricket: His Writings on the Game* edited by David Rayvern Allen first published by William Collins (Willow Books) 1984 © John Arlott 1984. *A Woman in Custody* by Audrey Peckham first published by Fontana Paperbacks 1985 © Audrey Peckham 1985. *Play Golf with Peter Alliss* by Peter Alliss published by the British Broadcasting Corporation 1977 © Peter Alliss and Renton Laidlaw 1977. Curtis Brown Ltd for: *The Pearl* by John Steinbeck first published by William Heinemann Ltd 1948 © John Steinbeck 1948. *An Unfinished History of the World* by Hugh Thomas first published in Great Britain by Hamish Hamilton Ltd 1979 © Hugh Thomas 1979, 1981. *The Winter of our Discontent* by John Steinbeck first published in Great Britain by William Heinemann Ltd 1961 © John Steinbeck 1961. *Burr* by Gore Vidal first published in Great Britain by William Heinemann Ltd 1974 © Gore Vidal 1974. *Doctor on the Job* by Richard Gordon first published by William Heinemann Ltd 1976 © Richard Gordon Ltd 1976. Andre Deutsch Ltd for: *How to be an Alien* by George Mikes first published by Andre Deutsch Ltd 1946 © George Mikes and Nicholas Bentley 1946. *Jaws* by Peter Benchley first published in Great Britain by Andre Deutsch Ltd 1974 © Peter Benchley 1974. *A Bend in the River* by V S Naipaul first published by Andre Deutsch Ltd 1979 © V S Naipaul 1979. *Couples* by John Updike first published by Andre Deutsch Ltd 1968 © John Updike 1968. *Games People Play* by Eric Berne published in Great Britain by Andre Deutsch Ltd 1966 © Eric Berne 1964. *The Age of Uncertainty* by John Kenneth Galbraith first published by The British Broadcasting Corporation and Andre Deutsche Ltd 1977 © John Kenneth Galbraith 1977. The Economist Newspaper Ltd for: *The Economist* (9-15 May 1981 and 22-28 August 1981) © published by The Economist Newspaper Ltd 1981. Faber & Faber Ltd for: *Lord of the Flies* by William Golding first published by Faber & Faber Ltd 1954 © William Golding 1954. *The Complete Book of Self-Sufficiency* by John Seymour first published in Great Britain by Faber & Faber Ltd 1976 © Text, John Seymour 1976, 1977 © Dorling Kindersley Ltd 1976, 1977. *Conversations with Igor Stravinsky* by Igor Stravinsky and Robert Craft first published by Faber & Faber Ltd 1959 © Igor Stravinsky 1958,1959. John Farquharson Ltd for: *The Moon's A Balloon* by David Niven published in Great Britain by Hamish Hamilton Ltd 1971 © David Niven 1971. John Gaselee for: 'Going it Alone' by John Gaselee in the *Illustrated London News* July 1981 and 'The Other Car's Fault' by John Gaselee in the *Illustrated London News* August 1981. Glidrose Publications Ltd for: *The Man with the Golden Gun* by Ian Fleming first published by Jonathan Cape Ltd © Glidrose Productions Ltd 1965. Victor Gollancz Ltd for: *The Next Horizon* by

Chris Bonnington published by Victor Gollancz Ltd 1976 © Chris Bonnington 1973. *Summerhill: A Radical Approach to Education* by A S Neill first published by Victor Gollancz Ltd 1962 © A S Neill 1926, 1932, 1937, 1953, 1961 (US permission by Hart Publishing Inc). *Lucky Jim* by Kingsley Amis first published by Victor Gollancz Ltd 1954 © Kingsley Amis 1953. *The Mighty Micro (The Impact of the Computer Revolution)* by Christopher Evans first published by Victor Gollancz Ltd 1979 © Christopher Evans 1979. *The Longest Day* by Cornelius Ryan published by Victor Gollancz Ltd 1960 © Cornelius Ryan 1959. *Asking for Trouble (Autobiography of a Banned Journalist)* by Donald Woods published by Victor Gollancz Ltd 1980 © Donald Woods 1980. *The Turin Shroud* by Ian Wilson first published in Great Britain by Victor Gollancz Ltd 1978 © Ian Wilson 1978. *Murdo and Other Stories* by Iain Crichton Smith published by Victor Gollancz Ltd 1981 © Iain Crichton Smith 1981. *The Class Struggle in Parliament* by Eric S Heffer published by Victor Gollancz Ltd 1973 © Eric S Heffer 1973. *A Presumption of Innocence (The Amazing Case of Patrick Meehan)* by Ludovic Kennedy published by Victor Gollancz Ltd 1976 © Ludovic Kennedy 1976. *The Treasure of Sainte Foy* by MacDonald Harris published by Victor Gollancz Ltd 1980 © MacDonald Harris 1980. *A Long Way to Shiloh* by Lionel Davidson first published by Victor Gollancz Ltd 1966 © Lionel Davidson 1966. *Education After School* by Tyrrell Burgess first published by Victor Gollancz Ltd 1977 © Tyrrell Burgess 1977. *The View From Serendip* by Arthur C Clarke published by Victor Gollancz Ltd 1978 © Arthur C Clarke 1967, 1968, 1970, 1972, 1974, 1976, 1977. *On Wings of Song* by Thomas M Disch published by Victor Gollancz Ltd 1979 © Thomas M Disch 1979. *The World of Violence* by Colin Wilson published by Victor Gollancz Ltd 1963 © Colin Wilson 1963. *The Lightning Tree* by Joan Aiken published by Victor Gollancz Ltd 1980 © Joan Aiken Enterprises 1980. *Russia's Political Hospitals* by Sidney Bloch and Peter Reddaway published by Victor Gollancz Ltd 1977 © Sidney Bloch and Peter Reddaway 1977. *Unholy Loves* by Joyce Carol Oates first published in Great Britain by Victor Gollancz Ltd 1980 © Joyce Carol Oates 1979. *Consenting Adults (or The Duchess will be Furious)* by Peter De Vries published by Victor Gollancz Ltd 1981 © Peter De Vries 1980. *The Passion of New Eve* by Angela Carter published by Victor Gollancz Ltd 1977 © Angela Carter 1977. Gower Publishing Co Ltd for: *Solar Prospects (The Potential for Renewable Energy)* by Michael Flood first published in Great Britain by Wildwood House Ltd in association with Friends of the Earth Ltd 1983 © Michael Flood. *Voiceless Victims* by Rebecca Hall first published in Great Britain by Wildwood House Ltd 1984 © Rebecca Hall 1984. Graham Greene and Laurence Pollinger Ltd for: *The Human Factor* by Graham Greene first published by The Bodley Head Ltd 1978 © Graham Greene 1978. Syndication Manager, The Guardian, for: *The Guardian* (12 May 1981, 7 September 1981 and 15 September 1981) © published by Guardian Newspapers Ltd 1981. Hamlyn for: *How to Play Rugby* by David Norrie published by The Hamlyn Publishing Group Ltd 1981 © The Hamlyn Publishing Group Ltd 1981. *How to Play Badminton* by Pat Davies first published by The Hamlyn Publishing Group Ltd 1979 © The Hamlyn Publishing Group Ltd 1979. Margaret Hanbury for: *Crisis and Conservation: Conflict in the British Countryside* by Charlie Pye-Smith and Chris Rose first published by Pelican/Penguin Books Ltd 1984 © Charlie Pye-Smith and Chris Rose 1984. Paul Harrison for: *Inside the Third World* by Paul Harrison first published in Great Britain by The Harvester Press Ltd 1980 © Paul Harrison 1979. A M Heath & Co Ltd for: *Rembrandt's Hat* by Bernard Malamud published by Chatto & Windus Ltd 1982 © Bernard Malamud 1968, 1972, 1973. William Heinemann Ltd for: *It's an Old Country* by J B Priestley first published in Great Britain by William Heinemann Ltd 1967 © J B Priestley 1967. Heinemann Educational Books Ltd and Gower Publishing Co Ltd for: *The Environmental Crisis (A Handbook for all Friends of the Earth)* edited by Des Wilson first published by Heinemann Educational Books Ltd 1984 © Foreword, David Bellamy 1984 © Individual Chapters, the Author of the Chapter 1984 © In the selection and all other matters Des Wilson 1984. The Controller, Her Majesty's Stationery Office, for: Department of Health and Social Security leaflets published by Her Majesty's Stationery Office 1981 © The Crown. David Higham Associates Ltd for: 'Two Peruvian Projects' by E R Chamberlain in the *Illustrated London News* September 1981. *Akenfield: Portrait of an English Village* by Ronald Blythe first published by Allen Lane, Penguin Books Ltd 1969 © Ronald Blythe1969. *The Far Pavillions* by M M Kaye first published by Allen Lane/Penguin Books Ltd 1978 © M M Kaye 1978. *Staying On* by Paul Scott first published by William Heinemann Ltd 1977 © Paul Scott 1977. *Let Sleeping Vets Lie* by James Herriot first published by Michael Joseph Ltd 1973 © James Herriot 1973. *The Midwich Cuckoos* by John Wyndham first published in Great Britain by Michael Joseph Ltd 1957 © The Estate of John Wyndham 1957. *The Girl in a Swing* by Richard Adams first published in Great Britain by Allen Lane in Penguin Books Ltd 1980 © Richard Adams 1980. Dr K B Hindley for: 'Hot Spots of the Deep' by Dr K B Hindley in the *Illustrated London News July* 1981. Hodder and Stoughton Ltd for: *Supernature* by Lyall Watson first published by Hodder & Stoughton Ltd 1973 © Lyall Watson 1973. *Tinker Tailor Soldier Spy* by John Le Carre first published by Hodder & Stoughton Ltd 1974 © Le Carre Productions 1974. The Editor, Homes and Gardens, for: *Homes and Gardens* (October 1981) (Number 4 Volume 63) © published by IPC Magazines Ltd 1981. Hughes Massie Ltd for: *Elephants Can Remember* by Agatha Christie first published by William Collins Sons & Co Ltd 1972 © Agatha Christie Mallowan. Hutchinson Publishing Group Ltd for: *An Autobiography* by Angela Davis published in Great Britain by Hutchinson & Co Publishers Ltd by arrangement with Bantam Books Inc 1975 © Angela Davis 1974. *The Day of the Jackal* by Frederick Forsyth published in Great Britian by Hutchinson & Co Publishers Ltd 1971 © Frederick Forsyth 1971. *Roots* by Alex Haley first published in Great Britain by Hutchinson & Co Publishers Ltd 1977 © Alex Haley 1976. *The Climate of Treason* by Andrew Boyle first published by Hutchinson & Co Publishers Ltd 1979 © Andrew Boyle 1979. *The Collapsing Universe: The Story of Black Holes* by Isaac Asimov first published by Hutchinson & Co Publishers Ltd 1977 © Isaac Asimov. *XPD* by Len Deighton published by Book Club Associates by arrangement with Hutchinson & Co Publishers Ltd 1981 © Len Deighton 1981. *Show Jumping with Harvey Smith* by Harvey Smith first published by Stanley Paul & Co Ltd 1979 © Tyne-Tees Television Ltd, A Member of the Trident Group 1979. *2001: A Space Odyssey* by Arthur C Clarke first published by Hutchinson & Co Publishers Ltd 1968 © Arthur C Clarke and Polaris Productions Inc 1968 © Epilogue material, Serendip BV 1982, 1983. The Illustrated London News and Sketch Ltd for: *The Illustrated London News* (July 1981, August 1981 and September 1981) © published by the Illustrated London News and Sketch Ltd 1981. The Editor, International Herald Tribune, for: *International Herald Tribune* (25-26 July 1981) © published by International Herald Tribune with The New York Times and The Washington Post 1981. Michael Joseph Ltd for: *Chronicles of Fairacre: Village School* by Miss Read first published in Great Britain by Michael Joseph Ltd 1964 © Miss Read 1955, 1964. *Fire Fox* by Craig Thomas first published in Great Britain by Michael Joseph Ltd 1977 © Craig Thomas 1977. William Kimber & Co Ltd for: *Exodus* by Leon Uris originally published in Great Britain by Alan Wingate Ltd 1959 © Leon Uris 1958. Kogan Page Ltd for: *How to Save the World (Strategy for World Conservation)* by Robert Allen first published by Kogan Page Ltd 1980 © IUCN-UNEP-WWF 1980. Marketing Department, Lloyds Bank PLC, for: *Lloyds Bank Leaflets* (1981) © published by Lloyds Bank PLC 1981. Macmillan Publishers Ltd for: *Appropriate Technology: Technology with a Human Face* by P D Dunn first published by the Macmillan Press Ltd 1978 © P D Dunn 1978. John Murray Publishers Ltd for: *A Backward Place* by Ruth Prawer Jhabvala first published by John Murray Publishers Ltd 1965 © R Prawer Jhabvala 1965. *Food For All The Family* by Magnus Pyke first published by John Murray Publishers Ltd 1980 © Magnus Pyke 1980. *Simple Movement* by Laura Mitchell and Barbara Dale first published by John Murray Publishers Ltd 1980 © Laura Mitchell and Barbara Dale 1980. *Civilisation: A Personal View* by Kenneth Clark first published by the British Broadcasting Corporation and John Murray Publishers Ltd 1969 © Kenneth Clark 1969. The Editor, National Geographic, for: *National Geographic* January, February and March (1980) © published by The National Geographic Society 1979, 1980. The National Magazine Co Ltd for: *Cosmopolitan* (May 1981 and July 1981) © published by the National Magazine Co Ltd 1981. Neilson Leisure Group Ltd for: *NAT Holidays' 'Caravans and Tents in the Sun'* (Summer 1983) holiday brochure. Newsweek Inc for: *Newsweek* (11 May 1981, 27 July 1981 and August 1981) © published by Newsweek Inc 1981. The Associate Editor, Now!, for: *Now!* (14-20 November 1980) © published by Cavenham Communications Ltd 1980. Harold Ober Associates Inc for: *The Boys from Brazil* by Ira Levin first published by Michael Joseph Ltd 1976 © Ira Levin 1976. Edna O'Brien and A M Heath & Co Ltd for: *August is a Wicked Month* by Edna O'Brien first published by Jonathan Cape Ltd 1965 © Edna O'Brien 1965. Pan Books Ltd for: *Dispatches* by Michael Herr first published in Great Britain by Pan Books Ltd 1978 © Michael Herr 1968, 1969, 1970, 1977. *Health and Safety at Work* by Dave Eva and Ron Oswald first published by Pan Books Ltd 1981 © Dave Eva, Ron Oswald and the Workers' Educational Association 1981. *Democracy at Work* by Patrick Burns and Mel Doyle first published by Pan Books Ltd 1981 © Patrick Burns,Mel Doyle and the Workers' Educational Association 1981. *Diet for Life (A Cookbook for Arthritics)* by Mary Laver and Margaret Smith first published by Pan Books Ltd 1981 © Mary Laver and Margaret Smith 1981. Penguin Books Ltd for: *Inside the Company: CIA Diary* by Philip Agee first published in Allen Lane/Penguin Books Ltd 1975 © Philip Agee 1975. Penguin Books Ltd and Spare Ribs Ltd for: *Spare Rib Reader* edited by Marsha Rowe first published in Penguin Books Ltd 1982 © Spare Ribs Ltd 1982. A D Peters & Co Ltd for: 'The Dark Side of Israel' by Norman Moss in Illustrated London News July 1981, 'Aftermath of Osirak' by Norman Moss in the *Illustrated London News* August 1981 and 'Turning Point for Poland' by Norman Moss in the *Illustrated London News* September 1981. 'Recent Fiction' by Sally Emerson in the *Illustrated London News* July 1981, August 1981 and September 1981. *The Complete Upmanship* by Stephen Potter first published in Great Britain by Rupert Hart-Davis Ltd 1970 © Stephen Potter. Elaine Pollard for: Personal Letters 1981 donated by Elaine Pollard. Laurence Pollinger Ltd for: *A Glastonbury Romance* by John Cowper Powys first published by MacDonald & Co Ltd 1933. Murray Pollinger for: *Kiss Kiss* by Roald Dahl published in Great Britain by Michael Joseph Ltd 1960 © Roald Dahl 1962. *Can You Avoid Cancer?* by Peter Goodwin first published by the British Broadcasting Corporation 1984 © Peter Goodwin 1984. Preston Travel Ltd for: Preston Sunroutes 'Camping and Self-Catering' (April to October 1983) holiday brochure. Punch Publications Ltd for: *Punch* (6 May 1981, 29 July 1981, 12 August 1981, 26 August 1981 and 9 September 1981) © published by Punch Publications Ltd 1981. Radala and associates for: *The Naked Civil Servant* by Quentin Crisp first published by Jonathan Cape Ltd 1968 © Quentin Crisp 1968. The Rainbird Publishing Group Ltd for: *The Making of Mankind* by Richard E Leakey first published in Great Britain by Michael Joseph Ltd 1981 © Sherma BV 1981. Robson Books Ltd for: *The Punch Book of Short Stories 3* selected by Alan Coren first published in Great Britain by Robson Books Ltd in association with Punch Publications Ltd 1981 © Robson Books Ltd 1981.*The Best of Robert Morley* by Robert Morley first published in Great Britain by Robson Books Ltd 1981 © Robert Morley 1981. Deborah Rogers Ltd for: 'Picasso's Late Works' by Edward Lucie-Smith in the *Illustrated London News* July 1981, 'David Jones at the Tate' by Edward Lucie-Smith in the *Illustrated London News* August 1981 and 'Further Light on Spanish Painting' by Edward Lucie-Smith in the *Illustrated London News* September 1981. *The Godfather* by Mario Puzo first published in Great Britain by William Heinemann Ltd 1969 © Mario Puzo 1969. Routledge & Kegan Paul Ltd for: *How To Pass Examinations* by John Erasmus first published by Oriel Press Ltd 1967 © Oriel Press Ltd 1980. *Daisy, Daisy* by Christian Miller first published by Routledge & Kegan Paul Ltd 1980 © Christian Miller 1980. *The National Front* by Nigel Fielding first published by Routledge & Kegan Paul Ltd 1981 © Nigel Fielding 1981. *The Myth of Home Ownership* by Jim Kemeny first published by Routledge & Kegan Paul Ltd 1980 © J Kemeny 1981. *Absent With Cause (Lessons of Truancy)* by Roger White first published by Routledge & Kegan Paul Ltd 1980 © Roger White 1980. *The Powers of Evil (in Western Religion, Magic and Folk Belief)* by Richard Cavendish first published by Routledge & Kegan Paul Ltd 1975 © Richard Cavendish 1975. *Crime and Personality* by H J Eysenck first published by Routledge & Kegan Paul Ltd 1964 © H J Eysenck 1964, 1977. Martin Secker & Warburg Ltd for: *Changing Places* by David Lodge first published in England by Martin Secker & Warburg Ltd 1975 © David Lodge 1975. *The History Man* by Malcolm Bradbury first published by Martin Secker & Warburg 1975 © Malcolm Bradbury 1975. *Humboldt's Gift* by Saul Bellow first published in England by The Alison Press/Martin Secker & Warburg Ltd 1975 © Saul Bellow 1973, 1974, 1975. *Wilt* by Tom Sharpe first published in England by Martin Secker & Warburg Ltd 1976 © Tom Sharpe 1976. *The Last Days of*

America by Paul E Erdman first published in England by Martin Secker & Warburg Ltd 1981 © Paul E Erdman 1981. *Autumn Manoeuvres* by Melvyn Bragg first published in England by Martin Secker & Warburg Ltd 1978 © Melvyn Bragg 1978. *The Act of Being* by Charles Marowitz first published in England by Martin Secker & Warburg Ltd 1978 © Charles Marowitz 1978. *As If By Magic* by Angus Wilson first published in England by Martin Secker & Warburg Ltd 1973 © Angus Wilson 1973. *All the President's Men* by Carl Bernstein and Bob Woodward first published in England by Martin Secker & Warburg Ltd 1974 © Carl Bernstein and Bob Woodward 1974. *The Myth of the Nation and the Vision of Revolution* by J L Talmon first published by Martin Secker & Warburg Ltd 1981 © J L Talmon 1980. *Animal Farm* by George Orwell first published by Martin Secker & Warburg 1945 © Eric Blair 1945. Anthony Sheil Associates Ltd for: *Daniel Martin* by John Fowles first published in Great Britain by Jonathan Cape Ltd 1977 © J R Fowles Ltd 1977. *Love Story* by Erich Segal published by Hodder & Stoughton Ltd 1970 © Erich Segal 1970. Sidgwick & Jackson Ltd for: *The Third World War* by General Sir John Hackett and others first published in Great Britain by Sidgwick & Jackson Ltd 1978 © General Sir John Hackett 1978. *Superwoman* by Shirley Conran first published by Sidgwick & Jackson Ltd 1975 © Shirley Conran 1975, 1977. *An Actor and His Time* by John Gielgud first published in Great Britain by Sidgwick & Jackson Ltd 1979 © John Gielgud, John Miller and John Powell 1979 © Biographical Notes, John Miller 1979. Simon & Schuster for: *Our Bodies Ourselves (A Health Book by and for Women)* by the Boston Women's Health Book Collective (British Edition by Angela Phillips and Jill Rakusen) published in Allen Lane and Penguin Books Ltd 1978 © The Boston Women's Health Collective Inc 1971, 1973, 1976 © Material for British Edition, Angela Phillips and Jill Rakusen 1978. Souvenir Press Ltd for: *The Bermuda Triangle* by Charles Berlitz (An Incredible Saga of Unexplained Disappearances) first published in Great Britain by Souvenir Press Ltd 1975 © Charles Berlitz 1974. Souvenir Press Ltd and Michael Joseph Ltd for: *Airport* by Arthur Hailey first published in Great Britain by Michael Joseph Ltd in association with Souvenir Press Ltd 1968 © Arthur Hailey Ltd 1968. Sunmed Holidays Ltd for: 'Go Greek' (Summer 1983) holiday brochure. Maurice Temple Smith Ltd for: *Friends of the Earth Pollution Guide* by Brian Price published by Maurice Temple Smith Ltd 1983 © Brian Price 1983. Maurice Temple Smith and Gower Publishing Co Ltd for: *Working the Land (A New Plan for a Healthy Agriculture)* by Charlie Pye-Smith and Richard North first published by Maurice Temple Smith Ltd 1984© Charlie Pye-Smith and Richard North 1984. Times Newspapers Ltd for: *The Sunday Times Magazine* (13 January 1980, 20 January 1980 and 11 May 1980) © published by Times Newspapers Ltd 1981. *The Times* (7 September 1981) © published by Times Newspapers Ltd 1981. Twenty's Holidays for: 'The Best 18-33 Holidays' (Winter 1982/83) holiday brochure. University of Birmingham for: Living in Birmingham (1984) © published by The University of Birmingham 1984. Birmingham University Overseas Student Guide © The University of Birmingham. Working with Industry and Commerce © published by The University of Birmingham 1984. University of Birmingham Prospectus (June 1985) © published by The University of Birmingham 1985. University of Birmingham Library Guide © published by The University of Birmingham. University of Birmingham Institute of Research and Development (1984) © published by the University of Birmingham 1984. Biological Sciences at The University of Birmingham (1985) © published by The University of Birmingham 1985. History at the University of Birmingham (1985) © published by the University of Birmingham 1985. Faculty of Arts Handbook (1984-85) © published by The University of Birmingham 1984. Virago Press Ltd for: *Benefits* by Zoe Fairbairns published by Virago Press Ltd 1979 © Zoe Fairbairns 1979. *Simple Steps to Public Life* by Pamela Anderson, Mary Stott and Fay Weldon published in Great Britain by Virago Press Ltd 1980 © Action Opportunities 1980. *Tell Me A Riddle* by Tillie Olsen published by Virago Press Ltd 1980 © this edition Tillie Olsen 1980. A P Watt (& Sons) Ltd for: *The Glittering Prizes* by Frederic Raphael first published in Great Britain by Penguin Books Ltd 1976 © Volatic Ltd 1976. *Then and Now* by W Somerset Maugham first published by William Heinemann Ltd 1946 © W Somerset Maugham 1946. *The Language of Clothes* by Alison Lurie published by William Heinemann Ltd 1981 © Alison Lurie 1981. 'Herschel Commemorative' by Patrick Moore in the *Illustrated London News* July 1981. 'The Outermost Giant' by Patrick Moore in the *Illustrated London News* August 1981. 'Cosmic Bombardment' by Patrick Moore in the *Illustrated London News* September 1981. Weidenfeld & Nicolson Ltd for: 'The Miraculous Toy' by Susan Briggs in the *Illustrated London News* August 1981. *The Needle's Eye* by Margaret Drabble first published by Weidenfeld & Nicolson Ltd 1972 © Margaret Drabble 1972. *Success Without Tears: A Woman's Guide to the Top* by Rachel Nelson first published in Great Britain by Weidenfeld & Nicolson Ltd 1979 © Rachel Nelson 1979. *Education in the Modern World* by John Vaizey published by Weidenfeld & Nicolson Ltd 1967 © John Vaizey 1967. *Rich Man, Poor Man* by Irwin Shaw first published in Great Britain by Weidenfield & Nicolson Ltd 1970 © Irwin Shaw 1969,1970. *Lolita* by Vladimir Nabokov first published in Great Britain by Weidenfeld & Nicolson Ltd 1959 © Vladimir Nabokov 1955, 1959, 1968, © G P Putnam's Sons 1963 © McGraw-Hill International Inc 1971. *The Third World* by Peter Worsley first published by Weidenfeld & Nicolson Ltd 1964 © Peter Worsley 1964, 1967. *Portrait of a Marriage* by Nigel Nicolson published by Weidenfeld & Nicolson Ltd 1973 © Nigel Nicolson 1973. *The Dogs Bark: Public People and Private Places* by Truman Capote first published in Great Britain by Weidenfeld & Nicolson Ltd 1974 © Truman Capote 1974. *Great Planning Disasters* by Peter Hall first published in Great Britain by George Weidenfeld & Nicolson Ltd 1980 © Peter Hall 1980. The Writers and Readers Publishing Co-operative Ltd for: *Working with Words, Literacy Beyond School* by Jane Mace published by The Writers and Readers Publishing Co-operative Ltd 1979 © Jane Mace 1979. *The Alienated: Growing Old Today* by Gladys Elder OAP published by The Writers and Readers Publishing Co-operative Ltd 1977 © Text, The Estate of Gladys Elder 1977 © Photographs, Mike Abrahams 1977. *Beyond the Crisis in Art* by Peter Fuller published by The Writers and Readers Publishing Co-operative Ltd 1980 © Peter Fuller 1980. *The War and Peace Book* by Dave Noble published by The Writers and Readers Publishing Co-operative Ltd 1977 © Dave Noble 1977. *Tony Benn: A Political Biography* by Robert Jenkins first published by The Writers and Readers Publishing Co-operative Ltd 1980 © Robert Jenkins 1980. *Nuclear Power for Beginners* by Stephen Croall and Kaianders Sempler first published by The Writers and Readers Publishing Co-operative Ltd 1978 © Text, Stephen Croall 1978,1980 © Illustrations Kaianders Sempler 1978, 1980. Yale University Press for: *Life in the English Country House: A Social and Architectural History* by Mark Girouard published by Yale University Press Ltd, London 1978 © Yale University 1978. The British Broadcasting Corporation for transcripts of radio transmissions of 'Kaleidoscope', 'Any Questions', 'Money Box' and 'Arts and Africa' 1981 and 1982. The British Broadcasting Corporation and Mrs Shirley Williams for transcripts of television interviews with Mrs Shirley Williams 1979. Dr B L Smith, School of Mathematics and Physical Sciences, University of Sussex for programmes on Current Affairs, Science and The Arts originally broadcast on Radio Sussex 1979 and 1980 © B L Smith. The following people in the University of Birmingham: Professor J McH Sinclair, Department of English, for his tapes of informal conversation (personal collection). Mr R Wallace, formerly Department of Accounting and Finance, and Ms D Houghton, Department of English, for transcripts of his accountancy lectures. Dr B K Gazey, Department of Electrical Engineering and Dr M Montgomery, University of Strathclyde, Department of English, for a transcript of Dr Gazey's lecture. Dr L W Poel, Department of Plant Biology, and Dr M Montgomery, University of Strathclyde, Department of English, for a transcript of Dr Poel's lecture. Professor J G Hawkes, formerly Department of Plant Biology, for recordings of his lectures. Dr M S Snaith, Department of Transportation for recordings of his lectures. Dr M P Hoey, Department of English, and Dr M Cooper, The British Council, for a recording of their discussion on discourse analysis. Ms A Renouf, Department of English, for recordings of job and academic interviews 1977. Mr R H Hubbard, formerly a B Phil (Ed) student, Faculty of Education, for his research recordings of expressions of uncertainty 1978-79. Mr A E Hare, formerly a B Phil (Ed) student, Faculty of Education, for his transcripts of telephone conversations 1978. Dr A Tsui, formerly Department of English, for her recordings of informal conversation. Mr J Couperthwaite, formerly Department of English, for a recording of informal conversation 1981. Ms C Emmott, M Litt student, Department of English, for a recording of informal conversation 1981. Mrs B T Atkins for the transcript of an account of a dream 1981. The British Council for 'Authentic Materials Numbers 1-28' 1981. Professor M Hammerton and Mr K Coghill, Department of Psychology, University of Newcastle-upon-Tyne, for tape recordings of their lectures 1981. Mr G P Graveson, formerly research student, University of Newcastle, for his recordings of teacher discussion 1977. Mr W R Jones, formerly research student, University of Southampton, for his recordings of classroom talk. Mr Ian Fisher, formerly BA student, Newcastle Polytechnic, for his transcripts of interviews on local history 1981. Dr N Coupland, formerly PhD student, Department of English, UWIST, for his transcripts of travel agency talk 1981. Professor D B Bromley, Department of Psychology, University of Liverpool, for his transcript of a research recording. Mr Brian Lawrence, formerly of Saffron Walden County High School, for a tape of his talk on 'The British Education System' 1979.

Every effort has been made to trace the copyright holders, but if any have been inadvertently overlooked the publishers will be pleased to make the necessary acknowledgments at the first opportunity.

A a

A, a /eɪ/, **A's, a's. A** is the first letter of the English alphabet. N COUNT

> **A stands for adjunct**
> Verbs which have the label +A in the Extra Column need an adjunct to complete their meaning. See the entry headed ADJUNCTS for more information.

a /eɪ/ or /ə/, **an** /æn/ or /ən/.
1 You use **a** or **an** at the beginning of noun groups when you are referring to someone or something and you do not want to say which particular person or thing you mean. EG *Tom could see a hallway... She wanted to be an actress.* DET

2 You can use **a** or **an** instead of the number 'one'. EG *...a year or two ago... ...in an hour's time.* DET

3 When you express rates, prices, and measurements, you can use **a** or **an** to say how many units apply to each of the items being measured. EG *He charges 100 dollars an hour.* DET

4 You can use **a** or **an** in front of uncount nouns when they are preceded by adjectives or followed by words that describe the uncount noun more fully. EG *...a happiness that he couldn't quite hide.* DET

5 You use **a** or **an** in front of the names of people when you are referring to someone who you do not know personally. EG *You don't know a Mrs Burton, do you?* DET

aback /əbæk/. See **take aback**.

abacus /æbəkəs/, **abacuses.** An **abacus** is a frame used for counting. It has rods with sliding beads on them. N COUNT

abandon /əbændən/, **abandons, abandoning, abandoned. 1** If you **abandon** a place, thing, or person, you leave it permanently or for a long time. EG *You're not supposed to abandon your car on the motorway.* V+O

2 If you **abandon** a plan, activity, or piece of work, you stop doing it before it is finished. EG *I abandoned the search.* V+O

3 If you **abandon** an idea or way of thinking, you stop thinking in that way. EG *I have abandoned the idea of consistency.* V+O

4 If you **abandon** yourself to an emotion, you think about it a lot and feel it strongly. EG *She abandoned herself to grief.* V-REFL+*to*

5 If you do something with **abandon**, you do it in a carefree way. EG *The food was consumed with joyous abandon.* N UNCOUNT

abandoned /əbændənd/. An **abandoned** place or building is no longer used or occupied. ADJ CLASSIF

abandonment /əbændənmə2nt/. **1** The **abandonment** of a place, thing, or person is the act of leaving it permanently or for a long time. EG *...the abandonment of the farms.* N UNCOUNT: USU+*of*

2 The **abandonment** of a piece of work or a plan is the act of stopping doing it before it is finished. N UNCOUNT: USU+*of*

abashed /əbæʃt/. If you are **abashed**, you feel embarrassed and ashamed. EG *The students looked guilty and abashed.* ADJ PRED

abate /əbeɪt/, **abates, abating, abated.** When something **abates**, it becomes much less strong or widespread. EG *My terror abated a little.* V Formal

abattoir /æbətwɑ:/, **abattoirs.** An **abattoir** is a place where animals are killed for meat. N COUNT

abbess /æbɪ2s/, **abbesses.** An **abbess** is a nun who is in charge of the other nuns in a convent. N COUNT

abbey /æbi1/, **abbeys.** An **abbey** is a church with buildings attached to it in which monks or nuns live or used to live. EG *...Westminster Abbey.* N COUNT

abbot /æbət/, **abbots.** An **abbot** is a monk who is in charge of the other monks in a monastery or abbey. N COUNT

abbreviate /ə3bri:vɪeɪt/, **abbreviates, abbreviating, abbreviated. 1** If you **abbreviate** a piece of writing or a speech you make it shorter. V+O
◇ **abbreviated.** EG *...an abbreviated version of a talk.* ◇ ADJ CLASSIF

2 A word or phrase that **is abbreviated** is made shorter by leaving out some of the letters or by using only the first letters of each word. EG *...the Ultra-Intelligent Machine (or UIM as it is abbreviated).* V+O: USU PASS

abbreviation /ə3bri:vɪeɪʃə0n/, **abbreviations.** An **abbreviation** is a short form of a word or phrase, made by leaving out some of the letters or by using only the first letters of each word. N COUNT

abdicate /æbdɪkeɪt/, **abdicates, abdicating, abdicated. 1** If a king or queen **abdicates**, he or she resigns. V ◇ **abdication** /æbdɪkeɪʃə0n/. EG *...the abdication crisis of 1936.* ◇ N UNCOUNT

2 If you **abdicate** your responsibility for something, you refuse to accept the responsibility for it any longer. V+O ◇ **abdication.** EG *...an abdication of political responsibility.* ◇ N UNCOUNT +SUPP

abdomen /æbdə6mən/, **abdomens.** Your **abdomen** is the part of your body below your chest where your stomach and intestines are. N COUNT ◇ **abdominal** /ə3bdɒmɪ1nə0l/. EG *...a patient suffering from abdominal pains.* ◇ ADJ CLASSIF

abduct /ə3bdʌkt/, **abducts, abducting, abducted.** If someone **abducts** another person, they take the person away, using force. V+O ◇ **abduction** /ə3bdʌkʃə0n/. EG *...the recent abduction of his son.* ◇ N UNCOUNT

aberration /æbəreɪʃə0n/, **aberrations.** An **aberration** is an action or way of behaving that is not normal. EG *This is a temporary aberration and will soon be put right.* N COUNT

abet /əbet/, **abets, abetting, abetted.** If you **abet** someone, you help them to do something wrong. EG *...aiding and abetting the enemy.* V+O

abhor /ə3bhɔ:/, **abhors, abhorring, abhorred.** If you **abhor** something, you hate it very much. EG *She abhors any form of cruelty.* V+O

abhorrent /ə3bhɒrənt/. If something is **abhorrent** to you, you hate it very much or consider it completely unacceptable. EG *...a ruthless and utterly abhorrent system.* ADJ QUALIT ◇ **abhorrence** /ə3bhɒrəns/. EG *...an abhorrence of war.* ◇ N UNCOUNT

abide /əbaɪd/, **abides, abiding, abided. 1** If you **can't abide** something, you dislike it very much. EG *He likes you but he can't abide Dennis.* PHRASE

2 If something **abides,** it continues to happen or exist for a long time. V ◇ **abiding.** EG *...a constant and abiding joy.* ◇ ADJ CLASSIF: ATTRIB

abide by. If you **abide by** a law, agreement, or decision, you do what it says you should do. EG *Both parties must agree to abide by the court's decision.* PHRASAL VB: V+PREP

ability /əbɪlə1ti1/, **abilities.** Your **ability** to do something is the quality or skill that you have which makes it possible for you to do it. EG *...the ability to see... ...his ability as a journalist.* N COUNT OR N UNCOUNT ● If you do something **to the best of** your **ability** or **to the best of** your **abilities**, you do it as well as you possibly can. ● PHRASE

-ability is added in place of '-able' at the end of adjectives to form nouns. These nouns are often not defined in this dictionary, but are treated with SUFFIX the related adjectives. EG *...the suitability of particular courses... ...their vulnerability to criticism.*

abject /æbdʒɛkt/. **1** You use **abject** to emphasize that a situation or quality is shameful or depressing. EG *...abject poverty.* ADJ CLASSIF: ATTRIB

2 Someone who is **abject** shows no self-respect or courage. EG *Even the most abject slaves joined in the revolt.* ADJ QUALIT

ablaze /əbleɪz/. **1** Something that is **ablaze** is burning fiercely. EG *In a moment the tents were ablaze.* ADJ PRED

2 If a place is **ablaze** with lights or colours, it is very bright because of them. ADJ PRED + *with*

able /eɪbə°l/, **abler, ablest. 1** If someone or something is **able** to do something, **1.1** they have the physical skill or the knowledge to do it. EG *The frog is able to jump three metres... I wasn't able to do these quizzes.* **1.2** they have enough freedom, power, time, or money to do it. EG *I thought I wouldn't be able to visit you this week... I was able to buy a caravan after a long search.* ADJ PRED + *to*-INF

2 Someone who is **able** is very clever or very good at doing something. EG *He was an unusually able detective.* ADJ QUALIT

-able is added to some verbs to form adjectives. These adjectives describe someone or something as able to have the thing done to them described by the verb. For example, something that is identifiable can be identified. EG *They are both immediately recognizable... Only the titles were readable.* SUFFIX

able-bodied /eɪbə°l bɒdɪd/. An **able-bodied** person is physically strong and healthy. ADJ CLASSIF

ably /eɪbli¹/ means skilfully and successfully. EG *They were ably supported by the Party members.* ADV

abnormal /æbnɔːmə°l/. Someone or something that is **abnormal** is unusual, especially in a way that is worrying. EG *Maybe my child is abnormal... ...an abnormal interest in food.* ADJ CLASSIF ◇ **abnormality** /æbnə⁸mælɪ¹ti¹/, **abnormalities.** EG *...an abnormality in the blood.* ◇ N COUNT OR N UNCOUNT

abnormally /æbnɔːmə°li¹/ means **1** to a much greater extent than usual. EG *...the abnormally warm day.* SUBMOD **2** in an unusual, often worrying way. EG *...people who are behaving abnormally.* ADV

aboard /əbɔːd/. If you are **aboard** a ship or plane, you are on or in it. EG *The plane crashed, killing all 271 aboard.* PREP OR ADV

abode /əbəʊd/, **abodes.** Your **abode** is the place where you live. EG *He took his new bride directly to their new abode.* N COUNT: OFT+POSS Formal

abolish /əbɒlɪʃ/, **abolishes, abolishing, abolished.** If you **abolish** a system or practice, you formally put an end to it. EG *They believed the death penalty should be abolished.* V+O ◇ **abolition** /æbəlɪʃə°n/. EG *...the abolition of slavery.* ◇ N UNCOUNT +SUPP

abominable /əbɒmɪnəbə°l/. Something that is **abominable** is very unpleasant or very bad. EG *They work in abominable conditions.* ADJ QUALIT ◇ **abominably.** EG *She had been treated abominably.* ◇ ADV

abort /əbɔːt/, **aborts, aborting, aborted. 1** If a woman's pregnancy **is aborted** or if she **aborts**, her pregnancy is ended deliberately and the baby dies. V+O :USU PASS; ALSO V

2 If you **abort** a process, plan, or activity, or if it **aborts**, you stop it before it has been completed. EG *Harris tried to abort the operation half-way through.* V-ERG

abortion /əbɔːʃə°n/, **abortions.** If a woman has an **abortion**, she ends her pregnancy deliberately and the baby dies. N COUNT OR N UNCOUNT

abortive /əbɔːtɪv/. An **abortive** attempt or action is unsuccessful. EG *...a year of demonstrations and abortive revolts.* ADJ CLASSIF: ATTRIB

abound /əbaʊnd/, **abounds, abounding, abounded.** If things **abound**, or if a place **abounds** with things, there are very large numbers of them. EG *Rumours abounded... Its hills abound with waterfalls.* V OR V+*with/in* Formal

about /əbaʊt/. **1** If you talk, write, or think **about** a particular thing, it is the subject of what you are saying, writing, or thinking. EG *I'll have to think about that... He had to talk about his profession... This is a book about India.* PREP

2 If you do something **about** a problem, you take action in order to solve it. EG *They knew they had to do something about their mother's unhappiness.* PREP

3 When you say that there is a particular quality **about** someone or something, you mean that they have this quality. EG *There's something peculiar about him.* PREP

4 About in front of a number means that the number is approximate, not exact. EG *We went about forty miles.* ADV

5 If someone or something moves **about**, they keep moving in different directions. EG *We saw them walking about... I stood waving my arms about.* ADV AFTER VB

6 About is used in phrasal verbs such as 'sit about' or 'mess about' to indicate that someone is not achieving very much. ADV AFTER VB

7 If someone or something is **about**, they are present or available. EG *There was no money about.* ADJ PRED

8 If you **are about to** do something, you are going to do it very soon. EG *Her father is about to retire.* PHRASE

about-turn, about-turns. An **about-turn** or an **about-face** is a complete change of attitude or opinion. EG *The Conservatives performed a swift about-turn.* N COUNT

above /əbʌv/. **1** If one thing is **above** another one, it is directly over it or higher than it. EG *...the branches above their heads... A noise was coming from the bedroom above.* PREP OR ADV

2 You use **above** in writing to refer to something that has already been mentioned. EG *All the above items can be obtained from Selfridges... The meanings of the terms used above are given in leaflet NI 12.* ADJ, ADV, OR *the*+N

3 If an amount or measurement is **above** a particular level, it is greater than that level. EG *...children above the age of 5... ...aged 15 and above.* PREP OR ADV

4 If someone is **above** you, they are in a position of authority over you. EG *He will have an executive above him to whom he reports.* PREP

5 If someone thinks that they are **above** a particular activity, they do not want to get involved in it because they do not approve of it. EG *They consider themselves above such mercenary transactions.* PREP

6 If someone is **above** criticism or suspicion, they cannot be criticized or suspected because of their good qualities or their position. PREP

above board. If an arrangement or deal is **above board**, it is completely honest. ADJ PRED

abrasion /əbreɪʒə°n/, **abrasions.** An **abrasion** is an area on a person's body where the skin has been scraped. EG *...abrasions to the side of the neck.* N COUNT Formal

abrasive /əbreɪsɪv/, **abrasives. 1** Someone who is **abrasive** is unkind and rude. EG *He could be abrasive and insensitive... ...an abrasive manner.* ADJ QUALIT

2 An **abrasive** substance is rough and can be used to clean hard surfaces. EG *...an abrasive cleaner.* ADJ CLASSIF

abreast /əbrɛst/. **1** If people or things walk or move **abreast**, they are next to each other, side by side. EG *...carts pulled by donkeys three abreast.* ADV

2 If you keep **abreast of** a subject, you know all the most recent facts about it. EG *The press kept abreast of each development.* PREP

abridged /əbrɪdʒd/. A book or play that is **abridged** has been made shorter by removing some parts of it. EG *...an abridged version of the novel.* ADJ CLASSIF

abroad /əbrɔːd/. **1** If you go **abroad**, you go to a foreign country. EG *...a holiday abroad... I just got back from abroad.* ADV

If someone told you something in absolute secrecy, would you tell other people?

2 If a story or feeling is **abroad**, people generally know about it or feel it. ADV

abrupt /əbrʌpt/. 1 If an action is **abrupt**, it is very sudden and often unpleasant. EG *It came to an abrupt end... ...an abrupt movement.* ◊ **abruptly**. EG *I had to apply the brakes abruptly.* ADJ QUALIT ◊ ADV

2 Someone who is **abrupt** is rather rude and unfriendly. EG *...David's abrupt and bullying manner.* ◊ **abruptly**. EG *I wouldn't have spoken so abruptly if I'd realized you were ill.* ADJ QUALIT ◊ ADV

abscess /æbsɪ[2]s/, **abscesses.** An **abscess** is a painful swelling on your skin, containing pus. N COUNT

abscond /ə[3]bskɒnd/, **absconds, absconding, absconded.** 1 If someone **absconds** with something, they run away with it. EG *He absconded with everyone's wages.* V+*with* Formal

2 If someone **absconds** from somewhere such as a prison, they run away from it. V: OFT+*from*

absence /æbsəns/, **absences.** 1 Someone's **absence** from a place is the fact of their not being there. EG *They remained in their seats during my absence... ...frequent absences from school.* N UNCOUNT OR N COUNT: +SUPP

2 The **absence** of something is the fact that it is not there. EG *The absence of electricity made matters worse.* N SING+SUPP

absent /æbsə[2]nt/. 1 If someone or something is **absent** from a place or situation, they are not there. EG *You have been absent twenty minutes... ...something which is still absent from your work.* ADJ CLASSIF: OFT+*from*

2 If someone appears **absent,** they are not paying attention because they are thinking about something else. EG *...an absent stare.* ◊ **absently**. EG *'Did you?' Boylan said absently.* ADJ CLASSIF ◊ ADV

absentee /æbsə[2]ntiː/, **absentees.** An **absentee** is a person who should be in a particular place but who is not there. EG *...absentees from school.* N COUNT

absent-minded. Someone who is **absent-minded** often forgets things. ◊ **absent-mindedly**. EG *...if you absent-mindedly drop a diamond ring down the sink.* ADJ QUALIT ◊ ADV

absolute /æbsə[6]luːt/, **absolutes. 1 Absolute** means total and complete. EG *...the necessity for absolute secrecy.* ADJ CLASSIF: ATTRIB

2 You use **absolute** to emphasize something that you are saying. EG *The script is an absolute mess.* ADJ CLASSIF: ATTRIB

3 An **absolute** ruler has complete power and authority over his or her country. ADJ CLASSIF

4 **Absolute** rules and principles are believed to be true or right for all situations. ADJ CLASSIF: ATTRIB

5 An **absolute** is a rule or principle that is believed to be true or right in all situations. EG *...rigid absolutes, such as 'divorce is always wrong'.* N COUNT

absolutely /æbsə[6]luːtli[1]/. 1 **Absolutely** means totally and completely. EG *That's an absolutely fascinating piece of work.* ADV OR SUBMOD

2 You say **absolutely** as an emphatic way of saying yes or agreeing with someone. EG *'She's excellent though.' – 'Absolutely.'* CONVENTION

absolution /æbsə[6]luːʃə[0]n/. If someone is given **absolution**, they are forgiven for something wrong that they have done. N UNCOUNT OR N COUNT Formal

absolve /ə[3]bzɒlv/, **absolves, absolving, absolved.** If someone **is absolved** from blame or responsibility, a formal statement is made that they are not guilty or are not to blame. EG *The captain is absolved from all blame and responsibility for the shipwreck... Before you die you're absolved of your sins.* V+O: USU PASS +*from/of*

absorb /ə[3]bsɔːb, -zɔːb/, **absorbs, absorbing, absorbed.** 1 If something **absorbs** a liquid, gas, light, or heat, it soaks it up or takes it in. EG *Frogs absorb water through their skins.* V+O

2 If a group **is absorbed** into a larger group, it becomes part of the larger group and loses its individuality. EG *Small businesses are absorbed by larger ones.* V+O: OFT+*into*

3 If a system or society **absorbs** changes or effects, it is able to deal with them without being badly affected. V+O

4 If you **absorb** information, you learn and understand it. V+O

5 If something **absorbs** you, it interests you very much and you pay a lot of attention to it. ◊ **absorbed**. EG *I was utterly absorbed in what I was doing.* ◊ **absorbing**. EG *The work is absorbing.* V+O ◊ ADJ QUALIT ◊ ADJ QUALIT

absorbent /ə[3]bsɔːbənt, -zɔː-/. **Absorbent** material soaks up liquid easily. ADJ QUALIT

absorption /ə[3]bsɔːpʃə[0]n, -zɔːp-/. 1 If you have an **absorption** in something, you are very interested in it. EG *...her growing absorption in the study of natural history.* N SING+SUPP

2 **Absorption** is the action of absorbing something. EG *...the absorption of foreign minorities.* N UNCOUNT +SUPP

abstain /ə[3]bsteɪn/, **abstains, abstaining, abstained.** 1 If you **abstain** from doing something enjoyable, you deliberately do not do it. EG *He abstained from eating for six days.* V: OFT+*from*

2 If you **abstain** during a vote, you do not vote. V

abstemious /ə[3]bstiːmɪəs/. Someone who is **abstemious** avoids doing too much of something enjoyable such as eating or drinking. ADJ QUALIT Formal

abstention /ə[3]bstenʃə[0]n/, **abstentions.** An **abstention** is a formal act of not voting either for or against a proposal. EG *There were 4 abstentions.* N COUNT OR N UNCOUNT

abstinence /æbstɪ[1]nəns/ is the practice of abstaining from something that you enjoy doing, especially from drinking alcoholic drinks. EG *He practised total abstinence for a month.* N UNCOUNT

abstract, abstracts, abstracting, abstracted; pronounced /æbstrækt/ when it is an adjective or a noun, and /ə[3]bstrækt/ when it is a verb.

1 An idea or argument that is **abstract** is based on general ideas rather than on particular things and events. EG *...our capacity for abstract reasoning... ...an abstract principle.* ADJ QUALIT

2 **Abstract** art is a style of art which uses shapes and patterns rather than representing people or things. EG *...abstract sculptures.* ADJ CLASSIF: ATTRIB

3 An **abstract** noun is a noun that describes a quality or idea rather than a physical object. ADJ CLASSIF: ATTRIB

4 An **abstract** of an article or speech is a short piece of writing that summarizes the main points of it. N COUNT

5 If you **abstract** information from an article or other piece of writing, you make a summary of the main points in it. V+O

abstracted /ə[3]bstræktɪ[2]d/. Someone whose behaviour is **abstracted** is thinking so deeply that they do not notice what is happening around them. EG *...a dreamy, abstracted stare.* ADJ QUALIT

abstraction /ə[3]bstrækʃə[0]n/, **abstractions.** 1 An **abstraction** is a general idea rather than one relating to a particular object, person, or situation. EG *...abstractions of philosophy and religion.* N COUNT

2 **Abstraction** is the state of being very deep in thought. N UNCOUNT

absurd /ə[3]bsɜːd/. Something that is **absurd** is ridiculous. EG *It seemed absurd to try to carry a twenty-five-pound camera about.* ◊ **absurdity** /ə[3]bsɜːdɪ[1]ti[1]/, **absurdities**. EG *...the oddities and absurdities of the language.* ◊ **absurdly**. EG *...an absurdly low rent.* ADJ QUALIT ◊ N COUNT OR N UNCOUNT ◊ ADV OR SUBMOD

abundance /əbʌndəns/. 1 An **abundance** of something is a large quantity of it. EG *...an abundance of evidence.* N PART: SING

2 If something is **in abundance**, there is a lot of it. EG *There was grass in abundance.* PHRASE

abundant /əbʌndə[2]nt/. Something that is **abundant** is present in large quantities. EG *...an abundant supply of food.* ADJ QUALIT

abundantly /əbʌndə[2]ntli[1]/. 1 If something is **abundantly** obvious, it is extremely obvious. EG *It has become abundantly clear that there is no time to lose.* SUBMOD

2 Something that occurs **abundantly** is present in large quantities. EG *...a plant growing abundantly at the edges of a road.* ADV

abuse, abuses, abusing, abused; pronounced /ə[3]bju:s/ when it is a noun and /ə[3]bju:z/ when it is a verb.

1 Abuse is rude and unkind things that people say when they are angry. EG *The girls shrieked abuse at the lawyers.* N UNCOUNT

2 Abuse of someone is cruel and violent treatment of them. EG *...found guilty of gross neglect and abuse.* N UNCOUNT +SUPP

3 Abuse of something is the use of it in a wrong way or for a bad purpose. EG *...the uses and abuses of power... ...drug abuse.* N UNCOUNT OR N COUNT : +SUPP

4 If you **abuse** something, you use it in a wrong way or for a bad purpose. V+O

5 If someone **abuses** you, **5.1** they say rude or unkind things to you. EG *He did not like to hear Elaine abused or criticized.* **5.2** they treat you cruelly and violently. EG *The patients were often physically abused.* V+O

abusive /ə[3]bju:sɪv/. Someone who is **abusive** says or writes rude or unkind things. EG *...abusive language.* ADJ QUALIT

abysmal /əbɪzmə[0]l/ means very bad or poor in quality. EG *...abysmal wages... ...an abysmal failure.* ADJ QUALIT
◊ **abysmally**. EG *He failed abysmally.* ◊ ADV

abyss /ə[3]bɪs/, **abysses. 1** An **abyss** is a very deep hole in the ground. EG *We looked down into the abyss.* N COUNT

2 A very frightening or threatening situation can be referred to as an **abyss**. EG *The world was teetering on the edge of the abyss of World War III.* N COUNT+SUPP Literary

AC is used to refer to an electric current that continually changes direction as it flows. **AC** is an abbreviation for 'alternating current'.

academic /ækədɛmɪk/, **academics. 1 Academic** work is work which is done in schools, colleges, and universities. EG *...the academic system.* ADJ CLASSIF : ATTRIB
◊ **academically**. EG *...people who are well qualified academically.* ◊ ADV

2 Someone who is **academic** is good at studying. ADJ QUALIT

3 An **academic** is a member of a university or college who teaches or does research. N COUNT

4 You also use **academic** to say that you think a particular point has no real effect on or relevance to what is happening. EG *It was all academic, because there were never any profits to share out.* ADJ QUALIT

academy /ə[3]kædə[2]mi[1]/, **academies.** Some schools or colleges are called **academies**, especially ones that specialize in a particular subject. EG *...the Royal Academy of Dramatic Art.* N COUNT

accede /ə[3]ksi:d/, **accedes, acceding, acceded.** If you **accede** to someone's request or opinion, you allow it or agree with it. V : USU+*to* Formal

accelerate /ə[3]ksɛləreɪt/, **accelerates, accelerating, accelerated. 1** When a process or the rate of something **accelerates**, it gets faster and faster. EG *Inflation rates began to accelerate.* V-ERG
◊ **acceleration** /ə[3]ksɛləreɪʃə[0]n/. EG *...the acceleration of economic growth.* ◊ N UNCOUNT

2 When moving vehicles **accelerate,** they go faster and faster. ◊ **acceleration**. EG *The acceleration of this car is very impressive.* V ◊ N UNCOUNT

accelerator /ə[3]ksɛləreɪtə/, **accelerators.** The **accelerator** in a car or other vehicle is the pedal which you press with your foot in order to make the vehicle go faster. See picture at CAR. N COUNT

accent, accents, accenting, accented; pronounced /æksə[2]nt/ when it is a noun and /æksɛnt/ when it is a verb.

1 Someone who speaks with a particular **accent** pronounces the words of a language in a distinctive way that shows which country, region, or social class they come from. EG *She has a strong Irish accent.* N COUNT : USU+SUPP

2 An **accent** is also a short line or other mark which is written above certain letters in some languages and which affects the way those letters are pronounced. N COUNT

3 If you say that the **accent** is on a particular feature of something, you mean that this feature is especially important. EG *The accent is on presentation in this contest.* N SING

4 If you **accent** a word or a musical note, you emphasize it, for example by making it louder. V+O

accentuate /ə[3]ksɛntʃʊeɪt/, **accentuates, accentuating, accentuated.** To **accentuate** something means to emphasize it or make it more noticeable. EG *These laws accentuate inequality and exploitation.* V+O

accept /ə[3]ksɛpt/, **accepts, accepting, accepted.**

1 If you **accept** something that you have been offered, you say yes to it or agree to take it. EG *He accepted our invitation... Her article has been accepted for publication.* V+O OR V

2 If you **accept** someone's advice or suggestion, you agree to do what they say. EG *I knew that they would accept my proposal.* V+O

3 If you **accept** a story or statement, you believe it. EG *The panel accepted her version of the story... The majority do not accept that there has been any discrimination.* V+O; ALSO V+REPORT : ONLY *that*

4 If you **accept** a difficult or unpleasant situation, you get used to it and recognize that it cannot be changed. EG *...unwillingness to accept bad working conditions... The astronaut accepts danger as being part of the job.* V+O

5 If you **accept** the blame or responsibility for something, you admit that you are responsible for it. V+O

6 When an institution or organization **accepts** someone, they give them a job or allow them to join. EG *I was accepted by the Open University.* V+O

7 If a group **accepts** you, they begin to think of you as part of the group. EG *The children gradually begin to accept her.* V+O

8 If a machine **accepts** a particular kind of thing, it is designed to take it and deal with it. EG *The ticket machine won't accept 20p pieces.* V+O

9 See also **accepted**.

acceptable /ə[3]ksɛptəbə[0]l/. **1** If something is **acceptable**, people generally approve of it or allow it to happen. EG *In war killing is acceptable.* ADJ QUALIT
◊ **acceptability** /əksɛptə[1]bɪlɪ[1]ti[1]/. EG *The proof of a doctrine is its acceptability to the man in the street.* ◊ **acceptably**. EG *...an acceptably low heat loss.* ◊ N UNCOUNT ◊ ADV

2 If you think that something is **acceptable**, you consider it to be good enough. EG *To my relief he found the article acceptable.* ADJ CLASSIF

acceptance /ə[3]ksɛptəns/, **acceptances. 1 Acceptance** of something that you have been offered is the act of taking it or agreeing to use it. EG *...the acceptance of foreign aid.* N UNCOUNT

2 If you receive an **acceptance** for a job or membership that you have applied for, you are offered the job or membership. EG *Within two days I had a letter of acceptance from the manager.* N COUNT OR N UNCOUNT

3 Acceptance of someone into a group is the act of beginning to think of them as part of the group, treating them in the same way as other members of it. N UNCOUNT

4 Acceptance of an idea is a general belief or agreement that it is true. EG *...their acceptance of his right to rule.* N UNCOUNT

5 Your **acceptance** of an unpleasant or difficult situation is your getting used to it and recognizing that you cannot change it. EG *...their acceptance of their plight.* N UNCOUNT

accepted /ə[3]ksɛptɪ[2]d/. **Accepted** ideas are generally agreed to be correct. EG *...the accepted wisdom about old age.* ADJ CLASSIF : ATTRIB

access /æksɛs/, **accesses, accessing, accessed.**

1 If you gain **access** to a building or other place, N UNCOUNT :

Do you think you are academic?

you succeed in getting into it. EG *The entrance door gives access to a living room.* OFT+to Formal

2 Access is also the opportunity or right to use or see something or someone. EG *I demanded access to a telephone... Has Donald got access to the child?* N UNCOUNT: OFT+to

3 If you **access** information from a computer, you get it. V+O

accessible /ə[3]ksɛsə[1]bə[0]l/. **1** If a place is **accessible**, you are able to reach it. EG *The hidden room was accessible only through a secret back entrance.* ◊ **accessibility** /əksɛsə[1]bɪlɪ[1]ti[1]/. EG *The site was picked because of its accessibility by rail.* ADJ QUALIT ◊ N UNCOUNT

2 If something is **accessible** to people, they are able to use it or buy it. EG *...computers cheap enough to be accessible to virtually everyone.* ADJ PRED+to

3 If a book, painting, or other work of art is **accessible** to people, they are able to understand it and appreciate it. ADJ PRED

accession /ə[3]ksɛʃə[0]n/ is the act of taking up a position as the ruler of a country. EG *...Queen Victoria's accession in 1837.* N UNCOUNT

accessory /ə[3]ksɛsəri[1]/, **accessories. 1 Accessories** are **1.1** extra parts added to a machine or tool in order to make it more efficient or able to perform extra jobs. EG *The car has an attractive range of extra accessories such as built-in tape decks and radios.* **1.2** articles, such as belts and handbags, which you wear or carry but which are not part of your main clothing. EG *...a grey silk suit and accessories to match.* N COUNT: USU PLURAL

2 A person who is an **accessory** to a crime knows that someone has committed the crime but does not tell the police. EG *They are all accessories to murder.* N COUNT Legal

accident /æksɪdə[2]nt/, **accidents. 1** An **accident** is **1.1** an event which happens completely by chance. EG *The fact that there is a university here is due to a historic accident.* **1.2** something unpleasant and unfortunate that happens and that often leads to injury or death. EG *He had an accident on his way home... She was killed in a motor accident.* N COUNT

2 If something happens **by accident**, it happens completely by chance. EG *I only came to Liverpool by accident.* PHRASE

accidental /æksɪdɛntə[0]l/. Something that is **accidental** happens by chance. EG *The evidence doesn't suggest accidental death.* ◊ **accidentally**. EG *We accidentally found an ideal solution.* ADJ CLASSIF ◊ ADV

accident-prone. Someone who is **accident-prone** keeps having accidents. ADJ QUALIT

acclaim /əkleɪm/, **acclaims, acclaiming, acclaimed. 1** If someone or something **is acclaimed**, they are praised enthusiastically. EG *He has been widely acclaimed for his paintings.* V+O: USU PASS Formal

2 Acclaim is praise for someone or something. EG *His book was published in 1919 and met with unusual acclaim.* N UNCOUNT Formal

acclimatize /əklaɪmətaɪz/, **acclimatizes, acclimatizing, acclimatized;** also spelled **acclimatise.** When you **acclimatize** to something or **acclimatize** yourself to it, you become used to it. EG *Once you've acclimatized to the heat you won't feel so tired.* V OR V-REFL

accolade /ækə[6]leɪd/, **accolades.** An **accolade** is praise or an award that is given publicly to someone who is greatly admired. EG *This was the highest accolade he could receive.* N COUNT+SUPP Formal

accommodate /əkɒmədeɪt/, **accommodates, accommodating, accommodated. 1** If you **accommodate** someone, **1.1** you provide them with a place where they can stay, live, or work. EG *She can't accommodate guests at the moment.* V+O: USU+A **1.2** you do something to help them. EG *The bank is accommodating its customers more than it used to.* V+O

2 If a place or building can **accommodate** a number of people or things, it has enough room for them. EG *The cottage could accommodate up to five people.* V+O

accommodating /əkɒmədeɪtɪŋ/. Someone who is **accommodating** is very willing to help you. EG *The warder was always accommodating in allowing visitors in.* ADJ QUALIT

accommodation /əkɒmədeɪʃə[0]n/ is a room or building to stay in, work in, or live in. EG *There is a shortage of accommodation.* N UNCOUNT

accompaniment /əkʌmpə[0]nɪmə[2]nt/, **accompaniments. 1** The **accompaniment** to a song or tune is the music that is played at the same time and that forms a background to it. EG *...a guitar accompaniment.* N UNCOUNT: USU+SUPP

2 An **accompaniment** to something is something else that happens or exists at the same time. EG *This sauce is often served as an accompaniment to fish.* N COUNT: OFT+to/of

accompanist /əkʌmpə[0]nɪst/, **accompanists.** An **accompanist** is a musician, especially a pianist, who plays one part of a piece of music while someone else sings or plays the main tune. N COUNT+SUPP

accompany /əkʌmpə[0]ni[1]/, **accompanies, accompanying, accompanied. 1** If you **accompany** someone, you go somewhere with them. EG *She asked me to accompany her to the church.* V+O: USU+A

2 If something **accompanies** something else, it happens or exists at the same time or as a result of it. EG *A high fever often accompanies a mild infection.* V+O

3 When you **accompany** a singer or a musician, you play one part of a piece of music while they sing or play the main tune. EG *Sarah sings and Bill accompanies her on the guitar.* V+O OR V-REFL

accomplice /əkɒmplɪs, əkʌm-/, **accomplices.** Someone's **accomplice** is a person who helps them to commit a crime. N COUNT

accomplish /əkɒmplɪʃ, əkʌm-/, **accomplishes, accomplishing, accomplished.** If you **accomplish** something, you succeed in doing it. EG *I never seem to accomplish anything.* V+O

accomplished /əkɒmplɪʃt, əkʌm-/. If someone is **accomplished** at something, they are very good at it. EG *...an accomplished cook.* ADJ QUALIT

accomplishment /əkɒmplɪʃmə[2]nt, əkʌm-/, **accomplishments. 1** A person of **accomplishment** has knowledge or skill to be able to do something well. EG *...actors of similar experience and accomplishment.* N UNCOUNT

2 The **accomplishment** of something is the fact of achieving or finishing it. EG *The accomplishment of this task filled him with satisfaction.* N UNCOUNT +SUPP

3 Your **accomplishments** are the things that you can do well. EG *One of her few accomplishments was the ability to do cartwheels.* N COUNT

4 An **accomplishment** is something remarkable that has been done or achieved. EG *This is no small accomplishment.* N COUNT+SUPP

accord /ə[3]kɔːd/, **accords, according, accorded. 1** When you do something **of** your **own accord**, you do it freely and because you want to. EG *She knew they would leave of their own accord.* PHRASE

2 If people are in **accord**, they agree about something. EG *There are few issues on which the two are in perfect accord.* N UNCOUNT

3 If you **accord** someone a particular kind of treatment, you treat them in that way. EG *Newsmen accorded her the kind of coverage normally reserved for film stars.* V+O+O OR V+O+to

4 If an idea, policy, or situation **accords** with something else, it fits in with it. EG *I rewrote the article because it didn't accord with our policy.* V+with Formal

accordance /ə[3]kɔːdəns/. If something is done **in accordance with** a particular rule or system, it is done in the way that the rule or system says that it should be done. EG *...in accordance with Islamic law.* PREP

accordingly /ə[3]kɔːdɪŋli[1]/. You use **accordingly** when you are saying that something happened as the result of something else. EG *Sometimes the press went too far, and suffered accordingly.* ADV

according to. 1 If you say that something is true **according to** a particular person, book, or document, you mean that you got the information from that person, book, or document. EG *According to Dr Santos, the cause of death was drowning... The road was some forty miles long according to my map.* — PREP

2 If something is done **according to** a particular principle or condition, this principle or condition is used as the basis for the way it has been done. EG *Each person was given tasks according to their skills... There are six classes organized according to age.* — PREP

3 If something happens **according to** a particular plan or system, it happens in the way that the plan or system says that it should be done. EG *Everything went according to plan.* — PREP

accordion /ə3kɔ:dɪən/, **accordions.** An **accordion** is a box-shaped musical instrument. You play it by pressing keys or buttons on either side while moving the two sides together and apart. — N COUNT

accost /əkɒst/, **accosts, accosting, accosted.** If you **accost** someone, especially a stranger, you stop them or go up to them and speak to them. EG *In the hall he was accosted by two men.* — V+O

account /əkaʊnt/, **accounts, accounting, accounted.** 1 An **account** is a written or spoken report of something that has happened. EG *There were accounts of the incident in the paper.* — N COUNT: OFT+*of*

2 **Accounts** are detailed records of all the money that a person or business receives and spends. EG *He had to submit accounts of his expenditure.* — N COUNT: USU PLURAL

3 If you have an **account** with a bank, you leave money with it and withdraw it when you need it. EG *I would like to open an account.* — N COUNT

4 If you have an **account** with a shop or company, you can get goods or services from the shop or company and pay for them at a later date, usually once a month. — N COUNT

5 **Account** is also used in these phrases. **5.1** If you **take** something **into account** or **take account of** it, you include it when you are thinking about a situation. EG *We'll certainly take your feelings into account.* **5.2** If you do something **on account of** something or someone, you do it because of that thing or person. EG *'Auntie told me not to run,' he explained, 'on account of my asthma.'... Don't abstain from smoking on my account.* **5.3** If you say that something should **on no account** be done, you mean that it should not be done under any circumstances. EG *On no account must strangers be let in.* **5.4** If something is **of no account**, it does not matter at all. EG *It's of no account to me whether you go or stay.* **5.5** If you **give a good account of** yourself, you behave in a way which brings you praise and respect from other people. EG *Your son gave a very good account of himself last night.* — PHRASES

account for. 1 If you **account for** something that has happened, you explain how it happened. EG *How do you account for the dent in the car?* — PHRASAL VB: V+PREP. 2 If something **accounts for** a part or proportion of something, it is what that part or proportion consists of. EG *Computer software accounts for some 70 per cent of our range of products.* — V+PREP

accountable /əkaʊntəbə0l/. If you are **accountable** to someone for something that you do, you are responsible for it and must be prepared to justify your actions to that person. EG *They cannot be held accountable for what they did... ...a public corporation fully accountable to Parliament.* — ADJ PRED
◊ **accountability**. EG *...the need for greater accountability of the police.* — ◊ N UNCOUNT

accountancy /əkaʊntənsi1/ is the work of keeping financial accounts. EG *...a career in accountancy.* — N UNCOUNT

accountant /əkaʊntənt/, **accountants.** An **accountant** is a person whose job is to keep financial accounts. — N COUNT

accredit /ə3krɛdɪt/, **accredits, accrediting, accredited.** If someone **is accredited** in a particular position or job, it is officially recognized that they have that position or job. EG *...an accredited shop steward.* — V+O: USU PASS

accumulate /ə3kju:mjə4leɪt/, **accumulates, accumulating, accumulated.** When you **accumulate** things or when they **accumulate**, they collect or gather over a period of time. EG *...the things I had accumulated over the last four years.* — V-ERG

accumulation /ə3kju:mjə4leɪʃə0n/, **accumulations.** 1 An **accumulation** is a large number of things which have been gathered together over a period of time. EG *...an accumulation of facts.* — N COUNT+SUPP

2 **Accumulation** is the collecting together of things over a period of time. EG *...the accumulation of wealth.* — N UNCOUNT +SUPP

accuracy /ækjə4rəsi1/ is 1 the ability to perform a task without making a mistake. EG *...the speed and accuracy with which she typed.* 2 the quality of being true or correct. EG *...the reputation of The Times for accuracy.* — N UNCOUNT

accurate /ækjə4rə1t/. 1 An account or description that is **accurate** gives a true idea of what someone or something is like. EG *...an accurate picture of social history.* — ADJ QUALIT
◊ **accurately**. EG *The story is accurately told.* — ◊ ADV

2 A person, device, or machine that is **accurate** is able to perform a task precisely and without making a mistake. EG *Missiles are becoming more accurate... She is accurate in punctuation and spelling.* — ADJ QUALIT
◊ **accurately**. EG *I have not drawn it accurately enough.* — ◊ ADV

accusation /ækjə4zeɪʃə0n/, **accusations.** 1 An **accusation** is a statement that someone has done something wrong or has committed a crime. EG *...accusations of cheating... He should defend himself against false accusations.* — N COUNT

2 **Accusation** is the quality of showing by your voice or behaviour that you think that someone has done something wrong. EG *Her eyes were full of accusation.* — N UNCOUNT

accuse /ə3kju:z/, **accuses, accusing, accused.** 1 If you **accuse** someone of something, you say that they have done something wrong. EG *He was accused of incompetence.* — V+O: OFT+*of*

2 If someone **is accused** of a crime, they have been charged with the crime and are on trial for it. EG *He is accused of killing ten young women.* — V+O: USU PASS+*of*

accused /ə3kju:zd/. **Accused** is both the singular and the plural.
The **accused** refers to the person or group of people being tried in a court for a crime. EG *Will the accused please stand.* — N COUNT: *the*+N

accusing /ə3kju:zɪŋ/. If your expression or tone of voice is **accusing**, it indicates that you think that someone has done something wrong. EG *She gave him an accusing look.* — ADJ QUALIT
◊ **accusingly**. EG *'You liked him,' he said accusingly.* — ◊ ADV

accustom /ə3kʌstəm/, **accustoms, accustoming, accustomed.** If you **accustom** yourself or someone else to something different, you make yourself or them used to it. EG *He sat very still, trying to accustom himself to the darkness.* — V-REFL+*to* OR V+O+*to*

accustomed /ə3kʌstəmd/. 1 If you are **accustomed** to something, you are used to it or familiar with it. EG *I am not accustomed to being interrupted... My eyes became accustomed to the dim lighting.* — ADJ PRED+*to*

2 **Accustomed** means usual. EG *He drove with his accustomed, casual ease.* — ADJ CLASSIF: ATTRIB

ace /eɪs/, **aces.** 1 An **ace** is a playing card which has a single symbol on it. EG *...the ace of spades.* — N COUNT

2 A person who is **ace** at something is extremely good at it. EG *...an ace marksman.* — ADJ CLASSIF Informal

ache /eɪk/, **aches, aching, ached.** 1 If you **ache** or if a part of your body **aches**, you feel a dull — V

Does an accountant have to be accurate?

steady pain. EG *I was tired, aching, and miserable... His leg ached.*

2 If you **ache** for something or **ache** to do something, you want it very much. EG *She was aching for a cigarette... I was aching to tell you all my news.* V+*for/with* OR *to*-INF

3 An **ache** is a dull steady pain in a part of your body. EG *...my usual aches and pains.* N COUNT

achieve /ə[3]tʃiːv/, **achieves, achieving, achieved.** If you **achieve** a particular aim or effect, you succeed in doing it or causing it to happen, usually after a lot of effort. EG *He will do anything in order to achieve his aim... The riots achieved nothing.* V+O

achievement /ə[3]tʃiːvmə[2]nt/, **achievements. 1** An **achievement** is something which someone has succeeded in doing, especially after a lot of effort. EG *It was an astonishing achievement.* N COUNT+SUPP

2 Achievement is the process of achieving something. EG *This fact did not lessen her sense of achievement.* N UNCOUNT

acid /æsɪd/, **acids. 1** An **acid** is a liquid with a pH value of less than 7. Strong acids can burn your skin and make holes in your clothes. N MASS

2 An **acid** substance or liquid has a pH value of less than 7. EG *...an acid soil.* ◇ **acidity** /ə[3]sɪdɪ[1]ti[1]/. EG *...the acidity of the wine.* ADJ CLASSIF ◇ N UNCOUNT

3 An **acid** fruit or drink has a sour or sharp taste. EG *These oranges are very acid.* ADJ QUALIT

4 An **acid** remark is very unkind or critical. EG *...her acid wit.* ◇ **acidity**. EG *I noticed a certain acidity in his comments.* ADJ QUALIT ◇ N UNCOUNT

5 If you say that something is **an acid test**, you mean that it is a way of proving whether something is true or not, or of good quality or not. EG *This venture is seen as an acid test of the alliance.* PHRASE

6 Acid is also the drug LSD. EG *One speaker was high on acid.* N UNCOUNT Informal

acidic /ə[3]sɪdɪk/. Something that is **acidic** contains acid or has a pH value of less than 7. ADJ CLASSIF

acknowledge /ə[3]knɒlɪdʒ/, **acknowledges, acknowledging, acknowledged. 1** If you **acknowledge** a fact or a situation, you accept or admit that it is true or that it exists. EG *Most people will now acknowledge that there is a crisis... He was acknowledged as America's finest writer.* V+O; ALSO V+REPORT: ONLY *that*

2 If you **acknowledge** someone, for example with a nod or a smile, you show that you have seen and recognized them. V+O: OFT+*with*

3 If you **acknowledge** a message, letter, or parcel, you tell the person who sent it that you have received it. EG *You have to sign here and acknowledge receipt.* V+O; ALSO V+REPORT: ONLY *that*

4 If you **acknowledge** applause, compliments, or something which is done for you, you show your appreciation. EG *The president stood up to acknowledge the cheers of the crowd.* V+O

acknowledgement /ə[3]knɒlɪdʒmə[2]nt/, **acknowledgements;** also spelled **acknowledgment. 1 Acknowledgement** of something is **1.1** accepting or admitting that it is true. EG *...his acknowledgement of his guilt.* **1.2** expressing your gratitude for it or appreciation of it. EG *...her acknowledgement of their offerings.* N UNCOUNT OR N COUNT: USU+SUPP

2 Acknowledgement of someone is showing that you have seen and recognized them. EG *One of the men raised an arm in acknowledgment.* N UNCOUNT

3 Acknowledgement of a message, letter, or parcel is telling the sender that you have received it. EG *...in acknowledgement of telephone orders.* N UNCOUNT: OFT+*of*

4 An **acknowledgement** is a letter or message telling the sender of a letter, message, or parcel that it has arrived. N COUNT

5 The **acknowledgements** at the beginning or end of a book are the short piece of writing in which the author thanks all the people who have helped him or her. N PLURAL

acne /ækni[1]/. If someone has **acne**, they have a lot of spots on their face and neck. Acne is common among teenagers. N UNCOUNT

acorn /eɪkɔːn/, **acorns.** An **acorn** is a pale oval nut that is the fruit of an oak tree. N COUNT

acoustic /əkuːstɪk/, **acoustics. 1 Acoustic** means relating to sound or hearing. EG *Acoustic contact had been made.* ADJ CLASSIF: ATTRIB

2 The **acoustics** of a room are the structural features which determine how well you can hear music or speeches in it. EG *The theatre was large, with good acoustics.* N PLURAL

acquaint /əkweɪnt/, **acquaints, acquainting, acquainted.** If you **acquaint** someone with something, you tell them about it or make them familiar with it. EG *I will acquaint you with the facts... They were well acquainted with modern farming methods.* V+O+*with* Formal

acquaintance /əkweɪntəns/, **acquaintances. 1** An **acquaintance** is someone who you have met but do not know well. EG *My cousin is an acquaintance of Lord Northcliffe.* N COUNT: USU+SUPP

2 If someone is **of** your **acquaintance,** you know them slightly, but not well. EG *...doctors of my acquaintance.* PHRASE

3 When you **make** someone's **acquaintance,** you meet them for the first time and get to know them a little. PHRASE

4 Your **acquaintance** with a subject is your knowledge or experience of it. EG *...her acquaintance with modern art.* N SING+SUPP

5 If you have a **nodding** or **passing acquaintance** with someone, you know them slightly but not very well. PHRASE

acquainted /əkweɪntɪ[2]d/. If you are **acquainted** with someone, you know them slightly but they are not a close friend. EG *Mrs Oliver is acquainted with my mother... The families were acquainted.* ADJ PRED: OFT+*with*

acquiesce /ækwiɛs/, **acquiesces, acquiescing, acquiesced.** If you **acquiesce** to something, you agree to do what someone wants or to accept what they do. EG *He acquiesced to the demand.* V: OFT+*to/in* Formal

◇ **acquiescence** /ækwi[1]ɛsə[0]ns/. EG *...passive acquiescence to the new arrangements.* ◇ N UNCOUNT: OFT+*to/in*

acquire /ə[3]kwaɪə/, **acquires, acquiring, acquired. 1** If you **acquire** something, you get it or buy it for yourself, or you are given it. EG *I tried to acquire the information I needed.* ◇ **acquired**. EG *...acquired wealth.* V+O ◇ ADJ CLASSIF

2 If you **acquire** a skill or habit, you learn it or develop it as you live your daily life or grow up. EG *It is a habit well worth acquiring.* ◇ **acquired**. EG *...hereditary and acquired characteristics.* V+O ◇ ADJ CLASSIF

acquisition /ækwɪ[1]zɪʃə[0]n/, **acquisitions. 1** An **acquisition** is something that you have obtained. EG *He invited me to inspect his latest acquisition.* N COUNT

2 Acquisition of something is getting it or being given it. EG *...the acquisition of land.* N UNCOUNT +SUPP

3 The **acquisition** of a skill or habit is the process of learning it or developing it. EG *...the acquisition of knowledge.* N UNCOUNT +SUPP

acquit /əkwɪt/, **acquits, acquitting, acquitted. 1** If someone **is acquitted** of a crime in a court of law, it is formally declared that they did not commit the crime. EG *The jury acquitted her of theft... Campbell was acquitted on all charges.* V+O: USU PASS

2 If you **acquit** yourself in a particular way, other people feel that you behave in that way. EG *She acquitted herself well.* V-REFL Formal

acquittal /əkwɪtə[0]l/, **acquittals. Acquittal** is a formal declaration in a court of law that someone who has been accused of a crime is innocent. N UNCOUNT OR N COUNT

acre /eɪkə/, **acres.** An **acre** is an area of land measuring 4840 square yards or 4047 square metres. EG *...an acre of orchard.* N PART

acrid /ækrɪd/. **1** An **acrid** smell or taste is strong and sharp, and usually unpleasant. EG *The room was filling with acrid smoke.* ADJ QUALIT

2 Acrid words or remarks are bitter and angry. EG *...an acrid attack on capitalism.* ADJ QUALIT

acrimonious /ækrɪ[1]məʊnɪəs/. **Acrimonious** words or quarrels are bitter and angry. EG *An acrimonious dispute broke out.* ADJ QUALIT Formal

acrimony /ækrɪ[1]məni[1]/ is bitterness and anger about something. EG *...acrimony over the involvement of the police.* N UNCOUNT Formal

acrobat /ækrə[6]bæt/, **acrobats.** An **acrobat** is an entertainer who performs difficult jumps, somersaults, and balancing acts. N COUNT

acrobatic /ækrə[6]bætɪk/, **acrobatics. 1** An **acrobatic** movement or display involves difficult jumps, somersaults, and balancing acts. ADJ QUALIT

2 Acrobatics are acrobatic movements. EG *He can do the most amazing acrobatics.* N PLURAL

acronym /ækrə[6]nɪm/, **acronyms.** An **acronym** is a word composed of the initial letters of the words in a phrase, especially when this is the name of something. An example of an acronym is AIDS. N COUNT

across /əkrɒs/. **1** If you go or look **across** a room or other place, you go or look from one side of it to the other. EG *We ran across the bridge... He turned his head and looked across at me... He wandered across Hyde Park.* PREP, OR ADV AFTER VB

2 Something that is situated or stretched **across** something else is situated or stretched from one side of it to the other. EG *...a banner stretched across the street... A straight line was ruled across the map.* PREP

3 Something that is situated **across** a street or river is on the other side of it. EG *He stared at the houses across the street.* PREP

4 Across is used to show the width of something. EG *The bomb blasted a hole 200 kilometres across.* ADV

acrylic /əkrɪlɪk/. **Acrylic** material is man-made, manufactured by a chemical process. EG *...acrylic blankets.* ADJ CLASSIF : ATTRIB

act /ækt/, **acts, acting, acted. 1** When you **act**, you do something for a particular purpose. EG *We have to act quickly... He acted alone in the shooting.* V : USU+A

2 If someone **acts** in a particular way, they behave in that way. EG *We acted as if we had never seen each other before... You're acting like a lunatic.* V+A

3 If one thing **acts** as another, it functions as that other thing. EG *The shark can twist its fins to act as brakes.* V+*as/like*

4 If you **act**, or **act** a part, in a play or film, you have a part in it. V OR V+O

5 An **act** is a single thing that someone does. EG *...an act of aggression... Sometimes the act of writing down the problems straightens out your thinking.* N COUNT+SUPP

6 If you say that someone's behaviour is an **act**, you mean that it does not express their real feelings. EG *She appeared calm and confident but it was just an act.* N SING

7 An **Act** is a law passed by the government. EG *...the 1944 Education Act.* N COUNT

8 An **act** in a play, opera, or ballet is one of the main parts into which it is divided. N COUNT

9 An **act** in a show is a short performance which is one of several in the show. EG *...comedy acts.* N COUNT

10 If you are **in the act of** doing something, you are doing it. EG *He saw Jones in the act of snatching a gun.* PHRASE

act up. 1 If something **is acting up**, it is not working properly. EG *Her car has started acting up again.* PHRASAL VB : V+ADV **2** If a child **is acting up**, he or she is behaving badly. V+ADV

acting /æktɪŋ/. **1 Acting** is the activity or profession of performing in plays or films. EG *...the brilliant acting of Hawtrey.* N UNCOUNT

2 You use **acting** before the title of a job to indicate that someone is only doing that job temporarily. EG *...Yassin, acting Director of Education.* ADJ CLASSIF : ATTRIB

action /ækʃə[0]n/, **actions. 1 Action** is doing something for a particular purpose. EG *The government was already taking action.* N UNCOUNT

2 An **action** is something that you do on a particular occasion. EG *Surely resigning was rather a rash action?* N COUNT

3 The **action** is all the important and exciting things that are happening in a situation. EG *They want to be where the action is... The whole action of the book takes place in one day.* N SING

4 Action is also fighting which takes place in a war. EG *...reports of military action... Henry had been killed in action.* N UNCOUNT

5 If you **put** an idea or policy **into action**, you begin to use it or cause it to operate. PHRASE

6 If something is **out of action**, it is damaged and cannot work or be used. EG *The trucks were out of action for three months.* PHRASE

activate /æktɪ[1]veɪt/, **activates, activating, activated.** To **activate** something means to cause it to start working. EG *...a device that activates a loud bell... The system is activated by computer.* V+O

active /æktɪv/. **1** An **active** person or animal is energetic and always busy or moving about. EG *...active and noisy children.* ADJ QUALIT

2 If someone is **active** in an organization or cause, they are involved in it and work for it. EG *He was active in drawing public attention to our problems.* ADJ QUALIT
◊ **actively.** EG *He had not actively participated in politics during his stay.* ◊ ADV

3 You use **active** to emphasize the energy or enthusiasm with which something is done. EG *The proposal is under active discussion.* ADJ CLASSIF : ATTRIB ◊ **actively.** EG *Such qualities were actively discouraged.* ◊ ADV

4 If a volcano is **active**, it has erupted quite recently or is expected to erupt quite soon. ADJ CLASSIF

activist /æktɪvɪst/, **activists.** An **activist** is a person who works to bring about political or social changes. EG *...a vigorous civil rights activist.* N COUNT

activity /æktɪvɪ[1]ti[1]/, **activities. 1 Activity** is a situation in which a lot of things are happening or being done. EG *There was a flurry of activity in the hall... ...periods of high economic activity.* N UNCOUNT

2 An **activity** is something that you spend time doing. EG *I find tennis a very enjoyable activity.* N COUNT

3 The **activities** of a group are the things that they do in order to achieve their aims. EG *...the activities of trade unions.* N PLURAL +SUPP

actor /æktə/, **actors.** An **actor** is someone whose job is acting in plays or films. 'Actor' in the singular usually refers to a man. EG *He was a fine actor.* N COUNT

actress /æktrɪ[2]s/, **actresses.** An **actress** is a woman whose job is acting in plays or films. N COUNT

actual /æktʃ[0]ʊəl/. **1** When you are emphasizing that a place, object, or person is real and not imaginary, you can say that it is an **actual** place, object, or person. EG *The predicted results and the actual results are very different.* ADJ CLASSIF : ATTRIB

2 When you want to emphasize that you are referring only to the specific thing mentioned and not to other things associated with it, you can talk about the **actual** thing. EG *The actual wedding procession starts at 10 a.m.* ADJ CLASSIF : ATTRIB

actuality /æktʃ[0]ʊælɪ[1]ti[1]/. When you want to emphasize that what you are saying is true, although it may be surprising, you can say that it is true **in actuality**. EG *The party in actuality contains only a small minority of extremists.* PHRASE

actually /æktʃ[0]ʊəli[1]/. **1** You use **actually** to indicate **1.1** that a situation exists in real life and not just in theory or in people's imaginations. EG *No one actually saw this shark.* **1.2** that you are giving correct or true details about a situation. EG *He actually died in exile, didn't he?* **1.3** that something is surprising or slightly shocking. EG *I was actually cruel sometimes.* ADV

2 You also use **actually** to introduce a new topic into a conversation. EG *Actually, Dan, before I forget, she asked me to give you this.* ADV SEN

Would an acting treasurer appear in a film or play?

3 You also use **actually** as a way of expressing things more politely **3.1** when you are stating an opinion. EG *I think that's pretty cheap actually.* **3.2** when you are correcting or contradicting someone. EG *I didn't mean it that way actually... Actually, it was more complicated than that.* **3.3** when you are giving instructions or advice. EG *Actually it might be a good idea to stop recording now.* ADV SEN

acumen /ækjʊmɛn/ is the ability to make good judgements and quick decisions. EG *...a man with big ideas and keen business acumen.* N UNCOUNT

acupuncture /ækjʊpʌŋktʃə/ is the treatment of a person's illness or pain by sticking small needles into their body. N UNCOUNT

acute /ə[3]kju:t/. **1** An **acute** situation, feeling, or illness is very severe or intense. EG *...acute staff shortages... ...acute anxiety... These problems have become more acute.* ADJ QUALIT

2 If your sight, hearing, or sense of smell is **acute**, it is sensitive and powerful. ADJ QUALIT

3 In geometry, an **acute** angle is less than 90°. ADJ CLASSIF

acutely /ə[3]kju:tli[1]/. **1** If you feel something **acutely**, you feel it very strongly. EG *They were acutely aware of the difficulties.* ADV

2 If a feeling or quality is **acutely** unpleasant, it is extremely unpleasant. EG *It was acutely embarrassing.* ADV

ad /æd/, **ads.** An **ad** is an advertisement. EG *...a newspaper ad.* N COUNT Informal

AD /eɪ di:/. You use **AD** in dates to indicate a number of years or centuries since the year in which Jesus Christ is believed to have been born. EG *...as early as AD 1200... ...2000 AD.*

adamant /ædəmənt/. If you are **adamant** about something, you are determined not to change your mind about it. EG *He is adamant that we must put less emphasis on nationalism.* ◊ **adamantly.** EG *He adamantly refused to be moved to a hospital.* ADJ CLASSIF ◊ ADV

Adam's apple /ædəmz æpə[0]l/, **Adam's apples.** Your **Adam's apple** is the lump that sticks out of the front of your neck below your throat. N COUNT

adapt /ə[3]dæpt/, **adapts, adapting, adapted. 1** If you **adapt** to a new situation or **adapt** yourself to it, you change your ideas or behaviour in order to deal with it successfully. EG *This book is about change and how we adapt to it... He cannot adapt himself to being free.* V OR V-REFL : OFT+*to*

2 If you **adapt** something, you change it to make it suitable for a new purpose or situation. EG *Reformers attempted to adapt traditional religion.* V+O : OFT+*to*

3 If you **adapt** a book or play, you change it so that it can be made into a film or a television programme. EG *Mortimer is adapting the novel for television.* V+O

4 See also **adapted**.

adaptable /ə[3]dæptəbə[0]l/. Someone who is **adaptable** is able to change their ideas or behaviour in order to deal with new situations. ◊ **adaptability** /ə[3]dæptəbɪlɪ[1]ti[1]/. EG *...adaptability to his environment.* ADJ QUALIT ◊ N UNCOUNT

adaptation /ædə[3]pteɪʃə[0]n/, **adaptations. 1** An **adaptation** of a story or novel is a play or film that is based on it. EG *...a new television adaptation of 'A Tale of Two Cities'.* N COUNT : OFT+*of*

2 **Adaptation** is the act of changing something to make it suitable for a new purpose or situation. EG *This windmill was designed for adaptation to different local requirements.* N UNCOUNT

adapted /ə[3]dæptɪ[2]d/. If something is **adapted** to a new situation or for a different purpose, it is especially suitable for it. EG *The cleaner is well adapted for use in the home and car.* ADJ PRED +*for/to*

adaptor /ə[3]dæptə/, **adaptors;** also spelled **adapter.** An **adaptor** is a device for connecting two or more electrical plugs to the same socket. N COUNT

add /æd/, **adds, adding, added. 1** If you **add** one thing to another, you put it in the same place as the other thing. EG *She added a tree to the picture.* V+O : OFT+*to*

2 If you **add** numbers or amounts together, you calculate their total. V+O OR V

3 If one thing **adds** to another, it makes the other thing greater in degree or amount. EG *He is given answers that only add to his confusion... This process can add £3 a barrel to the cost.* ◊ **added.** EG *There are added complications... This gave her an added charm.* V+*to* OR V+O+*to* ◊ ADJ CLASSIF : ATTRIB

4 If you **add** something when you are speaking, you say something more. EG *'Sorry,' he added... He added that the fee would be £100.* V-SPEECH

add up. 1 If you **add up** several numbers, you calculate their total. EG *What's the total when we add all the marks up?* **2** If facts or events **add up**, they make you realize or understand the true nature of the situation. EG *It all added up. I became aware that Halliday was the thief.* PHRASAL VB : V+O+ADV; V+ADV

add up to. If amounts **add up to** a particular total, they result in that total when they are put together. EG *This adds up to 75,000 miles of new streets.* PHRASAL VB : V+ADV+PREP

adder /ædə/, **adders.** An **adder** is a small poisonous snake. N COUNT

addict /ædɪkt/, **addicts.** An **addict** is **1** someone who takes harmful drugs and cannot stop taking them. **2** someone who is very fond of something or very interested in it. EG *He was a radio addict.* N COUNT; N COUNT+SUPP

addicted /ə[3]dɪktɪ[2]d/. **1** Someone who is **addicted** to a harmful drug cannot stop taking it. EG *He became addicted to drink.* ADJ PRED : OFT+*to*

2 If you are **addicted** to something, you like it very much and want it a lot. EG *He was addicted to chocolate.* ADJ PRED : OFT+*to*

addiction /ə[3]dɪkʃə[0]n/, **addictions. 1 Addiction** is the condition of taking harmful drugs and being unable to stop taking them. EG *...heroin addiction.* N UNCOUNT : OFT+*to*

2 An **addiction** to something is a very strong desire for it. EG *...an addiction to sweets.* N SING : OFT+*to*

addictive /ə[3]dɪktɪv/. If a drug is **addictive**, people who take it cannot stop taking it. ADJ QUALIT

addition /ə[3]dɪʃə[0]n/, **additions. 1** You use **in addition** when you want to add something to what you have already said. EG *In addition, there were meetings with trade unionists.* PHRASE

2 An **addition** to something is a thing which is added to it. EG *They can also award a weekly addition for extra heating.* N COUNT+SUPP

3 The **addition** of something is the fact that it is added as an extra. EG *These houses have been improved by the addition of bathrooms.* N UNCOUNT +SUPP

4 **Addition** is the process of calculating the total of two or more numbers. N UNCOUNT

additional /ə[3]dɪʃə[0]nəl, -ʃənə[0]l/. **Additional** things are extra things apart from the ones already present. EG *Additional troops were needed.* ADJ CLASSIF : OFT ATTRIB

additionally /ə[3]dɪʃə[0]nəli[1], -ʃənə[0]li[1]/. **1** You use **additionally** to introduce an extra fact. EG *Additionally, there was a substantial bill.* ADV SEN

2 If something happens **additionally**, it happens to a greater extent than before. EG *There was no point in additionally burdening her with this painful news.* ADV

additive /ædɪtɪv/, **additives.** An **additive** is a substance which is added to foods or other substances in order to improve them. N COUNT

address /ədrɛs/, **addresses, addressing, addressed. 1** Your **address** is the number of the house, the name of the street, and the town where you live or work. EG *The address is 70 Brompton Road, London SW1... He wrote down his name and address.* N COUNT : OFT+POSS

2 If a letter, envelope, or parcel **is addressed** to you, your name and address has been written on it. V+O : USU PASS

3 An **address** is also a formal speech. EG *He gave an address to the Psychological Association.* N COUNT

4 If you **address** a group of people, you give a speech to them. EG *He addressed a meeting in Bristol.* V+O

ADJECTIVES

An adjective (ADJ) tells you something about a noun – anything about it that is relevant. This includes its size, quality, colour, and type. For example, in the group of words *pretty blue dresses,* the word 'dresses' is a noun and 'pretty' and 'blue' are adjectives which tell you what kind of dresses they are.

There are two main things to notice about adjectives:

1 Their position
Most adjectives can have two positions in a clause. They can come before a noun, as in *the pretty blue dresses.* Or they can come after a verb such as **be, seem,** or **look,** as in *These dresses are expensive . . . She looks happy.*

A few adjectives occur in only one of these positions. Adjectives which only come before a noun are labelled ATTRIB (meaning 'attributive'), and adjectives which only come after a verb are labelled PRED (meaning 'predicative').

For example, 'classical', 'musical', and 'prospective' are examples of adjectives labelled ATTRIB, as in *Greek is a classical language . . . . . . a musical career . . . . . . 500 prospective students.*

On the other hand, 'alike', 'alive', and some meanings of 'dead' are examples of adjectives labelled PRED, as in *The twins are alike . . . My father is still alive . . . My foot has gone dead.*

2 Their meaning
There are two ways in which adjectives state the features that describe a noun. In some cases, it is possible to have more or less of the feature, and words such as **very** and **rather** are used to say how much. Adjectives of this kind are labelled QUALIT (meaning 'qualitative'). For example, *a very funny film . . . . . . a rather deep pool.*

Adjectives labelled QUALIT have comparative and superlative forms, which are formed either by adding the endings **-er** and **-est** to the word or by using **more** and **most** in front of it. Where an adjective has forms ending in **-er** and **-est,** these are given in the dictionary. For example, *small, smaller, smallest.*

If an adjective is labelled ADJ QUALIT, but no different forms are given, this means that you use **more** and **most.** For example, *important, more important, most important.* A few adjectives have forms which do not end in **-er** and **-est,** such as **good, better, best.** All three forms are given in the dictionary.

The second main way in which an adjective states a feature is to classify the noun as being of a particular type. Adjectives of this kind are labelled CLASSIF (meaning 'classifying'). For example, *. . . a French girl . . . . . . a wooden gate.*
Adjectives of this kind do not have comparative and superlative forms.

A very few adjectives are normally only used immediately following a noun (ADJ AFTER N). For example, **elect** is used after a noun, as in *. . . the President elect.*

Adjectives which are labelled COLOUR, such as **blue, red,** or **green,** can come either before a noun or after a verb, so you can say *Her father had a red beard . . . Roses are red.*

If there is more than one adjective in front of a noun, a qualitative adjective comes before a colour adjective, and a colour adjective comes before a classifying adjective, which comes nearest to the noun. So you could have a groups of words such as *. . . a small brown wooden gate,* although long strings of adjectives are not very common, especially in speech.

ADJUNCTS

An adjunct (A) is one of the main elements of a clause. It expresses ideas such as those of time, place, manner, and possibility. An adjunct tells you, for example, the time that something happens, the place where it happens, the way in which it happens, or how likely it is that it will happen. When A is used in the Extra Column, it shows that the structure of the word being explained is not complete without an adjunct.

V+A

There are a number of verbs which need an adjunct to complete their meaning. For example, the verbs **behave** and **belong** are nearly always followed by an adjunct. You say that someone 'behaves well', 'behaves badly', 'behaves in a strange way', but you hardly ever just say that they 'behave'. In the same way, you say that something 'belongs to someone'; you do not just say that it 'belongs'.

V+O+A

Some other verbs need both an object and an adjunct, see for example **put 1** and **empty 5**. This means that you can say that you 'put the book down', or that you 'put the book on the shelf', but you cannot just say 'put the book'. In the same way you say that you empty water out of a container; you do not say that you empty water.

Phrasal verbs

There are other associations between verbs and adjuncts. For example, in *he came to a decision,* the words 'to a decision' are closely associated with the particular meaning of 'came' and the whole clause means more or less the same as 'he decided'. Other examples of this can be found in the entry on PHRASAL VERBS.

Types of adjunct

A wide variety of words and phrases are used as adjuncts. Some of these are single words, for example adverbs such as **sadly**, **quickly**, **then**, and **down**. Some adjuncts are noun groups, such as **last night** and **yesterday morning**. Many other adjuncts are prepositional phrases, such as **in the evening**, **at school**, and **round the corner**.

Adjuncts can also be added to a clause in order to give extra information, even though the structure does not actually require them. For example, the sentence *The children sang* gives you one piece of information, but you can also say when they sang: *This morning the children sang.* You can say how they sang: *The children sang beautifully.* You can say where they sang: *The children sang at the school concert.* It is possible to have more than one adjunct in a sentence, and so you can combine these adjuncts to make the sentence: *This morning the children sang beautifully at the school concert.*

Sentence adverbs

There is another type of adjunct which shows how one clause or sentence is linked or joined to another. These are words like **therefore** and **however**. Words or phrases of this kind are called ADV SEN in this dictionary. See the entry for ADVERBS for more information about these words.

5 If you **address** a remark to someone, you say it to them. V+O+*to*

6 If you **address** a problem or task or if you **address** yourself to it, you try to understand it or deal with it. EG *He has not addressed the issue of the strike... We should address ourselves directly to this question.* V+O OR V-REFL+*to*

address book, address books. An **address book** is a book in which you write people's names and addresses. N COUNT

adept /ə³dɛpt/. Someone who is **adept** at something can do it skilfully. EG *They have become adept at filling in forms... ...an adept swimmer.* ADJ QUALIT: OFT+*at/in*

adequate /ædɪ¹kwə¹t/. **1** If the amount of something is **adequate**, there is just enough of it. EG *The pay was adequate... ...a country with adequate rainfall.* ◇ **adequately.** EG *The children are not being adequately fed.* ◇ **adequacy** /ædɪ¹kwəsi¹/. EG *...the adequacy of resources.* ADJ CLASSIF; ◇ ADV; ◇ N UNCOUNT

2 If something is **adequate**, it is good enough to be used or accepted. EG *She could not think of an adequate answer.* ◇ **adequately.** EG *This has never been adequately explained.* ◇ **adequacy.** EG *...his belief in the adequacy of Mr Hope's methods.* ADJ QUALIT; ◇ ADV; ◇ N UNCOUNT

adhere /ə³dhɪə/, **adheres, adhering, adhered. 1** If something **adheres** to something else, it sticks firmly to it. EG *This helps the plaster to adhere to the wall.* V+*to*

2 If you **adhere** to a rule or agreement, you act in the way that it says you should. EG *The fire regulations have been adhered to.* ◇ **adherence** /ə³dhɪərə²ns/. EG *Do they question our adherence to the treaty?* V+*to*; ◇ N UNCOUNT +*to*

3 If you **adhere** to an opinion or belief, you support or hold it. EG *She has adhered to the view that it is my responsibility.* ◇ **adherence.** EG *...their adherence to democratic systems.* V+*to*; ◇ N UNCOUNT +*to*

adhesive /ə³diːsɪv/, **adhesives. 1** An **adhesive** is a substance, such as glue, which is used to make things stick firmly together. EG *Make sure you stick them on with the correct adhesive.* N MASS

2 Something that is **adhesive** is able to stick firmly to something else. EG *...adhesive tape... ...adhesive plasters.* ADJ CLASSIF

ad hoc /æd hɒk/. An **ad hoc** activity or organization is done or formed only because a situation has made it necessary and was not planned in advance. EG *Rescue work continued on an ad hoc basis... The men agreed to set up an ad hoc committee.* ADJ CLASSIF: ATTRIB

> **ADJ** stands for **adjective**
> Words which have the label ADJ in the Extra Column are adjectives.
> For information about the different kinds of adjectives in English, see the entry headed ADJECTIVES.

adjacent /ə³dʒeɪsə⁰nt/. If one thing is **adjacent** to another, the two things are next to each other. EG *The bench was adjacent to the court... ...the adjacent room.* ADJ CLASSIF: OFT+*to*

> **ADJ AFTER N** stands for **adjective after noun**
> Adjectives which have the label ADJ AFTER N in the Extra Column are normally only used immediately following a noun.
> See the entry headed ADJECTIVES for more information.

> **ADJ CLASSIF** stands for **classifying adjective**
> Adjectives which have the label ADJ CLASSIF in the Extra Column classify a noun as being of a particular type. Classifying adjectives do not have comparative and superlative forms, and do not have words like 'very', 'more', or 'rather' in front of them.
> See the entry headed ADJECTIVES for more information.

> **ADJ COLOUR** stands for **colour adjective**
> Words which have the label ADJ COLOUR in the Extra Column show that the word describes a colour such as 'red', 'blue', and 'purple'.
> Colour adjectives can be used before a noun or after a verb. EG *Her father had a **red** beard... Roses are often **red**.*
> Colour adjectives can have other adjectives in front of them that describe the colour more accurately. EG *...**bright** yellow... ...**pale** green... ...**dark** blue.*
> Words which have the label ADJ COLOUR can also be used as nouns. EG *...a **blue** dress... ...a pretty shade of **blue**.*
> See the entry headed ADJECTIVES for more information about other kinds of adjectives.

adjective /ædʒəktɪv/, **adjectives.** An **adjective** is a word that describes a noun by telling you about its colour, size, or other qualities. See the entry headed ADJECTIVES for more information. N COUNT

adjoin /ə³dʒɔɪn/, **adjoins, adjoining, adjoined.** If one room, place, or object **adjoins** another, they are next to each other. EG *Her bedroom adjoined Guy's room.* ◇ **adjoining.** EG *The adjoining room is the office of Professor Marvin.* V+O Formal; ◇ ADJ CLASSIF: ATTRIB

adjourn /ə³dʒɜːn/, **adjourns, adjourning, adjourned.** If a meeting or trial **adjourns**, it is stopped for a short time. EG *He announced that the trial would be adjourned until the next morning.* ◇ **adjournment** /ə³dʒɜːnmə²nt/, **adjournments.** EG *An adjournment was called.* V-ERG; ◇ N COUNT

> **ADJ PRED** stands for **predicative adjective**
> Adjectives which have the label ADJ PRED in the Extra Column are normally only used after a verb such as 'be', 'become', 'feel', and 'seem'.
> See the entry headed ADJECTIVES for more information.

> **ADJ QUALIT** stands for **qualitative adjective**
> Adjectives which have the label ADJ QUALIT in the Extra Column describe features of a noun that can vary in amount or intensity, so that you can have more or less of the feature described. They can show this by comparative and superlative forms, or by words like 'very', 'more', and 'most'.
> See the entry headed ADJECTIVES for more information.

adjudged /ə³dʒʌdʒd/. You use **adjudged** to say what someone is considered to be. For example, if someone **is adjudged** a criminal, they are considered to be a criminal. V-PASS+C OR *to*-INF Formal

> If you administer something adequately, are you doing your job well?

adjudicate /ə^{3}dʒuːdɪkeɪt/, **adjudicates, adjudicating, adjudicated.** If you **adjudicate** on a dispute or problem, you make an official judgement or decision about it. EG *The boards adjudicate on the punishment of prisoners.* — V: OFT+*on* OR V+O

adjunct /ædʒʌŋkt/, **adjuncts. 1** An **adjunct** is something that is connected with a larger or more important thing. EG *Duncan's survey was an adjunct to the current population survey.* — N COUNT+*to/of*

2 In grammar, an **adjunct** is one of the main elements of a clause. See the entry headed ADJUNCTS for more information. — N COUNT

adjust /ə^{3}dʒʌst/, **adjusts, adjusting, adjusted. 1** When you **adjust** to a new situation, you get used to it by changing your behaviour or your ideas. EG *Couples do not give themselves time to adjust to marriage before a baby arrives.* ● See also **adjusted**. — V: OFT+*to*

2 If you **adjust** your clothing, a machine, or a device, you correct or alter its position or setting. EG *He spent several minutes adjusting his tie... I went to adjust the television set.* — V+O

adjustable /ə^{3}dʒʌstəbə^{0}l/. If something is **adjustable**, it can be changed to different positions. EG *...an adjustable spanner.* — ADJ CLASSIF

adjusted /ə^{3}dʒʌstɪ^{2}d/. A well **adjusted** person can control their behaviour and emotions and deal with the problems of life. A badly **adjusted** person cannot. EG *They grow up happy and well adjusted.* — ADJ QUALIT

adjustment /ə^{3}dʒʌstmə^{2}nt/, **adjustments.** An **adjustment** is **1** an alteration or correction made to something such as a machine. EG *He spent weeks making repairs and adjustments.* **2** a change in a person's behaviour or thinking. EG *Foreign students have problems of adjustment to living in Britain.* — N COUNT OR N UNCOUNT: OFT+*to*

ad-lib /ædlɪb/, **ad-libs, ad-libbing, ad-libbed. 1** If you **ad-lib** something in a play or a speech, you say something which has not been planned or prepared beforehand. EG *The commentator decided to ad-lib his way into the report.* — V OR V+O

2 If you say something **ad lib**, you have not planned or prepared it beforehand. EG *We discussed the result ad lib.* — ADV

administer /ə^{3}dmɪnɪstə/, **administers, administering, administered. 1** To **administer** a country, company, or institution means to be responsible for organizing and supervising it. EG *She had a huge department to administer.* — V+O

2 If you **administer** the law, a punishment, or a test, you organize it and make sure everything is done correctly. EG *Experts administer the tests and publish the results.* — V+O

3 If you **administer** a drug to someone, you give it to them to swallow. EG *The prison officers helped to administer a sedative to him.* — V+O Formal

administration /ə^{3}dmɪnɪstreɪʃə^{0}n/. **1 Administration** is the range of activities connected with organizing and supervising the way that a country, company, or institution functions. EG *They need to spend less on administration.* — N UNCOUNT

2 The **administration** of something is the process of administering something. EG *...the administration of justice.* — N UNCOUNT: OFT+*of*

3 The **administration** of a company or institution is the group of people who organize and supervise it. EG *...the University administration.* — N SING+SUPP

4 The **Administration** of a country, especially the United States, is its government. EG *...the Reagan Administration.* — N SING: *the*+N

administrative /ə^{3}dmɪnɪstrətɪv/. **Administrative** work involves organizing and supervising a country, company, or institution. EG *...the administrative head of the country.* — ADJ CLASSIF: USU ATTRIB

administrator /ə^{3}dmɪnɪstreɪtə/, **administrators.** An **administrator** is a person whose job involves helping to organize and supervise the way that a country, company, or institution functions. — N COUNT

admirable /ædmərəbə^{0}l/. A quality or action that is **admirable** deserves to be praised and admired. EG *The trains ran with admirable precision.* — ADJ QUALIT
◊ **admirably.** EG *It fulfils its purpose admirably.* — ◊ ADV

admiral /ædmərəl/, **admirals.** An **admiral** is a very senior officer who commands a navy or fleet of ships. — N COUNT

admiration /ædmə^{1}reɪʃə^{0}n/ is a feeling of great liking and respect for a person or thing. EG *Benson had enormous admiration for them all.* — N UNCOUNT: OFT+*for/of*

admire /ə^{3}dmaɪə/, **admires, admiring, admired.** If you **admire** someone or something, **1** you like and respect them very much. EG *I admire courage... They had been admired for their discipline.* **2** you look with pleasure at them. EG *He went along the lane admiring the crocuses.* — V+O

admirer /ə^{3}dmaɪə^{0}rə/, **admirers. 1** A woman's **admirers** are the men who are attracted to her. — N COUNT+POSS

2 If you are an **admirer** of someone, you like and respect them or their work very much. EG *I am not myself an admirer of Hogarth.* — N COUNT+POSS

admiring /ə^{3}dmaɪə^{0}rɪŋ/. An **admiring** expression indicates a person's liking and respect for someone or something. EG *She gave me one of her rare admiring looks.* ◊ **admiringly.** EG *Ralph glanced at them admiringly.* — ADJ QUALIT; ◊ ADV

admission /ə^{3}dmɪʃə^{0}n/, **admissions. 1 Admission** is **1.1** permission given to a person to enter a place or country. EG *No admission allowed after 10 pm... His Act tightened up the admission of immigrants into Britain.* — N UNCOUNT OR N COUNT **1.2** permission given to a person or a country to join an organization. EG *...the admission of China to the United Nations.* — N UNCOUNT: OFT+*of/to*

2 The **admission** fee at a park, museum, or other place is the amount of money that you pay to enter it. EG *They charge fifty cents admission.* — N UNCOUNT

3 An **admission** is a statement that something bad, unpleasant, or embarrassing is true. EG *He submitted his resignation, together with an admission of his guilt.* — N COUNT: OFT+*of* OR REPORT

admit /ə^{3}dmɪt/, **admits, admitting, admitted. 1** If you **admit** something bad, unpleasant, or embarrassing, you agree, often reluctantly, that it is true. EG *'I don't know,' he admitted... The President admitted taking bribes... He admitted that he had been disappointed by the failure.* — V-SPEECH, V+-ING, OR V+*to*

2 If you **admit defeat**, you accept that you cannot complete something which you have started. — PHRASE

3 If someone or something **is admitted** to a place, they are allowed to enter it. EG *Junior members of staff are not admitted.* — V+O: OFT PASS

4 If someone **is admitted** to hospital, they are kept there until they are well enough to go home. EG *He was admitted to hospital with an ulcerated leg.* — V+O: USU PASS+*to*

5 If someone **is admitted** to an organization or group, they are allowed to join it. EG *He was admitted to full membership of the academy.* — V+O: OFT PASS+*to/into*

admittance /ə^{3}dmɪtə^{0}ns/ is the act of entering a place or the right to enter it. EG *How was he to gain admittance?* — N UNCOUNT

admittedly /ə^{3}dmɪtɪ^{1}dli^1/. You use **admittedly** when you are saying something which weakens your previous statement or claim. EG *Admittedly, economists often disagree among each other.* — ADV SEN

admonish /ə^{3}dmɒnɪʃ/, **admonishes, admonishing, admonished.** If you **admonish** someone, you tell them sternly that they have done something wrong. EG *They are frequently admonished for their failure to act quickly.* — V+O Formal

ado /əduː/. If you do something **without further ado** or **without more ado**, you do it at once and do not discuss or delay it any longer. EG *So, without more ado, let me introduce tonight's guests.* — PHRASE Outdated

adolescence /ædə^{7}lesəns/ is the period of your life in which you develop from being a child into being an adult. EG *His adolescence was not a happy time for him.* — N UNCOUNT

adolescent /ædə^{7}lesə^{2}nt/, **adolescents.** An **adolescent** is a young person who is no longer a child but who has not yet become an adult. ▸ used as an adjective. EG *...a father with an adolescent son.* — N COUNT; ▸ ADJ CLASSIF: ATTRIB

adopt /ədɒpt/, **adopts, adopting, adopted. 1** If you **adopt** someone else's child, you take it into your own family and make it legally your son or daughter. ◇ **adopted.** EG *...the parents of adopted children.* ◇ **adoption** /ədɒpʃə[0]n/, **adoptions.** EG *...the shortage of children available for adoption.* — V+O; ◇ ADJ CLASSIF; ◇ N UNCOUNT OR N COUNT

2 If you **adopt** a new attitude, plan, or way of behaving, you begin to have it. EG *I had to adopt other methods of persuasion.* ◇ **adoption.** EG *That led to Labour's adoption of a radical foreign policy.* — V+O; ◇ N UNCOUNT +of

3 If you **adopt** a physical position, you move yourself into it. EG *Green adopts a golfing stance, his weight forward.* — V+O Formal

adorable /ədɔ:rəbə[0]l/. If you say that a child or animal is **adorable**, you think that it is very attractive and you feel great affection for it. — ADJ QUALIT

adoration /ædə[8]reɪʃə[0]n/ is a feeling of great admiration and love for someone or something. EG *He did not tell anyone of his adoration for her.* — N UNCOUNT

adore /ədɔ:/, **adores, adoring, adored. 1** If you **adore** someone, you feel great admiration and love for them. EG *She adored her sister.* ◇ **adoring.** EG *...listening with adoring concentration.* — V+O : NO CONT; ◇ ADJ QUALIT : ATTRIB

2 If you **adore** something, you like it very much. EG *People will adore this film.* — V+O : NO CONT Informal

adorn /ədɔ:n/, **adorns, adorning, adorned.** To **adorn** something means to add things to it in order to make it more beautiful. EG *Oil paintings adorned the walls... ...stalls adorned with candles.* — V+O Literary

adornment /ədɔ:nmə[2]nt/, **adornments. 1** An **adornment** is something that is used to make someone or something more beautiful. EG *...adornments such as make-up and jewellery.* — N COUNT

2 Adornment is making something more beautiful by adding something to it. EG *Styles of adornment have changed over the centuries.* — N UNCOUNT

adrenalin /ə[3]drɛnəlɪn/; also spelled **adrenaline. Adrenalin** is a substance which your body produces when you are angry, scared, or excited. It makes your heart beat faster and gives you more energy. EG *He felt the surge of adrenalin in his system.* — N UNCOUNT

adrift /ədrɪft/. If a boat is **adrift**, it is floating on the water and is not tied to anything or controlled by anyone. EG *The pirates would cut ships adrift at night.* — ADJ PRED

adroit /ə[3]drɔɪt/. Someone who is **adroit** is quick and skilful in their thoughts, behaviour, or actions. EG *Jamie was adroit at flattering others.* ◇ **adroitly.** EG *The young men picked the papers up adroitly.* — ADJ QUALIT Formal; ◇ ADV

adulation /ædjə[4]leɪʃə[0]n/ is very great and uncritical admiration and praise. EG *He was greeted with adulation.* — N UNCOUNT

adult /ædʌlt, ə[3]dʌlt/, **adults. 1** An **adult** is a mature, fully developed person or animal. EG *A happy home is one in which children and adults have equal rights... I spent all my adult life in England.* — N COUNT

2 An **adult** person or animal is fully developed and mature. EG *...adult insects.* — ADJ CLASSIF : ATTRIB

3 Something that is **adult** is suitable for, or typical of, adult people. EG *Children can assist in adult work at an early age.* — ADJ CLASSIF

adulterate /ə[3]dʌltəreɪt/, **adulterates, adulterating, adulterated.** If you **adulterate** drink or food, you make its quality worse by adding water or cheaper products to it. EG *The champagne had been adulterated.* — V+O

adultery /ə[3]dʌltə[0]ri[1]/. If a married person commits **adultery**, they have sex with someone that they are not married to. EG *Adultery was a ground for divorce.* — N UNCOUNT

adulthood /ædʌlthʊd/ is the state of being an adult. EG *...young Russians maturing to adulthood... There is no reason why she shouldn't survive into healthy adulthood.* — N UNCOUNT

ADV stands for **adverb**
Words which have only the label ADV in the Extra Column are of two kinds:
1. Some can be used with verbs, or adjectives, or other adverbs.
2. Some can only be used with verbs, but they can come before or after the verb.
The examples given for these adverbs will show you how they should be used.
See the entry headed ADVERBS for more information about these and about the other kinds of adverb noted in this dictionary as ADV AFTER VB, ADV BRD NEG, and ADV SEN.

ADV AFTER VB stands for **adverb used after verb**
Words which have the label ADV AFTER VB in the Extra Column are adverbs that can only be used after verbs.
See the entry headed ADVERBS for more information.

---

advance /ə[3]dvɑ:ns/, **advances, advancing, advanced. 1** To **advance** means **1.1** to move forward, often in order to attack someone. EG *She advanced on him, shouting and waving her ticket.* ◇ **advancing.** EG *...rows of advancing enemy tanks.* — V; ◇ ADJ CLASSIF

1.2 to make progress, especially in your knowledge of something. EG *This student has advanced in reading and writing.* ● See also **advanced.** — V

2 If you **advance** someone a sum of money, you lend it to them, or pay it to them earlier than arranged. EG *Axel advanced him the money for a suit.* — V+O+O

3 An **advance** is money which is lent to someone or paid to them before they are due to receive it. — N COUNT

4 If you make **advances** to someone, you try to start a sexual relationship with them. — N PLURAL Outdated

5 Advance in a particular subject or activity is progress in understanding it or in doing it well. EG *...radical advances in computer design.* — N COUNT OR N UNCOUNT

6 Advance booking, notice, or warning is done or given before an event happens. EG *There was no advance warning of the President's departure.* — ADJ CLASSIF : ATTRIB

7 If an idea or product is **in advance** of another one, it is more highly developed. EG *Their facilities were far in advance of anything in Europe.* — PHRASE

8 If you do something **in advance**, you do it before a particular date or event. EG *You should book well in advance, preferably six weeks before.* — PHRASE

advanced /ə[3]dvɑ:nst/. **1** An **advanced** student has already learned the basic facts of a subject and is doing more difficult work. — ADJ QUALIT

2 A country that is **advanced** has reached a high level of industrial or technological development. EG *Japan is becoming the most advanced country technologically.* — ADJ QUALIT

advancement /ə[3]dvɑ:nsmə[2]nt/. **1 Advancement** is promotion in your job, or to a higher social class. EG *...opportunity for personal advancement.* — N UNCOUNT

2 The **advancement** of something is the process of helping it to progress. EG *...the advancement of knowledge.* — N UNCOUNT +SUPP

advantage /ə[3]dvɑ:ntɪdʒ/, **advantages. 1** An **advantage** is **1.1** something that puts you in a better position than other people. EG *As a scientist I have* — N COUNT

What can you be advanced?

ADVERBS

An adverb is a word which gives more information about a verb, an adjective, or another adverb. There are several different kinds of adverbs.

1 Many adverbs (ADV) can be used with either a verb or an adjective. For example, in the sentence *Smoking can **seriously** damage your health,* the adverb 'seriously' tells you how much damage can be done. In *She was **seriously** ill,* the adverb tells you how ill she was. Occasionally, an adverb of this kind is used with another adverb, as in *I did not feel I knew her **sufficiently well**.*

2 Many adverbs (also ADV) can only be used with verbs. They can come either before or after the verb. So you can say *She grinned **happily** at him* and *He **happily** handed over ten pounds . . . They smiled **cheerfully** at each other* and *They **cheerfully** agreed to help.*

3 Many other adverbs (ADV AFTER VB) are used with verbs, but they can only come after the verb. These fall into two main groups.

The first group consists of some of the commonest adverbs in English, such as **back**, **up**, and **down**, and are used when you are describing, for example, where something happens and what direction something is going in. For example, *She nodded and looked down.* Very often adverbs of this kind are used with phrasal verbs. For more information about how they behave see the entry headed PHRASAL VERBS.

The second group consists of less common words which have a much more specific meaning, such as 'cross-legged', 'counter-clockwise', and 'barefoot'. For example, *She ran **barefoot** through the field.*

4 All of the groups of adverbs already mentioned can come after verbs. There is one group that cannot, and there are special rules about how these adverbs are used. This is a small group of adverbs which have a meaning close to the word 'not', but which are not quite negative (ADV BRD NEG). These are **hardly**, **scarcely**, **barely**, **rarely**, **seldom**, and **little**. So *He was hardly awake* means 'he was almost asleep'.

These adverbs can all be used as the first word in a clause, in order to emphasize their importance. So you can say *Hardly had I got into the house than the phone rang . . . Seldom did a week pass without a request for information . . . Rarely has so much time been wasted.* When one of these words begins a clause, notice that the rest of the clause has a word order that is similar to a question.

5 There is another kind of adverb (ADV SEN) that is used to comment on the whole sentence rather than just on part of it.

There are a number of words like **however**, **thus**, and **nevertheless** which help you to order and explain the argument you are putting forward in your statements. Here are some examples: *Most people think that David is nice. Not me, **however** . . . The new car is smaller and **therefore** cheaper . . . Life now is much less elaborate and, **consequently**, much less interesting than it used to be.*

6 The words that are labelled SUBMOD in this dictionary are often called adverbs. These are words like **very**, **rather** and **extremely**. See the entry headed SUBMOD for more information about these words.

a slight advantage over him. **1.2** a benefit or improvement that is likely to result from something. EG *The advantages of electricity are the lack of fumes and the ease of distribution.*

2 Advantage is used in these phrases. **2.1** If something is **to** your **advantage**, it will be useful for you or will benefit you. EG *It is to your advantage to keep him as happy as possible.* **2.2** If you **take advantage of** someone, you treat them unfairly for your own benefit. **2.3** If you **take advantage of** something, you make good use of it while you can. EG *Companies took advantage of favourable interest rates... You should take advantage of his generosity.* [PHRASES]

advantageous /ædvə[3]nteɪdʒəs/. Something that is **advantageous** to you is likely to benefit you. EG *Economic growth is inevitable and advantageous.* [ADJ QUALIT]

> **ADV BRD NEG** stands for **broad negative adverb**
> Words which have the label ADV BRD NEG in the Extra Column are used to make the sentence almost, but not quite, negative. Six words are labelled in this way: *hardly, scarcely, rarely, barely, seldom, little.*
> See the entry headed ADVERBS for more information.

advent /ædvə[2]nt/. The **advent** of something important is the fact of it starting or coming into existence. EG *...the advent of computers.* [N SING+POSS; Formal]

adventure /ə[3]dventʃə/, **adventures.** An **adventure** is a series of events that you become involved in that are unusual, exciting, and rather dangerous. EG *...my Arctic adventures... They were bored, and looking for adventure.* [N COUNT OR N UNCOUNT]

adventurer /ə[3]dventʃərə/, **adventurers.** An **adventurer** is a person who enjoys adventure. EG *...a daring band of adventurers.* [N COUNT]

adventurous /ə[3]dventʃərəs/. Someone who is **adventurous** is **1** willing to take risks and to try new methods. EG *I wish that he had been a bit more adventurous in his investigation.* **2** eager to visit new places and have new experiences. EG *The romance of the East had appealed to his adventurous spirit.* [ADJ QUALIT]

adverb /ædvɜːb/, **adverbs.** In grammar, an **adverb** is a word that adds information about a verb, about a following adjective or adverb, or about a following prepositional group. See the entry headed ADVERBS for more information. [N COUNT]

adversary /ædvəsə[2]ri[1]/, **adversaries.** Your **adversary** is someone you are competing with, or arguing or fighting against. EG *She had two potential political adversaries.* [N COUNT+SUPP]

adverse /ædvɜːs/. **Adverse** decisions, conditions, or effects are unfavourable to you. EG *Falling prices had an adverse effect on business... ...adverse weather conditions.* [ADJ QUALIT: ATTRIB] ◊ **adversely.** EG *The majority of children are adversely affected.* [◊ ADV]

adversity /ə[3]dvɜːsɪ[1]ti[1]/ is a very difficult or unfavourable situation. EG *They continue to fight in the face of adversity.* [N UNCOUNT]

advert /ædvɜːt/, **adverts.** An **advert** is the same as an advertisement. [N COUNT; Informal]

advertise /ædvətaɪz/, **advertises, advertising, advertised. 1** If you **advertise** something such as a product, an event, or a job, you tell people about it in newspapers, on television, or on posters in order to encourage them to buy the product, go to the event, or apply for the job. EG *...deodorants she had seen advertised on television... ...a leaflet advertising a fishing competition.* [V+O]

2 If you **advertise** for something or for someone to do a job, you announce in a newspaper, on television, or on a notice board that you want that thing or want a person to do that job. EG *The Council advertised for accountants.* [V: OFT+*for*]

advertisement /ə[3]dvɜːtɪsmə[2]nt/, **advertisements.** An **advertisement** is an announcement in a newspaper, on television, or on a poster about something such as a product, event, or job vacancy. EG *...an advertisement for Adler shoes... ...an advertisement for an assistant cashier.* [N COUNT]

advertiser /ædvətaɪzə/, **advertisers.** An **advertiser** is a person or company that pays for a product, event, or job vacancy to be advertised on television, in a newspaper, or on posters. [N COUNT]

advertising /ædvətaɪzɪŋ/ is the activity of telling people about products, events, or job vacancies, and making people want to buy the products, go to the events, or apply for the jobs. EG *Retailers spend a lot of money on advertising... ...an advertising agency.* [N UNCOUNT]

advice /ə[3]dvaɪs/. If you give someone **advice**, you tell them what you think they should do in a particular situation. EG *She promised to follow his advice... They want advice on how to do it.* [N UNCOUNT: USU+SUPP]

advisable /ə[3]dvaɪzəbə[0]l/. If a course of action is **advisable**, it is sensible or is likely to achieve the result you want. EG *It's advisable to ring up first to make an appointment.* [ADJ QUALIT]

advise /ə[3]dvaɪz/, **advises, advising, advised. 1** If you **advise** someone to do something, you tell them what you think they should do. EG *He advised me not to buy it... Their job involves advising people how to avoid this disease... I would strongly advise you against it.* [V+O+*to*-INF, REPORT, OR *against*]

2 If you **advise** people on a particular subject, you give them help and information on the subject. EG *A panel of bishops has been appointed to advise on matters of religious policy.* [V OR V+O: OFT +*on*]

advocate, advocates, advocating, advocated; pronounced /ædvə[6]keɪt/ when it is a verb and /ædvə[6]kət/ when it is a noun.

1 If you **advocate** a particular action or plan, you support it publicly. EG *He advocated the creation of a permanent United Nations... He advocated that Britain should join the alliance.* [V+O OR V+REPORT: ONLY *that*]

2 An **advocate** of a particular action or plan is someone who supports it publicly. EG *...the advocates of women's rights... ...a strong advocate of nuclear power.* [N COUNT+*of*]

3 An **advocate** is a lawyer who speaks in favour of someone or defends them in a court of law. [N COUNT; Legal]

> **ADV SEN** stands for **sentence adverb**
> Words and phrases which have the label ADV SEN in the Extra Column are used to comment on the whole sentence rather than on individual parts.
> See the entry headed ADVERBS for more information.

aerial /ɛərɪəl/, **aerials. 1** You use **aerial** to describe things that are fixed above the level of the ground or that happen in the air. EG *An aerial railway had been erected... ...aerial warfare.* [ADJ CLASSIF: ATTRIB]

2 Aerial photographs are photographs taken from aeroplanes of things on the ground. [ADJ CLASSIF: ATTRIB]

3 An **aerial** is a piece of wire that receives television or radio signals. Aerials are often fixed to buildings, cars, radios, and television sets. See picture at CAR. [N COUNT; British]

aerodynamic /ɛərə[6]daɪnæmɪk/. **Aerodynamic** effects and principles are concerned with the way in which objects move through the air. EG *...aerodynamic improvements in design.* [ADJ CLASSIF: ATTRIB]

> Is an adventurer likely to encounter adversity?

aeroplane /ɛərə[6]pleɪn/, **aeroplanes.** An **aeroplane** is a vehicle with wings and one or more engines that enable it to fly through the air.
N COUNT OR by+N British

aerosol /ɛərə[6]sɒl/, **aerosols.** An **aerosol** is a small container in which a liquid such as paint or deodorant is kept under pressure. When you press a button, the liquid is forced out as a fine spray or foam.
N COUNT

aesthetic /i[1]sθɛtɪk/; spelled **esthetic** in American English. **Aesthetic** means involving beauty or art, and people's appreciation of beautiful things. EG *...a purely aesthetic appeal.* ◊ **aesthetically.** EG *...aesthetically pleasing products.*
ADJ CLASSIF; ◊ ADV

afar /əfɑː/. **From afar** means from a long way away. EG *He saw me from afar.*
PHRASE Literary

affable /æfəbə[0]l/. Someone who is **affable** is pleasant and friendly. EG *Dominic was always affable with my friends.*
ADJ QUALIT Literary

affair /əfɛə/, **affairs. 1** You refer to an event or a situation as an **affair** when you are talking about it very generally. EG *The wedding was a quiet affair... An enquiry will be conducted into the whole affair.*
N COUNT +SUPP : USU SING

2 You can use **affairs** to refer to all the important facts or activities that are connected with a particular subject. EG *...a specialist in Eastern European affairs... ...affairs of state.* • See also **current affairs**, **state of affairs**.
N PLURAL +SUPP Formal

3 Your **affairs** are all the things connected with your life which you consider to be private and nothing to do with other people. EG *What had induced her to meddle in his affairs?*
N PLURAL +POSS

4 If someone says that something is your **affair**, they mean that they do not wish to know about it or become involved in it. EG *What went on behind that door was your own affair.*
N SING+POSS

5 If two people who are not married to each other are having an **affair**, they have a sexual relationship.
N COUNT

affect /ə[3]fɛkt/, **affects, affecting, affected. 1** When something **affects** someone or something else, it influences them or causes them to change in some way. EG *...the ways in which computers can affect our lives.*
V+O

2 When a disease **affects** someone, it causes them to become ill. EG *The disease primarily affected Jane's lungs.*
V+O

3 If you **affect** a particular characteristic or way of behaving, you pretend that it is natural for you. EG *She affected a lisp... He affected to despise every Briton he met.*
V+O OR V+to-INF Formal

affectation /æfɛkteɪʃə[0]n/, **affectations.** An **affectation** is an attitude or type of behaviour that is not genuine or natural, but which is intended to impress other people. EG *His film star affectations had disappeared.*
N COUNT OR N UNCOUNT

affected /ə[3]fɛktɪ[2]d/. Someone who is **affected** behaves in an unnatural way that is intended to impress other people. EG *He was affected and conceited.*
ADJ QUALIT

affection /ə[3]fɛkʃə[0]n/ is a feeling of fondness and caring that you have for another person or for an animal. EG *She gazed with deep affection at him.*
N UNCOUNT

affectionate /ə[3]fɛkʃənə[1]t/. If you are **affectionate**, you show your love or fondness for another person in the way that you behave towards them. EG *They were an affectionate couple... His tone was affectionate.* ◊ **affectionately.** EG *He stroked her affectionately.*
ADJ QUALIT; ◊ ADV

affinity /əfɪnɪ[1]ti[1]/, **affinities. 1** If you have an **affinity** with someone or something, you feel that you are similar to them and understand them very well. EG *I had this tremendous sense of affinity with the place.*
N COUNT OR N UNCOUNT : OFT+*with/for*

2 If people or things have an **affinity** with each other, they are similar in some ways. EG *In anatomical structure, Prehistoric Man has close affinities with modern humans.*
N COUNT

affirm /ə[3]fɜːm/, **affirms, affirming, affirmed. 1** If you **affirm** a fact, you state that it is definitely true. EG *I affirmed my innocence.*
V-SPEECH : ONLY *that* Formal

2 If you **affirm** an idea or belief, you indicate clearly that you have this idea or belief. EG *They affirm a policy of religious toleration.*
V+O Formal

affirmative /ə[3]fɜːmətɪv/. An **affirmative** word or gesture indicates that you agree with what someone has said or that the answer to a question is 'yes'. EG *...the affirmative nodding of my head.*
ADJ CLASSIF : ATTRIB Formal

• If you reply to a question **in the affirmative**, you say 'yes' or make a gesture that means 'yes'.
• PHRASE

afflict /ə[3]flɪkt/, **afflicts, afflicting, afflicted.** If pain, illness, or sorrow **afflicts** someone, it affects them and makes them suffer. EG *Cameron had been afflicted with blindness.*
V+O : OFT PASS+ *with/by*

affliction /ə[3]flɪkʃə[0]n/, **afflictions.** An **affliction** is something which causes physical or mental suffering. EG *...the horrors and afflictions of his time in prison.*
N COUNT OR N UNCOUNT

affluent /æfluənt/. If you are **affluent**, you have a lot of money and a high standard of living. EG *...affluent young professionals.* ◊ **affluence** /æfluəns/. EG *...the general affluence of a consumer society.*
ADJ QUALIT; ◊ N UNCOUNT Formal

afford /əfɔːd/, **affords, affording, afforded. 1** If you can **afford** something, you have enough money to pay for it. EG *...families who can afford cars... I can't afford to rent this flat.*
V+O OR V+to-INF

2 If you say that you cannot **afford** to do something or to allow it to happen, you mean that you must not do it or must try to prevent it happening because it would be harmful or embarrassing to you. EG *He could not afford to be associated with them... We can't afford another scandal.*
V+O OR V+to-INF

3 If something **affords** you support or an opportunity, it gives it to you. EG *...the protection afforded to the workers by the unions... They have been afforded some assistance.*
V+O+*to* OR V+O+O Formal

affront /əfrʌnt/, **affronts, affronting, affronted. 1** If you **are affronted** by something, you feel insulted and hurt because of it. EG *They were deeply affronted by their abrupt dismissal.*
V+O : USU PASS

2 If something is an **affront** to you, it is an obvious insult to you. EG *This is a serious affront to large numbers of citizens.*
N COUNT : OFT+*to*

afield /əfiːld/. If someone comes from **far afield**, they come from a long way away. EG *Groups from as far afield as Scotland have sent deputations.*
PHRASE

afloat /əfləʊt/. **1** When someone or something is **afloat**, they remain partly above the surface of water and do not sink. EG *By kicking constantly he could stay afloat.*
ADJ PRED

2 If you stay **afloat** or if you keep a business **afloat**, you have only just enough money to pay your debts or to run the business. EG *They have kept Vickers afloat during the recession.*
ADJ PRED

afoot /əfʊt/. If a plan or scheme is **afoot**, it is already happening or being planned, but you do not know much about it. EG *There was a plan afoot to have her sent to a camp.*
ADJ PRED

aforementioned /əfɔːmɛnʃənd/. When you refer to the **aforementioned** person or subject, you mean the person or subject that has already been mentioned. EG *...the works of all the aforementioned writers.*
ADJ CLASSIF : ATTRIB Formal

aforesaid /əfɔːsɛd/ means the same as aforementioned.
ADJ CLASSIF : ATTRIB

afraid /əfreɪd/. **1** If you are **afraid** of someone or **afraid** to do something, you are frightened because you think that something horrible is going to happen. EG *They were afraid of you... He was afraid even to turn his head... She suddenly looked afraid.*
ADJ PRED : OFT+*of* OR *to*-INF

2 If you are **afraid** that something unpleasant will happen, you are worried that it may happen and you want to avoid it. EG *She was afraid that I might be embarrassed... He was terribly afraid of offending anyone... Don't be afraid to ask questions.*
ADJ PRED +REPORT, *of*, OR *to*-INF

3 When you want to apologize to someone or to
CONVENTION

disagree with them in a polite way, you can begin by saying **I'm afraid**. EG *I'm afraid I can't agree... 'Can you come?' – 'I'm afraid not.'*

afresh /əfrɛʃ/. If you do something **afresh**, you do it again in a different way. EG *I'm too old to start afresh.* — ADV

African /æfrɪkən/, **Africans. 1 African** means 1.1 belonging or relating to the continent of Africa, or to its countries or peoples. **1.2** belonging or relating to black people who come from Africa. EG *He impressed people by the way he presented the African case.* — ADJ CLASSIF

2 An **African** is someone, usually black, who comes from Africa. EG *...civic rights for Africans... ...the African population of Johannesburg.* — N COUNT

after /ɑːftə/. **1** If something happens **after** a particular date or event, it happens during the period of time that follows it. EG *She arrived just after breakfast... Soon after, Faraday began his research into electricity... He was ill after eating the meal.* — PREP, ADV, OR CONJ

2 If you go **after** someone, you follow them. EG *She ran after him into the courtyard.* — PREP

3 If someone is **after** you, they are chasing you or searching for you. EG *The Germans were after him.* — PREP

4 If you are **after** something, you are trying to get it for yourself. EG *Those youngsters are after my job.* — PREP

5 If you call or look **after** someone, you call or look towards them when they are moving away from you. EG *'Hunter!' she called after him.* — PREP

6 If you clean up **after** someone, you clean up the mess which they have made. EG *Why do you spend your life cleaning up after him?* — PREP

7 If something is written **after** something else on a page, it is written following it or underneath it. — PREP

8 To be named **after** someone means to be given the same name as them. EG *...a street named after my grandfather.* — PREP

9 Americans use **after** when they are telling the time. If they say that it is, for example, ten **after** six, the time is ten minutes past six. EG *They met at twenty after eight.* — PREP American

10 If you do several things **one after the other** or **one after another**, you do them immediately following each other in time. EG *He begins opening bottles, one after another.* — PHRASE

11 If something happens **day after day** or **year after year**, it happens every day or every year. EG *Some jokes go round school year after year.* — PHRASE

12 After is also used in the phrasal verbs 'ask after', 'go after', 'look after', 'run after', and 'take after'. — ADV OR PREP

after-effect, after-effects. The **after-effects** of an activity or event are the conditions which result from it. EG *100,000 died from the after-effects of radiation over the next few decades.* — N COUNT: USU PLURAL

aftermath /ɑːftəmɑːθ, -mæθ/. The **aftermath** of an important event is the situation that results from it. EG *In the immediate aftermath of the accident, no one knew who had been hurt... ...the aftermath of war.* — N SING+POSS

afternoon /ɑːftənuːn/, **afternoons.** The **afternoon** is the part of each day which begins at lunchtime and ends at about six o'clock. EG *I'll do it this afternoon... ...my afternoon walk.* — N COUNT OR N UNCOUNT

after-shave /ɑːftəʃeɪv/ is a liquid with a pleasant smell that men sometimes put on their faces after they have shaved. — N UNCOUNT

afterthought /ɑːftəθɔːt/, **afterthoughts.** If you do or say something as an **afterthought**, you do or say it after something else as an addition, but without careful thought. EG *After a while she said as an afterthought, 'I could do that.'* — N COUNT: USU SING

afterwards /ɑːftəwədz/. The word **afterward** is also used, especially in American English. — ADV SEN

If you do something or if something happens **afterwards**, you do it or it happens after a particular event or time that has already been described. EG *Afterwards we all helped with the washing up... She died soon afterwards.*

again /əgɛn, əgeɪn/. **1** If you do something **again**, you do it once more or on another occasion. EG *Try again in half an hour... Let's do it, I may never have the chance again.* — ADV

● If you do something **again and again** or **time and again**, you do it many times or on many occasions. EG *This process is repeated again and again.* — ● PHRASE

2 When something is in a particular state or place **again**, it has returned to the state or place that it used to be in. EG *At last the assembly was silent again.* — ADV

3 When you are asking someone to repeat something that they have already told you, you can add **again** to the end of your question. EG *What's his name again?* — ADV SEN

4 You can use **again** when you want to emphasize that there is a similarity between the subject that you are talking about now and a previous subject. EG *My last question is again a personal one.* — ADV SEN

5 When you want to introduce a different point, often one that contradicts something that has just been said, you can say **'then again'**. EG *I don't think it should be an arts subject. But then again it's not really a science subject.* — ADV SEN

against /əgɛnst, əgeɪnst/. **1** If something is leaning or pressing **against** something else, it is touching it and leaning or pressing on it. EG *Ralph leaned against a tree... She was pressing her nose against the window.* — PREP

2 If you compete **against** someone in a game or other activity, you try to beat them or to do better than them. EG *He played in the first Test Match against Australia.* — PREP

3 If you do something **against** someone or something, you do something that might harm them. EG *They were not allowed to use arms against their enemies.* — PREP

4 If you are **against** an idea, policy, or system, you are opposed to it. EG *He was fanatically against American intervention in the war.* — PREP OR ADV

5 If something is **against** the law, there is a law which says that you must not do it. — PREP

6 If you take action **against** a possible future event, you try to prevent it or to make its effects less serious. EG *He has taken certain precautions against burglary.* — PREP

7 If you are moving **against** a current, tide, or wind, you are moving in the opposite direction to it. — PREP

8 The chances or odds **against** something happening are the chances or odds that it will not happen. — PREP OR ADV

age /eɪdʒ/, **ages, ageing** or **aging, aged. 1** Your **age** is the number of years that you have lived. EG *He is eighty years of age... He died at the age of forty... She thought I was her own age.* — N UNCOUNT +SUPP

2 Someone who is **under age** is not legally old enough to do something, for example to buy an alcoholic drink. EG *He had been under age when he joined the army.* — PHRASE

3 When someone **comes of age**, they become legally an adult. In Britain young people come of age when they are 18.

4 Age is the state of being old. EG *Her age and frailty are giving him cause for concern... ...medals stained with age.* — N UNCOUNT

5 When someone **ages**, they become or seem much older and less strong or less alert. EG *She was dismayed to see how much he had aged... The strain of looking after her had aged him.* — V-ERG

6 An **age** is a period in history. EG *...the great age of Greek sport... ...a detailed study of woman's role throughout the ages.* — N COUNT: IF SING, THEN+SUPP

7 You can say **an age** or **ages** to mean a very long — N SING: *an*+N,

Are you named after anyone?

time. EG *I've known him for ages... She took an age to dress.* OR N PLURAL Informal

8 See also **aged**, **ageing**.

> **AGE**
> There are a number of different ways of talking about age in English.
> The following examples show how to ask a person's age and how to say how old they are. EG *How old are you?... What age is she?... She is twenty-five years old... She must be nearly eighty... ...a young woman of sixteen... She died in 1816 at the age of 83... ...their three children, Andrea, aged 17, Julie, aged 16, and Paul, aged 13... ...a forty-year-old female... ...a class of 4-year-olds... ...nursery schools for the fives and under... My mother died just before my fourth birthday.*
> If you say that someone is in their twenties, you mean that they are between twenty and thirty years old. If you say that someone is in their early fifties, you mean that they are older than fifty, but younger than fifty-five; if you say that someone is in their late fifties, you mean that they are over fifty-five, but less than sixty.

aged; pronounced /eɪdʒd/ for paragraph 1 and /eɪdʒɪ^{2}d/ for paragraphs 2 and 3.
1 You use **aged** followed by a number to say how old someone is. EG *...men aged 60 and over.* ● See also **middle-aged**. ADJ PRED
2 Someone or something that is **aged** is very old. EG *...his aged aunt.* ADJ QUALIT
3 You can refer to all people who are very old as **the aged**. EG *...the care of the aged.* N PLURAL: the+N

ageing /eɪdʒɪŋ/; also spelled **aging. 1 Ageing** means becoming older and less attractive or efficient. EG *...an ageing film star.* ADJ CLASSIF
2 Ageing is the process of becoming old. N UNCOUNT

ageless /eɪdʒlɪ^{2}s/. If you describe someone or something as **ageless**, you mean that it is impossible to tell how old they are. EG *...an ageless ritual.* ADJ CLASSIF

agency /eɪdʒənsi^7/, **agencies.** An **agency** is **1** a business which provides services for another business. EG *...an advertising agency.* **2** an administrative organization run by a government. EG *...the Central Intelligence Agency.* N COUNT

agenda /ədʒɛndə/, **agendas.** An **agenda** is a list of the items that have to be discussed at a meeting. EG *What is on the agenda today?* N COUNT

agent /eɪdʒə^{2}nt/, **agents. 1** An **agent** is **1.1** someone who arranges business for someone else, especially someone who gets work for actors or musicians. EG *I phoned my agent in London about the job.* **1.2** someone who works for a country's secret service. EG *...an enemy agent.* N COUNT
2 If you refer to someone or something as the **agent** of a particular effect, you mean that they cause this effect. EG *...the agent of change.* N COUNT+SUPP

age-old. An **age-old** story, tradition, or connection has existed for longer than people can remember. ADJ CLASSIF: ATTRIB

aggravate /ægrəveɪt/, **aggravates, aggravating, aggravated. 1** If you **aggravate** a situation, you make it worse. EG *National poverty was aggravated by rapid population growth.* V+O
2 If someone or something **aggravates** you, they make you annoyed. EG *It's the little things that aggravate me.* V+O Informal

aggregate /ægrɪ^{2}gət/, **aggregates.** An **aggregate** is an amount that is made up of several smaller amounts. EG *He had spent an aggregate of fifteen years in various jails.* N COUNT: OFT+of

aggression /ə^{3}grɛʃə^{0}n/ is **1** a quality of anger and determination that makes you ready to attack other people. EG *Barbara defended herself with a sudden new aggression.* **2** violent and attacking behaviour. EG *...an act of aggression.* N UNCOUNT

aggressive /ə^{3}grɛsɪv/. **1** Someone who is **aggressive** shows aggression. EG *Mrs Zapp was in a highly aggressive mood.* ADJ QUALIT
2 People who are **aggressive** in their work or other activities behave in a forceful way because they are very eager to succeed. EG *...aggressive businessmen.* ADJ QUALIT

aggressor /ə^{3}grɛsə/, **aggressors.** The **aggressor** is the person, group, or country that starts a fight. N COUNT

aggrieved /ə^{3}griːvd/. If you feel **aggrieved**, you feel upset and angry because of the way in which you have been treated. ADJ QUALIT

aggro /ægrəʊ/ is aggressive or violent behaviour. EG *There wasn't a hint of aggro.* N UNCOUNT Informal

aghast /əgɑːst/. If you are **aghast**, you are filled with horror and surprise. EG *What she had learned had left her aghast.* ADJ PRED

agile /ædʒaɪl/. **1** Someone who is **agile** can move with surprising ease and speed. EG *He was as agile as a monkey.* ◇ **agility** /ədʒɪlɪ^{1}ti^1/. EG *He leaped out of the car with surprising agility.* ADJ QUALIT ◇ N UNCOUNT
2 If you have an **agile** mind, you think quickly and intelligently. ◇ **agility.** EG *...tests of mental agility.* ADJ QUALIT ◇ N UNCOUNT

aging /eɪdʒɪŋ/. See **age, ageing.**

agitate /ædʒɪteɪt/, **agitates, agitating, agitated.**
1 If you **agitate** for something, you talk and campaign enthusiastically in an attempt to get it. EG *...a group agitating against the use of chemical fertilizers.* ◇ **agitation** /ædʒɪteɪʃə^{0}n/. EG *...anti-imperialist agitation.* V+for/against ◇ N UNCOUNT
2 If something **agitates** you, it worries you and makes you unable to think clearly or calmly. EG *I don't want to agitate him unduly.* ◇ **agitated** /ædʒɪteɪtɪ^{2}d/. EG *He looked dishevelled and agitated.* ◇ **agitation.** EG *I saw Peter glancing at his watch in some agitation.* V+O ◇ ADJ QUALIT ◇ N UNCOUNT

agitator /ædʒɪteɪtə/, **agitators.** An **agitator** is someone who tries to bring about political or social change by making speeches and campaigning in public. EG *...political agitators.* N COUNT

agnostic /ægnɒstɪk/, **agnostics.** An **agnostic** believes that it is not possible to know whether God exists or not. ▸ used as an adjective. EG *She remained agnostic.* N COUNT ▸ ADJ CLASSIF

ago /əgəʊ/. You use **ago** to refer to past time. For example, if something happened one year **ago**, it is one year since it happened. If it happened a long time **ago**, it is a long time since it happened. EG *Five years ago, I went to the tropics... How long ago was that?* ADV

agog /əgɒg/. If you are **agog**, you are excited by something, and eager to know more about it. ADJ PRED

agonize /ægə^{7}naɪz/, **agonizes, agonizing, agonized;** also spelled **agonise.** If you **agonize** over something, you feel very anxious about it and spend a long time thinking about it. EG *He is agonizing over how to reply to the letter.* V

agonized /ægə^{7}naɪzd/; also spelled **agonised. Agonized** describes something that you say or do when you are in great physical or mental pain. EG *He could hear the prisoner's agonised moans.* ADJ CLASSIF

agonizing /ægə^{7}naɪzɪŋ/; also spelled **agonising.**
1 Something that is **agonizing** causes you to feel great physical or mental pain. EG *...agonizing feelings of shame and guilt.* ◇ **agonizingly.** EG *The sound was agonisingly painful.* ADJ QUALIT ◇ ADV
2 Agonizing decisions and choices are very difficult to make. ADJ QUALIT

agony /ægəni^1/, **agonies. Agony** is great physical or mental pain. EG *The blow made him scream in agony.* N UNCOUNT OR N PLURAL

agree /əgriː/, **agrees, agreeing, agreed. 1** If people **agree** with one another about something, they have the same opinion about it. EG *Do you agree with him about this?... People agree that the law is behind the times.* V OR V+with: RECIP

2 If you **agree** to do something, you say that you will do it. EG *She agreed to let us use her flat while she was away.* V: OFT+*to*-INF OR *to*

3 If people are **agreed** about something, they agree about it. EG *Are we agreed, gentlemen?* ADJ PRED

4 If you **agree** with an action or a suggestion, you approve of it. EG *I agree with what they are doing.* V+*with*

5 If two stories, accounts, or totals **agree**, they are the same as each other. EG *My theories and his do not always agree.* V

6 If food that you eat does not **agree** with you, it makes you feel ill. V+*with*

agreeable /əgriːəbə^{0}l/. 1 If something is **agreeable**, it is pleasant and you enjoy it. EG *...an agreeable sensation.* ADJ QUALIT

2 If someone is **agreeable**, they are pleasant and try to please people. EG *She always made a point of being agreeable to them.* ADJ QUALIT: OFT+*to*

3 If you are **agreeable** to something or if it is **agreeable** to you, you are willing to do it or to allow it to happen. EG *Get your secretary to do it if she is agreeable.* ADJ PRED: OFT+*to*

agreement /əgriːmə^{2}nt/, **agreements. 1** An **agreement** is a decision that two or more people have reached together. EG *Half of the land was given away under the same agreement.* N COUNT

2 **Agreement** is **2.1** the act of reaching a decision that is acceptable to everyone involved. EG *There was no general agreement on the timing.* N UNCOUNT: OFT+*on/about* **2.2** the act of saying or indicating that you will accept something or believe something. EG *They nodded agreement.* N UNCOUNT

3 If you are **in agreement** with someone, you have the same opinion as they have. EG *They were in complete agreement.* PHRASE

agriculture /ægrɪkʌltʃə/ is farming and the methods that are used to raise and look after crops and animals. EG *...areas that are unsuitable for agriculture.* ◊ **agricultural** /ægrɪkʌltʃə^{0}rəl/. EG *...modern agricultural methods.* N UNCOUNT; ◊ ADJ CLASSIF

aground /əgraʊnd/. If a ship runs **aground**, it touches the ground in a shallow part of a river, lake, or the sea. ADJ PRED

ah /ɑː/. When you want to express agreement, surprise, pleasure, or sympathy, you can say **'ah'**. EG *Ah, you poor fellow... Ah, Howard. Come in.*

aha /ɑːhɑː/. When you want to indicate that you understand, know, or have found something, you can say **'aha'**, especially when you are pleased about it. EG *I had a report here somewhere. Aha, here we are.*

ahead /əhed/. **1** If something is **ahead**, it is in front of you. EG *The road ahead is foggy... She stared ahead.* ADV

2 If you are **ahead** of someone in your work or achievements, you have made more progress than they have. EG *He is ten years ahead of the rest.* ADV: OFT+*of*

3 If a person or a team is **ahead** in a competition, they are winning. EG *Another goal put United ahead.* ADJ PRED

4 If someone goes **on ahead** or is sent **on ahead**, they leave for a place before other people or things. EG *Our parents had gone on ahead in father's car.* PHRASE

5 If someone arrives somewhere **ahead** of you, they arrive before you. ADV+*of*

6 If someone is **ahead** of you in a queue, they are in front of you. ADV+*of*

7 **Ahead** also means in the future. EG *I haven't had time to think far ahead.* ADV

8 See also **go ahead**.

aid /eɪd/, **aids, aiding, aided. 1 Aid** is money, equipment, or services that are provided for people in need. EG *...overseas aid for the less developed countries... ...food and medical aid.* N UNCOUNT +SUPP

2 An **aid** is something that makes things easier to do. EG *...a valuable aid to digestion.* N COUNT

3 If you **aid** a person or an organization, you help them by providing them with something that they need. EG *He crossed the border aided by a priest... ...state intervention to aid private industry.* V+O

4 **Aid** is also used in these phrases. **4.1** If an activity or event is **in aid of** a particular cause, it raises money for that cause. EG *...a cricket match in aid of cancer relief.* PREP **4.2** If you do something **with the aid of** someone or something, they help you to do it. EG *The programmes had been prepared with the aid of various broadcasters.* PREP **4.3** If you go **to the aid of** someone, you try to help them when they are in danger or difficulty. EG *They had rushed to her aid.* PHRASE

aide /eɪd/, **aides.** An **aide** is an assistant to someone who has an important job, especially in government or in the armed forces. N COUNT

AIDS /eɪdz/ is an illness which destroys the natural system of protection that the body has against disease. **AIDS** is an abbreviation for 'acquired immune deficiency syndrome'. N UNCOUNT

ailing /eɪlɪŋ/. **1** If someone is **ailing**, they are ill and are not getting better. EG *...his ailing wife.* ADJ CLASSIF

2 If an organization or society is **ailing**, it is in difficulty and is becoming weaker. ADJ CLASSIF

ailment /eɪlmə^{2}nt/, **ailments.** An **ailment** is an illness, especially one that is not very serious. EG *The crew began suffering a variety of ailments.* N COUNT

aim /eɪm/, **aims, aiming, aimed. 1** If you **aim** a weapon or object at something, you point it in the direction of the thing. EG *Roger picked up a stone, aimed it, and threw it at Henry... He lunged toward me as if he expected me to aim a gun at him.* V+O OR V: OFT +*at*
▸ used as a noun. EG *He leaned against a tree to steady his aim.* ▸ N UNCOUNT +SUPP

2 If you **take aim** at someone or something, you point a weapon or object at them, ready to shoot or throw. EG *He took careful aim at the centre and fired.* PHRASE

3 If you **aim** at something or **aim** to do something, you plan or hope to achieve it. EG *We are aiming at a higher production level... A good solid job is the thing to aim for.* V+*at/for* OR *to*-INF

4 If an action or plan **is aimed** at achieving something, it is intended to achieve it. EG *...policies aimed at securing mass support.* V-PASS+*at*

5 An **aim** is the thing that an action or plan is intended to achieve. EG *It is our aim to set up a workshop.* N COUNT+SUPP

6 If you **aim** an action at a particular person or group, you intend that they should notice it and be influenced by it. EG *This anti-smoking campaign is mainly aimed at young teenagers.* V+O+*at*: USU PASS

aimless /eɪmlɪ^{2}s/. A person or activity that is **aimless** has no clear purpose or plan. EG *...drawing aimless doodles in the sand.* ◊ **aimlessly.** EG *She wandered aimlessly along the beach.* ADJ QUALIT; ◊ ADV

ain't /eɪnt/ is used in nonstandard spoken English instead of 'am not', 'aren't', or 'isn't'.

air /ɛə/, **airs, airing, aired. 1 Air** is the mixture of gases which forms the earth's atmosphere and which we breathe. EG *She took a gulp of air... The air temperature was below freezing.* N UNCOUNT

2 The **air** is the space around things that is above the ground. EG *My dog was lying on the floor with its feet in the air... The smell of cooking filled the air.* N SING: *the*+N

3 **Air** is used to refer to travel in aircraft. EG *The fare by air from London to Luxembourg is £145 return... Philip was unaccustomed to air travel.* N UNCOUNT: *by*+N

4 If you say that someone or something has a particular **air**, you mean that they give this general impression. EG *He has a faintly old-fashioned air.* N SING+SUPP

5 If you **air** your opinions, you make them known to people. EG *He spoke on the radio, airing his views to the nation.* V+O

Can an aircraft run aground?

6 If you **air** a room or building, you let fresh air into it. V+O

7 If you **air** clothing or bedding, you put it somewhere warm in order to make sure that it is completely dry. V-ERG

8 Air is also used in these phrases. **8.1** If someone or something disappears **into thin air,** they disappear completely. **8.2** If someone or something appears **out of thin air**, they appear suddenly and mysteriously. EG *I can't simply conjure up the money out of thin air.* **8.3** If someone is **on the air**, they are broadcasting on radio or television. EG *The president went on the air to make a public statement.* PHRASES

9 See also **airing**.

airborne /ɛəbɔːn/. If something is **airborne**, it is in the air or it comes from the air. EG *...airborne attacks.* ADJ CLASSIF

air-conditioned. If a room is **air-conditioned**, the air in it is kept cool and dry by means of a special machine. ADJ CLASSIF

aircraft /ɛəkrɑːft/. **Aircraft** is both the singular and the plural. An **aircraft** is a vehicle which can fly, for example an aeroplane or a helicopter. N COUNT OR *by*+N

aircraft carrier, aircraft carriers. An **aircraft carrier** is a warship with a long, flat deck where aircraft can take off and land. N COUNT

airfield /ɛəfiːld/, **airfields.** An **airfield** is an area of ground where aircraft take off and land. It is smaller than an airport. N COUNT

air force, air forces. An **air force** is the part of a country's military organization that is concerned with fighting in the air. N COUNT

air hostess, air hostesses. An **air hostess** is a woman whose job is to look after the passengers in an aircraft. N COUNT

airing /ɛərɪŋ/. **1** If you give a room an **airing**, you let fresh air into it, often in order to remove unpleasant smells. N SING : *an*+N

2 If you give bedding or clothing an **airing**, you put it somewhere warm in order to make sure that it is completely dry. N SING : *an*+N

3 If you give your opinions an **airing**, you make them known to people. EG *Her views on sex and death regularly get an airing on television.* N SING : *an*+N

airless /ɛəlɪ²s/. If a room is **airless**, there is no fresh air in it. EG *...a small airless theatre crammed with children.* ADJ CLASSIF

airline /ɛəlaɪn/, **airlines.** An **airline** is a company which provides regular services carrying people or goods in aeroplanes. EG *There were no other airlines doing a direct flight to London.* N COUNT

airliner /ɛəlaɪnə/, **airliners.** An **airliner** is a large aeroplane that is used for carrying passengers. N COUNT

airmail /ɛəmeɪl/ is the system of sending letters, parcels, and goods by air. EG *She gave him a letter to post by airmail... ...an airmail envelope.* N UNCOUNT

airplane /ɛəpleɪn/, **airplanes.** An **airplane** is a vehicle with wings and one or more engines that enable it to fly through the air. N COUNT American

airport /ɛəpɔːt/, **airports.** An **airport** is a place where aircraft land and take off, usually with a lot of buildings and facilities. N COUNT

air raid, air raids. An **air raid** is an attack by enemy aircraft in which bombs are dropped. N COUNT

airship /ɛəʃɪp/, **airships.** An **airship** was an aircraft that was supported in the air by a large balloon filled with gas. Passengers sat in a compartment underneath the balloon. N COUNT

airsick /ɛəsɪk/. If you are **airsick**, the effects of flying in an aeroplane make you sick. ADJ QUALIT

airspace /ɛəspeɪs/. A country's **airspace** is the part of the sky that is over that country and is considered to belong to the country. EG *The plane crashed just after entering British airspace.* N UNCOUNT

air terminal, air terminals. An **air terminal** is a building in which passengers wait before they get on to their aeroplane. N COUNT

airtight /ɛətaɪt/. If a container is **airtight**, its lid fits so tightly that no air can get in or out. ADJ CLASSIF

air-traffic control is the group of people who organize routes for aircraft and who give instructions to pilots by radio about their routes. N UNCOUNT

airwaves /ɛəweɪvz/ are the radio waves which are used in radio and television broadcasting. N PLURAL

airy /ɛəri¹/, **airier, airiest. 1** If a building is **airy**, it is large and has plenty of fresh air inside. EG *The church was airy and light inside.* ADJ QUALIT

2 You can use **airy** to describe someone who is light-hearted and casual about things which should be taken seriously. EG *He applied in an airy way for the job of assistant manager.* ◊ **airily.** EG *People's jobs matter, yet you're talking airily of closing our company.* ADJ QUALIT; ◊ ADV

aisle /aɪl/, **aisles.** An **aisle** is a long narrow gap that people can walk along between rows of seats in a public building or between rows of shelves in a supermarket. N COUNT

ajar /ədʒɑː/. If a door is **ajar**, it is slightly open. ADJ PRED

akin /əkɪn/. If one thing is **akin** to another, it is similar to it in some way. EG *She had answered with something akin to anger.* ADJ PRED+*to* Formal

-al is added to nouns to form adjectives. For example, 'agricultural' means related to agriculture and 'departmental' means related to the work of a department. Adjectives like these are often not defined in this dictionary, but are treated with the related nouns. EG *There she stood in her bridal gown... They were still arguing about doctrinal matters.* SUFFIX

alacrity /əlækrɪ¹ti¹/. If you do something with **alacrity**, you do it quickly and eagerly. EG *He rose with alacrity to welcome her.* N UNCOUNT Formal

alarm /əlɑːm/, **alarms, alarming, alarmed. 1 Alarm** is a sudden feeling of fear or anxiety. EG *She looked round in alarm.* N UNCOUNT

2 An **alarm** is an automatic device that warns you of danger, for example by ringing a bell. EG *The alarm went off... ...a burglar alarm.* N COUNT

3 If you **sound** or **raise the alarm**, you warn people of danger. PHRASE

4 If something **alarms** you, it makes you suddenly afraid or anxious. EG *The sight of the school alarmed her... Even little things alarm them.* ◊ **alarmed.** EG *She looked alarmed.* V+O; ◊ ADJ QUALIT

alarm clock, alarm clocks. An **alarm clock** is a clock that you can set to make a noise so that it wakes you up at a particular time. N COUNT

alarming /əlɑːmɪŋ/. Something that is **alarming** makes you worried or concerned. EG *The world's forests are shrinking at an alarming rate.* ◊ **alarmingly.** EG *McPherson's sight had begun to deteriorate alarmingly.* ADJ QUALIT; ◊ ADV OR ADV SEN

alarmist /əlɑːmɪst/, **alarmists.** Someone or something that is **alarmist** causes unnecessary alarm. EG *Don't be too alarmist.* ADJ QUALIT

alas /ə³læs/. You use **alas** to say that you think that the facts you are talking about are sad, unfortunate, or regrettable. EG *There was, alas, no shortage of assassinations.* ADV SEN Formal

albatross /ælbətrɒs/, **albatrosses.** An **albatross** is a very large white seabird. N COUNT

albeit /ɔːlbiːɪt/. When you want to introduce a fact or a comment which contrasts with something that you have just said, you can use **albeit**. EG *It continues to publish, albeit irregularly, two journals.* CONJ Formal

albino /ælbiːnəʊ/, **albinos.** An **albino** is a person or animal with very white skin, white hair, and pink eyes. ▸ used as an adjective. EG *...an albino monkey.* N COUNT; ▸ ADJ CLASSIF

album /ælbəm/, **albums.** An **album** is **1** a record with about 25 minutes of music or speech on each side. EG *...an album sleeve.* **2** a special book in which you keep things such as photographs or stamps that you have collected. N COUNT; N COUNT+SUPP

alcohol /ælkə⁶hɒl/ is **1** drink such as beer, wine, and whisky that can make people drunk. EG *I never touch alcohol in any form.* **2** a colourless liquid that is found in drinks such as beer, wine, and whisky. It is also used as a solvent. N UNCOUNT

alcoholic /ælkə⁶hɒlɪk/, **alcoholics.** **1** An **alcoholic** drink contains alcohol. ADJ QUALIT

2 Someone who is an **alcoholic** is addicted to alcohol and continues drinking even though it makes them ill. N COUNT

alcoholism /ælkə⁶hɒlɪzə⁰m/ is a kind of poisoning caused by drinking too much alcohol over a long period of time. N UNCOUNT

alcove /ælkəʊv/, **alcoves.** An **alcove** is a small area of a room which is formed by one part of a wall being built further back than the rest of the wall. N COUNT

ale /eɪl/ is a kind of beer. N MASS

alert /əlɜːt/, **alerts, alerting, alerted.** **1** If you are **alert**, you are paying full attention to what is happening. EG *We have to be alert all the time and look for our opportunity.* ◇ **alertly.** EG *We were all watching Dixon alertly.* ◇ **alertness.** EG *The job requires constant alertness and vigilance.* ADJ QUALIT ◇ ADV ◇ N UNCOUNT

2 If you are **on the alert**, you are ready to deal with anything that might happen. PHRASE

3 If you are **alert** to something, you are fully aware of it. EG *They were both alert to the dangers in the grim business.* ADJ PRED : OFT+to

4 An **alert** is a situation in which people prepare themselves for something dangerous that might happen. EG *The city centre was on a nuclear alert.* N COUNT

5 If you **alert** someone, you warn them of danger or trouble. V+O

A level, A levels. An **A level** is an educational qualification in England, Wales, and Northern Ireland. Schoolchildren take A level examinations when they are seventeen or eighteen years old. People usually need A levels if they want to go to university in Britain. N COUNT

algebra /ældʒɪ²brə/ is a type of mathematics in which letters are used to represent possible quantities. N UNCOUNT

alias /eɪlɪəs/, **aliases.** **1** An **alias** is a false name, especially one used by a criminal. N COUNT

2 You use **alias** when you mention someone's false name. EG *Peter Lewis, alias John Lord, was convicted of fraud.* PREP

alibi /ælɪbaɪ/, **alibis.** If you have an **alibi**, you can prove that you were somewhere else when a crime was committed. EG *...his alibi for the night of the murder.* N COUNT : OFT+for

alien /eɪljən, eɪlɪən/, **aliens.** **1** Something that is **alien** belongs to a different country, race, or group. EG *...alien rulers... ...adjusting to an alien society.* ADJ CLASSIF : ATTRIB

2 If you describe something as **alien**, you mean that it seems strange and perhaps frightening, because it is not part of your normal experience. EG *...a totally alien and threatening environment.* ADJ QUALIT

3 If something is **alien** to your normal feelings or behaviour, it is not the way you would normally feel or behave. EG *Their system of parental care seems alien to us today.* ADJ CLASSIF : OFT+to

4 An **alien** is **4.1** someone who is not a legal citizen of the country in which they live. **4.2** a creature from outer space. EG *...an alien spacecraft.* N COUNT

alienate /eɪljəneɪt, eɪlɪə-/, **alienates, alienating, alienated.** **1** If you **alienate** someone, you make them become unfriendly or unsympathetic towards you. EG *I managed to alienate Dennis, who earlier on had been so very friendly.* ◇ **alienation** /eɪljəneɪʃə⁰n, eɪlɪə-/. EG *...alienation on the part of many workers.* V+O ◇ N UNCOUNT

2 If someone **is alienated** from something that they are normally linked with, they are emotionally or intellectually separated from it. EG *People have been alienated from their roots.* ◇ **alienation.** EG *...a growing feeling of despair and alienation.* V+O : USU PASS ◇ N UNCOUNT

alight /əlaɪt/, **alights, alighting, alighted.** **1** If something is **alight**, **1.1** it is burning. EG *...paraffin that has been set alight.* **1.2** it is very bright and colourful. EG *... bushes alight with glow-worms and fireflies.* ADJ PRED ; ADJ PRED : OFT+with

2 If you describe someone's face or expression as **alight**, you mean that they look excited. EG *She was looking at him, her eyes alight.* ADJ PRED

3 If a bird or insect **alights** somewhere, it lands there. EG *It flew across to the tree and alighted on a branch.* V : USU+A

4 When you **alight** from a train or bus, you get out of it after a journey. EG *He was photographed alighting from his private plane.* V : OFT+from Formal

align /əlaɪn/, **aligns, aligning, aligned.** **1** If you **align** yourself with a particular group or **are aligned** with them, you support them in the same political aim. EG *They have avoided aligning themselves with any one political party... The Soviet Union was aligned with the Western powers against the Nazis.* ◇ **alignment** /əlaɪnmə²nt/, **alignments.** EG *...political alignments with foreign powers.* V-REFL OR V-PASS : OFT+with /against ◇ N COUNT

2 If you **align** something, you place it in a certain position in relation to something else, usually parallel to it. EG *He aligned his papers in geometrical patterns on his desk.* ◇ **alignment.** EG *Something had slipped out of alignment.* V+O ◇ N UNCOUNT

alike /əlaɪk/. **1** If two or more things are **alike**, they are similar. EG *They all look alike to me.* ADJ PRED

2 **Alike** also means in a similar way. EG *The children are all treated alike... They did everything alike.* ADV

3 When you want to emphasize that you are referring to all of a group of people or things, you can use **alike** after you mention them. EG *The strike is damaging to managers and workers alike.* ADV

alimony /ælɪmənɪ¹/ is money that someone has to pay regularly to their former wife or husband after they have been divorced. N UNCOUNT

alive /əlaɪv/. **1** If people or animals are **alive**, they have life. EG *I think his father is still alive.* ADJ PRED

2 If you describe someone as **alive**, you mean that they are very lively and enjoy everything that they do. EG *Young people are so alive and exciting.* ADJ PRED

3 If an activity, organization, or situation is **alive**, it continues to exist or function. EG *Theatre outside London is very much alive.* ADJ PRED

4 If a place is **alive** with something, a lot of people or things are there and it seems busy or exciting. EG *The ditches beside the fields were alive with frogs... The church hall was alive with song.* ADJ PRED +with

5 If you are **alive** to a problem or situation, you are aware of it and realize how important it is. EG *They were fully alive to the danger.* ADJ PRED+to

6 If a story or description **comes alive**, it becomes interesting, lively, or realistic. EG *None of his characters actually comes alive.* PHRASE

7 If people or places **come alive**, they start to be active or lively again after a quiet or dull period. EG *The house had come alive.* PHRASE

alkali /ælkəlaɪ/, **alkalis.** An **alkali** is a substance with a pH value of more than 7. Alkalis form chemical salts when they are combined with acids. N MASS

all /ɔːl/. **1** You use **all** to refer to the whole of a particular group or thing. EG *All the girls think it's great... They carried all the stuff into the hall... All of the defendants were proved guilty... They all live together in the same house... All was quiet in the gaol.* PREDET OR PRON

2 You also use **all** **2.1** to emphasize that a quality is complete and total. EG *I say this in all seriousness.* DET
2.2 to emphasize that something happens or is true ADV

If your face is alight, is it burning?

to a very great extent. EG *He spilled coffee all over himself... I forgot all about him... I'm all alone.*

3 You can use **all** when you are emphasizing that something is the only thing that is important. EG *All you do is add water... Look, give me a chance. That's all I want.* PRON

4 You use **all** when you are talking about an equal score in a game. For example, if the score is three **all**, both players or teams have three points. ADV: NUMBER+ADV

5 **All** the more or **all** the better mean even more or even better than before. EG *You must work all the more quickly now.* PREDET

6 You say **above all** to emphasize that a particular thing is more important than other things. EG *Relax, and above all don't panic.* ADV SEN

7 You use **after all** **7.1** when you want to emphasize something that other people might have forgotten. EG *It had to be recognized, after all, that I was still a schoolboy.* **7.2** when you are saying that something that you thought was not true is in fact true. EG *Could it be true, after all, that money did not bring happiness?* ADV SEN

8 You use **all in all** to introduce a summary or generalization. EG *All in all, I'm not in favour.* ADV SEN

9 If you say that something is not **all that** good or not **all that** important, you mean that it is not very good or not very important. EG *I don't know him all that well.* PHRASE Spoken

10 If you say that something is **all very well**, you are suggesting that you do not really approve of it. EG *Look, it's all very well, but he scared the life out of me.* PHRASE

11 You use **at all** to emphasize a negative statement. EG *We didn't go there at all... Haven't you got any at all?* PHRASE

12 You use **for all** **12.1** to say that a particular fact does not affect or contradict what you are saying, although you know that it may seem to do so. EG *For all her sensitivity, she's extremely tough.* **12.2** in phrases such as 'for all I know', and 'for all he cares', to emphasize that something does not really matter. EG *It might have been tomato soup for all we knew.* PHRASE

13 **In all** means in total. EG *There were nine in all.* PHRASE

14 You use **of all** to emphasize the words 'first' or 'last', or a superlative adjective or adverb. EG *I asked them first of all if they were Welsh... This view is the best of all.* PHRASE

Allah /ælə/ is the name of God in Islam. N PROPER

allay /ə[3]leɪ/, **allays, allaying, allayed.** To **allay** an emotion means to cause it to be felt less strongly. EG *His efforts to allay her fears met with little success.* V+O Formal

all clear. The **all clear** is a signal that a dangerous situation has ended. EG *They eventually went back in after the all clear was sounded.* N SING

allegation /ælɪ[2]geɪʃə[0]n/, **allegations.** An **allegation** is a statement suggesting that someone has done something wrong. EG *...allegations of improper business dealings.* N COUNT

allege /ə[3]lɛdʒ/, **alleges, alleging, alleged.** If you **allege** that something is true, you say it but do not prove it. EG *The reports alleged that the motive was financial.* V+REPORT: ONLY *that*, OR V-PASS +*to*-INF

alleged /ə[3]lɛdʒd/. An **alleged** fact has been stated but has not been proved to be true. EG *...alleged police brutality.* ADJ CLASSIF: ATTRIB ◊ **allegedly.** EG *...the crimes he had allegedly committed.* ◊ ADV

allegiance /ə[3]liːdʒəns/, **allegiances.** Your **allegiance** is your support for and loyalty to a particular group, person, or belief. EG *...an oath of allegiance to his country... How can we win the allegiance of the masses?* N UNCOUNT OR N COUNT: OFT+*to*

allegorical /ælɪ[2]gɒrɪkə[0]l/. An **allegorical** story, poem, or painting uses allegory. ADJ CLASSIF

allegory /ælɪ[2]gə[0]ri[1]/, **allegories.** An **allegory** is a story, poem, or painting in which the characters and events are symbols of something else. Allegories are often moral, religious, or political. N COUNT OR N UNCOUNT

alleluia /ælɪluːjə/. See **hallelujah**.

allergic /ə[3]lɜːdʒɪk/. If you are **allergic** to something, you become ill or get a rash when you eat it, smell it, or touch it. EG *Are you allergic to dogs?... ...an allergic rash.* ADJ PRED+*to* OR ADJ CLASSIF: ATTRIB

allergy /ælədʒi[1]/, **allergies.** An **allergy** is an illness that you have when you eat, smell, or touch a substance which does not normally make people ill. EG *He had an allergy to milk.* N COUNT OR N UNCOUNT: OFT+*to*

alleviate /ə[3]liːvieɪt/, **alleviates, alleviating, alleviated.** If something **alleviates** pain or suffering, it makes it less intense or severe. EG *We want to help alleviate the national food shortage.* V+O
◊ **alleviation** /ə[3]liːvieɪʃə[0]n/. EG *...the alleviation of pain.* ◊ N UNCOUNT OFT+*of*

alley /æli[1]/, **alleys.** An **alley** or an **alleyway** is a narrow path or street. N COUNT

alliance /əlaɪəns/, **alliances.** An **alliance** is a relationship in which two or more people or groups work together for some purpose. EG *We met to discuss the strategies of a working alliance... This pleasant alliance between Mrs Bixby and the Colonel continued.* N COUNT

allied /ælaɪd/. **1** **Allied** countries, political parties, or other groups are united by a political or military agreement. EG *...allied leaders.* ADJ CLASSIF: ATTRIB

2 **Allied** describes things that are related to other things because they have particular qualities or characteristics in common. EG *The aircraft and allied industries were nationalized.* ADJ CLASSIF: ATTRIB

3 See also **ally**.

alligator /ælɪgeɪtə/, **alligators.** An **alligator** is a large animal, chiefly of the southern United States, similar to a crocodile. N COUNT

allocate /ælə[6]keɪt/, **allocates, allocating, allocated.** If something **is allocated** to a particular person or for a particular purpose, it is given to that person to use or is used for that purpose. EG *...money allocated to books and stationery... You've been allocated room 426.* V+O: OFT PASS+*to* ◊ **allocation** /ælə[6]keɪʃə[0]n/. EG *...the allocation of responsibilities.* ◊ N UNCOUNT

allot /ə[3]lɒt/, **allots, allotting, allotted.** If something **is allotted** to someone, it is given to them as their share. EG *She would be content to sleep in any corner that was allotted to her.* V+O: OFT PASS+*to* ◊ **allotted.** EG *We will spend our allotted sum of money on a larger swimming pool.* ◊ ADJ CLASSIF ATTRIB

allotment /ə[3]lɒtmə[3]nt/, **allotments. 1** An **allotment** is a small area of land in a town which a person rents to grow vegetables on. N COUNT British

2 An **allotment** of something is a share or amount of it that is given to someone. N SING+*of*

all-out. You use **all-out** to describe aggressive actions that are done in a very energetic and determined way. EG *...an all-out attack on trade unions.* ADJ CLASSIF: ATTRIB

allow /əlaʊ/, **allows, allowing, allowed. 1** If you **are allowed** to do something, it is all right for you to do it and you will not get into trouble. EG *No one is allowed here... He agreed to allow me to take the course.* V+O+*to*-INF OR V+A: USU PASS

2 If you **are allowed** something, you are given permission to have it. EG *Sometimes, we were allowed a special treat.* V+O+O: USU PASS

3 If you **allow** something to happen, you do not prevent it. EG *The further this process is allowed to go, the more difficult it will be to reverse it... You must not allow yourself to be upset.* V+O+*to*-INF OR V-REFL +*to*-INF

4 If something **allows** something to happen, it gives the opportunity for it to happen. EG *The creatures had warm blood, which allowed them to be active at night.* V+O+*to*-INF

5 When you are politely offering to do something for someone, you can say **'allow me'**. EG *Mr Smith jumped up and said, 'Allow me.'* CONVENTION

6 If you **allow** that something is true, you admit or agree that it is true. EG *He allowed that even world leaders could make mistakes.* V+REPORT: ONLY *that*

allow for. If you **allow for** certain problems or PHRASAL VB: V+PREP expenses, you include some extra time or money in your planning so that you can deal with them if they occur.

allowable /əlaʊəbəl/. If people decide that something is **allowable**, they let it happen without trying to stop it. EG *...allowable departures from the norms of behaviour.* ADJ CLASSIF

allowance /əlaʊəns/, **allowances. 1** An **allowance** is money that is given regularly to someone, in order to help them pay for the things that they need. EG *...a maternity allowance.* N COUNT+SUPP

2 If you **make allowances** for something, you take it into account in your plans or actions. EG *They make no allowances for a child's age.* PHRASE

all-powerful. Someone or something that is **all-powerful** has a great deal of power or influence. ADJ CLASSIF

all right; also spelled **alright. 1** If you say that someone or something is **all right**, you mean that you find them satisfactory or acceptable. EG *'Do you like this champagne?' – 'It's all right.'... Is everything all right?... He's getting on all right.* ADJ PRED OR ADV

2 If someone or something is **all right**, they are well or safe. EG *Someone should see if she's all right.* ADJ PRED

3 You say **'all right'** when you are agreeing to something. EG *'Can you help?' – 'All right. What do you want me to do?'* CONVENTION

4 If you say **'all right?'** to someone, you are checking that they have understood what you have just said. EG *If you feel dizzy again put your head in your hands, all right?* ADV SEN

5 Teachers and parents often say **'all right'** to indicate that they want you to end one activity and start another. EG *Alright team, let's move on to another question.* ADV SEN

all-rounder, all-rounders. Someone who is an **all-rounder** is good at a lot of different skills, academic subjects, or sports. N COUNT British

allude /əljuːd/, **alludes, alluding, alluded.** If you **allude** to something, you mention it in an indirect way. V+*to* Formal

allure /əljʊə/. The **allure** of something is the pleasing or exciting quality that it has. EG *...the allure of money.* N SING

alluring /əljʊərɪŋ/. Someone or something that is **alluring** is very attractive. EG *...alluring dark eyelashes.* ADJ QUALIT

allusion /əljuːʒən/, **allusions.** An **allusion** is a reference to someone or something in which they are not mentioned directly or in detail. EG *English literature is full of allusions to Latin and Greek authors.* N COUNT OR N UNCOUNT : OFT+*to*

ally, allies, allying, allied; pronounced /ælaɪ/ when it is a noun and /əlaɪ/ when it is a verb.

1 A country's **ally** is another country that has an agreement to support it, especially in war. EG *...our European allies.* N COUNT : OFT+POSS

2 Someone who is your **ally** helps and supports you, especially when other people are opposing you. EG *She wanted an ally so badly.* N COUNT : OFT+POSS

3 If you **ally** yourself with someone, you support them. EG *...countries who do not ally themselves with the super powers.* V-REFL+*with*

4 See also **allied**.

almighty /ɔːlmaɪtɪ/. **1** The **Almighty** is another name for God. EG *...the mercy of the Almighty.* N PROPER : *the*+N

▸ used as an adjective. EG *Almighty God appeared to Jacob in the land of Canaan.* ▸ ADJ CLASSIF : ATTRIB

2 An **almighty** row, problem, or mistake is a very great or serious one. EG *She made the most almighty fuss.* ADJ CLASSIF : ATTRIB Informal

almond /ɑːmənd/, **almonds.** An **almond** is a kind of pale oval nut. N COUNT

almost /ɔːlməʊst/ means very nearly. You can use it before nouns, adjectives, verbs, and adverbs, and before words such as 'anyone' and 'anything'. EG *I spent almost a month in China... He is almost blind... I had almost forgotten about the trip... The door opened almost before Brody had finished knocking... In Oxford Street, you can buy almost anything.* ADV

aloft /əlɒft/. Something that is **aloft** is in the air or off the ground. EG *Simon held his hands aloft.* ADV AFTER VB Literary

alone /ələʊn/. **1** When you are **alone**, **1.1** you are not with any other people. EG *I wanted to be alone... Barbara spent most of her time alone in the flat.* **1.2** you are amongst people who you do not know. EG *She was going all alone to Paris.* **1.3** you have no family or friends. EG *I had never felt so alone and without hope in my life.* ADJ PRED

2 If one person is **alone** with another person, or if two people are **alone**, they are together, without anyone else present. EG *I was alone with the attendant... We'd never spent such a long time alone together.* ADJ PRED

3 If you do something **alone**, you do it without help from other people. EG *I was left to bring up my two children alone.* ● When someone **goes it alone**, they do something without any help from other people. EG *He aimed to 'go it alone' politically.* ADV AFTER VB ● PHRASE Informal

4 If you **alone** do something, you are the only person who does it. EG *Simon alone knew the truth.* ADJ AFTER N

5 If something consists of one idea or feature **alone**, nothing else is involved. EG *Pride alone prevented her from giving up.* ADJ AFTER N

along /əlɒŋ/. **1** If you move or look **along** something such as a road, you move or look towards one end of it. EG *He was driving along a lane... She glanced along the corridor.* PREP

2 If something is situated **along** a road, river, or corridor, it is situated in it or beside it. EG *...an old house along the Lanark Road... Room 64 was half way along on the right.* PREP OR ADV

3 When someone or something moves **along**, they keep moving steadily and continuously. EG *I put my arm around him as we walked along.* ADV AFTER VB

4 If you say that something is going **along** in a particular way, you mean that it is progressing in that way. EG *It was going along nicely... His divorce is dragging along.* ADV AFTER VB

5 If you take someone **along** when you go somewhere, you take them with you. EG *He liked taking her along to parties... Why don't you come along too?* ADV AFTER VB

6 If something has existed or been true **all along**, it has existed or been true throughout a period of time. EG *Perhaps they had been mistaken all along.* PHRASE

7 If you do something **along with** someone else, you both do it. If you take one thing **along with** another, you take both things. EG *Along with thousands of others, he fled the country... The eggs were delivered along with the milk.* PREP

alongside /əlɒŋsaɪd/. **1** If something is **alongside** something else, it is next to it. EG *There was a butcher's shop alongside the theatre... A car drew up alongside.* PREP OR ADV

2 If several people are working **alongside** other people, they are working in the same place and are co-operating with each other. EG *The idea is to get them working on simple things alongside other people.* PREP

3 When you talk about one system or attitude existing **alongside** another one, you are comparing them and considering whether they can exist well or properly together. EG *I cannot imagine two political systems less likely to live at peace alongside each other.* PREP

aloof /əluːf/. **1** Someone who is **aloof** likes to be alone and does not talk much to other people. ADJ QUALIT

2 If someone stays **aloof** from something, they do not become involved with it. EG *The Emperor kept aloof from all political parties.* ADJ PRED : OFT+*from*

If you are not altogether aloof, do you talk much to other people?

aloud /əlaʊd/. When you speak or read **aloud**, you speak so that other people can hear you. EG *She read aloud to us from the newspaper.* ADV AFTER VB

alphabet /ælfəbɛt/, **alphabets.** The **alphabet** is the set of letters arranged in a fixed order which is used for writing the words of a language. N COUNT

alphabetical /ælfəbɛtɪkə^{0}l/ means arranged according to the normal order of the letters in the alphabet. EG *...an alphabetical list.* ADJ CLASSIF : ATTRIB
◇ **alphabetically.** EG *Books are catalogued alphabetically by author.* ◇ ADV

alpine /ælpaɪn/ means existing in or relating to mountains. EG *...alpine meadows.* ADJ CLASSIF : ATTRIB

already /ɔːlrɛdi^{1}/. If something has **already** happened, 1 it has happened before the present time, and therefore does not need to happen again. EG *I've had tea already, thank you.* 2 it has happened earlier than you expected. EG *By the time he got home, Julie was already in bed.* ADV

alright /ɔːlraɪt/. See **all right**.

also /ɔːlsəʊ/. You use **also** 1 when you are giving more information about a person or thing, or adding another relevant fact. EG *Tony Nuttall is Vice-Chancellor and also a Professor of English at Sussex... ...also available in blue and green.* 2 to say that the same fact applies to someone or something else. EG *His first wife was also called Margaret.* ADV

altar /ɒltə/, **altars.** An **altar** is a holy table in a church or temple. N COUNT : USU *the*+N

alter /ɒltə/, **alters, altering, altered.** If something **alters** or if you **alter** it, it changes. EG *The weather could alter violently... America must radically alter its economic policy.* V-ERG
◇ **alteration** /ɒltəreɪʃə^{0}n/, **alterations.** EG *It is not possible to make major alterations to existing arrangements.* ◇ N COUNT : USU+SUPP

altercation /ɒltəkeɪʃə^{0}n/, **altercations.** An **altercation** is a noisy argument. N COUNT Formal

alternate, alternates, alternating, alternated; pronounced /ɒltəneɪt/ when it is a verb and /ɒltɜːnət/ when it is an adjective.

1 When you **alternate** between two things, you regularly do or use one thing and then the other. EG *They alternated between patronising us and ignoring us.* V+*between*

2 When one thing **alternates** with another, the two things regularly occur after each other. EG *The Third World suffers from an annual cycle of drought alternating with flood.* V+*with*
◇ **alternation** /ɒltəneɪʃə^{0}n/. EG *...an alternation of right-wing and left-wing governments.* ◇ N UNCOUNT : USU+SUPP

3 **Alternate** actions, events, or processes regularly occur after each other. EG *...the alternate contraction and relaxation of muscles.* ADJ CLASSIF : ATTRIB
◇ **alternately.** EG *Each piece of material is washed alternately in soft water and coconut oil.* ◇ ADV

4 If something happens on **alternate** days, it happens on one day, then does not happen on the next day, then happens again on the day after it, and so on. In the same way, something can happen in **alternate** weeks, years, or other periods of time. EG *We saw each other on alternate Sunday nights.* ADJ CLASSIF : ATTRIB

alternative /ɒltɜːnətɪv/, **alternatives.** 1 An **alternative** is something that can exist instead of something else or that you can do instead of something else. EG *Are there alternatives to prison?* N COUNT : OFT+*to*
▸ used as an adjective. EG *But still people try to find alternative explanations.* ▸ ADJ CLASSIF : ATTRIB

2 **Alternative** is also used to describe something that is very different from the usual things of its kind, especially when it is simpler or more natural than normal. EG *...sources of alternative energy... ...alternative newspapers.* ADJ CLASSIF : ATTRIB

alternatively /ɒltɜːnətɪvli^{1}/. You use **alternatively** to suggest or mention something different from what has just been mentioned. EG *Alternatively, you can use household bleach.* ADV SEN

although /ɔːlðəʊ/. You use **although** to introduce subordinate clauses. It introduces 1 a clause which contains a statement that makes the main clause of the sentence seem surprising. EG *Although he was late he stopped to buy a sandwich... Gretchen kept her coat on, although it was warm in the room.* 2 a clause, often one that contains 'not', that modifies the main clause and corrects a wrong impression that someone might get from it. EG *I have a lot of my grandfather's features, although I'm not so tall as he was.* CONJ

altitude /æltɪtjuːd/, **altitudes.** If something is at a particular **altitude**, it is at that height above sea level. EG *The valley lies at an altitude of about 8,000 ft... ...an airliner flying at high altitude.* N UNCOUNT OR N COUNT

alto /æltəʊ/, **altos.** 1 An **alto** is a woman with a low singing voice. N COUNT

2 An **alto** musical instrument has a range of musical notes of medium pitch. EG *...an alto sax.* ADJ CLASSIF : ATTRIB

altogether /ɔːltəgɛðə/. 1 If something stops **altogether**, it stops completely. EG *The noise had stopped altogether... He abandoned his work altogether.* ADV AFTER VB

2 If one thing is **altogether** different from another, the two things are completely different. EG *...an altogether different kind of support.* ADV

3 If you say that you do **not altogether** trust someone, you mean that you do not trust them completely. PHRASE

4 If you say that something is **not altogether** true or **not altogether** satisfactory, you mean that it is not completely true or not completely satisfactory. PHRASE

5 You can use **altogether** to summarize something you have been saying. EG *Yes, it's quite a pleasant place altogether.* ADV SEN

6 If several amounts add up to a particular amount **altogether**, that amount is their total. EG *You will get £340 a week altogether... Altogether, he played in 44 matches.* ADV SEN

altruism /æltruːɪzə^{0}m/ is unselfish concern for other people's happiness and welfare. N UNCOUNT
◇ **altruistic** /æltruːɪstɪk/. EG *My invitation was not completely altruistic.* ◇ ADJ QUALIT

aluminium /æljə^{4}mɪnɪəm/; spelled **aluminum** /əluːmɪnəm/ in American English. **Aluminium** is a lightweight metal used for making cooking equipment and aircraft parts. EG *...an aluminium frying pan.* N UNCOUNT

always /ɔːlwɪ^{3}z/. 1 If you **always** do a particular thing, you do it all the time or on every possible occasion. EG *I shall always love you... You're always looking for faults... She always arrived before Watson.* ADV

2 If something is **always** the case, it is the case all the time. EG *I had always been poor... It's always raining.* ADV

3 If you say that someone can **always** take a particular course of action, you mean that they can try it if all other methods are unsuccessful or undesirable. EG *Oh well, I can always come back later.* ADV

am /æm/ is the first person singular of the present tense of **be.**

a.m. /eɪ ɛm/ after a number refers to a particular time between midnight and noon. EG *85 students were still in the hall at 2 a.m.* ADV

amalgamate /ə^{3}mælgəmeɪt/, **amalgamates, amalgamating, amalgamated.** When two or more organizations **amalgamate** or **are amalgamated**, they become one large organization. EG *...the Variety Artistes Federation, which has since amalgamated with Equity.* V OR V+*with* : RECIP
◇ **amalgamation** /ə^{3}mælgəmeɪʃə^{0}n/, **amalgamations.** EG *...the amalgamation of several large businesses.* ◇ N UNCOUNT OR N COUNT

amass /əmæs/, **amasses, amassing, amassed.** If you **amass** something such as money or information, you gradually get a lot of it. EG *They had amassed enough money to start a business.* V+O

amateur /æmətjʊə, -tʃə/, **amateurs. 1** An **amateur** is someone who does something as a hobby and not as a job. EG *It's a business for professionals not amateurs... ...a good amateur viola player.* N COUNT

2 Amateur can also mean the same as amateurish. ADJ QUALIT

amateurish /æmətjʊərɪʃ/. If you describe something as **amateurish**, you mean that it is not skilfully made or done. EG *Their publications were amateurish and inadequately researched.* ADJ QUALIT

amaze /əmeɪz/, **amazes, amazing, amazed.** If something **amazes** you, it surprises you very much. EG *She was amazed that I was only twenty... He was amazed by the response... It amazed them to learn that I was here.* ◇ **amazed.** EG *I saw her amazed look.* V+O; ◇ ADJ QUALIT

amazement /əmeɪzmənt/ is what you feel when something surprises you very much. EG *Her eyes were wide with amazement... To my amazement, he burst out laughing.* N UNCOUNT

amazing /əmeɪzɪŋ/. You say that something is **amazing** when it is very surprising and makes you feel pleasure, approval, or admiration. EG *New York is an amazing city... It's amazing how useful they are... Her general knowledge is amazing.* ◇ **amazingly.** EG *Our holiday was amazingly cheap.* ADJ QUALIT; ◇ SUBMOD

ambassador /æmbæsədə/, **ambassadors.** An **ambassador** is an important official who lives in a foreign country and represents his or her own country's interests there. EG *...the British Ambassador to Turkey.* N COUNT

amber /æmbə/. **1 Amber** is a hard yellowish-brown substance used for making jewellery. EG *...a dark amber necklace.* N UNCOUNT

2 Something that is **amber** is of an orange or yellowish-brown colour. EG *...clusters of amber berries... The lights constantly switch from red to amber and green.* ADJ COLOUR

ambience /æmbiəns/; also spelled **ambiance.** The **ambience** of a place is the character and atmosphere that it seems to have. EG *...the 'liberal' ambience of the average university.* N SING Literary

ambiguity /æmbɪgjuːɪti/, **ambiguities.** You say that there is **ambiguity** when something can be understood in more than one way. EG *...a speech which was a masterpiece of ambiguity.* N UNCOUNT OR N COUNT

ambiguous /æmbɪgjuəs/. Something that is **ambiguous** can be understood in more than one way. EG *There was nothing ambiguous in the message.* ◇ **ambiguously.** EG *The announcement was ambiguously worded.* ADJ QUALIT; ◇ ADV

ambition /æmbɪʃən/, **ambitions. 1** If you have an **ambition** to do or achieve something, you want very much to do it or achieve it in your life. EG *Her ambition was to be a teacher.* N COUNT

2 If someone has **ambition** or **ambitions**, they want to be successful, rich, or powerful. EG *...men of enterprise, energy, and ambition.* N UNCOUNT OR N PLURAL

ambitious /æmbɪʃəs/. **1** Someone who is **ambitious** wants to be successful, rich, or powerful. EG *...the President's ambitious wife.* ADJ QUALIT

2 An **ambitious** idea or plan is on a large scale and needs a lot of work to be carried out successfully. EG *She then attempted something more ambitious, a novel of 120,000 words.* ADJ QUALIT

ambivalent /æmbɪvələnt/. If you are **ambivalent** about something, you have, or seem to have, opposite feelings about it. EG *...an ambivalent attitude towards women.* ◇ **ambivalence** /æmbɪvələns/. EG *She was in a state of ambivalence about having children.* ADJ QUALIT; ◇ N UNCOUNT

amble /æmbəl/, **ambles, ambling, ambled.** When you **amble**, you walk slowly and in a relaxed manner. EG *I ambled home through the village.* ▸ used as a noun. EG *He slowed down to his usual steady amble.* V: USU+A; ▸ N SING

ambulance /æmbjələns/, **ambulances.** An **ambulance** is a vehicle for taking people to and from hospital. N COUNT

ambush /æmbʊʃ/, **ambushes, ambushing, ambushed.** If a group of people **ambush** a group of their enemies, they attack them after hiding and waiting for them. EG *Weyler's troops successfully ambushed a rebel force.* ▸ used as a noun. EG *A whole battalion got caught in an ambush.* V+O; ▸ N COUNT OR N UNCOUNT

amen /eɪmen, ɑːmen/ is said or sung by Christians at the end of a prayer. EG *This we ask in the name of Thy Son Jesus Christ, Amen.* CONVENTION

amenable /əmiːnəbəl/. If you are **amenable** to something, you are willing to do it or accept it. EG *She was amenable to whatever I suggested.* ADJ QUALIT

amend /əmend/, **amends, amending, amended.**
1 If you **amend** something that has been written or said, you change it. EG *Last year the regulations were amended to allow other awards to be made.* V+O

2 If you **make amends** when you have harmed someone, you show that you are sorry by doing something to please them. EG *He wanted to make amends for his former unkindness.* PHRASE

amendment /əmendmənt/, **amendments.** An **amendment** is **1** a section that is added to a law or rule in order to change it. EG *...amendments to the Industrial Relations Bill.* N COUNT OR N UNCOUNT **2** a correction to a piece of writing. N COUNT

amenity /əmiːnɪti/, **amenities.** An **amenity** is something such as a shopping centre or sports facility that is provided for people's convenience or enjoyment. EG *When you are young you want the amenities of the town... ...first class hotels with every amenity.* N COUNT

American /əmerɪkən/, **Americans. 1** An **American** person or thing belongs to or comes from the United States of America. EG *...an American accent... ...the American economy.* ADJ CLASSIF

2 An **American** is a person who comes from the United States of America. N COUNT

Americanism /əmerɪkənɪzəm/, **Americanisms.** An **Americanism** is an expression or custom that is typical of people living in the United States of America. N COUNT

amiable /eɪmɪəbəl/. Someone who is **amiable** is friendly and pleasant to be with. EG *...her amiable manner.* ◇ **amiably.** EG *He chatted amiably with Dorothy.* ADJ QUALIT; ◇ ADV

amicable /æmɪkəbəl/. When people have an **amicable** relationship, they are pleasant to each other and solve their problems without quarrelling. EG *We hope to settle the dispute in an amicable way.* ◇ **amicably.** EG *They parted amicably.* ADJ QUALIT; ◇ ADV

amid /əmɪd/. **1** If something happens **amid** other things, it happens while the other things are happening. EG *Suddenly, amid the cries, I heard some words.* PREP

2 If something is **amid** other things, it is surrounded by them. EG *Tombstones stood amid the swaying grass.* PREP Literary

amidst /əmɪdst/ means the same as amid.

amiss /əmɪs/. **1** If you say that something is **amiss**, you mean that there is something wrong. EG *I immediately sensed something amiss.* ADJ PRED

2 If someone **takes** something **amiss**, they are offended and upset by it. EG *You mustn't take anything I say amiss.* PHRASE

3 If you say that something would **not come amiss**, you mean that it would be welcome and useful. EG *A little calm wouldn't come amiss.* PHRASE

ammonia /əməʊnɪə, -njə/ is a colourless liquid or gas with a strong, sharp smell. It is used in making household cleaning substances. N UNCOUNT

Would you need an anaesthetic for an amputation?

ammunition /æmjə^{4}nɪʃə^{0}n/. **1 Ammunition** is bullets and rockets that are made to be fired from guns. N UNCOUNT

2 You can also use **ammunition** to mean information that you can use against someone. EG *The letters might be used as ammunition by reactionary groups.* N UNCOUNT

amnesia /æmniːzɪə/ is a person's loss of memory. N UNCOUNT

amnesty /æmnɪ^{2}sti^{1}/, **amnesties.** An **amnesty** is **1** an official pardon granted to a prisoner by the state. **2** a period of time during which people can confess to a crime or give up weapons without being punished. N COUNT

among /əmʌŋ/; the form **amongst** is also used.

1 A person or thing that is **among** a group of people or things is surrounded by them. EG *James wandered among his guests... We stood there among piles of wooden boxes... Among his baggage was a medicine chest.* PREP

2 If you are **among** a group of people, you are in their company. EG *I was among friends.* PREP

3 If you say that one person **among** others did something, you are saying that other people did it, and not just that one person. EG *Bluestone, among other union leaders, argued against a strike.* PREP

4 If an opinion, feeling, or state exists **among** a group of people, they have it or experience it. EG *He has always been popular among MPs... Unemployment amongst married women reached a peak.* PREP

5 If something is divided **among** three or more people, they all get a part of it. EG *The estate was divided among his brothers and sisters.* PREP

amongst /əmʌŋst/ means the same as among.

amoral /æmɒrəl, eɪ-/. Someone who is **amoral** does not care whether what they do is considered to be right or wrong; used showing disapproval. ADJ QUALIT

amorous /æmə^{8}rəs/. **Amorous** feelings and behaviour involve sexual desire. EG *...amorous affairs.* ADJ CLASSIF Literary

amorphous /əmɔːfəs/. Something that is **amorphous** has no clear shape or structure. EG *...an amorphous cloud... ...an amorphous society.* ADJ CLASSIF

amount /əmaʊnt/, **amounts, amounting, amounted. 1** The **amount** of something that you have, need, or get is how much of it you have, need, or get. EG *...the amount of potatoes that people buy... I was horrified by the amount of work I had to do.* N PART

2 If something **amounts** to a particular total, all the parts of it add up to that total. EG *...very high fees which amount to £2,000.* V+*to*

3 If an idea or feeling **amounts** to something else, it is almost the same as this other thing. EG *His attitude towards her amounted to loathing.* V+*to*

4 If something **amounts** to little, it is unimportant. If it **amounts** to a lot, it is important. EG *It is unlikely that the talks will amount to much.* V+*to*

amphibian /æmfɪbɪən/, **amphibians.** An **amphibian** is an animal such as a frog that can live both on land and in water. N COUNT

amphibious /æmfɪbɪəs/. An **amphibious** animal can live both on land and in water. ADJ CLASSIF

amphitheatre /æmfɪθɪətə/, **amphitheatres;** spelled **amphitheater** in American English. An **amphitheatre** is a large open area surrounded by rows of seats sloping upwards, and often used for performances of plays. N COUNT

ample /æmpə^{0}l/. **1** If there is an **ample** amount of something, there is enough of it and some extra. EG *This leaves her ample time to prepare... ...ample supplies of goods.* ◊ **amply.** EG *This has been amply demonstrated over the past few years.* ADJ QUALIT; ◊ ADV

2 Ample also means large. EG *There was provision for an ample lawn.* ADJ QUALIT : ATTRIB

amplifier /æmplɪfaɪə/, **amplifiers.** An **amplifier** is an electronic device in a radio or stereo system, which causes sounds or signals to become louder. N COUNT

amplify /æmplɪfaɪ/, **amplifies, amplifying, amplified. 1** If you **amplify** a sound, you make it louder. EG *These signals are then amplified.* ◊ **amplified.** EG *...an amplified electric guitar.* V+O; ◊ ADJ CLASSIF

2 If you **amplify** an idea, statement, or piece of writing, you explain it more fully. EG *They are simply rough ideas. They need amplifying, of course.* ◊ **amplification** /æmplɪfɪkeɪʃə^{0}n/. EG *His story needed confirmation and amplification.* V+O; ◊ N UNCOUNT

amputate /æmpjə^{4}teɪt/, **amputates, amputating, amputated.** If a surgeon **amputates** someone's arm or leg, he or she cuts part or all of it off. ◊ **amputation** /æmpjə^{4}teɪʃə^{0}n/. EG *Punishment for a thief was amputation of a hand.* V+O; ◊ N UNCOUNT

amuse /ə^{3}mjuːz/, **amuses, amusing, amused. 1** If something **amuses** you, it makes you want to laugh or smile. EG *He laughed as if the idea amused him.* V+O

2 If you **amuse** yourself, you do something in order to pass the time and not become bored. EG *Sam amused himself by throwing branches into the fire.* V-REFL OR V+O

amused /ə^{3}mjuːzd/. **1** If you are **amused** at or by something, it makes you want to laugh or smile. EG *I was highly amused by a comment Shaw made... ...an amused stare.* ADJ QUALIT

2 If you **keep** yourself **amused**, you find things to do which stop you from being bored. PHRASE

amusement /ə^{3}mjuːzmə^{2}nt/, **amusements. 1 Amusement** is **1.1** the feeling that you have when you think that something is funny. EG *She smiled in amusement.* **1.2** the pleasure that you get from being entertained or from doing something interesting. EG *Every kind of facility was laid on for their amusement.* N UNCOUNT

2 Amusements are **2.1** ways of passing the time pleasantly. EG *What amusements have you found to keep a young boy out of mischief?* **2.2** the games, rides on roundabouts, and other things that you can enjoy at a fairground or holiday resort. N COUNT : USU PLURAL; N PLURAL

amusing /ə^{3}mjuːzɪŋ/. Someone or something that is **amusing** makes you laugh or smile. EG *Francis was such a witty chap, so amusing... There was an amusing story in the paper.* ◊ **amusingly.** EG *He talked lightly and amusingly.* ADJ QUALIT; ◊ ADV

an /æn/ or /ən/. **An** is used instead of 'a', the indefinite article, in front of words that begin with vowel sounds: see **a.** DET

anachronism /ə^{3}nækrə^{7}nɪzə^{0}m/, **anachronisms.** You say that something is an **anachronism** when you think that it is out of date or old-fashioned. EG *The English public schools are an anachronism.* N COUNT

anachronistic /ə^{3}nækrə^{7}nɪstɪk/. You say that something is **anachronistic** when you think that it is out of date or old-fashioned. EG *...a peculiarly anachronistic view of communism.* ADJ QUALIT

anaemia /ə^{3}niːmɪə/; also spelled **anemia.** If you have **anaemia**, you have too few red cells in your blood, so that you feel tired and look pale. N UNCOUNT

anaemic /ə^{3}niːmɪk/; also spelled **anemic. 1** Someone who is **anaemic** suffers from anaemia. ADJ CLASSIF

2 If you describe something as **anaemic**, you mean that it is pale in an unpleasant or unhealthy way. EG *...pale, anaemic flowers.* ADJ QUALIT

anaesthesia /ænəsθiːzɪə/; also spelled **anesthesia. Anaesthesia** is **1** the use of anaesthetics in medicine and surgery. **2** a state in which you cannot feel anything in your body or in a part of your body. N UNCOUNT Technical

anaesthetic /ænəsθetɪk/, **anaesthetics;** also spelled **anesthetic.** An **anaesthetic** is a substance that stops you feeling pain, either in the whole of your body when you are unconscious, or in a part of your body when you are awake. EG *He was operated on without an anaesthetic.* N COUNT

anaesthetist /ə^{3}niːsθətɪst/, **anaesthetists;** also spelled **anesthetist.** An **anaesthetist** is a doctor who specializes in giving anaesthetics to patients. N COUNT

anaesthetize /ə^{3}niːsθətaɪz/, **anaesthetizes, anaesthetizing, anaesthetized;** also spelled **anaesthetise** or **anesthetize.** To **anaesthetize** someone means to make them unconscious by V+O giving them an anaesthetic. EG *The animals were anaesthetized for the experiment.*

anagram /ænəgræm/, **anagrams.** An **anagram** is a word or phrase that is formed by changing the order of the letters in another word or phrase. For example, 'triangle' is an anagram of 'integral'. N COUNT

anal /eɪnə^{0}l/ means relating to the anus of a person or animal. ADJ CLASSIF: ATTRIB

analogous /ənælə^{7}gəs/. If something is **analogous** to something else, the two things are similar in some way. ADJ CLASSIF: OFT+*to*

analogy /ənælə^{7}dʒi^1/, **analogies. 1** If you make or draw an **analogy** between two things, you show that they are alike in some way. EG *He made an analogy between parental and judicial discipline.* N COUNT

2 If you explain something **by analogy**, you explain it by describing something that is similar to it in some way. EG *The models are meant to show, by analogy, how matter is built up.* PHRASE

analyse /ænəlaɪz/, **analyses, analysing, analysed;** also spelled **analyze.** If you **analyse** something, you consider it or examine it in order to understand it or to find out what it consists of. EG *Specialists may analyse a situation and suggest solutions... He analysed the chemical structure of the molecules.* V+O

analysis /ənælɪ^{1}sɪs/, **analyses** /ənælɪ^{1}si:z/. **1 Analysis** is the process of considering something in order to understand it or to find out what it consists of. EG *...linguistic analysis... ...a chemical analysis of the poison.* N UNCOUNT OR N COUNT

2 An **analysis** is also an explanation or description that is the result of considering something. EG *He offers a calm analysis of the situation.* N COUNT

3 You use the expression **in the final analysis** or **in the last analysis** to indicate that the statement you are making is about the basic facts of a situation. EG *In the final analysis power rested in the hands of one man.* PHRASE

analyst /ænəlɪst/, **analysts.** An **analyst** is **1** a person whose job is to analyse a subject and give opinions about it. EG *...political analysts.* **2** someone who examines and treats people who are emotionally disturbed. N COUNT

analytic /ænəlɪtɪk/ or **analytical** /ænəlɪtɪkə^{0}l/ means using logical reasoning. EG *...her acute analytical powers.* ADJ QUALIT

analyze /ænəlaɪz/. See **analyse**.

anarchic /ænɑ:kɪk/ means without rules or laws. EG *The system is economically inefficient and politically anarchic.* ADJ CLASSIF

anarchism /ænəkɪzə^{0}m/ is the belief that the laws and power of governments should be replaced by people working together freely. ◇ **anarchist** /ænəkɪst/, **anarchists.** EG *Anarchists oppose the organised violence of war.* N UNCOUNT ◇ N COUNT

anarchy /ænəki^1/ is a situation where nobody seems to pay attention to rules or laws; used showing disapproval. EG *...his will to reverse the drift into anarchy and economic chaos.* N UNCOUNT

anathema /ə^{3}næθəmə/. If something is **anathema** to you, you dislike it strongly. EG *The idea of taking an exam was anathema to him.* N UNCOUNT: OFT+*to*

anatomical /ænətɒmɪkə^{0}l/ means relating to the structure of the bodies of people and animals. EG *...the anatomical features that animals have in common.* ADJ CLASSIF: ATTRIB

anatomy /ə^{3}nætə^{7}mi^1/, **anatomies. 1 Anatomy** is the study of the structure of the bodies of people or animals. N UNCOUNT

2 An animal's **anatomy** is the structure of its body. EG *...the anatomy of a fish.* N COUNT

-ance. -ance and **-ancy** are added to adjectives, usually in place of -ant, to form nouns. These nouns often refer to a quality or state. For example, 'brilliance' refers to the quality of being brilliant and 'buoyancy' refers to the state of being buoyant. Nouns like these are often not defined in this dictionary, but are treated with the related adjectives. EG *His arrogance was intolerable... We must maintain the constancy of family life.* SUFFIX

ancestor /ænsɛstə/, **ancestors. 1** Your **ancestors** are the people from whom you are descended. EG *The firm was founded by their ancestor, James Worthington.* N COUNT

2 An **ancestor** of something modern is an earlier thing from which it developed. EG *These creatures are the ancestors of modern man.* N COUNT

ancestral /ænsɛstrəl/ means relating to your family in former times. EG *...Gladstone's ancestral home at Hawarden.* ADJ CLASSIF: ATTRIB

ancestry /ænsɛstri^1/, **ancestries.** Your **ancestry** is the people from whom you are descended. EG *...American citizens of Japanese ancestry.* N COUNT

anchor /æŋkə/, **anchors, anchoring, anchored.**
1 An **anchor** is a heavy hooked object that is dropped from a boat into the water at the end of a chain in order to make the boat stay in one place. N COUNT

anchor

2 When a boat **anchors** or when you **anchor** it, its anchor is dropped into the water in order to make it stay in one place. V-ERG

3 If you **anchor** an object, you prevent it from moving. EG *We anchored his wheelchair to a huge stone.* V+O: OFT+*to*

ancient /eɪnʃənt/. You use **ancient** to describe things **1** that belong to the distant past. EG *...ancient Greece and Rome... ...ancient monuments.* **2** that have existed for a long time. EG *He came from an ancient Catholic family.* **3** that are very old. EG *...old men with ancient faces.* ADJ QUALIT

ancillary /ænsɪləri^1/. **1** The **ancillary** workers in an institution are the people such as the cleaners and cooks, whose work supports the main work of the institution. EG *...hospital ancillary workers.* ADJ CLASSIF: ATTRIB

2 Something that is **ancillary** to something else is additional to it. EG *Local resources were ancillary to a wider system of control.* ADJ CLASSIF Formal

-ancy. See **-ance**.

and /ə^{3}nd/. **1** You use **and 1.1** to link two or more words, groups, or clauses. EG *...my mother and father... I came here in 1972 and I have lived here ever since... He opened the car door and got out.* **1.2** to link two identical words or phrases in order to emphasize the degree of something or to suggest that something continues or increases over a period of time. EG *He became more and more annoyed... When Bill was happy, he laughed and laughed.* **1.3** to indicate that two numbers are to be added together. EG *Two and two is four.* CONJ

2 You also use **and** to interrupt yourself in order to make a comment on what you are saying. EG *Finally – and I really ought to stop in a minute – I wish to tell a little story.* CONJ

3 You use **and** in some numbers, especially when you say them. See the entry headed NUMBER. EG *...three hundred and fifty people... ...two and a half years.* CONJ

Could an animated conversation include anecdotes?

anecdotal /ænɪ²kdəʊtə⁰l/. **Anecdotal** speech or writing is full of anecdotes or is based on anecdotes. EG *...anecdotal evidence.* ADJ CLASSIF

anecdote /ænɪ²kdəʊt/, **anecdotes.** An **anecdote** is a short, entertaining account of something that has happened. EG *She told him anecdotes about the hospital and the patients.* N COUNT

anemia /əni:mɪə/. See **anaemia**.

anemic /əni:mɪk/. See **anaemic**.

anemone /ə³nɛməni¹/, **anemones.** An **anemone** is a garden plant with red, purple, or white flowers. N COUNT

anesthesia /ænəsθi:zɪə/. See **anaesthesia**.

anesthetic /ænəsθɛtɪk/. See **anaesthetic**.

anesthetist /ə³ni:sθətɪst/. See **anaesthetist**.

anesthetize /ə³ni:θətaɪz/. See **anaesthetize**.

anew /ə³nju:/. If you do something **anew**, you do it again, often in a different way from before. EG *...starting life anew in a fresh place.* ADV AFTER VB Literary

angel /eɪndʒə⁰l/, **angels. 1 Angels** are spiritual beings that some people believe are God's messengers and servants in heaven. N COUNT

2 You can call someone an **angel** when they have been very kind to you, or when you are very fond of them. EG *Thank you, you're an angel.* N COUNT

angelic /ændʒɛlɪk/. You can describe someone as **angelic** when they are, or seem to be, very good, kind, and gentle. ADJ QUALIT

anger /æŋgə/, **angers, angering, angered. 1 Anger** is the strong emotion that you feel when you think that someone has behaved in an unfair, cruel, or insulting way. EG *There was anger at the sufferings inflicted by the bombing... 'You're a fool.' – 'Am I?' he said, red with anger.* N UNCOUNT

2 If something **angers** you, it makes you feel angry. EG *His hostile attitude angered her.* V+O

angle /æŋgə⁰l/, **angles, angling, angled. 1** An **angle** is **1.1** the difference in direction between two lines or surfaces. Angles are measured in degrees. EG *The base angles of an isosceles triangle are equal... Oxford Road joins the High Street at an angle of ninety degrees.* ● See also **right angle**. **1.2** the shape that is created where two lines or surfaces join together. EG *He lay in the boat with his head against the angle of its bow.* **1.3** the direction from which you look at something. EG *He held the vase close to his face, peering at it from all angles.* N COUNT

2 If something is **at an angle**, it is not in a vertical or horizontal position. EG *...an old table leaning at an angle.* PHRASE

3 You can refer to a way of presenting something, for example in a play or a newspaper, as a particular **angle**. EG *The play's pacifist angle had a great appeal.* N COUNT+SUPP

4 If you **angle** for something, you try to make someone offer it to you without asking for it directly. EG *He got the invitation to Washington he had been angling for.* V+*for*

5 If you **angle** something in a particular way, you consider or present it in that way. EG *The whole thing was angled towards flirtation and amusement.* V+O : OFT +*towards/to*

6 See also **angling**.

angler /æŋglə/, **anglers.** An **angler** is someone who fishes with a fishing rod as a hobby. N COUNT

angling /æŋglɪŋ/ is the activity of fishing with a fishing rod. N ING

Anglo- forms adjectives which describe something connected with relations between Britain and another country. EG *...the 1921 Anglo-Irish treaty... ...Anglo-German friendship.* PREFIX

angry /æŋgri¹/, **angrier, angriest.** When you are **angry**, you feel or show strong emotion about something that you consider unfair, cruel, or insulting. EG *Are you angry with me?... He was angry at Sally for accusing him... She was always sending angry letters to the newspapers.* ◇ **angrily.** EG *The story was angrily denied by the dead man's family.* ADJ QUALIT ◇ ADV

anguish /æŋgwɪʃ/ is great mental suffering or physical pain. EG *...a quarrel which caused her intense unhappiness and anguish.* N UNCOUNT

anguished /æŋgwɪʃt/ means showing great mental suffering or physical pain. EG *The anguished cries continued.* ADJ QUALIT

angular /æŋgjə⁴lə/. **Angular** things have shapes that seem to contain a lot of straight lines and sharp points. EG *...his angular face... ...angular hats.* ADJ CLASSIF : ATTRIB

animal /ænɪmə⁰l/, **animals. 1** An **animal** is **1.1** a living creature such as a dog, lion, or rabbit, rather than a bird, fish, reptile, insect, or human being. EG *They used to hunt wild animals... ...domestic animals such as dogs and cats.* **1.2** any living thing that is not a plant, including people. EG *Man is a very weak animal... ...the animal kingdom.* N COUNT

2 If you refer to someone as an **animal**, you mean that their behaviour is unpleasant or disgusting. EG *Her husband was an animal.* N COUNT

3 Animal qualities, feelings, or abilities relate to someone's physical nature and instincts rather than to their mind. EG *Animal instinct warned me to tread carefully.* ADJ CLASSIF : ATTRIB

animate /ænɪmət/. Something that is **animate** has life, in contrast to things like stones and machines which do not have life. ADJ CLASSIF

animated /ænɪmeɪtɪ²d/. **1** Someone or something that is **animated** is lively and interesting. EG *The conversation was animated... He had an expressive, animated face.* ADJ QUALIT

2 An **animated** film has been filmed by means of animation. EG *...an animated cartoon.* ADJ CLASSIF

animation /ænɪmeɪʃə⁰n/. **1 Animation** is the process of making films in which drawings or puppets appear to move. N UNCOUNT

2 Someone with **animation** shows liveliness in the way that they speak, look, or behave. EG *She seemed to talk with animation.*

animosity /ænɪmɒsɪ¹ti¹/, **animosities. Animosity** is a feeling of strong dislike and anger. EG *Local animosities were forgotten in the face of this danger.* N UNCOUNT OR N COUNT

ankle /æŋkə⁰l/, **ankles.** Your **ankle** is the joint where your foot joins your leg. See picture at THE HUMAN BODY. EG *Rosa fell and sprained her ankle.* N COUNT

annals /ænə⁰lz/. If something is in the **annals** of a nation or society, it is recorded as part of its history. EG *...the most improbable soldiers in the annals of military history.* N PLURAL +SUPP

annex /ænɛks/, **annexes, annexing, annexed;** also spelled **annexe.**

1 An **annex** is a building which is joined to or next to a larger main building. EG *...the annexe to the Town Hall.* N COUNT

2 If a country **annexes** another country or an area of land, it seizes it and takes control of it. EG *The State was conquered and annexed in 1832.* V+O

◇ **annexation** /ænɛkseɪʃə⁰n/. EG *...the annexation of Hawaii.* ◇ N UNCOUNT

annihilate /ənaɪəleɪt/, **annihilates, annihilating, annihilated. 1** If something **is annihilated**, it is destroyed completely. EG *What would happen if the human race should be annihilated?* V+O : USU PASS

◇ **annihilation** /ənaɪəleɪʃə⁰n/. EG *...threatening the total annihilation of the planet.* ◇ N UNCOUNT

2 If you **annihilate** someone in a contest or argument, you defeat them completely. EG *The new party was annihilated in the 1931 election.* V+O

anniversary /ænə¹vɜ:sə⁰ri¹/, **anniversaries.** An **anniversary** is a date which is remembered or celebrated because a special event happened on that date in a previous year. EG *...the fiftieth anniversary of the Russian Revolution... It was his wedding anniversary.* N COUNT

announce /ə³naʊns/, **announces, announcing, announced.** If you **announce** something, **1** you tell people about it publicly or officially. EG *It was announced that the Prime Minister would speak on television... Mr Heath announced his decision.* **2** V-SPEECH

you say it in a deliberate and rather aggressive way. EG *'I am Mrs Jones,' she announced... He announced to his wife that he was leaving.*

announcement /ə[3]naʊnsmə[2]nt/, **announcements.** 1 An **announcement** is a public statement which gives information about something that has happened or that will happen. EG *The Government announcement gave details of small increases in taxes.* N COUNT

2 The **announcement** of something is the act of telling people about it. EG *...the events which follow the announcement of your resignation.* N SING

announcer /ə[3]naʊnsə/, **announcers.** An **announcer** is someone who introduces programmes on radio or television. N COUNT

annoy /ə[3]nɔɪ/, **annoys, annoying, annoyed.** If someone **annoys** you, they make you fairly angry. EG *You're just saying that to annoy me.* V+O

annoyance /ə[3]nɔɪəns/ is the feeling that you get when someone annoys you. EG *The Englishman showed no signs of his annoyance.* N UNCOUNT

annoyed /ə[3]nɔɪd/. If you are **annoyed**, you are fairly angry about something. EG *I got really annoyed because my father kept interrupting... She shook her head, annoyed with herself for forgetting.* ADJ PRED

annoying /ə[3]nɔɪɪŋ/. An **annoying** person or action makes you feel fairly angry and impatient. EG *It was annoying to be corrected by him all the time... ...her annoying habits.* ADJ QUALIT

annual /ænjʊ[0]əl/, **annuals. 1 Annual** means **1.1** happening or done once every year. EG *...the annual meeting of the Association... ...her annual holiday.* ADJ CLASSIF: ATTRIB

◊ **annually.** EG *Independence day is celebrated annually.* ◊ ADV **1.2** calculated over a period of one year. EG *...an annual income of twelve thousand dollars.* ADJ CLASSIF: ATTRIB

◊ **annually.** EG *They import 500 million tonnes of crude oil annually.* ◊ ADV

2 An **annual** is **2.1** a book or magazine that is published once a year. **2.2** a plant that grows and dies within one year. N COUNT

annul /ənʌl/, **annuls, annulling, annulled.** If a contract or marriage **is annulled**, it is declared invalid, so that legally it is considered never to have existed. V+O: USU PASS

annum /ænəm/. See **per annum**.

anomalous /ənɒmələs/. Something that is **anomalous** is different from what is normal or usual. EG *These calculations have given anomalous results.* ADJ CLASSIF Formal

anomaly /ənɒməli[1]/, **anomalies.** If a rule or practice is an **anomaly**, it is different from what is normal or usual. EG *We must correct these injustices and anomalies.* N COUNT Formal

anon. means anonymous; often written after poems or other writing whose author is not known.

anonymity /ænə[7]nɪmɪ[1]ti[1]/. **1 Anonymity** is the state of not having your name or identity known. EG *...a benefactor who insisted on anonymity.* N UNCOUNT

2 The **anonymity** of something is **2.1** the fact that it hides your identity. EG *...the anonymity of a typewritten letter... ...the anonymity of life in big cities.* **2.2** its lack of unusual or interesting features. EG *...the anonymity of a hotel room.* N UNCOUNT +SUPP

anonymous /ə[3]nɒnɪməs/. 1 If you remain **anonymous** when you do something, you do not let people know that you were the person who did it. EG *The donor prefers to remain anonymous... ...anonymous letters.* ADJ CLASSIF ◊ **anonymously.** EG *Anyone who wanted to make a complaint could do so anonymously.* ◊ ADV

2 Something that is **anonymous** **2.1** does not reveal who you are. EG *A taxi is anonymous. Nobody knows who's inside.* **2.2** has no unusual or interesting features. EG *...an anonymous little town.* ADJ CLASSIF

anorak /ænə[8]ræk/, **anoraks.** An **anorak** is a warm waterproof jacket, usually with a hood. N COUNT

another /ənʌðə/. **1 Another** thing or person means **1.1** an additional thing or person. EG *She finished her cigarette, then lit another one... We walked another hundred metres... ...a tin of pink paint and another of brown.* DET OR PRON: SING **1.2** a different thing or person. EG *They made it a crime to marry a person of another race... Parents say one thing and do another.* DET OR PRON

2 You use **one another** to indicate that each member of a group does something to or for the other members. EG *They didn't dare to look at one another... Members usually meet in one another's homes.* PHRASE

3 If you talk about **one** thing **after another**, you are referring to a series of repeated or continuous events. EG *She found one excuse after another to postpone it.* PHRASE

answer /ɑːnsə/, **answers, answering, answered. 1** When you **answer** someone who has asked you something, you say something back to them. EG *'Did he win?' – 'No,' I answered... I tried my best to answer her questions... He answered that the price would be three pounds... 'What's up?' said Sue. He didn't answer.* V-SPEECH: ONLY *that*; ALSO V

2 If you **answer** a letter or advertisement, you write to the person who wrote it. EG *She hadn't answered his letters.* V+O OR V

3 An **answer** is something that you say or write when you answer someone. EG *The answer to your question is no!... I got their answer to my letter.* N COUNT

4 When you **answer** the telephone, you pick it up when it rings. When you **answer** the door, you open it when you hear a knock or the bell. EG *A girl he didn't know answered the doorbell.* V+O OR V ▸ used as a noun. EG *I rang the doorbell, but there was no answer.* ▸ N COUNT

5 An **answer** to a problem is a possible solution to it. EG *There is no easy answer to the problem of pollution.* N COUNT: OFT+*to*

6 The **answer** to a question in a test is something that a student writes or says in an attempt to give the facts that are asked for. EG *I think the answer to No. 5 is fourteen.* N COUNT: OFT+*to* ▸ used as a verb. EG *You have to answer four questions.* ▸ V+O

7 If you say or do something **in answer** to something that someone else has said or done, you say it or do it as a response to what they have said or done. *She gave him a dreamy stare in answer.* PHRASE

answer back. If someone, especially a child, **answers** you **back** or **answers back**, they speak rudely to you when you speak to them. PHRASAL VB: V+O+ADV OR V+ADV

answer for. 1 If you say that someone **has a lot to answer for**, you mean that their actions have had a lot of bad results. PHRASE 2 If you say that you can or will **answer for** someone or for their qualities, you mean that you are sure that they will do what is wanted. EG *I can answer for his loyalty.* PHRASAL VB: V+PREP

answerable /ɑːnsə[0]rəbə[0]l/. 1 If you are **answerable** to someone, you have to report and explain your actions to them. EG *These three are answerable to the whole group.* ADJ PRED+*to*

2 If you are **answerable** for your actions or for someone else's actions, you are considered to be responsible for them. ADJ PRED+*for*

ant /ænt/, **ants. Ants** are small crawling insects that live in large groups. N COUNT

antagonism /æntægənɪzə[0]m/ is hatred or hostility. EG *...a mother who feels antagonism towards her children.* N UNCOUNT: OFT+*towards*

antagonist /æntægənɪst/, **antagonists.** Your **antagonist** is your opponent or enemy. N COUNT

antagonistic /æntægənɪstɪk/. Someone who is **antagonistic** shows hatred or hostility towards you. EG *Many of them are antagonistic towards the President.* ADJ QUALIT: OFT+ *towards/to*

antagonize /æntægənaɪz/, **antagonizes, antagonizing, antagonized;** also spelled **antagonise.** If V+O

Is it polite to answer back?

you **antagonize** someone, you make them feel angry or hostile towards you. EG *He had antagonized local tribesmen.*

antecedent /æntɪsiːdənt/, **antecedents. 1** An **antecedent** of something is something else that happened or existed before it and that was similar to it in some way. EG *...the prehistoric antecedents of the horse.* N COUNT: OFT+POSS

2 Your **antecedents** are your ancestors. N PLURAL

antelope /æntɪləʊp/, **antelopes.** The form **antelope** can also be used for the plural. N COUNT

An **antelope** is an animal with long legs and horns that looks like a deer.

antenna /æntenə/, **antennae** /ænteneɪ/ or **antennas.** For paragraph 2 the plural is usually **antennas**.

1 The **antennae** of something such as an insect or lobster are the two long, thin parts attached to its head that it uses to feel things with. N COUNT: USU PLURAL

2 An **antenna** is also a piece of wire that receives television or radio signals. Antennas are often fixed to buildings, cars, radios, and television sets. N COUNT American

anthem /ænθəm/, **anthems.** An **anthem** is a song or hymn written for a special occasion. • See also **national anthem**. N COUNT

anthology /ænθɒlədʒi¹/, **anthologies.** An **anthology** is a collection of writings by different writers published together in one book. EG *...an anthology of English poetry.* N COUNT

anthropology /ænθrəpɒlədʒi¹/ is the scientific study of people, society, and culture. N UNCOUNT

◊ **anthropologist, anthropologists.** EG *...an English anthropologist, Colin Turnbull.* ◊ N COUNT

◊ **anthropological.** EG *...anthropological research.* ◊ ADJ CLASSIF

anti- is used to form words that mean **1** opposed to a particular system, practice, or group of people. EG *...the anti-apartheid movement... ...anti-abortion campaigns... ...anti-American feelings.* **2** intended to prevent something from happening or to destroy something harmful. EG *...anti-freeze... ...anti-aircraft guns.* PREFIX PREFIX

antibiotic /ænti¹baɪɒtɪk/, **antibiotics. Antibiotics** are chemicals or drugs that are used in medicine to kill bacteria and to cure infections. N COUNT: USU PLURAL

anticipate /æntɪsɪpeɪt/, **anticipates, anticipating, anticipated. 1** If you **anticipate** an event, you realize in advance that it may happen and you are prepared for it. EG *The Secretary had anticipated the question... Incomes rose faster than anticipated... Some scientists anticipate that more food will be taken from the oceans.* ◊ **anticipation** /æntɪsɪpeɪʃ⁰n/. EG *Petrol coupons were issued in anticipation of rationing.* V+O OR V+REPORT ◊ N UNCOUNT

2 If you **anticipate** something pleasant or exciting that is going to happen, you look forward to it with pleasure. EG *She had often pleasurably anticipated the moment when she would hand in her resignation.* ◊ **anticipation.** EG *'Please!' the children cried, jumping up and down in anticipation.* V+O ◊ N UNCOUNT

anticlimax /ænti¹klaɪmæks/, **anticlimaxes.** If something is an **anticlimax**, it disappoints you because it is not as exciting as you expected, or because it happens after something that was very exciting. EG *Polling day was a bit of an anticlimax... ...a sense of anticlimax.* N COUNT OR N UNCOUNT

anti-clockwise /ænti¹klɒkwaɪz/. When something moves **anti-clockwise**, it moves in a circle in the opposite direction to the hands of a clock. EG *I gave it a sharp turn anti-clockwise.* ADV AFTER VB OR ADJ CLASSIF: ATTRIB British

antics /æntɪks/ are **1** funny and unusual ways of behaving. EG *She was smiling at the antics of the squirrels.* **2** actions which seem silly. EG *...the antics of the main political parties.* N PLURAL

antidote /ænti¹dəʊt/, **antidotes. 1** An **antidote** is a chemical substance that stops or controls the effect of a poison. N COUNT

2 An **antidote** to a difficult or unpleasant situation is something that helps you to overcome the situation. EG *Work is a wonderful antidote to misery.* N COUNT: OFT+*to*

antipathy /æntɪpəθi¹/ is a strong feeling of dislike or hostility. EG *...political antipathy to student radicalism.* N UNCOUNT: OFT+*to*

antiquarian /æntɪkweərɪən/ means concerned with old and rare objects. EG *...antiquarian bookshops.* ADJ CLASSIF: ATTRIB

antiquated /æntɪkweɪtɪ²d/. You describe something as **antiquated** when it is very old or old-fashioned. EG *...the clatter of the antiquated air-conditioning machine.* ADJ QUALIT

antique /æntiːk/, **antiques.** An **antique** is an old object, for example a piece of china or furniture, which is valuable because of its beauty or rarity. EG *His house was filled with antiques... ...antique furniture.* N COUNT

antiquity /æntɪkwɪ¹ti¹/, **antiquities. 1 Antiquity** is the distant past, especially the time of the ancient Egyptians, Greeks, and Romans. EG *...the great lost paintings of antiquity.* N UNCOUNT

2 Antiquities are interesting old buildings, statues, or other things that you can go and see. N COUNT: USU PLURAL

3 The **antiquity** of something is its great age. EG *...a famous landmark of great antiquity.* N UNCOUNT

anti-Semitism /ænti¹semɪ¹tɪzə⁰m/ is dislike for and prejudice against Jewish people. N UNCOUNT

antiseptic /ænti¹septɪk/ is a substance that kills germs and harmful bacteria. EG *I washed out the wound with antiseptic.* N MASS

anti-social. 1 Someone who is **anti-social** is unwilling to meet and be friendly with other people. ADJ QUALIT

2 Anti-social behaviour is annoying or upsetting to other people. EG *I don't like people phoning at this hour – it's anti-social.* ADJ QUALIT

antithesis /æntɪθə¹sɪs/, **antitheses** /æntɪθə¹siːz/. The **antithesis** of something is its exact opposite. EG *That is the antithesis of what he believes.* N COUNT Formal

antler /æntlə/, **antlers.** A male deer's **antlers** are the branched horns on its head. N COUNT: USU PLURAL

anus /eɪnəs/, **anuses.** A person's **anus** is the hole between their buttocks, from which faeces leave their body. N COUNT Medical

anvil /ænvɪl/, **anvils.** An **anvil** is a heavy iron block on which hot metals are beaten into shape. N COUNT

anxiety /æŋzaɪ¹ti¹/, **anxieties. 1 Anxiety** is a feeling of nervousness or worry. EG *'What do you think?' asked the Belgian with a touch of anxiety... ...their anxiety over what was to be done.* N UNCOUNT

2 An **anxiety** is something which causes you to feel nervous or worried. EG *...major financial anxieties.* N COUNT

anxious /æŋk⁰ʃəs/. **1** If you are **anxious**, you are nervous or worried about something. EG *It's time to be going home, your mother will be anxious... She was anxious about her job.* ◊ **anxiously.** EG *'I'm not boring you?' she asked anxiously.* ADJ QUALIT ◊ ADV

2 An **anxious** time or situation is one during which you feel nervous and worried. EG *You must have had an anxious day.* ADJ QUALIT: ATTRIB

3 If you are **anxious** to do something or **anxious** that something should happen, you very much want to do it or very much want it to happen. EG *...civil servants anxious for promotion... She's anxious to go abroad.* ADJ PRED +*to*-INF, REPORT, OR *for*

any /eni¹/. **1** You use **any** in negative statements, for example with 'not' or 'never', to mean none of a particular thing. EG *I hadn't had any breakfast and I was getting hungry... It won't do any good... I don't like any of this.* DET OR PRON

2 You use **any** in questions and conditional clauses to ask if there is some of a particular thing or to suggest that there might be. EG *Were you in any danger?... They will retaliate if any of their ships are attacked.* DET OR PRON

3 You use **any** in positive statements when you are referring to something or someone without saying exactly what, who, or which kind you mean. EG *Any big tin container will do... ...things that any man* DET OR PRON *might do under pressure... The meeting was different from any that had gone before.*

4 You can also use **any** to emphasize a comparative adjective or adverb in a negative statement. EG *I couldn't stand it any longer... He didn't want to express himself any more strongly than he had to.* ADV WITH NEG

anybody /ɛ̲nɪbɔ⁷di¹/. See **anyone**.

anyhow /ɛ̲nɪhaʊ/. 1 **Anyhow** means the same as anyway.

2 If you do something **anyhow**, you do it in a careless or untidy way. EG *They were all shoved in anyhow.* ADV

anyone /ɛ̲nɪwɔ⁹n/. The form **anybody** is also used.

1 You use **anyone** or **anybody** in negative statements, for example with 'not' or 'never', to say that nobody is present or involved in an action. EG *There wasn't anyone there.* PRON INDEF

2 You use **anyone** or **anybody** in questions and conditional clauses to ask or talk about whether someone is present or doing something. EG *Was there anyone behind you?... If anyone asks where you are I'll say you've just gone out.* PRON INDEF

3 You also use **anyone** and **anybody** to refer to a person or to people in general, when you do not want to say which particular person or people you are referring to. EG *Their laughter woke anyone who was not already up... He took longer than anybody else.* PRON INDEF

anything /ɛ̲nɪθɪŋ/. 1 You use **anything** in negative statements, for example with 'not' or 'never', to say that nothing is present or an action or event does not happen. EG *I did not say anything... They couldn't afford anything better.* PRON INDEF

2 You use **anything** in questions and conditional clauses to ask or talk about whether something is present or happening. EG *I've told her to come to you if she wants anything.* PRON INDEF

3 You can use **anything** to refer to a thing, an event, or an idea without saying exactly which one you mean. EG *The situation was very tense; anything might happen... Lemon gives a fresh flavour to almost anything.* PRON INDEF

4 You can use **anything** for emphasis, when you are saying that something is not at all like something else. EG *It didn't taste anything like soup.* ADV+*like/near*

5 You use **anything but** to emphasize that something is not the case. For example, if you say that someone or something is **anything but** attractive, you mean that they are not at all attractive. EG *The operation was anything but funny.*

anyway /ɛ̲nɪweɪ/. The form **anyhow** is also used. ADV SEN

You use **anyway** or **anyhow** 1 to indicate that a statement explains or supports a previous point. EG *We ought to spend less on the defence missiles, which I reckon are pretty useless anyway.* 2 to suggest that a statement is true or relevant in spite of other things that have been said. EG *'I can give you a lift.' – 'No, I'll walk. Thanks, anyway.'* 3 to correct or modify a statement, for example to limit it to what you definitely know to be true. EG *'All of them?' I asked. 'Some, anyway.'* 4 to change the topic or return to a previous topic. EG *What are you phoning for, anyway?... Anyway, I'll see you later.*

anywhere /ɛ̲nɪwɛɔ/. 1 You can use **anywhere** in negative statements, questions, and conditional clauses to refer to a place without saying exactly where you mean, for example because it does not matter about being exact. EG *I changed my mind and decided not to go anywhere... Is there an ashtray anywhere?* ADV

2 You can also use **anywhere** in positive statements 2.1 for emphasis with an expression that refers to a place or area. EG *They are the oldest rock paintings anywhere in North America... It is better in the kitchen than anywhere else.* ADV: OFT+PREP 2.2 to refer to a point within a stated range when you do not know what the point is. EG *...a time anywhere from zero to fifteen years from now.* ADV+*from/between*

apart /əpɑ̲:t/. 1 When something is **apart** from something else, there is a space between them. EG *I was sitting apart from the rest.* ADV+*from*

2 If two things are a particular distance **apart**, they are that distance from each other. EG *Their faces were a couple of inches apart.* ADJ PRED

3 If two things move **apart** or are pulled **apart**, they move away from each other. EG *I tried to pull the dogs apart.* ADV AFTER VB

4 If two people are **apart**, they are no longer living together or spending time together. EG *They could not bear to be apart.* ADJ PRED

5 If you take something **apart**, you separate it into the pieces that it is made of. If it comes or falls **apart**, its parts separate from each other. ADV AFTER VB

6 If something such as an organization or relationship falls **apart**, it can no longer continue because it has serious difficulties. EG *Their marriage began to fall apart.* ADV AFTER VB

7 If you **can't tell** two people or things **apart**, they look exactly the same to you. EG *He couldn't tell the boys apart.* PHRASE

8 You use **apart from** 8.1 when you are giving an exception to a general statement that you are making. EG *Apart from Ann, the car was empty... She had no money, apart from the five pounds that Christopher had given her.* 8.2 to say that you want to ignore one aspect of a situation so that you can talk about another aspect. EG *Quite apart from the expense, I don't think I would want to fly anyway.* PREP

apartheid /əpɑ̲:th⁰aɪt, -h⁰eɪt/ is a political system in South Africa in which people of different races are kept apart by law. N UNCOUNT

apartment /əpɑ̲:tmɔ²nt/, **apartments.** An **apartment** is 1 a set of rooms for living in, usually on one floor of a large building. EG *They pay 2,000 dollars a month for their three-bedroomed apartment.* 2 one of a set of large rooms used by an important person such as a king, queen, or president. EG *...splendid apartments of state.* N COUNT

apathetic /æ̲pəθɛ̲tɪk/. Someone who is **apathetic** is not interested in anything. EG *...bored, apathetic youngsters.* ◊ **apathetically.** EG *The onlookers applauded apathetically.* ADJ QUALIT; ◊ ADV

apathy /æ̲pəθi¹/ is a state of mind in which you are not interested in or enthusiastic about anything. EG *He began to lose his apathy and take a keen interest in sport.* N UNCOUNT

ape /eɪ̲p/, **apes, aping, aped.** 1 **Apes** are animals such as chimpanzees or gorillas. N COUNT

2 If you **ape** someone's speech or behaviour, you imitate it. EG *...aging television personalities who aped the fashions of the young.* V+O

aperitif /ɔ³pɛ̲rɪti¹f/, **aperitifs.** An **aperitif** is an alcoholic drink that you have before a meal. N COUNT

aperture /æ̲pətʃə/, **apertures.** An **aperture** is a narrow hole or gap, for example the opening in a camera through which light passes into it. EG *Into this aperture a drop of mercury was poured.* N COUNT

apex /eɪ̲pɛks/, **apexes.** The **apex** of something is its pointed top or end. EG *...the apex of the pyramid.* N COUNT: OFT+*of*

aphorism /æ̲fə⁸rɪzə⁰m/, **aphorisms.** An **aphorism** is a short, clever sentence which expresses a general truth. N COUNT

aphrodisiac /æfrɔ⁶dɪ̲ziæk/, **aphrodisiacs.** An **aphrodisiac** is a food, drink, or drug which makes people want to have sex. N COUNT

apiece /əpi̲:s/. If people have a particular number of things **apiece**, they have that number each. EG *He gave his daughters £200 apiece.* ADV

aplomb /əplɒ̲m/. If you do something with **aplomb**, you do it with great confidence. EG *She spoke with great aplomb.* N UNCOUNT

apolitical /eɪ̲pəlɪ̲tɪkɔ⁰l/. Someone who is **apolitical** is not interested in politics. ADJ QUALIT

Does something that is appalling appeal to you?

apologetic /əpɒlədʒɛtɪk/. If you are **apologetic**, you show or say that you are sorry that you have hurt someone or caused trouble for them. EG *'Oh, I'm sorry,' said the girl, immediately apologetic... He was apologetic about his behaviour at dinner.* ADJ QUALIT
◇ **apologetically.** EG *He smiled apologetically.* ◇ ADV

apologize /əpɒlədʒaɪz/, **apologizes, apologizing, apologized;** also spelled **apologise.** When you **apologize** to someone, you say that you are sorry that you have hurt them or caused trouble for them. EG *I apologise for my late arrival... 'Sorry I haven't called you yet,' he apologized.* V : OFT+*to/for* OR V+QUOTE

apology /əpɒlədʒi[1]/, **apologies.** An **apology** is something that you say or write in order to tell someone that you are sorry that you have hurt them or caused trouble for them. EG *He sent a letter of apology to the publisher... He phoned and was full of apologies.* N COUNT OR N UNCOUNT

apostrophe /əpɒstrəfi[1]/, **apostrophes.** An **apostrophe** is a mark written to indicate that one or more other letters have been omitted from a word, as in *can't* and *he'll.* An apostrophe is also written before or after an 's' at the end of a word to indicate that what follows belongs or relates to the word, as in *the cat's whiskers* and *the players' entrance.* N COUNT

appal /əpɔːl/, **appals, appalling, appalled;** spelled **appall** and **appalls** in American English. If something **appals** you, it shocks and disgusts you because it is so bad. EG *The architecture appalled her.* ◇ **appalled.** EG *I was absolutely appalled at the quality of the reporting.* V+O : USU PASS ◇ ADJ QUALIT : OFT+*at/by*

appalling /əpɔːlɪŋ/. **1** Something that is **appalling** is so bad or unpleasant that it shocks and disgusts you. EG *These people live in appalling conditions.* ADJ QUALIT
◇ **appallingly.** EG *He had behaved appallingly.* ◇ ADV
2 You can use **appalling** to emphasize that something is extremely bad. EG *I had the most appalling depression.* ADJ QUALIT : ATTRIB

apparatus /æpəreɪtəs/. **1 Apparatus** is the equipment, such as tools and machines, which is used to do a particular job or activity. EG *...large apparatus like slides and climbing frames.* N UNCOUNT
2 The **apparatus** of an organization or system is its structure and method of operation. EG *...the whole apparatus of the welfare state.* N UNCOUNT +SUPP

apparent /əpærənt/. **1** An **apparent** situation, quality, or feeling seems to exist, although you cannot be certain that it does exist. EG *...the apparent success of their marriage.* ADJ CLASSIF : ATTRIB
2 If something is **apparent** to you, it is clear and obvious to you. EG *It was becoming increasingly apparent to me that he disliked me... Everyone ran out for no apparent reason.* ADJ PRED : OFT+*to* OR REPORT

apparently /əpærəntli[1]/. You use **apparently 1** to indicate that the information that you are giving is something that you have heard but you are not certain that it is true. EG *Apparently she's living with them.* **2** to refer to something that seems to be the case although it may not be. EG *She was standing by the window, apparently quite calm and relaxed.* ADV SEN / ADV

apparition /æpərɪʃə[0]n/, **apparitions.** An **apparition** is something that you think you see but that is not really there. EG *He was visited by an apparition, a girl resembling his dead daughter.* N COUNT

appeal /əpiːl/, **appeals, appealing, appealed. 1** If you **appeal** for something that you need such as money or help, you make a serious and often urgent request for it. EG *He was appealing for funds to build a new school.* ▸ used as a noun. EG *A radio appeal she made, asking for money for cancer research, raised £75,000.* V+*for* OR V+QUOTE ▸ N COUNT
2 If you **appeal** to someone's honour, reason, or sense, you suggest that they should do what you ask if they want to seem honourable, reasonable, or sensible. EG *They are confident they can appeal to her sense of duty.* ▸ used as a noun. EG *...an appeal to her maternal feelings.* V+*to* ▸ N COUNT+*to*
3 If you **appeal** to someone in authority against a decision, you formally ask them to change it. EG *He successfully appealed against his conviction.* V+*to/against*
▸ used as a noun. EG *The Supreme Court turned down our appeal.* ▸ N COUNT
4 If something **appeals** to you, you find it attractive or interesting. EG *These books are designed to appeal to children... The idea appealed to him.* V+*to*
◇ **appealing.** EG *He has an appealing sense of humour.* ◇ ADJ QUALIT
5 The **appeal** of something is a quality that it has which people find attractive or interesting. EG *What is the main appeal of these cars?* N UNCOUNT +SUPP

appear /əpɪə/, **appears, appearing, appeared. 1** When something which you could not see before **appears**, it moves into a position where you can see it. EG *A glow of light appeared over the sea... Two men suddenly appeared.* V : USU+A
2 When something new **appears**, it begins to exist or becomes available. EG *...the newest political party to appear in Britain... His second novel appeared under the title 'Getting By'.* V : USU+A
3 When someone **appears** in a play or show, they take part in it. EG *He is currently appearing in the TV series 'Funny Man'.* V+*in*
4 When someone **appears** before a court of law, they go there in order to answer charges or to give information as a witness. V : USU+A
5 If you say that something **appears** to be the way that you describe it, you mean that you believe it to be that way. EG *Their offer appears to be the most attractive... He appears confident... It appears that he followed my advice.* V+*to*-INF OR C; ALSO V+REPORT : ONLY *that*

appearance /əpɪərəns/, **appearances. 1** The **appearance** of someone in a place is their arrival there, especially when it is unexpected. EG *The fight was soon stopped, thanks to the prompt appearance of the police.* N SING+SUPP
2 If you talk about the **appearance** of something new, you are referring to the fact that it has begun to exist. EG *With the appearance of credit cards more people got into debt.* N SING+SUPP
3 When you make an **appearance** in a play or show, you take part in it. EG *She has made several television appearances recently.* N COUNT
4 If you **put in an appearance** at an event, you go to it for a short time but do not stay. PHRASE
5 Someone or something's **appearance** is the way that they look to other people. EG *I had ceased to worry about my appearance... The building has changed the appearance of the whole area... The sisters were alike in appearance.* N UNCOUNT
6 If something is true **to all appearances** or **by all appearances**, it seems from what you know about it that it is true. EG *To all appearances he doesn't work hard.* PHRASE

appease /əpiːz/, **appeases, appeasing, appeased.** If you try to **appease** someone, you try to stop them being angry by giving them what they want. EG *He had ample funds to appease the king's anger.* ◇ **appeasement.** EG *...a gift of appeasement.* V+O Formal ◇ N UNCOUNT

appendicitis /əpendɪ[1]saɪtɪ[1]s/ is an illness in which your appendix is infected and painful. N UNCOUNT

appendix /ə[3]pɛndɪks/, **appendices** /ə[3]pɛndɪsiːz/ or **appendixes. 1** Your **appendix** is a small closed tube inside your body at the end of your digestive system. It has no particular function. N COUNT
2 An **appendix** to a book is extra information that is placed after the end of the main text. EG *A list of hotels is given in the Appendix.* N COUNT

appetite /æpə[1]taɪt/, **appetites. 1** Your **appetite** is your desire to eat and your feeling about how much you want to eat. EG *All that work has given me an appetite.* N COUNT OR N UNCOUNT
2 If you have an **appetite** for something, you have a strong desire for it. EG *...a repressed appetite for sensual pleasure.* N COUNT : OFT+*for*

appetizing /æpəˈtaɪzɪŋ/; also spelled **appetising.** Food that is **appetizing** looks and smells nice, and makes you want to eat it. ADJ QUALIT

applaud /əplɔːd/, **applauds, applauding, applauded. 1** When a group of people **applaud**, they clap their hands in order to show approval, for example when they have enjoyed a play or concert. EG *The whole assembly applauded him.* V OR V+O

2 When an action or attitude **is applauded**, people praise it. EG *These changes will be applauded.* V+O : USU PASS

applause /əplɔːz/ is an expression of praise or appreciation by a group of people, in which they clap their hands. EG *The delegates burst into loud applause.* N UNCOUNT

apple /æpəºl/, **apples.** An **apple** is a round fruit with a smooth skin and firm white flesh. EG *...apple pie... ...the apple tree.* N COUNT OR N UNCOUNT

appliance /əplaɪəns/, **appliances.** An **appliance** is a device or machine that does a particular job in your home. EG *...heating appliances.* N COUNT

applicable /æplɪkəbəºl, əplɪkə-/. Something that is **applicable** to a particular situation is relevant to it. EG *...a rule applicable to all cases... The following special regulations are applicable to overseas students.* ADJ QUALIT : OFT+*to*

applicant /æplɪkənt/, **applicants.** An **applicant** for a job or a place at a college is someone who formally asks to be given it. N COUNT

application /æplɪkeɪʃəºn/, **applications. 1** An **application** for a job or a place at a college is a formal written request to be given it. EG *The school receives up to 3,300 applications each year.* N COUNT OR N UNCOUNT

2 The **application** of a rule or piece of knowledge is the use of it in a particular situation. EG *Do the results have any practical application?* N UNCOUNT OR N COUNT

3 Application is hard work and concentration on what you are doing over a period of time. N UNCOUNT

applied /əˀplaɪd/. An **applied** subject of study has a practical use. EG *...applied psychology.* ADJ CLASSIF : ATTRIB

apply /əplaɪ/, **applies, applying, applied. 1** If you **apply** to have something or to do something, you write asking formally to be allowed to have it or do it. EG *I've applied for another job.* V : OFT+*for*

2 If you **apply** yourself to something, you concentrate hard on it. EG *He applied himself energetically to looking for work... He tried to apply his mind to Rose's problems.* V REFL OR V+O : OFT+*to*

3 If something **applies** to a person or a situation, it is relevant to the person or the situation. EG *The leaflet explains how the system will apply to you.* V : USU+*to*

4 If you **apply** a rule, system, or skill, you use it in a situation or activity. EG *...countries which have been the first to apply the death penalty... ...the capacity to develop and apply technology.* V+O

5 If you **apply** a name to someone or something, you refer to them by that name. EG *The label 'cold-blooded', so often applied to reptiles, is a very misleading one.* V+O : USU PASS

6 If you **apply** something to a surface, you put it or rub it on to the surface. EG *Apply a little wax polish.* V+O

7 See also **applied**.

appoint /əpɔɪnt/, **appoints, appointing, appointed. 1** If you **appoint** someone to a job or post, you formally choose them for it. EG *Ramsay MacDonald appointed him Secretary of State for India.* V+O : USU+A OR V+O+C

2 If you **appoint** a time or place for something to happen, you decide when or where it will happen. V+O Formal

◇ **appointed.** EG *I arrived at precisely the appointed time.* ◇ ADJ CLASSIF : ATTRIB

appointment /əpɔɪntməˀnt/, **appointments. 1** The **appointment** of a person to do a particular job is the choice of that person to do it. EG *Their duties include the appointment of all the staff.* N UNCOUNT : OFT+*of*

2 An **appointment** is a job or position of responsibility. EG *She applied for and got the appointment.* N COUNT

3 If you have an **appointment** with someone, you have arranged to see them at a particular time, usually in connection with their job. EG *I had an appointment with the editor of the Arkansas Gazette... The doctor's appointment was for 11 am.* N COUNT

4 If you do something **by appointment**, you arrange in advance to do it at a particular time. EG *They allow people to visit by appointment during the weekend.* PHRASE

appraisal /əpreɪzəºl/, **appraisals.** If you make an **appraisal** of something, you consider it carefully and form an opinion about it. N COUNT OR N UNCOUNT : OFT+*of*

appraise /əpreɪz/, **appraises, appraising, appraised.** If you **appraise** something, you consider it carefully and form an opinion about it. EG *Harris stood back and appraised his work.* V+O

appreciable /əpriːʃɪºəbəºl, -sɪ-/. An **appreciable** amount or effect is large enough to be important or clearly noticed. EG *...an appreciable percentage of the university's expenditure.* ◇ **appreciably.** EG *The following week it was appreciably colder.* ADJ CLASSIF : ATTRIB ◇ SUBMOD

appreciate /əpriːʃieɪt, -sɪ-/, **appreciates, appreciating, appreciated. 1** If you **appreciate** something, you like it because you recognize its good qualities. EG *He appreciated beautiful things.* V+O

2 If you **appreciate** a situation or problem, you understand it and know what it involves. EG *I appreciate the reasons for your anxiety... I appreciate that this is not a fair comparison.* V+O; ALSO V+REPORT : ONLY *that*

3 If you say that you **appreciate** something that someone has done for you, you mean that you are grateful to them for it. EG *We would much appreciate guidance from an expert.* V+O

4 If something **appreciates** over a period of time, its value increases. EG *These diamonds should appreciate in value.* V

appreciation /əpriːʃieɪʃəºn, -sɪ-/, **appreciations.**

1 Appreciation of something is recognition and enjoyment of its good qualities. EG *He had little appreciation of great plays.* N UNCOUNT : OFT+*of*

2 Your **appreciation** for something that someone has done for you is your gratitude for it. EG *...something to show their appreciation of his services.* N UNCOUNT : OFT+*of*

3 An **appreciation** of a situation or problem is an understanding of what it involves. EG *...a full appreciation of the implications.* N UNCOUNT

4 Appreciation in the value of something is the increase in its value over a period of time. N UNCOUNT

5 An **appreciation** of a person or a work of art is a discussion and evaluation of them. EG *...an appreciation of the life and work of Dame Flora Robson.* N COUNT : OFT+*of*

appreciative /əpriːʃɪºətɪv/. **1** An **appreciative** reaction, comment, or expression shows the pleasure that you are getting from something. EG *...appreciative laughter.* ADJ QUALIT

2 If you are **appreciative** of something, you are grateful for it. EG *She won't be appreciative of his efforts.* ◇ **appreciatively.** EG *'Want a lift?' she asked. I nodded appreciatively.* ADJ QUALIT ◇ ADV

apprehension /æprɪhenʃəºn/, **apprehensions. Apprehension** is a feeling of fear that something terrible may happen. EG *His mother trembled with apprehension.* N UNCOUNT OR N COUNT Formal

apprehensive /æprɪhensɪv/. Someone who is **apprehensive** is afraid that something terrible may happen. EG *I felt apprehensive about the whole operation.* ◇ **apprehensively.** EG *She looked up apprehensively.* ADJ QUALIT : OFT+*about* ◇ ADV

apprentice /əˀprentɪs/, **apprentices.** An **apprentice** is a young person who works with someone in order to learn their skill. EG *...an apprentice instrument maker.* N COUNT

apprenticeship /əˀprentɪsºʃɪp/, **apprenticeships.** Someone who has an **apprenticeship** works for a fixed period of time with a person who has a particular skill in order to learn the skill. EG *On leaving school he had an apprenticeship with his brother in leatherwork.* N COUNT OR N UNCOUNT

Is a valuable painting likely to appreciate?

approach /əprəʊtʃ/, **approaches, approaching, approached. 1** When someone **approaches** you, they come nearer to you. EG *He opened the door for her as she approached.* ▸ used as a noun. EG *The dogs began to bark as if aware of our approach.* — V+O OR V; ▸ N COUNT +SUPP

2 If you **approach** someone about something, you speak to them about it for the first time, often making a request or offer. EG *They had approached us about working with their party.* ▸ used as a noun. EG *I had an approach to join the staff of the Daily Mail.* — V+O : OFT+A; ▸ N COUNT

3 When you **approach** a situation or problem in a particular way, you think about it or deal with it in that way. EG *Governments must approach the subject of disarmament in a new spirit.* — V+O+A

4 When a future event or date **approaches** or when you **approach** it, it gradually becomes nearer as time passes. EG *As the end of the month approached, I was eating less and less... We are approaching the day of the race.* ▸ used as a noun. EG *...the approach of winter.* — V-ERG; ▸ N SING+SUPP

5 If something **approaches** a particular level or state, it almost reaches that level or state. EG *These rocket planes approached speeds of 4000 mph.* ◇ **approaching.** EG *...bills of approaching a million pounds.* — V+O; ◇ ADV

6 An **approach** to a place is a road or path that leads to it. — N COUNT : OFT+*to*

7 An **approach** to a situation or problem is a way of thinking about it or of dealing with it. EG *We need a new approach to this problem.* — N COUNT : OFT+*to*

approachable /əprəʊtʃəbə[0]l/. **1** Someone who is **approachable** is friendly and easy to talk to. EG *...a hotel with approachable staff.* — ADJ QUALIT

2 A place which is **approachable** by a particular route can be reached by that route. EG *The statue is approachable by steps inside the column.* — ADJ PRED +*by/from*

appropriate, appropriates, appropriating, appropriated; pronounced /ə[3]prəʊprɪət/ when it is an adjective and /ə[3]prəʊprɪeɪt/ when it is a verb.

1 Something that is **appropriate** is suitable or acceptable for a particular situation. EG *...the institutional structure appropriate to each country... It seemed appropriate to end with a joke.* — ADJ QUALIT : OFT+*to/for* OR *to*-INF

2 If you **appropriate** something which does not belong to you, you take it for yourself. EG *The materials are exported and other countries appropriate the profits.* — V+O Formal

approval /ə[3]pru:və[0]l/ is **1** agreement which is given to a plan or request. EG *The decision met with the committee's approval... He required his father's approval.* — N UNCOUNT +SUPP **2** admiration for someone. EG *Oliver looked at Simon with approval.* — N UNCOUNT

approve /ə[3]pru:v/, **approves, approving, approved. 1** If you **approve** of an action, event, or suggestion, you are pleased about it. EG *My grandfather did not approve of my father's marriage.* — V : USU+*of*

2 If you **approve** of someone or something, you like and admire them. EG *He did not approve of my pictures.* — V : USU+*of*

3 If someone in a position of authority **approves** a plan or idea, they formally agree to it and say that it can happen. EG *The firm's directors quickly approved the new deal.* — V+O

approved /ə[3]pru:vd/. **1** An **approved** method or course of action is generally or officially accepted as appropriate in a particular situation. — ADJ QUALIT

2 Someone who is **approved** in a particular position has been formally accepted in that position by people in authority. EG *...lists of approved candidates.* — ADJ CLASSIF

approving /ə[3]pru:vɪŋ/. An **approving** reaction or expression shows support for something, or satisfaction with it. EG *Cameron gave Scylla an approving nod.* ◇ **approvingly.** EG *His wife watched approvingly.* — ADJ QUALIT; ◇ ADV

approximate, approximates, approximating, approximated; pronounced /ə[3]prɒksə[1]mə[1]t/ when it is an adjective and /ə[3]prɒksə[1]meɪt/ when it is a verb.

1 An **approximate** number, time, or position is close to the correct number, time, or position but not exact. EG *...the approximate value of the property.* ◇ **approximately.** EG *We have approximately 40 pupils.* — ADJ QUALIT; ◇ ADV

2 An idea or description that is **approximate** is not intended to be precise or accurate. — ADJ QUALIT

3 If something **approximates** to a particular number or size, it is close to it. — V+*to*

4 If something **approximates** to something else, it is similar to it but not exactly the same. EG *Worsening social conditions approximate to those of the early thirties.* — V+*to* OR V+O

approximation /ə[3]prɒksɪ[1]meɪʃə[0]n/, **approximations.** An **approximation** is **1** a fact, object, or description which is similar to something else but which does not have all its features. EG *...an approximation to the truth.* **2** a number, calculation, or position that is not exact. EG *...a rough approximation of the proportions.* — N COUNT : OFT+*to/of*

apricot /eɪprɪkɒt/, **apricots.** An **apricot** is a small, soft, round fruit with yellowish-orange flesh and a stone inside. — N COUNT

April /eɪprə[1]l/ is the fourth month of the year in the Western calendar. EG *He will be seven next April... The Treaty was signed on 4 April 1949.* — N UNCOUNT

apron /eɪprən/, **aprons.** An **apron** is a piece of clothing that you put on over the front of your normal clothes and tie round your waist, especially when you are cooking, in order to prevent your clothes from getting dirty. — N COUNT

apt /æpt/. **1** Something that is **apt** is suitable. EG *...a very apt description.* ◇ **aptly.** EG *...as Dr Hochstadt so aptly remarked to his wife.* — ADJ QUALIT; ◇ ADV

2 If someone is **apt** to behave in a particular way, they usually behave in that way. EG *I was apt to fidget during a long performance.* — ADJ PRED +*to*-INF

aptitude /æptɪtju:d/, **aptitudes.** Someone's **aptitude** for a skill is their ability to learn it quickly and to do it well. EG *He had an aptitude for journalism.* — N COUNT : OFT+*for*

aquarium /əkwɛərɪəm/, **aquaria** /əkwɛərɪə/ or **aquariums.** An **aquarium** is **1** a glass tank filled with water, in which people keep fish. **2** a building, often in a zoo, where fish and underwater animals are kept. — N COUNT

aquatic /əkwætɪk/. **1** An **aquatic** animal or plant lives or grows in water. — ADJ CLASSIF : ATTRIB

2 Aquatic also means relating to water. EG *...aquatic sports.* — ADJ CLASSIF : ATTRIB

aqueduct /ækwɪ[1]dʌkt/, **aqueducts.** An **aqueduct** is a long bridge with many arches, which carries a water supply or a canal over a valley. — N COUNT

Arab /ærəb/, **Arabs.** An **Arab** is a member of a people who live in the Middle East and North Africa. ▸ used as an adjective. EG *The Ambassadors of several Arab countries were invited.* — N COUNT; ▸ ADJ CLASSIF

Arabian /əreɪbɪən/ means belonging or relating to Arabia, especially to Saudi Arabia. EG *...the Arabian peninsula.* — ADJ CLASSIF : ATTRIB

Arabic /ærəbɪk/. **1 Arabic** is a language that is spoken in the Middle East and in parts of North Africa. — N UNCOUNT

2 Something that is **Arabic** belongs or relates to the language, writing, or culture of the Arabs. — ADJ CLASSIF

3 An **Arabic** numeral is one of the written figures, such as 1, 2, 3, or 4. — ADJ CLASSIF : ATTRIB

arable /ærəbə[0]l/ is used to describe things relating to growing crops. EG *...arable farming... ...arable land... ...arable crops.* — ADJ CLASSIF

arbiter /ɑ:bɪtə/, **arbiters.** An **arbiter** is a person or institution that judges and settles a quarrel between two other people or groups. EG *The Court was an arbiter between the States and the Federal government... The state is the final arbiter of morality in these cases.* — N COUNT Formal

arbitrary /ɑ:bɪtrəri[1], ɑ:bɪtri[1]/. An **arbitrary** decision or action is taken without considering all its — ADJ QUALIT probable effects. EG *...the brutal and arbitrary expulsion of immigrants... It is difficult to discern the motive of this seemingly arbitrary attack.*

◊ **arbitrarily.** EG *The items are selected arbitrarily... ...laws that empowered them to close down any newspaper arbitrarily.* ◊ ADV

arbitrate /ɑːbɪtreɪt/, **arbitrates, arbitrating, arbitrated.** When someone **arbitrates** between two people who are in dispute, they consider all the facts and decide who is right. V OR V+O

arbitration /ɑːbɪtreɪʃəⁿn/ is the judging of a dispute between people or groups by someone who is not involved. EG *...arbitration between employers and unions.* N UNCOUNT

arc /ɑːk/, **arcs.** An **arc** is **1** a smoothly curving shape or line of movement. EG *The ball rose in an arc and landed about 150 yards away.* **2** a section of the line that forms the outside of a circle. N COUNT; Technical

arcade /ɑːkeɪd/, **arcades.** An **arcade** is a covered passageway where there are shops or market stalls. EG *...a shopping arcade.* N COUNT

arches

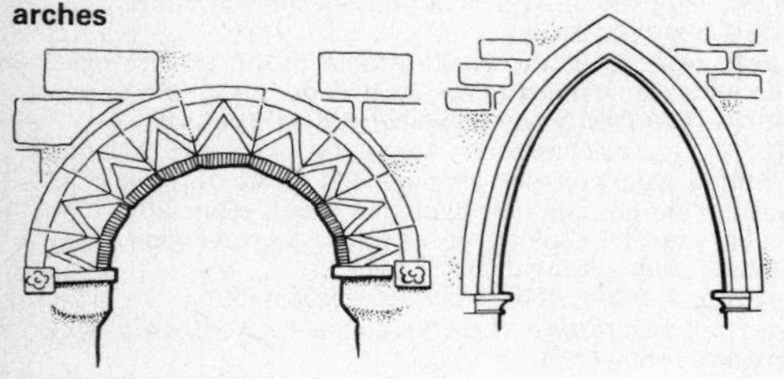

arch /ɑːtʃ/, **arches, arching, arched. 1** An **arch** is a structure that has a curved roof or top supported on either side by a pillar or wall, sometimes part of a bridge carrying a road or railway, or a doorway in a building. EG *...a house beneath the railway arches... We walked through an arch and into a huge square.* N COUNT

2 When something **arches**, it forms a curved shape or line. EG *She looked at him and her eyebrows arched... He arched his back.* V-ERG

3 An **arch** look is mysterious and mischievous. EG *She giggled and gave me an arch look.* ADJ QUALIT : ATTRIB

4 See also **arched.**

archaeology /ɑːkiˈɒlədʒiˈ/; also spelled **archeology,** especially in American English. N UNCOUNT

Archaeology is the study of the societies and peoples of the past, by examining the remains of their buildings, tools, and other things.

◊ **archaeologist, archaeologists.** EG *Archaeologists date the fragment between 4650 and 4500 BC.* ◊ N COUNT

◊ **archaeological.** EG *...dramatic archaeological discoveries.* ◊ ADJ CLASSIF

archaic /ɑːkeɪɪk/. Things that are **archaic** are very old or very old-fashioned. EG *...the archaic stove in the kitchen... ...archaic language.* ADJ QUALIT

archbishop /ɑːtʃbɪʃəp/, **archbishops.** An **archbishop** is a bishop of the highest rank, who is in charge of all the bishops and priests in a particular country or region. N COUNT

arched /ɑːtʃt/. **1** A roof, window, or doorway that is **arched** has a curved roof or top that is supported on either side by a pillar or wall. EG *...the arched roof over the staircase.* ADJ CLASSIF

2 Something that is **arched** curves upwards in the middle. EG *...his arched black eyebrows.* ADJ CLASSIF

archeology /ɑːkiɒlədʒiˈ/. See **archaeology.**

archer /ɑːtʃə/, **archers.** An **archer** is someone who shoots with a bow and arrow. N COUNT

archery /ɑːtʃəⁿriˈ/ is a sport in which people shoot at a target with a bow and arrow. N UNCOUNT

archetype /ɑːkiˈtaɪp/, **archetypes.** An **archetype** is something that is considered to be a perfect example of a particular kind of person or thing, because it has all their most important characteristics. EG *He is said to be the archetype of the modern journalist.* N COUNT : OFT+*of*

◊ **archetypal.** EG *...the archetypal Romantic heroes.* ◊ ADJ CLASSIF : ATTRIB

archipelago /ɑːkɪpeləgəʊ/, **archipelagos.** An **archipelago** is a group of small islands. EG *...the Philippine archipelago.* N COUNT

architect /ɑːkɪtɛkt/, **architects. 1** An **architect** is a person who designs buildings. N COUNT

2 The **architect** of an idea or event is the person who invented it or made it happen. EG *He was the real architect of the country's independence.* N COUNT : OFT+*of*

architectural /ɑːkiˈtɛktʃərəⁿl/ means relating to the design and construction of buildings. EG *...the architectural style suitable for government buildings.* ADJ CLASSIF : ATTRIB

architecture /ɑːkɪtɛktʃə/. **1 Architecture** is the art of planning, designing, and constructing buildings. N UNCOUNT

2 The **architecture** of a building is the style in which it is designed and constructed. EG *...the Late Victorian architecture of the Chapel.* N UNCOUNT +SUPP

archive /ɑːkaɪv/, **archives.** An **archive** or **archives** are a collection of documents and records that contain information about the history of a family, organization, or other group of people. EG *...the national archive of wills.* N COUNT OR N PLURAL

ardent /ɑːdəⁿnt/. Someone who is **ardent** about something has very enthusiastic or passionate feelings about it. EG *...an ardent religious faith... ...an ardent love-letter.* ADJ QUALIT

◊ **ardently.** EG *This is what he so ardently seeks.* ◊ ADV

ardour /ɑːdə/; spelled **ardor** in American English. **Ardour** is an intense and passionate feeling of love or enthusiasm for something. EG *...revolutionary ardour.* N UNCOUNT

arduous /ɑːdjuːəs/. Something that is **arduous** is tiring and involves a lot of effort. EG *...a long and arduous journey.* ADJ QUALIT

are /ɑː/ is the plural and the second person (singular and plural) of the present tense of the verb **be.**

area /ɛəriə/, **areas. 1** An **area** is **1.1** a particular part of a city, a country, or the world. EG *...a dry area that gets only a few months rain a year... ...all areas of Great Britain... ...the Brighton area.* N COUNT : USU+SUPP **1.2** a part of a surface that looks different from its surroundings. EG *...a pink area on the front of his thighs.* N COUNT+SUPP

2 A particular **area** of a room, building, or other place is a part of it that is used for a particular activity. EG *...an outdoor play area... ...a communal washing area.* N COUNT+SUPP

3 The **area** of a piece of land is the amount of ground that it covers, measured in a measurement such as square feet or square metres. EG *The farm was about 50 square kilometres in area.* N COUNT

4 An **area** of knowledge, interest, or activity is a particular kind of subject or activity. EG *His special interest lies in the area of literature.* N COUNT+SUPP

arena /əriːnə/, **arenas. 1** An **arena** is a place where sports and other public events take place, with seats around it where the public can sit and watch. N COUNT

2 A particular **arena** is the centre of attention in a particular situation. EG *He had come to the political arena late in life.* N COUNT+SUPP

aren't /ɑːnt/ is **1** the usual spoken form of 'are not'. EG *We aren't ready... They are coming, aren't they?* **2** the form that is usually used instead of 'am' in negative questions. EG *I'm right, aren't I?*

arguable /ɑːgjʊəbəⁿl/. **1** An idea, point, or comment that is **arguable** is not obviously true or correct and should be questioned. EG *Whether he was right or not is arguable.* ADJ CLASSIF

Is an archer armed?

2 If you say that it is **arguable** that something is true, you mean that it can be supported by evidence and is probably true. EG *It is arguable that the real damage will be seen much later.* ADJ CLASSIF: USU PRED

◊ **arguably.** EG *Deforestation is arguably the most serious environmental issue of our time.* ◊ ADV SEN

argue /ɑːgjuː/, **argues, arguing, argued. 1** If you **argue** with someone about something, you say things which show that you disagree with them about it, sometimes speaking angrily. EG *Don't argue with me, George, just do as you're told... They were arguing about who should sit in front.* V OR V+*with*: RECIP

2 If you **argue** that something is the case, you say that you think it is the case and give reasons why. EG *There are those who argue that the existence of nuclear weapons has helped to maintain peace... Bradbury argued the case for the opposition.* V+REPORT: ONLY *that*; ALSO V+O

3 If you **argue** for or **argue** against something, you give reasons why it should or should not happen and try to convince people that you are right. EG *Some politicians argued against giving women the vote.* V+*for/against*

4 If you **argue** someone **out of** doing something, you persuade them not to do it by talking to them. EG *He argued the man out of suicide.* PHRASE

argument /ɑːgjə⁴mə²nt/, **arguments. 1** An **argument** is a disagreement between two or more people, sometimes resulting in them shouting angrily at each other. EG *I said no and we got into a big argument over it... We accepted it without argument.* N COUNT OR N UNCOUNT

2 An **argument** is also a set of statements that you use in order to try to convince people that your opinion about something is correct. EG *There are strong arguments against these measures.* N COUNT: OFT+*for/against* OR REPORT

argumentative /ɑːgjə⁴mentə¹tɪv/. Someone who is **argumentative** is always ready to disagree with you. EG *'What did you mean by that?' he said in an argumentative tone.* ADJ QUALIT

aria /ɑːrɪə/, **arias.** An **aria** is a song for one of the leading singers in an opera or choral work. N COUNT

arid /ærɪd/. **1** Land that is **arid** is so dry that very few plants can grow on it. ADJ QUALIT

2 A subject or piece of writing that is **arid** is dull and uninteresting. ADJ QUALIT

arise /əraɪz/, **arises, arising, arose** /ərəʊz/, **arisen** /ərɪzə⁰n/. When something such as an opportunity, problem, or new state of affairs **arises**, it begins to exist. EG *A serious problem has arisen... He promised to help if the occasion arose... A whole community now arose.* V

aristocracy /ærɪ¹stɒkrəsi¹/, **aristocracies.** The **aristocracy** is a class of people in some countries who have a high social rank and special titles. N COLL

aristocrat /ærɪstə⁶kræt/, **aristocrats.** An **aristocrat** is someone whose family has a high social rank, especially someone who has a title. N COUNT

aristocratic /ærɪstə⁶krætɪk/. **1** Someone who is **aristocratic** belongs to the aristocracy. ADJ CLASSIF

2 Something that is **aristocratic** has characteristics which are considered to be typical of people of high social rank. EG *...his aristocratic features.* ADJ QUALIT

arithmetic /ə³rɪθmə²tɪk/ is the part of mathematics that is concerned with the addition, subtraction, multiplication, and division of numbers. EG *I blame the school for not making him learn arithmetic... ...simple arithmetic problems.* N UNCOUNT

arm /ɑːm/, **arms. 1** Your **arms** are the two long parts of your body that are attached to your shoulders and that have your hands at the end. See picture at THE HUMAN BODY. EG *She put her arm around his neck and kissed him.* N COUNT

2 The **arm** of a piece of clothing is the part of it that covers your arm. N COUNT

3 The **arm** of a chair is the part of it on which you rest your arm when you are sitting down. N COUNT

4 An **arm** of an organization is a section of it. EG *...the political arm of a trade union movement.* N COUNT+SUPP

5 **Arms** are weapons that are used in a war. N PLURAL

6 **Arm** is used in these phrases. **6.1** If you are walking **arm in arm** with someone, you are walking with your arm linked through their arm. **6.2** If you welcome someone **with open arms**, you hold your arms stretched out and apart, ready to hug them. **6.3** If you welcome an event or change **with open arms**, you are very pleased about it. **6.4** If you hold something **at arm's length**, you hold it at a distance from your body. EG *...holding the paper at arm's length to read it.* **6.5** If you **keep** someone **at arm's length**, you avoid becoming too friendly or involved with them. **6.6** If someone is **up in arms** about something, they are very angry about it and are protesting strongly. EG *Feminists are now up in arms over the new laws.* PHRASES

7 See also **armed.**

armada /ɑːmɑːdə/, **armadas.** An **armada** is a large fleet of warships. N COUNT

armament /ɑːməmə²nt/, **armaments. 1 Armaments** are weapons and military equipment belonging to an army or country. N PLURAL

2 **Armament** is the increase by a country in the number and effectiveness of its weapons. N UNCOUNT

armchair /ɑːmtʃeə/, **armchairs.** An **armchair** is a comfortable chair which has a support on each side for your arms. See picture at CHAIRS. N COUNT

armed /ɑːmd/. **1** Someone who is **armed** is carrying a weapon, usually a gun. ADJ CLASSIF

2 An **armed** attack or conflict involves people fighting with guns. EG *...armed assaults on homes.* ADJ CLASSIF: ATTRIB

3 If you are **armed** with something useful such as information or a skill, you have it. EG *Armed with secretarial skills, she will easily find a job.* ADJ PRED +*with*

armed forces. The **armed forces** of a country are its military forces, usually the army, navy, and air force. N PLURAL

armful /ɑːmfʊl/, **armfuls.** An **armful** of something is the amount of it that you can carry in one or both of your arms. EG *She came back with an armful of paperbacks.* N PART

armistice /ɑːmɪ¹stɪs/, **armistices.** An **armistice** is an agreement between countries who are at war with one another to stop fighting and to discuss ways of making a peaceful settlement. N COUNT OR N UNCOUNT

armour /ɑːmə/; spelled **armor** in American English. **1 Armour** is special metal clothing that soldiers used to wear for protection in battle. EG *...knights in armour.* N UNCOUNT

2 The **armour** of something is a hard covering that protects it against attack. EG *...the steel armour of a tank... The animal has an armour of horny scales.* N SING+SUPP

armoured /ɑːməd/; spelled **armored** in American English. An **armoured** vehicle is fitted with a hard metal covering in order to protect it from gunfire and other missiles. EG *...armoured cars.* ADJ CLASSIF

armpit /ɑːmpɪt/, **armpits.** Your **armpit** is the area of your body that is under your arm where your arm joins your shoulder. N COUNT

army /ɑːmi¹/, **armies. 1** An **army** is a large organized group of people who are armed and trained to fight on land in a war. EG *Both armies suffered thousands of wounded.* N COLL

2 An **army** of people, animals, or things is a large number of them, especially when they are regarded as a force of some kind. EG *...an army of ants.* N PART

aroma /ərəʊmə/, **aromas.** An **aroma** is a strong, pleasant smell. EG *The house was filled with the aroma of coffee.* N COUNT+SUPP

aromatic /ærə⁶mætɪk/. A plant or food that is **aromatic** has a strong, pleasant smell of spice or herbs. ADJ QUALIT

arose /ərəʊz/ is the past tense of **arise.**

around /əraʊnd/. **1 Around** can be an adverb or preposition, and is often used instead of **round** as the second part of a phrasal verb. Examples of these uses of **around** are explained at **round.** ADV AFTER VB, OR PREP

2 If someone or something **is around**, they are present or available. EG *He went back to see who* PHRASE

was around... It's a gadget which has been around for years.

3 If someone **has been around**, they have had a lot of experience of different people and situations. EG *I've been around and I know how to handle people like him.* PHRASE Informal

4 Around also means approximately. EG *He owns around 200 acres.* ADV

arousal /ərauzə^{0}l/. If something causes the **arousal** of a feeling, it causes you to begin to have this feeling. EG *...the arousal of interest... ...feelings of sexual arousal.* N UNCOUNT +SUPP

arouse /ərauz/, **arouses, arousing, aroused. 1** If something **arouses** a feeling in you, it causes you to begin to have this feeling. EG *It may arouse his interest in the subject... ...a move that would arouse opposition.* V+O

2 If something **arouses** people, it makes them feel angry. V+O

3 When people or things **arouse** you from sleep, they wake you up. V+O Literary

arr. is an abbreviation for 'arrives'. It is used on timetables to indicate what time a bus, train, or plane will reach a place.

arrange /ə^{3}reɪndʒ/, **arranges, arranging, arranged. 1** If you **arrange** an event or meeting, you make plans for it to happen. EG *Progressive Tours arrange holidays in Eastern Europe.* V+O

2 If you **arrange** with someone to do something, you make plans with them to do it. EG *We've arranged with somebody else to go to the cinema this evening... We had arranged to meet in the street outside... It was suddenly arranged that Celia should come to Switzerland.* V+*with* OR to-INF OR REPORT : ONLY *that*

3 If you **arrange** something for someone, you make it possible for them to have it or to do it. EG *We can arrange loans... I asked if it could be arranged for me to meet one of the leaders.* V+O OR V+*to*-INF : OFT+*for*

4 If you **arrange** things, such as flowers in a vase or books on a shelf, you put them in a particular position, usually in order to make them look attractive or tidy. EG *...four chairs arranged around the table.* V+O+A

arranged /ə^{3}reɪndʒd/. An **arranged** marriage is a marriage in which the parents choose the person who their son or daughter will marry. ADJ CLASSIF

arrangement /ə^{3}reɪndʒmə^{2}nt/, **arrangements. 1 Arrangements** are plans and preparations which you make so that something will happen or be possible. EG *I've made all the arrangements for the conference.* N PLURAL : OFT+*for*

2 An **arrangement** is **2.1** an agreement that you make with someone to do something. EG *He made an arrangement to rent the property.* **2.2** a plan for doing something. EG *What are the sleeping and eating arrangements?* N COUNT

3 An **arrangement** of things, for example flowers or furniture, is a group of them that have been set out in a particular position. EG *There was an arrangement of books in the window.* N COUNT+SUPP

array /əreɪ/, **arrays, arrayed. 1** An **array** of different things is a large number of them, especially when they are impressive. EG *They looked in the window at the array of cakes.* N COUNT : OFT+*of*

2 If things **are arrayed** somewhere, they are displayed there attractively. EG *Daggers and pistols were arrayed on the walls.* V-PASS+A Formal

arrears /ərɪəz/. **1 Arrears** are amounts of money that you owe. EG *He vanished leaving massive arrears.* N PLURAL

2 If someone is **in arrears** with their payments, they have not paid the regular amounts of money that they should have paid. EG *The council complained that his rent was in arrears.* PHRASE

3 If you are paid **in arrears**, your wages are paid to you at the end of the period of time in which you earned them. PHRASE

arrest /ərɛst/, **arrests, arresting, arrested. 1** If the police **arrest** someone, they catch them and take them somewhere in order to decide whether they should be charged with an offence. EG *A friend had been arrested for possession of explosives.* V+O : OFT+*for*

▸ used as a noun. EG *The riots led to the arrest of many union leaders... A number of arrests were made.* ▸ N UNCOUNT OR N COUNT ● If someone is **under arrest**, they have been caught by the police and are not allowed to go free. ● PHRASE

2 If you **arrest** something, you stop it happening. EG *He tried to arrest the course of destruction.* V+O Formal

3 If something **arrests** your attention, it interests or surprises you so that you look at it or listen to it carefully. V+O ◇ **arresting.** EG *...an arresting drawing of people turning into animals.* ◇ ADJ QUALIT

arrival /əraɪvə^{0}l/, **arrivals. 1** Your **arrival** at a place is the act of arriving there. EG *I apologize for my late arrival.* N UNCOUNT : USU+A

2 If you talk about the **arrival** of something new, you are referring to the fact that it has begun to exist or happen. EG *Industry has been revolutionized by the arrival of the computer.* N SING

3 The **arrival** of a baby is its birth. N SING

4 An **arrival** is someone who has just arrived at a place. EG *One of the new arrivals at the college was an old friend.* N COUNT

arrive /əraɪv/, **arrives, arriving, arrived. 1** When you **arrive** at a place, **1.1** you reach it at the end of a journey. EG *He arrived back at his hotel after midnight.* **1.2** you come to it for the first time in order to stay there or live there. EG *Since arriving in England in 1979, she has established herself as a major writer... ...newly arrived students.* V : USU+A

2 When a letter or piece of news **arrives**, it is brought or delivered to you. EG *Your card arrived on Monday... News arrived of an invasion in the south.* V : USU+A

3 When you **arrive** at an idea, decision, or conclusion, you reach it, make it, or decide on it. EG *It took us hours to arrive at a decision.* V+*at*

4 When a baby **arrives**, it is born. V : USU+A

5 When a moment, event, or new thing **arrives**, it begins to happen or exist. EG *Her wedding day arrived.* V

arrogant /ærəgənt/. Someone who is **arrogant** behaves in a proud, unpleasant way towards other people because they believe that they are more important than others. EG *I think it would be arrogant if I tried to give any advice.* ADJ QUALIT

◇ **arrogantly.** EG *The group had arrogantly assumed themselves to be in command.* ◇ ADV

◇ **arrogance** /ærəgəns/. EG *He had a reputation for arrogance.* ◇ N UNCOUNT

arrow /ærəʊ/, **arrows. 1** An **arrow** is a long thin weapon which is sharp and pointed at one end. An arrow is shot from a bow. N COUNT

2 An **arrow** is also a written sign that consists of a straight line with another line bent at a sharp angle at one end. The arrow points in a particular direction to indicate where something is. EG *The exit sign is marked with an arrow.* N COUNT

arsenic /ɑːsə^{0}nɪk/ is a very strong poison which can kill people. N UNCOUNT

arson /ɑːsə^{0}n/ is the crime of deliberately setting fire to a building. N UNCOUNT

art /ɑːt/, **arts. 1 Art** is **1.1** the creation of drawings, paintings, and sculpture, when these things are considered to be beautiful or to express a particular idea. EG *...the study of contemporary art.* **1.2** objects, such as paintings or pieces of sculpture, which are considered to be beautiful and which are part of a society's culture. EG *...sales of oriental art... ...an art collection.* N UNCOUNT

2 An **art** is an activity such as drama, poetry, or sculpture in which people try to create something N COUNT

What is the difference between 'artistic' and 'arty'?

beautiful or to express a particular idea. EG *The strongest 20th century art is film... ...the visual arts.*

3 The **arts** refers to the creation or performance of drama, music, poetry, or painting, especially in a particular country or region. EG *How much will they spend on sport, how much on the arts?* N PLURAL

4 **Arts** is used to refer to subjects such as history or languages in contrast to scientific subjects. EG *...an arts degree.* N PLURAL

5 You describe an activity as an **art** when it requires a lot of skill. EG *...the art of camouflage.* N SING

● If you **get** something **down to a fine art**, you are able to do it in a very skilled way because you have had a lot of experience of doing it. ● PHRASE

artefact /ɑ:tɪ^{1}fækt/, **artefacts;** also spelled **artifact.** An **artefact** is an ornament, tool, or other object that is made by a human being. N COUNT

artery /ɑ:təri^1/, **arteries.** Your **arteries** are the tubes in your body that carry blood from your heart to the rest of your body. N COUNT

artful /ɑ:tfʊl/. Someone who is **artful** is clever and skilful, often in a cunning way. EG *...the artful schemer.* ◊ **artfully.** EG *The lighting was artfully arranged to flatter people's faces.* ADJ QUALIT; ◊ ADV

arthritic /ɑ:θrɪtɪk/. A person who is **arthritic** has swollen and painful joints in their body. ADJ QUALIT

arthritis /ɑ:θraɪtɪ^{1}s/ is a condition in which the joints in someone's body are swollen and painful. N UNCOUNT

artichoke /ɑ:tɪtʃəʊk/, **artichokes. 1** An **artichoke** or a **globe artichoke** is a round, green vegetable that has a cluster of fleshy leaves, of which you can eat the bottom part. N COUNT

2 An **artichoke** or a **Jerusalem artichoke** is a small, yellowish-white vegetable that grows underground and looks like a potato. N COUNT

article /ɑ:tɪkə^{0}l/, **articles. 1** An **article** is **1.1** a piece of writing that has been written for publication in a newspaper or magazine. EG *...an article by J B Priestley in the New Statesman.* **1.2** a particular object or item. EG *He was ordered to pay for the articles he had stolen... ...an article of furniture.* N COUNT; N PART

2 An **article** of a formal agreement or document is a section of it which deals with a particular point. EG *The invasion contravened article 51 of the UN charter.* N COUNT

3 In grammar, the words 'a' and 'an' are sometimes called 'indefinite articles' and the word 'the' is called the 'definite article'. In this dictionary these words are called determiners (DET). See the entry headed DETERMINERS for more information about determiners in English. N COUNT

articulate, articulates, articulating, articulated; pronounced /ɑ:tɪkjə^{4}lə^{1}t/ when it is an adjective and /ɑ:tɪkjə^{4}leɪt/ when it is a verb.

1 If you are **articulate**, you are able to express yourself well. EG *He was the most articulate speaker.* ADJ QUALIT

2 When you **articulate** your ideas or feelings, you say in words what you think or how you feel. EG *I could not define or articulate the dissatisfaction I felt.* V+O Formal

articulated /ɑ:tɪkjə^{4}leɪtɪ^{2}d/. An **articulated** lorry is made in two sections which are joined together by a metal bar, so that the lorry can turn corners more easily. ADJ CLASSIF : ATTRIB

articulation /ɑ:tɪkjə^{4}leɪʃə^{0}n/. **1** The **articulation** of an idea or feeling is the expression of it, especially in words. N UNCOUNT : OFT+*of* Formal

2 The **articulation** of a sound or word is the way in which it is produced or spoken. N UNCOUNT

artifact /ɑ:tɪfækt/. See **artefact**.

artificial /ɑ:tɪfɪʃəl/. **1** An **artificial** state or situation is not natural and exists or happens because people have created it. EG *These results appear only in very artificial conditions.* ◊ **artificially.** EG *The government keeps prices artificially high.* ◊ **artificiality** /ɑ:tɪfɪʃi^{1}ælɪti^1/. EG *...the artificiality of a three hour written examination.* ADJ QUALIT; ◊ ADV; ◊ N UNCOUNT

2 **Artificial** objects or materials do not occur naturally and are created by people. EG *...artificial fibres... ...artificial flowers.* ADJ CLASSIF

3 An **artificial** arm or leg is made of metal or plastic and is fitted to someone's body when their own arm or leg has been removed. ADJ CLASSIF : ATTRIB

4 Someone who is **artificial** pretends to have attitudes and feelings which other people realize are not real. EG *They jumped at the suggestion with artificial enthusiasm.* ADJ QUALIT

artillery /ɑ:tɪləri^1/ consists of large, powerful guns which are transported on wheels and used by an army. EG *Artillery fire caused heavy losses.* N UNCOUNT

artist /ɑ:tɪst/, **artists.** An **artist** is **1** someone who draws, paints, or produces other works of art as a job or a hobby. EG *This abstract picture was painted by John Hoyland, an artist who emerged in the 1960's.* **2** someone who is very skilled at a particular activity. EG *He knew that he was good, that he was an artist.* **3** a performer such as a musician, actor, or dancer. EG *She has acted with great artists like Edith Evans.* N COUNT

artiste /ɑ:ti:st/, **artistes.** An **artiste** is a professional entertainer, for example a singer or a dancer. N COUNT

artistic /ɑ:tɪstɪk/. **1** Someone who is **artistic** is able to create good paintings, sculpture, or other works of art. EG *I talked to many artistic people: writers, dancers, and film makers.* ◊ **artistically.** EG *She is artistically gifted, especially in dance.* ADJ QUALIT; ◊ ADV

2 **Artistic** means relating to art or artists. EG *...artistic freedom... ...mediums of artistic expression.* ADJ CLASSIF

3 A design or arrangement that is **artistic** is attractive. EG *These are very artistic images.* ADJ QUALIT

artistry /ɑ:tɪstri^1/ is the creative skill of an artist, writer, actor, or musician. EG *He acted the final scenes with superb artistry.* N UNCOUNT

arty /ɑ:ti^1/. Someone who is **arty** seems to be very interested in painting, sculpture, and other works of art. ADJ QUALIT

as /ə^{3}z/. **1** If something happens **as** something else happens, it happens when the other thing happens. EG *She wept bitterly as she told her story... Parts are replaced as they grow old.* CONJ

2 You use the structure **as...as** when you are comparing things or saying that they are similar. EG *I'm as good a cook as she is... Treat the patient as soon as possible.*

3 You use **as** when you are describing someone's attitude or reaction to situations, people, or events. EG *You regard the whole thing as a joke... The sudden change had come as a shock to Castle.* PREP

4 You use **as** when you are specifying a feature or function that something or someone has. EG *He established his reputation as a radical with his very first speech... Over the summer she worked as a waitress... ...a story she had heard many times as a girl.* PREP

5 You use **as** when you are mentioning the way that something happens or is done. EG *I like the freedom to organise my day as I want to... He looked over his shoulder as Jack had done.* CONJ

6 You use **as** to introduce a comment that you are making. EG *As usual at the weekend, the club was almost empty... As you can see, we've got a problem with the engine.* PREP OR CONJ

7 You use **as** when you are explaining the reason for something. EG *She bought herself an iron, as she felt she couldn't keep borrowing Anne's.* CONJ

8 You use **as if** and **as though** when you are giving a possible explanation for something. EG *The furniture looked as though it had come out of somebody's attic... He looked at me as if I were mad.* CONJ

9 You use **as for** and **as to** at the beginning of a sentence in order to introduce a slightly different subject that is still connected to the previous one. EG *That's the answer. As for the cause, how do I know?* PREP

10 You also use **as to** to specify the particular subject that you are talking about. EG *John had been given no directions as to what to write.* PREP British

11 If you say that something will happen **as of** or **as from** a particular date or time, you mean that it will happen from that time onwards. EG *As of next week I'll be working at home.* PREP

12 You say **as it were** in order to make what you are saying sound less definite. EG *That was as it were part of the job.* ADV SEN

13 You use expressions such as **as it is, as it turns out**, and **as things stand** when you are making a contrast between a possible situation and what actually happened or is the case. EG *He could have been killed. As it was, he suffered severe back injuries.* ADV SEN

asbestos /æsbɛstɒs/ is a grey material which does not burn. EG *...an asbestos mat.* N UNCOUNT

ascend /əsɛnd/, **ascends, ascending, ascended.** **1** If something **ascends**, it moves or leads upwards. EG *The sound ascended to the room above... ...tiers of seats ascending to the roof.* V: USU+A Literary

2 If you **ascend** a hill or a staircase, you go up it. EG *He ascended the flight of narrow stairs to his bedroom.* V+O Literary

3 When someone **ascends the throne**, they become king or queen. EG *Queen Victoria ascended the throne in 1837.* PHRASE

4 See also **ascending**.

ascendancy /əsɛndənsi[1]/. If one group has **ascendancy** over another group, it has more power or influence than the other group. EG *...Unionist ascendancy over the Catholic minority.* N UNCOUNT: OFT+*over* Formal

ascendant /əsɛndənt/. Someone or something that is **in the ascendant** is increasing in power, influence, or popularity. EG *His party was now in the ascendant.* PHRASE

ascending /əsɛndɪŋ/. When a group of things is arranged in **ascending** order, each thing is higher in position or greater in amount or importance than the thing before it. EG *Arrange the four digits in ascending order... ...houses built on ascending levels on the slopes of hills.* ADJ CLASSIF: ATTRIB

ascent /əsɛnt/, **ascents. 1** An **ascent** is **1.1** an upward journey, for example when you climb a mountain. EG *The final ascent took an hour.* **1.2** an upward slope, especially one that you are walking up. EG *John toiled up the dusty ascent.* N COUNT

2 Someone's **ascent** is a process by which they become more important or advanced than before. EG *Nick and he had both succeeded, though Nick's ascent had been more honourable.* N UNCOUNT +SUPP Formal

ascertain /æsəteɪn/, **ascertains, ascertaining, ascertained.** If you **ascertain** that something is the case, you find out that it is the case. EG *I ascertained that Lo was still sound asleep.* V+REPORT OR V+O Formal

ascetic /əsɛtɪk/, **ascetics.** People who are **ascetic** have a way of life that is simple and strict, usually because of their religious beliefs. EG *He subjected himself to a strenuous ascetic discipline.* ADJ QUALIT
▸ used as a noun. EG *...a religious ascetic.* ▸ N COUNT

ascribe /ə³skraɪb/, **ascribes, ascribing, ascribed. 1** If you **ascribe** an event or state of affairs to a particular factor, you consider that it is caused by that factor. EG *It is wrong to ascribe all that has happened simply to the war... ...headaches which may be ascribed to stress.* V+O+*to*

2 If you **ascribe** a quality to someone, you consider that they possess it. EG *Husbands are often mistaken in the virtues they ascribe to their wives.* V+O+*to*

3 If you **ascribe** a work of art to someone, you say that they created it. EG *...a magnificent painted ceiling, doubtfully ascribed to Holbein.* V+O+*to*

asexual /eɪsɛksjʊ⁰əl/. Something that is **asexual** has no sex or involves no sexual activity. EG *...two methods of reproduction, sexual and asexual.* ADJ CLASSIF

ash /æʃ/, **ashes. 1 Ash** is the grey or black powdery substance that is left after something is burnt. EG *...cigarette ash... Ashes blew into Ralph's face from the dead fire.* N UNCOUNT OR N PLURAL

2 An **ash** is a kind of tree. N COUNT

ashamed /əʃeɪmd/. **1** If someone is **ashamed**, they feel embarrassed or guilty because of something that they have done. EG *She was ashamed of her tears... It's nothing to be ashamed of... You should be ashamed of yourself.* ADJ PRED: OFT+*of*

2 If someone is **ashamed** to do something, they do not want to do it because they feel embarrassed about it. EG *I bet that's what happened, only you're ashamed to admit it.* ADJ PRED +*to*-INF

3 If you are **ashamed** of someone, you feel embarrassed to be connected with them. EG *He was ashamed of her for writing such lies.* ADJ PRED+*of*

ashore /əʃɔː/. Something that comes **ashore** comes from the sea onto the shore. EG *He managed to swim ashore.* ADV AFTER VB

ashtray /æʃtreɪ/, **ashtrays.** An **ashtray** is a small dish in which people can put the ash from their cigarettes and cigars. N COUNT

Asian /eɪʃən, eɪʒən/, **Asians. 1** Someone or something that is **Asian** comes from Asia. EG *His philosophy is a mixture of both Western and Asian thought.* ADJ CLASSIF

2 An **Asian** is a person who comes from a country or region in Asia. N COUNT

aside /əsaɪd/, **asides. 1** If you move something **aside**, you move it to one side of you. EG *He threw the manuscript aside.* ADV AFTER VB

2 If you take or draw someone **aside**, you take them a little way away from a group of people in order to talk to them in private. ADV AFTER VB

3 If you move **aside**, you get out of someone's way. EG *She stepped aside, holding the door wide open.* ADV AFTER VB

4 If you brush or sweep a feeling or suggestion **aside**, you reject it. EG *She brushed his protests aside.* ADV AFTER VB

5 You use **aside** to indicate that you have finished talking about something, or that you are leaving it out of your discussion, and that you are about to talk about something else. EG *High technology aside, New England's economy is still largely based on fishing.* ADV AFTER N

6 An **aside** is **6.1** a comment that a character in a play makes to the audience, which the other characters are supposed not to be able to hear. **6.2** something that you say that is not directly connected with what you are talking about. EG *In an aside he said to his servant, 'See that man gets something to eat.'* N COUNT

ask /ɑːsk/, **asks, asking, asked. 1** If you **ask** someone something, you say something to them in the form of a question because you want to know something. EG *I asked him what he wanted... 'Why?' he asked... He started asking questions... Five or six years ago her sister asked me if I would paint her.* V+O+O, V+O+QUOTE; ALSO V-SPEECH OR V+O+REPORT: ONLY WH

2 If you **ask** someone to do something, you say to them that you want them to do it. EG *He asked her to marry him... He was asked to leave.* V+O: USU+*to*-INF

3 If you **ask** someone's permission or forgiveness, you try to obtain it by putting a question to them. EG *I asked permission to leave.* V+O OR V

4 If you **ask** someone somewhere, you invite them there. EG *I asked her to the party... She asked me in.* V+O+A

5 If something is yours **for the asking**, you can have it simply by saying that you would like it. PHRASE

6 You can say **'if you ask me'** to emphasize that you are stating your personal opinion. EG *The whole thing's stupid if you ask me.* ADV SEN

ask after. If you **ask after** someone, you ask how they are. EG *He asks after you a lot.* PHRASAL VB: V+PREP

ask for. 1 If you **ask for** someone, you say that you would like to speak to them. EG *He rang the office and asked for Cynthia.* **2** If you **ask for** PHRASAL VB: V+PREP V+PREP

If you ascribe a picture to Leonardo da Vinci, did he definitely paint it?

something, you say that you would like it. EG *She asked for a drink of water.* **3** If you say that someone **is asking for** trouble, you mean that they are behaving in a way that makes it very likely that they will get into trouble. V+PREP, USU CONT

askew /əskjuː/. Something that is **askew** is not straight or level. EG *His tie was askew.* ADJ PRED

asleep /əsliːp/. **1** Someone who is **asleep** is sleeping. ADJ PRED

2 When you **fall asleep**, you start sleeping. PHRASE

3 Someone who is **fast asleep** or **sound asleep** is sleeping deeply. PHRASE

asparagus /əspærəgəs/ is a vegetable with green shoots that you can cook and eat when they are young. N UNCOUNT

aspect /æspɛkt/, **aspects. 1** An **aspect** of something is one of the parts of its character or nature. EG *The most terrifying aspect of nuclear bombing is radiation... ...the influence which America had on many aspects of British cultural life.* N COUNT+SUPP

2 The **aspect** of a building or a window is the direction in which it faces. EG *...an office with a south-west aspect.* N COUNT+SUPP Formal

3 If something acquires a new **aspect**, it acquires a new appearance or quality. EG *The whole scheme began to take on a more practical aspect.* N COUNT+SUPP

aspersions /ə^{3}spɜːʃə^{0}nz/. If you **cast aspersions** on someone or something, you suggest that they are not very good in some way. PHRASE Formal

asphalt /æsfælt, -fɔːlt/ is a black substance used to make surfaces on things such as roads and playgrounds. N UNCOUNT

asphyxiate /æsfɪksɪeɪt/, **asphyxiates, asphyxiating, asphyxiated.** If someone **is asphyxiated** by smoke or a poisonous gas, they breathe it in and die. V+O

aspirant /æspə^{1}rənt, əspaɪərənt/, **aspirants.** Someone who is an **aspirant** to political power or to an important job has a strong desire to achieve it. N COUNT Formal

aspiration /æspə^{1}reɪʃə^{0}n/, **aspirations.** Someone's **aspirations** are their ambitions to achieve something. EG *Educational standards and aspirations have risen in recent years.* N COUNT OR N UNCOUNT

aspire /əspaɪə/, **aspires, aspiring, aspired.** If you **aspire** to something such as an important job, you have an ambition to achieve it. EG *She has always aspired to leadership.* ◊ **aspiring.** EG *...an aspiring concert pianist.* V+*to* OR *to*-INF; ◊ ADJ CLASSIF : ATTRIB

aspirin /æspɪ^{0}rɪn/, **aspirins. Aspirin** is a mild drug in the form of tablets which reduces pain and fever. EG *She gave me an aspirin for my headache.* N UNCOUNT OR N COUNT

ass /æs/, **asses. 1** An **ass** is an animal related to a horse but smaller and with long ears. N COUNT

2 If you say that someone is an **ass**, you mean that they say or do silly things. N COUNT Informal

assail /əseɪl/, **assails, assailing, assailed. 1** If you **assail** someone, you criticize them strongly. EG *He was assailed in the Press.* V+O Literary

2 If you **are assailed** by unpleasant thoughts or problems, you are greatly troubled or bothered by a large number of them. EG *They are assailed by doubts.* V+O : USU PASS Literary

assailant /əseɪlənt/, **assailants.** Someone's **assailant** is the person who physically attacks them. EG *He dared not take his eyes off his assailant for a second.* N COUNT Formal

assassin /əsæsɪn/, **assassins.** An **assassin** is a person who assassinates someone. N COUNT

assassinate /əsæsɪneɪt/, **assassinates, assassinating, assassinated.** When someone important **is assassinated**, they are murdered. V+O
◊ **assassination** /əsæsɪneɪʃə^{0}n/, **assassinations.** EG *...an assassination attempt.* ◊ N UNCOUNT OR N COUNT

assault /əsɔːlt/, **assaults, assaulting, assaulted.**
1 An **assault** by an army is a strong attack that is made on an area held by the enemy. EG *They responded with assaults against the enemy's bases.* N COUNT : OFT +*against/on*

2 An **assault** on a person is a physical attack on them. EG *He was threatened with assault in the street.* ▸ used as a verb. EG *She was found guilty of assaulting a police officer.* N COUNT OR N UNCOUNT; ▸ V+O

3 An **assault** on someone's beliefs is a strong criticism of them. EG *...an all-out assault on racism.* N COUNT

assemble /ə^{3}sɛmbə^{0}l/, **assembles, assembling, assembled. 1** When people or things **assemble** or **are assembled**, they gather together in a group, usually for a particular purpose. EG *The leaders assembled in Paris for a meeting... His job was to assemble the facts and evaluate them.* V-ERG
◊ **assembled.** EG *She announced to the assembled relatives that she intended to move abroad.* ◊ ADJ CLASSIF

2 To **assemble** something means to fit the parts of it together. EG *...a vast range of products that were assembled locally.* V+O

assembly /ə^{3}sɛmbli^1/, **assemblies. 1** An **assembly** is **1.1** a gathering of people or things. EG *...a great assembly of senators.* **1.2** a group of people who meet regularly to make laws for a region or country. N COUNT

2 Assembly is the gathering together of people for a particular purpose. EG *They are demanding rights of assembly.* N UNCOUNT

3 The **assembly** of the parts of a machine or device is the process of fitting them together. EG *...instructions for assembly of an outdoor barbecue.* N UNCOUNT

assembly line, assembly lines. An **assembly line** is an arrangement of workers and machines in a factory where the product passes from one worker to another until it is finished. N COUNT

assent /ə^{3}sɛnt/, **assents, assenting, assented.** If someone gives their **assent** to something that has been suggested, they agree to it. EG *Haldane acted with the full assent of the Foreign Office.* ▸ used as a verb. EG *They all assented to the proposition.* N UNCOUNT; ▸ V+*to* OR V+QUOTE

assert /ə^{3}sɜːt/, **asserts, asserting, asserted. 1** If someone **asserts** a fact or belief, they state it firmly. EG *The protesters asserted their right to be heard.* ◊ **assertion** /ə^{3}sɜːʃə^{0}n/, **assertions.** EG *I challenge that assertion.* V-SPEECH : ONLY *that*; ◊ N COUNT OR N UNCOUNT

2 If you **assert** your authority, you make it clear by your behaviour that you have authority. EG *He wished to assert his authority in his own house.* ◊ **assertion.** EG *...an assertion of power.* V+O; ◊ N UNCOUNT

3 If you **assert** yourself, you speak and act in a forceful way so that people take notice of you. EG *She had begun to assert herself strongly.* V-REFL

assertive /ə^{3}sɜːtɪv/. Someone who is **assertive** speaks and acts in a forceful way so that people take notice of them. ADJ QUALIT

assess /ə^{3}sɛs/, **assesses, assessing, assessed. 1** When you **assess** a person, feeling, or situation, you consider them and make a judgement about them. EG *They meet monthly to assess the current political situation... Ellen tried to assess how she felt.* V+O; ALSO V+REPORT : ONLY WH

2 When you **assess** the amount of money that something is worth or that should be paid, you calculate or estimate it. EG *She looked the house over and assessed its rough market value.* V+O

assessment /ə^{3}sɛsmə^{2}nt/, **assessments. 1** An **assessment** is a consideration of someone or something and a judgement about them. EG *There has to be a clear assessment of the country's social needs... ...the assessment of his academic progress.* N COUNT+SUPP

2 An **assessment** of the amount of money that something is worth or that should be paid is a calculation or estimate of the amount. N COUNT

asset /æsɛt/, **assets. 1** An **asset** is someone or something that is considered useful or that helps a person or organization to be successful. EG *He was a great asset to the committee... Her only asset was a gentle nature.* N COUNT : OFT+*to*

2 The **assets** of a company or a person are all the things that they own. N PLURAL

assiduous /əsɪdjuːəs/. Someone who is **assiduous** works hard at a particular task. EG *...an assiduous* ADJ QUALIT student. ◇ **assiduously.** EG *Throughout 1954 he assiduously studied law.* ◇ ADV

assign /əsaɪn/, **assigns, assigning, assigned. 1** If you **assign** a piece of work to someone, you give them the work to do. EG *She kept calling him up to assign some new task to him... She had been assigned to work in the fields.* V+O+*to* OR *to*-INF; ALSO V+O+O

2 If you **assign** something to someone, you say that it is for their use. EG *The bed which I'd been assigned was in Dormitory 2.* V+O+*to* OR V+O+O

3 If someone **is assigned** to a particular place, group, or person, they are sent there, usually in order to work there or for that person. EG *She was assigned to the men's wards.* V+O: USU PASS+*to*

4 If you **assign** a particular function or value to someone or something, you give it to them. EG *Mother and father play out the roles assigned to them.* V+O+*to* OR V+O+O

assignation /æsɪgneɪʃə0n/, **assignations.** An **assignation** is a secret meeting with someone, especially with a lover. N COUNT Formal

assignment /əsaɪnmə2nt/, **assignments. 1** An **assignment** is a task or piece of work that you are given to do, especially as part of your job or studies. EG *My first major assignment was to cover a large-scale riot.* N COUNT

2 You can refer to someone being given a particular task or job as their **assignment** to the task or job. EG *...the uproar about his assignment to the case.* N UNCOUNT +POSS

assimilate /əsɪmɪleɪt/, **assimilates, assimilating, assimilated. 1** If you **assimilate** ideas, customs, or techniques, you learn them and make use of them. EG *He was quick to assimilate new ideas.* V+O

◇ **assimilation** /ə3sɪmɪleɪʃə0n/. EG *...the rapid assimilation of new techniques in industry.* ◇ N UNCOUNT

2 When people such as immigrants **assimilate** or **are assimilated** into a community, they become an accepted part of it. ◇ **assimilation.** EG *...the assimilation of the new arrivals.* V-ERG: OFT+*into* ◇ N UNCOUNT

assist /əsɪst/, **assists, assisting, assisted. 1** If you **assist** someone, **1.1** you help them do something. EG *He was asked to assist in keeping the hotel under surveillance.* **1.2** you give them information, advice, or money. EG *We may be able to assist with the tuition fees.* V+O OR V: OFT+*with/in*

2 If something **assists** you with a task, it makes it easier for you. EG *With these clues to assist us, we can begin to identify the parents.* V+O OR V: OFT+*with/in*

assistance /əsɪstəns/. **1** If you give someone **assistance**, **1.1** you help them do something. EG *He thanked me for my assistance... They could not walk without assistance.* **1.2** you give them information, advice, or money. EG *The department provides special assistance to those with large families.* N UNCOUNT

2 Someone or something that is **of assistance** to you is helpful or useful to you. EG *I would be of little assistance in that kind of work.* PHRASE

assistant /əsɪstənt/, **assistants. 1 Assistant** is used in front of titles or jobs to indicate a slightly lower rank or title. For example, an **assistant** director is one rank lower than a director in an organization. ADJ CLASSIF: ATTRIB

2 Someone's **assistant** is a person who helps them in their work. N COUNT+POSS

3 An **assistant** or a **shop assistant** is a person who works in a shop selling things to customers. N COUNT

associate, associates, associating, associated; pronounced /ə3səʊsi1eɪt/ when it is a verb and /əsəʊsi1ət/ when it is a noun or adjective.

1 If you **associate** one thing with another, the two things are connected in your mind. EG *Dignity is the quality which I associate mostly with her... The smoking of pipes is often associated with old-fashioned 'masculine' values.* V+O+*with*

2 If one thing **is associated** with another, the two things are connected with each other. EG *Zuse worked on problems associated with aircraft design... ...the Executive and its associated committees.* V+O: USU PASS+*with*

3 If you **are associated** with a particular organization, cause, or point of view, or if you **associate** yourself with it, you support it publicly. EG *They became closely associated with the International Socialists.* V+O+*with* OR V-REFL+*with*

4 If you **associate** with a particular group of people, you spend a lot of time in their company; often used showing disapproval. EG *She spent her adolescence associating with criminals.* V+*with*

5 Your **associates** are your business colleagues. EG *The series is directed by my old associate Jack Good.* N COUNT

6 Associate is used before a rank or title to indicate a slightly different or lower rank or title. EG *Non-professional people could only be Associate Members.* ADJ CLASSIF: ATTRIB

association /ə3səʊsi1eɪʃə0n, -ʃi1-/, **associations. 1** An **association** is an official group of people with a common occupation, aim, or interest. EG *...the President of the British Medical Association.* N COUNT

2 Your **association** with a person, group, or organization is the connection that you have with them. EG *We shall do what we can while our business association lasts.* • If someone does something **in association with** someone else, they do it together. EG *The programme was made in association with Radio Brighton.* N UNCOUNT +SUPP • PREP

3 If something has a particular **association** for you, it is connected in your mind with a particular memory or feeling. EG *A number of tunes have a really strong association for individuals.* N COUNT+SUPP

assorted /ə3sɔːtɪ2d/. A group of **assorted** things or people is a group of similar things that have different sizes, colours, or other qualities. EG *...a bunch of assorted wild flowers.* ADJ CLASSIF: ATTRIB

assortment /əsɔːtmə2nt/, **assortments.** An **assortment** is a group of similar things that have different sizes, colours, or other qualities. EG *...an assortment of plastic bags.* N COUNT: OFT+*of*

assume /ə3sjuːm/, **assumes, assuming, assumed. 1** If you **assume** that something is true, you imagine that it is true, sometimes wrongly. EG *I assume you don't drive... I was mistakenly assumed to be a Welshman because of my surname.* V+REPORT: ONLY *that* OR V+O+*to*-INF

2 If someone **assumes** power or responsibility, they take power or responsibility. EG *Hitler assumed power in 1933.* V+O

3 If you **assume** a particular expression, quality, or way of behaving, you start to look or behave in this way. EG *He assumed an expression of resignation... Her eyes assumed a strange, indifferent look.* V+O

assuming /ə3sjuːmɪŋ/. You use **assuming** or **assuming that** when you are imagining that something is true, so that you can think about what the consequences would be. EG *Keep your goods (assuming that you have any) separate from those of your husband.* CONJ

assumption /ə3sʌmp0ʃə0n/, **assumptions. 1** If you make an **assumption**, you imagine that something is true, sometimes wrongly. EG *His suggestions are based on an assumption that the system is out of date.* N COUNT

2 Someone's **assumption** of power or responsibility is their taking of it. N UNCOUNT+*of*

assurance /ə3ʃʊərəns/, **assurances. 1** If you give someone an **assurance** that something is true or will happen, you say that it is definitely true or will definitely happen, in order to make them less worried. EG *One must be content with assurances that progress is being made... ...the assurance of full employment.* N COUNT OR N UNCOUNT

2 If you do something with **assurance**, you do it N UNCOUNT

What is the difference between an astrologer and an astronomer?

with a feeling of confidence and certainty. EG *'She'll like that,' said Lally with assurance.*

3 Assurance is also insurance that provides for certain events such as death. N UNCOUNT

assure /ə[3]ʃʊə/, **assures, assuring, assured. 1** If you **assure** someone that something is true or will happen, you tell them that it is definitely true or will definitely happen, often in order to make them less worried. EG *Kurt assured me that he was an excellent climber... I can assure you that this feeling will soon pass... Once assured of his daughter's safety, he was casual and relaxed.* V+O+QUOTE OR REPORT : ONLY *that*

2 If you **are assured** of something, it is certain that you will get it. EG *This film had assured him a place in movie history.* V+O+*of* OR V+O+O

3 You say **'rest assured'** when you want to reassure someone about something. EG *You can rest assured your son didn't die in vain.* PHRASE

assured /ə[3]ʃʊəd/. Someone who is **assured** is very confident and feels at ease. ADJ QUALIT

assuredly /ə[3]ʃʊərə[1]dli[1]/. If something is **assuredly** true, it is definitely true. EG *She would assuredly be back.* ADV OR ADV SEN

asterisk /æstə[0]rɪsk/, **asterisks.** An **asterisk** is the sign *. It is used, for example, to indicate that there is a comment at the bottom of the page. N COUNT

asthma /æsmə/ is a chest disease which makes breathing difficult. N UNCOUNT

asthmatic /æsmætɪk/. Someone who is **asthmatic** suffers from asthma. ADJ CLASSIF

astonish /ə[3]stɒnɪʃ/, **astonishes, astonishing, astonished.** If something or someone **astonishes** you, they surprise you very much. EG *You never cease to astonish me.* V+O

astonished /ə[3]stɒnɪʃt/. If you are **astonished**, you are very surprised about something. EG *They were astonished at the extraordinary beauty of the picture... ...groups of astonished customers.* ADJ QUALIT : USU PRED

astonishing /ə[3]stɒnɪʃɪŋ/. Something that is **astonishing** is very surprising. EG *The shape of their bodies changes with astonishing speed.* ADJ QUALIT

◇ **astonishingly.** EG *Birth rates there are astonishingly high.* ◇ SUBMOD OR ADV SEN

astonishment /ə[3]stɒnɪʃmə[2]nt/ is a feeling of great surprise. EG *John stared at him in astonishment... To the astonishment of his friends, he took off his shoes.* N UNCOUNT

astound /ə[3]staʊnd/, **astounds, astounding, astounded.** If something **astounds** you, you are amazed and perhaps shocked by it. EG *What newspapers will do for a story never fails to astound me.* V+O

◇ **astounded.** EG *Visitors to Sweden were astounded by its cleanliness... Everyone was astounded when Ruth quit.* ◇ ADJ QUALIT : USU PRED ◇ **astounding.** EG *It seemed an astounding decision.* ◇ ADJ QUALIT

astray /əstreɪ/. **1** If you **lead** someone **astray**, you make them behave in a bad or foolish way. PHRASE

2 If something **goes astray**, it gets lost while it is being taken or sent somewhere. PHRASE

astride /əstraɪd/. If you sit or stand **astride** something, you sit or stand with one leg on each side of it. EG *Karen sat astride a large white horse.* PREP

astringent /əstrɪndʒə[2]nt/, **astringents. 1** An **astringent** is a substance that makes your skin less greasy or that stops it bleeding. ▸ used as an adjective. EG *...an astringent lotion.* N COUNT OR N UNCOUNT ▸ ADJ CLASSIF

2 Astringent comments are forceful and critical. EG *...fierce and astringent attacks on the government.* ADJ QUALIT

astrologer /ə[3]strɒlədʒə/, **astrologers.** An **astrologer** is a person who uses astrology in order to tell you things about your character and your future. N COUNT

astrology /ə[3]strɒlədʒi[1]/ is the study of the movements of the planets, sun, moon, and stars in the belief that these movements can influence people's lives. ◇ **astrological.** EG *...astrological predictions.* N UNCOUNT ◇ ADJ CLASSIF

astronaut /æstrə[7]nɔːt/, **astronauts.** An **astronaut** is a person who is trained to fly in a spacecraft. N COUNT

astronomer /ə[3]strɒnəmə/, **astronomers.** An **astronomer** is a scientist who studies the stars, planets, and other natural objects in space. N COUNT

astronomical /æstrə[7]nɒmɪkə[0]l/. **1** If you describe a value, price, or amount as **astronomical**, you mean that it is very large indeed. EG *He was trying to sell the ranch at an astronomical price.* ADJ CLASSIF

2 Astronomical also means relating to astronomy. EG *...The Royal Astronomical Society.* ADJ CLASSIF

astronomy /ə[3]strɒnəmi[1]/ is the scientific study of the stars, planets, and other natural objects in space. N UNCOUNT

astute /ə[3]stjuːt/. Someone who is **astute** is clever and skilful at understanding behaviour and situations. EG *...an astute politician.* ADJ QUALIT

asylum /ə[3]saɪləm/, **asylums. 1** An **asylum** is a mental hospital. EG *They put him into an asylum.* N COUNT

2 Asylum is protection that is given by a government to foreigners who leave their own country for political reasons. N UNCOUNT

asymmetrical /eɪsɪmɛtrɪkə[0]l/. Something that is **asymmetrical** has two sides or halves that are different. EG *...an asymmetrical pattern.* ADJ CLASSIF

at /ə[3]t/. **1** If something happens or is situated **at** a place, that is the place where it happens or is situated. EG *The play takes place at a beach club... They've been away at a boarding school... There was a knock at his door.* PREP

2 If you look **at** someone or something or if you direct something **at** them, you look towards them or you direct the thing towards them. EG *They were staring at a garage roof... He grinned at Gretchen... Supporters threw petals at his car.* PREP

3 If something is **at** a distance from something else, or **at** an angle to something else, it is in that place in relation to it. EG *Place it at right angles to the door.* PREP

4 If something happens **at** a particular time, that is the time when it happens. EG *She leaves her house every day at 11 a.m... She had come in at dawn... You can come back at a later stage.* PREP

5 If something happens **at** a particular rate, that is how quickly or regularly it happens. EG *The high technology companies have grown at an astonishing rate... He hurtles through the air at 600 miles per hour.* PREP

6 If you buy or sell something **at** a particular price, you buy it or sell it for that price. EG *The book is published at $7.95.* PREP

7 If you are **at** lunch, dinner, or any other meal, you are eating it. PREP

8 If you are working or aiming **at** something, you are trying to do it or achieve it. EG *It means working harder at your thesis.* PREP

9 If something is done **at** someone's command or invitation, it is done as a result of it. EG *At the director's command, the people all left.* PREP

10 You also use **at 10.1** to say that someone or something is in a particular state or condition. EG *He remains at liberty... The two nations are at war.* **10.2** to say how something is being done. EG *He seemed to read at random... Guardsmen herded them back at gun point.* **10.3** to show that someone is doing something in a tentative way. EG *Rudolph sipped at his drink.* PREP

11 If you are good **at** something, you do it well. If you are bad **at** something, you do it badly. EG *They seemed to be very good at reading.* PREP

12 If you are delighted, pleased, or appalled **at** something, that is the effect it has on you. EG *I was appalled at the quality of the reporting.* PREP

ate /eɪt, ɛt/ is the past tense of **eat.**

atheism /eɪθi[1]ɪzə[0]m/ is the belief that there is no God. ◇ **atheist** /eɪθi[1]ɪst/, **atheists.** EG *He is a convinced atheist.* N UNCOUNT ◇ N COUNT

athlete /æθli:t/, **athletes.** An **athlete** is a person who takes part in athletics competitions. N COUNT

athletic /æθletɪk/, **athletics. 1 Athletics** consists of sports such as running, the high jump, and the javelin. EG *...an athletics meeting... He has retired from active athletics.* N UNCOUNT

2 Athletic means relating to athletes and athletics. EG *...athletic excellence.* ADJ CLASSIF : ATTRIB

3 An **athletic** person is fit, healthy, and active. EG *...athletic young men... ...his lean, athletic build.* ADJ QUALIT

-ation, -ations. -ation, -tion, and **-ion** are added to verbs to form nouns. These nouns usually refer to an action or to the result of an action. For example, 'alteration' can refer to the altering of something or to the result of altering something. Nouns like these are often not defined in this dictionary, but are treated with the related verbs. EG *He was annoyed by the cancellation of the visit... The majority of adoptions are highly successful.* SUFFIX

atlas /ætləs/, **atlases.** An **atlas** is a book of maps. N COUNT

atmosphere /ætməsfɪə/, **atmospheres. 1** A planet's **atmosphere** is the layer of air or other gas around it. EG *...the testing of nuclear weapons in the atmosphere.* N COUNT : USU *the*+N ◊ **atmospheric** /ætməsferɪk/. EG *...atmospheric pollution.* ◊ ADJ CLASSIF : ATTRIB

2 The **atmosphere** of a place is **2.1** the air that you breathe there. EG *...the polluted atmosphere of towns and cities.* N SING **2.2** the general impression that you get of the place. EG *It's got such a friendly atmosphere.* N SING+SUPP

3 If a place has **atmosphere**, it is interesting. EG *The place has no character, no atmosphere.* N UNCOUNT

atom /ætə⁰m/, **atoms. 1** An **atom** is the smallest amount of a substance that can take part in a chemical reaction. EG *...an atom of hydrogen... ...the nucleus of an atom.* N COUNT Technical

2 You can refer to a very small amount of something as an **atom** of it. EG *There's not one atom of romance in her.* N PART

atom bomb, atom bombs. An **atom bomb** or an **atomic bomb** is a bomb that causes an explosion by a sudden release of energy that results from splitting atoms. N COUNT

atomic /ə³tɒmɪk/ means **1** relating to power that is produced from the energy released by splitting atoms. EG *...atomic energy... ...atomic weapons.* **2** relating to the atoms of substances. ADJ CLASSIF : ATTRIB

atone /ətəʊn/, **atones, atoning, atoned.** If you **atone** for something that you have done, you do something to show that you are sorry you did it. EG *He has to atone for his sins.* V+*for* Formal

atrocious /ətrəʊʃəs/. Something that is **atrocious** is extremely bad. EG *...speaking French with an atrocious accent.* ADJ QUALIT ◊ **atrociously.** EG *The farm animals are treated atrociously.* ◊ ADV

atrocity /ətrɒsɪ¹ti¹/, **atrocities.** An **atrocity** is a very cruel, shocking action. EG *They were guilty of barbarous atrocities.* N COUNT OR N UNCOUNT

attach /ətætʃ/, **attaches, attaching, attached. 1** If you **attach** something to an object, you join it or fasten it to the object. EG *He attached some string to the can... Attached to the letter was a list of hotels.* V+O : OFT+*to*

2 If someone **is attached** to an organization or group of people, they are working with them, often only for a short time. EG *Hospital officers would be temporarily attached to NHS hospitals.* V+O : USU PASS+*to*

3 If one organization **is attached** to a larger one, it is part of the larger one and is controlled and administered by it. V+O : USU PASS+*to*

4 If you **attach** a quality to someone or something, or if it **attaches** to them, you consider that they have that quality. EG *Don't attach too much importance to what he said... No blame attaches to him.* V-ERG+*to*

5 See also **attached.**

attaché /ætæʃeɪ/, **attachés.** An **attaché** is a member of staff in an embassy. N COUNT

attaché case, attaché cases. An **attaché case** is a briefcase. N COUNT

attached /ətætʃt/. If you are **attached** to someone or something, you are very fond of them. EG *He had become attached to a student called Hilary.* ADJ PRED+*to*

attachment /ətætʃmə²nt/, **attachments. 1** If you have an **attachment** to someone or something, you are fond of them. EG *...a romantic attachment... ...their attachment to Western ways.* N COUNT : OFT+*to*

2 An **attachment** is a device that can be fixed onto a machine in order to enable it to do different jobs. EG *It has a special attachment for cleaning upholstery.* N COUNT

attack /ətæk/, **attacks, attacking, attacked. 1** If you **attack** someone, you try to hurt them or to get them in your power using physical violence. EG *He attacked and mutilated two women... She was attacked by a shark.* V+O OR V ▸ used as a noun. EG *There were more attacks on women going alone on the street... There were no defences against nuclear attack.* ▸ N COUNT OR N UNCOUNT

2 If you **attack** a person, belief, or idea, you criticize them strongly. EG *The senator attacked the press for misleading the public.* V+O ▸ used as a noun. EG *...attacks on apartheid... Burt's work came under violent attack.* ▸ N COUNT OR N UNCOUNT

3 If something such as a disease, a chemical, or an insect **attacks** something, it harms it or spoils it. EG *The venom attacks the nervous system.* V+O

4 If you **attack** a job or a problem, you start to deal with it with energy and enthusiasm. EG *He attacked his task with determination.* V+O

5 When players **attack** in a game such as football or hockey, they try to score a goal. V

6 An **attack** of an illness is a short period in which you suffer badly from it. EG *...an attack of smallpox.* N COUNT : OFT+*of*

attacker /ətækə/, **attackers.** Someone's **attacker** is the person who attacks them. EG *He described his attacker to the police.* N COUNT

attain /əteɪn/, **attains, attaining, attained.** If you **attain** something, you gain it or achieve it, often after a lot of effort. EG *...the qualities which enabled him to attain his ambitions... From 1976 to 1978 the party attained a position of prominence.* V+O

attainable /əteɪnəbə⁰l/. Something that is **attainable** can be achieved. EG *This kind of accuracy is attainable by modern techniques.* ADJ CLASSIF

attainment /əteɪnmə²nt/, **attainments. 1** The **attainment** of an aim is the achieving of it. EG *...the attainment of independence.* N UNCOUNT +SUPP Formal

2 An **attainment** is a skill you have learnt or an achievement you have made. EG *...your literary attainments.* N COUNT Formal

attempt /ə³tempt/, **attempts, attempting, attempted. 1** If you **attempt** something or **attempt** to do something, especially something difficult, you try to do it. EG *A long time had elapsed since I had attempted any serious study... Some of the crowd attempted to break through police cordons.* V+O OR V+*to*-INF

2 If you make an **attempt** at something, you try to do it, often without success. EG *...an attempt at a joke... ...in a vain attempt to have the report suppressed... The young birds manage to fly several kilometres at their first attempt.* N COUNT : OFT+*to*-INF OR *at*

3 An **attempt on** someone's **life** is an attempt to kill them. PHRASE

attempted /ə³temptɪ²d/. An **attempted** crime or other action is an unsuccessful effort to commit the crime. EG *He was charged with attempted murder.* ADJ CLASSIF : ATTRIB

attend /ə³tend/, **attends, attending, attended. 1** If you **attend** a meeting or other event, you are present at it. EG *I stopped off in London to attend a conference... The plays here are always well attended.* V+O

2 If you **attend** an institution such as a school, college, or church, you go to it regularly. V+O

What is an attaché attached to?

3 If you **attend** to something, you deal with it. EG *I had two items of business to attend to.* V+to

4 If you **attend** to something, you pay attention to it. EG *She was attending closely to the music.* V: OFT+to Formal

attendance /ə³tendəns/, **attendances.** 1 The **attendance** at a meeting is the number of people who are present at it. EG *At Easter, attendances at churches rose.* N COUNT OR N UNCOUNT

2 Someone's **attendance** at an event or an institution is the fact that they are present at the event or go regularly to the institution. EG *She was allowed to resume her attendance at the High School.* N UNCOUNT: OFT+at

attendant /ə³tendənt/, **attendants.** 1 An **attendant** is someone whose job is to serve people in a place such as a petrol station or a museum. N COUNT

2 You use **attendant** to describe something that results from a thing already mentioned or that is connected with it. EG *...nuclear energy and its attendant dangers.* ADJ CLASSIF: ATTRIB Formal

attention /ə³tenʃə⁰n/, **attentions.** 1 If you give something your **attention**, you look at it, listen to it, or think about it carefully. EG *When he felt he had their attention, he began... He switched his attention back to the magazine... They were listening with close attention... She was the centre of attention.* N UNCOUNT

2 If someone brings something important or interesting to your **attention** or draws your **attention** to it, they point it out to you. EG *I feel it is my duty to bring to your attention the following facts.* N UNCOUNT

3 If something **attracts** your **attention** or **catches** your **attention**, you suddenly notice it. EG *How can I attract the captain's attention?* PHRASE

4 **Attention** to something is dealing with it or caring for it. EG *They needed medical attention.* N UNCOUNT

5 If you **pay attention** to someone or something, 5.1 you watch them or listen to them carefully. EG *You must pay attention to his eyes.* 5.2 you show great interest in them and take notice of them. EG *There's far too much attention being paid to these hooligans.* PHRASE

6 If you **pay no attention** to someone or something, you behave as if you are not aware of them or as if they do not matter. EG *We didn't pay any attention to him.* PHRASE

7 **Attentions** that you pay to someone are things that you do to help them and to show your affection. N PLURAL

8 When soldiers or policemen **stand to attention**, they stand up straight with their feet together and their arms at their sides. ▸ **Attention!** is used as a command to stand in this way. PHRASE ▸ CONVENTION

attentive /ə³tentɪv/. Someone who is **attentive** 1 pays close attention to the person or thing that they are listening to or looking at. EG *...an attentive audience.* ◊ **attentively.** EG *He was listening attentively.* 2 is very helpful and polite to someone else, often because they like them very much. EG *He was unfailingly attentive.* ADJ QUALIT ◊ ADV ADJ QUALIT

attest /ə³test/, **attests, attesting, attested.** To **attest** something or to **attest** to something means to show or prove that it is true. EG *The perfection of their design is attested by the fact that they survived for thousands of years.* V+O OR V+to Formal

attic /ætɪk/, **attics.** An **attic** is a room at the top of a house just below the roof. N COUNT

attire /ə³taɪə/ is clothing. EG *Her whole attire was rich in appearance.* N UNCOUNT Formal

attired /ə³taɪəd/. Someone who is **attired** in a particular way is dressed that way. EG *He was elegantly attired in a cashmere coat.* ADJ CLASSIF: OFT+in Formal

attitude /ætɪtju:d/, **attitudes.** 1 Your **attitude** to something is the way that you think and feel about it. EG *They are adopting our attitude to life... She took the attitude that acting was a recreation.* N COUNT+SUPP

2 Your **attitude** to someone is the way that you behave when you are dealing with them. EG *I resented his attitude.* N COUNT+POSS

3 A particular **attitude** is a particular position in which you hold your body. EG *...with her arms flung out in an attitude of surrender.* N COUNT+SUPP

attorney /ə³tɜ:ni¹/, **attorneys.** An **attorney** is a lawyer. N COUNT American

attract /ə³trækt/, **attracts, attracting, attracted.** 1 If something **attracts** people or animals, it has features that cause them to come to it. EG *The show attracted large crowds this year... Moths are attracted to lights.* V+O: OFT+to

2 If someone or something **attracts** you, they have particular qualities which cause you to like or admire them. EG *She didn't attract me physically.* V+O

3 If a particular quality **attracts** you to a person or thing, it is the reason why you like them. EG *What attracted me to Valeria was her sense of humour.* V+O: OFT+to

4 If something **attracts** support or publicity, it receives support or publicity. EG *The women's movement has attracted a lot of publicity in the last decade.* V+O

5 If something **attracts** your attention, it makes you notice it. V+O

6 If something magnetic **attracts** an object, it causes the object to move towards it. V+O

attracted /ətræktɪ²d/. If you are **attracted** to someone or something, you like them and are interested in them. EG *I was becoming attracted to a girl from the next office... I'm not attracted to sociology.* ADJ PRED+to

attraction /ə³trækʃə⁰n/, **attractions.** 1 **Attraction** is 1.1 a feeling of liking someone, and often of being sexually interested in them. EG *He couldn't explain his attraction to her.* 1.2 a quality that something has of being interesting or desirable. EG *The attraction of the house lay in its simplicity.* N UNCOUNT: OFT+to N SING+SUPP

2 An **attraction** is 2.1 a feature which makes a thing or person interesting or desirable. EG *One of the main attractions of the city was its superb transport system.* 2.2 something that people can go to for interest or enjoyment, for example a famous building. EG *...to visit the tourist attractions.* N COUNT

attractive /ə³træktɪv/. 1 A person who is **attractive** is pretty or handsome. EG *...a remarkably attractive girl.* ◊ **attractiveness.** EG *...one's physical attractiveness.* ADJ QUALIT ◊ N UNCOUNT

2 Something that is **attractive** 2.1 has a pleasant appearance or sound. EG *...attractive illustrations... ...an attractive name.* 2.2 seems good to have or choose. EG *The company offers more time off and attractive pay.* ADJ QUALIT

> **ATTRIB** stands for **attributive adjective**
> Adjectives which are labelled ATTRIB in the Extra Column are normally only used in front of a noun. See the entry headed ADJECTIVES for more information.

attribute, attributes, attributing, attributed; pronounced /ə³trɪbju:t/ when it is a verb and /ætrɪbju:t/ when it is a noun.

1 If you **attribute** something to an event or situation, you think that it was caused by that event or situation. EG *Economists attributed the lack of progress to poor cooperation.* V+O+to

2 If you **attribute** a remark, a piece of writing, or a work of art to someone, you say that they said it, wrote it, or created it. EG *...a remark that was later attributed to Haldane.* V+O+to

3 If you **attribute** a particular quality or feature to someone or something, you think that they have got it. EG *Here we are attributing human feelings to animals.* ◊ **attribution** /ætrɪbju:ʃə⁰n/. EG *...the attribution of mysterious powers to these men.* V+O+to ◊ N UNCOUNT

4 An **attribute** is a quality or feature. EG *They appeared to possess all the attributes of a ruling class... ...her physical attributes.* N COUNT

attuned /ə[3]tjuːnd/. **1** If you are **attuned** to something, you can understand and appreciate it. EG *The public is not quite attuned to this kind of art.* ADJ PRED+*to*

2 If your ears are **attuned** to a sound, you can hear it and recognize it quickly. EG *Her ears were sharply attuned to any noise from the bedroom.* ADJ PRED+*to*

aubergine /əubəd[0]ʒiːn/, **aubergines.** An **aubergine** is a vegetable with a smooth, dark purple skin. N COUNT OR N UNCOUNT British

auburn /ɔːbə[0]n/. **Auburn** hair is reddish brown. ADJ COLOUR

auction /ɔːkʃə[0]n/, **auctions, auctioning, auctioned. 1** An **auction** is a public sale of goods where the goods are sold to the person who offers the highest price. N COUNT • If something is sold **by auction** or **at auction**, it is sold at an auction to the person who offers the highest price. EG *The big house was sold by auction.* PHRASE

2 If you **auction** something, you sell it in an auction. EG *Her car is going to be auctioned.* V+O

auction off. If you **auction off** a number of things, you get rid of them all by selling them at an auction. PHRASAL VB : V+O+ADV

auctioneer /ɔːkʃənɪə/, **auctioneers.** An **auctioneer** is a person in charge of an auction. N COUNT

audacious /ɔːdeɪʃəs/. **Audacious** behaviour is bold and sometimes cheeky. EG *...a series of audacious ventures.* ADJ QUALIT ◇ **audacity** /ɔːdæsɪ[1]ti[1]/. EG *He had the audacity to blame Baldwin for their failure.* ◇ N UNCOUNT

audible /ɔːdɪ[1]bə[0]l/. A sound that is **audible** is loud enough to be heard. EG *He spoke in a scarcely audible voice.* ADJ QUALIT ◇ **audibly.** EG *The clock ticked audibly.* ◇ ADV

audience /ɔːdɪəns/, **audiences. 1** An **audience** is **1.1** the group of people who are watching or listening to something such as a play, concert, or film. EG *Someone in the audience began to laugh... She spoke before an audience of schoolchildren.* **1.2** all the people who watch television or listen to the radio. **1.3** the people who read the books of a writer or hear about the ideas of a thinker. EG *...the need for intellectuals to communicate their ideas to a wider audience.* N COLL

2 If you have an **audience** with someone important, you have a formal meeting with them. EG *He stood up to show that the audience was over.* N COUNT

audio /ɔːdɪəʊ/. **Audio** equipment is used for recording and reproducing sound. ADJ CLASSIF : ATTRIB

audio-typist, audio-typists. An **audio-typist** is a typist who types letters and reports that have been dictated into a tape-recorder. N COUNT

audio-visual. Audio-visual teaching aids involve both recorded sound and pictures. ADJ CLASSIF : ATTRIB

audit /ɔːdɪt/, **audits, auditing, audited.** If an accountant **audits** an organization's accounts, he or she examines the accounts officially in order to make sure that they have been done correctly. V+O ▸ used as a noun. EG *We're going to conduct a full audit.* ▸ N COUNT

audition /ɔːdɪʃə[0]n/, **auditions, auditioning, auditioned. 1** An **audition** is a short performance that someone gives so that a director can decide if they are good enough to be in a play, film, or orchestra. N COUNT

2 If you **audition** or if someone **auditions** you, you perform an audition. EG *Are you going to audition for 'Stars of a Summer Night'?* V-ERG : OFT+*for*

auditor /ɔːdɪtə/, **auditors.** An **auditor** is an accountant who officially examines the accounts of organizations. N COUNT

auditorium /ɔːdɪtɔːrɪəm/, **auditoriums** or **auditoria** /ɔːdɪtɔːrɪə/. An **auditorium** is **1** the part of a theatre or concert hall where the audience sits. **2** a large building which is used for events such as public meetings and concerts. N COUNT Formal

augment /ɔːgment/, **augments, augmenting, augmented.** To **augment** something means to make it larger by adding something to it. EG *They hit upon another idea to augment their income.* V+O Formal

augur /ɔːgə/, **augurs, auguring, augured.** If something **augurs** well or badly for someone, it is a sign that things will go well or badly for them. EG *The start could not have augured better for success.* V+A : OFT+*for* Formal

august; pronounced /ɔːgəst/ when it is a noun and /ɔːgʌst/ when it is an adjective. It is spelled with a capital letter for paragraph 1.

1 August is the eighth month of the year in the Western calendar. EG *War broke out on August 4th... You start your new job in August.* N UNCOUNT

2 Someone or something that is **august** is dignified and impressive. EG *He was probably the most august figure in the House of Lords.* ADJ QUALIT Literary

aunt /ɑːnt/, **aunts.** Your **aunt** is the sister of your mother or father, or the wife of your uncle. EG *...Aunt Alice.* N COUNT

auntie /ɑːnti[1]/, **aunties;** also spelled **aunty.** Your **auntie** is your aunt. N COUNT Informal

au pair /əupɛə/, **au pairs.** An **au pair** is a young foreigner, usually a woman, who lives for a time with a family in order to learn the language and to help with the children and housework. N COUNT

aura /ɔːrə/, **auras.** An **aura** is a quality or feeling that seems to surround a person or place or to come from them. EG *European things acquired an aura of glamour and prestige.* N COUNT : OFT+*of*

aural /ɔːrəl/ means related to the sense of hearing. EG *I have used written and aural material.* ADJ CLASSIF

auspices /ɔːspɪsɪz/. If something is done **under the auspices of** a particular person or organization, it is done with their support and approval. PREP Formal

auspicious /ɔːspɪʃəs/. Something that is **auspicious** indicates that success is likely. EG *It was an auspicious start.* ADJ QUALIT Formal

austere /ɒstɪə/. **1** Something that is **austere** is plain and not decorated. EG *The interior of the church is sober and austere.* ADJ QUALIT ◇ **austerity** /ɒstɛrɪ[1]ti[1]/. EG *...the elegant austerity of her room.* ◇ N UNCOUNT

2 An **austere** person is strict and serious. EG *She was an austere religious woman.* ADJ QUALIT

3 An **austere** way of life is one that is simple and without luxuries. EG *In these austere times, we are all having to cut back.* ADJ QUALIT ◇ **austerity.** EG *...post-war austerity.* ◇ N UNCOUNT

Australian /ɒstreɪlɪən/, **Australians. 1** Something that is **Australian** belongs or relates to Australia, or to its people. EG *...the Australian novelist Patrick White.* ADJ CLASSIF

2 An **Australian** is someone who comes from Australia. N COUNT

authentic /ɔːθɛntɪk/. **1** If something such as a painting or piece of writing is **authentic**, it is genuine rather than being an imitation. ADJ CLASSIF ◇ **authenticity** /ɔːθɛntɪsɪ[1]ti[1]/. EG *...paintings of doubtful authenticity.* ◇ N UNCOUNT

2 If information or an account is **authentic**, it is reliable and accurate. EG *The book gives an authentic account of the war.* ADJ QUALIT ◇ **authenticity.** EG *...the authenticity of Haldane's account.* ◇ N UNCOUNT

authenticate /ɔːθɛntɪkeɪt/, **authenticates, authenticating, authenticated.** If you **authenticate** something, **1** you state officially that it is genuine after examining it. EG *He was responsible for authenticating the photographs.* **2** you prove or confirm that it is true. EG *These stories seem to be well authenticated.* V+O

author /ɔːθə/, **authors. 1** The **author** of a piece of writing is the person who wrote it. EG *...Bill Davies, author of a new book on money.* N COUNT : OFT+*of*

2 An **author** is a person whose occupation is writing books. EG *...Simone de Beauvoir, the French author.* N COUNT

authorise /ɔːθə[0]raɪz/. See **authorize**.

authoritarian /ɔːθɒrə[1]tɛəri[1]ən/, **authoritarians.** Someone who is **authoritarian** wants to control other people rather than letting them decide things ADJ QUALIT

Is an autobiography likely to be an authentic account of someone's life?

themselves; used showing disapproval. EG *...authoritarian parents... ...an authoritarian regime.* ▸ used as a noun. EG *The old rulers were authoritarians.* [▸ N COUNT]

authoritative /ɔːθɒrə^{1}tətɪv/. **1** Someone or something that is **authoritative** gives an impression of power and importance and is likely to be obeyed. EG *...a deep authoritative male voice.* [ADJ QUALIT] ◇ **authoritatively.** EG *'Don't do that,' he said authoritatively.* [◇ ADV]

2 Someone or something that is **authoritative** has a lot of knowledge of a particular subject. EG *...in his authoritative study of the Commonwealth.* [ADJ QUALIT]

authority /ɔːθɒrə^{1}ti^{1}/, **authorities. 1** The **authorities** are the people who have the power to make decisions, especially the government. EG *The authorities have got to clamp down on people like this.* [N PLURAL : *the*+N]

2 An **authority** is an official organization or government department that has the power to make decisions. EG *She sold the house to the local authority... ...the Regional Health Authorities.* [N COUNT+SUPP]

3 Authority is **3.1** the right to command and control other people. EG *He would be reported to those in authority... He made efforts to reassert his authority over them.* [N UNCOUNT : OFT+*over*] **3.2** a quality that someone has which makes other people take notice of what they say. EG *Her voice carried a note of authority.* [N UNCOUNT] **3.3** official permission to do something. EG *Have you been ordering taxis without signed authority?* [N UNCOUNT]

4 Someone who is an **authority** on a particular subject knows a lot about it. EG *He is an authority on India.* [N COUNT : OFT+*on*]

5 If you **have it on good authority** that something is true, you are fairly certain that it is true because you trust the person who told you about it. [PHRASE]

authorize /ɔːθəraɪz/, **authorizes, authorizing, authorized;** also spelled **authorise.** If someone in a position of authority **authorizes** something, they give their official permission for it to happen. EG *The president authorized the bombings... I am not authorized to approve payments.* [V+O : OFT+*to*-INF] ◇ **authorization** /ɔːθəraɪzeɪʃə^{0}n/. EG *They will have to phone your branch for authorization.* [◇ N UNCOUNT]

auto /ɔːtəʊ/, **autos.** An **auto** is a car. EG *...the U.S. auto industry.* [N COUNT American]

autobiographical /ɔːtə^{6}baɪəgræfɪkə^{0}l/. A piece of writing that is **autobiographical** relates to events in the life of the person who has written it. [ADJ CLASSIF]

autobiography /ɔːtə^{6}baɪɒgrəfi^{1}/, **autobiographies.** Your **autobiography** is an account of your own life, which you write yourself. EG *She describes in her autobiography a visit to Russia in 1909.* [N COUNT OR N UNCOUNT]

autocracy /ɔːtɒkrəsi^{1}/ is government or management by one person who has complete power. [N UNCOUNT]

autocrat /ɔːtə^{6}kræt/, **autocrats.** An **autocrat** is a person in authority who has complete power. [N COUNT]

autocratic /ɔːtə^{6}krætɪk/. Someone who is **autocratic** has complete power and makes decisions without asking anyone else's advice. [ADJ QUALIT]

autograph /ɔːtə^{6}grɑːf/, **autographs, autographing, autographed. 1** An **autograph** is the signature of someone famous; used especially when you have asked the person to write it for you. EG *...boys queueing to get his autograph.* [N COUNT : USU+POSS]

2 If someone famous **autographs** something, they put their signature on it. [V+O] ◇ **autographed.** EG *He gave me an autographed copy of his book.* [◇ ADJ CLASSIF]

automate /ɔːtə^{6}meɪt/, **automates, automating, automated.** To **automate** a factory, office, or industrial process means to install machines which can do the work instead of people. [V+O] ◇ **automation** /ɔːtə^{6}meɪʃə^{0}n/. EG *...an age of high technology and automation.* [◇ N UNCOUNT]

automatic /ɔːtə^{6}mætɪk/, **automatics. 1** An **automatic** machine is one which can perform a task without needing to be operated by a person. EG *...automatic washing machines... ...automatic data processing.* [ADJ CLASSIF] ◇ **automatically.** EG *The lights come on automatically.* [◇ ADV]

2 A gun, car, or washing machine that is automatic or partly automatic can be called an **automatic.** [N COUNT]

3 An **automatic** action is one that you do without thinking about it because it has become a habit. EG *...an automatic gesture.* [ADJ QUALIT] ◇ **automatically.** EG *Billy found himself automatically walking up to the house.* [◇ ADV]

4 If something such as an action or a punishment is **automatic,** it always happens as the normal result of something else. EG *These offences carry automatic fines.* [ADJ CLASSIF] ◇ **automatically.** EG *Once people retire they automatically cease to be union members.* [◇ ADV]

automaton /ɔːtɒmətɒn/, **automatons** or **automata** /ɔːtɒmətə/. If you say that someone is an **automaton,** you mean that they are so tired or bored that they act without thinking. [N COUNT]

automobile /ɔːtəmə^{6}biːl/, **automobiles.** An **automobile** is a car. [N COUNT American]

autonomous /ɔːtɒnəməs/. A country, organization, or group that is **autonomous** governs or controls itself rather than being controlled by anyone else. [ADJ QUALIT] ◇ **autonomy** /ɔːtɒnəmi^{1}/. EG *They wanted more autonomy.* [◇ N UNCOUNT]

autopsy /ɔːtɒpsi^{1}, ɔːtə^{7}p-/, **autopsies.** An **autopsy** is an examination of a dead body by a doctor who cuts it open in order to try to discover the cause of death. [N COUNT]

autumn /ɔːtəm/, **autumns. Autumn** is the season between summer and winter. In the autumn the weather becomes cooler. [N UNCOUNT OR N COUNT]

autumnal /ɔːtʌmnə^{0}l/. Something that is **autumnal** has features that are characteristic of autumn. EG *...autumnal browns and golds.* [ADJ CLASSIF]

> **AUX** stands for **auxiliary verb**
>
> English has three verbs which are used as auxiliaries: the verbs 'be', 'have', and 'do'.
>
> Auxiliaries are used before a main verb to show, for example, whether it is continuous or passive. They are also used in negative clauses, and are one of the ways of forming questions. So in the sentence *She* ***was*** *eating an apple*, 'was' is an auxiliary helping to form the past continuous tense. In *He* ***has*** *never been to London,*'has' is an auxiliary forming the present perfect tense. In *I* ***don't*** *like him*, 'do' is an auxiliary being used to form a negative clause, and in ***Do*** *you like Rome?* it is forming a question.
>
> AUX is used in the Extra Column in the entries for 'be', 'have', and 'do' to show you where the auxiliary uses are being explained.
>
> The modal verbs in English are also often called auxiliaries. In this dictionary we call them modal verbs, and their uses are explained in the entry headed MODAL VERBS.

auxiliary /ɔːgzɪljəri^{1}, -lə^{0}ri^{1}/, **auxiliaries. 1** An **auxiliary** is a person who is employed to help other people. Auxiliaries are often medical workers or members of the armed forces. EG *...nursing auxiliaries.* [N COUNT] ▸ used as an adjective. EG *...six auxiliary squadrons.* [▸ ADJ CLASSIF : ATTRIB]

2 Auxiliary equipment is extra equipment that is used when necessary. EG *...auxiliary scaffolding.* [ADJ CLASSIF : ATTRIB]

avail /əveɪl/, **avails, availing, availed. 1** If something that you do is **of no avail** or is done **to little avail,** it does not enable you to achieve what you want. EG *They were fighting to no avail... Speeches and protests were of no avail.* [PHRASE]

2 If you **avail** yourself of an offer or an opportunity, you accept the offer or make use of the opportunity. [V-REFL+*of* Formal]

available /əveɪləbəºl/. **1** If something is **available**, you are able to use it or obtain it. EG *...the amount of money available for spending... Will your accommodation be available next October?* ADJ CLASSIF
◊ **availability** /əveɪləbɪlɪ¹ti¹/. EG *Laws still controlled the availability of contraceptives.* ◊ N UNCOUNT : OFT+of/for
2 Someone who is **available** is not busy and is therefore free for you to talk to. EG *The MP was not available for comment yesterday.* ADJ CLASSIF

avalanche /ævəlɑːntʃ/, **avalanches. 1** An **avalanche** is a large mass of snow that falls down the side of a mountain. N COUNT
2 You can refer to a very large quantity of things that all arrive or happen at the same time as an **avalanche** of them. EG *...an avalanche of tourists.* N COUNT+SUPP

avant-garde /ævɒŋgɑːd/. **Avant-garde** art, theatre, and writing is very modern and experimental. ADJ QUALIT

avarice /ævərɪs/ is extreme greed for money. N UNCOUNT

avaricious /ævərɪʃəs/. Someone who is **avaricious** is very greedy for money. ADJ QUALIT

avenge /ə³vendʒ/, **avenges, avenging, avenged.** If you **avenge** a wrong or harmful act, you hurt or punish the person who has done it. EG *He was determined to avenge his father's death... ...a desire to avenge himself on all humanity.* V+O OR V-REFL

avenue /ævɪ¹njuː/, **avenues. 1 Avenue** is used in the names of some streets. EG *...Madison Avenue.*
2 An **avenue** is a wide road with trees on either side. N COUNT
3 You can also use **avenue** to mean a way of getting something done. EG *We are exploring a number of avenues.* N COUNT

average /ævəºrɪdʒ/, **averages, averaging, averaged. 1** An **average** is the result that you get when you add two or more numbers together and divide the total by the number of numbers you added together. EG *These pupils were examined in 39 subjects, an average of 6.5 subjects for each pupil.* N COUNT
▸ used as an adjective. EG *The average age of the group was thirty-nine years.* ▸ ADJ CLASSIF : ATTRIB
2 You use **average** to describe a person or thing in order to indicate that they are typical or normal. EG *Today the average American car owner drives 10,000 miles per year... ...a sheet of paper of average thickness.* ADJ CLASSIF : ATTRIB
3 An amount or quality that is the **average** is the normal amount or quality for a particular group of things or people. EG *They have long working hours - 50 a week is about the average... Their language development is below average.* N SING ▸ used as an adjective. EG *...above average inflation.* ▸ ADJ CLASSIF
4 Something that is **average** is neither very good nor very bad. EG *...an average piece of work.* ADJ QUALIT
◊ **averagely.** EG *...an averagely attractive woman.* ◊ ADV
5 To **average** a particular amount means to do, get, or produce that amount as an average over a period of time. EG *Price increases during these years averaged around 20%.* V+C
6 You say **on average** or **on an average** to indicate that a number is the average of several numbers. EG *We can discover how many words, on average, a person reads in a minute.* ADV SEN

average out. When you **average out** a set of numbers or when it **averages out** at a particular figure, you work out the average. PHRASAL VB : V+ADV OR V+O+ADV

averse /ə³vɜːs/. If you say that you are not **averse** to something, you mean that you quite like it or quite want to do it. EG *They were not averse to making a little extra money.* ADJ PRED+to Formal

aversion /ə³vɜːʃəºn/, **aversions. 1** If you have an **aversion** to someone or something, you dislike them very much. EG *She had a great aversion to children.* N COUNT : USU SING+to
2 An **aversion** is also something that you strongly dislike. EG *His current aversion is pop music.* N COUNT : USU+POSS

avert /ə³vɜːt/, **averts, averting, averted. 1** If you **avert** something unpleasant, you prevent it from happening. EG *There must be immediate action if total chaos is to be averted.* V+O
2 If you **avert** your eyes or gaze from someone or something, you look away from them. EG *Winifred averted her eyes from the figure in the bed.* V+O : OFT+from

aviary /eɪvjəri¹/, **aviaries.** An **aviary** is a large cage or covered area in which birds are kept. N COUNT

aviation /eɪvieɪʃəºn/ is the operation and production of aircraft. EG *...in the early days of aviation.* N UNCOUNT

avid /ævɪd/. **1** You use **avid** to describe someone who is very keen and enthusiastic about something. EG *...an avid reader of movie magazines.* ADJ QUALIT : ATTRIB ◊ **avidly.** EG *Sheila reads avidly... They listened avidly.* ◊ ADV
2 Someone who is **avid** for something is eager to get it. EG *The girls were avid for information.* ADJ PRED+for

avocado /ævə⁶kɑːdəʊ/, **avocados.** An **avocado** or an **avocado pear** is a tropical fruit in the shape of a pear with a dark green skin and a large stone inside it. N COUNT OR N UNCOUNT

avoid /əvɔɪd/, **avoids, avoiding, avoided. 1** If you **avoid** something, you take action in order to prevent it from happening. EG *...a book on how to avoid a heart attack.* V+O
2 If you **avoid** doing something, you make a deliberate effort not to do it. EG *Thomas turned his head, trying to avoid breathing in the smoke.* V+-ING
3 If you **avoid** someone or something, you keep away from them. EG *Joy tried to avoid her... They drive through the towns to avoid the motorway.* V+O

avoidable /ə³vɔɪdəbəºl/. Something that is **avoidable** can be prevented from happening. EG *Any avoidable risk should be avoided.* ADJ CLASSIF

avoidance /əvɔɪdəns/. **Avoidance** of someone or something is the act of avoiding them. EG *...the avoidance of responsibilities.* N UNCOUNT +SUPP

avowal /əvaʊəºl/, **avowals.** An **avowal** of something is an admission or declaration of it. EG *He made a shy avowal of love.* N COUNT OR N UNCOUNT Formal

avowed /əvaʊd/. **1** If you are an **avowed** supporter or opponent of something, you have declared that you support it or oppose it. EG *They were avowed enemies of the British.* ADJ CLASSIF : ATTRIB Formal
2 An **avowed** belief or aim is one that you hold very strongly. EG *The avowed aim of revolutionaries is to disrupt society.* ADJ CLASSIF : ATTRIB

avuncular /əvʌŋkjə⁴lə/. A man who is **avuncular** acts in a friendly and helpful way towards someone younger. EG *In my best avuncular fashion I put my arm round her shoulder.* ADJ QUALIT Formal

await /əweɪt/, **awaits, awaiting, awaited. 1** If you **await** someone or something, you wait for them. EG *I returned to the States to find the FBI awaiting me... Huey was awaiting trial for murder.* V+O
2 Something that **awaits** you is going to happen or come to you in the future. EG *...the adventures that awaited him.* V+O

awake /əweɪk/, **awakes, awaking, awoke** /əwəʊk/, **awoken** /əwəʊkəºn/. **1** Someone who is **awake** is not sleeping. EG *He lay awake all night.* ADJ PRED
● Someone who is **wide awake** is fully awake. ● PHRASE
2 When you **awake** or when something **awakes** you, you wake up. EG *I awoke from a deep sleep.* V-ERG Literary

awaken /əweɪkəºn/, **awakens, awakening, awakened. 1** To **awaken** a feeling in a person means to cause them to have this feeling. EG *My first visit to a theatre awakened an interest which never left me.* V+O Literary
2 When you **awaken** to a fact or when someone **awakens** you to it, you become aware of it. EG *Gradually people are awakening to their responsibilities.* V-ERG+to Literary
3 When you **awaken** or when something **awakens** you, you wake up. EG *He was awakened by the sound of singing.* V-ERG Literary

awakening /əweɪkəºnɪŋ/. **1** The **awakening** of a particular feeling or realization in someone is the N SING : USU+SUPP

Are women usually described as avuncular?

start of this feeling or realization in them. EG *...the awakening of love for another person.*

2 If you have a **rude awakening**, you are suddenly made aware of an unpleasant fact. PHRASE

award /əwɔːd/, **awards, awarding, awarded. 1** An **award** is **1.1** a prize or certificate that a person is given for doing something well. EG *He won the Current Affairs Award for his radio reporting.* **1.2** a sum of money that a court of law decides should be given to someone. N COUNT

2 To **award** someone something such as a prize or a mark means to give it to them. EG *This year's board awarded the top prize to reporter Carol Clay.* V+O+O OR V+O+*to*

3 If someone such as a judge or referee **awards** something to a person, they decide that the person will be given it. EG *It was the biggest libel settlement awarded up to that time.* V+O+*to*, V+O+O, OR V+O

aware /əwɛə/. **1** If you are **aware** of a fact, you know about it. EG *He was aware that he had drunk too much whisky... I was quite aware of this before we married... As far as I am aware, that's correct.* ADJ PRED : OFT+*of* OR REPORT

◇ **awareness.** EG *...the present public awareness of the need for conservation... ...an awareness that there was a problem.* ◇ N UNCOUNT +*of* OR REPORT

2 If you are **aware** of something, you realize that it is present or is happening because you hear it, see it, smell it, or feel it. EG *Ralph was aware of the heat for the first time that day.* ADJ PRED+*of* OR REPORT

3 Someone who is **aware** notices what is happening around them. EG *Some people are more politically aware than others.* ◇ **awareness.** EG *...the students' political awareness.* ADJ QUALIT : USU PRED ◇ N UNCOUNT

away /əweɪ/. **1** If you move **away** from a place, you move so that you are no longer there. EG *He rose and walked away... I kissed her goodbye and drove away.* ADV AFTER VB

2 If you look or turn **away** from something, you move your head so that you are no longer looking at it. EG *He turned away from the window.* ADV AFTER VB

3 If something is **away** from a person or place, it is at a distance from that person or place. EG *...a pleasant picnic spot away from the city... I was only four hours away from Oslo.* ADV : OFT+*from*

4 If you put something **away**, you put it in a safe place. EG *Tom put the book away... This work is ready to be filed away in the archives.* ADV AFTER VB

5 If you are **away**, you are not in the place, such as your home or office, where people expect you to be. EG *Is he at home or has he gone away?* ADV AFTER VB

6 You also use **away** to talk about future events. For example, if an event is a week **away**, it will happen in a week. EG *The debate on the Afghan crisis is only a fortnight away.* ADV

7 If you give something **away** or if someone takes it **away** from you, you no longer have it. EG *She gave a fortune away.* ADV AFTER VB

8 When a sports team plays an **away** game, it plays on its opponents' ground. ADJ CLASSIF : ATTRIB

9 You can use **away** to say that something slowly disappears, becomes less significant, or changes so that it is no longer the same. EG *The snow had all melted away... A murmur rose among the boys and died away... ...the shift away from crimes of theft.* ADV

10 You can also use **away** to emphasize a continuous or repeated action. EG *Howard was still working away in the university library... She was coughing away.* ADV AFTER VB

awe /ɔː/, **awes, awed. 1 Awe** is the feeling of respect and amazement that you have when you are faced with something wonderful and often rather frightening. EG *The child stared at him in silent awe.* N UNCOUNT

2 If you **are in awe of** someone or if you **stand in awe of** them, you have a lot of respect for them and are slightly afraid of them. PHRASE

3 If you **are awed** by someone or something, they make you feel amazed and often rather frightened. V+O : USU PASS

◇ **awed.** EG *...talking in an awed whisper... He took it reluctantly, awed by the value of the gift.* ◇ ADJ CLASSIF : OFT+*by*

awe-inspiring. Someone or something that is **awe-inspiring** is amazing and rather frightening. EG *It was an awe-inspiring sight.* ADJ QUALIT

awesome /ɔːsəm/. Something that is **awesome** is very impressive and frightening. EG *...an awesome responsibility... ...an awesome weapon.* ADJ QUALIT

awe-struck. If someone is **awe-struck**, they are very impressed and amazed by something. EG *...watching with awestruck interest.* ADJ QUALIT Formal

awful /ɔːfəˈl/. **1** If you say that something is **awful**, you mean that it is **1.1** not very good or not very nice. EG *Isn't the weather awful?* **1.2** very unpleasant, shocking, or bad. EG *...that awful war.* ADJ QUALIT

2 If you look or feel **awful**, you look or feel ill. ADJ PRED

3 You can use **awful** to emphasize how large an amount is. EG *It must have taken an awful lot of courage.* ◇ **awfully.** EG *She was awfully nice... I'm awfully sorry.* ADJ CLASSIF : ATTRIB ◇ SUBMOD

awhile /əwaɪl/ means for a short time. EG *Can't you just wait awhile?* ADV Literary

awkward /ɔːkwəd/. **1** An **awkward** movement or position is uncomfortable or clumsy. EG *...an awkward gesture.* ◇ **awkwardly.** EG *He fell and lay awkwardly, covered in mud.* ADJ QUALIT ◇ ADV

2 Someone who is **awkward 2.1** behaves in a shy or embarrassed way. EG *I hated the big formal dances and felt very awkward.* ◇ **awkwardly.** EG *Sonia patted her shoulder awkwardly.* ADJ QUALIT ◇ ADV

◇ **awkwardness.** EG *There was no awkwardness between them.* **2.2** is unreasonable and difficult to live with or deal with. ◇ N UNCOUNT ADJ QUALIT

3 A tool or machine that is **awkward** is difficult to use. A job that is **awkward** is difficult to do. EG *It is awkward to make this recipe.* ADJ QUALIT

4 A situation that is **awkward** is embarrassing and difficult to deal with. EG *The press conference came at an awkward time for me... He asked a lot of awkward questions... McPherson started making things awkward for him.* ADJ QUALIT

awning /ɔːnɪŋ/, **awnings.** An **awning** is a piece of material attached to a caravan or building which provides shelter from the rain or sun. N COUNT

awoke /əwəʊk/ is the past tense of **awake.**

awoken /əwəʊkəᵘn/ is the past participle of **awake.**

awry /əraɪ/. **1** If something is **awry**, it is not in its normal or proper position. EG *His tie was awry.* ADJ PRED

2 If something goes **awry**, it does not happen in the way it was planned and it goes wrong. EG *Here the plan began to go awry.* ADJ PRED

axe /æks/, **axes, axing, axed. 1** An **axe** is a tool used for cutting wood. It consists of a blade attached to the end of a long handle, at the side. N COUNT

2 If the government or a company **axes** something, it suddenly ends it or reduces it greatly. EG *After six months the project was axed.* V+O

axiom /æksɪəm/, **axioms.** An **axiom** is a statement or idea which people accept as being true. N COUNT Formal

axiomatic /æksɪəmætɪk/. If something is **axiomatic**, it seems to be obviously true. EG *It has come to be regarded as axiomatic that good nutrition must always imply eating expensively.* ADJ PRED Formal

axis /æksɪs/, **axes** /æksiːz/. **1** An **axis** is an imaginary line through the middle of something. EG *The earth's axis is tilted at an angle of about 23°.* N COUNT

2 An **axis** of a graph is one of the two lines on which the scales of measurement are marked. N COUNT

axle /æksəᵘl/, **axles.** An **axle** is a rod connecting a pair of wheels on a car or other vehicle. N COUNT

aye /aɪ/; also spelled **ay. 1 Aye** means yes. EG *'Surely that would help?' – 'Aye, we could do that.'* CONVENTION Scottish

2 If you vote **aye**, you vote in favour of something. ADV

azure /æʒʊᵘə, eɪ-/. Something that is **azure** is bright blue. EG *...the pure azure of the sky.* ADJ COLOUR Literary

B b

B, b /biː/, **Bs, b's. B** is the second letter of the English alphabet. N COUNT

B.A. /biː eɪ/, **B.A.s.** A **B.A.** is a degree in arts or social sciences. **B.A.** is an abbreviation for 'Bachelor of Arts'. EG *She took a B.A. in French... ...John Adams B.A.* N COUNT

babble /bæbᵊl/, **babbles, babbling, babbled. 1** If you **babble**, you talk in a confused or excited way. EG *He babbled on about old enemies... She babbled, 'Sonny, just send a car to bring me home.'* V : USU+A OR V+QUOTE
▸ used as a noun. EG *...the babble of women's voices.* ▸ N SING
2 When a stream **babbles**, it makes a low, bubbling sound. V : USU+A Literary

babe /beɪb/, **babes. 1** A **babe** is the same as a baby. N COUNT Outdated
2 Some people use **babe** as an affectionate way of addressing someone. EG *Take it easy, babe, be calm, she'll be all right.* VOCATIVE Informal American

baboon /bəbuːn/, **baboons.** A **baboon** is a type of monkey that lives in Africa. N COUNT

baby /beɪbi^1/, **babies. 1** A **baby** is a very young child, especially one that cannot yet walk or talk. N COUNT
2 Some people use **baby** as an affectionate way of addressing someone. EG *Con said, 'Don't worry, baby, I'll think of something.'* VOCATIVE Informal American

babyhood /beɪbi^{1}hʊd/. Your **babyhood** is the period of your life when you were a baby. N UNCOUNT

babyish /beɪbi^{1}ɪʃ/. Something that is **babyish** is suitable for a baby, or typical of a baby. EG *Don't think that a picture book is too babyish.* ADJ QUALIT

baby-sit, baby-sits, baby-sitting, baby-sat. If you **baby-sit** for someone, you look after their children while they are out. EG *Students occasionally baby-sit in the evenings.* V
◇ **baby-sitter.** EG *Can't you find a baby-sitter?* ◇ N COUNT
◇ **baby-sitting.** EG *Grandmother helps with washing and baby-sitting.* ◇ N UNCOUNT

bachelor /bætʃᵊlə/, **bachelors.** A **bachelor** is a man who has never married. N COUNT

Bachelor of Arts, Bachelors of Arts. A **Bachelor of Arts** is a person with a first degree, usually in an arts or social science subject. N COUNT

Bachelor of Science, Bachelors of Science. A **Bachelor of Science** is a person with a first degree in a science subject. N COUNT

back /bæk/, **backs, backing, backed. 1** If someone moves **back**, they move in the opposite direction to the one in which they are facing or in which they were moving before. EG *The child stepped back nervously... She pushed back her chair... Her head jerked back.* ADV AFTER VB
● If someone moves **back and forth**, they repeatedly move in one direction and then in the opposite direction. EG *Someone was pacing back and forth behind the curtains.* ● PHRASE
2 If someone or something goes **back** or is put **back**, they return to the place where they were before. EG *I went back to the kitchen... She put it back on the shelf.* ADV AFTER VB
3 If someone or something is **back** in a particular state, they were in that state before and are now in it again. EG *He went back to sleep... Things will soon get back to normal.* ADV AFTER VB
4 If you get something **back**, you get it again after not having it for a while. EG *You'll get the money back... They wanted their children back.* ADV AFTER VB
5 You use **back** after verbs such as 'write', 'look', and 'phone' to say that you write to, look at, or phone someone after they have done the same thing to you. EG *He looked at her, and the girl stared back... I shall make some enquiries and call you back.* ADV AFTER VB
6 If someone or something is kept or situated **back** from a place, they are at a distance away from it. EG *Police struggled to keep the crowd back... Stay back... The house is set back from the road.* ADV AFTER VB
7 If you talk or think about something that happened **back** in the past, you are talking or thinking about something that happened in the past. EG *I invested in the company way back in 1971... ...a law that goes back to the fifteenth century... Think back to what we've said.* ADV AFTER VB
8 Your **back** is the part of your body that is behind you, from your neck to the top of your legs. EG *We lay on our backs under the tree.* N COUNT : USU+POSS
9 The **back** of something is the side or part of it that is towards the rear or farthest from the front. The back of something is normally not used or seen as much as the front. EG *...the back of her hand... Sign on the back of the prescription form... He went to the small counter at the back of the store.* N COUNT+SUPP
▸ used as an adjective. EG *The back wheels were spinning in the mud.* ▸ ADJ CLASSIF : ATTRIB
10 The **back** of a chair is the part that you lean against when you sit on it. N COUNT+SUPP
11 A **back** road is small and has very little traffic on it. EG *...driving through back streets towards the outskirts of town.* ADJ CLASSIF : ATTRIB
12 Back is also used in these phrases. **12.1** If you are wearing something **back to front**, you are wearing it incorrectly, with the back of it on the front of your body. **12.2** If you do something **behind** someone's **back**, you do it without them knowing about it. EG *People used to laugh at him behind his back.* **12.3** If you tell someone to **get off** your **back**, you are telling them to stop criticizing you or putting pressure on you. EG *Just get off my back, will you?* **12.4** If you **put** someone's **back up**, you annoy them. **12.5** If you say that you will be glad to **see the back of** someone, you mean that you want them to leave. **12.6** If you **turn** your **back on** someone or something, you ignore them or refuse to help them. EG *We have turned our backs on the very principles we were elected to uphold.* PHRASES; 12.3 Informal; 12.4 Informal
13 If a building **backs** onto something, the back of it faces in that direction. EG *...the houses backing onto the park.* V+*onto*
14 When a car **backs** or when you **back** a car, it moves backwards. EG *She backed out of the driveway.* V-ERG : USU+A
15 If you **back** someone, you give them support or money. EG *The organization is backed by the U.N.* V+O
16 If you **back** a particular person, team, or horse in a competition, you bet money that they will win. V+O
17 See also **backing**.

back away. If you **back away**, you move away because you are nervous or frightened. PHRASAL VB : V+ADV

back down. If you **back down**, you withdraw a claim or demand that you made earlier. EG *They refused to back down.* PHRASAL VB : V+ADV

back off. If you **back off**, you move away in order to avoid problems or a fight. PHRASAL VB : V+ADV

back out. If you **back out**, you decide not to do something that you previously agreed to do. PHRASAL VB : V+ADV

back up. 1 If you **back up** a statement, you supply evidence to show it is true. EG *This claim is backed up by the fact that every year more and more money is being spent on arms.* PHRASAL VB : V+O+ADV
2 If you **back** someone **up**, **2.1** you help and support them. V+O+ADV
2.2 you confirm that what they are saying is true. EG *He had loyally backed up his boss.* V+O+ADV
3 See also **backup**.

backache /bækeɪk/ is a dull pain in your back. N UNCOUNT

backbencher /bækbentʃə/, **backbenchers.** A **backbencher** is an MP who is not a minister and who does not hold an official position in any party. N COUNT British

backbiting /bækbaɪtɪŋ/ is the saying of unpleasant or unkind things about someone who is not present. N UNCOUNT

backbone /bækbəʊn/, **backbones.** **1** Your **backbone** is the column of small linked bones along the middle of your back. N COUNT

2 The **backbone** of an organization or system is the part of it that gives it its main strength or unity. EG *Business people are the backbone of the nation.* N SING+SUPP

back-breaking work involves a lot of hard physical effort. ADJ QUALIT

backdate /bækdeɪt/, **backdates, backdating, backdated.** If an arrangement or document **is backdated**, it is valid from a date before the date when it is completed or signed. EG *...a 4% increase in basic pay backdated to last April.* V+O : USU PASS

backdoor /bækdɔː/. You use **backdoor** to describe something that is done or achieved in a secret, indirect, or dishonest way. EG *...charges of backdoor nationalization.* ADJ CLASSIF : ATTRIB

backer /bækə/, **backers.** A **backer** is someone who gives support or financial help to a person or project. EG *...the party's chief financial backers.* N COUNT+SUPP

backfire /bækfaɪə/, **backfires, backfiring, backfired.** **1** If a plan or project **backfires**, it has the opposite result to the one that was intended. V

2 When a motor vehicle or its engine **backfires**, it produces an explosion in the exhaust pipe. V

backgammon /bækgæmən/ is a game for two people. You throw dice and move pieces of wood or plastic around a board marked with long triangles. N UNCOUNT

background /bækgraʊnd/, **backgrounds.** **1** Your **background** is the kind of family you come from and the kind of education you have had. EG *...people from working-class backgrounds.* N COUNT+SUPP

2 The **background** to an event or situation consists of the facts that explain what caused it. EG *...against a background of poor housing conditions... ...background information.* N SING+SUPP

3 The **background** also refers to **3.1** the things, shapes, or colours in a picture or scene that are less noticeable or less important and are often partly hidden by the main things or people in it. EG *In the background is a tall cypress tree... ...blue flowers on a grey background.* **3.2** sounds, such as music, which you can hear but which you are not listening to with your full attention. EG *The TV set was blaring in the background... ...background music.* N SING

backhand /bækhænd/, **backhands.** A **backhand** is a shot in tennis or squash, which you make with your arm across your body. EG *...a backhand return.* N COUNT

backing /bækɪŋ/, **backings.** **1** If someone or something has the **backing** of an organization or an important person, they receive support or money from that organization or person in order to do something. EG *The bid has the backing of the directors... ...secret Government backing.* N UNCOUNT +SUPP

2 A **backing** is a layer of something such as cloth, that is put onto the back of something in order to strengthen or protect it. N COUNT OR N UNCOUNT

3 The **backing** of a popular song is the music which is sung or played to accompany the main tune. N SING

backlash /bæklæʃ/. A **backlash** is a sudden, strong reaction against a tendency or recent development in society or politics. EG *...a backlash against the Thatcher government.* N SING

backlog /bæklɒg/, **backlogs.** A **backlog** is a number of things which have not yet been done, but which need to be done. EG *There is a large backlog of cases to hear.* N COUNT : USU+*of*

backpack /bækpæk/, **backpacks.** A **backpack** is a rucksack. N COUNT American

back pay is money which an employer owes an employee for work that he or she did in the past. N UNCOUNT

back-seat driver, back-seat drivers. A **back-seat driver** is a passenger in a car who repeatedly gives advice to the driver without being asked for it. N COUNT

backside /bæksaɪd/, **backsides.** Your **backside** is the part of your body that you sit on. N COUNT Informal

backstage /bæksteɪdʒ/. In a theatre, **backstage** refers to the dressing rooms and other areas behind the stage. ▸ used as an adverb. EG *He went backstage.* N UNCOUNT ▸ ADV AFTER VB

backstreet /bækstriːt/. **Backstreet** activities are carried out unofficially, secretly, and often illegally. EG *...backstreet abortions.* ADJ CLASSIF : ATTRIB

backstroke /bækstrəʊk/ is a kind of swimming stroke that you do lying on your back. See picture at SWIMMING. N SING

back-up. **1 Back-up** is extra help or support from people or machines which you need in order to be able to achieve what you want. EG *...the computer back-up which each mission required.* N UNCOUNT

2 If you have something such as a second piece of equipment or set of plans as **back-up**, you have arranged for them to be available for use in case the first one does not work. EG *You can use a conventional heating system as back-up.* N UNCOUNT

backward /bækwəd/, **backwards.** When it is an adverb, the form **backwards** is normally used in British English and **backward** in American English or formal British English.

1 If you move or look **backwards**, you move or look in the direction that your back is facing. EG *He overbalanced and stepped backwards onto a coffee cup.* ▸ used as an adjective. EG *...a backward jerk of her head... Without a backward glance, he walked away.* ADV AFTER VB ▸ ADJ CLASSIF : ATTRIB

2 If someone moves **backwards and forwards**, they repeatedly move in one direction and then in the opposite direction. EG *He ran backwards and forwards along the cliff.* PHRASE

3 If you do something **backwards**, you do it in the opposite way to the usual way. EG *Listen to the tape backwards.* ADV AFTER VB

4 If you **know** something **backwards**, you know it very well. EG *He knew their history backwards.* PHRASE

5 A **backward** country or society does not have modern industries and machines. EG *...the backward regions of Africa and Asia.* ADJ QUALIT

6 A **backward** child has difficulty in learning. EG *I cannot make up my mind whether your son is backward or just lazy.* ADJ QUALIT

backward-looking attitudes, ideas, or actions are based on old-fashioned opinions or methods; used showing disapproval. EG *...their backward-looking suspicion of gadgets.* ADJ QUALIT

backwater /bækwɔːtə/, **backwaters.** A **backwater** is a place or an institution that is isolated from modern ideas or influences; often used showing disapproval. EG *...a cultural backwater.* N COUNT

backwoods /bækwʊdz/. Someone who lives in the **backwoods** lives a long way from large towns, and is isolated from modern life and modern ideas. EG *...his great familiarity with life in the backwoods.* ▸ used as an adjective. EG *...this tiny backwoods community.* N PLURAL ▸ ADJ CLASSIF : ATTRIB

back yard, back yards. A **back yard** is a small area of ground behind a house. N COUNT

bacon /beɪkən/ is salted or smoked meat which comes from the back or sides of a pig. EG *...bacon and eggs.* N UNCOUNT

bacteria /bæktɪərɪə/ are very small organisms. Some bacteria can cause disease. N PLURAL

bacteriology /bæktɪərɪɒlədʒi[1]/ is the science and study of bacteria. ◇ **bacteriological.** EG *...chemical and bacteriological warfare... ...the Bacteriological Research Institute.* N UNCOUNT ◇ ADJ CLASSIF : ATTRIB

bad /bæd/, **worse** /wɜːs/, **worst** /wɜːst/. **1** Something that is **bad** is **1.1** unpleasant, harmful, or undesirable. EG *I have some very bad news... Candy is bad for your teeth... The weather was bad.* **1.2** severe or great in degree. EG *Is the pain bad?* **1.3** of an unacceptably low standard, quality, or amount. ADJ QUALIT

EG *His flat is in bad condition... ...bad management... ...bad behaviour... The light's bad.*
2 Someone who is **bad** at doing something **2.1** is not very skilful at it. EG *I was bad at sports... ...a bad actor.* **2.2** fails to do it when they should do it. EG *Students are very bad at turning up for lectures.* ADJ QUALIT / ADJ PRED+*at*
3 Food that has gone **bad** has started to decay. EG *The milk's gone bad.* ADJ PRED
4 If you have a **bad** leg, heart, or eye, it is injured or there is something wrong with it. ADJ CLASSIF
5 If you call a child a **bad** boy or a **bad** girl, you mean that he or she is naughty and disobedient. ADJ QUALIT : ATTRIB
6 If you are in a **bad** mood, you are cross and behave unpleasantly to people. EG *The children were tired and bad-tempered.* ADJ QUALIT
7 If you say that something is **not bad**, you mean that it is quite good or acceptable. EG *It was an awful job, but the money wasn't bad.* ADJ PRED
8 If you **feel bad** about something, you feel rather sorry and sad about it. PHRASE
9 If you say **'too bad'**, you are indicating in a rather harsh way that nothing can be done to change the situation. EG *'I want to speak to the director.' – 'Too bad,' Castle said. 'You can't.'* CONVENTION
10 If a situation **goes from bad to worse**, it becomes even more unpleasant or unsatisfactory. PHRASE
11 **bad blood**: see **blood**. • **bad luck**: see **luck**.
• See also **worse, worst**.

bade /bæd, beɪd/ is a form of the past tense of **bid.**

badge /bædʒ/, **badges. 1** A **badge** is a small piece of metal or cloth which you attach to your clothes. Badges often have messages or designs on them. EG *...a shirt with a company badge on the pocket.* N COUNT
2 Any feature which is regarded as a sign of a particular quality can be referred to as a **badge** of that quality. EG *Wisdom is the badge of maturity.* N COUNT : USU+*of*

badger /bædʒə/, **badgers, badgering, badgered.**
1 A **badger** is a wild animal which has a white head with two wide black stripes on it. Badgers live underground and usually come up to feed at night. N COUNT
2 If you **badger** someone, you repeatedly tell them to do something or repeatedly ask them questions. EG *They badgered me to take them to the circus.* V+O

badly /bædli¹/, **worse** /wɜːs/, **worst** /wɜːst/. **1** If something is done **badly**, it is done with very little success or effect. EG *The party did badly in the election... The room was so badly lit I couldn't see what I was doing.* ADV
2 If someone or something is **badly** hurt or **badly** affected, they are severely hurt or affected. EG *The house was badly damaged... I cut myself badly.* ADV
3 If you need or want something **badly**, you need or want it very much. EG *We need the money badly... I am badly in need of advice.* ADV
4 You can use **badly** to say that something harms the reputation of someone or something. EG *The story reflected badly on Amity.* ADV
5 See also **worse, worst**.

badly off, worse off, worst off. 1 If you are **badly off** for something, you do not have enough of it. ADJ PRED : USU+*for*
2 If you are **badly off**, you do not have much money. EG *In the cities, the poor are as badly off as they were in the villages.* ADJ PRED

badminton /bædmɪntən/ is a game in which you use a racket to hit a small, feathered object called a shuttlecock over a high net to your opponent. N UNCOUNT

baffle /bæfə⁰l/, **baffles, baffling, baffled.** If you **are baffled** by something, you cannot understand it or explain it. EG *I was baffled by his refusal... The TV reporters looked slightly baffled.* ◇ **baffling.** EG *Some of these methods must be very baffling to a simple villager.* V+O : USU PASS / ◇ ADJ QUALIT

bag /bæg/, **bags. 1** A **bag** is **1.1** a container made of thin paper or plastic. EG *...a paper bag.* **1.2** a strong container with a handle or handles, used to carry things in. EG *He packed his bags and drove to the airport.* **1.3** a handbag. EG *She opened her bag and took out a handkerchief.* N COUNT

2 A **bag** of something can refer to either the bag and its contents or just to the contents. EG *Mrs Wilkins dropped her bag of plums... He ate a whole bag of sweets.* N PART
3 If you have **bags** under your eyes, you have folds of skin there, usually because you have not had enough sleep. N PLURAL
4 If you say there is **bags of** something, you mean that there is a large amount of it. If you say that there are **bags** of things, you mean that there are a large number of them. EG *There's bags of room... We've got bags of things to do before we leave.* N PART / Informal British
5 If you say that something is **in the bag**, you mean that you are certain that you will get it or achieve it. PHRASE / Informal
6 a **bag of bones**: see **bone**. • See also **mixed bag**.

baggage /bægɪdʒ/. Your **baggage** consists of the suitcases and bags that you take with you when you travel. EG *...a passenger who has lost his baggage.* N UNCOUNT

baggy /bægi¹/, **baggier, baggiest.** If a piece of clothing is **baggy**, it hangs loosely on your body. EG *...a pair of baggy trousers.* ADJ QUALIT

bagpipes /bægpaɪps/ are a musical instrument which you play by blowing air through a pipe into a leather bag, and then squeezing the bag to force the air out through other pipes. EG *...the sound of bagpipes... He played a few tunes on the bagpipes.* N PLURAL

bail /beɪl/, **bails, bailing, bailed;** also spelled **bale, bales, baling, baled** for paragraph 2 and for **bail out** 1.2 and 2.
1 Bail is **1.1** money that must be given to a law court before an arrested person can be released while they are waiting for their trial. EG *She was released on $2,500 bail.* **1.2** permission for an arrested person to be released after bail has been paid. EG *The judge refused to grant bail.* N UNCOUNT
2 If you **bail** water from a boat, you remove it using a container. V+O OR V : USU+A

bail out. 1 If you **bail** someone **out**, **1.1** you pay bail on their behalf. **1.2** you help them out of a difficult situation. **2** If you **bail out** of an aircraft, you jump out of it with a parachute because the aircraft is likely to crash. PHRASAL VB : V+O+ADV / V+ADV

bailiff /beɪlɪf/, **bailiffs.** A **bailiff** is **1** a law officer who makes sure that the decisions of a court are obeyed. EG *The bailiffs had arrived.* **2** a person who N COUNT / British

Should you drive a car if the tyres are bald?

is employed to look after land or property for the owner.

bait /beɪt/, **baits, baiting, baited.** 1 **Bait** is food which you put on a hook or in a trap in order to catch fish or animals. N UNCOUNT

2 When you **bait** a hook or trap, you put bait on it or in it. V+O

3 A person or thing that is being used as **bait** is being used to tempt or encourage someone to do something. EG *He's using my papers as a bait.* N SING

4 If you **bait** someone, you deliberately try to make them angry by teasing them. EG *Lucy seemed to take a delight in baiting him.* V+O

5 If you **rise to the bait** or **take the bait**, you react angrily to someone who is teasing you. EG *I knew that she, if anyone, would rise to the bait and argue.* PHRASE

baize /beɪz/ is a thick, green, woollen material used for covering snooker tables and card tables. N UNCOUNT

bake /beɪk/, **bakes, baking, baked.** 1 When you **bake** food or when it **bakes**, you cook it in an oven without using extra liquid or fat. EG *She said she would bake a cake... Mrs Burns was baking: it was Lionel's day off... ...while the souffle was baking.* V OR V-ERG

◊ **baked.** EG *...baked potatoes.* ◊ ADJ CLASSIF

2 When earth or clay **bakes**, it becomes hard and dry because of the heat of the sun. EG *The ground was baked hard.* V-ERG

3 See also **baking**.

baked beans are haricot beans cooked in tomato sauce. They are usually sold in tins. N PLURAL

baker /beɪkə/, **bakers.** 1 A **baker** is a person whose job is to bake and sell bread, rolls, and cakes. N COUNT

2 You can refer to a shop where bread and cakes are sold as the **baker** or the **baker's**. EG *I saw her at the baker's yesterday.* N SING

bakery /beɪkə⁰ri¹/, **bakeries.** A **bakery** is a building where bread, rolls, and cakes are baked. N COUNT

baking /beɪkɪŋ/. 1 **Baking** is the activity of making bread, rolls, and cakes. N UNCOUNT

2 If you say that a place is **baking**, you mean that it is very hot indeed. EG *He stared out across the baking roofs of Rome.* ADJ CLASSIF Informal

balance /bæləns/, **balances, balancing, balanced.** 1 If a person or thing **balances** or **is balanced**, they are steady and do not fall over. EG *An ashtray was balanced on the arm of her chair... Balancing on one leg is an excellent exercise.* V-ERG: OFT+*on*

2 **Balance** is 2.1 the steadiness that someone or something has when they are balanced on something. EG *She lost her balance.* N UNCOUNT 2.2 a situation in which all the different things involved are equal or correct in size, strength, or importance. EG *...the ecological balance of the lake... They had given the country a unique balance of freedom and order.* N SING+SUPP

3 If you **balance** one thing with another or if several things **balance** each other, each of the things has the same weight, strength, or importance. EG *Any escapism in the magazine is balanced by more practical items.* V+O OR V+O+*with*: RECIP

4 In a game or contest, if the **balance** swings in your favour, you start winning. EG *Competition was keen, and the balance swung this way and that.* N SING: *the*+N

5 To **balance** a budget or **balance** the books means to make sure that the amount of money that is spent is not greater than the amount that is received. EG *I just couldn't get the books to balance.* V-ERG

6 The **balance** in your bank account is the amount of money you have in it. N COUNT

7 **Balance** is also used in these phrases. 7.1 If you are **off balance**, you are in an unsteady position and about to fall. EG *I pulled her off balance and she slipped down.* 7.2 If a person or group **holds the balance of power** in a situation, that person or group will be able to win. 7.3 If something is **in the balance**, it is uncertain whether it will happen or continue. EG *The destiny of our race lies in the balance.* 7.4 You can say **on balance** to indicate that you are stating an opinion only after considering all the relevant facts or arguments. EG *On balance, he felt he had at least a month.* PHRASES

balanced /bælənst/. 1 A **balanced** account or report presents information in a fair and reasonable way. EG *...a balanced summary of the debate.* ADJ QUALIT

2 Something that is **balanced** is pleasing or beneficial because its parts have been used or arranged skilfully and in the correct proportions. EG *...a beautifully balanced play... ...a balanced diet.* ADJ QUALIT

balcony

balcony /bælkəni¹/, **balconies.** 1 A **balcony** is a platform which is on the outside of a building and has a wall or railing around it. EG *The Queen appeared on the balcony.* N COUNT

2 The **balcony** in a theatre or cinema is an area of seats upstairs. N COUNT

bald /bɔːld/, **balder, baldest.** 1 Someone who is **bald** has little or no hair on the top of their head. EG *You're going bald... He has a large bald patch.* ADJ QUALIT

◊ **baldness.** EG *I think you'll suffer from early baldness.* ◊ N UNCOUNT

2 A tyre that is **bald** has become very smooth and is no longer safe to use. ADJ QUALIT

3 A **bald** statement, question, or account has no unnecessary words in it. EG *The bald fact is that the first ten years were wasted.* ◊ **baldly.** EG *Stated baldly like this, these comments seem rather obvious.* ADJ QUALIT: ATTRIB ◊ ADV

balding /bɔːldɪŋ/. Someone who is **balding** is becoming bald. EG *...a trim, balding man in his early 60's.* ADJ CLASSIF

bale /beɪl/, **bales, baling, baled.** 1 A **bale** is a large quantity of something such as cloth, paper, or hay, tied into a tight bundle. EG *...bales of old newspaper.* N COUNT OR N PART

2 **Bale** can be used as a verb: see **bail.**

baleful /beɪlfʊl/. Something that is **baleful** is likely to have harmful effects, or expresses someone's harmful intentions. EG *We saw his baleful eye fixed on us.* ◊ **balefully.** EG *He glared at me balefully as I entered.* ADJ CLASSIF Literary ◊ ADV

balk /bɔːl⁰k/, **balks, balking, balked;** also spelled **baulk.** If you **balk** at something, you are very reluctant to do it or to let it happen. EG *I balked at cleaning the lavatory.* V: OFT+*at*

ball /bɔːl/, **balls.** 1 A **ball** is 1.1 a round object that is used in games such as tennis, cricket, and football. EG *...a golf ball.* N COUNT 1.2 something that has a round shape. EG *...a ball of wool... He rolled the socks into a ball.* N COUNT OR N PART

2 The **ball** of your foot or the **ball** of your thumb is the rounded part where your toes join your foot or where your thumb joins your hand. N COUNT+*of*

3 A **ball** is also a large, formal, social event at which people dance. N COUNT

4 **Ball** is used in these phrases. 4.1 If you **are having a ball**, you are having a very enjoyable PHRASES Informal

time. **4.2** If someone is **on the ball**, they are very alert and aware of what is happening. **4.3** If you are willing to **play ball** with someone, you are willing to do what they want you to do. **4.4** If you **start the ball rolling**, **set the ball rolling**, or **keep the ball rolling**, you start something happening or make sure that it keeps happening. EG *The banks set the ball rolling when they reduced their lending rates.*

ballad /bælәd/, **ballads.** A **ballad** is a long song or poem which tells a story in simple language. N COUNT

ballast /bælәst/ consists of a substance such as sand, iron, or water when it is used in ships or hot-air balloons to make them heavier and more stable. N UNCOUNT

ball bearing, ball bearings. Ball bearings are small metal balls placed between the moving parts of a machine to make the parts move smoothly. N COUNT

ballerina /bælәriːnә/, **ballerinas.** A **ballerina** is a woman ballet dancer. N COUNT

ballet /bæleɪ, bæleɪ/, **ballets. 1 Ballet** is a type of very skilled and artistic dancing with carefully planned movements. EG *...a ballet dancer.* N UNCOUNT

2 A **ballet** is an artistic work that is performed by ballet dancers. EG *...a ballet by Michel Fokine.* N COUNT

ball game, ball games. 1 A **ball game** is a baseball match. N COUNT American

2 If you say that a situation is **a whole new ball game**, you mean that it is completely different from the previous one or from any that you have ever experienced before. PHRASE Informal

ballistics /bә³lɪstɪks/. **Ballistics** is the study of the movement of objects that are shot or thrown through the air. N UNCOUNT

balloon /bәluːn/, **balloons, ballooning, ballooned. 1** A **balloon** is **1.1** a small, thin, rubber bag that you blow air into so that it becomes larger and rounder or longer. Balloons are used as toys or decorations. **1.2** a large, strong bag filled with gas or hot air, which can carry passengers in a basket or compartment underneath it. N COUNT

2 When something **balloons**, it quickly becomes bigger in size and rounder in shape. EG *She crossed the park, her skirt ballooning in the wind.* V

ballot /bælәt/, **ballots, balloting, balloted. 1** A **ballot** is a secret vote in which people select a candidate in an election, or express their opinion about something. • If someone is elected **by ballot**, they are chosen by the people voting in a ballot. EG *Committee members were picked by ballot.* N COUNT • PHRASE

2 If you **ballot** a group of people, you find out what they think about a subject by organizing a secret vote. ◊ **balloting.** EG *Balloting takes place next month.* V+O ◊ N UNCOUNT

ballot box, ballot boxes. 1 A **ballot box** is the box into which ballot papers are put after people have voted. N COUNT

2 You can also refer to the system of democratic elections as the **ballot box**. EG *Social change can be achieved through the ballot-box.* N SING : *the*+N

ballot paper, ballot papers. A **ballot paper** is a piece of paper on which you indicate your choice or opinion in a ballot. N COUNT

ballpoint /bɔːlpɔɪnt/, **ballpoints.** A **ballpoint** or a **ballpoint pen** is a pen with a small metal ball at the end which transfers the ink from the pen onto a surface. N COUNT

ballroom /bɔːlru⁴m/, **ballrooms.** A **ballroom** is a very large room that is used for dancing or for formal balls. N COUNT

ballroom dancing is a type of dancing in which a man and a woman dance together, using fixed sequences of steps and movements. N UNCOUNT

balustrade /bælәstreɪd/, **balustrades.** A **balustrade** is a railing or wall on a balcony or staircase. N COUNT

bamboo /bæmbuː/, **bamboos. 1 Bamboo** is a tall tropical plant with hard, hollow stems. The young shoots of the plant can be eaten. N UNCOUNT OR N COUNT

2 Bamboo also refers to the stems of the plant, which are used for making furniture and other things. EG *...a bamboo fence.* N UNCOUNT

bamboozle /bæmbuːzә⁰l/, **bamboozles, bamboozling, bamboozled.** If you **bamboozle** someone, you confuse them and often trick them. EG *Their sermons were intended to bamboozle the workers into obedience.* V+O : OFT+A Informal

ban /bæn/, **bans, banning, banned. 1** If something is **banned**, it is not allowed to be done, shown, or used. EG *His play was banned by the BBC... The treaty bans all nuclear tests.* ▸ used as a noun. EG *There was no ban on smoking.* V+O : USU PASS ▸ N COUNT : OFT+*on*

2 If you **are banned** from doing something, you are officially prevented from doing it. EG *He was banned from driving.* V+O : USU PASS+*from*

banal /bә³nɑːl/. Something that is **banal** is so ordinary that it is not at all effective or interesting. EG *Janis could make the most banal songs sound intensely personal.* ◊ **banality** /bә³nælɪ¹ti¹/. EG *Throughout the film, there are moments of banality.* ADJ QUALIT ◊ N UNCOUNT

banana /bәnɑːnә/, **bananas. 1** A **banana** is a long curved fruit with a yellow skin and cream-coloured flesh. EG *...a bunch of bananas.* N COUNT OR N UNCOUNT

2 If you say that someone is **bananas**, you mean that they are silly or mad. EG *You didn't save any of it? You must be bananas.* ADJ PRED Informal

band /bænd/, **bands, banding, banded. 1** A **band** is **1.1** a group of musicians who play jazz, rock, or pop music. EG *...a rock band.* **1.2** a group of musicians who play brass or percussion instruments. EG *He played the cornet in the school band.* **1.3** a group of people who have joined together because they share an interest or belief. EG *...a small band of revolutionaries.* N COUNT

2 A **band** is also **2.1** a flat, narrow strip of cloth which you wear round your head or wrists, or which forms part of a piece of clothing. EG *...a panama hat with a red band.* **2.2** a strip of something such as colour or light which contrasts with the areas on either side of it. EG *...a band of sunlight.* **2.3** a range of numbers or values within a system of measurement. EG *...a very wide band of radio frequencies.* N COUNT; N COUNT+SUPP; N COUNT+SUPP

band together. If people **band together,** they meet and act as a group in order to try and achieve something. EG *Everywhere women banded together to talk about liberation.* PHRASAL VB : V-ERG+ADV

bandage /bændɪdʒ/, **bandages, bandaging, bandaged. 1** A **bandage** is a long strip of cloth which is wrapped around a wounded part of someone's body to protect it. EG *She was wearing a bandage round her head.* N COUNT

2 If you **bandage** a wound or part of someone's body, you tie a bandage around it. ◊ **bandaged.** EG *...a man with a bandaged arm.* V+O ADJ CLASSIF

bandit /bændɪt/, **bandits.** A **bandit** is an armed robber. N COUNT Outdated

bandstand /bændstænd/, **bandstands.** A **bandstand** is a platform with a roof where a military band or a brass band can play in the open air. N COUNT

bandwagon /bændwægәn/. If you say that someone has **jumped on the bandwagon**, you mean that they have become involved in an activity or cause because it has become fashionable and they hope to gain some advantage from it. PHRASE

bandy /bændi¹/, **bandies, bandying, bandied.** If ideas or words **are bandied** about or around, they are mentioned or used by a lot of people. EG *Various suggestions were bandied around... The words dedication and loyalty are bandied about.* V+O+A : OFT PASS

bandy-legged. Someone who is **bandy-legged** has legs which curve outwards at the knees. ADJ QUALIT

If you have done everything bar the ironing, have you anything still to do?

bang /bæŋ/, **bangs, banging, banged. 1** A **bang** is a loud noise such as the noise of an explosion. EG *Walking across the street, we heard a bang... She slammed the drawer shut with a bang.* N COUNT
● **Bang** is used in speech and writing to represent a loud noise. EG *Bang! There's an explosion behind us... Bang! Bang! go the guns.* CONVENTION

2 If you **bang** a door or if it **bangs**, it closes violently with a loud noise. EG *She banged the door hard behind her... The door of the cafe banged shut.* V-ERG : OFT+A

3 If you **bang** on something or if you **bang** it, you hit it so that it makes a loud noise. EG *He banged on the door angrily... I banged the desk with my fist.* V+A OR V+O+A

4 If you **bang** part of your body against something, you accidentally knock into it and hurt yourself. EG *I bang my head against it every time.* V-ERG : USU+A ▸ used as a noun. EG *Did you suffer any bangs or bumps?* ▸ N COUNT

5 Bang is also used in these phrases. **5.1** If something goes **with a bang**, it is very successful. PHRASES Informal **5.2** If you say **bang goes** something, you mean that it is now obvious that it cannot succeed or be achieved. EG *Bang goes the Massachusetts vote!*

6 If you say that something is **bang** in a particular position, you mean that it is in exactly that position. EG *Emory University is bang in the middle of Atlanta.* ADV+PREP Informal

bang down. If you **bang** something **down**, you put it down violently so that it makes a loud noise. EG *He banged down the phone... I heard Marvin bang his files down hard onto the desk.* PHRASAL VB : V+O+ADV

banger /bæŋə/, **bangers.** A **banger** is **1** a sausage. EG *...bangers and mash.* **2** an old car that is in bad condition. **3** a small firework that makes a loud noise. N COUNT Informal British

bangle /bæŋgə^{0}l/, **bangles.** A **bangle** is a decorated bracelet or band that you can wear round your wrist or ankle. N COUNT

banish /bænɪʃ/, **banishes, banishing, banished.**
1 If someone **is banished**, they are punished by being sent away from the country where they live. V+O : USU PASS
◊ **banishment** /bænɪʃmə^{2}nt/. EG *They ordered the banishment of political and tribal leaders.* ◊ N UNCOUNT

2 If someone or something **is banished** from a place or situation, they are got rid of or are prevented from remaining in it. EG *The secretaries were banished to another room... Tobacco had been banished from polite society... Ignorance can be banished only by communication.* V+O+A : USU PASS

3 If you **banish** something from your thoughts, you stop thinking or worrying about it. EG *He could not banish his anxieties.* V+O

banister /bænɪstə/, **banisters;** also spelled **bannister.** A **banister** is a rail supported by posts and fixed along the side of a staircase. N COUNT

banjo /bændʒəʊ/, **banjos** or **banjoes.** A **banjo** is a musical instrument with a circular body and four or more strings. N COUNT

bank /bæŋk/, **banks, banking, banked. 1** A **bank** is a place where you can keep your money in an account. EG *You should ask your bank for a loan.* N COUNT

2 You use **bank** to mean a store of something. For example, a blood **bank** or a data **bank** is a store of blood or a store of data that is kept ready for use. N COUNT+SUPP

3 A **bank** is also **3.1** the raised ground along the edge of a river or lake. EG *...the river bank.* N COUNT **3.2** a long high row or mass of something. EG *...a bank of fog.* N COUNT+SUPP

bank on. If you **bank on** something happening, you expect it to happen and rely on it happening. EG *He may come, but I'm not banking on it.* PHRASAL VB : V+PREP

bank account, bank accounts. A **bank account** is an arrangement with a bank which allows you to keep your money in the bank and to withdraw it when you need it. N COUNT

banker /bæŋkə/, **bankers.** A **banker** is someone involved in banking at a senior level. N COUNT

bank holiday, bank holidays. A **bank holiday** is a public holiday. EG *...August Bank Holiday.* N COUNT British

banking /bæŋkɪŋ/ is the business activity of banks and similar institutions. N UNCOUNT

banknote /bæŋknəʊt/, **banknotes.** A **banknote** is a piece of paper money. EG *...a roll of banknotes.* N COUNT

bankrupt /bæŋkrə^{9}pt/, **bankrupts, bankrupting, bankrupted. 1** People or organizations that are **bankrupt** do not have enough money to pay their debts. EG *The company has gone bankrupt.* ADJ CLASSIF ◊ **bankruptcy** /bæŋkrə^{9}pt^{0}si^1/. EG *A really big strike will throw the firm into bankruptcy.* ◊ N UNCOUNT

2 To **bankrupt** a person or organization means to make them go bankrupt. EG *...contracts which would bankrupt the company.* V+O

3 A **bankrupt** is a person who has been legally declared bankrupt and is not allowed to take part in some kinds of business activities. N COUNT

4 Something that is **bankrupt** is completely lacking in a particular quality. EG *...the mindless, intellectually bankrupt leadership.* ADJ CLASSIF ◊ **bankruptcy.** EG *...the moral bankruptcy of our industrial economy.* ◊ N UNCOUNT : USU+SUPP

bank statement, bank statements. A **bank statement** is a list of all the money transactions into and out of a bank account. N COUNT

banner /bænə/, **banners.** A **banner** is a long strip of cloth with a message or slogan on it. Banners can be carried by people or stretched across a street. EG *Crowds filled the streets carrying banners.* N COUNT

bannister /bænɪstə/. See **banister**.

banquet /bæŋkwɪt/, **banquets.** A **banquet** is a grand formal dinner. N COUNT

banter /bæntə/ is teasing or joking talk that is amusing and friendly. N UNCOUNT

baptism /bæptɪzə^{0}m/, **baptisms.** A **baptism** is a Christian ceremony in which a person is baptized. N COUNT OR N UNCOUNT

baptize /bæptaɪz/, **baptizes, baptizing, baptized;** also spelled **baptise.** When someone **is baptized**, water is sprinkled on them or they are immersed in water as a sign that they have become a member of a Christian Church. V+O : USU PASS

bar /bɑː/, **bars, barring, barred. 1** A **bar** is **1.1** especially in America, a place where you can buy and drink alcoholic drinks. EG *Norris was drinking at a bar in San Francisco.* N COUNT **1.2** especially in Britain, a room in a pub or hotel where alcoholic drinks are served. EG *He called for the menu and ordered in the bar while they were finishing their drinks.* N COUNT : USU *the*+N **1.3** a counter on which alcoholic drinks are served. EG *Sally serves behind the bar.* N COUNT : USU *the*+N

2 A **bar** is also **2.1** a long, straight, rigid piece of metal. EG *...an iron bar... We beat on the bars of our cells.* N COUNT **2.2** a roughly rectangular piece of something. EG *...a bar of chocolate... ...a bar of soap.* N COUNT+SUPP

3 If you say that someone is **behind bars**, you mean that they are in prison. PHRASE Informal

4 If you **bar** someone's way, you prevent them from going somewhere or entering a place, by blocking their path. EG *I turned to go. Stryker barred my way... Once inside, we barred the door.* V+O

5 If you **bar** someone from a place or from doing something, you officially forbid them to go there or to do it. EG *Demands were made for the leader of the sect to be barred from Britain... ...restrictions barring the use of US-supplied weapons.* V+O : OFT+*from*

6 If something is a **bar** to doing a particular thing, it prevents someone from doing it. EG *This need not be a bar to success.* N COUNT+SUPP

7 You can use **bar** when you mean 'except'. For example, all the work **bar** the washing means all the work except the washing. EG *Every woman, bar the very young, can produce tales of this sort.* PREP Formal

8 In music, a **bar** is one of the several short parts of the same length into which a piece of music is divided. N COUNT

9 See also **barring**.

barb /bɑːb/, **barbs.** A **barb** is **1** a sharp curved point on the end of an arrow or fish-hook. N COUNT **2** an unkind remark. N COUNT : USU+SUPP

barbarian /bɑːbɛərɪən/, **barbarians. Barbarians** were members of wild and violent tribes in former times. N COUNT

barbaric /bɑːbærɪk/. If you describe a person or their behaviour as **barbaric**, you mean that they are extremely cruel. EG *...the barbaric sport of hunting.* ADJ QUALIT

barbarism /bɑːbərɪzəm/ is behaviour which is extremely rough or cruel. EG *War is barbarism.* N UNCOUNT

barbarous /bɑːbərəs/. Something that is **barbarous** is 1 rough and uncivilized. EG *Everything looked primitive and barbarous.* 2 extremely cruel. EG *...the most barbarous atrocities.* ADJ QUALIT

barbecue /bɑːbɪkjuː/, **barbecues.** A **barbecue** is 1 a grill that you use to cook food outdoors. 2 an outdoor party at which people eat food cooked on a barbecue. N COUNT

barbed /bɑːbd/. A **barbed** remark or joke seems humorous or polite, but contains a cleverly hidden criticism. EG *...a barbed compliment.* ADJ QUALIT

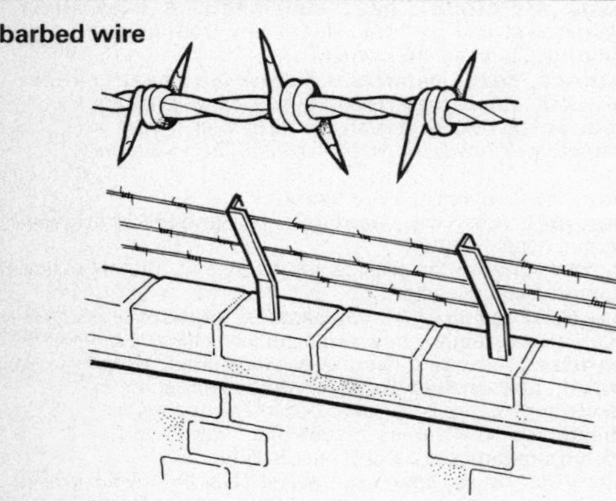

barbed wire is strong wire with sharp points sticking out of it, which is used to make fences. EG *This fence had barbed wire along the top and carried a metal notice.* N UNCOUNT

barber /bɑːbə/, **barbers.** 1 A **barber** is a man who cuts men's hair. N COUNT

2 You can refer to the shop or place where a barber works as the **barber's**. EG *He went to the barber's to please his mother.* N SING

bare /bɛə/, **barer, barest; bares, baring, bared.**

1 If a part of your body is **bare**, it is not covered by any clothing. EG *...her bare feet.* ● If someone does something **with** their **bare hands**, they do it without using any weapons or tools. EG *He killed those two men with his bare hands.* ADJ CLASSIF ● PHRASE

2 If a surface is **bare**, it is not covered or decorated with anything. EG *The doctor stood uneasily on the bare floor... The walls were bare.* ADJ CLASSIF

3 If a tree or a branch is **bare**, it has no leaves on it. EG *The trees were almost bare.* ADJ CLASSIF

4 If a room, cupboard, or shelf is **bare**, it is empty. EG *Inside the dairy, the counters and shelves were bare.* ADJ QUALIT

5 If you talk about the **bare** minimum or the **bare** essentials, you mean the very least that is necessary. EG *She packed the barest minimum of clothing.* ADJ QUALIT: ATTRIB

6 If you **bare** something, you uncover it. EG *She bared her teeth.* V+O

bareback /bɛəbæk/. If you ride **bareback**, you ride a horse without a saddle. EG *She galloped bareback down the road towards the village.* ADV AFTER VB

barefoot /bɛəfʊt/. Someone who is **barefoot** or **barefooted** is not wearing anything on their feet. EG *...a thin, barefooted boy with straw-coloured hair.* ▸ used as an adverb. EG *She ran barefoot through the field.* ADJ CLASSIF ▸ ADV AFTER VB

barely /bɛəli¹/. If something is **barely** true or possible, it is only just true or possible. EG *He was so drunk that he could barely stand... It was barely two months old.* ADV BRD NEG

bargain /bɑːgɪn/, **bargains, bargaining, bargained.** 1 A **bargain** is a business agreement in which two people or groups agree what each of them will do, pay, or receive. EG *We shook hands on the bargain.* N COUNT

2 When people **bargain** with each other, they discuss what each of them will do, pay, or receive. EG *Trade unions bargain with employers for better conditions.* ◊ **bargaining.** EG *...the kind of bargaining that goes on in industry.* V: OFT +*with/for* ◊ N UNCOUNT

3 A **bargain** is also something which is sold at a low price and which you think is good value for the money. EG *He couldn't resist a bargain... ...bargain prices.* N COUNT

4 When you are adding an extra piece of information to a statement and you want to emphasize it, you can say **into the bargain**. EG *She was an exceptional mathematician and an unusually beautiful one into the bargain.* PHRASE

bargain for. If you say that someone **had** not **bargained for** something, you mean that they did not expect it to happen. EG *They had not bargained for such opposition.* PHRASAL VB: V+PREP, HAS PASS

barge /bɑːdʒ/, **barges, barging, barged.** 1 If you **barge** into a place, you rush or push into it in a rough and rude way. EG *Arthur barged into the garden... ...barging his way through the crowd.* V+A OR V+O+A Informal

2 If you **barge** into someone, you bump against them roughly and rudely while you are walking. V+*into* Informal

3 A **barge** is a boat with a flat bottom. Barges are used for carrying heavy loads, especially on canals. N COUNT

barge in. If you **barge in**, you rudely interrupt what someone else is doing or saying. EG *I'm sorry to barge in on you like this.* PHRASAL VB: V+ADV Informal

barge pole. If you say that you **wouldn't touch** someone or something **with a barge pole,** you mean that you do not want to have anything to do with them because you think that they are untrustworthy or unreliable. PHRASE Informal British

baritone /bærɪtəʊn/, **baritones.** A **baritone** is a man with a fairly deep singing voice. N COUNT

bark /bɑːk/, **barks, barking, barked.** 1 When a dog **barks**, it makes a short, loud noise, once or several times. EG *The dogs began to bark.* ▸ used as a noun. EG *His spaniel gave a sudden bark.* V ▸ N COUNT

2 If you **bark** at someone, you shout at them in a loud, rough voice. EG *He barked an order at us... 'Shut up!' Caldwell barked.* V OR V+O: OFT+*at*; ALSO V+QUOTE

3 **Bark** is the tough material that covers the outside of a tree. N UNCOUNT

4 If you say that someone **is barking up the wrong tree**, you mean that they will not succeed in what they are trying to do. PHRASE Informal

5 If you say that someone's **bark is worse than** their **bite**, you mean that they are not as unpleasant or as hostile as they seem to be. PHRASE Informal

barley /bɑːli¹/ is 1 a tall, grass-like plant that is grown for food and for the production of beer and whisky. 2 the grain produced by this plant. N UNCOUNT

barmaid /bɑːmeɪd/, **barmaids.** A **barmaid** is a woman who serves drinks in a bar or pub. N COUNT

barman /bɑːmə³n/, **barmen.** A **barman** is a man who serves drinks in a bar or pub. N COUNT

barmy /bɑːmi¹/, **barmier, barmiest.** Someone or something that is **barmy** is slightly mad or very foolish. EG *The old woman's very rich and quite barmy... The whole scheme seems barmy to me.* ADJ QUALIT Informal British

barn /bɑːn/, **barns.** A **barn** is a large building on a farm in which crops or animal food can be kept. N COUNT

If your fridge is bare, what have you got in it?

barnacle /bɑːnəkə^{0}l/, **barnacles. Barnacles** are small shellfish that fix themselves tightly to rocks and the bottoms of boats. N COUNT

barometer /bərɒmə^{1}tə/, **barometers. 1** A **barometer** is an instrument that measures air pressure and shows when the weather is changing. N COUNT

2 When something indicates what people's feelings are about a situation, you can describe it as a **barometer** of their feelings. EG *The recent press statements have been the most telling barometer of the government's anxiety.* N COUNT+SUPP

baron /bærən/, **barons. 1** A **baron** is a man who is a member of the nobility. N COUNT

2 You can use **baron** to refer to someone who controls a large amount of a particular industry and who is therefore extremely powerful. EG *...the press barons... ...oil and wheat barons.* N COUNT+SUPP

baroness /bærənı^{2}s/, **baronesses.** A **baroness** is a woman who has the same rank as a baron, or who is the wife of a baron. N COUNT

baronet /bærənı^{2}t/, **baronets.** A **baronet** is a man who is given the honorary British title 'baronet' by the King or Queen, and can pass the title on to his son. N COUNT

baronial /bərəʊnıəl/ means belonging or relating to a baron or barons. ADJ CLASSIF : ATTRIB

baroque /bə^{3}rɒk, bə^{3}rəʊk/. **1 Baroque** art is an elaborate style of art that was used in Europe from the late 16th to the early 18th century. ADJ CLASSIF : ATTRIB

2 Baroque music is a style of European music that was written in the 18th century. ADJ CLASSIF : ATTRIB

barrack /bærək/, **barracks, barracking, barracked. 1** If you **barrack** someone, you shout loudly in order to interrupt them when they are making a speech. V OR V+O ◇ **barracking.** EG *The barracking was led by a bearded man in jeans.* ◇ N UNCOUNT

2 A **barracks** is a building or group of buildings where soldiers or other members of the armed forces live and work. The plural form is also **barracks.** EG *...soldiers from the nearby barracks.* N COUNT

barrage /bærɑːʒ/, **barrages.** If you get a lot of questions or complaints about something, you can say that you are getting a **barrage** of them. EG *His comments provoked a barrage of criticism... She faced a barrage of queries and complaints.* N COUNT+SUPP

barred /bɑːd/. **1 Barred** is the past tense and past participle of **bar.**

2 A **barred** window or door has bars on it to prevent people from getting into or out of a room. ADJ CLASSIF

barrel /bærə^{0}l/, **barrels. 1** A **barrel** is a round container for liquids. Barrels are wider in the middle than at the top and bottom and are usually made of wood. EG *...a wine barrel.* N COUNT

2 You can use **barrel** to refer to the contents of a barrel. EG *...a barrel of beer.* N PART

3 If you say that you are **scraping the barrel,** you mean you are having to use people or things of the poorest quality because all the better ones have already been used. PHRASE Informal

4 The **barrel** of a gun is the long, cylindrical part through which the bullet moves when the gun is fired. N COUNT

5 lock, stock, and barrel: see **lock.**

barren /bærə^{0}n/. **1 Barren** land has soil of such poor quality that plants cannot grow on it. ADJ CLASSIF

2 A **barren** woman is unable to have babies. EG *After twenty years of marriage, she remained barren.* ADJ CLASSIF Outdated

barricade /bærıkeıd/, **barricades, barricading, barricaded. 1** A **barricade** is a line of vehicles or other objects placed across a road or passage to stop people getting past. EG *They refused to man the barricades during the uprising.* N COUNT ▸ used as a verb. EG *They were barricading the house... ...barricaded roads.* ▸ V+O

2 If you **barricade** yourself inside a room or building, you put something heavy against the door so that other people cannot get in. EG *We rushed into the bedroom and barricaded ourselves in... They barricaded themselves behind concrete slabs.* V-REFL+A OR V+O+A

barrier /bærıə/, **barriers. 1** A **barrier** is a fence or wall that prevents people or things from moving from one area to another. EG *They were on different sides of a high barrier... Show your tickets at the barrier, please.* N COUNT

2 A **barrier** is also a problem that prevents two people or groups from agreeing or communicating with each other. EG *They have helped to break down the old barriers between the two parties.* N COUNT

3 A **barrier** to the happening or achievement of something is something that makes it difficult or impossible for it to happen or to be achieved. EG *Pollution is not a barrier to future economic growth.* N COUNT : OFT+*to*

barring /bɑːrıŋ/. You use **barring** to indicate that the person, thing, or event that you are mentioning is an exception to your general statement. EG *It is hard to imagine anyone, barring a lunatic, starting a war.* PREP

barrister /bærıstə/, **barristers.** A **barrister** is a lawyer who speaks in the higher courts of law on behalf of either the defence or the prosecution. N COUNT British

barrow /bærəʊ/, **barrows.** A **barrow** is **1** a wheelbarrow. **2** a cart from which fruit or other goods are sold in the street. N COUNT

bartender /bɑːtɛndə/, **bartenders.** A **bartender** is a person who serves drinks in a bar. N COUNT American

barter /bɑːtə/, **barters, bartering, bartered.** If you **barter** goods, you exchange them for other goods, rather than selling them for money. EG *They bring meat, grain, and vegetables to sell or barter.* V+O OR V ▸ used as a noun. EG *They send the fish for barter to the next village... Metal discs and chains were used for barter.* ▸ N UNCOUNT

base /beıs/, **bases, basing, based. 1** The **base** of something is **1.1** its lowest edge or part. EG *...at the base of a cliff... ...the switch on the lamp base.* **1.2** the part at which it is attached to something else. EG *...the scar at the base of his thumb... These birds have a large white mark near the base of the tail.* N COUNT : USU+SUPP

2 A position or thing that is a **base** for something is one from which that thing can be developed or achieved. EG *This innovation was regarded as a sensible base for teaching and research... The League had no real power base on which it could build.* N COUNT : OFT+SUPP

3 If you **base** one thing on another, you develop it from that thing. EG *The new agreement is based on the original United Nations proposal... ...movies based on British life.* V+O+*on/upon*

4 If you **are based** in a particular place, that is the place where you live or do most of your work. EG *I was based in London.* V+O+A : USU PASS

5 A military **base** is a place which part of an army, navy, or air force works from. EG *...the new air base at Buzaruto... The submarines abandoned the chase and returned to base.* N COUNT OR N UNCOUNT

6 Your **base** is the main place where you work, stay, or live. EG *The company made Luxembourg city their base... The best base for the visitor to London must be the West End.* N COUNT

baseball /beısbɔːl/ is a game played by two teams of nine players. Each player from one team hits a ball with a bat and then tries to run round all four bases before the other team can get the ball back. N UNCOUNT

baseless /beıslı^{2}s/. A story or belief that is **baseless** is not true and is not based on facts. EG *...baseless gossip.* ADJ CLASSIF

basement /beısmə^{2}nt/, **basements.** The **basement** of a building is a floor built partly or wholly below ground level. EG *They took the lift down to the basement of the hotel... It was horrible. There were rats in the basement!... ...a small basement flat.* N COUNT

bases is **1** the plural of **base,** pronounced /beısız/. **2** the plural of **basis,** pronounced /beısiːz/.

bash /bæʃ/, **bashes, bashing, bashed. 1** If you **bash** someone or something, you deliberately hit them hard. EG *She was bashing him over the head with a saucepan.* V+O : USU+A Informal

2 If you **bash** into something or against something, you hit it or bump into it accidentally with a lot of force. EG *He bashed into a tree... The cradle swayed and bashed against the walls.* ▸ used as a noun. EG *...a bash on the nose.* V+A Informal ▸ N COUNT

3 If you **have a bash** at something or if you **give it a bash**, you try to do it. EG *She was going to have a bash at swimming the Channel... Why don't you go and fetch the tools and we'll give it a bash.* PHRASE Informal

bashful /bæʃfʊl/. Someone who is **bashful** is shy and easily embarrassed. EG *Most new parents are bashful about asking questions.* ◊ **bashfully.** EG *He smiled bashfully when she said, 'You look lovely.'* ADJ QUALIT ◊ ADV

basic /beɪsɪk/, **basics. 1** You use **basic** to describe things which are the most important or the simplest parts of something. EG *The basic theme of these stories never varies... We never seem to solve the basic economic problems... ...people with only a basic education... We have taken this basic arrangement and elaborated it.* ADJ CLASSIF : ATTRIB

2 Something that is **basic** to the achievement or success of something else is necessary for it. EG *There are certain things that are absolutely basic to a good relationship.* ADJ PRED : OFT+*to*

3 You describe something as **basic** when it has only the most important features and no luxuries. EG *The people are having to move from luxury homes to basic two-roomed flats... The facilities are terribly basic.* ADJ QUALIT

4 The **basics** of a subject or activity are the simplest and most important aspects of it. EG *For a year I learnt the basics of journalism.* N PLURAL

basically /beɪsɪkə^{0}li^1/. You use **basically** when you are indicating what the most important feature of something is or when you are giving a general description of something complicated. EG *This was basically a political row... There are basically three types of vacuum cleaner... This is basically where we differ... Basically, I think Britain shouldn't have gone into the Common Market... To answer your question, I would say, basically, yes.* ADV SEN

basin /beɪsə^{0}n/, **basins. 1** A **basin** is **1.1** a deep bowl that you use for mixing or storing food. EG *Cover the basin with a clean cloth.* **1.2** a washbasin. N COUNT

2 The **basin** of a large river or lake is the area of land around it from which water and streams run down into it. EG *...the Amazon basin.* N COUNT

basis /beɪsɪs/, **bases** /beɪsiːz/. **1** The **basis** of something is the central and most important part of it, from which it can be further developed. EG *Many of the old actors used a script merely as a basis for improvization... This was the basis of the final design... Such dreams are the basis on which you later structure your life.* N COUNT : USU+SUPP

2 The **basis** for something is the thing that provides a reason for it. EG *There is no basis for this belief... ...arguments which had no logical basis.* N COUNT : USU+SUPP

3 If you make a decision **on the basis of** something, it provides the reason for making that decision. EG *I shall make up my own mind on the basis of the advice I've been given... The choice might have been made on the basis of convenience.* PHRASE

4 If something happens or is done **on a** particular **basis**, it happens or is done in that way or using that method. EG *We run the service on a voluntary basis... The results are checked on a daily basis... All the teachers work on a temporary basis at first.* PHRASE

bask /bɑːsk/, **basks, basking, basked. 1** If you **bask** in the sunshine, you lie in it and enjoy its warmth. EG *I want to spend the whole holiday just basking in the sun.* V : OFT+*in*

2 If you **bask** in someone's approval or favour, you get it and enjoy it. EG *The two journalists basked in the gratitude of the new rulers.* V+*in*

basket /bɑːskɪ^{2}t/, **baskets.** A **basket** is a container made of thin strips of cane woven together. EG *...a shopping basket... ...a basket of washing.* N COUNT : USU+SUPP

basketball /bɑːskɪ^{2}tbɔːl/ is a game in which two teams of five players each try to score goals by throwing a large ball through a circular net fixed to a metal ring at each end of the court. N UNCOUNT

bass /beɪs/, **basses. 1** A **bass** is a man with a very deep singing voice. N COUNT

2 A **bass** drum, guitar, or other musical instrument is one that produces a very deep sound. ADJ CLASSIF : ATTRIB

3 In popular music, a **bass** is a bass guitar or a double bass. EG *...with himself on trumpet and Kessler on bass... ...a new bass player.* N COUNT OR N UNCOUNT

bassoon /bəsuːn/, **bassoons.** A **bassoon** is a woodwind musical instrument which can produce a very deep sound. N COUNT

bastard /bɑːstəd, bæs-/, **bastards. 1** A **bastard** is someone whose parents were not married to each other at the time that he or she was born. EG *...the bastard son of the Marquis.* N COUNT Outdated

2 If you call someone a **bastard**, you are insulting them; an offensive use. N COUNT OR VOCATIVE

bastion /bæstɪən/, **bastions.** A **bastion** is something that protects a system or way of life from something that is likely to harm it. EG *They regard the wealth-producing system as a bastion of capitalistic privilege... Love is a bastion against loneliness.* N COUNT+SUPP Literary

bat /bæt/, **bats, batting, batted. 1** A **bat** is a specially shaped piece of wood that is used for hitting the ball in cricket, baseball, rounders, or table-tennis. EG *...a cricket bat.* N COUNT

2 When you **bat**, you have a turn at hitting the ball with a bat in cricket, baseball, or rounders. V

3 A **bat** is also a small flying animal that looks like a mouse with leathery wings. Bats fly at night. N COUNT

4 If someone does something **off** their **own bat**, they do it without anyone else suggesting it. PHRASE

5 If you say that someone did **not bat an eyelid**, you mean that they showed no sign of surprise. PHRASE

batch /bætʃ/, **batches.** A **batch** of things or people is a group of things or people of the same kind, especially a group that is dealt with at the same time. EG *Another batch of letters came in... ...the next batch of trainees.* N PART

bated /beɪtɪ^{2}d/. If you wait for something **with bated breath**, you are very anxious about it. PHRASE Literary

Find two words on these pages which have exactly the same meaning.

bath /bɑːθ/, **baths, bathing, bathed. 1** A **bath** is a long, rectangular container which you fill with water and sit in while you wash your body. N COUNT

2 When you have a **bath** or take a **bath**, you wash your body while sitting in a bath filled with water. EG *I must have a bath before we go.* N COUNT: USU SING

3 If you **bath** someone, you wash them in a bath. EG *She will show you how to bath the baby.* V+O

4 A public swimming pool is sometimes called the **baths**. EG *I take my older children to the baths once a week.* N PLURAL

bathe /beɪð/, **bathes, bathing, bathed. 1** When you **bathe**, you swim or play in a sea, river, or lake. EG *It is dangerous to bathe in the sea here.* ▸ used as a noun. EG *Let's go for a bathe.* ◊ **bathing.** EG *I know a place where we can go bathing.* V: OFT+*in* ▸ N SING: *a*+N ◊ N UNCOUNT

2 When you **bathe**, you have a bath. EG *After golf I would return to the flat to bathe and change.* V American

3 When you **bathe** a wound, you wash it gently. V+O

4 If a place **is bathed** in light, it is covered with light. EG *The room was bathed in sunlight.* V+O: USU PASS+*in*

bather /beɪðə/, **bathers.** A **bather** is a person who is swimming or playing in the sea, a river, or a lake. N COUNT

bathing costume /beɪðɪŋ kɒstjuːm/, **bathing costumes.** A **bathing costume** is the same as a bathing suit. N COUNT British

bathing suit /beɪðɪŋ sj^{0}uːt/, **bathing suits.** A **bathing suit** is a tight-fitting garment which a woman wears when she goes swimming. N COUNT American

bathing trunks /beɪðɪŋ trʌŋks/. **Bathing trunks** are the shorts that a man wears when he goes swimming. N PLURAL British

bathrobe /bɑːθrəʊb/, **bathrobes.** A **bathrobe** is **1** a loose piece of clothing made of towelling which you wear before or after you have a bath or a swim. **2** a dressing gown. N COUNT American

bathroom /bɑːθru^{4}m/, **bathrooms. 1** A **bathroom** is a room in a house that contains a bath or shower, a washbasin, and sometimes a toilet. See picture at HOUSE. EG *She went into the bathroom and took a shower.* N COUNT

2 People sometimes refer to a toilet as the **bathroom**. EG *Can I go to the bathroom, please?* N SING: USU *the*+N

bathtub /bɑːθtʌb/, **bathtubs.** A **bathtub** is a large, long container which you fill with water and sit in while you wash your body. N COUNT Outdated

baton /bætɒ^{0}n/, **batons.** A **baton** is **1** a light, thin stick used by a conductor to direct an orchestra or a choir. **2** a short stick that is passed from one runner to another in a relay race. **3** a short heavy stick used as a weapon by a policeman. N COUNT

baton charge, baton charges. A **baton charge** is an attacking forward movement made by a large group of policemen carrying batons. N COUNT

battalion /bətælɪ^{0}jən/, **battalions.** A **battalion** is a large group of soldiers that consists of three or more companies. N COUNT

batter /bætə/, **batters, battering, battered. 1** If someone **batters** a child or a woman, they injure them by hitting them many times. EG *Such parents have been known to batter their children.* ◊ **battered.** EG *Battered women may be protected one day.* V+O ◊ ADJ CLASSIF

2 To **batter** something means to hit it many times. EG *The ship was being battered by the waves... He was battering on the front door.* V+A OR V+O

3 Batter is a mixture of flour, eggs, and milk which you use to make things such as pancakes. N UNCOUNT

batter down. If you **batter down** a door, you hit it so hard that it breaks and falls down. PHRASAL VB: V+O+ADV

battered /bætəd/. Something that is **battered** is old, worn, and damaged as a result of being used a lot. EG *...a battered old hat.* ● See also **batter**. ADJ QUALIT

battering /bætə^{0}rɪŋ/, **batterings.** A **battering** is an experience in which someone suffers badly through being attacked. EG *The Eighth Army had taken the worst battering.* N COUNT

battery /bætə^{0}ri^1/, **batteries. 1** A **battery** is a device that produces the electricity in something such as a torch or radio. N COUNT

2 A **battery** of things, people, or events is a large number of them. EG *Batteries of cameras were set to record the event... We would undergo a battery of tests.* N PART

3 Battery hens are kept in small cages and made to produce large numbers of eggs. ADJ CLASSIF: ATTRIB

battle /bætə^{0}l/, **battles, battling, battled. 1** In a war, a **battle** is a fight between armies or between groups of ships or planes. EG *...the Battle of Balaclava... The general was killed in battle.* N COUNT OR N UNCOUNT

2 A **battle** is also **2.1** a process in which two people or two groups of people compete for power or try to achieve opposite things. EG *...the battle between the sexes... ...his battle for control of the administration.* N COUNT: USU +*between/for* **2.2** an attempt by a group of people to achieve something that is difficult and that can only be achieved slowly. EG *...the battle for women's liberation... ...the battle against inflation.* N COUNT: USU +*for/against*

3 Battle is used in these phrases. **3.1** When there is a **battle of wits**, people with opposing aims compete with each other using their intelligence. **3.2** If you say that something is **half the battle**, you mean that it is the most important step towards achieving something. **3.3** If you are **fighting a losing battle**, you are trying to achieve something but are not going to be successful. PHRASES

4 To **battle** means to fight very hard. EG *The males settle their problems by battling between themselves... Dad was soon battling for his life.* V+A

battlefield /bætə^{0}lfiːld/, **battlefields.** A **battlefield** is a place where a battle is fought. EG *...First World War battlefields.* N COUNT

battleground /bætə^{0}lgraʊnd/, **battlegrounds. 1** A **battleground** is a battlefield. N COUNT

2 You can also refer to a subject over which people disagree or compete as a **battleground**. EG *The theory of evolution is no longer a battleground.* N COUNT

battlements /bætə^{0}lmə^{2}nts/. The **battlements** of a castle or fortress consist of a wall built round the top, with gaps through which guns or arrows can be fired. N PLURAL

battleship /bætə^{0}lʃɪp/, **battleships.** A **battleship** is a very large, heavily armoured warship. N COUNT

batty /bæti^1/, **battier, battiest.** If you say that someone is **batty**, you think that they are rather strange or slightly mad. EG *She must be going batty.* ADJ QUALIT Informal

bauble /bɔːbə^{0}l/, **baubles.** A **bauble** is a small, cheap ornament or piece of jewellery. EG *...Christmas tree baubles.* N COUNT

baulk /bɔːl^{0}k/. See **balk**.

bawdy /bɔːdi^1/, **bawdier, bawdiest.** A **bawdy** story or joke contains humorous references to sex. EG *...bawdy songs.* ADJ QUALIT Outdated

bawl /bɔːl/, **bawls, bawling, bawled. 1** If you **bawl**, you shout or sing something loudly and harshly. EG *They bawl down the telephone at me... 'Truman,' he bawled, 'has been shot!'* V: OFT+A OR V+QUOTE

2 If a child **bawls**, it cries loudly. EG *Josephine started bawling.* V

bawl out. 1 If someone **bawls** you **out**, they scold you angrily for doing something wrong. EG *I was regularly bawled out at school for not doing homework.* PHRASAL VB: V+O+ADV Informal **2** If you **bawl** something **out**, you shout it or sing it very loudly. EG *...people bawling out, 'What about pensions?'* V-SPEECH+ADV

bay /beɪ/, **bays, baying, bayed. 1** A **bay** is a part of a coastline where the land curves inwards. EG *Hearst sailed from San Francisco across the bay to Oakland.* N COUNT

2 A **bay** is also a space or area that is used for a particular purpose. EG *...the corridor beyond the loading bay.* N COUNT: USU+SUPP

3 If you **keep** something that frightens or upsets you **at bay**, you prevent it from reaching you. EG *...lighting a fire to keep dangerous animals at bay.* PHRASE

BE

be /biː/ **am, are, is; was, were; being, been.**

There is a separate entry in this dictionary for each of the forms of **be** which will help you identify their shortened and negative forms.

'Be' as an auxiliary

1 In front of a present participle, it makes the continuous tense of verbs. For example: *. . . a problem which is getting worse and worse.*

2 In front of a past participle, it makes the passive voice of verbs. For example: *You have been warned.*

3 In front of an infinitive, it says something definite about a later event. For example: *You are to come back home by ten o'clock . . . The President is to appear on TV.*

'Be' with a complement

4 In front of a proper noun, it names a person or place. For example: *The head of the corporation is Sir Paul Simpson . . . This is London.*

'Be' with a complement or adjunct

5 In front of an adjective, a noun, or a prepositional phrase, it gives information about the subject, telling you about its features or qualities, or about things such as the identity of the subject or how old it is or where it is. For example: *The house was big and old . . . Rose Gibson is twenty-seven . . . The iron was in her left hand.*

'Be' with 'it' and 'there'

6 The subject of **be** can be 'it' or 'there'. These words do not refer to anything outside the sentence. The focus of the sentence is always on what follows **be**, and these words are just present to alert you to what follows.

6.1 With 'it' as subject, a feature or quality can be stated without any mention of what 'it' refers to. For example: *It's a pity . . . It's a lovely day . . . It was about four o'clock.*

6.2 With 'it' as subject, a statement like 'John bought the car yesterday' can be varied in emphasis by changing it to 'It was John who bought the car yesterday', or 'It was yesterday that John bought the car'.

In the same way, the statement can be introduced by a comment, as in: 'It was true that John bought the car', or 'It's unfortunate that John bought the car'.

6.3 With 'there' as subject, a noun or noun group can be stated without saying anything else about it. For example: *There was a rustling of papers.*

'Be' on its own

7 A form of **be** can be used without anything after it. This occurs in co-ordination and various kinds of responses and tags. For example:
Co-ordination: *She wasn't enjoying it but the children were.*
Response: *'Was she at the same hotel?' – 'No, she wasn't.'*
Tag: *'She's Welsh, isn't she?'*

4 When a dog or wolf **bays**, it makes a howling noise. V

bayonet /beɪənɪ^{2}t/, **bayonets.** A **bayonet** is a long, sharp blade that can be fixed to the end of a rifle and used as a weapon. N COUNT

bay window, bay windows. A **bay window** is a window that sticks out from the outside wall of a house. See picture at HOUSE. N COUNT

bazaar /bəzɑː/, **bazaars. 1** A **bazaar** is an area where there are many small shops and stalls, especially in the Middle East and India. EG *...the bazaars of old Delhi.* N COUNT

2 A **bazaar** is also a sale to raise money for charity. EG *Our local church is having a Christmas bazaar.* N COUNT

BC /biː siː/. You use **BC** in dates to indicate a number of years or centuries before the year in which Jesus Christ is believed to have been born. EG *...1600 BC... ...the fifth century BC.*

be. See the panel on the opposite page.

beach /biːtʃ/, **beaches.** A **beach** is an area of sand or pebbles beside the sea. *Tourists go there to walk on the beach.* N COUNT

beacon /biːkən/, **beacons.** A **beacon** is a light or a fire on a hill or tower, which acts as a signal or a warning. N COUNT

bead /biːd/, **beads. 1 Beads** are small pieces of coloured glass, wood, or plastic with a hole through the middle. Beads are often put together on a piece of string or wire to make necklaces, bracelets, and other jewellery. EG *...strings of beads.* N COUNT: USU PLURAL

2 A **bead** of liquid or moisture is a small drop of it. EG *Beads of perspiration began to form on his brow.* N PART

beady /biːdi^1/, **beadier, beadiest. Beady** eyes are small, round, and bright. ADJ QUALIT

beak /biːk/, **beaks.** A bird's **beak** is the hard curved or pointed part of its mouth. N COUNT: USU+POSS

beaker /biːkə/, **beakers.** A **beaker** is a plastic cup used for drinking, usually one with no handle. N COUNT

beam /biːm/, **beams, beaming, beamed. 1** If you **beam**, you smile because you are happy. EG *He beamed at Ralph... ...beaming faces.* ▸ used as a noun. EG *...a beam of satisfaction.* V: OFT+*at* ▸ N COUNT

2 A **beam** of light is a line of light that shines from an object such as a torch or the sun. EG *I could see the beam of his flashlight waving around in the dark.* N COUNT+SUPP

3 If you **beam** a signal or information to a place, you send it by means of radio waves. EG *We were able to beam pictures of the riots out to Denmark.* V+O+A

4 A **beam** is also a long thick bar of wood, metal, or concrete, especially one which is used to support the roof of a building. EG *...the low oak beams.* N COUNT

bean /biːn/, **beans. 1 Beans** are **1.1** the pods of a climbing plant, or the seeds that the pods contain, which are eaten as a vegetable. EG *...pork and beans... ...a garden where they grow beans.* **1.2** the seeds of various plants which are used for different purposes, for example to make drinks such as coffee or cocoa, or to produce oil. EG *...coffee beans.* N COUNT: USU PLURAL

2 If someone is **full of beans**, they are very lively and full of energy and enthusiasm. PHRASE Informal

3 If you **spill the beans**, you tell someone something that people have been trying to keep secret. PHRASE Informal

beansprouts /biːnsprauts/ or **beanshoots** are small shoots grown from beans. You can eat them raw or lightly cooked. N COUNT: USU PLURAL

bear /bɛə/, **bears, bearing, bore** /bɔː/, **borne** /bɔːn/. **1** A **bear** is a large, strong wild animal with thick fur and sharp claws. ● See also **polar bear**. ● **teddy bear**: see **teddy**. N COUNT

2 If you **bear** something somewhere, you carry it there or take it there. EG *Camels and donkeys bear those goods inland... She arrived bearing a large bunch of grapes.* V+O: USU+A Formal

3 If something **bears** the weight of something else, it supports the weight of that thing. EG *His ankle now felt strong enough to bear his weight.* V+O

4 If something **bears** a particular mark or characteristic, it has that mark or characteristic. EG *...a petition bearing nearly half a million signatures... The scene bore all the marks of a country wedding... The interpretation bore no relation to the actual words spoken.* V+O

5 If you **bear** something difficult, you accept it and are able to deal with it. EG *It was painful of course but I bore it... Their policies are putting a greater strain on the economic system than it can bear.* ● to **grin and bear it**: see **grin**. V+O

6 If you **can't bear** someone or something, you dislike them very much. EG *I can't bear weddings.* PHRASE

7 If you **bear** the responsibility for something, you accept responsibility for it. EG *It would be unjust for him to bear personally the great expenses involved.* V+O

8 When a plant or tree **bears** flowers, fruit, or leaves, it produces them. V+O

9 If you **bear** someone a feeling such as love or hate, you feel that emotion towards them. EG *He bore his children no malice.* V+O+O Formal

10 If you **bring** pressure or influence **to bear** on someone, you use it to try and persuade them to do something. PHRASE

11 If you **bear** left or **bear** right when you are driving or walking along, you turn slightly in that direction. EG *Bear right down the south side of the church.* V+A

bear down. If something large **bears down** on you, it moves quickly towards you in a threatening way. EG *We struggled to turn the boat as the wave bore down on us.* PHRASAL VB: V+ADV, USU+*on/upon*

bear out. If someone or something **bears** a person **out** or **bears out** what that person is saying, they support what that person is saying. EG *The claims are not borne out by the evidence.* PHRASAL VB: V+O+ADV

bear up. If you **bear up** when experiencing problems, you remain cheerful and show courage in spite of them. EG *You have to bear up under the strain.* PHRASAL VB: V+ADV

bear with. If you ask someone to **bear with** you, you are asking them to be patient. EG *I hope you'll bear with me as I explain.* PHRASAL VB: V+PREP

bearable /bɛərəbə^{0}l/. If something is **bearable**, you feel that you can accept it or deal with it. EG *The heat was just bearable... He hoped for some news that would make life more bearable.* ADJ QUALIT

beard /bɪəd/, **beards.** A man's **beard** is the hair that grows on his chin and cheeks. EG *He had a long grey beard.* ◇ **bearded** /bɪədɪ^{2}d/. EG *...a bearded man.* N COUNT ◇ ADJ CLASSIF

bearer /bɛərə/, **bearers. 1** A **bearer** is a person who carries a stretcher or coffin. EG *The four bearers lifted the coffin slowly.* N COUNT

2 The **bearer** of something such as a letter or a piece of news is the person who brings it to you. EG *...the bearer of the invitation.* N COUNT: OFT+*of*

3 The **bearer** of a document is the person who has it in their possession and who has the authority or right to possess it. EG *The identification document contains the bearer's fingerprints.* N COUNT Formal

4 The **bearer** of a name or title is the person who has it. N COUNT

bearing /bɛərɪŋ/, **bearings. 1** If something **has a bearing on** a situation or event, it is relevant to it. EG *That is all in the past. It has no bearing on what is happening today.* PHRASE

2 Someone's **bearing** is the way in which they move or stand. EG *Because of her bearing I realized that she was someone important.* N SING: USU POSS+N Formal

3 If you **get** or **find** your **bearings**, you find out where you are or what you should do next. If you **lose** your **bearings**, you do not know where you are or what you should do next. EG *They stopped to get their bearings... After a week in the job, she had got her bearings.* PHRASE

beast /biːst/, **beasts. 1** A **beast** is an animal, especially a large one. EG *...that most dangerous of all beasts – a maddened buffalo.* N COUNT

2 If you call someone a **beast**, you mean that they behave in a selfish, cruel, or unpleasant way. N COUNT Outdated

beastly /bi:stli1/, **beastlier, beastliest. 1** Something that is **beastly** is very unpleasant. EG *...a beastly smell... It's so beastly there.* ADJ QUALIT Outdated

2 Someone who is **beastly** is unkind, mean, and spiteful. EG *He was so beastly, you've no idea.* ADJ QUALIT Outdated

beat /bi:t/, **beats, beating, beaten.** The form **beat** is used in the present tense and is the past tense of the verb.

1 If you **beat** someone or something, you hit them very hard. EG *His stepfather used to beat him... The rain beat against the window.* V+O OR V: OFT+A

2 When a bird or insect **beats** its wings or when its wings **beat**, its wings move up and down. EG *It was trying to escape, frantically beating its wings.* V-ERG ▸ used as a noun. EG *Flies can move their wings at 1000 beats per second.* ▸ N COUNT

3 When your heart or pulse **is beating**, it is continually making movements with a regular rhythm. EG *His heart beat faster.* V ▸ used as a noun. EG *He could feel the beat of her heart.* ▸ N COUNT: USU+SUPP

4 The **beat** of a piece of music is the main rhythm that it has. N SING: *the*+N

5 If you **beat time** to a piece of music, you move your hand or foot up and down in time with the music. PHRASE

6 If you **beat** eggs, cream, or butter, you mix them thoroughly using a fork or whisk. V+O

7 If you **beat** someone in a game, race, or competition, you defeat them. EG *He's going to be a tough candidate to beat.* V+O

8 If someone or something **beats** a particular thing, they do better than it or are better than it. EG *He'll be trying to beat the world record... To my mind nothing beats a bowl of natural yogurt.* V+O

9 If you intend to do something but someone **beats** you **to it,** they do it before you do. EG *The Italians beat them to it by about 36 hours.* PHRASE

10 You use **beat** in expressions such as **'It beats me'** to indicate that you cannot understand or explain something. EG *What beats me is where they get the money from.* PHRASE Informal

11 A police officer **on the beat** is on duty, walking around the area for which he or she is responsible. PHRASE

12 If you tell someone to **beat it**, you are telling them to go away. CONVENTION Informal

13 to **beat about the bush**: see **bush**. • to **beat a retreat**: see **retreat**. • See also **beating**.

beat down. 1 When the sun **beats down**, it is very hot and bright. EG *...feeling the hot Alabama sun beat down.* PHRASAL VB: V+ADV **2** When the rain **beats down**, it rains very hard. EG *The soil absorbs only a fraction of the rain that beats down.* V+ADV **3** When you **beat down** a person who is selling you something, you force them to accept a lower price for it. V+O+ADV

beat up. If someone **beats** a person **up**, they hit or kick the person many times. EG *He told us that he had been beaten up by the police.* PHRASAL VB: V+O+ADV

beating /bi:tɪŋ/, **beatings. 1** If you are given a **beating**, you are hit hard many times, especially with something such as a stick. EG *She had left home after a savage beating.* N COUNT

2 If a team takes a **beating**, it is defeated by a large amount in a game or contest. N SING: *a*+N

3 If you say that something will **take some beating**, you mean that it is very good and it is unlikely that anything better will be done or made. PHRASE Informal

beating up, beatings up. A **beating up** is an attack on someone in which they are hit and kicked so that they are very badly hurt. EG *They gave him an awful beating up.* N COUNT

beatnik /bi:tnɪk/, **beatniks. Beatniks** were young people in the late 1950's who wore strange clothes and had unconventional beliefs. N COUNT

beautician /bju:tɪʃən/, **beauticians.** A **beautician** is a person whose job is giving people beauty treatments such as cutting and polishing their nails, treating their skin, and putting on their make-up. N COUNT

beautiful /bju:tɪfʊl/. **1** A **beautiful** woman is very attractive to look at. EG *...a very beautiful girl.* ADJ QUALIT

2 You say that something is **beautiful** when you find it very attractive or pleasant. EG *...beautiful music... ...a beautiful house... It's such a beautiful day.* ADJ QUALIT ◊ **beautifully.** EG *...beautifully dressed young men.* ◊ ADV

3 You can describe something that someone does as **beautiful** when they do it very skilfully. EG *It was a beautiful shot.* ADJ QUALIT ◊ **beautifully.** EG *Doesn't he play the piano beautifully?* ◊ ADV

beautify /bju:tɪfaɪ/, **beautifies, beautifying, beautified.** If you **beautify** something, you make it look more beautiful. EG *Charlotte went on beautifying her home.* V+O Formal

beauty /bju:ti1/, **beauties. 1 Beauty** is the state or quality of being beautiful. EG *Her beauty grew in her old age... ...the beauty of Kreisler's violin playing... She learned to appreciate beauty.* N UNCOUNT

2 A **beauty** is a beautiful woman. EG *Vita had turned into a beauty.* N COUNT

3 You can say that something is a **beauty** when you think it is very good. EG *My bike's a real beauty.* N COUNT Informal

4 The **beauties** of something are its attractive qualities or features. EG *...the beauties of nature... With him, I explored all the beauties of pre-war Warsaw.* N COUNT +SUPP: USU PLURAL

5 If you say that a particular feature is the **beauty** of something, you mean that this feature is what makes the thing so good. EG *That's the beauty of the plan – it's so simple.* N SING: *the*+N+*of*

6 Beauty is used to describe people, products, and activities that are concerned with making women look beautiful. EG *...beauty products... ...the magazine's beauty editor.* N MOD

beauty spot, beauty spots. A **beauty spot** is a place that is popular because of its beautiful countryside. EG *...Ashness Bridge, a popular beauty spot.* N COUNT

beaver /bi:və/, **beavers, beavering, beavered.** A **beaver** is a furry animal like a large rat with a big flat tail. Beavers build dams in streams. N COUNT

beaver away. If you **are beavering away** at something, you are working very hard at it. PHRASAL VB: V+ADV

became /bi1keɪm/ is the past tense of **become.**

because /bi1kɔ7z/. **1** You use **because** when stating the reason for something. EG *I couldn't see Helen's expression, because her head was turned... 'Why shouldn't I come?' – 'Because you're too busy.'* CONJ

2 You also use **because of** when stating the reason for something. EG *He retired last month because of illness.* PREP:

beck /bɛk/. If someone wants you to be **at** their **beck and call**, they want you to be constantly available and ready to do what they ask. PHRASE

beckon /bɛkə0n/, **beckons, beckoning, beckoned. 1** If you **beckon** to someone, you signal to them to come to you. EG *Claus beckoned to him excitedly... He beckoned and the girl came over... He beckoned me to follow him.* V: OFT+*to* OR V+O+*to*-IN

2 If something **beckons**, it is so attractive to someone that they feel they must become involved in it. EG *Vast countries beckon to young men in search of adventure... No restaurants beckoned late diners into the area.* V: OFT+*to* OR V+O

become /bi1kʌm/, **becomes, becoming, became** /bi1keɪm/. The form **become** is used in the present tense and is also the past participle.

1 If something **becomes** a particular thing, it starts being that thing. EG *The smell became stronger and stronger... It became clear that the Conservatives* V+C

Find two insects and an animal on these pages.

were not going to win... We became good friends at once.

2 If you wonder **what has become of** someone, you wonder where they are and what has happened to them. EG *He was an odd chap, Boon. I wonder what became of him.* PHRASE

becoming /biˈkʌmɪŋ/. A piece of clothing, a colour, or a hairstyle that is **becoming** makes the person who is wearing it look attractive. EG *She was dressed in an extremely becoming trouser suit.* ADJ QUALIT Outdated

bed /bɛd/, **beds, bedding, bedded. 1** A **bed** is a piece of furniture that you lie on when you sleep. EG *He sat down on the bed... He went to bed at ten... She had just got out of bed.* N COUNT OR N UNCOUNT ● When you **make** the **bed**, you neatly arrange the sheets and covers of a bed. ● PHRASE

2 If you **go to bed with** someone, you have sex with them. PHRASE

3 A flower **bed** is an area of earth in which you grow plants. EG *...beds of marigolds.* ● **not a bed of roses**: see **rose**. N COUNT+SUPP

4 The sea **bed** or a river **bed** is the ground at the bottom of the sea or of a river. N COUNT+SUPP

5 See also **bedding**.

bed down. If you **bed down** somewhere, you sleep there for the night, not in your own bed. PHRASAL VB : V+ADV+A

bed and breakfast is a system of accommodation in a hotel or guest house in which you pay for a room for the night and for breakfast the following morning. EG *...£15.50 a night for bed and breakfast.* N UNCOUNT

bedclothes /bɛdkləʊðz/ are the sheets and covers which you put over you when you get into bed. EG *Jamie pulled back the bedclothes and got into bed.* N PLURAL

bedding /bɛdɪŋ/ is sheets, blankets, and other covers that are used on beds. EG *She changed the bedding.* N UNCOUNT

bedevil /biˈdɛvəl/, **bedevils, bedevilling, bedevilled;** spelled **bedeviling, bedeviled** in American English. If you **are bedevilled** by something unpleasant, it causes you a lot of problems. EG *He has been bedevilled by injuries.* V+O : USU PASS Formal

bedfellow /bɛdfɛləʊ/, **bedfellows.** You refer to two things or people as **bedfellows** when they have become associated or related in some way. EG *The oddest of enemies might become bedfellows.* N COUNT

bedlam /bɛdləm/. If you say that a place or situation is **bedlam**, you mean that it is very noisy and disorderly. N UNCOUNT

bedraggled /biˈdrægəld/. Someone or something that is **bedraggled** is untidy and disorderly, because they have got wet or dirty. EG *She came in looking grubby and bedraggled.* ADJ QUALIT

bedridden /bɛdrɪdən/. Someone who is **bedridden** is so ill or disabled that they cannot get out of bed. ADJ CLASSIF

bedrock /bɛdrɒk/. The **bedrock** of something refers to all the principles, ideas, or facts on which it is based. EG *The Act reaffirmed family values as the moral bedrock of the nation.* N UNCOUNT : USU+SUPP Formal

bedroom /bɛdru⁴m/, **bedrooms.** A **bedroom** is a room which is used for sleeping in. See picture at HOUSE. EG *...a hotel bedroom... The bedroom door was closed.* N COUNT

bedside /bɛdsaɪd/. Your **bedside** is the area beside your bed. EG *An excellent breakfast had been left on the tray by his bedside... ...a bedside light.* N SING

bedsitter /bɛdsɪtə/, **bedsitters.** A **bedsitter** or **bedsit** is a single furnished room in a house, which you pay rent for and in which you live and sleep. Some bedsitters also have a washbasin and a small cooker. EG *A lot of students live off campus in flats, houses, and bedsitters.* N COUNT British

bedspread /bɛdsprɛd/, **bedspreads.** A **bedspread** is a decorative cover which is put over a bed, on top of the sheets and blankets. N COUNT

bedtime /bɛdtaɪm/. Your **bedtime** is the time when you usually go to bed. EG *It's long past bedtime.* N UNCOUNT

bee /biː/, **bees. 1** A **bee** is an insect that makes a buzzing noise as it flies and usually has a yellow-and-black striped body. Bees make honey, and live in large groups. N COUNT

2 If you **have a bee in** your **bonnet** about something, you are so enthusiastic or worried about it that you keep mentioning it or thinking about it. PHRASE

beech /biːtʃ/, **beeches.** A **beech** is a tree with a smooth grey trunk. EG *...under the shade of a huge beech... ...forests of ash, elm, and beech.* N COUNT OR N UNCOUNT

beef /biːf/ is the meat of a cow, bull, or ox. EG *...a joint of roast beef... ...beef sandwiches.* N UNCOUNT

beefy /biːfi¹/, **beefier, beefiest.** Someone, especially a man, who is **beefy** is strong and muscular. EG *Ronald was big, beefy, and aggressive.* ADJ QUALIT Informal

beehive /biːhaɪv/, **beehives.** A **beehive** is a structure in which bees are kept, which is designed so that the keeper can collect the honey that they produce. N COUNT

beeline /biːlaɪn/. If you **make a beeline for** a place, you go to it as quickly and directly as possible. EG *Three of them made a beeline for the pub.* PHRASE Informal

been /biːn, bɪn/. **1 Been** is the past participle of **be**.

2 You use **been** after the auxiliaries 'has', 'have', and 'had' in these ways. **2.1** If you **have been** to a place, you have gone to it or visited it. EG *She has not been to church for almost twenty years... I haven't been to Birmingham.* **2.2** If someone such as a postman or milkman **has been**, they have called at your house. EG *Has the milkman been yet?*

3 If you say that someone **has been and** done something, you are expressing surprise or horror at something that they have done. EG *Now you've been and set the whole box on fire!* PHRASE Informal

beer /bɪə/, **beers. 1 Beer** is a bitter alcoholic drink made from grain. EG *We drank a few pints of beer.* N MASS

2 A **beer** is a glass, bottle, or can containing beer. EG *He'd had two beers.* N COUNT

beet /biːt/ is a root vegetable that is used as food for animals, especially for cows. N UNCOUNT

beetle /biːtəl/, **beetles.** A **beetle** is an insect with a hard covering to its body. N COUNT

beetroot /biːtruːt/, **beetroots. Beetroot** is a dark red root vegetable which can be cooked or pickled, and eaten in salads. N UNCOUNT OR N COUNT

befall /biˈfɔːl/, **befalls, befalling, befell** /biˈfɛl/, **befallen.** If something bad or unlucky **befalls** you, it happens to you. EG *She knew no harm would ever befall her... A similar fate befell the British.* V+O Literary

befit /biˈfɪt/, **befits, befitting, befitted.** If something **befits** a person or thing, it is suitable for them or is expected of them. EG *He was courteous, as befitted a young man speaking to an older man.* V+O Formal

before /biˈfɔː/. **1** If something happens **before** a time or event, it happens earlier than that time or event. EG *We arrived just before two o'clock... Can I see you before you go, Helen?... A dozen ideas were considered before he decided on this plan.* PREP OR CONJ

2 You use **before** when you are talking about time. For example, if something happened the day **before** or the weekend **before**, it happened during the previous day or during the previous weekend. EG *It had rained the night before.* ADJ AFTER N

3 If someone has done something **before**, they have done it on a previous occasion. EG *Have you been to Greece before?* ADV

4 If someone is **before** something, they are in front of it. EG *He stood before the door to the cellar... He will appear before the magistrate.* PREP Formal

5 When you have a task or difficult situation **before** you, you have to deal with it. EG *Let's get started. I have a difficult job before me.* PREP+PRON

beforehand /biˈfɔːhænd/. If you do something [ADV] **beforehand**, you do it earlier than a particular event. EG *Kathleen got married without telling anyone beforehand.*

befriend /biˈfrend/, **befriends, befriending, befriended.** [V+O] If you **befriend** someone, you make friends with them. EG *I befriended a lonely little boy in the village.*

befuddle /biˈfʌdəᵊl/, **befuddles, befuddling, befuddled.** [V+O] If something **befuddles** you, it confuses you. EG *His words were sufficient to befuddle the girls.*

beg /beg/, **begs, begging, begged. 1** If you **beg** [V+O : OFT+*to*-INF, V+*for*, OR V+QUOTE] someone to do something, you ask them very anxiously or eagerly. EG *I begged him to stay, but he wouldn't... He begged for help... 'Tell me all the news,' I begged.*

2 When someone **begs**, they ask people to give [V : OFT+*for*, OR V+O : OFT+*for/from*] them food or money because they are very poor. EG *...children in the streets begging for money... Kids were begging milk from the governor.*

3 I beg your pardon: see **pardon**.

began /biˈgæn/ is the past tense of **begin.**

beget /biˈget/, **begets, begetting, begot** /biˈgɒt/, [V+O Formal] begotten /biˈgɒtəᵊn/. To **beget** something means to cause it to happen or be created. EG *Malnutrition begets disease.*

beggar /begə/, **beggars.** A **beggar** is someone [N COUNT] who lives by asking people for money or food.

begin /bɪˈgɪn/, **begins, beginning, began** /biˈgæn/, **begun** /biˈgʌn/. **1** If you **begin** to do [V+*to*-INF OR V+-ING] something, you start doing it. EG *The actors began to rehearse a scene... I began eating the grapes.*

2 When something **begins** or when you **begin** it, it [V-ERG OR V : OFT+A] takes place from a particular time onwards. EG *The concerts begin at 8 pm... Malcolm began his speech... They decided to begin by looking at the problems.*

3 You use the phrase **to begin with 3.1** when you [PHRASE] are talking about the first event or stage in a process. EG *To begin with, they just take your name and address.* **3.2** to introduce the first of several things that you want to say. EG *To begin with, the invitation for eight really means eight-thirty.*

4 When you want to emphasize that it is difficult [V+*to*-INF] for you to do something, you can say that you cannot **begin** to do it. EG *He could not begin to explain his feelings.*

5 If you say that a place or region **begins** some- [V+A] where, you are talking about or pointing to one of its edges. EG *The ocean begins here.*

beginner /biˈgɪnə/, **beginners.** A **beginner** is [N COUNT] someone who has just started learning to do something and cannot do it very well yet. EG *This is the sort of thing that beginners write.*

beginning /biˈgɪnɪŋ/, **beginnings. 1** If you refer [N COUNT : *the*+N] to the **beginning** or the **beginnings** of something, you mean the first part of it. EG *I say this at the beginning of my book... ...the beginnings of a new relationship.*

2 The **beginning** of a period of time is when it [N SING : *the*+N] starts. EG *I came back at the beginning of the term... The number had increased by the beginning of the following year.*

begot /biˈgɒt/ is the past tense of **beget.**

begotten /biˈgɒtəᵊn/ is the past participle of **beget.**

begrudge /bɪˈgrʌdʒ/ **begrudges, begrudging,** [V+O+O] **begrudged.** If you say that you do not **begrudge** someone something, you mean that you do not feel angry, upset, or jealous that they have got it. EG *I do not begrudge her that happiness... Let us not begrudge Shirley her victory.*

beguiling /biˈgaɪlɪŋ/. Something that is **beguiling** [ADJ QUALIT] seems attractive, but may be dangerous or harmful. EG *...this beguiling idea... The fruit is a beguiling red berry.*

begun /biˈgʌn/ is the past participle of **begin.**

behalf /biˈhɑːf/. If someone does something **on** [PHRASE] **your behalf**, they do it for you and as your representative. EG *Wilkins spoke on behalf of the Labour Party.*

behave /biˈheɪv/, **behaves, behaving, behaved.**
1 If you **behave** in a particular way, you act in that [V+A] way. EG *In New York, he had behaved in a very strange way... You are behaving like a silly child.*

2 If you **behave** yourself, you act in the way that [V OR V-REFL] people think is correct and proper. EG *Their startled boyfriends got warnings to behave... He's old enough to behave himself.*

behaviour /biˈheɪvjə/; spelled **behavior** in American English. **1** A person's **behaviour** is the [N UNCOUNT : OFT+SUPP] way they behave. EG *I had been puzzled by his behaviour... ...the obstinate behaviour of a small child.*

2 The **behaviour** of something is the way in which [N UNCOUNT : USU+SUPP] it acts, functions, or changes. EG *...the behaviour of the metal as we heat it.*

behead /biˈhed/, **beheads, beheading, beheaded.** [V+O : USU PASS] If someone **is beheaded**, their head is cut off. EG *Lady Jane Grey was beheaded in 1554.*

beheld /biˈheld/ is the past tense of **behold.**

behind /biˈhaɪnd/, **behinds. 1** If something is [PREP OR ADV] **behind** a thing or person, the back of that thing or person is facing it. EG *There were two boys sitting behind me... The sun went behind a cloud... Joe was limping along behind his wife... He followed a few paces behind.*

2 The reason or person **behind** something caused [PREP] that thing or is responsible for it. EG *These were the reasons behind Macleod's statement... ...the man behind the modernizing of the station.*

3 If you are **behind** someone, you support them. EG [PREP] *The country was behind the President.*

4 You say that you are **behind** when you have [ADV OR PREP] done less work than you should have done, or when you have been less successful than someone else. EG *I got more and more behind... The bus was badly behind schedule... In the Championship, he finished 11 strokes behind Watson.*

5 If an experience is **behind** you, it is finished. EG [PREP OR ADV] *...now that the war is behind us... We must leave adolescence behind and grow up.*

6 If you stay **behind**, you remain in a place after [ADV AFTER VB] other people have gone. EG *Susan asked me to stay behind.*

7 If you leave something **behind**, you do not take it [ADV AFTER VB] with you when you go. EG *Millie had left her cloak behind.*

8 Your **behind** is the part of your body that you sit [N COUNT] on.

behold /biˈhəʊld/, **beholds, beholding, beheld** /biˈheld/. **1** If you **behold** someone or something, [V+O Literary] you notice them or look at them. EG *She was a terrible sight to behold... I beheld with sorrow an old woman in tears.*

2 People sometimes say **'Behold'** to draw your [V : ONLY IMPER Literary] attention to something important or surprising that they are about to tell you or show you. EG *'Behold, I show you a mystery,' the Vicar read... And, behold, the Pentagon gave in.*

beholder /bɪhəʊldə/, **beholders.** The **beholder** of [N COUNT Outdated] something is the person who is looking at it. EG *The picture was very pleasing to beholders... Beauty is in the eye of the beholder.*

beige /beɪʒ/. Something that is **beige** is a very [ADJ COLOUR] pale brown colour. EG *...his pale beige summer coat.*

being /biːɪŋ/, **beings. 1 Being** is the present participle of **be**. EG *Julie, you're being unreasonable.*

2 Something that is **in being** exists. EG *...laws* [PHRASE] *already in being... The Polytechnic came into being in 1971.*

Do you apologize if you give someone a belated birthday present?

3 You can refer to any real or imaginary creature as a **being**. EG *Man is a rational being... ...the sight of these alien beings gliding down.* • See also **human being**. N COUNT: USU+SUPP Literary

belated /bi¹leɪtɪ²d/. A **belated** action happens later than it should have done. EG *Please accept my belated thanks for your kind gift... The Government is making a belated attempt to stop profiteering.* ◇ **belatedly.** EG *Bill belatedly agreed to call in the police.* ADJ QUALIT: ATTRIB Formal ◇ ADV

belch /bɛltʃ/, **belches, belching, belched. 1** If someone **belches**, they make a sudden noise in their throat because air has risen up from their stomach. EG *The baby drank his milk and belched.* ▸ used as a noun. EG *'Amazing,' said Brody, stifling a belch.* V ▸ N COUNT

2 If something **belches** smoke, fire, or loud sounds, it gives them out in large amounts. EG *Loudspeakers belched out deafening pop music... Smoke belched from the engine.* ▸ used as a noun. EG *...a belch of flame.* V+O OR V+A Literary ▸ N COUNT +SUPP

beleaguered /bi¹liːgəd/. **1** A **beleaguered** person is experiencing a lot of difficulties, opposition, or criticism. EG *The beleaguered prime minister explained this to an angry crowd.* ADJ CLASSIF: ATTRIB Formal

2 A **beleaguered** place or army is surrounded by its enemies. EG *...the distressed defenders of a beleaguered city.* ADJ CLASSIF: ATTRIB Formal

belfry /bɛlfri¹/, **belfries.** The **belfry** of a church is the top part of its tower or steeple, where the bells are. N COUNT

belie /bi¹laɪ/, **belies, belying, belied.** If one thing **belies** another, **1** it makes the other thing seem very surprising. EG *The young face belied the grey hair above it.* **2** it proves that the other thing is not genuine or true. EG *Their social attitudes belie their words.* V+O Formal

belief /bi¹liːf/, **beliefs. 1 Belief** is a feeling of certainty that something exists, is true, or is good. EG *...belief in God... It is my belief that more people could have been helped... ...the religious beliefs of her parents.* N COUNT OR N UNCOUNT: USU+SUPP

2 If you do something **in the belief that** something is true or will happen, you do it because you think this. EG *They put more and more demands on the system in the belief that it was indestructible.* PHRASE

3 You use **beyond belief** to emphasize that something is true or happened to a very great degree. EG *They are generous beyond belief.* PHRASE

believable /bi¹liːvəbə⁰l/. Something that is **believable** makes you think that it could be true or real. EG *...the only believable explanation for the disappearance of the plane.* ADJ CLASSIF

believe /bi¹liːv/, **believes, believing, believed. 1** If you **believe** that something is true, you think that it is true. EG *It is believed that two prisoners have escaped... I couldn't believe what I had heard... We believed him dead... I believed him to be right.* V+REPORT, V+O+C, OR V+O+*to*-INF

2 You can say **I believe** to indicate that you are not sure that what you are saying is correct. EG *He's very well known, I believe, in Germany.* PHRASE

3 If you **believe** someone, you accept that they are telling the truth. EG *He knew I didn't believe him... Don't believe a word he says.* V+O: NO CONT

4 You can say **'believe me'** to emphasize that what you are saying is true. EG *Believe me, it's important.* CONVENTION

5 You say **'believe it or not'** when you think that someone is going to be surprised by what you are saying. EG *Believe it or not, I'm feeling quite homesick.* ADV SEN

6 If you **believe** in things such as God, fairies, or miracles, you are sure that they exist or happen. EG *I don't believe in ghosts.* V+*in*

7 If you **believe** in something, you are in favour of it because you think it is good or right. EG *...all those who believe in democracy... He did not believe in educating women.* V+*in*

believer /bi¹liːvə/, **believers. 1** If you are a **believer** in something, you think that it is good, right, or beneficial. EG *...the true believer in democracy... Bob is a great believer in jogging.* N COUNT+*in*

2 A **believer** is someone who is sure that God exists or that their religion is true. EG *Of course you, as a believer, try to convert others?... We want to unite believers of all religions.* N COUNT

belittle /bi¹lɪtə⁰l/, **belittles, belittling, belittled.** If you **belittle** someone or something, you make them seem unimportant or not very good. EG *The press gave the election no publicity and belittled its significance... Don't think I'm trying to belittle Turner. He was a genius.* V+O

bell

bell /bɛl/, **bells. 1** A **bell** is **1.1** a device that makes a ringing sound and is used to give a signal or to attract people's attention. EG *He approached the front door and rang the bell.* **1.2** a hollow metal object shaped like a cup which has a piece hanging inside it that hits the sides and makes a sound. EG *In the distance a church bell was ringing.* N COUNT

2 If you say that something **rings a bell**, you mean that it reminds you of something else, but you cannot remember exactly what it is. EG *The name rings a bell.* PHRASE Informal

belligerent /bɪ²lɪdʒə⁰rənt/. If you are **belligerent**, you are eager to defend yourself or your opinions when you know that other people are likely to oppose you. EG *Not even the belligerent Leggett was willing to face that mob... The women were belligerent about their freedom not to have babies.* ◇ **belligerently.** EG *Mr Kidley looked at him belligerently.* ◇ **belligerence** /bɪ²lɪdʒə⁰rəns/. EG *'I wanted to teach him a lesson,' she said with sudden belligerence.* ADJ QUALIT ◇ ADV ◇ N UNCOUNT

bellow /bɛləʊ/, **bellows, bellowing, bellowed. 1** If someone **bellows**, they shout in a loud, deep voice. EG *The president bellowed with laughter... 'Thirty-two!' bellowed Mrs Pringle... Lionel bellowed his contribution from across the room.* ▸ used as a noun. EG *He raised his voice to a bellow.* V: OFT+QUOTE OR V+O ▸ N COUNT

2 When an animal **bellows**, it makes a loud, deep sound. EG *The cow charged across the farmyard with the bull bellowing after it.* V

3 A **bellows** is a device used for blowing air into a fire in order to make it burn more fiercely. The plural form is also **bellows**. EG *The blast can be provided by a bellows worked by hand, or by an electric air pump.* N COUNT

belly /bɛli¹/, **bellies. 1** Your **belly** is your stomach. EG *Their bellies were now filled with food... John was rather jolly, with a big belly and a pipe.* N COUNT Informal British

2 The **belly** of an animal is the lower part of its body. EG *...lions creeping on their bellies... ...fish with grey backs and white bellies.* N COUNT

belong /bi¹lɒŋ/, **belongs, belonging, belonged. 1** If something **belongs** to you, you own it or it is V+*to*

yours. EG *The land belongs to a big family... ...a myth belonging to some tribe in Western Australia.*
2 If someone or something **belongs** to a particular group, they are a member of that group. EG *She belongs to the Labour Party... ...bats belonging to eight different species.* V+*to*
3 If a person or thing **belongs** in a particular place, that is the place where they should be. EG *I don't belong here, mother, I am not like you... The plates don't belong in that cupboard.* V:OFT+A

belongings /bi[1]lɒŋɪŋz/. Your **belongings** are the things that you own and that you have with you or in your house. EG *She was tidying up her belongings... We packed the few belongings we had and left.* N PLURAL

beloved /bi[1]lʌvɪ[2]d/; also pronounced /bi[1]lʌvd/ when used after a noun or after the verb 'be'. A **beloved** person, thing, or place is one that you feel great affection for. EG *He withdrew to his beloved Kent... ...Marilyn Monroe, beloved of men in their millions.* ADJ CLASSIF: ATTRIB OR ADJ PRED+*of*

below /bi[1]ləʊ/. **1** If something is **below** something else, it is in a lower position. EG *The sun had just sunk below the horizon... ...a mile below the surface of the ocean... Their office is on the floor below... The fish attacked from below.* PREP OR ADV ● **Below ground** or **below the ground** means in the ground. EG *They spend their lives below ground.* ● PHRASE
2 You use **below** in a piece of writing to refer to something that is mentioned further on in it. EG *Get legal advice on how to do this (see below).* ADV
3 If something is **below** a particular amount, rate, or level, it is less than that amount, rate, or level. EG *The temperature was below freezing... Their reading ability is below average.* PREP
4 If someone is **below** you in an organization, they are lower in rank. EG *Below him are 14 Regional Health Authorities... Problems occur at the departmental level or below.* PREP OR ADV

belt /belt/, **belts, belting, belted. 1** A **belt** is a strip of leather or cloth that you fasten round your waist. EG *From his belt there dangled a large ring of keys.* ● See also **safety belt, seat-belt.** N COUNT
2 A **belt** is also a circular strip of rubber that is used in machines to drive moving parts or to move objects along. EG *A belt snapped in the vacuum cleaner.* ● See also **conveyor belt.** N COUNT
3 A **belt** of land or sea is a long, narrow area of it that has some special feature. EG *...the cotton belt of the USA.* N COUNT+SUPP
4 If someone **belts** you, they hit you very hard. EG *Her Dad belted her when she got home late.* V+O Informal
5 If you **belt** somewhere, you move or travel there very fast. EG *I came belting out of the woods.* V+A Informal
6 Belt is used in these phrases. **6.1** A comment or remark that is **below the belt** is cruel and unfair. **6.2** If you have something **under** your **belt**, you have already achieved it or done it. EG *You already had one university degree under your belt.* **6.3** When you **tighten** your **belt**, you have less money to spend than you used to. EG *We've all got to tighten our belts, you know.* PHRASES Informal

bemoan /bi[1]məʊn/, **bemoans, bemoaning, bemoaned.** If you **bemoan** something, you express sorrow or dissatisfaction about it. EG *The farmer bemoaned his loss... They were weeping and bemoaning their fate.* V+O Formal

bemused /bi[1]mjuːzd/. If you are **bemused**, you are puzzled or confused. ADJ QUALIT

bench /bentʃ/, **benches. 1** A **bench** is **1.1** a long seat of wood or metal that two or more people can sit on. EG *Rudolf sat on the bench and waited... ...a park bench.* **1.2** a long, narrow table in a factory or laboratory. EG *...the carpenter's bench... ...a work bench.* N COUNT
2 In Parliament, different groups sit on different **benches**. For example, the government sits on the government **benches**. N PLURAL

bend /bend/, **bends, bending, bent** /bent/. **1** When someone **bends**, they move the top part of their body towards the ground. EG *He bent down and undid his shoelaces... He was bending over the basin.* V:USU+A ◊ **bent.** EG *Dan is bent over the fireplace.* ◊ ADJ PRED
2 When you **bend** a part of your body such as your arm or leg, you change its position so that it is no longer straight. ◊ **bent.** EG *Keep your knees bent.* V-ERG ◊ ADJ CLASSIF
3 When you **bend** something that is flat or straight, you use force to make it curved or angular. EG *...pliers for bending wire.* V-ERG ◊ **bent.** EG *...two bent pipes.* ◊ ADJ CLASSIF
4 A **bend** in a road, river, or pipe is a curved part of it. EG *When I reached the first bend, I ran.* N COUNT
5 If you say that someone **is bending over backwards** to be helpful or kind, you mean that they are trying very hard to be helpful or kind. EG *We bend over backwards to keep young people out of prison.* PHRASE
6 If you say that someone or something is driving you **round the bend**, you mean that they are annoying you or upsetting you very much. PHRASE Informal
7 If you **bend the rules**, you interpret them in a way that allows you to do something that they really forbid. PHRASE
8 to **bend double** or to **be bent double**: see **double.** ● See also **bent.**

beneath /bi[1]niːθ/. **1** Something that is **beneath** another thing is under the other thing. EG *She concealed the bottle beneath her mattress... ...the soft ground beneath his feet... A trickle of sweat ran down his spine, beneath the loose cotton shirt.* PREP
2 If you talk about what is **beneath** the surface of something, you are talking about the aspects of it which are hidden or not obvious. EG *Beneath the veneer of civilization, he was a very vulgar man.* PREP

benefactor /benɪ[2]fæktə/, **benefactors.** A **benefactor** is a person who helps someone by giving them money. EG *He went to Long Beach to thank his benefactor.* N COUNT: OFT+POSS

beneficial /benɪ[1]fɪʃə[0]l/. Something that is **beneficial** helps people or improves their lives. EG *...the beneficial effects of exercise... Such a system will be beneficial to society.* ADJ QUALIT: OFT+*to*

beneficiary /benɪ[1]fɪʃə[0]ri[1]/, **beneficiaries. 1** A **beneficiary** of something is someone who is helped by it. EG *Who are the main beneficiaries of the changes?* N COUNT: OFT+POSS
2 The **beneficiaries** of a will legally receive money or property from someone when they die. EG *He wrote a will naming his children as beneficiaries.* N COUNT

benefit /benɪ[1]fɪt/, **benefits, benefiting, benefited. 1** A **benefit** is something that helps you or improves your life. EG *The industrial age has brought innumerable benefits... ...the benefits of modern technology.* N COUNT
2 If something is to your **benefit** or is of **benefit** to you, it helps you or improves your life. EG *This will be of benefit to the country as a whole.* N UNCOUNT
3 If you do something **for the benefit of** someone, you do it specially for them. EG *He smiled for the benefit of the reporters... They explained, for the benefit of the members, what they had done.* PHRASE
4 If something **benefits** you or if you **benefit** from it, it helps you or improves your life. EG *...a medical service which will benefit rich and poor... The firm benefited from his ingenuity.* V-ERG: IF V, THEN +*from/by*
5 If you have the **benefit** of something, it gives you an advantage. EG *I had the benefit of a good education.* N SING: *the*+N+*of*
6 If you **give** someone **the benefit of the doubt**, you accept what they say as true, because you cannot prove that it is not true. PHRASE
7 Benefit is money that is given by the govern- N UNCOUNT

What is the difference between a bend and a bent?

ment to people who are poor, ill, or unemployed. EG *You are entitled to child benefit... He is unemployed and receiving benefit.*

benevolent /bɪˈnɛvələnt/. Someone who is **benevolent** is kind, helpful, and tolerant. EG *My aunt and uncle were looking benevolent and prepared to forgive me... We live under a benevolent government.* ◇ **benevolently.** EG *He smiled benevolently.* ◇ **benevolence** /bɪˈnɛvələns/. EG *...the benevolence of the Vicar's smile.*
ADJ QUALIT / ◇ ADV / ◇ N UNCOUNT

benign /bɪˈnaɪn/. **1** Someone who is **benign** is kind, gentle, and harmless. EG *They are among the most benign people on earth... His face was calm and benign.* ◇ **benignly.** EG *The vicar smiled benignly.*
ADJ QUALIT / ◇ ADV

2 A **benign** disease or substance will not cause death or serious harm. EG *...women with benign breast disease.*
ADJ CLASSIF Technical

bent /bɛnt/. **1 Bent** is the past participle and past tense of **bend**.

2 If an object is **bent**, it is damaged and no longer has its correct shape. EG *...bent saucepans.*
ADJ QUALIT

3 If a person is **bent**, their body has become curved because of old age or disease. EG *He was bent with arthritis... ...old Mr Halliday, bent and white-haired.*
ADJ QUALIT

4 If you are **bent** on doing something, you are determined to do it. EG *They are bent on improving existing weapon systems.*
ADJ PRED +on/upon

5 If you have a **bent** for something, you have a natural interest in it or a natural ability to do it. EG *...a boy with a mechanical bent.*
N SING+SUPP

bequeath /bɪˈkwiːð/, **bequeaths, bequeathing, bequeathed. 1** If you **bequeath** your money or property to someone, you legally state that they should have it when you die. EG *He bequeathed his collection to the nation... ...bequeathing me an annual income of a thousand pounds.*
V+O+*to* OR V+O+O Formal

2 If you **bequeath** an idea or system, you leave it for other people to use or develop. EG *...the country your generation has bequeathed us... ...the economy bequeathed to the new President.*
V+O+O OR V+O+*to* Literary

bequest /bɪˈkwɛst/, **bequests.** A **bequest** is money or property which you legally leave to someone when you die. EG *Except for a few small bequests to relatives, he left all his property to charity.*
N COUNT Formal

bereaved /bɪˈriːvd/. A **bereaved** person is one who had a relative or close friend who has recently died. EG *His personal effects would be returned to the bereaved family.*
ADJ CLASSIF : USU ATTRIB Formal

bereavement /bɪˈriːvməˀnt/, **bereavements. Bereavement** is the experience you have or the state you are in when a relative or close friend dies. EG *...bereavement in old age... ...planning for the future after a bereavement.*
N UNCOUNT OR N COUNT Formal

bereft /bɪrɛft/. If a person or thing is **bereft** of something, they no longer have it. EG *They were bereft of speech... Her cheeks were bereft of colour... ...crumbling slums bereft of basic amenities.*
ADJ PRED+*of* Literary

beret /bɛreɪ/, **berets.** A **beret** is a circular, flat hat that is made of soft material and has no brim.
N COUNT

berry /bɛriˡ/, **berries.** A **berry** is a small, round fruit that grows on a bush or a tree. You can eat some berries.
N COUNT : USU PLURAL

berserk /bəzɜːk, -sɜːk/. If someone goes **berserk**, they lose control of themselves and become very violent. EG *One night she went berserk and wrecked her room.*
ADJ PRED

berth /bɜːθ/, **berths. 1** If you **give** someone or something **a wide berth**, you avoid them because they are unpleasant or dangerous. EG *One gives a wide berth to drunkards lying on the pavement.*
PHRASE

2 A **berth** is **2.1** a space in a harbour where a ship stays for a period of time. **2.2** a bed in a boat, train, or caravan. EG *...berths on the boat from Harwich... ...a twelve berth caravan.*
N COUNT

beseech /bɪˈsiːtʃ/, **beseeches, beseeching, besought** /bɪˈsɔːt/. The form **beseeched** is sometimes used for the past tense and past participle.
V+O+*to*-INF OR QUOTE Literary

If you **beseech** someone to do something, you ask them very insistently and desperately. EG *I beseech you to tell me... 'Cal, Cal!' his sister besought him, 'Remember your promise!'* ◇ **beseeching.** EG *She was staring at me with great beseeching eyes... Mary put a beseeching hand on my arm.* ◇ **beseechingly.** EG *Larsen looked beseechingly at Rudolph.*
◇ ADJ CLASSIF : USU ATTRIB / ◇ ADV

beset /bɪˈsɛt/, **besets, besetting.** The form **beset** is used in the present tense and is also the past tense and past participle.
V+O : USU PASS +by/with Formal

If someone or something **is beset** by problems or fears, they have many problems or fears which affect them severely. EG *She had been beset by doubts... The policy is beset with problems... ...the difficulties that beset the Africans.*

beside /bɪˈsaɪd/. **1** Something that is **beside** something else is at the side of it or next to it. EG *I sat down beside my wife... There right beside the road is a large grey house.*
PREP

2 If you are **beside yourself** with anger or excitement, you are extremely angry or excited.
PHRASE

3 See also paragraph 1 of **besides**. • **beside the point**: see **point**.

besides /bɪˈsaɪdz/. The form **beside** can be used for paragraph 1.

1 Besides something or **beside** it means in addition to it. EG *What languages do you know besides English?... He needed so much else besides.*
PREP OR ADV

2 You can use **besides** when you are making an additional point or giving an additional reason for something. EG *Would these figures prove anything? And besides, who keeps such statistics?*
ADV SEN

besiege /bɪˈsiːdʒ/, **besieges, besieging, besieged. 1** If you **are besieged** by people, many people want something from you and continually bother you. EG *I am besieged with visitors from abroad.*
V+O : USU PASS +by/with

2 If soldiers **besiege** a place, they surround it and wait for the people in it to surrender.
V+O : USU PASS

besought /bɪˈsɔːt/ is the past tense and past participle of **beseech.**

best /bɛst/. **1 Best** is **1.1** the superlative of **good**. EG *That was one of the best films I've seen... ...my best friend... I'm doing what is best for you... It's best to be as clear as possible... They told me it was best that I stay in New York... There were hills and trees and, best of all, a lake... I want her to have the very best. Private room. Special nurses. Everything.* **1.2** the superlative of **well**. EG *I think mine would suit her best.*
ADJ QUALIT : SUPERL / ADV : SUPERL

2 Your **best** is the greatest effort or the highest achievement that you are capable of. EG *They are trying their best to discourage them... The way to get the best out of a diesel is to drive it smoothly.*
N SING

3 If you like something **best** or like it the **best**, you prefer it. EG *Which did you like best – the Vivaldi or the Schumann?*
ADV OR ADJ : SUPERL

4 Best is also used in these phrases. **4.1** You use **at best** to indicate that even if you describe something as favourably as possible, it is still not very good. EG *At best the proposal was a lame compromise.* **4.2** If you **make the best of** an unsatisfactory situation, you accept it and try to be cheerful about it. EG *There is nowhere else to go, so make the best of it.* **4.3** If someone does something **as best** they **can**, they try as hard as they can to succeed in doing it. EG *I kept out of trouble as best I could.* **4.4** You can say **'All the best'** when you are saying goodbye to someone, or at the end of a letter.
PHRASE / PHRASE / PHRASE / CONVENTION

5 Best is also used to form the superlative of compound adjectives beginning with 'good' and 'well'. EG *...the best-looking women... ...the best-known author of books for children.*

6 to **do** your **best**: see **do**. • to **know best**: see **know**. • **the best part of** something: see **part**. • to **think the best of** someone: see **think**. • **the best**

of both worlds: see **world**. • See also **second-best**.

bestial /bɛstiəl/. You describe behaviour as **bestial** when it is very unpleasant or disgusting. EG *His habits are bestial... ...bestial violence.* ADJ CLASSIF Literary

bestow /bi'stəʊ/, **bestows, bestowing, bestowed.** If you **bestow** something on someone, you give it to them. EG *The Duke bestowed this property on him... ...the attention bestowed upon her son.* V+O: OFT+*on/upon* Formal

best-seller, best-sellers. You say that a book is a **best-seller** when a large number of copies of it have been sold. EG *It was soon a best-seller in Los Angeles.* N COUNT

bet /bɛt/, **bets, betting.** The form **bet** is used in the present tense and is the past tense and past participle of the verb.

1 If you **bet** on a future event, you make an agreement with someone that if what you say will happen does happen, they will give you a sum of money, and if you are wrong you will give them a sum of money. EG *I told him which horse to bet on... He bet me a hundred pounds that I wouldn't get through.* ◇ **betting.** EG *They spend their money on betting.* V+*on*, V+O: OFT+*on*, OR V+O+O ◇ N UNCOUNT

2 A **bet** is the act of betting on something, or the amount of money that you agree to give. EG *I didn't put a bet on.* N COUNT: OFT+*on*

3 You use **bet** in expressions such as 'I bet', 'I'll bet', and 'my bet is', to say that you are sure that something is true or will happen. EG *I bet nobody's been here before... My bet is he'll be right back.* PHRASE Informal

4 You say **'You bet'** as an emphatic way of saying 'yes' or of emphasizing a statement. EG *'Are you coming?' – 'You bet!'... You bet I'm getting out.* CONVENTION Informal

5 If you tell someone that something is **a good bet** or is their **best bet**, you are suggesting that it is the thing or course of action they should choose. EG *Your best bet is to go to Thomas Cook in the High Street.* PHRASE

betray /bi'treɪ/, **betrays, betraying, betrayed. 1** If you **betray** someone who thinks you support or love them, you do something which harms them, often by helping their enemies or opponents. EG *His best friend betrayed him... Daintry felt betrayed.* V+O

2 If you **betray** something such as a person's trust, you behave badly towards them when they trust you. EG *He would be betraying their trust if he ignored their wishes now.* V+O

3 If you **betray** a secret, you tell it to people who you should not tell it to. EG *The name was strictly private, never to be betrayed to a stranger.* V+O

4 If you **betray** a feeling or quality, you show it without intending to. EG *People learned never to betray their anger.* V+O

betrayal /bi'treɪə⁰l/, **betrayals.** If a person betrays something or someone, you refer to their action as a **betrayal**. EG *...the betrayal of socialist principles... Alex was filled with anger at Ned's betrayal of their secret sign.* N COUNT OR UNCOUNT: OFT+*of*

betrothed /bi'trəʊðd/. If you are **betrothed** to someone, you are engaged to be married to them. ADJ CLASSIF Outdated

better /bɛtə/. **1 Better** is **1.1** the comparative form of **good**. EG *The results were better than expected... I was better at mathematics than other subjects... Milk is much better for you than lemonade... It was better than nothing.* ADJ QUALIT: COMPAR **1.2** the comparative of **well**. EG *Some people can ski better than others... We are better housed than ever before.* ADV: COMPAR

2 If you like one thing **better** than another, you like it more. EG *I love this place better than anywhere else.* ADV: COMPAR

3 If you say that someone **had better** do something, you mean that they ought to do it. EG *I'd better go.* PHRASE

4 If someone **is better off**, they are in a pleasanter situation than before, often because they have more money than they had before. EG *They are much better off than they were two years ago... She will be better off in hospital... I'd be better off dead.* PHRASE

5 If something changes **for the better**, it improves. EG *The weather had changed for the better.* PHRASE

6 If something **gets the better of** you, you are unable to resist it. EG *My curiosity got the better of me.* PHRASE

7 If you are **better** after an illness or injury, you are feeling less ill. EG *Her cold was better.* ADJ PRED: COMPAR

8 You use **better** to form the comparative of compound adjectives beginning with 'good' or 'well.' EG *My husband was better-looking than that... She's much better known in Europe.*

9 to **know better**: see **know**. • **the better part of**: see **part.** • to **think better of it**: see **think**.

between /bi'twiːn/. **1** If something is **between** two things or is **in between** them, it has one of the things on one side of it and the other thing on the other side. EG *The island is midway between Sao Paolo and Porto Alegre... She put the cigarette between her lips and lit it... ...Penn Close, Court Road, and all the little side streets in between.* PREP OR ADV

2 If people or things are moving **between** two places, they are moving regularly from one place to the other and back again. EG *I have spent a lifetime commuting between Britain and the United States.* PREP

3 A relationship, discussion, or difference **between** two people, groups, or things is one that involves them both or relates to them both. EG *...marriages between Dutch men and African women... ...negotiations between Britain and Germany... ...a clash between the two gangs... I asked whether there was much difference between British and European law.* PREP

4 If something stands **between** you and what you want, it prevents you from having it. EG *These men stand between you and the top jobs.* PREP

5 If something is **between** or **in between** two amounts or ages, it is greater or older than the first one and smaller or younger than the second one. EG *...at temperatures between 36 and 39°C... ...a man aged between 20 and 25.* PREP

6 If something happens **between** or **in between** two times or events, it happens after the first time or event and before the second one. EG *The house was built between 1840 and 1852... Between sessions I spent my time with my husband.* PREP

7 If you must choose **between** two things, you must choose one thing or the other one. EG *The choice is between defeat or survival.* PREP

8 If people have a particular amount of something **between** them, this is the total amount that they have. EG *They have both been married before and have five children between them.* PREP

9 When something is divided or shared **between** people, they each have a share of it. EG *The land was divided equally between them.* PREP

beverage /bɛvə⁰rɪdʒ/, **beverages.** A **beverage** is a drink. N COUNT Formal

bevy /bɛvi¹/. A **bevy** of people or things is a group of them. EG *...a bevy of village girls... There are a whole bevy of reasons for this.* N PART: SING

beware /bi'wɛə/. If you tell someone to **beware** of a person or thing, you are warning them that the person or thing may harm them. EG *Beware of the dog!... I would beware of companies which depend on one product only.* V: USU IMPER

bewildered /bi'wɪldəd/. If you are **bewildered**, you are very confused and cannot understand something or decide what you should do. EG *His wife watched him, bewildered... I was bewildered by the volume of noise... ...bewildered and embarrassed tourists.* ADJ CLASSIF

bewildering /bi'wɪldə⁰rɪŋ/. Something that is **bewildering** is very confusing and difficult to understand or to make a decision about. EG *There is a* ADJ QUALIT

How many people do you know who are betrothed?

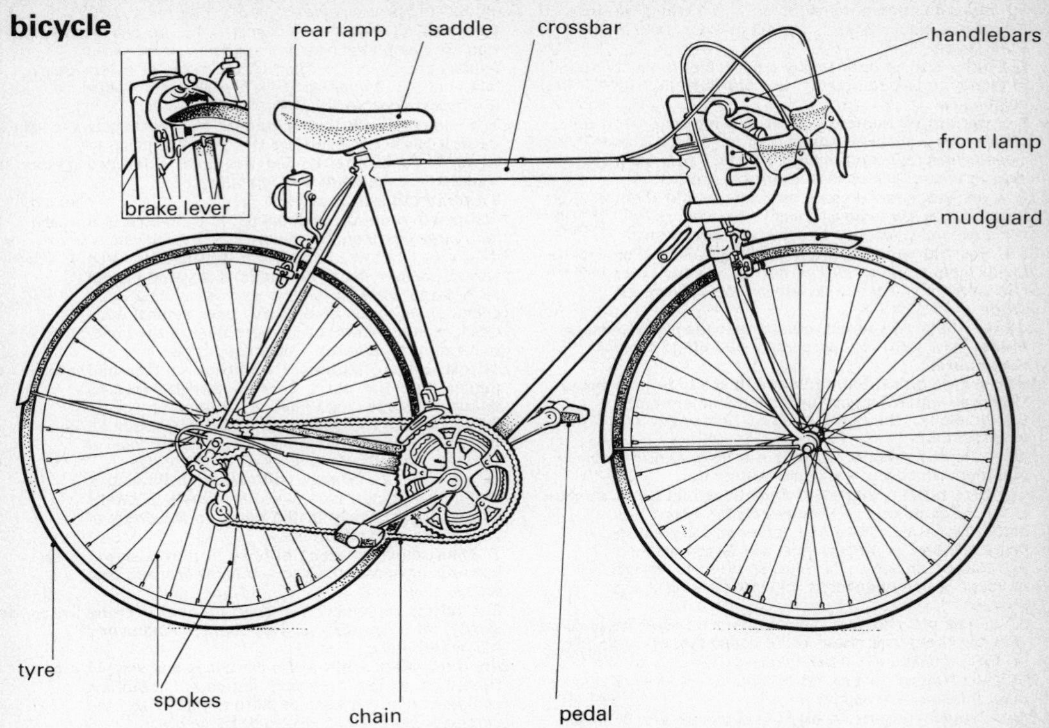

bewildering variety of activities... It was a bewildering and upsetting experience.

bewilderment /bi'wɪldəmə²nt/ is the feeling of being bewildered. EG *'But I just rented it,' Morris protested in bewilderment... To my complete bewilderment, she rang and offered to buy the place.* — N UNCOUNT

bewitch /bi'wɪtʃ/, **bewitches, bewitching, bewitched.** If someone or something **bewitches** you, you find them so attractive that you cannot think about anything else. EG *She had been bewitching the audience with her singing.* — V+O
◊ **bewitching.** EG *...a bewitching smile... ...the bewitching Mrs Paget.* — ◊ ADJ QUALIT

beyond /bi'jɒnd/. **1** If something is **beyond** a place, it is on the other side of it. EG *...a farm beyond Barnham... He indicated the street beyond.* — PREP OR ADV

2 If something extends, continues, or progresses **beyond** a particular thing or point, it extends, continues, or progresses further than that thing or point. EG *My responsibilities go beyond computers... Few children remain in the school beyond the age of 16... She was there for twenty years without progressing beyond her secretarial status.* — PREP

3 If someone or something is **beyond** understanding, control, or help, they have become impossible to understand, control, or help. EG *The situation has changed beyond recognition.* — PREP

4 If you say that something is **beyond** you, you mean that you cannot understand it. EG *How he managed to find us is beyond me.* — PREP

bias /baɪəs/, **biases.** Someone who shows **bias** is unfair in their judgements or decisions, because they allow themselves to be influenced by their own opinions, rather than considering the facts. EG *You're accusing me of bias in my marking... There's an intense bias against women.* — N UNCOUNT OR N COUNT

biased /baɪəst/. **1** Someone who is **biased** shows bias in their judgements or decisions. EG *I am biased in favour of Eisenhower.* — ADJ QUALIT

2 If something is **biased** towards one thing, it is more concerned with it than with other things. EG *The university is biased towards the sciences.* — ADJ PRED : USU +*towards*

bib /bɪb/, **bibs.** A **bib** is a piece of cloth or plastic which is worn by very young children while they are eating, to protect their clothes. — N COUNT

bible /baɪbə⁰l/, **bibles. 1** The **Bible** is the sacred book on which the Jewish and Christian religions are based. EG *...a new translation of the Bible.* — N PROPER : *the*+N
◊ **biblical** /bɪblɪkə⁰l/. EG *...the biblical account of creation.* — ◊ ADJ CLASSIF : ATTRIB

2 A **bible** is a copy of the Bible. EG *He took a bible from his pack and began reading.* — N COUNT

bibliography /bɪbli'ɒgrəfi¹/, **bibliographies.** A **bibliography** is **1** a list of books on a particular subject. EG *...a bibliography of basic works in philosophy.* **2** a list of the books and articles that are referred to in a particular book. — N COUNT

biceps /baɪsɛps/. Your **biceps** are the large muscles at the front of the upper part of your arms. **Biceps** is both the singular and the plural form. — N COUNT

bicker /bɪkə/, **bickers, bickering, bickered.** When people **bicker**, they argue or quarrel about unimportant things. EG *The girls were bickering over a packet of felt pens.* — V : USU+A
◊ **bickering.** EG *...after months of bickering and confusion.* — ◊ N UNCOUNT

bicycle /baɪsɪkə⁰l/, **bicycles.** A **bicycle** is a vehicle with two wheels which you ride by sitting on it and pushing two pedals with your feet. — N COUNT

bid /bɪd/, **bids, bidding; bade** /bæd, beɪd/, **bidden.** The form **bid** is used in the present tense for all the verbs, and is also the past tense and past participle for the verb in paragraph 3. The past tense of the verb in paragraphs 4 and 5 is **bade** and the past participle is **bidden**.

1 A **bid** is an attempt to obtain or do something. EG *He made a bid for power... Brandt failed in a bid to see Reagan.* N COUNT: OFT+*for* OR *to*-INF

2 A **bid** is also an offer to pay a particular amount of money to buy something. EG *...bids for other oil companies.* N COUNT: OFT+*for*

3 If you **bid** for something that is being sold, you offer to pay a particular amount of money for it. EG *...companies that want to bid for Conoco... He bid a quarter of a million pounds for the portrait.* V OR V+O: OFT+*for*

4 If you **bid** someone good morning or **bid** them farewell, you say hello or goodbye to them. EG *I bid you good night, young man... We bade her farewell.* V+O+O OR V+O+*to* Formal

5 If you **bid** someone do something, you ask or invite them to do it. EG *The holy man bade them rise from their knees... As bidden, Mrs Oliver sat down.* V+O+INF Literary

bidder /bɪdə/. If you sell something to the **highest bidder**, you sell it to the person who offers most money for it. PHRASE

bide /baɪd/, **bides, biding, bided.** If you **bide** your **time**, you wait for a good opportunity before doing something. EG *He never showed this anger but bided his time.* PHRASE

bidet /biːdeɪ/, **bidets.** A **bidet** is a low basin in a bathroom which you wash your bottom in. N COUNT

big /bɪg/, **bigger, biggest. 1** Something that is **big** is **1.1** large in size. EG *He was holding a big black umbrella... A big crowd had gathered.* **1.2** great in degree, extent, or importance. EG *I have noticed a big change in Sue... The biggest problem at the moment is unemployment... You're making a big mistake.* ADJ QUALIT

2 You can refer to your older brother or sister as your **big** brother or sister. EG *He hoped that his big brother would take him out again.* ADJ CLASSIF: ATTRIB Informal

biggish /bɪgɪʃ/ means fairly big. EG *He was a biggish fellow... ...a biggish town.* ADJ QUALIT: USU ATTRIB

bigot /bɪgət/, **bigots.** A **bigot** is someone who is bigoted. EG *...the religious bigots who put him on trial.* N COUNT

bigoted /bɪgəti²d/. Someone who is **bigoted** has strong and often unreasonable opinions and will not change them, even when they are proved to be wrong. EG *He was a bigoted, narrow-minded fanatic.* ADJ QUALIT

bigotry /bɪgətri¹/ is the possession or expression of strong and often unreasonable opinions. EG *...campaigns against bigotry and racism.* N UNCOUNT

bigwig /bɪgwɪg/, **bigwigs.** You can refer to an important person as a **bigwig**. EG *The bigwigs in Paris wanted to have a look at it.* N COUNT Informal

bijou /biːʒuː/. Small houses are sometimes described as **bijou** houses in order to make them sound attractive or fashionable. EG *...a bijou residence.* ADJ CLASSIF: ATTRIB

bike /baɪk/, **bikes.** A **bike** is a bicycle or a motorcycle. N COUNT Informal

bikini /bɪkiːni¹/, **bikinis.** A **bikini** is a two-piece swimming costume worn by women. N COUNT

bile /baɪl/ is a liquid produced by your liver which helps you to digest fat. N UNCOUNT

bilingual /baɪlɪŋgwəl/. **1 Bilingual** means involving or using two languages. EG *...bilingual dictionaries... ...bilingual street signs.* ADJ CLASSIF

2 Someone who is **bilingual** can speak two languages. EG *...a bilingual local farmer.* ADJ CLASSIF

bilious /bɪlɪəs/. **1 Bilious** means unpleasant and rather disgusting. EG *...a rather bilious green.* ADJ CLASSIF

2 If you feel **bilious**, you feel sick and have a headache. EG *...bilious attacks.* ADJ CLASSIF

bill /bɪl/, **bills, billing, billed. 1** A **bill** is a written statement of money that you owe for goods or services. EG *...an enormous electricity bill.* N COUNT: USU+SUPP

2 A **bill** is also a piece of paper money. EG *...a dollar bill.* N COUNT American

3 In parliament, a **bill** is a formal statement of a proposed new law that is discussed and then voted on. EG *The Bill was defeated by 238 votes to 145.* N COUNT

4 The **bill** of a show or concert is **4.1** the people who are appearing in it. EG *There were some famous names on the bill.* **4.2** the items of entertainment that it consists of. EG *The Chamber Opera is offering a double bill of Mozart and Haydn.* N SING: *the*+N; N SING

5 If someone **is billed** to appear at a particular show, it has been advertised that they are going to be in it. ◊ **billing.** EG *She was booked for two weeks at the Coliseum with top billing.* V+O: USU PASS ◊ N UNCOUNT

6 A bird's **bill** is its beak. N COUNT

billboard /bɪlbɔːd/, **billboards.** A **billboard** is a very large board on which posters are displayed. N COUNT

billiards /bɪliədz/. The form **billiard** is used before another noun. **Billiards** is a game played on a large table, in which you use a long stick called a cue to hit small heavy balls against each other or into pockets around the sides of the table. EG *...a game of billiards... ...a billiard table.* N UNCOUNT

billion /bɪljən/, **billions. 1** A **billion** is a thousand million. See the entry headed NUMBER. EG *...4.5 billion years ago... ...a £1 billion contract.* NUMBER

2 You can also use **billions** and **billion** to mean an extremely large amount. EG *...billions of tons of ice... They printed the papers off by the billion.* N PART

billow /bɪləʊ/, **billows, billowing, billowed. 1** When something made of cloth **billows**, it swells out and flaps slowly in the wind. EG *Hundreds of flags billowed in the breeze.* V

2 When smoke or cloud **billows**, it moves slowly upwards or across the sky. EG *Clouds of white dust billowed out.* V: USU+A

3 A **billow** of smoke is a large mass of it rising slowly into the air. EG *The flames illuminated billows of smoke.* N COUNT+SUPP

bin /bɪn/, **bins.** A **bin** is **1** a container that you put rubbish in. EG *She threw both letters in the bin.* **2** a container that you keep or store things in. EG *...the computer storage bin.* ● See also **litter bin**. N COUNT

binary /baɪnəᵒri¹/. The **binary** system expresses numbers using only the two digits 0 and 1. It is used especially in computing. ADJ CLASSIF: ATTRIB

bind /baɪnd/, **binds, binding, bound** /baʊnd/. **1** If you **bind** something, you tie a piece of string or rope tightly round it so that it is held firmly. EG *His hands were bound behind the post.* V+O: USU+A

2 If something **binds** people, it unites them. EG *We were bound together by our common grief... ...the ideology which binds members to the group.* V+O: USU+A Literary

3 If a duty or legal order **binds** you to a course of action, it forces you to do it. EG *This oath binds you to secrecy.* V+O: USU+A

4 When a book **is bound**, the pages are joined together and the cover is put on. V+O: USU PASS

5 If you say that something is a **bind**, you mean that it is unpleasant and boring to do. EG *It's a terrible bind to have to cook your own meals.* N SING: *a*+N Informal

6 See also **binding, bound**.

binder /baɪndə/, **binders.** A **binder** is a hard cover with metal rings inside, which is used to hold loose pieces of paper. N COUNT

binding /baɪndɪŋ/, **bindings. 1** If a promise or agreement is **binding**, it must be obeyed or carried out. EG *...a Spanish law that is still binding in California.* ADJ CLASSIF

2 The **binding** of a book is its cover. EG *...books in ugly economy bindings... ...durable leather binding.* N COUNT OR N UNCOUNT

3 **Binding** is a strip of material that you put round the edge of a piece of cloth or an object, in order to strengthen it or decorate it. N UNCOUNT OR N COUNT

binge /bɪndʒ/, **binges.** If you go on a **binge**, you go somewhere and drink a lot of alcohol. EG *Barber had gone on a monumental binge the night before.* N COUNT Informal

What nationality are you by birth?

bingo /bɪŋgəʊ/ is a game in which each player has a card with numbers on. Someone calls out numbers and if you are the first person to have all your numbers called out, you win the game. N UNCOUNT

binoculars

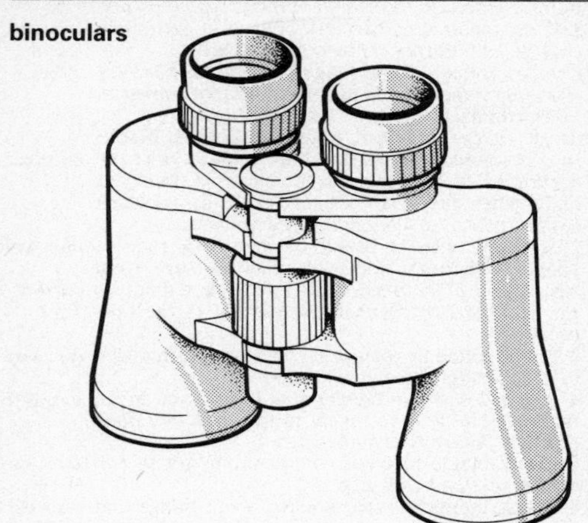

binoculars /bɪ[5]nɒkjə[4]ləz/ consist of two small telescopes joined together side by side, which you look through in order to see things that are a long way away. EG *He studied the house through his binoculars... ...a pair of binoculars.* N PLURAL

biochemistry /baɪə[6]kemɪstri[1]/ is the study of the chemistry of living things. N UNCOUNT

biographer /baɪɒgrəfə/, **biographers.** Someone's **biographer** is a person who writes an account of their life. N COUNT

biographical /baɪə[6]græfɪkə[0]l/. You use **biographical** to describe something which gives information about someone's life. EG *...a brief biographical sketch.* ADJ CLASSIF

biography /baɪɒgrəfi[1]/, **biographies. 1** A **biography** of someone is an account of their life, written by someone else. EG *...a biography of Dylan Thomas... I'm having my biography written.* N COUNT

2 Biography is the branch of literature which deals with accounts of people's lives. N UNCOUNT

biological /baɪəlɒdʒɪkə[0]l/. **1** A **biological** process, system, or product is connected with or produced by natural processes in plants, animals, and other living things. EG *...the effect of heat on biological activity.* ◊ **biologically.** EG *These beings were biologically different from man.* ADJ CLASSIF; ◊ ADV

2 Biological studies and discoveries are connected with research in biology. EG *...recent biological breakthroughs.* ADJ CLASSIF : ATTRIB

3 Biological weapons and **biological** warfare involve the use of organisms which damage living things. EG *...the stockpiling of biological weapons.* ADJ CLASSIF : ATTRIB

biology /baɪɒlədʒɪ/ is the science which is concerned with the study of living things. ◊ **biologist** /baɪɒlədʒɪst/, **biologists.** EG *This has puzzled biologists for a long time.* N UNCOUNT; ◊ N COUNT

birch /bɜːtʃ/, **birches. 1** A **birch** or a **birch tree** is a tall tree with thin branches. EG *...forests of pine and birch.* N COUNT OR N UNCOUNT

2 The **birch** is a punishment in which someone is hit with a wooden cane. EG *Some MPs think we should bring back the birch.* N SING : *the*+N

bird /bɜːd/, **birds. 1** A **bird** is a creature with feathers and wings. Female birds lay eggs. Most birds can fly. N COUNT

2 If you say that **a bird in the hand is worth two in the bush**, you mean that it is better to keep what you already have than to risk losing it by trying to achieve something else. PHRASE

3 If you say that something will **kill two birds with one stone**, you mean that it will have two good results, and not just one. PHRASE

4 Some men refer to young women as **birds**. Many women think that this is insulting. EG *There were some smashing birds there.* N COUNT Informal

birdcage /bɜːdkeɪdʒ/, **birdcages.** A **birdcage** is a cage in which a bird is kept. N COUNT

bird of prey, birds of prey. A **bird of prey** is a bird, such as an eagle or a hawk, that kills and eats other birds and animals. N COUNT

Biro /baɪrəʊ/, **Biros.** A **Biro** is a pen with a small metal ball at its tip which transfers the ink onto the paper. EG *Keep a notebook and a Biro handy.* N COUNT Trademark

birth /bɜːθ/, **births. 1** When a baby is born, you refer to this event as its **birth**. EG *...the birth of her first child... ...a girl deaf from birth... ...a birth certificate.* • When a woman **gives birth**, she produces a baby from her body. EG *Betta gave birth to our third child.* • See also **date of birth**. N UNCOUNT OR N COUNT; • PHRASE

2 If you are French **by birth**, you are French because your parents are French, or because you were born in France. EG *Dr Cort's father is a Russian by birth.* PHRASE

3 The country, town, or village **of** your **birth** is the place where you were born. PHRASE

4 You can refer to the beginning or origin of something as its **birth**. EG *...the birth of the Indonesian Republic... ...the birth of television.* N SING+SUPP

birth control is the same as contraception. N UNCOUNT

birthday /bɜːθdeɪ/, **birthdays.** Your **birthday** is the anniversary of the date on which you were born. EG *Happy birthday!... ...a birthday party.* N COUNT

birthplace /bɜːθpleɪs/, **birthplaces. 1** Your **birthplace** is the place where you were born. N COUNT+POSS

2 The **birthplace** of something is the place where it began or originated. EG *...the birthplace of the Renaissance.* N SING+POSS

birth rate, birth rates. The **birth rate** in a place is the number of babies born there for every 1000 people during a particular period of time. N COUNT

biscuit /bɪskɪt/, **biscuits.** A **biscuit** is a small, flat cake that is crisp and usually sweet. EG *Do you want a biscuit?... Have a chocolate biscuit.* N COUNT British

bisect /baɪsekt/, **bisects, bisecting, bisected.** If something long and thin **bisects** an area or line, it divides the area or line in half. EG *The main north-south road bisects the town.* V+O

bishop /bɪʃəp/, **bishops. 1** A **bishop** is a clergyman of high rank, especially in the Roman Catholic, Anglican, and Orthodox churches. EG *...the Bishop of Exeter.* N COUNT

2 In chess, a **bishop** is a piece that is moved diagonally across the board. N COUNT

bistro /biːstrəʊ/, **bistros.** A **bistro** is a small restaurant or bar. N COUNT

bit /bɪt/, **bits. 1** A **bit** of something is a small amount or piece of it. EG *There'll be a bit of sunshine... I was doing a bit of shopping... ...a little bit of cheese... I really enjoyed your letter, especially the bits about Dr O'Shea.* N PART Informal

2 Quite a bit of something is quite a lot of it. EG *...a rich Irishman who's made quite a bit of money.* PHRASE Informal

3 A **bit** is also an item or thing of a particular kind. EG *They charge for every bit of work... ...a bit of furniture.* N PART Informal

4 A bit means to a small extent or degree. EG *He was a bit deaf... You're a bit late, aren't you?* PHRASE Informal

5 You can also use **a bit** in these ways. **5.1** You can use **a bit of** to make a statement less extreme. For example, the statement 'It's a bit of a nuisance' is less extreme than 'It's a nuisance'. EG *Our room was a bit of a mess... This has all come as a bit of a shock.* **5.2** You use **not a bit** when you want to make a strong negative statement. EG *It was all very clean and tidy, not a bit like his back garden... You haven't changed a bit.* **5.3** If you do something PHRASES Informal; Informal; Informal

for a bit, you do it for a short period of time. EG *Why can't we stay here for a bit?* **5.4** You can say that someone's behaviour is **a bit much** when you are annoyed about it. EG *It's asking a bit much to expect a lift.* — Informal

6 You say that something is **every bit as** good, interesting, or worthwhile as something else to emphasize that it is just as good, interesting, or worthwhile. EG *She wanted to prove to them that she was every bit as clever as they were.* — PHRASE

7 If something is smashed or taken **to bits** or falls **to bits**, it is broken or comes apart so that it is in several pieces. EG *The dog was pulling the Christmas tree to bits.* — PHRASE

8 You can refer to a collection of different things as **bits and pieces**. EG *I saw her gathering up her bits and pieces for the move to the cabin.* — PHRASE

9 If you do something **bit by bit**, you do it in stages. EG *We eased the lid off, bit by bit.* — PHRASE

10 If you **do** your **bit**, you do something that, to a small or limited extent, helps to achieve something. EG *...having done his bit for king and country.* — PHRASE

11 In computing, a **bit** is the smallest unit of information that is held in a computer's memory. It is either 1 or 0. Several bits form a byte. — N COUNT

12 Bit is also the past tense of **bite**.

bitch /bɪtʃ/, **bitches, bitching, bitched. 1** If you call a woman a **bitch**, you mean that she behaves in a very unpleasant way; a rude and offensive use. — N COUNT

2 If someone **bitches**, they complain about something in a nasty way. EG *You haven't done a thing except bitch ever since we got here.* — V, Informal

3 A **bitch** is also a female dog. — N COUNT

bite /baɪt/, **bites, biting, bit** /bɪt/, **bitten** /bɪtə[o]n/.
1 When a person or animal **bites** something, they use their teeth to cut into it or through it. EG *My dog bit me... She bit into her cake... I have a habit of biting my nails.* ▸ used as a noun. EG *Madeleine took a bite. 'It's delicious.'* — V+O OR V+A; ▸ N COUNT

2 When an insect or a snake **bites** you, it pierces your skin and causes an area of your skin to be itchy or painful. EG *...what to do if someone is bitten by a viper.* ▸ used as a noun. EG *My hands are covered with mosquito bites.* — V+O; ▸ N COUNT

3 When an action or policy begins to **bite**, it begins to have a significant or harmful effect. EG *The sanctions are beginning to bite.* — V

4 If you have a **bite** to eat, you have a small meal or a snack. — N SING: *a*+N, Informal

biting /baɪtɪŋ/. **1** A **biting** wind is extremely cold. EG *...a biting east wind... ...a biting cold day.* — ADJ QUALIT

2 Biting speech or writing is sharp and clever in a way that makes people feel uncomfortable. EG *...biting sarcasm... ...a writer with a biting wit.* — ADJ QUALIT

bitten /bɪtə[o]n/ is the past participle of **bite.**

bitter /bɪtə/, **bitterest; bitters. 1** If someone is **bitter**, they feel angry and resentful. EG *He was a jealous, slightly bitter man.* ◇ **bitterly.** EG *'I'm glad somebody's happy,' he said bitterly.* ◇ **bitterness.** EG *He remembers with bitterness how his father was cheated.* — ADJ QUALIT; ◇ ADV; ◇ N UNCOUNT

2 If you have a **bitter** disappointment or experience, you feel angry or unhappy for a long time afterwards. EG *I have had long and bitter experience of dealing with people like that.* ● If you continue doing something difficult or unpleasant **to the bitter end**, you continue doing it until it is completely finished. EG *We have pursued everything to the bitter end.* — ADJ QUALIT: ATTRIB; ● PHRASE

3 In a **bitter** argument, war, or struggle, people argue or fight fiercely and angrily. EG *...a bitter struggle for supremacy.* — ADJ QUALIT

4 A **bitter** wind or **bitter** weather is extremely cold. EG *I had never known such bitter cold.* — ADJ QUALIT

5 Something that tastes **bitter** has a sharp, unpleasant taste. EG *It tasted faintly of bitter almonds.* — ADJ QUALIT

6 Bitter is a kind of British beer with a slightly bitter taste. EG *...two pints of bitter.* — N MASS

bitterly /bɪtəli[1]/. **1 Bitterly** means strongly and intensely. You use it to describe strong emotions such as anger, hatred, or shame. EG *No man could have hated the old order more bitterly... He was bitterly ashamed... She wept bitterly.* — ADV

2 If the weather is **bitterly** cold, it is extremely cold. EG *...a bitterly cold New Year's Day.* — ADV+ADJ

bizarre /bi[1]zɑː/. Something that is **bizarre** is very odd and strange. EG *He had some bizarre conversations with his landlady... ...bizarre gadgets.* — ADJ QUALIT

black /blæk/, **blacker, blackest; blacks, blacking, blacked. 1** Something that is **black** is of the darkest colour that there is, the colour of the sky at night when there is no light at all. EG *...a black leather coat... ...a woman dressed in black.* — ADJ COLOUR

2 Someone who is **black** belongs to a race of people with dark skins, especially a race from Africa. EG *...black musicians.* ▸ used as a noun. EG *He was the first black to be elected to the Congress.* — ADJ CLASSIF; ▸ N COUNT

3 Black coffee or tea has no milk or cream added to it. EG *...cups of strong black coffee.* — ADJ CLASSIF

4 If you describe a situation as **black**, you mean that it is bad and not likely to improve. EG *I don't think the future is as black as that.* — ADJ QUALIT

5 Black magic involves communicating with evil spirits. EG *...the black arts.* — ADJ CLASSIF: ATTRIB

6 Black humour involves jokes about things that are sad or unpleasant. EG *...a black comedy.* — ADJ QUALIT: ATTRIB

7 Someone who is **black and blue** is badly bruised. EG *He used to beat me black and blue.* — PHRASE

8 When a group **blacks** particular goods or people, it refuses to handle the goods or to have dealings with the people. EG *Their members had blacked these goods at the London Docks.* — V+O

black out. If you **black out**, you lose consciousness for a short time. ● See also **blackout**. — PHRASAL VB: V+ADV

black and white. 1 In a **black and white** photograph or film, everything is shown in black, white, and grey. EG *...black-and-white horror movies.* — ADJ COLOUR

2 You say that something is **in black and white** when it has been written or printed, and not just spoken. EG *He was surprised to see his conversation in black and white.* — PHRASE

blackberry /blækbəri[1]/, **blackberries.** A **blackberry** is a small black or dark purple fruit. — N COUNT

blackbird /blækbɜːd/, **blackbirds.** A **blackbird** is a common European bird with black or brown feathers. — N COUNT

blackboard /blækbɔːd/, **blackboards.** A **blackboard** is a dark-coloured board in a classroom, which teachers write on with chalk. — N COUNT

blackcurrant /blækkʌrənt/, **blackcurrants.** A **blackcurrant** is a very small dark purple fruit that grows in bunches. — N COUNT

blacken /blækən/, **blackens, blackening, blackened. 1** To **blacken** something means to make it black or very dark in colour. EG *His face was blackened with charcoal.* — V+O

2 If someone **blackens** your reputation, they make other people believe that you are a bad person. — V+O

black eye, black eyes. If you have a **black eye**, you have a dark-coloured bruise around your eye. — N COUNT

blackish /blækɪʃ/. Something that is **blackish** is very dark in colour. — ADJ COLOUR

blackmail /blækmeɪl/, **blackmails, blackmailing, blackmailed. Blackmail** is the action of threatening to do something unpleasant to someone, for example to reveal a secret about them, unless they give you money or behave in the way you want them to. EG *The statements amounted to blackmail.* ▸ used as a verb. EG *He tried to blackmail me.* ◇ **blackmailer** /blækmeɪlə/, **blackmailers.** EG *...the blackmailer's cruelty to his victim.* — N UNCOUNT; ▸ V+O; ◇ N COUNT

Can a blackbird be a brown bird?

black market, black markets. The **black market** is a system of buying and selling goods which is not legal. EG *He whispered that he could change money on the black market.* N COUNT

blackout /blækaʊt/, **blackouts. 1** A **blackout** is a period of time during a war in which a place is made dark for safety reasons. EG *We couldn't get home before the blackout.* N COUNT

2 If you have a **blackout**, you temporarily lose consciousness. N COUNT

black sheep. If you refer to someone as the **black sheep** of a group, you mean that everyone else in the group is good, but that person is bad. N SING

blacksmith /blæksmɪθ/, **blacksmiths.** A **blacksmith** is someone whose job is making things out of metal, for example horseshoes or farm tools. EG *...the village blacksmith.* N COUNT

bladder /blædə/, **bladders.** Your **bladder** is the part of your body where urine is held until it leaves your body. ● See also **gall bladder**. N COUNT

blade /bleɪd/, **blades. 1** The **blade** of a knife, axe, or saw is the sharp part. N COUNT

2 The **blades** of a propeller are the parts that turn round. N COUNT

3 The **blade** of an oar is the thin, flat part that you put into the water. N COUNT

4 A **blade** of grass is a single piece of grass. N COUNT

5 See also **razor blade**, **shoulder blade**.

blame /bleɪm/, **blames, blaming, blamed. 1** If you **blame** a person or thing for something bad, you think or say that they are responsible for it. EG *I was blamed for the theft... Violence at school is blamed on immigrants.* V+O : OFT+*for* ▸ used as a noun. EG *You haven't said a word of blame.* ▸ N UNCOUNT

2 The **blame** for something bad that has happened is the responsibility for causing it or letting it happen. EG *He had to take the blame for everything.* N UNCOUNT ● If you are **to blame** for something bad that has happened, you are responsible for it. ● PHRASE

3 If you say that you do not **blame** someone for doing something, you mean that it was a reasonable thing to do in the circumstances. EG *I can't really blame him for wanting to make me suffer.* V+O : WITH BROAD NEG

blameless /bleɪmlɪ^{2}s/. Someone who is **blameless** has not done anything wrong. EG *On that score, he was blameless... ...a blameless career.* ADJ QUALIT

blanch /blɑːntʃ/, **blanches, blanching, blanched.** If you **blanch**, you suddenly become very pale. EG *Eddie blanched and clutched my arm.* V

bland /blænd/, **blander, blandest. 1** Someone who is **bland** is calm, unexcited, and polite. EG *Manfred smiled his bland smile.* ADJ QUALIT ◊ **blandly.** EG *Mr Jones blandly dismissed their arguments.* ◊ ADV

2 Food that is **bland** has very little flavour. EG *...bland cheeses... The food was bland and unattractive.* ADJ QUALIT

3 You can describe something such as music or architecture as **bland** when it is dull and uninteresting. EG *...the bland facades of Belgravia.* ADJ QUALIT

blandishments /blændɪʃmə^{2}nts/ are pleasant things that you say to someone in order to persuade them to do something. EG *He remained impervious to all Nell's blandishments.* N PLURAL Formal

blank /blæŋk/, **blanker, blankest. 1** Something that is **blank** has nothing on it. EG *...a blank sheet of paper... ...a blank wall.* ● See also **point-blank**. ADJ QUALIT

2 If you look **blank**, your face shows no feeling, understanding, or interest. EG *Her face went blank.* ADJ QUALIT ◊ **blankly.** EG *I sat quietly, staring blankly ahead.* ◊ ADV

3 If your mind or memory is a **blank**, you cannot think of anything or remember anything. N SING : a+N

4 If you **draw a blank** when you are looking for someone or something, you fail to find them. PHRASE Informal

blanket /blæŋkɪ^{2}t/, **blankets, blanketing, blanketed. 1** A **blanket** is a large square or rectangular piece of thick cloth, especially one which you put on a bed to keep you warm. ● See also **wet blanket**. N COUNT

2 If something such as snow **blankets** an area, it covers it. EG *The streets were blanketed in a thin mist... Snow blanketed the plains.* V+O ▸ used as a noun. EG *...a blanket of cloud.* ▸ N PART

3 You use **blanket** to describe something which affects or refers to every person or thing in a group, without any exceptions. EG *...our blanket acceptance of everything they say.* ADJ CLASSIF : ATTRIB

blare /blɛə/, **blares, blaring, blared.** When something such as a siren or radio **blares**, it makes a loud, unpleasant noise. EG *The TV set was blaring in the background.* V ▸ used as a noun. EG *...the blare of conversation.* ▸ N SING : OFT+*of*

blare out. When a radio or record player **blares out** loud noise or when loud noise **blares out** of it, it produces this noise. EG *A radio was blaring out the news... Indian music had been blaring out all evening.* PHRASAL VB : V-ERG+ADV

blasé /blɑːzeɪ/. If you are **blasé** about something which other people find exciting, you show no excitement in it, because you have experienced it before. EG *You sound very blasé about it... He watched everything with a blasé air.* ADJ QUALIT

blaspheme /blæsfiːm/, **blasphemes, blaspheming, blasphemed.** If someone **blasphemes**, they say rude or disrespectful things about God, or they use God's name as a swear word. EG *He no longer felt afraid of blaspheming.* V OR V+QUOTE

blasphemous /blæsfə^{1}məs/. If someone says or does something that shows disrespect for God, you can say that they are being **blasphemous** or that what they are saying or doing is **blasphemous**. EG *She was foul-mouthed and blasphemous... ...a blasphemous poem.* ADJ QUALIT

blasphemy /blæsfə^{1}mi^1/, **blasphemies.** If someone says or does something that shows disrespect for God, you can say that what they are saying or doing is **blasphemy**. EG *Any attempt to violate that image is blasphemy.* N UNCOUNT OR N COUNT

blast /blɑːst/, **blasts, blasting, blasted. 1** A **blast** is a big explosion, especially one caused by a bomb. EG *Nobody had been hurt in the blast.* N COUNT

2 If you **blast** a hole in something, you make a hole in it with an explosion. EG *Tunnels have been blasted through bedrock beneath the city.* V+O

3 A **blast** is also **3.1** a sudden strong rush of air or wind. EG *...icy blasts.* **3.2** a short loud sound made by a whistle or a wind instrument. EG *Ralph blew a series of short blasts.* N COUNT : USU+SUPP

4 If a machine is on **at full blast**, it is producing as much sound or heat as it is able to. EG *She insists on having the radio on at full blast.* PHRASE

5 Blast is a mild swear word that people use when they are irritated or annoyed about something. EXCLAM

blast off. When a space rocket **blasts off**, it leaves the ground at the start of its journey. ● See also **blast-off**. PHRASAL VB : V+ADV

blasted /blɑːstɪ^{2}d/. You can use **blasted** to indicate that you are annoyed or irritated with someone or something. EG *...that blasted bank manager.* ADJ CLASSIF : ATTRIB

blast-off is the moment when a rocket or space shuttle leaves the ground and rises into the air. N UNCOUNT

blatant /bleɪtə^{0}nt/ is used to describe something bad which is very obvious and not concealed in any way. EG *...blatant discrimination... I wasn't quite as blatant as that.* ADJ QUALIT ◊ **blatantly.** EG *They blatantly ignored the truce agreement.* ◊ ADV

blaze /bleɪz/, **blazes, blazing, blazed. 1** When a fire **blazes**, it burns strongly and brightly. V

2 A **blaze** is a large fire in which things are damaged. EG *You never saw such a blaze.* N COUNT

3 If something **blazes** with light or colour, it is extremely bright. EG *The flower beds blazed with colour.* V : OFT+*with* ▸ used as a noun. EG *...a blaze of sunlight... ...the blaze of electric lights.* ▸ N COUNT +SUPP

4 If your eyes **are blazing**, they look very bright, because you are angry. EG *She turned and faced him, her eyes blazing.* V Literary

5 A **blaze** of publicity or attention is a great amount of it. EG *The School opened in a blaze of* N SING+*of*

publicity... She eventually retired in a blaze of glory.

blazer /bleɪzə/, **blazers.** N COUNT A **blazer** is a kind of jacket, especially one worn by schoolchildren or members of a sports team.

blazing /bleɪzɪŋ/. **1** ADJ CLASSIF: ATTRIB You use **blazing** to describe the weather or a place when it is very hot and sunny. EG *...the blazing beach... ...the blazing heat of the plain.* ● PHRASE **Blazing hot** means very hot indeed. EG *Already the square was blazing hot.*

2 ADJ CLASSIF: ATTRIB When people have a **blazing** row, they quarrel in a noisy and excited way. EG *She had a blazing row with her boss.*

bleach /bliːtʃ/, **bleaches, bleaching, bleached. 1** V-ERG To **bleach** material or hair means to make it white or pale in colour, either with a chemical or by leaving it in the sunlight. EG *He bleaches his hair... ...a pair of bleached jeans... I left the cloth in the sun to bleach.*

2 N UNCOUNT **Bleach** is a chemical that is used to make cloth white, or to clean things thoroughly and kill germs. EG *...a strong household bleach.*

bleak /bliːk/, **bleaker, bleakest. 1** ADJ QUALIT If a situation is **bleak**, it is bad, and seems unlikely to improve. EG *The future looked bleak.* ◊ N UNCOUNT ◊ **bleakness.** EG *...the bleakness of the post war years.*

2 ADJ QUALIT If a place is **bleak**, it looks cold, bare, and unattractive. EG *...the bleak coastline.*

3 ADJ QUALIT When the weather is **bleak**, it is cold, dull, and unpleasant. EG *...the bleak winters.*

4 ADJ QUALIT If someone looks or sounds **bleak**, they seem depressed, hopeless, or unfriendly. EG *...his bleak features.* ◊ ADV ◊ **bleakly.** EG *He stared bleakly ahead... 'What,' he asked bleakly, 'are these?'*

bleary /blɪəri¹/, **blearier, bleariest.** ADJ QUALIT If your eyes are **bleary**, they are red and watery, usually because you are tired. EG *We watched with bleary eyes.* ◊ ADV ◊ **blearily.** EG *He looked up blearily at Tom.*

bleat /bliːt/, **bleats, bleating, bleated. 1** V When a sheep or goat **bleats**, it makes the sound that sheep and goats usually make. ▸ N COUNT ▸ used as a noun. EG *...the bleat of a goat.*

2 V OR V+QUOTE When people **bleat**, they speak in a weak, high, complaining voice. EG *'Now?' Dixon bleated.*

bled /blɛd/ is the past tense and past participle of **bleed.**

bleed /bliːd/, **bleeds, bleeding, bled.** V When you **bleed**, you lose blood from your body as a result of injury or illness. EG *His feet had begun to bleed... He was bleeding heavily.* ◊ N UNCOUNT ◊ **bleeding.** EG *Has the bleeding stopped?* ● See also **nosebleed.**

blemish /blɛmɪʃ/, **blemishes, blemishing, blemished. 1** N COUNT A **blemish** is a mark that spoils the appearance of something. EG *There wasn't a blemish on his body.*

2 V+O If something **blemishes** your reputation, it spoils it. EG *I shall never teach again. My good character is blemished.*

blend /blɛnd/, **blends, blending, blended.**

1 V+O OR V+O+*with*: RECIP When you **blend** substances together, you mix them together so that they become one substance. EG *Blend the cornflour with a little cold water.* ▸ N COUNT ▸ used as a noun. EG *...a blend of different oils.*

2 N COUNT+SUPP If someone or something shows a **blend** of qualities, these qualities are combined together so that they produce a new effect. EG *...the company's blend of modern and classical dance.*

3 V OR V+*with*: RECIP When colours or sounds **blend**, they come together or are combined in a pleasing way. EG *...their voices blending marvellously as they sing in harmony.*

blend into. PHRASAL VB: V+ADV OR V+PREP If something **blends into** the background or **blends in**, it is so similar to the background in appearance or sound that it is difficult to see or hear it separately. EG *Tree snakes blend well into foliage.*

blender /blɛndə/, **blenders.** N COUNT A **blender** is a machine used in the kitchen for mixing liquids and soft foods together at high speed.

bless /blɛs/, **blesses, blessing, blessed, blest. Blessed** and **blest** are both used as the past tense and past participle.

1 V+O When a priest **blesses** people or things, he asks for God's favour and protection for them. EG *...bringing baskets of food to the church to be blessed.*

2 PHRASE If someone is **blessed with** a particular good quality or skill, they have it. EG *She is blessed with immense talent and boundless energy.*

3 CONVENTION When people say **God bless** or **bless you** to someone, they are expressing their affection, thanks, or good wishes. EG *Bless you, it's terribly good of you to come.*

4 CONVENTION You can say **bless you** to someone who has just sneezed.

blessed /blɛsɪ²d, blɛst/. ADJ CLASSIF: ATTRIB You use **blessed** to describe something that you think is wonderful, and that you are thankful for or relieved about. EG *...blessed freedom.* ◊ SUBMOD ◊ **blessedly.** EG *...the blessedly cool oasis of the airport.*

blessing /blɛsɪŋ/, **blessings. 1** N COUNT A **blessing** is something good that you are thankful for. EG *Health is a blessing that money cannot buy.*

2 N COUNT+POSS If something is done with someone's **blessing**, they approve of it and support it. EG *She did it with the full blessing of her parents.*

3 PHRASE If you say that something was **a blessing in disguise**, you mean that it caused problems and difficulties at first but later you realized that it was the best thing that could have happened.

4 PHRASE If you tell someone to **count** their **blessings**, you are saying that they should think about how lucky they are instead of complaining.

5 PHRASE If you say that a situation is a **mixed blessing**, you mean that it has disadvantages as well as advantages.

blew /bluː/ is the past tense of **blow.**

blight /blaɪt/, **blights, blighting, blighted.** N COUNT: USU SING You can refer to something as a **blight** when it causes great difficulties, and damages or spoils other things. EG *We think of pollution as a modern blight, but it is not.* ▸ V+O: USU PASS ▸ used as a verb. EG *Her career has been blighted by clashes with the authorities.*

blind /blaɪnd/, **blinds, blinding, blinded. 1** ADJ CLASSIF Someone who is **blind** is unable to see because their eyes are damaged. ◊ N UNCOUNT ◊ **blindness.** EG *Eye damage can result in temporary or permanent blindness.* ● See also **colour blind.**

2 N PLURAL: *the*+N You can refer to people who are blind as the **blind.** EG *...the help that's given to the blind.*

3 V+O If something **blinds** you, you become unable to see, either for a short time or permanently. EG *My eyes were momentarily blinded by flash bulbs.*

4 ADJ PRED+*to* If you are **blind** to a fact or situation, you take no notice of it or are unaware of it. EG *He was blind to everything except his immediate needs.*

5 V+O+*to* If something **blinds** you to a fact or situation, it prevents you from realizing that it exists. EG *We have to beware that missionary zeal doesn't blind us to the realities here.*

6 ADJ CLASSIF: ATTRIB You describe someone's beliefs or actions as **blind** when they take no notice of the facts or behave in an unreasonable way. EG *...her blind faith in the wisdom of her Church... ...their blind pursuit of their plans... She had driven him into a blind rage.*

7 PHRASE If you **turn a blind eye** to something that someone is doing, you pretend not to notice it. EG *He had often turned a blind eye to Barber's drinking sessions.*

8 ADJ CLASSIF A **blind** corner is one that you cannot see round because something is blocking your view.

9 PHRASE If you say that someone **is not taking a blind**

What could you make if you used a blender?

bit of notice, you are emphasizing that they are taking no notice at all. Informal

10 A **blind** is a roll of cloth or paper which you can pull down over a window in order to keep out the light. • See also **Venetian blind**. N COUNT

11 See also **blinding**, **blindly**.

blind alley, blind alleys. If you go up a **blind alley** when you are trying to achieve something, you do something which fails to help you to achieve it. N COUNT

blind date, blind dates. A **blind date** is an arrangement made for you to spend an evening with someone of the opposite sex who you have never met before. EG *We met on a blind date.* N COUNT

blindfold /blaɪndfəʊld/, **blindfolds, blindfolding, blindfolded. 1** A **blindfold** is a strip of cloth that is tied over someone's eyes so that they cannot see. EG *They pulled off his blindfold.* N COUNT

2 If you **blindfold** someone, you tie a blindfold over their eyes. V+O ◊ **blindfolded.** EG *He was shoved down into a canoe, still blindfolded.* ◊ ADJ CLASSIF

blinding /blaɪndɪŋ/. **1** A **blinding** light is extremely bright. EG *There came a blinding flash.* ADJ CLASSIF

2 You use **blinding** to emphasize that something is very obvious. EG *...the blinding obviousness of the advantage.* ADJ CLASSIF: ATTRIB ◊ **blindingly.** EG *Isn't it blindingly obvious?* ◊ SUBMOD

blindly /blaɪndli¹/. If you do something **blindly**, **1** you do it when you are unable to see properly. EG *He ran blindly across the clearing.* **2** you do it without having much information, or without thinking much about it. EG *With the information we have now, we can only speculate blindly.* ADV

blind spot, blind spots. 1 If you have a **blind spot** about something, you are unable to understand it. EG *Ford always had a terrible blind spot about these things.* N COUNT

2 A **blind spot** is a part of something that you cannot see properly, for example a part of the road when you are driving a car. N COUNT

blink /blɪŋk/, **blinks, blinking, blinked.**

1 When you **blink** or when you **blink** your eyes, you shut your eyes and very quickly open them again. EG *They looked at him without blinking... The girl blinked her eyes several times.* V OR V-ERG ▸ used as a noun. EG *It was his guilty blink that gave him away.* ▸ N COUNT

2 When a light **blinks**, it flashes on and off. EG *An amber light blinked down through the clouds.* V ▸ used as a noun. EG *There was a blink of bright light beyond the forest.* ▸ N COUNT

3 If a machine goes **on the blink**, it stops working properly. EG *The Hoover is on the blink again.* PHRASE Informal

blinkered /blɪŋkəd/. A **blinkered** view, attitude, or approach considers only a narrow point of view and does not take into account other people's opinions. EG *...blinkered self-interest.* ADJ CLASSIF British

blinkers /blɪŋkəz/. **1 Blinkers** are two pieces of leather which are placed at the side of a horse's eyes so that it can only see straight ahead. N PLURAL British

2 If you describe someone as wearing **blinkers**, you mean that they are considering only a narrow point of view and are not taking into account other people's opinions. N PLURAL British

bliss /blɪs/ is a state of complete happiness, or a time or situation in which you are very happy. EG *For a couple of months, weekends were bliss.* N UNCOUNT

blissful /blɪsful/. **1** A **blissful** situation or period of time is one in which you are extremely happy. EG *They sat there together in blissful silence... ...those blissful afternoons on the beach.* ADJ QUALIT ◊ **blissfully.** EG *His eyes shut blissfully and he smiled.* ◊ ADV

2 If someone is in **blissful** ignorance of something unpleasant or serious, they are totally unaware of it. ADJ CLASSIF: ATTRIB ◊ **blissfully.** EG *Most people remain blissfully unaware of the problem.* ◊ ADV+ADJ

blister /blɪstə/, **blisters, blistering, blistered. 1** A **blister** is a painful swelling containing clear liquid on the surface of your skin. N COUNT

2 When your skin **blisters** or **is blistered**, blisters appear on it as a result of burning or rubbing. EG *My feet were blistered and aching.* V-ERG

3 When paint or rubber **blisters**, small bumps appear on its surface. V-ERG

blistering /blɪstəʳrɪŋ/. **1** When the weather or the sun is **blistering**, it is extremely hot. EG *...the blistering days of midsummer.* ADJ QUALIT

2 A **blistering** remark or reply expresses great anger or sarcasm. EG *He wrote a blistering reply.* ADJ CLASSIF

blithe /blaɪð/. **1** You use **blithe** to indicate that something is done casually, without serious or careful thought. EG *I made a blithe comment about the fine weather.* ADJ QUALIT ◊ **blithely.** EG *...the blessing of good health which we blithely take for granted.* ◊ ADV

2 Someone who is **blithe** is carefree and cheerful. EG *I was feeling unusually blithe that day.* ADJ QUALIT Outdated

blizzard /blɪzəd/, **blizzards.** A **blizzard** is a very bad snowstorm with strong winds. N COUNT

bloated /bləʊtɪ²d/. **1** Something that is **bloated** is much larger than normal because it has a lot of liquid or gas inside it. EG *...bloated corpses.* ADJ QUALIT

2 If you feel **bloated** after eating a large meal, you feel very full and uncomfortable. ADJ QUALIT Informal

blob /blɒb/, **blobs. 1** A **blob** of thick or sticky liquid is a small amount of it. EG *...a blob of melted wax... ...the blob of blood on her wrist.* N PART

2 You describe something that you cannot see very clearly, for example because it is in the distance, as a **blob**. EG *He saw a white blob crossing the street... You see a blob of grey in the distance.* N COUNT

bloc /blɒk/, **blocs. 1** A **bloc** is a group of countries with similar political aims and interests acting together. EG *...an Eastern bloc country.* N COUNT+SUPP

2 See also **en bloc**.

block /blɒk/, **blocks, blocking, blocked. 1** A **block** of flats or offices is a large building containing them. EG *...a large office block.* N COUNT

2 A **block** in a town is an area of land with streets on all its sides. EG *The store was three blocks away.* N COUNT

3 A **block** of a substance is a large rectangular piece of it. EG *...a block of ice... ...blocks of stone.* N PART

4 To **block** a road, channel, or pipe means to put an object across it or in it so that nothing can get through. EG *They had blocked the land routes.* V+O ◊ **blocked.** EG *The road was completely blocked.* ◊ ADJ CLASSIF

5 If something **blocks** your view, it prevents you from seeing something by being between you and that thing. EG *The driver blocked his view.* V+O

6 If you **block** something that is being arranged, you prevent it from being done. EG *He couldn't block the deal... The Council blocked his plans.* V+O

7 If you have a mental **block** for a short period, you are unable to do something that you can normally do which involves using your brain or memory. EG *I must have had a block.* N COUNT

block out. 1 If someone **blocks out** a thought, they try not to think about it. EG *They attempt to withdraw from the world, to block it out.* PHRASAL VB: V+O+ADV **2** Something that **blocks out** light prevents it from reaching a place. EG *...tall buildings that block out sunlight.* V+O+ADV

block up. If you **block** something **up** or if it **blocks up**, it becomes completely blocked so that nothing can get through it. EG *Never block up ventilators... The sink keeps blocking up.* PHRASAL VB: V-ERG+ADV

blockade /blɒkeɪd/, **blockades, blockading, blockaded.** A **blockade** is an action that is taken to prevent goods from reaching a place. EG *...the blockade of Berlin.* N COUNT ▸ used as a verb. EG *The Atlantic Squadron promptly blockaded Santiago.* ▸ V+O

blockage /blɒkɪdʒ/, **blockages.** A **blockage** in a pipe, tube, or tunnel is something that is blocking it. EG *Perhaps there was a blockage in the fuel line.* N COUNT OR N UNCOUNT

block capitals or **block letters** are simple capital letters that are not decorated in any way. N PLURAL

bloke /bləʊk/, **blokes.** A **bloke** is a man. EG *I'm only an ordinary bloke... He's a good bloke... ...the bloke next door... ...a bloke called Robertson.* N COUNT Informal British

blonde /blɒnd/, **blondes;** also spelled **blond. 1** A **blonde** person has pale yellow-coloured hair. EG *...a tall, blond Englishman... ...her long blonde hair.* ADJ QUALIT

2 A **blonde** is a person, especially a woman, who has blonde hair. EG *...a plump blonde of about thirty.* N COUNT

blood /blʌd/. **1 Blood** is the red liquid that flows inside your body. EG *...the circulation of the blood... Her hand was covered with blood.* N UNCOUNT

2 If something **makes** your **blood boil**, it makes you very angry. PHRASE

3 Bad blood refers to feelings of hate and anger. EG *The rebels hoped to create bad blood between Spain and the United States.* PHRASE

4 If something violent and cruel is done **in cold blood**, it is done deliberately and in an unemotional way. EG *People were murdered in cold blood.* PHRASE

5 If something **makes** your **blood run cold**, it makes you feel very frightened. PHRASE

6 You can use **blood** to refer to the race or social class of someone's parents or ancestors. EG *There was eastern blood on her mother's side.* N UNCOUNT +SUPP

7 If a quality or talent is **in** your **blood**, it is part of your nature, and other members of your family have it too. EG *Music is in her blood.* PHRASE

8 New people who are introduced into an organization and whose fresh ideas are likely to improve it are referred to as **new blood**, **fresh blood**, or **young blood**. PHRASE

bloodbath /blʌdbɑːθ/, **bloodbaths.** If you describe an event as a **bloodbath**, you mean that a lot of people were killed very violently. N COUNT

bloodcurdling /blʌdkɜːdlɪŋ/. A **bloodcurdling** sound or story is very frightening and horrible. EG *...a bloodcurdling shriek.* ADJ CLASSIF : ATTRIB

blood donor, blood donors. Blood donors give blood from their bodies so that it can be used for transfusions or operations. N COUNT

bloodless /blʌdlɪ^{2}s/. **1** If you describe someone's face or skin as **bloodless**, you mean that it is very pale. EG *Lily wiped her bloodless lips.* ADJ CLASSIF

2 A **bloodless** coup or victory is one in which nobody is killed. ADJ CLASSIF

blood poisoning is a serious illness resulting from an infection in your blood. N UNCOUNT

blood pressure. Your **blood pressure** is a measure of the amount of force with which your blood flows around your body. EG *I have high blood pressure and heart trouble.* N UNCOUNT

bloodshed /blʌdʃɛd/ is violence in which people are killed or wounded. EG *There was no evidence of bloodshed or attack.* N UNCOUNT

bloodshot /blʌdʃɒt/. If your eyes are **bloodshot**, the parts that are usually white are red or pink. ADJ QUALIT

blood sport, blood sports. Blood sports are sports such as hunting in which animals are killed. N COUNT

bloodstained /blʌdsteɪnd/. Something that is **bloodstained** is covered with blood. EG *...bloodstained clothing.* ADJ CLASSIF

bloodstream /blʌdstriːm/, **bloodstreams.** Your **bloodstream** is your blood as it flows around your body. EG *...a drug that dissolves in the bloodstream.* N COUNT

bloodthirsty /blʌdθɜːsti^1/. Someone who is **bloodthirsty** is extremely eager to use violence or to see other people use violence. ADJ QUALIT

blood vessel, blood vessels. Blood vessels are the narrow tubes through which your blood flows. N COUNT

bloody /blʌdi^1/, **bloodier, bloodiest. 1 Bloody** is a swear word. You use 'bloody' to emphasize how annoyed or angry you are. EG *Bloody students!* ADJ CLASSIF : ATTRIB OR ADV British

2 A situation or event that is **bloody** is one in which there is a lot of violence and a lot of people are killed. EG *The effects will be violent, disruptive, and probably bloody.* ADJ QUALIT ◊ **bloodily.** EG *Helen was most horribly, most bloodily, killed.* ◊ ADV

3 Something that is **bloody** has a lot of blood on it. EG *...hands that were black and bloody.* ADJ QUALIT

bloody-minded. Someone who is being **bloody-minded** is deliberately making difficulties instead of being helpful. EG *You're just being bloody-minded.* ADJ QUALIT ◊ **bloody-mindedness.** EG *It's sheer bloody-mindedness on their part.* ◊ N UNCOUNT

bloom /bluːm/, **blooms, blooming, bloomed. 1** A **bloom** is the flower on a plant. EG *...great scarlet hibiscus blooms.* N COUNT ● A plant or tree that is **in bloom** has flowers on it. EG *...lovely almond trees in bloom.* ● PHRASE

2 When a plant or tree **blooms**, it produces flowers. When a flower **blooms**, the flower bud opens. EG *It has a beautiful orange flower which blooms in November.* V : USU+A

blossom /blɒsə^{0}m/, **blossoms, blossoming, blossomed. 1 Blossom** is the flowers that appear on a tree before the fruit. EG *The trees along the road were heavy with yellow blossoms.* N UNCOUNT OR N COUNT ● A tree that is **in blossom** has blossom on it. EG *...a cherry-tree in blossom.* ● PHRASE

2 When a tree **blossoms**, it produces blossom. V

3 You say that a person **blossoms** when they develop attractive qualities or abilities. EG *She had blossomed into a real beauty... Harold had suddenly blossomed at university.* V

blot /blɒt/, **blots, blotting, blotted. 1** A **blot** is a drop of liquid, especially ink, that has been spilled on a surface and has dried. N COUNT

2 If something is a **blot** on someone's reputation, it spoils their reputation. EG *...a blot on his career.* N SING+*on*

3 If you **blot** a surface, you remove liquid from it by pressing a piece of soft paper or cloth onto it. V+O

blot out. 1 If one thing **blots out** another thing, it is in front of the other thing and prevents it from being seen. EG *The resulting dust cloud blotted out the sun.* PHRASAL VB : V+O+ADV **2** If one thought or memory **blots out** other thoughts or memories, it becomes the only one that you can think about. If you try to **blot out** a memory, you try to forget it. V+O+ADV

blotch /blɒtʃ/, **blotches.** A **blotch** is a small area of colour, for example on someone's skin. EG *There were purple blotches around her eyes.* N COUNT : USU PLURAL

blotchy /blɒtʃi^1/. Something that is **blotchy** has blotches on it. EG *His skin was blotchy.* ADJ QUALIT

blotting paper is thick soft paper that you use for soaking up and drying ink on a piece of paper. N UNCOUNT

blouse /blaʊz/, **blouses.** A **blouse** is a kind of shirt worn by a girl or woman. See picture at CLOTHES. N COUNT

blow /bləʊ/, **blows, blowing, blew** /bluː/, **blown** /bləʊn/. **1** When a wind or breeze **blows**, the air moves. EG *The winds had been blowing from the west.* V : OFT+A

2 If something **blows** somewhere or if the wind **blows** it there, it is moved there by the wind. EG *The dust blew all over the decks... The wind blew his papers away.* V-ERG : USU+A

3 If you **blow**, you send out a stream of air from your mouth. EG *Eric put his lips close to the hole and blew softly.* V : USU+A

4 If you **blow** bubbles, you make them by blowing air out of your mouth through liquid. V+O

5 When you **blow** a whistle or a horn, you make a sound by blowing into it. EG *The conductor blew his whistle and the tram stopped.* V+O

6 When you **blow** your nose, you force air out of it through your nostrils in order to clear it. V+O

7 If you give someone a **blow**, you hit them. EG *He knocked Thomas unconscious with one blow of his fist... ...a blow on the back of the neck.* N COUNT : USU+SUPP ● If two people or groups **come to blows**, they start fighting. ● PHRASE

8 A **blow** is also something that happens which makes you very disappointed or unhappy. EG *It must have been a fearful blow to him.* N COUNT : OFT+*to* ● Something that **softens the blow** or **cushions the blow** makes an unpleasant piece of news easier to accept. ● PHRASE

9 A **blow** for a particular cause or principle is an N COUNT :

What is the difference between a blot and a blotch?

action that makes it more likely to succeed. A **blow** against it makes it less likely to succeed. EG *He struck a blow for liberty.* USU+*for/against*

10 If you **blow** something off, you violently remove or destroy it with an explosion. EG *He would have blown his hand off if he'd fired the gun... It blew a hole in the roof.* V+O+A

11 If you **blow** a large amount of money, you spend it quickly on things that you do not really need. V+O Informal

12 If you say '**Blow him**' or '**Blow the expense**', you mean that you do not care about what someone thinks or how much something costs. PHRASE Informal Outdated

blow out. If you **blow out** a flame or a candle, you blow at it so that it stops burning. EG *Rudolph blew out the candles... The pilot light had blown out.* PHRASAL VB: V-ERG+ADV

blow over. If something such as trouble or an argument **blows over**, it comes to an end. PHRASAL VB: V+ADV

blow up. 1 If you **blow** something **up** or if it **blows up**, it is destroyed by an explosion. EG *He was going to blow the place up... One of the submarines blew up.* PHRASAL VB: V-ERG+ADV **2** If you **blow up** something such as a balloon or a tyre, you fill it with air. V+O+ADV

blow-by-blow. A **blow-by-blow** account of an event describes every stage of it in detail. EG *...a blow-by-blow description of the trial.* ADJ CLASSIF: ATTRIB

blower /bləʊə/. The **blower** is the telephone. EG *Miss Callaghan was on the blower to Atkinson.* N SING: *the*+N Outdated

blown /bləʊn/ is the past participle of **blow**.

bludgeon /blʌdʒəⁿn/, **bludgeons, bludgeoning, bludgeoned. 1** If someone **bludgeons** you, they hit you several times with a heavy object. V+O Formal

2 If someone **bludgeons** you into doing something, they make you do it by bullying or threatening you. V+O+*into*

blue /bluː/, **bluer, bluest; blues. 1** Something that is **blue** is the colour of the sky on a sunny day. EG *She had bright blue eyes.* ADJ COLOUR

2 Something that happens **out of the blue** happens suddenly and unexpectedly. EG *She suddenly wrote out of the blue and asked me to go on holiday with her.* PHRASE

3 The **blues** is a type of music which is similar to jazz, but is always slow and sad. N UNCOUNT

4 Blue films, stories, or jokes are mainly about sex. ADJ QUALIT

bluebell /bluːbɛl/, **bluebells. Bluebells** are plants that have blue bell-shaped flowers on thin upright stems. N COUNT

blue-black. Something that is **blue-black** is very dark blue in colour. ADJ COLOUR

bluebottle /bluːbɒtəⁿl/, **bluebottles.** A **bluebottle** is a large fly with a shiny dark-blue body. N COUNT

blue-collar. Blue-collar workers work in industry, doing physical work, rather than in offices. ADJ CLASSIF

blueish /bluːɪʃ/. See **bluish**.

blueprint /bluːprɪnt/, **blueprints.** A **blueprint** for something is an original plan or description of how it is expected to work. EG *...a blueprint for a better world.* N COUNT: OFT+*of/for*

bluff /blʌf/, **bluffs, bluffing, bluffed. 1** A **bluff** is an attempt to make someone believe that you will do something when you do not really intend to do it. EG *The soldiers thought it was a bluff... His threats are merely bluff.* N COUNT OR N UNCOUNT ● If you **call** someone's **bluff**, you tell them to do what they have been threatening to do, because you are sure that they will not really do it. EG *It is time to call their bluff.* ● PHRASE

2 If you **bluff** or if you **bluff** someone, you make them believe that you will do something when you do not really intend to do it. EG *I was sure he was bluffing again.* V OR V+O

bluish /bluːɪʃ/; also spelled **blueish.** Something that is **bluish** is slightly blue in colour. EG *...bluish-grey water.* ADJ COLOUR

blunder /blʌndə/, **blunders, blundering, blundered. 1** If you **blunder**, you make a stupid or careless mistake. EG *Clearly, Alec had blundered badly.* V ▸ used as a noun. EG *I might have committed some dreadful blunder.* ▸ N COUNT

2 If you **blunder** somewhere, you move in a clumsy and careless way. EG *She blundered into a tree.* V+A

blunt /blʌnt/, **blunter, bluntest; blunts, blunting, blunted. 1** If you are **blunt**, you say exactly what you think without trying to be polite. EG *Let me ask a blunt question... To be blunt, you are no longer needed here.* ADJ QUALIT ◊ **bluntly.** EG *He told them bluntly what was acceptable.* ◊ ADV ◊ **bluntness.** EG *Other leaders have stated their views with equal bluntness.* ◊ N UNCOUNT

2 A **blunt** object has a rounded or flat end rather than a sharp one. EG *...a wooden spoon or similar blunt instrument.* ADJ QUALIT

3 A **blunt** knife is no longer sharp and does not cut well. ADJ QUALIT

4 If something **blunts** an emotion or feeling, it weakens it. EG *This side of his personality has been blunted by toil.* V+O

blur /blɜː/, **blurs, blurring, blurred. 1** A **blur** is a shape or area which you cannot see clearly because it has no distinct outline or because it is moving very fast. EG *Everything becomes a blur when you travel beyond a certain speed.* N COUNT: USU SING

2 When a thing **blurs** or when something **blurs** it, you cannot see it clearly because its edges are no longer distinct. V-ERG ◊ **blurred.** EG *...a blurred snapshot.* ◊ ADJ QUALIT

3 If an idea or a concept **blurs** or if something **blurs** it, it no longer seems clear. EG *...a determination to blur the line between art and reality.* V-ERG ◊ **blurred.** EG *The distinction between reform and revolution had become blurred in his mind.* ◊ ADJ QUALIT

blurt /blɜːt/, **blurts, blurting, blurted.** If you **blurt** something **out**, you say it suddenly, after trying hard to keep quiet or to keep it secret. EG *She suddenly blurted out, 'I'm not going.'* PHRASAL VB: V-SPEECH+ADV

blush /blʌʃ/, **blushes, blushing, blushed.** When you **blush**, your face becomes redder than usual because you are ashamed or embarrassed. EG *Philip blushed and laughed uneasily... I felt myself blushing.* V ▸ used as a noun. EG *'I made it myself,' Mr Solomon informed them with a modest blush.* ▸ N COUNT: USU SING

bluster /blʌstə/, **blusters, blustering, blustered.** When someone **blusters**, they speak angrily and aggressively because they are angry or offended. EG *They blustered and swore that the pictures were fakes.* V ▸ used as a noun. EG *She simply ignored his bluster.* ▸ N UNCOUNT

blustery /blʌstəⁿri¹/. **Blustery** weather is rough and windy. ADJ QUALIT

boa /bəʊə/, **boas.** A **boa** is a large snake that kills animals by squeezing them. N COUNT

boa constrictor /bəʊə kənstrɪktə/, **boa constrictors.** A **boa constrictor** is the same as a boa. N COUNT

boar /bɔː/, **boars. 1** A **boar** is a male pig. N COUNT

2 A **boar** or a **wild boar** is a wild pig. The plural can be 'boar' or 'boars'. N COUNT

board /bɔːd/, **boards, boarding, boarded. 1** A **board** is **1.1** a rectangular piece of wood on which something can be put, spread out, or cut. EG *He took a knife from a magnetic board on the wall... ...a chopping board.* **1.2** a square piece of wood or stiff cardboard that you use for playing games such as chess. **1.3** a long flat piece of wood which is used to make a floor, wall, or shelf. N COUNT

2 You can also refer to a blackboard, diving board, or notice board as a **board**. EG *I'll write the sum up on the board.* N COUNT

3 The **board** of a company or organization is the group of people who control it. EG *He was on the board of directors... ...board meetings.* N COUNT: OFT *the*+N

4 If you **board** a train, ship, or aircraft, you get on it in order to travel somewhere. V+O Formal

5 When you are **on board** a train, ship, or aircraft, you are on it or in it. PHRASE

6 Board is the food which is provided when you stay somewhere, for example in a hotel. EG *...the low price that my hostess was asking for board and bed.* N UNCOUNT

7 An arrangement or deal that is **above board** is legal and is being carried out honestly and openly. PHRASE

8 If a policy or a situation applies **across the board**, it affects everything or everyone in a particular group. EG *We're aiming for a 20% reduction across the board.* PHRASE

9 If an arrangement or plan **goes by the board** when something unexpected happens, it is not used or does not happen. PHRASE

10 If someone **sweeps the board** in a competition, they win everything. PHRASE

board up. If you **board up** a door or window, you fix pieces of wood over it so that it is covered up. PHRASAL VB : V+O+ADV

boarding house, boarding houses. A **boarding house** is a house where people pay to stay for a short time. N COUNT

boarding school, boarding schools. A **boarding school** is a school where the pupils live during the term. N COUNT

boardroom /bɔːdruːm, -rʊm/, **boardrooms.** The **boardroom** is **1** a room where the board of a company meets. EG *I got a summons to the boardroom on the top floor.* N COUNT **2** the people at the highest level of management in a company. EG *...the devolution of power from the boardroom to the shop floor.* N SING : *the*+N

boast /bəʊst/, **boasts, boasting, boasted.** If you **boast** about something that you have done or that you own, you talk about it in a way that shows that you are proud of it. EG *Williams boasted of his influence over the Prime Minister... British Rail can boast about their safety record... He's not all that exciting – even if he likes to boast that he is.* V : OFT+A, QUOTE, OR REPORT : ONLY *that*
▸ used as a noun. EG *It is his boast that he has read the entire works of Trollope.* ▸ N COUNT : OFT+REPORT

boastful /bəʊstfʊl/. If someone is **boastful**, they talk too proudly about something that they have done or that they own. EG *They are rather boastful about their equipment... ...his boastful laughter.* ADJ QUALIT

boat /bəʊt/, **boats. 1** A **boat** is a small vehicle which is used for travelling across water. EG *John took me down the river in the old boat... We are going by boat... ...a fishing boat.* N COUNT OR *by*+N

2 You can refer to a passenger ship as a **boat**. EG *She was intending to take the boat to Stockholm.* N COUNT Informal

3 Boat is used in these phrases. **3.1** If you say that someone is **rocking the boat**, you mean that they are upsetting a calm situation and causing trouble. PHRASES Informal **3.2** If two or more people are **in the same boat**, they are in the same unpleasant situation. EG *We are all in the same boat.*

boating /bəʊtɪŋ/ is travelling on a lake or river in a small boat for pleasure. EG *Uncle Jack once took me out boating... ...a number of boating accidents.* N ING

bob /bɒb/, **bobs, bobbing, bobbed. 1** If something **bobs**, it moves up and down, like something does when it is floating on water. EG *The toy boat bobbed gently on the ripples.* V+A

2 If you **bob** somewhere, you move there quickly. EG *The receptionist bobbed back into the rear office.* V+A

3 People used to refer to a shilling as a **bob**. The plural form was also **bob**. EG *They used to get four bob an hour.* N COUNT Informal

4 A **bob** is also a hair style in which a woman's hair is cut level with her chin. N COUNT

bobbed /bɒbd/. If a woman's hair is **bobbed**, it is cut in a bob. EG *...a girl with blonde bobbed hair.* ADJ CLASSIF

bode /bəʊd/, **bodes, boding, boded.** If something **bodes ill**, **bodes no good**, or **does not bode well**, it makes you think that something bad will happen. EG *This does not bode well for his chances against the champion... Her expression boded ill for somebody.* PHRASE Literary

bodice /bɒdɪs/, **bodices.** The **bodice** of a dress is the part above the waist. N COUNT

bodily /bɒdɪli[1]/. **1** Your **bodily** needs and functions are the needs and functions of your body. EG *They have no interests beyond their bodily needs... ...a general slowing up of the bodily functions.* ADJ CLASSIF : ATTRIB

2 You use **bodily** to refer to actions that involve the whole of someone's body. EG *He carried her bodily past the rows of empty seats... He hurled himself bodily at the Prince.* ADV

body /bɒdi[1]/, **bodies. 1** Someone's **body** is all their physical parts, or the main part and not their head, arms, and legs. EG *His whole body felt as if it were on fire... They respond with slow movements of their arms, legs, and bodies.* N COUNT : OFT+POSS

2 You can refer to a person's dead body as a **body**. EG *His body has not been found.* ● **over my dead body**: see **dead**. N COUNT

3 A **body** is also an organized group of people who deal with something officially. EG *...a unique body called the Inner London Education Authority... ...local voluntary bodies.* N COUNT : USU+SUPP

4 The **body** of a car or aeroplane is the main part of it, not including its engine, wheels, or wings. N COUNT : USU+SUPP

bodyguard /bɒdi[1]gɑːd/, **bodyguards.** A **bodyguard** is **1** a person who is employed to protect someone. EG *He came striding into the room followed by his two bodyguards.* N COUNT **2** a group of people who are employed to protect someone. EG *...one of the Rajah's personal bodyguard.*

bodywork /bɒdi[1]wɜːk/. The **bodywork** of a motor vehicle is the outside part of it. N UNCOUNT

bog /bɒg/, **bogs.** A **bog** is an area of land which is very wet and muddy. N COUNT

bogged down /bɒgd daʊn/. **1** If you are **bogged down** in something, it prevents you from making progress or getting something done. EG *Don't get bogged down in details... We had been bogged down in red tape.* ADJ PRED

2 If a vehicle is **bogged down** in mud or snow, it is stuck and cannot move. ADJ PRED

boggle /bɒgə[0]l/, **boggles, boggling, boggled.** If your mind **boggles** at something or if something **boggles** your mind, you find it difficult to imagine or understand. EG *The questions raised by the new biology simply boggle the mind.* V-ERG

boggy /bɒgi[1]/. **Boggy** land is very wet and muddy. ADJ QUALIT

bogus /bəʊgəs/. You say that something is **bogus** when someone is pretending that it is genuine and you know that it is not. EG *...bogus names... She was speaking with a terrible bogus accent.* ADJ CLASSIF

bohemian /bəʊhiːmɪən/, **bohemians.** A **bohemian** is someone who lives and dresses in a casual way that many people do not approve of. Bohemians are often connected with art, literature, or music. EG *Brian saw Tim as a romantic Bohemian.* N COUNT Outdated
▸ used as an adjective. EG *My parents disapproved of the bohemian life I led.* ▸ ADJ QUALIT

boil /bɔɪl/, **boils, boiling, boiled. 1** When a hot liquid **boils** or when you **boil** it, bubbles appear in it and it starts to change into steam or vapour. EG *When the water has boiled let it cool... Fill the teapot with boiling water.* V-ERG

2 When you **bring** a liquid **to the boil**, you heat it until it boils. When it **comes to the boil**, it begins to boil. PHRASE

3 When you **boil** a kettle, you heat it until the water inside it boils. When a kettle **is boiling**, the water inside it is boiling. EG *He boiled the kettle and made the tea.* V-ERG

4 When you **boil** food, you cook it in boiling water. EG *She didn't know how to boil an egg... ...boiled potatoes.* V+O

5 If something is **boiling** or **boiling** hot, it is very hot. EG *I immersed my boiling body in a cool pool.* ADJ CLASSIF

6 If you **are boiling** with anger, you are very angry. V : USU+*with*

7 A **boil** is a red, painful swelling on your skin. N COUNT

Would you be annoyed if someone was rocking the boat?

boil away. When a liquid **boils away**, all of it changes into steam or vapour. [PHRASAL VB: V+ADV]

boil down to. If you say that a situation or problem **boils down to** a particular thing, you mean that this is the most important aspect of it. EG *What it all seemed to boil down to was money... The question boils down to one of social priorities.* [PHRASAL VB: V+ADV+PREP]

boil over. 1 When a liquid that is being heated **boils over**, it rises and flows over the edge of the container. EG *The milk's boiling over.* [PHRASAL VB: V+ADV] 2 When someone's feelings **boil over**, they lose their temper or become violent. EG *George's temper promptly boiled over again.* [V+ADV]

boiler /bɔɪlə/, **boilers.** A **boiler** is a device which burns gas, oil, electricity, or coal in order to provide hot water, especially for the central heating in a building. [N COUNT]

boisterous /bɔɪstə¹rəs/. Someone who is **boisterous** is noisy, lively, and full of energy. [ADJ QUALIT]

bold /bəʊld/, **bolder, boldest.** 1 Someone who is **bold** is 1.1 not afraid to do things which involve risk or danger. EG *...the most ambitious, bold, and imaginative of Europe's citizens... ...a bold action.* [ADJ QUALIT] ◇ **boldly.** EG *...boldly going where no man had gone before.* [◇ ADV] ◇ **boldness.** EG *For any success, boldness is required.* [◇ N UNCOUNT] **1.2** not shy or embarrassed in the company of other people. EG *Mary was surprisingly bold for a girl who seemed so young... She had bold brown eyes.* [ADJ QUALIT] ◇ **boldly.** EG *He returned her gaze boldly.* [◇ ADV]

2 Bold lines or designs are painted or drawn in a clear, strong way. EG *...bold handwriting... She began to paint her lips with bold, defiant strokes.* [ADJ QUALIT]

3 A **bold** colour or pattern is very bright and noticeable. EG *...his bold black-and-white striped shirt.* [ADJ QUALIT]

4 If printed letters are in **bold** print or **bold** typeface, they are thicker and look blacker than ordinary printed letters. **This sentence is in bold type.** [ADJ CLASSIF: ATTRIB]

bollard /bɒlɑ:d, bɒləd/, **bollards. Bollards** are short thick posts that are used to prevent cars from going on to someone's land or on to part of a road. [N COUNT]

bolster /bəʊlstə/, **bolsters, bolstering, bolstered.** If you **bolster** someone's confidence or courage, you make them more confident or more courageous. EG *We arranged a daily routine that would bolster her sense of security.* [V+O]

bolster up. If you **bolster** something **up**, you help it or support it in order to make it stronger. EG *The industries provided the work that bolstered up the system... To bolster up their case, they quoted a speech by Ray Gunter.* [PHRASAL VB: V+O+ADV]

bolt /bəʊlt/, **bolts, bolting, bolted. 1** A **bolt** is a long metal object which screws into a nut and is used to fasten things together. EG *The bolts are all tight enough.* [N COUNT]

2 When you **bolt** one thing to another, you fasten them firmly together, using a bolt. EG *...an iron cot bolted to the floor.* [V+O: USU+A]

3 A **bolt** on a door or window is a metal bar that you can slide across in order to fasten the door or window. [N COUNT]

4 When you **bolt** a door or window, you slide the bolt across to fasten it. [V+O]

5 If a person or animal **bolts**, they suddenly start to run very fast, often because something has frightened them. [V]

6 If you **bolt** your food or **bolt** it down, you eat it so quickly that you hardly chew it or taste it. EG *Daniel bolted one slice of his mother's cake and rushed out.* [V+O OR V+O+A]

7 If someone is sitting or standing **bolt upright**, they are sitting or standing very straight. [PHRASE]

bomb /bɒm/, **bombs, bombing, bombed. 1** A **bomb** is a device which explodes and damages or destroys a large area. EG *...the bombs which destroyed these cities... They had planted the bomb beneath the house.* [N COUNT]

2 Nuclear weapons are sometimes referred to as the **bomb**. EG *Ban the bomb!* [N SING: *the*+N]

3 When people **bomb** a place, they attack it with bombs. EG *They bombed the airports in three cities... The premises were bombed in the Second World War.* [V+O] ◇ **bombing, bombings.** EG *It replaced the building destroyed by bombing in 1940... ...the current wave of bombings.* [◇ N UNCOUNT OR N COUNT]

bomb out. If a building **is bombed out**, it is destroyed by a bomb. If people **are bombed out**, their houses are destroyed by bombs. EG *Their factories were bombed out... These were people bombed out by the Allies.* [PHRASAL VB: V-PASS+ADV]

bombard /bɒmbɑ:d/, **bombards, bombarding, bombarded. 1** If you **bombard** someone with questions or criticism, you keep asking them a lot of questions or you keep criticizing them. [V+O: OFT+*with*]

2 When soldiers **bombard** a place, they attack it with continuous heavy gunfire or bombs. [V+O] ◇ **bombardment** /bɒmbɑ:dmə²nt/, **bombardments.** EG *...increasingly heavy artillery bombardment.* [◇ N COUNT OR N UNCOUNT]

bombastic /bɒmbæstɪk/. **Bombastic** statements or threats contain long and important sounding words, chosen to impress people rather than to express meaning clearly. EG *...bombastic threats of retaliation.* [ADJ QUALIT]

bomber /bɒmə/, **bombers.** A **bomber** is **1** an aircraft which drops bombs. **2** a person who causes a bomb to explode in a public place. [N COUNT]

bombshell /bɒmʃɛl/, **bombshells.** A **bombshell** is a sudden piece of bad or unexpected news. EG *She dropped her bombshell. 'I'm pregnant.'* [N COUNT]

bona fide /bəʊnəfaɪdi¹/, **bona fides. 1** If something is **bona fide**, it is genuine or real. EG *...bona fide applications to join the Service.* [ADJ CLASSIF: ATTRIB; Formal]

2 Your **bona fides** are your good or sincere intentions. EG *He wanted to check on my bona fides... They may have difficulty in establishing their bona fides.* [N PLURAL; Formal]

bonanza /bənænzə/, **bonanzas.** You can refer to a time or situation when people suddenly become much richer as a **bonanza**. EG *...an oil bonanza.* [N COUNT]

bond /bɒnd/, **bonds, bonding, bonded. 1** A **bond** between people is **1.1** a strong feeling of friendship, love, or shared beliefs that unites them. EG *...the bond between mother and child... ...bonds of friendship.* **1.2** a close connection that they have with each other as a result of an agreement. EG *Many people see marriage as a permanent bond.* [N COUNT: OFT+SUPP]

2 When people or animals **bond** or **are bonded**, they unite to help and protect each other. EG *Societies have always been bonded together by a threat from outside.* [V OR V-PASS]

3 A **bond** is a certificate issued by a government or company which shows that you have lent them money and that they will pay you interest. EG *Investors would refuse to buy the bonds at the low interest rate offered.* [N COUNT]

4 Bonds are feelings, duties, or customs that force you to behave in a particular way. EG *...the bonds of party discipline.* [N PLURAL +SUPP]

5 When you **bond** two things, you stick them together using glue. [V+O: OFT +*to/together*]

bondage /bɒndɪdʒ/ is the condition of belonging to someone as their slave. EG *They were kept in bondage.* [N UNCOUNT; Literary]

bone /bəʊn/, **bones, boning, boned. 1** Your **bones** are the hard parts inside your body which together form your skeleton. EG *...hip bones... Mary broke a bone in her back... Its eye sockets are encircled by bone.* [N COUNT OR N UNCOUNT]

2 If you **bone** a piece of meat or fish, you remove the bones from it before cooking it. EG *...boned sirloins of beef.* [V+O]

3 A **bone** tool or ornament is made of bone. EG *They fished with bone harpoons.* [ADJ CLASSIF]

4 Bone is used in these phrases. **4.1** If you **feel** or **know** something **in** your **bones**, you are certain [PHRASES; Informal] about it, although you cannot explain why. EG *He felt in his bones he could do it... James knew in his bones that she was the right girl for him.* **4.2** If you **make no bones** about doing something unpleasant or difficult, you do it without hesitation. EG *They made no bones about acknowledging their debt to him.* **4.3** When someone is very thin, you can say that they are **a bag of bones** or **all skin and bone**.

bonfire /bɒnfaɪə/, **bonfires.** A **bonfire** is a fire that is made outdoors, especially in order to burn rubbish from a garden. N COUNT

bonhomie /bɒnəmi¹/ is happy, jolly friendliness. EG *...the grin of bonhomie on his face.* N UNCOUNT Literary

bonnet /bɒnɪt/, **bonnets. 1** The **bonnet** of a car is the metal cover over the engine at the front. See picture at CAR. N COUNT British

2 A baby's or woman's **bonnet** is a hat tied under their chin. N COUNT

bonny /bɒni¹/; also spelled **bonnie.** Someone or something that is **bonny** is nice to look at. EG *She had a big bonny boy with fair hair.* ADJ QUALIT Scottish

bonus /bəʊnəs/, **bonuses.** A **bonus** is **1** an amount of money that is added to your usual pay, especially because you have worked very hard. EG *The farmer gave his men a five pound bonus.* **2** something good that you get in addition to something else. EG *Any sort of party after work was a bonus.* N COUNT

bony /bəʊni¹/. A **bony** person is very thin. EG *He was tall, thin, and bony... ...his long bony fingers.* ADJ QUALIT

boo /buː/, **boos, booing, booed.** If you **boo** a speaker or performer, you shout 'boo' to indicate that you do not like them, their opinions, or their performance. EG *By now most of the audience was booing.* ▸ used as a noun. EG *There were loud boos from the fans.* V+O OR V; ▸ N COUNT

boob /buːb/, **boobs.** A woman's **boobs** are her breasts; a rude word. N COUNT : USU PLURAL

booby prize /buːbi¹ praɪz/, **booby prizes.** The **booby prize** is a prize given to the person who comes last in a competition. EG *It looks as if you've got the booby prize.* N COUNT

booby-trap, /buːbi¹ træp/, **booby-traps, booby-trapping, booby-trapped. 1** A **booby-trap** is something such as a bomb which is hidden or disguised and which causes death or injury when it is touched. EG *They searched the ground for booby traps.* N COUNT

2 If something **is booby-trapped**, a booby-trap is placed in it or on it. EG *How do you know the building's not booby-trapped?* V+O : USU PASS

book /bʊk/, **books, booking, booked. 1** A **book** is a number of pieces of paper, usually with words printed on them, which are fastened together and fixed inside a cover of stronger paper or cardboard. Books contain information, stories, or poetry, for example. EG *...a book by John Fisher about Emily Hobhouse... ...a book on hypnotism... She opened the book and put the envelope between the pages.* N COUNT

2 A **book** of something such as stamps, matches, or tickets is a small number of them fastened together between thin cardboard or plastic covers. N PART

3 When you **book** something such as a hotel room or a ticket, you arrange to have it or use it at a particular time. EG *I'd like to book a table for four for tomorrow night.* ● See also **booking**. V+O : OFT+*for* OR V+O+O British

4 If a hotel, restaurant, or theatre is **booked up** or is **fully booked**, it has no rooms, tables, or tickets left for a particular time or date. PHRASE

5 A company's or organization's **books** are its records of money that has been spent and earned or of the names of people who belong to it. EG *He's going to help me go over my books and check the totals... His name is no longer on our books.* N PLURAL

6 If you are **in** someone's **bad books**, they are annoyed with you. If you are **in** their **good books**, they are pleased with you. PHRASE

book in or **book into.** When you **book into** a hotel or when you **book in**, you officially state that you have arrived to stay there, usually by signing your name in a register. EG *He booked in at the Hotel d'Angleterre.* PHRASAL VB : V+PREP OR V+ADV British

bookcase /bʊkkeɪs/, **bookcases.** A **bookcase** is a piece of furniture with shelves that you keep books on. N COUNT

booking /bʊkɪŋ/, **bookings.** A **booking** is the arrangement that you make when you book something such as a theatre seat or a hotel room. N COUNT

bookish /bʊkɪʃ/. Someone who is **bookish** spends a lot of time reading serious books. ADJ QUALIT

bookkeeping /bʊkkiːpɪŋ/ is the job of keeping an accurate record of the money that is spent and received by a business or other organization. N UNCOUNT

booklet /bʊklɛ¹t/, **booklets.** A **booklet** is a small book with a paper cover that gives you information about something. N COUNT

bookmaker /bʊkmeɪkə/, **bookmakers.** A **bookmaker** is a person whose job is to take your money when you bet and to pay you money if you win. N COUNT

bookmark /bʊkmɑːk/, **bookmarks.** A **bookmark** is a narrow piece of card or leather that you put between the pages of a book so that you can find a particular page easily. N COUNT

bookseller /bʊksɛlə/, **booksellers.** A **bookseller** is a person who sells books. N COUNT

bookshelf /bʊkʃɛlf/, **bookshelves.** A **bookshelf** is **1** a shelf on which you keep books. **2** a bookcase. N COUNT

bookshop /bʊkʃɒp/, **bookshops.** A **bookshop** is a shop where books are sold. N COUNT British

bookstall /bʊkstɔːl/, **bookstalls.** A **bookstall** is a small shop with an open front where books and magazines are sold. N COUNT

bookstore /bʊkstɔː/, **bookstores.** A **bookstore** is the same as a bookshop. N COUNT American

boom /buːm/, **booms, booming, boomed. 1** If there is a **boom** in something, there is a fast increase or development in it. EG *We must take advantage of the boom in world shipping... ...the population boom.* ▸ used as a verb. EG *The gardening industry is booming.* N COUNT+SUPP; ▸ V

2 When something such as a big drum, a cannon, or someone's voice **booms**, it makes a loud, deep, echoing sound. EG *The cannon boomed again... He had a booming voice... 'Nonsense!' boomed Mrs Pringle.* ▸ used as a noun. EG *The boom of the drum echoed along the street.* V OR V+QUOTE; ▸ N COUNT

boom out. When someone **booms out** a greeting or command, or when their voice **booms out**, they speak in a very loud, deep voice. EG *He boomed out: 'Good evening ladies and gentlemen!'... Hogan's voice boomed out of the telephone receiver.* PHRASAL VB : V+O+ADV OR V+ADV

boomerang /buːməræŋ/, **boomerangs.** A **boomerang** is a curved piece of wood which comes back to you if you throw it the correct way. Boomerangs were first used by Australian natives as weapons. N COUNT

boon /buːn/, **boons.** You say that something is a **boon** when it makes life better or easier for someone. EG *The bus service is a great boon to old people.* N COUNT

boor /bʊə/, **boors.** A **boor** is a boorish person. EG *...drunken boors.* N COUNT Outdated

boorish /bʊərɪʃ/. Someone who is **boorish** behaves in a rough, impolite, clumsy way. ADJ QUALIT

boost /buːst/, **boosts, boosting, boosted. 1** If one thing **boosts** another, it causes it to increase. EG *This new technology will boost food production... ...an auxiliary motor capable of boosting our speed to fifteen knots.* ▸ used as a noun. EG *This will be a great boost to the economy.* V+O; ▸ N COUNT

2 If something **boosts** your confidence or morale, it improves it. EG *There is nothing like winning to* V+O

Does a bookmaker produce books?

boost the morale of players. ▸ used as a noun. EG *...a boost to self-confidence.* ▸ N COUNT

3 If you **boost** someone or **boost** something that they have done, you praise them or publicize them in order to make them more popular. EG *Her books have been boosted in the Observer recently.* V+O

boot /buːt/, **boots, booting, booted. 1 Boots** are **1.1** shoes that cover your whole foot and the lower part of your leg. See picture at SHOES. EG *I put on my fur coat and boots.* **1.2** strong, heavy shoes which cover your ankle and which have thick soles. EG *I haven't got any climbing boots.* N COUNT: USU PLURAL

2 If you **boot** something such as a ball, you kick it hard. EG *She booted the ball back onto the pitch.* V+O: USU+A Informal

3 The **boot** of a car is a covered space at the back or front, in which you carry things such as luggage and shopping. See picture at CAR. N COUNT British

4 If someone **puts the boot in**, **4.1** they repeatedly kick someone who is lying on the ground. **4.2** they say something cruel to someone who is already feeling weak or upset. PHRASE Informal

5 If someone says that you **are getting too big for** your **boots**, they mean that you are becoming too proud and pleased with yourself. PHRASE Informal

6 If you **get the boot** or **are given the boot**, you are dismissed from your job. PHRASE Informal

7 You can say **to boot** when you have just added a further comment to something that you have said. EG *She was an unaccompanied female, and a foreigner to boot.* PHRASE Literary

boot out. If you **are booted out** of a job, organization, or place, you are forced to leave it. EG *I was a drunken swine. No wonder Gertrude booted me out.* PHRASAL VB: V+O+ADV Informal

booth /buːð/, **booths.** A **booth** is **1** a small area separated from a larger public area by screens or thin walls where, for example, you can make a telephone call. EG *He went into the booth and dialled the number.* **2** a small tent or stall, usually at a fair, in which you can buy goods or watch some form of entertainment. N COUNT

booty /buːti¹/ is a collection of valuable things taken from a place, especially by soldiers after a battle. EG *The victorious forces were laden with enemy booty.* N UNCOUNT Literary

booze /buːz/, **boozes, boozing, boozed. 1 Booze** is alcoholic drink. EG *You could smell the booze on his breath.* N UNCOUNT Informal

2 When people **booze**, they drink alcohol. EG *All these lads do is sit about and booze.* V Informal

boozer /buːzə/, **boozers. 1** A **boozer** is a person who drinks a lot of alcohol. N COUNT Informal

2 The **boozer** is a pub near to where you live or work. N COUNT Informal

boozy /buːzi¹/. A **boozy** person drinks a lot of alcohol. EG *...his boozy companions... ...boozy singing.* ADJ CLASSIF Informal

bop /bɒp/, **bops, bopping, bopped.** A **bop** is a dance. ▸ used as a verb. EG *There we were, bopping away till the small hours.* N COUNT ▸ V: USU+A Informal

border /bɔːdə/, **borders, bordering, bordered. 1** The **border** between two countries or regions is the dividing line between them. Sometimes the **border** also refers to the land close to this line. EG *He lives in the French Alps near the Swiss border... They crossed the border into Mexico.* N COUNT

2 If a country **borders** another country or **borders on** it, it is next to it. V+O OR V+*on*

3 A **border** is also **3.1** a strip or band around the edge of something. EG *It's painted in white with a gold border.* **3.2** a strip of ground planted with flowers along the edge of a lawn. N COUNT

4 If something **borders** something else, it forms a line along the edge of it. EG *Huge elm trees bordered the road.* V+O

border on. When you say that something **borders on** a particular state, you mean that it has almost reached that state. EG *I was in a state of excitement bordering on insanity... Their treatment of each other bordered on brutality.* PHRASAL VB: V+PREP

borderline /bɔːdəlaɪn/. **1** Something that is **borderline** is only just acceptable as a member of a class or group. EG *He is a borderline candidate for a special school... ...borderline cases.* ADJ CLASSIF

2 The **borderline** between two conditions or qualities is the division between them. EG *...the narrow borderline between laughter and tears.* N SING

bore /bɔː/, **bores, boring, bored. 1** If something **bores** you, you find it dull and uninteresting. EG *Most of the book had bored him... I won't bore you with the details.* V+O: OFT+*with* ● If something **bores** you **to tears**, **bores** you **to death**, or **bores** you **stiff**, it bores you very much indeed. ● PHRASE Informal

2 You describe someone as a **bore** when you think that they talk in a very uninteresting way. EG *Steve is the most frightful bore.* N COUNT

3 You can describe a situation as a **bore** when you find it annoying or a nuisance. N SING: *a*+N

4 If you **bore** a hole in something, you make a deep round hole in it using a special tool. EG *They were shown how to bore rivet holes in the sides of ships.* V+O: USU+A

5 If someone's eyes **bore** into you, they stare intensely at you. V+*into*

6 Bore is also the past tense of **bear**.

7 See also **bored, boring**.

bored /bɔːd/. When you are **bored**, you feel tired and impatient because you have lost interest in something or because you have nothing to do. EG *Tom was bored with the film... There is no chance of getting bored.* ADJ QUALIT: OFT+*with*

boredom /bɔːdə⁴m/ is the state of being bored. EG *Many of the audience walked out through sheer boredom.* N UNCOUNT

boring /bɔːrɪŋ/. Something that is **boring 1** is so dull and uninteresting that it makes people tired and impatient. EG *...a boring journey... Are all your meetings so boring?* **2** has been made in an uninteresting and unimaginative way. EG *The gardens were a bit boring.* ADJ QUALIT

born /bɔːn/. **1** When a baby **is born**, it comes out of its mother's body at the beginning of its life. EG *Mary was born in Glasgow in 1899... ...the village where she was born... It is a tragedy when a baby is born abnormal.* V-PASS: OFT+A OR C

2 You use **born** to talk about something that people can do very well and easily. For example, if you are a **born** cook, you have a natural ability to cook well. EG *...the curiosity and perception of the born reporter.* ADJ CLASSIF: ATTRIB

3 When a thought, idea, or organization **is born**, it comes into existence. EG *At that moment the concept of the computer was born.* V-PASS

-born combines with the name of a place or nationality to indicate where a person was born. EG *...South African-born Gus Calderwood.*

borne /bɔːn/ is the past participle of **bear.**

borough /bʌrə/, **boroughs.** A **borough** is a town, or a district within a large town, which has its own council. EG *...the London Borough of Lewisham.* N COUNT

borrow /bɒrəʊ/, **borrows, borrowing, borrowed.** If you **borrow** something that belongs to someone else, they allow you to have it or use it for a period of time. EG *Could I borrow your car?... I need to borrow five thousand pounds.* V+O: OFT +*from/off*

borrower /bɒrəʊə/, **borrowers.** A **borrower** is a person or organization that borrows money. EG *They increased the surcharge for big borrowers.* N COUNT

borrowing /bɒrəʊɪŋ/, **borrowings. Borrowing** is the activity of borrowing money by people or organizations. EG *Lowering interest rates will make borrowing cheaper.* N UNCOUNT

borstal /bɔːstə⁰l/, **borstals.** In Britain, a **borstal** is a prison for young criminals. EG *Most of the boys in borstals are from bad backgrounds... He was sent to borstal.* N COUNT OR N UNCOUNT

bosom /bʊzə⁰m/, **bosoms. 1** A woman's breasts are sometimes referred to as her **bosom**. EG *She* N COUNT Outdated *had a very large bosom... ...hugging the cat to her bosom.*

2 If you are in the **bosom** of your family or of a community, you are among people who love, accept, and protect you. EG *...torn from the bosom of his own family... ...acceptance into the bosom of the Establishment.* N SING+SUPP Literary ● If you **take** someone **to** your **bosom**, you accept them and treat them with great affection. ● PHRASE Literary

3 Strong feelings are sometimes described as being in your **bosom**. EG *...some dark, sinful passion you're nursing in your bosom.* N COUNT+POSS Literary

4 A **bosom** friend is a friend who you know and like very much indeed. EG *...the son of her bosom friend Klara.* N MOD

boss /bɒs/, **bosses, bossing, bossed.** 1 Your **boss** is the person in charge of the organization where you work. EG *I met his boss at a dinner party... The crisis occurred while the boss was away.* N COUNT

2 If you are the **boss** in a group or relationship, you are the person who makes all the decisions. EG *You're not the boss around here.* N COUNT: USU *the*+N Informal

3 If you **are** your **own boss**, you work for yourself or do not have to ask other people for permission to do something. EG *I'm my own boss now, thank God.* PHRASE

4 If someone **bosses** you, **bosses** you around, or **bosses** you about, they keep telling you what to do as if they had authority over you. EG *They've bossed us around enough... Some people like to be bossed and bullied.* V+O: OFT *+around/about*

bossy /bɒsi[1]/. A **bossy** person enjoys telling other people what to do; used showing disapproval. EG *...one of those large, bossy women.* ADJ QUALIT ◇ **bossiness.** EG *His bossiness didn't worry her unduly.* ◇ N UNCOUNT

botanic /bə[7]tænɪk/ means the same as botanical.

botanical /bə[7]tænɪkə[0]l/. **Botanical** books, research, and activities relate to the scientific study of plants. EG *...botanical drawings... ...botanical gardens.* ADJ CLASSIF: ATTRIB

botanist /bɒtənɪst/, **botanists.** A **botanist** is a scientist who studies plants. N COUNT

botany /bɒtəni[1]/ is the scientific study of plants. N UNCOUNT

botch /bɒtʃ/, **botches, botching, botched.** If you **botch** a piece of work or **botch** it up, you do it badly or clumsily. EG *I hope I don't do something stupid and botch it... ...a botched job.* V+O: OFT+*up* Informal ▸ used as a noun. EG *She's made a botch of it again.* ▸ N COUNT

both /bəʊθ/. 1 You use **both** when you are referring to two people or things and saying that something is true about each of them. EG *Both her parents were dead... Both policies make good sense.* PREDET OR QUANTIF ▸ used as a pronoun. EG *Most of them speak either English or German or both... He got angry with both of them... He's fond of you both... We were both young.* ▸ PRON: OFT+*of*

2 You use the structure **both...and** when you are giving two facts or alternatives and emphasizing that each of them is true or possible. EG *These are dangers that threaten both men and women... The prospects both excited and worried me.*

bother /bɒðə/, **bothers, bothering, bothered.** 1 If you do not **bother** to do something, you do not do it, because you think it is unnecessary or would involve too much effort. EG *I never bother to iron my shirts... Why bother learning all those facts?... Don't bother with the washing-up... Don't bother about the rug.* V: OFT *+to*-INF, -ING, OR *with/about*

2 If you say that you **can't be bothered** to do something, you mean that you are not going to do it because you think it is unnecessary or would involve too much effort. EG *I can't be bothered to cook for myself.* PHRASE

3 **Bother** is trouble, fuss, or difficulty. EG *We found the address without any bother.* N UNCOUNT

4 If a task or a person is a **bother**, they are boring or irritating. EG *Sorry to be a bother, but could you sign this for me?* N SING: *a*+N Informal

5 If something **bothers** you or if you **bother** about it, you are worried, concerned, or upset about it. EG *Is something bothering you?... You can come along too, if you like – it doesn't bother me... I didn't bother about what I looked like.* V+O OR V+*about* ◇ **bothered.** EG *She was bothered about Olive.* ◇ ADJ PRED

6 If you **bother** someone, you talk to them or interrupt them when they are busy. EG *I didn't want to bother him while he was working... Don't bother me with little things like that.* V+O: OFT+*with*

7 Some people say **'Bother'** when they are annoyed about something. EXCLAM British

bottle /bɒtə[0]l/, **bottles, bottling, bottled.** 1 A **bottle** is a container for keeping liquids in. Bottles are usually made of glass or plastic and are shaped like a cylinder with a narrow top. EG *She was screwing the top back on to her scent bottle.* N COUNT

2 You can also use **bottle** to refer to a full bottle and its contents, or to the contents only. EG *She drank half a bottle of whisky a day.* N PART

3 When people **bottle** wine or beer, they put it into bottles after it has been made. V+O

4 A **bottle** is also a drinking container used by babies. It has a special rubber part at the top through which they can suck their drink. EG *The baby went on sucking the bottle.* N COUNT

bottle up. If you **bottle up** strong feelings, you do not express them or show them. EG *...all the rage that had been bottled up in him for so long.* PHRASAL VB: V+O+ADV

bottled /bɒtə[0]ld/. **Bottled** drinks are sold in bottles. EG *...bottled beer... ...bottled water.* ADJ CLASSIF

bottom /bɒtə[0]m/, **bottoms, bottoming, bottomed.** 1 The **bottom** of something is the lowest part of it. EG *I stood there at the bottom of the steps... It sank to the bottom of the lake.* N COUNT: USU SING

2 The **bottom** thing or layer in a series of things or layers is the lowest one. EG *...the bottom button of my waistcoat.* ADJ CLASSIF: ATTRIB

3 The **bottom** of a place such as a street or garden is the end of it that is farthest away from the entrance. EG *...down at the bottom of the meadow.* N COUNT

4 The **bottom** of an organization or scale is the least powerful or important level in it or the lowest point on it. EG *Officials at the top make the decisions; men at the bottom carry them out.* N SING: *the*+N

5 If you are **bottom** of the class or come **bottom** in a test, you are the worst student in the class or get the lowest marks in the test. ADJ PRED

6 If you **get to the bottom of** something, you discover the real truth about it or the real cause of it. EG *I'm going to get to the bottom of this, once and for all.* PHRASE

7 The thing that is **at the bottom of** something is the real cause of it. EG *Greed lies at the bottom of our ecological predicament.* PHRASE

8 Your **bottom** is the part of your body that you sit on. See picture at THE HUMAN BODY. N COUNT

bottom out. When something that has been getting worse or lower **bottoms out**, it stops getting worse or lower, and remains at a particular level or amount. EG *Even if the recession has bottomed out, it will not help the unemployed.* PHRASAL VB: V+ADV

bottomless /bɒtəmlɪ[2]s/. If you describe a supply of something as **bottomless**, you mean that it seems so large that it will never run out. EG *...American millionaires with bottomless purses.* ADJ CLASSIF

bough /baʊ/, **boughs.** A **bough** is a large branch of a tree. EG *...leafy boughs.* N COUNT Literary

bought /bɔ:t/ is the past tense and past participle of **buy.**

boulder /bəʊldə/, **boulders.** A **boulder** is a large rounded rock. EG *...huge granite boulders.* N COUNT

boulevard /bu:lə[0]vɑ:d[0]/, **boulevards.** A **boulevard** is a wide street in a city, usually with trees along each side. N COUNT

What is the connection between a bouquet and a botanist?

bounce /baʊns/, **bounces, bouncing, bounced. 1** When an object such as a ball **bounces**, it moves upwards or away immediately after hitting something. EG *Enormous hailstones bounced off the pavements.* ▸ used as a noun. EG *She had not reached the ball before its second bounce.* V : OFT+A ▸ N COUNT

2 When you **bounce** a ball, you throw it hard against a surface so that it immediately moves away. EG *She bounced the ball twice before serving.* V+O

3 If sound or light **bounces** off a surface, it reaches the surface and is reflected back. EG *Its flickering light bounced off the walls.* V : OFT+A

4 You can say that something **bounces** when it swings or moves up and down. EG *The rucksack bounced and jingled on my shoulders.* V

5 If you **bounce** on something, you jump up and down on it repeatedly. EG *...bouncing on a trampoline.* V+A

6 If someone **bounces** somewhere, they move in an energetic way, because they are feeling happy. EG *He came bouncing in, grinning.* V+A

7 If a cheque **bounces** or if a bank **bounces** it, the bank refuses to accept it and pay out the money, because there is not enough money in the account. V-ERG

bounce back. If you **bounce back** after a bad experience, you return quickly to your previous level of activity, enthusiasm, or success. EG *You always bounce back.* PHRASAL VB : V+ADV

bouncer /baʊnsə/, **bouncers.** A **bouncer** is a man who is employed to stand at the door of a club, in order to prevent unwanted people from coming in and to throw people out if they cause trouble. N COUNT Informal

bouncy /baʊnsi¹/. Someone who is **bouncy** is very lively and enthusiastic. EG *...a bouncy little man.* ADJ QUALIT

bound /baʊnd/, **bounds, bounding, bounded. 1** If something is **bound** to happen, it is certain to happen. EG *We are bound to win.* ADJ PRED +to-INF

2 If you are **bound** by an agreement or law, you have a duty to obey it. EG *We are bound by the government's pay policy.* ADJ PRED : USU+by

3 You can say **'I am bound to say'** or **'I am bound to admit'** when mentioning a fact which you regret. EG *Sometimes, I'm bound to say, they are a hopeless muddle.* ADV SEN

4 If one thing is **bound up with** another, it is closely connected with the other thing. EG *All this was bound up with what was happening in Egypt.* PHRASE

5 If a vehicle is **bound** for a particular place, it is travelling towards it. EG *He put her aboard the steamer bound for New York.* ADJ PRED+for

6 Bounds are limits which restrict what can be done. EG *It is not outside the bounds of possibility.* N PLURAL

7 If a place is **out of bounds**, people are forbidden to go there. EG *The staff room at school was out of bounds.* PHRASE

8 If an area of land **is bounded** by something, that thing is situated around its edge. EG *The plantation was bounded by marsh.* V+O : USU PASS

9 When animals or people **bound**, they move quickly with large leaps. EG *Goats were bounding off in all directions.* ▸ used as a noun. EG *He advanced towards Alexandra with great bounds.* V : USU+A ▸ N COUNT

10 Bound is also the past tense and past participle of **bind**.

boundary /baʊndə⁰ri¹/, **boundaries. 1** The **boundary** of an area of land is an imaginary line that separates it from other areas. EG *...the boundary of the Snowdonia National Park... You have to stay within your county boundary.* N COUNT : USU+SUPP

2 The **boundaries** of something such as a subject or activity are the limits that people think that it has. EG *The old boundaries between subjects are collapsing.* N COUNT+SUPP

boundless /baʊndlɪ²s/. If you describe something as **boundless**, you mean that there seems to be no end or limit to it. EG *...her boundless energies.* ADJ CLASSIF

bountiful /baʊntɪful/. Something that is **bountiful** is provided in large amounts. EG *...a bountiful supply of Madame's favourite cigarettes.* ADJ QUALIT Literary

bounty /baʊnti¹/. **1** Someone's **bounty** is their generosity in giving something. EG *They must accept the colonel's bounty.* N SING+POSS Literary

2 You can refer to something that is provided in large amounts as **bounty**. EG *...potatoes and peas, ducks and turkeys, all the bounty of the freezer.* N UNCOUNT Literary

bouquet /bəukeɪ, bu:-/, **bouquets.** A **bouquet** is a bunch of flowers which is attractively arranged, especially one which is given as a present. EG *...a bouquet of roses.* N COUNT

bourbon /bɜ:bə⁰n/, **bourbons. Bourbon** is a type of whisky that is made mainly in America. N MASS

bourgeois /bʊəʒwa:/. **1** If you describe things, for example people's attitudes, as **bourgeois**, you mean that you consider them typical of fairly rich middle-class people; used showing disapproval. EG *They're the most conventional, dull, bourgeois people you've ever met.* ADJ QUALIT

2 Marxists use **bourgeois** when referring to the capitalist system and to the social class who own most of the wealth in that system. EG *She condemns modern bourgeois society.* ADJ CLASSIF

bourgeoisie /bʊəʒwɑ:zi:/. In Marxist theory, the **bourgeoisie** are the middle-class people who own most of the wealth in a capitalist system. N COLL

bout /baʊt/, **bouts. 1** If you have a **bout** of something such as an illness, you have it for a short period. EG *...a bout of malaria.* N COUNT : OFT+of

2 A **bout** of activity is a short time during which you put a lot of effort into doing something. EG *...frenzied bouts of writing.* N COUNT : OFT+of

3 A **bout** is also a boxing or wrestling match. N COUNT

boutique /bu:ti:k/, **boutiques.** A **boutique** is a small shop that sells fashionable clothes, shoes, or jewellery. N COUNT

bow, bows, bowing, bowed; pronounced /baʊ/ for paragraphs 1 to 4 and for the phrasal verbs, and /bəʊ/ for paragraphs 5, 6, and 7.

1 When you **bow** to someone, you briefly bend your body towards them as a formal way of greeting them or showing respect. EG *'Goodbye, Miss Drew,' he said, bowing to her.* ▸ used as a noun. EG *He opened the door with a bow.* V : OFT+to ▸ N COUNT

2 If you **bow** your head, you bend it downwards so that you are looking towards the ground. V+O

3 If you **bow** to someone's wishes or **bow** to pressure, you agree to do what someone wants you to do. EG *They bow to all her wishes regardless of their own.* V+to Formal

4 The **bow** of a ship is the front part of it. EG *...the spray about her bows.* N COUNT

bow

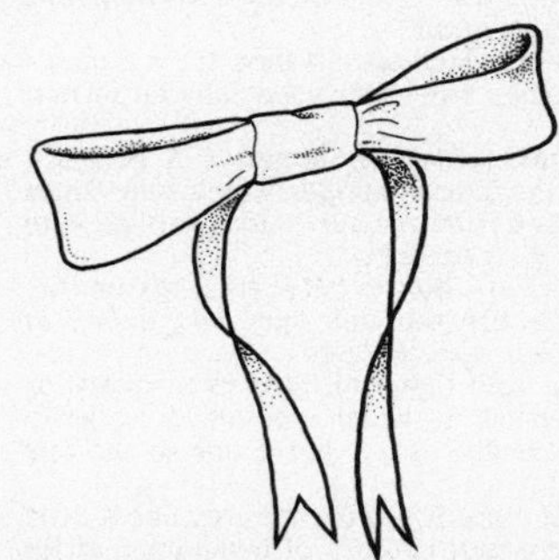

5 A **bow** is a knot with two loops and two loose ends that is used in tying shoelaces and ribbons. N COUNT

6 A **bow** is also a weapon for shooting arrows, consisting of a long piece of wood bent into a curve by a string attached to both its ends. N COUNT

7 The **bow** of a violin or other stringed instrument is a long thin piece of wood with horsehair N COUNT stretched along it, which you move across the strings of the instrument in order to play it.

bow down. If you **bow down**, you bow very low in order to show great respect. EG *Their people bowed down before them.* PHRASAL VB : V+ADV

bow out. If you **bow out** of something, you stop taking part in it. EG *We may do one more performance before we bow out.* PHRASAL VB : V+ADV

bowed; pronounced /bəʊd/ for paragraph 1 and /baʊd/ for paragraph 2.

1 Something that is **bowed** is curved. EG *He had slightly bowed legs.* ADJ QUALIT

2 If a person's body is **bowed**, it is bent forward. EG *...a man bent and bowed, walking slowly along.* ADJ QUALIT

bowel /baʊəl/, **bowels. 1** Your **bowels** are the tubes in your body through which digested food passes from your stomach to your anus. N PLURAL, OR N SING : *the*+N

2 You can refer to the parts deep inside something as the **bowels** of that thing. EG *...deep in the bowels of the earth.* N PLURAL +SUPP

bowl /bəʊl/, **bowls, bowling, bowled. 1** A **bowl** is a circular container with a wide, uncovered top. Bowls are used, for example, for serving food or mixing ingredients when cooking. N COUNT

2 You can also use **bowl** to refer to a bowl and its contents, or to the contents only. EG *...a bowl of water... I ate a big bowl of porridge.* N PART

3 The **bowl** of a lavatory, a tobacco pipe, or a spoon is the hollow, rounded part of it. N COUNT : USU+SUPP

4 When someone playing cricket **bowls** a ball, they throw it down the pitch towards the batsman. V+O OR V

5 Bowls is a game in which the players try to roll large wooden balls as near as possible to a small ball. N UNCOUNT

6 See **bowling**.

bowl over. 1 If you **bowl** someone **over**, you knock them down by accidentally hitting them when you are moving very quickly. EG *They leapt aside to avoid being bowled over by three boys as they raced past.* PHRASAL VB : V+O+ADV **2** If you **are bowled over** by something, you are very impressed or surprised by it. EG *I was bowled over by the beauty of Malawi.* V+O+ADV, USU PASS

bow-legged /bəʊ legɪd/. Someone who is **bow-legged** has legs that curve apart at the knees. ADJ CLASSIF

bowler /bəʊlə/, **bowlers. 1** The **bowler** in a game of cricket is the person who is bowling the ball. N COUNT

2 A **bowler** or a **bowler hat** is a round, stiff hat with a narrow curved brim. N COUNT

bowling /bəʊlɪŋ/ is **1** a game in which you roll a heavy ball down a long narrow track towards a group of wooden objects and try to knock down as many of them as possible. N ING **2** the action or activity of bowling the ball in cricket. EG *His bowling was generally disappointing.* N UNCOUNT

bow tie /bəʊ taɪ/, **bow ties.** A **bow tie** is a man's tie in the form of a bow, worn especially for formal occasions. N COUNT

box /bɒks/, **boxes, boxing, boxed. 1** A **box** is a square or rectangular container which sometimes has a lid. EG *...a cardboard box... ...boxes filled with old clothes... ...your tool box.* N COUNT

2 You can also use **box** to refer to a box and its contents, or to the contents only. EG *...a box of matches... ...a box of chocolates.* N PART

3 A **box** on a form that you fill in is a square or rectangular space in which you have to write something. EG *If you agree, put a tick in the box marked 'yes'.* N COUNT

4 A **box** in a theatre is a separate area like a little room where a small number of people can sit to watch the performance. EG *...the Royal Box.* N COUNT

5 You can refer to television as the **box**. EG *...eating, drinking, and watching the box... David Owen was on the box the other night.* N SING : *the*+N Informal

6 To **box** means to fight someone according to the rules of the sport of boxing. EG *He used to box, run, and swim for the school.* V

box in. If you **are boxed in**, you are unable to move from a particular place because you are surrounded by other people or cars. EG *Two other drivers boxed me in.* PHRASAL VB : V+O+ADV

boxer /bɒksə/, **boxers.** A **boxer** is a sportsman whose sport is boxing. N COUNT

boxing /bɒksɪŋ/ is a sport in which two men wearing large padded gloves fight according to special rules, by punching each other. N UNCOUNT

Boxing Day is the twenty-sixth of December, the day after Christmas Day. N UNCOUNT British

box office, box offices. 1 The **box office** in a theatre, cinema, or concert hall is the place where the tickets are sold. N COUNT

2 The **box office** is also used when referring to the degree of success of a film, play, or actor in terms of the number of people who go to watch it or them. EG *She was a very hot box office attraction indeed.* N SING : *the*+N OR N MOD

boy /bɔɪ/, **boys. 1** A **boy** is a male child. EG *There were hundreds of boys and girls on the lawn.* N COUNT

2 You can also refer to a young man as a **boy**. EG *...the boy you were going to marry... 'Poor boy,' said Molly.* N COUNT Informal

3 You can also refer to a group of men as **boys**. EG *We may need the help of the science boys... Take him away, boys.* N PLURAL Informal

4 Some people say **'Boy'** or **'Oh boy'** in order to express strong feelings such as excitement or admiration. EG *Boy oh boy, was that some party!* EXCLAM American

boycott /bɔɪkɒt/, **boycotts, boycotting, boycotted.** A **boycott** is a refusal to be involved with a country, organization, or event that you strongly disapprove of. EG *...an Olympic boycott... The boycott of British goods began in 1906.* N COUNT : OFT+SUPP ▸ used as a verb. EG *He urged all citizens to boycott the polls.* ▸ V+O

boyfriend /bɔɪfrend/, **boyfriends.** Someone's **boyfriend** is a man or boy with whom they are having a romantic or sexual relationship. EG *This is my boyfriend Oliver... She had lots of boyfriends.* N COUNT : USU+POSS

boyhood /bɔɪhʊd/ is the period of a male person's life during which he is a boy. EG *He began to talk about his boyhood in London.* N UNCOUNT : USU+POSS

boyish /bɔɪɪʃ/. **1** If you say that a man is **boyish**, you mean that he is like a boy in his appearance or behaviour. EG *...a boyish smile... This incident was not a boyish prank.* ADJ QUALIT ◊ **boyishly.** EG *He grinned boyishly.* ◊ ADV

2 If you say that a girl or woman is **boyish**, you mean that she looks or behaves like a boy, for example because she has short hair and small breasts. EG *...her boyish clothes.* ADJ QUALIT

bra /brɑː/, **bras.** A **bra** is a piece of underwear that women wear to support their breasts. N COUNT

brace /breɪs/, **braces, bracing, braced. 1** If you **brace** yourself for something unpleasant or difficult, you prepare yourself for it. EG *He braced himself for the task... She had braced herself to read the letter.* V-REFL : OFT+*for* OR *to*-INF

2 If you **brace** your body against something, you press against it in order to steady your body or to avoid falling. EG *The taxi swung round a bend and he braced himself with his foot.* V+O OR V-REFL

3 If you **brace** your shoulders or legs, you keep them stiffly in a particular position. EG *He stood to attention, his shoulders braced.* V+O

4 A **brace** is **4.1** a metal device that is sometimes fastened to a child's teeth in order to help them grow straight. **4.2** a device attached to a part of a person's body, for example to a weak leg, in order to strengthen or support it. N COUNT

5 Braces are a pair of straps that you can wear instead of a belt to prevent your trousers from falling down. The straps pass over your shoulders and are fastened to your trousers at the front and back. N PLURAL British

6 You can refer to two things of the same kind as a N PART

On these pages, how many things can you wear?

brace, especially two wild birds that have been killed for sport or food. The plural form is also **brace**. EG ...*a brace of pheasants.*

bracelet /breɪslɪ²t/, **bracelets.** A **bracelet** is a chain or band, usually made of metal, which you wear around your wrist as jewellery. See picture at JEWELLERY. N COUNT

bracing /breɪsɪŋ/. If you describe a place, climate, or activity as **bracing**, you mean that it makes you feel fit and full of energy. EG ...*mountain air, bracing and heady.* ADJ QUALIT

bracken /brækə⁰n/ is a plant like a large fern that grows on hills and in woods. N UNCOUNT

bracket /brækɪ²t/, **brackets, bracketing, bracketed. 1 Brackets** are **1.1** a pair of written marks such as ( ) that you place round a word, expression, or sentence in order to indicate that you are giving extra information. EG *The comments in brackets are the author's.* **1.2** a pair of marks that are placed around a series of symbols in a mathematical expression to indicate that the series functions as one item within the expression. N COUNT: USU PLURAL

2 If you **bracket** a word, expression, or sentence, you put brackets round it. EG ...*a bracketed question mark.* V+O

3 If you say that someone or something is in a particular **bracket**, you mean that they come within a particular range, for example a range of incomes, ages, or prices. EG ...*a professional in a high income bracket... ...the 14-16 age bracket.* N COUNT+SUPP

4 When you **bracket** two or more things or people together, you consider them as being similar or related in some way. EG *Should current affairs be bracketed with documentary?* V+O+ together/with

5 A **bracket** is also a piece of metal, wood, or plastic that is fastened to a wall to support something such as a shelf. N COUNT

brag /bræg/, **brags, bragging, bragged.** If you **brag**, you say in a very proud way that you have something or have done something; used showing disapproval. EG *I didn't brag about the salary... He bragged to two nurses that he had killed a man.* V: OFT+A, QUOTE, OR REPORT: ONLY *that*

braid /breɪd/, **braids, braiding, braided. 1 Braid** is a narrow piece of decorated cloth or twisted threads, which is used to decorate clothes or curtains. EG ...*a cap with gold braid on it.* N UNCOUNT

2 If you **braid** hair or a group of threads, you plait it. EG *They wore their hair braided in long pigtails.* V+O American

3 A **braid** is a length of hair which has been plaited and tied. EG *Carole was plump, with long braids.* N COUNT American

Braille /breɪl/ is a system of printing for blind people. The letters are printed as groups of raised dots that you can feel with your fingers. N UNCOUNT

brain /breɪn/, **brains. 1** Your **brain** is **1.1** the organ inside your head that enables you to think and to feel things such as heat and pain. EG ...*how the brain functions... ...brain damage.* **1.2** your mind and the way that you think. EG *He had one clear wish in his confused brain.* ● If someone **has** something **on the brain**, they keep thinking about it. N COUNT; ● PHRASE Informal

2 If you say that someone has **brains** or a good **brain**, you mean that they have the ability to learn and understand things quickly, to solve problems, and to make good decisions. EG *He'd got brains but wouldn't use them... She has a very capable business brain.* N COUNT

3 If you **pick** someone's **brains**, you ask them to help you with a problem because they know a lot about the subject involved. PHRASE Informal

4 Very clever people are sometimes referred to as **brains**. EG *Not even the great brains of Cambridge can solve his problem.* N COUNT Informal

5 The person who plans the activities of an organization can be referred to as the **brains** of that organization. EG *She was the brains of the company.* N SING: *the*+N Informal

6 to **rack** your **brains**: see **rack**.

brainchild /breɪntʃaɪld/. Someone's **brainchild** is an idea or invention that they have thought up or created. EG *The project was the brainchild of Max Nicholson.* N SING+POSS

brain drain. When people talk about a **brain drain**, they are referring to the movement of a large number of scientists or academics away from their own country to other countries where the conditions and salaries are better. N SING

brainless /breɪnlɪ²s/. If you say that someone is **brainless**, you mean that they are very silly. ADJ QUALIT

brainstorm /breɪnstɔːm/, **brainstorms.** If you have a **brainstorm**, you suddenly become unable to think sensibly. EG *I must have had a brainstorm.* N COUNT British

brainwash /breɪnwɒʃ/, **brainwashes, brainwashing, brainwashed.** If you **brainwash** someone, you force them to believe something by continually telling them that it is true, and preventing them from thinking about it properly. EG *The public continues to be brainwashed into believing that a nuclear war could be survived.* V+O: OFT+*into*

brainwave /breɪnweɪv/, **brainwaves.** A **brainwave** is a clever idea that you suddenly think of. EG *Then he had a brainwave.* N COUNT

brainy /breɪni¹/, **brainier, brainiest.** Someone who is **brainy** is clever and good at learning. ADJ QUALIT Informal

brake /breɪk/, **brakes, braking, braked. 1** The **brakes** of a vehicle are devices in it or on it that are used to make it go slower or stop. See picture at CAR. EG *There was a sudden screech of brakes... He took his foot off the brake.* N COUNT: USU PLURAL

2 When a vehicle **brakes**, the driver makes it slow down or stop by using the brakes. EG *Try to avoid sudden braking.* V

3 A **brake** is also something that slows down or stops action or progress. EG *Restrictive practices were putting a savage brake on enterprise.* N COUNT

bramble /bræmbə⁰l/, **brambles. Brambles** are wild, thorny bushes that produce blackberries. EG ...*a large house, all overgrown with brambles.* N COUNT: USU PLURAL

bran /bræn/ is the small brown flakes that are left when wheat grains have been used to make white flour. EG ...*breakfast cereals containing bran.* N UNCOUNT

branch /brɑːntʃ/, **branches, branching, branched. 1** The **branches** of a tree are the parts that grow out from its trunk and that have leaves, flowers, or fruit growing on them. EG *A bird flew across to the tree and alighted on a branch.* N COUNT

2 A **branch** of a business or other organization is one of the offices, shops, or local groups which belong to it. EG ...*the Ipswich branch of Marks and Spencer... All the organizations in this list have local branches.* N COUNT+SUPP

3 A **branch** of a subject is a part or type of it. EG ...*specialists in particular branches of medicine.* N COUNT+SUPP

4 A **branch** of government is a part or department with a particular function. EG ...*the executive branch of government.* N COUNT+SUPP

branch off. A road or path that **branches off** from another one starts from it and goes in a slightly different direction. EG *A dirt path branched off the main road.* PHRASAL VB: V+ADV/PREP

branch out. If you **branch out**, you do something different from your normal activities or work, especially something unusual or risky. EG *She decided to branch out alone and launch a campaign.* PHRASAL VB: V+ADV

brand /brænd/, **brands, branding, branded. 1** A **brand** of a product is the version of it that is made by one particular manufacturer. EG ...*a preference for one brand of soft drink rather than another.* N COUNT: OFT+SUPP

2 You can refer to a particular kind of thought, behaviour, or writing as a particular **brand** of it. EG ...*their brand of politics... ...a new brand of humour.* N COUNT+*of*

3 If you **are branded** as something bad, people decide and say that you are that thing. EG *His political supporters had been branded traitors... Hamburgers have been branded as junk food.* V+O+*as* OR V+O+C: OFT PASS

4 When an animal **is branded**, a permanent mark is burned on its skin, in order to indicate who it belongs to. V+O

brandish /brændɪʃ/, **brandishes, brandishing, brandished.** If you **brandish** something, especially a weapon, you wave it vigorously as a sign of aggression or triumph. EG *They sprang high into the air brandishing their spears.* V+O

brand name, brand names. The **brand name** of a product made by a particular manufacturer is the name that appears on it. N COUNT

brand-new. Something that is **brand-new** is completely new. EG *...a brand new religion.* ADJ CLASSIF

brandy /brændi^{1}/, **brandies. Brandy** is a strong alcoholic drink, usually made from wine. N MASS

brash /bræʃ/, **brasher, brashest.** If someone's behaviour is **brash**, they are being too confident and aggressive. EG *Jenny was alarmed by these brash children.* ADJ QUALIT

brass /brɑ:s/, **brasses. 1 Brass** is a yellow-coloured metal made from copper and zinc. It is used especially for making ornaments and musical instruments. EG *...brass buttons.* N UNCOUNT

2 Brasses are flat pieces of brass with writing or a picture cut into them, which are found in churches. N COUNT

3 The section of an orchestra which consists of brass wind instruments such as trumpets and horns is called the **brass**. See picture at MUSICAL INSTRUMENTS. N PLURAL : the+N

4 If you **get down to brass tacks**, you discuss the basic, most important facts of a situation. PHRASE

brassiere /bræsɪə, bræz-/, **brassieres.** A **brassiere** is the same as a bra. N COUNT Formal

brat /bræt/, **brats.** If you call a child a **brat**, you mean that he or she behaves badly or annoys you. EG *He's a spoilt brat.* N COUNT Informal

bravado /brəvɑ:dəʊ/ is an appearance of courage that someone shows in order to impress other people. EG *...some mad, defiant act of bravado.* N UNCOUNT

brave /breɪv/, **braver, bravest; braves, braving, braved. 1** Someone who is **brave** is willing to do things which are dangerous, and does not show fear in difficult or dangerous situations. EG *...the brave soldiers of your country... I think you were brave to defy convention.* ◇ **bravely.** EG *He fought bravely at the Battle of Waterloo.* ADJ QUALIT ◇ ADV

2 If you say that someone is **putting a brave face on** a difficult situation, you mean that they are pretending that they are happy or that they can deal with the situation easily. PHRASE

3 If you **brave** a difficult or dangerous situation, you deliberately experience it, in order to achieve something. EG *Farmers braved wintry conditions to rescue the sheep.* V+O Literary

bravery /breɪvə^{0}ri^{1}/ is brave behaviour or the quality of being brave. EG *Being a nurse requires infinite patience and bravery.* N UNCOUNT

bravo /brɑ:vəʊ/. Some people say **'Bravo'** to express appreciation when someone has done something well. EG *Kate applauded with the rest and shouted out 'Bravo!'* EXCLAM Outdated

brawl /brɔ:l/, **brawls, brawling, brawled.** A **brawl** is a rough fight or struggle. EG *His front teeth were knocked out in a brawl.* ▸ used as a verb. EG *They were brawling in the street.* N COUNT ▸ V

brawny /brɔ:ni^{1}/. Someone who is **brawny** is strong and muscular. EG *...a brawny worker.* ADJ QUALIT

bray /breɪ/, **brays, braying, brayed. 1** When a donkey **brays**, it makes the loud, harsh sound that donkeys typically make. ▸ used as a noun. EG *...the bray of a donkey.* V ▸ N COUNT

2 If you say that someone **brays**, you mean that they make a loud harsh sound or talk in a loud harsh way. EG *...her dreadful braying laughter.* V Literary

brazen /breɪzə^{0}n/, **brazens, brazening, brazened.** If you describe someone as **brazen**, you mean that they are very bold and do not care if other people think that they are behaving wrongly. EG *...a brazen whore... ...brazen claims.* ◇ **brazenly.** EG *No industry is more brazenly orientated towards quick, easy profits.* ADJ QUALIT ◇ ADV

brazen out. If you have done something wrong and you **brazen** it **out**, you behave confidently in order not to appear ashamed. EG *However, I had to brazen it out now, so I went up to him.* PHRASAL VB : V+O+ADV

brazier /breɪzɪə/, **braziers.** A **brazier** is a large metal container in which coal or charcoal is burned to keep people warm when they are outside in cold weather. N COUNT

breach /bri:tʃ/, **breaches, breaching, breached.**

1 If you **breach** an agreement or law, you do something that disobeys it. EG *...the ethical questions involved in breaching the confidentiality of patients.* ▸ used as a noun. EG *Does refusal to work on rest days constitute a breach of contract?* V+O Formal ▸ N COUNT OR N UNCOUNT

2 A **breach** in a relationship is a serious disagreement which often results in the relationship ending. EG *This was the most profound breach in our marriage.* N COUNT Formal

3 If you **step into the breach**, you do a job or task which someone else was supposed to do, because they are suddenly unable to do it. EG *Cooper loyally stepped into the breach as official Tory candidate.* PHRASE

4 A **breach** in a barrier is a gap or crack in it. EG *They rush to defend any breach in the walls.* N COUNT Formal

5 If you **breach** a barrier, you deliberately make a gap in it, especially in order to let someone through. EG *He breached the enemy barbed wire.* V+O Formal

bread /brɛd/ is a very common food made from flour, water, and often yeast. The mixture is made into a soft dough and baked in an oven. EG *...some bread and cheese... ...a loaf of bread... ...three slices of bread.* N UNCOUNT

breadcrumb /brɛdkrʌm/, **breadcrumbs. Breadcrumbs** are tiny pieces of bread. N COUNT : USU PLURAL

breadline /brɛdlaɪn/. Someone who is on or near the **breadline** is very poor indeed. EG *One family in four was on the breadline.* N SING : the+N

breadth /brɛdθ/. **1** The **breadth** of something is the distance between its two sides. EG *...six yards in breadth and fifty yards long.* N UNCOUNT

2 The **breadth** of something is also its quality of consisting of or involving many different things. EG *The very breadth of the subject gives it an added interest... ...his breadth of vision.* N UNCOUNT +SUPP

3 the **length and breadth** of somewhere: see **length.** ● See also **hair's breadth.**

breadwinner /brɛdwɪnə/, **breadwinners.** The **breadwinner** in a family is the person in it who earns the money that the family needs. N COUNT

break /breɪk/, **breaks, breaking, broke** /brəʊk/, **broken** /brəʊkə^{0}n/. **1** When an object **breaks** or when you **break** it, it suddenly separates into two or more pieces, often because it has been hit or dropped. EG *He has broken a window with a ball... She stepped backwards onto a cup, which broke into several pieces... The string broke... She's broken her ankle.* ▸ used as a noun, usually of bones. EG *That looks like a nasty break.* V-ERG ▸ N COUNT

2 When a tool or piece of machinery **breaks** or when you **break** it, it is damaged and no longer works. V-ERG

3 If you **break** a rule, promise, or agreement, you do something that disobeys it. EG *We're not breaking the law.* V+O

4 If you **break free** or **break** someone's **hold**, you free yourself by force from someone or something that is holding you. EG *He was thrashing to break free... I broke away from her and raced for the door... He had my hands behind my back in a hold that was impossible to break.* PHRASE

5 To **break** a connection or situation that has existed for some time means to end it suddenly. EG *Radio contact was broken... Everything you've tried has failed to break the deadlock... The stillness was broken by the barking of a dog... They cannot break the habit.* V+O

What is the difference between 'bravery' and 'bravado'?

6 If you **break** with a group of people or a way of doing things, you stop being involved with that group or stop doing things in that way. EG *The Chinese church broke with Rome in 1957... Two United Party senators broke away to form the Federal Party... He broke with precedent by making his maiden speech on a controversial subject.* V+A
▸ used as a noun. EG *...their break with the Labour Party in 1968.* ▸ N COUNT

7 If you **break** someone of a habit, you cause them to lose the habit. EG *...breaking a child of its bad habits.* V+O+*of*

8 To **break** someone means to destroy their success or their career. EG *...a prestigious competition which could make or break his career.* V+O

9 A **break** in a line, sound, or process is a gap or interruption in it. EG *...a break in routine.* N COUNT ▸ used as a verb. EG *The blue horizon encircled them, broken only by the mountain-top.* ▸ V+O

10 A **break** is also a short period of time when you have a rest or a change from what you are doing. EG *We all met in the pub during the lunch break... The doctors had worked without a break.* N COUNT ▸ used as a verb. EG *We broke for tea for an hour.* ▸ V : OFT+*for*

11 To **break** the force of something such as a blow or fall means to weaken its effect. EG *Fortunately, the tree broke her fall.* V+O

12 When someone **breaks** a piece of news or when a piece of news **breaks**, the news is told to people. EG *It was Ted who broke the news to me.* V-ERG

13 A **break** is also a lucky opportunity that someone gets to achieve something. EG *He has been running for 12 years, but his main break came last spring in Australia.* N COUNT Informal

14 If you **break** a record, you beat the previous record for a particular achievement. EG *Oliver Barrett was out to break his New York-Boston speed record.* V+O

15 When day **breaks**, it starts to grow light after the night has ended. V

16 When a wave **breaks**, the water at the top of it falls down, for example when it reaches the shore. V

17 When a company **breaks even**, it makes neither a profit nor a loss. PHRASE

18 If you **break** a secret code, you work out how to read it. V+O

19 When a boy's voice **breaks**, it becomes permanently deeper. V

20 In tennis, if you **break** your opponent's serve, you win a game in which your opponent is serving. V+O
▸ used as a noun. EG *Gomer is one break of serve up.* ▸ N COUNT

21 See also **broke**, **broken**.

break down. PHRASAL VB : V+ADV **1** When a machine or a vehicle **breaks down**, it stops working. EG *The car broke down three miles outside Winchester.* **2** When a system, plan, or discussion **breaks down**, it fails because of a problem or disagreement. EG *This efficient communication system started to break down... The talks broke down over differences on doctrine.* V+ADV **3** When a substance **breaks down** or when something **breaks** it **down**, it changes into a different form because of a chemical process. EG *Enzymes break down proteins by chemical action.* V-ERG+ADV
4 If someone **breaks down**, they start crying or laughing uncontrollably. EG *He had broken down and cried... They often broke down in chuckles.* V+ADV **5** If you **break down** a door or barrier, you hit it so hard that it falls to the ground. V+O+ADV **6** See also **breakdown**.

break in. PHRASAL VB : V+ADV **1** If someone **breaks in**, they get into a building by force. EG *They had broken in through the back.* **2** If you **break in** on someone's conversation or activity, you interrupt them. EG *'Don't look at me,' Etta broke in brusquely.* V+ADV **3** If you **break** someone **in**, you get them used to a new job or situation. EG *Chief Brody liked to break in his young men slowly.* V+O+ADV **4** See also **break-in**.

break into. PHRASAL VB : V+PREP **1** If someone **breaks into** a building, they get into it by force. EG *He broke into a shop one night.* **2** You can indicate that someone suddenly starts doing something by saying that they **break into** laughter or **break into** a run, for example. EG *When Rudolph saw her, he broke into a run... The boys broke into applause.* V+PREP **3** If you **break into** a new area of activity, especially an area of business, you become involved in it. EG *...women wanting to break into the labour market.* V+PREP, HAS PASS

break off. PHRASAL VB : V-ERG+ADV **1** When part of something **breaks off** or when you **break** it **off**, it comes off or is removed by being snapped off or torn away. EG *A little bit has broken off the left hand corner. Garroway broke off another piece of bread.* **2** If you **break off** when you are doing or saying something, you suddenly stop doing it or saying it. EG *He would break off the rehearsal... 'I thought – ' He broke off, then smiled. 'Sorry, not my business.'* V+ADV OR V+O+ADV
3 If someone **breaks off** a relationship, they end it. EG *She broke off her engagement.* V+O+ADV

break out. PHRASAL VB : V+ADV **1** If something such as a fight or disease **breaks out**, it begins suddenly. EG *Fierce fighting broke out between rival groups.* **2** If you **break out** in a rash or a sweat or if it **breaks out** on your body, it appears on your skin. EG *She felt the sweat break out on her forehead.* V+ADV, OFT+A

break through. PHRASAL VB : V+PREP **1** If you **break through** a barrier, you succeed in forcing your way through it. EG *I broke through the bushes.* **2** When something that was previously hidden or unseen **breaks through**, it appears. EG *Sometimes these impulses break through in your work... The sun managed to break through the clouds for a while.* V+ADV/PREP **3** See also **breakthrough**.

break up. PHRASAL VB : V-ERG+ADV **1** When something **breaks up** or when you **break** it **up**, it separates or is divided into several smaller parts. EG *The wood was so rotten that, when they pulled, it broke up into a shower of fragments.* **2** If you **break up** with your wife, husband, girlfriend, or boyfriend, your relationship with that person ends. EG *Tim and I broke up... Their marriage is breaking up.* V+ADV OR V+ADV+*with* : RECIP **3** If an activity **breaks up** or if you **break** it **up,** it is brought to an end. EG *The long drunken party had just broken up... The policemen broke the fight up.* V-ERG+ADV **4** When schools or the pupils in them **break up**, the school term ends and the pupils start their holidays. EG *We break up on Friday.* V+ADV **5** See also **break-up**.

breakable /breɪkəbə°l/. **Breakable** objects are easy to break by accident. EG *My wife let her play with breakable ornaments.* ADJ CLASSIF

breakage /breɪkɪdʒ/, **breakages. Breakage** is the act or result of breaking something. EG *Accidental breakage of your household glass will be covered by the policy... ...the cost of breakages.* N UNCOUNT OR N COUNT Formal

breakaway /breɪkəweɪ/. A **breakaway** group is a group of people who have separated from a larger group. EG *...a breakaway party.* ADJ CLASSIF : ATTRIB

breakdown /breɪkdaʊn/, **breakdowns. 1** The **breakdown** of a system, plan, or discussion is its failure or ending. EG *There was a serious breakdown of communications... ...the threat of social breakdown.* N COUNT OR N UNCOUNT +SUPP
2 If you suffer a **breakdown**, you become so depressed that you are unable to cope with your life. EG *I shall probably have another breakdown if I stay any longer in this house.* N COUNT
3 If you have a **breakdown** when travelling somewhere by car, your car stops working. N COUNT
4 A **breakdown** of something is a list of its separate parts: EG *I forget what the breakdown of hours is.* N COUNT

breaker /breɪkə/, **breakers. Breakers** are big sea waves. EG *...the roar of the breakers on the reef.* N COUNT : USU PLURAL

breakfast /brɛkfəst/, **breakfasts, breakfasting, breakfasted. 1 Breakfast** is the first meal of the day, which is usually eaten early in the morning. EG *I would get up early and eat my breakfast... ...men who hurry their breakfasts.* N UNCOUNT OR N COUNT

2 When you **breakfast**, you have breakfast. EG *She dressed early, and breakfasted.* V Formal

break-in, break-ins. When there is a **break-in**, someone gets into a building by force. EG *...the break-in at Blackburn Place.* N COUNT

breakneck /breɪknɛk/. Something that happens or travels at **breakneck** speed happens or travels very fast indeed. EG *The construction of other hotels proceeded at breakneck speed.* ADJ CLASSIF: ATTRIB

breakthrough /breɪkθruː/, **breakthroughs.** A **breakthrough** is an important development or achievement. EG *Scientists are hovering on the brink of a major breakthrough... ...a breakthrough in government-industry relations.* N COUNT

break-up, break-ups. When the **break-up** of a group, relationship, or system occurs, it comes to an end. EG *This caused the break-up of the coalition... All marriage break-ups are traumatic.* N UNCOUNT OR N COUNT

breakwater /breɪkwɔːtə/, **breakwaters.** A **breakwater** is a wooden or stone wall that extends from the shore into the sea and is built in order to protect a harbour or beach from the force of the waves. N COUNT

breast /brɛst/, **breasts.** 1 A woman's **breasts** are the two soft, round pieces of flesh on her chest that can produce milk to feed a baby. N COUNT

2 A person's **breast** is the upper part of his or her chest. EG *The bullet pierced Joel's breast.* N COUNT Literary

3 The **breast** is often considered to be the part of your body where your emotions are. EG *...the creation of national pride in the breasts of Frenchmen.* N COUNT+SUPP Literary

4 A bird's **breast** is the front part of its body. N COUNT

5 If you **make a clean breast of it**, you tell someone the truth about yourself or about something wrong that you have done. PHRASE

breastbone /brɛstbəʊn/, **breastbones.** Your **breastbone** is the long vertical bone in the centre of your chest. N COUNT

breast-feed, breast-feeds, breast-feeding, breast-fed. When a woman **breast-feeds** her baby, she feeds it with milk from her breasts, rather than from a bottle. ◇ **breast-feeding.** EG *A big advantage of breast-feeding is that the milk is always pure.* V+O OR V ◇ N UNCOUNT

breaststroke /brɛststrəʊk/ is a kind of swimming stroke which you do lying on your front, moving your arms and legs horizontally. See picture at SWIMMING. N UNCOUNT

breath /brɛθ/, **breaths.** 1 Your **breath** is the air which you take into and let out of your lungs when you breathe. EG *You could smell the whisky on his breath... Jenny paused for breath.* N COUNT OR N UNCOUNT

2 When you take a **breath**, you breathe in. EG *He took a deep breath and blew into the bag.* N COUNT

3 When you are **out of breath**, you breathe very quickly and with difficulty because you have been doing something energetic. PHRASE

4 When you **get** your **breath** back after doing something energetic, you start breathing normally again. PHRASE

5 If you **hold** your **breath**, you stop breathing for a short while. EG *We all held our breaths till the bomb burst.* PHRASE

6 If you say that something **takes** your **breath away**, you mean that it is extremely beautiful or amazing. PHRASE

7 If you say something **under** your **breath**, you say it in a very quiet voice. EG *I was cursing him under my breath.* PHRASE

8 If you tell someone to **save** their **breath** or say that they are **wasting** their **breath**, you mean that the person they are planning to say something to will not take any notice of them. PHRASE

9 If you go outside for **a breath of fresh air**, you go outside because it is stuffy indoors. PHRASE

breathalyze /brɛθəlaɪz/, **breathalyzes, breathalyzing, breathalyzed;** also spelled **breathalyse.** When the police **breathalyze** the driver of a car, they ask the driver to breathe into a special bag in order to see if he or she has drunk too much alcohol. V+O

breathe /briːð/, **breathes, breathing, breathed.** 1 When people or animals **breathe**, they take air into their lungs and let it out again. EG *I breathed deeply... When we breathed the air, it smelt sweet.* ◇ **breathing.** EG *He could hear her deep, regular breathing.* V OR V+O ◇ N UNCOUNT

2 If you **breathe** smoke or fumes over someone, you send smoke or fumes out of your mouth towards them. EG *...breathing whisky fumes all over my face.* V+O+A

3 When someone **breathes again** or **breathes** more **easily** after a frightening experience, they relax because the danger is over. EG *He breathed easier; he had made it.* PHRASE

4 If you say that someone **is breathing down** your **neck**, you mean that they are paying such careful attention to everything you do that you feel uncomfortable and unable to act freely. PHRASE

5 If someone says something very quietly, you can say that they **breathe** it. EG *'Frank,' she breathed. 'Help me, please.'* V+O OR V+QUOTE Literary

6 Someone who **breathes** life, confidence, or excitement into something gives this quality to it. EG *A teacher should try to breathe life into her subject.* V+O: OFT+*into* Literary

breathe in. When you **breathe in**, you take some air into your lungs. EG *Don't pant, breathe in slowly... He breathed in the cool crisp air.* PHRASAL VB: V+ADV OR V+O+ADV

breathe out. When you **breathe out**, you send air out of your lungs through your nose or mouth. EG *She breathed out through parted lips.* PHRASAL VB: V+ADV OR V+O+ADV

breather /briːðə/, **breathers.** If you take or have a **breather**, you stop what you are doing for a short time and have a rest. EG *I stopped and had another breather.* N COUNT Informal

breathing space. A **breathing space** is a short period of time between two activities in which you can recover from the first activity and prepare for the second one. N SING OR N UNCOUNT

breathless /brɛθlɪ²s/. If you are **breathless**, 1 you have difficulty in breathing properly, for example because you have been running. EG *She opened the door, a little breathless from climbing the stairs.* ◇ **breathlessly.** EG *'Miss Crabbe's on the telephone,' I said breathlessly.* ◇ **breathlessness.** EG *Obesity causes breathlessness.* 2 you are hardly able to breathe because you are so excited or afraid. EG *They followed the match with breathless interest.* ◇ **breathlessly.** EG *...waiting breathlessly for news.* ADJ QUALIT ◇ ADV ◇ N UNCOUNT ADJ CLASSIF ◇ ADV

breathtaking /brɛθteɪkɪŋ/. If you say that something is **breathtaking**, you mean that it is extremely beautiful or amazing. EG *...breathtaking scenery... We were travelling at breathtaking speed.* ◇ **breathtakingly.** EG *Fashion magazines display breathtakingly beautiful gowns.* ADJ QUALIT ◇ SUBMOD

bred /brɛd/ is the past tense and past participle of **breed.**

breeches /brɪtʃɪz/ are trousers which reach your knees. EG *...riding breeches.* N PLURAL

breed /briːd/, **breeds, breeding, bred** /brɛd/. 1 A **breed** of a pet animal or farm animal is a particular type of it. For example, terriers are a breed of dog. EG *Different breeds of sheep give wool of varying lengths.* N COUNT

2 If you **breed** animals or plants, you keep them for the purpose of producing more animals or plants with particular qualities, in a controlled way. EG *Strains of the plant have been bred that resist more diseases.* ◇ **breeding.** EG *We retain a small proportion of bulls for breeding purposes.* V+O ◇ N UNCOUNT

3 When animals **breed**, they mate and produce V

How many people are there on these pages?

offspring. ◇ **breeding.** EG *The breeding season is a very long one.* ◇ N UNCOUNT

4 If something **breeds** a particular situation or feeling, it causes it to develop. EG *Success breeds success, failure breeds failure... The rumours bred hope.* V+O

5 If someone **is bred** to do something, they are trained or taught to do it as they grow up. EG *They were bred to rule... Danny was bred for the sea.* V+O+*to*-INF OR *for*: USU PASS Formal

6 Someone who was **born and bred** in a particular place was born there and spent their childhood there. EG *I was born and bred in Edinburgh.* PHRASE

7 A particular **breed** of person is a particular type of person, with special qualities or skills. EG *This required a special skill and a whole new breed of actors.* N COUNT+SUPP

breeding /briːdɪŋ/. Someone who has **breeding** has been taught how to behave correctly and with good manners, and is often upper-class. EG *She certainly lacked breeding.* ● See also **breed**. N UNCOUNT

breeding ground, breeding grounds. 1 A place that is a **breeding ground** for a particular situation or activity is a place where it is very likely to develop. EG *...breeding grounds for passport forgery.* N COUNT+SUPP

2 A **breeding ground** of a particular type of animal is a place where this animal goes to breed. EG *Those cliffs are the finest bird breeding grounds in the Northern Hemisphere.* N COUNT

breeze /briːz/, **breezes, breezing, breezed. 1** A **breeze** is a gentle wind. EG *...a cool breeze.* N COUNT

2 If you **breeze** into a place, you enter it suddenly, in a very casual manner. EG *I just breezed into her room, flinging the door wide.* V+A

breezy /briːzi[1]/. **1** Someone who is **breezy** behaves in a brisk, casual, cheerful, and confident manner. ADJ QUALIT

2 When the weather is **breezy**, there is a fairly strong but pleasant wind blowing. ADJ QUALIT

brethren /breðrɪ[2]n/ is an old-fashioned plural form of **brother**.

brevity /brevɪ[1]ti[1]/. **1** The **brevity** of something is the fact that it lasts for only a short time. EG *...the brevity and frailty of human existence.* N UNCOUNT Formal

2 **Brevity** is the fact of saying something in only a few words. EG *Daniel delivered his message with telegraphic brevity.* N UNCOUNT Formal

brew /bruː/, **brews, brewing, brewed. 1** When you **brew** tea or coffee, you make it by pouring hot water over tea leaves or ground coffee. V+O

2 A **brew** is a drink made by mixing something such as tea with hot water. EG *...herbal brews.* N COUNT

3 When people **brew** beer, they make it. V+O

4 If an unpleasant situation **is brewing**, it is starting to develop. EG *A crisis was brewing.* V: USU CONT

brewer /bruːə/, **brewers.** A **brewer** is a person who makes beer or who owns a place where beer is made. N COUNT

brewery /brʊəri[1]/, **breweries.** A **brewery** is a company which makes beer, or a place where beer is made. N COUNT

briar /braɪə/, **briars.** A **briar** is a wild rose with long, thorny stems. N COUNT

bribe /braɪb/, **bribes, bribing, bribed. 1** A **bribe** is a sum of money or something valuable that someone gives to an official in order to persuade the official to do something. EG *The Vice President admitted taking bribes.* N COUNT

2 If someone **bribes** an official, they give the official a bribe. EG *The attempt to bribe the clerk had failed.* ◇ **bribery** /braɪbə[0]ri[1]/. EG *The court found Williams guilty of bribery.* V+O; ◇ N UNCOUNT

bric-a-brac /brɪkəbræk/ consists of small ornamental objects of no great value. N UNCOUNT

brick /brɪk/, **bricks, bricking, bricked. Bricks** are rectangular blocks of baked clay used for building walls. EG *...a brick wall.* N COUNT OR N UNCOUNT

brick up. If you **brick up** a hole, you close it with a wall of bricks. EG *Two workmen bricked up the window.* PHRASAL VB: V+O+ADV

bricklayer /brɪkleɪə/, **bricklayers.** A **bricklayer** is a person whose job is to build walls using bricks. N COUNT

brickwork /brɪkwɜːk/. You can refer to the bricks in the walls of a building as the **brickwork**. N UNCOUNT

bride /braɪd/, **brides.** A **bride** is a woman who is getting married or who has just got married. ◇ **bridal** /braɪdə[0]l/. EG *She was still wearing her bridal costume.* N COUNT; ◇ ADJ CLASSIF: ATTRIB

bridegroom /braɪdgru[4]m/, **bridegrooms.** A **bridegroom** is a man who is getting married. N COUNT

bridesmaid /braɪdzmeɪd/, **bridesmaids.** A **bridesmaid** is a woman or a girl who helps and accompanies a bride on her wedding day. N COUNT

bridge

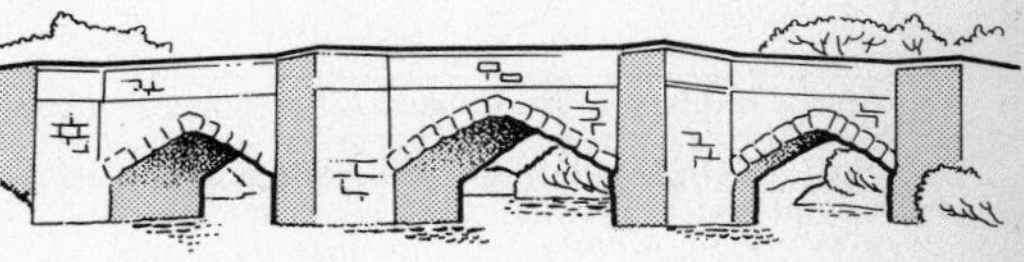

bridge /brɪdʒ/, **bridges, bridging, bridged. 1** A **bridge** is a structure that is built over a river, road, or railway so that people or vehicles can cross from one side to the other. EG *We walked across the railway bridge.* N COUNT

2 Something that is a **bridge** between two groups or things makes it easier for the differences between them to be overcome. EG *We need to build a bridge between East and West.* N COUNT

3 Something that **bridges** the gap between two groups or things makes it easier for the differences between them to be overcome. EG *...bridging the gap between what society needs and what the government can provide.* V+O

4 If someone mentions a possible problem and you say that you will **cross that bridge when you come to it**, you mean that you do not intend to think about it until it arises. PHRASE

5 The **bridge** of a ship is the high part from which the ship is steered. N COUNT

6 **Bridge** is a card game for four players. N UNCOUNT

bridle /braɪdə[0]l/, **bridles, bridling, bridled. 1** A **bridle** is a set of straps that is put around a horse's head and mouth so that the person riding or driving the horse can control it. N COUNT

2 When you **bridle** a horse, you put a bridle on it. V+O

3 If you **bridle**, you show that you are angry or displeased by moving your head and body upwards in a proud way. EG *Mrs Pringle bridled at the memory.* V: OFT+*at*

brief /briːf/, **briefer, briefest; briefs, briefing, briefed. 1** Something that is **brief** lasts for only a short time. EG *There was a brief scuffle... They started with a brief description of their work... As they talk, they exchange only the briefest of glances.* ● See also **briefly**. ADJ QUALIT

2 If you are **brief**, you say what you want to say in as few words as possible. EG *I shall have to be brief.* ADJ PRED

3 A **brief** skirt or pair of shorts is very short. ADJ QUALIT

4 **Briefs** are pants or knickers. N PLURAL

5 When you **brief** someone, you give them information that they need before they do something. EG *They had been well briefed about the political situation.* V+O

6 If someone gives you a **brief**, they officially give you the responsibility for dealing with a particular thing. EG *I was appointed and given the brief of developing local history research.* N COUNT

briefcase

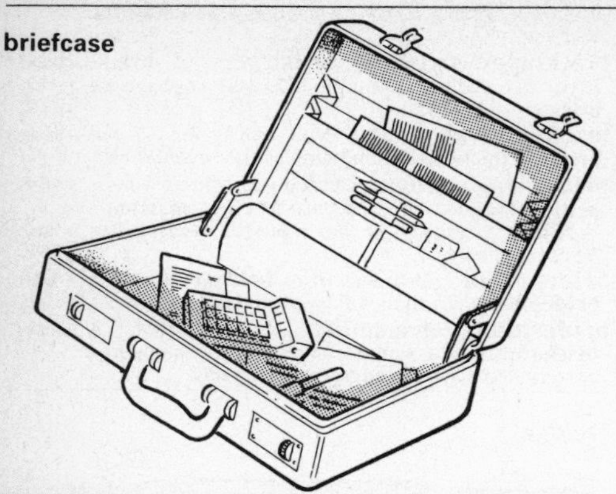

briefcase /briːfkeɪs/, **briefcases.** A **briefcase** is a case used for carrying documents in. N COUNT

briefing /briːfɪŋ/, **briefings.** A **briefing** is 1 a meeting at which information or instructions are given to people, especially before they do something. EG *We had a special briefing on what lies ahead.* N COUNT OR N UNCOUNT 2 the information or instructions that you get at a meeting. N COUNT

briefly /briːfli/. 1 Something that happens or is done **briefly** happens or is done for a very short period of time. EG *He smiled briefly.* ADV

2 If you say something **briefly**, you use very few words or give very few details. EG *She told them briefly what had happened.* ADV

3 You can say **briefly** to indicate that you are about to say something in as few words as possible. EG *The facts, briefly, are these.* ADV SEN

brigade /brɪgeɪd/, **brigades.** A **brigade** is one of the groups which an army is divided into. ● See also **fire brigade.** N COLL

brigadier /brɪgədɪə/, **brigadiers.** A **brigadier** is a senior officer in the army. N COUNT

bright /braɪt/, **brighter, brightest.** 1 A **bright** colour is strong and noticeable, and not dark. EG *Her eyes were bright blue.* ADJ QUALIT ◊ **brightly.** EG *...brightly coloured silk blouses.* ◊ ADV

2 A **bright** light, object, or place is shining strongly or is full of light. EG *The sun was bright and hot... ...a bright, sunlit room.* ADJ QUALIT ◊ **brightly.** EG *The sun shone brightly... ...the brightly lit room.* ◊ ADV ◊ **brightness.** EG *The stars were losing their brightness.* ◊ N UNCOUNT

3 Someone who is **bright** is quick at learning things. EG *They were the brightest girls in the school.* ADJ QUALIT

4 A **bright** idea is clever and original. EG *Then he had the bright idea of putting the engine at the back.* ADJ CLASSIF : ATTRIB

5 If someone looks or sounds **bright**, they look or sound cheerful. EG *'Good,' said Henry, looking brighter.* ADJ PRED ◊ **brightly.** EG *'Fine!' I said brightly.* ◊ ADV

6 If the future is **bright**, it is likely to be pleasant and successful. EG *The economic outlook is bright.* ADJ QUALIT

7 If you do something **bright and early**, you do it very early in the morning. EG *I was up bright and early, eager to be off.* PHRASE

brighten /braɪtən/, **brightens, brightening, brightened.** 1 If you **brighten**, you suddenly look happier. EG *Her face brightened. 'Oh, hi! It's you.'* V

2 If your eyes **brighten**, you suddenly look interested or excited. V

3 If someone or something **brightens** a situation, they make it more pleasant and enjoyable. EG *You girls brighten our Sundays.* V+O

4 When a light **brightens** a place or when a place **brightens**, it becomes brighter or lighter. EG *Stars brighten the night sky.* V-ERG

brighten up. 1 If you **brighten up**, you look happier. EG *She seemed to brighten up a bit at this.* PHRASAL VB : V+ADV

2 If you **brighten up** a place, you make it more colourful and attractive. EG *These flowers will brighten up your garden.* V+O+ADV 3 Someone or something that **brightens up** a situation makes it more pleasant and enjoyable. EG *The music brightened things up a little.* V+O+ADV

brilliant /brɪljənt/. 1 If you describe people or ideas as **brilliant**, you mean that they are extremely clever. EG *...a brilliant young engineer... It was a brilliant idea.* ADJ QUALIT ◊ **brilliantly.** EG *He acted brilliantly in a wide range of parts.* ◊ ADV ◊ **brilliance** /brɪljəns/. EG *...a writer of tremendous brilliance.* ◊ N UNCOUNT

2 You can say that something is **brilliant** when you are very pleased about it or think that it is very good. EG *'Did you enjoy your holiday?' – 'Yes, it was brilliant!'* ADJ QUALIT Informal British

3 A **brilliant** career or future is very successful. EG *He predicted a brilliant future for the child.* ADJ CLASSIF : ATTRIB ◊ **brilliantly.** EG *Sotheby's publicity stunt came off brilliantly.* ◊ ADV

4 A **brilliant** colour is extremely bright. EG *...a brilliant yellow flame... ...brilliant white marble.* ADJ QUALIT : ATTRIB ◊ **brilliantly.** EG *Many of them are brilliantly coloured.* ◊ ADV ◊ **brilliance.** EG *The painting has been restored to its former brilliance.* ◊ N UNCOUNT

5 You describe light, or something that reflects light, as **brilliant** when it shines very brightly. EG *The sea sparkled in the brilliant sunlight.* ADJ QUALIT ◊ **brilliantly.** EG *A downstairs window was brilliantly illuminated.* ◊ ADV ◊ **brilliance.** EG *...the brilliance of the lagoon.* ◊ N UNCOUNT

brim /brɪm/, **brims, brimming, brimmed.** 1 The **brim** of a hat is the wide part that sticks outwards at the bottom. N COUNT

2 If a container is filled **to the brim** with something, it is filled right up to the top. EG *The pool was full to the brim with brown water.* PHRASE

3 Someone or something that **is brimming** with things of a particular kind is full of them. EG *...a group of youngsters, all brimming with ideas... Her eyes brimmed with tears.* V : OFT+*with*

brim over. 1 When a container or the liquid in it **brims over**, the liquid spills out. EG *He poured wine into Daniel's glass until it brimmed over.* PHRASAL VB : V+ADV 2 If you **are brimming over** with a pleasant feeling, you behave in a way that shows how pleased you are. EG *She rushed to her mother, brimming over with joy and pride.* V+ADV

brine /braɪn/ is salty water, especially when it is used for preserving food. N UNCOUNT

bring /brɪŋ/, **brings, bringing, brought** /brɔːt/. 1 If you **bring** someone or something with you when you come to a place, they come with you or you have them with you. EG *He would have to bring Judy with him... Please bring your calculator to every lesson.* V+O : USU+A

2 If you **bring** something somewhere, you move it somewhere. EG *He opened the case and brought out a pair of glasses... Bring me a glass of wine... Sheldon brought his right hand to his head.* V+O+A OR V+O+O

3 To **bring** someone or something to a place means to cause them to come to the place. EG *The festival brings a great many people to Glastonbury... They were responsible for bringing jazz to Europe.* V+O+A

4 To **bring** someone or something into a particular state or condition means to cause them to be in that state or condition. EG *These ideas had brought him into conflict with Stalin... Printing brought the cost of books down... The wind had brought several trees down... He brought the car to a stop.* V+O+A

5 If something **brings** a particular feeling, situation, or quality, it makes people experience it or have it. EG *Could it be true that money did not bring* V+O : OFT+A

Give an example of something that you might bristle at.

happiness?... It will bring shame on the family... This generosity brought applause from the boys... The biting wind brought tears to her eyes.

6 If you cannot **bring** yourself to do something, you cannot make yourself do it. EG *I could not bring myself to touch him.* V-REFL+ *to*-INF : WITH BROAD NEG

7 If you **bring** a legal action against someone, you officially accuse them of doing something unlawful. EG *...a list of criminal charges brought against him by the government.* V+O : OFT+*against*

bring about. To **bring** something **about** means to cause it to happen. EG *The Administration helped bring about a peaceful settlement.* PHRASAL VB : V+O+ADV

bring along. If you **bring** someone or something **along**, you bring them with you when you come to a place. EG *Bring your friends along.* PHRASAL VB : V+O+ADV

bring back. **1** Something that **brings back** a memory makes you think about it. EG *Losing a husband can bring back memories of childhood loss.* PHRASAL VB : V+O+ADV **2** When people **bring back** a fashion or practice that existed at an earlier time, they introduce it again. EG *Many of the students appear to be trying to bring back the crew cut.* V+O+ADV

bring down. When people **bring down** a government or ruler, they cause the government or ruler to lose power. EG *A national strike would bring the government down.* PHRASAL VB : V+O+ADV

bring forward. **1** If you **bring forward** a meeting or lecture, you arrange for it to take place at an earlier date or time than had been planned. PHRASAL VB : V+O+ADV **2** If you **bring forward** an argument or proposal, you state it so that people can consider it. EG *He brought forward some very cogent arguments.* V+O+ADV

bring in. **1** When a government or organization **brings in** a new law or system, they introduce it. EG *Both Labour and Conservative administrations intend to bring in legislation to control their activities.* PHRASAL VB : V+O+ADV **2** Someone or something that **brings in** money makes it or earns it. EG *Tourism is a big industry, bringing in £7 billion a year.* V+O+ADV **3** If you **bring in** someone, you invite them to take part in an activity. EG *It would be fatal to bring in an outsider.* V+O+ADV

bring off. If you **bring off** something difficult, you do it successfully. EG *The most brilliant manoeuvre was brought off by Japan.* PHRASAL VB : V+O+ADV Informal

bring out. **1** When a person or company **brings out** a new product, especially a new book or record, they produce it and sell it. EG *I've just brought out a book on Dostoevski.* PHRASAL VB : V+O+ADV **2** Something that **brings out** a particular kind of behaviour or feeling in you causes you to show it although you do not normally show it. EG *These dreadful circumstances bring out the worst in everybody.* V+O+ADV

bring round or **bring to.** If you **bring round** someone who is unconscious or **bring** them **to**, you make them become conscious again. PHRASAL VB : V+O+ADV

bring up. **1** When someone **brings up** a child, they look after it until it is grown up, and try to give it particular attitudes. EG *Fathers are beginning to play a bigger role in bringing up their children... Tony was brought up strictly.* PHRASAL VB : V+O+ADV • You describe someone young as **well brought up** when you think that they behave well. • PHRASE **2** If you **bring up** a particular subject, you introduce it into a discussion or conversation. EG *I advised her to bring the matter up at the next meeting.* V+O+ADV **3** If you **bring up** food, you vomit. EG *I felt sick, coughed, and then brought up most of my dinner.* V+O+ADV

brink /brɪŋk/. If you are on the **brink** of something, usually something important, terrible, or exciting, you are just about to do it or experience it. EG *The country was on the brink of civil war... I was on the brink of losing my temper.* N SING : *the*+N

brisk /brɪsk/, **brisker, briskest.** **1** Someone who is **brisk** behaves in a busy, confident way which shows that they want to get things done quickly. EG *Lynn's tone was brisk.* ◇ **briskly.** EG *'We've been into that,' said Posy briskly.* ◇ **briskness.** EG *She adopted her usual briskness with him.* ADJ QUALIT ◇ ADV ◇ N UNCOUNT

2 A **brisk** action is done quickly and in an energetic way. EG *I went for a brisk swim.* ◇ **briskly.** EG *He walked briskly down the street.* ◇ **briskness.** EG *He was walking with unusual briskness.* ADJ QUALIT ◇ ADV ◇ N UNCOUNT

3 If trade or business is **brisk**, things are being sold very quickly and a lot of money is being made. EG *They are doing a brisk trade in cars.* ADJ QUALIT

4 If the weather is **brisk**, it is cold and refreshing. EG *It was one brisk April morning... ...brisk winds.* ADJ QUALIT

bristle /brɪsə⁰l/, **bristles, bristling, bristled.** **1** **Bristles** are **1.1** thick, strong animal hairs that are sometimes used to make brushes. **1.2** the short hairs that grow on a man's chin after he has shaved it. N COUNT OR N UNCOUNT

2 The **bristles** of a brush are the thick hairs or hair-like pieces of plastic which are attached to the handle. N PLURAL

3 If the hair on your body **bristles**, it rises away from your skin because you are cold, frightened, or angry. EG *I felt the hairs bristle along the back of my neck.* V

4 If you **bristle** at something, you react to it angrily, and show this in your expression or the way you move. EG *Eddie bristled at being called a 'girl'.* V : OFT+*at*

bristle with. If a place **bristles with** objects or people, there are a lot of them there. EG *The hill bristled with fortifications... The hotel was bristling with policemen.* PHRASAL VB : V+PREP

bristly /brɪsli¹/. **1** **Bristly** hair is rough, coarse, and thick. EG *...a bristly moustache.* ADJ QUALIT

2 If a man's chin is **bristly**, it is covered with bristles because he has not shaved recently. ADJ QUALIT

Brit /brɪt/, **Brits.** British people are sometimes referred to as **Brits.** N COUNT Informal

British /brɪtɪʃ/. **1** Someone or something that is **British** belongs or relates to Great Britain. EG *...my British friends... ...British textile companies.* ADJ CLASSIF

2 The **British** are the people who come from Great Britain. EG *The British are very good at sympathy.* N PLURAL

Britisher /brɪtɪʃə/, **Britishers.** Americans sometimes refer to British people as **Britishers.** N COUNT American

Briton /brɪtə⁰n/, **Britons.** A **Briton** is a person who comes from Great Britain. EG *The youth, a 17-year-old Briton, was searched and arrested.* N COUNT

brittle /brɪtə⁰l/, **brittler, brittlest.** **1** An object or substance that is **brittle** is hard but easily broken. EG *...dry sticks as brittle as candy.* ADJ QUALIT

2 Someone who is **brittle** says things which are likely to hurt other people's feelings. EG *...a brittle, humourless child.* ADJ QUALIT

3 A **brittle** sound is short, loud, and sharp. ADJ QUALIT

broach /brəʊtʃ/, **broaches, broaching, broached.** When you **broach** a subject, you mention it in order to start a discussion on it. EG *She first broached the idea of a partnership in 1985.* V+O

broad /brɔːd/, **broader, broadest.** **1** Something that is **broad** is wide. EG *The streets of this town are broad... He was tall, with broad shoulders... ...a broad grin.* ADJ QUALIT

2 You use **broad** to describe **2.1** something that includes or concerns a large number of different things or people. EG *She had a broader range of interests than Jane... This syllabus is a broad one... ...'cultural' in the broadest sense of the word.* ADJ QUALIT **2.2** something that is experienced by many people, or by people of many different kinds. EG *...a broad feeling that the West lacks direction... ...a youth organization with a broader appeal.* ADJ QUALIT : ATTRIB

3 A **broad** description or idea is general rather than detailed. EG *The book gives a broad introduction to linguistics.* ADJ QUALIT : ATTRIB

4 You use **broad** to describe a hint or sarcastic remark and indicate that its meaning is very obvious. EG *Broad hints were aired that the paper should be closed down.* ADJ QUALIT : ATTRIB

5 A **broad** accent is strong and noticeable. EG *He has a broad Wiltshire accent.* ADJ QUALIT

6 A crime that is done **in broad daylight** is done during the day, rather than at night. EG *Mugging in the streets, even in broad daylight, was common.* PHRASE

7 See also **broadly**.

broad bean, broad beans. Broad beans are flat, light green beans. N COUNT: USU PLURAL

broadcast /brɔ:dkɑ:st/, **broadcasts, broadcasting, broadcasted.** The past tense and past participle can be either **broadcasted** or **broadcast**.

1 A **broadcast** is something that you hear on the radio or see on television. EG *He was criticized for making these broadcasts.* N COUNT

2 To **broadcast** a programme means to send it out by radio waves, so that it can be heard on the radio or seen on television. EG *Episode One was broadcast last night.* V+O OR V

broadcaster /brɔ:dkɑ:stə/, **broadcasters.** A **broadcaster** is someone who gives talks or takes part in discussions on radio or television. EG *...Anthony Howard, the journalist and broadcaster.* N COUNT

broadcasting /brɔ:dkɑ:stɪŋ/ is the making and sending out of television and radio programmes. EG *...the purpose of educational broadcasting.* N UNCOUNT

broaden /brɔ:də[0]n/, **broadens, broadening, broadened.** 1 When something **broadens**, it becomes wider. EG *As the stream descends it broadens... Her smile broadened a little.* V

2 When you **broaden** something or when it **broadens**, 2.1 it includes or concerns a larger number of things or people. EG *Some members wished to broaden the scope of the campaign.* 2.2 it is experienced by or affects more people. EG *He made another attempt to broaden his appeal.* V-ERG

3 If an experience **broadens** your **mind**, it makes you more willing to accept other people's beliefs and customs. EG *Travel broadens the mind.* PHRASE

broaden out. When you **broaden** something **out** or when it **broadens out**, it includes or concerns a larger number of things or people. EG *...broadening out our political awareness.* PHRASAL VB: V-ERG+ADV

broadly /brɔ:dli[1]/. 1 You can say **broadly** or **broadly speaking** to mean that although there may be a few exceptions to what you are saying, it is true in almost all cases. EG *You can see that, broadly speaking, it is really quite straightforward.* ADV SEN

2 You can also use **broadly** to say that something is true to a large extent. EG *I was broadly in favour of it.* ADV+PREP

3 If someone smiles **broadly**, their mouth is stretched very wide because they are very pleased or amused. ADV

broadly-based. Something that is **broadly-based** involves many different kinds of things or people. EG *He wants it to be a broadly-based movement.* ADJ QUALIT

broadminded /brɔ:dmaɪndɪ[2]d/. Someone who is **broadminded** does not disapprove of actions or attitudes that many other people disapprove of. ADJ QUALIT

BROAD NEG stands for **broad negative**
Some words or phrases have the label WITH BROAD NEG in the Extra Column. This means that they are normally used in sentences which have a negative word such as 'not' or 'never' or which have the broad negative adverbs 'hardly', 'barely','scarcely', 'rarely', 'seldom', or 'little' in them.
For example, one meaning of the word 'bother' nearly always has one of these words: EG *I can't be bothered to write this... He never bothered to do his homework...She barely bothers to speak to me these days.*

brocade /brə[6]keɪd/ is a thick, expensive material, often made of silk, with a raised pattern on it. EG *She wore a dress of white brocade.* N UNCOUNT

broccoli /brɒkəli[1]/ is a vegetable with green stalks and green or purple flower buds. N UNCOUNT

brochure /brəʊʃj[0]ʊ[0]ə/, **brochures.** A **brochure** is a magazine or booklet with pictures that gives you information about a product or service. EG *...travel brochures... ...a brochure about retirement homes.* N COUNT

broil /brɔɪl/, **broils, broiling, broiled.** When you **broil** food, you grill it. EG *...trout broiled over charcoal.* V+O American

broke /brəʊk/. 1 **Broke** is the past tense of **break**.

2 If you are **broke**, you have no money. EG *He'd taken the job because he was broke.* ADJ PRED Informal

3 If a company **goes broke**, it loses money and is unable to continue in business. EG *The paper was going broke and would cease publication.* PHRASE Informal

broken /brəʊkə[0]n/. 1 **Broken** is the past participle of **break**.

2 An object that is **broken** has split into pieces or cracked, for example because it has been hit or dropped. EG *He sweeps away the broken glass under the window... He was rushed to hospital with a broken back.* ADJ CLASSIF

3 A tool or piece of machinery that is **broken** is damaged and no longer works. EG *...a broken television set... The telephone is broken.* ADJ CLASSIF

4 A line, sound, or process that is **broken** is interrupted or disturbed rather than continuous. EG *...a broken curve... ...broken, irregular screaming.* ADJ CLASSIF

5 A **broken** promise or contract has not been kept or obeyed. ADJ CLASSIF

6 A **broken** marriage has ended in divorce. EG *I came to hear a little about her broken marriage.* ADJ CLASSIF: ATTRIB

7 If someone talks in **broken** English, for example, or in **broken** French, they speak slowly and make a lot of mistakes because they do not know the language very well. ADJ QUALIT: ATTRIB

broken-down. 1 A **broken-down** vehicle or machine no longer works because it has something wrong with it. EG *...two men pushing a broken-down car.* ADJ CLASSIF

2 If a building is **broken-down**, it is in very bad condition or has partly fallen down. ADJ CLASSIF

broken-hearted. Someone who is **broken-hearted** is very sad and upset because they have had a serious disappointment. ADJ CLASSIF

broken home, broken homes. If you say that someone comes from a **broken home**, you mean that their family did not live together, because their parents were separated or divorced. N COUNT

broker /brəʊkə/, **brokers.** A **broker** is a person whose job is to buy and sell shares, foreign money, or goods for other people. EG *...an insurance broker.* N COUNT

brolly /brɒli[1]/, **brollies.** A **brolly** is the same as an umbrella. N COUNT British

bronchial tubes. Your **bronchial tubes** are the two tubes which connect your windpipe to your lungs. N PLURAL Medical

bronchitis /brɒŋkaɪtɪ[1]s/ is an illness like a very bad cough, in which your bronchial tubes become sore and infected. N UNCOUNT

bronze /brɒnz/, **bronzes. 1 Bronze** is a yellowish-brown metal which is a mixture of copper and tin. EG *...a large bronze statue.* N UNCOUNT

2 A **bronze** is 2.1 a statue or sculpture made of bronze. EG *...a modern bronze of Icarus.* 2.2 a bronze medal. N COUNT

3 Something that is **bronze** is yellowish-brown in colour. EG *...bronze hair.* ADJ COLOUR

bronzed /brɒnzd/. Someone who is **bronzed** is attractively sun-tanned. ADJ QUALIT

bronze medal, bronze medals. If you win a **bronze medal**, you come third in a competition, N COUNT

If you come from a broken home, does your house need rebuilding?

especially a sports contest, and are given a medal made of bronze as a prize.

brooch /brəʊtʃ/, **brooches.** A **brooch** is a small piece of jewellery with a pin at the back. You attach a brooch to a dress or a blouse. See picture at JEWELLERY. N COUNT

brood /bru:d/, **broods, brooding, brooded.** 1 A **brood** is a group of baby birds that a female bird has produced. EG *...a brood of ducklings.* N COLL

2 You can humorously refer to someone's children as their **brood.** EG *...a squabbling brood of children.* N COLL

3 If someone **broods** about something, they think about it a lot, seriously and often unhappily. EG *I slunk away to my room to brood... He brooded on his failure... Don't brood over your problems.* V : OFT+A

brooding /bru:dɪŋ/. Something that is **brooding** is disturbing and threatening. EG *The silent, brooding presence of the woman made him uncomfortable.* ADJ CLASSIF

broody /bru:di^1/. 1 You say that someone is **broody** when they are thinking a lot about something in an unhappy way. ADJ QUALIT

2 A **broody** hen is ready to lay or sit on eggs. ADJ CLASSIF

brook /brʊk/, **brooks.** A **brook** is a small stream. EG *...a mountain brook.* N COUNT

broom /bru^{4}m/, **brooms.** A **broom** is a kind of brush with a long handle. You use a broom for sweeping the floor. N COUNT

broomstick /bru^{4}mstɪk/, **broomsticks.** A **broomstick** is 1 the handle of a broom. 2 a broom which has a bundle of twigs at the end. Witches are said to fly on broomsticks. N COUNT

broth /brɒθ/ is soup. EG *...chicken broth.* N UNCOUNT

brothel /brɒθə^{0}l/, **brothels.** A **brothel** is a building where men pay to have sex with prostitutes. N COUNT

brother /brʌðə/, **brothers;** the old-fashioned form **brethren** /brɛðrɪ^{2}n/ is also used as the plural for paragraphs 2 and 3.

1 Your **brother** is a boy or a man who has the same parents as you. EG *I have two brothers and one sister... ...his brother Harold.* ● See also **half-brother, stepbrother.** N COUNT

2 You might describe as your **brother** a man who belongs to the same race, religion, profession, or trade union as you, or who has ideas that are similar to yours. EG *All men are our brothers... Both he and his brother judges had been amused.* N COUNT : USU PLURAL

3 **Brother** is a title given to a man who belongs to a religious institution such as a monastery. EG *...Brother Michael, one of the Anglican Chaplains... ...the Brethren of the Trinity.*

brotherhood /brʌðəhʊd/, **brotherhoods.** 1 **Brotherhood** is the affection and loyalty that you feel for people who you have something in common with. EG *...a deepening sense of brotherhood.* N UNCOUNT

2 A **brotherhood** is an organization whose members all have the same political aims and beliefs or the same job or profession. N COUNT : OFT+*of*

brother-in-law, brothers-in-law. Your **brother-in-law** is the brother of your husband or wife, or the man who is married to your sister or to your wife's or husband's sister. N COUNT

brotherly /brʌðəli^1/. **Brotherly** feelings are feelings of love and loyalty which you expect a brother to show. EG *...brotherly love.* ADJ CLASSIF : ATTRIB

brought /brɔ:t/ is the past tense and past participle of **bring.**

brow /braʊ/, **brows.** 1 Your **brow** is your forehead. EG *He mopped his sweating brow.* N COUNT

2 Your **brows** are your eyebrows. ● to **knit** your **brows**: see **knit.** N COUNT Formal

3 The **brow** of a hill is the top part of it. EG *I saw him disappear over the brow of the hill.* N COUNT : *the*+N+*of*

browbeat /braʊbi:t/, **browbeats, browbeating, browbeaten.** The form **browbeat** is used in the present tense and is also the past tense. V+O

If you **browbeat** someone, you bully them and try to force them to do what you want. EG *She browbeat her parents into letting her go.* ◇ **browbeaten.** EG *...his browbeaten wife.* ◇ ADJ CLASSIF

brown /braʊn/, **browner, brownest; browns, browning, browned.** 1 Something that is **brown** is the colour of earth or of wood. EG *His brown eyes twinkled at them... ...long brown hair... I never wear brown.* ADJ COLOUR

2 People are described as **brown** when 2.1 their skin is darker than usual because they have been in the sun. EG *His body was golden brown... ...her long brown legs.* ADJ COLOUR 2.2 they belong to a race of people who have brown-coloured skins. ADJ CLASSIF

3 When something **browns** or when you **brown** it, it becomes browner in colour. EG *Her hands had been browned by the sun.* V-ERG

brownish /braʊnɪʃ/. Something that is **brownish** is slightly brown in colour. EG *...a patch of brownish lawn... ...a brownish face.* ADJ COLOUR

browse /braʊz/, **browses, browsing, browsed.** 1 If you **browse** through a book or magazine, you look through it in a casual way. EG *He spent half an hour browsing through sections he had already read.* V : USU+A

2 If you **browse** in a shop, you look at things in a casual way, in the hope that you might find something you want. ▸ used as a noun. EG *I had a browse in the children's picture book section.* V : USU+A ▸ N COUNT +SUPP

3 When animals **browse**, they feed on plants. V : USU+A

bruise /bru:z/, **bruises, bruising, bruised.** A **bruise** is an injury produced when a part of your body is hit by something. Your skin is not broken but a purple mark appears on it. EG *I'm okay; just a few cuts and bruises.* ▸ used as a verb. EG *They were jostled, bruised, and scratched.* N COUNT ▸ V-ERG

brunette /bru:nɛt/, **brunettes.** A **brunette** is a white-skinned woman or girl with dark brown hair. N COUNT

brunt /brʌnt/. If someone **bears the brunt** or **takes the brunt** of something unpleasant, they suffer the main part or force of it. EG *Indian troops bore the brunt of the Burma campaigns.* PHRASE

brush /brʌʃ/, **brushes, brushing, brushed.** 1 A **brush** is an object which has a large number of bristles fixed to it. You use brushes for cleaning things, for painting, and for tidying your hair. N COUNT

2 If you **brush** something, you clean it or tidy it using a brush. EG *I'm going to brush my teeth... She began to brush her hair.* ▸ used as a noun. EG *Give the carpet a hard brush.* V+O ▸ N SING : *a*+N

3 If you **brush** something away, you remove it by pushing it lightly with your hand. EG *She brushed back the hair from her eyes.* V+O+A

4 To **brush** something or **brush** against it means to touch it lightly while passing it. EG *Something brushed against the back of the shelter... The girl's hair brushed his cheek.* V+O OR V+A

5 If you have a **brush** with someone, you have a small argument or fight with them. EG *His attitude has led to some brushes with authority.* N COUNT+*with*

brush aside. If you **brush aside** an idea, remark, or feeling, you refuse to consider it because you think it is not important. EG *She brushed his protests aside.* PHRASAL VB : V+O+ADV

brush up. If you **brush up** a subject or **brush up on** it, you revise or improve your knowledge of it. EG *They need to brush up their French.* PHRASAL VB : V+O+ADV OR V+ADV+PREP

brushwood /brʌʃwʊd/ consists of small branches and twigs that have broken off trees and bushes. EG *...a pile of brushwood and dead leaves.* N UNCOUNT

brusque /bru:sk, -ʊsk/. Someone who is **brusque** wastes no time when dealing with things and does not show much consideration for other people. EG *I made a brusque apology and left... She had a brusque manner.* ◇ **brusquely.** EG *'Sorry – no time to waste,' she said brusquely.* ADJ QUALIT ◇ ADV

brussels sprout, brussels sprouts; also spelled **brussel sprout. Brussels sprouts** are vegetables which look like very small cabbages. N COUNT : USU PLURAL

brutal /bru:tə^{0}l/. 1 Someone who is **brutal** is cruel and violent. EG *...the government's brutal treatment of political prisoners... ...a brutal killing.* ◇ **brutally.** EG *Richard II was brutally murdered.* ADJ QUALIT

brushes

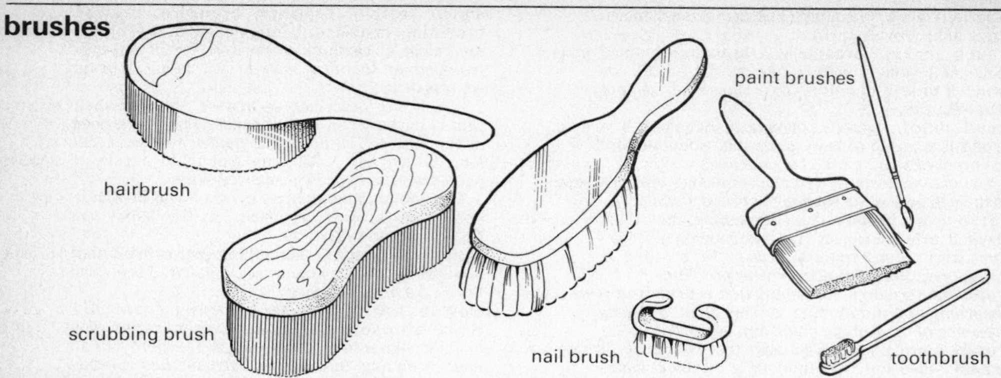

◇ **brutality** /bru:tælə¹ti¹/, **brutalities.** EG *There is so much brutality shown on the television screen... I abhor the brutalities of the regime.* ◇ N UNCOUNT OR N COUNT

2 If someone expresses something with **brutal** honesty or frankness, they express it in an unpleasantly clear and accurate way. EG *He spelled out with brutal clarity what the consequences would be... ...explained with brutal frankness.* ◇ **brutally.** EG *The photographer was brutally honest.* ADJ QUALIT : ATTRIB; ◇ ADV+ADJ

3 Brutal is used to emphasize an unpleasant or difficult quality. EG *...the brutal disenchantment of the people.* ◇ **brutally.** EG *We must ensure Britain's economic recovery in a brutally competitive world.* ADJ CLASSIF : ATTRIB; ◇ ADV+ADJ

brutalize /bru:tə⁰laɪz/, **brutalizes, brutalizing, brutalized;** also spelled **brutalise.** If an unpleasant experience **brutalizes** someone, it makes them cruel, violent, or uncaring. EG *Her childhood was so awful, it's a wonder she was not brutalized by it.* V+O

brute /bru:t/, **brutes. 1** A **brute** is **1.1** a rough and insensitive man. EG *Go ahead and hit me, you big brute... He's an ugly brute.* **1.2** a large animal, especially one that you feel sorry for. EG *...the poor half-starved brutes.* N COUNT

2 When you refer to **brute** strength or force, you are contrasting it with gentler methods or qualities. EG *We will never yield to brute force... In the end, he had to use brute strength and wrench the lock off.* ADJ CLASSIF : ATTRIB

brutish /bru:tɪʃ/. If you describe human conditions or actions as **brutish**, you mean that they seem to be like an animal's; used showing disapproval. EG *Man's life is nasty, brutish and short... His expression was brutish and mocking.* ADJ QUALIT

B.Sc. /bi: ɛs si:/, **B.Sc.s.** A **B.Sc.** is a science degree. **B.Sc.** is an abbreviation for 'Bachelor of Science'. EG *He's got a B.Sc... ...B.Sc. students... ...the final year of a B.Sc. course.* N COUNT

bubble /bʌbə⁰l/, **bubbles, bubbling, bubbled. 1** A **bubble** is **1.1** a ball of air in a liquid. EG *Tiny bubbles were rising from the dissolving tablets... A bubble of air escaped from the drowned woman's mouth.* **1.2** a hollow, delicate ball of soapy liquid that is floating in the air or standing on a surface. EG *Her elbows were covered in bubbles... She knows how to blow bubbles with washing-up liquid.* N COUNT

2 When a liquid **bubbles**, bubbles form in it, because it is boiling, is fizzy, or is moving quickly. EG *Cook the mixture until it bubbles... The champagne bubbled in her glass.* V

3 When something **bubbles**, it makes a sound like water boiling. EG *On the table an electric coffee percolator bubbled... ...low, bubbling laughter.* V

4 If you are **bubbling** with excitement, enthusiasm, or liveliness, for example, you are full of it. EG *She was bubbling with confidence... At the end of the day I was bubbling with excitement.* V : USU+*with*

bubble gum is chewing gum that you can blow out of your mouth in the shape of a bubble. N UNCOUNT

bubbly /bʌbli¹/, **bubblier, bubbliest. 1** A liquid that is **bubbly** is full of bubbles. EG *I like my mineral water bubbly rather than still.* ADJ QUALIT

2 Champagne is sometimes referred to as **bubbly.** EG *His wife opened a bottle of bubbly.* N UNCOUNT Informal

3 Someone who is **bubbly** is very lively and cheerful. EG *She's such a bubbly little girl.* ADJ QUALIT

buck /bʌk/, **bucks, bucking, bucked. 1** A **buck** is a US or Australian dollar. EG *It cost me four bucks for the taxi and ten bucks for the tickets.* N COUNT Informal

2 A **buck** is also the male of various animals, including the deer and rabbit. EG *The female deer attracts the buck with high-pitched sounds.* N COUNT

3 If an animal such as a horse **bucks**, it jumps into the air wildly with all four feet off the ground. EG *I fell off every time that stupid horse bucked.* V

4 When people **make a fast buck**, they make a lot of money quickly, especially by doing something dishonest. EG *Even some well-known politicians were making a fast buck at the expense of their innocent supporters.* PHRASE Informal

5 If you **pass the buck**, you refuse to accept responsibility for something, and say that someone else is responsible. EG *You're passing the buck! It was up to you to check!* PHRASE Informal

buck up. 1 If you **buck** someone **up** or if they **buck up**, they become more cheerful. EG *I need something to buck my spirits up today... He has bucked up the morale of the nation with his optimistic policies for social change.* **2** If you tell someone to **buck up**, you are telling them to hurry up. EG *Come on, Charlie, buck up or we'll be late!* PHRASAL VB : V-ERG+ADV; V+ADV Informal

bucket /bʌkɪt/, **buckets. 1** A **bucket** is a round metal or plastic container with a handle attached to its sides. Buckets are often used for holding and carrying water. EG *The hotel cleaner entered carrying a bucket and a mop.* N COUNT

2 You can use **bucket** to refer to a full bucket and its contents or just to the contents. EG *Dissolve the powder in a bucket of warm water.* N PART

3 You can use **buckets** to refer to large amounts of a liquid, especially rain. EG *We're going to get buckets of rain.* N PART : PLURAL Informal

bucketful /bʌkɪ²tfʊl/, **bucketfuls.** A **bucketful** is the amount contained in a bucket. EG *...a bucketful of cold water.* N PART

buckle /bʌkə⁰l/, **buckles, buckling, buckled. 1** A **buckle** is a piece of metal or plastic attached to one end of a belt or strap, which is used to fasten it. EG *...shoes fastened with big metal buckles.* N COUNT

Find the animals on these pages.

buckles

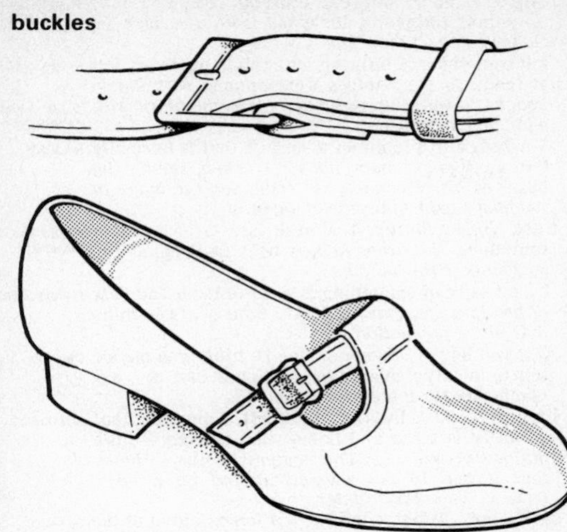

2 If you **buckle** a belt or strap, you fasten it. EG *The cuffs of the raincoat are tightly buckled... He buckled on his revolver.* V+O

3 If an object **buckles** or if something **buckles** it, it becomes bent as a result of severe heat or force. V-ERG

4 If your legs or knees **buckle**, they bend because they have become very weak or tired. EG *My knees were buckling under me.* V

buckle down. If you **buckle down** to something, you start working seriously at it. EG *I'm going to buckle down to the training course.* PHRASAL VB: V+ADV Informal

bud /bʌd/, **buds, budding, budded. 1** A **bud** is a small pointed lump that appears on a tree or plant and develops into a leaf or flower. EG *...when the bud opens.* ● When a tree or plant is **in bud**, it has buds on it. N COUNT ● PHRASE

2 When a tree or plant **buds**, buds appear on it. V

3 To **nip** something **in the bud** means to put an end to it at an early stage. EG *This incident very nearly nipped his political career in the bud.* PHRASE Informal

4 See also **budding**.

Buddhism /bʊdɪzəᵒm/ is a religion which teaches that the way to end suffering is by overcoming your desires. N UNCOUNT

Buddhist /bʊdɪst/, **Buddhists. 1** A **Buddhist** is a person whose religion is Buddhism. N COUNT

2 Buddhist means relating to Buddhism. EG *...Buddhist philosophy.* ADJ CLASSIF

budding /bʌdɪŋ/. A **budding** poet, artist, or musician is one who is just beginning to develop and be successful. EG *...a budding writer... ...budding doctors.* ADJ CLASSIF: ATTRIB

buddy /bʌdi¹/, **buddies. 1** A **buddy** is a close friend, especially a male friend of a man. EG *The two of them have become great buddies.* N COUNT Informal

2 Men sometimes address other men as **buddy**. EG *Keep going, buddy.* VOCATIVE American

budge /bʌdʒ/, **budges, budging, budged. 1** If someone will not **budge** on a matter, they refuse to change their mind or to compromise. EG *He refuses to budge on his design principles.* V: OFT +on/from

2 If you cannot move something, you can say that it will not **budge** or that you cannot **budge** it. EG *The screw just will not budge.* V-ERG

budgerigar /bʌdʒəᵒrɪgɑː/, **budgerigars. Budgerigars** are small, brightly-coloured birds that people keep in their houses as pets. N COUNT

budget /bʌdʒɪ²t/, **budgets, budgeting, budgeted.**

1 A **budget** is a plan showing how much money a person or organization has available and how it should be spent. EG *Work out a weekly budget... Education budgets have been cut.* N COUNT: USU+SUPP

2 If you **budget**, you plan carefully how much you are going to spend on each thing you want. EG *He could count on a regular salary and thus budget for the future.* ◇ **budgeting.** EG *Through careful budgeting they had equipped the entire school.* V: OFT+for ◇ N UNCOUNT

3 Budget is used in advertising to suggest that something is being sold cheaply. EG *...budget prices... ...budget travel.* ADJ CLASSIF: ATTRIB

budget for. If you **budget** for something, you take account of it in your budget. EG *These expenses can all be budgeted for.* PHRASAL VB: V+PREP, HAS PASS

budgetary /bʌdʒɪ²təᵒri¹/. A **budgetary** matter or policy is concerned with the amount of money that is available and how it is to be spent. EG *...disagreements over budgetary policies.* ADJ CLASSIF: ATTRIB Formal

budgie /bʌdʒi¹/, **budgies.** A **budgie** is the same as a budgerigar. N COUNT Informal

buff /bʌf/, **buffs. 1** Something that is **buff** is pale brown in colour. EG *...buff envelopes... ...She was wearing a buff uniform .* ADJ COLOUR

2 You can use **buff** to talk about people who know a lot about a particular subject. For example, someone who is a film **buff** knows a lot about films. EG *...chess buffs.* N COUNT+SUPP Informal

buffalo /bʌfələʊ/, **buffaloes.** A **buffalo** is a wild animal like a large cow with long curved horns. The plural of 'buffalo' is either 'buffaloes' or 'buffalo'. N COUNT

buffer /bʌfə/, **buffers, buffering, buffered. 1** A **buffer** is something that prevents something else from being harmed. EG *The world lacks the buffer of large international grain reserves... It acts as a buffer against harmful environmental change.* ▸ used as a verb. EG *When the fish bites, hold the rod high to buffer any sudden shocks.* N COUNT ▸ V+O

2 The **buffers** on a train or at the end of a railway line are two metal discs on springs that reduce the shock when they are hit. N COUNT: USU PLURAL

buffet, buffets, buffeting, buffeted; pronounced /bʊfeɪ/ for paragraph 1, and /bʌfət/ for paragraphs 2 and 3.

1 A **buffet** is **1.1** a café in a station. **1.2** a meal of cold food at a party or public occasion. Guests usually help themselves to the food and eat it standing up. EG *We found a huge buffet laid out... ...a buffet lunch.* N COUNT

2 If the wind or the sea **buffets** something, it pushes against it suddenly and violently. EG *The vessel was buffeted by huge waves.* ◇ **buffeting.** EG *...ships built to withstand the buffeting of the sea.* V+O ◇ N UNCOUNT

3 If you have a lot of shocks or unpleasant experiences, you can say that you **are buffeted** by them. EG *He is severely buffeted by events and forces beyond his control.* V+O: USU PASS Formal

buffet car /bʊfeɪ kɑː/, **buffet cars.** A **buffet car** is a carriage on a train where you can buy sandwiches, drinks, and other snacks. N COUNT

buffoon /bʌfuːn/, **buffoons.** You call someone a **buffoon** when they do silly things. ◇ **buffoonery** /bʌfuːnəᵒri¹/. EG *...a harmless piece of buffoonery.* N COUNT ◇ N UNCOUNT Outdated

bug /bʌg/, **bugs, bugging, bugged. 1** A **bug** is a tiny insect, especially one that causes damage. N COUNT

2 A **bug** is also a minor illness such as a cold that people catch from each other. EG *There must be a bug going around.* N COUNT Informal

3 If a place **is bugged**, tiny microphones are hidden there to secretly record what people are saying. EG *Don't speak in the bedrooms; they are bugged... ...electronic bugging devices.* V+O: USU PASS

4 If something **bugs** you, it worries or annoys you. EG *That's what bugs me about the whole business.* V+O Informal

5 You can say that someone **is bitten by** a **bug** when they suddenly become very enthusiastic about something. EG *She's been bitten by the skiing bug.* PHRASE Informal

bugle /bjuːgəᵒl/, **bugles.** A **bugle** is a simple brass instrument that looks like a small trumpet. N COUNT

build /bɪld/, **builds, building, built** /bɪlt/. **1** If you **build** a structure, you make it by joining things together. EG *John had built a house facing the river... They were building a bridge.* V+O, V+O+O, OR V+O+*for*

2 If people **build** an organization or a society, they gradually form it. EG *They struggled to build a more democratic society.* V+O

3 Your **build** is the shape that your bones and muscles give to your body. EG *She was in her early thirties, with a lean, athletic build.* N UNCOUNT +SUPP

4 See also **built**.

build into. 1 If you **build** something **into** a wall or object, you make it in such a way that it is in the wall or object, or is part of it. EG *There was a cupboard built into the whitewashed wall.* PHRASAL VB : V+O+PREP **2** If you **build** something **into** a policy, system, or product, you make it a part of it. EG *...the inequalities built into our system of financing.* V+O+PREP

build on or **build upon. 1** If you **build** an organization, system, or product **on** or **upon** something, you base it on it. EG *...the principles on which these organizations are built... ...an economy built upon manufacturing industry.* PHRASAL VB : V+O+PREP **2** If you **build on** or **upon** the success of something, you take advantage of this success in order to make further progress. EG *We must try to build on the success of these growth industries.* V+PREP, HAS PASS

build up. 1 If an amount of something **builds up** or if you **build** it **up**, it gradually gets bigger as a result of more being added to it. EG *Mud builds up in the lake... We're trying to build up a collection of herbs and spices.* PHRASAL VB : V-ERG+ADV **2** If you **build up** someone's trust or confidence, you gradually make them more trusting or more confident. EG *I found myself trying to reassure Ron, trying to build up his morale.* V+O+ADV **3** To **build** someone **up** means to cause them to be their normal weight again after they have been ill. EG *The patient badly needs building up.* V+O+ADV **4** See also **build-up**, **built-up**.

build upon. See **build on**.

builder /bɪldə/, **builders.** A **builder** is a person whose job is to build houses and other buildings. EG *Her father was a builder and decorator.* N COUNT

building /bɪldɪŋ/, **buildings.** A **building** is a structure that has a roof and walls, for example a house or a factory. EG *...a small farm building.* N COUNT

building society, building societies. In Britain, a **building society** is a business which will lend you money when you want to buy a house. You can also invest money in a building society, where it will earn interest. N COUNT

build-up, build-ups. A **build-up** is a gradual increase in something. EG *...a massive build-up of nuclear weapons.* N COUNT : USU SING+*of*

built /bɪlt/. **1 Built** is the past tense and past participle of **build**.

2 If you say that someone is **built** in a particular way, you are describing the kind of body they have. EG *He didn't look as if he was built for this kind of work.* • See also **well-built**. ADJ CLASSIF

built-in. Built-in devices or features are included in something as an essential part of it. EG *...a dishwasher with a built-in waste disposal unit... ...built-in safeguards.* ADJ CLASSIF : ATTRIB

built-up. A **built-up** area is an area where there are many buildings. EG *Such vehicles could not be brought into built-up areas.* ADJ QUALIT

bulb /bʌlb/, **bulbs. 1** A **bulb** is the glass part of an electric lamp, which gives out light when electricity passes through it. EG *The veranda was lit by a dim bulb... If it doesn't work it may need a new light bulb.* N COUNT

2 A **bulb** is also **2.1** a root shaped like an onion that grows into a flower or plant. EG *...tulip bulbs.* **2.2** something that has a round shape like a flower bulb. EG *...the bulb of the thermometer.* N COUNT

bulbous /bʌlbəs/. Something that is **bulbous** is round and fat in a rather ugly way. EG *...people with great bulbous noses.* ADJ CLASSIF

bulge /bʌldʒ/, **bulges, bulging, bulged. 1** If something **bulges**, it sticks out from a surface. EG *Guns bulged on their hips.* V : OFT+A

2 If something **is bulging** with things, it is very full of them. EG *The shelves were bulging with knick-knacks.* ◊ **bulging.** EG *He arrived in the office with a bulging briefcase.* V : OFT+*with* ◊ ADJ CLASSIF : ATTRIB

3 A **bulge** is a lump on a surface that is normally flat. EG *'What's under there?' I asked, seeing the bulge at his waistline... He could see the bulge of the body against the side of the tent.* N COUNT

bulk /bʌlk/, **bulks. 1** A **bulk** is a large mass of something. EG *Willie looked with loathing at the dark bulk of the building.* N COUNT : USU SING

2 The **bulk** of something is most of it. EG *The bulk of his days are spent quietly... ...the overwhelming bulk of the population.* N PART : SING

3 If you buy or sell something **in bulk**, you buy or sell it in large quantities. EG *Goods can be very much cheaper if they're sold in bulk.* PHRASE

bulky /bʌlki[1]/, **bulkier, bulkiest.** Something that is **bulky** is large and heavy, and therefore often difficult to move. EG *The equipment was so bulky that it had to be wheeled around on a large trolley... ...a bulky sweater.* ADJ QUALIT

bull /bʊl/, **bulls.** A **bull** is **1** a male animal of the cow family. **2** the male of some other animals, such as the elephant or the whale. EG *...a bull elephant.* N COUNT

bulldog /bʊldɒg/, **bulldogs.** A **bulldog** is a dog with a large square head and short hair. N COUNT

bulldoze /bʊldəʊz/, **bulldozes, bulldozing, bulldozed. 1** If people **bulldoze** something such as a building, they knock it down using a bulldozer. EG *Settlements have been bulldozed out of the way.* V+O

2 If people **bulldoze** earth, stone, or other heavy material, they move it using a bulldozer. V+O

bulldozer /bʊldəʊzə/, **bulldozers.** A **bulldozer** is a large, powerful tractor with a broad metal blade at the front, which is used for knocking down buildings or moving large amounts of earth. N COUNT

bullet /bʊlɪ[1]t/, **bullets.** A **bullet** is a small piece of metal with a pointed or rounded end, which is fired out of a gun. EG *...a bullet shot through the window... The car was covered with bullet holes.* N COUNT

bulletin /bʊlɪ[1]tɪn/, **bulletins.** A **bulletin** is **1** a short news report on the radio or television. **2** a regular newspaper or leaflet that is produced by an organization or group such as a school or church. EG *The Institute publishes a fortnightly bulletin.* N COUNT

bullet-proof. Something that is **bullet-proof** is made of a strong material that bullets cannot pass through. EG *...bullet-proof vests.* ADJ CLASSIF

bullfight /bʊlfaɪt/, **bullfights.** A **bullfight** is a public entertainment in which a man makes a bull angry by sticking short spears in it before trying to kill it with a sword. Bullfights are especially popular in Spain. N COUNT

bullfighter /bʊlfaɪtə/, **bullfighters.** A **bullfighter** is the man who tries to kill the bull in a bullfight. N COUNT

bullfighting /bʊlfaɪtɪŋ/ is the public entertainment in which men try to kill bulls in bullfights. N UNCOUNT

bullion /bʊlɪ[0]jən/ is gold or silver in the form of lumps or bars. N UNCOUNT

bullock /bʊlək/, **bullocks.** A **bullock** is a young bull that has been castrated. N COUNT

bull's-eye, bull's-eyes. 1 The **bull's-eye** is the small circular area at the centre of a target. EG *He hit the bull's-eye and won the prize.* N SING

2 A **bull's-eye** is a shot or throw of a dart that hits the bull's-eye. N COUNT

bullshit /bʊlʃɪt/ is a swear word. If you say **'bullshit!'**, you are telling someone that what they have said is nonsense or completely untrue. EXCLAM OR N UNCOUNT

If you buy something in bulk, is it bulky?

bully /bʊli¹/, **bullies, bullying, bullied. 1** A **bully** is someone who uses their strength or power to hurt or frighten other people. EG *There was a high proportion of sadists and bullies among the camp guards.* N COUNT

2 If someone **bullies** you, they use their strength or power to hurt or frighten you. EG *For the first month at my new school I was bullied constantly.* V+O

◇ **bullying.** EG *All cases of bullying will be severely dealt with.* ◇ N UNCOUNT

3 If someone **bullies** you into doing something, they make you do it by using force or threats. EG *He had been bullied into driving her home.* V+O: OFT+*into*

bulrush /bʊlrʌʃ/, **bulrushes. Bulrushes** are tall, stiff reeds that grow on the edges of rivers. N COUNT: USU PLURAL

bulwark /bʊlwək/, **bulwarks.** A **bulwark** is something strong that protects you against unpleasant or dangerous situations. EG *The fund is a bulwark against your benefits being cut.* N COUNT: OFT+*against*

bum /bʌm/, **bums. 1** A **bum** is a tramp. EG *If you were a bum, you would be free to do whatever you want.* N COUNT Informal American

2 You can say that someone is a **bum** when you think that they are worthless or irresponsible. EG *What an illiterate lot of bums you are!* N COUNT Informal American

3 Your **bum** is the part of your body which you sit on. EG *...sitting down on their big fat bums.* N COUNT Informal

bumble /bʌmbə⁰l/, **bumbles, bumbling, bumbled.** When someone **bumbles**, they behave in a confused, disorganized way and make a lot of mistakes. V ◇ **bumbling.** EG *Michael Hordern plays the bumbling Englishman yet again.* ◇ ADJ CLASSIF: ATTRIB

bumblebee /bʌmbə⁰bi:/, **bumblebees.** A **bumblebee** is a large hairy bee. N COUNT

bump /bʌmp/, **bumps, bumping, bumped. 1** If you **bump** into something, you accidentally hit it while you are moving. EG *He turned on the lamp so that he could find his way without bumping into anything.* V+A OR V+O

2 If a vehicle **bumps** over a surface, it travels in a rough, bouncing way because the surface is very uneven. EG *The jeep was bumping over stony ground... ...bumping along the dirt road.* V+A

3 If you have a **bump** while you are driving a car, you have a minor accident in which you hit something. EG *Her car got three bad bumps while she was in London.* N COUNT

4 If something makes a **bump** when it hits something, it makes a fairly gentle sound. EG *It slipped from his fingers and fell with a bump.* N COUNT

5 A **bump** on a road is a raised, uneven part. EG *If the motor cycle goes over a bump, the engine misfires.* N COUNT

6 If you have a **bump** on your body, you have a swollen shape there as a result of a blow. EG *You've got a bump on your forehead like an egg.* N COUNT

bump into. If you **bump into** someone you know, you meet them by chance. EG *I bumped into Mary an hour ago... We occasionally bump into one another.* PHRASAL VB: V+PREP Informal

bump off. To **bump** someone **off** means to kill them. PHRASAL VB: V+O+ADV

bumper /bʌmpə/, **bumpers. 1 Bumpers** are bars at the front and back of a vehicle which protect it if it bumps into something. See picture at CAR. N COUNT British ● If traffic is **bumper to bumper**, the vehicles are so close to one another that they are almost touching and are moving very slowly. ● PHRASE British

2 A **bumper** crop or harvest is one that is larger than usual. EG *We had a bumper crop of apples last year.* ADJ CLASSIF: ATTRIB

bumptious /bʌmpʃəs/. You say that someone is **bumptious** when they are continually expressing their own opinions and ideas in a self-important way. EG *I disliked these noisy bumptious types.* ADJ QUALIT

bumpy /bʌmpi¹/, **bumpier, bumpiest. 1** A road or path that is **bumpy** has a lot of bumps on it. EG *The track got bumpier and muddier the further we went.* ADJ QUALIT

2 If a journey in a vehicle is **bumpy**, it is uncomfortable and rough, because you are travelling over an uneven surface. EG *The ride was a bit bumpy.* ADJ QUALIT

bun /bʌn/, **buns. 1** A **bun** is a small cake or bread roll, often containing currants or spices. N COUNT

2 If a woman has her hair in a **bun**, it is fastened into a round shape at the back of her head. N COUNT

bunch /bʌntʃ/, **bunches, bunching, bunched. 1** A **bunch** of people is a group of them. EG *They're a bunch of tired old men... Ranchers are an independent bunch.* N PART Informal

2 A **bunch** of flowers is a number of them held or tied together. EG *...a big bunch of poppies.* N PART

3 A **bunch** of bananas, grapes, or other fruit is a group of them growing on the same stem. N PART

4 A **bunch** of similar things is a group of them situated, held, or fastened closely together. EG *...a big bunch of keys... ...holding a bunch of balloons.* N PART

5 If people **bunch** together or **bunch** up, they stay close together in a group. V: OFT +*together/up*

6 If you **bunch** things together or **bunch** them up, you gather them together to make a tight bundle. EG *She was holding her skirts bunched up over one arm.* V+O: OFT+A OR V+A

bundle /bʌndə⁰l/, **bundles, bundling, bundled. 1** A **bundle** is a number of things tied together or wrapped in a cloth so that they can be carried or stored. EG *He tied the wood into a bundle... He had his bundle of personal belongings under his arm.* N COUNT OR N PART

2 If you **bundle** someone or something somewhere, you push them there in a rough and hurried way. EG *He led her to the window and bundled her out... They bundled him into the ambulance.* V+O+A OR V+A

bundle off. If you **bundle** someone **off** somewhere, you send them there in a hurry. EG *Jack was bundled off to Ely to stay with friends.* PHRASAL VB: V+O+ADV, OFT+*to*

bundle up. If you **bundle up** a mass of things, you make them into a bundle by gathering or tying them together. EG *My mother bundled up all my comics and threw them out.* PHRASAL VB: V+O+ADV

bung /bʌŋ/, **bungs, bunging, bunged. 1** A **bung** is a round piece of wood, cork, or rubber which you use to close the hole in a container such as a barrel or flask. N COUNT

2 If you **bung** something somewhere, you put it there in a quick and careless way. EG *Just bung it in the oven... I bunged the books on the shelf.* V+O+A Informal

3 See also **bunged up**.

bungalow /bʌŋgələʊ/, **bungalows.** A **bungalow** is a house which has only one storey. N COUNT

bunged up. If a hole is **bunged up**, it is blocked. EG *The sink's bunged up... ...a bunged-up nose.* ADJ PRED Informal

bungle /bʌŋgə⁰l/, **bungles, bungling, bungled.** If you **bungle** something, you fail to do it properly, because you make mistakes or are clumsy. EG *They bungled the whole operation.* V OR V+O ◇ **bungled.** EG *...the bungled murder of Bernard Lustig.* ◇ ADJ CLASSIF ◇ **bungling.** EG *...this bungling administration.* ◇ ADJ CLASSIF

bunion /bʌnjən/, **bunions.** A **bunion** is a large painful lump on the first joint of a person's big toe. N COUNT

bunk /bʌŋk/, **bunks. 1** A **bunk** is a bed fixed to a wall, especially in a ship or caravan. EG *I ran to my cabin and threw myself on the bunk... Thomas was lying in the lower bunk.* N COUNT

2 If you describe something that someone has said or written as **bunk**, you mean that it is foolish or untrue. EG *That's all bunk – there can't be equality.* N UNCOUNT Informal

3 If you **do a bunk**, you suddenly leave a place without telling anyone. EG *The next thing I knew, the whole family had done a bunk.* PHRASE Informal

bunker /bʌŋkə/, **bunkers.** A **bunker** is **1** a place, usually underground, that has been built with strong walls to protect it against heavy gunfire and bombing. **2** a container for coal or other fuel. N COUNT

bunny /bʌni¹/, **bunnies.** Small children call a rabbit a **bunny** or a **bunny rabbit**. N COUNT

bunting /bʌntɪŋ/ consists of rows of small coloured flags that are used to decorate streets and N UNCOUNT buildings on special occasions. EG *The street was decorated with red, white and blue bunting.*

buoy /bɔɪ/, **buoys, buoying, buoyed.** A **buoy** is a floating object that shows ships and boats where they can go and that warns them of danger. N COUNT

buoy up. If you **buoy** someone **up**, you keep them cheerful in a situation in which they might feel depressed. EG *He did his best to buoy her up.* PHRASAL VB : V+O+ADV

buoyant /bɔɪənt/. **1** If you are **buoyant**, you feel cheerful and behave in a lively way. EG *He suddenly smiled, feeling buoyant and at ease... His mood became buoyant.* ◊ **buoyancy** /bɔɪənsi[1]/. EG *...a sensation of buoyancy and freedom.* ◊ **buoyantly.** EG *'I hope she will,' said Pratt buoyantly.* ADJ QUALIT; ◊ N UNCOUNT; ◊ ADV

2 Something that is **buoyant** floats on a liquid or in the air. EG *...a row of buoyant cylinders.* ◊ **buoyancy.** EG *New chambers were added to provide buoyancy.* ADJ QUALIT; ◊ N UNCOUNT

3 A **buoyant** economy is a successful one in which there is a lot of trade and economic activity. ADJ QUALIT

burble /bɜːbə[0]l/, **burbles, burbling, burbled.** If something **burbles**, it makes a low continuous bubbling sound. EG *Hot mud burbled down from a side valley... Lucy was making burbling noises.* V

burden /bɜːdə[0]n/, **burdens. 1** Something that is a **burden** causes you a lot of worry or hard work. EG *He was weighed down by the burden of state secrets he carried with him... This would relieve the initial burden on hospital staff.* N COUNT

2 A **burden** is also a heavy load that is difficult to carry. EG *Men and women came bearing heavy burdens of provisions.* N COUNT Formal

burdened /bɜːdə[0]nd/. If you are **burdened** with something, it causes you a lot of worry or hard work. EG *He was burdened with endless paperwork.* ADJ PRED +with/by

bureau /bjʊərəʊ/, **bureaux** or **bureaus. 1** A **bureau** is a writing desk with shelves and drawers and a lid that opens to form the writing surface. EG *He was going through the drawers of the bureau.* N COUNT British

2 A **bureau** is also **2.1** an office, organization, or government department that collects and distributes information. EG *The weather bureau promised a sunny weekend.* **2.2** an office of a company or organization which has its headquarters in another town or country. EG *...the Washington bureau of a Midwestern newspaper.* N COUNT American; American

bureaucracy /bjʊərɒkrəsi[1]/, **bureaucracies. 1** A **bureaucracy** is an administrative system operated by a large number of officials following rules and procedures. EG *Each industry is guided by massive bureaucracies... ...an inefficient bureaucracy.* N COUNT

2 Bureaucracy is all the rules and procedures followed by government departments and similar organizations; often used showing disapproval. EG *One of the problems is the bureaucracy the claimant has to face.* N UNCOUNT

bureaucrat /bjʊərə[6]kræt/, **bureaucrats.** A **bureaucrat** is an official who works in a bureaucracy, especially one who you think follows rules and procedures too strictly. EG *...endless paperwork dished out by bureaucrats.* N COUNT

bureaucratic /bjʊərə[6]krætɪk/. **Bureaucratic** rules and procedures are complicated ones which can cause long delays. ADJ QUALIT

bureaux /bjʊərəʊz/ is a plural form of **bureau.**

burglar /bɜːglə/, **burglars.** A **burglar** is a thief who breaks into a house and steals things. N COUNT

burglar alarm, burglar alarms. A **burglar alarm** is an electric device that makes a bell ring loudly if someone tries to break into a building. N COUNT

burglary /bɜːgləri[1]/, **burglaries.** If someone carries out a **burglary**, they break into a building and steal things. EG *Contact the police as soon as possible after a burglary... He was found guilty of burglary.* N COUNT OR N UNCOUNT

burgle /bɜːgə[0]l/, **burgles, burgling, burgled.** If someone **burgles** a building, they break into it and steal things. EG *She thought they might be criminals come to burgle the house.* V+O

burial /bɛri[1]əl/, **burials.** A **burial** is the ceremony that takes place when a dead body is put into a grave in the ground. EG *The bodies are brought home for burial... He read swiftly through the burial service.* N COUNT OR N UNCOUNT

burly /bɜːli[1]/, **burlier, burliest.** A **burly** man has a broad body and strong muscles. EG *...two burly Irish workers... ...his tall, burly frame.* ADJ QUALIT

burn /bɜːn/, **burns, burning, burned, burnt** /bɜːnt/. The past tense and past participle can be either **burned** or **burnt**.

1 If something **is burning**, it is on fire. EG *The stubble was burning in the fields.* ◊ **burning.** EG *There was a smell of burning.* ◊ **burnt.** EG *...a charred bit of burnt wood.* V; ◊ N UNCOUNT; ◊ ADJ CLASSIF

2 If you **burn** something, you destroy it with fire. EG *We couldn't burn the rubbish because it was raining.* ◊ **burning.** EG *...the burning of the Embassy during the riots.* V+O; ◊ N UNCOUNT

3 If you **burn** something that you are cooking or if it **burns**, you spoil it by using too great a heat. EG *I burnt the milk.* V-ERG

4 If you **burn** yourself, you are injured by fire or by something very hot. EG *'What's the matter with your hand?' – 'I burned it on my cigar.'* ▸ used as a noun. EG *Many had serious burns over much of their bodies.* V-REFL OR V+O; ▸ N COUNT

5 If your face **is burning**, it is red because you are embarrassed or upset. V : USU CONT

6 If you **are burning** with an emotion such as anger, you feel very angry. EG *...letters burning with indignation.* V+*with* : USU CONT

7 If the sun **burns** your skin, it makes your skin become red or brown. EG *Simon was burned by the sun to a deep tan... ...skin that usually burns in the sun.* V-ERG

8 You can say that something **burns** when it gives you a painful, hot feeling. EG *The whiskey he had drunk burned in his chest.* V

9 If something is extremely hot, you can say that it is **burning** or **burning hot**. EG *...burning deserts... ...burning hot irons.* ADJ CLASSIF : ATTRIB

burn down. If a building **burns down** or if someone **burns** it **down**, it is completely destroyed by fire. EG *My house was burnt down.* PHRASAL VB : V-ERG+ADV

burn out. 1 If a fire **burns** itself **out**, it stops burning because there is nothing left to burn. EG *All the fires had now burned themselves out.* **2** If you **burn** yourself **out**, you make yourself exhausted or ill by working too hard. **3** See also **burnt-out**. PHRASAL VB : V-REFL+ADV; V-REFL+ADV Informal

burn up. 1 If something **burns up**, it is completely destroyed by fire or strong heat. EG *The satellite had burned up on re-entering the atmosphere.* **2** If you say that an engine **burns up** fuel, you mean that it uses a lot of fuel. PHRASAL VB : V+ADV; V+O+ADV

burned-out. See **burnt-out**.

burner /bɜːnə/, **burners.** A **burner** is a device which produces heat or a flame, especially as part of a cooker or heater. N COUNT

burnish /bɜːnɪʃ/, **burnishes, burnishing, burnished.** When you **burnish** metal, you polish it so that it shines. V+O

burnished /bɜːnɪʃt/. You can describe something as **burnished** when it is bright or smooth. EG *...burnished leaves... ...her burnished skin.* ADJ CLASSIF Literary

burnt /bɜːnt/ is a past tense and past participle of **burn.**

burnt-out or **burned-out. Burnt-out** vehicles or buildings have been very badly damaged by fire. ADJ QUALIT

burp /bɜːp/, **burps, burping, burped.** When someone **burps**, they make a noise because air from their stomach has been forced up through

Can you burgle your own house?

their throat. ▸ used as a noun. EG *A slight burp interrupted her flowing speech.* ▸ N COUNT

burrow /bʌrəʊ⁰/, **burrows, burrowing, burrowed. 1** A **burrow** is a tunnel or hole in the ground that is dug by an animal such as a rabbit. N COUNT

2 When an animal **burrows**, it digs a tunnel or hole in the ground. EG *The fish burrows into the mud... ...earthworms burrowing their way through the soil.* V OR V+O: USU+A

3 When you **burrow** in a container or pile of things, you search there for something using your hands. EG *She began burrowing underneath the tissue paper.* V+A

bursary /bɜːsə⁰ri¹/, **bursaries.** A **bursary** is a sum of money which is given to someone to allow them to study in a college or university. N COUNT

burst /bɜːst/, **bursts, bursting.** The form **burst** is used in the present tense and is the past tense and past participle of the verb.

1 When something **bursts** or when you **burst** it, it suddenly breaks open or splits open, and the air inside or some other substance comes out. EG *As he braked a tyre burst... She burst the balloon... ...a burst water pipe.* V-ERG

2 When a door or lid **bursts** open, it opens very suddenly and violently because there is great pressure behind it. EG *I was sure the door was going to burst open any minute.* V+*open* OR V+O+*open*

3 If you **burst** into or through something, you suddenly go into it or through it with a lot of energy because you are in a great hurry. EG *O'Shea burst in through the opposite door... A woman burst her way through the guests at the buffet.* V+A OR V+O+A

4 If you say that someone is about to **burst** with an emotion such as pride or anger, you mean that they feel very proud or very angry. EG *I could have burst with pride... He felt himself about to burst with rage.* V: OFT+*with*

5 A **burst** of something is a sudden short period of it. EG *There was a burst of automatic rifle fire... ...capable of great bursts of speed.* N COUNT+*of*

burst in on. If you **burst in on** someone, you suddenly and quickly enter the room that they are in. EG *He suddenly burst in on me without warning.* PHRASAL VB: V+ADV+PREP

burst into. 1 If you **burst into** tears or laughter, you suddenly begin to cry or laugh. EG *I keep bursting into tears... The whole room burst into laughter.* PHRASAL VB: V+PREP **2** When plants **burst into** leaf, blossom, or flower, their leaves or flowers suddenly open. V+PREP **3** to **burst into flames**: see **flame**.

burst out. 1 If you **burst out** laughing or crying, you suddenly begin laughing or crying, usually loudly. PHRASAL VB: V+ADV+-ING **2** Writers use **burst out** to indicate that someone says something suddenly and loudly. EG *Then he burst out, 'Get into the car, Phil, can't you?'* V+ADV+QUOTE Written

bursting /bɜːstɪŋ/. **1** If a place is **bursting** with people or things, it is full of them. EG *...parks bursting with flowers.* ADJ PRED +*with* ● If you say that a place is **bursting at the seams**, you mean that it is very full indeed. EG *The psychiatric wards are bursting at the seams.* ● PHRASE Informal

2 Someone who is **bursting** with a feeling or quality is full of it. EG *Claud was bursting with pride and excitement... Jamie is bursting with energy.* ADJ PRED +*with*

3 Someone who is **bursting** to do something is very eager to do it. EG *I was bursting to tell someone... All the children were bursting to take part.* ADJ PRED +*to*-INF Informal

bury /beri¹/, **buries, burying, buried. 1** When a dead person **is buried**, their body is put into a grave and covered with earth. EG *She will be buried here in the churchyard.* V+O: USU+A

2 To **bury** something means to put it into a hole in the ground and cover it up, often in order to hide it. EG *Reptiles bury their eggs in holes... ...buried treasure.* V+O: USU+A

3 If you **are buried** under something that falls on top of you, you are completely covered and often cannot get out. EG *People were buried beneath mountains of rubble.* V+O: USU PASS+A

4 If you **bury** your face in something, you press your face against it in order to hide it. EG *She buried her face in her hands... She turned away, burying her face in the pillow.* V+O+A

5 If you **bury** a feeling, you try not to show it. If you **bury** a memory, you try to forget it. EG *The anger which had been buried inside me rose to the surface... ...buried memories.* V+O

6 If you **bury** yourself in something, you concentrate hard on it. EG *He buried himself deep in the wine list.* V-REFL+*in*

bury away. If something **is buried away** somewhere, you cannot easily find it or see it. EG *Buried away inside the paper, in a tiny paragraph, was an account of his visit.* PHRASAL VB: V+O+ADV, USU PASS

bus /bʌs/, **buses.** A **bus** is a large motor vehicle which carries passengers from one place to another. EG *I'm waiting for the bus back to town... I could go by bus... ...a bus driver.* N COUNT OR *by*+N

bus conductor, bus conductors. A **bus conductor** is an official on a bus who sells passengers their tickets. N COUNT

bush /bʊʃ/, **bushes. 1** A **bush** is a large plant which is smaller than a tree and has a lot of branches. EG *...a gorse bush... I peered through the bushes.* N COUNT

2 You can refer to the wild, uncultivated parts of some hot countries as the **bush**. EG *I went for a walk in the bush... ...a bush fire.* N SING: *the*+N

3 If you say to someone **'Don't beat about the bush'**, you mean that you want them to tell you something immediately and directly rather than trying to avoid doing so. PHRASE

bushy /bʊʃi¹/, **bushier, bushiest. Bushy** hair or fur grows very thickly. EG *...bushy eyebrows... ...a fox with a bushy tail.* ADJ QUALIT

busily /bɪzɪli¹/. If you do something **busily**, you do it in a very active way. EG *Some children were busily catching crabs... I went on writing busily.* ADV

business /bɪznɪs/, **businesses. 1 Business** is work relating to the production, buying, and selling of goods or services. EG *...firms that do business with Britain... There are good profits to be made in the hotel business... Are you in San Francisco for business or pleasure?... He had a business appointment.* N UNCOUNT

2 A **business** is an organization which produces and sells goods or which provides a service. EG *He set up a small travel business.* N COUNT

3 If a shop or company goes **out of business**, it has to stop trading because it is not making enough money. EG *Umbrella sellers went out of business.* PHRASE

4 If you have some **business** to deal with, you have something, especially something important, to deal with. EG *She got on with the business of clearing up... Let's get down to business now.* N UNCOUNT

5 If you say that something is your **business**, you mean that it concerns you personally and that other people have no right to get involved in it. EG *That's his business and no one else's... It's no business of mine what you choose to read.* N SING+POSS

6 If you say that someone **has no business** to do something, you mean that they have no right to do it. EG *She had no business to publish his letters.* PHRASE

7 If you say to someone **'Mind your own business'** or **'It's none of your business'**, you are telling them not to ask about something that does not concern them. EG *'Where were you last night?' – 'That's none of your business.'* PHRASE Informal

8 You use **business** to refer in a general way to an event, situation, or activity that you are talking about. EG *The whole business affected him profoundly... This assassination business has gone far enough.* N SING+SUPP

9 If someone **means business**, they are serious and determined about what they are doing. PHRASE Informal

businesslike /bɪznɪslaɪk/. Someone who is **businesslike** deals with things in an efficient way without wasting time. ADJ QUALIT

businessman /bɪznɪsmə^{3}n/, **businessmen.** 1 A **businessman** is a man who works in business, for example by running a firm. N COUNT

2 If you describe a man as a good **businessman** or a shrewd **businessman**, you mean that he knows how to deal with money and how to make good deals. N COUNT+SUPP

busker /bʌskə/, **buskers.** A **busker** is a person who plays music or sings for money in city streets or stations. N COUNT British

bus stop, bus stops. A **bus stop** is a place on a road where buses stop to let passengers on and off. EG *There were long queues at all the bus stops.* N COUNT

bust /bʌst/, **busts, busting, busted.** The form **bust** can be used as the past tense and past participle of the verb as well as the present tense.

1 When you **bust** something, you damage it so badly that it cannot be used. EG *She was furious about Jack busting the double bass.* V+O Informal

2 If something is **bust**, it is broken or very badly damaged. EG *The television's bust.* ADJ PRED Informal

3 If a company **goes bust**, it loses so much money that it is forced to close down. EG *The oil companies went bust.* PHRASE Informal

4 A **bust** is a statue of the head and shoulders of a person. EG *...a bust of Shakespeare.* N COUNT

5 A woman's **bust** is her breasts. N COUNT

bustle /bʌsə^{0}l/, **bustles, bustling, bustled.** 1 If someone **bustles** somewhere, they move there in a hurried and determined way, often because they are very busy. EG *I watched housewives bustle in and out of a supermarket... He was bustling around the kitchen cooking up a huge pot of stew.* V+A

◊ **bustling.** EG *...the bustling curator of the museum.* ◊ ADJ CLASSIF : ATTRIB

2 A place that **is bustling** is full of people and very busy and lively. EG *The station was bustling with activity... Fraserburgh is a bustling fishing town.* ADJ CLASSIF

3 **Bustle** is busy, noisy activity. EG *...the bustle of the airport.* N UNCOUNT

busy /bɪzi^1/, **busier, busiest; busies, busying, busied.** 1 When you are **busy**, you are working hard or concentrating on a task, so that you are not free to do anything else. EG *She's going to be busy till Friday... Not now, Jo, I'm busy.* ADJ QUALIT

2 A **busy** time is a period of time during which you have a lot of things to do. EG *I've had a busy day.* ADJ QUALIT

3 If you are **busy** doing something, it is taking all your attention. EG *She is too busy chasing after money to care about such things... Her assistant was busy putting the instruments away.* ADJ PRED+-ING

4 If you **busy** yourself with something, you occupy yourself by dealing with it. EG *I decided to busy myself with our untidy lawn.* V-REFL : USU+A

5 A **busy** place is full of people who are doing things or moving about. EG *...a busy office... Curzon Street is usually very busy.* ADJ QUALIT

busybody /bɪzi^{1}bɒdi^1/, **busybodies.** If you call someone a **busybody**, you mean that they interfere in other people's affairs. EG *...a detective whom some busybody had hired to see what I was up to.* N COUNT Informal

but /bʌt, bət/. 1 You use **but** to introduce a statement which contrasts with what you have just said. EG *We'll have a meeting. But not today... It was a long walk but it was worth it... ...a cheap but incredibly effective carpet cleaner.* CONJ

2 You also use **but** when you are about to add something further in a discussion or to change the subject. EG *Later I'll be discussing this with Dr Peter Unsworth. But first let me remind you of some of the issues.* CONJ

3 You also use **but** after you have made an excuse or apology for what you are just about to say. EG *I'm sorry, but she's not in at the moment... Forgive my ignorance, but just what is Arista?* CONJ

4 You use **but then** 4.1 before a remark which slightly contradicts what you have just said. EG *Iron would do the job better. But then you can't bend iron so easily.* 4.2 before a remark which suggests that what you have just said should not be regarded as surprising. EG *They're very close. But then, they've known each other for years and years.* ADV SEN

5 **But** also means 5.1 except. EG *It hurt nobody but himself... It could do everything but stop.* PREP 5.2 only. EG *Low cost and high speed are but two of the advantages of electronic data handling... When I first met her she had but recently divorced.* ADV Formal

6 You use **but for** to introduce the only factor that causes a particular thing not to happen or not to be completely true. EG *But for his ice-blue eyes, he looked like a bearded, wiry Moor.* CONJ

7 **anything but**: see **anything**.

butch /bʊtʃ/. If you describe a woman as **butch**, you mean that she behaves or dresses in a masculine way; an offensive word. ADJ QUALIT

butcher /bʊtʃə/, **butchers, butchering, butchered.** 1 A **butcher** is a shopkeeper who sells meat. N COUNT

2 You can refer to a shop where meat is sold as a **butcher** or a **butcher's**. EG *There's a family butcher at the end of our road.* N COUNT

3 To **butcher** a lot of people means to kill them in a cruel way. EG *He butchered tens of thousands of people.* V+O ◊ **butchery** /bʊtʃəri^1/. EG *...the butchery of two hundred innocent citizens.* ◊ N UNCOUNT

butler /bʌtlə/, **butlers.** A **butler** is the most important male servant in a house. N COUNT

butt /bʌt/, **butts, butting, butted.** 1 The **butt** of a weapon is the thick end of its handle. EG *...the padded butt of the rifle... ...the butt end of a spear.* N COUNT

2 The **butt** of a cigarette or cigar is the small part of it that is left when you have finished smoking it. N COUNT

3 A **butt** is a large barrel used for collecting or storing liquid. EG *...a water butt.* N COUNT

4 If you are the **butt** of teasing or criticism, people keep teasing you or criticizing you. EG *They made him the butt of endless practical jokes.* N SING : *the*+N

5 If you **butt** something, you hit it with your head. EG *He butted Stuart in the chest.* V+O

butt in. If you **butt in**, you rudely join in a private conversation or activity without being asked to. EG *You can't just butt in on someone else's discussion.* PHRASAL VB : V+ADV

butter /bʌtə/, **butters, buttering, buttered.** 1 **Butter** is a yellowish substance made from cream which you spread on bread or use in cooking. EG *...bread and butter... ...a shelf where the butter and cheese were kept.* N UNCOUNT

2 When you **butter** bread or toast, you spread butter on it. EG *She buttered herself a piece of bread.* V+O OR V-REFL+O

3 If you say that **butter wouldn't melt in** someone's **mouth**, you mean that they look very innocent but you know that they have done something wrong or they are intending to. PHRASE

butter up. If you **butter** someone **up**, you praise them or try to please them, because you want to ask them a favour. PHRASAL VB : V+O+ADV Informal

buttercup /bʌtəkʌp/, **buttercups.** A **buttercup** is a small plant with bright yellow flowers. N COUNT

butterfly /bʌtəflaɪ/, **butterflies.** 1 A **butterfly** is a type of insect with large colourful wings and a thin body. N COUNT

2 If you have **butterflies in** your **stomach**, you are very nervous about something. EG *I could feel the butterflies in my stomach as I waited.* PHRASE Informal

3 **Butterfly** is a kind of swimming stroke which you do lying on your front, bringing your arms over your head together. See picture at SWIMMING. N UNCOUNT

buttock /bʌtə^{0}k/, **buttocks.** Your **buttocks** are the part of your body that you sit on. N COUNT : USU PLURAL

button /bʌtə^{0}n/, **buttons, buttoning, buttoned.** 1 **Buttons** are small hard objects sewn on to shirts, N COUNT

Find words on these pages which apply only to men or only to women.

coats, or other pieces of clothing. You fasten the clothing by pushing the buttons through holes called buttonholes. EG *She opened the top two buttons of her dress.*

2 If you **button** a shirt, coat, or other piece of clothing, you fasten it by pushing its buttons through the buttonholes. V+O

3 A **button** is also a small object on a machine or electrical device that you press in order to operate the machine or device. EG *I couldn't remember which button turns it off... The gate slid open at the push of a button.* N COUNT

button up. If you **button up** a shirt, coat, or other piece of clothing, you fasten it completely by pushing all its buttons through the buttonholes. PHRASAL VB : V+O+ADV

buttonhole /bʌtənhəʊl/, **buttonholes, buttonholing, buttonholed. 1** A **buttonhole** is **1.1** a hole that you push a button through in order to fasten a shirt, coat, or other piece of clothing. N COUNT **1.2** a flower that you wear on the collar or lapel of your jacket. British

2 If you **buttonhole** someone, you stop them and make them listen to you. EG *I was just on my way out and he buttonholed me.* V+O

buttress /bʌtrɪs/, **buttresses, buttressing, buttressed. 1 Buttresses** are supports, usually made of stone or brick, that support a wall. N COUNT

2 To **buttress** a wall means to support it with buttresses. V+O

3 To **buttress** an argument or system means to give support and strength to it. EG *The present system serves to buttress the social structure in Britain.* V+O

buxom /bʌksəm/. If you describe a woman as **buxom**, you mean that she looks healthy and attractive and has a rather large body. ADJ QUALIT

buy /baɪ/, **buys, buying, bought** /bɔːt/. **1** If you **buy** something, you obtain it by paying money for it. EG *Let me buy you a drink.* V+O, V+O+O, OR V+O+*for*

2 If something is a good **buy**, it is of good quality and you can buy it cheaply. EG *Other good buys include cameras and toys.* N COUNT : MOD+N

buy out. If you **buy** someone **out**, you buy their share of something that you previously owned together. EG *He sold off the shops to buy out his partner.* PHRASAL VB : V+O+ADV

buy up. If you **buy up** land or property, you buy large quantities of it, or all that is available. PHRASAL VB : V+O+ADV

buyer /baɪə/, **buyers. 1** A **buyer** is a person who is buying something or who intends to buy it. EG *I have a buyer for the house.* N COUNT

2 A **buyer** who works in a large store decides what goods will be bought from manufacturers to be sold in the store. EG *She is the chief fashion buyer for Sparks & Fraser.* N COUNT

buzz /bʌz/, **buzzes, buzzing, buzzed. 1** A **buzz** is a continuous sound, like the sound of a bee when it is flying. EG *...the buzz of an insect.* ▸ used as a verb. EG *Bees buzzed outside.* N COUNT ▸ V

2 If thoughts **are buzzing** round your head, you are thinking about a lot of things, usually in a confused way. EG *Anne's head buzzed with angry, crazy thoughts.* V+A

3 If a place **is buzzing** with conversation, it is filled with the sound of a lot of people talking. EG *The room buzzed with excited questions.* ▸ used as a noun. EG *...the buzz of conversation around her.* V : OFT+*with* ▸ N SING : USU+SUPP

buzz off. If you say **'buzz off'** to someone, you are telling them rudely to go away. PHRASAL VB : V+ADV Informal

buzzard /bʌzəd/, **buzzards.** A **buzzard** is a large bird of prey. N COUNT

buzzer /bʌzə/, **buzzers.** A **buzzer** is a device that makes a buzzing sound and that is used, for example, in alarm clocks and office telephones. EG *Press the buzzer... The intercom buzzer sounded.* N COUNT

by /baɪ/. **1** If something is done **by** a person or thing, that person or thing does it or causes it. EG *He was brought up by an aunt... I was startled by his anger... ...the use of pocket calculators by schoolchildren.* PREP

2 If you achieve one thing **by** doing another thing, your action enables you to achieve the first thing. EG *By bribing a nurse I was able to see some files... They were making a living by selling souvenirs to the tourists.* PREP+-ING

3 If you do something **by** a particular thing, you do it using that thing. EG *The money will be paid by cheque... We heard from them by phone... I always go home by bus.* PREP

4 If something happens **by** chance or **by** accident, it happens although you did not intend it. EG *They had met by chance.* PREP

5 If you say what someone means **by** a particular word or expression, you are saying what they intend the word or expression to refer to. EG *By 'John' I assumed he meant John Fletcher.* PREP

6 If you say that something such as a book, a piece of music, or a painting is **by** a particular person, you mean that this person wrote it or created it. EG *...three books by a great Australian writer.* PREP

7 Someone or something that is **by** something else is beside it and close to it. EG *I sat by her bed.* PREP

8 When a person or vehicle passes **by** you, they move past you without stopping. EG *People rushed by us... They watched the cars whizzing by.* PREP, OR ADV AFTER VB

9 If something happens **by** a particular time, it happens at or before that time. EG *He can be out by seven... By 1940 the number had grown to 185 millions.* PREP

10 If you do something **by** day, you do it during the day. If you do it **by** night, you do it during the night. PREP

11 If something happens **by** law, it happens according to the law. If something is the case **by** particular standards, it is the case according to the standards. EG *Each year, by law, state pensions must be reviewed... He is rich by Chinese standards.* PREP

12 If you are **by yourself**, you are alone. EG *He was standing by himself in a corner of the room.* PHRASE

13 If you do something **by yourself**, you succeed in doing it without anyone helping you. EG *She did not think she could manage by herself.* PHRASE

14 In arithmetic, you use **by** before the second number in a multiplication or division sum. EG *Twelve divided by three is four... Multiply it by three.* PREP

15 You use **by** to talk about measurements of area. For example, if a room is twenty feet **by** fourteen feet, it measures twenty feet in one direction and fourteen feet in the other direction. PREP

16 Things that are made or sold **by** the million or **by** the dozen are made or sold in those quantities. EG *Books can be mailed by the dozen.* PREP

17 You use **by** to talk about things that happen gradually, not all at once. EG *The university gets bigger year by year... The children had one by one fallen asleep.* PREP

18 If something increases or decreases **by** a particular amount, that amount is gained or lost. EG *Its grant is to be cut by more than 40 per cent.* PREP

19 If you hold someone or something **by** a particular part of them, you hold that part. EG *My mother took me firmly by the hand and led me downstairs.* PREP

20 If someone is a particular type of person **by** nature or **by** profession, they are that type of person because of their nature or their profession. EG *By trade he was a dealer in antique furniture.* PREP

bye /baɪ/. **'Bye'** and **'bye-bye'** are informal ways of saying goodbye. CONVENTION

bye-law /baɪlɔː/. See **by-law**.

by-election, by-elections. A **by-election** is an election that is held to choose a new member of parliament when a member has resigned or died. N COUNT

bygone /baɪgɒn/, **bygones. 1 Bygone** means happening or existing a very long time ago. EG *...empires established in bygone centuries.* ADJ CLASSIF : ATTRIB

2 If you say to someone **'let bygones be bygones'**, you are suggesting that you should both forget PHRASE about unpleasant things that have happened between you in the past.

by-law, by-laws; also spelled **bye-law.** A **by-law** is a law which is made by a local authority and which applies only in their area. N COUNT

bypass /baɪpɑːs/, **bypasses, bypassing, bypassed. 1** If you **bypass** someone in authority, you avoid asking their permission to do something. EG *This is what happens when the worker by-passes his foreman.* V+O

2 If you **bypass** a difficulty, you avoid discussing it or getting involved in it. EG *It's no good trying to bypass the issue.* V+O

3 A **bypass** is a main road which takes traffic round the edge of a town rather than through its centre. EG *...the Oxford bypass.* N COUNT

4 If you **bypass** a place, you go round it rather than through it. EG *We drove through Kilmarnock but bypassed Ayr.* V+O

5 A **bypass** operation is a surgical heart operation in which the flow of blood is redirected so that it does not flow through a part of the heart which is diseased or blocked. N MOD

by-product, by-products. 1 A **by-product** is something which is made during the manufacture or processing of another product. EG *Oxygen is released as a by-product of the photosynthesis.* N COUNT: USU+SUPP

2 A **by-product** of an event or situation is something that happens as a result of it, especially something that was not expected or planned. EG *They see truancy as a by-product of compulsory education.* N COUNT: USU+SUPP

bystander /baɪstændə/, **bystanders.** A **bystander** is a person who is present when something happens and who sees it but does not take part in it. EG *...curious bystanders watching from a distance.* N COUNT

byte /baɪt/, **bytes.** A **byte** is a unit of storage in a computer. N COUNT Technical

byway /baɪweɪ/, **byways.** A **byway** is a small road which is not used by many cars or people. N COUNT: USU PLURAL

byword /baɪwɜːd/, **bywords. 1** Someone or something that is a **byword** for a particular quality is well known for having that quality. EG *The department had become a byword for ignorance, obstinacy and brutality.* N COUNT+*for*

2 A **byword** is a word or phrase which people often use. EG *Internal redesign has become a byword in Washington.* N COUNT

C c

C, c /siː/, **C's, c's. 1 C** is the third letter of the English alphabet. N COUNT

2 C is an abbreviation for 'century' or 'centuries'. You put 'C' before or after a number which refers to a particular century. EG *...living in the C14... ...the 14th C.*

3 c. is written in front of a date or number to indicate that it is approximate. EG *He was born c. 834 A.D.*

4 C is also an abbreviation for 'centigrade'.

> **C** stands for **complement**
> Verbs which have the label +C in the Extra Column are verbs which have a complement.
> See the entry headed COMPLEMENTS for more information.

cab /kæb/, **cabs. 1** A **cab** is a taxi. EG *Morris hurried off eagerly to get a cab.* N COUNT OR *by*+N

2 The **cab** of a lorry is the front part in which the driver sits. N COUNT

cabaret /kæbəreɪ/, **cabarets.** A **cabaret** is a show that is performed in a restaurant or nightclub, and that consists of dancing, singing, or comedy acts. EG *The cabaret was just finishing... ...a cabaret artiste.* N COUNT OR N UNCOUNT

cabbage /kæbɪdʒ/, **cabbages.** A **cabbage** is a vegetable which looks like a large ball of green leaves. N COUNT OR N UNCOUNT

cabin /kæbɪn/, **cabins.** A **cabin** is **1** a small room in a ship or boat. **2** one of the areas inside a plane. EG *...the First Class cabin.* **3** a small wooden house. N COUNT

cabinet /kæbɪ[1]nɪ[2]t/, **cabinets. 1** A **cabinet** is a cupboard used for storing things such as medicine or alcoholic drinks. EG *...a cocktail cabinet... ...a glass cabinet with Chinese things in it.* • See also **filing cabinet**. N COUNT

2 The **Cabinet** is a group of the most senior ministers in a government, who meet regularly to decide policies. EG *...a former cabinet minister.* N COLL: *the*+N

cable /keɪbə[0]l/, **cables.** A **cable** is **1** a very strong, thick rope. EG *...the suspension cables of the bridge.* N COUNT

2 a bundle of wires inside a rubber or plastic covering, along which electricity flows. EG *...ten metres of electrical cable.* N UNCOUNT OR N COUNT

cable car, cable cars. A **cable car** is a cabin suspended from a wire, pulled by a moving cable. It is used to take passengers up mountains. N COUNT OR *by*+N

cable television is a television system in which signals are sent along wires, rather than by radio waves. N UNCOUNT

cache /kæʃ/, **caches.** A **cache** is a quantity of things, for example weapons or drugs, that have been hidden. EG *...an arms cache.* N COUNT

cackle /kækə[0]l/, **cackles, cackling, cackled.** If you **cackle**, you laugh in a loud unpleasant way. EG *She cackled with delight... 'Fools!' she cackled.* V OR V+QUOTE
▸ used as a noun. EG *He gave a malicious cackle.* ▸ N COUNT

cacophony /kəkɒfəni[1]/. A **cacophony** is a loud, unpleasant noise that consists of a lot of different sounds together. EG *...a cacophony of squeaks and rattles.* N SING Formal

cactus /kæktəs/, **cactuses** or **cacti** /kæktaɪ/. A **cactus** is a thick fleshy plant that grows in deserts. Cacti have no leaves and many of them are covered in spikes. N COUNT

cadaverous /kədævə[0]rəs/. Someone who is **cadaverous** is extremely thin and pale. EG *He was tall and spare, with a cadaverous face.* ADJ QUALIT Formal

cadence /keɪdə[0]ns/, **cadences.** A **cadence** is the way your voice gets higher and lower as you speak. EG *His voice had an unfamiliar cadence.* N COUNT Formal

cadet /kədet/, **cadets.** A **cadet** is a young man or woman who is being trained in the army, navy, air force, or police. N COUNT

cadge /kædʒ/, **cadges, cadging, cadged.** If you **cadge** food, money, or help from someone, you ask them for it and succeed in getting it. EG *He only came to cadge free drinks... ...living by cadging off relatives and doing odd jobs.* V OR V+O: OFT +*from/off* Informal British

Caesarean /si[1]zeərɪən/, **Caesareans.** A **Caesarean** or a **Caesarean section** is an operation in which a baby is lifted out of a woman's womb through an opening cut in her abdomen. N COUNT

café /kæfeɪ/, **cafés.** A **café** is a place where you can buy drinks and light meals or snacks. In Britain cafés do not serve alcoholic drinks. N COUNT

cafeteria /kæfɪ[1]tɪərɪə/, **cafeterias.** A **cafeteria** is a restaurant where you choose your food from a N COUNT counter and carry it to your table yourself after paying for it.

caffeine /kæfi:n/; also spelled **caffein. Caffeine** is a chemical substance found in coffee, tea, and cocoa, which makes your brain and body more active. N UNCOUNT

cage /keɪdʒ/, **cages.** A **cage** is a structure of wire or metal bars in which birds or animals are kept. N COUNT

caged /keɪdʒd/. A **caged** bird or animal is inside a cage. ADJ CLASSIF

cagey /keɪdʒi¹/. When people are being **cagey**, they are being careful not to give much information. EG *They were so cagey about Lucy and her new job.* ADJ QUALIT

cagoule /kəgu:l/, **cagoules.** A **cagoule** is a waterproof jacket that you wear over other clothes to prevent them getting wet. N COUNT

cahoots /kəhu:ts/. If someone is **in cahoots with** someone else, they are planning something with them; used showing disapproval. EG *Halliday was in cahoots with the person who was so handy with poison.* PHRASE

cajole /kədʒəʊl/, **cajoles, cajoling, cajoled.** If you **cajole** someone into doing something, you persuade them to do it by flattering or praising them. EG *McKinley and Sherman were cajoled into coming with us.* V+O : USU+A Formal

cake /keɪk/, **cakes. 1** A **cake** is **1.1** a sweet food made by baking a mixture of flour, eggs, sugar, and fat in an oven. EG *She cut the cake and gave me a piece... ...a slice of cake.* N COUNT OR N UNCOUNT **1.2** a food that is formed into a flat, round shape before it is cooked. EG *...fish cakes.* N COUNT+SUPP

2 A **cake** of something such as soap or wax is a small block of it. N PART OR N COUNT

3 Cake is used in these phrases. **3.1** If you say that something is **a piece of cake**, you mean that it is very easy to do. **3.2** If things are **selling like hot cakes**, people are buying a lot of them. **3.3** If someone says that **you can't have your cake and eat it**, they mean that people cannot have both alternatives that are available, but will have to choose only one. **3.4 the icing on the cake**: see **icing**. PHRASES Informal

caked /keɪkt/. **1** If something is **caked**, it has changed from a thick liquid into a dry layer or lump. EG *He sat slumped forward, with dried blood caked in his hair.* ADJ CLASSIF

2 If a surface is **caked** with something such as mud, it is covered with it. EG *...heavy farm shoes caked with mud.* ADJ PRED

calamitous /kəlæmɪ¹təs/. Something that is **calamitous** is very unfortunate indeed. EG *I'm always expecting something calamitous to happen.* ADJ CLASSIF Formal

calamity /kəlæmɪ¹ti¹/, **calamities.** A **calamity** is an event that causes a great deal of damage, destruction, or personal distress. EG *...the glee with which the media report scientific calamities... ...the awareness of approaching calamity.* N COUNT OR N UNCOUNT Formal

calcium /kælsɪəm/ is a soft white element which is found in bones and teeth, and also in limestone, chalk, and marble. N UNCOUNT

calculate /kælkjə⁴leɪt/, **calculates, calculating, calculated. 1** If you **calculate** a number or amount, you work it out by doing some arithmetic. EG *The number of votes cast will then be calculated... She was busy calculating.* V+O OR V

2 If you **calculate** the effects of something, you think about its effects and form an opinion about them. EG *...actions whose consequences can in no way be calculated... She calculated that the risks were worth taking.* V+O OR V+REPORT

3 If something **is calculated** to have a particular effect, it is specially done or arranged in order to have that effect. EG *I adopted a cool dignified attitude that was calculated to discourage familiarity.* V-PASS+*to*-INF ◇ **calculated.** EG *...the deliberate, calculated use of violence.* ◇ ADJ QUALIT

calculating /kælkjə⁴leɪtɪŋ/. A person who is **calculating** arranges situations and controls people in order to get what he or she wants; used showing disapproval. EG *...the most calculating and selfish men in the community.* ADJ QUALIT

calculation /kælkjə⁴leɪʃəⁿn/, **calculations. 1** A **calculation** is something that you think about and work out mathematically. EG *'How long will it take me?' I did a rapid calculation. 'About ten years,' I said... ...a technique for quick calculation.* N COUNT OR N UNCOUNT

2 Calculation is behaviour in which someone thinks only of themselves and not of other people; used showing disapproval. EG *His behaviour seems free of all calculation.* N UNCOUNT Formal

calculator /kælkjə⁴leɪtə/, **calculators.** A **calculator** is a small electronic device that you use for doing mathematical calculations. N COUNT

calendar /kælɪ¹ndə/, **calendars. 1** A **calendar** is a chart which shows a particular year divided up into months, weeks, and days, and shows what the date of each day is in that year. EG *He glanced up at the wall calendar – today was Thursday.* N COUNT

2 A **calendar** month is one of the twelve named periods of time that a year is divided into. A **calendar** year is a period of 365 days, or 366 days in a leap year. EG *It costs one hundred dollars per calendar month.* ADJ CLASSIF : ATTRIB

3 A **calendar** is also **3.1** a system for dividing up time, which establishes year zero, numbers the years, and arranges the days into months and years. EG *...the Muslim calendar.* N COUNT : USU SING+SUPP **3.2** a list of dates within a particular year that are important for an organization or kind of activity. EG *...a major event in the theatrical calendar.*

calf /kɑ:f/, **calves** /kɑ:vz/. **1** A **calf** is a young cow. N COUNT

2 Some other young animals, including elephants, giraffes, whales, and seals, are also called **calves**. N COUNT

3 Your **calf** is the thick part at the back of your leg between your ankle and your knee. See picture at THE HUMAN BODY. N COUNT

calibre /kælɪbə/, **calibres;** spelled **caliber** in American English. **1** The **calibre** of a person is the quality or standard of their ability or intelligence, especially when this is high. EG *...directors of the right calibre.* N UNCOUNT +SUPP

2 The **calibre** of a gun is the width of the inside of its barrel. N COUNT+SUPP Technical

call /kɔ:l/, **calls, calling, called. 1** If someone or something **is called** by a particular name, that is their name or title. EG *She had a boyfriend called David... ...a novel called 'Memoirs of a Survivor'... All his friends call him Jo.* V+O+C

2 Call is used to refer to ways of describing things or people by using a particular word or phrase. For example, if you call someone a liar, you say that they are a liar. EG *President Nixon called his opponents traitors... I wouldn't call it awful, but it wasn't very well written.* V+O+C

3 If you **call** someone's name, you say it in a loud voice, because you are trying to attract their attention. EG *'Edward!' she called. 'Edward! Lunch is ready!'... I could hear a voice calling my name... Children are as likely to call for their father as for their mother.* V+O, V+QUOTE, OR V+A

4 If you **call** someone, **4.1** you telephone them. EG *He promised to call me soon... 'I want to speak to Mr Landy, please.' – 'Who is calling?'* V+O OR V **4.2** you ask them to come to you by shouting to them or telephoning them. EG *The editor called me to his office to tell me the news... When Margaret collapsed, I called the doctor.* V+O

5 When you make a phone **call**, you phone someone. EG *There have been two telephone calls for you.* N COUNT

6 If you **call** something such as a meeting or a rehearsal, you arrange for it to take place at a particular time. EG *He called a press conference to explain his proposals.* V+O

7 If you **call** somewhere, you make a short visit there. EG *We called at the Vicarage.* V+A

8 If you pay a **call** on someone, you visit them briefly. EG *We went to pay a call on some people I know... Doctors have no time these days to make regular calls.* N COUNT

9 A **call** for something is a demand or desire for it to be done or to be provided. EG *Labour MPs renewed their call for the abolition of the House of Lords... There is little call for his services.* N COUNT OR N UNCOUNT

10 The **call** of a bird is the short sound that it makes. N COUNT

11 to **call it a day**: see **day**. • to **call a halt**: see **halt**.

call for. 1 If you **call for** someone or something, you go to the building where they are in order to collect them. EG *I'll call for you about eight... I called at the station for my luggage.* PHRASAL VB : V+PREP, HAS PASS 2 If you **call for** something, you demand that it should happen. EG *The declaration called for an immediate cease-fire.* V+PREP, HAS PASS 3 If something **calls for** a particular action or quality, it needs it in order to be successful. EG *Controlling a class calls for all your skill as a teacher.* V+PREP, HAS PASS

call in. If you **call** someone **in**, you ask them to come and help you or do something for you. EG *We called in the police.* PHRASAL VB : V+O+ADV

call off. If you **call off** an event that has been planned, you cancel it. EG *We had to decide whether classes should be called off.* PHRASAL VB : V+O+ADV

call on or **call upon.** 1 If you **call on** someone to do something or **call upon** them to do it, you appeal to them to do it. EG *The Opposition called on the Prime Minister to stop the arms deal.* PHRASAL VB : V+PREP 2 If you **call on** someone, you pay them a short visit. V+PREP

call out. 1 If you **call** something **out**, you shout it. EG *The driver didn't stop or even call out thank you... 'Where shall I put them?' I called out... She turned into the yard, calling out to the porter that she'd arrived.* PHRASAL VB : V-SPEECH+ADV OR V+ADV 2 If you **call** someone **out**, you order them to come to help, especially in an emergency. EG *The National Guard has been called out.* V+O+ADV

call up. 1 If you **call** someone **up**, you telephone them. EG *Many of my friends called me up to congratulate me.* PHRASAL VB : V+O+ADV 2 If someone **is called up**, they are ordered to join the army, navy, or air force. EG *I was lucky not to be called up at the time.* V+O+ADV

call upon. See **call on**.

call box, call boxes. A **call box** is a telephone box. N COUNT

caller /kɔ:lə/, **callers.** A **caller** is 1 a person who comes to see you for a short visit. EG *I had a lot of callers when I came home from hospital.* 2 a person who is making a telephone call. EG *The telephone rang and the caller asked to speak to my mother.* N COUNT

call girl, call girls. A **call girl** is a prostitute who makes appointments by telephone. N COUNT

calling /kɔ:lɪŋ/. A **calling** is a profession or career, especially one which involves helping other people. EG *Teaching is said to be a worthwhile calling.* N SING

callous /kæləs/. Someone who is **callous** is very cruel and shows no concern for other people's feelings. EG *She was selfish, arrogant and often callous... ...a shocking act of callous irresponsibility.* ADJ QUALIT

calm /kɑ:m/, **calmer, calmest; calms, calming, calmed.** 1 Someone who is **calm** does not show any worry or excitement. EG *Gary was a calm and reasonable man... Sit down and keep calm... Her voice was calm.* ADJ QUALIT ◇ **calmly.** EG *She calmly wiped the blood away with her hand.* ◇ ADV ◇ **calmness.** EG *A great sense of calmness began to settle upon her.* ◇ N UNCOUNT

2 **Calm** is a state of quietness and peacefulness. EG *...the peace of the countryside, the calm of the vicarage.* N UNCOUNT

3 A sea or lake that is **calm** does not have any big waves. EG *He was not afraid, for the water was calm.* ADJ QUALIT

4 Weather that is **calm** is very still without any wind. EG *It was a calm, sunny evening.* ADJ QUALIT

5 If you **calm** someone or **calm** their fears, you do something to make them less upset, less worried, or less excited. EG *Mitchell tried to calm her, but she didn't hear him... To calm himself he walked over to the window.* V+O OR V-REFL

calm down. If you **calm down** or if someone **calms** you **down**, you become less upset, excited, or lively. EG *'Please, Mrs Kinter,' said Brody. 'Calm down. Let me explain.'... An officer tried to calm them down but had no success.* PHRASAL VB : V-ERG+ADV

Calor gas /kælə gæs/ is gas that is sold in portable metal containers. You can use it for cooking and heating. EG *...a little Calor gas stove.* N UNCOUNT Trademark

calorie /kæləri[1]/, **calories.** A **calorie** is a unit of measurement for the energy value of food. EG *He was put on a diet of only 1,700 calories a day.* N COUNT

calve /kɑ:v/, **calves, calving, calved.** 1 When a cow **calves**, it gives birth to a calf. V

2 **Calves** is the plural of **calf**.

camaraderie /kæmərɑ:dəri[1]/ is a feeling of trust and friendship among a group of people. EG *There was a camaraderie between the girls.* N UNCOUNT

came /keɪm/ is the past tense of **come.**

camel /kæmə[0]l/, **camels.** A **camel** is a large animal that lives in deserts. Camels have long necks and one or two humps on their backs. N COUNT

cameo /kæmɪəʊ/, **cameos.** 1 A **cameo** is a short description or piece of acting which expresses cleverly and neatly the nature of a situation, event, or person's character. EG *She has starred in several small but delightful cameo parts... He gave cameos of debates with exquisite touches of irony.* N COUNT

2 A **cameo** is also a piece of jewellery, usually oval in shape, consisting of a raised stone figure or design fixed on to a flat stone of another colour. N COUNT

camera /kæmə[0]rə/, **cameras.** A **camera** is a piece of equipment that is used for taking photographs, making films, or producing television pictures. EG *I took a camera and photographed some of the buildings... The press and television cameras were gathered.* N COUNT

cameraman /kæmə[0]rəmə[3]n/, **cameramen.** A **cameraman** is a person who operates a camera for television or film making. N COUNT

camouflage /kæməflɑ:ʒ/, **camouflages, camouflaging, camouflaged.** 1 **Camouflage** consists of things such as leaves, branches, or brown and green paint, which are used to make it difficult for an enemy to see military forces and equipment. N UNCOUNT ▸ used as a verb. EG *The gun crews were in camouflaged bunkers at the end of the beach.* ▸ V+O

2 **Camouflage** is also the way in which some animals are coloured and shaped to blend in with their natural surroundings. EG *The snake's skin has the colours and patterns necessary for perfect camouflage.* N UNCOUNT

camp /kæmp/, **camps, camping, camped.** 1 A **camp** is a place where people live in tents or stay in tents on holiday. EG *The camp had a beautiful view of the mountains... We set up camp near the bay.* N COUNT OR N UNCOUNT

2 If you **camp** somewhere, you stay or live there for a short time in a tent or a caravan. EG *That night I camped in the hills.* V : USU+A ◇ **camping.** EG *I don't like camping at all... ...camping equipment.* ◇ N UNCOUNT

3 A **camp** is also a collection of huts and other buildings that has been specially built for people such as soldiers, refugees, or prisoners. EG *Three fifths of the refugees in the camp were starving.* N COUNT

4 You can also use **camp** to refer to a group of people who all support a particular idea, person, or belief. EG *The realignment produced two clear-cut camps, reformists and reactionaries.* N COUNT+SUPP

Name three callings.

cameras

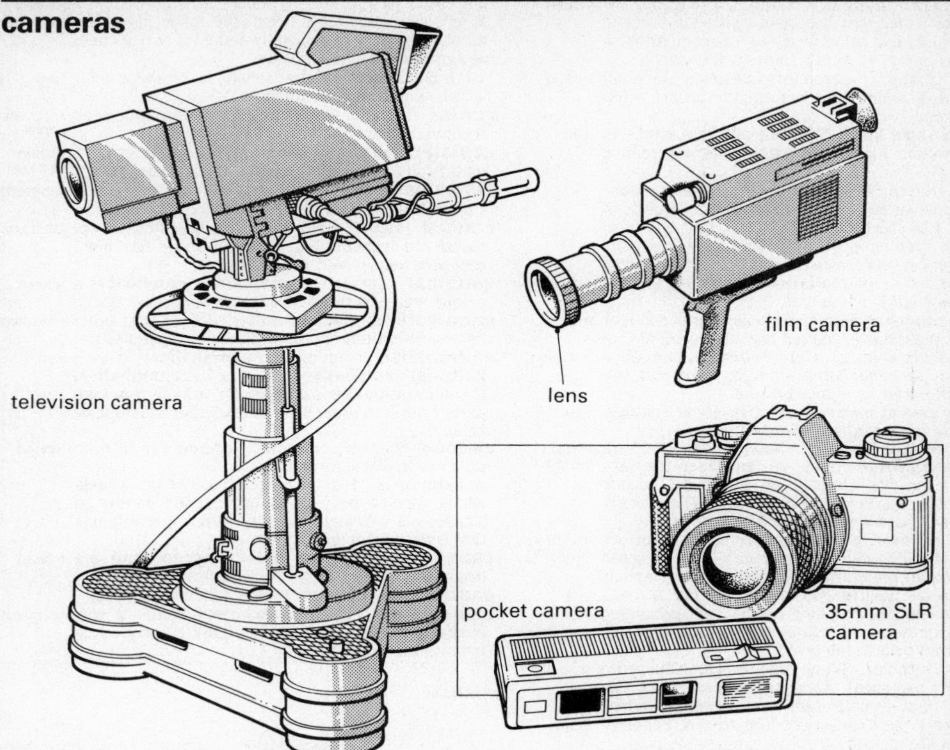

camp out. If you **camp out**, you sleep outdoors in a tent. PHRASAL VB : V+ADV

campaign /kæmpeɪn/, **campaigns, campaigning, campaigned.** 1 A **campaign** is a planned set of activities that people carry out over a period of time, in order to achieve something such as social or political change. EG *...Labour's election campaign... ...the campaign against world hunger.* N COUNT
▸ used as a verb. EG *He campaigned for political reform.* ▸ V+A ◊ **campaigner, campaigners.** EG *...anti-apartheid campaigners.* ◊ N COUNT
2 In a war, a **campaign** is a series of planned movements carried out by armed forces. EG *...bombing campaigns.* N COUNT

camp bed, camp beds. A **camp bed** is a small bed that you can fold up. N COUNT

camper /kæmpə/, **campers.** A **camper** is 1 a person who goes camping. EG *...equipment for hunters, campers and fishermen.* 2 a van which is equipped with beds and cooking equipment so that you can live, cook, and sleep in it. N COUNT

campsite /kæmpsaɪt/, **campsites.** A **campsite** is a place where people who are on holiday can stay in tents. N COUNT

campus /kæmpəs/, **campuses.** A **campus** is the area of land that contains the main buildings of a university. EG *...the university campus... How many students live on campus?* N COUNT OR N UNCOUNT

can, cans, canning, canned. In paragraphs 1 to 5, **can** is pronounced /kæn/or /kən/; in paragraphs 6 and 7, it is always pronounced /kæn/. The form **canned** is used as the past tense and past participle of the verb in paragraph 7. **Could** is sometimes considered to be the past form of the modal **can**, but in this dictionary the two words are dealt with separately. See **could**.
1 If you **can** do something, **1.1** it is possible for you to do it. EG *Anybody can become a qualified teacher... Many elderly people cannot afford telephones... 'Will you stay for lunch?' – 'I can't,' the colonel said.* **1.2** you have the skill or ability to do it. EG *Some people can ski better than others... My wife can't sew.* **1.3** you are allowed to do it. Some speakers of English think that it is incorrect to use 'can' instead of 'may' with this meaning. EG *You can borrow that pen if you want to... Can I speak to Nicky please?* MODAL
2 You ask someone if they **can** do something as a polite way of asking them to do it. EG *Can you tell me the time?... Can you do me a favour?* MODAL
3 You say that someone **cannot** do something as a way of saying that they should not do it. EG *We can't stop now. We've got to keep on struggling... A secretary can hardly be regarded as a status symbol.* MODAL WITH BROAD NEG
4 If you say to someone **can't you** do something, you are suggesting that they do it or asking them to do it. EG *Can't we talk about it?... For goodness sake! Can't you keep your voice down?* MODAL+*not*
5 If you say that something **cannot** be true or **cannot** happen, you mean that you feel sure that it is not true or will not happen. EG *This cannot be the whole story... The repression can't last... He can hardly have read the report with much care... He can't have said that. He just can't.* MODAL WITH BROAD NEG
6 A **can** is a metal container in which something such as food, drink, or paint is put. The container is usually sealed to keep the contents fresh. EG *...cans of beans... ...beer cans.* N COUNT
7 When food or drink **is canned**, it is put into a metal container and sealed so that it will remain fresh. ◊ **canned.** EG *...canned beer.* V+O ◊ ADJ CLASSIF
8 See also **canned**.

canal /kənæl/, **canals.** A **canal** is a long, narrow stretch of water that has been made for boats to travel along or to bring water to a particular area. EG *...the canals of Venice... ...irrigation canals.* N COUNT

canary /kənɛəri¹/, **canaries. Canaries** are small yellow birds which sing beautifully and are often kept as pets. N COUNT

can-can /kæn kæn/. The **can-can** is a dance in which women kick their legs in the air to fast music. N SING

cancel /kænsəl/, **cancels, cancelling, cancelled;** spelled **canceling, canceled** in American English. **1** If you **cancel** something that has been arranged, you stop it from happening. EG *The performances were cancelled because the leading man was ill.* V+O ◇ **cancellation** /kænsə¹leɪʃə⁰n/. EG *...the cancellation of the tour.* ◇ N UNCOUNT

2 If you **cancel** something such as a hotel room or a seat at the theatre, you tell the management that you no longer want it. V+O ◇ **cancellation, cancellations.** EG *...a cancellation charge... I've had two cancellations already this morning.* ◇ N COUNT

3 If you **cancel** a cheque or a business arrangement, you cause it to be no longer valid. V+O

cancel out. If two things **cancel** each other **out**, they have opposite effects, so that when they are combined no real effect is produced. EG *The one effect tends to cancel the other out... These political factions cancelled each other out.* PHRASAL VB: V+O+ADV

cancer /kænsə/, **cancers. Cancer** is a serious disease in which cells in a person's body increase rapidly in an uncontrolled way, producing abnormal growths. EG *He had cancer of the throat... Nicholas was dying of lung cancer... Most cancers are preventable.* N UNCOUNT OR N COUNT ◇ **cancerous** /kænsərəs/. EG *...cancerous cells in the blood.* ◇ ADJ CLASSIF

candid /kændɪd/. When you are **candid** with someone, you speak honestly to them. EG *I was entirely candid with him... ...a candid smile.* ADJ QUALIT ◇ **candidly.** EG *Charlie got him to talk candidly about his life.* ◇ ADV

candidacy /kændɪdəsi¹/. Someone's **candidacy** is their position of being a candidate in an election. EG *He had already formally announced his candidacy.* N UNCOUNT +SUPP

candidate /kændɪdeɪt, -də¹t/, **candidates.** A **candidate** is **1** someone who is being considered for a position, for example in an election or for a job. EG *...a parliamentary candidate... We're prepared to take candidates from any academic discipline.* **2** someone who is taking an examination. EG *Sixty per cent of the candidates failed their examinations.* **3** a person or thing that is regarded as being suitable for a particular purpose. EG *Small companies are likely candidates for take-over.* N COUNT

candle /kændə⁰l/, **candles.** A **candle** is a stick of hard wax with a piece of string called a wick through the middle. You light the wick in order to give a steady flame that provides light. EG *I blew out my candle and went to sleep.* N COUNT

candlelight /kændə⁰llaɪt/ is the light that a candle produces. EG *She was reading by candlelight.* N UNCOUNT

candlelit /kændə⁰llɪt/. A room or table that is **candlelit** is lit by the light of candles. EG *...a little candlelit restaurant.* ADJ CLASSIF

candlestick /kændə⁰lstɪk/, **candlesticks.** A **candlestick** is a narrow object with a hole at the top which holds a candle. N COUNT

candour /kændə/; spelled **candor** in American English. **Candour** is the quality of speaking honestly and openly about things. EG *They were talking of personal matters with unusual candour.* N UNCOUNT

candy /kændi¹/, **candies.** A **candy** is a sweet. EG *There was a bowl of candies on his desk... You eat too much candy. It's bad for your teeth.* N COUNT OR N UNCOUNT American

cane /keɪn/, **canes, caning, caned. 1 Cane** is **1.1** the long, hollow stems of a plant such as bamboo. EG *...sugar cane.* **1.2** strips of cane that are used for weaving things such as baskets or chairs. EG *...cane chairs.* N UNCOUNT

2 A **cane** is a long narrow stick. N COUNT

3 At school, when children used to be given the **cane**, they were punished by being hit with a cane. EG *I got the cane for smoking.* N SING: *the*+N

4 If a child **was caned** at school, he or she was hit with a cane as a punishment. V+O

canine /keɪnaɪn, kæn-/ means relating to dogs or resembling a dog. ADJ CLASSIF: ATTRIB

canister /kænɪstə/, **canisters.** A **canister** is a metal container. EG *...a canister of shaving cream.* N COUNT OR N PART

cannabis /kænəbɪs/ is a drug which some people smoke. Cannabis is illegal in many countries. N UNCOUNT

canned /kænd/. **Canned** music, laughter, or applause on a television or radio show has been recorded beforehand. ● See also **can.** ADJ CLASSIF

cannibal /kænɪbə⁰l/, **cannibals.** A **cannibal** is a person who eats the flesh of other human beings. N COUNT

cannibalism /kænɪ¹bəlɪzə⁰m/. People who practise **cannibalism** eat the flesh of other people. N UNCOUNT

cannibalize /kænɪ¹bəlaɪz/, **cannibalizes, cannibalizing, cannibalized;** also spelled **cannibalise.** If you **cannibalize** a machine or vehicle, you take parts from it in order to repair another machine or vehicle. V+O

cannon /kænən/, **cannons. Cannon** can also be used as the plural form. N COUNT

A **cannon** is **1** a large gun, usually on wheels, which used to be used in battles. See picture at WEAPONS. **2** a heavy automatic gun, especially one that is fired from an aircraft.

cannon ball, cannon balls. A **cannon ball** is a heavy metal ball that was fired from a cannon. N COUNT

cannot /kænɒt, kænɒt/ means 'can not': see **can.**

canny /kæni¹/, **cannier, canniest.** Someone who is **canny** is clever and able to think quickly. EG *...a canny smile.* ADJ QUALIT

canoe

canoe /kənuː/, **canoes.** A **canoe** is a small, narrow boat that you row using a paddle. N COUNT

canoeing /kənuːɪŋ/ is the sport of racing and performing tests of skill in canoes. EG *...facilities for rock climbing, sailing, and canoeing.* N ING

canon /kænən/, **canons. 1** A **canon** is a member of the clergy who is on the staff of a cathedral. N COUNT

2 A **canon** is also a general rule or principle. EG *...the traditional canons of literary and artistic judgement.* N COUNT+SUPP Formal

canonize /kænənaɪz/, **canonizes, canonizing, canonized;** also spelled **canonise.** If a dead person **is canonized**, it is officially announced that he or she is a saint; used especially in the Catholic Church. EG *Two years after his death the bishop was canonised.* V+O: USU PASS

canopy /kænəpi¹/, **canopies.** A **canopy** is **1** a decorated cover, often made of cloth, which is placed above something such as a bed or a throne. EG *There was a large bed with a silk canopy over it.* N COUNT

2 a layer of something that spreads out and covers N COUNT+SUPP

If you can can-can, what can you do?

an area, for example the branches and leaves that spread out at the top of trees in a forest. EG *The leaves created a dense canopy that cut out much of the light.*

can't /kɑːnt/ is the usual spoken form of 'cannot'.

cantankerous /kə^{3}ntæŋkə^{0}rəs/. Someone who is **cantankerous** is always finding things to argue or complain about. EG *Their boredom made them quarrelsome and cantankerous.* ADJ QUALIT Formal

canteen /kæntiːn/, **canteens.** A **canteen** is a place in a factory or other place of work where the people who work there can eat. EG *I had a cup of tea in the canteen.* N COUNT

canter /kæntə/, **canters, cantering, cantered.** When a horse **canters**, it moves at a speed that is slower than a gallop but faster than a trot. ▸ used as a noun. EG *It broke into an easy canter.* V; ▸ N COUNT

canvas /kænvəs/, **canvases. 1 Canvas** is strong, heavy cloth. It is used for making things such as tents, sails, and bags. N UNCOUNT

2 If you are living and sleeping **under canvas**, you are living and sleeping in a tent. PHRASE

3 A **canvas** is **3.1** a piece of canvas or similar material on which an oil painting can be done. EG *...oil paintings on canvas.* N COUNT OR N UNCOUNT **3.2** a painting that is done on canvas. EG *...the canvases of Hieronymus Bosch.* N COUNT

canvass /kænvəs/, **canvasses, canvassing, canvassed. 1** If you **canvass** for a particular person or political party, you go round an area trying to persuade people to vote for that person or party. EG *He had canvassed for Mr Foot in the leadership election.* V: USU+A ◊ **canvassing.** EG *...house-to-house canvassing.* ◊ N UNCOUNT

2 If you **canvass** public opinion, you find out how people feel about a particular subject by asking them. V+O

canyon /kænjən/, **canyons.** A **canyon** is a long, narrow valley with very steep sides. EG *The cold wind sweeps down the canyon.* N COUNT

cap

cap /kæp/, **caps, capping, capped. 1** A **cap** is **1.1** a soft, flat hat which is usually worn by men or boys. EG *On his head he wore a brown cloth cap.* N COUNT **1.2** a special hat which is worn as part of a uniform. EG *...my school cap.* **1.3** a small flat lid on a bottle or container. EG *Brody grabbed the bottle, twisted off the cap, and sniffed.* **1.4** a contraceptive device consisting of a small round object that a woman places inside her vagina.

2 If you go to someone **cap in hand**, you go to them very humbly, because you are asking them for something. EG *It's bad enough having to go cap in hand to ask for a rise.* PHRASE Informal

3 If you **cap** one thing with another, you put the second thing on top of the first thing. EG *...sweets coated with chocolate and capped with a cherry.* V+O+*with*

4 If you **cap** an action, you do something that is better or more exciting. EG *He capped his performance by telling the funniest joke I have ever heard.* V+O

5 A **cap** is also a small amount of explosive that is wrapped in paper. Caps are often used in toy guns. N COUNT

capability /keɪpəbɪlə^{1}ti^{1}/, **capabilities. 1** If you have the **capability** or the **capabilities** to do something, you have the ability or the qualities that are necessary to do it. EG *The work may be beyond his capability or endurance... She may worry about her capabilities as a parent.* N UNCOUNT+ SUPP OR N COUNT

2 A country's military **capability** is its ability to fight in a war. EG *The French nuclear capability might never be used.* N UNCOUNT

capable /keɪpəbə^{0}l/. **1** If a person or thing is **capable** of doing something, they have the ability to do it. EG *...a man capable of killing the President... ...a mind capable of original ideas.* ADJ PRED+*of*

2 Someone who is **capable** has the skill or qualities necessary to do a particular thing well. EG *Basil proved a capable cricketer... She was extremely capable and dependable.* ADJ QUALIT ◊ **capably.** EG *...a capably performed dance.* ◊ ADV

capacious /kəpeɪʃəs/. Something that is **capacious** has a lot of space to put things in. EG *...her capacious pockets.* ADJ QUALIT

capacity /kəpæsə^{1}ti^{1}/, **capacities. 1** The **capacity** of something is the largest amount that it can hold, produce, or carry. EG *The pipeline has a capacity of 1.2m barrels a day.* N UNCOUNT +SUPP ● If something is filled **to capacity**, it is as full as it can possibly be. EG *The ship set sail with her hold filled to capacity.* ● PHRASE

2 A **capacity** crowd or audience completely fills a theatre, sports ground, or other place. N MOD

3 The **capacity** of a person, society, or system is the power or ability that they have to do a particular thing. EG *This society demands of everyone the capacity to read and write... People have different capacities for learning.* N COUNT+SUPP

4 Someone's **capacity** for food or drink is the amount that they can eat or drink. EG *His capacity for brandy was phenomenal.* N UNCOUNT +SUPP

5 If you say that someone does something **in a** particular **capacity,** you mean that they do it as part of their duties. EG *I was involved in an advisory capacity.* PHRASE

6 Capacity in a factory or industry is the quantity of things that can be produced. EG *We need to raise productivity and expand capacity.* N UNCOUNT Technical

cape /keɪp/, **capes.** A **cape** is **1** a large piece of land that sticks out into the sea from the coast. EG *...Cape Horn.* **2** a short cloak. EG *Waving a red cape, Delgado provoked the bull to charge.* N COUNT

caper /keɪpə/, **capers, capering, capered. 1 Capers** are the flower buds of a type of bush, which are pickled and used to season food. EG *...wild duck in caper sauce.* N COUNT: USU PLURAL

2 If you **caper** about, you dance or leap about energetically. EG *The little girl capered towards Bill.* V: USU+A

3 A **caper** is a light-hearted practical joke or trick. N COUNT

capillary /kəpɪləri^{1}/, **capillaries. Capillaries** are tiny blood vessels in your body. N COUNT

capital /kæpɪtə^{0}l/, **capitals. 1 Capital** is a large sum of money which you use to start or expand a business, or which you invest in order to make more money. EG *He gained overall control by putting up most of the capital.* N UNCOUNT

2 Capital investment or expenditure is money which is spent on equipment and buildings in a business or industry. EG *...substantial increases in capital expenditure on telephone exchanges.* N MOD

3 If you **make capital of** or **out of** a situation, you use the situation to gain some advantage for yourself. EG *At the time much political capital was made of the intention to increase top people's salaries.* PHRASE Formal

4 The **capital** of a country is the city or town where its government or parliament is. N COUNT

5 The **capital** of a particular industry, product, or activity is the place which is most famous for it. EG *...the peach capital of America... Rome was, I suppose, the capital of the art world.* N COUNT+SUPP

6 A **capital** or a **capital** letter is the written form of a letter which is used at the beginning of a sentence or a name. 'T', 'B', and 'F' are capital letters. N COUNT

car

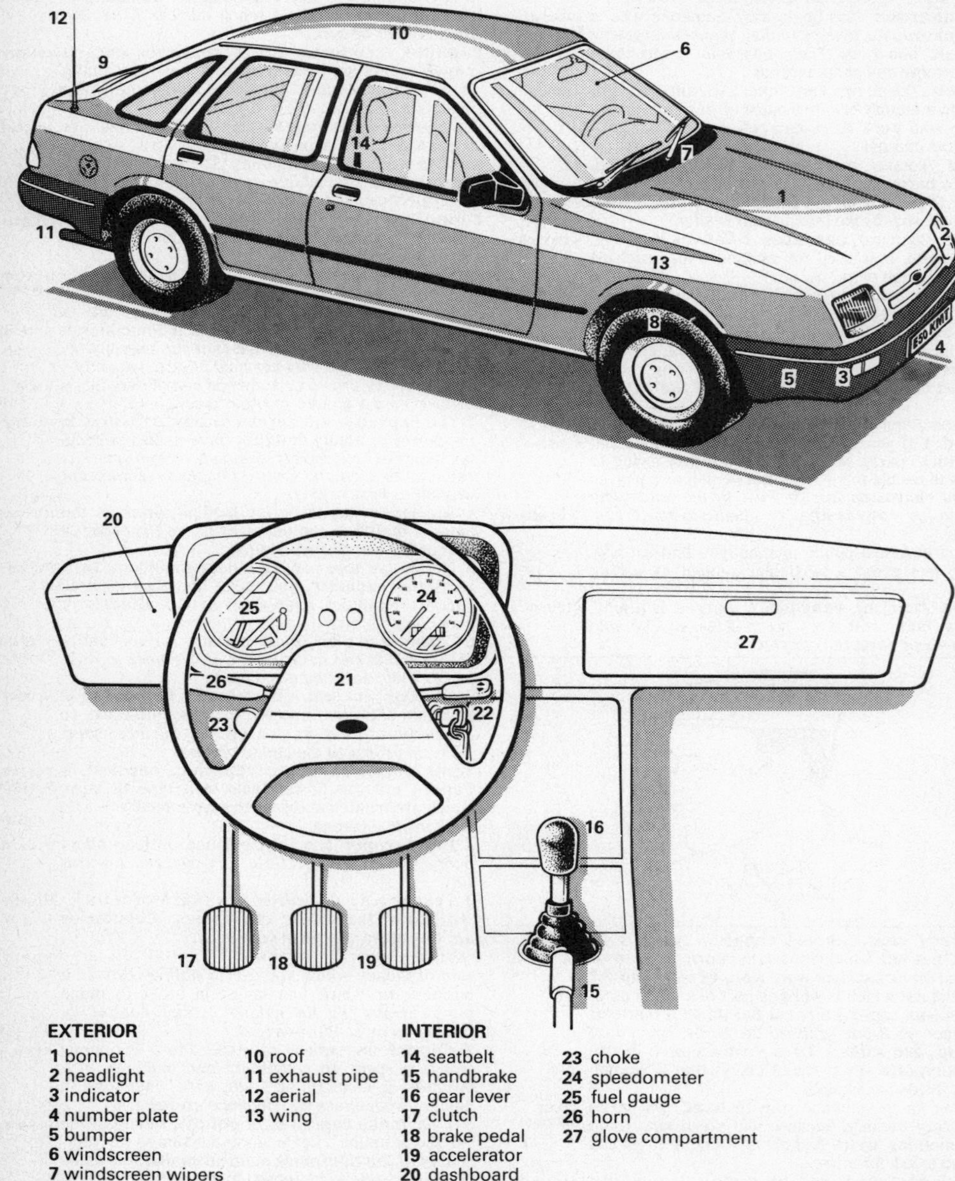

EXTERIOR

1 bonnet
2 headlight
3 indicator
4 number plate
5 bumper
6 windscreen
7 windscreen wipers
8 tyre
9 boot
10 roof
11 exhaust pipe
12 aerial
13 wing

INTERIOR

14 seatbelt
15 handbrake
16 gear lever
17 clutch
18 brake pedal
19 accelerator
20 dashboard
21 steering wheel
22 ignition
23 choke
24 speedometer
25 fuel gauge
26 horn
27 glove compartment

7 A **capital** offence is one that is so serious that the person who commits it can be punished by death. EG *...the capital offence of murder.* ADJ CLASSIF: ATTRIB

capitalise /kæpɪtəlaɪz/. See **capitalize**.

capitalism /kæpɪtəlɪzm/ is an economic and political system in which property, business, and industry are owned by private individuals and not by the state. EG *...modern industrial capitalism.* N UNCOUNT

capitalist /kæpɪtəlɪst/, **capitalists. 1** A **capitalist** country or society is one which supports capitalism. EG *...the enormous strength and influence of capitalist America... ...capitalist societies.* ADJ CLASSIF

2 A **capitalist** system or economy is based on the principles of capitalism. EG *Japan successfully built up a modern capitalist economy.* ADJ CLASSIF

3 A **capitalist** is **3.1** someone who believes in and supports the principles of capitalism. **3.2** someone who owns a business. EG *Capitalists are encouraged to put their wealth into new industries.* N COUNT

capitalistic /kæpɪtəlɪstɪk/ means supporting or based on the principles of capitalism; often used showing disapproval. EG *...the economic crisis in the capitalistic world.* ADJ CLASSIF

capitalize /kæpɪtəlaɪz/, **capitalizes, capitalizing, capitalized;** also spelled **capitalise.** If you **capitalize** on a situation, you use it to gain some advantage for yourself. EG *Mr Healey has been capitalising on the anxiety expressed throughout the House.* V: OFT +*on/upon*

capital punishment is punishment which involves the legal killing of a person who has committed a serious crime such as murder. N UNCOUNT

capitulate /kəpɪtjə[4]leɪt/, **capitulates, capitulating, capitulated.** If you **capitulate**, you stop resisting and do what someone else wants you to do. EG *Economic pressures finally forced the Government to capitulate to our demands.* V: OFT+*to*

◇ **capitulation** /kəpɪtjə[4]leɪʃə[0]n/. EG *...the capitulation of the city without a struggle.* ◇ N UNCOUNT

caprice /kə[3]priːs/, **caprices.** A **caprice** is an unexpected action or decision which has no strong reason or purpose. EG *Newspapers became subject to the whims and caprices of their owners... His drawings could be hideous or comical according to caprice.* N COUNT OR N UNCOUNT Formal

capricious /kə[3]prɪʃəs/. **1** Someone who is **capricious** often changes their mind unexpectedly. EG *Authoritarian rulers are typically capricious.* ADJ QUALIT

2 Something that is **capricious** often changes unexpectedly. EG *...a capricious postal system... ...a capricious summer breeze.* ADJ QUALIT

capsize /kæpsaɪz/, **capsizes, capsizing, capsized.** If you **capsize** a boat or if it **capsizes**, it turns upside down in the water. EG *Ships capsize when struck by these waves... ...a capsized boat.* V-ERG

capsule /kæpsjʊl/, **capsules.** A **capsule** is **1** a very small, round container with powdered medicine in it, which you swallow. **2** a small strong container used for storing or carrying things. **3** the part of a spacecraft in which people travel and in which they return to earth. N COUNT

captain /kæptɪn/, **captains, captaining, captained. 1** The **captain** of a ship is the officer in charge of it. EG *...the captain of a battleship.* N COUNT

2 In the army, a **captain** is an officer of middle rank. N COUNT

3 The **captain** of an aeroplane is its pilot. N COUNT

4 The **captain** of a sports team is its leader. N COUNT

5 If you **captain** a group or team of people, you are their leader. EG *Willis is probably the best player to have captained England.* V+O

caption /kæpʃə[0]n/, **captions.** A **caption** is the words printed underneath a picture or cartoon which explain what it is about. EG *Underneath was a caption that said: 'The greatest power on this earth'.* N COUNT

captivate /kæptə[1]veɪt/, **captivates, captivating, captivated.** If you **are captivated** by someone or something, you find them fascinating and attractive. EG *At eighteen he had been captivated by a charming brunette.* ◇ **captivating.** EG *Roosevelt was a captivating speaker.* V+O; ◇ ADJ QUALIT

captive /kæptɪv/, **captives. 1** A **captive** is a prisoner. EG *The troops took the women and children as captives.* ▸ used as an adjective. EG *...a wounded captive bird.* N COUNT Literary; ▸ ADJ CLASSIF

2 If you **take** someone **captive**, you take them as a prisoner. EG *Nine Indians were taken captive.* PHRASE

3 A **captive audience** is a group of people who cannot leave a place and so have to watch or listen to someone. EG *Give him a captive audience, and he can sell anything.* PHRASE

captivity /kæptɪvɪ[1]ti[1]/ is the state of being kept as a captive. EG *...wild birds raised in captivity.* N UNCOUNT

capture /kæptʃə/, **captures, capturing, captured. 1** If you **capture** someone, you take them prisoner, especially in a war or after a struggle. EG *They had been captured and thrown in chains.* ▸ used as a noun. EG *He hadn't eaten anything since the night before his capture.* V+O; ▸ N UNCOUNT: USU+POSS

2 When military forces **capture** a town or a country, they take control of it by force. EG *The city took 24 days to capture.* ▸ used as a noun. EG *...the capture of the city.* V+O; ▸ N UNCOUNT +SUPP

3 If you **capture** an animal, you catch it. V+O

4 To **capture** something also means to gain control of it. EG *In August, overseas firms captured almost 41 per cent of the market.* V+O

5 If someone **captures** something such as the atmosphere or quality of something, they represent it successfully in pictures, music, or words. EG *With his camera he tried to capture changes as they took place before his eyes.* V+O

car /kɑː/, **cars. 1** A **car** is a motor vehicle with room for a small number of passengers. EG *He parked the car about a hundred yards from the gates... They usually go by car.* N COUNT OR *by*+N

2 In America, a **car** is also a railway carriage. N COUNT

3 In Britain, railway carriages are called **cars** when they are used for a particular purpose. EG *...passengers in the dining car.* N COUNT+SUPP

4 See also **cable car**.

carafe /kəræf, -rɑːf/, **carafes.** A **carafe** is a glass container in which you serve water or wine. EG *...a carafe of house wine.* N COUNT OR N PART

caramel /kærəmə[0]l, -mel/, **caramels. 1** A **caramel** is a chewy sweet made from sugar, butter, and milk. N COUNT

2 Caramel is burnt sugar used for colouring and flavouring food. N UNCOUNT

carat /kærət/, **carats.** A **carat** is **1** a unit for measuring the weight of diamonds and other precious stones. It is equal to 0.2 grams. **2** a unit for measuring the purity of gold. The purest gold is 24-carat gold. N COUNT

caravan /kærəvæn/, **caravans.** A **caravan** is **1** a vehicle with beds and other equipment inside, in which people live or spend their holidays. Caravans are usually pulled by a car. EG *He went on a caravan holiday.* **2** a group of people and animals who travel together in places such as deserts. EG *Once we were part of a caravan of twelve thousand camels.* N COUNT

caravanning /kærəvænɪŋ/ is the activity of having a holiday in a caravan. EG *We went caravanning in North Wales.* N ING

carbohydrate /kɑːbəʊhaɪdreɪt/, **carbohydrates. Carbohydrate** is a substance found in food such as sugar and bread, that gives you energy. EG *Most fish are free from carbohydrate... ...our diet, with its high intake of carbohydrates and fat.* N UNCOUNT OR N COUNT

carbon /kɑːbə[0]n/ is a chemical element that diamonds and coal are made of. All living things contain carbon. N UNCOUNT

carbon copy, carbon copies. A **carbon copy** is a copy of a piece of writing that is made using carbon paper. EG *I kept a carbon copy of my letter.* N COUNT

carbon dioxide /kɑːbən daɪɒksaɪd/ is a gas. Animals and people breathe out carbon dioxide. N UNCOUNT

carbon monoxide /kɑːbən mə⁷nɒksaɪd/ is a poisonous gas that is produced especially by the engines of vehicles. N UNCOUNT

carbon paper is thin paper with a dark substance on one side. You use it to make copies of letters, bills, and other papers. N UNCOUNT

carcass /kɑːkəs/, **carcasses;** also spelled **carcase.** A **carcass** is the body of a dead animal. EG *...rotting carcasses of cattle.* N COUNT

card /kɑːd/, **cards. 1** A **card** is **1.1** a piece of stiff paper that you write information on. EG *Put all the details on the card... ...report cards.* N COUNT OR N UNCOUNT **1.2** a piece of cardboard or plastic with your name, photograph, or signature on it. EG *...a membership card... Did you ask to see his card?* N COUNT+SUPP **1.3** a piece of stiff paper with a picture and a message printed on it, which you send to someone on a special occasion. EG *...a Christmas card.* N COUNT **1.4** a postcard. EG *Send me a card when you get there.* N COUNT

2 Cards are thin pieces of cardboard with numbers or pictures printed on them which are used to play various games. EG *He shuffled the cards and dealt them.* N COUNT: USU PLURAL

3 If you are playing **cards**, you are playing a game using cards. N PLURAL

4 You can use **card** to refer to something that gives you an advantage in a particular situation. EG *Her chief card was her perfect memory... This placed all the cards in the hands of the landowners.* N COUNT

cardboard /kɑːdbɔːd/ is thick, stiff paper that is used to make boxes and other containers. EG *...a large cardboard box.* N UNCOUNT

cardiac /kɑːdɪæk/ means relating to the heart. EG *...death caused by cardiac failure... ...a relaxation of the cardiac muscle.* ADJ CLASSIF: ATTRIB Medical

cardigan /kɑːdɪgən/, **cardigans.** A **cardigan** is a knitted woollen sweater that you fasten at the front with buttons or a zip. See picture at CLOTHES. N COUNT

cardinal /kɑːdɪnə⁰l/, **cardinals. 1** A **cardinal** is a priest of high rank in the Catholic church. N COUNT

2 Cardinal means extremely important. EG *...a cardinal part of the scheme... ...a fact of cardinal importance.* ADJ QUALIT: ATTRIB Formal

cardinal sin, cardinal sins. If you refer to an action as a **cardinal sin**, you are indicating in a humorous way that some people strongly disapprove of it. EG *I had committed the cardinal sin of shutting the window.* N COUNT

card-index, card-indexes. A **card-index** is a set of cards with information on them. The cards are arranged in alphabetical order. EG *The students were just names in the card index.* N COUNT

care /kɛə/, **cares, caring, cared. 1** If you **care** about something, you feel that it is important or interesting and are concerned about it. EG *...people who care about the environment.* V: USU+A

2 If you do not **care** about something, it does not matter to you. EG *She couldn't care less what they thought... You can go with Roger for all I care... Who cares where she is?* V, WITH BROAD NEG

3 If you **care** for someone or something, you look after them and keep them in a good state or condition. EG *You must learn how to care for children.* ▸ used as a noun. EG *...the care of mental patients... She needed a lot of care... ...the children in her care.* V+*for* ▸ N UNCOUNT

4 To **care** for someone also means to love them. EG *Do you think she still cares for him?* V+*for* Outdated

5 If you say that you do not **care** for something, you mean that you do not like it. EG *I didn't much care for the way he looked at me.* V+*for*, WITH BROAD NEG Outdated

6 To **care** to do something means to want or choose to do it. EG *It's wrong whichever way you care to look at it... It's not a problem I'd care to face myself.* V+*to*-INF Formal

7 If you do something with **care**, you do it with great attention because you do not want to make any mistakes or cause any damage. EG *He chose every word with care... The label on the crate said 'Glass. Handle with care.'* N UNCOUNT

8 Cares are worries. EG *...without a care in the world.* N COUNT

9 Children who are **in care** are being looked after by the state, because their parents are dead or are unable to look after them properly. PHRASE

10 You use **take care** in these ways. **10.1** If you **take care of** something or someone, you look after them and prevent them from being harmed or damaged. EG *He takes good care of my goats.* PHRASE **10.2** You can say **'Take care'** when saying goodbye to someone or at the end of a letter. CONVENTION Informal **10.3** If you **take care** to do something, you make sure that you do it. EG *Take care not to spill the mixture.* PHRASE **10.4** If you **take care of** a task or situation, you deal with it. EG *They can take care of their own breakfast.* PHRASE

career /kərɪə/, **careers, careering, careered. 1** A **career** is a type of job or profession that someone does for a long period of their life. EG *...a career in accountancy... ...careers like teaching and medicine... ...a political career.* N COUNT: USU+SUPP

2 Your **career** is the part of your life that you spend working. EG *Her early career was not a great success... I did it for the sake of my husband's career.* N COUNT: USU+SUPP

3 Careers advisers give people information and help them to decide what kind of work they want to do. N MOD

4 If a person or vehicle **careers** somewhere, they move fast and in an uncontrolled way. EG *He careered into a wall.* V+A

carefree /kɛəfriː/. If someone is **carefree**, they have no problems, worries, or responsibilities. EG *She had been lively and carefree... ...his normally carefree attitude.* ADJ QUALIT

careful /kɛəfʊl/. **1** If you say **'Be careful'** to someone, you are warning them of a danger or a problem. EG *Be careful or you'll fall!... Please be careful with the washing machine.* CONVENTION

2 If you are **careful**, **2.1** you do something with a lot of attention and thought. EG *This law will encourage more careful driving... He had to be careful about what he said.* ADJ QUALIT ◇ **carefully.** EG *He walked carefully around the broken glass.* ◇ ADV **2.2** you do something thoroughly and make sure that all the details are correct. EG *He made a careful copy of the notes... ...careful preparation.* ADJ QUALIT ◇ **carefully.** EG *Now listen carefully everybody.* ◇ ADV

careless /kɛəlɪ²s/. **1** If you are **careless**, you do not pay enough attention to what you are doing, and so you make mistakes or produce unsatisfactory results. EG *We are rather careless about the way we cook... I had been careless and let him wander off on his own.* ADJ QUALIT ◇ **carelessly.** EG *...a gate left carelessly ajar.* ◇ ADV ◇ **carelessness.** EG *They severely criticized Crook for his carelessness.* ◇ N UNCOUNT

2 You do something in a **careless** way when you are relaxed or confident. EG *...a careless laugh... ...her simplicity and careless grace.* ADJ CLASSIF ◇ **carelessly.** EG *'I'll give him a ring later,' Rudolph said, carelessly.* ◇ ADV ◇ **carelessness.** EG *She handled it with the carelessness of an expert.* ◇ N UNCOUNT

caress /kərɛs/, **caresses, caressing, caressed.** If you **caress** someone, you stroke them gently and affectionately. EG *I caressed her hair and we kissed.* ▸ used as a noun. EG *...a loving caress.* V OR V+O: RECIP ▸ N COUNT

caretaker /kɛəteɪkə/, **caretakers.** A **caretaker** is a person who looks after a large building such as a school or a block of flats and deals with small repairs to it. N COUNT

cargo /kɑːgəʊ/, **cargoes.** The **cargo** of a ship or plane is the goods that it is carrying. EG *...a cargo of wool... The port is still handling cargo.* N COUNT OR N UNCOUNT

Are you a carnivore?

caricature /kærɪkətjʊə/, **caricatures, caricaturing, caricatured. 1** A **caricature** of someone is a drawing or description of them that exaggerates their appearance or behaviour. EG *...a caricature of Max Beerbohm... He was a master of caricature.* ▸ used as a verb. EG *Lawson caricatured his boss in his cartoons.* N COUNT OR N UNCOUNT ▸ V+O

2 If you describe something as a **caricature** of an event or situation, you mean that it is a very exaggerated account of it. EG *...an outrageous caricature of the truth.* N COUNT: OFT+of

caring /kɛərɪŋ/. **1** If someone is **caring**, they are affectionate, helpful, and sympathetic. EG *...a caring parent... We need a more caring society.* ADJ QUALIT

2 Caring is behaviour that is affectionate, helpful, and sympathetic. EG *...love and caring between a man and a woman.* N UNCOUNT

carnage /kɑːnɪdʒ/. When there is **carnage**, a lot of people are killed, especially in a war. EG *Refugees crossed the border to escape the carnage.* N UNCOUNT Literary

carnal /kɑːnə⁰l/ means involving sexual feelings or activity; used showing disapproval. EG *...carnal desires.* ADJ CLASSIF: ATTRIB Literary

carnation /kɑːneɪʃə⁰n/, **carnations.** A **carnation** is a plant with white, pink, or red flowers. EG *...a bouquet of pink carnations.* N COUNT

carnival /kɑːnɪvə⁰l/, **carnivals.** A **carnival** is a public festival during which people play music and sometimes dance in the streets. N COUNT

carnivore /kɑːnɪvɔː/, **carnivores.** A **carnivore** is an animal that eats meat rather than plants. N COUNT Formal
◇ **carnivorous** /kɑːnɪvə⁰rəs/. EG *Snakes are carnivorous.* ◇ ADJ CLASSIF

carol /kærəl/, **carols. Carols** are Christian religious songs that are sung especially at Christmas. EG *After the carols, presents were distributed.* N COUNT

carp /kɑːp/, **carps, carping, carped. 1** A **carp** is a kind of large fish that lives in lakes and rivers. The plural form is also **carp**. N COUNT

2 If you **carp**, you keep criticizing or complaining about someone or something. EG *To carp about his leadership seems almost churlish... There's no point in carping.* V: OFT +about/at Literary

car park, car parks. A **car park** is an area or building where people can leave their cars. EG *...the entrance to the multi-storey car park.* N COUNT British

carpenter /kɑːpɪntə/, **carpenters.** A **carpenter** is a person whose job is making and repairing wooden things. N COUNT

carpentry /kɑːpɪntri¹/ is the skill or the work of a carpenter. N UNCOUNT

carpet /kɑːpɪt/, **carpets. 1** A **carpet** is a thick, flat piece of cloth which is used to cover the floors and stairs in a building. EG *...an old brown carpet.* N COUNT
◇ **carpeted** /kɑːpɪtɪ²d/. EG *The corridor was carpeted.* ◇ ADJ CLASSIF

2 A **carpet** of something is a layer of it which covers the ground. EG *There was a carpet of snow everywhere.* ◇ **carpeted.** EG *The ground was carpeted with flowers.* N COUNT+SUPP ◇ ADJ CLASSIF

carriage /kærɪdʒ/, **carriages.** A **carriage** is **1** one of the separate sections of a train that carries passengers. **2** an old-fashioned vehicle which is pulled by horses. EG *...a procession of eight carriages led by the Queen.* N COUNT British; N COUNT

carried away /kæri¹d əweɪ/. If you are **carried away**, you are so enthusiastic about something that you behave in a foolish way. EG *She can get so carried away making the designs that she forgets the time.* ADJ PRED

carrier /kærɪə/, **carriers. 1** A **carrier** is a vehicle or device that is used for carrying things. EG *...a new luggage carrier for bicycles... ...a troop carrier.* ● See also **aircraft carrier**. N COUNT: USU+SUPP

2 A **carrier** is also someone who is infected with a disease and can make other people ill. EG *...mothers identified from blood tests as carriers.* N COUNT

carrier bag, carrier bags. A **carrier bag** is a bag made of paper or plastic which you carry shopping in. N COUNT British

carrion /kærɪən/ is the decaying flesh of dead animals. EG *These birds live by scavenging carrion.* N UNCOUNT

carrot /kærət/, **carrots. 1** A **carrot** is a long, thin, orange-coloured vegetable that grows under the ground. EG *She served us beef with carrots and potatoes... ...carrot juice.* N COUNT OR N UNCOUNT

2 You use **carrot** to refer to something that is offered to people in order to persuade them to do something. The word 'stick' is used to refer to harsher methods of persuasion. EG *The free cottage is the carrot which makes him accept his low wage... Their policy is all sticks and no carrots.* N COUNT

carry /kæri¹/, **carries, carrying, carried. 1** If you **carry** something, **1.1** you take it with you, holding it so that it does not touch the ground. EG *He picked up his suitcase and carried it into the bedroom.* **1.2** you have it with you wherever you go. EG *I always carry a gun.* V+O: USU+A; V+O

2 If something **carries** a person or thing somewhere, it takes them there. EG *A gentle current carried him slowly to the shore... ...trucks that carried casualties.* V+O: USU+A

3 If someone or something **carries** a disease, they are infected with it and can pass it on to people or animals. EG *Rats carry very nasty diseases.* V+O

4 If an action or situation **carries** a particular quality or consequence, it has it or involves it. EG *Any job carries with it daily periods of boredom... Adultery in those cultures carried the death penalty.* V+O: NO PASS, NO CONT

5 If you **carry** an idea or a method to a particular extent, you use or develop it to that extent. EG *George carried this idea one step further.* V+O+A

6 If a newspaper or poster **carries** a picture or a piece of writing, it contains it or displays it. EG *A poster carried a portrait of Churchill.* V+O

7 If a proposal or motion **is carried** in a debate, a majority of people vote in favour of it. EG *The motion was carried by 259 votes to 162.* V+O: USU PASS

8 If a sound **carries**, it can be heard a long way away. EG *Sound seems to carry better in the still evening air.* V

9 If a woman **is carrying** a child, she is pregnant. V+O

10 If a person or their opinion **carries weight**, they are respected by other people and influence them. EG *What I think doesn't carry much weight around here.* PHRASE

carry on. 1 If you **carry on** doing something, you continue to do it. EG *I carried on without their support... The speaker carried on reading from his prepared manuscript.* **2** If you **carry on** an activity, you take part in it. EG *Our work is carried on in an informal atmosphere... She could not carry on a sensible conversation.* PHRASAL VB: V+ADV OR V+ADV+O; V+O+ADV

carry out. 1 If you **carry out** a task, you do it. EG *They also have to carry out many administrative duties... The experiments were carried out by Dr Preston.* **2** If you **carry out** an order, you do what you are told to do. EG *He was simply carrying out the instructions he had received.* PHRASAL VB: V+O+ADV; V+O+ADV

carry over. If you **carry** something **over** from one situation to another, you make it continue to exist in the new situation. EG *The habit of obedience is carried over from the war.* PHRASAL VB: V+O+ADV

carry through. If you **carry** a plan **through**, you put it into practice. EG *...the task of carrying through the necessary reforms.* PHRASAL VB: V+O+ADV

carrycot /kæri¹kɒt/, **carrycots.** A **carrycot** is a cot for small babies which has handles for carrying it. N COUNT British

cart /kɑːt/, **carts, carting, carted. 1** A **cart** is an old-fashioned wooden vehicle that is used for transporting goods or people. Some carts are pulled by animals. EG *...a cart loaded with hay... ...a donkey cart.* N COUNT

2 If you **cart** things or people somewhere, you V+O+A Informal carry them or transport them there, often with difficulty. EG *It took several trips to cart it all back up the stairs... He was carted off to hospital.*

carte blanche /kɑ:t blɑ:nt^{0}ʃ/. If someone gives you **carte blanche**, they give you the authority to do whatever you think is right. EG *They gave him carte blanche to publish his proposals.* — N UNCOUNT, Formal

cartilage /kɑ:tı^{0}lıdʒ/ is a strong, flexible substance in your body, especially around your joints. EG *...the cartilage on the inside of the kneecap.* — N UNCOUNT

carton /kɑ:tə^{0}n/, **cartons.** A **carton** is **1** a plastic or cardboard container in which food or drink is sold. EG *...a loaf of bread and a carton of milk.* **2** a large, strong cardboard box in which goods are packed for storage and transport. EG *He was putting metal bands round cartons.* — N COUNT OR N PART; American

cartoon /kɑ:tu:n/, **cartoons.** A **cartoon** is **1** a humorous drawing or series of drawings in a newspaper or magazine. EG *The Telegraph had a very funny cartoon about the demonstration.* **2** a film in which all the characters and scenes are drawn rather than being real people or objects. — N COUNT

cartoonist /kɑ:tu:nıst/, **cartoonists.** A **cartoonist** is a person whose job is to draw cartoons for newspapers and magazines. — N COUNT

cartridge /kɑ:trıdʒ/, **cartridges.** A **cartridge** is a metal or cardboard tube containing a bullet and an explosive substance. Cartridges are used in guns. — N COUNT

cartwheel /kɑ:twi:l/, **cartwheels.** If you turn a **cartwheel**, you do a fast, circular movement with your body. You fall sideways, put your hands on the ground, swing your legs over, and return to a standing position. — N COUNT

carve /kɑ:v/, **carves, carving, carved. 1** If you **carve** an object, you make it by cutting it out of stone or wood. EG *The statue was carved by John Gibson.* ◇ **carved.** EG *Pat loved the carved Buddhas... ...a big, cracked mirror with little, carved Cupids in each corner.* — V+O : USU+A; ◇ ADJ CLASSIF : ATTRIB

2 If you **carve** writing or a design on an object, you cut it into the surface of the object. EG *He begins to carve his initials on the tree.* — V+O OR V : USU+A

3 If you **carve** a cooked piece of meat, you cut slices from it at a meal. EG *He knew how to carve a goose.* — V+O OR V

carve out. If you **carve out** something for yourself, you create or obtain it, often with difficulty. EG *The company is carving out a huge slice of the electronics market.* — PHRASAL VB : V+O+ADV

carve up. If you **carve** something **up**, you divide it into smaller areas or pieces. EG *They prepared to carve up the British Empire.* — PHRASAL VB : V+O+ADV

carving /kɑ:vıŋ/, **carvings. 1** A **carving** is an object that has been cut out of a substance such as stone or wood. EG *...a stone carving from central Europe.* — N COUNT

2 Carving is the art of carving objects or carving designs on them. EG *Here you can see English carving at its best.* — N UNCOUNT

carving knife, carving knives. A **carving knife** is a large, sharp knife that you use to cut cooked meat. — N COUNT

cascade /kæskeıd/, **cascades, cascading, cascaded. 1** A **cascade** is a waterfall. EG *The river fell in a series of cascades down towards the Hudson.* — N COUNT, Literary

2 If you refer to a **cascade** of something, you mean a large amount or quantity of it. EG *Around her face fell cascades of curls.* — N PART, Literary

3 When water **cascades**, it pours downwards very fast and in large quantities. EG *The water is cascading through the air.* — V+A

4 If people or things **cascade** somewhere, they move or arrive there in large quantities. EG *Telegrams of protest cascaded onto his desk... The crowd cascaded down a flight of stairs.* — V+A, Literary

case /keıs/, **cases. 1** A **case** is a particular situation or instance, or an event or situation of a particular kind. EG *In Catherine's case, it led to divorce... In some cases, they burst into flames... ...cases where both partners have been married before... All cases of bullying will be severely dealt with.* — N COUNT+SUPP

2 Case is also used in these phrases. **2.1** You say **in that case** or **in which case** to indicate that you are assuming that a previous statement is correct or true. EG *'The bar is closed,' the waiter said. 'In that case,' McFee said, 'I'll go to another hotel'.* **2.2** If you say that something **is the case**, you mean that it is true or correct. EG *Paul argued that this was the case.... ...if it is prohibited (as is the case in Britain).* **2.3** If you say that a job or task **is a case of** doing a particular thing, you mean that that is what it consists of. EG *There's very little work involved. It's just a case of drafting the summons.* **2.4** If you say that something **is a case in point**, you mean that it is a good example of a general statement you have just made. EG *Britain is a case in point. 75% of the population now have washing machines.* **2.5** You say **as the case may be** or **whatever the case may be** to indicate that the statement you are making applies equally to situations that are different in a minor way from the one first mentioned. EG *They say that the hat is red (or green, as the case may be).* — PHRASES

3 You say **in any case 3.1** when you are adding another reason for something you have said or done. EG *I couldn't ask him all the time, and in any case he wasn't always there.* **3.2** after talking about things that you are not sure about, to emphasize that you are sure about your next statement. EG *Perhaps he did nothing. In any case, there was a brief fight.* — ADV SEN

4 You say **in case** to indicate that you have something or are doing something because a particular thing might happen or might have happened. EG *Do you want me to hold them just in case?... I've got the key in case we want to go inside... I have a phone number in case of emergency.* — CONJ OR PHRASE

5 Doctors sometimes refer to a patient as a **case**. EG *...road accident cases.* — N COUNT : USU+SUPP

6 Police and detectives refer to a crime or mystery that they are investigating as a **case**. EG *...one of Sherlock Holmes's cases.* — N COUNT

7 In an argument or debate, the **case** for or against a plan or idea consists of the facts and reasons used to support it or oppose it. EG *...a book arguing the case for better adult education... He stated his case.* — N COUNT : USU SING +*for/against*

8 In law, a **case** is a trial or other legal inquiry. EG *He had lost the case.* — N COUNT

9 A **case** is also **9.1** a container that is specially designed to hold or protect something. EG *...scissors in a leather case.* **9.2** a suitcase. EG *They unload their trunks and cases.* — N COUNT

case history, case histories. A person's **case history** is the record of past events or problems that have affected them. EG *They had no case history of illness... She was making out a case-history for each child.* — N COUNT, Formal

cash /kæʃ/, **cashes, cashing, cashed. 1 Cash** is money in the form of notes and coins rather than cheques. EG *How much cash do you have?... ...four hundred dollars in cash.* — N UNCOUNT

2 If you **cash** a cheque, you exchange it at a bank for the amount of money that it is worth. EG *Cheques up to 50 pounds may be cashed at any of our branches.* — V+O

cash in. If you **cash in** on a situation, you use it to gain an advantage, often in an unfair or dishonest way. EG *They cashed in on the public's growing suspicion.* — PHRASAL VB : V+ADV, OFT+*on*

Would you do a carving with a carving knife?

cashier /kə³ʃɪə/, **cashiers.** A **cashier** is a person that customers pay money to or get money from in a shop, bank, or garage. N COUNT

cashmere /kæʃmɪə/ is a kind of very fine, soft wool. EG *...her cashmere shawl.* N UNCOUNT

casing /keɪsɪŋ/, **casings.** A **casing** is a substance or object that covers something and protects it. EG *...the outer casing of a vacuum flask.* N COUNT

casino /kəsiːnəʊ/, **casinos.** A **casino** is a building or room where people play gambling games such as roulette. N COUNT

cask /kɑːsk/, **casks.** A **cask** is a wooden barrel that is used for storing things, especially alcoholic drink. EG *...a four-gallon cask... ...a cask of beer.* N COUNT

casket /kɑːskɪ²t/, **caskets.** A **casket** is **1** a small box in which you keep valuable things. EG *...her exquisite jewel casket.* **2** a coffin. N COUNT; American

casserole /kæsərəʊl/, **casseroles.** A **casserole** is **1** a dish that you make by cooking food in liquid in an oven. EG *Use this stock in soups or casseroles... There's lamb casserole for dinner.* **2** a large, heavy container with a lid which is used to cook food. EG *Cook this in a casserole for one and a half hours.* N COUNT OR N UNCOUNT; N COUNT

cassette /kə³set/, **cassettes.** A **cassette** is a small, flat rectangular plastic container with magnetic tape inside which is used for recording and playing back sounds. EG *Some libraries have cassettes of stories... ...a cassette player.* N COUNT

cassette recorder, cassette recorders. A **cassette recorder** is a machine that is used for recording and listening to cassettes. N COUNT

cast /kɑːst/, **casts, casting. Cast** is used in the present tense and is the past tense and past participle of the verb.

1 The **cast** of a play or film is all the people who act in it. EG *Who was in the cast?... The whole cast worked wonderfully together.* N COLL

2 To **cast** an actor in a play or film means to choose them to act a particular role in it. EG *I was cast as the husband.* V+O: OFT+*as*

3 If you **cast** your eyes or **cast** a look in a particular direction, you look in that direction. EG *He cast a quick glance at his friend.* V+O+A

4 If you **cast** your **mind back**, you think about things in the past or try to remember them. EG *He cast his mind back over the day.* PHRASE

5 If something **casts** light or shadows somewhere, it causes them to appear there. EG *The fire cast a faint glow over the bed.* V+O+A Literary

6 If you **cast** doubt or suspicion on something, you cause other people to be unsure about it. EG *He had cast doubt on our traditional beliefs.* V+O: OFT +*on/upon*

7 When you **cast** your vote in an election, you vote. EG *Will had cast his vote for the President.* V+O: OFT+A

8 If you **cast** something somewhere, you throw it there. EG *He casts his clothes on to the bench... She cast her jewels into the lake.* V+O: USU+A Literary

9 To **cast** an object means to make it by pouring hot, liquid metal into a specially shaped container and leaving it there until it becomes hard. EG *...a statue of Achilles, cast in bronze.* V+O

cast about or **cast around.** If you **cast about** or **cast around** for something, you look for it. EG *I cast around for some place to hide.* PHRASAL VB: V+ADV, OFT+*for* Literary

cast aside. If you **cast** someone or something **aside**, you get rid of them because you no longer need them; used showing disapproval. EG *His country cast him aside and disgraced him.* PHRASAL VB: V+O+ADV Formal

cast off. 1 If you **cast** something **off**, you get rid of it or no longer use it. EG *Organizations must cast off old-fashioned practices in order to survive.* • See also **cast-off**. **2** If you are on a boat and you **cast off**, you untie the rope that is keeping the boat in a fixed position. EG *We cast off as quietly as we could... Hendricks cast off the bow line and walked to the stern.* PHRASAL VB: V+O+ADV Formal; V+ADV OR V+O+ADV Technical

caste /kɑːst/, **castes. 1** A **caste** is one of the social classes into which people in a society are divided, especially in India. EG *Sushma came from a lower caste.* N COUNT

2 Caste is the system of dividing people in a society into different social classes. EG *Duties were determined by caste.* N UNCOUNT

caster /kɑːstə/. See **castor**.

castigate /kæstɪgeɪt/, **castigates, castigating, castigated.** If you **castigate** someone or something, you scold them or criticize them severely. EG *He castigated me for my mistakes... They castigated the report as inadequate.* ◊ **castigation** /kæstɪgeɪʃə⁰n/. EG *...his castigation of their reckless utterances.* V+O Formal; ◊ N UNCOUNT

casting /kɑːstɪŋ/ is the activity or job of choosing actors to play particular roles in films or plays. EG *...people doing the casting for films... ...the casting director.* N UNCOUNT

cast-iron. 1 Cast-iron objects are made of a special type of iron which contains carbon. EG *...a cast-iron stove... ...cast-iron gates.* ADJ CLASSIF: ATTRIB

2 A **cast-iron** excuse, guarantee, or solution is one that is absolutely certain to be effective. EG *We offer no cast-iron solutions to the problems.* ADJ CLASSIF: ATTRIB

castle /kɑːsə⁰l/, **castles. 1** A **castle** is a large building with thick, high walls. Castles were built by kings, queens and other important people in former times, especially for protection during wars and battles. EG *...Windsor Castle... ...a ruined castle.* N COUNT

2 In chess, a **castle** is a piece that is moved forwards, backwards, or sideways. N COUNT

cast-off, cast-offs. Cast-off things, especially clothes, are ones which you no longer use and which you give to someone else or throw away. EG *They were wearing cast-off jackets.* ▸ used as a noun. EG *They dressed up in Winifred's cast-offs.* ADJ CLASSIF: ATTRIB; ▸ N COUNT: USU PLURAL

castor /kɑːstə/, **castors;** also spelled **caster. Castors** are small wheels fitted to a piece of furniture so that it can be moved more easily. N COUNT

castrate /kæstreɪt/, **castrates, castrating, castrated.** To **castrate** a male animal means to remove its testicles so that it cannot reproduce. EG *The two bulls had to be castrated.* ◊ **castration** /kæstreɪʃə⁰n/. EG *They used castration of men as a form of punishment.* V+O Formal; ◊ N UNCOUNT

casual /kæʒjʊ⁰əl/, **casuals. 1** If you are **casual**, you are relaxed and do things without great attention or concentration. EG *He tried to appear casual as he asked her to dance... ...a casual glance.* ◊ **casually.** EG *...saying goodbye as casually as I could.* ◊ **casualness.** EG *...working with apparent casualness.* ADJ QUALIT; ◊ ADV; ◊ N UNCOUNT

2 A **casual** event or situation happens by chance or without planning. EG *...a casual friendship... It is not open to casual visitors.* ◊ **casually.** EG *...any casually assembled group of men.* ADJ CLASSIF; ◊ ADV

3 Casual clothes are ones that you normally wear at home or on holiday, and not for work or formal occasions. EG *She wears casual clothes in bright colours.* ▸ used as a noun. EG *...smart casuals.* ◊ **casually.** EG *The students dress casually, in jeans and sweat shirts.* ADJ CLASSIF: ATTRIB; ▸ N PLURAL; ◊ ADV

4 Casual work is done for short periods and not permanently or regularly. EG *He was doing casual jobs for two years... ...a casual labourer.* ADJ CLASSIF: ATTRIB

casualty /kæʒjʊ⁰əlti¹/, **casualties. 1** A **casualty** is **1.1** a person who is injured or killed in a war or in an accident. EG *No casualties were reported... There were heavy casualties on both sides.* **1.2** a person or a thing that has suffered badly as a result of a particular event or situation. EG *She was one of the casualties of the system.* N COUNT: USU PLURAL; N COUNT: USU+*of*

2 The **casualty** ward or department of a hospital is the place where people who have severe injuries or sudden illness are taken for emergency treatment. ADJ CLASSIF: ATTRIB

cat /kæt/, **cats. 1** A **cat** is **1.1** a small, furry animal with a tail, whiskers, and sharp claws, which is often kept as a pet. EG *The cat was lying on the sofa.* **1.2** a larger animal that is a type of cat, such N COUNT as a lion or tiger. EG *Lions will hunt as a team – the only cats that do so.*

2 If you talk about a **game of cat and mouse**, you are referring to a situation in which someone uses their greater strength, skill, or authority to treat another person in an unfair or cruel way. EG *There followed a game of cat and mouse with my tormentor.* PHRASE

cataclysm /kætəklɪsə^{0}m/, **cataclysms.** A **cataclysm** is an event that causes great change or harm. EG *Europe is approaching a terrible cataclysm.* N COUNT Literary
◊ **cataclysmic** /kætəklɪsmɪk/. EG *...a cataclysmic effect on British politics.* ◊ ADJ QUALIT

catalogue /kætəlɒg/, **catalogues, cataloguing, catalogued;** spelled **catalog** in American English.
1 A **catalogue** is a list of things such as the goods you can buy from a particular company, the objects in a museum, or the books in a library. EG *...expensive illustrated catalogues... ...catalogues from publishers.* N COUNT
▸ used as a verb. EG *Books are catalogued on white cards filed alphabetically.* ▸ V+O

2 A **catalogue** of similar things is a number of them considered or discussed one after another. EG *Mrs Zapp recited a catalogue of her husband's sins.* N COUNT+*of*
▸ used as a verb. EG *They had been cataloguing the many discomforts of life in India.* ▸ V+O

catalyst /kætəlɪst/, **catalysts.** A **catalyst** is 1 something that causes a change or event to happen. EG *Nuclear power served as a catalyst for the emergence of the Greens as a political force.* 2 a substance that causes a chemical reaction to take place more quickly. 1 N COUNT Formal; 2 Technical

cataract /kætərækt/, **cataracts. 1** A **cataract** is a layer that has grown over a person's eye because of old age or illness and that prevents them from seeing properly. EG *He had a cataract removed.* N COUNT

2 A **cataract** is also a large waterfall. EG *The river comes roaring down in a foaming cataract.* N COUNT Literary

catastrophe /kətæstrəfi^{1}/, **catastrophes.** A **catastrophe** is an unexpected event that causes great suffering or damage. EG *Unemployment is a personal catastrophe... ...an overwhelming sense of catastrophe.* N COUNT OR N UNCOUNT

catastrophic /kætəstrɒfɪk/ means extremely bad or serious, often causing great suffering or damage. EG *The impact on Belgium has already been catastrophic... ...catastrophic mistakes.* ADJ QUALIT

catcall /kætkɔːl/, **catcalls.** A **catcall** is a loud noise that someone makes to show that they disapprove of something. EG *In the street, the whistles and cat-calls began.* N COUNT

catch /kætʃ/, **catches, catching, caught** /kɔːt/. **1** If you **catch** an animal or person, you capture them after pursuing them, or by using a trap, net, or other device. EG *I went fishing and caught a nice little trout... ...a wild otter caught in a trap... We can get six months in prison if they catch us.* V+O

2 If you **catch** an object which is moving through the air, you seize it with your hands. EG *Tom flipped a toffee in the air and Claude caught it.* V+O
▸ used as a noun. EG *...a magnificent catch.* ▸ N COUNT

3 If you **catch** someone doing something wrong or doing something secretly, you notice them when they are doing it. EG *A gardener was sacked if he was caught smoking... Don't let him catch you at it.* V+O: USU+-ING OR A

4 If something **catches** something else, it hits it with a lot of force. EG *The wave caught the trawler on her bow.* V+O: USU+A

5 If something **catches** on an object or **is caught** between two things, it becomes attached to the object or becomes trapped. EG *There was a bit of rabbit's fur caught on the fence... He caught his fingers in the spokes of the wheel.* V-ERG: USU+A

6 If you **catch** a bus, train, or plane, you get on it in order to travel somewhere. EG *She caught a train to Boston.* V+O

7 If you **catch** something that someone has said, you manage to hear it. EG *She whispered something he could not catch.* V+O

8 If something **catches** your interest or your imagination, you notice it or become interested in it. EG *A poster caught her attention.* V+O

9 If you **catch sight** of someone or something, or **catch** a glimpse of them, you suddenly notice them or get a quick look at them. EG *I walked slowly, hoping she would catch sight of me... I caught a glimpse of two men in uniform.* PHRASE

10 If you **catch the post**, you succeed in putting a letter or parcel in a post-box before it is emptied. PHRASE

11 If you **are caught** in a storm or other unpleasant situation, it happens when you cannot avoid its effects. V-PASS+*in*

12 If you **catch** a cold or a disease, you become ill with it. V+O

13 To **catch** a liquid which falls from somewhere means to collect it in a container. EG *There were pots and bowls everywhere catching water-drops that fell from the ceiling.* V+O: USU+A

14 If something **catches** the light or if the light **catches** it, it reflects the light and looks bright or shiny. EG *The grass is sparkling where the sunlight catches small drops from the rain.* V+O

15 If the wind or water **catches** something, it carries or pushes it along. EG *The wind caught her hat.* V+O

16 A **catch** on a window or door is a device that fastens it. EG *He put his hand through the hole in the glass and released the catch.* N COUNT

17 A **catch** is also a hidden problem or difficulty in a plan or course of action. EG *'There's a catch in this.' – 'There's no catch, Gordon. I swear it.'* N SING

18 When people have been fishing, their **catch** is the total number of fish that they have caught. EG *They won't be able to land their catches at the home port.* N COUNT

19 **Catch** is **19.1** a game in which children throw a ball to each other and catch it. **19.2** a game in which one child chases other children and tries to touch or catch one of them. N UNCOUNT

20 to **catch** someone's **eye**: see **eye**. • to **catch fire**: see **fire**.

catch at. If you **catch at** something, you quickly take hold of it. EG *The children caught at my skirts and tugged me back.* PHRASAL VB: V+PREP

catch on. 1 If you **catch on** to something, you understand it, or realize that it is happening. EG *You were expected to catch on quick... They finally caught on to our game.* PHRASAL VB: V+ADV, OFT+*to* **2** If something **catches on**, it becomes popular. EG *Ballroom dancing caught on... If the machine had been cheaper, it might well have caught on.* V+ADV

catch out. If you **catch** someone **out**, you make them make a mistake, often by an unfair trick. EG *Are you trying to catch me out?* PHRASAL VB: V+O+ADV

catch up. 1 If you **catch up** with someone who is in front of you, you reach them by walking faster than they are walking. EG *Tim had just reached the corner when Judy caught up with him... She stood still, allowing him to catch her up.* PHRASAL VB: V+ADV, USU+*with*, OR V+O+ADV **2** To **catch up** with someone also means to reach the same standard or level that they have reached. EG *Most leaders were obsessed with catching up with the West.* V+ADV, OFT+*with* **3** If you **catch up** on an activity that you have not had much time to do, you spend time doing it. EG *They went to the office to catch up on correspondence... I was catching up on my sleep.* V+ADV, OFT+*on/with* **4** If you **are caught up** in something, you are involved in it, usually unwillingly. EG *He was determined not to get caught up in any publicity nonsense.* V-PASS +ADV+*in*

catch up with. 1 When people **catch up with** someone who has done something wrong, they succeed in finding them in order to arrest or punish them. EG *When Birmingham authorities* PHRASAL VB: V+ADV+PREP

Which words on these pages are spelled differently in British and American English?

finally caught up with her, she had spent all the money. **2** If something **catches up with** you, you find yourself in an unpleasant situation which you have been able to avoid but which you are now forced to deal with. EG *I am sure that the truth will catch up with him.* V+ADV+PREP

catchment area /kætʃmənt ɛərɪə/, **catchment areas.** The **catchment area** of a school or hospital is the area that it serves. N COUNT British

catch-phrase, catch-phrases. A **catch-phrase** is a sentence or phrase which becomes popular or well-known for a while because it is often used by a famous person. N COUNT

catchy /kætʃi¹/, **catchier, catchiest.** If you describe a tune as **catchy**, you mean that it is easy to remember. EG *The songs are irresistibly catchy.* ADJ QUALIT

categorical /kætə¹gɒrɪkə⁰l/. If you are **categorical** about something, you state your views with certainty and firmness. EG *I don't see how you can be so categorical.* ◇ **categorically.** EG *The proposals had been categorically rejected by Donovan.* ADJ QUALIT ◇ ADV

categorize /kætə¹gəraɪz/, **categorizes, categorizing, categorized;** also spelled **categorise.** If you **categorize** people or things, you divide them into sets or you say which set they belong to. EG *Animals can be categorised according to the food they eat.* ◇ **categorization** /kætɪgə⁰raɪzeɪʃə⁰n/, **categorizations.** EG *Today, this three-way categorization is no longer adequate.* V+O: OFT+*as* ◇ N UNCOUNT OR N COUNT

category /kætə¹gərɪ⁰/, **categories.** If people or things are divided into **categories**, they are divided into groups in such a way that the members of each group are similar to each other in some way. EG *They divided the nation into six social categories... There are three categories of machine.* N COUNT

cater /keɪtə/, **caters, catering, catered.** To **cater** for a person or group means to provide all the things that they need or want. EG *We can cater for all age groups... ...theatres catering to a white middle-class audience.* V+*for/to*

caterer /keɪtərə/, **caterers.** A **caterer** is a person or a company that provides food and drink for people in a particular place or on a special occasion. EG *...a hotel caterer.* N COUNT

catering /keɪtə⁰rɪŋ/ is the activity or business of providing food and drink for people. EG *'Who did the catering?' - 'A firm in Arundel.'* N UNCOUNT

caterpillar /kætəpɪlə/, **caterpillars.** A **caterpillar** is a small, worm-like animal that feeds on plants and eventually develops into a butterfly or moth. N COUNT

catharsis /kə³θɑːsɪs/ is getting rid of strong emotions or unhappy memories by expressing them in some way. EG *The catharsis of the confession had left her exhausted.* N UNCOUNT Literary

cathedral /kəθiːdrə⁰l/, **cathedrals.** A **cathedral** is a very large and important church which has a bishop in charge of it. EG *...Westminster Cathedral.* N COUNT

cathode-ray tube, cathode-ray tubes. A **cathode-ray tube** is a device used in televisions and computer terminals which sends an image onto the screen. N COUNT Technical

Catholic /kæθə⁰lɪk/, **Catholics.** A **Catholic** is someone who belongs to the branch of the Christian church which accepts the Pope as its leader. EG *She was a devout Catholic... ...the Catholic Church.* N COUNT

Catholicism /kəθɒlɪsɪzə⁰m/ is the set of Christian beliefs that are held by Catholics. N UNCOUNT

cattle /kætə⁰l/ are cows and bulls. EG *...herds of cattle.* N PLURAL

catty /kæti¹/, **cattier, cattiest.** If you say that a woman or girl is being **catty**, you mean she is being unpleasant and spiteful. EG *Miss Haynes was capable of being catty and jealous.* ADJ QUALIT

caucus /kɔːkəs/, **caucuses.** A **caucus** is a group of people within an organization who share similar aims and interests or who have a lot of influence. EG *...the California caucus at the National Convention.* N COUNT: USU+SUPP Formal

caught /kɔːt/ is the past tense and past participle of **catch.**

cauldron /kɔːldrən/, **cauldrons;** spelled **caldron** in American English. A **cauldron** is a very large, round metal pot used for cooking over a fire. EG *...the cauldron in which she prepared the soup.* N COUNT

cauliflower

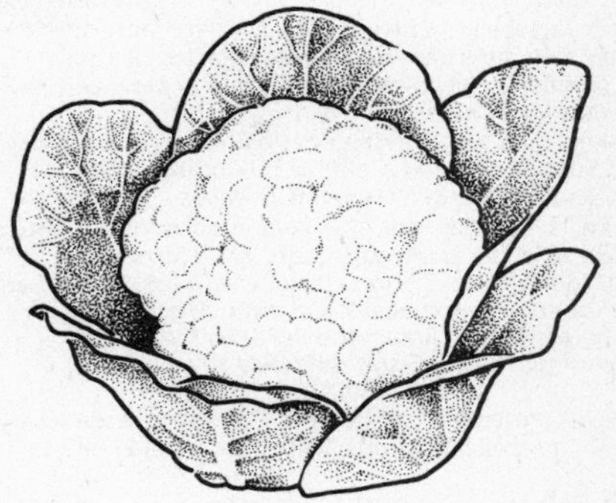

cauliflower /kɒlɪflaʊə/, **cauliflowers.** A **cauliflower** is a vegetable with green leaves around a large white ball of flower buds. N COUNT OR N UNCOUNT

causal /kɔːzə⁰l/ means connected by a relationship of cause and effect. EG *There may be no causal link.* ADJ CLASSIF: ATTRIB

causality /kɔːzælɪ¹ti¹/ is the relationship of cause and effect. EG *...simple models of causality.* N UNCOUNT Formal

causation /kɔːzeɪʃə⁰n/. The **causation** of something is its cause or causes. EG *...a problem, the actual causation of which is unknown.* N UNCOUNT Formal

cause /kɔːz/, **causes, causing, caused. 1** The **cause** of an event is the thing that makes it happen. EG *Nobody knew the cause of the explosion... The argument seems to confuse cause and effect... The men died of natural causes.* N COUNT OR N UNCOUNT: USU+SUPP

2 If you have **cause** for a particular feeling or action, you have good reasons for feeling it or doing it. EG *Years of training gave him every cause for confidence... I have no cause to go back.* N UNCOUNT +*for* OR *to*-INF

3 To **cause** something means to make it happen. EG *...difficulties caused by price increases... What's causing you so much concern?... The sound caused her to step aside.* V+O: OFT+*to*-INF OR V+O+O

4 A **cause** is also an aim or principle which a group of people supports or is fighting for. EG *He is sympathetic to our cause... ...the cause of world peace.* N COUNT: USU+SUPP

causeway /kɔːzweɪ/, **causeways.** A **causeway** is a raised path or road that crosses water or marsh. N COUNT

caustic /kɔːstɪk/. **1 Caustic** chemical substances are very powerful and can dissolve other substances. EG *Do not use a caustic cleaner on enamel.* ADJ CLASSIF

2 A **caustic** remark is extremely critical, cruel, or bitter. EG *...her caustic sense of humour.* ADJ QUALIT: USU ATTRIB

caution /kɔːʃə⁰n/, **cautions, cautioning, cautioned. 1 Caution** is great care which you take in order to avoid possible danger. EG *You must proceed with extreme caution.* N UNCOUNT

2 If someone **cautions** you, they warn you about problems or danger. EG *I cautioned him not to reveal too much to anyone.* ▸ used as a noun. EG *...a word of caution.* V+O OR V+QUOTE ▸ N UNCOUNT

3 When the police **caution** someone who they have arrested, they warn them that anything that they say may be used as evidence in a trial. EG *He cautioned her, and read out the warrant.* V+O

cautionary /kɔːʃənə^{0}ri^{1}/. A **cautionary** story or tale is intended to give a warning to people. ADJ CLASSIF: ATTRIB

cautious /kɔːʃəs/. Someone who is **cautious** acts very carefully in order to avoid possible danger. EG *Her husband is reserved and cautious.* ADJ QUALIT
◇ **cautiously.** EG *We moved cautiously forward.* ◇ ADV

cavalier /kævəlɪə/. Someone who is **cavalier** in their behaviour does not consider other people's feelings or the seriousness of a situation. EG *Farmers were adopting a cavalier attitude to very dangerous substances.* ADJ QUALIT

cavalry /kævəlri^{1}/. The **cavalry** is **1** the part of an army that uses fast armoured vehicles. **2** the group of soldiers in an army who ride horses. EG *...the Household Cavalry.* N SING

cave /keɪv/, **caves, caving, caved.** A **cave** is a large hole in the side of a cliff or hill, or under the ground. EG *The cliffs are riddled with caves.* N COUNT

cave in. 1 When a roof or a ceiling **caves in**, it collapses into the house or room. EG *In order to prevent the sides caving in, it is lined with bricks.* PHRASAL VB: V+ADV **2** If you **cave in**, you suddenly stop arguing or resisting, especially under pressure. EG *I more or less caved in, though I still defended my explanation.* V+ADV

caveman /keɪvmæn/, **cavemen. Cavemen** were people in prehistoric times who lived mainly in caves. N COUNT

cavern /kævə^{0}n/, **caverns.** A **cavern** is a large deep cave. N COUNT

cavernous /kævənəs/. A **cavernous** building is very large inside, so that it reminds you of a cave. EG *The engine noise boomed in the cavernous building.* ADJ CLASSIF

caviar /kævɪɑː, kævɪɑː/; also spelled **caviare. Caviar** is the salted eggs of a fish called the sturgeon. N UNCOUNT

cavity /kævə^{1}ti^{1}/, **cavities.** A **cavity** is **1** a space or hole in something such as a solid object or a person's body. EG *...the nasal cavity.* **2** a hole in a tooth, caused by decay. N COUNT

cavort /kə^{3}vɔːt/, **cavorts, cavorting, cavorted.** When people **cavort**, they leap about in a noisy and excited way. EG *...children cavorting in an adventure playground.* V

cc /siː siː/ is an abbreviation for 'cubic centimetres'. You use 'cc' when referring to the volume or capacity of something. EG *...500cc motorbikes.*

CD /siː diː/, **CDs. CD** is an abbreviation for 'compact disc'. EG *...a CD player.*

cease /siːs/, **ceases, ceasing, ceased. 1** If something **ceases**, it stops happening or existing. EG *Hostilities must cease at once.* V Formal

2 If you **cease** to do something, you stop doing it. EG *Once people retire they automatically cease to be union members... The vicar sighed as he ceased speaking.* V+to-INF OR -ING Formal

3 If you **cease** something that you are producing or providing, you stop producing or providing it. EG *They threatened to cease financial support to the university... Existing units must cease production by 1991.* V+O Formal

ceasefire /siːsfaɪə/, **ceasefires.** A **ceasefire** is an arrangement in which countries that are fighting each other agree to stop fighting. EG *...the cease-fire agreement.* N COUNT

ceaseless /siːslɪ^{2}s/ means happening for a long time without stopping or changing. EG *...his ceaseless rebellion against discipline... ...the ceaseless traffic.* ADJ CLASSIF: ATTRIB Formal ◇ **ceaselessly.** EG *Clarissa was talking ceaselessly.* ◇ ADV

cedar /siːdə/, **cedars.** A **cedar** is a kind of large evergreen tree. EG *...cedar wood.* N COUNT

cede /siːd/, **cedes, ceding, ceded.** If you **cede** something to someone, you let them have it, often as part of an official agreement. EG *The Louisiana colony was ceded to Spain in 1762.* V OR V+O: OFT+to Formal

ceiling /siːlɪŋ/, **ceilings. 1** A **ceiling** is the horizontal surface that forms the top part inside a room. EG *...a large room with a high ceiling.* N COUNT

2 You use **ceiling** to refer to an official upper limit on prices or wages. EG *...a ceiling on business rate increases.* N COUNT: OFT+on

celebrate /sɛlə^{1}breɪt/, **celebrates, celebrating, celebrated. 1** If you **celebrate** or if you **celebrate** something, you do something enjoyable because of a special occasion or to honour someone's success. EG *We ought to celebrate; let's have a bottle of champagne... His victory was celebrated with music and dancing.* V OR V+O ◇ **celebration** /sɛlə^{1}breɪʃə^{0}n/, **celebrations.** EG *We ought to have a little celebration... ...a time of celebration.* ◇ N COUNT OR N UNCOUNT

2 If an organization or country **is celebrating** an anniversary, it has existed for that length of time and is doing something special because of it. EG *The company was celebrating its fiftieth birthday.* V+O
◇ **celebrations.** EG *...its tenth anniversary celebrations.* ◇ N PLURAL

3 When priests **celebrate** Holy Communion or Mass, they officially perform the actions and ceremonies that are involved. V+O

celebrated /sɛlə^{1}breɪtɪ^{2}d/. Someone or something that is **celebrated** is famous. EG *Her mother was a celebrated actress... ...Churchill's celebrated remark.* ADJ QUALIT

celebrity /sə^{1}lɛbrɪ^{1}ti^{1}/, **celebrities.** A **celebrity** is someone who is famous, especially in acting or show business. EG *Lots of celebrities have stayed here.* N COUNT

celery /sɛləri^{1}/ is a vegetable with long pale green stalks. It is often eaten raw in salads. N UNCOUNT

celestial /sɪ^{2}lɛstɪəl/ is used to describe things connected with heaven. EG *They had no hope of admission to the celestial kingdom.* ADJ CLASSIF: ATTRIB Formal

celibate /sɛlɪbə^{1}t/, **celibates.** Someone who is **celibate 1** does not marry or have sex, because of their religious beliefs. EG *The celibate life was beginning to appeal to him.* ADJ CLASSIF Formal ◇ **celibacy** /sɛlə^{1}bəsi^{1}/. EG *We are still required to take vows of poverty and celibacy and obedience.* ◇ N UNCOUNT **2** does not have sex during a particular period of their life. EG *For once I had to spend a celibate night.* ADJ CLASSIF Formal
◇ **celibacy.** EG *A month of enforced celibacy can't be good for anyone.* ◇ N UNCOUNT

cell /sɛl/, **cells. 1** A **cell** is the smallest part of an animal or plant. Every animal or plant is made up of millions of cells. EG *...the cell walls of plants.* N COUNT

2 A **cell** is also **2.1** a small room in which a prisoner is locked. EG *There were four bunks in the cell.* **2.2** a small room in which a monk or nun lives. N COUNT

3 You can refer to a small group of people within a larger organization as a **cell**. EG *...a Trotskyist cell within the Labour organisation.* N COUNT: USU+SUPP

cellar /sɛlə/, **cellars.** A **cellar** is **1** a room in the ground underneath a building, often used for storing things in. **2** a place where wine is stored. EG *He orders wine from the firm's cellars each week.* N COUNT

cello /tʃɛləʊ/, **cellos.** A **cello** is a musical instrument that looks like a large violin. You hold it upright and play it sitting down. N COUNT

cellophane /sɛlə^{6}feɪn/ is a thin, strong, transparent material that is used to wrap things in. EG *...cheese and biscuits wrapped in cellophane.* N UNCOUNT

cellular /sɛljə^{4}lə/. **1 Cellular** means relating to the cells of animals or plants. EG *...basic cellular structures.* ADJ CLASSIF: ATTRIB

2 Cellular blankets, clothes, or fabrics are very loosely woven and keep you very warm. ADJ CLASSIF: ATTRIB

celluloid /sɛljə^{4}lɔɪd/. **1 Celluloid** is a type of plastic. EG *He wore a celluloid collar.* N UNCOUNT

2 You can use **celluloid** to refer to films and the cinema. EG *...the celluloid world of Hollywood.* N UNCOUNT Literary

Find the one word after 'cavort' which does not begin with the sound /s/.

Celsius /sɛlsɪəs/ is a scale for measuring temperature, in which water freezes at 0 degrees and boils at 100 degrees. It is represented by the symbol °C. N UNCOUNT

cement /sɪmɛnt/, **cements, cementing, cemented. 1 Cement** is **1.1** a grey powder which is mixed with sand and water in order to make concrete. EG *...a sack of cement.* **1.2** the same as concrete. EG *...a little cement courtyard.* N UNCOUNT

2 Cement is also a type of glue. EG *...a tube of cement.* N UNCOUNT

3 If you **cement** an area, you cover it with cement. EG *The floor has been cemented over.* V+O

4 To **cement** something to something else means to stick or glue the two things together. EG *The lumps were cemented to the reef with coral... ...a large heap of stones cemented together by lead.* V+O +to/together

5 If you **cement** a relationship, agreement, or position, you make it stronger or more official. EG *We would do the company some good by cementing relationships with business contacts.* V+O

cemetery /sɛməˈtri¹/, **cemeteries.** A **cemetery** is a place where dead people are buried. N COUNT

censor /sɛnsə/, **censors, censoring, censored. 1** If someone **censors** letters or newspaper articles, they officially examine them and cut out any information that is regarded as secret. EG *Believe it or not they censor your letters here.* V+O

2 If someone **censors** a book, play, or film, they officially examine it and cut out any parts that are considered to be immoral. V+O

3 A **censor** is a person who has been officially appointed to examine plays, films, and books and to cut out any parts that are considered to be immoral. EG *A film critic complained that the censor was being too tolerant.* N COUNT

censorious /sɛnsɔːrɪəs/. When someone is **censorious**, they strongly criticize someone else's behaviour. EG *There is no need to be censorious about such activities... She had had to put up with a number of censorious comments.* ADJ QUALIT Formal

censorship /sɛnsəʃɪp/. When there is **censorship**, books, plays, and films are censored because they are considered to be immoral, or letters and newspaper reports are censored because they are thought to reveal important secrets. EG *...the censorship of bad news in wartime.* N UNCOUNT

censure /sɛnʃə/, **censures, censuring, censured.** If you **censure** someone for something that they have done, you tell them that you strongly disapprove of it. EG *He had been censured for showing cowardice in the battle.* ▸ used as a noun. EG *The result exposed him to official censure... Grimes seems to have escaped any severe censure.* V+O Formal ▸ N UNCOUNT

census /sɛnsəs/, **censuses.** A **census** is an official survey of the population of a country that is carried out in order to find out how many people live there and to obtain details of such things as people's ages and occupations. N COUNT

cent /sɛnt/, **cents.** A **cent** is a small unit of money worth one hundredth of the main unit of money in many countries. ● See also **per cent**. N COUNT

centenary /sɛntiːnəⁿri¹/, **centenaries.** A **centenary** is a year in which people celebrate something important that happened exactly one hundred years earlier. EG *1928 was the centenary of Ibsen's birth.* N COUNT

center /sɛntə/. See **centre**.

centigrade /sɛntɪgreɪd/ is a scale for measuring temperature, in which water freezes at 0 degrees and boils at 100 degrees. It is represented by the symbol °C. N UNCOUNT

centimetre /sɛntɪmiːtə/, **centimetres;** spelled **centimeter** in American English. A **centimetre** is a unit of length in the metric system equal to ten millimetres or one-hundredth of a metre. N COUNT

centipede /sɛntɪpiːd/, **centipedes.** A **centipede** is a long, thin insect with a lot of legs. N COUNT

central /sɛntrəl/. **1** Something that is **central** is in the middle of a place or area. EG *The houses are arranged around a central courtyard... ...a film about central Poland.* ◊ **centrally.** EG *The pin is centrally positioned on the circle.* ADJ CLASSIF ◊ ADV

2 A place that is **central** is easy to reach because it is in the centre of a city. ◊ **centrally.** EG *...a centrally located flat.* ADJ QUALIT ◊ ADV

3 A **central** group or organization makes all the important decisions that are followed throughout a larger organization or a country. EG *Their activities are strictly controlled by a central committee... ...local and central government.* ◊ **centrally.** EG *France has a centrally organized system.* ADJ CLASSIF : ATTRIB ◊ ADV

4 The **central** person or thing in a particular situation is the most important one. EG *The central character was played by William Hurt... These statistics were central to the debate.* ADJ CLASSIF : OFT+to

central heating is a heating system for buildings. Air or water is heated in one main tank and travels round a building through pipes and radiators. N UNCOUNT

centralize /sɛntrəlaɪz/, **centralizes, centralizing, centralized;** also spelled **centralise.** To **centralize** a country or state means to create a system of government in which one central group of people gives instructions to regional groups. ◊ **centralized.** EG *We believe in a strong centralized state.* ◊ **centralization** /sɛntrəlaɪzeɪʃəⁿn/. EG *Large-scale technology brings centralization.* V+O : USU PASS ◊ ADJ CLASSIF ◊ N UNCOUNT

centrally heated. A building that is **centrally heated** has central heating. ADJ CLASSIF

centre /sɛntə/, **centres, centring, centred;** spelled **center, centers, centering, centered** in American English. **1** The **centre** of something is the middle of it. EG *He moved the table over to the centre of the room.* ▸ used as an adjective. EG *...a black wig with a centre parting... The centre section was coloured pink.* N COUNT : OFT SING+of ▸ ADJ CLASSIF : ATTRIB

2 A **centre** is a building where people have meetings, get help of some kind, or take part in a particular activity. EG *...a new arts centre... Treatment is available from the university's health centre.* N COUNT : USU+SUPP

3 If an area or town is a **centre** for an industry or activity, that industry or activity is very important there. EG *The region began as a centre for sheep-farming.* N COUNT+SUPP

4 The **centre** of an event or activity is the most important thing involved. EG *The Workers' movement was at the centre of the 1972 strike... Smith was right in the centre of the action.* N COUNT+SUPP

5 If something is the **centre** of attention or interest, people are giving it a lot of attention. EG *The television screen remained the centre of attention.* N COUNT+SUPP

6 In politics, the **centre** refers to political groups and beliefs that are considered to be neither left-wing nor right-wing. ▸ used as an adjective. EG *In addition, there is one relatively small centre party called the Free Democrats.* N SING : the+N ▸ ADJ CLASSIF : ATTRIB

7 Someone or something that is **centred** in a particular place is based there. EG *They were now centred in the new Royal Observatory at Greenwich.* ADJ CLASSIF : OFT+in

centre around or **centre on.** If something **centres around** a person or thing or **centres on** them, that person or thing is the main feature or subject of attention. EG *The workers' demands centred around pay and conditions... Attention was for the moment centred on Michael Simpson.* PHRASAL VB : V-ERG+PREP

century /sɛntʃəri¹/, **centuries.** A **century** is **1** a period of a hundred years that is used when stating a date. For example, the 19th century was the period from 1801 to 1900. EG *...Italian paintings of the fifteenth century.* **2** any period of a hundred years. EG *...a century of progress... ...a book written centuries ago.* N COUNT

ceramic /sɪˈræmɪk/, **ceramics. 1 Ceramic** objects are made of clay that has been heated to a very high temperature. EG *...ceramic tiles.* ADJ CLASSIF : ATTRIB

2 Ceramics are ceramic objects. EG *...Chinese ceramics.* N COUNT: USU PLURAL

cereal /sɪərɪəl/, **cereals.** A **cereal** is **1** a plant such as wheat, maize, or rice that produces grain. EG *...cereal crops.* **2** a food made from grain, usually mixed with milk and eaten for breakfast. EG *...a box of cereal.* N COUNT OR N UNCOUNT

cerebral /sɛrə¹brəl/ means **1** relating to thought or reasoning rather than to emotions. EG *...the cerebral challenge of police work.* **2** relating to the brain. EG *Her father died later of a cerebral hemorrhage.* ADJ QUALIT Formal; ADJ CLASSIF: ATTRIB Technical

ceremonial /sɛrə¹məʊnɪəl/, **ceremonials. 1** Something that is **ceremonial** is used in a ceremony or relates to a ceremony. EG *...a ceremonial robe from Africa... ...ceremonial dances.* ◊ **ceremonially.** EG *The bride is then ceremonially shown to the crowd.* ADJ CLASSIF; ◊ ADV

2 Ceremonial consists of all the impressive things that are done, said, and worn on very formal occasions. EG *...the splendid ceremonial of Whitehall on great occasions... As a child, he loved parades and ceremonials.* N UNCOUNT OR N COUNT: OFT+SUPP

ceremonious /sɛrə¹məʊnɪəs/. You describe behaviour as **ceremonious** when it is excessively polite and formal. EG *He bid her an unusually ceremonious farewell.* ◊ **ceremoniously.** EG *He filled all their glasses ceremoniously.* ADJ QUALIT; ◊ ADV

ceremony /sɛrə¹məni¹/, **ceremonies. 1** A **ceremony** is **1.1** a formal event such as a wedding or a coronation. EG *...a coronation ceremony.* **1.2** an action that is done in a very formal and polite way. EG *The waiter gave them fresh glasses and there was the ceremony of tasting the wine once more.* N COUNT; N COUNT: USU SING

2 Ceremony consists of **2.1** the special things that are said and done on very formal occasions. **2.2** very formal and polite behaviour. EG *At the BBC she was received with respectful ceremony.* N UNCOUNT

3 If you do something **without ceremony**, you do it quickly and in a casual way. EG *He produced the book, without ceremony, from under his bed.* PHRASE

certain /sɜːtə⁰n/. **1** If you are **certain** about something, you have no doubt about it. EG *He felt certain that she would disapprove... I'm absolutely certain of that... We're not quite certain how much there is.* ● If you know something **for certain**, you have no doubt at all about it. EG *It is not known for certain where they are now.* ADJ PRED: USU+REPORT; ● PHRASE

2 If something is **certain** to happen, it will definitely happen. EG *She's certain to be late... It is almost certain that he will be elected... Such a vote would mean the certain defeat of the government.* ADJ CLASSIF: OFT+to-INF

3 Something that is **certain** is known to be true or correct. EG *It was poison, that's certain... ...if you want to get on with something in the certain knowledge that you will not be interrupted.* ADJ CLASSIF

4 When you **make certain** that something happens, you take action to ensure that it happens. EG *We need to make certain that governments adhere to disarmament agreements.* PHRASE

5 You use **certain 5.1** to indicate that you are referring to one particular thing, person, or group, although you are not saying exactly which it is. EG *She arranged to meet him at three o'clock on a certain afternoon... Certain areas in Sussex are better than others for keeping bees.* ▸ used as a pronoun. EG *Certain of our judges have claimed that this is the case.* **5.2** before the name of a person in order to indicate that you do not know them. EG *...a certain Mrs Wendy Smith who worked for a large company in Leeds.* **5.3** to suggest that a quality or condition is noticeable. EG *He wore a tweed overcoat which gave him a certain distinction.* ADJ CLASSIF: ATTRIB; ▸ PRON+of Formal; ADJ CLASSIF: ATTRIB; ADJ CLASSIF: ATTRIB

6 If something is done or achieved **to a certain extent**, it is only partly done or achieved. EG *That takes care of my anxieties to a certain extent.* PHRASE

certainly /sɜːtə⁰nli¹/. **1** You use **certainly** to emphasize what you are saying **1.1** when you are making a statement. EG *If nothing is done there will certainly be an economic crisis... It certainly looks wonderful, doesn't it?* **1.2** when you are agreeing with what someone has said. EG *'Would you agree that it is still a difficult world for women to live in?' – 'Oh certainly.'* **1.3** when you are agreeing with a proposal or suggestion. EG *He asked me if he could use my pen. I said, 'Certainly.'* ADV; ADV SEN OR CONVENTION; CONVENTION OR ADV SEN

2 You say **certainly not** when you want to say 'no' in a strong way. EG *'Had you forgotten?' – 'Certainly not.'* CONVENTION

certainty /sɜːtə⁰nti¹/, **certainties. 1 Certainty** is **1.1** the state of having no doubts at all about something. EG *Answers to such questions would never be known with certainty.* **1.2** the fact of something being certain to happen. EG *...the certainty of death in battle.* N UNCOUNT

2 A **certainty** is something that nobody has any doubts about. EG *It's not a certainty that we'll win.* N COUNT

certificate /sətɪfɪ¹kə¹t/, **certificates.** A **certificate** is **1** an official document stating that particular facts are true. EG *...a medical certificate... ...your birth certificate.* **2** an official document that you receive when you have successfully completed a course of study or training. N COUNT: USU+SUPP; N COUNT

certify /sɜːtɪfaɪ/, **certifies, certifying, certified. 1** To **certify** something means to declare formally that it is true. EG *...a piece of paper certifying the payment of his taxes... ...papers certifying that he was a good friend of the United States.* V+O OR V+REPORT

2 To **certify** someone means **2.1** to give them a certificate stating that they have successfully completed a course of training. EG *The pilots are certified by the navy.* **2.2** to officially declare that they are insane. EG *Her father was certified insane.* V+O OR V+O+C; V+O+C OR V+O+as

cessation /sɛseɪʃə⁰n/. The **cessation** of something is the stopping of it. EG *...a cessation of hostilities.* N UNCOUNT +SUPP Formal

chafe /tʃeɪf/, **chafes, chafing, chafed. 1** When your skin **chafes** or **is chafed** by something, it becomes sore as a result of something rubbing against it. EG *Baby powder helps to avoid chafing.* V OR V-ERG

2 If you **chafe** at something such as a restriction, you feel annoyed about it. EG *He chafed at the delay.* V+at/under Formal

chaff /tʃæf/ consists of the outer parts of grain such as wheat that are removed before the grain is used as food. N UNCOUNT

chagrin /ʃægrɪn/ is a feeling of annoyance or disappointment. EG *Thomas discovered to his great chagrin that he was too late.* N UNCOUNT Formal

chain /tʃeɪn/, **chains, chaining, chained. 1** A **chain** consists of metal rings connected together in a line. EG *She wore a silver chain around her neck... ...a length of chain... ...bicycle chains.* See picture at BICYCLE. N COUNT OR N UNCOUNT

chain

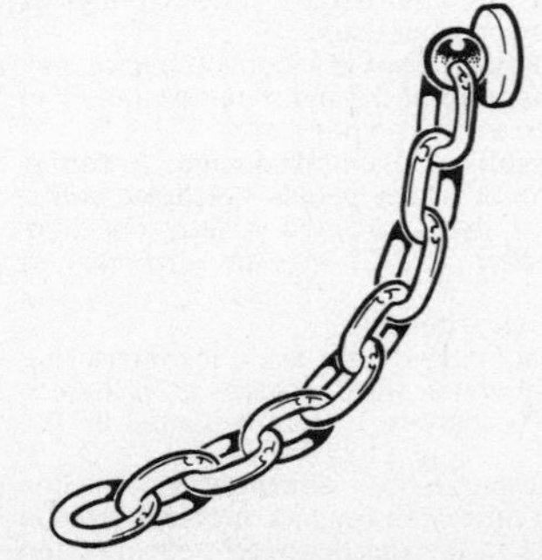

Does a chambermaid clean chambers?

2 When you **chain** a person or thing to something, you fasten them to it using a chain. EG *They chained themselves to the fence.* V+O : USU+A

3 A **chain** of things is a group of them existing or arranged in a line. EG *...the island chains of the Pacific.* N COUNT+SUPP

4 A **chain** of shops or hotels is a number of them owned by the same person or company. EG *...a chain of 970 food stores.* N COUNT+SUPP

5 A **chain** of events is a series of them happening one after another. EG *...the brief chain of events that led up to her death... ...a nuclear chain reaction.* N COUNT+SUPP

chain-smoke, chain-smokes, chain-smoking, chain-smoked. Someone who **chain-smokes** smokes cigarettes or cigars continuously. V OR V+O

chain store, chain stores. A **chain store** is one of several similar shops that are owned by the same person or company. N COUNT

chairs

chair /tʃɛə/, **chairs, chairing, chaired. 1** A **chair** is a piece of furniture for one person to sit on, with a back and four legs. EG *I sat in low chair by the fire, reading.* N COUNT

2 At a university, a **chair** is the post of professor. EG *He was extraordinarily young to get the Chair.* N COUNT

3 If you **chair** a meeting, you are the chairman or chairwoman. EG *The commission was chaired by Professor Lunt.* V+O

chairman /tʃɛəmə³n/, **chairmen. 1** The **chairman** of a meeting or debate is the person in charge, who decides when each person is allowed to speak. N COUNT

2 The **chairman** of a committee, organization, or company is the head of it. EG *...the Chairman of British Rail.* N COUNT

chairmanship /tʃɛəmə³nʃɪp/. Someone's **chairmanship** is the fact that they are chairman, or the period during which they are chairman. EG *...the efforts of the Spartacus League, under the chairmanship of Peter Gowan.* N SING+POSS

chairperson /tʃɛəpɜːsə⁰n/, **chairpersons.** The **chairperson** of a meeting, committee, or organization is the person in charge of it. N COUNT

chairwoman /tʃɛəwʊmən/, **chairwomen.** The **chairwoman** of a meeting, committee, or organization is the woman in charge of it. N COUNT

chalet /ʃæleɪ/, **chalets.** A **chalet** is a small wooden house, especially in a mountain area or a holiday camp. N COUNT

chalk /tʃɔːk/, **chalks, chalking, chalked. 1 Chalk** is a soft white rock. You can use small pieces of it for writing or drawing with. EG *...the chalk uplands of Wiltshire... He took a piece of chalk from his pocket.* N UNCOUNT

2 Chalks are small pieces of chalk used for writing or drawing with. N PLURAL

3 If you **chalk** something, you draw or write it using a piece of chalk. EG *...a young man chalking on the blackboard.* V+O OR V+A

chalk up. If you **chalk up** a success or victory, you achieve it. EG *The company has recently chalked up its most outstanding success.* PHRASAL VB : V+O+ADV

chalky /tʃɔːki¹/, **chalkier, chalkiest.** Something that is **chalky** contains chalk or is covered with chalk. EG *...the white, chalky road.* ADJ QUALIT

challenge /tʃælɪ²ndʒ/, **challenges, challenging, challenged. 1** A **challenge** is **1.1** something new and difficult which requires great effort and determination. EG *...the challenge of the unknown... Mount Everest presented a challenge to Hillary.* N COUNT OR N UNCOUNT

1.2 a suggestion from someone that you should compete or argue with them. EG *Her smile held a tiny hint of a challenge.* N COUNT **1.3** a questioning of the truth or value of something, or of a person's right to do something. EG *...the challenge to authority... There will inevitably be challenges to the existing order.* N COUNT OR N UNCOUNT

2 If you **challenge** someone, **2.1** you invite them to fight or compete with you. EG *They had challenged and beaten the best teams in the world.* **2.2** you question whether they have the right to do something, or whether what they are saying is true. EG *The idea has never been challenged... He challenged the minister to produce evidence.* V+O : OFT+*to*-INF OR *to*

challenger /tʃælɪ²ndʒə/, **challengers.** A **challenger** is someone who competes with you for a position or title that you already have, for example a sports championship. EG *...a challenger to Mitterrand's leadership.* N COUNT

challenging /tʃælɪ²ndʒɪŋ/. **1** A **challenging** task or job requires great effort and determination. EG *Life as a housewife does not seem very challenging to the highly educated girl.* ADJ QUALIT

2 If you do something in a **challenging** way, you seem to be inviting people to argue with you or compete against you in some way. EG *...a suspicious challenging look.* ◊ **challengingly.** EG *He looked challengingly at the Doctor.* ADJ QUALIT ◊ ADV

chamber /tʃeɪmbə/, **chambers. 1** A **chamber** is **1.1** a large room that is used for formal meetings. EG *...the Council Chamber... Labour MPs left the Chamber in protest.* N COUNT **1.2** a room designed and equipped for a particular purpose. EG *...a built-in echo chamber... He led the way to the torture chamber.* N COUNT+SUPP

2 A **Chamber** of Commerce or **Chamber** of Trade is a group of business people who work together to improve business in their town. N COUNT+*of*

3 Chambers are rooms used by judges and barristers. EG *All the barristers in Chambers seemed to be out.* N PLURAL

chambermaid /tʃeɪmbəmeɪd/, **chambermaids.** A **chambermaid** is a woman who cleans and tidies the bedrooms in a hotel. N COUNT

chamber music is classical music written for a small number of instruments. N UNCOUNT

chameleon /kəmiːlɪən/, **chameleons.** A **chameleon** is a lizard whose skin changes colour to match the colour of its surroundings. N COUNT

chamois leather /ʃæmi¹ leðə/, **chamois leathers.** A **chamois leather** or a **chamois** is a soft leather cloth used for cleaning and polishing. N COUNT

champagne /ʃæmpeɪn/ is an expensive French white wine that has lots of bubbles in it. N UNCOUNT

champion /tʃæmpɪən/, **champions, championing, championed. 1** A **champion** is someone who has won the first prize in a competition, contest, or fight. EG *...the school tennis champion.* N COUNT

2 If you are a **champion** of a person, a cause, or a principle, you support or defend them. EG *...a champion of liberty.* N COUNT+SUPP ▸ used as a verb. EG *He went on to champion the rights of accused criminals to have access to their lawyers.* ▸ V+O

championship /tʃæmpɪənʃɪp/, **championships.** A **championship** is **1** a competition to find the best player or team in a particular sport. EG *...the first round of the U.S open golf championship.* N COUNT **2** the title or status of someone who has won a sports championship. EG *...the heavyweight championship of the world.* N COUNT+SUPP

chance /tʃɑːns/, **chances, chancing, chanced. 1** If there is a **chance** of something happening, it is possible. EG *I think we've got a good chance of winning... There's little chance that the situation will improve... What are her chances of getting the job?* N COUNT OR N UNCOUNT +SUPP ● If you say that someone doesn't **stand a chance** of achieving something, you mean that they cannot possible achieve it. ● PHRASE

2 If you have a **chance** to do something, you have the opportunity to do it. EG *He gave me no chance to reply to this.* N COUNT: USU+*to*-INF OR *of*

3 When you take a **chance**, you try to do something although there is a large risk of danger or failure. EG *We may lose a lot of support, but that's a chance we'll have to take.* N COUNT

4 Something that happens by **chance** was not planned by anyone. EG *Almost by chance I found myself talking to him... ...a chance meeting... It was pure chance.* N UNCOUNT

5 You can say **by any chance** when you are asking something politely or when you think the answer to your question will probably be 'no'. EG *You aren't by any chance related to David Howe, are you?* ADV SEN Formal

6 If you **chance** to do something, you do it although you had not planned or tried to do it. EG *I chanced to overhear them.* V+*to*-INF Formal

chandelier /ʃændəˈlɪə/, **chandeliers.** A **chandelier** is a circular frame which holds light bulbs or candles and hangs from the ceiling. N COUNT

change /tʃeɪndʒ/, **changes, changing, changed.**
1 If there is a **change** in something, it becomes different. EG *...a radical change in attitudes... ...the changes that had taken place since he had left China... There had been little change.* N COUNT OR N UNCOUNT

2 If you say that an experience **makes a change**, you mean that it is enjoyable because it is different from what you are used to. EG *Being out in the country made a refreshing change.* PHRASE

3 If you say that something is happening **for a change**, you mean that it is different from what usually happens. EG *They were glad to leave their cars and walk for a change... Its nice to see you with your books for a change.* PHRASE

4 When something **changes** or when you **change** it, it becomes different. EG *Her disdain changed to surprised respect... They can be used to change uranium into plutonium... A bird changes direction by dipping one wing and lifting the other.* V-ERG
◊ **changed.** EG *He returned to parliament a changed man... Their changed status is reflected in their clothes.* ◊ ADJ CLASSIF ◊ **changing.** EG *They are anachronisms in a changing world... ...a report on changing fashions in food.* ◊ ADJ CLASSIF

5 To **change** something also means to replace it with something new or different. EG *I changed the bulb... His doctor advised that he change his job.* V+O

6 If there is a **change** of something, it is replaced. EG *...a change of government... That motorcycle needs a change of oil.* N COUNT+SUPP

7 When you **change** your clothes, you take them off and put on different ones. EG *I want to change my socks... She changed into her street clothes.* V+O, OR V: OFT+*into/out of*

8 A **change** of clothes is an extra set of clothes that you take with you when you go to stay somewhere. N COUNT+*of*

9 When you **change** a baby or **change** its nappy, you take off its dirty nappy and put on a clean one. V+O

10 When you **change** buses or trains, you get off one bus or train and get on to another in order to continue your journey. EG *Don't forget to change at Crewe.* V+O OR V

11 Your **change** is the money that you receive when you pay for something with more money than it costs because you do not have exactly the right amount of money. EG *Morris handed Hooper his change.* N UNCOUNT

12 Change is coins, rather than notes. EG *We only had 80p in change.* N UNCOUNT

13 If you have **change** for a note or a large coin, you have the same amount of money in smaller notes or coins. EG *Have you got change for a fiver?* N UNCOUNT+*for*

14 When you **change** money, you exchange it for the same amount of money in different coins or notes. EG *Can anyone change a ten pound note?... Do you change foreign currency?* V+O

15 to **change hands**: see **hand.** ● to **change** your **mind**: see **mind.**

change over. If you **change over** from one thing to another, you stop being or doing one thing and start being or doing the other. EG *They had been Liberal till several years ago, then they changed over to Conservative.* ● See also **changeover.** PHRASAL VB: V+ADV, OFT+*from/to*

changeable /tʃeɪndʒəbəl/. Someone or something that is **changeable** is likely to change many times. EG *He was as changeable as the weather.* ADJ QUALIT

changeover /tʃeɪndʒəʊvə/, **changeovers.** A **changeover** is a change from one activity or system to another. EG *The changeover had taken place in the Easter vacation.* N COUNT

channel /tʃænəl/, **channels, channelling, channelled;** spelled **channeling** and **channeled** in American English. **1** A **channel** is a wavelength on which television or radio programmes are broadcast. EG *He switched to the other channel.* N COUNT

2 If you say that something has been done through particular **channels**, you are referring to the people who arranged for it to be done. EG *I notified the authorities through the normal channels.* N COUNT: USU+SUPP

3 If you **channel** money or resources into something, you arrange for them to be used for that thing. EG *...the need to channel North Sea oil revenues into industry.* V+O: USU+A

4 A **channel** is also **4.1** a passage along which water flows. EG *...irrigation channels.* **4.2** a route used by boats. EG *The main channels had been closed by enemy submarines.* N COUNT

5 The **Channel** or the **English Channel** is the narrow area of water between England and France. N PROPER: *the*+N

chant /tʃɑːnt/, **chants, chanting, chanted. 1** A **chant** is **1.1** a word or group of words that is repeated over and over again. EG *The assembly broke into a chant: 'What's your name? What's your name?'* **1.2** a religious song or prayer that is sung on only a few notes. N COUNT

2 If you **chant** or if you **chant** something, **2.1** you repeat the same words over and over again. EG *They marched to their coach chanting slogans... She chanted, 'Johnny never hurt me, Johnny never hurt me.'* V, V+O, OR V+QUOTE **2.2** you sing a religious song or prayer. V+O OR V

chaos /keɪɒs/ is a state of complete disorder and confusion. EG *Chaos began to develop on the roads... ...economic chaos.* N UNCOUNT

If you do something that is out of character, is it characteristic of you?

chaotic /keɪɒtɪk/. Something that is **chaotic** is in a state of complete disorder and confusion. EG *...a chaotic jumble of motor vehicles.* ADJ QUALIT

chap /tʃæp/, **chaps.** You can use **chap** to refer to a man or boy. EG *The chap she danced with was a very good friend of mine.* N COUNT Informal

chapel /tʃæpə^{0}l/, **chapels.** A **chapel** is **1** a part of a church which has its own altar and which is used for private prayer. **2** a small church attached to a school, hospital, or prison. **3** a building used for worship by members of some Protestant churches. EG *...a Methodist chapel.* N COUNT

chaperone /ʃæpərəʊn/, **chaperones, chaperoning, chaperoned;** also spelled **chaperon. 1** **Chaperones** were women who used to accompany young unmarried women on social occasions, especially when men were present. N COUNT

2 If you **chaperone** young people, you accompany them, to make sure that they are safe and that they behave properly. EG *We went to France with one of the mistresses to chaperone us.* V+O

chaplain /tʃæplɪn/, **chaplains.** A **chaplain** is a member of the Christian clergy who does religious work in a hospital, school, or prison. EG *...a hospital chaplain.* N COUNT

chapped /tʃæpt/. If your skin is **chapped**, it is dry, cracked, and sore. EG *His lips were all chapped and rough.* ADJ QUALIT

chapter /tʃæptə/, **chapters. 1** A **chapter** is one of the parts that a book is divided into. EG *I'd nearly finished chapter 8.* N COUNT OR N+NUMBER

2 You can refer to a part of your life or a period in history as a **chapter** when it begins or ends with a major event. EG *A new chapter of my career as a journalist was about to commence.* N COUNT+SUPP Literary

character /kærə^{3}ktə/, **characters. 1** The **character** of a person or place consists of all the qualities they have that make them distinct from other people or places. EG *There was another side to his character... ...the character of New York.* N COUNT : USU+POSS

2 If you say that what someone does is **in character**, you mean that it is what you would expect them to do, knowing what kind of person they are. If what they do is **out of character**, it is not what you would expect them to do. EG *It's quite in character for Carey to use a word like that... Her reading glasses had bright green frames, which seemed out of character.* PHRASE

3 If something has a particular **character**, it has a particular quality. EG *We need to emphasize the radical character of our demands... Concessions are not always purely negative in character.* N UNCOUNT : USU+SUPP

4 The **characters** in a film, book, or play are the people that it is about. EG *...the tensions that develop between the two main characters.* N COUNT

5 You use **character** to say what kind of person someone is. EG *He's a strange character, Evans... Another colourful character regularly in the bar was the local plumber.* N COUNT : OFT ADJ+N Informal

6 If you say that someone is a **character**, you mean that they are interesting, unusual, or amusing. EG *She was a real character.* N COUNT : OFT ADJ+N Informal

7 A **character** is also a letter, number, or other symbol that is written or printed. N COUNT Technical

characteristic /kærə^{3}ktərɪstɪk/, **characteristics. 1** A **characteristic** is a quality or feature that is typical of someone or something and that makes that person or thing easy to recognize. EG *Ambition is a characteristic of all successful businessmen.* N COUNT : OFT+SUPP

2 Something that is **characteristic** of someone or something is typical of that person or thing. EG *...those large brick tiles so characteristic of East Anglia.* ◇ **characteristically.** EG *He proposed a characteristically brilliant solution.* ADJ QUALIT : OFT+*of* ◇ ADV

characterize /kærə^{3}ktəraɪz/, **characterizes, characterizing, characterized;** also spelled **characterise. 1** If something **characterizes** a period of history or a place, it is very typical of it. EG *...the incessant demand for change that characterizes our time.* V+O

2 If you **characterize** someone or something, you describe them by saying what their characteristics are. EG *The revolutionaries characterize the seventies as an era of attack... How would you characterize a shanty town from that picture?* V+O : OFT+*as*

charade /ʃərɑːd/, **charades.** A **charade** is a pretence which is so obvious that nobody is deceived by it. EG *...a charade of negotiations with the government.* N COUNT

charcoal /tʃɑːkəʊl/ is a black substance obtained by burning wood without much air. It can be burned as a fuel, and small sticks of it are used for drawing with. EG *...glowing charcoal fires... ...a charcoal drawing.* N UNCOUNT

charge /tʃɑːdʒ/, **charges, charging, charged. 1** If you **charge** someone an amount of money, you ask them to pay that amount for something that you have sold to them or done for them. EG *'How much do you charge?' – '£6 a night.'... You can be sure he's going to charge you something for the service.* V+O+O OR V+O : OFT+A

2 If you **charge** goods or services to a person or organization, you tell the people providing the goods or services to send the bill to that person or organization. V+O+*to*

3 A **charge** is the price that you have to pay for a service or for something you buy. EG *...increases in postal and telephone charges... No charge is made for repairs.* ● If something is **free of charge**, it does not cost anything. EG *They're happy to give their services free of charge.* N COUNT ● PHRASE

4 A **charge** is also a formal accusation that someone has committed a crime. EG *The police arrested her on a charge of conspiracy to murder... ...a murder charge.* N COUNT

5 When the police **charge** someone, they formally accuse them of having done something illegal. EG *He was arrested and charged with a variety of offences.* V+O : OFT+*with*

6 If you have **charge** of something or someone, you have responsibility for them and control over them. EG *She intended to take charge of the boy herself.* ● If you are **in charge** of something or someone, you have responsibility for them and control over them. EG *You had left me in charge, John... He was minister in charge of government business.* N UNCOUNT +SUPP ● PHRASE

7 If you **charge** towards someone or something, you move quickly and aggressively towards them. EG *Hendricks charged into the station house.* V : USU+A

8 When you **charge** a battery, you pass an electrical current through it in order to make it more powerful or to make it last longer. V+O

charged /tʃɑːdʒd/ means filled with emotion and therefore very tense or excited. EG *...a highly charged silence... His voice was charged with suppressed merriment.* ADJ QUALIT : OFT+*with*

chariot /tʃærɪət/, **chariots. Chariots** were fast-moving vehicles with two wheels that were pulled by horses in ancient times. N COUNT

charisma /kərɪzmə/. You say that someone has **charisma** when they can attract, influence, and inspire people by their personal qualities. N UNCOUNT
◇ **charismatic** /kærɪzmætɪk/. EG *...a charismatic politician.* ◇ ADJ CLASSIF

charitable /tʃærɪtəbə^{0}l/. **1** Someone who is **charitable** is kind or tolerant towards other people. EG *She was being unusually charitable to me... ...a charitable remark.* ◇ **charitably.** EG *He charitably chose to ignore her impertinence.* ADJ QUALIT ◇ ADV

2 A **charitable** organization or activity helps and supports people who are ill, handicapped, or very poor. EG *...charitable donations.* ADJ CLASSIF : ATTRIB

charity /tʃærɪ^{1}ti^1/, **charities. 1** A **charity** is an organization which raises money in order to help people who are ill, handicapped, or very poor. EG *The proceeds will go to local charities.* N COUNT

2 Charity is **2.1** a kind, helpful and generous attitude towards other people. EG *She found the charity in her heart to forgive them.* **2.2** money or gifts which are given to poor people. EG *He's far too proud to accept charity.* N UNCOUNT Formal

charlatan /ʃɑːlətəⁿn/, **charlatans.** A **charlatan** is someone who pretends to have skills or knowledge that he or she does not really possess. EG *The doctor was either a charlatan or a shrewd old rogue.* N COUNT Formal

charm /tʃɑːm/, **charms, charming, charmed. 1 Charm** is the quality of being attractive and pleasant. EG *He bowed with infinite grace and charm... ...the charms of the exotic.* N UNCOUNT OR N COUNT

2 If you **charm** someone, you please them by being charming. EG *I was charmed by his courtesy.* V+O

3 A **charm** is **3.1** a small ornament that is fixed to a bracelet or necklace. **3.2** an act, saying, or object that is believed to have magic powers. N COUNT

charmer /tʃɑːmə/, **charmers.** You refer to someone as a **charmer** when they behave in a very charming but rather insincere way. EG *They're both tremendous charmers in their different ways.* N COUNT

charming /tʃɑːmɪŋ/. If someone or something is **charming**, they are very pleasant and attractive. EG *Celia is a charming girl.* ◇ **charmingly.** EG *The house has a charmingly medieval atmosphere.* ADJ QUALIT ◇ ADV

charred /tʃɑːd/. Something that is **charred** is partly burnt and made black by fire. ADJ QUALIT

chart /tʃɑːt/, **charts, charting, charted. 1** A **chart** is **1.1** a diagram, picture, or graph which makes information easy to understand. EG *...large charts illustrating world poverty.* **1.2** a map of the sea or stars. N COUNT

2 The **charts** are the official lists that show which pop records have sold the most copies each week. N PLURAL: *the*+N

3 If you **chart** something, you observe it and record it carefully. EG *We charted their movements.* V+O

charter /tʃɑːtə/, **charters, chartering, chartered. 1** A **charter** is a formal document describing the rights, aims, or principles of an organization or group of people. EG *...the Working Women's Charter... It contravened article 51 of the UN charter.* N COUNT: USU+SUPP Formal

2 A **charter** plane or boat is hired for use by a particular person or group. EG *He is travelling on a charter flight.* ADJ CLASSIF: ATTRIB

3 If you **charter** a plane, boat, or other vehicle, you hire it for your private use. EG *We plan to charter a special train for London.* V+O

chartered /tʃɑːtəd/ is used to describe people who have formally qualified in their profession. EG *...a chartered accountant... ...the Royal Institute of Chartered Surveyors.* ADJ CLASSIF: ATTRIB

chase /tʃeɪs/, **chases, chasing, chased. 1** If you **chase** someone, you run after them or follow them quickly in order to catch them. EG *Youngsters chase one another up trees... A dozen soldiers chased after the car.* ▸ used as a noun. EG *They abandoned the chase and returned home.* V+O OR V+*after* ▸ N COUNT

2 If you **chase** someone from a place, you force them to leave by using threats or violence. EG *They were chased from the village.* V+O+A

3 If you **chase** something such as work or money, you spend a lot of time and effort trying to get it. EG *We are getting more and more applicants chasing fewer and fewer jobs... Joe was away in Bombay, chasing after some film job.* V+O OR V+*after*

chasm /kæzəⁿm/, **chasms. 1** A **chasm** is a very deep crack in rock, earth, or ice. N COUNT

2 If you say that there is a **chasm** between two things or between two groups of people, you mean that there is a very large difference between them. EG *...the chasm between rich and poor... She became increasingly aware of the chasm between men and women that rigid sex roles create.* N COUNT: OFT +*between*

chaste /tʃeɪst/. Someone who is **chaste** does not have sex with anyone, or only has sex with their husband or wife; used showing approval. ◇ **chastity** /tʃæstɪ¹ti¹/. EG *A monk makes vows of poverty, chastity and obedience.* ADJ CLASSIF Outdated ◇ N UNCOUNT

chasten /tʃeɪsəⁿn/, **chastens, chastening, chastened.** If you **are chastened** by something, it makes you regret that you have behaved badly or foolishly. EG *I left the cafe secretly chastened.* V+O: USU PASS Formal

chastise /tʃæstaɪz/, **chastises, chastising, chastised.** If you **chastise** someone, **1** you scold them. EG *He chastised members at the Conference for not taking things seriously enough.* **2** you punish them by beating them. EG *Dr O'Shea chastised his son with the end of his belt.* V+O Formal Outdated

chat /tʃæt/, **chats, chatting, chatted.** When people **chat**, they talk in an informal and friendly way. EG *We sat by the fire and chatted all evening... She chatted amiably enough about the children.* ▸ used as a noun. EG *We had a nice long chat about our schooldays... The chat goes on all day and night... ...popular subjects for lunchtime chat.* V: OFT+A ▸ N COUNT OR N UNCOUNT

chat up. If a man **chats** a woman **up**, he talks to her in a friendly way because he is attracted to her. EG *Hughie queued up for coffee and chatted up the women serving it.* PHRASAL VB: V+O+ADV Informal British

château /ʃætəʊ/, **châteaux.** A **château** is a large country house or castle in France. N COUNT

chatter /tʃætə/, **chatters, chattering, chattered. 1** If you **chatter**, you talk quickly and continuously, usually about things which are not important. EG *Off we set, with Bill chattering away all the time.* ▸ used as a noun. EG *At teatime there was much excited chatter.* V: OFT+A ▸ N UNCOUNT

2 When birds and small animals **chatter**, they make a series of short, quick, high-pitched noises. EG *The monkeys chattered high up in the trees.* ▸ used as a noun. EG *The wood was noisy with the song of birds and the chatter of squirrels.* V ▸ N UNCOUNT +SUPP

3 You say that objects **chatter** when they make repeated rattling or clicking sounds. EG *His teeth chattered uncontrollably because of the cold.* ▸ used as a noun. EG *...the chatter of the typewriters... From the floor below came the continuous whirr and chatter of machinery.* V: OFT+A ▸ N UNCOUNT +SUPP

chatterbox /tʃætəbɒks/, **chatterboxes.** A **chatterbox** is someone who talks a lot. N COUNT Informal

chatty /tʃæti¹/, **chattier, chattiest.** Someone who is **chatty** talks a lot in a friendly, informal way. EG *The taxi driver was chatty and merry... ...a nice chatty letter.* ADJ QUALIT

chauffeur /ʃəʊfə, ʃəʊfɜː/, **chauffeurs, chauffeuring, chauffeured. 1** The **chauffeur** of a rich or important person is someone who is employed to look after their car and drive them around in it. N COUNT

2 If you **chauffeur** someone somewhere, you drive them there in a car, usually as part of your job. EG *You can't expect him to chauffeur you everywhere... ...chauffeured limousines.* V+O

chauvinism /ʃəʊvɪnɪzəⁿm/ is a strong and unreasonable belief that your own country is more important and morally better than other people's. ◇ **chauvinist.** EG *...chauvinist pride.* ● See also **male chauvinism.** N UNCOUNT ◇ N COUNT OR N MOD

chauvinistic /ʃəʊvɪnɪstɪk/. Someone who is **chauvinistic** believes that their own country is more important and morally better than other people's; used showing disapproval. EG *...chauvinistic nationalism and ethnic prejudice.* ADJ QUALIT

cheap /tʃiːp/, **cheaper, cheapest. 1** When goods or services are **cheap**, they cost less money than usual. EG *...cheap plastic buckets... A solid fuel cooker is cheap to run.* ◇ **cheaply.** EG *He decorated my home cheaply and efficiently.* ADJ QUALIT ◇ ADV

2 If you do or buy something **on the cheap**, you spend less money on it than you should; used PHRASE Informal

How many ways can you pronounce 'ch' in English?

showing disapproval. EG *...a clever way of running a college on the cheap.*

3 You describe a person's behaviour or remarks as **cheap** when they say unkind things about someone in an unnecessary way. EG *He could not resist making cheap jokes at their expense.* ADJ QUALIT

cheat /tʃiːt/, **cheats, cheating, cheated. 1** When someone **cheats**, they lie or behave dishonestly in order to get or achieve something. EG *We all used to cheat in exams.* ◇ **cheating.** EG *...accusations of cheating.* V; ◇ N UNCOUNT

2 If someone **cheats** you out of something, they get it from you by behaving dishonestly. EG *His father was cheated of his land... She cheated her sister out of some money.* V+O : OFT *+of/out of*

3 If you **feel cheated**, you feel that you have been treated wrongly or unfairly. EG *He will compare your life-style with his own and feel cheated.* PHRASE

4 If you call someone a **cheat**, you mean that they behave dishonestly in order to get what they want. N COUNT

check /tʃɛk/, **checks, checking, checked. 1** If you **check** something, you make sure that it is satisfactory, safe, or correct. EG *Did you check the engine?... Tony came in from time to time, to check on my progress... He needed a chance to check with Hooper to see if his theory was plausible... He checked that both rear doors were safely shut... Check when the bill will have to be paid.* V+O, V+*on/with*, OR V+REPORT

▸ used as a noun. EG *Checks on cars and televisions are thorough... ...security checks.* ▸ N COUNT : OFT+*on*

2 To **check** something also means to stop it from continuing or spreading. EG *The destruction of the bridge checked the enemy's advance.* V+O

3 If you **check** yourself or if something **checks** you, you suddenly stop what you are doing or saying. EG *He began to saunter off, then checked himself and turned back... Sudhir held up his hand to check him.* V-REFL OR V+O

4 If you keep something or someone **in check**, you keep them under control. EG *He had not conquered inflation but he had held it in check.* PHRASE

5 In a restaurant, your **check** is your bill. EG *The waiter brought him his check.* N COUNT American

6 Check is a pattern consisting of squares, usually of two colours. EG *...the simplest of stripes and checks.* ▸ used as an adjective. EG *...a tall fair-haired man in a check suit.* N UNCOUNT OR N COUNT; ▸ ADJ CLASSIF

7 See also **cheque**.

check in or **check into. 1** When you **check** into a hotel or **check in**, you fill in the necessary forms before staying there. EG *He checked into a small boarding house... I checked in at the Gordon Hotel.* PHRASAL VB : V+ADV OR V+PREP

2 When you **check in** at an airport, you arrive and show your ticket before going on a flight. EG *He had already checked in for his return flight when the news reached him.* ● See also **check-in**. V+ADV

check out. 1 When you **check out** of the hotel where you have been staying, you pay the bill and leave. EG *The following morning he checked out of the hotel... Mr Leonard checked out this afternoon, Miss.* PHRASAL VB : V+ADV, OFT+*of* **2** If you **check** something **out**, you find out about it or examine it. EG *It might be difficult to transfer your money, so check it out with the manager.* V+O+ADV **3** See also **checkout**.

check up. If you **check up** on someone or something, you obtain information about them, often secretly. EG *He had been asked to check up on a woman suspected of drug smuggling.* ● See also **check-up**. PHRASAL VB : V+ADV, OFT+*on*

checkered /tʃɛkəd/. See **chequered**.

check-in. At an airport, a **check-in** counter or desk is a place where you check in. ADJ CLASSIF

checkmate /tʃɛkmeɪt/. In chess, **checkmate** is a situation in which you cannot stop your king being captured and so you lose the game. N UNCOUNT

checkout /tʃɛkaʊt/, **checkouts.** In a supermarket, a **checkout** is a counter where you pay for the things that you have bought. N COUNT

checkpoint /tʃɛkpɔɪnt/, **checkpoints.** A **checkpoint** is **1** a place where traffic has to stop in order to be checked. **2** one of the items in a list of things that you can check, in order to make sure that you have done something correctly or completely. N COUNT

check-up, check-ups. A **check-up** is an examination by a doctor to see if your health is all right. N COUNT Informal

cheek /tʃiːk/, **cheeks, cheeking, cheeked. 1** Your **cheeks** are the sides of your face below your eyes. See picture at THE HUMAN BODY. EG *She kissed him on both cheeks.* N COUNT

2 You say that someone has **cheek** when you are annoyed about something unreasonable that they have done. EG *You've got a cheek, coming in here.* N UNCOUNT Informal

3 If you **cheek** someone, you are rude or disrespectful to them. EG *Charlie cheeked his dad today.* V+O Informal

cheekbone /tʃiːkbəʊn/, **cheekbones.** Your **cheekbones** are the two bones in your face just below your eyes. N COUNT

cheeky /tʃiːki¹/, **cheekier, cheekiest.** If someone is **cheeky**, they behave in a rude or disrespectful way. EG *They're such cheeky boys.* ADJ QUALIT

cheer /tʃɪə/, **cheers, cheering, cheered. 1** When you **cheer**, you make a loud noise with your voice to show your approval of something or to encourage someone who is taking part in a game. EG *The home crowd cheered their team enthusiastically... His speech was cheered.* ▸ used as a noun. EG *I heard a great cheer go up.* V OR V+O; ▸ N COUNT

2 If you **are cheered** by something, it makes you happier or less worried. EG *We were cheered by her warmth and affection.* ◇ **cheering.** EG *It was very cheering to have her here.* V+O : USU PASS; ◇ ADJ QUALIT

3 People say **'Cheers'** just before they drink an alcoholic drink. CONVENTION

cheer on. If you **cheer** someone **on**, you cheer loudly in order to encourage them. EG *Students stood on the roof, cheering the rioters on.* PHRASAL VB : V+O+ADV

cheer up. When you **cheer up** or when something **cheers** you **up**, you stop feeling depressed and become more cheerful. EG *She cheered up a little... Her friends tried to cheer her up.* PHRASAL VB : V-ERG+ADV

cheerful /tʃɪəful/. **1** Someone who is **cheerful** is happy and joyful and shows this in their behaviour. EG *She remained cheerful throughout the trip.* ◇ **cheerfully.** EG *He smiled cheerfully at everybody.* ◇ **cheerfulness.** EG *They worked with great energy and cheerfulness.* ADJ QUALIT; ◇ ADV; ◇ N UNCOUNT

2 Something that is **cheerful** is pleasant and makes you feel happy. EG *...literature of a more cheerful nature.* ADJ QUALIT

3 You describe someone's attitude as **cheerful** when they are not worried about something, and you think that they should be worried. EG *...the cheerful conviction that no one will ever start a nuclear war.* ◇ **cheerfully.** EG *They live on irreplaceable capital, which they cheerfully treat as income.* ADJ QUALIT : ATTRIB; ◇ ADV

cheerio /tʃɪəriəʊ/ is an informal way of saying 'goodbye'. CONVENTION

cheerless /tʃɪəlɪ²s/. Something that is **cheerless** is gloomy and depressing. EG *It was a cold, cheerless sort of morning.* ADJ QUALIT

cheery /tʃɪəri¹/, **cheerier, cheeriest.** If someone is **cheery**, they are cheerful and happy. EG *Mr Phillips was a cheery man... I wrote cheery letters home.* ◇ **cheerily.** EG *'Hello!' I shouted cheerily.* ADJ QUALIT Outdated; ◇ ADV

cheese /tʃiːz/, **cheeses. Cheese** is a solid food made from milk. It is usually white or yellow. EG *You can't live on bread and cheese... I made a nice cheese omelette.* N MASS

cheesecake /tʃiːzkeɪk/, **cheesecakes. Cheesecake** is a dessert that consists of biscuit covered with a soft mixture containing cream cheese. EG *Have some more cheesecake... ...a delicious creamy cheesecake.* N UNCOUNT OR N COUNT

cheetah /tʃiːtə/, **cheetahs.** A **cheetah** is a wild animal that looks like a large cat with black spots on its body. Cheetahs can run very fast. N COUNT

chef /ʃɛf/, **chefs.** A **chef** is a cook in a restaurant or hotel. N COUNT

chemical /kɛmɪkəºl/, **chemicals. 1 Chemical** means concerned with chemistry or made by a process in chemistry. EG *...the chemical composition of the atmosphere... ...chemical fertilizers.* ADJ CLASSIF : ATTRIB

◊ **chemically.** EG *Chemically, this substance is similar to cellulose.* ◊ ADV OR ADV SEN

2 A **chemical** is a substance that is used in a chemical process or made by a chemical process. N COUNT

chemist /kɛmɪst/, **chemists. 1** A **chemist** or a **chemist's** is a shop where you can buy medicine, cosmetics, and some household goods. EG *I found her buying bottles of vitamin tablets at the chemist's.* N SING British

2 In Britain, a **chemist** is someone who is qualified to sell medicines prescribed by a doctor. N COUNT British

3 A **chemist** is also a scientist who does research in chemistry. N COUNT

chemistry /kɛmɪstri¹/. **1 Chemistry** is the scientific study of the characteristics and composition of substances and of the way that they react with other substances. EG *She did a degree in chemistry... ...a new chemistry lab.* N UNCOUNT

2 If you talk about the **chemistry** of a substance, you are referring to its characteristics and composition and the way that it reacts with other substances. N UNCOUNT+*of*

cheque /tʃɛk/, **cheques;** spelled **check** in American English. A **cheque** is a printed piece of paper that you can use instead of money. You write on it the name of the person you are paying and the amount of money that you are paying them, and then you sign it. N COUNT ● If you **pay by cheque**, you give someone a cheque to pay for something, rather than giving them cash. ● PHRASE

chequebook /tʃɛkbʊk/, **chequebooks;** spelled **checkbook** in American English. A **chequebook** is a book of cheques. N COUNT

chequered /tʃɛkəd/; spelled **checkered** in American English. If a person or organization has had a **chequered** career or history, they have had a varied past with both good and bad parts. EG *The Journal was a paper with a chequered history.* ADJ QUALIT : ATTRIB

cherish /tʃɛrɪʃ/, **cherishes, cherishing, cherished. 1** If you **cherish** something such as a hope or a memory, you keep it in your mind so that it gives you happy feelings. EG *I cherish a hope that one day we will be reunited.* V+O ◊ **cherished.** EG *...cherished memories.* ◊ ADJ QUALIT

2 If you **cherish** someone, you care for them lovingly and tenderly. EG *Comfort and cherish those you love.* V+O

3 If you **cherish** a right or a privilege, you regard it as important and try hard to keep it. EG *Can he preserve the values he cherishes in his own culture?* V+O ◊ **cherished.** EG *One of our cherished privileges is the right of free speech.* ◊ ADJ QUALIT

cherry /tʃɛri¹/, **cherries. 1 Cherries** are small, round fruit with red or black skins. N COUNT

2 A **cherry** or a **cherry tree** is a tree that cherries grow on. EG *...a cherry orchard.* N COUNT

chess /tʃɛs/ is a game for two people, played on a chessboard. Each player has 16 pieces, including a king. The aim is to move your pieces so that your opponent's king cannot escape being taken. N UNCOUNT

chessboard /tʃɛsbɔːd/, **chessboards.** A **chessboard** is a square board that you play chess on. It is divided into 64 black and white squares. N COUNT

chest /tʃɛst/, **chests. 1** Your **chest** is the top part of the front of your body, where your ribs, lungs, and heart are. See picture at THE HUMAN BODY. EG *He folded his arms on his chest... She has severe pains in her chest.* N COUNT

2 A **chest** is a large, heavy box used for storing things. EG *...an oak chest... ...a medicine chest stuffed with drugs.* N COUNT

3 If you **get** something **off** your **chest**, you say what you have been worrying about. PHRASE Informal

chestnut /tʃɛsnʌt/, **chestnuts. 1** A **chestnut** is a type of reddish-brown nut. N COUNT

2 A **chestnut** or a **chestnut tree** is a tree on which chestnuts grow. N COUNT

3 Something that is **chestnut** or **chestnut-brown** is dark reddish-brown in colour. EG *He was riding a chestnut mare.* ADJ COLOUR

chest of drawers, chests of drawers. A **chest of drawers** is a piece of furniture with drawers. N COUNT

chew /tʃuː/, **chews, chewing, chewed. 1** When you **chew** food, you use your teeth to break it up in your mouth, so that it becomes easier to swallow. EG *He had started to chew a piece of meat... He broke off another piece of bread and chewed at it.* V+O; ALSO V : OFT+*at*

2 If you **chew** your fingernails, you keep biting them because you are nervous. EG *He sat and chewed his fingernails.* V+O; ALSO V : OFT+*at*

3 If an animal **chews** a hole in something, it makes a hole in it by biting it with its teeth. V+O+A OR V+A

4 If you **chew** on or **chew** over a problem, you think carefully about it. EG *He chewed on this new complication... We chew over problems and work out possible solutions.* V+*on/over* Informal

5 If you say that someone **has bitten off more than** they **can chew**, you mean that they are trying to do something which is too difficult for them. PHRASE Informal

chewing gum is a kind of sweet which you chew for a long time but do not swallow. N UNCOUNT

chic /ʃiːk, ʃɪk/. Something or someone that is **chic** is fashionable and sophisticated. EG *...a very chic Art College.* ADJ QUALIT ▸ used as a noun. EG *Vermont and New Hampshire have acquired a rural chic.* ▸ N UNCOUNT

chick /tʃɪk/, **chicks.** A **chick** is a baby bird. N COUNT

chicken /tʃɪkɪn/, **chickens, chickening, chickened. 1 Chickens** are birds which are kept on a farm for their eggs and for their meat. N COUNT

2 Chicken is the meat of a chicken. EG *There was fried chicken for dinner.* N UNCOUNT

3 If you describe a situation as **a chicken and egg situation**, you mean that it is impossible to decide which of two things caused the other one. PHRASE Informal

4 You call someone a **chicken** when they are afraid to do something. EG *I was too much of a chicken to fight.* N COUNT Informal

chicken out. If you **chicken out** of something, you decide not to do it because you are afraid. EG *I chickened out at the last moment.* PHRASAL VB : V+ADV Informal

chickenpox /tʃɪkɪnpɒks/ is a disease which gives you a high temperature and red spots that itch. N UNCOUNT

chicory /tʃɪkəri¹/ is a vegetable with crunchy, sharp-tasting leaves. N UNCOUNT

chide /tʃaɪd/, **chides, chiding, chided.** If you **chide** someone, you scold them. EG *Maurice chided him for his carelessness... 'Fusspot,' chided Clarissa.* V+O : OFT+*f*[or] OR V+QUOTE Outdated

chief /tʃiːf/, **chiefs. 1** The **chief** of an organization is the person who is in charge of it. EG *...the current CIA chief... ...the chief of the Presidential Security Corps.* N COUNT

2 The **chief** of a tribe is its leader. EG *He was the last of the Apache chiefs.* N COUNT

3 Chief is used to describe the most important worker of a particular kind in an organization. EG *Mr Zuckermann summoned his chief cashier.* ADJ CLASSIF : ATTRIB

4 The **chief** cause, part, or member of something is the most important one. EG *The 1902 Education Act was the chief cause of the Progressives' downfall... I was his chief opponent.* ADJ CLASSIF : ATTRIB

chiefly /tʃiːfli¹/. **1** You use **chiefly** to indicate the most important cause or feature of something. EG *The experiment was not a success, chiefly because the machine tools were of poor quality... They were chiefly interested in making money.* ADV OR ADV SEN

2 If something is done **chiefly** in a particular way ADV

In what way are 'chilli' and 'chilly' opposite in meaning?

or place, it is done mainly in that way or place. EG *They lived chiefly by hunting... The film was made in Scotland, chiefly in Glasgow.*

chieftain /tʃiːftəˈn/, **chieftains.** A **chieftain** is the leader of a tribe. N COUNT

chiffon /ʃɪfɒn, ʃɪfɒn/ is a kind of very thin silk or nylon cloth that you can see through. EG *...a green chiffon scarf.* N UNCOUNT

chilblain /tʃɪlbleɪn/, **chilblains. Chilblains are** painful red swellings which people get on their fingers or toes in cold weather. N COUNT

child /tʃaɪld/, **children** /tʃɪldrən/. **1** A **child** is a human being who is not yet an adult. EG *...a child of fourteen... ...a family with young children.* N COUNT

2 Someone's **children** are their sons and daughters of any age. EG *He has a wife and four children... Their children are all married.* N PLURAL

childbearing /tʃaɪldbɛərɪŋ/ is the process of giving birth to babies. EG *...muscles strained in childbearing... ...women of childbearing age.* N UNCOUNT

childbirth /tʃaɪldbɜːθ/ is the act of giving birth to a child. EG *His mother died in childbirth.* N UNCOUNT

childhood /tʃaɪldhʊd/. A person's **childhood** is the time when they are a child. EG *Her early childhood had been very happy... ...childhood games.* N UNCOUNT

childish /tʃaɪldɪʃ/. You describe someone as **childish** when you think that they behave in a silly and immature way. EG *I thought her nice but rather childish.* ◊ **childishly.** EG *'It's too hot here,' he complained childishly.* ADJ QUALIT ◊ ADV

childless /tʃaɪldlɪˀs/. Someone who is **childless** has no children. EG *...childless couples.* ADJ CLASSIF

childlike /tʃaɪldlaɪk/. You describe someone as **childlike** when they seem like a child in their appearance or behaviour. EG *Her voice was fresh and childlike.* ADJ QUALIT

childminder /tʃaɪldmaɪndə/, **childminders.** A **childminder** is someone whose job is to look after other people's children when their parents are not at home. N COUNT

children /tʃɪldrən/ is the plural of **child.**

chili /tʃɪliˡ/. See **chilli**.

chill /tʃɪl/, **chills, chilling, chilled. 1** When you **chill** something, you lower its temperature so that it becomes colder but does not freeze. EG *White wine should be slightly chilled.* V-ERG

2 When something **chills** you, **2.1** it makes you feel very cold. EG *A bank clerk is more easily chilled outside than a farmer.* ◊ **chilling.** EG *A chilling wind swept round them... He was exhausted after a chilling swim in the lake.* **2.2** it frightens you very much. EG *She was chilled by his callousness.* ◊ **chilling.** EG *The thought was chilling... It was one of the most chilling articles I have ever read.* V+O : USU PASS ◊ ADJ QUALIT V+O ◊ ADJ QUALIT

3 A **chill** is **3.1** a mild illness which can give you a slight fever and headache. **3.2** a sudden feeling of anxiety. EG *The sound sent a chill down my spine.* N COUNT

4 Chill weather is cold and unpleasant. EG *It was a chill autumn day when I left London.* ▸ used as a noun. EG *Barnabas led the way home, feeling the chill of the night through his shirt.* ADJ QUALIT ▸ N UNCOUNT +SUPP

chilli /tʃɪliˡ/, **chillies;** also spelled **chili. Chillies** are small red or green seed pods, which have a hot, spicy taste and are used in cooking. N COUNT OR N UNCOUNT

chilly /tʃɪliˡ/, **chillier, chilliest. 1** Something that is **chilly** is rather cold and unpleasant. EG *A draught of chilly air entered the room.* ADJ QUALIT

2 If you feel **chilly**, you feel cold. EG *Light the fire if you feel chilly.* ADJ PRED

chime /tʃaɪm/, **chimes, chiming, chimed.** When church bells or clocks **chime**, they make ringing sounds, especially to show what time it is. EG *The cathedral bells were chiming through the night... The clock chimed eight-thirty.* ▸ used as a noun. EG *...the silvery chime of the old stable clock.* V OR V+O ▸ N COUNT

chime in. If someone **chimes in**, they say something just after someone else has spoken. EG *Bill chimed in with 'This is an emergency situation.'* PHRASAL VB : V+ADV+ QUOTE, OFT+*with*

chimney /tʃɪmniˡ/, **chimneys.** A **chimney** is a pipe through which smoke goes up into the air, usually through the roof of a building. See picture at HOUSE. EG *I sat watching the sparks fly up the chimney... ...factory chimneys.* N COUNT

chimney pot, chimney pots. A **chimney pot** is a short pipe on top of a chimney stack. N COUNT

chimney stack, chimney stacks. A **chimney stack** is the brick or stone part of a chimney that is above the roof of a building. N COUNT British

chimney sweep, chimney sweeps. A **chimney sweep** is a person whose job is to clean the soot out of chimneys. N COUNT

chimpanzee /tʃɪmpəˀnziː/, **chimpanzees.** A **chimpanzee** is a kind of small African ape. N COUNT

chin /tʃɪn/, **chins.** Your **chin** is the part of your face that is below your mouth and above your neck. See picture at THE HUMAN BODY. N COUNT

china /tʃaɪnə/. **1 China** or **china clay** is a kind of very thin clay from which cups, saucers, plates, and ornaments are made. EG *...china cups and saucers.* N UNCOUNT

2 Cups, saucers, plates, and ornaments made of china are referred to as **china**. EG *She laid out a small tray with the best china.* N UNCOUNT

chink /tʃɪŋk/, **chinks, chinking, chinked. 1** A **chink** is a very narrow opening. EG *Through a chink she could see a bit of blue sky.* N COUNT

2 When objects **chink**, they touch each other, making a short, light, ringing sound. EG *Empty bottles chinked as the milkman put them into his crate.* ▸ used as a noun. EG *...the chink of money.* V ▸ N SING+*of*

chintz /tʃɪnts/ is a cotton fabric with bright patterns on it. EG *...chintz curtains.* N UNCOUNT

chip /tʃɪp/, **chips, chipping, chipped. 1** In Britain, **chips** are long, thin pieces of potato fried in oil or fat. EG *...fish and chips.* N COUNT : USU PLURAL

2 In America, **chips** or **potato chips** are very thin slices of potato that have been fried until they are hard and crunchy. EG *...a packet of potato chips.* N COUNT : USU PLURAL

3 A **chip** is a very small piece of silicon with electric circuits on it which is part of a computer. EG *The entire contents of a book will be located on a single silicon chip.* N COUNT

4 When you **chip** something, you accidentally damage it by breaking a small piece off it. ◊ **chipped.** EG *...a chipped mug... Deirdre saw that the varnish was slightly chipped.* V+O ◊ ADJ QUALIT

5 A **chip** is also a small piece which has been broken off something. EG *...granite chips.* N COUNT

6 Chips are also plastic counters used in gambling to represent money. N COUNT : USU PLURAL

7 You use the expression **when the chips are down** to refer to a serious situation which must be dealt with, and which shows how well or badly someone or something is able to deal with it. EG *It's difficult to tell who is 'average' and who is not until the chips are down.* PHRASE Informal

8 If someone has **a chip on** their **shoulder**, they behave rudely and aggressively because they feel inferior or think that they have been treated unfairly. PHRASE Informal

chip in. 1 When a number of people **chip in**, each person gives some money so that they can pay for something together. EG *They all chipped in to pay the doctor's bill.* **2** If someone **chips in** during a conversation, they interrupt it in order to say something. EG *'Come on, back to work,' chipped in the supervisor.* PHRASAL VB : V+ADV Informal V+ADV, OFT+QUOTE Informal

chiropodist /kɪrɒpədɪst/, **chiropodists.** A **chiropodist** is a person whose job is to treat and care for people's feet. N COUNT

chirp /tʃɜːp/, **chirps, chirping, chirped.** When a bird or insect **chirps**, it makes short high-pitched sounds. EG *Birds had begun to chirp among the trees.* V

chisel /tʃɪzəˀl/, **chisels, chiselling, chiselled;** spelled **chiseling, chiseled** in American English.
1 A **chisel** is a tool that has a long metal blade with N COUNT

a sharp edge at the end. It is used for cutting and shaping wood and stone.

2 If you **chisel** wood or stone, you cut and shape it using a chisel. EG *The men chisel the blocks out of solid rock.* V+O : OFT+A

chivalrous /ʃɪvəlrəs/. A man who is **chivalrous** is polite, kind, and unselfish, especially towards women. EG *They were treated with chivalrous consideration.* ◊ **chivalrously.** EG *'A pleasure,' said Colonel Cameron chivalrously.* ADJ QUALIT ◊ ADV

chivalry /ʃɪvəlri¹/ is polite, kind, and unselfish behaviour, especially by men towards women. N UNCOUNT

chlorine /klɔːriːn/ is a strong-smelling gas that is used to disinfect water and to make cleaning products. N UNCOUNT

chlorophyll /klɒrəfɪl/ is a green substance in plants which enables them to use the energy from sunlight in order to grow. N UNCOUNT

chocolate /tʃɒkə⁰lə¹t/, **chocolates. 1 Chocolate** is **1.1** a sweet, hard, brown food made from cocoa beans, which is eaten as a sweet. EG *...a bar of chocolate... ...chocolate cake.* **1.2** a hot drink made from a powder containing chocolate. N UNCOUNT

2 A **chocolate** is a sweet or nut covered with a layer of chocolate. EG *...a box of chocolates.* N COUNT

choice /tʃɔɪs/, **choices; choicer, choicest. 1** If there is a **choice** of things, there are several of them and you can choose the one you want. EG *There's a choice of eleven sports... The choice was very limited... ...the choice between peace and war.* N COUNT : USU SING

2 Your **choice** is the thing or things that you choose from a range of things. EG *He congratulated the chef on his choice of dishes.* N COUNT

3 The thing or person **of** your **choice** is the one that you choose. EG *They could attend the church of their choice... She was prevented from marrying the man of her choice.* PHRASE

4 If you **have no choice** but to do something, you cannot avoid doing it. EG *The President had no choice but to agree.* PHRASE

5 You use **choice** to describe things that are of high quality. EG *...choice cuts of meat.* ADJ QUALIT : ATTRIB

choir /kwaɪə/, **choirs.** A **choir** is a group of people who sing together, for example in a church. N COUNT

choirboy /kwaɪəbɔɪ/, **choirboys.** A **choirboy** is a boy who sings in a church choir. N COUNT

choke /tʃəʊk/, **chokes, choking, choked. 1** When you **choke** or when something **chokes** you, you cannot breathe properly because you cannot get enough air into your lungs. EG *Philip choked on his drink... The pungent smell of sulphur choked him.* ◊ **choking.** EG *They were enveloped in a cloud of choking dust.* V-ERG : IF V, OFT+*on* ◊ ADJ QUALIT

2 If someone **chokes** someone else, they squeeze their neck until they are dead. EG *An old woman was found choked to death.* V+O

3 If a place **is choked** with things or people, it is full of them and they prevent movement in it. EG *The centre of the city was choked with cars.* V+O : USU PASS+*with*

4 The **choke** in a car, lorry, or other vehicle is a device that reduces the amount of air going into the engine and makes it easier to start; also used of the button on the dashboard which operates the device. See picture at CAR. N COUNT

choke back. If you **choke back** a strong emotion, you force yourself not to show it. EG *I choked back my sobs.* PHRASAL VB : V+O+ADV

choked /tʃəʊkt/. If you say something in a **choked** voice, your voice does not have its full sound, because you are upset or afraid. EG *He let out a choked scream.* ADJ QUALIT : ATTRIB

cholera /kɒlərə/ is a serious disease that affects your digestive organs. EG *His parents died of cholera.* N UNCOUNT

choose /tʃuːz/, **chooses, choosing, chose** /tʃəʊz/, **chosen** /tʃəʊzə⁰n/. **1** If you **choose** something from several things that are available, you decide to have it. EG *I chose a yellow dress... They were choosing sweets from one of the stalls... I had been chosen to be trained as editor.* ◊ **chosen.** EG *They undergo training in their chosen professions... He met them at a chosen rendezvous on the Common.* V+O : OFT+A OR *to*-INF ◊ ADJ CLASSIF : ATTRIB

2 If you **choose** to do something, you do it because you want to or because you feel that it is right. EG *He chose to ignore her impertinence... They could fire employees whenever they chose.* V : USU+*to*-INF

3 If there is **little to choose between** things or **not much to choose between** them, it is difficult to decide which is better or more suitable. EG *There's nothing to choose between the two countries.* PHRASE

choosy /tʃuːzi¹/. You say that someone is **choosy** when they are difficult to please, because they will only accept something if it is exactly what they want or if it is of very high quality. EG *I'm very choosy about my whisky... It's not like you to be so choosy.* ADJ QUALIT

chop /tʃɒp/, **chops, chopping, chopped. 1** If you **chop** something, you cut it into pieces by hitting it with an axe or a knife. EG *I don't like chopping wood... Peel, slice, and chop the apple.* V+O : USU+A

2 A **chop** is a small piece of meat cut from the ribs of a sheep or pig. EG *...lamb chops.* N COUNT

3 If something is **for the chop**, it is going to be stopped or closed. EG *The small theatres will be first for the chop.* PHRASE Informal British

4 When people **chop and change**, they keep changing their minds about what to do or how to act. PHRASE Informal

chop down. If you **chop down** a tree, you cut through its trunk with an axe so that it falls to the ground. PHRASAL VB : V+O+ADV

chop up. If you **chop** something **up** you chop it into small pieces. EG *Chop up some tomatoes and add them to the onion.* PHRASAL VB : V+O+ADV

chopper /tʃɒpə/, **choppers.** A **chopper** is **1** a helicopter. EG *Above the house a chopper buzzed and circled... These days we usually go by chopper.* N COUNT Informal

2 an axe. EG *We broke open the crate with a blow from the chopper.* Informal

choppy /tʃɒpi¹/, **choppier, choppiest.** When water is **choppy**, there are a lot of small waves on it. EG *The sea suddenly turned from smooth to choppy.* ADJ QUALIT

chopstick /tʃɒpstɪk/, **chopsticks. Chopsticks** are a pair of thin sticks which people in China and the Far East use to eat their food with. N COUNT

choral /kɔːrəl/. **Choral** music is sung by a choir. EG *...the pleasures of choral singing.* ADJ CLASSIF : ATTRIB

chord /kɔːd/, **chords. 1** A **chord** is a number of musical notes played or sung at the same time with a pleasing or satisfying effect. EG *He played some random chords.* N COUNT

2 If something **strikes a chord** with you, it makes you feel sympathy or enthusiasm. EG *The idea struck a chord... Her story may strike a chord for other women in the same situation.* PHRASE

chore /tʃɔː/, **chores.** A **chore** is a task that you find unpleasant or boring. EG *Does your husband do his fair share of the household chores?* N COUNT : USU PLURAL

choreograph /kɒrɪəgræf/, **choreographs, choreographing, choreographed.** When someone **choreographs** a ballet or other dance, they invent the steps and movements and tell the dancers how to perform them. ◊ **choreographer** /kɒrɪɒgrəfə/, **choreographers.** EG *He joined the company as a choreographer in 1975.* V+O ◊ N COUNT

choreography /kɒrɪɒgrəfi¹/ is the art of inventing the steps and movements of ballets or other dances. EG *Our studies include choreography.* N UNCOUNT

chortle /tʃɔːtə⁰l/, **chortles, chortling, chortled.** When someone **chortles**, they laugh with pleasure or amusement. EG *She chortled with delight.* V OR V+QUOTE

chorus /kɔːrəs/, **choruses, chorusing, chorused.** **1** A **chorus** is **1.1** a large group of people who sing N COUNT

Find two words on these pages which mean 'laugh'.

together. **1.2** a piece of music written to be sung by a large group of people. EG *...the Soldiers' Chorus from Faust.* **1.3** a part of a song which is repeated after each verse. **1.4** a group of singers or dancers who perform together in a show, in contrast to the soloists. EG *...the girls who danced in the chorus.*

2 You can use **chorus** to talk about attitudes expressed by a lot of people at the same time. For example, you can talk about a **chorus** of disapproval or a **chorus** of satisfaction. EG *In recent weeks the chorus of complaint has been growing.* N COUNT: USU+*of*

3 When people **chorus** something, they say it or sing it together. EG *'Shall I tell you a story?' – 'Please!' the children would chorus.* V+O OR V+QUOTE Literary

chose /tʃəʊz/ is the past tense of **choose.**

chosen /tʃəʊzəⁿn/ is the past participle of **choose.**

christen /krɪsəⁿn/, **christens, christening, christened. 1** When a baby **is christened**, he or she is given a name during the Christian ceremony of baptism. EG *She was christened Victoria Mary... Charles II was christened in this church.* V+O OR V+O+C: USU PASS

2 To **christen** a place or an object means to choose a name for it and to start calling it by that name. EG *The crew christened the hot geysers the 'black smokers'.* V+O+C Informal

christening /krɪsəⁿnɪŋ/, **christenings.** A **christening** is a Christian ceremony in which a baby is made a member of the Christian church and is officially given his or her name. N COUNT

Christian /krɪstʃən/, **Christians. 1** A **Christian** is a person who believes in Jesus Christ and follows his teachings. ▸ used as an adjective. EG *...a Christian missionary... Charity is the greatest of Christian virtues.* N COUNT ▸ ADJ CLASSIF

2 People are sometimes described as **Christian** when they are very good and kind. EG *She was a really Christian woman... I wouldn't call that a very Christian attitude.* ADJ QUALIT: ATTRIB

Christianity /krɪstɪænɪˡtiˡ/ is a religion that is based on the teachings of Jesus Christ and the belief that he was the son of God. N UNCOUNT

Christian name, Christian names. A person's **Christian name** is a name that is given to them when they are born or when they are christened. EG *Do all your students call you by your Christian name?* N COUNT

Christmas /krɪsməs/, **Christmases. Christmas** is the Christian festival when the birth of Jesus Christ on the 25th of December is celebrated. EG *Merry Christmas and a Happy New Year!... ...the Christmas holidays... The past few Christmases have been very quiet.* N UNCOUNT OR N COUNT

Christmas Day is the 25th of December, when Christmas is celebrated. N UNCOUNT

Christmas Eve is the 24th of December, the day before Christmas Day. N UNCOUNT

Christmas tree, Christmas trees. A **Christmas tree** is a fir tree, or an artificial tree that looks like a fir tree, which people put in their houses at Christmas and decorate with coloured lights and balls. N COUNT

chrome /krəʊm/ is a hard silver-coloured metal. EG *...chrome bath taps.* N UNCOUNT

chromium /krəʊmɪəm/ is the same as chrome. N UNCOUNT

chromosome /krəʊməsəʊm/, **chromosomes.** A **chromosome** is a part of a cell in an animal or plant. It contains genes which determine what characteristics the animal or plant will have. N COUNT Technical

chronic /krɒnɪk/. **1** A **chronic** illness lasts for a very long time. EG *Her father was dying of chronic asthma.* ◇ **chronically.** EG *...pensions for the chronically sick.* ADJ CLASSIF: USU ATTRIB ◇ ADV+ADJ

2 You describe someone's bad habits or behaviour as **chronic** when they have behaved like that for a long time and do not seem to be able to stop themselves. EG *...chronic drunkenness.* ADJ CLASSIF: ATTRIB

3 A **chronic** situation or problem is very severe and unpleasant. EG *...chronic food shortages.* ◇ **chronically.** EG *...an education service that is chronically short of finance.* ADJ CLASSIF: USU ATTRIB ◇ SUBMOD

chronicle /krɒnɪkəˡl/, **chronicles, chronicling, chronicled. 1** If you **chronicle** a series of events, you write about them in the order in which they happened. EG *Xenophon chronicled the Persian Wars.* V+O Formal

2 A **chronicle** is a formal account or record of a series of events. N COUNT Formal

chronological /krɒnəlɒdʒɪkəˡl/. If you describe a series of events in **chronological** order, you describe them in the order in which they happened. ◇ **chronologically.** EG *The collection is arranged chronologically.* ADJ CLASSIF ◇ ADV

chrysalis /krɪsəlɪs/, **chrysalises.** A **chrysalis** is **1** a butterfly or moth in the stage between being a larva and an adult. **2** the hard, protective covering that a chrysalis has. N COUNT

chrysanthemum /krɪsænθəməm/, **chrysanthemums.** A **chrysanthemum** is a large garden flower with many long, thin petals. N COUNT

chubby /tʃʌbiˡ/, **chubbier, chubbiest.** A **chubby** child is rather fat and round. EG *...chubby little fingers.* ADJ QUALIT

chuck /tʃʌk/, **chucks, chucking, chucked. 1** When you **chuck** something somewhere, you throw it there in a casual or careless way. EG *Chuck my tights across, please.* V+O+A Informal

2 If you **chuck** someone out of a place, you force them to leave. EG *We were chucked out of the meeting.* V+O+A Informal

chuck away or **chuck out.** If you **chuck** something **away** or **chuck** it **out**, you throw it away, because you do not need it or cannot use it. EG *The clock had to be chucked away because it didn't work.* PHRASAL VB: V+O+ADV Informal

chuckle /tʃʌkəˡl/, **chuckles, chuckling, chuckled.** When people **chuckle**, they laugh quietly. EG *They were chuckling over the photographs.* ▸ used as a noun. EG *He shook his head with a soft chuckle.* V OR V+QUOTE ▸ N COUNT

chug /tʃʌg/, **chugs, chugging, chugged.** When a vehicle or engine **chugs**, it makes short thudding sounds. EG *A small fishing boat comes chugging towards them.* V: OFT+A

chum /tʃʌm/, **chums. 1** Your **chum** is your friend. EG *I had my chum with me... In Dublin he met an old school chum.* N COUNT Outdated Informal

2 Men sometimes address each other as **chum**, usually in a slightly aggressive or unfriendly way. EG *You've had it, chum.* VOCATIVE Outdated Informal

chunk /tʃʌŋk/, **chunks. 1** A **chunk** of something solid is a piece of it. EG *...a great chunk of meat.* N PART

2 A **chunk** is also a large amount or part of something. EG *Research and development now take up a sizeable chunk of the military budget.* N PART Informal

chunky /tʃʌŋkiˡ/. **1** You describe people as **chunky** when they are broad and heavy. EG *A chunky waitress came waddling towards him.* ADJ QUALIT

2 A **chunky** object is large and thick. EG *...great chunky cardigans.* ADJ QUALIT

church /tʃɜːtʃ/, **churches. 1** A **church** is a building in which Christians worship. EG *There were no services that day, and the church was empty... His parents go to church now and then.* N COUNT OR N UNCOUNT

2 A **Church** is one of the groups of people within the Christian religion, for example Catholics. EG *Jane had been received into the Church a month previously.* N COUNT

churchman /tʃɜːtʃməˢn/, **churchmen.** A **churchman** is the same as a clergyman. N COUNT Formal

churchyard /tʃɜːtʃjɑːd/, **churchyards.** A **churchyard** is an area of land around a church where people are buried. N COUNT

churlish /tʃɜːlɪʃ/. **Churlish** behaviour is unfriendly, bad-tempered, or impolite. EG *It seemed churlish to send him away.* ADJ QUALIT

churn /tʃɜːn/, **churns, churning, churned. 1** A **churn** is a container which is used for making milk or cream into butter. N COUNT

2 When someone **churns** milk or cream, they stir it vigorously in order to turn it into butter. V+O

3 If something **churns** mud or water, it moves it about violently. EG *The bulldozers were churning the mud... He could see the water churning about under the propellers.* V-ERG

4 If you say that your stomach **is churning**, you mean that you feel sick. EG *My stomach churned when I saw them together.* V Informal

churn out. To **churn** things **out** means to produce large numbers of them very quickly. EG *His organization began churning out tracts and posters... My brain was churning out objections at an incredible speed.* PHRASAL VB: V+O+ADV Informal

churn up. When something **churns up** mud or water, it moves it about violently. EG *The wind churned up the water into a swirling foam.* PHRASAL VB: V+O+ADV

chute /ʃuːt/, **chutes.** A **chute** is a steep, narrow slope down which objects such as coal or parcels can slide so that they do not have to be carried. N COUNT

chutney /tʃʌtni^1/ is a strong-tasting mixture of fruit, vinegar, sugar, and spices which you eat with meat or cheese. EG *...mango chutney.* N UNCOUNT

cider /saɪdə/ is an alcoholic drink made from apples. N UNCOUNT

cigar /sɪgɑː/, **cigars. Cigars** are rolls of dried tobacco leaves which people smoke. N COUNT

cigarette /sɪgə^{0}ret/, **cigarettes. Cigarettes** are small tubes of paper containing tobacco which people smoke. EG *Boylan lit a cigarette.* N COUNT

cinch /sɪntʃ/. If you say that something **is a cinch**, you mean that it is very easy to do. EG *Beating Rangers should be a cinch.* PHRASE Informal

cinder /sɪndə/, **cinders. 1 Cinders** are the pieces of material that are left after wood or coal has burned. N COUNT: USU PLURAL

2 If you burn something **to a cinder**, you burn it until it is black. PHRASE

cinema /sɪnə^{1}mə/, **cinemas. 1** A **cinema** is a place where people go to watch films. N COUNT

2 **Cinema** is the business and art of making films. EG *...one of the classic works of Hollywood cinema.* N UNCOUNT

cinematic /sɪnə^{1}mætɪk/ means relating to films made for the cinema. ADJ CLASSIF: ATTRIB

cinnamon /sɪnəmən/ is a spice used for flavouring sweet food. N UNCOUNT

cipher /saɪfə/, **ciphers;** also spelled **cypher.** A **cipher** is a secret system of writing that you use to send messages. EG *The necessary codes and ciphers will be included in your orders... They had been corresponding with one another in cipher.* N COUNT OR *in*+N

circa /sɜːkə/ in front of a year means that this is the approximate date when something happened or was made. EG *...an old British newspaper, circa 1785.* PREP

circle /sɜːkə^{0}l/, **circles, circling, circled. 1** A **circle** is a curved line completely surrounding an area. Every part of the line is the same distance from the centre of the area. See picture at SHAPES. EG *The students sit in a circle on the floor.* N COUNT

2 A **circle** of something is a round, flat piece or area of it. EG *Stand the paint tin on a circle of aluminium foil.* N COUNT: USU+SUPP

3 If a bird or aircraft **circles**, it moves round in a circle in the air. EG *Hawks circled overhead looking for prey.* V: OFT+A

4 If something **circles** something else, it moves round it. EG *Galileo saw four moons circling Jupiter in 1610.* V+O

5 You can refer to a group of people as a **circle.** EG *I have widened my circle of acquaintances... This proposal caused an uproar in parliamentary circles.* N COUNT+SUPP

6 The **circle** in a theatre or cinema is an area of seats on the upper floor. N SING: *the*+N

7 If you say that someone **is going round in circles**, you mean that they are not achieving anything because they keep coming back to the same point or problem. PHRASE Informal

8 If you say that something **has come full circle**, you mean that after a long series of events or changes the same situation exists as at the beginning. PHRASE

circuit /sɜːkɪt/, **circuits. 1** An electrical **circuit** is a complete route which an electric current can flow around. N COUNT

2 A **circuit** is also a series of places that are visited regularly by a person or group. EG *...the American college lecture circuit.* N COUNT+SUPP

3 A racing **circuit** is a track on which cars, motorbikes, or cycles race. N COUNT

circuitous /sə^{5}kjuːɪtəs/. A **circuitous** route or journey is long and complicated rather than simple and direct. EG *After a long and circuitous journey by train and boat, we finally arrived.* ADJ QUALIT: USU ATTRIB Formal

circular /sɜːkjə^{4}lə/, **circulars. 1** Something that is **circular** is shaped like a circle. EG *...a circular pond.* ADJ CLASSIF

2 A **circular** journey or route is one in which you go to a place and return by a different route. ADJ CLASSIF

3 A **circular** argument or theory is not valid because it uses a statement to prove the conclusion and the conclusion to prove the statement. ADJ CLASSIF Formal

◇ **circularity** /sɜːkjə^{4}lærɪ^{1}ti^1/. EG *My argument suffered from circularity.* ◇ N UNCOUNT

4 A **circular** is an official letter or advertisement that is sent to a large number of people at the same time. N COUNT

circulate /sɜːkjə^{4}leɪt/, **circulates, circulating, circulated. 1** When a piece of writing **circulates** or **is circulated**, copies of it are passed round among a group of people. EG *The report was circulated to all the members... A union newspaper was circulating at the congress.* V-ERG: USU+A

2 If something such as a joke or a rumour **circulates** or **is circulated**, the people in a place tell it to each other. EG *Stories about him circulated at his club... A wicked rumour had been circulated that she was a secret drinker.* V-ERG: USU+A

3 If a substance **circulates** or **is circulated**, it moves easily and freely within a closed place or system. EG *We are governed by the hormones that circulate around our bodies.* V-ERG: USU+A

4 If you **circulate** at a party, you move among the guests and talk to different people. V

circulation /sɜːkjə^{4}leɪʃə^{0}n/, **circulations. 1 Circulation** refers to the process by which a piece of writing is passed round among a group of people. EG *...the circulation of illegal books.* N UNCOUNT

2 The **circulation** of a newspaper or magazine is the number of copies that are sold each time it is produced. EG *The local paper had a circulation of only six thousand.* N COUNT+SUPP

3 The **circulation** of a substance is the process by which it moves freely within a place or system. EG *...the circulation of air.* N UNCOUNT

4 Your **circulation** is the movement of blood through your body. EG *He stamped his feet from time to time to keep the circulation going.* N SING: USU+SUPP

5 Money that is in **circulation** is being used by the public. N UNCOUNT

circumcise /sɜːkəmsaɪz/, **circumcises, circumcising, circumcised.** To **circumcise** a man or boy means to cut off the loose skin at the end of his penis for religious or medical reasons. V+O

◇ **circumcision** /sɜːkəmsɪʒə^{0}n/. EG *...the rite of circumcision.* ◇ N UNCOUNT

circumference /səkʌmfə^{0}rəns/, **circumferences.** The **circumference** of a circle, place, or round object is **1** its edge. EG *He went jogging around the circumference of the reservoir.* **2** the distance around its edge. EG *The area has a circumference of 54 miles.* N COUNT+SUPP

Could cider cause cirrhosis?

circumscribe /sɜːkəmskraɪb/, **circumscribes, circumscribing, circumscribed.** If someone's power or freedom **is circumscribed**, it is limited or restricted. — V+O : USU PASS; Formal

circumspect /sɜːkəmspɛkt/. If you are **circumspect**, you are cautious and avoid taking risks. EG *Physicians are now more circumspect about making recommendations for surgery.* — ADJ QUALIT; Formal
◊ **circumspectly.** EG *He would have to behave circumspectly.* — ◊ ADV

circumstance /sɜːkəmstə^{3}ns/, **circumstances.**
1 **Circumstances** are the conditions which affect what will happen in a particular situation. EG *In normal circumstances I would have resigned immediately... Under the circumstances Dolores had better stay away... ...the political and economic circumstances that exist in Ireland.* — N PLURAL +SUPP
2 You can emphasize that something must not or will not happen by saying that it must not or will not happen **under any circumstances**. EG *Under no circumstances whatsoever will I support Mr Baldwin.* — PHRASE
3 If someone describes the **circumstances** of an event, they describe how it happened. EG *She died without ever learning the circumstances of her grandfather's death.* — N PLURAL +SUPP
4 Your **circumstances** are the conditions of your life, especially the amount of money that you have. EG *...the change in George's circumstances.* — N PLURAL +POSS
5 Events and situations which cannot be controlled are sometimes referred to as **circumstance**. EG *...a victim of circumstance... Ambitions are thwarted by circumstance.* — N UNCOUNT; Literary

circumstantial /sɜːkəmstænʃə^{0}l/. **Circumstantial** evidence makes it seem likely that something happened, but does not prove it. EG *The circumstantial evidence is overwhelming.* — ADJ CLASSIF; Formal

circus /sɜːkəs/, **circuses.** A **circus** is a show performed in a large tent, with animals, clowns, and acrobats. EG *...the trainers from a nearby circus... We were going to take the children to the circus.* — N COUNT

cirrhosis /sɪrəʊsɪs/ is a serious disease which destroys a person's liver. It is often caused by drinking too much alcohol. — N UNCOUNT; Medical

cissy /sɪsi^{1}/. See **sissy**.

cistern /sɪstən/, **cisterns.** A **cistern** is 1 a container which holds the water that is used to flush a toilet. 2 a large tank in the roof of a house in which water is stored. — N COUNT

citadel /sɪtədə^{2}l/, **citadels.** A **citadel** is a strongly fortified building in a city. — N COUNT

citation /saɪteɪʃə^{0}n/, **citations.** A **citation** is 1 an official document or speech which praises a person for something brave or special that they have done. EG *The three policemen subsequently received citations.* 2 a quotation from a book or other piece of writing. — N COUNT; Formal; Formal

cite /saɪt/, **cites, citing, cited.** 1 If you **cite** something, you quote it from a written work or you mention it, especially as an example or proof of what you are saying. EG *The most commonly cited example of a primitive device is the abacus.* — V+O; Formal
2 To **cite** someone or something in a legal action means to officially name them. EG *...the woman who was cited in his divorce action.* — V+O; Formal

citizen /sɪtɪzən/, **citizens.** 1 If someone is a **citizen** of a particular country, they are legally accepted as belonging to that country. EG *...a Swedish citizen.* — N COUNT+SUPP
2 The **citizens** of a town or city are the people who live there. EG *...the citizens of Bristol.* — N COUNT+SUPP
3 See also **senior citizen**.

citizenship /sɪtɪzənʃɪp/ refers to the country that you legally belong to. For example, if you have Portuguese **citizenship**, you are legally accepted as belonging to Portugal. — N UNCOUNT +SUPP

citrus fruit /sɪtrəs fruːt/, **citrus fruits.** A **citrus fruit** is a juicy, sharp-tasting fruit such as an orange, lemon, or grapefruit. — N COUNT OR N UNCOUNT

city /sɪti^{1}/, **cities.** 1 A **city** is a large town. EG *...overcrowded cities... ...the city of Birmingham... ...a modern city centre.* — N COUNT
2 The **City** is the part of London where many important financial institutions have their main offices. EG *...a City banker.* — N PROPER : *the*+N

civic /sɪvɪk/. You use **civic** to describe 1 people or things that have an official status in a town or city. EG *...the civic centre... ...a civic leader from the local Pakistani community.* 2 the duties or feelings that people have because they belong to a particular community. EG *She was determined to carry out her civic responsibilities... ...civic pride.* — ADJ CLASSIF : ATTRIB

civil /sɪvə^{0}l/. 1 You use **civil** to describe 1.1 events that happen within a country and that involve the different groups of people in it. EG *...a society in which wars or civil disturbances happen.* 1.2 people or things in a country that are not connected with its armed forces. EG *...the civil authorities... ...a supersonic civil airliner named the Concorde.* 1.3 the rights that people have within a society. EG *...the defence of civil liberties and human rights.* — ADJ CLASSIF : ATTRIB
2 Someone who is **civil** is polite. EG *He'd been careful to be civil to everyone.* ◊ **civilly.** EG *He was somewhat upset but he answered civilly enough.* ◊ **civility** /sɪvɪlɪ^{1}ti^{1}/. EG *She was treated with civility and consideration.* — ADJ QUALIT; ◊ ADV; ◊ N UNCOUNT

civilian /sɪvɪljən/, **civilians.** A **civilian** is anyone who is not a member of the armed forces. EG *They tried to avoid bombing civilians.* — N COUNT

civilise /sɪvɪ^{1}laɪz/. See **civilize**.

civilization /sɪvɪ^{1}laɪzeɪʃə^{0}n/, **civilizations;** also spelled **civilisation.** 1 A **civilization** is a human society which has its own highly developed social organization, culture, and way of life which makes it distinct from other societies. EG *...the entire history of Western civilisation.* — N COUNT OR N UNCOUNT
2 **Civilization** is the state of having a high level of social organization, culture, and a comfortable way of life. EG *The Romans brought civilization to much of Europe.* — N UNCOUNT

civilize /sɪvɪ^{1}laɪz/, **civilizes, civilizing, civilized;** also spelled **civilise.** To **civilize** a person or society means to educate them so that they can improve their social organization, culture, or way of life. EG *He treated them as savages to be tamed and civilised.* — V+O

civilized /sɪvɪ^{1}laɪzd/; also spelled **civilised.**
1 A society that is **civilized** has a highly developed culture, technology, and system of government. EG *They aim to create an orderly and civilised society.* — ADJ QUALIT
2 If you describe a person as **civilized**, you mean that they are polite and reasonable in their attitudes and behaviour. EG *...a civilized discussion.* — ADJ QUALIT

civil servant, civil servants. A **civil servant** is a person who works in the Civil Service. — N COUNT

Civil Service. The **Civil Service** of a country consists of all the government departments and all the people who work in them. — N COLL : *the*+N

civil war, civil wars. A **civil war** is a war which is fought between different groups of people who live in the same country. EG *His brother was killed in the Spanish Civil War... There might be civil war again in this area.* — N COUNT OR N UNCOUNT

clad /klæd/. If you are **clad** in particular clothes, you are wearing them. EG *...beggars clad in dirty white rags.* — ADJ CLASSIF : USU PRED+*in*; Literary

claim /kleɪm/, **claims, claiming, claimed.** 1 You use **claim** to report what someone says when you want to indicate that you are not sure whether what they are saying is true or not. EG *He claimed that he found the money in the forest... They claimed to have shot down twenty-two planes... The marines were invited, it is claimed, by the government.* — V+QUOTE, REPORT OR *to*-INF

2 If someone **claims** responsibility or credit for something, they say that they are responsible for it, although they might not be telling the truth. EG *The rebels claimed responsibility for the bombing.* V+O

3 If you **claim** something, you ask for it because you have a right to it, or think that you have. EG *Voluntary workers can claim travelling expenses... Don't forget to claim for a first-class rail ticket to London... ...claiming back land lost by his father.* V+O OR V+A

4 If you say that a fight or disaster **claims** someone's life, you mean that they are killed in it. EG *The wave of bombings and street clashes is claiming new lives every day.* V+O Formal

5 A **claim** is 5.1 something which someone says which they cannot prove and which may be false. EG *Forecasts do not support the government's claim that the economy is picking up.* N COUNT: OFT+REPORT 5.2 a demand for something that you think you have a right to. EG *...a pay claim... ...a claim for compensation.* N COUNT 5.3 the right to have something. EG *They denied her rightful claim to the property... Henry Cooper's chief claim to fame is that he knocked down Mohammed Ali.* N COUNT: OFT+*to*

6 If you have a **claim** on someone, you have the right to demand things from them. EG *She realized that she had no claims on the man.* N COUNT +*on/upon*

7 If you **lay claim to** something, you say that it is yours. EG *Both countries laid claim to the territory.* PHRASE Formal

● to **stake a claim**: see **stake**.

claimant /kleɪmənt/, **claimants.** A **claimant** is someone who asks to be given something which they think they are entitled to, especially money. EG *It is not always clear whether a claimant is entitled to benefit.* N COUNT

clairvoyant /klɛəvɔɪənt/, **clairvoyants.** Someone who is **clairvoyant** is believed to know about future events or to be able to communicate with dead people. ADJ CLASSIF ▸ used as a noun. EG *I'm like a clairvoyant receiving messages from another world.* ▸ N COUNT ◇ **clairvoyance** /klɛəvɔɪəns/. EG *...the power of magic and clairvoyance.* ◇ N UNCOUNT

clam /klæm/, **clams, clamming, clammed.** A **clam** is a kind of shellfish. N COUNT

clam up. If someone **clams up**, they stop talking. EG *Then I clammed up and said nothing for the rest of the meal.* PHRASAL VB: V+ADV Informal

clamber /klæmbə/, **clambers, clambering, clambered.** If you **clamber** somewhere, you climb there with difficulty, usually using your hands as well as your feet. EG *We clambered up the hill.* V+A

clammy /klæmi[1]/, **clammier, clammiest.** Something that is **clammy** is unpleasantly damp and sticky. EG *His handshake is cold and clammy.* ADJ QUALIT

clamour /klæmə/, **clamours, clamouring, clamoured;** spelled **clamor** in American English.

1 If people **clamour** for something, they demand it noisily or angrily. EG *...changes in the law for which people are clamouring.* V+*for* Formal

2 When large groups of people **clamour**, they all talk and shout together loudly. EG *The clamouring crowd was spreading.* V Literary ▸ used as a noun. EG *The clamour of voices from the living-room seemed louder than ever.* ▸ N UNCOUNT +SUPP

clamp /klæmp/, **clamps, clamping, clamped.** 1 A **clamp** is a device that holds two things firmly together. EG *...containers which are sealed with metal clamps.* N COUNT

2 When you **clamp** one thing to another, you fasten the two things together with a clamp. EG *...trays that were clamped to the arm of a chair.* V+O: OFT +*to/together*

3 To **clamp** something in a particular place means to put it or hold it there firmly and tightly. EG *He picked up his bowler hat and clamped it upon his head... They clamped handcuffs around my wrists.* V+O+A

clamp down. To **clamp down** on people or activities means to take strong official action to stop or control them. EG *The authorities have got to clamp down on these trouble-makers.* PHRASAL VB: V+ADV, OFT+*on*

clan /klæn/, **clans.** A **clan** is a group of families that are related to each other. EG *...a power struggle between two Somali clans.* N COLL

clandestine /klændɛstɪ[5]n/. Something that is **clandestine** is hidden or kept secret, often because it is illegal. EG *...a clandestine radio station... We had to ensure that no clandestine operations were under way.* ADJ CLASSIF: USU ATTRIB Formal

clang /klæŋ/, **clangs, clanging, clanged.** When a large metal object **clangs**, it makes a loud, deep noise. EG *...the sound of the bells clanging... She clanged the gates behind her.* V-ERG ▸ used as a noun. EG *The door opened with a heavy clang.* ▸ N COUNT: USU SING

clank /klæŋk/, **clanks, clanking, clanked.** When metal objects **clank**, they make a loud noise because they are crashing together or against something hard. EG *All about him he heard chains clanking.* V ▸ used as a noun. EG *...the clank of metal upon stone.* ▸ N COUNT: USU SING

clap /klæp/, **claps, clapping, clapped.** 1 When people **clap**, they hit their hands together several times, usually in order to express appreciation. EG *The audience clapped enthusiastically and called for more.* V

2 If you **clap** your hands, you hit your hands together once, usually in order to attract someone's attention. EG *The vicar clapped his hands for silence.* V+O ▸ used as a noun. EG *He called them to order with a clap of his hands.* ▸ N COUNT

3 If you **clap** an object or your hand onto something, you put it there quickly and firmly. EG *He claps his hands to his head.* V+O+A

4 If you **clap** someone on the back or on the shoulder, you hit their back or shoulder with your hand in a friendly way. EG *He clapped her on the back and laughed.* V+O+A ● to **clap eyes on** someone: see **eye**.

5 A **clap** of thunder is a sudden loud noise of thunder. N COUNT+*of*

clapped-out. A machine that is **clapped-out** is old and no longer working properly. EG *The last car was a clapped-out old Ford.* ADJ QUALIT Informal British

claptrap /klæptræp/. If you describe something that someone says as **claptrap**, you mean that it is stupid or foolish. EG *A lot of claptrap is talked about the 'dignity of labour'.* N UNCOUNT Informal

claret /klærət/, **clarets. Claret** is a type of red French wine. N MASS

clarify /klærɪfaɪ/, **clarifies, clarifying, clarified.** To **clarify** something means to make it easier to understand. EG *If you don't understand, ask the speaker to clarify the point.* V+O ◇ **clarification** /klærɪfɪkeɪʃə[0]n/. EG *We must wait for clarification of the situation.* ◇ N UNCOUNT

clarinet /klærɪnɛt/, **clarinets.** A **clarinet** is a woodwind instrument with a straight tube and a single reed in its mouthpiece. See picture at MUSICAL INSTRUMENTS. N COUNT

clarity /klærɪ[1]ti[1]/ is 1 the quality of being well explained and easy to understand. EG *...the clarity of her explanation.* N UNCOUNT +SUPP 2 the ability to think clearly. EG *She was forcing me to think with more clarity about what I had seen.*

clash /klæʃ/, **clashes, clashing, clashed.** 1 If someone **clashes** with someone else or if two people **clash**, they fight, argue, or disagree with each other. EG *Youths clashed with police in the streets around the ground... The delegates clashed from the first day of the congress.* V OR V+*with*: RECIP ▸ used as a noun. EG *...the first public clash between the two party leaders.* ▸ N COUNT

2 Beliefs, ideas, or qualities that **clash** with each other are very different from each other and therefore are opposed to each other. EG *This belief clashes with all that we know about human psy-* V OR V+*with*: RECIP

Which words on these pages can refer to sounds?

chology... In a situation like this, moral values or principles may clash. ▸ used as a noun. EG *...a personality clash.* ▸ N COUNT

3 If two events **clash**, they happen at the same time so that you cannot attend both of them. EG *A religious convention had clashed with a flower show.* V OR V+*with*: RECIP

4 When two or more colours or styles **clash**, they look ugly together. EG *She was wearing a pink jacket which clashed violently with the colour of her hair.* V OR V+*with*: RECIP

5 When metal objects **clash**, they make a lot of noise by being hit together. ▸ used as a noun. EG *...a clash of cymbals.* V ▸ N COUNT

clasp /klɑːsp/, **clasps, clasping, clasped. 1** If you **clasp** someone or something, you hold them tightly in your hands or arms. EG *The woman was standing clasping the sleeping baby in her arms.* V+O

2 A **clasp** is a small device that fastens something. EG *...a black bag with a silver clasp.* N COUNT

class /klɑːs/, **classes, classing, classed. 1** A **class** is **1.1** a group of pupils or students who are taught together. EG *If classes were smaller, children would learn more.* N COUNT **1.2** a short period of teaching in a particular subject. EG *Peggy took evening classes in French.* N COUNT ● If you do something **in class**, you do it during a lesson in school. EG *You're not supposed to eat in class.* ● PHRASE

2 Class is used to refer to the way that the people in a society are divided into groups according to their social status. Each group is referred to as a particular **class**. EG *...the ruling class... ...other children of the same age and class... ...the British class system.* ● See also **middle class, upper class, working class.** N COUNT OR N UNCOUNT

3 A **class** of things is a group of them with similar characteristics. EG *We can identify several classes of fern.* N COUNT+SUPP

4 If you say that someone is **in a class of** their **own**, you mean that they have more of a particular skill or quality than anyone else. PHRASE

5 If you say that someone or something has **class**, you mean that they are elegant and sophisticated. N UNCOUNT Informal

6 If you **class** someone or something as a particular thing, you consider them as belonging to that group of things. EG *At nineteen you're still classed as a teenager.* V+O+*as/with*

-class is added to words like 'first' and 'executive' to indicate that a service or product is of a particular official standard. EG *I prefer to travel first class.*

classic /klæsɪk/, **classics. 1** A **classic** example of a thing or situation has all the features which you expect such a thing or situation to have. EG *London is the classic example of the scattered city... This statement was a classic illustration of British politeness.* ADJ CLASSIF: ATTRIB

2 You use **classic** to describe something such as a film or a piece of writing when it is of very high quality and has become a standard against which similar things are judged. EG *...one of the classic works of the Hollywood cinema.* ADJ CLASSIF: ATTRIB

3 A **classic** is a book which is well-known and considered to be of a very high literary standard. EG *...a great classic of Brazilian literature.* N COUNT

4 Classics is the study of the ancient Greek and Roman civilizations, especially their languages, literature, and philosophy. N UNCOUNT

classical /klæsɪkᵊl/. You use **classical** to describe **1** something that is traditional in form, style, or content. EG *We offer tuition in classical ballet, modern ballet, and ballroom dancing... ...the classical Hindu scheme of values.* ADJ CLASSIF: USU ATTRIB **2** music that is considered to be serious and of lasting value, as opposed to pop or jazz. EG *...classical pianists.* ADJ CLASSIF: ATTRIB **3** something that relates to ancient Greek or Roman civilization. EG *...plays set in classical times.* ADJ CLASSIF: ATTRIB

classification /klæsɪfɪkeɪʃᵊn/, **classifications. 1** The **classification** of things is the activity or process of classifying them into different types. EG *The cataloguing and classification of the plants on the island took several months.* N UNCOUNT

2 A **classification** is **2.1** a system of classifying things. EG *The broad outlines of most classifications are quite similar.* N COUNT **2.2** a division or category in a classifying system. EG *Your insurance group classification changes when you buy a bigger car.*

classified /klæsɪfaɪd/. Something that is **classified** is officially secret. EG *...a man suspected of passing on classified information.* ADJ CLASSIF

classify /klæsɪfaɪ/, **classifies, classifying, classified.** To **classify** things such as animals, plants, or books means to divide them into groups so that things with similar characteristics are in the same group. EG *Pastimes may be classified in different ways... Twenty-two of these plants are now classified as rare... The books have been classified according to subject.* V+O: USU PASS+*as*

classless /klɑːslɪ²s/. A **classless** society is one in which all people have the same social and economic status. ADJ CLASSIF: USU ATTRIB

classmate /klɑːsmeɪt/, **classmates.** Your **classmates** are students who are in the same class as you at school or college. N COUNT

classroom /klɑːsru⁴m/, **classrooms.** A **classroom** is a room in a school where lessons take place. N COUNT

classy /klɑːsi¹/, **classier, classiest.** If you describe someone or something as **classy**, you mean they are stylish and sophisticated. EG *...eating out in classy places.* ADJ QUALIT Informal

clatter /klætə/, **clatters, clattering, clattered.** A **clatter** is a continuous series of short, loud sounds made by hard things hitting each other. EG *...the clatter of dishes being washed.* ▸ used as a verb. EG *My sister was clattering the forks back into the drawer... The door clattered open.* N COUNT: USU SING+SUPP ▸ V-ERG: USU+A

clause /klɔːz/, **clauses. 1** A **clause** is a section of a legal document. EG *He included a clause in the contract that allowed him to buy the house back at the original price.* N COUNT

2 In grammar, a **clause** is a group of words containing a verb. Sentences contain one or more clauses. N COUNT

claustrophobia /klɒstrə⁶fəʊbɪə, klɔːs-/. Someone who suffers from **claustrophobia** is afraid of being in small or enclosed places. N UNCOUNT

claustrophobic /klɒstrə⁶fəʊbɪk, klɔː-/. **1** If you feel **claustrophobic**, you feel uncomfortable or frightened when you are in a small or enclosed place. EG *Leave the door open. I get very claustrophobic.* ADJ QUALIT

2 You describe a place or situation as **claustrophobic** when it makes you feel uncomfortable and unhappy because you are enclosed or restricted. EG *...a small claustrophobic restaurant... Life can seem claustrophobic.* ADJ QUALIT

claw /klɔː/, **claws, clawing, clawed. 1** The **claws** of a bird or animal are the thin, hard, curved nails at the end of its feet. EG *...a cat sharpening its claws.* N COUNT

2 The **claws** of a lobster, crab, or scorpion are two pointed parts at the end of one of its legs which are used for grasping things. N COUNT

3 If an animal **claws** something, it scratches or damages it with its claws. EG *...a tiger clawing the back of a water buffalo.* V+O

claw at. When people or animals **claw at** something, they try to get hold of it or damage it by using their nails or claws. EG *His cats were clawing at his trousers.* PHRASAL VB: V+PREP, HAS PASS

clay /kleɪ/ is a substance in the ground that is soft when it is wet and hard when it is dry. Clay is used to make things such as pots. EG *...clay pots... ...modelling in clay.* N UNCOUNT

clean /kliːn/, **cleaner, cleanest; cleans, cleaning, cleaned. 1** Something that is **clean** is free from dirt and unwanted substances or marks. EG ADJ QUALIT

...*clean white shirts... Knives should be wiped clean after use.*

2 You say that people or animals are **clean** when they keep themselves or their surroundings clean. ADJ QUALIT

3 If you **clean** something, you make it free from dirt and unwanted substances or marks, for example by washing or wiping it. EG *Clean the bathroom and lavatory thoroughly... ...the industrial fluid used to clean grease from the hands.* ▸ used as a noun. EG *The windows could do with a clean.* V+O ▸ N SING : *a*+N

4 To **clean** means to make the inside of a house or other building and the furniture in it free from dirt and dust. ◇ **cleaning.** EG *We have a landlady who does our cooking and our cleaning.* V ◇ N UNCOUNT

5 If you describe humour as **clean**, you mean that it is morally acceptable and not offensive. EG *...clean jokes.* ADJ CLASSIF : ATTRIB

6 If someone's reputation or record is **clean**, they have never done anything illegal or wrong. EG *Applicants must have a clean driving licence.* ADJ CLASSIF

7 If you **come clean** about something that you have been keeping secret, you admit it. EG *She decided to come clean.* PHRASE Informal

8 Clean also means **8.1** smoothly and immediately. EG *The ninth shot went clean through the forehead.* ADV+PREP Informal **8.2** completely or thoroughly. EG *The thief got clean away... I'd clean forgotten.* ADV Informal

clean out. 1 If you **clean out** somewhere such as a cupboard, room, or house, you take everything out of it, often before cleaning it. EG *I was cleaning out my desk.* PHRASAL VB : V+O+ADV **2** If you **clean** someone **out**, you take all the money they have. If you **clean out** a place, you take everything of value that is in it. EG *Thomas thought idly of cleaning out the cash register.* V+O+ADV Informal

clean up. If you **clean up** something or someone, you clean them, usually after they have just become dirty. EG *Clean up food spills at once... I cleaned up Allen as best I could.* PHRASAL VB : V+O+ADV

clean up after. If you **clean up after** someone, you clean or tidy a place that they have made dirty or untidy. PHRASAL VB : V+ADV+PREP

clean-cut. Someone who is **clean-cut** has a neat, tidy appearance. EG *...a clean-cut American girl.* ADJ QUALIT

cleaner /kliːnə/, **cleaners. 1** A **cleaner** is **1.1** someone who is employed to clean the rooms and furniture inside a building. N COUNT **1.2** someone whose job is to clean a particular type of thing. EG *...our window cleaner.* N COUNT : USU+SUPP **1.3** a substance or device used for cleaning things. EG *...a spray oven cleaner... Never use lavatory cleaner in the bath.* ● See also **vacuum cleaner**. N COUNT OR N UNCOUNT

2 The **cleaner** or the **cleaner's** is a shop where things such as clothes and curtains are dry-cleaned. EG *She collected the curtains from the cleaner's.* N SING

cleanliness /klenlɪnəˀs/ is the habit of keeping yourself and your surroundings clean. N UNCOUNT

cleanly /kliːnli¹/. If something is done **cleanly**, it is done smoothly and completely, without making a mess. EG *The porcelain top of the ornament broke cleanly off.* ADV

cleanse /klenz/, **cleanses, cleansing, cleansed. 1** To **cleanse** a place or a person means to make them free from something dirty, unpleasant, or evil. EG *...his vow to cleanse Washington of subversives.* V+O : OFT+*of/from* Formal

2 If you **cleanse** your skin or a wound, you clean it, especially with disinfectant. V+O

cleanser /klenzə/, **cleansers.** A **cleanser** is a liquid that you use for cleaning something. EG *Use a gentle cleanser.* N MASS

clean-shaven. If a man is **clean-shaven**, he does not have a beard or a moustache. ADJ CLASSIF

clear /klɪə/, **clearer, clearest; clears, clearing, cleared. 1** Something that is **clear** is **1.1** easy to understand, see, or hear. EG *I gave a clear, frank account of the incident... The line of its footprints is still clear... ...a clear voice.* ◇ **clearly.** EG *They've got to clearly define their policies... Make sure that all your luggage is clearly labelled... I couldn't see him clearly.* ADJ QUALIT ◇ ADV **1.2** obvious and impossible to be mistaken about. EG *They are faced with clear alternatives... It was clear from his letter that he was not interested.* ◇ **clearly.** EG *Whoever owned the house was clearly not expecting us... Clearly, it is very important for a solution to be found quickly.* ADJ QUALIT ◇ ADV OR ADV SEN

2 If you are **clear** about something, you understand it completely. EG *I'm not clear from what you said whether you support the idea or not.* ADJ PRED

3 If you **make** something **clear** or **make** yourself **clear**, you say something in a way that makes it impossible for there to be any doubt about your meaning, wishes, or intentions. EG *It is important to make clear your wishes about the funeral... All of them made it clear they would support my decision.* PHRASE

4 If your mind or your way of thinking is **clear**, you are able to think sensibly, reasonably, and logically. ◇ **clearly.** EG *Wait until you can think more clearly.* ADJ QUALIT ◇ ADV

5 If a substance is **clear**, you can see through it. EG *...a clear glue... ...a small creek with cold, clear water.* ADJ CLASSIF

6 If someone's eyes are **clear**, they are attractive and shining. EG *...clear brown eyes.* ADJ QUALIT

7 If a surface or place is **clear**, it is free of obstructions or unwanted objects. EG *The road was clear... ...a patch of floor that has been swept clear.* ADJ QUALIT

8 If it is a **clear** day or if the sky is **clear**, there is no mist, rain, or cloud. EG *On a clear day you can see the Welsh hills.* ADJ QUALIT

9 If your skin is **clear**, it is healthy and free from spots. ADJ QUALIT

10 If your conscience is **clear**, you do not feel guilty about anything. ADJ CLASSIF

11 If something is **clear** of something else, it is not touching it. EG *Raise the jack until the wheel is clear of the ground.* ADJ PRED : OFT+*of*

12 If you **stay clear** or **steer clear** of a person or place, you do not go near them. EG *He took special care to stay clear of any place where Sally might be.* PHRASE

13 If someone is **in the clear**, they are free from blame, suspicion, or danger. PHRASE Informal

14 When you **clear** an area or place, you remove things from it that you do not want to be there. EG *The children were helping me clear weeds from the pond... Will you clear the table when you've finished eating?... The princess's aides advanced before her to clear a passage.* V+O : OFT+A

15 To **clear** your mind or your head means to free it from confused thoughts or from the effects of alcohol. EG *He went for a walk to clear his mind.* V+O

16 If an animal or person **clears** a fence, wall, or hedge, they jump over it without touching it. V+O

17 When you **clear** your **throat**, you cough slightly in order to make it easier to speak. EG *He cleared his throat and spoke.* PHRASE

18 When fog or mist **clears**, it gradually disappears. EG *Outside the fog had cleared a little.* V

19 If a course of action **is cleared**, people in authority give permission for it to happen. V+O

20 If someone **is cleared**, they are proved to be not guilty of a crime or mistake. EG *The tribunal cleared all the people who had been accused.* V+O

21 the coast is clear: see **coast**. ● **loud and clear**: see **loud**. ● See also **clearing**.

clear away. When you **clear away**, you put away the things that you have been using. EG *We cleared away and helped with the washing-up... Brody began to clear away the soup bowls.* PHRASAL VB : V+ADV OR V+O+ADV

clear off. If you say **'clear off'** to someone, you are telling them in a rude way to go away. EG *Clear off and leave me alone!* PHRASAL VB : V+ADV Informal

What is the word for a group of clients?

clear out. 1 If you **clear out** of a place or if you **clear out**, you leave. EG *I've got to clear out of my place by next week... Just clear out and leave me in peace!* 2 If you **clear out** a cupboard, room, or house, you tidy it and throw away the things in it that you no longer want. EG *It's time I cleared out the kitchen cupboards.* PHRASAL VB : V+ADV, OFT+*of* Informal; V+O+ADV

clear up. 1 When you **clear up** or **clear** a place **up**, you tidy things and put them away. EG *I was too exhausted to clear up properly... Go and clear up your room.* 2 When a problem, disagreement, or misunderstanding **is cleared up**, it is settled or a satisfactory explanation is given. EG *I'm assuming that the misunderstanding will be cleared up soon.* PHRASAL VB : V+ADV OR V+O+ADV; V+O+ADV

3 When bad weather **clears up**, it stops raining or being cloudy. EG *If it clears up tomorrow, why don't we do some walking?* V+ADV

clearance /klɪərəns/. 1 **Clearance** is the removal of old buildings, trees, or other things that are not wanted from an area. EG *He was responsible for slum clearance and rehousing programmes.* N UNCOUNT

2 If you get **clearance** for something, you get official approval or permission for it. N UNCOUNT

clear-cut. Something that is **clear-cut** is easy to understand and quite distinct from other things. EG *It was a clear-cut decision... ...clear-cut economic groups.* ADJ QUALIT

clear-headed. Someone who is **clear-headed** is sensible and thinks clearly, especially in a difficult situation. ADJ QUALIT

clearing /klɪərɪŋ/, **clearings.** A **clearing** is a small area of grass or bare ground in a wood or forest. EG *They are alone in a clearing in the forest.* N COUNT

clear-sighted. Someone who is **clear-sighted** is able to understand situations well and to make sensible judgements and decisions about them. EG *He was too clear-sighted not to see what problems would follow.* ADJ QUALIT

cleavage /kliːvɪdʒ/, **cleavages.** 1 A woman's **cleavage** is the space between her breasts. N COUNT : USU+POSS

2 A **cleavage** between two people or things is a division or disagreement between them. EG *There is no distinct cleavage between the classes.* N COUNT : OFT +*between* Formal

clef /klɛf/, **clefs.** A **clef** is a symbol at the beginning of a line of a piece of music that indicates the range of the written notes. N COUNT

cleft /klɛft/, **clefts.** A **cleft** in a rock or in the ground is a narrow opening in it. EG *He could see the valley through a cleft in the rocks.* N COUNT : OFT +*in/between* Literary

clemency /klɛmənsi[1]/ is kind treatment that a person receives, especially from someone who has authority to punish them. EG *...appeals for clemency by the lawyers of the condemned men.* N UNCOUNT Formal

clench /klɛntʃ/, **clenches, clenching, clenched.**
1 When you **clench** your fist, you curl your fingers up tightly, usually because you are very angry. V+O

2 When you **clench** your teeth, you squeeze them together firmly, usually because you are angry or upset. EG *She hissed through clenched teeth, 'Get out of here.'* V+O

3 If you **clench** something in your hand or in your teeth, you hold it tightly with your hand or your teeth. EG *There he sat, pipe clenched in his mouth, typing away.* V+O : OFT+A

clergy /klɜːdʒi[1]/. The **clergy** are the officially appointed leaders of the religious activities of a particular church or temple. N PLURAL

clergyman /klɜːdʒɪmə[3]n/, **clergymen.** A **clergyman** is a male member of the clergy. N COUNT

cleric /klɛrɪk/, **clerics.** A **cleric** is a member of the clergy. N COUNT Outdated

clerical /klɛrɪkə[0]l/. 1 **Clerical** jobs, skills, and workers are concerned with work that is done in an office. EG *...clerical skills.* ADJ CLASSIF

2 **Clerical** also means relating to the clergy. EG *...a priest in a clerical grey suit with a dog collar.* ADJ CLASSIF Formal

clerk /klɑːk/, **clerks.** A **clerk** is a person who works in an office, bank, or law court and whose job is to look after the records or accounts. N COUNT

clever /klɛvə/, **cleverer, cleverest.** 1 Someone who is **clever** is intelligent and able to understand things easily or plan things well. EG *My sister was very clever and passed all her exams at school... He's a clever rogue... How clever of you to know that.* ◇ **cleverly.** EG *They had gone about the scheme cleverly... Mr White very cleverly analyzed this game without any assistance.* ◇ **cleverness.** EG *Some men don't like cleverness in a woman.* ADJ QUALIT; ◇ ADV; ◇ N UNCOUNT

2 An idea, book, or invention that is **clever** is extremely effective and shows the skill of the people involved. EG *This is a very clever way of running a college... It's such a clever gadget.* ADJ QUALIT

cliché /kliːʃeɪ/, **clichés;** also spelled **cliche.** A **cliché** is an idea or phrase which has been used so much that it is no longer original or effective. EG *...sentimental clichés about 'peace' and 'the open air'.* N COUNT

click /klɪk/, **clicks, clicking, clicked.** 1 When something **clicks** or when you **click** it, it makes a short, sharp sound. EG *His camera was clicking away... He clicked the switch on the radio.* ▸ used as a noun. EG *The lock opened with a click.* V-ERG; ▸ N COUNT

2 When you suddenly understand something, you can say that it **clicks.** V Informal

client /klaɪənt/, **clients.** A **client** of a professional person or organization is a person or company that receives a service from them in return for payment. EG *...a solicitor and his client.* N COUNT

clientele /kliːɒntɛl/. The **clientele** of a place or organization are its customers or clients. EG *...a restaurant with a predominantly upper-class clientele.* N COLL

cliff /klɪf/, **cliffs.** A **cliff** is a high area of land with a very steep side, especially one next to the sea. N COUNT

climactic /klaɪmæktɪk/. A **climactic** moment in a situation is one in which a very exciting or important event occurs. EG *He keeps it secret from her until a climactic point in the story.* ADJ CLASSIF Formal

climate /klaɪmə[1]t/, **climates.** 1 The **climate** of a place is the general weather conditions that are typical of it. EG *...the English climate... ...changes in climate... In very cold climates you cannot grow winter beans.* ◇ **climatic** /klaɪmætɪk/. EG *...favourable climatic conditions... The world was experiencing tremendous climatic change.* N COUNT OR N UNCOUNT; ◇ ADJ CLASSIF : ATTRIB

2 You can use **climate** to refer to people's attitudes or opinions at a particular time. EG *...this changing climate of public opinion... ...the prevailing political climate at Oxford.* N COUNT+SUPP

climax /klaɪmæks/, **climaxes.** The **climax** of a process, book, or piece of music is the most exciting or important moment in it, usually near the end. EG *This proved to be the climax of his political career... The climax of the book happens in Egypt.* N COUNT : USU+SUPP

climb /klaɪm/, **climbs, climbing, climbed.** 1 If you **climb** something tall such as a tree, mountain, or ladder, you move towards the top of it, often with some effort or difficulty. EG *We started to climb the hill... We climbed to the top of the mountain... I climbed up the ladder.* ▸ used as a noun. EG *We were still out of breath from the climb.* V+O, OR V : OFT+*to/up*; ▸ N COUNT

2 If you **climb** somewhere, you move there carefully, and often rather awkwardly, for example because you are moving into a small space or trying to avoid falling. EG *She climbed into her car... Four men climbed down through the hatch.* V+A OR V+O

3 When something **climbs,** 3.1 it moves gradually upwards to a higher position. EG *The plane climbed steeply and banked.* 3.2 it increases in value or amount. EG *The cost has climbed to a staggering £35 billion.* V : OFT+A

climber /klaɪmə/, **climbers.** 1 A **climber** is someone who climbs rocks or mountains as a sport or a hobby. EG *...a party of Swiss climbers en route to Everest.* N COUNT

2 You use **climber** to say how good a person or N COUNT+SUPP

animal is at climbing. For example, if you say that someone is a good **climber**, you mean that they are good at climbing. EG *He was an excellent climber... Chimpanzees are adept climbers.*
3 A **climber** is also a plant that grows upwards by attaching itself to other plants or objects. N COUNT
climbing /klaɪmɪŋ/ is the activity of climbing rocks or mountains. EG *...a pair of climbing boots.* N ING
clime /klaɪm/, **climes.** You use **clime** to refer to a place that has a particular kind of climate. For example, a warm **clime** is a place with a warm climate. EG *He retreats to sunny climes, leaving the winter behind.* N COUNT+SUPP Literary
clinch /klɪntʃ/, **clinches, clinching, clinched.** If you **clinch** an agreement or an argument, you settle it in a definite way. EG *The salesman was in Columbia trying to clinch a deal for his employer.* V+O Informal
cling /klɪŋ/, **clings, clinging, clung. 1** If you **cling** to someone or something, you hold onto them tightly with your arms. EG *The human baby is too weak to cling to its mother for hours on end... I clung to the door to support myself.* V: OFT+*to/on*
2 Clothes that **cling** to you stay pressed against your body when you move, because they are wet or very tight. EG *The dress clung tight to Etta's waist.* V: OFT+A
3 If you **cling** to someone you are fond of, you do not allow them to have enough freedom or independence. EG *A working woman is not so likely to cling to her children when they leave home.* V+*to*
◊ **clinging.** EG *There was something weak and clinging in his nature.* ◊ ADJ QUALIT
4 If you **cling** to an idea or way of behaving, you continue to believe in its value or importance, even though it may no longer be valid or useful. EG *They cling to all the old, inefficient methods of doing things.* V+*to*
clinic /klɪnɪk/, **clinics.** A **clinic** is a building where people go to receive medical advice or treatment. EG *...dental clinics... ...the family planning clinic.* N COUNT: USU+SUPP
clinical /klɪnɪkəˀl/. **1 Clinical** work, teaching, and examination relates to the direct medical treatment of patients rather than to theoretical research. EG *Doctors are hoping to start clinical tests next month.* ◊ **clinically.** EG *On examination she looked well and was not clinically anaemic.* ADJ CLASSIF: ATTRIB Medical ◊ ADV+ADJ
2 You use **clinical** to describe thought or behaviour which is very logical and detached and does not show any emotion or personal involvement; used showing disapproval. EG *She adopted an icy, impersonal, clinical attitude.* ADJ QUALIT
3 A room or building that is **clinical** is designed to look very plain, or is kept too neat and clean, so that people do not enjoy being in it. EG *...tiny offices painted clinical white.* ADJ QUALIT
clink /klɪŋk/, **clinks, clinking, clinked.** When objects made of glass, pottery, or metal **clink** or when you **clink** them, they touch each other and make a short, light sound. EG *The milk bottles clinked... She clinked her glass against Rudolph's.* V-ERG
▸ used as a noun. EG *...the clink of glasses... There was a clink as he put the cups into their saucers.* ▸ N COUNT
clip /klɪp/, **clips, clipping, clipped. 1** A **clip** is a small device, usually made of metal or plastic, that is specially shaped for holding things together. EG *He wore three pencils held by metal clips in his top pocket... ...hair clips.* N COUNT
2 When something **clips** to something else or when you **clip** it there, it fastens to it by means of one or more clips. EG *Keep the list clipped to that notebook.* V-ERG+A
3 If you **clip** something, you cut small pieces from it, especially in order to shape it. EG *Mr Willet had come to clip the hedges.* V+O
4 A **clip** of a film or television programme is a short piece of it that is shown separately. EG *Medical students were shown film clips depicting murders.* N COUNT: USU+SUPP
5 See also **clipping, clipped.**

clipboard /klɪpbɔːd/, **clipboards.** A **clipboard** is a board with a clip at the top. You use it to hold together pieces of paper that you need to carry around. It also provides a firm base so that you can write on the papers while you are standing. N COUNT
clipped /klɪpt/. **1** If a man's hair or moustache is **clipped**, it is neatly trimmed. EG *...a handsome man with a clipped moustache.* ADJ CLASSIF
2 If you have a **clipped** way of speaking, you speak with quick, short sounds. EG *He talked with a clipped, upper-class accent.* ADJ QUALIT
clippers /klɪpəz/ are a tool used for cutting small amounts from something. EG *...a pair of nail clippers.* N PLURAL
clipping /klɪpɪŋ/, **clippings.** A **clipping** is an article, picture, or advertisement that has been cut from a newspaper or magazine. EG *Dawlish read the newspaper clipping I gave him.* N COUNT: OFT+SUPP
clique /kliːk, klɪk/, **cliques.** A **clique** is a small group of people who spend a lot of time together and are unfriendly towards other people. EG *They had made a small, superior, isolated clique.* N COLL
cloak /kləʊk/, **cloaks, cloaking, cloaked. 1** A **cloak** is a wide, loose coat that fastens at the neck and does not have sleeves. See picture at CLOTHES. N COUNT
2 You can refer to something that someone does or says as a **cloak** when it is intended to hide the truth. EG *He could be using the story as a cloak for more sinister activities.* N COUNT+SUPP
3 To **cloak** something means to cover it or hide it. EG *The hills were cloaked by thick mists.* V+O: USU PASS+*in*
cloakroom /kləʊkruᵘm/, **cloakrooms.** In a public building, a **cloakroom** is **1** a place where you can leave your coat and hat. **2** a room containing toilets and washbasins. N COUNT
clobber /klɒbə/, **clobbers, clobbering, clobbered. 1** You can refer to someone's belongings as their **clobber**. EG *...bits of old army clobber.* N UNCOUNT Informal
2 If you **clobber** someone, you hit them. EG *If that dog bites me I'll clobber it.* V+O Informal
clock /klɒk/, **clocks, clocking, clocked. 1** A **clock** is an instrument, for example in a room or on the outside of a building, that shows you what time of day it is. EG *...the ticking of the clock... The church clock struck eleven.* N COUNT
2 If you work **round the clock**, you work all day and all night without stopping. PHRASE
3 To **put** or **turn the clock back** means to return to ideas or situations that existed a long time ago; used showing disapproval. EG *This government seems to want to see the clock put back.* PHRASE
4 A **clock** or a time **clock** on a machine or system is a device that causes things to happen automatically at particular times. EG *Set the time clock on your central heating system to give heat only when it is needed.* N COUNT
5 The **clock** in a car is an instrument that shows the number of miles or kilometres that the car has travelled. EG *...a Mini with 5,000 miles on the clock.* N COUNT
clock in. 1 When workers **clock in** at a factory or office, they record the time that they arrive by putting a special card into a device. EG *When they are late clocking in for factory work they may lose pay.* PHRASAL VB: V+ADV **2** If someone or something **clocks in** at a particular weight, they register that weight when they are weighed. EG *The truck clocked in at about two thousand pounds.* V+ADV, OFT+*at*
clock up. To **clock up** a large number or total means to reach that total. EG *He has clocked up more than 171,750 miles in a lifetime of cycling.* PHRASAL VB: V+ADV+O
clockwise /klɒkwaɪz/. When something moves in a **clockwise** direction, it moves in a circle and in the same direction as the hands on a clock. EG *He pushed the bolt back in and twisted it clockwise.* ADJ CLASSIF: ATTRIB OR ADV

What words for clothes are there on these pages?

clockwork /klɒkwɜːk/. **1 Clockwork** is the machinery in some types of toys or models that makes them move or operate when they are wound up with a key. N UNCOUNT

2 If you say that something happens **like clockwork**, you mean that it happens without any problems or delays. EG *That summer the work of the farm went like clockwork.* PHRASE

clod /klɒd/, **clods.** A **clod** is a large lump of earth. N COUNT

clog /klɒg/, **clogs, clogging, clogged. 1** When something **clogs** a hole, it blocks it so that nothing can pass through. V+O ◇ **clogged.** EG *My nose and throat felt clogged... His rifle was clogged with sand.* ◇ ADJ CLASSIF

2 Clogs are heavy leather or wooden shoes with thick wooden soles. See picture at SHOES. N COUNT: USU PLURAL

clog up. When something **clogs up** or **is clogged up**, it becomes blocked and no longer works properly. EG *Their lungs may progressively clog up... If the cooling unit gets clogged up with ice it can't do its job efficiently.* PHRASAL VB: V-ERG+ADV, OFT+*with*

cloister /klɔɪstə/, **cloisters.** A **cloister** is a paved and covered area round a square in a monastery or a cathedral. N COUNT

cloistered /klɔɪstəd/. If you have a **cloistered** way of life, you live quietly and are not involved in the normal busy life of the world around you. EG *...cloistered academic solitude.* ADJ QUALIT

clone /kləʊn/, **clones, cloning, cloned. 1** A **clone** is an animal or plant that has been produced artificially, for example in a laboratory, from the cells of another animal or plant. A clone is identical to the original animal or plant. N COUNT

2 To **clone** an animal or plant means to produce it as a clone. V+O

close, closes, closing, closed; closer, closest; pronounced /kləʊz/ when it is a verb and also in paragraph 4, and /kləʊs/ when it is an adjective or adverb and also in paragraphs 18 and 20.

1 When something such as a door or a lid **closes** or when you **close** it, it moves so that it covers or fills a hole or a gap. EG *He opened the door and closed it behind him... It took a bit of pressure to make the lid close.* V-ERG

2 When a place **closes** or **is closed**, people cannot use it, or all work stops there. EG *Many libraries close on Saturdays at 1 p.m... Shotton Steelworks was closed with the loss of nearly 8,000 jobs.* V-ERG

3 To **close** a conversation, event, or matter means to bring it to an end. EG *He spoke as though he wanted to close the conversation... The case is closed.* V+O

4 The **close** of a period of time or an activity is the end of it. EG *The view is best of all towards the close of the day... The war in Europe drew to a close.* N SING: OFT+*of* Formal

5 If you **close** on someone or something that you are following, you get nearer and nearer to them. EG *The shark closed on the woman... The boat was about 200 yards away from us but closing fast.* V: OFT+*on*

6 Something that is **close** to something else is near to it. EG *Their two heads were close together... I got close enough to see what the trouble was.* ▸ used as an adverb. EG *He moved a bit closer... The children followed close behind them.* ◇ **closely.** EG *The crowd moved in more closely around him.* ADJ PRED ▸ ADV ◇ ADV

7 Something that is **close by** or **close at hand** is near to you. EG *There was a small lamp on the table close by.* PHRASE

8 If you look at something **close up** or **close to**, you look at it when you are very near to it. EG *Close up, they should look even bigger... It was my first glimpse of him close to.* PHRASE

9 You say that people are **close** to each other when they like each other very much and know each other very well. EG *They felt very close to each other... Father and I are very close... Not even my closest friends had any idea that something was wrong.* ◇ **closeness.** EG *They felt a new closeness in relationships with their friends.* ADJ QUALIT ◇ N UNCOUNT

10 Your **close** relatives are the members of your family who are most directly related to you, for example your parents and your brothers or sisters. ADJ QUALIT: ATTRIB

11 Close contact or co-operation involves seeing or communicating with someone often. EG *My sons have maintained extremely close ties with a college friend... ...his closest advisers.* ◇ **closely.** EG *Every doctor works closely with the Child Health Service.* ADJ QUALIT: ATTRIB ◇ ADV

12 If there is a **close** link or resemblance between two things, they are strongly connected or are very similar. EG *...the close link between love and fear.* ◇ **closely.** EG *Status was closely linked with wealth... ...a creature that closely resembles a newt.* ADJ QUALIT ◇ ADV

13 Close inspection or observation of something is careful and thorough. EG *These events deserve closer examination.* ◇ **closely.** EG *He studied the photographs very closely.* ADJ QUALIT: ATTRIB ◇ ADV

14 When a competition or election is **close**, it is only won by a small amount. EG *The vote was close.* ADJ QUALIT

15 If you are **close** to laughter or **close** to tears, you are likely to laugh or cry soon. ADJ PRED+*to*

16 If an event is **close**, it will happen soon. EG *An agreement seems close.* ADJ PRED

17 Something such as an opinion or emotion that is **close** to something else is almost the same as it. EG *She regarded Lomax with something that was close to fear.* ADJ PRED+*to*

18 If something is **close to** or **close on** a particular amount or distance, it is slightly less than that amount or distance. EG *The Thompsons face a bill of close to £8,000 for a new roof... The pile of wood was close on ten feet in height.* PREP

19 If the atmosphere is **close**, it is uncomfortably warm with not enough air. EG *The room was hot and close and full of smoke.* ADJ QUALIT British

20 Close is used in the names of some streets. EG *...7 Winchester Close.*

21 If you describe an event as **a close shave**, **a close thing**, or **a close call**, you mean that an accident or a disaster very nearly happened. EG *It was a very close shave. The car only just missed me.* PHRASE

22 See also **closed, closing**.

close down. If someone **closes down** a factory or a business or if it **closes down**, all work or activity stops there, usually for ever. EG *The mines had been closed down... The magazine was forced to close down.* PHRASAL VB: V-ERG+ADV

close in. If a group of people **close in** on a person or place, they come nearer and nearer to them and gradually surround them. EG *As the enemy closed in, the resistance of the villagers shrank to nothing.* PHRASAL VB: V+ADV: OFT+*on/upon*

closed /kləʊzd/. **1** If something such as a door or a lid is **closed**, it is covering or filling a hole or gap. EG *I fell asleep with my window closed tight... He was sitting in his wheelchair with closed eyes.* ADJ CLASSIF

2 If a shop or a public building is **closed**, people cannot use it. EG *It was Sunday and the garage was closed.* ADJ CLASSIF

3 A **closed** group of people is restricted to only a few people. EG *He had a fairly closed circle of friends... Britain dearly loves its little closed societies.* ADJ QUALIT: ATTRIB

4 If people do something **behind closed doors**, they do it in secret. EG *On the whole these debates take place behind closed doors.* PHRASE

closed-circuit television, closed-circuit televisions. Closed-circuit television is a television system that is used inside a building, for example to film customers in a shop so that shoplifters can be identified. N UNCOUNT OR N COUNT

closed shop, closed shops. A **closed shop** is a factory, shop, or other business in which employees must be members of a particular trade union. N COUNT

clothes

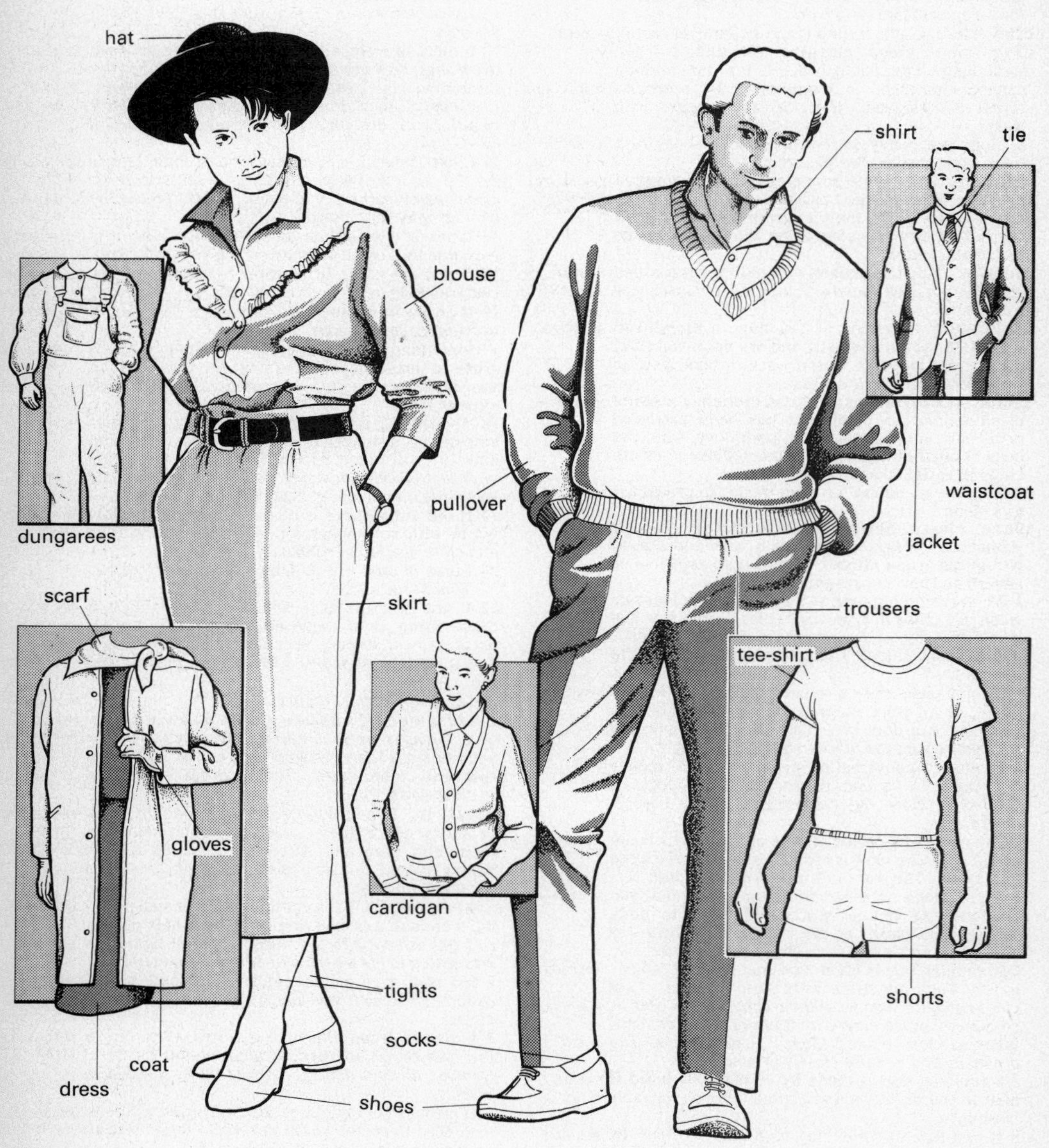
hat
shirt
tie
blouse
dungarees
pullover
waistcoat
jacket
scarf
skirt
trousers
tee-shirt
gloves
cardigan
tights
socks
coat
dress
shoes
shorts

close-knit /kləʊs nɪt/. If a group of people are **close-knit**, they are closely linked and share similar beliefs or activities. EG *It's a very close-knit community.* ADJ QUALIT

close-set /kləʊs set/. If someone's eyes are **close-set**, they are very near to each other. ADJ QUALIT

closet /klɒzɪt/, **closets, closeting, closeted. 1** A **closet** is a cupboard. N COUNT American

2 If you **are closeted** with someone, you are talking privately to them. EG *Judith is still closeted with those two lawyers.* V+O: USU PASS+*with*

3 You use **closet** to describe beliefs, habits, or feelings that people keep private and secret, often because they are embarrassed about them. EG *...closet fears... ...closet alcoholics.* ADJ CLASSIF: ATTRIB

close-up /kləʊs ʌp/, **close-ups.** A **close-up** is a photograph or film that shows a lot of detail because it is taken very near to the subject. EG *The team anxiously awaited close-ups of the moon.* N COUNT ● If you see something **in close-up**, you see it in great detail on a photograph or film which has been taken very near to the subject. EG *...a portrait of the chairman, huge and in close-up.* ● PHRASE

closing /kləʊzɪŋ/. The **closing** part of an activity or period of time is the final part of it. EG *...the closing stages of the election campaign.* ADJ CLASSIF: ATTRIB

closure /kləʊʒə/, **closures. 1** The **closure** of a business or factory is the permanent shutting of it. EG *...newspapers that are threatened with closure.* N UNCOUNT OR N COUNT

2 The **closure** of a road or border is the blocking of it in order to prevent people from using it. EG *...the closure of the Suez Canal.* N UNCOUNT +SUPP

clot /klɒt/, **clots, clotting, clotted. 1** A **clot** is a sticky lump that forms when blood dries up and becomes thicker. EG *...a blood clot.* N COUNT

2 When blood **clots**, it becomes thick and forms a lump. V-ERG

3 You call someone a **clot** when they have done or said something stupid. EG *That's what it's supposed to look like, you clot.* N COUNT OR VOCATIVE Informal British

cloth /klɒθ/, **cloths. 1 Cloth** is fabric which is made by weaving, knitting, or some other similar process. Cloth is used especially for making clothes. EG *...strips of cotton cloth.* N MASS

2 A **cloth** is a piece of cloth which you use for a particular purpose, such as cleaning. EG *Clean with a soft cloth dipped in warm soapy water.* N COUNT

clothe /kləʊð/, **clothes, clothing, clothed. 1 Clothes** are the things that people wear, such as shirts, coats, trousers, and dresses. EG *I took off all my clothes... They hadn't got any clothes on.* N PLURAL

2 If you **are clothed** in something, you are dressed in it. EG *Mrs Travers was clothed in green.* V+O: USU PASS+*in*

3 To **clothe** someone means to provide them with clothes to wear. EG *Are we not better fed, better clothed, and better housed than ever before?* V+O: USU PASS

clothes line, clothes lines. A **clothes line** is a rope on which you hang washing so that it can dry. N COUNT

clothes peg, clothes pegs. A **clothes peg** is a small wooden or plastic device which you use to fasten clothes to a clothes line. See picture at PEGS. N COUNT

clothing /kləʊðɪŋ/. **1 Clothing** is the clothes people wear. EG *...loans to pay for food and clothing... ...waterproof clothing.* N UNCOUNT

2 You use **clothing** to describe something which is concerned with the business of designing, manufacturing, or selling clothes. EG *...a clothing factory.* ADJ CLASSIF: ATTRIB

clotted cream is very thick cream that is made mainly in the south-west of England. N UNCOUNT

cloud /klaʊd/, **clouds, clouding, clouded. 1** A **cloud** is a mass of water vapour that floats in the sky. Clouds are usually white or grey. EG *There were little white clouds high in the blue sky... There will be heavy cloud over many areas.* N COUNT OR N UNCOUNT

2 A **cloud** of smoke or dust is a mass of it floating in the air. EG *...billowing clouds of thick black smoke.* N PART

3 If something such as a room **clouds** or if you **cloud** it, it becomes less easy to see through. EG *He lit a cigar and soon clouded the room in smoke.* V-ERG

4 If one thing **clouds** another, **4.1** it confuses things so that you cannot understand a situation or judge it properly. EG *His explanations clouded the issue.* **4.2** it makes a situation more unpleasant. EG *Insanity clouded the last years of his life.* V+O

5 If you are **under a cloud**, you are in disgrace and people have a poor opinion of you. EG *I was already under a cloud at the office.* PHRASE Informal

cloud over. 1 If your face or eyes **cloud over**, you suddenly look sad or angry. EG *The vicar's face clouded over and his mouth fell open.* PHRASAL VB: V+ADV **2** If it **clouds over**, the sky becomes covered with clouds. V+ADV

cloudless /klaʊdlɪ²s/. If the sky is **cloudless**, there are no clouds in it. ADJ CLASSIF

cloudy /klaʊdi¹/. **1** If it is **cloudy**, there are a lot of clouds in the sky. EG *It was a cloudy day.* ADJ QUALIT

2 If a liquid is **cloudy**, it is less clear than it should be. EG *...cloudy water.* ADJ QUALIT

3 Ideas or opinions that are **cloudy** are confused or uncertain. EG *Their policies seem fairly cloudy.* ADJ QUALIT

clout /klaʊt/, **clouts, clouting, clouted. 1** If you **clout** someone, you hit them. EG *Then he clouted me across the face.* V+O: OFT+A Informal ▸ used as a noun. EG *...a clout on the head.* ▸ N COUNT

2 Someone who has **clout** has influence and power. EG *The commission lacks the clout to force him to resign... ...political clout.* N UNCOUNT Informal

clove /kləʊv/, **cloves. 1 Cloves** are small dried flower buds which are used as a spice. N COUNT: USU PLURAL

2 A **clove** of garlic is a small part of a garlic bulb. N COUNT

clover /kləʊvə/ is a small plant with pink or white ball-shaped flowers. N UNCOUNT

clown /klaʊn/, **clowns, clowning, clowned. 1** A **clown** is a performer in a circus who wears funny clothes and bright make-up, and does silly things in order to make people laugh. N COUNT

2 If you **clown**, you do silly things in order to make people laugh. EG *He clowned and joked with the children.* V

3 You can describe someone as a **clown** when you have no respect for them. EG *Any clown with a PhD should be able to teach English.* N COUNT Informal

cloying /klɔɪɪŋ/. You use **cloying** to describe something that you find unpleasant because it is too sweet and sickly, or too sentimental. EG *...the cloying scent of flowers... ...cloying sentimentality.* ADJ QUALIT

club /klʌb/, **clubs, clubbing, clubbed. 1** A **club** is **1.1** an organization of people who are all interested in a particular activity or subject. EG *Have you joined the Swimming Club?* N COUNT: USU+SUPP **1.2** a place where the members of a club meet. EG *I'll see you at the club.* N COUNT

2 A **club** is also **2.1** a thick heavy stick that can be used as a weapon. **2.2** a long thin stick which a player uses to hit the ball in golf. N COUNT

3 If you **club** someone, you hit them hard with something blunt and heavy. EG *They were going to club him to death.* V+O: OFT+A

clubs

4 Clubs is one of the four suits in a pack of playing cards. Each card in the suit is marked with one or more black symbols in the shape of a leaf with three rounded parts. N UNCOUNT

5 A **club** is also one of the thirteen playing cards in the suit of clubs. N COUNT

club together. If people **club together** for something, they all give money in order to share PHRASAL VB: V+ADV, USU+*to*-INF the cost of it. EG *We all clubbed together to buy her a present.*

cluck /klʌk/, **clucks, clucking, clucked. 1** When a hen **clucks**, it makes the noise that hens typically make. V

2 If you **cluck** over someone or something, you say things in a disapproving or fussy way. EG *The women clucked disapprovingly over her hair.* V: OFT+*over*

clue /klu:/, **clues. 1** A **clue** is **1.1** something that provides information about a problem that you are trying to solve. EG *The clue to solving our energy problem lies in conservation... The police searched all the houses but found no clues.* N COUNT: OFT+SUPP **1.2** a short piece of writing in a crossword or game, giving information which helps you to work out the answer to a question. N COUNT

2 If you **haven't a clue** about something, for example what it is or where it is, you do not know much about it. EG *I hadn't got a clue how to spell it.* PHRASE

clump /klʌmp/, **clumps, clumping, clumped. 1** A **clump** of plants, people, or buildings is a small group of them growing or standing together. EG *...a clump of thistles... ...clumps of young fir trees.* N COUNT+SUPP

2 If someone **clumps** about, they walk with heavy clumsy footsteps. EG *My sister came clumping back in her wellingtons.* V+A

clumsy /klʌmzi¹/, **clumsier, clumsiest. 1** Someone who is **clumsy** moves or handles things in a careless, awkward way, often so that things are knocked over or broken. EG *I wanted to dance, but I felt stupid and clumsy and afraid to get up... I held the tweezers, but by fingers were too clumsy to handle them properly.* ◊ **clumsily**. EG *She stumbled clumsily, as though drunk, and sat down.* ◊ **clumsiness**. EG *The older boys would laugh loudly at his clumsiness.* ADJ QUALIT; ◊ ADV; ◊ N UNCOUNT

2 A **clumsy** action or statement is tactless and likely to upset people. EG *Haldane's efforts at reconciliation were clumsy and naive.* ◊ **clumsily**. EG *...a clumsily phrased apology.* ADJ QUALIT; ◊ ADV

3 An object that is **clumsy** is not neat in design or appearance, and is often awkward to use. EG *Mechanical switches are often clumsy and unreliable... ...a clumsy weapon.* ◊ **clumsily**. EG *The furniture was clumsily designed.* ADJ QUALIT; ◊ ADV

clung /klʌŋ/ is the past tense and past participle of **cling.**

clunk /klʌŋk/, **clunks.** A **clunk** is a sound made by heavy objects hitting against each other. EG *There was a metallic clunk as the gun struck the table.* N COUNT

cluster /klʌstə/, **clusters, clustering, clustered.**
1 A **cluster** of people or things is a small group of them close together. EG *There was a little cluster of admirers round the guest speaker... ...a cluster of cottages... ...clusters of white flowers.* N PART

2 If people or things **cluster** together, they gather together or are found together in a small group. EG *Many of the guests immediately clustered around the table... ...a hill where the white buildings clustered together.* ◊ **clustered**. EG *They were clustered round a radio.* V: USU+A; ◊ ADJ PRED +A

clutch /klʌtʃ/, **clutches, clutching, clutched. 1** If you **clutch** something, you hold it tightly, usually because you are afraid or anxious. EG *Myra came in, clutching her handbag... Her pony stumbled, and she clutched at the reins.* ● to **clutch at straws**: see **straw**. V+O OR V+A

2 If someone is in the **clutches** of another person, that person has captured them or has power over them. EG *He escaped the clutches of the law.* N PLURAL Informal

3 In a car, the **clutch** is the pedal that you press before you change gear, and the mechanism that it operates. See picture at CAR. N COUNT

4 A **clutch** is **4.1** a group of eggs laid by a bird at one time. N PART **4.2** a small group of people or things. EG *Mrs Thatcher was there with a clutch of cabinet ministers.* Literary

clutter /klʌtə/, **clutters, cluttering, cluttered. 1** **Clutter** is a lot of things in an untidy state, especially things that are not useful or necessary. EG *The rooms were full of clutter.* N UNCOUNT

2 If things **clutter** a place, they fill it untidily. EG *Cluttering the table were papers, books, and ashtrays.* ◊ **cluttered**. EG *He glanced around the small, cluttered room.* V+O: OFT+*up*; ◊ ADJ QUALIT

cm is an abbreviation for 'centimetre'. EG *...two rolls of sterile bandage 5 cm wide.*

c/o. You write **c/o** before an address on an envelope when you are sending it to someone who is staying or working at that address, often for only a short time. **c/o** is an abbreviation for 'care of'. EG *Mr A D Bright, c/o Sherman Ltd, 62 Burton Road, Bristol 8.*

co- /kəʊ/ is used to form words that refer **1** to people sharing things or doing things together. EG *...co-ownership schemes... The two countries have continued to coexist peacefully.* **2** to people who share the same job. EG *...the co-author of a cookery book... He sat behind the pilot and co-pilot.* PREFIX

Co. /kəʊ/. **1 Co.** is used as an abbreviation for 'company' in the names of companies. EG *...Morris, Marshall, Faulkner & Co.*

2 You can use **and co.** to refer to a group of people associated with a particular person; used showing disapproval. EG *The time may be coming for Mrs Thatcher and co. to redeem themselves.* PHRASE Informal

coach /kəʊtʃ/, **coaches, coaching, coached. 1** A **coach** is **1.1** a comfortable bus that carries passengers on long journeys. EG *The coach leaves Cardiff at twenty to eight... We usually go there by coach... ...a coach journey.* N COUNT OR *by*+N British **1.2** one of the separate sections of a train that carries passengers. N COUNT **1.3** an enclosed four-wheeled vehicle pulled by horses, in which people used to travel. Coaches are still used for ceremonial events. N COUNT OR *by*+N

2 If you **coach** someone, you help them to become better at a particular sport or subject. EG *She had been coached by a former Wimbledon champion.* V+O OR V

3 A **coach** is also someone who coaches a person or a sports team. EG *...a famous football coach.* N COUNT

coachload /kəʊtʃləʊd/, **coachloads.** A **coachload** of people is a group of people who travel somewhere together in a coach. EG *...coachloads of tourists.* N PART

coagulate /kəʊægjə⁴leɪt/, **coagulates, coagulating, coagulated.** When a liquid such as paint or blood **coagulates**, it becomes very thick. V-ERG

coal /kəʊl/, **coals. 1 Coal** is a hard black substance that is taken from under the earth and burned as fuel. EG *...a lump of coal... ...coal, oil, and gas... ...the coal mining industry.* N UNCOUNT

2 Coals are burning pieces of coal. EG *...chestnuts roasting over glowing coals.* N COUNT: USU PLURAL

coalesce /kəʊəlɛs/, **coalesces, coalescing, coalesced.** If two or more things **coalesce**, they come together and form a larger group or system. EG *There is a tendency for industrial systems to coalesce into large units.* V OR V+*with*: RECIP Formal

coalface /kəʊlfeɪs/, **coalfaces.** In a coal mine, the **coalface** is the part where the coal is being cut out of the rock. N COUNT

coalfield /kəʊlfi:ld/, **coalfields.** A **coalfield** is a region where there is coal under the ground. N COUNT

coalition /kəʊəlɪʃə⁰n/, **coalitions.** A **coalition** is **1** a government consisting of people from two or more political parties. EG *...the fall of Asquith's Coalition Government.* **2** a group consisting of people from different political or social groups who are cooperating to achieve a particular aim. EG *...a broad coalition of community groups in the area.* N COUNT

coalman /kəʊlmə³n/, **coalmen.** A **coalman** is a person who delivers coal to people's houses. N COUNT British

Does a coat of arms have sleeves?

coalminer /kəʊlmaɪnə/, **coalminers.** A **coalminer** is a person whose job is mining coal. N COUNT

coal scuttle, coal scuttles. A **coal scuttle** is a special kind of bucket for keeping coal in. N COUNT

coarse /kɔ:s/, **coarser, coarsest. 1** Something that is **coarse** has a rough texture which consists of thick strands or large pieces. EG *...coarse white cloth... ...coarse black hair... ...coarse grass.* ADJ QUALIT

2 Someone who is **coarse** talks and behaves in a rude and offensive way. EG *He objected to her coarse remarks.* ◊ **coarsely.** EG *She speaks rather coarsely.* ◊ **coarseness.** EG *With deliberate coarseness, he wiped his mouth with the back of his hand.* ADJ QUALIT ◊ ADV ◊ N UNCOUNT

coarsen /kɔ:sə^{0}n/, **coarsens, coarsening, coarsened.** If someone **coarsens** or **is coarsened**, they become less polite. EG *My whole nature had coarsened in a way that horrified me.* V-ERG

coast /kəʊst/, **coasts, coasting, coasted. 1** The **coast** is an area of land that is next to the sea. EG *...a trawler fishing off the coast of Portugal... We had made up our minds to stay on the East Coast.* N COUNT: USU the+N

2 If you say that **the coast is clear**, you mean that there is nobody around to see you or catch you. PHRASE

coastal /kəʊstə^{0}l/ means in the sea or on the land near a coast. EG *Sea lions inhabit the coastal waters... ...the coastal plain.* ADJ CLASSIF: ATTRIB

coaster /kəʊstə/, **coasters.** A **coaster** is a small mat that you put underneath a glass or mug. N COUNT

coastguard /kəʊstgɑ:d/, **coastguards. 1** A **coastguard** is an official who watches the sea near a coast, in order to get help for sailors when they need it, and to prevent smuggling. N COUNT

2 The **coastguard** is the organization to which coastguards belong. N SING: the+N

coastline /kəʊstlaɪn/, **coastlines.** A country's **coastline** is the edge of its coast. EG *...a rocky and treacherous coastline.* N COUNT

coat /kəʊt/, **coats, coating, coated. 1** A **coat** is a piece of clothing with long sleeves which you wear over your other clothes when you go outside. See picture at CLOTHES. N COUNT

2 An animal's **coat** is the fur or hair on its body. EG *It has a long shaggy coat.* N COUNT: USU+SUPP

3 If you **coat** something with a substance, you cover it with a thin layer of the substance. EG *The sweets are then coated with chocolate.* ◊ **coated.** EG *My face was coated with dust.* V+O: USU PASS+with ◊ ADJ QUALIT

4 A **coat** of paint or varnish is a thin layer of it on a surface. N COUNT

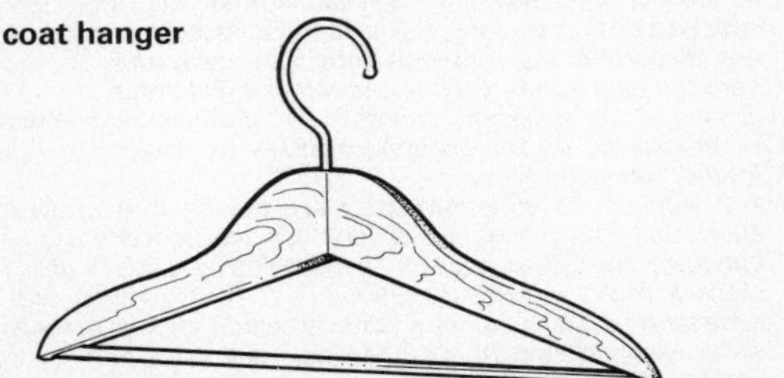

coat hanger

coat hanger, coat hangers. A **coat hanger** is a curved piece of wood, metal, or plastic that you hang a piece of clothing on. N COUNT

coating /kəʊtɪŋ/, **coatings.** A **coating** of a substance is a thin layer of it spread over a surface. EG *...a coating of dust.* N COUNT+SUPP

coat of arms, coats of arms. A **coat of arms** is a design in the form of a shield that is used as an emblem by a family, a town, or an organization. N COUNT

co-author, co-authors. The **co-authors** of a book are the people who have written it together. N COUNT

coax /kəʊks/, **coaxes, coaxing, coaxed.** If you **coax** someone to do something, you gently try to persuade them to do it. EG *You just coax them into doing it... 'It won't hurt you,' Marsha coaxed.* V+O: USU+A OR V+QUOTE

cobalt /kəʊbɒlt, -bɔ:lt/. **Cobalt** or **cobalt blue** is a deep blue colour. ADJ COLOUR Literary

cobble /kɒbə^{0}l/, **cobbles, cobbling, cobbled.** **Cobbles** are the same as cobblestones. N COUNT: USU PLURAL

cobble together. If you **cobble** something **together**, you make it roughly or quickly; used showing disapproval. EG *Its author has cobbled together a guide to the islands.* PHRASAL VB: V+O+ADV

cobbled /kɒbə^{0}ld/. A **cobbled** street has a surface made of cobblestones. ADJ CLASSIF

cobbler /kɒblə/, **cobblers.** A **cobbler** is a person whose job is to make or mend shoes. N COUNT Outdated

cobblestone /kɒbə^{0}lstəʊn/, **cobblestones.** **Cobblestones** are stones with a rounded upper surface which were once used for making streets. N COUNT: USU PLURAL

cobra /kəʊbrə/, **cobras.** A **cobra** is a kind of poisonous snake. N COUNT

cobweb /kɒbwɛb/, **cobwebs.** A **cobweb** is the net which a spider makes for catching insects. ◊ **cobwebbed** /kɒbwɛbd/. EG *...the dusty cobwebbed bulb.* N COUNT OR N UNCOUNT ◊ ADJ CLASSIF

cocaine /kə^{6}keɪn/ is a drug which people take for pleasure, but which they can become addicted to. In most countries it is illegal to take cocaine. N UNCOUNT

cock /kɒk/, **cocks, cocking, cocked. 1** A **cock** is an adult male chicken. EG *Cocks began to crow.* N COUNT British

2 A **cock** bird is a male bird. EG *...a cock pheasant.* N COUNT

3 If you **cock** a part of your body in a particular direction, you lift it or point it in that direction. EG *He stepped back, his head cocked to one side, to admire his work... A stray dog cocked his leg against a lamp-post.* V+O: USU+A

4 If you **keep** your **ears cocked**, you listen very carefully for something. EG *She kept her ears cocked for any mention of her name.* PHRASE

cock up. If you **cock** something **up**, you ruin it by doing something wrong; a rude expression. EG *We don't want to cock the whole thing up.* • See also **cock-up.** PHRASAL VB: V+O+ADV Informal British

cockatoo /kɒkətu:, kɒkətu:/, **cockatoos.** A **cockatoo** is a kind of parrot which has a crest on its head. N COUNT

cockerel /kɒkə^{0}rəl/, **cockerels.** A **cockerel** is a young cock. N COUNT

cockeyed /kɒkaɪd/. If an idea or scheme is **cockeyed**, it is stupid and very unlikely to succeed. EG *That sounds a cockeyed way of going about things.* ADJ QUALIT

cockle /kɒkə^{0}l/, **cockles.** **Cockles** are a kind of small shellfish. N COUNT: USU PLURAL

cockney /kɒkni^{1}/, **cockneys. 1** A **cockney** is a person who was born in the East End of London. N COUNT

2 **Cockney** is the dialect and accent of the East End of London. EG *...a cockney accent.* N UNCOUNT

cockpit /kɒkpɪt/, **cockpits.** A **cockpit** is **1** the part of a small plane where the pilot sits. **2** the part of a racing car where the driver sits. N COUNT

cockroach /kɒkrəʊtʃ/, **cockroaches.** A **cockroach** is a large brown insect that is often found in dirty rooms. N COUNT

cocksure /kɒkʃʊə, -ʃɔ:/. If someone is **cocksure**, they are too confident; used showing disapproval. ADJ QUALIT

cocktail /kɒkteɪl/, **cocktails.** A **cocktail** is **1** an alcoholic drink which contains several ingredients. EG *...a champagne cocktail... ...a cocktail party.* N COUNT **2** something which is made by combining a number of different things. EG *...a shrimp cocktail.* N COUNT+SUPP

cock-up /kɒkʌp/, **cock-ups.** A **cock-up** is a mistake that prevents something being done successfully; a rude word. EG *There has been a series of cock-ups.* N COUNT Informal British

cocky /kɒki^{1}/, **cockier, cockiest.** Someone who is **cocky** is very self-confident and rather cheeky. EG *Don't be too cocky, you were only third.* ADJ QUALIT Informal

cocoa /kəʊkəʊ/ is **1** a brown powder made from the seeds of a tropical tree, which is used in making chocolate. **2** a hot drink made from cocoa powder and milk or water. EG *...a cup of cocoa.* N UNCOUNT

coconut /kəʊkənʌt/, **coconuts.** A **coconut** is a very large nut with a hairy shell, which has white flesh and milky juice inside it. N COUNT

cocoon /kəkuːn/, **cocoons. 1** A **cocoon** is a covering of silky threads that the larvae of moths and other insects make for themselves before they grow into adults. N COUNT

2 You can use **cocoon** to describe an environment in which someone feels protected and safe. EG *I lived in a cocoon of love and warmth.* N COUNT+SUPP

cocooned /kəkuːnd/. **1** If someone is **cocooned** in blankets or clothes, they are completely wrapped in them. ADJ CLASSIF

2 If you say that someone is **cocooned**, you mean that they are isolated and protected from everyday life and problems. EG *A historian cocooned in Oxford can easily lose touch with reality.* ADJ CLASSIF

cod /kɒd/. **Cod** is the singular and the plural form. **Cod** is a kind of fish. EG *Their diet centres upon cod and fried chicken.* N COUNT OR N UNCOUNT

coddle /kɒdəᵒl/, **coddles, coddling, coddled.** If you **coddle** someone, you treat them too kindly or you protect them too much. EG *Teachers shouldn't coddle their pupils.* V+O

code /kəʊd/, **codes, coding, coded. 1** A **code** is a set of rules about how people should behave. EG *...accepted codes of behaviour... ...the IBA's code of advertising standards and practice.* N COUNT: USU+SUPP

2 A **code** is also **2.1** a system of replacing the letters or words in a message with other letters or words, so that nobody can understand it unless they know the system. EG *It is a code that even I can crack... The messages were typed in code.* N COUNT OR N UNCOUNT **2.2** a group of numbers or letters which is used to identify something, such as an educational course or a postal address. EG *My university course code is E5L21.* N COUNT **2.3** any system of signs or symbols that has a meaning. EG *We invented a code of telephone rings.* N COUNT

3 If you **code** a message, **3.1** you replace the letters or words in it with other letters or words, so that nobody can understand it unless they know the system. V+O ◇ **coded.** EG *For several hours now coded messages had been going out by telephone.* ◇ ADJ CLASSIF **3.2** you express it in a rather indirect way, because it would be dangerous or embarrassing to express it more plainly. V+O ◇ **coded.** EG *The letters were full of coded threats.* ◇ ADJ CLASSIF **3.3** you identify it by a group of numbers or letters. V+O

code name, code names. A **code name** is a name used for someone or something in order to keep their identity secret. EG *He is listed in the files by his code-name, the Jackal.* N COUNT

code-named. If a police or military operation is **code-named** a particular name, it is known by that name to the people involved in it. EG *It was code-named Operation Pegasus.* ADJ PRED+N

codify /kəʊdɪfaɪ, kɒ-/, **codifies, codifying, codified.** If you **codify** a set of rules, you define them or present them in a clear and ordered way. V+O ◇ **codified.** EG *...a codified system of criminal law.* ◇ ADJ CLASSIF

co-ed /kəʊɛd/. A **co-ed** school is the same as a co-educational school. ADJ CLASSIF: ATTRIB

co-educational /kəʊɛdjə⁴keɪʃəᵒnəl, -ʃənəᵒl/. A **co-educational** school is a school which is attended by both boys and girls. ADJ CLASSIF

coerce /kəʊɜːs/, **coerces, coercing, coerced.** If you **coerce** someone into doing something, you make them do it, although they do not want to. EG *They tried to coerce me into changing my appearance.* V+O: OFT+*into* Formal ◇ **coercion** /kəʊɜːʃəᵒn/. EG *No one was using coercion.* ◇ N UNCOUNT

coexist /kəʊɪ²gzɪst/, **coexists, coexisting, coexisted.** If two or more things **coexist**, they exist together at the same time or in the same place. EG *Large numbers of species coexist here.* V OR V+*with*: RECIP ◇ **coexistence** /kəʊɪ²gzɪstəns/. EG *...the need for peaceful coexistence.* ◇ N UNCOUNT

coffee /kɒfi¹/, **coffees. 1 Coffee** is **1.1** a hot brown drink that you make by pouring boiling water onto the roasted and ground seeds of a tropical tree, or onto a powder. EG *...a cup of coffee.* N MASS **1.2** the roasted seeds or powder from which the drink is made.

2 A **coffee** is a cup of coffee. N COUNT

coffee bar, coffee bars. A **coffee bar** is a small café where drinks and snacks are sold. N COUNT

coffee morning, coffee mornings. A **coffee morning** is a social event that takes place in the morning in someone's house, and is usually intended to raise money for charity. N COUNT

coffee pot, coffee pots. A **coffee pot** is a tall narrow container with a spout and a lid, in which coffee is made or served. N COUNT

coffee table, coffee tables. A **coffee table** is a small, low table in a living-room. N COUNT

coffers /kɒfəz/. When people refer to the **coffers** of an organization, they are talking about the amount of money it has. EG *...the flow of taxes into the government's coffers.* N PLURAL: USU+SUPP Formal

coffin /kɒfɪn/, **coffins. 1** A **coffin** is a box in which a dead body is buried or cremated. N COUNT

2 If one thing is a **nail in** another thing's **coffin**, it will help bring about its end or failure. EG *Credit cards are the first nails in the coffin of traditional financial methods.* PHRASE

cog /kɒg/, **cogs. 1** A **cog** is a wheel with square or triangular teeth around the edge, which is used in a machine to turn another wheel or part. N COUNT

2 If you describe someone as **a cog in a machine**, you mean that they have no importance or power within a large organization or group. EG *Workers on the production line feel that they are small cogs in the industrial machine.* PHRASE

cogent /kəʊdʒənt/. A reason, argument, or example that is **cogent** has the power to make you believe or accept it. EG *He put forward a cogent objection to our analysis.* ADJ QUALIT Formal ◇ **cogently.** EG *His opinions were always cogently expressed.* ◇ ADV

cognac /kɒnjæk/, **cognacs. Cognac** is a kind of brandy. N MASS

cognitive /kɒgnɪtɪv/ means relating to the mental process of learning. EG *...a study of the cognitive functions in learning to read.* ADJ CLASSIF: ATTRIB Technical

cohabit /kəʊhæbɪt/, **cohabits, cohabiting, cohabited.** If two people **are cohabiting**, they are living together and have a sexual relationship, but are not married. V OR V+*with*: RECIP Formal ◇ **cohabitation.** EG *We were thinking of marriage, or at least cohabitation.* ◇ N UNCOUNT

coherent /kəʊhɪərənt/. **1** If something is **coherent**, its parts fit together well so that it is clear and easy to understand. EG *They can offer no coherent answer... ...a coherent theory.* ADJ QUALIT ◇ **coherence** /kəʊhɪərəns/. EG *The theory possesses a certain intellectual coherence.* ◇ N UNCOUNT

2 If someone is **coherent**, they are talking in a clear and calm way. EG *At last his sister was coherent enough to explain.* ADJ QUALIT ◇ **coherently.** EG *Is she able to talk coherently now?* ◇ ADV

cohesion /kəʊhiːʒəᵒn/ is a state in which all the parts of something fit together well and form a united whole. EG *We lack a sense of national purpose and social cohesion.* N UNCOUNT

cohesive /kəʊhiːsɪv/. Something that is **cohesive** consists of parts that fit together well and form a united whole. EG *The poor do not see themselves as a cohesive group.* ADJ QUALIT

coil /kɔɪl/, **coils, coiling, coiled. 1** A **coil** of rope or wire is a length of it that has been wound into a series of loops. N COUNT: OFT+*of*

2 A **coil** is a single loop that is one of a series into which something has been wound. EG *Pythons kill* N COUNT

Do you burn coke or drink it?

by tightening their coils so that their victim cannot breathe.

3 If you **coil** something or if it **coils**, it curves into a series of loops or into the shape of a ring. EG *Pythons coil themselves around their prey and kill it... Thick smoke coiled up over the fields.* V-ERG : OFT+A

◇ **coiled.** EG *The base is made of coiled springs.* ◇ ADJ CLASSIF

coil up. If you **coil** something **up**, you wind it into a continuous series of loops. EG *He coiled up the hose.* PHRASAL VB : V+O+ADV

coin /kɔɪn/, **coins, coining, coined. 1** A **coin** is a small piece of metal which is used as money. EG *...a 10p coin... ...notes and coins.* N COUNT

2 If you **coin** a word or a phrase, you invent it. EG *Schumacher coined the slogan 'Small is beautiful'.* V+O

● You say **'to coin a phrase'** when you realize that you have just used a cliché or are just about to use one. EG *It was, to coin a phrase, an offer I couldn't refuse.* ● ADV SEN

3 If you say that two things are **two sides of the same coin**, you mean that they are two different aspects of the same situation. PHRASE Formal

coinage /kɔɪnɪdʒ/ consists of the coins which are used in a country. EG *...decimal coinage.* N UNCOUNT

coincide /kəʊɪnsaɪd/, **coincides, coinciding, coincided. 1** If two or more events **coincide**, they happen at about the same time. EG *Macmillan's departure coincided with Benn's return.* V OR V+*with* : RECIP

2 If the opinions or ideas of two or more people **coincide**, they are the same. EG *On the whole their views coincided.* V OR V+*with* : RECIP

3 If two or more lines or points **coincide**, they are in exactly the same place. EG *The boundary of the L.E.A. coincides with a county boundary.* V OR V+*with* : RECIP

coincidence /kəʊɪnsəˈdəns/, **coincidences.** A **coincidence** is what happens when two or more things occur at the same time by chance. EG *It was quite a coincidence that my sister was on the same train.* N COUNT OR N UNCOUNT

coincidental /kəʊɪnsɪdentəˈl/. Something that is **coincidental** is the result of a coincidence and has not been deliberately arranged. EG *Any similarity to real people is purely coincidental.* ADJ QUALIT

◇ **coincidentally** /kəʊɪnsɪdentəˈliˈ/. EG *These players, coincidentally, are all left-handed.* ◇ ADV SEN

coke /kəʊk/, **cokes. 1 Coke** is a solid black substance that is produced from coal and is burned as a fuel. N UNCOUNT

2 Coke is the name of a brown, fizzy, non-alcoholic drink. N MASS Trademark

colander /kɒləndə, kʌl-/, **colanders.** A **colander** is a bowl-shaped container with holes in it which you wash or drain food in. N COUNT

cold /kəʊld/, **colder, coldest; colds. 1** Something that is **cold** has a very low temperature or a lower temperature than is normal or acceptable. EG *Wash delicate fabrics in cold water... Your food is getting cold... This coffee's cold.* ADJ QUALIT

2 If it is **cold**, the temperature of the air is very low. EG *It's bitterly cold... ...a cold winter's day... The building was cold and draughty.* ADJ QUALIT

3 The **cold** is cold weather or a low temperature. EG *My fingers are so stiff from the cold.* N SING : *the*+N

4 If you are **cold**, your body is at an unpleasantly low temperature. EG *Can I light the fire? I'm cold.* ADJ PRED

5 Someone who is **cold** does not show much emotion, especially affection. EG *She seemed cold and uncaring.* ADJ QUALIT ◇ **coldly.** EG *'It's yours,' I said, politely, but coldly.* ◇ ADV ◇ **coldness.** EG *Kay was stunned by the coldness in his voice.* ◇ N UNCOUNT

6 If something **leaves** you **cold**, it fails to excite or interest you. EG *Her performance left me cold.* PHRASE

7 If you **have** or **get cold feet** about something that you were intending to do, you are now frightened of doing it. PHRASE

8 A **cold** is a mild, very common illness which makes you sneeze a lot and gives you a sore throat or a cough. N COUNT ● If you **catch cold**, you become ill with a cold. ● PHRASE

9 in cold blood: see **blood.** ● to **make** your **blood run cold**: see **blood.** ● to **throw** or **pour cold water on** something: see **water.**

cold-blooded. Someone who is **cold-blooded** does not show any pity or emotion. EG *...a cold-blooded murderer.* ADJ QUALIT

cold sweat. If you are in a **cold sweat**, you are sweating and feel cold, because you are very afraid or nervous. EG *He awoke trembling and in a cold sweat.* N SING : *a*+N

cold war is a state of extreme political unfriendliness between two countries, although they are not actually fighting each other. EG *...the cold war years of the 1950s.* N UNCOUNT, OR N SING : *the*+N

coleslaw /kəʊlslɔː/ is a salad of chopped cabbage, carrots, onions, and other vegetables, mixed together in mayonnaise. N UNCOUNT

colic /kɒlɪk/. If a baby has **colic**, it has pain in its stomach and bowels. N UNCOUNT

collaborate /kəlæbəreɪt/, **collaborates, collaborating, collaborated. 1** When people **collaborate**, they work together, especially on a book or on some research. EG *Antony and I are collaborating on a paper... The university hopes to collaborate with industry.* V OR V+*with* : RECIP ◇ **collaboration** /kəlæbəreɪʃəⁿn/. EG *...photographs published by Collins in collaboration with the Imperial War Museum.* ◇ N UNCOUNT ◇ **collaborator** /kəlæbəreɪtə/, **collaborators.** EG *My collaborator Roy Lewis and I did a series of articles for Radio 4.* ◇ N COUNT

2 If someone **collaborates** with enemies who have taken control of their country by force, he or she helps them; used showing disapproval. V OR V+*with* : RECIP

◇ **collaborator.** EG *They committed treason as collaborators of the invaders.* ◇ N COUNT

collaborative /kəlæbəˀrətɪv/. A **collaborative** piece of work is done by two or more people working together. EG *The project is a collaborative one.* ADJ CLASSIF : ATTRIB Formal

collage /kəˀlɑːʒ, kɒlɑːʒ/, **collages.** A **collage** is a picture that has been made by sticking pieces of coloured paper and cloth onto paper. N COUNT

collapse /kəlæps/, **collapses, collapsing, collapsed. 1** If a building **collapses**, it suddenly falls down. EG *These flimsy houses are liable to collapse in a heavy storm.* V ▸ used as a noun. EG *The collapse of buildings trapped thousands of people.* ▸ N UNCOUNT

2 If something **collapses**, it falls inwards and becomes smaller or flatter. EG *One of my lungs had collapsed.* V

3 If a system or institution **collapses**, it fails completely and suddenly. EG *Their marriage had collapsed.* V ▸ used as a noun. EG *...a company on the verge of collapse.* ▸ N UNCOUNT

4 If you **collapse, 4.1** you suddenly fall down because you are very tired, weak, or ill. EG *As we walked into the hotel, Jane collapsed.* V ▸ used as a noun. EG *Upon her collapse she was rushed to hospital.* ▸ N UNCOUNT **4.2** you sit down very suddenly, for example because you feel tired. EG *The music stopped and they collapsed onto cushions.* V : USU+A

collapsible /kəlæpsəˈbəˀl/. A **collapsible** object is designed to be folded flat when it is not being used. EG *...a collapsible bed.* ADJ CLASSIF

collar /kɒlə/, **collars, collaring, collared. 1** The **collar** of a shirt or coat is the part which fits round the neck and is usually folded over. N COUNT

2 A **collar** is also a leather band which is put round the neck of a dog or cat. N COUNT

3 If someone **collars** you, they catch you. EG *I was collared by the police.* V+O Informal

collarbone /kɒləbəʊn/, **collarbones.** Your **collarbone** is one of the two long bones which run from the base of your neck to your shoulder. N COUNT

collate /kəˀleɪt/, **collates, collating, collated.** When you **collate** pieces of information, you gather them all together and examine them. EG *All the new evidence had been collated.* V+O

collateral /kə^{6}lætərəl/ is money or property which is used as a guarantee that someone will repay a loan. EG *They have nothing to offer as collateral.* N UNCOUNT Formal

colleague /kɒli:g/, **colleagues.** Your **colleagues** are the people you work with, especially in a professional job. EG *I talked to a colleague of yours recently.* N COUNT

collect /kəlɛkt/, **collects, collecting, collected.**
1 If you **collect** a number of things, you bring them together from several places. EG *They're collecting wood for the fire.* V+O
2 If you **collect** things, for example stamps or books, as a hobby, you get a large number of them because you are interested in them. EG *Do you collect antiques?* V+O
3 When you **collect** someone, you go and get them from a place where they are waiting for you. EG *I have to collect the children from school.* V+O: OFT+*from*
4 When things **collect** in a place, they gather there over a period of time. EG *Damp leaves collect in gutters.* V+A
5 If you **collect** for a charity or for a present for someone, you ask people to give you money for it. EG *How much have you collected so far?* V OR V+O: OFT+*for*
6 If you **collect** yourself or **collect** your thoughts, you make an effort to calm yourself or prepare yourself mentally. EG *I had five minutes in which to collect my thoughts before the interview.* V-REFL OR V+O
collect up. If you **collect up** things, you collect them all together. EG *They collected up their gear.* PHRASAL VB: V+O+ADV

collected /kəlɛktı^{2}d/. Someone's **collected** works or letters are all their works or letters published as one book or as a set of books. EG *...the collected works of Proust.* ADJ CLASSIF

collecting /kəlɛktıŋ/. **1 Collecting** is the hobby of collecting a particular type of thing. EG *...stamp collecting... ...art collecting.* N UNCOUNT: USU+SUPP
2 A **collecting** tin or box is one that is used to collect money for charity. ADJ CLASSIF: ATTRIB

collection /kəlɛkʃə^{0}n/, **collections. 1** A **collection** of things is **1.1** a group of things you have acquired over a period of time. EG *Davis had a large collection of pop records.* **1.2** a number of stories, poems or articles published in one book. EG *...a collection of Scott Fitzgerald's short stories.* **1.3** a group of things. EG *...a collection of old ruins.* N PART
2 Collection is the act of collecting something from a place or from people. EG *...the collection of national taxes... Your curtains are ready for collection.* N UNCOUNT OR N COUNT
3 A **collection** is also **3.1** the organized collecting of money from people for charity. EG *They organized dances and collections which raised £450.* N COUNT OR N UNCOUNT **3.2** money that is given by people in church during some Christian services. N COUNT

collective /kəlɛktıv/ means shared by or involving every member of a group of people. EG *It was a collective decision.* ADJ CLASSIF: ATTRIB

collectively /kəlɛktıvli^{1}/. **1** If people do something **collectively**, they do it together. EG *They were collectively responsible.* ADV
2 You use **collectively** when you are referring to a group of things as a whole. EG *...a small group of marsupials called, collectively, rat-kangaroos.* ADV OR ADV SEN

collector /kəlɛktə/, **collectors. 1** A **collector** is a person who collects things of a particular type as a hobby. EG *...an art collector.* N COUNT+SUPP
2 You can also use **collector** to refer to someone whose job is to take something such as money or tickets from people. For example, a rent **collector** collects rent from tenants. N COUNT+SUPP

college /kɒlıdʒ/, **colleges. 1** A **college** is **1.1** an institution where students study after they have left school. EG *...the local technical college... What do you plan to do after college?* N COUNT OR N UNCOUNT **1.2** one of the institutions which some British universities are divided into. EG *...Jesus College, Cambridge.* N COUNT
2 College is **2.1** used in the titles of some secondary schools. EG *...Milton Ladies' College.* **2.2** used in the titles of some organized groups of people. EG *...the Royal College of Physicians.*

collide /kəlaɪd/, **collides, colliding, collided.** If a moving person or object **collides** with something, they hit it. EG *The two vehicles collided.* V OR V+*with*: RECIP

collie /kɒli^{1}/, **collies.** A **collie** or **collie dog** is a dog used by farmers for controlling sheep. N COUNT

colliery /kɒljəri^{1}/, **collieries.** A **colliery** is a coal mine. N COUNT British

collision /kəlıʒə^{0}n/, **collisions. 1** A **collision** occurs when a moving object hits something. EG *...a mid-air collision... A meteor is on a collision course with the Earth.* N COUNT OR N UNCOUNT: OFT+*with*
2 A **collision** of cultures or ideas occurs when two very different cultures or people meet and conflict. EG *...a collision of egos... This put them on a collision course with their elders.* N COUNT OR N UNCOUNT

colloquial /kələʊkwıəl/. **Colloquial** words and phrases are informal and are used especially in conversation. EG *...an intensive course in colloquial Greek.* ADJ QUALIT ◊ **colloquially.** EG *This game is colloquially known as 'Buzz off, Buster'.* ◊ ADV

collude /kə^{7}lu:d/, **colludes, colluding, colluded.** If you **collude** with someone, you cooperate with them secretly or illegally; used showing disapproval. EG *Some groups have colluded with the unions in avoiding holding a ballot.* V OR V+*with*: RECIP ◊ **collusion** /kə^{7}lu:ʒə^{0}n/. EG *She was in collusion with Christopher for financial reasons.* ◊ N UNCOUNT: OFT+*with/of*

cologne /kələʊn/ is a kind of weak perfume. N UNCOUNT

colon /kəʊlə^{7}n/, **colons. 1** A **colon** is a punctuation mark (:), which you can use in several ways. For example, you can put it before a list of things or before reported speech. N COUNT
2 Your **colon** is the part of your intestine above your rectum. N COUNT

colonel /kɜ:nə^{0}l/, **colonels.** A **colonel** is a senior officer in an army or air force. N COUNT

colonial /kələʊnıəl/ means relating to countries that are colonies, or to colonialism. EG *...the liberation of oppressed peoples from colonial rule.* ADJ CLASSIF: ATTRIB

colonialism /kələʊnıəlızə^{0}m/ is the practice by which a powerful country directly controls less powerful countries. EG *The politics of the Third World had their origins in colonialism.* N UNCOUNT

colonialist /kələʊnıəlıst/ means relating to colonialism. EG *Many people think of Northern Ireland as a colonialist situation.* ADJ CLASSIF

colonist /kɒlə^{7}nıst/, **colonists.** A **colonist** is someone who starts a colony. EG *...the Australian colonists.* N COUNT

colonize /kɒlə^{7}naız/, **colonizes, colonizing, colonized;** also spelled **colonise. 1** When people **colonize** a foreign country, they go to live there and take control of it. EG *...the Europeans who colonized North America.* V+O
2 When animals **colonize** a place, they move into it and make it their home. EG *The plains of North America were colonised by ant-eaters and other species.* V+O

colony /kɒlə^{7}ni^{1}/, **colonies.** A **colony** is **1** a country which is controlled by a more powerful country. EG *...the newly established colony of Australia.* N COUNT **2** a place where a particular group of people lives. EG *...a leper colony.* N COUNT **3** a group of insects or animals that live together. EG *...a colony of bees.* N COUNT

color /kʌlə/. See **colour.**

coloration /kʌləreıʃə^{0}n/. The **coloration** of an animal or a plant is the colours and patterns on it. N UNCOUNT

colossal /kəlɒsə^{0}l/. Something that is **colossal** is very large. EG *...colossal sums of money.* ADJ QUALIT

colour /kʌlə/, **colours, colouring, coloured;** spelled **color** in American English. **1** The **colour** of something is the appearance that it has as a result N COUNT OR N UNCOUNT

Would you be pleased if someone described your personality as colourless?

of reflecting light. Red, blue, and green are colours. EG *I don't know what colour her eyes are... All the rooms were painted different colours... His face was greyish in colour.*

2 Someone's **colour** is the normal colour of their skin, for example brown. EG *It was illegal to discriminate on the grounds of colour.* N UNCOUNT

3 A **colour** television, photograph, or picture is one that shows things in all their colours, and not just in black, white, and grey. EG *...marvellous colour illustrations.* ADJ CLASSIF : ATTRIB

4 If something such as a film or a television programme is **in colour**, it has been made in all colours, and not just in black, white, and grey. PHRASE

5 **Colour** is also a quality that makes something especially interesting or exciting. EG *The audiences liked the romance and colour of 'The Lady's Not for Burning'.* N UNCOUNT

6 If something **colours** your mind or opinion, it affects the way that you think about something. EG *Anger had coloured her judgement.* V+O

7 If you achieve something **with flying colours**, you achieve it in an extremely successful way. PHRASE

8 See also **coloured**, **colouring**.

colour in. If you **colour in** a drawing, you give it different colours using crayons. PHRASAL VB : V+O+ADV

colour blind. Someone who is **colour blind** cannot distinguish between colours, especially between red and green. ◇ **colour blindness.** EG *Colour blindness is a serious problem for pilots.* ADJ CLASSIF ◇ N UNCOUNT

coloured /kʌləd/, **coloureds;** spelled **colored** in American English. 1 Something that is **coloured** a particular colour has that colour. EG *The sky was mauve-coloured... The centre section was coloured pink... ...vividly coloured birds.* ADJ CLASSIF

2 Something that is **coloured** has a colour such as blue or red rather than being just white or black. EG *He drew patterns on the floor in coloured chalks.* ADJ CLASSIF

3 A person who is **coloured** belongs to a race of people who do not have white or pale skins. ADJ CLASSIF

colourful /kʌləful/; spelled **colorful** in American English. 1 Something that is **colourful** has bright colours. EG *...colourful posters of Paris and Venice.* ADJ QUALIT

2 A **colourful** story is full of exciting details. EG *Many colourful stories were told about him.* ADJ QUALIT

3 Someone who is described as **colourful** behaves in an interesting and amusing way; used showing approval. EG *He is one of the most colourful Parliamentary figures of his age.* ADJ QUALIT

colouring /kʌlərɪŋ/; **colourings;** spelled **coloring** in American English. 1 The **colouring** of something is the colours that it has. EG *...its rounded fins and distinctive green colouring.* N UNCOUNT

2 Someone's **colouring** is the colour of their hair, skin, and eyes. N SING+POSS

3 **Colouring** is a substance that is used to give colour to food. N MASS

colourless /kʌləlɪ²s/; spelled **colorless** in American English. Something that is **colourless** 1 is dull and uninteresting. EG *He spoke in the same colourless, plodding voice.* 2 has no colour at all. EG *...a colourless and tasteless liquid.* ADJ QUALIT / ADJ CLASSIF

colour supplement, colour supplements. In Britain, a **colour supplement** is a magazine that you get free when you buy a Sunday newspaper. N COUNT

colt /kɒlt/, **colts.** A **colt** is a young male horse. N COUNT

column /kɒləm/, **columns.** 1 A **column** is 1.1 a tall solid cylinder, usually used to support or decorate part of a building. 1.2 something that has a tall narrow shape. EG *...columns of smoke.* 1.3 a group of people or animals which moves in a long line. EG *Behind the brass band came a column of workers.* N COUNT

2 In a newspaper or magazine, a **column** is a vertical section of writing, especially one that is always written by the same person or is always about the same topic. EG *Bill used to write a column for the Bristol Evening News.* N COUNT

columnist /kɒləmnᵒɪst/, **columnists.** A **columnist** is a journalist who writes a regular article in a newspaper or magazine. EG *...gossip columnists.* N COUNT

coma /kəʊmə/, **comas.** Someone who is in a **coma** is in a state of deep unconsciousness. N COUNT

comatose /kəʊmətəʊs, -təʊz/. A person who is **comatose** is in a coma. ADJ CLASSIF Technical

comb /kəʊm/, **combs, combing, combed.** 1 A **comb** is a flat piece of plastic or metal, which you use to tidy your hair. N COUNT

comb

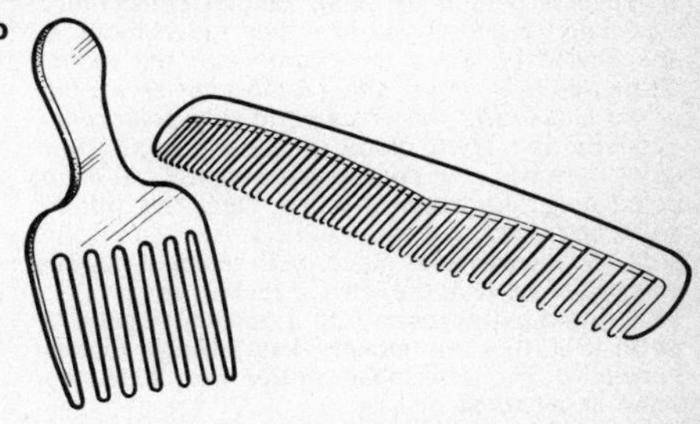

2 When you **comb** your hair, you tidy it using a comb. V+O

3 If you **comb** a place, you search everywhere in it in order to find someone or something. EG *It might amuse her to comb the town for antiques.* V+O : OFT+*for*

combat /kɒmbæt/, **combats, combating, combated.** 1 **Combat** is fighting that takes place in a war. EG *He was awarded the Military Cross for gallantry in combat.* N UNCOUNT

2 A **combat** is a battle, or a fight between two people. EG *...the mighty combats between the West and the East.* N COUNT Formal

3 If people in authority **combat** something, they try to stop it happening. EG *The basic problem is that of combating poverty.* V+O

combatant /kɒmbətᵊnt, kʌm-/, **combatants.** A **combatant** is someone who takes part in the fighting in a war. N COUNT

combination /kɒmbɪneɪʃᵊn/, **combinations.** A **combination** is 1 a mixture of things. EG *All actors use a combination of these techniques... Perhaps it was a combination of all these reasons.* 2 a series of letters or numbers that is used to open a combination lock. EG *I can't remember the combination.* N COUNT OR N UNCOUNT / N COUNT

combination lock, combination locks. A **combination lock** is a lock which can only be opened by turning a dial according to a particular series of letters or numbers. N COUNT

combine, combines, combining, combined; pronounced /kə⁷mbaɪn/ when it is a verb, and /kɒmbaɪn/ when it is a noun.

1 If you **combine** two or more things or if they **combine**, 1.1 they exist together. EG *We would all prefer to combine liberty with order.* 1.2 they join together to make a single thing. EG *Later the two teams were combined.* V-ERG; ALSO V OR V+*with* : RECIP

2 A **combine** is a group of people or organizations that are working or acting together. EG *...a newspaper combine.* N COUNT

3 If someone or something **combines** two qualities or features, they have both those qualities or features at the same time. EG *Carbon fibre combines flexibility with immense strength.* V+O OR V+O+*with* : RECIP

4 If someone **combines** two activities, they do them both at the same time. EG *It's difficult to combine family life with a career.* V+O OR V+O+*with* : RECIP

combined /kə⁷mbaɪnd/. 1 If someone or something has one quality or feature **combined** with another, they have both those qualities or features. EG *...a perfect example of professional expertise combined with personal charm... His eyes were wide with amazement and adoration combined.* ADJ PRED +*with*, OR ADJ AFTER N

2 A **combined** effort or attack is made by groups of people at the same time. EG *The combined efforts of police and military were at last successful.* ADJ CLASSIF : ATTRIB

combustion /kəmbʌstʃəⁿn/ is the act of burning something or the process of burning. EG *The ball of paper was heated to combustion point.* N UNCOUNT Formal

come /kʌm/, **comes, coming, came** /keɪm/. The form **come** is used in the present tense and is the past participle of the verb.

1 When a person or thing **comes** somewhere, especially to where you are, they move there. EG *She looked up when they came into the room... Come and look... She came clambering over a pile of old junk... The waiter came to take the order... Can you and Myra come to a party next Saturday?... Are you ever coming back home?... You can come over tomorrow at four... Then this woman came up to me.* V : OFT+A OR to-INF

2 If you **come** to a place, you reach it. EG *She eventually came to the town of Pickering.* V+to

3 If something **comes** up to a particular point or down to it, it is tall enough, deep enough, or long enough to reach that point. EG *Her hair came right down to her waist.* V+A

4 If something **comes** apart or **comes** to pieces, it breaks into pieces. If something **comes** off or **comes** away, it becomes detached from something else. EG *It just came apart in my hands... All the wallpaper's coming off... Ordinary sticky tape comes unstuck.* V+A

5 If someone or something **comes** to or into a particular state, they enter or reach that state. EG *They had come to power ten years earlier... The elevator came to a stop... Christianity came into being in a hostile environment... Some people stared at me when I came into sight.* V+to/into

6 If someone **comes** to do something, they gradually start doing it over a period of time. EG *I have come to like him quite a lot.* V+to-INF

7 When a particular time or event **comes**, it arrives or happens. EG *The time has come for a full campaign against the government's spending cuts.* V : USU+A

8 **Come** is used in expressions such as 'come the spring' and 'come the election' to mean when the time or event mentioned arrives or happens. EG *Come tomorrow you'll feel better about things.* PHRASE

9 When you refer to a time **to come** or an event **to come**, you are referring to a future time or event. EG *He hoped to play a significant role in the Parliamentary battle to come... Our income is going to be strictly limited for some time to come.* PHRASE

10 If a memory, thought, or idea **comes** to you, you suddenly remember or realize it. EG *The answer came to him just before noon... It came to me suddenly that what was wrong was that I was tired.* V+to

11 You say **'Come to think of it'** to indicate that you have suddenly realized something, often something obvious. EG *Come to think of it, why should I apologize?* ADV SEN

12 If something **comes** to a particular number or amount, it adds up to it. EG *My income now comes to £65 a week.* V+to

13 If someone or something **comes** from a particular place or thing, it is their source or starting point. EG *'Where do you come from?' – 'India.'... Information coming out of the country was unreliable... This extract comes from a conversation I had with her recently... Did you know the word 'idea' comes from Greek?* V+from/out of

14 Something that **comes** from something else is the result of it. EG *...the warm glow that comes from working co-operatively... You're always reading. No good will come of it, you'll see!* V+from/of

15 If someone or something **comes** first, next, or last, they are first, next, or last in a series, list, or competition. EG *What comes next then?... I was never in any race in which I didn't come last.* V+C

16 If a type of thing **comes** in a particular range of colours, styles, or sizes, it can have any of those colours, styles, or sizes. EG *The van came in two colours, medium brown or medium grey.* V : USU+in

17 The word **come** is also used in expressions such as 'It came as a surprise', which indicate a person's reaction to something. EG *It comes as no surprise to discover that Americans usually love Britain.* PHRASE

18 In a discussion, the next subject that you **come** to is the one that you talk about next. EG *Now we come to the most important thing.* V+to

19 If you say that you **do not know whether** you **are coming or going**, you mean that you are so busy that you are rather confused. PHRASE

20 See also **coming**.

come about. When you say how something **came about**, you say how it happened. EG *The discovery of adrenalin came about through a mistake... How did the invitation come about?* PHRASAL VB : V+ADV

come across. 1 If you **come across** someone or something, you meet them or find them by chance. EG *I came across a letter from Brunel the other day.* PHRASAL VB : V+PREP 2 If someone who is speaking **comes across** in a particular way, or if what they are saying **comes across** in that way, they make that impression on their audience. EG *He wasn't coming across as the idiot I had expected him to be.* V+ADV+A

come along. 1 You say **'come along'** to someone 1.1 to encourage them to do something they do not really want to do. EG *Come along, now, drink this.* 1.2 to encourage them to hurry up. PHRASE 2 When something **comes along**, it arrives or happens by chance. EG *A new generation of planners came along who were much more scientifically based.* PHRASAL VB : V+ADV 3 If something **is coming along**, it is developing or making progress. EG *There are even cookers which tell you how the meat is coming along.* V+ADV : ONLY CONT Informal

come at. If a person or animal **comes at** you, they move towards you in a threatening way and attack you. EG *The bear came at me.* PHRASAL VB : V+PREP

come back. 1 If you **come back** to a topic or point, you talk about it again later. EG *We'll come back to that question a little later.* PHRASAL VB : V+ADV+to 2 If something that you had forgotten **comes back** to you, you remember it. EG *It was all coming back to him. She was the girl from the sweet shop.* V+ADV, USU+to 3 When something **comes back**, it becomes fashionable again. EG *She was pleased to see that mini skirts were coming back.* V+ADV 4 See also **comeback**.

come by. To **come by** something means to find it or obtain it. EG *Jobs were hard to come by... He had not come by these things through his own labour.* PHRASAL VB : V+PREP, HAS PASS

come down. 1 If the cost, level, or amount of something **comes down**, it becomes less than it was before. EG *Inflation is starting to come down.* PHRASAL VB : V+ADV 2 If something **comes down**, it falls to the ground. EG *In the storm a tree came down.*

come down on. If you **come down on** someone, you criticize them severely. EG *Social workers like me come down harder on parents than on their children.* PHRASAL VB : V+ADV+PREP

come down to. If a problem, decision, or question **comes down to** a particular thing, that thing is the most important factor involved. EG *Your final choice of kitchen may well come down to cost.* PHRASAL VB : V+ADV+PREP

come down with. If you **come down with** an illness, you get it. EG *She came down with pneumonia and was taken to hospital.* PHRASAL VB : V+ADV+PREP

come for. If someone **comes for** you, they move towards you quickly in a threatening way, in order to attack you. EG *Jake was coming for me with a knife.* PHRASAL VB : V+PREP

come forward. If someone **comes forward**, they offer to do what is required. EG *More coloured men are now coming forward to join the police.* PHRASAL VB : V+ADV

come in. 1 If information or a report **comes in**, it PHRASAL VB :

What would you do if a lion came at you?

is received. EG *Reports are coming in from Mexico of a major earthquake.* V+ADV **2** If you have some money **coming in**, you receive it regularly as your income. V+ADV **3** If someone **comes in** on a discussion or an arrangement, they join in. EG *He should come in on the deal.* V+ADV, USU+A **4** If you ask where something or someone **comes in**, you are asking how they are involved in a particular matter. EG *Where does your husband come in?* V+ADV

come in for. If someone or something **comes in for** criticism or blame, they receive it. EG *British industry does come in for a great deal of criticism.* PHRASAL VB: V+ADV+PREP

come into. **1** If someone **comes into** some money, some property, or a title, they inherit it. EG *She was going to come into some more money on her mother's death.* PHRASAL VB: V+PREP **2** If someone **comes into** their **own**, they begin to perform or work really well because the circumstances are just right. EG *Brooke came into his own when he was appointed Home Secretary.* PHRASE **3** If you say that something **comes into it**, you mean that it is an important aspect of the situation you are talking about. EG *Prestige comes into it as much as other factors.* PHRASE

come off. **1** If something **comes off**, it is successful or effective. EG *Sotheby's publicity stunt came off brilliantly.* PHRASAL VB: V+ADV **2** If you **come off** well when something happens, you are in a good position as a result of it. If you **come off** badly, you are in a bad position as a result of it. EG *They came off better than the British.* V+ADV+ADV **3** You say **'come off it'** to someone to show them that you think what they are saying is untrue. CONVENTION Informal

come on. **1** You say **'Come on'** to someone PHRASE **1.1** to encourage them to do something they do not really want to do. EG *Come on, Wendy, you say something.* **1.2** to encourage them to hurry up. **1.3** when you think that what they are saying is silly or unreasonable. **2** If you have got a cold or a headache **coming on**, it is just starting. EG *I felt a cold coming on.* PHRASAL VB: V+ADV **3** If something **is coming on**, it is developing or making progress. EG *My new book is coming on quite well.* V+ADV **4** When something such as a machine or system **comes on**, it starts working or functioning. EG *The lights came on.* V+ADV

come on to. When you **come on to** a particular topic, you start discussing it. EG *I want to come on to the question of disease in a minute.* PHRASAL VB: V+ADV+PREP

come out. **1** If a fact **comes out**, it becomes known to people. EG *All the facts came out after Seery's death... Something that comes out very clearly in interviews is how predictable people's answers are.* PHRASAL VB: V+ADV **2** When a new product **comes out**, it becomes available to the public. EG *Over the summer his book had come out and done well.* V+ADV **3** To **come out** in a particular way means to be in the position or state described at the end of a process or event. EG *Who do you think will come out on top?... The press was coming out of the affair very badly.* V+ADV, USU+A OR C **4** If you **come out** for something, you declare that you support it. If you **come out** against something, you declare that you do not support it. EG *He came out in support of the claim.* V+ADV+A **5** If a photograph **comes out**, it is successful and all the details can be seen. V+ADV **6** When the sun, moon, or stars **come out**, they appear in the sky. V+ADV

come out in. If you **come out in** spots, you become covered with them. PHRASAL VB: V+ADV+PREP

come over. If a feeling **comes over** you, it affects you. EG *I don't know what came over me.* PHRASAL VB: V+PREP

come round. **1** If you **come round** to an idea, you eventually change your mind and accept it or agree with it. EG *He knew I would have to come round to his way of thinking in the end.* PHRASAL VB: V+ADV, USU+*to* **2** When something **comes round**, it happens as a regular or predictable event. EG *Don't wait for April to come round before planning your vegetable garden.* V+ADV **3** When someone who is unconscious **comes round**, they recover consciousness. V+ADV

come through. **1** If you **come through** a dangerous or difficult situation, you survive it. EG *Most of the troops came through the fighting unharmed.* PHRASAL VB: V+ADV/PREP **2** If something **comes through**, **2.1** it is clearly shown by what is said or done. EG *I think the teacher's own personality has got to come through.* V+ADV **2.2** it arrives, especially after some procedure has been carried out. EG *Has my visa come through yet?*

come to. When someone who is unconscious **comes to**, they recover consciousness. EG *That's about all I remember, until I came to in a life-raft.* PHRASAL VB: V+ADV

come under. **1** If something **comes under** a particular authority, it is managed or controlled by that authority. EG *Day Nurseries come under the Department of Health and Social Security.* PHRASAL VB: V+PREP **2** If you **come under** criticism or attack, you are criticized or attacked. EG *The premier came under severe criticism... British produce came under pressure from foreign competition.* **3** If something **comes under** a particular heading, it is in the category mentioned. EG *Records and tapes come under published material.*

come up. **1** If something **comes up** in a conversation or meeting, it is mentioned or discussed. EG *His name came up at a buffet lunch.* PHRASAL VB: V+ADV **2** If something **is coming up**, it is about to happen or take place. EG *There's a royal wedding coming up.* V+ADV **3** If something **comes up**, it happens unexpectedly. EG *I can't see you tonight. Something's come up.* V+ADV **4** When someone or something **comes up** for election or review, the time arrives when they have to be considered or dealt with. EG *A third of my colleagues will come up for election next May.* V+ADV, USU+*for* **5** When the sun or moon **comes up**, it rises. EG *The sun comes up in the East.* V+ADV **6** In law, when a case **comes up**, it is heard in a court of law. V+ADV

come up against. If you **come up against** a problem or difficulty, you are faced with it and have to deal with it. EG *Everyone comes up against discrimination sooner or later.* PHRASAL VB: V+ADV+PREP

come upon. **1** If you **come upon** someone or something, you meet them or find them by chance. EG *They rounded a turn and came upon a family of lions.* PHRASAL VB: V+PREP **2** If an attitude or feeling **comes upon** you, it begins to affect you. EG *His new outlook on life had come upon him gradually.* Literary

come up to. To **be coming up to** a time or state means to be getting near to it. EG *Some of them are coming up to retirement... It was just coming up to ten o'clock.* PHRASAL VB: V+ADV+PREP

come up with. If you **come up with** a plan or idea, you think of it and suggest it. EG *I hope to come up with some of the answers.* PHRASAL VB: V+ADV+PREP

comeback /kʌmbæk/, **comebacks.** If something or someone makes a **comeback**, they become popular or successful again. EG *Wigs and elaborate hairstyles made a comeback.* N COUNT

comedian /kəmiːdɪən/, **comedians.** A **comedian** is an entertainer whose job is to make people laugh, especially by telling jokes or funny stories. N COUNT

comedienne /kəmiːdɪɛn/, **comediennes.** A **comedienne** is a female comedian. N COUNT

comedy /kɒmə^{1}di^1/, **comedies.** **1** A **comedy** is an amusing play or film. EG *...a revival of Maugham's comedy 'Caroline'.* N COUNT

2 You can refer to amusing things in a play or film as **comedy**. EG *The play had plenty of excitement as well as comedy... ...her rare gift for comedy on the stage.* N UNCOUNT

comely /kʌmli^1/, **comelier, comeliest.** A woman who is **comely** is attractive. ADJ QUALIT Outdated

comet /kɒmɪ^{2}t/, **comets.** A **comet** is an object that travels around the sun leaving a bright trail behind it. N COUNT

come-uppance /kʌmʌpəns/. When someone gets their **come-uppance**, they are justly punished for something wrong that they have done. EG *It is difficult not to be pleased at his come-uppance.* N SING+POSS

comfort /kʌmfət/, **comforts, comforting, comforted. 1 Comfort** is **1.1** the state of being physically relaxed. EG *She longed to stretch out in comfort... ...a hard narrow chair not made for comfort.* **1.2** a pleasant style of life in which you have everything you need. EG *She wanted a life of reasonable comfort.* **1.3** a feeling of relief from worries or unhappiness. EG *I found comfort in his words.* N UNCOUNT

2 You can refer to a person, thing, or idea that helps you to stop worrying as a **comfort**. EG *It will be a comfort to know that you are standing by.* N COUNT

3 You can use **comfort** in a phrase such as **too close for comfort** to mean that you are worried because something is closer than you would like it to be. EG *Her comments were a little too revealing for comfort.* PHRASE

4 Comforts are things which make your life easier and more pleasant. EG *I longed for the comforts of home.* N COUNT: USU PLURAL

5 To **comfort** someone means to make them feel less worried or unhappy. EG *Jeannie came to comfort him.* V+O
◊ **comforting.** EG *It's a comforting thought that we have a few days before it starts.* ◊ ADJ QUALIT

comfortable /kʌmfə°təbə°l/. **1** Something that is **comfortable** makes you feel physically relaxed when you are using it. EG *That chair is quite comfortable... The hotel was large and comfortable.* ADJ QUALIT

2 If you are **comfortable**, or if you **make yourself comfortable**, you are physically relaxed and at ease. EG *Sit down and make yourself comfortable.* ADJ QUALIT OR PHRASE
◊ **comfortably.** EG *They were too cold to sleep comfortably.* ◊ ADV

3 If you say that someone is **comfortable**, you mean that they have enough money to be able to live without financial problems. EG *She was comfortable, even wealthy by old standards.* ADJ QUALIT Outdated
◊ **comfortably.** EG *She has been living quite comfortably since her husband died.* ◊ ADV

4 If you feel **comfortable** in a particular situation, you feel confident and are not worried, afraid, or embarrassed. EG *He did not feel comfortable with strangers.* ADJ QUALIT: USU PRED

5 When a person who has been ill or injured is said to be **comfortable**, they are in a stable physical condition. ADJ PRED

6 A **comfortable** job or task is quite easy to do. EG *It's a comfortable two hours' walk from here.* ADJ QUALIT
◊ **comfortably.** EG *I can manage the work comfortably.* ◊ ADV

7 A **comfortable** opinion or belief ignores the difficult or unpleasant aspects of something; used showing disapproval. EG *...the comfortable belief that nothing is likely to go wrong.* ADJ QUALIT

comic /kɒmɪk/, **comics. 1** Something that is **comic** amuses you and makes you want to laugh. EG *...a story rich in comic and dramatic detail.* ADJ QUALIT

2 A **comic** is a person who tells jokes in order to make people laugh. EG *When the comic comes on they'll all laugh.* N COUNT

3 A **comic** is also a magazine that contains stories told in pictures. EG *He saw me reading a comic.* N COUNT British

comical /kɒmɪkə°l/. Someone or something that is **comical** makes you want to laugh. EG *There is something slightly comical about him.* ADJ QUALIT
◊ **comically.** EG *David looked comically astonished.* ◊ ADV

comic strip, comic strips. A **comic strip** is a series of drawings that tell a story. N COUNT

coming /kʌmɪŋ/, **comings. 1** A **coming** event or time is an event or time that will happen soon. EG *The real struggle will take place in the coming weeks.* ADJ CLASSIF: ATTRIB

2 Comings and goings are the arrivals and departures of people at a particular place. EG *...the comings and goings of the guests.* PHRASE

comma /kɒmə/, **commas.** A **comma** is the punctuation mark (,) which is used to separate parts of a sentence or items in a list. N COUNT

command /kəmɑːnd/, **commands, commanding, commanded. 1** If you **command** someone to do something, you order them to do it. EG *'Stay here!' he commanded... She commanded me to lie down and relax.* V+O+*to*-INF OR QUOTE; ALSO V
▸ used as a noun. EG *They waited for their master's command.* ▸ N COUNT OR N UNCOUNT

2 If you **command** something, **2.1** you order it. EG *The king had commanded his presence at court.* V+O
2.2 you obtain it as a result of being popular or important. EG *She was no longer in a position to command obedience or admiration.*

3 An officer who **commands** part of an army, navy, or air force is responsible for controlling and organizing it. EG *He commanded a regiment of cavalry in Algiers.* V+O
▸ used as a noun. EG *He had been in command of HMS Churchill for a year.* ▸ N UNCOUNT

4 Someone who is **second in command** of an organization or group is the second most important person in charge of the organization or group. PHRASE

5 Command is control over a particular situation. EG *Lady Sackville took command... He was looking more relaxed and in command than ever before.* N UNCOUNT
● If you are **in command** of yourself, you are able to react and behave in the way that you want to. EG *She felt happy and in command of herself.* ● PHRASE

6 Your **command** of something is your knowledge of it and your ability to use this knowledge. EG *...a good command of spoken English.* N UNCOUNT+OI
● If you have a particular skill **at** your **command**, you have it and can use it fully. EG *...a writer who has both elegance and passion at his command.* ● PHRASE

commandant /kɒməndænt/, **commandants.** A **commandant** is an army officer in charge of a particular place or group of people. N COUNT

commandeer /kɒməndɪə/, **commandeers, commandeering, commandeered. 1** If the army **commandeer** a building or vehicle, they officially take it from someone so that they can use it. V+O

2 If you **commandeer** something, you take it from someone who is less important or powerful than you; used showing disapproval. EG *...a tiny office that he has commandeered from a secretary.* V+O

commander /kəmɑːndə/, **commanders.** A **commander** is **1** an officer in charge of a military operation or organization. EG *Montgomery was a cautious commander who never took risks.* **2** an officer in the Royal Navy. N COUNT

commander-in-chief, commanders-in-chief. A **commander-in-chief** is an officer in charge of all the forces in a particular area. N COUNT

commanding /kəmɑːndɪŋ/. **1** If you are in a **commanding** position or situation, you are able to control people and events. EG *Britain had lost her commanding position in the world.* ADJ QUALIT: ATTRIB

2 If you have a **commanding** voice or manner, you seem powerful and confident. EG *He gave orders in a commanding voice.* ADJ QUALIT
◊ **commandingly.** EG *He speaks confidently and commandingly of his views.* ◊ ADV

3 A building that has a **commanding** position is high up and has good views of the surrounding area. EG *The University stands in a commanding position overlooking the bay.* ADJ QUALIT: ATTRIB

commandment /kəmɑːndmə²nt/, **commandments.** The Ten **Commandments** are the ten rules of behaviour which, according to the Old Testament of the Bible, God says that people should obey. N COUNT

commando /kəmɑːndəʊ/, **commandos.** A **commando** is **1** a small group of specially trained soldiers. EG *...the side road where the second commando of OAS men waited.* **2** a soldier who is a N COUNT

Find a word on these pages which means 'an advertisement'.

member of a commando. EG *The commandos headed across the bridges.*

commemorate /kəmɛməreɪt/, **commemorates, commemorating, commemorated. 1** An object that **commemorates** a person or an event is intended to make people remember the person or event. EG *...a monument commemorating a great soldier.* ◊ **commemorative** /kəmɛmə^{0}rətɪv/. EG *...a commemorative plaque.* V+O ◊ ADJ CLASSIF : ATTRIB

2 If you **commemorate** an event, you do something special to show that you remember it. EG *...a Jewish holiday commemorating the destruction of the Temple.* ◊ **commemoration** /kəmɛməreɪʃə^{0}n/. EG *...the commemoration of the fiftieth anniversary of the revolution.* V+O ◊ N UNCOUNT : OFT+*of*

commence /kəmɛns/, **commences, commencing, commenced. 1** When something **commences**, it begins. EG *He had been in prison for nine months when his trial commenced.* ◊ **commencement** /kəmɛnsmə^{2}nt/, **commencements**. EG *...the commencement of the present century.* V Formal ◊ N UNCOUNT : USU+SUPP

2 If you **commence** doing something, you begin doing it. EG *Laurie commenced running in his late twenties... I commenced a round of visits.* V+-ING OR V+O Formal

commend /kəmɛnd/, **commends, commending, commended. 1** If you **commend** someone, you praise them formally. EG *I was commended for my reports.* ◊ **commendation** /kɒmɛndeɪʃə^{0}n/, **commendations**. EG *His action earned the personal commendation of the prime minister.* V+O : OFT+*for* ◊ N UNCOUNT OR N COUNT

2 If you **commend** something to someone, you tell them that it is very good. EG *Rothermere commended Baldwin to his readers as a great man.* V+O : OFT+*to*

3 If something **commends** itself to you, you approve of it. EG *The defence would scarcely commend itself even to other lawyers.* V-REFL+*to*

commendable /kəmɛndəbə^{0}l/. Behaviour that is **commendable** is admired and praised. EG *The committee acted with commendable fairness and understanding.* ADJ QUALIT

commensurate /kəmɛnsərə^{1}t, -ʃə-/. If an amount is **commensurate** with another amount, it is in proportion to the other amount. EG *The house brings in a return commensurate with its current market value.* ADJ PRED +*with* Formal

comment /kɒmɛnt/, **comments, commenting, commented. 1** If you **comment** on something, you give your opinion about it or you give an explanation for it. EG *Both girls commented on Chris's size... 'It needs washing,' she commented... Someone commented that Brian changes his mind every day.* V : USU+*on/upon*; ALSO V+QUOTE OR REPORT : ONLY *that*

2 A **comment** is something that you say which expresses your opinion of something or which gives an explanation of it. EG *People in the town started making rude comments... Well, this isn't a fair comment on the situation... He was not available for comment yesterday.* N COUNT OR N UNCOUNT : OFT+*on/upon*

3 People say **'no comment'** as a way of refusing to answer a question during an interview. EG *'Do you intend to keep them in prison?' – 'No comment.'* CONVENTION

commentary /kɒməntə^{0}ri^1/, **commentaries. 1** A **commentary** is a description of an event that is broadcast on radio or television while the event is taking place. EG *We were gathered round a radio to hear the commentary.* N COUNT

2 A **commentary** is also a book or article which explains or discusses something. EG *...a series of political commentaries.* N COUNT OR N UNCOUNT

commentator /kɒmənteɪtə/, **commentators. 1** A **commentator** is a broadcaster who gives a radio or television commentary on an event. N COUNT

2 A **commentator** is also someone who often writes or broadcasts about a particular subject. EG *...Peter Jenkins, an experienced commentator on political affairs.* N COUNT+SUPP

commerce /kɒmɜːs/ is the activities and procedures involved in buying and selling things. EG *...the world of industry and commerce.* N UNCOUNT

commercial /kəmɜːʃə^{0}l/, **commercials. 1 Commercial** means involving or relating to commerce and business. EG *...commercial and industrial organisations.* ADJ CLASSIF : ATTRIB

2 A **commercial** activity involves producing goods in large quantities in order to make a profit. EG *...commercial agriculture... ...a big commercial bakery.* ◊ **commercially**. EG *Slate was quarried commercially here.* ADJ CLASSIF : ATTRIB ◊ ADV

3 Commercial television and radio are paid for by the broadcasting of advertisements between programmes. ADJ CLASSIF : ATTRIB

4 A **commercial** is an advertisement that is broadcast on television or radio. N COUNT

commercialized /kəmɜːʃəlaɪzd/; also spelled **commercialised.** Something that is **commercialized** is mainly concerned with making money; used showing disapproval. EG *The ceremonies have degenerated into vulgar, commercialized spectacles.* ADJ QUALIT

commiserate /kəmɪzəreɪt/, **commiserates, commiserating, commiserated.** If you **commiserate** with someone, you show them pity or sympathy when something unpleasant has happened to them. EG *I commiserated with him over the recent news.* ◊ **commiseration** /kəmɪzəreɪʃə^{0}n/. EG *She gave him a look of commiseration.* V : OFT+*with* ◊ N UNCOUNT

commission /kəmɪʃə^{0}n/, **commissions, commissioning, commissioned. 1** If you **commission** something or **commission** someone to do something, you formally arrange for someone to do a piece of work for you. EG *The Times commissioned a Public Opinion Poll... I was immediately commissioned to write another book.* V+O OR V+O+*to*-INF

2 A **commission** is a piece of work that someone is asked to do and is paid for. EG *Red House was Webb's first commission as an architect.* N COUNT

3 Commission is a sum of money paid to a salesman for every sale that he or she makes. EG *They get commission on top of their basic salary.* N UNCOUNT OR N COUNT

4 A **commission** is also a group of people who have been appointed to find out about something or to control something. EG *A commission was appointed to investigate the assassination of the President.* N COLL

commissionaire /kəmɪʃənɛə/, **commissionaires.** A **commissionaire** is a man employed by a hotel, theatre, or cinema to open doors and help customers. Commissionaires usually wear uniform. N COUNT

commissioner /kəmɪʃə^{0}nə/, **commissioners.** A **commissioner** is an important official in an organization. EG *...the Church Commissioners.* N COUNT : USU+SUPP

commit /kəmɪt/, **commits, committing, committed. 1** If someone **commits** a crime or a sin, they do it. EG *He has committed a criminal offence... Margaret had no intention of committing suicide.* V+O

2 If you **commit** money or resources to something, you decide to use them for a particular purpose. EG *Rolls Royce must commit its entire resources to the project.* V+O : OFT+*to*

3 If you **commit** yourself to a course of action, you definitely decide that you will do it. EG *I really wouldn't like to commit myself.* V-REFL : OFT+*to*

4 If someone **is committed** to a hospital or prison, they are officially sent there for a time. EG *She was committed to a nursing home.* V+O : USU PASS+*to*

5 If you **commit** something **to memory**, you memorize it. EG *You'll need these figures so often that you must commit them to memory.* PHRASE

commitment /kəmɪtmə^{2}nt/, **commitments. 1 Commitment** is a strong belief in an idea or system. EG *There is no doubting his enthusiasm or his commitment.* N UNCOUNT

2 A **commitment** is something which regularly N COUNT : USU PLURAL takes up some of your time. EG *She's got family commitments.*

3 If you give a **commitment** to something, you promise faithfully that you will do it. EG *He gave a clear commitment to reopen disarmament talks.* N COUNT Formal

committal /kəmɪtə^{0}l/ is the process of officially sending someone to prison or to hospital. EG *One hundred and ten days may elapse between committal and trial.* N UNCOUNT

committee /kəmɪti^1/, **committees.** A **committee** is a group of people who represent a larger group or organization and who make decisions or plans for that group or organization. EG *A special committee has been set up... The whole Committee are very grateful to you.* N COLL

commodious /kəməʊdɪəs/. A room or house that is **commodious** is large and has plenty of space. EG *...a commodious building suitable for conversion.* ADJ QUALIT Formal

commodity /kəmɒdɪti^1/, **commodities.** A **commodity** is something that is sold for money. EG *He dealt in all domestic commodities – clothes, hardware, and furniture.* N COUNT Formal

common /kɒmən/, **commoner, commonest; commons. 1** If something is **common**, it is found in large numbers or it happens often. EG *Durand is a common name there... It was quite common for dogs to be poisoned this way.* ◇ **commonly.** EG *The most commonly used argument is that clients do not like long delays.* ADJ QUALIT ◇ ADV

2 If something is **common** to two or more people, it is possessed, done, or used by them all. EG *We shared a common language... It suppressed the desire for freedom common to all people.* ADJ CLASSIF: IF PRED THEN+*to*

3 If two or more things have something **in common**, they have the same characteristic or feature. EG *What have these names in common?... In common with many other companies, we advertise in the local press.* ● If two or more people have something **in common**, they share the same interests or experiences. EG *You two have got a lot in common.* PHRASE ● PHRASE

4 Common is also used to indicate that something is of the ordinary kind and not special in any way. EG *Sodium chloride is better known as common salt.* ADJ CLASSIF: ATTRIB

5 If something is **common** knowledge or is the **common** belief, it is known about or believed to be true by people in general. EG *It was common knowledge that he lived alone in the mansion.* ◇ **commonly.** EG *Chauffeurs, it is commonly agreed, know more about what is going on than their employers think.* ADJ CLASSIF: ATTRIB ◇ ADV

6 Someone who is **common** behaves in a way that shows lack of taste, education, and good manners; used showing disapproval. ADJ QUALIT

7 A **common** is an area of grassy land in or near a village where the public is allowed to go. N COUNT

8 Common is also used in these phrases. **8.1 Common or garden** things are ordinary and not special in any way. EG *These are common or garden transistors.* **8.2** If something is done **for the common good**, it is done for the benefit of everyone in the community. **8.3 Common ground** is something which two or more people or groups agree about. EG *There is no common ground upon which dialogue can be based.* PHRASES

commoner /kɒmənə/, **commoners.** A **commoner** is a person who is not a member of the nobility. N COUNT

common-law. A **common-law** relationship is regarded as a marriage because it has lasted a long time, although no official marriage contract has been signed. EG *...common-law marriage... ...his common-law wife.* ADJ CLASSIF: ATTRIB

Common Market. The **Common Market** is an organization of West European countries, including the UK, who make decisions together about their trade, agriculture, and other policies. N PROPER: *the*+N

commonplace /kɒmənpleɪs/. Something that is **commonplace** is not surprising because it happens often or is often found. EG *Air travel has now become commonplace.* ADJ QUALIT

common room, common rooms. A **common room** is a room in a university or school where people can sit, talk, and relax. N COUNT

common sense is a person's natural ability to make good judgements and to behave in a practical and sensible way. EG *Use your common sense... This precaution is simply common sense.* ▸ used as an adjective. EG *Take a few common-sense steps to help the situation.* N UNCOUNT ▸ ADJ CLASSIF: ATTRIB

commotion /kəməʊʃə^{0}n/. A **commotion** is a lot of noise, confusion, and excitement. EG *Suddenly there was a commotion at the other end of the bar.* N SING OR N UNCOUNT

communal /kɒmjə^{4}nə^{0}l/. Something that is **communal** is shared by a group of people. EG *...a communal dining-room... ...a communal style of life.* ◇ **communally.** EG *The mills are owned communally.* ADJ CLASSIF ◇ ADV

commune, communes, communing, communed; pronounced /kɒmju:n/ when it is a noun, and /kəmju:n/ when it is a verb.

1 A **commune** is a group of people who live together and share everything. EG *...a women's commune.* N COLL

2 If you **commune** with nature or some other power or spirit, you feel that you have a very close relationship with it. EG *...a beautiful spot where one communed with God and Nature.* V+*with* Literary

communicate /kəmju:nɪkeɪt/, **communicates, communicating, communicated. 1** If you **communicate** with another person or place, **1.1** you use signals such as speech, radio signals, or body movements to give them information. EG *He communicates with Miami by radio... Through signs she communicated that she wanted a drink.* **1.2** you write a letter to them or you telephone them. EG *Anthony and I hadn't communicated for years.* V OR V+*with*: RECIP; ALSO V+REPORT: ONLY *that* — V OR V+*with*: RECIP

2 If you **communicate** an idea or a feeling to someone, you make them aware of it. EG *...the failure of intellectuals to communicate their ideas to a wider audience.* V+O: OFT+*to*

3 If people **communicate**, they can understand each other's feelings or attitudes. EG *Cliff talked to me a few times but we couldn't really communicate.* V OR V+*with*: RECIP

communicating /kəmju:nɪkeɪtɪŋ/. **Communicating** doors link one room directly to another. EG *The two rooms were next to each other, with a communicating door.* ADJ CLASSIF: ATTRIB

communication /kəmju:nɪkeɪʃə^{0}n/, **communications. 1 Communication** is the activity or process of giving information to other people or to other living things. EG *Insects such as ants have a highly effective system of communication.* N UNCOUNT

2 Communications are the systems and processes that are used to communicate or broadcast information, especially by means of electricity or radio waves. EG *...large numbers of communications satellites.* N PLURAL

3 A **communication** is a letter or telephone call. EG *...a secret communication from the Foreign Minister.* N COUNT Formal

communicative /kəmju:nɪkətɪv/. **1** Someone who is **communicative** is able to talk to people easily. EG *He was as friendly and communicative as taxi-drivers commonly are.* ADJ QUALIT

2 Communicative means relating to the ability to communicate. EG *...sounds whose communicative function can be understood.* ADJ CLASSIF

communion /kəmju:njən/. **1 Communion** is the sharing of thoughts or feelings. EG *Society has lost all communion with the elementary sources of life.* N UNCOUNT Literary

2 Communion is also the Christian ceremony in which people eat bread and drink wine as a symbol N UNCOUNT

What is the difference between 'compact' and 'commodious'?

of Christ's death and sacrifice. EG *He started going to Communion.*

communiqué /kəmjuːnɪkeɪ/, **communiqués.** A **communiqué** is an official statement or announcement. EG *On his desk were a dozen communiqués from various government departments.* — N COUNT

communism /kɒmjə4nɪzə0m/ is the political belief that the state should control the means of producing everything, and that there should be no private property. EG *But Communism still commands great respect in many countries.* — N UNCOUNT

communist /kɒmjə4nɪst/, **communists.** A **communist** is someone who believes in Communism. EG *...a young communist from Cleveland, Ohio.* — N COUNT
▸ used as an adjective. EG *I know you had some Communist friends.* — ▸ ADJ CLASSIF

community /kəmjuːnɪ1ti1/, **communities. 1** A **community** is made up of the people who live in a particular area. EG *Members are drawn from all sections of the local community... ...community affairs.* — N COLL
2 A particular **community** is a particular group of people in society who are alike in some way. EG *...the black community in Britain.* — N COLL+SUPP

community service is unpaid work that criminals sometimes do as a punishment instead of being sent to prison. — N UNCOUNT

commute /kəmjuːt/, **commutes, commuting, commuted.** If you **commute**, you travel a long distance every day between your home and your place of work. EG *...the 120,000 workers who commute from nearby towns.* — V : USU+A
◇ **commuter** /kəmjuːtə/, **commuters.** EG *...a crowd of commuters on the London Underground.* — ◇ N COUNT

compact, compacts, compacting, compacted; pronounced /kɒmpækt/ or /kə7mpækt/ when it is an adjective, /kə7mpækt/ when it is a verb, and /kɒmpækt/ when it is a noun.
1 Something that is **compact** takes up very little space. EG *The kitchen was small, compact, and immaculately clean... ...smaller, more compact computers.* — ADJ QUALIT
2 To **compact** something means to press it so that it becomes more dense. EG *The tractor wheels compact the soil to a damaging extent.* — V+O Formal
◇ **compacted.** EG *...compacted soil.* — ◇ ADJ CLASSIF
3 A **compact** is a small, flat, round case that contains face-powder and a mirror. — N COUNT

compact disc /kɒmpækt dɪsk/, **compact discs.** A **compact disc** is a type of record that has a very high quality of sound reproduction. Compact discs have to be played on a special machine. — N COUNT

companion /kə7mpænjən/, **companions.** A **companion** is someone who you spend time with or who you are travelling with. EG *He saw Vita as the companion of a lifetime.* — N COUNT

companionable /kəmpænjənəbə0l/. A person who is **companionable** is friendly and pleasant to be with. — ADJ QUALIT

companionship /kəmpænjənʃɪp/ is being with someone you know and like, rather than being on your own. EG *She missed her mother's companionship and love.* — N UNCOUNT

company /kʌmpəni1/, **companies. 1** A **company** is **1.1** a business organization that makes money by selling goods or services. EG *He is a geologist employed by an oil company.* **1.2** a group of actors, opera singers, or dancers who work together. EG *...the Royal Shakespeare Company.* — N COLL
2 If you have **company**, you have a friend or visitor with you. EG *Are you expecting company?... She preferred his company to that of most people.* — N UNCOUNT
3 If you **keep** someone **company**, you spend time with them and stop them feeling lonely or bored. — PHRASE
4 If you **part company** with someone, you end your association with them or disagree with them. EG *In 1911, Adler parted company with Freud... Even those who usually agree with the headmaster would part company with him on this point.* — PHRASE

> **COMPAR** stands for **comparative**
> Adjectives which have the label COMPAR in the Extra Column are in the comparative form. A few adverbs are also labelled COMPAR.
> See the entry headed ADJECTIVES for more information.

comparable /kɒmpərəbə0l/. Something that is **comparable** to something else is **1** as good, as big, or as important as the other thing. EG *At that moment there seemed nothing in the world comparable to sleep... The sums of money involved were not, of course, comparable.* **2** similar to the other thing, and therefore able to be compared with it. EG *They have much lower fuel consumption than comparable petrol-engined cars.* — ADJ QUALIT : OFT+*to/with*; ADJ CLASSIF : OFT+*to/with*
◇ **comparability** /kɒmpərəbɪlɪti1/. EG *There are problems over the comparability of data.* — ◇ N UNCOUNT

comparative /kə7mpærə1tɪv/, **comparatives. 1** You use **comparative** to say that you are judging something by the standards of what is normally the case. For example, **comparative** peace or silence is a state which is fairly peaceful or silent compared with what is normal. EG *He hoped they could spend the night in comparative safety.* — ADJ CLASSIF : ATTRIB
◇ **comparatively.** EG *There was comparatively little pressure for change.* — ◇ SUBMOD
2 A **comparative** study is a study that involves the comparison of two or more things of the same kind. EG *...a comparative study of Indian and Western food.* — ADJ CLASSIF : ATTRIB
3 In grammar, the **comparative** form of an adjective or adverb is the form, usually ending in *-er*, that indicates that there is an increase in quality, size, or amount. See the entry headed ADJECTIVES for more information. — ADJ CLASSIF OR N COUNT

compare /kə7mpɛə/, **compares, comparing, compared. 1** When you **compare** things, you consider them and discover the differences or similarities between them. EG *It's interesting to compare the two prospectuses... ...studies comparing Russian children with those in Britain.* — V+O OR V+O+*with/to* : RECIP
◇ **compared.** EG *The fee is low, compared with that at many other independent schools... Breast milk always looks thin, compared to cow's milk.* — ◇ ADJ PRED +*with/to*
2 If you **compare** one person or thing to another, you say that they are like the other person or thing. EG *As an essayist he is compared frequently to Paine and Hazlitt.* — V+O+*to*
3 If one thing **compares favourably** with another, it is better than the other thing. If it **compares unfavourably**, it is worse than the other thing. EG *Japanese children have an education which compares favourably with some other countries.* — PHRASE
4 If you say that something **does not compare** with something else, you mean that it is much worse than it. EG *His intelligence doesn't compare with that of the average Londoner.* — PHRASE

comparison /kə7mpærɪsən/, **comparisons. 1** When you make a **comparison**, you consider two or more things and discover the differences between them. EG *Here, for comparison, is the French version... We have to find out more before we can make a proper comparison.* — N COUNT OR N UNCOUNT
2 If you say that something is large or small **in comparison with** or **in comparison to** something else, you mean that it is larger or smaller than the other thing. EG *Their possessions were few in comparison to those of the older men.* — PHRASE
3 If something is large or small **in comparison** or **by comparison**, it is large or small when it is compared to something that has just been mentioned. EG *He made me look, in comparison, a good, calm, reasonable person.* — ADV SEN

compartment /kə⁷mpɑ:tmə²nt/, **compartments.** N COUNT
A **compartment** is 1 one of the separate spaces into which a railway carriage is divided. EG *I had a first-class compartment to myself.* 2 one of the separate parts of an object that is used for keeping things in. EG *He tucked the ticket into the inner compartment of his wallet.*

compartmentalize /kɒmpɑ:tmentəlaɪz/, **compartmentalizes, compartmentalizing, compartmentalized;** also spelled **compartmentalise.** V+O
To **compartmentalize** something means to divide it into separate sections. EG *I have found it best to compartmentalize my contracts.*

compass /kʌmpəs/, **compasses. 1** A **compass** is an instrument that you use for finding directions. It has a dial and a magnetic needle that always points to the north. EG *I set off clutching my map and compass.* N COUNT

compass

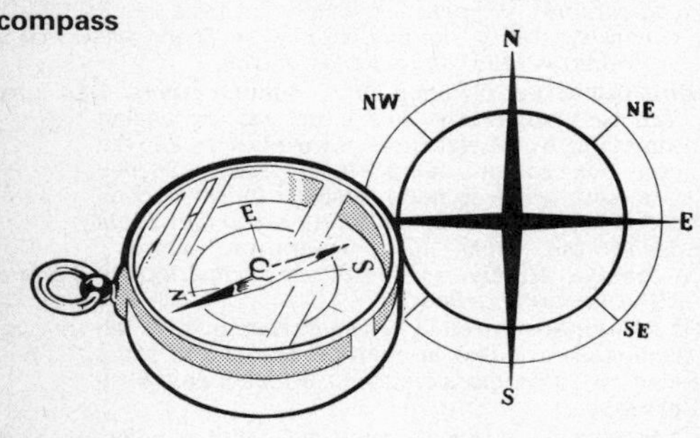

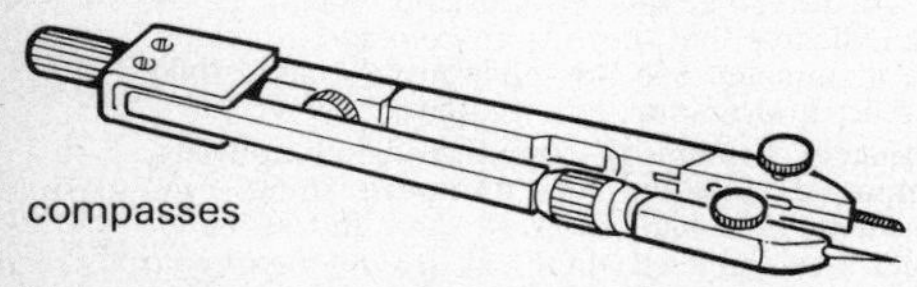

compasses

2 Compasses are a hinged V-shaped instrument that you use for drawing circles. N PLURAL

3 The **compass** of something is the range over which it can operate. EG *...reality beyond the mind's normal compass.* N COUNT+SUPP Formal

compassion /kə⁷mpæʃə⁰n/ is a feeling of pity and sympathy for someone who is suffering. EG *The suffering of the Cubans aroused their compassion.* N UNCOUNT

compassionate /kə⁷mpæʃənə¹t/. Someone who is **compassionate** feels or shows pity and sympathy for other people when they are suffering. EG *She was among the most compassionate of women.* ADJ QUALIT
◇ **compassionately.** EG *Liz looked at her compassionately.* ◇ ADV

compatible /kə⁷mpætəbə⁰l/. If people or things are **compatible**, they can live or exist together happily or safely. EG *These programs no longer seem compatible with European society... We assumed that all these objectives were compatible.* ADJ QUALIT : OFT+*with*
◇ **compatibility** /kə⁷mpætəbɪlɪti¹/. EG *They failed to achieve any compatibility of planning aims.* ◇ N UNCOUNT : OFT+SUPP

compatriot /kə⁷mpætrɪət/, **compatriots.** Your **compatriots** are people from your own country. N COUNT

compel /kə⁷mpel/, **compels, compelling, compelled. 1** If someone or something **compels** you to do something, they force you to do it. EG *...illnesses which compel people to change their diet... He felt compelled to intervene in the dispute.* V+O+*to*-INF

2 To **compel** an attitude, feeling, or action means to make people have it or do it. EG *His appearance was so bizarre that it compelled attention.* V+O Formal

compelling /kə⁷mpelɪŋ/. An argument or reason that is **compelling** convinces you that something is true or that something should be done. EG *I had ended a man's life for no compelling reason.* ADJ QUALIT

compensate /kɒmpə²nseɪt/, **compensates, compensating, compensated. 1** To **compensate** someone for something means to pay them money so that they can replace something that has been lost, damaged, or destroyed. EG *The allowance should be paid to compensate people for loss of earnings.* V OR V+O : OFT+*for*

2 To **compensate** for the bad effect of something means to do something that cancels out this effect. EG *Fish can compensate for the tiniest variation of current by moving their fins.* V : OFT+*for*

compensation /kɒmpə²nseɪʃə⁰n/, **compensations. 1 Compensation** is money that you claim from a person or organization that is responsible for something unpleasant that has happened to you. EG *If you were killed, your dependants could get compensation.* N UNCOUNT

2 A **compensation** is **2.1** an action that cancels out another action that has had a bad effect. EG *Look for some of the compensations your body has to make.* **2.2** an event or fact that makes you feel better in spite of something bad that has happened to you. EG *Letters that began to arrive from Nell were some compensation.* N COUNT OR N UNCOUNT

compensatory /kɒmpə²nseɪtə⁰ri¹/. Something that is **compensatory 1** involves the payment of compensation. EG *There must be compensatory payments to the farmers.* **2** is designed to help people who have special problems or disabilities. EG *...compensatory education.* ADJ CLASSIF : ATTRIB

compere /kɒmpeə/, **comperes, compering, compered.** A **compere** is the person on a radio or television show who introduces the guests and performers. ▸ used as a verb. EG *Esther Rantzen agreed to compere the Miss World contest.* N COUNT ▸ V+O

compete /kə⁷mpi:t/, **competes, competing, competed. 1** When one firm **competes** with another firm, it tries to get people to buy its own goods in preference to the other firm's goods. EG *This would enable British shipbuilders to compete with foreign yards.* V OR V+*with/against* : RECIP

2 If you **compete** with someone for something, you try to get it for yourself. EG *Senior members of staff competed eagerly for the honour of representing the company.* V OR V+*with/against* : RECIP

3 If you **compete** in a contest or a game, you take part in it. EG *Dave Moorcroft has now competed in two Olympics.* V+A

4 If two statements or ideas **compete**, they cannot both be right, or cannot both be accepted. V OR V+*with* : RECIP
◇ **competing.** EG *Various competing theories are compared and discussed.* ◇ ADJ CLASSIF : ATTRIB

competent /kɒmpə¹tənt/. Someone who is **competent** can do something in an efficient and effective way. EG *He was a competent amateur pilot... It was a highly competent piece of work.* ADJ QUALIT
◇ **competently.** EG *He carved the bird roughly, but competently.* ◇ ADV ◇ **competence** /kɒmpə¹təns/. EG *He will be expected to show competence in the relevant methods of research.* ◇ N UNCOUNT

competition /kɒmpə¹tɪʃə⁰n/, **competitions. 1 Competition** is **1.1** a situation in which two or more people or groups are trying to get something which not everyone can have. EG *Competition for admission to the college is keen... The two parties were not in competition with each other.* **1.2** an activity involving two or more firms, in which each firm tries to get people to buy its own goods in preference to the other firms' goods. EG *Part of the reason for the drop in sales is competition from overseas suppliers.* N UNCOUNT

2 A **competition** is an event in which many people take part in order to find out who is best at a N COUNT

If people are compatible, are they likely to complement each other?

COMPLEMENTS

The complement (c) is one of the major elements in the structure of a clause. It takes the form of an adjective group or a noun group. It comes after a verb and gives information about the subject or object of the verb. For example, in the sentence *She is happy,* 'happy' is the complement. It is an adjective and it tells you something about the subject 'she'. In the sentence *She made him happy,* 'happy' is again the complement and tells you something about 'him', the object of the clause.

Where the complement is a noun, it refers to the same person or thing as the subject or object of the verb. In the sentence *Harold is a teacher,* 'a teacher' is the complement and gives you some information about the subject 'Harold'. Compare *Harold is a teacher* and *Harold met a teacher.* In the second example 'a teacher' is the object of the clause and is obviously not the same person as 'Harold'. In the sentence *We made Harold chairman,* 'chairman' is the complement and refers to the same person as the object 'Harold'.

A complement can occur with or without an object. For example, the verbs **be, seem,** and **look** have a complement but no object (v+c), as in *Her name is* ***Melanie*** *. . . He seemed* ***nice*** *. . . You look* ***very pale.*** Other verbs which have a complement are transitive and so they do have an object (v+o+c). Examples are **make, call,** and **leave,** as in *The women made her* ***welcome*** *. . . We called our son* ***Iain*** *. . . Who left the gates* ***open?***

particular activity. EG *...the Segovia International Guitar Competition.*

competitive /kə⁷mpɛtɪtɪv/. **1** Something that is **competitive** involves people or firms competing with each other. EG *...a highly competitive society.* ADJ QUALIT

2 A person who is **competitive** is eager to be more successful than other people. EG *I realize how awfully competitive I am.* ◇ **competitively.** EG *It's running for fitness as opposed to running competitively.* ◇ **competitiveness.** EG *Why should we put such an emphasis on individualism and competitiveness?* ADJ QUALIT ◇ ADV ◇ N UNCOUNT

3 Goods that are **competitive** are likely to be bought, because they are less expensive than other goods of the same kind. EG *...a competitive car for the 1980s.* ◇ **competitively.** EG *...competitively priced newspapers.* ADJ QUALIT ◇ ADV

competitor /kə⁷mpɛtɪtə/, **competitors. 1** Someone who is your **competitor** is trying to sell goods or services to the same people as you are. EG *...Austin-Rover's challenge to its foreign competitors.* N COUNT

2 A **competitor** is also a person who takes part in a competition or contest. N COUNT

compilation /kɒmpɪleɪʃə⁰n/, **compilations. 1** A **compilation** is a book, record, or programme that contains many different parts that have been gathered together. EG *...a compilation of Victorian poetry.* N COUNT

2 Compilation is the act of compiling something. EG *One of the first steps was the compilation of a report.* N UNCOUNT

compile /kəmpaɪl/, **compiles, compiling, compiled.** When you **compile** a book, report, or film, you produce it by collecting and putting together many pieces of information. EG *The programme was compiled and presented by Dr Brian Smith.* V+O

complacent /kə⁷mpleɪsənt/. If you are **complacent**, you do not feel that you need to worry or do anything about a situation; used showing disapproval. EG *We cannot afford to be complacent about the energy problem.* ◇ **complacently.** EG *Her mother smiled complacently.* ◇ **complacency** /kə⁷mpleɪsənsi¹/. EG *No one has any cause for complacency.* ADJ QUALIT: OFT+*about* ◇ ADV ◇ N UNCOUNT

complain /kə⁷mpleɪn/, **complains, complaining, complained.** If you **complain, 1** you express the fact that you are not satisfied with a particular situation. EG *People had complained to Uncle Harold about his fights... Women complain of pressure on them to get jobs... 'He never told me, sir,' Watson complained... He complained that the office was not 'businesslike'.* **2** you say that you are feeling pain or feeling ill. EG *He complained of pain in the chest.* V: OFT+A, QUOTE, OR REPORT: ONLY *that* / V+*of* OR REPORT: ONLY *that*

complaint /kə⁷mpleɪnt/, **complaints. 1** A **complaint** is **1.1** a statement in which you express your dissatisfaction with a particular situation. EG *There were the usual complaints of violence... She wrote a letter of complaint to the manufacturer.* **1.2** a reason for complaining. EG *As always, the main complaint is that people don't read the instructions.* N COUNT OR N UNCOUNT / N COUNT

2 A **complaint** is also an illness, often one which is not very serious. EG *It turned out to be a minor urinary complaint.* N COUNT

complement /kɒmplə¹mə²nt/, **complements, complementing, complemented. 1** If one person or thing **complements** another, they increase each other's good qualities when they are brought together. EG *Crisp pastry complements the juicy fruit of an apple pie.* ▸ used as a noun. EG *The exercises are an ideal complement to my usual rehearsal methods.* V+O / ▸ N COUNT: OFT+*to*

2 When you are talking about the number of people you work with, you can refer to the **complement** of them. EG *Forty four of the original complement of 150 were dead... ...the ship's complement.* N COUNT +SUPP Formal

3 The **full complement** of a group or set is every item or person that it normally includes. EG *The birds all have their full complement of feathers.* PHRASE

4 In grammar, a **complement** is one of the elements of clause structure. See the entry headed COMPLEMENTS for more information. N COUNT

complementary /kɒmplə¹mɛntə⁰ri¹/. Two or more different things are **complementary** if they form a complete or better unit when they are brought together. EG *These two approaches are complementary... The roles of the sexes are complementary to one another.* ADJ CLASSIF : OFT+*to*

complete /kə⁷pliːt/, **completes, completing, completed.** 1 You use **complete** to emphasize that something is as great in extent, degree, or amount as it possibly can be. EG *You need a complete change of diet... ...a complete break from my children... They were in complete agreement.* ADJ QUALIT : USU ATTRIB
◇ **completely.** EG *He was completely bald.* ◇ ADV
2 If something is **complete**, 2.1 it has been finished. EG *The harvesting was complete.* ADJ PRED 2.2 it contains all the parts that it should contain. EG *This is not a complete list... ...an almost complete skeleton of a dinosaur.* ADJ QUALIT
3 If you **complete** something, you finish doing, making, or producing it. EG *The cathedral was begun in 1240 and completed forty years later... Give yourself plenty of time to complete a job.* V+O
4 If something **completes** a group or set, it is the last item that is needed to make it a full group or set. EG *A black silk tie completed the outfit.* V+O
5 If you **complete** a form or questionnaire, you write down the answers to the questions on it. V+O
6 Something that is **complete with** a particular thing has that thing as an extra part. EG *He bought a lovely mansion, complete with swimming pool.* PREP

completion /kə⁷mpliːʃə⁰n/ is the finishing of a piece of work. EG *The house was due for completion in 1983.* N UNCOUNT

complex /kɒmplɛks/, **complexes.** 1 Something that is **complex** has many different parts, and is therefore often difficult to understand. EG *...complex lace patterns... It is a complex problem.* ADJ QUALIT
2 A **complex** is 2.1 a group or system of things that are connected with each other in a complicated way. EG *...a complex of little roads... Conflicts usually develop out of a complex of causes.* N COUNT+SUPP 2.2 a group of buildings or a large building divided into several areas. EG *...a splendid new sports and leisure complex.*
3 If someone has a **complex**, they have a mental or emotional problem because of an unpleasant experience in the past which continues to influence them. EG *I am developing a guilt complex about it.* N COUNT : OFT+*about*

complexion /kə⁷mplɛkʃə⁰n/, **complexions.** 1 Your **complexion** is the natural quality of the skin on your face. EG *He said I had a good complexion.* N COUNT
2 The **complexion** of something is its general nature or character. EG *...the political complexion of the press.* N UNCOUNT +SUPP Formal

complexity /kə⁷mplɛksɪ¹ti¹/, **complexities.** 1 **Complexity** is the state of having many different parts connected or related to each other in a complicated way. *...problems of varying complexity.* N UNCOUNT
2 The **complexities** of something are its many connected parts, which make it difficult to understand or deal with. EG *...the complexities of tax law.* N PLURAL

compliance /kə⁷mplaɪəns/ is the act of doing what you have been asked to do. EG *I was surprised by Melanie's compliance with these terms.* N UNCOUNT Formal

complicate /kɒmplɪkeɪt/, **complicates, complicating, complicated.** To **complicate** something means to make it more difficult to understand or deal with. EG *Just to complicate matters, I have to be back by the end of the month.* V+O

complicated /kɒmplɪkeɪtɪ²d/. Something that is **complicated** has so many parts or aspects that it is difficult to understand or deal with. EG *I find the British legal system extremely complicated... The situation is much more complicated than that.* ADJ QUALIT

complication /kɒmplɪkeɪʃə⁰n/, **complications.** A **complication** is a circumstance that makes a situation harder to deal with. EG *Finally, there is the complication that wages help to determine the level of inflation.* N COUNT

complicity /kə⁷mplɪsɪ¹ti¹/ is involvement with other people in an illegal activity or plan. EG *She suspected him of complicity in Ashok's escape.* N UNCOUNT Formal

compliment /kɒmplə¹mə²nt/, **compliments, complimenting, complimented.** 1 A **compliment** is something that you say to someone to show that you admire them. EG *He had just been paid a great compliment.* N COUNT ● If you **take** something that someone does or says **as a compliment**, you regard it as an indication that they admire you. EG *She took his acceptance as a great compliment.* ● PHRASE
2 If you **compliment** someone, you tell them how much you admire something that they own or something that they have done. EG *He complimented Morris on his new car... I was complimented for my opposition to the treaty.* V+O : OFT+*on/for*
3 **Compliments** is used in some expressions when you want to formally express good wishes or respect. EG *The Secretary of State presents his compliments and regrets that he is unable to attend.* N PLURAL : USU+POSS Formal

complimentary /kɒmplə¹mɛntə⁰ri¹/. 1 If you are **complimentary** about something, you express admiration for it. EG *In Russia a rhythmic slow handclap can be highly complimentary.* ADJ QUALIT
2 A **complimentary** seat, ticket, or book is given to you free. ADJ CLASSIF : ATTRIB

comply /kə⁷mplaɪ/, **complies, complying, complied.** If you **comply** with an order or set of rules, you do what you are required or expected to do. EG *New vehicles must comply with certain standards.* V : OFT+*with*

component /kə⁷mpəʊnənt/, **components.** The **components** of something are the parts that it is made of. EG *The factory makes components for cars... ...electronic components... ...the component parts of the rifle.* N COUNT

compose /kə⁷mpəʊz/, **composes, composing, composed.** 1 If something **is composed** of particular things or people, it has those things or people as its parts or members. EG *The book is composed of essays written over the last twenty years... The National Committee was composed of 22 manual workers and 6 white-collar workers.* V-PASS+*of*
2 If a number of things **compose** something, they are the parts that it consists of. EG *...the elements which compose his individuality.* V+O Formal
3 When someone **composes** a piece of music, they write it. EG *Mozart composed his first symphony in 1764.* V+O OR V
4 If you **compose** a letter, poem, or speech, you write it. EG *Mr Morris sat down to compose his letter of resignation.* V+O
5 If you **compose** yourself, you succeed in becoming calm after being angry, excited, or upset. EG *She lay on her bed and cried and then she composed herself and went downstairs.* V-REFL

composed /kə⁷mpəʊzd/. If someone is **composed**, they are calm and able to control their feelings. EG *I felt calmer and more composed than I had in a long time.* ADJ QUALIT

composer /kə⁷mpəʊzə/, **composers.** A **composer** is a person whose job is writing music, especially classical music. N COUNT

composite /kɒmpəzɪt/, **composites.** You use **composite** to describe something that is made up of several different things, parts, or substances. EG *...the composite annual fee.* ADJ CLASSIF : ATTRIB Formal ▸ used as a noun. EG *He works in a composite of styles.* ▸ N COUNT

composition /kɒmpəzɪʃə⁰n/, **compositions.** 1 The **composition** of something is the things that it N UNCOUNT : USU+SUPP

Should you comply with something compulsory?

consists of and the way in which these things are arranged. EG *...the chemical composition of the atmosphere.*

2 A **composition** is a piece of written work that you write at school. EG *The composition had to be at least three pages long.* — N COUNT

3 A composer's **compositions** are the pieces of music that he or she has written. EG *...another of his finer compositions – the B minor Sonata.* — N COUNT

4 **Composition** is also the act of composing something such as a piece of music or a poem. EG *He began by reading a poem of his own composition.* — N UNCOUNT

compost /kɒmpɒst/ is a mixture of decaying plants and manure, which is added to the soil to help plants grow. EG *...a compost heap.* — N UNCOUNT

composure /kə7mpəʊʒə/. Someone's **composure** is their ability to stay calm and to control their feelings. EG *He had recovered his composure... She looked out over the auditorium with grave composure.* — N UNCOUNT, Formal

compound, compounds, compounding, compounded; pronounced /kɒmpaʊnd/ when it is a noun, and /kə7mpaʊnd/ when it is a verb.

1 A **compound** is an enclosed area of land that is used for a particular purpose. EG *He led the men into the prison compound.* — N COUNT

2 In chemistry, a **compound** is a substance that consists of two or more elements. — N COUNT

3 If something is a **compound** of different things, it consists of those things. EG *The new threat was a compound of nationalism and social revolution.* — N COUNT

4 If something **is compounded** of different things, it is made by mixing those things together. EG *They specialize in local dishes compounded of fresh fish and vegetables.* — V-PASS : OFT + *of/from*, Formal

5 To **compound** a problem, difficulty, or mistake means to make it worse by adding to it. EG *Her uncertainty was now compounded by fear.* — V+O, Formal

comprehend /kɒmprɪhɛnd/, **comprehends, comprehending, comprehended.** If you cannot **comprehend** something, you cannot fully understand or appreciate it. EG *...a failure to comprehend the huge power of computers... They did not comprehend how hard he had struggled.* — V+O, V+REPORT, OR V, Formal

comprehensible /kɒmprɪhɛnsə1bə0l/. Something that is **comprehensible** can be easily understood. EG *The object is to make our research readable and comprehensible.* — ADJ QUALIT

comprehension /kɒmprɪhɛnʃə0n/, **comprehensions. 1 Comprehension** is the ability to understand or appreciate something fully. EG *The problems of solar navigation seem beyond comprehension... Richard looked from face to face with dawning comprehension.* — N UNCOUNT

2 A **comprehension** is an exercise to find out how well you understand a piece of spoken or written language. — N COUNT

comprehensive /kɒmprɪhɛnsɪv/, **comprehensives. 1** Something that is **comprehensive** includes everything that is needed or relevant. EG *...a comprehensive list of all the items in stock.* — ADJ CLASSIF

2 A **comprehensive** or a **comprehensive school** is a school in which children of all abilities are taught together. — N COUNT, British

compress /kə7mprɛs/, **compresses, compressing, compressed. 1** When you **compress** something or when it **compresses**, it is pressed or squeezed so that it takes up less space. EG *I could feel my lips compress into a white line... ...compressed air.* — V-ERG ◊ **compression** /kə7mprɛʃə0n/. EG *...the compression of air by the piston.* — ◊ N UNCOUNT

2 If you **compress** something such as a piece of writing or a description, you make it shorter. EG *I soon finished a paper, which I compressed to minimum length.* — V+O : USU PASS ◊ **compression.** EG *...the compression of information.* — ◊ N UNCOUNT

comprise /kə7mpraɪz/, **comprises, comprising, comprised. 1** If something **comprises** a number of things or people, it has them as its parts or members. EG *The Privy Council comprised 283 members... The fountain was comprised of three stone basins.* — V+C OR V-PASS +*of*, Formal

2 If a number of things or people **comprise** something, they are the parts or members that it consists of. EG *Farmers comprise just 1.2 per cent of the country's population.* — V+C, Formal

compromise /kɒmprəmaɪz/, **compromises, compromising, compromised. 1** A **compromise** is an agreement between two people in which they both give up something that they originally wanted. EG *It was necessary for members to make compromises to ensure party unity... Delegates predict that some compromise will be reached.* — N COUNT OR N UNCOUNT

2 If you **compromise**, you reach an agreement with another person or group in which you both give up something that you originally wanted. EG *The best thing to do is to compromise.* — V

3 If you **compromise** yourself or your beliefs, you do something which causes people to doubt how sincere, moral, or honest you are. EG *The Government had compromised its principles... They claim he has already compromised himself.* — V-REFL OR V+O

◊ **compromising.** EG *There were photos and compromising letters.* — ◊ ADJ QUALIT

compulsion /kə7mpʌlʃə0n/, **compulsions. 1** A **compulsion** is a strong desire to do something, which you find difficult to control. EG *She feels a compulsion to tidy up all the time.* — N COUNT : OFT + *to*-INF

2 If someone uses **compulsion** in order to get you to do something, they force you to do it, for example by threatening to punish you if you do not do it. EG *We are not entitled to use compulsion... Pressed into rugby under compulsion, I began to enjoy the game.* — N UNCOUNT

compulsive /kə7mpʌlsɪv/. **1** You use **compulsive** to describe people who keep doing something wrong or harmful and who cannot prevent themselves from doing it. For example, a **compulsive** liar is someone who cannot stop lying. EG *...a compulsive gambler.* — ADJ CLASSIF ◊ **compulsively.** EG *He steals compulsively.* — ◊ ADV

2 If a book or television programme is **compulsive**, it is so interesting that you do not want to stop reading or watching it. — ADJ QUALIT ◊ **compulsively.** EG *The book is compulsively readable.* — ◊ ADV+ADJ

compulsory /kə7mpʌlsə0ri1/. If something is **compulsory**, you must do it. EG *In most schools, sports are compulsory... ...his compulsory retirement at the age of 60.* — ADJ CLASSIF

computation /kɒmpjə4teɪʃə0n/, **computations. Computation** is mathematical calculation. EG *There had been a sudden advance in the field of automatic computation... He sat over his adding machine making rapid computations.* — N UNCOUNT OR N COUNT

compute /kə7mpjuːt/, **computes, computing, computed.** To **compute** a quantity or number means to calculate it. EG *It is difficult to compute the loss in revenue.* ● See also **computing**. — V+O

computer /kə7mpjuːtə/, **computers.** A **computer** is an electronic machine that can quickly make calculations, store, rearrange, and retrieve information, or control another machine. EG *Portable computers can be plugged into TV sets... ...computer games.* — N COUNT ● If you do something **by computer**, you do it using a computer. EG *The entire process is done by computer.* — ● PHRASE

computerize /kə7mpjuːtəraɪz/, **computerizes, computerizing, computerized;** also spelled **computerise. 1** To **computerize** a system, process, or type of work means to arrange for a lot of the work to be done by computers. EG *We are currently computerizing the Inland Revenue.* — V+O

◊ **computerized.** EG *He had just introduced a computerized filing system into the office.* — ◊ ADJ CLASSIF

◊ **computerization** /kə7mpjuːtəraɪzeɪʃə0n/. EG *...the economic benefits of computerization.* — ◊ N UNCOUNT

2 To **computerize** information means to store or process it in a computer. — V+O

computing /kə7mpju:tɪŋ/ is the activity of using a computer and writing programs for it. EG *...the impact of computing on routine office work.* N UNCOUNT

comrade /kɒmrɪ3d, -æd/, **comrades. 1** Socialists or communists call each other **comrade**, especially in meetings. EG *This is what I propose, Comrades.* VOCATIVE

2 Someone's **comrades** are their friends or companions. N COUNT Outdated

con /kɒn/, **cons, conning, conned. 1** If someone **cons** you, they persuade you to do something or believe something by telling you things that are not true. EG *A lot of people are conned into thinking that they can't fight back.* V+O: OFT+*into* Informal

2 A **con** is a trick in which someone deceives you by telling you something that is not true. EG *The whole thing was a big con.* N COUNT Informal

3 See also **mod cons.** • **pros and cons**: see **pro.**

concave /kɒŋ1keɪv, kɒŋ1keɪv/. A surface that is **concave** curves inwards in the middle. EG *...a concave valley.* ADJ QUALIT

conceal /kə7nsi:l/, **conceals, concealing, concealed. 1** If you **conceal** something, you cover it or hide it carefully. EG *She concealed the bottle beneath her mattress.* V+O

2 If you **conceal** a piece of information or a feeling, you do not let other people know about it. EG *He might be concealing a secret from me.* V+O: OFT+*from*

3 If something **conceals** an object, it covers it and prevents it from being seen. EG *The scarf concealed a revolver.* V+O

concealment /kə7nsi:lmə2nt/ is the state of being hidden or the act of hiding something. EG *The trees offered concealment and protection... ...the concealment of truth.* N UNCOUNT

concede /kə7nsi:d/, **concedes, conceding, conceded. 1** If you **concede** something, you admit, often unwillingly, that it is true or correct. EG *The company conceded that an error had been made... They reluctantly conceded the point... I'll concede you that.* V-SPEECH OR V +O+O

2 If you **concede** defeat, you accept that you have lost a struggle. EG *The government was forced to concede defeat.* V OR V+O

conceit /kə7nsi:t/ is very great pride in your abilities or achievements; used showing disapproval. EG *His recent movies have shown signs of arrogance and conceit.* N UNCOUNT

conceited /kə7nsi:tɪ2d/. Someone who is **conceited** is very proud of their abilities or achievements; used showing disapproval. EG *...a conceited old fool.* ADJ QUALIT

conceivable /kə7nsi:vəbə0l/. If something is **conceivable**, you can imagine it or believe it. EG *Jenny learned every conceivable recipe for pasta... It is conceivable that he drowned.* ◇ **conceivably.** EG *She brought it because she thought it might conceivably be useful to me.* ADJ QUALIT ◇ ADV SEN

conceive /kə7nsi:v/, **conceives, conceiving, conceived. 1** If you can **conceive** of something, you can imagine it or believe it. EG *He could never conceive of such a thing happening to himself... We could not conceive where the energy came from.* V+*of* OR REPORT

2 If you **conceive** something as a particular thing, you consider it to be that thing. EG *A politician conceives the world as a variety of conflicts.* V+O: USU+*as*

3 If you **conceive** a plan or idea, you think of it and work out how it can be done. EG *A Prices and Incomes policy was boldly conceived.* V+O

4 When a child **is conceived** or when a woman **conceives**, the woman becomes pregnant. EG *The boy had been conceived on their honeymoon.* V+O OR V

concentrate /kɒnsə2ntreɪt/, **concentrates, concentrating, concentrated. 1** If you **concentrate** on something, you give all your attention to it. EG *Concentrate on your driving... He believed governments should concentrate more on education.* V: OFT+*on*

2 If something **concentrates the mind**, it makes you think clearly and carefully. EG *The prospect of death concentrates the mind wonderfully.* PHRASE

3 When an amount of something **is concentrated** in a small space, there is a lot of it there. EG *Modern industry has been concentrated in a few large urban centres.* V+O

concentrated /kɒnsə2ntreɪtɪ2d/. **1** A liquid that is **concentrated** has been increased in strength by having water removed from it. EG *...concentrated orange juice.* ADJ CLASSIF

2 A **concentrated** activity is directed with great intensity in one place. EG *...a heavily concentrated attack.* ADJ QUALIT

concentration /kɒnsə2ntreɪʃə0n/, **concentrations. 1 Concentration** on something is giving all your attention to it. EG *It requires considerable concentration... ...his concentration on civil rights.* N UNCOUNT: OFT+*on*

2 A **concentration** of something is a large amount of it or large numbers of it in a small area. EG *...the concentration of power in the hands of a single group.* N COUNT OR N UNCOUNT

concentration camp, concentration camps. A **concentration camp** is a prison for political prisoners, especially in Germany during the Second World War. N COUNT

concentric /kə7nsentrɪk/. **Concentric** circles or rings have the same centre. EG *...concentric circles of stones.* ADJ CLASSIF: ATTRIB

concept /kɒnsept/, **concepts.** A **concept** is an idea or abstract principle. EG *...the concept of trade unionism... Of course, it's a difficult concept.* N COUNT

conception /kə7nsepʃə0n/, **conceptions. 1** A **conception** is an idea that you have in your mind. EG *He had a definite conception of how he wanted things arranged.* N COUNT

2 Conception is **2.1** the forming of an idea for something in your mind. EG *The plan was very imaginative in conception.* **2.2** the process in which a woman becomes pregnant. EG *...the nine months between conception and birth.* N UNCOUNT

conceptual /kə7nseptʃʊ0əl/ means related to ideas and concepts formed in the mind. EG *Most people have little conceptual understanding of computers.* ADJ CLASSIF: ATTRIB Formal

concern /kə7nsɜ:n/, **concerns, concerning, concerned. 1 Concern** is worry about a situation. EG *...the growing public concern over Britain's poor economic performance... My concern is that many of these cases are going unnoticed.* N UNCOUNT OR N COUNT +SUPP

2 If something **concerns** you, it worries you. EG *One of the things that concerns me is the rise in vandalism.* ◇ **concerned.** EG *He was concerned about the level of unemployment.* V+O ◇ ADJ QUALIT

3 If you **concern** yourself with something, you give attention to it because you think that it is important. EG *I don't want you to concern yourself with it.* ◇ **concerned.** EG *We are more concerned with efficiency than expansion.* V-REFL OR V+O: OFT+*with* ◇ ADJ PRED

4 If something is **of concern** to you, it is important to you. EG *This was of no concern to businessmen.* PHRASE

5 Your **concern for** someone is a feeling that you want them to be happy, safe, and well. EG *She shows a true concern for others.* N UNCOUNT +SUPP

6 If a situation, event, or activity **concerns** you, it affects or involves you. V+O

7 If a situation or problem is your **concern**, it is something that you have a duty to be involved with. EG *That's your concern, I'm afraid... This quarrel is no concern of ours.* N SING+POSS

8 You say **as far as** something **is concerned** to indicate the subject that you are talking about. EG *We have rather a poor record as far as regional studies are concerned.* PHRASE

9 You say **'as far as I'm concerned'** to indicate that you are giving your own opinion. EG *This is all rubbish as far as I'm concerned.* PHRASE

10 The people **concerned** are the people who take ADJ AFTER N

Which meaning of 'concrete' is the opposite of 'conceptual'?

part in something or are affected by it. EG *It was a perfect arrangement for all concerned.*

11 If a book, speech, or piece of information **concerns** a particular subject or **is concerned** with it, it is about that subject. EG *This chapter is concerned with changes that are likely to take place.* V+O OR V-PASS +*with*

12 A **concern** is also a company or business. EG *...the giant West German chemical concern, Hoechst.* N COUNT Formal

concerning /kə[7]nsɜːnɪŋ/. You use **concerning** to indicate what a question, story or letter is about. EG *He refused to answer questions concerning his private life... I will now destroy some myths concerning these animals.* PREP

concert /kɒnsət/, **concerts. 1** A **concert** is a performance of music given by musicians. EG *...pop concerts... ...a concert hall.* N COUNT ● When pop groups are **in concert**, they are giving a concert. ● PHRASE

2 If a number of people do something **in concert**, they do it together. EG *Sanctions will be more effective if they are undertaken in concert by a group of countries.* PHRASE Formal

concerted /kə[7]nsɜːtɪ[2]d/. A **concerted** action is done by several people working together. EG *Everyone makes a concerted effort to help.* ADJ CLASSIF : ATTRIB

concerto /kə[7]ntʃeətəʊ/, **concertos.** A **concerto** is a piece of music written for a solo instrument and an orchestra. N COUNT

concession /kə[7]nsɛʃə[0]n/, **concessions.** A **concession** is **1** something that you agree to let someone do or have, especially in order to end an argument. EG *The Prime Minister had been urged to make a concession by the government.* **2** a special right or privilege that is given to someone. EG *Foreign oil companies were granted concessions.* N COUNT

conciliate /kə[7]nsɪlieɪt/, **conciliates, conciliating, conciliated.** If you **conciliate**, you try to end a disagreement with someone. V OR V+O Formal

◇ **conciliation** /kə[7]nsɪlieɪʃə[0]n/. EG *Did you make any efforts at conciliation?* ◇ N UNCOUNT

conciliatory /kə[7]nsɪljətri[1]/. When you are **conciliatory**, you are willing to end a disagreement with someone. EG *She spoke in a conciliatory tone.* ADJ QUALIT

concise /kə[7]nsaɪs/. Something that is **concise** says everything that is necessary without using any unnecessary words. EG *...a concise survey of English literature.* ADJ QUALIT ◇ **concisely.** EG *Write clearly and concisely.* ◇ ADV

conclude /kə[7]ŋ[1]kluːd/, **concludes, concluding, concluded. 1** If you **conclude** that something is true, you decide that it is true because you know that other things are true. EG *Darwin concluded that men were descended from apes... What do you conclude from all that?.* V+REPORT : ONLY *that*, OR V+*from*

2 When you **conclude**, you say the last thing that you are going to say. EG *'That,' he concluded, 'is why we're so poor.'* V+QUOTE Formal ◇ **concluding.** EG *...his concluding remark.* ◇ ADJ CLASSIF : ATTRIB

3 When you **conclude** something, you end it. EG *I will conclude this chapter with a quotation from Orwell.* V-ERG Formal

4 If you **conclude** a treaty or business deal, you arrange or settle it finally. V+O Formal

conclusion /kə[7]ŋ[1]kluːʒə[0]n/, **conclusions. 1** A **conclusion** is something that you decide is true after you have thought about it carefully. EG *I came to the conclusion that I didn't really like civil engineering.* N COUNT : OFT +REPORT ● If you **jump to a conclusion**, you decide too quickly that something is true, when you do not know all the facts. EG *Some people jumped rashly to the conclusion that something must be wrong.* ● PHRASE

2 The **conclusion** of something is its ending. EG *We tried an experiment which had an interesting conclusion.* N SING : USU+SUPP ● You can describe something that seems certain to happen as a **foregone conclusion**. EG *The result should be a foregone conclusion.* ● PHRASE

3 The **conclusion** of a treaty or a business deal is its final settlement. N SING : USU+SUPP

conclusive /kə[7]ŋ[1]kluːsɪv/. Facts or evidence that are **conclusive** show that something is certainly true. EG *The evidence is not conclusive.* ADJ QUALIT ◇ **conclusively.** EG *This has been difficult to prove conclusively.* ◇ ADV

concoct /kə[7]ŋ[1]kɒkt/, **concocts, concocting, concocted. 1** If you **concoct** an excuse or explanation, you invent one. EG *He had to hastily concoct an excuse.* V+O

2 If you **concoct** something, you make it by mixing several things together. EG *Nancy had concocted a red wine sauce.* V+O

concoction /kə[7]ŋ[1]kɒkʃə[0]n/, **concoctions.** A **concoction** is something that has been made out of several things mixed together. EG *Chutney is a concoction of almost any fruit or vegetable you like.* N COUNT

concomitant /kə[7]ŋ[1]kɒmɪtənt/. Something that is **concomitant** with another thing happens at the same time and is connected with it. EG *...the growth of bureaucracy, with its concomitant dangers of corruption.* ADJ CLASSIF : OFT+*with* Formal

concord /kɒŋ[1]kɔːd/ is the state of living or working together in peaceful agreement. EG *...this religion of peace and concord.* N UNCOUNT Formal

concrete /kɒŋ[1]kriːt/, **concretes, concreting, concreted. 1 Concrete** is a substance used for building which is made by mixing together cement, sand, small stones, and water. EG *...a modern tower made of concrete and steel.* N UNCOUNT

2 When you **concrete** something such as a path, you cover it with concrete. V+O

3 You use **concrete** to describe something that is **3.1** definite and not general or vague. EG *There were no specific, concrete proposals placed before the people.* ADJ QUALIT **3.2** real and physical rather than abstract. EG *There were many concrete reminders of his existence.* ADJ CLASSIF

concur /kə[7]ŋ[1]kɜː/, **concurs, concurring, concurred.** When you **concur**, you agree with someone or with their opinion. EG *The judge concurred with earlier findings... Baghdad residents all concur that food shortages are acute.* V : OFT+*with* OR REPORT : ONLY *that* Formal

concurrence /kə[7]ŋ[1]kʌrəns/. **1** Someone's **concurrence** is their agreement to something. EG *The French President gave his instant concurrence.* N UNCOUNT +SUPP Formal

2 If there is a **concurrence** of two or more things, they happen at the same time. EG *...a bizarre concurrence of events.* Formal

concurrent /kə[7]ŋ[1]kʌrənt/. If two things are **concurrent**, they happen at the same time. ADJ CLASSIF : OFT+*with* ◇ **concurrently.** EG *Two subjects will be studied concurrently.* ◇ ADV

concussed /kə[7]ŋ[1]kʌst/. If you are **concussed** by a blow to your head, it causes you to lose consciousness or to feel sick or confused. ADJ CLASSIF

concussion /kə[7]ŋ[1]kʌʃə[0]n/. If you suffer **concussion** after a blow to your head, you lose consciousness or feel sick or confused. EG *She was in Newcastle Infirmary with concussion.* N UNCOUNT

condemn /kə[7]ndɛm/, **condemns, condemning, condemned. 1** If you **condemn** something, you say that it is very bad and unacceptable. EG *He condemned the report as partial and inadequate... I did not condemn him for what he had done.* V+O : OFT+ *for/as* ◇ **condemnation** /kɒndɛmneɪʃə[0]n/, **condemnations.** EG *...their strong condemnation of her conduct.* ◇ N UNCOUNT OR N COUNT

2 If someone **is condemned** to a punishment, they are given this punishment. EG *Susan was condemned to death.* V+O+*to* OR *to*-INF

3 If circumstances **condemn** you to an unpleasant situation, they make it certain that you will suffer in that way. EG *Most of the applicants are condemned to spend all morning waiting to be seen.* V+O+*to* OR *to*-INF

4 If authorities **condemn** a building, they officially decide that it is not safe and must be pulled down. V+O

condemned /kə⁷ndɛmd/. A **condemned** man or woman is going to be executed. EG *...the condemned prisoners.* ADJ CLASSIF: ATTRIB

condensation /kɒndɛnseɪʃə⁰n/ consists of small drops of water which form when warm water vapour or steam touches a cold surface such as a window. N UNCOUNT

condense /kə⁷ndɛns/, **condenses, condensing, condensed. 1** If you **condense** a piece of writing or speech, you make it shorter, usually by including only the most important parts. EG *I tried to condense every report into as few words as possible.* V+O

2 When a gas or vapour **condenses**, it changes into a liquid. V-ERG

condescend /kɒndɪsɛnd/, **condescends, condescending, condescended. 1** If you **condescend** to people, you behave in a way which shows them that you think you are superior to them. EG *He never condescended, never spoke down to me.* V: OFT+*to* Formal

◊ **condescending** /kɒndɪsɛndɪŋ/. EG *She addressed him with the same condescending tone.* ◊ ADJ QUALIT

2 If you **condescend** to do something, you agree to do it, but in a way which shows that you think you are doing people a favour. EG *She did not condescend to have dinner with him.* V+*to*-INF

condescension /kɒndɪsɛnʃə⁰n/ is condescending behaviour or qualities. EG *He spoke to the labourers with no condescension.* N UNCOUNT

condition /kə⁷ndɪʃə⁰n/, **conditions, conditioning, conditioned. 1** The **condition** of someone or something is the state that they are in. EG *You can't go home in that condition... Families had only intervened when the condition of hunger strikers became critical... Keep your car exterior in good condition.* N SING+SUPP

2 The **conditions** in which people live or do things are the qualities or factors that affect their comfort, safety, or success. EG *These experiments were carried out under almost unimaginable conditions... ...adverse weather conditions... ...appalling living conditions.* N PLURAL +SUPP

3 A **condition** is something which must happen in order for something else to be possible. EG *You have to live there as a condition of your job.* N COUNT: OFT+*of/for*

4 When you agree to do something **on condition that** something else happens, you mean that you will only do it if this other thing happens or is agreed to first. EG *He has agreed to come on condition that there won't be any publicity.* CONJ

5 You can refer to an illness or other medical problem as a particular **condition**. EG *He has a heart condition.* N COUNT+SUPP

6 If someone is **out of condition**, they are unhealthy and unfit. PHRASE

7 If someone **is conditioned** by their upbringing or environment to do or think a particular thing, they are influenced by it over a period of time so that they do or think that thing. EG *Men had been conditioned to regard women as their inferiors.* V+O: USU PASS +*to*-INF

◊ **conditioning.** EG *It is very difficult to overcome your early conditioning.* ◊ N UNCOUNT

conditional /kə⁷ndɪʃə⁰nəl, -ʃənə⁰l/. If a situation or agreement is **conditional** on something, it will only happen or be accepted if this thing happens. EG *Their support is conditional upon further reduction in public expenditure... ...conditional acceptance.* ◊ **conditionally.** EG *She said yes, conditionally.* ADJ CLASSIF: OFT+*on/upon* ◊ ADV SEN

conditioner /kə⁷ndɪʃə⁰nə/, **conditioners.** A **conditioner** is 1 a substance which you can put on your hair after washing it in order to make it softer. 2 a thick liquid which you can use when you wash clothes in order to make them feel softer. N MASS

condolence /kə⁷ndəʊləns/, **condolences. Condolence** is sympathy that you express for someone when one of their friends or relatives has died. EG *...letters of condolence... She wished to offer her condolences.* N UNCOUNT OR N PLURAL

condom /kɒndə⁷m/, **condoms.** A **condom** is a covering made of rubber which a man wears on his penis during sexual intercourse as a contraceptive. N COUNT

condone /kə⁷ndəʊn/, **condones, condoning, condoned.** If someone **condones** behaviour that is morally wrong, they accept it and allow it to happen. EG *We cannot condone the daily massacre of innocent people.* V+O

conducive /kə⁷ndjuːsɪv/. If one thing is **conducive** to another thing, it makes the other thing likely to happen. EG *Competition is not conducive to human happiness.* ADJ PRED+*to*

conduct, conducts, conducting, conducted; pronounced /kə⁷ndʌkt/ when it is a verb and /kɒndʌkt/ when it is a noun.

1 When you **conduct** an activity or task, you organize it and carry it out. EG *We have been conducting a survey of the region.* ▸ used as a noun. EG *Secrets are essential to the conduct of a war.* V+O ▸ N UNCOUNT

2 If you **conduct** yourself in a particular way, you behave in that way. EG *He instructed them in how to conduct themselves inside the mosque.* ▸ used as a noun. EG *The minister had several good reasons for his conduct.* V-REFL+A Formal ▸ N UNCOUNT: USU+POSS

3 When someone **conducts** an orchestra or choir, they stand in front of it and direct its performance. V+O OR V

4 If something **conducts** heat or electricity, it allows heat or electricity to pass through it or along it. V+O OR V

conductor /kə⁷ndʌktə/, **conductors.** A **conductor** is 1 a person who sells tickets on a bus. 2 a person who stands in front of an orchestra or choir and conducts it. N COUNT

cone /kəʊn/, **cones.** A **cone** is 1 a shape with a circular base and smooth curved sides ending in a point at the top. See picture at SHAPES. EG *...a cone-shaped hill.* 2 the fruit of a tree such as a pine or fir which consists of a cluster of woody scales containing seeds. 3 an ice cream cornet. N COUNT

confectionery /kə⁷nfɛkʃənə⁰ri¹/. You can refer to sweets and chocolates as **confectionery**. N UNCOUNT

confederate /kə⁷nfɛdə⁰rə¹t/, **confederates.** Someone's **confederates** are the people they are working with in a secret activity. N COUNT

confederation /kə⁷nfɛdəreɪʃə⁰n/, **confederations.** A **confederation** is an organization or alliance of groups of people for political or business purposes. EG *We are in favour of a loose confederation of states.* N COUNT

confer /kə⁷nfɜː/, **confers, conferring, conferred. 1** When you **confer** with someone, you discuss something with them in order to make a decision. EG *He went home to confer with his wife.* V OR V+*with*: RECIP

2 If something **confers** an advantage, it gives that advantage. EG *The system had conferred great benefits.* V+O: OFT+*on/upon* Formal

conference /kɒnfə⁰rəns/, **conferences. 1** A **conference** is a meeting at which formal discussions take place. EG *The Managing Director has daily conferences with the other staff members.* ● If someone is **in conference**, they are having a formal meeting. EG *...the time he must spend in conference listening to reports.* N COUNT ● PHRASE

2 A **conference** is also a meeting about a particular subject, often lasting a few days. EG *...a conference on nuclear disarmament in London.* N COUNT

confess /kə⁷nfɛs/, **confesses, confessing, confessed. 1** If you **confess** something that you are ashamed of, you admit it. EG *Perhaps I shouldn't confess this, but I did on one occasion forge Tony's signature... I confess to a certain weakness for puddings.* V-SPEECH, V+*to*, OR V-REFL+C

2 You say **'I must confess'** to emphasize that you PHRASE

Would you tell a confidence to a confidante?

are being honest about something. EG *I must confess that I find him a bore.*
3 If you **confess** to a crime, you admit that you have committed that crime. EG *Bianchi had confessed to five of the murders... He had confessed his guilt.* V: OFT+*to* OR V+O

confessed /kə^{7}nfest/. You use **confessed** to describe someone who openly admits that they have a particular fault or weakness. EG *He was self-indulgent and cynical, a confessed failure.* ADJ CLASSIF: ATTRIB

confession /kə^{7}nfeʃə^{0}n/, **confessions. 1** A **confession** is a statement that you make in which you admit that you have committed a crime or done something wrong. EG *I have a confession to make... The moment you sign a confession, you can have all the sleep you want.* N COUNT
2 Confession is **2.1** the act of confessing something. EG *...a torrent of confession.* **2.2** a religious act in which you tell a priest about your sins and ask for forgiveness. EG *He had gone to confession.* N UNCOUNT

confetti /kə^{7}nfeti^1/ is small pieces of coloured paper that people throw over the bride and groom at a wedding. N UNCOUNT

confidant /kɒnfɪdænt/, **confidants.** Someone's **confidant** is a man who they discuss their private problems with. N COUNT Formal

confidante /kɒnfɪdænt/, **confidantes.** Someone's **confidante** is a woman who they discuss their private problems with. N COUNT Formal

confide /kə^{7}nfaɪd/, **confides, confiding, confided.** If you **confide** a secret to someone, you tell it to them. EG *I never confided my fear to anyone... He had confided to me that he wasn't an Irishman at all.* ◊ **confiding** /kə^{7}nfaɪdɪŋ/. EG *At first she was suspicious, then she became confiding.* V-SPEECH: ONLY *that*, OFT +*to* ◊ ADJ QUALIT
confide in. If you **confide in** someone, you tell them about a private problem or some other secret matter. EG *May I confide in you?* PHRASAL VB: V+PREP, HAS PASS

confidence /kɒnfɪdəns/, **confidences. 1** If you have **confidence** in someone, you feel that you can trust them. EG *I have a lot of confidence in him.* N UNCOUNT
2 If you have **confidence**, you feel sure about your abilities, qualities, or ideas. EG *I was full of confidence.* N UNCOUNT
3 Confidence is also a situation in which you tell someone a secret. EG *I'm telling you this in the strictest confidence... ...a breach of confidence.* N UNCOUNT
4 If you **take** someone **into** your **confidence**, you tell them a secret. PHRASE
5 A **confidence** is a secret that you tell someone. EG *Edith was used to receiving confidences.* N COUNT

confident /kɒnfɪdənt/. **1** If you are **confident** about something, you are certain that it will happen in the way you want it to. EG *He said he was very confident that the scheme would be successful.* ◊ **confidently.** EG *One could confidently rely on him.* ADJ QUALIT ◊ ADV
2 People who are **confident** feel sure of their own abilities, qualities, or ideas. EG *...a witty, young and confident lawyer.* ◊ **confidently.** EG *I strode confidently up the hall.* ADJ QUALIT ◊ ADV

confidential /kɒnfɪdenʃə^{0}l/. **1** Information that is **confidential** is meant to be kept secret. EG *This arrangement is to be kept strictly confidential.* ◊ **confidentially.** EG *I wrote to you confidentially on 30th September 1987.* ◊ **confidentiality** /kɒnfɪdenʃi^{1}ælə^{1}ti^1/. EG *Please respect the confidentiality of this information.* ADJ QUALIT ◊ ADV ◊ N UNCOUNT
2 If you talk to someone in a **confidential** way, you talk to them quietly because what you are saying is secret. EG *He became very confidential.* ◊ **confidentially.** EG *She leaned forward and whispered to him confidentially.* ADJ QUALIT ◊ ADV

configuration /kə^{7}nfɪgjə^{4}reɪʃə^{0}n/, **configurations.** A **configuration** is an arrangement of a group of things. EG *The blades collapse into an arrow-head configuration.* N COUNT Formal

confine, confines, confining, confined; pronounced /kə^{7}nfaɪn/ when it is a verb and /kɒnfaɪnz/ when it is a noun.
1 If something **is confined** to only one place, situation, or person, it only exists there or only affects that person. EG *The problem appears to be confined to the tropics.* V+O: USU PASS+*to*
2 If you **confine** yourself to something, you do only that thing and are involved with nothing else. EG *They confine themselves to discussing the weather... Confine your messages to official business.* V-REFL+*to* OR V+O+*to*
3 To **confine** someone means to keep them in prison or some other place which they cannot leave. EG *William was confined to an institution for some years.* V+O: USU+A
4 The **confines** of an area are the boundaries enclosing it. EG *...within the confines of the Gallery.* N PLURAL Formal

confined /kə^{7}nfaɪnd/. A **confined** space or area is small and enclosed by walls. ADJ CLASSIF

confinement /kə^{7}nfaɪnmə^{2}nt/ is the state of being forced to stay in a prison or another place which you cannot leave. EG *...his many years in confinement.* N UNCOUNT

confirm /kə^{7}nfɜːm/, **confirms, confirming, confirmed. 1** If something **confirms** what you believe, it shows that it is definitely true. EG *My suspicions were confirmed... He glanced round to confirm that he was alone... They have confirmed what I suspected long ago.* ◊ **confirmation** /kɒnfəmeɪʃə^{0}n/. EG *This discovery was a confirmation of Darwin's proposition.* V+O OR V+REPORT ◊ N UNCOUNT
2 If you **confirm** something, you say that it is true. EG *She asked me if it was my car and I confirmed that it was... There is no one to confirm whether these memories are correct.* ◊ **confirmation.** EG *She turned to Jimmie for confirmation and he nodded.* V+O OR V+REPORT ◊ N UNCOUNT
3 If you **confirm** an arrangement or appointment, you say that it is definite, usually in a letter or on the telephone. EG *...a letter confirming that they expect you on the twelfth.* ◊ **confirmation.** EG *All times are approximate and subject to confirmation.* V+O OR V+REPORT ◊ N UNCOUNT
4 When someone **is confirmed**, they are formally accepted as a member of a Christian church. ◊ **confirmation, confirmations.** EG *...the confirmation service.* V+O: USU PASS ◊ N UNCOUNT OR N COUNT

confirmed /kə^{7}nfɜːmd/. You use **confirmed** to describe someone who has a particular habit or belief that they are very unlikely to change. EG *I am a confirmed non-smoker.* ADJ CLASSIF: ATTRIB

confiscate /kɒnfɪskeɪt/, **confiscates, confiscating, confiscated.** If you **confiscate** something from someone, you take it away from them, often as a punishment. EG *We had special instructions to confiscate all their cameras.* ◊ **confiscation** /kɒnfɪskeɪʃə^{0}n/. EG *I faced two years' jail plus the confiscation of the tapes.* V+O ◊ N UNCOUNT

conflagration /kɒnfləgreɪʃə^{0}n/, **conflagrations.** A **conflagration** is a large fire. N COUNT Formal

conflict, conflicts, conflicting, conflicted; pronounced /kɒnflɪkt/ when it is a noun and /kə^{7}nflɪkt/ when it is a verb.
1 Conflict is **1.1** serious disagreement and argument about something important. EG *...the familiar conflict between government and opposition... They often came into conflict with the islanders... ...a number of conflicts in the engineering industry.* N UNCOUNT OR N COUNT
1.2 a state of mind in which you find it impossible to make a decision. EG *Frequently he is in a state of conflict or indecision.* N UNCOUNT
2 A **conflict** is **2.1** a serious difference between two or more beliefs, ideas, or interests. EG *Conflicts of loyalty arose.* **2.2** fighting between countries or groups of people. EG *A conventional conflict might escalate to a nuclear confrontation.* N COUNT OR N UNCOUNT
3 If ideas, interests, or accounts **conflict**, they are very different from each other and it seems impossible for them to exist together or to both be true. EG *There is some research that conflicts with this view.* ◊ **conflicting.** EG *There are too many* V OR V+*with*: RECIP ◊ ADJ QUALIT

conflicting interests... The evidence seems to be conflicting.

conform /kə^{7}nfɔ:m/, **conforms, conforming, conformed. 1** If you **conform**, you behave in the way that you are expected to behave. EG *You must be prepared to conform.* — V

2 If something **conforms to** a law, regulation, or wish, it is of the type or quality that is required or desired. EG *Such a change would not conform to the wishes of the great majority of people.* — V+*to/with*

conformist /kə^{7}nfɔ:mɪst/, **conformists.** A **conformist** is someone who behaves or thinks like everyone else rather than doing things that are original; often used showing disapproval. ▸ used as an adjective. EG *The school had grown more conformist and cautious.* — N COUNT; ▸ ADJ QUALIT

conformity /kə^{7}nfɔ:mɪ^{1}ti^1/ is behaviour, thought, or appearance that is the same as that of most other people. EG *All that seems to be required of us is conformity.* — N UNCOUNT

confound /kə^{7}nfaʊnd/, **confounds, confounding, confounded.** If something **confounds** you, it makes you feel confused or surprised. EG *...speaking French to confound their friends.* — V+O

confront /kə^{7}nfrʌnt/, **confronts, confronting, confronted. 1** If you **are confronted** with a problem or task, you have to deal with it. EG *I was confronted with the task of designing the system... ...typical problems that confront Germans learning English... We will soon have to confront a fundamental question.* — V+O: OFT+*with*

2 If you **confront** someone, **2.1** you meet them face to face, especially when you are going to fight them. EG *The two men confronted each other... They were confronted by a line of guardsmen.* — V+O **2.2** you present facts or evidence to them in order to accuse them of something. EG *I decided to confront her with the charges of racism.* — V+O+*with*

confrontation /kɒnfrənteɪʃə^{0}n/, **confrontations.** A **confrontation** is a dispute, fight, or battle between two groups of people. EG *Every now and then there is a confrontation between the pickets and police.* — N COUNT OR N UNCOUNT

confuse /kə^{7}nfju:z/, **confuses, confusing, confused. 1** If you **confuse** two things, you get them mixed up, so that you think one of them is the other one. EG *You seem to confuse the words 'satire' and 'satyr' in your paper... You must be confusing me with someone else.* — V+O: OFT+*with*

2 To **confuse** someone means to make it difficult for them to know exactly what to do. EG *You're trying to confuse me.* — V+O

3 To **confuse** a situation means to make it complicated or difficult to understand. EG *To confuse matters further, her sister is married to her husband's uncle.* — V+O

confused /kə^{7}nfju:zd/. **1** Something that is **confused** does not have any order or pattern and is difficult to understand. EG *...a confused dream about the end of the world... My thoughts were confused.* — ADJ QUALIT

2 If you are **confused**, you do not understand what is happening or you do not know what to do. EG *She was bewildered and confused.* — ADJ QUALIT

confusing /kə^{7}nfju:zɪŋ/. Something that is **confusing** makes it difficult for people to know exactly what is happening. EG *The plot is fairly confusing.* — ADJ QUALIT

confusion /kə^{7}nfju:ʒə^{0}n/, **confusions. 1 Confusion** is **1.1** making a mistake about a person or thing and thinking that they are another person or thing. EG *There is danger of confusion between them.* — N UNCOUNT **1.2** a situation where it is not clear what is happening. EG *In all the confusion, both men managed to grab me.* — N UNCOUNT OR N COUNT

2 If your mind is in a state of **confusion**, you do not know what to believe or what you should do. EG *Her answers to his questions have only added to his confusion.* — N UNCOUNT

congeal /kə^{7}ndʒi:l/, **congeals, congealing, congealed.** When a liquid **congeals**, it becomes very thick and sticky and almost solid. EG *The blood had already congealed.* — V-ERG

congenial /kə^{7}ndʒi:njəl, -nɪəl/. Someone or something that is **congenial** is pleasant. EG *A pub would be more congenial than a boarding house... ...congenial company.* — ADJ QUALIT Formal

congenital /kə^{7}ndʒɛnɪtə^{0}l/. A **congenital** disease or medical condition is one that a person has had from birth, but not one that is inherited. EG *The brain damage was congenital.* ◇ **congenitally.** EG *She is congenitally disabled.* — ADJ CLASSIF Medical; ◇ ADV

congested /kə^{7}ndʒɛstɪ^{2}d/. A road or area that is **congested** is so crowded with traffic or people that normal movement there is impossible. — ADJ QUALIT

congestion /kə^{7}ndʒɛstʃə^{0}n/. **1** If there is **congestion** in a place, the place is so crowded with traffic or people that normal movement is impossible. EG *...traffic congestion in urban areas.* — N UNCOUNT

2 Congestion in a part of the body is a medical condition in which the part becomes blocked. EG *...nasal congestion.* — N UNCOUNT +SUPP

conglomerate /kə^{7}nglɒmərə^{1}t/, **conglomerates.** A **conglomerate** is a large business firm consisting of several different companies. — N COUNT

conglomeration /kə^{7}nglɒməreɪʃə^{0}n/, **conglomerations.** A **conglomeration** is a group of many different things. EG *...a conglomeration of white buildings.* — N COUNT+SUPP

congratulate /kəngrætjə^{4}leɪt/, **congratulates, congratulating, congratulated. 1** If you **congratulate** someone, you praise them for something that they have done. EG *Friends came to congratulate the parents and to see the baby... I must congratulate you on a successful interview.* — V+O: OFT+*on* ◇ **congratulation** /kə^{7}ngrætjə^{4}leɪʃə^{0}n/. EG *...a letter of congratulation.* — ◇ N UNCOUNT

2 If you **congratulate** yourself, you are pleased about something that you have done or that has happened to you. EG *I congratulated myself on not looking my age.* — V-REFL: OFT+*on*

congratulations /kə^{7}ngrætjə^{4}leɪʃə^{0}nz/. You say **'congratulations'** to someone in order to congratulate them. EG *'Congratulations,' the doctor said. 'You have a son.'... I offered him my heartiest congratulations.* — CONVENTION

congratulatory /kə^{7}ngrætjə^{4}lətri^1/. Something that is **congratulatory** expresses congratulations. EG *...a congratulatory smile.* — ADJ CLASSIF

congregate /kɒŋgrɪ^{2}geɪt/, **congregates, congregating, congregated.** When people **congregate**, they gather together and form a group. EG *The crowds congregated around the pavilion.* — V: USU+A

congregation /kɒŋgrɪ^{2}geɪʃə^{0}n/, **congregations.** The people who attend a church service are referred to as the **congregation**. EG *There were only ten in the congregation.* — N COLL

congress /kɒŋgrɛs/, **congresses.** A **congress** is a large meeting that is held to discuss ideas and policies. EG *...the second Congress of Negro Writers and Artists.* — N COUNT

conical /kɒnɪkə^{0}l/. Something that is **conical** is shaped like a cone. EG *...a small conical shell.* — ADJ CLASSIF

conifer /kəʊnɪfə, kɒn-/, **conifers.** A **conifer** is a tree that has needle-like leaves and produces brown cones. — N COUNT

> **CONJ stands for conjunction**
> Words which have the label CONJ in the Extra Column are conjunctions, such as 'and' or 'although'.
> See the entry headed CONJUNCTIONS for more information.

conjecture /kə^{7}ndʒɛktʃə/, **conjectures. Conjecture** is the formation of ideas or opinions from — N UNCOUNT OR N COUNT Formal

CONJUNCTIONS

A conjunction is a word that joins together words, groups, or clauses. There are two main kinds of conjunction.

Coordinating conjunctions

There are a few words which we call coordinating conjunctions (CONJ). These are **and**, **but**, **yet**, **or**, and **nor**. They come between the two parts of a sentence, and these two parts are the same grammatical type. So they join words, as in *Jack **and** Jill*, groups of words, as in *We went to the Tower of London **and** Westminster Abbey*, and clauses, as in *I told them they should get on the bus outside the university **and** get off five stops later.*

As you can see from this last example, you do not need to repeat the subject of the second verb when it is the same as the first. You can also omit the second verb or part of it when it is the same as the first, as in the last example, where the word 'should' is omitted. Also in *Karen likes pop music but Liz doesn't,* where the form 'does' is used instead of 'likes'.

Here are some more examples of sentences with coordinating conjunctions in them: *John **and** Helen have just quarrelled . . .   We had a choice of home-made icecream **or** fresh fruit salad . . .   All the girls went swimming **but** none of the boys did . . .   She doesn't like school, **nor** do I.*

Subordinating conjunctions

There is a larger group of words which join subordinate clauses to main clauses. These are called subordinating conjunctions (also CONJ), and they are words such as **although**, **unless**, **if**, and **because**. A subordinating conjunction is usually the first word in the subordinate clause, although an adverb such as 'even' or 'especially' can sometimes be used in front of it.

Here are some examples of clauses joined by subordinating conjunctions: *He went to the party **although** he was very tired . . .   **Although** she is only fourteen, she thinks she is very grown-up . . .   I'll come for you at seven, **unless** you phone me before that . . .   **If** there's time, we could go to the cinema as well . . .   I like Americans **because** they are optimistic.*

incomplete or doubtful information. EG *The exact figure is a matter for conjecture.*

conjugal /kɒndʒə[4]gə[0]l/ means relating to marriage and the relationship between a husband and wife, especially their sexual relationship. EG *...conjugal happiness.* ADJ CLASSIF: ATTRIB Formal

conjunction /kə[7]ndʒʌŋk[0]ʃə[0]n/, **conjunctions. 1** A **conjunction** of things, characteristics, or features is a combination of them. EG *The cause of suicide is a nasty conjunction of personal and social factors.* N COUNT: OFT+*of* Formal

2 If two or more things are done **in conjunction**, they are done together rather than separately. EG *This course can only be taken in conjunction with course 234.* PHRASE

3 In grammar, a **conjunction** is a word or a group of words that joins together words, groups, or clauses. See the entry headed CONJUNCTIONS for more information. N COUNT

conjure /kʌndʒə/, **conjures, conjuring, conjured. 1** If you **conjure** something into existence, you make it appear by magic or by a trick. EG *He appeared with a small bucket he'd apparently conjured from nowhere.* V+O: USU+A

2 If you say that a particular name is **a name to conjure with**, you mean that it is a very important and influential name. PHRASE

conjure up. If you **conjure up** a memory, picture, or idea, you create it in your mind. EG *To many people, the name Kalahari conjures up images of a desert of unrelenting aridity.* PHRASAL VB: V+O+ADV

conjurer /kʌndʒə[0]rə/, **conjurers;** also spelled **conjuror.** A **conjurer** is a person who entertains people by doing magic tricks. N COUNT

conjuring trick, conjuring tricks. A **conjuring trick** is a trick in which something is made to appear or disappear as if by magic. N COUNT

conker /kɒŋkə/, **conkers. Conkers** are round brown nuts which come from horse chestnut trees. N COUNT

con-man, con-men. A **con-man** is a man who persuades people to give him their money or property by lying to them. N COUNT

connect /kə[7]nɛkt/, **connects, connecting, connected. 1** To **connect** one thing to another means to join the two things to each other. EG *Connect the fishing line to the hook.* V+O: OFT+*to*

2 If a piece of equipment **is connected**, it is joined by a wire or cable to an electricity supply or to another piece of equipment. EG *...a telephone line connected to their terminal.* V+O: USU PASS+*to*

3 If a telephone operator **connects** you, he or she enables you to speak to another person by telephone. EG *I'm trying to connect you, sir.* V+O

4 If a door or corridor **connects** two rooms or buildings, it joins them and makes it possible to walk between them. ◊ **connecting.** EG *The rooms had connecting doors between them.* V+O ◊ ADJ CLASSIF: ATTRIB

5 If a train, plane, or bus **connects** with another form of transport, it arrives at a time which allows passengers to change to the other form of transport in order to continue their journey. V: OFT+*with*

6 If you **connect** a person or thing with something, you realize that there is a relationship or link between them. EG *There is no evidence to connect Griffiths with the murder... Do you connect the two events?* V+O: OFT+*to/with*

connected /kə[7]nɛktɪ[2]d/. If one thing is **connected** with another, there is a relationship or link between them. EG *There are serious questions connected with radioactive waste disposal.* ADJ CLASSIF: USU PRED+*with*

connection /kə[7]nɛkʃə[0]n/, **connections;** also spelled **connexion. 1** A **connection** is a relationship between two things. EG *I do not think there is any logical connection between the two halves of the question.* N COUNT: OFT +*between/with*

2 If you talk or write to someone **in connection with** something, you talk or write to them about that thing. EG *The police wanted to interview him in connection with the murder.* PREP

3 A **connection** is also the joint where two wires or pipes are joined together. EG *There must be a loose connection.* N COUNT

4 If you get a **connection** at a station or airport, you catch a train, bus, or plane after having got off another train, bus, or plane so that you can continue your journey. EG *I missed my connection.* N COUNT

5 Your **connections** are the people who you know. EG *He's one of her husband's business connections.* N COUNT: USU PLURAL

connive /kənaɪv/, **connives, conniving, connived. 1** If you **connive** at something, you allow it to happen even though you know that it is wrong. EG *He was assisted by his mother who connived at his laziness.* ◊ **connivance** /kə[7]naɪvəns/. EG *He kept out of jail with the connivance of corrupt police.* V+*at* ◊ N UNCOUNT: USU+SUPP

2 If you **connive**, you secretly try to achieve something which is to your advantage. EG *He believes that Cal and Fanny connived together to do the deed.* V OR V+*with*: RECIP

connoisseur /kɒnə[1]sɜː/, **connoisseurs.** A **connoisseur** is someone who knows a lot about the arts, food, drink, or some other subject. *...a connoisseur of Italian operatic music.* N COUNT: OFT+*of*

connotation /kɒnə[6]teɪʃə[0]n/, **connotations.** The **connotations** of a particular word or name are the ideas or qualities which it makes you think of. EG *'Intermediate' has connotations of the inferior and the second rate.* N COUNT+SUPP

conquer /kɒŋkə/, **conquers, conquering, conquered. 1** If one country or group of people **conquers** another, they take complete control of their land. EG *...the white people who had conquered their land.* ◊ **conqueror** /kɒŋkərə/, **conquerors.** EG *...the European conquerors of Mexico.* V+O OR V ◊ N COUNT

2 If you **conquer** something difficult or dangerous, you succeed in destroying it or getting control of it. EG *...a tremendous international effort to conquer cancer.* V+O

conquest /kɒŋ[1]kwɛst/, **conquests. 1 Conquest** is the act of conquering a country or group of people. EG *Negotiations are preferable to conquest.* N UNCOUNT

2 A **conquest** is land that has been conquered in war. N COUNT

3 If you make a **conquest**, you succeed in winning the love or admiration of someone. EG *...stories of his conquests of bored housewives.* N COUNT+SUPP

4 The **conquest** of something difficult or dangerous is success in getting control of it. EG *...the conquest of space.* N SING: *the*+N+*of*

conscience /kɒnʃəns/, **consciences. 1** Your **conscience** is the part of your mind that tells you whether what you are doing is right or wrong. EG *My conscience told me to vote against the others... ...a matter which has been on my conscience for a long time.* N COUNT

2 If you have a guilty **conscience**, you feel guilty because you have done something wrong. EG *When I got your letter it revived my guilty conscience.* N UNCOUNT

3 Conscience is doing what you believe is right even though it might be unpopular, difficult, or dangerous. EG *In all conscience, I couldn't make things difficult for him.* N UNCOUNT

conscience-stricken. Someone who is **conscience-stricken** feels very guilty about something wrong that they have done. ADJ QUALIT

conscientious /kɒnʃiɛnʃəs/. Someone who is **conscientious** is very careful to do their work properly. ◊ **conscientiously.** EG *He'd been doing his job conscientiously for many years.* ADJ QUALIT ◊ ADV

conscious /kɒnʃəs/. **1** If you are **conscious** of something, **1.1** you notice or realize what is happening. EG *She became conscious of Rudolph looking at her... I was conscious that he had changed his tactics.* **1.2** you think about it a lot ADJ PRED+*of* OR REPORT

> Find two words on these pages which have the same pronunciation.

because of the special way in which it affects you. EG *Tony was very conscious of his ancestry.*

2 Conscious is used in expressions such as 'socially conscious' and 'politically conscious' to describe someone who believes that a particular aspect of life is important. EG *Hundreds of women had become politically conscious.* ADJ QUALIT

3 A **conscious** action or effort is done deliberately. EG *He made a conscious effort to look as though he was enjoying himself.* ◇ **consciously.** EG *She couldn't believe that Mr Foster would ever consciously torment her.* ADJ CLASSIF : ATTRIB ◇ ADV

4 Someone who is **conscious** is awake rather than asleep or unconscious. EG *The patient was fully conscious during the operation.* ADJ PRED

consciousness /kɒnʃəsnɪ^{2}s/. **1** Your **consciousness** is your mind and your thoughts. EG *Doubts were starting to enter into my consciousness.* N UNCOUNT : USU+POSS

2 The **consciousness** of a group of people is all the ideas, attitudes, and beliefs shared by the group. EG *This is a novel that has become imprinted on the English consciousness.* N UNCOUNT +SUPP

3 Consciousness is an interest in and knowledge of a particular subject or idea. EG *...the awakening political consciousness of Africans.* N UNCOUNT

4 If you lose **consciousness**, you are unconscious rather than awake. If you have regained **consciousness**, you are awake again rather than unconscious. N UNCOUNT

conscript, conscripts, conscripting, conscripted; pronounced /kə^{7}nskrɪpt/ when it is a verb and /kɒnskrɪpt/ when it is a noun.

1 If someone **is conscripted, 1.1** they are officially made to join the armed forces of a country. EG *Nine countries decided to let women be conscripted.* V+O : USU PASS

◇ **conscription** /kə^{7}nskrɪpʃə^{0}n/. EG *The president has ended conscription.* ◇ N UNCOUNT **1.2** they are officially forced to work for a country or group of people. EG *Workers were conscripted into forced labour gangs to build the railways.* ◇ **conscripted.** EG *...conscripted labourers from Indo-China.* V+O : USU PASS ◇ ADJ CLASSIF

2 A **conscript** is a person who has been made to join the armed forces of a country. N COUNT

consecrate /kɒnsɪ^{2}kreɪt/, **consecrates, consecrating, consecrated.** When a building, place, or object **is consecrated**, it is officially declared to be holy. EG *King Edward consecrated the original church here in 1065.* ◇ **consecrated.** EG *He was refused burial in consecrated ground.* V+O ◇ ADJ CLASSIF

◇ **consecration** /kɒnsɪ^{2}kreɪʃə^{0}n/. EG *...the consecration of the church.* ◇ N UNCOUNT

consecutive /kə^{7}nsɛkjə^{4}tɪv/. Periods of time or events that are **consecutive** happen one after the other and are not interrupted. EG *I had been away for forty-two consecutive days... ...three consecutive victories.* ADJ CLASSIF

consensus /kə^{7}nsɛnsəs/ is general agreement amongst a group of people. EG *There was some consensus of opinion.* N UNCOUNT

consent /kə^{7}nsɛnt/, **consents, consenting, consented. 1 Consent** is **1.1** permission given to someone to do something. EG *She had threatened to marry without her parents' consent.* **1.2** agreement about something between two or more people or groups. EG *By common consent they stopped.* N UNCOUNT : USU+POSS; N UNCOUNT +SUPP

2 If you **consent** to something, you agree to do it or to allow it to be done. EG *He consented to the removal of the flags.* V : USU+*to* OR *to*-INF

consequence /kɒnsɪkwəns/, **consequences. 1** A **consequence** of a situation or event is a result or effect of it. EG *...the economic consequences of the computer revolution.* N COUNT

2 If one thing happens and then another thing happens **in consequence**, the second thing happens as a result of the first. EG *These jobs are considered suitable for females, and are usually badly paid in consequence.* PHRASE

3 Someone or something that is of **consequence** is important or valuable. Someone or something that is of little **consequence** is not important. N UNCOUNT Formal

consequent /kɒnsɪkwənt/ means happening as a direct result of an event or situation. EG *...the non-publication of the report and the consequent absence of public discussion.* ◇ **consequently.** EG *Absolute secrecy is essential. Consequently, the fewer who are aware of the plan the better.* ADJ CLASSIF : ATTRIB Formal ◇ ADV SEN

consequential /kɒnsɪkwɛnʃə^{0}l/ means happening as a direct result of a particular event or situation. EG *...overcrowding and the consequential lack of privacy.* ADJ CLASSIF : ATTRIB Formal

conservation /kɒnsəveɪʃə^{0}n/ is the preservation and protection of the environment. EG *...the present public awareness of the need for conservation.* N UNCOUNT

conservationist /kɒnsəveɪʃənɪst/, **conservationists.** A **conservationist** is someone who cares greatly about conservation. N COUNT

conservatism /kə^{7}nsɜːvətɪzə^{0}m/ is unwillingness to accept changes and new ideas. EG *He has been much criticized for his aesthetic conservatism.* N UNCOUNT

conservative /kə^{7}nsɜːvətɪv/, **conservatives. 1** Someone who is **conservative 1.1** is unwilling to accept changes and new ideas. EG *Publishers in Britain are more conservative than their continental counterparts.* ◇ **conservatively.** EG *He dresses conservatively.* **1.2** has right-wing views. EG *...a conservative politician... ...conservative voters.* ▸ used as a noun. EG *...leading conservatives in the Senate.* ADJ QUALIT ◇ ADV ADJ QUALIT ▸ N COUNT

2 A **conservative** estimate or guess is very cautious. EG *How long will it last? Three hundred years at a fairly conservative estimate.* ADJ QUALIT

conservatory /kə^{7}nsɜːvətri^1/, **conservatories.** A **conservatory** is a room with glass walls and a glass roof in which plants are kept and which is usually attached to a house. N COUNT

conserve /kə^{7}nsɜːv/, **conserves, conserving, conserved. 1** If you **conserve** a supply of something, you use it carefully so that it lasts for a long time. EG *They made themselves wait quietly, conserving their strength.* V+O

2 To **conserve** something means to keep it in its original form and protect it from harm, loss, or change. EG *Such laws exist only to conserve the privilege of this selfish minority.* V+O

consider /kə^{7}nsɪdə/, **considers, considering, considered. 1** If you **consider** a person or thing to be something, you have the opinion that this is what they are. EG *They consider themselves to be very lucky... They do not consider a child as important... Some British generals considered the attack a mistake... You always consider that I do nothing.* V+O+*to*-INF OR as, V+O+C, OR V+REPORT

2 If you **consider** something, you think about it carefully. EG *He had no time to consider the matter... I had begun to consider the possibility of joining a new company.* V+O

3 You say **all things considered** to indicate that you are making a judgement after taking all the facts into account. EG *He's okay, all things considered.* ADV SEN

4 If you **consider** a person's needs, wishes, or feelings, you pay attention to them. EG *I've got a family to consider.* V+O

5 See also **consideration**, **considered**, **considering**.

considerable /kə^{7}nsɪdə^{0}rəbə^{0}l/. Something that is **considerable** is great in amount or degree. EG *The building suffered considerable damage.* ADJ QUALIT

◇ **considerably.** EG *His work had improved considerably... Large windows make the car feel considerably bigger.* ◇ ADV

considerate /kə^{7}nsɪdə^{0}rə^{1}t/. Someone who is **considerate** pays attention to the needs, wishes, or feelings of other people. ADJ QUALIT

consideration /kə^{7}nsɪdəreɪʃə^{0}n/, **considerations. 1 Consideration** is **1.1** careful thought about something. EG *After careful consideration,* N UNCOUNT *her parents gave her permission.* **1.2** attention that you pay to the needs, wishes, or feelings of other people. EG *He showed no consideration for his daughters.*

2 A **consideration** is something that should be thought about, especially when you are planning or deciding something. EG *An important consideration is the amount of time it will take.* N COUNT

3 If you **take** something **into consideration**, you think about it because it is relevant to what you are doing. EG *The first thing one has to take into consideration is the cost.* PHRASE

4 Something that is **under consideration** is being discussed. EG *The case was still under consideration.* PHRASE

considered /kə⁷nsɪdəd/. A **considered** opinion or way of behaving is one that you have as a result of careful thought. EG *...a considered change of mind.* ADJ CLASSIF : ATTRIB

considering /kə⁷nsɪdə⁰rɪŋ/. You use **considering** to indicate that you are taking a particular fact into account when making a judgement or giving an opinion. EG *Considering that he received no help, his results are very good... Considering her dislike of Martin, it was surprising that she invited him.* CONJ OR PREP

consign /kə⁷nsaɪn/, **consigns, consigning, consigned.** **1** If you **consign** something to a particular place, you get rid of it by putting it there. EG *I discovered some wheels that had been consigned to the loft.* V+O+*to* Formal

2 If someone or something **is consigned** to a situation, they are put in that situation. EG *Such a policy would consign the poor to indefinite poverty.* V+O+*to* Formal

consignment /kə⁷nsaɪnmə²nt/, **consignments.** A **consignment** of goods is a load that is being delivered to a place or person. EG *The shop announced the arrival of a new consignment of dress materials.* N COUNT : OFT+SUPP

consist /kə⁷nsɪst/, **consists, consisting, consisted.** **1** Something that **consists** of particular things is formed from them. EG *The committee consists of scientists and engineers... Each convoy consisted of twelve ships.* V+*of*

2 Something that **consists** in something else has that thing as its main or only part. EG *Nineteenth-century trade consisted principally in luxuries such as silk, spices and ivory.* V+*in*

consistency /kə⁷nsɪstənsi¹/. **1 Consistency** is the condition of being consistent. EG *...consistency and continuity in government policy.* N UNCOUNT

2 The **consistency** of a substance is its degree of thickness or smoothness. EG *Small children dislike food with a sticky consistency.* N UNCOUNT

consistent /kə⁷nsɪstənt/. **1** Someone who is **consistent** never changes their behaviour or attitudes towards people or things. EG *Brook was Baldwin's most dangerous and consistent adversary.* ADJ QUALIT

◇ **consistently.** EG *Hearst consistently opposed Roosevelt's policies.* ◇ ADV

2 An idea or argument that is **consistent** is organized so that each part of it agrees with all the other parts. ADJ QUALIT : OFT+*with*

console, consoles, consoling, consoled; pronounced /kə⁷nsəʊl/ when it is a verb and /kɒnsəʊl/ when it is a noun.

1 If you **console** someone who is unhappy about something, you try to make them feel more cheerful. EG *She tried to console me by saying that I'd probably be happier in a new job.* V+O : OFT+*by/with* ◇ **consoling.** EG *It is a consoling thought... Dad laid a consoling hand on his shoulder.* ◇ ADJ QUALIT ◇ **consolation** /kɒnsəleɪʃə⁰n/, **consolations.** EG *...a few words of consolation... My only consolation is that nobody knows.* ◇ N UNCOUNT OR N COUNT

2 A **console** is a panel with a number of switches or knobs that you use to operate a machine. N COUNT

consolidate /kə⁷nsɒlɪdeɪt/, **consolidates, consolidating, consolidated.** **1** If you **consolidate** power or a plan, you strengthen it so that it becomes more effective or secure. EG *The new middle class consolidated its wealth and power.* V+O OR V

◇ **consolidation** /kə⁷nsɒlɪdeɪʃə⁰n/. EG *...the long-term consolidation of party power.* ◇ N UNCOUNT

2 To **consolidate** a number of small groups or firms means to make them into one large organization. EG *British rule consolidated the states of the north into a unified Northern Region.* V-ERG

◇ **consolidation.** EG *...a dangerous trend toward consolidation that could destroy small businesses.* ◇ N UNCOUNT

consonant /kɒnsənənt/, **consonants.** A **consonant** is a sound such as 'p' or 'm' which you pronounce by stopping the air flowing freely through your mouth. Most words are pronounced with a combination of consonants and vowels. N COUNT

consort, consorts, consorting, consorted; pronounced /kə⁷nsɔːt/ when it is a verb and /kɒnsɔːt/ when it is a noun. **1** If someone **consorts** with a particular person or group, they spend a lot of time with them; often used showing disapproval. EG *Daddy would never approve of her consorting with drug addicts.* V+*with* Formal

2 A **consort** is the wife or husband of the ruling monarch. N COUNT

consortium /kə⁷nsɔːtɪəm/, **consortia** /kə⁷nsɔːtɪə/ or **consortiums.** A **consortium** is a group of people or firms who have agreed to work in cooperation with each other. EG *...a newly formed consortium of Rummidge businessmen.* N COLL

conspicuous /kə⁷nspɪkjʊəs/. If something is **conspicuous**, people can see or notice it very easily. EG *Her freckles were more conspicuous than usual... She felt conspicuous.* ADJ QUALIT ◇ **conspicuously.** EG *He had been conspicuously successful.* ◇ ADV

conspiracy /kə⁷nspɪrəsi¹/, **conspiracies. Conspiracy** is the secret planning by a group of people to do something illegal, usually for political reasons. EG *The police arrested her on a charge of conspiracy to murder... Very few people knew the details of the conspiracy.* N UNCOUNT OR N COUNT

conspirator /kə⁷nspɪrətə/, **conspirators.** A **conspirator** is a person who joins a conspiracy. N COUNT

conspiratorial /kə⁷nspɪrətɔːrɪəl/. **1** If you are **conspiratorial**, you behave as if you are sharing a secret with someone. EG *...a conspiratorial nod.* ADJ QUALIT

2 Something that is **conspiratorial** is secret and illegal, often with a political purpose. EG *...a conspiratorial group.* ADJ CLASSIF

conspire /kə⁷nspaɪə/, **conspires, conspiring, conspired.** **1** If you **conspire**, you secretly agree with other people to do something illegal or harmful. EG *Anarchists were conspiring to kill the ruler... My enemies are conspiring against me.* V OR V+*with* RECIP, USU+*to*-INF OR *against*

2 If events **conspire** towards a particular result, they seem to work together to cause this result. EG *Everything had conspired to make him happy.* V Literary

constable /kʌnstəbə⁰l/, **constables.** A **constable** is a police officer of the lowest rank in Britain. N COUNT

constabulary /kənstæbjə⁴ləri¹/, **constabularies.** A **constabulary** is the police force of a particular area. EG *...the Wiltshire Constabulary.* N COUNT British

constant /kɒnstənt/. **1** Something that is **constant** happens all the time or is always there. EG *He was in constant pain... He is my constant companion.* ADJ CLASSIF : USU ATTRIB ◇ **constantly.** EG *The world around us is constantly changing.* ◇ ADV

2 An amount or level that is **constant** stays the same over a particular period of time. EG *...a constant voltage.* ADJ CLASSIF ◇ **constancy** /kɒnstənsi¹/. EG *...the constancy of the temperature.* ◇ N UNCOUNT

3 If you are **constant**, you are always faithful to a particular person or idea. ADJ CLASSIF ◇ **constancy.** EG *I might have known not to expect constancy from you.* ◇ N UNCOUNT

constellation /kɒnstɪ²leɪʃə⁰n/, **constellations.** A **constellation** is a group of stars which form a pattern and have a name. N COUNT

If a speech sound is not a vowel, what is it likely to be?

consternation /kɒnstəneɪʃə^{0}n/ is a feeling of anxiety or fear. EG *We looked at each other in consternation.* N UNCOUNT

constipated /kɒnstɪpeɪtɪ^{2}d/. Someone who is **constipated** is unable to defecate. ADJ QUALIT

constipation /kɒnstɪpeɪʃə^{0}n/ is a medical condition which makes people unable to defecate. N UNCOUNT

constituency /kə^{7}nstɪtjʊənsi^1/, **constituencies.** A **constituency** is a town or area which is officially allowed to elect someone to represent them in parliament. EG *There were about 14,000 voters in the constituency.* N COUNT

constituent /kə^{7}nstɪtjʊənt/, **constituents.** A **constituent** is 1 someone who lives in a particular constituency, especially someone who is able to vote in an election. EG *An MP is the servant of his constituents.* 2 one of the things that a mixture, substance, or system is made from. EG *Nitrogen is one of the essential constituents of living matter... What are the constituent parts of an atom?* N COUNT

constitute /kɒnstɪtju:t/, **constitutes, constituting, constituted.** 1 If something **constitutes** a particular thing, it can be regarded as being that thing. EG *These questions constitute a challenge to established attitudes... Conifers constitute about a third of the world's forests.* V+C : NO CONT

2 To **constitute** something means to form it from a number of parts or elements. EG *...the recently constituted board of directors.* V+O Formal

constitution /kɒnstɪtju:ʃə^{0}n/, **constitutions.** 1 The **constitution** of a country or organization is the system of laws which formally states people's rights and duties. EG *...the US constitution.* N COUNT

2 Your **constitution** is your health. EG *He has a strong constitution.* N COUNT

3 The **constitution** of something is what it is made of, and how its parts are arranged. EG *Questions were asked concerning the constitution and scope of the proposed commission.* N SING : the+N+of

constitutional /kɒnstɪtju:ʃə^{0}nəl, -ʃənə^{0}l/ means relating to the constitution of a particular country or organization. EG *...a major constitutional change... ...constitutional privileges.* ADJ CLASSIF : USU ATTRIB

constrain /kə^{7}nstreɪn/, **constrains, constraining, constrained.** 1 If someone or something **constrains** you, they force you to act in a particular way. EG *Papa had told her that he would not constrain her in any way... ...the need to constrain groups to work together.* V+O : OFT+*to*-INF Formal

2 To **constrain** something means to prevent it from developing freely. EG *The housing regulations constrain variety and diversity.* V+O Formal

constrained /kə^{7}nstreɪnd/. 1 If you feel **constrained** to do something, you feel forced or obliged to do it. EG *He felt constrained to apologize.* ADJ PRED : OFT +*to*-INF Formal

2 If you feel **constrained** by the situation you are in, you feel that you are not able to behave in the way that you want to. EG *In the end, he felt constrained by the lack of privacy.* ADJ PRED : OFT +*by* Formal

constraint /kə^{7}nstreɪnt/, **constraints.** 1 A **constraint** is something that limits or controls the way you behave. EG *The constraint on most doctors is lack of time.* N COUNT : OFT+*on/of* Formal

2 **Constraint** is control over the way you behave which prevents you from doing what you want to do. EG *The list of instructions and guidelines brings with it a flavour of constraint.* N UNCOUNT Formal

constrict /kə^{7}nstrɪkt/, **constricts, constricting, constricted.** 1 To **constrict** something, for example a part of the body, means to squeeze it tightly. EG *He rubbed his ankles where the bindings had constricted him.* V+O ◇ **constricting.** EG *Her dress was too constricting.* ◇ ADJ QUALIT ◇ **constriction** /kə^{7}nstrɪkʃə^{0}n/. EG *Some snakes kill, not by constriction, but by poison.* ◇ N UNCOUNT

2 If something **constricts** you, it limits your actions so that you cannot do what you want to do. V+O ◇ **constricting.** EG *...the constricting structure of schools.* ◇ ADJ QUALIT ◇ **constriction, constrictions.** EG *...the constrictions of family life.* ◇ N COUNT : USU PLURAL

construct, constructs, constructing, constructed; pronounced /kə^{7}nstrʌkt/ when it is a verb and /kɒnstrʌkt/ when it is a noun.

1 If you **construct** a building, vehicle, road, or machine, you build or make it. EG *We constructed a raft... ...a building constructed of brick.* V+O

2 If you **construct** an idea, piece of writing, or system, you create it by putting different parts together. EG *It's a beautifully constructed book.* V+O

3 A **construct** is 3.1 a complex idea. EG *...theoretical constructs.* 3.2 something that is built, made, or created. EG *These machines are vast constructs of cogs, screws, and wheels.* N COUNT Formal

construction /kə^{7}nstrʌkʃə^{0}n/, **constructions.** 1 **Construction** is the building or creating of something. EG *...the construction of the Panama Canal... ...the careful construction of a theory by logical means.* N UNCOUNT

2 A **construction** is an object that has been made or built. EG *These wigs are complicated constructions of real and false hair.* N COUNT

3 You use the word **construction** to talk about how things have been built. For example, if something is **of** simple **construction**, it is simply built. EG *The main walls of the building are of solid brick construction.* PHRASE

constructive /kə^{7}nstrʌktɪv/. A piece of advice or criticism that is **constructive** is useful and helpful. EG *...constructive criticism... I did not have anything constructive to say.* ADJ QUALIT ◇ **constructively.** EG *You must channel your anger constructively.* ◇ ADV

construe /kə^{7}nstru:/, **construes, construing, construed.** If you **construe** a situation, event, or statement in a particular way, you interpret its meaning in that way. EG *Any show of emotion would be construed as a weakness.* V+O : USU PASS+*as* Formal

consul /kɒnsə^{0}l/, **consuls.** A **consul** is an official who is sent by his or her government to live in a foreign city in order to look after all the people there that belong to his or her own country. N COUNT ◇ **consular** /kɒnsjə^{4}lə/. EG *...the British Consular authorities in Barcelona.* ◇ ADJ CLASSIF : ATTRIB

consulate /kɒnsjə^{4}lə^{1}t/, **consulates.** A **consulate** is the place where a consul works. N COUNT

consult /kə^{7}nsʌlt/, **consults, consulting, consulted.** 1 If you **consult** someone, you ask them for their opinion and advice. EG *If your baby is losing weight, you should consult your doctor promptly.* V+O

2 If two or more people **consult** each other, they talk and exchange ideas and opinions. EG *We needed to consult each other nearly every day... They would have to consult with their allies.* V+O OR V+*with* : RECIP

3 If you **consult** a book or a map, you refer to it for information. V+O

consultancy /kə^{7}nsʌltənsi^1/, **consultancies.** A **consultancy** is a group of people who set up a company to give expert advice on a particular subject. EG *You can start your own consultancy.* N COUNT

consultant /kə^{7}nsʌltə^{2}nt/, **consultants.** A **consultant** is 1 an experienced doctor who specializes in one area of medicine. EG *I was the first woman consultant on the staff of Charing Cross Hospital.* 2 a person who gives expert advice to people who need professional help. EG *...a firm of public relations consultants.* N COUNT

consultation /kɒnsə^{0}lteɪʃə^{0}n/, **consultations.** 1 A **consultation** is a meeting which is held to discuss something. N COUNT : OFT +*about/with*

2 **Consultation** is 2.1 discussion between people, especially when advice is being given. EG *This is a matter for the Prime Minister to decide in consultation with the Ministry of Defence.* N UNCOUNT : OFT+*with/about* 2.2 reference to a book or other source of information. EG *I keep my car handbook near me for frequent consultation.* N UNCOUNT

consultative /kə^{7}nsʌltətɪv/. A **consultative** committee or document is formed or written in order to give advice about something. ADJ CLASSIF: ATTRIB Formal

consulting room, consulting rooms. A **consulting room** is a room in which a doctor sees patients. N COUNT

consume /kə^{7}nsj^{0}u:m/, **consumes, consuming, consumed. 1** If you **consume** something, you eat or drink it. EG *They spend their evenings consuming vodka.* V+O Formal

2 To **consume** an amount of fuel, energy, or time means to use it up. EG *The ship consumed a great deal of fuel.* V+O

3 If a feeling or desire **consumes** you, it affects you very strongly indeed. EG *His hatred of them consumed him.* V+O Literary

consumer /kə^{7}nsj^{0}u:mə/, **consumers.** A **consumer** is a person who buys things or uses services. EG *The consumer is entitled to products that give value for money... ...consumer advice... ...gas consumers.* N COUNT

consuming /kə^{7}nsj^{0}u:mɪŋ/. A **consuming** passion or interest is more important to you than anything else. EG *Politics is the consuming passion of half the town.* ADJ CLASSIF: ATTRIB

consummate, consummates, consummating, consummated; pronounced /kɒnsj^{0}ə^{4}meɪt/ when it is a verb and /kɒnsj^{0}ə^{4}mət/ when it is an adjective.

1 If two people **consummate** a marriage or relationship, they make it complete by having sex. V+O Formal
◇ **consummation.** EG *...the consummation of their marriage.* ◇ N UNCOUNT

2 To **consummate** something means to do something which makes it complete. EG *We need to consummate what we have so far achieved.* V+O Formal
◇ **consummation.** EG *This expedition was the consummation of what he regarded as his life's work.* ◇ N UNCOUNT

3 You use **consummate 3.1** to describe someone who is extremely skilful. EG *He was a fighter of consummate skill.* **3.2** to emphasize that something is a perfect or extreme example of a particular thing. EG *We were both consummate snobs.* ADJ CLASSIF: ATTRIB Formal

consumption /kə^{7}nsʌmpʃə^{0}n/. **1** The **consumption** of fuel or energy is **1.1** the amount of it that is used up. EG *Oil used to make up 10% of our total energy consumption.* **1.2** the act of using it up. EG *...our consumption of energy.* N UNCOUNT +SUPP

2 Consumption is **2.1** the act of eating or drinking something. EG *The water was unfit for consumption.* **2.2** the act of buying and using things. EG *...new patterns of consumption.* N UNCOUNT Formal

3 If you say that information or a remark is **for** a particular person's **consumption**, you mean that it is intended for that person. EG *That prim declaration was strictly for George's consumption.* PHRASE

> **CONT** stands for **continuous tenses**
> A few verbs have the label USU CONT in the Extra Column. This means that they are normally only used in continuous tenses. An example of a verb that is labelled USU CONT is **burn 6**. You say *I am burning with indignation.* You do not usually say 'I burn with indignation'.
> A few other verbs have the label NO CONT in the Extra Column. This means that they are not normally used in continuous tenses. An example of a verb that is labelled NO CONT is **know 1**. You say *I do not know her address.* You do not usually say 'I am not knowing her address'.

contact /kɒntækt/, **contacts, contacting, contacted. 1** If you are in **contact** with someone, you regularly meet them, talk to them, or write to them, often as a part of your work. EG *I'm in contact with a number of schools... ...everyone who came into contact with her... We have many contacts with local people.* N UNCOUNT OR N COUNT

2 When people or things are in **contact**, they are touching each other. EG *Close physical contact is important for a baby... My hand came into contact with a small lump.* N UNCOUNT

3 If you **make contact** with someone, you find out where they are and talk or write to them. EG *I finally made contact with my friend.* PHRASE

4 If you **lose contact** with someone you know, you no longer meet or write to each other. PHRASE

5 If you **contact** someone, you telephone them or write to them. EG *As soon as we find out, we'll contact you.* V+O

6 A **contact** is a person in an organization or profession who you get special help or information from, often unofficially. EG *He had contacts in America... ...business contacts.* N COUNT

contact lens, contact lenses. Contact lenses are two small pieces of plastic that you put on your eyes to make you see better, instead of wearing glasses. N COUNT

contagious /kə^{7}nteɪdʒəs/. **1** A **contagious** disease is one that you can catch by touching people or things that are infected with it. EG *It was as contagious as smallpox.* ADJ QUALIT

2 A feeling or attitude that is **contagious** spreads quickly among a group of people. EG *Quint's confidence was contagious.* ADJ QUALIT

contain /kə^{7}nteɪn/, **contains, containing, contained. 1** If something such as a box or room **contains** things, those things are inside it. EG *...a basket containing groceries... The urban areas contain several million people.* V+O

2 If a substance **contains** something, that thing is a part of it. EG *...chemical compounds containing mercury.* V+O

3 If writing, speech, or film **contains** particular information, ideas, or images, it includes them. EG *...the stories contained in the book.* V+O

4 If something **contains** a particular quality, it indicates or expresses it. EG *The letter contained an element of nastiness.* V+O

5 If you **contain** something, you control it and prevent it from increasing. EG *He could hardly contain his eagerness to leave... ...measures to contain population growth.* V+O Formal

container /kə^{7}nteɪnə/, **containers. 1** A **container** is something such as a box or bottle that is used to hold or store things in. EG *...a soap container... ...cheap plastic containers.* N COUNT

2 Container ships and lorries transport goods in very large sealed metal boxes. N MOD

contaminate /kə^{7}ntæmɪneɪt/, **contaminates, contaminating, contaminated.** If something **is contaminated** by dirt, chemicals, or radiation, it becomes impure, unhealthy, or harmful. EG *Many wells have been contaminated by chemicals... ...foods that are easily contaminated with poisonous bacteria.* ◇ **contaminated.** EG *The men died from drinking contaminated water.* V+O ◇ ADJ QUALIT
◇ **contamination** /kə^{7}ntæmɪneɪʃə^{0}n/. EG *...infections caused by the contamination of milk.* ◇ N UNCOUNT

contemplate /kɒntə^{2}mpleɪt/, **contemplates, contemplating, contemplated. 1** If you **contemplate** an action, you think about doing it. EG *Lawrence contemplated publishing the book.* V+O OR V+-ING

2 If you **contemplate** an idea or subject, you think about it carefully and for a long time. EG *We have to pause and contemplate what we are talking about.* V+O OR V+REPORT
◇ **contemplation** /kɒntə^{2}mpleɪʃə^{0}n/. EG *...religious contemplation.* ◇ N UNCOUNT

3 If you **contemplate** something, you look at it V+O OR V

> What word do you use to describe a disease that is spread by contact?

quietly for a long time. EG *They contemplated each other in silence.* ◊ **contemplation.** EG *She returned to the contemplation of the sunset.* ◊ N UNCOUNT

contemplative /kə[7]ntɛmplətɪv/. When you are **contemplative**, you think deeply in a serious and calm way. EG *...the contemplative civilizations of the Far East.* ADJ CLASSIF

contemporary /kə[7]ntɛmprəri[1]/, **contemporaries.** **1 Contemporary** people or things **1.1** are alive or happening now. EG *...contemporary writers... ...life in contemporary America.* **1.2** were alive or happening in the past, at the same time as something else you are talking about. EG *...a contemporary account of the trial.* ADJ CLASSIF: ATTRIB

2 Someone's **contemporary** is a person who is or was alive at the same time as them. EG *...Darwin's contemporary, Sir James Simpson.* N COUNT: USU+POSS

contempt /kə[7]ntɛmpt/. **1** If you have **contempt** for someone or something, you have no respect for them or think that they are unimportant. EG *The women would often look at us with contempt... ...his contempt for the truth.* N UNCOUNT

2 If you **hold** someone or something **in contempt**, you feel contempt for them. EG *...the contempt in which he held professional politicians.* PHRASE

contemptible /kə[7]ntɛmptəbə[0]l/. If you feel that someone or something is **contemptible**, you feel strong dislike and disrespect for them. EG *You are showing a contemptible lack of courage.* ADJ QUALIT

contemptuous /kə[7]ntɛmptjuəs/. If you are **contemptuous** of someone or something, you do not like or respect them at all. EG *Hamilton gave me a contemptuous look.* ◊ **contemptuously.** EG *He tossed the paper contemptuously on to the table.* ADJ QUALIT: OFT+*of* Formal ◊ ADV

contend /kə[7]ntɛnd/, **contends, contending, contended.** **1** If you have to **contend** with a problem or difficulty, you have to deal with it or overcome it. EG *The girls had problems of their own at home to contend with.* V+*with*

2 If you **contend** that something is true, you state or argue that it is true. EG *She contended that the report was deficient.* V+REPORT: ONLY *that* Formal

3 If you **contend** with someone for something, you compete with them in order to get it. EG *Three parties are contending for power.* ◊ **contending.** EG *Those decisions were fought out between contending groups.* V OR V+*with*: RECIP ◊ ADJ CLASSIF: ATTRIB

contender /kə[7]ntɛndə/, **contenders.** A **contender** in a competition is someone who takes part in it. EG *...a contender in the Presidential election.* N COUNT

content, contents, contenting, contented; pronounced /kɒntɛnt/ for paragraphs 1 to 4, and /kə[7]ntɛnt/ for paragraphs 5 to 8.

1 The **contents** of something such as a box or room are the things that are inside it. EG *He drank the contents of his glass in one gulp... ...pouring out the contents of the bag.* N PLURAL

2 The **contents** of something such as a document or tape are the things written in it or recorded on it. EG *He knew by heart the contents of the note.* N PLURAL

3 The **content** of a piece of writing, a speech, or a television programme is its main subject and the ideas and opinions expressed in it. EG *I was disturbed by the content of some of the speeches.* N UNCOUNT

4 You can use **content** to refer to the amount or proportion of something that a substance contains, for example its moisture **content** or its fibre **content**. EG *No other food has so high an iron content.* N SING+SUPP

5 If you are **content** to do something or if you are **content** with something, you are willing to do, have, or accept it. EG *A few teachers were content to pay the fines... Children are not content with glib explanations.* ADJ PRED +*to*-INF OR *with*

6 If you are **content**, you are fairly happy or satisfied. EG *However hard up they were, they stayed content.* ADJ PRED

7 If you **content** yourself with something, you are satisfied with doing or having that thing and do not try to do or have other things. EG *She didn't take part in the discussion, but contented herself with smoking cigarettes.* V-REFL+*with*

8 to your **heart's content**: see **heart**.

contented /kə[7]ntɛntɪ[2]d/. If you are **contented**, you are happy and satisfied. EG *My father was the most contented man I ever met... ...firms with a loyal and contented labour force.* ◊ **contentedly.** EG *She plays contentedly by herself.* ADJ QUALIT ◊ ADV

contention /kə[7]ntɛnʃə[0]n/, **contentions.** **1** Someone's **contention** is the idea or opinion that they are expressing in an argument or discussion. EG *My main contention is that we must offer all our children the same opportunities.* N COUNT Formal

2 Contention is disagreement or argument about something. EG *This is an issue of great contention at the moment.* N UNCOUNT Formal

3 If you are **in contention** in a contest, you have a chance of winning it. EG *Rees was in contention to win the title.* PHRASE Formal

contentious /kə[7]ntɛnʃəs/. A subject or opinion that is **contentious** causes a lot of disagreement or arguments. EG *...his contentious view that mental illness is in fact a myth.* ADJ QUALIT Formal

contentment /kə[7]ntɛntmə[2]nt/ is a feeling of quiet happiness and satisfaction. EG *I sighed with contentment.* N UNCOUNT

contest, contests, contesting, contested; pronounced /kɒntɛst/ when it is a noun and /kə[7]ntɛst/ when it is a verb.

1 A **contest** is **1.1** a competition or game in which people try to win. EG *...a fishing contest.* **1.2** a struggle to win power or control. EG *He won the contest for the deputy leadership.* N COUNT

2 If someone **contests** an election or competition, they take part in it and try to win it. EG *There was an election contested by six candidates.* V+O

3 If you **contest** a statement or decision, you object to it formally because you think it is wrong or unreasonable. EG *We hotly contest the idea that any of them were ours.* V+O Formal

contestant /kə[7]ntɛstənt/, **contestants.** A **contestant** in a competition or quiz is a person who takes part in it. EG *...the contestants in the world championship.* N COUNT

context /kɒntɛkst/, **contexts.** **1** The **context** of an idea or event is the general information about the time, place, and situation in which it occurred, which you need to know in order to understand it fully. EG *We need to place present events in some kind of historical context... ...the relevance of these ideas in the context of Britain.* N COUNT OR N UNCOUNT

2 The **context** of a word or sentence consists of the words or sentences before and after it which help to make its meaning clear. EG *What do we mean by 'growth' and 'power' in this context?... This remark was taken completely out of context.* N COUNT OR N UNCOUNT

continent /kɒntɪnənt/, **continents.** **1** A **continent** is a very large area of land, such as Africa or Asia. EG *...the North American continent.* N COUNT

◊ **continental** /kɒntɪnɛntə[0]l/. EG *Defence should be organized on a continental scale.* ◊ ADJ CLASSIF: ATTRIB

2 In Britain, the mainland of Europe is sometimes referred to as the **Continent**. EG *British artists are very well known on the Continent.* ◊ **Continental.** EG *...West Germany and other Continental countries... ...a Continental holiday.* N PROPER: *the*+N ◊ ADJ CLASSIF: ATTRIB

contingency /kə[7]ntɪndʒənsi[1]/, **contingencies.** A **contingency** is something that might happen in the future. EG *He had anticipated all contingencies... ...contingency plans for nuclear attack.* N COUNT Formal

contingent /kə[7]ntɪndʒənt/, **contingents.** **1** A **contingent** is **1.1** a group of people representing a country or organization at a meeting or other event. EG *...a contingent of European scientists.* **1.2** a group of police, soldiers, or military vehicles. EG *Police contingents were ordered into the area.* N COUNT: USU+SUPP Formal; Formal

2 If something is **contingent** on something else, it ADJ PRED+*on* Formal depends on it in order to happen or exist. EG *The raid was contingent on the weather.*

continual /kə7ntɪnjʊ0əl/ means **1** happening all the time without stopping. EG *...a continual movement of air... The figures show an almost continual increase.* ◇ **continually.** EG *We are continually learning from experience.* **2** happening again and again. EG *He ignored the continual warnings of his nurse.* ◇ **continually** EG *Tom was continually asking me questions.*
ADJ CLASSIF: ATTRIB · ◇ ADV · ADJ CLASSIF: ATTRIB · ◇ ADV

continuance /kə7ntɪnjʊəns/. The **continuance** of something is its continuation. EG *...the continuance of the war.*
N UNCOUNT: USU+SUPP Formal

continuation /kə7ntɪnju:eɪʃə0n/, **continuations. 1** The **continuation** of something is the fact that it continues to happen or exist. EG *People take for granted the continuation of economic growth.*
N UNCOUNT: USU+SUPP

2 If something is a **continuation** of something else, it is situated next to it or happens after it and forms an extra part of it. EG *The carpet seemed a continuation of the lawn.*
N COUNT: USU+SUPP

continue /kə7ntɪnju:/, **continues, continuing, continued. 1** If you **continue** to do something, you keep doing it and do not stop. EG *The orchestra continued to play... He continued talking.*
V+to-INF OR -ING

2 If something **continues** or if you **continue** it, **2.1** it does not stop happening. EG *If the trend continues, the area will be ruined... They want to continue their education... The battle continued for an hour.* **2.2** it starts again after stopping for a period of time. EG *The next day the performance continued... He arrived in Norway, where he continued his campaign.*
V OR V-ERG · V OR V-ERG

3 If you **continue** with something, you keep doing it or using it. EG *The girls should continue with their mathematics.*
V+with

4 If you **continue**, you begin speaking again after a pause or interruption. EG *'May I continue?' – 'Go on.'... 'I mean Phil,' she continued, 'It's for him.'*
V OR V+QUOTE

5 If you **continue** in a particular direction, you keep walking or travelling in that direction. EG *I continued up the path... She continued on her way.*
V+A

continuity /kɒntɪnju:ɪ1ti1/. The **continuity** of something is the fact that it is happening, existing, or developing without stopping or changing suddenly. EG *...the importance of continuity in government policy... ...the continuity of this tradition.*
N UNCOUNT

continuous /kə7ntɪnju:əs/. **1** Something that is **continuous** happens or exists without stopping. EG *...the continuous increase in their military capacity.* ◇ **continuously.** EG *The volcano had been erupting continuously since March.*
ADJ CLASSIF: USU ATTRIB · ◇ ADV

2 A **continuous** line or surface has no gaps or holes in it.
ADJ CLASSIF: ATTRIB

3 In English grammar, the **continuous** form of verbs is formed by the auxiliary 'be' and the present participle of a verb. When a verb typically occurs in the continuous or when it is rarely used in the continuous, this is mentioned in the Extra Column. See the entry headed CONT for more information.
ADJ CLASSIF

continuum /kə7ntɪnjʊəm/. A **continuum** is a series of events that are considered as a single thing or process. EG *...the continuum of the seasons.*
N SING Formal

contort /kə7ntɔ:t/, **contorts, contorting, contorted.** When something **contorts** or **is contorted**, it moves into an unnatural and unattractive shape or position. EG *His face contorted with hatred.* ◇ **contorted.** EG *...his mad contorted smile.*
V-ERG · ◇ ADJ CLASSIF

contortion /kə7ntɔ:ʃə0n/, **contortions.** A **contortion** is a movement of your body into an unusual shape or position. EG *...the child's ceaseless contortions.*
N COUNT OR N UNCOUNT

contour /kɒntʊə/, **contours. 1** The **contours** of something are its outer shape or outline. EG *Pain altered the contours of his face.*
N COUNT: USU PLURAL Literary

2 A **contour** on a map is a line joining points of equal height and indicating hills, valleys, and the steepness of slopes. EG *...the 300ft contour line.*
N COUNT: USU N MOD

contraband /kɒntrəbænd/ refers to goods that are taken into or out of a country illegally. EG *He might be carrying contraband.*
N UNCOUNT

contraception /kɒntrəsɛpʃə0n/. The various methods of preventing pregnancy are called **contraception.** EG *...safe, easy methods of contraception.*
N UNCOUNT

contraceptive /kɒntrəsɛptɪv/, **contraceptives.** A **contraceptive** is a device or pill that prevents a woman from becoming pregnant during sexual intercourse. EG *There are clinics where women can be fitted with contraceptives... ...contraceptive pills.*
N COUNT

contract, contracts, contracting, contracted; pronounced /kɒntrækt/ when it is a noun, and /kə7ntrækt/ when it is a verb.

1 A **contract** is a written legal agreement between people which usually involves buying something or doing work for a stated sum of money. EG *We won a contract to build fifty-eight planes... I did not sign a contract with them... ...a marriage contract.*
N COUNT

2 If you **contract** with someone to do something, you legally agree to do it. EG *They contracted to supply us with horses.*
V+ to-INF Formal

3 When something **contracts**, it becomes smaller or shorter. EG *Metals expand with heat and contract with cold.* ◇ **contraction**/kə7ntrækʃə0n/, **contractions.** EG *She first acted under the name of Terson (a contraction of Terry and Neilson).*
V-ERG · ◇ N COUNT OR N UNCOUNT

4 If you **contract** an illness, you become ill with it. EG *She then contracted breast cancer.*
V+O Formal

contractor /kɒntræktə, kəntræk-/, **contractors.** A **contractor** is a person or company that does work for other people or companies. EG *...houses built by private contractors.*
N COUNT

contractual /kə7ntræktjʊ0əl/. A **contractual** relationship involves a legal agreement between people. EG *The union had a contractual agreement with the company.*
ADJ CLASSIF: ATTRIB Formal

contradict /kɒntrədɪkt/, **contradicts, contradicting, contradicted. 1** If you **contradict** someone, you say that they are wrong and that the opposite of what they have said is correct or true. EG *I took care not to contradict her... 'No,' contradicted her sister, 'it's because he doesn't care.'*
V+O OR V+QUOTE

2 If one fact or statement **contradicts** another, it suggests or indicates that the second one is wrong. EG *Research evidence contradicts this idea... Perfectly reputable books may contradict each other.*
V+O

contradiction /kɒntrədɪkʃə0n/, **contradictions.**

1 If there is a **contradiction** in something, it has features which are completely different from each other and so make it confused or difficult to understand. EG *There is a contradiction between the two laws... I hate to admit all these contradictions in myself... There is no contradiction in this approach.*
N COUNT OR N UNCOUNT

2 If you say that something is a **contradiction in terms**, you mean that it is described as having a quality that it cannot have. EG *A rational religion is almost a contradiction in terms.*
PHRASE

contradictory /kɒntrədɪktə0ri1/. If two facts, ideas, or statements are **contradictory**, they say that opposite things are true. EG *The government had made two contradictory promises.*
ADJ QUALIT

contralto /kə7ntræltəʊ/, **contraltos.** A **contralto** is a woman with a low singing voice.
N COUNT Technical

contraption /kə7ntræpʃə0n/, **contraptions.** You can describe a device or machine as a **contraption**, especially when it looks strange or you do not know what it is used for. EG *Over his door was a contraption with a sliding shutter.*
N COUNT: USU+SUPP

contrary /kɒntrəri1/. **1** You say **on the contrary** to emphasize that your next statement is true even though it contradicts what has just been said. EG
ADV SEN

If you carry contraband, are you contravening the law?

There was nothing ugly about her dress: on the contrary, it had a certain elegance... 'You'll get tired of it.' – 'On the contrary. I shall enjoy it.'

2 Ideas, attitudes, or reactions that are **contrary** to each other are completely different from each other. EG *They happily tolerated the existence of opinions contrary to their own... ...contrary impulses.* ADJ CLASSIF : OFT+*to*

3 If you say that something is true **contrary to** other people's beliefs, you are emphasizing that it is true and that they are wrong. EG *Contrary to what is generally assumed, the adjustment is easily made.* PREP

4 If you talk about evidence **to the contrary**, you mean evidence that contradicts what you are saying or what someone else has said. EG *This method, despite statements to the contrary, has no damaging effects.* PHRASE

contrast, contrasts, contrasting, contrasted; pronounced /kɒntrɑ:st/ when it is a noun, and /kə7ntrɑ:st/ when it is a verb.

1 A **contrast** is a great difference between two or more things which is clear when you compare them. EG *...the contrast between his public image and his private life.* N COUNT : OFT +*between/with*

2 You say **by contrast** or **in contrast** to emphasize the difference between one thing and another that you have already mentioned. EG *By contrast, our use of oil has increased enormously... This second movement, in contrast, reached a membership of 100,000 in two years.* ADV SEN

3 If one thing is **in contrast** to another, it is very different from it. EG *He thought of her idleness in contrast to his own busy life.* PHRASE

4 If something is a **contrast** to or with something else, it is very different from it. EG *The atmosphere of the Second War was a complete contrast to that of the First.* N COUNT : OFT+*to/with*

5 If you **contrast** things, you explain or emphasize the differences between them. EG *The book contrasts the methods used in America and Russia... He contrasted America with the older European countries.* V+O : OFT+ *with/to*

6 If one thing **contrasts** with another, it is very different from it. EG *This gesture contrasts oddly with her clothes.* ◊ **contrasting.** EG *...their contrasting attitudes... ...contrasting colours.* V OR V+*with* : RECIP ◊ ADJ CLASSIF : ATTRIB

contravene /kɒntrəvi:n/, **contravenes, contravening, contravened.** If someone **contravenes** a law or rule, they do something that is forbidden by the law or rule. EG *They contravened the drug laws.* V+O Formal

◊ **contravention** /kɒntrəvɛnʃə0n/, **contraventions.** EG *The advert was in contravention of the Race Relations Act.* ◊ N UNCOUNT OR N COUNT

contribute /kə7ntrɪbju:t/, **contributes, contributing, contributed.** **1** If you **contribute** to something, **1.1** you do things to help to make it successful. EG *The elderly have much to contribute to the community.* V OR V+O : OFT+*to* **1.2** you give money to help pay for something. EG *She persuaded friends to contribute $5,000 to the fund.* V OR V+O : OFT+*to* ◊ **contributor** /kə7ntrɪbjə4tə/, **contributors.** EG *...contributors to a fund to save the house.* ◊ N COUNT : OFT+*to*

2 If something **contributes** to an event or situation, it is one of the causes of it. EG *Soaring land prices contribute to the high cost of housing.* V+*to/towards*

3 If you **contribute** to a magazine or book, you write things that are published in it. EG *Distinguished writers had contributed to its pages.* ◊ **contributor, contributors.** EG *...a contributor of short stories to a national weekly.* V OR V+O : OFT+*to* ◊ N COUNT : OFT+*to*

contribution /kɒntrɪbju:ʃə0n/, **contributions.** **1** If you make a **contribution** to something, you do something to help make it successful. EG *...the BBC's contribution to the adult literacy campaign.* N COUNT : OFT+*to*

2 A **contribution** is also **2.1** a sum of money that you give in order to help pay for something. EG *The United Kingdom had to make a contribution of £1,000 million to the EEC budget.* N COUNT : OFT+*to* **2.2** something that you write which is published in a book or magazine. EG *...pamphlets with contributions from trade unionists.* N COUNT

contributory /kəntrɪbjə4tə0ri1/. A **contributory** cause or factor of something is one of several things which cause it to happen. EG *The inefficient use of oil was a major contributory factor.* ADJ CLASSIF : USU ATTRIB Formal

contrite /kə7ntraɪt, kɒntraɪt/. If you are **contrite**, you are very ashamed and apologetic because you have done something wrong. EG *I tried to look contrite.* ◊ **contrition** /kə7ntrɪʃə0n/. EG *They tell lies and show no sign of contrition.* ADJ QUALIT Literary ◊ N UNCOUNT

contrivance /kə7ntraɪvəns/, **contrivances.** **1** A **contrivance** is a device or machine that looks strange and seems to have been quickly built. EG *...a contrivance of wood and wire.* N COUNT

2 A **contrivance** is also an unfair or dishonest scheme to gain an advantage for yourself. EG *...a contrivance to raise prices.* N COUNT

contrive /kə7ntraɪv/, **contrives, contriving, contrived.** **1** If you **contrive** to do something difficult, you succeed in doing it. EG *I shall contrive to see you again... Mike contrived to grin without taking his cigar out of his mouth.* V+*to*-INF Formal

2 If you **contrive** an event or situation, you succeed in making it happen, often by tricking someone. EG *Confidential talks with professors were contrived by reporters posing as students.* V+O Formal

contrived /kə7ntraɪvd/. **Contrived** behaviour is false and artificial. EG *Olivia displayed her contrived smile.* ADJ QUALIT

control /kə7ntrəʊl/, **controls, controlling, controlled.** **1** **Control** of a country or an organization is the power to make all the important decisions about the way that it is run. EG *The bank took control of a television station... ...political control over colonies.* N UNCOUNT : OFT+*of/over*

2 If you have **control** of something, you are able to make it behave exactly as you want. EG *You should have control of your vehicle at all times.* N UNCOUNT : OFT+*of/over*

3 If you show **control**, you are able to prevent yourself behaving in an excited or emotional way. EG *He told himself that he mustn't lose control if he wanted to save his strength.* N UNCOUNT

4 **Control** is also used in these phrases. **4.1** If something is **beyond** your **control** or **outside** your **control**, you do not have any power to affect it or change it. EG *The service is being withdrawn for reasons outside anyone's control.* **4.2** If you are **in control** of something, you decide or influence the way it develops. EG *Those who begin the revolution rarely stay in control to complete the process.* **4.3** If something is **out of control**, nobody has any power over it. EG *Inflation got out of control.* **4.4** If something harmful is **under control**, it is being dealt with successfully and is unlikely to cause any more harm. EG *The fever was brought under control.* **4.5** If something is **under** your **control**, you have the power to decide what will happen to it. EG *...when a village is under enemy control.* PHRASES

5 The people who **control** a country or an organization have the power to take all the important decisions about the way that it is run. EG *The Australians controlled the island.* ◊ **controlling.** EG *The family had a controlling interest in the firm.* V+O ◊ ADJ CLASSIF : ATTRIB

6 To **control** a machine, process, or system means to make it work in the way that is required. EG *Computer systems control the lighting and heating.* ◊ **controlled.** EG *...the controlled release of water from reservoirs.* V+O ◊ ADJ QUALIT

7 When a government **controls** wages, prices, or the activities of a particular group, it uses its power to restrict them. EG *...a law to control incomes.* V+O

8 If you **control** yourself, you make yourself behave calmly when you are feeling angry, excited, or upset. V-REFL OR V+O

9 To **control** something dangerous means to prevent it from becoming worse or from spreading. EG *...a way of controlling cancer.* V+O

CONVENTIONS

People often use ready-made phrases in conversation, and in this dictionary these are called CONVENTIONS. They are often used in situations where you are expected to say something, as for example when you meet someone for the first time. Here are some examples:

Meeting someone:	*Hello.*	Response:	*Hello.*
Leaving someone:	*Goodbye.*	Response:	*Goodbye. See you soon.*
Congratulating someone:	*Congratulations.*	Response:	*Thanks.*
Thanking someone:	*Thank you.*	Response:	*Oh, that's all right.*

You can of course often slightly vary the words that you use. The important thing is that there is a convention for you to use if you want to.

So, one important use of conventions is as the first utterance in a very common situation that you find yourself in. Another important use of conventions is that you can use them as responses to ordinary utterances. Here are some examples:

And this is your room, I suppose.	Response:	*Yes, it is.*
Would you like a coffee?	Response:	*Thanks very much.*
How about coming for a meal tomorrow?	Response:	*That'd be nice.*
I'll be back in the middle of August.	Response:	*See you then.*
Could you check this for me?	Response:	*No problem.*
I've got my French exam tomorrow.	Response:	*The best of luck.*

10 A **control** is a device which you use in order to operate a machine. EG *Just turn the volume control.* N COUNT

11 Controls are the methods that a government uses to restrict increases, for example in prices or wages. EG *...government price controls.* N PLURAL: USU+SUPP

controller /kə[7]ntrəʊlə/, **controllers.** A **controller** is a person who has responsibility for a particular task or for a section of an organization. EG *...an air traffic controller... ...the financial controller.* N COUNT: USU+SUPP

controversial /kɒntrəvɜːʃə[0]l/. Someone or something that is **controversial** causes a lot of discussion, argument, and strong feelings of anger or disapproval. EG *Many of the new taxes are controversial... He is a controversial politician.* ADJ QUALIT

controversy /kɒntrəvɜːsi[1], kə[7]ntrɒvəsi[1]/, **controversies. Controversy** is a lot of discussion and argument about something, often involving strong feelings of anger or disapproval. EG *The government tried to avoid controversy... ...a violent controversy over a commercial treaty.* N UNCOUNT OR N COUNT

conundrum /kənʌndrəm/, **conundrums.** A **conundrum** is a difficult or confusing problem. EG *The belief in reincarnation poses some conundrums.* N COUNT Formal

conurbation /kɒnə[5]beɪʃə[0]n/, **conurbations.** A **conurbation** is a large urban area formed by several towns that have spread towards each other. EG *...major industrial conurbations.* N COUNT Formal

convalesce /kɒnvəlɛs/, **convalesces, convalescing, convalesced.** If you **are convalescing**, you are resting and regaining your health after an illness or operation. EG *The fever is gone and the child is convalescing.* V

convalescence /kɒnvəlɛsəns/ is the period or process of becoming healthy and well again after an illness or operation. EG *Clem wasn't allowed to visit me during my convalescence.* N UNCOUNT

convalescent /kɒnvəlɛsənt/ means relating to convalescence. EG *...a convalescent home in the country.* ADJ CLASSIF: ATTRIB

convene /kə[7]nviːn/, **convenes, convening, convened. 1** If you **convene** a meeting or conference, you arrange for it to take place. EG *Roland convened a small meeting to discuss the issue.* V+O Formal

2 If a group of people **convene**, they come together for a meeting. EG *The grand jury did not convene until February.* V Formal

convenience /kə[7]nviːnɪəns/, **conveniences. 1 Convenience** is the state or quality of being easy to use or making something easy to do. EG *We use frozen food for convenience.* N UNCOUNT

2 If something is done for your **convenience**, it is done in a way that is useful or suitable for you. EG *The entire event had been arranged for their convenience.* N UNCOUNT +POSS

3 If you describe something as a **convenience**, you mean that it is very useful. EG *It's a great convenience to have a separate room for the twins... ...a house with every modern convenience.* N COUNT

convenience food, convenience foods. Convenience food is frozen, dried, or tinned food that can be cooked quickly without any preparation. N MASS

convenient /kə[7]nviːnɪənt/. Something that is **convenient** is very useful or suitable for a particular purpose. EG *It will be more convenient to stick to a three-hour timetable... ...a convenient place to live.* ADJ QUALIT

◊ **conveniently.** EG *The amount of fuel is displayed conveniently on a gauge.* ◊ ADV

convent /kɒnvə[2]nt/, **convents.** A **convent** is **1** a building in which a community of nuns live. **2** a school that is run by nuns. N COUNT

convention /kə[7]nvɛnʃə[0]n/, **conventions. 1** A **convention** is **1.1** a way of behaving that is considered to be correct or polite by most people in a society. EG *...the everyday conventions and rules of behaviour... ...his arrogance and rejection* N COUNT OR N UNCOUNT

What is convenient about convenience food?

of convention. **1.2** a traditional method or style that is used in art or literature. EG *...the conventions of the novel.* N COUNT

2 A **convention** is also **2.1** an official agreement between countries or groups of people. EG *They signed the convention in 1905.* **2.2** a large meeting of an organization or political group. EG *He left New York before the convention ended.* N COUNT

conventional /kə⁷venʃə⁰nəl, -ʃənə⁰l/. **1** Someone who is **conventional** behaves in an ordinary and normal way. EG *They're the most conventional, dull people... ...the conventional housewife.* ADJ QUALIT
◊ **conventionally.** EG *...a more conventionally acceptable life.* ◊ ADV

2 A **conventional** method or product has been used or produced for a long time in the same way. EG *...the abolition of conventional examinations... ...conventional fuels.* ◊ **conventionally.** EG *...conventionally educated students.* ADJ CLASSIF: ATTRIB ◊ ADV

3 Conventional wars and weapons do not involve nuclear explosives. ADJ CLASSIF: ATTRIB

converge /kə⁷vɜːdʒ/, **converges, converging, converged. 1** When roads or lines **converge**, they meet or join at a particular place. EG *The paths converge under the trees.* V: USU+A

2 When people or vehicles **converge** on a place or a person, they move towards them from different directions. EG *The guards converged on her and flung her to the ground.* V: OFT +*on/upon*

3 When different ideas, forces, or societies **converge**, they gradually become similar to each other. EG *Two radically different types of society were converging through economic evolution.* V Formal
◊ **convergence** /kə⁷vɜːdʒəns/. EG *There was some convergence of views.* ◊ N UNCOUNT

conversant /kə⁷vɜːsə⁰nt/. If you are **conversant** with something, you are familiar with it and able to deal with it. EG *The designer must be conversant with all the aspects of the problem.* ADJ PRED +*with* Formal

conversation /kɒnvəseɪʃə⁰n/, **conversations. 1** If you have a **conversation** with someone, you talk to them. EG *Roger and I had a conversation about the risks... He spent some hours in conversation with me.* N COUNT OR N UNCOUNT

2 If you have to **make conversation**, you have to talk to someone in order to be polite and not because you really want to. EG *He didn't like having to make conversation.* PHRASE

conversational /kɒnvəseɪʃə⁰nəl, -ʃənə⁰l/ means used in conversation or in casual and informal talk. EG *...their brilliant conversational powers.* ADJ CLASSIF: ATTRIB
◊ **conversationally.** EG *'Tell me,' she said conversationally, 'does he bite?'* ◊ ADV

converse, converses, conversing, conversed; pronounced /kə⁷vɜːs/ when it is a verb and /kɒnvɜːs/ when it is a noun or an adjective.

1 If you **converse** with someone, you talk to them. EG *I consider it a privilege to have conversed with you.* V OR V+*with*: RECIP Formal

2 The **converse** of a statement is its opposite or reverse. EG *If you can do it, a machine can, at least in theory, also do it. The converse, however, is not true.* ▸ used as an adjective. EG *Political power is used to win economic power. But the converse process is just as common.* N SING: *the*+N ▸ ADJ CLASSIF: ATTRIB Formal

conversely /kə⁷vɜːsli¹/. You say **conversely** to indicate that the statement you are about to make is the opposite or reverse of the one you have just made. EG *You can use beer yeast for bread-making. Conversely, you can use bread yeast in beer-making.* ADV SEN

conversion /kə⁷vɜːʃə⁰n/, **conversions. 1** A **conversion** is the act or process of changing something into a different state or form. EG *...the conversion of coal into oil and gas.* N COUNT OR N UNCOUNT

2 Someone's **conversion** is the process of changing their religious or political beliefs. EG *...his recent conversion to Christianity.* N COUNT OR N UNCOUNT: OFT+*to/from*

convert, converts, converting, converted; pronounced /kə⁷vɜːt/ when it is a verb, and /kɒnvɜːt/ when it is a noun.

1 To **convert** something into something else means to change it into a different form. EG *A solar cell takes radiation from the sun and converts it into electricity... ...prams that convert into push-chairs... ...the formula for converting kilometres to miles.* V-ERG: OFT+*into/to*

2 If someone **converts** a building, they alter it in order to use it for a different purpose. EG *The house has been converted into two apartments.* V+O: OFT+ *into/to* OR *to*-INF
◊ **converted.** EG *The theatre is a converted squash court.* ◊ ADJ CLASSIF: ATTRIB

3 If you **convert** a vehicle or a system, you change it so that it can use a different fuel. EG *They would convert the entire country to coal gas.* V+O: OFT+*to/from*

4 If someone **converts** you, they persuade you to change your religious or political beliefs. EG *Birch became converted to communism.* V+O: OFT+*to/from*

5 A **convert** is someone who has changed their religious or political beliefs. EG *...a Catholic convert... ...new converts to Trotskyism.* N COUNT

convertible /kə⁷vɜːtəbə⁰l/, **convertibles. 1** A **convertible** is a car with a soft roof that can be folded down or removed. EG *The red convertible was following us.* N COUNT

2 Money that is **convertible** can be easily exchanged for other forms of money. EG *The loan is freely convertible into dollars.* ADJ CLASSIF

convex /kɒnvɛks, kɒnvɛks/. Something that is **convex** curves outwards at its centre. EG *...a convex lens.* ADJ QUALIT Technical

convey /kə⁷veɪ/, **conveys, conveying, conveyed. 1** To **convey** information or feelings means to cause them to be known or understood by someone. *Newspapers convey the impression that the war is over... ...trying to convey that it did not really matter.* V+O: OFT+*to* OR V+REPORT

2 To **convey** someone or something to a place means to carry or transport them there. EG *...the truck conveying Daniel and the work crew.* V+O: USU+A Formal

conveyance /kə⁷veɪəns/, **conveyances.** A **conveyance** is a vehicle. EG *The conveyance had drawn up at her door.* N COUNT Outdated

conveyor belt /kə⁷veɪə bɛlt/, **conveyor belts.** A **conveyor belt** is a continuously moving strip of rubber or metal which is used in factories for moving objects along. EG *Slabs of toffee pass along a conveyor belt.* N COUNT

convict, convicts, convicting, convicted; pronounced /kə⁷vɪkt/ when it is a verb, and /kɒnvɪkt/ when it is a noun.

1 To **convict** someone of a crime means to find them guilty of it in a court of law. EG *He was convicted of spying.* ◊ **convicted.** EG *...convicted criminals.* V+O: OFT+*of* ◊ ADJ CLASSIF

2 A **convict** is someone who is in prison. EG *...an escaped convict.* N COUNT Outdated

conviction /kə⁷vɪkʃə⁰n/, **convictions. 1** A **conviction** is a strong belief or opinion. EG *...his conviction that he could run a newspaper.* N COUNT: USU+REPORT

2 If you have **conviction**, you have great confidence and certainty in your beliefs or opinions. EG *'Yes,' I said without much conviction.* N UNCOUNT

3 A **conviction** is also the act of finding someone guilty in a court of law. EG *...the trial and conviction of Ward... ...his record of previous convictions.* N COUNT OR N UNCOUNT

convince /kə⁷vɪns/, **convinces, convincing, convinced.** If someone or something **convinces** you, **1** they make you believe that something is true or necessary. EG *It took them a few days to convince me that it was possible... This had convinced her of the problems.* **2** they persuade you to do something. EG *You can convince people to buy almost anything.* V+O: OFT + REPORT OR *of/about* V+O+*to*-INF

convinced /kə⁷vɪnst/. If you are **convinced** of something, you are sure that it is true or genuine. ADJ PRED: OFT+*of* OR REPORT

EG *He was convinced that her mother was innocent... I am convinced of your loyalty.*

convincing /kə⁷nvɪnsɪŋ/. 1 Something that is **convincing** causes you to believe that it is true, correct, or genuine. EG *...a more convincing explanation.* ADJ QUALIT

2 Someone who is **convincing** is able to make you believe that something is true. EG *He was a convincing liar.* ◊ **convincingly.** EG *She must speak more convincingly.* ADJ QUALIT ◊ ADV

convivial /kə⁷nvɪvɪəl/. 1 A social event that is **convivial** is enjoyable and friendly. EG *The meal was not a convivial one.* ADJ QUALIT Formal

2 **Convivial** people are friendly and pleasant to be with. EG *...a happy and convivial group.* ADJ QUALIT

convoluted /kɒnvəlu:tɪ²d/. A **convoluted** sentence or idea is complicated and difficult to understand. ADJ QUALIT Formal

convoy /kɒnvɔɪ/, **convoys.** A **convoy** is a group of vehicles or ships travelling together. EG *...a convoy of police cars.* • If a group of vehicles or ships are travelling **in convoy**, they are all travelling somewhere together. EG *...eight trucks moving in convoy.* N COUNT • PHRASE

convulse /kə⁷nvʌls/, **convulses, convulsing, convulsed.** If someone **convulses** or if something **convulses** them, their body moves suddenly in an uncontrolled way. EG *He convulsed in pain... A quiver convulsed his body.* V-ERG Formal

convulsion /kə⁷nvʌlʃə⁰n/, **convulsions.** If someone has a **convulsion** or **convulsions**, they suffer uncontrollable movements of their muscles. EG *Another convulsion shook him... Convulsions are rare after the first day of fever.* N COUNT OR N UNCOUNT

convulsive /kə⁷nvʌlsɪv/. A **convulsive** movement or action is sudden and cannot be controlled. EG *I gave his hand a sudden convulsive squeeze.* ◊ **convulsively.** EG *He shivered convulsively.* ADJ CLASSIF ◊ ADV

coo /ku:/, **coos, cooing, cooed.** 1 When a dove or pigeon **coos**, it makes the soft sound that doves and pigeons typically make. V

2 When someone **coos**, they speak in a very soft, quiet voice. EG *'Tell me all about it,' she cooed.* V OR V+QUOTE

cook /kʊk/, **cooks, cooking, cooked.** 1 When you **cook** food, you prepare it for eating and then heat it, for example in an oven or in a saucepan. EG *We cooked the pie in the oven... I could smell vegetables cooking in the kitchen... Mildred cooks remarkably well... Cook us a bit of supper... I cook for myself.* V-ERG, V, V+O+O, V+O+*for*, OR V+*for*

2 A **cook** is a person who prepares and cooks food, often as a job. EG *Are you a good cook?... Margaret employed a cook.* N COUNT

3 See also **cooking**.

cook up. If someone **cooks up** a dishonest scheme, they plan it. EG *They cook up all sorts of little deals.* PHRASAL VB : V+O+ADV Informal

cooker /kʊkə/, **cookers.** A **cooker** is a large metal box-shaped device for cooking food in the kitchen using gas or electricity. EG *The milk was warming in a saucepan on the cooker.* N COUNT

cookery /kʊkə⁰ri¹/ is the activity of preparing and cooking food. EG *...cookery demonstrations.* N UNCOUNT

cookie /kʊki¹/, **cookies.** A **cookie** is the same as a biscuit. EG *...homemade oatmeal cookies.* N COUNT American

cooking /kʊkɪŋ/ is 1 the activity of preparing and cooking food. EG *My mother was fond of cooking.* 2 cooked food. EG *She loves your cooking.* N UNCOUNT; N UNCOUNT +SUPP

cool /ku:l/, **cooler, coolest; cools, cooling, cooled.** 1 Something that is **cool** has a temperature which is low but not cold. EG *The air was cool and fresh... ...a cool drink.* ◊ **coolness.** EG *...the coolness of the room.* ADJ QUALIT ◊ N UNCOUNT

2 Clothing that is **cool** is made of thin material. EG *I'll just change into a cooler frock.* ADJ QUALIT

3 When something **cools** or when you **cool** it, it becomes lower in temperature. EG *The water began to cool... Cool your feet in the stream.* V-ERG

4 If someone's behaviour is **cool**, it is 4.1 calm and unemotional. EG *Keep cool and reasonable when complaining.* ◊ **coolly.** EG *He drove coolly and carefully.* ◊ **coolness.** EG *I admired the coolness with which he dealt with a crisis.* 4.2 unfriendly or unenthusiastic. EG *Should she be cool and withdrawn, or warm and welcoming?* ◊ **coolly.** EG *'I'm not asking you,' she informed him coolly.* ◊ **coolness.** EG *Hagen was hurt by my coolness.* ADJ QUALIT ◊ ADV ◊ N UNCOUNT ADJ QUALIT ◊ ADV ◊ N UNCOUNT

5 When anger **cools**, it becomes less powerful. EG *Their tempers had cooled.* V-ERG

6 If you **play it cool**, you deliberately behave in a calm and unemotional way. EG *They agreed to play it cool if they saw the boys again.* PHRASE Informal

7 If you **keep** your **cool**, you control your temper and remain calm. If you **lose** your **cool**, you become angry or excited. EG *He struggled to keep his cool.* PHRASE Informal

cool down. 1 If something **cools down** or if you **cool** it **down**, it becomes cooler and reaches the temperature that you want it to be at. EG *The engine will take half an hour to cool down.* PHRASAL VB : V-ERG+ADV

2 If someone **cools down** or if you **cool** them **down**, they become less angry. EG *I had great difficulty in cooling him down.* V-ERG+ADV

cool off. If someone or something **cools off**, they become cooler after having been hot. EG *We cooled off with a refreshing swim.* PHRASAL VB : V-ERG+ADV

co-op /kəʊɒp/, **co-ops.** A **co-op** is a co-operative. EG *I'm in the food co-op... ...a co-op house.* N COUNT Informal

cooped up /ku:pt ʌp/. If someone is **cooped up** in a place, they are kept in a place which is too small or which does not give them much freedom. EG *I hate being cooped up in the flat every day.* ADJ PRED

co-operate /kəʊɒpəreɪt/, **co-operates, co-operating, co-operated.** 1 If people **co-operate**, they work or act together for a purpose. EG *The workers cooperated with the management and the police.* ◊ **co-operation** /kəʊɒpəreɪʃə⁰n/. EG *...co-operation between staff and parents.* V OR V+*with* : RECIP ◊ N UNCOUNT

2 If you **co-operate**, you do what someone asks you to do. EG *You're not co-operating!* ◊ **co-operation.** EG *Thank you for your co-operation.* V ◊ N UNCOUNT

co-operative /kəʊɒpə⁰rətɪv/, **co-operatives.** 1 A **co-operative** is a business or organization run by the people who work for it, who share its benefits and profits. EG *...a food co-operative.* N COUNT

2 A **co-operative** activity is done by people working together. EG *...cooperative forms of ownership.* ◊ **co-operatively.** EG *The work is carried on co-operatively.* ADJ CLASSIF ◊ ADV

3 Someone who is **co-operative** does what you ask them to. EG *Her children are considerate and co-operative.* ◊ **co-operatively.** EG *She pushed me, and I rolled over cooperatively.* ADJ QUALIT ◊ ADV

co-opt /kəʊɒpt/, **co-opts, co-opting, co-opted.** If the people in an official group **co-opt** you, they make you a member of their group. EG *Committees can always co-opt members.* V+O Formal

co-ordinate, co-ordinates, co-ordinating, co-ordinated; pronounced /kəʊɔ:dɪneɪt/ when it is a verb, and /kəʊɔ:dɪnət/ when it is a noun.

1 If you **co-ordinate** an activity, you organize the people and things involved in it. EG *They were asked to coordinate the election campaign.* ◊ **co-ordinated.** EG *...an effective and co-ordinated attack.* ◊ **co-ordination** /kəʊɔ:dɪneɪʃə⁰n/. EG *...the co-ordination of public transport.* ◊ **co-ordinator** /kəʊɔ:dɪneɪtə/, **co-ordinators.** EG *...the co-ordinator of a project in Cornwall.* V+O ◊ ADJ QUALIT ◊ N UNCOUNT ◊ N COUNT : USU+SUPP

2 If you **co-ordinate** the parts of your body, you make them work together efficiently to perform particular movements. EG *The children could not* V+O

If you cook up something with the cops and then play it cool, what kind of language are you using?

co-ordinate their movements. ◇ **co-ordination.** EG *His arms moved in perfect co-ordination.* ◇ N UNCOUNT

3 The **co-ordinates** of a point on a map or graph are the two sets of numbers or letters that you need in order to find it. N COUNT: USU PLURAL Technical

cop /kɒp/, **cops, copping, copped.** A **cop** is a policeman or policewoman. N COUNT Informal

cop out. If someone **cops out**, they do not do what they should do; used showing disapproval. EG *I simply and shamefully copped out.* ● See also **cop-out.** PHRASAL VB: V+ADV Informal

cope /kəʊp/, **copes, coping, coped. 1** If you **cope** with a problem or task, you deal with it successfully. EG *John and Sally coped with all their problems cheerfully... ...a computer capable of coping with domestic requirements.* V: USU+*with*

2 If you have to **cope** with an unpleasant situation, you have to accept it or endure it. EG *Poor families have to cope with a lot of strain.* V: USU+*with*

co-pilot, co-pilots. The **co-pilot** of an aeroplane is a pilot who assists the chief pilot. N COUNT

copious /kəʊpɪəs/. Something that is **copious** exists or happens in large amounts or quantities. EG *Plants need copious sunshine... She made copious notes.* ◇ **copiously.** EG *He cried copiously.* ADJ QUALIT ◇ ADV

cop-out, cop-outs. If you say that something is a **cop-out**, you think that someone is not doing what they should do. EG *Such international co-operation is often merely a cop-out.* N COUNT Informal

copper /kɒpə/, **coppers. 1 Copper** is a soft, reddish brown metal. EG *...a copper mine... ...copper wire.* N UNCOUNT

2 A **copper** is a policeman or policewoman. EG *Wait here till the coppers turn up.* N COUNT Informal

3 A **copper** is also a brown metal coin of low value. EG *It only cost a few coppers.* N COUNT Informal

copse /kɒps/, **copses.** A **copse** is a small group of trees growing very close to each other. EG *...pretty meadows and copses.* N COUNT

copulate /kɒpjə⁴leɪt/, **copulates, copulating, copulated.** When animals **copulate**, they have sex. ◇ **copulation** /kɒpjə⁴leɪʃə⁰n/. EG *...the act of copulation.* V OR V+*with*: RECIP ◇ N UNCOUNT Formal

copy /kɒpi¹/, **copies, copying, copied. 1** A **copy** is something that is made to look exactly the same as something else. EG *I will send you a copy of the letter.* N COUNT

2 If you **copy** something that someone has written or said, you write it down exactly. EG *...a comment she had copied from his notes.* V+O

3 If you **copy** a person or their ideas, you try to behave like them because you admire them. EG *Our scheme has been copied by other universities.* V+O

4 A **copy** of a book, newspaper, or record is one of the many identical ones that have been printed or produced. EG *Sixty thousand copies of the record were sold.* N COUNT

copy down. If you **copy down** what someone has written or said, you write it down exactly. EG *I shouldn't bother to copy these figures down.* PHRASAL VB: V+O+ADV

copy out. If you **copy out** a piece of writing, you write it all down exactly. EG *I remember copying out the whole play.* PHRASAL VB: V+O+ADV

copyright /kɒpi¹raɪt/, **copyrights.** The **copyright** on a piece of writing or music is the legal right of the writer or publisher to be asked for permission and paid before anyone else can reproduce it or perform it. EG *Who holds the copyright of the song?* N COUNT OR N UNCOUNT

coral /kɒrə⁰l/, **corals. 1 Coral** is a hard substance formed from the skeletons of very small sea animals. It is often used to make jewellery. EG *...a coral necklace.* N UNCOUNT

2 A **coral** is a very small sea animal. EG *...primitive creatures like jellyfish and corals.* N COUNT

cord /kɔːd/, **cords. 1 Cord** is **1.1** strong, thick string. EG *She tied a cord around her box... ...a piece of cord.* N COUNT OR N UNCOUNT **1.2** wire covered in rubber or plastic which connects electrical equipment to an electricity supply. EG *...a small electric heater on a long cord.* N COUNT

2 Cords are trousers made of corduroy. EG *...a pair of grey cords.* N PLURAL

cordial /kɔːdɪəl/, **cordials 1** Someone who is **cordial** is warm and friendly. EG *Relations between the two men were far from cordial.* ◇ **cordially.** EG *She shook hands cordially with Charley.* ◇ **cordiality** /kɔːdɪælɪ¹ti¹/. EG *They greeted me with genuine cordiality.* ADJ QUALIT Formal ◇ ADV ◇ N UNCOUNT

2 Cordial is a sweet drink made from fruit juice. EG *...lime juice cordial.* N MASS

cordon /kɔːdə⁰n/, **cordons, cordoning, cordoned.** A **cordon** is a line or ring of police, soldiers, or vehicles preventing people from entering or leaving an area. EG *The crowd attempted to break through the police cordons.* N COUNT

cordon off. If police or soldiers **cordon off** an area, they prevent people from entering or leaving it, usually by forming a line or ring. EG *The area surrounding the office had been cordoned off.* PHRASAL VB: V+O+ADV

corduroy /kɔːdə⁰rɔɪ, kɔːdə⁰rɔɪ/ is thick cotton cloth with parallel raised lines on the outside. EG *...a corduroy jacket.* N UNCOUNT

core /kɔː/, **cores. 1** The **core** of a fruit is its hard central part which contains seeds or pips. EG *...the core of an apple.* N COUNT

2 The **core** of an object, building, or city is its central part. EG *The planet probably has a molten core.* N COUNT: USU+SUPP

3 A **core** of people in an organization or system is an important group within it. EG *...a student body led by a core of academics.* N SING

4 The **core** of a situation or problem is its most important part. EG *...the core of industry's problems.* N SING: USU+SUPP Formal

cork /kɔːk/, **corks. 1 Cork** is a soft, light substance which forms the bark of a type of Mediterranean tree. It floats on water and is not easily damaged by heat or liquids. EG *...cork table mats... ...a floor covering such as cork.* N UNCOUNT

2 A **cork** is a piece of cork or plastic that is pushed into the end of a bottle to close it. EG *He removed the cork from the wine bottle.* N COUNT

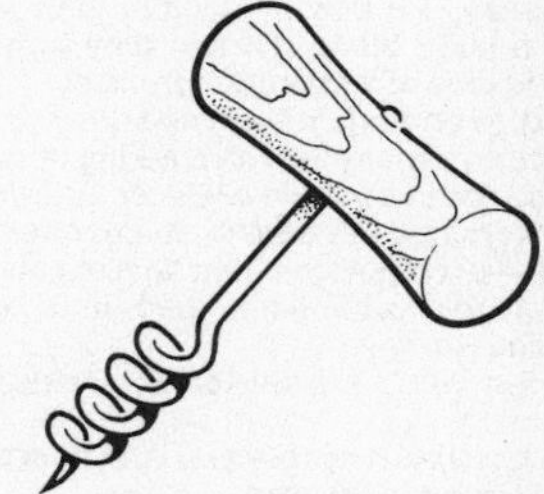

corkscrew /kɔːkskruː/, **corkscrews.** A **corkscrew** is a device for pulling corks out of bottles. N COUNT

corn /kɔːn/, **corns. 1 Corn** is used to refer to crops such as wheat and barley, or the seeds from these plants. EG *...a field of corn... ...sacks of corn.* N UNCOUNT British

2 Corn is also the same as maize. EG *...corn bread.* N UNCOUNT

3 A **corn** is a small, painful area of hard skin which can form on your foot, especially near your toes. N COUNT

corned beef is beef which has been cooked and preserved in salt water. N UNCOUNT

corner /kɔːnə/, **corners, cornering, cornered. 1** A **corner** of something is a point or an area where two or more of its edges, sides, or surfaces join. EG *He signed his name on the lower right-hand corner of the drawing... There was a television set in the corner of the room... Out of the corner of my eye I caught a glimpse of two men in uniform.* N COUNT: OFT+SUPP

2 A **corner** is also **2.1** a place where two streets join. EG *There's a telephone box on the corner.* **2.2** a N COUNT sharp bend in a road. EG *The lorry took the corner too fast.*

3 Places that are far away or difficult to get to are sometimes referred to as the **corners** of the world or of a country. EG *You have carried Britain's fame to the remotest corners of the earth.* N COUNT : USU PLURAL Literary

4 If you are in a **corner**, you are in a situation that is difficult to escape from or to deal with. EG *Laing talked himself into a corner.* N COUNT : USU a+N Informal

5 If you **corner** a person or animal, you get them into a place or situation which they cannot escape from. EG *The police pursued and cornered the wrong car.* V+O
◊ **cornered.** EG *She had me cornered between the front porch and her car.* ◊ ADJ CLASSIF

6 If you **corner** a market or some other area of activity, you gain control over it so that no one else can have any success in that area. EG *He had a crazy scheme to corner the champagne market.* V+O

7 If you **cut corners**, you do something quickly by doing it in a less thorough way than you should. PHRASE

cornerstone /kɔːnəstəʊn/, **cornerstones.** The **cornerstone** of something is the basic part which its existence, success, or truth depends on. EG *Mathematics is the cornerstone of scientific certainty... The trade union movement was the cornerstone of Labour's economic strategy.* N COUNT : USU+*of* Formal

cornet /kɔːnɪ^{2}t/, **cornets. 1** A **cornet** is a small trumpet. N COUNT

2 An ice cream **cornet** is a soft thin biscuit shaped like a cone with ice cream in it. N COUNT

cornflakes /kɔːnfleɪks/ are a breakfast cereal made from maize. N PLURAL

cornflour /kɔːnflaʊə/ is a fine white flour made from maize. N UNCOUNT

cornucopia /kɔːnjʊkəʊpɪə/. A **cornucopia** of good things is a large number of them. N PART : SING Formal

corny /kɔːni^1/, **cornier, corniest.** Something that is **corny** is very obvious or sentimental and not at all subtle or original. EG *Ben loves corny old jokes.* ADJ QUALIT

corollary /kərɒləri^1/, **corollaries.** A **corollary** of something is an idea, argument, or fact which is the direct result of it. EG *This change is the inevitable corollary of the social revolution I have just described.* N COUNT : OFT+*of/to* Formal

coronary /kɒrənə^{0}ri^1/, **coronaries.** If someone has a **coronary**, the flow of blood to their heart is blocked by a large blood clot and they suffer a lot of pain. EG *He died of a massive coronary.* N COUNT

coronation /kɒrəneɪʃə^{0}n/, **coronations.** A **coronation** is the ceremony at which a king or queen is crowned. EG *...the coronation of Queen Elizabeth.* N COUNT

coroner /kɒrənə/, **coroners.** A **coroner** is an official who is responsible for investigating the deaths of people who have died in a sudden, violent, or unusual way. N COUNT

coronet /kɒrənɪ^{2}t/, **coronets.** A **coronet** is a small crown. N COUNT

corporal /kɔːpə^{0}rəl/, **corporals.** A **corporal** is an officer of low rank in the army. N COUNT

corporal punishment is the punishment of people by beating them. N UNCOUNT

corporate /kɔːpə^{0}rə^{1}t/ means owned or shared by all the members of a group or organization. EG *...a corporate identity.* ADJ CLASSIF : ATTRIB

corporation /kɔːpəreɪʃə^{0}n/, **corporations.** A **corporation** is **1** a large business or company. N COUNT **2** an organization that is responsible for running a particular town or city. EG *A petition was sent from the mayor and corporation.* British

corps /kɔː/. **Corps** is both the singular and the plural.
A **corps** is **1** a part of the army which has special duties. EG *...the Royal Army Ordnance Corps.* N COUNT **2** a small group of people who do a special job. EG *...the diplomatic corps.* N COUNT+SUPP

corpse /kɔːps/, **corpses.** A **corpse** is a dead body, especially the body of a human being. N COUNT

corpulent /kɔːpjə^{4}lənt/. Someone who is **corpulent** is fat. EG *...his corpulent figure.* ADJ QUALIT Formal

corpuscle /kɔːpʌsə^{0}l/, **corpuscles.** A **corpuscle** is a red or white blood cell. N COUNT

correct /kərɛkt/, **corrects, correcting, corrected. 1** Something that is **correct** is accurate and has no mistakes. EG *That's the correct answer.* ADJ CLASSIF
◊ **correctly.** EG *I hope I pronounced his name correctly.* ◊ ADV ◊ **correctness.** EG *This confirmed the correctness of my decision.* ◊ N UNCOUNT

2 If you are **correct**, what you have said or thought is true. EG *Jenkins is correct. We've got to change our strategy.* ADJ PRED

3 The **correct** thing is the thing that is required or is most suitable in a particular situation. EG *Make sure you ask for the correct fuse.* ADJ CLASSIF : ATTRIB ◊ **correctly.** EG *Rice, correctly cooked and prepared, is delicious.* ◊ ADV

4 If you **correct** a mistake, problem, or fault, you do something which puts it right. EG *I wish to correct a false impression which may have been created... They are studying ways of correcting the imbalance between the rich and poor countries.* V+O

5 If you **correct** someone, you say something which you think is more accurate or appropriate than what they have just said. EG *I suspect – though correct me if I'm wrong – that this is their view too... 'I'm a fighter like your dad is – or was,' Mr Cupples corrected himself.* V+O OR V-REFL : OFT+QUOTE; ALSO V+QUOTE

6 When someone **corrects** a piece of writing, they look at it and mark the mistakes in it. EG *Miss Lennox was seated at her desk correcting papers.* V+O

7 Correct behaviour is considered to be morally or socially acceptable. EG *Charter's dealings with him have been wholly correct.* ADJ QUALIT ◊ **correctly.** EG *We tried to behave correctly.* ◊ ADV ◊ **correctness.** EG *Such a person should be treated with polite correctness.* ◊ N UNCOUNT

correction /kərɛkʃə^{0}n/, **corrections. 1** A **correction** is something which puts right something that has been wrongly done, said, written, or believed. EG *We'll make the necessary corrections... A couple of mistakes need correction.* N COUNT OR N UNCOUNT

2 Correction is the changing of something so that it is no longer faulty or unsatisfactory. EG *Deaf children need speech correction.* N UNCOUNT OR N COUNT

corrective /kərɛktɪv/, **correctives. Corrective** measures or techniques are intended to put right something that is wrong. EG *...corrective surgery.* ADJ CLASSIF : USU ATTRIB
▸ used as a noun. EG *This analysis provides an important corrective to the traditional view.* ▸ N COUNT : OFT+*to*

correlate /kɒrə^{1}leɪt/, **correlates, correlating, correlated.** If two things **correlate** or if they **are correlated**, they always exist or happen together. EG *In Britain, class and region are strongly correlated.* V-ERG; ALSO V OR V+*with* : RECIP ◊ **correlation** /kɒrə^{1}leɪʃə^{0}n/, **correlations.** EG *There's no correlation between mental ability and physical strength.* ◊ N UNCOUNT OR N COUNT

correspond /kɒrɪspɒnd/, **corresponds, corresponding, corresponded. 1** If one thing **corresponds** with or to another thing, it is similar to it. EG *His job in Moscow corresponds to your father's position here... ...a professional qualification corresponding to a first degree.* V OR V+*with/to* : RECIP

2 If two numbers or amounts **correspond**, they are the same. EG *The date of her birth corresponded with the date of her father's affair in Paris.* V OR V+*with/to* : RECIP

3 If two people **correspond**, they write letters to each other. EG *I've been corresponding with Tim Johns... Elizabeth and I corresponded regularly.* V OR V+*with* : RECIP

4 See also **correspondig**.

correspondence /kɒrɪspɒndəns/, **correspondences. 1 Correspondence** is **1.1** the act of writing letters to someone. EG *The judges' decision is final and no correspondence will be entered into.* N UNCOUNT : OFT+*with* **1.2** the letters that someone receives. EG *The letter had been among his correspondence that morning.* N UNCOUNT

2 If there is a **correspondence** between two things, there is a close relationship or similarity N UNCOUNT OR N COUNT

How valuable is costume jewellery?

between them. EG *In African languages there is a close correspondence between sounds and letters.*

correspondent /kɒrɪspɒndənt/, **correspondents.** A **correspondent** is a newspaper reporter or television reporter. EG *...the Economics correspondent of the Guardian.* N COUNT: USU+SUPP

corresponding /kɒrɪspɒndɪŋ/. You use **corresponding** 1 to describe a change which is the result of a change in something else. EG *Any increase in complexity brings with it a corresponding probability of error.* ◇ **correspondingly.** EG *The new edition is bigger and correspondingly more expensive.* 2 to describe something which is similar to something else. EG *In France they study to the same standard and take the corresponding examinations.* ADJ CLASSIF: ATTRIB Formal; ◇ ADV SEN; ADJ CLASSIF: ATTRIB

corridor /kɒrɪdə^{8}/, **corridors.** A **corridor** is a long passage in a building or train, with doors and rooms on one or both sides. N COUNT

corroborate /kərɒbəreɪt/, **corroborates, corroborating, corroborated.** If someone or something **corroborates** an idea, account, or argument, they provide evidence or information that supports it. EG *Abrams and Rose corroborated this view in their influential study of the subject.* ◇ **corroboration** /kərɒbəreɪʃə^{0}n/. EG *Evangelina's story was later published without corroboration.* V+O Formal; ◇ N UNCOUNT

corrode /kərəʊd/, **corrodes, corroding, corroded.** When metal **corrodes**, it is gradually destroyed by a chemical or by rust. EG *Vinegar will corrode metal.* ◇ **corroded.** EG *The generator was badly corroded.* V-ERG; ◇ ADJ QUALIT

corrosion /kərəʊʒə^{0}n/ is the damage that is caused when something is corroded. EG *Check that the terminals of the battery are free from dirt and corrosion.* N UNCOUNT

corrosive /kərəʊsɪv/. 1 A substance that is **corrosive** is able to destroy solid materials by a chemical reaction. EG *...a corrosive poison.* ADJ QUALIT

2 Something that is **corrosive** has a harmful effect over a period of time. EG *...the corrosive effects of inflation.* ADJ QUALIT Literary

corrugated /kɒrə^{4}geɪtɪ^{2}d/. **Corrugated** metal or cardboard has been folded into a series of small parallel folds to make it stronger. EG *...a corrugated iron roof.* ADJ CLASSIF: ATTRIB

corrupt /kərʌpt/, **corrupts, corrupting, corrupted.** 1 Someone who is **corrupt** behaves in a way that is morally wrong, especially by doing dishonest or illegal things in return for money or power. EG *...corrupt politicians... ...corrupt practices.* ADJ QUALIT

2 To **corrupt** someone means **2.1** to cause them to become dishonest and unjust. EG *Power and wealth corrupted him... Young people in prison are corrupted by hardened criminals.* **2.2** to stop them from caring about moral standards. EG *I doubt that any film ever corrupted anyone.* V+O OR V

corruption /kərʌpʃə^{0}n/. 1 **Corruption** is dishonesty and illegal behaviour by people in positions of authority or power. EG *...police corruption.* N UNCOUNT

2 The **corruption** of someone is the process of making them behave in a way that is considered morally wrong. EG *His whole life seemed dedicated to the corruption of the young.* N UNCOUNT

corset /kɔːsɪ^{2}t/, **corsets.** A **corset** is a stiff piece of underwear worn by some women. It fits tightly around their hips and waist and makes them appear slimmer. N COUNT

cos /kə^{7}s/ is a very informal way of saying 'because'. EG *You'd better make a note of that, cos I haven't.* CONJ Spoken

cosmetic /kɒzmetɪk/, **cosmetics.** 1 **Cosmetics** are substances such as lipstick or powder, which people put on their face to make themselves look more attractive. N COUNT: USU PLURAL

2 **Cosmetic** measures or changes improve the appearance of something but do not change its basic character. EG *It was a purely cosmetic measure.* ADJ CLASSIF

cosmetic surgery is surgery which is done to people in order to make them look more attractive. N UNCOUNT

cosmic /kɒzmɪk/ means belonging or relating to the universe. EG *The other great cosmic reality is time.* ADJ CLASSIF: ATTRIB Formal

cosmonaut /kɒzmə^{6}nɔːt/, **cosmonauts.** A **cosmonaut** is a Soviet astronaut. N COUNT

cosmopolitan /kɒzmə^{6}pɒlɪtə^{0}n/. Something that is **cosmopolitan** has been influenced by many different countries and cultures. EG *It remains a cosmopolitan street... ...his cosmopolitan wife.* ADJ QUALIT

cosmos /kɒzmɒs/. You can refer to the universe as the **cosmos**. EG *...the creation of the cosmos.* N SING: the+N

cosset /kɒsɪt/, **cossets, cosseting, cosseted.** If you **cosset** someone, you do everything possible for them and protect them from anything unpleasant. EG *We all yearn to be cosseted.* V+O

cost /kɒst/, **costs, costing.** The form **cost** is used in the present tense and is the past tense and past participle of the verb.

1 The **cost** of something is the amount of money that is needed in order to buy, do, or make it. EG *The total cost of the holiday was £300... The building was restored at a cost of £500,000... ...the huge increases in fuel costs.* N COUNT

2 You use **cost** to talk about the amount of money that you have to pay for things. For example, if something **costs** £5, you have to pay £5 for it. EG *Those books cost £2.95 each... A two-day stay there cost me $125... A freezer doesn't cost much to run.* V+O OR V+O+O

3 The **cost** of something is also the loss, damage, or injury that is involved in trying to achieve it. EG *The cost in human life had been enormous.* N SING

4 If an event or mistake **costs** you something, you lose that thing as the result of it. EG *A single error here could cost you your life.* V+O+O OR V+O

5 If you say that something must be done **at all costs**, you mean that it must definitely be done, even if it requires a lot of effort or money. EG *This right must be protected at all costs.* PHRASE

co-star, co-stars, co-starring, co-starred. 1 An actor or actress who **co-stars** in a film has one of the most important parts in it. EG *...Jackson Florentine, who co-starred in Gold-Diggers of 1984.* V OR V+with: RECIP

2 An actor or actress who is a **co-star** of a film has one of the most important parts in it. EG *...a photograph of her with her co-star, Gerard Depardieu.* N COUNT+SUPP

cost-effective. Something that is **cost-effective** saves or makes a lot of money in comparison with the costs involved. EG *We urgently need more cost-effective methods of production.* ADJ QUALIT

costly /kɒstli^{1}/, **costlier, costliest.** Something that is **costly** 1 is very expensive. EG *It proved a costly mistake.* 2 uses up a lot of time or effort. EG *That route will be too costly in time.* ADJ QUALIT

cost of living. The **cost of living** is the average amount of money that each person in a country needs to spend on food, housing, and clothing. EG *In Britain today the cost of living is still rising rapidly.* N SING: the+N

costume /kɒstjuːm/, **costumes.** 1 A **costume** is a set of clothes worn by an actor. EG *...theatrical costumes.* N COUNT

2 The clothes worn by people at a particular time in history or in a particular country are referred to as a particular type of **costume**. EG *...17th-century costume.* N UNCOUNT

costume jewellery is jewellery made from cheap materials. N UNCOUNT

cosy /kəʊzi^{1}/, **cosier, cosiest; cosies;** spelled **cozy** in American English.

1 A house or room that is **cosy** is comfortable and warm. EG *They were beginning to miss the cosy flat in St John's Wood.* ADJ QUALIT

2 If you are **cosy**, you are comfortable and warm. EG *A hot water bottle will make you feel cosier.* ADJ QUALIT

◇ **cosily.** EG *We were all sitting cosily in the recreation room.* ◇ ADV

3 You use **cosy** to describe activities that are pleasant and friendly. EG *I had a cosy chat with him... We had quite a few cosy evenings together.* ADJ QUALIT

◇ **cosily.** EG *We spent the afternoon cosily gossiping.* ◇ ADV

4 A **cosy** is a soft cover which you put over a teapot to keep it warm. EG *...tea cosies.* N COUNT+SUPP

cot /kɒt/, **cots.** A **cot** is **1** a bed for a baby, with bars or panels round it so that the baby cannot fall out. **2** a small, narrow bed. N COUNT British American

cottage /kɒtɪdʒ/, **cottages.** A **cottage** is a small house in the country. N COUNT

cottage cheese is soft white lumpy cheese made from sour milk. N UNCOUNT

cotton /kɒtə⁰n/, **cottons, cottoning, cottoned. 1 Cotton** is **1.1** a natural cloth made from the soft fibres that are produced by the cotton plant. EG *...a cotton dress.* **1.2** a tall plant that is used to produce this cloth. EG *...cotton fields.* N MASS N UNCOUNT

2 Cotton is also thread that is used for sewing. EG *...reels of cotton.* N MASS British

cotton on. If you **cotton on** to something, you understand it or realize it, especially without people telling you about it. EG *At long last he has cottoned on to the fact that I don't want him!.* PHRASAL VB : V+ADV, OFT+*to* Informal

cotton wool is soft, fluffy cotton, used especially for applying liquids or creams to your skin. N UNCOUNT

couch /kaʊtʃ/, **couches, couching, couched. 1** A **couch** is **1.1** a long piece of furniture which more than one person can sit on. **1.2** a bed in a doctor's consulting room, which patients lie on while they are being examined or treated. N COUNT

2 If you **couch** a statement in a particular style of language, you express it in that style of language. EG *Here was a resolution couched in forthright terms.* V+O : USU PASS+*in* Formal

cough /kɒf/, **coughs, coughing, coughed. 1** When you **cough**, you force air out of your throat with a sudden, harsh noise, often because you are not well. EG *Mr Willet coughed nervously.* ▸ used as a noun. EG *There was a muffled cough outside the study door.* ◇ **coughing.** EG *They suffered abdominal pains and intense coughing.* V ▸ N COUNT ◇ N UNCOUNT

2 If you **cough** blood or phlegm, you force it out of your throat with a sudden, harsh noise. EG *He started coughing blood.* V+O

3 A **cough** is also an illness in which you cough often and your chest or throat hurts. EG *I had a terrible cough every winter.* N COUNT

cough up. 1 If you **cough up** money, you give someone money. EG *They'll cough up the hundred million... How can he persuade the authorities to cough up for the private education of his children?* PHRASAL VB : V+ADV OR V+O+ADV Informal

2 If you **cough up** blood or phlegm, you force it out of your throat with a sudden, harsh noise. EG *She coughed up some phlegm.* V+O+ADV

could /kʊd, kəd/. **Could** is sometimes considered to be the past form of **can**, but in this dictionary the two words are dealt with separately. See **can**.

1 If you **could** do something, you were able to do it. EG *They complained that they couldn't sleep... When I was young you could buy a packet for two shillings... We just could not understand why he'd failed.* MODAL

2 You use **could** in indirect speech to indicate that someone has given permission for something or that something is possible. EG *She said I could go... I asked if we could somehow get a car.* MODAL

3 If you say that something **could** happen, **3.1** you mean that it is possible that it will happen. EG *The river could easily overflow, couldn't it?... It could be disastrous.* **3.2** you mean that it is possible to do. EG *We could do a great deal more in this country to educate people.* MODAL

4 If you say that something **could** have happened, you mean that it was possible although it did not actually happen. EG *You were lucky. It could have been awful.* MODAL

5 If you say that something **could** be the case, you mean that it is possibly the case. If you say that something **could** have been the case, you mean that it was possibly the case. EG *It could be a symbol, couldn't it?... It couldn't possibly be poison... It could have been an axe... He didn't carry a dinghy, so he couldn't have rowed away.* MODAL

6 If you say that someone **could** do something, you mean that it is possible for them to do it and that it might be a good thing to do. EG *You could phone her... Couldn't you just build more factories?... I could ask her, I suppose.* MODAL

7 If you say that you **could** do something, you mean that you would like to do it. If you say that you **could** have done something, you mean that you would have liked to do it. EG *I could kill you... I could have screamed... I could have easily spent the whole year on it.* MODAL

8 If you ask someone if they or you **could** do something, you are politely asking them if they will do it or allow it. EG *Could you just switch the projector on behind you?... Could we put this fire on?... Could I speak to Sue, please?* MODAL

9 If you say to someone that they **could** do something, you mean that they ought to do it, and you are angry with them because they have not. If you say that they **could** have done something, you mean that they should have done it, and you are angry with them because they did not. EG *You could at least apologize... You could have told me!* MODAL

10 You use **could** after 'if' when you are imagining a situation or action, in order to consider what the likely consequences might be. EG *If one could measure this sort of thing, one might understand it better.* MODAL

11 If you say that you **could not** do something, you mean that you find it unacceptable or unreasonable. EG *I couldn't let you do it on your own.* MODAL+*not*

couldn't /kʊdə⁰nt/ is the usual spoken form of 'could not'.

could've /kʊdə⁰v/ is the usual spoken form of 'could have', especially when 'have' is an auxiliary verb.

council /kaʊnsə¹l/, **councils. 1** A **council** is **1.1** a group of people who are elected to run a town, borough, city, or county. EG *...Wiltshire County Council... ...council meetings.* **1.2** a group of people who give advice about a particular subject or who run a particular organization. EG *...the Arts Council.* N COLL British

2 A **council** house or flat is owned by the local council. You pay rent to live in it. EG *...council estates... ...a council tenant.* ADJ CLASSIF : ATTRIB

3 A **council** is also a specially organized meeting. EG *That afternoon a council of ministers and generals was held at No. 10.* N COUNT

councillor /kaʊnsə⁰lə/, **councillors.** A **councillor** is a member of a local council. N COUNT

counsel /kaʊnsəl/, **counsels, counselling, counselled;** spelled **counseling** and **counseled** in American English.

1 Counsel is serious or careful advice. EG *His voice had been heard before, giving counsel in times of stress.* N UNCOUNT Formal

2 If you **counsel** someone to do something, you advise them to do it. EG *'Ignore them,' Mrs Jones counselled... Some wanted to fight. Others counselled caution.* V+O : OFT +TO-INF OR V +QUOTE Formal

3 If you **counsel** people, you give them advice about their problems. EG *Part of her work is to counsel families when problems arise.* V+O

◇ **counselling.** EG *...psychiatric counselling.* ◇ N UNCOUNT

4 A **counsel** is a lawyer who gives advice on a legal case and fights the case in court. EG *...counsel* N COUNT OR N UNCOUNT

Who is a count married to?

for the defence... You should take the advice of counsel.

counsellor /kaʊnsəºlə/, **counsellors;** spelled **counselor** in American English. A **counsellor** is a person whose job is to give advice to people who need it. EG *The hospital has trained counsellors who are used to dealing with depressed patients.* N COUNT

count /kaʊnt/, **counts, counting, counted. 1** When you **count**, you say all the numbers one after another up to a particular number. EG *I'm going to count up to three... After counting sixty the rest set off in pursuit.* V: OFT +to/up to OR V+O

2 If you **count** all the things in a group, you add them up in order to find how many there are. EG *He withdrew to his office to count the money.* V+O

3 A **count** is a number that you get by counting a particular set of things. EG *The official government count has now risen to eight million.* N COUNT: USU SING

4 If you **keep count** of a number of things, you keep a record of how many have occurred. If you **lose count** of a number of things, you cannot remember how many have occurred. EG *Keep count of the unforeseen difficulties you encounter... I've lost count of the number of boyfriends she's had.* PHRASE

5 The thing that **counts** in a particular situation is the thing that is most important in that situation. EG *What counts is how you feel about yourself.* V

6 If you say that a particular thing **counts** for something, you mean that it is valuable or important. EG *I felt that all my years there counted for nothing.* V+*for*

7 If something **counts** as a particular thing, it is regarded as being that thing, especially in particular circumstances. EG *These benefits do not count as income for tax purposes... They can hardly be counted as friends.* V-ERG: USU+*as*

8 If you **count** something when you are making a calculation, you include it in that calculation. EG *We must count the infected trees as well as the healthy ones... ...36,600,000 Americans (not counting children less than one year old).* V+O

9 You can also use **count** to refer to one or more points that you are considering. For example, if something is wrong on two counts, it is wrong for two reasons. EG *The use of these tests is criticized on two counts.* N COUNT: USU PLURAL

10 A **count** is also a European nobleman with the same rank as an English earl. N COUNT

count against. If something **counts against** you, it may cause you to be punished or rejected. EG *It would count heavily against me if I got the Director into trouble.* PHRASAL VB: V+PREP

count on or **count upon. 1** If you **count on** something or **count upon** it, you expect it to happen and include it in your plans. EG *Doctors could now count on a regular salary.* PHRASAL VB: V+PREP **2** If you **count on** someone or **count upon** them, you rely on them to support you or help you. EG *You can count on me.* V+PREP

count out. If you **count out** a sum of money, you count the notes or coins as you put them in a pile one by one. PHRASAL VB: V+O+ADV

count up. If you **count up** all the things in a group, you add them up in order to find out how many there are. EG *I counted up my years of teaching experience.* PHRASAL VB: V+O+ADV

count upon. See **count on.**

countable noun /kaʊntə¹bəºl naʊn/, **countable nouns.** A **countable noun** is the same as a count noun. N COUNT

countdown /kaʊntdaʊn/, **countdowns.** A **countdown** is the counting aloud of numbers in reverse order before something happens, especially before a spacecraft is launched. N COUNT

countenance /kaʊntɪ²nəns/, **countenances.** Someone's **countenance** is their face. EG *He saw the boyish countenance of Tom Barter before him.* N COUNT Literary

counter /kaʊntə/, **counters, countering, countered. 1** A **counter** is a long, narrow table or flat surface in a shop, where goods are displayed or sold. EG *There was a long queue at the medicine counter.* N COUNT

2 If you **counter** something that is being done, you act in a way that makes it less effective. EG *He argued that Labour should counter this propaganda with a series of press statements.* V+O: OFT+*by/with*

3 If you **counter** something that has just been said, you say something in reaction to it or in opposition to it. EG *I countered by enquiring whether she actually knew this man.* V+*by/with*; ALSO V-SPEECH: ONLY *that* Formal

4 If one thing **runs counter to** another, it is in direct contrast with it. EG *The ideology of modern nationalism often runs counter to older ideology.* PHRASE Formal

5 A **counter** is also a small, flat, round object used in board games. N COUNT

counteract /kaʊntərækt/, **counteracts, counteracting, counteracted.** To **counteract** something means to reduce its effect by doing something that produces an opposite effect. EG *We added malt to counteract the bitterness of the taste.* V+O

counter-attack, counter-attacks, counter-attacking, counter-attacked. If you **counter-attack**, you attack someone who has attacked you. V OR V+O
▸ used as a noun. EG *...counter-attacks against enemy civilians.* ▸ N COUNT OR N UNCOUNT

counterbalance /kaʊntəbæleºns/, **counterbalances, counterbalancing, counterbalanced.** To **counterbalance** something means to balance or correct it with an equal effect, force, or amount. EG *Political power counterbalances the other influences in society.* V+O

counterclockwise /kaʊntəklɒkwaɪz/ means the same as anti-clockwise. EG *...a large counterclockwise circulation of air.* ADV AFTER VB, OR ADJ CLASSIF: ATTRIB American

counterfeit /kaʊntəfi¹t/, **counterfeits, counterfeiting, counterfeited. 1** Something that is **counterfeit** is not genuine, but has been made to look exactly like something that is genuine, in order to deceive people. EG *...a counterfeit coin.* ADJ CLASSIF

2 To **counterfeit** something means to make an object that looks exactly like a genuine object, in order to deceive people. V+O

counterfoil /kaʊntəfɔɪl/, **counterfoils.** A **counterfoil** is the part of a cheque or receipt that you keep when you have paid for something. N COUNT

countermand /kaʊntəmɑːnd/, **countermands, countermanding, countermanded.** If you **countermand** an order, you cancel it, usually by giving a different order. V+O Formal

counterpane /kaʊntəpeɪn/, **counterpanes.** A **counterpane** is a decorative cover on a bed. N COUNT Formal

counterpart /kaʊntəpɑːt/, **counterparts.** The **counterpart** of a person or thing is another person or thing that has a similar function or position in a different place. EG *...the English merchant bank and its American counterpart, the Wall Street investment bank.* N COUNT+POSS

counter-productive. Something that is **counter-productive** achieves the opposite result from the one that you want to achieve. ADJ QUALIT

countertenor /kaʊntətɛnə/, **countertenors.** A **countertenor** is a man who sings with a high voice that is similar to a low female singing voice. N COUNT Technical

countess /kaʊntɪ²s/, **countesses.** A **countess** is a woman who has the same rank as a count or earl, or who is married to a count or earl. N COUNT

countless /kaʊntlɪ²s/ means very many. EG *He sent countless letters to the newspapers.* ADJ CLASSIF: ATTRIB

count noun, count nouns. A **count noun** is a noun that has a singular and a plural form and is always used after a determiner in the singular. In this dictionary count nouns have N COUNT in the Extra Column. See the entry headed NOUNS for more information. N COUNT

country /kʌntri¹/, **countries. 1** A **country** is one of the political areas which the world is divided into. A country has its own government, people, language, culture, and land. EG *The level of unemployment in this country is too high... Forests cover about one third of the country... ...small East European countries, like Hungary.* N COUNT

2 You can also refer to the people who live in a particular country as the **country**. EG *The country was stunned.* N SING : *the*+N

3 The **country** is also land which is away from towns and cities. EG *We live in the country... There was a big move of people away from the country to the towns.* N SING : *the*+N ▸ used as an adjective. EG *...lonely country roads... I'm just a country boy.* ▸ ADJ CLASSIF : ATTRIB

4 A particular kind of **country** is an area of land which has particular characteristics or is connected with a particular person. EG *We were in mountain country... This is Max Ernst country.* N UNCOUNT +SUPP

5 Country music is the same as country and western music. ADJ CLASSIF : ATTRIB

country and western is a style of popular music from the USA. N UNCOUNT

country dancing is traditional dancing in which people dance in rows or circles. N UNCOUNT

country house, country houses. A **country house** is a large, attractive house in the country, owned by a rich or noble family. N COUNT

countryman /kʌntrɪmə³n/, **countrymen.** Your **countrymen** are people from your own country. EG *I hope this doesn't shock my fellow countrymen.* N COUNT : USU+POSS

countryside /kʌntrɪsaɪd/. The **countryside** is land which is away from towns and cities. EG *...the English countryside... It's very nice countryside around there.* N SING : *the*+N OR N UNCOUNT

county /kaʊnti¹/, **counties.** A **county** is a region of Britain, Ireland, or the USA which has its own local government. EG *I was a long way from home, on the other side of the county.* N COUNT

coup /kuː/, **coups.** A **coup** is **1** the same as a coup d'état. EG *A coup displaced the regime that had imprisoned him.* **2** an achievement which is thought to be especially brilliant because it was very difficult. EG *Brooke went on to bigger things, his next notable coup being the case of Robert Scott.* N COUNT

coup d'état /kuː deɪtɑː/, **coups d'état.** The plural is pronounced the same as the singular. A **coup d'état** is an attempt to get rid of the president or government of a country. EG *Here governments are generally replaced by coups d'état.* N COUNT OR N UNCOUNT

couple /kʌpə⁰l/, **couples, coupling, coupled. 1** A **couple** is **1.1** two people who are married, living together, or having a sexual relationship. EG *...married couples.* **1.2** two people who you see together on a particular occasion. EG *He watched a couple on the dance floor.* N COLL

2 A **couple** of people or things means two people or things. EG *...a couple of Washington newspaper reporters... He met her a couple of years ago.* N PART

3 If one thing **is coupled** with another, the two things are done or dealt with together. EG *Strong protests were made, coupled with demands for an international inquiry.* V+O+*with* : USU PASS

coupon /kuːpɒn/, **coupons.** A **coupon** is **1** a piece of printed paper which allows you to pay less money than usual for something. EG *This coupon is worth five pounds.* **2** a small form, for example in a newspaper or magazine, which you send to an organization to ask for information about their products or services. **3** a form which you fill in in order to enter a competition. EG *Every Thursday they fill in pools coupons.* N COUNT

courage /kʌrɪdʒ/. **1 Courage** is the quality shown by someone who decides to do something difficult or dangerous, even though they may be afraid; used showing approval. EG *She would never have had the courage to defy him.* N UNCOUNT

2 If you **have the courage of** your **convictions**, you have the confidence to do what you believe is right, even though other people may not agree or approve. PHRASE

3 If you **take courage**, you begin to feel hopeful and confident about something. EG *I take courage from Robert Oppenheimer's vision.* PHRASE

courageous /kəreɪdʒəs/. Someone who is **courageous** shows courage. EG *...his courageous attempt to get the facts published.* ◊ **courageously.** EG *She fought courageously for her principles.* ADJ QUALIT ◊ ADV

courgette /kʊəʒet/, **courgettes.** A **courgette** is a type of small vegetable marrow. N COUNT

courier /kʊərɪə/, **couriers.** A **courier** is **1** a person employed by a travel company to look after people who are on holiday. **2** a person who is paid to take a special letter from one place to another. N COUNT

course /kɔːs/, **courses, coursing, coursed. 1** You say **of course 1.1** when you are saying something that you expect other people already realize or understand. EG *There is of course an element of truth in this argument.* **1.2** when you are talking about an event or situation that does not surprise you. EG *He never writes to me, of course.* ADV SEN

2 You also use **of course 2.1** as a polite way of giving permission or agreeing with someone. EG *'Could I make a telephone call?' he said. 'Of course,' Boylan said.* CONVENTION **2.2** in order to emphasize a statement that you are making, especially when you are agreeing or disagreeing with someone. EG *'Do you love him, Dolly?' – 'Of course I do. He's wonderful.'* ADV SEN

3 Of course not is an emphatic way of saying no. EG *'Do you think he was killed?' – 'No, no, of course not.'* CONVENTION

4 A **course** is a series of lessons or lectures on a particular subject. It usually includes reading and written work that a student has to do. EG *They have computer-science courses.* N COUNT

5 A **course** of medical treatment is a series of treatments that a doctor gives someone. EG *Another course of injections was prescribed.* N COUNT+*of*

6 A **course** in a meal is one of the sections of the meal. EG *...a three-course dinner... He didn't even finish his main course.* N COUNT

7 A **course** or a **course of action** is one of the things that you can do in a particular situation. EG *The company has a choice of three courses of action.* N COUNT OR PHRASE

8 The **course** of a ship or aircraft is the route that it takes. EG *I set a course for the rock.* N COUNT ● If a ship or aircraft is **on course**, it is travelling along the correct route. If it is **off course**, it is no longer travelling along the correct route. EG *He was at the wheel again, with the Morning Rose back on course.* ● PHRASE

9 You can refer to the way that events develop as the **course** of history, nature, or events. EG *It was one of those ideas that change the course of history.* N SING : *the*+N+*of*

10 If something happens **in the course of** a particular period of time, it happens during that period of time. EG *I hope that in the course of the next two or three weeks they'll make up their minds.* PREP ● **in due course**: see **due**.

11 If you do something **as a matter of course**, you do it as part of your normal work or way of life. EG *Harry now flies overseas as a matter of course.* PHRASE

12 If something **runs its course** or **takes its course**, it develops naturally and comes to a natural end. EG *The illness was allowed to run its course.* PHRASE

13 If a liquid **courses** somewhere, it flows quickly. EG *Tears coursed down my face.* V : USU+A Literary

Which words on these pages have a 'p' that is not pronounced?

14 See also **golf course**, **racecourse**.

court /kɔ:t/, **courts, courting, courted.** 1 A **court** is a place where legal matters are decided by a judge and jury or by a magistrate. EG *...divorce courts.* N COUNT
● If someone is **in court**, they are in a court while a trial is taking place. EG *...evidence for possible use in court.* ● PHRASE

2 You can also refer to the people in a court, especially the judge, jury, or magistrates, as the **court**. EG *The court dismissed the charges.* N COUNT: the+N

3 If you **go to court** or **take** someone **to court**, you take legal action against them. EG *I told them I could take them to court.* PHRASE

4 A **court** is also an area in which you play a game such as tennis, badminton, or squash. EG *...an indoor court.* N COUNT
● When tennis players are **on court**, they are playing tennis. When they are **off court**, they are not playing. ● PHRASE

5 The **court** of a king or queen is the place where he or she lives and carries out ceremonial or administrative duties. N COUNT
● When someone is **at court**, they are present at the king's or queen's residence. ● PHRASE

6 If a man and a woman **are courting**, they are spending a lot of time together, because they are intending to marry each other. V Outdated

courteous /kɜ:tɪəs/. Someone who is **courteous** is polite, respectful, and considerate. EG *He was the kindest, most courteous gentleman to work for.* ADJ QUALIT
◇ **courteously.** EG *The jailer received me courteously.* ◇ ADV

courtesy /kɜ:tɪsi^{1}/, **courtesies. 1 Courtesy** is behaviour that is polite, respectful, and considerate. EG *He replied with promptness and courtesy.* N UNCOUNT

2 Courtesies are polite and respectful things that you say or do. EG *There was a brief exchange of courtesies with Elizabeth.* N PLURAL Formal

3 If something is done **by courtesy of** someone, they have given their permission for it to be done. If something happens **by courtesy of** a situation, it happens because the situation makes it possible for it to happen. EG *He was Prime Minister by courtesy of an uneasy alliance with the Liberals.* PREP

courthouse /kɔ:thaʊs/, **courthouses.** A **courthouse** is a building in which a court of law meets. N COUNT American

courtier /kɔ:tɪə/, **courtiers. Courtiers** were noblemen and women who spent a lot of time at the court of a king or queen. N COUNT

court-martial, court-martials, court-martialling, court-martialled. To **court-martial** a member of the armed forces means to try them in a military court. V+O Technical
▸ used as a noun. EG *They arrested General Lee for disobedience, and ordered a court-martial.* ▸ N COUNT

court of appeal, courts of appeal. A **court of appeal** is a court which deals with appeals against legal judgements. N COUNT

court of inquiry, courts of inquiry. A **court of inquiry** is 1 an official investigation into a serious accident or incident. 2 a group of people who are officially appointed to investigate a serious accident or incident. EG *A court of inquiry sharply criticized the local authority.* N COUNT

courtroom /kɔ:tru^{4}m/, **courtrooms.** A **courtroom** is a room in which a legal court meets. N COUNT

courtship /kɔ:tʃɪp/ is the activity of courting or the time during which a man and a woman are courting. EG *...the romance of courtship.* N UNCOUNT Formal

court shoe, court shoes. Court shoes are ladies' shoes that have high heels and are made of plain leather with no design. See picture at SHOES. N COUNT

courtyard /kɔ:tjɑ:d/, **courtyards.** A **courtyard** is a flat open area of ground surrounded by buildings or walls. It is often paved. N COUNT

cousin /kʌzə^{0}n/, **cousins.** Your **cousin** is the child of your uncle or aunt. N COUNT

cove /kəʊv/, **coves.** A **cove** is a small bay on the coast. EG *...Fisherman's Cove.* N COUNT

covenant /kʌvə^{0}nənt/, **covenants.** A **covenant** is a formal written promise to pay a sum of money each year for a fixed period, especially to a charity. N COUNT

cover /kʌvə/, **covers, covering, covered. 1** If you **cover** something, you place something else over it in order to protect it or hide it. EG *She covered her face with her hands... The tray was covered with a starched white cloth.* V+O: OFT+*with*

2 If something **covers** something else, it forms a layer over it. EG *Her hand was covered with blood.* V+O

3 If you **cover** a particular distance, you travel that distance. EG *I covered approximately twenty miles a day.* V+O

4 An insurance policy that **covers** a person or thing guarantees that money will be paid by the insurance company in relation to that person or thing. EG *Many people are covered by private health insurance.* V+O

5 If a law **covers** a particular set of people, things, or situations, it applies to them. EG *Workers in factories are already covered by the Factories Act.* V+O

6 If you **cover** a particular topic, you discuss it in a lecture, course, or book. EG *We've covered a wide range of subjects today.* V+O

7 If reporters, newspapers, or television companies **cover** an event, they report on it. V+O

8 If a sum of money **covers** something, it is enough to pay for it. EG *I'll give you a cheque to cover the cost of your journey.* V+O

9 A **cover** is something which is put over an object, usually in order to protect it. EG *She put the cover on her typewriter.* N COUNT

10 Something that is a **cover** for secret or illegal activities seems respectable or normal, but is intended to hide the activities. EG *...a cover for murder.* N COUNT: OFT+SUPP

11 The **covers** on your bed are the sheet, blankets, and bedspread that you have on top of you. N PLURAL: the+N

12 The **cover** of a book or a magazine is the outside part of it. EG *On the front cover was a picture of a woman.* N COUNT

13 Cover is trees, rocks, or other places where you shelter from the weather or hide from someone. EG *They crossed to the other side of the stream in search of cover.* N UNCOUNT

14 Insurance **cover** is a guarantee from an insurance company that money will be paid by them if it is needed. EG *This policy gives unlimited cover for hospital charges.* N UNCOUNT: OFT+*for*

15 Cover is also used in these phrases. **15.1** If you **take cover**, you shelter from the weather or from gunfire. **15.2** If you are **under cover**, you are under something that protects you from the weather. EG *I've got to put the car under cover.* **15.3** If you do something **under cover of** a particular condition, you are able to do it without being noticed because of this condition. EG *The attack usually takes place under cover of darkness... Under cover of the general panic, the assassin escaped.* PHRASES

16 See also **covering**.

cover up. 1 If you **cover** something **up**, you put something else over it in order to protect it or hide it. EG *Cover yourself up with this sheet.* PHRASAL VB: V+O+ADV
2 If you **cover up** something that you do not want people to know about, you hide it from them. EG *There is a great deal to cover up in this case... She tried to cover up for Willie.* ● See also **cover-up**. V+O+ADV OR V+ADV

coverage /kʌvə^{0}rɪdʒ/. The **coverage** of something in the news is the reporting of it. EG *They put an immediate ban on all television coverage of their operations.* N UNCOUNT

covering /kʌvə^{0}rɪŋ/, **coverings.** A **covering** is a layer of something over something else. EG *Kitchen floor covering should be non-slip.* N COUNT OR N UNCOUNT

covering letter, covering letters. A **covering letter** is a letter that you send with a parcel or with another letter in order to give extra information. N COUNT

coverlet /kʌvəlɪ[2]t/, **coverlets.** A **coverlet** is a decorative cover which is put over a bed. N COUNT Formal

covert /kʌvət/. Something that is **covert** is secret or hidden, and not done or shown openly. EG *...a covert involvement in activist politics.* ◊ **covertly.** EG *She watched Marina covertly.* ADJ QUALIT Formal ◊ ADV

cover-up, cover-ups. A **cover-up** is an attempt to hide a crime or mistake. EG *He denied that he took any part in the cover-up.* N COUNT

covet /kʌvə[1]t/, **covets, coveting, coveted.** If you **covet** something, you strongly want to have it for yourself. EG *It was an honour he had long coveted.* V+O Formal

covetous /kʌvə[1]təs/. **Covetous** feelings and actions involve a strong desire to possess something. EG *The United States Steel Corporation was casting covetous eyes at his company.* ADJ QUALIT : ATTRIB Formal

cow /kaʊ/, **cows, cowing, cowed. 1** A **cow** is **1.1** a large female animal that is kept on farms for its milk. **1.2** any animal of this species, either male or female. You can refer to a number of these animals as 'cattle'. EG *...a herd of cows.* N COUNT

2 If you describe a woman as a **cow**, you mean that she is very unpleasant; an offensive use. N COUNT Informal

3 If someone **is cowed**, they are made afraid, or made to behave in a particular way because they have been frightened or oppressed. EG *People shouldn't allow themselves to be cowed into this.* V+O : USU PASS Formal

◊ **cowed.** EG *...his tragically cowed and battered wife.* ◊ ADJ QUALIT

coward /kaʊəd/, **cowards.** If you say that someone is a **coward**, you mean that they are easily frightened and avoid dangerous or difficult situations; used showing disapproval. EG *I was basically a dreadful coward.* N COUNT

cowardice /kaʊədɪs/ is cowardly behaviour. EG *He despised them for their cowardice and ignorance.* N UNCOUNT

cowardly /kaʊədli[1]/. If you describe someone as **cowardly**, you mean that they avoid doing dangerous or difficult things because they are afraid; used showing disapproval. EG *...corrupt and cowardly generals... ...a cowardly refusal to face reality.* ADJ QUALIT

cowboy /kaʊbɔɪ/, **cowboys. 1** A **cowboy** is **1.1** a man employed to look after cattle in America. **1.2** a male character in a Western. EG *...cowboy films.* N COUNT

2 You can refer to someone who runs a business as a **cowboy** if they run it dishonestly or are not experienced, skilful, or careful in their work. EG *...cowboy building contractors.* N COUNT British

cower /kaʊə/, **cowers, cowering, cowered.** If you **cower**, you bend forward and downwards or move back because you are very frightened. EG *Bernadette cowered in her seat.* V : USU+A

cowshed /kaʊʃɛd/, **cowsheds.** A **cowshed** is a building where cows are kept or milked. N COUNT

coy /kɔɪ/. If someone is **coy**, **1** they pretend to be shy and modest. EG *...a coy little smile.* ◊ **coyly.** EG *They were looking at us coyly through their elegant lashes.* ◊ **coyness.** EG *There is no false modesty or coyness about her.* **2** they are unwilling to say something, in a way that people find slightly irritating. EG *Let us not be coy about the identity of this great man.* ADJ QUALIT ◊ ADV ◊ N UNCOUNT ADJ QUALIT

cozy /kəʊzi[1]/. See **cosy**.

crab

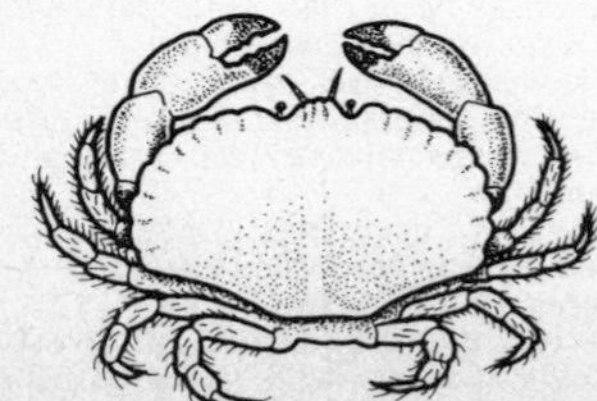

crab /kræb/, **crabs.** A **crab** is a sea creature with a flat round body covered by a shell, and five pairs of legs with large claws on the front pair. Crabs usually move sideways. N COUNT

crack /kræk/, **cracks, cracking, cracked. 1** If something **cracks** or if you **crack** it, **1.1** it becomes slightly damaged, with lines appearing on its surface. EG *If you hold a glass under the hot tap, it may crack.* **1.2** it makes a sharp sound like the sound of a piece of wood breaking. EG *The whips began to crack over their heads.* V-ERG

2 If someone **cracks**, they finally give in or have a nervous breakdown. EG *I thought I might crack if I didn't get away soon.* V Informal

3 If you **crack** a problem or a code, you solve it, especially after a lot of thought. V+O

4 If you **crack** a joke, you tell it. V+O

5 A **crack** is **5.1** a very narrow gap between two things. EG *...the cracks between the boards of the ceiling... I felt a gust of wind through a crack in the wall... I opened the door a crack.* **5.2** a line that appears on the surface of something when it is slightly damaged. EG *She found a crack in one of the tea-cups.* N COUNT : OFT +between/in N COUNT : OFT+in

6 A **crack** is also a slightly rude or cruel joke. EG *There were the routine cracks about the Prime Minister.* N COUNT

7 A **crack** soldier or sportsman is highly trained and very skilful. EG *...a crack British regiment.* ADJ CLASSIF : ATTRIB

8 If you do something **at the crack of dawn**, you do it very early in the morning. EG *He always got up at the crack of dawn.* PHRASE

9 If you **have a crack at** something, you make an attempt to do it. PHRASE Informal

10 See also **cracked, cracking.**

crack down. If people in authority **crack down** on a group of people, they become stricter in making the group obey rules or laws. EG *Her first reaction to the riots was to crack down hard... They have cracked down on thieves and vandals.* PHRASAL VB : V+ADV, OFT+on

● See also **crackdown**.

crack up. 1 If someone **cracks up**, they are under such a lot of emotional strain that they become mentally ill. EG *I'd crack up if there wasn't someone I could talk to.* **2** If you say that something is **not all it's cracked up to be**, you mean that it is not as good as other people have said it is. EG *Marriage is not all it's cracked up to be.* PHRASAL VB : V+ADV Informal PHRASE Informal

crackdown /krækdaʊn/, **crackdowns.** A **crackdown** is strong official action that is taken to punish people who break laws. EG *...a crackdown on criminals.* N COUNT : OFT+on

cracked /krækt/. **1** An object that is **cracked** has lines on its surface because it has been damaged. EG *...the big, cracked mirror.* ADJ QUALIT

2 A voice or musical instrument that is **cracked** sounds rough and unsteady. EG *...a high, cracked voice.* ADJ QUALIT

cracker /krækə/, **crackers. 1** A **cracker** is a thin, crisp biscuit which is often eaten with cheese. N COUNT

2 A **cracker** is also a hollow cardboard tube covered with coloured paper. It can be pulled apart and usually contains a small toy and a paper hat. Children often pull crackers at parties. N COUNT

cracking /krækɪŋ/. **1** If you tell someone to **get cracking**, you are telling them to start doing something immediately. EG *Get cracking or we'll never finish in time.* PHRASE Informal

2 If you walk at **a cracking pace**, you walk very quickly. EG *Gillian used to go at a cracking pace.* PHRASE Informal

crackle /krækə[0]l/, **crackles, crackling, crackled.** If something **crackles**, it makes a rapid series of short, harsh noises. EG *The loudspeaker crackled.* V

▸ used as a noun. EG *...the crackle of the fire.* ▸ N COUNT

If a place is crawling with people, are they on their hands and knees?

◊ **crackling.** EG *The crackling became louder and louder.* ◊ N SING

crackpot /krækpɒt/, **crackpots.** You call someone a **crackpot** when you think that they have strange and crazy ideas. EG *Every crackpot in the world writes to him.* ▸ used as an adjective. EG *...a crackpot letter.* N COUNT Informal ▸ ADJ CLASSIF: ATTRIB

cradle /kreɪdəᵒl/, **cradles, cradling, cradled.** 1 A **cradle** is a small box-shaped bed for a baby. N COUNT

2 A place that is referred to as the **cradle** of something is the place where it began. EG *New England saw itself as the cradle of American technology.* N SING: the+N+of Literary

3 If you **cradle** something in your arms or hands, you hold it carefully. EG *She cradled a child in her arms.* V+O

craft /krɑːft/, **crafts.** 1 A **craft** is 1.1 an activity such as weaving, carving, or pottery that involves making things skilfully with your hands. EG *...traditional crafts such as thatching and weaving... ...a craft festival.* 1.2 any activity or job that involves doing something skilfully. EG *He was still learning his journalistic craft.* N COUNT

2 You can refer to a boat, a spacecraft, or an aircraft as a **craft**. The plural form is also **craft**. EG *There were eight destroyers and fifty smaller craft... My little boat was too frail a craft to weather these storms.* N COUNT

craftsman /krɑːftsmən/, **craftsmen.** A **craftsman** is a man whose job is making things skilfully using his hands. EG *The equipment could be manufactured cheaply by local craftsmen.* N COUNT

craftsmanship /krɑːftsmənʃɪp/ is 1 the skill that someone uses when they make beautiful things with their hands. EG *...Bernini's great craftsmanship.* 2 the quality that something has when it is beautiful and has been very carefully made. EG *I bent down to examine the exquisite craftsmanship.* N UNCOUNT N UNCOUNT

crafty /krɑːftiˡ/, **craftier, craftiest.** Someone who is **crafty** obtains or achieves things by deceiving people in a clever way. EG *...the crafty tactics of journalists... ...the craftiest of all politicians.* ADJ QUALIT

◊ **craftily.** EG *Several ploys are being craftily developed.* ◊ **craftiness.** EG *He shows the same craftiness as his brother.* ◊ ADV ◊ N UNCOUNT

crag /kræg/, **crags.** A **crag** is a steep, rocky cliff or part of a mountain. EG *...a 200 foot high crag.* N COUNT

craggy /krægiˡ/. 1 A **craggy** mountain or cliff is steep and rocky. EG *...the craggy heights of Mount Rushmore.* ADJ QUALIT

2 A **craggy** face has large features and deep lines. ADJ QUALIT

cram /kræm/, **crams, cramming, crammed.** 1 If you **cram** people or things into a place, you put more of them into it than there is room for. EG *Thirty of us were crammed into a small dark room... He crammed the bank notes into his pockets.* V+O+A

2 If you **are cramming** for an examination, you are learning as much as possible in a short time just before you take the examination. V: OFT+*for*

crammed /kræmd/. If something is **crammed** with things or people, it is very full of them, so that there is hardly room for anything or anyone else. EG *The rooms were crammed with congressmen... ...a concrete bunker crammed full of radio equipment.* ADJ PRED+A

cramp /kræmp/, **cramps, cramping, cramped.** 1 If you have **cramp** or **cramps**, you feel a strong pain caused by a muscle suddenly contracting. EG *I had the most excruciating cramp in my leg... She had severe stomach cramps.* N UNCOUNT OR N PLURAL

2 If your behaviour **cramps** someone's **style**, it prevents them from impressing other people. EG *He was always butting in and saying the wrong thing and cramping her style.* PHRASE Informal

cramped /kræmpt/. A **cramped** room or building is not big enough for the people or things in it. EG *...bringing up children in cramped high-rise flats.* ADJ QUALIT

crane /kreɪn/, **cranes, craning, craned.** 1 A **crane** is a large machine that moves heavy things by lifting them in the air. N COUNT

2 A **crane** is also a kind of large bird with a long neck and long legs. N COUNT

3 If you **crane** your neck or head, you stretch your head in a particular direction in order to see or hear something better. EG *He craned his neck out of the window.* V OR V+O: USU+A

crank /kræŋk/, **cranks, cranking, cranked.** 1 If you call someone a **crank**, you mean that they have peculiar ideas and behave in a strange way. EG *I didn't want to be thought a crank.* N COUNT

2 A **crank** is also a device that you turn in order to make something move. EG *Brody began to turn the crank to reel in the fish.* N COUNT

3 If you **crank** something, you make it move by turning a handle. EG *She cranked down the window.* V+O: USU+A

cranky /kræŋkiˡ/, **crankier, crankiest.** If you describe ideas or ways of behaving as **cranky**, you mean that they are strange and slightly mad. EG *...a bachelor of cranky habits... ...a cranky old woman.* ADJ QUALIT Informal

cranny /kræniˡ/, **crannies.** A **cranny** is a very narrow opening in a wall or rock. EG *The fish have underwater crannies where they hide.* ● **every nook and cranny**: see **nook**. N COUNT

crash /kræʃ/, **crashes, crashing, crashed.** 1 A **crash** is an accident in which a moving car or other vehicle hits something and is badly damaged or destroyed. EG *Her mother was killed in a car crash.* N COUNT

2 If a moving car or other vehicle **crashes**, it hits something and is badly damaged or destroyed. EG *The plane crashed within seconds of taking off.* V OR V-ERG

3 If something **crashes** somewhere, it hits something else violently, making a loud noise. EG *The door crashed open.* V: USU+A

4 A **crash** is also a sudden, loud noise. EG *...a terrific crash of thunder.* N COUNT

5 The **crash** of a business or financial institution is its serious failure. EG *...one of the most spectacular financial crashes of the decade.* N COUNT: USU+SUPP

crash helmet, crash helmets. A **crash helmet** is a helmet that motor cyclists wear in order to protect their heads if they have an accident. N COUNT

crass /kræs/. Behaviour that is **crass** is stupid and insensitive. EG *I'm sorry I was so crass... Most Hollywood movies seemed crass and trivial.* ADJ QUALIT

crate /kreɪt/, **crates.** A **crate** is a large box used for transporting or storing things. EG *...a crate of oranges.... ...a crate of beer.* N COUNT OR N PART

crater /kreɪtə/, **craters.** A **crater** is a very large hole in the ground, which has been caused by something hitting it or by an explosion. EG *...bomb craters... ...the craters of the moon.* N COUNT

cravat /krəvæt/, **cravats.** A **cravat** is a piece of cloth which a man wears wrapped around his neck and tucked inside the collar of his shirt. N COUNT

crave /kreɪv/, **craves, craving, craved.** If you **crave** something or **crave** for it, you want to have it very much. EG *She craved luxury... ...finding the absolute security for which he had always craved.* V+O OR V+*for*

◊ **craving** /kreɪvɪŋ/, **cravings.** EG *Both the sisters had a craving for sweets... ...their powerful craving to succeed.* ◊ N COUNT: OFT+*for* OR *to*-INF

crawl /krɔːl/, **crawls, crawling, crawled.** 1 When you **crawl**, you move forward on your hands and knees. EG *Her baby is crawling about now.* V: USU+A

2 When an insect or a vehicle **crawls**, it moves very slowly. EG *A spider was crawling up my leg... The train crawled deeper into Russia.* V: USU+A

3 If you say that a place **is crawling** with people or things, you mean that it is full of them. EG *The forecourt was crawling with security men.* V: OFT+*with*; ONLY CONT

4 If something **makes** your **skin crawl**, it makes you feel horrified or revolted. EG *...a noise that made my skin crawl.* PHRASE Informal

5 If you **crawl** to someone, you try to please them in order to gain some advantage for yourself. V: OFT+*to* Informal

6 The **crawl** is a kind of swimming stroke which you do lying on your front, swinging one arm over your head, and then the other arm. See picture at SWIMMING. N SING : *the*+N

crayon /kreɪə^{7}n/, **crayons.** A **crayon** is a pencil containing coloured wax or clay. EG *...a box of crayons... They wanted to draw in crayon.* N COUNT OR N UNCOUNT

craze /kreɪz/, **crazes.** A **craze** is something that a lot of people show a strong interest in for a short time. EG *...the latest dance craze from America.* N COUNT : USU+SUPP

crazed /kreɪzd/. **Crazed** behaviour is wild and uncontrolled. EG *She fought with crazed ferocity.* ADJ QUALIT : ATTRIB

crazy /kreɪzi^{1}/, **crazier, craziest. 1** You say that someone is **crazy** when they talk or behave in a very strange or foolish way. EG *...a crazy American... My fellow students thought I was crazy... It's crazy to have a picnic in October.* ◇ **crazily.** EG *A man rushed past him shouting crazily.* ADJ QUALIT Informal ◇ ADV

2 If you are **crazy** about something, you are very enthusiastic about it. EG *They are crazy about football.* ADJ PRED +*about* OR ADJ AFTER N Informal

3 If something makes you **crazy** or drives you **crazy**, it makes you extremely annoyed or upset. EG *The tourists were beginning to drive me crazy.* ADJ PRED Informal

creak /kri:k/, **creaks, creaking, creaked.** If something **creaks**, it makes a harsh sound when it moves. EG *The door creaked... The lift creaks its way up the central tower.* ▸ used as a noun. EG *The creak of the mattress did not wake her.* ◇ **creaking.** EG *There was silence except for the creaking of the carriage.* V OR V+O+A ▸ N COUNT +SUPP ◇ N UNCOUNT OR N COUNT

creaky /kri:ki^{1}/, **creakier, creakiest.** Something that is **creaky** creaks when it moves. EG *He was careful on the creaky stairs.* ADJ QUALIT

cream /kri:m/, **creams, creaming, creamed. 1** **Cream** is a thick, yellowish-white liquid that is taken from milk. You can use it in cooking or pour it on fruit or puddings. EG *...strawberries and cream.* N UNCOUNT

2 Cream is also **2.1** an artificial substance that looks and tastes like cream. EG *...chocolates with cream fillings.* N UNCOUNT **2.2** a substance that you rub into your skin in order to make it soft. EG *She wiped the cream off her face.* N MASS

3 Something that is **cream** is of a yellowish-white colour. EG *The shell was deep cream touched here and there with pink.* ADJ COLOUR

4 You can refer to the best people or things in a group as the **cream** of the group. EG *They were the cream of their generation.* N SING : *the*+N +SUPP

cream off. If you **cream off** part of a group of people, you take them away and treat them in a special way, because you think that they are better than the others. EG *The best pupils would be creamed off and given a superior training.* PHRASAL VB : V+O+ADV

creamy /kri:mi^{1}/, **creamier, creamiest. 1** Something that is **creamy** is of a yellowish-white colour. EG *...a house made of creamy limestone.* ADJ COLOUR

2 Food or drink that is **creamy** contains a lot of cream. EG *...a nice cup of creamy coffee... ...rich creamy pastries.* ADJ QUALIT

crease /kri:s/, **creases, creasing, creased. 1** **Creases** are irregular lines that appear in cloth or paper when it has been crushed. EG *She smoothed down the creases in her dress.* N COUNT : USU PLURAL

2 If you **crease** cloth or paper or if it **creases**, lines appear in it because it has been crushed. ◇ **creased.** EG *His suit had become creased.* V-ERG ◇ ADJ QUALIT

3 If your face **creases** or if something **creases** it, lines appear on it because you are frowning. EG *A wrinkle of doubt creased her forehead.* ◇ **creased.** EG *His face was creased in thought.* V-ERG ◇ ADJ CLASSIF

create /kri:eɪt/, **creates, creating, created. 1** To **create** something means to cause it to happen or exist. EG *His work created enormous interest in England... They opened windows and doors to create a draught.* V+O

2 When someone **creates** a new product or process, they invent it or design it. EG *The industry responded by creating a new textile.* V+O

3 If you say that something **creates** a thought or feeling, you mean that it gives you this thought or feeling. EG *Your words create the most beautiful images.* V+O

creation /kri:eɪʃə^{0}n/, **creations. 1** The **creation** of something is the act of bringing it into existence. EG *They proposed the creation of Welsh and Scottish parliaments... ...a job creation scheme... ...the creation of visual images.* N UNCOUNT : OFT+*of*

2 In the Bible, the **Creation** is the making of the universe, earth, and creatures by God. N PROPER : *the*+N

3 People sometimes refer to the entire universe as **creation**. EG *They look upon everything in creation as material for exploitation.* N UNCOUNT

4 A **creation** is **4.1** something that has been made, especially a work of art. EG *...his ceramic creations.* **4.2** a thought or image produced in your mind. EG *...the creations of a frightened imagination.* N COUNT Literary

creative /kri:eɪtɪv/. **1** Someone who is **creative** has the ability to invent and develop original ideas, especially in art. **Creative** activities involve the inventing and developing of these ideas. EG *He has more time to be creative... I'd like to get involved in something creative... ...creative writing.* ◇ **creativity** /kri:eɪtɪvɪ^{1}ti^{1}/. EG *...adults who want to express their own creativity.* ADJ QUALIT ◇ N UNCOUNT

2 If you use something in a **creative** way, you use it in a new way that produces interesting and unusual results. ◇ **creatively.** EG *...the desire to use mathematics creatively.* ADJ QUALIT ◇ ADV

creator /kri:eɪtə/, **creators. 1** The **creator** of something is the person who made it or invented it. EG *The police were known as Peelers in honour of their creator, Sir Robert Peel... ...Kit Williams, the creator of the book 'Masquerade'.* N COUNT : USU+POSS

2 God is sometimes referred to as the **Creator**. EG *...a song of praise to the Creator.* N PROPER : *the*+N

creature /kri:tʃə/, **creatures. 1** A **creature** is a living thing that can move about, such as an animal, a bird, or an insect. EG *The opossum is a large rat-like creature... Worms are very simple creatures.* N COUNT

2 You can also use **creature** to talk about people. For example, if you call someone a stupid **creature** or a spiteful **creature**, you are emphasizing that they are stupid or spiteful. EG *She was a weak and helpless creature... ...a voluptuous creature with blonde bobbed hair.* N COUNT+SUF

crèche/kreʃ/, **crèches.** A **crèche** is a place where small children can be left and looked after while their parents are working. N COUNT

credence /kri:də^{0}ns/. If something gives or lends **credence** to a theory or story, it makes it easier to believe. EG *These latest discoveries give credence to Burke's ideas.* N UNCOUNT Formal

credentials /krɪ^{2}denʃə^{0}lz/. Your **credentials** are **1** your previous achievements, training, and general background, which indicate that you are qualified to do something. EG *I think he has established his credentials... His credentials as a journalist were beyond dispute.* N PLURAL : USU+SUPP Formal **2** a letter or certificate that proves your identity or qualifications. EG *Didn't you ask for his credentials?* N PLURAL Formal

credibility /kredɪ^{1}bɪlɪ^{1}ti^{1}/. If someone or something has **credibility**, people believe in them and trust them. EG *He felt that he had lost credibility... ...doubts about the credibility of the nuclear deterrent.* N UNCOUNT

credible /kredɪ^{1}bə^{0}l/. **1** Something that is **credible** can be believed. EG *His latest statements are hardly credible.* ADJ QUALIT

2 Someone who is **credible** is able to convince you that they can be trusted. EG *No politicians seem credible these days.* ADJ QUALIT

Do you think that a crematorium at night would be creepy?

credit /krɛdɪt/, **credits, crediting, credited. 1** If you are allowed **credit**, you are allowed to pay for goods or services several weeks or months after you have received them. EG *...the availability of cheap long-term credit... They sold grain on credit during times of famine.* N UNCOUNT

2 If someone or their bank account is **in credit**, their bank account has money in it. PHRASE

3 If you get the **credit** for something, people praise you for it. EG *Some of the credit should go to Nick... He deserves great credit for keeping them together.* N UNCOUNT: OFT+*for*

4 Credit is also used in these phrases. **4.1** If you say that something **does** someone **credit**, you mean that they should be respected or admired for it. EG *Your concern for us all does you the greatest credit.* **4.2** If someone says that something is **to** your **credit**, they mean that you deserve praise for it. EG *Price, to his credit, denounced in private the brutalities of the regime.* **4.3** If you already have one or more achievements **to** your **credit**, you have achieved them. EG *She already had several London successes to her credit.* PHRASES

5 If you **are credited** with an achievement or if it **is credited** to you, people believe that you were responsible for it. EG *...the woman who is often credited with originating the movement.* V+O +*with/to*: USU PASS

6 If you **give** someone **credit for** a good quality, you believe that they have it. EG *The public are more tolerant than they are often given credit for being.* PHRASE

7 If you cannot **credit** something, you cannot believe that it is true. EG *There must be many of you who find this case hard to credit.* V+O: NO CONT Formal

8 The list of people who helped to make a film, a record, or a television programme is called the **credits**. N PLURAL

creditable /krɛdɪtəbə⁰l/. **1** Something that is **creditable** is of a reasonably high standard. EG *He polled a creditable 44.8 per cent.* ADJ QUALIT

2 If you describe someone's behaviour as **creditable**, you mean that it should be respected or admired. EG *That, I think, was creditable on his part.* ADJ QUALIT

credit card, credit cards. A **credit card** is a plastic card that you can use to allow you to buy goods on credit or to borrow money. N COUNT

creditor /krɛdɪtə/, **creditors.** Your **creditors** are the people who you owe money to. N COUNT

credulity /krɪ²dju:lɪ¹ti¹/ is a willingness to believe that something is real or true. EG *Don't stretch my credulity too far.* N UNCOUNT Formal

credulous /krɛdjə⁴ləs/. If you are **credulous**, you are always ready to believe what people tell you, and are easily deceived. EG *...a well-meaning, credulous British officer.* ADJ QUALIT

creed /kri:d/, **creeds. 1** A **creed** is a set of beliefs, principles, or opinions that strongly influence the way people live or work. EG *They never embraced any particular creed... ...the free enterprise creed.* N COUNT

2 A **creed** is also a religion. EG *...the Christian creed.* N COUNT Formal

creek /kri:k/, **creeks.** A **creek** is **1** a narrow inlet where the sea comes a long way into the land. EG *...the muddy creeks of my home coast.* **2** a small stream or river. EG *By early summer the creek was almost dry.* N COUNT American

creep /kri:p/, **creeps, creeping, crept** /krɛpt/. **1** When people or animals **creep** somewhere, they move quietly and slowly. EG *I heard my landlady creeping stealthily up to my door.* V+A

2 If something **creeps** somewhere, it moves very slowly, so that you hardly notice that it is moving. EG *Here and there, little breezes crept over the water.* V+A Literary

3 If someone or something **gives** you **the creeps**, they make you feel uncomfortable, or rather frightened. EG *The thought gives me the creeps.* PHRASE Informal

4 If you call someone a **creep**, you mean that you dislike them very much, especially because they flatter people. EG *She's a cunning little creep.* N COUNT Informal

creep in. If something such as a custom **creeps in**, it gradually becomes used. EG *New gestures do occasionally manage to creep in.* PHRASAL VB: V+ADV

creep up on. 1 If you **creep up on** someone, you move slowly closer to them without being seen by them. **2** If a feeling or state **creeps up on** you, you hardly notice that you are about to experience it. EG *Senility is creeping up on me, I guess.* PHRASAL VB: V+ADV+PREP V+ADV+PREP

creeper /kri:pə/, **creepers.** A **creeper** is a plant with long stems that wind themselves around objects. EG *...an impenetrable tangle of creepers and trees.* N COUNT

creepy /kri:pi¹/, **creepier, creepiest.** Something that is **creepy** gives you a strange, unpleasant feeling of fear. EG *It was very creepy in the woods... We've found a creepy caravan where a witch lives.* ADJ QUALIT Informal

cremate /krɪ¹meɪt/, **cremates, cremating, cremated.** When someone **is cremated**, their dead body is burned, usually as part of a funeral service. EG *Her husband will be cremated.* V+O: USU PASS

cremation /kri¹meɪʃə⁰n/, **cremations. 1** A **cremation** is a funeral service during which a dead body is cremated. N COUNT

2 Cremation is the process of burning a dead body at a funeral. N UNCOUNT

crematorium /krɛmətɔ:rɪəm/, **crematoria** /krɛmətɔ:rɪə/ or **crematoriums.** A **crematorium** is a building in which the bodies of dead people are burned as part of a funeral service. N COUNT

crepe /kreɪp/ is **1** a thin fabric made of cotton, silk, or wool with an uneven, ridged surface. EG *...a pink crepe evening gown.* **2** a type of rubber with a rough surface. EG *...shoes with crepe soles.* N UNCOUNT

crept /krɛpt/ is the past tense and past participle of **creep.**

crescendo /krɪ²ʃɛndəʊ/, **crescendos.** A **crescendo** is **1** a noise that is getting louder or that is very loud. EG *The ovation rose in a new crescendo... The noise reached a crescendo.* **2** the time when something is at its most intense. EG *The clamour in the press was reaching a crescendo.* N COUNT Literary

crescent /krɛsə⁰nt, -zə⁰nt/, **crescents.** A **crescent** is **1** a street or row of houses that is built in a curve. EG *...Grosvenor Crescent.* **2** a curved shape that is wider in the middle than at its ends, like the shape of the moon during its first and last quarters. See picture at SHAPES. EG *There was a scar on her right arm, a jagged crescent of white.* N COUNT

crest /krɛst/, **crests. 1** The **crest** of a hill or a wave is the highest part of it. EG *We had reached the crest of the hill.* N COUNT: USU+POSS

2 A **crest** on a bird is a tuft of feathers on the top of its head. EG *The birds' crests are raised.* N COUNT

3 A **crest** is also a small picture or design that is the sign of a noble family, a town, or an organization. N COUNT

crestfallen /krɛstfɔ:lən/. Someone who looks **crestfallen** looks sad and disappointed about something. ADJ PRED

cretin /krɛtɪn/, **cretins.** If you call someone a **cretin**, you mean that they are very stupid; an offensive word. N COUNT

crevice /krɛvɪs/, **crevices.** A **crevice** is a narrow crack or gap in a rock. EG *Most of the year the insects are hidden in rock crevices.* N COUNT

crew /kru:/, **crews. 1** The people who work on and operate a ship, an aeroplane, or a spacecraft are called the **crew**. EG *The Captain ordered his crew to prepare for action... The 'Maine' carried a crew of three hundred and fifty.* N COLL

2 You also use **crew** to refer to people with special technical skills who work together on a task or project. EG *The TV crews couldn't film at night.* N COLL

crew cut, crew cuts. A **crew cut** is a man's hairstyle in which his hair is cut very short. EG *...an ex-colonel with a bushy moustache and a crew cut.* N COUNT

crewman /kru:mə[3]n/, **crewmen.** A **crewman** is a member of a crew. EG *One of the crewmen died... ...TV crewmen.*
N COUNT

crib /krɪb/, **cribs, cribbing, cribbed. 1** If you **crib**, you copy something that someone else has written and pretend that it is your own work. EG *The teacher thought we'd cribbed off each other.*
V OR V+O: OFT+*off/from* Informal

2 A **crib** is written information that someone uses dishonestly to help them in an examination.
N COUNT Outdated

3 A **crib** is also a baby's cot. EG *She used to throw her toys out of her crib.*
N COUNT American

crick /krɪk/, **cricks, cricking, cricked. 1** If you have a **crick** in your neck or in your back, you have a pain there caused by muscles becoming stiff.
N COUNT: USU SING

2 If you **crick** your neck or back, you injure it so that it becomes stiff and hurts.
V+O

cricket /krɪkɪt/, **crickets. 1 Cricket** is an outdoor game played between two teams. Players try to score points, called runs, by hitting a ball with a wooden bat. EG *I spent the afternoon watching cricket.*
N UNCOUNT

2 A **cricket** is a small jumping insect that produces sharp sounds by rubbing its wings together. EG *We lay in our tent listening to the crickets.*
N COUNT

cricketer /krɪkɪtə/, **cricketers.** A **cricketer** is a person who plays cricket.
N COUNT

crime /kraɪm/, **crimes. 1** A **crime** is an illegal action for which a person can be punished by law. EG *A crime has been committed... ...the crime of murder... ...a life of crime.*
N COUNT OR N UNCOUNT

2 You can also refer to an action which is morally wrong as a **crime**. EG *To waste good food is a crime against nature.*
N COUNT: OFT+*against*

criminal /krɪmɪnə[0]l/, **criminals. 1** A **criminal** is a person who has committed a crime. EG *...one of the country's ten most wanted criminals.*
N COUNT

2 Something that is **criminal** is **2.1** connected with crime. EG *He had done nothing criminal... ...a criminal offence.* ◊ **criminally.** EG *...the care of the criminally insane... ...criminally responsible for the loss of lives.* **2.2** morally wrong. EG *To refuse medical aid would be criminal.* ◊ **criminally.** EG *The pay was criminally poor.*
ADJ CLASSIF / ◊ SUBMOD / ADJ QUALIT / ◊ SUBMOD

criminology /krɪmɪnɒləd͡ʒi[1]/ is the scientific study of crime and criminals. ◊ **criminologist, criminologists.** EG *Death was caused by what the criminologists call a solid object.*
N UNCOUNT / ◊ N COUNT

crimson /krɪmzə[0]n/, **crimsons. 1** Something that is **crimson** is of a dark, purplish-red colour. EG *She was wearing a crimson dress.*
ADJ COLOUR

2 If a person goes **crimson**, their face becomes red because they are angry or embarrassed.
ADJ PRED

cringe /krɪnd͡ʒ/, **cringes, cringing, cringed. 1** If you **cringe**, you move away from someone or something because you are afraid of them. EG *She cringed against the wall.*
V: USU+A

2 You also say that people **cringe** when they are very embarrassed. EG *Cringing under the stares of passers-by, I tried to read my newspaper.*
V: USU+A

crinkle /krɪŋkə[0]l/, **crinkles, crinkling, crinkled.**

1 When something **crinkles** or when you **crinkle** it, it becomes slightly creased or folded. EG *His face crinkled into a smile.* ◊ **crinkled.** EG *...brown crinkled leaves.*
V-ERG / ◊ ADJ QUALIT

2 Crinkles are small creases or folds. EG *There were crinkles at the outer corners of his eyes.*
N COUNT: USU PLURAL

crinkly /krɪŋkli[1]/. Something that is **crinkly** has many small creases or folds. EG *Her bodice was made of crinkly material.*
ADJ QUALIT

cripple /krɪpə[0]l/, **cripples, crippling, crippled.**

1 If someone is a **cripple**, they cannot move their body properly because it is weak, injured, or affected by a disease.
N COUNT

2 If something **cripples** you, it seriously injures you so that you can never move properly again.
V+O

3 If something **cripples** an organization or system, it prevents it from working properly. EG *The government had done much to cripple national enterprise.*
V+O

crippled /krɪpə[0]ld/. Someone who is **crippled** cannot move their body properly because it is weak, injured, or affected by disease. EG *...his crippled mother... They will be crippled for life.*
ADJ CLASSIF

crippling /krɪplɪŋ/. **1** A **crippling** illness or disability severely damages your health or your body. EG *...the dread of crippling disablement.*
ADJ QUALIT: ATTRIB

2 Crippling prices or taxes have a serious harmful effect on a person's or country's financial situation.
ADJ QUALIT

crisis /kraɪsɪs/, **crises** /kraɪsi:z/. **1** A **crisis** is a serious or dangerous situation which could cause death or hardship to many people. *I was in Munich during the 1938 crisis... They've still got an economic crisis on their hands.*
N COUNT OR N UNCOUNT: OFT+SUPP

2 A **crisis** in someone's life is a time when they have serious personal problems and are extremely unhappy. EG *The anxiety of this personal crisis turned his hair white... Who can you turn to in time of crisis?*
N COUNT OR N UNCOUNT: OFT+SUPP

crisp /krɪsp/, **crisper, crispest; crisps. 1** Something that is **crisp** is hard or stiff, usually in a pleasant way. EG *...crisp bacon... ...crisp new bank notes... ...her crisp white blouse.*
ADJ QUALIT

2 Crisps are very thin slices of potato that have been fried until they are hard and crunchy. EG *...a packet of crisps.*
N COUNT: USU PLURAL British

3 You describe the air or the weather as **crisp** when it is pleasantly fresh, cold, and dry. EG *...a crisp October morning.*
ADJ QUALIT

4 You describe what someone says or writes as **crisp** when they do not say unnecessary things and sound efficient and perhaps unfriendly. EG *He sent off two crisp telegrams.* ◊ **crisply.** EG *'What did she want?' Etta said crisply. 'Money?'*
ADJ QUALIT / ◊ ADV

criss-cross /krɪskrɒs/, **criss-crosses, criss-crossing, criss-crossed. 1** If things **criss-cross**, they create a pattern of crossed lines. EG *Dozens of searchlights criss-crossed to pick out possible targets... ...the freeways that criss-cross the whole of Los Angeles.*
V OR V+O

2 A **criss-cross** pattern or design has lines crossing each other. EG *...light brown boots with criss-cross laces up the front.*
ADJ CLASSIF: ATTRIB

criterion /kraɪtɪərɪən/, **criteria** /kraɪtɪərɪə/. A **criterion** is a standard by which you judge or decide something. EG *My own criterion of success is the ability to work joyfully... Little agreement exists on the criteria for defining mental illness.*
N COUNT: OFT+*for/of*

critic /krɪtɪk/, **critics. 1** A **critic** is a person who writes reviews and expresses opinions about books, films, music, and art. EG *What did the New York critics have to say about the production?... ...television critics.*
N COUNT

2 Someone who is a **critic** of a person or system disapproves of them and criticizes them publicly. EG *The Minister returned to London to face his parliamentary critics... ...critics of the Trade Union Movement.*
N COUNT+SUPP

critical /krɪtɪkə[0]l/. **1** A **critical** time or situation is **1.1** extremely important. EG *This was a critical moment in his career... The twelve weeks of summer were critical to most of the restaurants and pubs.* ◊ **critically.** EG *The distribution of resources is critically important.* **1.2** very serious and dangerous. EG *...the critical state of the economy.* ◊ **critically.** EG *He became critically ill.*
ADJ QUALIT: OFT+*to* / ◊ ADV / ADJ CLASSIF / ◊ ADV

2 If you are **critical**, **2.1** you criticize something or someone. EG *He had long been critical of Conservative policy... Whole groups of nations adopted a more critical attitude towards apartheid.* ◊ **critically.** EG *She had mentioned the book critically to friends.* **2.2** you examine and judge something carefully. EG *...each player regarding the*
ADJ QUALIT: OFT+*of* / ◊ ADV / ADJ QUALIT: ATTRIB

On these pages, find two kinds of food.

other with critical interest. ◇ **critically.** EG *Eva looked at the picture critically... The problem should be analysed more critically.* ◇ ADV

criticism /krɪtɪsɪzəm/, **criticisms. 1 Criticism** is the expression of disapproval of someone or something. EG *The Government came in for severe criticism... Some fierce public criticism of the plan had been voiced.* N UNCOUNT

2 Criticism of a book, play, or other work of art is a serious examination and judgement of it. EG *She would write vivid and constructive criticism.* N UNCOUNT: OFT+SUPP

3 A **criticism** is a comment in which you say that someone or something has a particular fault. EG *One of the main criticisms against him is that he is lazy... I don't mean this as a criticism.* N COUNT

criticize /krɪtɪsaɪz/, **criticizes, criticizing, criticized;** also spelled **criticise.** If you **criticize** someone or something, you express your disapproval of them by saying what you think is wrong with them. EG *Please don't get angry if I criticize you... I criticized the path the government was taking... He was criticized for pursuing a policy of conciliation.* V+O: OFT+*for*

critique /krɪtiːk/, **critiques.** A **critique** is a written examination and judgement of a situation or of a person's work or ideas. EG *...an intelligent and incisive critique of our society.* N COUNT Formal

croak /krəʊk/, **croaks, croaking, croaked. 1** When animals or birds **croak**, they utter harsh, low sounds. EG *A bullfrog was croaking in the distance.* V
▸ used as a noun. EG *...the croak of a raven.* ▸ N COUNT

2 When someone **croaks** something, they say it in a hoarse, rough voice. EG *'Brandy,' he croaked... He croaked her name.* ▸ used as a noun. EG *His voice was a weak croak.* V, V+O, OR V+QUOTE ▸ N COUNT

crochet /krəʊʃɪ/, **crochets, crocheting, crocheted. Crochet** is a way of making clothes out of thread by using a needle with a small hook at the end. ▸ used as a verb. EG *She would patiently crochet complex patterns.* N UNCOUNT ▸ V+O OR V

crock /krɒk/, **crocks.** A **crock** is an earthenware pot or jar. N COUNT Outdated

crockery /krɒkəri/. The plates, cups, and saucers that you use at mealtimes are referred to as **crockery**. EG *...a sink overflowing with dirty crockery.* N UNCOUNT

crocodile /krɒkədaɪl/, **crocodiles.** A **crocodile** is a large reptile with a long body. Crocodiles live in rivers and eat meat. N COUNT

crocus /krəʊkəs/, **crocuses. Crocuses** are small white, yellow, or purple flowers that are grown in parks and gardens in the early spring. N COUNT

croissant /krwʌsɒŋ/, **croissants.** A **croissant** is a type of small bread-like cake that is eaten for breakfast. N COUNT

crony /krəʊni/, **cronies.** Your **cronies** are the friends who you spend a lot of time with. EG *He had a farewell drink with his cronies.* N COUNT: USU+POSS Informal

crook /krʊk/, **crooks, crooking, crooked. 1** A **crook** is a criminal. N COUNT Informal

2 If you call someone a **crook**, you mean that they are dishonest. EG *The accountants turned out to have been crooks... She called me a lousy crook.* N COUNT

3 The **crook** of your arm or leg is the soft inside part where you bend your elbow or knee. EG *She buried her face in the crook of her arm.* N COUNT: USU SING+*of*

4 If you **crook** your arm or finger, you bend it. V+O

5 A **crook** is also a long pole with a large hook at the end. EG *...a shepherd's crook.* N COUNT Outdated

crooked /krʊkɪd/. **1** Something that is **crooked** is bent or twisted. EG *My back is so crooked and painful that I cannot stand upright.* ADJ QUALIT

2 A **crooked** smile or grin is uneven and bigger on one side than the other. EG *He showed his small pearly teeth in a crooked grin.* ◇ **crookedly.** EG *The grey-haired man smiled crookedly.* ADJ QUALIT ◇ ADV

3 Someone who is **crooked** is dishonest or a criminal. EG *...a crooked cop.* ADJ QUALIT

croon /kruːn/, **croons, crooning, crooned. 1** If you **croon** something, you say it in a gentle voice. EG *'You little charmer,' he crooned.* V OR V+QUOTE

2 To **croon** also means to sing or hum quietly and gently. V OR V+O

crop /krɒp/, **crops, cropping, cropped. 1 Crops** are plants such as wheat and potatoes that are grown in large quantities for food. EG *The population is dependent upon a simple crop, wheat... ...vast fields of crops.* N COUNT: USU PLURAL

2 The plants that are collected at harvest time are referred to as a **crop**. EG *They get two crops of rice a year.* N COUNT: OFT+*of*

3 You can also refer to a group of people or things that have appeared together as a **crop**. EG *What do you think of the current crop of school-leavers?* N PART Informal

4 If your hair **is cropped**, it is cut very short. EG *Her grey hair was cropped close to her skull.* V+O: USU PASS
◇ **cropped.** EG *...a boy with closely cropped hair.* ◇ ADJ CLASSIF

5 When an animal such as a cow **crops** grass or leaves, it eats them. EG *Our goat was cropping the hedge.* V+O

crop up. If something **crops up**, it happens or appears unexpectedly. EG *I can come now, unless any other problems crop up... Has anything cropped up that we should talk about?* PHRASAL VB: V+ADV Informal

cropper /krɒpə/. If you say that someone **has come a cropper**, you mean that they have had an unexpected and embarrassing failure. PHRASE Informal

croquet /krəʊkɪ/ is a game in which the players use long-handled wooden mallets to hit balls through metal arches stuck in a lawn. N UNCOUNT

cross /krɒs/, **crosses, crossing, crossed; crosser, crossest. 1** If you **cross** something such as a room, a road, or an area of land, you move or travel to the other side of it. EG *He crossed the room slowly... I wanted to prove that a woman could cross a desert.* V+O

2 If you **cross** to a place, you go across an area of land or water in order to reach the place. EG *He stood up at once and crossed to the door... Where and how did you cross into Swaziland?* V: USU+A

3 Lines or roads that **cross** meet and go across each other. V+O OR V

4 If an expression **crosses** someone's face, it appears briefly on their face. EG *A flicker of unconcealed distaste crossed his features.* V+O Literary

5 If a thought **crosses** your **mind**, you think of it. EG *It had not crossed my mind to tell them I was leaving.* PHRASE

6 A **cross** is **6.1** a shape that consists of a vertical line with a shorter horizontal line across it. It is the most important Christian symbol. EG *She wore a tiny golden cross.* **6.2** a written mark in the shape of an X. You can use it, for example, to indicate that an answer to a question is wrong, or to mark the position of something on a map. See picture at SHAPES. EG *The reader has to indicate the answer with a cross or a tick.* N COUNT

7 If you **cross** your arms, legs, or fingers, you put one of them on top of the other. EG *She sat back and crossed her legs.* ● If you say that you **are crossing** your **fingers** about something, you mean that you are hoping that everything will happen as you want it to. EG *She just has to cross her fingers and hope.* V+O ● PHRASE Informal

8 Someone who is **cross** is rather angry. EG *He was looking very red and rather cross... We all get cross with our children.* ◇ **crossly.** EG *'Don't ask me,' the post office lady replied, crossly.* ADJ QUALIT: USU PRED ◇ ADV

9 Something that is a **cross** between two things is neither one thing nor the other, but a mixture of both. EG *A Barbary duck is a cross between a wild duck and an ordinary duck.* N COUNT +*between*: USU SING

cross off. If you **cross off** words on a list, you draw a line through them to indicate that they no longer belong on the list. EG *...crossing off those who were no longer interested.* PHRASAL VB: V+O+ADV/PREP

cross out. If you **cross out** words on a page, you PHRASAL VB: V+O+ADV draw a line through them, usually because they are wrong. EG *She saw her name and crossed it out.*

crossbar /krɒsbɑː/, **crossbars.** A **crossbar** is **1** a horizontal piece of wood attached to two upright pieces, for example the top part of the goal in the game of football. N COUNT **2** the horizontal metal bar between the handlebars and the saddle on a man's or boy's bicycle. See picture at BICYCLE.

cross-country. 1 If you go somewhere **cross-country**, you use paths or less important roads or railway lines, rather than the main routes. EG *...a cross-country bicycle trip... He walked cross-country to the hospital.* ADJ CLASSIF: ATTRIB, OR ADV AFTER VB

2 Cross-country is the sport of running across open countryside rather than along roads or around a running track. EG *He won a cup for cross-country in 1944... I'm in training for a cross-country run.* N UNCOUNT

cross-examine, cross-examines, cross-examining, cross-examined. If you **cross-examine** someone during a trial in a court of law, you question them about the evidence that they have already given. V+O ◇ **cross-examination, cross-examinations.** EG *Mr Fairbairn, in cross-examination, took the matter further.* ◇ N UNCOUNT OR N COUNT

cross-eyed. A person who is **cross-eyed** has eyes that seem to look towards each other. ADJ QUALIT

crossing /krɒsɪŋ/, **crossings. 1** A **crossing** is a journey by boat or ship to a place on the other side of a sea. EG *...the night ferry crossing to Esbjerg.* N COUNT

2 A **crossing** is also the same as a pedestrian crossing. EG *...light-controlled crossings.* N COUNT

cross-legged /krɒslɛgɪ¹d, krɒslɛgd/. If someone is sitting **cross-legged**, they are sitting on the floor with their legs bent so that their knees point outwards and their feet point inwards. ADV AFTER VB, OR ADJ CLASSIF

cross-purposes. If people are **at cross-purposes**, there is a misunderstanding between them because they are talking about different things without realizing it. EG *They are bound to be at cross-purposes.* PHRASE

cross-reference, cross-references. A **cross-reference** is a note in a book which tells you that there is relevant or more detailed information in another part of the book. N COUNT

crossroads /krɒsrəʊdz/. The plural form is also **crossroads**.

1 A **crossroads** is a place where two roads meet and cross each other. EG *You could change buses at Polegate crossroads.* N COUNT

2 If you say that something is **at a crossroads**, you mean that it has reached a very important stage in its development. EG *Ecology stands at a cross-roads at present.* PHRASE

cross-section, cross-sections. 1 A **cross-section** of something such as a group of people is a typical or representative sample. EG *It attracts a remarkable cross-section of the public.* N COUNT: USU SING+*of*

2 A **cross-section** of an object is what you would see if you could cut straight through the middle of it. EG *...a cross-section of a human brain.* N COUNT+SUPP

crossword /krɒswɜːd/, **crosswords.** A **crossword** or **crossword puzzle** is a word game in which you work out the answers to clues, and write the answers in the white squares of a pattern of small black and white squares. EG *I do the crossword on the back page first.* N COUNT

crotch /krɒtʃ/, **crotches. 1** Your **crotch** is the part of your body between the tops of your legs. EG *He is carrying a stack of books, which reach from the level of his crotch to just under his chin.* N COUNT

2 The **crotch** of a pair of trousers or pants is the part that covers the area between the tops of your legs. EG *There were grains of sand in the crotch of her swimming costume.* N COUNT: OFT+*of*

crotchety /krɒtʃɪ²ti¹/. Someone who is **crotchety** is grumpy and easily irritated. EG *...the most crotchety judge in Cape Town.* ADJ QUALIT Informal

crouch /kraʊtʃ/, **crouches, crouching, crouched. 1** If you **are crouching**, your legs are bent under you so that you are close to the ground and leaning forward slightly. EG *He crouched down among the tangled foliage... There was an enormous cat crouching on the counter.* V: USU+A

2 If you **crouch** over something, you bend over it so that you are very near to it. EG *Her stout form crouched over a typewriter.* V: USU+A

crow /krəʊ/, **crows, crowing, crowed. 1** A **crow** is a kind of large black bird which makes a loud, harsh noise. N COUNT

2 If you say that a place is a particular distance away **as the crow flies**, you mean that it is that distance away measured in a straight line. EG *It was only about eight miles as the crow flies.* PHRASE

3 When a cock **crows**, it utters a loud sound early in the morning. EG *The cocks crowed again.* V

4 If someone **crows** about something or **crows** over it, they keep telling people proudly about it; often used showing disapproval. EG *Now perhaps that is something to crow about.* V: USU +*about/over* Informal

crowbar /krəʊbɑː/, **crowbars.** A **crowbar** is a heavy iron bar which is used as a lever. N COUNT

crowd /kraʊd/, **crowds, crowding, crowded. 1** A **crowd** is **1.1** a large group of people who have gathered together. EG *The crowd was silent... She vanished into the crowd... ...crowds of tourists.* N COUNT OR N PART **1.2** a group of friends, or a set of people who share the same interests or occupation. EG *They were mostly women, the usual crowd.* N COUNT+SUPP Informal

2 When people **crowd** round someone or something, they gather closely together around them. EG *The boys crowded round him... We crowded round eagerly.* V+*round*

3 If a group of people **crowd** a place or **crowd** into it, they fill it completely. EG *Mobs of movie stars were crowding the bar... The TV men crowded in, examining our equipment.* V+O OR V+*in/into*

4 If you **crowd** things into a place, you put them into a space which is really too small for them. EG *He helped his dad crowd the animals into a truck.* V+O+*in/into*

crowded /kraʊdɪ²d/. **1** If a place is **crowded, 1.1** it is full of people. EG *The bar was very crowded... ...crowded pavements... The centre of Birmingham was crowded with shoppers.* ADJ QUALIT: OFT+*with* **1.2** a lot of people live there. EG *...crowded urban areas.* ADJ QUALIT

2 If your mind is **crowded**, it is full of thoughts or memories. EG *His mind was crowded with memories of his mother.* ADJ QUALIT: OFT+*with*

crown /kraʊn/, **crowns, crowning, crowned. 1** A **crown** is a circular ornament for the head, usually made of gold and precious jewels. Kings and queens wear crowns at official ceremonies. N COUNT

2 The monarchy of a particular country is referred to as the **Crown** when it is regarded as an institution rather than as an individual king or queen. EG *...a senior Minister of the Crown.* N PROPER: *the*+N

3 When someone **is crowned**, a crown is placed on their head as part of a ceremony in which they are officially made king or queen. EG *The Emperor was crowned by the Pope.* V+O OR V+O+C: USU PASS

4 If something **crowns** something else, it is on the top of it. EG *...the shattered rocks that crowned the hill.* V+O Literary

5 Your **crown** is the top part of your head, at the back. EG *The crown of his head is completely bald.* N COUNT: USU+POSS

6 An achievement, event, or quality that **crowns** something is the most successful, exciting, or beautiful part of it. EG *The evening was crowned by a dazzling performance from Maria Ewing.* V+O ◇ **crowning.** EG *...the crowning achievement of 16 years of research.* ◇ ADJ CLASSIF: ATTRIB

crucial /kruːʃə⁰l/. Something that is **crucial** is extremely important. EG *Success or failure here* ADJ QUALIT

What cross-references are there on these pages?

would be crucial to his future prospects. ◊ **crucially.** EG *The answer will depend crucially on the kind of data collected.* ◊ ADV

crucifix /kru:sıfıks/, **crucifixes.** A **crucifix** is a cross with a figure of Christ on it. N COUNT

crucifixion /kru:sıfıkʃəⁿn/, **crucifixions. 1 Crucifixion** is a way of killing people which was common in the Roman Empire, in which they were tied or nailed to a cross and left there to die. N UNCOUNT OR N COUNT

2 The **Crucifixion** was the death of Christ by this method. N PROPER: the+N

crucify /kru:sıfaı/, **crucifies, crucifying, crucified.** If someone **is crucified**, they are killed by being tied or nailed to a cross and left there to die. V+O

crude /kru:d/, **cruder, crudest. 1** Something that is **crude** is simple and unsophisticated. EG *...crude methods of administration.* ◊ **crudely.** EG *...crudely sewn shirts... The situation can be expressed, crudely, by a mathematical equation.* ◊ **crudity** /kru:dıti¹/. EG *...the crudity of the draughtsmanship in these sketches.* ADJ QUALIT; ◊ ADV; ◊ N UNCOUNT

2 Someone who is **crude** speaks or behaves in a rude and often offensive way. EG *Do you have to be so crude?* ADJ QUALIT

crude oil is oil that is in a natural state and has not yet been processed. N UNCOUNT

cruel /kru:əl/, **crueller, cruellest. 1** Someone who is **cruel** deliberately causes pain or distress to people or animals. EG *He was cruel to her... She had cruel parents.* ◊ **cruelly.** EG *They treated him cruelly.* ADJ QUALIT: OFT+*to*; ◊ ADV

2 A situation or action that is **cruel** is very harsh and causes people pain or distress. EG *They don't have the ability to survive in this cruel world.* ADJ QUALIT

cruelty /kruəlti¹/, **cruelties. Cruelty** is behaviour that deliberately causes pain or distress to people or animals. EG *...cruelty to animals... They suffered beatings and other cruelties.* N UNCOUNT OR N PLURAL

cruise /kru:z/, **cruises, cruising, cruised. 1** A **cruise** is a holiday during which you travel on a ship and visit a number of places. ▸ used as a verb. EG *They spent the summer cruising in the Greek islands.* N COUNT; ▸ V: USU+A

2 If a car or ship **cruises**, it moves at a constant speed that is comfortable and unhurried. EG *The taxi cruised off down the Cromwell Road.* V: USU+A

cruise missile, cruise missiles. A **cruise missile** is a missile which carries a nuclear warhead and which is guided by a computer. N COUNT

cruiser /kru:zə/, **cruisers.** A **cruiser** is **1** a motor boat which has a cabin for people to live or sleep in. **2** a large fast warship. N COUNT

crumb /krʌm/, **crumbs. 1 Crumbs** are very small pieces of bread, cake, or biscuit. N COUNT: USU PLURAL

2 A **crumb** of information or knowledge is a very small amount of it. EG *They eagerly gathered each crumb of information that he let drop.* N PART

crumble /krʌmbəⁿl/, **crumbles, crumbling, crumbled. 1** If you **crumble** something soft or brittle or if it **crumbles**, it breaks into a lot of little pieces. EG *The bread crumbled in my fingers... The flakes can be easily crumbled into small pieces.* V-ERG

2 When a building or cliff **crumbles**, it breaks into a lot of small pieces because it is old and is decaying. EG *The villages are crumbling into ruin.* V

3 When a society, organization, or relationship **crumbles**, it begins to fail or come to an end. EG *His first Labour Government crumbled.* ◊ **crumbling.** EG *We live in an age of crumbling values.* V; ◊ ADJ CLASSIF

crumbly /krʌmbli¹/, **crumblier, crumbliest.** Something that is **crumbly** is easily broken into a lot of little pieces. EG *...crumbly pastries.* ADJ QUALIT

crummy /krʌmi¹/, **crummier, crummiest.** If you say that something is **crummy**, you mean that it is of very bad quality. EG *...a crummy little flat.* ADJ QUALIT Informal

crumpet /krʌmpıt/, **crumpets.** A **crumpet** is a round, flat, bread-like cake with holes in one side. You toast crumpets and eat them with butter and jam. N COUNT

crumple /krʌmpəⁿl/, **crumples, crumpling, crumpled. 1** If you **crumple** paper or cloth or if it **crumples**, it is squashed and becomes full of untidy creases and folds. EG *He took the letter and crumpled it in his hand.* ◊ **crumpled.** EG *He was dressed in crumpled clothes.* V-ERG; ◊ ADJ QUALIT

2 If someone or something **crumples**, they collapse suddenly in an untidy and helpless way. EG *He crumpled into a heap... Daddy's face crumpled when she told him.* V: USU+A

crumple up. If you **crumple up** a piece of paper, you crush it into a ball. EG *She crumpled it up and threw it into the wastebasket.* PHRASAL VB: V+O+ADV

crunch /krʌntʃ/, **crunches, crunching, crunched. 1** If you **crunch** something hard such as a sweet, you crush it noisily between your back teeth. EG *He put seven or eight pieces into his mouth and began crunching them.* V+O

2 If you **crunch** gravel or glass or if it **crunches**, it makes a breaking or crushing noise when you step on it. EG *I crunched a wine glass underfoot.* ▸ used as a noun. EG *She could hear the crunch of footsteps on the gravel.* V-ERG; ▸ N COUNT +SUPP

3 You can say **'if it comes to the crunch'** or **'when the crunch comes'**, when you are considering what you would do if the situation became so serious that you were forced to take action. EG *When the crunch comes, we can cope alone.* PHRASE

crunchy /krʌntʃi¹/, **crunchier, crunchiest. 1** Food that is **crunchy** is hard or crisp so that it makes a noise when you eat it. EG *...crunchy vegetables.* ADJ QUALIT

2 Gravel or snow that is **crunchy** makes a noise when you step on it. ADJ QUALIT

crusade /kru:seıd/, **crusades, crusading, crusaded.** A **crusade** is a set of activities that you carry out over a period of time in support of a cause that you feel strongly about. EG *...the great crusade to fight and conquer cancer.* ▸ used as a verb. EG *We must crusade for better communication.* N COUNT+SUPP; ▸ V: USU+A

crusader /kru:seıdə/, **crusaders.** A **crusader** is someone who is involved in activities in support of a cause that they feel strongly about. EG *...a communist crusader.* N COUNT+SUPP

crush /krʌʃ/, **crushes, crushing, crushed. 1** If you **crush** something, **1.1** you press it very hard so that you break it or destroy its shape. EG *The jaws snapped shut, crushing bones and flesh.* **1.2** you make it into a powder by pressing and grinding it. EG *To get the oil out you will have to crush the seeds.* V+O

2 To **crush** an army or a political organization means to defeat it completely. EG *The government still think they can crush the unions.* ◊ **crushing.** EG *It was a crushing result for the Labour Party.* V+O; ◊ ADJ CLASSIF: ATTRIB

3 If an event or a piece of news **crushes** someone, it shocks them or upsets them very much. EG *He has been crushed by the experience.* ◊ **crushed.** EG *She saw that he was hurt and crushed.* ◊ **crushing.** EG *The lecture was interrupted by the crushing news of President Kennedy's death.* V+O; ◊ ADJ CLASSIF; ◊ ADJ CLASSIF: ATTRIB

4 If you **are crushed** against other people or things, you are pushed or pressed against them. EG *Women were crushed up against men.* V+O: USU PASS

5 A **crush** is a dense crowd of people. EG *A reporter made his way through the crush.* N COUNT

6 If you have a **crush** on someone, you have a strong feeling of attraction for them that does not usually last very long. EG *I had a crush on the violin master.* N COUNT: OFT+*on* Informal

crust /krʌst/, **crusts. 1** The **crust** on a loaf of bread is the hard, crispy outside part of it. N COUNT OR N UNCOUNT

2 A **crust** is also a hardened layer of something, especially on top of a softer or wetter substance. EG *The snow had a fine crust on it.* N COUNT: USU SING

3 The earth's **crust** is the outer layer of its surface. EG ...*movements of the earth's crust.* N COUNT+SUPP

crusted /krʌstɪ²d/. Something that is **crusted** with a substance is covered with a hard layer of it. EG *The lane was crusted with cow dung.* ADJ PRED: OFT+*with*

crusty /krʌstiˈ/, **crustier, crustiest.** Something that is **crusty** has a hard, crisp outside layer. EG ...*crusty bread.* ADJ QUALIT

crutch /krʌtʃ/, **crutches.** 1 A **crutch** is a support like a stick, which you lean on in order to help you to walk when you have injured your foot or leg. EG *She came walking in on crutches, her foot still in a cast.* N COUNT

2 If you refer to someone or something as a **crutch**, you mean that they give you help or support. EG *The book was simply a crutch to my memory.* N COUNT

3 A **crutch** is also the same as a crotch. N COUNT

crux /krʌks/. The **crux** of a problem or argument is the most important or difficult part of it which affects everything else. EG *Here we come to the crux of the matter.* N SING: USU *the*+N+*of*

cry /kraɪ/, **cries, crying, cried.** 1 When you **cry**, 1.1 you produce tears in your eyes, usually because you are unhappy or hurt. EG *Helen began to cry... 'Oh don't cry,' said Florrie.* ▸ used as a noun. EG *I think she had a good cry, for her eyes were rather red.* 1.2 you shout or say something loudly. EG *'Come on!' he cried... 'Oh look!' she cried, seeing the ticket.* V; ▸ N SING; V+QUOTE

2 A **cry** is 2.1 a loud, high sound that you make with your voice and that expresses a strong emotion such as fear, pain, or pleasure. EG *Claud let out a cry of horror.* 2.2 a shout, usually made in order to attract someone's attention. EG ...*battle cries... I heard a cry for help.* 2.3 the sound that some birds make. EG *A sea bird flapped upwards with a hoarse cry.* N COUNT: OFT+*of*; N COUNT+SUPP; N COUNT

3 Something that is **a far cry** from something else is very different from it. EG *The tropical grasslands are a far cry from the lush green pastures of Ireland.* PHRASE

cry off. If you **cry off**, you decide not to do something that you had arranged to do. EG *I'm afraid I cried off at the last moment.* PHRASAL VB: V+ADV Informal

cry out. If you **cry out**, 1 you call out loudly because you are frightened, unhappy, or in pain. EG *I heard Mary cry out in fright.* 2 you speak loudly. EG *'Father! You must stop that!' he suddenly cried out.* PHRASAL VB: V+ADV; V+ADV, OFT+QUOTE

cry out for. If you say that one thing **is crying out for** another, you mean that it needs that thing very much. EG *There is a vast surplus of workers crying out for employment.* PHRASAL VB: V+ADV+PREP

crypt /krɪpt/, **crypts.** A **crypt** is an underground room beneath a church or cathedral. N COUNT

cryptic /krɪptɪk/. A **cryptic** remark or message contains a hidden meaning or is difficult to understand. EG *I didn't ask what this cryptic remark was intended to convey.* ADJ QUALIT

crystal /krɪstəºl/, **crystals.** 1 A **crystal** is a mineral that has formed naturally into a regular symmetrical shape. EG *Pure copper is made up of layers of crystals.* N COUNT

2 **Crystal** is 2.1 a rock that is transparent like ice, often used in jewellery or ornaments. EG *The throne has a beautiful inlay of agate, onyx, and crystal.* 2.2 very high quality glass, usually with its surface cut so that it twinkles in the light. EG ...*a shimmering crystal chandelier.* N UNCOUNT

crystal clear. Something that is **crystal clear** is 1 absolutely clear and transparent like glass. EG ...*blue skies and crystal clear air.* 2 very easy to understand. EG *He challenged every point which he did not find crystal clear.* ADJ CLASSIF

crystallize /krɪstəºlaɪz/, **crystallizes, crystallizing, crystallized;** also spelled **crystallise.** 1 If you **crystallize** an opinion or idea or if it **crystallizes**, it becomes fixed and definite in your mind. EG *This involvement has helped me to crystallize my criticisms of the women's movement.* V-ERG

◊ **crystallization** /krɪstəºlaɪzeɪʃəºn/. EG ...*the crystallisation of our beliefs.* ◊ N UNCOUNT

2 If a substance **crystallizes**, it turns into crystals. EG *Eventually the sugar crystallises.* V

cub /kʌb/, **cubs.** A **cub** is a young wild animal such as a lion, wolf, or bear. EG ...*a two-month-old leopard cub.* N COUNT

cubby-hole /kʌbiˈ həʊl/, **cubby-holes.** A **cubby-hole** is a very small room or space for storing things. N COUNT Outdated

cube /kju:b/, **cubes, cubing, cubed.** 1 A **cube** is a solid object with six square surfaces which are all the same size. See picture at SHAPES. EG ...*cubes of bread.* N COUNT

2 The **cube** of a number is another number that is produced by multiplying the first number by itself twice. For example, the cube of 2 is 8. N COUNT: USU *the*+N+*of*

3 When a number **is cubed**, it is multiplied by itself twice; for example, 3 cubed is 3 x 3 x 3, which is 27. 3 cubed is usually written as 3^3. V+O: USU PASS

cubic /kju:bɪk/. You use **cubic** in units of volume to indicate that you are measuring length, width, and height. For example, a cubic metre is the equivalent of something a metre long, a metre high, and a metre wide. ADJ CLASSIF: ATTRIB

cubicle /kju:bɪkəºl/, **cubicles.** A **cubicle** is a small enclosed area in a public building such as a sports centre, which people use for dressing and undressing. N COUNT

cuckoo /kʊku:/, **cuckoos.** A **cuckoo** is a grey bird that has an easily recognizable call of two quick notes, and that lays its eggs in other birds' nests. N COUNT

cucumber /kju:kʌmbə/, **cucumbers.** A **cucumber** is a long, thin vegetable, often used raw in salads, that has a green skin and is white and moist inside. N COUNT

cud /kʌd/. When animals such as cows or sheep **chew the cud**, they slowly chew their partly digested food over and over again in their mouth before finally swallowing it. PHRASE

cuddle /kʌdəºl/, **cuddles, cuddling, cuddled.** If you **cuddle** someone, you put your arms round them and hold them close as a way of showing your affection. EG *A baby must be cuddled a lot.* ▸ used as a noun. EG *Give them a few cuddles and talk nicely to them.* V OR V+O: RECIP; ▸ N COUNT

cuddle up. If you **cuddle up** to someone, you sit or lie as near to them as possible and you hold them. EG *Jenny was cuddled up against me.* PHRASAL VB: V+ADV, USU+A Informal

cuddly /kʌdliˈ/. People, animals, or toys that are **cuddly** are soft or furry so that you want to cuddle them. EG ...*cuddly toys.* ADJ CLASSIF

cudgel /kʌdʒəºl/, **cudgels.** 1 A **cudgel** is a thick, short stick used for hitting people. N COUNT Outdated

2 If you **take up the cudgels** for someone or something, you speak or fight in support of them. EG *Brown took up the cudgels on his behalf.* PHRASE

cue /kju:/, **cues, cueing, cued.** 1 A **cue** is 1.1 something that is said or done by a performer that is a signal for another performer to begin speaking or doing something. EG *The violinist was late for her cue.* 1.2 anything that serves as a signal for some action. EG *The Director General stood up. It was Stuart's cue to depart.* N COUNT+SUPP

2 If you **take** your **cue** from someone, you use their behaviour as an indication of what you should do in a particular situation. EG *Michael took his cue from the Duke's tone.* PHRASE

3 If you say that something happened **on cue**, you are emphasizing that it happened just when it was expected to happen. EG *Then, right on cue, the coach broke down.* PHRASE

4 A **cue** that is used in games such as snooker, N COUNT

Is a culprit culpable?

billiards, and pool is a long, thin wooden stick with a leather tip at one end.

cuff /kʌf/, **cuffs, cuffing, cuffed. 1** A **cuff** is **1.1** the end part of a sleeve which is thicker than the rest of the sleeve. **1.2** the bottom part of a trouser leg, which is turned up. N COUNT; American

2 If you are speaking **off the cuff**, you are speaking spontaneously, without preparing what you are going to say. EG *I can't answer that question off the cuff.* PHRASE

3 If you **cuff** someone, you hit them with your hand, usually in a light, friendly way. EG *Sally cuffed my head lightly.* ▸ used as a noun. EG *...a cuff on the head.* V+O; ▸ N COUNT; Informal

cufflink /kʌflɪŋk/, **cufflinks. Cufflinks** are small decorative objects used for holding together shirt cuffs around the wrist. N COUNT : USU PLURAL

cuisine /kwɪzi:n/. **1** The **cuisine** of a country or district is the style of cooking which is characteristic of that area. EG *...the delights of the Paris cuisine.* N UNCOUNT +SUPP

2 The **cuisine** of a restaurant is the range of food that is served in it. N UNCOUNT +POSS

cul-de-sac /kʌldəsæk, kʊl-/, **cul-de-sacs.** A **cul-de-sac** is a short road which is closed at one end. N COUNT

culinary /kʌlɪnə^{0}ri^1/ means concerned with kitchens or cooking. EG *...their culinary skills.* ADJ CLASSIF : ATTRIB

cull /kʌl/, **culls, culling, culled. 1** If you **cull** ideas or information, you gather them together and choose which of them you need. EG *...materials that I'd culled from all sorts of places.* V+O : OFT+*from*

2 To **cull** animals means to kill the weaker animals in a group in order to reduce their numbers. EG *They start to cull the herds in dry years.* ▸ used as a noun. EG *...a big elephant cull in Zimbabwe.* V+O; ▸ N COUNT

culminate /kʌlmɪneɪt/, **culminates, culminating, culminated.** If a situation or process **culminates** in something, this thing happens after the situation or process has gradually developed. EG *The struggle between King and Parliament had culminated in the Civil War.* V+*in*

culmination /kʌlmɪneɪʃə^{0}n/. The **culmination** of a situation or process is what happens as its final result. EG *Marriage is seen as the culmination of a successful relationship.* N UNCOUNT : USU *the*+N+*of*

culpable /kʌlpəbə^{0}l/. If someone is **culpable**, they are responsible for something wrong or unpleasant that has happened. EG *Was Hearst culpable? To what extent?* ADJ PRED; Formal

culprit /kʌlprɪt/, **culprits. 1** A **culprit** is someone who has committed a crime or done something wrong. EG *The main culprits were caught and heavily sentenced.* N COUNT

2 If you say that a particular thing is the **culprit**, you mean that it is the cause of problems or trouble. EG *Fat is a major culprit in causing cancers of the bowel.* N COUNT

cult /kʌlt/, **cults. 1** A **cult** is a religious group which worships a particular person or performs particular rituals, especially one which is considered strange or unnatural. EG *The 'Moonies' cult gained adherents at an alarming rate.* N COUNT : USU SING+*of*

2 A particular person, object, or activity that is a **cult** has become very popular or fashionable. EG *The Beatles became the heroes of a world-wide cult.* N COUNT : USU SING

cultivate /kʌltɪveɪt/, **cultivates, cultivating, cultivated. 1** If you **cultivate** land, you prepare it and grow crops on it. EG *He retired to his estate near Bordeaux to cultivate his vineyard.* V+O
◇ **cultivated.** EG *Only 1 per cent of the cultivated area was under irrigation.* ◇ ADJ CLASSIF
◇ **cultivation** /kʌltɪveɪʃə^{0}n/. EG *Some extra land is being brought under cultivation in Asia.* ◇ N UNCOUNT

2 If you **cultivate** a feeling, idea, or attitude, you try hard to develop it and make it stronger. EG *He was anxious to cultivate the trust of moderate Tories.* ◇ **cultivation.** EG *...the cultivation of good taste.* V+O; ◇ N UNCOUNT +*of*

3 If you **cultivate** someone, you try hard to develop a friendship with them. EG *Their cooperation is vital, so cultivate them assiduously.* V+O

cultivated /kʌltɪveɪtɪ^{2}d/. **1** Someone who is **cultivated** has had a good education, and shows this in their behaviour. EG *...his cultivated Southern English accent.* ADJ QUALIT

2 Cultivated plants have been developed for growing on farms or in gardens. EG *...cultivated wheat... ...cultivated mushrooms.* ADJ CLASSIF : ATTRIB

cultural /kʌltʃə^{0}rəl/ means **1** relating to a particular society and its ideas, customs, and art. EG *... cultural traditions of great antiquity.* ◇ **culturally.** EG *They had little in common culturally with us.* ADJ CLASSIF : ATTRIB; ◇ ADV **2** involving or concerning the arts. EG *...cultural activities such as plays, concerts, and poetry readings.* ◇ **culturally.** EG *...an elegant and culturally vital life.* ADJ CLASSIF : ATTRIB; ◇ ADV+ADJ

culture /kʌltʃə/, **cultures. 1 Culture** consists of the ideas, customs, and art that are produced by a particular society. EG *He was specially interested in culture and history... ...African culture.* N UNCOUNT OR N COUNT : OFT+SUPP

2 A **culture** is a particular society or civilization, especially considered in relation to its ideas, art, or way of life. EG *We must respect the practices of cultures different from our own.* N COUNT+SUPP

3 In science, a **culture** is a group of bacteria or cells which are grown in a laboratory as part of an experiment. EG *...blood cultures.* N COUNT : USU+SUPP

cultured /kʌltʃəd/. Someone who is **cultured** has good manners, is well educated, and knows a lot about the arts. EG *...a highly cultured man.* ADJ QUALIT

culture shock is a feeling of anxiety, loneliness, and confusion that people sometimes experience when they first arrive in another country. N UNCOUNT

-cum- is placed between two words to form a compound noun describing something or someone as being partly one thing and partly another. EG *...a dining-cum-living room.*

cumbersome /kʌmbəsəm/. **1** Something that is **cumbersome** is large and heavy and therefore difficult to carry, wear, or handle. EG *...a cumbersome piece of machinery.* ADJ QUALIT

2 An activity, process, or system that is **cumbersome** is very complicated and inefficient. EG *The process is cumbersome and inflexible.* ADJ QUALIT

cumulative /kju:mjə^{4}lətɪv/. Something that is **cumulative** keeps increasing steadily in quantity or degree. EG *It was an accelerating, cumulative process.* ADJ CLASSIF

cunning /kʌnɪŋ/. **1** Someone who is **cunning** has the ability to plan things cleverly, often by deceiving other people. EG *He knew nothing of the cunning means employed to get him out of his job.* ADJ QUALIT

2 Someone who has **cunning** has the ability to plan things cleverly, often by deceiving other people. EG *They achieved their aim by stealth and cunning.* N UNCOUNT

cup /kʌp/, **cups, cupping, cupped. 1** A **cup** is a small, round container, usually with a handle, from which you drink liquids such as tea and coffee. EG *...a china cup.* N COUNT

2 You can use **cup** to refer to the contents of a cup, as in a **cup** of tea or a **cup** of coffee. EG *I've just made some tea. Would you like a cup?... I had a cup of hot flavourless coffee.* N PART

3 A **cup** is also **3.1** something which is small, round, and hollow in shape like a cup. EG *....an egg cup... She tipped a pile of raisins into the cup of his hand.* N COUNT : USU+SUPP **3.2** a prize of a large metal cup that is given to the person or team that wins a game or competition. EG *...runner-up for the King's Cup.* N COUNT

4 If you **cup** something in your hands, you hold it with your hands touching all round it. EG *....his hands were cupped around his lighter.* V-ERG : USU+A

cupboard /kʌbəd/, **cupboards.** A **cupboard** is a piece of furniture which has one or two doors at the front and usually shelves inside it. It is used for keeping things in. EG *...a well-stocked kitchen cupboard.* N COUNT

cupful /kʌpfʊl/, **cupfuls.** A **cupful** is the amount which one cup can hold. EG *...a cupful of rice.* N PART

curable /kjʊərəbə°l/. If a disease or illness is **curable**, it can be cured. ADJ CLASSIF

curate /kjʊərə¹t/, **curates.** A **curate** is a clergyman in the Church of England who helps the vicar or rector of a parish. N COUNT

curative /kjʊərətɪv/ is used to describe something that can cure people's illnesses or problems. EG *...the curative power of herbal remedies.* ADJ CLASSIF: ATTRIB

curator /kjʊə°reɪtə/, **curators.** A **curator** is someone who is in charge of the objects or works of art in a museum or art gallery. N COUNT: OFT+*of*

curb /kɜːb/, **curbs, curbing, curbed. 1** If you **curb** something, you control it and keep it within fixed limits. EG *...proposals to curb the powers of the Home Secretary.* V+O ▸ used as a noun. EG *This requires a curb on public spending.* ▸ N COUNT: OFT+*on*

2 If you **curb** someone, you act firmly to control them and make them behave properly. EG *Children whose instincts are to rebel often get curbed by their teachers.* V+O

3 See also **kerb**.

curd /kɜːd/, **curds. Curds** are the thick white substance which is formed when milk turns sour. N COUNT: USU PLURAL

curdle /kɜːdə°l/, **curdles, curdling, curdled.** If milk **curdles** or if something **curdles** it, it becomes sour. • See also **bloodcurdling**. V-ERG

cure /kjʊə/, **cures, curing, cured. 1** If doctors or medical treatments **cure** an illness or injury, they make it end or disappear. EG *There are few diseases that these modern drugs cannot cure.* V+O ▸ used as a noun. EG *I'm interested in the cure of cancer.* ▸ N COUNT: OFT+*of*

2 If doctors or medical treatments **cure** a person, they make the person well again after an illness or injury. EG *Her patients appear to be cured.* V+O

3 A **cure** for an illness is a medicine or other treatment that cures people suffering from the illness. EG *There's no known cure for a cold.* N COUNT: OFT+*for*

4 If someone or something **cures** a problem, they remove it. EG *The bishop had done nothing to cure the widespread lack of faith.* V+O ▸ used as a noun. EG *The only cure for her unhappiness was to leave home.* ▸ N COUNT: OFT+*for*

5 If an action or event **cures** someone of a habit or an attitude, it makes them give it up. EG *The shock of losing my purse cured me of my former carelessness.* V+O+*of*

6 If food, tobacco, or animal skin **is cured**, it is treated by being dried, smoked, or salted so that it will last for a long time. V-ERG ◇ **cured.** EG *...cured ham.* ◇ ADJ CLASSIF

cure-all, cure-alls. A **cure-all** is something that people think will solve all their problems. EG *Lowering of interest rates has been presented by the media as a kind of universal cure-all.* N COUNT

curfew /kɜːfjuː/, **curfews. 1** A **curfew** is a law stating that people must stay inside their houses after a particular time at night, for example during a war. EG *An emergency curfew was enforced.* N COUNT

2 Curfew is the time after which you will be punished if you are found outside your house when there is a curfew. EG *He had gone into a shop ten minutes after the curfew to buy some tobacco.* N UNCOUNT OR N COUNT

curio /kjʊərɪəʊ/, **curios.** A **curio** is an object such as a small ornament which is unusual and fairly rare. N COUNT

curiosity /kjʊərɪɒsɪ¹ti¹/, **curiosities. 1 Curiosity** is a desire that someone has to know about things and to learn as much as possible about them. EG *She looked at me, eyes wide open and full of curiosity... She showed an insatiable curiosity for my past.* N UNCOUNT

2 A **curiosity** is something that is unusual, interesting, and fairly rare. EG *...old but natural curiosities like fossils... ...a little curiosity shop.* N COUNT

curious /kjʊərɪəs/. **1** Someone who is **curious** is interested in things and eager to learn as much as possible about them. EG *She was curious to see what would happen... He seemed awfully curious about Robertson's day-to-day routine.* ADJ QUALIT ◇ **curiously.** EG *They stopped and looked at her curiously.* ◇ ADV

2 Something that is **curious** is **2.1** unusual and interesting. EG *Not long after our arrival, a curious thing happened.* ADJ QUALIT ◇ **curiously.** EG *She had a curiously husky voice.* ◇ ADV **2.2** difficult to explain because you cannot understand why it happens or what causes it. EG *It is curious how two such different problems can be solved so similarly.* ADJ QUALIT ◇ **curiously.** EG *Curiously, Hearst worked energetically during his mental breakdown.* ◇ ADV SEN

curl /kɜːl/, **curls, curling, curled. 1 Curls** are lengths of hair that are shaped in tight curves and circles. EG *...a little girl with golden curls.* N COUNT: USU PLURAL

2 Hair that has **curl** has waves or curls in it. EG *He now wore his hair shorter and it had lost its curl.* N UNCOUNT

3 A **curl** is a curved, spiral shape. EG *...curls of smoke.* N COUNT: USU+SUPP

4 If something **curls** or if you **curl** it, it has tight curves in it or it becomes tightly curved. EG *Her hair curled about her head like a child's... The bark was curling and falling away from the trunk... Her hands were curled around the cup.* V-ERG: OFT+A

5 If something **curls** somewhere, it moves in circles or spirals. EG *Smoke was curling out of kitchen chimneys.* V+A

6 If an animal **curls** itself **into a ball**, it moves into a position which makes a rounded shape. PHRASE

curl up. 1 If you **curl up**, you lie down and bring your arms, legs, and head in towards your stomach. EG *He was lying curled up with his back to us.* PHRASAL VB: V+ADV **2** When something flat such as a leaf or a piece of paper **curls up**, its edges bend up or towards the centre, usually because it is old. V+ADV

curler /kɜːlə/, **curlers. Curlers** are small plastic or metal tubes that women roll their hair round in order to make it curly. EG *She took her curlers out.* N COUNT: USU PLURAL

curly /kɜːli¹/, **curlier, curliest. 1** Hair that is **curly** is full of curls. ADJ QUALIT

2 Something that is **curly** is curved, circular, or spiral in shape. EG *What are these curly bits of paper for?* ADJ QUALIT Informal

currant /kʌrənt/, **currants. 1 Currants** are small dried grapes, used especially in cakes. N COUNT: USU PLURAL

2 You use **currant** to refer to several different soft fruits, such as blackcurrants or redcurrants. EG *The currant bushes were heavy with fruit.* N COUNT

currency /kʌrənsi¹/, **currencies. 1** The **currency** of a country is **1.1** the system of money that is used in it. EG *Sterling has once again become one of the stronger currencies.* N COUNT: USU+SUPP **1.2** the coins and banknotes that are used in it. EG *Do you change foreign currency?* N UNCOUNT

2 If ideas, expressions, and customs have **currency**, they are used and accepted by many people at a particular time. EG *They have seen many of their basic ideas gain wide currency.* N UNCOUNT Formal

current /kʌrənt/, **currents. 1** A **current** is **1.1** a steady and continuous flowing movement of some of the water in a river, lake, or sea. EG *The child had been swept out to sea by the current.* N COUNT **1.2** a steady flowing movement of air. N COUNT

2 An electric **current** is a flow of electricity through a wire or circuit. EG *There was a powerful electric current running through the wires.* N COUNT

3 A **current** of opinion or behaviour is a general tendency within a group of people to adopt a particular opinion or way of behaving. EG *...the fickle currents of fashion.* N COUNT+SUPP

4 Something that is **current** is happening, being done, or being used at the present time. EG *Our current methods of production are too expensive... The conversation shifted onto what is current in art and music.* ADJ CLASSIF ◇ **currently.** EG *...experiments currently in progress.* ◇ ADV

What currency is used in your country?

5 Ideas, expressions, and customs that are **current** are generally accepted and used by most people. EG *The words 'light pollution' are in current use only among astronomers.* ADJ CLASSIF

current account, current accounts. A **current account** is a personal bank account which you can take out money from at any time using your cheque book or cheque card. N COUNT British

current affairs are political and social events which are discussed in newspapers and on television and radio programmes. EG *...the BBC's current affairs programmes.* N PLURAL

curriculum /kərɪkjə[4]ləm/, **curriculums** or **curricula** /kərɪkjə[4]lə/. A **curriculum** is 1 all the different courses of study that are taught in a school, college, or university. EG *Social studies have now been added to the curriculum.* 2 one particular course of study that is taught in a school, college, or university. EG *...our English curriculum.* N COUNT

curriculum vitae /kərɪkjə[4]ləm viːtaɪ/. Your **curriculum vitae** is a brief written account of your personal details, your education, and the jobs you have had. You are often asked to send a curriculum vitae when you are applying for a job. N SING : OFT+POSS

curried /kʌrɪd/. **Curried** food has been flavoured with hot spices. EG *...curried eggs.* ADJ CLASSIF : ATTRIB

curry /kʌri[1]/, **curries. Curry** is an Indian dish made with hot spices. EG *...a vegetable curry.* N MASS

curse /kɜːs/, **curses, cursing, cursed. 1** If you **curse**, you swear or say rude words because you are angry about something. EG *He missed the ball and cursed violently.* V ▸ used as a noun. EG *With a curse he disentangled his head from the netting.* ▸ N COUNT

2 If you **curse** someone, you say insulting things to them because you are angry with them. EG *I was cursing him under my breath for his carelessness.* V+O : OFT+*for*

3 If you **curse** something, you complain angrily about it, especially using rude language. EG *Cursing my plight, I tried to find shelter for the night.* V+O

4 If you say that there is a **curse** on someone, you mean that there seems to be a supernatural power causing unpleasant things to happen to them. EG *There is a curse on this family.* N COUNT : OFT+*on/upon*

5 You can also refer to something or someone that causes a great deal of trouble or harm as a **curse**. EG *Loneliness in old age is the curse of modern society.* N COUNT+SUPP

cursed /kɜːsɪd, kɜːst/. **1** Someone who is **cursed** is suffering as the result of a curse. EG *The descendants of Ham were cursed for ever.* ADJ CLASSIF

2 If you are **cursed** with something, you are very unlucky in having it. EG *...a land cursed with almost continuous rainfall.* ADJ PRED +*with*

cursory /kɜːsə[0]ri[1]/. A **cursory** glance or examination is a brief one in which you do not pay much attention to detail. EG *They signed with only a cursory glance at what I had written.* ADJ QUALIT : USU ATTRIB

curt /kɜːt/, **curter, curtest.** If someone is **curt**, they speak in a brief and rather rude way. EG *He had been curt with Gertrude.* ADJ QUALIT ◇ **curtly.** EG *Marsha said curtly, 'You're supposed to be on watch.'* ◇ ADV ◇ **curtness.** EG *His tone was characterised by curtness and dryness.* ◇ N UNCOUNT

curtail /kə[5]teɪl/, **curtails, curtailing, curtailed.**

1 If you **curtail** something, you reduce it. EG *Countries are under pressure to curtail public expenditure.* V+O

2 If you **curtail** someone's power or freedom, you restrict it. EG *...further legislation to curtail basic union rights.* V+O

curtailment /kə[5]teɪlmə[2]nt/. The **curtailment** of something is the act of reducing or restricting it. EG *...the curtailment of military aid from the US.* N UNCOUNT +SUPP Formal

curtain /kɜːtə[0]n/, **curtains, curtaining, curtained. 1** A **curtain** is a piece of material which hangs from the top of a window. You pull it across the window when you want to keep light out or prevent people from seeing you. EG *He drew the curtains.* N COUNT : USU PLURAL

2 In a theatre, the **curtain** is the large piece of material that hangs in front of the stage until a performance begins. EG *There was a burst of applause as the curtain went up.* N SING : *the*+N

3 You can refer to something as a **curtain** when it hangs down thickly and is difficult to see through or get past. EG *A dense curtain of reeds stretches across the water... ...an impenetrable curtain of blonde hair.* N UNCOUNT +SUPP

curtain off. If you **curtain off** part of a room, you separate it from the rest of the room by hanging a curtain across the room. PHRASAL VB : V+O+ADV

curtained /kɜːtə[1]nd/. A **curtained** window, door, or other opening has a curtain hanging across it. EG *The curtained stage was empty.* ADJ CLASSIF

curtsy /kɜːtsi[1]/, **curtsies, curtsying, curtsied;** also spelled **curtsey.** When a woman or a girl **curtsies**, she lowers her body briefly, bending her knees and holding her skirt with both hands, as a way of showing respect for an important person. EG *The ladies curtsied deeply to him.* V : OFT+*to* ▸ used as a noun. EG *I bobbed him a curtsy.* ▸ N COUNT

curve /kɜːv/, **curves, curving, curved. 1** A **curve** is a smooth, gradually bending line, for example part of the edge of a circle. EG *The beach stretched away before them in a gentle curve.* N COUNT

2 When something **curves, 2.1** it has the shape of a curve. EG *The lane curved round to the right.* **2.2** it moves in a curve, for example through the air. EG *The missile curved gracefully towards its target.* V+A

curved /kɜːvd/. A **curved** object has the shape of a curve. EG *...the curved tusks of a walrus.* ADJ QUALIT

curvy /kɜːvi[1]/ means the same as curved. EG *...a settee with only one curvy end.* ADJ QUALIT

cushion /kʊʃə[0]n/, **cushions, cushioning, cushioned. 1** A **cushion** is **1.1** a fabric case filled with soft material, which you put on a seat to make it more comfortable. N COUNT **1.2** a soft pad or barrier, especially one that stops something hitting something else violently. EG *The device floats on a cushion of air.* N COUNT+SUPP

2 If objects **cushion** a collision, they are between the things that hit each other and therefore make the collision less violent. EG *The pile of branches cushioned his fall.* V+O

3 To **cushion** the effect of something unpleasant means to reduce it. EG *A cut in income tax would cushion the blow of sharp price increases.* V+O ▸ used as a noun. EG *...that reassuring cushion of economic growth.* ▸ N COUNT +SUPP

cushy /kʊʃi[1]/, **cushier, cushiest.** A **cushy** job or task is very easy. EG *...that nice cushy job in the bank.* ADJ QUALIT Informal

custard /kʌstəd/ is a sweet yellow sauce made from milk and eggs or from milk and a powder. You eat custard with fruit and puddings. EG *...jelly and custard.* N UNCOUNT

custodial /kʌstəʊdɪəl/ means relating to the custody of people in prison. EG *...offences which called for custodial sentences.* ADJ CLASSIF Formal

custodian /kʌstəʊdɪən/, **custodians.** A **custodian** is someone who is in charge of a building or the objects in a building such as a museum. N COUNT

custody /kʌstədi[1]/. **1 Custody** is the legal right to keep and look after a child, especially the right given to the child's father or mother when they become divorced. EG *Divorce courts usually award custody to mothers.* N UNCOUNT

2 Someone who is **in custody** has been arrested and is being kept in prison until they can be tried in a court. EG *...people who have been quite wrongly held in custody.* PHRASE

custom /kʌstə[0]m/, **customs. 1** A **custom** is **1.1** a traditional activity or festivity. EG *My wife likes all the old English customs.* N COUNT **1.2** something that the people of a society always do in particular circumstances because it is regarded as the right thing to do. EG *It is the custom to take chocolates or fruit when visiting a patient in hospital.* N COUNT OR N UNCOUNT **1.3** something N COUNT : USU+POSS that someone usually does in a particular situation or at a particular time. EG *It is Howard's custom to take his class for coffee afterwards.*

2 **Customs** is the place at a border, airport, or harbour where people arriving from a foreign country have to declare goods that they bring with them. EG *At Kennedy airport I went through the customs... ...a customs officer.* N UNCOUNT OR N MOD

3 **Custom** is the practice of regularly buying things from a particular shop or tradesman. EG *Many local services depend on the University's custom.* N UNCOUNT Formal

customary /kʌstəmə^{r}ri^1/. 1 Something that is **customary** is usually done in a particular situation or at a particular time. EG *...the customary Christmas party.* ◇ **customarily.** EG *...the civil exchange of letters which customarily marks the departure of a minister.* ADJ CLASSIF ◇ ADV

2 Someone's **customary** behaviour is their usual behaviour. The **customary** way of doing something is the usual way of doing it. EG *Peter had never seen her so shaken out of her customary calm... She was rewarded in the customary way.* ADJ CLASSIF : ATTRIB

3 The **customary** time for something is the time at which it usually happens or is usually done. EG *At the customary hour the doctor knocked on my door.* ADJ CLASSIF : ATTRIB

customer /kʌstəmə/, **customers.** 1 A **customer** is someone who buys something, especially from a shop. EG *She's one of our regular customers.* N COUNT

2 You can use **customer** when you are describing someone's behaviour. For example, if you describe someone as an awkward **customer**, you mean that you think they deliberately behave in a way which causes other people trouble. N COUNT : ADJ+N Informal

custom-made. Something that is **custom-made** is made for you according to your special requirements. EG *...custom-made cars.* ADJ CLASSIF

cut /kʌt/, **cuts, cutting.** The form **cut** is used in the present tense and is the past tense and past participle of the verb.

1 If you **cut** something, you push a knife or a similar tool into it in order to remove a piece of it or to mark it or damage it. EG *She cut the cake and gave me a piece... His wife killed herself by cutting her wrists.* ▸ used as an adjective. EG *...thinly cut rye bread.* ▸ used as a noun. EG *He made a deep cut in the wood.* V+O ▸ ADJ CLASSIF ▸ N COUNT

2 If you **cut** yourself, you accidentally injure yourself on a sharp object so that you bleed. EG *Robert cut his knee quite badly.* ▸ used as a noun. EG *I had some cuts and bruises but I'm OK.* V-REFL OR V+O ▸ N COUNT

3 To **cut** through something means to move or pass through it easily. EG *The big canoe was cutting through the water.* V+*through*

4 If you **cut** across or through a place, you go through it because it is the shortest route to another place. EG *I cut across country for the next hundred miles.* V+*across/through*

5 If you **cut** the amount of something, you reduce it. EG *She cut her costs by half.* ▸ used as a noun. EG *...a tax cut... ...large cuts in government spending.* V+O ▸ N COUNT : USU+SUPP

6 If you **cut** part of something that someone has written, you do not print or broadcast it. EG *Her publishers insisted on cutting several stories out of her memoirs.* ▸ used as a noun. EG *He agreed to make a few minor changes and cuts in the play.* V+O : USU+A ▸ N COUNT : USU PLURAL

7 If you **cut** something, especially someone's hair, you shorten it using scissors or another tool. EG *Tell him to get his hair cut.* ▸ used as a noun. EG *He is having a cut and blow-dry.* V+O ▸ N COUNT

8 Well **cut** clothes have been well designed and well made. EG *He wears beautifully cut suits.* ADJ CLASSIF

9 If you **cut** a pack of playing cards, you divide it into two. V+O

10 A **cut** of meat is a large piece of meat which is ready for cooking. N COUNT

11 A person or thing that is **a cut above** other people or things of the same kind is better than them. EG *The meals they serve are a cut above most pub food.* PHRASE

12 See also **cutting.**

cut across. If an issue or problem **cuts across** the division between two groups of people, it affects or matters to people in both groups. EG *Issues, however, tended to cut across party lines.* PHRASAL VB : V+PREP

cut back. If you **cut back** something such as expenditure or **cut back on** it, you reduce it. EG *Congress cut back the funds... Other countries have cut back on high-priced oil.* ● See also **cutback.** PHRASAL VB : V+O+ADV, V+ADV+PREP, OR V+ADV

cut down. 1 If you **cut down** on an activity, you do it less often. EG *She had cut down on smoking... Heavy drinkers must be prepared to cut down.* 2 If you **cut** a tree **down**, you cut through its trunk so that it falls to the ground. PHRASAL VB : V+ADV, OFT+*on* V+O+ADV

cut in. If you **cut in** on someone, you interrupt them when they are speaking. EG *Mrs Travers began a reply, but Mrs Patel cut in again.* PHRASAL VB : V+ADV, OFT+QUOTE

cut off. 1 If you **cut** something **off**, you remove it by cutting it. EG *Lexington cut off a small piece of meat... ...egg sandwiches with the crusts cut off.* 2 To **cut** someone or something **off** means to separate them from things that they are normally connected with. EG *The town was cut off... We have cut ourselves off from the old ways of thinking.* ▸ used as an adjective. EG *Mary feels cut off from the central life of the village... She is completely cut off from friends.* 3 If a supply of something **is cut off**, it stops being provided. EG *Gas supplies had now been cut off... They are threatening to cut off funds.* 4 If you **cut** someone **off** when they are having a telephone conversation, you disconnect them. 5 See also **cut-off.** PHRASAL VB : V+O+ADV; V+O+ADV, OFT+*from*; ▸ ADJ PRED : OFT+*from*; V+O+ADV; V+O+ADV

cut out. 1 If you **cut out** part of something, you remove it using a tool with a sharp edge. EG *Badly decayed timber should be cut out and replaced.* 2 If you **cut out** something that you are doing or saying, you stop doing or saying it. EG *Cut out waste... He's cut out the drinking altogether.* 3 If you **cut** someone **out** of an activity or event, you do not allow them to be involved in it. EG *I don't think I should be cut out of the trip.* 4 If an object **cuts out** the light, it is between you and the light so that you are in the dark. 5 If an engine **cuts out,** it suddenly stops working. EG *It keeps cutting out when I stop.* 6 If you are **cut out** for a particular type of work, you have the qualities that will make you able to do it. EG *I'm not really cut out for this job.* 7 See also **cut-out.** ● to **have your work cut out**: see **work.** PHRASAL VB : V+O+ADV; V+O+ADV; V+O+ADV, OFT+*of*; V+O+ADV; V+ADV; PHRASE

cut up. If you **cut** something **up**, you cut it into several pieces. EG *She cut up her piece of cheese.* ● See also the separate entry **cut up.** PHRASAL VB : V+O+ADV

cut-and-dried. A **cut-and-dried** answer or solution is clear and obvious. EG *There is no cut-and-dried formula which can answer these questions.* ADJ QUALIT

cutback /kʌtbæk/, **cutbacks.** A **cutback** is a reduction in something, especially in the number of people that a firm or organization employs. EG *In the defence industries sudden cutbacks are common... ...the cutback in public services.* N COUNT : OFT+*in*

cute /kju:t/, **cuter, cutest.** If you describe someone or something as **cute**, you mean that you think they are very pretty or attractive. EG *What a cute little girl.* ADJ QUALIT American

cut glass is glass that has patterns cut into its surface. EG *...a cut-glass bowl.* N UNCOUNT OR N MOD

cutlery /kʌtləri^1/. The knives, forks, and spoons that you eat your food with are referred to as **cutlery.** N UNCOUNT

cutlet /kʌtlə^{2}t/, **cutlets.** A **cutlet** is 1 a small piece of meat which is usually fried or grilled. EG *...veal cutlets.* 2 vegetables or nuts that are fried or grilled together in a small lump. EG *...a nut cutlet.* N COUNT

Would you be cut up by a cutting remark?

cut-off, cut-offs. A **cut-off** or a **cut-off** point is the level or limit at which you decide that something should stop happening. N COUNT OR N MOD

cut-out, cut-outs. 1 A **cut-out** is an automatic device that turns off a motor, for example because there is something wrong with it. EG *...a cut-out to prevent the battery from overcharging.* N COUNT
2 A cardboard **cut-out** is a shape that has been cut from card. EG *...a cut-out of a girl.* N COUNT

cut-price. You use **cut-price** to describe something that is for sale at a reduced price. EG *We enjoy going shopping and taking advantage of cut-price offers.* ADJ CLASSIF

cutter /kʌtə/, **cutters.** A **cutter** or a pair of **cutters** is a tool that you use for cutting through something. EG *...a glass cutter... ...a pair of wire cutters.* N PLURAL OR N COUNT

cut-throat. You use **cut-throat** to describe situations in which people all want the same thing and do not care if they harm each other in getting it. EG *...cut-throat competition... ...a cut-throat advertising battle.* ADJ QUALIT

cutting /kʌtɪŋ/, **cuttings. 1** A **cutting** is a piece of writing which has been cut from a newspaper or magazine. EG *...press cuttings.* N COUNT
2 A **cutting** from a plant is a part of the plant, for example a leaf, that you cut and use in order to grow a new plant. EG *They are easy roses to grow from cuttings.* N COUNT
3 A **cutting** remark is unkind and likely to hurt someone's feelings. EG *Does this sound cutting? It's not meant to be.* ADJ QUALIT

cut up. If you are **cut up** about something that has happened, you are very unhappy because of it. EG *She's still terribly cut up about his death.* • See also the phrasal verb **cut up** at the entry for **cut**. ADJ PRED Informal

CV /siː viː/, **CV's. CV** is an abbreviation for 'curriculum vitae'.

cwt, cwts. cwt can also be used as the plural form. **cwt** is an abbreviation for 'hundredweight'. EG *...75 cwt of wheat.*

cyanide /saɪənaɪd/ is a highly poisonous substance. N UNCOUNT

cycle /saɪkəᵒl/, **cycles, cycling, cycled. 1** If you **cycle**, you ride a bicycle. EG *I decided to cycle into town.* ◇ **cycling.** EG *We recommend cycling as a good form of exercise.* V: USU+A ◇ N UNCOUNT
2 A **cycle** is **2.1** a bicycle. **2.2** a motorcycle. N COUNT
3 A **cycle** is also **3.1** a series of events or processes that is repeated again and again, always in the same order. EG *...the endless cycle of the seasons.* N COUNT+SUPP
3.2 a single complete series of movements in an electrical, electronic, or mechanical process. EG *...50 cycles per second.* N COUNT **3.3** a series of songs or poems that are intended to be performed or read one after the other. N COUNT+SUPP

cyclic /saɪklɪk, sɪklɪk/ means the same as cyclical. EG *...a cyclic process.* ADJ CLASSIF

cyclical /sɪklɪkəᵒl/. A **cyclical** process happens again and again in cycles. EG *...cyclical fluctuations in investment.* ADJ CLASSIF

cyclist /saɪklɪst/, **cyclists.** A **cyclist** is someone who rides a bicycle. N COUNT

cyclone /saɪkləʊn/, **cyclones.** A **cyclone** is a violent storm in which air circulates rapidly in a clockwise direction. N COUNT

cygnet /sɪgnəˀt/, **cygnets.** A **cygnet** is a young swan. N COUNT

cylinder /sɪlɪndə/, **cylinders.** A **cylinder** is **1** a shape or an object with flat circular ends and long straight sides. See picture at SHAPES. **2** a piece of machinery with this shape, especially one in an engine in which a piston moves backwards and forwards. EG *...a five cylinder engine.* N COUNT

cylindrical /sɪlɪndrɪkəᵒl/. Something that is **cylindrical** is in the shape of a cylinder. EG *...a cylindrical pipe.* ADJ CLASSIF

cymbal /sɪmbəᵒl/, **cymbals.** A **cymbal** is a flat circular brass object that is used as a musical instrument. You hit it with a stick or hit two cymbals together, making a loud noise. See picture at MUSICAL INSTRUMENTS. EG *...the clashing of the cymbals.* N COUNT: USU PLURAL

cynic /sɪnɪk/, **cynics.** A **cynic** is someone who believes that people always behave in a selfish way. EG *Pareto was a cynic, disillusioned by the society of his day.* N COUNT

cynical /sɪnɪkəᵒl/. Someone who is **cynical** or who has **cynical** attitudes believes that people always behave in a selfish way. EG *You are taking a rather cynical view of marriage.* ◇ **cynically.** EG *Grant smiled cynically.* ADJ QUALIT ◇ ADV

cynicism /sɪnɪsɪzəᵒm/ is an attitude towards people in which you always expect them to act in a selfish way. EG *The mood of political cynicism and despair deepened.* N UNCOUNT

cypher /saɪfə/. See **cipher**.

cypress /saɪprəs/, **cypresses.** A **cypress** is a type of evergreen tree. N COUNT

cyst /sɪst/, **cysts.** A **cyst** is a growth containing liquid that appears inside your body or under your skin. N COUNT

D d

D, d /diː/, **Ds, d's. 1 D** is the fourth letter of the English alphabet. N COUNT
2 d was a written form of 'penny' or 'pence' in Britain before decimal currency was introduced in 1971.

-'d. In spoken English and in informal written English, **-'d** is **1** a short form of 'would'. EG *She'd be sure to see it... I knew there'd be trouble.* **2** a short form of 'had', especially when 'had' is an auxiliary verb. EG *I'd heard it many times.*

dab /dæb/, **dabs, dabbing, dabbed. 1** If you **dab** a substance onto a surface, you put it there with quick, light, strokes. If you **dab** a substance from a surface, you remove it with quick, light strokes. EG *She dabbed some powder on her nose... He dabbed the cuts with disinfectant... He gently dabbed the sweat from Joe's upper lip.* V+O+A
2 A **dab** of something is a small amount of it that is put onto a surface. EG *She returned wearing a dab of rouge on each cheekbone.* N PART
3 If you are a **dab hand** at something, you are very good at doing it. EG *She is a dab hand at finding excuses for their mistakes.* PHRASE Informal British

dabble /dæbəᵒl/, **dabbles, dabbling, dabbled.** If you **dabble** in an activity or subject, you take part in it or study it a bit, but not very seriously. EG *They dabble in politics.* V+*in*

dad /dæd/, **dads.** People often call their father **dad**. EG *Hey, Dad, what's for dinner?... My dad doesn't like her.* VOCATIVE OR N COUNT Informal

daddy /dædi¹/, **daddies.** Children often call their father **daddy**. EG *Daddy, why do we grow old?... My daddy is a policeman.* VOCATIVE OR N COUNT Informal

daffodil /dæfədɪl/, **daffodils.** A **daffodil** is a yellow trumpet-shaped flower that blooms in the spring. N COUNT

daft /dɑːft/, **dafter, daftest.** Someone or something that is **daft** is stupid or not sensible. EG *Don't be daft.* ADJ QUALIT Informal

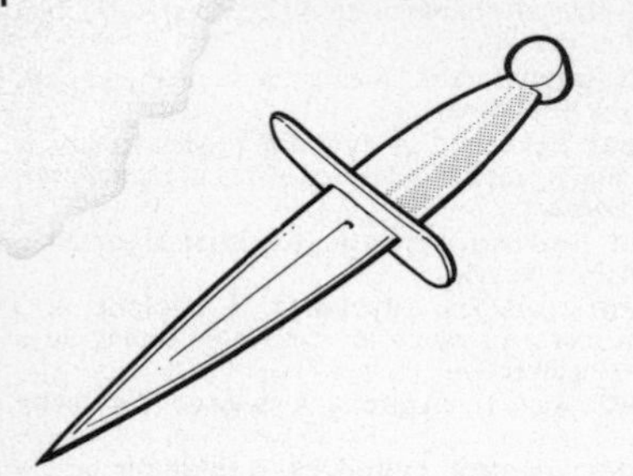

dagger /dægə/, **daggers.** A **dagger** is a weapon like a knife with two sharp edges. N COUNT

daily /deɪli¹/, **dailies. 1** If something happens **daily**, it happens every day. EG *He wrote to her almost daily... Fights are a daily hazard... ...Margaret's daily visits.* ADV OR ADJ CLASSIF : ATTRIB

2 Daily also means relating to a single day or to one day at a time. EG *Daily wage rates were around two dollars... ...the daily routine of the jail.* ADJ CLASSIF : ATTRIB

3 A **daily** newspaper or a **daily** is a newspaper that is published every day of the week except Sunday. ADJ CLASSIF : ATTRIB OR N COUNT

dainty /deɪnti¹/, **daintier, daintiest.** A **dainty** movement, person, or object is small, neat, or pretty. EG *...walking with neat, dainty steps... ...a dainty little girl... ...a dainty cup with flowers painted on it.* ◊ **daintily.** EG *She raised a plump arm, fingers daintily extended.* ADJ QUALIT ◊ ADV

dairy /deəri¹/, **dairies. 1** A **dairy** is **1.1** a shop or company that sells milk, butter, and cheese. **1.2** a building on a farm where milk is kept or where cream, butter, and cheese are made. N COUNT

2 Dairy is used to refer to **2.1** foods such as butter and cheese that are made from milk. EG *...dairy products.* **2.2** the use of cattle to produce milk rather than meat. EG *He owns a dairy herd of 105 cattle.* N MOD

dais /deɪɪs/. A **dais** is a raised platform in a hall. EG *As I stepped up on the dais, the Chief rose to greet me.* N SING

daisy /deɪzi¹/, **daisies.** A **daisy** is a small wild flower with a yellow centre and white petals. N COUNT

dam /dæm/, **dams, damming, dammed. 1** A **dam** is a wall that is built across a river in order to stop the flow of the water and make a lake behind it. N COUNT

2 To **dam** a river means to build a dam across it. V+O

dam up. To **dam up** a river means to dam it or block it. PHRASAL VB : V+O+ADV

damage /dæmɪdʒ/, **damages, damaging, damaged. 1** To **damage** something means **1.1** to harm or spoil it physically, for example by breaking it. EG *A fire had severely damaged part of the school.* V+O **1.2** to have a harmful effect on it, for example by making it weaker or less successful. EG *Unofficial strikes were damaging the British economy.* V+O ◊ **damaging.** EG *The incident was damaging to his career and reputation.* ◊ ADJ QUALIT : OFT+*to/for*

2 Damage is **2.1** physical harm that is caused to something. EG *It can cause lethal damage to the liver.* **2.2** a harmful effect that something has on something else. EG *He could not repair the damage done to the party's standing and credibility.* N UNCOUNT : OFT+*to*

3 When a court of law awards **damages** to someone, it orders money to be paid to them by a person who has harmed their reputation or property, or who has injured them. EG *He finally got £4,000 in damages.* N PLURAL

damask /dæməsk/ is a type of heavy cloth with a pattern woven into it. N UNCOUNT

dame /deɪm/, **dames. 1** A **dame** is a woman. EG *The dame wore a veil... Remember, some of these dames are very powerful in movies, they can get you work.* N COUNT Informal American

2 In Britain, **Dame** is a title given to a woman as a special honour because of important service or work that she has done. EG *...Dame Flora Robson.*

dammit /dæmɪt/. See **damn**.

damn /dæm/. **1 Damn, damn it**, and **dammit** are swear words which people sometimes use to express anger or annoyance. EXCLAM

2 The swear word **damn** is also used for emphasis. EG *I knew damn well what he was going to say.* SUBMOD ▸ used as an adjective. EG *We kept tripping over pieces of wood which some damn fool had left lying about.* ▸ ADJ CLASSIF : ATTRIB Informal

3 If you say that someone does not **give a damn** or does not **care a damn** about something, you mean that they do not care about it at all. PHRASE Informal

damnation /dæmneɪʃəⁿn/. According to some religions, if someone suffers **damnation**, they are condemned to stay in hell for ever after death because of their sins. EG *...eternal damnation.* N UNCOUNT

damned /dæmd/. **1 Damned** is a swear word that some people use, especially when they are angry, to emphasize what they are saying. EG *I don't know what you're talking about, and I'm damned sure you don't either.* ▸ used as an adjective. EG *He's a damned nuisance.* SUBMOD ▸ ADJ CLASSIF : ATTRIB

2 If you say that you **are damned if** you are going to do something, you mean that you do not intend to do it and think it is unreasonable for someone to expect you to do it. PHRASE Informal

3 You can say **I'll be damned** or **Well, I'm damned** when you are expressing surprise at something. EXCLAM Informal

4 According to some religions, the **damned** are people who have been condemned to stay in hell for ever after they have died. N PLURAL : *the*+N

damning /dæmɪŋ/. Something that is **damning** suggests very strongly that someone is guilty of a crime or error. EG *I was getting the type of damning evidence I was looking for.* ADJ QUALIT

damp /dæmp/, **damper, dampest; damps, damping, damped. 1** Something that is **damp** is slightly wet. EG *The building was cold and draughty and damp... She wiped the table with a damp cloth.* ◊ **dampness.** EG *...the cold and dampness of winter.* ADJ QUALIT ◊ N UNCOUNT

2 Damp is slight wetness in the air or on the inside walls of a house. EG *The paint had not fully covered the damp on the walls.* N UNCOUNT

damp down. To **damp** something **down** means to reduce its liveliness, violence, or urgency. EG *Neighbouring countries had been of no help in damping down the crisis.* PHRASAL VB : V+O+ADV

dampen /dæmpəⁿn/, **dampens, dampening, dampened. 1** To **dampen** something means to reduce its energy, liveliness, or violence. EG *The prospect of an election in no way dampened his spirits.* V+O

2 If you **dampen** something, you make it slightly wet. EG *He dampens his face, then dries it.* V+O

damson /dæmzəⁿn/, **damsons.** A **damson** is a small, sour purple plum. N COUNT

dance /dɑːns/, **dances, dancing, danced. 1** When you **dance**, you move around in time to music. EG *John danced with Julie... ...girls dancing the can-can.* ◊ **dancing.** EG *The music and dancing lasted for hours.* V OR V+O ◊ N UNCOUNT

2 A **dance** is **2.1** a series of steps and rhythmic movements which you do in time to music. EG *Before we knew it, we were doing this dance.* **2.2** a N COUNT

What is the difference between a place that is damp and a place that is dank?

piece of music which people can dance to. **2.3** a social event where people can dance with each other. EG *I hated the big formal dances at college.* ● to make a **song and dance** about something: see **song**.

3 Dance is the activity of performing dances, especially as a public entertainment. EG *They are supreme artists of dance and theatre.* N UNCOUNT

4 If you **dance** from one place to another, you jump and skip as you go along, usually because you are happy or excited. EG *Ralph danced out into the street.* V+A

5 If you say that something **dances**, you mean that it moves about lightly and quickly. EG *The little metal boxes dance and vibrate.* ◇ **dancing.** EG *The fires cast dancing shadows upon their faces.* V : USU+A; ◇ ADJ CLASSIF : ATTRIB

dancer /dɑːnsə/, **dancers. 1** A **dancer** is a person who earns money by dancing, or a person who is dancing. EG *He always wanted to be a dancer.* N COUNT

2 If someone is a good **dancer**, they dance well. N COUNT

dandelion /dændə[1]laɪən/, **dandelions.** A **dandelion** is a wild plant which has yellow flowers first, then fluffy balls of seeds. N COUNT

dandruff /dændrə[9]f/ refers to small white pieces of dead skin that are in someone's hair or that fall from their hair. EG *Miss Travers has dandruff.* N UNCOUNT

danger /deɪndʒə/, **dangers. 1 Danger** is the possibility that someone may be harmed or killed. EG *The child is too young to understand danger... My friends were round me. I was in no danger.* N UNCOUNT

2 A **danger** is something or someone that can hurt or harm you. EG *Cigarette smoking is a danger to health... They warned us of the dangers of making assumptions.* N COUNT

3 If there is a **danger** that something unpleasant will happen, it is possible that it will happen. EG *There was a danger that she might marry the wrong man... There is no danger of fire.* N UNCOUNT +SUPP

dangerous /deɪndʒə[0]rəs/. Something that is **dangerous** is able or likely to hurt or harm you. EG *...a dangerous animal... It is dangerous to drive with a dirty windscreen.* ◇ **dangerously.** EG *She was dangerously close to the fire.* ADJ QUALIT; ◇ ADV

dangle /dæŋgə[0]l/, **dangles, dangling, dangled.** When something **dangles** or when you **dangle** it, it hangs or swings loosely. EG *Huge wooden earrings dangled from her ears... Charlie was leaning across my desk dangling the long roll of paper.* V-ERG

dank /dæŋk/, **danker, dankest.** A place that is **dank** is unpleasantly damp and cold. EG *I slept in the dank basement room.* ADJ QUALIT

dapper /dæpə/. A man who is **dapper** has a very neat and clean appearance, and is small or slim. ADJ QUALIT

dappled /dæpə[0]ld/. Something that is **dappled** has dark or light patches on it, or is made up of patches of light and shade. EG *...dappled leafy sunlight.* ADJ CLASSIF Literary

dare /dɛə/, **dares, daring, dared. Dare** is used both as a main verb and as a semi-modal. For information about semi-modals, see the entry headed SEMI-MODALS.

1 If you **dare** to do something, you have enough courage to do it. EG *She did not dare to look at him... He dared not show that he was pleased... I can't do that – I simply wouldn't dare.* V+*to*-INF, OR SEMI-MODAL : USU WITH BROAD NEG

2 If you say **don't you dare** do something, you are angrily telling someone not to do it. EG *Don't you dare throw it away.* PHRASE

3 You say **how dare you** when you are very shocked and angry about something that someone has done. EG *How dare you speak to me like that!* PHRASE

4 If you say **I dare say** or **I daresay**, you mean that you think something is probably true. EG *I daresay you've spent all your money by now... It's worth a few pounds, I dare say, but no more.* PHRASE

5 If you **dare** someone to do something dangerous or frightening, you suggest that they do it to show how brave they are. EG *He looked round fiercely, daring them to contradict.* V+O : USU+*to*-INF

6 A **dare** is a challenge which one person makes to another to do something dangerous or frightening. EG *It was many years since James had accepted a dare.* N COUNT : USU SING

daren't /dɛənt/ is the usual spoken form of 'dare not'.

daresay /dɛəseɪ/. See paragraph 4 of **dare**.

daring /dɛərɪŋ/. **1** Someone who is **daring** does things which might be dangerous or which might shock people. EG *He was the most daring of contemporary writers of fiction... ...a daring raid.* ◇ **daringly.** EG *One of the boys very daringly bent down and touched it.* ADJ QUALIT; ◇ ADV

2 Daring is the courage to do things which might be dangerous or which might shock people. EG *...the efficiency and daring shown by our armed forces.* N UNCOUNT

dark /dɑːk/, **darker, darkest. 1** When it is **dark**, there is not enough light to see properly. EG *Luckily it was too dark for anyone to see me blushing... The room was dark and empty.* ◇ **darkness.** EG *The lights went out and the hall was plunged into darkness.* ADJ QUALIT; ◇ N UNCOUNT

2 The **dark** is the lack of light in a place. EG *He was sitting in the dark at the back of the theatre.* N SING : *the*+N

3 If you do something **before dark**, you do it before the sun sets. If you do something **after dark**, you do it when night has begun. EG *I want to get there before dark.* PHRASE

4 Something that is **dark** is a colour that is quite near black. EG *...a man in an elegant dark suit... ...long dark hair... ...dark red curtains.* ADJ QUALIT

5 Someone who is **dark** has brown or black hair, and often brown skin as well. EG *He was a tall, dark, and undeniably handsome man.* ADJ QUALIT

6 A **dark** period of time is unpleasant or frightening. EG *...the dark days of high unemployment.* ADJ QUALIT : ATTRIB

7 Dark looks or remarks make you think that the person giving them wants to harm you or that something horrible is going to happen. ◇ **darkly.** EG *Another of the men hinted darkly that there would be violence.* ADJ QUALIT : ATTRIB; ◇ ADV

8 If you are **in the dark** about something, you do not know anything about it. PHRASE

darken /dɑːkə[0]n/, **darkens, darkening, darkened. 1** If a place or the sky **darkens** or **is darkened**, it becomes darker, for example because it is nearly night. EG *The autumn sky darkened.* V-ERG

2 When you **darken** something or when it **darkens**, it becomes darker in colour. EG *Rub in linseed oil to darken the wood... His hair was darkened by the rain.* V-ERG

3 If someone's face **darkens**, they suddenly look angry. V+O

darkened /dɑːkə[0]nd/. A **darkened** building has no lights on inside it. ADJ CLASSIF

dark glasses. Dark glasses are glasses which have dark-coloured lenses to protect your eyes in the sunshine. N PLURAL

darkish /dɑːkɪʃ/ means quite dark in colour. ADJ CLASSIF

darkroom /dɑːkru[4]m/, **darkrooms.** A **darkroom** is a room which is lit only by red light, so that photographs can be developed there. N COUNT

darling /dɑːlɪŋ/, **darlings. 1** You call someone **darling** if you love them or like them very much. EG *You're looking marvellous, darling.* VOCATIVE

2 In some parts of Britain, people call other people **darling** as a sign of friendliness. VOCATIVE

3 You can use **darling** to describe someone that you love or like very much. EG *...her darling baby brother.* ADJ CLASSIF : ATTRIB

4 You describe someone as a **darling** when you are fond of them and think that they are nice. EG *The poor darling doesn't have a car.* N COUNT

5 The **darling** of a group of people is someone who is especially liked by that group. EG *She quickly became the darling of the crowds.* N COUNT+POSS

darn /dɑːn/, **darns, darning, darned. 1** When you **darn** something made of cloth, you mend a hole in it by sewing stitches across the hole and then V+O OR V weaving stitches in and out of them. EG *I offered to darn Sean's socks... She started darning.*

2 A **darn** is a part of a piece of clothing that has been darned. EG *Her jumper had a darn at the bottom.* N COUNT

3 People sometimes use **darn** or **darned** to emphasize what they are saying, often when they are annoyed. EG *It's darned hot in here.* SUBMOD OR ADJ CLASSIF : ATTRIB Informal

dart /dɑːt/, **darts, darting, darted. 1** If a person or animal **darts** somewhere, they move there suddenly and quickly. EG *...butterflies darting from one flower to another.* V : USU+A

2 If you **dart** a glance at someone or something, you look at them very quickly. V+O+A

3 A **dart** is a small, narrow object with a sharp point which can be thrown or shot. EG *They killed the elephants with tiny poisoned darts.* N COUNT

4 **Darts** is a game in which you throw darts at a round board which has numbers on it. N UNCOUNT

dash /dæʃ/, **dashes, dashing, dashed. 1** If you **dash** somewhere, you run or go there quickly and suddenly. EG *People dashed out into the street to see what was happening.* ▸ used as a noun. EG *He made a dash for the door.* V+A ▸ N COUNT

2 If you say that you **have to dash** or you **must dash**, you mean that you are in a hurry and have to leave. PHRASE Informal

3 A **dash** of a liquid is a small quantity of it which you add when you are preparing food or mixing a drink. EG *Some soups are delicious served cold with a dash of cream.* N PART

4 If you **dash** something somewhere, you throw it or push it violently. EG *She picked up his photograph and dashed it to the ground.* V+O+A

5 If your hopes **are dashed**, something happens that makes it impossible for you to get what you hope for. V+O

6 A **dash** is also a short horizontal line (–) that is used in writing, for example before and after a sentence that occurs within another sentence. N COUNT

dash off. If you **dash off** a letter or other piece of writing, you write it very quickly and without thinking about it very much. PHRASAL VB : V+O+ADV

dashboard /dæʃbɔːd/, **dashboards.** The **dashboard** in a car is the panel facing the driver's seat where most of the instruments and switches are. See picture at CAR. N COUNT

dashing /dæʃɪŋ/. Someone who is **dashing** or who wears **dashing** clothes is very stylish and attractive. EG *She felt very dashing in her yellow suit.* ADJ QUALIT

data /deɪtə, dɑːtə/ is information, usually in the form of facts or statistics that you can analyse. EG *The data was being processed at the Census Office... It isn't present in the data when they are received.* N UNCOUNT OR N PLURAL

database /deɪtəbeɪs/, **databases.** A **database** is a collection of data that is stored in a computer and that can easily be used and added to. N COUNT

date /deɪt/, **dates, dating, dated. 1** A **date** is a particular day, for example 7th April 1988, or the year in which something happened or will happen, for example 1066. EG *No date was announced for the talks.* N COUNT

2 When you **date** something, you give the date when it began or when it was made. EG *How can we date these fossils?* V+O

3 When you **date** something such as a letter or a cheque, you write the day's date on it. EG *The letter was dated September 18 1952.* V+O OR V+O+O

4 At a particular **date** means at a particular time or stage. EG *The matter may be worth pursuing at a later date.* N SING

5 If something has happened or been true **to date**, it has happened or been true until the present time. EG *Their effects to date have been limited.* PHRASE

6 If something **dates**, it goes out of fashion. ● See also **dated**. V

7 A **date** is also an appointment to meet someone or to go out with them, especially someone of the opposite sex. EG *Sorry I can't come – I have a date with Jill.* N COUNT : OFT+*with*

8 Your **date** is a person of the opposite sex that you have a date with. EG *Her date says that he doesn't know either.* N COUNT : USU+POSS American

9 If you **are dating** someone of the opposite sex, you go out regularly with them. V+O American

10 A **date** is also a small, sticky, dark brown fruit. Dates grow on palm trees. N COUNT

11 See also **out of date, up-to-date**.

date back. If something **dates back** to a particular time, it started or was made at that time. EG *The present city hall dates back to the 1880s.* PHRASAL VB : V+ADV, USU+*to*

date from. If something **dates from** a particular time, it started or was made at that time. EG *...a manuscript dating from the eleventh century.* PHRASAL VB : V+PREP

DATE

This entry gives some of the ways in which you can express dates.

A date can be written as 'July 10', 'July 10th', '10 July' or '10th July', but is usually pronounced 'July the tenth' or 'the tenth of July'. However, 'July 10' is sometimes pronounced 'July ten' in American English. The year and the month are often left out of dates when it is clear which year or month you are referring to. The day of the week is usually mentioned before the rest of the date, and the year is usually mentioned after the day and month. EG *'What date is it?' – 'It's the 30th today.'... ...Tuesday May the thirteenth... ...Monday the fifth of April... They married on December 9, 1913... Labour was defeated in the General Election of 19 June 1970... The case was heard in the High Court in February 1910... Where were you on the night of February 4th?*

In British English, you can mention the month either after or before the day, but in American English it is more common to mention the month first. This is especially important when dates are written as a series of numbers, since a date such as 10/7/86 usually means July 10th 1986 in British English, but it means October 7th 1986 in American English.

In British English, you usually say that something happens **on** a particular day, for example 'It happened on Thursday', but in American English you can also leave out 'on' and say 'It happened Thursday'.

If you refer to the twenties, you are referring to the years between 1920 and 1929. If you refer to the 1840's, you are referring to the years between 1840 and 1849. The early sixties are the years between 1960 and 1965, and the late sixties are the years between 1965 and 1969. EG *...Stockholm in the thirties... I went on a computer training course in the nineteen fifties.*

In the following examples, the speaker is referring to things that usually happen on a particular day. EG *I'm terribly busy on Saturdays... On Monday nights, the pupils go to the local cinema... ...every Tuesday for the next few months... I've never worked on a Saturday.*

If you dash somewhere, do you dawdle on the way?

dated /deɪtɪ²d/. Something that is **dated** seems old-fashioned, although it may once have been fashionable. EG *...dated clothes.* ADJ QUALIT

date of birth, dates of birth. Your **date of birth** is the exact date on which you were born, including the year. EG *Give your name, age, and date of birth.* N COUNT: USU+POSS

daub /dɔːb/, **daubs, daubing, daubed.** When you **daub** a substance such as mud or paint on something, you carelessly spread it on the thing. EG *He had mud daubed on his boots... ...daubing walls with paint.* V+O+A

daughter /dɔːtə/, **daughters.** Someone's **daughter** is their female child. EG *She is the daughter of a retired Army officer.* N COUNT

daughter-in-law, daughters-in-law. Someone's **daughter-in-law** is the wife of their son. N COUNT

daunt /dɔːnt/, **daunts, daunting, daunted.** If something **daunts** you, it makes you feel slightly afraid or worried about whether you can succeed in doing it. EG *They may be daunted by the size of the task.* ◇ **daunting.** EG *It is a daunting prospect for a party so recently formed.* V+O; ◇ ADJ QUALIT

dawdle /dɔːdə⁰l/, **dawdles, dawdling, dawdled.** If you **dawdle**, you spend more time than is necessary doing something or going somewhere. EG *Billy dawdled behind her, balancing on the cracks in the pavement.* V

dawn /dɔːn/, **dawns, dawning, dawned. 1 Dawn** is the time of day when light first appears in the sky, before the sun rises. EG *Tom woke me at dawn... They worked from dawn till dusk.* N UNCOUNT OR N COUNT

2 When a day **dawns**, the sky begins to grow light after the night. EG *The first day of the holidays dawned bright and fair.* V Written

3 The **dawn** of a period of time or a situation is the beginning of it. EG *This marked the dawn of a new era in human history.* N SING: the+N+of Literary

4 If something **is dawning**, it is beginning to develop or appear. EG *The age of the answering machine is just dawning.* ◇ **dawning.** EG *She wrote of the dawning hopes of reconciliation in Western Europe.* V Literary; ◇ ADJ CLASSIF: ATTRIB

dawn on or **dawn upon.** If a fact or idea **dawns on** you or **dawns upon** you, you realize it. EG *Then it dawned on me that they were speaking Spanish.* PHRASAL VB: V+PREP

day /deɪ/, **days. 1** A **day** is **1.1** one of the seven twenty-four hour periods of time in a week. EG *The attack occurred six days ago... Can you go any day of the week? What about Monday?* N COUNT **1.2** the time when it is light, or the time when you are awake and doing things. EG *They had waited three days and nights for this opportunity... They hunt by day... ...a typical working day.* N COUNT OR N UNCOUNT

2 You can refer to a particular period in history as a particular **day**. EG *This is the main problem of the present day... ...in the early days of the republic... Are students interested in religion these days?* N COUNT+SUPP

3 If you **call it a day**, you decide to stop what you are doing and you leave it to be finished later. PHRASE

4 If something happens **day and night** or **night and day**, it happens all the time without stopping. EG *The factories were working continuously day and night throughout the year.* PHRASE

5 In this day and age means in modern times. EG *Even in this day and age the old attitudes persist.* PHRASE

6 If something **makes** your **day**, it makes you feel very happy. EG *Her smile somehow makes my day.* PHRASE Informal

7 One day or **some day** or **one of these days** means at some future time. EG *We're all going to be old one day.* PHRASE

8 If it is a month or a year **to the day** since a particular thing happened, it is exactly a month or a year since it happened. PHRASE

daybreak /deɪbreɪk/ is the time in the morning when light first appears. EG *They had to leave at daybreak.* N UNCOUNT

daydream /deɪdriːm/, **daydreams, daydreaming, daydreamed. 1** A **daydream** is a series of pleasant thoughts, especially about things that you would like to happen. EG *He drifted off into another daydream.* N COUNT

2 When you **daydream**, you think about pleasant things for a period of time. EG *Boys and girls daydream about what they want to be.* V: OFT +about/of

daylight /deɪlaɪt/ is **1** the light that there is during the day before it gets dark. EG *We've got at least two more hours of daylight... It looks different in daylight.* **2** the time of day when it begins to get light. EG *The ship sailed into harbour before daylight on 1 September 1942.* ● **in broad daylight**: see **broad**. N UNCOUNT

day off, days off. A **day off** is a day when you do not have to go to work even though it is usually a working day. EG *'Where's Cynthia?' – 'It's her day off.'* N COUNT

day return, day returns. A **day return** is a train or bus ticket which allows you to go somewhere and come back on the same day for a lower price than an ordinary return ticket. N COUNT British

daytime /deɪtaɪm/ is the part of a day between the time when it gets light and the time when it gets dark. EG *The forests were dark even in the daytime... He held a daytime job as a shop assistant.* N UNCOUNT OR N SING: the+N

day-to-day means happening every day as part of ordinary life. EG *This is very much part of the day-to-day life of all human beings.* ADJ CLASSIF: ATTRIB

daze /deɪz/, **dazed. 1** If someone is **in a daze**, they are feeling very confused or upset. EG *I left the ranch in a daze.* PHRASE

2 If someone **is dazed** by a sudden physical injury or other unexpected event, they are unable to think clearly. EG *She was dazed by the news.* ◇ **dazed.** EG *He seemed dazed and bewildered.* V-PASS; ◇ ADJ QUALIT

dazzle /dæzə⁰l/, **dazzles, dazzling, dazzled. 1** If someone or something **dazzles** you, you are extremely impressed by their skill, qualities, or beauty. EG *She had clearly been dazzled by the evening's performance.* ◇ **dazzling.** EG *She gave him a dazzling smile... ...his dazzling political career.* V+O: USU PASS; ◇ ADJ QUALIT

2 The **dazzle** of a light is its sudden brightness that makes it impossible for you to see properly for a short time. EG *They both blinked in the sudden dazzle.* N UNCOUNT

3 The **dazzle** of something is a quality it has, such as beauty or skill, which is impressive and attractive. EG *...the dazzle of high technology.* N UNCOUNT

4 If a bright light **dazzles** you, it makes you unable to see properly for a short time. ◇ **dazzling.** EG *Marsha shut her eyes against the dazzling sun.* V+O; ◇ ADJ CLASSIF

DC /diː siː/ is used to refer to an electric current that always flows in the same direction. **DC** is an abbreviation for 'direct current'.

DDT /diː diː tiː/ is a poisonous substance which is used for killing insects. N UNCOUNT

dead /ded/. **1** A person, animal, or plant that is **dead** is no longer living. EG *He was shot dead in a gunfight... Mary threw away the dead flowers.* ADJ CLASSIF

2 The **dead** are people who are dead. EG *I try to forget the dead.* N PLURAL: the+N

3 If a part of your body goes **dead**, you lose the sense of feeling in it. ADJ PRED

4 If a telephone or a piece of electrical equipment is **dead**, it is not functioning. EG *The phone went dead.* ADJ PRED

5 Dead can mean complete or absolute, especially with the words 'silence', 'centre', and 'stop'. EG *There was dead silence... The table was placed in the dead centre of the room.* ADJ CLASSIF: ATTRIB

6 Dead also means **6.1** precisely or exactly. EG *I was staring dead ahead.* **6.2** very or very much. EG *It's dead easy... They were dead against the idea.* SUBMOD Informal

7 If something stops **dead**, it stops quickly and suddenly. ADV AFTER VB

8 The **dead** of night is the middle part of it, when it is very dark and quiet. EG *They came at dead of night.* N UNCOUNT+of

9 If someone is **dead to the world**, they are sound asleep. PHRASE Informal

10 If you say **'Over my dead body'** when someone has just mentioned a future event, you mean that you feel very strongly that it should not happen, and that you will do everything you can to prevent it. EG *'Roger and I are going to get married.' – 'Over my dead body!'* CONVENTION Informal

11 If you say that you **wouldn't be seen dead** doing a particular thing, you mean that you would never do that thing because you think it is unfashionable or awful. EG *I wouldn't be seen dead in a skirt like that.* PHRASE Informal

deaden /dɛdə^{0}n/, **deadens, deadening, deadened.** If something **deadens** a feeling or a sound, it makes it less strong so that you feel it less or hear it less. EG *Drugs deaden the pangs of hunger.* V+O

dead end, dead ends. 1 If a street is a **dead end**, there is no way out at one end of it. N COUNT

2 A job or course of action that is a **dead end** does not lead to further developments. EG *The investigation has reached a dead end... ...a dead-end job.* N COUNT

deadening /dɛdə^{0}nɪŋ/. Something that is **deadening** destroys people's enthusiasm and creativity. EG *...degrading, deadening tasks.* ADJ QUALIT

dead heat, dead heats. If a race ends in a **dead heat**, two or more competitors reach the finishing line first at exactly the same time. N COUNT

deadline /dɛdlaɪn/, **deadlines.** A **deadline** is a time or date before which a particular task must be finished. EG *We must meet the deadline.* N COUNT

deadlock /dɛdlɒk/ is a state of affairs in an argument or dispute in which neither side is willing to give in at all and so no agreement can be reached. EG *The meeting between management and unions ended in deadlock.* N UNCOUNT

deadly /dɛdli^{1}/, **deadlier, deadliest. 1** Something that is **deadly** is likely or able to cause someone's death. EG *This is one of nature's deadliest poisons... ...deadly spiders.* ADJ QUALIT

2 You use **deadly** to emphasize the extent to which something has an unpleasant or serious quality. EG *The air was deadly cold... He was deadly serious.* SUBMOD

3 **Deadly** also means very great in degree and therefore very effective, especially at hurting someone. EG *This was the deadliest insult he could think of... ...deadly accuracy.* ADJ QUALIT

deadpan /dɛdpæn/. If you do something **deadpan** or if you look **deadpan**, you appear to be serious and are hiding the fact that you are joking or teasing someone. EG *She looked at me deadpan.* ADV
▸ used as an adjective. EG *He speaks in a deadpan way.* ▸ ADJ CLASSIF

dead weight, dead weights. A **dead weight** is a load which is surprisingly heavy and difficult to lift. N COUNT

deaf /dɛf/, **deafer, deafest. 1** Someone who is **deaf** is unable to hear anything or unable to hear very well. EG *...a school for deaf children... He was very deaf.* ◊ **deafness.** EG *They finally diagnosed her deafness when she was thirteen.* ADJ QUALIT ◊ N UNCOUNT

2 The **deaf** are people who are deaf. EG *The deaf know it perfectly well, but we choose to ignore that fact.* N PLURAL: the+N

3 If someone is **deaf** to something, they refuse to pay attention to it. EG *He was deaf to the public's complaints.* ADJ PRED+to

4 If you **turn a deaf ear** to something that someone says, you refuse to pay attention to it. EG *Young people sometimes seem to turn a deaf ear to the words of their anxious parents.* PHRASE

deafen /dɛfə^{0}n/, **deafens, deafening, deafened.** If you **are deafened** by a noise, it is so loud that you cannot hear anything else at the same time. EG *She was momentarily deafened by the din.* ◊ **deafening.** EG *The noise was deafening.* V+O: USU PASS ◊ ADJ QUALIT

deal /di:l/, **deals, dealing, dealt** /dɛlt/. **1 A good deal** or **a great deal** of something is a lot of it. EG *There was a great deal of concern about energy shortages... They talked a great deal... The teaching of the older children is a good deal better.* QUANTIF

2 A **deal** is an agreement or arrangement that is made, especially in business. EG *He certainly hadn't done badly on the deal.* N COUNT

3 If someone has had a bad **deal**, they have been unfortunate or have been treated unfairly. N COUNT: ADJ+N

4 You can say **'Big deal'** when you are expressing scorn, because you are not impressed by what someone has just told you. EG *'I once knew all Keats's poems.' – 'Big deal.'* EXCLAM Informal

5 If you **deal** someone or something a blow, you inflict it or give it. EG *The growth of modern industry had dealt a heavy blow to their way of life... This woman dealt him an alarming series of blows.* V+O+to OR V+O+O

6 When you **deal** cards, you give them out to the players in a game of cards. EG *Deal seven cards to each player... You've dealt me eight cards!... Whose turn is it to deal?* V+O: OFT+to, V+O+O, OR V

7 See also **dealing** and **wheeling and dealing**.

deal in. To **deal in** a particular type of goods means to sell those goods. EG *The shop deals only in trousers.* PHRASAL VB: V+PREP

deal out. When you **deal out** cards, you give them out to the players in a game of cards. EG *Deal the cards out first, then I'll explain the points system.* PHRASAL VB: V+O+ADV

deal with. 1 When you **deal with** a situation or problem, you do what is necessary to achieve the result you want. EG *They learned to deal with any sort of emergency.* **2** If a book, speech, or film **deals with** a particular subject, it is concerned with it. EG *The film deals with a strange encounter between two soldiers.* PHRASAL VB: V+PREP, HAS PASS; V+PREP, HAS PASS

dealer /di:lə/, **dealers.** A **dealer** is a person whose business involves buying and selling things. EG *...a dealer in antique furniture.* N COUNT: USU+SUPP

dealing /di:lɪŋ/, **dealings. 1** Your **dealings** with a person or organization are the relations that you have with them or the business that you do with them. EG *Ford insists that Carter's dealings with him have been totally correct... He was questioned about his past business dealings.* N PLURAL: OFT+with

2 You use **dealing** to talk about someone's job. For example, drug **dealing** is selling drugs and antique **dealing** is selling antiques. N UNCOUNT

dealt /dɛlt/ is the past tense and past participle of **deal.**

dean /di:n/, **deans.** A **dean** is **1** an important administrator at a university or college. **2** a priest who is the main administrator of a large church. N COUNT

dear /dɪə/, **dearer, dearest; dears. 1** You can call someone **dear** as a sign of affection. EG *How are you, dear?... Now, my dears, come with me.* VOCATIVE

2 You can use **dear** in expressions such as 'my **dear** fellow' or 'my **dear** Richard', to address someone that you are quite fond of. EG *My dear fellow, I really am sorry.* ADJ CLASSIF: ATTRIB Outdated

3 **Dear** is usually written at the beginning of a letter, followed by the name or title of the person you are writing to. EG *Dear Mum, I was glad to get your letter... Dear Sir, I regret to inform you that I cannot accept your kind invitation.* ADJ CLASSIF: ATTRIB

4 You use **dear** to describe someone or something that you feel affection for. EG *...dear old Aunt Elizabeth... ...a dear friend.* ADJ QUALIT: ATTRIB

5 If something is **dear** to you, you care very deeply about it. EG *Sussex was very dear to him... ...a cause that is very dear to her heart.* ADJ PRED+to Formal

6 You say **'Oh dear'** when you are sad or upset about something. EG *Oh dear, I'm late.* EXCLAM

7 Something that is **dear** costs a lot of money. EG *Firewood is getting dearer, as supplies dwindle.* ADJ PRED Outdated

If you are in someone's debt, do you owe them money?

dearest /dɪərɪ^{2}st/. 1 You can call someone **dearest** when you are very fond of them. EG *It's too late now, my dearest.* — VOCATIVE Outdated

2 You use **dearest** to describe something that is very important to you. EG *His dearest wish was to become a civil servant.* — ADJ SUPERL Formal

dearly /dɪəli^1/. 1 If you love someone **dearly**, you love them very much. If you would **dearly** like to do or have something, you would very much like to do it or have it. EG *I loved him dearly... I dearly wish I had more money.* — ADV Formal

2 If you **pay dearly** for doing something, you suffer a lot as a result. EG *He paid dearly for his mistake.* — PHRASE Formal

dearth /dɜ:θ/. If there is a **dearth** of something, there is not enough of it. EG *There is a dearth of good children's plays.* — N SING : USU+*of*

death /dɛθ/, **deaths. 1 Death** is the end of the life of a person or animal. EG *...after the death of her parents... He bled to death... The two deaths could have been prevented.* — N UNCOUNT OR N COUNT

2 If someone is **at death's door**, they are very ill indeed. — PHRASE Informal

3 If something **frightens** or **worries** you **to death**, it frightens or worries you very much. EG *He was frightened to death of her.* — PHRASE Informal

4 If you say that you are **sick to death** of something, you mean that you feel very angry about it. EG *The Town Council are sick to death of waiting for your report!* — PHRASE Informal

5 If someone **is put to death**, they are executed. EG *Because she had loved a slave, she was put to death.* — PHRASE Formal

deathbed /dɛθbɛd/, **deathbeds.** Someone's **deathbed** is the bed that they are lying in when they are about to die. EG *On his deathbed he asked her forgiveness.* — N COUNT : USU+POSS

deathly /dɛθli^1/ is used to describe something that is characteristic of a dead person in some way, for example as cold, pale, or quiet as a dead person. EG *A deathly hush lay in the streets.* ▸ used as an adverb. EG *Her feet were deathly cold.* — ADJ CLASSIF : ATTRIB; ▸ ADV+ADJ

death penalty. The **death penalty** is the punishment of death used in some countries for people who have committed very serious crimes. — N SING : *the*+N

debacle /deɪbɑ:kə^{0}l, dɪ-/, **debacles;** also spelled **débâcle.** A **debacle** is an event or attempt that is a complete failure. EG *I couldn't afford to ask them again after the debacle of the TV series.* — N COUNT

debar /di^{1}bɑ:/, **debars, debarring, debarred.** If you **are debarred** from doing something, you are prevented from doing it by a law or rule. EG *He was debarred from attending the meetings.* — V+O : OFT+*from* Formal

debase /di^{1}beɪs/, **debases, debasing, debased.** If something **is debased**, its value or quality is reduced. EG *The quality of life can only be debased by such a system.* — V+O : USU PASS Formal

debatable /di^{1}beɪtəbə^{0}l/. A statement or fact that is **debatable** is not definitely true or not definitely known. EG *'They won't notice it's gone.' – 'Well. That's debatable.'* — ADJ QUALIT

debate /di^{1}beɪt/, **debates, debating, debated. 1** A **debate** is a discussion in which people express different opinions about a subject. EG *...a debate on education... There was a great deal of debate about the national health service.* — N COUNT OR N UNCOUNT : OFT+*on/about*

2 When people **debate** something, they discuss it fairly formally, putting forward different views. EG *These issues have been widely debated... They debated the motion that capital punishment should be re-introduced.* — V+O OR V+REPORT

3 If you **debate** what to do, you think about possible courses of action before deciding what to do. EG *He turned round, debating whether to go back... He debated heating up the stew.* — V+REPORT OR -ING

4 If something is **open to debate**, it has not been proved to be true. EG *Whether they actually are safer is open to debate.* — PHRASE

debauchery /di^{1}bɔ:tʃəri^1/ is excessive drunkenness or excessive sexual activity. — N UNCOUNT Formal

debilitated /dɪ^{1}bɪlɪteɪtɪ^{2}d/. A person, country, or organization that is **debilitated** has been made weak. EG *...the shabby and debilitated economy.* — ADJ QUALIT Formal

debilitating /dɪ^{1}bɪlɪteɪtɪŋ/. A **debilitating** illness, feeling, or action makes a person, country, or organization weak and unable to take action. EG *...the debilitating effects of the fast... ...economically debilitating subsidies.* — ADJ QUALIT Formal

debility /dɪ^{1}bɪlɪti^1/ is physical or mental weakness, especially weakness caused by an illness. EG *...the debility produced by old age.* — N UNCOUNT : USU+SUPP Formal

debit /dɛbɪt/, **debits, debiting, debited. 1** When your bank **debits** your account, money is taken from it, usually in order to pay for something. — V+O

2 A **debit** is a record of the money which is taken out of your bank account, for example when you write a cheque. EG *...a statement showing all the credits and debits.* — N COUNT

debonair /dɛbə^{7}nɛə/. A man who is **debonair** is well-dressed, charming, and confident. — ADJ QUALIT

debris /deɪbri^1, dɛbri^1/ consists of pieces of things that have been destroyed, or rubbish that is lying around. EG *Two people were killed by flying debris... She began clearing up the debris.* — N UNCOUNT

debt /dɛt/, **debts. 1** A **debt** is a sum of money that you owe someone. EG *You must spend less until your debts are paid off.* — N COUNT

2 **Debt** is the state of owing money. EG *He began getting deeper and deeper into debt.* — N UNCOUNT

3 A **debt** is also a feeling of gratitude towards someone for something that they have done for you, and a feeling that you owe them something. EG *...a debt that could never be repaid.* — N COUNT+SUPP Formal

4 If you are **in** someone's **debt**, you are grateful to them for something that they have done for you, and you feel that you must do something for them in return. — PHRASE Formal

debtor /dɛtə/, **debtors.** A **debtor** is a person who owes money. — N COUNT

debunk /di:bʌŋk/, **debunks, debunking, debunked.** If you **debunk** an idea or belief, you show that it is false or not important. — V+O

debut /deɪbju:, dɛbju:/, **debuts.** The **debut** of a singer, musician, footballer, or other performer is his or her first public performance or recording. EG *She made her debut in this theatre.* — N COUNT

decade /dɛkeɪd, dɪ^{2}keɪd/, **decades.** A **decade** is a period of ten years, especially one that begins with a year ending in 0, for example 1980 to 1989. EG *By the end of the decade he had acquired international fame.* — N COUNT

decadent /dɛkədə^{2}nt/. If you say that someone or something is **decadent**, you mean that they show low standards, especially low moral standards. EG *The gaudy casinos seemed even more decadent.* — ADJ QUALIT

◇ **decadence** /dɛkədə^{2}ns/. EG *...moral decadence.* — ◇ N UNCOUNT

decaffeinated /di^{1}kæfə^{1}neɪtɪ^{2}d/. Coffee that is **decaffeinated** has had most of the caffeine removed from it. — ADJ CLASSIF

decant /dɪ^{2}kænt/, **decants, decanting, decanted.** If you **decant** port or sherry, you pour it slowly from its bottle into another container before serving it. — V+O

decanter /dɪ^{2}kæntə/, **decanters.** A **decanter** is a glass container that you use for serving port or sherry. — N COUNT

decapitate /di^{1}kæpɪteɪt/, **decapitates, decapitating, decapitated.** To **decapitate** someone means to cut off their head. — V+O : USU PASS Formal

decathlon /dɪ^{2}kæθlə^{7}n/, **decathlons.** A **decathlon** is a competition in which athletes compete in ten different sporting events. — N COUNT

decay /dɪ^{2}keɪ/, **decays, decaying, decayed. 1** When something such as a plant or a piece of meat **decays**, it rots and starts to fall apart. EG *The body had already started to decay.* — V

◇ **decayed.** EG *...black, decayed leaves... A decayed tooth may* — ◇ ADJ QUALIT *cause pain.* ◊ **decaying.** EG *...a smell of decaying meat.* ◊ ADJ CLASSIF

2 If buildings **decay**, their condition becomes worse because they have not been looked after and repaired. EG *The old palace decayed badly during Cromwell's time.* ◊ **decayed.** EG *...slums and decayed factories... ...a decayed cloth-mill by the stream.* ◊ **decaying.** EG *...decaying urban centres.* V; ◊ ADJ QUALIT; ◊ ADJ CLASSIF

3 If something such as a society or an institution **decays**, it gradually becomes weaker or more corrupt. EG *Working class culture was decaying.* ◊ **decaying.** EG *...a corrupt, decaying society... ...images of decaying imperial Rome.* V; ◊ ADJ CLASSIF : ATTRIB

4 Decay refers to **4.1** the process or result of something such as a plant or a piece of meat rotting and falling apart. EG *...toothpaste that helps to prevent dental decay.* **4.2** the process or result of buildings becoming worse in condition because they have not been looked after and repaired. EG *...saving houses from falling into decay.* **4.3** the process or result of a society or institution gradually becoming weaker or more corrupt. EG *...a religion in the final stages of decay.* N UNCOUNT

deceased /di'si:st/. **1** A person who has recently died can be referred to as the **deceased**. EG *...the property of the deceased.* N SING : the+N Formal

2 A **deceased** person is one who has recently died. EG *...the relatives of the deceased couple.* ADJ CLASSIF Formal

deceit /dɪsi:t/, **deceits. Deceit** is lying, or behaviour that is intended to make people believe something which is not true. EG *...marriages in which deceit was commonplace.* N UNCOUNT OR N COUNT

deceitful /dɪsi:tfʊl/. Someone who is **deceitful** lies or tries to make other people believe things that are not true. ADJ QUALIT

deceive /dɪsi:v/, **deceives, deceiving, deceived.**
1 If you **deceive** someone, you deliberately make them believe something that is not true. EG *He tried to deceive me... ...the man he had been deceived into calling 'father'.* V+O : OFT+into

2 If you **deceive** yourself, you do not admit to yourself something that you know is true. EG *They try to deceive themselves that everything is all right.* V-REFL

3 If something **deceives** you, it causes you to believe something that is not true. EG *His unkempt appearance deceived the staff into believing that he was a student.* V+O : OFT+into

December /di'sɛmbə/ is the twelfth and last month of the year in the Western calendar. EG *We gave a party early in December.* N UNCOUNT

decency /di:sə⁰nsi¹/ is **1** the quality of being sensible and following accepted moral standards. EG *They tried to restore some sense and decency to the Administration.* **2** behaviour that shows kindness towards people. EG *Why hadn't they had the decency to ask him if he'd like to join in?* N UNCOUNT

decent /di:sə⁰nt/. **1** You use **decent** to describe something which is **1.1** considered to be of an acceptable standard or quality. EG *...decent wages... It was several weeks before I got a decent night's rest.* ◊ **decently.** EG *The farm animals are decently treated and killed as humanely as possible.* **1.2** morally correct or acceptable. EG *He would marry her as soon as a decent amount of time had elapsed.* ◊ **decently.** EG *They only want the chance to live their lives decently.* ADJ QUALIT; ◊ ADV; ADJ CLASSIF : ATTRIB; ◊ ADV

2 Decent people are honest and respectable and behave morally. EG *...decent, hard-working citizens.* ADJ QUALIT : ATTRIB

decentralize /di'sɛntrəlaɪz/, **decentralizes, decentralizing, decentralized;** also spelled **decentralise.** V+O
To **decentralize** a large organization means to move some departments of it away from the main administrative area, or to give more power to local departments. EG *He accused the Minister of seeking to decentralise the Commission.* ◊ **decentralized.** EG *...a decentralized health service.* ◊ ADJ CLASSIF

◊ **decentralization** /di'sɛntrəlaɪzeɪʃə⁰n/. EG *...the decentralization of government.* ◊ N UNCOUNT

deception /di'sɛpʃə⁰n/, **deceptions. 1** A **deception** is something that you say or do which is intended to deceive someone. EG *He would quickly have seen through Mary's deceptions.* N COUNT

2 Deception is the act of deceiving someone or the state of being deceived by someone. EG *...his part in the deception of the British public... This made Tim sadder than his deception.* N UNCOUNT

deceptive /di'sɛptɪv/. If something is **deceptive**, it might cause you to believe something which is not true. EG *Its fragile appearance was deceptive.* ◊ **deceptively.** EG *It all looks deceptively simple... It was deceptively presented as a scientific study.* ADJ QUALIT; ◊ SUBMOD OR ADV

decibel /dɛsɪbɛl/, **decibels.** A **decibel** is a unit of measurement relating to how loud a sound is. EG *He lowered his voice a few decibels.* N COUNT

decide /di'saɪd/, **decides, deciding, decided. 1** If you **decide** to do something, you choose to do it, usually after you have thought carefully about the other possibilities. EG *What made you decide to get married?... She decided that she would leave... He has a month to decide whether he's going to stay... I'm glad you decided against a career as a waiter.* V+to-INF, REPORT, OR A

2 When something **is decided**, people choose what something should be like or what should be done. EG *The case is to be decided by the International Court.* V+O

3 If an event or fact **decides** something, it makes it certain that there will be a particular result or choice. EG *It was this that decided the fate of the company.* ◊ **deciding.** EG *I suppose cost shouldn't be a deciding factor.* V+O; ◊ ADJ CLASSIF : ATTRIB

4 If you **decide** that something is the case, you form that opinion after considering the facts. EG *He decided that the doorbell was broken... I couldn't decide whether she was joking or not.* V+REPORT

decide on or **decide upon.** If you **decide on** something or **decide upon** it, you choose it from two or more possibilities. EG *He decided on a career in the army.* PHRASAL VB : V+PREP, HAS PASS

decided /di'saɪdɪ²d/ means clear and definite. EG *This gave them a decided advantage over their opponents.* ADJ QUALIT : ATTRIB

decidedly /di'saɪdɪ²dli¹/. **1 Decidedly** means to a great extent and in a way that is very obvious. EG *The men looked decidedly uncomfortable.* SUBMOD

2 If you say something **decidedly**, you say it in a way that suggests that you are unlikely to change your mind. EG *'It's time things were altered,' said Mrs Moffat decidedly.* ADV

deciduous /di'sɪdju:əs/. A tree that is **deciduous** loses its leaves in autumn every year. ADJ CLASSIF

decimal /dɛsɪmə⁰l/, **decimals. 1** A **decimal** system involves counting in units of ten. EG *...the new decimal currency.* ADJ CLASSIF : ATTRIB

2 A **decimal** is a fraction that is written in the form of a dot followed by one or more numbers which represent tenths, hundredths, and so on: for example .5, .51, .517. N COUNT

decimal point, decimal points. A **decimal point** is the dot that occurs before a fraction that is expressed as a decimal. N COUNT

decimate /dɛsɪmeɪt/, **decimates, decimating, decimated.** To **decimate** a group of people or animals means to destroy a very large number of them. EG *The soldiers would be decimated long before they reached the beaches.* V+O

decipher /di'saɪfə/, **deciphers, deciphering, deciphered.** If you **decipher** a piece of writing, you work out what it says, even though it is very difficult to read or understand. EG *Archaeologists labour to decipher clay tablets.* V+O

In Britain, does a deciduous tree have leaves on it in December?

decision /dɪ'sɪʒə°n/, **decisions.** **1** A **decision** is a choice that you make about what should be done or about which is the best of various alternatives. EG *I think that I made the wrong decision... ...a decision on the issue might not be necessary... He has to make some difficult decisions about where he wants to go.* [N COUNT: OFT+*on/about*]

2 Decision is **2.1** the act of deciding something. EG *Philip laced up his shoes slowly, delaying the moment of decision.* [N UNCOUNT] **2.2** the ability to decide quickly and definitely what to do. EG *...a man of decision and action.*

decisive /dɪ'saɪsɪv/. **1** If a fact, action, or event is **decisive**, it makes it certain that there will be a particular result or that the result will be a definite one. EG *...a decisive battle... This promise was not a decisive factor in the election.* [ADJ CLASSIF] ◇ **decisively.** EG *Thornton was decisively defeated.* [◇ ADV]

2 If someone is **decisive**, they have the ability to make quick decisions. EG *...a decisive leader... How could a girl be so decisive?* [ADJ QUALIT] ◇ **decisively.** EG *'Can I see him?' Edgar shook his head decisively.* [◇ ADV] ◇ **decisiveness.** EG *The sight of the body had robbed her of her usual decisiveness.* [◇ N UNCOUNT]

deck /dɛk/, **decks, decking, decked. 1** A **deck** on a bus or ship is a downstairs or upstairs area on it. EG *They got on the bus and sat on the top deck.* [N COUNT]

2 The **deck** of a ship is the top part of it that forms a floor in the open air which you can walk on. EG *I'm going back up on deck.* See picture at YACHT. [N SING: *the*+N, OR *on*+N]

3 A record **deck** is a piece of equipment on which you play records. [N COUNT]

4 A **deck** of cards is a pack of playing cards. [N COUNT]

5 If you **deck** something with pretty things, you decorate it. EG *The graves are decked with flowers.* [V+O+*with*; Written]

deck out. If you **deck** someone or something **out**, you decorate them or make them look attractive, usually for a special occasion. EG *I decked myself out in a suit and tie.* [PHRASAL VB: V+O+ADV; Written]

deckchair /dɛktʃɛə/, **deckchairs.** A **deckchair** is a simple folding chair which is used out of doors. [N COUNT]

declaration /dɛkləreɪʃə°n/, **declarations.** A **declaration** is **1** a firm, emphatic statement. EG *He seemed embarrassed by her declaration of love... ...his earlier declarations that things were improving.* [N COUNT: OFT+*of* OR REPORT] **2** an official announcement or statement. EG *...the day after the declaration was signed... ...formal declarations of war.* [N COUNT: OFT+SUPP]

declare /dɪ'klɛə/, **declares, declaring, declared. 1** If you **declare** that something is the case, you say it in a firm, deliberate way. EG *'I like it,' she declared... They were heard to declare that they would never steal again.* [V+QUOTE OR REPORT: ONLY *that*]

2 If you **declare** an attitude or intention or if you **declare** yourself as having this attitude or intention, you make it known to people that you have it. EG *He declared his intention to fight... Mr Bell has declared his support... He declared himself strongly in favour of the project.* [V+O OR V-REFL+C] ◇ **declared.** EG *...his declared intention to resign.* [◇ ADJ CLASSIF: ATTRIB]

3 If you **declare** something, you state it officially. EG *...when the French declared war on England... At his trial he was declared innocent.* [V+O OR V+O+C]

4 If you **declare** goods that you have bought abroad or money that you have earned, you tell customs or tax officials about it so that you can pay tax on it. [V+O]

decline /dɪ'klaɪn/, **declines, declining, declined. 1** If something **declines**, it becomes smaller, weaker, or worse. EG *The number of congress members declined from 371 to 361... Since 1971 the party's influence has declined.* [V] ◇ **declining.** EG *...declining industries.* [◇ ADJ CLASSIF: ATTRIB]

2 If there is a **decline** in something, it becomes smaller, weaker, or worse. EG *...a decline in standards... ...the decline of the motor industry.. The city's population is in decline.* [N COUNT OR N UNCOUNT]

3 If something is **on the decline**, it is declining. EG *Organized religion seems to be on the decline.* [PHRASE]

4 If you **decline** something or **decline** to do something, you politely refuse to accept it or do it. EG *He has declined the invitation... Mr Santos declined to comment on the news... On each occasion, he declined.* [V+O, V+*to*-INF, OR V; Formal]

decode /di:kəʊd/, **decodes, decoding, decoded.** If you **decode** a message that has been written or spoken in code, you change it into ordinary language. [V+O]

decompose /di:kə'mpəʊz/, **decomposes, decomposing, decomposed.** When something that has died **decomposes**, it changes chemically and begins to rot. EG *Shellfish decompose very quickly after death.* [V] ◇ **decomposition** /di:kɒmpəzɪʃə°n/. EG *...the decomposition of organic matter.* [◇ N UNCOUNT]

decor /deɪkɔ:/. The **decor** of a house or room is the style in which it is furnished and decorated. EG *...the pine decor of the kitchen.* [N UNCOUNT: USU+SUPP]

decorate /dɛkə'reɪt/, **decorates, decorating, decorated. 1** If you **decorate** something, you make it look more attractive by adding things to it. EG *The walls were all decorated with posters.* [V+O]

2 If you **decorate** a building or room, you put new paint or wallpaper on the walls, ceiling, and woodwork. [V+O OR V] ◇ **decorating.** EG *We said we would do the decorating.* [◇ N UNCOUNT]

decoration /dɛkə'reɪʃə°n/, **decorations. 1 Decoration** is **1.1** something that is added to something else in order to make it look more attractive. EG *...dresses that are white and plain, free of all decoration... ...Christmas decorations.* **1.2** the furniture, wallpaper, and ornaments of a room or building. EG *...the style of decoration typical of the 1920s... I like the interior decorations.* [N UNCOUNT OR N COUNT]

2 A **decoration** is a medal which is given to someone as an official honour. [N COUNT]

decorative /dɛkə°rətɪv/. Something that is **decorative** is intended to look pretty or attractive. EG *...decorative objects.* [ADJ QUALIT]

decorator /dɛkəreɪtə/, **decorators.** A **decorator** is a person whose job is to paint houses or put wallpaper on the walls. [N COUNT]

decorous /dɛkə'rəs/. Behaviour that is **decorous** is polite and correct and does not offend people. EG *He gave his wife a decorous kiss.* [ADJ QUALIT; Formal] ◇ **decorously.** EG *...teenage lovers strolling decorously.* [◇ ADV]

decorum /dɪ'kɔ:rəm/ is behaviour that people consider to be correct and polite. EG *She was expected to behave with decorum.* [N UNCOUNT; Formal]

decoy /di:kɔɪ/, **decoys, decoying, decoyed. 1** A **decoy** is a person or object that you use to lead someone away from where they intended to go, especially so that you can catch them. EG *They chased the decoys down to the place of ambush.* [N COUNT]

2 If you **decoy** someone, you lead them away from where they intended to go, often by means of a trick. EG *Eight of the missiles were decoyed away from targets.* [V+O+A]

decrease /dɪ'kri:s/, **decreases, decreasing, decreased. 1** When something **decreases** or **is decreased**, it becomes smaller or weaker. EG *Over a seven-year period the number of marriages has decreased by forty per cent... To save money, decrease the temperature.* [V-ERG] ◇ **decreasing.** EG *...a life of increasing labour and decreasing leisure.* [◇ ADJ CLASSIF: ATTRIB]

2 A **decrease** is a reduction in the quantity, size, or strength of something. EG *The decrease in size was gradual.* [N COUNT: OFT+*in/of*]

decree /dɪ'kri:/, **decrees, decreeing, decreed. 1** If someone in authority **decrees** that something must happen, they order this officially. EG *The minister decreed that there should be a full investigation.* [V+REPORT: ONLY *that*]

2 A **decree** is an official order, especially one made by the ruler of a country. [N COUNT]

decrepit /dɪ'krɛpɪt/. Something that is **decrepit** is very old and in bad condition. EG *...decrepit houses.* [ADJ CLASSIF]

decry /di^{1}kraɪ/, **decries, decrying, decried.** If you **decry** something, you say that it is bad. EG *We decry their absence of principle.* V+O Formal

dedicate /dɛdɪkeɪt/, **dedicates, dedicating, dedicated. 1** If you **dedicate** yourself to something, you decide to devote a lot of time and effort to it because you think that it is important. EG *...a man who had dedicated himself to his work.* V-REFL+*to*

2 If you **dedicate** something such as a book or a piece of music to someone, you say that the work is written for them, as a way of showing affection or respect. EG *She dedicated her first book to her husband.* V+O+*to*

dedicated /dɛdɪkeɪtɪ^{2}d/. If you are **dedicated** to something, you believe that it is right and worthwhile, and give a lot of time and effort to it. EG *...people dedicated to social or political change... ...a dedicated surgeon.* ADJ QUALIT

dedication /dɛdɪkeɪʃə^{0}n/, **dedications. 1** If you show **dedication** to something, you work hard at it, because you believe it is important or worthwhile. EG *I admired her dedication to her family.* N UNCOUNT

2 A **dedication** is a message which is written at the beginning of a book or said before a piece of music is performed, as a sign of affection or respect for someone. N COUNT

deduce /dɪdju:s/, **deduces, deducing, deduced.** If you **deduce** that something is true, you reach that conclusion because of facts that you know to be true. EG *Morris deduced that he was in the presence of the Head of Department... What do you deduce from all this?* V+REPORT OR V+O

deduct /di^{1}dʌkt/, **deducts, deducting, deducted.** When you **deduct** an amount from a total, you reduce the total by that amount. EG *Tax will be deducted automatically from your wages.* V+O

deduction /di^{1}dʌkʃə^{0}n/, **deductions. 1** A **deduction** is a conclusion that you reach about something because of facts that you know to be true. EG *That seems a reasonable deduction... If the battery is dead the horn will not work; that is deduction.* N COUNT OR N UNCOUNT

2 A **deduction** is also an amount that has been subtracted from a total. EG *...tax and national insurance deductions.* N COUNT OR N UNCOUNT

deed /di:d/, **deeds. 1** A **deed** is something that is done, especially something very good or very bad. EG *...the brave deeds his son would do when he grew up.* N COUNT: USU+SUPP Literary

2 A **deed** is also a legal document containing an agreement or contract. N COUNT+SUPP

deem /di:m/, **deems, deeming, deemed.** If you **deem** something to be the case, you consider that it is the case. EG *This was deemed to detract from the dignity of the republic... He said he would take what measures he deemed necessary.* V+O+*to*-INF OR V+O+C: USU PASS Formal

deep /di:p/, **deeper, deepest. 1** If something is **deep**, it extends a long way down from the surface. EG *The sea is not very deep there... They dug deep down into the earth.* ◊ **deeply.** EG *His face was deeply lined.* ADJ QUALIT OR ADV ◊ ADV

2 You use **deep** to talk about measurements. For example, if something is two feet **deep**, it measures two feet from the top to the bottom, or from the front to the back. EG *...a crater over 300 feet deep.* ADJ AFTER N

3 Something that is **deep** in an area is a long way inside it. EG *...deep in the forest... Guerrilla forces were advancing deep into enemy territory.* ADJ CLASSIF OR ADV

4 You use **deep** to emphasize the degree or intensity of something. EG *This was a matter of deep concern... Our hearts go out to you in deepest sympathy.* ◊ **deeply.** EG *...deeply religious people.* ADJ QUALIT: ATTRIB ◊ ADV+ADJ

5 If you feel something **deep down** or **deep inside** you, you feel it very strongly although you may not show it. EG *Deep down they're still frustrated adolescents.* PHRASE

6 If you are in a **deep** sleep, you are sleeping peacefully and it is difficult to wake you. ADJ QUALIT: ATTRIB

7 A **deep** breath or sigh uses the whole of your lungs. EG *He took a few deep breaths before jumping into the foaming water.* ◊ **deeply.** EG *She sighed deeply.* ADJ QUALIT: ATTRIB ◊ ADV

8 A **deep** colour is strong and fairly dark. EG *...deep blue eyes... The sky was a deep purple.* ADJ QUALIT

9 A **deep** sound is a low one. EG *He sang in a deep voice... ...fits of deep, hoarse coughing.* ADJ QUALIT

10 Deep thoughts are serious thoughts about important things. ADJ QUALIT

11 Deep is also used in these phrases. **11.1** If you are **deep in thought**, you are thinking very hard about something. **11.2** If you say that something **goes** or **runs deep**, you mean that it is very serious and hard to change. EG *The crisis in the prisons goes deep.* **11.3** If you **are thrown in at the deep end**, you are asked to do something new and difficult without being given any help. PHRASES

deepen /di:pə^{0}n/, **deepens, deepening, deepened. 1** If people **deepen** something, they cause it to become greater in measurement from the surface to the bottom. EG *The authority wants to spend £7 million to widen and deepen the River Soar.* V+O

2 Where a river or a sea **deepens**, the bottom begins to slope downwards and the water gets deeper. V

3 If a situation or emotion **deepens** or **is deepened**, it becomes stronger and more intense. EG *The crisis deepened... The incident deepened my commitment to Richard.* V-ERG

4 If you **deepen** your knowledge of a subject, or if your knowledge **deepens**, you learn more about it. EG *Their object was to deepen man's understanding of tne universe.* V-ERG

5 When a sound **deepens** or when you **deepen** it, it becomes lower in tone. V-ERG

deep freeze, deep freezes. A **deep freeze** is a large container used for storing food. The temperature inside it is always kept below freezing point. N COUNT

deep-rooted. An idea or feeling that is **deep-rooted** or **deeply rooted** is so firmly fixed in a person or a society that it is difficult to change or remove. EG *...a deep-rooted prejudice.* ADJ QUALIT

deep-sea. Deep-sea activities take place in areas of the sea that are a long way from the coast. EG *...deep-sea diving.* ADJ CLASSIF: ATTRIB

deep-seated. A **deep-seated** feeling or problem is very strong or basic, and is very difficult to change. EG *...deep-seated fears.* ADJ CLASSIF

deer /dɪə/. **Deer** is both the singular and the plural. N COUNT

A **deer** is a large wild animal that eats grass and leaves. Male deer usually have large, branching horns.

deface /di^{1}feɪs/, **defaces, defacing, defaced.** If someone **defaces** something such as a wall or a notice, they deliberately spoil it by writing or drawing things on it. EG *...books with pages torn out or defaced with graffiti.* V+O

defamation /dɛfəmeɪʃə^{0}n/ is the damaging of someone's reputation by saying something bad and untrue about them. EG *...defamation of character, slander, and libel.* N UNCOUNT Formal Legal

default /di^{1}fɔ:lt/, **defaults, defaulting, defaulted. 1** If you **default**, you fail to do something that you are legally supposed to do, such as make a payment that you owe. EG *He said he had been right to default on that loan.* ▸ used as a noun. EG *...default of payment.* V: OFT+*on/in* ▸ N UNCOUNT

2 If something happens **by default**, it happens only because something else which might have prevented it has not happened. EG *He is responsible either through bad design or by default.* PHRASE

defeat /di^{1}fi:t/, **defeats, defeating, defeated. 1** If you **defeat** someone, you win a victory over them in a battle, game, or contest. EG *Arsenal were* V+O

Which word on these pages has the same form in the singular and the plural?

defeated on Saturday... Labour was defeated in the General Election of 19 June 1970.

2 If a proposal or a motion in a debate **is defeated**, more people vote against it than vote for it. EG *The motion was defeated by 221 votes to 152.* V+O : USU PASS

3 If a task or a problem **defeats** you, it is so difficult that you cannot do it or solve it. EG *...a complex sum which defeats many adults as well as children.* V+O

4 If someone or something **defeats** something else, they cause it to fail. EG *Moral instruction thus defeats its own purpose... He would like to see the strike defeated.* V+O

5 **Defeat** is **5.1** the state of being beaten in a battle, game, or contest. EG *The bad weather contributed to the defeat of the navy... These defeats came as a setback for Thorne.* **5.2** failure to achieve something. EG *He would never admit defeat... Her friend finally gave up in defeat.* N UNCOUNT OR N COUNT

defeatism /diˈfiːtɪzə°m/ is a way of thinking or talking which suggests that you expect to be unsuccessful. EG *We were accused of defeatism.* N UNCOUNT
◇ **defeatist** /diˈfiːtɪst/, **defeatists.** EG *I was in a defeatist mood.* ◇ N COUNT : OFT N MOD

defecate /dɛfəˈkeɪt/, **defecates, defecating, defecated.** When you **defecate**, you get rid of waste matter from your body through your anus. V Formal

defect, defects, defecting, defected; pronounced /diːfɛkt/ when it is a noun and /diˈfɛkt/ when it is a verb.

1 A **defect** is a fault or imperfection in a person or thing. EG *They were not blind to the defects of Western society.* N COUNT : OFT+*of/in*

2 If you **defect**, you leave your own country, political party, or other group, and join an opposing one. EG *Several of the Labour MPs defected to the new party.* V : OFT+*to* ◇ **defection** /diˈfɛkʃə°n/, **defections.** EG *The number of defections has increased in recent years.* ◇ N COUNT OR N UNCOUNT ◇ **defector, defectors.** EG *...defectors from the Liberal Party.* ◇ N COUNT : USU+SUPP

defective /diˈfɛktɪv/. If a piece of machinery is **defective**, there is something wrong with it and so it does not work properly. EG *One of the engines was found to be defective.* ADJ CLASSIF

defence /diˈfɛns/, **defences;** also spelled **defense** in American English. **1 Defence** is **1.1** action that is taken to protect someone or something against attack. EG *They carried sticks for defence rather than aggression... ...the defence of civil liberties.* **1.2** a country's armies and weapons, and their activities. EG *...the Ministry of Defence... ...defence spending... ...the defence forces.* N UNCOUNT

2 A **defence** is something that people or animals can use or do to protect themselves. EG *The jellyfish has had to develop this deadly poison as a defence... He had found coldness his only defence against despair.* N COUNT : OFT+*against*

3 In a court of law, a person's **defence** is their denial of a charge against them. EG *He decided to conduct his own defence.* N COUNT : USU+SUPP

4 A **defence** is also something that you say in support of ideas or actions that have been criticized. EG *His economists have drawn up a defence of his policy.* N COUNT ● If you say something **in defence**, you say it in order to support ideas or actions that have been criticized. EG *Brown, in defence, said that it was his boss who was violent.* ● PHRASE

5 The **defence** is **5.1** the case that is presented by a lawyer for the person in a trial who has been accused of a crime. EG *He gave evidence for the defence in the Hennessy case.* **5.2** the lawyers for this person. N SING : *the*+N

6 The **defences** of a country or region are its armed forces and weapons. N PLURAL

7 In a sports team, the **defence** is the group of players who try to stop the opposing team scoring a goal or a point. EG *The English defence were weak.* N COLL

defenceless /diˈfɛnsləs/; also spelled **defenseless** in American English. If someone is **defenceless**, they are weak and unable to defend themselves. EG *...attacks on defenceless civilians.* ADJ QUALIT

defend /diˈfɛnd/, **defends, defending, defended.**

1 If you **defend** someone or something, **1.1** you do something in order to protect them. EG *The village had to defend itself against raiders.* V+O OR V-REFL **1.2** you argue in support of them when they have been criticized. EG *The bank has defended its actions in these cases.* V+O OR V-REFL
◇ **defender, defenders.** EG *...a defender of right-wing views.* ◇ N COUNT : USU+SUPP

2 In a court of law, when a lawyer **defends** a person who has been accused of a crime, he or she tries to prove that the charges are not true or that there was an excuse for the crime. V+O

3 If a sports champion **defends** his or her title, he or she plays a match or a game against someone who will become the new champion if they win. V+O OR V

defendant /diˈfɛndənt/, **defendants.** The **defendant** in a trial is the person who has been accused of a crime. N COUNT

defense /diˈfɛns/. See **defence.**

defensible /diˈfɛnsəˈbə°l/. An opinion, system, or action that is **defensible** is one that people can argue is right or good. EG *He gave a very defensible definition of socialism.* ADJ QUALIT

defensive /diˈfɛnsɪv/. **1** You use **defensive** to describe things that are intended to protect someone or something. EG *...defensive weapons... ...defensive measures... ...formidable defensive air cover.* ADJ CLASSIF : ATTRIB

2 If you are **on the defensive**, you are trying to protect yourself or your interests because you feel that you are being threatened. PHRASE

3 Someone who is **defensive** is behaving in a way that shows that they feel unsure or threatened. EG *I shuffled my feet and mumbled something defensive.* ADJ QUALIT ◇ **defensively.** EG *'I'm in no hurry,' said Rudolph defensively.* ◇ ADV

defer /diˈfɜː/, **defers, deferring, deferred. 1** If you **defer** an event or action, you arrange that it will take place at a later date than was planned. EG *They offered to defer his appointment for a year.* V+O OR V+-ING Formal

2 If you **defer** to someone, you accept their opinion or you do what they want because you respect them. V+*to* Formal

deference /dɛfə°rəns/ is a polite and respectful attitude to someone. EG *She is treated with deference... I refused to discuss the matter out of deference to my employer.* N UNCOUNT : OFT+*to*

deferential /dɛfərɛnʃə°l/. Someone who is **deferential** is polite and respectful. EG *I made every effort to be pleasant and deferential to Mr Thoms.* ADJ QUALIT
◇ **deferentially.** EG *'What work do you do, sir?' he asked deferentially.* ◇ ADV

defiance /diˈfaɪəns/. **1 Defiance** is behaviour which shows that you are not willing to obey someone or are not worried about their disapproval. EG *In a gesture of defiance, I wore a black miniskirt.* N UNCOUNT

2 If you do something **in defiance of** a person or a rule, you do it even though it has been forbidden. EG *The houses were erected in defiance of all building regulations.* PREP

defiant /diˈfaɪənt/. If you are **defiant**, you refuse to obey someone or you ignore their disapproval of you. EG *The girl sat down with a defiant look at Judy.* ADJ CLASSIF ◇ **defiantly.** EG *She announced defiantly that she intended to stay.* ◇ ADV

deficient /diˈfɪʃənt/. **1** If someone or something is **deficient** in a particular thing, they do not have as much of it as they need. EG *...old people deficient in vitamin C.* ADJ CLASSIF : USU PRED+*in* ◇ **deficiency** /diˈfɪʃənsiˈ/, **deficiencies.** EG *...vitamin deficiency... Calcium deficiency causes acid soil.* ◇ N COUNT OR N UNCOUNT +SUPP

2 Something that is **deficient** is not good enough. EG *...increasingly deficient public services.* ADJ QUALIT Formal
◇ **deficiency.** EG *The deficiency of the answers* ◇ N COUNT OR N UNCOUNT

was obvious to everybody... ...Lowell's deficiencies as an observer.

deficit /dɛfɪsɪt/, **deficits.** A **deficit** is the amount by which the money received by a country or organization is less than the money it has spent. EG *The Post Office's deficit totalled 150m pounds.* N COUNT

defile /di'faɪl/, **defiles, defiling, defiled.** If you **defile** something precious, you spoil it or damage it. EG *...secret thoughts which defiled her purity.* V+O

definable /di'faɪnəbə⁰l/. Something that is **definable** can be described clearly. EG *The most important definable group is the community... The magic has gone, and for no definable reason.* ADJ CLASSIF

define /di'faɪn/, **defines, defining, defined.** If you **define** something, you say exactly what it is. EG *Roland Buck asked Dr Kossou to define the problems discussed by the ministers... Each object had clearly defined functions... My dictionary defines 'crisis' as a 'turning point'.* V+O

definite /dɛfɪnɪt/. **1** If something is **definite**, **1.1** it is firm and clear, and unlikely to be changed. EG *They have very definite views on this topic... There's a definite date for the wedding.* **1.2** it is true rather than being someone's opinion or guess. EG *There was no definite evidence.* ADJ QUALIT

2 Someone who is **definite** behaves or talks in a firm, confident way. ADJ QUALIT

definite article, definite articles. In grammar, the word 'the' is sometimes called the **definite article**. In this dictionary 'the' is called a determiner (DET). See the entry headed DETERMINERS for more information. N COUNT

definitely /dɛfɪnɪtli¹/. **1** You use **definitely** to emphasize that something is certainly the case. EG *They were definitely not for sale... Yes, we definitely need a car park.* ADV SEN

2 If something has **definitely** been decided, the decision will not be changed. EG *I haven't definitely decided on going to law school.* ADV

definition /dɛfɪnɪʃə⁰n/, **definitions. 1** A **definition** is a statement giving the meaning of a word, especially in a dictionary. EG *There is no clear definition of schizophrenia.* N COUNT ● If you say that something has a particular quality **by definition**, you mean that it has this quality simply because of what it is. EG *Street life is, by definition, a life lived in public.* ● PHRASE

2 Definition is the quality of being clear and distinct. EG *They lack definition and identity as a class.* N UNCOUNT

definitive /də²fɪnɪtɪv/. **1** Something that is **definitive** provides a firm conclusion that cannot be questioned. EG *...a definitive verdict.* ADJ CLASSIF ◇ **definitively.** EG *'Hearts of Darkness' will definitively establish McCullin as a writer.* ◇ ADV

2 A book or performance that is **definitive** is thought to be the best of its kind that has ever been done or that will ever be done. EG *He has written the definitive study of Hooker.* ADJ CLASSIF

deflate /di'fleɪt/, **deflates, deflating, deflated. 1** If you **deflate** someone, you say or do something which makes them appear less important or makes them less confident. EG *...a mischievous desire to deflate the reputation of some contemporary.* V+O ◇ **deflated.** EG *If that left us feeling deflated, worse was to come.* ◇ ADJ CLASSIF

2 When a tyre or balloon **deflates**, or when you **deflate** it, all the air comes out of it. V-ERG

deflation /di'fleɪʃə⁰n/ is a reduction in economic activity in a country that leads to lower industrial output and lower prices. N UNCOUNT

deflect /di'flɛkt/, **deflects, deflecting, deflected. 1** If you **deflect** something such as someone's attention or criticism, you cause them to turn their attention to something else or to do something different. EG *Their main purpose was to deflect attention from the Government's proposals.* V+O

2 When something moving **is deflected**, it starts going in a slightly different direction from the way it was going before, often because it has hit something. EG *The two streams of water are deflected.* V-ERG

deform /di'fɔːm/, **deforms, deforming, deformed.** If something **deforms** a person's body or an object, it causes it to have an unnatural shape or appearance. EG *Badly fitting shoes can deform the feet.* V+O ◇ **deformed.** EG *The drug may have caused deformed babies.* ◇ ADJ QUALIT

deformity /di'fɔːmɪ'ti¹/, **deformities. 1** A **deformity** is a part of someone's body which is the wrong shape because of injury or illness. N COUNT

2 Deformity is the condition of having a deformity. N UNCOUNT

defrost /diːfrɒst, di'frɒst/, **defrosts, defrosting, defrosted. 1** When you **defrost** a fridge or freezer or when it **defrosts**, you switch it off so that the ice inside it can melt. V-ERG

2 When you **defrost** frozen food or when it **defrosts**, you allow it to become unfrozen so that you can eat it. V-ERG

deft /dɛft/. A **deft** action is skilful and often quick. EG *...cutting the edges away with deft movements of the knife... The deft fingers massaged his scalp.* ADJ QUALIT ◇ **deftly.** EG *He deftly slit open the envelope.* ◇ ADV

defunct /dɪfʌŋkt/. If something is **defunct**, it no longer exists or it is no longer functioning. EG *...long defunct local authorities.* ADJ CLASSIF

defuse /di'fjuːz/, **defuses, defusing, defused. 1** If you **defuse** a dangerous or tense situation, you make it less dangerous or tense. EG *Lester's casual attitude defused the situation.* V+O

2 If someone **defuses** a bomb, they remove the fuse from it so that it cannot explode. V+O

defy /di'faɪ/, **defies, defying, defied. 1** If you **defy** people or laws, you refuse to obey them. EG *...people who are intending to defy the law.* V+O

2 If you **defy** someone to do something, you challenge them to do it when you think that they will be unable to do it or will be too frightened to do it. EG *I defy anyone to disprove it.* V+O+*to*-INF

3 If something **defies** description or understanding, it is so strange or surprising that it is almost impossible to describe or understand. EG *...forces within the human character which defy rational analysis.* V+O

degenerate, degenerates, degenerating, degenerated; pronounced /di'dʒɛnəreɪt/ when it is a verb and /di'dʒɛnərə¹t/ when it is an adjective or a noun.

1 If someone or something **degenerates**, they become worse. EG *The discussion degenerated into a row.* V: OFT +*into/to* ◇ **degeneration** /dɪdʒɛnəreɪʃə⁰n/. EG *This disease causes physical and mental degeneration.* ◇ N UNCOUNT

2 If someone is **degenerate**, they show low standards of morality. EG *...the less degenerate men of earlier times.* ADJ QUALIT ◇ **degeneracy** /dɪdʒɛnərəsi¹/. EG *...the degeneracy of the age.* ◇ N UNCOUNT

3 A **degenerate** is someone who behaves in a way that many people find shocking or disgusting. N COUNT

degradation /dɛgrədeɪʃə⁰n/ is a state of poverty and dirt. EG *They forgot the squalor and degradation around them.* N UNCOUNT

degrade /di'greɪd/, **degrades, degrading, degraded.** If something **degrades** someone, it causes people to have less respect for them. EG *...films that degrade women.* V+O ◇ **degrading.** EG *He denounced the 'vicious and degrading cult of violence'.* ◇ ADJ QUALIT

degree /di'griː/, **degrees. 1** A **degree** is the amount of a feeling or quality that someone or something has or the extent to which something happens. EG *She admits to a degree of prejudice... This has been tried with varying degrees of success... The number of police carrying guns has increased to an alarming degree.* N COUNT+SUPP ● If something ● PHRASE

How many words on these pages could you use when talking about food?

happens **by degrees**, it happens slowly and gradually.

2 A **degree** is also **2.1** a unit of measurement that is used when expressing temperatures; often written as '°', for example 23°. EG *The temperature was 23 degrees centigrade.* **2.2** a unit of measurement that is used when expressing angles and also latitude and longitude; often written as '°', for example 50°. N COUNT

3 If you take a **degree**, you take a course of study at a university or polytechnic. If you have a **degree**, you have gained a qualification by passing a course like this. EG *He had taken a degree in music at Cambridge.* N COUNT

dehydrate /diːhaɪdreɪt/, **dehydrates, dehydrating, dehydrated. 1** When something such as food **is dehydrated**, all the water is removed from it, often in order to preserve it. ◊ **dehydrated.** EG *...packets of dehydrated soup.* V+O : USU PASS ◊ ADJ CLASSIF

2 If you **are dehydrated**, you have lost too much water from your body so that you feel weak or ill. V+O : USU PASS

deign /deɪn/, **deigns, deigning, deigned.** If you **deign** to do something, you do it even though you think you are really too important to do such a thing. EG *...plays that no regular reviewer would deign to go to.* V+to-INF Formal

deity /diːɪtɪ, deɪ-/, **deities.** A **deity** is a god or goddess. EG *...Roman deities... ...Blake's visions of the Deity.* N COUNT Formal

dejected /di¹dʒɛktɪ²d/. If you are **dejected**, you feel unhappy or disappointed about something. EG *He has a dejected, saddened look... He walked off, dejected in defeat.* ◊ **dejectedly.** EG *'I can't do it,' said the girl dejectedly.* ADJ QUALIT Formal ◊ ADV

dejection /di¹dʒɛkʃə⁰n/ is unhappiness and disappointment about something. EG *There was general dejection over the siege of Jerusalem.* N UNCOUNT Formal

delay /di¹leɪ/, **delays, delaying, delayed. 1** If you **delay** doing something, you do not do it until a later time. EG *Try and persuade them to delay some of the changes... She will delay starting for six months... Don't delay.* V+-ING, V+O, OR V

2 To **delay** someone means to make them late or to make them slow down. EG *I'm afraid I was slightly delayed.* V+O

3 To **delay** something means to make it happen later than was planned or expected. EG *The shock of the operation delayed his recovery.* V+O

4 If there is a **delay**, something does not happen until later than was planned or expected. EG *The delays were caused by events beyond our control... We shall inform you without delay.* N COUNT OR N UNCOUNT

delectable /di¹lɛktəbə⁰l/. **1** If you say that someone is **delectable**, you mean that they are very attractive. EG *...the delectable Miss Haynes.* ADJ QUALIT Literary

2 Food that is **delectable** is very pleasant and tasty. ADJ QUALIT Literary

delegate, delegates, delegating, delegated; pronounced /dɛləgə¹t/ when it is a noun and /dɛləgeɪt/ when it is a verb.

1 A **delegate** is a person who is chosen to make decisions on behalf of a group of other people, especially at a meeting. EG *...delegates to the annual party conference.* N COUNT

2 If you **delegate** someone to do something, you formally ask them to do it on your behalf. EG *The Bishop delegated me to approach the local press.* V+O : USU+to-INF

3 If you **delegate** duties or responsibilities, you tell someone to do them on your behalf. EG *I employ staff and delegate all household tasks.* V+O OR V

delegation /dɛlɪ²geɪʃə⁰n/, **delegations.** A **delegation** is a group of people who have been sent somewhere to speak or act on behalf of a larger group of people. EG *There was also a delegation from the British Isles.* N COUNT

delete /di¹liːt/, **deletes, deleting, deleted.** If you **delete** something that has been written down, you cross it out or remove it. EG *...a narrative from which some words have been deleted.* V+O

deliberate, deliberates, deliberating, deliberated; pronounced /di¹lɪbərə¹t/ when it is an adjective and /di¹lɪbəreɪt/ when it is a verb.

1 If something that you do is **deliberate**, you planned or intended to do it, rather than doing it by accident. EG *It was a deliberate lie.* ◊ **deliberately.** EG *I've never deliberately hurt anyone.* ADJ CLASSIF ◊ ADV

2 An action or movement that is **deliberate** is done slowly and carefully. EG *His manner was quiet, his speech deliberate.* ◊ **deliberately.** EG *He climbed the stairs slowly and deliberately.* ADJ QUALIT ◊ ADV

3 If you **deliberate**, you think about something carefully before making a decision. EG *We had been waiting for two days while the jury deliberated.* V

deliberation /dɪ¹lɪbəreɪʃə⁰n/, **deliberations. 1** **Deliberation** is careful consideration of a subject. EG *After considerable deliberation, I decided to accept the job.* N UNCOUNT

2 If you do something **with deliberation**, you do it slowly and carefully. EG *John, with great deliberation, put his books into his briefcase.* PHRASE

3 **Deliberations** are formal discussions. EG *I left the committee to its deliberations.* N PLURAL

delicacy /dɛlɪkəsi¹/, **delicacies. 1** If something has **delicacy**, it is graceful and attractive. EG *...the ravishing beauty and delicacy of their features.* N UNCOUNT

2 If you do or say something with **delicacy**, you do it or say it carefully and tactfully because you do not want to offend someone. EG *With great delicacy, they refrained from asking the sex of his friend.* N UNCOUNT

3 A **delicacy** is a rare or expensive food that is considered especially nice to eat. EG *...artichokes, smoked fish, and other delicacies.* N COUNT

delicate /dɛlɪkə¹t/. **1** Something that is **delicate** is narrow and graceful or attractive. EG *She had long delicate fingers.* ◊ **delicately.** EG *...delicately veined pale skin.* ADJ QUALIT ◊ ADV

2 A colour, taste, or smell that is **delicate** is pleasant and not strong or intense. EG *...a delicate pale cream colour.* ADJ QUALIT

3 A **delicate** object is fragile and needs to be handled carefully. EG *...delicate china.* ADJ QUALIT

4 A **delicate** movement is gentle, controlled, and not at all clumsy. EG *...delicate ballet steps.* ◊ **delicately.** EG *The princess took the pot delicately from him.* ADJ QUALIT ◊ ADV

5 Someone who is **delicate** is often ill. EG *She was a very delicate child.* ADJ QUALIT

6 If someone is **delicate** in their speech, they choose their words carefully in order to avoid offending people. ◊ **delicately.** EG *She had delicately hinted at his inadequacy.* ADJ QUALIT ◊ ADV

7 A **delicate** situation or problem needs very careful and tactful treatment. EG *...the delicate sphere of race relations.* ◊ **delicately.** EG *...highly sensitive and delicately balanced economic systems.* ADJ QUALIT ◊ ADV

8 A **delicate** sense or scientific instrument is capable of noticing very small changes or differences. EG *Bees have a delicate sense of smell.* ADJ QUALIT

delicatessen /dɛlɪkətɛsə⁰n/, **delicatessens.** A **delicatessen** is a shop that sells unusual foods such as foreign cheeses and cold meats. N COUNT

delicious /dɪ²lɪʃəs/. **1** Food that is **delicious** has a very pleasant taste. EG *...a delicious cake.* ADJ QUALIT

2 Something or someone that is **delicious** is very nice or pleasant. EG *It is a delicious feeling.* ◊ **deliciously.** EG *The sun felt deliciously warm.* ADJ QUALIT Informal ◊ ADV+ADJ

delight /di¹laɪt/, **delights, delighting, delighted.**

1 **Delight** is a feeling of very great pleasure. EG *Frank discovered to his delight that the gun was real.* N UNCOUNT

2 If someone **takes a delight** or **takes delight** in doing something, they get a lot of pleasure from doing it. EG *...sadistic friends who take delight in breaking bad news.* PHRASE

3 You can refer to someone or something that gives you great joy or pleasure as a **delight**. EG N COUNT: OFT+SUPP

That was when I first discovered the delights of the city... Mrs Travers was a delight to interview.

4 If something **delights** you, it gives you a lot of pleasure. EG *The thought of divorce neither distressed nor delighted her.* V+O

5 If you **delight** in something, you get a lot of pleasure from it. EG *Morris delighted in hard manual work.* V+*in/at*

delighted /di[1]laɪtɪ[2]d/. If you are **delighted**, you are extremely pleased and excited about something. EG *He was delighted with his achievement... He was delighted to meet them again.* ADJ QUALIT
◊ **delightedly.** EG *She laughed delightedly.* ◊ ADV

delightful /dɪlaɪtfʊl/. Someone or something that is **delightful** is very pleasant. EG *Her children really are delightful... ...a delightful room.* ADJ QUALIT
◊ **delightfully.** EG *...a delightfully smooth soup.* ◊ ADV+ADJ

delinquent /dɪ[2]lɪŋkwənt/, **delinquents.** You use **delinquent** to describe young people who are always committing minor crimes. EG *...families with delinquent children... ...delinquent behaviour.* ADJ CLASSIF
▸ used as a noun. EG *A few months of this may deter some potential delinquents.* ▸ N COUNT ◊ **delinquency** /dɪ[2]lɪŋkwənsi[1]/. EG *...children taken into care because of their delinquency.* ◊ N UNCOUNT Formal ● See also **juvenile delinquent**.

delirious /dɪlɪrɪəs/. 1 Someone who is **delirious** is unable to think or speak in a rational way, usually because they have a fever. ADJ CLASSIF ◊ **delirium** /dɪlɪrɪəm/. EG *We heard him babble in delirium.* ◊ N UNCOUNT

2 You can also describe someone who is extremely excited and happy as **delirious**. EG *He sang before delirious crowds in a theatre.* ADJ QUALIT

deliver /dɪ[2]lɪvə/, **delivers, delivering, delivered.** 1 If you **deliver** something, 1.1 you take it to someone's house or office. EG *He delivered newspapers as a boy.* V+O 1.2 you give it to someone. EG *Chance delivered his enemy into his hands.* V+O+A Formal

2 If you **deliver** a lecture or speech, you give it. V+O

3 When someone **delivers** a baby, they help the woman who is giving birth to the baby. V+O

4 If you say that someone has **delivered the goods**, you mean that they have done something that they promised to do. EG *The Department failed to deliver the goods.* PHRASE

delivery /dɪ[2]lɪvə[0]ri[1]/, **deliveries. 1 Delivery** is the bringing of letters, parcels, or goods to someone's house or office. EG *All goods must be paid for before delivery.* N UNCOUNT

2 A **delivery** is something that is delivered to someone. EG *We ordered an extra delivery of coal.* N COUNT

3 Someone's **delivery** is the way in which they give a speech. EG *His delivery was slow and ponderous.* N UNCOUNT: USU+SUPP

4 **Delivery** is also the process of giving birth to a baby. EG *It was a simple, routine delivery.* N COUNT OR N UNCOUNT

delta /deltə/, **deltas.** A **delta** is an area of flat land where a river spreads out into several smaller rivers before entering the sea. N COUNT

delude /di[1]lj[0]u:d/, **deludes, deluding, deluded.** If you **delude** someone, you make them believe something that is not true. EG *They are not deluded by our talk of freedom... It was no good deluding myself that he loved me.* V+O OR V-REFL

deluge /delju:dʒ/, **deluges, deluging, deluged. 1** A **deluge** is a sudden, very heavy fall of rain. EG *The rain turned to a deluge.* N COUNT

2 A **deluge** of things is a very large number of them which arrive at the same time. EG *...a deluge of petitions to the King.* N PART

3 If you **are deluged** with things, a very large number of them arrive at the same time. EG *They were deluged with requests to play the song.* V+O: USU PASS+*with*

delusion /di[1]lu:ʒən/, **delusions.** A **delusion** is a false belief. EG *...the delusion that slaughter in Britain is humane.* N COUNT

de luxe /di[1] lʌks/. You use **de luxe** to describe things that are better and more expensive than other things of the same kind. EG *...a de luxe version of the Ford Escort.* ADJ CLASSIF

delve /delv/, **delves, delving, delved. 1** If you **delve** into something, you try to discover more information about it. EG *One must delve more deeply to find the reasons.* V+A

2 If you **delve** inside something such as a cupboard or a bag, you search inside it. V+A

demagogue /deməgɒg/, **demagogues.** A **demagogue** is a political leader who tries to win support by appealing to people's emotions rather than by using rational arguments; used showing disapproval. N COUNT

demand /di[1]mɑ:nd/, **demands, demanding, demanded. 1** If you **demand** something, **1.1** you ask for it very forcefully. EG *They are demanding higher wages... I demand to see a doctor... She had been demanding that he visit her.* V+O, V+*to*-INF, OR V+REPORT **1.2** you ask a question in a forceful way. EG *'What have I done?' he demanded.* V+QUOTE

2 If a job or situation **demands** something, that thing is necessary for it. EG *He has most of the qualities demanded of a leader.* V+O

3 A **demand** is a firm request for something. EG *They feared what might happen if they refused his demands... ...his demand for stronger armed forces.* N COUNT +SUPP OR REPORT

4 If there is **demand** for something, a lot of people want to buy it or have it. EG *The demand for health care is unlimited.* N UNCOUNT: OFT+*for* ● If something is **in demand**, a lot of people want to buy it or have it. ● PHRASE

5 The **demands** of something are the things that have to be done or provided for it. EG *The system has always made heavy demands on those working in it.* N COUNT: USU PLURAL

6 If something is available **on demand**, you can have it whenever you ask for it. EG *Your money is available on demand.* PHRASE

demanding /di[1]mɑ:ndɪŋ/. **1** A **demanding** job or task requires a lot of time, energy, or attention. EG *...women who are involved in demanding careers.* ADJ QUALIT

2 People who are **demanding** are not easily satisfied. EG *...an impatient and demanding public.* ADJ QUALIT

demarcation /di:mɑ:keɪʃə[0]n/ is the action of showing or stating exactly where two things are separated or are different. EG *...the demarcation lines between ethnic groups.* N UNCOUNT

demean /di[1]mi:n/, **demeans, demeaning, demeaned.** If you **demean** yourself or **demean** something, you do something which makes people have less respect for you or for that thing. EG *They all agreed that the President had demeaned himself as a man... He had demeaned his office by lying.* V-REFL OR V+O Formal ◊ **demeaning** /di[1]mi:nɪŋ/. EG *They regard these jobs as demeaning and degrading.* ◊ ADJ QUALIT

demeanour /di[1]mi:nə/; spelled **demeanor** in American English. Your **demeanour** is the way you behave, which gives people an impression of your character and feelings. EG *...his usual calm demeanour... ...the vulgarity of his demeanour.* N UNCOUNT: USU+POSS Formal

demented /di[1]mentɪ[2]d/. Someone who is **demented** behaves in a wild or violent way, often because they are mad. ADJ CLASSIF

demise /di[1]maɪz/. The **demise** of something or someone is their end or death. EG *...the demise of the British Empire.* N SING+SUPP Formal

democracy /dɪ[2]mɒkrəsi[1]/, **democracies. 1 Democracy** is a system of government or organization in which people choose leaders or make important decisions by voting. N UNCOUNT

2 A **democracy** is a country in which the people choose their government by voting for it. N COUNT

democrat /deməⁱkræt/, **democrats.** A **democrat** is a person who believes in the ideals of democracy, personal freedom, and equality. N COUNT

What different style labels are used in the Extra Column on these pages?

democratic /dɛmə[6]krætɪk/. A **democratic** country, organization, or system is one in which leaders are chosen or decisions are made by voting. EG *...democratic government.* ◊ **democratically.** EG *...a democratically elected government.*
ADJ CLASSIF; ◊ ADV

demolish /di[1]mɒlɪʃ/, **demolishes, demolishing, demolished. 1** When a building **is demolished**, it is knocked down, often because it is old or dangerous. EG *The old prison was demolished in 1890.* ◊ **demolition** /dɛməlɪʃə[0]n, di:-/. EG *...the demolition of the old YMCA building.*
V+O; ◊ N UNCOUNT

2 If you **demolish** someone's idea, argument, or belief, you prove that it is completely wrong. EG *A week in Moscow demolished the myth that their stage productions are not exciting.* ◊ **demolition.** EG *...the demolition of a beloved theory.*
V+O; ◊ N UNCOUNT

demon /di:mə[0]n/, **demons.** A **demon** is an evil spirit. EG *...a demon of wrath.*
N COUNT

demonic /di[1]mɒnɪk/. Something that is **demonic** is evil. EG *...demonic forces.*
ADJ CLASSIF

demonstrable /dɪ[2]mɒnstrəbə[0]l/. Something that is **demonstrable** can be shown to exist or to be true. EG *The economic advantages are clearly demonstrable.* ◊ **demonstrably.** EG *Their vehicles are demonstrably more reliable than ours.*
ADJ CLASSIF; ◊ ADV : OFT+ADJ

demonstrate /dɛmənstreɪt/, **demonstrates, demonstrating, demonstrated. 1** To **demonstrate** a fact or theory means to make it clear to people. EG *Her latest book demonstrates how important freedom is.*
V+O OR V+REPORT

2 If you **demonstrate** something to someone, you show them how to do it or how it works. EG *She is demonstrating a new kind of cooker... She has been demonstrating how you make bread.*
V+O : OFT+*to* OR V+REPORT

3 If you **demonstrate** a particular skill, quality, or feeling, you show that you have it. EG *She has not demonstrated much generosity.*
V+O

4 When people **demonstrate**, they take part in a march or a meeting to show their opposition to something or their support for it. ◊ **demonstrator, demonstrators.** EG *...crowds of demonstrators.*
V; ◊ N COUNT

demonstration /dɛmənstreɪʃə[0]n/, **demonstrations. 1** A **demonstration** is a public meeting or march which is held by people to show their opposition to something or their support for it. EG *There was a series of demonstrations against the visit.*
N COUNT

2 A **demonstration** of something is a talk by someone who shows you how to do it or how it works. EG *...a demonstration of the new machinery.*
N COUNT

3 A **demonstration** of something such as a fact is a proof by someone that it exists or is true. EG *It was an unforgettable demonstration of the power of reason.*
N COUNT OR N UNCOUNT

4 Demonstration of a quality or feeling is an expression of it. EG *...spontaneous demonstrations of affection.*
N COUNT OR N UNCOUNT

demonstrative /di[2]mɒnstrətɪv/. Someone who is **demonstrative** shows affection freely and openly. EG *...a demonstrative and sympathetic mother.*
ADJ QUALIT

demoralize /di[1]mɒrəlaɪz/, **demoralizes, demoralizing, demoralized;** also spelled **demoralise.** If something **demoralizes** you, it makes you lose confidence in what you are doing and makes you feel depressed. EG *People are demoralized by the present climate of public opinion.* ◊ **demoralized.** EG *...the stream of desperate and demoralized people seeking work.* ◊ **demoralization** /di[1]mɒrəlaɪzeɪʃə[0]n/. EG *...the growing national mood of doubt and demoralisation.*
V+O; ◊ ADJ QUALIT; ◊ N UNCOUNT

demote /di[1]məʊt/, **demotes, demoting, demoted.** If someone in authority **demotes** you, they reduce your rank, often as a punishment. EG *He was demoted to the rank of ordinary soldier.*
V+O

demur /dɪmɜ:/, **demurs, demurring, demurred.** If you **demur**, you say that you do not agree with something or will not do something. EG *Morris invited her out for a meal. She demurred.*
V; Formal

demure /di[1]mjʊə/. Someone, especially a young woman, who is **demure** is quiet and rather shy, and behaves very correctly. EG *...a demure, sweet-faced girl.* ◊ **demurely.** EG *She sat demurely by her mother.*
ADJ QUALIT; ◊ ADV

den /dɛn/, **dens.** The **den** of a fox or wolf is its home.
N COUNT

denial /dɪ[2]naɪəl/, **denials. 1** If you make a **denial** of something such as an accusation, you say that it is not true. EG *He made a personal denial of all the charges against him.*
N COUNT OR N UNCOUNT

2 If there is a **denial** of something that people think they have a right to, someone in authority refuses to let them have it. EG *They protested against the continued denial of civil liberties.*
N UNCOUNT : OFT+*of*

denigrate /dɛnɪ[2]greɪt/, **denigrates, denigrating, denigrated.** If you **denigrate** someone or something, you criticize them unfairly. EG *To assert this is to denigrate the effectiveness of the police.*
V+O; Formal

denim /dɛnɪm/, **denims. 1 Denim** is a thick cotton cloth which is used to make clothes. EG *...denim jeans... ...a skirt made of black denim.*
N UNCOUNT : USU N MOD

2 Denims are trousers made of denim.
N PLURAL

denomination /di[1]nɒmɪneɪʃə[0]n/, **denominations.** A **denomination** is a religious group within a particular religion. EG *...young people of all denominations.*
N COUNT

denote /di[1]nəʊt/, **denotes, denoting, denoted. 1** If one thing **denotes** another, it is a sign or indication of it. EG *My identity was denoted by a plastic label on my wrist.*
V+O OR V+REPORT; Formal

2 What a word or name **denotes** is what it means or refers to. EG *'Basic', as its name denotes, is a very straightforward set of computer instructions.*
V+O; Formal

denounce /di[1]naʊns/, **denounces, denouncing, denounced.** If you **denounce** someone or something, you criticize them severely and publicly. EG *A mass meeting at Carnegie Hall denounced him as a traitor.*
V+O : OFT+*as*

dense /dɛns/, **denser, densest. 1** Something that is **dense** contains a lot of things or people in a small area. EG *...a dense crowd... ...dense forest.* ◊ **densely.** EG *...the most densely populated region in the country.*
ADJ QUALIT; ◊ ADV

2 Dense fog or smoke is thick and difficult to see through.
ADJ QUALIT

3 If you say that someone is **dense**, you think that they are stupid and take a long time to understand simple things.
ADJ PRED; Informal

density /dɛnsɪ[1]ti[1]/, **densities. 1** The **density** of something in a place is the extent to which it fills the place. EG *Australia has a very low population density... Traffic density was increasing.*
N UNCOUNT OR N COUNT

2 The **density** of a substance or object is the relation of its mass to its volume. EG *...the density of water.*
N UNCOUNT OR N COUNT; Technical

dent /dɛnt/, **dents, denting, dented. 1** If you **dent** something, you damage its surface by hitting it and causing a bit of it to curve inwards. EG *He pulled back the covers and dented the pillow a little.* ◊ **dented.** EG *...some dented oil drums.*
V+O; ◊ ADJ CLASSIF

2 A **dent** is a hollow made in the surface of something, which has been caused by hitting it. EG *...car owners searching for dents and scratches.*
N COUNT

dental /dɛntə[0]l/ is used to describe things that relate to teeth. EG *...free dental treatment... Maggie has a dental appointment.*
ADJ CLASSIF : ATTRIB

dentist /dɛntɪst/, **dentists. 1** A **dentist** is a person who is qualified to treat people's teeth.
N COUNT

2 You refer to the place where a dentist works as the **dentist's** or the **dentist**. EG *He's at the dentist's.*
N SING : *the*+N

dentures /dɛntʃəz/ are artificial teeth used by people who no longer have all their own teeth.
N PLURAL

denude /di[1]nju:d/, **denudes, denuding, denuded.** If something **is denuded**, everything is taken off it or from it. EG *The Christmas tree was soon denuded of its parcels.*
V+O : USU PASS, OFT+*of*; Formal

denunciation /di1nʌnsieɪʃən/, **denunciations.** **Denunciation** of someone or something is severe public criticism of them. EG *...his denunciations of the errors of the previous government.* N UNCOUNT OR N COUNT : USU+SUPP

deny /dɪ2naɪ/, **denies, denying, denied. 1** If you **deny** something, you say that it is not true. EG *He denied that he was involved... Green denied doing anything illegal.* V+O, V+-ING, OR V+REPORT : ONLY *that*

2 If you **deny** someone something that they want, you do not let them have it. EG *He has denied you access to information... Freedom is denied to the young for the same reason.* V+O+O OR V+O+*to*

deodorant /di:əʊdə0rənt/ **deodorants. Deodorant** is a pleasant-smelling liquid that you put on your body, in order to reduce the smell of perspiration. N MASS

depart /di1pɑ:t/, **departs, departing, departed. 1** When someone or something **departs** from a place, they leave it. EG *She prepared to depart for Italy... The Express was scheduled to depart at six.* V : USU+A

2 If you **depart** from the normal way of doing something, you do something slightly different. EG *...their unwillingness to depart from traditional practice... We departed from the script to produce a startling finish.* V+*from*

departed /di1pɑ:tɪ2d/. If you talk about **departed** friends or relatives, you mean the ones who have died. ADJ CLASSIF Formal

department /di1pɑ:tmə2nt/, **departments.** A **department** is one of the sections in a large shop or an organization such as a university. EG *...a Professor in the English department... ...the cosmetics department of Harrods... ...the local office of the Department of Health.* N COUNT+SUPP ◊ **departmental** /di:pɑ:tmɛntə0l/. EG *...a departmental meeting.* ◊ ADJ CLASSIF : ATTRIB

department store, department stores. A **department store** is a large shop which sells many different kinds of goods. N COUNT

departure /di1pɑ:tʃə/, **departures. 1 Departure** is the act of leaving a place. EG *...the signal for departure... ...the week before their departure.* N COUNT OR N UNCOUNT

2 If an action is a **departure** from what was previously planned or what is usually done, it is different from it. EG *Does the budget represent a departure from stated Government policy?* N COUNT : OFT+*from*

depend /di1pɛnd/, **depends, depending, depended. 1** If you **depend** on someone or something, you need them in order to be able to survive. EG *...the two persons on whom the child depended for survival... These factories depend upon natural resources.* V+*on/upon*

2 If you can **depend** on someone or something, you know that they will help you when you need them. EG *I knew I could depend on you.* V+*on/upon*

3 If you say that something **depends** on something else, you mean that it will only happen if the circumstances are right. EG *The success of the meeting depends largely on whether the chairman is efficient.* V : OFT+*on* OR V+REPORT : ONLY WH

4 You use an expression such as **'It depends'** to indicate that you are not sure what will happen or what is the best answer to give. EG *'What will you do?' – 'I don't know. It depends.'* PHRASE

5 You use **depending on** to say that what happens varies according to the circumstances. EG *This training takes a variable time, depending on the chosen speciality.* PREP

dependable /di1pɛndəbə0l/. If someone or something is **dependable**, you know that they will always do what you need or expect them to do. EG *She was remarkably self-confident and dependable for her age... ...a dependable sort of car.* ADJ QUALIT

dependant /di1pɛndənt/, **dependants;** also spelled **dependent.** Your **dependants** are the people who you support financially, such as your children. EG *Were you to be killed, your dependants could get compensation.* N COUNT

dependence /di1pɛndəns/; also spelled **dependance. Dependence** is a constant and regular need that someone has for something in order to be able to live or work properly. EG *...the increasing dependence of police forces on computers... ...dependence on pain-killing drugs.* N UNCOUNT +*on/upon*

dependent /di1pɛndənt/. **1** If you are **dependent** on someone or something, you need them in order to be able to survive. EG *West Europe was still heavily dependent on Middle Eastern oil.* ADJ QUALIT : OFT+*on/upon*

2 See also **dependant.**

depict /di1pɪkt/, **depicts, depicting, depicted.** If you **depict** someone or something, **1** you draw them in a painting or cartoon. EG *Haselden's cartoon depicted the British lion roaring triumphantly.* V+O

2 you describe them. EG *Women are constantly depicted as inferior to men.* V+O : OFT+*as*

depiction /di1pɪkʃə0n/, **depictions.** A **depiction** of something is a picture of it or a written description of it. EG *...the depiction of Christ.* N COUNT OR N UNCOUNT

deplete /di1pli:t/, **depletes, depleting, depleted.** If you **deplete** something, you reduce the amount of it that is available to be used. EG *We must be careful as we deplete our stocks of resources.* V+O ◊ **depletion** /di1pli:ʃə0n/. EG *...the depletion of raw material reserves.* ◊ N UNCOUNT : USU+SUPP

deplorable /di1plɔ:rəbə0l/. If you say that something is **deplorable**, you mean that it is extremely bad or unpleasant. EG *How did these deplorable conditions come about?* ADJ QUALIT Formal

deplore /di1plɔ:/, **deplores, deploring, deplored.** If you **deplore** something, you think that it is wrong or immoral. EG *We deplore waste.* V+O Formal

deploy /di1plɔɪ/, **deploys, deploying, deployed.** When a country **deploys** troops, resources, or equipment, it organizes them so that they are ready for immediate action. V+O ◊ **deployment** /di1plɔɪmə2nt/. EG *...the deployment of nuclear weapons.* ◊ N UNCOUNT

deport /di1pɔ:t/, **deports, deporting, deported.** When a government **deports** foreigners, it sends them out of the country because they have committed a crime or because they do not have official permission to be there. V+O ◊ **deportation** /di:pɔ:teɪʃə0n/, **deportations.** EG *They were prepared to risk prison or deportation.* ◊ N UNCOUNT OR N COUNT

deportment /di1pɔ:tmə2nt/. Your **deportment** is the way you behave, especially the way you walk and move. N UNCOUNT Formal

depose /di1pəʊz/, **deposes, deposing, deposed.** If a ruler or leader **is deposed**, they are removed from their position by force. V+O : USU PASS

deposit /di1pɒzɪt/, **deposits, depositing, deposited. 1** If a substance **is deposited** somewhere, it is left there as a result of a chemical or geological process. EG *Layers of sand were deposited on top of the peat.* V+O : USU PASS+A

2 If you **deposit** something somewhere, you put it there, often so that it will be safe until it is needed again. EG *He deposited the case in the left luggage office.* V+O : USU+A

3 A **deposit** is an amount of a substance that has been left somewhere as a result of a chemical or geological process. EG *...rich mineral deposits.* N COUNT

4 When talking about money, a **deposit** is **4.1** a sum of money which you put in a bank account or other savings account. **4.2** part of the price of something which you pay when you agree to buy it. EG *We've saved enough for the deposit on a house.* **4.3** a sum of money which you give a person you rent or hire something from. The money is returned to you if you do not damage what you have rented. N COUNT

depot /dɛpəʊ/, **depots.** A **depot** is **1** a place where goods and vehicles are kept when they are not being used. EG *...airfields and supply depots.* **2** a bus station or a railway station. N COUNT; American

On these pages, which noun is often used in front of another noun?

depraved /di^{1}preɪvd/. If you describe someone as **depraved**, you think that they are morally bad. EG *Few mothers are depraved enough to kill their children.* ◊ **depravity** /di^{1}prævɪ^{1}ti^1/. EG *...a world of depravity and torture.* — ADJ QUALIT; ◊ N UNCOUNT Formal

deprecating /dɛprəkeɪtɪŋ/. A **deprecating** gesture or remark shows that you think something is not very good. EG *Tom waved a deprecating hand.* — ADJ QUALIT Formal

depreciate /di^{1}priːʃɪeɪt/, **depreciates, depreciating, depreciated.** When something **depreciates**, it loses some of its value. EG *Property rarely depreciates.* ◊ **depreciation** /di^{1}priːsi^{1}eɪʃə^{0}n/. EG *...the depreciation of currency.* — V; ◊ N UNCOUNT +SUPP

depress /di^{1}prɛs/, **depresses, depressing, depressed. 1** If something **depresses** you, it makes you feel sad and disappointed. EG *She lost the case, which depressed her enormously.* — V+O

2 If something **depresses** prices or wages, it causes them to drop in value. EG *The current oil glut has depressed prices still more.* — V+O

depressed /di^{1}prɛst/. **1** If you are **depressed**, you feel sad and disappointed. — ADJ QUALIT

2 A place that is **depressed** does not have as much business or employment as it used to. EG *...the effects of living in depressed city areas.* — ADJ QUALIT

depressing /di^{1}prɛsɪŋ/. Something that is **depressing** makes you feel sad and disappointed. EG *This was depressing news.* ◊ **depressingly.** EG *It was all depressingly clear.* — ADJ QUALIT; ◊ ADV+ADJ

depression /di^{1}prɛʃə^{0}n/, **depressions. 1 Depression** is great sadness and disappointment. — N UNCOUNT OR N COUNT

2 A **depression** is a time when there is very little economic activity, which results in a lot of unemployment. EG *...during the depression of the 1930's.* — N COUNT

3 On a surface, a **depression** is an area which is lower than the rest of the surface. EG *...shallow depressions in the ground.* — N COUNT

deprive /di^{1}praɪv/, **deprives, depriving, deprived.** If you **deprive** someone of something, you take it away from them or prevent them from having it. EG *...to deprive a peasant of his land.* ◊ **deprivation** /dɛprɪ^{2}veɪʃə^{0}n/, **deprivations.** EG *...suffering years of deprivation and poverty.* — V+O+*of*; ◊ N UNCOUNT OR N COUNT

deprived /di^{1}praɪvd/. If you describe someone as **deprived**, you think that they do not have the things that are essential in life. EG *...deprived children.* — ADJ QUALIT

dept is a written abbreviation for 'department'; mainly used as part of a name. EG *...Dept of English.*

depth /dɛpθ/, **depths. 1** The **depth** of something is **1.1** the distance between its top and bottom surfaces. EG *None of the lakes was more than a few yards in depth.* **1.2** the distance between the front and the back of it. EG *...things buried in the depths of your store cupboard.* — N UNCOUNT OR N COUNT

2 The **depth** of a situation or emotion is its great degree or intensity. EG *The depth of his concern was evident enough.* — N UNCOUNT +SUPP

3 The **depths** of the ocean are the parts of it which are a long way below the surface. — N PLURAL : *the*+N

4 If you are in the **depths** of despair, you are extremely unhappy. — N PLURAL +SUPP

5 In the **depths** of winter means in the middle of winter, when it is coldest. — N PLURAL +SUPP

6 If you deal with a subject **in depth**, you deal with it very thoroughly and consider all the aspects of it. — PHRASE

7 If you are **out of** your **depth**, you are trying to deal with something that is too difficult for you to cope with or understand. — PHRASE

deputation /dɛpjə^{4}teɪʃə^{0}n/, **deputations.** A **deputation** is a small group of people who have been asked to speak to someone on behalf of a larger group of people, usually in order to make a complaint. — N COUNT

deputize /dɛpjə^{4}taɪz/, **deputizes, deputizing, deputized;** also spelled **deputise.** If you **deputize** for someone, you do something on their behalf, for example attend a meeting. — V : OFT+*for*

deputy /dɛpjə^{4}ti^1/, **deputies.** A **deputy** is the second most important person in an organization or department. A deputy often acts on behalf of the boss when the boss cannot be present. EG *He and his deputy co-operated well... ...the Deputy Chairman of the Commission.* — N COUNT OR N MOD

deranged /di^{1}reɪndʒd/. Someone who is **deranged** behaves in a wild or strange way, often as a result of mental illness. — ADJ QUALIT

derelict /dɛrə^{1}lɪkt/. A **derelict** building or area of land has not been used for some time and is in a bad condition. — ADJ CLASSIF

deride /di^{1}raɪd/, **derides, deriding, derided.** If you **deride** someone or something, you unkindly laugh at them, saying that they are stupid or of no value. EG *His sense of superiority makes him deride her opinions.* — V+O

derision /di^{1}rɪʒə^{0}n/. If you speak of someone or something with **derision**, you show that you have contempt for them, believing that they are stupid or have no value. EG *They speak with derision of amateurs.* — N UNCOUNT

derisive /di^{1}raɪsɪv/. A **derisive** noise, expression, or remark shows the contempt that you have for someone or something. EG *Maureen rocked with derisive laughter.* ◊ **derisively.** EG *Desiree snorted derisively.* — ADJ QUALIT; ◊ ADV

derisory /di^{1}raɪzərɪ/. Something that is **derisory** is so small or inadequate that it seems silly or not worth considering. EG *Fines for cruelty to animals are derisory.* — ADJ QUALIT

derivation /dɛrə^{1}veɪʃə^{0}n/, **derivations.** The **derivation** of a word is the original word or expression that it comes from. — N COUNT

derivative /dɪrɪvətɪv/, **derivatives. 1** A **derivative** is something which has developed from something else. EG *...the modern derivative of the fairy story.* — N COUNT

2 A work or idea that is **derivative** is not new or original, but copies ideas that have been used before; used showing disapproval. — ADJ QUALIT

derive /di^{1}raɪv/, **derives, deriving, derived. 1** If you **derive** a particular feeling from someone or something, you get it from them. EG *They derive enormous pleasure from their grandchildren.* — V+O : OFT+*from* Formal

2 If you say that something **derives** or **is derived** from another thing, you mean that it comes from that thing. EG *The word 'detergent' is derived from the Latin word for 'cleaner'... Wealth derives from political power.* — V-ERG+*from*

derogatory /dɪrɒgətə^{0}ri^1/. A **derogatory** remark expresses your low opinion of someone or something. — ADJ CLASSIF

descend /di^{1}sɛnd/, **descends, descending, descended. 1** If you **descend** or if you **descend** something, you move downwards from a higher to a lower level. EG *The valley becomes more exquisite as we descend... They descended the stairs.* — V OR V+O Formal

2 If silence or unhappiness **descends** on people or places, it occurs or starts to affect them. EG *A sinister silence descended upon the office.* — V : OFT +*on/upon* Literary

3 If you **descend** on a place, you arrive suddenly and often unexpectedly. EG *...the prospect of millions of pilgrims descending on Turin.* — V : OFT +*on/upon*

4 If you **descend** to something, you behave in a way that is considered unacceptable or unworthy of you. EG *Gareth was vexed that he should descend to such a stupid remark.* — V+*to*

5 See also **descended, descending**.

descendant /di^{1}sɛndə^{2}nt/, **descendants.** Someone's **descendants** are the people in later generations who are related to them. — N COUNT

descended /di^{1}sɛndɪ^{2}d/. A person who is **descended** from someone who lived a long time ago is related to them. EG *His family were descended from kings.* — ADJ PRED +*from*

descending /di^{1}sɛndɪŋ/. When a group of things is arranged in **descending** order, each thing is smaller in size or less in importance than the thing — ADJ CLASSIF : ATTRIB before it. EG *Arrange the numbers in descending order.*

descent /di'sent/, **descents. 1** A **descent** is a movement from a higher to a lower level. EG *He saw an aircraft making a very steep descent.* N COUNT: USU SING

2 Your **descent** is the nationality or social status of the people that you are descended from. EG *...Americans of Irish descent.* N UNCOUNT +SUPP

describe /dɪ²skraɪb/, **describes, describing, described.** When you **describe** a person, thing, or event, you say what they are like or you say what happened. EG *Can you describe your son?... His ideas could hardly be described as original... He described how he was kidnapped.* V+O: OFT+*as*; ALSO V+REPORT: ONLY WH

description /dɪ²skrɪpʃə⁰n/, **descriptions. 1** A **description** is an account of what someone or something is like. EG *...a detailed description of the house... His description was remarkably accurate.* N COUNT: OFT+*of*

2 Description is the act of saying what someone or something is like. EG *The relationships in his family are so complex that description is almost impossible.* N UNCOUNT

3 Something of a particular **description** is something of that kind. EG *Her dress was too tight to have concealed a weapon of any description.* N SING

descriptive /dɪ²skrɪptɪv/. Writing that is **descriptive** describes what something is like. EG *...a descriptive article about Venice.* ADJ QUALIT

desecrate /dɛsɪkreɪt/, **desecrates, desecrating, desecrated.** If someone **desecrates** something that is considered to be sacred or special, they deliberately damage it. EG *The men in Rodez had desecrated the church.* ◇ **desecration** /dɛsəkreɪʃə⁰n/. EG *...the desecration of religious sites in Nigeria.* V+O ◇ N UNCOUNT

desert, deserts, deserting, deserted; pronounced /dɛzət/ when it is a noun and /di'zɜːt/ when it is a verb.

1 A **desert** is a large area of land where there is very little water or rain and very few plants. EG *...the Sahara Desert.* N COUNT

2 You can refer to any place where there is nothing good or interesting as a **desert**. EG *Our modern towns are concrete deserts created by modern planning.* N COUNT+SUPP

3 If people **desert** a place, they all leave it and it becomes empty. ◇ **deserted.** EG *...a deserted village.* V+O ◇ ADJ CLASSIF

4 If someone **deserts** you, they leave you and no longer help or support you. EG *She deserted her family and ran away with him.* ◇ **desertion** /di'zɜːʃə⁰n/. EG *She could get a divorce on the grounds of desertion.* V+O ◇ N UNCOUNT

5 If you **desert** a political party or idea, you stop supporting it. EG *Owen deserted the Labour Party.* V+O

6 If someone **deserts** their job in the armed forces or if they **desert**, they leave their job without permission. ◇ **desertion.** EG *...the desertion of young conscripts.* ◇ **deserter** /di'zɜːtə/, **deserters.** EG *...a deserter from the British army.* V+O OR V ◇ N UNCOUNT ◇ N COUNT

deserve /di'zɜːv/, **deserves, deserving, deserved.** If you say that someone **deserves** a particular reward or punishment, you mean that they should be given this reward or punishment because of their qualities or actions. EG *These people deserve recognition for their talents... He deserves to get the sack.* V+O OR V+*to*-INF

deserved /di'zɜːvd/. If you say that something is **deserved**, you mean that the person getting it is worthy of it. EG *It was a richly deserved honour.* ◇ **deservedly.** EG *The first prize was won, most deservedly, by Mrs Jones.* ADJ QUALIT ◇ ADV

deserving /di'zɜːvɪŋ/. **1** If you describe someone or something as **deserving**, you mean that you think they should be helped. EG *Let us not forget the deserving poor... The proceeds will be given to a deserving charity.* ADJ QUALIT Formal

2 If someone is **deserving of** particular treatment, they have qualities or have done something which makes it right for them to be treated in that way. EG *...those who see their behaviour as deserving of punishment.* PREP Formal

design /di'zaɪn/, **designs, designing, designed.**
1 When you **design** something, **1.1** you plan it in your mind and make a detailed drawing of it from which it can be built or made. EG *The house was designed by local builders... Who designed the costumes?* **1.2** you plan, prepare, and decide on all the details of it. EG *Tests have been designed to assess mathematical ability.* V+O; V+O: USU PASS +*to*-INF

2 Design is the process and art of planning and making detailed drawings of something. EG *...graphic and industrial design.* N UNCOUNT

3 The **design** of something is the way in which it has been planned and made. EG *The awkward design of the handles made it difficult to use.* N UNCOUNT

4 A **design** is **4.1** a drawing which someone produces to show how they would like something to be built or made. EG *He is submitting a design for the new building.* **4.2** a pattern of lines, flowers, or shapes which is used to decorate something. EG *They painted floral designs on the walls.* **4.3** the intention that someone has in their mind when they are doing something. EG *He failed in his design to become Prime Minister.* ● If something happens or is done **by design**, someone does it deliberately, rather than by accident. N COUNT; N COUNT: USU+SUPP; N COUNT Formal; ● PHRASE

5 If something **is designed** for a purpose, it is intended for that purpose. EG *The laws were designed to protect women.* V-PASS+*for* OR+*to*-INF

designate, designates, designating, designated; pronounced /dɛzɪ²gneɪt/ when it is a verb, and /dɛzɪ²gnət/ when it is an adjective.

1 When you **designate** someone or something, **1.1** you formally give them a particular description or name. EG *The area was designated a national monument.* **1.2** you formally choose them to do a particular job. EG *I had been designated to read the lesson.* V+O OR V+O+C; V+O OR *to*-INF ALSO V+O+C

2 Designate is used to describe someone who has been formally chosen to do a particular job, but has not yet started doing it. EG *Mr Bell had been Attorney General designate.* ADJ AFTER N

designation /dɛzɪgneɪʃə⁰n/, **designations.** A **designation** is a description or name that is given to a person or thing. EG *No one would dare to apply the designation 'OAP' to a retired judge.* N COUNT OR N UNCOUNT Formal

designer /di'zaɪnə/, **designers.** A **designer** is a person whose job is to design things by making drawings of them. EG *She wants to be a dress designer.* N COUNT

desirable /di'zaɪərəbə⁰l/. **1** Something that is **desirable** is worth having or doing because it is useful, necessary, or popular. EG *After an injury an X-ray is often desirable... ...one of the most desirable residences in London.* ◇ **desirability** /di'zaɪrəbɪlɪ'ti'/. EG *...decisions about the desirability of an official policy.* ADJ QUALIT ◇ N UNCOUNT USU+SUPP

2 Someone who is **desirable** is sexually attractive. ADJ QUALIT

desire /di'zaɪə/, **desires, desiring, desired. 1** If you **desire** something, you want it. EG *He passionately desired to continue his career in politics.* ▸ used as a noun. EG *He had not the slightest desire to go on holiday.* ◇ **desired.** EG *This did not produce the desired effect... ...their desired goals.* V+O OR V+*to*-INF: NO CONT; ▸ N COUNT; ADJ CLASSIF

2 Desire for someone is a strong feeling of wanting to have sex with them. EG *Their desire for each other was as eager as ever.* ▸ used as a verb. EG *He still desired her, after all these years.* N UNCOUNT OR N COUNT; ▸ V+O: NO CONT

3 If you say that something **leaves a lot to be desired** or **leaves a great deal to be desired**, you mean that it is not as good as it should be. EG *His work left much to be desired.* PHRASE

What are you desperate for if you are destitute?

desist /dɪzɪst, -sɪst/, **desists, desisting, desisted.** If you **desist** from doing something, you stop doing it. EG *They ought to desist from such foolish activities.* — V: OFT+*from* Formal

desk /dɛsk/, **desks.** A **desk** is a table, often with drawers, which you sit at in order to write or work. EG *...a beautiful mahogany desk.* — N COUNT

desolate /dɛsə^{7}lət/. **1** A place that is **desolate** is empty of people and looks depressing. EG *The house looked desolate, ready to be torn down.* — ADJ QUALIT

2 If someone is **desolate**, they feel very lonely and depressed. — ADJ QUALIT

desolation /dɛsə^{7}leɪʃə^{0}n/ is **1** a quality of a place which makes it seem empty and frightening. EG *...the horror and desolation of the camp.* **2** a feeling of great unhappiness and despair. — N UNCOUNT

despair /dɪ^{2}spɛə/, **despairs, despairing, despaired. 1 Despair** is the feeling that everything is wrong and nothing can improve. EG *I was in despair, all hope gone.* — N UNCOUNT

2 If you **despair**, you feel that everything is wrong and that nothing will improve. EG *She despaired at the thought of it.* — V: OFT+*at*

3 If you **despair** of something, you feel that there is no hope that it will happen or improve. EG *She had despaired of completing her thesis.* — V+*of*

despatch /dɪspætʃ/. See **dispatch**.

desperate /dɛspə^{0}rə^{1}t/. **1** If you are **desperate**, you are in such a bad or frightening situation that you will try anything to change it. EG *She was desperate with fright.* — ADJ QUALIT ◊ **desperation** /dɛspəreɪʃə^{0}n/. EG *Sam's desperation grew worse as the day approached.* — ◊ N UNCOUNT

2 A **desperate** action is one that you take when you are in such a bad or frightening situation that you feel it is the only thing that you can try. EG *She killed him in a desperate attempt to free herself.* — ADJ QUALIT ◊ **desperately.** EG *He will fight even more desperately if trapped.* — ◊ ADV

3 If you are **desperate** for something or **desperate** to do something, you want to have it or do it very much indeed. EG *She was desperate to find a job... I was desperate for the money.* — ADJ PRED: OFT+*for* OR *to*-INF ◊ **desperately.** EG *I desperately wanted to be on my own.* — ◊ ADV

4 A **desperate** situation is very difficult or dangerous. EG *The situation had become desperate; we were rapidly running out of money.* — ADJ QUALIT

despicable /dɛspɪkəbə^{0}l, dɪspɪk-/. A person or action that is **despicable** is extremely nasty or evil. EG *He is too nice a man to do anything as despicable as murder.* — ADJ QUALIT

despise /dɪ^{2}spaɪz/, **despises, despising, despised.** If you **despise** someone or something, you have a very low opinion of them and so dislike them. EG *They despise them for their cowardice and ignorance.* — V+O

despite /dɪ^{2}spaɪt/. **1** You use **despite** to introduce a fact which makes the other part of the sentence surprising. EG *Despite the difference in their ages they were close friends.* — PREP

2 If you do something **despite** yourself, you do it although you did not really intend or expect to. EG *Rose, despite herself, had to admit that she was impressed.* — PREP

despondent /dɪ^{2}spɒndə^{2}nt/. If you are **despondent**, you are unhappy because you have difficulties that you think you will not be able to overcome. EG *They grew increasingly despondent about securing any improvement.* — ADJ QUALIT ◊ **despondently.** EG *Fanny sighed despondently.* — ◊ ADV ◊ **despondency** /dɪ^{2}spɒndə^{2}nsi^1/. EG *He was unable to hide his despondency.* — ◊ N UNCOUNT

despot /dɛspɒt/, **despots.** A **despot** is a ruler or other person who has a lot of power and uses it unfairly or cruelly. — N COUNT Formal

despotic /də^{2}spɒtɪk/ is used to describe people or their behaviour when they use their power in an unfair or cruel way. EG *...oppression by despotic governments.* — ADJ QUALIT Formal

dessert /dɪzɜ:t/, **desserts. Dessert** is something sweet, such as fruit or a pudding, that you eat at the end of a meal. EG *For dessert there was ice cream.* — N UNCOUNT OR N COUNT

dessert spoon, dessert spoons. 1 A **dessert spoon** is a spoon which is about twice as big as a teaspoon. You use it to eat puddings with. — N COUNT

2 A **dessert spoon** of food or liquid is the amount that a dessert spoon will hold. EG *Add two dessert spoons of salt.* — N PART

destination /dɛstɪneɪʃə^{0}n/, **destinations.** The **destination** of someone or something is the place to which they are going. EG *I reached my destination around half-past two.* — N COUNT

destined /dɛstɪnd/. **1** If something is **destined** to happen, it is planned and will definitely happen. EG *The station was destined for demolition... She felt she was destined to be unhappy for the rest of her life.* — ADJ CLASSIF: USU PRED +*to*-INF OR+*for*

2 If you are **destined** for a particular place, you are travelling towards it. EG *...passengers destined for New York.* — ADJ CLASSIF: USU PRED+*for*

destiny /dɛstɪ^{1}ni^1/, **destinies. 1** Someone's **destiny** is everything that will happen to them during their life, especially when it is considered to be controlled by someone or something else. EG *We know we are in control of our own destiny.* — N COUNT+SUPP

2 Destiny is the force which some people believe controls the things that happen to you in your life. — N UNCOUNT

destitute /dɛstɪtju:t/. Someone who is **destitute** has no money or possessions. EG *...destitute immigrants.* — ADJ QUALIT ◊ **destitution** /dɛstɪtju:ʃə^{0}n/. EG *The peasantry hovered on the brink of destitution.* — ◊ N UNCOUNT Formal

destroy /dɪ^{2}strɔɪ/, **destroys, destroying, destroyed. 1** To **destroy** something means **1.1** to cause so much damage to it that it is completely ruined. EG *Several buildings were destroyed by the bomb.* **1.2** to cause it not to exist any more. EG *They want to destroy the State... I don't wish to destroy a life-long friendship.* — V+O

2 If you **destroy** an animal, you kill it because it is dangerous or very ill. EG *During the epidemic farmers had to destroy entire herds of cattle.* — V+O

3 If someone or something **destroys** you, they ruin your life by making you so depressed that there seems to be no hope for you in the future. EG *The loss of his business and of his wife finally destroyed him.* — V+O

destroyer /dɪ^{2}strɔɪə/, **destroyers. 1** A **destroyer** is a small warship with a lot of guns. — N COUNT

2 You can refer to anything that destroys things or people as a **destroyer**. EG *Sunshine is a potent destroyer of many bacteria.* — N COUNT

destruction /dɪ^{2}strʌkʃə^{0}n/ is the act of destroying something. EG *It will cause pollution and the destruction of our seas and rivers.* — N UNCOUNT

destructive /dɪ^{2}strʌktɪv/. Something that is **destructive** causes great damage or distress. EG *This rocket has sufficient destructive power to blow a battleship to pieces... Jealousy is destructive and undesirable.* — ADJ QUALIT ◊ **destructiveness.** EG *...a monster of great potential destructiveness.* — ◊ N UNCOUNT

desultory /dɛsəltə^{0}rɪ/. Something that is **desultory** is done without enthusiasm and in an unplanned and disorganized way. EG *There were some desultory attempts to defend him.* — ADJ QUALIT Formal

> **DET stands for determiner**
> A small group of words, such as 'a', 'the', 'this', and 'every', have the label DET in the Extra Column. See the entry headed DETERMINERS for information about this group of words.

detach /di^{1}tætʃ/, **detaches, detaching, detached. 1** If you **detach** one thing from another — V+O: OFT+*from*

DETERMINERS

When you use a noun in English, you have to say how the noun relates to objects, events, or concepts in the real world. This is usually done by putting a determiner (DET) in front of the noun. The most typical, most common determiners are **the** (often called the 'definite article') and **a** or **an** (the 'indefinite article').

The definite article tells you that you should already know what the noun refers to. So that when someone says *I bought the table yesterday,* you know which table they are talking about. See the entry for **the** for more details about this.

The indefinite article tells you that you probably do not know what the noun refers to. So that when someone says *I bought a table yesterday,* you do not know which table they are talking about. See the entry for **a** for more details about this.

The determiners **all**, **some**, **any**, **another**, **each**, **every**, **either**, **neither**, and **no** are like **a** – they do not refer to specific items that you can identify individually.

The determiners **this**, **that**, **these**, and **those**, and the possessive determiners (DET POSS) **my**, **your**, **his**, **her**, **its**, **our**, and **their** are like **the**. In various ways these words tell you that you should be able to identify exactly what the noun refers to. You use **this** and **these** to refer to things that you consider to be relatively close to you. You use **that** and **those** to refer to things that you consider to be relatively far from you. The possessive determiners tell you who something belongs to. So that 'your book' belongs to you and 'my book' belongs to me.

When you want to refer very generally to something, you can use some nouns without a determiner. Uncountable nouns (N UNCOUNT), such as **rice**, **chemistry**, and **disappointment** are usually used without a determiner, unless you want to specify something very precisely. So you normally say *I like rice,* when you are thinking about rice in general, although you can also say *I cooked **this** rice for longer than usual,* when you are referring to the rice that you are eating. Plural countable nouns (N COUNT) such as **boys**, **parties**, and **lessons** are also often used without a determiner, unless you want to be more specific. So you can say *I like parties,* when you are thinking of parties in general, or you can say *I like **the** parties that my boss gives,* when you are thinking of particular kinds of parties.

Most determiners can be used with any noun, whether it is singular or plural or uncountable. There are, however, some which cannot. The determiners **a**, **another**, **each**, **every**, **either**, and **neither** are normally used with singular countable nouns, as in *She poured herself **another** cup of tea* and *I kept records on **each** child. **These*** and **those** are normally used with nouns in the plural, as in *Who are **those** men over there?* **This** and **that** are used with uncountable nouns or singular countable nouns, as in *I've used **that** information many times since then* and ***That** night Kunta slept well.* The determiner **some** can be used with uncountable nouns or plural countable nouns, as in *I bought **some** meat for dinner* and *We've got **some** friends coming.*

There can only be one determiner in a noun group, and it is usually the first word in the group. But occasionally a predeterminer (PREDET) can come in front of the determiner. The words that are labelled as predeterminers in this dictionary are: **all**, **both**, **half**, **double**, **treble**, **quadruple**, **twice**, **such**, and **what**. As with the determiners, these words have other uses. The words **such** and **what** come in front of the determiner **a**, as in *There was **such** a noise in the room* and ***What** a mess!* The other predeterminers are usually used in front of words with a more specific meaning, such as **the**, **those**, and the possessive determiners. So you can say *He looked at **all** my paintings, They charged us **double** the price they should have done,* and ***Both** her parents are dead.*

thing that it is fixed to, you remove it. EG *The handle of the saucepan can be detached.*

2 If you **detach** yourself from something, you feel less involved in it. EG *...learning to detach ourselves from the world.* V-REFL : OFT+*from*

detachable /di^{1}tætʃəbə^{0}l/. Something that is **detachable** is made so that it can be removed from a larger object. EG *...detachable collars.* ADJ CLASSIF

detached /di^{1}tætʃt/. **1** A **detached** house is one that is not joined to any other house. ADJ CLASSIF

2 Someone who is **detached** is not personally involved in something. EG *...the detached view that writers must take.* ADJ QUALIT

detachment /di^{1}tætʃmə^{2}nt/ is the feeling that you have of not being personally involved in something. EG *...his strange detachment from the world about him.* N UNCOUNT

detail /di:teɪl/, **details, detailing, detailed. 1** A **detail** is **1.1** an individual fact or feature which you notice when you look at something carefully, or which you remember when you think about it. EG *I can still remember every single detail of that night... He described it down to the smallest detail.* N COUNT : OFT+*of*

1.2 a fact or comment that is not of major importance to what is being discussed. EG *But those were details; what was important was that the rate of work failed to increase.* N COUNT

2 Detail consists of all the small features which are often not noticed when people first look at something or think about it. EG *Attention to detail is vital in this job.* N UNCOUNT

3 If you **go into detail** or **go into details** about something, you explain it thoroughly, including all the small pieces of information. EG *I don't want to go into detail about the actual methods used.* PHRASE

4 If you examine or discuss something **in detail**, you do it thoroughly. EG *His theory is examined in detail in chapter 12.* PHRASE

5 Details about someone or something are facts or pieces of information about them. EG *You can get details of nursery schools from the local authority... He was interested in every detail about you.* N PLURAL : OFT+*about/of*

6 If you **detail** things, you list them and give information about them. EG *I carefully detailed the areas of the Avenue that I could see.* V+O Formal

detailed /di:teɪld/. Something that is **detailed** contains a lot of details. EG *...a detailed map of the area... They gave a detailed account of what they had seen.* ADJ QUALIT

detain /di^{1}teɪn/, **detains, detaining, detained.** If you **detain** someone, **1** you force them to stay in a place. EG *We shall be obliged to detain you here while we continue the investigation.* **2** you delay them, for example by talking to them. EG *Well, I needn't detain you any longer.* V+O

detect /di^{1}tɛkt/, **detects, detecting, detected.** If you **detect** something, **1** you notice it, often when it is not very obvious. EG *These animals seem able to detect a shower of rain falling five miles away.* **2** you find it. EG *The submarines had to be detected and destroyed.* V+O

detection /di^{1}tɛkʃə^{0}n/ is **1** the act of noticing something. EG *The main detection device is sonar.* **2** the discovery of something in a place, especially when it is supposed to be hidden. EG *The submarines were able to withdraw without detection.* N UNCOUNT

detective /di^{1}tɛktɪv/, **detectives.** A **detective** is someone whose job is to discover what has happened in a crime or other situation and to find the people involved. Some police officers are detectives. EG *He was being followed by a private detective.* N COUNT

detector /di^{1}tɛktə/, **detectors.** A **detector** is an instrument which is used to find or measure something. EG *...a metal detector.* N COUNT : USU+SUPP

detente /deɪtɒnt/; also spelled **détente. Detente** is a state of friendly relations between two countries when previously there had been problems between them. N UNCOUNT Formal

detention /di^{1}tɛnʃə^{0}n/ is the arrest or imprisonment of someone, especially for political reasons. EG *It was obvious to his colleagues that his detention was politically motivated.* N UNCOUNT

deter /di^{1}tɜ:/, **deters, deterring, deterred.** To **deter** someone means to persuade them not to do something or to prevent them from doing it. EG *Such discrimination may deter more women from seeking work.* V+O : OFT+*from*

detergent /di^{1}tɜ:dʒə^{2}nt/, **detergents. Detergent** is a chemical substance, usually a powder or liquid, which is used for washing things such as clothes or dishes. EG *Wash it with hot water and detergent.* N MASS

deteriorate /di^{1}tɪərɪəreɪt/, **deteriorates, deteriorating, deteriorated.** If something **deteriorates, 1** it becomes worse in condition. EG *His sight had begun to deteriorate.* V ◇ **deterioration** /di^{1}tɪərɪəreɪʃə^{0}n/. EG *She had suffered progressive deterioration of health.* ◇ N UNCOUNT **2** it becomes more difficult or unpleasant. EG *The weather had deteriorated.* V

◇ **deterioration.** EG *This speeded the deterioration of our relationship.* ◇ N UNCOUNT

determination /di^{1}tɜ:mɪneɪʃə^{0}n/. **1 Determination** is the quality that you show when you have decided to do something and you will not let anything stop you. EG *Seeing my determination to leave, she demanded her money.* N UNCOUNT

2 The **determination** of something is the deciding or settling of it. EG *She is responsible for the determination of wage levels within this company.* N UNCOUNT +SUPP

determine /di^{1}tɜ:mɪn/, **determines, determining, determined. 1** If something **determines** a situation or result, it controls it or causes it. EG *Economic factors determine the progress which a society can make.* V+O

2 If you **determine** something, **2.1** you find out the facts about it. EG *It was in the public interest to determine exactly what happened... An X ray determined that no bones were broken.* **2.2** you decide it or settle it. EG *The date of the match is yet to be determined.* V+O

3 If you **determine** to do something, you make a firm decision to do it. EG *He determined to become commander-in-chief of the forces.* V+*to*-INF Formal

determined /di^{1}tɜ:mɪnd/. If you are **determined** to do something, you have made a firm decision to do it and will not let anything stop you. EG *He is determined to win in the end.* ◇ **determinedly.** EG *She determinedly kept the conversation going.* ADJ QUALIT : USU+*to*-INF ◇ ADV

deterrence /di^{1}tɛrəns/ is the prevention of war by having weapons that are so powerful that people will not dare to attack you. EG *They believe that NATO's policy of deterrence is justified.* N UNCOUNT

deterrent /di^{1}tɛrənt/, **deterrents. 1** A **deterrent** is **1.1** a thing that prevents you from doing something by making you afraid of what will happen if you do it. EG *Severe punishment is the only true deterrent.* **1.2** a weapon or set of weapons that are intended to prevent enemies from attacking by making them afraid to do so. EG *...the nuclear deterrent.* N COUNT

2 If something has a **deterrent** effect, it discourages people from doing something they might want to do. EG *...the deterrent effect of nuclear weapons.* ADJ CLASSIF : ATTRIB

detest /di^{1}tɛst/, **detests, detesting, detested.** If you **detest** someone or something, you dislike them very much. EG *They detest the thought of living elsewhere.* V+O

detestable /di^{1}tɛstəbə^{0}l/. If you say that someone or something is **detestable**, you mean that you dislike them very strongly. EG *...a step-son he thought altogether detestable.* ADJ QUALIT

detonate /dɛtə^{7}neɪt/, **detonates, detonating, detonated.** If you **detonate** a bomb or if it **detonates**, it explodes. EG *...land mines which could be detonated from inside the camp.* V-ERG ◇ **detonation** /dɛtə^{7}neɪʃə^{0}n/. EG *...the possible detonation of a nuclear weapon.* ◇ N UNCOUNT

detour /diːtʊə/, **detours.** A **detour** is a route which is not the shortest way from one place to another. You often make a detour because you want to avoid a traffic jam or because you want to see the countryside. EG *He made a detour to pass the house where Miss Lenaut lived.* N COUNT

> **DET POSS** stands for **possessive determiner**
> The words 'my', 'your', 'his', 'her', 'its', 'our', and 'their' have the label DET POSS in the Extra Column. See the entry headed DETERMINERS for more information.

detract /dɪˈtrækt/, **detracts, detracting, detracted.** If one thing **detracts** from another, it makes the other thing seem less good than people thought or than it really is. EG *This fact did not detract from her sense of achievement.* V+*from*

detriment /dɛtrəˈməˀnt/. If something happens **to** the **detriment** of someone or something, it causes harm or damage to them. EG *This discovery has been exploited to the detriment of the poor peasants.* PHRASE Formal

detrimental /dɛtrɪmɛntəˀl/. Something that is **detrimental** has harmful or damaging effects. EG *...actions which may be detrimental to the company.* ADJ QUALIT : OFT+*to* Formal

deuce /djuːs/ is the score in a game of tennis when both players have forty points. N UNCOUNT

devalue /diːvæljuː/, **devalues, devaluing, devalued. 1** If you **devalue** someone or something, you think that they are unimportant and so you do not give them the respect that they deserve. EG *Scientific expertise has been devalued.* V+O

2 To **devalue** the currency of a country means to reduce its value in relation to other currencies. EG *The President has devalued the dollar.* V+O Technical

◇ **devaluation** /diːvæljuːeɪʃəˀn/. EG *...the devaluation of sterling in November 1967.* ◇ N UNCOUNT

devastate /dɛvəsteɪt/, **devastates, devastating, devastated.** If something **devastates** a place, it destroys it or damages it very badly. EG *A hurricane had devastated the plantation.* V+O : OFT PASS ◇ **devastation** /dɛvəsteɪʃəˀn/. EG *...the threat of nuclear devastation.* ◇ N UNCOUNT

devastated /dɛvəsteɪtɪˀd/. If you are **devastated** by something, you are very shocked and upset by it. EG *We were devastated by her decision.* ADJ PRED

devastating /dɛvəsteɪtɪŋ/. **1** Something that is **devastating** destroys or severely damages something. EG *...devastating bombing raids.* ADJ QUALIT

2 Devastating remarks indicate strongly that a point of view that has been expressed is wrong. EG *He thought of the devastating witticisms with which he would destroy his opponents.* ADJ QUALIT

3 If you find something **devastating**, it makes you feel very shocked and upset. EG *It was a devastating announcement.* ADJ QUALIT

4 You can also use **devastating** to describe things that are very good or beautiful. EG *That's her most devastating insight.* ADJ QUALIT ◇ **devastatingly.** EG *She was devastatingly beautiful.* ◇ ADV+ADJ

develop /dɪvɛləp/, **develops, developing, developed. 1** When something **develops**, it grows or changes over a period of time into a better or more complete form. EG *The bud develops into a flower... Her friendship with Harold developed slowly... We had hopes of developing tourism on a big scale.* V-ERG : USU+A

2 If a problem **develops**, it starts to exists and gradually becomes more severe. EG *A new crisis began to develop.* V

3 If a country **develops**, it changes from being a poor or agricultural country to being an advanced industrial country. V ◇ **developing.** EG *Several industrialized nations are supplying developing countries with new technology.* ◇ ADJ CLASSIF : ATTRIB

4 To **develop** an area of land means to build houses or factories on it. V+O

5 To **develop** a characteristic, illness, or fault means to begin to have it. EG *She developed an enormous appetite... Write to the manufacturer if the machine develops the same fault again.* V+O

6 If someone **develops** a new machine, they produce it by improving the original design. EG *Their new engine was developed from a petrol motor.* V+O

7 If you **develop** an argument or idea, you begin to understand it better by saying more about it. EG *The rationale he developed was very interesting.* V+O

8 When a photographic film **is developed**, prints or negatives are made from it. V+O

developer /dɪvɛləˀpə/, **developers. 1** A **developer** is a person or a company that buys land in order to build new houses or factories on it. EG *Villagers are protesting about the destruction of their beautiful landscape by the developers.* N COUNT

2 If a child is an early **developer**, he or she develops physically or mentally earlier than others of the same age. A late **developer** develops later than others of the same age. N COUNT+SUPP

development /dɪvɛləˀpməˀnt/, **developments. 1 Development** is **1.1** the gradual growth or formation of something. EG *This can harm a child's psychological development... Some people expect rapid economic development in Pakistan.* N UNCOUNT +SUPP **1.2** the process or result of improving a basic design. EG *...research and development... What have been the major developments in aircraft engines in the last decade?* N UNCOUNT OR N COUNT **1.3** the process of making an area of land or water more useful or profitable. EG *...Japanese ventures for the development of Siberia.* N UNCOUNT +SUPP

2 A **development** is an event which is likely to have an effect on the situation in a particular place or field of activity. EG *Recent developments in Latin America suggest that the situation may be improving.* N COUNT

3 A **development** is also an area of houses or buildings which have been built by property developers. EG *Many people live in new housing developments.* N COUNT

deviant /diːvɪənt/, **deviants.** A **deviant** is someone whose behaviour or beliefs are not considered by most people to be acceptable. N COUNT ▸ used as an adjective. EG *To light a cigarette in company is becoming a deviant act.* ▸ ADJ QUALIT

deviate /diːvɪeɪt/, **deviates, deviating, deviated.** If you **deviate**, you change your ideas or behaviour so that they are different from what they used to be or from what people usually consider to be acceptable. EG *He has not deviated from his view that war can never be justified.* V : OFT+*from*

deviation /diːvɪeɪʃəˀn/, **deviations. Deviation** is a difference in behaviour or belief from what people consider to be normal or acceptable. EG *There was to be no deviation from the ruling ideology.* N UNCOUNT OR N COUNT

device /dɪˈvaɪs/, **devices. 1** A **device** is an object that has been made or built for a particular purpose, for example for recording or measuring something. EG *A computer is a device for handling or processing information... Firemen carry a little alarm device in their pocket... ...pumps and other devices.* N COUNT : USU+SUPP

2 A **device** is also a method of getting what you want or of getting something done. EG *They used television advertising as a device for stimulating demand.* N COUNT : USU+SUPP

3 If you **leave** someone **to their own devices**, they have to find something to occupy them because you do not give them anything to do. EG *The children were left to their own devices.* PHRASE

If you devour a book, do you eat it?

devil /dɛvəˡl/, **devils.** 1 In Christianity, the **Devil** is the most powerful evil spirit. N PROPER: the+N
2 You can use **devil** to refer to any evil spirit. N COUNT
3 You can also use **devil** to talk about people. For example, if you call someone a silly **devil**, you are saying that you think that they are silly. EG *You lucky devil!... The poor devil died of a heart attack.* N COUNT+SUPP Informal
4 When you want to emphasize how annoyed or surprised you are, you can start your sentence with a phrase such as **who the devil, where the devil,** or **why the devil.** EG *Where the devil did you get that cat?* PHRASE

devilish /dɛvəˡlɪʃ/. A **devilish** idea or action is cruel or unpleasant. EG *What devilish impulse moved you to this?* ADJ QUALIT

devious /diːvɪəs/. 1 Someone who is **devious** is dishonest and does things in a secretive, often complicated way. EG *...consultants who are prepared to use devious means to justify their actions.* ADJ QUALIT
2 A **devious** route or path to a place involves many changes in direction rather than going in the straightest possible line. EG *She led him by devious ways to the meeting place.* ADJ QUALIT

devise /diˡvaɪz/, **devises, devising, devised.** If you **devise** a plan, system, or machine, you have the idea for it and you work out how you could create it. EG *It has been necessary to devise a system of universal schooling.* V+O

devoid /diˡvɔɪd/. If someone or something is **devoid** of a quality, they have none of it at all. EG *He was devoid of any talent whatsoever.* ADJ PRED+*of* Formal

devolution /diːvəˡluːʃəˡn/ is the transfer of authority or power from a central organization or government to smaller organizations or government departments. N UNCOUNT

devolve /diˡvɒlv/, **devolves, devolving, devolved.** If a responsibility or privilege **devolves** or **is devolved** upon a person or group, it is transferred to them from a more important or powerful person or group. EG *The necessity for making decisions devolves upon him.* V-ERG +*upon/on/to* Formal

devote /diˡvəʊt/, **devotes, devoting, devoted.** If you **devote** yourself, your time, or your energy to something, you spend a lot of your time or energy on it. EG *They have devoted all their time to helping the sick... He devoted himself to his studies.* V+O OR V-REFL+*to*

devoted /diˡvəʊtiˡd/. 1 If you are **devoted** to someone, you love them very much. EG *He's devoted to his mother.* ADJ QUALIT: OFT+*to*
2 You use **devoted** to describe activities which have involved a lot of someone's time and energy. EG *...years of devoted research.* ADJ QUALIT: ATTRIB

devotee /dɛvəˡtiː/, **devotees.** A **devotee** of a subject or activity is someone who is very enthusiastic about it. EG *The building has an enormous appeal for devotees of history.* N COUNT: OFT+SUPP

devotion /diˡvəʊʃəˡn/ is 1 great love and affection for someone. EG *Their devotion to their children is plain to see.* 2 the giving of a lot of your time or energy to a particular activity. EG *It demands total devotion to the cause.* 3 strong religious feeling. EG *We watched them kneel in devotion.* N UNCOUNT: OFT+*to* / N UNCOUNT: OFT+*to* / N UNCOUNT

devour /diˡvaʊə/, **devours, devouring, devoured.** 1 When one animal **devours** another, it eats it. EG *We came upon a black snake devouring a large frog.* V+O Formal
2 If you **devour** something, you eat it quickly and eagerly. EG *He sat by the fire, devouring beef and onions.* V+O Formal
3 If you **devour** a book or magazine, you read it quickly and eagerly. EG *As a boy I devoured Scott's novels.* V+O Formal

devout /diˡvaʊt/. Someone who is **devout** believes in God or a religion very deeply. EG *She was a devout Catholic.* ADJ QUALIT

dew /djuː/ is small drops of water that form on the ground and other surfaces outdoors during the night. N UNCOUNT

dexterous /dɛkstrəs/; also spelled **dextrous.** Someone who is **dexterous** is very skilful with their hands. ◊ **dexterity** /dɛkstɛrɪˡtiˡ/. EG *...weaving in and out with great dexterity.* ADJ QUALIT Formal ◊ N UNCOUNT

diabetes /daɪəbiːtɪs, -tiːz/ is an illness in which someone's body is unable to control the level of sugar in their blood. N UNCOUNT

diabetic /daɪəbɛtɪk/, **diabetics.** 1 A **diabetic** is a person who suffers from diabetes. N COUNT
2 **Diabetic** medicines or conditions are intended for or affect people who have diabetes. EG *...in a diabetic coma... ...diabetic chocolate.* ADJ CLASSIF: ATTRIB

diabolical /daɪəbɒlɪkəˡl/. You use **diabolical** to emphasize how bad or unpleasant you think something is. EG *It gave men the pretext for all sorts of diabolical behaviour.* ADJ CLASSIF Informal

diagnose /daɪəgnəʊz/, **diagnoses, diagnosing, diagnosed.** When a doctor **diagnoses** an illness that someone has, he or she identifies exactly what is wrong. EG *The doctor has diagnosed it as rheumatism.* V+O: OFT+*as*

diagnosis /daɪəgnəʊsɪs/, **diagnoses** /daɪəgnəʊsiːz/. **Diagnosis** is identifying what is wrong with someone who is ill. EG *Joan's fever led to a diagnosis of pneumonia.* N UNCOUNT OR N COUNT

diagnostic /daɪəgnɒstɪk/. **Diagnostic** equipment or methods are used for discovering what is wrong with people who are ill. EG *...medical diagnostic devices.* ADJ CLASSIF

diagonal /daɪægənəˡl/, **diagonals.** 1 A **diagonal** line goes in a slanting direction. EG *There was a diagonal red line on the label.* ◊ **diagonally.** EG *We drove diagonally across the airfield.* ADJ CLASSIF ◊ ADV
2 A **diagonal** is a straight line that joins two opposite corners in a flat four-sided shape such as a square. N COUNT Technical

diagram /daɪəgræm/, **diagrams.** A **diagram** is a simple drawing consisting mainly of lines, often one which is used to explain how something works. EG *...a simple diagram showing compass directions.* ◊ **diagrammatic** /daɪəgrəmætɪk/. EG *The factors can be shown in diagrammatic form.* N COUNT: USU+SUPP ◊ ADJ CLASSIF

dial /daɪl/, **dials, dialling, dialled;** spelled **dialing** and **dialed** in American English. 1 On an instrument such as a clock or a meter, the **dial** is an indicator which shows you the time or a measurement. EG *...the luminous dial of his watch... The figures on the dial can be seen.* N COUNT
2 On a piece of equipment such as a radio or a time switch, the **dial** is the controlling part which you move in order to change the radio frequency or the timing. N COUNT
3 On some telephones, the **dial** is the circle that has holes in it and numbers behind the holes. You move the dial to ring the telephone number that you want to call. N COUNT
4 If you **dial** a number, you move the circle or press the buttons on the front of a telephone in order to phone someone. EG *Jim dialled his home number.* V+O OR V

dialect /daɪəlɛkt/, **dialects.** A **dialect** is a form of a language that is spoken by people living in a particular area. It has different pronunciations and words from other forms of the language. EG *...old ballads written in northern dialect.* N COUNT OR N UNCOUNT

dialogue /daɪəlɒg/, **dialogues;** spelled **dialog** in American English. 1 **Dialogue** is communication or discussion between people or groups. EG *The union continued to seek dialogue with the authorities.* N UNCOUNT OR N COUNT
2 A **dialogue** is a conversation between two people, especially one in a book, film, or play. EG *...500 words of movie dialogue... Their dialogue was interrupted by Philip's voice.* N COUNT OR N UNCOUNT

diameter /daɪæməˡtə/, **diameters.** The **diameter** of a round object is the length of a straight line that can be drawn through the middle of it. EG *...a giant planet over 30,000 miles in diameter.* N COUNT

diametrically /daɪəmetrɪkli[1]/. If you say that two things are **diametrically opposed** or **diametrically opposite**, you are emphasizing that they are completely different from each other. EG *The two systems are diametrically opposed.* PHRASE

diamond /daɪəmənd/, **diamonds. 1** A **diamond** is a hard, bright, precious stone that consists of pure carbon. Diamonds are used especially in jewellery. EG *...diamond brooches.* N COUNT

2 If something has the shape of a **diamond**, it has four straight sides of equal length, but the sides are not at right angles to each other as they are in a square. See picture at SHAPES. N COUNT

3 Diamonds is one of the four suits of cards in a pack of playing cards. Each card in the suit is marked with one or more red symbols in the shape of a diamond. N UNCOUNT

4 A **diamond** is also one of the thirteen playing cards in the suit of diamonds. N COUNT

diaper /daɪəpə/, **diapers.** A **diaper** is a piece of soft towel or absorbent paper, which you put round a baby's bottom until it is old enough to use a toilet. N COUNT American

diaphragm /daɪəfræm/, **diaphragms. 1** Your **diaphragm** is a muscle between your lungs and your stomach. It is used especially when you breathe deeply. N COUNT

2 A **diaphragm** is a small, round contraceptive device that a woman places inside her vagina. N COUNT

diarrhoea /daɪərɪə/; also spelled **diarrhea. Diarrhoea** is an illness in which people get rid of a lot of faeces which are much more liquid than usual. N UNCOUNT

diary /daɪəri[1]/, **diaries.** A **diary** is a book which has a separate space for each day of the year. You use a diary to write down your appointments and things you have to do in the future, or to record what happens in your life day by day. EG *Her diary gives an account of what happened.* N COUNT: USU+POSS

dice

dice /daɪs/, **dices, dicing, diced. Dice** is both the singular and the plural form of the noun.

1 A **dice** is a small cube made of wood or plastic, which has from one to six spots on each of its six sides. You throw dice in games to decide, for example, who will start the game first or how many moves you can make. EG *They roll dice to see who will go first.* N COUNT

2 When you **dice** food, you cut it into small cubes. V+O
◊ **diced.** EG *...diced potatoes.* ◊ ADJ CLASSIF

dicey /daɪsi[1]/. Something that is **dicey** is slightly dangerous or uncertain. EG *Hitch-hiking's a bit dicey in this area.* ADJ QUALIT Informal

dichotomy /daɪkɒtə[7]mi[1]/, **dichotomies.** If there is a very great difference between two things, you can say that there is a **dichotomy** between them. EG *The clearest dichotomy is between the winners and the losers.* N COUNT Formal

dictate, dictates, dictating, dictated; pronounced /dɪkteɪt/ when it is a verb and /dɪkteɪt/ when it is a noun.

1 If you **dictate** something, you say it aloud for someone else to write down. EG *It took him a long time to dictate this letter.* V+O OR V

2 If you **dictate** to someone, you tell them what they must do. EG *The unions are hardly in a position to dictate to the Labour party... The printers tried to dictate how he should run his business... The law dictated that his right hand be cut off.* V+*to*, V+O, OR V+REPORT

3 A **dictate** is an order which you have to obey. EG *They obeyed the union's dictates and went on strike.* N COUNT

dictation /dɪkteɪʃə[0]n/, **dictations. 1 Dictation** is **1.1** the speaking aloud of words for someone else to write down. EG *Jill took down a story from Frank's dictation.* **1.2** the giving of orders in a forceful and commanding way. EG *The group resented dictation from above.* N UNCOUNT

2 A **dictation** is a test of your knowledge of a foreign language, in which you have to write down a text that is read aloud to you. N COUNT OR N UNCOUNT

dictator /dɪkteɪtə/, **dictators.** A **dictator** is a ruler who has complete power in a country; used showing disapproval. N COUNT

dictatorial /dɪktətɔːrɪəl/. **1 Dictatorial** means caused, controlled, or used by a dictator. EG *...dictatorial regimes.* ADJ QUALIT

2 Dictatorial power or behaviour involves giving orders to people in a forceful and often unfair way. EG *...the dictatorial power of central committees.* ADJ QUALIT

dictatorship /dɪkteɪtə[8]ʃɪp/, **dictatorships. 1 Dictatorship** is government by a dictator. EG *Democracy soon gave way to dictatorship.* N UNCOUNT

2 A country that is a **dictatorship** is ruled by a dictator. N COUNT

diction /dɪkʃə[0]n/. You refer to how clearly someone speaks or sings as their **diction.** EG *What was so striking was her magnificent diction.* N UNCOUNT

dictionary /dɪkʃənə[0]rɪ/, **dictionaries.** A **dictionary** is **1** a book in which the words of a language are listed alphabetically and their meanings are explained. N COUNT **2** a book in which words in one language are listed alphabetically and are followed by words which have the same meaning in another language. EG *...an English-French dictionary.* N COUNT **3** an alphabetically ordered reference book on a particular subject. EG *...the Dictionary of National Biography.* N COUNT+SUPP

did /dɪd/ is the past tense of **do.**

didactic /dɪ[5]dæktɪk/. Something that is **didactic** is intended to teach people a moral lesson. EG *...authoritarian, didactic teaching.* ADJ QUALIT Formal

didn't /dɪdə[0]nt/ is the usual spoken form of 'did not'.

die /daɪ/, **dies, dying, died. 1** When people, animals, and plants **die**, they stop living. EG *He died of a heart attack.* V ● If someone **dies a** violent or unnatural **death**, they die in a violent or unnatural way. EG *I don't believe Davis died a natural death.* ● PHRASE

2 If someone **is dying**, they are so ill or so badly injured that they will not live much longer. EG *...an old woman dying of cancer.* V: ONLY CONT

3 When emotions **die**, they become less intense and disappear. EG *True love never dies.* V Literary

4 If you say that you are **dying for** something or **dying to do** something, you mean that you want very much to have it or to do it. EG *I'm dying for a drink... They were all dying to go to Paris.* PHRASE Informal

5 If an idea or custom **dies hard**, it changes or disappears very slowly. EG *Colonial traditions die hard.* PHRASE

6 See also **dying.**

die away. If a sound **dies away**, it gradually becomes fainter and finally disappears. EG *Now that the cheers had died away, it seemed oddly quiet.* PHRASAL VB: V+ADV

die down. If something **dies down**, it becomes quieter or less intense. EG *She waited until the laughter had died down... The wind has died down.* PHRASAL VB: V+ADV

die out. If something **dies out**, it becomes less and less common and eventually disappears. EG *He* PHRASAL VB: V+ADV

If you are diffident, do you behave in a dictatorial way?

thought the custom had died out a long time ago... Many species died out.

diesel /di:zəl/, **diesels. 1** A **diesel** is a vehicle which has an engine in which a mixture of air and heavy oil is made to burn by pressure rather than by an electric spark. N COUNT

2 Diesel or **diesel oil** is the heavy oil used in a diesel engine. N UNCOUNT

diet /daɪət/, **diets, dieting, dieted. 1** A **diet** is the food that a person or animal eats regularly. EG *Her diet consisted of bread and lentils... Correct diet is important.* N COUNT OR N UNCOUNT ◇ **dietary.** EG *We are working on changing dietary habits.* ◇ ADJ CLASSIF : ATTRIB

2 If you are on a **diet**, you are eating special kinds of food because you want to lose weight. EG *'Have a biscuit.' – 'No thanks, I'm on a diet.'* N COUNT ▸ used as an adjective. EG *Saccharin is the main sweetener for diet drinks.* ▸ ADJ CLASSIF : ATTRIB

3 If you **are dieting**, you are eating special kinds of food because you want to lose weight. V

differ /dɪfə/, **differs, differing, differed. 1** If things **differ**, they are unlike each other in some way. EG *Modern cars differ from the early ones in many ways... Although our looks differ, we are both attractive.* V OR V+*from* : RECIP

2 If people **differ** about something, they disagree with each other about it. EG *We differ about moral standards.* V

difference /dɪfərəns/, **differences. 1** The **difference** between things is the way in which they are different from each other. EG *There is an essential difference between computers and humans... Look at their difference in size.* N COUNT OR N UNCOUNT : USU+SUPP

2 If you say that something **doesn't make any difference**, you mean that it does not change the situation in any way. EG *It makes no difference whether he is a citizen or not.* PHRASE

3 If you say that something **makes all the difference**, you mean that it is very important in helping you to achieve what you are trying to do. EG *That extra money would have made all the difference.* PHRASE

4 The **difference** between two amounts is the amount by which they differ. N SING : OFT *between*

5 If people have their **differences**, they disagree about things. N COUNT : USU PLURAL

different /dɪfərənt/. **1** If one thing is **different** from another, it is unlike the other thing in some way. EG *The meeting was different from any that had gone before... His message is very different to theirs.* ADJ QUALIT : OFT+*from/to/than* ◇ **differently.** EG *...people who feel very differently about things.* ◇ ADV

2 When you refer to two or more **different** things of a particular kind, you mean two or more separate things of that kind. EG *I visited 21 different schools.* ADJ CLASSIF : ATTRIB

differentiate /dɪfərenʃieɪt/, **differentiates, differentiating, differentiated. 1** If you **differentiate** between things or **differentiate** one thing from another, you recognize or show the difference between them. EG *How can you differentiate between moral and religious questions?* V+*between*; ALSO V+O : OFT+*from*

2 If a quality or aspect **differentiates** one thing from another, it makes the two things different. EG *What differentiates a sculpture from an object?* V+O : OFT+*from*

◇ **differentiation** /dɪfərenʃieɪʃən/. EG *...the differentiation of classes.* ◇ N UNCOUNT

difficult /dɪfɪkəlt/. **1** Something that is **difficult** is not easy to do, understand, or solve. EG *Many youngsters find it difficult to get jobs... That's a very difficult question... This is bad for a child, making it difficult for him to adjust.* ADJ QUALIT : OFT+*to-INF* OR *for*

2 Someone who is **difficult** behaves in an unreasonable and unhelpful way. EG *...a difficult baby.* ADJ QUALIT

difficulty /dɪfɪkəlti/, **difficulties. 1** A **difficulty** is something that is a problem for you. EG *There are lots of difficulties that have to be overcome.* N COUNT

2 If you have **difficulty** doing something, you are not able to do it easily. EG *I was having difficulty breathing... She spoke with difficulty.* N UNCOUNT

3 If you are **in difficulty** or **in difficulties**, you are in a situation in which you are having a lot of problems. EG *He went to the aid of a swimmer in difficulty.* PHRASE

diffident /dɪfɪdənt/. Someone who is **diffident** is nervous and lacks confidence. EG *...a rather diffident, uncommunicative man.* ADJ QUALIT ◇ **diffidently.** EG *He approached the desk diffidently.* ◇ ADV ◇ **diffidence** /dɪfɪdəns/. EG *She walked up with some diffidence.* ◇ N UNCOUNT

diffuse, diffuses, diffusing, diffused; pronounced /dɪfju:z/ when it is a verb and /dɪfju:s/ when it is an adjective.

1 When light **diffuses** or when something **diffuses** it, the light spreads in a lot of directions and shines faintly over a wide area. EG *The light was diffused by leaves.* V-ERG Formal

2 If you **diffuse** knowledge or information or if it **diffuses**, it spreads to a lot of people over a wide area. EG *Fashion trends diffuse themselves rapidly around the globe.* V-ERG Formal ◇ **diffusion** /dɪfju:ʒən/. EG *...the diffusion of scientific knowledge.* ◇ N UNCOUNT

3 Something that is **diffuse** is **3.1** vague and not easy to understand. EG *Modern anarchism has become increasingly diffuse.* ADJ QUALIT Formal **3.2** spread out over a large area rather than concentrated in one place. EG *...a broad, diffuse organization... ...a faint and diffuse glow of light.* Formal

dig /dɪg/, **digs, digging, dug** /dʌg/. **1** If you **dig**, you make a hole in the ground, using your hands or a spade. EG *I was digging my garden... He dug a little hole in the ground.* V OR V+O

2 If you **dig** into something, you search in it for something with your hand. EG *Thomas dug into the bag and pulled out a sandwich.* V+A

3 If you **dig** one thing into another, you press the first thing hard into the second. EG *She dug her needle into her sewing... My corset was digging into my stomach.* V-ERG+A

4 A **dig** is an unpleasant remark which is intended to hurt or embarrass someone. EG *Whenever she can, she takes a dig at me.* N COUNT : OFT+*at*

5 Your **digs** are a room in someone else's house which you pay to live in. EG *When I was working in Sheffield, I lived in digs.* N PLURAL : OFT *in*+N British

dig out. 1 If you **dig** someone or something **out** of somewhere, you get them out with some effort or difficulty. EG *They worked all night, digging people out of the rubble.* PHRASAL VB : V+O+ADV, OFT+*of* **2** If you **dig** something **out**, you find it after it has been hidden or stored for a long time. EG *We dug out our tour books and maps for the holiday.* V+O+ADV

dig up. 1 If you **dig** something **up**, you remove it from the ground where it has been buried. EG *...digging up potatoes in the vegetable garden.* PHRASAL VB : V+O+ADV **2** If you **dig up** information that is not widely known, you discover it. EG *Journalists have dug up some hair-raising facts about the company.* V+O+ADV

digest, digests, digesting, digested; pronounced /dɪdʒest/ when it is a verb and /daɪdʒest/ when it is a noun.

1 When you **digest** food, you stomach removes the substances that your body needs and gets rid of the rest. V+O

2 If you **digest** information, you think about it and understand it. EG *I had heard it without having actually digested what was said.* V+O

3 A **digest** is a collection of pieces of writing, which are published together in a shorter form than they originally appeared in. N COUNT : USU+SUPP

digestion /dɪdʒestʃən/, **digestions. 1 Digestion** is the process of digesting food. EG *A good walk aids digestion.* N UNCOUNT

2 Your **digestion** is the system in your body which digests your food. EG *His digestion had always been poor.* N COUNT

digestive /dɪdʒestɪv/ means relating to the digestion of food. EG *...the digestive system.* ADJ CLASSIF : ATTRIB

digit /dɪdʒɪt/, **digits.** A **digit** is **1** a written symbol for any of the ten numbers from 0 to 9. EG *11 is a* N COUNT *two digit number.* **2** a finger, thumb, or toe. Formal

digital /dɪdʒə1tə0l/. **Digital** watches or clocks show the time by displaying numbers rather than by using hands on a traditional clock face. ADJ CLASSIF : ATTRIB

dignified /dɪgnɪfaɪd/. Someone who is **dignified** is calmly impressive and worthy of respect. EG *She was tall, handsome, very dignified... ...a cool, dignified attitude... He composed a dignified letter to accompany his cheque.* ADJ QUALIT

dignify /dɪgnɪfaɪ/, **dignifies, dignifying, dignified.** Something that **dignifies** a place makes it impressive. EG *They stood admiring the broad steps that dignified the front of the mansion.* V+O : NO IMPER

dignitary /dɪgnɪtə0ri1/, **dignitaries.** A **dignitary** is someone who has a high rank in government or in the Church. N COUNT : USU PLURAL

dignity /dɪgnɪti1/. **1** If someone has **dignity** or if they show **dignity**, their behaviour or appearance is serious, calm, and controlled. EG *There was something impressive about Julia's quiet dignity.* N UNCOUNT : USU+SUPP

2 Dignity is also the quality of being worthy of respect. EG *Don't discount the importance of human dignity.* N UNCOUNT : USU+SUPP

digress /daɪgrɛs/, **digresses, digressing, digressed.** If you **digress**, you move away from the subject you are talking or writing about and talk or write about something different for a while. EG *I will digress slightly at this stage.* ◇ **digression** /daɪgrɛʃə0n/, **digressions.** EG *This long digression has led me away from my main story.* V ◇ N COUNT OR N UNCOUNT

dike /daɪk/. See **dyke**.

dilapidated /di1læpɪdeɪtɪ2d/. A building that is **dilapidated** is old and in bad condition. ADJ QUALIT

dilate /dɪ5leɪt/, **dilates, dilating, dilated.** When your eyes **dilate**, the pupils of your eyes become wider or bigger. ◇ **dilated.** EG *She smiled, her eyes bright and dilated.* V-ERG ◇ ADJ QUALIT

dilemma /dɪ5lɛmə/, **dilemmas.** A **dilemma** is a difficult situation in which you have to choose between two or more alternatives. EG *It put me in a difficult moral dilemma.* N COUNT

diligent /dɪlɪ2dʒə2nt/. Someone who is **diligent** works hard and carefully, and tries to do everything that they are expected to do. EG *I have no doubt that diligent research will produce results.* ADJ QUALIT

◇ **diligently.** EG *He read the Bible diligently.* ◇ ADV

◇ **diligence** /dɪlɪ2dʒə2ns/. EG *I had been hoping to impress my new boss with my diligence.* ◇ N UNCOUNT

dilute /daɪlj0u:t/, **dilutes, diluting, diluted.** When you **dilute** a liquid, you add water or another liquid to it in order to make it weaker. V+O

dim /dɪm/, **dimmer, dimmest; dims, dimming, dimmed. 1** Something that is **dim** is **1.1** rather dark because there is not much light in it. EG *The room was dim.* ◇ **dimly.** EG *...the dimly lit department store.* ◇ **dimness.** EG *...in the dimness of the church.* **1.2** not very easy to see. EG *Bernard peered at the dim figure by the bus-stop.* ADJ QUALIT ◇ ADV ◇ N UNCOUNT ADJ QUALIT

2 If your memory of something is **dim**, you can hardly remember it at all. EG *I only have a dim recollection of the production.* ADJ QUALIT

3 If you describe someone as **dim**, you mean that they are stupid. ADJ QUALIT Informal

4 If a light **dims** or if you **dim** it, it becomes less bright. V-ERG

dime /daɪm/, **dimes.** A **dime** is an American coin worth ten cents. N COUNT

dimension /dɪ5mɛnʃə0n/, **dimensions. 1** A particular **dimension** of a situation is a fact or event that affects the way you understand the situation. EG *Most of us were Catholic, and this added an extra dimension to the tension.* N COUNT : USU+SUPP

2 The **dimensions** of a situation or problem are the extent or importance of it. EG *...a growing awareness of the true dimensions of the threat.* N COUNT : USU PLURAL

3 A **dimension** is a measurement in space such as length, width, or height. EG *...a dimension of six metres.* N COUNT

4 You can refer to the size of something as its **dimensions**. EG *These plants grew to magnificent dimensions.* N COUNT : USU PLURAL

diminish /dɪmɪnɪʃ/, **diminishes, diminishing, diminished.** When something **diminishes** or **is diminished**, it becomes reduced in size, importance, or intensity. EG *As she turned the knob, the sound diminished.* ◇ **diminished.** EG *...clear evidence of diminished social tension.* ◇ **diminishing.** EG *...the diminishing importance of universities.* V-ERG ◇ ADJ QUALIT ◇ ADJ QUALIT

diminutive /dɪmɪnju:tɪv/ means very small indeed. EG *...Mrs Bradley, a diminutive figure in black.* ADJ CLASSIF Literary

dimple /dɪmpə0l/, **dimples.** A **dimple** is a small hollow in someone's cheek or chin, often one that you can see when they smile. N COUNT

dimpled /dɪmpə0ld/. Something that is **dimpled** has small hollows in it. EG *...the child's dimpled cheeks.* ADJ CLASSIF

din /dɪn/. A **din** is a very loud and unpleasant noise that lasts for a long time. EG *They were unable to sleep because of the din coming from the bar.* N SING Informal

dine /daɪn/, **dines, dining, dined.** When you **dine**, you have dinner. EG *They arrived at seven, in time to dine at a splendid Hungarian restaurant.* V Formal

dine out. If you **dine out**, you have dinner away from your home, usually at a restaurant. PHRASAL VB : V+ADV

diner /daɪnə/, **diners.** A **diner** is **1** someone who is having dinner in a restaurant. **2** a small, cheap restaurant. N COUNT American

dinghy /dɪŋi1/, **dinghies.** A **dinghy** is a small boat that you sail or row. N COUNT

dingy /dɪndʒi1/, **dingier, dingiest. 1** A building or place that is **dingy** is rather dark and depressing. EG *We drove through some of the dingiest streets of the town.* ADJ QUALIT

2 Clothes or curtains that are **dingy** are dirty or faded. ADJ QUALIT

dining room, dining rooms. A **dining room** is the room in a house where people have their meals, or a room in a hotel where meals are served. N COUNT

dinner /dɪnə/, **dinners. 1 Dinner** is the main meal of the day. EG *I haven't had dinner yet.* N UNCOUNT OR N COUNT

2 A **dinner** is a formal social event in the evening at which a meal is served. EG *Mrs Thatcher attended a dinner at the Mansion House last night.* N COUNT

dinner jacket, dinner jackets. A **dinner jacket** is a black jacket that a man wears with a bow tie at formal social events. N COUNT

dinner party, dinner parties. A **dinner party** is a social event where a small group of people are invited to have dinner and spend the evening at someone's house. EG *How about giving a dinner-party next week?* N COUNT

dinosaur /daɪnəsɔ:/, **dinosaurs. Dinosaurs** were large reptiles which lived in prehistoric times and which are now extinct. N COUNT

diocese /daɪə7sɪs/, **dioceses.** A **diocese** is the area over which a bishop has control. N COUNT

dip /dɪp/, **dips, dipping, dipped. 1** If you **dip** something into a liquid or powder, you put it into the liquid or powder and then quickly take it out again. EG *He dipped his pen in the ink.* V+O : OFT +*in/into*

2 If something **dips**, it makes a downward movement. EG *The plane's nose dipped.* V

3 If a road **dips**, it goes down quite suddenly to a lower level. EG *The railway dips between thick forests.* V

4 A **dip** in a surface is a place in it that is lower than the rest of the surface. EG *...a small dip in the ground.* N COUNT

5 A **dip** is a thick creamy mixture which you eat by scooping it up with raw vegetables or biscuits. EG *...tasty cheese dips.* N COUNT OR N UNCOUNT

When your eyes dilate, does the size of your pupils diminish?

6 If you have a **dip**, you go for a quick swim. N COUNT

diphtheria /dɪpθɪərɪə, dɪf-/ is a dangerous infectious disease. N UNCOUNT

diploma /dɪpləʊmə/, **diplomas.** A **diploma** is a qualification which is awarded to students by a university or college. A diploma is not as high as a degree. EG *She studied for a diploma in theology.* N COUNT

diplomacy /dɪpləʊməsi[1]/ is **1** the management of relations between countries. EG *The crisis developed into a matter of high-level diplomacy between the two embassies.* **2** the skill of saying or doing things without offending people. EG *You will need to employ a great deal of tact and diplomacy to put him politely in his place.* N UNCOUNT

diplomat /dɪplə[6]mæt/, **diplomats.** A **diplomat** is **1** a senior government official who negotiates with another country on behalf of his or her own country. Diplomats usually work as members of an embassy. N COUNT

2 You can also refer to someone who is skilful at saying and doing things that do not offend people as a **diplomat**. N COUNT

diplomatic /dɪplə[6]mætɪk/. **1 Diplomatic** means relating to diplomacy and diplomats. EG *The government was reluctant to endanger its diplomatic links with Britain.* ADJ CLASSIF : ATTRIB

2 Someone who is **diplomatic** is able to be tactful and say or do things without offending people. EG *The secretary was diplomatic on the telephone.* ADJ QUALIT

dire /daɪə/ is used to emphasize how serious or terrible a situation is. EG *...countries in dire misery... ...the dire consequences of his actions.* ADJ CLASSIF : USU ATTRIB

direct /dɪ[5]rɛkt/, **directs, directing, directed. 1 Direct** means going or aimed straight towards a place or object. EG *Are there any direct flights to Athens?... Why hadn't he gone direct to the lounge?* ADJ CLASSIF; ALSO ADV : USU+PREP
◊ **directly.** EG *She turned her head and looked directly at them.* ◊ ADV

2 You use **direct** to emphasize that no other person or situation is involved. EG *...the direct intervention of the managing director... ...as a direct result of this information... Some of the money comes direct from industry.* ◊ **directly.** EG *They negotiated directly with the leaders.* ADJ CLASSIF : ATTRIB OR ADV; ◊ ADV

3 A **direct** attack or challenge is one made openly so that there is no doubt about what is being done. EG *This move is a direct challenge to the government.* ADJ CLASSIF : ATTRIB

4 Someone who is **direct** makes their opinions and wishes known in a very clear, open way. ADJ QUALIT
◊ **directly.** EG *She never directly asked for money.*
◊ **directness.** EG *Such directness embarrassed Ian.* ◊ N UNCOUNT

5 Something that **is directed** at a particular person or thing is aimed at them or is intended to affect them. EG *...a question that John had evidently directed at me... This is a fundamental question to which we should all be directing our attention.* V+O+A

6 If you **direct** someone somewhere, you tell them how to get there. EG *Can you direct me to the cemetery?* V+O : OFT+*to* Formal

7 If someone **directs** a project or a group of people, they organize it and are in charge of it. EG *No one seemed to be directing the operation.* V+O

8 If someone **directs** a film, play, or television programme, they decide how it should be made and performed. V+O OR V

9 If you **direct** someone to do something, you tell them to do it. EG *She directed me to sit in the waiting room.* V+O+*to*-INF Formal

10 Someone who is a **direct** descendant of a particular person is descended from that person through their parents, grandparents and so on, rather than through uncles, aunts, or cousins. ADJ CLASSIF : ATTRIB

11 See also **directly**.

direction /dɪ[5]rɛkʃə[0]n/, **directions. 1** A **direction** is **1.1** the general line that someone or something is moving or pointing in. EG *We ended up going in the opposite direction from them... Pieces of jagged metal are sent flying in all directions.* **1.2** the general way in which something develops or progresses. EG *The government has to guide the general direction of the economy.* N COUNT : USU+SUPP

2 Directions are instructions that tell you what to do or how to get to a place. EG *Follow the directions that your doctor gives you... I asked a policeman for directions to the hospital.* N PLURAL

3 The **direction** of a film, play, or television programme is the work that the director does while it is being made. N UNCOUNT

4 If you do something **under** someone else's **direction**, they tell you what to do. PHRASE

directive /dɪ[5]rɛktɪv/, **directives.** A **directive** is an official instruction that is given by someone in authority. EG *The government is obliged to take action because of EEC directives.* N COUNT Formal

directly /dɪ[5]rɛktli[1]/. **1** If something is **directly** above, below, or in front of something, it is in exactly that position. EG *The sun was almost directly overhead... I saw him pass directly in front of the window.* ADV

2 If you say something will happen **directly**, you mean that it will happen very soon. EG *She's in a meeting at the moment but she will be here directly.* ADV

3 You use **directly** to say that one thing happens immediately after another thing. EG *Newly married girls go directly to live in the village of their new husband... Directly he heard the door close he picked up the telephone.* ADV

4 See also **direct**.

director /dɪ[5]rɛktə/, **directors.** A **director** is **1** someone who is responsible for organizing and leading a group of people who are working together. EG *He became artistic director of the Sadlers Wells ballet in 1978.* **2** someone who is on the board of a company or in charge of a government organization. **3** someone who decides how a film, play, or television programme is made or performed. N COUNT

directory /dɪ[5]rɛktə[0]ri[1]/, **directories.** A **directory** is a book which gives lists of information such as people's names, addresses, and telephone numbers, usually arranged in alphabetical order. EG *...the Birmingham telephone directory.* N COUNT

dirge /dɜːdʒ/, **dirges.** A **dirge** is a slow, sad song or piece of music, often performed at funerals. N COUNT

dirt /dɜːt/ is **1** dust or mud on something which is usually kept clean. EG *...sweeping up the dirt.* **2** the earth on the ground. EG *...rough dirt roads.* N UNCOUNT

dirty /dɜːti[1]/, **dirtier, dirtiest; dirties, dirtying, dirtied. 1** Something that is **dirty** has dust, mud, or stains on it and needs to be cleaned. EG *The children were hot, dirty, and exhausted... ...dirty marks on the walls.* ADJ QUALIT

2 To **dirty** something means to make it dirty. EG *She didn't like dogs; they dirtied her clothes.* V+O

3 A **dirty** action is unfair or dishonest. EG *They will use any dirty trick.* ADJ QUALIT : ATTRIB

4 Dirty jokes, books, or language refer to sex in a way that many people find offensive. ADJ QUALIT

disability /dɪsəbɪlə[1]ti[1]/, **disabilities.** A **disability** is a physical injury or mental illness that severely affects your life. EG *...the disabilities suffered by the elderly.* N COUNT OR N UNCOUNT Formal

disable /dɪseɪbə[0]l/, **disables, disabling, disabled.** If something **disables** you, it injures you physically or mentally and severely affects your life. EG *...if you are disabled by an accident at work.* V+O

disabled /dɪseɪbə[0]ld/. **1** Someone who is **disabled** has a physical injury or mental illness that severely affects their life. EG *She has to look after a disabled relative.* ADJ QUALIT

2 The **disabled** are people who have a physical injury or mental illness that severely affects their lives. EG *...the variety of help available to the disabled.* N PLURAL : *the*+N

disablement /dɪseɪbə[0]lmə[2]nt/ is the state of being disabled or the act of becoming disabled. EG *...un-* N UNCOUNT Formal *able to work because of disablement caused by an accident.*

disadvantage /dɪsəʳdvɑːntɪdʒ/, **disadvantages.** 1 A **disadvantage** is a part of a situation which causes problems. EG *...the disadvantages of living in cities.* N COUNT

2 If you are **at a disadvantage** in a situation, you cannot succeed easily because you have a problem that other people do not have. EG *These restrictions put banks at a disadvantage.* PHRASE

3 If something is **to** your **disadvantage**, it causes problems for you or puts you in a worse position than other people. EG *The treaty was to our disadvantage.* PHRASE

disadvantaged /dɪsəʳdvɑːntɪdʒd/. People who are **disadvantaged** live in bad conditions and cannot easily improve their situation. EG *...disadvantaged children.* ADJ QUALIT

disadvantageous /dɪsædvɑːnteɪdʒəs/. Something that is **disadvantageous** causes problems or puts someone in a worse position than other people. EG *This made the 1976 agreement disadvantageous to the British.* ADJ QUALIT: OFT+*to*

disaffected /dɪsəfɛktɪᵊd/. People who are **disaffected** are dissatisfied with an organization or idea and no longer support it. EG *Our party gained four disaffected UP members.* ADJ QUALIT

disaffection /dɪsəfɛkʃᵊn/ is a feeling of dissatisfaction that people have with an organization or idea, so that they no longer support it. EG *They were worried about the possibility of disaffection in the army.* N UNCOUNT Formal

disagree /dɪsəgriː/, **disagrees, disagreeing, disagreed.** 1 If you **disagree** with a person or idea, you have a different opinion of what is true or correct. EG *I disagree completely with John Taylor... He and I disagree about it.* V: OFT+*with/about*

2 If you **disagree** with an action or decision, you disapprove of it. EG *Benn disagreed with the abandonment of the project.* V+*with*

3 If food or drink **disagrees** with you, it makes you feel ill after you have eaten or drunk it. V+*with* Informal

disagreeable /dɪsəgriːəbᵊl/. 1 Something that is **disagreeable** is unpleasant or annoying. EG *...a very disagreeable smell.* ADJ QUALIT

2 Someone who is **disagreeable** is unfriendly or bad-tempered. ADJ QUALIT ◇ **disagreeably.** EG *'I hate it,' she said disagreeably.* ◇ ADV

disagreement /dɪsəgriːməᵊnt/, **disagreements.** 1 **Disagreement** is a situation in which people have different opinions and cannot reach a decision. EG *There was little disagreement over what needed to be done... The experts find themselves in total disagreement.* N UNCOUNT

2 A **disagreement** is an argument between people. EG *We had a serious disagreement about business.* N COUNT: USU+SUPP

disallow /dɪsəlaʊ/, **disallows, disallowing, disallowed.** If an action or claim **is disallowed**, it is not accepted or not approved by people in authority. EG *The appeals were disallowed by the court.* V+O Formal

disappear /dɪsəpɪə/, **disappears, disappearing, disappeared.** 1 If someone or something **disappears**, 1.1 they go where you can no longer see them. EG *I saw him disappear round the corner.* V: OFT+A 1.2 they go where nobody can find them. EG *I shall disappear. You will not hear from me again.* V

◇ **disappearance** /dɪsəpɪərəns/, **disappearances.** EG *...the mysterious disappearance of Halliday.* ◇ N UNCOUNT OR N COUNT

2 If something **disappears**, it stops existing or happening. EG *Some newspapers are going to disappear as a result of this strike.* V ◇ **disappearance.** EG *...the disappearance of the dinosaurs.* ◇ N UNCOUNT

disappoint /dɪsəpɔɪnt/, **disappoints, disappointing, disappointed.** If things or people **disappoint** you, they do not satisfy you, because they are not as good as you had hoped, or do not do what you want. EG *The results disappointed him... We must not disappoint the hopes of the people.* V+O

disappointed /dɪsəpɔɪntɪᵊd/. If you are **disappointed**, you are sad because something that you wanted has not happened or because it is not as good as you hoped it would be. EG *She was disappointed that Ted had not come... My father was bitterly disappointed in me.* ADJ QUALIT

disappointing /dɪsəpɔɪntɪŋ/. Something that is **disappointing** is not as good or not as much as you expected it to be. EG *...a disappointing book.* ADJ QUALIT

◇ **disappointingly.** EG *...the disappointingly small crowd.* ◇ ADV

disappointment /dɪsəpɔɪntməᵊnt/, **disappointments.** 1 **Disappointment** is the state of feeling disappointed. EG *To my disappointment, she came with her mother.* N UNCOUNT: USU+SUPP

2 A **disappointment** is something which makes you feel disappointed. EG *That defeat was a surprise and a disappointment.* N COUNT

disapproval /dɪsəpruːvᵊl/. If you express **disapproval** of someone or something, you indicate that you do not like them or that you think they are wrong. EG *...his disapproval of the President's policy.* N UNCOUNT

disapprove /dɪsəpruːv/, **disapproves, disapproving, disapproved.** If you **disapprove** of someone or something, you feel or show that you do not like them or that you think they are wrong. EG *The other teachers disapproved of his methods.* V: OFT+*of*

disapproving /dɪsəpruːvɪŋ/. A **disapproving** action or expression indicates that you do not like someone or something or that you think they are wrong. EG *...a disapproving glance... My parents were slightly disapproving of Ellen.* ADJ QUALIT

◇ **disapprovingly.** EG *He shook his head disapprovingly.* ◇ ADV

disarm /dɪsɑːm/, **disarms, disarming, disarmed.** 1 If you **disarm** people, you take away their weapons. EG *The officer captured and disarmed the two men.* V+O

2 If a country **disarms**, it gives up the use of weapons, especially nuclear weapons. V

3 If you **disarm** someone or **disarm** their anger or hostility, you cause them to feel less angry or hostile. EG *They were so kind that it surprised and disarmed her.* V+O

disarmament /dɪsɑːməməᵊnt/ is a process in which countries agree to reduce the number of weapons that they have, especially nuclear weapons. N UNCOUNT

disarming /dɪsɑːmɪŋ/. If someone is **disarming**, they cause you to feel less angry or hostile. EG *...Harriet's disarming friendliness... ...a disarming smile.* ADJ QUALIT

disarrange /dɪsəreɪndʒ/, **disarranges, disarranging, disarranged.** To **disarrange** something means to make it untidy. EG *The wind was disarranging her hair.* V+O Formal

disarray /dɪsəreɪ/. 1 If a group of people is **in disarray** or has been thrown **into disarray**, they have become confused and disorganized. EG *The Democratic Party was in disarray.* PHRASE Formal

2 If things or places are **in disarray**, they are very untidy. EG *...books in disarray.* PHRASE Formal

disassociate /dɪsəsəʊʃieɪt/, **disassociates, disassociating, disassociated.** If you **disassociate** yourself from a person or situation, you state or show that you are not involved with them, in order to avoid trouble or blame. EG *Democratic politicians wanted to disassociate themselves from the President.* V-REFL+*from* Formal

disaster /dɪzɑːstə/, **disasters.** 1 A **disaster** is an unexpected event which causes a lot of damage or N COUNT

On these pages which adjective is always used in front of a noun?

suffering. EG *...a natural disaster, an earthquake or a typhoon.*

2 If you say that something was a **disaster**, you mean that you think it was very unsuccessful or unpleasant. EG *The last day at the hotel was a disaster.* N COUNT

3 **Disaster** is something which affects you very badly. EG *They had led the country into economic disaster.* N UNCOUNT

disastrous /dɪzɑːstrəs/. 1 A **disastrous** event causes a lot of damage or suffering. EG *...disastrous floods.* ◇ **disastrously.** EG *These diseases have increased disastrously.* ADJ QUALIT ◇ ADV

2 If you say that something is **disastrous**, you mean that it is very unsuccessful or unpleasant. EG *...a disastrous holiday.* ◇ **disastrously.** EG *The team performed disastrously.* ADJ QUALIT ◇ ADV

disband /dɪsbænd/, **disbands, disbanding, disbanded.** If someone **disbands** an organization or group of people, the organization or group officially ceases to exist. EG *The regiment had been disbanded... They began to disband.* V-ERG

disbelief /dɪsbə¹liːf/ is not believing that something is true or real. EG *He shook his head in disbelief... I looked at it with disbelief.* N UNCOUNT

disbelieve /dɪsbə¹liːv/, **disbelieves, disbelieving, disbelieved.** If you **disbelieve** someone, you think that they are telling lies. EG *There is no reason to disbelieve him.* V+O Formal

disc /dɪsk/, **discs;** spelled **disk** in American English. A **disc** is 1 a flat, circular shape or object. EG *...a metal disc with a number stamped on it.* 2 a thin, circular piece of cartilage between the bones in your spine. 3 a gramophone record. N COUNT

discard /dɪskɑːd/, **discards, discarding, discarded.** If you **discard** something, you get rid of it or leave it because it is old, useless, or unwanted. EG *Pull off and discard the outer leaves.* V+O
◇ **discarded.** EG *...discarded newspapers.* ◇ ADJ CLASSIF

discern /dɪsɜːn/, **discerns, discerning, discerned.** If you **discern** something, 1 you can see it by looking carefully. EG *I could dimly discern his figure.* V+O Formal 2 you can notice it or understand it by careful thought or study. EG *Posy had not discerned the real reason... He is unable to discern what is actually happening.* V+O OR V+REPORT Formal

discernible /dɪsɜːnəbə⁰l/. If something is **discernible**, 1 you can see it by looking carefully. EG *Each pebble was clearly discernible.* ADJ QUALIT 2 you can notice it or understand it by careful thought or study. EG *An element of envy is discernible in his attitude.* ADJ QUALIT : OFT+*in*

discerning /dɪsɜːnɪŋ/. Someone who is **discerning** is good at judging the quality of something. EG *...discerning readers.* ADJ QUALIT

discharge, discharges, discharging, discharged; pronounced /dɪstʃɑːdʒ/ when it is a verb and /dɪstʃɑːdʒ/ when it is a noun.

1 When someone **is discharged** from hospital, prison, or the armed forces, they are officially allowed to leave. ▸ used as a noun. EG *...from the time of his discharge until his re-arrest.* V+O : USU PASS ▸ N UNCOUNT : USU+POSS

2 If someone **discharges** their duties or responsibilities, they carry them out satisfactorily. EG *He is unable to discharge the duties of his office.* V+O Formal

3 To **discharge** an object or substance means to send it out from a place or container. EG *The city's sewage is discharged into huge lakes.* ▸ used as a noun. EG *...the discharge of mercury from industrial premises.* V+O Formal ▸ N COUNT OR N UNCOUNT : USU+SUPP

4 A **discharge** is also a substance that comes out from a place. EG *...a discharge from the nose.* N COUNT Formal

disciple /dɪsaɪpə⁰l/, **disciples.** A **disciple** is someone who believes, supports, and uses the ideas of their leader or superior. EG *...Jesus and his disciples.* N COUNT

disciplinarian /dɪsɪplɪnɛərɪən/, **disciplinarians.** If someone in authority is a **disciplinarian**, they are strict and insist that people obey the rules. N COUNT

disciplinary /dɪsɪplɪnəri¹/ matters are concerned with rules, making sure that people obey them, and punishing people who do not. EG *...forcing them to take disciplinary action against their own members.* ADJ CLASSIF : ATTRIB

discipline /dɪsɪplɪn/, **disciplines, disciplining, disciplined.** 1 **Discipline** is 1.1 the practice of making people obey rules and punishing them when they do not. EG *She was a harsh mother and imposed severe discipline.* 1.2 the quality of always behaving or working in a controlled way. EG *They admired our patience and discipline.* N UNCOUNT

2 The **discipline** of a particular activity is the system of rules or methods that is used in it. EG *...the discipline of dancing... ...military discipline.* N UNCOUNT OR N COUNT

3 If you **discipline** someone, 3.1 you train them to behave or work in a controlled way. EG *They will have to discipline themselves.* V+O OR V-REFL 3.2 you punish them for behaving badly or breaking a rule. EG *They could be disciplined by the union if they refused to strike.* V+O

4 A **discipline** is a subject that is studied at colleges and universities. EG *...graduates of all disciplines.* N COUNT Formal

disciplined /dɪsɪplɪnd/. Someone who is **disciplined** behaves or works in a controlled way. EG *Baker lives a disciplined life.* ADJ QUALIT

disc jockey, disc jockeys. A **disc jockey** is someone whose job is to play and introduce pop records on the radio or at a disco. N COUNT

disclaim /dɪskleɪm/, **disclaims, disclaiming, disclaimed.** If you **disclaim** knowledge of something or **disclaim** responsibility for it, you say that you did not know about it or are not responsible for it. EG *Tess disclaimed any knowledge of it... She disclaimed any wish to impose censorship on television.* V+O Formal

disclose /dɪskləʊz/, **discloses, disclosing, disclosed.** If you **disclose** new or secret information, you tell it to someone. EG *I had no intention of disclosing their names... The English newspaper disclosed that the treaty had been signed.* V+O OR V+REPORT
◇ **disclosure** /dɪskləʊʒə/, **disclosures.** EG *He feared it might lead to the disclosure of his visit to Rome... There were more disclosures about Casey in the press.* ◇ N UNCOUNT OR N COUNT Formal

disco /dɪskəʊ/, **discos.** A **disco** is a place or event at which young people dance to pop records. EG *...going out to a disco or a pub.* N COUNT

discolour /dɪskʌlə/, **discolours, discolouring, discoloured;** spelled **discolor** in American English.

If something **discolours** or if it **is discoloured** by something else, it changes its original colour and looks unattractive. EG *The pans may discolour inside.* ◇ **discoloured.** EG *...discoloured teeth.* V-ERG ◇ ADJ QUALIT

discomfort /dɪskʌmfə⁸t/, **discomforts.** 1 **Discomfort** is 1.1 an unpleasant or painful feeling in a part of your body. EG *He was conscious only of physical discomfort.* 1.2 a feeling of worry or embarrassment. EG *I no longer experienced discomfort in their presence.* N UNCOUNT

2 **Discomforts** are conditions which make you feel pain or unease. EG *...the discomforts of life in India.* N PLURAL +SUPP

disconcert /dɪskə⁷nsɜːt/, **disconcerts, disconcerting, disconcerted.** If something **disconcerts** you, it makes you feel worried or embarrassed. EG *Her cold stare disconcerted me.* V+O : USU PASS Formal

disconcerting /dɪskə⁷nsɜːtɪŋ/. Something that is **disconcerting** makes you feel worried or embarrassed. EG *...his disconcerting habit of pausing before he spoke.* ◇ **disconcertingly.** EG *Harold laughed disconcertingly loudly.* ADJ QUALIT ◇ SUBMOD OR ADV

disconnect /dɪskə⁷nɛkt/, **disconnects, disconnecting, disconnected.** 1 If you **disconnect** things that are joined, you pull them apart. EG *Can you disconnect all these tubes?* V+O

2 If you **disconnect** a piece of equipment, you V+O

detach it from its source of power, such as a gas or electricity supply. EG *I bent down to disconnect the plug.*

3 If a gas, electricity, water, or telephone company **disconnects** you, it turns off the connection to your house. EG *His telephone had been disconnected.* — V+O : USU PASS

4 If a telephone operator **disconnects** you, he or she suddenly ends a call you are making. — V+O

disconnected /dɪskə[2]nɛktɪ[2]d/. **Disconnected** things are not linked in any way. EG *...a series of disconnected events... She gave disconnected answers.* — ADJ CLASSIF

disconsolate /dɪskɒnsələ[1]t/. Someone who is **disconsolate** is very unhappy or disappointed. EG *...disconsolate passengers standing around.* — ADJ QUALIT Formal

◇ **disconsolately.** EG *He walked disconsolately down the path.* — ◇ ADV

discontent /dɪskə[7]ntɛnt/ is the feeling of not being satisfied with your situation. EG *...their discontent with pay and conditions.* — N UNCOUNT : USU+SUPP

discontented /dɪskə[7]ntɛntɪ[2]d/. If you are **discontented**, you are not satisfied with your situation. EG *Most of the people he saw looked discontented.* — ADJ QUALIT

discontinue /dɪskə[7]ntɪnju:/, **discontinues, discontinuing, discontinued.** If you **discontinue** an activity, you stop doing it. EG *Fanny wanted to discontinue her visits.* — V+O Formal

discord /dɪskɔ:d/, **discords. 1 Discord** is disagreement and unpleasantness between people. EG *He's been a source of discord and worry.* — N UNCOUNT Literary

2 A **discord** is an unpleasant combination of musical notes. — N COUNT Technical

discordant /dɪskɔ:də[0]nt/. **1** Things that are **discordant** are different from each other in an unexpected or unpleasant way. EG *...the discordant state of industrial relations.* — ADJ QUALIT Formal

2 A sound that is **discordant** is unpleasant to listen to. — ADJ QUALIT Formal

discotheque /dɪskə[6]tɛk/, **discotheques.** A **discotheque** is a disco. — N COUNT Formal

discount, discounts, discounting, discounted; pronounced /dɪskaʊnt/ when it is a noun and /dɪskaʊnt/ when it is a verb.

1 A **discount** is a reduction in the usual price of something. EG *Our clients receive a 50% discount.* — N COUNT

2 If you **discount** someone or something, you reject or ignore them because you think they are not important. EG *I decided to discount the risks.* — V+O

discourage /dɪskʌrɪdʒ/, **discourages, discouraging, discouraged. 1** If someone or something **discourages** you, they cause you to lose your enthusiasm or become unwilling to do something. EG *Don't let friends discourage you.* — V+O

◇ **discouraging.** EG *...a difficult and discouraging task.* — ◇ ADJ QUALIT ◇ **discouraged.** EG *Whenever I feel discouraged, I read that letter.* — ◇ ADJ QUALIT ◇ **discouragement** /dɪskʌrɪdʒmə[2]nt/, **discouragements.** EG *The submarines were a constant discouragement to naval movements.* — ◇ N COUNT

2 To **discourage** an action or to **discourage** someone from doing it means to try and persuade them not to do it. EG *She wanted to discourage him from marrying the girl.* — V+O : OFT+*from* ◇ **discouragement.** EG *When I first started, I encountered opposition and discouragement.* — ◇ N UNCOUNT

discourse, discourses, discoursing, discoursed; pronounced /dɪskɔ:s/ when it is a noun and /dɪskɔ:s/ when it is a verb.

1 A **discourse** is a talk or piece of writing that teaches or explains something. EG *They listened to his discourse on human relations.* — N COUNT ▸ used as a verb. EG *Jeff discoursed impressively on Newton's theory of gravity.* — ▸ V+*on/upon* Formal

2 Discourse is spoken or written communication between people. EG *Let us switch the area of discourse to politics.* — N UNCOUNT Formal

discover /dɪskʌvə/, **discovers, discovering, discovered. 1** When you **discover** a fact that you did not know, you find out about it. EG *We discovered a way to get rid of it... I discovered that Zapp is Melanie's father.* — V+O OR V+REPORT

2 If you **discover** someone or something, you find them accidentally or by searching for them. EG *He was dead before anyone discovered him.* — V+O

3 If someone **discovers** something that nobody knew about before, they are the first person to find it or find out about it. EG *Herschel discovered a new planet.* — V+O ◇ **discoverer** /dɪskʌvərə/, **discoverers.** EG *...the discoverer of penicillin, Sir Alexander Fleming.* — ◇ N COUNT

4 If you **discover** a feeling, you experience it for the first time. EG *She discovered the joy of writing.* — V+O

5 If an artist or athlete **is discovered**, someone realizes how talented they are and helps them to become famous. — V+O : USU PASS

discovery /dɪskʌvə[0]ri[1]/, **discoveries.** A **discovery** is **1** the finding of an object or fact that nobody knew about. EG *New scientific discoveries are being made every day... ...the Chinese discovery of paper-making.* — N COUNT OR N UNCOUNT : USU+SUPP **2** the finding of an object or fact that you did not know about. EG *...the discovery that he wanted to hurt her.* — N COUNT : USU+SUPP

discredit /dɪskrɛdɪt/, **discredits, discrediting, discredited. 1** To **discredit** someone means to cause them to lose the trust or respect of other people. EG *...efforts to discredit the government.* — V+O Formal

◇ **discredited.** EG *...the discredited ambassador.* — ◇ ADJ QUALIT

2 To **discredit** an idea or belief means to make it appear false or doubtful. EG *Scientific discoveries have discredited religious belief.* — V+O Formal ◇ **discredited.** EG *...discredited theories.* — ◇ ADJ QUALIT

3 Discredit is shame or disapproval. EG *It may bring discredit to our city.* — N UNCOUNT Formal

4 If something is **to** your **discredit**, it causes people to lose respect for you. EG *To Monty's discredit, he refused.* — PHRASE

discreet /dɪskri:t/. **1 Discreet** behaviour involves being careful not to cause embarrassment or difficulties for someone. EG *Make discreet enquiries at his place of employment.* — ADJ QUALIT ◇ **discreetly.** EG *The king came discreetly up the back stairs.* — ◇ ADV

2 If you are **discreet**, you do not talk about secret or private matters. EG *I'll certainly be most discreet in my conversation.* — ADJ QUALIT

3 Something that is **discreet** is intended not to attract a lot of attention. EG *...discreet advertisements in the newspapers.* — ADJ QUALIT ◇ **discreetly.** EG *...the discreetly shaded light.* — ◇ ADV

discrepancy /dɪskrɛpənsi[1]/, **discrepancies.** A **discrepancy** is a surprising difference between things that ought to be similar or the same. EG *...discrepancies between school records and examination results... ...discrepancies in Mr Casey's accounts.* — N COUNT : OFT +*between/in*

discrete /dɪskri:t/. A **discrete** thing is separate and different from similar things. EG *...the two discrete hemispheres of the brain... ...mobility between discrete social classes.* — ADJ CLASSIF : ATTRIB Formal

discretion /dɪskrɛʃə[0]n/. **1 Discretion** is **1.1** the quality of not causing embarrassment or difficulties or of not revealing secrets. EG *The plan was carried out with maximum speed and discretion.* — N UNCOUNT **1.2** the ability to judge a situation and to take suitable decisions or actions. EG *Use your discretion!*

2 If a decision is **at the discretion of** someone in authority, it depends on them and not on a fixed rule. EG *The issue of these cards is at the discretion of your bank manager.* — PHRASE

discretionary /dɪskrɛʃənə[0]rɪ/ matters are not fixed by rules but are decided by the people in authority. EG *The University has funds for discretionary awards in special cases.* — ADJ CLASSIF

Which word on these pages is spelled differently in British English and American English?

discriminate /dɪskrɪmɪneɪt/, **discriminates, discriminating, discriminated. 1** If you can **discriminate** between two things, you can recognize and understand the difference between them. EG *...to discriminate between right and wrong.* — V : OFT+ *between*

2 To **discriminate** against someone or in favour of them means to unfairly treat them worse or better than other people. EG *The law discriminated against women.* — V : OFT +*against/ favour of*

discriminating /dɪskrɪmɪneɪtɪŋ/. Someone who is **discriminating** recognizes and likes things that are of good quality. EG *We offer choices to discriminating readers.* — ADJ QUALIT

discrimination /dɪskrɪmɪneɪʃə^{0}n/ is **1** the practice of unfairly treating someone worse or better than other people. EG *...discrimination against women.* — N UNCOUNT : USU+SUPP **2** the ability to recognize and understand the difference between two things. EG *...discrimination between the important and the trivial problems.* — N UNCOUNT : USU+SUPP **3** the ability to recognize and like things that are of good quality. EG *There was in Julie a coarseness and a lack of discrimination.* — N UNCOUNT

discursive /dɪskɜːsɪv/. If speech or writing is **discursive**, the ideas in it are not carefully arranged and include unnecessary details. EG *They complained that my writing was becoming too discursive.* — ADJ QUALIT Formal

discus /dɪskəs/, **discuses.** A **discus** is a heavy, circular object that is thrown as a sport. — N COUNT

discuss /dɪskʌs/, **discusses, discussing, discussed.** If you **discuss** something, you talk about it seriously with other people. EG *They said they had an important matter to discuss with you.* — V+O

discussion /dɪskʌʃə^{0}n/, **discussions. 1 Discussion** is the act of talking seriously about something with other people. EG *Ten hours were spent in discussion of Boon's papers... There was much discussion between those inside and outside the party.* — N UNCOUNT

2 A **discussion** is a serious conversation between people. EG *I had been involved in discussions about this with Ken and Frank... We're having a discussion on leisure activities.* — N COUNT

3 If something is **under discussion**, it is being talked about and no decision about it has been reached yet. EG *...the weapons system under discussion.* — PHRASE

disdain /dɪsdeɪn/, **disdains, disdaining, disdained. 1** If you feel **disdain** for someone or something, you think that they have little value or importance. EG *He spoke of the rebels with disdain.* — N UNCOUNT : OFT+*for* Formal
◊ **disdainful** /dɪsdeɪnfʊl/. EG *They tend to be disdainful of their colleagues.* — ◊ ADJ QUALIT ◊ **disdainfully.** EG *She looked away disdainfully.* — ◊ ADV

2 If you **disdain** something or **disdain** to do something, you reject it or refuse to do it because you think that it is not important or is not good enough for you. EG *...disdaining the help of his son... Claire disdained to reply.* — V+O OR V+*to*-INF Formal

disease /dɪziːz/, **diseases. 1** A **disease** is an illness in living things that is caused by infection or by a fault inside them. EG *I have a rare eye disease... ...conditions that cause disease and starvation.* — N COUNT OR N UNCOUNT

2 You can refer to an attitude or habit that you consider to be unnatural or harmful as a **disease**. EG *You've caught the disease of the profession, suspicion.* — N COUNT+SUPP

diseased /dɪziːzd/. **1** Someone or something that is **diseased** is affected by a disease. EG *...an old diseased tree.* — ADJ CLASSIF

2 If you say that someone has a **diseased** mind, you mean that they have strange or shocking ideas. — ADJ QUALIT

disembark /dɪsɪ^{2}mbɑːk/, **disembarks, disembarking, disembarked.** When you **disembark** from a ship or aeroplane, you get off it at the end of your journey. — V : OFT+*from* Formal

disenchanted /dɪsɪntʃɑːntɪ^{2}d/. If you are **disenchanted** with something, you no longer think that it is good or worthwhile. EG *Some young people are disenchanted with school.* — ADJ QUALIT Formal

disenchantment /dɪsɪntʃɑːntmə^{2}nt/ is the feeling of being disappointed with something and no longer thinking that it is good or worthwhile. EG *...public disenchantment with the war.* — N UNCOUNT Formal

disengage /dɪsɪ^{2}ngeɪdʒ/, **disengages, disengaging, disengaged.** If you **disengage** things that are connected, you separate them. EG *Don't break or disengage the rope... Melanie attempted to disengage her arms from his grip... He disengaged himself and jumped up.* — V+O OR V-REFL : OFT+*from* Formal

disentangle /dɪsɪ^{2}ntæŋgə^{0}l/, **disentangles, disentangling, disentangled.** If you **disentangle** something, you separate it from other things that it has become mixed with or attached to. EG *She disentangled her jacket from the coat-hanger... Tom disentangled himself himself from his wife's arms.* — V+O OR V-REFL : OFT+*from*

disfavour /dɪsfeɪvə/; spelled **disfavor** in American English.

Disfavour is **1** dislike or disapproval of someone or something. EG *...looking with disfavour at the glass in his hand.* — N UNCOUNT : USU+POSS **2** the state of being disliked or disapproved of by someone in authority. EG *He was in disfavour with his employer.* — N UNCOUNT

disfigure /dɪsfɪgə/, **disfigures, disfiguring, disfigured.** To **disfigure** someone or something means to spoil their appearance. EG *His nose was disfigured in an accident.* — V+O : USU PASS Formal

disgrace /dɪsgreɪs/, **disgraces, disgracing, disgraced. 1 Disgrace** is a state in which people disapprove of someone or stop respecting them. EG *My uncle brought disgrace on the family.* — N UNCOUNT ● If someone is **in disgrace**, other people disapprove of them or stop respecting them. EG *He was sent back to his village in disgrace.* — ● PHRASE

2 You say that something is a **disgrace** when you find it totally unacceptable. EG *They are destroying the country – it's a disgrace!* — N SING : *a*+N

3 You say that someone is a **disgrace** to someone else when their behaviour makes the other person feel ashamed. EG *You're a disgrace to the Italians.* — N SING : *a*+N+*to*

4 If you **disgrace** someone, you behave in a way that causes them to be disapproved of by other people. EG *Fanny disgraced herself in London.* — V+O OR V-REFL

disgraceful /dɪsgreɪsfʊl/. If you say that something is **disgraceful**, you think it is totally unacceptable. EG *...the disgraceful state of the prisons.* — ADJ CLASSIF
◊ **disgracefully.** EG *She behaved disgracefully.* — ◊ ADV

disgruntled /dɪsgrʌntə^{0}ld/. If you are **disgruntled**, you are cross and dissatisfied about something. EG *The disgruntled passengers were guided to another plane.* — ADJ QUALIT

disguise /dɪsgaɪz/, **disguises, disguising, disguised. 1** A **disguise** is clothing or a change in your appearance that is intended to prevent people from recognizing you. EG *...the disguise he wore when he escaped.* — N COUNT

2 If you are **in disguise**, you have changed your clothes or appearance to prevent people recognizing you. EG *The Emperor came aboard the ship in disguise.* — PHRASE

3 If you **disguise** yourself or if you **are disguised** as someone else, you dress like them and behave like them in order to deceive other people. EG *I disguised myself as a French priest.* — V-REFL : OFT+*as*

4 If you **disguise** something, **4.1** you change it so that people do not recognize it. EG *He tried to disguise his voice.* **4.2** you prevent other people knowing about it. EG *It proved difficult to disguise her anxiety.* — V+O

disgust /dɪsgʌst/, **disgusts, disgusting, disgusted. 1 Disgust** is a feeling of strong dislike or disapproval. EG *Many expressed disgust at the use of such weapons.* — N UNCOUNT ● If you do something **in disgust**, you do it because of a strong feeling of dislike or disapproval. EG *He returned downstairs in disgust.* — ● PHRASE

2 Something that **disgusts** you causes you to have — V+O a strong feeling of dislike or disapproval. EG *The attitudes of the tourists disgusted him even more.*

disgusted /dɪsgʌstɪ[2]d/. If you are **disgusted**, you have a strong feeling of dislike or disapproval. EG *She was disgusted with herself.* ADJ QUALIT

disgusting /dɪsgʌstɪŋ/. If you say that something is **disgusting**, you mean that it is extremely unpleasant. EG *The food was disgusting... ...his disgusting behaviour.* ◊ **disgustingly.** EG *She was disgustingly fat.* ADJ QUALIT; ◊ SUBMOD

dish /dɪʃ/, **dishes, dishing, dished. 1** A **dish** is **1.1** a shallow container used for cooking or serving food. N COUNT **1.2** food that is prepared in a particular style or combination. EG *...the traditional British dish of eggs and bacon.* N COUNT: USU+SUPP

2 The **dishes** are all the objects that have been used to cook, serve, and eat a meal. EG *Rudolph stayed to dry the dishes after his mother had washed them.* N PLURAL: USU *the*+N ● If you **do the dishes**, you wash the objects that have been used to cook, serve, and eat a meal. ● PHRASE

dish out. If you **dish out** something, you give it to people. EG *...dishing out presents at Christmas.* PHRASAL VB: V+O+ADV

dish up. If you **dish up** food, you serve it to people. PHRASAL VB: V+O+ADV

dishcloth /dɪʃklɒθ/, **dishcloths.** A **dishcloth** is a cloth that you use for washing objects that have been used to cook, serve, and eat a meal. N COUNT

disheartened /dɪshɑːtə[0]nd/. If you are **disheartened**, you feel disappointed and have less hope or confidence. EG *He became disheartened after losing the money.* ADJ QUALIT Formal

disheartening /dɪshɑːtə[0]nɪŋ/. If something is **disheartening**, it makes you feel disappointed and have less hope or confidence. EG *Such a defeat is inevitably disheartening.* ADJ QUALIT Formal

dishevelled /dɪʃɛvə[0]ld/; spelled **disheveled** in American English. ADJ QUALIT
If someone is **dishevelled**, their appearance is very untidy. EG *...dirty and dishevelled travellers.*

dishonest /dɪsɒnɪ[2]st/. **1** Someone who is **dishonest** lies, cheats, or does illegal things, and cannot be trusted. ADJ QUALIT ◊ **dishonesty** /dɪsɒnə[1]sti[1]/. EG *The moneylender dare not admit his dishonesty.* ◊ N UNCOUNT

2 A **dishonest** action involves lying, cheating, or doing illegal things. EG *It would be dishonest to claim that.* ADJ QUALIT

dishonour /dɪsɒnə/, **dishonours, dishonouring, dishonoured;** spelled **dishonor** in American English.

1 Dishonour is a state in which people disapprove of you and have no respect for you. EG *There are men who prefer death to dishonour.* N UNCOUNT Formal

2 If you **dishonour** someone, you do something that causes people to disapprove of them and to have no respect for them. EG *He taught her never to dishonour her family.* V+O Formal

dishwasher /dɪʃwɒʃə/, **dishwashers.** A **dishwasher** is a machine that washes objects that have been used to cook, serve, and eat a meal. N COUNT

disillusion /dɪsə[1]luːʒə[0]n/, **disillusions, disillusioning, disillusioned. 1** If something **disillusions** you, it makes you feel disappointed because it is not as good as you expected. EG *They were bitterly disillusioned by the performance.* V+O ◊ **disillusioning.** EG *...the disillusioning failure of the unit.* ◊ ADJ QUALIT

2 Disillusion is the same as disillusionment. EG *...her growing disillusion with her husband.* N UNCOUNT

disillusioned /dɪsə[1]luːʒə[0]nd/. If you are **disillusioned**, you feel disappointed because someone or something is not as good as you expected. EG *My father was thoroughly disillusioned with me.* ADJ QUALIT

disillusionment /dɪsə[1]luːʒə[0]nmə[2]nt/ is a feeling of disappointment that you have when you discover that something is not as good as you expected it to be. EG *...public disillusionment with politics.* N UNCOUNT

disinclination /dɪsɪŋklɪneɪʃə[0]n/ is a feeling that you do not want to do something. EG *...a disinclination to go out on winter evenings.* N UNCOUNT: USU+*to*-INF

disinclined /dɪsɪŋklaɪnd/. If you are **disinclined** to do something, you do not want to do it. EG *He was disinclined to talk about that.* ADJ PRED: USU+*to*-INF

disinfect /dɪsɪnfɛkt/, **disinfects, disinfecting, disinfected.** If you **disinfect** something, you clean it using a liquid that kills germs. EG *Wash the cuts and disinfect them.* V+O

disinfectant /dɪsɪnfɛktənt/ is a liquid which contains chemicals that kill germs. N MASS

disinherit /dɪsɪnhɛrɪt/, **disinherits, disinheriting, disinherited.** If someone **disinherits** their son or daughter, they legally arrange that, when they die, the son or daughter will not receive any of their money or property. V+O Formal

disintegrate /dɪsɪntɪ[2]greɪt/, **disintegrates, disintegrating, disintegrated. 1** If an object **disintegrates**, it breaks into many small pieces. EG *There was an explosion and the boat disintegrated.* V

2 If a relationship or organization **disintegrates**, it becomes very weak and unsuccessful. EG *They had seen marriages disintegrate under such pressure.* V: OFT+A ◊ **disintegration** /dɪsɪntɪ[2]greɪʃə[0]n/. EG *...the disintegration of the army.* ◊ N UNCOUNT

disinterest /dɪsɪntə[0]rɪ[2]st/ is a lack of interest or enthusiasm. EG *...the Government's disinterest in conservation.* N UNCOUNT

disinterested /dɪsɪntə[0]rɪ[2]stɪ[2]d/. Someone who is **disinterested** is **1** not involved in a situation and can make fair decisions or judgments about it. EG *I'm a disinterested observer.* ADJ QUALIT **2** not interested in something. Some people think that it is not correct to use **disinterested** with this meaning. EG *Her mother had always been a little disinterested in her, preferring her brother's company.* ADJ QUALIT

disjointed /dɪsdʒɔɪntɪ[2]d/ words or ideas are not connected in a sensible way and are difficult to understand. EG *...a number of disjointed statements.* ADJ QUALIT

disk /dɪsk/. See **disc**.

dislike /dɪslaɪk/, **dislikes, disliking, disliked. 1** If you **dislike** someone or something, you think that they are unpleasant and do not like them. EG *I dislike him intensely.* V+O

2 Dislike is the feeling of not liking someone or something. EG *...their dislike of authority.* N UNCOUNT: OFT+*of/for*

3 If you **take a dislike to** someone or something, you begin to dislike them. EG *This caused Brody to take an instant dislike to the man.* PHRASE

4 Your **dislikes** are the things that you do not like. EG *She has her likes and dislikes, as we all have.* N PLURAL

dislocate /dɪslə[7]keɪt/, **dislocates, dislocating, dislocated. 1** If you **dislocate** a part of your body, it is forced out of its normal position and causes you pain. EG *I had a nasty fall and dislocated my arm.* V+O

2 If a process **is dislocated**, something stops it from continuing normally. EG *The accident had dislocated the flow of vehicles.* V+O Formal ◊ **dislocation** /dɪslə[7]keɪʃə[0]n/. EG *...the serious dislocation to business.* ◊ N UNCOUNT

dislodge /dɪslɒdʒ/, **dislodges, dislodging, dislodged.** To **dislodge** someone or something from a place means to cause them to move from it. EG *Burr put his feet on the table, dislodging papers and books.* V+O

disloyal /dɪslɔɪə[0]l/. If you are **disloyal** to your friends, family, or country, you do not support them. EG *You wanted me to be disloyal to Gareth.* ADJ QUALIT: OFT+*to* ◊ **disloyalty** /dɪslɔɪə[0]lti[1]/. EG *...Haldane's disloyalty to the nation.* ◊ N UNCOUNT: OFT+*to*

dismal /dɪzmə[0]l/. Something that is **dismal 1** is rather unattractive and depressing. EG *...one dark, dismal day.* ADJ QUALIT ◊ **dismally.** EG *It's a dismally dull* ◊ ADV+ADJ

What is the difference between 'dishevelled' and 'disordered'?

place. **2** is unsuccessful and makes people lose hope or confidence. EG *Their record over the last decade has been dismal.* ADJ QUALIT

dismantle /dɪsmæntə[0]l/, **dismantles, dismantling, dismantled.** If you **dismantle** a machine or structure, you separate it into its parts. EG *The gun had to be dismantled and carried.* V+O

dismay /dɪsmeɪ/, **dismays, dismaying, dismayed. 1 Dismay** is a strong feeling of fear, worry, or disappointment. EG *I realised with dismay that he had gone... To their dismay, few companies were keen... They looked at each other in dismay.* N UNCOUNT

2 If something **dismays** you, it makes you feel afraid, worried, or disappointed. V+O ◇ **dismayed.** EG *Barbara seemed dismayed at my views.* ◇ ADJ QUALIT
◇ **dismaying.** EG *...the dismaying complexity of the problems.* ◇ ADJ QUALIT

dismember /dɪsmɛmbə/, **dismembers, dismembering, dismembered.** To **dismember** a person or animal means to tear their body to pieces. EG *...a wild animal dismembering its prey.* V+O Formal

dismiss /dɪsmɪs/, **dismisses, dismissing, dismissed. 1** If you **dismiss** someone or something, **1.1** you decide or say that they are not important or not good enough. EG *This plan was dismissed as foolish.* **1.2** you stop thinking about them. EG *She dismissed him from her mind.* V+O

2 If you **are dismissed** from your job, your employers get rid of you. EG *They were dismissed for refusing to join a union.* V+O : USU PASS

3 If someone in authority **dismisses** you, they give you permission to go away. EG *Dismissing the other children, she told me to wait.* V+O

dismissal /dɪsmɪsə[0]l/, **dismissals. Dismissal** is **1** the act of getting rid of an employee. EG *They discussed the dismissal of a teacher... ...a tribunal dealing with unfair dismissals.* N UNCOUNT OR N COUNT **2** the act of stating that someone or something is not important or not good enough. EG *...this dismissal of the computer's potential.* N UNCOUNT

dismissive /dɪsmɪsɪv/. If you are **dismissive** of someone or something, your attitude indicates that you think they are not important or not good enough. EG *She is dismissive of the school.* ADJ QUALIT : OFT+*of* Formal

dismount /dɪsmaʊnt/, **dismounts, dismounting, dismounted.** If you **dismount** from a horse or a vehicle, you get down from it. EG *The police officer dismounted from his bicycle.* V : OFT+*from* Formal

disobedience /dɪsə[6]biːdɪəns/ is deliberately not doing what a person in authority or a rule says that you should do. EG *She would tolerate no argument or disobedience.* N UNCOUNT

disobedient /dɪsə[6]biːdɪənt/. If you are **disobedient**, you deliberately do not do what a person in authority or a rule says that you should do. EG *...a disobedient child.* ADJ QUALIT

disobey /dɪsə[6]beɪ/, **disobeys, disobeying, disobeyed.** If you **disobey** a person in authority or an order, you deliberately do not do what you have been told to do. EG *It never occurred to them that they could disobey their parents... If he disobeys, he will be killed.* V+O OR V

disorder /dɪsɔːdə/, **disorders. 1** Something that is in **disorder 1.1** is very untidy. EG *The room was in dreadful disorder.* **1.2** is badly prepared or badly organized. EG *They rushed after them in disorder.* N UNCOUNT

2 Disorder is a situation in which many people behave violently. EG *...a serious risk of public disorder.* N UNCOUNT

3 A **disorder** is a problem or illness which affects a person's mind or body. EG *...painful stomach disorders.* N COUNT OR N UNCOUNT : USU+SUPP

disordered /dɪsɔːdəd/. **1** Something that is **disordered** is untidy and not neatly arranged. EG *...the small disordered room.* ADJ QUALIT

2 Someone who is mentally **disordered** has an illness which affects their mind. EG *...the care of mentally disordered patients.* ADJ CLASSIF

disorderly /dɪsɔːdəli[1]/. **1** Something that is **disorderly** is very untidy. EG *...their disorderly bedroom.* ADJ QUALIT

2 People who are **disorderly** behave in an uncontrolled or violent way. EG *...disorderly assemblies of soldiers.* ADJ QUALIT

disorganized /dɪsɔːgənaɪzd/; also spelled **disorganised. 1** Something that is **disorganized** is in a confused and badly prepared state. EG *Everything was disorganised because he had got back late.* ADJ QUALIT

2 If you are **disorganized**, you do not plan or arrange things well. EG *She is inclined to be disorganised and indecisive.* ADJ QUALIT

disorientated /dɪsɔːrɪə[2]nteɪtɪ[2]d/ means the same as disoriented. EG *I stood there, feeling disorientated.* ADJ QUALIT

disorientation /dɪsɔːrɪə[2]nteɪʃə[0]n/ is a feeling of extreme confusion. N UNCOUNT

disoriented /dɪsɔːrɪə[2]ntɪ[2]d/. If you are **disoriented**, you are confused or lost and are not sure where you are. EG *I woke up that afternoon, totally disoriented.* ADJ QUALIT

disown /dɪsəʊn/, **disowns, disowning, disowned.** If you **disown** someone or something, you formally end your connection with them. EG *If it happened again her family would disown her.* V+O

disparage /dɪspærɪdʒ/, **disparages, disparaging, disparaged.** If you **disparage** someone or something, you talk about them with disapproval or lack of respect. V+O Formal ◇ **disparagement** /dɪspærɪdʒmə[2]nt/. EG *...Bernstein's disparagement of the myth.* ◇ N UNCOUNT

disparaging /dɪspærɪdʒɪŋ/. A **disparaging** remark or comment is critical and scornful of someone or something. EG *The newspaper had made disparaging remarks about his wife.* ADJ QUALIT
◇ **disparagingly.** EG *She spoke disparagingly of the new house.* ◇ ADV

disparate /dɪspərə[1]t/ is used to describe things that are very different from each other. EG *...disparate social groups... ...a range of entirely disparate reasons.* ADJ QUALIT Formal

disparity /dɪspærə[1]ti[1]/, **disparities.** A **disparity** between things is a surprising or unfair difference between them. EG *...the disparity between rich and poor... ...the regional disparities in unemployment.* N COUNT OR N UNCOUNT : OFT+ *between/in* Formal

dispassionate /dɪspæʃə[0]nə[1]t/. Someone who is **dispassionate** is calm, reasonable, and not influenced by their emotions. EG *...a dispassionate observer.* ADJ QUALIT ◇ **dispassionately.** EG *I shall judge your problems dispassionately.* ◇ ADV

dispatch /dɪspætʃ/, **dispatches, dispatching, dispatched;** also spelled **despatch** in British English.

1 If you **dispatch** someone or something to a place, you send them there. EG *Troops were dispatched to the north coast.* V+O : USU+A Formal

2 A **dispatch** is an official report that is sent to a person or organization by their representative in another place. EG *...a dispatch from their office in Rome.* N COUNT Formal

dispel /dɪspɛl/, **dispels, dispelling, dispelled.** To **dispel** an idea or feeling that someone has means to stop them believing in it or feeling it. EG *Jenny tried to dispel her illusions... All such doubts were now dispelled.* V+O

dispensable /dɪspɛnsəbə[0]l/. Someone or something that is **dispensable** is not really needed. EG *These were dispensable luxuries.* ADJ QUALIT

dispensation /dɪspɛnseɪʃə[0]n/, **dispensations.** A **dispensation** is special permission to do something that is normally not allowed. EG *For centuries royal dispensation was required to hunt here.* N COUNT OR N UNCOUNT Formal

dispense /dɪspɛns/, **dispenses, dispensing, dispensed. 1** To **dispense** something means to give it to people. EG *...a clinic at which advice was dispensed.* V+O Formal

2 Someone who **dispenses** medicine prepares it and gives it to people. EG *...a dispensing chemist.* V+O

dispense with. If you **dispense with** some- PHRASAL VB : V+PREP thing, you stop using it or get rid of it because you no longer need it. EG *We decided to dispense with the services of Mrs Baggot.*

dispenser /dɪspɛnsə/, **dispensers.** A **dispenser** is a machine or container from which you can get things. EG *...cash dispensers... ...paper napkins from the dispenser.*
N COUNT+SUPP

disperse /dɪspɜːs/, **disperses, dispersing, dispersed. 1** When a group of people **disperse** or when someone **disperses** them, they go away in different directions. EG *Police used tear gas to disperse the mob.*
V-ERG

2 When something **disperses** or when you **disperse** it, it spreads over a wide area. EG *Most of the pieces had dispersed.*
V-ERG

dispirited /dɪspɪrɪtɪ^{2}d/. If you are **dispirited**, you have lost your confidence or enthusiasm.
ADJ QUALIT

displace /dɪspleɪs/, **displaces, displacing, displaced. 1** If one thing **displaces** another, it forces the other thing out of its position and occupies that position itself. EG *London displaced Antwerp as the commercial capital of Europe.*
V+O: NO IMPER

2 If someone **is displaced**, they are forced to move away from the area or country where they live. ◇ **displacement** /dɪspleɪsmə^{2}nt/. EG *...the displacement of large masses of people.*
V+O: NO IMPER; ◇ N UNCOUNT

display /dɪspleɪ/, **displays, displaying, displayed. 1** If you **display** something, you put it in a place where people can easily see it. EG *...a small museum where they could display the collection.* ▸ used as a noun. EG *He has all his tools on display.*
V+O; ▸ N UNCOUNT

2 If you **display** a quality or emotion, you behave in a way which shows that you have it. EG *...the hostility displayed by trade unions.* ▸ used as a noun. EG *...a spontaneous display of affection.*
V+O; ▸ N COUNT: USU+SUPP

3 A **display** is **3.1** an arrangement of things that is intended to attract people's attention. EG *...displays of sausages and cheese.* **3.2** a public event that is intended to entertain people. EG *...a firework display.*
N COUNT: USU+SUPP

displease /dɪspliːz/, **displeases, displeasing, displeased.** If someone or something **displeases** you, they make you dissatisfied, annoyed, or upset. EG *What he saw did not displease him.* ◇ **displeased.** EG *'Why are you displeased with me?' I pleaded.*
V+O; ◇ ADJ PRED +*with*

displeasure /dɪsplɛʒə/ is a feeling of dissatisfaction or annoyance. EG *Professor Aitken looked at me with displeasure.*
N UNCOUNT

disposable /dɪspəʊzəbə^{0}l/. Something that is **disposable** is designed to be thrown away after it has been used. EG *...disposable nappies... ...disposable paper tissues.*
ADJ CLASSIF

disposal /dɪspəʊzə^{0}l/. **1** If you have something **at** your **disposal**, you can use it at any time and for any purpose. EG *...a cottage put at her disposal by a friend.*
PHRASE

2 Disposal is the act of getting rid of something. EG *...the safe disposal of radioactive waste.*
N UNCOUNT: USU+SUPP

dispose /dɪspəʊz/, **disposes, disposing, disposed.** If you **dispose of** something that you no longer want or need, you get rid of it, for example by throwing it away or by selling it. EG *He could dispose of the house and car.*
PHRASAL VB: V+PREP, HAS PASS

disposed /dɪspəʊzd/. **1** If you are **disposed** to do something, you are willing to do it. EG *He seemed disposed to chat.*
ADJ PRED +*to*-INF Formal

2 If you are **well disposed** to someone, you feel friendly towards them.
PHRASE Formal

disposition /dɪspəzɪʃə^{0}n/, **dispositions. 1** Someone's **disposition** is their character or mood. EG *Waddell was of a cheerful disposition.*
N COUNT

2 If you show a **disposition** to do something, you show a willingness to do it or a tendency to do it. EG *Adam showed no disposition to move... Dixon had been showing a disposition to tremble and stagger.*
N UNCOUNT +*to*-INF Formal

dispossess /dɪspə^{6}zɛs/, **dispossesses, dispossessing, dispossessed.** If you **are dispossessed** of land or property, it is taken away from you. EG *Landowners could not be legally dispossessed.*
V+O: USU PASS

disproportionate /dɪsprəpɔːʃə^{0}nə^{1}t/. Something that is **disproportionate** is surprising or unreasonable in amount or size. EG *A disproportionate number of people die shortly after retiring.* ◇ **disproportionately.** EG *There were disproportionately high costs.*
ADJ QUALIT; ◇ ADV

disprove /dɪspruːv/, **disproves, disproving, disproved.** If you **disprove** an idea or belief, you show that it is not true. EG *They can neither prove nor disprove that it is genuine.*
V+O OR V+REPORT: ONLY *that*

dispute, disputes, disputing, disputed; pronounced /dɪspjuːt/ when it is a noun and /dɪspjuːt/ when it is a verb.

1 A **dispute** is a disagreement or quarrel between people or groups. EG *...disputes between unions and employers... There is some dispute about this.*
N COUNT OR N UNCOUNT

2 If people are **in dispute**, they disagree with each other. EG *We're not really in dispute over this, actually.*
PHRASE

3 If something is **in dispute**, people disagree about it.
PHRASE

4 If you **dispute** an opinion or action, you say that you think it is untrue or incorrect. EG *I don't dispute that children need love.* ◇ **disputed.** EG *...a disputed decision.*
V+O OR V+REPORT; ◇ ADJ CLASSIF

5 When people or animals **dispute** something, they fight for control of it. EG *They continued to dispute the ownership of the territory.* ◇ **disputed.** EG *...the disputed provinces.*
V+O; ◇ ADJ CLASSIF

disqualify /dɪskwɒlɪfaɪ/, **disqualifies, disqualifying, disqualified.** If someone **is disqualified**, they are officially stopped from doing something because they have broken a law or rule. EG *Seven of them were disqualified from driving.* ◇ **disqualification** /dɪskwɒlɪfɪkeɪʃə^{0}n/, **disqualifications.** EG *He is liable to disqualification from all official events.*
V+O: USU PASS+*from*; ◇ N UNCOUNT OR N COUNT

disquiet /dɪskwaɪət/ is a feeling of worry or anxiety. EG *Many physicists expressed extreme disquiet about the idea.*
N UNCOUNT Formal

disregard /dɪsrɪ^{2}gɑːd/, **disregards, disregarding, disregarded.** If you **disregard** something, you ignore it or do not consider it seriously. EG *Men who disregarded the warning were beaten severely.* ▸ used as a noun. EG *The centre was built with an obvious disregard for cost.*
V+O; ▸ N UNCOUNT: OFT+*for/of*

disrepair /dɪsrɪ^{2}pɛə/. If something is **in disrepair**, it is broken or has not been looked after properly. EG *His cycle is in disrepair.*
PHRASE Formal

disreputable /dɪsrɛpjə^{4}təbə^{0}l/. If someone or something is **disreputable**, they are considered to be not respectable or not to be trusted. EG *...Ash and his disreputable friends.*
ADJ QUALIT

disrepute /dɪsrɪ^{2}pjuːt/. If something is brought **into disrepute** or falls **into disrepute**, it loses its good reputation and is disapproved of. EG *He brought his profession into disrepute.*
PHRASE Formal

disrespect /dɪsrɪ^{2}spɛkt/. If someone shows **disrespect** for a person, law, or custom, they do not behave in a correct or acceptable way. ◇ **disrespectful** /dɪsrɪ^{1}spɛkt^{0}fə^{4}l/. EG *They are arrogant and disrespectful to me.*
N UNCOUNT: OFT+*for*; ◇ ADJ QUALIT

disrupt /dɪsrʌpt/, **disrupts, disrupting, disrupted.** To **disrupt** an activity or system means to prevent it from continuing normally. EG *...attempts to disrupt meetings organized by their opponents.* ◇ **disruption** /dɪsrʌpʃə^{0}n/, **disruptions.** EG *...the disruption of rail communications... ...disruptions in routine.* ◇ **disruptive** /dɪsrʌptɪv/. EG *...children who are disruptive in school.*
V+O; ◇ N COUNT OR N UNCOUNT; ◇ ADJ QUALIT

dissatisfaction /dɪssætɪsfækʃə^{0}n/. If you feel **dissatisfaction** with something, you are not contented or are not pleased with it. EG *There is wide-*
N UNCOUNT: OFT+*with*

Find five words on these pages which mean the opposite if you take off the prefix 'dis-'.

spread dissatisfaction with the existing political parties.

dissatisfied /dɪssætɪsfaɪd/. If you are **dissatisfied**, you are not contented, or are not pleased with something. EG *All of them had been dissatisfied with their lives.* ADJ QUALIT : USU PRED +*with*

dissect /dɪ^{5}sɛkt/, **dissects, dissecting, dissected.** If someone **dissects** the body of a dead person or animal, they cut it up carefully in order to examine it. V+O ◊ **dissection** /dɪ^{5}sɛkʃə^{0}n/. EG *...the dissection of the earthworm.* ◊ N UNCOUNT

disseminate /dɪsɛmɪneɪt/, **disseminates, disseminating, disseminated.** To **disseminate** information means to distribute it to many people. EG *...disseminating information among the villages.* V+O Formal ◊ **dissemination** /dɪsɛmɪneɪʃə^{0}n/. EG *...the printing and dissemination of news.* ◊ N UNCOUNT : USU+SUPP

dissension /dɪsɛnʃə^{0}n/ is disagreement and argument. EG *It would create dissension in the home.* N UNCOUNT Formal

dissent /dɪsɛnt/, **dissents, dissenting, dissented. 1 Dissent** is strong disagreement with established ideas. EG *Healthy societies can tolerate dissent.* N UNCOUNT Formal

2 If someone **dissents**, they express strong disagreement with established ideas. EG *...anyone dissenting from the prevailing view.* V Formal ◊ **dissenting.** EG *There have been dissenting voices.* ◊ ADJ CLASSIF : ATTRIB

dissenter /dɪsɛntə/, **dissenters.** A **dissenter** is someone who expresses disagreement with established ideas. EG *...political and religious dissenters.* N COUNT Formal

dissertation /dɪsəteɪʃə^{0}n/, **dissertations.** A **dissertation** is a long, formal piece of writing on a particular subject, especially for a university degree. EG *She wrote a dissertation on industrial development.* N COUNT Formal

disservice /dɪssɜːvɪs/. If you do someone a **disservice**, you do something that harms them. EG *They are guilty of a disservice to their community.* N COUNT : USU SING+*to* Formal

dissident /dɪsɪdə^{2}nt/, **dissidents.** A **dissident** is someone who criticizes their government or organization. EG *...political dissidents.* N COUNT Formal

dissimilar /dɪsɪmɪlə/. If two things are **dissimilar**, they are different from each other. EG *...a proposal not dissimilar to that now adopted by the Government.* ADJ QUALIT : OFT+*to* Formal

dissipate /dɪsɪpeɪt/, **dissipates, dissipating, dissipated. 1** If something **dissipates** or **is dissipated** by something else, it gradually becomes less or disappears. EG *The heat was dissipated by cooling systems.* V-ERG Formal

2 If someone **dissipates** money, time, or effort, they waste it in a foolish way. EG *He rapidly dissipated his fortune.* V+O Formal

dissociate /dɪsəʊʃɪeɪt, -sɪ-/, **dissociates, dissociating, dissociated. 1** If you **dissociate** yourself from someone or something, you try to deny or end any connection with them. EG *He did all he could to dissociate himself from the Government.* V-REFL+*from*

2 If you **dissociate** one thing from another, you consider the two things separately. EG *It is often difficult to dissociate cause from effect.* V+O+*from*

dissolution /dɪsəluːʃə^{0}n/. The **dissolution** of an organization or legal relationship is the act of officially ending it. EG *...the dissolution of the village council.* N UNCOUNT : OFT+SUPP Formal

dissolve /dɪzɒlv/, **dissolves, dissolving, dissolved. 1** If you **dissolve** a solid substance or if it **dissolves**, you mix it with a liquid until it disappears. EG *Dissolve the sugar in the water.* V-ERG

2 To **dissolve** an organization or legal relationship means to officially end it. EG *They wish to dissolve their union with the United States.* V+O Formal

dissolve in or **dissolve into.** If you **dissolve into** tears or laughter, you begin to cry or laugh, because you cannot control yourself. EG *Kiri dissolved in tears.* PHRASAL VB : V+PREP Literary

dissuade /dɪsweɪd/, **dissuades, dissuading, dissuaded.** If you **dissuade** someone from doing something, you persuade them not to do it. EG *I tried to dissuade David from going.* V+O : OFT+*from* Formal

distance /dɪstəns/, **distances, distancing, distanced. 1** The **distance** between two places is the amount of space between them. EG *The town is some distance from the sea... Farmers were travelling long distances to get supplies.* N COUNT OR N UNCOUNT +SUPP

2 Distance is the fact of being far away from something in space or time. EG *...cut off from the next community by distance.* N UNCOUNT

3 If you are **at a distance** from something, or if you see it or remember it **from a distance**, you are a long way away from it in space or time. EG *From a distance, he heard Jack's whisper.* PHRASE

4 If you can hear or see something **in the distance,** you can hear or see something that is far away from you. EG *In the distance, she sees a cloud of smoke.* PHRASE

5 If something **distances** you from someone or something, it causes you to feel less friendly towards them or less involved with them. EG *...distancing young people from their families.* V+O : OFT+*from* Formal

distant /dɪstənt/. **1** Something that is **distant** is far away. EG *...a distant country... The planes were distant from each other.* ADJ QUALIT

2 An event or time that is **distant** is far away in the past or future. EG *He may return in the not too distant future.* ADJ QUALIT

3 A **distant** relative is one that you are not closely related to. ADJ QUALIT ◊ **distantly.** EG *...an Italian family to whom he was distantly related.* ◊ ADV

4 Someone who is **distant** is **4.1** unfriendly. EG *Boylan was polite but distant.* ADJ QUALIT **4.2** not paying attention because they are thinking about something else. EG *His eyes took on a distant look.* ◊ **distantly.** EG *Jennifer looked at herself, smiling distantly.* ◊ ADV AFTER VB

distaste /dɪsteɪst/ is a feeling of dislike or disapproval. EG *She looked at him with distaste... ...his distaste for money.* N SING+SUPP

distasteful /dɪsteɪstfʊl/. If you say that something is **distasteful**, you dislike it or disapprove of it. EG *...work that is distasteful to him.* ADJ QUALIT : OFT+*to*

distended /dɪstɛndɪ^{2}d/. If a part of someone's body is **distended**, it is swollen and unnaturally large. EG *He had a grossly distended stomach.* ADJ QUALIT Formal

distil /dɪstɪl/, **distils, distilling, distilled;** spelled **distill** in American English.

1 When a liquid **is distilled**, it is purified or concentrated by being heated until it becomes steam and then being cooled until it becomes liquid again. V+O ◊ **distilled.** EG *Top up the car battery with distilled water.* ◊ ADJ CLASSIF ◊ **distillation** /dɪstɪleɪʃə^{0}n/. EG *Separate the alcohol from the water by distillation.* ◊ N UNCOUNT

2 If you **distil** information from something, you obtain it by careful study. EG *The record had been distilled from conversations and correspondence.* V+O : OFT+*from* Formal

distinct /dɪstɪŋkt/. **1** If something is **distinct** from another thing, there is an important difference between them. EG *Our interests were quite distinct from those of the workers... The word is used in three distinct senses.* ADJ QUALIT : OFT+*from* ● If you refer to one thing **as distinct from** another, you are indicating exactly which thing you mean by contrasting it with the other. EG *...parliamentary (as distinct from presidential) systems.* ● PREP

2 If something is **distinct**, you hear or see it clearly. EG *...a small but distinct voice.* ADJ QUALIT ◊ **distinctly.** EG *Jones was distinctly seen at the back door.* ◊ ADV

3 You can use **distinct** to emphasize that something is great enough in amount or degree to be noticeable or important. EG *...a distinct possibility of war.* ADJ QUALIT : ATTRIB ◊ **distinctly.** EG *...a distinctly different picture.* ◊ SUBMOD

distinction /dɪstɪŋkʃə^{0}n/, **distinctions. 1** A **distinction** is a difference between similar things. EG *Remember the distinction between those words.* N COUNT : OFT +*between*

2 If you **draw** or **make a distinction** between two PHRASE things, you say that the two things are different. EG *I must make a distinction here between travellers and tourists.*

3 **Distinction** is the quality of being excellent. EG *He is a man of distinction.* N UNCOUNT

4 A **distinction** is also something that causes someone to be respected or admired. EG *...the distinction of being Gerran's son-in-law.* N UNCOUNT OR N COUNT

distinctive /dɪstɪŋktɪv/. Something that is **distinctive** has special qualities that make it easily recognizable. EG *Irene had a very distinctive voice.* ADJ QUALIT
◇ **distinctively.** EG *...a distinctively African culture.* ◇ ADV

distinguish /dɪstɪŋgwɪʃ/, **distinguishes, distinguishing, distinguished. 1** If you can **distinguish** one thing from another, you can see or understand the difference between them. EG *He had never been capable of distinguishing between his friends and his enemies... ...animals that cannot distinguish colours.* V+O OR V+*between*

2 If a feature or quality **distinguishes** one thing from another, it causes the things to be recognized as different. EG *...the characteristics that distinguish birds from other animals.* ◇ **distinguishing.** EG *He had no scars or distinguishing marks.* V+O+*from* ◇ ADJ CLASSIF : ATTRIB

3 If you can **distinguish** something, you are just able to see it, hear it, or taste it. EG *The photograph was poor and few details could be distinguished.* V+O

4 If you **distinguish** yourself, you do something that causes other people to admire you. EG *...prisoners who had distinguished themselves in battle.* V-REFL

distinguishable /dɪstɪŋgwɪʃəbə⁰l/. If one thing is **distinguishable** from another, you can see or understand the difference between them. ADJ PRED : OFT+*from*

distinguished /dɪstɪŋgwɪʃt/. A **distinguished** person is very successful, famous or important. EG *...rushing to meet the distinguished visitors.* ADJ QUALIT

distort /dɪstɔːt/, **distorts, distorting, distorted. 1** To **distort** a fact or idea means to change it so much that it becomes incorrect or untrue. EG *You're distorting his argument.* ◇ **distorted.** EG *They get a distorted picture of what's going on.* V+O ◇ ADJ QUALIT
◇ **distortion** /dɪstɔːʃə⁰n/, **distortions.** EG *...this distortion of history... The report contained a number of distortions.* ◇ N UNCOUNT OR N COUNT

2 If something **distorts** or **is distorted**, it becomes twisted into a different shape. EG *The objects were scorched and distorted.* ◇ **distorted.** EG *...her distorted limbs.* ◇ **distortion.** EG *...the distortion of his face.* V-ERG : USU PASS ◇ ADJ QUALIT ◇ N UNCOUNT OR N COUNT

distract /dɪstrækt/, **distracts, distracting, distracted. 1** If something **distracts** you or your attention, it makes you stop concentrating on what you are doing. EG *It distracted them from their work.* ◇ **distracting.** EG *...irrelevant or distracting details.* V+O : OFT+*from* ◇ ADJ QUALIT

2 If you try to **distract** someone, you try to stop them feeling upset or worried. EG *Distract her with a toy if you can.* V+O OR V-REFL

distracted /dɪstræktɪ²d/. If you are **distracted**, you are very worried or are thinking about something else. EG *During classes he was distracted and strangely troubled.* ◇ **distractedly.** *She began looking distractedly about her.* ADJ QUALIT ◇ ADV

distraction /dɪstrækʃə⁰n/, **distractions. 1** A **distraction** is 1.1 something that takes your attention away from what you are doing. EG *It would be a distraction from his political labours... She needed to work without interruption or distraction.* 1.2 an object or activity that is intended to entertain people. EG *...the various distractions provided for them.* N COUNT OR N UNCOUNT : OFT+*from*; N COUNT OR N UNCOUNT

2 If someone or something **drives** you **to distraction**, they annoy you continually. EG *They were driven to distraction by the flies.* PHRASE

distraught /dɪstrɔːt/. If someone is **distraught**, they are extremely upset or worried and cannot think clearly. EG *'What can we do?' she asked, turning a distraught face to me.* ADJ QUALIT

distress /dɪstres/, **distresses, distressing, distressed. 1 Distress** is 1.1 extreme anxiety, sorrow, or pain. EG *Delays may cause distress to your family... He was breathing fast and in obvious distress.* 1.2 the state of being in extreme danger and needing urgent help. EG *...an aircraft in distress... ...a distress signal.* N UNCOUNT

2 If someone or something **distresses** you, they cause you to be upset or worried. EG *I hate to distress you like this, but it is important.* V+O
◇ **distressing** /dɪstresɪŋ/. EG *It was a distressing experience for me.* ◇ **distressed** /dɪstrest/. EG *She was distressed about having to leave home.* ◇ ADJ QUALIT ◇ ADJ QUALIT

distribute /dɪstrɪbjuːt, dɪstrɪbjuːt/, **distributes, distributing, distributed. 1** If you **distribute** things, you hand them to people. EG *The leaflets were distributed by students.* V+O

2 When goods **are distributed**, they are supplied to the shops or businesses that use or sell them. EG *They needed trucks to distribute their produce over New York City.* ◇ **distribution** /dɪstrɪbjuːʃə⁰n/. EG *...the manufacture and distribution of products.* V+O : USU+A ◇ N SING : USU the+N+OF

3 To **distribute** something also means to share it among the members of a group. EG *Profits should be distributed between employers and workers.* ◇ **distribution.** EG *...a fairer distribution of wealth.* V+O ◇ N UNCOUNT

distributor /dɪstrɪbjə⁴tə/, **distributors.** A **distributor** is a person or company that supplies goods to shops or other businesses. N COUNT

district /dɪstrɪkt/, **districts.** A **district** is 1 an area of a town or country. EG *...doctors in country districts... ...a working class district of Paris.* 2 an administrative area of a town or country. EG *...district councils... ...the Southall district of London.* N COUNT+SUPP

distrust /dɪstrʌst/, **distrusts, distrusting, distrusted.** If you **distrust** someone or something, you think that they are not honest, reliable, or safe. EG *He keeps his savings under his mattress because he distrusts the banks.* ▸ used as a noun. EG *...their distrust of politicians.* V+O ▸ N UNCOUNT

distrustful /dɪstrʌstfʊl/. If you are **distrustful** of someone or something, you think that they are not honest, reliable, or safe. EG *Both parties were distrustful of his policies.* ADJ QUALIT : OFT+*of*

disturb /dɪstɜːb/, **disturbs, disturbing, disturbed. 1** If you **disturb** someone, you interrupt what they are doing and cause them inconvenience. EG *Sorry to disturb you... If she's asleep, don't disturb her.* V+O

2 If something **disturbs** you, it makes you feel upset or worried. EG *I was disturbed by some of the speeches.* V+O

3 To **disturb** something means to change its position or appearance. EG *The sand had not been disturbed.* V+O

4 To **disturb** a situation means to cause it to become less peaceful or organized. EG *...people who disturb public order.* V+O

disturbance /dɪstɜːbəns/, **disturbances. 1** A **disturbance** is an event in which people behave violently in public. EG *...violent disturbances in Liverpool.* N COUNT

2 **Disturbance** is the act of making a situation less peaceful, organized, or stable. EG *This would cause disturbance to the public... ...a disturbance of the social order.* N UNCOUNT OR N COUNT

3 You can use **disturbance** when you are talking about extreme unhappiness or mental illness in a person. EG *This often causes serious emotional disturbance.* N UNCOUNT OR N COUNT

disturbed /dɪstɜːbd/. **1** Someone who is **disturbed** is 1.1 extremely unhappy or mentally ill. EG *...emotionally disturbed youngsters.* 1.2 very ADJ QUALIT

On these pages, which verb has a different past tense in British English and American English?

worried about something. EG *They appeared disturbed by their powerlessness.*
2 If you say that a period of time is **disturbed**, you mean that the people involved are unhappy. EG *...his disturbed childhood.* ADJ QUALIT

disturbing /dɪstɜːbɪŋ/. Something that is **disturbing** makes you feel worried or upset. EG *She has written two disturbing books.* ◇ **disturbingly.** EG *The radiation levels are disturbingly high.* ADJ QUALIT ◇ SUBMOD

disuse /dɪsjuːs/ is the state of being no longer used. EG *These methods have fallen into disuse.* N UNCOUNT

disused /dɪsjuːzd/. A **disused** place or building is empty and no longer used. EG *...a disused airfield near Lincoln.* ADJ CLASSIF

ditch /dɪtʃ/, **ditches, ditching, ditched. 1** A **ditch** is a long narrow channel cut into the ground at the side of a road or field. EG *...a muddy ditch.* N COUNT
2 If you **ditch** someone, you end a relationship with them. EG *She ditched him for an older man.* V+O Informal
3 If you **ditch** something that is no longer of any use to you, you get rid of it. EG *He had decided to ditch the car.* V+O Informal

dither /dɪðə/, **dithers, dithering, dithered.** If you **are dithering**, you are hesitating because you are unable to make a quick decision. EG *After dithering about helplessly for a bit, he picked up the phone... You mustn't dither.* V : OFT+*about*

ditto /dɪtəʊ/. You use **ditto** to represent the word or phrase that you have just used in order to avoid repeating it. In written lists, **ditto** can be represented by a symbol (,,) underneath the word or phrase that you want to repeat. EG *...a cupboard door with mirror, a bathroom door ditto.*

divan /dɪvæn/, **divans.** A **divan** or a **divan bed** is a bed that has a thick base under the mattress. N COUNT

dive /daɪv/, **dives, diving, dived.** In American English, the form **dove** /dəʊv/ is sometimes used as the past tense.
1 If you **dive**, **1.1** you jump head-first into water with your arms held straight above your head. EG *She dived into the water and swam away.* ▸ used as a noun. EG *Ralph did a dive into the pool.* **1.2** you go under the surface of the sea or a lake, using special breathing equipment. EG *No one had ever dived there before.* ◇ **diving.** EG *...deep-sea diving.* V : OFT+*into* ▸ N COUNT V : USU+A ◇ N UNCOUNT
2 When birds and animals **dive**, they go quickly downwards, head-first, through the air or through water. EG *The fish dived down toward the reef.* V : USU+A
3 If you **dive** forwards or to one side, you jump or rush in that direction, for example in order to catch something. EG *He dived after the ball.* ▸ used as a noun. EG *He made a dive for the bag.* V+A ▸ N COUNT +SUPP
4 If you **dive** into something such as a bag, you put your hands into it quickly in order to get something out. EG *He suddenly dived into the chest and produced a shirt.* V+A

diver /daɪvə/, **divers.** A **diver** is a person who works under water, usually in the sea, using special breathing equipment. N COUNT

diverge /daɪvɜːdʒ/, **diverges, diverging, diverged. 1** If two things **diverge**, they are different or become different from one another. EG *...countries whose history and circumstances widely diverge... Their interests diverge from those of pensioners.* V OR V+*from*
2 Where two roads or paths **diverge**, they start leading in different directions. V : OFT+*from*

divergent /daɪvɜːdʒənt/. Things that are **divergent** are different from each other. EG *...widely divergent religious groups.* ◇ **divergence** /daɪvɜːdʒəns/, **divergences.** EG *...a sharp divergence of opinion.* ADJ QUALIT ◇ N UNCOUNT OR N COUNT

diverse /daɪvɜːs, daɪvɜːs/. People or things that are **diverse** are very different from each other. EG *...celebrities as diverse as Bob Dylan, Bob Hope, and Ronald Reagan... ...a man of diverse talents.* ADJ QUALIT

diversify /daɪvɜːsəˈfaɪ/, **diversifies, diversifying, diversified.** When a company or organization **diversifies**, it increases the variety of the things that it makes or does. EG *Many car manufacturers are diversifying as rapidly as they can.* ◇ **diversification** /daɪvɜːsəˈfɪkeɪʃəⁿn/. EG *...the diversification of the range of studies.* V OR V+O ◇ N UNCOUNT

diversion /daɪvɜːʃəⁿn/, **diversions. 1** A **diversion** is an action that attracts your attention away from what you are doing. EG *Billy created a welcome diversion by bringing in a shrew.* N COUNT
2 A **diversion** is also a special route arranged for traffic when the normal route cannot be used. EG *You can't go on, there's a diversion.* N COUNT
3 The **diversion** of something involves **3.1** changing its course or destination. EG *Possible diversions of the troop convoys were considered.* **3.2** changing the thing that it is used for. EG *Inflation and diversion of investment were having a bad effect.* N UNCOUNT OR N COUNT

diversity /daɪvɜːsəˈtiˈ/ is a range of different conditions, qualities, or types. EG *...the rich diversity of cultures and societies in the world.* N UNCOUNT

divert /daɪvɜːt/, **diverts, diverting, diverted. 1** If you **divert** something, **1.1** you change its course or destination. EG *The police were diverting the traffic.* **1.2** you cause it to be used for a different purpose. EG *We feel it desirable to divert funds from armaments to health and education.* V+O : USU+A V+O+A
2 If you **divert** someone's attention, you attract their attention away from a particular thing. EG *...diverting attention from the making of lethal weapons.* V+O : OFT+A

divest /daɪvest/, **divests, divesting, divested. 1** If you **divest** yourself of something, you get rid of it. EG *She divested herself of her bag.* V-REFL+*of* Formal
2 If you **divest** someone or something of a position or quality, you cause them to lose it. EG *...divesting public housing of its welfare role.* V+O+*of* Formal

divide /dɪˈvaɪd/, **divides, dividing, divided. 1** When something **divides** or **is divided**, it becomes separated into smaller parts. EG *...an attempt to divide the country into two social classes... The cells begin to divide rapidly.* V-ERG
2 If something **is divided** into several distinct parts, it consists of these parts. EG *The houses in Florence St are all divided into flats... The children are divided into three age groups.* V-PASS+*into*
3 If you **divide** something among a number of people, you give each of them part of it. EG *He divided his property among his brothers and sisters... The land was divided between the two brothers.* V+O : OFT +*among/between*
4 If something **divides** two areas or **divides** an area into two, it forms a barrier or boundary which keeps the two areas separate from each other. EG *A line of rocks seemed to divide the cave into two.* V+O : USU+A
5 If people **divide** over something or if something **divides** people, it causes strong disagreement between them. EG *This question is dividing the people of Wales.* ◇ **divided.** EG *The conference was divided on many issues.* V-ERG ◇ ADJ CLASSIF
6 If you **divide** a larger number by a smaller number, you calculate how many times the smaller number can go exactly into the larger number. EG *Divide 35 by 7... Divide 7 into 35... 35 divided by 7 is 5.* V+O+*by/into*
7 A **divide** is a significant difference between two groups, especially one that causes conflict. EG *The divide between rich and poor was great... ...the religious divide.* N COUNT

divide up. If you **divide** something **up**, **1** you separate it into different parts. EG *We're dividing our group up.* **2** you share it out among a number of people. EG *The proceeds had to be divided up among about four hundred people.* PHRASAL VB : V+O+ADV V+O+ADV

dividend /dɪvɪdəˀnd/, **dividends. 1** A **dividend** is part of a company's profits which is paid to people who have shares in the company. N COUNT
2 If something **pays dividends**, it brings advantages at a later date. EG *The time she had spent learning German now paid dividends.* PHRASE

divine /di'vaɪn/, **divines, divining, divined.** 1 Something that is **divine** belongs or relates to a god or goddess. EG *These men had been operating under divine inspiration.* ◊ **divinely.** EG *...a divinely appointed prophet.* ADJ CLASSIF / ◊ ADV
2 If you **divine** something, you guess it correctly. EG *She had divined something about me... She seemed to divine that it would be unpopular.* V+O OR V+REPORT Literary

diving board, diving boards. A **diving board** is a board high above a swimming pool from which people can dive into the water. N COUNT

divinity /dɪvɪnɪ'ti'/, **divinities.** 1 **Divinity** is the study of the Christian religion. EG *...a degree in divinity.* N UNCOUNT
2 **Divinity** is also the quality of being divine. EG *The divinity of the Pharoah was not doubted.* N UNCOUNT
3 A **divinity** is a god or goddess. N COUNT

divisible /dɪvɪzə'bəl/. A number that is **divisible** by another number can be divided by that number. EG *24 is divisible by 3.* ADJ PRED: OFT+*by*

division /dɪvɪʒən/, **divisions.** 1 The **division** of something is 1.1 the act of separating it into two or more different parts. EG *...the division of physical science into chemistry and physics.* N UNCOUNT: OFT+*into* 1.2 the sharing of it among a number of people. EG *...the division of responsibility.* N UNCOUNT
2 **Division** is the mathematical process of dividing one number by another. N UNCOUNT
3 A **division** is a difference or conflict that exists between two groups. EG *...class divisions... ...political divisions between North and South... ...a division of opinion.* N COUNT
4 A **division** is also 4.1 a department in a large organization. EG *...the BBC's engineering division.* N COUNT 4.2 one of the groups of teams which make up a football league or other sports league. The teams in each division are considered to be about the same standard. EG *United are top of the First Division.*

division sign, division signs. A **division sign** is the symbol (÷) which is used between two numbers to show that the first number has to be divided by the second. N COUNT

divisive /di'vaɪsɪv/. Something that is **divisive** causes hostility between people. EG *...the Government's divisive policy of confrontation.* ADJ QUALIT Formal

divorce /dɪvɔ:s/, **divorces, divorcing, divorced.**
1 A **divorce** is the formal ending of a marriage by law. EG *I want a divorce... Divorce is on the increase.* N COUNT OR N UNCOUNT
2 When someone **divorces** their husband or wife or when a married couple **divorce**, their marriage is legally ended. EG *I divorced him for cruelty.* V+O OR V: RECIP
◊ **divorced.** EG *...a divorced lady with two children... ...when my parents got divorced.* ◊ ADJ CLASSIF
3 If you **divorce** one thing from another, you consider or treat the two things as different and separate from each other. EG *I don't think it is possible to divorce sport from politics.* V+O: OFT+*from* Formal

divorcee /di'vɔ:si:/, **divorcees.** A **divorcee** is a person, especially a woman, who is divorced. N COUNT

divulge /daɪvʌldʒ/, **divulges, divulging, divulged.** If you **divulge** a piece of information, you tell someone about it. EG *I shall divulge the details to no one.* V+O OR V+REPORT Formal

D.I.Y. /di: aɪ waɪ/ is the activity of making or repairing things yourself, especially in your home. **D.I.Y.** is an abbreviation for 'do-it-yourself'. EG *...D.I.Y. experts.* N UNCOUNT

dizzy /dɪzi'/. 1 If you feel **dizzy**, you feel that you are losing your balance and are about to fall. EG *I felt dizzy and weak... I can't climb trees – I get dizzy.* ◊ **dizziness.** EG *She was overcome by nausea and dizziness.* ADJ QUALIT / ◊ N UNCOUNT
2 If you say that something has reached **dizzy** heights, you mean that it is at a very high level indeed. EG *...the dizzy heights of success.* ADJ QUALIT: ATTRIB Literary

do /du:/, **does** /dʌz/, **doing, did** /dɪd/, **done** /dʌn/. **Do** is both a main verb and an auxiliary verb. The meanings of **do** as an auxiliary are given in paragraph 1.
1 **Do** is used as an auxiliary in the following ways: AUX
1.1 to form the negative of main verbs, by putting 'not' or '-n't' after the auxiliary and before the main verb in its infinitive form. EG *You don't have to go.* 1.2 to form questions, by putting the subject after the auxiliary and before the main verb in its infinitive form. EG *What did he say?... Do you think that's possible?* 1.3 to stand for, and refer back to, a previous verbal group. EG *She meets lots more people than I do... I like cooking and so does John.* 1.4 in question tags. EG *She made a lot of mistakes, didn't she?... You don't know her, do you?* 1.5 to give emphasis to the main verb when there is no other auxiliary. EG *I did buy a map but I must have lost it... Do sit down.* 1.6 with a negative to tell someone not to behave in a certain way. EG *Don't speak to me like that.*
2 When you **do** something, you perform an action, activity, or task. EG *What are you doing?... I do the cooking and Brian does the cleaning... I've got to do some work this morning.* V+O
3 You can use **do** with a noun referring to a thing when you are talking about performing an action or task involving that thing. For example, if someone **does** their teeth, they brush their teeth. EG *She had done her hair for the party... We have a man to do the garden.* V+O
4 If you **do** something about a problem, you take action to try to solve it. EG *They promised that they were going to do something about immigration... There's nothing I can do about it.* V+O: OFT+about
5 You can use **do** to say that an action or event has a particular result or effect. EG *Their policies have done more harm for the working class than ours... They are afraid of what it might do to the children.* V+O
6 If you ask someone what they **do**, you are asking what their job is. EG *What do you want to do when you leave school?* V+O
7 If someone **does** well or badly, they are successful or unsuccessful. EG *I didn't do very well in my exams... It all depends how the Labour Party do at this next election.* V+A
8 If a person or organization **does** a particular service, they provide that service. EG *They do ferry bookings to Ireland.* V+O
9 If you **do** a subject, you study it at school or college. EG *I'm doing biology.* V+O
10 You can use **do** when referring to the speed or rate that something or someone achieves or can achieve. EG *The car's already doing 70 miles per hour.* V+NUMBER
11 If you say that something will **do** or will **do** you, you mean that it is good enough for you. If you say that something will not **do**, you mean that it is not suitable or satisfactory. EG *No other school will do... Two thousand will do me very well.* V OR V+O
12 **How do you do** is used as a formal way of greeting someone when you meet them. When one person says 'How do you do', the other person says 'How do you do' in reply. CONVENTION
13 **Do** is used in these phrases. 13.1 If you **do** your **best** to achieve something, you try as hard as you can to achieve it. EG *We do our best to make sure it's up to date information.* 13.2 If you ask someone **what** they **did with** something, you are asking them where they put it. EG *What did you do with the keys?* 13.3 If you say that something is **the thing to do** or **the best thing to do**, you mean that it would be a very good idea to do it. EG *The best thing to do is come in tomorrow morning.* 13.4 If you ask **what** someone **is doing** in a particular place, you are showing that you are surpised that they are there. EG *What are you doing here, Francis? I* PHRASES

Do you say 'How do you do?' to someone you know very well?

thought you were still in London. **13.5** If you say that someone **would do well** to do something, you mean that they ought to do it. EG *She would do well to steer clear of men.* **13.6** If you say that one thing **has to do with** or **is to do with** another thing, you mean that the first thing is connected or concerned with the second thing. EG *The basic argument has nothing to do with agriculture... It's got something to do with an economic crisis.* **13.7** If you say that you **could do with** something, you mean that you need it. EG *I think we could all do with a good night's sleep... The staff could probably do with some more money.* PHRASE

14 A **do** is a party, dinner party, or other social event. The plural is 'dos'. EG *We're going to a formal do tonight.* N COUNT Informal

15 Do's and don'ts are things which you must and must not do in a particular situation. EG *...lists of do's and don'ts for fitness.* PHRASE

16 See also **doings**, **done**.

do away with. If someone or something **does away with** a thing, they get rid of it. EG *Modern medicines have not done away with disease.* PHRASAL VB: V+ADV+PREP

do down. If someone **does** you **down**, they criticize you in order to make other people think that you are unpleasant or unsuccessful. PHRASAL VB: V+O+ADV Informal

do for. If something **does for** you or if you **are done for**, your life is ruined or ended. EG *She couldn't open the door. She was done for.* PHRASAL VB: V+PREP, HAS PASS Informal

do in. To **do** someone **in** means to kill them. EG *They might do you in one night while you're sleeping.* PHRASAL VB: V+O+ADV Informal

do out of. If you **do** someone **out of** something, you unfairly cause them not to have it. EG *He did me out of £500.* PHRASAL VB: V+O+ADV +PREP Informal

do up. 1 If you **do** something **up**, you fasten it. EG *He did his shoelaces up... Make sure you do your tie up.* PHRASAL VB: V+O+ADV **2** If you **do up** an old building, you repair and decorate it. EG *The theatre was horrible, done up as cheaply as possible.* V+O+ADV Informal **3** If something **is done up** in a parcel or bundle, it is wrapped in something or tied with something. EG *I gave her a box, nicely done up in flowered paper.* V+O+ADV, USU PASS

do without. If you **do without** something, you manage or survive in spite of not having it. EG *Many Victorian households did without a bathroom altogether.* PHRASAL VB: V+PREP, HAS PASS

docile /dəʊsaɪl/. A person or animal that is **docile** is quiet and easily controlled. ADJ QUALIT

dock /dɒk/, **docks, docking, docked. 1** A **dock** is an area in a harbour where ships go to be loaded, unloaded, or repaired. EG *...London Docks.* N COUNT

2 When a ship **docks** or when it **is docked**, it comes into a dock at the end of a voyage. EG *They docked at Southampton.* V OR V-ERG: USU+A

3 In a law court, the **dock** is the place where the person accused of a crime stands or sits. EG *...the people who should have been in the dock.* N SING: *the*+N

4 If you **dock** someone's wages or money, you take some of the money away. EG *He docked her pocket money until the debt was paid off.* V+O

docker /dɒkə/, **dockers.** A **docker** is a person who works in the docks. N COUNT

doctor /dɒktə/, **doctors, doctoring, doctored. 1** A **doctor** is someone who is qualified in medicine and treats people who are ill. EG *She felt so ill we had to call the doctor... ...Doctor Barker.* N COUNT

2 When you go to the **doctor's**, you go to the surgery or clinic where a doctor works. N SING: *the*+N

3 The title **Doctor** is also given to someone who has been awarded the highest academic degree by a university. EG *...Doctor Brian Smith, Physics Building... He is a doctor of philosophy.* N COUNT

4 If someone **doctors** something, they deliberately change it, usually in order to deceive people. EG *The despatch from Davis had been doctored.* V+O

5 If someone **doctors** food or drink, they add a poison or drug to it. V+O

doctorate /dɒktəºrə¹t/, **doctorates.** A **doctorate** is the highest degree awarded by a university. EG *...a doctorate in art.* N COUNT

doctrinaire /dɒktrɪnɛə/. Someone who is **doctrinaire** insists on principles or theories without allowing arguments against them. EG *Their attitudes were condemned as doctrinaire.* ADJ QUALIT Formal

doctrine /dɒktrɪn/, **doctrines.** A **doctrine** is a principle or belief, or a set of principles or beliefs. EG *...the doctrine of permanent revolution... ...Christian doctrine.* ◇ **doctrinal** /dɒktraɪnəºl/. EG *...doctrinal arguments between rival factions.* N COUNT OR N UNCOUNT ◇ ADJ CLASSIF: ATTRIB

document /dɒkjəmə²nt/, **documents, documenting, documented. 1** A **document** is an official piece of paper with writing on it. EG *...documents relating to the nineteenth century... ...travel documents.* N COUNT

2 If you **document** something, you write down facts and details about it, or record them on film or tape. EG *The films document the development of the railways.* V+O

documentary /dɒkjə⁴mɛntəºri¹/, **documentaries. 1** A **documentary** is a radio or television programme, or a film, which provides information about a particular subject. EG *...a television documentary on the lives of the Royal Family.* N COUNT

2 Documentary evidence consists of documents rather than things that people say. EG *There is plenty of documentary evidence on the Roman Empire.* ADJ CLASSIF: ATTRIB

documentation /dɒkjə⁴mɛnteɪʃəºn/ is documents that provide proof or evidence of something. EG *His story was backed by massive documentation.* N UNCOUNT

doddle /dɒdəºl/. Something that is a **doddle** is very easy to do. EG *Don't worry about it. It'll be a doddle.* N SING: a+N Informal British

dodge /dɒdʒ/, **dodges, dodging, dodged. 1** If you **dodge**, you move suddenly in order to avoid being hit, caught, or seen. EG *He dodged into the post office.* V: USU+A

2 If you **dodge** something, **2.1** you avoid it by quickly moving aside. EG *The Minister had to dodge flying tomatoes.* **2.2** you avoid thinking about it or dealing with it. EG *We cannot dodge this accusation... This issue should not be dodged.* V+O

dodgy /dɒdʒi¹/. Something that is **dodgy** seems rather risky, dangerous, or unreliable. EG *It's a rather dodgy plan, but it might just work... Relying on the conscience of your rulers is a dodgy thing.* ADJ QUALIT Informal British

doe /dəʊ/, **does.** A **doe** is an adult female deer, rabbit, or hare. N COUNT

does /dʌz/ is the third person singular of the present tense of **do.**

doesn't /dʌzəºnt/ is the usual spoken form of 'does not'.

dog /dɒg/, **dogs, dogging, dogged. 1** A **dog** is **1.1** an animal that is often kept as a pet or used to guard or hunt things. EG *Their dog started barking at me.* **1.2** a male dog or fox. N COUNT

2 If you **dog** someone, you follow them very closely and never leave them. EG *He's been dogging me all day.* V+O: OFT+A

3 If problems or injuries **dog** you, they keep affecting you. EG *The project has been dogged by a number of technical problems... Bad luck has dogged me all year... Last winter's cricket tour was dogged by injuries to our best players.* V+O

4 If you say that a particular way of life is **a dog's life**, you mean that it is very unpleasant. EG *It's a dog's life being a football manager.* PHRASE

5 See also **dogged**.

dog-collar, dog-collars. A **dog-collar** is a white collar that is worn by priests and ministers of the Christian Church. N COUNT Informal

dog-eared. A book or piece of paper that is **dog-eared** has been used so much that the corners of the pages are turned down or crumpled. ADJ QUALIT

dogged /dɒgɪd/ means showing determination to continue with something, even if it is very difficult. ADJ CLASSIF: ATTRIB

EG ...*his dogged refusal to admit defeat.* ◇ **doggedly.** EG *Karen doggedly continued to search... They persisted doggedly in their campaign against the law.* ◇ ADV

doggerel /dɒgə[0]rəl/, is poetry which is silly or funny, often written quickly and not intended to be serious. EG *She wrote some doggerel about it.*

dogma /dɒgmə/, **dogmas.** A **dogma** is a belief or a system of beliefs which a particular religious or political group has. EG *He had no time for political or other dogmas... ...Christianity in the early days when there was less dogma.* N COUNT OR N UNCOUNT : USU+SUPP

dogmatic /dɒgmætɪk/. Someone who is **dogmatic** about something is convinced that they are right about it and does not consider other points of view. EG *He was so dogmatic about it that I almost believed him... She was not impressed by his dogmatic assertions.* ◇ **dogmatically.** EG *He argued so dogmatically... 'This stone,' he said dogmatically, 'is far older than the rest.'* ADJ QUALIT; ◇ ADV

dogsbody /dɒgzbɒdi[1]/, **dogsbodies.** A **dogsbody** is someone who has to do all the boring jobs that nobody else wants to do. EG *I was employed as a general dogsbody on the project.* N COUNT Informal British

doings /du:ɪŋz/. Someone's **doings** are their activities. EG *...a magazine about the doings of royalty... He gave an admiring account of Larry's doings.* N PLURAL

do-it-yourself is the activity of making or repairing things yourself, especially in your home. EG *You can get them from good do-it-yourself shops.* N UNCOUNT

doldrums /dɒldrəmz/. If an area of activity is **in the doldrums,** it is very quiet and nothing new or exciting is happening. EG *The American market is in the doldrums... By and large, athletics were in the doldrums in the 1960s.* PHRASE Informal

dole /dəʊl/, **doles, doling, doled.** The **dole** is money that is given regularly by the government to people who are unemployed. EG *...dole money... ...lengthening dole queues.* ● Someone who is **on the dole** is unemployed and receives money regularly from the government. EG *He's spent the last year on the dole... They made him redundant but he wouldn't go on the dole.* N SING : *the*+N British; ● PHRASE

dole out. If you **dole** something **out,** you give a certain amount of it to each person in a group. EG *The food was doled out.* PHRASAL VB : V+O+ADV

doleful /dəʊlfʊl/. A **doleful** expression or manner is depressed and miserable. EG *...a doleful sigh.* ◇ **dolefully.** EG *'You're hopeless,' she said dolefully.* ADJ QUALIT; ◇ ADV

doll /dɒl/, **dolls.** A **doll** is a child's toy which looks like a small person or baby. N COUNT

dollar /dɒlə/, **dollars.** A **dollar** is a unit of money used in the USA, Canada, and some other countries. EG *They spent half a million dollars on the campaign... Ethel gave him a dollar bill... The pound fell more than 25 per cent against the dollar.* N COUNT

dolled up /dɒld ʌp/. When a woman gets **dolled up,** she puts on smart clothes in order to look attractive. EG *She was all dolled up in the latest fashion.* ADJ PRED Informal

dollop /dɒləp/, **dollops.** A **dollop** of soft or sticky food is a small amount of it served in a lump. EG *...a dollop of ice-cream... ...stew with beans, topped up with a dollop of mashed potato.* N PART Informal

dolphin /dɒlfɪn/, **dolphins.** A **dolphin** is a mammal which lives in the sea and looks like a large fish. N COUNT

dolt /dəʊlt/, **dolts.** If you call someone a **dolt,** you mean that you think that they have done something stupid. EG *You would have to be a complete dolt to miss the turn-off.*

domain /də[7]meɪn/, **domains.** A **domain** is **1** a particular area of activity or interest. EG *This question comes into the domain of philosophy... The ultimate responsibility in this domain, as in all others, lay with the chairman.* **2** an area over which someone has control or influence. EG *His domain extended to New York.* N COUNT+SUPP; N COUNT+POSS

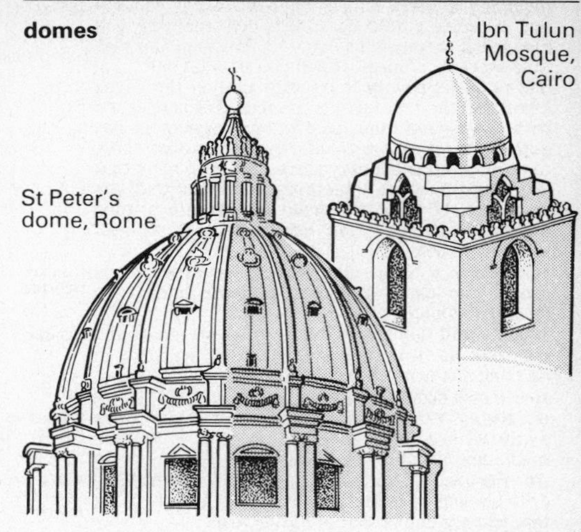

dome /dəʊm/, **domes.** A **dome** is a round roof. EG *...the dome of St Peter's.* N COUNT

domestic /də[6]mɛstɪk/. **1 Domestic** activities, events, and situations happen or exist within one particular country. EG *...foreign and domestic policy.* ADJ CLASSIF : ATTRIB

2 Domestic duties and activities are concerned with your home and family. EG *...domestic chores... ...domestic responsibilities.* ADJ CLASSIF : ATTRIB

3 Someone who is **domestic** enjoys doing things in their home, for example cooking and cleaning. EG *She was never a very domestic sort of person.* ADJ QUALIT

4 Domestic items and services are used in people's homes rather than in factories or offices. EG *...domestic appliances... ...a domestic water supply... ...coal for industrial and domestic use.* ADJ CLASSIF : ATTRIB

5 Domestic animals are not wild, and are kept as pets or are kept on farms to produce food. ADJ CLASSIF

domesticate /də[6]mɛstɪkeɪt/, **domesticates, domesticating, domesticated.** When people **domesticate** wild animals or plants, they bring them under control and use them for work or for food. ◇ **domesticated.** EG *There were no domesticated animals for ploughing.* V+O; ◇ ADJ CLASSIF

domesticity /dəʊmɛstɪsɪ[1]ti[1], dɒm-/ is the habit of spending a lot of time at home with your family. EG *I had put off settling down to such domesticity.* N UNCOUNT Formal

dominance /dɒmɪnəns/. **1** If someone has **dominance** over a person, place, or group, they have power or control over them. EG *Their dominance over the party was eroded... The treaty gave them dominance of the sea routes.* N UNCOUNT : OFT+*over*

2 The **dominance** of something is the fact that it is more important than other similar things. EG *...the dominance of economics in social sciences.* N UNCOUNT : USU+SUPP

dominant /dɒmɪnənt/. Someone or something that is **dominant** is more powerful, important, or noticeable than other similar things. EG *The dominant personality in our firm was John Brown.* ADJ QUALIT

dominate /dɒmɪneɪt/, **dominates, dominating, dominated. 1** If someone or something **dominates** a situation or event, they are the most powerful or important thing in it. EG *These issues dominated the election.* ◇ **domination** /dɒmɪneɪʃə[0]n/. EG *...the company's increasing domination of the UK market.* V+O; ◇ N UNCOUNT

2 If one country **dominates** another, it has power V+O

On these two pages, find two animals and a mammal that is like a large fish.

over it. ◊ **domination.** EG *...the domination of Europe over the rest of the world.* ◊ N UNCOUNT

3 If something **dominates** an area, it is so large that it can be seen from all over that area. EG *The valley was dominated by the huge Benedictine abbey.* V+O

dominating /dɒmɪneɪtɪŋ/. Someone who is **dominating** has a very strong personality and influences other people a great deal. ADJ QUALIT

domineering /dɒmɪnɪərɪŋ/. Someone who is **domineering** tries to control other people. EG *...domineering husbands.* ADJ QUALIT

dominion /dəʊmɪnjən/, **dominions. 1 Dominion** is control or authority that someone has over other people. EG *They now had dominion over a large part of southern India.* N UNCOUNT: OFT+*over* Formal

2 A **dominion** is an area of land that is controlled by a ruler. EG *...Britain's imperial dominions.* N COUNT Formal

domino /dɒmɪnəʊ/, **dominoes. 1 Dominoes** are small rectangular blocks marked with two groups of spots on one side. Dominoes are used for playing games. N COUNT

2 Dominoes is a game played using dominoes. N UNCOUNT

don /dɒn/, **dons, donning, donned. 1** A **don** is a lecturer at a university, especially Oxford or Cambridge. N COUNT

2 If you **don** a piece of clothing, you put it on. EG *The two men donned white cotton gloves.* V+O Literary

donate /dəʊneɪt/, **donates, donating, donated.** If you **donate** something to a charity or other organization, you give it to them. EG *The van was donated to us by a local firm.* V+O: OFT+*to*

donation /dəʊneɪʃən/, **donations.** A **donation** is an amount of money that is given to a charity or other organization. EG *They received a large donation from one of the unions.* N COUNT

done /dʌn/. **1 Done** is the past participle of **do**.

2 A task that is **done** has been completed. EG *When her errand was done she ran home.* ADJ PRED

3 If you say that a situation or task is **over and done with**, you mean that it is finished and you can forget about it. PHRASE

4 You say **'Done'** when you are accepting a deal or a bet. EG *'Shall we say two hundred pounds?' – 'Done.'* CONVENTION

donkey /dɒŋki/, **donkeys. 1** A **donkey** is an animal which is like a horse, but smaller and with longer ears. N COUNT

2 If you say that something has been happening for **donkey's years**, you mean that it has been happening for a very long time. EG *She's been there donkey's years.* PHRASE Informal

donor /dəʊnə/, **donors.** A **donor** is **1** someone who lets a doctor take an organ or some blood from their body so that it can be given to a patient who needs it. EG *...kidney donors.* **2** someone who gives something such as money to a charity or other organization. EG *About half this amount comes from individual donors.* N COUNT: USU+SUPP; N COUNT

don't /dəʊnt/ is the usual spoken form of 'do not'.

doodle /duːdəl/, **doodles, doodling, doodled. 1** A **doodle** is a pattern or picture that you draw when you are thinking about something else or when you are bored. N COUNT

2 When someone **doodles**, they draw doodles. EG *I used to doodle on my papers.* V

doom /duːm/ a terrible state or event in the future which you cannot prevent. EG *I felt as if I were going to my doom.* N UNCOUNT

doomed /duːmd/. **1** If someone or something is **doomed** to an unpleasant or undesirable experience, they are certain to suffer it. EG *They are doomed to failure... He was doomed to be killed in a car crash.* ADJ PRED+*to* OR *to*-INF

2 Something that is **doomed** is certain to fail or be destroyed. EG *They informed the Prime Minister that his government was doomed.* ADJ CLASSIF

doomsday /duːmzdeɪ/. **1 Doomsday** is the end of the world. N UNCOUNT

2 If you say that something will or could happen **until Doomsday**, you mean that it will or could go on for ever. EG *I could have knocked until Doomsday and Antonio would not have heard me.* PHRASE

door /dɔː/, **doors. 1** A **door** is **1.1** a swinging or sliding piece of wood, glass, or metal, which is used to open and close the entrance to a building, room, cupboard, or vehicle. EG *My friend knocked on the door... There was a knock at the door... He opened the car door and got out.* **1.2** the space in a wall which a door can close and through which you enter a building or room. EG *As they passed through the door, they saw Tom at the end of the room.* N COUNT

2 Door is used in these phrases. **2.1** The person who lives **next door** to you lives in the house that is next to yours. EG *She put a notice in the shop next door... ...our next-door neighbour, Joan.* **2.2** When you are **out of doors**, you are not inside a building, but are in the open air. **2.3** If you **lay** the blame for something **at** someone's **door**, you blame that person for it. EG *Responsibility for the strike was laid at the door of the employers.* **2.4** An event which **opens the door to** something makes that thing possible. EG *This new discovery will open the doors to prosperity.* **2.5 at death's door**: see **death**. PHRASES

doorbell /dɔːbɛl/, **doorbells.** A **doorbell** is a bell on the outside of a house, which you ring when you want the people inside to open the door. N COUNT

doorknob /dɔːnɒb/, **doorknobs.** A **doorknob** is a round handle on a door. N COUNT

doormat /dɔːmæt/, **doormats.** A **doormat** is a mat by a door which people can wipe their shoes on before coming into the house. N COUNT

doorstep /dɔːstɛp/, **doorsteps. 1** A **doorstep** is a step in front of a door on the outside of a building. N COUNT

2 If a place is **on your doorstep**, it is very near to where you live. PHRASE

door-to-door. Door-to-door activities involve going from one house to another along a street, often in order to try and sell something. ADJ CLASSIF: ATTRIB

doorway /dɔːweɪ/, **doorways.** A **doorway** is a space in a wall which a door can close. EG *A child stood in the doorway.* N COUNT

dope /dəʊp/, **dopes, doping, doped. 1 Dope** is a drug, often an illegal drug such as cannabis. EG *Others sat around smoking dope.* N UNCOUNT Informal

2 If someone **dopes** you, they put a drug into your food or drink in order to make you unconscious. EG *She'd been heavily doped.* V+O

3 If you call someone a **dope**, you mean that you think they are stupid. N COUNT Informal

dopey /dəʊpi/. **1** Someone who is **dopey** is sleepy, especially because they have taken drugs or alcohol. EG *The pill had already made her dopey.* ADJ QUALIT

2 If you describe someone as **dopey**, you mean that they are stupid. ADJ QUALIT Informal

dormant /dɔːmənt/. Something that is **dormant** has not been active or been used for a long time. EG *The idea had lain dormant in Britain during the fifties.* ADJ CLASSIF

dormitory /dɔːmətəri/, **dormitories.** A **dormitory** is **1** a large bedroom where several people sleep, for example in a boarding school. **2** a building where students live, in an American college. N COUNT

dormouse /dɔːmaʊs/, **dormice** /dɔːmaɪs/. A **dormouse** is a small furry animal. People think of it as being a very sleepy animal. N COUNT

dosage /dəʊsɪdʒ/, **dosages.** The **dosage** of a medicine or drug is the total amount of it that should be taken over a period of time. EG *...a daily dosage of 150 mg.* N COUNT

dose /dəʊs/, **doses, dosing, dosed. 1** A **dose** of a medicine or drug is a measured amount of it. EG *This is lethal to rats in small doses.* N PART

2 A **dose** of something is an amount of it which you get or need. EG *What we needed was a large dose of courage.* N PART

3 If you **dose** someone, you give them a medicine or drug. EG *He dosed himself with pills.* V+O, OR V-REFL : OFT+*with*

doss /dɒs/, **dosses, dossing, dossed.** If you **doss down** somewhere, you sleep there because you have nowhere else to sleep. PHRASAL VB : V+ADV Informal

dossier /dɒsɪeɪ, -sɪə/, **dossiers.** A **dossier** is a collection of papers containing information on a particular subject. EG *We have a hefty dossier on his exploits in the war.* N COUNT

dot /dɒt/, **dots, dotting, dotted. 1** A **dot** is a very small round mark. EG *She painted black dots for the clown's eyes.* N COUNT

2 If things **dot** an area, they are scattered or spread all over it. EG *Countless fishing villages dot the coast... The hills are dotted with trees.* V+O

3 If you arrive somewhere **on the dot**, you arrive there at exactly the right time. PHRASE

dote /dəʊt/, **dotes, doting, doted.** If you **dote** on someone, you love them very much and cannot see their faults. ◊ **doting.** EG *...doting relatives who keep spoiling them with presents.* V+*on/upon*; ◊ ADJ CLASSIF : ATTRIB

dotted /dɒtɪ²d/. **Dotted** lines are lines which are made of a row of dots. EG *The boundaries are shown on the map by dotted lines.* ADJ CLASSIF : ATTRIB

dotty /dɒti¹/, **dottier, dottiest.** Someone who is **dotty** is slightly mad. ADJ QUALIT Informal

double /dʌbə⁰l/, **doubles, doubling, doubled. 1** If one thing is **double** the amount or size of another thing, it is twice as large. EG *He needs to eat double that amount... We paid her double what she was getting before.* PREDET OR QUANTIF

2 You use **double** to describe **2.1** something that is twice the normal size. EG *I asked for a double gin.* **2.2** something that consists of two things of the same kind. EG *The double doors were open.* **2.3** something that is intended to be used by two people. EG *...a double bed.* ADJ CLASSIF : ATTRIB

3 You say **double** before a number or letter to indicate that it occurs twice. EG *My phone number is nine, double three, two, four.* ADJ CLASSIF : ATTRIB

4 If something **doubles** or if you **double** it, it becomes twice as large as it was. EG *The world population is doubling every thirty-five years.* V-ERG

5 If someone or something **doubles** as something else, they have a second job or use as well as their main one. EG *This bedroom doubles as a study.* V+*as*

6 Doubles is a game of tennis or badminton in which two people play against two other people. EG *Don't use this shot in mixed doubles.* N UNCOUNT

7 If you **bend double**, you bend right over. If you **are bent double**, you are bent right over. PHRASE

double up. If you **double up**, you bend your body quickly. EG *He doubled up with laughter, holding his stomach.* ◊ **doubled up.** EG *I was doubled up in pain.* PHRASAL VB : V+ADV; ◊ ADJ PRED

double bass, double basses. A **double bass** is a large stringed instrument shaped like a violin, which you play standing up. See picture at MUSICAL INSTRUMENTS. N COUNT

double-breasted. A **double-breasted** jacket or coat has two very wide sections at the front which overlap when you button them up. ADJ CLASSIF

double-check, double-checks, double-checking, double-checked. If you **double-check** something, you examine or test it a second time to make sure that it is completely correct or safe. EG *The facts will be double-checked by more senior persons.* V+O OR V

double chin, double chins. Someone who has a **double chin** has a fold of fat under their chin. N COUNT

double cream is very thick cream. N UNCOUNT

double-cross, double-crosses, double-crossing, double-crossed. If someone **double-crosses** you, they pretend that they are doing what you had planned together, when in fact they are doing the opposite. EG *You want me to double-cross the man I work for?* V+O Informal

double-dealing is behaviour which is deliberately deceitful. EG *They dismissed him for suspected double-dealing.* N UNCOUNT

double-decker, double-deckers. A **double-decker** is a bus that has two floors. N COUNT

double-glazing is an extra layer of glass which can be fitted to the windows in a house in order to keep the house warmer or quieter. EG *...a house with double-glazing.* N UNCOUNT

doubly /dʌbli¹/. You use **doubly 1** to say that there are two aspects or features that have an effect or make something true. EG *...doubly handicapped children.* **2** to emphasize that something happens or is true to a greater degree than usual. EG *It was doubly difficult for Dora at her age.* ADV+ADJ

doubt /daʊt/, **doubts, doubting, doubted. 1** A **doubt** about something is a feeling of uncertainty about it, for example about whether it is true or possible. EG *Frank had no doubts about the outcome of the trial... I had moments of doubt.* N COUNT : USU PLURAL +*about*, OR N UNCOUNT

2 Doubt is used in these phrases. **2.1** If you say **there is no doubt** about something or you **have no doubt** about it, you mean that you feel certain it is true. EG *There's no doubt that it's going to be difficult... Rose was mad, there was no doubt about it.* **2.2 No doubt** means probably or almost certainly. EG *As Jennifer has no doubt told you, we are leaving tomorrow.* **2.3** You say **without doubt** or **without a doubt** to emphasize that you think that what you are saying is definitely true. EG *Hugh Scanlon became without doubt one of the most powerful men in Britain.* **2.4** If something is shown to be true **beyond a doubt**, it is shown to be definitely true. EG *We have established the ownership beyond all doubt.* **2.5** If something is **in doubt** or is **open to doubt**, it is considered to be uncertain or unreliable. EG *Devaluation had put Concorde's future in doubt.* **2.6** To **cast doubt** on something means to cause people to suspect that it might not be true. EG *The new evidence cast doubt on Christine's story.* **2.7** If you are **in doubt** about something, you feel unsure about it. EG *If in doubt, call the doctor... He left us in no doubt that he wanted results.* **2.8** to **give** someone **the benefit of the doubt**: see **benefit**. PHRASE; ADV SEN; ADV SEN; ADV SEN; PHRASE; PHRASE; PHRASE

3 If you **doubt** whether something is true or possible, you think that it is probably not true or possible. EG *I doubt if they will ever want vanilla pudding again... Maybe he changed his mind, but I doubt it.* V+REPORT

4 If you **doubt** something, you think that it might not be true or might not exist. EG *...men who never doubt their own superiority.* V+O

5 If you **doubt** someone or **doubt** their word, you think that they may not be telling the truth. EG *I apologized for having doubted his word.* V+O

doubtful /daʊtful/. **1** Something that is **doubtful** seems unlikely or uncertain. EG *The organisation has a doubtful future... It is doubtful whether the Chairman would approve.* ADJ QUALIT

2 If you are **doubtful** about something, you are unsure about it. EG *I was a little doubtful about accepting the job... He was doubtful of his talents.* ◊ **doubtfully.** EG *Ralph looked at him doubtfully.* ADJ QUALIT : USU PRED +*about/of*; ◊ ADV

doubtless /daʊtlɪ²s/ means probably or almost certainly. EG *Over 2,500 species are known and doubtless more are still to be discovered.* ADV SEN

dough /dəʊ/. **1 Dough** is a mixture of flour and water, and sometimes also sugar and fat, which can be cooked to make bread, pastry, or biscuits. EG *Shape the dough into rolls.* N UNCOUNT

2 You can refer to money as **dough**. EG *Twenty million bucks is a lot of dough.* N UNCOUNT Informal

doughnut /dəʊnʌt/, **doughnuts.** A **doughnut** is a lump or ring of sweet dough cooked in hot fat. N COUNT

If you have doubts about something, would you double-check?

dour /dʊə/. Someone who is **dour** has a severe and unfriendly manner. EG *She faced me with her usual dour expression.* ◊ **dourly.** EG *'Yes,' said Christopher, smiling dourly.* ADJ QUALIT ◊ ADV

douse /daʊs/, **douses, dousing, doused;** also spelled **dowse. 1** If you **douse** a fire or a light, you stop it burning or shining. V+O
2 If you **douse** someone or something with liquid, you throw the liquid over them. EG *She had doused herself with perfume.* V+O

dove, doves; pronounced /dʌv/ for paragraph 1 and /dəʊv/ for paragraph 2.
1 A **dove** is a type of pigeon. Doves are often used as a symbol of peace. N COUNT
2 In American English, **dove** is a past tense of **dive.**

dowager /daʊədʒə/, **dowagers.** A **dowager** is an old lady, especially a grand-looking one. N COUNT Literary

dowdy /daʊdi[1]/, **dowdier, dowdiest.** Someone who is **dowdy** is wearing dull and unfashionable clothes. ADJ QUALIT

down /daʊn/, **downs, downing, downed. 1 Down** means towards the ground or a lower level, or in a lower place. EG *They walked down the steps... Shall I lift your suitcase down?... The rain came down in sheets... ...the house down below.* PREP, OR ADV AFTER VB
2 You use **down** with verbs such as 'fall' or 'pull' to say that something is destroyed or falls to the ground. EG *The house fell down a week later... He burnt down his school.* ADV AFTER VB
3 If you put something **down**, you put it onto a surface. EG *Put that book down.* ADV AFTER VB
4 If you go **down** a road or river, you go along it. EG *He walked down the road reading a newspaper... I'm just going down to the shops... The library is halfway down the street.* PREP OR ADV
5 Down also means in the south or towards the south. EG *There's a man down in Baltimore who does that... Did you have a good trip down?* ADV
6 If one thing has another thing **down** it, it has the other thing on its surface from the top towards the bottom. EG *...a girl with a pigtail down her back.* PREP
7 If an amount of something goes **down**, it decreases. EG *Sheila was trying to get her weight down... Tourism is down 40 percent.* ADV AFTER VB
8 If something is **down** on paper, it has been written on the paper. EG *That date wasn't down on our news sheet.* ADJ PRED
9 Down to a particular detail means including everything, even that detail. EG *Successful suicides seem to have been planned down to the last detail.* ADV+*to*
10 If you are **down** with an illness, you have that illness. EG *She's down with the flu.* ADV+*with* Informal
11 If you are feeling **down**, you are feeling unhappy or depressed. ADJ PRED Informal
12 If you **down** a drink, you drink it quickly. EG *I poured him a whisky and he downed it at a gulp.* V+O
13 Down is the small, soft feathers on young birds. Down is used to make pillows or quilts. N UNCOUNT
14 Down is also used in phrasal verbs such as 'bring down' and 'calm down.'
15 up and down, ups and downs: see **up**.

downcast /daʊnkɑːst/. **1** If you are **downcast**, you are feeling sad and pessimistic. ADJ QUALIT Formal
2 If your eyes are **downcast**, you are looking towards the ground, usually because you are feeling sad or embarrassed. EG *The girl could only nod, her eyes downcast.* ADJ CLASSIF Formal

downfall /daʊnfɔːl/. **1** The **downfall** of a successful or powerful person or institution is their loss of success or power. EG *...the downfall of a dictator.* N UNCOUNT: USU+POSS
2 The thing that was a person's **downfall** caused them to fail or lose power. EG *Bad publicity was our downfall.* N UNCOUNT: USU+POSS

downgrade /daʊngreɪd/, **downgrades, downgrading, downgraded.** If you **downgrade** something, you give it less importance than it used to have or should have. EG *They were reluctant to downgrade the nuclear element of their defence.* V+O

downhearted /daʊnhɑːtɪ[2]d/. If you are **downhearted**, you are feeling sad and discouraged. ADJ QUALIT Outdated

downhill /daʊnhɪl/. **1** If something is moving **downhill**, it is moving down a slope. EG *The children were racing downhill on their sledges... ...a downhill slope.* ADV AFTER VB OR ADJ CLASSIF: ATTRIB
2 If something is going **downhill**, it is becoming worse or less successful. EG *Journalism is going downhill nowadays.* ADV AFTER VB
3 If you say that a task or situation is **downhill** after a particular stage or time, you mean that it is easy to deal with after that stage or time. EG *It was downhill all the way after that.* ADJ PRED

downpour /daʊnpɔː/, **downpours.** When there is a **downpour**, a lot of rain falls fast and heavily. N COUNT

downright /daʊnraɪt/. You use **downright** to emphasize that something is unpleasant or bad in some way. EG *Some of the jobs were downright disgusting... That's a downright lie.* SUBMOD OR ADJ CLASSIF: ATTRIB

Down's syndrome. If a baby is born with **Down's syndrome**, it has less than normal intelligence and develops a flat face and sloping eyes. N UNCOUNT

downstairs /daʊnstɛəz/. **1** If you go **downstairs** in a building, you go down a staircase towards the ground floor. EG *He went downstairs and into the kitchen.* ADV AFTER VB
2 If someone or something is **downstairs** in a building, they are on the ground floor. EG *Arthur isn't downstairs; he is asleep in bed... ...the photograph on the piano downstairs.* ADV AFTER VB OR ADV AFTER N
3 A **downstairs** room or object is situated on the ground floor of a building. EG *...the downstairs phone.* ADJ CLASSIF: ATTRIB

downstream /daʊnstriːm/. Something that is moving **downstream** is moving towards the mouth of a river, from a point further up the river. EG *The soil is washed downstream.* ADV

down-to-earth. Someone who is **down-to-earth** is concerned with practical things and actions, rather than with abstract theories. EG *...his warm, down-to-earth manner.* ADJ QUALIT

downtown /daʊntaʊn/ means in or towards the centre of a large town or city. EG *We went downtown to buy a pair of shoes... ...downtown Belfast.* ADV OR ADJ CLASSIF: ATTRIB

downtrodden /daʊntrɒdə[0]n/. People who are **downtrodden** are treated very badly by people with power, and do not have the ability or the energy to rebel. ADJ QUALIT

downturn /daʊntɜːn/, **downturns.** If there is a **downturn** in something such as a country's economy, it becomes worse or less successful. EG *...a downturn in manufacturing and industry.* N COUNT: USU SING

downward /daʊnwəd/, **downwards.** When it is an adverb, the form **downwards** is normally used in British English and **downward** in American English.
1 If you move or look **downwards**, you move or look towards the ground or a lower level. EG *It glides gently downwards... My dad was lying face downward.* ▸ used as an adjective. EG *...a downward glance.* ADV AFTER VB OR ADV AFTER N ▸ ADJ CLASSIF: ATTRIB
2 If an amount or rate moves **downwards**, it decreases. EG *The long term trend in the suicide rate is downwards.* ▸ used as an adjective. EG *Prices started a downward plunge.* ADV AFTER VB ▸ ADJ CLASSIF: ATTRIB
3 When you want to emphasize that a statement applies to everyone in an organization, you can say that it applies **from** its leader **downwards**. EG *The entire crew from Captain Imrie downwards believed that we were sinking.* PHRASE

downwind /daʊnwɪnd/. If something moves **downwind**, it moves in the same direction as the wind. EG *The sparks drifted downwind.* ADV AFTER VB

downy /daʊni[1]/. Something that is **downy** is **1** filled or covered with small soft feathers. EG *...thick downy feather beds.* **2** covered with very fine hairs. EG *...the downy head of the sleeping baby.* ADJ CLASSIF

dowry /daʊəri[1]/, **dowries.** A woman's **dowry** is money or goods which her father gives to the man that she marries, in some countries. [N COUNT]

dowse /daʊs/. See **douse**.

doze /dəʊz/, **dozes, dozing, dozed.** When you **doze**, you sleep lightly or for a short period. EG *Thomas dozed in the armchair.* ▸ used as a noun. EG *I had a short doze at ten o'clock.* [V; ▸ N COUNT]

doze off. If you **doze off**, you fall into a light sleep. EG *He dozed off in front of the fire.* [PHRASAL VB: V+ADV]

dozen /dʌz[ə]n/, **dozens.** **1** If you have a **dozen** things, you have twelve of them. See the entry headed NUMBER. EG *...a dozen eggs... ...a few dozen mats.* [NUMBER]

2 You can use **dozens** to refer vaguely to a large number. EG *There had been dozens of attempts at reform.* [N PART: USU PLURAL]

dozy /dəʊzi[1]/. If you are **dozy**, you are feeling sleepy and not very alert. [ADJ QUALIT]

Dr, Drs. Dr is a written abbreviation for 'Doctor'. EG *Dr Franz was an economist of some standing.*

drab /dræb/. Something that is **drab** is dull and not attractive or exciting. EG *...the drab old building... ...a drab brown dress.* ◊ **drabness.** EG *...the ugliness and drabness of most people's surroundings.* [ADJ QUALIT; ◊ N UNCOUNT]

draconian /drə[3]kəʊnɪən/. **Draconian** laws or measures are extremely harsh or drastic. EG *There has been an overall growth in population, despite some draconian efforts to contain it.* [ADJ CLASSIF: ATTRIB]

draft /drɑːft/, **drafts, drafting, drafted.** **1** A **draft** of a letter, book, or speech is an early version of it. EG *...the change from the first draft to the final printed version.* [N COUNT: USU+SUPP]

2 When you **draft** a letter, book, or speech, you write the first version of it. EG *They sat down and drafted a letter to the local newspaper.* [V+O]

3 If you **are drafted**, you are ordered to serve in one of the armed forces of your country. EG *I was drafted into the navy.* [V+O: USU PASS; American]

4 If you **draft** people somewhere, you move them to another place so that they can do a specific job. EG *Extra staff were drafted from Paris to Rome.* [V+O: OFT+A]

5 See also **draught**.

draftsman /drɑːftsmən/. See **draughtsman**.

drafty /drɑːfti[1]/. See **draughty**.

drag /dræg/, **drags, dragging, dragged.** **1** If you **drag** a heavy object somewhere, you pull it along the ground with difficulty. EG *He listened as the body was dragged up the stairs.* [V+O: USU+A]

2 If you **drag** someone somewhere, **2.1** you pull them there roughly. EG *She grabbed her husband by the wrist and dragged him away.* **2.2** you make them go there. EG *I'm sorry to drag you to the telephone, but something awful has happened.* [V+O+A]

3 If you **drag** yourself somewhere, you move there slowly because you feel ill or weak or because you do not want to go there. EG *I was able to drag myself shakily to my feet.* [V-REFL+A]

4 If an event or a period of time **drags**, it is very boring and seems to last a long time. EG *The part of the play which drags is the last half-hour.* [V]

5 If a man, especially an entertainer, is **in drag**, he is wearing women's clothes. [PHRASE]

6 If you take a **drag** on a cigarette or pipe, you suck air through it. [N COUNT; Informal]

drag down. If something **drags** you **down**, it makes you feel less able to succeed or progress. [PHRASAL VB: V+O+ADV]

drag into. If you **drag** something **into** a discussion or situation, you mention it or involve it when it is not necessary or not desirable. EG *It was the politicians who were dragging politics into sport, not the sportsmen.* [PHRASAL VB: V+O++PREP]

drag on. If an event or process **drags on**, it progresses very slowly and lasts a long time. EG *Some legal cases have dragged on for years.* [PHRASAL VB: V+ADV]

drag out. **1** If you **drag** something **out**, you make it last for longer than is necessary. EG *How could we prevent them from dragging out the talks?* **2** If you **drag** something **out** of someone, you persuade them with great difficulty to tell it to you. EG *The truth had to be dragged out of him.* [PHRASAL VB: V+O+ADV; V+O+ADV]

dragon /drægən/, **dragons.** In stories and legends, a **dragon** is an animal like a big lizard. It has wings and claws, and breathes out fire. [N COUNT]

dragonfly /drægənflaɪ/, **dragonflies.** A **dragonfly** is a brightly-coloured insect which is often found near water. [N COUNT]

drain /dreɪn/, **drains, draining, drained.** **1** If you **drain** something or if it **drains**, liquid gradually flows out of it or off it. EG *...the complex problem of draining the marshes... Put those plates on the rack to drain.* [V-ERG]

2 If a liquid **drains** somewhere, it flows there gradually. EG *The sewage drains off into the river.* [V-ERG+A]

3 If you **drain** a glass, you drink the whole of its contents. EG *I picked up the glass and drained it.* [V+O]

4 If a feeling **drains** out of you, it gradually becomes less strong until you no longer feel it. EG *He felt the tension drain out of him.* [V+A]

5 If something **drains** your strength or resources, it gradually uses up your strength or resources and leaves you weaker. EG *The project is already draining the charity's funds.* ◊ **drained.** EG *She looked tired and drained.* [V+O; ◊ ADJ QUALIT]

6 If something is a **drain** on your resources, it gradually uses them up. EG *The banks are facing a very large drain on their funds.* [N SING: a+N]

7 A **drain** is **7.1** a pipe that carries water or sewage away from a place. **7.2** a metal grid in a road, through which rainwater can flow away into pipes. [N COUNT]

8 If you say that something goes **down the drain**, you mean that it is wasted or ruined. EG *That's just money down the drain.* [PHRASE; Informal]

drainage /dreɪnɪdʒ/ is **1** a system of pipes or ditches that are used for draining water or other liquids away from a place. EG *There is no drainage of any sort... Massive big drainage ditches take the water away.* **2** the process of draining water away, or the way in which a place drains. EG *Good drainage doesn't mean dry soil.* [N UNCOUNT]

draining board, draining boards. A **draining board** is the place next to the sink where you put cups, plates, and cutlery to drain after washing them up. [N COUNT]

drainpipe /dreɪnpaɪp/, **drainpipes.** A **drainpipe** is a pipe attached to the side of a building, through which water flows from the roof into a drain. [N COUNT]

drake /dreɪk/, **drakes.** A **drake** is a male duck. [N COUNT]

drama /drɑːmə/, **dramas.** **1** A **drama** is a serious play for the theatre, television, or radio. EG *I remember her acting in a drama called The Garden Party.* [N COUNT]

2 You refer to plays in general and to all work in the theatre as **drama**. EG *...an expert on modern drama.* [N UNCOUNT]

3 You can refer to an exciting real-life situation as a **drama**. EG *...the dramas of this village life.* [N COUNT]

4 You can refer to the exciting aspects of a situation or activity as its **drama**. EG *...the drama of politics.* [N UNCOUNT +SUPP]

dramatic /drəmætɪk/, **dramatics.** **1** A **dramatic** change happens suddenly and is very noticeable. EG *I expect to see dramatic improvements.* ◊ **dramatically.** EG *The way in which information is transmitted has changed dramatically.* [ADJ QUALIT; ◊ ADV]

2 You can describe something as **dramatic** when it is very exciting or impressive. EG *Landing on the moon was one of the most dramatic scientific adventures of this century.* [ADJ QUALIT]

3 If you say or do something **dramatic**, you are trying to surprise and impress people. EG *...a dramatic gesture.* ◊ **dramatically.** EG *He paused* [ADJ QUALIT; ◊ ADV]

On these pages, which words can be spelled differently in British and American English?

dramatically... She stared into the distance, sighing dramatically.

4 Dramatic art or writing is connected with plays and the theatre. EG *...Browning's dramatic works.* ADJ CLASSIF : ATTRIB

5 Dramatics is the performing of plays. EG *...amateur dramatics.* N UNCOUNT

6 You can refer to emotional behaviour which is intended to impress people as **dramatics**; used showing disapproval. EG *George's dramatics were beginning to irritate me.* N PLURAL

dramatist /dræmətɪst/, **dramatists.** A **dramatist** is someone who writes plays. N COUNT

dramatize /dræmətaɪz/, **dramatizes, dramatizing, dramatized;** also spelled **dramatise.**

1 If you **dramatize** a book or story, you rewrite it as a play. EG *His ambition is to dramatise the great works of literature.* ◇ **dramatization** /dræmətaɪzeɪʃəⁿn/, **dramatizations.** EG *...a dramatization of the story of Ali Baba.* V+O; ◇ N COUNT

2 If you **dramatize** an event or situation, you try to make it seem more serious or exciting than it really is. EG *The conflict has been dramatized in the newspapers.* V+O

drank /dræŋk/ is the past tense of **drink.**

drape /dreɪp/, **drapes, draping, draped. 1** If you **drape** a piece of cloth somewhere, you place it there so that it hangs down. EG *He began to drape the shawl carefully over Gertrude's shoulders.* V+O+A

2 If something **is draped** with a piece of cloth, it is covered by it. EG *The walls were draped with banners... ...coffins draped with American flags.* V+O : OFT PASS+ *with/in*

3 Drapes are curtains. EG *The drapes were drawn... Kitty pulled back the drapes.* N PLURAL American

drapery /dreɪpəⁿriˡ/, **draperies. 1** You can refer to cloth or clothing hanging in folds as **drapery** or **draperies.** EG *...fold upon fold of thick drapery... They wore layers of enfolding draperies.* N UNCOUNT OR N PLURAL

2 Drapery is also cloth that you buy in a shop. EG *She works in the drapery department.* N UNCOUNT British

drastic /dræstɪk/. **1** A **drastic** course of action is extreme and is usually taken urgently. EG *This may force the Government to take drastic measures.* ADJ QUALIT

2 A **drastic** change is very significant and noticeable. EG *...the drastic decline in flat-building.* ◇ **drastically.** EG *Because of the snow, visibility was drastically reduced.* ADJ QUALIT; ◇ ADV

draught /drɑːft/, **draughts;** spelled **draft** in American English. **1** A **draught** is a current of air coming into a room or a vehicle. EG *The draught from the window stirred the papers on her desk.* N COUNT

2 A **draught** of liquid or air is a large amount that you swallow or breathe in. EG *He gulped the brandy down in one draught.* N COUNT : USU+SUPP

3 Draught beer is served from barrels rather than bottles. ADJ CLASSIF : ATTRIB

4 Draughts is a game for two people, played with round pieces on a board. In America, draughts is called 'checkers'. N UNCOUNT British

draughtsman /drɑːftsmən/, **draughtsmen;** spelled **draftsman** in American English. A **draughtsman** is someone whose job is to prepare technical drawings. EG *My father worked as a draughtsman in a shipyard.* N COUNT

draughty /drɑːftiˡ/, **draughtier, draughtiest;** spelled **drafty** in American English. If a room or building is **draughty**, it has currents of cold air blowing through it. ADJ QUALIT

draw /drɔː/, **draws, drawing, drew** /druː/, **drawn. 1** If you **draw** a picture, pattern, or diagram, you make it using a pencil, pen, or crayon. EG *She used to draw funny pictures of everybody... He drew a rough sketch on his pad.* V+O OR V

2 When vehicles or people **draw** away or **draw** near, they move away or move near. EG *The cab drew away from the kerb... Jack and Roger drew near... The slave drew back in fear.* V+A

3 When an event or period of time **draws to an end** or **draws to a close**, it finishes. PHRASE

4 If you **draw** someone or something in a particular direction, you pull them there smoothly or gently. EG *He draws the document from its folder... She drew the comb lightly through her hair.* V+O+A

5 When an animal **draws** a cart or other vehicle, it moves along pulling the vehicle behind it. V+O

6 If you **draw** a curtain or blind, you pull it across a window to cover it or uncover it. V+O

7 If someone **draws** a gun, sword, or knife, they pull it out of its holder so that it is ready to use. V+O OR V

8 If you **draw** a deep breath, you breathe in deeply. V+O

9 If you **draw** money out of a bank or building society, you take it out so that you can use it. V+O+A

10 If something **is drawn** from a particular thing or place, it is obtained from that thing or place. EG *The committee members are drawn from all sections of the local community.* V+O : USU PASS + *from*

11 If you **draw** a conclusion from facts that you know, you decide that it is the correct conclusion. EG *Unfortunately, they drew the wrong conclusions.* V+O

12 If you **draw** a distinction, comparison, or parallel between two things, you point out that it exists. V+O

13 If something that you do **draws** a particular reaction, that is the way that people react to it. EG *The mayor drew criticism for these excesses... The police drew praise for their handling of the riots.* V+O

14 If you **draw** people's **attention** to something, you make them aware of it. EG *He drew attention to the rising unemployment rates.* PHRASE

15 If something or someone **draws** you, they attract or interest you. EG *She was shy, and perhaps he was drawn to her for that reason.* V+O

16 In a game or competition, if one person or team **draws** with another one, they get the same number of points and nobody wins. V OR V+ *with* : RECIP

17 A **draw** is the result of a game or competition in which two people or teams draw. N COUNT

18 See also **drawing, drawn.**

draw into. If you **draw** someone **into** something, you cause them to become involved in it. EG *She refused to be drawn into the conversation.* PHRASAL VB : V+O+PREP

draw on. 1 If you **draw on** something, you make use of it in order to do something. EG *...the kind of information an expert draws on... He was able to draw on vast reserves of talent.* **2** When someone **draws on** a cigarette, they breathe in through it and inhale the smoke. PHRASAL VB : V+PREP, HAS PASS; V+PREP

draw up. 1 When you **draw up** a document, list, or plan, you prepare it and write it out. EG *I was busy drawing up plans for the new course.* **2** When a vehicle **draws up**, it comes to a particular place and stops. EG *Just before eleven a bus drew up.* PHRASAL VB : V+O+ADV; V+ADV

draw upon. If you **draw upon** something, you make use of it in order to do something. EG *One had to draw upon some knowledge of human psychology.* PHRASAL VB : V+PREP, HAS PASS

drawback /drɔːbæk/, **drawbacks.** A **drawback** is a difficult or unpleasant aspect of something that makes it less acceptable or less desirable. EG *The major drawback of the system is that the funds are administered centrally.* N COUNT : USU+SUPP

drawer /drɔːəⁿ/, **drawers.** A **drawer** is a box-shaped part of a desk or other piece of furniture. You pull it towards you to open it, so that you can take things out of it or put things in. EG *The letter had always been kept in a drawer in his study.* N COUNT

drawing /drɔːɪŋ/, **drawings. 1** A **drawing** is a picture made with a pencil, pen, or crayon. EG *On the cover was a drawing of five students.* N COUNT

2 Drawing is the skill or work of drawing pictures. EG *She had a passion for drawing and painting.* N UNCOUNT

drawing pin, drawing pins. A **drawing pin** is a short nail with a broad, flat top which you use for attaching papers to a vertical surface. See picture at PINS. N COUNT British

drawl /drɔːl/, **drawls, drawling, drawled.** If someone **drawls**, they speak slowly, with long vowel sounds. ▸ used as a noun. EG *McCord spoke in a soft drawl.* V OR V+QUOTE; ▸ N SING+SUPP

drawn /drɔːn/. **1 Drawn** is the past participle of **draw**.

2 A **drawn** curtain or blind has been pulled over a window to cover it. ADJ CLASSIF

3 If someone looks **drawn** or if their face looks **drawn**, they look very tired or ill. EG *There was a drawn and haggard look about his eyes.* ADJ QUALIT

drawn-out. You describe something as **drawn-out** when it lasts longer than you think it should. EG *He was tired of the long drawn-out arguments.* ADJ QUALIT

dread /drɛd/, **dreads, dreading, dreaded. 1** If you **dread** something which is going to happen or which may happen, you feel very worried about it because you think that it will be very unpleasant. EG *She had begun to dread these excursions... Fanny dreaded seeing Thomas again, but felt that she had to... What woman does not dread that a lump will turn out to be cancer?* V+O, V+-ING, OR V+REPORT : ONLY *that* ▸ used as a noun. EG *Her dread of returning to school gets stronger... ...his dread that the child would be infected with the disease.* ▸ N UNCOUNT : OFT+*of* OR REPORT

2 If you say that you **dread to think** what is happening, you mean that you think that it is probably unpleasant or undesirable. EG *I dread to think what goes on in these schools.* PHRASE

dreaded /drɛdɪ[2]d/ means terrible and greatly feared. EG *Consumption was the most dreaded disease of the time... ...the dreaded General van den Bergh.* ADJ CLASSIF : ATTRIB

dreadful /drɛdfʊl/. **1** If you say that something is **dreadful**, you mean that it is **1.1** very bad or unpleasant. EG *The weather was dreadful... ...that dreadful man!* ADJ QUALIT ◇ **dreadfully.** *Ian was behaving dreadfully.* ◇ ADV **1.2** of very poor quality. EG *She spoke dreadful English.* ADJ QUALIT

2 You can use **dreadful** to emphasize the degree or extent of something bad. EG *I was a dreadful coward... It'll be a dreadful waste.* ADJ QUALIT : ATTRIB ◇ **dreadfully.** EG *The girls were dreadfully dull companions.* ◇ SUBMOD

dream /driːm/, **dreams, dreaming, dreamed** or **dreamt. Dreamed** and **dreamt** are both used as the past tense and past participle of the verb.

1 A **dream** is **1.1** an imaginary series of events that you experience in your mind while you are asleep. EG *In his dream he was sitting in a theatre watching a play... I had a strange dream about you last night.* N COUNT

1.2 a situation or event which you often think about because you would very much like it to happen. EG *His dream of being champion had come true... ...a dream world.* N COUNT : OFT+SUPP

2 When you **dream**, **2.1** you see imaginary pictures and events in your mind while you are asleep. EG *That night I dreamt that I was beaten up by Ernest Hemingway.* V : OFT+*of/about* OR REPORT : ONLY *that* **2.2** you think about a particular situation or event that you would very much like to happen. EG *He dreamed of having a car.*

3 If you say that you **would not dream of** doing something, you are emphasizing that you would not do it. EG *A lot of the boys would never dream of going away for residential courses.* PHRASE

4 If you say that you **never dreamed** that something would happen, you are emphasizing that you did not think it would happen. EG *It all seemed so permanent; we never dreamed that it was about to end.* PHRASE

5 If you describe your house or job as a **dream** house or a **dream** job, you mean that you are very pleased with it. ADJ CLASSIF : ATTRIB

dream up. If someone **dreams up** a plan, they invent it. EG *He would never dream up a desperate scheme like that on his own.* PHRASAL VB : V+ADV+O

dreamer /driːmə/, **dreamers.** Someone who is a **dreamer** looks forward to pleasant things that may never happen, rather than being realistic and practical. N COUNT

dreamily /driːmɪli[1]/. If you do something **dreamily**, you do it without concentrating, because you are thinking about something else. EG *He stared dreamily around him.* ADV

dreamt /drɛmt/ is a past tense and past participle of **dream.**

dreamy /driːmi[1]/, **dreamier, dreamiest. 1** If someone has a **dreamy** expression, they look as if they are thinking about something very pleasant. EG *...a dreamy smile of content... A dreamy look came into her eyes.* ADJ QUALIT

2 See also **dreamily**.

dreary /drɪəri[1]/, **drearier, dreariest.** If something is **dreary**, it is so dull that it makes you feel bored or depressed. EG *They don't realise how dull and dreary their world is... I spent a dreary hour with him... They do only the dreariest jobs.* ADJ QUALIT ◇ **drearily.** EG *He was dressed drearily in grey.* ◇ ADV

dredge /drɛdʒ/, **dredges, dredging, dredged.** To **dredge** a harbour or a river means to clear a channel by removing mud from the bottom using a special machine. V+O

dregs /drɛgz/. **1** The **dregs** of a liquid are the last drops left at the bottom of a container, together with any solid bits that have sunk to the bottom. EG *She had drunk her coffee down to the dregs.* N PLURAL

2 If you talk about the **dregs** of a society or community, you are referring to the worst or most useless people in it. EG *...the dregs of humanity.* N PLURAL +SUPP

drenched /drɛntʃt/. If people or things are **drenched**, they have become very wet. EG *Joseph was drenched with sweat... ...scores of drenched people waiting for the bus.* ADJ QUALIT

dress /drɛs/, **dresses, dressing, dressed. 1** A **dress** is a piece of clothing worn by a woman or girl. It covers her body and extends down over her legs. See picture at CLOTHES. EG *She was wearing a short black dress.* N COUNT

2 You can refer to clothes worn by men or women as **dress**. EG *He was in evening dress.* N UNCOUNT

3 When you **dress** or **dress** yourself, you put on your clothes. EG *When he had shaved and dressed, he went down to the kitchen.* V OR V-REFL

4 If you are **dressed**, you are wearing clothes rather than being naked, or wearing ordinary clothes rather than pyjamas or a nightdress. EG *Both men were fully dressed... Get dressed.* ADJ PRED

5 If you are **dressed** in a particular way, you are wearing clothes of a particular kind or colour. EG *He was dressed in a black suit.* ADJ PRED : USU+*in*

6 You say that someone **dresses** in a particular way when they usually wear that style of clothes. EG *He still dressed like a bank manager.* V+A

7 If you **dress** someone, for example a child, you put clothes on them. V+O

8 See also **dressing**.

dress up. If you **dress up** or **dress** yourself **up**, you put on different clothes, in order to make yourself look smarter than usual or to disguise yourself. EG *That evening they dressed themselves up in fancy clothes.* PHRASAL VB : V+ADV OR V-REFL+ADV ◇ **dressed up.** EG *She was glad that she was all dressed up.* ◇ ADJ CLASSIF

dresser /drɛsə/, **dressers. 1** A **dresser** is **1.1** a piece of furniture with cupboards or drawers in the lower part and shelves in the top part. N COUNT British **1.2** a chest of drawers, usually with a mirror on the top. American

2 You also use **dresser** to refer to the kind of clothes that a person wears. For example, if you say that someone is a neat dresser, you mean that they dress neatly. EG *Fisher was a smart dresser.* N COUNT+SUPP

dressing /drɛsɪŋ/, **dressings. 1** A **dressing** is a covering that is put on a wound to protect it while it heals. N COUNT

2 A **salad** dressing is a mixture of oil, vinegar, and herbs, which you pour over a salad. N MASS

dressing-down. If someone gives you a **dressing-down**, they speak angrily to you because you have done something bad or foolish. N SING

What kind of thing do *you* dream about?

dressing gown, dressing gowns. A **dressing gown** is a loose-fitting coat which you wear over pyjamas or a nightdress when you are not in bed. N COUNT

dressing room, dressing rooms. A **dressing room** is a room in a theatre where performers can get dressed and put on their make-up. N COUNT

dressing table, dressing tables. A **dressing table** is a small table in a bedroom. It has drawers underneath and a mirror on top. N COUNT

dressmaker /drɛsmeɪkə/, **dressmakers.** A **dressmaker** is a woman who is paid to make women's or children's clothes. N COUNT

drew /druː/ is the past tense of **draw.**

dribble /drɪbə[0]l/, **dribbles, dribbling, dribbled.**
1 When a liquid **dribbles** down a surface, it moves down it in a thin stream. EG *Condensation dribbled down the glass.* V-ERG : USU+A
2 A **dribble** of liquid is a small amount of it dribbling somewhere. EG *...dribbles of blood.* N PART
3 When a person or animal **dribbles**, saliva trickles from their mouth. V

dried /draɪd/. **1 Dried** is the past tense and past participle of **dry**.
2 Dried food is food that has been preserved by having liquid removed from it. EG *...dried milk... ...pieces of dried fruit.* ADJ CLASSIF : ATTRIB

drier /draɪə/. See **dryer**.

drift /drɪft/, **drifts, drifting, drifted. 1** When something **drifts** somewhere, it is carried there by the wind or by water. EG *The clouds drifted away... A tiny fishing boat was drifting slowly along.* V+A
2 A **drift** is the same as a snowdrift. EG *There were two-foot drifts in some places.* N COUNT
3 When people **drift** somewhere, they move there slowly or gradually. EG *The crowd started to drift away.* V+A
4 To **drift** towards a bad situation means to slowly reach the stage where you are in this situation. EG *We are drifting towards disaster.* ▸ used as a noun. EG *...the drift to violence.* V+A ▸ N SING+SUPP
5 When someone **drifts** or **drifts** around, they travel from place to place without a settled way of life. EG *They had drifted around in search of their great chance.* ◇ **drifter** /drɪftə/, **drifters.** EG *She was a drifter with no family and no close friends.* V : USU+A ◇ N COUNT
6 Someone's **drift** is the general line of argument in what they are saying. EG *I was able to follow his drift pretty well.* N COUNT
drift off. If you **drift off** to sleep, you gradually fall asleep. PHRASAL VB : V+ADV

driftwood /drɪftwʊd/ is wood which is floating on the sea or a river, or which has been carried by the water onto the shore. N UNCOUNT

drill /drɪl/, **drills, drilling, drilled. 1** A **drill** is a tool or machine that you use for making holes. EG *...an electric drill.* N COUNT
2 When you **drill** into something or **drill** a hole in something, you make a hole in it using a drill. V OR V+O : OFT+A
3 When people **drill** for oil or water, they search for it by drilling deep holes in the ground or in the bottom of the sea. V : OFT+*for*
4 A **drill** is also **4.1** a way of teaching people to do something by making them repeat it many times. EG *...spelling drills.* **4.2** a routine exercise that is intended to save people's lives by showing them what to do in a dangerous situation. EG *...a fire drill.* N COUNT; N COUNT+SUPP
5 If you **drill** people, you teach them to do something by making them repeat it many times. EG *He was not pleased at having to drill a squad of new recruits.* V+O : OFT+*in*

drily /draɪli[1]/. See **dry**.

drink /drɪŋk/, **drinks, drinking, drank** /dræŋk/, **drunk** /drʌŋk/. **1** When you **drink** a liquid, you take it into your mouth and swallow it. EG *We sat drinking coffee... He drank eagerly.* V+O OR V
2 To **drink** also means to drink alcohol. EG *She said she didn't drink... You shouldn't drink and drive.* V
3 A **drink** is **3.1** an amount of a liquid which you drink. EG *I asked for a drink of water.* **3.2** an alcoholic drink. EG *He poured himself a drink.* N COUNT
4 Drink is alcohol, for example beer, wine, or whisky. EG *We are trying to keep him away from drink... He eventually died of drink.* N UNCOUNT
drink to. If you **drink to** someone or something, you raise your glass and say their name before drinking, as a way of showing that you hope they will be happy or successful. EG *They agreed on their plan and drank to it.* PHRASAL VB : V+PREP

drinker /drɪŋkə/, **drinkers. 1** A **drinker** is someone who drinks a lot of alcohol. EG *She had become a secret drinker.* N COUNT
2 You can use **drinker** to say what kind of drink someone regularly drinks. For example, a coffee drinker is someone who regularly drinks coffee. EG *...a tea drinker... ...a beer drinker.* N COUNT+SUPP

drinking /drɪŋkɪŋ/ is the activity of drinking alcohol. EG *There had been some heavy drinking at the party.* N UNCOUNT

drip /drɪp/, **drips, dripping, dripped. 1** When liquid **drips**, it falls in small drops. EG *The rain was dripping down our necks.* V-ERG
2 When something **drips**, drops of liquid fall from it. EG *...the dripping of the cold water tap.* V
3 Drips are drops of liquid falling from a place. EG *She placed a cup under the leak to catch the drips.* N COUNT

drive /draɪv/, **drives, driving, drove** /drəʊv/, **driven** /drɪvə[0]n/. **1** When you **drive** a vehicle, you operate it and control it so that it goes where you want it to go. EG *It is her turn to drive the car... They drove to the temple... I have never learned to drive.* V+O OR V : OFT+A
2 If you **drive** someone somewhere, you take them there in a car. EG *Can I drive you to the airport?* V+O+A
3 A **drive** is a journey in a vehicle such as a car. EG *It'll be a thirty mile drive.* N COUNT
4 The **drive** to someone's house is a private road that leads from a public road to the house. EG *There were several cars parked in the drive.* N COUNT
5 If something **drives** a machine, it supplies the power that makes it work. EG *Steam can be used to drive generators.* V+O
6 If you **drive** a post or a nail into something, you force it in by hitting it with a hammer. EG *...a stake driven into the gravel.* V+O+A
7 If people or animals **are driven** somewhere, they are forced to go there. EG *Half a million people had been driven out... We smoked constantly to drive away the mosquitoes.* V+O+A
8 To **drive** someone into a particular state or situation means to force them into it. EG *The farming venture drove the company into debt... The tourists were beginning to drive me crazy.* V+O+A OR V+O+C
9 If someone **is driven** by a feeling or need, this is what makes them behave as they do. EG *...a man driven by greed or envy.* V+O : USU PASS
10 If someone has **drive**, they have energy and determination. EG *Northcliffe had great ability and drive.* N UNCOUNT
11 A **drive** is also a special effort made by a group of people in order to achieve something. EG *The Poles launched a tremendous investment drive.* N SING+SUPP
12 If you understand **what** someone **is driving at**, you understand what they are trying to say. EG *She knew at once what I was driving at.* PHRASE
13 See also **driving, drove**.

drivel /drɪvə[0]l/. You can describe something that someone has said or written as **drivel** when you think that it is very silly. EG *I've never heard such drivel.* N UNCOUNT

driven /drɪvə[0]n/ is the past participle of **drive.**

driver /draɪvə/, **drivers. 1** A **driver** is someone who drives a motor vehicle. EG *I hate being behind middle-aged drivers.* N COUNT
2 A bus **driver** or a taxi **driver** is someone whose job is to drive a bus or a taxi. N COUNT+SUPP

driveway /draɪvweɪ/, **driveways.** A **driveway** is a private road that leads from a public road to a N COUNT house or garage. EG *The car turned into a dark driveway.*

driving /draɪvɪŋ/. 1 **Driving** is the activity of driving a car, or the way that you drive it. EG *I love driving... She was found guilty of dangerous driving.* N UNCOUNT

2 You describe something as the **driving** force behind something else when it is the main cause of it. EG *The union is the driving force behind the revolution.* ADJ CLASSIF : ATTRIB

driving licence, driving licences. A **driving licence** is a card showing that you are qualified to drive because you have passed a driving test. N COUNT British

drizzle /drɪzəl/, **drizzles, drizzling, drizzled.** 1 **Drizzle** is light rain falling in very small drops. EG *He walked back through the fine drizzle.* N UNCOUNT

2 If it **is drizzling**, it is raining lightly. V

drone /drəʊn/, **drones, droning, droned.** 1 If something **drones**, it makes a low, continuous humming noise. EG *The engine droned on and on.* V

▸ used as a noun. EG *...the drone of a bee... ...the steady drone of the traffic.* ▸ N SING+SUPP

2 A **drone** is a male bee. N COUNT

drone on. If someone **drones on**, they keep talking about something or reading something aloud in a boring way. EG *He droned on through several more pages of information.* PHRASAL VB : V+ADV

drool /druːl/, **drools, drooling, drooled.** 1 If someone **drools**, they let saliva fall from their mouth, without being able to stop it. V

2 If you **drool** over someone or something, you look at them with uncontrolled pleasure; used showing disapproval. EG *Gaskell's drooling over you all the time.* V : OFT+*over/at* Informal

droop /druːp/, **droops, drooping, drooped.** If something **droops**, it hangs or leans downwards with no strength or firmness. EG *His shoulders drooped... His eyelids drooped as though he was on the verge of sleep.* V ◇ **drooping.** EG *...drooping purple flowers... ...a drooping moustache.* ◇ ADJ CLASSIF

drop /drɒp/, **drops, dropping, dropped.** 1 If you **drop** something, you let it fall deliberately or by mistake. EG *Planes dropped huge quantities of incendiary bombs... He collided with a chair and dropped his cigar.* V+O

2 If something **drops**, it falls straight down. EG *Ash dropped from his cigarette.* V : USU+A

3 If a level or amount **drops**, it quickly becomes less. EG *The temperature of their bodies dropped ten degrees.* V : OFT+A ▸ used as a noun. EG *...a drop in income... ...a voltage drop.* ▸ N COUNT +SUPP

4 If your voice **drops** or if you **drop** your voice, you speak more quietly. V-ERG

5 If someone **drops dead**, they die suddenly. EG *The minister dropped dead at a public meeting.* PHRASE Informal

6 If you **drop** something that you are doing or dealing with, you stop doing it or dealing with it. EG *Most of the charges against him were dropped... I was certain he would drop everything to help.* V+O

7 If you **drop** a hint, you give someone a hint in a casual way. EG *Don't drop hints about promotion.* V+O

8 If the driver of a vehicle **drops** you somewhere, he or she stops the vehicle and you get out. EG *He ordered his taxi to drop him at the corner of the street.* V+O+A

9 If you **drop** someone **a line**, you write them a short letter. PHRASE Informal

10 A **drop** of a liquid is a very small amount of it shaped like a little ball. EG *A drop of blood slid down his leg.* N COUNT OR N PART

11 A **drop** of an alcoholic drink is a small amount of it in a glass. EG *A little drop of scotch would be very welcome.* N PART Informal

12 **Drops** are a kind of medicine which you put drop by drop into your ears, eyes, or nose. N COUNT : USU PLURAL

13 You use **drop** to talk about vertical distances. For example, a thirty-foot **drop** is a distance of thirty feet between the top of a cliff or wall and the bottom of it. N COUNT+SUPP

drop by. If you **drop by**, you visit someone informally. EG *If there's anything you want to see, just drop by.* PHRASAL VB : V+ADV

drop in. If you **drop in** on someone, you visit them informally, usually without having arranged it before. EG *I thought I'd just drop in and see how you were.* PHRASAL VB : V+ADV, OFT+*on* Informal

drop off. 1 If you **drop off** to sleep, you go to sleep. EG *I was feeling tired enough to drop off to sleep at any moment.* PHRASAL VB : V+ADV 2 If the driver of a vehicle **drops** you **off** somewhere, he or she stops the vehicle and you get out. EG *I can drop Daisy off on my way home.* V+O+ADV

drop out. If you **drop out** of college or university, you leave it without finishing your course. EG *Some students drop out after a relatively short time.* PHRASAL VB : V+ADV : OFT+*of*

drop-out, drop-outs. 1 **Drop-outs** are people who reject the accepted ways of a society, for example by not having a regular job and by dressing in an untidy way; used showing disapproval. N COUNT Informal

2 **Drop-outs** are also young people who have left school or college before they have finished their studies. EG *...a high-school dropout.* N COUNT Informal

droppings /drɒpɪŋz/ are the faeces of birds and small animals. EG *...mouse droppings.* N PLURAL

drought /draʊt/, **droughts.** A **drought** is a long period of time during which no rain falls. EG *...the effects of famine and drought... Local problems include diseases and periodic droughts.* N UNCOUNT OR N COUNT

drove /drəʊv/, **droves.** 1 **Drove** is the past tense of **drive**.

2 **Droves** of people are very large numbers of them. EG *They came in droves to see Australia's natural wonder.* N PLURAL

drown /draʊn/, **drowns, drowning, drowned.** 1 When someone **drowns** or **is drowned**, they die because they have gone under water and cannot breathe. EG *A man fell from a bridge and drowned... I couldn't make myself drown the poor creature.* V-ERG

2 If something **drowns** a sound, it is louder than the sound and makes it impossible to hear it. EG *...the heckling which drowned his speech.* V+O : USU PASS

3 If you say that someone **is drowning** their **sorrows**, you mean that they are drinking a lot of alcohol in order to forget an unhappy experience. PHRASE Informal

drowse /draʊz/, **drowses, drowsing, drowsed.** If you **drowse**, you are almost asleep or just asleep. EG *She drowsed in the sun.* V

drowsy /draʊzi[1]/, **drowsier, drowsiest.** If you are **drowsy**, you feel sleepy and cannot think clearly. EG *I became pleasantly drowsy.* ADJ QUALIT

◇ **drowsiness.** EG *The sound of the waves lulled me into drowsiness... I must shake off this drowsiness.* ◇ N UNCOUNT ◇ **drowsily.** EG *I shook my head drowsily.* ◇ ADV

drudge /drʌdʒ/, **drudges.** You can refer to someone as a **drudge** when they have to do a lot of very uninteresting work. N COUNT

drudgery /drʌdʒəri[1]/ is uninteresting work that must be done. EG *...the drudgery of housework.* N UNCOUNT

drug /drʌg/, **drugs, drugging, drugged.** 1 A **drug** is a chemical which is given to people in order to treat or prevent an illness or disease. EG *This drug is prescribed to treat hay fever.* N COUNT

2 **Drugs** are also substances that some people smoke or inject into their blood because of their stimulating effects. In most countries, these uses of drugs are illegal. EG *He was on drugs... She takes drugs... ...drug addiction.* N COUNT : USU PLURAL

3 If you **drug** a person or animal, you give them a chemical substance in order to make them sleepy or unconscious. V+O ◇ **drugged.** EG *She spoke as if she was half asleep or drugged.* ◇ ADJ CLASSIF

4 If food or drink **is drugged**, a chemical substance is added to it in order to make someone unconscious when they eat or drink it. EG *The sweets she had given them were drugged.* V+O : USU PASS

> If an English film is dubbed into your language, what language would you hear?

drugstore /drʌgstɔː/, **drugstores.** In America, a **drugstore** is a shop where you can buy medicines and other goods and also get drinks and snacks. N COUNT

drum /drʌm/, **drums, drumming, drummed. 1** A **drum** is a musical instrument consisting of a skin stretched tightly over a round frame. You play a drum by beating it rhythmically with sticks or with your hands. See picture at MUSICAL INSTRUMENTS. N COUNT

2 A **drum** is also a large cylindrical container in which fuel is kept. EG *...oil drums.* N COUNT

3 If you **drum** your fingers, you hit a surface with them, making a continuous beating sound. EG *He drummed his fingers on the desk.* V+O OR V

4 If something **is drumming** on a surface, it is hitting it regularly, making a continuous beating sound. EG *We sat listening to the rain drumming on the roof.* V

drum into. If you **drum** something **into** someone, you keep saying it to them until they understand it or remember it. EG *These facts had been drummed into him.* PHRASAL VB : V+O+PREP

drum up. If you **drum up** support, you succeed in getting it. EG *...the patriotic fervour Hamilton had drummed up.* PHRASAL VB : V+ADV+O

drummer /drʌmə/, **drummers.** A **drummer** is a person who plays a drum or drums in a band or group. N COUNT

drunk /drʌŋk/, **drunks. 1 Drunk** is the past participle of **drink**.

2 If someone is **drunk**, they have drunk so much alcohol that they cannot speak clearly or behave sensibly. EG *He was never going to get drunk again... He was so drunk he couldn't write a word.* ADJ QUALIT

3 A **drunk** is someone who is drunk or who often gets drunk. EG *San Francisco has a lot of drunks.* N COUNT

drunkard /drʌŋkəd/, **drunkards.** A **drunkard** is someone who often gets drunk. N COUNT

drunken /drʌŋkəⁿn/. **1 Drunken** behaviour is clumsy, noisy, or foolish behaviour by someone who is drunk. EG *A long drunken party had just broken up... ...drunken whoops of laughter.* ADJ CLASSIF : ATTRIB
◇ **drunkenly.** EG *Their parents fought drunkenly with each other.* ◇ ADV ◇ **drunkenness** /drʌŋkənnəˀs/. EG *They acquired a reputation for drunkenness and crime.* ◇ N UNCOUNT

2 A **drunken** person is drunk. EG *...stiffer penalties for drunken drivers.* ADJ QUALIT : ATTRIB

dry /draɪ/, **drier** or **dryer, driest; dries, drying, dried. 1** Something that is **dry** has no water or other liquid on it or in it. EG *They threw onto the fire some dry branches... He was rubbing himself dry with a towel.* ADJ QUALIT ◇ **dryness.** EG *...the dryness of the air.* ◇ N UNCOUNT

2 When you **dry** something or when it **dries**, it becomes dry. EG *He dried his feet with the towel... The washing hung drying in the sun.* V-ERG

3 When the weather is **dry**, there is no rain. EG *The night was dry and clear.* ADJ QUALIT

4 If you are on **dry land**, you are on the shore, rather than in a ship or boat. PHRASE

5 Dry humour is subtle and sarcastic. EG *I enjoyed her dry accounts of her work experiences.* ADJ QUALIT ◇ **drily** or **dryly.** EG *'Thank you,' I said drily. 'It must be nice to be so culturally enlightened.'* ◇ ADV

6 Dry sherry or wine does not taste sweet. ADJ CLASSIF

7 See also **dried, dryer**.

dry out. If something **dries out**, it becomes completely dry. EG *The material gets as hard as a brick when it dries out.* PHRASAL VB : V-ERG+ADV

dry up. 1 If something **dries up**, it loses all its water or moisture. EG *The pool dried up in the late summer... My mouth always dries up when I'm nervous.* PHRASAL VB : V+ADV ◇ **dried-up.** EG *...a dried-up piece of cake.* ◇ ADJ CLASSIF

2 When you **dry up** after a meal or **dry** the dishes **up**, you wipe the water off the cutlery, plates, and cups when they have been washed. EG *Would you like me to dry up?... I started to dry up the cups.* V+ADV OR V+O+ADV

3 If a supply or series of things **dries up**, it stops. EG *Orders dried up and costs continued to rise.* V+ADV

dry-clean, dry-cleans, dry-cleaning, dry-cleaned. When clothes **are dry-cleaned**, they are cleaned with a liquid chemical rather than with water. V+O : USU PASS ◇ **dry-cleaning.** *...dry-cleaning fluid... I'm taking a load of things to the dry-cleaning shop.* ◇ N UNCOUNT

dryer /draɪə/, **dryers;** also spelled **drier. 1** A **dryer** is a machine for drying clothes. N COUNT

2 Dryer and **drier** are also the comparative forms of **dry**.

dual /djuːəl/ means having two parts, functions, or aspects. EG *The committee has a dual function... ...dual nationality... ...dual purpose furniture.* ADJ CLASSIF : ATTRIB

dual carriageway, dual carriageways. A **dual carriageway** is a road which has a strip of grass or concrete down the middle to separate traffic going in opposite directions. N COUNT OR N UNCOUNT British

dub /dʌb/, **dubs, dubbing, dubbed. 1** If something **is dubbed** a particular name, it is given that name. EG *London was dubbed 'the insurance capital of the world'.* V+O+C : USU PASS

2 If a film **is dubbed**, the voices on the soundtrack are not those of the actors, but those of other actors speaking in a different language. EG *The series is dubbed into six languages.* V+O : USU PASS

dubious /djuːbɪəs/. **1** You describe something as **dubious** when you think that it is not completely honest, safe, or reliable. EG *...goods of dubious origin... Here Halliday carried on his dubious trade.* ADJ QUALIT

2 If you are **dubious** about something, you are not sure about it. EG *He was dubious about Baker's choice of pilot.* ADJ PRED ◇ **dubiously.** EG *They looked at him dubiously, not knowing how much to believe.* ◇ ADV

duchess /dʌtʃɪˀs/, **duchesses.** A **duchess** is a woman who has the same rank as a duke, or who is a duke's wife or widow. EG *...the Duchess of Marlborough.* N COUNT

duck /dʌk/, **ducks, ducking, ducked. 1** A **duck** is a very common water bird with short legs, webbed feet, a short neck, and a large flat beak. The plural form of 'duck' is either 'ducks' or 'duck'. N COUNT

2 Duck also refers to the meat of a duck when it is cooked and eaten. EG *Gerald had ordered duck.* N UNCOUNT

3 If you **take to** something **like a duck to water**, you discover that you are naturally good at it or that you like doing it. PHRASE Informal

4 If you **duck** your head or **duck**, you move your head quickly downwards in order to avoid being seen or hit by something. EG *A gull flew so close that she ducked.* V+O OR V

5 If you **duck** into a place, you move there quickly, especially in order to escape danger. EG *I ducked into the shrubbery.* V+A

6 If you **duck** a duty or responsibility, you avoid it. V+O

duck out. If you **duck out** of something that you are supposed to do, you avoid doing it. EG *I once ducked out of an appointment I couldn't face.* PHRASAL VB : V+ADV, OFT+*of*

duckling /dʌklɪŋ/, **ducklings.** A **duckling** is a young duck. N COUNT

duct /dʌkt/, **ducts.** A **duct** is **1** a pipe, tube, or channel through which a liquid or gas is sent. **2** a tube in your body that a liquid such as tears or bile can pass through. EG *...an obstructed tear duct.* N COUNT : OFT+SUPP

dud /dʌd/, **duds.** You say that something is **dud** or a **dud** when it does not work properly. EG *...dud light bulbs... The new system is a dud.* ADJ CLASSIF OR N COUNT Informal

due /djuː/, **dues. 1** If a situation, event, or state of affairs is **due to** something else, it happens or exists as a result of it. EG *Over 40 per cent of deaths were due to this disease... There's still a good deal of disruption due to the strike.* PREP

2 If something is **due** at a particular time, it is expected to happen or to arrive at that time. EG *We were due in at 2 a.m... What time is the bus due?... The committee was due to meet on 22 August.* ADJ PRED : USU+A OR *to*-INF

3 If you say that something will happen **in due course**, you mean that it will happen eventually, PHRASE Formal when the time is right. EG *All will be attended to in due course.*

4 Dues are sums of money that you pay regularly to an organization that you belong to. N PLURAL

5 If some money is **due** to you, you have a right to it. EG *You may get slightly less pension than the full amount due to you.* ADJ PRED: OFT+*to*

6 If you give something **due** consideration or **due** attention, you give it the amount of consideration or attention that it deserves. EG *After due consideration of the evidence, the meeting decided that no one had been to blame.* ADJ CLASSIF: ATTRIB

7 You say **'to give** them their **due'** when you are saying something good about people who have been criticized. EG *To give him his due, he had no idea that he was breaking the rules.* ADV SEN

8 You use **due** to talk about exact compass directions. For example, if a place is **due** north, it is exactly to the north of where you are. EG *They were travelling due east.* ADV

duel /djuːəl/, **duels. 1** A **duel** is a fight between two people in which they use guns or swords in order to settle a quarrel. EG *Feelings were so intense that they fought a duel.* N COUNT

2 You can refer to any conflict between two people as a **duel.** EG *The enemy pilot had fired too soon in the high-speed duel.* N COUNT

duet /djuːɛt/, **duets.** A **duet** is a piece of music sung or played by two people. N COUNT

duffel coat /dʌfə[0]l kəʊt/, **duffel coats;** also spelled **duffle coat.** A **duffel coat** is a heavy coat with rod-shaped buttons and a hood. N COUNT

dug /dʌg/ is the past tense and past participle of **dig.**

duke /djuːk/, **dukes.** A **duke** is a nobleman with a rank just below that of a prince. EG *...the Duke of York... I was in the Duke's service.* N COUNT

dulcet /dʌlsɪ[2]t/. **Dulcet** sounds are gentle and pleasant to listen to; often used humorously. EG *I wake up to the dulcet tones of the Radio Four news.* ADJ CLASSIF: ATTRIB Literary

dull /dʌl/, **duller, dullest; dulls, dulling, dulled.**

1 Something or someone that is **dull** is not interesting in any way. EG *I thought the book dull and unoriginal... It will be so dull here without you.* ADJ QUALIT

◊ **dullness.** EG *...the dullness of his life.* ◊ N UNCOUNT

2 You can say that someone is **dull** when they show no interest in anything. ◊ **dully.** EG *They stared dully down at the ground.* ADJ QUALIT ◊ ADV

3 A **dull** colour or light is not bright. EG *The sea had been a dull grey... On the opposite wall was a dull electric sign.* ◊ **dully.** EG *The lights of the houses gleamed dully.* ADJ QUALIT: ATTRIB ◊ ADV

4 You say that the weather is **dull** when it is rather cloudy. EG *It was a dull morning.* ADJ QUALIT

5 A **dull** sound is not clear or loud. EG *...a dull thud.* ADJ CLASSIF

6 Dull feelings are weak and not intense. EG *The dull ache in her side began again... I stared at her in dull discomfort.* ◊ **dully.** EG *His ankle throbbed dully.* ADJ CLASSIF: ATTRIB ◊ ADV

7 If something **dulls** a pain or feeling, it causes it to seem less intense. EG *In her experience, the taking of food dulled pain.* V+O

8 If something **dulls** or **is dulled,** it becomes less bright. EG *His eyes dulled.* V-ERG Literary

duly /djuːli[1]/. **1** If something is **duly** done, it is done in the correct way. EG *She was declared duly elected to Parliament.* ADV Formal

2 If something happens that was expected to happen, you can say that it **duly** happened. EG *De Gaulle duly attended the ceremony at the appointed time.* ADV

dumb /dʌm/, **dumber, dumbest. 1** Someone who is **dumb** is completely unable to speak. EG *She was deaf and dumb from birth.* ADJ CLASSIF

2 If someone is **dumb** on a particular occasion, they cannot speak because they are angry, shocked, or surprised. EG *We were struck dumb with horror.* ADJ PRED

3 Dumb also means stupid; an offensive use. EG *Get out of the way, you dumb idiot.* ADJ QUALIT

4 You can describe attitudes or feelings as **dumb** when they are expressed without words. EG *Silence can upset some people who interpret it as dumb insolence.* ADJ CLASSIF: ATTRIB

dumbfounded /dʌmfaʊndɪ[2]d/. If you are **dumbfounded,** you are so surprised that you cannot speak. EG *He was watching, dumbfounded.* ADJ CLASSIF

dumbly /dʌmli[1]/. If you do something **dumbly,** you do it without saying anything. EG *He stared dumbly at the wall.* ADV

dummy /dʌmi[1]/, **dummies. 1** A baby's **dummy** is a rubber or plastic object that you give to it to suck so that it feels comforted and stays quiet. N COUNT British

2 A tailor's **dummy** is a large model that looks like a human being and that is used to display clothes in a shop. EG *...dummies dressed in military uniforms.* N COUNT

3 You use **dummy** to describe things that are not real. For example, a **dummy** car is not a real car, but one that has been made to look or behave like a real car. EG *...dummy doors... ...experiments with dummy animals.* ADJ CLASSIF: ATTRIB

dump /dʌmp/, **dumps, dumping, dumped.**

1 When unwanted waste matter **is dumped,** it is put somewhere and is intended to remain there for ever. EG *...chemicals dumped in unsuitable places.* V+O: USU+A

◊ **dumping.** EG *...the dumping of acid wastes in the North Sea.* ◊ N UNCOUNT

2 If you **dump** something somewhere, you put it there quickly and in a careless way. EG *She dumped her bag on Judy's table.* V+O: USU+A

3 A **dump** or a **rubbish dump** is a place where rubbish is left, for example on open ground outside a town. EG *...a large municipal dump.* N COUNT

4 You refer to a place as a **dump** when it is unattractive and unpleasant to live in. EG *She'll never want to endure that squalid little dump again... What a dump!* N COUNT Informal

5 If you are **in the dumps,** you feel depressed and miserable. PHRASE Informal

dumping ground, dumping grounds. If you refer to a place as a **dumping ground,** you mean that things are left there, usually in large quantities. EG *The house has become a dumping ground for stolen goods.* N COUNT+*for*

dumpling /dʌmplɪŋ/, **dumplings.** A **dumpling** is a small lump of dough that is cooked with meat and vegetables. N COUNT

dumpy /dʌmpi[1]/, **dumpier, dumpiest.** Someone who is **dumpy** is short and fat. ADJ QUALIT

dun /dʌn/. Something that is **dun** is a dull grey-brown colour. ADJ COLOUR

dunce /dʌns/, **dunces.** You call someone a **dunce** when they cannot learn what someone is trying to teach them. EG *I was such a dunce at school.* N COUNT

dune /djuːn/, **dunes.** A **dune** or a sand **dune** is a hill of sand near the sea or in a desert. N COUNT

dung /dʌŋ/ is faeces from large animals. N UNCOUNT

dungarees /dʌŋgə[0]riːz/ are trousers attached to a piece of cloth which covers your chest and has straps going over your shoulders. See picture at CLOTHES. N PLURAL

dungeon /dʌndʒə[0]n/, **dungeons.** A **dungeon** is a dark underground prison in a castle. N COUNT

dunk /dʌŋk/, **dunks, dunking, dunked.** If you **dunk** something in a liquid, you put it in it for a short time. EG *I dunked my bread in the cocoa.* V+O+*in* Informal

dupe /djuːp/, **dupes, duping, duped. 1** If someone **dupes** you, they trick you. EG *I was duped into expressing my thoughts.* V+O: USU PASS+*into*

2 A **dupe** is someone who has been tricked. N COUNT

duplicate, duplicates, duplicating, duplicated; pronounced /djuːplɪkeɪt/ when it is a verb and /djuːplɪkə[1]t/ when it is a noun or an adjective.

Are a dustman's clothes likely to be dusty?

1 If you **duplicate** a piece of writing or a drawing, you make exact copies of it using a machine. EG *The story was typed and duplicated.* — V+O

2 A **duplicate** is something that is identical to something else. EG *In the room was a duplicate of the display panel.* ▸ used as an adjective. EG *...a duplicate key... My bag contained the duplicate typescript of the book.* — N COUNT; ▸ ADJ CLASSIF : ATTRIB

3 If you have something **in duplicate**, you have two identical copies of it. EG *Usually we ask for a draft in duplicate.* — PHRASE

4 When an activity **is duplicated**, two people or two groups do the same thing. ◇ **duplication** /djuːplɪkeɪʃəⁿn/. EG *We try to avoid duplication of work.* — V+O; ◇ N UNCOUNT

durable /djʊəᵒrəbəᵒl/. Something that is **durable** is strong and lasts a long time. EG *...well-finished and durable products.* ◇ **durability** /djʊəᵒrəbɪlɪ¹ti¹/. EG *...the durability of their love.* — ADJ QUALIT; ◇ N UNCOUNT

duration /djʊreɪʃəⁿn/. The **duration** of something is the length of time during which it happens or exists. EG *He was prepared to do this for the duration of the campaign.* — N SING : *the*+N+*of*

duress /djʊəᵒrɛs/. If you do something under **duress**, you are forced to do it, and do it very unwillingly. EG *...a decision made early in life under duress.* — N UNCOUNT

during /djʊəᵒrɪŋ/. Something that happens **during** a period of time **1** happens continuously or several times in that period. EG *She heated the place during the winter with a huge wood furnace... Fred had worked a great deal with her at Oxford during the war.* **2** happens at some point in that period. EG *He had died during the night.* — PREP

dusk /dʌsk/ is the time just before night when it is not completely dark. — N UNCOUNT

dusky /dʌski¹/. Something that is **dusky** is rather dark. EG *...her dusky cheeks... ...the dusky room.* — ADJ QUALIT

dust /dʌst/, **dusts, dusting, dusted. 1 Dust** on a road or in the air consists of many tiny particles of earth or sand. EG *Each car threw up a cloud of white dust.* — N UNCOUNT

2 Dust in a building consists of many tiny particles of dirt. EG *...the dust on the coffee table.* — N UNCOUNT

3 Gold **dust** or chalk **dust** is fine powder consisting of tiny particles of gold or chalk. — N UNCOUNT

4 When you **dust** furniture or other objects, you remove dust from them using a duster. EG *She lifted the jugs one by one as she dusted the shelf.* — V+O OR V

5 If you **dust** a surface with a powder, you cover it lightly with the powder. EG *She put on lipstick and dusted her face with powder.* — V+O : OFT+*with*

dustbin /dʌstbɪn/, **dustbins.** A **dustbin** is a large container that you put rubbish in. You keep it outside your house. — N COUNT; British

duster /dʌstə/, **dusters.** A **duster** is a cloth that you use for removing dust from furniture and other objects. — N COUNT

dustman /dʌstməⁿn/, **dustmen.** A **dustman** is a person whose job is to take away the rubbish that people keep in their dustbins. — N COUNT; British

dustpan /dʌstpæn/, **dustpans.** A **dustpan** is a small flat container for sweeping dust and dirt into. — N COUNT

dust-up, dust-ups. A **dust-up** is a quarrel or fight. EG *Another dust-up took place on the public beach.* — N COUNT; Informal

dusty /dʌsti¹/, **dustier, dustiest.** Something that is **dusty** is covered with dust. EG *We rode along a dusty mountain track... ...a room full of dusty, broken furniture.* — ADJ QUALIT

dutiful /djuːtɪfʊl/. If you are **dutiful**, you do everything that you are expected to do. EG *He was a dutiful son.* ◇ **dutifully.** EG *The audience dutifully applauded.* — ADJ QUALIT; ◇ ADV

duty /djuːti¹/, **duties. 1 Duty** is the work that you have to do as your job. EG *He reported for duty at the manager's office.* — N UNCOUNT

2 When policemen, doctors, or nurses are **on duty**, they are working. When they are **off duty**, they are not working. EG *A police constable on duty became suspicious... You can go off duty now.* — PHRASE

3 Your **duties** are the tasks which you do as part of your job. EG *Nursing auxiliaries help qualified nurses with their basic duties.* — N PLURAL

4 If you say that something is your **duty**, you mean that you ought to do it because it is your responsibility. EG *As a doctor, it was my duty to preserve life... I've always tried to do my duty.* — N SING+POSS

5 Duties are taxes which you pay to the government on goods that you buy. EG *The government increased the duty on petrol.* — N COUNT

duty-bound. If you are **duty-bound** to do something, you must do it because it is your duty. EG *You are duty-bound to stay by her sick bed.* — ADJ PRED +*to*-INF; Formal

duty-free. Duty-free goods are goods that you buy at airports or on planes or ships at a cheaper price than usual because you do not have to pay taxes on them. EG *...duty-free whisky.* — ADJ CLASSIF

duvet /duːveɪ/, **duvets.** A **duvet** is a large bag filled with feathers or similar material, which you use to cover yourself in bed. — N COUNT; British

dwarf /dwɔːf/, **dwarfs, dwarfing, dwarfed. 1** If one thing **dwarfs** another thing, it is much bigger than the other thing and makes it look small. EG *David was dwarfed by a huge desk... Commercial buildings are beginning to dwarf the city churches.* — V+O : USU PASS

2 Dwarf plants or animals are much smaller than other plants or animals of the same kind. EG *...dwarf wheat.* — ADJ CLASSIF : ATTRIB

3 A **dwarf** is a person who is much smaller than most people. — N COUNT

dwell /dwɛl/, **dwells, dwelling, dwelled, dwelt** /dwɛlt/. **Dwelled** and **dwelt** are both used as the past tense and past participle of the verb. — V+A; Outdated

If you **dwell** somewhere, you live there. EG *They still dwelt in their old abode.*

dwell on. If you **dwell on** something or **dwell upon** it, you think, speak, or write about it a great deal. EG *She began to dwell on memories of her mother... So far we have dwelt upon the negative elements in the situation.* — PHRASAL VB : V+PREP, HAS PASS

dweller /dwɛlə/, **dwellers.** You use **dweller** to say where someone lives. For example, a city **dweller** is someone who lives in a city. EG *...slum dwellers... ...cave dwellers.* — N COUNT+SUPP

dwelling /dwɛlɪŋ/, **dwellings.** A **dwelling** is a house or other place where someone lives. EG *They were five miles from the nearest dwelling.* — N COUNT; Formal

dwelt /dwɛlt/ is the past tense and past participle of **dwell.**

dwindle /dwɪndəᵒl/, **dwindles, dwindling, dwindled.** If something **dwindles**, it becomes smaller or less strong. EG *Their small hoard of money dwindled... The stream had dwindled to a trickle.* ◇ **dwindling.** EG *...an area of rapidly dwindling forest.* — V : OFT+A; ◇ ADJ QUALIT

dye /daɪ/, **dyes, dyeing, dyed. 1** If you **dye** something such as hair or cloth, you change its colour by soaking it in a coloured liquid. ◇ **dyed.** EG *...a woman with dyed red hair.* — V+O; ◇ ADJ CLASSIF

2 A **dye** is a substance which is mixed into a liquid and is used to change the colour of something such as cloth or hair. — N MASS

dying /daɪɪŋ/. **1 Dying** is the present participle of **die.**

2 The **dying** are people who are so ill or so badly injured that they are likely to die soon. EG *She cared for the poor, the diseased and the dying.* — N PLURAL : *the*+N

3 A **dying** tradition or industry is becoming less important and is likely to finish altogether. EG *Coal is by no means a dying industry.* — ADJ CLASSIF : ATTRIB

dyke /daɪk/, **dykes;** also spelled **dike.** A **dyke** is a thick wall that prevents water flooding onto land from a river or from the sea. — N COUNT

dynamic /daɪnæmɪk/, **dynamics. 1** Someone who is **dynamic** is full of energy. EG *The new President is a dynamic and able man.* ◇ **dynamically.** EG *We* — ADJ QUALIT; ◇ ADV *would like to see them participate more dynamically.*

2 The **dynamics** of a society or a situation are the forces that cause it to change. EG *...the dynamics of industrial development.* N PLURAL

dynamism /daɪnəmɪzə^{0}m/. Someone's **dynamism** is their energy or ability to produce new ideas. N UNCOUNT

dynamite /daɪnəmaɪt/, **dynamites, dynamiting, dynamited. 1 Dynamite** is an explosive. EG *...rebels wielding sticks of dynamite.* N UNCOUNT

2 If you **dynamite** something, you blow it up using dynamite. EG *They dynamited the houses.* V+O

dynamo /daɪnəməʊ/, **dynamos.** A **dynamo** is a device that uses the movement of a machine or vehicle to produce electricity. N COUNT

dynasty /dɪnəsti^{1}/, **dynasties.** A **dynasty** is a series of rulers of a country who all belong to the same family. N COUNT

d'you is a short form of 'do you' used in questions in spoken English. EG *D'you know what I found?*

dysentery /dɪsə^{0}ntri^{1}/ is an infection that causes severe diarrhoea. N UNCOUNT

dyslexia /dɪslɛksɪə/ is difficulty with reading, caused by a slight disorder of the brain. N UNCOUNT
◇ **dyslexic** /dɪslɛksɪk/. EG *Her younger daughter was dyslexic... ...dyslexic pupils.* ◇ ADJ CLASSIF

E e

E, e /iː/, **E's, e's. 1 E** is the fifth letter of the English alphabet. N COUNT

2 E is a written abbreviation for 'east'.

each /iːtʃ/. **1** If you refer to **each** thing or **each** person in a group, you are referring to every member of the group and considering them as individuals. EG *Each county is subdivided into several districts... Each day Kunta felt a little worse... There were peaches and pears. I opened two tins of each... They were all just sitting there, each of them thinking private thoughts.* DET; ALSO PRON : OFT+*of*

2 You use **each** to emphasize that you are referring to every individual thing or person in a group. EG *He offered me the tin of biscuits and my sister and I had one each... They cost eight pounds each.* PRON

3 You use **each other** when you are saying that each member of a group does something to the others or has a particular connection with the others. EG *She and John looked at each other... We know each other's minds very well.* PRON

eager /iːgə/. If you are **eager** to do something, you want to do it very much. EG *The majority were eager to express their opinions... ...people eager for a quick cure.* ◇ **eagerly.** EG *They began to talk eagerly.* ◇ **eagerness.** EG *...my eagerness to learn... ...an eagerness for total freedom.* ADJ QUALIT : OFT+*to*-INF OR *for*; ◇ ADV; ◇ N UNCOUNT

eagle/iːgə^{0}l/, **eagles.** An **eagle** is a large bird that lives by eating small animals. N COUNT

ear /ɪə/, **ears. 1** Your **ears** are the two parts of your body, one on each side of your head, with which you hear sounds. See picture at THE HUMAN BODY. N COUNT

2 You can use **ear** to refer to a person's willingness to listen to what someone is saying. EG *He tried to give a sympathetic ear at all times.* N SING+SUPP

3 The **ears** of a cereal plant such as wheat or barley are the parts at the top of the stem, which contain the seeds or grains. N COUNT

4 Ear is used in these phrases. **4.1** If you **keep** or **have** your **ear to the ground**, you make sure that you are well informed about what is happening. **4.2** If can you **play** a piece of music **by ear**, you can play it when you hear it or have heard it in the past, rather than by reading printed music. **4.3** If you **turn a deaf ear** to something that is being said, you take no notice of it. EG *Young people sometimes seem to turn a deaf ear to the words of their anxious parents.* **4.4** When someone forgets what you tell them, you can say that it **goes in one ear and out the other**. PHRASES; Informal; Informal; Informal

eardrum /ɪədrʌm/, **eardrums.** Your **eardrums** are thin pieces of tightly stretched skin inside your ears, which vibrate so that you can hear sounds. N COUNT

earl /ɜːl/, **earls.** An **earl** is a British nobleman. N COUNT

earlier /ɜːli^{1}ə/ is the comparative of **early.** It is also used to refer to a point or period in time before the present or before the one that you are talking about. EG *Her parents had died of cholera four years earlier... ...as I said earlier... ...in earlier times, when this fashion was popular.* ● **Earlier on** means the same as 'earlier'. *I mentioned that problem earlier on.* ADV AFTER VB, OR ADJ QUALIT : COMPAR; ● PHRASE

earlobe /ɪələʊb/, **earlobes.** Your **earlobes** are the soft parts at the bottom of your ears. N COUNT

early /ɜːli^{1}/, **earlier, earliest. 1 Early** means near the beginning of a period of time, a process, or a piece of work. EG *I got up early... ...very early in the morning... ...early last week... ...in the early 1980s... The men realized this quite early on in their lives... ...in those early chapters, when he's writing about his family.* ADV OR ADJ QUALIT : ATTRIB

2 If someone or something arrives or happens **early**, they arrive or happen before the time that was arranged or expected. EG *The day's practice ended early because of bad light... He knew he was three minutes early.* ADV AFTER VB OR AFTER N

3 You also use **early** to describe things that happen before the normal time. EG *...her husband's early death... Everyone went to sleep early.* ADJ QUALIT : ATTRIB OR ADV AFTER VB

4 As early as means at a particular time or period that is surprisingly early. EG *As early as 1978 the United States had taken steps to counteract this.* PHRASE

5 At the earliest means not before the date or time mentioned. EG *No developments were expected before August at the earliest.* PHRASE

6 If you say that it is **early days**, you mean that it is too soon for you to be completely sure about something. EG *Well, it's early days yet to say whether it works.* PHRASE

7 bright and early: see **bright.** ● **early night**: see **night.** ● See also **earlier.**

earmark /ɪəmɑːk/, **earmarks, earmarking, earmarked.** If something **is earmarked** for a particular purpose, it has been reserved for that purpose. EG *The fund contained more than $300,000 earmarked for sensitive political projects.* V+O : USU PASS+*for*

earn /ɜːn/, **earns, earning, earned. 1** If you **earn** money, you receive it in return for work that you do. EG *...the average worker, earning $15,058... They have to earn a living somehow.* ◇ **earner** /ɜːnə/, **earners.** EG *Most wage earners can afford it.* V+O; ◇ N COUNT +SUPP

2 If something **earns** money, it produces money as profit. EG *Something is uneconomic when it fails to earn an adequate profit.* V+O

3 If you **earn** something such as praise, you get it V+O because you deserve it. EG *He has earned his place in history... They earn acclaim wherever they go.*

earnest /ɜːnɪ²st/. **1** People who are **earnest** are very serious in what they say and do. EG *She was approached by an earnest young man from the University... It is my earnest wish that you use this money to further your research.* ◊ **earnestly.** EG *He was in a corner of the room talking earnestly to Julie.* ◊ **earnestness.** EG *...speaking with great earnestness.* ADJ QUALIT / ◊ ADV / ◊ N UNCOUNT

2 If you are **in earnest**, you are sincere in your intentions. EG *Is the President in earnest about the desire to negotiate?* PHRASE

3 If something happens **in earnest**, it happens to a much greater extent and more seriously than before. EG *Work on the tunnel began in earnest soon after.* PHRASE

earnings /ɜːnɪŋz/. Your **earnings** are the money that you earn by working. EG *...a tax form which shows your earnings in the previous year.* N PLURAL

earphone /ɪəfəʊn/, **earphones. Earphones** are equipment which you wear over your ears, so that you can listen to a radio or a cassette recorder in private. N COUNT : USU PLURAL

earplug /ɪəplʌg/, **earplugs. Earplugs** are small pieces of soft material which you put into your ears to keep out noise, water, or cold air. N COUNT : USU PLURAL

earring /ɪərɪŋ/, **earrings. Earrings** are pieces of jewellery which you attach to your earlobes. See picture at JEWELLERY. N COUNT

earshot /ɪəʃɒt/. If you are **within earshot** of something, you are close enough to be able to hear it. If you are **out of earshot**, you are too far away to hear it. EG *There was no one within earshot... Keep him out of earshot if possible.* PHRASE

ear-splitting. An **ear-splitting** noise is very loud. EG *...an ear-splitting shriek.* ADJ CLASSIF

earth /ɜːθ/, **earths. 1** The **earth** is **1.1** the planet on which we live. EG *The earth moves around the sun... ...man's life on Earth.* **1.2** the land surface on which we live and move about. EG *For twenty minutes the earth shook.* N PROPER / N SING : the+N

2 Earth is the substance on the land surface of the earth in which plants grow. EG *Beyond the pines were clumps of sand and earth... He was pulling dead roots from the earth.* N UNCOUNT

3 An **earth** is a wire which passes from a piece of electrical equipment into the ground and makes the equipment safe. N COUNT : USU SING

4 You use **on earth** for emphasis **4.1** with words such as 'how', 'why', 'what', or 'where', or with negatives, usually in order to suggest that there is no obvious answer to a question or problem. EG *How on earth do we raise half a million dollars?... He was wondering what on earth he should do.* **4.2** after a noun group that contains a superlative adjective in order to emphasize the adjective. EG *He regarded film-making as the most glamorous job on earth.* PHRASE

5 If you say that something costs **the earth**, you mean that it costs a very large amount of money. EG *If you go to a commercial photographer he'll charge the earth for it.* PHRASE Informal

6 the salt of the earth: see **salt**. • See also **down-to-earth**.

earthen /ɜːθəᵒn/. **1 Earthen** pots or bowls are made of baked clay. ADJ CLASSIF : ATTRIB

2 An **earthen** floor is made of hard earth. EG *The earthen floor was covered with rugs and cushions.* ADJ CLASSIF : ATTRIB

earthenware /ɜːθəᵒnwɛə/. **Earthenware** pots or bowls are made of baked clay. EG *...a big earthenware jar.* ▸ used as a noun. EG *...bowls of glazed earthenware.* ADJ CLASSIF : ATTRIB / ▸ N UNCOUNT

earthly /ɜːθli¹/. **1 Earthly** means happening in the material world of our life on earth and not in any spiritual life or life after death. EG *She believed that our earthly life is all that matters.* ADJ CLASSIF : ATTRIB

2 If you say that there is no **earthly** reason for something, you are emphasizing that there is no reason at all for it. ADJ CLASSIF : ATTRIB

earthquake /ɜːθkweɪk/, **earthquakes.** An **earthquake** is a shaking of the ground caused by movement of the earth's crust. N COUNT

earthworm /ɜːθwɜːm/, **earthworms.** An **earthworm** is a kind of worm that lives under the ground. N COUNT

earthy /ɛːθi¹/. **1** Someone who is **earthy** does not mind talking openly about things such as sex that other people feel embarrassed about. EG *...a buxom, earthy, attractive girl.* ADJ QUALIT

2 Something that is **earthy** looks, smells, or feels like earth. EG *...the subtle, earthy fragrance of wild thyme.* ADJ QUALIT

ease /iːz/, **eases, easing, eased. 1 Ease** is lack of difficulty. EG *She performed this trick with ease... The boxes are designed to fit one inside the other for ease of transportation.* N UNCOUNT

2 If you have a life of **ease**, you have plenty of money and live comfortably. EG *I remember being astounded by the quietness and ease of the place.* N UNCOUNT Formal

3 If you are **at ease**, you feel confident and comfortable. If you are **ill at ease**, you are anxious or worried. EG *He was at ease with strangers... Brody felt ill at ease and patronized... My smiling face set her at ease.* PHRASE

4 If something **eases** a problem or an unpleasant situation, it makes it less difficult or less unpleasant. EG *The bungalows were built in 1946 to ease the housing shortage... ...a powder which eased the pain.* V+O

5 You say that something **eases** when it becomes less in degree, quantity, or intensity. EG *The snow had eased... He had taken the drugs to ease the pain.* V-ERG

6 If you **ease** something somewhere, you move it there slowly and carefully. EG *I eased the back door open.* V+O+A

ease off. If something **eases off**, it becomes less in degree, quantity, or intensity. EG *The rain had eased off.* PHRASAL VB : V+ADV

easel /iːzəᵒl/, **easels.** An **easel** is a wooden frame that supports a picture which an artist is painting. N COUNT

easily /iːzɪli¹/. **1** You use **easily** **1.1** to emphasize that something is very likely to happen. EG *She might easily decide to cancel the whole thing.* **1.2** to emphasize that there can be no doubt that something is the case. EG *This car is easily the most popular model.* **1.3** to say that something happens more quickly than is usual or normal. EG *He tired very easily.* ADV

2 See also **easy**.

east /iːst/; often spelled with a capital letter. **1** The **east** is **1.1** the direction which you look towards in order to see the sun rise. EG *Ben noticed the first faint streaks of dawn in the east.* **1.2** the part of a place or country which is towards the east. EG *...the east of the country.* N SING : the+N

2 East means towards the east or to the east of a place or thing. EG *They were heading almost due east... There were areas of open country east of the river.* ADV AFTER VB

3 The **east** part of a place or country is the part which is towards the east. EG *...East Africa... ...the east coast of South America.* ADJ CLASSIF

4 An **east** wind blows from the east. EG *There was a cold blue sky and a biting east wind.* ADJ CLASSIF : ATTRIB

5 The **East** is also used to refer to **5.1** the countries in the southern and eastern part of Asia, including India, China, and Japan. EG *He was deeply interested in meditation, the East, and yoga.* **5.2** the USSR and other communist countries in the eastern part of Europe. EG *...a breakthrough in East-West relations.* N SING : the+N

6 See also **Far East, Middle East**.

Easter /iːstə/ is a religious festival in March or April when Christians celebrate the death and resurrection of Christ. N UNCOUNT

Easter egg, Easter eggs. An **Easter egg** is a chocolate egg that is given as a present at Easter. N COUNT

easterly /i:stəli[1]/. **1** The most **easterly** of a group of things or places is the one that is farthest to the east. EG *Greenwich is the most easterly of the Thames-side places.* ADJ QUALIT
2 An **easterly** wind blows from the east. ADJ CLASSIF

eastern /i:stə[5]n/. **Eastern** means **1** in or from the east of a region or country. EG *...a small town in Eastern Portugal.* **2** coming from or associated with the people or countries of the East, such as India, China, and Japan. EG *...Eastern philosophy.* **3** coming from or associated with the countries in the east of Europe and the USSR. EG *...the Eastern bloc.* ADJ CLASSIF : ATTRIB

eastward /i:stwəd/, **eastwards. Eastward** or **eastwards** means towards the east. EG *They travelled eastwards.* ▸ **Eastward** is also used as an adjective. EG *...a grassy eastward slope.* ADV AFTER VB; ▸ ADJ CLASSIF : ATTRIB

easy /i:zi[1]/, **easier, easiest. 1** Something that is **easy** can be done without difficulty or effort. EG *The house is easy to keep clean... How easy is it for novelists to get their work published?... This new dancing looked easy.* ◊ **easily.** EG *A baby buggy can be easily carried on a bus or in a car.* ADJ QUALIT; ◊ ADV
2 You can say **easier said than done** to indicate that it is difficult to do what someone has just suggested. EG *'Just relax.' – 'Easier said than done.'* CONVENTION
3 Easy also means relaxed. EG *They have a natural, easy confidence.* ◊ **easily.** EG *...a friendly man who talked freely and easily.* ADJ QUALIT; ◊ ADV
4 An **easy** life or time is comfortable and without any problems. EG *I wanted to make life easier for you.* ADJ QUALIT
5 If you **take it easy** or **take things easy**, you relax and do not do very much. PHRASE Informal
6 If you **go easy on** something, you avoid using too much of it. EG *I suggested to him that he should go easy on publicity for a while.* PHRASE Informal
7 See also **easily**.

easy chair, easy chairs. An **easy chair** is a large, comfortable chair in which you can relax. N COUNT

easy-going. Someone who is **easy-going** is not easily annoyed, worried, or upset. EG *My father was a gentle, easy-going person.* ADJ QUALIT

eat /i:t/, **eats, eating, ate** /eɪt, ɛt/, **eaten.** When you **eat** something, you put it into your mouth, chew it, and swallow it. EG *He began to eat his sandwich... He said he would eat at his hotel.* V+O OR V

eat into. If a substance such as acid or rust **eats into** something, it destroys the surface of the thing. PHRASAL VB : V+PREP

eat out. When you **eat out**, you have a meal at a restaurant. PHRASAL VB : V+ADV

eat up. If you **eat up** your food, you eat it all. EG *He gave her a spoon to eat up the cream with... 'Eat up, girl, that's it,' he said.* PHRASAL VB : V+O+ADV OR V+ADV

eater /i:tə/, **eaters.** You use **eater** to refer to someone who eats in a particular way or eats a particular thing. EG *Tim was a slow eater... ...a meat eater.* N COUNT+SUPP

eau-de-cologne /əʊdə[1]kələʊn/ is a fairly weak, sweet-smelling perfume. N MASS

eaves /i:vz/. The **eaves** of a house are the lower edges of its roof. N PLURAL : the+N

eavesdrop /i:vzdrɒp/, **eavesdrops, eavesdropping, eavesdropped.** If you **eavesdrop**, you listen secretly to what other people are saying. EG *I don't like eavesdropping on people talking on the phone.* V : OFT+on
◊ **eavesdropper** /i:vzdrɒpə/, **eavesdroppers.** EG *There was an eavesdropper on the landing.* ◊ N COUNT

ebb /ɛb/, **ebbs, ebbing, ebbed. 1** If a feeling or a person's strength **ebbs**, it becomes weaker. EG *Only then did the strength ebb from his fingers.* V Literary
2 If something is **at a low ebb**, it is not being very successful or profitable. EG *George's fortunes at this time were at a low ebb.* PHRASE
3 When the tide or the sea **ebbs**, its level falls. ▸ used as a noun. EG *...the stormy ebb and flow of the sea.* V; ▸ N SING : the+N
4 You can talk about **the ebb and flow of** something when you want to describe a situation in which periods of progress and success are followed by periods of trouble or difficulty. EG *...the ebb and flow of political struggle.* PHRASE

ebony /ɛbəni[1]/, **ebonies. 1 Ebony** is a very hard, dark-coloured wood. N UNCOUNT
2 Something that is **ebony** is a very deep black colour. EG *...ebony eyes.* ADJ COLOUR

ebullient /i[1]bʌli[1]ənt/. Someone who is **ebullient** is lively and full of enthusiasm. ADJ QUALIT Formal

eccentric /ɪ[2]ksɛntrɪk/ , **eccentrics. 1** Someone who is **eccentric** has habits or opinions that other people think strange. EG *...a slightly eccentric Frenchman... ...eccentric right-wing views.* ADJ QUALIT
◊ **eccentricity** /ɛksɛntrɪsɪ[1]ti[1]/, **eccentricities.** EG *...the eccentricity of Rose's behaviour... ...her husband's eccentricities.* ◊ N UNCOUNT OR N COUNT
2 An **eccentric** is a person who has habits or opinions which other people think strange. EG *...a bunch of harmless eccentrics.* N COUNT

ecclesiastical /ɪ[2]kli:ziæstɪkə[0]l/ means belonging to or connected with the Christian Church. ADJ CLASSIF

echelon /ɛʃə[0]lɒn/, **echelons.** An **echelon** is a level of power or responsibility in an organization. EG *...the higher echelons of the party.* N COUNT+SUPP Formal

echo /ɛkəʊ/, **echoes, echoing, echoed. 1** An **echo** is **1.1** a sound which is caused when a loud, sharp noise is reflected off a surface such as a wall. EG *Judy listened to the echo of her shoes clicking on the marble floors.* N COUNT **1.2** an expression of an attitude or opinion which has already been expressed by someone else. EG *The echo of public sentiment in Congress was inevitable.* N COUNT : USU+of **1.3** a small detail or feature which reminds you of something else. EG *...echoes of the past.* N COUNT+SUPP
2 A sound that **echoes** is reflected off a surface such as a wall so that it can be heard again after the original sound has stopped. EG *The cry echoed back from the mountain.* V : USU+A
3 A place that **echoes** is one in which a sound continues or is repeated after the original sound has stopped. EG *The bamboo grove echoed with the screams of monkeys.* ◊ **echoing.** EG *...echoing halls.* V : USU+A; ◊ ADJ CLASSIF
4 If you **echo** something that someone has said, you repeat it. EG *'They lived in the open air, simply under a tree.' – 'Under a tree,' echoed Etta.* V+O OR V+QUOTE

éclair /i[2]klɛə/, **éclairs.** An **éclair** is a long thin cake made of very light pastry, which is filled with cream and usually has chocolate on top. N COUNT

eclectic /ɪ[2]klɛktɪk/ means using what seems to be best or most useful from several different sets of ideas or beliefs. EG *...a doctrine that drew upon an eclectic mixture of both Western and Asian thought.* ADJ QUALIT Formal

eclipse /i[1]klɪps/, **eclipses, eclipsing, eclipsed. 1** When there is an **eclipse** of the sun, the moon comes between the earth and the sun, so that for a short time you cannot see part or all of the sun. When there is an **eclipse** of the moon, the earth comes between the sun and the moon, so that for a short time the earth's shadow covers the moon. N COUNT
2 If someone or something suffers an **eclipse**, they lose some or all of their importance or influence. EG *...the eclipse of the national radical press.* N SING : USU+POSS
3 If something **eclipses** something else, the first thing is more important or influential than the second thing, so that the second thing is no longer noticed. EG *Less talented artists were totally eclipsed.* V+O

ecologist /i[1]kɒlə[7]dʒɪst/, **ecologists.** An **ecologist** is **1** a person who studies the pattern and balance of relationships between plants, animals, people, and their environment. EG *Ecologists estimate that* N COUNT

Would you be pleased if your mother eavesdropped on your conversation?

half of the ancient woodlands in Britain are in danger of extinction. **2** a person who believes that the environment and natural resources should be used properly and be preserved.

ecology /i[1]kɒlədʒi[1]/. **1** When you talk about the **ecology** of a place, you are referring to the pattern and balance of relationships between all the plants, animals, and people there. EG *...the delicate ecology of the rainforest.* ◊ **ecological** /iːkəlɒdʒɪkə[0]l/. EG *Use of nitrogen fertilizers has damaged the ecological balance in the lake.* ◊ **ecologically.** EG *...an ecologically sound system of farm management.* — N UNCOUNT; ◊ ADJ CLASSIF : ATTRIB; ◊ SUBMOD

2 Ecology is the study of the relationships between plants, animals, people, and their environment, and the balances between these relationships. EG *...the most recent research in ecology.*

economic /iːkənɒmɪk, ɛk-/, **economics. 1 Economic** means concerned with the organization of the money, industry, and trade of a country, region, or social group. EG *What has gone wrong with the economic system during the last ten years?... ...a period of economic and industrial crisis.* — ADJ CLASSIF : ATTRIB

◊ **economically.** EG *Katanga was extremely unevenly developed economically.* — ◊ ADV

2 A business that is **economic** produces a profit. EG *We have to keep fares high enough to make it economic for the service to continue.* — ADJ QUALIT

3 Economics is the study of the way in which money, industry, and trade are organized in a society. EG *...a degree in economics.* — N UNCOUNT

4 The **economics** of a society or industry is the system of organizing money and trade in it. EG *...the economics of the timber trade.* — N UNCOUNT +SUPP

economical /iːkənɒmɪkə[0]l, ɛk-/. **1** Something that is **economical** does not require a lot of money to operate. EG *This system was extremely economical because it ran on half-price electricity.* — ADJ QUALIT

◊ **economically.** EG *This courier service could be most economically operated.* — ◊ ADV

2 If someone is **economical**, they spend money carefully and sensibly. ◊ **economically.** EG *We live very economically.* — ADJ QUALIT; ◊ ADV

3 Economical also means using the minimum amount of something that is necessary. EG *She spoke in short, economical sentences.* — ADJ QUALIT

◊ **economically.** EG *The book is very economically written.* — ◊ ADV

economist /i[1]kɒnəmɪst/, **economists.** An **economist** is a person who studies, teaches, or writes about economics. — N COUNT

economize /i[1]kɒnəmaɪz/, **economizes, economizing, economized;** also spelled **economise.** If you **economize**, you save money by spending it very carefully and not buying expensive things. EG *The loss of business was so great that they had to economize on staff.* — V

economy /i[1]kɒnəmi[1]/, **economies. 1** The **economy** of a country or region is **1.1** the system according to which money, industry, and trade are organized there. EG *New England's economy is still largely based on manufacturing.* **1.2** the wealth that it gets from business and industry. EG *Unofficial strikes were damaging the British economy.* — N COUNT : USU SING

2 Economy is careful spending or the careful use of things in order to save money. EG *His seaside shack was small, for reasons of economy.* — N UNCOUNT

3 If you make **economies**, you save money, by not spending it on unnecessary things. — N PLURAL

ecstasy /ɛkstəsi[1]/, **ecstasies. 1 Ecstasy** is a feeling of very great happiness. EG *On both faces were expressions of ecstasy.* — N UNCOUNT

2 If you go **into ecstasies** about something, you show how delighted you are about it. EG *Her mere proximity would send him into ecstasies.* — PHRASE

ecstatic /ɪ[2]kstætɪk/. If you are **ecstatic**, you feel very enthusiastic and happy. EG *Eddie was ecstatic over his new rifle... ...a wild ecstatic happiness.* — ADJ QUALIT

◊ **ecstatically.** EG *...children jumping ecstatically up and down.* — ◊ ADV

ecumenical /iːkjuːmɛnɪkə[0]l, ɛk-/ is used to describe activities, ideas, and movements which try to unite different Christian Churches. EG *...an ecumenical institute.* — ADJ CLASSIF; Formal

-ed. 1 -ed is used to form the past tense and past participle of many verbs. EG *He blinked in the bright light... Tim dodged round the car... They had arrived two hours earlier.* — SUFFIX

2 -ed is also added to nouns to form adjectives. These adjectives describe someone or something as having a particular feature or features. For example, a bearded man is a man with a beard and a fenced area is an area with a fence round it. Adjectives like these are often not defined in this dictionary, but are treated with the related nouns. EG *She put on a feathered hat.* — SUFFIX

eddy /ɛdi[1]/, **eddies, eddying, eddied.** If water or wind **eddies**, it moves round and round in no particular direction. EG *The wind whipped and eddied around the buildings.* ▸ used as a noun. EG *...every trick and eddy of the tide.* — V : USU+A; ▸ N COUNT

edge /ɛdʒ/, **edges, edging, edged. 1** The **edge** of something is the place or line where it stops and another thing begins. EG *Little children played in the sand at the water's edge... They lived in a cottage on the edge of the moors.* — N COUNT : USU+SUPP

2 The **edge** of a flat, solid object is its narrow side. EG *...the edge of a ruler.* — N COUNT : USU+SUPP

3 If something **is edged** with a particular thing, it has that thing along its edge. EG *...a beautiful garden edged with flowering trees.* — V+O : USU PASS+*with*

4 If you **edge** somewhere, you move there very slowly. EG *He edged away from the thug... I edged my way to the window.* — V+A OR V+O+A

5 If people are on the **edge** of an event or situation, it is likely to happen to them soon. EG *The world had been brought to the edge of war.* — N SING : *the*+N

6 If you say that there is an **edge** to someone's voice, you mean that they sound angry or bitter. — N SING : *an*+N

7 If you are **on edge**, you are tense, nervous, and unable to relax. EG *She was worried that the prospect was setting his nerves on edge.* — PHRASE

8 If you have an **edge** over someone, you have an advantage that makes you more likely to be successful than them. — N SING : OFT+*over*

edgeways /ɛdʒweɪz/. If you say that you **cannot get a word in edgeways**, you mean that you are unable to say anything because someone else is talking too much. — PHRASE; Informal

edging /ɛdʒɪŋ/, **edgings.** An **edging** is something that is put along the sides of something else in order to make it look attractive. EG *...a blouse trimmed with bows and lace edgings.* — N COUNT

edgy /ɛdʒi[1]/. When you are **edgy**, you are nervous and anxious. EG *Rick seemed very edgy.* — ADJ QUALIT

edible /ɛdɪ[1]bə[0]l/. Something that is **edible** is safe to eat and not poisonous. EG *...edible mushrooms.* — ADJ CLASSIF

edict /iːdɪkt/, **edicts.** An **edict** is a command given by someone in authority. EG *I told the factory inspector we would defy his edict... ...banned by government edict.* — N COUNT; Formal

edifice /ɛdɪfɪs/, **edifices.** An **edifice** is **1** a large and impressive building. EG *...a huge Victorian edifice.* **2** a system of beliefs or a traditional institution. EG *The whole edifice of modern civilization is beginning to sway.* — N COUNT; Formal; N COUNT : USU+SUPP; Formal

edify /ɛdɪfaɪ/, **edifies, edifying, edified.** If something **edifies** you, it teaches you something useful or interesting. EG *...a series of popular talks intended to edify and entertain.* ◊ **edifying.** EG *He may come out with all sorts of edifying sentiments.* — V+O : NO IMPER; Formal; ◊ ADJ QUALIT

◊ **edification** /ɛdɪfɪkeɪʃə[0]n/. EG *...books bought for instruction or edification.* — ◊ N UNCOUNT

edit /ɛdɪt/, **edits, editing, edited. 1** If you **edit** a text, you examine it and make corrections to it so that it is suitable for publication. ◊ **edited.** EG *This is the edited text.* — V+O OR V; ◊ ADJ CLASSIF

2 If you **edit** a book, you collect several pieces of writing by different authors and prepare them for — V+O publication. EG *...'The Save and Prosper Book of Money,' edited by Margaret Allen.*

3 If you **edit** a film or a television or radio programme, you choose some of the material that has been filmed or recorded and arrange it in a particular order. V+O

4 Someone who **edits** a newspaper or magazine is in charge of it. V+O

edition /ɪ[2]dɪʃə[0]n/, **editions.** An **edition** is **1** a particular version of a book, magazine, or newspaper that is printed at one time. EG *...the city edition of the New York Times.* N COUNT+SUPP **2** a single television or radio programme that is one of a series. EG *...tonight's edition of Kaleidoscope.*

editor /ɛdɪtə/, **editors.** An **editor** is **1** a person who is in charge of a newspaper or magazine. EG *....the editor of a local newspaper.* N COUNT **2** a journalist who is responsible for a particular section of a newspaper or magazine. EG *...the foreign editor.* N COUNT: OFT+SUPP **3** a person whose job is to check texts and make changes and corrections before they are published. N COUNT

4 a person who prepares a film or a radio or television programme by selecting some of what has been filmed or recorded and putting it in a particular order. N COUNT

editorial /ɛdɪtɔːrɪəl/, **editorials. 1 Editorial** means **1.1** involved in preparing a newspaper, magazine, or book for publication. EG *Hearst expanded his editorial staff.* ADJ CLASSIF: ATTRIB **1.2** involving the attitudes, opinions, and contents of a newspaper, magazine, or television programme. EG *...the paper's editorial policy.*

2 An **editorial** is an article in a newspaper which gives the opinion of the editor or publisher on a topic or item of news. N COUNT

editorship /ɛdɪtə[8]ʃɪp/. The **editorship** of a newspaper or magazine is the position and authority of its editor. EG *The paper was considerably improved under McPherson's editorship.* N SING: USU+POSS

educate /ɛdjə[4]keɪt/, **educates, educating, educated. 1** When someone, especially a child, **is educated**, he or she is taught at a school or college. EG *He was educated at Eton.* V+O

2 Educated people have reached a high standard of learning. EG *...an educated man.* ADJ QUALIT

3 To **educate** people also means to teach them better ways of doing something or a better way of living. EG *Not enough is being done to educate smokers about the benefits of stopping the habit.* V+O

education /ɛdjə[4]keɪʃə[0]n/ consists of teaching people various subjects at a school or college. EG *...the government's policy on higher education.* N UNCOUNT

educational /ɛdjə[4]keɪʃə[0]nəl, -ʃənə[0]l/ means concerned with and related to education. EG *...an educational institution.* ADJ CLASSIF ◊ **educationally.** EG *...a school for the educationally subnormal.* ◊ ADV

educationalist /ɛdjə[4]keɪʃə[0]nəlɪst/, **educationalists.** An **educationalist** is a specialist in the theories and methods of education. N COUNT

educator /ɛdjə[4]keɪtə/, **educators.** An **educator** is a person who educates people. EG *He was a distinguished educator.* N COUNT Formal

EEC /iː iː siː/. The **EEC** is an organization of Western European countries, including the UK, that have joint policies on matters such as trade and agriculture. 'EEC' is an abbreviation for 'European Economic Community'. N PROPER: *the*+N

eel /iːl/, **eels.** An **eel** is a long, thin, snake-like fish. N COUNT

eerie /ɪəri[1]/. Something that is **eerie** is strange and frightening. EG *...the eerie feeling that someone was watching me.* ADJ QUALIT ◊ **eerily.** EG *The lights gleamed eerily.* ◊ ADV

efface /ɪ[1]feɪs/, **effaces, effacing, effaced.** To **efface** something means to rub it out or remove it. EG *In the sand, all the footprints had effaced one another... He hoped to efface the memory of an embarrassing speech.* V+O Formal

effect /ɪ[1]fɛkt/, **effects, effecting, effected. 1** An **effect** is **1.1** a change or event that is caused by something or is the result of something. EG *This has the effect of separating students from teachers... ...the effect of noise on people in the factories... These measures did have some effect on rural poverty.* N COUNT OR N UNCOUNT: OFT+*on* **1.2** an impression that a speaker or artist deliberately creates. EG *Don't move, or you'll destroy the whole effect.* N COUNT ● If you do something **for effect**, you do it in order to impress people. EG *...a pause for effect.* ● PHRASE

2 You add **in effect** to a statement to indicate that it is not precisely accurate but it is a reasonable description or summary of a situation. EG *In effect he has no choice.* ADV SEN

3 You use **to this effect**, **to that effect**, or **to the effect that** when you are summarizing what someone has said, rather than repeating their actual words. EG *...a rumour to the effect that he had been drunk... He said, 'No, you fool, the other way!' or words to that effect.* PHRASE

4 When something **takes effect** or **is put into effect**, it starts to happen or to have some result. EG *The tax cuts take effect on July 1st... Signing the agreement was one thing, putting it into effect was another.* PHRASE

5 If you **effect** something, you succeed in causing it to happen. EG *Production was halted until repairs could be effected.* V+O Formal

6 See also **sound effect**.

effective /ɪ[1]fɛktɪv/. **1** Something that is **effective** works well and produces the results that were intended. EG *...the most effective ways of reducing pollution... In order to be effective we need your support.* ADJ QUALIT ◊ **effectiveness.** EG *Methods vary in effectiveness.* ◊ N UNCOUNT

2 Effective also means having a particular role or result in practice, though not officially. EG *He assumed effective command of the armed forces.* ADJ CLASSIF: ATTRIB

3 When a law or an agreement becomes **effective**, it begins officially to apply or be valid. EG *...a ceasefire, to become effective as soon as possible.* ADJ PRED

effectively /ɪ[1]fɛktɪvli[1]/. **1** If something works **effectively**, it works well. EG *...an attempt to make the system work more effectively.* ADV

2 You can also use **effectively** to indicate that what you are saying is a reasonable summary of a situation, although it is not precisely accurate. EG *The television was on, effectively ruling out conversation.* ADV

effeminate /ɪ[1]fɛmɪnə[1]t/. When people describe a man or a boy as **effeminate**, they mean that he behaves, looks, or sounds like a woman or girl; an offensive word. ADJ QUALIT

effete /ɪ[1]fiːt/. Someone who is **effete** is weak and powerless. EG *...an effete middle-class aesthete.* ADJ QUALIT Formal

efficient /ɪ[1]fɪʃə[0]nt/. A person, machine, or organization that is **efficient** does a job well and successfully, without wasting time or energy. EG *Engines and cars can be made more efficient... You need a very efficient production manager.* ADJ QUALIT ◊ **efficiently.** EG *You must work more efficiently.* ◊ ADV ◊ **efficiency** /ɪ[1]fɪʃə[0]nsi[1]/. EG *...an increase in business efficiency.* ◊ N UNCOUNT

effigy /ɛfɪ[1]dʒi[1]/, **effigies.** An **effigy** is **1** a roughly made figure that represents someone you strongly dislike. EG *The students burned effigies of the president.* N COUNT **2** a statue or carving of a famous person. EG *...unusually good fifteenth-century alabaster effigies.* Formal

effluent /ɛfluənt/, **effluents. Effluent** is liquid waste material that comes out of factories or sewage works. EG *Our rivers are being poisoned by industrial waste and untreated effluent.* N UNCOUNT OR N COUNT Formal

effort /ɛfət/, **efforts. 1** If you make an **effort** to do something, you try very hard to do it. EG *Little effort has been made to investigate this claim...* N UNCOUNT OR N COUNT

What kind of place would you describe as eerie?

...*the efforts of governments to restrain inflation...* ...*a waste of effort.*

2 If you do something with **effort**, it is difficult for you to do. EG *Robert spoke with effort.* N UNCOUNT

3 If you describe an object or an action as a poor **effort** or a feeble **effort**, you mean that it has not been well made or well done. EG *It was a rather amateurish effort.* N COUNT : ADJ+N

4 If you say that an action is an **effort**, you mean that an unusual amount of physical or mental energy is needed to do it. EG *Getting up was an effort.* N SING : *an*+N

5 If you **make the effort** to do something, you use the extra energy that is needed to do it, even though you may not really want to. EG *Having made the effort to find them, I was unwilling to let them go.* PHRASE

6 If you say that something is **worth the effort**, you mean that it will justify the energy that you have spent or will spend on it. EG *It's not worth the effort to get them to do the washing up.* PHRASE

effortless /ɛfətlɪ²s/. You describe an action as **effortless** when it is achieved very easily. EG *His rise in politics appears to have been effortless.* ADJ QUALIT
◊ **effortlessly.** EG *He finished his MA thesis almost effortlessly.* ◊ ADV

effrontery /i¹frʌntə⁰ri¹/ is bold, rude, or cheeky behaviour. EG *He has the effrontery to use my office without asking.* N UNCOUNT Formal

effusive /i¹fjuːsɪv/. A person who is **effusive** expresses pleasure, gratitude, or approval enthusiastically. EG *Mrs Schiff was effusive in her congratulations... ...an effusive welcome.* ADJ QUALIT Formal
◊ **effusively.** EG *The doctor thanked him effusively.* ◊ ADV

EFL /iː ɛf ɛl/ is used to describe things that are connected with the teaching of English to people whose first language is not English. **EFL** is an abbreviation for 'English as a Foreign Language'. EG *...EFL dictionaries... ...an EFL teacher.*

e.g. /iː dʒiː/ is an abbreviation that means 'for example'. It is used before a noun, or to introduce another sentence. EG *...woollens and other delicate fabrics (e.g. lace)... He specialised in trivial knowledge, e.g. that three MPs had glass eyes.*

egalitarian /i¹gælɪtɛərɪən/. In an **egalitarian** system or society, all people are equal and have the same rights. EG *...a more egalitarian educational system... ...egalitarian principles.* ADJ QUALIT Formal

egg /ɛg/, **eggs, egging, egged.** An **egg** is **1** the rounded object produced by a female bird from which a baby bird later emerges. Some other creatures also lay eggs. EG *...birds' eggs... The alligator then lays her eggs... These eggs hatch into larvae.* N COUNT **2** a hen's egg considered as food. EG *...a dozen eggs... ...bacon and egg.* N COUNT OR N UNCOUNT

egg on. If you **egg** someone **on**, you encourage them to do something daring or foolish. EG *Egged on by Iago, Othello makes up his mind to kill Desdemona.* PHRASAL VB : V+O+ADV

eggcup /ɛgkʌp/, **eggcups.** An **eggcup** is a small container in which you put a boiled egg while you eat it. N COUNT

eggplant /ɛgplɑːnt/, **eggplants.** An **eggplant** is an aubergine. EG *I've made you that eggplant dip you like.* N COUNT OR N UNCOUNT American

eggshell /ɛgʃɛl/, **eggshells.** An **eggshell** is the hard covering round an egg. N COUNT OR N UNCOUNT

egg-timer, egg-timers. An **egg-timer** is a device that helps you measure the time needed to boil an egg. N COUNT

ego /iːgəʊ, ɛgəʊ/, **egos.** Your **ego** is your opinion of your own worth. EG *It was a blow to my ego, and meant I would have to look for a new job.* N COUNT

egoism /iːgəʊɪzə⁰m, ɛg-/ is the same as egotism. N UNCOUNT

egoist /iːgəʊɪst, ɛg-/, **egoists.** An **egoist** is the same as an egotist. N COUNT

egoistic /iːgəʊɪstɪk, ɛg-/ means the same as egotistic. ADJ QUALIT

egotism /iːgətɪzə⁰m, ɛg-/ is behaviour which shows that you only care about yourself, or that you believe that you are more important than other people. EG *It was a piece of blatant egotism.* N UNCOUNT

egotist /iːgətɪst, ɛg-/, **egotists.** An **egotist** is a person who acts selfishly and believes that he or she is more important than other people. N COUNT

egotistic /iːgətɪstɪk, ɛg-/. If you are **egotistic** or **egotistical**, you believe that you are more important than other people. EG *Success makes a man egotistic.* ADJ QUALIT

eh /eɪ/. You say **eh 1** when you are asking someone to reply to you or to agree with you. EG *Looks good, eh?... Who knows we're here? Eh?* **2** when you are asking someone to repeat what they have just said because you did not hear it the first time. EG *'Well, I still have a chequebook.' - 'Eh?' - 'I said I still have a chequebook.'*

eiderdown /aɪdədaʊn/, **eiderdowns.** An **eiderdown** is a bed covering that is filled with small soft feathers or warm material. N COUNT

eight /eɪt/ **eights. Eight** is the number 8: see the entry headed NUMBER. EG *...eight months of exile.* NUMBER

eighteen /eɪtiːn/ **eighteens. Eighteen** is the number 18: see the entry headed NUMBER. NUMBER

eighteenth /eɪtiːnθ/ **eighteenths.** The **eighteenth** item in a series is the one that you count as number eighteen: see the entry headed NUMBER. EG *...the early eighteenth century.* ORDINAL

eighth /eɪtθ/, **eighths. 1** The **eighth** item in a series is the one that you count as number eight: see the entry headed NUMBER. EG *...his room on the eighth floor.* ORDINAL

2 An **eighth** is one of eight equal parts of something. EG *It was about an eighth of an inch thick.* N COUNT : USU+*of*

eightieth /eɪti¹ɪθ/ **eightieth.** The **eightieth** item in a series is the one that you count as number eighty: see the entry headed NUMBER. EG *I saw him at his eightieth birthday party.* ORDINAL

eighty /eɪti¹/ **eighties. Eighty** is the number 80: see the entry headed NUMBER. NUMBER

either /aɪðə, iːðə/. **1** You use **either 1.1** in front of the first of two or more alternatives, when you are stating the only possibilities or choices that there are. The other alternative is introduced by 'or'. EG *I was expecting you either today or tomorrow... You either love him or you hate him... Either you eat your spinach or you go without ice cream.* **1.2** in a negative statement in front of the first of two alternatives, when you are emphasizing that the negative statement refers to both the alternatives. EG *Dr Kirk, you're not being either frank or fair... I wouldn't dream of asking either Mary or my mother to take on the responsibility.* CONJ

2 You can also use **either 2.1** to refer to one of two possible things, people, or situations, when you want to say that it does not matter which one is chosen or considered. EG *One speech by either of them stating the facts would have ended his uncertainty... Either is acceptable... Either way, I can't lose.* PRON OR DET **2.2** in a negative statement to refer to each of two things, people, or situations, when you are emphasizing that the negative statement includes both of them. EG *'Which one do you want?' - 'I don't want either.'... There was no sound from either of the flats... She could not see either man.* PRON OR DET : WITH BROAD NEG

3 You can use **either** by itself at the end of a negative statement **3.1** to indicate that there is a similarity between a person or thing that you have just mentioned and one that was mentioned earlier, for example that the same fact is true about both of them. EG *'I haven't got that address.' - 'No, I haven't got it either'... I can't play golf either.* **3.2** to indicate that you are adding an extra piece of information. EG *Not only was he ugly, he was not very interesting to talk to either.* ADV : WITH BROAD NEG

4 You can use **either** before a noun that refers to each of two things when you are talking about both of them. EG *The two ladies sat in large armchairs* DET *on either side of the stage... In either case the answer is the same.*

eject /i[1]dʒɛkt/, **ejects, ejecting, ejected. 1** To **eject** something means to push or send it out, usually with force. EG *The machine ejected a handful of cigarettes.* V+O

2 If you **eject** someone from a place, you force them to leave. *We reserve the right to eject any objectionable person.* V+O

eke /i:k/, **ekes, eking, eked. 1** If you **eke** something **out**, you make your supply of it last as long as possible. EG *Migrants send home cash that helps eke out low village incomes.* PHRASAL VB : V+O+ADV

2 If you **eke out** a living, you manage to survive with very little money. EG *In his early days he eked out a precarious living from designing book jackets.* PHRASAL VB : V+O+ADV

elaborate, elaborates, elaborating, elaborated; pronounced /i[1]læbərə[1]t/ when it is an adjective and /i[1]læbəreɪt/ when it is a verb.

1 Something that is **elaborate** is very complex because it has a lot of different parts. *...the elaborate network of canals... ...an elaborate ceremony.* ADJ QUALIT

◇ **elaborately.** EG *Every inch of its surface was elaborately decorated.* ◇ ADV

2 If you **elaborate** on an idea, or if you **elaborate** it, you give more details about it. EG *It isn't a statement I want to elaborate on... Some of these points will have to be further elaborated as we go along.* V+*on* OR V+O ◇ **elaboration** /i[1]læbəreɪʃə[0]n/, **elaborations.** EG *An elaboration of this idea will follow in Chapter 12.* ◇ N COUNT OR N UNCOUNT

3 To **elaborate** something also means to make it more complex. EG *This type of plan could be elaborated.* V+O

elapse /i[1]læps/, **elapses, elapsing, elapsed.** When a period of time **elapses**, it passes. EG *Too much time had elapsed since I had attempted any serious study.* V Formal

elastic /i[1]læstɪk/. **1 Elastic** is a rubber material that stretches when you pull it and returns to its original size and shape when you let it go. EG *It snapped back like a piece of elastic.* N UNCOUNT

2 Something that is **elastic** is able to stretch easily and then return to its original size and shape. EG *...a softer, more elastic and lighter material.* ADJ QUALIT

◇ **elasticity** /i:læstɪsɪ[1]ti[1], ɪlæstɪsɪ[1]ti[1]/. EG *The skin eventually loses its elasticity.* ◇ N UNCOUNT : USU+SUPP

3 Elastic ideas and policies can change in order to suit new circumstances. EG *Liberal policy was sufficiently elastic to accommodate both views.* ADJ QUALIT

elastic band, elastic bands. An **elastic band** is the same as a rubber band. N COUNT

elated /i[1]leɪtɪ[2]d/. If you are **elated**, you are extremely happy and excited. EG *The members left the meeting elated.* ADJ QUALIT

elation /i[1]leɪʃə[0]n/ is a feeling of great happiness and excitement. EG *This little incident filled me with elation.* N UNCOUNT

elbow /ɛlbəʊ/, **elbows, elbowing, elbowed. 1** Your **elbow** is the part in the middle of your arm where your arm bends. See picture at THE HUMAN BODY. EG *She sat with her elbows on the table.* N COUNT

2 The **elbow** on a sleeve is the part that covers your elbow. EG *...an old suit whose jacket had worn through at the elbows.* N COUNT

3 If you **elbow** someone away, you use one of your elbows to push them out of the way. EG *Ralph elbowed him to one side.* V+O+A

elder /ɛldə/, **elders. 1** The **elder** of two people is the one who was born first. EG *...his elder brother... Posy was the elder of the two.* ADJ QUALIT : COMPAR

2 Your **elders** are people who are older than you. EG *Their father had taught them to show respect towards their elders.* N COUNT : USU+POSS Formal

3 The **elders** of a tribe are the older members who have influence and authority. N COUNT

4 The **elders** of some Christian churches are people who hold positions of responsibility in these churches. N COUNT

5 An **elder** is also a bush or small tree with small white flowers and red or black berries. N COUNT

elderly /ɛldəli[1]/. **1 Elderly** people are old. EG *The coach was full of elderly ladies.* ADJ QUALIT

2 You can refer to old people in general as the **elderly**. EG *...unless the elderly are adequately cared for.* N PLURAL : *the*+N

3 Something that is **elderly** is rather old or old-fashioned. EG *...elderly oil-fired steam engines.* ADJ QUALIT

eldest /ɛldɪ[2]st/. The **eldest** person in a group is the one who was born before all the others. EG *Her eldest son was killed in the First War... Gladys was the eldest of four children.* ADJ QUALIT : SUPERL

elect /i[1]lɛkt/, **elects, electing, elected. 1** When people **elect** someone, they choose that person to represent them, by voting. EG *They met to elect a president... Why should we elect him Mayor?... You could be elected as an MP.* V+O : OFT+*as/to*; ALSO V+O+C ◇ **elected.** EG *...a democratically elected government.* ◇ ADJ CLASSIF : ATTRIB

2 If you **elect** to do something, you choose to do it. EG *...the questions he had elected to answer.* V+*to*-INF Formal

election /i[1]lɛkʃə[0]n/, **elections. 1** An **election** is an organized process in which people vote to choose a person or group of people to hold an official position or to represent them in government. EG *Labour did badly in the election... I may vote for her at the next election.* ● See also **by-election, general election.** N COUNT OR N UNCOUNT

2 When you talk about the **election** of a person or a political party, you are referring to their success in winning an election. EG *...within two months of her election as Tory leader... ...after the election of Mr Heath's government in 1970.* N SING : USU+POSS

elector /i[1]lɛktə/, **electors.** The **electors** are the people who have the right to vote in an election. N COUNT

electoral /i[1]lɛktə[0]rəl/ means intended for an election, happening in an election, or resulting from an election. EG *...a contribution to their electoral funds... ...electoral success.* ADJ CLASSIF : ATTRIB

electorate /i[1]lɛktə[0]rə[1]t/, **electorates.** The **electorate** of a country or area is all the people in it who have the right to vote in an election. EG *The Government was responsible to the electorate as a whole.* N COUNT : USU *the*+N

electric /i[1]lɛktrɪk/. **1** An **electric** device or machine works by means of electricity. EG *...an electric fan.* ADJ CLASSIF

2 Electric is used to describe other things that relate to electricity. EG *...electric current.* ADJ CLASSIF : ATTRIB

3 If you describe a situation as **electric**, you mean that people are very excited. EG *When Drew arrived, the atmosphere was already electric.* ADJ CLASSIF

electrical /i[1]lɛktrɪkə[0]l/. **1 Electrical** devices or machines work by means of electricity. EG *...electrical equipment.* ADJ CLASSIF ◇ **electrically.** EG *...electrically operated windows.* ◇ ADV

2 Electrical engineers and industries are involved in the production or maintenance of electricity or electrical goods. ADJ CLASSIF : ATTRIB

electric chair. The **electric chair** is a method of execution, used in some parts of the United States, in which a person is strapped to a special chair and killed by a powerful electric current. N SING : *the*+N

electrician /ɪlɛktrɪʃə[0]n, i:lɛk-/, **electricians.** An **electrician** is a person whose job is to install and repair electrical equipment. N COUNT

electricity /ɪlɛktrɪsɪ[1]ti[1], i:lɛk-/ is a form of energy that is used for heating and lighting, and to provide power for machines in houses and factories. EG *They generate the electricity in power stations... There were no telephones and no electricity.* N UNCOUNT

electric shock, electric shocks. An **electric shock** is a sudden painful feeling that you get when N COUNT

> If you have to eke out your money, are you likely to feel elated?

you touch something which is connected to a supply of electricity.

electrify /iˈlɛktrɪfaɪ/, **electrifies, electrifying, electrified.** 1 If something **electrifies** you, it excites you a lot. EG *...the news that had electrified the world.* ◊ **electrifying.** EG *...an electrifying speech.* V+O ◊ ADJ QUALIT

2 When something **is electrified**, it is altered so that it operates by electricity or is connected to a supply of electricity. EG *British Rail plans to electrify over 50 per cent of its network.* ◊ **electrified.** EG *...electrified wire netting.* V+O : USU PASS ◊ ADJ CLASSIF : ATTRIB

electrocute /iˈlɛktrəˈkju:t/, **electrocutes, electrocuting, electrocuted.** If you **electrocute** yourself or if you **are electrocuted**, you are killed or badly injured by touching something that is connected to a source of electricity. EG *Don't touch that wire, you'll electrocute yourself!... He fell and was electrocuted on the rails.* V+O OR V-REFL

electrode /iˈlɛktrəʊd/, **electrodes.** An **electrode** is a small piece of metal or other substance that is used to take an electric current to or from a source of power or to or from a piece of equipment. N COUNT

electron /iˈlɛktrɒn/, **electrons.** An **electron** is a tiny particle of matter that is smaller than an atom. N COUNT Technical

electronic /ɪlɛktrɒnɪk, i:lɛk-/, **electronics.** 1 An **electronic** device has transistors, silicon chips, or valves which control and change the electric current passing through it. EG *...electronic equipment.* ADJ CLASSIF

2 An **electronic** process or activity involves the use of electronic devices. EG *...electronic surveillance.* ◊ **electronically.** EG *Each vehicle might be electronically tracked.* ADJ CLASSIF : ATTRIB ◊ ADV

3 **Electronics** is 3.1 the technology of using transistors, silicon chips, or valves, especially in the manufacture of devices such as radios, televisions, and computers. EG *...the British electronics industry.* N UNCOUNT 3.2 equipment that consists of electronic devices. EG *The boat carries a mass of sophisticated electronics.* N PLURAL

elegant /ɛlɪgənt/. 1 Someone or something that is **elegant** is pleasing and graceful in appearance. EG *...a tall, elegant woman... ...the little church with its elegant square tower.* ◊ **elegantly.** EG *...an elegantly dressed woman.* ◊ **elegance** /ɛlɪgəns/. EG *The street had retained some of its old elegance.* ADJ QUALIT ◊ ADV ◊ N UNCOUNT

2 You can say that an idea or plan is **elegant** when it is simple, clear, and clever. EG *His proposal has an elegant simplicity.* ADJ QUALIT

elegiac /ɛlɪdʒaɪək/. Something that is **elegiac** expresses or shows sadness. EG *...an elegiac mood.* ADJ CLASSIF Literary

elegy /ɛlɪdʒiˈ/, **elegies.** An **elegy** is a sad poem, often about someone who has died. N COUNT

element /ɛləˈmənt/, **elements.** 1 An **element** of something is a single part which combines with others to make up a whole. EG *...the different elements in the play... ...the basic elements of a job... Surprise would be an essential element in any such action.* N COUNT+SUPP

2 The **elements** of a subject are the first and most important things that you need to know about it. EG *...the elements of reading.* N PLURAL +SUPP

3 When you talk about **elements** within a society or organization, you are referring to groups of people who have similar aims, beliefs, or habits. EG *...sympathetic elements outside the party.* N COUNT+SUPP

4 If something has an **element** of a particular quality or emotion, it has a certain amount of this quality or emotion. EG *It contains an element of truth... ...to add an element of suspense and mystery to my novels.* N PART

5 An **element** is a substance that consists of only one type of atom. For example, gold, oxygen, and carbon are elements. N COUNT

6 The **element** in an electric fire or water heater is the metal part which changes the electric current into heat. N COUNT

7 You can refer to the weather, especially when it is stormy, as the **elements**. EG *Her raincoat was buttoned tight against the elements.* N PLURAL : the+N

8 If you say that someone is **in** their **element**, you mean that they are doing something that they enjoy and do well. PHRASE

elemental /ɛləˈmɛntəˈl/. **Elemental** feelings and behaviour are simple, basic, and forceful. EG *...outbursts of elemental rage.* ADJ QUALIT Literary

elementary /ɛləˈmɛntəˈri/. Something that is **elementary** 1 is very simple and straightforward. EG *Most towns had taken some elementary precautions.* 2 is of a simple or basic standard. EG *...elementary maths.* ADJ QUALIT

elephant /ɛlɪˈfənt/, **elephants.** An **elephant** is a very large animal with a long trunk. Elephants are found in Africa and India. N COUNT

elephantine /ɛlɪfæntaɪn/. Something that is **elephantine** is large and clumsy. EG *...Amelia's elephantine foot... ...an elephantine attempt at gallantry.* ADJ CLASSIF Literary

elevate /ɛlɪveɪt/, **elevates, elevating, elevated.** 1 When people or things **are elevated**, they are given greater status or importance. EG *Someone described cricket as 'male idleness elevated into religion'.* V+O+*to/into* : NO IMPER

2 To **elevate** something means to raise it to a higher level. EG *Earth movements elevated great areas of the seabed.* V+O

elevated /ɛlɪveɪtɪˈd/. 1 A person or a job or role that is **elevated** is very important or of very high rank. EG *...some elevated person like the Home Secretary.* ADJ QUALIT : ATTRIB

2 If thoughts or ideas are **elevated**, they are on a high level morally or intellectually. EG *Let's discuss it on a slightly more elevated plane.* ADJ QUALIT

3 You say that land or a building is **elevated** when it is higher than the surrounding area. ADJ CLASSIF

elevation /ɛliˈveɪʃəˈn/, **elevations.** 1 The **elevation** of someone or something is the act of raising them to a position of greater importance or higher rank. EG *...the elevation of the standards of the average man... ...his elevation to the peerage.* N UNCOUNT +POSS Formal

2 The **elevation** of a place is its height above sea level. EG *...a fairly flat plateau at an elevation of about a hundred feet.* N COUNT Formal

elevator /ɛləˈveɪtə/, **elevators.** An **elevator** is a device that moves up and down inside a tall building and carries people from one floor to another. N COUNT American

eleven /ɪlɛvəˈn/ **elevens. Eleven** is the number 11: see the entry headed NUMBER. EG *The flight had been postponed until eleven o'clock.* NUMBER

eleventh /iˈlɛvəˈnθ/, **elevenths.** 1 The **eleventh** item in a series is the one that you count as number eleven: see the entry headed NUMBER. EG *...the eleventh floor of the building.* ORDINAL

2 An **eleventh** is one of eleven equal parts of something. N COUNT : USU+*of*

eleventh hour. The **eleventh hour** is the last possible moment before something happens. EG *I was asked, at the eleventh hour, to step in and direct the play.* N SING : *the*+N

elicit /iˈlɪsɪt/, **elicits, eliciting, elicited.** 1 If you **elicit** a response or a reaction, you cause it to happen by saying or doing something. EG *Threats to reinstate the tax elicited jeers from the opposition.* V+O : OFT+*from* Formal

2 If you **elicit** a piece of information, you find it out by asking careful questions. EG *In five minutes she had elicited all the Herriard family history.* V+O Formal

eligible /ɛlɪdʒəˈbəˈl/. 1 Someone who is **eligible** for something is qualified or suitable for it. EG *You may be eligible for a grant to help you study.* ◊ **eligibility** /ɛlɪdʒəbɪlɪtiˈ/. EG *...the eligibility of applicants.* ADJ CLASSIF : OFT+*for* OR *to*-INF ◊ N UNCOUNT

2 An **eligible** man or woman is not yet married but is considered to be a suitable marriage partner. EG *...an eligible bachelor.* ADJ QUALIT

eliminate /iˈlɪmɪˈneɪt/, **eliminates, eliminating, eliminated.** 1 To **eliminate** something means to V+O remove it completely, especially when it is something that you do not want or need. EG *Poverty must be eliminated.* ◊ **elimination** /i^{1}lɪmɪneɪʃə^{0}n/. EG *...the elimination of spelling errors.* ◊ N UNCOUNT : OFT+SUPP

2 When a person or team **is eliminated** from a competition, they are defeated and so take no further part in the competition. EG *Four minor candidates were eliminated in the first round.* V+O : USU PASS

elite /ɪ^{3}liːt/, **elites.** **1** An **elite** is a group of the most powerful, rich, or talented people in a place or community. EG *...a small intellectual elite.* N COLL

2 Elite people or organizations are considered to be the best of their kind. EG *...a small group of elite investment bankers... ...elite training establishments.* ADJ CLASSIF : ATTRIB

elitism /ɪ^{3}liːtɪzə^{0}m/ is the belief that a society or country should be ruled by a small group of people who are considered to be superior to everyone else. EG *This kind of elitism is even more marked in public schools.* N UNCOUNT ◊ **elitist** /ɪ^{3}liːtɪst/, **elitists.** EG *Conservationists are often branded as elitists... It had been a very elitist society.* ◊ N COUNT OR ADJ QUALIT

elixir /ɪ^{2}lɪksɪə/, **elixirs.** An **elixir** is a liquid that is considered to have magical powers. N COUNT

ellipse /i^{1}lɪps/, **ellipses.** An **ellipse** is an oval shape like a flattened circle. N COUNT

elm /ɛlm/, **elms.** An **elm** is a kind of tree with broad leaves which it loses in winter. EG *...a house surrounded by tall elms.* N COUNT OR N UNCOUNT

elocution /ɛləkjuːʃə^{0}n/ is the art of speaking clearly in public with a standard accent. EG *He taught elocution at a junior college.* N UNCOUNT

elongated /iːlɒŋgeɪtɪ^{2}d/. Something that is **elongated** is very long and thin. ADJ QUALIT

elope /i^{1}ləʊp/, **elopes, eloping, eloped.** When two people **elope**, they go away secretly together in order to get married, usually without their parents' permission. EG *Is it true you eloped with her to Florida?* V OR V+*with* : RECIP

eloquent /ɛləkwə^{2}nt/. People who are **eloquent** express themselves well when they are speaking and can persuade other people to do things. EG *He was tall, eloquent, and had fine manners... ...detailed and eloquent descriptions.* ADJ QUALIT ◊ **eloquently.** EG *They spoke eloquently of their concern.* ◊ ADV

◊ **eloquence** /ɛləkwəns/. EG *He may have inherited his eloquence from his father.* ◊ N UNCOUNT

else /ɛls/. **1** You use **else** after words such as 'anywhere', 'someone', and 'what' to refer in a vague way to another place, person, or thing. EG *Let's go somewhere else... I had nothing else to do... ...someone else's house... Who else was there?* ADV

2 You use **or else** **2.1** to introduce a statement that indicates the unpleasant results that will occur if someone does something. EG *You've got to be very careful or else you'll miss the turn-off into our drive.* **2.2** to introduce the second of two possibilities, when you are sure that there are only two but you do not know which one is true. EG *I think I was at school, or else I was staying with a school friend during the vacation.* CONJ

elsewhere /ɛlswɛə/ means in other places or to another place. EG *...in Europe and elsewhere... He can go elsewhere.* ADV

ELT /iː ɛl tiː/ is an abbreviation for 'English Language Teaching'.

elucidate /i^{1}lj^{0}uːsɪdeɪt/, **elucidates, elucidating, elucidated.** If you **elucidate** something, you make it easier to understand by explaining it fully. EG *...a lesson elucidating the points that have been made in the previous lecture.* V+O Formal ◊ **elucidation** /i^{1}lj^{0}uːsɪdeɪʃə^{0}n/. EG *These are issues which deserve more thorough elucidation.* ◊ N UNCOUNT

elude /i^{1}luːd/, **eludes, eluding, eluded.** **1** If a fact or idea **eludes** you, you cannot understand it or remember it. EG *She tried to remember the shape of his face, but it eluded her.* V+O : NO PASS Formal

2 If you **elude** someone or something, you avoid them or escape from them. EG *...the problems of eluding the police.* V+O Formal

elusive /i^{1}luːsɪv/. Something or someone that is **elusive** is difficult to find, achieve, describe, or remember. EG *Happiness is an elusive quality... Rommel remained as elusive as ever.* ADJ QUALIT Formal

emaciated /i^{1}meɪsɪeɪtɪ^{2}d/. Someone who is **emaciated** is extremely thin and weak because of illness or lack of food. ADJ QUALIT

emanate /ɛməneɪt/, **emanates, emanating, emanated.** If a quality, idea, or feeling **emanates** from you, or if you **emanate** a feeling, it comes from you or was originally started by you. EG *These ideas are said to emanate from Henry Kissinger... He emanates concern.* V+*from* OR V+O Formal

emancipate /i^{1}mænsɪpeɪt/, **emancipates, emancipating, emancipated.** To **emancipate** someone means to free them from unpleasant social, political, or legal restrictions. EG *...a government determined to emancipate the poor.* V+O Formal

◊ **emancipation** /i^{1}mænsɪpeɪʃə^{0}n/. EG *Marx spoke of the emancipation of mankind.* ◊ N UNCOUNT : OFT+SUPP

embalm /ɪ^{2}mbɑːm/, **embalms, embalming, embalmed.** When a dead person **is embalmed**, their body is preserved using spices, oils, or chemicals. V+O

embankment /ɛmbæŋkmə^{2}nt/, **embankments.** An **embankment** is a thick wall built of earth, often supporting a railway line. EG *The car ran up an embankment covered with grass... ...a railway embankment.* N COUNT

embargo /ɛmbɑːgəʊ/, **embargoes.** An **embargo** is an order that is made by a government to stop trade with another country. EG *The states imposed an embargo on oil shipments... ...a trade embargo.* N COUNT : OFT+*on*

embark /ɪ^{2}mbɑːk/, **embarks, embarking, embarked.** **1** If you **embark** on something new, difficult, or exciting, you start doing it. EG *Peru embarked on a massive programme of reform.* V+*on/upon* : HAS PASS

2 When you **embark** on a ship, you go on board before the start of a voyage. EG *She had embarked on the S.S. Gordon Castle at Tilbury.* V : USU+A

◊ **embarkation** /ɛmbɑːkeɪʃə^{0}n/. EG *They returned to their port of embarkation, Toulon.* ◊ N UNCOUNT

embarrass /ɪ^{2}mbærəs/, **embarrasses, embarrassing, embarrassed.** **1** If something **embarrasses** you, it makes you feel shy or ashamed. EG *It embarrasses me even to think about it... He had been highly embarrassed by this confession.* V+O

2 If something **embarrasses** a politician or political party, it causes political problems for them. EG *The march could embarrass the government.* V+O

embarrassed /ɪ^{2}mbærəst/. If you are **embarrassed**, you feel shy or ashamed. EG *I felt really embarrassed about it... She had been too embarrassed to ask her friends... They were met with embarrassed silence.* ADJ QUALIT : USU PRED

embarrassing /ɪ^{2}mbærəsɪŋ/. Something that is **embarrassing** makes you feel embarrassed. EG *He said something that would be embarrassing for me to repeat.* ADJ QUALIT ◊ **embarrassingly.** EG *Their possessions were embarrassingly few.* ◊ SUBMOD

embarrassment /ɪ^{2}mbærəsmə^{2}nt/, **embarrassments.** **1 Embarrassment** is a feeling of shyness or shame. EG *His cheeks were hot with embarrassment... ...her embarrassment at having to visit me.* N UNCOUNT

2 Someone or something that embarrasses people can be referred to as an **embarrassment**. EG *For Labour, it was a political embarrassment... He was an embarrassment to so many people.* N COUNT : USU+SUPP

embassy /ɛmbəsi^1/, **embassies.** An **embassy** is **1** a group of government officials, headed by an ambassador, who represent their government in a foreign country. EG *She was attached to the Canadian embassy.* **2** the building in which an ambassador and his or her officials work. N COUNT

Do eloquent people elucidate things well?

embattled /ɪ^{2}mbætə^{0}ld/. An **embattled** person or group is having a lot of problems or difficulties. EG *...supporting an embattled Labour Government.* ADJ CLASSIF

embedded /ɪ^{2}mbedɪd/. **1** If an object is **embedded** in something, it is fixed there firmly and deeply. EG *The boat lay with its rudder embedded in mud.* ADJ PRED+*in*

2 If something such as an attitude or feeling is **embedded** in a society or in someone's personality, it has become a permanent feature of it. EG *...a deeply embedded feeling of guilt.* ADJ CLASSIF

embellish /ɪ^{2}mbelɪʃ/, **embellishes, embellishing, embellished. 1** If something **is embellished** with other things such as decorations, they are added to it to make it more attractive. EG *...a dress embellished with tiny circular mirrors.* V+O : USU PASS+*with* Formal

◇ **embellishment** /ɪ^{2}mbelɪʃmə^{2}nt/, **embellishments.** EG *...the embellishment of the church at Chambery.* ◇ N COUNT OR N UNCOUNT

2 If you **embellish** a story or account, you make it more interesting by adding details which are possibly untrue. EG *...embellished accounts of the day's events.* ◇ **embellishment.** EG *...copying articles from other papers and repeating them with embellishments.* V+O Formal ◇ N COUNT

ember /embə/, **embers.** The **embers** of a fire are the small hot pieces of wood or coal that remain and glow after the fire has finished burning. N COUNT : USU PLURAL

embezzle /ɪ^{2}mbezə^{0}l/, **embezzles, embezzling, embezzled.** If someone **embezzles** money, they steal it from an organization that they work for. EG *For years he'd been embezzling large sums of money from the company.* ◇ **embezzlement.** EG *He was prosecuted for embezzlement.* V+O ◇ N UNCOUNT

embitter /ɪ^{2}mbɪtə/, **embitters, embittering, embittered.** If someone **is embittered** by what happens to them, they feel angry and resentful because of it. ◇ **embittered.** EG *...a disappointed and embittered man.* ◇ **embittering.** EG *...an embittering experience.* V+O : USU PASS ◇ ADJ QUALIT ◇ ADJ QUALIT

emblazoned /ɪ^{2}mbleɪzə^{0}nd/ If designs or letters are **emblazoned** on something, they are clearly drawn, printed, or sewn on it. EG *...a flag on which the imperial eagle was emblazoned... ...sweatshirts emblazoned with the name of their college.* ADJ PRED : OFT +*on/with*

emblem /embla^{2}m/, **emblems.** An **emblem** is **1** a design that represents a country or organization. EG *The bald eagle remains the proud emblem of the USA.* **2** something that represents a quality or idea. EG *...a ruler's staff, an emblem of kingship.* N COUNT : USU+SUPP N COUNT+SUPP

embodiment /ɪ^{2}mbɒdi^{1}mə^{2}nt/. If you describe someone or something as the **embodiment** of a quality, principle, or idea, you mean that they have that quality, principle, or idea as their main feature or as the basis for all they do. EG *She was the embodiment of loyalty.* N SING : OFT+SUPP Formal

embody /ɪ^{2}mbɒdi^1/, **embodies, embodying, embodied. 1** To **embody** a quality, principle, or idea means to have it as your main feature or basis. EG *...the institutions which embody traditional values.* V+O

2 If something **embodies** a particular thing, it contains or consists of that thing. EG *These proposals were embodied in the Industrial Relations Act.* V+O

emboldened /ɪ^{2}mbəʊldə^{0}nd/ If you are **emboldened** by something that happens, it makes you feel confident enough to do something. EG *Emboldened by this success, he had begged a further favour.* ADJ PRED : OFT +*by*

embossed /ɛmbɒst/. An **embossed** design or word sticks up slightly from the surface it has been added to. EG *...embossed writing paper.* ADJ CLASSIF

embrace /ɪ^{2}mbreɪs/, **embraces, embracing, embraced. 1** When you **embrace** someone, you put your arms around them in order to show your affection for them. EG *We embraced each other.* V OR V+O : RECIP

▸ used as a noun. EG *They greeted us with warm embraces.* ▸ N COUNT

2 If something **embraces** a group of people, things, or ideas, it includes them. EG *The course embraces elements of chemistry, physics, and engineering.* V+O Formal

3 If you **embrace** a religion, political system, or idea, you start believing wholeheartedly in it. EG *She embraced the Catholic faith.* V+O Formal

embroider /ɪ^{2}mbrɔɪdə/, **embroiders, embroidering, embroidered.** If you **embroider** something made of cloth, you sew a decorative design onto it. ◇ **embroidered.** EG *...an embroidered shirt... ...a veil embroidered with red flowers.* V+O OR V ◇ ADJ CLASSIF

embroidery /ɪ^{2}mbrɔɪdə^{0}ri^1/ is **1** designs sewn on cloth. EG *...fine linen, decorated with embroidery.* **2** cloth on which designs have been sewn. **3** the activity of sewing designs on cloth. EG *...Jane's first attempts at embroidery.* N UNCOUNT

embroil /ɪ^{2}mbrɔɪl/, **embroils, embroiling, embroiled.** When someone **is embroiled** in an argument or fight, they become deeply involved in it. EG *It would be foolish to become embroiled in this struggle.* V+O : USU PASS+*in*

embryo /embrɪəʊ/, **embryos. 1** An **embryo** is an animal or human being which has not yet been born and which is in the very early stages of development. N COUNT

2 Something that is **in embryo** is at a very early stage of its development. EG *The electron microscope has been around, in embryo at any rate, for a long time.* PHRASE

embryonic /embrɪɒnɪk/ means in a very early stage of development. EG *Embryonic peasant movements began to emerge.* ADJ CLASSIF : ATTRIB Formal

emerald /emə^{0}rəld/, **emeralds. 1** An **emerald** is a precious stone which is clear and bright green. N COUNT

2 Something that is **emerald** is bright green in colour. EG *...over the emerald turf.* ADJ COLOUR

emerge /i^{1}mɜːdʒ/, **emerges, emerging, emerged. 1** When you **emerge**, you come out from a place where you could not be seen. EG *I saw the woman emerge from a shop.* V : OFT+*from/out of*

2 When you **emerge** from a situation or state, you stop being in it or experiencing it. EG *Few emerge from the experience unscathed.* V+*from*

3 If a fact **emerges** from a discussion or investigation, it becomes known as a result of it. EG *It emerged that she had been drinking.* V+*from* OR REPORT : ONLY *that*

4 When something such as an industry or a political movement **emerges**, it comes into existence. EG *Large-scale industry emerged only gradually.* V

◇ **emergence** /i^{1}mɜːdʒəns/. EG *...the emergence of new ideas.* ◇ N SING

emergency /i^{1}mɜːdʒənsi^1/, **emergencies. 1** An **emergency** is an unexpected and dangerous situation, which must be dealt with quickly. EG *The bells were only used in emergencies... ...what to do in case of emergency.* N COUNT OR N UNCOUNT

2 Emergency action is taken immediately, because an emergency has occurred. EG *The plane made an emergency landing.* ADJ CLASSIF : ATTRIB

3 Emergency equipment or supplies are intended for use in an emergency. EG *...emergency supplies of food.* ADJ CLASSIF : ATTRIB

emergent /i^{1}mɜːdʒənt/. An **emergent** country, political group, or way of life is becoming powerful or is coming into existence. ADJ CLASSIF : ATTRIB Formal

emigrate /emɪgreɪt/, **emigrates, emigrating, emigrated.** If you **emigrate**, you leave your native country to live in another country. EG *He received permission to emigrate to Canada.* V : OFT+*to/from*

◇ **emigration** /emɪgreɪʃə^{0}n/. EG *...the encouragement given to peasant emigration.* ◇ N UNCOUNT

émigré /emɪgreɪ/, **émigrés.** An **émigré** is someone who has left their country for political reasons. EG *...revolutionary émigrés from Russia.* N COUNT Formal

eminent /emɪnənt/. An **eminent** person is important and highly respected, especially because they are very good at their profession. EG *...one of the most eminent scientists in Britain.* ◇ **eminence** /emɪnə^{2}ns/. EG *...a statesman of great eminence.* ADJ QUALIT ◇ N UNCOUNT

eminently /emɪnəntli^1/ means very, or to a great degree. EG *Children are eminently practical.* SUBMOD Formal

emissary /ɛmɪsə⁰ri¹/, **emissaries.** An **emissary** is a messenger or representative who is sent by one government or leader to another. N COUNT Formal

emission /i¹mɪʃə⁰n/, **emissions.** When there is an **emission** of gas or radiation, it is released into the atmosphere. EG *...emissions of sulphur.* N COUNT OR N UNCOUNT Formal

emit /i¹mɪt/, **emits, emitting, emitted.** To **emit** a sound, a smell, a substance, heat, or light means to produce it or send it out. EG *He was heard to emit heartbroken sighs... ...the rays of heat that are emitted by the warm earth.* V+O Formal

emotion /i¹məʊʃə⁰n/, **emotions.** An **emotion** is a feeling such as fear, love, anger, or jealousy. EG *It wasn't proper for a man to show his emotions... She looked around her without emotion.* N COUNT OR N UNCOUNT

emotional /i¹məʊʃə⁰nəl, -ʃənə⁰l/. **1 Emotional** means relating to your emotions. EG *...the emotional needs of children.* ◇ **emotionally.** EG *He felt physically and emotionally exhausted.* ADJ CLASSIF ◇ ADV

2 When someone is **emotional**, they experience a strong emotion and show it openly, especially by crying. EG *Nell was far more emotional about it than he was.* ADJ QUALIT

emotive /i¹məʊtɪv/. Something that is **emotive** is likely to make people feel strong emotions. EG *Sir John used extremely emotive language.* ADJ QUALIT

empathy /ɛmpəθi¹/ is the ability to share another person's feelings as if they were your own. N UNCOUNT Formal

emperor /ɛmpə⁰rə/, **emperors.** An **emperor** is a man who rules an empire. EG *...the Emperor of Austria.* N COUNT

emphasis /ɛmfəsɪs/, **emphases** /ɛmfəsi:z/. **Emphasis** is **1** special importance that is given to an activity or to a part or aspect of something. EG *Too much emphasis is being placed on basic research... The army has always laid great emphasis on the use of helicopters.* N UNCOUNT OR N COUNT **2** extra force that you put on a word when you are speaking in order to make it seem more important. EG *'They had four cars,' he repeated with emphasis.* N UNCOUNT OR N COUNT

emphasize /ɛmfəsaɪz/, **emphasizes, emphasizing, emphasized;** also spelled **emphasise.** To **emphasize** something means to indicate that it is particularly important or true. EG *John went on to emphasise a point I'd already made... Mr Thompson was at pains to emphasize that he was threatening nobody.* V+O OR V+REPORT

emphatic /ı²mfætɪk/. **1** An **emphatic** statement is one that is made forcefully and clearly. EG *...an emphatic refutation.* ADJ QUALIT

2 If you are **emphatic**, you use forceful language, showing that you believe that what you are saying is important. EG *But Wendy was emphatic. 'You must do it,' she said.* ADJ PRED

3 An **emphatic** way of speaking is one in which you speak slowly, adding extra stress to many words in order to make them sound more important. ADJ CLASSIF : ATTRIB

emphatically /ı²mfætɪkə⁰li¹/. **1** If you say something **emphatically**, you say it in a way that shows that you feel strongly about what you are saying. EG *'I hope it does,' she said emphatically.* ADV

2 You also use **emphatically** to indicate that something is definitely true. EG *She is emphatically not a recluse.* ADV

empire /ɛmpaɪə/, **empires.** An **empire** is **1** a number of nations that are all controlled by one country. EG *...the British Empire.* **2** a large group of companies which is controlled by one person. EG *His publishing empire was flourishing.* N COUNT

empirical /ı²mpɪrɪkə⁰l/. **Empirical** knowledge or study comes from or involves practical experience rather than theories. EG *...the empirical study of anatomy.* ◇ **empirically.** EG *The theory could be tested empirically.* ADJ CLASSIF Formal ◇ ADV OR ADV SEN

empiricism /ɛmpɪrɪsɪzə⁰m/ is the belief that people should rely on practical experience rather than theories as a basis for knowledge and action. N UNCOUNT Technical

employ /ı²mplɔɪ/, **employs, employing, employed. 1** If you **employ** someone, you pay them to work for you. EG *He was employed as a research assistant.* V+O : USU PASS+*as*

2 To **employ** something means to use it. EG *If nuclear weapons are employed the world will be destroyed... You will need to employ a great deal of tact.* V+O Formal

employee /ɛmplɔɪi:, ı²mplɔɪi:/, **employees.** An **employee** is a person who is paid to work for an organization or for another person. EG *...a BBC employee.* N COUNT

employer /ı²mplɔɪə/, **employers.** Your **employer** is the person or organization that you work for. EG *The university is a major employer in the area.* N COUNT

employment /ı²mplɔɪmə²nt/ is the position of having a paid job. EG *He had retired from regular employment.* N UNCOUNT

empower /ı²mpaʊə/, **empowers, empowering, empowered.** When someone **is empowered** to do something, they are given the authority or power to do it. EG *The police are empowered to stop anyone to search for illegal drugs.* V+O+*to*-INF : USU PASS Formal

empress /ɛmprı²s/, **empresses.** An **empress** is a woman who rules an empire, or the wife of an emperor. N COUNT

emptiness /ɛmp⁰ti¹nı²s/. **1** A feeling of **emptiness** is an unhappy or frightening feeling that nothing is worthwhile. EG *She showed no sign of the inner sense of emptiness she felt.* N UNCOUNT

2 The **emptiness** of a place is the fact that it has nothing in it. EG *...the largely unexplored emptiness of the Indian Ocean.* N UNCOUNT

empty /ɛmp⁰ti¹/, **emptier, emptiest; empties, emptying, emptied. 1** A place, vehicle, or container that is **empty** has no people or things in it. EG *The room was empty... ...two empty bottles.* ADJ QUALIT

2 A gesture, threat, or relationship that is **empty** has no real value, meaning, or effectiveness. EG *They ignored his threats as empty rhetoric.* ADJ QUALIT

3 If you describe a person's life or a period of time as **empty**, you mean that it has nothing interesting or important in it. EG *How shall I exist during the empty days ahead?* ADJ QUALIT

4 If you **empty** a container, you remove its contents. EG *She picked up an ashtray and emptied it into a wastepaper basket.* V+O : USU+A

5 If you **empty** a substance or object out of a container, you pour or tip it out of the container. EG *You ought to empty the water out of those boots.* V+O+A

6 If a room or container **empties**, everyone or everything that is in it goes out of it. EG *The play was over and the auditorium began to empty.* V

empty-handed. If you come back from somewhere **empty-handed**, you have failed to get what you intended to get. EG *They were punished severely if they came back empty-handed.* ADJ PRED

emulate /ɛmjə⁴leɪt/, **emulates, emulating, emulated.** If you **emulate** someone or something, you imitate them because you admire them. EG *...a system that has been envied and emulated.* V+O Formal

enable /ı²neɪbə⁰l/, **enables, enabling, enabled.** If someone or something **enables** you to do something, they make it possible for you to do it. EG *...the feathers that enable a bird to fly.* V+O+*to*-INF Formal

enact /ı²nækt/, **enacts, enacting, enacted. 1** When a government **enacts** a proposal, they make it into a law. V+O Technical

2 If people **enact** a story or play, they act it. EG *They enacted tales of feudal princes.* V+O Formal

enamel /i¹næmə⁰l/ is **1** a substance like glass which can be heated and put onto metal, glass, or pottery in order to decorate it. ◇ **enamelled** /i¹næmə⁰ld/. EG *...scissors with enamelled handles.* N UNCOUNT ◇ ADJ CLASSIF

What do you call the wife of an emperor?

2 the hard white substance that forms the outer part of a tooth. N UNCOUNT

enamoured /ɪ²næməd/; spelled **enamored** in American English. If you are **enamoured** of someone or something, you like them very much. EG *I was, of course, always enamoured of the theatre.* ADJ PRED : USU +of

en bloc /ɒn blɒk/. If several people or things do something **en bloc**, they do it as a group. EG *...a system which teaches the young, en bloc, a number of beliefs.* ADV Formal

encapsulate /ɪ²ŋ¹kæpsjə⁴leɪt/, **encapsulates, encapsulating, encapsulated.** If something **encapsulates** facts or ideas, it contains or represents them in a very small space or in a single object or event. EG *A play was written, encapsulating the main arguments.* V+O Formal

encase /ɪ²ŋ¹keɪs/, **encases, encasing, encased.** If something **is encased** in a container or material, it is completely enclosed within it or covered by it. EG *Her feet were encased in a pair of old baseball boots.* V+O : USU PASS+in

-ence. -ence and **-ency** are added to adjectives, usually in place of -ent, to form nouns. These nouns refer to states, qualities, attitudes, or behaviour. For example, 'affluence' is the state of being affluent, and 'complacency' is the attitude of someone who is complacent. Nouns like these are often not defined in this dictionary, but are treated with the related adjective. EG *...his abhorrence of war... ...the prevention of delinquency.* SUFFIX

enchanted /ɪ²ntʃɑːntɪd/. **1** If you are **enchanted** by something, you think that it is lovely or delightful. EG *Sheila was enchanted by the prospect of a journey.* ADJ QUALIT

2 If you describe a place or event as **enchanted**, you mean that it seems as lovely or strange as something in a fairy story. EG *...an enchanted island.* ADJ CLASSIF

enchanting /ɪ²ntʃɑːntɪŋ/. Something that is **enchanting** is lovely or delightful. EG *...the most enchanting smile.* ADJ QUALIT

encircle /ɪ²nsɜːkə⁰l/, **encircles, encircling, encircled.** If something **encircles** something else, it completely surrounds it or encloses it. EG *The M5 and M6 motorways encircle Birmingham.* V+O

enclave /ɛŋ¹kleɪv/, **enclaves.** You can refer to a place as an **enclave** when it is surrounded by other places which are different, for example because they are inhabited by people of a different culture. EG *...the cloistered enclaves of academic life.* N COUNT : USU+SUPP Formal

enclose /ɪ²ŋ¹kləʊz/, **encloses, enclosing, enclosed. 1** If an object **is enclosed** by something solid, it is completely surrounded by it. EG *The statue is enclosed in a heavy glass cabinet.* V+O : OFT+in/with

◇ **enclosed.** EG *The reaction takes place extremely rapidly within an enclosed space.* ◇ ADJ CLASSIF

2 If you **enclose** something with a letter, you put it in the same envelope. EG *I enclose a small cheque.* V+O

◇ **enclosed.** EG *The enclosed list gives details of the courses available.* ◇ ADJ CLASSIF

enclosure /ɪ²ŋ¹kləʊʒə/, **enclosures.** An **enclosure** is an area of land that is surrounded by a wall or fence and that is used for a special purpose. EG *...the public enclosure of a racecourse.* N COUNT

encode /ɪ²ŋ¹kəʊd/, **encodes, encoding, encoded.** If you **encode** a message or some information, you put it into code. V+O

encompass /ɪ²ŋ¹kʌmpəs/, **encompasses, encompassing, encompass.** If something or someone **encompasses** certain things, they have a wide range that includes all those things. EG *...a policy which encompasses all aspects of conservation.* V+O Formal

encore /ɒŋkɔː/, **encores.** An audience shouts **'Encore!'** at the end of a concert when they want the performer to perform an extra item. ▸ An **encore** is this extra item. EG *...and lastly, for the encore, a Brahms waltz.* CONVENTION ▸ N COUNT

encounter /ɪ²ŋ¹kaʊntə/, **encounters, encountering, encountered. 1** If you **encounter** someone, you meet them. EG *On their journey they encountered an English couple.* ▸ used as a noun. EG *That was my first encounter with the great man.* V+O : NO CONT Formal ▸ N COUNT : OFT+with

2 If you **encounter** something, you experience it. EG *They've never encountered any discrimination.* ▸ used as a noun. EG *In their earliest encounters with stories, children want action.* V+O ▸ N COUNT : OFT+with

encourage /ɪ²ŋ¹kʌrɪdʒ/, **encourages, encouraging, encouraged. 1** If you **encourage** someone to do something, you tell them that you think that they should do it, or that they should continue doing it. EG *Her husband encouraged her to get a car.* ◇ **encouragement** /ɪ²ŋ¹kʌrɪdʒmə²nt/. EG *Many people sent messages of encouragement.* V+O : OFT+to-INF ◇ N UNCOUNT

2 If you **encourage** a particular activity, you support it actively. EG *Group meetings in the factory were always encouraged.* V+O : USU PASS

3 If something **encourages** an attitude or a kind of behaviour, it makes it more likely to happen. EG *Could the Scarman Report encourage racism?* V+O

4 Something that is **encouraging** gives you hope or confidence. EG *...a piece of encouraging news.* ADJ QUALIT

◇ **encouragingly.** EG *Rachel smiled encouragingly.* ◇ ADV

encroach /ɪ²ŋ¹krəʊtʃ/, **encroaches, encroaching, encroached. 1** To **encroach** on something means to take away part of it or to take more and more of it. EG *The new law doesn't encroach on the rights of the citizen.* ◇ **encroachment** /ɪ²ŋ¹krəʊtʃmə²nt/, **encroachments.** EG *...the Establishment's encroachments on traditional rights and liberties.* V : OFT +on/upon ◇ N COUNT OR N UNCOUNT

2 If someone or something **encroaches** on an area of land, they gradually occupy more and more of it. EG *They would not try to encroach in any way on the estate.* ◇ **encroachment.** EG *...justifiable concern about the encroachment on farming land that might occur.* V : OFT +on/upon ◇ N COUNT OR N UNCOUNT

encrusted /ɪ²ŋ¹krʌstɪ²d/. If a surface is **encrusted** with something, it is covered with it. EG *The statues are encrusted with jewels.* ADJ QUALIT : OFT+with

encumber /ɪ²ŋ¹kʌmbə/, **encumbers, encumbering, encumbered.** If something **encumbers** you, it makes it difficult for you to move or to take some action. EG *...passengers who were encumbered with suitcases.* V+O : USU PASS+with Formal

encumbrance /ɪ²ŋ¹kʌmbrəns/, **encumbrances.** An **encumbrance** is something or someone that encumbers you. EG *They are both encumbrances and I don't want them around.* N COUNT Formal

-ency. See **-ence.**

encyclopedia /ɪ²nsaɪklə⁶piːdɪə/, **encyclopedias;** also spelled **encyclopaedia.** An **encyclopedia** is a book or set of books in which many facts are arranged for reference, usually in alphabetical order. N COUNT

end /ɛnd/, **ends, ending, ended. 1** The **end** of a period of time, an event, or a piece of writing is the last part of it. EG *...at the end of August... ...one afternoon near the end of my stay... She read the first draft from beginning to end.* N SING : the+N

2 If something puts an **end** to an activity or situation, the activity or situation stops. EG *He urged an immediate end to all armed attacks.* N SING : OFT+to/of

3 The **end** of something long and narrow is one of its two extreme points, or the place that is furthest away from the point where it is attached to something else. EG *Sharpen a stick at both ends... The end of its tail quivered.* N COUNT+SUPP

4 You can refer to one of the two extreme points of a scale as one **end** of the scale. EG *...at the other end of the social scale.* N COUNT+SUPP

5 The other **end** is one of two places that are connected because people are communicating with each other by telephone or in writing. EG *The phone at the other end rang.* N COUNT+SUPP

6 An **end** is also the purpose for which something is done. EG *...their use of industrial power for political ends.* ● If you consider something to be an N COUNT : USU+SUPP ● PHRASE

end in itself, you consider it to be desirable, even though you do not achieve anything by it.
7 Someone's **end** is their death. EG *He did not deserve such a cruel end.* N COUNT Literary
8 When a situation or activity **ends** or when you **end** it, it stops. EG *The current agreement ends on November 24... ...a desperate initiative which ended in failure... He refused to end his nine-week-old hunger strike.* ◊ **ending.** EG *...the ending of all manufacture of nuclear weapons.* V-ERG ◊ N UNCOUNT
9 If a piece of writing or a performance **ends** in a particular way or if the writer or performer **ends** it in that way, its final part consists of the thing mentioned. EG *The play ends with all the children playing and reciting.* V OR V-ERG+ *with/on*
10 An object that **ends** with or in something has that thing on its tip, or as its last part. EG *Each finger ends with a sharp claw.* V+*with/in*
11 A journey, road, or area that **ends** at a particular place stops there and goes no further. EG *The trail ends one mile from Bakewell.* V : USU+A
12 **End** is also used in these phrases. **12.1** If something is **at an end**, it is finished and will not continue. EG *The service was nearly at an end.* **12.2** If something **comes to an end**, it stops and does not continue. EG *And here the story comes to an end.* **12.3** You say **at the end of the day** when you are talking about what appears to be the case after you have considered the relevant facts. EG *The question at the end of the day is whether the house is actually worth that amount.* **12.4 In the end** means finally, after a considerable time. EG *She went back to England in the end.* **12.5** If you manage to **make ends meet**, you have just enough money to buy necessary things. EG *Many were finding it difficult to make ends meet, especially those with young children.* **12.6 No end** means a lot. EG *It upset me no end... She had no end of trouble at school.* **12.7** When something happens for days or weeks **on end**, it happens continuously for that amount of time. EG *I don't see anybody for weeks on end.* PHRASES Informal Informal
13 to **get the wrong end of the stick**: see **stick**. • **at a loose end**: see **loose**. • See also **dead end**, **ending**, and **odds and ends**.

end up. If you **end up** in a particular place or situation, you are in that place or situation after a series of events, even though you did not intend to be. EG *Many of their friends have ended up in prison... We ended up taking a taxi there.* PHRASAL VB : V+ADV+A OR V+ADV+-ING

endanger /ɪ²ndeɪndʒə/, **endangers, endangering, endangered.** If you **endanger** someone or something, you cause them to be in a dangerous situation in which they might be seriously harmed. EG *They claimed the herbicides did not endanger human life.* ◊ **endangered.** EG *...endangered species of animals.* V+O ◊ ADJ QUALIT

endear /ɪ²ndɪə/, **endears, endearing, endeared.** If someone's behaviour **endears** them to you, it makes you fond of them. EG *This sort of talk did not endear him to Mr Lincoln.* V+O+*to* OR V-REFL+*to* Formal

endearing /ɪ²ndɪərɪŋ/. If someone's behaviour is **endearing**, it makes you fond of them. EG *...an endearing smile.* ◊ **endearingly.** EG *...endearingly childish behaviour.* ADJ QUALIT Formal ◊ ADV

endearment /ɪ²ndɪəmə²nt/, **endearments. Endearments** are words or phrases that you use to show affection. EG *He held me close to him, murmuring endearments.* N COUNT OR N UNCOUNT Formal

endeavour /ɪ²ndɛvə/, **endeavours, endeavouring, endeavoured**; spelled **endeavor** in American English.
If you **endeavour** to do something, you try to do it. EG *He endeavoured to adopt a positive but realistic attitude.* ▸ used as a noun. EG *...this exciting new field of endeavour... We must wish him good fortune in his endeavours.* V+*to*-INF ▸ N UNCOUNT OR N COUNT Formal

endemic /ɛndɛmɪk/. A condition or illness that is **endemic** in a particular place is found naturally or commonly among the people there. EG *Until the 1940's, malaria was endemic in Ceylon.* ADJ CLASSIF : OFT+*in* Formal

ending /ɛndɪŋ/, **endings.** The **ending** of something such as a story or a play is the last part of it. EG *The best kind of story is the one with a happy ending.* N COUNT

endless /ɛndlɪ²s/. If you describe something as **endless**, 1 you mean that it lasts so long that it seems as if it will never end. EG *They spend their time in an endless search for food.* ◊ **endlessly.** EG *She used to nag me endlessly about the family's money.* 2 you mean that it is very large or long, with no variation. EG *...an endless sandy waste.* ADJ CLASSIF ◊ ADV ADJ CLASSIF

endorse /ɪ²ndɔːs/, **endorses, endorsing, endorsed.** If you **endorse** someone or something, you say publicly that you support or approve of them. EG *The Germans and Italians endorsed the plan.* ◊ **endorsement** /ɪ²ndɔːsmə²nt/, **endorsements.** EG *...their public endorsement of Liberal candidates.* V+O ◊ N COUNT OR N UNCOUNT

endow /ɪ²ndaʊ/, **endows, endowing, endowed. 1** If someone or something **is endowed** with a quality, they have it or are given it. EG *O'Neill had been endowed with film star looks.* V+O : USU PASS+*with* Formal
2 If someone **endows** an institution, they give it a large amount of money to invest or use. V+O

endowment /ɪ²ndaʊmə²nt/, **endowments. 1** An **endowment** is a gift of money that is made to an institution such as a school or hospital. N COUNT
2 Someone's **endowments** are their natural qualities and abilities. N COUNT Formal

end product. The **end product** of an activity or process is the thing that it produces. N SING

end result. You can describe the result of a lengthy process or activity as the **end result** of it. EG *This sense of one's own worth is the end result of years of loving care.* N SING

endure /ɪ²ndjʊ⁰ə/, **endures, enduring, endured.**
1 If you **endure** a painful or difficult situation, you bear it calmly and patiently. EG *It was more than I could endure.* ◊ **endurance** /ɪ²ndjʊ⁰ərəns/. EG *They admired the troops for their courage and endurance.* V+O ◊ N UNCOUNT
2 If something **endures**, it continues to exist. EG *...a city which will endure for ever.* ◊ **enduring.** EG *...hopes for an enduring peace.* V ◊ ADJ QUALIT

enemy /ɛnəmi¹/, **enemies. 1** You can describe someone who intends to harm you as your **enemy**. EG *I have many enemies... ...an enemy of society.* N COUNT
2 In a war, the **enemy** is the army or country that your country is fighting. EG *After a fierce battle the enemy had been forced back... ...enemy aircraft.* N COLL : SING, *the*+N

energetic /ɛnədʒɛtɪk/. **1** Someone who is **energetic 1.1** shows a lot of enthusiasm and determination. EG *He is an energetic campaigner in the cause of road safety.* ◊ **energetically.** EG *This right is not merely questioned but energetically denied.* ADJ QUALIT ◊ ADV
1.2 is lively and physically active. EG *...energetic young children.* ◊ **energetically.** EG *...acrobats energetically tumbling across the stage.* ADJ QUALIT ◊ ADV
2 An **energetic** activity involves a lot of physical movement. EG *Do something energetic, play golf, swim, or ski.* ADJ QUALIT

energy /ɛnədʒi¹/, **energies. 1 Energy** is the ability and willingness to do lots of active things, because you do not feel at all tired. EG *He has neither the time nor the energy to play with the children... ...a woman of energy and ambition.* N UNCOUNT
2 Your **energies** are your effort and attention, which you direct towards a particular aim. EG *Men like Muhammed Abdu poured their energies into religious reform.* N COUNT+POSS
3 **Energy** is also power that is obtained from sources such as electricity, coal, or water, and that N UNCOUNT

If a meeting seems endless, do you find it enjoyable?

makes machines work or provides heat. EG *...nuclear energy.*

enfold /ɪ^{2}nfəʊld/, **enfolds, enfolding, enfolded. 1** If you **enfold** something in your hand or in your arms, you put your hand or your arms around it. EG *Their arms reached out to enfold him.* V+O : OFT+*in* Formal

2 You can say that something **enfolds** you when it is all around you. EG *...this darkness that continually enfolds me.* V+O Literary

enforce /ɪ^{2}nfɔːs/, **enforces, enforcing, enforced. 1** If people in a position of authority **enforce** a law or rule, they make sure that it is obeyed. EG *...officials who refused to enforce the immigration laws.* V+O ◇ **enforcement** /ɪ^{2}nfɔːsmə^{2}nt/. EG *...the enforcement of public laws and regulations.* ◇ N UNCOUNT : OFT+SUPP

2 If you **enforce** a particular condition, you force it to be done or to happen. EG *He enforced high standards.* V+O ◇ **enforced.** EG *...a life of enforced inactivity... ...the enforced discipline of working life.* ◇ ADJ CLASSIF : ATTRIB ◇ **enforcement** /ɪ^{2}nfɔːsmə^{2}nt/. EG *...the enforcement of discipline.* ◇ N UNCOUNT : OFT+SUPP

enforceable /ɪ^{2}nfɔːsəbə^{0}l/. A rule or agreement that is **enforceable** can be enforced. EG *...a civil contract enforceable by law.* ADJ CLASSIF : OFT+*by*

engage /ɪ^{2}ŋ^{1}geɪdʒ/, **engages, engaging, engaged. 1** If you **engage** in an activity, you do it. If you **are engaged** in it, you are doing it. EG *It was considered inappropriate for a former President to engage in commerce... The work we're engaged on is a study of heat transfer.* V+*in/on* OR V-PASS+*in/on* Formal

2 If something **engages** you or **engages** your attention or interest, it keeps you interested in it and thinking about it. EG *Boredom has a chance to develop if the child's interest is not engaged.* V+O Formal

3 If you **engage** someone **in conversation**, you have a conversation with them. EG *This allowed him to engage the woman in further conversation.* PHRASE Formal

4 If you **engage** someone to do a particular job, you appoint them to do it. EG *No continental opera would engage an English singer.* V+O

engaged /ɪ^{2}ŋ^{1}geɪdʒd/. **1** When two people are **engaged**, they have agreed to marry each other. EG *A week later, Tony became engaged to Caroline.* ADJ CLASSIF : OFT+*to*

2 If a telephone or telephone line is **engaged**, it is already being used, so you cannot speak to the person you are trying to phone. ADJ CLASSIF : USU PRED

3 If a public toilet is **engaged**, it is already being used by someone else. ADJ PRED

engagement /ɪ^{2}ŋ^{1}geɪdʒmə^{2}nt/, **engagements.** An **engagement** is **1** an arrangement that you have made to do something at a particular time. EG *I phoned my wife to cancel our lunch engagement.* N COUNT Formal **2** an arrangement that has been made for a performer to perform somewhere on a particular occasion. EG *He is much in demand in America for television engagements.* **3** an agreement that two people have made with each other to get married. EG *Their engagement was officially announced on 5th August.* **4** the period of time during which two people are engaged. EG *...a letter which she wrote to Harold during their engagement.*

engaging /ɪ^{2}ŋ^{1}geɪdʒɪŋ/. Someone who is **engaging** is pleasant and charming. EG *Peter was an engaging personality.* ADJ QUALIT

engender /ɪ^{2}ndʒɛndə/, **engenders, engendering, engendered.** If someone or something **engenders** a particular feeling, atmosphere, or situation, they cause it to occur. EG *This engenders a sense of responsibility.* V+O Formal

engine /ɛndʒɪn/, **engines. 1** The **engine** of a car or other vehicle is the part that produces the power which makes the vehicle move. EG *He couldn't get his engine started.* N COUNT

2 An **engine** is also the large vehicle that pulls a railway train. EG *...a steam engine.*

engineer /ɛndʒɪ^{1}nɪə/, **engineers, engineering, engineered. 1** An **engineer** is **1.1** a skilled person who uses scientific knowledge to design and construct machinery, electrical devices, or roads and bridges. N COUNT **1.2** a person who repairs mechanical or electrical devices. EG *...a telephone engineer.* **1.3** a person who is responsible for the engine of a ship while it is at sea.

2 If you **engineer** an event or situation, you cause it to happen, in a clever or indirect way. EG *It was Dr Martin who had engineered Miss Jackson's dismissal.* V+O

engineering /ɛndʒɪ^{1}nɪ^{1}ərɪŋ/ is the work involved in designing and constructing machinery, electrical devices, or roads and bridges. N UNCOUNT

English /ɪŋglɪʃ/. **1 English** means belonging or relating to England, or to its people or language. EG *...the English language.* ADJ CLASSIF

2 English is the language that is spoken by people who live in Great Britain and Ireland, the United States, Canada, Australia, and many other countries. EG *Half the letter was in Swedish and the rest in English.* N UNCOUNT

3 The **English** are the people who live in England. N PLURAL

Englishman /ɪŋglɪʃmə^{3}n/, **Englishmen.** An **Englishman** is a man who comes from England or Great Britain. N COUNT

Englishwoman /ɪŋglɪʃwʊmən/, **Englishwomen.** An **Englishwoman** is a woman who comes from England or Great Britain. N COUNT

engrave /ɪ^{2}ŋ^{1}greɪv/, **engraves, engraving, engraved. 1** If you **engrave** something with a design or inscription or if you **engrave** a design on it, you cut the design into its surface. EG *They engraved on it, 'Dedicated to the Lord'.* V+O : USU PASS +*with*; ALSO V+O+*on* ◇ **engraved.** EG *...engraved copper trays.* ◇ ADJ CLASSIF

2 If you say that something **is engraved** on your mind, memory, or heart, you mean that you will never forget it. EG *This episode remains sharply engraved on my mind.* V+O+*on* : USU PASS Literary

engraving /ɪ^{2}ŋ^{1}greɪvɪŋ/, **engravings.** An **engraving** is a picture or design that has been either cut into a surface or printed from an engraved plate. N COUNT

engrossed /ɪ^{2}ŋ^{1}grəʊst/. If you are **engrossed** in something, it holds your attention completely. EG *She was engrossed in her book.* ADJ PRED : OFT +*in*

engulf /ɪ^{2}ŋ^{1}gʌlf/, **engulfs, engulfing, engulfed. 1** To **engulf** something means to completely cover and hide it. EG *The town was quickly engulfed in volcanic ash.* V+O Literary

2 If something such as a feeling **engulfs** you, you are affected by it to a very great degree. EG *Panic engulfed him... ...a world engulfed in hatred and intolerance.* V+O Literary

enhance /ɪ^{2}nhɑːns/, **enhances, enhancing, enhanced.** To **enhance** something means to improve it. EG *It would enhance his standing in the community.* V+O

enigma /ɪ^{2}nɪgmə/, **enigmas.** Someone or something that is an **enigma** is mysterious and difficult to understand. EG *Mrs Yule remains an enigma, revealing nothing of herself.* N COUNT

enigmatic /ɛnɪgmætɪk/. Someone or something that is **enigmatic** is mysterious and difficult to understand. EG *...an enigmatic smile.* ADJ QUALIT ◇ **enigmatically.** EG *'You can try,' he said enigmatically.* ◇ ADV

enjoy /ɪ^{2}ndʒɔɪ/, **enjoys, enjoying, enjoyed. 1** If you **enjoy** something, **1.1** you find pleasure and satisfaction in doing it or experiencing it. EG *I enjoyed the holiday enormously... Painting is something that I really enjoy doing.* V+O OR V+-ING **1.2** you are lucky enough to have it. EG *They enjoyed exceptional living standards.* V+O

2 If you **enjoy** yourself, you do something you like doing or you take pleasure in what you are doing. EG *He is thoroughly enjoying himself.* V-REFL

enjoyable /ɪ^{2}ndʒɔɪəbə^{0}l/. Something that is **enjoyable** gives you pleasure. EG *We had an enjoyable day at Poole.* ADJ QUALIT

enjoyment /ɪ^{2}ndʒɔɪmə^{2}nt/, **enjoyments. 1 Enjoyment** is the feeling of pleasure that you have N UNCOUNT when you do or experience something you like. EG *...the enjoyment that reading brings.*

2 An **enjoyment** is an activity that gives you pleasure. EG *His enjoyments in life are limited to fighting and drinking.* N COUNT

enlarge /ɪ2nlɑːdʒ/, **enlarges, enlarging, enlarged. 1** If you **enlarge** something, you make it bigger. When something becomes bigger, you can say that it **enlarges**. EG *The original windows were enlarged by Christopher Wren... The pores enlarge and secrete more oil.* V-ERG ◇ **enlarged.** EG *...abnormally enlarged tonsils.* ◇ ADJ QUALIT

2 When a photograph **is enlarged**, a bigger print of it is made. V+O

enlarge on or **enlarge upon.** If you **enlarge on** or **enlarge upon** a subject, you give more details about it. EG *He enlarged on the glorious future he had in mind.* PHRASAL VB : V+PREP, HAS PASS Formal

enlargement /ɪ2nlɑːdʒmə2nt/, **enlargements. 1** **Enlargement** is the process or result of making something larger. EG *...the enlargement of crowded hospitals... The X-ray showed moderate enlargement of the heart.* N UNCOUNT

2 An **enlargement** is a photograph that has been made bigger. EG *Patrick is still looking at the enlargements.* N COUNT

enlighten /ɪ2nlaɪtə0n/, **enlightens, enlightening, enlightened.** To **enlighten** someone means to give them more knowledge about something. EG *The object is to amuse and enlighten the reader.* V+O Formal ◇ **enlightening.** EG *It was a most enlightening book.* ◇ ADJ QUALIT ◇ **enlightenment** /ɪ2nlaɪtə0nmə2nt/. EG *The talks were intended to bring culture and enlightenment to the hearers.* ◇ N UNCOUNT

enlightened /ɪ2nlaɪtə0nd/. If you describe someone as **enlightened**, you mean that they have sensible, modern attitudes and ways of dealing with things. EG *Our enlightened social policies are much admired.* ADJ QUALIT

enlist /ɪ2nlɪst/, **enlists, enlisting, enlisted. 1** If someone **enlists**, they join the army, navy, or air force. EG *He had enlisted in the Marines.* V-ERG : OFT+*in/into*

2 If you **enlist** someone or **enlist** their help, you persuade them to help you. EG *He should try to enlist the help of a doctor with an interest in sport.* V+O

enliven /ɪ2nlaɪvə0n/, **enlivens, enlivening, enlivened.** If something **enlivens** an event or situation, it makes it more lively or cheerful. EG *The journey was enlivened by noisy goings-on in the next carriage.* V+O

en masse /ɒn mæs/. If a group of people do something **en masse**, they all do it together. EG *They threatened to resign en masse.* ADV

enmeshed /ɪ2nmɛʃt/. If you are **enmeshed** in a situation, you are involved in it and find it difficult to escape from it. EG *At the time I was enmeshed in a controversy over abortion.* ADJ PRED : USU +*in* Formal

enmity /ɛnmɪ1ti1/, **enmities. Enmity** is a long-lasting feeling of hatred towards someone. EG *It had earned him the enduring enmity of the farmers.* N UNCOUNT OR N COUNT Formal

ennoble /ɪ2nəʊbə0l/, **ennobles, ennobling, ennobled.** To **ennoble** someone or something means to make them more noble and dignified. EG *Suffering does not ennoble people.* V+O Formal

ennui /ɒnwiː/ is a feeling of tiredness, boredom, and dissatisfaction. N UNCOUNT Literary

enormity /i1nɔːmɪ1ti1/. The **enormity** of something such as a problem or difficulty is its very large size or extent and its seriousness. EG *Smith did not grasp the enormity of the danger involved.* N SING : *the*+N+*of*

enormous /i1nɔːməs/. **1** Something that is **enormous** is extremely large in size or amount. EG *...an enormous cat... We do an enormous amount of research.* ADJ QUALIT

2 Enormous is also used to emphasize the great degree or extent of something. EG *To his enormous delight he was elected... ...an enormous success.* ADJ QUALIT : ATTRIB ◇ **enormously.** EG *I admired her enormously... ...an enormously long room.* ◇ ADV

enough /i1nʌf/. **1 Enough** means as much as you need. EG *I haven't enough room... I don't think I've really got enough information... I've got five thousand dollars – I hope it's enough... I had not seen enough of his work.* DET, OR PRON OFT+*of* ▸ used after a noun. EG *The fact that he did so much is proof enough.* ▸ ADJ AFTER N Formal

2 If you say that something is **enough**, you mean that you do not want it to continue any longer or get any worse. EG *I didn't want to stay any longer. Two years was enough... I've had enough of the both of you. Get out... Don't tell me. I've got enough problems.* PRON : OFT+*of* OR DET ▸ used as an adverb. EG *No. This thing is complicated enough already.* ▸ ADV AFTER VB

3 You use **enough** to say that someone or something has the necessary amount of a quality, or that something is happening to the necessary extent. EG *He was old enough to understand... The student isn't trying hard enough.* ADV AFTER ADJ/ADV/VB

4 You can also use **enough** to say that something is the case to a moderate or fairly large degree. EG *He was a nice enough boy.* ADV AFTER ADJ/ADV

5 You use expressions such as **strangely enough** and **interestingly enough** to indicate that you think a fact is strange or interesting. EG *Oddly enough, I do believe you.* ADV SEN

6 If you say **'Enough is enough'**, you mean that you want something that is happening to stop. CONVENTION

7 fair enough: see **fair.** ● **sure enough**: see **sure.**

enquire /ɪ2n1kwaɪə/. See **inquire.**

enquiry /ɪ2n1kwaɪəri1/. See **inquiry.**

enrage /ɪ2nreɪdʒ/, **enrages, enraging, enraged.** If something **enrages** you, it makes you very angry. EG *She was enraged by these remarks.* V+O ◇ **enraged.** EG *Letters flooded in to MPs from enraged constituents.* ◇ ADJ QUALIT

enrich /ɪ2nrɪtʃ/, **enriches, enriching, enriched. 1** To **enrich** something means to improve its quality by adding something else to it. EG *He enriched drab lives.* V+O ◇ **enriched.** EG *...enriched breakfast cereals.* ◇ ADJ QUALIT ◇ **enrichment** /ɪ2nrɪtʃmə2nt/. EG *...the enrichment of human experience.* ◇ N UNCOUNT

2 To **enrich** someone means to make them richer. EG *The purpose of the colonies was to enrich the colonists.* V+O Formal ◇ **enrichment.** EG *...the pursuit of personal enrichment.* ◇ N UNCOUNT

enrol /ɪ2nrəʊl/, **enrols, enrolling, enrolled;** spelled **enroll** in American English.
If you **enrol** or **are enrolled** on a course, you officially join it and pay a fee. EG *I was enrolled at the University of Vienna.* V-ERG ◇ **enrolment** /ɪ2nrəʊlmə2nt/. EG *...the enrolment of pupils.* ◇ N UNCOUNT

en route /ɒn ruːt/. If you are **en route** to a place, you are travelling there. EG *You'll see plenty to interest you en route.* ADV

enshrined /ɪ2nʃraɪnd/. If something such as an idea or a right is **enshrined** in a society or a law, it is permanent and protected. EG *The universities' autonomy is enshrined in their charters.* ADJ CLASSIF Formal

enslave /ɪ2nsleɪv/, **enslaves, enslaving, enslaved. 1** To **enslave** someone means to make them into a slave. EG *He was enslaved and ill-treated.* V+O : USU PASS ◇ **enslaved.** EG *...slave-owning governments and enslaved peoples.* ◇ ADJ CLASSIF ◇ **enslavement** /ɪ2nsleɪvmə2nt/. EG *...the enslavement of the whole population.* ◇ N UNCOUNT

2 To **enslave** people also means to keep them in a situation from which they cannot escape. EG *Men were enslaved by developing industrialism.* V+O : USU PASS ◇ **enslavement.** EG *...enslavement to the state.* ◇ N UNCOUNT

ensue /ɪ2nsj0uː/, **ensues, ensuing, ensued.** If something **ensues**, it happens immediately after something else. EG *A shouting match ensued between us and the bus driver.* V Formal ◇ **ensuing.** EG *He killed a policeman in the ensuing fight... ...the ensuing months.* ◇ ADJ CLASSIF ATTRIB

If you entertain people at your house, are you an entertainer?

ensure /ɪ^{2}nʃʊə, -ʃɔː/, **ensures, ensuring, ensured;** also spelled **insure** /ɪnʃʊə, -ʃɔː/in American English. To **ensure** that something happens means to make certain that it happens. EG *The first duty of the state is to ensure that people are protected from crime... The door did not lock, but at least it ensured a reasonable amount of privacy... I shall try to insure that your stay is a pleasant one.* — V+REPORT OR V+O

entail /ɪ^{2}nteɪl/, **entails, entailing, entailed.** If something **entails** something else, it necessarily involves it or causes it. EG *The move entailed radical changes in lifestyle... ...my romantic notions of what parenthood entailed.* — V+O

entangled /ɪ^{2}ntæŋgə^{0}ld/. **1** If something becomes **entangled** in something such as a rope or a net, it is caught and held by it. EG *The oar got entangled in the weeds.* — ADJ PRED : OFT +*in*

2 If you are **entangled** in a difficult situation, you are involved in it and you find it hard to escape from. EG *The country became entangled in a grave economic crisis.* — ADJ PRED : OFT +*in*

3 If you are **entangled** with someone, you are involved in a relationship with them that causes you problems. EG *She got entangled with a pretty awful crook.* — ADJ PRED : OFT +*with*

entanglement /ɪ^{2}ntæŋgə^{0}lmə^{2}nt/, **entanglements.** An **entanglement** is a relationship with someone, often a sexual one, which you wish to escape from. EG *For years Uncle Tom had avoided entanglements. Then he met Effie Mansell.* — N COUNT OR N UNCOUNT

enter /ɛntə/, **enters, entering, entered. 1** When you **enter** a place, you come into it or go into it. EG *They stopped talking as soon as they saw Brody enter... Tom timidly entered the bedroom.* — V OR V+O

2 When you **enter** an organization, institution, or profession, you become a member of it or become involved in it. EG *He decided to enter college... She entered politics.* — V+O

3 When a new quality or feature **enters** something, it appears in it. EG *A note of resolution entered the bishop's voice... A new factor has unfortunately entered trade union negotiations.* — V+O

4 When something **enters** a new period in its development or history, it begins this period. EG *The industry entered a period of lower growth.* — V+O

5 If you **enter** a competition or race or if you **enter** for it, you take part in it. EG *I entered one or two competitions and won prizes.* — V+O OR V+*for*

6 When you **enter** something in a written set of records or a computer, you write it down or type it in. EG *Enter it in the cash book.* — V+O : OFT+*in*

enter into. 1 When you **enter into** something important or complicated, you start doing it or being involved in it. EG *The Labour Government refused to enter into negotiations.* — PHRASAL VB : V+PREP, HAS PASS **2** Something that **enters into** something else is a factor in it or is involved in it. EG *Obviously personal relationships enter into it.* — V+PREP, HAS PASS

enterprise /ɛntəpraɪz/, **enterprises. 1** An **enterprise** is **1.1** a company or business. EG *...large industrial enterprises.* **1.2** something new, difficult, or important that you do or try to do. EG *He had doubts about the whole enterprise.* — N COUNT : USU+SUPP

2 Enterprise is **2.1** a system of business, especially one in a particular country. EG *...private enterprise.* **2.2** willingness to try out new ways of doing and achieving things. EG *...men of enterprise, energy, and ambition.* — N UNCOUNT : USU+SUPP

enterprising /ɛntəpraɪzɪŋ/. Someone who is **enterprising** is willing to try out new ways of doing and achieving things. EG *You are no longer the enterprising cook that once you were.* — ADJ QUALIT

entertain /ɛntəteɪn/, **entertains, entertaining, entertained. 1** To **entertain** people means **1.1** to do something that amuses or interests them and gives them pleasure. EG *We entertained the guests with a detailed description of the party.* **1.2** to give them food and hospitality, for example at your house. EG *She never entertained.* — V+O OR V

2 If you **entertain** an idea or suggestion, you consider it. EG *I wondered what could have led me to entertain so ludicrous a suspicion.* — V+O : NO IMPER Formal

entertainer /ɛntəteɪnə/, **entertainers.** An **entertainer** is a person whose job is to entertain audiences, for example by telling jokes, singing, or dancing. — N COUNT

entertaining /ɛntəteɪnɪŋ/. **1** People or things that are **entertaining** are amusing or interesting and give people pleasure. EG *Films should be entertaining.* — ADJ QUALIT

2 Entertaining involves giving guests food and talking to them. EG *...business entertaining.* — N UNCOUNT

entertainment /ɛntəteɪnmə^{2}nt/, **entertainments. 1 Entertainment** consist of performances or activities that give an audience pleasure. EG *...the entertainment business... This was not Morris's idea of an evening's entertainment.* — N UNCOUNT

2 An **entertainment** is a performance which people watch for pleasure. EG *...extravagant musical entertainments.* — N COUNT

enthral /ɪ^{2}nθrɔːl/, **enthrals, enthralling, enthralled;** spelled **enthraling** and **enthraled** in American English.
To **enthral** someone means to hold their attention and interest completely. ◊ **enthralled.** EG *400 people listened enthralled to an account of their journey.* ◊ **enthralling.** EG *...an enthralling story.* — V+O : USU PASS; ◊ ADJ QUALIT; ◊ ADJ QUALIT

enthuse /ɪ^{2}nθj^{0}uːz/, **enthuses, enthusing, enthused.** If you **enthuse** over something, you say excitedly how wonderful or pleasing it is. EG *...enthusing over a weekend spent in the Lake District... 'Brilliant,' he enthused.* — V+*over/about* OR V+QUOTE

enthusiasm /ɪ^{2}nθj^{0}uːzɪæzə^{0}m/, **enthusiasms. 1 Enthusiasm** is great eagerness to do something or to be involved in something. EG *He had embarked with great enthusiasm on an ambitious project... ...her enthusiasm for the theatre.* — N UNCOUNT

2 An **enthusiasm** is an activity or subject that interests you a great deal. EG *Pop music and football are her chief enthusiasms.* — N COUNT : USU+SUPP Literary

enthusiast /ɪ^{2}nθj^{0}uːzɪæst/, **enthusiasts.** An **enthusiast** is a person who is very interested in a particular activity or subject. EG *...a great soccer enthusiast.* — N COUNT : USU+SUPP

enthusiastic /ɪ^{2}nθj^{0}uːzi^{1}æstɪk/. If you are **enthusiastic** about something, you want to do it very much or like it very much, and show this in an excited way. EG *Sarah is very enthusiastic about learning to read.* ◊ **enthusiastically.** EG *I responded very enthusiastically.* — ADJ QUALIT : OFT+*about*; ◊ ADV

entice /ɪ^{2}ntaɪs/, **entices, enticing, enticed.** If you **entice** someone away from a place or activity or **entice** them into it, you tempt them away from it or into it. EG *An attempt is being made to entice otters back to the river.* — V+O

enticing /ɪ^{2}ntaɪsɪŋ/. Something that is **enticing** is extremely attractive. EG *Tanya's invitation seemed too enticing to refuse.* — ADJ QUALIT Literary

entire /ɪ^{2}ntaɪə/ is used to refer to the whole of something. EG *We've covered the entire wall with postcards... He had spent his entire career on Wall Street.* — ADJ CLASSIF : ATTRIB

entirely /ɪ^{2}ntaɪəli^1/ means completely, and not just partly. EG *It was entirely my own fault... I must say I agree entirely... McGovern had told them something entirely different.* — ADV

entirety /ɪ^{2}ntaɪərɪ^{1}ti^1/. If something happens to something **in** its **entirety**, it happens to all of it. EG *If published, it must be published in its entirety.* — PHRASE Formal

entitle /ɪ^{2}ntaɪtə^{0}l/, **entitles, entitling, entitled. 1** If something **entitles** you to have or do something, it gives you the right to have it or do it. EG *Their qualifications entitle them to a higher salary... Women aged 60 and over are entitled to free prescriptions.* — V+O+*to* OR *to*-INF

2 If something such as a book, film, or painting is **entitled** 'Sunrise', its title is 'Sunrise'. EG *...a report entitled 'Attitudes Towards Geriatrics'.* — ADJ PRED+N PROPER

entitlement /ɪ2ntaɪtə0lmə2nt/, **entitlements. Entitlement** to something is the right to have it or do it. EG *...entitlements to welfare and tax benefits.* N UNCOUNT OR N COUNT Formal

entity /ɛntɪ1ti1/, **entities.** An **entity** is something that exists separately from other things and has a clear identity. EG *Increasingly, inner cities and suburbs are separate entities.* N COUNT: USU+SUPP Formal

entomology /ɛntə6mɒlədʒi1/ is the study of insects. N UNCOUNT

entourage /ɒntʊrɑːʒ/, **entourages.** The **entourage** of someone famous or important is the group of assistants, servants, or other people who travel with them. EG *Among his entourage was a retired general.* N COUNT: USU+POSS

entrails /ɛntreɪlz/. The **entrails** of people or animals are their intestines. N PLURAL Literary

entrance, entrances, entrancing, entranced; pronounced /ɛntrəns/ when it is a noun, and /ɪ2ntrɑːns/ when it is a verb.

1 An **entrance** is a way into a place, for example a door or gate. EG *...the entrance to the National Gallery.* N COUNT

2 Someone's **entrance** is their arrival in a room. EG *She had only broken off to acknowledge our entrance... Her father would make a sudden entrance.* N COUNT: USU+POSS

3 If you gain **entrance** to a particular place, you are able to go into it. EG *I denied him entrance.* N UNCOUNT

4 If you gain **entrance** to a profession, society, or institution, you are accepted as a member of it. EG *Entrance to the professions is open to many more people.* N UNCOUNT

5 If something **entrances** you, it causes you to feel delight and wonder. EG *The man was so entranced and amused by the whole idea that he said he would return.* V+O: USU PASS ◇ **entranced.** EG *Everyone sat entranced.* ◇ ADJ QUALIT ◇ **entrancing.** EG *...the most entrancing singers.* ◇ ADJ QUALIT

entrant /ɛntrənt/, **entrants.** An **entrant** is **1** a person who has recently become a member of an institution such as a university. **2** a person who is taking part in a competition. EG *Each entrant plays the music of their choice.* N COUNT

entrenched /ɪ2ntrɛntʃt/. If something such as power, a custom, or an idea is **entrenched**, it is firmly established, so that it would be difficult to change it. EG *...strongly entrenched ideas.* ADJ QUALIT Formal

entrepreneur /ɒntrəprənɜː/, **entrepreneurs.** An **entrepreneur** is a person who sets up businesses. N COUNT

entrust /ɪ2ntrʌst/, **entrusts, entrusting, entrusted.** If you **entrust** something important to someone or if you **entrust** them with it, you make them responsible for looking after it or dealing with it. EG *Children are too young to be entrusted with family money... It was a task the Foreign Secretary had entrusted to him.* V+O+*to/with*

entry /ɛntri1/, **entries. 1** An **entry** is **1.1** something that you do in order to take part in a competition, for example a piece of work or the answers to a set of questions. EG *Here are some extracts from the five winning entries.* **1.2** something written in a diary, account book, dictionary, or encyclopedia. EG *Let me look up the entries for mid-June.* **1.3** a way into a place, for example a door or gate. EG *...the pretty screen at the entry to Hyde Park.* N COUNT

2 A person's **entry** is their arrival in a room. EG *At Derek's entry a few heads turned.* N COUNT+POSS

3 If you are allowed **entry** into a country, building, or enclosure, you are allowed to go in it. EG *Many of his associates were refused entry to Britain.* N UNCOUNT

4 The words **no entry** are used on signs to indicate that you are not allowed to go through a particular door or gate.

5 Someone's **entry** into a society or group is the act of joining it. EG *...her entry into national politics.* N UNCOUNT: OFT+*into/to*

6 Entry, in a competition, is the act of taking part in it. EG *Entry is free to all readers... ...the entry form.* N UNCOUNT

entwine /ɪ2ntwaɪn/, **entwines, entwining, entwined.** If you **entwine** something with something else, you twist it in and around it. EG *One second later her fingers were entwined in my own.* V-ERG: OFT PASS+*in/with* Formal

enumerate /ɪ1njuːməreɪt/, **enumerates, enumerating, enumerated.** When you **enumerate** a list of things, you name each one in turn. V+O Formal

enunciate /ɪ1nʌnsɪeɪt/, **enunciates, enunciating, enunciated. 1** When you **enunciate** a word or part of a word, you pronounce it clearly. V+O OR V Formal

2 When you **enunciate** a thought, idea, or plan, you express it clearly and formally. EG *I enunciated a general principle.* V+O OR V+QUOTE Formal

envelop /ɪ2nvɛləp/, **envelops, enveloping, enveloped.** If something soft **envelops** something else, it covers or surrounds it completely. EG *Mist was rising, enveloping the grey tree trunks.* V+O

envelope /ɛnvələʊp, ɒn-/, **envelopes.** An **envelope** is the rectangular paper cover in which you send a letter or card to someone through the post. EG *...a sealed envelope.* N COUNT

enviable /ɛnvɪəbə0l/. You describe something such as a quality as **enviable** when someone else has it and you wish that you had it yourself. EG *She learned to speak foreign languages with enviable fluency.* ADJ QUALIT

envious /ɛnvɪəs/. Someone who is **envious** of someone else envies them. EG *Ralph watched them, envious and resentful.* ADJ QUALIT ◇ **enviously.** EG *They were watched enviously by the rest of the crowd.* ◇ ADV

environment /ɪ2nvaɪrən0mə2nt/, **environments.**

1 Someone's **environment** is everything that affects their daily life, for example the place where they live, the people around them, and the things that they experience. EG *Could the college provide a stimulating environment?... Are we more influenced by environment or heredity?* N COUNT OR N UNCOUNT: USU+SUPP

2 The **environment** is the natural world of land, sea, air, plants, and animals that exists around towns and cities. EG *We are fighting pollution to protect the environment.* N SING: *the*+N

environmental /ɪ2nvaɪrən0mɛntə0l/ means **1** concerned with or relating to the natural world. EG *...environmental pollution.* **2** relating to the surroundings in which a person or animal lives. EG *Corals are very demanding in their environmental requirements.* ADJ CLASSIF: ATTRIB

environmentalist /ɪ2nvaɪrən0mɛntəlɪst/, **environmentalists.** An **environmentalist** is a person who wants to protect and preserve the natural environment, for example by preventing pollution. N COUNT

environs /ɪ2nvaɪrənz/. If you talk about a place and its **environs**, you are referring to the place and the area immediately surrounding it. EG *...Fleet Street and its environs.* N PLURAL +POSS Formal

envisage /ɪ2nvɪzɪdʒ/, **envisages, envisaging, envisaged.** If you **envisage** a situation or event, you imagine it, or think that it is likely to happen. EG *The last forecast envisaged inflation falling to about 10 per cent... The party envisages that socialism can come without civil war.* V+O OR V+REPORT Formal

envoy /ɛnvɔɪ/, **envoys.** An **envoy** is a diplomat sent to a foreign country. N COUNT

envy /ɛnvi1/, **envies, envying, envied.** If you **envy** someone, you wish that you had things or qualities that they have. EG *It would be unfair to envy him his good fortune.* V+O OR V+O+O ▸ used as a noun. EG *Her undisputed good looks caused envy and admiration.* ▸ N UNCOUNT

● If you have something that other people wish they had, you can say that it is **the envy of** these people. EG *It has a robust economy that is the envy of its neighbours.* ● PHRASE

Where might you see the words 'no entry'?

ephemeral /iˈfɛməºrəl/. Something that is **ephemeral** lasts only for a short time. EG *...the ephemeral nature of fads and fashions.* ADJ QUALIT Literary

epic /ɛpɪk/, **epics. 1** An **epic** is a long book, poem, or film which usually tells a story of heroic deeds. EG *...the latest James Bond epic.* N COUNT

2 Something that is described as **epic** is considered to be very impressive or ambitious. EG *...his triumphant return after his epic voyage.* ADJ CLASSIF

epidemic /ɛpɪdɛmɪk/, **epidemics.** An **epidemic** is an occurrence of a disease which affects a large number of people and which spreads quickly. EG *...an influenza epidemic.* N COUNT: OFT+SUPP

epilepsy /ɛpɪlɛpsiˈ/ is a brain condition which causes a person to suddenly lose consciousness and sometimes to have fits. N UNCOUNT

epileptic /ɛpɪlɛptɪk/, **epileptics. 1** Someone who is **epileptic** suffers from epilepsy. ▸ used as a noun. EG *He is an epileptic.* ADJ CLASSIF ▸ N COUNT

2 Epileptic also means caused by epilepsy. EG *...an epileptic fit.* ADJ CLASSIF: ATTRIB

epilogue /ɛpɪlɒg/, **epilogues.** An **epilogue** is a passage or speech which is added to the end of a book or play as a conclusion. N COUNT

episcopal /iˈpɪskəpəºl/ means belonging or relating to a bishop. EG *...dressed in his episcopal vestments.* ADJ CLASSIF: ATTRIB Formal

episode /ɛpɪsəʊd/, **episodes. 1** An **episode** is an important or memorable event or series of events. EG *A wartime episode had demonstrated his judgement of men.* N COUNT: OFT+SUPP

2 An **episode** of a drama series on television or radio is one of the programmes or parts that it consists of. EG *...the end of the first episode.* N COUNT

epitaph /ɛpɪtɑːf, -tæf/, **epitaphs.** An **epitaph** is something written on a person's gravestone, or a sentence or short poem that sums up a dead person's character. N COUNT

epithet /ɛpɪθɛt/, **epithets.** An **epithet** is an adjective or a short descriptive phrase. EG *No one could have denied to him the epithet of handsome.* N COUNT: OFT+SUPP Formal

epitome /iˈpɪtəmiˈ/. If you say that someone or something is the **epitome** of a particular thing, you mean that they are a perfect example of it. EG *He was considered the epitome of a gentleman.* N SING: *the*+N+*of* Formal

epitomize /iˈpɪtəmaɪz/, **epitomizes, epitomizing, epitomized;** also spelled **epitomise.** If you say that someone or something **epitomizes** a particular thing, you mean that they are a perfect example of it. EG *His failure epitomizes that of the whole movement.* V+O

epoch /iːpɒk/, **epochs.** An **epoch** is a long period of time in history. EG *We are at the end of one historical epoch, and at the dawn of another.* N COUNT+SUPP Formal

equable /ɛkwəbəºl/. Someone who is **equable** is calm and reasonable, and does not get angry quickly. EG *'Oh yes, sir.' Bond's voice was patient, equable.* ◇ **equably.** EG *'It suits me,' I said equably.* ADJ QUALIT ◇ ADV

equal /iːkwəl/, **equals, equalling, equalled;** spelled **equaling** and **equaled** in American English.

1 If two things are **equal** or if one thing is **equal** to another, they are the same, usually in size, amount, or degree. EG *The cake was divided into twelve equal parts... This creed is held with equal fervour by all political parties... They paid fines of 250 rupees each (equal to about three months' wages).* ADJ CLASSIF: OFT+*to*

2 If people have **equal** rights, they have the same rights as each other. EG *There is a trend towards equal opportunities for men and women.* ADJ CLASSIF: ATTRIB

3 If you say that people are **equal**, you mean that everyone has or should have the same rights and opportunities as each other. ADJ PRED

4 Someone who is your **equal** has the same ability, status, or rights that you have. EG *We treat our enemies as equals.* N COUNT+POSS

5 If two people do something **on equal terms**, neither person has any advantage over the other. EG *This law enables British shipbuilders to compete on equal terms with foreign yards.* PHRASE

6 If something **equals** a particular amount, it is the exact equivalent of it. EG *79 minus 14 equals 65.* V+C

7 To **equal** something or someone means to be as good or as great as them. EG *There are few film artists who can equal this man for sheer daring... Your folly is only equalled by your ignorance.* V+O

8 If someone is **equal** to a job or situation, they have the necessary abilities, strength, or courage to deal successfully with it. EG *The staff are not equal to all these demands.* ADJ PRED+*to* Formal

equality /iˈkwɒlɪˈtiˈ/ is the same status, rights, and opportunities for all the members of a society or group. EG *...equality between men and women.* N UNCOUNT

equally /iːkwəliˈ/. **1 Equally** means **1.1** in sections, amounts, or spaces that are the same size as each other. EG *On his death the land was divided equally between them.* **1.2** to the same degree or extent. EG *...two equally qualified men... Are parents meant to love all their children equally?* **1.3** to the same degree or extent as someone or something else that has just been mentioned. EG *He was a superb pianist. Irene was equally brilliant... This applies equally to partnerships of a less emotional nature.* ADV / SUBMOD OR ADV / SUBMOD OR ADV

2 Equally is also used to introduce a comment which balances or contrasts with another comment that has just been made. EG *Each country must find its own solution to unemployment. Equally, each must find its own way of coping with inflation.* ADV SEN

equals sign, equals signs. An **equals sign** is the sign (=), which is used in arithmetic to indicate that two numbers or sets of numbers are equal. N COUNT

equanimity /ɛkwənɪmɪˈtiˈ/ is a calm state of mind. EG *They were content to accept their defeat with equanimity.* N UNCOUNT Formal

equate /iˈkweɪt/, **equates, equating, equated.** If you **equate** one thing with another, you say or believe that it is the same thing. EG *It is imperative that war should on no account be equated with glory.* V+O+*with/to* Formal

equation /iˈkweɪʒəºn/, **equations.** An **equation** is a mathematical statement saying that two amounts or values are the same, for example 6 x 4 = 12 x 2. N COUNT

equator /iˈkweɪtə/. The **equator** is an imaginary line round the middle of the earth at an equal distance from the North Pole and the South Pole. N PROPER

equatorial /ɛkwətɔːrɪəl/ is used to describe places and conditions near or at the equator. EG *...the equatorial lands in the Amazon and Congo basins.* ADJ CLASSIF: ATTRIB

equestrian /ɪ²kwɛstrɪən/ means connected with the activity of riding horses. EG *...an equestrian statue of the Duke of Wellington.* ADJ CLASSIF: ATTRIB Formal

equidistant /iːkwɪdɪstənt/. A place that is **equidistant** from two other places is the same distance away from each of them. ADJ PRED

equilibrium /iːkwɪlɪbrɪəm/ is a balance between several different forces, groups, or aspects of a situation. EG *I believe this state of equilibrium will be maintained.* N UNCOUNT Formal

equine /ɛkwaɪn/ means connected with or relating to horses. EG *...research into equine health.* ADJ CLASSIF Formal

equip /ɪ²kwɪp/, **equips, equipping, equipped. 1** If you **equip** yourself with something, or if someone **equips** you with it, you obtain it for a particular purpose. EG *They equip themselves with a great variety of gadgets... The enemy troops were equipped with tanks, aircraft and missiles.* V-REFL OR V+O: OFT+*with*

◇ **equipped.** EG *...a large and well equipped army... By contrast, their competitors were superbly equipped.* ◇ ADJ QUALIT: USU ADV+ADJ

2 If something **is equipped** with a particular thing or device, it has it. EG *The card will be equipped with a built-in computer chip.* V+O: USU PASS+*with*

3 If something **equips** you for a task or experi- V+O:

ence, it prepares you mentally for it. EG *Kindness will not equip your children to stand on their own feet... Little in their history has equipped them for coping with this problem.* OFT+for OR to-INF ◇ **equipped.** EG *They were ill equipped to deal with the situation... They are not equipped to face reality in any shape or form.* ◇ ADJ QUALIT : USU ADV+ADJ

equipment /i[1]kwɪpmə[2]nt/ consists of the things which are needed for a particular activity. EG *...kitchen equipment... ...fire-fighting equipment.* N UNCOUNT

equitable /ɛkwɪtəbə[0]l/. In an **equitable** system or arrangement, everyone is treated equally. EG *...economic growth of a more balanced and equitable kind.* ADJ QUALIT Formal ◇ **equitably.** EG *...spreading work and its benefits equitably through society.* ◇ ADV

equivalence /i[1]kwɪvələns/. If there is **equivalence** between two things, they have the same use, function, size, or value. N UNCOUNT

equivalent /i[1]kwɪvələ[2]nt/, **equivalents.** If things are **equivalent**, they have the same use, function, size, or value. EG *Women were paid less than men doing equivalent work... His job was roughly equivalent to that of the State Department's chief.* ADJ CLASSIF
▸ used as a noun. EG *A good quilt is the equivalent of at least three blankets.* ▸ N COUNT : OFT+of

equivocal /i[1]kwɪvəkə[0]l/. **1** If something that you say is **equivocal**, it is deliberately vague or ambiguous because you want to avoid speaking the truth. EG *He limited himself to an equivocal grunt.* ADJ QUALIT Formal

2 Equivocal behaviour, attitudes, and events are difficult to understand or explain. EG *...equivocal and complex situations.* ADJ QUALIT Formal

equivocate /i[1]kwɪvəkeɪt/, **equivocates, equivocating, equivocated.** When someone **equivocates**, they deliberately use vague and ambiguous language in order to deceive people or to avoid speaking the truth. EG *The temptation to equivocate was especially strong.* V

er /ə, ɜː/ is used in writing to represent the sound that people make **1** when they hesitate while they are deciding what to say next. EG *...and it was not until 1845 that, er, Texas became part of the USA.* **2** when they want to attract someone's attention before speaking. EG *Er, ladies and gentlemen, dinner is served.*

-er, -ers. 1 You add **-er** to adjectives that have one or two syllables in order to form comparative adjectives. You also add it to some adverbs that do not end in -ly in order to form comparative adverbs. EG *They are faced with a much harder problem... Alf kept putting bigger and bigger locks on the door... He apologized for not returning sooner.* SUFFIX

2 -er is used in the following ways to form nouns. These nouns are often not defined in this dictionary, but are treated at the related words. **2.1 -er** is added to verbs to form nouns that refer to people or things that do a particular action. For example, a reader is someone who reads, and a money-saver is something that saves money. EG *I think I know what the questioner is getting at.* **2.2 -er** is used to form nouns that refer to a person who does a particular job. EG *My grandfather was a miner... She joined the theatre as a choreographer.* **2.3 -er** is used to form nouns that refer to a particular kind of person. For example, a pensioner is someone who is entitled to a pension. SUFFIX

era /ɪərə/, **eras.** An **era** is a period of time that is considered as a single unit because it has a particular feature that makes it remarkable in some way. EG *...the post-war era... Her candidacy marked the beginning of a new era for the party.* N COUNT : USU+SUPP

eradicate /ɪrædɪkeɪt/, **eradicates, eradicating, eradicated.** To **eradicate** something means to destroy it or remove it completely. EG *...the failure of the welfare state to eradicate poverty... ...efforts to eradicate every trace of discrimination.* V+O Formal
◇ **eradication** /ɪ[2]rædɪkeɪʃə[0]n/. EG *...pest eradication... ...the eradication of apartheid.* ◇ N UNCOUNT

erase /ɪreɪz/, **erases, erasing, erased. 1** If you **erase** a thought or feeling, you destroy it so that you can no longer remember it or feel it. EG *He cannot erase the memories of childhood... Your fears must be erased.* V+O

2 If you **erase** writing, you remove it by rubbing it with a rubber or cloth. V+O

3 To **erase** something also means to destroy or remove it completely so that it no longer exists. EG *...a campaign to erase hunger from the world.* V+O Formal

eraser /ɪreɪzə/, **erasers.** An **eraser** is a piece of rubber which is used for rubbing out writing. N COUNT American

erect /ɪrɛkt/, **erects, erecting, erected. 1** If you **erect** something, **1.1** you build it. EG *It would be splendid to erect a memorial to the regiment.* V+O Formal
◇ **erection** /ɪrɛkʃə[0]n/. EG *...the erection of a gravestone... The building was badly damaged shortly after its erection.* ◇ N UNCOUNT **1.2** you fit the pieces of it together so that it is ready to be used. EG *Thirty beds had to be erected... This kind of tent is easily erected or folded away.* V+O

2 People or things that are **erect** are straight and upright. EG *In the door, small but erect, stood an old man... She held herself erect.* ADJ QUALIT ◇ **erectly.** EG *Each plant begins by growing erectly.* ◇ ADV

erode /i[1]rəʊd/, **erodes, eroding, eroded. 1** If something **erodes** or **is eroded**, it is gradually destroyed or removed. EG *Confidence in the dollar has eroded... Our freedom is being eroded.* V-ERG : USU PASS

2 If rock or soil **erodes** or **is eroded** by the weather, sea, or wind, it is gradually destroyed or removed. EG *The river has eroded the rocks... The cliffs have become eroded by wind and water.* V-ERG : USU PASS

erosion /i[1]rəʊʒə[0]n/. **1 Erosion** is the gradual destruction or removal of something. EG *...the erosion of individual freedom.* N UNCOUNT : USU+SUPP

2 When the **erosion** of rock or soil takes place, it is gradually destroyed or removed by the weather, sea, or wind. EG *...the loss of farmland by erosion.* N UNCOUNT : USU+SUPP

erotic /i[1]rɒtɪk/. **1 Erotic** feelings and activities involve sexual pleasure or desire. EG *...erotic dreams... ...an erotic experience.* ADJ QUALIT ◇ **erotically.** EG *He found her loose dress erotically appealing.* ◇ ADV

2 Erotic paintings, books, and films are intended to produce feelings of sexual pleasure. EG *...an anthology of erotic verse... ...erotic photographs.* ADJ QUALIT

eroticism /i[1]rɒtɪsɪzə[0]m/ is **1** the erotic quality of something such as a book, picture, or sculpture. EG *The powerful eroticism of his painting was a revelation.* **2** sexual interest and excitement. EG *...the helpless rapture of adolescent eroticism.* N UNCOUNT

err /ɜː/, **errs, erring, erred. 1** If you **err**, you make a mistake. EG *Undoubtedly we have erred in giving such low status to our nurses.* V Formal ● If someone says **to err is human**, they mean that it is natural for human beings to make mistakes. ● PHRASE

2 If you **err on the side of** a particular way of behaving, you tend to behave that way rather than the opposite way. EG *Often one finds that advisers err on the side of caution.* PHRASE

errand /ɛrənd/, **errands.** If you go on an **errand** or run an **errand** for someone, you go a short distance in order to do something for them, for example to buy something from a shop. EG *It was the children's job to run errands.* N COUNT

erratic /ɪ[2]rætɪk/. Something that is **erratic** does not follow a regular pattern, but happens at unexpected times or moves in an irregular way. EG *...the country's erratic attempts to move into the future... I made my erratic way through the dining room.* ADJ QUALIT
◇ **erratically.** EG *Gaskell steered the boat erratically towards the harbour.* ◇ ADV

erroneous /ɪ[2]rəʊnɪəs/. **Erroneous** beliefs or opinions are incorrect. EG *...the erroneous belief that every man is a responsible human being.* ADJ QUALIT Formal

Does an escalator escalate?

◇ **erroneously.** EG *Some drinkers erroneously imagined that they had become wiser.*

error /ɛrə/, **errors.** 1 An **error** is a mistake. EG *The doctor committed an appalling error of judgement... ...errors in grammar.* N COUNT OR N UNCOUNT

2 If you do something **in error** or if something happens **in error**, it happens because of a mistake. EG *Another village had been wiped out in error.* PHRASE

3 **trial and error**: see **trial**.

erudite /ɛrju:daɪt/. People who are **erudite** show great academic knowledge. EG *...the erudite scholar Herbert Thurston.* ADJ QUALIT

erupt /ɪ¹rʌpt/, **erupts, erupting, erupted.** 1 When something **erupts**, it happens suddenly and in an unexpected way. EG *The Cuban Missile Crisis had erupted... Spontaneous discussion erupted about colour prejudice.* V

2 When the people in a place suddenly become angry or violent, you can say that they **erupt** or that the place **erupts**. EG *The inhabitants had erupted in massive protests... The room erupted.* V+A

3 When war or fighting **erupts**, it suddenly begins. EG *...the urban riots that erupted this summer in Britain.* ◇ **eruption** /ɪ¹rʌpʃə⁰n/, **eruptions.** EG *This may have stopped the eruption of a major war between the superpowers.* V; ◇ N UNCOUNT OR N COUNT

4 When a volcano **erupts**, it throws out lava, ash, and steam. EG *Six other volcanoes were still erupting.* ◇ **eruption.** EG *...the most violent eruption of Mount Etna... ...a volcano on the point of eruption.* V : NO IMPER; ◇ N UNCOUNT OR N COUNT

escalate /ɛskəleɪt/, **escalates, escalating, escalated.** If an unpleasant situation **escalates**, it becomes worse. EG *There is a danger that the conflict might escalate to a nuclear confrontation.* V-ERG

◇ **escalation** /ɛskəleɪʃə⁰n/. EG *...the risk of escalation... ...a steady escalation of violence.* ◇ N UNCOUNT

escalator /ɛskəleɪtə/, **escalators.** An **escalator** is a moving staircase on which people can go up or down. EG *They got on the wrong escalator.* N COUNT

escapade /ɛskəpeɪd/, **escapades.** An **escapade** is an exciting and rather dangerous adventure. EG *She enjoyed the escapade... The whole school knew every detail of this mad escapade.* N COUNT

escape /ɪ²skeɪp/, **escapes, escaping, escaped.** 1 If you **escape** from something or someone that you do not like, you succeed in avoiding them or in getting away from them. EG *How does one escape from the influence of such ideas?... Ralph was thankful to have escaped responsibility... They cannot escape their enemies.* V : OFT+*from*; ALSO V+O : NO PASS

2 If you **escape** from a place such as a prison, you succeed in getting away from it. EG *On 7 October Eva escaped from prison... He escaped to Britain.* ▸ used as a noun. EG *They were now able to make their escape... The chances of escape were not high... ...escape stories.* ◇ **escaped.** EG *He had shot and killed two escaped convicts... He pretended to be the escaped officer.* V : OFT +*from/to*; ▸ N UNCOUNT OR N COUNT; ◇ ADJ CLASSIF : ATTRIB

3 You can also say that you **escape** when you survive something such as an attack or an accident. EG *Fortunately we all escaped unhurt... The minister escaped without a scratch.* V+C OR V+A

4 If something **escapes** you or **escapes** your notice, you do not know about it, do not remember it, or do not notice it. EG *I doubt that such tactics escaped their notice... Their names escaped him.* V+O

5 You can describe a way of avoiding difficulties or responsibilities as an **escape**. EG *Reading is an escape from reality.* N COUNT OR N UNCOUNT : OFT+*from*

6 When a gas or liquid **escapes**, it leaks from a pipe or container. EG *...air escaping from a tyre.* V

7 See also **fire escape**.

escapism /ɪ²skeɪpɪzə⁰m/ consists of thoughts or activities that involve pleasant or fantastic ideas instead of the uninteresting or unpleasant aspects of your life. EG *Thinking about the future is a form of escapism.* ◇ **escapist** /ɪ²skeɪpɪst/. EG *...an escapist fantasy... His pleasures are mostly escapist.* N UNCOUNT; ◇ ADJ QUALIT

escort, escorts, escorting, escorted; pronounced /ɛskɔ:t/ when it is a noun, and /ɪ²skɔ:t/ when it is a verb. ◇ ADV

1 An **escort** is a person who goes somewhere with you in order to protect you or guard you. EG *...a police escort.* ● If someone is taken somewhere **under escort**, they are accompanied by guards, either because they have been arrested or because they are very important. N COUNT; ● PHRASE

2 If you **escort** someone, you go somewhere with them, usually in order to make sure that they leave a place or get to their destination. EG *He escorted me to the door.* V+O+A

ESL /i: ɛs ɛl/ is used to describe things that are connected with the teaching of English to people whose first language is not English, and who need to speak and write English because they are living in a country where English is an important language or the official language. **ESL** is an abbreviation for 'English as a second language'.

esoteric /ɛsəutɛrɪk/. Something that is **esoteric** is understood by only a small number of people who have special knowledge of it. EG *It is written in an esoteric script that few people can read.* ADJ QUALIT Formal

ESP /i: ɛs pi:/ is the teaching of English to students who need it for a particular purpose. **ESP** is an abbreviation for 'English for specific purposes' or 'English for special purposes'.

especial /ɪ²spɛʃə⁰l/ means the same as special. EG *He took especial care to vary his routine.* ADJ QUALIT : ATTRIB

especially /ɪ²spɛʃə⁰li¹/. 1 You use **especially** to indicate that what you are saying applies more to one thing or situation than to any other. EG *He was kind to his staff, especially those who were sick or in trouble... Children's bones, especially, are very sensitive to radiation... Double ovens are a good idea, especially if you are cooking several meals at once.* ADV SEN

2 You use **especially** to emphasize a quality. For example, if you say that something is **especially** good, you mean that it is very good indeed. EG *He found his host especially irritating... They didn't find it especially hard to do these exams.* SUBMOD

espionage /ɛspɪənɑ:ʒ/ is the activity of finding out the political, military, or industrial secrets of your enemies or rivals by using spies. EG *The Swiss threatened to throw them in jail for espionage.* N UNCOUNT

espouse /ɪ²spauz/, **espouses, espousing, espoused.** If you **espouse** a policy, cause, or plan, you become interested in it and support it. EG *The ideas she espoused were incomprehensible to me.* V+O Formal

Esq. is sometimes written after a man's name if he has no other title. It is an abbreviation for 'esquire'. EG *...a postcard addressed to James Dickson, Esq.*

essay /ɛseɪ/, **essays.** An **essay** is a short piece of writing on a particular subject. Students write essays for their tutors to mark, and authors write them for publication. EG *I had to produce an essay on Herrick for my tutor... ...a volume of essays.* N COUNT

essayist /ɛseɪɪst/, **essayists.** An **essayist** is someone who writes essays for publication. EG *...the best political essayist in the country.* N COUNT

essence /ɛsə⁰ns/. 1 The **essence** of something is its basic, central, and most important characteristic which gives it an individual identity. EG *Competition is the essence of all games.* N SING : USU+POSS

2 You use **in essence** to indicate that you are talking about the most important or central aspect of an idea, situation, or event. EG *But this is not in essence a book about religion.* ADV SEN Formal

essential /ɪ¹sɛnʃə⁰l/, **essentials.** 1 Something that is **essential** is absolutely necessary. EG *Land is essential for food and for work... A degree is by no means an essential qualification for a journalist... It is essential to set your targets realistically...* ▸ used as a noun. EG *...other essentials such as fuel and clothing... I had only the bare essentials.* ADJ QUALIT : OFT+*for/to* OR *to*-INF; ▸ N COUNT : USU PLURAL

2 The **essential** aspects of something are its most basic or important aspects. EG *...the essential fea-* ADJ QUALIT : ATTRIB

ture of the situation... The people around me translated the essential points of the lectures into English.

3 Essentials are the most important principles, ideas, or facts involved in a particular subject. EG *Their laws deal with essentials, not appearances.* N PLURAL

essentially /ɪ[1]sɛnʃə[0]li[1]/. You use **essentially 1** to emphasize a particular feature or quality that something or someone has, and to say that this feature or quality is their most important one. EG *Phyllis was essentially a soft, caring person... ...a country not essentially different from our own... Essentially, what you're saying is that a teacher shouldn't be afraid to admit ignorance.* ADV OR ADV SEN **2** to indicate that what you are saying is true in general terms, and that other, more detailed factors are not necessary for you to be able to make your point. EG *Such theories are essentially correct.* ADV

-est. You add **-est** to adjectives that have one or two syllables to form superlatives. You also add it to some adverbs that do not end in -ly. EG *...the hardest rock in the world... ...the prettiest girl she had ever seen... Children love simple toys best and play with them longest.* SUFFIX

establish /ɪ[2]stæblɪʃ/, **establishes, establishing, established. 1** If you **establish** something such as an organization or a system, you create it and make it begin to operate. EG *He had set out to establish his own business.* V+O ◊ **established.** EG *...the established institutions of society... This was a well-established custom among the prisoners.* ◊ ADJ CLASSIF : ATTRIB

2 If you **establish** contact with a group of people, you start to have discussions with them. EG *We tried to establish contact with pressure groups.* V+O : OFT+*with*

3 If you **establish** that something is the case, you discover facts which show that it is definitely the case. EG *A court of enquiry established that there were faults on both sides... So far they have been unable to establish the cause of death.* V+REPORT OR V+O

4 If you **establish** yourself as something, or **establish** your reputation as something, you get a reputation for being that thing. EG *The Liberals established themselves as the major alternative... He quickly established his reputation as a radical.* V-REFL OR V+O : OFT+*as*

establishment /ɪ[2]stæblɪʃmə[2]nt/, **establishments. 1** The **establishment** of an organization or system is the process by which it is created and begins to operate. EG *...the establishment of free trade unions.* N SING : *the*+N+*of*

2 An **establishment** is a shop or business. EG *At least one establishment in Savile Row now sells clothes off-the-peg.* N COUNT+SUPP

3 You refer to a group of people as the **establishment** when they have special power and influence in the running of a country or an organization. EG *It taught me more about the British Establishment... ...the university establishment.* N SING : *the*+N

estate /ɪ[2]steɪt/, **estates. 1** An **estate** is a large area of land in the country which is owned by one person or organization. EG *The colonel returned to his estate in Somerset.* N COUNT

2 A housing **estate** or factory **estate** is a large area of land, usually in or near a city, which has houses or factories on it. EG *...Singapore's industrial estates.* ● See also **real estate**. N COUNT+SUPP

3 Someone's **estate** is all the money and property that they leave when they die. EG *She left her estate to her grandchildren.* N COUNT

estate agent, estate agents. An **estate agent** is someone who works for a company that sells houses and land. N COUNT British

estate car, estate cars. An **estate car** is a car with a long body, a door at the rear, and space behind the back seats. N COUNT British

esteem /ɪ[2]sti:m/ is admiration and respect. EG *I know the high esteem you feel for our colleague here... Zapp had no great esteem for his fellow lecturers.* N UNCOUNT Formal ● If you **hold** someone or something **in high esteem**, you admire and respect them very much. EG *The organization was one which he held in high esteem.* ● PHRASE

esteemed /ɪ[2]sti:md/ is used to describe someone who you greatly admire and respect. EG *...our esteemed employer, Otto Gerran.* ADJ QUALIT Outdated

esthetic /ɛsθɛtɪk/. See **aesthetic**.

estimate, estimates, estimating, estimated; pronounced /ɛstɪmeɪt/ when it is a verb, and /ɛstɪmə[1]t/ when it is a noun.

1 If you **estimate** something such as an amount or a quantity, you calculate it approximately. EG *They were not able to estimate the cost... He estimated he would do the hundred miles by noon.* V+O OR V+REPORT ◊ **estimated.** EG *In 1975 there were an estimated 6,000 children in community homes.* ◊ ADJ CLASSIF

2 An **estimate** is **2.1** an approximate calculation, or the result obtained by such a calculation. EG *According to some estimates the number of farms has increased by 50 per cent.* N COUNT **2.2** a judgement which you make about a person or a situation. EG *Thomas wasn't living up to my estimate of him.*

3 If you get an **estimate** from someone such as a builder or plumber, they give you a written statement of how much a job is likely to cost. N COUNT

estimation /ɛstɪmeɪʃə[0]n/, **estimations. 1** Your **estimation** of a person or situation is the opinion that you have formed about them. EG *His comments were, in my estimation, correct and most useful.* N SING : USU+POSS

2 An **estimation** is an approximate calculation, or the result obtained by such a calculation. EG *...an estimation of the speed of the air leaving the lungs.* N COUNT : USU+SUPP

estranged /ɪ[2]streɪndʒd/. **1** If you are **estranged** from your husband or wife, you are no longer living with him or her. EG *He was estranged from his second wife... ...her estranged husband.* ADJ CLASSIF

2 If you are **estranged** from your family or friends, you have quarrelled with them and do not meet them or speak to them. EG *He knows I am estranged from my father.* ADJ PRED : OFT+*from*

estuary /ɛstjʊə[0]ri[1]/, **estuaries.** An **estuary** is the wide part of a river where it joins the sea. N COUNT

etc /ɪ[2]tsɛtə[0]rə/ is used at the end of a list to indicate that there are other items which you could mention if you had enough time or space. EG *...window frames, floorboards, beams, etc... She had to cook, do the cleaning, make beds etc, etc.*

etch /ɛtʃ/, **etchs, etching, etched. 1** If you **etch** a design or pattern on a surface, you cut it into the surface by using acid or something sharp such as a knife. EG *The artists must have spent many hours etching the images on the walls.* V+O OR V

2 If something **is etched** on your memory, it has made such a strong impression on you that you cannot forget it. EG *His face will remain permanently etched on my memory.* V+O : USU PASS +*on*

etching /ɛtʃɪŋ/, **etchings.** An **etching** is a picture printed from a metal plate that has had a design cut into it. EG *His etchings and drawings never went out of fashion.* N COUNT

eternal /ɪ[1]tɜ:nə[0]l/. **1** If something is **eternal**, it lasts for ever. EG *...the promise of eternal bliss.* ADJ CLASSIF ◊ **eternally.** EG *Something remained eternally unspoiled in him.* ◊ ADV

2 You can also describe something as **eternal** when it seems to last for ever, because it is boring or annoying. EG *He was annoying me with his eternal whining.* ADJ CLASSIF

3 Eternal truths and values never change and are believed to be true and relevant in all situations. EG *...a society which lives by eternal principles.* ADJ CLASSIF

eternity /ɪ[1]tɜ:nɪ[1]ti[1]/, **eternities. 1 Eternity** is time without an end, or a state of existence that is outside time, especially the state which some people believe they will pass into after they have died. EG *The preacher promised us eternity.* N UNCOUNT

If you say that something is essentially correct, is it completely correct?

2 You can refer to a period of time as an **eternity** when it seems very long indeed because you are having a boring or unpleasant experience. EG *I lay there for an eternity, coughing and gasping.* N COUNT : USU SING Informal

ethic /ɛθɪk/, **ethics. 1** A particular **ethic** is an idea or moral belief that influences the behaviour, attitudes, and philosophy of life of a group of people. EG *...the American ethic of expansion and opportunity... ...the Protestant work ethic.* N SING+SUPP

2 Ethics are moral beliefs and rules about right and wrong. EG *...a rational, scientific code of ethics.* N PLURAL

ethical /ɛθɪkə^{0}l/ means influenced by or based on a system of moral beliefs about right and wrong. EG *...an ethical problem... He had no ethical objection to drinking.* ◊ **ethically.** EG *I found Captain Imrie's proposal ethically objectionable.* ADJ CLASSIF : ATTRIB ◊ SUBMOD

ethnic /ɛθnɪk/ means connected with or relating to different racial groups of people. EG *...the ethnic composition of the voters of New York... ...ethnic minorities.* ADJ CLASSIF : ATTRIB

ethos /iːθɒs/. The **ethos** of a group of people or of a type of activity is the set of ideas and attitudes that is associated with it. EG *...the working-class ethos of 'togetherness'... ...the prevailing social ethos.* N SING : USU+SUPP

etiquette /ɛtɪkɛt/ is a set of customs and rules for polite behaviour. EG *...problems of etiquette... ...a book on etiquette.* N UNCOUNT

eulogy /juːlə^{7}dʒi^1/, **eulogies.** A **eulogy** is a speech or piece of writing that praises someone or something. EG *Countless eulogies have been written about her... ...a eulogy to the Queen Mother.* N COUNT Formal

euphemism /juːfɪ^{1}mɪzə^{0}m/, **euphemisms.** A **euphemism** is a polite word or expression that people use when they are talking about something which they or other people find unpleasant or embarrassing, such as death or sex. N COUNT OR N UNCOUNT

euphemistic /juːfɪ^{1}mɪstɪk/. **Euphemistic** language consists of polite words or expressions for things that people find unpleasant or embarrassing. ◊ **euphemistically.** EG *Then came what the French euphemistically call 'the events of May' – the student revolution.* ADJ QUALIT ◊ ADV

euphoria /juːfɔːrɪə/ is a feeling of great happiness. EG *She shared Dan's euphoria over the play.* N UNCOUNT

euphoric /juːfɒrɪk/. If you are **euphoric**, you are extremely happy. EG *...a euphoric moment... ...a feeling of euphoric triumph.* ADJ QUALIT

European /jʊərəpɪən/, **Europeans. 1 European** means coming from or relating to Europe. ADJ CLASSIF

2 A **European** is a person who comes from Europe. EG *She was the only European living in the neighbourhood.* N COUNT

euthanasia /juːθəneɪzɪə/ is the practice of painlessly killing someone who is ill in order to relieve their suffering when there is nothing more that can be done to help them. N UNCOUNT

evacuate /i^{1}vækju^{4}eɪt/, **evacuates, evacuating, evacuated.** If people **evacuate** a place or if they **are evacuated** from it, they move out of it for a period of time, because it has become dangerous. EG *The entire complex was being evacuated... I was evacuated to Swindon in 1941.* ◊ **evacuation** /i^{1}vækju^{4}eɪʃə^{0}n/, **evacuations.** EG *Orders went out to prepare for the evacuation of the city.* V+O : USU PASS ◊ N UNCOUNT OR N COUNT

evade /i^{1}veɪd/, **evades, evading, evaded. 1** If you **evade** something that you do not want to be involved with, you succeed in not becoming involved with it. EG *I evaded the issue... He had found a way of evading responsibility.* V+O

2 If you **evade** someone or something that is moving towards you, you succeed in not being touched or hit by them. EG *Tim tried to catch her arm but she evaded him.* V+O

3 If something such as success or love **evades** you, you never manage to achieve it. EG *Military glory had evaded him throughout his long career.* V+O

evaluate /i^{1}vælju^{4}eɪt/, **evaluates, evaluating, evaluated.** If you **evaluate** something, you decide how significant or valuable it is after carefully studying its good and bad features. EG *He was asked to evaluate the situation... Football performance can never be truly evaluated.* V+O

evaluation /i^{1}vælju^{4}eɪʃə^{0}n/, **evaluations.** An **evaluation** is a decision about how significant or valuable something is, based on a careful study of its good and bad features. EG *...a realistic evaluation of the working of Britain's economy... They can help develop our powers of critical evaluation.* N COUNT OR N UNCOUNT

evaporate /i^{1}væpəreɪt/, **evaporates, evaporating, evaporated. 1** When a liquid **evaporates**, it changes into a gas, usually because it has been heated. EG *All the water has evaporated.* ◊ **evaporation** /i^{1}væpəreɪʃə^{0}n/. EG *Be careful not to lose too much liquid by evaporation.* V ◊ N UNCOUNT

2 If a feeling or attitude **evaporates**, it gradually becomes less and eventually disappears altogether. EG *My nervousness evaporated.* V

evasion /i^{1}veɪʒə^{0}n/, **evasions. Evasion** consists of deliberately not doing something that you ought to do or of deliberately avoiding talking about something. EG *He is guilty of gross tax evasion... ...an evasion of our responsibilities... He continued with his evasions and lies.* N UNCOUNT OR N COUNT

evasive /i^{1}veɪsɪv/. **1** If you are being **evasive**, you are deliberately not talking about something. EG *Victor became evasive... ...an evasive answer.* ◊ **evasively.** EG *The Count had answered evasively.* ◊ **evasiveness.** EG *There was a certain evasiveness in Mary's replies.* ADJ QUALIT ◊ ADV ◊ N UNCOUNT

2 If a ship or plane **takes evasive action**, it changes its position or course to avoid being hit by something that is coming towards it. PHRASE

eve /iːv/, **eves.** The **eve** of an event or occasion is the day before it. EG *...a devastating attack on the eve of the election.* ● See also **Christmas Eve, New Year's Eve**. N COUNT : USU+SUPP

even /iːvə^{0}n/, **evens, evening, evened. 1** You use **even 1.1** to emphasize that what comes just after or just before it in the sentence is surprising. EG *Even Anthony enjoyed it... She liked him even when she was quarrelling with him... I often lend her money even now... No one dared even to whisper.* ADV SEN **1.2** to emphasize the fact that something is, for example, bigger, better, or worse than something else. EG *Barber had something even worse to tell me... ...an even brighter light... I must be even more tired than I thought.* ADV+COMPAR

2 You use **even if** or **even though** to indicate that a fact would not make what you are saying untrue or does not make it untrue. EG *Even if you disagree with her, she's worth listening to... I was always rather afraid of men, even though I had lots of boyfriends.* CONJ

3 You use **even so** to introduce a fact which seems surprising after what you have just said. EG *Their feathers are regularly shed and renewed. Even so they need constant care.* ADV SEN

4 When a measurement or rate is **even**, it stays at about the same level. EG *...an even body temperature.* ◊ **evenly.** EG *Mary was breathing quietly and evenly.* ADJ QUALIT ◊ ADV

5 Surfaces that are **even** are smooth and flat. EG *The road wasn't very even.* ADJ QUALIT

6 If there is an **even** distribution of something, each person, group, or area involved has an equal amount or share. EG *The distribution of land was much more even than in Latin America.* ◊ **evenly.** EG *Opinion seems to be fairly evenly divided.* ADJ QUALIT ◊ ADV

7 If a contest or competition is **even**, the people taking part are all as strong, skilful, or successful as each other. ◊ **evenly.** EG *Government and rebel soldiers are evenly matched.* ADJ QUALIT ◊ ADV

8 If you say that you are going to **get even** with someone, you mean that you are going to harm them because they have harmed you. EG *I always knew that one day I would get even with her.* PHRASE Informal

9 If you say that there is an **even** chance of ADJ CLASSIF something happening, you mean that it is equally likely to happen or not to happen. EG *She would have had only an even chance of being saved.*

10 An **even** number can be divided exactly by the number two. EG *Houses with even numbers are on the right, those with odd numbers on the left.* ADJ CLASSIF

even out. When an amount of something **evens out** or when you **even** it **out**, each person, group, or area begins to receive an equal share of it. EG *Irrigation systems help to even out the supply of water over the growing season.* PHRASAL VB : V-ERG+ADV

evening /iːvnɪŋ/, **evenings.** The **evening** is the part of each day between the end of the afternoon and the time when you go to bed. EG *He arrived about six in the evening... Each evening he runs 5 miles... He was silently finishing his evening meal.* N COUNT OR N UNCOUNT

evening class, evening classes. An **evening class** is a course for adults that is taught in the evening rather than during the day. N COUNT

event /i¹vɛnt/, **events. 1** An **event** is something that happens, especially something unusual or important. EG *Next day the newspapers reported the event... ...the most important event in family life.* N COUNT

2 You can refer to all the things that are happening in a particular situation as **events**. EG *Events now moved swiftly... The authorities were quite unable to control events.* N PLURAL

3 In sport, an **event** is one of a series of races or other activities that are part of an organized occasion. EG *Lord Exeter presented the medals for this event.* N COUNT

4 You use an expression such as **in the event that** when you are talking about something that might happen in the future. *In the unlikely event that they give you any real trouble, give me a ring... In that event, we would take the matter to court.* PHRASE Formal

5 You say **at all events** or **in any event** when you are pointing out that something is definitely true, although there may be uncertainty about other things that you have mentioned. EG *In any event, it was something that had to be done.* ADV SEN

6 You say **in the event** when you are stating what actually happened, after you have been discussing what might have happened. EG *In the event, it turned out to be fun.* PHRASE Formal

eventful /i¹vɛntfʊl/. An **eventful** period of time is full of interesting, exciting, or important events. EG *...the most exhausting and eventful day of his life.* ADJ QUALIT

eventual /i¹vɛntʃ⁰ʊ⁰əl/. The **eventual** result of a process or series of events is what happens or what has been achieved at the end of it. EG *...the company's eventual collapse in 1971... ...anxiety about the eventual outcome.* ADJ CLASSIF : ATTRIB

eventuality /i¹vɛntʃʊælɪ¹ti¹/, **eventualities.** An **eventuality** is a possible future event. EG *He was ready for any eventuality... We are insured against all eventualities.* N COUNT Formal

eventually /i¹vɛntʃʊ⁰əli¹/. If something happens **eventually**, **1** it happens after a lot of delays, caused for example by problems or arguments. EG *Rodin eventually agreed that Casson was right... Eventually they got through to the hospital.* ADV OR ADV SEN **2** it happens at the end of a process or series of events, or as the final result of it. EG *The three firms eventually became Imperial Airways.* ADV

ever /ɛvə/. **1 Ever** means at any time. EG *I don't think I'll ever be homesick here... ...one of the best novels ever written... I am happier than I have ever been... The news is as awful as ever.* ADV

2 Ever also means all the time. You use it **2.1** in expressions like 'ever-increasing' and 'ever-present' to indicate that something exists all the time or continues doing something or being something all the time. EG *...an ever-increasing prison population... ...an ever-present sense of danger.* **2.2** to indicate someone's usual behaviour or character. EG *Ever unpredictable, James could be angry one moment and calm the next.* ADV

3 You also use **ever** in questions when you want to emphasize how surprised or shocked you are. EG *'I'm sorry. I'd rather not say.' - 'Why ever not?'... Who ever would have thought that?* ADV AFTER WH

4 You use **ever since** to emphasize that something has been true all the time since the time mentioned, and is still true now. EG *'How long have you lived here?' - 'Ever since I was married.'... They were formed in the seventeenth century and have continued ever since.* CONJ, ADV, OR PREP

5 You use **ever so** and **ever such** to emphasize the degree of something. EG *They are ever so kind... I had ever such a nice letter from her.* PHRASE Informal

evergreen /ɛvəgriːn/, **evergreens.** An **evergreen** is a tree or bush which has green leaves all the year round. EG *...forests of evergreens.* N COUNT

everlasting /ɛvəlɑːstɪŋ/. Something that is **everlasting** continues to exist or to happen, and never ends. EG *...the everlasting snows of the mighty Himalayas.* ◊ **everlastingly.** EG *He was everlastingly optimistic.* ADJ CLASSIF Literary ◊ ADV

every /ɛvri¹/. **1** You use **every** to indicate that you are referring to all the members of a group or all the parts of something and not only some of them. EG *She spoke to every person at the party... I have answered every single question... I loved every minute of it.* DET

2 You also use **every** **2.1** in order to indicate that something happens at regular intervals. EG *They met every day... I visit her once every six months.* **2.2** in expressions such as 'every now and then' in order to indicate that something happens occasionally. EG *Every now and then she would cry out... Every so often, she spends a weekend in London.* DET

3 You use **every** to say how often something happens. For example, if something happens **every second** day or **every other** day, it happens on one day in each period of two days. If something happens **every third** day or **every fourth** year, it happens on one day in each period of three days or in one year in each period of four years. EG *We only save enough money to take a real vacation every other year... He shaved only every second day.* PHRASE

4 You use **every** in front of a number when you are saying what proportion of people or things something happens to or applies to. EG *One woman in every two hundred is a sufferer... Since 1976, nine women have lost jobs for every five men.* DET

5 If you say that something shows **every** sign of happening, or if you say that there is **every** chance that something will happen, you mean that it is very likely that it will happen. EG *They show every sign of continuing to succeed.* DET

6 If you say that someone has **every** reason to do something, you mean that they would be justified in doing it. EG *She had every reason to be pleased.* DET

everybody /ɛvrɪbɒdi¹/. See **everyone**.

everyday /ɛvrɪdeɪ/. You use **everyday** to describe something which **1** is part of normal life, and is not especially interesting or unusual. EG *People could resume a normal everyday life... ...their role in everyday affairs.* **2** happens or is used each day. EG *Exercise is part of my everyday routine.* ADJ CLASSIF : ATTRIB

everyone /ɛvrɪwə⁹n/. The form **everybody** is also used.

You use **everyone** or **everybody** **1** to refer to all the people in a particular group. EG *Everybody in the office laughed... She was genuinely interested in everyone she met.* **2** to refer to all the people in the world. EG *Everyone has their own ideas about it... Everyone knows that.* PRON INDEF

everything /ɛvrɪθɪŋ/. You use **everything** **1** to refer to all the objects, actions, activities, or facts in a particular situation. EG *I don't agree with everything he says... I will arrange everything.* **2** to PRON INDEF

Is an ex-President still a President?

refer to all possible or likely actions, activities, or situations. EG *That's your answer to everything... You think of everything.* **3** to refer to a whole situation or to life in general. EG *Is everything all right?... Everything went on just as before.*

everywhere /ɛvrɪwɛə/. You use **everywhere** **1** to refer to a whole area or to all the places in a particular area. EG *Everywhere in Asia it is the same... People everywhere are becoming aware of the problem.* **2** to refer to all the places that someone goes to. EG *Everywhere I went, people were angry or suspicious... She always carried a gun with her everywhere.* ADV

evict /ɪ¹vɪkt/, **evicts, evicting, evicted.** When people **are evicted**, they are officially forced to leave the house where they are living. EG *If evicted, they would have nowhere else to go.* V+O : USU PASS
◇ **eviction** /ɪ¹vɪkʃə⁰n/, **evictions.** EG *The family faces eviction for non-payment of rent... She described the evictions as 'an outrage'.* ◇ N UNCOUNT OR N COUNT

evidence /ɛvɪdəns/. **1 Evidence** is anything that you see, experience, read, or are told which causes you to believe that something is true or has really happened. EG *We saw evidence everywhere that a real effort was being made to promote tourism... There was no evidence of quarrels between them.* N UNCOUNT : USU+SUPP
2 If you **give evidence** in a court of law, you officially say what you know about something. EG *The doctor gave evidence at the inquest.* PHRASE
3 If you say that someone or something is **in evidence**, you mean that they are present and can be clearly seen. EG *Violence was particularly in evidence in the towns.* PHRASE

evident /ɛvɪdənt/. If it is **evident** that something exists or that something is true, people can easily see that it exists or is true. EG *It was evident that his faith in the Government was severely shaken... She took a sip with evident enjoyment.* ADJ QUALIT

evidently /ɛvɪdəntli¹/. You use **evidently** **1** to say that something appears to be true. EG *They said it would come, but evidently they failed to send it.* **2** to say that something is obviously true. EG *I found her in bed, evidently in great pain.* ADV SEN

evil /iːvə⁰l/, **evils. 1 Evil** is all the wicked and bad things that happen in the world. EG *...the conflict between good and evil.* N UNCOUNT
2 The **evils** of a situation or activity are all the things that are bad or harmful about it. EG *...a sermon on the evils of drink.* N COUNT : USU+SUPP
3 Someone who is **evil** is wicked and enjoys doing things that harm other people. ADJ QUALIT
4 Something that is **evil** causes a great deal of harm to people. EG *Slavery was the most evil system of labour ever devised.* ADJ QUALIT

evocation /iːvəkeɪʃə⁰n/, **evocations.** An **evocation** of a place or a past event is an experience in which you remember or think about this place or event. EG *...evocations of rural America... It was disturbing, this evocation of her youth.* N COUNT OR N UNCOUNT : USU+SUPP Formal

evocative /ɪ¹vɒkətɪv/. Something that is **evocative** makes you remember or think about a place or a past event. EG *...an evocative description.* ADJ QUALIT
◇ **evocatively.** EG *Old photographs are evocatively displayed round the building.* ◇ ADV

evoke /ɪ¹vəʊk/, **evokes, evoking, evoked.** If something **evokes** an emotion, memory, or response, it causes it to be felt, remembered, or expressed. EG *The quarrel seemed to evoke the bitterest passions.* V+O Formal

evolution /iːvəluːʃə⁰n/. **1 Evolution** is a process of gradual change that takes place over many generations, during which animals and plants change some of their characteristics and sometimes develop into new species. EG *The processes of evolution are still going on.* N UNCOUNT ◇ **evolutionary** /iːvəluːʃənə⁰ri¹/. EG *...evolutionary theory... These variations can produce evolutionary change.* ◇ ADJ CLASSIF : ATTRIB
2 You can use **evolution** to refer to any gradual process of change and development. EG *Social evolution has now become extremely rapid... ...the evolution of parliamentary democracy.* N UNCOUNT +SUPP

evolve /ɪ¹vɒlv/, **evolves, evolving, evolved. 1** When animals and plants **evolve**, they gradually change and develop into different forms. EG *The earliest fish have evolved into some 30,000 different species.* V : OFT +*into/from*
2 When something **evolves**, it gradually develops from something simpler. EG *It was fascinating to see how the film evolved... How did Giotto evolve his very personal and original style?* V-ERG

ewe /juː/, **ewes.** A **ewe** is an adult female sheep. N COUNT

ex- is added to nouns to indicate that someone or something is no longer the thing referred to by the noun. For example, an ex-farmer is someone who is no longer a farmer. EG *...an ex-serviceman... ...his ex-wife.* PREFIX

exacerbate /ɪ²gzæsəbeɪt, ɪ²ksæs-/, **exacerbates, exacerbating, exacerbated.** If something **exacerbates** a bad situation, it makes it worse. EG *Withholding aid only exacerbates the problem... ...inadequacy exacerbated by muddle.* V+O Formal

exact /ɪ²gzækt/, **exacts, exacting, exacted. 1** Something that is **exact** is **1.1** correct or accurate, rather than approximate. EG *He noted the exact time... He searched for the exact word to define his feelings.* ADJ CLASSIF ◇ **exactness.** EG *He expressed himself with great exactness.* ◇ N UNCOUNT **1.2** correct and complete in every detail. EG *...an exact replica of Hamburg airport.* ADJ CLASSIF
2 You say **to be exact** when you want to indicate that you are giving more detailed information or are slightly correcting what you have said. EG *I thought that this would be possible, or to be more exact, I could see no reason why it should not be so.* ADV SEN
3 If someone **exacts** something from you, they demand and obtain it from you, because they are more powerful than you are. EG *They exacted absolute obedience from their followers.* V+O : OFT+*from* Formal

exacting /ɪ²gzæktɪŋ/. **1** If something is **exacting**, you have to work very hard to do it well. EG *...an exacting job... The task proved to be exacting.* ADJ QUALIT
2 If someone is **exacting**, they insist that you work very hard or with very great care. EG *Both were exacting bosses... The state of repair failed to measure up to their exacting standards.* ADJ QUALIT

exactly /ɪ²gzæktli¹/. **1 Exactly** means precisely, and not just approximately. EG *You've exactly one hour to do this... That's exactly what they told me... I don't know exactly where it is, but it's in the south of France.* ADV
2 If you do something **exactly**, you do it very accurately or precisely. EG *Sam answered the owl's cry, imitating it exactly... He did exactly as he was told.* ADV
3 You can use **exactly** to emphasize how similar something is to something else. EG *He's exactly like a little baby.* ADV
4 You can say **'Exactly'** to express agreement with what has just been said or to confirm that it is true. EG *'Do you mean that we are stuck here?' – 'Exactly, my dear.'* CONVENTION
5 You can use **not exactly** to indicate that something is not true, but is almost true. EG *He didn't exactly block me, but he didn't move either... 'She's taken the day off.' – 'Is she sick?' – 'Not exactly.'* ADV OR CONVENTION

exaggerate /ɪ²gzædʒəreɪt/, **exaggerates, exaggerating, exaggerated. 1** If you **exaggerate**, you make the thing that you are talking about seem bigger, better, or worse than it actually is. EG *I am exaggerating a little... She did not exaggerate about the height of the tower... It is impossible to exaggerate the horrors of the system.* V OR V+O ◇ **exaggeration** /ɪ²gzædʒəreɪʃə⁰n/, **exaggerations.** EG *Isn't that a bit of an exaggeration?... One can speak, without exaggeration, of a peaceful revolution.* ◇ N COUNT OR N UNCOUNT
2 If something **exaggerates** a quality or feature, it makes it seem more obvious or more important V+O

than it really is. EG *Ballet exaggerates ordinary body movements.*

3 An **exaggerated** expression or gesture is more noticeable than it needs to be. EG *Brody heaved an exaggerated sigh.* ◊ **exaggeratedly.** EG *...an exaggeratedly intense smile.* — ADJ QUALIT; ◊ ADV

exalted /ɪ2gzɔːltɪ2d/. Someone who is **exalted** is very important. EG *I had never met so exalted a person... ...someone in his exalted position.* — ADJ QUALIT

exam /ɪ2gzæm/, **exams.** An **exam** is the same as an examination in paragraph 1. — N COUNT Informal

examination /ɪ2gzæmɪneɪʃə0n/, **examinations. 1** An **examination** is a formal test that you take to show your knowledge or ability in a particular subject. EG *...a three-hour written examination.* — N COUNT

2 If you make an **examination** of something, you look at it carefully. EG *Mrs Oliver devoted herself to an examination of the address book... The weapon was taken away for examination.* — N UNCOUNT OR N COUNT

3 When you have a medical **examination**, a doctor looks at your body in order to check how healthy you are. EG *A full examination of the chest failed to reveal anything wrong.* — N UNCOUNT OR N COUNT

4 When there is **examination** of an idea, proposal, or plan, it is considered very carefully. EG *...an important case which deserves closer examination.* — N UNCOUNT OR N COUNT

examine /ɪ2gzæmɪn/, **examines, examining, examined. 1** If you **examine** something, you look at it carefully. EG *I examined the lighter, then handed it back... Government experts were still examining the wreckage of the plane.* — V+O

2 If a doctor **examines** you, he or she looks at your body in order to check how healthy you are. EG *Each child is medically examined.* — V+O

3 If you **examine** an idea, proposal, or plan, you consider it very carefully. EG *They agreed immediately without having examined the proposition.* — V+O; N UNCOUNT OR N COUNT

4 If a teacher **examines** you, he or she finds out how much you know by asking you questions or by making you take an examination. — V+O

examiner /ɪ2gzæmɪnə/, **examiners.** An **examiner** is a person who sets or marks an examination. — N COUNT

example /ɪ2gzɑːmpə0l/, **examples. 1** An **example** of a particular kind of thing is a thing of that kind, which can be mentioned or pointed out in order to show the characteristics of that kind of thing. EG *It's a very fine example of traditional architecture... Could you give me an example of an application of this principle?* — N COUNT

2 You use **for example** to show that you are giving an example of a particular kind of thing. EG *Japan, for example, has two languages... In our library we have quite a lot of newspapers - The Times, for example, and the New York Times.* — ADV SEN

3 If you say that someone is an **example** to other people or sets an **example**, you mean that they behave in a way that other people copy or should copy. EG *They are a shining example to progressive people everywhere... She set such a good example to us all.* ● If you **follow** someone's **example**, you behave in the same way that they do. EG *A number of people followed Shuttleworth's example and were subsequently arrested.* — N COUNT; ● PHRASE

4 If you **make an example of** someone, you punish them severely so that other people will not behave in the same way. EG *It was decided to make an example of some of the top conspirators.* — PHRASE

exasperate /ɪ2gzɑːspəreɪt/, **exasperates, exasperating, exasperated.** If someone or something **exasperates** you, they annoy you and make you feel frustrated or upset. EG *She frequently exasperates her friends.* ◊ **exasperated.** EG *He had an exasperated look on his face... ...overworked and exasperated teachers.* ◊ **exasperating.** EG *I have seldom had a more exasperating day... She could be a most exasperating child.* ◊ **exasperation** /ɪ2gzɑːspəreɪʃə0n/. EG *He looked at the little boy in exasperation.* — V+O; ◊ ADJ QUALIT; ◊ ADJ QUALIT; ◊ N UNCOUNT

excavate /ɛkskəveɪt/, **excavates, excavating, excavated.** When people **excavate** a piece of land, they remove earth carefully from it and look for the remains of pots, bones, or buildings, in order to discover information about the past. ◊ **excavation** /ɛkskəveɪʃə0n/, **excavations.** EG *...the excavation of a Neolithic village... Post-war excavations revealed the foundations of an earlier church.* — V+O OR V; ◊ N COUNT OR N UNCOUNT

exceed /ɪ2ksiːd/, **exceeds, exceeding, exceeded.**

1 If something **exceeds** a particular amount or number, it is greater than that amount or number. EG *Average annual temperatures exceed 20° centigrade.* — V+O

2 If you **exceed** a limit or rule, you go beyond it. EG *A motorist was caught exceeding the speed limit... The company is not allowed to exceed its budget.* — V+O

exceedingly /ɪ2ksiːdɪŋli1/ means very much indeed. For example, someone who is exceedingly rich is very rich indeed. EG *The Colonel was exceedingly wealthy... Doug is an exceedingly amiable fellow.* — SUBMOD Outdated

excel /ɪ2ksɛl/, **excels, excelling, excelled.** If someone **excels** at something or **excels** in it, they are very good at it. *He excels at sports... It is in this area of running that women excel.* — V: OFT+*at/in*

excellence /ɛksələns/. **1 Excellence** is the quality of being extremely good at something. EG *Sport is an area in which excellence is still treasured.* — N UNCOUNT

2 See also **par excellence**.

Excellency /ɛksələnsi1/, **Excellencies.** People say **Your Excellency**, **His Excellency**, or **Excellency** when they are referring to or addressing important officials such as ambassadors. EG *His Excellency desires to see you... I shall do my best, Your Excellency.*

excellent /ɛksələnt/. Something that is **excellent** is very good indeed. EG *I think the teaching here is excellent... That's an excellent idea.* ◊ **excellently.** EG *The system works excellently... There are some excellently preserved fossils here.* — ADJ QUALIT; ◊ ADV

except /ɪ2ksɛpt/. You use **except** or **except for** to introduce the only thing or person that a statement does not apply to. EG *All the boys except Piggy started to giggle... The classroom was silent, except for the busy scratching of pens on paper... There was little I could do except wait.* — PREP OR CONJ

excepted /ɪ2ksɛptɪd/. You use **excepted** after you have mentioned a person or thing to show that you do not include them in the statement you are making. EG *...a gentleman for whom other people - Rhoda excepted - put on their biggest smiles... It is more worth seeing than any city I ever saw, London excepted.* — PREP AFTER N

excepting /ɪ2ksɛptɪŋ/. You use **excepting** to introduce the only thing or person that prevents a statement from being completely true. EG *He was the only human male for miles around (excepting an old handyman).* — PREP

exception /ɪ2ksɛpʃə0n/, **exceptions. 1** An **exception** is a thing, person, or situation that is not included in a general statement. EG *Women, with a few exceptions, are not involved in politics... They are all, with the exception of one Swedish coin, of Portuguese origin... There is no exception to this rule.* — N COUNT: OFT+*of/to*

2 You use **without exception** to indicate that the statement you are making is true in all cases. EG *Almost without exception, the fastest-growing cities are in Africa.* — ADV SEN

3 If you **take exception to** something, you feel offended or annoyed by it, and usually complain about it. EG *There are three things you've just said that I take exception to.* — PHRASE

> Do you make an example of someone who sets a good example?

exceptional /ɪ²ksɛpʃə⁰nəl, -ʃənə⁰l/. **1** Someone who is **exceptional** is unusually talented, clever, or gifted. EG *She was an exceptional teacher... My brother isn't exceptional; there are plenty of youngsters like him.* ADJ QUALIT

2 Exceptional situations, incidents, or events are unusual and only likely to happen very rarely. EG *Permission will be granted only in very exceptional circumstances.* ADJ QUALIT

exceptionally /ɪ²ksɛpʃə⁰nəli¹/. You use **exceptionally 1** to emphasize how very good, important, or bad something is. EG *...an exceptionally fine meal... February had been exceptionally wet.* **2** to indicate that what you are talking about is unusual and is only likely to happen very rarely. EG *Exceptionally, with the approval of the University, a degree will be awarded to a candidate who did not take all the exams.* SUBMOD; ADV SEN

excerpt /ɛksɜːpt/, **excerpts.** An **excerpt** is a short piece of writing or music which is taken from a larger piece. EG *Here are a few excerpts from her diary... You'll hear the oboe in this final excerpt.* N COUNT: OFT+*from*

excess, excesses; pronounced /ɛksɛs/ when it is an adjective, and either /ɪ²ksɛs/ or /ɛksɛs/ when it is a noun.

1 An **excess** of something is a larger amount than is needed, allowed, or usual. EG *Inflation results from an excess of demand over supply... This report should discourage us all from eating an excess of fat.* ▸ used as an adjective. EG *The body gets rid of excess water through the urine.* N SING: *an*+N; ▸ ADJ CLASSIF: ATTRIB

2 If something is **in excess of** an amount, it is more than that amount. EG *...interest rates in excess of 20 per cent.* PREP Formal

3 If you do something **to excess**, you do it too much. EG *He spent all his time in the flat, cleaning and tidying it to excess.* PHRASE

4 Excesses are acts which are very extreme, irresponsible, cruel, or immoral. EG *...the worst excesses of the French Revolution.* N PLURAL

excessive /ɪ²ksɛsɪv/. If you describe something as **excessive**, you mean that it is too large or too extreme. EG *Their profits were excessive... ...excessive pessimism.* ◇ **excessively.** EG *He walked excessively fast.* ADJ QUALIT; ◇ ADV

exchange /ɪ²kstʃeɪnd⁰ʒ/, **exchanges, exchanging, exchanged. 1** If two or more people **exchange** things, they give them to each other at the same time. EG *The three of us exchanged addresses... Gertie and Dolly exchanged glances.* ▸ used as a noun. EG *...an exchange of information.* V+O; ▸ N COUNT

2 If you **exchange** one thing for another, you replace it with it, because the other thing is more satisfactory or more useful. EG *The sales girl refused to exchange the sweater... She exchanged the jewels for money.* V+O: OFT+*for*

3 If you **exchange** your house or job with someone, you live or work in the place where they normally live or work, while they live or work in the place where you normally live or work. EG *The Ingrams exchanged houses with some friends who live in London.* ▸ used as a noun. EG *...the exchange of visiting teachers.* V+O: OFT+*with*; ▸ N COUNT

4 An **exchange** is also a brief conversation. EG *Throughout these exchanges I had a curious feeling of detachment.* N COUNT Formal

5 If you give something to someone **in exchange for** something else, you give it to them because they are giving the other thing to you. EG *They sold textiles in exchange for agricultural products.* PHRASE

6 See also **stock exchange**, **telephone exchange**.

exchange rate, exchange rates. The **exchange rate** is the rate at which a sum of money of your country's currency is exchanged for an equivalent sum of money of another country's currency. N COUNT

excise /ɛksaɪz/ is a tax that the government of a country puts on goods which are produced for sale in that country. EG *...excise duties.* N UNCOUNT

excitable /ɪ²ksaɪtəbə⁰l/. If someone is **excitable**, they become excited very easily. EG *They were both very excitable... ...a highly excitable man.* ADJ QUALIT

excite /ɪ²ksaɪt/, **excites, exciting, excited. 1** If something **excites** you, it makes you very interested and enthusiastic. EG *The idea of journalism excited me.* V+O

2 If something excites a feeling, emotion, or reaction, it causes it to happen. EG *These rumours excited suspicion.* V+O

excited /ɪ²ksaɪtɪ²d/. If you are **excited**, you are so happy that you are full of energy and cannot relax, usually because you are looking forward to something and cannot stop thinking about it. EG *He was so excited he could hardly sleep... There were hundreds of excited children to meet us.* ◇ **excitedly.** EG *They were excitedly discussing plans for the weekend... They turned to each other, laughing excitedly.* ADJ QUALIT; ◇ ADV

excitement /ɪ²ksaɪtmə²nt/, **excitements. 1 Excitement** is the state of being excited. EG *Struggling to conceal his excitement, he accepted her invitation.* N UNCOUNT

2 Excitements are things that cause you to feel excited. EG *...all the excitements of London.* N COUNT Literary

exciting /ɪ²ksaɪtɪŋ/. Something that is **exciting** causes you to feel excited. EG *Growing up in the heart of London was exciting... It did not seem a very exciting idea.* ◇ **excitingly.** EG *Life was excitingly unpredictable.* ADJ QUALIT; ◇ ADV

exclaim /ɪ²kskleɪm/, **exclaims, exclaiming, exclaimed.** When you **exclaim**, you say something suddenly and emphatically because you are excited, shocked, or angry. EG *'Oh, you poor child!' exclaimed Mrs Socket... All of the women exclaimed at how well formed the baby was.* V: OFT +*at/over*; ALSO V+QUOTE

> **EXCLAM** stands for **exclamation**
> Words and phrases which have the label EXCLAM in the Extra Column are exclamations such as **Oh dear!** and **Help!** which you use to show that you are angry, worried, and so on.

exclamation /ɛkskləmeɪʃə⁰n/, **exclamations.** An **exclamation** is a sound, word, or sentence that is spoken suddenly and emphatically in order to express excitement, admiration, shock, or anger. EG *He drew back with a sharp exclamation... They embraced him with exclamations of joy.* N COUNT

exclamation mark, exclamation marks. An **exclamation mark** is the sign (!). It is used in writing to show that a word, phrase, or sentence is an exclamation. N COUNT

exclude /ɪ²ksklu:d/, **excludes, excluding, excluded. 1** If you **exclude** something from an activity or a piece of work, you deliberately do not include that thing in it. EG *For the moment we will exclude the special case of the religious wars.* V+O: OFT+*from*

2 If you **exclude** a possibility, you reject it after considering it carefully. EG *A fake call from some local phone box was not excluded.* V+O

3 If you **exclude** someone from a place or activity, you prevent them from entering the place or taking part in the activity. EG *...jobs from which the majority of workers are excluded.* V+O: OFT+*from*

excluding /ɪ²ksklu:dɪŋ/. You use **excluding** before you mention a person or thing to show that you are not including them in a statement that you are making. EG *We are open seven days a week, excluding Christmas Day.* PREP

exclusion /ɪ²ksklu:ʒə⁰n/. **1** When someone is prevented from entering a place or from taking part in an activity, you can refer to this as their **exclusion** from this place or activity. EG *...the laws relating to the admission and exclusion of aliens.* N UNCOUNT: USU+POSS

2 The **exclusion** of something from a speech, piece of writing, or activity is the act of deliberate- N UNCOUNT ly not including it. EG *...the exclusion of any mention of her good qualities.*

3 You say that something happens **to the exclusion of** other things when it happens to such a great extent that there is no chance for anything else to be considered or to be present. EG *...the ability to concentrate on a problem to the exclusion of all other matters.* PREP

exclusive /ɪ[2]ksklu:sɪv/. **1** Something that is **exclusive** is **1.1** available only to people who are rich or who belong to a high social class. EG *...an exclusive residential district.* ADJ QUALIT **1.2** used or owned by only one person or group, and not shared with anyone else. EG *They have exclusive use of the machine.* ADJ CLASSIF : ATTRIB

2 If two things are mutually **exclusive**, they cannot exist together. EG *There is no reason why these two functions should be mutually exclusive.* ADJ CLASSIF

exclusively /ɪ[2]ksklu:sɪvli[1]/. You use **exclusively** to refer to situations or activities that involve only the things mentioned, and nothing else. EG *...young people who devote their lives exclusively to sport.* ADV

excrement /ɛkskrɪ[1]mə[2]nt/ is the solid waste matter that is passed out of your body through your bowels. N UNCOUNT Formal

excrete /ɪ[2]kskri:t/, **excretes, excreting, excreted.** When you **excrete** waste matter from your body, you get rid of it, usually by going to the lavatory or by sweating. V+O OR V

excruciating /ɪ[2]kskru:ʃieɪtɪŋ/. **1 Excruciating** pain is very painful indeed. EG *I had the most excruciating cramp in my leg.* ADJ QUALIT ◊ **excruciatingly.** EG *Walking was excruciatingly painful.* ◊ SUBMOD

2 An **excruciating** situation or experience is extremely difficult to bear. EG *...excruciating unhappiness.* ADJ QUALIT ◊ **excruciatingly.** EG *It was an excruciatingly humiliating experience.* ◊ SUBMOD

excursion /ɪ[2]ksk3:ʃə[0]n/, **excursions. 1** An **excursion** is a short journey, especially one that you make for a particular purpose. EG *...a shopping excursion... ...excursions to deserted beaches.* N COUNT

2 An **excursion** into something such as a new topic or a new experience is an attempt to develop it or understand it. EG *...a rare excursion into contemporary music.* N COUNT : OFT+*into*

excusable /ɪ[2]kskju:zəbə[0]l/. If a mistake or wrong action is **excusable**, you can forgive it, because of the circumstances in which it was made. EG *He made an excusable mistake.* ADJ QUALIT

excuse, excuses, excusing, excused; pronounced /ɪ[2]kskju:s/ when it is a noun and /ɪ[2]kskju:z/ when it is a verb.

1 An **excuse** is a reason which you give in order to explain why something has been done, has not been done, or will not be done. EG *You don't have to make any excuses to me... There is no excuse for this happening in a new building.* N COUNT

2 If you **excuse** yourself or **excuse** something wrong that you have done, you say why you did it, in an attempt to make yourself seem less bad. EG *I'm not going to try and excuse myself... The Vice-President admitted taking bribes, excusing it as a momentary weakness.* V-REFL OR V+O

3 If you **excuse** someone for something wrong that they have done, you forgive them for it. EG *Such delays cannot be excused... I excused him much of his prejudice because I liked him.* V+O : OFT+*for*, ALSO V+O+O

4 If you **excuse** someone from a duty or responsibility, you free them from it. EG *...a certificate excusing him from games at school.* V+O : OFT+*from*

5 If you ask someone to **excuse** you, you are asking them to allow you to leave. EG *Will you excuse me just a second?* V+O

6 You say **excuse me** to show politeness in these ways: **6.1** to get someone's attention, especially when you want to ask them a question. EG *Excuse me, but is there a fairly cheap restaurant near here?* PHRASE **6.2** before correcting someone. EG *Excuse me, but I think you have misunderstood.* PHRASE **6.3** to apologize for disturbing or interrupting someone, or for doing something slightly impolite such as burping or hiccupping. EG *Excuse me butting in.* PHRASE **6.4** to indicate that you are about to leave the room. CONVENTION **6.5** to ask someone to repeat what they have just said. CONVENTION American

execrable /ɛksɪkrəbə[0]l/. If you say that something is **execrable**, you mean that it is very bad or very unpleasant. EG *The food is execrable.* ADJ QUALIT Formal

execute /ɛksɪkju:t/, **executes, executing, executed. 1** To **execute** someone means to kill them as a punishment. EG *...the last woman to be executed in Britain.* V+O : USU PASS ◊ **execution** /ɛksɪkju:ʃə[0]n/, **executions.** EG *...the execution of Charles I.* ◊ N COUNT OR N UNCOUNT

2 If you **execute** a plan, you carry it out. EG *...a carefully executed crime.* V+O ◊ **execution.** EG *...obstructing an officer in the execution of his duty.* ◊ N UNCOUNT Formal

3 If you **execute** a difficult action or movement, you perform it. EG *The pilot began to execute a series of aerobatics.* V+O

executioner /ɛksɪkju:ʃə[0]nə/, **executioners.** An **executioner** is a person who has the job of executing criminals. N COUNT

executive /ɪ[2]gzɛkjə[4]tɪv/, **executives. 1** An **executive** is someone who is employed by a company at a senior level. EG *...a senior executive.* N COUNT

2 The **executive** sections and tasks of an organization are concerned with making important decisions. EG *...our executive board.* ADJ CLASSIF : ATTRIB

3 Executive goods are expensive and fashionable. EG *...an executive chair.* ADJ CLASSIF : ATTRIB

4 The **executive** of an organization such as a political party is a committee within that organization which has the authority to make important decisions. EG *...the executive of the National Union of Teachers.* N COLL

executor /ɪ[2]gzɛkjə[4]tə/, **executors.** Your **executor** is the person who you appoint to deal with your affairs after your death. N COUNT Legal

exemplary /ɪ[2]gzɛmpləri[1]/. If you describe someone or something as **exemplary**, you mean that they are excellent. EG *He had been an exemplary father.* ADJ QUALIT Formal

exemplify /ɪ[2]gzɛmplɪfaɪ/, **exemplifies, exemplifying, exemplified. 1** If you say that someone or something **exemplifies** a situation or quality, you mean that they are a typical example of it. EG *He exemplified the new liberalism.* V+O

2 If you **exemplify** something, you give an example of it. EG *I'm going to exemplify one or two of these points.* V+O

exempt /ɪ[2]gzɛmp[0]t/, **exempts, exempting, exempted. 1** If you are **exempt** from a rule or duty, you do not have to obey it or perform it. EG *Harold was exempt from military service.* ADJ PRED : USU+*from*

2 To **exempt** a person from a rule or duty means to state officially that they do not have to obey it or perform it. EG *Farmers were exempted from rates.* V+O : OFT+*from* ◊ **exemption** /ɪ[2]gzɛmp[0]ʃə[0]n/, **exemptions.** EG *...exemption from jury service.* ◊ N UNCOUNT OR N COUNT

exercise /ɛksəsaɪz/, **exercises, exercising, exercised. 1 Exercises** are **1.1** energetic movements which you do in order to become fit or remain healthy. EG *...gymnastic exercises.* N COUNT : USU PLURAL **1.2** repeated actions which you do in order to practise for something such as playing a musical instrument. **1.3** operations or manoeuvres that are performed by a section of the army, navy, or air force. EG *...peacetime exercises and training.*

2 Exercise is energetic movement that you do to keep healthy or to train for a sport. EG *I have had all the exercise I need for one day.* N UNCOUNT

3 An **exercise** is a short piece of work that you do, for example in school, which is designed to help you learn something. EG *...grammatical exercises.* N COUNT

4 An **exercise** in something is an activity which is N COUNT

Does exertion exhaust you?

planned to achieve a particular purpose. EG *The rally was organized by the state as an exercise in patriotism.*

5 When you **exercise**, you move your body energetically in order to become fit and to remain healthy. EG *I could not fall asleep unless I exercised first.* V

6 If you **exercise** authority, rights, or responsibilities, you use them. EG *They exercise considerable influence in all western countries... They had no intention of exercising restraint.* ▸ used as a noun. EG *..the exercise of personal responsibility.* V+O Formal ▸ N SING : *the*+N+*of*

7 If something **exercises** your mind, you think or talk about it a great deal. EG *This problem has exercised the minds of academics and politicians.* V+O Formal

exercise book, exercise books. An **exercise book** is a small book with blank pages that pupils and students use for doing their schoolwork. N COUNT

exert /ɪ²gzɜːt/, **exerts, exerting, exerted. 1** If you **exert** influence or pressure, you use it in order to achieve something. EG *These departments exert pressure on the schools to get them to agree.* V+O : USU+A

2 If you **exert** yourself, you make a physical or mental effort to do something. EG *He had to exert himself to make conversation with the visitor.* V-REFL

exertion /ɪ²gzɜʃə⁰n/, **exertions. Exertion** is physical effort or exercise. EG *He was panting with exertion... I was weakened by my exertions.* N UNCOUNT OR N COUNT

exhale /ɪ²gzh⁰eɪl/, **exhales, exhaling, exhaled.** When you **exhale**, you breathe out. EG *He exhaled slowly and smiled.* ◇ **exhalation** /ɛgzəleɪʃə⁰n/, **exhalations.** EG *...a soft exhalation of breath.* V OR V+O Formal ◇ N UNCOUNT OR N COUNT

exhaust /ɪ²gzɔːst/, **exhausts, exhausting, exhausted. 1** If something **exhausts** you, it makes you very tired. EG *She exhausted Nell both nervously and physically.* ◇ **exhausted.** EG *All three men were hot, dirty, and exhausted.* ◇ **exhausting.** EG *...a difficult and exhausting job.* V+O ◇ ADJ QUALIT ◇ ADJ QUALIT

2 If you **exhaust** money or food, you use or finish it all. EG *They soon exhausted the food resources of the surrounding area.* V+O

3 If you **exhaust** a subject, you talk about it so much that there is nothing else to say about it. EG *...when the subject had been thoroughly exhausted.* V+O

4 An **exhaust** or an **exhaust pipe** is a pipe which carries the gas out of the engine of a motor vehicle. See picture at CAR. N COUNT

5 Exhaust is the gas that is produced when the engine of a motor vehicle is running. N UNCOUNT

exhaustion /ɪ²gzɔːstʃə⁰n/ is the state of being so tired that you have no energy left. EG *She was almost fainting with exhaustion.* N UNCOUNT

exhaustive /ɪ²gzɔːstɪv/. An **exhaustive** study or search is very thorough. EG *This list is by no means exhaustive.* ◇ **exhaustively.** EG *...exhaustively researched evidence.* ADJ QUALIT ◇ ADV

exhibit /ɪ²gzɪbɪt/, **exhibits, exhibiting, exhibited. 1** If you **exhibit** an ability or feeling, it can be easily seen by other people. EG *He still exhibited signs of stress.* V+O Formal

2 When something **is exhibited**, it is put in a public place so that people can come to look at it. EG *The paintings are exhibited in chronological sequence.* V+O : USU PASS

3 An **exhibit** is **3.1** something that is put on show to the public in a museum or art gallery. EG *Our local museum has over a thousand exhibits.* **3.2** something that a lawyer shows in court as evidence. EG *Exhibit number two is a diary belonging to the accused.* N COUNT

exhibition /ɛgzɪbɪʃə⁰n/, **exhibitions. 1** An **exhibition** is a collection of pictures, sculptures, or other things displayed in a public place. EG *Did you see the Shakespeare exhibition?* N COUNT

2 Exhibition is the showing of pictures, sculptures, or other things in a public place. EG *The film was refused a licence for public exhibition.* N UNCOUNT

3 If you **make an exhibition of** yourself, you behave very stupidly or rudely in public. PHRASE

exhibitionism /ɛgzɪbɪʃə⁰nɪzə⁰m/ is a type of behaviour in which someone tries to get people's attention all the time; used showing disapproval. ◇ **exhibitionist, exhibitionists.** EG *As a child I was inclined to be an exhibitionist.* N UNCOUNT Formal ◇ N COUNT

exhibitor /ɪ²gzɪbɪtə/, **exhibitors.** An **exhibitor** is a person whose work is being shown in a public exhibition. N COUNT

exhilarate /ɪ²gzɪləreɪt/, **exhilarates, exhilarating, exhilarated.** If you **are exhilarated** by something, it gives you a strong feeling of happiness and excitement. EG *The refugees were exhilarated by the news.* ◇ **exhilarated.** EG *He felt exhilarated.* ◇ **exhilarating.** EG *...an exhilarating experience.* ◇ **exhilaration** /ɪ²gzɪləreɪʃə⁰n/. EG *There was a sense of exhilaration about being alone on the beach.* V+O : USU PASS ◇ ADJ QUALIT ◇ ADJ QUALIT ◇ N UNCOUNT

exhort /ɪ²gzɔːt/, **exhorts, exhorting, exhorted.** If you **exhort** someone to do something, you try hard to persuade them to do it. EG *I exhorted the men not to drink too much.* ◇ **exhortation** /ɛgzɔːteɪʃə⁰n/, **exhortations.** EG *...fervent exhortations to revolutionary action.* V+O : OFT+*to*-INF Formal ◇ N COUNT OR N UNCOUNT

exhume /ɛksh⁰juːm/, **exhumes, exhuming, exhumed.** When a body **is exhumed**, it is taken out of the ground where it is buried. V+O Formal

exile /ɛgzaɪl, ɛksaɪl/, **exiles, exiling, exiled. 1** If someone lives in **exile**, they live in a foreign country because they cannot live in their own country, usually for political reasons. EG *...eight whole months of exile.* N UNCOUNT

2 If someone **is exiled**, they are sent away from their own country and are not allowed to return there. EG *I was exiled from Ceylon for a year.* ◇ **exiled.** EG *...the exiled King.* V+O ◇ ADJ CLASSIF

3 An **exile** is someone who lives in exile. EG *...political exiles.* N COUNT

exist /ɪ²gzɪst/, **exists, existing, existed.** If something **exists**, it is present in the world as a real, living, or actual thing. EG *That word doesn't exist in English... Nobody can actually know if God exists.* V : NO CONT

existence /ɪ²gzɪstəns/, **existences. 1 Existence** is the state of existing. EG *Do you believe in the existence of God?* N UNCOUNT

2 You refer to someone's way of life as an **existence** when they live under difficult conditions. EG *The family lived a more or less vagabond existence.* N COUNT+SUPP

existential /ɛgzɪstɛnʃə⁰l/ means relating to human existence and experience. ADJ CLASSIF Formal

existentialism /ɛgzɪstɛnʃə⁰lɪzə⁰m/ is a philosophical belief which stresses the importance of human experience and says that everyone is responsible for the results of their own actions. ◇ **existentialist** /ɛgzɪstɛnʃə⁰lɪst/, **existentialists.** EG *...the writings of the existentialists.* N UNCOUNT ◇ N COUNT

existing /ɪ²gzɪstɪŋ/. You use **existing** to describe something which is now in use or in operation. EG *We have to find ways of making the existing system work better.* ADJ CLASSIF : ATTRIB

exit /ɛgzɪt, ɛksɪt/, **exits, exiting, exited. 1** An **exit** is **1.1** a door in a public building through which you can leave. EG *He hurried towards the exit.* **1.2** a place on a motorway where traffic can leave the motorway. N COUNT

2 When someone leaves a room, you can say that they make an **exit**. EG *He made a hasty exit from the Men's Room.* N SING

3 If you **exit** from a room, you leave it. EG *I exited from the surgery.* V : IF+PREP THEN *from*

exodus /ɛksədəs/. When there is an **exodus**, a lot of people leave a place together. EG *...the massive exodus of refugees from the North.* N SING

exonerate /ɪ²gzɒnəreɪt/, **exonerates, exonerating, exonerated.** To **exonerate** someone means to show that they are not responsible for something wrong that has happened. EG *...to exonerate me from the crimes they had charged me with.* V+O : OFT+*from* Formal

exorbitant /ɪ[2]gzɔ:bɪtənt/. If you describe something as **exorbitant**, you mean that it is much more expensive than it should be. EG *...an exorbitant rent.* ADJ QUALIT

exorcism /ɛksɔ:sɪzə[0]m/ is the removing of evil spirits from a place or person by using prayer. N UNCOUNT OR N COUNT
◊ **exorcist** /ɛksɔ:sɪst/, **exorcists.** EG *They felt they had to call in an exorcist.* ◊ N COUNT

exorcize /ɛksɔ:saɪz/, **exorcizes, exorcizing, exorcized;** also spelled **exorcise.** To **exorcize** an evil spirit or to **exorcise** a place or person means to force the spirit to leave the place or person by means of prayers and religious ceremonies. V+O

exotic /ɪ[2]gzɒtɪk/. Something that is **exotic** is unusual and interesting because it comes from a distant country. EG *...rich exotic foods.* ADJ QUALIT

expand /ɪ[2]kspænd/, **expands, expanding, expanded.** If something **expands** or if you **expand** it, **1** it becomes greater in number or amount. EG *The city's population expanded by 12 per cent... ...major measures to expand the Royal Air Force.* **2** it becomes larger in size. EG *Natural materials expand with heat... His business expanded rapidly.* V-ERG

expand on or **expand upon.** If you **expand on** or **expand upon** something, you give more information or details about it. EG *Perhaps you could expand on this a little bit.* PHRASAL VB : V+PREP, HAS PASS

expanse /ɪ[2]kspæns/, **expanses.** An **expanse** of sea, sky, or land is a very large amount of it. EG *...the wide expanse of snowy fields.* N COUNT+*of* Written

expansion /ɪ[2]kspænʃə[0]n/ is the process of becoming greater in size or amount. EG *...the rapid expansion of British agriculture.* N UNCOUNT

expansionism /ɪ[2]kspænʃə[0]nɪzə[0]m/ is the policy of expanding the economy of a country or increasing the amount of land that it rules. N UNCOUNT ◊ **expansionist.** EG *...expansionist policies.* ◊ ADJ CLASSIF

expansive /ɪ[2]kspænsɪv/. If you are **expansive**, you talk a lot, because you are happy and relaxed. EG *That week had made him jovial and expansive.* ADJ QUALIT

expatriate /ɛkspætri[1]ət/, **expatriates.** An **expatriate** is someone who is living in a country which is not their own. EG *...British expatriates.* N COUNT

expect /ɪ[2]kspɛkt/, **expects, expecting, expected.**
1 If you **expect** something to happen, you believe that it will happen. EG *Nobody expected the strike to succeed... He didn't expect to be so busy... When do you expect that this material will be available?* V+O+*to*-INF, V+*to*-INF, OR V+REPORT ONLY *that*
2 If you **expect** something, **2.1** you believe that it is going to happen or arrive. EG *We are expecting rain... Dr Willoughby was expecting him.* V+O
◊ **expected.** EG *We would resist this expected attack.* ◊ ADJ CLASSIF **2.2** you believe that it is your right to get it or have it. EG *We expect sincerity from our politicians... I expect to be treated with respect.* V+O, OR V : OFT+*to*-INF
3 If you **expect** someone to do something, you require them to do it as a duty or obligation. EG *He is expected to put his work before his family.* V+O+*to*-INF
4 If a woman **is expecting**, she is pregnant. EG *She's expecting her third baby.* V OR V+O : ONLY CONT
5 If you say **'I expect'**, you mean that you think that what you are saying is likely to be correct. EG *I expect he was trying to make me feel sorry for him.* PHRASE
6 If you say **'What do you expect?'** you mean that there is nothing surprising about a person's behaviour or a situation. EG *What could you expect from a family like that?* PHRASE

expectancy /ɪ[2]kspɛktənsi[1]/ is the feeling that something exciting or interesting is about to happen. ● See also **life expectancy**. N UNCOUNT

expectant /ɪ[2]kspɛktənt/. **1** If you are **expectant**, you are excited because you think something interesting is going to happen. EG *The assembly, sensing a crisis, was tensely expectant.* ADJ QUALIT ◊ **expectantly.** EG *She looked at him expectantly.* ◊ ADV
2 An **expectant** mother or father is someone whose baby is going to be born soon. EG *Good nutrition is important to an expectant mother.* ADJ CLASSIF : ATTRIB

expectation /ɛkspɛkteɪʃə[0]n/, **expectations.** An **expectation** is **1** a strong hope that something will happen. EG *The plan has succeeded beyond our expectations... Living standards and expectations are increasing.* **2** a belief that something is likely to happen or should happen. EG *I was watched in the expectation that I would go too far... ...women with expectations of old-fashioned gallantry.* N COUNT

expediency /ɪ[2]kspi:dɪənsi[1]/ is behaviour in which you do what is convenient, rather than what is morally right. EG *The government is torn between principle and expediency.* N UNCOUNT Formal

expedient /ɪ[2]kspi:dɪənt/, **expedients. 1** An **expedient** is an action or plan that achieves a particular purpose, but that may not be morally acceptable. EG *Incomes controls were used only as a short-term expedient.* N COUNT Formal
2 If it is **expedient** to do something, it is useful or convenient to do it. EG *The President did not find it expedient to attend the meeting.* ADJ QUALIT Formal

expedition /ɛkspɪ[1]dɪʃə[0]n/, **expeditions.** An **expedition** is **1** an organized journey that is made for a particular purpose such as exploration. EG *...the British expedition to Mount Everest... ...a hunting expedition.* **2** a short journey or outing that you make for pleasure. EG *...a shopping expedition.* N COUNT

expel /ɪ[2]kspɛl/, **expels, expelling, expelled. 1** If someone **is expelled** from a school or organization, they are officially told that they no longer belong to it, because they have behaved badly. EG *He had been expelled from his previous school for stealing.* V+O : USU PASS
2 When people **are expelled** from a place, they are made to leave it, usually by force. EG *Peasants were expelled from their villages.* V+O : USU PASS+A
3 If a gas or liquid **is expelled** from a place, it is forced out of it. EG *Water is sucked in at one end and expelled at the other.* V+O Formal

expend /ɪ[2]kspɛnd/, **expends, expending, expended.** To **expend** energy, time, or money means to spend it or use it. EG *They expend large sums of money to maintain this beach.* V+O Formal

expendable /ɪ[2]kspɛndəbə[0]l/, **expendables.** Something or someone that is **expendable** is no longer needed and can be got rid of. EG *My part would be played and I would become expendable.* ADJ CLASSIF Formal

expenditure /ɪ[2]kspɛndɪtʃə/, **expenditures. Expenditure** is **1** the total amount of money that is spent on something. EG *We restricted our expenditure on food... ...public expenditure.* N UNCOUNT OR N COUNT **2** the using of energy or time for a particular purpose. EG *This was done with a minimum expenditure of energy.* N UNCOUNT +SUPP

expense /ɪ[2]kspɛns/, **expenses. 1 Expense** is the money that something costs. EG *...the roads they're building at vast expense... ...household expenses.* N UNCOUNT OR N COUNT
● If you **go to great expense** to do something, you spend a lot of money on it. EG *The Government has gone to great expense to set up procedures.* ● PHRASE
2 Your **expenses** are the money that you spend while doing something connected with your work, and which is paid back to you afterwards. EG *...travelling expenses.* N PLURAL
3 The phrase '**at** someone's **expense**' is used in these ways: **3.1** If you do something **at** someone's **expense**, they provide the money for you to do it. EG *He circulated the document at his own expense.* **3.2** If you make a joke **at** someone's **expense**, you do it to make fun of them or to make them seem foolish. **3.3** If you achieve something **at** someone's **expense**, you do it in a way that harms them. EG *They increase their own income at the expense of the rural masses.* PHRASE, PREP

expensive /ɪ[2]kspɛnsɪv/. Something that is **expensive** costs a lot of money. EG *...expensive clothes.* ADJ QUALIT

If you say 'I expect it's true', do you feel sure that it is true?

◊ **expensively.** EG *We can do that fairly easily and not too expensively.* ◊ ADV

experience /ɪ²kspɪərɪəns/, **experiences, experiencing, experienced. 1 Experience** is **1.1** the fact of having worked at a particular kind of job for a period of time. EG *I had no military experience... She's had nine months experience.* **1.2** the act of seeing, doing, or feeling something or the fact of being affected by it. EG *...his experience of nature and natural forms... The new countries have no experience of democracy.* **1.3** the things that have happened to you or that you have done. EG *Everyone learns best from his own experience... ...speaking from personal experience.* N UNCOUNT: USU+SUPP

2 An **experience** is something that happens to you or something that you do, especially something unusual. EG *Moving house can be a traumatic experience... I was enjoying the experience of working with Tony.* N COUNT+SUPP

3 If you **experience** a situation or feeling, it happens to you or you are affected by it. EG *Similar problems have been experienced by other students... Few of the soldiers had experienced combat... They experienced a mild burning sensation.* V+O

experienced /ɪ²kspɪərɪənst/. You describe someone as **experienced** when they are skilled at a particular job because they have done it for a long time. EG *...an experienced lecturer.* ADJ QUALIT

experiment /ɪ²kspɛrə¹mə²nt/, **experiments, experimenting, experimented. 1** An **experiment** is **1.1** a scientific test which is done in order to prove or discover something. EG *...experiments in physics.* **1.2** the trying out of a new idea or method to see what effect it has. EG *...the failure of this great experiment in industrial democracy.* N COUNT OR N UNCOUNT

2 If you **experiment** with something or **experiment** on it, you do a scientific test on it in order to prove or discover something. EG *He experimented with young white rats.* ◊ **experimentation** /ɪ²kspɛrə¹mɛnteɪʃə⁰n/. EG *...a place for medical experimentation.* ◊ **experimenter** /ɪ²kspɛrə¹mɛntə/, **experimenters.** EG *Experimenters have licences granted by the Home Office.* V: USU+A ◊ N UNCOUNT ◊ N COUNT

3 To **experiment** also means to try out a new idea or method to see what effects it has. EG *...small businesses anxious to experiment with computers.* V: USU+A

◊ **experimentation.** EG *...experimentation with cut-out shapes.* ◊ N UNCOUNT

experimental /ɪ²kspɛrə¹mɛntə⁰l/. **1 Experimental** means **1.1** involving the use of new ideas or methods. EG *...experimental forms of teaching.* ADJ QUALIT

◊ **experimentally.** EG *...the first parking meters, introduced experimentally in 1958.* **1.2** relating to scientific experiments. ◊ **experimentally.** EG *These are then measured experimentally and the results compared.* ◊ ADV; ADJ CLASSIF; ◊ ADV

2 An **experimental** action is done in order to see what effects it has. EG *He gave an experimental tug at Clarissa's bag.* ◊ **experimentally.** EG *He took the rifle and held it experimentally to his shoulder.* ADJ CLASSIF; ◊ ADV

expert /ɛkspɜːt/, **experts. 1** An **expert** is **1.1** a person who is very skilled at doing something. EG *Experts were called in to dismantle the bomb.* **1.2** a person who has studied a particular subject and knows a lot about it. EG *...an expert on Eastern philosophy.* N COUNT

2 Someone who is **expert** at doing something is very skilled at it. EG *...expert acrobats... Get expert treatment from a specialist.* ◊ **expertly.** EG *Burke drove expertly.* ADJ QUALIT; ◊ ADV

expertise /ɛkspɜːtiːz/ is special skill or knowledge. EG *...jobs which require a great deal of managerial expertise.* N UNCOUNT: USU+SUPP

expiate /ɛkspɪeɪt/, **expiates, expiating, expiated.** If you **expiate** guilty feelings or bad behaviour, you do something to indicate that you are sorry for what you have done. EG *He hoped to expiate his guilt over leaving her.* ◊ **expiation** /ɛkspɪeɪʃə⁰n/. EG *He sought expiation by demanding punishment.* V+O Formal; ◊ N UNCOUNT

expire /ɪ²kspaɪə/, **expires, expiring, expired. 1** When something **expires**, it reaches the end of the period of time for which it is valid. EG *My passport is due to expire in three months.* ◊ **expiration** /ɛkspɪreɪʃə⁰n/. EG *...expiration of the legal waiting period.* ◊ **expiry** /ɪ²kspaɪəri¹/. EG *The French licences have no expiry date.* V Formal; ◊ N UNCOUNT; ◊ N UNCOUNT

2 When someone **expires**, they die. EG *The old lady expired within the hour.* V Literary

explain /ɪ²ksplerɪn/, **explains, explaining, explained.** If you **explain** something, **1** you give details about it so that it can be understood. EG *John went on to explain the legal situation... I explained that I was trying to write a book... Let me explain to you about Jackie.* **2** you give people reasons for it. EG *He never wrote to me to explain his decision... Just a minute. Let me explain.* V+O: OFT+to; ALSO V+REPORT OR QUOTE; V+O, V-REFL, OR V

explain away. If you **explain away** a mistake, you try to indicate that it is not very important or that it is not really your fault. EG *...explaining away his department's latest blunder.* PHRASAL VB: V+O+ADV

explanation /ɛksplәneɪʃə⁰n/, **explanations.** If you give an **explanation**, **1** you say why something happened. EG *There was no reasonable explanation for her decision... Enclose a note of explanation with the parcel... The time for lengthy explanations was over.* **2** you describe something in detail. EG *...a scientific explanation of the universe.* N COUNT OR N UNCOUNT; N COUNT

explanatory /ɪ²ksplænətə⁰ri¹/. **Explanatory** statements are intended to make people understand something by describing it or giving the reasons for it. EG *They produce free explanatory leaflets on heating.* ADJ CLASSIF Formal

explicable /ɛksplɪkəbə⁰l, ɪ²ksplɪk-/. Something that is **explicable** can be explained and understood. EG *For no explicable reason your mind goes blank.* ADJ QUALIT Formal

explicit /ɪ²ksplɪsɪt/. **1** Something that is **explicit** is shown or expressed clearly and openly, without any attempt to hide anything. EG *...the explicit support of the Prime Minister.* ◊ **explicitly.** EG *...explicitly violent scenes.* ADJ QUALIT; ◊ ADV

2 If you are **explicit** about something, you express yourself clearly and openly about it. EG *She was not explicit about what she really felt.* ◊ **explicitly.** EG *This was explicitly admitted by the Premier.* ADJ QUALIT; ◊ ADV

explode /ɪ²ksplәʊd/, **explodes, exploding, exploded. 1** When a bomb **explodes**, it bursts loudly and with great force, often causing a lot of damage. EG *A bomb had exploded in the next street... They exploded a nuclear device.* V-ERG

2 When something increases suddenly and rapidly, you can say that it **explodes**. EG *The population was still exploding.* V

3 You can say that a person **explodes** when they express strong feelings suddenly and violently. EG *She exploded with rage.* V+A

4 If you **explode** a theory, you prove that it is wrong or impossible. EG *I could explode some of the myths about him.* V+O

exploit, exploits, exploiting, exploited; pronounced /ɪksplɔɪt/ when it is a verb and /ɛksplɔɪt/ when it is a noun. **1** If someone **exploits** you, they treat you unfairly by using your work or your ideas and giving you very little in return. EG *Adults exploit children far too often.* ◊ **exploitation** /ɛksplɔɪteɪʃə⁰n/. EG *...to protect the public from commercial exploitation.* V+O; ◊ N UNCOUNT

2 If you **exploit** something such as a raw material or an idea, you develop it in order to make money out of it. EG *Everyone is seeking to exploit opportunities for improving efficiency.* ◊ **exploitation.** EG *...the exploitation of the Earth's resources.* V+O; ◊ N UNCOUNT

3 Someone's **exploits** are the brave or interesting things that they have done. EG *...his exploits in the War.* N COUNT: USU PLURAL

exploitative /ɪ²ksplɔɪtətɪv/. If you describe a person or organization as **exploitative**, you mean that they treat people unfairly because they are interested only in making money. EG *...exploitative employment agencies.* ADJ QUALIT Formal

exploiter /ɪ²ksplɔɪtə/, **exploiters.** You refer to people as **exploiters** when they use other people or things in order to make money in an uncaring way. EG *...the misuse of power by property-hungry exploiters.* N COUNT

exploratory /ɪ²ksplɒrətə⁰ri¹/. **Exploratory** actions are done in order to discover something or to learn something. EG *An early exploratory expedition had failed.* ADJ CLASSIF Formal

explore /ɪ²ksplɔː/, **explores, exploring, explored.** **1** If you **explore** a place, you travel in it in order to find out what it is like. EG *He explored three continents by canoe.* V+O ◇ **exploration** /ɛkspləreɪʃə⁰n/, **explorations.** EG *...voyages of exploration... He had become fascinated by the great explorations of the past.* ◇ N UNCOUNT OR N COUNT ◇ **explorer** /ɪ²ksplɔːrə/, **explorers.** EG *...an Arctic explorer.* ◇ N COUNT

2 If you **explore** something with your hands, you touch it so that you can feel what it is like. EG *With widespread hands he explored the wet grass.* V+O

3 If you **explore** an idea, you think about it carefully in order to decide whether it is a good one. EG *The conference explored the possibility of closer trade links.* V+O ◇ **exploration.** EG *...a fundamental exploration of the main alternatives.* ◇ N UNCOUNT OR N COUNT

explosion /ɪ²kspləʊʒə⁰n/, **explosions.** An **explosion** is **1** a sudden, violent burst of energy, for example one caused by a bomb. EG *Twenty men were killed in the explosion.* N COUNT **2** a large and rapid increase in something. EG *...the population explosion.* N COUNT+SUPP **3** a sudden and violent expression of anger. EG *...an explosion of rage.* N COUNT **4** an outbreak of protest or violence. EG *...the explosion of mass protest.* N COUNT

explosive /ɪ²kspləʊsɪv/, **explosives.** **1** An **explosive** is a substance or device that can explode. N COUNT OR N UNCOUNT

2 Something that is **explosive** **2.1** is capable of exploding or is likely to explode. EG *...a powerful explosive device.* ADJ CLASSIF **2.2** involves an explosion or results from an explosion. EG *Modern bullets produce an explosive effect upon impact.* ADJ CLASSIF **2.3** happens suddenly and makes a loud noise. EG *The final applause was explosive.* ADJ QUALIT

3 An **explosive** situation is likely to have serious or dangerous effects. EG *Unemployment has become the most explosive political issue.* ADJ QUALIT

exponent /ɪ²kspəʊnənt/, **exponents.** **1** An **exponent** of an idea, theory, or plan is someone who supports it. EG *...the leading exponents of apartheid.* N COUNT+SUPP

2 An **exponent** of a particular skill or activity is someone who is good at it. EG *...the supreme exponent of the English humorous essay.* N COUNT+SUPP Formal

exponential /ɛkspə⁶nɛnʃə⁰l/ means growing or increasing very rapidly. EG *Computer technology is embarking on a period of exponential growth.* ADJ CLASSIF Formal
◇ **exponentially.** EG *Money spent by Education Authorities has risen exponentially.* ◇ ADV

export, exports, exporting, exported; pronounced /ɛkspɔt/ when it is a noun and /ɪ²kspɔt/ when it is a verb.

1 To **export** products or raw materials means to sell them to another country and send them there. EG *Africa is exporting beef to Europe.* V+O OR V ▸ used as a noun. EG *They grow coffee and bananas for export.* ▸ N UNCOUNT

2 **Exports** are products or raw materials which are sold and sent to another country. N COUNT

3 To **export** ideas or values means to introduce them into other countries. EG *The values of today's Europeans are now exported by them to all parts of the world.* V+O

exporter /ɛkspɔːtə/, **exporters.** An **exporter** is a country, firm, or person that sells and sends goods to another country. N COUNT

expose /ɛkspəʊz/, **exposes, exposing, exposed.** **1** To **expose** something means to uncover it and make it visible. EG *The rocks are exposed at low tide.* V+O

2 If you **are exposed** to something dangerous or unpleasant, you are put in a situation in which it might harm you. EG *They had been exposed to radiation.* V+O+*to*

3 If you **are exposed** to an idea or feeling, you experience it. EG *We are all exposed to grief.* V+O+*to*: USU PASS

4 To **expose** a person or situation means to reveal the truth about them, especially when it involves dishonest or shocking behaviour. EG *He was eventually exposed in the perjury case.* V+O

5 An **exposed** place has no natural protection against bad weather or enemies. EG *The house is in a very exposed position.* ADJ QUALIT

exposé /ɛkspəʊzeɪ/, **exposés.** An **exposé** is a piece of writing which reveals the truth about a situation or person, especially when it involves dishonest or shocking behaviour. EG *...a lucid exposé of the hypocrisy surrounding the payment.* N COUNT

exposition /ɛkspə⁶zɪʃə⁰n/, **expositions.** An **exposition** is a detailed explanation of an idea or a discussion of a problem. EG *...a clear exposition of the theory of evolution.* N COUNT Formal

expostulate /ɪ²kspɒstjə⁴leɪt/, **expostulates, expostulating, expostulated.** If you **expostulate**, you express strong disagreement with someone. EG *Sir William expostulated against this policy of suppression.* V OR V+QUOTE Formal

exposure /ɪ²kspəʊʒə/, **exposures.** **1** **Exposure** to something is **1.1** a situation in which you are affected or influenced by something. EG *He was suffering from exposure to nuclear radiation... ...receiving maximum exposure to new ideas.* N UNCOUNT **1.2** the publicity given to something. EG *...the widest possible exposure to scenes of casualties and damage.*

2 The **exposure** of someone or something is the revealing of the truth about them, especially when it involves dishonest or shocking behaviour. EG *...the public exposure of a president.* N UNCOUNT

3 **Exposure** is the harmful effect on your body caused by very cold weather. EG *The group's leader died of exposure.* N UNCOUNT

4 In photography, an **exposure** is a single photograph. EG *...a camera capable of taking a hundred exposures before the film needs changing.* N COUNT Technical

expound /ɪ²kspaʊnd/, **expounds, expounding, expounded.** If you **expound** an idea or opinion, you give a clear and detailed explanation of it. EG *He expounded his latest theory.* V+O Formal

express /ɪ²ksprɛs/, **expresses, expressing, expressed.** **1** When you **express** an idea or feeling or when you **express** yourself, you show people what you think or feel by saying or doing something. EG *They hooted their car horns to express their disapproval... I expressed myself better in French.* V+O OR V-REFL

2 If an idea or feeling **expresses** itself in some way, it can be clearly seen in someone's actions or in its effects on a situation. EG *That increased confidence expressed itself in other ways.* V-REFL : USU+ Formal

3 If you **express** a quantity in a particular form, you write it down in that form. EG *Here it is expressed as a percentage.* V+O : USU+A Technical

4 An **express** command or order is one that is clearly stated. EG *This may not be published save by the express direction of the School.* ADJ CLASSIF : ATTRIB Formal
◇ **expressly.** EG *Jefferson had expressly asked her to invite Freeman.* ◇ ADV

5 An **express** intention or purpose is a deliberate and specific one. EG *She came with the express purpose of causing trouble.* ADJ CLASSIF : ATTRIB ◇ **expressly.** EG *They bought the house expressly for her.* ◇ ADV

6 An **express** service is one in which things are ADJ CLASSIF :

If your face is expressionless, do people know what you are thinking?

sent or done faster than usual. EG *...an express letter.* ATTRIB

7 An **express** is a fast train or coach which stops at very few places. N COUNT

expression /ɪ^{2}kspreʃə^{0}n/, **expressions. 1** An **expression** is a word or phrase that is usually used in a particular situation or by particular people, and that you are quoting, explaining, or commenting on. EG *...slang expressions... The expression is 'fly in the ointment'.* N COUNT

2 The **expression** of ideas or feelings is **2.1** the act of putting them into words by speaking or writing. EG *We parted with many expressions of goodwill.* N UNCOUNT OR N COUNT : OFT+*of*

2.2 the act of showing them through your actions or through artistic activities. EG *His carvings have become one of the finest expressions of African art.* N COUNT : OFT+*of*

3 Your **expression** is the way that your face shows what you are thinking or feeling. EG *He couldn't see the expression on her face... Anthony's face showed no expression.* N COUNT +SUPP OR N UNCOUNT

4 Expression is the showing of feeling when you are acting, singing, or playing a musical instrument. EG *The playing was flat, without expression.* N UNCOUNT

expressionless /ɪ^{2}kspreʃə^{0}nlɪ^{2}s/. If someone's face or voice is **expressionless**, it shows no feelings. EG *His face was completely expressionless.* ADJ QUALIT

expressive /ɪ^{2}kspresɪv/. **1** Something that is **expressive** indicates clearly a person's feelings or intentions. EG *She had given Lynn an expressive glance.* ◊ **expressively.** EG *He drew a finger expressively across his throat.* ADJ QUALIT ◊ ADV

2 Someone's **expressive** ability is their ability to speak or write clearly and interestingly. EG *...evaluating the child's expressive powers.* ADJ CLASSIF

expressway /ɪ^{2}kspresweɪ/, **expressways.** An **expressway** is a wide road that is specially designed so that a lot of traffic can move along it very quickly. EG *...a four-lane expressway.* N COUNT American

expropriate /ɛksprəʊprɪeɪt/, **expropriates, expropriating, expropriated.** If someone **expropriates** something, they take it away from the person who it belongs to. EG *The surplus will be expropriated by the government.* V+O Formal

expulsion /ɪ^{2}kspʌlʃə^{0}n/, **expulsions. Expulsion** is **1** the expelling of someone from a school or organization. EG *...his expulsion from the university.* N UNCOUNT OR N COUNT Formal

2 the act of forcing people to leave a place. EG *...the expulsion of military advisers.* **3** the act of forcing something out of a container or out of your body. EG *...with each expulsion of breath.* Formal Formal

exquisite /ɪ^{2}kskwɪzɪt, ɛkskwɪzɪt/. You describe something as **exquisite 1** when it is extremely beautiful in appearance. EG *She has the most exquisite face... ...exquisite jewellery.* ◊ **exquisitely.** EG *Their children were exquisitely dressed.* **2** when it is very pleasant or satisfying. EG *...sipping the water slowly with exquisite relief.* ◊ **exquisitely.** EG *...his exquisitely polite voice.* ADJ QUALIT ◊ ADV ADJ QUALIT ◊ ADV

extant /ɛkstænt, ɛkstənt/. Something that is **extant** still exists although it is very old. EG *...one Spanish law that is still extant in California.* ADJ CLASSIF Formal

extend /ɪ^{2}kstend/, **extends, extending, extended. 1** If something **extends** for a particular distance, it continues for that distance from a point or central area. EG *The road now extends two kilometres beyond the River.* V+A

2 If something **extends** from a surface or object, it sticks out from it. EG *...metal slabs extending from the wall.* V+A

3 If something **extends** for a period of time, it continues for that time. EG *His working day often extends well into the evening.* V+A

4 If something **extends** to other people or things, it includes or affects them. EG *The consequences of unemployment extend well beyond the labour market.* V+A

5 If you **extend** something, **5.1** you make it bigger or longer. EG *Have you ever thought of extending your house?* **5.2** you cause it to exist or be valid for a longer period of time. EG *The authorities extended her visa.* ◊ **extended.** EG *...extended news bulletins.* **5.3** you cause it to include or affect more people or things. EG *Congress wants the law extended to cover all states.* V+O V+O ◊ ADJ CLASSIF V+O

6 If you **extend** a part of your body, you straighten it or stretch it out. EG *He extended his hand, and Brody shook it.* V+O

7 If you **extend** something to someone, you offer it to them in a polite or friendly way. EG *The invitation she had extended was promptly accepted.* V+O : OFT+*to* Formal

extension /ɪ^{2}kstenʃə^{0}n/, **extensions. 1** An **extension** is a new room or building which is added to an existing building. EG *...a new extension to the library.* N COUNT

2 An **extension** is also **2.1** an extra period of time for which something continues to exist or be valid. EG *He asked for extension of his residence permit.* N COUNT OR N UNCOUNT

2.2 a development that includes or affects more people, ideas, or activities. EG *Nationalist leaders demanded the extension of democratic rights.*

3 A telephone **extension** is a telephone that is connected to the switchboard of an organization, and that has a special number. N COUNT

extensive /ɪ^{2}kstensɪv/. Something that is **extensive 1** covers a large area. EG *...an extensive Roman settlement in north-west England.* **2** is very great in effect. EG *Many buildings suffered extensive damage in the blast.* ◊ **extensively.** EG *The aircraft were extensively modified.* **3** contains many details, ideas, or items on a particular subject. EG *We had fairly extensive discussions.* ◊ **extensively.** EG *I have quoted extensively from it in the following pages.* ADJ QUALIT ADJ QUALIT ◊ ADV ADJ QUALIT ◊ ADV

extent /ɪ^{2}kstent/. **1** The **extent** of something is its length, area, or size. EG *...to expand the empire to its largest extent.* N SING+POSS

2 The **extent** of a situation or difficulty is its size or scale. EG *The full extent of the problem is not yet known.* N SING+POSS

3 You use phrases such as **to a large extent, to some extent**, or **to a certain extent** in order to indicate that something is partly true, but not entirely true. EG *Well I think to a certain extent it's true.* ADV SEN

4 You use phrases such as **to what extent, to that extent**, or **to the extent that** when you are discussing how true a statement is. EG *To what extent are diseases linked with genes?... A computer is intelligent only to the extent that it can store information.* PHRASE

5 You use phrases such as **to the extent of, to the extent that**, or **to such an extent that** in order to indicate that a situation has reached a particular stage. EG *Sanitary conditions had deteriorated to such an extent that there was widespread danger of disease.* PHRASE

exterior /ɪ^{2}kstɪərɪə/, **exteriors. 1** The **exterior** of something is its outside surface. EG *Keep your car exterior in good condition.* N COUNT

2 Your **exterior** is your usual appearance or behaviour, especially when it is very different from your character. EG *Beneath his professional doctor's exterior, he was wildly fun-loving and reckless.* N COUNT+SUPP

3 You use **exterior** to describe something that is situated or happening outside something or someone. EG *Exterior drains must be kept clear.* ADJ CLASSIF : ATTRIB

exterminate /ɪ^{2}kstɜːmɪneɪt/, **exterminates, exterminating, exterminated.** When a group of animals or people **is exterminated**, they are all killed. EG *Fishing must stop before the species is completely exterminated.* ◊ **extermination** /ɪ^{2}kstɜːmɪneɪʃə^{0}n/. EG *...a way to prevent the extermination of these animals.* V+O : USU PASS ◊ N UNCOUNT

external /ɪ^{2}kstɜːnə^{0}l/, **externals. 1 External** means happening, coming from, or existing outside a place, person, or area of activity. EG *...the exter-* ADJ CLASSIF : USU ATTRIB

nal walls of the chimneys... They did it in response to external pressures. ◇ **externally.** EG *It should be applied externally.*
◇ ADV

2 External is used to describe people who come into an organization from outside in order to do a job there. EG *Their accounts are audited by a firm of external auditors.*
ADJ CLASSIF : ATTRIB

3 When you talk about the **externals** of a situation, you are referring to features that are obvious but not very important. EG *The popular historian is concerned only with externals.*
N PLURAL Formal

extinct /ɪ^{2}kstɪŋkt/. **1** A species of animals that is **extinct** no longer has any living members. EG *The wolf is now nearly extinct... The dodo became extinct about 300 years ago.*
ADJ CLASSIF

2 An **extinct** volcano does not erupt or is very unlikely to erupt.
ADJ CLASSIF

extinction /ɪ^{2}kstɪŋk^{0}ʃə^{0}n/ is The **extinction** of a species of animal is the death of all its remaining members. EG *Apes are in danger of extinction.*
N UNCOUNT

extinguish /ɪ^{2}kstɪŋgwɪʃ/, **extinguishes, extinguishing, extinguished. 1** If you **extinguish** a fire or a light, you stop it burning or shining. EG *...a new method of extinguishing forest fires.*
V+O Formal

2 If someone or something **extinguishes** an idea or feeling, they destroy it. EG *We have to extinguish the memory of the defeat.*
V+O Formal

extinguisher /ɪ^{2}kstɪŋgwɪʃə/. See **fire extinguisher**.

extol /ɪ^{2}kstəʊl/, **extols, extolling, extolled.** If you **extol** something, you praise it enthusiastically, often in order to persuade other people to like it or approve of it. EG *Only a week or two later he was extolling the virtues of female independence.*
V+O Formal

extort /ɪ^{2}kstɔːt/, **extorts, extorting, extorted.** If someone **extorts** money from you, they get it from you by using force or threats. EG *They extorted every penny from us.* ◇ **extortion** /ɪ^{2}kstɔːʃə^{0}n/. EG *He faces trial on extortion charges.*
V+O : OFT+*from*
◇ N UNCOUNT

extortionate /ɪ^{2}kstɔːʃə^{0}nət/. You describe something as **extortionate** when it is bigger or more costly than you consider to be fair. EG *...a worker making extortionate demands upon the employer.*
ADJ QUALIT

extra /ɛkstrə/, **extras. 1** An **extra** thing, person, or amount is a thing, person, or amount that is added to others of the same kind. EG *Take an extra pair of shoes... You have to pay extra for breakfast.*
QUANTIF, OR ADV AFTER VB

2 Extras are **2.1** things that are not necessary but that make something more comfortable, useful, or enjoyable. EG *With the extras, the car cost £4,000.*
N COUNT : USU PLURAL
2.2 additional amounts of money which are added to the price that you have to pay for something. EG *There are no hidden extras.*

3 An **extra** is a person who plays an unimportant part in a film.
N COUNT

4 If you are **extra** polite or **extra** careful, you are more polite or careful than usual. EG *He was extra polite to his superiors.*
SUBMOD

extra- is used to form adjectives that describe something as being outside something else. For example, extra-parliamentary activities are political activities that take place outside parliament. EG *He was preoccupied with extra-theatrical problems.*
PREFIX Formal

extract, extracts, extracting, extracted; pronounced /ɪ^{2}kstrækt/ when it is a verb and /ɛkstrækt/ when it is a noun.

1 If you **extract** something from a place, you take it out or pull it out. EG *Mrs Oliver extracted a small notebook from her bag... He tried to extract his pole from the mud.*
V+O : OFT+*from* Formal

2 To **extract** a raw material means to get it from the ground or from another substance. EG *The Japanese extract ten million tons of coal each year.*
V+O

3 If you **extract** information from someone, you get it from them with difficulty. EG *Sir James had extracted from Francis a fairly detailed account.*
V+O : OFT+*from*

4 If someone **extracts** an advantage from a situation, they use the situation in order to gain the advantage. EG *They will extract the maximum propaganda value from this affair.*
V+O+*from* Formal

5 An **extract** from a piece of writing or music is a small part of it that is printed or played separately. EG *I would like to quote two extracts from the book.*
N COUNT

extraction /ɪ^{2}kstrækʃə^{0}n/. **1** Your **extraction** is the country or people that your family originally comes from. EG *Alistair was of Scottish extraction.*
N UNCOUNT Formal

2 The **extraction** of something from a place is the act or process of removing it. EG *...industries involved in mineral extraction.*
N UNCOUNT

extractor /ɪ^{2}kstræktə/, **extractors.** An **extractor** or **extractor fan** is a device that is fixed to a window or wall in order to draw steam or hot air out of a room or building.
N COUNT

extra-curricular /ɛkstrə kərɪkjə^{4}lə/. **Extra-curricular** activities are activities for students that are not part of the course that they are doing. EG *We offer a wide range of extracurricular activities... ...informal, extra-curricular discussions about politics.*
ADJ CLASSIF Formal

extradite /ɛkstrədaɪt/, **extradites, extraditing, extradited.** To **extradite** someone means to officially send them back to their own country so that they can be tried there for a crime that they have been accused of. ◇ **extradition** /ɛkstrədɪʃə^{0}n/, **extraditions.** EG *France requested their extradition from the United States.*
V+O Formal
◇ N UNCOUNT OR N COUNT

extramarital /ɛkstrəmærɪtə^{0}l/. You use **extramarital** to describe a sexual relationship between a married person and another person who is not their husband or wife. EG *...an extramarital affair.*
ADJ CLASSIF Formal

extra-mural. You use **extra-mural** to refer to courses in a college or university which are involved mainly with part-time students. EG *...the Department of Extra-mural Studies.*
ADJ CLASSIF : ATTRIB

extraneous /ɪ^{2}kstreɪnɪəs/. Something that is **extraneous** happens or concerns things outside the situation or subject that you are talking about. EG *We must avoid all extraneous issues.*
ADJ CLASSIF Formal

extraordinary /ɪ^{2}kstrɔːdə^{0}nə^{0}ri^1/. **1** If you describe someone or something as **extraordinary**, you mean that they have some very special or extreme qualities. EG *My grandfather was a most extraordinary man.* ◇ **extraordinarily.** EG *...an extraordinarily beautiful girl.*
ADJ QUALIT
◇ SUBMOD

2 You can also say that something is **extraordinary** when it is unusual or surprising in a particular situation. EG *What an extraordinary thing to say.* ◇ **extraordinarily.** EG *...extraordinarily high levels of radiation.*
ADJ QUALIT
◇ SUBMOD

3 An **extraordinary** meeting is arranged specially to deal with a particular situation or problem.
ADJ CLASSIF : ATTRIB

extravagance /ɪ^{2}kstrævə^{1}gəns/, **extravagances.**

1 Extravagance is the spending of more money than is reasonable or than you can afford. EG *It is easy to criticize governments for extravagance and waste.*
N UNCOUNT

2 An **extravagance** is something that you spend money on which you cannot really afford. EG *It was a little extravagance of my father to buy new plants every year.*
N COUNT

extravagant /ɪ^{2}kstrævə^{1}gənt/. **1** Someone who is **extravagant 1.1** spends more money than is reasonable or than they can afford. EG *He was extravagant and liked to live well.* ◇ **extravagantly.** EG *I lived extravagantly, taking cabs everywhere.*
ADJ QUALIT
◇ ADV
1.2 uses more of something than is reasonable. EG *She considered him extravagant with electricity.*
ADJ QUALIT

2 Something that is **extravagant 2.1** costs more money than is reasonable or than you can afford. EG *...extravagant gifts.* ◇ **extravagantly.** EG *...merchandise known to be extravagantly priced.*
ADJ QUALIT
◇ SUBMOD
2.2 uses more of something than is reasonable. EG
ADJ QUALIT

Does an extravaganza cost an extortionate amount of money?

...machines that are extravagant in their requirements of energy.

3 Extravagant behaviour is extreme and is done to create a particular effect. EG *He raised his eyebrows in extravagant surprise.* ◇ **extravagantly.** EG *Harold was extravagantly affectionate with his daughters.* — ADJ QUALIT; Formal; ◇ SUBMOD

4 Extravagant ideas are unrealistic and impractical. EG *...extravagant expectations.* — ADJ QUALIT; Formal

5 Extravagant entertainments or designs are elaborate and impressive. ◇ **extravagantly.** EG *...extravagantly elaborate funerals.* — ADJ QUALIT; ◇ SUBMOD

extravaganza /ɪ[2]kstrævəgænzə/, **extravaganzas.** An **extravaganza** is a very elaborate and expensive public activity or performance. — N COUNT

extreme /ɪ[2]kstri:m/, **extremes. 1 Extreme** means very great in degree or intensity. EG *He died in extreme poverty... You must proceed with extreme caution.* ◇ **extremely.** EG *...an extremely difficult task... Ralph and I always got on extremely well.* — ADJ QUALIT : ATTRIB; ◇ SUBMOD

2 Things that are **extreme**, for example opinions, beliefs, or behaviour, are very severe, unusual, or unreasonable. EG *People are capable of surviving in extreme conditions... Their methods may seem extreme to many parents... ...the extreme Right Wing of the Party.* — ADJ QUALIT

3 The **extreme** point, edge, or end of something is its furthest point, edge, or end. EG *...the extreme south of the country.* — ADJ CLASSIF : ATTRIB

4 An **extreme** of behaviour is one in which you show a quality or attitude to an unacceptable degree. EG *There's now a danger that we're going to the other extreme and being too lenient.* — N COUNT

5 If you say that someone **is going to extremes**, or **is taking** something **to extremes**, you mean that their behaviour is extreme and unacceptable. — PHRASE

6 You use **in the extreme** to emphasize how bad or undesirable something is. EG *I thought the suggestion dangerous in the extreme.* — PHRASE; Formal

extremism /ɪ[2]kstri:mɪzə[0]m/ is the behaviour or beliefs of extremists. EG *...political extremism.* — N UNCOUNT

extremist /ɪ[2]kstri:mɪst/, **extremists.** An **extremist** is a person who wishes to bring about political or social change by using methods that other people consider too severe or unreasonable. EG *...a bomb planted by Nationalist extremists.* ▸ used as an adjective. EG *...political parties with extremist views.* — N COUNT; ▸ ADJ CLASSIF

extremity /ɪ[2]kstremɪ[1]ti[1]/, **extremities. 1** The **extremities** of something are its furthest ends or edges. EG *...the northern extremity of the cathedral.* — N COUNT : USU+POSS; Formal

2 Your **extremities** are the outermost parts of your body, especially your hands and feet. EG *The warmth spread outwards till it reached his extremities.* — N PLURAL

3 An **extremity** is a very serious situation. EG *She tried to remember how things had ever reached such an extremity.* — N COUNT; Formal

4 If you think that someone talks or behaves in an extreme way, you can talk about the **extremity** of their views or behaviour. — N UNCOUNT; Formal

extricate /ɛkstrɪkeɪt/, **extricates, extricating, extricated. 1** If you **extricate** someone from a difficult or serious situation, you free them from it. EG *She found it impossible to extricate herself from the relationship.* — V+O OR V-REFL : OFT+*from*

2 If you **extricate** someone from a place where they are trapped or caught, you succeed in freeing them. EG *It was exceedingly difficult to extricate her from the hole.* — V+O OR V-REFL : OFT+*from*

extrovert /ɛkstrəvɜ:t/, **extroverts.** An **extrovert** is a person who is very active, lively, and sociable. ▸ used as an adjective. EG *...a rather extrovert student.* — N COUNT; ▸ ADJ QUALIT

extrude /ɪ[2]kstru:d/, **extrudes, extruding, extruded.** When something **extrudes** or **is extruded**, it is forced or squeezed out through a small opening. EG *As the eggs are extruded, the male fertilizes them.* — V-ERG; Formal

exuberant /ɪ[2]gzju:bə[0]rənt/. Someone who is **exuberant** is full of energy, excitement, and cheerfulness. EG *...the exuberant director of the Theatre Royal.* ◇ **exuberantly.** EG *Children danced exuberantly around the tree.* ◇ **exuberance** /ɪ[2]gzju:bə[0]rəns/. EG *She always greeted him with the same exuberance.* — ADJ QUALIT; ◇ ADV; ◇ N UNCOUNT

exude /ɪ[2]gzju:d/, **exudes, exuding, exuded. 1** If you say that someone **exudes** a quality or feeling, you mean that they seem to have it to a great extent. EG *She exuded vitality, enthusiasm, and generosity.* — V+O; Formal

2 If something **exudes** a liquid or a smell, the liquid or smell comes out of it. EG *Some frogs exude a poisonous chemical from their skins.* — V-ERG; Formal

exult /ɪ[2]gzʌlt/, **exults, exulting, exulted.** If you **exult**, you feel and show great happiness and pleasure because of some triumph or success that you have had. EG *I exulted at my fortune... 'I've never played golf like I did last week,' he exulted.* ◇ **exultation** /ɪ[2]gzəlteɪʃə[0]n/. EG *He spoke with an air of exultation.* — V : USU+A OR V+QUOTE; ◇ N UNCOUNT

exultant /ɪ[2]gzʌltənt/. If you are **exultant**, you feel very happy and triumphant. EG *Her voice was loud and exultant.* ◇ **exultantly.** EG *She laughed again, exultantly.* — ADJ QUALIT; Formal; ◇ ADV

eye /aɪ/, **eyes, eyeing** or **eying, eyed. 1** Your **eyes** are the two things in your face that you see with. See picture at THE HUMAN BODY. EG *She opened her eyes.* — N COUNT

2 If you say that someone has an **eye** for something, you mean that they can recognize it and make good judgements about it. EG *...a marvellous eye for detail.* — N SING+*for*

3 If you **eye** something, you look at it carefully or suspiciously. EG *Posy was eyeing the man thoughtfully.* — V+O : NO IMPER

4 Eye is also used in these phrases. **4.1** If you say that something happened **before** your **eyes**, you mean that you actually saw it happen. EG *Her father was murdered before her very eyes.* **4.2** If you **cast** or **run** your **eye over** something, you look quickly at every part of it. EG *He ran his eye over the article.* **4.3** If something **catches** your **eye**, you suddenly notice it. EG *The flowers in your window caught my eye.* **4.4** If you try to **catch** someone's **eye**, you try to attract their attention. **4.5** If you **clap**, **lay**, or **set eyes on** someone, you see them. EG *She was the most extraordinary person I had ever laid eyes on.* (Outdated) **4.6** If you **cry** your **eyes out**, you cry a lot. **4.7** If someone **has** their **eye on** you, they are watching you and making judgements about you. **4.8** If you say that something is true **in** a particular person's **eyes**, you mean that this is that person's opinion. EG *Her children could do no wrong in her eyes.* **4.9** If you **keep** your **eyes open** or if you **keep an eye out for** something, you are looking or watching for it carefully. EG *You'll have to keep your eyes open for trouble tonight.* (Informal) **4.10** If you **keep an eye on** someone or something, you watch them and make sure that they are safe. EG *Can you keep an eye on the baby while I go shopping?* **4.11** If you say that there is **more** to a situation **than meets the eye**, you mean that it is more complicated than you originally thought. **4.12** If an event **opens** your **eyes**, it makes you aware that something is different from the way you thought it was. **4.13** If you don't **see eye to eye** with someone, you don't agree with them. **4.14** If you **shut** or **close** your **eyes to** something, you ignore it. EG *It is foolish to shut our eyes to the effects of unemployment.* **4.15** If you are **up to** your **eyes in** something, you are extremely busy dealing with it. EG *Sal is still up to her eyes in kids and housework.* **4.16** to **turn a blind eye**: see **blind**. — PHRASES

eyeball /aɪbɔːl/, **eyeballs.** Your **eyeballs** are the parts of your eyes that are like white balls. N COUNT

eyebrow /aɪbraʊ/, **eyebrows.** Your **eyebrows** are the lines of hair which grow in an arch above each of your eyes. See picture at THE HUMAN BODY. N COUNT

● If something causes you to **raise an eyebrow** or to **raise** your **eyebrows**, it causes you to feel surprised, shocked, or disapproving. EG *Eyebrows were raised at their behaviour.* ● PHRASE

eye-catching. Something that is **eye-catching** is very noticeable. EG *...an eye-catching poster.* ADJ QUALIT

eyelash /aɪlæʃ/, **eyelashes.** Your **eyelashes** are the hairs which grow on the edges of your upper and lower eyelids. N COUNT

eyelid /aɪlɪd/, **eyelids. 1** Your **eyelids** are the two flaps of skin which cover your eyes when they are closed. N COUNT

2 If you **don't bat an eyelid** when something happens, you remain completely calm and are not at all shocked or surprised. EG *She didn't bat an eyelid when she was given the bill.* PHRASE Informal

eye-opener. If you say that something is an **eye-opener**, you mean that you find it very surprising and that you have learned something from it which you did not know before. EG *The book is quite an eye-opener.* N SING : *an*+N Informal

eye-shadow is a substance which women put on their eyelids in order to make them a different colour. N UNCOUNT

eyesight /aɪsaɪt/. Your **eyesight** is your ability to see. EG *His eyesight was excellent.* N UNCOUNT

eyesore /aɪsɔː/, **eyesores.** If you say that something is an **eyesore**, you mean that it is extremely ugly. EG *It's an architectural eyesore.* N COUNT

eye-witness /aɪwɪtnɪ^{1}s/, **eye-witnesses.** An **eye-witness** is a person who has seen an event and can therefore describe it, for example in a law court. EG *'Planes plunged down from the skies,' recalled one eyewitness.* N COUNT

F f

F, f /ɛf/, **Fs, f's. 1 F** is the sixth letter of the English alphabet. N COUNT

2 F is an abbreviation for 'Fahrenheit'.

fable /feɪbə^{0}l/, **fables.** A **fable** is a traditional story that is intended to teach a moral lesson and often has animals as its main characters. EG *...a children's fable.* N COUNT

fabric /fæbrɪk/, **fabrics. 1** A **fabric** is a type of cloth or material. EG *...silks and other soft fabrics... ...a bit of fabric.* N MASS

2 The **fabric** of a society or system is its structure and the customs that make it work successfully. EG *...the priests who upheld the fabric of Roman society.* N SING : *the*+N+*of* Formal

3 The **fabric** of a building is its walls, roof, and other parts. EG *This amount was enough to maintain the fabric of the house.* N SING : *the*+N+*of* Formal

fabricate /fæbrɪkeɪt/, **fabricates, fabricating, fabricated. 1** If you **fabricate** information, you invent it in order to deceive people. EG *They fabricated evidence and threatened witnesses.* V+O Formal

◊ **fabrication** /fæbrɪkeɪʃə^{0}n/, **fabrications.** EG *The story was a fabrication... ...how truth differs from falsehood and fabrication.* ◊ N COUNT OR N UNCOUNT

2 When objects **are fabricated**, they are made. EG *New parts had to be fabricated out of scrap iron.* V+O Formal

◊ **fabrication.** EG *...the fabrication of metals and alloys.* ◊ N UNCOUNT

fabulous /fæbjə^{4}ləs/. **1** If you say that something is **fabulous**, you are expressing your admiration or approval of it. EG *What a fabulous place this is!* ADJ QUALIT Informal

2 If you talk about someone's **fabulous** wealth or **fabulous** beauty, you mean that they are extremely wealthy or beautiful. EG *...a woman of fabulous beauty.* ◊ **fabulously.** EG *...a fabulously rich family.* ADJ CLASSIF : ATTRIB ◊ SUBMOD

3 Fabulous is also used to describe things that occur in traditional stories but are not real or true. EG *...fabulous beasts.* ADJ CLASSIF : ATTRIB Formal

facade /fə^{3}sɑːd/, **facades;** also spelled **façade.**

1 The **facade** of a large building is the outside surface of its front wall. EG *...the ornate facade of the Palace.* N COUNT

2 You say that something is a **facade** when it gives a wrong impression of the true nature of a situation. EG *...the grim facts behind the facade of gaiety... The unity of the Party was a facade.* N SING

face /feɪs/, **faces, facing, faced. 1** Your **face** is the front of your head from your chin to your forehead. EG *Her face was sad... ...the expression on her face... The wind blew snow in her face.* N COUNT

2 The **face** of a cliff or a mountain is a side of it. EG *...the north face of the Eiger.* N COUNT : USU+SUPP

3 The **face** of a clock or watch is the surface with numbers on it, which shows the time. N COUNT

4 The **face** of a place or organization is its appearance or nature. EG *The face of a city can change completely in a year.* N SING : *the*+N+*of* Literary

5 If someone or something **faces** a particular thing, person, or direction, their front is towards that thing, person, or direction. EG *The two boys faced each other... The seats face forward.* V+O OR V+A

6 If you **face** something difficult or unpleasant, or if you **are faced** with it, it is going to affect you or you have to deal with it. EG *It is the biggest problem he has ever faced... They face a sentence of ten years in prison... You are faced with a choice.* V+O

7 If you cannot **face** something, you do not feel able to do it or cope with it because it seems so unpleasant. EG *She could not face speaking to them.* V+O OR V+-ING : WITH BROAD NEG

8 If you **face** the truth, you accept it, although it is unpleasant. EG *We simply must face facts... Let's face it, we all cheat.* V+O

9 Face is also used in these phrases. **9.1** If someone or something is **face down**, their face or front points downwards. If they are **face up**, their face or front points upwards. EG *Philip lay face down on the floor.* **9.2** If two people are **face to face**, they are looking directly at each other. EG *I suddenly came face to face with Karen.* **9.3** If you are brought **face to face** with an unpleasant fact, you cannot avoid it and have to deal with it. EG *It brings patients face to face with their problems.* **9.4** If you cannot **look** someone **in the face**, you are too ashamed or embarrassed to look at them directly. **9.5** If you say something **to** someone's **face**, you say it directly to them, rather than when they are not there. **9.6** To **show** your **face** some- PHRASES where means to go there. EG *She never showed her face in the town again.* **9.7** If you **make** or **pull a face**, you put on an ugly expression to show that you dislike something or to annoy someone. EG *She made monstrous faces at me.* **9.8** If you **lose face**, people lose respect for you. EG *He is afraid that he will lose face with the boss.* **9.9** If you do something to **save face**, you do it in order to avoid losing people's respect. **9.10** If you do something **in the face of** a particular problem or difficulty, you do it even though this problem or difficulty exists. EG *They carry on smiling in the face of adversity.* **9.11** If an action or belief **flies in the face of** accepted ideas, it seems to oppose or contradict them. EG *This proposal flies in the face of so many British political traditions.* **9.12** If you talk about **the face of the earth** or **the face of the world**, you mean the whole world. EG *...if men were to disappear from the face of the earth.* **9.13** You say **on the face of it** to indicate that you are describing what something seems to be like and that its real nature may be different. EG *On the face of it, it sounds like a good idea.* **9.14 at face value**: see **value**. Literary

face up to. If you **face up to** a difficult situation, you accept it and deal with it. EG *They had to face up to many setbacks.* PHRASAL VB : V+ADV+PREP

faceless /feɪslɪ^{2}s/. If you describe people as **faceless**, you mean that they are dull and boring and have no character or individuality. EG *...faceless bureaucrats in the Civil Service.* ADJ CLASSIF : ATTRIB

face-saving. A **face-saving** action is done in order to avoid losing people's respect. EG *As a face-saving gesture the British let the prisoner go.* ADJ CLASSIF : ATTRIB

facet /fæsɪ^{2}t/, **facets. 1** A **facet** of something is a part or aspect of it. EG *...every facet of their lives... ...an interesting facet of his character.* N COUNT

2 The **facets** of an object, especially a precious stone, are the flat surfaces on its outside. N COUNT

facetious /fəsiːʃəs/. You say that someone is being **facetious** when they make humorous remarks in a serious situation. EG *Mrs Pringle ignored this facetious interruption.* ◇ **facetiously.** EG *Frank suggested facetiously that we all go home.* ADJ QUALIT ◇ ADV

facial /feɪʃə^{0}l/ is used to describe things that relate to your face. EG *...facial muscles... ...changes in facial expression.* ADJ CLASSIF : ATTRIB

facile /fæsaɪl/. A **facile** remark or argument is a simple and obvious one, rather than one that has been carefully thought about. EG *It would be facile to call it a conspiracy.* ADJ QUALIT

facilitate /fəsɪlɪteɪt/, **facilitates, facilitating, facilitated.** To **facilitate** an action or process means to make it easier for it to happen or be done. EG *...legislation to facilitate the sale of homes.* V+O Formal

facility /fəsɪlɪ^{1}ti^{1}/, **facilities. 1 Facilities** are buildings or pieces of equipment which are provided for a particular purpose. EG *...the lack of play facilities for young children.* N COUNT : USU PLURAL +SUPP

2 A **facility** is an additional feature or service which is useful but not essential. EG *This tape recorder has a tape-slide facility.* N COUNT+SUPP

3 If you have a **facility** for something, you find it easy to do it well. EG *Meehan began to learn German and, having a facility for languages, was soon fluent in it.* N COUNT OR N UNCOUNT Formal

facsimile /fæksɪmɪli^{1}/, **facsimiles.** A **facsimile** of something is an exact model or copy of it. EG *The Morning Star produced a facsimile of the letter.* N COUNT

fact /fækt/, **facts. 1** A **fact** is **1.1** a statement or piece of information that is true. EG *The report is full of facts and figures... He told me a few facts about her.* **1.2** a situation that exists or something that happened. EG *There was little warmth, owing to the fact that Smithy had left the door open... ...the fact of belonging to a certain race... ...to investigate the facts of the killing.* N COUNT

2 If you say that a story or statement is **fact**, you mean that it is true. EG *How much of the novel is fiction and how much is fact?* N UNCOUNT

3 You say **in fact**, **in point of fact**, **in actual fact**, or **as a matter of fact 3.1** to emphasize that something really happened or is true. EG *This is, in fact, what happened... In actual fact, we don't have all that much more leisure time than we used to.* **3.2** to introduce some information, especially more precise information. EG *It was terribly cold weather – a blizzard in fact... I don't think she mentioned it. In fact I don't think she knew... As a matter of fact, I just got it this afternoon.* ADV SEN

4 You say **the fact is** before reluctantly telling someone something true. EG *The fact is, we are rivals... The fact is that child rearing is a long, hard job.* PHRASE

5 You say **the fact remains** to emphasize what you think is important in a situation or argument. EG *We may have forgotten their true meaning but the fact remains that they exist.* PHRASE

6 If you say that you know something **for a fact**, you are emphasizing that you know that it is true. EG *I know for a fact that there's a place free.* PHRASE

faction /fækʃə^{0}n/, **factions.** A **faction** is an organized group of people within a larger group, who oppose some of the ideas of the larger group. EG *...arguments between rival factions.* N COLL

factor /fæktə/, **factors.** A **factor** is one of the things that affects an event, decision, or situation. EG *Confidence is the key factor in any successful career... ...social and economic factors.* N COUNT+SUPP

factory /fæktə^{0}ri^{1}/, **factories.** A **factory** is a large building or group of buildings where machines are used to make goods in large quantities. EG *...a furniture factory... ...factory workers.* N COUNT

factual /fæktʃʊ^{0}əl/. Something that is **factual** contains or refers to facts and not theories or opinions. EG *...a factual account... ...an enormous amount of factual information.* ◇ **factually.** EG *...a factually accurate pamphlet.* ADJ CLASSIF ◇ ADV

faculty /fækə^{0}lti^{1}/, **faculties. 1** Your **faculties** are your physical and mental abilities. EG *She was in full command of all her faculties... ...the faculty of imagination.* N COUNT

2 A **faculty** in a university or college is a group of related departments. EG *...the Arts Faculty... ...the Faculty of Engineering.* N COUNT

fad /fæd/, **fads.** A **fad** is something which is very popular for a short period of time. EG *The interest in things Japanese is not just a passing fad.* N COUNT

fade /feɪd/, **fades, fading, faded. 1** When a coloured object **fades**, it gradually becomes paler in colour. EG *The wallpaper may have faded.* ◇ **faded.** EG *...an old man in a faded blue shirt.* V-ERG ◇ ADJ QUALIT

2 When something that you are looking at **fades**, it slowly becomes less bright or clear until you cannot see it any longer. EG *Already the mountains are fading in the evening light.* V

3 When the light **fades**, it becomes darker, because the sun is going down. EG *The afternoon light was fading.* V

4 When a sound **fades**, it slowly becomes less loud until you cannot hear it. EG *The applause faded.* V

5 When a feeling, memory, or quality **fades**, it slowly becomes less intense. EG *My anger faded... Interest in the story will fade.* V

6 When someone's smile **fades**, they slowly stop smiling. V

fade away or **fade out.** When something **fades away** or **fades out**, it slowly becomes less intense or strong until it ends completely. EG *Your enthusiasm for running will soon fade away... The sound of the chopper had faded out... This sort of protest tends to fade out quickly.* PHRASAL VB : V+ADV

faeces /fiːsiːz/; spelled **feces** in American English. **Faeces** is the solid waste that people get rid of from their body when they go to the toilet. N UNCOUNT Formal

fag /fæg/, **fags. 1** In British English, a **fag** is a cigarette. EG *...a packet of fags.* N COUNT Informal

2 In American English, a **fag** is a homosexual man; an offensive use. N COUNT Informal

faggot /fægət/, **faggots.** In American English, a **faggot** is a homosexual man; an offensive use. N COUNT Informal

Fahrenheit /færənh(ə)aɪt/ is a scale for measuring temperature, in which water freezes at 32 degrees and boils at 212 degrees. EG *...a temperature of 50° Fahrenheit.* N UNCOUNT

fail /feɪl/, **fails, failing, failed.** 1 If someone **fails** to do something that they were trying to do, they do not succeed in doing it. EG *Their party failed to win a single seat... The attempt to bribe the clerk had failed.* ◇ **failed.** EG *He was a failed novelist and poet.* V : USU + *to*-INF ◇ ADJ CLASSIF : ATTRIB

2 If someone **fails** to do something that they should have done, they do not do it. EG *He was fined for failing to complete the census form.* V + *to*-INF

3 If someone **fails** a test or examination, they do not reach the standard that is required. EG *I passed the written part but failed the oral section.* V + O OR V

4 If something **fails**, it stops working or functioning properly. EG *Her lighter failed... ...people whose sight is failing.* V

5 If someone **fails** you, they do not do what you expected or trusted them to do. EG *Our leaders have failed us.* V + O

6 If a quality or ability that you have **fails** you, you lose it just when you need it. EG *At the last minute his courage failed him... His usually inventive imagination had failed for once.* V + O OR V

failing /feɪlɪŋ/, **failings.** 1 A **failing** is a fault or unsatisfactory feature. EG *The present system has many failings... Being rude was one of Cindy's failings.* N COUNT

2 If someone has **failing** health or **failing** eyesight, their health or eyesight is getting worse. EG *He had given up his job because of failing health.* ADJ CLASSIF : ATTRIB

3 You say **'failing that'** to introduce an alternative, in case what you previously said is not possible. EG *Wear your national dress or, failing that, a suit.* ADV SEN

failure /feɪljə/, **failures.** 1 **Failure** is a lack of success in doing or achieving something. EG *...a desperate initiative which ended in failure.* N UNCOUNT

2 Someone who is a **failure** has not succeeded at something or at anything. EG *I felt such a failure.* N COUNT

3 If something is a **failure**, it is unsuccessful. EG *The meeting was a failure.* N COUNT

4 Someone's **failure** to do something is the fact that they do not do it although they were expected to. EG *His friends remarked on his failure to appear at the party.* N UNCOUNT + *to*-INF

5 When there is a **failure**, something stops working or does not do what it is supposed to do. EG *...engine failure... ...the failure of the bank where he kept his money.* N UNCOUNT OR N COUNT + SUPP

6 If you have a **failure** of an ability or quality that you normally have, you lose it. EG *...a failure of imagination... ...a sudden failure of nerve.* N UNCOUNT OR N COUNT + SUPP

faint /feɪnt/, **fainter, faintest; faints, fainting, fainted.** 1 Something that is **faint** is not at all strong or intense. EG *There was a faint smell of gas... Her cries grew fainter... ...a faint hope.* ADJ QUALIT

2 A **faint** action is one that is done without much effort or enthusiasm. EG *...a few faint protests... Her lips parted in a faint smile.* ADJ QUALIT

3 If you **faint**, you lose consciousness for a short time. EG *He nearly fainted from the pain.* V

4 Someone who feels **faint** feels dizzy and unsteady. ADJ QUALIT

5 You can use **faintest** in negative sentences to emphasize the total absence of something. EG *He didn't have the faintest idea what to do... I never felt the faintest desire to cry.* ADJ QUALIT : SUPERL, ONLY ATTRIB

faintly /feɪntli[1]/. 1 You can use **faintly** to indicate that something is true only to a very slight degree. EG *It was faintly possible.* ADV + ADJ

2 If something happens **faintly**, it happens with very little strength or intensity. EG *She turned and smiled faintly.* ADV

fair /fɛə/, **fairer, fairest; fairs.** 1 Something or someone that is **fair** is reasonable, right, and just. EG *It wouldn't be fair to disturb the children... This isn't fair on anyone... ...a fairer share of profits... She won't get a fair trial.* ● You can say **to be fair** before making a statement which corrects a previous unfavourable and exaggerated one. EG *Well, to be fair, it only happened once.* ADJ QUALIT ● PHRASE

2 You say **fair enough** 2.1 to indicate that you accept what has been said or done so far, but that you think more needs to be said or done. EG *All this is fair enough, but it touches only the surface of the problem.* 2.2 to indicate that you agree to what someone has just said. EG *...Thursday, yes, fair enough.* PHRASE; CONVENTION

3 **Fair** also means 3.1 quite large. EG *We've got a fair number of postgraduate students... ...a fair-sized bedroom.* 3.2 quite good. EG *I've think I've got a fair chance of evading them altogether.* ADJ CLASSIF : ATTRIB; ADJ QUALIT : USU ATTRIB

4 A **fair** guess or idea is one that is likely to be correct. EG *I had a pretty fair idea of the answer to this question.* ADJ QUALIT : ATTRIB

5 Someone who is **fair** or who has **fair** hair has light, gold-coloured hair. EG *She was fair and blue-eyed.* ADJ QUALIT

6 **Fair** skin is pale in colour. EG *Unprotected fair skin gets sunburned quickly.* ADJ QUALIT

7 When the weather is **fair**, it is not cloudy or rainy. EG *It will be fair and warm.* ADJ CLASSIF Formal

8 A **fair** is 8.1 an event held in a park or field at which people pay to ride on various machines for amusement or try to win prizes in games. EG *...the doll I won at the fair.* 8.2 an event at which people display or sell goods. EG *...the Leipzig Trade Fair.* N COUNT British; British

9 See also **fair play**.

fairground /fɛəgraʊnd/, **fairgrounds.** A **fairground** is an area of land where a fair is being held. N COUNT

fairly /fɛəli[1]/. 1 **Fairly** means to quite a large degree. EG *The information was fairly accurate... I wrote the first part fairly quickly.* SUBMOD

2 If something is said or done **fairly**, the statement or action is reasonable and just. EG *The car could fairly be described as sluggish and noisy... We want it to be fairly distributed.* ADV

fairness /fɛənəs/. 1 **Fairness** is the quality of being reasonable and just. EG *Even a child sees the fairness of reasonable penalties.* N UNCOUNT

2 You say **in all fairness**, or **in fairness to** someone, before a statement that corrects or balances a previous unfavourable one. EG *In all fairness, I must say that I was not the only one... Yet in fairness to him, one must add that he was often correct.* ADV SEN

fair play. If you want **fair play**, you want everyone to be treated in a reasonable and just way. EG *They appealed to his sense of fair play.* N UNCOUNT

fairy /fɛəri[1]/, **fairies. Fairies** are small, imaginary creatures with magical powers. They are usually said to look like tiny girls with wings. N COUNT

fairy tale, fairy tales. A **fairy tale** or a **fairy story** is a story for children involving magical events and imaginary creatures such as fairies. N COUNT

fait accompli /feɪt ə[3]kɒmpliː/. If something is a **fait accompli**, it has already been done and cannot be changed. EG *You've presented us with a fait accompli.* N SING Formal

faith /feɪθ/, **faiths.** 1 If you have **faith** in someone or something, you feel confident and hopeful about their ability or goodness. EG *I had faith in Alan – I knew he could take care of me.* N UNCOUNT : USU + *in*

2 A **faith** is a particular religion, such as Christianity or Buddhism. EG *...its tolerant attitude to other faiths.* N COUNT

If you fall into a particular group, do you hurt yourself?

3 Faith is also strong religious belief. EG *...the power of faith... ...her deep religious faith.* — N UNCOUNT

4 If you break **faith** with someone, you fail to behave in the way that you promised or were expected to. If you keep **faith** with them, you continue to behave as you promised or were expected to. EG *They were forced to break faith with millions of decent, hard working citizens.* — N UNCOUNT

5 If you do something **in good faith**, you sincerely believe that it is the right thing to do in the circumstances. EG *The two doctors were acting in good faith.* — PHRASE

faithful /feɪθfʊl/. **1** If you are **faithful** to a person, organization, or idea, you remain firm in your support for them. EG *Bond remained faithful to his old teacher.* — ADJ QUALIT ◇ **faithfully.** EG *The party rallied round him faithfully.* — ◇ ADV

2 People who firmly support a particular religion or political party are sometimes referred to as the **faithful**. EG *The bishop was condemned because he had led the faithful astray.* — N PLURAL: the+N

3 Someone who is **faithful** to their husband, wife, or lover does not have a sexual relationship with anyone else. EG *She has been a faithful wife to him.* — ADJ CLASSIF

4 A **faithful** account, translation, or adaptation of a book represents the facts or the original book accurately. EG *Do you think the film was faithful to the book?* — ADJ QUALIT ◇ **faithfully.** EG *Their activities were faithfully described in the newspapers.* — ◇ ADV

faithfully /feɪθfə[4]li[1]/. You write **Yours faithfully** before your signature at the end of a formal letter, when you have started the letter with 'Dear Sir' or 'Dear Madam'. — CONVENTION

fake /feɪk/, **fakes, faking, faked. 1** A **fake** is something that is made to look like something valuable or real in order to deceive people. EG *They swore that the pictures were fakes.* — N COUNT ▸ used as an adjective. EG *...a fake passport.* — ▸ ADJ CLASSIF

2 If someone **fakes** something, they make it look like something valuable or real in order to deceive people. EG *...faking the fine furniture of the century before.* — V+O ◇ **faked.** EG *...faked pictures.* — ◇ ADJ CLASSIF

3 Someone who is a **fake** is not the type of person that they pretend to be. EG *I admit I'm a fake.* — N COUNT

4 If you **fake** a feeling or reaction, you pretend that you are experiencing it when you are not. EG *Thomas faked a yawn.* — V+O

falcon /fɔːl[0]kən/, **falcons.** A **falcon** is a bird of prey that can be trained to hunt other birds and animals. — N COUNT

fall /fɔːl/, **falls, falling, fell** /fel/, **fallen** /fɔːlən/. **1** If someone or something **falls**, they move quickly downwards onto or towards the ground. EG *The cup fell from her hand and shattered on the floor... Tears fell from Mother's eyes... Part of the ceiling fell down... A bomb had fallen on the school.* — V: USU+A ▸ used as a noun. EG *He was rushed to hospital after a 40-foot fall.* — ▸ N SING

2 If someone or something that is standing **falls**, they accidentally move or are pushed from their upright position so that they end up lying on the ground. EG *She lost her balance and fell... He tripped and fell down... ...a falling tree.* — V ▸ used as a noun. EG *He asked her if she had had a fall.* — ▸ N COUNT ◇ **fallen.** EG *...to rescue people trapped inside fallen buildings.* — ◇ ADJ CLASSIF: ATTRIB

3 When rain or snow **falls**, it comes down from the sky. EG *The snow was still falling.* — V

4 If people in a position of power **fall**, they suddenly lose that position. EG *The regime had fallen.* — V ▸ used as a noun. EG *This led to the Government's fall.* — ▸ N SING+POSS

5 If a place **falls** in a war or election, an enemy army or a different political party takes control of it. EG *Greater London will fall to Labour.* — V ▸ used as a noun. EG *...the fall of France.* — ▸ N SING+POSS

6 If someone **falls** in battle, they are killed. EG *...the brave young men who have fallen in the struggle.* — V: USU+A Literary

7 If something **falls** in amount, value, or strength, it decreases. EG *The value of the dollar has fallen... Their voices could be heard rising and falling.* — V ▸ used as a noun. EG *...a fall in moral standards.* — ▸ N SING ◇ **falling.** EG *Some nations were uneasy about their falling birth rates.* — ◇ ADJ CLASSIF

8 If silence or a feeling of sadness or tiredness **falls** on a group of people, they become silent, sad, or tired. EG *An expectant hush fell on the gathering.* — V: USU+A Written

9 When light or shadow **falls** on something, it covers it. EG *A shadow fell over her book and she looked up.* — V+A

10 When night or darkness **falls**, night begins and it becomes dark. — V

11 You can use **fall** to show that someone or something passes into another state. For example, if someone **falls** ill, they become ill. EG *After a while I fell asleep... The crowd fell silent... Their ideas had fallen into disuse... He fell in love with her.* — V+C OR V+A

12 If you say that something **falls** into a particular group or category, you mean that it belongs in that group or category. EG *Human beings fall into two types.* — V+A

13 You can refer to a waterfall as the **falls**. EG *...Niagara Falls.* — N PLURAL

14 Fall is the season between summer and winter. In the fall the weather becomes cooler. EG *In the fall of 1941 he appointed a committee.* — N UNCOUNT OR N COUNT American

15 Fall is also used in these phrases. **15.1** If something **falls to bits** or **falls to pieces**, it breaks into pieces because it is old or badly made. EG *The boots had all fallen to bits.* **15.2** If something **falls open**, it opens accidentally. EG *Ellen's mouth fell open and she began to snore.* **15.3** If someone's **face falls**, they suddenly look upset or disappointed. **15.4** to **fall flat**: see **flat**. ● to **fall into place**: see **place**. — PHRASES

fall about. If you say that people **are falling about**, you mean that they are very amused by something. EG *When he complained, they fell about laughing.* — PHRASAL VB: V+ADV Informal

fall apart. 1 If something **falls apart**, it breaks into pieces because it is old or badly made. EG *...cheap beds that fell apart.* — PHRASAL VB: V+ADV **2** If an organization or system **falls apart**, it becomes disorganized and unable to work effectively. EG *The nation is falling apart.* — V+ADV

fall away. If something **falls away** from the surface that it is attached to, it breaks off. EG *Patches of plaster had fallen away between the windows.* — PHRASAL VB: V+ADV

fall back. If you **fall back**, you move quickly away from someone or something. EG *I saw my husband fall back in horror.* — PHRASAL VB: V+ADV

fall back on. If you **fall back on** something, you do it or use it after other things have failed. EG *Often you give up and fall back on easier solutions.* — PHRASAL VB: V+ADV+PREP

fall behind. If you **fall behind**, you do not make progress or move forward as fast as other people. EG *...children who fall behind with their reading.* — PHRASAL VB: V+ADV

fall for. 1 If you **fall for** someone, you are strongly attracted to them and start loving them. EG *Richard fell for her the moment he set eyes on her.* — PHRASAL VB: V+PREP **2** If you **fall for** a lie or trick, you believe it even though it is not true. EG *The working class were not going to fall for this one.* — V+PREP Informal

fall in. If a roof or ceiling **falls in**, it collapses and falls to the ground. — PHRASAL VB: V+ADV

fall in with. If you **fall in with** an idea, plan, or system, you accept it and do not try to change it. EG *Instead of challenging the lie, she falls in with it.* — PHRASAL VB: V+ADV+PREP

fall off. If the degree, amount, or rate of something **falls off**, it decreases. EG *We knew that the numbers of overseas students would fall off drastically.* ● See also **falling-off**. — PHRASAL VB: V+ADV

fall on or **fall upon.** If your eyes **fall on** something or **fall upon** it, you suddenly see or notice it. EG *His gaze fell on a small white bundle.* — PHRASAL VB: V+PREP

fall out. 1 If something such as a person's hair or — PHRASAL VB: V+ADV a tooth **falls out**, it becomes loose and separates from their body. EG *After about two weeks, the victim's hair starts to fall out.* **2** If you **fall out** with someone, you have an argument and stop being friendly with them. EG *I've fallen out with certain members of the band.* **3** See also **fallout**. V+ADV OR V+ADV+*with*: RECIP

fall over. 1 If someone or something that is standing **falls over**, they accidentally move or are pushed from their upright position so that they end up lying on the ground. EG *He pushed back his chair so hard that it fell over.* PHRASAL VB: V+ADV **2** If you **are falling over yourself** to do something, you are very keen to do it. EG *Producers were falling over themselves to hire girls who had acting experience.* PHRASE Informal

fall through. If an arrangement **falls through**, it fails to happen. EG *We wanted to book a villa but it fell through.* PHRASAL VB: V+ADV

fall to. If a responsibility or duty **falls to** someone, it becomes their responsibility or duty. EG *It fell to Philip Crow to act the part of host.* PHRASAL VB: V+PREP Formal

fall upon. See **fall on.**

fallacious /fəleɪʃəs/. A **fallacious** idea or argument is wrong because it is based on incorrect information or a fault in logic. EG *This point of view is exposed as fallacious by Emerson.* ADJ CLASSIF Formal

fallacy /fæləsi[1]/, **fallacies.** A **fallacy** is an idea or argument which is incorrect or illogical. EG *It is a fallacy that women are more pure-minded than men... I spotted the fallacy in the argument.* N COUNT Formal

fallen /fɔːlən/ is the past participle of **fall.**

fallible /fælɪ[1]bə[0]l/. **1** If you say that someone is **fallible**, you mean that their judgement or knowledge is not perfect and they may make mistakes. ADJ QUALIT Formal

2 If you say that something is **fallible**, you mean that it is not perfect and may be wrong or unreliable. EG *Mary was conscious how fallible this method was.* ADJ QUALIT Formal

falling-off. If there is a **falling-off** in something, it decreases. EG *A falling-off in business was expected.* N SING

fallout /fɔːlaʊt/ is the radiation that affects an area after a nuclear explosion. N UNCOUNT

fallow /fæləʊ/. If land is lying **fallow**, it has been dug or ploughed but no crops have been planted in it, so that the soil has a chance to rest and improve. EG *...plots of fallow land.* ADJ CLASSIF

false /fɒls, fɔːls/. **1** If a statement is **false**, it is not true. EG *What you're saying is false.* ◇ **falsely.** EG *...falsely accusing him of a crime.* ADJ CLASSIF ◇ ADV

2 If an idea or action is **false**, it is based on wrong information or beliefs. EG *I had a false impression of him... ...to save her from false imprisonment.* ADJ CLASSIF

3 False things are **3.1** made so that they appear real although they are not. EG *...false teeth... ...false eyelashes.* **3.2** intended to deceive people. EG *She travelled under a false name.* ● **under false pretences**: see **pretence.** ADJ CLASSIF: USU ATTRIB

4 Behaviour that is **false** is not sincere and is often intended to deceive people. EG *...a false smile... ...false modesty.* ◇ **falsely.** EG *She laughed, falsely, to cheer him up.* ADJ QUALIT ◇ ADV

false alarm, false alarms. When you are warned of something dangerous and it does not happen, you say that the warning was a **false alarm.** N COUNT

falsehood /fɒlshʊd, fɔːl-/, **falsehoods. 1** The **falsehood** of something is the fact that it is untrue. EG *We must establish the truth or falsehood of the various rumours.* N UNCOUNT Formal

2 A **falsehood** is a lie. EG *...exaggerations and falsehoods about the Indians.* N COUNT Formal

false start, false starts. A **false start** is **1** an attempt to start something which fails because you were not properly ready to begin. EG *...natural speech with all its hesitations and false starts.* **2** a beginning of a race when one competitor moves before the starter has given the signal. N COUNT

falsetto /fɒlsetəʊ/, **falsettos.** If a man speaks or sings in a **falsetto**, he uses a high-pitched voice. EG *I heard him singing in a clear, high falsetto... ...a falsetto whine.* N COUNT

falsify /fɒlsɪfaɪ, fɔːl-/, **falsifies, falsifying, falsified.** If someone **falsifies** information, they change it so that it is no longer true or correct, in order to deceive people. EG *The facts concerning my birth have been falsified.* ◇ **falsification** /fɒlsɪfɪkeɪʃə[0]n, fɔːl-/, **falsifications.** EG *...falsification of accounts.* V+O ◇ N UNCOUNT OR N COUNT

falsity /fɒlsɪ[1]ti[1], fɔːl-/. The **falsity** of something is the fact that it is untrue. EG *...the falsity of this evidence.* N UNCOUNT

falter /fɒltə, fɔːltə/, **falters, faltering, faltered. 1** If something **falters**, it becomes weaker or slower in an uneven way and may stop completely. EG *The engines faltered and the plane lost height... The organization's progress faltered.* V

2 If you **falter**, **2.1** you lose confidence in what you are doing. EG *From that moment onwards he never faltered in his resolve.* V: OFT+*in* **2.2** you stop saying something, because you are nervous or unhappy. EG *'Would you – ' Rey faltered.* V OR V+QUOTE **2.3** you stop moving easily and start moving slowly and with difficulty. EG *Looking to his left, he saw Percy faltering.* V

fame /feɪm/. If you achieve **fame**, you become well known and admired by many people. EG *She was jealous of Ellen's fame... He rose rapidly to fame.* N UNCOUNT

famed /feɪmd/. If you are **famed** for something, you are well known and admired because of it. EG *The women there were famed for the pots they made... ...a great church, famed for its flower festivals.* ADJ QUALIT: OFT+*for* Literary

familial /fəmɪlɪəl/ means concerning families in general or one particular family. EG *...social and familial influences.* ADJ CLASSIF: ATTRIB Formal

familiar /fəmɪljə/. **1** If someone or something is **familiar** to you, you recognize them or know them well because you have seen, heard, or experienced them before. EG *His name was familiar to me... ...my pleasure at seeing all the familiar faces again.* ADJ QUALIT: OFT+*to* ◇ **familiarity** /fəmɪlɪærɪ[1]ti[1]/. EG *...the familiarity of the surroundings.* ◇ N UNCOUNT

2 If you are **familiar** with something, you know it well. EG *I am of course familiar with your work.* ADJ PRED +*with* ◇ **familiarity.** EG *...his familiarity with the system gave him a considerable advantage.* ◇ N UNCOUNT +*with*

3 If you behave in a **familiar** way towards someone, you treat them very informally like a close friend, so that you may offend them if they are not a close friend. EG *...disliking intensely the burly man's familiar tone.* ADJ QUALIT ◇ **familiarly.** EG *He spoke of them casually and familiarly by their first names.* ◇ ADV ◇ **familiarity.** EG *They greeted him with familiarity.* ◇ N UNCOUNT

familiarize /fəmɪljəraɪz/, **familiarizes, familiarizing, familiarized;** also spelled **familiarise.** If you **familiarize** yourself with something, or if someone **familiarizes** you with it, you learn all about it and get to know it. EG *He had to familiarize himself with the ship.* V-REFL+*with* OR V+O+*with*

family /fæmɪ[0]li[1]/, **families. 1** A **family** is a group of people who are related to each other, especially parents and their children. EG *...an English family on holiday... ...the Barrett family... He showed me photographs of his family... ...help offered by family and friends.* N COLL OR N UNCOUNT

2 When people talk about their **family**, they can also mean **2.1** their children. EG *...raising a family... ...mothers with large families... She has no family of her own.* N COLL OR N UNCOUNT **2.2** one line of their ancestors. EG *Her mother's family had lived there for generations.* N COLL

3 You can use **family** to describe **3.1** things that belong to a particular family. EG *Ben worked in the family business.* N MOD **3.2** things that are designed to be

Do you plant a family tree?

used or enjoyed by both parents and children. EG *...a family car... ...family entertainment.*

4 A **family** of animals or plants is a group of related species. EG *It is a member of the sparrow family.* N COUNT+SUPP

family planning is the practice of using contraception to control the number of children in a family. EG *...family planning clinics.* N UNCOUNT

family tree, family trees. A **family tree** is a chart that shows all the people in your family over many generations and their relationships with one another. N COUNT

famine /fæmɪn/, **famines. Famine** is a serious shortage of food in a country, which may cause many deaths. EG *...the effects of famine and drought... ...a severe famine.* N UNCOUNT OR N COUNT

famished /fæmɪʃt/. If you say that you are **famished**, you mean that you are very hungry. ADJ CLASSIF Informal

famous /feɪməs/. Someone or something that is **famous** is very well known. EG *...a famous writer... California is famous for raisins.* ADJ QUALIT : OFT+*for*

fan /fæn/, **fans, fanning, fanned. 1** If you are a **fan** of someone or something, you admire them and support them. EG *I was a Beatles fan... ...football fans.* N COUNT : USU+SUPP

2 A **fan** is also **2.1** a flat object that you hold in your hand and wave in order to move the air and make yourself cooler. **2.2** a piece of electrical equipment with revolving blades which keeps a room or machine cool or gets rid of unpleasant smells. N COUNT

3 If you **fan** yourself when you are hot, you wave a fan or other flat object in order to move the air and make yourself cooler. EG *She took up some sheets of paper and fanned herself with them.* V-REFL OR V+O

4 To **fan** a fire means to create a current of air so that the fire burns more strongly. EG *The rush of air fed and fanned the fires.* V+O

5 To **fan** fear, hatred, or passion means to cause people to feel it more strongly. EG *Public hysteria fanned fears of an invasion.* V+O

fan out. When people or things **fan out**, they move forwards together from the same point, while moving further apart from each other. EG *The five of us fanned out at intervals of not more than fifteen feet.* PHRASAL VB : V+ADV

fanatic /fənætɪk/, **fanatics. 1** A **fanatic** is **1.1** a person with strong religious or political beliefs who behaves in an extreme or violent way. **1.2** a person who is very enthusiastic about a subject or activity. EG *...a sports fanatic.* N COUNT

2 Fanatic means the same as fanatical. EG *...a fanatic hunter.* ADJ QUALIT

fanatical /fənætɪkə[0]l/. Someone who is **fanatical** feels very strongly about something and behaves in an extreme way because of this. EG *...fanatical rebels... Bill inspired fanatical devotion in his pupils.* ◊ **fanatically.** EG *He was fanatically against intervention in the war.* ADJ QUALIT ◊ ADV

fanaticism /fənætɪsɪzə[0]m/ is fanatical behaviour. EG *He took to abstract painting with an obsessive fanaticism.* N UNCOUNT

fanciful /fænsɪfʊl/. **1 Fanciful** ideas or stories are based on someone's imagination and not on facts or reality. EG *He had heard fanciful tales about their work... It would not be fanciful to say that he hissed.* ADJ QUALIT

2 Something that is **fanciful** is unusual and elaborate rather than plain and simple; used showing disapproval. EG *...fanciful architecture... He considered this name far too fanciful.* ADJ QUALIT

fancy /fænsi[1]/, **fancies, fancying, fancied; fancier, fanciest. 1** If you **fancy** something, you want to have it or do it. EG *She fancied a flat of her own... I don't fancy going back alone.* V+O OR V+-ING Informal

2 If you **fancy** someone, you feel attracted to them in a sexual way. V+O Informal

3 If you **fancy** yourself, you think that you are very clever, attractive, or good at something, or think that you would be good at something if you tried it; used showing disapproval. EG *I've heard that this man Bond fancies himself with a pistol... We all fancied ourselves as leaders.* V-REFL Informal

4 If you **take a fancy to** someone or something, you start liking them, usually for no understandable reason. PHRASE Informal

5 If something **takes** your **fancy**, you like it quite a lot when you see it or think of it. EG *He paid £50 for a painting that had taken his fancy.* PHRASE Informal

6 You say **'fancy'** when you want to express surprise. EG *Fancy seeing you here!... 'You're in hospital.' – 'Well, fancy that.'* EXCLAM Informal

7 If you **fancy** that something is the case, you think or suppose that it is. EG *I fancied I could hear a baby screaming.* V+REPORT : ONLY *that* Formal

8 A **fancy** is an idea that is unlikely or untrue. EG *His mind was filled with weird fancies... It is difficult to separate fact from fancy... ...indulging in a flight of fancy.* N COUNT OR N UNCOUNT Formal

9 Something that is **fancy** is special, unusual, and elaborate. EG *...fancy hats... ...good plain food: nothing fancy.* ADJ QUALIT Informal

fancy dress is clothing that you wear for a party at which everyone tries to look like a person from a story, from history, or from a particular profession. EG *...ladies in fancy dress... ...a fancy dress ball.* N UNCOUNT

fanfare /fænfɛə/, **fanfares.** A **fanfare** is a short, loud tune played on trumpets to announce a special event. EG *The Queen's arrival was greeted with a fanfare.* N COUNT

fang /fæŋ/, **fangs.** An animal's **fangs** are its long, sharp teeth. EG *Most snakes withdraw their fangs after striking.* N COUNT

fanlight /fænlaɪt/, **fanlights.** A **fanlight** is a small window above a door. N COUNT

fantasize /fæntəsaɪz/, **fantasizes, fantasizing, fantasized;** also spelled **fantasise.** If you **fantasize**, you think imaginatively about something that you would like to happen but that is unlikely to happen. EG *...fantasizing about ripping down the iron bars of the jail... She had fantasized that she and Wendy would live in this house.* V : OFT +*about* OR V+REPORT : ONLY *that*

fantastic /fæntæstɪk/. **1** People say that something is **fantastic** when they like it or admire it very much. EG *He chewed it and said, 'Fantastic!'... He scored the most fantastic goal I have ever seen.* ADJ QUALIT Informal

2 You use **fantastic** when you want to emphasize the size, amount, or degree of something. EG *...a fantastic amount of time... ...her fantastic power.* ◊ **fantastically.** EG *They were fantastically strict.* ADJ QUALIT : ATTRIB ◊ SUBMOD

3 You can describe something as **fantastic** when it looks strange and wonderful. EG *...fantastic images of gods.* ◊ **fantastically.** EG *...fantastically shaped islands.* ADJ QUALIT ◊ SUBMOD

4 If you say that a statement or story is **fantastic**, you mean that it is very strange and difficult to believe. EG *He was in love with her – fantastic though that may seem.* ADJ QUALIT

fantasy /fæntəsi[1]/, **fantasies. 1** A **fantasy** is a situation or event that you think about or imagine, although it is unlikely to happen or be true. EG *That's supposed to be every schoolgirl's fantasy... ...fantasies about suicide.* N COUNT

2 Fantasy refers to **2.1** stories or situations that people create from their imagination and that are not based on reality. EG *To a child, fantasy and reality are very close to each other... His novels were fantasies.* **2.2** the activity of imagining things. EG *Everyone should indulge in fantasy on occasions.* N UNCOUNT OR N COUNT; N UNCOUNT

far /fɑː/, **farther** /fɑːðə/ or **further** /fɜːðə/, **farthest** /fɑːðɪ[2]st/ or **furthest** /fɜːðɪ[2]st/. See separate entries for **further** and **furthest**. **Farther** and **farthest** are used mainly when talking about distance.

1 If one place, thing, or person is **far** away from another, there is a great distance between them. EG *He sat far away from the others... ...a villa not far* ADV *from Hotel Miranda... ...clouds drifting far above... ...a little farther south.*

2 If you ask how **far** away a place is, you are asking how great a distance away it is. If you ask how **far** someone went, you are asking what distance they travelled or what place they reached. EG *How far is Amity from here?... Vita went as far as Bologna.* ADV

3 When there are two similar things somewhere, the **far** one is the one that is a greater distance away from you. EG *...the far end of the room.* ADJ CLASSIF : ATTRIB

4 You can use **far** to refer to the part of an area that is the greatest distance from the centre in a particular direction. For example, the **far** north of a country is the part that is the greatest distance to the north. EG *...on the far right of the page.* ADJ CLASSIF : ATTRIB

5 If something happens **far and wide**, it happens in a lot of places or over a large area. EG *People would come from far and wide to hear him.* PHRASE

6 A time or event that is **far** in the future or the past is a long time from the present. EG *The Fourth of July isn't far off... ...as far back as the twelfth century.* ADV+ADV OR ADV+PREP

7 You can use **far** to indicate the extent or degree to which something happens. EG *Prices will not come down very far... None of us would trust them very far... ...using her methods as far as possible.* ADV

8 If you ask or say how **far** someone or something gets or goes, you are talking about their level of achievement or progress. EG *How far have you got in developing this?... Selling programmes, that's about as far as it goes.* ADV

9 If you say that someone is going **too far**, you mean that they are behaving in an unacceptable or extreme way. EG *The press went too far and suffered accordingly.* PHRASE

10 If you say that someone **goes so far as** to do something, you mean that what they do is surprising or extreme. EG *He went so far as to spit over the wall.* PHRASE

11 You can use **far** to emphasize that something is much greater or better than something else, or has much more of a particular quality. EG *...a far greater problem... It was far more than I expected... The firm had far outstripped its rivals.* ADV

12 You can use **by far** or **far and away** to emphasize that something is the best, or has more of a particular quality than anything else. EG *She was by far the camp's best swimmer... This is far and away the most important point.* PHRASE

13 Someone or something that is **not far wrong**, **not far out**, or **not far off** is almost correct. EG *...an answer that's not far wrong... He hadn't been so far out, for Antonio had died.* PHRASE

14 You can use **far from** to emphasize that something is the opposite of what it should be, could be, or was expected to be. EG *His hands were far from clean... Far from speeding up, the tank slithered to a halt... It is not that you are ungenerous. Far from it.* PHRASE

15 You use **far** in expressions such as 'as far as I know' and 'so far as I remember' to indicate that you are not absolutely sure and may be wrong. EG *We only had one paper as far as I remember... As far as they could see, the room was empty.* ADV SEN

16 **So far** means up until the present point in time or the present stage in a situation. EG *What do you think of the town so far?... So far only two bodies have been discovered.* PHRASE

17 You say **'So far so good'** when what you are doing has been successful or satisfactory up until the time when you are speaking. EG *I tied him quickly to a tree. So far so good.* CONVENTION

18 You can use **in so far as** or **insofar as** to introduce a statement that limits the extent of another statement or gives a reason for it. EG *Liberty is cherished only in so far as it costs nothing.* CONJ Formal

19 **as far as** something **is concerned**: see **concern**. • **few and far between**: see **few**.

faraway /fɑːr°əweɪ/. **1** A **faraway** place or sound is a long distance away from you. EG *...news from far-away villages... ...the faraway sound of a waterfall.* ADJ CLASSIF : ATTRIB

2 If someone has a **faraway** expression, they look as if they are thinking deeply about something and are not paying attention to what is happening. EG *She had a faraway look in her eyes.* ADJ CLASSIF : ATTRIB

farce /fɑːs/, **farces. 1** A **farce** is a humorous play in which the characters become involved in unlikely and complicated situations. N COUNT

2 If you say that something is a **farce**, you mean that it is very disorganized or unsatisfactory. EG *His education had been a farce.* N COUNT

farcical /fɑːsɪkə°l/. If you say that something is **farcical**, you mean that it is ridiculous, disorganized, or unsatisfactory. EG *The next ten minutes were farcical... ...this farcical voyage to somewhere she did not want to go.* ADJ QUALIT

fare /fɛə/, **fares, faring, fared. 1** The **fare** is the money that you pay for a journey in a vehicle such as a taxi, train, or aeroplane. EG *Coach fares are cheaper than rail fares... What is the fare to Weymouth?* N COUNT

2 The **fare** served at a place such as a restaurant is the food that is served there. EG *Army kitchens serve better fare than some hotels.* N UNCOUNT Outdated

3 If you **fare** badly in a particular situation, you are unsuccessful or are treated badly. If you **fare** well, you are successful or are treated well. EG *How did you fare with Sir Hugo?... They fared badly in the 1978 elections.* V+A : OFT WITH BROAD NEG Outdated

Far East. The **Far East** consists of all the countries of Eastern Asia, including China and Japan. N PROPER : *the*+N

farewell /fɛəwel/, **farewells. Farewell** means goodbye. EG *Farewell, my dear child... He bade farewell to his family.* ▸ used as a noun. EG *...tearful farewells... ...the farewell party.* CONVENTION Outdated ▸ N COUNT

far-fetched. If you say that a statement, idea, or plan is **far-fetched**, you mean that it is exaggerated, unlikely, or impossible. EG *The theory is too far-fetched to be considered.* ADJ QUALIT

far-flung. 1 Far-flung places are a very long distance away. EG *...some far-flung corner of the world.* ADJ CLASSIF : ATTRIB

2 A **far-flung** empire or organization extends to distant places. EG *...the produce of a far-flung empire.* ADJ CLASSIF : ATTRIB

farm /fɑːm/, **farms, farming, farmed. 1** A **farm** is an area of land consisting of fields and some buildings, which is used for growing crops or raising animals. EG *My father worked on a farm... ...farm buildings.* N COUNT

2 If you **farm** an area of land, you grow crops or raise animals on it. EG *The hill land is farmed by Mike Keeble... ...those who have farmed for generations.* V+O OR V

farmer /fɑːmə/, **farmers.** A **farmer** is a person who owns or manages a farm. N COUNT

farmhand /fɑːmhænd/, **farmhands.** A **farmhand** is a person who is employed by a farmer to work on a farm. N COUNT

farmhouse /fɑːmhaʊs/, **farmhouses.** A **farmhouse** is a house on a farm, especially one where a farmer lives. N COUNT

farming /fɑːmɪŋ/ is the activity of growing crops or raising animals on a farm. EG *...an economy based on farming and tourism... ...sheep farming.* N UNCOUNT

farmland /fɑːmlænd/ is land which is farmed or is suitable for farming. EG *...1500 acres of forest and farmland.* N UNCOUNT

On these pages, what coin is no longer used in Britain?

farmyard /fɑːmjɑːd/, **farmyards.** A **farmyard** is an area on a farm surrounded by buildings or walls. N COUNT

far-off. 1 A **far-off** place is a long distance away. EG *...a far-off country.* ADJ QUALIT

2 A **far-off** time is a long time away in the future or the past. EG *...looking back at that far-off day.* ADJ QUALIT

far-reaching means affecting something greatly, in many ways, and for a long time. EG *It could have far-reaching implications for the economy.* ADJ QUALIT

far-sighted. If you say that someone is **far-sighted**, you mean that they are good at foreseeing what will happen in the future and making suitable plans or decisions. ADJ QUALIT

farther /fɑːðə/ is a comparative of **far.**

farthest /fɑːðɪ^{2}st/ is a superlative of **far.**

farthing /fɑːðɪŋ/, **farthings.** In old British currency, a **farthing** was a coin that was worth a quarter of a penny. N COUNT

fascinate /fæsɪneɪt/, **fascinates, fascinating, fascinated.** If something or someone **fascinates** you, you find them very interesting. EG *I love history, it fascinates me... I was fascinated by the people dressed in white.* V+O ◇ **fascinated.** EG *He became fascinated with their whole way of life.* ◇ ADJ QUALIT ◇ **fascinating.** EG *It's a fascinating book.* ◇ **fascination** /fæsɪneɪʃə^{0}n/. EG *...Taylor's fascination with bees... Mildred was staring with fascination at the scene.* ◇ N UNCOUNT

fascist /fæʃɪst/, **fascists.** If you call someone a **fascist**, you mean that their opinions are very right-wing, and that they believe in strong government and do not care about people's rights. EG *I fought a war to get rid of Fascists like you.* N COUNT ▸ used as an adjective. EG *...those fascist parents of yours.* ▸ ADJ CLASSIF

fashion /fæʃə^{0}n/, **fashions, fashioning, fashioned.** 1 If you do something in a particular **fashion**, you do it in that way. EG *We talked in an animated fashion... He greeted us in his usual friendly fashion.* N SING+SUPP

2 **Fashion** is the area of activity that involves styles of clothing and appearance. EG *...hints on fashion and cookery... ...the fashion industry.* N UNCOUNT

3 A **fashion** is a style of clothing or a way of behaving that is popular at a particular time. EG *...the latest Parisian fashions... The Beatles set the fashion for a generation.* N COUNT

4 If something is **in fashion**, it is popular and approved of at a particular time. If it is **out of fashion**, it is not popular or approved of. EG *Exotic fruits are coming into fashion... She never wears a hat. They're out of fashion.* PHRASE

5 If you **fashion** something, you make it. EG *The crew fashioned a raft from the wreckage.* V+O Outdated

6 See also **old-fashioned.**

fashionable /fæʃə^{0}nəbə^{0}l/. Something that is **fashionable** is popular or approved of at a particular time. EG *...the striped shirts that were fashionable in 1963... ...the less fashionable parts of the city.* ADJ QUALIT ◇ **fashionably.** EG *...fashionably dressed ladies.* ◇ ADV

fast /fɑːst/, **faster, fastest; fasts, fasting, fasted.**
1 If something or someone is **fast**, they move, do something, or happen with great speed. EG *...a fast car... ...producing goods at a faster rate.* ADJ QUALIT ▸ used as an adverb. EG *I ran as fast as I could... We are fast becoming a nation fed on canned food.* ▸ ADV

2 If you ask how **fast** something is moving, you want to know the speed at which it is moving. ADV

3 If something happens **fast**, it happens very soon and without any delay. EG *She needed medical help fast... Treat stains as fast as posible.* ADV

4 If a watch or clock is **fast**, it is showing a time that is later than the real time. ADJ PRED

5 If you **hold fast** to an idea or course of action, you firmly continue believing it or doing it. EG *He was determined to hold fast to his beliefs.* PHRASE

6 Someone who is **fast asleep** is completely asleep. PHRASE

7 If you **fast**, you eat no food for a period of time, usually for religious reasons. EG *He fasts for a whole day every week.* V ▸ used as a noun. EG *During my fast I lost fifteen pounds.* ▸ N COUNT

8 to **make a fast buck**: see **buck.** ● **thick and fast**: see **thick.** ● See also **hard and fast.**

fasten /fɑːsə^{0}n/, **fastens, fastening, fastened.** 1 If you **fasten** something, you fix it in a closed position with a button, strap, or other device. EG *He fastened his seat-belt... The case fastened at the top.* V-ERG

2 If you **fasten** one thing to another, you attach the first thing to the second thing. EG *The bench had been fastened to the pavement.* V+O+A

3 If you **fasten** your hands or teeth around or onto something, you grasp it firmly with your hands or teeth. EG *He fastened his hands round the spear... The snake's fangs fastened on the Count's arm.* V-ERG+A

fasten on. If you **fasten on** to someone or something, you concentrate your attention on them. EG *Once she had fastened on to a scheme she did not let go.* PHRASAL VB : V+ADV : OFT+*to*

fastening /fɑːsə^{0}nɪŋ/, **fastenings.** A **fastening** is a device that keeps something in a fixed or closed position. EG *...the fastenings of her gown.* N COUNT

fast food is hot food that is prepared and served quickly after you order it. EG *...fast-food restaurants.* N UNCOUNT

fastidious /fæstɪdiəs/. Someone who is **fastidious** is fussy and likes things to be clean, tidy, and properly done. EG *...with noses wrinkled in fastidious distaste.* ADJ QUALIT ◇ **fastidiously.** EG *The process was fastidiously checked.* ◇ ADV ◇ **fastidiousness.** EG *I want you to overcome your fastidiousness.* ◇ N UNCOUNT

fat /fæt/, **fatter, fattest; fats.** 1 A **fat** person has a lot of flesh on their body. EG *...a small fat man... Henry has grown fat.* ADJ QUALIT ◇ **fatness.** EG *He was embarrassed to hear her discussing his fatness.* ◇ N UNCOUNT

2 **Fat** is 2.1 the layer of flesh in the bodies of animals and people which is used to store energy and to keep them warm. N UNCOUNT 2.2 a substance used in cooking which is obtained from vegetables or the flesh of animals. EG *...a smell of fried fat.* N MASS 2.3 a substance contained in many foods and used by your body to produce energy. EG *...a diet containing protein, fats, carbohydrates, and vitamins.* N MASS

3 A **fat** object is very thick or wide. EG *...one fat volume of a report... ...a fat briefcase.* ADJ QUALIT

4 A **fat** profit or fee is a large one. EG *The shoes made a fat profit for the manufacturer.* ADJ QUALIT : ATTRIB

5 You use **a fat lot** to mean 'not any' or 'nothing'. For example, if you say that something is **a fat lot** of good or **a fat lot** of use, you mean that it is completely useless. EG *A fat lot of good that would be!... A fat lot that'll prove!* PHRASE Informal

fatal /feɪtə^{0}l/. 1 A **fatal** action has very undesirable results. EG *I made the fatal mistake of letting her talk... It would be fatal to bring in an outsider.* ADJ CLASSIF ◇ **fatally.** EG *Their leaders are fatally mistaken.* ◇ ADV

2 A **fatal** accident or illness causes someone's death. EG *...Pollock's fatal car crash.* ADJ CLASSIF ◇ **fatally.** EG *Four men were fatally stabbed.* ◇ ADV

fatalism /feɪtəlɪzə^{0}m/ is the belief that people cannot prevent or control events. EG *...the fatalism of the masses.* N UNCOUNT ◇ **fatalist, fatalists.** EG *I've always been a fatalist.* ◇ N COUNT

fatalistic /feɪtəlɪstɪk/. Someone who is **fatalistic** believes that people cannot prevent or control events. EG *They're so fatalistic, they don't even bother to vote.* ADJ QUALIT

fatality /fətælɪ^{1}ti^{1}/, **fatalities.** 1 A **fatality** is a person's death that is caused by an accident or by violence. EG *Fatalities from the use of pesticide are rare.* N COUNT

2 **Fatality** is the feeling or belief that people cannot prevent or control events. EG *The modern world is dominated by a sense of fatality.* N UNCOUNT Formal

fate /feɪt/, **fates.** 1 **Fate** is a power that is believed by some people to control everything that happens. EG *Fate was against me.* N UNCOUNT

2 Someone's **fate** is what happens to them. EG *Several other companies suffered a similar fate.* N COUNT+SUPP

fated /feɪtɪ^{2}d/. If you say that someone is **fated** to do something, or that an event is **fated**, you mean that nothing can be done to avoid or change what will happen. EG *We were fated to dislike one another.* ADJ CLASSIF: USU+*to*-INF

fateful /feɪtfʊl/. If you describe an action or event as **fateful**, you mean that it had important, and often bad, effects on later events. EG *...when the President made his fateful announcement.* ADJ QUALIT: ATTRIB

father /fɑːðə/, **fathers, fathering, fathered. 1** Your **father** is the man who is one of your parents. N COUNT OR VOCATIVE

2 When a man **fathers** a child, he makes a woman pregnant and their child is born. EG *He fathered two children.* V+O Literary

3 The man who invented or started something is sometimes referred to as its **father**. EG *Chaucer is often said to be the father of English poetry.* N SING: *the*+N+*of*

4 In some Christian churches, priests are addressed or referred to as **Father**. EG *Good afternoon, Father... ...Father Drew.*

5 Christians often refer to God as our **Father** or address him as **Father**. EG *Heavenly Father, hear our prayers.* N PROPER OR VOCATIVE

Father Christmas is an imaginary old man with a long white beard and a red coat. Young children believe that he brings them their presents at Christmas. N PROPER

fatherhood /fɑːðəhʊd/ is the state of being a father. EG *Attitudes to fatherhood are changing.* N UNCOUNT

father-in-law, fathers-in-law. Someone's **father-in-law** is the father of their husband or wife. N COUNT

fatherless /fɑːðəlɪ^{2}s/. You describe children as **fatherless** when their father has died or does not live with them. ADJ CLASSIF

fatherly /fɑːðəli^{1}/. You say that someone behaves in a **fatherly** way when they behave like a kind father. EG *Let me give you some fatherly advice.* ADJ QUALIT: ATTRIB

fathom /fæðə^{0}m/, **fathoms, fathoming, fathomed. 1** A **fathom** is a measurement of 1.8 metres or 6 feet, used when describing the depth of the sea. N COUNT Technical

2 If you **fathom** something or **fathom** it out, you understand it as a result of thinking about it carefully. EG *I couldn't fathom the meaning of her remarks... She couldn't fathom why McCurry was causing such a scene.* V+O: OFT+*out*; ALSO V+WH

fatigue /fətiːg/, **fatigues, fatiguing, fatigued. 1 Fatigue** is a feeling of extreme physical or mental tiredness. EG *He was dizzy with hunger and fatigue.* N UNCOUNT

2 If something **fatigues** you, it makes you extremely tired. EG *Some people say eating fatigues them.* ◊ **fatigued.** EG *She was utterly fatigued.* V+O Formal ◊ ADJ QUALIT

3 Fatigue in metal is a weakness caused by repeated stress. It can sometimes cause the metal to break. N UNCOUNT

fatten /fætə^{0}n/, **fattens, fattening, fattened.** If you **fatten** an animal or if it **fattens**, it becomes fatter as a result of eating more. EG *Soya is excellent for fattening pigs.* V-ERG

fatten up. If you **fatten up** an animal, you feed it more food so that it reaches the weight that you want it to be. EG *Their cattle take twice as long to fatten up as European cattle.* PHRASAL VB: V+O+ADV

fattening /fætə^{0}nɪŋ/. Food that is **fattening** tends to make people fat. ADJ QUALIT

fatty /fæti^{1}/, **fatties. 1** A fat person is sometimes called a **fatty**; an offensive use. EG *Shut up, Fatty.* N COUNT OR VOCATIVE

2 Fatty food contains a lot of fat. ADJ QUALIT

fatuous /fætjʊəs/. If you say that a remark, action, or plan is **fatuous**, you mean that it is very silly indeed. ADJ QUALIT

faucet /fɔːsɪt/, **faucets.** A **faucet** is a device that you turn in order to control the flow of a liquid or gas from a pipe or container. Sinks and baths have faucets attached to them. N COUNT American

fault /fɔːlt/, **faults, faulting, faulted. 1** If a bad or undesirable situation is your **fault**, you are the cause of it or are responsible for it. EG *It was entirely my own fault... It's all the fault of a girl called Sarah.* N SING+POSS

2 If you are **at fault**, you have done something wrong or have made a mistake. EG *It was 1976, I believe, if my memory is not at fault.* PHRASE

3 A **fault** in a person's character or in a system is a weakness or imperfection in it. EG *She is forever telling me what my faults are.* N COUNT

4 A **fault** in a machine or structure is a broken part or a mistake in the way it was made. EG *Computer faults are commonplace.* N COUNT

5 If you say that you cannot **fault** someone, you mean that they are doing something so well that you cannot criticize them for it. EG *You can't fault their psychology... I couldn't fault him on that one.* V+O: OFT+*on*

6 If you **find fault** with something, you complain about it. PHRASE

7 A **fault** is also a large crack in the surface of the earth. N COUNT Technical

8 In tennis, a **fault** is a service that is wrong according to the rules. N COUNT

faultless /fɔːltlɪ^{2}s/. Something that is **faultless** has no mistakes in it. EG *...two men who spoke to him in faultless German.* ADJ CLASSIF

faulty /fɔːlti^{1}/. A machine or piece of equipment that is **faulty** is not working properly. EG *We traced the trouble to a faulty transformer.* ADJ CLASSIF

fauna /fɔːnə/. The **fauna** in a place are all the animals, birds, fish, and insects there. EG *...the flora and fauna of Africa.* N PLURAL Formal

faux pas /fəʊ pɑː/. A **faux pas** is a socially embarrassing action or mistake. The plural form is also **faux pas**. EG *They behaved as if they were fearful of committing a faux pas.* N COUNT Formal

favour /feɪvə/, **favours, favouring, favoured;** spelled **favor** in American English.

1 If you regard something or someone with **favour**, you like or support them. EG *I think the company will look with favour on your plan... Is this just an attempt to win his favour?* N UNCOUNT

2 In favour is used in these ways. **2.1** If you are **in favour** of something, you support it and think that it is a good thing. EG *They are in favour of reforming the tax laws.* **2.2** If you make a judgement **in** someone's **favour**, you say that they are right. EG *The umpire ruled in her favour.* **2.3** Something that is **in** someone's **favour** gives them an advantage. EG *The system is biased in favour of young people.* **2.4** If something is rejected **in favour of** something else, the second thing is done or chosen instead of the first one. EG *The plans for a new airport have been scrapped in favour of an extension to the old one.* PHRASES

3 If something is **out of favour**, people no longer like it or support it. If something is **in favour**, people like it or support it. EG *Their views are very much out of favour now.* PHRASE

4 If you do someone a **favour**, you do something for them even though you do not have to. EG *I've come to ask a favour.* N COUNT

5 If you **favour** something, you like that thing more than the other choices available. EG *...those who favour disarmament.* V+O

6 Something that **favours** a person or event make it easier for that person to do something or for that event to happen. EG *The weather favoured the attacking army.* V+O

7 If you **favour** someone, you treat them better or more kindly than you treat other people. EG *Parents may favour the youngest child in the family.* V+O

8 If you **favour** someone with something such as your attention or your presence, you give them V+O+*with* Formal

If you are fed up, have you had enough to eat?

that thing. EG *I cannot say why he believes this, for he does not favour us with his reasoning.*

favourable /feɪvə°rəbə°l/; spelled **favorable** in American English. **1** If you are **favourable** to something, you agree with it or approve of it. EG *Most people were favourable to the idea... Her request met with a favourable response.* — ADJ QUALIT: OFT+*to*
◊ **favourably.** EG *Many reacted favourably to the plan.* — ◊ ADV

2 If something makes a **favourable** impression on you, you like it or approve of it. ◊ **favourably.** EG *Her application had impressed him very favourably.* — ADJ QUALIT; ◊ ADV

3 If you present something in a **favourable** light, you try to make people like it or approve of it. EG *We must try to present our profession in a more favourable light.* — ADJ QUALIT

4 Favourable conditions make something more likely to succeed. EG *This creates an atmosphere favourable to expansion.* — ADJ QUALIT

5 If you make a **favourable** comparison between one thing and another, you say that the first thing is at least as good as the second. ◊ **favourably.** EG *...an education service which compares favourably with that of other countries.* — ADJ QUALIT; ◊ ADV

favourite /feɪvə°rɪt/, **favourites;** spelled **favorite** in American English. **1** Your **favourite** thing of a particular type is the one that you like most. EG *What is your favourite television programme?... She's one of my favourite writers.* — ADJ CLASSIF

2 The **favourite** in a race or contest is the person or animal that is expected to win. — N COUNT

favouritism /feɪvə°rɪtɪzm/; spelled **favoritism** in American English. **Favouritism** is the practice of unfairly helping or supporting one person or group more than another. EG *There must be no favouritism in the allocation of contracts.* — N UNCOUNT

fawn /fɔːn/, **fawns, fawning, fawned. 1** Something that is **fawn** is a pale yellowish brown colour. — ADJ COLOUR

2 A **fawn** is a very young deer. — N COUNT

3 If people **fawn** on a powerful or rich person, they flatter him or her, usually in order to get some advantage for themselves. — V: OFT+*on*

fear /fɪə/, **fears, fearing, feared. 1 Fear** is the unpleasant feeling that you have when you think that you are in danger. EG *They huddled together, quaking with fear... She was brought up with no fear of animals.* — N UNCOUNT

2 If you **fear** someone or something, you are frightened because you think that they will harm you. EG *He fears nothing.* — V+O

3 If you **fear** something unpleasant, you think that it might happen, or might have happened, and feel worried about this. EG *An epidemic of plague was feared... The new countries fear that their newfound independence might be lost.* — V+O OR V+REPORT: ONLY *that*

4 A **fear** is a thought that something unpleasant might happen or might have happened. EG *My worst fears were quickly realized.* — N COUNT

5 If you **fear** for something, you think that it might be in danger and are very worried. EG *Morris began to fear for the life of Mrs Reilly.* ▸ used as a noun. EG *They had fears for their health.* — V+*for*; ▸ N COUNT OR N UNCOUNT

6 If you do not take a particular course of action **for fear** of something happening, you do not take it because you do not wish that thing to happen. EG *They did not mention it for fear of offending him.* — PHRASE

7 If you say that you **fear** that something is the case, you mean that you are sorry or sad that it is the case. EG *It is usually, I fear, the parents who are responsible.* — V: OFT+REPORT, ONLY *that* Formal

fearful /fɪəful/. **1** Someone who is **fearful** is afraid. EG *They are fearful of letting their feelings take over.* ◊ **fearfully.** EG *The boys looked at each other fearfully.* — ADJ QUALIT; ◊ ADV

2 Something that is **fearful** is very unpleasant or bad. EG *...the fearful risks of the operation.* — ADJ QUALIT

fearless /fɪəlɪ²s/. Someone who is **fearless** is not afraid at all. EG *...fearless reporters.* ◊ **fearlessly.** EG *If provoked, it defended itself fearlessly.* — ADJ QUALIT; ◊ ADV

fearsome /fɪəsəm/. Something that is **fearsome** is terrible or frightening. EG *The dog had a fearsome set of teeth.* — ADJ QUALIT Formal

feasible /fiːzəbə°l/. Something that is **feasible** can be done, made, or achieved. EG *The electric car is technically feasible.* ◊ **feasibility** /fiːzəbɪlɪti¹/. EG *...the technical feasibility of a supersonic aircraft.* — ADJ QUALIT; ◊ N UNCOUNT

feast /fiːst/, **feasts, feasting, feasted. 1** A **feast** is a large and special meal. EG *...a wedding feast.* — N COUNT

2 If you **feast**, you take part in a feast. EG *The poor starve while the rich feast... He sprawled there, feasting off cold roast duck.* ◊ **feasting.** EG *The feasting went on for hours.* — V: OFT+*off/on*; ◊ N UNCOUNT

3 If you **feast** your **eyes** on something, you look at it for a long time because you like it very much. EG *I feasted my eyes upon her lovely face.* — PHRASE

feat /fiːt/, **feats.** A **feat** is an impressive and difficult act or achievement. EG *...a brilliant feat of engineering.* — N COUNT+SUPP

feather /fɛðə/, **feathers.** A bird's **feathers** are the light, soft things that cover its body. EG *...ostrich feathers.* ◊ **feathered** /fɛðəd/. EG *...girls in feathered head-dresses.* — N COUNT; ◊ ADJ CLASSIF: ATTRIB

feathery /fɛðə°ri¹/. Something that is **feathery** has an edge divided into lots of thin parts so that it looks soft. EG *...feathery palm trees.* — ADJ QUALIT

feature /fiːtʃə/, **features, featuring, featured. 1** A **feature** of something is some part or characteristic that it has. EG *The most important feature of our work must be parental involvement... Every car will have built-in safety features.* — N COUNT+SUPP

2 Your **features** are your eyes, nose, mouth, and other parts of your face. — N PLURAL

3 When a film or exhibition **features** someone or something, they are an important part of it. EG *This film features two of my favourite actors.* — V+O

4 If you **feature** in something, you are an important and noticeable part of it. EG *This is not the first time he has featured in allegations of violence.* — V+*in*

5 A geographical **feature** is something noticeable in a particular area of country, for example a hill or a river. EG *...the natural features of the landscape.* — N COUNT+SUPP

6 A **feature** is also **6.1** a special article in a newspaper or magazine. EG *The local newspaper ran a feature on drug abuse.* **6.2** a special programme on radio or television. — N COUNT

7 You can also refer to a full-length film in a cinema as a **feature** or a **feature** film. — N COUNT

February /fɛbruəri¹/ is the second month of the year in the Western calendar. — N UNCOUNT

feces /fiːsiːz/. See **faeces**. — N UNCOUNT

feckless /fɛklɪ²s/. Someone who is **feckless** lacks strength of character, and cannot run their life properly. EG *...children with drunken or feckless parents.* — ADJ QUALIT Formal

fed /fɛd/ is the past tense and past participle of **feed.** ● See also **fed up**.

federal /fɛdə°rəl/. In a **federal** country or system of government, a group of states is controlled by a central government. EG *...the Federal Republic of Germany... ...a federal court.* — ADJ CLASSIF: ATTRIB

federation /fɛdəreɪʃə°n/, **federations.** A **federation** is **1** a group of organizations with a common interest. EG *...the National Federation of Women's Institutes.* **2** a federal country. EG *...the proposal to form a federation out of Northern and Southern Rhodesia.* — N COUNT

fed up. Someone who is **fed up** is bored or annoyed. EG *You sound a bit fed up... They're getting pretty fed up with him.* — ADJ PRED Informal

fee /fiː/, **fees.** A **fee** is **1** a sum of money that you pay to be allowed to do something. EG *...an entrance fee.* **2** the amount of money that a person or organization is paid for a particular job or service. EG *Agencies charge a fee to find an au pair.* — N COUNT

feeble /fi:bə[9]l/, **feebler, feeblest. 1** Someone or something that is **feeble** has very little power, strength, or energy. EG *The creature is physically feeble, with poor vision and dull senses... ...the feeble light of the bulb in the hallway.* — ADJ QUALIT
◇ **feebly.** EG *It feebly beat its wings.* — ◇ ADV

2 You can describe something that someone says as **feeble** when it is not effective, good, or convincing. EG *...feeble excuses... ...a feeble joke.* — ADJ QUALIT
◇ **feebly.** EG *'They seemed all right to me,' I explained feebly.* — ◇ ADV

feed /fi:d/, **feeds, feeding, fed** /fɛd/. **1** If you **feed** a baby or an animal, you give it food. EG *He had just come back from feeding the ponies... She fed the baby some milk.* — V+O: OFT+A; ALSO V+O+O
▸ used as a noun. EG *What time is his next feed?* — ▸ N COUNT

2 When an animal or baby **feeds**, it eats something. EG *Not all bats feed on insects.* — V: OFT+*on/off*

3 Feed is food that is given to an animal. — N MASS

4 If you **feed** your family or a community, you supply or prepare food for them. EG *The farmers grew too little to feed even their own families.* — V+O OR V-REFL

5 If something **feeds** on something else or **is fed** by it, it grows stronger as a result of it. EG *Once the process has been started, it feeds on itself... The fires were being fed by escaping gas.* — V+*on* OR V+O: USU PASS

6 If you **feed** something into an object, you put it gradually into the object. EG *Extra gas was fed into the pipeline... This data is fed into the computer.* — V+O: USU PASS+A

feedback /fi:dbæk/. When you get **feedback**, you get comments about something that you have done or made. EG *The more feedback we get from viewers, the better.* — N UNCOUNT

feel /fi:l/, **feels, feeling, felt** /fɛlt/. **1** If you **feel** a particular emotion or sensation, you experience it. EG *Mrs Oliver felt a sudden desire to burst out crying... I felt angry... I was feeling hungry and sleepy... She felt a fool... I felt like a murderer.* — V+O, V+C, OR V+A

2 If you **feel** that something is the case, it is your opinion that it is the case. EG *He felt I was making a terrible mistake... I felt obliged to invite him in... He felt it necessary to explain why he had come.* — V+REPORT: ONLY *that*; ALSO V+C, OR V+O+C: NO CONT

3 If you **feel** a particular way about something, you have that attitude or reaction to it. EG *She knew how I felt about totalitarianism.* — V+A: OFT+*about*; NO CONT

4 If you **feel like** doing something or having something, you want to do it or have it. EG *Whenever I felt like talking they were ready to listen... I feel like a stroll.* — PHRASE

5 You use **feel** when describing something that you are touching or holding. For example, if something **feels** heavy, it seems heavy when you pick it up. EG *It looks and feels like a normal fabric.* — V+C OR V+*like*: NO CONT
▸ used as a noun. EG *...the cool feel of armchair leather.* — ▸ N SING+SUPP

6 If you talk about how an experience **feels**, you are talking about the emotions and sensations that you have when you have the experience. EG *It felt good to be back... What does it feel like to watch yourself on TV?* — V+C OR V+*like*

7 If you **feel** something, **7.1** you are aware that it is touching you or happening to your body. EG *They felt the wind on their damp faces... She felt his hand pat hers... Rudolph could feel himself blushing.* — V+O, OR V-REFL +-ING OR INF
7.2 you are aware of it, even though you cannot see or hear it. EG *He had felt Binta's presence in the hut.* — V+O

8 If you **feel** the effect or result of something, you experience it. EG *We shan't feel the effect of the change for some years.* — V+O

9 If you **feel** a physical object, you touch it deliberately, in order to find out what it is like. EG *Eric felt his face. 'I'm all rough. Am I bleeding?'* — V+O

10 If you **feel** for an object, you try to find it using your hands rather than your eyes. EG *She felt in her bag for her key.* — V+*for*

11 The **feel** of something, for example a place, is the general impression that it gives you. EG *The Brazilian Amazon has the feel of a tropical wild west.* — N SING+SUPP

12 If you **do not feel yourself**, you feel slightly ill. — PHRASE

13 See also **feeling, felt**.

feeling /fi:lɪŋ/, **feelings. 1** A **feeling** is an emotion or attitude. EG *A feeling of panic was rising in him... She tried to hide her feelings... She cried out in a voice rich in real feeling, 'It means so much to me!'* — N COUNT OR N UNCOUNT: USU+SUPP

2 A **feeling** of, for example, hunger or tiredness is a physical sensation that you experience. EG *...an itchy feeling... ...feelings of nausea.* — N COUNT+SUPP

3 If you have no **feeling** in a part of your body, you cannot tell when that part is being touched. — N UNCOUNT

4 If you have a **feeling** that something is the case, you think that it is probably the case. EG *My feeling is that it would work very well... I have a nasty feeling you're right.* — N COUNT: OFT +REPORT

5 Feeling for someone or something is affection for them. EG *He may be moved by feeling for his fellow-citizens.* — N UNCOUNT

6 If you **hurt** someone's **feelings**, you upset them. — PHRASE

7 Bad feeling is resentment or hostility which exists between people. — PHRASE

8 If you have no **hard feelings** towards someone who has quarrelled with you or upset you, you do not feel angry with them. — PHRASE

feet /fi:t/ is the plural of **foot**.

feign /feɪn/, **feigns, feigning, feigned.** If you **feign** a feeling, you pretend that you are experiencing it. EG *She knew that her efforts to feign cheerfulness weren't convincing.* — V+O Literary
◇ **feigned.** *'I thought you must know,' Dixon said with feigned surprise.* — ◇ ADJ CLASSIF

feint /feɪnt/, **feints, feinting, feinted.** A **feint** is a misleading action or movement, especially in boxing, which is intended to deceive your opponent. — N COUNT
▸ used as a verb. EG *Green feinted with his right.* — ▸ V

feline /fi:laɪn/. **1 Feline** means belonging or relating to the cat family. — ADJ CLASSIF

2 If you describe someone as **feline**, you mean that they look or move like a cat. EG *...her feline charm.* — ADJ QUALIT

fell /fɛl/, **fells, felling, felled. 1 Fell** is the past tense of **fall**.

2 If you **fell** a tree, you cut it down. — V+O

3 If you **fell** someone, you knock them down. EG *This blow would have felled most men.* — V+O Literary

fellow /fɛləʊ/, **fellows. 1** A **fellow** is a man. EG *Doug is an exceedingly amiable fellow... My dear fellow, I really am sorry.* — N COUNT Informal

2 You use **fellow** to describe people who have something in common with you. EG *I've always trusted my fellow men... I had a conversation with a fellow passenger.* — ADJ CLASSIF: ATTRIB
▸ used as a plural noun. EG *He sought the approval of his fellows.* — ▸ N PLURAL +POSS

3 A **fellow** of a society or academic institution is a member of it. EG *...Sir George Porter, Fellow of the Royal Society.* — N COUNT

fellowship /fɛlə[6]ʃɪp/, **fellowships. 1 Fellowship** is a feeling of friendship that people have when they are doing something together. EG *...the atmosphere of cheerful good fellowship.* — N UNCOUNT

2 A **fellowship** is a group of people that join together for a common purpose or interest. EG *...the Socialist Fellowship.* — N COUNT+SUPP

felony /fɛləni[1]/, **felonies.** A **felony** is a very serious crime such as murder or armed robbery. — N COUNT Legal

felt /fɛlt/. **1 Felt** is the past tense and past participle of **feel**.

2 Felt is a type of thick cloth made by pressing short threads together. — N UNCOUNT

felt-tip. A **felt-tip** pen has a rod of fibres for a nib. — ADJ CLASSIF

female /fi:meɪl/, **females. 1** You can refer to any creature that can produce babies from its body or lay eggs as a **female**. EG *The male fertilizes the female's eggs.* — N COUNT
▸ used as an adjective. EG *...a female toad.* — ▸ ADJ CLASSIF

2 Women and girls are sometimes referred to as — N COUNT

Do you ever have to fend for yourself?

females. Some people find this use offensive. EG ...*a lone female staying at a hotel.* ▸ used as an adjective. EG *There are only nineteen female members of parliament.* ▸ ADJ CLASSIF

3 Something that is **female** concerns, relates to, or affects women rather than men. EG ...*female inventions... ...traditionally female areas of work.* ADJ CLASSIF : ATTRIB

feminine /fɛmɪnɪn/. Something that is **feminine** relates to or is considered typical of women, in contrast to men. EG *Society hasn't regarded science or engineering as feminine occupations... ...feminine clothes.* ADJ QUALIT

femininity /fɛmɪnɪnɪ[1]ti[1]/. 1 A woman's **femininity** is the fact that she is a woman. N UNCOUNT

2 **Femininity** is also the qualities that are considered to be typical of women. EG *The fashion industry responded to the new mood of femininity.* N UNCOUNT

feminism /fɛmɪnɪzə[0]m/ is the belief that women should have the same rights, power, and opportunities as men. N UNCOUNT

feminist /fɛmɪnɪst/, **feminists.** A **feminist** is a person who believes in and supports feminism. EG *Claudia thought of herself as a feminist.* ▸ used as an adjective. EG ...*the feminist response to the new law.* N COUNT ▸ ADJ CLASSIF

fence /fɛns/, **fences, fencing, fenced.** 1 A **fence** is a barrier made of wood or wire supported by posts. N COUNT

2 If you **fence** an area of land, you surround it with a fence. ◊ **fenced.** EG ...*a fenced enclosure.* V+O ◊ ADJ CLASSIF

3 If you **sit on the fence**, you avoid supporting any side in a discussion or argument. PHRASE

fence in. If you **fence** something **in**, you surround it completely with a fence. PHRASAL VB : V+O+ADV

fence off. If you **fence off** an area of land, you build a fence round it. PHRASAL VB : V+O+ADV

fencing /fɛnsɪŋ/. 1 **Fencing** is a sport in which two competitors fight each other using very thin swords. N UNCOUNT

2 You can also refer to materials that are used to make fences as **fencing**. EG ...*cedar wood fencing.* N UNCOUNT : USU+SUPP

fend /fɛnd/, **fends, fending, fended.** If you **fend for yourself**, you look after yourself without relying on help from anyone else. EG *Grown up children should leave home and fend for themselves.* PHRASE

fend off. 1 If you **fend off** someone who is attacking you, you use your arms or a stick to defend yourself. 2 If you **fend off** questions or requests, you avoid answering them. EG *She fended off all these claims.* PHRASAL VB : V+O+ADV; V+ADV+O

ferment, ferments, fermenting, fermented; pronounced /fɜːmɛnt/ when it is a noun and /fə[5]mɛnt/ when it is a verb.

1 **Ferment** is excitement and unrest caused by change or uncertainty. EG *Portugal was in ferment... ...the present ferment in education.* N UNCOUNT

2 When wine, beer, or fruit **ferments** or **is fermented**, a chemical change takes place in it. ◊ **fermented.** EG *He smelt the whiff of fermented apples.* ◊ **fermentation** /fɜːmɛnteɪʃə[0]n/. EG ...*the fermentation of wines.* V-ERG ◊ ADJ CLASSIF ◊ N UNCOUNT

fern /fɜːn/, **ferns.** A **fern** is a plant that has long stems with feathery leaves and no flowers. N COUNT

ferocious /fərəʊʃəs/. A **ferocious** animal, person, or action is fierce and violent. EG ...*two years of ferocious fighting.* ◊ **ferociously.** EG *The buck shook his antlers ferociously.* ADJ QUALIT ◊ ADV

ferocity /fərɒsɪ[1]ti[1]/. When something is done with **ferocity**, it is done in a fierce and violent way. EG *The attack was resumed with a new ferocity.* N UNCOUNT

ferret /fɛrɪt/, **ferrets, ferreting, ferreted.** A **ferret** is a small, white, fierce animal. Ferrets are used for hunting rabbits and rats. N COUNT

ferret out. If you **ferret out** information, you discover it by searching thoroughly. EG ...*ferreting out the details of their private lives.* PHRASAL VB : V+O+ADV Informal

ferry /fɛri[1]/, **ferries, ferrying, ferried.** 1 A **ferry** is a boat that carries passengers or vehicles across a river or a narrow bit of sea. EG ...*car ferries... We got back to London by train and ferry.* N COUNT OR *by*+N

2 To **ferry** people or goods somewhere means to transport them there. EG *They were ferried from one building to another.* V+O : USU+A

fertile /fɜːtaɪl/. 1 You describe land or soil as **fertile** when plants grow easily in it. ◊ **fertility** /fɜːtɪlɪti[1]/. EG ...*soil fertility.* ADJ QUALIT ◊ N UNCOUNT

2 If someone has a **fertile** mind or imagination, they produce a lot of good or original ideas. ADJ QUALIT : ATTRIB

3 You describe a place or situation as **fertile** ground when you think that something is likely to succeed or develop there. EG *Britain is not fertile ground for news magazines.* ADJ QUALIT

4 A woman who is **fertile** can have babies. ◊ **fertility.** EG *Fertility rates have declined.* ADJ QUALIT ◊ N UNCOUNT

fertilize /fɜːtɪlaɪz/, **fertilizes, fertilizing, fertilized;** also spelled **fertilise.** 1 When an egg or a plant **is fertilized**, sperm reaches the egg, or pollen reaches the reproductive part of the plant, so that young animals or plants can start to be produced. ◊ **fertilized.** EG *The fertilised egg remains where it is for one more week.* ◊ **fertilization** /fɜːtɪlaɪzeɪʃə[0]n/. EG ...*the small amount of pollen necessary for fertilization.* V+O : USU PASS ◊ ADJ CLASSIF ◊ N UNCOUNT

2 To **fertilize** land means to spread manure or chemicals on it in order to make plants grow well. V+O

fertilizer /fɜːtɪlaɪzə/, **fertilizers;** also spelled **fertiliser. Fertilizer** is a substance that you spread on the ground in order to make plants grow more successfully. N MASS

fervent /fɜːvənt/. Someone who is **fervent** about something has strong and enthusiastic feelings about it. EG ...*a fervent belief in God... He had been one of Lily's most fervent admirers.* ◊ **fervently.** EG *'Oh, I am glad!' Scylla said fervently.* ADJ QUALIT ◊ ADV

fervour /fɜːvə/; spelled **fervor** in American English. **Fervour** is a very strong feeling in favour of something. EG *She was swept to power on a tide of patriotic fervour... 'She's marvellous,' said Mrs Moffatt with fervour.* N UNCOUNT Formal

fester /fɛstə/, **festers, festering, festered.** 1 When a wound **festers**, it becomes infected. EG ...*a painful, festering sore.* V

2 If an unpleasant situation, feeling, or thought **festers**, it grows worse. EG ...*the bitter row still festering between them.* V

festival /fɛstɪvə[0]l/, **festivals.** A **festival** is 1 an organized series of events such as musical concerts or drama productions. EG ...*the Edinburgh Festival... ...the London Film Festival.* 2 a day or time of the year when people have a holiday from work and celebrate some special event, especially a religious event. N COUNT

festive /fɛstɪv/. Something that is **festive** is full of colour and happiness, especially because of a holiday or celebration. EG ...*a festive occasion... They were in a festive mood.* ADJ QUALIT

festivity /fɛstɪvɪ[1]ti[1]/, **festivities.** 1 **Festivity** is the celebrating of something in a happy way. EG ...*four days of festivity.* N UNCOUNT

2 **Festivities** are things that people do in order to celebrate something. EG *The week is crammed with festivities.* N PLURAL

festooned /fɛstuːnd/. If something **is festooned** with objects, the objects are hanging over it in large numbers. EG *The counters were festooned with rainbow-coloured scarves.* V-PASS+*with*

fetch /fɛtʃ/, **fetches, fetching, fetched.** 1 If you **fetch** something or someone, you bring them from a place by going there in order to get them. EG *He fetched a bucket of water from the pond.* V+O : OFT+A; ALSO V+O+O

2 If something **fetches** a particular amount of money, it is sold for that amount. EG *His pictures fetch very high prices.* V+O

3 See also **far-fetched.**

fetch up. If you **fetch up** somewhere, you arrive there, usually without intending to. EG *She fell* PHRASAL VB : V+ADV American *through the rotten floorboards, finally fetching up on the ground floor.*

fetching /fɛtʃɪŋ/. If you say that a woman looks **fetching**, you mean that she looks attractive. EG *Melanie looked remarkably fetching in a white dress.* ADJ QUALIT

fête /feɪt/, **fêtes, fêting, fêted;** also spelled **fete. 1** A **fête** is an event that is held out of doors and includes competitions, entertainments, and the selling of homemade goods. EG *...the church fête.* N COUNT

2 If someone important **is fêted**, a public welcome is provided for them. EG *In New York, Karen Blixen was being fêted by everyone who knew her work.* V+O : USU PASS

fetid /fɛtɪd, fiː-/. **Fetid** water or air has a strong, unpleasant smell. ADJ CLASSIF Formal

fetter /fɛtə/, **fetters, fettering, fettered. 1** If something **fetters** you, it prevents you from behaving in a free and natural way. EG *...the forces that fetter our souls.* V+O Literary

2 Fetters are things that prevent you from behaving in a free and natural way. EG *...freed from the fetters of control.* N COUNT : USU PLURAL Literary

fetus /fiːtəs/. See **foetus**.

feud /fjuːd/, **feuds, feuding, feuded.** A **feud** is a long-lasting and bitter dispute. EG *His feud with the Premier proceeded remorselessly.* ▸ used as a verb. EG *They are constantly feuding amongst themselves... He feuded with the formidable Ernest Bevin.* N COUNT ▸ V OR V+*with* : RECIP

feudal /fjuːdəᵒl/ means relating to the system of feudalism. EG *...a feudal society.* ADJ CLASSIF : ATTRIB

feudalism /fjuːdəᵒlɪzəᵒm/ was a system in which people were given land or protection by people of higher rank, and worked and fought for them in return. N UNCOUNT

fever /fiːvə/, **fevers. 1** If you have a **fever**, your temperature is higher than usual because you are ill. • See also **hay fever**, **scarlet fever**, **yellow fever**. N COUNT OR N UNCOUNT

2 You can also refer to extreme excitement or agitation as a **fever**. EG *He stayed calm through the fever of the campaign.* N COUNT : USU+SUPP

feverish /fiːvəᵒrɪʃ/. **1 Feverish** emotion or activity shows great excitement or agitation. EG *...the feverish excitement in his voice... ...a feverish race against time.* ◊ **feverishly.** EG *They worked feverishly.* ADJ QUALIT ◊ ADV

2 If you are **feverish**, you are suffering from a fever. ADJ QUALIT

few /fjuː/, **fewer, fewest. 1 Few** is used **1.1** to refer to a small number of things or people. EG *The window opened a few inches... During the first few weeks, I didn't understand a word... A few were smoking.* **1.2** to indicate that the number of things or people that you are referring to is smaller than is desirable or than was expected. EG *Very few people survived... There are fewer trains at night... Few of them ever reach their potential.* QUANTIF OR PRON

2 You use **no fewer than** to suggest that a number is surprisingly large. EG *No fewer than five cameramen lost their lives.* PHRASE

3 You use **quite a few** and **a good few** when you are referring to quite a lot of things or people. EG *We had quite a few friendly arguments... I spent a good few years of my life there.* QUANTIF

4 Things that are **few and far between** are very rare or uncommon. PHRASE

fiancé /fiˈɒnseɪ/, **fiancés.** A woman's **fiancé** is the man to whom she is engaged to be married. N COUNT

fiancée /fɪˈɒnseɪ/, **fiancées.** A man's **fiancée** is the woman to whom he is engaged to be married. N COUNT

fiasco /fiˈæskəʊ/, **fiascos** or **fiascoes.** When something fails completely, you can describe it as a **fiasco**. EG *The meeting was a fiasco.* N COUNT

fib /fɪb/, **fibs, fibbing, fibbed. 1** A **fib** is a small lie which is not very important. N COUNT Informal

2 If you **are fibbing**, you are telling lies. EG *It isn't true! You're fibbing!* V Informal

fibre /faɪbə/, **fibres;** spelled **fiber** in American English. **1** A **fibre** is a thin thread of a natural or artificial substance, especially one that is used to make cloth or rope. N COUNT

2 Fibre consists of the parts of plants or seeds that your body cannot digest. EG *Scientists are recommending people to eat more fibre.* N UNCOUNT

3 A **fibre** is also a thin piece of flesh like a thread which connects nerve cells in your body or which muscles are made of. EG *...nerve fibres.* N COUNT

fibreglass /faɪbəglɑːs/; spelled **fiberglass** in American English. **Fibreglass** is plastic strengthened with short threads of glass. N UNCOUNT

fibrous /faɪbrəs/. Something that is **fibrous** contains a lot of fibres. EG *They eat a great deal of fibrous twigs and woody material.* ADJ CLASSIF

fickle /fɪkəᵒl/. Someone who is **fickle** keeps changing their mind about what they like or want. ◊ **fickleness.** EG *This serves to demonstrate the fickleness of public taste.* ADJ QUALIT ◊ N UNCOUNT

fiction /fɪkʃəᵒn/, **fictions. 1 Fiction** consists of books and stories about imaginary people and events. EG *I enjoy reading fiction... ...a fiction writer.* N UNCOUNT

2 A **fiction** is something that you pretend is true, although you know that it is not true. EG *We had to keep up the fiction of being a normal couple... ...the replacement of facts by comforting fictions.* N UNCOUNT OR N COUNT

fictional /fɪkʃəᵒnəl, -ʃənəᵒl/. **1 Fictional** people and events occur in stories, plays, and films, and never actually existed or happened. EG *...a fictional composer called Moony Shapiro.* ADJ CLASSIF

2 Fictional means relating to fiction. EG *...the fictional treatment of adultery.* ADJ CLASSIF : ATTRIB

fictitious /fɪktɪʃəs/. Something that is **fictitious** is false or does not exist. EG *They bought the materials under fictitious names.* ADJ CLASSIF

fiddle /fɪdəᵒl/, **fiddles, fiddling, fiddled. 1** If you **fiddle** with something, you keep moving it or touching it with your fingers. EG *He sat nervously fiddling with his spectacles.* V : OFT+*with*

2 When people **fiddle** an account or bill, they alter it dishonestly or arrange it so that they get money for themselves. EG *He had fiddled the figures in the transaction.* ◊ **fiddling.** EG *A lot of fiddling goes on in these companies.* V+O Informal ◊ N UNCOUNT

3 A **fiddle** is a dishonest action or scheme in which a person gets money for himself or herself. EG *Laing had worked some fiddle.* N COUNT Informal

4 A **fiddle** is also a violin. N COUNT

5 If you **play second fiddle** to someone, your position is less important than theirs in something that you are doing together. PHRASE

fiddle about or **fiddle around.** If you **fiddle about** or **fiddle around** with something, you keep moving it or touching it with your fingers. PHRASAL VB : V+ADV, OFT+*with*

fiddly /fɪdliˈ/. You say that something is **fiddly** when it is difficult to do or use, because it involves small or complicated objects. EG *It is a very fiddly job.* ADJ QUALIT Informal

fidelity /fɪdɛlɪˈtiˈ/. **1** When you talk about the **fidelity** of a person or an animal, you are referring to the fact that they continue to be faithful or loyal to someone. EG *There's nothing like a dog's fidelity.* N UNCOUNT : OFT+*to* Formal

2 When you talk about the **fidelity** of a report, translation, or adaptation, you are referring to its degree of accuracy. EG *...fidelity to the author's intentions.* N UNCOUNT : OFT+*to* Formal

fidget /fɪdʒɪt/, **fidgets, fidgeting, fidgeted.** When people **fidget**, they keep moving their hands or feet or changing their position slightly, because they are nervous or bored. EG *The children are starting to fidget.* V

fidgety /fɪdʒɪtiˈ/. Someone who is **fidgety** keeps fidgeting. ADJ QUALIT

Which words on these pages can be spelled in two ways?

field /fiːld/, **fields, fielding, fielded.** 1 A **field** is an area of land on which a crop is grown, or an area of grass where animals are kept. EG *...fields of wheat... We pitched our tent in a field.* N COUNT

2 A sports **field** is an area of grass where a sport is played. EG *...a football field.* N COUNT

3 A magnetic or gravitational **field** is an area in which magnetism or gravity is strong enough to have an effect. N COUNT+SUPP

4 Your **field** of vision or **field** of view is the whole area that you can see from a particular position or without turning your head. EG *A brown figure dressed in red crept into her field of vision.* N COUNT+SUPP

5 In a war, fighting takes place in the **field** or on the **field** of battle. EG *They needed a more effective way of using military forces in the field.* N SING: *the*+N

6 A particular **field** is a particular subject or area of activity or interest. EG *He doesn't seem to have done much in the political field... She is an expert in this field.* N COUNT+SUPP

7 A **field** trip or a **field** study involves research that is done in a real, natural environment rather than in a theoretical way. ADJ CLASSIF: ATTRIB

8 Something that is studied or tested **in the field** is studied or tested in a real, natural environment. PHRASE

9 The team that **is fielding** in a game of cricket, baseball, or rounders is the team that is trying to catch the ball, rather than batting. V: USU CONT

10 If you **have a field day**, you have a very pleasant time doing something that you have been given an opportunity to do. EG *The local papers had a field day.* PHRASE

field-glasses are binoculars. N PLURAL

field marshal, field marshals. A **field marshal** is an officer in the army who has the highest possible rank. EG *...Field Marshal Montgomery.* N COUNT

fiend /fiːnd/, **fiends.** 1 If you call someone a **fiend**, you mean that they are very wicked or cruel. EG *I have no idea who this murderous fiend may be.* N COUNT Literary

2 You can use **fiend** to describe someone who is very interested in a particular thing or likes it very much. For example, if you say that someone is a health **fiend**, you mean that they are very interested in good health. N COUNT+SUPP Informal

fiendish /fiːndɪʃ/. 1 Someone who is **fiendish** is very cruel. EG *...a fiendish despot.* ADJ QUALIT

2 A **fiendish** problem or task is very difficult. EG *...a task of fiendish complexity.* ◊ **fiendishly.** EG *This effect is fiendishly hard to achieve.* ADJ QUALIT ◊ SUBMOD Informal

fierce /fɪəs/, **fiercer, fiercest.** 1 A **fierce** person or animal is very aggressive or angry. EG *...fierce dogs.* ◊ **fiercely.** EG *'Don't assume anything!' said Martha fiercely.* ADJ QUALIT ◊ ADV

2 Something that is **fierce** 2.1 involves strong feelings or great activity. EG *...a fierce battle... ...the fierce loyalty of these people.* ◊ **fiercely.** EG *...a fiercely dedicated group of people.* 2.2 is very strong or intense. EG *...fierce heat... ...a fierce storm.* ◊ **fiercely.** EG *The fire was blazing fiercely.* ADJ QUALIT ◊ ADV ADJ QUALIT ◊ ADV

fiery /faɪəri¹/, **fierier, fieriest.** 1 Something that is **fiery** 1.1 is burning strongly or contains fire. EG *...clouds of fiery gas.* 1.2 is bright red in colour. EG *The tonsils become fiery red and swollen.* ADJ CLASSIF ADJ QUALIT

2 A **fiery** person behaves or speaks in an angry way. EG *...this fiery young man... ...a fiery speech.* ADJ QUALIT

fifteen /fɪftiːn/, **fifteens. Fifteen** is the number 15: see the entry headed NUMBER. EG *We were married for fifteen years.* NUMBER

fifteenth /fɪftiːnθ/ **fifteenths.** The **fifteenth** item in a series is the one that you count as number fifteen: see the entry headed NUMBER. EG *The palace is supposed to have been built in the late fifteenth century.* ORDINAL

fifth /fɪfθ/, **fifths.** 1 The **fifth** item in a series is the one that you count as number five: see the entry headed NUMBER. EG *We were sent to another office on the fifth floor.* ORDINAL

2 A **fifth** is one of five equal parts of something. EG *Only one fifth of the surface area of Africa is farmland.* N COUNT: USU+*of*

fiftieth /fɪfti¹əθ/ **fiftieths.** The **fiftieth** item in a series is the one that you count as number fifty: see the entry headed NUMBER. EG *...the fiftieth anniversary of the Russian Revolution.* ORDINAL

fifty /fɪfti¹/, **fifties. Fifty** is the number 50: see the entry headed NUMBER. EG *He pointed to some low buildings about fifty yards away.* NUMBER

fifty-fifty. 1 When something is divided **fifty-fifty** between two people, each person gets half of it. EG *Profits were to be split fifty-fifty between us.* ADV AFTER VB, OR ADJ CLASSIF

2 If the chances of something happening are **fifty-fifty**, it is equally likely to happen as not to happen. EG *We have little better than a fifty-fifty chance of survival.* ADJ CLASSIF

fig /fɪg/, **figs.** A **fig** is a soft, sweet fruit full of tiny seeds. Figs grow on trees in hot countries. N COUNT

fig., figs. Fig. is used to refer to a particular diagram. It is an abbreviation for 'figure'. EG *The piston moves into a horizontal position (see fig. 3).*

fight /faɪt/, **fights, fighting, fought** /fɔːt/. 1 If you **fight** something, you try in a determined way to prevent it or stop it. EG *We must fight discrimination... You can't fight against progress.* ▸ used as a noun. EG *...the fight against illegal drugs.* V+O; ALSO V: OFT+*against* ▸ N COUNT

2 If you **fight** for something, you try in a determined way to get it or achieve it. EG *They will fight for their rights... Workers will have to fight to participate in the country's economic growth.* ▸ used as a noun. EG *...the fight for equality.* V: OFT+*for* OR *to*-INF ▸ N COUNT

3 When people **fight**, they try to hurt each other physically. EG *I learned how to fight other boys... He had fought in the First World War... The men were going off to fight a battle.* ▸ used as a noun. EG *There would be fights sometimes between the workers.* ◊ **fighting.** EG *We were only metres away from the fighting.* V OR V+O ▸ N COUNT ◊ N UNCOUNT

4 When people **fight** about something, they quarrel. EG *They fought about money... It's nice not having to fight you about housework.* V OR V+O: OFT +*about/over*

5 If you **put up a fight**, you fight strongly against someone who is stronger than you are. PHRASE

6 When politicians **fight** an election, they try to win it. V+O

7 If you **fight** your **way** somewhere, you get there with great difficulty, for example because there are a lot of people in your way. PHRASE

8 When you **fight** an emotion or desire, you try very hard not to feel it, show it, or act on it. EG *He fought the urge to cry.* V+O

9 to **fight a losing battle**: see **battle**.

fight back. 1 If you **fight back** against someone who has attacked you or made difficulties for you, you try to protect yourself and stop them or beat them. EG *The importing countries could fight back with laws of their own.* 2 When you **fight back** an emotion or a desire, you try very hard not to feel it, show it, or act on it. EG *She fought back the tears.* PHRASAL VB: V+ADV V+ADV+O

fight off. 1 If you **fight off** something, for example an illness or an unpleasant feeling, you succeed in getting rid of it. EG *We can fight off most minor ailments.* 2 If you **fight off** someone who has attacked you, you succeed in driving them away by fighting them. PHRASAL VB: V+O+ADV V+O+ADV

fight out. When two people or groups **fight** something **out**, they fight or argue until one of them wins. EG *...while the European nations were fighting it out on the battlefield.* PHRASAL VB: V+O+ADV

fighter /faɪtə/, **fighters.** 1 A **fighter** or a **fighter plane** is a fast military aircraft that is used for destroying other aircraft. N COUNT

2 A **fighter** is also someone who fights. N COUNT

figment /fɪgmə²nt/, **figments.** If you say that something is a **figment** of someone's imagination, you mean that it does not really exist and they are imagining it. EG *I thought this man Broum was another figment of your imagination.* N COUNT: USU+*of*

figuratively /fɪgəʳrətɪvli¹/. When someone is speaking **figuratively**, they are using a word or expression with a more abstract or imaginative meaning than its usual one. EG *'She said I killed him.' – 'She was speaking figuratively.'* ADV

figure /fɪgə/, **figures, figuring, figured. 1** A **figure** is **1.1** a particular amount expressed as a number, especially a statistic. EG *...unemployment figures... The figure for 1983 was as low as 23 per cent.* **1.2** any of the ten written symbols from 0 to 9 that are used to represent a number. EG *...a three-figure number.* N COUNT

2 An amount or number that is in **double figures** is between ten and ninety-nine. An amount or number that is in **single figures** is between nought and nine. EG *The rate of inflation remains in double figures.* PHRASE

3 When you **put a figure on** an amount, you say exactly how much it is. EG *They said defence spending should be raised but put no figure on the increase they wanted.* PHRASE

4 You refer to someone that you can see as a **figure** when you cannot see them clearly, for example because they are a long way away. EG *I could see a small female figure advancing towards us.* N COUNT

5 Someone who is referred to as a particular type of **figure** is well-known and important in some way. EG *He was a key figure in the independence struggle... ...one of the great theatrical figures of our time.* N COUNT+SUPP

6 Someone who is regarded as, for example, a mother **figure** or a hero **figure** is regarded as the type of person stated or suggested. EG *...authority figures.* N COUNT+SUPP

7 Your **figure** is the shape of your body. EG *She's got a fabulous figure.* N COUNT

8 A **figure** is also a drawing or diagram in a book. EG *The original design was modified (see Figure 4.)* N COUNT

9 If you **figure** that something is the case, you think or guess that it is the case. EG *They figured it was better to stay where they were.* V+REPORT: ONLY *that* Informal

10 A thing or person that **figures** in something appears in it or is included in it. EG *Loneliness figures quite a lot in his conversation.* V: USU+*in*

figure out. If you **figure out** a solution to a problem or the reason for something, you work it out. EG *She had not yet figured out what she was going to do... We thought you'd figured it out by now.* PHRASAL VB: V+ADV+O OR V+ADV+REPORT Informal

figurehead /fɪgəhɛd/, **figureheads.** If you refer to the leader of a movement or organization as a **figurehead**, you mean that he or she has little real power. EG *The president had become merely a figurehead.* N COUNT

figure of speech, figures of speech. A **figure of speech** is an expression or word that is used with a more abstract or imaginative meaning than its original one. N COUNT

filament /fɪləmə²nt/, **filaments.** A **filament** is a very thin piece or thread of something. N COUNT

filch /fɪltʃ/, **filchs, filching, filched.** If someone **filches** something, they steal it. EG *The letters had been filched from the private files of John D. Archbold.* V+O Informal

file /faɪl/, **files, filing, filed. 1** A **file** is **1.1** a box or a folded piece of card in which someone keeps documents that belong together. EG *He closed the file and looked up at Rodin.* **1.2** a collection of information about a particular person or thing. EG *Get me the personal file on Viktor Kowalski.* N COUNT

2 Something that is **on file** or **on the files** is recorded in a collection of information. EG *The police had both men on their files.* PHRASE

3 If you **file** a document, you put it in the correct file. EG *Bills are not filed under B; but under U for unpleasant.* V+O: OFT+*under*

4 In computing, a **file** is a set of related data that has its own name. N COUNT

5 When you **file** a formal accusation, complaint, or request, you make it officially. EG *Adoption papers were duly filed by Mr and Mrs White in May 1974... I'm filing for divorce.* V+O OR V+*for*

6 When a group of people **files** somewhere, they walk one behind the other in a line. EG *They filed out in silence.* V+A

7 A group of people who are moving along **in single file** are in a line, one behind the other. PHRASE

8 A **file** is also a hand tool with rough surfaces which is used for rubbing hard objects to make them smooth, shape them, or cut through them. N COUNT

9 If you **file** an object, you smooth it, shape it, or cut it with a file. EG *Kitty sat at the kitchen table filing her fingernails.* V+O

filial /fɪljəl/ means relating to the status or duties of a son or daughter. EG *...a sense of filial obligation.* ADJ CLASSIF Formal

filing cabinet, filing cabinets. A **filing cabinet** is a piece of office furniture with deep drawers in which files are kept. N COUNT

fill /fɪl/, **fills, filling, filled. 1** If you **fill** a container or area, you put a large amount of something into it, with the result that it is full. EG *Fill the teapot with boiling water.* V+O: OFT+*with*

2 If an amount of things or an object **fills** a space or area, it is so large that there is very little room left. EG *Enthusiastic crowds filled the streets.* V+O
◇ **filled.** EG *They entered a large hall filled with rows of desks.* ◇ ADJ PRED +*with*

3 If a thing or a place **fills**, it becomes full of things, people, or a substance. EG *Madeleine's eyes filled with tears... The place of assembly filled quickly.* V: OFT+*with*

4 If something **fills** you with an emotion or if an emotion **fills** you, you experience this emotion strongly. EG *His son's lies filled him with anger and contempt... A wave of panic filled her.* V+O: OFT+*with*

5 If something **fills** a need or a gap, it puts an end to this need or gap by existing or being active. EG *The Alliance filled the political vacuum.* V+O

6 Something that **fills** a role or position performs a particular function or has a particular place within a system. EG *It has filled this role in a most satisfactory way for many years.* V+O

7 If you **have had your fill of** something, you do not want to experience it or do it any more. EG *I'd had my fill of storms.* PHRASE

8 See also **filling**.

fill in. 1 When you **fill in** a form, you write information in the spaces on it. EG *Fill in your name and address.* PHRASAL VB: V+O+ADV **2** If you **fill** someone **in**, you give them detailed information about something. EG *I'll fill you in on the details now.* V+O+ADV **3** If you **fill in** for someone else, you do the work that they normally do because they are unable to do it on that day. V+ADV, OFT+*for* **4** If you **are filling in time**, you are doing something to use up some spare time while waiting for something else to happen. PHRASE

fill out. 1 When you **fill out** a form, you write information in the spaces on it. EG *I've filled out the death certificate.* PHRASAL VB: V+O+ADV **2** If a fairly thin person **fills out**, he or she becomes fatter. V+ADV

fill up. 1 If you **fill up** a container, you put a large amount of something into it, with the result that it is full. EG *Fill up his seed bowl twice a day.* PHRASAL VB: V+O+ADV **2** If a place **fills up**, it becomes full of things or people. EG *His office began to fill up with people.* V+ADV, OFT+*with*

fillet /fɪlɪt/, **fillets.** A **fillet** of fish or meat is a piece that has no bones in it. N COUNT OR N UNCOUNT

filling /fɪlɪŋ/, **fillings. 1** A **filling** is a small amount of metal or plastic that a dentist puts in a hole in a tooth. N COUNT

2 The **filling** in a cake, pie, chocolate, or sandwich is the mixture inside it. EG *...delicious chocolates with cream fillings.* N MASS

Which word on these pages is an informal word meaning 'to steal'?

3 Food that is **filling** makes you feel full when you have eaten it. ADJ QUALIT

filling station, filling stations. A **filling station** is a place where you can buy petrol and oil for your car. N COUNT

film /fɪlm/, **films, filming, filmed. 1** A **film** consists of moving pictures that have been recorded so that they can be shown in a cinema or on television. EG *Shall we go and see a film?... The film was shot largely on location... The broadcast began with close-up film of babies crying.* N COUNT OR N UNCOUNT

2 If you **film** someone or something, you use a camera to take moving pictures which can be shown in a cinema or on television. EG *Joan ran ahead to film us... The TV crews couldn't film at night.* V+O OR V

3 A **film** is also the roll of thin plastic that you use in a camera to take photographs. EG *...a roll of film.* N COUNT OR N UNCOUNT

4 A **film** of powder, liquid, or grease is a very thin layer of it. N COUNT: USU+SUPP

filming /fɪlmɪŋ/ is the activity of making a film, including the acting, directing, and operating of the cameras. EG *I found filming terribly exhausting.* N UNCOUNT

filter /fɪltə/, **filters, filtering, filtered. 1** To **filter** a substance means to pass it through a device which is designed to remove particles from it. EG *Water would have to be filtered many times to remove any radioactive matter.* V+O

2 A **filter** is a device through which something is filtered. N COUNT

3 When light or sound **filters** into a place, it comes in faintly. EG *...with the morning light already filtering through the curtains.* V+A

4 When news or information **filters** through to people, it gradually reaches them. EG *Disturbing rumours filtered back from the East.* V+A

filter out. To **filter out** something from a substance means to remove it by passing the substance through a filter. EG *First we would have to filter out some of the tar particles.* PHRASAL VB: V+O+ADV

filth /fɪlθ/. **1 Filth** is a disgusting amount of dirt. EG *...the filth and decay of the villages.* N UNCOUNT

2 People refer to words or pictures as **filth** when they think that they describe or represent sex or nudity in a disgusting way. EG *...the filth the press printed about him.* N UNCOUNT

filthy /fɪlθi¹/, **filthier, filthiest. 1** Something that is **filthy** is very dirty indeed. EG *...a really filthy oven... Her sandals were filthy.* ADJ QUALIT

2 People describe words or pictures as **filthy** when they think that they describe or represent sex or nudity in a disgusting way. EG *I caught her reading a filthy book.* ADJ QUALIT

fin /fɪn/, **fins.** A fish's **fins** are flat objects like small wings sticking out of its body. Fins help the fish to swim and to keep its balance. N COUNT

final /faɪnə⁰l/, **finals. 1** In a series of events, things, or people, the **final** one is the last one. EG *...on the final morning of the festival... We made our final attempt to beat the record.* ADJ CLASSIF: ATTRIB

2 Final also means **2.1** happening at the end of an event or series of events. EG *The final applause was explosive.* **2.2** the greatest or most severe that is possible. EG *He paid the final penalty for his crime.* ADJ CLASSIF: ATTRIB

3 If a decision is **final**, it cannot be changed or questioned. EG *The judges' decision is final... You'd be insane to let him have the final say.* ADJ CLASSIF

4 The **final** of a competition or sporting event is the last game or contest. The winner of the final wins the whole competition or event. EG *I'm trying to get tickets for the Cup Final.* N COUNT+SUPP

5 When university students take their **finals**, they take the last and most important examinations in their course. N PLURAL

finale /fɪnɑːli¹/, **finales.** The **finale** of a show or piece of music is the last section of it. EG *...the Finale of Beethoven's Violin Concerto.* N COUNT

finalise /faɪnəlaɪz/. See **finalize**.

finalist /faɪnəlɪst/, **finalists.** A **finalist** is someone who takes part in the final of a competition or sporting event. EG *...an Olympic finalist.* N COUNT

finality /faɪnælɪ¹ti¹/. If you say or do something with **finality**, you say or do it in a way that makes it clear that you will not say or do anything else relating to that matter. EG *Margaret said quietly but with finality: 'Well, we'll just have to disagree over this.'* N UNCOUNT

finalize /faɪnəlaɪz/, **finalizes, finalizing, finalized;** also spelled **finalise.** If you **finalize** something that you are arranging or organizing, you complete the arrangements for it. EG *I'm hoping to finalize things with the builders next week.* V+O

finally /faɪnəli¹/. **1** If you say that something **finally** happened, you mean that it happened after a long delay. EG *One of them stared at me for a long time and finally asked whether I was Angela Davis... They finally realized that the whole thing was a joke.* ADV

2 You use **finally** to indicate that something is the last in a series. EG *Trotsky lived in Turkey, France, Norway and finally Mexico.* ADV

3 You also use **finally** to introduce a final point, question, or topic. EG *Finally, Carol, are you encouraged by the direction education is taking?... Let's come finally to the question of pensions.* ADV SEN

finance /fɪnæns, faɪnæns/, **finances, financing, financed. 1** When someone **finances** a project or purchase, they provide the money that is needed to pay for it. EG *A private company will finance and build the pipeline.* V+O

2 Finance for a project or purchase is the money that is needed to pay for it. EG *The Group raises finance for oil drilling... Obtaining finance may be difficult.* N UNCOUNT

3 Finance is also the management of money, loans, credit, and investment, especially on a national level. EG *...public-sector finance... ...a successful job in high finance.* N UNCOUNT

4 You can refer to the amount of money that you have as your **finances**. EG *Whether it can be done depends, of course, on your finances.* N PLURAL

financial /fɪ⁵nænʃə⁰l/ means relating to or involving money. EG *The company was in deep financial difficulties... Let's talk in purely financial terms.* ADJ CLASSIF

◊ **financially.** EG *The venture was not financially successful.* ◊ ADV+ADJ

financier /fɪ⁵nænsɪə/, **financiers.** A **financier** is a person who provides money for projects or enterprises. N COUNT

finch /fɪntʃ/, **finches.** A **finch** is a small bird with a short strong beak. N COUNT

find /faɪnd/, **finds, finding, found** /faʊnd/. **1** If you **find** something, often something that you are looking for, you discover it, see it, or learn where it is. EG *Put things in a place where you can find them quickly... She found a crack in one of the tea-cups... She looked up to find Tony standing there.* V+O

2 If you **find** something that you need or want, you succeed in getting it. EG *He cannot find work... I had not yet found the answer... They don't guarantee to find me a job.* V+O, V+O+O, OR V+O+*for*

3 If you **find** that something is the case, you become aware that it is the case. EG *When I got back, I found that the reading lamp would not work... They found it impossible to get a bank loan.* V+REPORT: ONLY *that*; ALSO V+O+C: OFT+*to*-INF

4 You can use **find** when describing your reaction to something. For example, if you say that you **find** something frustrating, you mean that you think it is frustrating. EG *I don't find that funny at all... I found him a disappointment... Others may find them of value.* V+O+C OR V+O+A

5 If you **find** yourself doing something, you do it without intending to. EG *He found himself giggling uncontrollably.* V-REFL+-ING OR A

6 If you say that something **is found** in a particular place, you mean that it exists in that place. EG *Four different species of lungfish are found in Africa.* V+O: USU PASS+A

7 If you **find** your **way** somewhere, you get there by choosing the right way to go. PHRASE

8 If something **finds** its **way** somewhere, it eventually gets there. EG *I doubt whether much of the money found its way to Bernadette.* PHRASE

9 If you **find** the time to do something, you manage to do it even though you are busy. EG *How do you find time to write these books?* V+O : OFT+ to-INF OR for

10 If someone who is on trial **is found** guilty or **is found** not guilty, the court or the jury decides that they are guilty or innocent. EG *He was found guilty of murder.* V+O+C : USU PASS

11 If you describe something that has been discovered as a **find**, you mean that it is interesting, good, or useful. EG *Among the finds so far are pottery and jewellery... Liz Pym, who plays the heroine, is a real find.* N COUNT

12 to **find fault**: see **fault**.

find out. 1 If you **find out** a fact that you did not already know, you learn it, often by making a deliberate effort. EG *I found out the train times... We found out that she was wrong.* PHRASAL VB : V+ADV+O OR V+ADV+REPORT **2** If you **find** someone **out**, you discover that they have been doing something dishonest. V+O+ADV

finding /faɪndɪŋ/, **findings.** Someone's **findings** are the information they get or the conclusions they come to as the result of an investigation or some research. EG *...the findings of the committee... His findings were both surprising and significant.* N COUNT : USU PLURAL

fine /faɪn/, **finer, finest; fines, fining, fined. 1** You use **fine** to describe something that is very good. EG *From the top there is a fine view... It is, I believe, the finest English painting of its time.* ADJ QUALIT : USU ATTRIB

2 If you say that something is **fine**, you mean that it is satisfactory or acceptable. EG *'Do you want it stronger than that?' - 'No, that's fine.'... If you want to come, that's fine.* ▸ used as an adverb. EG *We get on fine.* ADJ PRED ▸ ADV

3 If you say that you are **fine**, you mean that you are in good health and quite happy. EG *'How are you?' - 'Fine, thanks.'* CONVENTION

4 Something that is **fine** is very narrow or consists of very narrow threads or pieces. EG *...fine string... ...fine hair.* ADJ QUALIT

5 A **fine** substance consists of very small bits or particles. EG *...handfuls of fine sand.* ◇ **finely.** EG *...finely chopped meat.* ADJ QUALIT ◇ ADV

6 A **fine** adjustment, detail, or distinction is very delicate, small, or exact. EG *Their eyes are trained to see the fine detail.* ◇ **finely.** EG *...finely balanced systems.* ADJ QUALIT ◇ ADV

7 You describe the weather as **fine** when it is not raining, especially when it is also sunny. EG *...a fine summer's day.* ADJ CLASSIF

8 A **fine** is a punishment in which a person is ordered to pay a sum of money. EG *He paid a £10,000 fine for income tax evasion.* N COUNT

9 If you **are fined**, you are punished by being ordered to pay a fine. EG *The demonstrators were fined £5 each for breach of the peace.* V+O : USU PASS

fine art, fine arts. 1 You can refer to the producing of objects which are beautiful rather than useful as **fine art** or the **fine arts**. EG *...a fine art course.* N UNCOUNT OR N PLURAL

2 to **get** something **down to a fine art**: see **art**.

finery /faɪnə⁰ri¹/ is clothing and jewellery that is beautiful and impressive. EG *The ladies were dressed up in all their finery.* N UNCOUNT

finesse /fɪnɛs/. If you do something with **finesse**, you do it with great skill and elegance or subtlety. N UNCOUNT

finger /fɪŋgə/, **fingers, fingering, fingered. 1** Your **fingers** are the four long jointed parts at the end of your hand. You can also use **fingers** to refer to your fingers and your thumb, although **finger** in the singular never refers to your thumb. See picture at THE HUMAN BODY. EG *She ran her fingers through the cool grass... He held the handkerchief between his finger and thumb.* N COUNT

2 If you **finger** something, you touch it or feel it with your finger. EG *Eric fingered his split lip.* V+O

3 **Finger** is also used in these phrases. **3.1** If you **put** your **finger on** something such as a problem, you succeed in identifying it. EG *He immediately put his finger on what was wrong.* **3.2** If you say that someone did not **lay a finger on** someone else, you mean that they did not touch or harm them. EG *Stop yelling! He didn't lay a finger on you.* **3.3** If you say that someone did not **lift a finger** or **raise a finger** to help someone else, you mean that they did nothing at all to help them. EG *He's never raised a finger to help you with the baby.* **3.4** If you **point the finger** or **point a finger** at someone, you blame them or accuse them of something. **3.5** to **cross** your **fingers**: see **cross**. ● to have **green fingers**: see **green**. PHRASES

fingernail /fɪŋgəneɪl/, **fingernails.** Your **fingernails** are the thin hard areas on the ends of your fingers. N COUNT

fingerprint /fɪŋgəprɪnt/, **fingerprints, fingerprinting, fingerprinted. 1** A **fingerprint** is a mark made by your finger which shows the lines on the skin. EG *He was careful, leaving no fingerprints.* ● When the police **take** your **fingerprints**, they make you press your fingers onto an inky pad and then onto paper, so that they can see what your fingerprints look like. N COUNT ● PHRASE

2 If the police **fingerprint** you, they take your fingerprints. V+O

fingertip /fɪŋgətɪp/, **fingertips. 1** Your **fingertips** are the ends of your fingers. EG *I probed through his hair with my fingertips.* N COUNT : USU PLURAL

2 If you say that someone is professional or an artist **to** their **fingertips**, you mean that they are professional or an artist in every way possible. PHRASE

3 If you have something **at your fingertips**, you can reach it or make use of it quickly and easily. EG *The task is easier now, with calculators and computers at your fingertips.* PHRASE

4 If you have some information **at your fingertips**, you know it very well and can easily pass it on. EG *Mrs Leach had the facts at her fingertips.* PHRASE

finicky /fɪnɪki¹/. Someone who is **finicky** is fussy. EG *He was a very finicky eater.* ADJ QUALIT

finish /fɪnɪʃ/, **finishes, finishing, finished. 1** When you **finish** something that you are making or doing, you make or do the last part of it, so that there is no more for you to do. EG *The building was finished in 1962... I've finished reading your book.* ● When you put the **finishing touches** to something, you do the last things that are needed in order to make it complete. EG *She had been putting the finishing touches to her make-up.* V+O; ALSO V : OFT+-ING ● PHRASE

2 When something **finishes**, it does not continue any longer. EG *The course starts in October and finishes in June.* V : USU+A

3 The **finish** of something is the end or the last part of it. N SING

4 If you **finish** work or school at a particular time, you stop working or studying at that time. EG *I finish work at 3.* V+O : USU+A

5 When you **finish** something that you have been eating, drinking, or smoking, you eat, drink, or smoke the last part of it. EG *Brody finished his sandwich.* V+O

6 The position that someone taking part in a race or competition **finishes** in is the position they are in at the end of the race or competition. EG *He finished fifth in the 1967 US Open.* V+A OR V+C

7 An object's **finish** is the appearance or texture of its surface. EG *Metallic finish is standard on this car.* N UNCOUNT OR N COUNT

8 See also **finished**.

finish off. 1 When you **finish off** something that you are doing, you do the last part of it. EG *He* PHRASAL VB : V+O+ADV

If you make a fine distinction, are you being finicky?

finished off his thesis. **2** When you **finish off** something that you have been eating or drinking, you eat or drink the last part of it. EG *He finished off the wine with a couple of swallows.* V+O+ADV

finish up. 1 If you **finish up** in a particular place or situation, you are in that place or situation at the end of doing something. EG *She'll be going on tour, starting in Southampton and finishing up in London... They finished up serving in a shop.* **2** If you **finish up** some food or drink that is left, you eat or drink it all. PHRASAL VB : V+ADV+A OR V+ADV+-ING; V+O+ADV

finish with. When you **finish with** someone or something, you stop dealing with them or being involved with them. EG *I haven't finished with you yet.* PHRASAL VB : V+PREP, HAS PASS

finished /fɪnɪʃt/. **1** If you are **finished** with something, you are no longer doing it or dealing with it, or are no longer interested in it. EG *He won't be finished for at least half an hour... He was finished with marriage.* ADJ PRED : OFT +*with*

2 Something that is **finished** no longer exists or is no longer happening. EG *All that is finished now.* ADJ PRED

3 You also say that people or things are **finished** when they are no longer important or effective. EG *If that happens, Richard is finished.* ADJ PRED

finishing school, finishing schools. A **finishing school** is a private school where rich or upper-class young women are taught behaviour and skills that are considered to be suitable for them. N COUNT OR N UNCOUNT

finite /faɪnaɪt/. Something that is **finite** has a definite boundary beyond which it does not exist or a limit beyond which it cannot increase or develop. EG *...a finite but unbounded universe... We have a finite number of places.* ADJ CLASSIF Formal

fir /fɜː/, **firs.** A **fir** or a **fir tree** is a tall, pointed tree that grows mainly in cool countries. N COUNT

fire /faɪə/, **fires, firing, fired. 1 Fire** is the hot, bright flames produced by things that are burning. N UNCOUNT

2 A **fire** is **2.1** an occurrence of uncontrolled burning which destroys things. EG *A fire had severely damaged part of the school... His neighbour's house is not insured against fire.* N COUNT OR N UNCOUNT **2.2** a burning pile of wood or coal that you have set light to, often in order to keep yourself warm. EG *He lit a fire and cooked a meal.* N COUNT **2.3** a device that uses electricity or gas to give out heat and warm a room. EG *She switched on the electric fire.* N COUNT

3 Fire is used in these phrases relating to burning. PHRASES **3.1** Something that is **on fire** is burning and is being destroyed. EG *Two vehicles were on fire.* **3.2** If something **catches fire**, it starts burning. EG *Will the house catch fire?* **3.3** If you **set fire to** something, you start it burning in order to destroy it. EG *He set fire to the church.*

4 If someone **fires** a gun or **fires** a bullet, they cause a bullet to be sent from the gun that they are using. People can also **fire** missiles and arrows. EG *I fired three or four times in quick succession.* V OR V-ERG

◊ **firing.** EG *The firing stopped.* ◊ N SING

5 Shots fired from a gun or guns are referred to as **fire**. EG *There was a burst of automatic rifle fire... We climbed up the hill under fire.* N UNCOUNT ● If you **open fire** on someone, you start shooting at them. ● PHRASE

6 If you **fire** questions or suggestions at someone, you say a lot of them quickly, one after another. V+O : OFT+*at*

7 If your employer **fires** you, he or she dismisses you from your job. EG *Graffman fired him for incompetence.* V+O Informal

firearm /faɪərɑːm/, **firearms. Firearms** are guns, especially the sort that you can carry. EG *He got a fourteen-year sentence for illegal possession of firearms.* N COUNT : USU PLURAL

firebrand /faɪəbrænd/, **firebrands.** You describe someone as a **firebrand** when they are very active in politics and try to make other people take strong action. EG *He is represented by the media as a dangerous firebrand.* N COUNT

fire brigade, fire brigades. The **fire brigade** is an organization which puts out fires. EG *Smother the flames with a coat or blanket and call the fire brigade.* N COUNT

firecracker /faɪəkrækə/, **firecrackers.** A **firecracker** is a firework that makes several loud bangs when you light it. EG *People set off strings of firecrackers.* N COUNT

fire engine, fire engines. A **fire engine** is a large vehicle that carries firemen and equipment for putting out fires. N COUNT

fire escape, fire escapes. A **fire escape** is a metal staircase or ladder on the outside of a building down which people can escape if there is a fire. N COUNT

fire extinguisher, fire extinguishers. A **fire extinguisher** is a metal cylinder which contains water or chemicals at high pressure for putting out fires. N COUNT

fire-fighting is the work of putting out fires. EG *...fire-fighting equipment.* N UNCOUNT

fireguard /faɪəgɑːd/, **fireguards.** A **fireguard** is a screen made of strong wire mesh that you put in front of a fire so that people cannot accidentally burn themselves. N COUNT

fire hydrant /faɪə haɪdrənt/, **fire hydrants.** A **fire hydrant** is a pipe in the street from which firemen can obtain water that they can use to put out a fire. N COUNT

firelight /faɪəlaɪt/ is the light that comes from a fire. EG *His face looked ruddy in the firelight.* N UNCOUNT

fireman /faɪəməⁿn/, **firemen.** A **fireman** is a person whose job is to put out fires. Firemen also rescue people or animals when they are trapped, for example in burning buildings or cars. EG *Firemen turned their hoses on the flames.* N COUNT

fireplace /faɪəpleɪs/, **fireplaces.** A **fireplace** is an opening in the wall of a room where you can light a fire. EG *There was a portrait of his wife over the fireplace.* N COUNT

firepower /faɪəpaʊə/. The **firepower** of an army, ship, tank, or aircraft is the amount of ammunition it can fire. EG *They have greatly increased the firepower of their fleet.* N UNCOUNT

fireproof /faɪəpruːf/. Something that is **fireproof** cannot be damaged by fire. EG *...fireproof clothing.* ADJ CLASSIF

fireside /faɪəsaɪd/, **firesides.** If you sit by the **fireside** in a room, you sit near the fire. EG *...sitting comfortably by his fireside... ...a fireside chat.* N COUNT : USU SING

fire station, fire stations. A **fire station** is a building where fire engines are kept, and where firemen wait until they are called to put out a fire. N COUNT

firewood /faɪəwʊd/ is wood that has been cut into pieces so that it can be burned on a fire. EG *...a bundle of firewood.* N UNCOUNT

firework /faɪəwɜːk/, **fireworks. Fireworks** are small objects with chemicals inside them that burn with coloured sparks or smoke when you light them. Some fireworks make loud noises. Fireworks are lit to entertain people. EG *A few fireworks went off... I had gone to watch the fireworks... ...a firework display.* N COUNT

firing squad, firing squads. A **firing squad** is a group of soldiers who are ordered to shoot dead a person who has been found guilty of committing a crime. N COUNT ● If someone is executed **by firing squad**, they are shot by a firing squad. EG *He faces death by firing squad.* ● PHRASE

firm /fɜːm/, **firms; firmer, firmest. 1** A **firm** is an organization which sells or produces something or which provides a service which you pay for. EG *He was a partner in a firm of solicitors.* N COUNT

2 Something that is **firm 2.1** does not change its shape much when you press it, although it is not completely hard. EG *...a firm mattress.* ADJ QUALIT **2.2** does not shake or move when you put pressure on it. EG *...a firm ladder.* ADJ QUALIT ◊ **firmly.** EG *Each block rested firmly on the block below it.* ◊ ADV

3 If you have a **firm** grasp of something, you are holding it tightly. EG *I took a firm hold on the rope.* ADJ QUALIT

◊ **firmly.** EG *She grasped the cork firmly.* ◊ ADV

4 A **firm** push or pull is done with quite a lot of force but is controlled. EG *...firm pressure.* ◇ **firmly.** EG *She closed the door firmly.* ADJ QUALIT ◇ ADV

5 A **firm** decision or opinion is definite and unlikely to change. EG *...a person with firm views.* ◇ **firmly.** EG *His sister was firmly of the belief that he was crazy.* ADJ QUALIT ◇ ADV

6 **Firm** evidence or information is definitely true. EG *No firm evidence had come to light... By the weekend came firm news.* ADJ QUALIT

7 Someone who is **firm** behaves in a way that shows that they will not change their mind or that they are in control. EG *Our present state of affairs demands firm leadership... 'No,' said Mother in a firm voice.* ◇ **firmly.** EG *I shall tell her quite firmly that it is not any business of hers.* ◇ **firmness.** EG *She treated the children with kindliness and firmness.* ADJ QUALIT ◇ ADV ◇ N UNCOUNT

8 If you **stand firm**, you refuse to change your mind. EG *The Government should stand firm against such threats.* PHRASE

9 If something relating to finance and trade is **firm**, it is not decreasing in value or amount. EG *Investment remained firm despite the average 1.8% growth rate.* ADJ CLASSIF

first /fɜːst/ **firsts.** 1 The **first** thing, person, event, or period of time is the one that happens or comes before all the others of the same kind: see the entry headed NUMBER. EG *...the first man in space... ...the first two years of life.* ORDINAL

2 If you do something **first**, **2.1** you do it before anyone else does it. EG *Ralph spoke first.* **2.2** you do it before you do other things. EG *We sent her a letter first... First I went to see the editor of the Dispatch.* ADV; ADV OR ADV SEN

3 When something happens to you for the **first** time, it has never happened to you before. When you do something for the **first** time, you have never done it before. EG *For the first time in our lives something really exciting has happened... Vita and Harold first met in the summer of 1910.* ORDINAL OR ADV

4 An event that is described as a **first** has never happened before and is important or exciting. N SING : *a*+N

5 The **first** you hear of something or the **first** you know about it is the time when you first become aware of it. EG *The first Mr Walker knew about it was when he saw it in the local paper.* PRON

6 You use **at first** when you are talking about what happens in the early part of an event or experience, in contrast to what happens later. EG *At first I was reluctant.* PHRASE

7 You say **first** when you are about to mention the first in a series of items. EG *There were several reasons for this. First, four submarines had been sighted.* ADV SEN

8 The **first** thing, person, or place in a line is the one that is nearest to you or nearest to something else. EG *They took their seats in the first three rows.* ORDINAL

9 You use **first** to refer to the best or most important thing or person of a particular kind. EG *She won first prize... The first duty of the state is to ensure that law and order prevail.* ORDINAL

10 If you put someone or something **first**, you treat them as more important than anything else. EG *Put your career first... Your family must always come first.* ADV

11 **First** is also used in these phrases. **11.1** If you experience something **at first hand**, you experience it yourself rather than being told about it by other people. **11.2** If you do something **first thing**, you do it at the beginning of the day, before you do anything else. EG *I'll tell her first thing tomorrow.* **11.3** If you say **'first things first'**, you mean that a particular thing should be dealt with before anything else because it is the most important thing. **11.4** If you say that you **do not know the first thing about** something, you mean that you know absolutely nothing about it. PHRASES

first aid is simple medical treatment which is given as soon as possible to a person who is injured or who has suddenly become ill. EG *The wounded were given first aid... ...my first-aid kit.* N UNCOUNT

first-born. You can refer to someone's first child as their **first-born** or their **first-born** child. EG *We'll stand by you. You are our first-born... ...his first-born son.* N SING OR ADJ CLASSIF : ATTRIB Literary

first-class. 1 If you describe something or someone as **first-class**, you mean that they are excellent and of the highest quality. EG *...a first-class administrator.* ADJ QUALIT

2 A **first-class** degree is a degree of the highest class. EG *...a first class honours degree in applied chemistry.* ADJ CLASSIF : ATTRIB

3 A **first-class** ticket allows you to travel in the best type of accommodation on a train, aircraft, or ship. EG *...a first-class rail ticket.* ▸ used as an adverb. EG *...the privilege of flying first class.* ADJ CLASSIF ▸ ADV AFTER VB

4 **First-class** postage is the quicker and more expensive type of postage. ADJ CLASSIF, OR ADV AFTER VB

first floor. The **first floor** of a building is 1 the floor immediately above the ground floor. EG *...on the first floor of the Museum... ...a first-floor suite.* 2 the ground floor. N SING : *the*+N British; American

first-hand. First-hand information or experience is gained directly, rather than from other people or from books. EG *They have first-hand experience of charitable organizations.* ▸ used as an adverb. EG *This sort of experience can only be gained first-hand.* ADJ CLASSIF : ATTRIB ▸ ADV

firstly /fɜːstli[1]/. You use **firstly** when you are about to mention the first in a series of items or reasons. EG *There are two reasons. Firstly I have no evidence that the original document has been destroyed.* ADV SEN

first name, first names. Your **first name** is the first of the names that you were given when you were born. You can also refer to all of your names except your surname as your **first names.** EG *Nobody called Daintry by his first name because nobody knew it.* N COUNT

first night, first nights. The **first night** of a show or play is the first public performance of it. N COUNT

first-rate. If you describe someone or something as **first-rate**, you mean that they are excellent and of the highest quality. EG *...a first-rate golfer... ...first-rate performances.* ADJ CLASSIF

first school, first schools. A **first school** is a school for children aged between five and eight or nine. N COUNT British

fiscal /fɪskə[0]l/ is used to describe something that relates to government money, especially taxes. EG *...fiscal controls.* ADJ CLASSIF : ATTRIB Technical

fish /fɪʃ/, **fishes, fishing, fished. Fish** is the most common form for the plural of the noun, but **fishes** is also sometimes used.

1 A **fish** is a creature that lives in water and that has a tail and fins. EG *We didn't catch any fish.* N COUNT

2 **Fish** is the flesh of a fish eaten as food. EG *...fish and chips.* N UNCOUNT

3 If you **fish**, you try to catch fish, either for food or as a sport or hobby. EG *They went fishing and caught half a dozen trout.* V

4 If you **fish** a particular area of water, you try to catch fish in it. EG *It was the first trawler ever to fish those waters.* V+O

5 If you **fish** for information or praise, you try to get it in an indirect way. EG *I think he was just fishing for compliments.* V+*for*

6 If you **fish** something out of a liquid or a container, you take it out or pull it out. EG *More bodies have been fished out of the canal... She fished out her cigarettes.* V+O+A Informal

Name some of the fittings you might find in an office.

fisherman /fɪʃəmə^{3}n/, **fishermen.** A **fisherman** is a man who catches fish as a job or for sport. N COUNT

fishery /fɪʃə^{0}ri^{1}/, **fisheries.** A **fishery** is an area of the sea where fish are caught in large quantities. N COUNT

fishing /fɪʃɪŋ/ is the sport, hobby, or business of catching fish. EG *Fishing has been a profitable industry lately... ...a small fishing boat.* N UNCOUNT

fishing rod, fishing rods. A **fishing rod** is a long thin pole with a line and hook attached to it which is used for catching fish. N COUNT

fishmonger /fɪʃmʌŋgə/, **fishmongers.** A **fishmonger** is a shopkeeper who sells fish. N COUNT British

fishy /fɪʃi^{1}/. **1** If something smells or tastes **fishy**, it smells or tastes like fish. EG *It had a fishy flavour.* ADJ QUALIT
2 If something seems **fishy** to you, you feel that someone is not telling the truth or not behaving honestly. EG *It all sounded very fishy to her.* ADJ QUALIT Informal

fission /fɪʃə^{0}n/. Nuclear **fission** is the splitting of the nucleus of an atom to produce a large amount of energy or to cause a large explosion. N UNCOUNT

fissure /fɪʃə/, **fissures.** A **fissure** is a deep crack in something, especially in rock or in the ground. N COUNT Formal

fist /fɪst/, **fists.** You refer to someone's hand as their **fist** when they have bent their fingers towards their palm. EG *She hit me with her fist... I shook my fist... The Marine held it tightly in his fist.* N COUNT

fistful /fɪstfʊl/, **fistfuls.** A **fistful** of things is the number of them that you can hold in your fist. EG *He handed me a fistful of letters.* N PART

fit /fɪt/, **fits, fitting, fitted; fitter, fittest.** In American English the form **fit** can also be used for the past tense and past participle of the verb.
1 If something **fits**, it is the right size and shape to go onto a particular person's body or onto a particular object. EG *The boots fitted Rudolph perfectly... Does the lid fit?... The metal cover fits over the tap.* V OR V+O: OFT+A
2 If something is a good **fit**, it fits. N SING
3 If something **fits** into something else, it is small enough to be able to go in it. EG *All my clothes fit into one suitcase.* V+A
4 If you **fit** something into the right space or place, you put it there. EG *Philip fitted his key into the lock.* V+O+A
5 If you **fit** a piece of equipment or an extra part to something, you fix it to it. EG *Castors can be fitted to a bed to make it easier to pull... The kitchen has been fitted with a stainless steel sink.* V+O: OFT+*to/with*
6 You can also say that something **fits** a person or thing when it is suitable for them. EG *The description fits women better than it fits men... ...the attempt to make the punishment fit the crime.* V+O
7 If someone or something is **fit** for a particular purpose, they are good enough for that purpose. EG *The houses are now fit for human habitation... She regarded herself as fit to be a governess.* ADJ PRED+*for* OR *to*-INF
8 If someone **sees fit** or **thinks fit** to do something, they decide that it is the right thing to do. EG *The present government has seen fit to cut back on spending.* PHRASE Formal
9 Someone who is **fit** is healthy and able to do physical activities without getting tired. EG *She works hard at keeping fit.* ◇ **fitness.** EG *They were trained to a peak of physical fitness.* ADJ QUALIT ◇ N UNCOUNT
10 If you say that someone is as **fit as a fiddle**, you mean that they are very fit. PHRASE Informal
11 If someone has a **fit**, they suddenly lose consciousness and their body makes uncontrollable movements. EG *...an epileptic fit.* ● If you say that someone will **have a fit** when they hear about something, you mean that they will be very angry or shocked. N COUNT ● PHRASE Informal
12 If you have a **fit** of coughing or laughter, you suddenly start coughing or laughing in an uncontrollable way. EG *She had a coughing fit.* N COUNT+SUPP
13 If you do something in a **fit** of anger or panic, you are very angry or afraid when you do it. EG *In a fit of rage, he had flung Paul's violin out of the window.* N COUNT+*of*
14 Something that happens **in fits and starts** keeps happening and then stopping again. PHRASE
15 not in a fit state: see **state.** ● See also **fitted, fitter, fitting.**

fit in or **fit into. 1** If you **fit** something **in** or **fit** it **into** your schedule, you find time to do it or deal with it. EG *You seem to fit in an enormous amount every day.* **2** If you **fit in** or **fit into** a group, you are similar to the other people in the group. EG *These children are unable to fit into ordinary society when they leave school.* PHRASAL VB: V+O+ADV OR V+O+PREP; V+ADV OR V+PREP

fitful /fɪtfʊl/. Something that is **fitful** happens for irregular periods of time, rather than being continuous. EG *He dozed off into a fitful sleep.* ◇ **fitfully.** EG *A pallid moon shone fitfully between the clouds.* ADJ CLASSIF ◇ ADV

fitted /fɪtɪ^{2}d/ **1** If you are **fitted** to something or **fitted** to do something, you have the right qualities for it. EG *Those best fitted to their surroundings will survive.* ADJ PRED+*to* OR *to*-INF Formal
2 A **fitted** piece of clothing is designed so that it is the same size and shape as your body. EG *Dolly wore a grey dress with a fitted bodice.* ADJ CLASSIF: ATTRIB
3 A **fitted** carpet is cut to the same shape as a room so that it covers the floor completely. ADJ CLASSIF: ATTRIB
4 A **fitted** piece of furniture, for example a cupboard, is designed to fill a particular space and is fixed in place. EG *...fitted wardrobes.* ADJ CLASSIF: ATTRIB

fitter /fɪtə/, **fitters.** A **fitter** is a person whose job is to put together, adjust, or install machinery or equipment. EG *He got a job as an electrical fitter.* N COUNT

fitting /fɪtɪŋ/, **fittings. 1** If you say that something is **fitting**, you mean that it is right or suitable. EG *She said that I was the eldest and that it was fitting that I should go first.* ◇ **fittingly.** EG *The speech was fittingly solemn.* ADJ QUALIT ◇ ADV Formal
2 A **fitting** is one of the smaller parts on the outside of a piece of equipment or furniture, for example a handle or a tap. EG *They make fittings for car dashboards... ...light fittings.* N COUNT
3 Fittings are things such as cookers or electric fires that are fixed inside a building but can be removed to another building. EG *Make sure you know what fixtures and fittings will be left at your new home.* N PLURAL
4 If someone has a **fitting**, they try on a piece of clothing that is being made for them, to see if it fits. EG *Rhoda had been for several fittings for the fur coat.* N COUNT

five /faɪv/, **fives. Five** is the number 5: see the entry headed NUMBER. EG *Five inches of snow had fallen.* NUMBER

fiver /faɪvə/, **fivers.** A **fiver** is five pounds, or a note worth five pounds. EG *You owe me a fiver... She took a fiver from her purse.* N COUNT Informal

fix /fɪks/, **fixes, fixing, fixed. 1** If you **fix** something to something else, you attach it firmly to the other thing. EG *He had the sign fixed to the gate... She fixed a jewelled brooch on her dress.* V+O+A
2 If you **fix** your eyes or attention on something, you look at it or think about it with complete attention. EG *She fixed her brown eyes upon him.* V+O+*on/upon*
3 If you **fix** the date or amount of something, you decide exactly what it will be. EG *All that remained was to fix the date of the wedding.* V+O
4 If you **fix** something which is damaged or which will not work properly, you repair it. EG *I learned how to fix radios in the Army... He spent the afternoon getting his car fixed.* V+O
5 To **fix** something also means to arrange for it to happen. EG *Leave it to me. I'll fix it.* V+O
6 If you say that a race or a competition **was fixed**, you mean that someone unfairly arranged for a particular competitor to win or lose. V+O: USU PASS Informal
7 If you **fix** a drink or food for someone, you prepare it for them. EG *Would you like me to fix you a drink?... She fixed herself a plate of food.* V+O, V+O+O, OR V-REFL+O Informal
8 A **fix** is an injection of a drug such as heroin. EG *He inquired if I was in need of a fix.* N COUNT Informal

9 See also **fixed**.

fix up. 1 If you **fix** someone **up** with something they need, you provide it for them. EG *They told me that they could fix me up with tickets.* 2 If you **fix** something **up**, you arrange it. EG *The holiday is all fixed up.* — PHRASAL VB: V+O+ADV; V+O+ADV

fixation /fɪkseɪʃə^{0}n/, **fixations.** If you have a **fixation** on someone or something, you think about them to an excessive degree. EG *...fixations on brothers or sisters... ...the sport fixation of the British.* — N COUNT: USU+SUPP

fixed /fɪkst/. 1 A **fixed** amount, position, pattern, or method always stays the same. EG *The signal goes on sounding at fixed intervals... ...a fixed pattern of behaviour.* — ADJ CLASSIF

2 If you say that someone has **fixed** ideas or opinions, you mean that their ideas or opinions never change. EG *Children can be raised without fixed ideas and prejudices.* — ADJ QUALIT

3 You can say that something is **fixed** in your mind or brain when you remember it very well. EG *The scene was firmly fixed in all our minds.* — ADJ PRED

fixedly /fɪksə^{1}dli^{1}/. If you stare **fixedly** at someone or something, you look at them steadily and continuously for a period of time. — ADV

fixture /fɪkstʃə/, **fixtures.** 1 A **fixture** is a piece of furniture or equipment, for example a bath or sink, which is fixed inside a house or other building and which is left in place when you move. EG *Make sure you know what fixtures and fittings will be left at your new home... ...the light fixture on the ceiling.* — N COUNT

2 If you say that something or someone is a **fixture** in a particular place or group, you mean that they are always there and it seems likely that they will always remain there. EG *Pool seems likely to become a fixture in working-class pubs.* — N COUNT

3 In sport, a **fixture** is a match or competition which has been arranged to take place on a particular date. EG *We had to cancel a lot of fixtures... Most athletic clubs produce their own fixture lists.* — N COUNT, British

fizz /fɪz/, **fizzes, fizzing, fizzed.** If a liquid, especially a drink, **fizzes**, it produces lots of little bubbles of gas and makes a hissing sound. — V

fizzle /fɪzə^{0}l/, **fizzles, fizzling, fizzled.** If something **fizzles out**, it ends in a weak or disappointing way. EG *The strike fizzled out after three days.* — PHRASAL VB: V+ADV

fizzy /fɪzi^{1}/. A **fizzy** drink or other liquid is full of little bubbles of gas and makes a hissing sound. EG *...fizzy lemonade.* — ADJ QUALIT

flabbergasted /flæbəgɑːstɪ^{2}d/. If you are **flabbergasted**, you are extremely surprised. EG *I stared at him, flabbergasted.* — ADJ CLASSIF

flabby /flæbi^{1}/. **Flabby** people are fat and have loose flesh on their bodies. EG *He was a flabby, pale-faced bachelor... ...her flabby arms.* — ADJ QUALIT

flaccid /flæsɪd/. Something that is **flaccid** is soft and loose or limp, rather than firm. EG *Her lips went flaccid, her eyes glazed over.* — ADJ QUALIT, Formal

flag /flæg/, **flags, flagging, flagged.** 1 A **flag** is a piece of coloured cloth which can be attached to a pole and which is used as a sign, signal, or symbol of something, especially of a country. EG *...a ship flying a foreign flag... The guard blew his whistle and waved his flag.* — N COUNT

2 If you **flag** or if your spirits **flag**, you begin to lose enthusiasm or energy. EG *They showed signs of flagging... Your spirits may flag when faced with this new task.* ◇ **flagging.** EG *She tried to revive their flagging energies.* — V; ◇ ADJ CLASSIF

flag down. If you **flag down** a vehicle, especially a taxi, you wave at it as a signal for the driver to stop. — PHRASAL VB: V+O+ADV

flagon /flægə^{0}n/, **flagons.** A **flagon** is 1 a wide bottle in which cider or wine is sold. 2 a jug with a narrow neck in which wine is served. — N COUNT

flagpole /flægpəʊl/, **flagpoles.** A **flagpole** is a tall pole on which a flag can be displayed. — N COUNT

flagrant /fleɪgrənt/ is used to describe bad actions or situations which are not concealed in any way. EG *...a flagrant violation of human rights... ...flagrant injustices.* ◇ **flagrantly.** EG *This legislation remains flagrantly unenforced.* — ADJ QUALIT: ATTRIB; ◇ ADV

flagship /flægʃɪp/, **flagships.** A **flagship** is the most important ship in a fleet, especially the one on which the commander of the fleet sails. EG *...a replica of Christopher Columbus's flagship.* — N COUNT

flagstaff /flægstɑːf/, **flagstaffs.** A **flagstaff** is the same as a flagpole. — N COUNT

flagstone /flægstəʊn/, **flagstones. Flagstones** are big, flat, square pieces of stone which are used for paving. — N COUNT

flail /fleɪl/, **flails, flailing, flailed.** If you **flail** your arms or legs about or if they **flail**, they wave about in a wild, uncontrolled way. EG *The baby flailed her little arms... ...his flailing arms.* — V-ERG

flair /flɛə/. 1 If you have a **flair** for doing something, you have a natural ability to do it. EG *He had a flair for this branch of law... Wilson was impressed by his political flair.* — N SING: OFT+*for*, OR N UNCOUNT

2 **Flair** is also the ability to do things in an original, interesting, and stylish way. EG *She showed her usual flair and cunning.* — N UNCOUNT

flak /flæk/. 1 **Flak** is a large number of explosive shells being fired at planes from the ground. EG *I saw one of the Dakotas hit by flak.* — N UNCOUNT

2 You can also refer to severe criticism as **flak**. EG *The President has already run into murderous political flak over his decision.* — N UNCOUNT, Informal

flake /fleɪk/, **flakes, flaking, flaked.** 1 A **flake** is 1.1 a small thin piece of something that has broken off a larger piece. EG *...flakes of burnt paper from a bonfire.* 1.2 a snowflake. EG *The first flakes began to flutter down.* — N COUNT

2 If something such as paint **flakes**, small thin pieces of it come off. EG *The paint was flaking off the walls.* — V: OFT+A

flake out. If you **flake out**, you collapse, go to sleep, or lose consciousness, usually because you are very tired. — PHRASAL VB: V+ADV, Informal

flamboyant /flæmbɔɪənt/. 1 Someone who is **flamboyant** behaves in a very noticeable, confident, and exaggerated way. EG *He has been accused of being too flamboyant on stage... My father was capable of flamboyant generosity.* — ADJ QUALIT

2 Something that is **flamboyant** is very brightly coloured or of a very noticeable shape or design. EG *...a flamboyant quilted bathrobe.* — ADJ QUALIT

flame /fleɪm/, **flames.** 1 A **flame** is a quantity of hot, bright, burning gas that comes in a pointed stream from something that is burning. EG *The flames and smoke rose hundreds of feet into the air... The aircraft disappeared in a ball of flame.* — N COUNT OR N UNCOUNT

2 If something is **in flames**, it is on fire. EG *My parents' home was in flames.* — PHRASE

3 If something **bursts into flames**, it suddenly starts burning fiercely. EG *The satellite burst into flames and disintegrated.* — PHRASE

4 An **old flame** is someone who you once had a romantic relationship with. — PHRASE, Outdated

flamenco /flə^{3}mɛŋkəʊ/, **flamencos.** A **flamenco** is a Spanish dance that is danced to a special type of guitar music. — N COUNT OR N UNCOUNT

flaming /fleɪmɪŋ/. 1 **Flaming** is used to describe things that are burning and producing a lot of flames. EG *...planes diving down with flaming wings.* — ADJ CLASSIF: ATTRIB

2 You describe something as **flaming**, **flaming red**, or **flaming orange** when it is bright red or bright orange in colour. EG *...gorgeous flaming sunsets... She had flaming red hair.* — ADJ CLASSIF: USU ATTRIB

3 Some people use **flaming** as a mild swear word when they are annoyed. EG *The flaming car's locked.* — ADJ CLASSIF: ATTRIB, Informal

What is the difference between a flask and a flagon?

flamingo /flə^{3}mɪŋgəʊ/, **flamingos** or **flamingoes.** A **flamingo** is a bird with pink feathers, long thin legs, and a curved beak. N COUNT

flammable /flæməbə^{0}l/. Something that is **flammable** can catch fire and burn easily. ADJ QUALIT

flan /flæn/, **flans.** A **flan** is a kind of tart which has a base and sides of pastry or sponge cake, and which is filled with fruit or something savoury. EG *...onion flan.* N COUNT OR N UNCOUNT

flank /flæŋk/, **flanks, flanking, flanked. 1** If something **is flanked** by things, it has them on both sides of it, or sometimes on one side of it. EG *Billy was seated at the table, flanked by the two women.* V+O : USU PASS *+by/with*

2 An animal's **flanks** are its sides. EG *Their legs gripped the flanks of the ponies.* N COUNT

3 The **flank** of an army or fleet is one side of it when it is organized ready for battle. EG *...the weaknesses of NATO's south-east flank.* N COUNT

flannel /flænə^{0}l/, **flannels. 1 Flannel** is a lightweight cloth used for making clothes. EG *...a grey flannel suit.* N UNCOUNT

2 Flannels are men's trousers made of flannel. EG *...a pair of pressed grey flannels.* N PLURAL

3 A **flannel** is a small cloth that you use for washing yourself. N COUNT British

flap /flæp/, **flaps, flapping, flapped. 1** If a piece of cloth or paper **flaps** or if you **flap** it, it moves quickly up and down or from side to side, often making a snapping sound. EG *His long robes flapped in the breeze.* V-ERG

2 When a bird **flaps** its wings, it moves them quickly up and down. EG *Its wings flapped weakly... The pheasant flapped around for a few seconds.* V-ERG OR V+A

3 If you **flap** your arms or hands, you move them quickly up and down as if they were wings. V+O

4 A **flap** is a flat piece of something that can move freely up and down or from side to side because it is attached by only one edge. EG *...looking out through a tent flap... The men wore black shiny caps, with broad flaps at the back.* N COUNT

5 Someone who is **in a flap** is in a state of great excitement or panic. PHRASE Informal

flare /fleə/, **flares, flaring, flared. 1** A **flare** is a small device that produces a bright flame. Flares are used as signals. EG *He stood ready to fire a warning flare.* N COUNT

2 If a flame or fire **flares**, the flame or flames suddenly become larger. EG *The candle flared to a bright light.* V : OFT+*up*

3 If something such as violence, conflict, or anger **flares**, it starts or becomes more violent. EG *From time to time violence flared... Fury flared up in his mind.* V : OFT+*up*

4 If something such as a dress **flares**, it spreads outwards at one end to form a wide shape. EG *She pirouetted, making the skirt flare out.* V : OFT+*out*

flared /fleəd/. **Flared** skirts or trousers become wider towards the hem or towards the bottom of the legs. ADJ CLASSIF : ATTRIB

flash /flæʃ/, **flashes, flashing, flashed. 1** A **flash** of light is a very bright light which appears suddenly and then disappears immediately. EG *Suddenly there was a flash of lightning.* N COUNT : USU+SUPP

2 If a light **flashes** or if you **flash** it, it shines brightly once or several times. EG *I'll flash my headlights to make sure he sees us.* V-ERG

3 If you say that something **flashes** past you, you mean that it moves very fast. EG *Something white flashed past the van.* V+A

4 In a flash means very quickly. EG *I was out of the room in a flash.* PHRASE Written

5 Quick as a flash means immediately and quickly. EG *Quick as a flash, Claud pulled the paper bag out of his pocket.* PHRASE Written

6 If something **flashes** through your mind, you think of it suddenly and briefly. EG *It flashed through his mind that he might never get back.* V+*through*

7 If you have a **flash** of intuition or insight, you suddenly guess or realise something. N COUNT+SUPP

8 If you **flash** a look or a smile at someone, you look or smile at them quickly and briefly. EG *He flashed a conspiratorial grin at them.* V+O+*at* Literary

9 If you say that someone's eyes **flash**, you mean that their eyes seem bright because they are experiencing a strong emotion. EG *Her eyes flashed as she demanded to know what I was laughing at.* V Literary

flashback /flæʃbæk/, **flashbacks.** A **flashback** is a scene in a film or a part of a novel or play in which the plot suddenly changes to events in the past. N COUNT

flashbulb /flæʃbʌlb/, **flashbulbs.** A **flashbulb** is a small lightbulb that can be fixed to a camera. It makes a bright flash of light so that you can take photographs indoors. N COUNT

flashlight /flæʃlaɪt/, **flashlights.** A **flashlight** is a torch, especially a large one. N COUNT

flashy /flæʃi^{1}/, **flashier, flashiest.** You describe something as **flashy** when it looks smart, bright, and expensive in a rather vulgar way. EG *...a flashy sports car.* ◊ **flashily.** EG *He was dressed rather more flashily than usual.* ADJ QUALIT Informal ◊ ADV

flask /flɑːsk/, **flasks.** A **flask** is **1** a small, flat bottle that you use for carrying alcoholic drink around with you. **2** a Thermos flask. EG *...a flask of coffee.* N COUNT

flat /flæt/, **flats; flatter, flattest. 1** A **flat** is a set of rooms for living in, usually on one floor of a large building. EG *...a block of flats.* N COUNT British

2 Something that is **flat 2.1** is not sloping or curved, or has no raised parts. EG *Every flat surface in our house is covered with junk... He took the handkerchief and smoothed it flat.* **2.2** is not as round, pointed, or tall as things of its kind usually are. EG *...a huge man with a broad flat nose... ...a flat box.* ADJ QUALIT

3 If something is **flat** against a surface, all of it is touching the surface. EG *She let the blade of her oar rest flat upon the water.* ADV+PREP

4 A **flat** tyre does not have enough air inside it. ADJ CLASSIF

5 A **flat** refusal, denial, or rejection is definite and firm. EG *Their earnest request met with a flat refusal.* ◊ **flatly.** EG *She has flatly refused to go.* ADJ CLASSIF : ATTRIB ◊ ADV

6 If someone says something in a **flat** voice, they do not show any emotion in their voice. ◊ **flatly.** EG *'She is dead,' said Ash flatly.* ADJ QUALIT ◊ ADV

7 If something is done in a particular amount of time **flat**, it is done in exactly that amount of time. EG *They will be able to hit the targets in four minutes flat.* ADV AFTER N

8 If an event or an attempt to do something **falls flat**, it is unsuccessful. PHRASE

9 In music, a **flat** is a note that is a semitone lower than the note which is described by the same letter. It can be represented by the symbol 'b' after the letter. EG *...the Sonata in B flat minor.* N COUNT, OR ADJ AFTER N

10 If a musical note is played or sung **flat**, it is slightly lower in pitch than it should be. ADV OR ADJ QUALIT

11 A **flat** charge or fee is the same for everyone whatever the circumstances are. ADJ CLASSIF : ATTRIB

12 A **flat** battery has lost some or all of its electrical power. ADJ CLASSIF

13 If you do something **flat out**, you do it as fast or as hard as you can. EG *Our staff are working flat out.* PHRASE Informal

flatmate /flætmeɪt/, **flatmates.** Someone's **flatmate** is the person who shares a flat with them. N COUNT

flatten /flætə^{0}n/, **flattens, flattening, flattened.**

1 If you **flatten** something or if it **flattens**, it becomes flat or flatter. EG *The steel rod had been slightly flattened.* V-ERG

2 If you **flatten** buildings or crops, you destroy them by knocking or pushing them down. EG *Huge areas of Queen Victoria Street were flattened by bombs.* V+O

3 If you **flatten** yourself against something, you press yourself flat against it, for example in order V-REFL+A not to be seen. EG *She flattened herself against the door.*

4 If you **flatten** someone, you make them fall by hitting them violently. EG *I watched Carpentier flatten Wells in 73 seconds.* V+O Informal

flatten out. If you **flatten** something **out** or if it **flattens out**, it becomes flat or flatter. EG *The lump had flattened out, almost.* PHRASAL VB : V-ERG+ADV

flattened /flætə⁰nd/. A **flattened** object 1 has been squashed flat. EG *...flattened paper cups.* 2 has a flatter shape than usual. EG *...a grotesque creature with a flattened body.* ADJ CLASSIF : USU ATTRIB

flatter /flætə/, **flatters, flattering, flattered.** 1 If you **flatter** someone, you say or imply that they are more attractive, important, or clever than they really are in order to please them or to persuade them to do something. EG *Ginny knew that he was saying all this just to flatter her.* V+O

2 If you **are flattered** by something that someone says or does, you are pleased because it makes you feel more important. EG *I was flattered that he remembered my name... I'm all the more flattered to be invited to your home.* V-PASS : OFT+REPORT : ONLY *that*

3 If you **flatter** yourself that something is the case, you believe, perhaps wrongly, something good about yourself or your abilities. EG *I rather flatter myself I've been reserved for a better fate.* V-REFL +REPORT : ONLY *that*

flattering /flætərɪŋ/. If you say that something is **flattering**, you mean that it makes someone appear more attractive or important than they really are. EG *...clothing which is stylish, well made or flattering... It is not a flattering picture.* ADJ QUALIT

flattery /flætə⁰ri¹/ is flattering words or behaviour. EG *He was immune to the flattery of political leaders.* N UNCOUNT

flaunt /flɔːnt/, **flaunts, flaunting, flaunted.** If you **flaunt** something desirable that you possess, you display it in a very obvious way. EG *They flaunt their engagement rings... The leader of the group wanted to flaunt his authority.* V+O

flavour /fleɪvə/, **flavours, flavouring, flavoured;** spelled **flavor** in American English.

1 The **flavour** of a food or drink is its taste. EG *...the flavour of the honey... Do you think that improves the flavour?* N COUNT OR N UNCOUNT

2 If you **flavour** food or drink, you add something to it to give it a particular taste. EG *Milk can be flavoured with vanilla.* V+O : OFT+ *with*

3 You can refer to a special quality that something has as its **flavour**. EG *Pimlico has its own peculiar flavour and atmosphere... ...drama with an African flavour.* N UNCOUNT

flavouring /fleɪvə⁰rɪŋ/, **flavourings;** spelled **flavoring** in American English. N MASS

Flavouring is a substance that you add to food or drink to give it a particular taste.

flaw /flɔː/, **flaws.** 1 If there is a **flaw** in something, there is something wrong with it which makes it ineffective, invalid, or unsatisfactory. EG *There is a flaw in this policy. We have no money to lend them... The law contained a flaw which made it unworkable.* N COUNT

2 A **flaw** in someone's character is an undesirable quality which they have, especially the only one they have. N COUNT

3 A **flaw** in a material such as cloth or glass or in a pattern is a small mark or damaged area that should not be there. N COUNT

flawed /flɔːd/. Something that is **flawed** has a flaw of some kind. EG *We are all flawed in some way... ...flawed arguments.* ADJ CLASSIF

flawless /flɔːlɪ²s/. Something that is **flawless** is perfect and has no flaws. EG *...a flawless performance... ...her flawless complexion.* ADJ CLASSIF

flax /flæks/ is a plant whose stem is used for making thread, rope, and cloth. N UNCOUNT

flaxen /flæksə⁰n/. **Flaxen** hair is pale yellow in colour. ADJ COLOUR Literary

flay /fleɪ/, **flays, flaying, flayed.** When someone **flays** a dead animal, they cut off its skin. V+O

flea /fliː/, **fleas.** 1 A **flea** is a very small jumping insect that feeds on the blood of humans and animals. N COUNT

2 If you send someone away **with a flea in** their **ear**, you speak to them angrily and reject their suggestion or attempt to do something. EG *Don't blame me if you come back with a flea in your ear!* PHRASE

fleck /flɛk/, **flecks. Flecks** are small marks on a surface, or objects that look like small marks. EG *...the grey flecks in his eyes... Little flecks of white powder floated on top.* N COUNT

flecked /flɛkd/. If a surface is **flecked** with small marks, it is covered with them. EG *Her eyes were dull grey, and flecked with dots of milky white.* ADJ PRED+ *with*

fled /flɛd/ is the past tense and past participle of **flee.**

fledgling /flɛdʒlɪŋ/, **fledglings.** 1 A **fledgling** is a young bird. N COUNT

2 You use **fledgling** to describe an inexperienced person or a new organization. EG *...fledgling industries.* ADJ CLASSIF : ATTRIB Literary

flee /fliː/, **flees, fleeing, fled** /flɛd/. 1 If you **flee**, you run away from someone or something. EG *Local tribesmen fled in fear... He had to flee to Tanzania... The gazelle fled from him.* V : OFT+A

2 If you **flee** a place, you leave it quickly because you are in danger. EG *He fled the country.* V+O : NO PASS

fleece /fliːs/, **fleeces, fleecing, fleeced.** 1 A sheep's **fleece** is its wool. N COUNT

2 A **fleece** is a sheep's wool when it is cut off in one piece. N COUNT

3 If you **are fleeced**, someone gets a lot of money from you by tricking you or overcharging you. EG *The pensioners feel they are being fleeced.* V+O : USU PASS Informal

fleet /fliːt/, **fleets.** 1 A **fleet** is a group of ships organized to do something together. EG *Britain had to increase her battle fleet... ...a trawling fleet.* N COUNT

2 You can also refer to a group of vehicles as a **fleet**. EG *Fleets of buses take them the rest of the way.* N COUNT

fleeting /fliːtɪŋ/ is used to describe things which last for only a very short time. EG *I got only fleeting glimpses of them.* ◇ **fleetingly.** EG *...a way to assert power, however fleetingly.* ADJ QUALIT : ATTRIB ◇ ADV

flesh /flɛʃ/, **fleshes, fleshing, fleshed.** 1 Your **flesh** is the substance your body is made of, which comes between your bones and your skin. EG *The fangs are driven into the victim's flesh.* N UNCOUNT

2 You can also refer to a person's skin as their **flesh**. EG *...the whiteness of her flesh.* N UNCOUNT

3 Someone who is your **own flesh and blood** is a member of your own family. ● See also **flesh-and-blood**. PHRASE

4 If you see someone **in the flesh**, you actually see them rather than, for example, seeing them in a film or on television. PHRASE

5 The **flesh** of a fruit or vegetable is the soft inner part. N UNCOUNT

flesh out. If you **flesh** something **out**, you add more details to it. EG *We're now seeing the proposal fleshed out for the first time.* PHRASAL VB : V+O+ADV

flesh-and-blood means real and alive, rather than imaginary or artificial. EG *...a game between a computer and a flesh-and-blood chess master.* ADJ CLASSIF : ATTRIB

fleshy /flɛʃi¹/, **fleshier, fleshiest.** 1 **Fleshy** people have a lot of flesh on their bodies. EG *...a fleshy middle-aged official... ...her fleshy arms.* ADJ QUALIT

2 **Fleshy** leaves or stalks are thick. ADJ QUALIT

flew /fluː/ is the past tense of **fly.**

flex /flɛks/, **flexes, flexing, flexed.** 1 A **flex** is a long, flexible plastic tube with two or three wires inside. It is used to carry electricity from a plug to an electrical appliance. EG *...a length of flex.* N COUNT OR N UNCOUNT

If you are fleshy, are you fat?

2 If you **flex** a muscle or a part of your body, you bend, move, or stretch it for a short time in order to exercise it. V+O

flexible /flɛksɪbəᵊl/. **1** A **flexible** object or material can be bent easily without breaking. EG *The tube is flexible but tough.* ADJ QUALIT

2 A **flexible** system or arrangement can be changed and adapted to different conditions or circumstances. EG *We need a more flexible decision-making system... ...flexible working hours.* ADJ QUALIT

◇ **flexibility** /flɛksəbɪlɪ¹ti¹/. EG *This called for some flexibility of approach.* ◇ N UNCOUNT

flick /flɪk/, **flicks, flicking, flicked. 1** If something **flicks** in a particular direction or if you **flick** it, it moves with a short, sudden movement. EG *Its tongue flicks in and out of its tiny mouth... ...flicking its tail backwards and forwards.* ▸ used as a noun. EG *...a quick upward flick of the arm.* V-ERG+A ▸ N COUNT

2 If you **flick** something away or **flick** it off something else, you remove it with a quick movement of your finger or hand. EG *He flicked the dust from his suit... She sat there, flicking ash into the ashtray.* V+O+A

3 If you **flick** something such as a whip or a towel, you hold one end and move your hand quickly up and then forward, so that the other end moves or hits something. EG *He flicked their bare arms with a tea towel.* ▸ used as a noun. EG *He gave a flick of the whip.* V+O: OFT+*with* ▸ N COUNT: OFT+*of*

4 If you **flick** pages over or **flick** through a book or magazine, you turn the pages quickly. EG *He flicked through the passport, not understanding a word.* ▸ used as a noun. EG *...a quick flick through the pages.* V+O: OFT+A; ALSO V+A ▸ N COUNT +SUPP

5 You also **flick** something when you hit it sharply with your fingernail by pressing the fingernail against your thumb and suddenly releasing it. EG *I flicked the hollow door with my finger.* V+O

6 If you **flick** a switch or catch, you press it sharply so that it moves into a different position. EG *He flicked a couple of light switches... She flicked on the lamp.* V+O: OFT +*on/off*

7 Some people refer to the cinema as the **flicks**. EG *Sometimes she just went to the flicks... What's on at the flicks?* N PLURAL: *the*+N Informal

flicker /flɪkə/, **flickers, flickering, flickered. 1** If a light or flame **flickers**, it shines unsteadily, with sudden changes in strength and brightness. EG *The candle flickered by the bed.* ▸ used as a noun. EG *...a faint flicker of lightning.* V ▸ N COUNT

2 A **flicker** of a feeling happens or is noticeable only briefly. EG *There was a flicker of fear in the man's eyes.* ▸ used as a verb. EG *A rather sad smile flickered across her face.* N COUNT ▸ V+A

3 You can also say that something **flickers** when it moves lightly and quickly, especially up and down or backwards and forwards. EG *Her eyelids flickered and closed again.* V

flier /flaɪə/. See **flyer**.

flight /flaɪt/, **flights. 1** A **flight** is **1.1** a journey made by flying, especially in an aeroplane. EG *It had been his first flight.* **1.2** an aeroplane that takes you on a particular journey. EG *Can you tell me what time Flight No. 172 arrives?* N COUNT

2 Flight is the action of flying. EG *...a bird in flight... Supersonic flight is very expensive.* N UNCOUNT

3 A **flight** of birds is a group of them flying together. EG *...a flight of duck.* N PART

4 Flight is also the act of running away from a place or situation which you feel is dangerous or unpleasant. EG *He was born at sea during his parents' flight from the revolution.* N UNCOUNT: USU+SUPP

5 A **flight** of steps or stairs is a row of them leading from one level to another without changing direction. EG *She led the way down a short flight of steps.* N COUNT: USU+*of*

6 You can refer to an idea that is imaginative but not practical as a **flight** of fancy or a **flight** of the imagination. EG *Despite his occasional flights of fancy, he is an astute politician.* N COUNT+*of*

flighty /flaɪti¹/. People, especially women, are described as **flighty** when they are not serious, steady, or reliable. EG *...the disrespectful way in which these flighty females carry out their duties.* ADJ QUALIT Outdated

flimsy /flɪmzi¹/, **flimsier, flimsiest. 1** Something that is **flimsy** is easily damaged because it is badly made or made of a weak material. EG *Poor people can afford only flimsy houses of mud and straw.* ADJ QUALIT

2 Flimsy cloth or clothing is thin and does not give much protection. EG *They stood shivering in flimsy white muslin gowns.* ADJ QUALIT

3 A **flimsy** excuse or **flimsy** evidence is not very good or convincing. ADJ QUALIT

flinch /flɪntᵊʃ/, **flinches, flinching, flinched. 1** If you **flinch** when you are startled or hurt, you make a small, sudden movement without meaning to. EG *The children flinched as the cold rain splashed them.* V

2 If you **flinch** from something unpleasant, you are unwilling to do it or think about it. EG *They flinched from the prospect of starting again.* V: OFT+*from*

fling /flɪŋ/, **flings, flinging, flung** /flʌŋ/. **1** If you **fling** something somewhere, you throw or move it there suddenly and not at all carefully. EG *She took off her hat, flinging it on the grass... She was flinging a few things into her handbag... The woman flung her arms around him.* V+O+A

2 If you **fling** yourself somewhere, you move or jump there with a lot of force. EG *He flung himself down at Jack's feet.* V-REFL+A

3 If you have a **fling**, **3.1** you enjoy yourself briefly in an energetic way. EG *...a last fling at the disco.* **3.2** you have a brief romantic or sexual relationship. EG *She had a brief fling while her husband was away.* N COUNT Informal

flint /flɪnt/, **flints. 1 Flint** is a very hard, greyish-black stone. EG *...the grey flint parish church... ...a wall made of flints.* N UNCOUNT OR N COUNT

2 A **flint** is also a small piece of flint which can be struck to produce sparks and used to light a fire. N COUNT

flip /flɪp/, **flips, flipping, flipped. 1** If you **flip** through a book or file, you turn the pages or documents quickly. V+*through*

2 If you **flip** a switch or **flip** a light or machine on or off, you turn it on or off quickly. EG *He flipped off the outside light.* V+O: OFT +*on/off*

3 If you **flip** something into a different position, you turn it or move it into that position with a quick push. EG *He flipped open his notebook.* V+O+A

4 If you **flip** something somewhere, you hit it sharply so that it moves there through the air. EG *He tore off the metal tab and flipped it into the garbage can.* V+O+A

flippant /flɪpənt/. You say that someone is being **flippant** when they make remarks which show that they are not taking something seriously, although they ought to. EG *John was offended by the doctor's flippant attitude.* ◇ **flippancy** /flɪpənsi¹/. EG *'This is no time for flippancy,' he said angrily.* ADJ QUALIT ◇ N UNCOUNT

flipper /flɪpə/, **flippers. 1** The **flippers** of an animal such as a seal are the two or four flat limbs that it uses for swimming. N COUNT: USU PLURAL

2 Flippers are also flat pieces of rubber that you can wear on your feet to help you swim more quickly, especially underwater. N COUNT: USU PLURAL

flirt /flɜːt/, **flirts, flirting, flirted. 1** If you **flirt** with someone, you behave as if you are sexually attracted to them, in a not very serious way. EG *She never even flirted with other men.* ◇ **flirtation** /flɜːteɪʃəᵊn/, **flirtations.** EG *He had a mild flirtation with two Danish blondes.* V OR V+*with*: RECIP ◇ N COUNT OR N UNCOUNT

2 If you describe someone as a **flirt**, you mean that they flirt a lot. N COUNT

3 If you **flirt** with the idea of doing or having something, you consider doing or having it, without making any definite plans. EG *Burlington has flirted for years with the idea of a wood-burning electrical generator.* V+*with*

flirtatious /flɜːteɪʃəs/. Someone who is **flirtatious** behaves towards someone as if they are sexually attracted to them, in a not very serious way. EG *She kept giving him flirtatious looks.* ADJ QUALIT

flit /flɪt/, **flits, flitting, flitted. 1** To **flit** about means to fly or move quickly from one place to another with small, light movements. EG *Bats flitted about in the darkening sky.* V+A

2 If an expression **flits** across your face or an idea **flits** through your mind, it is there for a short time and then goes again. EG *An expression of pain flitted across her face.* V+A

float /fləʊt/, **floats, floating, floated. 1** If something **is floating** in a liquid, it is lying or moving slowly along on the surface. EG *There was seaweed floating on the surface of the water.* V:OFT+A

2 Something that **floats** through the air moves slowly through it, because it is very light. EG *Six dollar bills floated down on to the table.* V:USU+A

3 If a sound **floats** somewhere, it can be heard faintly there. EG *Their voices floated across the graveyard.* V+A Literary

4 A **float** is a light object that is used to help someone or something float in water. N COUNT

5 A **float** is also a lorry on which people and displays are carried in a festival procession. N COUNT

floating /fləʊtɪŋ/. A **floating** voter is a person who is not a firm supporter of any political party. ADJ CLASSIF: ATTRIB

flock /flɒk/, **flocks, flocking, flocked. 1** A **flock** of birds, sheep, or goats is a group of them. EG *...a flock of seagulls... Shepherds moved with their flocks to lowland pastures.* N PART

2 Someone's **flock**, especially a clergyman's, is the group of people that they are responsible for. EG *He looked severely at his flock.* N COLL+POSS Outdated

3 If people **flock** to a place or event, a lot of them go there, because it is pleasant or interesting. EG *Many thousands had flocked to Rome for the festival... Crowds flocked to see the treasures.* V+A OR *to*-INF

flog /flɒg/, **flogs, flogging, flogged. 1** If you **flog** something, you sell it. V+O OR V+O+O Informal

2 To **flog** someone means to hit them hard with a whip or stick as a punishment. EG *Frequently slaves were flogged.* ◇ **flogging, floggings.** EG *He was sentenced to receive a public flogging.* V+O ◇ N UNCOUNT OR N COUNT

flood /flʌd/, **floods, flooding, flooded. 1** If there is a **flood**, a large amount of water covers an area which is usually dry, for example when a river overflows. EG *In 1975, floods in north-eastern India made 233,000 people homeless.* N COUNT

2 If something **floods** a place that is usually dry or if the place **floods**, it becomes covered with water. EG *When we took the plug out the kitchen flooded.* V-ERG
◇ **flooding.** EG *There has been heavy rain in many areas, resulting in widespread flooding.* ◇ N UNCOUNT

3 If a river **floods**, it overflows, usually after very heavy rain. V

4 A **flood** of things is a large number of them that come or occur. EG *She received a flood of grateful letters.* N PART

5 If people or things **flood** into a place, large numbers of them come there. EG *This brought more and more migrants flooding into the cities.* V+A

6 If you **flood** a place with things, you fill it with so many of them that it cannot hold or deal with any more. EG *Manufacturers have been flooding India with imports from Britain.* V+O: OFT+*with*

7 If memories or anxieties come **flooding** back, you suddenly remember them or feel them again very strongly. EG *The memories flooded back as we passed the old school.* V+O OR V+A

8 If light **floods** a place or **floods** into it, it suddenly fills it. EG *Daylight flooded the room.* V+O OR V+*into*

floodgates /flʌdgeɪtz/. If someone or something **opens the floodgates**, they make it possible for a large number of people to do something for the first time. EG *They were afraid of opening the floodgates to mass democracy.* PHRASE

floodlight /flʌdlaɪt/, **floodlights, floodlighting, floodlit. 1 Floodlights** are powerful lamps which are used to light sports grounds and the outsides of public buildings when it is dark. N COUNT: USU PLURAL

2 If a building or place **is floodlit**, it is lit by floodlights. EG *The cathedral is floodlit at night.* V+O: USU PASS

floor /flɔː/, **floors, flooring, floored. 1** The **floor** of a room is the flat part of it that you walk on. EG *The book fell to the floor.* N COUNT

2 The **floor** of a valley or forest, or of the sea, is the ground at the bottom of it. EG *Fifty yards farther out, the ocean floor dropped steeply.* N COUNT+SUPP

3 A **floor** of a building is all the rooms that are on a particular level. EG *My office is on the second floor.* N COUNT

4 If a remark or question **floors** you, you are so surprised or confused by it that you are completely unable to answer it. V+O

5 See also **shop floor**.

floorboard /flɔːbɔːd/, **floorboards. Floorboards** are the long pieces of wood that a floor is made of. EG *The floorboards creaked.* N COUNT: USU PLURAL

flop /flɒp/, **flops, flopping, flopped. 1** If you **flop** onto something, you sit or lie down suddenly and heavily because you are tired. EG *She flopped into an armchair.* V+A

2 If something **flops** somewhere, it falls there untidily. EG *She tipped the pan over and a fish flopped out.* V+A

3 Something that is a **flop** is a total failure. EG *His first play was a disastrous flop... So the brilliant invention was a flop economically.* ▸ used as a verb. EG *One of their space projects flopped.* N COUNT Informal ▸ V

floppy /flɒpi[1]/. Something that is **floppy** is loose rather than stiff, and tends to hang downwards. EG *...ladies in floppy hats.* ADJ QUALIT

flora /flɔːrə/. The **flora** in a place are all the plants there. EG *...the unnecessary destruction of the flora and fauna of our countryside.* N PLURAL Formal

floral /flɔːrəl/. **1 Floral** cloth, paper, or china has a pattern of flowers on it. EG *...floral dresses.* ADJ CLASSIF: ATTRIB

2 You also use **floral** to describe something that is made of flowers. EG *...floral decorations.* ADJ CLASSIF: ATTRIB

florid /flɒrɪd/. **1** Something that is **florid** is complicated and extravagant rather than plain and simple. EG *...florid verse.* ADJ QUALIT Literary

2 Someone who is **florid** has a red face. EG *...a large man with a florid complexion.* ADJ QUALIT

florist /flɒrɪst/, **florists.** A **florist** is a shopkeeper who sells indoor plants and bunches of flowers. N COUNT

flounce /flaʊns/, **flounces, flouncing, flounced.** When people, especially women, **flounce** somewhere, they walk there quickly in a way which suggests that they are angry. EG *She flounced into the bedroom, slamming the door behind her.* V+A

flounder /flaʊndə/, **flounders, floundering, floundered. 1** If you **flounder** when you are in water, you move in an energetic, uncontrolled way, trying not to sink. EG *Ahead, men were floundering in the dark swamps.* V: USU+A

2 You can also say that someone **is floundering** when they cannot think what to say or do. EG *Suddenly she asked me: 'What do you think?' I floundered for a moment.* V

flour /flaʊə/ is a white or brown powder that is made by grinding grain. It is used to make bread, cakes, and pastry. N UNCOUNT

flourish /flʌrɪʃ/, **flourishes, flourishing, flourished. 1** When you say that something **is flourishing**, you mean that it is active or successful, or is developing quickly and strongly. EG *Democracy cannot possibly flourish in such circumstances.* V
◇ **flourishing.** EG *...flourishing industries.* ◇ ADJ QUALIT

2 If a plant or animal **flourishes**, it grows well or is healthy because the conditions are right for it. EG *In these waters, bacteria flourish.* V

Find two words on these pages with the same pronunciation.

3 If you **flourish** an object, you wave it about so that people notice it. EG *She rushed in flourishing a document.* V+O

4 If you do something with a **flourish**, you do it with a bold waving or sweeping movement. EG *Jack drew his knife with a flourish.* N COUNT

flout /flaʊt/, **flouts, flouting, flouted.** If you **flout** a law, order, or rule of behaviour, you deliberately disobey it. EG *We're prepared to flout their laws if necessary.* V+O

flow /fləʊ/, **flows, flowing, flowed. 1** If a liquid, gas, or electrical current **flows** somewhere, it moves there steadily and continuously. You can also say that a number of people or things **flow** somewhere. EG *The river flows south-west to the Atlantic Ocean... European scientists are flowing into the United States.* ▸ used as a noun. EG *The blood flow is cut off... There's a good flow of information.* V+A; ▸ N COUNT +SUPP

2 If someone's hair or clothing **flows** about them, it hangs freely and loosely. EG *She let her hair down so that it flowed over her shoulders.* ◊ **flowing.** EG *...women in long flowing robes.* V+A; ◊ ADJ CLASSIF

3 If a quality or situation **flows** from something, it comes from it or results naturally from it. EG *The love for one another flows from that unity.* V+*from* Literary

4 If there is a **flow** of conversation, people are talking without stopping. EG *She can keep up a non-stop flow of baby talk.* N SING+SUPP

5 the ebb and flow of something: see **ebb.**

flower /flaʊə/, **flowers, flowering, flowered. 1** The **flowers** on a plant are the coloured or white parts that grow on its stems. EG *The hawthorn has white flowers in June.* N COUNT

2 Flowers are small plants that are grown for their flowers, as opposed to trees, shrubs, and vegetables. EG *He planted flowers on the banks... ...a bunch of flowers.* N COUNT: USU PLURAL

3 When a plant or tree **flowers**, its flowers appear and open. V

4 When an idea, artistic style, or political movement **flowers**, it develops fully and becomes successful. EG *Liberties need to grow and flower in times of peace.* ◊ **flowering.** EG *...the flowering of socialist thought.* V; ◊ N UNCOUNT: OFT+SUPP

flowerbed /flaʊəbɛd/, **flowerbeds.** A **flowerbed** is an area of earth in which you grow plants. N COUNT

flowered /flaʊəd/. **Flowered** cloth, paper, or china has a pattern of flowers on it. EG *...a flowered skirt.* ADJ CLASSIF

flowering /flaʊə⁰rɪŋ/. **Flowering** shrubs, trees, or plants produce flowers. ADJ CLASSIF: ATTRIB

flowerpot /flaʊəpɒt/, **flowerpots.** A **flowerpot** is a small container which a plant is grown in. N COUNT

flowery /flaʊə⁰ri¹/. **1** Something that is **flowery 1.1** has a sweet smell. EG *...a flowery perfume.* **1.2** has a pattern of flowers on it. EG *...a flowery apron.* ADJ QUALIT; ADJ CLASSIF

2 Flowery speech or writing contains long, complicated words and literary expressions. ADJ QUALIT

flown /fləʊn/ is the past participle of **fly.**

flu /flu:/ is an illness which is like a bad cold. When you have flu, you feel weak and your muscles ache. N UNCOUNT

fluctuate /flʌktjʊeɪt/, **fluctuates, fluctuating, fluctuated.** If something **fluctuates**, its amount, level, or nature keeps changing. EG *Prices fluctuated between 1970 and 1972... Friendships blossomed, fluctuated, and died.* ◊ **fluctuating.** EG *...fluctuating opinions.* ◊ **fluctuation** /flʌktjʊeɪʃə⁰n/, **fluctuations.** EG *...fluctuations in temperature... ...sharp fluctuations in policy.* V; ◊ ADJ CLASSIF; ◊ N COUNT OR N UNCOUNT

flue /flu:/, **flues.** A **flue** is a chimney or a pipe that acts as a chimney. N COUNT

fluent /flu:ənt/. **1** Someone who is **fluent** in a language can speak or write it easily and correctly. EG *She was fluent in Spanish... ...people who spoke fluent Portuguese.* ◊ **fluently.** EG *He spoke both languages fluently.* ◊ **fluency** /flu:ənsi¹/. EG *She could speak German with great fluency.* ADJ QUALIT: OFT+*in*; ◊ ADV; ◊ N UNCOUNT

2 Someone whose speech, reading, or writing is **fluent** speaks, reads, or writes easily and clearly with no hesitation or mistakes. ◊ **fluently.** EG *By the time she was six she could read fluently.* ADJ QUALIT; ◊ ADV

fluff /flʌf/, **fluffs, fluffing, fluffed. 1 Fluff** is **1.1** the small masses of soft, light thread that you find on clothes or in dusty corners of a room. EG *He brushed some fluff from his jacket.* **1.2** soft, newly grown hair or fur. EG *...a tiny creature covered with black fluff.* N UNCOUNT

2 If you **fluff** something or **fluff** it out, you shake it or brush it in order to make it seem larger and lighter. EG *...birds fluffing their feathers... She fluffed her hair out in big waves.* V+O: OFT+*up/out*

3 If you **fluff** something that you are trying to do, you do it badly. EG *My co-star used to get very cross if I fluffed my lines.* V+O Informal

fluffy /flʌfi¹/. Something that is **fluffy** is very soft and furry. EG *...a fluffy kitten... ...fluffy white robes.* ADJ QUALIT

fluid /flu:ɪd/, **fluids. 1** A **fluid** is a substance that can flow, especially a liquid. EG *...petrol and cleaning fluids.* ▸ used as an adjective. EG *After a month it was still completely fluid at the centre.* N COUNT OR N UNCOUNT; ▸ ADJ PRED

2 Fluid movements are relaxed, smooth, and graceful. ADJ QUALIT

3 A situation, idea, or arrangement that is **fluid** is not fixed and is likely to change often. EG *Opinion in the trade unions is very fluid as regards this question.* ◊ **fluidity** /flu:ɪdɪ¹ti¹/. EG *...the fluidity of the situation.* ADJ QUALIT; ◊ N UNCOUNT

fluid ounce, fluid ounces. A **fluid ounce** is a measurement of liquid. There are twenty fluid ounces in a British pint, and sixteen in an American pint. N COUNT

fluke /flu:k/, **flukes.** If something good that happens is a **fluke**, it happens accidentally rather than because of someone's skill or plan. EG *The police have stumbled on this man by a fluke.* N COUNT: USU SING Informal

flung /flʌŋ/ is the past tense of **fling.**

fluorescent /flʊərɛsə⁰nt/. **1** Something that is **fluorescent** looks very bright when light is shone on it, as if it is shining itself. EG *...a fluorescent orange circle fixed to a belt.* ADJ CLASSIF

2 A **fluorescent** light shines with a very hard, bright light. ADJ CLASSIF: ATTRIB

fluoride /flʊəraɪd/ is a mixture of chemicals that is sometimes added to a water supply or to toothpaste because it is thought to be good for people's teeth. N UNCOUNT

flurry /flʌri¹/, **flurries. 1** A **flurry** of activity or speech is a short, vigorous amount of it. EG *There was the usual flurry of activity in the hall... The decision raised a flurry of objections.* N COUNT: USU+*of*

2 A **flurry** of snow or wind is a small amount of it that moves suddenly and quickly along. EG *The wind came at them in a flurry... ...snow flurries.* N COUNT: OFT+*of*

flush /flʌʃ/, **flushes, flushing, flushed. 1** If you **flush**, your face goes red because you are embarrassed or because you feel hot. ▸ used as a noun. EG *There was a flush in his cheeks.* ◊ **flushed.** EG *Her face was hot and flushed... ...her flushed cheeks.* V; ▸ N SING; ◊ ADJ QUALIT

2 When you **flush** a toilet or when it **flushes**, the handle is pressed or pulled and water flows into the toilet bowl. V-ERG

3 If you **flush** something down the toilet, you put it into the toilet bowl and operate the handle so that it is washed away. V+O+A

4 If you **flush** people or animals out of a place, you force them to come out. EG *They went into the area to flush out guerrillas who were sheltering there.* V+O+A

5 If you are **in the first flush** of something, you are in the first stages of experiencing it. EG *...in the first fine flush of liberation.* PHRASE Literary

6 If something is **flush** with a surface, it is level with it and does not stick up. ADJ PRED: OFT+*with*

flushed /flʌʃt/. Someone who is **flushed** with success or pride is very pleased and excited as a result of achieving something. EG *He hurried flushed with victory into the office.* ADJ PRED: OFT+*with*

fluster /flʌstə/, **flusters, flustering, flustered.** If something or someone **flusters** you, they make you feel nervous and confused. V+O : USU PASS ▸ used as a noun. EG ...*doing several things at once and not getting in a fluster.* ▸ N SING : a+N ◊ **flustered.** EG *He was so flustered he forgot to close the door.* ◊ ADJ QUALIT

flute /flu:t/, **flutes.** A **flute** is a musical instrument in the shape of a long tube with holes in it. You play it by blowing over a hole near one end while holding it sideways to your mouth. See picture at MUSICAL INSTRUMENTS. N COUNT

fluted /flu:tɪ^{2}d/. Something that is **fluted** has long grooves cut or shaped into it. EG ...*fluted columns.* ADJ CLASSIF

flutter /flʌtə/, **flutters, fluttering, fluttered. 1** If something **flutters** or if you **flutter** it, it waves up and down or from side to side with small quick movements. EG *His long robe fluttered in the wind... Courting male birds flutter their wings like chicks.* V-ERG
▸ used as a noun. EG *He let her pass after one flutter of her long dark eyelashes.* ▸ N SING
2 If something light such as a bird or a piece of paper **flutters** somewhere, it moves through the air with small quick movements. EG *The pieces of paper flutter down like butterflies.* V : USU+A
3 A **flutter** of panic or excitement is a slight feeling of panic or excitement. EG *He felt a flutter of panic.* N SING : OFT+SUPP
4 If your heart or stomach **flutters**, you feel excited, worried, or afraid. EG *His heart fluttered with fear.* V : USU+A

flux /flʌks/. If something is in a state of **flux**, it is changing constantly. EG ...*years of political flux and turmoil.* N UNCOUNT

fly /flaɪ/, **flies, flying, flew** /flu:/, **flown** /fləʊn/. **1** A **fly** is a small insect with two wings. EG ...*the flies that buzzed around their bodies.* N COUNT
2 When a bird, insect, or aircraft **flies**, it moves through the air. EG *My canary flew away.* V : USU+A
3 If you **fly** somewhere, you travel there in an aircraft. EG *You can fly from Cardiff to Ostend.* V : USU+A
4 When someone **flies** an aircraft, they control its movement in the air. V+O OR V ◊ **flying.** EG *Why don't you take up flying?* ◊ N UNCOUNT
5 If you **fly** someone or something somewhere, you send them there by plane. EG *Exotic fruits were specially flown in for the occasion.* V+O+A
6 If something **flies** about, it moves about freely and loosely. EG *He jumped onto the platform with his cloak flying.* V : USU+A
7 When a flag **is flying** or when people **fly** a flag, it is displayed at the top of a pole. V-ERG
8 If something **flies** in a particular direction, it moves there with a lot of speed or force. EG *His glasses flew off and smashed on the rocks... Pieces of jagged metal are sent flying in all directions.* V+A
9 If you say that **time flies**, you mean that it seems to pass very quickly. PHRASE
10 If you **fly** at someone or **let fly** at them, you attack them, either by hitting them or by insulting them. EG *One day the man flew at me in a temper.* V+*at*, OR PHRASE
11 The front opening on a pair of trousers is referred to as the **fly** or the **flies.** N COUNT
12 See also **flying.** • **as the crow flies**: see **crow.** • to **fly in the face of** something: see **face.** • to **fly off the handle**: see **handle.** • **a fly in the ointment**: see **ointment.**

fly into. If you **fly into** a rage or a panic, you suddenly become very angry or anxious, and show this in your behaviour. EG *She flies into a temper if I make a mistake.* PHRASAL VB : V+PREP

flyer /flaɪə/, **flyers;** also spelled **flier. 1** If a bird or insect is a skilled **flyer**, it can fly well or quickly. EG *Hawkmoths are among the swiftest insect flyers.* N COUNT : USU+SUPP
2 People who fly aircraft are sometimes referred to as **flyers.** EG ...*dashing young flyers.* N COUNT

flying /flaɪɪŋ/. **1** If you take a **flying** leap or jump, you run forward and jump. EG *She took a flying leap at the fence.* ADJ CLASSIF : ATTRIB
2 A **flying** animal is able to fly. EG ...*flies and other flying insects.* ADJ CLASSIF : ATTRIB
3 If you **get off to a flying start**, you start something very well, for example a race or a new job. PHRASE
4 A **flying** visit is a visit that lasts for a very short time. ADJ CLASSIF : ATTRIB
5 See also **fly.** • **with flying colours**: see **colour.**

flying saucer, flying saucers. Flying saucers are round flat spacecraft from other planets, which some people say they have seen. N COUNT

flyover /flaɪəʊvə/, **flyovers.** A **flyover** is a structure which carries one road over the top of another one. N COUNT

foal /fəʊl/, **foals.** A **foal** is a very young horse. N COUNT

foam /fəʊm/, **foams, foaming, foamed. 1 Foam** consists of a mass of small bubbles. It is formed when air and a liquid are mixed together violently. EG *She could see the line of white foam where the waves broke on the beach.* N UNCOUNT
2 Foam or **foam rubber** is soft rubber full of small holes which is used, for example, to make mattresses and cushions. EG ...*foam mattresses.* N UNCOUNT
3 If a liquid **is foaming**, it has lots of small bubbles in it or on its surface. V : USU+A ◊ **foaming.** EG *He poured foaming champagne into her glass.* ◊ ADJ CLASSIF

fob /fɒb/, **fobs, fobbing, fobbed.** If you ask for something and you **are fobbed off** with something else, the thing that you are given is not very good or is not really what you want. EG *He may try to fob you off with a prescription for pills.* PHRASAL VB : V+O+ADV, USU+*with*

focal point /fəʊkə^{0}l pɔɪnt/. The **focal point** of people's interest or activity is the thing they concentrate on or the place they are active in most. EG *Dinner was the focal point of my day... The focal point of these celebrations was the local church.* N SING

focus /fəʊkəs/, **focuses, focusing, focused.** The spellings **focusses, focussing,** and **focussed** are also used.
1 When you **focus** a camera or telescope or **focus** your eyes on something, you adjust it or them so that you can clearly see the thing you want to look at. EG ...*when he saw me focusing the camera on him... His eyes would not focus.* V-ERG OR V : OFT+*on*
2 If a photograph or a camera or telescope is **in focus**, the photograph or the thing you are looking at is clear and sharp. If it is **out of focus**, the photograph or the thing you are looking at is blurred. EG *The only part of the picture which was in clear focus was a small child.* PHRASE
3 If you **focus** a ray of light, you make it narrower or direct it towards a particular point. EG *I focused the beam of the spotlight on them.* V+O : OFT+*on*
4 If you **focus** your attention on something, you look at it or concentrate on it. EG *As we cannot study all resources, I propose to focus attention on one... Attention focused on the election.* V-ERG : USU+*on*
5 If special attention is being paid to someone or something, you can say that they are the **focus** of interest or attention. EG *Changes in the urban environment are the focus of public interest and discussion.* N UNCOUNT
6 The **focus** on a particular person or thing is the fact that special attention is being paid to them. EG *The focus on money and position tends to foster rivalry.* N UNCOUNT

fodder /fɒdə/ is food that is given to animals such as cows or horses. N UNCOUNT

foe /fəʊ/, **foes.** Your **foe** is your enemy. EG *Friends became foes.* N COUNT Outdated

foetus /fi:təs/, **foetuses;** also spelled **fetus.** A **foetus** is an unborn animal or human being in its later stages of development. N COUNT

fog /fɒg/, **fogs.** When there is **fog**, there are tiny drops of water in the air which form a thick cloud N UNCOUNT OR N COUNT

Do you believe in flying saucers?

and make it difficult to see things. EG *The only accident I've ever had was in fog... Around midday, the fog lifted.*

foggy /fɒgi¹/, **foggier, foggiest.** 1 When it is **foggy**, there is fog. EG *...a foggy day.* ADJ QUALIT

2 When people say they **haven't the foggiest idea**, they are emphasizing that they do not know something. EG *I haven't the foggiest idea what it is.* PHRASE Informal

foghorn /fɒghɔːn/, **foghorns.** A **foghorn** is a loud horn that is used when it is foggy to warn ships about the position of land and other ships. N COUNT

foible /fɔɪbəºl/, **foibles.** A **foible** is a habit or tendency which is rather strange or foolish, but not serious. EG *She knows his moods and foibles.* N COUNT

foil /fɔɪl/, **foils, foiling, foiled.** 1 **Foil** is metal in the form of a sheet as thin as paper. It is used especially to wrap food in and keep it fresh. EG *...the foil wrapper of a bar of chocolate.* N UNCOUNT

2 If you **foil** someone's plan or attempt at something, you prevent them from being successful. EG *Their attempt to recapture Calais was foiled by a traitor.* V+O

3 Something that is a good **foil** for something else contrasts with it and makes its good qualities more noticeable. EG *She had bronzed skin, for which her yellow swimsuit was a perfect foil.* N SING: USU+*for/to*

foist /fɔɪst/, **foists, foisting, foisted.** If you **foist** something on someone, you force them to have it or experience it. EG *They were out to foist their views on the people.* V+O+*on*

fold /fəʊld/, **folds, folding, folded.** 1 If you **fold** a piece of paper or cloth, you bend it so that one part of it covers another part. EG *Fold the sheet and blankets back at the top.* V+O: OFT+A

2 If you **fold** something, you make it into a smaller shape by folding it several times. EG *They folded the tent neatly.* V+O

3 A **fold** is 3.1 one of the curved shapes that are formed in a piece of cloth when it is not lying flat. EG *Snow had collected in the folds of my clothes.* 3.2 a bend that you make in a piece of paper or cloth when you fold it. N COUNT

4 If you **fold** a piece of furniture or equipment, you change its shape by bending or closing parts of it. EG *The bed can be easily erected or folded away... The rear seat folds down.* V-ERG: USU+A

5 If you **fold** your arms or hands, you bring them together and cross them or link them. EG *He sat with his arms folded across his chest.* V+O

6 If a business or organization **folds**, it is unsuccessful and has to close. EG *The project folded.* V

7 You can refer to an organization or group as the **fold** when you are talking about its members leaving it or returning to it. EG *They wanted to entice the conservatives back to the fold.* N SING: *the*+N Literary

8 See also **folding**.

fold up. 1 If you **fold** something **up**, you make it into a smaller shape by folding it several times. EG *She folded up some shirts.* 2 If a business or organization **folds up**, it is unsuccessful and has to close. PHRASAL VB: V+O+ADV; V+ADV

-fold combines with a number 1 to indicate that something has a particular number of kinds or parts. EG *The problems were two-fold: it was difficult to get finance, and there weren't enough trained people available.* 2 to indicate that something is multiplied a particular number of times. EG *Even if we multiplied it ten-fold, that would still only be thirty per cent.*

folder /fəʊldə/, **folders.** A **folder** is a thin piece of cardboard folded into the shape of a container or cover, in which you can keep documents. EG *He took a sealed envelope from the folder on his desk.* N COUNT

folding /fəʊldɪŋ/. A **folding** table, bicycle, or other object is designed so that you can fold it into a smaller shape to make it easier to carry or store. EG *...folding chairs... ...folding steps.* ADJ CLASSIF: ATTRIB

foliage /fəʊliˈɪdʒ/. The leaves of plants and trees are referred to as **foliage**. EG *...the dense foliage of the forest.* N UNCOUNT

folk /fəʊk/, **folks.** 1 You can refer to people as **folk**. EG *...old folk... ...country folk.* N PLURAL: OFT+SUPP

2 Your **folks** are your close relatives, especially your parents. EG *I don't even have time to write letters to my folks.* N PLURAL Informal American

3 You can use **folks** to address a group of people. EG *That's all for tonight, folks.* VOCATIVE Informal

4 **Folk** music, art, and customs are considered to be traditional or typical of a particular community or nation. EG *...Russian folk songs.* ADJ CLASSIF: ATTRIB

folklore /fəʊklɔː/. The traditional stories and customs of a community or nation are referred to as its **folklore**. EG *...a flourishing oral tradition of folklore and song.* N UNCOUNT

follow /fɒləʊ/, **follows, following, followed.** 1 If you **follow** someone, 1.1 you move along behind them. EG *He followed Sally into the yard... Lynn got up and made for the stairs. Marsha followed.* 1.2 you go to the place that they have recently gone to. EG *He followed them to Venice.* V+O OR V

2 An event or period of time that **follows** a particular event happens or comes after it. EG *In the days that followed, Keith and his mates could talk of nothing else... ...outings to the cinema followed by tea at Lyons Corner House... Famine and disease follow close behind.* V+O OR V

3 If you say that something **follows**, you mean that 3.1 it is true as a logical result of something else being true. EG *Just because they are old, it doesn't follow that they have to be patronized.* 3.2 it comes next in a piece of writing or speech. EG *I learned most of what follows from a parlourmaid called Louise.* V: OFT +REPORT, ONLY *that*; V OR V+O

4 You use **as follows** to introduce 4.1 a list of things. EG *The contents are as follows: one black desk, one grey wastepaper bin, two red chairs.* 4.2 a description of the way that something is done. EG *File your correspondence roughly as follows.* PHRASE

5 If you **follow** something with your eyes, you watch it as it moves. EG *Its eyes followed her everywhere she moved.* V+O: USU+A

6 If you **follow** a path, river, or route, you go along it. EG *We followed a path up along the creek.* V+O: USU+A

7 If you **follow** someone's instructions, advice, or example, you do what they say or do what they have done. EG *She promised to follow his advice.* V+O

8 If you **follow** a particular course of action, you do a particular thing, in a planned way. EG *This forced them to follow a tight money policy.* V+O

9 If you manage to **follow** an explanation or the plot of a story, you manage to understand it. EG *They were having some difficulty in following the plot... He didn't quite follow.* V+O OR V: USU WITH BROAD NEG

10 If you **follow** a series of events or a television serial, you take an interest in it and keep informed about what happens. EG *...the thousands of American couples who followed the case with great interest.* V+O

11 to **follow suit**: see **suit**. ● See also **following**.

follow up. 1 If you **follow** something **up**, you try to find out more about it. EG *It's an idea which has been followed up by a group of researchers at Birmingham.* 2 If you **follow** one thing **up** with another, you do the second thing after you have done the first. EG *He followed up this criticism with a personal attack on the Prime Minister.* 3 See also **follow-up**. PHRASAL VB: V+O+ADV; V+O+ADV, OFT+*with*

follower /fɒləʊə/, **followers.** The **followers** of a person or belief are the people who support the person or belief. EG *...Freud and his followers... ...the followers of Chinese communism.* N COUNT: USU+POSS

following /fɒləʊɪŋ/. 1 The **following** day, week, or year is the day, week, or year that comes after the one that you have just mentioned. EG *He died the following day... She intended to come on the following Friday.* ADJ CLASSIF: ATTRIB; *the*+ADJ

2 Following a particular event means after that event. EG *...the election of Harold Wilson to the leadership following Gaitskell's death.* PREP

3 You can refer to the things that you are about to mention as the **following** things. EG *This could be achieved in the following way.* ADJ CLASSIF : ATTRIB; *the*+ADJ

4 A person or organization that has a **following** has a group of people who support their beliefs or actions. EG *This religion is too stark to attract a large following.* N SING

follow-up, follow-ups. Follow-up work or action is done as a continuation or second part of something that has been done previously. EG *He needed follow-up treatment from a specialist doctor... ...a follow-up survey.* ADJ CLASSIF : ATTRIB ▸ used as a noun. EG *This conference is a follow-up to an earlier one in Gabon.* ▸ N COUNT

folly /fɒliˈ/, **follies.** If you say that an action or way of behaving is **folly** or a **folly**, you mean that it is foolish. EG *It would be folly to continue... ...to protect others against their follies or vices.* N UNCOUNT OR N COUNT

fond /fɒnd/, **fonder, fondest. 1** If you are **fond** of someone, you like them and have a feeling of affection for them. EG *I'm very fond of you.* ADJ PRED+*of*

2 If you are **fond** of something, you like it. If you are **fond** of doing something, you like doing it. EG *I am not fond of salad... Etta was fond of shopping.* ADJ PRED+*of*
◇ **fondness.** EG *...my fondness for red wine and black olives.* ◇ N UNCOUNT

3 You use **fond** to describe people or their actions or expressions when they show affection for someone or something. EG *His fond parents looked on with a smile... ...looking at me with fond eyes.* ADJ QUALIT : ATTRIB
◇ **fondly.** EG *He used to gaze at the old car fondly.* ◇ ADV

4 Fond hopes, wishes, or expectations are unlikely to be fulfilled. EG *One fond dream has been to harness the sun's rays.* ADJ CLASSIF : ATTRIB ◇ **fondly.** EG *He had fondly imagined that it would be a simple matter.* ◇ ADV

fondle /fɒndəˈl/, **fondles, fondling, fondled.** If you **fondle** someone, you touch them or stroke them gently, usually to show your affection for them. EG *I began fondling her neck.* V+O

font /fɒnt/, **fonts.** The **font** in a church is a bowl which holds the water used for baptisms. N COUNT

food /fu:d/, **foods. Food** is what people and animals eat. EG *...money for food or clothing... ...food supplies... ...health foods.* N MASS

foodstuff /fu:dstʌf/, **foodstuffs. Foodstuffs** are substances which people eat. EG *They produce sugar and other basic foodstuffs.* N COUNT : USU PLURAL

fool /fu:l/, **fools, fooling, fooled. 1** If you call someone a **fool**, you mean that they are silly or have done something silly. EG *Just look what you've done! You stupid fool!... She was sharp-witted and no fool.* N COUNT OR VOCATIVE

2 If you **make a fool of** someone, you make them appear silly by telling people about something silly that they have done, or by tricking them in some way. EG *They threatened to publish his letters to her and make a fool of him before the world.* PHRASE

3 If you **make a fool of** yourself, you behave in a way that makes you appear silly. EG *He had never learned to dance and was not prepared to make a fool of himself.* PHRASE

4 If you **play the fool**, you behave in a playful, childish, and silly way. PHRASE

5 If you **fool** someone, you deceive or trick them. EG *He fooled them with false promises... Do not be fooled into thinking that the system is perfect.* V+O

fool about or **fool around.** If you **fool about** or **fool around**, you behave in a playful, childish, and silly way. EG *He was always fooling about.* PHRASAL VB : V+ADV

foolhardy /fu:lhɑ:diˈ/. **Foolhardy** behaviour is foolish because it involves taking risks. EG *It was considered foolhardy for him to quit his job.* ADJ QUALIT Outdated

foolish /fu:lɪʃ/. **1** If you say that someone's behaviour is **foolish**, you mean that it is not sensible and shows a lack of good judgement. EG *It would be foolish to tell such things to a total stranger... How foolish I was not to have bought it.* ADJ QUALIT ◇ **foolishly.** EG *They have acted a little foolishly... Foolishly, we said we would do the decorating.* ◇ ADV OR ADV SEN ◇ **foolishness.** EG *Have I killed him by my foolishness?* ◇ N UNCOUNT

2 You can also say that people or things are **foolish** when they are so silly that they make you want to laugh. EG *They looked foolish... ...the foolish stick that he carried.* ADJ QUALIT ◇ **foolishly.** EG *Would the whole thing appear foolishly melodramatic?* ◇ ADV

foolproof /fu:lpru:f/. A plan, system, or machine that is **foolproof** is so good or easy to use that it cannot go wrong or be used wrongly. EG *...foolproof safety devices.* ADJ QUALIT

foot /fʊt/, **feet; foots, footing, footed.** The plural of the noun is **feet. Foots** is the third person singular of the verb in the phrase in paragraph 8.

1 Your **feet** are the parts of your body that are at the ends of your legs and that you stand on. See picture at THE HUMAN BODY. EG *It fell to the floor at her feet.* N COUNT

2 If you go somewhere **on foot**, you walk, rather than using any form of transport. EG *The city should be explored on foot.* PHRASE

3 When you are **on** your **feet**, you are standing up. PHRASE

4 If you get **to** your **feet,** you stand up. EG *He rose hurriedly to his feet and ran from the room.* PHRASE

5 The **foot** of something is the bottom or lower end of it. EG *...at the foot of the stairs... We camped at the foot of some hills... He sat at the foot of her bed.* N SING

6 A **foot** is a unit for measuring length, equal to 12 inches or 30.48 centimetres. The plural can be **foot** or **feet**. EG *We were a few feet away from the edge... ...a 40-foot fall.* N COUNT

7 Foot or **feet** is also used in these phrases. PHRASES **7.1** To **set foot** in a place means to go there. EG *It was a long time before I set foot in a theatre again.* Formal **7.2** When someone or something is **on** their **feet** again after an illness or a difficult period of time, they have recovered. EG *...an economic programme to put the country back on its feet.* **7.3** If you **put** your **feet up**, you relax by sitting or lying with your feet supported by something. **7.4** If someone in authority **puts** their **foot down**, they say that something must not happen or continue. **7.5** If you **put** your **foot in it**, you cause embarrassment by doing or saying something tactless. Informal **7.6** If someone has to **stand on** their **own two feet**, they have to be independent and manage their lives without help from other people.

8 If you **foot the bill** for something, you pay for it. EG *They may no longer be willing to foot the bills.* PHRASE

9 to **have** or **get cold feet**: see **cold**.

football /fʊtbɔ:l/, **footballs. 1 Football** is a game played between two teams of eleven players who kick a ball around a field in an attempt to score goals. EG *The children are playing football... ...a football match.* N UNCOUNT

2 A **football** is the large ball which is used in the game of football. N COUNT

footballer /fʊtbɔ:lə/, **footballers.** A **footballer** is a person who plays football, especially as a profession. N COUNT

foothills /fʊthɪlz/ are hills at the base of a mountain or range of mountains. EG *...exploring the foothills of the Himalayas.* N PLURAL

foothold /fʊthəʊld/, **footholds. 1 Footholds** are ledges or hollows where you can put your feet when you are climbing. EG *He cut footholds in the side of the ravine.* N COUNT

2 If a person or animal gets a **foothold** on a vertical surface, they hold on to it with their feet or claws without slipping or falling. EG *They keep their foothold on the bark with their claws.* N SING

3 You can also say that you get a **foothold** when you establish yourself in a strong position from N SING

Are you forbearing with people you are fond of?

which you can make progress. EG *I tried to find a way to gain a foothold in the organization.*

footing /fʊtɪŋ/. **1** If you lose your **footing**, your feet slip, and you fall. EG *He lost his footing, and stumbled to the floor... She regained her footing.* N UNCOUNT: USU+POSS

2 When an activity goes on in a particular way, you can say that it is on that kind of **footing**. EG *We've had to get this on a more official footing.* N SING+SUPP

3 If you are on a particular kind of **footing** with someone, you have that kind of relationship with them. EG *The school's constitution puts parents on an equal footing with staff.* N SING: OFT+*with*

footman /fʊtmə³n/, **footmen.** A **footman** is a male servant who does jobs such as opening doors or serving food. N COUNT

footnote /fʊtnəʊt/, **footnotes.** A **footnote** is a note at the bottom of a page in a book which provides more information about something that is mentioned on the page. N COUNT

footpath /fʊtpɑːθ/, **footpaths.** A **footpath** is a path for people to walk on, especially in the countryside. N COUNT

footprint /fʊtprɪnt/, **footprints. Footprints** are the marks that your feet leave in soft ground or when they are wet. EG *...footprints in the snow.* N COUNT: USU PLURAL

footstep /fʊtstɛp/, **footsteps. 1** Your **footsteps** are the sounds that your feet make when you walk. EG *They heard footsteps and turned.* N COUNT: USU PLURAL

2 If you **follow in** someone's **footsteps**, you do the same things as they did earlier. EG *I'd have liked to have followed in my father's footsteps and been a gamekeeper.* PHRASE

footwear /fʊtwɛə/ refers to things that people wear on their feet, for example shoes, boots, and sandals. EG *...the footwear industry.* N UNCOUNT

for /fɔː/. **1** If something is intended or done **for** someone, they are intended to have it, use it, or benefit from it. EG *He left a note for her on the table... I am doing everything I can for you... He often cooked for himself.* PREP

2 If you work **for** someone, you are employed by them. EG *He works for British Rail.* PREP

3 You use **for** when you state **3.1** the purpose of something. EG *...a Stanley knife for cutting linoleum, etc... I walked two miles for a couple of pails of water... We met for lunch.* **3.2** the reason for something or the cause of it. EG *Money is the primary reason for a young man's leaving the village... This area is famous for its spring flowers.* PREP

▸ used as a conjunction. EG *This was where he spent his free time, for he had nowhere else to go.* ▸ CONJ

4 For is the preposition that you use after many nouns, adjectives, and verbs in order to introduce more information. EG *...their reputation for being fierce and warlike... ...his designs for the engine... You had to be ready for any emergency... They were aiming for a double share by 1985.* PREP

5 You use **for** when you say how something affects or relates to someone or what their attitude to it is. EG *I knew it was difficult for him to talk like this... It was a frightening experience for a boy.* PREP

6 You use **for** when you say that an aspect of someone or something is surprising in relation to other aspects of them. EG *She wore rather too much make-up for her age.* PREP

7 If you feel a particular emotion **for** someone, **7.1** you feel it about them. EG *I felt sorry for my wife... ...Kurt's contempt for people.* **7.2** you feel it on their behalf. EG *I'm delighted for you.* PREP

8 You use **for** after words such as 'time', 'space', or 'money' when you say how much of it there is and what use could be made of it. EG *There was room for a table... He didn't have the concentration required for doing the job.* PREP

9 If something lasts or continues **for** a period of time, that is how long it lasts or continues. EG *I have known you for a long time... ...for three days.* PREP

10 If something extends **for** a particular distance, that is how far it extends. EG *Black cliffs rose sheer out of the water for a hundred feet or more.* PREP

11 If you give someone something **for** their birthday or **for** some other occasion, you give it on that occasion. EG *She had given him a dog for his birthday... What did you get for Christmas?* PREP

12 If something is planned **for** a particular time, it is planned to happen then. EG *The meeting has been scheduled for August 30.* PREP

13 You use expressions such as **for the first time** and **for the second time** when you are talking about how often something has happened. EG *The guide returned for the third time.* PHRASE

14 If you leave **for** a place or if you take a train, plane, or boat **for** a place, you are going there. EG *...one morning, before he left for the fields.* PREP

15 If something is bought, sold, or done **for** a particular amount of money, that is the cost of buying, selling, or doing it. EG *You can buy the paperback for about two pounds.* PREP

16 If you are **for** something, you are in favour of it. **For** is usually stressed when it is used with this meaning. EG *There was a majority of 294 for war, with only 6 voting against.* PREP ● If you are **all for** something, you are very much in favour of it. ● PHRASE

17 You use **for** after words such as 'argue' and 'vote' in order to introduce the thing that is being supported. EG *I had to vote for him on principle... This looked like a good case for the existence of telepathy.* PREP

18 You use **for** when you state the second part of a ratio. EG *About nine women have lost jobs for every five men.* PREP

19 If one word or expression has the same meaning as another one, you can say that the first one is another word or expression **for** the second one. EG *'Carte' is the French word for card.* PREP

20 for all: see **all.** ● **as for:** see **as.** ● **but for:** see **but.**

forage /fɒrɪdʒ/, **forages, foraging, foraged. 1** When animals **forage**, they search for food. V

2 If you **forage** for something, you search busily for it. EG *She couldn't resist foraging around for paintings.* V+A

foray /fɒreɪ/, **forays. 1** If a group of soldiers make a **foray** into an area, they make a quick attack, usually in order to steal supplies. N COUNT

2 If you make a **foray** somewhere, you go there briefly, usually in order to obtain something. EG *From time to time he made forays to the pavement booksellers.* N COUNT

3 If you make a **foray** into a particular area of activity, you try it for a short while. EG *It was his first foray into politics.* N COUNT+*into*

forbade /fəbæd, -beɪd/ is the past tense of **forbid.**

forbearance /fɔːbɛərəns/ is patience and kindness. N UNCOUNT Formal

forbearing /fɔːbɛərɪŋ/. Someone who is **forbearing** is patient and kind. ADJ QUALIT Formal

forbid /fə⁸bɪd/, **forbids, forbidding, forbade** /fəbæd, -beɪd/, **forbidden. 1** If you **forbid** someone to do something, you order them not to do it. EG *I forbid you to tell her... They had obtained a court order forbidding the sale.* V+O: OFT+*to*-INF

2 If something **forbids** an event or course of action, it makes it impossible for it to happen. EG *Mexico City's altitude forbids such exertions.* V+O Formal

3 If you say **God forbid** or **Heaven forbid** that a particular thing should happen, you mean that you hope that it will not happen. EG *God forbid that anything should happen to my father.* PHRASE

forbidden /fə⁸bɪdə⁰n/. **1** If something is **forbidden**, you are not allowed to do it or have it. EG *It is forbidden to bathe in the sea here... Indoor football is forbidden.* ADJ PRED

2 A **forbidden** place is one that you are not allowed to visit or enter. EG *...forbidden ground.* ADJ CLASSIF

3 A **forbidden** subject is one that you are not allowed to mention. ADJ CLASSIF

forbidding /fəʳbɪdɪŋ/. Someone or something that is **forbidding** has a severe and unfriendly appearance. EG *...a bleak, forbidding stretch of grey water.* ADJ QUALIT

force /fɔːs/, **forces, forcing, forced. 1** If you **force** someone to do or to have something, you make them do it or have it, although they are very unwilling to. EG *They forced him to resign... She forced herself to kiss her mother's cheek... ...the campaign to force the closure of the factory... ...the missiles which they are forcing upon Britain.* V+O OR V-REFL : OFT+*to*-INF OR A

2 If a situation or event **forces** you to do something, it makes it necessary for you to do it. EG *Weekend gales forced him to change his plans... This forces us into specialization.* V+O+*to*-INF OR A

3 If you **force** something into a particular position, you use a lot of strength to make it move there. EG *I forced his head back.* V+O+A

4 If you **force** a lock, a door, or a safe, you break the lock in order to open it. V+O

5 If you **force** your **way** through or into a place, you have to push or break things that are in your way in order to get there. PHRASE

6 If something is done by **force**, strong and violent physical action is used in order to do it. EG *We have renounced the use of force to settle our disputes.* N UNCOUNT

7 Force is power or strength. EG *I hit him with all the force I could muster.* N UNCOUNT

8 Someone or something that is referred to as a **force** has a great effect or influence on a situation. EG *Britain is re-establishing itself as a powerful force in world affairs.* N COUNT : USU+SUPP

9 A **force** in physics is the pulling or pushing effect that something has on something else. EG *...magnetic forces.* N COUNT OR N UNCOUNT

10 If something happens **by force of** a particular quality or action, it happens because of the nature or intensity of that quality or action. EG *By sheer force of will, he fought the urge to go after them.* PHRASE

11 If you do something from **force of habit**, you do it because you have always done it in the past. PHRASE

12 A law or system that is **in force** exists or is being used. EG *...when the system comes into force.* PHRASE

13 A **force** is an organized group of soldiers or other armed people. EG *...the United States armed forces... ...a guerrilla force.* N COUNT : USU PLURAL

14 If you **join forces** with someone, you work together in order to achieve a common aim or purpose. PHRASE

forced /fɔːst/. **1** A **forced** action is one that you only do because you have to do it. EG *They promised to abolish forced labour... ...a forced landing.* ADJ CLASSIF : ATTRIB

2 Something that is **forced** is done with an effort rather than being genuine and spontaneous. EG *...a forced smile... The conversations had been stiff, forced, and uncomfortable.* ADJ QUALIT

forceful /fɔːsfʊl/. **1** Someone who is **forceful** expresses their opinions in a strong and confident way. EG *...a forceful and assertive man.* ADJ QUALIT
◊ **forcefully.** EG *Her views were forcefully expressed.* ◊ ADV

2 Something that is **forceful** causes you to think or feel something very strongly. EG *...a forceful reminder of the risks involved.* ◊ **forcefully.** EG *It forcefully struck the bishop that this was very unusual.* ADJ QUALIT, ◊ ADV

3 A **forceful** point or argument in a discussion is good and convincing. ADJ QUALIT

forceps /fɔːsɪᵊps/ are an instrument consisting of two long narrow arms. They are used by a doctor for holding things. EG *...a pair of forceps.* N PLURAL

forcible /fɔːsəbᵊl/. **1 Forcible** actions involve physical force or violence. EG *...the forcible imposition of military control.* ◊ **forcibly.** EG *Children were taken forcibly from their mothers.* ADJ CLASSIF : ATTRIB, ◊ ADV

2 A **forcible** reminder, example, or lesson is very powerful. EG *...a forcible reminder of the continuing strife there.* ◊ **forcibly.** EG *This was brought home to me forcibly by a personal experience.* ADJ QUALIT : ATTRIB, ◊ ADV

3 A **forcible** expression of an opinion or wish is strong and emphatic. EG *The survey made certain very forcible recommendations.* ◊ **forcibly.** EG *This point has been forcibly expressed by Tories.* ADJ QUALIT : ATTRIB, ◊ ADV

ford /fɔːd/, **fords.** A **ford** is a shallow place in a river or stream where you can cross safely on foot. N COUNT

fore /fɔː/. When something or someone comes **to the fore**, they suddenly become important or popular. EG *Andrew Young came to the fore during the 1960s.* PHRASE

forearm /fɔːrɑːm/, **forearms.** Your **forearms** are the parts of your arms between your elbows and your wrists. N COUNT

forebear /fɔːbeə/, **forebears.** Your **forebears** are your ancestors. EG *...the lands from which their forebears had been driven.* N COUNT : USU PLURAL Formal

foreboding /fɔːbəʊdɪŋ/, **forebodings. Foreboding** is a strong feeling that something terrible is going to happen. EG *Tim's absence filled her with foreboding... ...beset by dismal forebodings.* N UNCOUNT OR N COUNT

forecast /fɔːkɑːst/, **forecasts, forecasting, forecasted.** The forms **forecast** and **forecasted** are both used as the past tense and past participle of the verb.

1 A **forecast** is a prediction or statement of what is expected to happen in the future. EG *...forecasts of military involvement in British politics... ...the weather forecast.* N COUNT : USU+SUPP

2 If you **forecast** future events, you say what you think is going to happen. EG *It is almost impossible to forecast the future development of a very young child... Some warm weather had been forecast.* V+O

forecourt /fɔːkɔːt/, **forecourts.** The **forecourt** of a large building is an open area at the front of it. N COUNT

forefather /fɔːfɑːðə/, **forefathers.** Your **forefathers** are your ancestors, especially your male ancestors. N COUNT : USU PLURAL Formal

forefinger /fɔːfɪŋgə/, **forefingers.** Your **forefinger** is the finger next to your thumb. N COUNT

forefront /fɔːfrʌnt/. Someone or something that is in the **forefront** of an activity is advanced, active, or important. EG *This was to place the company in the forefront of computer manufacture.* N SING : *the*+N

forego /fɔːgəʊ/, **foregoes, foregoing** /fɔːgəʊɪŋ/, **forewent** /fɔːwent/, **foregone** /fɔːgɒn/; also spelled **forgo.** If you **forego** something, you give it up or do not insist on having it. EG *Lilian agreed to forego her holiday.* V+O Formal

foregoing /fɔːgəʊɪŋ/. You can refer to something that has just been said as the **foregoing**. EG *In the foregoing we have seen how people differ in their approach to problems.* ▸ used as an adjective. EG *...the foregoing analysis.* N SING : *the*+N Formal, ▸ ADJ CLASSIF ATTRIB

foregone /fɔːgɒn/. If you say that the result of something is **a foregone conclusion**, you mean that it is certain what the result will be. EG *The outcome was assumed to be a foregone conclusion.* PHRASE

foreground /fɔːgraʊnd/. The **foreground** of a picture is the part that seems nearest to you. N SING : *the*+N

forehand /fɔːhænd/, **forehands.** A **forehand** is a shot in a game such as tennis in which the palm of your hand faces the direction in which you are hitting the ball. N COUNT

forehead /fɒrɪd, fɔːhed/, **foreheads.** Your **forehead** is the flat area at the front of your head above your eyebrows and below where your hair grows. See picture at THE HUMAN BODY. EG *He wiped his forehead with the back of his hand... He kissed her forehead.* N COUNT

foreign /fɒrɪᵊn/. **1** Something that is **foreign** belongs to or relates to a country that is not your own. EG *...a policy of restricting foreign imports... ...children from foreign countries.* ADJ CLASSIF

2 A **foreign** minister is a government minister who deals with matters that involve other countries besides his own. EG *...the Belgian Foreign* ADJ CLASSIF : ATTRIB

What does the prefix 'fore-' mean in words like 'forerunner', 'foresight', and 'forewarn'?

Minister... ...the Foreign Secretary... ...the Foreign Office.

3 A **foreign** object or substance is one that has got into something else, usually by accident, and should not be in it. EG *...food containing foreign matter.* — ADJ CLASSIF: ATTRIB Formal

4 You can say that something is **foreign** to a person or thing when it is not typical of them. EG *...that strange gloomy mood that was so foreign to him.* — ADJ QUALIT: OFT+*to* Formal

foreigner /fɒrɪ^{1}nə/, **foreigners.** You refer to someone as a **foreigner** when they belong to a country that is not your own. EG *More than a million foreigners visit the USA every year.* — N COUNT

foreman /fɔːmə^{3}n/, **foremen.** A **foreman** is a person, especially a man, who is in charge of a group of workers. — N COUNT

foremost /fɔːməʊst/. **1** The **foremost** of a group of things is the most important or the best. EG *...India's foremost centre for hand-made shoes.* — ADJ CLASSIF

2 First and foremost means more than anything else. EG *Rugby is first and foremost a team game.* — ADV SEN

forename /fɔːneɪm/, **forenames.** Your **forename** is your first name. — N COUNT Formal

forensic /fərensɪk/. When a **forensic** analysis is done, objects are examined scientifically in order to discover information about a crime. EG *...the forensic department... ...the standard forensic tests for detecting the presence of blood.* — ADJ CLASSIF: ATTRIB

forerunner /fɔːrʌnə/, **forerunners.** The **forerunner** of someone or something is a similar thing or person that existed before them. EG *...the forerunners of the International Socialists.* — N COUNT: OFT+SUPP

foresee /fɔːsiː/, **foresees, foreseeing, foresaw** /fɔːsɔː/, **foreseen** /fɔːsiːn/. If you **foresee** something, you believe that it is going to happen. EG *Do you foresee any problems with the new system?... It was possible to foresee that the coming winter would be a hard one.* — V+O OR V+REPORT

foreseeable /fɔːsiːəbə^{0}l/. **1** When you talk about **the foreseeable future**, you are referring to the period of time in the future during which it is possible to predict what will happen. EG *Nobody is likely to find a cure in the foreseeable future.* — PHRASE

2 Something that is **foreseeable** can be expected to happen, and should not be a surprise. EG *...a perfectly foreseeable catastrophe.* — ADJ QUALIT

foreshadow /fɔːʃædəʊ/, **foreshadows, foreshadowing, foreshadowed.** If one thing **foreshadows** another, it suggests that the other thing will happen. EG *These later movements had been foreshadowed in much of the work of the late 1950s.* — V+O

foresight /fɔːsaɪt/ is the ability to see what is likely to happen in the future, which is shown in the action that someone takes. EG *He showed remarkable foresight... ...a lack of foresight.* — N UNCOUNT

forest /fɒrɪ^{2}st/, **forests.** A **forest** is a large area where trees grow close together. A forest is usually larger than a wood. EG *...a clearing in the forest.* — N COUNT OR N UNCOUNT

forestall /fɔːstɔːl/, **forestalls, forestalling, forestalled.** If you **forestall** someone, you realize what they were intending to do and prevent them from doing it. — V+O

forestry /fɒrɪstri^1/ is the science or skill of growing and taking care of trees in forests. — N UNCOUNT

foretaste /fɔːteɪst/. You say that something is a **foretaste** of something that is going to happen when it is similar to it and shows you what it will be like. EG *The episode was a foretaste of the bitter struggle that was to come.* — N SING+*of*

foretell /fɔːtel/, **foretells, foretelling, foretold** /fɔːtəʊld/. If you **foretell** something, you say correctly that it will happen in the future. EG *Who could ever foretell that Paul would turn traitor?* — V+O OR V+REPORT Literary

forethought /fɔːθɔːt/ is the practice of thinking carefully about what will be needed, or about what the consequences of something will be. EG *With a bit of forethought, life can be made a lot easier.* — N UNCOUNT

forever /fə^{8}revə/. The form **for ever** is also used, except in paragraph 4.

1 Something that will happen or continue **forever** will always happen or continue. EG *They thought that their empire would last forever.* — ADV

2 Something that has gone **forever** has disappeared completely and permanently. EG *This innocence is lost forever.* — ADV

3 People say that something takes **for ever** or lasts **for ever** when they want to emphasize that it takes or lasts a very long time. EG *The next minutes lasted for ever.* — ADV Informal

4 If you say that someone or something is **forever** doing a particular thing, you mean that they do it very often. EG *Babbage was forever spotting errors in their calculations.* — ADV+-ING Informal

forewarn /fɔːwɔːn/, **forewarns, forewarning, forewarned.** If you **forewarn** someone, you warn them that something is going to happen. EG *We were forewarned that the food would be unusual.* — V+O: OFT+REPORT, ONLY *that*

foreword /fɔːwɜːd/, **forewords.** The **foreword** to a book is an introduction either by the author or by someone else. — N COUNT

forfeit /fɔːfɪt/, **forfeits, forfeiting, forfeited.** If you **forfeit** something, you have to give it up because you have broken a rule or done something wrong. EG *He has forfeited the right to be the leader of this nation.* — V+O

forgave /fɔːgeɪv/ is the past tense of **forgive.**

forge /fɔːdʒ/, **forges, forging, forged. 1** If someone **forges** banknotes, documents, or paintings, they copy them or make false ones in order to deceive people. EG *I learnt how to forge someone else's signature.* — V+O

2 If you **forge** an alliance or relationship, you succeed in creating it. EG *They forged links with the French Communist Party.* — V+O

3 A **forge** is a place where metal things such as horseshoes are made. — N COUNT

forge ahead. If you **forge ahead** with something, you make a lot of progress. EG *They forged ahead, leaving countries like Britain behind.* — PHRASAL VB: V+ADV

forger /fɔːdʒə/, **forgers.** A **forger** is someone who forges things such as banknotes, documents, or paintings. — N COUNT

forgery /fɔːdʒə^{0}ri^1/, **forgeries. 1 Forgery** is the crime of forging things such as banknotes, documents, or paintings. EG *...passport forgery.* — N UNCOUNT

2 You can refer to a forged banknote, document, or painting as a **forgery**. — N COUNT

forget /fəget/, **forgets, forgetting, forgot** /fəgɒt/, **forgotten** /fəgɒtə^{0}n/. **1** If you **forget** something or **forget** how to do something, you cannot think of it or think how to do it, although you knew it or knew how to do it in the past. EG *I never forget a face... She had forgotten how to ride a bicycle.* — V+O OR V+REPORT: NO CONT

◊ **forgotten.** EG *...a forgotten event in her past.* — ◊ ADJ CLASSIF

2 If you **forget** something or **forget** to do something, you do not remember to consider it or do it. EG *I meant to see her on Friday, but I forgot all about it... I forgot to mention that John is a musician.* — V+O; ALSO V: OFT+REPORT OR *to*-INF

3 If you **forget** something that you had intended to bring, you do not bring it because you did not think about it at the right time. EG *Sorry to disturb you – I forgot my key.* — V+O

4 You can also say that someone **forgets** something or someone when they deliberately do not think about them any more. EG *If you want my advice I think you ought to forget her.* — V+O

5 If you **forget** yourself, you behave in an uncontrolled or unacceptable way, which is not the way in which you usually behave. EG *'Oh darling!' cried Judy, forgetting herself.* — V-REFL Formal

forgetful /fəgetfʊl/. **1** Someone who is **forgetful** often forgets things. EG *Be sure to remind your uncle – you know how forgetful he is.* — ADJ QUALIT

◊ **forgetfulness.** EG *...his growing forgetfulness.* — ◊ N UNCOUNT

2 Someone who is **forgetful** of a particular thing does not think about it or notice it. EG *Fiona, forgetful of the time, was still working away in the library.* ADJ PRED+*of*

forgettable /fəgetəbə^{0}l/. Something that is **forgettable** is not unusual or special in any way. EG *...forgettable men working at obscure jobs.* ADJ QUALIT

forgivable /fəgɪvəbə^{0}l/. If you say that something is **forgivable**, you mean that you can understand it and can forgive it. EG *Her lack of sympathy was perhaps forgivable.* ADJ CLASSIF

forgive /fəgɪv/, **forgives, forgiving, forgave** /fɔ:geɪv/, **forgiven. 1** If you **forgive** someone who has done something wrong, you stop being angry with them. EG *I'll never forgive you for what you did... I forgave him everything.* V+O : OFT+*for*, ALSO V+O+O

2 You use **forgive** in polite expressions like 'forgive me' and 'forgive the language' to apologize for saying something that might seem rude, silly, or too complicated. EG *Forgive my ignorance, but who is Jane Fonda?* PHRASE

3 If you say that someone could **be forgiven** for doing something, you mean that such behaviour would be reasonable in the circumstances. EG *We could be forgiven for thinking that we were still in London.* V-PASS : MODAL+V+*for*

forgiveness /fəgɪvnɪ^{2}s/. If you ask someone for their **forgiveness**, you are asking them to forgive you for something wrong that you have done. N UNCOUNT

forgiving /fəgɪvɪŋ/. Someone who is **forgiving** is willing to forgive people. EG *...a forgiving father.* ADJ QUALIT

forgo /fɔ:gəʊ/. See **forego**.

forgot /fəgɒt/ is the past tense of **forget.**

forgotten /fəgɒtə^{0}n/ is the past participle of **forget.**

fork

fork /fɔ:k/, **forks, forking, forked. 1** A **fork** is **1.1** a tool that you eat food with. It consists of three or four prongs on the end of a handle. **1.2** a large tool that you dig your garden with. It consists of three or four long prongs attached to a long handle. See picture at TOOLS. N COUNT

2 A **fork** in a road, path, or river is the point at which it divides into two parts in the shape of a 'Y'. N COUNT
▸ used as a verb. EG *...where the road forks.* ▸ V

fork out. If you **fork out** for something, you pay for it. EG *...the fortune I had already had to fork out on her education.* PHRASAL VB : V+ADV OR V+O+ADV Informal

forked /fɔ:kt/. Something that is **forked** divides into two parts in the shape of a 'Y'. EG *...an adder's forked tongue.* ADJ CLASSIF

forlorn /fəlɔ:n/. **1** If you are **forlorn**, you are lonely and unhappy. EG *The child looked very forlorn... ...a forlorn cry.* ADJ QUALIT ◇ **forlornly.** EG *He was standing forlornly by the ticket office.* ◇ ADV

2 A **forlorn** place looks deserted and not cared for. EG *...this grimy, forlorn industrial town.* ADJ QUALIT

3 A **forlorn** attempt or hope has no chance of success. EG *...the forlorn hope of achieving full employment.* ADJ CLASSIF : ATTRIB

form /fɔ:m/, **forms, forming, formed. 1** A particular **form** of something is a type or kind of it. EG *He begged for any form of transport that would take him to the ferry... I never touch alcohol in any form... ...money, in the form of coins, notes, or cheques... The broadcast took the form of an interview.* N COUNT+SUPP

2 When people or things **form** a particular shape, they move or are arranged so that this shape is made. EG *They formed a ring... Long queues had formed... The men formed themselves into a line.* V-ERG OR V-REFL : OFT+

3 The **form** of something is its shape. EG *The middle finger was touching the end of the thumb in the form of a letter O.* N COUNT

4 You can refer to someone or something that you see as a **form**. EG *She gazed with deep affection at his slumbering form.* N COUNT Literary

5 If you say that a particular thing **forms** something with a particular structure or function, you mean that it has this structure or function. EG *The black leather chair folds back to form a couch... ...red rocks forming a kind of cave.* V+C

6 The things or people that **form** a particular thing are the things or people that it consists of. EG *The contents of the house will form the basis of a major exhibition.* V+C

7 If you **form** an organization, group, or company, you start it. EG *The League was formed in 1959.* V+O

8 When something natural **forms** or **is formed**, it begins to exist. EG *The islands are volcanic and were formed comparatively recently.* V-ERG

9 If you **form** an idea, relationship, or habit, you begin to have it. EG *He formed the habit of taking long solitary walks.* V+O

10 A **form** is a piece of paper with questions on it. You write the answers on the same piece of paper. EG *Fill in this form... ...application forms.* N COUNT

11 In a school, a **form** is a class, or all the classes containing children of a similar age. EG *...the fifth form.* N COUNT

12 Someone who is **on form** is performing their usual activity very well. Someone who is **off form** is not performing as well as they usually do. PHRASE

13 If someone's behaviour is **true to form**, it is typical of them. EG *Watson, true to form, made an instant decision.* PHRASE

formal /fɔ:mə^{0}l/. **1 Formal** speech or behaviour is very correct and serious rather than relaxed and friendly, and is used especially in official situations. In this dictionary, language of this kind is indicated by the use of the word 'Formal' in the Extra Column. EG *The letter was stiff and formal.* ADJ QUALIT
◇ **formally.** EG *Everyone was formally lined up to meet the king.* ◇ ADV ◇ **formality** /fə^{8}mælɪ^{1}ti^{1}/. EG *The elders conversed with strict formality.* ◇ N UNCOUNT

2 A **formal** statement or action is an official one. EG *No formal declaration of war had been made.* ADJ CLASSIF : ATTRIB
◇ **formally.** EG *He had already formally announced his candidacy.* ◇ ADV

3 **Formal** occasions are ones at which people wear smart clothes and behave correctly rather than in a casual way. EG *...a formal dinner at Buckingham Palace... ...a formal dance.* ADJ QUALIT

4 **Formal** clothes are very smart clothes that are suitable for formal occasions. ◇ **formally.** EG *He dressed rather formally.* ADJ QUALIT ◇ ADV

5 A **formal** garden or room is arranged in a very neat, regular way. EG *...formal flowerbeds.* ADJ CLASSIF

6 **Formal** education or training is given officially, usually in a school or college. EG *Faraday had no formal education... ...formal qualifications.* ADJ CLASSIF : ATTRIB

formality /fə^{8}:mælɪti^{1}/, **formalities. 1 Formalities** are formal actions that are carried out on particular occasions. EG *The pre-funeral formalities had to be attended to.* N COUNT

2 If you say that an action or procedure is just a **formality**, you mean that it must be done, although it will not have any effect on what is being N COUNT

Has a forlorn place been forsaken?

decided or arranged. EG *He knew the interview was just a formality.*

3 See also **formal**.

formalize /fɔːməlaɪz/, **formalizes, formalizing, formalized;** also spelled **formalise.** If you **formalize** a plan, idea, or arrangement, you make it clear and official. EG *Their marriage vows will be formalized.* V+O

format /fɔːmæt/, **formats.** The **format** of something is the way in which it is arranged and presented. EG *They're producing material in all kinds of different formats.* N COUNT

formation /fɔ⁸meɪʃə⁰n/, **formations. 1** The **formation** of something is its start or creation. EG *He had played a major role in the formation of the United Nations... ...the physical process of rock formation... ...the formation of new ideas.* N UNCOUNT +SUPP

2 If things are in a particular **formation**, they are arranged in a particular pattern. EG *...aircraft flying in formation.* N COUNT OR N UNCOUNT

3 A rock **formation** or a cloud **formation** is rock or clouds of a particular shape. N COUNT

formative /fɔːmətɪv/. A **formative** period in your life has an important and lasting influence on your character and attitudes. EG *...where I spent my formative years.* ADJ CLASSIF : ATTRIB

former /fɔːmə/. **1 Former** is used to describe **1.1** someone who used to have a particular job or position, but no longer has it. EG *...former President Theodore Roosevelt.* **1.2** something which someone used to have or which used to be a particular thing. EG *...their former home... The college was in fact a former mansion.* **1.3** a situation or period of time which came before the present one. EG *...a selection of items published in former years.* ADJ CLASSIF : ATTRIB

2 When two people or things have just been mentioned, you can refer to the one that was mentioned first as the **former**. EG *The former believe in a strong centralized government.* ▸ used as an adjective. EG *Lack of space forbids the former alternative.* N SING OR N PLURAL : the+N ▸ ADJ CLASSIF : the+ADJ+N

formerly /fɔːməli¹/. If something happened or was true **formerly**, it happened or was true in the past. EG *Some of my salesmen formerly worked for this company.* ADV

formidable /fɔːmɪdəbə⁰l, fɔ⁸mɪdəbə⁰l/. Something that is **formidable** is **1** rather frightening because it is difficult to deal with or overcome. EG *He had earned the reputation of being a formidable opponent.* **2** very impressive because it is so good or great. EG *...the formidable army of brains that are at the Prime Minister's disposal.* ◊ **formidably.** EG *The jeeps came with army drivers, each formidably armed.* ADJ QUALIT ◊ ADV

formless /fɔːmlɪ²s/. Something that is **formless** does not have a clear shape or structure. EG *...a group of formless shapes... ...formless chaos.* ADJ CLASSIF Formal

formula /fɔːmjə⁴lə/, **formulae** /fɔːmjə⁴liː/ or **formulas.** A **formula** is **1** a group of letters, numbers, or other symbols which represents a scientific or mathematical rule. EG *He knew the formula for converting kilometres into miles.* **2** a list of substances which tells you what amounts to mix together in order to make another substance. **3** a plan that is devised as a way of dealing with a problem. EG *...a peace formula.* N COUNT

formulate /fɔːmjə⁴leɪt/, **formulates, formulating, formulated. 1** If you **formulate** a plan or proposal, you invent it, thinking about the details carefully. EG *We had formulated our own strategy.* ◊ **formulation** /fɔːmjə⁴leɪʃə⁰n/, **formulations.** EG *...the formulation of policy.* V+O ◊ N UNCOUNT OR N COUNT

2 If you **formulate** a thought or opinion, you express it in words. V+O

forsake /fə⁸seɪk/, **forsakes, forsaking, forsook** /fə⁸sʊk/, **forsaken. 1** If you **forsake** someone, you stop helping them or stop looking after them. EG *Their leaders have forsaken them.* V+O Literary

2 If you **forsake** something, you stop doing it or having it. EG *...if you forsake religion.* V+O Literary

forsaken /fə⁸seɪkə⁰n/. A **forsaken** place is no longer lived in or no longer looked after. EG *...a dusty, forsaken prairie village... ...a forsaken garden.* ADJ CLASSIF Literary

fort /fɔːt/, **forts. 1** A **fort** is a strong building that is used as a military base. N COUNT

2 If you **hold the fort** for someone, you look after things for them while they are somewhere else. PHRASE Informal

forte /fɔːteɪ/, **fortes.** You can say that an activity is your **forte** if you are very good at it. EG *Cooking is hardly my forte.* N COUNT+SUPP

forth /fɔːθ/. **1** When someone goes **forth** from a place, they leave it. EG *The goats came bounding forth from their pens.* ADV AFTER VB Formal

2 When something is brought **forth**, it is brought out into a place where you can see it. EG *He reached into his briefcase and brought forth a file.* ADV AFTER VB Formal

3 back and forth: see **back**. • **and so forth**: see **so**.

forthcoming /fɔːθkʌmɪŋ/. **1** A **forthcoming** event is planned to happen soon. EG *...the forthcoming presidential election.* ADJ CLASSIF : ATTRIB Formal

2 When something such as help or information is **forthcoming**, it is provided or is made available. EG *No evidence was forthcoming.* ADJ PRED Formal

3 You say that a person is **forthcoming** when they willingly give you information. EG *He was not forthcoming on the way in which he had risen to power.* ADJ PRED Formal

forthright /fɔːθraɪt/. Someone who is **forthright** shows clearly and strongly what they think and feel. EG *...his forthright opposition to the war.* ADJ QUALIT

forthwith /fɔːθwɪθ, -wɪð/ means immediately. EG *He would take up his new duties forthwith.* ADV Formal

fortieth /fɔːtɪɪ²θ/, **fortieths.** The **fortieth** item in a series is the one that you count as number forty: see the entry headed NUMBER. EG *...the fortieth president of the United States.* ORDINAL

fortification /fɔːtɪfɪkeɪʃə⁰n/, **fortifications. 1 Fortifications** are buildings, walls, or ditches that are built to protect a place against attack. N COUNT : USU PLURAL

2 The **fortification** of a place is the act of fortifying it. EG *...the fortification of Florence.* N UNCOUNT Formal

fortify /fɔːtɪfaɪ/, **fortifies, fortifying, fortified. 1** If people **fortify** a place, they make it better able to resist an attack, often by building a wall or ditch round it. EG *...the tiny fortified town.* V+O

2 Things, such as food or drinks, that **fortify** you make you feel stronger and more full of energy. V+O

fortitude /fɔːtɪtjuːd/. If someone shows **fortitude** when in pain or in danger, they do not complain and remain brave and calm. EG *Cal bore his pain with commendable fortitude.* N UNCOUNT Formal

fortnight /fɔːtnaɪt/, **fortnights.** A **fortnight** is a period of two weeks. EG *I went to Rothesay for a fortnight.* N COUNT : USU SING

fortnightly /fɔːtnaɪtli¹/. A **fortnightly** event or magazine happens or appears once a fortnight. EG *...a fortnightly newspaper... The therapy group meets fortnightly.* ADJ CLASSIF : ATTRIB OR ADV AFTER VB

fortress /fɔːtrɪ²s/, **fortresses.** A **fortress** is a castle or other large strong building which is difficult for enemies to enter. N COUNT

fortuitous /fə⁸tjuːɪtəs/. You describe an event as **fortuitous** when it happens by chance and helps someone. EG *...a fortuitous discovery.* ADJ QUALIT Formal

fortunate /fɔːtʃə⁴nə¹t/. **1** Someone who is **fortunate** is lucky. EG *...those who are fortunate enough to get jobs.* ADJ QUALIT

2 You say that an event is **fortunate** when it is lucky for someone. EG *It was fortunate for Mr Fox that he decided to wait.* ◊ **fortunately** /fɔːtʃə⁴nətli¹/. EG *Fortunately she didn't mind.* ADJ QUALIT ◊ ADV SEN

fortune /fɔːtʃə⁴n/, **fortunes. 1 Fortune** or good **fortune** is good luck. Ill **fortune** is bad luck. EG *He has since had the good fortune to be promoted.* N UNCOUNT

2 If you talk about someone's **fortunes**, you are N PLURAL +POSS referring to the extent to which they are doing well or being successful. EG *In the following years, Victor's fortunes improved considerably.*

3 When someone **tells** your **fortune**, they look at something such as playing cards and tell you what will happen to you in the future. PHRASE

4 Someone who has a **fortune** has a very large amount of money. EG *His father left him an immense fortune.* N COUNT

5 You can refer to any large sum of money as a **fortune**. EG *She earns a fortune.* N SING : *a*+N Informal

fortune-teller, fortune-tellers. A **fortune-teller** is someone who tells people's fortunes, often in exchange for money. N COUNT

forty /fɔ:ti¹/, **forties. Forty** is the number 40: see the entry headed NUMBER. EG *We have a nursery school for forty children.* NUMBER

forum /fɔ:rəm/, **forums.** A **forum** is a place or event in which people exchange ideas and discuss things. EG *...Parliament's role as a forum for debate.* N COUNT

forward /fɔ:wəd/, **forwards, forwarding, forwarded. 1** If someone moves or faces **forward** or **forwards**, they move or face in a direction that is in front of them. EG *Suddenly she leaned forward... ...his forward movement.* ● **backwards and forwards**: see **backwards.** ADV AFTER VB OR ADJ CLASSIF : ATTRIB

2 Forward or **forwards** is also used to indicate that something progresses or becomes more modern. EG *Obviously it's a great step forward for you... ...moving society forward into a better world.* ADJ AFTER N, OR ADV

3 If you look **forward** in time, you look into the future. EG *When I was your age I could only look forward... ...forward planning.* ● to **look forward to** something: see **look.** ADV AFTER VB OR ADJ CLASSIF : ATTRIB

4 If you put a clock or watch **forward**, you alter it so that it shows a later time. ADV AFTER VB

5 If you **forward** a letter that has been sent to someone who has moved, you send it to them at the place where they are now living. V+O

forwarding address, forwarding addresses. A **forwarding address** is an address that you give to someone when you go and live somewhere else so that they can send your mail on to you. EG *She had gone to Spain, leaving no forwarding address.* N COUNT

fossil /fɒsə⁰l/, **fossils.** A **fossil** is the hardened remains of a prehistoric animal or plant, or a print that it leaves in rock. N COUNT

fossil fuel, fossil fuels. Fossil fuels are fuels such as coal, oil, and peat that are formed from the decayed remains of plants and animals. N MASS

fossilize /fɒsılaız/, **fossilizes, fossilizing, fossilized;** also spelled **fossilise.** When the remains of an animal or plant **fossilize** or **are fossilized**, they become hard, or leave a print, and form a fossil. EG *...fossilised bones.* V-ERG : USU PASS

foster /fɒstə/, **fosters, fostering, fostered. 1 Foster** parents are people who officially take someone else's child into their family for a period of time, without becoming the child's legal parents. The child is referred to as their **foster** child. ADJ CLASSIF : ATTRIB
▸ used as a verb. EG *When they are fostered, boys have more behaviour problems than girls.* ▸ V+O OR V

2 If you **foster** a feeling, an activity, or an idea, you help it to develop. EG *The local council has a policy of fostering music, drama, and crafts.* V+O

fought /fɔ:t/ is the past tense of **fight.**

foul /faul/, **fouler, foulest; fouls, fouling, fouled.**
1 You say that something is **foul** when it is dirty or smells unpleasant. EG *The water in the pools became tepid and foul.* ADJ QUALIT

2 Foul language contains swear words or rude words. ADJ QUALIT

3 If someone has a **foul** temper, they become angry or violent suddenly and easily. ADJ QUALIT

4 If you **fall foul of** someone or something, you accidentally do something which gets you into trouble with them. EG *He was found drowned in a river after falling foul of local poachers.* PHRASE

5 If you **foul** something, you make it dirty. EG *The deck would soon be fouled with blood.* V+O

6 In a game or sport, a **foul** is an action that is against the rules. EG *The team's record of fouls was among the worst.* N COUNT

foul up. If you **foul up** something such as a plan, you spoil it by doing something wrong or stupid. EG *So many good projects have been fouled up by elementary mistakes.* PHRASAL VB : V+O+ADV Informal

foul play is criminal violence or activity that results in a person's death. EG *There was no evidence of foul play.* N UNCOUNT

found /faund/, **founds, founding, founded. 1 Found** is the past tense and past participle of **find.**

2 If someone **founds** an institution or organization, they create it, often by providing the necessary money. EG *The Constituency Labour Party was founded in 1918 by Walter Ayles and others.* V+O
◊ **founding.** EG *He opposed the founding of the National Gallery.* ◊ N SING : *the*+N+*of*

3 If someone **founds** a town, important building, or other place, they cause it to be built. EG *The theatre was founded in 1720.* V+O

4 If something **is founded** on a particular thing, it is based on it. EG *...a political system founded on force.* ● See also **well-founded.** V+O+*on/upon* : USU PASS

foundation /faundeıʃə⁰n/, **foundations. 1** The **foundation** of something such as a belief or way of life is the basic idea, attitude, or experience on which it is built. EG *Respect for the law is the foundation of civilised living.* N COUNT+SUPP

2 The **foundations** of a building or other structure are the layers of bricks or concrete below the ground that it is built on. N PLURAL

3 When a new institution or organization is created, you can refer to this event as the **foundation** of the institution or organization. EG *...since the foundation of the university.* N SING : *the*+N+*of*

4 A **foundation** is an organization which provides money for a special purpose such as research or a charity. EG *...the National Foundation for Educational Research.* N COUNT

5 If you say that a story, idea, or argument has no **foundation**, you mean that there are no facts to support it and prove that it is true. EG *The suggestion is absurd and without foundation.* N UNCOUNT : USU WITH BROAD NEG

founder /faundə/, **founders, foundering, foundered. 1** The **founder** of an institution, organization, or building is the person who created it or caused it to be built. EG *...Thomas Kemp, the founder of Kemp Town.* N COUNT : USU+POSS

2 If something **founders**, it fails. EG *Without their assistance the arrangement would have foundered pretty quickly.* V

3 If a ship **founders**, it fills with water and sinks. V : USU+A

founder member, founder members. A **founder member** of a club, group, or organization is one of the original members. N COUNT

foundry /faundri¹/, **foundries.** A **foundry** is a place where metal or glass is melted and formed into particular shapes. N COUNT

fount /faunt/. If you describe a person or thing as the **fount** of something, you mean that they are the best source or supply of it. EG *...the Encyclopaedia Britannica, the fount of all knowledge.* N SING+*of* Literary

fountain /fauntın/, **fountains.** A **fountain** is an ornamental feature in a pool which consists of a spray or jet of water that is forced up into the air by a pump. N COUNT

fountain pen, fountain pens. A **fountain pen** is a pen that has a container inside which you fill with ink. N COUNT

four /fɔ:/, **fours. 1 Four** is the number 4: see the entry headed NUMBER. EG *His mother died when he was four... ...a four-mile walk.* NUMBER

Might you get a fracture in a fracas?

2 If you are **on all fours**, you are crawling or leaning on your hands and knees. EG *Claud slipped through the hedge on all fours.* PHRASE

four-letter word, four-letter words. Four-letter words are short words that people consider to be rude or offensive, usually because they refer to sex or other bodily functions. N COUNT

foursome /fɔːsəm/, **foursomes.** A **foursome** is a group of four people. EG *We functioned well as a foursome.* N COUNT

fourteen /fɔːtiːn/, **fourteens. Fourteen** is the number 14: see the entry headed NUMBER. EG *He was the eldest of a family of fourteen children.* NUMBER

fourteenth /fɔːtiːnθ/, **fourteenths.** The **fourteenth** item in a series is the one that you count as number fourteen: see the entry headed NUMBER. EG *...their son's fourteenth birthday.* ORDINAL

fourth /fɔːθ/, **fourths. 1** The **fourth** item in a series is the one that you count as number four: see the entry headed NUMBER. EG *My mother died just before my fourth birthday.* ORDINAL

2 A **fourth** is one of four equal parts of something. EG *They conceded him three-fourths or more of the spending cuts he sought.* N COUNT: USU+*of*

fowl /faʊl/, **fowls. Fowl** can also be used as the plural form. N COUNT OR N UNCOUNT
A **fowl** is a bird, especially one that can be eaten as food.

fox /fɒks/, **foxes, foxing, foxed. 1** A **fox** is a wild animal which looks like a dog and has reddish-brown fur. N COUNT

2 If something **foxes** you, you cannot understand it or solve it. EG *We were foxed by the calculations... Ah, now you've foxed me.* V+O Informal

fox-hunting is a sport in which people riding horses chase foxes across the countryside. N UNCOUNT

foyer /fɔɪeɪ, fɔɪə/, **foyers.** The **foyer** of a theatre, cinema, or hotel is the large area just inside the main doors where people meet or wait. N COUNT

fracas /frækɑː/. A **fracas** is a rough, noisy quarrel or fight. EG *They got involved in another fracas.* N SING Formal

fraction /frækʃəⁿn/, **fractions. 1** You can refer to a small amount or proportion of something as a **fraction** of it. EG *For a fraction of a second, I hesitated... The door opened a fraction.* N PART

2 In arithmetic, a **fraction** is an exact division of a number. For example, ½ and ⅓ are fractions of 1. N COUNT

fractionally /frækʃəⁿnəli¹, -ʃənəⁿli¹/. **Fractionally** means very slightly. EG *They're only fractionally different.* ADV

fracture /fræktʃə/, **fractures, fracturing, fractured. 1** A **fracture** is a crack or break in something, especially a bone. EG *...a fracture of the left shoulder blade.* N COUNT

2 If something such as a bone **fractures** or **is fractured**, it breaks. EG *...a fractured ankle.* V-ERG

fragile /frædʒaɪl/. **Fragile** things are easily spoilt, harmed, or broken. EG *...constructions built of fragile materials... ...extremely fragile economies.* ◇ **fragility** /frəᶟdʒɪlɪ¹ti¹/. EG *...the fragility of their communication links.* ADJ QUALIT ◇ N UNCOUNT

fragment, fragments, fragmenting, fragmented; pronounced /frægməᶟnt/ when it is a noun and /frægment/ when it is a verb.
1 A **fragment** of something is a small piece or part of it. EG *...a small fragment of bone... This was only a fragment out of a long conversation with John.* N COUNT

2 If something **fragments** or **is fragmented**, it breaks or separates into small pieces. EG *Farms are constantly being fragmented into smaller holdings.* V-ERG
◇ **fragmentation** /frægmenteɪʃəⁿn/. EG *This led to its fragmentation into eight independent parties.* ◇ N UNCOUNT Formal

fragmentary /frægməᶟntəⁿri¹/. Something that is **fragmentary** is made up of small or unconnected pieces. EG *...the fragmentary evidence for this story.* ADJ QUALIT

fragmented /frægmentɪd/. Something that is **fragmented** consists of a lot of different parts which seem unconnected with each other. EG *It's a book that is very fragmented in its structure.* ADJ QUALIT

fragrance /freɪgrəns/, **fragrances.** You can refer to a sweet or pleasant smell as a **fragrance**. EG *...a deep, musky fragrance.* N COUNT OR N UNCOUNT

fragrant /freɪgrənt/. Something that is **fragrant** has a sweet or pleasant smell. EG *...fragrant flowers.* ADJ QUALIT

frail /freɪl/, **frailer, frailest. 1** Someone who is **frail** is not strong or healthy. EG *...a frail old man.* ADJ QUALIT

2 Something that is **frail** is easily broken or damaged. EG *...a frail structure.* ADJ QUALIT

frailty /freɪlti¹/, **frailties. 1** If you talk about the **frailties** or **frailty** of people, you are referring to their weaknesses. EG *...our vanities and frailties.* N PLURAL OR N UNCOUNT

2 **Frailty** is also the condition of being weak in health. EG *...the advanced age and frailty of some of the inhabitants.* N UNCOUNT

frame /freɪm/, **frames, framing, framed. 1** A **frame** is **1.1** a hollow structure inside which you can fit something such as a window, door, or picture. EG *...gold-painted picture frames.* **1.2** an arrangement of bars that give an object its shape and strength. EG *...a bunk made of canvas laced to a steel frame.* N COUNT

2 The **frames** of a pair of glasses are the wire or plastic part which holds the lenses in place. EG *...sunglasses with black frames.* N PLURAL

3 Your **frame** is your body. EG *His big frame was gaunt and weak.* N COUNT Literary

4 If you **frame** a picture or photograph, you put it in a frame. EG *Are you having your picture professionally framed?* ◇ **framed.** EG *...a framed photograph of her mother.* V+O: USU PASS ◇ ADJ CLASSIF

5 If something **is framed** by a particular thing, it is surrounded by that thing, and is noticeable or attractive as a result. EG *She stood framed in the doorway of the dining-room.* V+O: USU PASS Written

6 If you **frame** something in a particular kind of language, you express it in that way. EG *Laws are invariably framed in tortuous jargon.* V+O+A

7 If you **are framed** by someone, they make it seem that you have committed a crime, although you haven't. EG *I was framed by the authorities.* V+O Informal

frame of mind. Your **frame of mind** is the mood that you are in at a particular time. EG *I'm not in the right frame of mind for riddles, Tana.* N SING

framework /freɪmwɜːk/, **frameworks. 1** A **framework** is a structure that forms a support or frame for something. EG *There are nine large panels set in a richly carved framework.* N COUNT

2 A **framework** is also a set of rules, ideas, or beliefs which you use in order to decide what to do. EG *They were able to absorb these changes within the framework of traditional institutions and ideas.* N COUNT+SUPP

franchise /fræntʃaɪz/, **franchises. 1** The **franchise** is the right to vote in an election, especially one in which people elect a parliament. EG *...a policy of universal franchise.* N SING

2 A **franchise** is an authority that is given by a company to someone, allowing them to sell its goods or services. EG *...a farm equipment franchise.* N COUNT

frank /fræŋk/, **franker, frankest.** If someone is **frank**, they state things in an open and honest way. EG *John was perfectly frank with him... ...a frank discussion.* ◇ **frankness.** EG *He seemed to be speaking with complete frankness.* ADJ QUALIT ◇ N UNCOUNT

frankly /fræŋkli¹/. **1** You use **frankly** when boldly stating a feeling or opinion. EG *Frankly, this has all come as a bit of a shock.* ADV SEN

2 If you say or do something **frankly**, you say or do it in an open and honest way. EG *He asked me to tell him frankly what I wished to do.* ADV

frantic /fræntɪk/. **1** If you are **frantic**, you are behaving in a wild and desperate way because you are frightened or worried. EG *We were frantic with worry.* ◇ **frantically.** EG *...frantically searching for David.* ADJ QUALIT ◇ ADV

2 When there is **frantic** activity, things are being done hurriedly and in a rather disorganized way. EG ADJ QUALIT

...a frantic week of high-level discussions.
◊ **frantically.** EG *They worked frantically throughout the day.* ◊ ADV

fraternal /frə[3]tɜːnə[0]l/ means having strong links of friendship with another group of people. EG *Fraternal greetings were received from the Communist Party of the Soviet Union.* ADJ CLASSIF Formal

fraternity /frə[3]tɜːnɪti[1]/, **fraternities. 1 Fraternity** refers to feelings of friendship between groups of people. N UNCOUNT Formal

2 You can refer to a group of people who have the same profession or interests as a particular **fraternity**. EG *...the banking fraternity.* N COUNT: OFT+SUPP Formal

fraternize /frætənaɪz/, **fraternizes, fraternizing, fraternized;** also spelled **fraternise.** If you **fraternize** with someone, you associate with them in a friendly way. EG *We fraternized with their sons and grandsons.* V OR V+*with*: RECIP

fraud /frɔːd/, **frauds. 1 Fraud** is the crime of gaining money by deceit or trickery. EG *His closest adviser is under indictment for fraud.* N UNCOUNT

2 A **fraud** is something that deceives people in a way that is illegal or immoral. N COUNT

3 Someone who is a **fraud** is not the person they pretend to be or does not have the abilities or status they pretend to have. N COUNT

fraudulent /frɔːdjə[4]lənt/. Something that is **fraudulent** is deliberately deceitful, dishonest, or untrue. EG *The promise Mrs Haze had made was a fraudulent one.* ADJ CLASSIF

fraught /frɔːt/. **1** If you say that something is **fraught** with problems or difficulties, you mean that it is full of them. EG *Any further moves would be fraught with danger.* ADJ PRED +*with*

2 Someone who is **fraught** is very worried or anxious. EG *Everyone's rather tense and fraught tonight.* ADJ QUALIT

fray /freɪ/, **frays, fraying, frayed. 1** If something such as cloth or rope **frays**, its threads or strands become worn and it is likely to tear or break. EG *His shirts were frayed.* V-ERG

2 If your nerves **fray** or your temper **frays**, you feel irritable and nervous because of mental strain and anxiety. V-ERG

3 You can refer to an exciting activity or argument that you are involved in as the **fray**. EG *I returned to the fray with renewed vigour.* N SING: *the*+N

freak /friːk/, **freaks, freaking, freaked. 1** People call someone a **freak 1.1** when their behaviour or attitudes are very unusual. EG *A woman is considered a freak if she puts her career first.* **1.2** when they are physically abnormal in some way. EG *...hair-raising freaks, including a two-headed Indian.* N COUNT

2 You can also describe someone as a **freak** when they are very enthusiastic about something. EG *He was a real cleanliness freak.* N COUNT+SUPP Informal

3 A **freak** event or action is very unusual and very unlikely to happen. EG *My mother died in a freak accident, struck by lightning at a picnic.* N MOD

freakish /friːkɪʃ/. You describe something as **freakish** when it is very unusual. EG *...an isolated, freakish event... ...freakish-looking people.* ADJ QUALIT

freckled /frɛkə[0]ld/. Someone who is **freckled** has freckles. EG *...her freckled face.* ADJ CLASSIF

freckles /frɛkə[0]lz/ are small, light brown spots on someone's skin, especially on their face. EG *She had red hair and freckles.* N PLURAL

free /friː/, **freer** /friːə/, **freest** /friːɪ[2]st/; **frees, freeing, freed. 1** Someone or something that is **free** is not restricted, controlled, or limited. EG *Within the EEC there is free movement of labour... We are free to regard such a view as mistaken... ...a free press.* ADJ QUALIT

2 Someone who is **free** is no longer a prisoner or a slave. EG *I wish to return to London, this time as a free man... One prisoner in seven had been set free.* ADJ CLASSIF OR ADV AFTER VB

3 If you **free** a prisoner or a slave, you let them go or release them from prison. EG *Her sister was also arrested but was freed after three weeks.* V+O

4 If you **free** someone of something that is unpleasant or restricting, you remove it from them. EG *...the attempt to free France of the Dictator.* V+O OR V-REFL: OFT+A

5 A person or thing that is **free** of something unpleasant does not have it or is not affected by it. EG *The area will be free of pollution by the year 2000.* ADJ PRED +*of/from*

6 If you **free** someone or something, you cause them to become available for a task or purpose. EG *We could cut defence expenditure, freeing vital resources for more useful purposes.* V+O

7 If you have a **free** period of time or are **free** at a particular time, you are not busy then. EG *They don't have much free time... Are you free for lunch?* ADJ CLASSIF

8 A place, seat, or machine that is **free** is not occupied or not being used by anyone. ADJ CLASSIF

9 If something is **free**, you can have it or use it without paying for it. EG *...free school meals.* ADJ CLASSIF

10 If you do something or get something **for free**, you do it without being paid or you get it without having to pay for it. EG *I said I'd work for free.* PHRASE

11 Something that is moved **free** is moved so that it is no longer attached to or trapped by something. EG *I shook my jacket free and hurried off.* ADV AFTER VB

12 If you **free** something, you remove or loosen it from the place in which it has been fixed or trapped. EG *He freed his arms.* V+O

13 When someone is using one of their hands to hold or do something, you can refer to their other hand as their **free** hand. EG *...buttoning his overcoat with his free hand.* ADJ CLASSIF: ATTRIB

14 You say **'Feel free'** to someone as an informal way of giving your permission. EG *'Is it OK if I take this one?' – 'Yeah, feel free.'* PHRASE Informal

15 **free of charge**: see **charge**. • to give someone **a free hand**: see **hand**.

-free combines with nouns to form adjectives that indicate that something does not have the thing mentioned. EG *Each submarine reported a trouble-free launch... ...error-free computer programs.*

free agent, free agents. You say that someone is a **free agent** when they can do whatever they want because they are not responsible to anyone. N COUNT

free-and-easy. Free-and-easy people and things are casual and informal. EG *...a free-and-easy relationship.* ADJ QUALIT

freebie /friːbi[1]/, **freebies.** A **freebie** is something that you are given without having to pay for it, usually by a company. N COUNT Informal

freedom /friːdəm/, **freedoms. 1 Freedom** is the state of being allowed to do or say what you want to. EG *Political freedom is still rare... ...freedom of speech... ...the erosion of basic freedoms.* N UNCOUNT OR N COUNT

2 When slaves or prisoners escape or are released, they gain their **freedom**. EG *Many slaves buy their freedom with what they save from farming.* N UNCOUNT

3 When someone or something has **freedom** of movement, they can move about. N UNCOUNT

4 When there is **freedom** from something unpleasant, people are not affected by it. EG *...freedom from hunger and starvation.* N UNCOUNT +*from*

freedom fighter, freedom fighters. Freedom fighters are people who are trying to overthrow the government of their country using violent methods; used showing approval. N COUNT

free enterprise is an economic system in which businesses compete for profit without much government control. N UNCOUNT

free-for-all, free-for-alls. A **free-for-all** is a disorganized fight, argument, or attempt to get something, in which everybody joins in. EG *The* N COUNT

Do you find French windows only in France?

fight turned into a free-for-all... This would result in a free-for-all on wage bargaining.

free kick, free kicks. When there is a **free kick** in a game of football or rugby, the ball is given to a member of one side to kick without opposition because a member of the other side has broken a rule. N COUNT

freelance /fri:lɑ:ns/, **freelances.** A **freelance** journalist or photographer is not employed by one organization, but is paid for each piece of work that they do by the organization that they do it for. EG *...freelance writing... I work freelance.* ▸ used as a noun. EG *'Are you employed by Collins?' – 'No, I'm a freelance.'* ADJ CLASSIF OR ADV; ▸ N COUNT

freely /fri:li[1]/. **1** You say that something is done **freely** when it is done often or in large quantities. EG *He spends fairly freely... ...perspiring freely.* ADV

2 Someone or something that can move or act **freely** is not restricted, controlled, or limited by anything or anyone. EG *British goods were allowed to move freely from one state to another.* ADV

3 If you can talk **freely**, you do not need to be careful about what you say. EG *We are all comrades here and I may talk freely.* ADV

4 Something that is **freely** available can be obtained easily. EG *These drugs are freely available in most cities.* ADV+ADJ

5 Something that is given or done **freely** is given or done willingly. EG *...freely given affection.* ADV

freer /fri:ə/ is the comparative of **free.**

free-range. Free-range eggs are produced by hens that can move and feed freely on an area of open ground. ADJ CLASSIF

freest /fri:ɪ[2]st/ is the superlative of **free.**

freestyle /fri:staɪl/. **Freestyle** is used to describe sports competitions, especially in swimming, wrestling, and skiing, in which competitors can use any style or method they like. EG *She won the 100 metres freestyle.* N SING

freeway /fri:weɪ/, **freeways.** A **freeway** is a road which has several lanes and controlled places where vehicles join it, so that people can travel quickly. EG *He turned off the freeway.* N COUNT American

free will. 1 If you believe in **free will**, you believe that people have a choice in what they do and that their actions have not been decided in advance by God or Fate. N UNCOUNT

2 If you do something **of** your **own free will**, you do it by choice and not because you are forced to do it. EG *He has come back of his own free will.* PHRASE

freeze /fri:z/, **freezes, freezing, froze** /frəʊz/, **frozen** /frəʊzə[0]n/. **1** When a liquid **freezes** or when something **freezes** it, it becomes solid because it is very cold. EG *The water froze in the wells.* V-ERG

2 If you **freeze** food, you preserve it by storing it at a temperature below freezing point. V-ERG

3 If you say that it will **freeze**, you mean that the temperature outside will fall below freezing point. ▸ used as a noun. EG *...the forecasting of storms, freezes, and droughts.* V; ▸ N COUNT

4 If you **freeze**, you become very cold. EG *You'll freeze to death out there.* V

5 You can also say that someone **freezes** when they suddenly stop moving and become completely still and quiet, for example because they have seen something dangerous. EG *Then she sensed something moving about. She froze.* V

6 To **freeze** something such as wages or prices means to state officially that they will not be allowed to increase for a fixed period of time. EG *Various attempts to control or freeze wages have failed.* ▸ used as a noun. EG *...a freeze in the nuclear arms race.* V+O; ▸ N COUNT +SUPP

7 See also **deep freeze, freezing, frozen**.

freezer /fri:zə/, **freezers.** A **freezer** is a large container in which you can store food for long periods of time, because the temperature inside is kept below freezing point. N COUNT

freezing /fri:zɪŋ/. **1** If you say that something is **freezing**, you mean that it is very cold indeed. EG *It's freezing outside... The water was black and freezing.* ADJ CLASSIF

2 If you say that you are **freezing**, you mean that you feel unpleasantly cold. ADJ PRED

3 Freezing is the same as freezing point. EG *The air temperature was now well below freezing.* N UNCOUNT

freezing point, freezing points. 1 Freezing point is 0° Celsius, the temperature at which water freezes. EG *The temperature was well above freezing point.* N UNCOUNT

2 The **freezing point** of a particular substance is the temperature at which it freezes. N COUNT

freight /freɪt/ refers to **1** the transportation of goods by lorries, trains, ships, or aeroplanes. EG *...one section going by air freight... ...freight charges.* **2** the goods transported by lorries, trains, ships, or aeroplanes. EG *...eight thousand tons of freight.* N UNCOUNT

freighter /freɪtə/, **freighters.** A **freighter** is a ship or aeroplane that is designed to carry goods rather than people. N COUNT

freight train, freight trains. A **freight train** is a train that carries goods rather than people. N COUNT American

French fries /frɛnt[0]ʃ fraɪz/ are long, thin pieces of potato fried in oil or fat. EG *...hamburgers and French fries.* N PLURAL

French window /frɛnt[0]ʃ wɪndəʊ/, **French windows. French windows** are glass doors which you go through into a garden or onto a balcony. N COUNT: USU PLURAL

frenetic /frɪ[2]nɛtɪk/. **Frenetic** activity or behaviour is fast, energetic, and often confused or uncontrolled. ADJ QUALIT

frenzied /frɛnzɪd/. **Frenzied** actions are wild, excited, and uncontrolled. EG *...frenzied cheers... ...a frenzied mob of students.* ◊ **frenziedly.** EG *I scrambled frenziedly to the cave.* ADJ QUALIT; ◊ ADV

frenzy /frɛnzi[1]/, **frenzies.** You say that someone is in a **frenzy** when they are very excited and their behaviour is violent or uncontrolled. EG *It would drive Thomas into a frenzy... There was an element of frenzy and desperation in the singing.* N COUNT OR N UNCOUNT

frequency /fri:kwənsi[1]/, **frequencies. 1** The **frequency** of an event is the number of times that it happens during a particular period. EG *Serious disasters appear to be increasing in frequency... ...the frequency of their appearance.* N UNCOUNT

2 The **frequency** of a sound or radio wave is the rate at which it vibrates. A high frequency sound wave produces a high-pitched sound. N COUNT OR N UNCOUNT Technical

frequent, frequents, frequenting, frequented; pronounced /fri:kwənt/ when it is an adjective, and /fri[1]kwɛnt/ when it is a verb.

1 You say that something is **frequent** when it often happens. EG *George's absences were frequent... They move at frequent intervals... Etta was a frequent visitor there.* ◊ **frequently.** EG *This question is frequently asked.* ADJ QUALIT; ◊ ADV

2 If you **frequent** a place, you go there often and spend a lot of time there. EG *Jo liked to frequent the bars... The restaurant was frequented by workmen.* V+O

fresco /frɛskəʊ/, **frescoes.** A **fresco** is a picture that is painted on a plastered wall while the plaster is still wet. N COUNT Technical

fresh /frɛʃ/, **fresher, freshest. 1** A **fresh** thing or amount replaces or is added to a previous one. EG *He poured himself a fresh drink... Rose had given him fresh instructions.* ADJ CLASSIF: ATTRIB

2 Something that is **fresh** has been done or experienced recently. EG *...fresh footprints in the snow... Memories of the war are fresh in both countries.* ADJ QUALIT

3 If food is **fresh**, it has been made or got recently, and has not been tinned or frozen. EG *...fresh vegetables.* ADJ QUALIT

4 If you describe something as **fresh**, you mean that it is **4.1** different in a new and exciting way. EG *He has a fresh approach.* ◊ **freshness.** EG *This gives the novel freshness and charm.* **4.2** pleasant ADJ QUALIT; ◊ N UNCOUNT; ADJ QUALIT

and clean in appearance. EG *...the fresh dawn light.*
◇ **freshness.** EG *...the freshness of the curtains.* ◇ N UNCOUNT

5 If something smells, tastes, or feels **fresh**, it is pleasant and refreshing. EG *The air is cool and fresh... A piece of lemon gives it a fresh flavour.* ADJ QUALIT

6 **Fresh** water is water that is not salty, for example the water in streams and lakes. ADJ CLASSIF

7 If the weather is **fresh**, it is fairly cold and windy. ADJ QUALIT

8 If you are **fresh** from a place or experience, you have been to the place or had the experience very recently. EG *...coming fresh from the junior school.* ADJ PRED+PREP

freshen /frɛʃə^{0}n/, **freshens, freshening, freshened. 1** If you **freshen** something, you make it cleaner and more pleasant. EG *Keith freshened himself with a wash... The air freshened his lungs.* V+O

2 If the wind **freshens**, it increases and becomes fairly strong. V

freshen up. If you **freshen up**, you have a quick wash and make yourself look neat and tidy. EG *Sarah and Barry returned to their hotel to freshen up.* PHRASAL VB : V+ADV

fresher /frɛʃə/, **freshers.** A **fresher** is a student who has just started university or college. N COUNT British

freshly /frɛʃli^{1}/. You say that something is **freshly** made or done when it has been recently made or done. EG *...freshly cooked food... ...a freshly painted room.* ADV

freshwater /frɛʃwɔːtə/. **1** A **freshwater** lake or pool contains water that is not salty. ADJ CLASSIF : ATTRIB

2 A **freshwater** fish lives in a river, lake, or pool that is not salty. ADJ CLASSIF : ATTRIB

fret /frɛt/, **frets, fretting, fretted.** If you **fret** about something, you worry about it. EG *Daniel was fretting about money... 'Don't fret,' she said. 'He'll be all right.* V : OFT+ *about/over*

fretful /frɛtfʊl/. You say that someone is **fretful** when they behave in a way that shows that they are worried or unhappy about something. EG *...fretful babies.* ADJ QUALIT

friar /fraɪə/, **friars.** A **friar** is a member of a Catholic religious order. Friars travel around preaching Christianity. N COUNT

friction /frɪkʃə^{0}n/, **frictions. 1 Friction** is **1.1** the force that prevents things from moving freely when they are touching each other. **1.2** the rubbing of one thing against another. EG *She rubbed her hands as if trying to warm them by friction.* N UNCOUNT

2 **Friction** between people is disagreement and quarrels. EG *...friction between Healy and his colleagues... ...family frictions.* N UNCOUNT OR N PLURAL

Friday /fraɪdi^{1}/, **Fridays. Friday** is the day after Thursday and before Saturday. EG *I came here on Friday... Try and finish that by next Friday.* N UNCOUNT OR N COUNT

fridge /frɪdʒ/, **fridges.** A **fridge** is a large metal container in which you store food to keep it fresh. Fridges are kept cool by electricity. EG *He put the milk back in the fridge.* N COUNT British

friend /frɛnd/, **friends. 1** Your **friends** are the people who you know well and like to spend time with. EG *He was my best friend at Oxford... ...an old friend of the family.* N COUNT

2 If you are **friends** with someone, you like each other and enjoy spending time together. EG *You used to be friends with him, didn't you?* N PLURAL : OFT+*with*

3 If you **make friends** with someone, you begin a friendship with them. EG *Karen made friends with some young Chinese girls.* PHRASE

4 The people who help and support a cause or a country are often referred to as its **friends**. EG *All friends of Ireland should support us.* N PLURAL : OFT+*of*

5 You can refer to an object that you know well or use a lot as your **friend**. EG *Use your old friend the microscope.* N COUNT

friendless /frɛndlɪ^{2}s/. Someone who is **friendless** has no friends. EG *She remained friendless and miserable.* ADJ CLASSIF

friendly /frɛndli^{1}/, **friendlier, friendliest; friendlies. 1** If you are being **friendly** to someone, you are behaving in a kind and pleasant way to them. EG *The women had been friendly to Lyn... ...a friendly smile.* ADJ QUALIT ◇ **friendliness.** EG *The friendliness was gone from his voice.* ◇ N UNCOUNT

2 If you are **friendly** with someone, you like each other and enjoy spending time together. EG *I became friendly with a young engineer.* ADJ QUALIT

3 A **friendly** place or object makes you feel comfortable and relaxed. EG *...a small room lit by friendly lamps.* ADJ QUALIT

4 A **friendly** fight or argument is one in which people are only amusing themselves and do not intend to harm or offend each other. ADJ QUALIT

5 A **friendly** is a sports match that is played for practice and not as part of a competition. N COUNT

friendship /frɛndʃɪp/, **friendships. 1** A **friendship** is a relationship between two people who like each other and enjoy spending time together. EG *My friendship with her had taught me a great deal... ...the ability to form friendships.* N COUNT

2 **Friendship** is the state of being friends with someone. EG *Friendship is based on shared interests... He lost Britten's friendship.* N UNCOUNT

3 **Friendship** between countries is a relationship in which they help and support each other. EG *...his efforts to promote Anglo-German friendship... ...our friendship with America.* N UNCOUNT

frieze /friːz/, **friezes.** A **frieze** is a long, narrow strip of decoration, carving, or pictures along the top of the walls of a room or on the outside walls of a building. N COUNT

frigate /frɪgə^{1}t/, **frigates.** A **frigate** is a small, fast ship used by the navy to protect other ships. N COUNT

fright /fraɪt/, **frights. 1 Fright** is a sudden feeling of fear. EG *I heard Amy cry out in fright... He was paralysed with fright.* N UNCOUNT

2 If someone **takes fright**, they experience a sudden feeling of fear. EG *The animals took fright and ran away.* PHRASE

3 A **fright** is an experience which gives you a sudden feeling of fear. EG *She gave me a nasty fright with those rabbits.* N COUNT

frighten /fraɪtə^{0}n/, **frightens, frightening, frightened.** If something **frightens** you, it makes you feel afraid or nervous. EG *Rats and mice don't frighten me... The threat of prison did not frighten them.* V+O

frighten away. If you **frighten** someone **away**, you make them feel afraid so that they go away and do not harm you. EG *He waved his torch to frighten away some animal.* PHRASAL VB : V+O+ADV

frighten into. If you **frighten** someone **into** doing something that they do not want to do, you make them do it by making them afraid not to do it. EG *They tried to frighten me into talking.* PHRASAL VB : V+O+PREP

frighten off. To **frighten** a person **off** means to make them unwilling to become involved with someone or something. EG *Cliff was less encouraging, seeking to frighten him off.* PHRASAL VB : V+O+ADV

frightened /fraɪtə^{0}nd/. If you are **frightened**, **1** you are afraid because of something that has happened or that may happen. EG *The men led their frightened families to safety... When you were a child, were you frightened of the dark?* ADJ QUALIT **2** you are worried or nervous about something. EG *I was frightened of making a fool of myself... I am frightened to look... They were frightened that you might talk to the police.* ADJ PRED

frightening /fraɪtə^{0}nɪŋ/. Something that is **frightening** makes you feel afraid or worried. EG *...the most frightening sight he had ever seen... It is frightening to think what a complete search would reveal.* ADJ QUALIT ◇ **frighteningly.** EG *It was happening frighteningly fast.* ◇ ADV

frightful /fraɪtfʊl/. **1** If you say that something is **frightful**, you mean that it is very bad or unpleas- ADJ QUALIT Informal

If you fritter your time away, are you frivolous?

ant. EG *The smell was frightful.* ◇ **frightfully.** EG *She had behaved frightfully.* ◇ ADV

2 You can also use **frightful** to emphasize what you are saying. EG *It seems a frightful nuisance.* ADJ CLASSIF : ATTRIB
◇ **frightfully.** EG *I'm frightfully sorry.* ◇ SUBMOD

frigid /frɪdʒɪd/. If a woman is **frigid**, she does not easily become sexually aroused. ADJ QUALIT

frill /frɪl/, **frills.** 1 A **frill** is a long, narrow strip of cloth or paper with many folds, which is attached to something as a decoration. EG *...a white pillow with a blue frill round it.* ◇ **frilled** /frɪld/. EG *...a white frilled blouse.* N COUNT ◇ ADJ CLASSIF

2 If you say that something has no **frills**, you mean that it is simple and has no unnecessary additions. EG *...a house with no frills... ...the necessities of life but none of the frills.* N PLURAL

frilly /frɪli^1/. **Frilly** clothes or objects are decorated with many frills. EG *...a frilly nightdress.* ADJ QUALIT

fringe /frɪndʒ/, **fringes.** 1 A **fringe** is **1.1** hair which is cut so that it hangs over your forehead. EG *Her hair was rather short and had a fringe in front.* **1.2** a decoration attached to clothes and other objects, consisting of a row of hanging strips or threads. EG *...silk shawls with fringes.* N COUNT

2 The **fringes** of a place are the parts that are farthest from its centre. EG *...on the western fringe of London... ...from the desert fringes of Mali right across to Sudan.* N COUNT

3 The **fringes** of an activity or organization are the parts that are least typical, or most unusual or extreme. EG *...the radical fringe of the Labour Party... ...Julie's work in fringe theatre... Benn remained on the fringes of the debate.* N COUNT : USU+SUPP

fringed /frɪnd^{0}ʒd/. 1 If clothes or other objects are **fringed**, they are decorated with a fringe. EG *...a fringed leather jacket.* ADJ CLASSIF

2 If a place or object is **fringed** with things, they form a border around it or are situated along its edges. EG *Her eyes were large, fringed with long eyelashes... ...a bay of blue water fringed by palm trees.* ADJ PRED+ *with/by*

frisk /frɪsk/, **frisks, frisking, frisked.** 1 If someone **frisks** you, they search you with their hands in order to see if you are hiding a weapon or something else in your clothes. EG *Two policemen grabbed his arms while another one frisked him.* V+O Informal

2 When animals **frisk**, they run around in a happy, energetic way. EG *...his nine dogs frisking round him.* V

frisky /frɪski^1/, **friskier, friskiest.** A **frisky** animal or person is energetic and wants to have fun. EG *...frisky young ponies... ...the frisky schoolboy lurking underneath.* ADJ QUALIT

fritter /frɪtə/, **fritters, frittering, frittered.** **Fritters** consist of fruit, vegetables, or other food dipped in batter and fried. EG *...corn fritters... ...banana fritters.* N COUNT

fritter away. If you **fritter away** time or money, you waste it gradually on unimportant or unnecessary things. EG *She would not fritter away her vacation on reading.* PHRASAL VB : V+O+ADV

frivolity /frɪvɒlɪ^{1}ti^1/ is rather silly, light-hearted behaviour. EG *Harry tolerated the younger man's frivolity.* N UNCOUNT

frivolous /frɪvələs/. 1 Someone who is **frivolous** behaves in a silly or light-hearted way, especially when they should be serious or sensible. EG *Forgive me. I didn't mean to sound frivolous... She is seen as rather a frivolous writer.* ADJ QUALIT

2 **Frivolous** objects and activities are amusing or silly, rather than useful or important. EG *I spend a lot of my salary on frivolous things.* ADJ QUALIT

frizzy /frɪzi^1/, **frizzier, frizziest.** **Frizzy** hair has a lot of stiff, wiry curls. EG *...a youth with a mop of frizzy hair.* ADJ QUALIT

fro /frəʊ/. **to and fro**: see **to**.

frock /frɒk/, **frocks.** A **frock** is a woman's or girl's dress. N COUNT Outdated

frog

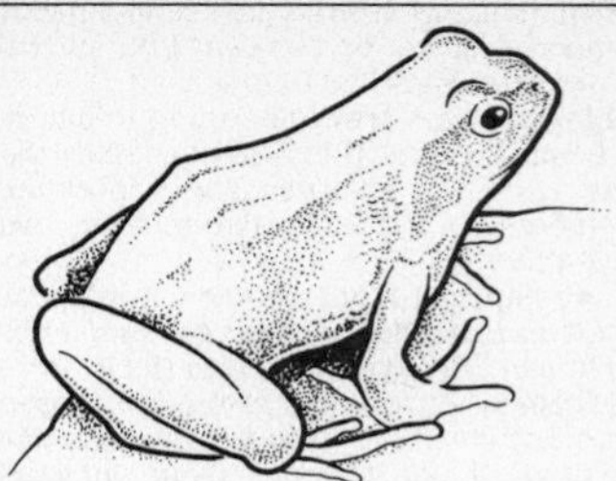

frog /frɒg/, **frogs.** 1 A **frog** is a small creature with smooth skin, big eyes, and long back legs which it uses for jumping. Many frogs live near water. N COUNT

2 If you **have a frog in** your **throat**, you cannot speak properly because your throat is partly blocked by phlegm, for example when you have a cold. PHRASE Informal

frogman /frɒgmə^{3}n/, **frogmen.** A **frogman** is a person whose job is to work underwater, wearing special rubber clothing and breathing equipment. N COUNT

frog-march, frog-marches, frog-marching, frog-marched. If you **are frog-marched** somewhere, you are forced to walk there by two people, each holding one of your arms. EG *I was frog-marched down to the police station.* V+O : USU+A

frolic /frɒlɪk/, **frolics, frolicking, frolicked.** When animals or children **frolic**, they run around and play in a lively way. EG *The children frolicked on the sand.* ▸ used as a noun. EG *What started as a frolic might turn into something different.* V : USU+A ▸ N COUNT

from /frɒm/. 1 You use **from** to say what the source of something is, or where it began. EG *...wisps of smoke from a small fire... She came from Ilford... Get the leaflet from a post office... She got a postcard from them yesterday... ...a song from his latest film... He was always sure of sympathy from his mother.* PREP

2 A person who is **from** a particular organization works for that organization. EG *This is Mr Castle from the bank.* PREP

3 If someone or something moves or is moved **from** a place, they leave it or are removed, so that they are no longer there. EG *They drove down from Leeds... We scrambled from our trucks and ran after them... We went around clearing rubbish from the fields.* PREP

4 If something is taken **from** you, it is removed or stolen, and you no longer have it. PREP

5 If you take something **from** an amount, you reduce the amount by that much. EG *This will be deducted from your pension.* PREP

6 If you are away **from** a place, you are not there. EG *They were away from home.* PREP

7 If you return **from** doing something, you return after doing it. EG *The men had not yet come back from fishing.* PREP

8 If you see or hear something **from** a particular position, you are in that position when you see it or hear it. EG *From the top of the bus you could look down on people below.* PREP

9 If something hangs or sticks out **from** an object, it is attached to it or held by it. EG *...buckets hanging from a bamboo pole.* PREP

10 You can use **from** when giving distances. For example, if a place is fifty miles **from** another place, the distance between the two places is fifty miles. PREP

11 If a road goes **from** one place to another, you can travel along it between the two places. EG *...on the main road from Paris to Marseilles.* PREP

12 If something is made **from** a particular substance, that substance is used to make it. EG *The shafts were cut from heavy planks of wood.* PREP

13 If something happens **from** a particular time, it begins to happen then. EG *She was deaf from birth... We had no rain from March to October.* PREP

14 If something changes **from** one thing to another, it stops being the first thing and becomes the second thing. EG *They enlarged the committee from 17 members to 30... ...translating from one language to another.* PREP

15 If one thing happens **from** another, it happens as a result of it. EG *From nervousness she said a few more stupid things... My eyes hurt from the wind.* PREP

16 You use **from** when you are giving the reason for an opinion. EG *I could see from her face that she felt disappointed... I am speaking from personal experience.* PREP

17 You say **from** one thing to another when you are stating the range of things that are possible. EG *The process takes from two to five weeks... The flowers may be anything from pink to crimson.* PREP

frond /frɒnd/, **fronds.** **Fronds** are long leaves with lots of spiky edges. EG *...palm fronds... ...huge fronds of seaweed.* N COUNT

front /frʌnt/, **fronts, fronting, fronted. 1** The **front** of something is the part of it that faces you or faces forward, or that you normally see or use. EG *...jackets with six buttons down the front... The policeman searched the front of the car.* N COUNT: USU SING+SUPP ▸ used as an adjective. EG *...the front gate... One of his front teeth was gone.* ▸ ADJ CLASSIF: ATTRIB

2 If a person or thing is **in front**, they are ahead of other ones in a moving group, or further forward than other ones. EG *Jay walked in front and Simon and Val behind him... ...a lady in the row in front.* PHRASE

3 If you are **in front** in a competition or contest, you are winning. PHRASE

4 If someone or something is **in front of** a particular thing, they are facing it, ahead of it, or close to the front part of it. EG *A car was drawing up in front of the house... There was a man standing in front of me.* PREP

5 If you do something **in front of** someone else, you do it when they are present. EG *I couldn't tell you in front of Sam.* PREP

6 In a war, the **front** is the place where two armies are fighting. N COUNT: *the*+N

7 If you say that something happens on a particular **front**, you mean that it happens with regard to a particular situation or activity. EG *On the intellectual front, little advance has been made.* N COUNT: USU SING+SUPP

8 If someone puts on a **front**, they pretend to have a feeling or quality which they do not have. EG *...presenting a united front to the world.* N SING: *a*+N

9 In meteorology, a **front** is the line where a mass of cold air meets a mass of warm air. N COUNT Technical

10 A building that **fronts** a place is next to it and faces it. EG *This beach has two restaurants fronting it.* V+O

frontage /frʌntɪdʒ/, **frontages.** The **frontage** of a building is the wall which faces the street. EG *...the Victorian frontage of the Treasury.* N COUNT

frontal /frʌntə^{0}l/. **1** A **frontal** attack is direct and obvious. EG *...a frontal attack on the unions.* ADJ CLASSIF: ATTRIB

2 **Frontal** also means concerning the front of something. EG *...a frontal view.* ADJ CLASSIF: ATTRIB

frontier /frʌntɪə/, **frontiers. 1** A **frontier** is a border between two countries. EG *...the frontier between the United States and Canada.* N COUNT

2 The **frontiers** of a subject or activity are the limits to which it can be known or done, or the boundary between it and something else. EG *They are doing work on the frontiers of discovery... ...crossing social frontiers.* N COUNT+SUPP

frontispiece /frʌntɪspi:s/, **frontispieces.** The **frontispiece** of a book is a picture at the beginning, opposite the page with the title on. N COUNT

front line, front lines. The **front line** is the place where two armies are fighting each other. EG *We came to within a mile of the front line... ...front-line troops.* N COUNT

front-page. **Front-page** articles or pictures are printed on the front page of a newspaper because they are very important or interesting. EG *Several papers carried front-page stories about the murdered girl.* ADJ CLASSIF: ATTRIB

frost /frɒst/, **frosts. 1** When there is a **frost**, the temperature outside falls below freezing point and the ground is covered with ice crystals. EG *There was a touch of frost this morning... Even into April the frosts continued.* N COUNT OR N UNCOUNT

2 **Frost** is the thin layer of ice crystals that forms on the ground when there is a frost. EG *The lawn was sparkling with frost.* N UNCOUNT

frostbite /frɒstbaɪt/ is a condition caused by extreme cold which can damage your fingers, toes, and ears. EG *He was crippled with frostbite.* N UNCOUNT

frosted /frɒstɪ^{2}d/. **Frosted** glass has a rough surface that you cannot see through. EG *...the frosted glass pane in the door.* ADJ CLASSIF: ATTRIB

frosty /frɒsti^{1}/, **frostier, frostiest. 1** If the weather is **frosty**, the temperature is below freezing. EG *...a still and frosty night.* ADJ QUALIT

2 If you say that someone is **frosty**, you mean that they are unfriendly or disapproving. EG *...a frosty glance.* ◇ **frostily.** EG *He smiled frostily.* ADJ QUALIT ◇ ADV

froth /frɒθ/, **froths, frothing, frothed. 1** **Froth** is a mass of small bubbles on the surface of a liquid. N UNCOUNT

2 If a liquid **froths**, it has lots of small bubbles in it or on its surface. EG *...the water frothing at his feet.* V: USU+A

frothy /frɒθi^{1}/. A **frothy** liquid has lots of bubbles on its surface. EG *...frothy beer.* ADJ QUALIT

frown /fraʊn/, **frowns, frowning, frowned.** When someone **frowns**, they move their eyebrows towards each other because they are annoyed, worried, or concentrating on something. EG *He frowned as though deep in thought... She frowned at him. 'What others?'* V: OFT+*at* ▸ used as a noun. EG *...a frown of disappointment.* ▸ N COUNT

frown on or **frown upon.** If something **is frowned on** or **is frowned upon**, people disapprove of it. EG *Non-membership of a union is frowned upon.* PHRASAL VB: V+PREP, OFT PASS

froze /frəʊz/ is the past tense of **freeze.**

frozen /frəʊzə^{0}n/ **1** **Frozen** is the past participle of **freeze.**

2 If a lake or river is **frozen** or **frozen over**, its surface has turned into ice because the weather is very cold. EG *...the frozen canal... The Missouri was frozen over.* ADJ CLASSIF

3 **Frozen** food has been preserved by freezing. EG *...a packet of frozen peas... ...a frozen chicken.* ADJ CLASSIF: USU ATTRIB

4 If you are **frozen**, you are very cold. EG *'Poor Oliver,' she said. 'You're frozen.'* ADJ QUALIT

5 If you stand or sit **frozen**, you keep still or cannot move because of danger or fear. EG *The men sat frozen with terror.* ADJ PRED: USU +*with*

frugal /fru:gə^{0}l/. **1** People who are **frugal** eat very little and spend very little money on themselves. EG *She lived a careful, frugal life.* ◇ **frugally.** EG *He ate frugally.* ◇ **frugality** /fru:gælɪ^{1}ti^{1}/. EG *...the tendency towards frugality and simplicity.* ADJ QUALIT ◇ ADV ◇ N UNCOUNT

2 A **frugal** meal is small and inexpensive. EG *...his frugal breakfast.* ADJ QUALIT

fruit /fru:t/, **fruits.** The plural can be either **fruit** or **fruits**, but it is usually **fruit.**

1 A **fruit** is something which grows on a tree or a bush and which contains seeds or a stone covered by a substance that you can eat. Apples, oranges, grapes, and bananas are all fruit. N COUNT OR N UNCOUNT

2 The **fruit** or the **fruits** of an action or activity are its results or products, especially good or pleasant ones. EG *...the fruit of his visits to China... The fruits of our labours were tremendous.* N UNCOUNT OR N PLURAL: USU+*of* ● If an action **bears fruit**, it produces good results. EG *The good work of this year will continue to bear fruit.* ● PHRASE Formal

Do you get fruit from a fruit machine?

fruitcake /fru:tkeɪk/, **fruitcakes.** A **fruitcake** is a cake that contains dried fruit. N COUNT OR N UNCOUNT

fruitful /fru:tfʊl/. Something that is **fruitful** produces good and useful results. EG *...hours of fruitful discussion... ...the fruitful use of funds.* ADJ QUALIT

fruition /fru:ɪʃə°n/. If something comes to **fruition**, it starts to succeed and produce the results that were intended or hoped for. EG *At last his efforts were coming to fruition.* N UNCOUNT Formal

fruitless /fru:tlɪ^{2}s/. Something that is **fruitless** does not produce any results or achieve anything. EG *...making fruitless inquiries... ...their fruitless search for the plane.* ADJ QUALIT

fruit machine, fruit machines. A **fruit machine** is a machine used for gambling. You put in a coin and then press buttons to try and get particular patterns of symbols on a screen in order to win money. N COUNT British

fruity /fru:ti^{1}/, **fruitier, fruitiest. 1** Something that is **fruity** smells or tastes of fruit. EG *...cheap, fruity wines.* ADJ QUALIT

2 A **fruity** laugh or voice is rich and deep; used showing approval. ADJ QUALIT

frustrate /frʌstreɪt/, **frustrates, frustrating, frustrated. 1** If a situation **frustrates** you, it makes you feel upset and angry because you are unable to do what you would like to do. EG *The lack of money and facilities depressed and frustrated him.* V+O ◇ **frustrated.** EG *...the sobbing wife and the angry, frustrated husband... ...a job in which you feel frustrated.* ◇ ADJ QUALIT ◇ **frustrating.** EG *It was frustrating to live at the sea's edge and be unable to swim.* ◇ ADJ QUALIT ◇ **frustration** /frʌstreɪʃə°n/, **frustrations.** EG *...screaming with frustration... ...the frustrations of poverty.* ◇ N UNCOUNT OR N COUNT

2 If someone or something **frustrates** a plan or hope, they prevent the event that was planned or hoped for from taking place. EG *The government have frustrated further advance towards European union.* V+O ◇ **frustrated.** EG *...frustrated desires... Many frustrated poets end up as teachers.* ◇ ADJ CLASSIF ◇ **frustration.** EG *...the frustration of hopes.* ◇ N UNCOUNT

fry /fraɪ/, **fries, frying, fried. 1** When you **fry** food, you cook it in a pan that contains hot fat or oil. EG *Ellen was frying an egg... ...the smell of frying onions.* V-ERG ◇ **fried.** EG *...fried potatoes.* ◇ ADJ CLASSIF

2 See also **small fry**.

frying pan, frying pans. 1 A **frying pan** is a flat, metal pan with a long handle, in which you fry food. N COUNT

2 If you say that doing something is jumping **out of the frying pan into the fire**, you mean that doing it puts you in just as bad a position as you were in before. PHRASE

ft is a written abbreviation for 'foot' or 'feet' in measurements. EG *...cages less than 4 ft high and 2 ft wide... ...age 35, height 6 ft 3 in.*

fudge /fʌdʒ/, **fudges, fudging, fudged. 1 Fudge** is a soft, brown sweet made from butter, milk, and sugar. N UNCOUNT

2 If you **fudge** something, you avoid making clear or definite decisions or statements about it. EG *...an attempt to fudge this issue by concealing the facts.* V+O

fuel /fjʊəl/, **fuels, fuelling, fuelled;** also spelled **fueling, fueled** in American English.

1 Fuel is a substance such as wood, coal, or petrol that is burned to supply heat or power. EG *The cost of fuel is a worry for old people... ...the increase in world fuel consumption.* ● See also **fossil fuel**. N MASS

2 A machine or vehicle that **is fuelled** by a particular substance works by burning that substance. EG *...boilers fuelled by coal.* V+O : USU PASS

3 If something **fuels** a situation or feeling, it causes it to increase in intensity or scale. EG *Hugh's anger was fuelled by resentment.* V+O

4 If something **adds fuel to** a conflict or an unpleasant situation, it makes the situation worse. EG *The trouble will add fuel to the class war.* PHRASE

fugitive /fju:dʒɪtɪv/, **fugitives. 1** A **fugitive** is someone who is running away from or hiding from their enemies, from the police, or from an unpleasant situation. EG *...political fugitives from Algeria... ...the hunt for a fugitive American.* N COUNT OR N MOD

2 Fugitive also means lasting for only a very short time. EG *...a fugitive smile... ...fugitive visits.* ADJ CLASSIF Literary

-ful, -fuls. -ful is used to form nouns that refer to the quantity of a substance that an object contains or can contain. For example, a handful of sand is the amount of sand that you can hold in your hand. EG *...two cupfuls of sugar... ...every mouthful of food.* SUFFIX

fulcrum /fʌlkrəm, fʊlkrəm/. The **fulcrum** of something that is balancing or being used as a lever is the point at which it is supported or fixed. N SING Technical

fulfil /fʊlfɪl/, **fulfils, fulfilling, fulfilled;** also spelled **fulfill, fulfills** in American English.

1 If you **fulfil** a promise, request, or hope, you do what was promised, asked, or hoped. EG *They failed to fulfil their promises to revive the economy... I had fulfilled many of my ambitions.* V+O

2 If what you are doing **fulfils** you or if you **fulfil** yourself, you feel happy and satisfied with what you are doing. EG *This way of life no longer fulfils the individuals concerned.* V+O OR V-REFL ◇ **fulfilling.** EG *Jobs should be made as creative and fulfilling as possible.* ◇ ADJ QUALIT ◇ **fulfilled.** EG *The children gain if both parents are living fulfilled lives.* ◇ ADJ QUALIT

3 If someone or something **fulfils** a role or function, they do whatever is required by it. EG *He could no longer fulfil his function as breadwinner for the family... Helicopters fulfilled a variety of roles.* V+O

fulfilment /fʊlfɪlmə^{2}nt/; also spelled **fulfillment** in American English.

1 Fulfilment is a feeling of satisfaction that you get from doing or achieving something. EG *People find fulfilment in working for a common goal.* N UNCOUNT

2 When something happens that has been promised or hoped for, you can refer to this event as the **fulfilment** of the promise or hope. EG *...the fulfilment of their dreams.* N UNCOUNT : USU+*of*

full /fʊl/, **fuller, fullest. 1** Something that is **full** contains as much of a substance or as many objects as it can. EG *The bucket's almost full... All the car parks are absolutely full.* ADJ QUALIT

2 If you say that something is **full** of things or people, you mean that it contains a large number of them. EG *...a garden full of pear and apple trees.* ADJ PRED+*of*

3 If you say that someone or something is **full** of a feeling or quality, you mean that they have a lot of it. EG *I was full of confidence.* ADJ PRED+*of*

4 You can use **full** to indicate the greatest extent or amount of something that is possible. EG *...a return to full employment... Make full use of your brains... The radio was playing at full volume.* ADJ CLASSIF : ATTRIB

5 You say that something has been done **in full** when everything that is necessary has been done. EG *The bill has been paid in full.* PHRASE

6 Something that is done **to the full** is done to as great an extent as is possible. EG *She wanted to exploit that opportunity to the full.* PHRASE

7 You can use **full** to emphasize **7.1** that you are referring to the whole of something, or to a complete thing. EG *I haven't got his full name... ...my last full day in Warsaw.* ADJ CLASSIF : ATTRIB **7.2** the degree of a quality that something has. EG *...the full squalor of the buildings.* ADJ CLASSIF : ATTRIB **7.3** the directness and force with which a person or thing hits or looks at something. EG *My skis struck a woman full in the face.* ADV+PREP

8 When machinery or equipment is **full** on, it is working at its greatest power or intensity. EG *The gas fire was full on.* ADV AFTER VB

9 If someone has a **full** life, they are always busy. ADJ QUALIT

10 If you describe a part of someone's body as **full**, you mean that it is rounded and rather large. EG *...her full red lips.* ADJ QUALIT

11 When there is a **full** moon, the moon appears as a bright circle. ADJ CLASSIF

12 If you say that you know something **full well**, PHRASE

you are emphasizing that you are totally sure about it. EG *We know full well that Congress will spend every penny.*
13 to be **full of beans**: see **bean**. • to **come full circle**: see **circle**.

full-blooded. Full-blooded is used to describe things that are intense or complete. EG *...without the full-blooded support of the Opposition parties.* ADJ CLASSIF : ATTRIB

full-blown. Full-blown things are as intense as possible or have all the features they could have. EG *...a full-blown military operation.* ADJ CLASSIF : ATTRIB

full board. If you stay at a hotel that provides **full board**, you can get all your meals there. N UNCOUNT

full-length. 1 A **full-length** novel, film, or play is the normal length, rather than being shorter than normal. ADJ CLASSIF : ATTRIB
2 A **full-length** skirt or coat is quite long, rather than being short. ADJ CLASSIF : ATTRIB
3 A **full-length** mirror or portrait shows the whole of a person. ADJ CLASSIF : ATTRIB
4 Someone who is lying **full-length** is lying down flat and stretched out. ADV AFTER VB

full marks. 1 If you get **full marks** in a test or exam, you answer every question correctly. N PLURAL
2 If you say that someone gets **full marks** for something, you are praising them. EG *Mr Jenkins gets full marks for courage.* N PLURAL

fullness /fʊlnɪ²s/. **1** If you talk about the **fullness** of something, you mean that it is very strong or rich, or full of many things. EG *...the fullness of her love... ...life in all its fullness.* N UNCOUNT Literary
2 If you say that something will happen **in the fullness of time**, you mean that it will eventually happen, but probably after a long time. EG *The inspector's report, in the fullness of time, would reach headquarters.* PHRASE

full-page. A **full-page** advertisement, picture, or article covers a whole page of a newspaper or magazine. ADJ CLASSIF : ATTRIB

full-scale is used to describe things that have all the features they could have and that are done to the greatest extent possible. EG *It could turn into a full-scale war.* ADJ CLASSIF : ATTRIB

full-size. Full-size or **full-sized** things **1** have finished growing and will not become any larger. EG *...full-size trees.* ADJ CLASSIF **2** are the same size as the thing they represent. EG *...a full-size model of a vehicle.* ADJ CLASSIF : ATTRIB

full stop, full stops. A **full stop** is the dot (.) which you put as a punctuation mark at the end of a sentence when it is not a question or an exclamation. N COUNT British

full-time. 1 Full-time work or study takes up the whole of each normal working week rather than just part of it. EG *...a full-time job... ...full-time students... Bob and I worked full time.* ADJ CLASSIF, OR ADV AFTER VB
2 If you say that an activity or task is **a full-time job**, you mean that it takes up a lot of your time. EG *Answering letters was a full-time job.* PHRASE
3 In some sports such as football, hockey, and rugby, **full time** is the end of a match. N UNCOUNT

full up. If you say that something is **full up**, you are emphasizing that it contains as much of a substance or as many objects as it can. EG *The town's full up.* ADJ PRED

fully /fʊli¹/. **1 Fully** means to the greatest degree or extent possible. EG *The secrets of its success are still not fully understood... ...fully automatic washing machines.* ADV
2 You use **fully** to indicate that a process is completely finished. EG *It was weeks before he fully recovered... Barber isn't fully trained yet.* ADV
3 If you do something **fully**, you do not leave out or forget any details or aspects of it. EG *She answered his questions fully.* ADV
4 You can use **fully** to emphasize how great an amount is. EG *Fully one-quarter of the workers are Turks.* ADV+N

fully-fledged /fʌli¹flɛdʒd/ means having completely developed into the type of thing or person mentioned. EG *...fully-fledged members of the association.* ADJ CLASSIF : ATTRIB

fulsome /fʊlsəm/. **Fulsome** apologies or expressions of gratitude or admiration are very exaggerated or excessive. EG *...with fulsome compliments and extravagant gifts.* ADJ QUALIT Formal

fumble /fʌmbə⁰l/, **fumbles, fumbling, fumbled.**
1 If you **fumble** with an object or **fumble** in a container, you handle the object or search for something clumsily. EG *His awkwardness made him fumble with the key... He fumbled in his pocket for his whistle.* V : USU+A
2 If you **fumble** when you are trying to say something, you talk in a confused and unclear way. EG *Brody fumbled for words.* V OR V+O

fume /fjuːm/, **fumes, fuming, fumed. 1 Fumes** are strong and unpleasant or harmful gases, smells, or smoke. EG *...the exhaust fumes of a car... ...tobacco fumes.* N PLURAL
2 If you **fume**, you show or express impatience and anger. EG *I was fuming with rage... He fumed: 'I have answered every question.'* V OR V+QUOTE

fun /fʌn/. **1** If you say that an activity is **fun**, you mean that it is enjoyable or amusing. EG *It's fun working for him... Tests are no fun.* N UNCOUNT
2 If you have **fun**, you enjoy yourself. EG *We had great fun on the beach... She wanted a bit more fun out of life.* N UNCOUNT
3 If you say that someone is **fun**, you mean that you enjoy being with them because they say and do interesting or amusing things. EG *She was great fun... He was fun to be with.* N UNCOUNT
4 If you say that something is a **fun** thing, you mean that you enjoy it. EG *Those were fun times.* ADJ CLASSIF Informal
5 If you do something **for fun** or **for the fun of it**, you do it in order to enjoy yourself and not because it is important or necessary. EG *...things that you do for fun in your spare time... You don't come to work just for the fun of it.* PHRASE
6 If you **make fun of** someone or something or **poke fun at** them, you tease them or make jokes about them. EG *Don't make fun of my father.* PHRASE

function /fʌŋk⁰ʃə⁰n/, **functions, functioning, functioned. 1** The **function** of something or someone is the useful thing that they do or are intended to do. EG *The essential function of trade unions is to bargain with employers... The brain performs three functions: recording, recalling, and analysing... What is your main function in life?* N COUNT
2 If a machine or system **is functioning**, it is working or operating. EG *The phone didn't function at all... Only one hospital is functioning... ...an idea of how the civil service functions.* V
3 If someone or something **functions** as a particular thing, they do the work or fulfil the purpose of that thing. EG *The room had previously functioned as a playroom... I found myself functioning as an ambassador.* V+as
4 If you say that one thing is a **function** of another, you mean that its amount or nature depends on the other thing. EG *The supply of money was a function of the amount of gold discovered.* N COUNT : OFT SING+of Formal
5 A **function** is also a large formal dinner or party. EG *He had been invited to a function at the college.* N COUNT

functional /fʌŋk⁰ʃə⁰nəl, -ʃənə⁰l/. **1** Something that is **functional 1.1** is intended to be useful rather than attractive. EG *...functional modern furniture.* ADJ QUALIT **1.2** is working or operating. EG *How long has the machine been functional?* ADJ CLASSIF
2 Functional also means relating to the way something works. EG *...a functional description of the motorcycle... ...functional efficiency.* ADJ CLASSIF

functionary /fʌŋk⁰ʃənə⁰ri¹/, **functionaries.** A **functionary** is a person who has an official admin- N COUNT Formal

If you poke fun at someone, are you being funny?

istrative job in an organization, especially in a government or a political party.

fund /fʌnd/, **funds, funding, funded. 1 Funds** are amounts of money that are available for spending. EG *...how to raise funds for a commercial project.* N PLURAL

2 A **fund** is an amount of money that is collected for a particular purpose. EG *He made a generous donation to our campaign fund.* N COUNT

3 If you have a **fund** of something, you have a lot of it. EG *...a large fund of scientific knowledge.* N PART

4 When a person or organization **funds** something, they provide money for it. EG *The work is being funded both by governments and private industry.* V+O

◇ **funding.** EG *They provide funding in the form of loans.* ◇ N UNCOUNT

fundamental /fʌndəmentəˀl/, **fundamentals. 1** If you describe something as **fundamental**, you mean that it is very important or basic. EG *...the fundamental principles on which it is based... The differences are in some respects fundamental.* ADJ CLASSIF

2 The **fundamentals** of a subject or activity are its most important and basic parts. EG *...the fundamentals of police work... Their test really gets down to fundamentals.* N PLURAL

fundamentalism /fʌndəmentəlɪzəˀm/ is belief in the original form of a religion, without accepting any later ideas. ◇ **fundamentalist** /fʌndəmentəlɪst/, **fundamentalists.** EG *...a fundamentalist Christian.* N UNCOUNT; ◇ N COUNT OR N MOD

fundamentally /fʌndəmentəli[1]/. You use **fundamentally 1** to indicate that you are talking about the real or basic nature of something. EG *Our criminal code is based fundamentally on fear... Fundamentally, we are not a part of the community.* **2** to indicate the extreme degree or extent of something. EG *I disagreed fundamentally with the Party.* ADV OR ADV SEN; ADV

fund-raising is the activity of collecting money for a particular purpose or organization. N UNCOUNT

funeral /fju:nəˀrəl/, **funerals.** A **funeral** is the ceremony that is held when the body of someone who has died is buried or cremated. EG *Both actresses attended the funeral... ...a funeral service.* N COUNT

funereal /fju:nɪərɪəl/. If you describe something as **funereal**, you mean that it is very sad, serious, and depressing. EG *The atmosphere in the cabin was almost funereal.* ADJ QUALIT Literary

fungus /fʌŋgəs/, **fungi** /fʌngaɪ/. **Fungi** are plants such as mushrooms, toadstools, and mould which have no leaves or green colouring. N COUNT OR N UNCOUNT

funk /fʌŋk/ is a style of music based on jazz and blues, with a strong, repeated bass part. N UNCOUNT

funky /fʌŋki[1]/. **Funky** jazz, blues, or pop music has a very strong, repeated bass part. ADJ QUALIT

funnel

funnel /fʌnəˀl/, **funnels, funnelling, funnelled;** also spelled **funneling, funneled** in American English.

1 A **funnel** is an object with a wide, circular top and a short tube at the bottom, which is used when pouring liquids, powders, or very small things into a container. EG *Fill a bottle through a funnel.* N COUNT

2 A **funnel** is also a chimney on a ship or railway engine powered by steam. EG *...a ship with a yellow funnel.* N COUNT

3 If something **funnels** or **is funnelled** somewhere, it is directed through a narrow space. EG *...gales funnelling between the islands.* V-ERG : USU+A

4 If you **funnel** money, information, or goods somewhere, you cause them to be sent there from several sources. EG *...funneling aid to the resistance groups.* V+O+A

funnily /fʌnɪli[1]/. You say **funnily enough** to indicate that, although something is surprising, it is true or it really did happen. EG *Funnily enough, old people seem to love bingo... Well, funnily enough, all seven of us went there, but separately.* ADV SEN

funny /fʌni[1]/, **funnier, funniest. 1** You say that something is **funny 1.1** when it is strange, surprising, or puzzling. EG *...a funny little white hat... It's a funny thing to write... It was funny that you met the same people... The funny thing is, we went to Arthur's house just yesterday.* **1.2** when it is amusing and makes you smile or laugh. EG *She laughed. 'What's funny?' he asked... It did look funny upside down... He told funny stories and made everyone laugh.* ADJ QUALIT

2 If you feel **funny**, you feel slightly ill. EG *I just feel a bit funny, it's difficult to describe.* ADJ PRED

fur /fɜ:/, **furs. 1 Fur** is **1.1** the thick hair that grows on the bodies of many animals. EG *Moles have short silky fur.* N UNCOUNT **1.2** the fur-covered skin of an animal that is used to make clothing or rugs. EG *...a jacket edged with white fur... ...a fur coat.* N MASS **1.3** a soft, artificial material that looks like fur and is used to make clothing, rugs, toys, and seat covers. N UNCOUNT

2 A **fur** is a coat made from real or artificial fur, or a piece of fur worn round a woman's neck. EG *Many women refused to buy furs... You can get a genuine fur in Jenners.* N COUNT

furious /fjʊərɪəs/. **1** Someone who is **furious** is extremely angry. EG *I was furious and told them to get out of my house... She was furious with him.* ADJ QUALIT

◇ **furiously.** EG *'Who is this man?' the Prince exclaimed furiously.* ◇ ADV

2 You can use **furious** to indicate that something happens with great energy, speed, or violence. EG *...a furious battle... ...the furious efforts they were making.* ◇ **furiously.** EG *She ran furiously up the hill.* ADJ CLASSIF : ATTRIB; ◇ ADV

furled /fɜ:ld/. If something such as an umbrella or a sail is **furled**, it is rolled or folded up because it is not being used. EG *...a ship with its sails furled.* ADJ CLASSIF

furnace /fɜ:nɪ[1]s/, **furnaces. 1** A **furnace** is a container in which a very hot fire is used to melt metal, burn rubbish, or produce steam. EG *He kicked the furnace door open and began shovelling coal... Gradually, coal furnaces were replaced by gas and electric ones.* N COUNT

2 You can describe a room or vehicle as a **furnace** when it is very hot inside it. EG *The car was a furnace when we got in again.* N COUNT

furnish /fɜ:nɪʃ/, **furnishes, furnishing, furnished. 1** When you **furnish** a room or building, you put furniture, carpets, curtains, and other things into it. EG *Do you enjoy decorating and furnishing a house?* V+O

2 To **furnish** something means to provide it or supply it. EG *They were not prepared to furnish the necessary troops... Luckily, they have furnished us with a translation.* V+O : OFT+with Formal

furnished /fɜ:nɪʃt/. **1** A **furnished** room or house is rented with furniture already in it. EG *They were living in a furnished flat near Finchley Station.* ADJ CLASSIF

2 When you say how a room or house is **furnished**, you are describing the kind or amount of furniture that it has in it. EG *The bedroom was scantily furnished... ...a large room furnished with low tables and cushions.* ADJ CLASSIF

furnishings /fɜːnɪʃɪŋz/. The **furnishings** of a room or house are the furniture, carpets, curtains, and decorations. EG *The tables and stools were the sole furnishings of the room.* N PLURAL

furniture /fɜːnɪtʃə/ consists of the large, movable objects such as tables, chairs, or beds that are used in a room. EG *She arranged the furniture... The only piece of furniture was an old wardrobe.* N UNCOUNT

furore /fjʊəʳrɔːri¹, fjʊərɔː/; also spelled **furor** /fjʊərɔː/ in American English. A **furore** is a very angry or excited reaction by people to something. EG *The lecture caused an enormous furore... ...the present furore over drugs.* N SING

furrow /fʌrəʊ/, **furrows, furrowing, furrowed.** N COUNT

1 A **furrow** is **1.1** a long line in the earth which a farmer makes in order to plant seeds in or to allow water to flow along. EG *...a field with parallel furrows running down it.* **1.2** a deep fold or line in the skin of someone's face. EG *...the deep furrows in his cheeks.*

2 When you **furrow** your brow or forehead or when it **furrows**, it has deep folds because you are frowning. EG *The pain caused him to furrow his brow.* V-ERG

furry /fɜːri¹/, **furrier, furriest. 1** A **furry** animal is covered with thick, soft hair. EG *It had a long furry tail.* ADJ QUALIT

2 Something that is **furry** has a soft texture like fur. EG *...a furry coat.* ADJ QUALIT

further /fɜːðə/, **furthers, furthering, furthered. Further** is a comparative form of **far**, and is also a verb.

1 Further means to a greater degree or extent. EG *The situation was further complicated by uncertainty about the future... He sank further into debt.* ADV

2 If someone or something goes **further** or takes something **further**, they progress to a more advanced stage. EG *They never got any further... He hoped the new offer would develop matters a stage further.* ADV

3 If you say you will go **further** in a discussion, you mean you will make a more extreme or more detailed statement. EG *I shall go further and say that Len was lying.* ADV

4 A **further** thing or amount is an additional one. EG *We need a further five hundred pounds... Do you have nothing further to say?* ADJ CLASSIF, OR ADJ AFTER N

5 Further to is used in business letters to indicate that you are referring to a previous letter or conversation. EG *Further to your enquiry of the 16th, I am happy to enclose the new contract.* PREP Formal

6 Further means a greater distance than before or than something else. EG *I walked further than I intended.* ● If something is **further on**, it is further in the direction that you are going. EG *I found a tree a little further on.* ADV ● PHRASE

7 If you tell someone that a piece of information must **not go any further**, you mean that they must not tell it to anyone else. EG *'This mustn't go any further.' – 'No, of course.'* PHRASE

8 You can use expressions such as '**further** back' and '**further** on' to refer to a time that is before or after the time you are talking about. EG *It has its origins much further back... Three years further on, Linda has no regrets.* ADV+ADV

9 If you **further** something, you help it to progress, to be successful, or to be achieved. EG *...a plot by Morris to further his career... ...furthering the cause of liberation.* V+O

furtherance /fɜːðəʳrəns/. If you do something in **furtherance** of something else, you do it in order to help this other thing to be achieved. EG *He did it solely in the furtherance of his own interests... ...acting in furtherance of a lawful trade dispute.* N UNCOUNT +SUPP Formal

further education is the education of people who have left school and want more qualifications, at a lower level than a degree. EG *The state is pouring money into further education... We can give advice on further education courses throughout Britain.* N UNCOUNT British

furthermore /fɜːðəmɔː/ is used to introduce a piece of information or an opinion that adds to or supports the previous one. EG *He carried out orders without questioning them. Furthermore, he was not bothered by hard work... It is nearly dark, and furthermore it's going to rain.* ADV SEN

furthest /fɜːðɪ²st/. **Furthest** is a superlative form of **far**.

1 Furthest means to a greater extent or degree than ever before or than anything or anyone else. EG *...countries where commercialized farming has advanced furthest... ...the furthest limits of democracy.* ADV OR ADJ QUALIT : SUPERL

2 The **furthest** one of a number of things is the one that is the greatest distance away from a particular place. EG *She sat near the furthest window... ...the fields which lay furthest from his farm.* ADJ CLASSIF OR ADV

furtive /fɜːtɪv/. You say that someone's behaviour is **furtive** when they seem to be trying to do something secretly. EG *They suddenly looked furtive... ...a furtive glance.* ◊ **furtively.** EG *He furtively handed over the letter... He looked round, furtively.* ADJ QUALIT ◊ ADV

fury /fjʊəri¹/. **1 Fury** is violent or very strong anger. EG *He clenched his fists in fury... There was fury in Miss Lenaut's dark eyes... He looked up at us with fury.* N UNCOUNT

2 If you are **in a fury**, you are very angry. EG *The women jumped on Willie in a fury... He flew into a fury.* PHRASE

fuse /fjuːz/, **fuses, fusing, fused. 1** A **fuse** is a safety device in an electric plug or circuit. It contains a piece of wire which melts when there is a fault so that the flow of electricity stops. EG *...to switch off the lamp and mend the fuse... Have you checked the fuse?* N COUNT

2 When an electric device **fuses**, it stops working because of a fault. EG *Several of the street lamps had fused.* V-ERG

3 A **fuse** is also a device on a bomb or firework which delays the explosion and gives people time to move away to a safe distance. N COUNT

4 When objects **fuse** or **are fused**, they join together physically because of heat or a biological process. EG *During fertilization the sperm and egg fuse.* V-ERG

5 If you **fuse** two ideas, methods, or systems, you combine them. EG *...the attempt to fuse new and old.* V-ERG

fuselage /fjuːzɪlɑːʒ/, **fuselages.** The **fuselage** of an aeroplane, missile, or rocket is its main part. EG *The big jet was still stuck, its fuselage and tail blocking runway three.* N COUNT

fusion /fjuːʒəʳn/, **fusions. 1** When two ideas, methods, or systems are combined, you can say that there is a **fusion** of these ideas, methods, or systems. EG *...the fusion of radical and socialist ideals... The painting is a rich fusion of several elements.* N UNCOUNT OR N COUNT

2 The process in which atomic particles combine and produce nuclear energy is called nuclear **fusion**. N UNCOUNT Technical

fuss /fʌs/, **fusses, fussing, fussed. 1** If you say that someone is making a **fuss** about something, you mean that they are behaving in an unnecessarily anxious, excited, or angry way. EG *They're making a fuss about the wedding... He accepted the statement without fuss.* N SING OR N UNCOUNT : OFT+*about/over*

2 If you **make a fuss of** someone, you pay a lot of PHRASE

What is the difference between 'furniture' and 'furnishings'?

attention to them. EG *They like to be flattered and made a fuss of.*

3 When people **fuss**, they behave in an unnecessarily anxious or excited way. EG *Stop fussing, mother... Ted fussed with his camera.* V

fuss over. If you **fuss over** someone or something, you pay too much attention to them or worry about them too much. EG *She was inclined to fuss over her health.* PHRASAL VB : V+PREP, HAS PASS

fussy /fʌsi¹/, **fussier, fussiest. 1** Someone who is **fussy** is excessively nervous, concerned with details, or careful in choosing things. EG *I am very fussy about my food... ...a fat and fussy lady... He's not fussy who he rents his room to.* ◇ **fussily.** EG *...fumbling fussily with his papers.* ADJ QUALIT : OFT+*about* ◇ ADV

2 If you describe clothes or furniture as **fussy**, you mean that they are too elaborate or have too much decoration. EG *...fussy lace curtains.* ◇ **fussily.** EG *She was fussily dressed.* ADJ QUALIT ◇ ADV

futile /fju:taɪl/. If you describe an action or attempt as **futile**, you mean that it will not be successful or was not successful. EG *...a series of costly and futile wars... Lucy knew how futile it was to argue with her father.* ◇ **futility** /fju:tɪlɪ¹ti¹/. EG *...the futility of their attempts.* ADJ QUALIT ◇ N UNCOUNT

future /fju:tʃə/, **futures. 1** The **future** is the period of time that will come after the present, or the things that will happen then. EG *It might be possible in the future... What plans do you have for the future?* N SING : *the*+N

2 You use **in future** when you are telling someone what you want or expect to happen from now on. EG *Be more careful in future... More hospital officers will in future be temporarily attached to hospitals.* ADV SEN

3 Future things will happen or exist after the present time. EG *Let's meet again at some future date... ...future generations.* ADJ CLASSIF : ATTRIB

4 Your **future** is your life or career after the present time. EG *I decided that my future lay in medicine.* N COUNT : OFT+POSS

5 If something has a **future**, it is likely to be successful and to continue to exist. EG *Does the engine have a future?* N SING : *a*+N

future tense. In grammar, the **future tense** is used to refer mainly to things that will come after the present, or the things that will happen then. N SING : *the*+N

futuristic /fju:tʃərɪstɪk/. You describe something as **futuristic** when it looks or seems unusual, like something from the future. EG *...the futuristic shape of the buildings.* ADJ QUALIT

fuzz /fʌz/. **1 Fuzz** is a mass of short curly hairs or threads. EG *...the light, blond fuzz on his cheeks.* N UNCOUNT

2 Some people refer to the police as **the fuzz**. EG *We thought you were the fuzz.* N SING : *the*+N Informal

fuzzy /fʌzi¹/, **fuzzier, fuzziest. 1 Fuzzy** hair sticks up in a soft, curly mass. ADJ QUALIT

2 If something looks **fuzzy**, its shape is blurred rather than being sharp and clear. EG *These photographs were less fuzzy.* ADJ QUALIT

3 If you or your thoughts are **fuzzy**, you are confused and cannot think clearly. EG *My mind was tired and a bit fuzzy.* ADJ QUALIT

G g

G, g /dʒi:/, **Gs, g's. 1 G** is the seventh letter of the English alphabet. N COUNT

2 g is used after a number as an abbreviation for 'gram'. EG *...257g.*

gab /gæb/. If you say that someone has **the gift of the gab**, you mean that they have the ability to speak easily, confidently, and in a persuasive way. PHRASE Informal

gabble /gæbə⁰l/, **gabbles, gabbling, gabbled.** If you **gabble**, you say things so quickly that it is difficult for people to understand you. EG *'Look here,' he gabbled, 'It's about the Harvest Festival.'* V, V+QUOTE, OR V+O

▸ used as a noun. EG *There was a gabble of conversation in the pub.* ▸ N UNCOUNT

gable /geɪbə⁰l/, **gables.** A **gable** is the triangular part at the top of the end wall of a building, between the two sloping sides of the roof. N COUNT

◇ **gabled** /geɪbə⁰ld/. EG *...small gabled houses.* ◇ ADJ CLASSIF

gadget /gædʒɪ²t/, **gadgets.** A **gadget** is a small machine or device. EG *...household gadgets.* N COUNT

gaffe /gæf/, **gaffes.** A **gaffe** is something that you say or do which is considered to be socially incorrect. EG *I had no idea of the gaffe which I was committing.* N COUNT

gag /gæg/, **gags, gagging, gagged. 1** A **gag** is a piece of cloth that is tied round or put inside someone's mouth in order to stop them from speaking. N COUNT

2 If someone **gags** you, they tie a piece of cloth round your mouth. EG *She was gagged and blindfolded.* V+O

3 If you **gag**, you choke and nearly vomit. EG *Dr. Hutchinson suddenly gagged. 'Too much wine. Forgive me.'* V

4 A **gag** is also a joke, especially one told by a professional comedian. EG *Where do you get all these gags?* N COUNT Informal

gaga /gɑ:gɑ:/. Someone who is **gaga** is senile. EG *She's seventy-seven and rather gaga.* ADJ QUALIT Informal

gaggle /gægə⁰l/, **gaggles.** You can use **gaggle** to refer to a group of people. EG *...a gaggle of little girls.* N PART

gaiety /geɪə²ti¹/ is a feeling or attitude of liveliness and fun. EG *...fresh youthful gaiety.* N UNCOUNT

gaily /geɪli¹/. **1** If you do something **gaily**, you do it in a lively, happy way. EG *Off we set, with Pam chattering gaily all the way.* ADV

2 Something that is **gaily** coloured or decorated is coloured or decorated in a bright, pretty way. EG *...donkeys pulling gaily painted carts.* ADV

gain /geɪn/, **gains, gaining, gained. 1** If you **gain** a quality, you gradually get more of it. EG *The speaker began to gain confidence... ...if the baby fails to gain weight... The opposition party is gaining in popularity.* V+O OR V+*in*

2 If you **gain** from something, you get some advantage or benefit from it. EG *It is not only banks who will gain from the coming of electronic money... What has Britain gained by being a member of the EEC?* V OR V+O : USU+A

3 A **gain** is an improvement, or something that is achieved. EG *The company has made notable gains in productivity.* N COUNT

4 If you do something for **gain**, you do it in order to get some profit for yourself. EG *He did it for financial gain.* N UNCOUNT Formal

5 If a clock or watch **gains**, it shows a time that is later than the real time. V OR V+O

gain on. If you **are gaining on** someone or something that you are chasing, you are gradually catching them up. PHRASAL VB : V+PREP

gait /geɪt/, **gaits.** Someone's **gait** is the way that they walk. EG *He moves with the slow confident gait of a successful man.* N COUNT : USU SING+SUPP Formal

gala /gɑ:lə/, **galas.** A **gala** is a special public celebration, entertainment, or performance. EG *...the special guest on a gala occasion.* N COUNT

galactic /gəlæktɪk/ means relating to galaxies in space. ADJ CLASSIF : ATTRIB

galaxy /gæləksi[1]/, **galaxies.** A **galaxy** is a huge group of stars and planets that extends over many millions of miles. N COUNT

gale /geɪl/, **gales.** A **gale** is a very strong wind. N COUNT

gall /gɔːl/, **galls, galling, galled. 1** If you say that someone has the **gall** to do something dangerous or dishonest, you mean that they have the courage to do it. EG *They haven't the gall to steal.* N SING : the+N Formal

2 If something **galls** you, it makes you angry or annoyed. EG *It galled him to have to ask permission.* V+O Formal

gallant /gælənt/; also pronounced /gəlænt/ in rather old-fashioned English for paragraph 2.

1 Someone who is **gallant** is very brave and honourable when they are in danger or difficulty. EG *They have put up a gallant fight over the years.* ADJ QUALIT
◊ **gallantly.** EG *Gallantly they battled on.* ◊ ADV

2 A man who is **gallant** is kind, polite, and considerate towards women. ◊ **gallantly.** EG *He gallantly offered to carry her cases to the car.* ADJ QUALIT ◊ ADV

gallantry /gæləntri[1]/ is **1** bravery that is shown by someone who is in danger, especially in a war. EG *He was awarded the Military Cross for gallantry in combat.* **2** polite and considerate behaviour by men towards women. N UNCOUNT

gall bladder, gall bladders. Your **gall bladder** is the organ in your body which contains bile and is next to your liver. N COUNT

gallery /gælə[0]ri[1]/, **galleries. 1** A **gallery** is **1.1** a building or room that has exhibitions of works of art in it. EG *...pictures in the National Gallery.* **1.2** a place where works of art are displayed and sold. **1.3** a raised area at the back or the sides of a large room or hall. EG *...the public gallery at Parliament.* N COUNT

2 The **gallery** in a theatre is a raised area like a large balcony that usually contains the cheapest seats. EG *She always sat in the gallery.* N COUNT

galley /gæli[1]/, **galleys.** A **galley** is a small kitchen, especially in a ship or an aircraft. N COUNT

gallon /gælən/, **gallons.** A **gallon** is a unit of volume that is equal to eight pints. EG *...three gallons of water.* N PART

gallop /gæləp/, **gallops, galloping, galloped. 1** When a horse **gallops**, it runs very fast so that all four legs are off the ground at the same time in each stride. EG *The horse galloped down the road.* V : USU+A
▸ used as a noun. EG *All the animals broke into a gallop.* ▸ N SING

2 If you **gallop**, you ride a horse that is galloping. EG *He swung onto his horse, saluted, and galloped off.* V OR V+O : USU+A

3 A **gallop** is also a ride on a horse that is galloping. EG *...a brisk morning's gallop.* N COUNT

galloping /gæləpɪŋ/ is used to describe something that is increasing or developing very fast and is difficult to control. EG *The oil crisis brought galloping inflation on an international scale.* ADJ CLASSIF : ATTRIB

gallows /gæləʊz/. **Gallows** is both the singular and the plural form.
A **gallows** is a wooden frame used to execute criminals by hanging. N COUNT

galore /gəlɔː/ means existing in very large numbers. EG *...restaurants and night clubs galore.* ADJ AFTER N Outdated

galoshes /gəlɒʃɪz/ are waterproof shoes which people wear over their ordinary shoes to prevent them getting wet. EG *...a pair of galoshes.* N PLURAL

galvanize /gælvənaɪz/, **galvanizes, galvanizing, galvanized;** also spelled **galvanise.** To **galvanize** someone means to cause them to do something suddenly by making them feel excited, afraid, or angry. EG *The lecture galvanized several others into action.* V+O : OFT+*into*

galvanized /gælvənaɪzd/; also spelled **galvanised. Galvanized** metal has been covered with zinc in order to protect it from rust. EG *...a barn made out of galvanized iron.* ADJ CLASSIF : ATTRIB

gambit /gæmbɪt/, **gambits.** A **gambit** is something that you do or say for a particular purpose. EG *...a good gambit for attracting attention... ...a conversational gambit.* N COUNT

gamble /gæmbə[0]l/, **gambles, gambling, gambled. 1** A **gamble** is a risky action or decision that you take in the hope of gaining money or success. EG *We took a gamble, and lost... ...a gamble that paid off for us.* ▸ used as a verb. EG *I was gambling on the assumption that the file had been lost.* N COUNT : USU SING ▸ V OR V+O : OFT+*on*

2 If you **gamble**, you bet money in a game such as cards or on the result of a race or competition. EG *He gambled heavily on the horses.* ◊ **gambling.** EG *He used the firm's money to pay off gambling debts.* ◊ **gambler, gamblers.** EG *...a compulsive gambler.* V OR V+O : OFT +*on* ◊ N UNCOUNT ◊ N COUNT

gambol /gæmbə[0]l/, **gambols, gambolling, gambolled;** spelled **gamboling** and **gamboled** in American English.
If animals or people **gambol**, they run or jump about in a playful way. EG *...with his dogs gambolling round him.* V : USU+A

game /geɪm/, **games. 1** A **game** is **1.1** an activity or sport involving skill, knowledge, or chance, in which you follow rules and try to win against an opponent or try to solve a puzzle. EG *You need two people to play this game... ...a game like tennis... ...word games.* **1.2** a particular occasion on which a game is played. EG *Did you go to the baseball game?... This was our last game, which we lost 6 – 3.* **1.3** a part of a match, consisting of a fixed number of points. EG *Becker leads by four games to one.* **1.4** the equipment that you need to play a particular indoor game, for example a specially marked board, dice, or special cards. EG *...a box of toys and games.* **1.5** a way of behaving in which a person uses a particular plan, especially in order to gain an advantage. EG *...these games that politicians play... ...the power game.* N COUNT

2 Game is used in these phrases. **2.1** If you beat someone **at** their **own game**, you use the same methods that they have used, but more successfully, so that you gain an advantage over them. EG *The Japanese were beating the West at its own game.* **2.2** If you say **the game is up**, you mean that someone's secret plans or activities have been discovered. EG *The British realized that the game was up.* **2.3** If someone or something **gives the game away**, they reveal something such as information which is secret. EG *I always give the game away – you've only got to look at my face.* PHRASES

3 Game is wild animals or birds that are hunted for sport and sometimes cooked and eaten. EG *The men had gone to hunt wild game.* N UNCOUNT

4 If you describe someone as **game**, you mean that they are willing to do something new, unusual, or risky. ◊ **gamely.** EG *The vicar rose gamely to the challenge.* ADJ CLASSIF ◊ ADV

5 Games are **5.1** an organized event in which competitions in several sports take place. EG *...the Olympic Games.* **5.2** organized sports activities that children do at school. EG *I was hopeless at games at school.* N PLURAL

gamekeeper /geɪmkiːpə/, **gamekeepers.** A **gamekeeper** is a person who takes care of the wild animals or birds that are kept on someone's land for hunting. N COUNT

gammon /gæmən/ is meat from a pig which has been smoked or salted like ham. N UNCOUNT

gamut /gæmə[4]t/. The **gamut** of something is the wide variety of things that can be included in it. EG *...the entire gamut of London politics... Fathers can participate in the whole gamut of domestic work.* N SING : USU+OF Literary
● If you **run the gamut** of something, you experience or express the wide variety of things that can be included in it. EG *She ran the gamut of all the illnesses that babies can have.* ● PHRASE

What kinds of food are mentioned on these pages?

gang /gæŋ/, **gangs, ganging, ganged.** A **gang** is 1 a group of criminals who work together to commit crimes. EG *...a gang of terrorists.* 2 a group of people who go around together. EG *They stood around in gangs... ...fights with rival gangs.* N COLL

gang up. If people **gang up**, they unite against someone else, for example in a fight or argument. EG *National groups are ganging up to claim their rights.* PHRASAL VB : V+ADV Informal

gangling /gæŋglɪŋ/. You use **gangling** to describe a young person who is tall, thin, and clumsy. EG *...a gangling twenty-year-old by the name of Pyle.* ADJ CLASSIF Written

gangrene /gæŋgri:n/ is bad decay that can occur in a part of a person's body if the blood stops flowing to it, for example as a result of illness or injury. N UNCOUNT

gangster /gæŋstə/, **gangsters.** A **gangster** is a member of an organized group of violent criminals. EG *...a gangster film.* N COUNT

gangway /gæŋweɪ/, **gangways.** A **gangway** is 1 a passage left between rows of seats, for example in a theatre or aircraft, for people to walk along. 2 a short bridge or platform leading onto a ship. EG *...walking down the gangway to the wharf.* N COUNT British

gaol /dʒeɪl/. See **jail**.

gaoler /dʒeɪlə/. See **jailer**.

gap /gæp/, **gaps.** A **gap** is 1 an empty space or hole in the middle of something solid or between two things. EG *...a narrow gap in the mountains... She had gaps in her teeth... ...a gap in the hedge.* N COUNT : USU+SUPP 2 a period of time when you are not busy or not doing something that you normally do. EG *After a gap of two years, she went back to college.* N COUNT : USU+SUPP 3 the absence of something in a situation that prevents it from being satisfactory or complete. EG *This book fills a major gap... You may not get a pension if there are gaps in your record.* N COUNT : USU+SUPP 4 a great difference between two things, people, or ideas. EG *The gap between rich and poor regions widened.* • See also **generation gap**. N COUNT : USU+*between*

gape /geɪp/, **gapes, gaping, gaped.** 1 If you **gape**, you look at someone or something in surprise, with your mouth open. EG *Jackson gaped in astonishment at the result.* ◇ **gaping.** EG *...gaping tourists.* V : OFT+*at* ◇ ADJ CLASSIF

2 If something **gapes**, it opens wide or comes apart. EG *The front door gaped open... The shirt gaped to reveal his chest.* ◇ **gaping.** EG *The dressing gown had a gaping hole in it.* V OR V+C ◇ ADJ CLASSIF : ATTRIB

garage /gærɑ:ʒ, -rɪdʒ/, **garages.** A **garage** is 1 a building in which you keep a car. See picture at HOUSE. 2 a place where you can get your car repaired, buy a car, or buy petrol. EG *It was Sunday and the garage was closed.* N COUNT

garb /gɑ:b/. Someone's **garb** is the clothes that they are wearing, especially clothes that are in a particular style or are part of a uniform. EG *...a convict in striped prison garb... ...his habitual winter garb of cloak and gloves.* N UNCOUNT +SUPP Formal

garbage /gɑ:bɪdʒ/. 1 **Garbage** is rubbish, especially waste from a kitchen. EG *...the garbage in the streets.* N UNCOUNT American

2 You can refer to ideas and opinions that are stupid or of no value as **garbage**. EG *He talked a lot of garbage on the subject.* N UNCOUNT Informal

garbled /gɑ:bə^{0}ld/. If a message or explanation is **garbled**, the details are confused or wrong. EG *I got a garbled telephone message.* ADJ QUALIT

garden /gɑ:də^{0}n/, **gardens, gardening.** 1 A **garden** is a piece of land next to someone's house where they grow flowers, vegetables, or other plants, and which often includes a lawn. EG *...sitting in the back garden... ...the vegetable garden.* N COUNT

2 If you **are gardening**, you are doing work in your garden such as weeding or planting. ◇ **gardening.** EG *It is too hot to do any gardening... ...gardening gloves.* V : USU CONT ◇ N UNCOUNT

3 **Gardens** are a place like a park that has areas of plants, trees, and grass. EG *...Kensington Gardens... ...the botanical gardens.* N COUNT : USU PLURAL

gardener /gɑ:də^{0}nə/, **gardeners.** A **gardener** is 1 a person who is paid to work in someone else's garden. 2 someone who enjoys working in their garden as a hobby. EG *He was not a keen gardener.* N COUNT

garden party, garden parties. A **garden party** is a formal party that is held in a large private garden, usually in the afternoon. N COUNT

gargantuan /gɑ:gæntju^{4}ən/. Something that is **gargantuan** is very large. EG *...a gargantuan meal.* ADJ QUALIT Literary

gargle /gɑ:gə^{0}l/, **gargles, gargling, gargled.** When you **gargle**, you wash your mouth by filling it with liquid, tilting your head back, and breathing out through your mouth, making a bubbling noise. V OR V+O

garish /geərɪʃ/. Something that is **garish** is very bright in colour and harsh to look at. EG *...a garish yellow tie.* ADJ QUALIT

garland /gɑ:lənd/, **garlands.** A **garland** is a decoration in the shape of a circle made of flowers and leaves, which is worn round someone's neck or head. EG *He hung a garland of flowers round my neck.* N COUNT

garlic /gɑ:lɪk/ is the small round white bulb of an onion-like plant. Garlic has a very strong smell and taste and is used in cooking. EG *Add a crushed clove of garlic.* N UNCOUNT

garment /gɑ:mə^{2}nt/, **garments.** A **garment** is a piece of clothing, for example a shirt, dress, skirt, or pair of trousers. EG *She wore a long smock-like garment in scarlet linen.* N COUNT Formal

garner /gɑ:nə/, **garners, garnering, garnered.** If you **garner** information, you collect it, often with some difficulty. EG *A certain amount can be garnered from the British press.* V+O Formal

garnish /gɑ:nɪʃ/, **garnishes, garnishing, garnished.** 1 A **garnish** is a small amount of food that you use to decorate food. EG *...a garnish of parsley.* N COUNT OR N UNCOUNT

2 If you **garnish** food, you decorate it with small amounts of a different food. EG *Garnish the fish with cucumber slices.* V+O : OFT+*with*

garret /gærɪ^{2}t/, **garrets.** A **garret** is a very small room at the top of a house. N COUNT

garrison /gærɪsə^{0}n/, **garrisons.** A **garrison** is a group of soldiers whose job is to guard a town or building. N COUNT

garrulous /gærə^{4}ləs/. Someone who is **garrulous** talks a lot. EG *She's only a foolish, garrulous woman.* ADJ QUALIT

garter /gɑ:tə/, **garters.** A **garter** is a piece of elastic worn round the top of a stocking or sock in order to prevent it slipping down. N COUNT

gas /gæs/, **gases; gasses, gassing, gassed.** The form **gases** is the plural of the noun; **gasses** is the 3rd person singular, present tense of the verb.

1 **Gas** is 1.1 a substance like air that is neither liquid nor solid and burns easily. It is used as a fuel for fires, cookers, and central heating in people's homes. EG *He remembered to turn the gas off before leaving home.* N UNCOUNT 1.2 any substance that is neither liquid nor solid, for example oxygen or hydrogen. EG *Helium is a gas at room temperature... ...deadly nerve gases.* • See also **tear gas**. N COUNT OR N UNCOUNT

2 **Gas** fires and **gas** cookers use gas as a fuel. N MOD

3 **Gas** is also the same as petrol. EG *Sorry I'm late. I had to stop for gas.* N UNCOUNT American

4 To **gas** a person or animal means to kill them by making them breathe poisonous gas. EG *She tried to gas herself.* V+O OR V-REFL

gas chamber, gas chambers. A **gas chamber** is a room that can be filled with poisonous gas in order to kill people or animals. N COUNT

gaseous /gæsɪəs, geɪʃəs/ is used to describe substances which are neither solid nor liquid. EG *...liquid or gaseous fuels.* ADJ CLASSIF : ATTRIB Formal

gash /gæʃ/, **gashes, gashing, gashed.** 1 A **gash** is a long, deep cut in something. EG *Zeleika had a large gash in her head.* N COUNT : USU+SUPP

2 If you **gash** something, you make a long, deep cut in it. EG *He gashed his arm on a window last night.* V+O

gas mask, gas masks. A **gas mask** is a device that you wear over your face to protect you from breathing poisonous gases. N COUNT

gasoline /gæsəli[1]n/ is the same as petrol. EG *...soaring gasoline prices.* N UNCOUNT American

gasp /gɑːsp/, **gasps, gasping, gasped.** A **gasp** is a short quick breath of air that you take in through your mouth, especially when you are surprised or in pain. EG *I listened to him breathing in short gasps... ...a gasp of horrified surprise.* N COUNT ▸ used as a verb. EG *He was gasping for air... 'Call the doctor!' she gasped.* ▸ V OR V+QUOTE

gas station, gas stations. A **gas station** is a place where petrol is sold. N COUNT American

gastric /gæstrɪk/ is used to describe processes, pains, or illnesses that occur in your stomach. EG *...a gastric ulcer.* ADJ CLASSIF : ATTRIB

gastronomic /gæstrə[6]nɒmɪk/ means concerned with good food. EG *...the gastronomic reputation of France.* ADJ CLASSIF : ATTRIB Formal

gate /geɪt/, **gates.** A **gate** is **1** a structure like a door that is used at the entrance to a field, a garden, or the grounds of a building. EG *The prison gates closed behind him... The taxi swung in through the gates of the vicarage.* **2** an official exit in a large airport which passengers go through on their way to the aeroplane. EG *Passengers on flight BA504 should proceed to gate four.* N COUNT

gateau /gætəʊ/, **gateaux;** also spelled **gâteau.** A **gateau** is a rich cake, usually with cream in it. EG *...chocolate gateau.* N COUNT OR N UNCOUNT

gatecrash /geɪtkræʃ/, **gatecrashes, gatecrashing, gatecrashed.** If someone **gatecrashes** a party, they go to it, even though they have not been invited. V+O OR V Informal

gatepost /geɪtpəʊst/, **gateposts.** A **gatepost** is a post in the ground which a gate is fastened to. N COUNT

gateway /geɪtweɪ/, **gateways. 1** A **gateway** is an entrance where there is a gate. EG *They passed through an arched gateway.* N COUNT

2 A **gateway** to somewhere is a place which you go through because it leads you to a much larger place. EG *...Sheremetyevo, the gateway to Moscow.* N COUNT+*to*

3 If something is a **gateway** to a job, career, or other activity, it gives you the opportunity to progress into that job or activity. EG *...a world in which examinations are the gateways to some professions.* N COUNT+*to*

gather /gæðə/, **gathers, gathering, gathered. 1** When people **gather** somewhere, they come together in a group. EG *The villagers gathered around him... He whistled to gather the whole squad in a group.* V-ERG : USU+A ◊ **gathered.** EG *All the family were gathered to hear the solicitor read the will.* ◊ ADJ PRED

2 If you **gather** together a number of things that you have spread out, you bring them together again. EG *I gathered my maps together and tucked them into the folder.* V+O : USU+A

3 If you **gather** things, you collect them from a number of different places. EG *They gathered berries and nuts... The team worked for about a year and a half to gather data.* V+O

4 If you say that something **is gathering dust**, you mean that it is not being used regularly. EG *My briefcase was already beginning to gather dust.* PHRASE

5 If something **gathers** speed, momentum, or force, it gradually becomes faster or more powerful. EG *The train gathered speed as it left the town.* V+O

6 If you **gather** that something is true, you learn from what someone says that it is true. EG *I gathered that they were not expected to eat with us... His wife had been ill, I gather, for some time.* V+REPORT : ONLY *that*

7 If you **gather** a piece of cloth, you make a row of very small pleats in it by sewing a thread through it and then pulling the thread tight. EG *...a long white dress gathered under the bosom.* V+O

gather up. If you **gather up** a number of things, you bring them together into a group. EG *She watched Willie gather up the papers.* PHRASAL VB : V+O+ADV

gathering /gæðə[0]rɪŋ/, **gatherings. 1** A **gathering** is a group of people who are meeting for a particular purpose. EG *...political and social gatherings.* N COUNT

2 If you talk about the **gathering** dusk, you mean that it is gradually getting darker, usually because it is nearly night. EG *We walked up the long Main Street in the gathering dusk.* ADJ CLASSIF : ATTRIB

gauche /gəʊʃ/. Someone who is **gauche** is awkward and uncomfortable in the company of other people. EG *She seemed rather gauche and fat and to have grown much shyer.* ADJ QUALIT

gaudy /gɔːdi[1]/. Something that is **gaudy** is very brightly coloured; used showing disapproval. EG *...young men in gaudy shirts.* ADJ QUALIT

gauge /geɪdʒ/, **gauges, gauging, gauged. 1** If you **gauge** an amount or quantity, you measure or calculate it. EG *With a modern machine, you can gauge the number of stitches... I could usually gauge how many members were present.* V+O OR V+REPORT

2 If you **gauge** people's feelings or actions, you carefully consider and judge them. EG *...gauging what the people wanted... I couldn't gauge how it would affect me.* V+O OR V+REPORT

3 A **gauge** is **3.1** a device that measures the amount of something and shows the amount measured. EG *The fuel gauge dropped swiftly towards zero.* See picture at CAR. **3.2** a fact that can be used to judge a situation or a person's feelings. EG *The increase in attendance was used as a gauge of the course's success.* N COUNT : OFT+SUPP

gaunt /gɔːnt/. **1** Someone who is **gaunt** looks very thin and unhealthy. EG *She looked very weak, her face gaunt and drawn.* ADJ QUALIT

2 Something that is **gaunt** looks bare and unattractive. EG *...the gaunt outlines of the houses opposite.* ADJ QUALIT

gauntlet /gɔːntlɪ[2]t/, **gauntlets. 1 Gauntlets** are long, thick gloves that are worn for protection, for example by motorcyclists. N COUNT : USU PLURAL

2 If you **throw down the gauntlet** to someone, you say or do something that challenges them to argue, compete, or fight with you. If you **pick up the gauntlet**, you accept their challenge. EG *Wendy now had to pick up the gauntlet thrown down by her mother.* PHRASE

3 If you **run the gauntlet**, you go through an unpleasant experience in which a lot of people criticize or attack you. EG *In research, academics run the gauntlet of their professional peers.* PHRASE

gauze /gɔːz/ is a light, soft cloth with tiny holes in it. N UNCOUNT

gave /geɪv/ is the past tense of **give.**

gawky /gɔːki[1]/. Someone who is **gawky** stands and moves awkwardly and clumsily. EG *...a gawky young woman.* ADJ QUALIT

gawp /gɔːp/, **gawps, gawping, gawped.** If you are **gawping** at someone or something, you are staring at them in a rude or stupid way. EG *Don't stand there gawping, come away.* V : OFT+*at*

gay /geɪ/, **gays; gayer, gayest. 1** A person who is **gay** is homosexual. EG *I've told them I'm gay.* ADJ CLASSIF ▸ used as a noun. EG *...a holiday spot for gays.* ▸ N COUNT

2 Gay organizations and magazines are for homosexual people. EG *They have an active Gay Group.* ADJ CLASSIF : ATTRIB

3 In slightly more old-fashioned English, a person who is **gay** is lively and enjoyable to be with. EG *Well, he's not the gayest of companions... ...a gay, carefree young woman.* ADJ QUALIT Outdated

4 A place or a piece of music that is **gay** is lively and pleasant. EG *What gay and exciting place are you taking me to?* ADJ QUALIT

5 Something that is **gay** is brightly coloured and pretty. EG *Her dress was gay and flowered.* ADJ QUALIT

6 See also **gaiety** and **gaily.**

> Would you be pleased if someone referred to you as gauche?

gaze /geɪz/, **gazes, gazing, gazed.** If you **gaze**, you look steadily at someone or something for a long time. EG *She turned to gaze admiringly at her husband... He gazed down into the water.* ▸ used as a noun. EG *He sat without shifting his gaze from the television.* V+A; ▸ N COUNT: USU SING

gazelle /gəˈzel/, **gazelles.** A **gazelle** is a kind of small antelope. N COUNT

GCE /dʒiː siː iː/, **GCEs. 1 GCE** is an abbreviation for 'General Certificate of Education'. The **GCE** is an examination in Britain which is usually taken at Ordinary level when leaving school and at Advanced level before going to University: see also **A level** and **O level.** EG *...good grades in GCE subjects.*

2 A **GCE** is a pass in an Ordinary level GCE examination for a particular subject. N COUNT

GCSE /dʒiː siː es iː/ is an abbreviation for 'General Certificate of Secondary Education'. The **GCSE** is an examination in Britain introduced to replace the GCE Ordinary level examination in 1988.

gear /gɪə/, **gears, gearing, geared. 1** A **gear** in a machine or vehicle is **1.1** a device or system which controls the rate at which energy is converted into motion. Gears usually consist of moving wheels and levers which fit together. See picture at CAR. EG *...interlocking cogs and gears... John checked the gear on the bicycle.* N COUNT **1.2** one of the different ranges of speed or power which a machine or vehicle has. EG *We slow down to first gear and ten miles an hour.* N COUNT OR N UNCOUNT

2 The **gear** for a particular activity is the equipment and special clothes that you use. EG *...camping gear.* N UNCOUNT: USU+SUPP

3 If someone or something **is geared** to a particular purpose, they are organized or designed to be suitable for that purpose. EG *They were not geared to armed combat... ...a policy geared towards rehabilitation.* V+O+A: USU PASS

gear up. If someone **is geared up** to do something, they are prepared and able to do it. EG *Hotels like this are not geared up to cater for parties like ours.* PHRASAL VB: V+ADV OR V-REFL+ADV

gearbox /gɪəbɒks/, **gearboxes.** A **gearbox** is the system of gears in an engine or vehicle. N COUNT

gee /dʒiː/. Some people say **gee** when they are surprised or excited. EG *Gee, what fun!* EXCLAM American

geese /giːs/ is the plural of **goose.**

gel /dʒel/, **gels, gelling, gelled;** also spelled **jell. 1** If a liquid **gels**, it changes into a thicker, firmer substance rather like jelly. V

2 If an unclear shape, thought, or idea **gels**, you can see or understand it more clearly and definitely. EG *After talking to you things really began to gel.* V

3 Gel is a thick oily substance, especially one that you use to keep your hair in a particular style. N MASS

gelatine /dʒelətiˈn/ is a clear, tasteless powder that is used to make liquids become firm. Gelatine is often used in cooking. N MASS

gelignite /dʒelɪgnaɪt/is an explosive substance that is similar to dynamite. N UNCOUNT

gem /dʒem/, **gems. 1** A **gem** is a jewel that is used in jewellery. EG *...a bracelet of solid gold, studded with gems.* N COUNT

2 If you refer to someone or something as a **gem**, you think they are especially good or pleasing. EG *...this gem of wisdom... This house is a gem.* N COUNT

gender /dʒendə/, **genders.** A person's **gender** is the sex that they belong to. Men belong to the male gender and women belong to the female gender. EG *...differences of race or gender.* N UNCOUNT OR N COUNT

gene /dʒiːn/, **genes. Genes** are parts of cells which control the physical characteristics, growth, and development of living things. Genes are passed on from one generation to another. N COUNT: USU PLURAL

genealogy /dʒiːniˈælədʒiˈ/, **genealogies. 1 Genealogy** is the study of the history of families. ◇ **genealogist, genealogists.** EG *...an amateur genealogist attempting to trace the family of his wife.* N UNCOUNT Formal; ◇ N COUNT

2 A **genealogy** is the history of a particular family, describing who each person married and who their children were. N COUNT Formal

genera /dʒenərə/ is the plural of **genus.**

general /dʒenəᵒrəl/, **generals. 1** You use **general 1.1** when describing something that belongs or relates to the whole of something rather than to its details or parts. EG *Their cost rose despite a general decline in their quality... The general standard of education there is very high... His general attitude suggested that he regarded me as a fool.* ADJ CLASSIF: ATTRIB ◇ **generally.** EG *His account was generally accurate... Wool and cotton blankets are generally cheapest.* ◇ ADV OR ADV SEN **1.2** when describing several items or activities, when there are too many of them or when they are not important enough to mention separately. EG *Put down telephone calls as part of your general business expenses.* ADJ CLASSIF: ATTRIB ◇ **generally.** EG *It's wonderful for information on things generally.* ◇ ADV SEN

2 You also use **general 2.1** to describe something that involves or affects most people in a group. EG *There was a general movement to leave the table at this point... ...a topic of general interest.* ADJ QUALIT ◇ **generally.** EG *When will this material become generally available?* ◇ ADV **2.2** to describe a statement that involves only the main features of something and not its details. EG *Principles have to be stated in very general terms.* ADJ QUALIT ◇ **generally.** EG *I'll say a few words generally on grants... Generally speaking, your pronunciation of English is very good.* ◇ ADV OR ADV SEN **2.3** to describe a statement or opinion that is true or suitable in most situations. EG *As a general rule, consult the doctor if the baby has a temperature.* ADJ CLASSIF: ATTRIB **2.4** to describe an organization or business that offers a variety of services or goods. EG *...a general hospital... ...a general grocery store.* ADJ CLASSIF: ATTRIB **2.5** to describe a person's job, to indicate that they have complete responsibility for the administration of an organization. EG *...the general manager of the hotel... ...the General Secretary.* ADJ CLASSIF: ATTRIB **2.6** to describe a person who does a variety of jobs which require no special skill or training. EG *...unskilled general labourers.* ADJ CLASSIF: ATTRIB

3 You say **in general 3.1** when you are talking about the whole of a situation without going into details. EG *They want shorter shifts, and shorter working hours in general.* PHRASE **3.2** when you are referring to most people or things in a group. EG *...his contemptuous attitude to society in general.* PHRASE **3.3** to indicate that a statement is true in most cases. EG *The industrial processes, in general, are based on man-made processes.* ADV SEN

4 A **general** is an officer who holds a high rank in the armed forces, usually in the army. EG *...General Ravenscroft.* N COUNT

general election, general elections. A **general election** is an election at which all the citizens of a country vote for people to represent them in the national parliament. EG *A general election was called.* N COUNT

generality /dʒenəræliˈtiˈ/, **generalities.** A **generality** is something that you say that is general and not very detailed. EG *She spoke in short simple generalities.* N COUNT OR N UNCOUNT Formal

generalize /dʒenəᵒrəlaɪz/, **generalizes, generalizing, generalized;** also spelled **generalise.** If you **generalize**, you say that something is true in most situations or for most people, especially when you have very little evidence for it. EG *I don't think you can generalize about that.* V ◇ **generalization, generalizations.** EG *It is easy to make sweeping generalizations about someone else's problems.* ◇ N COUNT OR N UNCOUNT

generalized /dʒenəᵒrəlaɪzd/; also spelled **generalised. Generalized** means **1** involving a large number of people or things. EG *The problem is one of generalized human needs.* **2** applying to a variety of situations or subjects. EG *...generalised remarks about the futility of love.* ADJ QUALIT

general knowledge is knowledge about many different things, rather than about one particular subject. EG *Her general knowledge is amazing.* — N UNCOUNT

general practice, general practices. 1 General practice is the work of a doctor who treats people at a surgery or in their homes, not in a hospital, and who does not specialize in particular illnesses or methods of treatment. — N UNCOUNT British

2 A **general practice** is a place where such a doctor works. EG *Some hospital doctors are also attached to general practices.* — N COUNT

general practitioner. See **GP**.

general public. The **general public** is all the people in a society. EG *The lecture will interest both musicians and members of the general public.* — N COLL : *the*+N

generate /dʒɛnəreɪt/, **generates, generating, generated. 1** To **generate** something means to cause it to begin and develop. EG *This book will continue to generate excitement for a long time... Tourism will generate new jobs.* — V+O Formal

2 To **generate** energy means to produce it from fuel or from another source of power such as water. EG *...improved methods of generating electricity.* — V+O

generation /dʒɛnəreɪʃə0n/, **generations. 1** A **generation** is **1.1** all the people in a group or country who are of a similar age. EG *...an older generation of intellectuals... Few actresses of her generation could play the part well... Property is handed on from generation to generation.* — N COUNT+SUPP **1.2** the period of time, usually considered to be about thirty years, that it takes for children to grow up and become adults and have children of their own. EG *We have had a generation of peace in Europe.* — N COUNT **1.3** a stage of development in the design and manufacture of machines or equipment. EG *...the new generation of missiles.* — N COUNT+SUPP

2 The **generation** of energy is its production from fuel or from another source of power such as water. EG *Electric power generation had ceased.* — N UNCOUNT

generation gap. A **generation gap** is a difference in attitude and behaviour between older people and younger people. — N SING

generator /dʒɛnəreɪtə/, **generators.** A **generator** is a machine which produces electricity. — N COUNT

generic /dʒɪ²nɛrɪk/ means referring to or shared by a whole group of similar things. EG *Software is a generic term for the sets of programs which control a computer.* — ADJ CLASSIF : ATTRIB Formal

generosity /dʒɛnərɒsɪ¹ti¹/ is the quality of being generous, especially in doing or giving more than is usual or expected. EG *You shouldn't take advantage of his generosity... ...the generosity with which she had shared her ideas.* — N UNCOUNT

generous /dʒɛnə⁰rəs/. **1** Someone who is **generous 1.1** gives more of something, especially money, than is usual or expected. EG *That's very generous of you... They aren't very generous with pensions.* — ADJ QUALIT ◇ **generously.** EG *She was paid generously to look after the children.* — ◇ ADV **1.2** is friendly, helpful, and willing to see the good qualities in people or things. EG *She was a kind and generous soul... The most generous interpretation is that he didn't know.* — ADJ QUALIT

2 Something that is **generous** is much larger in quantity than is usual or necessary. EG *...a generous donation to our campaign fund... ...a generous measure of cognac.* — ADJ QUALIT ◇ **generously.** EG *He was providing for them generously in his will.* — ◇ ADV

genetic /dʒɪ²nɛtɪk/, **genetics. 1 Genetics** is the study of how characteristics are passed from one generation to another by means of genes. — N UNCOUNT

2 Something that is **genetic** is concerned with genetics or with genes. EG *...genetic defects.* — ADJ CLASSIF ◇ **genetically.** EG *...genetically programmed behaviour.* — ◇ ADV

genial /dʒi:nɪəl/. Someone who is **genial** is kind and friendly. EG *...a genial smile.* — ADJ QUALIT ◇ **genially.** EG *He waved genially to people as they passed.* — ◇ ADV

◇ **geniality** /dʒi:nɪælɪ¹ti¹/. EG *...his general air of geniality.* — ◇ N UNCOUNT

genital /dʒɛnɪtə⁰l/, **genitals. 1** Someone's **genitals** are their external sexual organs. — N PLURAL

2 Genital means relating to a person's external sexual organs. — ADJ CLASSIF : ATTRIB

genius /dʒi:nɪəs/, **geniuses. 1 Genius** is **1.1** very great ability or skill in something. EG *...his genius for improvisation.* — N UNCOUNT **1.2** an excellent quality which makes something distinct from everything else. EG *That is the genius of the system.*

2 Someone who is a **genius** has very great natural ability and talent, especially for a particular subject or activity. EG *Beethoven was a genius.* — N COUNT

genocide /dʒɛnə⁶saɪd/ is the murder of a whole community or race. — N UNCOUNT Formal

genre /ʒɑ:nrə/, **genres.** A **genre** is a particular style of literature, art, or music. EG *...a whole new genre of sentimental fiction.* — N COUNT Formal

gent /dʒɛnt/, **gents. 1** A **gent** is the same as a gentleman. EG *They are very tough gents.* — N COUNT Informal

2 A **gents** or the **gents** is a public toilet for men. EG *The gents was situated in a small yard outside.* — N SING British

genteel /dʒɛnti:l/. Someone who is **genteel** is polite, respectable, and refined. EG *He came from a genteel family.* — ADJ QUALIT

gentle /dʒɛntə⁰l/, **gentler, gentlest. 1** Someone who is **gentle** is kind, mild, and pleasantly calm. EG *...a gentle, sweet man... She had very gentle blue eyes.* — ADJ QUALIT ◇ **gently.** EG *'You have nothing to worry about,' he said gently.* — ◇ ADV ◇ **gentleness.** EG *...the virtues of gentleness and compassion.* — ◇ N UNCOUNT

2 Movements that are **gentle** are even and calm. EG *...the gentle rocking of his mother's chair... There was a gentle breeze.* — ADJ QUALIT ◇ **gently.** EG *I shook her gently and she opened her eyes.* — ◇ ADV

3 Scenery that is **gentle** has soft shapes and colours that people find pleasant and relaxing. EG *...a gentle little landscape... The beach stretched away in a gentle curve.* — ADJ QUALIT ◇ **gently.** EG *...gently sloping hills.* — ◇ ADV

4 Gentle jokes or hints are quite kind and not intended to hurt people. EG *...a very gentle parody of American life... I gave a gentle hint.* — ADJ QUALIT : ATTRIB

gentleman /dʒɛntə⁰lmə³n/, **gentlemen. 1** A **gentleman** is **1.1** a man who comes from a family of high social standing. EG *...a country gentleman.* — N COUNT **1.2** a man who is well behaved, educated, and refined. EG *He was a terribly nice man – a real gentleman.*

2 You can refer politely to men as **gentlemen**. EG *...the gentlemen of the Press... Good afternoon, ladies and gentlemen.* — N COUNT

gentlemanly /dʒɛntə⁰lmə³nli¹/. A man who is **gentlemanly** has perfect manners and is very well-behaved. EG *...a courteous, gentlemanly gesture.* — ADJ QUALIT

gentry /dʒɛntri¹/. The **gentry** are people of high social status. — N PLURAL Formal

genuine /dʒɛnjuɪn/. **1** Something that is **genuine** is real and exactly what it appears to be. EG *...genuine Ugandan food... She looked at me in genuine astonishment.* — ADJ CLASSIF ◇ **genuinely.** EG *...genuinely democratic countries.* — ◇ ADV : OFT+ADJ

2 If you describe a person as **genuine**, you mean that they are honest and sincere. EG *They seemed nice, genuine fellows.* — ADJ QUALIT

genus /dʒi:nəs/, **genera** /dʒɛnərə/. A **genus** is a class or group of similar animals or plants. — N COUNT Technical

geographic /dʒi:ə⁶græfɪk/ or **geographical** /dʒi:ə⁶græfɪkə⁰l/. Something that is **geographic** or **geographical** involves geography. EG *...geographic and political boundaries... ...the characteristics of any geographical region.* — ADJ CLASSIF ◇ **geographically.** EG *...geographically separated species.* — ◇ ADV OR ADV SEN

Do you think that a geologist should know something about geography?

geography /dʒɪɒgrəfi[1]/. **1 Geography** is the study of the countries of the world and of such things as land formations, seas, climate, towns, and population. N UNCOUNT ◇ **geographer, geographers.** EG *...professional geographers.* ◇ N COUNT

2 The **geography** of a place is the way that its physical features are arranged within it. EG *...the geography of the United States.* N UNCOUNT: OFT+SUPP

geology /dʒɪɒlədʒi[1]/. **1 Geology** is the scientific study of substances such as rock and soil in order to find out about the origin, structure, and history of the earth. N UNCOUNT ◇ **geological** /dʒiːə[6]lɒdʒɪkə[0]l/. EG *...an interesting geological site.* ◇ ADJ CLASSIF ◇ **geologist, geologists.** EG *For many years these questions puzzled geologists.* ◇ N COUNT

2 The **geology** of an area is the structure of its land. N UNCOUNT: OFT+SUPP

geometric /dʒiːə[6]metrɪk/ or **geometrical** /dʒiːə[6]metrɪkə[0]l/. Something that is **geometric** or **geometrical** involves geometry or consists of regular shapes and lines. EG *...geometric blocks of concrete... ...a geometrical problem... ...abstract geometrical designs.* ADJ CLASSIF: ATTRIB

geometry /dʒɪɒmɪ[2]tri[1]/ is a mathematical science concerned with the measurement of lines, angles, curves, and shapes. N UNCOUNT

geranium /dʒɪ[2]reɪnɪəm/, **geraniums.** A **geranium** is a plant with small red, pink, or white flowers. N COUNT

geriatric /dʒeri[1]ætrɪk/ is used to describe very old people, their illnesses, and their treatment. EG *...a geriatric ward.* ADJ CLASSIF Technical

germ /dʒɜːm/, **germs. 1** A **germ** is a very small organism that causes disease. EG *...a flu germ.* N COUNT

2 The **germ** of something is the beginning of it which may develop or become more important. EG *It contains the germ of an idea which might save us.* N COUNT: USU SING+*of*

German measles is a disease which gives you red spots and a sore throat. N UNCOUNT

germinate /dʒɜːmɪneɪt/, **germinates, germinating, germinated. 1** If a seed **germinates** or **is germinated**, it starts to grow. EG *You need cool, moist weather for the seed to germinate.* V-ERG ◇ **germination** /dʒɜːmɪneɪʃə[0]n/. EG *Temperature is most important for seed germination.* ◇ N UNCOUNT

2 If an idea, plan, or feeling **germinates**, or if someone or something **germinates** it, it comes into existence and begins to develop. EG *New concepts germinate before your eyes.* V-ERG Formal

gestation /dʒesteɪʃə[0]n/ is **1** the process in which babies grow inside their mother's body before they are born. EG *...the shortest gestation period in any mammal.* N UNCOUNT Technical **2** the process in which an idea or plan develops. EG *The road had been sixty years in gestation.* Literary

gesticulate /dʒestɪkjə[4]leɪt/, **gesticulates, gesticulating, gesticulated.** If you **gesticulate**, you make movements with your arms or hands, often while you are talking. EG *We sometimes gesticulate even when talking on the telephone... Stuart gesticulated angrily.* V Formal ◇ **gesticulation** /dʒestɪkjə[4]leɪʃə[0]n/, **gesticulations.** EG *...the gesticulations that accompany conversation.* ◇ N UNCOUNT OR N COUNT

gesture /dʒestʃə/, **gestures, gesturing, gestured.** A **gesture** is **1** a movement that you make with your hands or your head to express emotion or to give information. EG *She made an angry gesture with her fist.* N COUNT ▸ used as a verb. EG *She gestured that I ought to wait... He gestured to me to lie down... She gestured towards the bookshelves.* ▸ V+REPORT OR V+A **2** something that you say or do in order to express your attitude or intentions. EG *The demonstration is a gesture of defiance... She thanked him for his thoughtful gesture.* N COUNT: USU+SUPP

get /get/, **gets, getting, got** /gɒt/. The form **gotten** /gɒtə[0]n/ is often used in American English for the past participle. In most of its uses **get** is a fairly informal word.

1 Get often has the same meaning as 'become'. For example, if someone **gets** bored, they become bored. If something **gets** cold, it becomes cold. EG *She began to get suspicious... If things get worse, you'll have to come home.* V+C

2 If you **get** into a particular state or situation, you allow or cause yourself to be in that state or situation. EG *He got into trouble with the police... I began to get in a panic.* V+A

3 If you **get** someone or something into a particular state or situation, you cause them to be in that state or situation. EG *The girl finally got the door open... He got her pregnant.* V+A OR C

4 If you **get** someone to do something, you cause them to do it by asking them or telling them to do it. EG *She gets Stuart to help her.* V+O+*to*-INF

5 If you **get** something done, you cause it to be done. EG *I got safety belts fitted.* V+O +PAST PART

6 If you **get** somewhere, **6.1** you move there. EG *When the train stopped, he got off... Brody got out of bed... Nobody can get past.* V+A **6.2** you arrive there. *When we got to Firle Beacon we had a rest... What time do they get back?*

7 If you **get** someone or something into or out of a place, you succeed in moving them there. EG *I got Allen into his bunk.* V+O+A

8 If you **get** someone something, you bring it to them. EG *Get me a glass of water.* V+O+O OR V+O+*for*

9 Get is often used instead of 'be' to form passives. EG *Suppose someone gets killed... He failed to get re-elected.* AUX+PAST PART: FORMS PASS

10 If you **get** something, **10.1** you obtain it. EG *He's trying to get a flat... Get advice from your local health department... I am going to get a divorce... He got her a job with the telephone company.* V+O, V+O+O, OR V+O+*for* **10.2** you receive it. EG *I got the anorak for Christmas... He was with us when we got the news... She ought to get at least eight pounds for it.* V+O: NO IMPER, NO PASS

11 If you **get** the time or the opportunity to do something, you have the time or the opportunity to do it. EG *We get little time for sewing.* V+O: OFT+*to*-INF OR *for*

12 If you **get** an idea or feeling, you come to have it as the result of an experience. EG *She got a lot of fun out of sweeping the front porch... I got the impression he'd had a sleepless night.* V+O: OFT+A

13 If you **get** an illness or disease, you become ill with it. EG *She got chicken pox.* V+O: NO PASS

14 If you **get** to do something, **14.1** you eventually do it. EG *The Prime Minister got to hear of the rumours... I got to like the whole idea.* V+*to*-INF **14.2** you eventually succeed in doing it. EG *We never got to see the play.*

15 If you **get** moving or **get** going, you begin to move or to do something. EG *We can't seem to get moving.* V+-ING

16 If you **get** to a particular stage in something, you reach that stage. EG *You have got to an important stage in your career... I got as far as dismantling the plug.* V+A

17 When it **gets** to a particular time, it is that time. EG *It's getting late.* V+A

18 If you **get** a joke or **get** the point of something, you understand it. EG *I don't really get the point of the story.* V+O: NO IMPER, NO PASS

19 When you **get** a train or bus, you leave a place on it. EG *We got the train to Colchester.* V+O: NO PASS

20 If you **get** a person or an animal, you catch them or shoot them. EG *The police got him in the end.* V+O

21 If you say that something **is getting** to you, you mean that it is making you suffer physically or mentally. EG *The fatigue and backache are getting to me now.* V+*to*

22 If you say that someone's behaviour **gets** you, you mean that it annoys you. EG *What gets me is the way Janet implies that I'm lazy.* V+O: NO CONT Informal

23 You can use **you get** instead of 'there is' or 'there are' to say that something exists, happens, or PHRASE can be experienced. EG *You get some rather curious effects.*

24 If you say that you are **getting somewhere**, you mean that you are making progress. If you say that you are **getting nowhere**, you mean that you are making no progress. PHRASE

25 See also **got**. • to **get used to** something: see **used**. • to **get** your **way**: see **way**.

get about or **get around. 1** If you **get about** or **get around**, you go to a lot of different places as part of your way of life. PHRASAL VB : V+ADV **2** If news **gets about** or **gets around**, it is told to lots of people and becomes well known. V+ADV : OFT+REPORT **3** See also **get around**.

get across. If you **get** an idea or argument **across**, you succeed in making people understand it. EG *We managed to get our message across.* PHRASAL VB : V-ERG+ADV

get ahead. If you **get ahead**, you are successful in your career. PHRASAL VB : V+ADV

get along. If you **get along** with someone, you have a friendly relationship with them. EG *They just can't get along together.* PHRASAL VB : V+ADV OR V+ADV+*with* : RECIP

get around or **get round. 1** If you **get around** a difficulty or restriction or **get round** it, you overcome it. EG *To help get around this problem, some tanks are now equipped with radar.* PHRASAL VB : V+PREP, HAS PASS **2** If news **gets around** or **gets round**, it is told to lots of people and becomes well known. EG *The word got round that Morris was going to England.* V+ADV : OFT+REPORT **3** When you eventually **get around** to doing something or **get round** to it, you do it, when you were previously too busy to do it or were reluctant to do it. EG *I only got around to doing this a few days ago.* V+ADV+*to* **4** See also **get about**.

get at. 1 If you manage to **get at** something, you manage to reach it. EG *The goats bent down to get at the short grass.* PHRASAL VB : V+PREP **2** If you ask someone what they **are getting at**, you are asking them to explain what they mean. EG *I don't know what you are getting at.* V+PREP **3** If you say that someone **is getting at** you, you mean that they are criticizing you or teasing you in an unkind way. V+PREP, HAS PASS Informal

get away. 1 If you **get away**, **1.1** you succeed in leaving a place or person. EG *Last year, he was always trying to get away by five in the evening.* PHRASAL VB : V+ADV, OFT+*from* **1.2** you go away to have a holiday. EG *Is there any chance of you getting away this summer?* V+ADV • If you **get away from it all**, you have a holiday in a place that is very different from the place where you live and work. • PHRASE **2** If you **get** someone **away** or if they **get away**, they escape. EG *They got away through Mrs Barnett's garden.* • See also **getaway**. PHRASAL VB : V-ERG+ADV

get away with. If you **get away with** something that you should not have done, you are not punished for doing it. EG *He bribed her – and got away with it.* PHRASAL VB : V+ADV+PREP

get back. 1 If you **get back** to your previous state or situation, you return to it. EG *Eddie wanted to get back to sleep... Things would soon get back to normal.* PHRASAL VB : V+ADV+*to* **2** If you **get back** to what you were doing or talking about before, you start doing it or talking about it again. EG *He got back to work again.* V+ADV+*to/into* **3** If you **get back** something that you used to have, you then have it again. EG *He would get back his old job.* V+O+ADV **4** If you tell someone to **get back**, you are telling them to move away from something or someone. V+ADV

get by. If you **get by**, you succeed in surviving and having a fairly satisfactory life. EG *He had managed to get by without much reading or writing.* PHRASAL VB : V+ADV, OFT+A

get down. If a situation **gets** you **down**, it makes you unhappy. EG *It isn't just the work that gets her down.* PHRASAL VB : V+O+ADV Informal

get down to. When you **get down to** something, you start doing it. EG *I got down to work.* PHRASAL VB : V+ADV+PREP

get in. 1 When a political party or a politician **gets in**, they are elected. EG *What would Labour do if they got in, then?* PHRASAL VB : V+ADV **2** When a train, bus, or plane **gets in**, it arrives somewhere. EG *What time does the coach get in?* V+ADV **3** If you **get** a remark **in**, you eventually succeed in making it when other people are talking continuously. EG *'What I wanted to say,' I finally got in, 'is that I've a set of instructions at home.'* V+O+ADV; ALSO V+ADV +QUOTE

get in on. If you **get in on** an activity, you start taking part in it. EG *'He even gets in on the photography shows,' she said indignantly.* PHRASAL VB : V+ADV+PREP Informal

get into. 1 If you **get into** an activity, you start being involved in it. EG *I always get into arguments with people... He was determined to get into politics.* PHRASAL VB : V+PREP **2** If you **get into** a particular habit, you start having it. EG *She'd got into the habit of sulking.* V+PREP **3** If you **get into** a school, college, or university, you are accepted there as a pupil or student. V+PREP **4** If you ask what has **got into** someone, you mean that they are behaving in an unexpected way. V+PREP Informal

get off. 1 If someone is given a very small punishment for breaking a law or rule, you can say that they **got off** with this punishment. EG *He expressed relief that he had got off so lightly.* PHRASAL VB : V-ERG+ADV **2** If you **get** something **off**, you remove it. EG *...stains you can't get off your skin... Get your shirt off.* V+O+ADV/PREP **3** If you say **'Get off'** or **'Get your hands off'**, you are telling someone not to touch you, or not to touch something. PHRASE

get off with. If you **get off with** someone, you begin a romantic or sexual relationship with them. EG *Mike thinks I'm trying to get off with his girlfriend.* PHRASAL VB : V+ADV+PREP Informal

get on. 1 If you **get on** with someone, you have a friendly relationship with them. EG *Mother and I get on very well... It is very important to get on with your employer.* PHRASAL VB : V+ADV OR V+ADV+*with* : RECIP **2** If you **get on** with something, you continue doing it or start doing it. EG *Perhaps we can get on with the meeting now.* V+ADV, OFT+*with* **3** If someone who is doing a task **is getting on** well, they are making good progress. EG *I always get on far better if I can draw a diagram.* V+ADV+A **4** If you **get on**, you are successful in your career. EG *She's got to study to get on.* V+ADV **5** If you say that someone **is getting on**, you mean that they are old. EG *She must be getting on now, I suppose.* V+ADV Informal **6** If you **get** a piece of clothing **on**, you put it on. EG *Get your coat on.* V+O+ADV **7 Getting on for** means the same as nearly. EG *They have getting on for a hundred stores.* PHRASE Informal

get on to. 1 If you **get on to** a particular topic, you start talking about it in a lecture or conversation. EG *Somehow we got on to grandparents.* PHRASAL VB : V+ADV+PREP **2** If you **get on to** someone, you contact them. EG *I'll get on to her right away.* V+ADV+PREP

get out. 1 If you **get out** of an organization, you withdraw from it. EG *The Common Market? The sooner we get out the better.* PHRASAL VB : V+ADV **2** If you **get out** of doing something, you avoid doing it. EG *She always got out of washing up.* V+ADV+*of* **3** If news or information **gets out**, it becomes known. EG *The word got out that he would go ahead with the merger.* V+ADV **4** If you **get** something **out**, you take it out of the thing in which it is kept or in which it is being carried. EG *He got out a book and read.* V+O+ADV **5** If you **get** a stain **out**, you remove it. V+O+ADV

get over. 1 If you **get over** an unpleasant experience or an illness, you recover from it. EG *Have you got over the shock?* PHRASAL VB : V+PREP **2** If you **get over** a problem, you overcome it. EG *One mother got over this problem by leaving her baby with someone else.* V+PREP

get over with. If you decide to **get** something unpleasant **over with**, you decide to do it or undergo it. EG *Can we just get this questioning over with?* PHRASAL VB : V+O+ADV+PREP

get round. See **get around**.

get through. 1 If you **get through** a task, you succeed in completing it. EG *It is extremely difficult* PHRASAL VB : V+PREP

Do people get together when they have a get-together?

to get through this amount of work in such a short time. **2** If you **get through** an unpleasant experience or period of time, you succeed in living through it. EG *They helped me to get through that time.* **3** If you **get through** a large amount of something, you completely use it up. EG *I got through about six pounds worth of drink.* **4** If you **get through** to someone, **4.1** you succeed in making them understand what you are trying to tell them. EG *Howard, how do I get through to you?* **4.2** you succeed in contacting them on the telephone. EG *I finally got through at twenty past ten.* V+PREP, HAS PASS / V+PREP, HAS PASS / V+ADV+*to* / V+ADV

get together. **1** When people **get together**, they meet in order to discuss something or to spend time together. EG *I want a team of experts to be got together.* • See also **get-together**. **2** If you **get** something **together**, you make it or organize it. EG *He's spent a whole afternoon trying to get the thing together.* PHRASAL VB : V-ERG+ADV, OFT+*with* / V+O+ADV

get up. **1** When you **get up**, **1.1** you rise to a standing position after you have been sitting or lying down. EG *The woman got up from her chair with the baby in her arms.* **1.2** you get out of bed. EG *You've got to get up at eight o'clock.* **2** See also **get-up**. PHRASAL VB : V+ADV, OFT+A / V+ADV OR V+O+ADV

get up to. When you talk about what someone **gets up to**, you are referring to what they do, especially when it is something that you do not approve of. EG *When I found out what they used to get up to I was horrified.* PHRASAL VB : V+ADV+PREP

getaway /getəweɪ/, **getaways.** When someone makes a **getaway**, they leave a place in a hurry, often after committing a crime. EG *Duffield was already making his getaway down the stairs.* N COUNT

get-together, get-togethers. A **get-together** is an informal meeting or party. EG *We must have a get-together some evening.* N COUNT

get-up, get-ups. A **get-up** is a strange or unusual set of clothes. EG *...Albert Finney in a Mexican get-up.* N COUNT

geyser /giːzə/, **geysers.** A **geyser** is **1** a hole in the Earth's surface from which hot water and steam are forced out. **2** a device for providing hot water in a bathroom or kitchen. N COUNT / British

ghastly /gɑːstli¹/. **1** You describe things or people as **ghastly** when you dislike them very much because of their appearance or behaviour. EG *...ghastly office blocks... ...those ghastly Hewson-Smarts.* ADJ QUALIT

2 A **ghastly** experience or situation is very unpleasant. EG *We wouldn't be in this ghastly mess if you had kept quiet... ...the ghastly news of the murder.* ADJ QUALIT

3 You also describe something as **ghastly** when it looks strange or evil and makes you feel afraid. EG *The great fangs gleamed a ghastly white.* ADJ QUALIT

4 You can say that someone looks **ghastly** when they look very ill. ADJ PRED Informal

ghetto /getəʊ/, **ghettos** or **ghettoes.** A **ghetto** is a part of a city in which many people of a particular race, religion, or nationality live. EG *...a black kid growing up in the ghetto.* N COUNT

ghost /gəʊst/, **ghosts.** **1** When people think that they see a **ghost**, they think that they can see a dead person behaving as if they were still alive. EG *...the ghost of Mrs Dowell... I don't believe in ghosts.* N COUNT

2 A **ghost** of something is a faint trace of it. EG *We haven't the ghost of a chance... ...a ghost of a smile.* N COUNT+*of* Literary

ghostly /gəʊstli¹/. Something that is **ghostly** is frightening because it does not seem real or natural. EG *...ghostly rumbling noises.* ADJ QUALIT

ghost town, ghost towns. A **ghost town** is a town which used to be busy and prosperous but which people no longer live in. N COUNT

ghoulish /guːlɪʃ/. Something that is **ghoulish** is concerned with torture or death. EG *Tim took a ghoulish interest in the murders.* ADJ QUALIT

GI /dʒiː aɪ/, **GIs.** A **GI** is a soldier in the United States army. N COUNT

giant /dʒaɪənt/, **giants.** **1** A **giant** is an imaginary person who is very big and strong, especially one mentioned in myths and children's stories. EG *...stories of cruel giants and wicked witches.* N COUNT

2 Large business organizations are sometimes referred to as **giants**. EG *...the electronics giant, Hitachi.* N COUNT+SUPP

3 Something that is much larger than usual can be referred to as a **giant**. EG *...a giant of a man.* ▸ used as an adjective. EG *...giant Christmas trees.* N COUNT / ▸ ADJ CLASSIF : ATTRIB

gibber /dʒɪbə/, **gibbers, gibbering, gibbered.** When people **gibber**, they talk very fast in a confused manner. EG *...men gibbering in their terror.* V OR V+QUOTE

gibberish /dʒɪbə⁰rɪʃ/. You describe what someone says as **gibberish** when it does not make any sense. EG *He was talking gibberish.* N UNCOUNT

gibbon /gɪbən/, **gibbons.** A **gibbon** is an ape with very long arms. N COUNT

gibe /dʒaɪb/. See **jibe**.

giblets /dʒɪblɪ²ts/ are the parts such as the heart and liver that you remove from inside a chicken or other bird before you cook it. N PLURAL

giddy/gɪdi¹/, **giddier, giddiest.** **1** If you feel **giddy**, you feel that you are about to fall over, usually because you are not well. ◇ **giddiness.** EG *...a sensation of extreme giddiness.* ADJ QUALIT / ◇ N UNCOUNT

2 If something makes you **giddy**, **2.1** you find it very confusing. EG *It made me giddy to hear so much analysis.* **2.2** it makes you happy and excited. EG *The news made me giddy with excitement.* ADJ QUALIT

gift /gɪft/, **gifts.** **1** A **gift** is something that you give someone as a present. EG *...a gift from the Russian ambassador to Charles II... ...the gift of a handful of primroses.* N COUNT

2 If you say that someone has a **gift** for doing something, you mean that they have a natural ability for doing it. EG *John has a real gift for conversation... ...his gifts as a story-teller.* N COUNT : USU SING +*for/of*

gifted /gɪftɪ²d/. **1** Someone who is **gifted** has a natural ability to do something well. EG *She was a gifted actress.* ADJ QUALIT

2 A **gifted** child is extremely intelligent. ADJ QUALIT

gig /gɪg/, **gigs.** A **gig** is a performance by pop musicians. EG *They started out doing free gigs in bars.* N COUNT Informal

gigantic /dʒaɪgæntɪk/. Something that is **gigantic** is extremely large. EG *...a gigantic rubbish heap... ...a gigantic effort.* ◇ **gigantically.** EG *The company got away with gigantically inflated profits.* ADJ QUALIT / ◇ ADV

giggle /gɪgə⁰l/, **giggles, giggling, giggled.** **1** If you **giggle**, you make quiet laughing noises, because you are amused or because you are nervous or embarrassed. EG *The absurd sound made her giggle... 'Oh dear,' she giggled, 'I forgot.'* ▸ used as a noun. EG *...a nervous giggle.* V OR V+QUOTE / ▸ N COUNT

2 If someone has got the **giggles**, they cannot stop giggling. N PLURAL Informal

gilded /gɪldɪd/. If something is **gilded**, it has been covered with a thin layer of gold or gold paint. EG *...the ornate gilded mirror.* ADJ CLASSIF

gill /gɪl/, **gills. Gills** are the organs on the sides of a fish through which it breathes. N COUNT : USU PLURAL

gilt /gɪlt/. Something that is **gilt** is covered with a thin layer of gold or gold paint. EG *...paintings in dark gilt frames.* ▸ used as a noun. EG *The gilt had been chipped.* ADJ CLASSIF / ▸ N UNCOUNT

gimmick /gɪmɪk/, **gimmicks.** A **gimmick** is an unusual action, object, or device which is intended to attract attention or publicity. EG *The manufacturer needed a new sales gimmick.* N COUNT

gin /dʒɪn/, **gins. Gin** is a colourless alcoholic drink. EG *A gin and tonic, please.* N MASS

ginger /dʒɪndʒə/. **1 Ginger** is the root of a plant, sometimes sold in the form of a powder, which has a spicy hot flavour and is used in cooking. N UNCOUNT

2 Something that is **ginger** is a bright orange- ADJ COLOUR brown colour. EG ...*a man with ginger hair... ...a ginger cat.*

ginger ale, ginger ales. Ginger ale is a fizzy non-alcoholic drink flavoured with ginger, which you usually add to an alcoholic drink such as whisky. N MASS

ginger beer, ginger beers. Ginger beer is a fizzy drink flavoured with ginger and sometimes slightly alcoholic, which you drink by itself. N MASS

gingerly /dʒɪndʒəli¹/. If you do something **gingerly**, you do it in a careful, hesitant, and often nervous manner. EG *They walked gingerly over the rotten floorboards.* ADV

gingham /gɪŋəm/ is cloth made of cotton which has a pattern of small squares or stripes. EG ...*a pink gingham shirt.* N UNCOUNT

gipsy /dʒɪpsi¹/. See **gypsy**. N COUNT

giraffe /dʒəˈrɑːf, -ræf/, **giraffes.** A **giraffe** is a large African animal with a very long neck, long legs, and dark patches on its yellowish body. N COUNT

gird /gɜːd/, **girds, girding, girded.** If you say that someone is **girding** their **loins** or **girding up** their **loins**, you mean that they are preparing to do something difficult or dangerous. PHRASE Outdated

girder /gɜːdə/, **girders.** A **girder** is a long, thick piece of steel or iron that is used in the framework of buildings and bridges. N COUNT

girdle /gɜːdəºl/, **girdles.** A **girdle** is a piece of woman's underclothing that fits tightly around her stomach and hips. N COUNT

girl /gɜːl/, **girls. 1** A **girl** is a female child. EG ...*a girl of eleven... ...when you were a little girl... ...a girls' school.* N COUNT

2 You can also refer to a young woman as a **girl**. EG ...*a girl of nineteen... There were a lot of pretty girls there.* N COUNT

3 Someone's daughter can be referred to as their **girl**. EG *She has two girls and a boy.* N COUNT

4 You can refer to a group of women as **girls**. EG *Come on, girls... ...the other girls at work.* N PLURAL

5 Older people sometimes address a woman or female child as **my girl**. EG *My dear girl, what does it matter?* VOCATIVE Outdated

girlfriend /gɜːlfrɛnd/, **girlfriends. 1** A man's or boy's **girlfriend** is a girl or woman with whom he is having a romantic or sexual relationship. EG *His girlfriend walked out on him.* N COUNT: USU+POSS

2 A woman's **girlfriend** is a female friend. EG *She went to the movies with some girlfriends.* N COUNT

girlhood /gɜːlhʊd/ is the time during which a female person is a girl. EG *She had a healthy and happy girlhood.* N UNCOUNT

girlish /gɜːlɪʃ/. If you say that a woman's behaviour is **girlish**, you mean that she behaves like a young girl. EG *She felt a surge of girlish nervousness... ...a girlish laugh.* ADJ QUALIT

giro /dʒaɪrəʊ/, **giros. 1 Giro** is a system by which a bank or post office can transfer money from one account to another. N UNCOUNT British

2 A **giro** or a **giro cheque** is a cheque that is given by the government to a person who is unemployed or ill. N COUNT British

girth /gɜːθ/, **girths.** The **girth** of something is the measurement around it. EG ...*a 52-inch girth.* N COUNT Formal

gist /dʒɪst/. The **gist** of a speech, conversation, or piece of writing is its general meaning. EG *We began to get the gist of her remarks.* N SING: USU the+N+of

give /gɪv/, **gives, giving, gave** /geɪv/, **given. Give** is one of the most common English verbs. It is often used with nouns to form expressions referring to an action. For example, 'She gave a smile' means almost the same as 'She smiled'. Paragraphs 1 to 3 show how **give** is used in this way.

1 You use **give** to refer to an action, especially a physical action. EG *Jill gave an immense sigh... She gave Etta a quick, shrewd glance... She gave the door a push... Any aircraft carrying the Prime Minister is given a thorough check.* V+O OR V+O+O

2 If you **give** a speech or a performance, you speak or perform in public. EG *He was due to give a lecture that evening.* V+O, V+O+*to*, OR V+O+O

3 If something **is given** attention or thought, people concentrate on it, deal with it, or think about it. EG *She hadn't bothered to give it particular thought.* V+O+O, OR V+O+*o*

4 You use **give** to say that a person does something for someone else. For example, if you **give** someone help, you help them. EG *He gave her a lift back to London... ...a tutor who came to give lessons to my son.* V+O+O OR V+O+*to*

5 You use **give** to say that a person tells someone something or tells them to do something. For example, if you **give** someone some news, you tell them some news. EG *That's the best advice I can give... Castle gave the porter the message... Marsha gave her name... 13% gave bad housing as their main source of worry.* V+O, V+O+O, OR V+O+*to*

6 If you **give** someone something, **6.1** you offer it to them as a present. EG *They gave me a handsome little wooden box.* V+O+O OR V+O+*to* **6.2** you hand it over it to them. EG *Give me your key... Joe, give the Colonel another coffee.* V+O+O OR V+O+*to* **6.3** you provide them with it or let them have it. EG ...*without having been given the opportunity to defend himself.* V+O+O

7 If something **gives** a person or thing a particular feeling, quality, idea, or right, it causes that person or thing to have it or experience it. EG *Working on the car has given me an appetite... What gave you that idea?... His leadership gives him the right to command.* V+O+O, V+O, OR V+O+*to*

8 If you **give** a party, you organize it. EG *Every year he gives a lunch for his family and friends.* V+O, V+O+O, OR V+O+*for*

9 If you **give** something a value, you estimate that it has that value. EG *The polls had given the President a 10 to 15 point lead.* V+O, V+O+O, OR V+*to*

10 If something **gives**, it collapses or breaks under pressure. EG *His legs gave beneath him.* V

11 If you say that you **are given** to believe or understand something, you mean that someone has told it to you. EG *We are given to believe that patience is a virtue.* PHRASE Formal

12 If you say that you would **give** your **right arm** or **give anything** to have or do something, you are emphasizing how very keen you are to have it or do it. EG *She said she would give anything to stay in China.* PHRASE

13 People use **give** in expressions such as 'I don't give a damn' to emphasize that they do not care about something. EG *He didn't give a damn about his passengers.* V+O Informal

14 If someone **gives as good as** they **get**, they fight or argue as well as the person they are fighting or arguing with. PHRASE

15 Give or take is used to indicate that an amount is approximate. For example, if you say that something is fifty years old **give or take** a few years, you mean that it is approximately fifty years old. PHRASE

16 Give way is used in these ways. **16.1** If something **gives way** to something else, it is replaced by it. EG *Her look of joy gave way to one of misery.* **16.2** If a structure **gives way**, it collapses. EG *The floor gave way.* **16.3** If you **give way** to someone, you agree to allow them to do something, although you do not really want them to do it. EG *In the long run it proved easier to give way to his demands.* **16.4** If you **give way** when you are driving a car, you slow down or stop in order to allow other traffic to go in front of you. PHRASE

17 See also **given**.

give away. 1 If you **give** something **away**, you give it to someone, often because you no longer want it. EG *She has given away jewellery worth millions of pounds.* PHRASAL VB: V+O+ADV **2** If you **give away** information V+O+ADV

If you glare at someone, will they be pleased?

that should be kept secret, you reveal it to other people.

give back. If you **give** something **back**, you return it to the person who gave it to you. EG *If I didn't need the money, I would give it back again.* PHRASAL VB: V+O+ADV

give in. If you **give in**, **1** you admit that you are defeated or that you cannot do something. EG *We mustn't give in to threats.* PHRASAL VB: V+ADV **2** you allow something to happen that you do not want to happen, or agree to do something that you do not want to do. EG *We mustn't give in to threats.* V+ADV, OFT+*to*

give off. If something **gives off** heat, smoke, or a smell, it produces it and sends it out into the air. EG *...the tremendous heat given off by the fire.* PHRASAL VB: V+O+ADV

give out. If you **give out** a number of things, you distribute them among a group of people. EG *Howard gave out drinks to his guests.* PHRASAL VB: V+O+ADV

give over. If something **is given over** to a particular use, it is used for that purpose. EG *...land given over to agriculture.* PHRASAL VB: V+O+ADV, USU PASS+*to*

give up. 1 If you **give up** something, you stop doing it or having it. EG *He gave up smoking to save money... She never completely gave up hope.* PHRASAL VB: V+ADV+O **2** If you **give up**, you admit that you cannot do something and stop trying to do it. EG *I don't know. I give up. What is it?* V+ADV **3** If you **give up** your job, you resign from it. V+O+ADV

give up on. If you **give up on** something, you decide that you will never succeed in doing it, understanding it, or changing it, and you stop trying to. PHRASAL VB: V+ADV+PREP

give-and-take is a willingness to listen to other people's opinions and to make compromises. EG *...a give-and-take relationship.* N UNCOUNT

give-away. A **give-away** is something that reveals a truth that someone is trying to hide. EG *The give-away is the slight droop of the head... ...a give-away remark.* N SING

given /gɪvəⁿn/. **1 Given** is the past participle of **give**.

2 A **given** date or time is one that has been fixed or decided on previously. EG *At a given moment we all cheered.* ADJ CLASSIF: ATTRIB

3 If you talk about **any given** society or **any given** time, you mean any society or time that can be mentioned. EG *One cannot look at the problems of any given society in isolation from the rest of the world.* PHRASE

4 If you say that something is the case **given** a particular thing, you mean that it is the case if you take that thing into account. EG *This was the best place to study, given my interest in Kant, Hegel, and Marx... It seemed churlish to send him away, given that he only wanted to take photographs.* PREP OR CONJ

5 If you say that someone is **given** to doing something, you mean that they often do it. EG *He was given to claiming that he was related to the Queen.* ADJ PRED+*to* Formal

glacial /gleɪsjəⁿl/ means relating to glaciers or ice. EG *...a glacial landscape.* ADJ CLASSIF: ATTRIB

glacier /glæsjə/, **glaciers.** A **glacier** is a huge mass of ice which moves very slowly, often down a mountain valley. N COUNT

glad /glæd/, **gladder, gladdest. 1** If you are **glad** about something, you are happy and pleased about it. EG *I'm so glad that your niece was able to use the tickets... Ralph was glad of a chance to change the subject.* ADJ PRED+ *to*-INF, REPORT, OR PREP ◊ **gladly.** EG *He gladly accepted their invitation.* ◊ ADV

2 If you say that you are **glad** to do something, you mean that you are willing to do it. EG *Many people would be glad to work half time.* ADJ PRED +*to*-INF ◊ **gladly.** EG *We will gladly do it if it is within our power.* ◊ ADV

gladden /glædəⁿn/, **gladdens, gladdening, gladdened.** If something **gladdens** you, it makes you happy and pleased. EG *It gladdened him to be home.* V+O

glade /gleɪd/, **glades.** A **glade** is a grassy space without trees in a wood or forest. EG *...a forest glade.* N COUNT Literary

glamorous /glæmərəs/. People, places, or jobs that are **glamorous** are attractive and exciting. EG *...the most glamorous star in motion pictures.* ADJ QUALIT

glamour /glæmə/; spelled **glamor** in American English. People, places, or jobs that have **glamour** are attractive and exciting. EG *Acapulco has lost much of its glamour... ...the superficial glamour of television.* N UNCOUNT

glance /glɑːns/, **glances, glancing, glanced. 1** If you **glance** at something, you look at it very quickly and then look away immediately. EG *Jacqueline glanced at her watch... Rudolph glanced around to make sure nobody was watching.* V+A ▸ used as a noun. EG *He cast a quick glance at his friend.* ▸ N COUNT: OFT+SUPP

2 If you **glance** through or **glance** at a newspaper or book, you spend a short time looking at it without reading it carefully. EG *During breakfast he glances through the morning paper.* V+*through/at*

3 If you can see or recognize something **at a glance**, you can see or recognize it immediately. EG *She can tell at a glance whether they are married to each other.* PHRASE

4 If you say that something seemed to be true **at first glance**, you mean that it seemed to be true when you first saw it or thought about it, but that your first impression was probably wrong. EG *At first glance the bullets looked the same as the others.* PHRASE

glance off. If an object **glances off** something, it hits it at an angle and bounces away in another direction. EG *The ball glanced off my fingertips.* PHRASAL VB: V+ADV/PREP

glancing /glɑːnsɪŋ/. A **glancing** blow hits something at an angle rather than from directly in front. EG *The glass hit him a glancing blow on the forehead.* ADJ CLASSIF: ATTRIB

gland /glænd/, **glands. Glands** are organs in your body that make substances for your body to use or allow substances to pass out of it. EG *...the thyroid gland.* N COUNT ◊ **glandular** /glændjəˀlə/. EG *...glandular changes.* ◊ ADJ CLASSIF: ATTRIB

glare /glɛə/, **glares, glaring, glared. 1** If you **glare** at someone, you look at them with an angry expression on your face. EG *The two brothers glared at each other.* V: OFT+*at* ▸ used as a noun. EG *He shot a suspicious glare at me.* ▸ N COUNT: USU+SUPP

2 If a light **glares**, it shines very brightly and makes it difficult for you to look in a particular direction. V: USU+A ▸ used as a noun. EG *The windows were tinted to reduce the glare.* ▸ N UNCOUNT ◊ **glaring.** EG *...the glaring lights of the fairground.* ◊ ADJ CLASSIF

3 If you are in the **glare** of publicity or public attention, you are constantly being watched and talked about by a lot of people. EG *At home he can relax once he's away from the glare of publicity.* N SING: *the*+N

glaring /glɛərɪŋ/. If you refer to something bad as **glaring**, you mean that it is very obvious. EG *...glaring inequalities of wealth.* ADJ QUALIT ◊ **glaringly.** EG *It was glaringly obvious that he had no idea what he was doing.* ◊ ADV: USU+ADJ

glass /glɑːs/, **glasses. 1 Glass** is the hard transparent substance that windows and bottles are made from. EG *He sweeps away the broken glass... They crept up to the glass doors and peeped inside.* N UNCOUNT

2 A **glass** is a container made from glass which you can drink from. Glasses do not have handles. EG *I put down my glass and stood up.* N COUNT

3 You can use **glass** to refer to the contents of a glass, as in a **glass** of water or a **glass** of milk. EG *He poured Ellen a glass of wine.* N PART

4 Glass objects that you have in your house can be referred to as **glass**. EG *...a house crammed with beautiful furniture, glass and china.* N UNCOUNT

5 Glasses are two lenses in a frame that some people wear in front of their eyes in order to help them to see better. EG *...a girl with glasses... ...a pair of glasses.* N PLURAL

6 See also **dark glasses, magnifying glass.**

glasshouse /glɑːshaʊs/, **glasshouses.** A **glasshouse** is a large greenhouse. N COUNT

glassy /glɑ:si¹/. **1** Something that is **glassy** is very smooth and shiny, like glass. EG *The boat lay motionless on the glassy sea.* ADJ CLASSIF Literary

2 If you describe someone's eyes as **glassy**, you mean that they show no feeling or understanding in their expression. EG *He gazed at the street with dull, glassy eyes.* ADJ QUALIT

glaze /gleɪz/, **glazes, glazing, glazed.** A **glaze** is a thin layer of a hard shiny substance on a piece of pottery. N COUNT

glaze over. If someone's eyes **glaze over**, they become dull in appearance, usually because the person is no longer interested in what they are looking at or being told. EG *I can see people's eyes start to glaze over at the mention of Chomsky.* PHRASAL VB : V+ADV

glazed /gleɪzd/. **1** If you describe someone's eyes as **glazed**, you mean that their expression is dull or dreamy, because they are tired or are having difficulty concentrating on something. EG *His eyes took on a slightly glazed, distant look.* ADJ QUALIT

2 If a piece of pottery is **glazed**, it is covered with a thin layer of a hard shiny substance. EG *...glazed clay pots.* ADJ CLASSIF

3 A **glazed** window or door has glass in it. ADJ CLASSIF

gleam /gli:m/, **gleams, gleaming, gleamed. 1** If an object or a surface **gleams**, it shines brightly because it is reflecting light. EG *He polished the gold until it gleamed.* ▸ used as a noun. EG *...a gleam of water.* ◊ **gleaming.** EG *...the gleaming brass on the altar.* V ▸ N COUNT ◊ ADJ CLASSIF

2 When a small light shines brightly, you can say that it **gleams**. EG *The lighthouses of the islands gleam and wink above the surf.* V

3 If your face or eyes **gleam** with a particular feeling, they show it. EG *His eyes gleamed with pleasure.* ▸ used as a noun. EG *A gleam of triumph crossed the woman's face.* V : OFT+*with* ▸ N COUNT : USU SING+*of*

glean /gli:n/, **gleans, gleaning, gleaned.** If you **glean** information about something, you obtain it slowly and with difficulty. EG *Much of the information he gleaned was of no practical use.* V+O : OFT+*from*

glee /gli:/ is a feeling of joy and excitement. EG *...the glee with which the media report scientific calamities.* N UNCOUNT

gleeful /gli:fʊl/. Someone who is **gleeful** is full of joy and excitement, often because of someone else's foolishness or failure. ◊ **gleefully.** EG *He gleefully rubbed his hands.* ADJ QUALIT ◊ ADV

glen /glen/, **glens.** A **glen** is a deep, narrow valley, especially in Scotland or Ireland. N COUNT

glib /glɪb/. You describe someone's behaviour as **glib** when they talk too quickly and confidently, often making difficult situations sound easy, so that you feel that you cannot trust them. EG *MacIver was always ready with glib promises.* ◊ **glibly.** EG *They still talk glibly of a return to full employment.* ADJ QUALIT ◊ ADV

glide /glaɪd/, **glides, gliding, glided. 1** If you **glide** somewhere, you move there smoothly and silently. EG *Tim glided to the door and down the stairs... The canoes glided by.* V : USU+A

2 When birds or aeroplanes **glide**, they float on air currents. EG *...an owl gliding silently over the fields.* V : USU+A

glider /glaɪdə/, **gliders.** A **glider** is an aircraft without an engine. Gliders fly by floating on air currents. N COUNT

glimmer /glɪmə/, **glimmers, glimmering, glimmered. 1** If something **glimmers**, it produces a faint, often unsteady light. EG *The pearl glimmered faintly as she moved.* ▸ used as a noun. EG *The sky was pink with the first, far-off glimmer of the dawn.* ◊ **glimmering.** EG *...the glimmering night sky.* V ▸ N COUNT : OFT+*of* ◊ ADJ CLASSIF

2 A **glimmer** or a **glimmering** of something is a faint sign of it. EG *He showed no glimmer of interest in them... ...the first glimmering of hope.* N COUNT+SUPP

glimpse /glɪmp⁰s/, **glimpses, glimpsing, glimpsed. 1** If you **glimpse** something, you see it very briefly and not very well. EG *...a village they had glimpsed through the trees.* ▸ used as a noun. EG *...the first glimpse I caught of Fanny.* V+O ▸ N COUNT : OFT+*of*

2 You can also say that you **glimpse** something when you experience or think about it briefly, especially when this makes you understand it better. EG *She glimpses something of what life ought to be about.* ▸ used as a noun. EG *...glimpses of his kindness.* V+O ▸ N COUNT : OFT+*of*

glint /glɪnt/, **glints, glinting, glinted. 1** If something **glints**, it produces or reflects a quick flash of light. EG *His spectacles glinted in the sunlight... The sun glinted on the walls.* ▸ used as a noun. EG *...a glint of metal.* ◊ **glinting.** EG *...a city of glinting glass and high towers.* V : OFT+A ▸ N COUNT ◊ ADJ CLASSIF

2 If someone's eyes **glint**, they shine and express a particular emotion. EG *Her green eyes glinted with mockery.* ▸ used as a noun. EG *There was an ironic glint in his eyes.* V ▸ N COUNT

glisten /glɪsə⁰n/, **glistens, glistening, glistened.** If something **glistens**, it shines or sparkles, because it is smooth, wet, or oily. EG *His face glistened with sweat.* ◊ **glistening.** EG *...glistening lips.* V : OFT+A ◊ ADJ CLASSIF

glitter /glɪtə/, **glitters, glittering, glittered. 1** If something **glitters**, it shines in a sparkling way. EG *Her jewellery glittered under the spotlight... Stars glittered in a clear sky.* ▸ used as a noun. EG *...the glitter of the sea.* ◊ **glittering.** EG *...glittering Christmas trees... ...a charming dress glittering with diamonds.* V : OFT+A ▸ N UNCOUNT ◊ ADJ CLASSIF

2 If someone's eyes **glitter**, they are very bright and shiny because they are feeling a particular emotion. EG *Her eyes glittered as she described these wonders.* ▸ used as a noun. EG *He noticed a slight glitter in the whites of her eyes.* ◊ **glittering.** EG *Tony gazed with glittering eyes around him.* V : OFT+A ▸ N SING ◊ ADJ QUALIT

3 You can describe something as **glittering** when it is very impressive. EG *...a glittering career.* ADJ QUALIT : ATTRIB

gloat /gləʊt/, **gloats, gloating, gloated.** When someone **gloats**, they show great pleasure at their own success or at other people's failure. EG *They were gloating over my bankruptcy.* ◊ **gloating.** EG *...gloating self-satisfaction.* V : OFT+*over* ◊ ADJ CLASSIF : ATTRIB

global /gləʊbə⁰l/ means concerning or including the whole world. EG *...protests on a global scale.* ◊ **globally.** EG *This accounts for about half the wheat sold globally.* ADJ CLASSIF ◊ ADV

globe /gləʊb/, **globes. 1** You can refer to the Earth as the **globe**. EG *...television pictures seen all over the globe... ...countries on the far side of the globe.* N SING : *the*+N

2 A **globe is** a spherical object, usually fixed on a stand, with a map of the world on it. N COUNT

3 Any object shaped like a ball can be referred to as a **globe**. EG *...the orange globe of the sun.* N COUNT : USU+SUPP

globule /glɒbju:l/, **globules.** A **globule** is a tiny round particle of a substance, especially of a liquid. EG *...a globule of blood.* N PART Formal

gloom /glu:m/. **1 Gloom** is partial darkness in which there is still a little light. EG *He peered through the gloom at the dim figure... ...the gloom of their cell.* N SING : *the*+N

2 Gloom is also **2.1** a feeling of unhappiness or despair. EG *He viewed the future with gloom.* **2.2** the quality that something has of making people feel depressed. EG *...the pervading gloom of the place.* N UNCOUNT

gloomy /glu:mi¹/, **gloomier, gloomiest. 1** If a place is **gloomy**, it is almost dark so that you cannot see very well. EG *...the gloomy prison.* ADJ QUALIT

2 You say that the weather is **gloomy** when it is cloudy and rather dark. ADJ QUALIT

3 If someone is **gloomy**, they are unhappy and have no hope. EG *He looked gloomy... There was a* ADJ QUALIT

Which words on these pages refer to lights shining?

gloomy silence. ◊ **gloomily.** EG *'Trouble,' Rudolph said gloomily.* ◊ ADV

4 If a situation is **gloomy**, it does not give you much hope of success or happiness. EG *He could only see the gloomy possibilities of modern science.* ADJ QUALIT

glorified /glɔ:rɪfaɪd/ is used to say that something is not as important or impressive as its name suggests. For example, if you say that a lake is a glorified pond, you mean that it is not much bigger than a pond. ADJ CLASSIF : ATTRIB

glorify /glɔ:rɪfaɪ/, **glorifies, glorifying, glorified.** If you **glorify** someone or something, you praise them or make them seem important. EG *His newspapers glorified his charitable donations.* V+O

◊ **glorification** /glɔ:rɪfɪkeɪʃəⁿn/. EG *...the glorification of war.* ◊ N UNCOUNT : *the*+N+*of*

glorious /glɔ:rɪəs/. 1 Something that is **glorious** is very beautiful and impressive. EG *...the most glorious flowers I have ever seen.* ◊ **gloriously.** EG *...gloriously embroidered pictures.* ADJ QUALIT ◊ ADV

2 **Glorious** events and experiences 2.1 make you very happy. EG *...a glorious carefree feeling of joy.* ADJ QUALIT

◊ **gloriously.** EG *We got gloriously drunk.* 2.2 involve great fame or success. EG *...the glorious future opening before them.* ADJ QUALIT

3 If you describe the weather as **glorious**, you mean that it is hot and sunny. EG *We had glorious sunshine.* ◊ **gloriously.** EG *The first few days were gloriously hot.* ADJ QUALIT ◊ ADV

glory /glɔ:ri[1]/, **glories, glorying, gloried.** 1 **Glory** is the fame and admiration that you get by achieving something. EG *The warriors valued glory and honour above life itself... I did it for the theatre, not for my own personal glory.* N UNCOUNT

2 The **glory** of something is its great beauty or impressiveness. EG *...the glory of the classical theatre.* N UNCOUNT +SUPP

3 The **glories** of a person or group of people are the occasions on which they have done something famous or admirable. EG *...a shrine to the glories of the French Army.* N PLURAL +SUPP

4 The **glories** of a culture or place are the things that people find most attractive about it. EG *...the glories of Venice.* N PLURAL +POSS

glory in. If you **glory in** a situation or activity, you enjoy it very much. EG *The women were glorying in this new-found freedom.* PHRASAL VB : V+PREP, HAS PASS

gloss /glɒs/, **glosses, glossing, glossed.** A **gloss** is a bright shine on the surface of something. EG *The wood has a high gloss.* N SING

gloss over. If you **gloss over** a problem, a mistake, or an embarrassing moment, you try and make it seem unimportant by ignoring it or by dealing with it very quickly. EG *Truffaut glosses over such contradictions.* PHRASAL VB : V+ADV+O

glossary /glɒsəⁿri[1]/, **glossaries.** The **glossary** of a book or a subject is an alphabetical list of the special or technical words used in it, with explanations of their meanings. N COUNT

glossy /glɒsi[1]/. 1 Something that is **glossy** is smooth and shiny. EG *She had glossy brown hair.* ADJ QUALIT

2 **Glossy** magazines and photographs are produced on expensive, shiny paper. EG *...the fashion models you see in glossy magazines.* ADJ QUALIT : ATTRIB

glove /glʌv/, **gloves.** A **glove** is a piece of clothing which covers your hand and wrist and has individual sections for each finger. See picture at CLOTHES. EG *He pulled his gloves on... Wear rubber gloves or you may scald yourself.* N COUNT : USU PLURAL

glove compartment, glove compartments. The **glove compartment** in a car is a small cupboard or shelf below the front windscreen. See picture at CAR. N COUNT

glow /gləʊ/, **glows, glowing, glowed.** 1 A **glow** is a dull, steady light, for example the light produced by a fire when there are no flames. EG *...the blue glow of a police station light.* N COUNT : USU SING

2 A **glow** on someone's face is the pink colour that it has when they are excited or when they have done some exercise. EG *The conversation brought a glow to her cheeks.* N SING

3 A **glow** is also a strong feeling of pleasure or satisfaction. EG *I felt a glow of pleasure.* N SING : USU+SUPP

4 If something **glows**, 4.1 it produces a dull, steady light. EG *A cluster of stars glowed above us... They blew into the charcoal until it glowed red.* 4.2 it looks bright by reflecting light. EG *...children's faces glowing in the light of the fire.* 4.3 it is bright, attractive, and colourful. EG *The Church glowed with colourful African patterns and fabrics.* V OR V+C; V OR V+C; V

5 If someone **glows** or their face **glows**, their face is pink as a result of excitement or physical exercise. EG *Aunt Agnes glowed with joy... Her face glowed with a healthy red sheen.* V : OFT+*with*

6 See also **glowing**.

glower /glaʊə/, **glowers, glowering, glowered.** If you **glower** at someone or something, you look at them angrily. EG *He glowered resentfully at Ash.* V : USU+A

glowing /gləʊɪŋ/. A **glowing** description of someone or something praises them very highly. EG *...the book, of which I had read such glowing reports.* ADJ QUALIT

glow-worm, glow-worms. A **glow-worm** is a beetle which produces a greenish light from its body. N COUNT

glucose /glu:kəʊz, -əʊs/ is a type of sugar that gives you energy. It is produced in your body from the food that you eat and you can also buy it in the form of a powder or tablets. N UNCOUNT

glue /glu:/, **glues, glueing** or **gluing, glued.** 1 **Glue** is a sticky substance used for joining things together. EG *The hat seems to be stuck on with glue.* N MASS

2 If you **glue** one object to another, you stick them together using glue. EG *A new piece was glued into place.* V+O+A

3 If you say that something is **glued** to something else by a substance that is not glue, you mean that it is firmly fixed to it. EG *...a chop glued to the plate by a thick sauce.* ADJ PRED+*to*

4 If you say that someone is **glued** to the television or radio, you mean that they are giving it all their attention. EG *They were glued to their TV sets watching the latest news.* ADJ PRED+*to*

5 If you say that someone's eyes are **glued** to something, you mean that they are watching it with all their attention. EG *Their eyes were glued to the scene below.* ADJ PRED+*to/on*

glum /glʌm/, **glummer, glummest.** Someone who is **glum** is sad and quiet, because they are disappointed or unhappy. EG *Don't look so glum... ...his glum face.* ◊ **glumly.** EG *'It's no use,' Eddie said glumly.* ADJ QUALIT ◊ ADV

glut /glʌt/, **gluts.** A **glut** is a situation in which there is too much of something, especially goods or raw materials, so that not all of it can be sold or used. EG *The oil glut has forced price cuts.* N COUNT

glutinous /glu:tɪnəs/. Something that is **glutinous** is very sticky. EG *...glutinous rice.* ADJ QUALIT

glutton /glʌtəⁿn/, **gluttons.** 1 Someone who is a **glutton** eats too much in a greedy way. N COUNT

2 If you say that someone is a **glutton** for something, you mean that they enjoy or need it very much. EG *The British must be gluttons for satire.* N COUNT+*for*

gluttony /glʌtəⁿni[1]/ is the act or habit of eating too much. N UNCOUNT

glycerine /glɪsəⁿri[1]n/; spelled **glycerin** in American English. **Glycerine** is a thick, colourless liquid that is used in making medicine, explosives, and antifreeze. N UNCOUNT

gnarled /nɑ:ld/. 1 A **gnarled** tree is twisted and rough because it is old. ADJ QUALIT

2 A **gnarled** person has rough swollen skin, as a result of old age or hard physical work. EG *...gnarled peasant's hands.* ADJ QUALIT

gnash /næʃ/, **gnashes, gnashing, gnashed.** If you **gnash** your teeth, you bite and rub them together hard because you are angry or in pain. EG *I lay gnashing my teeth in despair.* V+O

gnat /næt/, **gnats.** A **gnat** is a small flying insect that bites people. N COUNT

gnaw /nɔː/, **gnaws, gnawing, gnawed. 1** If animals or people **gnaw** something or **gnaw** at it, they bite it repeatedly. EG *...watching her puppy gnaw a bone... The ant tried to gnaw through the thread.* V+O OR V+A

2 If a feeling **gnaws** at you or **gnaws** away at you, it causes you to worry or suffer and is hard to get rid of. EG *These desires gnaw away at us constantly.* V+*at/away* Literary

◊ **gnawing.** EG *...gnawing doubts about the future of civilisation.* ◊ ADJ CLASSIF : ATTRIB

gnome /nəʊm/, **gnomes.** A **gnome** is an imaginary creature in children's stories that is like a tiny old man with a beard and pointed hat. People sometimes have small statues of gnomes in their gardens. N COUNT

go /gəʊ/, **goes, going, went** /went/, **gone** /gɒn/. In most cases the past participle of **go** is 'gone', but occasionally you use 'been': see **been**.

1 When you **go** somewhere, you move or travel there. EG *I went to Stockholm... She went into the sitting-room... He went to get some fresh milk... A car went by.* V : USU+A

2 When you **go**, you leave the place where you are. EG *'I must go,' she said... Our train went at 2.25.* V

3 You use **go** to say that someone leaves the place where they are and takes part in an activity. EG *Let's go fishing... They went for a walk.* V+-ING OR *for* ● If you advise someone not to **go** doing something, you mean that they should not do it. EG *Don't go hiding in the attic.* ● V+-ING : WITH BROAD NEG Informal

4 If you **go** and do a particular thing, you move from one place to another in order to do the thing, and you do it. EG *I'll go and see him in the morning.* V+*and*+INF : NO CONT

● If you say that someone **has gone and** done something, you are expressing annoyance at what they have done. EG *That idiot Antonio has gone and locked our door.* ● PHRASE Informal

5 If you **go** to school, church, or work, you attend it regularly. EG *She went to London University.* V+*to*

6 You can use **go** to say that someone is in a particular state. For example, if someone **goes** naked, they are not wearing any clothes, and if they **go** unarmed, they are not carrying any weapons. V+C

7 You can also use **go** to say that something does not have something done to it. For example, if someone's words **go** unheard, they are not heard. EG *Halliday's absence had gone unnoticed... Her decision went unchallenged.* V+C

8 You can also use **go** to mean become. For example, if someone's hair **is going** grey, it is becoming grey. EG *The village thought we had gone crazy.* V+C

9 If you say that a period of time **goes** quickly or **goes** slowly, you mean that it seems to pass quickly or slowly. V+A

10 If an event or activity **goes** well, it is successful. If it **goes** badly, it is unsuccessful. EG *Everything went pretty smoothly... How did school go?... The way things are going, it'll be dark before we've finished.* V+A

11 If a machine or device **is going**, it is working. EG *The tape recorder was still going.* V : OFT+A

12 You talk about how a story, song, saying, or piece of writing **goes** just before quoting it or singing it. EG *As the song goes: I fell in love with eyes of blue.* V : OFT+QUOTE

13 You use **go** before the word that represents a noise that something makes. EG *...American sirens which instead of going 'Ow-wow' go 'Whoop-whoop'.* V+QUOTE

14 When a bell or alarm **goes**, it makes a noise. V

15 If you say that money **goes** in, into, or on something, you mean that it is used for that purpose. EG *Most of the aid has gone into urban projects... 40% of his income goes on rent.* V+*in/into/on*

16 If something **goes** to someone, it is given to them. EG *The job is to go to a private contractor.* V+*to*

17 If you say that someone or something **has got to go**, you mean that they must be got rid of. EG *The last to be hired had to be the first to go.* PHRASE

18 If you say that there is a particular thing **to go**, you mean that it remains to be dealt with. If there is a particular period of time **to go**, that period of time remains to pass. EG *Eight down and two to go... There are still two years to go.* PHRASE

19 If someone's sight or hearing **is going**, it is getting worse. V

20 If two things **go** together, **20.1** they look nice when they are placed together. EG *I got the shoes to go with my coat.* **20.2** they are appropriate or suitable together. EG *White wine goes with fish.* V OR V+*with* : RECIP, NO CONT

21 If something **goes** in a particular place, **21.1** it fits in that place. EG *The silencer went on easily.* **21.2** it belongs there, because that is where you normally keep it. EG *Where do the pans go?* V+A

22 When you talk about where a road or path **goes**, you are referring to the place it leads to or passes through. EG *There's a little road that goes off to the right.* V+A

23 You say **'here goes'** just before you do something difficult, exciting, or dangerous. CONVENTION Informal

24 You say **there goes** a particular thing to express disappointment when something happens to prevent you getting it. EG *There goes my chance of a job.* PHRASE Informal

25 If someone asks **'Where do we go from here?'** when a problem has not been solved satisfactorily, they mean 'What shall we do next?' PHRASE

26 If you do something **as** you **go along**, you do it without preparing it beforehand. EG *I was making it up as I went along.* PHRASE Informal

27 If you say that something **goes to show** or **goes to prove** something interesting, you mean that it shows or proves it. EG *All of which goes to show that people haven't changed.* PHRASE

28 A **go** is an attempt at doing something. EG *He passed the test first go... I'll have a go at mending it.* N COUNT ● If you **have a go at** someone, you criticize them. ● PHRASE Informal

29 If you say that something happened **from the word go**, you mean that it happened from the very beginning of a situation. EG *She complained from the word go.* PHRASE

30 If you say that someone **is making a go** of a business or relationship, you mean that they are being successful. PHRASE Informal

31 If you say that someone is always **on the go**, you mean that they are busy and active. PHRASE Informal

32 See also **going, gone.** ● to **go easy on**something: see **easy.** ● to **go so far as** to do something: see **far.** ● to **go hungry**: see **hungry.** ● to **go without saying**: see **say.** ● **there you go**: see **there.**

go about. 1 If you **go about** a task in a particular way, you deal with it in that way. EG *She told me how to go about it.* PHRASAL VB : V+PREP **2** If you **go about** your usual activities, you continue doing them. EG *He wanted to be left alone to go about his business.* V+PREP **3** See also **go around.**

go after. If you **go after** something, you try to get it. EG *My husband had gone after a job.* PHRASAL VB : V+PREP

go against. 1 If something **goes against** an idea, it conflicts with it. EG *When things go against my wishes, I threaten to resign... The teaching of the Bible clearly goes against it.* PHRASAL VB : V+PREP, HAS PASS **2** If you **go against** someone's advice or wishes, you do something different from what they want you to do. EG *She went against the advice of her Cabinet and called a general election.* V+PREP **3** If a decision **goes against** someone, for example in a court of law, they lose. V+PREP

If you go along with a decision, do you agree with it?

go ahead. [PHRASAL VB : V+ADV, OFT+*with*] 1 If someone **goes ahead** with something they have planned or suggested, they begin to do it or make it. EG *They are going ahead with the missile... 'Would you like to hear it?' – 'Go ahead.'* [V+ADV] 2 If an organized event **goes ahead**, it takes place. EG *The May day marches could go ahead.* 3 See also **go-ahead**.

go along with. [PHRASAL VB : V+ADV+PREP] If you **go along with** a decision, policy, or idea, you accept it and obey it. EG *How could you go along with such a plan?*

go around, go round, or **go about.** [PHRASAL VB : V+ADV+-ING] 1 If you **go around**, **go round**, or **go about** doing something, often something that other people disapprove of, you have the habit of doing it. EG *I don't go around deliberately hurting people's feelings.* [V+ADV OR V+ADV+*with* : RECIP] 2 If you **go around**, **go round**, or **go about** with a person or group of people, you regularly meet them and go to different places with them. EG *He had no intention of letting her go around with those scruffy students.* [V+ADV/PREP] 3 If a piece of news or a joke **is going around, is going round**, or **is going about**, it is being told by many people.

go back on. [PHRASAL VB : V+ADV+PREP] If you **go back on** a promise or agreement, you do not do what you promised or agreed to do.

go back to. [PHRASAL VB : V+ADV+PREP] 1 If you **go back to** a task or activity, you start doing it again. EG *She had gone back to staring out of the window.* [V+ADV+PREP] 2 If you **go back to** something that was mentioned earlier in a discussion or talk, you discuss it again. EG *Going back to your point about standards, I agree that they have fallen.* [V+ADV+PREP] 3 If something **goes back to** a particular time in the past, it was made, built, or started at that time. EG *The shop goes back to 1707.*

go before. [PHRASAL VB : V+ADV] Something that **has gone before** has happened or been discussed at an earlier time. EG *The meeting was unlike any that had gone before.*

go by. [PHRASAL VB : V+ADV] 1 If a period of time **has gone by**, it has passed. EG *Eight years went by and the children grew up.* [V+PREP] 2 If you **go by** something, you use it as a basis for a judgement or action. EG *I try to go by reason as far as possible.*

go down. [PHRASAL VB : V+ADV] 1 If a price, amount, or level **goes down**, it becomes lower. EG *The average age of farmers has gone down.* [V+ADV+A] 2 If a speech or performance **goes down** well, people like it and are impressed by it. [V+ADV] 3 When the sun **goes down**, it sets.

go down with. [PHRASAL VB : V+ADV+PREP] If you **go down with** an illness, you catch it.

go for. [PHRASAL VB : V+PREP] 1 If you **go for** a particular type of product or way of doing something, you choose it. EG *...a tendency to go for grand projects.* [V+PREP] 2 If you **go for** someone, you attack them. EG *He went for me with the bread-knife.* [V+PREP] 3 If you say that a statement you have made about one person or thing **goes for** another person or thing, you mean that it is also true of this other person or thing. EG *The same goes for Bardolph.*

go in for. [PHRASAL VB : V+ADV+PREP] If you **go in for** something, 1 you decide to do it as your job. EG *I thought of going in for teaching.* [V+ADV+PREP] 2 you often do it or have it. EG *They go in for vintage port.*

go into. [PHRASAL VB : V+PREP] 1 If you **go into** something, 1.1 you describe it in detail. EG *I won't go into what I've suffered.* [V+PREP, HAS PASS] 1.2 you examine or investigate it thoroughly. EG *My solicitors are going into the question of my jewellery.* [V+PREP] 1.3 you decide to do it as your career. EG *Have you ever thought of going into journalism?* [V+PREP] 2 The amount of time, effort, or money that **goes into** something is the amount that is used to produce it. EG *Three years of research went into the making of those films.* [V+PREP] 3 If a vehicle **goes into** a particular kind of movement, it starts moving in that way. EG *The plane went into a nose dive.*

go off. [PHRASAL VB : V+ADV+O] 1 If you **go off** someone or something, you stop liking them. EG *He's suddenly gone off the idea.* [V+ADV] 2 If something **goes off**, 2.1 it explodes. EG *I could hear the bombs going off.* [V+ADV] 2.2 it makes a sudden loud noise. EG *The alarm went off.* [V+ADV] 2.3 it stops operating. EG *The light only goes off at night.* [V+ADV+A] 3 If an organized event **goes off** well, it is successful. EG *The meeting went off well.*

go off with. [PHRASAL VB : V+ADV+PREP] If someone **goes off with** something that belongs to someone else, they take it away with them. EG *She had let him go off with her papers.*

go on. [PHRASAL VB : V+ADV+-ING OR *with*] 1 If you **go on** doing something, you continue to do it. EG *I went on writing... They can't go on with their examinations... There's no need to go on arguing about it.* [V+ADV+*to*-INF] 2 If you **go on** to do something, you do it after you have done something else. EG *He went on to get his degree.* [V+ADV+A] 3 If you **go on** to a place, you go to it from the place that you have reached. EG *We had gone on to Clare's house.* [V+ADV, USU+QUOTE] 4 If you **go on**, you continue talking. EG *'You know,' he went on, 'it's extraordinary.'... 'Sounds serious,' I said. 'Go on.'* [V+ADV : OFT+*about/at* Informal] 5 If you **go on** about something or **go on** at someone, you talk about the same thing for a long time in an annoying way. EG *Don't go on about it... I went on at my father to have safety belts fitted.* [V+ADV] 6 If you say that a particular activity **is going on**, you mean that it is taking place. EG *There's a big argument going on... A lot of cheating goes on.* • See also **goings-on**. [V+ADV] 7 As time **goes on** means as time passes. EG *I get more depressed, as time goes on.* [V+ADV, ONLY IMPER] 8 You say **'Go on'** to someone to persuade or encourage them to do something. EG *Go on, have a biscuit.* [V+PREP, HAS PASS] 9 If you **go on** a piece of information, you base an opinion or judgement on it. EG *It's not much to go on.* [V+ADV] 10 If a device or machine **goes on**, it begins operating. EG *The light goes on automatically.*

go out. [PHRASAL VB : V+ADV OR V+ADV+*with* : RECIP] 1 If you **go out** with someone, you spend time with them socially and often have a romantic or sexual relationship with them. EG *My parents wouldn't let me go out with boys... I went out with him a long time ago.* [V+ADV] 2 If a light **goes out**, it stops shining. EG *The lights went out in the big tent.* [V+ADV] 3 If a fire or a flame **goes out**, it stops burning. EG *The fire went out... My cigar's gone out.* [V+ADV] 4 If something **goes out**, it stops being popular or stops being used. EG *Steam went out and diesel was introduced.*

go over. [PHRASAL VB : V+PREP] If you **go over** something, you examine, discuss, or think about it very carefully. EG *He went over this in his mind.*

go over to. [PHRASAL VB : V+ADV+PREP] 1 If someone **goes over to** a different way of doing things, they change to it. EG *We went over to the American system.* [V+ADV+PREP] 2 If you **go over to** a group of people, you join them after previously belonging to a group with very different aims or ideas. EG *Anyone joining the police is going over to the other side.*

go round. [PHRASAL VB : V+ADV/PREP, NO CONT] If there is enough of something to **go round**, there is enough of it for everyone in a group to have some. • See also **go around**.

go through. [PHRASAL VB : V+PREP] 1 If you **go through** an event or a period of time, especially an unpleasant one, you experience it. EG *I'm too old to go through that again.* [V+PREP, HAS PASS] 2 If you **go through** a number of things, you look at them in turn, especially in order to find a particular item. EG *Go through the files again.* [V+PREP, HAS PASS] 3 If you **go through** a list, story, or plan, you say it or describe it from beginning to end. EG *You'd better go through the names.* [V+ADV/PREP] 4 If a law, agreement, or official decision **goes through**, it is approved and becomes official. EG *The adoption went through.*

go through with. [PHRASAL VB : V+ADV+PREP] If you **go through with** something, you do it even though it is difficult or unpleasant for you or other people. EG *Would he go through with the assassination?*

go towards. [PHRASAL VB : V+PREP] If an amount of money **goes towards** something, it is used as part of the cost of that thing. EG *It will go towards a deposit on the flat.*

go under. [PHRASAL VB : V+ADV] If a business or project **goes under**, it fails.

go up. [PHRASAL VB : V+ADV] 1 If a price, amount, or level **goes up**, it becomes higher than it was. EG *The price of food will go up.* **2** When a building or other structure **goes up**, it is built. **3** If something **goes up**, it explodes or starts to burn fiercely. EG *In seconds it had gone up in flames.* **4** If a shout or a cheer **goes up**, it is made by a lot of people together. V+ADV V+ADV V+ADV

go with. If one thing **goes with** another, you always get the second thing if you get the first one. EG *The house went with the job.* PHRASAL VB : V+PREP, NO CONT

go without. If you **go without** something, you do not get it. EG *If they couldn't get coal, they had to go without... The family went without food all day.* PHRASAL VB : V+ADV/PREP

goad /gəʊd/, **goads, goading, goaded.** If you **goad** someone, you make them feel a strong emotion such as anger, often causing them to react by doing something. EG *She was being goaded into denouncing her own friend.* V+O : USU+A

goad on. If you **goad** someone **on**, you encourage them. EG *...the spontaneous uprising of masses goaded on by student activists.* PHRASAL VB : V+O+ADV, USU PASS

go-ahead. 1 If you give someone the **go-ahead**, you give them permission or approval to start doing something. EG *He gave the go-ahead for the Manhattan Project.* N SING : *the*+N

2 A **go-ahead** person or organization is ambitious and tries hard to succeed, often by using new methods. ADJ QUALIT

goal /gəʊl/, **goals. 1** A **goal** in some games such as football or hockey is **1.1** the space into which the players try to get the ball in order to score a point for their team. **1.2** an instance in which a player succeeds in getting the ball into the goal, and the point they score by doing this. N COUNT

2 Something that is your **goal** is something that you hope to achieve. EG *They had at last achieved their goal of landing a man on the Moon.* N COUNT+SUPP

goalkeeper /gəʊlkiːpə/, **goalkeepers.** A **goalkeeper** is the player in a sports team whose job is to guard the goal. N COUNT

goalpost /gəʊlpəʊst/, **goalposts.** A **goalpost** is one of the two upright wooden posts that are connected by a crossbar and form the goal in games like football and hockey. N COUNT

goat /gəʊt/, **goats.** A **goat** is an animal with horns and a short tail. Goats are found in mountain areas or are kept on farms. N COUNT

gob /gɒb/, **gobs.** Someone's **gob** is their mouth; often used in a rude way. EG *You shut your gob!* N COUNT Informal

gobble /gɒbəºl/, **gobbles, gobbling, gobbled.** If you **gobble** food, you eat it quickly and greedily. EG *Still hungry, I gobbled a second sandwich.* V+O

gobble down or **gobble up.** If you **gobble** food **down** or **gobble** it **up**, you eat all of it very quickly. EG *He gobbled down the eggs with satisfaction.* PHRASAL VB : V+ADV+O

gobbledygook /gɒbəºldi¹guːk/; also spelled **gobbledegook. Gobbledygook** is language, often in official statements, which you cannot understand at all. EG *He talked complicated gobbledygook.* N UNCOUNT Informal

go-between, go-betweens. A **go-between** is a person who takes messages between people who are unable or unwilling to meet each other. EG *Fortunately I was there to act as a go-between.* N COUNT

goblet /gɒblɪ²t/, **goblets.** A **goblet** is a type of cup without handles and usually with a long stem, which is used for drinking wine out of. N COUNT

goblin /gɒblɪn/, **goblins.** A **goblin** is a small ugly creature in fairy stories. N COUNT

god /gɒd/, **gods. 1** The name **God** is given to the spirit or being who is worshipped as the creator and ruler of the world, especially by Christians, Jews, and Muslims. N PROPER

2 People sometimes use **God** in exclamations to emphasize something that they are saying, or to express surprise, fear, or excitement. Some people find this offensive. EG *My God, John, what are you doing here?* EXCLAM

3 The word **God** is also used in these phrases. **3.1** If you say **God help** someone, you mean that you hope they will not have to experience something unpleasant or dangerous, often when you are warning them. EG *He spoke sharply: 'God help them if that's whom they follow.'* **3.2** If you say **God forbid**, you are expressing your hope that something will not happen. EG *God forbid that anything should happen to my father.* **3.3** If you say **God knows**, you are emphasizing that you don't know something or that you find a fact very surprising. EG *He was interested in shooting and God knows what else... God knows how they knew I was coming.* **3.4** You use **to God** in expressions like **I pray to God** and **I hope to God** to emphasize what you are saying. EG *I hope to God she'll be happy.* **3.5 for God's sake**: see **sake**. ● **thank God**: see **thank**. PHRASES Formal Informal

4 A **god** is **4.1** one of the spirits or beings that are believed in many religions to have power over a particular part of the world or nature. EG *...the Saxon god of war.* **4.2** someone who you admire very much and think is more important than anyone else. EG *When I was eight years old, my uncles were my gods.* N COUNT

godchild /gɒdtʃaɪld/, **godchildren** /gɒdtʃɪldrən/. If someone is your **godchild**, you are their godparent, which means that you agreed to take responsibility for their religious upbringing when they were baptized in a Christian church. N COUNT

goddaughter /gɒddɔːtə/, **goddaughters.** A **goddaughter** is a female godchild. N COUNT

goddess /gɒdɪ²s/, **goddesses.** A **goddess** is a female spirit or being that is believed in many religions to have power over a particular part of the world or nature. N COUNT

godfather /gɒdfɑːðə/, **godfathers.** A **godfather** is a male godparent. N COUNT

god-fearing. Someone who is **god-fearing** is religious and behaves according to the moral rules of their religion. ADJ QUALIT

god-forsaken. A **god-forsaken** place is not at all interesting and is very depressing. EG *The ranch was a lonely run-down god-forsaken place.* ADJ CLASSIF : ATTRIB

godless /gɒdlɪ²s/. A **godless** person does not believe in God and has no religion; often used showing disapproval. EG *These men were dirty, drunken, and both godless and lawless.* ADJ CLASSIF

godly /gɒdli¹/. Someone who is **godly** is deeply religious and shows obedience to the rules of their religion. ADJ QUALIT

godmother /gɒdmʌðə/, **godmothers.** A **godmother** is a female godparent. N COUNT

godparent /gɒdpɛərənt/, **godparents.** Someone's **godparent** is a man or woman who agrees to take responsibility for their religious upbringing when they are baptized in a Christian church. N COUNT

godsend /gɒdsɛnd/. If you describe something as a **godsend**, you mean that it helps you very much. EG *The extra twenty dollars a week was a godsend.* N SING : *a*+N

godson /gɒdsʌn/, **godsons.** A **godson** is a male godchild. N COUNT

-goer /gəʊə/, **-goers. -goer** is added to words such as 'theatre' and 'church' to form nouns that refer to people who regularly go to a particular place or event. EG *They were both enthusiastic playgoers.*

goggle /gɒgəºl/, **goggles, goggling, goggled. 1** If you **goggle** at something, you stare at it with your eyes wide open. EG *She goggled at the dreadful suit.* V : OFT+*at* Informal

2 Goggles are large glasses that fit closely to your face around your eyes to protect them from such things as water, wind, or sparks. EG *She was wearing big green-tinted snow goggles.* N PLURAL

going /gəʊɪŋ/. **1** If you say that something **is going to** happen, **1.1** you mean that it will happen in the future, especially soon. EG *She told him she was going to leave her job.* **1.2** you mean that you are determined that it will happen. EG *I'm not going to be made a scapegoat.* PHRASE

Do polite people gobble their food?

2 If you **get going**, you start doing something, especially after a delay. PHRASE

3 If you **keep going**, you continue doing something, especially something difficult or tiring. PHRASE

4 The **going** is the conditions that affect your ability to do something. EG *...when the going gets tough... It was hard going at first.* N UNCOUNT

5 You say **'That's good going'** or **'That's not bad going'** when something has been done more quickly or more successfully than expected. PHRASE Informal

6 The **going** rate for something is the usual amount of money that you expect to pay or receive for it. EG *The going rate is about £1,000 a head.* ADJ CLASSIF : ATTRIB

7 If you **have** something **going for** you, you have a particular advantage or useful quality. EG *She had so much going for her in the way of wealth and success.* PHRASE

8 See also **go.** • **comings and goings**: see **coming**.

goings-on. You refer to activities that you think are strange or amusing, or that you do not approve of, as **goings-on**. EG *...an amusing story about goings-on at Harry's Bar.* N PLURAL

gold /gəʊld/, **golds. 1 Gold** is **1.1** a valuable yellow-coloured metal that is used for making jewellery, and as an international currency. EG *...gold bracelets.* **1.2** jewellery and other things that are made of gold. EG *They stole an estimated 12 million pounds worth of gold and jewels.* N UNCOUNT

2 Something that is **gold** is bright yellow in colour. EG *...a cap with gold braid all over it.* ADJ COLOUR

3 If you say that someone has **a heart of gold**, you mean that they are very good, kind, and considerate. PHRASE

4 If you say that a child or an animal is **as good as gold**, you mean that it behaves very well. PHRASE

5 A **gold** is a gold medal. EG *He won the gold at Amsterdam in 1928.* N COUNT

golden /gəʊldə^{0}n/. **1** Something that is **golden** is **1.1** bright yellow in colour and looks rather like gold. EG *...a girl with bright golden hair.* ADJ COLOUR **1.2** made of gold. EG *She wore a golden cross.* ADJ CLASSIF

2 You use **golden** to describe something that you think will be successful or the best of its kind. EG *It's a golden opportunity.* ADJ QUALIT

goldfish /gəʊldfɪʃ/. **Goldfish** is both the singular and the plural form.
A **goldfish** is a small orange-coloured fish. People keep goldfish in garden ponds or in a bowls. N COUNT

gold medal, gold medals. If you win a **gold medal**, you come first in a competition, especially a sports contest, and are given a medal made of gold as a prize. N COUNT

goldmine /gəʊldmaɪn/, **goldmines.** If you call a business or activity a **goldmine**, you mean that it is very successful and produces large profits. EG *The company has bought Cosmopolitan, a future goldmine.* N COUNT

gold-plated. Something that is **gold-plated** is covered with a very thin layer of gold. EG *...a bath with gold-plated taps.* ADJ CLASSIF

golf /gɒlf/ is a game in which you use long sticks called clubs to hit a small, hard ball into holes that are spread out over a large area of grassy land. N UNCOUNT

golf club, golf clubs. A **golf club** is **1** a long, thin, metal stick with a piece of wood or metal at one end that you use to hit the ball in golf. **2** an organization whose members play golf. **3** a place where people play golf. N COUNT

golf course, golf courses. A **golf course** is a large area of grassy land that is specially prepared for playing golf on. N COUNT

golfer /gɒlfə/, **golfers.** A **golfer** is a person who plays golf for pleasure or as a profession. N COUNT

golfing /gɒlfɪŋ/ is the activity of playing golf. EG *...a golfing holiday.* N UNCOUNT

gone /gɒn/. **1 Gone** is the past participle of **go.**

2 Someone or something that is **gone** is no longer present or no longer exists. EG *He turned the corner and was gone... The days are gone when women worked for half pay.* ADJ PRED

3 If it is **gone** a particular time, it is later than that time. EG *It's gone tea-time.* PREP

gong /gɒŋ/, **gongs.** A **gong** is a flat, circular piece of metal that you hit with a hammer to make a sound like a loud bell. N COUNT

gonna /gɒnə/ is used in written English to represent the words 'going to' pronounced informally or in a particular accent. EG *What are we gonna do?*

goo /guː/. You can use **goo** to refer to any thick, sticky substance, for example mud or paste. EG *...animals sinking in the goo offshore.* N UNCOUNT Informal

good /gʊd/, **better** /bɛtə/, **best** /bɛst/; **goods.** See also separate entries at **better** and **best**.

1 Something that is **good** is **1.1** pleasant and enjoyable. EG *They had a good time... That's good news... Hello! It's good to see you.* **1.2** of a high quality or standard. EG *...a very good school... ...good agricultural land... She speaks good English.* **1.3** satisfactory or successful. EG *Develop a good relationship with the staff... Both policies make good sense.* ADJ QUALIT

2 If you say that a situation or idea is **good**, you mean it is desirable, acceptable, or right. EG *It's good that there are places like this... She takes on more work than is good for her... 'How is he?' – 'He's fine.' – 'Good.'* • If you say **it's a good thing** or **it's a good job** that something is the case, you mean it is fortunate that it is the case. EG *It's a good thing I wasn't there.* ADJ QUALIT • PHRASE

3 Someone who is in a **good** mood is cheerful and pleasant to be with. ADJ QUALIT : ATTRIB

4 If you are **good** at something, you are skilful and successful at doing it. EG *Alex is a good swimmer... Marcus was good with his hands... You were never any good at Latin.* ADJ QUALIT

5 Someone who is **good** is **5.1** kind and thoughtful. EG *He's always been good to me... It's good of you to come.* **5.2** morally correct in their attitudes and behaviour. EG *There was no trace of evil in her – she was good.* ADJ QUALIT

6 A child or animal that is **good** is well-behaved and obedient. EG *Were the kids good?* ADJ QUALIT

7 Good is what is considered to be right according to moral standards or religious beliefs. EG *...the conflict between good and evil.* N UNCOUNT

8 If something is done for the **good** of a person or organization, it is done in order to benefit them. EG *Casey should quit for the good of the agency... It was for her own good.* N SING+POSS

9 If you say that something will **do** someone **good**, you mean that it will benefit them or improve them. EG *It'll do you good to get a bit of fresh air!* PHRASE

10 You use **good** with a negative to say that something will not succeed or be of any use. EG *It's no good worrying any more tonight... Even if I came, what good would it do?* N UNCOUNT : WITH BROAD NEG

11 People say **'Good for you'** to express approval of your actions. CONVENTION

12 You use **good** to emphasize the great extent or degree of something. EG *He took a good long look at it... ...a good while ago... Take good care of it, won't you?* ADJ QUALIT : ATTRIB

13 If something happens **for good**, the situation never changes back to what it was before. EG *They had gone for good.* PHRASE

14 You use **as good as** before an adjective or a verb to indicate that something is almost true or almost the case. EG *Without her glasses she was as good as blind... He had as good as abdicated.* PHRASE

15 If you **make good** some damage or a loss, you try to repair the damage or replace what has been lost. PHRASE

16 Goods are things that are made to be sold. EG *...a wide range of electrical goods.* N PLURAL

17 If you **deliver the goods** or **come up with the goods**, you do what is expected or required of you. PHRASE Informal

EG *Such an unwieldy banking system is unable to deliver the goods.*
18 so far so good: see **far.** • **in good time**: see **time**.

good afternoon. You say **'Good afternoon'** in the afternoon when you are greeting someone. EG *Good afternoon. Could I speak to Mr Duff, please.* CONVENTION Formal

goodbye /gʊdbaɪ/, **goodbyes. 1** You say **'Good-bye'** to someone when you or they are leaving, or at the end of a telephone conversation. EG *We said good-bye to Charlie and walked back.* CONVENTION
2 A **goodbye** is the act of saying goodbye. EG *They said their good-byes at the front door.* N COUNT

good evening. You say **'Good evening'** in the evening when you are greeting someone, or sometimes instead of 'Goodbye'. EG *Good evening, Mr Castle. I'm sorry I'm late.* CONVENTION Formal

good-humoured. Someone who is **good-humoured** is pleasant and cheerful in their attitude and behaviour. EG *The crowds were patient and good-humoured.* ADJ QUALIT

goodie /gʊdi[1]/. See **goody**.

good-looking. Someone who is **good-looking** has an attractive face. ADJ QUALIT

good morning. You say **'Good morning'** in the morning when you are greeting someone. EG *Good morning, darling. Another beautiful day.* CONVENTION

good-natured. A person or animal that is **good-natured** is friendly and pleasant and does not easily get angry. ADJ QUALIT

goodness /gʊdnɪ[2]s/. **1** People say **'My goodness'** or **'Goodness'** to express surprise. EG *My goodness, this is a difficult one.* • **thank goodness**: see **thank**. EXCLAM
2 Goodness is the quality of being kind and considerate. EG *...a belief in the goodness of human nature.* N UNCOUNT

goodnight /gʊdnaɪt/, **goodnights. 1** You say **'Goodnight'** to someone late in the evening, before going home or going to sleep. EG *We all said good night and went to our rooms.* CONVENTION
2 A **goodnight** is the act of saying goodnight. EG *They just left. Not even a goodnight or a thank you.* N COUNT

goods train, goods trains. A **goods train** is a train that transports goods and not people. N COUNT

good-tempered. Someone who is **good-tempered** is cheerful and does not easily get angry. ADJ QUALIT

goodwill /gʊdwɪl/ is kind feelings and helpful behaviour towards other people. EG *...the goodwill and cooperation of all who are involved.* N UNCOUNT

goody /gʊdi[1]/, **goodies;** also spelled **goodie. 1** People, especially children, say **'goody'** to express their pleasure about something. EG *Oh goody, there's some cake!* EXCLAM Informal
2 A **goody** is **2.1** a person, especially in a film or book, who works or fights for people or ideas that you approve of. **2.2** something pleasant, exciting, or attractive. EG *She opened the bag of goodies.* N COUNT: USU PLURAL Informal

gooey /guːi[1]/. A **gooey** substance is very soft and sticky. EG *...gooey fudge.* ADJ QUALIT Informal

goof /guːf/, **goofs, goofing, goofed.** If you **goof**, you make a foolish mistake. EG *They had their chance, and they goofed.* V Informal

goose /guːs/, **geese** /giːs/. A **goose** is a large bird that has a long neck and webbed feet and makes a loud noise. N COUNT

gooseberry /gʊzbə[0]ri[1]/, **gooseberries. 1** A **gooseberry** is a small, round, green fruit that grows on a bush, has a sharp taste, and is covered with tiny hairs. N COUNT
2 If you say that someone is **playing gooseberry**, you mean that they are an unwelcome third person in the company of two people who are in love with each other and who want to be alone together. EG *I'd hate to play gooseberry to you and your boyfriend.* PHRASE

gooseflesh /guːsflɛʃ/ or **goose pimples** refers to a condition of your skin when you are cold or scared. The hairs on the skin stand up so that it is covered with tiny bumps. EG *The sudden chill raised gooseflesh on the girl's arms.* N UNCOUNT

gore /gɔː/, **gores, goring, gored. 1** If an animal **gores** someone, it wounds them badly with its horns or tusks. EG *...if a bull gores someone to death.* V+O
2 Gore is unpleasant-looking blood from a person or animal, for example after they have been in an accident. EG *...lie dying in a pool of black gore.* N UNCOUNT

gorge /gɔːdʒ/, **gorges, gorging, gorged. 1** A **gorge** is a deep, narrow valley with very steep sides, usually where a river passes through mountains. EG *The road winds through rocky gorges and hills.* N COUNT
2 If you **gorge** or **gorge** yourself, you eat very greedily until you are so full that you cannot eat any more. EG *They gorged themselves on rich food.* V OR V-REFL

gorgeous /gɔːdʒəs/. **1** If you say that something is **gorgeous**, you mean that you find it extremely pleasant or enjoyable. EG *'Look what David gave me.' – 'Oh it's absolutely gorgeous.'... Isn't it a gorgeous day?* ADJ QUALIT Informal
2 If you say that someone is **gorgeous**, you mean that you find them extremely attractive. ADJ QUALIT Informal

gorilla /gərɪlə/, **gorillas.** A **gorilla** is an animal which looks like a very large monkey with a black face and black fur. Gorillas live in African forests. N COUNT

gorse /gɔːs/ is a dark green bush that grows wild and has sharp prickles and small yellow flowers. N UNCOUNT

gory /gɔːri[1]/. **Gory** situations involve people being injured or dying in a horrible way. EG *The film contains no gory violence.* ADJ QUALIT

gosh /gɒʃ/. You say **'Gosh'** to indicate how surprised or shocked you are about something. EG *Thirteen pounds! Gosh that's a lot.* EXCLAM Informal

gosling /gɒzlɪŋ/, **goslings.** A **gosling** is a baby goose. N COUNT

go-slow, go-slows. A **go-slow** is a protest by workers in which they deliberately work slowly in order to cause problems for their employers. N COUNT

gospel /gɒspə[0]l/, **gospels. 1** The **Gospels** are the four books of the Bible which describe the life and teachings of Jesus Christ. EG *...the Gospel according to St Mark.* N COUNT
2 A **gospel** is also a set of ideas that someone believes in very strongly and that they urge others to accept. EG *They continue to preach their gospel of self-reliance.* N COUNT+SUPP
3 If you regard something as **gospel** or as **gospel** truth, you believe that it is completely true. EG *You can take it as gospel truth that he is busy.* ADJ CLASSIF
4 Gospel music is a style of religious music that uses strong rhythms and people singing in harmony. It is especially popular among black Christians in the southern United States. ADJ CLASSIF: ATTRIB

gossamer /gɒsəmə/. **1 Gossamer** is the very light, fine thread that spiders use to make cobwebs. N UNCOUNT
2 You use **gossamer** to describe cloth that is very thin and delicate. EG *...a gossamer handkerchief.* N MOD Literary

gossip /gɒsɪp/, **gossips, gossiping, gossiped. 1 Gossip** is informal conversation or information about other people, often including comments about their private affairs. EG *...spreading scandal and gossip about their colleagues.* N UNCOUNT
2 A **gossip** is **2.1** a person who enjoys talking about the private affairs of other people. EG *According to the gossips, Mrs Ede is absolutely furious.* **2.2** an informal conversation, especially about other people or local events. EG *...friendly gossips over our garden gates.* N COUNT
3 If you **gossip**, you talk informally with someone, especially about other people or local events. EG *I mustn't stay gossiping with you any longer.* V: USU+A

Find three words beginning with 'good' which have nearly the same meaning.

gossip column, gossip columns. A **gossip column** is a part of a newspaper or magazine where the activities and private affairs of famous people are discussed. N COUNT

gossipy /gɒsɪpi¹/. 1 A **gossipy** person enjoys gossiping; used showing disapproval. EG *...a lot of gossipy old women.* ADJ QUALIT

2 Speech or writing that is **gossipy** is informal and full of news about your own affairs or about other people. ADJ QUALIT

got /gɒt/. 1 **Got** is the past tense and past participle of **get**.

2 **Got** is often used in spoken English after the verb 'have' in the expression **have got**, when 'have' alone would be correct but more formal. The form **have got** is used with the same meanings as the main verb 'have', in the senses of owning or possessing things: see **have**. EG *We haven't got a car... Have you got any brochures on Holland?... I've got nothing to hide... That door's got a lock on it.* V+O

3 **Got** is also used in the expression **have got to**, which is an informal way of saying 'have to' or 'must'. It is used mainly to indicate that it is necessary that something should be done. EG *We've got to get up early tomorrow... There's got to be some motive.* V+*to*-INF

gotta /gɒtə/ is used in written English to represent the words 'got to' pronounced informally or in a particular accent. It is an informal way of saying 'have to' or 'must'. EG *I've gotta get back.*

gotten /gɒtə⁰n/ is often used for the past participle of **get** in American English.

gouge /gaʊdʒ/, **gouges, gouging, gouged.** If you **gouge** something, you make a hole in it with a pointed object. EG *...gouging a trough in the lawn.* V+O : USU+A

gouge out. If you **gouge** something **out**, you force it out of a hole using your fingers or a sharp instrument. EG *...gouging out the dirt with a knife.* PHRASAL VB : V+O+ADV

gourd /gʊəd/, **gourds.** A **gourd** is a large fruit that is similar to a marrow. N COUNT

gourmet /gʊəmeɪ/, **gourmets.** A **gourmet** is a person who knows a lot about good cooking and wine, and who enjoys eating good food. N COUNT

gout /gaʊt/ is a disease which causes someone's joints to swell painfully, especially in their toes. N UNCOUNT

govern /gʌvə⁰n/, **governs, governing, governed.** 1 Someone who **governs** a country rules the country, for example by making and revising the laws, managing the economy, and controlling public services. EG *Many civil servants are sure that they can govern better than the politicians.* V OR V+O

2 Something that **governs** an event or situation has control and influence over it. EG *Poverty governed our lives... ...rules governing the conduct of students.* V+O

governess /gʌvənɪ²s/, **governesses.** A **governess** is a woman who is employed by a family to live with them and educate their children. N COUNT

government /gʌvən⁰mə²nt/, **governments.** 1 A **government** is the group of people who are responsible for governing a country or state. EG *The Wilson Government came to power in 1964... The government has had to cut back on public expenditure.* N COLL

2 **Government** is 2.1 the departments, ministries, and committees that carry out the decisions of the political leaders of a country. EG *...a cut in government spending.* N UNCOUNT : USU N MOD 2.2 the activities and methods involved in governing a country or state. EG *Most of his ministers had no previous experience of government... ...the principle of government by the majority.* N UNCOUNT

governor /gʌvə⁰nə/, **governors.** A **governor** is 1 a person who is responsible for the political administration of a region, especially of a state in the United States of America. EG *...former Governor John Connally of Texas.* 2 a person who is on a committee which controls an institution such as a school or a hospital. EG *...the Board of Governors.* 3 the person who is in charge of the administration of a prison. N COUNT

gown /gaʊn/, **gowns.** A **gown** is 1 a long dress which women wear on formal occasions. EG *...a wedding gown.* 2 a loose piece of clothing like a long cloak, which is usually black and is worn on formal occasions by people such as judges and lawyers. N COUNT

GP, GPs. A **GP** is a doctor who does not specialize in any particular area of medicine, but who has a medical practice in which he or she treats all types of illness. **GP** is an abbreviation for 'general practitioner'. EG *...the GP's surgery.* N COUNT

grab /græb/, **grabs, grabbing, grabbed.** 1 If you **grab** something, you take it or pick it up suddenly and roughly. EG *She grabbed my arm.* V+O

2 If you **grab** at something, you try to take it or pick it up. EG *She fell on her knees to grab at the money.* V+*at* ▸ used as a noun. EG *He made a grab for the knife.* ▸ N COUNT

3 If you **grab** some food or sleep, you get it quickly, usually because you do not have much time. EG *I'll grab a sandwich before I go.* V+O

4 If you **grab** a chance or opportunity, you take advantage of it eagerly. EG *Why didn't you grab the chance to go to New York?* V+O OR V+*at*

grace /greɪs/, **graces, gracing, graced.** 1 If you refer to someone's **grace**, you are referring to the smooth, controlled, and attractive way they move. EG *She moved with an extraordinary grace.* N UNCOUNT

2 If you do something unpleasant **with good grace**, you do it without complaining. EG *They accept unhappiness with stoic good grace.* PHRASE

3 If you say that someone **had the grace** to do something, you mean that what they did showed that they were ashamed of something bad that they had done earlier; used showing approval. EG *At least he had the grace to drop his smile and look away from me.* PHRASE

4 If you say that something **graces** a place, you mean that it makes the place more pleasant or attractive. EG *...the plants that grace our conservatories.* V+O Formal

5 If you say that someone important will **grace** an event, you mean that they have kindly agreed to be present at it. EG *He had been invited to grace a function at the college.* V+O Formal

6 You use expressions such as **Your Grace** and **Her Grace** when you are addressing or referring to a duke, duchess, or archbishop. EG *His Grace will receive you now.*

graceful /greɪsfʊl/. 1 Someone or something that is **graceful** moves in a smooth and controlled way which is attractive to watch. EG *They're very graceful animals.* ◇ **gracefully.** EG *Learn how to move gracefully on a stage.* ADJ QUALIT ◇ ADV

2 Something that is **graceful** is attractive because it has a pleasing shape or style. EG *...graceful curves... ...graceful writing.* ADJ QUALIT

3 If a person's behaviour is **graceful**, it is polite, kind, and pleasant, especially in a difficult situation. EG *She turned with graceful solicitude to Anthea.* ◇ **gracefully.** EG *He accepted gracefully and gratefully.* ADJ QUALIT ◇ ADV

graceless /greɪslɪ²s/. 1 Something that is **graceless** is unattractive and not very interesting. EG *...a large, graceless industrial city.* ADJ QUALIT

2 If you describe someone as **graceless**, you mean that they behave impolitely. EG *He was so graceless, so eager to shock.* ADJ QUALIT Formal

gracious /greɪʃəs/. 1 If you say that someone is **gracious**, you mean that they are polite and pleasant, especially in the way that they treat people who have a lower social position than them. ADJ QUALIT ◇ **graciously.** EG *She accepted the tribute graciously.* ◇ ADV Formal

2 You use **gracious** to describe the comfortable ADJ QUALIT : ATTRIB

way of life of wealthy people, especially in former times. EG *...places of recreation and gracious living.*

3 People use phrases such as **'Good gracious!'** and **'Goodness gracious!'** to express surprise or annoyance. EG *Good gracious! I never knew that... 'You're short of money?' – 'Good gracious no!'* EXCLAM Informal Outdated

gradation /grədeɪʃən/, **gradations.** A **gradation** is a small change, or one of the stages in the process of change. EG *...white bread and wholemeal bread, and many gradations between the two.* N COUNT+SUPP

grade /greɪd/, **grades, grading, graded. 1** If you **grade** a number of things, you judge or measure their quality and give each of them a number or name that indicates how good or bad it is. EG *The reports are graded 1 to 6.* V+O : USU PASS

2 The **grade** of a product is its quality, usually when this has been officially judged or measured. EG *...ordinary grade petrol.* N COUNT : OFT+SUPP

3 Your **grade** in an examination or piece of written work is the mark that you get. EG *She passed the exams with good grades.* N COUNT

4 Your **grade** in a company or organization is your level of importance or your rank. EG *...separate dining rooms for different grades of staff.* N COUNT+SUPP

5 A **grade** in an American school is a class or a group of classes in which all the children are of a similar age. EG *She had entered the sixth grade at eleven.* N COUNT

6 If you **make the grade**, you succeed in something by reaching the standard that is required. EG *She couldn't make the grade.* PHRASE Informal

graded /greɪdɪd/ is used to describe something that is gradually sloping or changing. EG *...a nicely graded curve.* ADJ CLASSIF : ATTRIB

gradient /greɪdɪənt/, **gradients.** A **gradient** is a slope or the degree of steepness of a slope. EG *The floor has a minimum gradient of one in five... ...roads with sharp bends and varying gradients.* N COUNT

gradual /grædjʊəl/. Something that is **gradual** happens over a long period of time rather than suddenly. EG *It's a process of gradual development.* ADJ QUALIT

◇ **gradually.** EG *Things change gradually in engineering.* ◇ ADV

graduate, graduates, graduating, graduated; pronounced /grædjʊət/ when it is a noun and /grædjʊeɪt/ when it is a verb.

1 A **graduate** is **1.1** a student who has successfully completed a first degree at a university or college. EG *...a psychology graduate of Stanford University.* N COUNT

1.2 in the United States, a student who has successfully completed high school. N COUNT+SUPP

2 Graduate means the same as postgraduate. EG *...graduate students in the philosophy department.* N MOD

3 When a student **graduates**, he or she has successfully completed a degree course at a university or college and receives a certificate that shows this. EG *She recently graduated from law school.* V : USU+A

4 In the United States, when someone **graduates**, they have successfully completed high school and receive a certificate or diploma that shows this. V : USU+A

5 If you **graduate** from one thing to another, you go from a less important job or position to a more important one. EG *Start on a local paper, and then graduate to a provincial paper.* V : OFT+*from/to*

graduated /grædʊeɪtɪd/ is used to describe something that increases by regular amounts or grades. EG *...graduated pensions.* ADJ CLASSIF

graduation /grædjʊeɪʃən/ is **1** the successful completion of a course of study at a university or college, for which you receive a degree or diploma. EG *He should get a good job after graduation.* **2** a ceremony at university or college, at which degrees and diplomas are given to students who have successfully completed their studies. EG *He had just attended his daughter's graduation.* N UNCOUNT

graffiti /grəfiːtiː/. **Graffiti** is words or pictures that are written or drawn on walls, signs, and posters in public places. Graffiti is usually rude, funny, or contains a political message. EG *...walls covered with graffiti.* N UNCOUNT OR N PLURAL

graft /grɑːft/, **grafts, grafting, grafted. 1** If you **graft** a part of one plant on to another plant, you join them together so that they will grow together and become one plant. V+O : OFT+*onto*

2 If you **graft** one idea or system on to another, you try to join one to the other. EG *...modern federal structures grafted on to ancient cultural divisions.* V+O : OFT +*on/upon*

3 If doctors **graft** a piece of healthy skin or bone or a healthy organ to a damaged part of your body, they attach it by a medical operation in order to replace the damaged part. EG *...new veins grafted to his heart.* V+O : OFT +*to/onto*

4 A **graft** is a piece of healthy skin or bone, or a healthy organ, which is attached to a damaged part of your body by a medical operation in order to replace it. EG *Laverne had skin grafts on her thighs.* N COUNT : OFT+SUPP

5 Graft means hard work. EG *...the hard graft of the working men.* N UNCOUNT British

6 Graft is also the act of obtaining money dishonestly by using your position of political power. EG *...graft and corruption.* N UNCOUNT

grain /greɪn/, **grains. 1** A **grain** of wheat, rice, or other cereal crop is a seed from it. EG *...no bigger than grains of rice.* N PART OR N COUNT

2 Grain is a cereal crop, especially wheat or corn, that has been harvested to be used for food. EG *We had surplus grain.* N MASS

3 A **grain** of sand or salt is a tiny hard piece of it. N PART

4 A **grain** of a quality is a very small amount of it. EG *He did not have a grain of humour... ...a grain of truth.* N PART Literary

5 The **grain** of a piece of wood is the natural pattern and direction of lines on its surface. N COUNT

6 If you say that an idea or action **goes against the grain**, you mean that it is very difficult for you to accept it or do it, because it conflicts with your ideas or beliefs. EG *However much it goes against the grain, we are compelled to concede that their methods may succeed.* PHRASE

grained /greɪnd/ is used after adjectives and adverbs to describe substances that consist of particles of a particular size. EG *...a coarse grained clay.* ADJ CLASSIF

grainy /greɪni/. Something that is **grainy** has a rough surface or texture. EG *...the grainy wood of the table.* ADJ CLASSIF : ATTRIB

gram /græm/, **grams;** also spelled **gramme.** A **gram** is a very small unit of weight. One thousand grams are equal to one kilogram. EG *...500 grams of flour.* N COUNT OR N PART

grammar /græmə/, **grammars. 1 Grammar** is **1.1** the rules of a language, relating to the way in which you can put words together in order to make sentences. **1.2** the way in which someone either obeys or does not obey the rules of grammar when they write or speak. EG *I'm constantly having to correct their grammar.* N UNCOUNT

2 A **grammar** is **2.1** a book that describes the rules of a language. EG *...an old French grammar.* **2.2** a theory that is intended to explain the rules of a language. EG *...the theory of Case Grammar.* N COUNT; N COUNT OR N UNCOUNT

grammar school, grammar schools. A **grammar school** is a school in Britain for children aged between eleven and eighteen who have a high academic ability. N COUNT

grammatical /grəmætɪkəl/. **1 Grammatical** is used to describe something that relates to grammar. EG *This sentence is very complex in its grammatical structure.* ◇ **grammatically.** EG *His English was usually grammatically correct.* ADJ CLASSIF : ATTRIB; ◇ ADV

2 If someone's language is **grammatical**, it is correct because it obeys the rules of grammar. EG *He speaks perfectly grammatical English.* ADJ QUALIT

Do grapefruit grow on grapevines?

gramme /græm/. See **gram**.

gramophone /græməfəʊn/, **gramophones.** A **gramophone** is an old-fashioned type of record player. N COUNT

gran /græn/, **grans.** Your **gran** is your grandmother. N COUNT OR VOCATIVE

granary /grænəri[1]/, **granaries.** A **granary** is a building in which grain is stored. N COUNT

grand /grænd/, **grander, grandest. 1** Buildings that are **grand** are splendid or impressive in size and appearance. EG *...a grand palace... ...grand architecture.* ◊ **grandly.** EG *Its interior is grandly elegant.* ADJ QUALIT; ◊ ADV

2 Plans and actions that are **grand** are intended to achieve important results. EG *...the grand plot that you two are hatching.* ADJ QUALIT : ATTRIB

3 People, jobs, or appearances that are **grand** seem important or socially superior. EG *...all sorts of grand people... The job isn't as grand as it sounds.* ◊ **grandly.** EG *He announced grandly that he 'had no time for women.'* ADJ QUALIT; ◊ ADV

4 Grand moments or activities are exciting and important. EG *Finally, the grand moment comes when you make your first solo flight.* ADJ QUALIT : ATTRIB

5 If you describe an experience as **grand**, you mean that it is very pleasant and enjoyable. EG *We've had some grand times together, haven't we?* ADJ QUALIT Informal Outdated

6 A **grand** total is the final amount of something. EG *In 1886 Levers, the soap firm, spent a grand total of 50 pounds on advertising.* ADJ CLASSIF : ATTRIB

7 A **grand** is a thousand dollars or pounds. EG *That still leaves you with fifty grand.* NUMBER Informal

grandad /grændæd/, **grandads;** also spelled **granddad.** Your **grandad** is your grandfather. N COUNT OR VOCATIVE

grandchild /grænd[0]tʃaɪld/, **grandchildren** /grænd[0]tʃɪldrən/. Someone's **grandchild** is the child of their son or daughter. N COUNT

granddaughter /grændɔ:tə/, **granddaughters.** Someone's **granddaughter** is the daughter of their son or daughter. N COUNT

grandeur /grændʒə/ is **1** the quality in something, for example in a building or in scenery, which makes it seem impressive and often elegant. EG *...the grandeur of Lansdowne House.* **2** great importance and social status that a person has. EG *His wealth gave him grandeur.* N UNCOUNT

grandfather /grænd[0]fɑ:ðə/, **grandfathers.** Your **grandfather** is the father of your father or mother. N COUNT

grandfather clock, grandfather clocks. A **grandfather clock** is a clock in a tall wooden case which stands upright on the floor. N COUNT

grandiose /grændɪəʊs/ is used to describe something which is bigger or more elaborate than necessary and therefore seems ridiculous. EG *...grandiose architecture... ...grandiose schemes to recycle everything.* ADJ QUALIT

grandma /grænd[0]mɑ:/, **grandmas.** Your **grandma** is your grandmother. N COUNT OR VOCATIVE

grandmother /grænd[0]mʌðə/, **grandmothers.** Your **grandmother** is the mother of your father or mother. N COUNT

grandpa /grænd[0]pɑ:, græmpɑ:/, **grandpas.** Your **grandpa** is your grandfather. N COUNT OR VOCATIVE

grandparent /grænd[0]peərənt/, **grandparents.** Your **grandparents** are the parents of your father or mother. N COUNT : USU PLURAL

grand piano, grand pianos. A **grand piano** is a large flat piano. See picture at MUSICAL INSTRUMENTS. N COUNT

grandson /grænd[0]sʌn/, **grandsons.** Someone's **grandson** is the son of their son or daughter. N COUNT

grandstand /grænd[0]stænd/, **grandstands.** A **grandstand** is a covered stand with several rows of seats which provide a good view, for example at racecourses or football grounds. N COUNT

granite /grænɪt/ is a very hard rock which is often used in building. N UNCOUNT

granny /græni[1]/, **grannies;** also spelled **grannie.** Your **granny** is your grandmother. N COUNT OR VOCATIVE

grant /grɑ:nt/, **grants, granting, granted. 1** A **grant** is an amount of money that the government gives to a person or to an organization for a particular purpose such as education, welfare, or home improvements. EG *You may be eligible for a grant to help you study.* N COUNT

2 If someone in authority **grants** you something such as a sum of money, they give it to you. EG *Proposals have been made to grant each displaced family £25,000... He was finally granted a visa.* V+O+O OR V+O+*to*

3 If you **take it for granted** that something is true, you believe that it is true without thinking about it or looking for proof. EG *It is taken for granted that every child should learn mathematics.* PHRASE

4 If you **take** someone **for granted**, you benefit from them without showing that you are grateful. EG *He just takes me absolutely for granted.* PHRASE

5 If you **grant** that something is true, you admit that it is true. EG *That joy ride, I grant you, was a silly stunt.* ● You use **granted** or **granting** to say that something is true, before you make a comment about it. EG *Granted that he's in hospital, he can't do us much harm.* V+REPORT : ONLY *that* OR V+O; ● CONJ Formal

granulated /grænjə[4]leɪtɪ[2]d/. **Granulated** sugar is sugar which is in the form of coarse grains. ADJ CLASSIF : ATTRIB

granule /grænjə[4]l/, **granules.** A **granule** is a small round piece of something. EG *...sea salt sold in the form of granules.* N COUNT

grape /greɪp/, **grapes.** A **grape** is a small, round fruit, green or purple in colour, which is eaten raw, used for making wine, or dried to make raisins, sultanas, or currants. EG *...a bunch of grapes.* N COUNT : USU PLURAL

grapefruit /greɪpfru:t/, **grapefruits. Grapefruit** can also be used as the plural form.
A **grapefruit** is a large, round, yellow fruit, similar to an orange, that has a sharp, sour taste. N COUNT OR N UNCOUNT

grapevine /greɪpvaɪn/, **grapevines. 1** A **grapevine** is a climbing plant on which grapes grow. N COUNT

2 If people hear news on the **grapevine**, the news is passed from one person to another in casual conversation. EG *She heard something intriguing on the grapevine.* N SING : *the*+N

graph /grɑ:f, græf/, **graphs.** A **graph** is a mathematical diagram, usually a line or curve, which shows how two or more sets of numbers or measurements are related. EG *...a temperature graph.* N COUNT

graphic /græfɪk/, **graphics. 1** Descriptions or accounts that are **graphic** are very clear and detailed. EG *...his graphic stories of persecution.* ◊ **graphically.** EG *The cruelty of this is graphically described by the old farmer.* ADJ QUALIT; ◊ ADV

2 Something that is **graphic** is concerned with drawing, especially the use of strong lines and colours. EG *...graphic and industrial design.* ADJ CLASSIF : ATTRIB

3 Graphics are drawings and pictures that are made using simple lines and sometimes strong colours. EG *...computer generated graphics.* N PLURAL

graphite /græfaɪt/ is a hard black substance that is a form of carbon. It is used to make the centre part of pencils. N UNCOUNT

grapple /græpə[0]l/, **grapples, grappling, grappled. 1** If you **grapple** with someone, you take hold of them and struggle or fight with them. EG *We grappled with him and took the guns from him.* V : OFT+*with*

2 If you **grapple** with a problem, you try hard to solve it. EG *I grappled with this moral dilemma.* V+*with*

grasp /grɑ:sp/, **grasps, grasping, grasped. 1** If you **grasp** something, you take it with your hand and hold it firmly. EG *Edward grasped Castle's arm.* ● See also **grasping**. V+O OR V+*for/at*

2 A **grasp** is a firm hold or grip. EG *The animal had a powerful grasp.* N SING+SUPP

3 If you **grasp** something complicated, you understand it. EG *The concepts were difficult to grasp... I grasped quite soon what was going on.* V+O OR V+REPORT

4 If you have a **grasp** of something, you have an N SING+SUPP understanding of it. EG *He had a sound grasp of tactics.*

5 If something is **within** your **grasp**, it is likely that you will achieve it. EG *A peaceful solution was within his grasp.* PHRASE

6 If something is **in** your **grasp**, you hold it or control it. If something escapes or slips **from** your **grasp**, you no longer hold it or control it. EG *They regretted letting her slip from their grasp.* PHRASE

grasping /grɑːspɪŋ/. Someone who is **grasping** wants to get as much money as possible; used showing disapproval. ADJ QUALIT

grass /grɑːs/ is a very common plant with narrow leaves that forms a layer covering an area of ground. EG *They lay on the grass.* N UNCOUNT

grasshopper /grɑːshᵒɒpə/, **grasshoppers.** A **grasshopper** is an insect which has long back legs and can jump high into the air. Grasshoppers make a high, vibrating sound. N COUNT

grassland /grɑːslə³nd/, **grasslands. Grassland** is land which is covered with wild grass. N UNCOUNT OR N COUNT

grass roots. The **grass roots** of an organization are the ordinary people in it, rather than its leaders. EG *...to strengthen democracy at the grass roots... ...grass-roots support for the new party.* N PLURAL

grassy /grɑːsi¹/. A **grassy** area of land is covered in grass. ADJ QUALIT

grate /greɪt/, **grates, grating, grated. 1** A **grate** is a framework of metal bars in a fireplace, which holds the coal or wood. EG *A fire was burning in the grate.* N COUNT

2 When you **grate** food such as cheese or carrot, you rub it over a metal tool so that it is shredded into very small pieces. EG *...grated lemon peel.* V+O

3 When something **grates** or when you **grate** it, it makes a harsh, unpleasant sound because two surfaces are rubbing hard against each other. EG *He could hear her shoes grating on the steps.* V-ERG

4 If a noise or someone's behaviour **grates** on you, it irritates you. EG *That shrill laugh grated on her mother.* V: OFT+*on*

5 See also **grating**.

grateful /greɪtful/. If you are **grateful** for something that someone has given you or done for you, you have friendly feelings towards them and wish to thank them. EG *I am ever so grateful to you for talking to me... I'd be so grateful if you could do it.* ADJ QUALIT

◇ **gratefully.** EG *He accepted the money gratefully.* ◇ ADV

grater /greɪtə/, **graters.** A **grater** is a metal tool with sharp, raised parts on its surface which is used for grating food. N COUNT

gratify /grætɪfaɪ/, **gratifies, gratifying, gratified. 1** If you **are gratified** by something, it gives you pleasure or satisfaction. EG *He was gratified that his guess had been proved right.* V+O Formal

◇ **gratifying.** EG *It was gratifying to see so many people present... It makes a gratifying change.* ◇ ADJ QUALIT

◇ **gratification** /grætɪfɪkeɪʃəⁿn/. EG *To my immense gratification, he fell into the trap.* ◇ N UNCOUNT

2 If you **gratify** a desire, you do what is necessary to please the person who has that desire. EG *His smallest wish must be gratified... Do gratify our curiosity.* ◇ **gratification.** EG *...action directed towards the gratification of desire.* V+O Formal ◇ N UNCOUNT

grating /greɪtɪŋ/, **gratings. 1** A **grating** is a flat metal frame with rows of bars across it which is fastened over a window or over a hole in a wall or in the ground. N COUNT

2 A **grating** sound is harsh and unpleasant. EG *...a repulsive woman with a grating voice.* ADJ QUALIT

gratitude /grætɪtjuːd/ is the state of feeling grateful. EG *People wish to show their gratitude for the help he has given them... I must express my gratitude to the BBC.* N UNCOUNT

gratuitous /grətjuːɪtəs/. An action that is **gratuitous** is unnecessary, and usually harmful or upsetting. EG *...gratuitous acts of vandalism.* ADJ QUALIT Formal

◇ **gratuitously.** EG *She had no wish to wound his feelings gratuitously.* ◇ ADV

grave /greɪv/, **graves; graver, gravest. 1** A **grave** is a place where a dead person is buried. EG *Flowers had been put on the grave.* N COUNT

2 You can refer to death as the **grave**. EG *He drank himself into an early grave.* N COUNT

3 If you say that someone who is dead would **turn in** their **grave** if something happened, you mean that they would be very shocked or upset if they were alive. EG *Crewe would turn in his grave if that building came down.* PHRASE

4 A situation or event that is **grave** is very serious and worrying. EG *...grave mistakes... I had the gravest suspicions about the whole enterprise.* ADJ QUALIT

◇ **gravely.** EG *His father was gravely ill.* ◇ ADV

5 A person who is **grave** is quiet and serious. ◇ **gravely.** EG *Roger nodded gravely.* ADJ QUALIT ◇ ADV

gravel /grævəⁿl/ consists of very small stones. It is often used to make paths. EG *...the sound of his feet on the gravel.* N UNCOUNT

gravelled /grævəⁿld/; spelled **graveled** in American English. A **gravelled** path or road has a surface made of gravel. ADJ CLASSIF

gravelly /grævəⁿli¹/. An area of land that is **gravelly** is covered in small stones. ADJ QUALIT

gravestone /greɪvstəʊn/, **gravestones.** A **gravestone** is a large piece of stone with words carved into it, which is placed by or on a grave. N COUNT

graveyard /greɪvjɑːd/, **graveyards.** A **graveyard** is an area of land, often near a church, where dead people are buried. N COUNT

gravitate /grævɪteɪt/, **gravitates, gravitating, gravitated.** If you **gravitate** towards a particular place or activity, you are attracted by it and go to it or get involved in it. EG *The best reporters gravitate towards the centres of power.* V+*towards/to* Formal

gravitation /grævɪteɪʃəⁿn/ is the force which causes objects to be attracted towards each other because they have mass. ◇ **gravitational** /grævɪteɪʃəⁿnəl, -ʃənəⁿl/. EG *...the earth's gravitational force.* N UNCOUNT Technical ◇ ADJ CLASSIF: ATTRIB

gravity /grævɪ¹ti¹/. **1 Gravity** is the force which causes things to fall to the ground when you drop them, and to remain on the ground instead of floating in the air. N UNCOUNT

2 The **gravity** of a situation or event is its extreme importance and seriousness. EG *...the gravity of the threat to shipping.* N UNCOUNT +SUPP

gravy /greɪvi¹/ is a thin savoury sauce that is served with meat. N UNCOUNT

gray /greɪ/. See **grey**.

graze /greɪz/, **grazes, grazing, grazed. 1** When an animal **grazes** or when someone **grazes** it somewhere, it eats the grass that is growing there. EG *The horses graze peacefully... The people of the town fought for the right to graze cattle on the Common... ...land grazed by sheep and cattle.* V-ERG OR V+O

2 If you **graze** a part of your body, you injure the skin by scraping against something. EG *I grazed my legs as he pulled me up.* V+O

3 A **graze** is a small wound caused by scraping against something. EG *...cuts and grazes.* N COUNT

4 If something **grazes** you, it touches you lightly as it passes you. EG *Jones's shot only grazed him.* V+O

grease /griːs/, **greases, greasing, greased. 1 Grease** is **1.1** a thick, oily substance which is put on the moving parts of machines in order to make them work smoothly. **1.2** an oily substance that is produced by your skin. **1.3** animal fat that is produced by cooking meat. N UNCOUNT

2 If you **grease** something, you put grease or fat on it. EG *Clean and grease the valve thoroughly.* V+O

If you grieve, do you have a grievance?

greaseproof paper /griːspruːf peɪpə/ is a kind of paper which does not allow grease to pass through it and is used especially in cooking. N UNCOUNT

greasy /griːsi¹, -zi¹/. Something that is **greasy** is covered with grease or contains a lot of grease. EG *...greasy tools... ...greasy hamburgers.* ADJ QUALIT

great /greɪt/, **greater, greatest. 1** You use **great** to describe something that is **1.1** very large in size. EG *...a great black cloud of smoke.* ADJ QUALIT **1.2** large in amount or degree. EG *There is a great amount of conflict... He had great difficulty in selling his house... The heat was so great I took off my sweater.* ADJ QUALIT **1.3** important, famous, or exciting. EG *...the great cities of the Rhineland... ...the great issues of the day.* ADJ CLASSIF: USU ATTRIB ◊ **greatness.** EG *...the greatness of Germany.* ◊ N UNCOUNT

2 A person who is described as **great** is successful, famous, and respected. EG *...a great actor.* ADJ QUALIT ◊ **greatness.** EG *...Boltzmann's greatness as a physicist.* ◊ N UNCOUNT

3 If you say that something is **great**, you mean that you think it is very good or nice. EG *It's a great idea.* ADJ QUALIT Informal ▸ used as an exclamation. EG *Great! Thanks very much.* ▸ EXCLAM

4 If you feel **great**, you feel very healthy and energetic. ADJ PRED Informal

5 You also use **great** to emphasize the size or degree of a quality that something has. EG *...a great big gaping hole... He was a great friend of Huxley.* ADV+ADJ, OR ADJ QUALIT: ATTRIB

great- is used before nouns that refer to relatives, such as 'aunt' or 'grandson', to indicate that a relative is one generation further away than the one that the noun refers to. For example, someone's great-aunt is the aunt of their mother or father, and someone's great-grandson is the grandson of their son or daughter. EG *...our great-great-grandparents.* PREFIX

greatly /greɪtli¹/. You use **greatly** to emphasize the degree or extent of something. EG *I was greatly influenced by Sullivan... He was not greatly surprised.* ADV Formal

greed /griːd/ is an eager desire for more of something such as food, money, or power than it is necessary or fair for you to have. N UNCOUNT

greedy /griːdi¹/, **greedier, greediest.** Someone who is **greedy** wants more of something such as food, money, or power than it is necessary or fair for them to have. EG *People got richer and also greedier.* ADJ QUALIT ◊ **greedily.** EG *He slurped the soup greedily.* ◊ ADV

green /griːn/, **greener, greenest; greens. 1** Something that is **green** is the colour of grass or leaves. EG *She had blonde hair and green eyes.* ADJ COLOUR

2 A place that is **green** is covered with grass and trees and not with buildings; used showing approval. ADJ COLOUR

3 A **green** is **3.1** an area of grass in a town or village. EG *...the village green.* **3.2** a smooth, flat area of grass around a hole on a golf course. N COUNT

4 You can refer to cooked cabbage as **greens**. N PLURAL

5 If someone is **green** with envy, they are very envious indeed. ADJ PRED +*with*

6 If you describe someone as **green**, you mean that they have had very little experience. EG *...green recruits, new to the traditions.* ADJ QUALIT

7 Green is also used of political movements whose members are particularly concerned about protecting the environment. ADJ CLASSIF

8 Greens are members of green political movements. EG *...the success of the Greens in Germany.* N COUNT: USU PLURAL

9 If you say that someone has **green fingers** or, in American English, **a green thumb**, you mean that they are very good at gardening. PHRASE

10 If someone in authority gives you a **green light**, they give you permission to do something. PHRASE

greenery /griːnəᵒri¹/. Plants or leaves that make a place look attractive are referred to as **greenery**. EG *...the lush greenery of the region.* N UNCOUNT

greengrocer /griːngrəʊsə/, **greengrocers. 1** A **greengrocer** is a shopkeeper who sells fruit and vegetables. N COUNT British

2 You refer to a shop that sells fruit and vegetables as the **greengrocer's** or the **greengrocer**. N SING: *the*+N

greenhouse /griːnhaʊs/, **greenhouses.** A **greenhouse** is a glass building in which you grow plants that need to be protected from cold weather, wind, or frost. N COUNT

greenish /griːnɪʃ/ means slightly green in colour. EG *...a greenish blue.* ADJ COLOUR

greet /griːt/, **greets, greeting, greeted. 1** When you meet someone, you **greet** them by saying something such as 'Hello' or 'How are you?', as a way of being friendly. V+O

2 If you **greet** something in a particular way, you express your reaction to it. EG *The news will be greeted with shock and surprise.* V+O: USU+A

3 If something **greets** you, it is the first thing you notice in a place. EG *The smell of coffee greeted us as we entered.* V+O Literary

greeting /griːtɪŋ/, **greetings.** A **greeting** is something that you say or do as a way of expressing friendliness when you meet someone. EG *...a friendly greeting... She smiled in greeting.* N COUNT OR N UNCOUNT

gregarious /grɪ²gɛərɪəs/. Someone who is **gregarious** enjoys being with other people. ADJ QUALIT Formal

grenade /grɪ²neɪd/, **grenades.** A **grenade** is a small bomb containing explosive that can be thrown by hand or fired from a gun. N COUNT

grew /gruː/ is the past tense of **grow.**

grey /greɪ/, **greyer, greyest; greys, greying;** spelled **gray** in American English.

1 Something that is **grey** is the colour of ashes or of clouds on a rainy day. EG *...a grey suit... ...the grey-haired driver.* ADJ COLOUR

2 If someone **is greying** or **is going grey**, their hair is becoming grey. EG *She went grey in about a year.* V: ONLY CONT OR PHRASE ◊ **greying.** EG *...a small, greying man... A strand of greying hair fell over her eyes.* ◊ ADJ CLASSIF: ATTRIB

3 If someone looks **grey**, their face is pale because they are tired, ill, or worried. ADJ QUALIT ◊ **greyness.** EG *There was an awful greyness about his face.* ◊ N UNCOUNT

4 If the weather is **grey**, the sky is very cloudy and the light is dull. EG *...a grey April afternoon.* ADJ QUALIT

grey area, grey areas. A **grey area** is a situation or aspect of something that does not seem to belong to any particular category, and so people are not sure how to deal with it. N COUNT

greyhound /greɪhaʊnd/, **greyhounds.** A **greyhound** is a thin dog that can run very fast. Greyhounds sometimes run in races. N COUNT

greyish /greɪɪʃ/; spelled **grayish** in American English. **Greyish** means slightly grey in colour. ADJ COLOUR

grid /grɪd/, **grids.** A **grid** is a pattern or object which consists of straight lines that cross over each other and form a series of squares. EG *...a grid of small streets.* N COUNT

grief /griːf/. **1 Grief** is extreme sadness. EG *That helped to ease his grief.* N UNCOUNT Formal

2 If someone or something **comes to grief**, they fail or are harmed. EG *I ran away once but came to grief.* PHRASE Formal

3 Some people say **'Good grief'** to express surprise or exasperation. EXCLAM

grievance /griːvəns/, **grievances.** A **grievance** is **1** a complaint that you make about something which you feel is unfair. EG *They may well have a genuine grievance.* **2** a feeling that something that has been done is unfair. EG *...my family's grievance against Mr Geard.* N COUNT OR N UNCOUNT

grieve /griːv/, **grieves, grieving, grieved. 1** If you **grieve**, you feel very sad about something that has happened. EG *She was grieving for the dead baby.* V: OFT+*for/over* Formal

2 If something **grieves** you, it makes you feel very sad. EG *It grieves me to say this, but you must leave now.* V+O: OFT+*to*-INF Formal

grievous /gri:vəs/. Something that is **grievous** is extremely serious or worrying in its effects. EG *...a grievous mistake.* ◊ **grievously.** EG *He had been grievously wounded.* ADJ QUALIT ◊ ADV Formal

grill /grɪl/, **grills, grilling, grilled. 1** When you **grill** food, you cook it using strong heat directly above or below it. ◊ **grilled.** EG *...a grilled chop.* V-ERG ◊ ADJ CLASSIF

2 A **grill** is **2.1** a part of a cooker that consists of a metal shelf where food is cooked by strong heat from above. N COUNT **2.2** a flat frame of metal bars on which you cook food over a fire. N COUNT **2.3** a dish which consists of food that has been grilled. N COUNT OR N UNCOUNT

3 If you **grill** someone about something, you ask them many questions for a long period of time. EG *At the police station, she was grilled for twenty-four hours.* V+O Informal

grille /grɪl/, **grilles.** A **grille** is a framework of metal bars or wire which is placed in front of something such as a window or a piece of machinery, in order to protect it or to protect people. EG *...the protective grille at the back of the set.* N COUNT

grim /grɪm/, **grimmer, grimmest. 1** A situation or piece of information that is **grim** is unpleasant, difficult to accept, and worrying. EG *...the grim facts... ...the grim aftermath of World War I.* ADJ QUALIT

2 A place that is **grim** is unattractive and depressing in appearance. ADJ QUALIT

3 If someone is **grim**, they are very serious or stern, especially because they are worried or angry about something. EG *...his grim determination not to cry... ...grim-faced guards.* ◊ **grimly.** EG *'Smoke,' Eddie announced grimly.* ADJ QUALIT ◊ ADV

grimace /grɪmeɪs, grɪmə[1]s/, **grimaces, grimacing, grimaced.** A **grimace** is an expression that you make by twisting your face in an ugly way because you are displeased, disgusted, or in pain. EG *Thomas made a little grimace. Perhaps he thought the wine was sour.* ▸ used as a verb. EG *She made a bad gear-change and grimaced.* N COUNT ▸ V

grime /graɪm/ is dirt which gathers on the surface of something. EG *The windows were thick with grime.* N UNCOUNT

grimy /graɪmi[1]/. Something that is **grimy** is very dirty. EG *...a grimy office.* ADJ QUALIT

grin /grɪn/, **grins, grinning, grinned. 1** If you **grin**, you smile broadly. EG *He grinned at her.* ▸ used as a noun. EG *The pilot was unhurt and climbed out with a cheerful grin.* V : OFT+*at* ▸ N COUNT

2 If you say you will **grin and bear it**, you mean that you will accept a difficult or unpleasant situation without complaining because there is nothing you can do to make things better. EG *I'd just have to grin and bear it for the next two hours.* PHRASE Informal

grind /graɪnd/, **grinds, grinding, ground** /graʊnd/. **1** If you **grind** something such as corn or pepper, you crush it between two hard surfaces or in a machine until it becomes a fine powder. EG *...freshly ground black pepper.* V+O

2 If you **grind** something into a surface, you press it hard into the surface with small circular or sideways movements. EG *He ground his cigarette in the ashtray.* V+O+A

3 If a machine **grinds**, it makes a harsh scraping noise. EG *The lift grinds in the shaft.* V

4 If something large **grinds to a halt** or **comes to a grinding halt**, it stops. EG *The huge coal cart would grind to a halt at our front door... Why doesn't the whole economy grind to a halt?* PHRASE

5 You can refer to routine work which you have to do and which is tiring or boring as the **grind**. EG *They then begin the long and tiresome grind of preparing themselves for college entrance.* N SING

6 See also **grinding**.

grind down. If you **grind** someone **down**, you treat them very harshly, with the result that they do not have the will to resist you. EG *See how the working people of Britain are ground down.* PHRASAL VB : V+O+ADV

grind up. If you **grind** something **up**, you crush it until it becomes a fine powder, especially in a machine. PHRASAL VB : V+O+ADV

grinder /graɪndə/, **grinders.** A **grinder** is a machine or device which crushes something into small pieces. EG *...a coffee grinder.* N COUNT

grinding /graɪndɪŋ/. You use **grinding** to describe a situation that never seems to change or end, and that makes you feel unhappy, tired, or bored. EG *...grinding poverty.* ADJ CLASSIF : ATTRIB

grip /grɪp/, **grips, gripping, gripped. 1** If you **grip** something, you take hold of it with your hand and continue to hold it firmly. EG *Lomax gripped the boy's arm.* V+O

2 A **grip** is a firm, strong hold on something. EG *I tightened my grip on the handrail.* N COUNT : USU SING

3 A **grip** on someone or something is power and control over them. EG *He now took a firm grip on the management side of the newspaper... She felt herself in the grip of a sadness she could not understand.* N SING+SUPP

4 If something **grips** you, **4.1** it suddenly affects you strongly. EG *He seemed to be gripped by a powerful desire to laugh.* V+O : USU PASS **4.2** it keeps your attention concentrated on it. EG *I was really gripped by the first few pages.* ◊ **gripping.** EG *...a gripping film.* V+O : USU PASS ◊ ADJ QUALIT

5 If tyres or shoes have **grip**, they do not slip. N UNCOUNT

6 A **grip** is also a bag that you use when you are travelling. N COUNT

7 Grip is also used in these phrases. **7.1** If you **get** or **come to grips with** a problem or situation, you consider it seriously, and start taking action to deal with it. EG *It's taken us eighteen years to get to grips with our inadequacies.* **7.2** If you **get** or **take a grip on** yourself, you make an effort to control yourself. **7.3** If you **are losing** your **grip**, you are becoming less efficient and less confident, and less able to deal with things. EG *I could see they thought I was losing my grip.* PHRASES

gripe /graɪp/, **gripes, griping, griped.** If you **gripe** about something, you keep complaining about it. EG *I guess you think I'm just griping because I wasn't elected captain.* V : OFT+*about* Informal

grisly /grɪzli[1]/. Something that is **grisly** is extremely nasty and horrible. EG *...a grisly experiment.* ADJ QUALIT

grist /grɪst/. If you say that something is **grist to the mill**, you mean that it is something that can be used. EG *All this conflict was grist to the mill for the various Left groups.* PHRASE

gristle /grɪsə[0]l/ is a tough, rubbery substance found in meat. Gristle is unpleasant to eat. N UNCOUNT

grit /grɪt/, **grits, gritting, gritted. 1 Grit** consists of very small pieces of stone. N UNCOUNT

2 If people **grit** a road, they put grit on it in order to make it less slippery in icy or snowy weather. V+O

3 Grit is also determination and courage. EG *He has grit.* N UNCOUNT

4 If you **grit** your **teeth**, **4.1** you press your upper and lower teeth tightly together. EG *She nodded at me sternly. I gritted my teeth, but she didn't notice my anger.* **4.2** you decide to carry on in a difficult situation. EG *We must just grit our teeth and carry on.* PHRASE

gritty /grɪti[1]/. **1** Something that is **gritty** is covered with grit or has a texture like grit. EG *...the gritty carpet.* ADJ QUALIT

2 Someone who is **gritty** is strong, determined, and courageous. EG *...a gritty upholder of the law.* ADJ QUALIT

groan /grəʊn/, **groans, groaning, groaned. 1** If you **groan**, you make a long, low sound because you are in pain or unhappy, or because you disapprove of something. EG *'I'm sick,' he groaned.* ▸ used as a noun. EG *...the groans of the wounded... A chorus of groans greeted his joke.* V, V+QUOTE, OR V+O ▸ N COUNT

Is a grotto grotty?

2 If something made of wood **groans**, it makes a loud creaking sound. EG *The wind roared, and the trees groaned.* V

grocer /grəʊsə/, **grocers. 1** A **grocer** is a shopkeeper who sells foods such as flour, sugar, and tinned foods. N COUNT

2 You refer to a shop where groceries are sold as the **grocer's** or the **grocer**. N SING : *the*+N

grocery /grəʊsəʳri¹/, **groceries. 1** A **grocery** is a grocer's shop. N COUNT American

2 **Groceries** are foods such as flour, sugar, and tinned foods. EG *...a shopping-basket containing groceries.* N PLURAL

groggy /grɒgi¹/. If you feel **groggy**, you feel weak and ill. EG *I expect you're feeling a bit groggy with the injections.* ADJ QUALIT Informal

groin /grɔɪn/, **groins.** Your **groin** is the part of your body where your legs meet. N COUNT

groom /gru⁴m/, **grooms, grooming, groomed. 1** A **groom** is **1.1** a person whose job is to look after the horses in a stable. **1.2** the same as a bridegroom. EG *The wedding feast went on until midnight but the bride and groom left before that.* N COUNT

2 If you **groom** an animal, you clean its fur, usually by brushing it. V+O

3 If you **groom** a person for a special job, you prepare them for it by teaching them the skills they will need. EG *I had been chosen to be groomed as editor.* V+O : OFT+ *for/as*

groomed /gruːmd/. Someone who is well **groomed** is clean and smart in appearance. ADJ QUALIT : USU WITH ADV

groove /gruːv/, **grooves.** A **groove** is a deep line cut into a surface. EG *...a steel plate with grooves cut in it.* N COUNT ◇ **grooved** /gruːvd/. EG *...the grooved rock.* ◇ ADJ QUALIT

grope /grəʊp/, **gropes, groping, groped. 1** If you **grope** for something that you cannot see, you try to find it by moving your hands around in order to feel it. EG *I groped for the timetable I had in my pocket.* V : OFT+*for*

2 If you **grope** your way to a place, you move there holding your hands in front of you and feeling the way because you cannot see anything. EG *I groped my way out of bed and downstairs.* V+O+A OR V+A

3 If you **grope** for something such as the solution to a problem, you try to think of it, when you have no real idea what it could be. EG *We are groping for ways to get the communities together... 'I mean...' She groped for words.* V : OFT+*for*

gross /grəʊs/, **grosser, grossest; grosses, grossing, grossed. 1** You use **gross** to describe something unacceptable or unpleasant that is very great in amount or degree. EG *...children whose parents are guilty of gross neglect... ...gross inequalities in wealth, power and privilege.* ADJ CLASSIF : ATTRIB

◇ **grossly.** EG *...grossly unfair social conditions... They were both grossly overweight.* ◇ ADV : OFT+ADJ

2 Speech or behaviour that is **gross** shows lack of taste, or is very rude. EG *He felt he had said something gross, indecent.* ADJ QUALIT

3 Something that is **gross** is very large and ugly. EG *...the gross architecture of the Piccadilly frontages.* ADJ QUALIT

4 **Gross** is also used to describe **4.1** someone's total earnings, before any necessary deductions are made. EG *His gross income will very likely exceed $900,000 this year.* ADJ CLASSIF : ATTRIB OR ADV **4.2** the total amount of something, after all the relevant amounts have been added together. EG *...the gross national product.* ADJ CLASSIF : ATTRIB **4.3** the total weight of something, including its container or wrapping. EG *...8,000 merchant ships with a gross tonnage of 20 million.* ADJ CLASSIF : ATTRIB OR ADV

5 If you **gross** an amount of money, you earn that amount money in total. EG *The film grossed a quarter of a billion dollars in America.* V+O Formal

6 A **gross** is a group of 144 things. The plural is also **gross**. EG *He bought them by the gross.* N COUNT

grotesque /grəʊtesk/. Something that is **grotesque** is **1** very exaggerated so that it is ridiculous or frightening. EG *...grotesque comedy.* ADJ QUALIT

◇ **grotesquely.** EG *I knew I had been perfectly ridiculous, over-acting grotesquely.* ◇ ADV **2** very ugly in appearance. EG *...grotesque figures carved into the stonework.* ADJ QUALIT

grotto /grɒtəʊ/, **grottoes** or **grottos.** A **grotto** is a small attractive cave. N COUNT

grotty /grɒti¹/. Something that is **grotty** is unpleasant or of poor quality. EG *...a grotty little building.* ADJ QUALIT Informal

grouchy /graʊtʃi¹/. Someone who is **grouchy** is bad-tempered and complains a lot. ADJ QUALIT Informal

ground /graʊnd/, **grounds, grounding, grounded. 1** The **ground** is the surface of the earth. EG *He set down his bundle carefully on the ground... He keeled over unconscious and fell to the ground.* N SING : *the*+N

2 **Ground** is land. EG *...a rocky piece of ground... They spend their lives below ground.* N UNCOUNT

3 A **ground** is **3.1** an area of land or sea which is used for a particular purpose. EG *...a burial ground... ...fishing grounds.* N COUNT+SUPP **3.2** an area of land where sport is played. EG *...football grounds.*

4 The **grounds** of a building are the land which surrounds it and which is owned by the same people. EG *...the school grounds.* N PLURAL : USU+SUPP

5 A particular type of **ground** is **5.1** a place or situation in which ideas, attitudes, or organizations can develop. EG *Britain is not fertile ground for news magazines.* N COUNT OR N UNCOUNT +SUPP **5.2** a subject or range of subjects. EG *This course covers the same ground as the undergraduate degree in Social Administration.* N UNCOUNT +SUPP

6 Something that is **grounds** or a **ground** for something else is a reason or justification for it. EG *You have no real grounds for complaint... Adultery was a ground for divorce.* N COUNT OR N UNCOUNT +SUPP Formal ● You can use **on grounds of**, **on the grounds of**, and **on the grounds that** to introduce the reason for a particular action. EG *He was always declining their invitations on grounds of ill health... She was prohibited from speaking on the grounds that it would stir up trouble.* ● PHRASE

7 If you gain **ground**, you make progress or get an advantage. EG *Godley's views are gaining political ground... He tried to regain lost ground.* N UNCOUNT

8 If aircraft or pilots **are grounded**, they have to remain on the ground. V+O

9 If an argument or opinion **is grounded** in or on something, it is based on that thing or results from it. EG *...a delusion grounded in fear.* V+O : OFT+*in/on*

10 **Ground** is also the past tense and past participle of **grind**.

11 **Ground** is also used in these phrases. PHRASES **11.1** If you **go to ground**, you hide somewhere for a period of time. EG *All the people involved have gone to ground in cheap hotels.* **11.2** If you **run** someone or something **to ground**, you find them after a long and difficult search. EG *It was run to ground in the nearby woods.* **11.3** If you **break fresh ground** or **break new ground**, you make a new discovery or start a new activity. **11.4** If you **get** something **off the ground**, you get it started. EG *There was a hurry to get the new film off the ground.* **11.5** If you **stand** your **ground** or **hold** your **ground**, you do not retreat or give in when people are opposing you; used showing approval. EG *Laing held his ground. 'We seek only to reverse the discrimination which already exists.'* **11.6** If you **cut** or **dig the ground from under** someone's **feet**, you do something that destroys their chance of success.

12 to **have** your **ear to the ground**: see **ear**. ● **thin on the ground**: see **thin**. ● See also **home ground**.

ground floor. The **ground floor** of a building is the floor that is level with the ground outside. EG *There's a bathroom on the ground floor.* N SING British

grounding /graʊndɪŋ/. A **grounding** in a subject is a course of instruction in the basic facts or principles of the subject. EG *Schools must provide a* N SING : OFT+*in* *firm grounding in the basics, reading, writing, arithmetic.*

groundless /graʊndlɪ²s/. A fear, suspicion, or claim that is **groundless** is not based on reason or evidence. EG *Your fears are groundless... His allegations, when investigated, prove groundless.* ADJ QUALIT Formal

ground level is used to refer to the ground or to the floor of a building which is at the same level as the ground. EG *...an explosion at ground level.* N UNCOUNT

ground rules. The **ground rules** for something are the basic principles on which future action will be based. EG *They sat down to work out the ground rules for the project.* N PLURAL

groundsheet /graʊndʃiːt/, **groundsheets.** A **groundsheet** is a piece of waterproof material which you put on the ground to sleep on when you are camping. N COUNT

groundsman /graʊndzmən/, **groundsmen.** A **groundsman** is a person whose job is to look after a park or sports ground. N COUNT

groundswell /graʊndswɛl/. A **groundswell** is the rapid growth of a feeling or opinion about something in a society or group of people. EG *There was a groundswell of outrage against him.* N SING+SUPP

groundwork /graʊndwɜːk/ is early work on something which forms the basis for further work or study. EG *The previous president had already provided the groundwork for economic progress.* N SING

group /gruːp/, **groups, grouping, grouped. 1** A **group** is **1.1** a number of people or things which are together in one place at one time. EG *...a small group of boys... ...a group of buildings... They were all standing in a group in the centre of the room.* N COLL OR N PART
1.2 a set of people or things which have something in common. EG *...children of his age group... We feel it's wrong for one group of people to take land from another... A parents' action group has accused the local authority of breaking the law.* N COLL+SUPP **1.3** a number of musicians who perform pop music together. EG *...a pop group.* N COUNT **1.4** See also **pressure group**.
2 When you **group** a number of things or people together or when they **group** together, they all come together in one place or within one organization. EG *They encouraged workers and consumers to group together... Occupations are grouped into separate categories.* V-ERG : USU+A

grouping /gruːpɪŋ/, **groupings.** A **grouping** is a set of people or things which have something in common. EG *Lawyers and government officials were the largest groupings.* N COUNT+SUPP

grouse /graʊs/, **grouses, grousing, groused.** **Grouse** is both the singular and the plural form of the noun.
1 A **grouse** is a small fat bird. Grouse are often shot for sport and can be eaten. N COUNT
2 If you **grouse**, you complain. EG *It was a sad end to her career but she never grumbled or groused.* V OR V+QUOTE

grove /grəʊv/, **groves.** A **grove** is a group of trees that are close together. EG *...an olive grove.* N COUNT

grovel /grɒvə⁰l/, **grovels, grovelling, grovelled;** spelled **groveling** and **groveled** in American English.
If you **grovel**, **1** you behave very humbly towards someone, for example because they are important or because you are frightened of them; used showing disapproval. V ◊ **grovelling.** EG *He sent a letter of grovelling apology to the publisher.* ◊ ADJ QUALIT **2** you crawl on the floor, for example in order to find something. EG *He was grovelling under his desk for a dropped pencil.* V+A

grow /grəʊ/, **grows, growing, grew** /gruː/, **grown. 1** When people, animals, or plants **grow**, they increase in size. EG *Babies who are small at birth grow faster... ...fast-growing weeds.* V : USU+A
2 If a plant or tree **grows** in a particular place, it is alive there. EG *An oak tree grew at the edge of the lane... ...an old brick wall with things growing up it.* V : USU+A
3 When you **grow** plants, you put seeds or young plants in the ground and look after them as they develop. EG *The district grew peas on a large scale.* V+O ◊ **grower, growers.** EG *My father was a great rose grower.* ◊ N COUNT +SUPP
4 If a man **grows** a beard or a moustache, he allows the beard or moustache to develop by not shaving. V+O
5 If someone or something **grows** into a particular state or condition, they change gradually until they are in that state or condition. EG *The sun grew so hot that they were forced to stop working... I grew to dislike working for the cinema.* V+C, V+*to*-INF, OR V+A
6 If an idea, feeling, amount, or problem **grows**, it gradually becomes stronger or greater. EG *There is a growing awareness of the difficulties... Jobs in industry will grow by 11 per cent... Refugees were posing a growing problem.* V
7 If one idea, plan, or policy **grows** out of another, it develops from it. EG *Out of this would grow a broad socialist programme.* V : OFT+*out of/from*
8 If a place or organization **grows**, it increases in size, wealth, or importance. EG *...the fast-growing New York investment bank.* V
9 See also **grown**.

grow apart. If people **grow apart**, they gradually start to have different interests and opinions from each other. PHRASAL VB : V+ADV

grow into. When children **grow into** a piece of clothing that is too big for them, they become bigger so that it fits them properly. PHRASAL VB : V+PREP

grow on. If someone or something **grows on** you, you start to like them more and more. EG *She was someone whose charm grew very slowly on you.* PHRASAL VB : V+PREP Informal

grow out of. 1 If you **grow out of** a type of behaviour or an interest, you stop behaving in that way or having that interest. EG *I've rather grown out of my taste for the bizarre.* PHRASAL VB : V+ADV+PREP **2** If a child **grows out of** a piece of clothing, they become so big that it no longer fits them properly. V+ADV+PREP

grow up. 1 When someone **grows up**, they gradually change from being a child into being an adult. EG *They grew up in the early days of television.* PHRASAL VB : V+ADV **2** If something **grows up**, it starts to exist and becomes stronger. EG *The idea has grown up that science cannot be wrong.* V+ADV **3** If you tell someone to **grow up**, you are telling them to stop being silly or childish. V+ADV **4** See also **grown-up**.

growl /graʊl/, **growls, growling, growled. 1** When a dog or other animal **growls**, it makes a low rumbling noise, usually because it is angry. EG *The dog growled at me.* V ▸ used as a noun. EG *He did not hear the growl of the leopard.* ▸ N COUNT
2 If someone **growls** something, they say it in a low, rough, and rather angry voice. EG *'There's a visitor here,' he growled.* V+O, V+QUOTE, OR V ▸ used as a noun. EG *'Yeah,' said John in a low growl.* ▸ N COUNT
3 If something **growls**, it makes a deep rumbling noise. EG *The thunder still growled in the distance.* V Literary ▸ used as a noun. EG *The engine's pitch changed from a low murmur to an urgent growl.* ▸ N COUNT

grown /grəʊn/. A **grown** man or woman is a physically and mentally mature adult. EG *It requires a child's spontaneity and a grown man's decisiveness.* ● See also **grow**. ADJ CLASSIF : ATTRIB

grown-up, grown-ups. 1 A **grown-up** is the same as an adult; used especially by children. EG *Until the grown-ups come to fetch us we'll have fun.* N COUNT Informal
2 If you say that someone is **grown-up**, you mean **2.1** that they are physically and mentally mature. EG *...older couples with grown-up children.* ADJ CLASSIF **2.2** that they behave in an adult way, especially when they are in fact still a child. EG *Your brother's awfully grown-up for his age.* ADJ QUALIT

Which words on these pages can you use to talk about people complaining or being angry?

growth /grəʊθ/, **growths. 1** The **growth** of something such as an industry or organization is its development in size, wealth, or importance. EG *Its economic growth rate is second only to Japan's... ...the growth of political opposition... Computing remains a growth area.* N UNCOUNT: USU+SUPP

2 A **growth** in an amount of something is an increase in it. EG *...India's population growth... ...a growth in research expenditure.* N UNCOUNT +SUPP

3 Growth in a person, animal, or plant is the process of increasing in size and development. EG *He noticed that this drug seemed to inhibit bacterial growth.* N UNCOUNT: USU+SUPP

4 A **growth** is an abnormal lump that grows inside or on a person, animal, or plant. EG *...an ache where a growth was removed.* N COUNT

grub /grʌb/, **grubs, grubbing, grubbed. 1** A **grub** is a young insect which has just come out of an egg and looks like a short fat worm. N COUNT

2 Grub is food. EG *It sounds fun. Can I come? I'll bring my own grub.* N UNCOUNT Informal

3 If you **grub** about for something, you search for it by moving things or digging. EG *The fish grubs around on the river bed.* V: OFT+ *about/around*

grubby /grʌbi^{1}/, **grubbier, grubbiest.** A person or object that is **grubby** is rather dirty. EG *...grubby clothes... ...their grubby hands.* ADJ QUALIT

grudge /grʌdʒ/, **grudges, grudging, grudged. 1** If you have a **grudge** against someone, you have unfriendly feelings towards them because they have upset you or harmed you in the past. EG *They had to do it, and I bear them no grudge... It isn't in her nature to hold grudges.* N COUNT: OFT+*against*

2 If you **grudge** someone something, you give it to them very unwillingly or you are displeased that they have it. EG *We need not grudge them their mindless pleasures... Not that I grudge the use of my kitchen to you.* V+O+O OR V+O+*to*

grudging /grʌdʒɪŋ/. A **grudging** feeling or action is one that you feel or do very unwillingly. EG *Others stood watching with grudging respect.* ADJ QUALIT

◊ **grudgingly.** EG *'Okay,' he said grudgingly, 'I suppose I was to blame.'* ◊ ADV

gruel /grʊəl/ is a cheap food made by boiling oats with water or milk. N UNCOUNT

gruelling /grʊəlɪŋ/; spelled **grueling** in American English. Something that is **gruelling** is extremely difficult and tiring. EG *I was exhausted after a gruelling week.* ADJ QUALIT

gruesome /gruːsəm/. Something that is **gruesome** involves death or injury and is very unpleasant and shocking. EG *...gruesome tales of child murder.* ADJ QUALIT

gruff /grʌf/. If someone's voice is **gruff**, they speak in a low, rough, unfriendly voice. EG *He hid his feelings behind a kind of gruff abruptness.* ADJ QUALIT

◊ **gruffly.** EG *She said gruffly, 'Put on your clothes.'* ◊ ADV

grumble /grʌmbə^{0}l/, **grumbles, grumbling, grumbled.** If you **grumble**, you complain about something, usually in a low voice and not forcefully. EG *They will grumble about having to do the work... 'It's awful,' Posy grumbled.* V, V+*about*, OR V+QUOTE ▸ used as a noun. EG *There were angry grumbles from the British ranks.* ▸ N COUNT ◊ **grumbling.** EG *There was more grumbling at the Cabinet's decision.* ◊ N UNCOUNT

grumpy /grʌmpi^{1}/. Someone who is **grumpy** is bad-tempered and rather miserable. EG *Don't be so grumpy and cynical about it.* ADJ QUALIT

grunt /grʌnt/, **grunts, grunting, grunted. 1** If you **grunt**, you make a low rough noise, usually because you are uninterested or disapproving. EG *His father looked up and grunted, then went back to his work.* V, V+QUOTE, OR V+O ▸ used as a noun. EG *He gave a sceptical grunt.* ▸ N COUNT

2 When a pig **grunts**, it makes a low rough noise. V ▸ used as a noun. EG *It sounded like a pig's grunt.* ▸ N COUNT

guarantee /gærəntiː/, **guarantees, guaranteeing, guaranteed. 1** If something **guarantees** something else, it is certain to cause that thing to happen. EG *Equality does not guarantee happiness in love... This method guarantees success.* V+O

2 If you **guarantee** something, you promise that it will definitely happen, or that you will do or provide it. EG *I'm not guaranteeing that this will work... They guarantee to hold interest rates down until next year... Advertisers were guaranteed a weekly circulation of 250,000.* V+O: OFT+ REPORT OR *to*-INF; ALSO V+O+O

3 If you say that you **guarantee** that something will happen, or that it **is guaranteed** to happen, you mean that you are certain that it will happen. EG *You should have one evening off a week, but you can't guarantee it... This state of affairs is guaranteed to continue indefinitely.* V+REPORT: ONLY *that*, V+O, OR V-PASS+*to*-INF

4 Something that is a **guarantee** of something else makes it certain that it will happen or that it is true. EG *There is no guarantee that they are telling the truth... The jury system is one of the guarantees of democracy.* N COUNT: USU+REPORT OR *of*

5 A **guarantee** is also **5.1** a promise that something will definitely happen. EG *We want some guarantee that an enquiry will be held... They gave guarantees of full employment.* N COUNT: USU+REPORT OR *of* **5.2** a written promise by a company that if their product or work has any faults within a particular time, it will be repaired or replaced free of charge. EG *How long does the guarantee last?* N COUNT

6 If a company **guarantees** their product or work, they give a written promise that if it has any faults within a particular time it will be repaired or replaced free of charge. V+O

guard /gɑːd/, **guards, guarding, guarded. 1** If you **guard** a place, person, or object, you watch and protect them. EG *Scotland Yard sent an officer to guard his house.* V+O

2 If you **guard** someone, you watch them to stop them from escaping. EG *She had been locked in her room and was guarded night and day.* V+O

3 A **guard** is **3.1** a person who is guarding a person, place, or object. N COUNT **3.2** an organized group of soldiers or policemen that protect or watch someone or something. EG *They will give him an armed guard.* N COLL **3.3** a railway official on a train. N COUNT

4 If you **guard** something important or secret, you protect or hide it. EG *The contents of the lists were a closely guarded secret.* V+O

5 A **guard** is also a device which covers a dangerous part of something. EG *When the guard is taken off the motor the machine can't start.* N COUNT

6 Guard is also used in these phrases. PHRASES **6.1** If you **stand guard**, you stand near a person or place and watch or protect them. EG *You will be expected to stand guard over the village.* **6.2** Someone who is **on guard** is on duty and responsible for guarding a particular place or person. **6.3** If you are **on** your **guard**, you are being very careful because you think a situation might become difficult or dangerous. EG *Busy parents have to be on their guard against being bad-tempered with their children.* **6.4** If you **catch** someone **off guard**, you surprise them by doing something when they are not expecting it. EG *I didn't want to be caught off guard in the middle of the night.*

guard against. If you **guard against** something, you are careful to avoid it happening, or to avoid being affected by it. EG *...ideas which the trained mind of a judge knows to guard against.* PHRASAL VB: V+PREP, HAS PASS

guarded /gɑːdɪ^{2}d/. Someone who is **guarded** is careful not to show their feelings or give away information about something. EG *The play got very guarded reviews.* ADJ QUALIT ◊ **guardedly.** EG *'Do you ever hear from your sister?' – 'Sometimes,' Rudolph said guardedly.* ◊ ADV

guardian /gɑːdɪən/, **guardians.** A **guardian** is **1** someone who has been legally appointed to look after a child, usually when the child's parents have died. EG *He became the legal guardian of his brother's daughter.* N COUNT: OFT+POSS **2** someone who is considered to protect or defend a person or thing. EG ...*guardians of morality.*

guerrilla /gərɪlə/, **guerrillas;** also spelled **guerilla.** A **guerrilla** is a person who fights as part of an unofficial army. EG ...*guerilla attacks.* N COUNT

guess /gɛs/, **guesses, guessing, guessed. 1** If you **guess** something, **1.1** you give an answer or an opinion about something when you do not know whether it is correct. EG *She guessed that she was fifty yards from shore... We can only guess at the number of deaths it has caused.* V-SPEECH, V+*at*, OR V **1.2** you give the correct answer to a problem or question when you did not know it for certain. EG *How did you guess?... I had guessed the identity of her lover.* V OR V+O

2 A **guess** is an attempt to give the right answer to something when you do not know it. EG *I don't know the name but I'll take a guess at it... I'll give you two guesses.* N COUNT

3 You say **I guess 3.1** to indicate that you think that something is true or likely. EG *I guess I got the news a day late... 'What's that?' - 'Some sort of blackbird, I guess.'... 'Sure?' - 'I guess so.'* PHRASE Informal American **3.2** to indicate what you are thinking, especially when you have made a decision. EG *I guess I won't wake him up yet.* Informal American

4 If you **keep** someone **guessing**, you do not tell them what they want to know. EG *'Have you told them where you are living?' - 'Not yet. Let's keep them guessing a while longer.'* PHRASE

5 You say **'guess what'** to draw attention to something exciting, surprising, or interesting that you are about to tell someone. EG *Guess what, you're going to be a granny!* CONVENTION Informal

6 If you say that something is **anyone's guess** or **anybody's guess**, you mean that nobody can be certain about what is really the case. EG *What would have happened is anyone's guess.* PHRASE Informal

guesswork /gɛswɜːk/ is the process or result of trying to guess something without knowing all the facts. EG *This is pure guesswork at this stage.* N UNCOUNT

guest /gɛst/, **guests.** A **guest** is **1** someone who is staying in your home or is at an occasion because you have invited them. EG ...*wedding guests.* **2** someone who is staying in a hotel. **3** someone who visits a place or appears on a radio or television show because they have been invited. EG *We're here as guests of the National Theatre.* N COUNT

guest house, guest houses. A **guest house** is a small hotel. N COUNT

guest of honour, guests of honour; spelled **guest of honor** in American English.
The **guest of honour** is the most important guest at a dinner or other social occasion. N COUNT

guest-room, guest-rooms. A **guest-room** is a bedroom in someone's house for visitors to sleep in. N COUNT

guffaw /gəfɔː/, **guffaws, guffawing, guffawed.** A **guffaw** is a very loud laugh. EG *Martin let out a delighted guffaw.* ▸ used as a verb. EG *He guffawed and thumped his friend on the shoulder.* N COUNT ▸ V

guidance /gaɪdəᵒns/ is help and advice. EG *We would appreciate guidance from an expert in this field.* N UNCOUNT

guide /gaɪd/, **guides, guiding, guided. 1** A **guide** is **1.1** someone who shows places such as cities or museums to tourists. N COUNT **1.2** someone who shows people the way to a place in a difficult or dangerous region. N COUNT **1.3** the same as a guidebook. EG ...*a guide to New York City.* N COUNT **1.4** a book which gives you information or instructions to help you do or understand something. EG *This book is meant to be a practical guide to healthy living.* N COUNT **1.5** something that can be used to help you plan your actions. EG *As a rough guide, 1 cubic foot stores 25lb frozen food.* N SING : *a*+N

2 A **guide** or a **girl guide** is a girl who belongs to the Girl Guides Association, an organization which encourages girls to become disciplined and to learn practical skills. N COUNT British

3 If you **guide** someone round a city, museum, or building, you show it to them and explain points of interest. ◇ **guided.** EG *We went on a guided tour of Paris.* V+O : USU+A ◇ ADJ CLASSIF : ATTRIB

4 To **guide** someone or something means to cause them to move in the right direction. EG *He took Julie's arm and guided her through the doorway... Men crossing the ocean would use the stars to guide them.* V+O

5 If you **guide** someone, you influence their actions or decisions. EG *Politicians will in the end always be guided by changes in public opinion.* ◇ **guiding.** EG *The guiding principle of the family was Catholicism.* V+O ◇ ADJ CLASSIF : ATTRIB

guidebook /gaɪdbʌk/, **guidebooks.** A **guidebook** is a book which gives information for tourists about a town, area, or country. N COUNT

guideline /gaɪdlaɪn/, **guidelines.** A **guideline** is a piece of advice about how to do something. EG ...*government pay guidelines... ...guidelines for the control of dogs in public places.* N COUNT : USU PLURAL

guild /gɪld/, **guilds.** A **guild** is an organization of people who do the same job or share an interest. N COUNT Formal

guile /gaɪl/ is the quality of being very cunning and good at deceiving people. N UNCOUNT Literary

guillotine /gɪlətiːn/, **guillotines.** A **guillotine** is **1** a device consisting of a blade in a large frame which was used to execute people, especially in France in the past. **2** a device used for cutting and trimming paper. N COUNT

guilt /gɪlt/ is **1** an unhappy feeling that you have because you believe that you have done something wrong. EG *I had agonizing feelings of shame and guilt.* **2** the fact that you have done something wrong or have broken a law. EG *He at last made a public admission of his guilt.* N UNCOUNT

guiltless /gɪltlɪ²s/. If someone is **guiltless**, they have not done anything wrong. EG *Nor were governments guiltless in this matter.* ADJ CLASSIF Formal

guilty /gɪlti¹/. **1** If you feel **guilty**, you feel unhappy because you believe that you have done something wrong. EG *They feel guilty about seeing her so little.* ◇ **guiltily.** EG *I blushed and looked away guiltily.* ADJ QUALIT ◇ ADV

2 You use **guilty** to describe an action or fact that you feel guilty about. EG ...*a guilty secret.* ADJ CLASSIF : ATTRIB

3 If you have a **guilty conscience**, you feel guilty about something that you have done. EG *Some children get a guilty conscience about not learning enough.* PHRASE

4 If someone is **guilty**, **4.1** it is officially stated that they have committed a crime or offence. EG *He was found guilty of passing on secret papers to a foreign power.* ADJ CLASSIF : OFT+*of* **4.2** they have done something wrong. EG *He was guilty of an important misjudgment.*

guinea /gɪni¹/, **guineas.** A **guinea** is an old British unit of money that was worth 21 shillings. N COUNT

guinea pig, guinea pigs. A **guinea pig** is **1** a small furry animal without a tail. Guinea pigs are often kept as pets. **2** a person that is used in an experiment. EG ...*experimentation on human guinea pigs.* N COUNT

guise /gaɪz/, **guises.** You use **guise** to refer to the outward appearance or form of something. EG *They will form new political groupings, or old ones in new guises... A lot of nonsense was talked, under the guise of philosophy.* N COUNT+SUPP

guitar /gɪtɑː/, **guitars.** A **guitar** is a wooden musical instrument with six strings. You play the guitar by plucking or strumming the strings. See picture at MUSICAL INSTRUMENTS. N COUNT

guitarist /gɪtɑːrᵒɪst/, **guitarists.** A **guitarist** is someone who plays the guitar. N COUNT

Would you see a gymnast at a gymkhana?

gulf /gʌlf/, **gulfs.** A **gulf** is **1** an important or significant difference between two people, things, or groups. EG *The gulf between the cultures was too great to be easily bridged.* N COUNT: OFT+*between* **2** a large area of sea which extends a long way into the surrounding land. EG *...the Gulf of Mexico.* N COUNT

gull /gʌl/, **gulls.** A **gull** is a common sea bird. N COUNT

gullet /gʌlɪ^{2}t/, **gullets.** Your **gullet** is the tube which goes from your mouth to your stomach. N COUNT

gullible /gʌləbə^{0}l/. Someone who is **gullible** is easily tricked because they are too trusting. ADJ QUALIT

gully /gʌli^{1}/, **gullies.** A **gully** is a long narrow valley with steep sides. N COUNT

gulp /gʌlp/, **gulps, gulping, gulped. 1** If you **gulp** something, you drink or eat it very fast by swallowing large quantities of it at once. EG *She gulped her coffee.* V+O ▸ used as a noun. EG *She took a gulp of whisky... He finished his drink in one gulp.* ▸ N COUNT

2 If you **gulp**, you swallow air, because you are nervous. V ▸ used as a noun. EG *I gave a little gulp.* ▸ N COUNT

gulp down. If you **gulp** something **down**, you quickly drink or eat it all by swallowing large quantities of it at a time. EG *The old man gulped down his coffee.* PHRASAL VB: V+O+ADV

gum /gʌm/, **gums, gumming, gummed. 1 Gum** is **1.1** a kind of sweet which you chew for a long time but do not swallow. **1.2** a type of glue that you use to stick paper together. N UNCOUNT

2 If you **gum** something to something else, you stick it to something else. EG *...false eyelashes gummed together by lumps of mascara.* V+O+A

3 Your **gums** are the areas of firm, pink flesh inside your mouth, above your top teeth and below your bottom teeth. N COUNT: USU PLURAL

gumboot /gʌmbu:t/, **gumboots. Gumboots** are long rubber boots which you wear to keep your feet dry. N COUNT: USU PLURAL

gun /gʌn/, **guns, gunning, gunned. 1** A **gun** is a weapon consisting mainly of a metal tube from which bullets are fired. N COUNT

2 If you **jump the gun**, you do something before the proper time. EG *Newspapers began to jump the gun and talk about resignations.* PHRASE Informal

3 If you **stick to** your **guns**, you continue to have your own opinion about something even though other people tell you that you are wrong. EG *People who lean towards strictness should stick to their guns and raise their children that way.* PHRASE Informal

gun down. If you **gun** someone **down**, you shoot them and injure them severely or kill them. PHRASAL VB: V+O+ADV

gunboat /gʌnbəʊt/, **gunboats.** A **gunboat** is a small ship which has several large guns fixed on it. N COUNT

gunfire /gʌnfaɪə/ is the repeated shooting of guns, especially in a battle. EG *...listening for the bursts of gunfire.* N UNCOUNT

gunge /gʌnd^{0}ʒ/ is a soft or sticky mass of something. EG *It's solidifying into a sort of brown gunge.* N UNCOUNT Informal

gunman /gʌnmə^{3}n/, **gunmen.** A **gunman** is someone who uses a gun to commit a crime. N COUNT

gunner /gʌnə/, **gunners.** A **gunner** is a member of the armed forces who is trained to use guns. N COUNT

gunpoint /gʌnpɔɪnt/. If someone does something to you **at gunpoint**, they are threatening to shoot you if you do not obey them. EG *He held the three men at gunpoint.* PHRASE

gunpowder /gʌnpaʊdə/ is an explosive substance. N UNCOUNT

gunshot /gʌnʃɒt/, **gunshots.** A **gunshot** is the firing of a gun. EG *...the sound of gunshots.* N COUNT

gurgle /gɜ:gə^{0}l/, **gurgles, gurgling, gurgled. 1** When water **gurgles**, it makes a rippling, bubbling sound. EG *The waves swept back with a gurgling, sucking sound.* V

2 When a baby **gurgles**, it makes a bubbling sound in its throat. EG *Kicking and gurgling, his little brother looked up at him.* V OR V+QUOTE ▸ used as a noun. EG *...gurgles of pleasure.* ▸ N COUNT

guru /gu^{4}ru:/, **gurus.** A **guru** is **1** a spiritual leader and teacher, especially in Hinduism. **2** an adviser whom a group of people respect greatly. EG *She has become the guru of many a modern mother-to-be.* N COUNT

gush /gʌʃ/, **gushes, gushing, gushed. 1** When liquid or gas **gushes** out of something, it flows out very quickly and in large quantities. EG *Blood gushed from the wounds.* V+A ▸ used as a noun. EG *...a gush of smoke.* ▸ N SING: OFT+*of*

2 If someone **gushes**, they express their admiration or pleasure in a very exaggerated way. EG *'Amy!' he gushed. 'How good to see you again.'* V OR V+QUOTE ◊ **gushing.** EG *He arrived in the company of a large gushing female.* ◊ ADJ QUALIT

gust /gʌst/, **gusts. 1** A **gust** is a short, strong, sudden rush of wind. EG *...a sudden gust of wind.* N COUNT: OFT+*of*

2 If you feel a **gust** of emotion such as anger, you feel the emotion suddenly and intensely. EG *A gust of pure happiness swept through her.* N SING+*of*

gusto /gʌstəʊ/. If you do something with **gusto**, you do it very energetically and enthusiastically. EG *We ate with gusto.* N UNCOUNT

gusty /gʌsti^{1}/ is used to describe weather in which there are very strong, irregular winds. EG *...gusty winds.* ADJ QUALIT

gut /gʌt/, **guts, gutting, gutted. 1** Your **guts** are your internal organs, especially your intestines. N PLURAL

2 When someone **guts** a dead fish, they remove all the organs from inside it. V+O

3 The **gut** is the tube inside your body through which food passes while it is being digested. N SING Formal

4 Guts is courage. EG *Sam hasn't got the guts to leave his dad.* N UNCOUNT Informal

5 A **gut** feeling or reaction is based on instinct or emotion rather than on reason. EG *My immediate gut reaction was to refuse.* N MOD

6 If a building **is gutted**, the inside of it is destroyed. EG *The whole house was gutted by fire.* V+O: USU PASS

7 If you **hate** someone's **guts**, you dislike them very intensely. PHRASE Informal

gutter /gʌtə/, **gutters.** A **gutter** is **1** the edge of a road next to the pavement, where rain water collects and flows away. EG *The motorbike lay on its side in the gutter.* **2** a plastic or metal channel fixed to the edge of the roof of a building, which rain water drains into. N COUNT

guttering /gʌtə^{0}rɪŋ/ consists of the plastic or metal channels fixed to the edge of the roof of a building, which rain water drains into. N UNCOUNT

guttural /gʌtə^{0}rəl/. **Guttural** sounds are harsh sounds that are produced at the back of a person's throat. EG *...a strange, loud, guttural cry.* ADJ QUALIT

guy /gaɪ/, **guys. 1** A **guy** is a man. EG *...the guy who drove the bus... He's a nice guy.* N COUNT Informal

2 Americans sometimes address a group of people as **guys** or **you guys**. VOCATIVE Informal

guzzle /gʌzə^{0}l/, **guzzles, guzzling, guzzled.** If you **guzzle** something, you drink or eat it quickly and greedily. EG *The wine was being guzzled like lemonade.* V+O OR V Informal

gym /dʒɪm/, **gyms. 1** A **gym** is a gymnasium. EG *He was always at the gym.* N COUNT

2 Gym means gymnastics. EG *We did an hour of gym... She wore white gym shoes.* N UNCOUNT

gymkhana /dʒɪmkɑ:nə/, **gymkhanas.** A **gymkhana** is an event in which people ride horses in competitions. N COUNT

gymnasium /dʒɪmneɪzɪəm/, **gymnasiums.** A **gymnasium** is a building or large room which is used for physical exercise and usually has equipment such as bars and ropes in it. N COUNT

gymnast /dʒɪmnæst/, **gymnasts.** A **gymnast** is someone who is trained in gymnastics. N COUNT

gymnastic /dʒɪmnæstɪk/, **gymnastics. 1 Gymnastics** are physical exercises, often using equipment such as bars and ropes, which develop your strength and agility. N PLURAL

2 Gymnastic is used to describe things relating to gymnastics. EG *He shows great gymnastic ability.* ADJ CLASSIF: ATTRIB

gynaecology /gaɪnəkɒlədʒi[1]/; also spelled **gynecology. Gynaecology** is the branch of medical science which deals with diseases and medical conditions that only women have. N UNCOUNT Technical
◊ **gynaecologist, gynaecologists.** EG *...an eminent gynaecologist.* ◊ N COUNT ◊ **gynaecological.** EG *...the gynaecological ward.* ◊ ADJ CLASSIF

gypsy /dʒɪpsi[1]/, **gypsies;** also spelled **gipsy.** A **gypsy** is a member of a race of people who travel from place to place in caravans rather than living in one place. N COUNT

gyrate /dʒaɪreɪt/, **gyrates, gyrating, gyrated.** If something **gyrates**, it turns round and round in a circle, usually very fast. EG *...a small gyrating plastic advertisement for a brand of lager.* V Formal
◊ **gyration** /dʒaɪreɪʃə[0]n/, **gyrations.** EG *...their bodily gyrations and contortions.* ◊ N COUNT OR N UNCOUNT

H h

H, h /eɪtʃ/, **Hs, h's** /eɪtʃɪz/. **H** is the eighth letter of the English alphabet. N COUNT

ha /h[0]ɑː/; also spelled **hah.** You say **ha** to show that you are very surprised, pleased, or annoyed about something. EG *'Ha!' she said, 'Isn't that wonderful?'... Hah! Scared you, didn't I?* ● See also **ha ha.** EXCLAM Informal

haberdashery /hæbədæʃə[0]ri[1]/ is **1** buttons, zips, thread, and other small things that you need for sewing. N UNCOUNT British **2** men's clothing sold in a shop. American

habit /hæbɪt/, **habits. 1** A **habit** is **1.1** something that you do often or regularly. EG *I got into the habit of studying at the library... More out of habit than anything else, I stopped and went in.* N COUNT OR N UNCOUNT : OFT+SUPP **1.2** an action that someone has done many times before and finds difficult to stop, especially when this action is considered to be bad. EG *He had a nervous habit of biting his nails.* N COUNT : OFT+SUPP

2 If you are **in the habit of** doing something, or if you **make a habit** of doing it, you do it regularly and often. EG *Once a month Castle was in the habit of taking Sarah for an excursion... They made a habit of lunching together twice a week.* PHRASE

3 A **habit of mind** is the kind of thought, feeling, or attitude that someone generally has. EG *Resistance is a natural habit of mind in people who have been oppressed.* PHRASE

4 A drug **habit** is an addiction to a drug. EG *Groups exist to help those who want to kick the marijuana habit.* N COUNT+SUPP

5 A **habit** is also a piece of clothing shaped like a long loose dress, which a nun or monk wears. N COUNT

habitable /hæbɪtəbə[0]l/. If a place is **habitable**, it is good enough for people to live in. EG *A few flats were made habitable.* ADJ CLASSIF

habitat /hæbɪtæt/, **habitats.** The **habitat** of an animal or plant is the natural environment in which it normally lives. EG *...the open woodland that is their natural habitat.* N COUNT+SUPP

habitation /hæbɪteɪʃə[0]n/, **habitations. 1 Habitation** is the human activity of living somewhere. EG *...to see whether the houses are fit for human habitation.* N UNCOUNT

2 A **habitation** is a place where people live. EG *...squalid human habitations.* N COUNT Formal

habitual /hə[3]bɪtjʊ[0]əl/. **1** A **habitual** action is one that someone usually or often does. EG *'Sorry I'm late,' David said with his habitual guilty grin.* ADJ CLASSIF
◊ **habitually.** EG *Anybody who habitually keeps his office door shut is suspect.* ◊ ADV

2 A **habitual** criminal or liar commits crimes or tells lies very often. ADJ CLASSIF : ATTRIB

hack /hæk/, **hacks, hacking, hacked. 1** If you **hack** something, you cut it using a sharp tool, such as an axe or knife, with strong, rough strokes. EG *They were ambushed and hacked to death... ...hacking away at the branches.* V+O OR V+A

2 A **hack** is a professional writer who produces work fast, without worrying very much about the quality of it. EG *...a hack writer, scribbling madly to keep to the deadline.* N COUNT Informal

3 When someone **hacks** a computer system, **3.1** they write programs for the system. V+A OR V+O **3.2** they try to break into the system, especially in order to get secret or confidential information that is stored there. V+O

hack through. If you **hack through** something such as jungle, you move through it by cutting down branches and bushes. PHRASAL VB : V+PREP

hacker /hækə/, **hackers.** A computer **hacker** is **1** someone who uses a computer a lot, especially so much that they have no time to do anything else. **2** someone who tries to break into computer systems, especially in order to get secret or confidential information that is stored there. N COUNT

hackneyed /hæknɪd/. An expression that is **hackneyed** is boring because it has been used many times before. EG *'Of course I love you. With all my heart.' The hackneyed phrase came unintended to his lips.* ADJ QUALIT

hacksaw /hæksɔː/, **hacksaws.** A **hacksaw** is a small saw used for cutting metal. N COUNT

had /hæd/ is the past tense and past participle of **have.**

haddock /hædək/. **Haddock** is both the singular and the plural form. N COUNT OR N UNCOUNT
A **haddock** is a kind of sea fish. EG *Would you like smoked haddock this evening?*

hadn't /hædə[0]nt/ is the usual spoken form of 'had not'.

haemoglobin /hiːmə[6]gləʊbɪn, hem-/; also spelled **hemoglobin. Haemoglobin** is a substance that carries oxygen in red blood cells. N UNCOUNT Technical

haemophilia /hiːmə[6]fɪlɪə, hem-/; also spelled **hemophilia. Haemophilia** is an inherited disease, usually affecting men, in which a person's blood does not clot properly, so that they continue to bleed for a long time if they are injured. N UNCOUNT

haemophiliac /hiːmə[6]fɪlɪæk, hem-/, **haemophiliacs;** also spelled **hemophiliac.** A **haemophiliac** is a person who suffers from haemophilia. N COUNT

haemorrhage /hemə[0]rɪdʒ/, **haemorrhages, haemorrhaging, haemorrhaged;** also spelled **hemorrhage.** A **haemorrhage** is serious bleeding inside a person's body. EG *He had died of a brain haemorrhage.* N COUNT OR N UNCOUNT ▸ used as a verb. EG *She began to haemorrhage badly.* ▸ V

haemorrhoids /hemə[0]rɔɪdz/; also spelled **hemorrhoids. Haemorrhoids** are painful swellings that appear in the veins inside a person's anus. N PLURAL Medical

hag /hæg/, **hags.** If you call a woman a **hag**, you mean that you think she is ugly and unpleasant; an offensive word. N COUNT

haggard /hægəd/. Someone who is **haggard** looks very tired and worried. EG *There was a haggard look about his eyes.* ADJ QUALIT

haggis /hægɪs/ is a Scottish dish made with oatmeal and the internal organs of a sheep or calf. N UNCOUNT

haggle /hæge[0]l/, **haggles, haggling, haggled.** If you **haggle**, you argue about the cost of something V OR V+*with* : RECIP that you are buying. EG *They haggled with shopkeepers in the bazaar.*

hah /hɑ:/. See **ha**.

ha ha /hɑ: hɑ:/. **1 Ha ha** is used in writing to represent the sound that people make when they laugh. CONVENTION

2 You sometimes say **ha ha** sarcastically, when you are not amused and are only pretending to laugh. EG *I watched as the man made mistakes. 'Ha ha,' I sneered to myself.* CONVENTION

hail /heɪl/, **hails, hailing, hailed. 1 Hail** consists of tiny balls of ice that fall like rain from the sky. EG *The hail battered on the windows.* N SING

2 When it **hails**, hail falls from the sky. EG *It hailed all afternoon.* V

3 A **hail** of small objects is a large number of them that fall down on you at the same time with great force. EG *He was dead, killed in a hail of bullets.* N PART

4 If you **hail** someone, you call to them. EG *A voice hailed him from the steps.* V+O Literary

5 If you **hail** a taxi, you wave at it in order to stop it and ask the driver to take you somewhere. V+O

6 If you **hail** a person, event, or achievement as important or successful, you praise them publicly. EG *They were hailed as heroes... The discovery was hailed as the scientific sensation of the century.* V+O+*as*

hailstone /heɪlstəun/, **hailstones. Hailstones** are tiny balls of ice that fall from the sky when it hails. N COUNT

hailstorm /heɪlstɔ:m/, **hailstorms.** A **hailstorm** is a storm during which it hails. N COUNT

hair /hɛə/, **hairs. 1 Hairs** are the long, fine, thread-like things that grow in large numbers on your head and on other parts of your body. EG *...black hairs on the back of his hands.* N COUNT

2 Your **hair** is the large number of hairs that grow in a mass on your head. See picture at THE HUMAN BODY. EG *...a young woman with long blonde hair.* N UNCOUNT

3 Hairs are also very fine thread-like pieces of material that grows on some insects and plants. EG *The adult beetle has silken hairs on its body.* N COUNT

4 Hair is used in these phrases. **4.1** Something that **makes** your **hair stand on end** shocks or horrifies you. EG *She did it with an ease that made his hair stand on end.* **4.2** If you **let** your **hair down**, you relax completely and enjoy yourself. **4.3** If you say that someone is **splitting hairs**, you mean that they are making very fine distinctions that are not necessary. EG *Am I splitting hairs here? I think not, because this is an important distinction.* PHRASES

hairbrush /hɛəbrʌʃ/, **hairbrushes.** A **hairbrush** is a brush that you use to brush your hair. See picture at BRUSHES. N COUNT

haircut /hɛəkʌt/, **haircuts. 1** If you have a **haircut**, someone cuts your hair for you. EG *He needed a haircut.* N COUNT

2 A **haircut** is also the style in which your hair has been cut. EG *The girls had short, neat haircuts.* N COUNT

hairdo /hɛədu:/, **hairdos.** A **hairdo** is the style in which your hair has been cut and arranged. EG *I went to a salon and had a new hairdo.* N COUNT Informal

hairdresser /hɛədrɛsə/, **hairdressers. 1** A **hairdresser** is a person who cuts, washes, and styles people's hair. N COUNT

2 A **hairdresser** or a **hairdresser's** is a shop where a hairdresser works. EG *...going to the hairdresser.* N COUNT

hairdryer /hɛədraɪə/, **hairdryers;** also spelled **hairdrier.** A **hairdryer** is a machine that you use to dry your hair. N COUNT

hairless /hɛəlɪ²s/. A part of your body that is **hairless** has no hair on it. EG *...his hairless chest.* ADJ CLASSIF

hairline /hɛəlaɪn/, **hairlines. 1** Your **hairline** is the edge of the area where your hair grows on the front part of your head. EG *His hairline was receding.* N COUNT

2 A **hairline** crack or gap is very narrow or fine. EG *...a tiny hairline fracture.* ADJ CLASSIF: ATTRIB

hairnet /hɛənɛt/, **hairnets.** A **hairnet** is a small net that some women wear over their hair in order to keep it tidy. N COUNT

hairpin /hɛəpɪn/, **hairpins. 1** A **hairpin** is a thin piece of bent metal that women use to hold their hair in position. N COUNT

2 A **hairpin** bend is a very sharp bend in a road, where the road turns back in the opposite direction. N COUNT

hair-raising. Something that is **hair-raising** is very frightening or disturbing. EG *The ride was bumpy and at times hair-raising.* ADJ QUALIT

hair's breadth. A **hair's breadth** is a very small degree or amount. EG *A national strike has been averted by no more than a hair's breadth.* N SING: a+N

hair slide, hair slides. A **hair slide** is a decorative clip that girls and women put in their hair to hold it in position. N COUNT

hairstyle /hɛəstaɪl/, **hairstyles.** Your **hairstyle** is the style in which your hair has been cut or arranged. EG *...a new hairstyle.* N COUNT

hairy /hɛəri¹/, **hairier, hairiest. 1** Someone or something that is **hairy** is covered with hair. EG *...a big, hairy man.* ADJ QUALIT

2 If you describe a situation as **hairy**, you mean that it is exciting, worrying, and rather frightening. EG *It got a little hairy when we drove him to the station with less than two minutes to spare.* ADJ QUALIT Informal

halcyon /hælsɪən/. A **halcyon** time is a peaceful or happy one. EG *...the halcyon days of his late teens.* ADJ CLASSIF: ATTRIB Formal

hale /heɪl/. If you describe someone as **hale**, you mean that they are healthy. EG *They had hale old parents who lived on farms in the country.* ADJ QUALIT Literary

half /hɑ:f/, **halves** /hɑ:vz/. **1 Half** of an amount or object is one of the two equal parts that together make up the amount or object. EG *Roughly half are French... The house was half a mile away... ...half a million men... Half his front teeth are missing... ...the two halves of the brain... I went to Poland four and a half years ago.* PRON, PREDET, OR N COUNT

2 You can also use **half** to describe a half of something. EG *...a half chicken... The picture wouldn't end for another half hour.* ADJ CLASSIF: ATTRIB

3 Half is also used in these phrases. **3.1** If something is divided **in half**, it is divided into two equal parts. EG *He tore it in half.* **3.2** If you increase something **by half**, half of the original amount is added to it. If you decrease it **by half**, half of the original amount is taken away from it. EG *She reckoned she cut her costs by half.* **3.3** If you say that someone is **too** clever **by half** or **too** arrogant **by half**, you mean that you dislike their cleverness or arrogance. **3.4** If two people **go halves**, they divide the cost of something equally between them. PHRASES Informal

4 A **half** is **4.1** half a pint of beer, lager, or cider. EG *...a half of lager.* **4.2** a half-price ticket on a bus or train, especially one for a child. N PART N COUNT

5 You also use **half** to say that something is only partly the case or happens to only a limited extent. EG *He half expected to see Davis there... His eyes were half-closed... ...his half empty glass.* ADV

6 You can use **half** to say that someone has parents of different nationalities. For example, if you are **half** German, one of your parents is German. ADV +ADJ CLASSIF

7 You use **half** to refer to a time that is thirty minutes after a particular hour. For example, if it is **half** past two, thirty minutes have passed since two o'clock. See the entry headed TIME. ADV

8 half the battle: see **battle**.

half-baked. Ideas, opinions, or plans that are **half-baked** have not been properly thought out, and so are usually stupid or impractical. EG *...your half-baked political opinions.* ADJ QUALIT

half board. If you stay at a hotel and have **half board**, you have your breakfast and evening meal at the hotel, but not your lunch. N UNCOUNT

half-brother, half-brothers. Your **half-brother** is a boy or man who has the same mother or the same father as you have. N COUNT

half-caste. Someone who is **half-caste** has parents who come from different races. EG *Half-caste children were taken forcibly from their parents and sold as slaves.* ADJ CLASSIF

half-day, half-days. A **half-day** is a day when you work only in the morning or in the afternoon, but not all day. EG *Saturday is his half-day.* N COUNT

half-hearted. Someone or something that is **half-hearted** shows no real effort, interest, or enthusiasm. EG *She made a half-hearted attempt to break away.* ◊ **half-heartedly.** EG *I stayed home, studying half-heartedly.* ADJ QUALIT ◊ ADV

half-life, half-lives. The **half-life** of a radioactive substance is the amount of time that it takes to lose half its radioactivity. EG *...a half-life of 30 years.* N COUNT Technical

half-mast. If a flag is flying **at half-mast**, it is flying from the middle of the mast as a sign that someone important has died. PHRASE

halfpenny /heɪpni^1/, **halfpennies** or **halfpence.** A **halfpenny** is a small British coin which used to be worth one half of a penny. N COUNT

half-price. If something is **half-price**, it costs only half what it usually costs. EG *...half-price electricity.* ADJ CLASSIF

half-sister, half-sisters. Your **half-sister** is a girl or woman who has the same mother or the same father as you have. N COUNT

half-term is a short holiday in the middle of a school term. EG *It's half-term next week.* N UNCOUNT

half-timbered. Buildings that are **half-timbered** have wooden beams showing in the brick and plaster walls. ADJ CLASSIF

half-time is the short period of time between the two parts of a sports match, when the players have a short rest. N UNCOUNT

halfway /hɑːfweɪ/. **1 Halfway** means **1.1** at the middle of a place or of a distance between two points. EG *She was half-way up the stairs.* **1.2** at the middle of a period of time or of an event. EG *Dr O'Shea usually fell asleep halfway through the programme.* ADV : OFT+PREP OR+ADV

2 If you **meet** someone **halfway**, you accept some of the points they are making so that you can come to an agreement. PHRASE

half-yearly. A **half-yearly** event happens twice a year, with six months between each event. ADJ CLASSIF : ATTRIB

hall /hɔːl/, **halls. 1** A **hall** is **1.1** the area just inside the front door of a house. EG *We began bringing down our suitcases and putting them in the hall.* N COUNT

1.2 a large building or a room in a building which is used for public events such as concerts, exhibitions, and meetings. EG *We organized a concert in the village hall.* N COUNT **1.3** a building where a local government authority has its main offices. EG *...the town hall.* N COUNT+SUPP

2 Students who live **in hall** live in university or college accommodation. PHRASE

3 A **hall** is also a large house on a country estate. EG *'I don't own Barrett Hall,' I said.* N COUNT

hallelujah /hælɪ^{2}luːjə/; also spelled **halleluiah** and **alleluia.** Some Christians say **hallelujah** in church as an exclamation of praise and thanks to God. CONVENTION

hallmark /hɔːlmɑːk/, **hallmarks.** A **hallmark** is **1** the most typical quality or feature of something or someone. EG *...the kind of subtlety that was the hallmark of Elgar.* N COUNT+SUPP **2** an official mark put on things made of gold, silver, or platinum that indicates the quality of the metal and where the object was made. N COUNT

hallo /hə^{3}ləʊ/. See **hello.**

hall of residence, halls of residence. Halls of residence are blocks of rooms or flats, usually built by universities or colleges, in which students live. N COUNT

hallowed /hæləʊd/. If something is **hallowed**, it is respected and revered, usually because it is old or important. EG *...those hallowed offices on State Street.* ADJ QUALIT

Halloween /hæləʊiːn/; also spelled **Hallowe'en. Halloween** is October 31st. It is traditionally said to be the night on which ghosts and witches can be seen, and so children often dress up as ghosts and witches. N UNCOUNT

hallucinate /hə^{3}luːsɪneɪt/, **hallucinates, hallucinating, hallucinated.** If you **hallucinate**, you see things that are not really there, either because you are ill or because you have taken a drug. EG *She barked at me and I knew she must be hallucinating.* V

hallucination /hə^{3}luːsɪneɪʃə^{0}n/, **hallucinations.** A **hallucination** is what you see when you are hallucinating. EG *...a bizarre hallucination.* N COUNT OR N UNCOUNT

hallway /hɔːlweɪ/, **hallways.** A **hallway** is the entrance hall of a house or other building. N COUNT

halo /heɪləʊ/, **haloes** or **halos.** A **halo** is a circle of light that is drawn in pictures round the heads of saints or angels to show that they are holy. N COUNT

halt /hɒlt/, **halts, halting, halted. 1** When you **halt** or when something **halts** you, you stop moving and stand still. EG *He took a step and halted... He tried to push past, but the girl halted him.* V-ERG

2 When growth, development, or activity **halts** or when you **halt** it, it stops completely. EG *...if population growth were to halt overnight... The firm ran into foreign exchange problems which halted its imports of nylon.* V-ERG

3 If someone or something comes **to a halt**, they stop moving. EG *The car slowed, and came to a halt opposite her.* PHRASE

4 If growth, development, or activity comes **to a halt**, it stops completely. EG *The comment brought conversation to a halt.* PHRASE

5 If you **call a halt** to something, you decide not to continue with it. EG *Surely it is time to call a halt to these practices?* PHRASE

halting /hɒltɪŋ, hɔːl-/. If you speak in a **halting** way, you speak uncertainly with a lot of pauses. EG *...his halting admission of guilt.* ◊ **haltingly.** EG *He answered haltingly.* ADJ QUALIT ◊ ADV

halve /hɑːv/, **halves, halving, halved. 1** When you **halve** something or when it **halves**, it is reduced to half its previous size or amount. EG *This could halve rail fares... If that happened, sales would halve overnight.* V-ERG

2 If you **halve** something, you divide it into two equal parts. EG *Halve the avocado pears and remove the stones.* V+O

3 Halves is the plural of **half.**

ham /hæm/, **hams, hamming, hammed. 1 Ham** is salted meat from a pig's leg. EG *...legs of ham hanging behind the counter... ...a ham sandwich.* N UNCOUNT

2 If actors or actresses **ham it up**, they exaggerate every emotion and gesture when they are acting. EG *She was obviously hamming it up for the benefit of the watching tourists.* PHRASE

hamburger /hæmbɜːgə/, **hamburgers.** A **hamburger** is minced meat which has been shaped into a flat disc. Hamburgers are fried or grilled and often eaten in a bread roll. N COUNT

hamlet /hæmlɪ^{2}t/, **hamlets.** A **hamlet** is a very small village. N COUNT

hammer /hæmə/, **hammers, hammering, hammered. 1** A **hammer** is **1.1** a tool that you use for hitting things. It consists of a heavy piece of metal at the end of a handle. See picture at TOOLS. **1.2** a heavy weight attached to a piece of wire, that is thrown as a sport. N COUNT

2 If you **hammer** something such as a nail, you hit it with a hammer. V+O

Will you find a hallmark in a hall?

3 If you **hammer** a surface or **hammer** on it, you make a noise by hitting it several times with your fist. EG *Men used to hammer on our door late at night.* V+O OR V+A

4 If you **hammer** an idea into people, you keep repeating it forcefully so that it will have an effect on them. EG *...ideas hammered into their heads by a stream of movies.* V+O+A

hammer away. If you **hammer** away at some work or activity, you work at it constantly and with great energy. EG *They all hammer away at their thesis.* PHRASAL VB : V+ADV, OFT+*at*

hammer out. If you **hammer** something **out**, you reach an agreement about it after a long or difficult discussion. EG *...procedures hammered out over recent years.* PHRASAL VB : V+O+ADV

hammock /hæmək/, **hammocks.** A **hammock** is a piece of strong cloth which is hung between two supports and is used as a bed. N COUNT

hamper /hæmpə/, **hampers, hampering, hampered. 1** If you **hamper** a person or their actions, you restrict them by making their development, progress, or movement difficult. EG *They were hampered by a constant stream of visitors.* V+O

2 A **hamper** is a large basket with a lid, used especially for carrying food in. EG *We packed a big wicker hamper and went for a picnic.* N COUNT

hamstring /hæmstrɪŋ/, **hamstrings, hamstringing, hamstrung. 1** A **hamstring** is a tendon behind your knee which joins the muscles of your thigh to the bones of your lower leg. EG *...a hamstring injury.* N COUNT

2 If you **hamstring** someone, you make it very difficult for them to take any action. EG *If you made the law too precise, you would so hamstring the medical profession that patients would go untreated.* V+O Formal

hand /hænd/, **hands, handing, handed. 1** Your **hands** are the parts of your body at the end of your arms. Each hand has four fingers and a thumb. See picture at THE HUMAN BODY. EG *He took her hand and squeezed it.* N COUNT

2 If someone has a **hand** in an action or situation, they are actively involved in it. EG *I had a hand in drafting the appeal... The hand of the military in shaping government policy was obvious.* N SING

3 If you ask someone for a **hand** with something, you are asking them to help you. EG *Give me a hand with this desk, will you?* ● to **lend a hand**: see **lend.** N SING : *a*+N

4 A **hand** is someone who is employed to do hard physical work. N COUNT

5 The **hands** of a clock or watch are the thin pieces of metal or plastic that point to the numbers in order to show what time it is. N COUNT

6 If you **hand** something to someone, you give it to them. EG *Could you hand me that piece of wood?... I examined the lighter, then handed it back.* V+O+*to* OR V+O+O

7 Hand is used in the following ways after different prepositions. **7.1** Something that is **at hand** or that is **close at hand** is very near in time or place. EG *I picked up a book that happened to lie at hand.* **7.2** If you do something **by hand**, you do it using your hands rather than using a machine. **7.3** If you have some time **in hand**, you have some time free. EG *He arrived with half an hour in hand and went for a walk.* **7.4** The job or problem **in hand** is the one that you are dealing with at the moment. EG *Let's get on with the job in hand.* **7.5** If someone is **on hand**, they are near and ready to help. **7.6** If you reject an idea **out of hand**, you reject it immediately and completely. **7.7** If you have something **to hand**, you have it ready to use when needed. EG *...using the material most readily to hand.* PHRASES

8 Hand is also used in these phrases. **8.1** If someone gives you **a free hand**, they allow you to do a particular task exactly as you want. **8.2** You use **on the one hand** when mentioning one aspect of a situation. Then you use **on the other hand** when mentioning another, contrasting aspect. EG *John had great difficulties playing cricket. But on the other hand, he was an awfully good rugby player.* **8.3** Two people who are **hand in hand** are holding each other's hand. **8.4** Two things that **go hand in hand** are closely connected. EG *Military superiority went hand in hand with organizational superiority.* **8.5** If you **force** someone's **hand**, you force them to act sooner than they want to. **8.6** If a person or a situation **gets out of hand**, you are no longer able to control them or it. **8.7** If you **know** a place **like the back of** your **hand**, you know it extremely well. **8.8** If you **take** someone **in hand**, you take control over them, especially in order to improve them. **8.9** If you **try** your **hand** at a new activity, you attempt to do it. EG *I had tried my hand at milking years ago.* PHRASES

9 Hands is used in these phrases. **9.1** You say **'Hands off'** to tell someone not to touch something. **9.2** If you receive bad treatment **at** someone's **hands**, they treat you badly. EG *...brutality at the hands of angry parents.* **9.3** If something is **in the hands** of a particular person, the person has it, or has power or responsibility over it. EG *This law leaves too much power in the hands of the judges.* **9.4** If you have a responsibility or problem **on** your **hands**, you have to deal with it. When it is **off** your **hands**, it is no longer your responsibility. EG *They've still got an economic crisis on their hands.* **9.5** If a possession **changes hands**, it is sold or given from one person to another. **9.6** If you **get** or **lay** your **hands on** something, you manage to find it or obtain it. EG *I wondered how I could lay my hands on the money to buy equipment.* **9.7** If you **have** your **hands full**, you are very busy. **9.8** Two people who **are holding hands** are holding each other's hand. **9.9** If you **wash** your **hands** of someone or something, you refuse to take any more responsibility for them. PHRASES

hand down. If you **hand** something **down**, you give it or leave it to people who belong to a younger generation. EG *Such knowledge was handed down from father to son.* PHRASAL VB : V+O+ADV, USU PASS

hand in. If you **hand in** something you have written, you give it to someone in authority. EG *I haven't yet marked the work you handed in... I was tempted to hand in my resignation at once.* PHRASAL VB : V+O+ADV

hand on. If you **hand** something **on** to someone, you give it or leave it to them. EG *Property is something handed on from generation to generation.* PHRASAL VB : V+O+ADV, OFT+*to*

hand out. 1 If you **hand out** a set of things, you give one to each person in a group. EG *Hand out the books.* PHRASAL VB : V+O+ADV **2** When people in authority **hand out** advice or punishment, they give it to people. EG *Family doctors handed out information on treatment.* V+O+ADV **3** See also **handout.**

hand over. 1 If you **hand** something **over** to someone, you give it to them. EG *Samuel was clearly about to hand over large sums of money to this man.* PHRASAL VB : V+O+ADV, OFT+*to* **2** If you **hand over** to someone, you give them the responsibility for dealing with something which you were previously responsible for. EG *Sir John handed over to his deputy and left.* V+ADV OR V+O+ADV, OFT+*to*

handbag /hændbæg/, **handbags.** A **handbag** is a small bag in which a woman carries things such as her money and keys. See picture at BAGS. N COUNT

handbook /hændbʊk/, **handbooks.** A **handbook** is a book that gives you advice and instructions about something. EG *...the official handbook for the airport.* N COUNT : OFT+SUPP

handbrake /hændbreɪk/, **handbrakes.** A **handbrake** is a brake which is operated by the hand of the person driving a vehicle. See picture at CAR. EG *Mr Boggis released the handbrake.* N COUNT

handclap /hændklæp/. A **slow handclap** is slow rhythmic clapping by an audience to show that they do not like what they are seeing or hearing. PHRASE British

handcuff /hændkʌf/, **handcuffs, handcuffing, handcuffed. 1 Handcuffs** are two metal rings which are joined by a short chain and which can be locked round someone's wrists, usually by the police. N PLURAL

2 If you **handcuff** someone, you put handcuffs around their wrists. EG *They were searched and handcuffed.* V+O: USU PASS

handful /hændfʊl/, **handfuls. 1** A **handful** of something is the amount of it that you can hold in your hand. EG *Roger gathered a handful of stones.* N PART

2 If there is only a **handful** of people or things, there are not very many of them. EG *The firm employs only a handful of workers.* N PART: SING

3 If you describe a child as a **handful**, you mean that he or she is difficult to control. N COUNT Informal

handicap /hændɪkæp/, **handicaps, handicapping, handicapped. 1** A **handicap** is **1.1** a physical or mental disability which prevents you from living a totally normal life. EG *These changes have made the campus an easier place for people with handicaps.* **1.2** an event or situation that makes it difficult for you to do something. EG *His chief handicap is that he comes from a broken home.* N COUNT

2 If an event or a situation **handicaps** someone, it makes it difficult for them to do something. EG *We were handicapped by the darkness.* V+O

3 A **handicap** is also a disadvantage that is given to someone who is good at a particular sport, in order to make the competition between them and the other competitors more equal. N COUNT

handicapped /hændɪkæpt/. **1** Someone who is **handicapped** has a physical or mental disability that prevents them living a totally normal life. EG *A friend of his had a handicapped daughter.* ADJ QUALIT

2 You can refer to people who are handicapped as **the handicapped**. EG *...establishments for the mentally or physically handicapped.* N PLURAL: *the*+N

handicraft /hændɪkrɑ:ft/, **handicrafts. Handicrafts** are **1** activities such as embroidery and pottery which involve making things with your hands in a skilful way. EG *She teaches handicrafts.* **2** the objects that are produced by people doing handicrafts. EG *Handicrafts were produced by families to be sold in local shops.* N COUNT: USU PLURAL

handiwork /hændɪwɜ:k/. If you refer to something as your **handiwork**, you mean that you made it yourself. EG *He stood back and surveyed his handiwork.* N UNCOUNT +POSS

handkerchief /hæŋkətʃɪ^{1}f/, **handkerchiefs.** A **handkerchief** is a small square piece of fabric which you use for blowing your nose. N COUNT

handle /hændə^{0}l/, **handles, handling, handled. 1** A **handle** is **1.1** a lever or other small object that is attached to a door or window and is used for opening and closing it. EG *He tugged at the metal handle.* **1.2** the part of an object that you hold in order to carry it or use it. EG *...a broom handle.* N COUNT

2 If you **fly off the handle**, you suddenly and completely lose your temper. PHRASE Informal

3 When you **handle** something, you hold it and move it about in your hands. EG *Glass. Handle with Care.* V+O

4 When you **handle** something such as a weapon, car, or horse, you use or control it effectively. EG *She had handled a machine gun herself... This car handles very nicely.* V-ERG: IF V THEN+A

5 If you **handle** a problem or difficult situation, you deal with it successfully. EG *You don't have to come. Hendricks and I can handle it.* ◇ **handling.** EG *His handling of these important issues was condemned by the opposition.* V+O ◇ N UNCOUNT: USU+*of*

6 If you **handle** a particular area of work, you have responsibility for it. EG *He handles all the major accounts.* V+O

7 If you can **handle** people, you establish a good relationship with them so that they respect you and do what you want them to. EG *The principal was a genius in the way he handled us.* V+O

handlebar /hændə^{0}lbɑ:/, **handlebars.** The **handlebars** of a bicycle consist of a curved metal bar with handles at each end. The handlebars are attached to the front of the bicycle and are turned in order to steer it. See picture at BICYCLE. N COUNT: USU PLURAL

handler /hændlə/, **handlers.** A **handler** is **1** someone who is in charge of an animal as part of their work. **2** someone who deals with a particular type of object as part of their work. EG *...baggage handlers.* N COUNT+SUPP

handmade /hændmeɪd/. If something is **handmade**, it is made by someone without using machines. EG *...beautiful handmade clothes.* ADJ CLASSIF

handout /hændaʊt/, **handouts. 1** A **handout** is money, clothing, or food which is given free to poor people. EG *We said that we wouldn't be relying on handouts from anyone for our future.* N COUNT

2 A **handout** is also **2.1** a document which gives information about a particular company or event, and is used to publicize the company or event. EG *...a pile of unread public relations handouts and shiny magazines.* **2.2** a summary of the information in a lecture or talk, which is given to the audience. N COUNT

hand-picked. If someone is **hand-picked**, they have been very carefully chosen for a particular purpose or for a particular job. EG *Each of the officers had been hand-picked by the general.* ADJ CLASSIF

handrail /hændreɪl/, **handrails.** A **handrail** is a long piece of metal or wood which is fixed near stairs or high places, which people can hold for support as they walk. EG *I had to cling with both hands to the handrails.* N COUNT

handshake /hændʃeɪk/, **handshakes.** If you give someone a **handshake**, you take their right hand with your right hand and hold it firmly or move it up and down. You do this as a sign of greeting or to show that you have agreed about something. EG *He came to the door to welcome me with a handshake.* N COUNT

handsome /hænsəm/. **1** A man who is **handsome** has an attractive face with regular features. EG *He was a tall, dark, and undeniably handsome man.* ADJ QUALIT

2 A woman who is **handsome** has an attractive, smart appearance, usually with features that are large and regular rather than small and delicate. EG *...a strikingly handsome woman.* ADJ QUALIT

3 A building or garden that is **handsome** is large and well made with an attractive appearance. EG *...handsome big apartment buildings.* ◇ **handsomely.** EG *...handsomely sized rooms.* ADJ QUALIT ◇ ADV

4 A **handsome** sum of money is a large or generous amount. EG *The rate of return on these farmers' outlay was a handsome 57 per cent.* ADJ CLASSIF: ATTRIB

handstand /hændstænd/, **handstands.** If you do a **handstand**, you balance upside down on your hands with your body and legs straight up in the air. N COUNT

hand-to-hand. A **hand-to-hand** fight is one in which people are fighting very close together, with their hands or sometimes with knives. ADJ CLASSIF: ATTRIB OR ADV

hand-to-mouth. A **hand-to-mouth** existence is a way of life in which you have hardly enough food or money to live on. ADJ CLASSIF: ATTRIB OR ADV

handwriting /hændraɪtɪŋ/. Someone's **handwriting** is their style of writing with a pen or pencil rather than with a typewriter. EG *He looked at his son's laborious handwriting.* N UNCOUNT

handwritten /hændrɪtə^{0}n/. A piece of writing that is **handwritten** is one that has been written using a pen or pencil. ADJ CLASSIF

handy /hændi^{1}/, **handier, handiest. 1** Something that is **handy** is useful and easy to use. EG *An electric kettle is very handy.* ● If you say that something will **come in handy**, you mean that it ADJ QUALIT ● PHRASE Informal will be useful. EG *Rick's raft came in handy for shipping camera gear up the river.*

2 Someone who is **handy** with a particular tool is skilful at using it. EG *He was handy with an axe.* — ADJ QUALIT, Informal

3 A thing or place that is **handy** is nearby and convenient. EG *I looked to see whether there was a glass handy.* — ADJ QUALIT, Informal ● If you **keep** something **handy**, you keep it easily available so that you can use it when you need it. — ● PHRASE

handyman /hændi^{1}mæn/, **handymen.** A **handyman** is a man who is good at making things or repairing things. — N COUNT

hang /hæŋ/, **hangs, hanging, hung** /hʌŋ/, **hanged. Hung** is the past tense and past participle of the verb, except in paragraph 3, where the form **hanged** is used.

1 If you **hang** something on a hook or rail, you place it so that its highest part is supported and the rest of it is not. EG *He was hanging his coat in the hall.* — V+O+A

2 If something **is hanging** somewhere, the top of it is attached to something and the rest of it is free and unsupported. EG *...some washing hanging on a line.* — V+A

3 To **hang** someone means to kill them by tying a rope around their neck and taking away the support from under their feet so that they hang in the air. EG *Rebecca Smith was hanged in 1849... He tried to hang himself.* — V+O OR V-REFL

4 If a future event or a possibility **hangs** over you, it worries you. EG *...the threat of universal extinction hanging over all the world today.* — V+*over*

5 If you **get the hang of** something, you begin to understand how to do it. EG *Once you have got the hang of it, you'll be alright.* — PHRASE, Informal

6 See also **hanging**.

hang about or **hang around.** If you **hang about** or **hang around** somewhere, you stay in a particular place doing nothing, often because you are waiting for someone. EG *We would have to hang around for a while... I enjoyed hanging around Parliament listening to debates.* — PHRASAL VB: V+ADV/PREP, Informal

hang on. 1 If you ask someone to **hang on**, you mean you want them to wait for a moment or stop what they are doing or saying. EG *Hang on a minute.* — CONVENTION, Informal **2** If you **hang on**, you manage to survive until the situation you are in improves. EG *I can't keep hanging on here much longer.* — PHRASAL VB: V+ADV **3** If something **hangs on** something else, it depends on it. EG *Everything hangs on money at the moment.* — V+PREP

hang onto. If you **hang onto** something, **1** you hold it very tightly. EG *Claude hung on to Tom's shoulder.* — PHRASAL VB: V+PREP **2** you keep it or try to keep it. EG *Fear is a powerful motive for hanging on to power.* — V+PREP

hang out. When you **hang out** washing, you hang it on a clothes line to dry. — PHRASAL VB: V+O+ADV

hang round. See **hang around**.

hang up. 1 If you **hang** something **up**, you place it so that its highest part is supported and the rest of it is not. EG *Howard hangs up his scarf on the hook behind the door.* — PHRASAL VB: V+ADV **2** Something that **is hanging up** somewhere has been put there so that it does not touch the ground. EG *There are some old tools hanging up in the shed.* — V+ADV **3** When you **hang up** at the end of a phone call, you put back the receiver. — V+ADV OR V+O+ADV

hang up on. If you **hang up on** someone, you end a phone call to them suddenly and unexpectedly by putting back the receiver. — PHRASAL VB: V+ADV+PREP

hangar /hæŋə/, **hangars.** A **hangar** is a large building in which aircraft are kept. — N COUNT

hanger /hæŋə/, **hangers.** A **hanger** is the same as a coat hanger. EG *He took off his shirt, put it on a hanger, and hung it in the wardrobe.* — N COUNT

hanger-on, hangers-on. A **hanger-on** is a person who tries to be friendly with a richer or more important person or group, especially for his or her own advantage. EG *...a small group of writers, artists and assorted hangers-on.* — N COUNT

hang-glider, hang-gliders. A **hang-glider** is a type of large kite, which someone can hang from and use to help them fly through the air. — N COUNT

hang-gliding is the activity of flying in a hang-glider. — N ING

hanging /hæŋɪŋ/, **hangings. 1 Hanging** is the practice of executing people by hanging them. EG *Every one of them was in favour of hanging.* — N UNCOUNT

2 A **hanging** is the act or occasion of killing a person by hanging them. EG *The crowds at Tyburn used to find a hanging entertaining.* — N COUNT OR N UNCOUNT

3 A **hanging** is also a large piece of cloth that you put as a decoration on a wall or as a curtain over a window. EG *...silk and damask hangings.* — N COUNT: OFT+SUPP

hangman /hæŋmə^{3}n/, **hangmen.** A **hangman** is a man whose job is to execute people by hanging them. — N COUNT

hangover /hæŋəʊvə/, **hangovers. 1** A **hangover** is a headache and feeling of sickness that you have in the morning if you have drunk a lot of alcohol the night before. — N COUNT

2 A **hangover** from the past is something that results from ideas or attitudes which people had in the past but which are no longer generally held. EG *This feeling should be attributed to habit, a hangover from earlier, more primitive times.* — N COUNT+SUPP

hang-up, hang-ups. If you have a **hang-up** about something, you have a feeling of fear, embarrassment, or worry about it. EG *He's got a hang-up about flying.* — N COUNT, Informal

hank /hæŋk/, **hanks.** A **hank** is an amount of wool, rope, or string that has been loosely wound. — N COUNT, Technical

hanker /hæŋkə/, **hankers, hankering, hankered.** If you **hanker** after something or for something, you have a great desire for it. EG *We always hankered after a bungalow of our own.* — V+*after/for*

hankering /hæŋkə^{0}rɪŋ/, **hankerings.** A **hankering** for something is a great desire for it. EG *If you give way to this hankering for food you will become fat.* — N COUNT+*for*

hanky /hæŋki^1/, **hankies;** also spelled **hankie.** A **hanky** is the same as a handkerchief. — N COUNT, Informal

haphazard /hæphæzəd/. Something that is **haphazard** is not organized or not arranged according to a plan. EG *It was done on a haphazard basis.* — ADJ QUALIT ◇ **haphazardly.** EG *...all the papers haphazardly strewn on desks.* — ◇ ADV

hapless /hæplɪ^{2}s/. A **hapless** person is very unlucky. EG *...the hapless victim of a misplaced murder attempt.* — ADJ CLASSIF: ATTRIB, Literary

happen /hæpə^{0}n/, **happens, happening, happened. 1** When something **happens**, it occurs or is done without being planned. EG *The explosion had happened at one in the morning... ...a court of inquiry into what happened.* — V: OFT+A

2 When something **happens** to someone or something, it takes place and affects them, often in an unpleasant way. EG *...all the ghastly things that had happened to him.* — V+*to*

3 If you **happen** to do something, you do it as a result of chance. EG *He happened to be at their base when the alert began.* — V+*to*-INF

4 You say **as it happens** before a statement in order to introduce a new fact. EG *As it happens, I brought the note with me.* — ADV SEN

happening /hæpə^{0}nɪŋ/, **happenings.** A **happening** is something that happens, often in a way that is unexpected or hard to explain. EG *...some very bizarre happenings in Europe.* — N COUNT

happy /hæpi^1/, **happier, happiest. 1** Someone who is **happy** has feelings of pleasure, often because something nice has happened. EG *...a happy smile... The old man's not very happy.* — ADJ QUALIT ◇ **happily.** EG *We laughed and chatted happily together.* — ◇ ADV ◇ **happiness.** EG *Money did not bring happiness.* — ◇ N UNCOUNT

2 A time or place that is **happy** has an atmosphere in which people feel happy. EG *...a happy childhood... ...the happiest time of their lives.* — ADJ QUALIT

3 If you are **happy** about a situation or arrange- — ADJ PRED +*about/with*

ment, you are satisfied with it. EG *We are not too happy about this turn of events... Are you happy with that, Diana?*

4 If you say you are **happy** to do something, you mean that you are very willing to do it. EG *I was happy to work with George.* ADJ PRED +*to*-INF

5 You use **happy** in greetings to say that you hope someone will enjoy a special occasion. EG *Happy birthday!... Happy New Year!* ● **many happy returns**: see **return**. ADJ QUALIT : ATTRIB

6 You use **happy** to describe something that is very suitable, appropriate, or fortunate. EG *I appreciate that this is not a happy comparison.* ADJ QUALIT : ATTRIB Formal

◇ **happily.** EG *That trend reversed itself, happily.* ◇ ADV SEN

happy-go-lucky. Someone who is **happy-go-lucky** enjoys life and does not worry about the future. ADJ QUALIT

harangue /hə^{r}ræŋ/, **harangues, haranguing, harangued.** A **harangue** is a long, forceful speech that someone makes in order to persuade other people to accept their opinions. EG *...blazing harangues about the wickedness of the Government.* N COUNT

▸ used as a verb. EG *Smith harangued his fellow students and persuaded them to walk out.* ▸ V+O

harass /hærəs/, **harasses, harassing, harassed.** If you **harass** someone, you trouble them or annoy them. EG *Some governments have chosen to harass and persecute the rural poor.* V+O

harassed /hærəst/. Someone who is **harassed** feels worried and under pressure because they have too much to do. EG *As the pressure gets worse, people get more harassed and work is rushed.* ADJ QUALIT

harassing /hærəsıŋ/. Something that is **harassing** makes you feel worried and under pressure because you have too many jobs to do or too many problems to cope with. EG *I have had a particularly busy and harassing day.* ADJ QUALIT

harassment /hærəsm^{ə}nt/ is behaviour which is intended to trouble or annoy someone. EG *...alleged police brutality and harassment.* N UNCOUNT

harbinger /hɑːbındʒə/, **harbingers.** A person or thing that is a **harbinger** of something is a sign that it is going to happen in the future. EG *The sudden oil price rise was a harbinger of future problems.* N COUNT : USU+*of* Formal

harbour /hɑːbə/, **harbours, harbouring, harboured;** spelled **harbor** in American English. **1** A **harbour** is an area of water at the coast which is protected from the sea by land or strong walls, so that boats can be left there safely. N COUNT

2 If you **harbour** a strong emotion, you have it in your mind over a long period of time. EG *I was unable to dismiss the fears I harboured for my safety.* V+O Literary

3 If you **harbour** someone who is wanted by the police, you hide them secretly in your house. EG *You could get into trouble for harbouring her.* V+O

hard /hɑːd/, **harder, hardest. 1** If something feels **hard** when you touch it, it is very firm and is not easily bent, cut, or broken. EG *The green fruits were as hard as rocks... The ground was baked hard.* ADJ QUALIT

◇ **hardness.** EG *We gave them cushions to ease the hardness of the benches.* ◇ N UNCOUNT

2 If something is **hard** to do or to understand, it is difficult. EG *He found it hard to make friends... That is a very hard question to answer.* ADJ QUALIT

3 If you try **hard** to do something or if you concentrate **hard**, you make a great effort or pay great attention. EG *I cannot stand upright, no matter how hard I try... He had worked hard all his life... Think hard about what I'm offering.* ADV

4 Hard work involves a lot of effort. EG *This has been a long hard day.* ADJ QUALIT

5 Hard also means **5.1** with a lot of force. EG *She slammed the door hard.* **5.2** with great severity. EG *The government's first reaction to the riots was to clamp down hard.* ADV

6 Someone who is **hard** shows no kindness or sympathy. EG *His hard grey eyes began to soften a little.* ADJ QUALIT

7 If you are **hard** on someone, you treat them severely or unkindly. EG *Don't be hard on her.* ADJ PRED+*on*

8 If something is **hard** on a person or thing, it causes them suffering or damage. EG *This arrangement seemed rather hard on the women... This work's hard on the feet.* ADJ PRED+*on*

9 If your life is **hard**, it is difficult and unpleasant. ADJ QUALIT

10 A **hard** winter or **hard** frost is very cold or severe. ADJ QUALIT

11 Hard facts are definitely true. EG *We have no hard evidence to indicate that he is the culprit.* ADJ CLASSIF : ATTRIB

12 Hard drugs are very strong illegal drugs such as heroin or cocaine. ADJ CLASSIF : ATTRIB

13 You can refer to very extreme members of political parties as the **hard** left or the **hard** right. ADJ CLASSIF : ATTRIB

14 If you are **hard pushed**, **hard put**, or **hard pressed** to do something, you have great difficulty doing it. EG *One would be hard put to think of a better plan.* ● See also **hard-pressed**. PHRASE

15 If you feel **hard done by**, you feel that you have not been treated fairly. PHRASE

16 to **follow hard on the heels of** something: see **heel**.

hard and fast. Hard and fast rules cannot be changed and should be obeyed. EG *There isn't any hard and fast rule about this.* ADJ CLASSIF : ATTRIB

hardback /hɑːdbæk/, **hardbacks.** A **hardback** is a book which has a stiff hard cover. EG *...a hardback edition... The book was published in hardback.* N COUNT OR *in*+N

hardboard /hɑːdbɔːd/ is a material made by pressing small pieces of wood very closely together. You buy it in thin, flexible sheets. N UNCOUNT

hard-boiled. A **hard-boiled** egg has been boiled in its shell until the yolk and the white are hard. ADJ CLASSIF

hard cash is money in the form of notes and coins as opposed to a cheque or a credit card. N UNCOUNT

hard core. The **hard-core** members of a group are the ones who are most involved with the activities of the group. N MOD OR N SING

harden /hɑːd^{ə}n/, **hardens, hardening, hardened. 1** When something **hardens** or when you **harden** it, it becomes stiff or firm. EG *The glue dries very fast and hardens in an hour.* V-ERG

2 When you **harden** your ideas or attitudes or when they **harden**, they become fixed and you become determined not to change them. EG *The organization has hardened its attitude to the crisis.* V-ERG

◇ **hardening.** EG *It would almost certainly result in a hardening of Allied opposition and determination.* ◇ N UNCOUNT

3 When events **harden** people or when people **harden**, they become less sympathetic and gentle than they were before. EG *Life in the camp had hardened her considerably.* V-ERG

hard-headed. Someone who is **hard-headed** does not allow emotion to affect their actions. EG *...this hard-headed brother of mine.* ADJ QUALIT

hard-hearted /hɑːd hɑːtıd/. Someone who is **hard-hearted** has no sympathy for people and does not care if they are hurt or unhappy. EG *I'm not a hard-hearted man.* ADJ QUALIT

hard labour; spelled **hard labor** in American English. **Hard labour** is hard physical work which people have to do as punishment for a crime. EG *He was condemned to six months hard labour.* N UNCOUNT

hard line. If someone takes a **hard line** on something, they have a firm policy which they refuse to change. EG *He applauded the president's hard line on the issue.* N SING

hard luck. You can say **'Hard luck'** to someone to say that you are sorry they have not got something that they wanted. CONVENTION Informal

What phrase might you use to show sympathy with someone?

hardly /hɑːdli¹/. **1** You use **hardly** to say that something is only just true. EG *I was beginning to like Sam, though I hardly knew him... The boy was hardly more than seventeen... She had hardly any money... Her bedroom was so small that she could hardly move in it.* ADV BRD NEG

2 If you say **hardly** had one thing happened when something else happened, you mean that the first event was followed immediately by the second. EG *Hardly had he uttered the words when he began laughing.* ADV BRD NEG

3 You can use **hardly** in an ironic way to emphasize that something is certainly not true. EG *In the circumstances, it is hardly surprising that he resigned.* ADV BRD NEG

hard of hearing. If someone is **hard of hearing**, they are deaf. ADJ QUALIT

hard-pressed. If someone is **hard-pressed**, they are under a great deal of strain and worry. EG *...hard-pressed clergymen.* ADJ QUALIT

hardship /hɑːdʃɪp/, **hardships. Hardship** is the situation someone is in when they are suffering from great difficulties and problems in life, often because they do not have enough money. EG *...a period of considerable hardship and unhappiness... You know the hardships we have suffered.* N UNCOUNT OR N COUNT

hard shoulder. The **hard shoulder** is the area at the side of a motorway where you are allowed to stop if your car has broken down. N SING : *the*+N

hard-up. If you are **hard-up**, you have very little money. EG *I know we're all hard up, but everybody can afford a drink now and then.* ADJ QUALIT

hardware /hɑːdwɛə/. **1 Hardware** is tools and equipment for use in the home and garden. N UNCOUNT

2 Computer **hardware** is the machinery of a computer as opposed to the programs that are written for it. EG *Computer technology in all its phases from hardware to software has become less expensive.* N UNCOUNT

hard-wearing. Something that is **hard-wearing** is strong and well made so that it lasts for a long time. EG *These blankets are hard-wearing, but not so warm as wool.* ADJ QUALIT

hardy /hɑːdi¹/, **hardier, hardiest. 1** People and animals that are **hardy** are strong and able to endure difficult conditions. EG *Their children are remarkably hardy.* ADJ QUALIT

2 Plants that are **hardy** are able to survive frost and cold weather. EG *Strawberries are hardy and easy to grow in all soils.* ADJ QUALIT

hare /hɛə/, **hares, haring, hared. 1** A **hare** is an animal like a large rabbit with long ears, long legs, and a small tail. N COUNT

2 If you **hare** off or **hare** away somewhere, you run off very fast. EG *They took one look at him and hared off.* V+A

harebrained /hɛəbreɪnd/. Plans or ideas that are **harebrained** are foolish and not likely to succeed. EG *...harebrained schemes.* ADJ QUALIT

harem /hɛərəm, hɑːriːm/, **harems.** A **harem** is a group of wives or mistresses belonging to one man, especially in Muslim societies. EG *...a harem of more than a hundred wives.* N COUNT

haricot /hærɪkəʊ/, **haricots. Haricots** or **haricot beans** are small, pale beans. They are usually sold dried. N COUNT : USU PLURAL

hark /hɑːk/, **harks, harking, harked.** If someone or something **harks back** to an event or situation in the past, they remember it or remind you of it. EG *Increasingly she harked back to our 'dear little cottage'.* PHRASAL VB : V+ADV+*to*

harlequin /hɑːlɪkwɪn/ means having a lot of different colours. EG *...a harlequin jacket.* ADJ CLASSIF : ATTRIB

harm /hɑːm/, **harms, harming, harmed. 1** To **harm** someone means to cause them physical injury. EG *I stood very still, hoping they wouldn't harm my sister and me.* ▸ used as a noun. EG *He went in danger of physical harm.* V+O ▸ N UNCOUNT

2 To **harm** something means to damage it or make it less effective or successful. EG *Washing cannot harm the fabric... This can harm a child's psychological development.* ▸ used as a noun. EG *Much harm has been done to the earth's environment... Do prisons do more harm than good?* V+O ▸ N UNCOUNT

3 If you say that someone or something will **come to no harm** or that **no harm will come** to them, you mean that they will not be hurt or damaged. PHRASE

4 If you say that someone or something is **out of harm's way**, you mean that they are in a safe place. EG *The presents were now hidden under the sink, out of harm's way.* PHRASE

5 If you say **there is no harm in** doing something, you mean that you want to do it and you do not think that you will be blamed for doing it. EG *There's no harm in asking.* PHRASE

harmful /hɑːmfʊl/. Something that is **harmful** has a bad effect on someone or something else. EG *...the harmful effects of eating too many eggs... Too much salt can be harmful to a young baby.* ADJ QUALIT

harmless /hɑːmlɪ²s/. **1** Something that is **harmless** is safe to use, touch, or be near. EG *...harmless butterflies.* ◇ **harmlessly.** EG *The rocket thudded harmlessly to the ground.* ADJ QUALIT ◇ ADV

2 An action or activity that is **harmless** is unlikely to annoy other people or make them worried or upset. EG *Singing in the bath gives him a little harmless pleasure.* ◇ **harmlessly.** EG *His column deals harmlessly with the antics of film stars.* ADJ QUALIT ◇ ADV

harmonica /hɑːmɒnɪkə/, **harmonicas.** A **harmonica** is a small musical instrument. You play it by moving it across your lips and blowing and sucking air through it. N COUNT

harmonious /hɑːməʊnɪəs/. **1** A relationship, agreement, or discussion that is **harmonious** is friendly and peaceful. EG *...a generally harmonious debate.* ◇ **harmoniously.** EG *Harold and I worked harmoniously together.* ADJ QUALIT ◇ ADV

2 Something that is **harmonious** has parts which go well together and which are in proportion to each other. EG *The different parts of the garden fit together in a harmonious way.* ADJ QUALIT

3 Musical notes that are **harmonious** produce a pleasant sound when played together. EG *...a harmonious musical chord.* ADJ QUALIT

harmonize /hɑːmənaɪz/, **harmonizes, harmonizing, harmonized;** also spelled **harmonise.** If two or more things **harmonize** with each other, they fit in well with each other. EG *Such events harmonized with one's view of society.* V OR V+*with* : RECIP

harmony /hɑːməni¹/, **harmonies. 1** If people are living in **harmony** with each other, they are in a state of peaceful agreement and co-operation. EG *Industry and the universities have worked together in harmony... ...people living in harmony with their environment.* N UNCOUNT

2 Harmony is the pleasant combination of different notes of music played at the same time. EG *They sing in harmony... ...the harmonies of Ravel and Debussy.* N UNCOUNT OR N COUNT

3 The **harmony** of something is the way in which its parts are combined into a pleasant arrangement. EG *...the harmony of nature.* N UNCOUNT +SUPP

harness /hɑːnɪ²s/, **harnesses, harnessing, harnessed. 1** If you **harness** something such as a natural source of energy, you bring it under your control and use it. EG *Techniques harnessing the energy of the sun are being developed.* V+O

2 A **harness** is **2.1** a set of straps which fit under a person's arms and round their body in order to hold equipment in place or to prevent them from moving too much. EG *A seat and harness for a child are essential in a family car.* **2.2** a set of leather straps and metal links fastened round a horse's head or body so that the horse can pull a carriage, cart, or plough. N COUNT

3 If you **harness** a horse or other animal, you put a harness on it. EG *...a dog harnessed to a sledge.* V+O : OFT+*to*

harp /hɑ:p/, **harps, harping, harped.** A **harp** is a large musical instrument consisting of a row of strings stretched from the top to the bottom of a frame, which you play by picking at the strings with your fingers. See picture at MUSICAL INSTRUMENTS. N COUNT

harp on. If you **harp on** about something, you keep on talking about it; used showing disapproval. EG *She continued to harp on the theme of her wasted life.* PHRASAL VB : V+ADV/PREP

harpoon /hɑ:pu:n/, **harpoons.** A **harpoon** is a spear with a long rope attached to it, which is fired by people hunting whales. N COUNT

harpsichord /hɑ:psɪkɔ:d/, **harpsichords.** A **harpsichord** is a musical instrument which looks like a small piano. When you press the keys, strings are plucked mechanically rather than hit by hammers as in a piano. N COUNT

harrowing /hærəʊɪŋ/. A situation or event that is **harrowing** is very upsetting or disturbing. EG *...a harrowing experience... The film is deeply harrowing.* ADJ QUALIT

harry /hæri[1]/, **harries, harrying, harried.** If you **harry** someone, you constantly tell them what to do, so that they feel anxious or annoyed. EG *He set to work harrying people for donations.* ◊ **harried.** EG *...a waiter with a full tray and a harried expression.* V+O Formal ◊ ADJ QUALIT

harsh /hɑ:ʃ/, **harsher, harshest.** **1** A condition or way of life that is **harsh** is severe and difficult. EG *His family wouldn't survive the harsh winter.* ◊ **harshness.** EG *...the harshness of their nomadic life.* ADJ QUALIT ◊ N UNCOUNT

2 Behaviour and actions that are **harsh** are cruel and unkind. EG *...her harsh, cold, contemptuous attitude.* ◊ **harshly.** EG *He thinks you've marked his essay rather harshly.* ◊ **harshness.** EG *Disobedience is treated with special harshness.* ADJ QUALIT ◊ ADV ◊ N UNCOUNT

3 Something such as a light or a sound that is **harsh** is very bright or loud, so as to be unpleasant. EG *Harsh daylight fell into the room... She spoke in a harsh whisper.* ◊ **harshly.** EG *'What is it?' he said harshly.* ADJ QUALIT ◊ ADV

harvest /hɑ:vɪ[2]st/, **harvests, harvesting, harvested.** **1** The **harvest** is the cutting or picking of crops at the time of year when they are ripe. EG *Their stock of rice wouldn't last until the harvest.* ▸ used as a verb. EG *We harvested what we could before the rains came.* N SING : *the*+N ▸ V+O

2 A **harvest** is a year's crops that have ripened so that they can be cut or picked. EG *Their sons always came home to help bring in the harvest.* N COUNT

has /hæz/ is the third person singular of the present tense of **have.**

has-been, has-beens. A **has-been** is a person who was once important or successful, but who is now thought to be unimportant. EG *She was no longer dismissed as a political has-been.* N COUNT Informal

hash /hæʃ/. **1** If you **make a hash of** a job, you do the job very badly. EG *At first I thought I would make a terrible hash of it.* PHRASE Informal

2 Hash is a dish made from small lumps of meat fried with onions, potatoes, or other ingredients. EG *...corned beef hash.* N UNCOUNT

hasn't /hæzə[0]nt/ is the usual spoken form of 'has not'.

hassle /hæsə[0]l/, **hassles, hassling, hassled.** **1** If you say that something is a **hassle**, you mean that it is difficult and annoying to do. EG *Washing is a real hassle in a house with one cold tap.* N COUNT OR N UNCOUNT Informal

2 A **hassle** is also an argument. EG *I didn't want any hassle from the other women.* N COUNT OR N UNCOUNT

3 If someone **hassles** you, they keep annoying you, for example by telling you to do things that you do not want to do. EG *Oh God, she's back again to hassle me.* V+O Informal

haste /heɪst/. **1 Haste** is the quality of doing things quickly. EG *I immediately regretted my haste... The old men began interrupting each other in their haste to explain what had happened.* N UNCOUNT

2 If you do something **in haste**, you do it in a hurry. EG *It was written quickly and published in haste.* PHRASE

3 To **make haste** means to act quickly in doing something. EG *Make haste, all of you, and get ready.* PHRASE Outdated

hasten /heɪsə[0]n/, **hastens, hastening, hastened.** **1** If you **hasten** something, you make it happen faster or sooner. EG *Two factors hastened the formation of the new party.* V+O Formal

2 If you **hasten** to do something, you are quick to do it. EG *He hastened to remark that he was not against television.* V+*to*-INF

3 If you **hasten** somewhere, you hurry there. EG *He hastened back into the forest.* V+A Literary

hasty /heɪsti[1]/, **hastier, hastiest.** **1** If you are **hasty**, you do things suddenly and quickly, often without thinking properly about them. EG *Don't be hasty. It's not so easy to find another job... He made a hasty, unsuitable marriage.* ◊ **hastily.** EG *Philip hastily changed the subject.* ADJ QUALIT ◊ ADV

2 A **hasty** action is done quickly because you do not have much time. EG *...a hasty meal.* ◊ **hastily.** EG *He dressed himself hastily.* ADJ QUALIT ◊ ADV

hat /hæt/, **hats.** **1** A **hat** is a covering that you wear on your head, especially when you are out of doors. See picture at CLOTHES. N COUNT

2 Hat is used in these phrases. **2.1** If you ask someone to **keep** something **under** their **hat**, you are asking them to keep it secret. **2.2** If you describe something as **old hat**, you mean that it is so well-known and familiar that it has become uninteresting and boring. **2.3** If you say that someone **is talking through** their **hat**, you mean that they are talking nonsense. PHRASES

hatch /hætʃ/, **hatches, hatching, hatched.** **1** When a baby bird, insect, or other animal **hatches** or when it **is hatched**, it comes out of its egg by breaking the shell. EG *The larva hatches out and lives in the soil... ...newly hatched chicks.* V-ERG : IF V OFT+*out*

2 When an egg **hatches**, it breaks open and a baby bird, insect, or other animal comes out. EG *After ten days, the eggs hatch.* V

3 If you **hatch** a plot or a scheme, you think of it and work it out. EG *I've heard about the grand plot that you two gentlemen are hatching.* V+O

4 A **hatch** is **4.1** an opening in the deck of a ship, which is used for people to come on deck or go below, or during loading and unloading cargo. EG *Hendricks poked his head through the forward hatch.* **4.2** an opening in a wall, especially one between a kitchen and a dining room, which you use to pass food through. N COUNT

hatchback /hætʃbæk/, **hatchbacks.** A **hatchback** is a car with an extra door at the back which opens upwards. N COUNT

hatchet /hætʃɪ[2]t/, **hatchets.** **1** A **hatchet** is a small axe. N COUNT

2 If two people **bury the hatchet**, they become friendly again after a quarrel or disagreement. EG *Now that our fight was over we were glad to bury the hatchet.* PHRASE

hate /heɪt/, **hates, hating, hated.** **1** If you **hate** someone, you have an extremely strong feeling of dislike for them. EG *You really hate her, don't you?... She was aware of what she was doing and she hated herself for it.* ◊ **hated.** EG *...the most hated man in America.* V+O ◊ ADJ QUALIT

2 If you say that you **hate** something, you mean that you find it very unpleasant. EG *I used to hate going to lectures... I hate milk... I would hate to move to another house.* V+O, V+-ING, OR V+*to*-INF

3 Hate is a strong feeling of dislike for someone or something. EG *He was a violent bully, destructive* N UNCOUNT

Do you use a musical instrument to harp on about something?

and full of hate... ...highly charged scenes of love and hate.

4 You can use an expression such as **'I hate to disturb you'**, or **'I hate to trouble you'** when you are apologizing to someone for what you are going to say next. EG *I hate to wake you up, but there's something urgent I've got to tell you.* PHRASE

5 You say **'I hate to say it'** to introduce something that you regret having to say because you feel that it is unpleasant or unfair. EG *There is unfortunately – I hate to say it – a substantial amount of racism in our cities.* PHRASE

hateful /heɪtful/. Someone or something that is **hateful** is extremely unpleasant. EG *It was going to be a hateful week.* ADJ QUALIT Outdated

hatred /heɪtrɪ²d/ is an extremely strong feeling of dislike for someone or something. EG *...their hatred of technology... She felt hatred towards his sister.* N UNCOUNT: USU+SUPP

haughty /hɔːti¹/, **haughtier, haughtiest.** Someone who is **haughty** is very proud and thinks that they are better than other people; used showing disapproval. EG *He had an air of haughty aloofness.* ADJ QUALIT

◇ **haughtily.** EG *'Very well,' he replied haughtily.* ◇ ADV

haul /hɔːl/, **hauls, hauling, hauled. 1** If you **haul** a heavy object somewhere, you pull it there using a lot of effort. EG *They hauled the pilot clear of the wreckage... Ralph hauled himself onto the platform.* V+O+A OR V-REFL+A

2 If you say that a journey or a struggle is a **long haul**, you mean that it takes a long time and a big effort. EG *We began the long haul up the cobbled street... ...as women begin the long haul to equality.* PHRASE

haul up. If someone **is hauled up** before a court of law, they are made to appear before the court. EG *He got hauled up in court for assaulting a student.* PHRASAL VB: V+O+ADV: OFT PASS

haunch /hɔːntʃ/, **haunches.** Your **haunches** are your buttocks and the tops of your legs. EG *He squatted down on his haunches.* N COUNT: USU PLURAL

haunt /hɔːnt/, **haunts, haunting, haunted. 1** If a place **is haunted**, people believe that a ghost appears there regularly. EG *The building was supposed to be haunted by the ghost of a leper.* V+O: USU PASS

2 If something unpleasant **haunts** you, you keep thinking about it or worrying about it over a long period of time. EG *...a mystery that had haunted me for most of my life.* V+O

3 A problem that **haunts** a person or organization regularly causes difficulties for them over a period of time. EG *Lack of money haunted successive projects.* V+O Literary

4 Someone's **haunt** is a place which they often visit. EG *The pottery seems to be a favourite haunt among the children... Their old haunts have been ruined by becoming too popular.* N COUNT+SUPP

haunted /hɔːntɪ²d/. **1** A **haunted** building or other place is one where people believe that a ghost regularly appears. EG *...a haunted house.* ADJ CLASSIF

2 Someone who has a **haunted** expression looks very worried or troubled. EG *Her face took on a haunted quality.* ADJ QUALIT

haunting /hɔːntɪŋ/. Something that is **haunting** has a quality such as great beauty or sadness that makes a strong impression on you and remains in your thoughts. EG *He repeated the haunting melody.* ADJ QUALIT

have. See the entry on the next two pages.

haven /heɪvə⁰n/, **havens.** You can refer to a place where people feel safe and secure as a **haven**. EG *They have made the park a haven for weary Londoners.* N COUNT

haven't /hævə⁰nt/ is the usual spoken form of 'have not'.

haversack /hævəsæk/, **haversacks.** A **haversack** is a canvas bag that you wear on your back and use to carry things in when you are out walking. N COUNT

havoc /hævək/. **1 Havoc** is a state of great disorder. EG *After the havoc of the war, England had to be rebuilt.* N UNCOUNT

2 If one thing **plays havoc with** another, it causes a lot of disorder and confusion. EG *The anxieties of the last few days had played havoc with his working hours.* PHRASE

hawk /hɔːk/, **hawks, hawking, hawked. 1** A **hawk** is a large bird with a short hooked bill and sharp claws. Hawks eat small birds and animals. EG *A hawk hovered, motionless, in the blue sky.* N COUNT

2 If you **watch** someone **like a hawk**, you watch them very carefully so that you will know if they do something wrong. PHRASE

3 If you **hawk** something around, you try to sell it by taking it around to various people who might be interested in buying it; often used showing disapproval. EG *His writings were being hawked round German publishers.* V+O: USU+A

hawthorn /hɔːθɔːn/, **hawthorns.** A **hawthorn** is a small tree which has sharp thorns and white flowers. N COUNT OR N UNCOUNT

hay /heɪ/ is grass which has been cut and dried so that it can be used to feed animals. EG *About 30 or 40 bales of hay were scattered over the barn.* N UNCOUNT

hay fever is an illness similar to a cold, in which people sneeze a lot. People get hay fever in the summer because they are allergic to some types of pollen. N UNCOUNT

haystack /heɪstæk/, **haystacks. 1** A **haystack** is a large pile of hay in a field, which has been built into a stack. N COUNT

2 If you say that trying to find something is like looking for **a needle in a haystack**, you mean that it is extremely difficult to find so you are very unlikely to find it. PHRASE

haywire /heɪwaɪə/. If something goes **haywire**, it becomes completely disordered or out of control. ADJ PRED Informal

hazard /hæzəd/, **hazards, hazarding, hazarded.**

1 A **hazard** is something which could be dangerous to you. EG *...a natural hazard, like an earth tremor... Drinking alcohol is a real health hazard if carried to excess.* N COUNT

2 If you **hazard** a guess, you make a suggestion which is only a guess and which might be wrong. EG *'How much do you think he makes a year?' – 'Fifteen thousand,' Rudolph hazarded... As to the author of the letter, I will hazard a guess that it is Howard.* V+QUOTE OR V+O

hazardous /hæzədəs/. Something that is **hazardous** is dangerous to people's health or safety. EG *...hazardous chemicals... Breathing smoky air may be hazardous to health.* ADJ QUALIT

haze /heɪz/ is a kind of mist caused by heat or dust in the air. EG *...in the golden morning haze... The room became cloudy with a blue haze of smoke.* N UNCOUNT +SUPP

hazel /heɪzə⁰l/, **hazels. 1** A **hazel** is a kind of small tree which produces nuts. N COUNT OR N UNCOUNT

2 Hazel eyes are greenish-brown in colour. ADJ COLOUR

hazelnut /heɪzə⁰lnʌt/, **hazelnuts. Hazelnuts** are nuts from a hazel tree. N COUNT

hazy /heɪzi¹/, **hazier, haziest. 1** When the sky or a view is **hazy**, you cannot see it clearly because there is haze in the air. EG *...a hazy blue view beyond railings on a mountain pass.* ADJ QUALIT

2 If you are **hazy** about things or if your thoughts are **hazy**, you are unclear or confused about them. EG *She was hazy about her mother's origins... The details are getting a bit hazy in my mind now.* ADJ PRED

he /hiː/ is used as the subject of a verb. You use **he** **1** to refer to a man, boy, or male animal who has already been mentioned, or whose identity is known. EG *Bill had flown back from New York and he and his wife took me out to dinner.* **2** to refer to a person whose sex is not known or is not stated. EG *A teacher should do whatever he thinks best.* PRON: SING Outdated

head /hɛd/, **heads, heading, headed. 1** Your **head** is the part of your body which has your eyes, mouth, and brain in it. See picture at THE HUMAN BODY. EG *She shook her head.* N COUNT

2 The **head** of something is the top or most N SING+SUPP

HAVE

have /hæv/, **has, having, had.**

Have is one of the most important verbs in English. It is very common and has a large number of different uses, the most important of which are explained here.

In speech, and very informal writing, **have** is reduced to the sound /v/ spelled **'ve**.

'Have' as an auxiliary

1 When you want to show that an event that happened in the past is still important at the time you are speaking or writing, you use **have** followed by the past participle form of a verb. For example: *It hasn't rained for a month . . . She has never been to Rome . . . They have just bought a new car.*

2 The use of **had** as an auxiliary shows that an action happened earlier than another action which was also in the past. For example: *I had just finished when you arrived . . . Officials said that the two men had at last signed an agreement.*

3 The use of **having** as an auxiliary shows that one action had already happened before another action began. For example: *We were home by 8, having come straight from the station . . . Having been warned beforehand, I knew how he would react.*

'Have' meaning 'must'

4 When you want to say that something must be done or must happen, you can use **have** followed by the to-infinitive of another verb. For example: *We had to learn it in school . . . He had to sit down because he felt dizzy . . . I have to speak to your father . . . You have to be careful of your facts.*

'Have' with nouns

5 When you want to talk about something that happens as if it were an event, instead of using a verb you can use **have** followed by a noun. So that, instead of saying: *I* ***strolled*** *round the garden this morning,* you can say *I had a stroll round the garden this morning.*

Other examples of this are:
She ***was invited*** *to the party / She* ***had an invitation*** *to the party . . .*
A lot of people ***commented*** *on my work / I* ***had a lot of comments*** *on my work.*

You also find this use of **have** with nouns which do not have a corresponding verb, as in: *The children are having a party . . . What effect will this have on transport?*

'Have' replacing 'be'

6 You can make some statements more personal by using **have** instead of **be**. So that instead of saying: *There is no alternative,* you can say *You have no alternative*; and instead of: *There were students living with us,* you can say *We had students living with us.*

'Have' replacing other verbs

7 In normal speech or writing you can often use **have** where in more restricted or more formal language you would use a more specific verb. So you are more likely to say: *I have a sandwich every lunchtime,* than *I eat a sandwich every lunchtime.*

Other examples are:
I had a boring afternoon, rather than *I spent a boring afternoon.*
I had an operation last year, rather than *I underwent an operation last year.*

This feature of the use of **have** is particularly common where it is very obvious from the context what the meaning of the whole phrase is. Where doubt or confusion could be caused, speakers will probably choose the more specific verb, if it is important to be understood!

'Have' meaning 'own'

8 You can use **have** to make statements about things that you possess or about people and things that are closely associated with you. For example: *What is the point of having a mink coat?... He had a small hotel... She had a successful career.*

The following sentences with **have** would be equally correct with **have got**, especially in spoken English: *They don't have any money... We had no regrets at all... They have one daughter... I have lots of friends.*

'Have' in phrases

9 **Have** is often followed by an object and a verb which can be either a past participle or a to-infinitive.

When it is followed by a past participle, it can mean that you arrange for something to happen. For example: *You should have your car cleaned... Make sure you have that shirt washed for next Monday... Isn't it time you had your hair cut?*

Or it can mean that something happens to you without you doing anything about it: *She had her purse stolen... Children love to have stories read to them.*

When **have** is followed by a to-infinitive, it means that you are responsible for something. For example: *She had a huge department to administer... They have a lot of shopping to do... I've never had so much work to finish.*

10 Here are a number of expressions which use **have**:

If you **have it in for someone**, you want to make life difficult for them because you dislike them or they have upset you.

If you **have been had**, you have been deliberately tricked by someone, who has, for example, sold you something at too high a price.

If you are **had up for something**, you appear in court for a crime that you have committed.

If you say that you **have had it**, you mean that you are too exhausted to continue doing something.

If you **have on** something such as a dress or a shirt, you are wearing it.

If you **are having** someone **on**, you are teasing them.

important end of it. EG *Howard stood at the head of the stairs... ...standing at the head of the queue.*

3 When you toss a coin and it comes down **heads**, you can see the side of the coin which has a person's head on it. ADV AFTER VB

4 The **head** of a company or organization is the person in charge of it. EG *...the head of the English department.* ▸ used as an adjective. EG *...the head gardener.* N COUNT+SUPP ▸ ADJ CLASSIF : ATTRIB

5 In a school, the **head** is the head teacher. EG *I had coffee with the head after school.* N COUNT

6 If you **head** an organization, you are in charge of it. EG *The firm is headed by John Murray.* V+O

7 If something **heads** a list, it is at the top of it. V+O

8 You can mention the title of a piece of writing by saying how it **is headed**. EG *...an article headed 'An Open Letter to the Prime Minister.'* V+O+C : USU PASS

9 If you **head** in a particular direction, you go in that direction. EG *Julie headed for the cupboard.* V+A

10 If you **are heading** for an unpleasant situation, you are behaving in a way that makes the situation more likely. EG *You may be heading for disaster.* V+*for* : ONLY CONT

11 When you **head** a ball, you hit it with your head. V+O

12 Head is also used in these phrases. **12.1** The cost or amount **a head** or **per head** is the cost or amount for each person. EG *The meal will cost £9 a head.* **12.2** If you say something **off the top of your head**, you say it without thinking about it before you speak. **12.3** If someone says to you **'On your own head be it'**, they mean that any unpleasant or bad results of your action will be your responsibility. **12.4** If you are laughing, crying, or shouting your **head off**, you are doing it very noisily. EG *It woke up and started screaming its head off.* **12.5** If you **bite** or **snap** someone's **head off**, you speak to them very angrily. **12.6** If something **comes** or **is brought to a head**, it reaches a state where you have to do something urgently about it. EG *Anti-British feeling came to a head in the 1890's.* **12.7** If you **get** a fact or idea **into** your **head**, you start thinking that it is true. If you **get** a fact or idea **into** someone else's **head**, you make them think that it is true. **12.8** If alcohol **goes to** your **head**, it makes you drunk. **12.9** If praise or success **goes to** your **head**, it makes you conceited. **12.10** If you **keep** your **head**, you stay calm. If you **lose** your **head**, you panic. **12.11** If you say you could not **make head nor tail of** something, you mean you could not understand it at all. **12.12** When people **put** their **heads together**, they try to solve a problem together. **12.13** If you say that someone is **off** their **head**, you mean that they are behaving in a very stupid way. PHRASES; Informal (12.4); Informal (12.5); Informal (12.11); Informal (12.13)

13 See also **heading**.

headache /hɛdeɪk/, **headaches. 1** A **headache** is a pain that you feel in your head. EG *She took an aspirin to relieve her headache.* N COUNT

2 If you say that something is a **headache**, you mean that it causes you difficulty or worry. EG *Rivalry between the two industries presents a big headache for government.* N COUNT

headdress /hɛddrɛs/, **headdresses.** A **headdress** is something that people sometimes wear on their heads for decoration. EG *The dancers wore face masks and tall head-dresses.* N COUNT

head-first. If you fall somewhere **head-first**, your head is the part of your body that is furthest forward as you fall. EG *He had fallen head-first into the ditch.* ADV AFTER VB

headgear /hɛdgɪə/. You can refer to hats or other things worn on people's heads as **headgear**. N UNCOUNT

heading /hɛdɪŋ/, **headings.** A **heading** is the title of a piece of writing, written or printed at the top of it. EG *The figures were put forward under the heading 'World Fuel Requirements in the 1990's'.* N COUNT

headlamp /hɛdlæmp/, **headlamps.** A **headlamp** is a headlight. N COUNT

headland /hɛdlə³nd/, **headlands.** A **headland** is a narrow piece of land which sticks out into the sea. EG *A road was built across the headland.* N COUNT

headless /hɛdlɪ²s/. A **headless** body has no head. ADJ CLASSIF

headlight /hɛdlaɪt/, **headlights.** A car's **headlights** are the large bright lights at the front of it. See picture at CAR. EG *All the cars had their headlights on.* N COUNT : USU+POSS

headline /hɛdlaɪn/, **headlines. 1** A **headline** is the title of a newspaper story, printed in large letters at the top of the story. EG *The headlines that day were full of news of the kidnapping.* N COUNT

2 The **headlines** are also the main points of the news which are read on radio or television. EG *And now for the main headlines again.* N PLURAL

headlong /hɛdlɒŋ/. **1** If you move **headlong** in a particular direction, you move there very quickly. EG *The frightened elephants ran headlong through the forest.* ADV AFTER VB

2 If you rush **headlong** into something, you do it quickly without thinking carefully about it. EG *Don't rush headlong into buying new furniture... ...a headlong rush to sell.* ADV AFTER VB OR ADJ CLASSIF

headmaster /hɛdmɑːstə/, **headmasters.** A **headmaster** is a man who is the head teacher of a school. N COUNT

headmistress /hɛdmɪstrɪ²s/, **headmistresses.** A **headmistress** is a woman who is the head teacher of a school. N COUNT

head of state, heads of state. A **head of state** is the leader of a country, for example a president, king, or queen. N COUNT

head-on. 1 If two vehicles hit each other **head-on**, they hit each other with their front parts pointing towards each other. EG *The motor cycle ran head-on into the lorry... ...a head-on collision.* ADV AFTER VB OR ADJ CLASSIF : ATTRIB

2 A **head-on** disagreement is firm and direct and has no compromises. EG *...a head-on confrontation with the unions... It had to meet the threat head-on.* ADJ CLASSIF : ATTRIB, OR ADV AFTER VB

headphones /hɛdfəʊnz/ are small speakers which you wear over your ears in order to listen to music or speech without other people hearing it. N PLURAL

headquarters /hɛdkwɔːtəz/. The **headquarters** of an organization are the main offices where the leaders of the organization work. EG *The bank had its headquarters in Paris... Captain Meadows was ordered to report to headquarters the following day.* N PLURAL

headroom /hɛdru⁴m/ is the amount of space below a roof or a bridge. EG *Maximum headroom 2.6 metres.* N UNCOUNT

headscarf /hɛdskɑːf/, **headscarves.** A **headscarf** is a scarf which is worn on the head by women. N COUNT

headstand /hɛdstænd/, **headstands.** If you do a **headstand**, you balance upside down with your head and your hands on the ground and your legs up in the air. N COUNT

head start, head starts. If you have a **head start** on other people, you have an advantage over them in a competition or race. EG *A university degree would give you a head start in getting a job.* N COUNT

headstone /hɛdstəʊn/, **headstones.** A **headstone** is a large stone at one end of a grave, usually with the name of the dead person carved on it. N COUNT

headstrong /hɛdstrɒŋ/. Someone who is **headstrong** is determined to do what they want and will not let anyone stop them. EG *Luce was stubborn and headstrong.* ADJ QUALIT

head teacher, head teachers. A **head teacher** is a teacher who is in charge of a school. N COUNT

headway /hɛdweɪ/. If you **make headway**, you make progress towards achieving something. EG *The emergency services began to make some headway in restoring order to the devastated area.* PHRASE

Is it safe to believe in hearsay?

headwind /hedwɪnd/, **headwinds.** A **headwind** is a wind which blows in the opposite direction to the one in which you are moving. N COUNT

heady /hedi¹/. **1** A **heady** experience makes you feel very excited and full of energy. EG *...the heady days of the sixties.* ADJ QUALIT : ATTRIB

2 A **heady** drink or atmosphere strongly affects your physical senses, for example by making you feel drunk or excited. EG *...heady perfumes.* ADJ QUALIT

heal /hi:l/, **heals, healing, healed. 1** When an injury **heals** or when something **heals** it, it becomes healthy and normal again. EG *His leg needs support while the bone is healing.* V-ERG

2 If someone **heals** you when you are ill, they make you well again. ◇ **healer, healers.** EG *Some were treated by traditional healers.* V+O ◇ N COUNT

3 When a process or the passage of time **heals** something that has been damaged, it restores it. EG *...damage to the ecology that would take a hundred years to heal.* V+O

heal up. When an injury **heals up**, it becomes completely healthy again. EG *His hoof had healed up.* PHRASAL VB : V+ADV

health /helθ/. **1** Your **health** is the condition of your body. EG *Cigarette smoking is dangerous to your health... My mother was in poor health.* N UNCOUNT

2 Health is a state in which you are fit and well and not ill. EG *They were glowing with health... ...a soldier who was nursed back to health.* N UNCOUNT

3 When you **drink to** someone's **health** or **drink** their **health**, you have a drink as a sign of wishing that they will be healthy and happy. PHRASE

4 The **health** of an organization or system is the success that it has and the fact that it is working well. EG *...the health of the British film industry.* N UNCOUNT : USU+SUPP

health food is food which has been made or grown without any chemicals, and which some people eat because they believe it is better for their health than ordinary food. N MASS

healthy /helθi¹/, **healthier, healthiest. 1** Someone who is **healthy** is well and is not suffering from any illness. EG *...a healthy baby... As a result of the diet, he feels fitter and healthier.* ◇ **healthily.** EG *It is perfectly possible to live healthily on a meat-free diet.* ADJ QUALIT ◇ ADV

2 If a feature or quality that you have is **healthy**, it shows that you are well. EG *The children have healthy appetites... ...healthy skin.* ◇ **healthily.** EG *...the dreamless slumber of the healthily tired man.* ADJ QUALIT ◇ ADV+ADJ

3 Something that is **healthy** is good for you and likely to make you healthy. EG *...healthy seaside air.* ADJ QUALIT

4 An organization or system that is **healthy** is successful. EG *...a healthy economy.* ADJ QUALIT

5 A **healthy** amount of something is a large amount that is a sign of success. EG *...healthy profits.* ADJ QUALIT

heap /hi:p/, **heaps, heaping, heaped. 1** A **heap** of things is an untidy pile of them. EG *Brody picked up the heap of papers and piled them on top of a radiator... ...a compost heap.* ● If someone collapses **in a heap**, they fall heavily and do not move. N COUNT OR N PART ● PHRASE

2 If you **heap** things in a pile, you arrange a lot of them in a large pile. EG *...food heaped on platters... We sat on cushions heaped on the floor.* V+O+A

3 If you **heap** praise or criticism on someone or something, you give them a lot of praise or criticism. EG *Burgin heaped scorn on such styles of painting and sculpture.* V+O+*on/upon*

4 Heaps of something or a **heap** of something is a large quantity of it. EG *We've got heaps of time.* N PART Informal

heap up. If you **heap** things **up**, you make them into a pile. *Heap up the flour round the sides of the bowl.* PHRASAL VB : V+O+ADV

heaped /hi:pt/. **1** A **heaped** spoonful is so full that its contents rise higher than the top of its sides. EG *Add one heaped tablespoon of salt.* ADJ CLASSIF

2 If a surface is **heaped** with things, it has a lot of them on it in a pile. EG *The desk was heaped with magazines.* ADJ CLASSIF : OFT+*with*

hear /hɪə/, **hears, hearing, heard** /hɜ:d/. **1** When you **hear** sounds, you are aware of them because they reach your ears. EG *He heard a distant voice shouting... Etta hated to hear Mrs Hochstadt talk like that... She could hear clearly.* V+O OR V : NO IMPER

2 When a judge or a court **hears** a case or **hears** evidence, they listen to it officially in order to make a decision about it. V+O

3 If you **hear** from someone, you receive a letter or a telephone call from them. EG *They'll be delighted to hear from you again.* V+*from* : NO CONT, NO IMPER

4 If you **hear** some news or information, you learn it because someone tells it to you or it is mentioned on the radio or television. EG *I was glad to hear that things are quietening down... My first meeting with the woman confirmed everything I had heard about her... When he came to hear of their difficulties, he volunteered help.* V+O, V+REPORT, OR V+*about/of*

5 If you **have heard of** someone or something, you know that they exist, but you do not know any details about them. EG *The vast majority of these students had never heard of the Marshall plan.* PHRASE

6 If you **won't hear of** someone doing something, you refuse to let them do it. EG *Her father had refused to hear of such a thing.* PHRASE

hearer /hɪərə/, **hearers.** Your **hearers** are the people who are listening to you speak. EG *He was shocked by the violent reactions of some of his hearers.* N COUNT Formal

hearing /hɪərɪŋ/, **hearings. 1 Hearing** is the sense which people and animals have that makes it possible for them to be aware of sounds. EG *Her limbs were weak, her hearing almost gone.* ● See also **hard of hearing**. N UNCOUNT

2 If you are **in** or **within** someone's **hearing**, you are so close to them that they can hear what you are saying. EG *She began to grumble about it within his hearing.* PHRASE

3 A **hearing** is an official meeting held to collect facts about an incident or problem. EG *I wish these hearings had been televised.* N COUNT

4 If you get **a hearing** or **a fair hearing**, you have the opportunity to give your opinion about something. EG *She believed in giving a fair hearing to all sides of the question.* PHRASE

hearing aid, hearing aids. A **hearing aid** is an instrument that helps deaf people to hear better. N COUNT

hearsay /hɪəseɪ/ is information which you have been told indirectly, but which you do not personally know to be true. EG *'Everything else I know is hearsay,' she said.* N UNCOUNT

hearse /hɜ:s/, **hearses.** A **hearse** is a large car that carries the coffin at a funeral. N COUNT

heart /hɑ:t/, **hearts. 1** Your **heart** is the organ in your chest that pumps the blood around your body. EG *She could hear her heart beating... ...the first successful human heart transplant.* N COUNT

2 You can also talk about someone's **heart 2.1** when you are referring to their emotions. EG *...the troubled heart of the younger man... She knew all the secrets of my heart.* **2.2** when you are describing their character and attitudes. EG *He's got a very soft heart.* N COUNT : USU+POSS Literary; N COUNT OR N UNCOUNT

3 Heart is also used in various expressions to refer to courage and determination. EG *It was a bad time and people were losing heart... No one had the heart to tell her.* N UNCOUNT

4 The **heart** of something is the most central and important part of it. EG *...the heart of the problem... ...lyrics that get right to the heart of the matter.* N SING+*of*

5 The **heart** of a place is its centre. EG *Thousands of protesters marched into the heart of San Francisco.* N SING+*of*

6 The **heart** of a vegetable such as a cabbage or lettuce is the group of leaves in its centre. N COUNT+SUPP

7 A **heart** is also a shape with an outline made up of two curves going upwards and then meeting at a N COUNT point at the bottom. It is often coloured red or pink and is used to represent love. See picture at SHAPES.

8 **Hearts** is one of the four suits in a pack of playing cards. Each card in the suit is marked with one or more red symbols in the shape of a heart. N UNCOUNT

9 A **heart** is also one of the thirteen playing cards in the suit of hearts. N COUNT

10 **Heart** is also used in these phrases. **10.1** If you say that someone is a particular kind of person **at heart**, you mean that this is what they are really like. EG *He was at heart a kindly man.* **10.2** If you know something such as a poem **by heart**, you have learnt it so well that you can remember it perfectly. EG *...learning by heart the dates of battles.* **10.3** If you have a **change of heart**, your feelings about something change and you act in a different way. EG *He has declared his change of heart on this matter.* **10.4** If you say something **from the heart** or **from the bottom of** your **heart**, you are being sincere. **10.5** If your **heart isn't in** what you are doing, you have very little enthusiasm for it. EG *The children soon sensed that his heart was not in it.* **10.6** What you think or feel **in** your **heart of hearts** is what you secretly really think or feel. EG *In his heart of hearts, he didn't trust the authorities.* **10.7** If someone can do something **to** their **heart's content**, they can do it as much as they want. EG *Jack could talk and plan to his heart's content.* **10.8** If someone **breaks** your **heart**, they make you very unhappy, for example because you love them and they do not love you. EG *She said that I had broken her heart.* **10.9** If something **breaks** your **heart**, it makes you very sad. EG *Though it breaks my heart to say it, the American ship is prettier.* **10.10** If something is **close to** or **dear to** your **heart**, you care deeply about it. **10.11** If your **heart leaps**, you suddenly feel very excited and happy. If your **heart sinks**, you suddenly feel very disappointed or unhappy. EG *I found there were six of us auditioning and my heart sank.* **10.12** If you have **set** your **heart on** something, you want it very much. EG *She had set her heart on going.* **10.13** If you **take** an experience **to heart**, you are deeply affected and upset by it. PHRASES

heart attack, heart attacks. If someone has a **heart attack**, their heart begins to beat irregularly or fails to pump blood properly, so that it causes them a lot of pain. People often die of heart attacks. N COUNT

heartbeat /hɑːtbiːt/, **heartbeats.** 1 Your **heartbeat** is the regular movement of your heart as it pumps blood around your body. EG *He could hear the pounding rhythm of her heartbeat.* N SING

2 A **heartbeat** is one of the movements of your heart. N COUNT

heartbreak /hɑːtbreɪk/ is very great sadness or unhappiness. EG *All of Allen's work is about heartbreak.* N UNCOUNT

heartbreaking /hɑːtbreɪkɪŋ/. Something that is **heartbreaking** makes you feel extremely sad and upset. EG *...a heartbreaking letter from an American friend whose wife had died.* ADJ QUALIT

heartbroken /hɑːtbrəʊkə^{0}n/. Someone who is **heartbroken** is extremely sad and upset. EG *Sylvia would be heartbroken if one of her cats died.* ADJ QUALIT

hearten /hɑːtə^{0}n/, **heartens, heartening, heartened.** When something such as good news **heartens** you, it encourages you and makes you cheerful. EG *I am very heartened by her success in the last election.* V+O : USU PASS ◊ **heartening.** EG *...some heartening news.* ◊ ADJ QUALIT

heartfelt /hɑːtfelt/. You use **heartfelt** to describe something that someone feels or believes deeply and sincerely. EG *...a heartfelt wish that it will never happen.* ADJ CLASSIF : ATTRIB

hearth /hɑːθ/, **hearths.** A **hearth** is the floor of a fireplace. EG *A bright fire was burning in the hearth.* N COUNT

heartland /hɑːtlænd/, **heartlands.** The **heartland** or **heartlands** of a country, region, or continent are the most central parts of it. EG *...the industrial heartlands of western Europe.* N COUNT OR N PLURAL +SUPP

heartless /hɑːtlɪ^{2}s/. Someone who is **heartless** is cruel and unkind. EG *...a heartless cynic... She sat there, mocking me with her heartless eyes.* ADJ QUALIT ◊ **heartlessly.** EG *...defenceless creatures being heartlessly destroyed.* ◊ ADV

heartrending /hɑːtrendɪŋ/. Something that is **heartrending** makes you feel great sadness and pity. EG *Isabel's sigh was heartrending.* ADJ QUALIT

hearty /hɑːti^1/, **heartier, heartiest.** 1 Someone or something that is **hearty** is loud, cheerful, and energetic. EG *He had a big hearty laugh... ...hearty soccer fans.* ADJ QUALIT ◊ **heartily** /hɑːtɪli^1/. EG *Etta laughed heartily... 'Now then,' she cried heartily, 'who's for a lovely drink?'* ◊ ADV

2 **Hearty** feelings or opinions are strongly felt or held. EG *I have a hearty hatred of all examinations.* ADJ CLASSIF : ATTRIB ◊ **heartily.** EG *Why should one pretend to like people one actually heartily dislikes?* ◊ ADV

heat /hiːt/, **heats, heating, heated.** 1 When you **heat** something, you raise its temperature by using a flame, a cooker, or other special piece of equipment. EG *Don't heat more water than you need... ...accommodation that is difficult to heat.* V+O

2 **Heat** is **2.1** warmth or the quality of being hot. EG *Water retains heat much longer than air... ...loss of body heat.* N UNCOUNT **2.2** the temperature of something that is warm. EG *It should be equivalent to blood heat.* N UNCOUNT +SUPP **2.3** a source of heat, for example a cooking ring on a stove. EG *Don't put pans straight on to a high heat.* N SING

3 The **heat** is very hot weather. EG *You shouldn't go out in this heat.* N SING

4 You also use **heat** to refer to a state of strong emotional feeling, especially anger or excitement. EG *'You're a fool,' Boylan said, without heat.* N UNCOUNT +SUPP

5 The **heat** of a particular activity or time is the point at which there is the greatest activity and excitement. EG *Last week, in the heat of the election campaign, the Prime Minister left for Venice.* N SING : *the+N+of*

6 A **heat** is a race or competition whose winners take part in the next one with winners of similar races or competitions. This continues until there is the right number of competitors for a final race or competition. • See also **dead heat**. N COUNT

7 See also **heated, heating**.

heat up. 1 When something **heats up**, it gradually becomes hotter. EG *The air over the great land mass heats up in the summer.* PHRASAL VB : V+ADV 2 When you **heat up** food that has already been cooked, you make it hot again. EG *He debated heating up the pot roast.* V+O+ADV

heated /hiːtɪ^{2}d/. If someone is **heated** about something, they are angry and excited about it. EG *He became quite heated... ...a heated argument.* ADJ QUALIT ◊ **heatedly.** EG *Naturalists argued heatedly about the issue for nearly a century.* ◊ ADV

heater /hiːtə/, **heaters.** A **heater** is a piece of equipment which is used to warm the air in a room or to heat water. EG *...a water heater... Mel had left the car heater on.* • See also **immersion heater**. N COUNT

heath /hiːθ/, **heaths.** A **heath** is an area of open land covered with rough grass or heather. N COUNT

heathen /hiːðə^{0}n/, **heathens.** Christians used to refer to people from other countries who were not Christian as **heathens**. EG *He was sent out to convert the heathens.* N COUNT Outdated ▸ used as an adjective. EG *...the ancient heathen inhabitants of this place.* ▸ ADJ CLASSIF

heather /heðə/ is a plant with small flowers that grows wild on hills and moorland. N UNCOUNT

heating /hiːtɪŋ/ is the process, system, or equipment involved in keeping a room or building warm. EG *The rent was £7 a week including heating.* • See also **central heating**. N UNCOUNT

When is a hedge not a hedgerow?

heatwave /hiːtweɪv/, **heatwaves.** A **heatwave** is a period of time when the weather is much hotter than usual. N COUNT

heave /hiːv/, **heaves, heaving, heaved. 1** If you **heave** something that is heavy or difficult to move, you push, pull, or lift it using a lot of effort. EG *I threw the rope around the tree and heaved with all my might... Lee heaved himself with a groan from his chair.* V OR V+O ▸ used as a noun. EG *With one single determined heave I pulled everything down.* ▸ N COUNT

2 If something **heaves**, it moves up and down or in and out with large regular movements. EG *I staggered across the heaving deck... His shoulders heaved silently.* V

3 To **heave** also means to vomit or feel sick. EG *The sight of the soapy scum made her stomach heave.* V

4 If you **heave a sigh**, you give a big sigh. EG *They all heaved a sigh of relief when he finally departed.* PHRASE

heaven /hɛvə^{0}n/, **heavens. 1 Heaven** is where God is believed to live, and where good people are believed to go when they die. N PROPER

2 If you say that a place or a situation is **heaven**, you mean that it gives you a lot of pleasure. EG *Mrs Duncan's cottage is just heaven... Kelmscott is a heaven on earth.* N UNCOUNT Informal

3 The **heavens** are the sky. EG *The moon was high in the heavens... The man continued to gesticulate sadly towards the heavens.* N PLURAL : the+N Literary

4 You say **'heaven knows'** to emphasize that you do not know something or that you find something very surprising. EG *Heaven knows what I would do without it... He ended up, heaven knows why, in the Geological Museum.* PHRASE

5 You say **'good heavens'** or **'heavens'** to express surprise or to emphasize that you agree or disagree with someone. EG *Heavens, is that the time?... 'Oh, good heavens, no,' said Etta with a light laugh.* EXCLAM

• **thank heavens**: see **thank.** • **for heaven's sake**: see **sake.**

heavenly /hɛvə^{0}nli^1/. **1** You use **heavenly** to describe things relating to heaven. EG *The heavenly spirits were displeased with the people.* ADJ CLASSIF : ATTRIB

2 If you describe something as **heavenly**, you mean that it is very pleasant and enjoyable. EG *...a big steaming pot of the most heavenly stew.* ADJ QUALIT Informal

heaven-sent. Something that is **heaven-sent** is unexpected but very welcome because it happens at just the right time. EG *...the latest heaven-sent triumph of advanced technology.* ADJ CLASSIF

heavenward /hɛvə^{0}nwəd/; also **heavenwards. Heavenward** means up towards the sky or to heaven. EG *Mr Menzies turned his eyes heavenward... The old lady's husband had departed heavenwards during the night.* ADV Literary

heavily /hɛvɪli^1/. If someone says something **heavily**, they say it in a slow way which shows a feeling such as sadness, tiredness, or annoyance. EG *'I don't understand you,' he said heavily.* ADV

heavy /hɛvi^1/, **heavier, heaviest. 1** Something that is **heavy 1.1** weighs a lot. EG *He dumped the heavy suitcases by the door.* ADJ QUALIT **1.2** is great in amount, degree, or intensity. EG *There would be heavy casualties... ...a heavy responsibility.* ADJ QUALIT ◇ **heavily.** EG *It began to rain more heavily... He smoked heavily all his life.* ◇ ADV **1.3** has a solid, thick appearance rather than being light and delicate. EG *...spectacles with heavy black frames... He had a heavy, sullen face.* ADJ QUALIT ◇ **heavily.** EG *I've never seen anyone so heavily built move quite so fast.* ◇ ADV

2 If you ask how **heavy** something is, you are asking how much it weighs. ADJ PRED

3 Something that is **heavy** with things is full of them or loaded with them. EG *The trees were heavy with fruit and blossoms.* ADJ PRED +with Literary

4 If a person's breathing is **heavy**, it is very loud and deep. EG *She lay sleeping, her breathing heavy.* ADJ QUALIT ◇ **heavily.** EG *She sighed heavily.* ◇ ADV

5 A **heavy** substance or material is thick and solid in texture. EG *...heavy clay soil... ...a heavy tweed coat.* ADJ QUALIT

6 A **heavy** movement or action is done with a lot of force or pressure. EG *A heavy blow with a club knocked him senseless.* ADJ QUALIT : ATTRIB ◇ **heavily.** EG *He sat down heavily.* ◇ ADV

7 You say that a period of time or a schedule is **heavy** when it involves a lot of work. EG *I've had a heavy week.* ADJ QUALIT

8 Heavy work requires a lot of strength or energy. ADJ QUALIT

9 If you are **heavy** on something, you use too much of it. EG *You've been a bit heavy on the mascara, haven't you?* ADJ PRED+on Informal

10 Air or weather that is **heavy** is unpleasantly still, hot, and damp. ADJ QUALIT

11 If your heart is **heavy**, you are sad about something. ADJ QUALIT

12 to **make heavy weather** of something: see **weather.**

heavy-duty. A **heavy-duty** machine is strong and can be used a lot or used to do very hard work. ADJ CLASSIF : ATTRIB

heavy-handed. Someone who is **heavy-handed** acts or speaks forcefully and without any care or thought. EG *We are incensed at the government's heavy-handed economic policies.* ADJ QUALIT

heavy industry, heavy industries. Heavy industry is industry in which large machines are used to produce a raw material such as steel, or to make large objects. N UNCOUNT OR N COUNT

heavy metal is a style of rock music with a strong, fast beat, which is played very loudly on electric guitars and drums. N UNCOUNT

heavyweight /hɛvi^{1}weɪt/, **heavyweights.** A **heavyweight** is a boxer or wrestler in the heaviest class. EG *...a heavyweight boxing champion.* N COUNT

heck /hɛk/. **1** Some people use **the heck** in questions after words such as 'how', 'why', or 'what', to emphasize that they are angry or surprised. EG *Why the heck is she so polite?* EXCLAM Informal

2 People use **a heck of** to emphasize the amount or size of something. EG *Jean has done a heck of a lot for us.* PHRASE Informal

heckle /hɛkə^{0}l/, **heckles, heckling, heckled.** If people **heckle** public speakers or performers, they interrupt them by making loud, unfriendly remarks. EG *He went to heckle at their meetings.* V OR V+O ◇ **heckling.** EG *Despite the heckling, the meeting was a success.* ◇ N UNCOUNT ◇ **heckler, hecklers.** EG *There was already a crowd of hecklers there when I arrived.* ◇ N COUNT

hectic /hɛktɪk/. A situation that is **hectic** is very busy and involves a lot of rushed activity. EG *It's been pretty hectic at the office.* ADJ QUALIT

he'd /hiːd/ is **1** the usual spoken form of 'he had', especially when 'had' is an auxiliary verb. EG *He said he'd told them.* **2** a spoken form of 'he would'. EG *He said that he'd give me a lift.*

hedge /hɛdʒ/, **hedges, hedging, hedged. 1** A **hedge** is a row of bushes along the edge of a garden, field, or road. N COUNT

2 If you **hedge**, you avoid answering a question or committing yourself to something. EG *Politicians are known for hedging on promises.* V : OFT+on

3 If something **is hedged** about, **hedged** around, or **hedged** in with things, it is affected by things which prevent or restrict its freedom or development. EG *The concessions were hedged around with many restrictions... We feel hedged in by fear.* V-PASS+A : OFT+with

4 If you **hedge** your **bets**, you avoid the risk of losing a lot by supporting more than one person or thing in a situation. PHRASE Informal

hedgehog /hɛdʒhɒg/, **hedgehogs.** A **hedgehog** is a small brown animal with sharp spikes covering its back. N COUNT

hedgerow /hɛdʒrəʊ/, **hedgerows.** A **hedgerow** is a row of bushes, trees, and plants, usually growing along a country lane or between fields. N COUNT

hedonism /hiːdə^{0}nɪzə^{0}m, hɛd-/ is the belief that gaining pleasure is the most important thing in life. N UNCOUNT Formal

◊ **hedonistic** /hiːdə⁰nɪstɪk, hɛd-/. EG *...lives of unending hedonistic delight.* ◊ ADJ CLASSIF

heed /hiːd/, **heeds, heeding, heeded.** 1 If you **heed** someone's advice or warning, you pay attention to it and do what they suggest. EG *David wished that he had heeded his father's warnings.* V+O Formal

2 If you **take heed of** what someone says or if you **pay heed** to them, you consider carefully what they say. EG *Take heed of these warnings.* PHRASE

heedless /hiːdlɪ²s/. If you are **heedless** of someone or something, you do not take any notice of them. EG *She stood glued to the radio, heedless of the bustle about her... ...heedless passers-by hurrying through the market place.* ADJ CLASSIF: OFT+*of* Formal

heel /hiːl/, **heels.** 1 Your **heel** is 1.1 the back part of your foot, just below your ankle. See picture at THE HUMAN BODY. EG *One of his heels had got blistered on the walk.* 1.2 the raised part on the bottom of your shoe at the back. EG *All I could hear was the click of my own heels on the linoleum.* N COUNT

2 **Heel** is used in these phrases. 2.1 If you **dig** your **heels in**, you refuse to do something such as change your opinions or plans. EG *Organizations employing volunteers are beginning to dig their heels in about the new regulations.* 2.2 If one event or situation **follows hard on the heels of** another, it happens very quickly after it. EG *Cultural isolation has followed quickly on the heels of economic recession.* 2.3 If you **turn** or **swing on** your **heel**, you suddenly turn round, often because you are angry or surprised. EG *He swung round upon his heel and surveyed the young man.* 2.4 If you **take to** your **heels**, you run away. PHRASES; Literary

hefty /hɛfti¹/, **heftier, heftiest.** Someone or something that is **hefty** is very large in size, weight, or amount. EG *...a broad, hefty Irish nurse... We sell them at a hefty profit.* ADJ QUALIT Informal

heifer /hɛfə/, **heifers.** A **heifer** is a young cow. N COUNT

height /haɪt/, **heights.** 1 The **height** of a person or thing is its measurement from the bottom to the top. EG *The redwood grows to 100 metres in height... He was of medium height... This enables them to grow to considerable heights.* N UNCOUNT OR N COUNT +SUPP

2 **Height** is the quality of being tall. EG *You'll recognize her because of her height.* N UNCOUNT

3 A particular **height** is the distance that something is above the ground. EG *The aircraft reaches its maximum height of 80,000 feet in about ten minutes... The bag had been dropped from about shoulder height.* N UNCOUNT OR N COUNT +SUPP ● If something **gains height**, it moves to a higher position above the ground. If it **loses height**, it moves to a lower position. EG *The plane began to lose height on its approach to Heathrow.* ● PHRASE

4 You use **heights** to refer to the top of a hill or cliff. EG *...fierce fighting on the heights above the bay.* N PLURAL

5 Something that is at its **height** is at its most successful, powerful, or intense. EG *The group had at its height 500 members... It is the height of the tourist season.* N SING+POSS

6 You can use **height** to emphasize how extreme a quality is. For example, if you say that something is the **height** of absurdity, you mean that it is extremely absurd. EG *It seemed to me the height of luxury.* N SING: *the*+N+*of* Formal

7 If something reaches great **heights**, it becomes very extreme or intense. EG *Love must soar to the greatest heights of sacrifice.* N PLURAL +SUPP

heighten /haɪtə⁰n/, **heightens, heightening, heightened.** When something **heightens** a feeling or state or when it **heightens**, it increases in degree or intensity. EG *We should try to calm people's fears rather than heighten them through uncertainty... As their hardship heightened, so did their desperation and anger.* V-ERG ◊ **heightened.** EG *She is in a state of heightened emotion.* ◊ ADJ CLASSIF: ATTRIB

heinous /heɪnəs, hiː-/ means extremely evil. EG *...heinous crimes.* ADJ QUALIT Formal

heir /ɛə/, **heirs.** Someone's **heir** is the person who will inherit their money, property, or title when they die. EG *...Thompson's son and heir... The Prince of Wales is heir to the throne.* N COUNT

heiress /ɛərɪ²s/, **heiresses.** An **heiress** is a woman who will inherit property, money, or a title. N COUNT

heirloom /ɛəluːm/, **heirlooms.** An **heirloom** is an ornament or other object that has belonged to a family for a very long time. EG *...jewels and other family heirlooms.* N COUNT

held /hɛld/ is the past tense and past participle of **hold.**

helicopter /hɛlɪkɒptə/, **helicopters.** A **helicopter** is an aircraft with large blades which rotate above it rather than wings. N COUNT

hell /hɛl/. 1 **Hell** is the place where wicked people are believed to go when they die. N PROPER

2 If you say that a situation is **hell**, you mean that it is extremely unpleasant. EG *War is hell... I don't know how I've stuck it. It's been hell.* N UNCOUNT Informal ● If you say that all hell broke loose, you mean that there was suddenly a lot of arguing or fighting. EG *When Darwin asserted that men were descended from apes, all hell broke loose.* ● PHRASE

3 **Hell** is a swear word used by some people to express annoyance or to emphasize what they are saying. EXCLAM

4 **Hell** is also used in these phrases. 4.1 If someone **gives** you **hell**, they are very severe and cruel to you. EG *I bet these ladies gave their secretaries hell.* PHRASES Informal 4.2 Something that **plays hell** with something else has a bad effect on it. EG *The new extension will play hell with the plumbing.* Informal 4.3 Some people say **'go to hell'** when they are angrily telling someone to go away; a rude expression. Informal 4.4 If you **get the hell out** of a place, you leave it very quickly. EG *Get the hell out of here!* Informal 4.5 If someone says **'to hell with'** something, they are saying that they do not care about it and do not want any more to do with it. EG *To hell with university.* Informal 4.6 Some people use **the hell** in questions after words such as 'how', 'why', or 'what', to emphasize how angry or surprised they are. EG *How the hell should I know?* Informal 4.7 If someone does something **for the hell of it**, they do it for fun or for no particular reason. EG *I don't want to offend people for the hell of it.* Informal 4.8 People use **a hell of** or **one hell of** to emphasize the amount or size of something. EG *There was a hell of a lot of traffic... The government was in one hell of a mess.* Informal 4.9 Some people use **like hell** to emphasize how strong an action or quality is. EG *It was beginning to hurt like hell... It's cold as hell out here.* Informal

he'll /hiːl/ is the usual spoken form of 'he will'. EG *He'll have to go to hospital, won't he?*

hellish /hɛlɪʃ/. If you describe something as **hellish**, you mean that it is extremely unpleasant. EG *It's hellish being a student without a grant.* ADJ QUALIT Informal

hello /hə²ləʊ/, **hellos;** also spelled **hallo** and **hullo.** 1 You say **'Hello'** when you are greeting someone or starting a telephone conversation, for example. EG *'Hello,' Lynn said. 'Hello,' said the girl... He lifted the receiver and said 'Hello,' but no one replied.* CONVENTION ▸ used as a noun. EG *Do come over and say hello to the group.* ▸ N COUNT

2 You can call **'hello'** to attract someone's attention. EG *'Hello, can I come in?' I called. 'Is anyone here?'* CONVENTION

helmet /hɛlmɪt/, **helmets.** A **helmet** is a type of hard hat which you wear to protect your head. N COUNT

help /hɛlp/, **helps, helping, helped.** 1 If you **help** someone, you make it easier for them to do something, for example by doing part of the work or by giving them advice or money. EG *Something went wrong with his machine so I helped him fix it... The* V+O OR V: OFT+INF OR *to*-INF

Which words on these pages refer only to women?

courier helped everyone out of the coach... This organization may be able to help you with such information.

2 If something **helps**, it makes it easier for you to get something, do something, or bear something. EG *I've got 40 pence, will that help?* V OR V+O: OFT+INF OR *to*-INF

3 If something **helps** to achieve a particular result, it is one of the things that together achieve it. EG *One of the things that can help to keep prices down is high productivity... Having a job helps keep them off the streets.* V+*to*-INF OR -INF; ALSO V+O+*to*-INF OR -INF

4 If you **help** yourself, you serve yourself some food or drink. EG *Mr Stokes helped himself to some more rum.* V-REFL: OFT+*to*

5 If you can't **help** the way you feel or the way you behave, you cannot change it or stop it happening. EG *You can't help who you fall in love with... I can't help feeling that it was a mistake to let him go.* V+O OR V+-ING

6 If you give **help** to someone, you help them. EG *The organization gives help to single women.* N UNCOUNT

7 If you say that someone or something is a **help**, you mean that they help you to do something. EG *He was a great help with some of the problems.* N SING: *a*+N

8 If something **is of help**, it makes things easier or better. EG *Having a sober mind around might prove to be of some help.* PHRASE

9 Help is also the assistance that someone gives when they go to rescue a person who is in danger. EG *I thought I'd better yell for help.* N UNCOUNT

10 You shout **'Help!'** when you are in danger, in order to attract someone's attention. EXCLAM

help out. If you **help out** or **help** someone **out**, you help them by doing some work for them or lending them money. PHRASAL VB: V+ADV OR V+O+ADV

helper /hɛlpə/, **helpers.** A **helper** is a person who helps another person or group with a job. EG *All the helpers for this organization are voluntary.* N COUNT

helpful /hɛlpfʊl/. **1** If someone is **helpful**, they help you by doing work for you or by giving you advice or information. EG *They were all very pleasant and extremely kind and helpful.* ADJ QUALIT

◊ **helpfully.** EG *Doctor Percival said helpfully, 'I'd advise you not to go'.* ◊ ADV ◊ **helpfulness.** EG *I was greatly impressed by the efficiency and helpfulness of the stage crew.* ◊ N UNCOUNT

2 Something that is **helpful** makes a situation more pleasant or more easy to tolerate. EG *It is often helpful during an illness to talk to other sufferers... None of these suggestions is very helpful.* ADJ QUALIT

helping /hɛlpɪŋ/, **helpings.** A **helping** of food is the amount of it that you get in a single serving. EG *I gave him a second helping of pudding.* N PART

helpless /hɛlplɪ[2]s/. If you are **helpless**, you are unable to do anything useful or unable to protect yourself, for example because you are very weak. EG *He was helpless to resist... ...a helpless baby... Sam raised his arms in a helpless gesture.* ADJ QUALIT

◊ **helplessly.** EG *She stood there helplessly crying... His wrist hung helplessly at his side.* ◊ ADV

◊ **helplessness.** EG *She took advantage of my utter helplessness.* ◊ N UNCOUNT

hem /hɛm/, **hems, hemming, hemmed. 1** The **hem** of a skirt or dress is the bottom edge of it, which is folded over and sewn. N COUNT

2 If you **hem** a piece of cloth, you sew the edge of it to make it neat and prevent it fraying. V OR V+O

hem in. If you **are hemmed in** by something, you are completely surrounded by it so that you cannot move. EG *The Princess's car was hemmed in by the crowd.* PHRASAL VB: V+O+ADV

hemisphere /hɛmɪsfɪə/, **hemispheres.** A **hemisphere** is one half of the earth. EG *...the greatest empires in the western hemisphere.* N COUNT Formal

hemoglobin /hiːmə[6]gləʊbɪn, hɛm-/. See **haemoglobin.**

hemophilia /hiːmə[6]fɪlɪə, hɛm-/. See **haemophilia.**

hemorrhage /hɛmə[0]rɪdʒ/. See **haemorrhage.**

hemorrhoids /hɛmə[0]rɔɪdz/. See **haemorrhoids.**

hen /hɛn/, **hens.** A **hen** is **1** a female chicken. People often keep hens for their eggs. **2** the female of any bird. EG *...a hen pheasant.* N COUNT

hence /hɛns/. **1 Hence** means for the reason just mentioned or as a result of the fact just mentioned. EG *The computer has become smaller and cheaper and hence more available to a greater number of people.* ADV SEN Formal

2 If you say that something will happen a number of hours, days, or years **hence**, you mean that it will happen that number of hours, days, or years after the time when you are speaking. EG *The tunnel will open in 1993, seven years hence.* ADV AFTER N Formal

henceforth /hɛnsfɔːθ/ means from this time on. EG *Henceforth his life would never be the same again.* ADV SEN Formal

henchman /hɛntʃmə[3]n/, **henchmen.** The **henchmen** of a powerful person are people employed by that person to do violent or dishonest work; used showing disapproval. EG *He signed the papers and left it to his henchmen to do the work.* N COUNT

hepatitis /hɛpətaɪtɪs/ is a serious disease which causes a person's liver to become inflamed. N UNCOUNT

her /hɜː/. **1 Her** is used as the object of a verb or preposition. You use **her** to refer to a woman, girl, or female animal who has already been mentioned, or whose identity is known. **Her** is also sometimes used to refer to a nation, ship, or car. EG *I knew your mother. I was at school with her... They gave her the job.* PRON: SING

2 You also use **her** to indicate that something belongs or relates to a woman, girl, or female animal who has already been mentioned, or whose identity is known. **Her** is also sometimes used to indicate that something belongs or relates to a nation, ship, or car. EG *Her face was very red... Britain must, of course, expand her air power.* DET POSS

3 You also use **her** in some titles when you are referring to a woman with that title. EG *...Her Majesty the Queen.*

herald /hɛrəld/, **heralds, heralding, heralded. 1** Something that **heralds** a future event or situation is a sign that it is going to happen or appear. EG *His rise to power heralded the end of the liberal era.* V+O

▸ used as a noun. EG *The festival was the herald of a new age.* ▸ N COUNT+*of*

2 If an important event or action **is heralded**, announcements have been made about it so that everyone knows about it. EG *Every reduction in taxation is heralded as a new achievement... ...the royal couple's much heralded world tour.* V+O: USU PASS+*as*

herb /hɜːb/, **herbs.** A **herb** is a plant which is used to add flavour to food, or as a medicine. EG *...dried herbs and spices... ...herb tea.* N COUNT ◊ **herbal** /hɜːbə[0]l/. EG *...herbal medicine.* ◊ ADJ CLASSIF: ATTRIB

herculean /hɜːkjə[4]liːən/. A **herculean** task or effort requires great strength or effort. EG *You must make a herculean effort not to talk to them about it.* ADJ CLASSIF: ATTRIB Literary

herd /hɜːd/, **herds, herding, herded. 1** A **herd** is a large group of animals of one kind that live together. EG *...a herd of goats.* N PART

2 If you **herd** people or animals, you make them move together to form a group. EG *...men herding cattle... The chained people were herded back into the dark cellar.* V+O: OFT+A

here /hɪə/. **1** You use **here** **1.1** when you are referring to the place where you are or to a place which has been mentioned. EG *She left here at eight o'clock... Elizabeth, come over here... You've been here for a number of years.* **1.2** when you are pointing to a place that is near you, in order to draw someone's attention to it. EG *You have to sign here and acknowledge the receipt.* **1.3** to indicate that the person or thing that you are talking about is near you or being held by you. EG *What can you do with this thing here?... I have here a very important message that has just arrived.* ADV

2 You can also use **here** to refer to the time, situation, or subject that you have come to or that you are dealing with. EG *I think that what we're talking about here is role-playing... The autumn's really here at last.* ADV

3 You use **here is** or **here are** to draw attention to something or to introduce something. EG *Now here is the News... Here she is... Here's how it's done.* PHRASE

4 You say **'Here'** or **'Here you are'** when you are offering or giving something to someone. EG *He pushed a piece of paper across the table. 'Here you are. My address.'... Here, hold this while I go and get a newspaper.* CONVENTION

5 You say **'Here we are'** when you have just found something that you have been looking for. CONVENTION

6 Something that is happening **here and there** is happening in several different places. EG *Panic here and there was only to be expected.* PHRASE

7 You say **'Here's to us'** or **'Here's to your new job'**, for example, as a toast in order to wish success or happiness to someone. CONVENTION

hereby /hɪəbaɪ/. You use **hereby** in formal statements and documents to emphasize that a statement or declaration is official. EG *I hereby resign.* ADV Formal

hereditary /hɪ2rɛdɪtə0ri1/. **1** A characteristic or illness that is **hereditary** is passed on to a child from its parents before it is born. EG *...a progressive, hereditary disease of certain glands.* ADJ CLASSIF

2 A title or position in society that is **hereditary** is passed on as a right from parent to child. EG *...the hereditary right to belong to the House of Lords.* ADJ CLASSIF

heredity /hɪ2rɛdɪ1ti1/ is the process by which characteristics are passed on from parents to their children before the children are born. EG *Do you think we are influenced more by environment or heredity?* N UNCOUNT

heresy /hɛrə1si1/, **heresies. Heresy** is **1** a belief, opinion, or way of behaving that disagrees with beliefs that are generally accepted. EG *...bitter complaints about the heresies of the group.* **2** a belief, opinion, or way of behaving that seriously disagrees with the principles of a particular religion. EG *He was tried for heresy in the ecclesiastical courts.* N UNCOUNT OR N COUNT

heretic /hɛrə1tɪk/, **heretics.** A **heretic** is **1** a person who has beliefs or opinions that most people think are wrong. EG *His views are portrayed as those of an unrealistic leftist heretic.* **2** a person who belongs to a particular religion, but whose beliefs seriously disagree with the principles of that religion. EG *They were denounced as heretics and burned at the stake.* N COUNT

heretical /hɪ2rɛtɪkə0l/. A belief or action that is **heretical 1** disagrees with beliefs that are generally accepted. EG *...heretical opinions.* **2** seriously disagrees with the principles of a particular religion. EG *The bishops jailed him for heretical and blasphemous words.* ADJ CLASSIF

heritage /hɛrɪtɪdʒ/. A country's **heritage** is all the qualities and traditions that have continued over many years, especially when they are considered to be of historical importance. EG *...a building that may one day be part of Britain's national heritage.* N SING+POSS

hermit /hɜːmɪt/, **hermits.** A **hermit** is a person who lives alone, away from people and society. N COUNT

hero /hɪərəʊ/, **heroes. 1** A **hero** is **1.1** the main male character in a book, play or film, who is admired or respected for his good qualities. EG *Robert Powell plays Alec, the hero of the play.* **1.2** someone who has done something brave or good and is admired by a lot of people. EG *...one of the heroes of the Battle of Britain.* N COUNT

2 If you describe someone as your **hero**, you mean that you admire them greatly. EG *Bill Hook was my first rugby hero.* N COUNT+POSS

heroic /hɪ2rəʊɪk/, **heroics. 1** Actions that are **heroic 1.1** are brave and courageous. EG *...truly heroic work by army engineers.* ◇ **heroically.** EG *They fought heroically.* **1.2** involve great effort and determination to succeed. EG *...a heroic stand against undemocratic provocation.* ◇ **heroically.** EG *The boys heroically kept the secret even from their parents.* ADJ QUALIT ◇ ADV ADJ QUALIT ◇ ADV

2 Heroic people are very brave and courageous. EG *They are heroic figures in the fight against cancer.* ADJ CLASSIF : ATTRIB

heroin /hɛrəʊɪn/ is a powerful drug which some people take for pleasure, but which they can become addicted to. EG *...an overdose of heroin.* N UNCOUNT

heroine /hɛrəʊɪn/, **heroines.** A **heroine** is **1** the main female character in a book, play or film, who is admired or respected for her good qualities. EG *...Adah, the heroine of the book.* **2** a woman who has done something brave or good and is admired by a lot of people. EG *...the heroine of their great 1967 election triumph.* N COUNT

heroism /hɛrəʊɪzə0m/ is great courage and bravery. EG *...an act of heroism.* N UNCOUNT

heron /hɛrən/, **herons.** A **heron** is a kind of large bird which eats fish. N COUNT

herring /hɛrɪŋ/, **herrings. Herring** can also be used as the plural form. N COUNT

A **herring** is a kind of long silver-coloured fish that lives in the sea. ● See also **red herring**.

hers /hɜːz/. You use **hers** to indicate that something belongs or relates to a woman, girl, or female animal who has already been mentioned, or whose identity is known. **Hers** is also sometimes used to indicate that something belongs or relates to a nation, ship, or car. EG *He laid his hand on hers... You were an old friend of hers.* PRON POSS : SING

herself /hə5sɛlf/. **1** You use **herself** as the object of a verb or preposition to refer to the same woman, girl, or female animal who is mentioned as the subject of the clause, or as a previous object in the clause. **Herself** is also sometimes used in relation to a nation, ship, or car. EG *She groaned and stretched herself out flat on the sofa... Barbara stared at herself in the mirror... On the way home Rose bought herself a piece of cheese for lunch.* PRON REFL : SING

2 You also use **herself** to emphasize the female subject or object of a clause, and to make it clear who you are referring to. EG *Sally herself came back... How strange that he should collide with Melanie Byrd herself... Their audience was of middle-aged women like herself.* PRON REFL : SING

3 If a girl or woman does something **herself**, she does it without any help or interference from anyone else. EG *She had printed the little card herself.* PRON REFL : SING

he's /hiːz/ is the usual spoken form of 'he is' or 'he has', especially when 'has' is an auxiliary verb. EG *He's a reporter... I hope he's got some money left.*

hesitancy /hɛzɪtənsi1/ is unwillingness to do something. EG *...an air of childlike hesitancy.* N UNCOUNT

hesitant /hɛzɪtə0nt/. If you are **hesitant** about doing something, you do not do it quickly or immediately, for example because you are uncertain, embarrassed, or worried about it. EG *He seemed hesitant to confirm the bad news... ...a hesitant, almost boyish smile.* ◇ **hesitantly.** EG *'Maybe you could teach me,' said Marsha hesitantly.* ADJ QUALIT ◇ ADV

hesitate /hɛzɪteɪt/, **hesitates, hesitating, hesitated. 1** If you **hesitate**, you pause slightly while you are doing something or just before you do it, usually because you are uncertain, embarrassed, or worried about it. EG *She put her hand on the phone, hesitated for a moment, then picked up the receiver... I said: 'What was all that about?' He hesitated. 'I'm sorry. I'd rather not say.'* V

2 If you **hesitate** to do something, you are unwilling to do it because you are not certain whether it is correct or right. EG *I would hesitate to say* V+to-INF

What is the name for a female hero?

precisely what a fantasy is... Don't hesitate to go to a doctor if you have any unusual symptoms.

hesitation /hezɪteɪʃə0n/, **hesitations. 1 Hesitation** is **1.1** a pause or slight delay in something that you are doing. EG *'Well, no,' Karen said, with some hesitation... ...a slight hesitation.* **1.2** an unwillingness to do something. EG *After some hesitation he agreed to allow me to write the article... The calm voice of authority overrode the teacher's hesitations.* N UNCOUNT OR N COUNT

2 If you **have no hesitation in** saying something, you are certain that you are right to say it. EG *They had no hesitation in describing the situation as ridiculous.* PHRASE

heterogeneous /hetə0rə6dʒiːnɪəs/. Something that is **heterogeneous** consists of many different types of things. EG *Arts and sciences are contained in one heterogeneous collection, the South Kensington Museum.* ADJ QUALIT Formal

heterosexual /hetə0rə6seksjuə0əl/. **1** A **heterosexual** relationship is a sexual relationship between a man and a woman. ADJ CLASSIF

2 Someone who is **heterosexual** is sexually attracted to people of the opposite sex. ADJ CLASSIF

het up /het ʌp/. If you get **het up**, you get very excited or anxious about something. EG *...when he gets all het up about some business problem.* ADJ PRED Informal

hew /hjuː/, **hews, hewing, hewed, hewn** /hjuːn/. If someone **hews** stone, they cut large pieces out of it roughly. EG *...hewn stone.* V+O Formal

hey /heɪ/. You say or shout **'hey'** to attract someone's attention or show how surprised, interested, or annoyed you are. EG *'Hey, Ben!' he called. There was no reply... Hey, Dad, what's for dinner?* CONVENTION Informal

heyday /heɪdeɪ/. The **heyday** of a person, nation, or organization is the time when they are most powerful, successful, or popular. EG *...the heyday of Christianity.* N SING+POSS

hi /haɪ/. You say **'hi' 1** when you are greeting someone. EG *'Hi, Uncle Harold,' Thomas said... Hi, there, Mr Swallow, good to see you.* **2** when you are trying to attract someone's attention. EG *Ralph jumped to his feet. 'Hi! You two!'* CONVENTION Informal Outdated

hiatus /haɪeɪtəs/. A **hiatus** is a pause in which nothing happens. EG *There came a pause, a hiatus. He stared out of the window.* N SING Formal

hibernate /haɪbəneɪt/, **hibernates, hibernating, hibernated.** Animals that **hibernate** spend the winter in a state like a deep sleep. EG *Squirrels don't hibernate.* ◇ **hibernation** /haɪbəneɪʃə0n/. EG *...a brown bear emerging from hibernation.* V ◇ N UNCOUNT

hiccup /hɪkʌp/, **hiccups, hiccupping, hiccupped;** also spelled **hiccough. Hiccups** are repeated little choking sounds in your throat. You sometimes get hiccups if you have been eating or drinking too quickly. ▸ used as a verb. EG *She turned over on her side, hiccupped once or twice and went to sleep.* N COUNT: USU PLURAL ▸ V

hid /hɪd/ is the past tense of **hide.**

hidden /hɪdə0n/. **1 Hidden** is the past participle of **hide**.

2 Something that is **hidden** is not easily noticed. EG *...the hidden disadvantages of a cheque book.* ADJ CLASSIF

3 A place that is **hidden** is difficult to find. EG *...hidden valleys.* ADJ CLASSIF

hide /haɪd/, **hides, hiding, hid** /hɪd/, **hidden** /hɪdə0n/. **1** If you **hide** something, you put it in a place where it cannot easily be seen or found. EG *The women managed to steal and hide a few knives.* V+O

2 If you **hide** or if you **hide** yourself, you go somewhere where you cannot easily be seen or found. EG *There was nowhere to hide.* V OR V-REFL

3 If you **hide** your feelings or information, you keep it a secret, so that no one knows about it. EG *I couldn't hide this fact from you.* V+O

4 If something **hides** an object, it covers it and prevents it from being seen. EG *Much of his face was hidden by a beard.* V+O

5 A **hide** is the skin of a large animal, which is used for making leather. N MASS

6 See also **hidden, hiding**.

hideous /hɪdi1əs/. Something that is **hideous** is extremely unpleasant or ugly. EG *They're not like dogs, they're ugly, hideous brutes... ...the hideous conditions of trench warfare.* ◇ **hideously.** EG *...hideously mutilated bodies... ...a hideously difficult task.* ADJ QUALIT ◇ SUBMOD

hiding /haɪdɪŋ/, **hidings. 1** If someone is in **hiding**, they have secretly gone somewhere where they cannot be seen or found. EG *He has not been heard from since going into hiding in June.* N UNCOUNT

2 If you give someone a **hiding**, you hit them many times as a punishment. EG *He told us to stop, or else we'd get a good hiding.* N COUNT Informal

hierarchy /haɪərɑːki1/, **hierarchies. 1** A **hierarchy** is a system in which people have different ranks or positions depending on how important they are. EG *...the hierarchy of the Episcopal Church.* ◇ **hierarchical** /haɪərɑːkɪkə0l/. EG *...ancient hierarchical societies.* N COUNT Formal ◇ ADJ QUALIT

2 The **hierarchy** is the group of people who have the power in an organization. EG *The university hierarchy decided that it was best to ignore the situation.* N COUNT Formal

hieroglyphics /haɪərəglɪfɪks/ are written symbols or words which you cannot understand. EG *On the blackboards were hieroglyphics which I was told were called logarithms.* N COUNT

hi-fi /haɪfaɪ/, **hi-fis.** A **hi-fi** is a set of equipment which you use to play records and tapes, and which produces stereo sound of good quality. EG *...listening to classical music on the hi-fi.* N COUNT

high /haɪ/, **higher, highest; highs. 1** A **high** structure or mountain measures a great amount from the bottom to the top. EG *...the high walls of the prison.* ADJ QUALIT

2 You use **high** to say how much something measures from the bottom to the top. EG *...a low mud wall about 10 centimetres high... ...a 200 foot high crag.* ADJ AFTER N

3 If something is **high**, it is a long way above the ground, above sea level, or above a person. EG *The bookshelf was too high for him to reach... I threw the shell high up into the air.* ADJ QUALIT

4 High also means great in amount, degree, or intensity. EG *Ceramic materials will withstand high temperatures... Her works fetch high prices... ...areas of high unemployment.* ADJ QUALIT

5 You can use **high** with numbers. For example, if a number or level is **in the high** eighties, it is more than eighty-five, but not as much as ninety. PHRASE

6 If someone has a **high** position in a profession or society, they have an important position in it. EG *She is high enough up in the company to be able to help you... ...high social status.* ADJ QUALIT

7 If people have a **high** opinion of you, they respect you very much. ADJ QUALIT

8 If the quality or standard of something is **high**, it is very good indeed. EG *...high-quality colour photographs.* ADJ QUALIT

9 If someone has **high** principles or standards, they are morally good. ADJ QUALIT

10 A **high** sound is close to the top of a particular range of notes. EG *...a high squeaky voice.* ADJ QUALIT

11 If your spirits are **high**, you are happy and confident about the future. EG *They were not at all depressed, but in high spirits.* ADJ QUALIT

12 If you are **high** on drugs, you are under the influence of drugs. ADJ QUALIT Informal

13 A **high** is the greatest level or amount that something reaches or has reached. EG *Prices on the stock exchange reached another record high last week.* N COUNT+SUPP

14 High also means advanced or complex. EG *...a successful job in high finance... The questions he'd asked were at a higher level than other people's.* ADJ CLASSIF: ATTRIB

15 If you say that **it is high time** something was PHRASE done, you mean that it should be done now, and that it should have been done before now. EG *It's high time that we did something about improving the situation.*

highbrow /haɪbraʊ/. If you describe something as **highbrow**, you mean that it is intellectual, academic, and difficult to understand. EG *...highbrow radio programmes.* ADJ QUALIT

high-class. Something that is **high-class** is of very good quality and of high social status. EG *...big hotels and high-class restaurants.* ADJ QUALIT

higher /haɪə/. **1 Higher** is the comparative form of **high**.

2 A **higher** exam or qualification is of an advanced standard or level. EG *They have their first degrees and are studying for higher degrees.* ADJ CLASSIF : ATTRIB

higher education is education at universities, colleges, and polytechnics. EG *...the government's policy on higher education.* N UNCOUNT

high-heeled /haɪ hiːld/. **High-heeled** shoes have a narrow high heel at the back. They are usually worn by women. ADJ CLASSIF

high heels are high-heeled shoes. N PLURAL

highlands /haɪləndz/ are mountainous areas of land. EG *...the highlands of New Guinea.* N PLURAL

highlight /haɪlaɪt/, **highlights, highlighting, highlighted. 1** If you **highlight** a point or problem, you draw attention to it. EG *The survey highlighted the needs of working women.* V+O

2 A **highlight** is the most interesting or exciting part of something. EG *This visit provided the real highlight of the morning.* N COUNT+SUPP

3 Highlights in a person's hair are thin streaks of lighter colour that have been made by dyeing the hair. EG *...blonde highlights.* N PLURAL

highly /haɪli¹/. **1** You use **highly 1.1** to emphasize that a particular quality exists to a great degree. EG *The report is highly critical of these policies... It is highly improbable that they will accept... ...highly-educated people.* **1.2** to indicate that something is very important. EG *...a highly placed negotiator... ...a very highly classified document.* ADV+ADJ

2 If you praise someone **highly** or speak **highly** of them, you praise them a lot. EG *They spoke highly of Harold... Ross Thompson obviously thought very highly of him.* ADV

highly-strung. Someone who is **highly-strung** is very nervous and easily upset. ADJ QUALIT

high-minded. Someone who is **high-minded** has strong moral principles. EG *...high-minded idealists from overseas.* ADJ QUALIT

Highness /haɪnɪ²s/, **Highnesses.** You use expressions such as **Your Highness** and **His Highness** when you are addressing or referring to a prince or princess. EG *...Her Royal Highness, Princess Alexandra.*

high-pitched. A sound that is **high-pitched** is very high and shrill. EG *...a high-pitched whine.* ADJ QUALIT

high point, high points. The **high point** of an event or period of time is the most exciting or enjoyable part of it. EG *His speech was the high point of the evening.* N COUNT+SUPP

high-powered. 1 A machine or piece of equipment that is **high-powered** is very powerful and efficient. EG *...high-powered microscopes.* ADJ QUALIT

2 An activity that is **high-powered** is very advanced and successful. EG *...high-powered advertising... The course is high-powered.* ADJ QUALIT

high-rise. High-rise buildings are very tall modern buildings. EG *...high-rise flats.* ADJ CLASSIF : ATTRIB

high school, high schools. A **high school** is **1** a school in Britain for people aged between eleven and eighteen. **2** a school in the United States for people aged between fifteen and eighteen. N COUNT OR N UNCOUNT

high-spirited. Someone who is **high-spirited** is very lively. ADJ QUALIT

high street, high streets. The **high street** of a town is the main street where most of the shops and banks are. EG *They had a little flat off Kensington High Street.* N COUNT

high tea is a large meal that some people eat in the late afternoon, often with tea to drink. N UNCOUNT British

high technology is the practical use of advanced scientific research and knowledge, especially in relation to electronics and computers. EG *...a new leap forward into an age of high technology... ...high-technology equipment.* N UNCOUNT

high tide is the time at which the sea is at its highest level at the coast each day before it starts to fall again. EG *...a pool which the sea only reached at high tide.* N UNCOUNT

highway /haɪweɪ/, **highways.** A **highway** is **1** a large road that connects towns or cities. EG *...interstate highways.* **2** a main road. EG *She was charged with obstructing the highway.* N COUNT American Formal

hijack /haɪdʒæk/, **hijacks, hijacking, hijacked.** If someone **hijacks** a plane, they illegally take control of it by force while it is on a journey. EG *A Pan Am aircraft was hijacked on its way to Singapore.* V+O

hike /haɪk/, **hikes, hiking, hiked. 1** A **hike** is a long walk in the country. EG *We're going on a four mile hike tomorrow.* N COUNT

2 If you **hike**, you go on long country walks for pleasure. EG *She was in Switzerland, hiking.* V
◇ **hiker, hikers.** EG *I watched the hikers scrambling up the gully.* ◇ N COUNT ◇ **hiking.** EG *We have maps of the area where we hope to do some hiking.* ◇ N UNCOUNT

hilarious /hɪlɛərɪəs/. Something that is **hilarious** is extremely funny and makes you laugh a lot. EG *...the hilarious tale of how Uncle Harold got stuck in a lift.* ◇ **hilariously.** EG *These words are now hilariously old-fashioned.* ADJ QUALIT ◇ SUBMOD

hilarity /hɪlærɪ¹ti¹/ is great amusement and laughter. EG *The noise of hilarity in the restaurant below kept him awake until the small hours.* N UNCOUNT

hill /hɪl/, **hills.** A **hill** is an area of land that is higher than the land that surrounds it, but not as high as a mountain. EG *I started to walk up the hill... ...the Malvern Hills of Worcestershire.* N COUNT

hillock /hɪlək/, **hillocks.** A **hillock** is a small hill. EG *The view was broken up into many little valleys and small hillocks.* N COUNT Literary

hillside /hɪlsaɪd/, **hillsides.** A **hillside** is the side of a hill. EG *...the steep hillsides of North Wales... ...a hillside town.* N COUNT

hilltop /hɪltɒp/, **hilltops.** A **hilltop** is the top of a hill. EG *...the hilltop village of Combe.* N COUNT

hilly /hɪli¹/, **hillier, hilliest.** Land that is **hilly** has many hills. EG *They drove around the hilly area behind the town.* ADJ QUALIT

hilt /hɪlt/, **hilts. 1** The **hilt** of a sword, dagger, or knife is its handle. N COUNT

2 If you support or defend someone **to the hilt**, you give them all the support that you can. EG *She had backed me to the hilt in all my projects.* PHRASE Informal

him /hɪm/ is used as the object of a verb or preposition. You use **him** to refer to a man, boy, or male animal who has already been mentioned or whose identity is known, or to someone whose sex is not known or stated. EG *He asked if you'd ring him back when you got in... There's no need for him to worry.* PRON : SING

himself /hɪmsɛlf/. **1** You use **himself** as the object of a verb or preposition to refer to the same man, boy, male animal, or person who is mentioned as the subject of the clause, or as a previous object in the clause. EG *Mr Boggis introduced himself... ...his lack of confidence in himself.* PRON REFL : SING

2 You also use **himself** to emphasize the male subject or object of a clause, and to make it clear who you are referring to. EG *Forman himself became Minister of International Affairs... It was* PRON REFL : SING

If you hire something, does it belong to you?

easy for a clever young man like himself to make a good living.

3 If a man or boy does something **himself**, he does it without any help or interference from anyone else. PRON REFL : SING

hind /ha̱ɪnd/. The **hind** legs of an animal are at the back of its body. EG *Kangaroos' hind legs are enormously powerful.* ADJ CLASSIF : ATTRIB

hinder /hɪ̱ndə/, **hinders, hindering, hindered.** If something **hinders** you, it makes it more difficult for you to do something. EG *Her career was not hindered by the fact that she had three children.* V+O

hindrance /hɪ̱ndrəns/, **hindrances. 1** A **hindrance** is a person or thing that makes it more difficult for you to do something. EG *New ideas may be more of a hindrance than an asset.* N COUNT

2 Hindrance is the act of hindering someone or something. EG *Now they can construct tunnel systems without hindrance.* N UNCOUNT

hindsight /ha̱ɪndsaɪt/. If you can understand something with **hindsight**, you can understand it after it has happened. EG *With the benefit of hindsight, what lessons could we learn from their mistakes?* N UNCOUNT

Hindu /hɪ̱ndu:, hɪndu̱:/, **Hindus. 1** A **Hindu** is a person who believes in Hinduism. N COUNT

2 Something that is **Hindu** belongs or relates to Hinduism. EG *...Hindu civilization.* ADJ CLASSIF

Hinduism /hɪ̱ndu:ɪzᵊm/ is an Indian religion. Hinduism has many gods and teaches that people live again after they die. N UNCOUNT

hinge /hɪ̱ndʒ/, **hinges, hinging, hinged.** A **hinge** is a piece of metal, wood or plastic that is used to join two things together so that one of them can swing freely. EG *The door was ripped from its hinges.* N COUNT

hinge on or **hinge upon.** If something **hinges on** or **hinges upon** a fact or event, it depends on it. EG *Everything hinged on what happened to the United States economy.* PHRASAL VB : V+PREP

hinged /hɪ̱ndᵊʒd/. Something that is **hinged** is joined to something by means of a hinge. EG *...the hinged flap of the counter.* ADJ CLASSIF

hink /hɪ̱ŋk/, **hinks, hinking, hinked.** If you **hink**, you think hopefully and unrealistically about something. V OR V+REPORT

hint /hɪ̱nt/, **hints, hinting, hinted. 1** A **hint** is a suggestion about something that is made in an indirect way. EG *As yet no hint had appeared as to who was going to be the next Foreign Secretary.* N COUNT

• If you **drop a hint**, you suggest something in an indirect way. EG *He had dropped several hints that he knew where Mary was.* ● PHRASE • If you **take a hint**, you understand something that someone is suggesting indirectly to you. EG *She may take the hint and become more organized.* ● PHRASE

2 If you **hint** at something, you suggest something in a very indirect way. EG *Harold hinted at what she had already guessed... I tried to hint that I deserved an increase in salary.* V+*at*, OR V+REPORT : ONLY *that*

3 A **hint** is also a helpful piece of advice. EG *The magazine had the usual hints on fashion and cookery.* N COUNT : USU PLURAL

4 A **hint** of something is a very small amount of it. EG *There was a hint of disapproval in her face.* N PART

hip /hɪ̱p/, **hips.** Your **hips** are the two areas at the sides of your body between the tops of your legs and your waist. EG *Her waist was slender, her hips curved... She put her hand on her hip.* N COUNT

hippie /hɪ̱pi^{1}/, **hippies;** also spelled **hippy.** N COUNT
A **hippie** is someone who has rejected conventional ideas about dress and social values and wants to live a different kind of life based on love. EG *...hippies in a commune... ...the hippy generation.*

hippo /hɪ̱pəʊ/, **hippos.** A **hippo** is a hippopotamus. N COUNT

hippopotamus /hɪ̱pəpɒ̱təməs/, **hippopotamuses** or **hippopotami.** A **hippopotamus** is a large animal with short legs and thick, wrinkled skin. Hippopotamuses live near rivers in Africa. N COUNT

hippy /hɪ̱pi^{1}/. See **hippie**.

hire /ha̱ɪə/, **hires, hiring, hired. 1** If you **hire** something, you pay money to use it for a period of time. EG *We hired a car and drove across the island.* V+O
▸ used as a noun. EG *Hire of a van costs about £30 a day.* ▸ N UNCOUNT +SUPP

2 If something is **for hire**, you can hire it. EG *...boats for hire.* PHRASE

3 If you **hire** someone, you pay them to do a job for you. EG *You've got to hire a private detective to make enquiries.* V+O

hire out. If you **hire out** something, you allow it to be used in return for payment. EG *Holborn library hires out pictures.* PHRASAL VB : V+O+ADV

hire purchase is a way of buying goods gradually. You make regular payments to the seller until you have paid the full price and the goods belong to you. EG *Have you bought anything on hire purchase?* N UNCOUNT

his /hɪ̱z/. **1** You use **his** to indicate that something belongs or relates to a man, boy, or male animal who has already been mentioned or whose identity is known, or to someone whose sex is not known or stated. EG *His name was Simon.* ▸ used as a pronoun. EG *Willie had a job on a new magazine that a friend of his had just started.* DET POSS ▸ PRON POSS : SING

2 You also use **his** in some titles when you are referring to a man with that title. EG *...his Lordship.* DET POSS

hiss /hɪ̱s/, **hisses, hissing, hissed. 1** To **hiss** means to make a sound like a long 's'. EG *If you shove a hot frying pan into water it will hiss and buckle.* ▸ used as a noun. EG *...the soft hiss of roasting meat.* V ▸ N COUNT

2 If you **hiss**, you say something in a strong, angry whisper. EG *He pointed a shaking finger at my friend and hissed through clenched teeth: 'You, you get out!'* V+QUOTE

3 When an audience **hisses** a performance, they express their dislike of it by making long loud 's' sounds. EG *His public appearances were frequently hissed.* V+O OR V

historian /hɪstɔ̱:rɪən/, **historians.** A **historian** is a person who studies history. EG *...art historians.* N COUNT

historic /hɪstɒ̱rɪk/. Something that is **historic** is important in history. EG *What we are talking about was a historic change.* ADJ QUALIT

historical /hɪstɒ̱rɪkᵊl/. **1 Historical** people or situations existed in the past and are considered to be a part of history. EG *...actual historical events... ...autographs and manuscripts of historical interest.* ADJ CLASSIF : ATTRIB
◊ **historically.** EG *Historically, Labour was strongly opposed to the powers of the Lords.* ◊ ADV SEN OR ADV

2 Historical books and pictures describe or represent real people or things that existed in the past. EG *...historical novels.* ADJ CLASSIF : ATTRIB

history /hɪ̱stᵊri^{1}/, **histories. 1** You can refer to the events of the past as **history**. EG *...one of the most dramatic moments in Polish history... Each city has its own history and character.* • Someone who **makes history** does something very important and significant. • If you **go down in history**, people in the future remember you because of things that you have done. N UNCOUNT ● PHRASE ● PHRASE

2 History is also a subject studied in schools, colleges, and universities that deals with the past. EG *I adored history and hated geography... ...a history book, not a novel.* • See also **natural history**. N UNCOUNT

3 A **history** is a description of the important events that have happened in a particular subject. EG *...a television history of the United States.* N COUNT+SUPP

4 If someone has a **history** of something, that thing has happened frequently in their life. EG *There is a family history of coronary heart disease... Both he and Nick have similar histories of success.* N COUNT+*of*

5 The **history** of a person or thing is a set of facts that are known about their past. EG *I'd like to look at his medical history.* N COUNT : USU+POSS

histrionic /hɪstri¹ɒnɪk/. **Histrionic** behaviour is very dramatic and seems full of emotion, but is not sincere. EG *...a flamboyant, histrionic gesture.* ADJ QUALIT: ATTRIB Formal
◇ **histrionically.** EG *She sighed histrionically.* ◇ ADV

hit /hɪt/, **hits, hitting.** The form **hit** is used in the present tense and is the past tense and past participle of the verb.
1 If you **hit** someone or something, you deliberately touch them with a lot of force using your hand or an object. EG *He hit the burglar on the head with a candlestick... He never hit the ball very far.* V+O
2 When something **hits** something else, it touches it with a lot of force. EG *The truck had hit a wall... Enormous hailstones hit the roof of the car.* V+O
3 If a bomb or other missile **hits** its target, it reaches it. EG *Three ships were hit.* ▸ used as a noun. EG *The tanks were designed to withstand anything except a direct hit.* V+O ▸ N COUNT
4 If something **hits** a person, place, or thing, it affects them very badly. EG *Spectator sport has been badly hit by the increase in ticket prices.* V+O
5 When a feeling or an idea **hits** you, it suddenly affects you or comes into your mind. EG *The shock of her death kept hitting me afresh... Suddenly it hit me: my diary had probably been read by everyone in the office.* V+O
6 A **hit** is a record, play, or film that is very popular and successful. EG *The play became a tremendous hit... ...a hit single.* N COUNT
7 If you **hit the roof**, you react to something very angrily. PHRASE Informal
8 If two people **hit it off**, they like each other and become friendly as soon as they meet. PHRASE Informal
hit back. If you **hit back** at someone who has criticized or harmed you, you criticize or harm them in return. PHRASAL VB: V+ADV, OFT+*at*
hit on or **hit upon.** If you **hit on** an idea or **hit upon** it, you think of it. EG *He hit on the idea of cutting a hole in the door to allow the cat to get in and out.* PHRASAL VB: V+PREP, HAS PASS

hit and miss. Something that is **hit and miss** happens in an unplanned way, so that you never know what the result will be. EG *The service here is very hit and miss, isn't it?* ADJ QUALIT

hit-and-run. A **hit-and-run** car accident is one in which the driver does not stop. EG *...killed in a hit-and-run accident.* ADJ CLASSIF: ATTRIB

hitch /hɪtʃ/, **hitches, hitching, hitched. 1** A **hitch** is a slight problem or difficulty. EG *There had also been one or two technical hitches.* N COUNT
2 If you **hitch** or **hitch** a lift, you hitch-hike. EG *He hitched south towards Italy.* V OR V+O: OFT+A
3 If you **hitch** something onto something else, you hook it or fasten it there. EG *...ponies hitched to rails.* V+O+A
hitch up. If you **hitch up** a piece of clothing, you pull it up into a higher position. EG *He hitched up his trousers.* PHRASAL VB: V+O+ADV

hitch-hike, hitch-hikes, hitch-hiking, hitch-hiked. If you **hitch-hike**, you travel by getting lifts in other people's cars, which you ask for by standing at the side of the road with your thumb held out. EG *She went off with a friend intending to hitch-hike to Turkey.* ◇ **hitch-hiker, hitch-hikers.** EG *...foreign hitch-hikers in Sardinia.* V: USU+A ◇ N COUNT

hi tech /haɪ tek/. Something that is **hi tech** uses very modern methods and equipment. ADJ QUALIT

hither /hɪðə/ is used to describe movement towards the place where you are at present. EG *...my journey hither.* ● Something that moves **hither and thither** moves in all directions. EG *She ran hither and thither in the orchard.* ADV Literary ● PHRASE Literary

hitherto /hɪðətuː/. If something has been happening **hitherto**, it has been happening until now. EG *She had hitherto been relatively nice to me.* ADV Formal

hit list, hit lists. A **hit list** is a list that terrorists have of the people they intend to kill. N COUNT

hit or miss. Something that is **hit or miss** happens in an unplanned way, so that you never know what the result will be. EG *We are working on a rather hit-or-miss basis at the moment.* ADJ QUALIT

hive /haɪv/, **hives. 1** A **hive** is a beehive. EG *There must be sixty thousand bees in that hive.* N COUNT
2 You describe a place as a **hive** of activity when there is a lot of activity there. EG *Calcutta is a hive of industry and trade.* N COUNT+*of*

h'm; also spelled **hm.** You say **'h'm'** when you are hesitating, for example because you are thinking about something.

HMS is used before the names of ships in the British Royal Navy. **HMS** is an abbreviation for 'Her Majesty's Ship' or 'His Majesty's Ship'. EG *...HMS Churchill.*

hoard /hɔːd/, **hoards, hoarding, hoarded. 1** If you **hoard** things, you save or store them, often in secret. EG *Is it better to spend your money today or hoard every penny in the bank for tomorrow?* V+O
2 A **hoard** is a store of things you have saved. EG *...a small hoard of coins.* N PART

hoarding /hɔːdɪŋ/, **hoardings.** A **hoarding** is a very large notice board that stands at the sides of roads and is used for displaying advertisements and posters. EG *I scanned the hoardings for election posters.* N COUNT: USU PLURAL

hoarse /hɔːs/, **hoarser, hoarsest.** If your voice is **hoarse**, it sounds rough and unclear. EG *When he spoke his voice was hoarse with rage.* ◇ **hoarsely.** EG *'Go in there,' he whispered hoarsely.* ◇ **hoarseness.** EG *I noticed a peculiar hoarseness in Johnny's voice.* ADJ QUALIT ◇ ADV ◇ N UNCOUNT

hoary /hɔːri¹/. **1** Something that is **hoary** is greyish white. EG *...a clump of hoary juniper bushes.* ADJ QUALIT Literary
2 A **hoary** problem or subject is old and familiar. EG *They discussed the hoary old problem.* ADJ QUALIT

hoax /həʊks/, **hoaxes.** A **hoax** is a trick in which someone tells people something that is not true. EG *It wasn't a hoax, there really was a fire.* N COUNT

hob /hɒb/, **hobs.** A **hob** is a surface on top of a cooker which can be heated. EG *The stew simmered on the hob.* N COUNT

hobble /hɒbəᵒl/, **hobbles, hobbling, hobbled. 1** If you **hobble**, you walk in an awkward way with small steps, for example because your feet are injured. EG *He hobbled along as best he could.* V: USU+A
2 If you **hobble** an animal, you tie its legs together so that it cannot run away. EG *They were hobbled by straps around their legs.* V+O

hobby /hɒbi¹/, **hobbies.** A **hobby** is something that you enjoy doing in your spare time, such as collecting stamps or painting. EG *Music is his chief hobby.* N COUNT

hock /hɒk/ is a type of dry white wine from Germany. EG *...a glass of hock.* N MASS

hockey /hɒki¹/ is an outdoor game, played between two teams of 11 players who use long curved sticks to hit a small ball and try to score goals. ● See also **ice hockey**. N UNCOUNT

hoe /həʊ/, **hoes, hoeing, hoed. 1** A **hoe** is a gardening tool with a long handle and a small square blade, which is used to remove small weeds. N COUNT
2 If you **hoe** a field, you use a hoe on the weeds or soil there. V OR V+O

hog /hɒg/, **hogs, hogging, hogged. 1** A **hog** is a male pig that has been castrated. N COUNT
2 If you **hog** something, you take all of it in a selfish or impolite way. EG *...a huge lorry hogging the centre of the road.* V+O Informal
3 If you **go the whole hog**, you do something bold or extravagant in the most complete way possible. PHRASE Informal

ho ho /həʊ həʊ/ is used, especially in writing, to represent laughter. CONVENTION

hoist /hɔɪst/, **hoists, hoisting, hoisted. 1** If you **hoist** something heavy somewhere, you lift it or V+O+A

If you hit the roof, do you touch it?

pull it up there. EG *She hoisted the child onto her shoulder.*

2 If you **hoist** a flag or a sail, you pull it up to its correct position by means of ropes. EG *The American flag was hoisted.* V+O

3 A **hoist** is a machine for lifting heavy things. EG *...an electric hoist.* N COUNT

hold /həʊld/, **holds, holding, held** /hɛld/. **1** When you **hold** something, you have your fingers or arms firmly round it. You can also **hold** things with other parts of your body, for example your mouth. EG *He was holding a bottle of milk... I held the picture up to the light... He held her in his arms.* V+O : USU+A

▸ used as a noun. EG *She resumed her hold on the rope.* ▸ N SING

● If you **hold tight**, you hold something very firmly, especially so that you do not fall. ● PHRASE

2 If you **hold** someone or **hold** them prisoner, you keep them as a prisoner. EG *I was held overnight in a cell.* V+O : USU+A; ALSO V+O+C

3 If you **hold** your body or part of your body in a particular position, you keep it in that position. EG *Etta held her head back... Mrs Patel held herself erect.* V+O+A OR V-REFL+A

4 If you **hold** power or office, you have it. EG *...one of the greatest Prime Ministers who ever held office.* V+O

5 If you **hold** a qualification, licence, or other official document, you have it. V+O

6 If you **hold** an event such as a meeting or a party, you organize it and it takes place. EG *He had promised he would hold elections in June.* V+O

7 If you **hold** a conversation with someone, you talk with them. V+O

8 If something **holds** a particular quality or characteristic, it has it. EG *These legends hold a romantic fascination for many Japanese... We will have to see what the future holds.* V+O

9 If you **hold** a particular opinion or belief, you have it. EG *People who hold this view are sometimes dismissed as cranks... Marxists hold that people are all naturally creative.* V+O OR V+REPORT : ONLY *that*

10 You can also use **hold** to say that you consider someone or something to have a particular quality. For example, if you **hold** someone responsible for something, you consider them responsible for it. EG *The government is destroying every institution and value they hold dear.* V+O+A OR V+O+C

11 If someone asks you to **hold** the line when you have made a telephone call, they are asking you to wait until they can connect you. V+O OR V

12 If you **hold** someone's interest or attention, you do or say something which keeps them interested. V+O

13 If a group of fighters **hold** a place, they prevent it from being captured. V+O

14 Something that **holds** something else keeps it fixed or supported in position. EG *There was just a rail holding it... There were tremendous pillars holding up high ceilings.* V OR V+O

15 If something **holds** a particular amount of something, it can contain that amount. EG *The theatre itself can hold only a limited number of people.* V+O

16 If an offer or invitation still **holds**, it is still available for you to accept. V

17 If your luck **holds** or if the weather **holds**, it remains good. EG *If my luck continues to hold, I think I've got a fair chance.* V

18 The **hold** of a ship or aeroplane is the place where cargo or luggage is stored. N COUNT

19 If you have a **hold** over someone, **19.1** you know something about them that you can use in order to make them do something for you. N SING+*over* **19.2** you have power or control over them. EG *The party tightened its hold on the union.* N SING : OFT+*on/over*

20 If you take **hold** of something, you put your hand tightly round it. EG *She took hold of my wrist... He still had hold of my jacket.* N UNCOUNT : OFT+*of*

21 When something takes **hold**, it starts to have a great effect. EG *Then the fire took hold.* N UNCOUNT

22 If you **get hold of** something or someone, you manage to get them or find them. EG *Can you get hold of a car this weekend?* PHRASE

23 Hold is also used in these phrases. **23.1** If you say to people **'Hold it'** or **'Hold everything'**, you are telling them to stop what they are doing. **23.2** If you **hold still** or **hold steady**, you do not move. EG *'Oh! do hold still!' she cried.* **23.3** If you **hold** your **own**, you are not defeated by someone or do not do worse than them. EG *She was still able to hold her own with the Prime Minister.* PHRASES

hold against. If someone has done something wrong and you **hold** it **against** them, you treat them more severely because they did it. EG *His refusal to cooperate will be held against him.* PHRASAL VB : V+O+PREP

hold back. 1 If you **hold back** or if something **holds** you **back**, you hesitate before you do something because you are not sure whether it is the right thing to do. EG *Police have held back from going into such a holy place.* PHRASAL VB : V-ERG+ADV **2** If you **hold** someone or something **back**, you prevent them from advancing or increasing. EG *If she is ambitious, don't try to hold her back... The rise in living standards has been held back for so long.* V+O+ADV **3** If you **hold** something **back**, you do not tell someone the full details about something. V+O+ADV

hold down. If you **hold down** a job, you manage to keep it. EG *He was surprised to find her holding down a successful job in high finance.* PHRASAL VB : V+O+ADV

hold off. 1 If you **hold off** something such as an army, you prevent it from coming too close to you. PHRASAL VB : V+O+ADV **2** If the rain **holds off**, it does not rain although you had expected it to. V+ADV

hold on. 1 If you **hold on**, you put or keep your hand firmly round something. EG *He tried to pull free but she held on tight.* PHRASAL VB : V+ADV **2** If you ask someone to **hold on**, you are asking them to wait for a short time. EG *Hold on a moment, please.* V+ADV, OFT+A

hold onto. If you **hold onto** something, **1** you put or keep your hand firmly round it. EG *He has to hold onto something to steady himself.* PHRASAL VB : V+PREP **2** you keep it. EG *Politicians want to hold on to power at all costs.* V+PREP

hold out. 1 If you **hold out** your hand or something that you have in your hand, you move it away from your body, usually towards someone. EG *'John?' Esther held out the phone.* PHRASAL VB : V+O+ADV **2** If you **hold out** for something, you want it and refuse to accept anything else. EG *Women all over the country are holding out for more freedom.* V+ADV, OFT+*for* **3** If you **hold out**, you manage to resist an enemy or opponent. EG *I can't hold out forever.* V+ADV

hold up. 1 If someone or something **holds** you **up**, they delay you. EG *The whole thing was held up about half an hour.* PHRASAL VB : V+O+ADV **2** If you **hold up** something as being good or bad, you mention it to other people in order to influence their opinions. EG *Their ways are held up to scorn... What do you hold up to the children as being desirable goals?* V+O+ADV+A **3** See also **hold-up**.

hold with. If you do not **hold with** something, you do not approve of it. EG *...a man who did not hold with these notions.* PHRASAL VB : V+PREP, WITH BROAD NEG

holdall /həʊldɔːl/, **holdalls.** A **holdall** is a large bag in which you carry things. N COUNT

holder /həʊldə/, **holders.** A **holder** is **1** a container in which you put an object, usually in order to protect it or to keep it in place. EG *The cup was held in a brown plastic holder.* N COUNT : OFT+SUPP **2** someone who owns something or has control of it. EG *I require the licence number and the full name of the holder... ...ticket-holders.* **3** someone who has a particular opinion. EG *...holders of anti-government opinions.*

holding /həʊldɪŋ/, **holdings. 1** If you have a **holding** in a company, you own shares in it. EG *We should sell the government holding in British Gas.* N COUNT+SUPP

2 A **holding** is also an area of farm land which is rented or owned by the person who cultivates it. EG *78 per cent of holdings are below 5 hectares.* N COUNT

3 You use **holding** to describe a temporary action ADJ CLASSIF : ATTRIB which is intended to prevent a situation from becoming worse. EG *The rest of the campaign was a holding operation.*

hold-up, hold-ups. A **hold-up** is 1 a situation in which someone is threatened with a weapon in order to make them hand over money. EG *...the victim of a masked hold-up.* 2 something which causes a delay. EG *He may be delayed by some hold-up in the department... ...traffic hold-ups.* N COUNT

hole /həʊl/, **holes, holing, holed. 1** A **hole** is **1.1** a hollow space in something solid, with an opening on one side. EG *What do you recommend for filling holes and cracks?... ...a deep hole in the ground.* **1.2** an opening in something that goes right through it. EG *He was wearing grey socks with holes in them.* N COUNT

2 If you **pick holes in** an argument or theory, you find weak points in it. EG *...when someone really picks holes in their argument.* PHRASE Informal

3 You can describe an unpleasant place as a **hole**. EG *Why don't you leave this awful hole and come to live with me.* N COUNT Informal

4 If a building or a ship **is holed**, holes are made in it by guns or other weapons. EG *The buildings were holed by shells.* V+O : USU PASS

hole up. If you **hole up** somewhere, you hide yourself there. EG *San Francisco was where she holed up.* PHRASAL VB : V+ADV+A Informal

holiday /hɒlɪdɪ³/, **holidays, holidaying, holidayed.** A **holiday** is **1** a period of time during which you are relaxing and enjoying yourself away from home. EG *I went to Marrakesh for a holiday... Remember to turn off the gas when you go on holiday.* N COUNT OR N UNCOUNT **2** a period of time during which you are not working or attending school, college, or university. EG *New Year's Day is a national holiday.* ● See also **bank holiday**. N COUNT OR N UNCOUNT

holiday camp, holiday camps. A **holiday camp** is a place which provides holiday accommodation and entertainment for large numbers of people. N COUNT

holidaymaker /hɒlɪdɪ³meɪkə/, **holidaymakers.** A **holidaymaker** is a person who is away from home on holiday. EG *The sundeck was crowded with holidaymakers.* N COUNT

holiness /həʊlɪnɪ²s/. **1 Holiness** is the state or quality of being holy and dedicated to God. EG *She could feel the holiness of the place.* N UNCOUNT

2 You use expressions such as **Your Holiness** and **His Holiness** when you are addressing or referring to the Pope or to leaders of some other religions.

holler /hɒlə/, **hollers, hollering, hollered.** If you **holler**, you shout or weep loudly. EG *You should have heard him holler!... 'Fishing?' she hollered. 'On Sunday?'* V : OFT+QUOTE Informal American

hollow /hɒləʊ/, **hollows, hollowing, hollowed. 1** Something that is **hollow** has a hole or space inside it. EG *...a hollow tube... ...a large hollow container.* ADJ CLASSIF

2 A surface that is **hollow** or **hollowed** curves inwards or downwards. EG *...a lean, hollow-cheeked man... ...a cadaverous face, hollowed by illness.* ADJ QUALIT

3 A **hollow** is an area that is lower than the surrounding surface. EG *Davis hid in a hollow surrounded by bracken.* N COUNT

4 A situation or opinion that is described as **hollow** has no real value, worth, or effectiveness. EG *Their independence is hollow... His outward optimism rang hollow.* ◇ **hollowness.** EG *...the hollowness of his victory.* ADJ QUALIT Formal ◇ N UNCOUNT +SUPP

5 If someone gives a **hollow** laugh, they laugh in a way that shows that they do not really find something funny. ◇ **hollowly.** EG *He laughed hollowly. 'And what a mess we made of that!'* ADJ CLASSIF : ATTRIB ◇ ADV

6 A **hollow** sound goes on for some time after it has been made, like an echo. ◇ **hollowly.** EG *His footsteps sounded hollowly on the uncarpeted stairs.* ADJ QUALIT ◇ ADV

hollow out. If you **hollow** something **out**, you remove the inside part of it. EG *The kids had hollowed out tunnels through the maize.* PHRASAL VB : V+ADV

holly /hɒli¹/ is a kind of small evergreen tree with hard, prickly leaves and red berries. N UNCOUNT

holocaust /hɒləkɔːst/, **holocausts.** A **holocaust** is very great destruction and loss of life, especially in war or by fire. EG *He claimed that the world was about to be consumed in a nuclear holocaust.* N COUNT OR N UNCOUNT

hologram /hɒlə⁶græm/, **holograms.** A **hologram** is a three-dimensional photographic image created by laser beams. N COUNT

holster /həʊlstə/, **holsters.** A **holster** is a holder for a gun, which is worn on a belt round someone's waist or on a strap below their arm. N COUNT

holy /həʊli¹/, **holier, holiest. 1** Something that is **holy** relates to God or to a particular religion. EG *...holy pictures and statues.* ADJ QUALIT

2 Someone who is **holy** leads a pure and good life which is dedicated to God or to a religion. ADJ QUALIT

homage /hɒmɪdʒ/ is a way of behaving towards someone which shows that you respect or honour them very much. EG *The young soldiers gathered to pay homage to the new heroes.* N UNCOUNT : USU+*to*

home /həʊm/, **homes, homing, homed. 1** Your **home** is **1.1** the place where you live and feel that you belong. EG *The old man wants to die in his own home... ...a normal home life... He stayed at home to care for the children.* N UNCOUNT OR N COUNT **1.2** the area or country where you were born or where your home is. EG *For most English children, home is a town or city... My own home town is thousands of miles away.* N UNCOUNT

2 Home means to or at the place where you live. EG *I want to go home... Here we are, home at last.* ADV AFTER VB

3 You can use **at home** to refer to things that happen in your own country, rather than in a foreign country. EG *Newspapers both at home and abroad ignored the incident.* PHRASE

4 If you are **at home** in a particular situation, you feel comfortable and relaxed in it. EG *I felt at home at once, because I recognized familiar faces.* ● If you say to a guest **'Make yourself at home'**, you are inviting them to feel relaxed in your home. EG *Make yourself at home. I'll be back in half an hour.* PHRASE ● CONVENTION

5 Home also means relating to your own country rather than to foreign countries. EG *The government had promised to maintain an expanding home market.* ADJ CLASSIF : ATTRIB

6 If you **make** your **home** somewhere, you start living there. EG *Tramps have made their homes in warehouses on the river bank.* PHRASE

7 When someone **leaves home**, they leave their parents' home and go to live somewhere else. PHRASE

8 A **home** is also a building where people who cannot look after themselves live and are looked after by other people. EG *...a children's home... ...a home for the elderly.* N COUNT : USU+SUPP

9 The **home** of something is the place where it began or where it is found. EG *...that home of free enterprise, the United States.* N SING+SUPP

10 If you **bring** or **drive** something **home to** someone, you make them understand how important or serious it is. EG *We must bring home to everyone the dangers of any other course of action... He raised his voice to drive home the point.* PHRASE

11 A **home** game is played on your team's own ground. EG *They watched every single game, home or away.* ADJ CLASSIF : ATTRIB

12 See also **homing**.

home in. If a missile **homes in** on something, it finds it. EG *It can thus home in on the target with pinpoint accuracy.* PHRASAL VB : V+ADV+PREP

home-brew is beer made in someone's home rather than in a brewery. N UNCOUNT

homecoming /həʊmkʌmɪŋ/, **homecomings.** Your **homecoming** is your return to your home or your country after you have been away for a long N COUNT OR N UNCOUNT

If you are homesick, do you need a holiday?

time. EG *There were 120,000 people at his homecoming.*

home economics is a subject studied at school and college in which students are taught how to run a house well and efficiently. N UNCOUNT

home ground, home grounds. 1 If you are **on home ground**, **1.1** you are near where you live and so know where you are. **1.2** you are discussing a subject that you know about. PHRASE

2 A sports team's **home ground** is their own playing field. N COUNT

home-grown fruit and vegetables have been grown in your own garden, area, or country. ADJ CLASSIF

home help, home helps. A **home help** is a person employed by a local government authority to help people who are old or ill with their housework. N COUNT

homeland /həʊmlə3nd/, **homelands.** Your **homeland** is your native country. N COUNT

homeless /həʊmlɪ2s/. **1** If people are **homeless**, they have nowhere to live. EG *Floods in north-eastern India made 233,000 people homeless.* ADJ CLASSIF

◇ **homelessness.** EG *For a growing number of young people, homelessness is becoming a way of life.* ◇ N UNCOUNT

2 You can refer to people who are homeless as **the homeless**. EG *We were running homes for the homeless.* N PLURAL : the+N

homely /həʊmli1/. **1** If something is **homely**, it is simple and ordinary. EG *We stayed in the Hotel Claravallis, a homely and comfortable establishment.* ADJ QUALIT

2 If someone is **homely**, they are not very attractive to look at. EG *Paul is a homely, shy, stammering boy.* ADJ QUALIT American

home-made. Something that is **home-made** has been made in somebody's home, rather than in a shop or factory. EG *...homemade bread.* ADJ CLASSIF

homeopath /həʊmi1ə6pæθ/, **homeopaths;** also spelled **homoeopath.** A **homeopath** is someone who treats illness by homeopathy. N COUNT

homeopathy /həʊmi1ɒpəθi1/; also spelled **homoeopathy. Homeopathy** is a way of treating illness in which the patient is given very small amounts of drugs. N UNCOUNT ◇ **homeopathic** /həʊmi1ə6pæθɪk/. EG *...homeopathic remedies.* ◇ ADJ CLASSIF

homeowner /həʊməʊnə/, **homeowners.** A **homeowner** is someone who owns their own home. N COUNT

homesick /həʊmsɪk/. If you are **homesick**, you are feeling unhappy because you are away from home. EG *The smell of the grass made her homesick for her parents' farm.* ADJ QUALIT ◇ **homesickness.** EG *...a sudden spasm of homesickness.* ◇ N UNCOUNT

homespun /həʊmspʌn/. Beliefs, opinions, or comments that are **homespun** are simple and uncomplicated. EG *They believed in simple living and homespun virtues.* ADJ CLASSIF

homestead /həʊmstɛd/, **homesteads.** A **homestead** is a farmhouse and the land around it. N COUNT American

home truth, home truths. Home truths are unpleasant facts that you learn about yourself, usually from someone else. N COUNT : USU PLURAL

homeward /həʊmwəd/ means going towards home. EG *The tank blew up on its homeward journey.* ADJ CLASSIF : ATTRIB ▸ **Homeward** or **homewards** is also used as an adverb. EG *The time had come to drive the goats homewards.* ▸ ADV AFTER VB

homework /həʊmwɜ:k/ is **1** work that teachers give to pupils to do at home. EG *He never did any homework and he got terrible results in school.* **2** research that someone does, usually in preparation for a written article or speech. EG *Aiken did his homework and worked out a convincing commercial case.* N UNCOUNT

homicidal /hɒmɪsaɪdə0l/. Someone who is **homicidal** is likely to kill someone. EG *...homicidal maniacs.* ADJ CLASSIF

homicide /hɒmɪsaɪd/, **homicides. Homicide** is the crime of murder. EG *...countries where theft and homicide are unknown today.* N UNCOUNT OR N COUNT American

homily /hɒmɪli1/, **homilies.** A **homily** is a speech in which someone complains about something or tells people how they ought to behave. EG *We listened to her homily about the rising cost of living.* N COUNT Formal

homing /həʊmɪŋ/. **1** A weapon that has a **homing** system is able to guide itself to a particular position. EG *Even small missiles have built-in homing devices.* ADJ CLASSIF : ATTRIB

2 An animal that has a **homing** instinct has the ability to remember and return to a place where it has been in the past. ADJ CLASSIF : ATTRIB

homoeopath /həʊmi1ə6pæθ/. See **homeopath.**

homogeneity /hɒmə6dʒɪni:ɪ1ti1, həʊ-/ is the quality of being homogeneous. EG *...emphasis on the unity of the nation and the homogeneity of society.* N UNCOUNT : USU+SUPP

homogeneous /hɒmə6dʒi:nɪəs, həʊ-/. A thing or group that is **homogeneous** has parts or members which are all the same. EG *The working class is not very homogeneous.* ADJ QUALIT

homogenous /həmɒdʒənəs/ means the same as homogeneous. ADJ QUALIT

homosexual /həʊmə6sɛksjʊ0əl, hɒm-/, **homosexuals.** Someone who is **homosexual** is sexually attracted to someone of the same sex. ADJ CLASSIF ▸ used as a noun. EG *...clubs and bars for homosexuals.* ▸ N COUNT

◇ **homosexuality** /həʊmə6sɛksju:ælɪti1, hɒm-/. EG *...the reform of the laws on homosexuality.* ◇ N UNCOUNT

honest /ɒnɪst/. **1** Someone who is **honest** about something is completely truthful about it and does not hide anything. EG *At least you're honest about why you want the money... To be perfectly honest, up until three weeks ago I had never set foot in a nightclub... Not all scientists are as honest as Pasteur was.* ADJ QUALIT ◇ **honestly.** EG *Philip had answered them honestly.* ◇ ADV

2 You say **'honest'** to emphasize that you are telling the truth. EG *It's true as I'm sitting here, Mabel, honest it is.* ADV SEN Informal

3 Someone who is **honest** does not cheat or break the law and can be trusted with money and other valuable things. EG *He's very honest in money matters.* ADJ QUALIT ◇ **honestly.** EG *If he couldn't get rare shrubs honestly, he would steal them.* ◇ ADV

4 Some people say **'honest to God'** or **'honest to goodness'** to express annoyance or impatience. EG *Honest to God, how can you believe such rubbish?* ADV SEN Outdated

honestly /ɒnɪ2stli1/. You use **honestly 1** to emphasize that you are telling the truth. EG *He didn't honestly think he would miss them... I'll go if you like. I don't mind, honestly.* ADV OR ADV SEN **2** to indicate that you are annoyed or impatient. EG *Honestly, Flora, this is getting ridiculous.* CONVENTION OR ADV SEN

honesty /ɒnɪ2sti1/ is the quality of being honest. EG *I sat quietly admiring Claudia's honesty.* N UNCOUNT ● If you say something **in all honesty**, you are being completely truthful. EG *In all honesty he had to admit that he was glad.* ● ADV SEN

honey /hʌni1/. **1 Honey** is a sweet sticky yellowish substance that is made by bees. EG *...tea sweetened with honey.* N UNCOUNT

2 You can call someone **honey** as a sign of affection. EG *Hi there, honey.* VOCATIVE American

honeybee /hʌni1bi:/, **honeybees.** A **honeybee** is a bee that makes honey. N COUNT

honeycomb /hʌni1kəʊm/, **honeycombs.** A **honeycomb** is a wax structure made by bees. It contains lots of six-sided holes where the bees store honey. N COUNT OR N UNCOUNT

honeyed /hʌnɪd/. If someone speaks **honeyed** words or speaks with a **honeyed** voice, what they say is soft and pleasant to listen to. EG *She was soothed by his honeyed words.* ADJ CLASSIF

honeymoon /hʌnɪmu:n/, **honeymoons.** A **honeymoon** is **1** a holiday taken by a man and a woman who have just got married. EG *They spent their* N COUNT *honeymoon at Petersburg, Florida.* **2** a period of time after the start of a new job or new government when everyone is pleased with the person or people concerned. EG *The honeymoon period is over.*

honeysuckle /hʌnɪsʌkə^{0}l/ is a climbing plant with sweet-smelling flowers. N UNCOUNT

honk /hɒŋk/, **honks, honking, honked.** If you **honk** the horn of a vehicle or if it **honks**, it produces a short loud sound. V-ERG

honor /ɒnə/. See **honour**.

honorable /ɒnə^{0}rəbə^{0}l/. See **honourable**.

honorary /ɒnə^{0}rəri^1/. **1** An **honorary** title or **honorary** membership of a group is given to someone for a special reason without them needing to have the qualifications that are usually necessary. EG *...an honorary degree.* ADJ CLASSIF : ATTRIB

2 An **honorary** job is an official job that is done without payment. EG *...the honorary Treasurer.* ADJ CLASSIF : ATTRIB

honour /ɒnə/, **honours, honouring, honoured;** spelled **honor** in American English. **1 Honour** is a feeling of pride that you have when you behave in the best way so that people admire or respect you. EG *A debt is a thing of family honour... He was able to withdraw from the battle with honour.* N UNCOUNT

2 An **honour** is a special award or job that is given to someone. EG *It was a richly deserved honour.* N COUNT

3 If you describe something that has happened to you as an **honour**, you mean that you are very pleased and proud about it. EG *He is one of the most interesting people I have had the honour of meeting... She did me the honour of attending my exhibition.* N SING Formal

4 If something is arranged **in** your **honour**, it is arranged specially for you. EG *I arranged to give a party in her honour.* PHRASE

5 If something is arranged **in honour of** an event, it is arranged to celebrate the event. EG *The ceremony was held in honour of the Queen's birthday.* PREP

6 You address a judge in court as **your honour**. EG *Is there any evidence of this, your honour?* VOCATIVE American

7 Honours is a type of university degree which is of a higher standard than an ordinary degree. EG *...a first class honours degree in French.* N UNCOUNT British

8 If you **do the honours** at a social occasion, you pour drinks for people or serve food. PHRASE Informal

9 If you **honour** someone, **9.1** you give them public praise or a medal because they have done something good or brave. EG *The people came to honour their leader... In 1949, he was honoured by the Grand Cross.* **9.2** you treat them with special attention and respect. ◇ **honoured.** EG *Rose was the honoured guest.* V+O ◇ ADJ CLASSIF : ATTRIB

10 If you **honour** an arrangement or promise, you keep to it and do not change your mind. EG *The government has solemn commitments and must honour them.* V+O Formal

honourable /ɒnə^{0}rəbə^{0}l/; spelled **honorable** in American English. **1** Someone or something that is **honourable** is honest and worthy of respect. EG *...an honourable man... Major Vane had always tried to do the honourable thing.* ◇ **honourably.** EG *He served his master honourably until his death.* ADJ QUALIT ◇ ADV

2 Honourable is used as part of a title. EG *...the Honourable Miss Sparrow.* ADJ CLASSIF : ATTRIB

hood /hʊd/, **hoods.** A **hood** is **1** a part of a coat or cloak which you pull up to cover your head. EG *He held both sides of the parka hood closed against the snow.* **2** a covering on a vehicle or a piece of equipment, which is usually curved and can be moved. EG *...a pram which had its hood folded down.* **3** the bonnet of a car. N COUNT American

hooded /hʊdɪ^{2}d/. **1** A **hooded** piece of clothing has a hood. EG *...a hooded duffel coat.* ADJ CLASSIF : ATTRIB

2 Someone with **hooded** eyes has large eyelids that are partly closed. ADJ CLASSIF : ATTRIB

hoodwink /hʊdwɪŋk/, **hoodwinks, hoodwinking, hoodwinked.** If you **hoodwink** someone, you trick or deceive them. EG *He is too often hoodwinked by flashy external appearances.* V+O

hoof /hu:f/, **hoofs** or **hooves** /hu:vz/. The **hooves** of an animal such as a horse are the hard parts of its feet. N COUNT : USU PLURAL

hook /hʊk/, **hooks, hooking, hooked. 1** A **hook** is a bent piece of metal or plastic that is used for holding things. EG *Howard hangs up his coat on the hook behind the door... ...curtain hooks.* N COUNT

2 If you **hook** one thing onto another, you attach it there using a hook. EG *One after the other they were hooked to the moving cable.* • See also **hooked**. V+O+A

3 If you **hook** your arm, leg, or foot round an object, you place it like a hook round the object in order to move it or hold it. EG *She hooked her foot under a cane stool, drawing it nearer.* V+O+A

4 Hook is used in these phrases. **4.1** If you take the phone **off the hook**, you take the receiver off the part that it normally rests on, so that the phone will not ring. **4.2** If someone **gets off the hook**, they manage to get out of a difficult or dangerous situation. EG *He felt he had got off the hook perhaps too easily.* PHRASES

hook up. If you **hook up** a computer or other electronic machine, you connect it to other similar machines or to a central power supply. • See also **hook-up**. PHRASAL VB : V+O+ADV, USU PASS

hook and eye, hooks and eyes. A **hook and eye** is a small metal hook and bar that together form a fastening for clothes such as dresses or skirts. N COUNT

hooked /hʊkt/. **1** Something that is **hooked** is shaped like a hook. EG *...huge hooked claws.* ADJ CLASSIF

2 A **hooked** nose is large and curved. ADJ CLASSIF

3 If you are **hooked** on something, **3.1** you like it or enjoy it so much that it takes up a lot of your interest and attention. EG *They're the sweetest kids ever. I'm really hooked on those kids.* **3.2** you are addicted to it. EG *...hooked on heroin.* ADJ PRED : OFT+*on*

hooker /hʊkə/, **hookers.** In American English, a **hooker** is a prostitute; an offensive use. N COUNT Informal

hook-up, hook-ups. A **hook-up** is an electronic or radio connection between computers, satellites, or radios. N COUNT

hooligan /hu:lɪgən/, **hooligans.** A **hooligan** is a young person who behaves in a noisy and violent way in public places. ◇ **hooliganism** /hu:lɪgənɪzə^{0}m/. EG *...football hooliganism.* N COUNT ◇ N UNCOUNT

hoop /hu:p/, **hoops.** A **hoop** is a large ring made of wood, metal, or plastic. EG *...boys holding hoops, kites, and marbles.* ◇ **hooped** /hu:pt/. EG *...hooped earrings.* N COUNT ◇ ADJ CLASSIF

hooray /hə^{4}reɪ/. People sometimes shout **'Hooray!'** when they are very happy and excited. EXCLAM

hoot /hu:t/, **hoots, hooting, hooted. 1** If you **hoot** the horn on a vehicle or if it **hoots**, it makes a loud noise. EG *Tug boats hooted at it... He hoots the horn.* ▸ used as a noun. EG *I heard a hoot and saw Martin driving by.* V OR V-ERG ▸ N COUNT

2 If you **hoot**, you make a loud high-pitched noise, for example when you are laughing. EG *They pointed and hooted with enjoyment.* ▸ used as a noun. EG *At this Etta gave a hoot of laughter.* V : USU+A Literary ▸ N COUNT

3 When an owl **hoots**, it makes a sound like a long 'oo'. EG *Outside, an owl hooted among the pines.* ▸ used as a noun. EG *He heard the hoot of an owl.* V ▸ N COUNT

hooter /hu:tə/, **hooters. 1** A **hooter** on a car or other vehicle is a device such as a horn or a siren. N COUNT

2 In British English, you can refer to someone's nose as their **hooter**, especially if it is very large. N COUNT Informal

hoover /hu:və/, **hoovers, hoovering, hoovered. 1** A **Hoover** is a vacuum cleaner. EG *There was no Hoover for the carpets.* N COUNT Trademark

2 If you **hoover** a carpet, you clean it using a V OR V+O

Find two things that make the same sort of noise, and two noises that they make.

vacuum cleaner. EG *She began the daily round of washing and hoovering.*

hooves /hu:vz/ is a plural of **hoof.**

hop /hɒp/, **hops, hopping, hopped. 1** If you **hop**, you move along jumping on one foot. ▸ used as a noun. EG *They began jumping up and down together in short hops.* V: USU+A ▸ N COUNT

2 When birds and some small animals **hop**, they move in small jumps using both feet together. EG *A hare hopped straight into the doorway.* ▸ used as a noun. EG *...a bird so heavy that it could make only short, low hops through the brush.* V: USU+A ▸ N COUNT

3 If you **hop** somewhere, you move there quickly or suddenly. EG *He hopped out of bed... Let's hop in my car and drive out there.* V+A Informal

4 Hops are flowers that are dried and used for making beer. EG *...the hop gardens of Sussex.* N COUNT: USU PLURAL

5 Someone who is **hopping mad** is very angry or annoyed. PHRASE Informal

hope /həʊp/, **hopes, hoping, hoped. 1** If you **hope** that something is true or will happen, you want it to be true or to happen and usually believe that it is possible. EG *She hoped she wasn't going to cry... I sat down, hoping to remain unnoticed... He paused, hoping for evidence of interest... I hope I didn't wake you... 'You haven't lost the ticket, have you?' - 'I hope not.'* V+REPORT: ONLY *that*; ALSO V+*to*-INF OR *for*

2 Hope is a feeling of confidence that what you want to happen might happen. EG *She never completely gave up hope... Do you see any cause for hope for a settlement?... ...his hopes of a reconciliation.* N UNCOUNT OR N COUNT

3 If there is a **hope** of something desirable happening, there is a chance that it will happen. EG *Technical co-operation is the only hope for progress... There is no hope of regular employment as an agricultural labourer.* N SING+SUPP

4 Hope is also used in these phrases. **4.1** If you **hope for the best**, you hope that everything will happen in the way that you want it to. **4.2** If you do something **in the hope** of achieving a particular thing, you do it because you hope to achieve that thing. EG *Tourists were waiting outside the palace in the hope of getting a look at the king.* **4.3** If you **hold out hope**, you tell someone that what they want to happen might happen. **4.4** If something **raises** your **hopes**, it gives you a stronger feeling that what you want to happen will happen. EG *The new agreement raised hopes for conditions of prosperity.* PHRASES

hopeful /həʊpfʊl/, **hopefuls. 1** If you are **hopeful**, you are fairly confident that something that you want to happen will happen. EG *He sounded hopeful that she would come.* ADJ QUALIT

2 Something that is **hopeful** gives you the feeling that what you want to happen will happen. EG *...the most astonishing and hopeful results.* ADJ QUALIT

3 If you refer to someone as a **hopeful**, you mean that they have an ambition that they want to achieve and that there is a possibility that they will achieve it. EG *Almost a hundred hopefuls stood in a queue outside the theatre.* N COUNT

hopefully /həʊpfəli[1]/. **1** If you do something **hopefully**, you do it in a way which shows that you are fairly confident that what you want to happen will happen. EG *He smiled hopefully in their direction.* ADV

2 You say **hopefully** when mentioning something that you hope and are fairly confident will happen. Some careful speakers of English think that this use of **hopefully** is not correct, but it is very frequently used. EG *The new legislation, hopefully, will lead to some improvements.* ADV SEN

hopeless /həʊplɪ[2]s/. **1** If you feel **hopeless**, you feel desperate because there seems to be no possibility of comfort or success. EG *I walked away in an agony of hopeless grief and pity.* ◊ **hopelessly.** EG *She shook her head hopelessly.* ◊ **hopelessness.** EG *...the hopelessness of the poor.* ADJ QUALIT ◊ ADV ◊ N UNCOUNT

2 Something that is **hopeless** is certain to fail or to be unsuccessful. EG *I knew my love was as hopeless as ever... The situation was hopeless.* ADJ CLASSIF

3 If someone is **hopeless** at something, they do it very badly. EG *He was hopeless at games.* ADJ QUALIT Informal

4 You use **hopeless** to emphasize how bad an event or situation is. EG *Her room is in a hopeless muddle.* ◊ **hopelessly.** EG *She was hopelessly impulsive.* ADJ CLASSIF: ATTRIB ◊ SUBMOD

horde /hɔ:d/, **hordes.** A **horde** is a large crowd of people. EG *...hordes of screaming children... ...rioting hordes.* N COUNT OR N PART

horizon /həraɪzə[0]n/, **horizons. 1** The **horizon** is the line in the far distance where the sky seems to touch the land or the sea. EG *...the smoke on the horizon.* N COUNT

2 If you say that something is **on the horizon**, you mean that it is almost certainly going to happen or appear soon. EG *A new type of drug is on the horizon.* PHRASE

3 Your **horizons** are the limits of what you want to do or of what you are interested or involved in. EG *...the spontaneous expansion of human horizons.* N COUNT: USU PLURAL

horizontal /hɒrɪzɒntə[0]l/. Something that is **horizontal** is flat and level with the ground, rather than at an angle to it. EG *...horizontal stripes.* ◊ **horizontally.** EG *The lower branches spread out almost horizontally.* ADJ CLASSIF ◊ ADV

hormone /hɔ:məʊn/, **hormones.** A **hormone** is a chemical that is produced in your body. EG *...the male hormone testosterone.* ◊ **hormonal** /hɔ:məʊnə[0]l/. EG *...hormonal changes.* N COUNT ◊ ADJ CLASSIF

horn /hɔ:n/, **horns. 1** The **horn** on a car or other vehicle is the thing that makes a loud noise as a signal or warning; also used of the button that you press in order to operate it. See picture at CAR. EG *A car passed him at top speed, sounding its horn.* N COUNT

2 Horns are the hard pointed things that stick out of the heads of cows, deer, and some other animals. EG *...the horns of a bull.* N COUNT: USU PLURAL

3 Horn is the hard substance that the horns of animals are made of. People use horn to make objects such as spoons or ornaments. N UNCOUNT

4 A **horn** or a **French horn** is a brass musical instrument that you play by blowing into it. It consists of a long metal tube wound round in a circle with a funnel at one end. N COUNT

horn-rimmed /hɔ:n rɪmd/ spectacles have plastic frames that look as though they are made of horn. EG *She wore enormous horn-rimmed glasses.* ADJ CLASSIF

horoscope /hɒrəskəʊp/, **horoscopes.** Your **horoscope** is a forecast of events that will happen to you in the future. Horoscopes are based on the position of the stars when you were born. N COUNT

horrendous /hə[7]rɛndəs/. Something that is **horrendous** is very unpleasant and shocking. EG *...the horrendous murder of a prostitute.* ADJ QUALIT

horrible /hɒrə[1]bə[0]l/. **1** Something that is **horrible** **1.1** is very unpleasant. EG *The hotel was horrible... I've never had such a horrible meal.* **1.2** causes you to feel great shock, fear, and disgust. EG *...an imaginary torture, perhaps, but all the more horrible.* ◊ **horribly.** EG *The man had begun to scream horribly.* ADJ QUALIT Informal ◊ ADV

2 You use **horrible** to emphasize how bad something is. EG *Everything's in a horrible muddle... I've got a horrible suspicion this thing won't work.* ◊ **horribly.** EG *I am horribly timid... Everything has gone horribly wrong.* ADJ QUALIT: ATTRIB ◊ SUBMOD Informal

horrid /hɒrɪd/. **1** Something that is **horrid** is very unpleasant. EG *Tea always tastes horrid out of Thermos flasks... ...a horrid little flat.* ADJ QUALIT Informal

2 If you describe a person as **horrid**, you mean that they behave in a very unpleasant way. EG *...her horrid parents... I don't mean to be horrid to you.* ADJ QUALIT Informal

horrific /hə[7]rɪfɪk/. Something that is **horrific** is so unpleasant that people are horrified and shocked by it. EG *It was one of the most horrific experiences of my life.* ADJ QUALIT

horrify /hɒrɪfaɪ/, **horrifies, horrifying, horrified.** If you **are horrified** by something, it makes you feel very alarmed and upset. EG *He was horrified by their poverty... Both Mr Faulds and his daughter were horrified at the proposal.* V+O: USU PASS

◊ **horrifying.** EG *...horrifying stories... ...brutal beatings and horrifying torture sessions.* ◊ ADJ QUALIT

horror /hɒrə/, **horrors. 1 Horror** is a strong feeling of alarm caused by something extremely unpleasant. EG *The boys shrank away in horror... These policies arouse in many people a horror and an anger that cannot be suppressed.* N UNCOUNT

2 If you have a **horror** of something, you are afraid of it or dislike it strongly. EG *Despite a horror of violence, John allowed himself to be drafted into the army.* N SING: a+N+of

3 You can refer to extremely unpleasant experiences as **horrors**. EG *Sometimes his mind would dwell on the horrors he had been through.* N COUNT: USU PLURAL

4 If you talk about the **horror** of something unpleasant, you are emphasizing that it is very unpleasant. EG *They will never forget the blood and horror of the battle.* N SING: the+N+of

5 A **horror** film or story is intended to be very frightening and is often about ghosts, witches, or imaginary monsters. N MOD

hors d'oeuvre /ɔːdɜːv/, **hors d'oeuvres. Hors d'oeuvres** are dishes of cold food that you eat before the main course of a meal. N COUNT: USU PLURAL

horse /hɔːs/, **horses.** A **horse** is a large animal which you can ride. Some horses are used for pulling ploughs and carts. EG *He was seen riding a horse through the streets of London.* N COUNT

horseback /hɔːsbæk/. If you are **on horseback**, you are riding a horse. EG *The crowds were dispersed by policemen on horseback.* PHRASE

horseman /hɔːsmə^{3}n/, **horsemen. 1** A **horseman** is a man who is riding a horse. N COUNT

2 If you say that a man is a good **horseman**, you mean that he can ride a horse well. N COUNT: ADJ+N

horseshoe /hɔːsʃuː/, **horseshoes.** A **horseshoe** is a piece of metal shaped like a U which is fixed to a horse's hoof. N COUNT

horticulture /hɔːtɪkʌltʃə/ is the study and practice of growing flowers, fruit, and vegetables. N UNCOUNT

◊ **horticultural** /hɔːti^{1}kʌltʃərəl/. EG *...the Royal Horticultural Society.* ◊ ADJ CLASSIF

hose /həʊz/, **hoses, hosing, hosed. 1** A **hose** is a long, flexible pipe made of rubber or plastic, along which water is carried. N COUNT

2 If you **hose** something, you wash it or spread water on it using a hose. EG *Hose the soil well immediately after planting rose bushes.* V+O

hose down. If you **hose** something **down**, you clean it using a hose. EG *Could you not get the sanitation department to hose the place down?* PHRASAL VB: V+O+ADV

hosiery /həʊzɪ^{0}əri^1/ is garments such as tights and stockings that are for sale in a shop. N UNCOUNT Formal

hospice /hɒspɪs/, **hospices.** A **hospice** is a hospital where dying people receive special care. N COUNT

hospitable /hɒspɪtəbə^{0}l, hɒspɪt-/. If you are **hospitable**, you are friendly and welcoming to guests or strangers. EG *Mr Steinberg was a good-natured and hospitable man... She behaved in a generous and hospitable fashion.* ADJ QUALIT

◊ **hospitably.** EG *'You must have a drink!' cried Bill hospitably.* ◊ ADV

hospital /hɒspɪtə^{0}l/, **hospitals.** A **hospital** is a place where sick people are looked after by doctors and nurses. EG *I was working at the hospital... ...a psychiatric hospital... I used to visit him in hospital.* N COUNT OR N UNCOUNT

hospitality /hɒspɪtæli^{1}ti^1/ is friendly, welcoming behaviour towards guests or strangers. EG *I thanked him for his hospitality.* N UNCOUNT

hospitalize /hɒspɪtəlaɪz/, **hospitalizes, hospitalizing, hospitalized.** If someone **is hospitalized**, they are sent to hospital. EG *She contracted pneumonia and had to be hospitalized.* V+O: USU PASS American

◊ **hospitalization** /hɒspɪtəlaɪzeɪʃə^{0}n/. EG *...the first 60 days of hospitalization.* N UNCOUNT

host /həʊst/, **hosts. 1** The **host** at a party is the person who has invited the guests. EG *Drinks were being prepared by the host... We ended up having a tremendous row with our host.* N COUNT

2 A **host** country or organization provides the facilities for an event, or gives people from another country a place to live. EG *...the attitude of the host community to the refugees... Within a week his host country had supplied him with accommodation.* N COUNT: USU N MOD

3 The **host** of a radio or television show is the person who introduces it and talks to the people who appear in it. N COUNT

4 A **host** of things is a lot of them. EG *I'm sure the audience has a host of questions for our team of experts.* N PART Formal

hostage /hɒstɪdʒ/, **hostages.** A **hostage** is someone who has been captured by a person or organization and who may be killed or injured if people do not do what the person or organization wants. EG *An agreement was reached that freed the 52 hostages.* ● If someone **is taken hostage** or **is held hostage**, they are captured and kept as a hostage. EG *He had been taken hostage by terrorists... They are being held hostage until our demands are met.* N COUNT; ● PHRASE

hostel /hɒstə^{0}l/, **hostels.** A **hostel** is a house where people can stay cheaply for a short time. Hostels are usually owned by local government authorities or charities. N COUNT

hostess /həʊstɪ^{2}s/, **hostesses. 1** The **hostess** at a party is the woman who has invited the guests. EG *My hostess greeted me with unexpected warmth.* N COUNT

2 A **hostess** at a night club or dance hall is a woman who is paid by a man to be his companion for the evening. N COUNT

hostile /hɒstaɪl/. **1** Someone who is **hostile** is unfriendly and aggressive. EG *Frank was a reserved, almost hostile person... I was in a depressed and hostile mood.* ADJ QUALIT

2 If you are **hostile** to someone or something, you disagree with them or disapprove of them. EG *...a new government that is hostile to us.* ADJ QUALIT

3 Hostile situations and conditions make it difficult for you to achieve something. EG *...hostile weather... ...the problem of running machinery in hostile environments.* ADJ QUALIT

hostility /hɒstɪlɪ^{1}ti^1/, **hostilities. 1 Hostility** is **1.1** unfriendly and aggressive behaviour. EG *Their friendship is regarded with suspicion and hostility.* **1.2** opposition to something that you do not approve of. EG *American spokesmen made clear their hostility to the new proposals.* N UNCOUNT

2 You can refer to fighting between two countries or groups as **hostilities**. EG *Both sides wanted a cessation of hostilities.* N PLURAL Formal

hot /hɒt/, **hotter, hottest; hots, hotting, hotted. 1** Something that is **hot** has a high temperature. EG *The metal is so hot I can't touch it... ...hot water.* ADJ QUALIT

2 If it is **hot**, the temperature of the air is high. EG *...a fine, hot August day.* ADJ QUALIT

3 If you are **hot**, your body is at an unpleasantly high temperature. EG *Hot and perspiring, John toiled up the hill.* ADJ PRED

4 Food that is **hot** has a strong, burning taste caused by spices. EG *...hot curries.* ADJ QUALIT

5 If you say that someone is **hot** on something, you mean that they know a lot about it. EG *I'm not so hot on linguistic theory.* ADJ PRED: OFT+on Informal

6 Someone who has a **hot** temper gets angry very easily. ADJ QUALIT

hot up. When an event **hots up**, there begins to PHRASAL VB:

Would you expect a hostile person to give you hospitality?

house

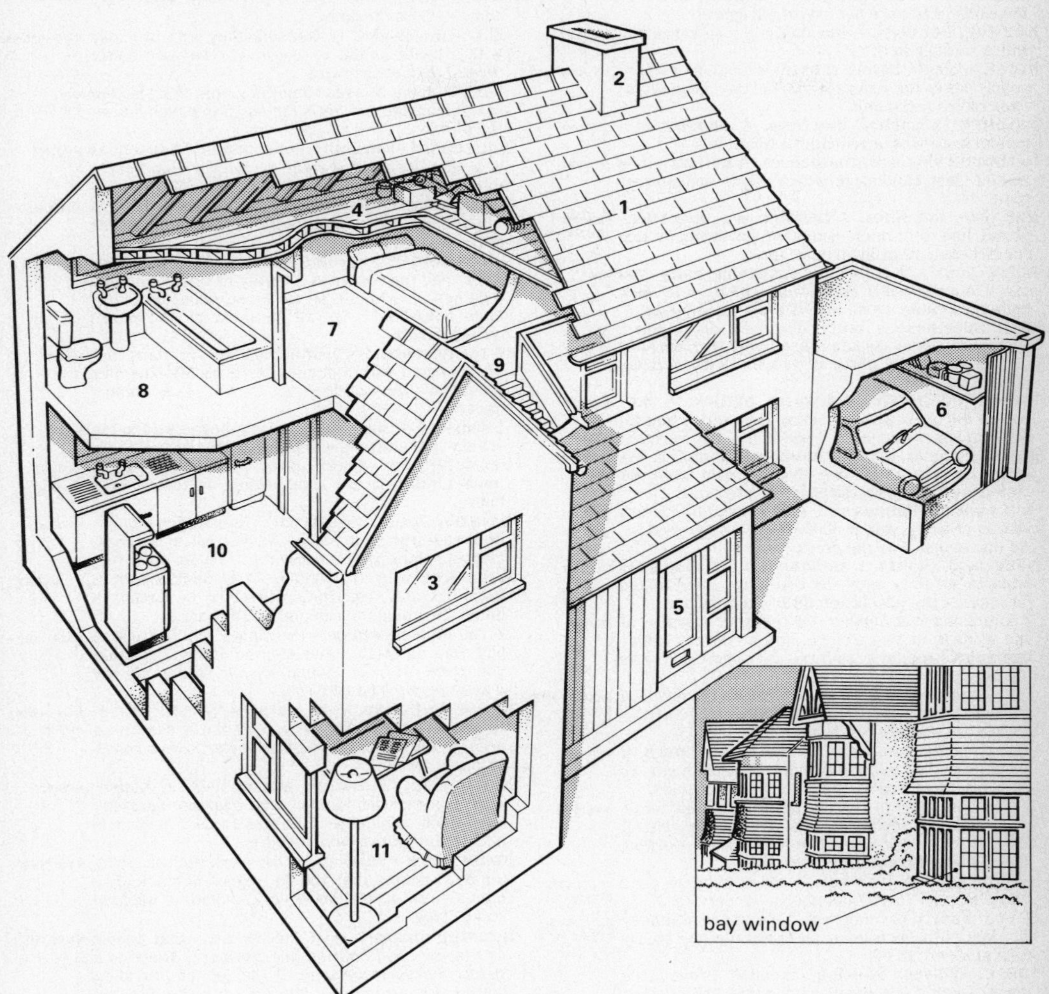

1 roof
2 chimney
3 window
4 loft
5 front door
6 garage
7 bedroom
8 bathroom
9 staircase
10 kitchen
11 sitting room/living room

be a lot of activity and excitement. EG *Now the pace really began to hot up.* — V-ERG+ADV Informal

hotbed /hɒtbɛd/, **hotbeds.** If you say that a place is a **hotbed** of a particular kind of activity, you mean that a lot of this activity happens there. EG *The universities are hotbeds of intrigue.* — N COUNT+*of*

hot dog, hot dogs. A **hot dog** is a long bread roll with a sausage in it. — N COUNT

hotel /h^{ə}ʊtɛl/, **hotels.** A **hotel** is a building where people stay, for example on holiday, paying for their rooms and meals. — N COUNT

hotelier /h^{ə}ʊtɛlɪə/, **hoteliers.** A **hotelier** is a person who owns or manages a hotel. — N COUNT

hothouse /hɒthaʊs/, **hothouses.** A **hothouse** is a heated glass building in which plants and flowers grow. — N COUNT

hot line, hot lines. A **hot line** is a direct telephone line by which heads of government can contact each other in an emergency. — N COUNT: USU *the*+N

hotly /hɒtli^{1}/. **1** If you say something **hotly**, you say it angrily. EG *'I don't mind going,' said Jack hotly... ...a claim which the USA has hotly denied.* — ADV

2 If something is **hotly** discussed or disputed, people discuss or dispute it in a lively way, because they feel strongly about it. EG *...the hotly debated question of abortion.* — ADV

hot-water bottle, hot-water bottles. A **hot-water bottle** is a rubber container which you fill with hot water and put in a bed to make it warm. — N COUNT

hound /haʊnd/, **hounds, hounding, hounded. 1** A **hound** is a type of dog that is often used for hunting or racing. EG *...large packs of hounds.* — N COUNT

2 If someone **hounds** you, they constantly disturb you or criticize you; used showing disapproval. EG *He was hounded by the press.* — V+O

hour /aʊə/, **hours. 1** An **hour** is a period of sixty minutes. EG *They slept for two hours... We talked for hours.* • See also **lunch hour**, **rush-hour**. — N COUNT

2 Something that happens **on the hour** happens at one o'clock, at two o'clock, and so on at regular intervals of one hour. EG *Buses for London leave on the hour.* — PHRASE

3 You can refer to a particular time in the day as a particular **hour**. EG *There was little traffic at this hour.* • See also **eleventh hour**. — N COUNT+SUPP Literary

4 If something happens in **the small hours**, it happens in the early morning after midnight. EG *The noise kept him awake until the small hours.* — PHRASE

5 You can refer to the period of time that something happens each day as the **hours** that it happens. EG *...our demands for shorter working hours.* • See also **opening hours**. — N PLURAL

hourly /aʊəli^{1}/. **1** An **hourly** event happens once every hour. EG *There is an hourly bus service.* — ADJ CLASSIF: ATTRIB

2 Your **hourly** earnings are the amount of money that you earn each hour. EG *Their average hourly earnings were £5.00.* — ADJ CLASSIF: ATTRIB

house, houses, housing, housed; pronounced /haʊs/ when it is a singular noun and /haʊz/ when it is a verb. The plural of the noun is pronounced /haʊzɪ^{1}z/.

1 A **house** is **1.1** a building in which people live. EG *He has a house in Pimlico... It only takes 35 minutes from my house.* • See also **boarding house**, **public house**. — N COUNT **1.2** a company, especially one which publishes books, lends money, or designs clothes. EG *...a University Publishing House.* — N COUNT+SUPP

2 If someone tells you to **set** or **put** your **own house in order**, they mean that you should arrange your own affairs properly before you tell others how to arrange theirs. • to **set up house**: see **set up**. — PHRASE

3 The group of people who make a country's laws are often referred to as a **House**. EG *...the House of Assembly... ...twenty-two members drawn from both Houses.* — N COUNT Formal

4 In a theatre or cinema, the **house** is the part where the audience sits. EG *We stood at the back of the packed house.* — N COUNT • If a performance **brings the house down**, the audience claps and cheers loudly for a long time. EG *There was one scene which never failed to bring the house down.* — • PHRASE Informal

5 If you are given something at a restaurant **on the house**, you do not have to pay for it. EG *You try some – it's on the house.* — PHRASE Informal

6 When someone **is housed**, they are provided with a house or flat to live in. EG *They are better housed than ever before.* — V+O: USU PASS

7 If a building **houses** something, that thing is kept in the building. EG *This is the building which houses the library.* — V+O Formal

houseboat /haʊsbəʊt/, **houseboats.** A **houseboat** is a small boat on a river or canal which people live in. — N COUNT

housebound /haʊsbaʊnd/. Someone who is **housebound** is unable to go out of their house because they are ill or old. — ADJ CLASSIF

household /haʊshəʊld/, **households. 1** A **household** is all the people in a family or group who live together in a house. EG *He loved being part of a huge household... Only 8 per cent of households owned a fridge.* — N COUNT

2 The **household** is your home and everything that is connected with looking after it. EG *My daughter managed the entire household... ...household chores.* — N SING

3 Someone or something that is a **household** name is very well known and often talked about. — N MOD

householder /haʊshəʊldə/, **householders.** A **householder** is the legal owner or tenant of a house. — N COUNT

housekeeper /haʊski:pə/, **housekeepers.** A **housekeeper** is a person whose job is to cook, clean and look after a house for its owner. — N COUNT

housekeeping /haʊski:pɪŋ/. **1 Housekeeping** is the work and organization involved in running a home, including the cooking and cleaning. — N UNCOUNT

2 The **housekeeping** is the money that you use to buy food, cleaning materials, and other things that you need in your home. EG *She spent all the housekeeping on a new coat.* — N SING: *the*+N

house-to-house. If the police carry out a **house-to-house** search, they search all the houses in an area. EG *We've not got the manpower to do a house-to-house check.* — ADJ CLASSIF: ATTRIB

housewife /haʊswaɪf/, **housewives.** A **housewife** is a married woman who does not normally have a job outside her home. EG *I was a housewife and mother of two small children.* — N COUNT

housework /haʊswɜ:k/ is the work such as cleaning and cooking that you do in your home. EG *The men shared all the housework, including washing and ironing.* — N UNCOUNT

housing /haʊzɪŋ/ is **1** the buildings that people live in. EG *...bad housing and poverty... There is a severe housing shortage.* **2** the job of providing houses for people to live in. EG *...the housing department.* — N UNCOUNT

housing estate, housing estates. A **housing estate** is a large number of houses or flats built close together at the same time. — N COUNT

hovel /hʌv^{ə}l, hɒv-/, **hovels.** A **hovel** is a small hut that people live in and that is in bad condition. EG *They lived in overcrowded hovels.* — N COUNT

hover /hɒvə/, **hovers, hovering, hovered. 1** When a bird or insect **hovers**, it stays in the same position in the air by moving its wings very quickly. — V

2 If someone **is hovering**, **2.1** they are waiting in one place, for example because they cannot decide what to do. EG *A figure hovered uncertainly in the doorway... His hand was hovering over the telephone.* — V: OFT+A **2.2** they are unable to make a decision

Would you like to live in a hovel?

about something. EG *We hovered between the two possibilities.*

hovercraft /hɒvəkrɑ:ft/, **hovercrafts. Hovercraft** can also be the plural form. N COUNT
A **hovercraft** is a vehicle that can travel across land and water by floating on a cushion of air.

how /haʊ/. **1** You use **how** in questions when you are asking someone about the way or manner in which something is done. EG *How did you know about this?... How did they behave towards me?* WH : ADV
2 If you talk about **how** something is done, **2.1** you are talking about the way or manner in which it is done. EG *Tell me how to get there... A lot depends on how the Americans handle the situation.* **2.2** you are talking about the fact that it is done. EG *Do you remember how you and I planned to live in Venice?* WH : CONJ
3 You use **how** **3.1** when you are asking someone whether something is or was successful or enjoyable. EG *'How did school go?' – 'It was all right.'... How was Paris?* **3.2** when you are asking about someone's health, or referring to it. EG *'How are you?' – 'Fine, thanks.'... I'm going to see how Davis is.* ● **'How do you do?'** is a polite way of greeting someone when you meet them for the first time. WH : ADV ● CONVENTION
4 You can use **how** to emphasize an adjective, adverb, or statement. EG *How pretty you look!... How I dislike that man!* WH : ADV
5 You use **how** when you are asking someone to tell you something such as a measurement or a person's age. EG *How old are you?... How far is Amity from here?* ● If you ask **how much** something is, you are asking what its price is, because you want to buy it. EG *How much is it?* WH : ADV ● PHRASE
6 You can say '**How can** you' or '**How could** you' to indicate that you are surprised at what someone has done or said. EG *'I'm bored.' – 'How can you be bored?'* PHRASE
7 You can say **how about** something or **how would you** like something when you are making a suggestion or an offer. EG *If there isn't a playgroup locally, how about starting one?... How would you fancy a few months on the continent?* PHRASE
8 You can say **'How about you?'** when you are asking someone what they think or want. EG *How about you, Dorothy, what do you want?* CONVENTION

however /haʊevə/. **1** You use **however** when you are adding a comment which is surprising or which contrasts with what has just been said. EG *I felt that I would not be sufficiently experienced. However Jenkins seemed to have confidence in me... Losing at games doesn't seem to matter to some women. Most men, however, can't stand it.* ADV SEN
2 You can use **however** to emphasize that the degree of something, for example size or effort, cannot change a situation. EG *She could not remember, however hard she tried.* WH : ADV
3 You can use **or however many** or **or however much** at the beginning of a clause to indicate that you do not know the exact quantity or size of something, and that it is not important. EG *...the twelve or eleven people on the jury or however many there are.* PHRASE Informal

howl /haʊl/, **howls, howling, howled. 1** If an animal such as a wolf or a dog **howls**, it utters a long, loud, crying sound. EG *Jackals howled among the ruins.* ◊ **howling.** EG *He could hear the howling of hyenas.* V ◊ N UNCOUNT
2 If someone **howls**, they weep loudly because they are very unhappy or in pain. EG *I put back my head and howled.* ▸ used as a noun. EG *He gave a howl of pain.* ◊ **howling.** EG *...the endless howling of their children.* V ▸ N COUNT ◊ N UNCOUNT
3 When the wind **howls**, it blows hard and makes a loud noise. ◊ **howling.** EG *...torrential rain and howling winds.* V ◊ ADJ CLASSIF
howl down. If people **howl** you **down**, they shout loudly in order to prevent you from speaking. EG *He was howled down by monarchists.* PHRASAL VB : V+O+ADV

HP is an abbreviation for 'hire purchase'.

HQ, HQs. HQ is an abbreviation for 'headquarters'.

hr, hrs. hr is a written abbreviation for 'hour'. EG *He won the Cardiff run in 2hrs 26mins 4secs... ...a 6hr sea crossing.*

HRH is an abbreviation for 'His Royal Highness' or 'Her Royal Highness'. It is used as part of the title of a prince or princess. EG *...HRH Prince Charles.*

hub /hʌb/, **hubs. 1** The **hub** of a wheel is the part which is at the centre. EG *...the hub of a bicycle wheel.* N COUNT
2 If you describe a place as the **hub** of a district, you mean that it is the most important area of the district. EG *Amity would one day be the hub of commerce on Long Island.* N COUNT+*of*

huddle /hʌdə°l/, **huddles, huddling, huddled. 1** If you **huddle** somewhere, you sit, stand, or lie there holding your arms and legs close to your body, because you are cold or frightened. EG *She huddled among the untidy bedclothes.* ◊ **huddled.** EG *In the evening he would sit huddled near the stove.* V+A ◊ ADJ CLASSIF
2 If people **huddle** together or **huddle** round something, they stand, sit, or lie close to each other, because they are cold or frightened. EG *The people huddled around their fires.* ◊ **huddled.** EG *We sat huddled together.* V+A ◊ ADJ CLASSIF
3 A **huddle** of people or things is a small group standing or sitting close together. EG *They flopped down in a huddle... ...a huddle of huts.* N COUNT

hue /hju:/, **hues.** A **hue** is a colour. EG *Mrs Partridge's face took on a deeper hue.* N COUNT Literary

huff /hʌf/, **huffs, huffing, huffed. 1** If someone is **in a huff**, they are behaving in a bad-tempered way because they are annoyed or offended. EG *The people all left in a huff.* PHRASE
2 If someone **is huffing and puffing**, they are expressing their annoyance or dissatisfaction in a silly and unnecessary way. EG *The politicians still huffed and puffed, but were ignored.* PHRASE

hug /hʌg/, **hugs, hugging, hugged. 1** When you **hug** someone, you put your arms around them and hold them tightly because you like them or are pleased to see them. EG *During our infancy, our parents cuddle and hug us... In an instant we were hugging and kissing.* ▸ used as a noun. EG *He greeted his mother with a hug.* V OR V+O : RECIP ▸ N COUNT
2 If you **hug** something, you hold it close to your body with your arms tightly round it. EG *...a basket of provisions which she hugged tight on her lap.* V+O

huge /hju:dʒ/. Something that is **huge** is extremely large in size, amount, or degree. EG *Huge wooden earrings dangled from her ears... A huge industry has been built up... Huge numbers of children are leaving school.* ◊ **hugely.** EG *...a hugely expensive machine... He was having a hugely enjoyable time.* ADJ QUALIT ◊ ADV

huh /hʌ, hə/. Some people say **'huh?'** at the end of a question. EG *'You been away, huh?' – 'Yes,' I said.* American Informal

hulk /hʌlk/, **hulks.** You can refer to something or someone that is large, clumsy, and heavy as a **hulk**. EG *Her pupils were raw-boned hulks with red hair and freckles... The Abbey is a great cross-shaped, blackish hulk.* N COUNT

hulking /hʌlkɪŋ/. A **hulking** person is extremely large and heavy. ADJ CLASSIF : ATTRIB

hull /hʌl/, **hulls.** The **hull** of a boat or ship is the main part of its body. See picture at YACHT. N COUNT

hullabaloo /hʌləbəlu:/, **hullabaloos.** If you make a **hullabaloo**, you make a lot of noise or fuss about something. EG *You can't imagine what a hullabaloo they've been making about it at College.* N COUNT Outdated

hullo /hə°ləʊ/. See **hello**.

hum /hʌm/, **hums, humming, hummed. 1** If something **hums**, it makes a low continuous noise. EG *The air-conditioning hummed.* ▸ used as a noun. EG *The only sound she heard was the hum of a machine in the basement.* V ▸ N COUNT
2 When you **hum**, you sing a tune with your lips closed. EG *I began to hum... She continued to hum the song.* V OR V+O

human body

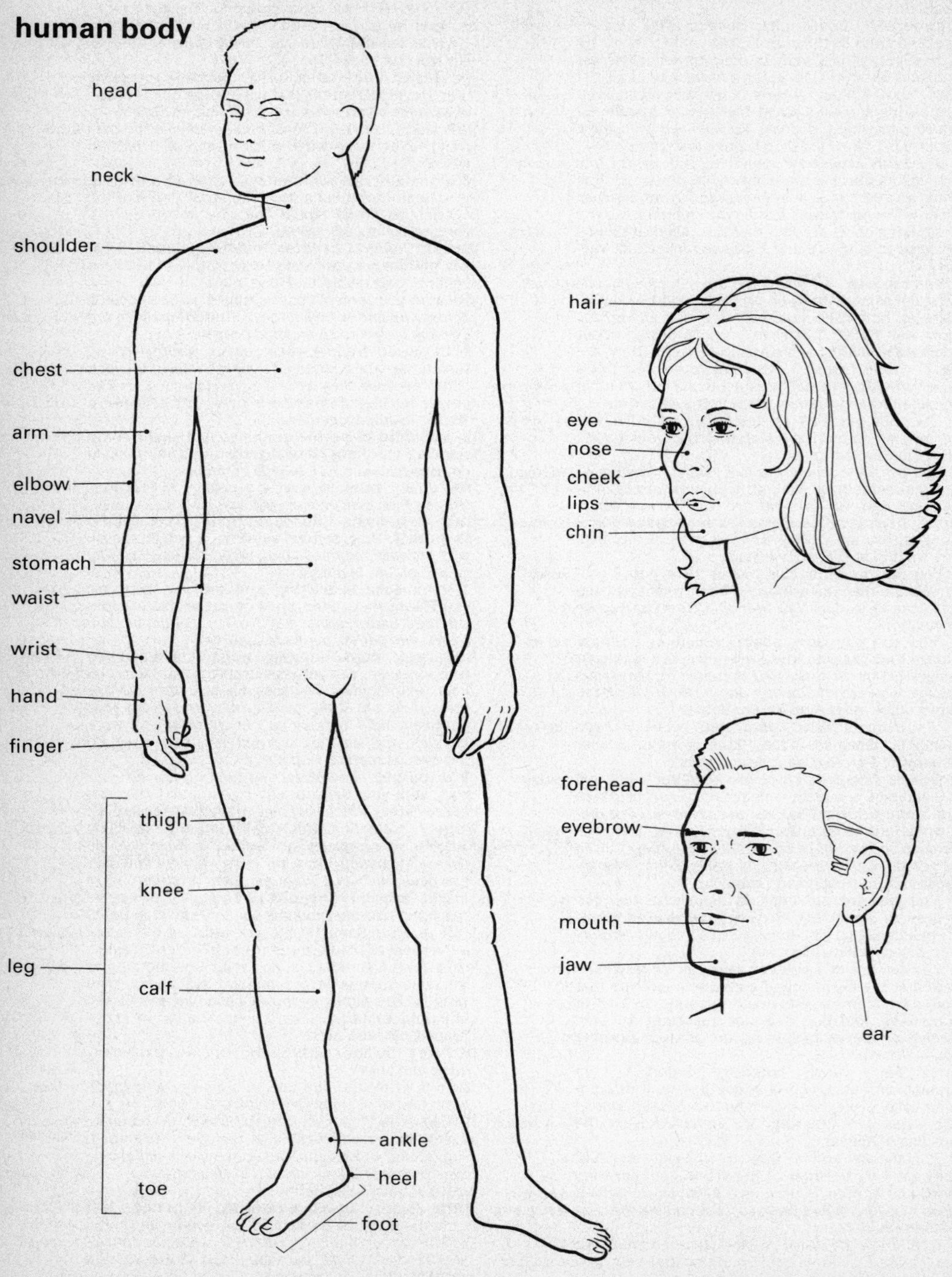
head
neck
shoulder
chest
arm
elbow
navel
stomach
waist
wrist
hand
finger
thigh
knee
leg
calf
toe
ankle
heel
foot
hair
eye
nose
cheek
lips
chin
forehead
eyebrow
mouth
jaw
ear

3 If you say that a place is **humming** with something, you mean that it is full of activity. EG *The area is usually humming with shoppers.* ADJ PRED : OFT+with

human /hju:mən/, **humans. 1 Human** means relating to or concerning people. EG *He had no regard for human life... ...the human body... ...one of the most exciting periods in human history.* ADJ CLASSIF

2 You can refer to people as **humans** when you are comparing them with animals or machines. EG *Could a computer ever beat a human at chess?* N COUNT

human being, human beings. A **human being** is a man, woman, or child. EG *A dog eats far more meat than a human being.* N COUNT

humane /hju:meɪn/. Someone who is **humane** is kind, thoughtful, and sympathetic. EG *He's one of the most humane people I have ever worked with... ...the humane treatment of psychiatric patients.* ADJ QUALIT
◊ **humanely.** EG *Animals must be killed humanely.* ◊ ADV
◊ **humaneness.** EG *...the moral necessity for humaneness towards all people.* ◊ N UNCOUNT

humanism /hju:mənɪzə⁰m/ is the belief that people can achieve happiness and fulfilment without having a religion. ◊ **humanist, humanists.** EG *...the humanist's belief in man.* N UNCOUNT ◊ N COUNT

humanitarian /hju:mænɪtɛərɪən/, **humanitarians.** A **humanitarian** is someone who works to improve the welfare of mankind and to end suffering and pain. ▸ used as an adjective. EG *...liberal and humanitarian opinions.* N COUNT ▸ ADJ CLASSIF

humanity /hju:mænɪ¹ti¹/, **humanities. 1 Humanity** is the same as mankind. EG *...a crime against humanity... ...a triumph for humanity.* N UNCOUNT

2 A person's **humanity** is their state of being a human being, rather than an animal or an object. EG *They denied him his humanity.* N UNCOUNT Formal

3 Humanity is also the quality of being kind, thoughtful, and sympathetic. EG *...a man of remarkable humanity.* N UNCOUNT

4 The **humanities** are subjects such as literature, philosophy, and history which are concerned with human ideas and behaviour. EG *She has a background in humanities and modern languages.* N PLURAL

humanly /hju:mənli¹/. If something is **humanly possible**, it is possible for people to do it. EG *People were asked to reply within twenty-four hours whenever this was humanly possible.* PHRASE

human nature is the natural qualities and ways of behaviour that most people have. EG *You can't change human nature.* N UNCOUNT

human race. You can refer to the whole of mankind as the **human race**. EG *The future of the human race might now be at stake.* N SING : the+N

human rights are the basic rights which most nations agree that all people should have. EG *...a violation of human rights.* N PLURAL

humble /hʌmbə⁰l/, **humbler, humblest. 1** Someone who is **humble** is not proud and does not believe that they are better or more important than other people. EG *We were taught to be humble, truthful, and generous... Jim bore this with humble patience.* ◊ **humbly.** EG *'You know much more about it, Sir, than I do,' said John humbly.* ADJ QUALIT ◊ ADV

2 People with low social status are sometimes described as **humble**. EG *...men and women from very humble backgrounds.* ADJ QUALIT

3 People use **humble** in expressions such as **my humble opinion** when they are expressing an opinion politely but firmly. EG *My humble opinion is that an analysis would be very useful.* ADJ QUALIT

humbug /hʌmbʌg/, **humbugs. 1** A **humbug** is a hard striped sweet that tastes of peppermint. N COUNT

2 If you describe speech or writing as **humbug**, you mean that you think it is dishonest and intended to deceive people. EG *...parliamentary humbug.* N UNCOUNT Outdated

humdrum /hʌmdrʌm/. Something that is **humdrum** is ordinary and dull. EG *...their humdrum lives.* ADJ QUALIT

humid /hju:mɪd/. In **humid** places, the weather is hot and damp. EG *...humid jungles... Singapore was dank and humid.* ADJ QUALIT

humidity /hju:mɪdɪ¹ti¹/ is dampness in the air. EG *...diseases and weeds, encouraged by heat and humidity.* N UNCOUNT

humiliate /hju:mɪlieɪt/, **humiliates, humiliating, humiliated.** If you **humiliate** someone, you do or say something that makes them feel ashamed or stupid. EG *She had humiliated him in front of his friends.* ◊ **humiliated.** EG *I could die. I feel so humiliated.* V+O ◊ ADJ QUALIT

humiliating /hju:mɪlieɪtɪŋ/. Something that is **humiliating** embarrasses you and makes you feel ashamed and stupid. EG *He said it was humiliating for him that his wife should go out to work.* ADJ QUALIT

humiliation /hju:mɪlieɪʃə⁰n/, **humiliations. 1 Humiliation** is the embarrassment that you feel when you are made to appear helpless or stupid. EG *The prisoners suffered constant public humiliation.* N UNCOUNT

2 A **humiliation** is an experience in which you are humiliated. EG *Taylor's humiliations had taken place in public.* N COUNT

humility /hju:mɪlɪ¹ti¹/. Someone who has **humility** is not proud and does not believe that they are better or more important than other people. EG *He has sufficient humility to acknowledge his own imperfections.* N UNCOUNT

humor /hju:mə/. See **humour**.

humorist /hju:mərɪst/, **humorists.** A **humorist** is an entertainer or writer who makes jokes or writes in a humorous way. N COUNT

humorous /hju:mərəs/. **1** Something that is **humorous** is amusing. EG *...humorous books.* ADJ QUALIT

2 Someone who is **humorous** is amusing and witty. EG *They were imaginative, quick, and humorous.* ◊ **humorously.** EG *They often humorously referred to themselves as caretakers.* ADJ QUALIT ◊ ADV

humour /hju:mə/, **humours, humouring, humoured;** spelled **humor** in American English.

1 Humour is the ability to see when something is funny and to say amusing things. EG *My grandmother had a kind of heavy humour... ...a great sense of humour.* N UNCOUNT

2 If something has **humour**, it is funny and makes you want to laugh. EG *She could appreciate the humour of the remark.* N UNCOUNT

3 Humour is also things that people say or write which make you laugh. EG *...the difference between English and American humour.* N UNCOUNT

4 If you are in a good **humour**, you are cheerful and behave pleasantly to people. If you are in a bad **humour**, you are unhappy and behave unpleasantly. EG *This put Etta into a good humour... The work was proceeding with efficiency and good humour... I am in a bad humour today.* N UNCOUNT +SUPP

5 If you **humour** someone who is behaving strangely or unreasonably, you try to please them, so that they will not become upset or behave unpleasantly. EG *He had bought it to humour Julie... Maybe if I humor him he'll go away.* V+O

humourless /hju:məlɪ²s/; spelled **humorless** in American English. Someone who is **humourless** is very serious about everything and does not find things amusing. ADJ CLASSIF

hump /hʌmp/, **humps, humping, humped. 1** A **hump** is a small hill or raised piece of ground. EG *...the humps and hollows of the old golf course.* N COUNT

2 A camel's **hump** is the large lump on its back. N COUNT

3 If you **hump** something heavy somewhere, you carry it there with difficulty. EG *You will probably have to hump your own luggage.* V+O Informal

humpbacked /hʌmpbækt/. A **humpbacked** animal has a hump on its back. ADJ CLASSIF : ATTRIB

hunch /hʌnt⁰ʃ/, **hunches, hunching, hunched. 1** If you have a **hunch** that something is true, you feel strongly that it is true, although you have no proof. EG *Morris had a hunch that she was a good cook... Watson frequently acted on a hunch.* N COUNT Informal

2 If you **hunch** somewhere, you draw your shoulders towards each other and lower your chin towards your chest. EG *She hunched down in her seat... I was cold as I hunched over my meagre fire.* V: USU+A
◇ **hunched.** EG *His eyes fell on Laing, hunched in a corner.* ◇ ADJ CLASSIF

hundred /hʌndrə¹d/, **hundreds. 1** A **hundred** or one **hundred** is the number 100. See the entry headed NUMBER. EG *There are more than two hundred languages spoken in Nigeria.* NUMBER
2 You can use **hundreds** to mean an extremely large number. EG *He handed me hundreds of forms.* N PART: PLURAL
3 If you say that something is **a hundred per cent** true or **a hundred per cent** accurate, you mean that it is completely true or accurate. EG *Your assessment of Otto is a hundred per cent wrong... I agree one hundred per cent with Carol.* PHRASE Informal

hundredth /hʌndrədθ/, **hundredths. 1** The **hundredth** item in a series is the one that you count as number one hundred. See the entry headed NUMBER. EG *...the hundredth anniversary of tennis championships at Wimbledon.* ORDINAL
2 A **hundredth** is one of a hundred equal parts of something. EG *...one hundredth of a second... These simple organisms are no more than one or two hundredths of a millimetre across.* N COUNT: USU+of

hundredweight /hʌndrədweɪt/, **hundredweights.** The plural can be either **hundredweight** or **hundredweights**. N COUNT OR N PART
A **hundredweight** is a unit of weight that is equal to 112 pounds in Britain and to 100 pounds in the United States. EG *The tenor bell in St Paul's Cathedral weighs sixty-two hundredweight.*

hung /hʌŋ/ is the past tense and past participle for most of the senses of **hang.**

hunger /hʌŋgə/, **hungers, hungering, hungered. 1 Hunger** is **1.1** the feeling of weakness or discomfort that you get when you need something to eat. EG *Babies show their hunger by waking up to be fed.* **1.2** a serious lack of food which causes suffering or death. EG *There were families dying of hunger and disease.* N UNCOUNT
2 If you **hunger** for or **hunger** after something, you want it very much. EG *...Spaniards who hunger for Flamenco music.* ▸ used as a noun. EG *What gives people the hunger for power?* V+for/after Formal ▸ N UNCOUNT: OFT+for

hungry /hʌŋgri¹/, **hungrier, hungriest. 1** When you are **hungry**, you want food. EG *I'm tired and hungry and I want some supper... ...a hungry baby.* ADJ QUALIT
◇ **hungrily.** EG *I ate hungrily.* ◇ ADV
2 If people **go hungry**, they suffer from hunger. EG *...sad reports of children going hungry.* PHRASE
3 If you are **hungry** for something, you want it very much. EG *They were hungry for news.* ADJ QUALIT: OFT+for

hung up. If you are **hung up** on something or **hung up** about it, you are anxious about it. EG *You're hung up about your father.* ADJ QUALIT Informal

hunk /hʌŋk/, **hunks.** A **hunk** of something is a large piece of it. EG *...a hunk of brown bread.* N PART

hunt /hʌnt/, **hunts, hunting, hunted. 1** When people **hunt**, they chase wild animals in order to kill them, either for food or as a sport. Some wild animals also **hunt** other animals for food. EG *The men had gone to the forest to hunt wild game... Hyenas usually hunt at night.* ▸ used as a noun. EG *They sighted a zebra and the hunt began.* V OR V+O ▸ N COUNT
◇ **hunting.** EG *...communities who live by hunting... ...a hunting expedition.* ◇ N UNCOUNT
2 In Britain, when people **hunt**, they chase and kill foxes as a sport. ◇ **hunting.** EG *The squire was killed in a hunting accident.* V ◇ N UNCOUNT
3 If you **hunt** a criminal or an enemy, you search for them in order to catch or defeat them. EG *Two helicopters were hunting a submarine.* V+O
4 If you **hunt** for something, you try to find it. EG *The kids hunted for treasure... She began hunting frantically in the back of the car... I'm still job hunting.* ▸ used as a noun. EG *...the hunt for the missing child.* V: USU+for ▸ N COUNT: USU SING

hunt down. If you **hunt** someone or something **down**, you succeed in finding them after you have been searching for them. EG *It was obvious that they had hunted down their victims.* PHRASAL VB: V+O+ADV

hunter /hʌntə/, **hunters. 1** A **hunter** is a person who hunts wild animals for food or as a sport. N COUNT
2 People who search for things of a particular kind are often referred to as **hunters**. EG *...bargain hunters... ...fossil hunters.* N COUNT+SUPP

huntsman /hʌntsmən/, **huntsmen.** A **huntsman** is a person who hunts wild animals, especially one who hunts foxes using dogs. N COUNT

hurdle /hɜːdə⁰l/, **hurdles. 1** A **hurdle** is a difficulty that you must overcome in order to achieve something. EG *The Government had got over their first important hurdle.* N COUNT
2 Hurdles are fences that runners jump over in some races. N COUNT

hurl /hɜːl/, **hurls, hurling, hurled. 1** If you **hurl** something, you throw it with a lot of force. EG *I took all his books and hurled them out of the window.* V+O: USU+A
2 If you **hurl** abuse or insults at someone, you shout abuse or insults at them. EG *Abuse was hurled at the police.* V+O: USU+A

hurray /hərеɪ/ and **hurrah** /hərɑː/ mean the same as hooray. CONVENTION

hurricane /hʌrɪkə⁰n, -keɪn/, **hurricanes.** A **hurricane** is an extremely violent wind or storm. EG *The island is in the path of the hurricane.* N COUNT

hurried /hʌrɪd/. Something that is **hurried** is done very quickly or suddenly. EG *...a hurried lunch... ...a hurried glance.* ◇ **hurriedly.** EG *He had dressed hurriedly.* ADJ QUALIT ◇ ADV

hurry /hʌri¹/, **hurries, hurrying, hurried. 1** If you **hurry** somewhere, you go there quickly. EG *He hurried off down the street... The people hurried home.* V: USU+A
2 If you **hurry** to do something, you start doing it as soon as you can. *They hurried to help him.* V: USU+to-INF
3 If you **hurry** someone or something, you try to make them do something more quickly. EG *Efforts to hurry them only make them angry.* V+O OR V+O+A
4 If you are in a **hurry**, you need to do something quickly. If you do something in a **hurry**, you do it quickly. EG *She was always in a hurry... Otto had to leave in a great hurry... In the middle of all this hurry, he dropped the bag.* N SING
5 Hurry is used in these phrases. **5.1** If you say to someone **'There's no hurry'** or **'I'm in no hurry'**, you are telling them that there is no need to do something immediately. EG *There's no hurry. You've got until nine o'clock.* **5.2** If you say **'What's the hurry?'**, you want to know why something must be done quickly. EG *'Drink up, Sarah!' – 'What's the hurry?'* **5.3** You can also say that you are **in no hurry** to do something when you are very unwilling to do it. EG *He was in no hurry to confront Abraham Chase.* CONVENTION Informal; CONVENTION Informal; PHRASE Informal

hurry up. If you tell someone to **hurry up**, you are telling them to do something more quickly. EG *Hurry up, it's getting late... You can hurry the process up by leaving the door open.* PHRASAL VB: V+ADV OR V+O+ADV

hurt /hɜːt/, **hurts, hurting.** The form **hurt** is used in the present tense and is also the past tense and past participle of the verb.
1 If you **hurt** yourself or **hurt** a part of your body, you injure yourself. EG *How did you hurt your finger?* V-REFL OR V+O
2 If a part of your body **hurts**, you feel pain there. EG *My leg was beginning to hurt.* V
3 If you **hurt** someone else, you cause them to feel pain. EG *Did I hurt you?... Stop it! You're hurting!* V+O
4 If you **hurt** someone or **hurt** their feelings, you make them unhappy by being unkind to them. EG V+O

If someone called you a hypocrite, would you feel hurt?

She was easily hurt by an unkindness... He didn't want to hurt her feelings.
5 If you are **hurt**, **5.1** you have been injured. EG *The soldier was obviously badly hurt.* **5.2** you are upset because of something that someone has said or done. EG *His mother was deeply hurt... ...a tone of hurt surprise.* ADJ QUALIT
6 **Hurt** is the damage to someone's feelings when they think that they have been treated badly. EG *...feelings of anger and hurt.* N UNCOUNT
7 You can say that something **hurts** someone or something when it has a bad effect on them. EG *These policies could destroy small businesses and hurt consumers.* V+O

hurtful /hɜ:tfʊl/. Something that is **hurtful** is unkind and makes you feel unhappy and upset. EG *Some of the things they say are hurtful.* ADJ QUALIT

hurtle /hɜ:tə^{0}l/, **hurtles, hurtling, hurtled.** If something **hurtles**, it moves very quickly, often in a dangerous way. EG *He didn't like hurtling along rough dirt roads at fifty miles an hour... He watched the plane as it hurtled down the runway.* V: USU+A

husband /hʌzbənd/, **husbands.** A woman's **husband** is the man she is married to. N COUNT: OFT+POSS

hush /hʌʃ/, **hushes, hushing, hushed. 1** If you say **'Hush!'** to someone, you are telling them to be quiet. CONVENTION
2 You say that there is **hush** or a **hush** when it is quiet and peaceful. EG *An expectant hush fell on the gathering.* N SING
hush up. If people in authority **hush** something **up**, they prevent the public from knowing about it. EG *The police had hushed the matter up.* PHRASAL VB: V+O+ADV

hushed /hʌʃt/. **1** A **hushed** place is quiet and peaceful. EG *We walked in silence through the hushed valley.* ADJ QUALIT Literary
2 If you say something in a **hushed** voice, you say it very quietly. EG *In the hotel lobby, people were talking in hushed tones.* ADJ QUALIT Literary

husk /hʌsk/, **husks. Husks** are the outer coverings of grains or seeds. N COUNT

husky /hʌski^{1}/, **huskier, huskiest.** If someone's voice is **husky**, it sounds rough or hoarse. ADJ QUALIT

hustle /hʌsə^{0}l/, **hustles, hustling, hustled.** If you **hustle** someone somewhere, you make them move there quickly, usually by pulling or pushing them. EG *He hustled Fanny through the door.* V+O: USU+A

hut /hʌt/, **huts.** A **hut** is **1** a small house with only one or two rooms which is usually made of wood, mud, or grass. **2** a small shed or shelter. N COUNT

hyacinth /haɪəsɪnθ/, **hyacinths.** A **hyacinth** is a plant with a lot of small, sweet-smelling flowers growing closely around a single stem. N COUNT

hybrid /haɪbrɪd/, **hybrids. 1** A **hybrid** is an animal or plant that has been bred from two different types of animal or plant. ▸ used as an adjective. EG *...hybrid roses.* N COUNT Technical ▸ ADJ CLASSIF
2 Anything that is a mixture of two different things can be called a **hybrid**. EG *...a hybrid of business and art.* ▸ used as an adjective. EG *...hybrid systems of heat storage.* N COUNT ▸ ADJ CLASSIF

hydro-electric /haɪdrəʊ ɪ^{1}lɛktrɪk/. **Hydro-electric** power is electrical power obtained from the energy of running water. *...a hydro-electric project.* ADJ CLASSIF: ATTRIB

hydrogen /haɪdrədʒə^{2}n/ is the lightest gas and the simplest chemical element in nature. Hydrogen and oxygen make water. N UNCOUNT

hygiene /haɪdʒi:n/ is the practice of keeping yourself and your surroundings clean, especially in order to prevent illness or the spread of diseases. EG *...personal hygiene.* N UNCOUNT

hygienic /haɪdʒi:nɪk/. Something that is **hygienic** is clean and unlikely to cause illness. EG *It's more hygienic to use disposable paper tissues.* ADJ QUALIT

hymn /hɪm/, **hymns.** A **hymn** is a song that Christians sing in order to praise God. N COUNT

hyper- is used to form adjectives that describe someone as having too much of a particular quality. For example, someone who is hyper-cautious is too cautious. EG *I find that a bit hypercritical... Emily is fastidious and hypersensitive.* PREFIX

hypermarket /haɪpəmɑ:kɪt/, **hypermarkets.** A **hypermarket** is a very large supermarket. N COUNT

hyphen /haɪfə^{0}n/, **hyphens.** A **hyphen** is a sign used to join words together to make compounds. The word 'left-handed' has a hyphen in the middle of it. Hyphens can also be used to indicate that the first part of a word is at the end of one line and the second part is at the beginning of the next line. N COUNT

hypnosis /hɪpnəʊsɪs/. **1 Hypnosis** is the practice or skill of hypnotizing people. N UNCOUNT
2 If you are **under hypnosis**, you have been hypnotized. EG *Is it true that a person could be made to commit a crime under hypnosis?* PHRASE

hypnotic /hɪpnɒtɪk/. Something that is **hypnotic** makes you feel as if you are hypnotized. EG *The rhythmic clapping was having a hypnotic effect on Ginny.* ADJ QUALIT

hypnotism /hɪpnətɪzə^{0}m/ is the same as hypnosis. N UNCOUNT
◇ **hypnotist, hypnotists.** EG *Some hypnotists can hypnotize people who are not prepared for it.* ◇ N COUNT

hypnotize /hɪpnətaɪz/, **hypnotizes, hypnotizing, hypnotized;** also spelled **hypnotise.**
1 If someone **hypnotizes** you, they put you into a state in which you seem to be asleep but in which you can see or hear certain things and respond to some things that are said to you. EG *I was able to hypnotize him into doing things against his own will.* V+O
2 If you **are hypnotized** by something, you are so fascinated by it that you cannot think of anything else. EG *The child was hypnotized by the machine.* V+O: USU PASS

hypochondriac /haɪpəkɒndrɪæk/, **hypochondriacs.** A **hypochondriac** is someone who continually worries about their health, often when there is nothing wrong with them. EG *He was a bit of a hypochondriac.* N COUNT

hypocrisy /hɪpɒkrəsi^{1}/ is behaviour in which someone pretends to have beliefs, principles, or feelings that they do not really have; used showing disapproval. EG *...social injustice and official hypocrisy... Many people have dismissed his criticism as hypocrisy.* N UNCOUNT

hypocrite /hɪpəkrɪt/, **hypocrites.** If you call someone a **hypocrite**, you mean that they are pretending to have beliefs, principles, or feelings that they do not really have; used showing disapproval. EG *They were nothing but a lot of hypocrites.* N COUNT

hypocritical /hɪpəkrɪtɪkə^{0}l/. If someone is being **hypocritical**, they are pretending to have beliefs, principles, or feelings that they do not really have; used showing disapproval. EG *They send you their love. It would be hypocritical of me to do the same.* ADJ QUALIT

hypodermic /haɪpədɜ:mɪk/. A **hypodermic** needle or syringe is a medical instrument with a hollow needle, which is used to inject drugs into a person's body. See picture at NEEDLES. ADJ CLASSIF

hypothesis /haɪpɒθɪ^{1}sɪs/, **hypotheses** /haɪpɒθɪ^{1}si:z/. A **hypothesis** is an idea which is suggested as a possible explanation for something, but which has not yet been proved to be correct. EG *People have proposed all kinds of hypotheses about what these things are.* N COUNT Formal

hypothetical /haɪpəθɛtɪkə^{0}l/. Something that is **hypothetical** is based on possible situations rather than actual ones. EG *Let me put a hypothetical question to you.* ADJ CLASSIF Formal

hysteria /hɪstɪərɪə/. **1 Hysteria** among a group of people is a state of uncontrolled excitement, anger, or panic. EG *...a growing climate of hysteria and racialism... ...this current hysteria about shortage of petrol.* N UNCOUNT
2 A person who is suffering from **hysteria** is in a state of violent and disturbed emotion as a result of shock. EG *...her thin shoulders shaking convulsively in hysteria.* N UNCOUNT Medical

hysterical /hɪstɛrɪkəºl/. **1** Someone who is **hysterical** is **1.1** in a state of uncontrolled excitement, anger, or panic. EG *...a mob of hysterical vigilantes... ...Farlow's hysterical letter.* **1.2** in a state of violent and disturbed emotion as a result of shock. EG *...stress leading to irrational and hysterical behaviour.* ◇ **hysterically.** EG *A man was screaming hysterically.* ADJ QUALIT; ADJ CLASSIF; ◇ ADV

2 Hysterical laughter is loud and uncontrolled. ◇ **hysterically.** EG *We laughed hysterically at their startled expressions.* ADJ CLASSIF; ◇ ADV

3 If you describe something as **hysterical**, you mean that it is extremely funny. ◇ **hysterically.** EG *...jokes which people find hysterically funny.* ADJ QUALIT; ◇ ADV+ADJ; Informal

hysterics /hɪstɛrɪks/. If someone is in **hysterics** or having **hysterics**, **1** they are in a state of uncontrolled excitement, anger, or panic. EG *If she didn't get home early, there would probably be hysterics from her mother.* **2** they are laughing loudly in an uncontrolled way. EG *The audience was in hysterics.* N PLURAL; Informal

I i

I, i /aɪ/, **I's, i's. I** is the ninth letter of the English alphabet. N COUNT

I /aɪ/ is used as the subject of a verb. A speaker or writer uses **I** to refer to himself or herself. EG *I like your dress... He and I were at school together.* PRON : SING

-ibility, -ibilities. -ibility is added in place of '-ible' at the end of adjectives to form nouns. These nouns are often not defined in this dictionary, but are treated with the related adjectives. EG *...the need to provide flexibility... ...the impossibility of any change.* SUFFIX

ice /aɪs/, **ices, icing, iced. 1 Ice** is **1.1** water that has frozen and become solid. **1.2** pieces of ice that you use to keep food or drink cool. EG *...two tall glasses of pineapple juice, soda and ice.* N UNCOUNT

2 If you **ice** cakes, you cover them with icing. V+O

3 An **ice** is an ice cream. EG *He bought ices and lollipops for the children.* N COUNT

4 If you do something to **break the ice**, you make people feel relaxed and comfortable, for example at the beginning of a party. EG *A cigarette was often the means of breaking the ice.* PHRASE

5 See also **iced, icing**.

ice over or **ice up.** If something **ices over** or **ices up**, it becomes covered with a layer of ice. EG *The road becomes treacherous when it is iced over.* PHRASAL VB : V+ADV

iceberg /aɪsbɜːg/, **icebergs.** An **iceberg** is a large, tall mass of ice floating in the sea. ● **tip of the iceberg**: see **tip**. N COUNT

ice-box, ice-boxes. An **ice-box** is a large metal container in which you store food to keep it fresh. Ice-boxes are kept cool by electricity. N COUNT; American

ice-cold. Something that is **ice-cold** is very cold indeed. EG *...ice-cold beer.* ADJ CLASSIF

ice cream, ice creams. 1 Ice cream is a very cold, sweet-tasting food. EG *For dessert there was vanilla ice cream.* N UNCOUNT

2 An **ice cream** is a portion of ice cream, usually wrapped in paper or in a container. EG *They spent all their pocket money on sweets and ice-creams.* N COUNT

ice cube, ice cubes. An **ice cube** is a small square block of ice that you put into a drink to make it cold. N COUNT

iced /aɪst/. **1** An **iced** drink has been made very cold. EG *...an iced beer.* ADJ CLASSIF : ATTRIB

2 An **iced** cake is covered with icing. ADJ CLASSIF

ice hockey is a game played on ice by two teams. Each team tries to score goals by using long sticks to hit a small, flat object called the puck into a goal. N UNCOUNT

ice lolly, ice lollies. An **ice lolly** is a piece of flavoured ice or ice cream on a stick. N COUNT

ice-skate, ice-skates, ice-skating, ice-skated. 1 Ice-skates are shoes with a metal bar attached to them that you wear when you skate on ice. N COUNT

2 If you **ice-skate**, you move about on ice wearing ice-skates. ◇ **ice-skating.** EG *I like to watch soccer and ice-skating.* V; ◇ N UNCOUNT

icicle /aɪsɪkəºl/, **icicles.** An **icicle** is a long pointed piece of ice that hangs down from a surface in cold weather. EG *Huge gleaming icicles hung halfway down her windows.* N COUNT

icing /aɪsɪŋ/. **1 Icing** is a sweet substance made from powdered sugar that is used to cover cakes as a decoration. EG *...cake covered in chocolate icing.* N UNCOUNT

2 If you describe something as **the icing on the cake**, you mean that it is an extra unnecessary detail that has been added to something. EG *All further changes are icing on the cake.* PHRASE

icon /aɪkɒn/, **icons;** also spelled **ikon.** An **icon** is a picture of Christ or of a saint painted on a wooden panel. Icons are regarded as holy by many Orthodox Christians. EG *...an icon of the face of Christ.* N COUNT

icy /aɪsi¹/. **1 Icy** air or water is extremely cold. EG *As I opened the door a gust of icy air struck me... ...an icy shower.* ADJ QUALIT

2 An **icy** road has ice on it. EG *We made our way along the icy, muddy lanes.* ADJ QUALIT

3 If someone's manner or way of speaking is **icy**, they indicate their dislike or anger in a quiet, controlled way. EG *Bowman spoke with an icy calm.* ◇ **icily.** EG *'That is quite out of the question,' said Thomas icily.* ADJ QUALIT; ◇ ADV

I'd /aɪd/ is **1** the usual spoken form of 'I had', especially when 'had' is an auxiliary verb. EG *I'd just had a letter from her.* **2** the usual spoken form of 'I would'. EG *I'd like to make my views clear.*

idea /aɪdɪə/, **ideas. 1** An **idea** is **1.1** a plan, suggestion, or possible course of action. EG *That's a good idea... I suddenly had the idea of cutting a hole in the door... It's a good idea to get some instruction... I don't like the idea of going to ask for money.* **1.2** an opinion or belief about what something is like or should be like. EG *They had many ideas on how films should be made... People had some odd ideas about village children... ...the idea of happiness... What's your idea of a good party?* N COUNT

2 If you have an **idea** of something or an **idea** that something is true, you know about it to some extent. EG *He has a good idea of how the Civil Service functions... Have you any idea how much it would cost?... My friends had an idea that something was wrong.* N SING OR N UNCOUNT +SUPP

3 If you **have no idea** about something, you do not know about it at all. EG *'How much does he earn?' – 'I've no idea.'... They'd no idea it was there.* PHRASE

4 If someone **gets the idea**, they understand how to do something or they understand what you are telling them. PHRASE; Informal

5 The **idea** of a particular course of action is its aim or purpose. EG *The idea is to try and avoid further expense.* N SING : the+N

ideal /aɪdɪəl/, **ideals. 1** An **ideal** is a principle, idea, or standard that seems perfect to you so that N COUNT you try to achieve it. EG *He believed in parliamentary democracy as an ideal... ...the ideal of marriage as a permanent bond.*

2 Your **ideal** of something is the person or thing that seems to you to be the best possible example of it. EG *He idolizes her as his feminine ideal.* N SING

3 The **ideal** person or thing for a particular purpose is the best one for it. EG *He is the ideal person for the job.* ADJ CLASSIF: OFT+*for*

4 An **ideal** society or world is the best possible kind of society or world that you can imagine. EG *That would be the simplest solution in an ideal world.* ADJ CLASSIF: ATTRIB

idealise /aɪdɪəlaɪz/. See **idealize.**

idealism /aɪdɪəlɪzə[0]m/ is the behaviour and beliefs of someone who has ideals. EG *...the idealism and action of the young people of Britain.* N UNCOUNT

◇ **idealist** /aɪdɪəlɪst/ **idealists.** EG *He was a romantic idealist, almost a dreamer.* ◇ N COUNT

idealistic /aɪdɪəlɪstɪk/. An **idealistic** person has ideals, and bases their behaviour on these ideals. EG *We need to attract idealistic young people into politics... Teachers are often very idealistic.* ADJ QUALIT

idealize /aɪdɪəlaɪz/, **idealizes, idealizing, idealized;** also spelled **idealise.** If you **idealize** someone or something, you think of them or represent them as being perfect or much better than they really are. EG *Romantic love and motherhood are sentimentally idealized.* ◇ **idealized.** EG *The boy yearned to be like his idealized father.* V+O OR V; ◇ ADJ CLASSIF

ideally /aɪdɪəli[1]/. **1** If you say that **ideally** something should happen, you mean that you would like it to happen in this way, although it may not be possible. EG *The government should ideally be run by the people... Ideally, we would like to start at the beginning.* ADV SEN

2 If you say that someone or something is **ideally** suited or **ideally** located, you mean that they are in the best possible situation or position. EG *He considered himself ideally suited for the job of Prime Minister.* ADV+PAST PART

identical /aɪdentɪkə[0]l/. Things that are **identical** are **1** exactly the same in every detail. EG *...two women in identical pinafores... Chemically, it is almost identical to limestone... India's internal structure can never be identical with Europe's.* ADJ CLASSIF

◇ **identically.** EG *All of them were identically dressed for the occasion.* ◇ ADV **2** very similar indeed. EG *The houses in this colony were all identical.* ADJ CLASSIF

identical twin, identical twins. Identical twins are twins who are the same sex and look exactly like each other. N COUNT: USU PLURAL

identifiable /aɪdentɪfaɪəbə[0]l/. Something that is **identifiable 1** can be easily recognized because it has a particular quality. EG *...a much more easily identifiable hand signal.* ADJ CLASSIF **2** can be named. EG *They were convinced that certain identifiable groups were threatening them.* ADJ QUALIT

identification /aɪdentɪfɪkeɪʃə[0]n/. **1** The **identification** of people and things is the process of recognizing or choosing them because they have a particular quality. EG *...the identification of requirements and resources.* N UNCOUNT

2 Your **identification** of a particular person or thing is your ability to name them because you know them. EG *...the identification, examination, and disposal of a dead body.* N UNCOUNT

3 If someone asks you for **identification**, they are asking you for something such as a driving licence, passport, or identity card, which proves who you are. EG *Could I ask you to show me some identification?* N UNCOUNT

4 Identification with someone or something is a feeling of sympathy and support for them. EG *These conditions gave us a strong identification with our people and our history.* N UNCOUNT +*with*

identify /aɪdentɪfaɪ/, **identifies, identifying, identified. 1** If you can **identify** someone or something, you can recognize them or name them. EG *An individual bird can identify the call of its own species... The guard had been identified as Victor Kowalski.* V+O

2 Something that **identifies** you makes you easy to recognize, because it makes you different in some way. EG *Wear on your third finger an iron ring, which will identify you.* V+O

3 If you **identify** facts, you notice them and realize that they are important. EG *The report does clearly identify the fact that there is racial inequality.* V+O

4 If you **identify** with someone or something, you feel that you understand them. EG *He couldn't identify with other people's troubles.* V+O: OFT+*with*

5 If you **are identified** with someone or something, you are very closely involved with them. EG *During the 1950's he was identified with certain radical causes.* V+O: USU PASS+*with*

6 If you **identify** one thing with another, you consider them to be the same thing. EG *If I protested he would at once identify me with his stern father.* V+O+*with* Formal

identity /aɪdentɪ[1]ti[1]/, **identities.** Your **identity** is **1** who you are. EG *I had guessed the identity of her lover... Glenn whipped off the mask to reveal his identity.* N COUNT+POSS **2** all the qualities, beliefs, and ideas which make you feel that you belong to a particular group. EG *...our identity as black people.... ...a region with its own cultural identity.* N COUNT OR N UNCOUNT

identity card, identity cards. Your **identity card** is a card that has your name, photograph, age, address, and other information on it. In some countries you have to carry an identity card in order to prove who you are. N COUNT

ideological /aɪdɪəlɒdʒɪkə[0]l/. Something that is **ideological** relates to principles or beliefs. EG *...the ideological aspects of the dispute... ...ideological assertions of national solidarity.* ADJ CLASSIF ◇ **ideologically.** EG *I was ideologically attracted to Liberalism.* ◇ ADV

ideology /aɪdi[1]ɒlədʒi[1]/, **ideologies.** An **ideology** is a set of beliefs, especially the political beliefs on which people, parties, or countries base their actions. EG *...the capitalist ideology of the West.* N COUNT +SUPP OR N UNCOUNT

idiocy /ɪdɪəsi[1]/, **idiocies.** The **idiocy** of something is the total stupidity of it. EG *...the idiocy of the plan... ...her contempt for parliamentary idiocy.* N UNCOUNT OR N COUNT Formal

idiom /ɪdɪəm/, **idioms. 1** The **idiom** of something such as speech, writing, or music is its particular style. EG *The Beatles changed for ever the idiom of popular music... ...a church in the idiom of the thirteenth century.* N COUNT+SUPP Formal

2 An **idiom** is a group of words which have a different meaning when used together from the one they would have if you took the meaning of each word individually. EG *The idiom 'ladies' man' is untranslatable into Japanese.* N COUNT

idiomatic /ɪdi[1]ə[6]mætɪk/. Language that is **idiomatic** uses words in a way that sounds natural to native speakers of the language. EG *Her English was fluent and idiomatic.* ADJ QUALIT

idiosyncrasy /ɪdi[1]ə[6]sɪnkrəsi[1]/, **idiosyncrasies.** Someone's **idiosyncrasies** are their own rather unusual habits or likes and dislikes. EG *She adjusted magnificently to her husband's many idiosyncrasies.* N COUNT

idiosyncratic /ɪdi[1]ə[6]sɪnkrætɪk/. If someone's behaviour or likes and dislikes are **idiosyncratic**, they are personal to them, and are often rather unusual. EG *...Michelangelo's highly idiosyncratic style of painting.* ADJ QUALIT

idiot /ɪdɪət/, **idiots.** If you call someone an **idiot**, you mean that you think they have done something very stupid. EG *That idiot Antonio has gone and locked our door.* N COUNT

idiotic /ɪdi[1]ɒtɪk/. If you describe someone or something as **idiotic**, you mean that they are extremely stupid. EG *It was an idiotic question to ask... It was just one of his idiotic jokes.* ADJ QUALIT

idle /aɪdə[0]l/. **1** Someone who is **idle 1.1** is not doing anything, especially when they should be doing ADJ QUALIT something. EG *A healthy child cannot be idle; he has to be doing something all day long.* ◊ **idly.** EG *...those who sit idly by while you slave over a hot stove.* ◊ ADV ◊ **idleness.** EG *No one can afford to pay troops to sit about in idleness.* ◊ N UNCOUNT **1.2** does not have a job. EG *There are 13,000 idle in a workforce of 170,000.* ADJ PRED

2 Machines or factories that are **idle** are not working or being used. EG *The machinery could not be converted, and so stood idle.* ADJ PRED

3 If you say that it is **idle** to do something, you mean that it is not worth doing it, because no useful result would be achieved. EG *It would be idle to look for a solution at this stage.* ADJ CLASSIF Formal

4 You use **idle** to describe **4.1** something that you do for no particular reason, often simply because you have nothing better to do. EG *Sudhir and Judy carried on long, idle conversations.* ADJ CLASSIF: ATTRIB ◊ **idly.** EG *She glanced idly down the list of contents.* ◊ ADV **4.2** something that someone has said or done that you do not treat seriously. EG *This is no idle bluff.* ADJ CLASSIF: ATTRIB

idle away. If you **idle away** a period of time, you spend it doing very little. EG *...three old men, idling away the summer afternoon under the trees.* PHRASAL VB: V+O+ADV

idler /aɪdlə/, **idlers.** If you call someone an **idler**, you mean that they are lazy and should be working. EG *...a state full of idlers.* N COUNT

idol /aɪdəl/, **idols.** **1** An **idol** is someone such as a film star or pop star, who is greatly admired or loved by the public. EG *...young pop idols... Django Reinhardt is evidently Chris Goddard's idol.* N COUNT

2 An **idol** is also a statue that is worshipped by people who believe that it is a god. EG *They set up stone pillars for idol worship.* N COUNT

idolatry /aɪdɒlətri/. Someone who practises **idolatry** worships idols. N UNCOUNT Formal

idolize /aɪdəlaɪz/, **idolizes, idolizing, idolized;** also spelled **idolise.** If you **idolize** someone such as a film star or pop star, you admire them or love them very much. EG *They idolize Bob Dylan.* V+O

idyll /ɪdɪl/, **idylls.** An **idyll** is a situation which is idyllic. EG *...the myth of an unchanging idyll of rural England.* N COUNT

idyllic /ɪdɪlɪk/. Something that is **idyllic** is extremely pleasant and peaceful without any difficulties. EG *...an idyllic place to raise a young child... ...an idyllic country holiday.* ADJ QUALIT

i.e. /aɪ iː/ is used to introduce a word or sentence which gives more information about the meaning of what you have just said. EG *To keep a dog costs twice as much, i.e. £110 a year.*

if /ɪf/. **1** You use **if** to mention an event or situation that might happen, might be happening, or might have happened. EG *If all goes well, Voyager 2 will head on to Uranus... If unemployment remains at present levels for a few more years, democracy could become unworkable... If any questions occur to you, then don't hesitate to write... If I could afford it I would buy a boat.* CONJ

2 You use **if** in indirect questions. EG *I asked her if I could help her... I wonder if you'd give the children a bath?* CONJ

3 You can use **if** in sentences in which you mention a possible exception to a general statement you have already made. EG *It was an excellent concert. If I had any disappointment at all it was the end.* CONJ

4 You can use **if** to introduce a comment or make a request. EG *If you don't mind my saying so, I think you are partly responsible... If you can sign that for me. Thank you.* CONJ

5 You use **if not** **5.1** to suggest that an amount, degree, or time might be even bigger, better, or sooner than the one you have mentioned. EG *They have hundreds of thousands if not millions of pounds of investment... I'd like to see you tonight, if not sooner.* **5.2** to mention a state of affairs that does not exist, when saying that a less extreme one does. EG *Her voice was, if not perfect, at least nearly so.* CONJ

6 You say **'if I were you'** to someone when you are giving them advice. EG *If I were you I'd take the money.* ADV SEN

7 You use **'if anything'** after a negative statement to say that something different is true. EG *It certainly wasn't an improvement. We were, if anything, worse off than before.* ADV SEN

8 You use **if ever** to emphasize the description of a person or thing that you are giving. EG *She was a hopeless figure if ever I saw one.* CONJ

9 You use **if only** **9.1** to introduce one reason for doing something, when you realize it may not be a very good one. EG *I'll have a glass myself, if only to stop you from drinking it all.* **9.2** to express a wish or desire, especially one that cannot be fulfilled. EG *If only she could have lived a little longer.* CONJ

10 You use **as if** **10.1** when describing the way that something is done. EG *She folded her arms as if she were cold.* **10.2** to emphasize that something is not the case, for example that something is not important. EG *He keeps worrying about what wine to buy. As if it mattered!* CONJ

igloo /ɪgluː/, **igloos.** An **igloo** is a dome-shaped house made out of blocks of snow. N COUNT

ignite /ɪgnaɪt/, **ignites, igniting, ignited.** When you **ignite** something or when it **ignites**, it starts burning or it explodes. EG *The device was supposed to ignite the fireworks.* V-ERG

ignition /ɪgnɪʃən/ **ignitions.** **1** The **ignition** in a car is the part of the engine where the fuel is ignited, and which starts the engine when you start the car; also used of the keyhole in the dashboard in which you put the key to start it. See picture at CAR. EG *Have you switched the ignition on?* N COUNT: USU SING

2 **Ignition** is the process by which a car engine is started. EG *...electronic ignition.* N UNCOUNT

ignoble /ɪgnəʊbəl/. An **ignoble** person behaves in a way that is considered dishonourable. EG *There's something cowardly and ignoble about such an attitude.* ADJ QUALIT Formal

ignominious /ɪgnəmɪnɪəs/. **Ignominious** behaviour is considered shameful or morally unacceptable. EG *The marriage was considered especially ignominious since she was of royal descent.* ADJ QUALIT Formal ◊ **ignominously.** EG *They were ignominiously defeated in the general election.* ◊ ADV

ignorant /ɪgnərənt/. Someone who is **ignorant** of something does not know about it. EG *The masses were largely ignorant of the options open to them... ...his idea that ordinary people are ignorant.* ADJ QUALIT: OFT+*of* ◊ **ignorance** /ɪgnərəns/. EG *Individuals suffer through ignorance of their rights.* ◊ N UNCOUNT: OFT+*of*

ignore /ɪgnɔː/, **ignores, ignoring, ignored.** **1** If you **ignore** someone or something that you have seen, heard, or experienced, you act as if they are not there, or as if the event has not happened. EG *Ralph ignored Jack's question... The President cannot rudely ignore any head of state who chooses to come here... I ignored him and looked at Judith.* V+O

2 If you **ignore** something that you have been advised or told to do, you deliberately do not do it. EG *The Government ignored his advice.* V+O

3 Something that **ignores** an important aspect of a situation fails to take it into account. EG *These proposals ignore the court's existing power.* V+O

ikon /aɪkɒn/. See **icon**.

ill /ɪl/, **ills.** **Worse** /wɜːs/ and **worst** /wɜːst/ are often used as the comparative and superlative of **ill** when it is an adjective or adverb.

1 Someone who is **ill** is suffering from a disease or health problem which makes them unable to work or to live normally. EG *I feel ill... Don't refreeze food. It could make you ill... She is ill with cancer.* ADJ QUALIT: USU PRED

● If you **fall ill** or **are taken ill**, you become ill ● PHRASE

Can you read something that is illegible?

suddenly. EG *She was taken ill on holiday and they had to find a doctor.*

2 Difficulties or problems can be referred to as **ills**. EG *...the necessary ills of old age... No ill had yet come to Sarah's child.* [N UNCOUNT OR N PLURAL Literary]

3 If something **bodes ill** or **augurs ill** for you, it gives you a reason to fear that something harmful might happen. EG *She had a sullen expression which might bode ill.* [PHRASE Literary]

4 You can use **ill** to describe something that is done badly. EG *The programme was ill researched.* [ADV Literary]

5 If you **speak ill of** someone, you criticize them. EG *Don't expect me to speak ill of my employer.* [PHRASE]

6 You can use **ill** to describe harmful or unpleasant things. EG *Did you get any ill effects when you had your blood transfusion?... ...protection against ill fortune and disaster.* [ADJ CLASSIF : ATTRIB]

I'll /aɪl/ is the usual spoken form of 'I will' or 'I shall'. EG *I'll ring you tomorrow morning.*

ill- is added to words, especially adjectives and past participles, to add the meaning 'badly' or 'inadequately'. For example, 'ill-written' means badly written, and 'ill-judged' means judged with insufficient care or judgement.

ill-advised. An action that is **ill-advised** is not sensible or wise. EG *It is ill-advised to attempt competition.* [ADJ QUALIT]

ill at ease. Someone who is **ill at ease** feels uncomfortable or embarrassed. EG *He was ill at ease with people whom he didn't understand.* [ADJ PRED]

illegal /ɪliːgə^{0}l/. 1 If an activity or possession is **illegal**, the law says that you are not allowed to do it or have it. EG *It is illegal in many countries for women to work on night shifts... Marijuana is illegal in the United States.* [ADJ CLASSIF] ◊ **illegally.** EG *...illegally parked cars.* [◊ ADV]

2 An **illegal** organization is one which a government says must not exist. EG *...the Haganah, the illegal Jewish defence force.* [ADJ CLASSIF]

3 An **illegal** action or system is one which breaks an international law or agreement. EG *...the illegal colonial regime.* [ADJ CLASSIF] ◊ **illegally.** EG *Their country had been illegally occupied for many years.* [◊ ADV]

4 An **illegal** immigrant is a person who has entered a country without an official permit. [ADJ CLASSIF : ATTRIB]

illegible /ɪledʒɪbə^{0}l/. Writing that is **illegible** is so unclear that you cannot read it. EG *...a suitcase with illegible labels.* [ADJ QUALIT]

illegitimate /ɪlɪdʒɪtɪmə^{1}t/. 1 A person who is **illegitimate** was born of parents who were not legally married to each other. EG *...an illegitimate child.* [ADJ CLASSIF] ◊ **illegitimacy** /ɪlɪdʒɪtɪməsi^1/. EG *Victoria was not told of her illegitimacy until she was 25.* [◊ N UNCOUNT]

2 An **illegitimate** activity is not allowed or approved of by law or social customs. EG *All parties regarded the treaty as illegitimate and not binding.* [ADJ CLASSIF]

ill-equipped. Someone who is **ill-equipped** to do something does not have the ability, the qualities, or the equipment necessary to do it. EG *The police were plainly ill-equipped to deal with the riot.* [ADJ QUALIT]

ill-fated. If you describe something as **ill-fated**, you mean that it has a tragic or unlucky outcome. EG *Alice recounted the story of her ill-fated boating expedition.* [ADJ CLASSIF]

ill-health. If you are in a state of **ill-health**, you have an illness. EG *Throughout his career he had suffered from ill-health.* [N UNCOUNT]

illicit /ɪlɪsɪt/. An **illicit** activity or substance is not allowed or not approved of by the laws and social customs of a country. EG *They were prosecuted for illicit liquor selling.* [ADJ CLASSIF : ATTRIB]

illiterate /ɪlɪtərə^{1}t/, **illiterates.** Someone who is **illiterate** does not know how to read or write. EG *40 per cent of the country is reckoned to be illiterate.* [ADJ CLASSIF] ▸ used as a noun. EG *...the teaching of adult illiterates.* [▸ N COUNT] ◊ **illiteracy** /ɪlɪtə^{0}rəsi^1/. EG *...adult illiteracy.* [◊ N UNCOUNT]

illness /ɪlnɪ^{2}s/, **illnesses.** 1 **Illness** is the experience of being ill for a period of time. EG *During his last illness we only saw him twice.* [N UNCOUNT OR N COUNT]

2 An **illness** is a particular disease that people can suffer from, such as a cold, measles, or pneumonia. EG *She died of a mysterious illness.* [N COUNT]

illogical /ɪlɒdʒɪkə^{0}l/. If a feeling or action is **illogical**, it is not reasonable or sensible, because you are not considering properly all the aspects of a situation. EG *...the illogical reactions of the male sex... It is clearly illogical to maintain such a proposition.* [ADJ QUALIT] ◊ **illogically.** EG *I felt illogically that my own years there counted for nothing.* [◊ ADV]

ill-treat, ill-treats, ill-treating, ill-treated. If someone **ill-treats** you, they treat you cruelly. EG *The man had been ill-treated in prison.* [V+O]

illuminate /ɪluːmɪneɪt/, **illuminates, illuminating, illuminated.** 1 If you **illuminate** something, you shine light on it. EG *Lamps were arranged to illuminate his work.* [V+O] ◊ **illuminated.** EG *...illuminated advertising.* [◊ ADJ CLASSIF]

2 If you **illuminate** something that is difficult to understand, you make it easier to understand by explaining it or giving examples. EG *Their doctrine illuminates much that might seem obscure in the Muslim teaching.* [V+O] ◊ **illuminating.** EG *...Basil Spence, in his illuminating book on the subject.* [◊ ADJ QUALIT]

illumination /ɪluːmɪneɪʃə^{0}n/, **illuminations.** 1 **Illumination** is the lighting that a place has. EG *The dusty bulb gave barely adequate illumination.* [N UNCOUNT]

2 **Illuminations** are coloured lights which are put up in towns, especially at Christmas, as a decoration. [N PLURAL]

illusion /ɪluːʒə^{0}n/, **illusions.** An **illusion** is 1 an idea or belief which you think is true but which is in fact false. EG *We have an illusion of freedom.* [N COUNT OR N UNCOUNT] 2 something that looks like one thing but is really another thing or is not there at all. EG *The garden through the windows was merely a clever optical illusion.* [N COUNT] 3 a magic trick in which the audience is fooled by the skill of the magician's actions. [N COUNT]

illusory /ɪluːzəri^1/. Something that is **illusory** seems to be true or possible, but is false or impossible in reality. EG *...illusory hopes that he would soon find a new job.* [ADJ CLASSIF Formal]

illustrate /ɪləstreɪt/, **illustrates, illustrating, illustrated.** 1 If you **illustrate** a point that you are making, you make it clear by using examples, stories, or diagrams. EG *The Muslims tell a story to illustrate the fact that power changes people... Nothing illustrates his selfishness more clearly than his behaviour to his wife.* [V+O]

2 If you **illustrate** a book, you put pictures or diagrams into it. [V+O] ◊ **illustrated.** EG *...illustrated books of fairy tales.* [◊ ADJ CLASSIF]

illustration /ɪləstreɪʃə^{0}n/, **illustrations.** 1 An **illustration** of a point is an example or a story which is used to make the point clear. EG *I've included a few specific examples as illustrations of the difficulty of our work.* [N COUNT : OFT+*of*]

2 An **illustration** in a book is a picture or diagram. EG *...a cookery book with marvellous colour illustrations.* [N COUNT]

3 **Illustration** is the activity or process of illustrating. EG *...evening classes in drawing and illustration.* [N UNCOUNT]

illustrative /ɪləstrətɪv/. An **illustrative** picture or action is an example or explanation of something. EG *These incidents are illustrative of the range of political actions being undertaken.* [ADJ CLASSIF Formal]

illustrator /ɪləstreɪtə/, **illustrators.** An **illustrator** is an artist who draws pictures and diagrams for books and magazines. EG *...an illustrator of children's books.* [N COUNT]

illustrious /ɪlʌstrɪəs/. An **illustrious** person is extremely well known and famous. EG *He was determined not to be outdone by his more illustrious partner... ...a long and illustrious career as a radio producer.* [ADJ QUALIT : ATTRIB]

ill-will is a feeling of hostility towards someone. EG *He assured me he felt no ill-will toward me.* [N UNCOUNT]

I'm /aɪm/ is the usual spoken form of 'I am'. EG *I'm not blaming you... I'm afraid I can't come.*

image /ɪmɪdʒ/, **images. 1** If you have an **image** of someone or something, you have a picture or idea of them in your mind. EG *To most people, the term 'industrial revolution' conjures up images of smoky steel mills or clanking machines... They feel under pressure to conform to our image of them.* N COUNT: USU+SUPP

2 The **image** of a person or organization is the way that they appear to other people. EG *His attempts to improve the Post Office's image were criticised as 'gimmicks'.* N COUNT: USU+POSS

3 An **image** is also **3.1** a picture or theme in a work of art such as a painting or a book. EG *He was one of the few painters who produced convincing images of life in contemporary America.* **3.2** a picture that you see of someone or something. EG *...a musical sound track accompanying the visual image... He began to dress, never taking his eyes off his image in the mirror.* N COUNT

imagery /ɪmɪdʒri[1]/ is **1** the mental pictures that are created in your mind by poetic language. EG *He argued that Shakespeare's plays were patterns of imagery.* **2** ideas or themes that are represented in visual art such as pictures and statues. N UNCOUNT

imaginable /ɪmædʒɪnəbə[0]l/. You use **imaginable** when referring to the most extreme example of a particular thing that you can think of. EG *...the narrowest imaginable range of interests... ...every bit of information imaginable.* ADJ CLASSIF: ATTRIB, OR ADJ AFTER N

imaginary /ɪmædʒɪnə[0]ri[1]/. Something that is **imaginary** exists only in your mind and not in real life. EG *Many children develop fears of imaginary dangers... He was playing an imaginary trumpet.* ADJ CLASSIF

imagination /ɪmædʒɪneɪʃə[0]n/, **imaginations.** Your **imagination** is **1** the ability that you have to form ideas of new or exciting things. EG *He has a marvellous imagination... These plans reveal a complete failure of imagination.* N COUNT OR N UNCOUNT **2** the part of your mind which you use to form pictures or ideas of things that do not necessarily exist in real life. EG *They are creations of our imagination.* N COUNT: USU+POSS **3** something that you think of that does not exist in real life or that never happened. EG *There's nothing there – it's just your imagination.* N UNCOUNT +POSS

imaginative /ɪmædʒɪnətɪv/. Someone who is **imaginative** is easily able to form ideas of new or exciting things in their mind. EG *...an imaginative writer... ...imaginative and original theories.* ADJ QUALIT

◊ **imaginatively.** EG *...an imaginatively designed bathroom.* ◊ ADV

imagine /ɪmædʒɪn/, **imagines, imagining, imagined. 1** If you **imagine** something, **1.1** you think about it and your mind forms a picture or idea of it. EG *Not one of us could imagine what he'd meant... Try to imagine you're sitting on a cloud... Can you imagine standing up there and giving a speech?* V+O, V+REPORT, OR V+-ING **1.2** you think that you have seen or heard something, although actually you haven't. EG *'I saw a thing on the mountain.' – 'You only imagined it.'... He imagined he saw things.* V+O OR V+REPORT

2 If you **imagine** that something is true, you think that it is true. EG *I should imagine he wants you to hold his hand... He was much more generous than people imagined.* V+REPORT: ONLY *that*, NO CONT

imbalance /ɪmbæləns/, **imbalances.** If there is an **imbalance** in a situation, things are not evenly or fairly arranged. EG *...the imbalance between the rich and poor countries.* N COUNT OR N UNCOUNT

imbecile /ɪmbɪsi:l, -saɪl/, **imbeciles.** If you call someone an **imbecile**, you are saying that you think that they are stupid; an offensive word. EG *For two years that imbecile spent his money like water.* N COUNT

imbibe /ɪmbaɪb/, **imbibes, imbibing, imbibed. 1** If you **imbibe** alcohol, you drink it. EG *He had imbibed some much stronger beers in his young days in Manchester.* V+O OR V Formal

2 If you **imbibe** ideas or arguments, you listen to them and believe that they are right or true. EG *You have been imbibing too many of their doctrines.* V+O Formal

imbue /ɪmbju:/, **imbues, imbuing, imbued.** If you **imbue** something or someone with a particular quality, you give them that quality so that they become filled with it. EG *...Mondrian's desire to imbue his art with mystical properties.* V+O ◊ **imbued.** EG *...a unified society deeply imbued with Marxist convictions.* ◊ ADJ PRED +*with*

imitate /ɪmɪteɪt/, **imitates, imitating, imitated. 1** If you **imitate** a person, group, or society, you behave in the same way as they do. EG *Other societies have begun to imitate the wastefulness of the West... The University of London imitated the German tradition of scholarship.* V+O

2 If you **imitate** a person or animal, you copy the way they speak or behave, often in order to be amusing. EG *'Sidney, you'll kill him,' he said, trying to imitate the girl's voice.* V+O

imitation /ɪmɪteɪʃə[0]n/, **imitations. 1** An **imitation** is **1.1** something which is a copy of something else. EG *Computers so far are just bad imitations of our brains.* **1.2** something that you do in order to copy the way someone else speaks or behaves. EG *'Come here, my dear,' she said, giving a reasonable imitation of Isabel Travers.* N COUNT

2 Imitation is behaviour which is modelled on someone else's behaviour. EG *Boys can be seen to pat one another on the head in imitation of what their fathers do.* N UNCOUNT

3 Imitation things are not genuine but are made to look as if they are genuine. EG *...a pocket diary bound in black imitation leather.* ADJ CLASSIF: ATTRIB

imitative /ɪmɪtətɪv/. Behaviour that is **imitative** copies someone else's behaviour. ADJ QUALIT Formal

imitator /ɪmɪteɪtə/, **imitators.** An **imitator** of someone is a person who copies them or behaves in the same way as them. EG *...successful designers and their imitators.* N COUNT

immaculate /ɪmækjə[4]lə[1]t/. Something that is **immaculate** is **1** absolutely clean or tidy. EG *Her apartment was immaculate.* ADJ CLASSIF ◊ **immaculately.** EG *Sir Oswald was immaculately dressed.* ◊ ADV **2** perfect, with no mistakes at all. EG *Your timing and technique will have to be immaculate.* ADJ CLASSIF

immaterial /ɪmətɪərɪəl/. Something that is **immaterial** is not important or not relevant. EG *The price was immaterial.* ADJ CLASSIF

immature /ɪmətjʊə, -tʃʊə/. **1** Something that is **immature** is not yet fully developed. EG *...an immature organism... ...the baby's immature digestive system.* ADJ CLASSIF

2 If you describe someone as **immature**, you mean that they are not sensible enough to behave properly. EG *I was too immature to understand.* ADJ QUALIT

◊ **immaturity** /ɪmətjʊərɪ[1]ti[1]/. EG *There were complaints about my immaturity and lack of judgement.* ◊ N UNCOUNT

immeasurable /ɪmɛʒə[0]rəbə[0]l/. An amount or distance that is **immeasurable** is too large to be measured or counted. EG *The gap between them now seems immeasurable.* ADJ CLASSIF

immeasurably /ɪmɛʒə[0]rəbli[1]/. You use **immeasurably** to emphasize that something has a particular quality to a very great extent. EG *Paul Getty had always been immeasurably wealthy.* ADV+ADJ

immediacy /ɪmi:dɪəsi[1]/. When you talk about the **immediacy** of something, you mean that it seems to be happening now or that it makes you feel directly involved with it. EG *It is the immediacy of events which makes television so popular.* N UNCOUNT Formal

immediate /ɪmi:dɪət/. **1 Immediate** means **1.1** happening without any delay. EG *They called for an immediate meeting of the Security Council... My immediate reaction was one of relief.* ADJ CLASSIF: USU ATTRIB **1.2** actually existing now, and needing to be dealt with quickly. EG *...the immediate needs of people in western* ADJ CLASSIF: ATTRIB

What is the difference between an imaginary diamond and an imitation one?

society... He was occupied with more immediate matters.

2 You use **immediate** to describe someone or something that is very near in time or position to another person or thing. EG *Charlie was more honest than his immediate predecessor... To the immediate south we can see the mountains.* — ADJ CLASSIF: ATTRIB

3 Your **immediate** family are the people who are very closely related to you, such as your parents, children, brothers, and sisters. — ADJ CLASSIF: ATTRIB

immediately /ɪmiːdɪətlɪ[1]/. **1** If something happens **immediately**, it happens without any delay. EG *I have to go to Brighton immediately. It's very urgent... She finished her cigarette, then lit another one immediately.* — ADV

2 You use **immediately 2.1** when talking about something that can be understood or used without any delay. EG *The connection was not immediately apparent.* — ADV **2.2** when talking about something that is closely and directly involved in a situation. EG *The countries most immediately threatened are those to the south.* — ADV **2.3** when talking about someone or something that is very near in time or position to another person or thing. EG *The church is immediately on your right... The sequence of events immediately preceding the tragedy is uncertain.* — ADV+PREP

3 You also use **immediately** when you are saying what happens or is done as soon as something else has happened. EG *Immediately I finish the show I get changed and go home.* — CONJ

immemorial /ɪmɪ[2]mɔːrɪəl/. **1** If something has been happening **from time immemorial**, it has been happening for longer than anyone can remember. EG *Indian villages have governed themselves from time immemorial.* — PHRASE

2 You use **immemorial** to describe something that is so old that nobody can remember a time when it did not exist. EG *...the immemorial custom of all Western societies.* — ADJ CLASSIF: ATTRIB

immense /ɪmɛns/. Something that is **immense** is extremely large. EG *Squids grow to an immense size... This development has been of immense importance.* — ADJ QUALIT

immensely /ɪmɛnslɪ[1]/ means to a very great extent or degree. EG *The issue is immensely complex... I enjoyed the course immensely.* — ADV

immensity /ɪmɛnsɪ[1]tɪ[1]/. The **immensity** of something is the very large size or extent of it. EG *...the immensity of the building.* — N UNCOUNT +SUPP

immerse /ɪmɜːs/, **immerses, immersing, immersed. 1** If you **immerse** yourself in something, you become completely involved in it. EG *That year I immersed myself totally in my work.* — V-REFL+*in*
◊ **immersed.** EG *He became immersed in the activities of the union.* — ◊ ADJ PRED ◊ **immersion** /ɪmɜːʃə[0]n/. EG *...their total immersion in European history.* — ◊ N UNCOUNT

2 If you **immerse** something in a liquid, you put it into the liquid so that it is completely covered. EG *Ebony hairbrushes shouldn't be immersed in water.* — V+O: USU+*in* ◊ **immersion.** EG *Treat sprained ankles by immersion in cold water.* — ◊ N UNCOUNT

immersion heater, immersion heaters. An **immersion heater** is an electric heater which is used to provide hot water. — N COUNT

immigrant /ɪmɪgrənt/, **immigrants.** An **immigrant** is a person who has come to live in a country from another country. EG *...a Russian immigrant... ...immigrant communities in London.* — N COUNT

immigration /ɪmɪgreɪʃə[0]n/ is **1** the coming of people into a country in order to live and work there. EG *...government controls on immigration.* — N UNCOUNT **2** the control section at a port, airport or international border, where officials check the passports of people who wish to come into the country. — N UNCOUNT

imminent /ɪmɪnənt/. Something that is **imminent** is certain to happen very soon. EG *I believed that war was imminent... ...his imminent departure.* — ADJ CLASSIF
◊ **imminence** /ɪmɪnəns/. EG *They seemed unaware of the imminence of the invasion.* — ◊ N UNCOUNT +*of*

immobile /ɪməʊbaɪl/. Someone or something that is **immobile** is **1** completely still. EG *Boylan sat immobile, staring straight ahead.* — ADJ PRED ◊ **immobility** /ɪməʊbɪlɪ[1]tɪ[1]/. EG *She had drugged herself into immobility with sleeping pills.* — ◊ N UNCOUNT **2** unable to move. EG *Sea-snakes have fangs that are short and immobile.* — ADJ CLASSIF

immobilize /ɪməʊbɪlaɪz/, **immobilizes, immobilizing, immobilized;** also spelled **immobilise. 1** If you **immobilize** something, you completely stop it from moving. EG *When you ring the alarm it immobilizes the lift.* — V+O

2 Something that **immobilizes** someone stops them from working efficiently. EG *They must cast off those bureaucratic practices that immobilize them.* — V+O

immodest /ɪmɒdɪst/. **1** Behaviour that is **immodest** shocks or embarrasses some people because they think that it is rude. EG *Breast feeding in public may seem immodest to some people.* — ADJ QUALIT

2 Someone who is **immodest** often says that they are very clever or important. EG *He said it might be immodest for him to quote the next two lines of the review.* — ADJ QUALIT

immoral /ɪmɒrəl/. If you describe someone or their behaviour as **immoral**, you mean that they are morally wrong. EG *...the cruel and immoral use of animals in medical research... ...an immoral seducer of youth.* — ADJ QUALIT ◊ **immorality** /ɪmə[7]rælɪ[1]tɪ[1]/. EG *...the immorality of apartheid.* — ◊ N UNCOUNT

immortal /ɪmɔːtə[0]l/. Someone or something that is **immortal 1** is famous and will be remembered for a long time. EG *The play contained one immortal line.* — ADJ CLASSIF ◊ **immortality** /ɪmɔ[8]tælɪ[1]tɪ[1]/. EG *You're not going to achieve immortality by writing a book like that.* — ◊ N UNCOUNT **2** lives for ever and never dies. EG *...old legends of immortal creatures.* — ADJ CLASSIF

immortalize /ɪmɔːtə[0]laɪz/, **immortalizes, immortalizing, immortalized;** also spelled **immortalise.** If someone or something **is immortalized**, for example in a book or film, they are remembered for a very long time. EG *We talked about her gangster parts immortalised on film.* — V+O: USU PASS+A

immovable /ɪmuːvəbə[0]l/. **1** Something that is **immovable** is fixed and cannot be moved. EG *...an immovable pillar.* — ADJ CLASSIF

2 Feelings or opinions that are **immovable** are firm and will not change. EG *...fossilised ways and immovable conservatism.* — ADJ CLASSIF

immune /ɪmjuːn/. **1** If you are **immune** to a particular disease, you cannot be made ill by it. EG *She thought that women might be immune to lung cancer.* — ADJ PRED+*to* ◊ **immunity** /ɪmjuːnɪ[1]tɪ[1]/. EG *Babies receive immunity to a variety of infections... ...the immunity of some crops against pests and diseases.* — ◊ N UNCOUNT: OFT+*to*/*against*

2 If you are **immune** to a situation or to people's behaviour, you are not affected by it. EG *He was immune to the flattery of political leaders.* — ADJ PRED: OFT+*to*
◊ **immunity.** EG *This immunity to criticism is built into them.* — ◊ N UNCOUNT: OFT+*to*

3 Someone or something that is **immune** from a process or situation is able to escape it. EG *...targets that the West had considered immune from air attack.* — ADJ PRED: OFT+*from* ◊ **immunity, immunities.** EG *He had been granted immunity from prosecution.* — ◊ N UNCOUNT OR N COUNT

immunize /ɪmjə[4]naɪz/, **immunizes, immunizing, immunized;** also spelled **immunise.** — V+O: OFT+*against*
If you **are immunized** against a disease, you are made immune to it, usually by being given an injection. EG *They should have their children immunised against diphtheria.* ◊ **immunization** /ɪmjə[4]naɪzeɪʃə[0]n/, **immunizations.** EG *Measles can be prevented by immunization.* — ◊ N UNCOUNT OR N COUNT

immutable /ɪmjuːtəbə[0]l/. Something that is **immutable** will never change. EG *...behaving according to a set of immutable rules.* — ADJ CLASSIF Formal

impact /ɪmpækt/, **impacts. 1** If something has an **impact** on a situation or person, it has a great effect on them. EG *...the impact of computing on* — N COUNT+SUPP *routine office work... British authors make relatively little impact abroad.*

2 Impact is **2.1** the action of one object hitting another. EG *Many modern bullets produce an explosive effect upon impact.* **2.2** the force with which one object hits another. EG *Hill 402 seemed to crumble with the impact of enemy artillery fire.* — N UNCOUNT

impacted /ɪmpæktɪ^{2}d/. An **impacted** tooth is unable to grow through your gum properly. EG *...an impacted wisdom tooth that had to be taken out.* — ADJ CLASSIF: USU ATTRIB

impair /ɪmpɛə/, **impairs, impairing, impaired.** If you **impair** something, you damage or weaken it so that it stops working properly. EG *His digestion had been impaired by his recent illness.* — V+O
◇ **impaired.** EG *...children with impaired hearing.* — ◇ ADJ CLASSIF

impale /ɪmpeɪl/, **impales, impaling, impaled.** If you **impale** something, you pierce through it with a sharp pointed object. EG *He cut off a piece of the meat and impaled it on his fork.* — V+O OR V-REFL: OFT+A Formal

impart /ɪmpɑːt/, **imparts, imparting, imparted.**
1 If you **impart** information to people, you tell it to them. EG *He had a terrible piece of news to impart.* — V+O: OFT+*to* Formal
2 If something **imparts** a particular quality, it gives that quality to another thing. EG *Peas and carrots impart a delicious flavour to stews.* — V+O Formal

impartial /ɪmpɑːʃə^{0}l/. Someone who is **impartial** is able to act fairly because they are not involved in a particular situation. EG *He gave an impartial view of the state of affairs in Northern Ireland.* — ADJ CLASSIF
◇ **impartially.** EG *These men will judge the people impartially.* — ◇ ADV
◇ **impartiality** /ɪmpɑːʃɪælɪ^{1}ti^{1}/. EG *...the impartiality of the law.* — ◇ N UNCOUNT

impassable /ɪmpɑːsəbə^{0}l/. A road or path that is **impassable** is impossible to travel over because it is blocked or in bad condition. — ADJ CLASSIF

impasse /ɒmpæs/. An **impasse** is a difficult situation in which it is impossible to make any progress. EG *The government had reached an impasse... I see no way out of this impasse.* — N SING Formal

impassioned /ɪmpæʃənd/. When you speak in an **impassioned** way, you express powerful emotion. EG *After three hours of impassioned debate the motion was defeated.* — ADJ QUALIT Formal

impassive /ɪmpæsɪv/. If your face is **impassive**, it does not show any emotion. EG *Ruth smiled her usual impassive smile and said nothing.* — ADJ CLASSIF
◇ **impassively.** EG *He looked at me impassively.* — ◇ ADV

impatient /ɪmpeɪʃənt/. **1** Someone who is **impatient 1.1** is annoyed because they have had to wait too long for something, or because they are not getting what they want. EG *He became impatient. 'Well, can you do it?'* — ADJ QUALIT
◇ **impatiently.** EG *Oliver stood waiting impatiently.* — ◇ ADV
◇ **impatience** /ɪmpeɪʃəns/. EG *Chris watched me with some impatience.* — ◇ N UNCOUNT
1.2 is easily irritated by people or situations. EG *He was very impatient with students who could not follow him.* — ADJ QUALIT: OFT+*with*
◇ **impatiently.** EG *'I know, I know,' Vaughan said impatiently.* — ◇ ADV
◇ **impatience.** EG *There was increasing impatience with the reluctance of the party to grant these reforms.* — ◇ N UNCOUNT
2 If you are **impatient** to do something or **impatient** for something to happen, you are eager to do it or for it to happen and do not want to wait. EG *Philip was impatient to inspect his place of work.* — ADJ QUALIT: OFT+*to*-INF OR *for*
◇ **impatiently.** EG *He looked forward impatiently to Kumar's next visit.* — ◇ ADV
◇ **impatience.** EG *There is always a certain impatience to try out an idea to see if it works... He was awaiting the outcome with impatience.* — ◇ N UNCOUNT +SUPP

impeccable /ɪmpɛkəbə^{0}l/. Something that is **impeccable** is perfect. EG *He had impeccable manners... He stood before them, impeccable as ever in his elegant suit.* — ADJ CLASSIF
◇ **impeccably.** EG *As usual, he was impeccably dressed.* — ◇ ADV

impede /ɪmpiːd/, **impedes, impeding, impeded.** To **impede** someone or something means to make their movement or development difficult. EG *Their advance was seriously impeded by the bad weather... ...procedures that would impede an effective investigation.* — V+O Formal

impediment /ɪmpɛdɪmə^{2}nt/, **impediments. 1** Something that is an **impediment** to a person or thing makes their movement or development difficult. EG *The new taxes were a major impediment to economic growth.* — N COUNT: OFT+*to* Formal
2 A speech **impediment** is a disability such as a stammer which makes speaking difficult. — N COUNT: USU+SUPP

impel /ɪmpɛl/, **impels, impelling, impelled.** When an emotion **impels** you to do something, it affects you so strongly that you feel forced to do it. EG *I feel impelled to express grave doubts about the project... What were the motives that impelled Geoffrey to act?* — V+O: USU+*to*-INF Formal

impending /ɪmpɛndɪŋ/. You use **impending** to describe something that is going to happen very soon. EG *We were well aware of impending disaster.* — ADJ CLASSIF: ATTRIB Formal

impenetrable /ɪmpɛnɪtrəbə^{0}l/. Something that is **impenetrable** is **1** solid and impossible to get through. EG *...an impenetrable wall... ...immense tracts of impenetrable jungle.* **2** impossible or very difficult to understand. EG *The law seems mysterious and impenetrable.* — ADJ QUALIT

> **IMPER** stands for **imperative**
> The imperative form of the verb is used when you are giving a command or making a suggestion to someone, such as *Keep off the grass* or *Come at about 6 o'clock*.
> The verb is used without inflections, and there is no need for a subject, because you are talking or writing directly to someone.
> In a verb entry some meanings have the label ONLY IMPER in the Extra Column. This means that for these meanings the imperative is normally the only form used. An example of a verb meaning labelled ONLY IMPER is **see 20**. You say *See p. 19* when you are telling readers that they should look at p. 19 for further details of something.
> Some meanings of verbs have the label NO IMPER in the Extra Column. This means that they are not normally used in the imperative. An example of a verb meaning labelled NO IMPER is **see 1**. You do not usually say to someone 'See me' although you can, of course, say 'Look at me' and 'Watch me'.

imperative /ɪmpɛrətɪv/, **imperatives. 1** Something that is **imperative** is extremely important and needs to be dealt with before anything else. EG *It's imperative that we take care of Liebermann immediately.* — ADJ QUALIT: USU PRED
► used as a noun. EG *Any species' first imperative is to survive.* — ► N COUNT Formal
2 In grammar, an **imperative** is a verb in the form that is typically used for giving orders. — N COUNT

imperceptible /ɪmpəsɛptɪbə^{0}l/. Something that is **imperceptible** happens or exists without being felt or noticed. EG *...an almost imperceptible sensation.* — ADJ CLASSIF
◇ **imperceptibly.** EG *Gradually, almost imperceptibly, the sun warmed us up.* — ◇ ADV

imperfect /ɪmpɜːfɪ^{2}kt/. **1** Something that is **imperfect** has faults or problems. EG *We live in an imperfect society... The examination system is imperfect.* — ADJ QUALIT
2 In grammar, the **imperfect** or the **imperfect** tense is used in describing continuous or repeated actions in the past. — N SING: *the*+N

imperfection /ɪmpə^{5}fɛkʃə^{0}n/, **imperfections. 1** An **imperfection** in someone or something is a fault or weakness that they have. EG *...his human* — N UNCOUNT OR N COUNT

If something is impending, when will it happen?

imperfection... Americans do not tolerate such imperfections in themselves.

2 An **imperfection** in something is a small mark or damaged area which may spoil its appearance. EG *...an imperfection on the surface.* — N COUNT

imperfectly /ɪmpɜːfɪ2ktli1/. If you do something **imperfectly**, you do not do it completely or perfectly. EG *...a world which we only imperfectly understand.* — ADV

imperial /ɪmpɪərɪəl/. 1 **Imperial** is used 1.1 to describe an empire. EG *...the decline of Britain as an imperial power.* 1.2 to describe something that relates to an emperor or empress. EG *...the Imperial Palace.* — ADJ CLASSIF : ATTRIB

2 The **imperial** system of measurement is the system where length is measured in inches, feet, and yards, weight is measured in ounces and pounds, and the volume of liquids is measured in pints and gallons. — ADJ CLASSIF : ATTRIB

imperialism /ɪmpɪərɪəlɪzə0m/ is a system of rule in which a rich and powerful country controls other countries in order to become richer and more powerful. EG *...British imperialism in India.* — N UNCOUNT

◇ **imperialist** /ɪmpɪərɪəlɪst/. EG *...the imperialist ruling classes.* — ◇ ADJ CLASSIF

imperil /ɪmperɪ1l/, **imperils, imperilling, imperilled;** spelled **imperiling** and **imperiled** in American English. — V+O Formal

Something that **imperils** you puts you in danger. EG *...a political crisis which had imperilled the future of the party.*

imperious /ɪmpɪərɪəs/. An **imperious** person is proud and expects to be obeyed. EG *All his imperious orders were obeyed.* — ADJ QUALIT Formal

imperishable /ɪmperɪʃəbə0l/. Something that is **imperishable** cannot disappear or be destroyed. EG *There was a certain quality which was imperishable.* — ADJ CLASSIF Formal

impersonal /ɪmpɜːsənə0l/. 1 A place or an activity that is **impersonal** makes you feel that you are not important and do not matter. EG *...the rules and regulations of a vast, impersonal organization... ...dull, repetitive, impersonal work.* — ADJ QUALIT

2 An **impersonal** feeling or action does not relate to any particular person. — ADJ CLASSIF ◇ **impersonally.** EG *...written examinations marked impersonally and with no knowledge of the candidate.* — ◇ ADV

impersonate /ɪmpɜːsəneɪt/, **impersonates, impersonating, impersonated.** If you **impersonate** someone, 1 you pretend that you are that person, usually by disguising yourself. EG *I ought to be arrested for impersonating an officer.* — V+O 2 you imitate them in order to be amusing or as an entertainment. EG *...Senator Johnson was brilliantly impersonated by an actor.* — V+O ◇ **impersonation** /ɪmpɜːsəneɪʃə0n/, **impersonations.** EG *...Harry's impersonation of a Russian prince.* — ◇ N COUNT OR N UNCOUNT

impertinent /ɪmpɜːtɪnənt/. Someone who is **impertinent** speaks or behaves rudely. EG *...impertinent questions.* — ADJ QUALIT ◇ **impertinence** /ɪmpɜːtɪnəns/. EG *They might be offended by such impertinence.* — ◇ N UNCOUNT

impervious /ɪmpɜːvɪəs/. 1 If you are **impervious** to someone's actions, you are not affected or influenced by them. EG *I became impervious to influence of any kind... They were impervious to any outside pressures.* — ADJ QUALIT : USU PRED+*to*

2 Something that is **impervious** to water does not allow water to pass through it. EG *The upper walls are impervious to water.* — ADJ CLASSIF : USU PRED+*to*

impetuous /ɪmpetjʊəs/. Someone who is **impetuous** acts quickly and suddenly without thinking. EG *I thought scientists were never impetuous.* — ADJ QUALIT

impetus /ɪmpɪ2təs/ is an important effect which strongly influences a situation and causes something to happen. EG *The present conflict might provide fresh impetus for peace talks.* — N UNCOUNT +SUPP Formal

impinge /ɪmpɪndʒ/, **impinges, impinging, impinged.** Something that **impinges** on you has an effect on you, often by restricting the way that you can behave. EG *Your political opinions will necessarily impinge on your public life.* — V+*on/upon* Formal

implacable /ɪmplækəbə0l/. Someone who is **implacable** has a strong feeling of anger, disapproval, or resentment that you are unable to change. EG *...our most implacable opponent... ...the implacable hatred that workers feel for their employers.* — ADJ QUALIT

◇ **implacably.** EG *They are implacably hostile.* — ◇ ADV

implant, implants, implanting, implanted; pronounced /ɪmplɑːnt/ when it is a verb, and /ɪmplɑːnt/ when it is a noun.

1 If someone **implants** something into a person's body, they put it there by means of an operation. EG *They implanted electrodes in the skull of a bull.* — V+O : OFT+*in/into*

2 An **implant** is something that is implanted into a person's body. EG *...hormone implants.* — N COUNT

3 If you **implant** an idea or attitude in people, you make it become accepted or believed. EG *...parents requiring teachers to implant religious attitudes in their children.* — V+O : OFT+*in/into*

implausible /ɪmplɔːzə1bə0l/. Something that is **implausible** is not easy to believe, and therefore unlikely to be true or genuine. EG *It's an extremely likeable but very implausible romantic thriller.* — ADJ QUALIT

implement, implements, implementing, implemented; pronounced /ɪmplɪ1mə2nt/ when it is a verb, and /ɪmplɪ1mənt/ when it is a noun.

1 If you **implement** a plan, system, or law, you carry it out. EG *...policies that they would like to see implemented in the next parliament.* — V+O

◇ **implementation** /ɪmplɪ1mə2nteɪʃə0n/. EG *...the implementation of the desired reforms.* — ◇ N UNCOUNT

2 An **implement** is a tool or other piece of equipment. EG *...producing basic agricultural implements for underdeveloped areas.* — N COUNT

implicate /ɪmplɪkeɪt/, **implicates, implicating, implicated.** If you **implicate** someone in an unpleasant event or situation, you show that they have been involved in it. EG *He was implicated in the horrendous murder of a teacher.* — V+O : OFT PASS+*in*

implication /ɪmplɪkeɪʃə0n/, **implications.** 1 An **implication** is something that is suggested or implied by a particular situation, event, or statement. EG *Spencer began to query the political implications of Macaulay's statement.* — N COUNT

2 If something appears to be the case **by implication**, you think that it is probably true because of another fact that you have just mentioned. *Many are saying her policies have failed and, by implication, so has she.* — PHRASE

implicit /ɪmplɪsɪt/. 1 Something that is **implicit** is expressed in an indirect way. EG *...advertisements containing implicit racial prejudice... Although it wasn't spoken, it was implicit in her attitude that she thought I had failed.* — ADJ CLASSIF ◇ **implicitly.** EG *Nobody questioned the implicitly accepted dogma.* — ◇ ADV

2 If you have an **implicit** belief or faith in something, you believe it completely and have no doubts about it. — ADJ QUALIT ◇ **implicitly.** EG *I believe implicitly in the concept of Europe.* — ◇ ADV

implore /ɪmplɔː/, **implores, imploring, implored.** If you **implore** someone to do something, you desperately beg them to do it. EG *She telephoned me to implore me to come.* — V+O+*to*-INF OR V+QUOTE Formal

imply /ɪmplaɪ/, **implies, implying, implied.** 1 If you **imply** that something is true, you suggest that it is true without actually saying so. EG *At one point she implied she would marry me... In Malta this gesture implies heavy sarcasm.* — V+REPORT OR V+O ◇ **implied.** EG *...implied criticism.* — ◇ ADJ CLASSIF

2 When one situation **implies** another, it suggests that the second situation is true as a consequence of the first one being true. EG *All these requirements imply a reduction in government spending... These discoveries imply that the sea-bed is rich in fossil fuels.* — V+O OR V+REPORT ONLY *that*

impolite /ɪmpəlaɪt/. Someone who is **impolite** is rather rude and offends people. EG *It was very impolite of him to ask.* — ADJ QUALIT

import, imports, importing, imported; pronounced /ɪmpɔːt/ when it is a verb, and /ɪmpɔːt/ when it is a noun.

1 If you **import** goods or services, you buy them from another country and have them sent to your own country. EG *The government had an interest in importing scientific equipment... ...imported sugar.* V+O

▸ used as a noun. EG *The import of cotton goods went up sharply in 1859.* ▸ N UNCOUNT ◊ **importation** /ɪmpɔːteɪʃə^{0}n/. EG *...the illegal importation of drugs into Britain.* ◊ N UNCOUNT

2 An **import** is a product or raw material which you buy from another country for use in your own country. EG *They blamed the closure on cheap imports and the recession.* N COUNT

important /ɪmpɔːtənt/. 1 Something that is **important** is very significant, valuable, or necessary. EG *This is the most important part of the job... It is important to get on with your employer and his wife... Your child's health is more important than the doctor's feelings.* ADJ QUALIT ◊ **importantly.** EG *The problems the Chinese face differ importantly from those facing Africa.* ◊ ADV ◊ **importance** /ɪmpɔːtəns/. EG *Here I would stress the importance of mathematics to the whole of science... ...an attempt to assess Stonehenge's historic importance.* ◊ N UNCOUNT +SUPP

2 Things that are **important** to you have great significance for you and you consider them very seriously. EG *I realize how important it is for me to have a job... It was important to me to know.* ADJ QUALIT

3 Someone who is **important** has influence or power. EG *He wasn't anyone important in the firm... ...the list of important people who are coming on state visits.* ADJ QUALIT ◊ **importance.** EG *Was he related to anyone of importance?* ◊ N UNCOUNT

importer /ɪmpɔːtə/, **importers.** An **importer** is a person, country, or firm which buys goods or services from another country for use in its own country. EG *Many western countries have ceased to be major food importers.* N COUNT

impose /ɪmpəʊz/, **imposes, imposing, imposed.**

1 If you **impose** something on people, you use your authority to force people to accept it. EG *She was a harsh mother and imposed severe discipline on her children... ...the proposal to impose a 20p admission charge for museums... ...parents who impose religion on their children.* V+O: OFT+*on/upon* ◊ **imposition** /ɪmpəzɪʃə^{0}n/. EG *...the imposition of a wages freeze.* ◊ N UNCOUNT: USU+*of*

2 If something **imposes** an unpleasant effect, it causes this effect. EG *...the restraint imposed on them by the government... Overcrowding imposes mental strains.* V+O: OFT+*on/upon*

3 If someone **imposes** on you, they unreasonably expect you to do something for them when you do not really want to. EG *She would hate to feel that she was imposing on anyone.* V OR V-REFL: OFT+*on* ◊ **imposition, impositions.** EG *I'd be so grateful, though really it's an imposition.* ◊ N COUNT

4 If something **imposes** itself on a situation or activity, it becomes noticeable as a strong factor in the situation. EG *The logic of party organization imposes itself even on anarchic movements.* V-REFL: OFT+*on*

imposing /ɪmpəʊzɪŋ/. Someone or something that is **imposing** has an impressive appearance or manner. EG *Mrs Sabawala's house was large and imposing.* ADJ QUALIT

impossible /ɪmpɒsə^{1}bə^{0}l/. 1 Something that is **impossible** cannot be done, cannot happen, or cannot be believed. EG *It was an impossible task... Staying awake all night was virtually impossible.* ADJ QUALIT

◊ **impossibly.** EG *He had impossibly thin legs.* ◊ ADV+ADJ

◊ **impossibility** /ɪmpɒsəbɪlɪ^{1}ti^1/, **impossibilities.** EG *...the impossibility of change.* ◊ N UNCOUNT OR N COUNT

2 A situation that is **impossible** is one that you find very difficult and are unable to decide on or improve. EG *They are in an impossible position on this matter.* ADJ QUALIT ◊ **impossibly.** EG *Flats make life impossibly restrictive for energetic young children.* ◊ ADV+ADJ

3 If you describe someone as **impossible**, you mean that they are very difficult to deal with, usually because of their bad behaviour or strong views. EG *...my impossible daughter... You're an impossible man to please.* ADJ QUALIT ◊ **impossibly.** EG *She was impossibly rude to Miss Cormorant.* ◊ ADV+ADJ

impostor /ɪmpɒstə/, **impostors;** also spelled **imposter.** If someone is an **impostor**, they are dishonestly pretending to be someone else in order to get something that they want. EG *This is not Doctor Malcolm, he is an impostor.* N COUNT

impotent /ɪmpətənt/. 1 Someone who is **impotent** has no power to influence people or events. EG *Those who do not conform must be rendered impotent.* ADJ QUALIT Formal ◊ **impotence** /ɪmpətəns/. EG *...the impotence and inactivity of the left-wing parties in Europe.* ◊ N UNCOUNT

2 If a man is **impotent**, he is unable to reach an orgasm when having sex. ADJ CLASSIF ◊ **impotence.** EG *...impotence and frigidity in adults.* ◊ N UNCOUNT

impound /ɪmpaʊnd/, **impounds, impounding, impounded.** If policemen or other officials **impound** something that you own, they take legal possession of it. EG *Security Police had come to our house and impounded all our belongings.* V+O Formal

impoverish /ɪmpɒvə^{0}rɪʃ/, **impoverishes, impoverishing, impoverished.** To **impoverish** someone or something means to make them poor. EG *They were impoverished by a prolonged spell of unemployment.* V+O ◊ **impoverished.** EG *...an impoverished Third World country... ...a spiritually impoverished way of life.* ◊ ADJ QUALIT ◊ **impoverishment** /ɪmpɒvə^{0}rɪʃmə^{2}nt/. EG *...a period of very severe impoverishment.* ◊ N UNCOUNT

impracticable /ɪmpræktɪkəbə^{0}l/. A course of action that is **impracticable** is impossible to do. EG *It would be impracticable to ban all food additives.* ADJ CLASSIF

impractical /ɪmpræktɪkə^{0}l/. An idea or course of action that is **impractical** is not sensible, realistic, or practical. EG *...a totally impractical view... To expect automatic protection is impractical.* ADJ QUALIT

imprecise /ɪmprɪsaɪs/. Something that is **imprecise** is not clear or accurate. EG *My ideas about it were imprecise... ...imprecise data.* ADJ QUALIT

impregnable /ɪmprɛgnəbə^{0}l/. 1 Something that is **impregnable** is so strong or solid that it cannot be broken into. EG *They will establish impregnable fortresses to defend themselves.* ADJ CLASSIF

2 A person or group that is **impregnable** cannot be affected or overcome by anyone. EG *They are virtually impregnable to attack from any other party.* ADJ CLASSIF

impregnate /ɪmprɛgneɪt/, **impregnates, impregnating, impregnated.** If you **impregnate** something with a substance, you make the substance pass into it and spread through it. EG *...paper that has been impregnated with chemicals.* V+O: OFT+*with*

impresario /ɪmprɪ^{2}sɑːri^{1}əʊ/, **impresarios.** An **impresario** is a person whose job is to manage a theatre or music company. EG *...a successful West End impresario.* N COUNT

impress /ɪmprɛs/, **impresses, impressing, impressed.** 1 If you do something that **impresses** someone, you make them admire you and respect you. EG *I was hoping to impress my new boss with my diligence... I was greatly impressed by the pianist.* V+O: OFT+A

2 If you **impress** something on someone, you make them understand the importance of it. EG *She impressed on the Government the danger of making too many cuts.* V+O+*on/upon* Formal

impression /ɪmprɛʃə^{0}n/, **impressions.** 1 An **impression** that you have of someone or something is the way that they look or seem to you. EG *The immediate impression of the bedroom is one of sheer 1950s Hollywood.* N COUNT: USU+SUPP

If you are impudent, what kind of impression do you make?

2 Your **impression** of a situation, place, or person is the opinion that you have about it. EG *My impression is that contemporary British authors have a lot to learn from American writing... Reporters wanted my personal impressions of China.* — N COUNT: USU+SUPP

3 When something gives a particular **impression**, it causes people to believe that something is true, often when it is not actually true. EG *They give the impression of not working... I had the impression that he didn't trust me.* — N SING: USU+SUPP ● If you are **under the impression** that something is true, you believe that it is true. EG *They were under the impression I had come to stay.* — ● PHRASE

4 The **impression** that something makes on people is the effect that it has on their ideas or attitudes. EG *I left thinking that I had created quite a good impression.* — N COUNT: USU+SUPP ● If you **make an impression**, you have a strong effect on people when you meet them, causing them to notice you and remember you. EG *She did not fail to make an impression.* — ● PHRASE

5 An **impression** by someone is an amusing imitation of a well-known person. EG *Have you seen her impressions of the TV newscasters?* — N COUNT

impressionable /ɪmprɛʃə^{0}nəbə^{0}l/. Someone who is **impressionable** is easy to influence. EG *...an impressionable young girl.* — ADJ QUALIT

impressive /ɪmprɛsɪv/. Someone or something that is **impressive** impresses you, usually because they are very important. EG *She was a very impressive woman... ...an impressive international reputation... The list of speakers was impressive.* — ADJ QUALIT
◇ **impressively.** EG *The Mysore Palace was impressively elegant and massive.* — ◇ ADV

imprint, imprints, imprinting, imprinted; pronounced /ɪmprɪnt/ when it is a noun, and /ɪmprɪnt/ when it is a verb.

1 If something leaves an **imprint** on your mind or on a place, it has a strong effect on it. EG *These things have left a deep imprint on our thinking... The town still bears the imprint of its industrial origins.* — N COUNT: USU+SUPP

2 If something **is imprinted** on your memory, it is so firmly fixed in your memory that you will not forget it. EG *This is a sunset that will be forever imprinted in the mind.* — V+O+A: USU PASS

3 An **imprint** is a mark or outline made by pressure of an object on a surface. EG *In its centre was the imprint of his hand.* — N COUNT

4 If an object **is imprinted** onto a surface, it is pressed hard onto the surface so that it leaves a mark or an outline. EG *...the hand imprinted in the sand.* — V+O+A: USU PASS

imprison /ɪmprɪzə^{0}n/, **imprisons, imprisoning, imprisoned.** 1 If someone **imprisons** you, they lock you up in prison. — V+O

2 A condition or situation that **imprisons** you restricts your freedom. EG *...the conditions that imprison the industrial worker today.* — V+O

imprisonment /ɪmprɪzə^{0}nmə^{2}nt/ is the state of being imprisoned. EG *They were sentenced to life imprisonment.* — N UNCOUNT

improbable /ɪmprɒbəbə^{0}l/. 1 Something that is **improbable** is unlikely to be true or to happen. EG *His explanation seems highly improbable.* — ADJ QUALIT

2 If you describe something as **improbable**, you mean that you find it strange, unusual, or ridiculous. EG *...the gaudiest and most improbable water wheel the world has ever seen.* — ADJ QUALIT

impromptu /ɪmprɒmptju:/. An **impromptu** action is done without planning or organizing it in advance. EG *I got drawn into a kind of impromptu party downstairs.* — ADJ CLASSIF: USU ATTRIB Formal

improper /ɪmprɒpə/. 1 If you describe someone's behaviour as **improper**, you mean that it is rude or shocking because it is not the correct way to behave. EG *Charlotte thought my mirth improper.* — ADJ QUALIT

2 **Improper** activities are illegal or dishonest. EG *...allegations of improper business dealings.* — ADJ CLASSIF
◇ **improperly.** EG *There were charges that Hugel had improperly provided them with cash.* — ◇ ADV

3 **Improper** conditions or methods of treatment are not suitable or adequate for a particular purpose. EG *...the cruel and improper treatment of cattle.* — ADJ CLASSIF ◇ **improperly.** EG *Bottled milk, improperly handled, is a lethal carrier of disease.* — ◇ ADV

improve /ɪmpru:v/, **improves, improving, improved.** 1 If something **improves** or if you **improve** it, it gets better. EG *The weather improved later in the day... These houses have been improved by the addition of bathrooms.* — V-ERG ◇ **improved.** EG *In underdeveloped countries, improved health and education are urgently needed.* — ◇ ADJ CLASSIF

2 If you **improve** at a skill or in an area of knowledge, you get better at it by practising or studying. EG *She went to the club to improve her tennis... His French was improving.* — V-ERG

3 If you **improve** after an illness or an injury, your health gets better. EG *She may improve with medical treatment.* — V

4 If something **improves** someone, it changes them so that they have a better character or a better social status. EG *He is enjoying his job, getting on and improving himself.* — V+O OR V-REFL

5 If you **improve** on an achievement, you achieve a better standard or result than the previous one. EG *He thinks he's improving on my work... Our techniques are already far advanced and being improved on daily.* — V+*on/upon*: HAS PASS

improvement /ɪmpru:vmə^{2}nt/, **improvements.** **Improvement** in someone or something is a change which improves their quality or condition. EG *The Company made a significant improvement in the wages of its employees... ...the gradual improvement of relations between East and West... Life there would be such an improvement on Paris.* — N UNCOUNT OR N COUNT

improvise /ɪmprəvaɪz/, **improvises, improvising, improvised.** 1 If you **improvise** something, you make it or do it using whatever you have or without planning it in advance. EG *We had to improvise as we went along... The sisters helped me improvise a curtain in front of the toilet.* — V OR V+O
◇ **improvised.** EG *Tanks were crossing the river on improvised bridges.* — ◇ ADJ CLASSIF

2 When musicians **improvise**, they play music without set music, using their imagination. When actors **improvise**, they act without set words, using their imagination. EG *He could improvise quite ambitiously on classical themes.* — V OR V+O
◇ **improvisation** /ɪmprəvaɪzeɪʃə^{0}n/, **improvisations.** EG *...actors playing out improvisations.* — ◇ N UNCOUNT OR N COUNT

imprudent /ɪmpru:dənt/. **Imprudent** behaviour is not sensible or carefully thought out. EG *It would be imprudent of you to make enemies of those who can help you.* — ADJ QUALIT

impudent /ɪmpjə^{4}dənt/. Someone who is **impudent** behaves or speaks rudely or disrespectfully. EG *The impudent child extended her legs across my lap.* — ADJ QUALIT ◇ **impudently.** EG *...somebody who impudently defies my orders.* — ◇ ADV

impulse /ɪmpʌls/, **impulses.** 1 If you have an **impulse** to do something, you have a sudden desire to do it. EG *I had a sudden impulse to turn around and walk out.* — N COUNT ● If you do something **on impulse**, you do it suddenly without planning. EG *On a sudden impulse, he went into the library.* — ● PHRASE

2 An **impulse** is a short electrical signal that is sent along a wire or nerve or through the air. — N COUNT

impulsive /ɪmpʌlsɪv/. Someone who is **impulsive** does things suddenly without thinking about them carefully first. EG *Alice's overdose was an impulsive act.* — ADJ QUALIT ◇ **impulsively.** EG *She kissed him impulsively on the mouth.* — ◇ ADV

impunity /ɪmpju:nɪ^{1}ti^{1}/. If you do something wrong **with impunity**, you are not punished for doing it. EG *Landlords were simply ignoring the law with impunity.* — PHRASE Formal

impure /ɪmpjʊə/. 1 A substance that is **impure** is not of good quality because it has other substances mixed with it. ADJ CLASSIF

2 **Impure** thoughts and actions are concerned with sex and are regarded as sinful. ADJ CLASSIF

impurity /ɪmpjʊərɪ'ti'/, **impurities.** An **impurity** is a substance that is present in another substance making it of a low quality. EG *There are traces of impurities in the gold.* N COUNT

in /ɪn/. 1 Something that is **in** something else is enclosed by it or surrounded by it. EG *We put them away in a big box... We've just found a body in the water... She opened her bag and put her diary in.* PREP, OR ADV AFTER VB

2 If something is **in** a place, it is there. EG *I wanted to play in the garden... She locked herself in the bathroom... In Hamburg the girls split up... I could not sleep because of the pain in my feet.* PREP

3 If you are **in**, you are present at your home or place of work. EG *He's never in when I phone.* ADV AFTER VB

4 When someone comes **in**, they enter a room or building. EG *There was a knock at Howard's door. 'Come in,' he shouted... He had his meals brought in... The children run in and out all the time.* ADV AFTER VB

5 If a train, boat, or plane is **in** or has come **in**, it has arrived somewhere. EG *The train's not in yet.* ADV AFTER VB

6 Something that is **in** a window, especially a shop window, is just behind the window so that you can see it from outside. EG *How much is the hat in the window?* PREP

7 When you see something **in** a mirror, you see its reflection. PREP

8 If you are **in** a piece of clothing, you are wearing it. EG *Martin was in his pyjamas.* PREP

9 If something is **in** a book, film, play, or picture, you can read it or see it there. EG *She dies in the last act... In Chapter 7 this point is discussed in detail.* PREP, OR ADV AFTER VB

10 If something is **in** a group or collection, it is part of it. EG *She waited in the queue.* PREP

11 If you are **in** something such as a play or a race, you are one of the people taking part. EG *She took part in a marathon.* PREP

12 You also use **in** when you are talking about time. **12.1** If something happens **in** a particular year, month, or season, it happens during that time. EG *In 1872, Chicago was burned to the ground... It'll be warmer in the spring.* **12.2** If you do something **in** a particular period of time, that is how long it takes you to do it. EG *I told him the money would be paid back in six months.* **12.3** If something will happen **in** a particular length of time, it will happen after that length of time. EG *In another five minutes it'll be pitch dark.* PREP

13 If something happens **in** a particular situation, it happens during it or when it is going on. EG *He escaped in the confusion... In these circumstances prices and profits would remain stable.* PREP

14 If you are **in** a particular state or situation, that is your present state or situation. EG *We are in a position to advise our Indian friends... We might be in a state of near chaos again... You can't go home in all this rain.* PREP

15 You use **in** to say that an emotion, desire, or reaction causes someone to do something. For example, if you do something **in** surprise, you do it because you are surprised. EG *He shook his head in admiration... In his excitement, Billy had forgotten the letter... In an effort to conceal my thinness, I had worn two layers of clothing.* PREP

16 You use **in** to specify a general subject or field of activity. EG *...recent advances in mathematics... He plans to make his career in music.* PREP

17 You use **in** to indicate how many people or things do something. EG *Students flocked to the SDP in considerable numbers.* PREP

18 You use **in** to give someone's approximate age. For example, if someone is **in** their fifties, they are between 50 and 59 years old. EG *In her twenties and thirties she had had no difficulty in finding jobs.* PREP

19 You use **in** to indicate how someone is expressing something. EG *I need your complaints in writing... She spoke in a calm, friendly voice... They were speaking in French.* PREP

20 You use **in** to describe the arrangement or shape of something. For example, if things are **in** a row, they are arranged to form a row. If something is **in** a ball, its shape is that of a ball. EG *The students sit in a circle on the floor.* PREP

21 If something is **in** a particular colour, it has that colour. EG *We put up curtains in yellow and orange.* PREP

22 You use **in** to specify what something relates to. EG *It grew to eight metres in length... We need a change in direction... She was dismissed for slackness in her duties.* PREP

23 You use **in** to express a ratio, proportion, or probability. EG *Only one acre in five was previously uncultivated... He has only a one in ten chance of being reunited with his family.* PREP

24 Something that is **in** or that is the **in** thing is fashionable. EG *Bright colours are in this year.* ADJ CLASSIF Informal

25 When the sea or tide comes **in**, the sea moves towards the shore rather than away from it. ADV AFTER VB

26 You use **in** with a present participle to indicate that when you do something, something else happens as a consequence. EG *Babbage rejected the obvious, and in doing so achieved his magnificent insight.* PREP+-ING

27 If you say that someone **is in for** a shock or a surprise, you mean that they are going to experience it. PHRASE

28 If you **have it in for** someone, you dislike them and try to cause problems for them. PHRASE Informal

29 If you are **in on** something, you are involved in it or know about it. EG *I'd like to be in on the scheme.* PHRASE

30 You use **in that** to explain a statement you have just made. EG *He's a good listener in that he never interrupts you with thoughts of his own.* CONJ

in. is a written abbreviation for 'inch'. The plural can be **in.** or **ins.** EG *...6 x 4 ins.*

in- is added to some adjectives, adverbs, and nouns to form other adjectives, adverbs, and nouns that have the opposite meaning. For example, something that is incorrect is not correct. EG *He was obviously insincere... 'No, Father,' she said, almost inaudibly... ...a source of political instability.* PREFIX

inability /ɪnəbɪlɪ'ti'/. If you refer to someone's **inability** to do something, you are referring to the fact that they are unable to do it. EG *She despises her husband for his inability to work.* N UNCOUNT +*to*-INF

inaccessible /ɪnə³ksɛsə'bə⁰l/. If something is **inaccessible**, 1 it is impossible to reach or very difficult to reach. EG *...the most inaccessible reaches of the jungle.* ◇ **inaccessibility** /ɪnə³ksɛsə'bɪlɪ'ti'/. EG *The hilltop church attracted good congregations, in spite of its inaccessibility.* 2 you are unable to understand or appreciate it. EG *The music of Bartok is considered inaccessible by many people.* ADJ QUALIT; ◇ N UNCOUNT; ADJ QUALIT Formal

inaccuracy /ɪnækjə⁴rəsi'/, **inaccuracies.** 1 The **inaccuracy** of something is the fact that it is inaccurate. EG *...the inaccuracy of my estimates.* N UNCOUNT

2 An **inaccuracy** is a statement that is inaccurate. EG *The report contained a number of inaccuracies.* N COUNT

inaccurate /ɪnækjə⁴rə't/. Something that is **inaccurate** is not correct or precise. EG *...a wildly inaccurate editorial.* ADJ QUALIT

inaction /ɪnækʃə⁰n/. If you refer to someone's **inaction**, you are referring to the fact that they are doing nothing. EG *We do not accept this as an excuse for government inaction.* N UNCOUNT

inactive /ɪnæktɪv/. A person, animal, or thing that is **inactive** is not doing anything. EG *Crocodiles are inactive for long periods.* ◇ **inactivity** ADJ CLASSIF; ◇ N UNCOUNT

What is the difference between an inborn quality and an inbred one?

/ɪnæktɪvɪ¹ti¹/. EG *The dry season was traditionally a time of inactivity.*

inadequacy /ɪnædɪ¹kwəsi¹/, **inadequacies.** 1 The **inadequacy** of something is the fact that there is not enough of it or that it is not good enough. EG *Parents are complaining at the inadequacy of education facilities in Britain.* — N UNCOUNT OR N COUNT

2 If someone has feelings of **inadequacy**, they feel that they do not have the qualities and abilities necessary to do something or to cope with life. — N UNCOUNT

3 An **inadequacy** is a weakness or fault in a person or thing. EG *...the inadequacies of a superficial education.* — N COUNT

inadequate /ɪnædɪ¹kwə¹t/. 1 If something is **inadequate**, there is not enough of it or it is not good enough. EG *His income is inadequate to meet his basic needs... ...an inadequate and hurried lunch.* — ADJ QUALIT

◇ **inadequately.** EG *Many elderly people live in inadequately heated accommodation.* — ◇ ADV

2 If someone feels **inadequate**, they feel that they do not have the qualities or abilities necessary to do something or to cope with life. EG *He makes me feel totally inadequate.* — ADJ QUALIT

inadvertently /ɪnə³dvɜːtəntli¹/. If you do something **inadvertently**, you do it without intending to do it. EG *...a dog that has been kicked inadvertently by a friend.* — ADV

inadvisable /ɪnə³dvaɪzəbə⁰l/. A course of action that is **inadvisable** is not sensible and should not be done. EG *It is inadvisable to plant lettuces too early.* — ADJ QUALIT : USU PRED

inalienable /ɪneɪljənəbə⁰l/. An **inalienable** right is one that cannot be taken away. EG *...the inalienable right to do anything you want.* — ADJ CLASSIF : USU ATTRIB Formal

inane /ɪneɪn/. **Inane** remarks or actions are silly. EG *She sat through the lesson making inane remarks.* ◇ **inanely.** EG *He smiled rather inanely.* — ADJ QUALIT; ◇ ADV

inanimate /ɪnænɪmə¹t/. An **inanimate** object has no life. — ADJ CLASSIF

inappropriate /ɪnəprəʊprɪə¹t/. Something that is **inappropriate** is not suitable. EG *...a small suitcase full of inappropriate clothes.* — ADJ CLASSIF

inarticulate /ɪnɑːtɪkjə⁴lə¹t/. If you are **inarticulate**, you are unable to express yourself easily or well in speech. EG *He became inarticulate in his anger... ...inarticulate sounds.* — ADJ QUALIT

inasmuch /ɪnə³zmʌtʃ/; also spelled **in as much.** You use **inasmuch as** when you are giving the reason for something. EG *The outcome of this was important inasmuch as it showed just what human beings were capable of.* — CONJ Formal

inattention /ɪnətenʃə⁰n/ is lack of attention to what is being said or done. EG *...scolding the maid for inattention.* — N UNCOUNT

inattentive /ɪnətentɪv/. Someone who is **inattentive** is not paying attention to what is being said or done. EG *...children who are inattentive and doing poorly in school.* — ADJ QUALIT

inaudible /ɪnɔːdə¹bəl/. A sound that is **inaudible** is not loud enough to be heard. EG *Her voice became inaudible.* — ADJ CLASSIF

inaugural /ɪnɔːgj⁰ərəl/. An **inaugural** meeting or speech is the first one of a new organization or leader. EG *...his inaugural address as President.* — ADJ CLASSIF : ATTRIB

inaugurate /ɪnɔːgj⁰əreɪt/, **inaugurates, inaugurating, inaugurated.** 1 When new leaders **are inaugurated**, they are officially established in their new position at a special ceremony. — V+O

◇ **inauguration** /ɪnɔːgj⁰əreɪʃə⁰n/. EG *...the inauguration of a new President.* — ◇ N UNCOUNT : USU+SUPP

2 If you **inaugurate** a system or organization, you start it. EG *They undertook to inaugurate measures to control and protect shipping.* — V+O Formal

inborn /ɪm¹bɔːn/. **Inborn** qualities are believed to be natural ones with which you are born. EG *...our inborn hatred for freaks and outcasts.* — ADJ CLASSIF

inbred /ɪm¹bred/. 1 An **inbred** quality is an inborn one. EG *...the inbred suspicion of strangers.* — ADJ CLASSIF Formal

2 People who are **inbred** have ancestors who are all closely related to each other. EG *...the inbred royal family.* — ADJ CLASSIF

inbuilt /ɪm¹bɪlt/. An **inbuilt** quality is one that someone or something has from the time they were born or produced. EG *The child has got an inbuilt feeling of inferiority.* — ADJ CLASSIF

incalculable /ɪŋ¹kælkjələbə⁰l/. Something that is **incalculable** is so great that it cannot be estimated. EG *The loss to the race as a whole is incalculable.* — ADJ CLASSIF

incantation /ɪŋ¹kænteɪʃə⁰n/, **incantations.** An **incantation** is a series of words that a person says or sings as a magic spell. — N COUNT

incapable /ɪŋ¹keɪpəbə⁰l/. 1 Someone who is **incapable** of doing something is unable to do it. EG *She is incapable of grasping what self-discipline means.* — ADJ PRED+*of*

2 An **incapable** person is weak and helpless or stupid. EG *He's both incapable and dishonest.* — ADJ CLASSIF

incapacitate /ɪŋ¹kə³pæsɪteɪt/, **incapacitates, incapacitating, incapacitated.** If you **are incapacitated** by something, it weakens or harms you so much that you become unable to do things. EG *...those not yet incapacitated by seasickness.* — V+O : USU PASS Formal

incapacity /ɪŋ¹kə³pæsɪ¹ti¹/. The **incapacity** of a person, society, or system is their inability to do something. EG *Growing incapacity is expected with increasing age... ...her incapacity to forgive herself.* — N UNCOUNT Formal

incarcerate /ɪŋ¹kɑːsəreɪt/, **incarcerates, incarcerating, incarcerated.** If someone **is incarcerated**, they are put in prison. — V+O Formal ◇ **incarceration** /ɪŋ¹kɑːsəreɪʃə⁰n/. EG *...the incarceration of political dissenters.* — ◇ N UNCOUNT

incarnation /ɪŋ¹kɑːneɪʃə⁰n/, **incarnations.** 1 You can describe someone as the **incarnation** of a particular quality to emphasize that they have that quality very strongly. EG *...Miss Lenaut, that incarnation of feminine beauty.* — N COUNT+*of*

2 An **incarnation** is an instance of being alive on earth in a particular form. Some religions believe that people have several incarnations. EG *Perhaps they were lovers in a previous incarnation.* — N COUNT

incautious /ɪŋ¹kɔːʃəs/. Someone who is **incautious** does not take enough care over what they say or do. EG *...an incautious remark.* — ADJ QUALIT

incendiary /ɪnsendjəri¹/. **Incendiary** attacks or weapons involve setting fire to something. EG *...a huge incendiary bomb that exploded in the street.* — ADJ CLASSIF : ATTRIB

incense, incenses, incensing, incensed; pronounced /ɪnsens/ when it is a noun and /ɪnsens/ when it is a verb.

1 **Incense** is a substance that is burned for its sweet smell, often during a religious ceremony. — N UNCOUNT

2 Something that **incenses** you makes you extremely angry. EG *The proposed pay freeze has incensed the men.* — V+O ◇ **incensed.** EG *Korean businessmen are particularly incensed at the government's new policy.* — ◇ ADJ QUALIT : USU PRED

incentive /ɪnsentɪv/, **incentives.** An **incentive** is something that encourages you to do something. EG *Money is being used as an incentive... He has no incentive to make permanent improvements.* — N COUNT OR N UNCOUNT

inception /ɪnsepʃə⁰n/. The **inception** of an institution or activity is the start of it. EG *He has been associated with Everyman Opera since its inception in 1952.* — N UNCOUNT +POSS Formal

incessant /ɪnsesənt/. An **incessant** activity continues without stopping. EG *...long centuries of almost incessant warfare.* — ADJ QUALIT ◇ **incessantly.** EG *She drank tea incessantly.* — ◇ ADV

incest /ɪnsest/ is a crime in which someone has sex with a person they are closely related to, for example their brother or sister. — N UNCOUNT

incestuous /ɪnsestjʊəs/. 1 An **incestuous** relationship is one involving incest. — ADJ CLASSIF

2 An **incestuous** group of people is a small group of people who all know each other well and do not associate with anyone outside the group. — ADJ QUALIT

inch /ɪntʃ/, **inches, inching, inched.** 1 An **inch** is an unit for measuring length, approximately equal — N COUNT to 2.54 centimetres. There are twelve inches in a foot. EG *A standard bed is 6 feet 3 inches long... Five inches of snow had fallen... ...searching every inch of the car.*

2 If you **inch** somewhere, you move there very slowly and carefully. EG *You can only enter the caves by inching through a narrow tunnel on your stomach... Howard inched the van forward.* V-ERG+A

incidence /ɪnsɪdəns/. The **incidence** of something is how often it occurs. EG *There is a high incidence of heart disease among middle-aged men.* N SING+*of*

incident /ɪnsɪdənt/, **incidents.** An **incident** is an event, especially one involving violence or something unpleasant. EG *...a succession of bizarre incidents... ...a shooting incident... ...the recent smallpox incident.* N COUNT Formal

incidental /ɪnsɪdentəºl/. Something that is **incidental** happens or exists in connection with something else that is more important. EG *...incidental expenses... ...incidental music for a film.* ADJ CLASSIF: ATTRIB

incidentally /ɪnsɪdentəºli¹/. You use **incidentally** when you add something to what you are saying or when you change the subject. EG *Incidentally, I suggest that you have the telephone moved to the sitting-room.* ADV SEN

incinerate /ɪnsɪnəreɪt/, **incinerates, incinerating, incinerated.** If you **incinerate** something, you burn it completely. EG *Tons of paper are incinerated every year.* V+O Formal

incinerator /ɪnsɪnəreɪtə/, **incinerators.** An **incinerator** is a furnace for burning rubbish. N COUNT

incipient /ɪnsɪpɪənt/. An **incipient** condition or quality is one that is starting to happen or appear. EG *...a good way of curing incipient baldness.* ADJ CLASSIF: ATTRIB Formal

incision /ɪnsɪʒəºn/, **incisions.** An **incision** is a careful cut made in something, for example by a surgeon. EG *...an incision between the fifth and sixth ribs.* N COUNT Formal

incisive /ɪnsaɪsɪv/. Speech or writing that is **incisive** is clear and forceful. EG *...an incisive critique of our society.* ADJ QUALIT

incite /ɪnsaɪt/, **incites, inciting, incited.** If you **incite** someone to behave in a particular way or **incite** particular behaviour, you encourage someone to behave in that way. EG *...inciting people to acts of violence... He was accused of inciting violence.* ◇ **incitement** /ɪnsaɪtməˀnt/. EG *I have been convicted of incitement to murder.* V+O: OFT+*to*-INF OR A; ◇ N UNCOUNT: USU+*to*

inclination /ɪŋ¹klɪneɪʃəºn/, **inclinations.** An **inclination** is a feeling that makes you act or want to act in a particular way. EG *People decide on their aims in life according to their inclinations... Some parents have no time or inclination to play with their children.* N COUNT OR N UNCOUNT

incline, inclines, inclining, inclined; pronounced /ɪŋ¹klaɪn/ when it is a noun and /ɪŋ¹klaɪn/ when it is a verb.

1 An **incline** is land that slopes at an angle. EG *They walked down a steep incline.* N COUNT

2 If you **incline** your head, you bend your neck so that your head is leaning forward. V+O Formal

inclined /ɪŋ¹klaɪnd/. **1** If you are **inclined** to behave in a particular way, **1.1** you often behave in that way. EG *My father was inclined to be very moody.* **1.2** you want to behave in that way. EG *Only do the dusting when you feel inclined.* ADJ PRED +*to*-INF; ADJ PRED

2 If you say that you are **inclined** to have a particular opinion, you are saying that you have this opinion. EG *I'm inclined to agree with you.* ADJ PRED +*to*-INF Formal

3 Someone who is mathematically **inclined** or artistically **inclined**, for example, has a natural ability to do mathematics or art. ADJ PRED

4 Something that is **inclined** in a particular direction is sloping in this direction. EG *The southern hemisphere is inclined towards the sun.* ADJ CLASSIF+A

include /ɪŋ¹klu:d/, **includes, including, included. 1** If one thing **includes** another, it has the other thing as one of its parts. EG *The four-man crew included one Briton... The proposals included the nationalization of major industries.* V+O

2 If you **include** one thing in another, you make it part of the other thing. EG *Carpets and curtains are to be included in the purchase price.* V+O+A

included /ɪŋ¹klu:dɪ²d/. You use **included** to emphasize that someone or something is part of the group of people or things that you are referring to. EG *All of us, myself included, had been totally committed to the project.* ADJ AFTER N

including /ɪŋ¹klu:dɪŋ/. You use **including** to say that someone or something is part of the group of people or things that you are referring to. EG *Nine persons were injured, including two wounded by gunfire... ...a home with 5 rooms (not including the bathroom).* PREP

inclusion /ɪŋ¹klu:ʒəºn/. The **inclusion** of one thing in another is the act of making it a part of the other thing. EG *...the inclusion of the Old Testament in the Christian Bible.* N UNCOUNT

inclusive /ɪŋ¹klu:sɪv/. **1** A price that is **inclusive** includes all the goods and services that are being offered. EG *It's a fully inclusive price... ...£168 (inclusive of tax).* ADJ CLASSIF

2 You use **inclusive** to say that you are including the things mentioned when you refer to a series of things. EG *...ages 17 to 27 inclusive.* ADJ AFTER N

incognito /ɪŋ¹kɒgni:təʊ/. Someone famous who is travelling **incognito** is travelling in disguise or using another name so that they will not be recognized. ADV AFTER VB

incoherent /ɪŋ¹kəʊhɪərənt/. If someone is **incoherent**, they are talking in an unclear way. EG *He moved among his guests, stammering incoherent apologies... He was quite incoherent with joy.* ◇ **incoherently.** EG *Marcus stood up, muttering incoherently.* ADJ QUALIT; ◇ ADV

income /ɪŋ¹kəºm/, **incomes.** A person's **income** is the money that they earn or that they get from other sources such as investments. N COUNT

incoming /ɪŋ¹kʌmɪŋ/. **1** An **incoming** tide or wave is going towards the shore. ADJ CLASSIF: ATTRIB

2 An **incoming** plane, vehicle, or passenger is arriving at a place. ADJ CLASSIF: ATTRIB

3 An **incoming** message, report, or phone call is one that you receive. ADJ CLASSIF: ATTRIB

4 An **incoming** official or government has just been appointed or elected. ADJ CLASSIF: ATTRIB

incomparable /ɪŋ¹kɒmpəºrəbəºl/. Something that is **incomparable** is very good or great in degree. EG *...a movement of incomparable grace... ...a writer of incomparable prose.* ◇ **incomparably.** EG *The private schoolboy enjoys an incomparably superior education.* ADJ CLASSIF Formal; ◇ SUBMOD

incompatible /ɪŋ¹kəmpætə¹bəºl/. Two things that are **incompatible** are unable to exist together because they are completely different. EG *Their styles of life were incompatible... ...his actions are totally incompatible with the group's safety.* ◇ **incompatibility** /ɪŋ¹kəmpætə¹bɪlɪti¹/. EG *There is a fundamental incompatibility between the management and the unions.* ADJ CLASSIF: OFT+*with*; ◇ N UNCOUNT

incompetent /ɪŋ¹kɒmpɪtənt/. Someone who is **incompetent** does their job badly or does a particular thing badly. EG *Our secret services and our navy are completely incompetent.* ◇ **incompetence** /ɪŋ¹kɒmpɪtəns/. EG *Graffman fired him for incompetence.* ADJ QUALIT; ◇ N UNCOUNT

incomplete /ɪŋ¹kəmpli:t/. Something that is **incomplete 1** does not have all the parts that it should have. EG *...a short and incomplete account of my life.* **2** is not as great in extent, degree, or amount as it could be. EG *...the consequences of incomplete military success.* ◇ **incompletely.** EG *...incompletely cooked meat.* ADJ QUALIT; ADJ CLASSIF; ◇ ADV

If you were travelling incognito, would you try to be inconspicuous?

incomprehensible /ɪŋ1kɒmprɪhensə1bə0l/. ADJ CLASSIF Something that is **incomprehensible** is impossible to understand. EG *A great deal of Caine's language was incomprehensible to me.*

incomprehension /ɪŋ1kɒmprɪhenʃə0n/ is the N UNCOUNT state of being unable to understand something. EG *He went on staring in incomprehension.*

inconceivable /ɪŋ1kənsi:vəbə0l/. If you describe ADJ QUALIT something as **inconceivable**, you mean that you cannot believe that it could possibly be true. EG *He found it inconceivable that Belov was insane.*

inconclusive /ɪŋ1kənklu:sɪv/. **1** If a discussion is ADJ QUALIT **inconclusive**, it does not lead to any decision.

2 If evidence, an experiment, or a result is **incon-** ADJ CLASSIF **clusive**, it has not proved anything.

incongruous /ɪŋ1kɒŋgru:əs/. Something that is ADJ QUALIT **incongruous** seems strange because it does not fit in with the rest of the situation. EG *He was an incongruous figure among the tourists.*
◊ **incongruously.** ◊ ADV EG *...a fat lady, dressed incongruously in black satin.* ◊ **incongruity** ◊ N UNCOUNT OR N COUNT /ɪŋ1kɒŋgru:ɪti1/, **incongruities.** EG *We were both conscious of the incongruity of the situation... ...looking for contradictions and incongruities.*

inconsequential /ɪŋ1kɒnsi1kwenʃə0l/. Something ADJ QUALIT that is **inconsequential** is not very important. EG *...some inconsequential conversation.*

inconsiderable /ɪŋ1kənsɪdə0rəbə0l/. If you de- ADJ CLASSIF scribe something as not **inconsiderable**, you mean that it is large. EG *The country's not inconsiderable army was mobilized.*

inconsiderate /ɪŋ1kənsɪdə0rə1t/. People who are ADJ QUALIT **inconsiderate** do not care how their behaviour affects other people.

inconsistent /ɪŋ1kənsɪstənt/. **1** Someone who is ADJ QUALIT **inconsistent** behaves differently in a particular situation each time it happens; used showing disapproval. EG *The blame was laid on an inconsistent government... They're such an inconsistent lot, young people.* ◊ **inconsistency** /ɪŋ1kə7nsɪstənsi1/, ◊ N UNCOUNT OR N COUNT **inconsistencies.** EG *His life was full of inconsistencies.*

2 If you say things that are **inconsistent**, they ADJ QUALIT contradict each other. EG *Some of your answers are rather inconsistent.* ◊ **inconsistency, inconsist-** ◊ N UNCOUNT OR N COUNT **encies.** EG *...the complete inconsistency between the two views expressed by John.*

3 Something that is **inconsistent** with a particular ADJ PRED +*with* set of ideas, beliefs, or values is not in accordance with them. EG *...a monarch whose behaviour they judged to be inconsistent with Hindu religious values.*

inconspicuous /ɪŋ1kənspɪkju:əs/. Something that ADJ QUALIT is **inconspicuous** is not at all noticeable. EG *I have asked the children to make themselves as inconspicuous as possible.* ◊ **inconspicuously.** ◊ ADV EG *He slipped into the nearest bar as inconspicuously as he could.*

incontinent /ɪŋ1kɒntɪnənt/. Someone who is **in-** ADJ CLASSIF **continent** is unable to control their bladder or bowels. ◊ **incontinence** /ɪŋ1kɒntɪnəns/. ◊ N UNCOUNT EG *Incontinence can become a real problem in old age.*

incontrovertible /ɪŋ1kɒntrəvɜ:tə1bə0l/. **Incon-** ADJ CLASSIF Formal **trovertible** evidence or proof shows that something is definitely true. EG *His picture collection was incontrovertible evidence of his wealth.*

inconvenience /ɪŋ1kənvi:njəns, -vi:nɪəns/, **inconveniences, inconveniencing, inconvenienced. 1** N UNCOUNT OR N COUNT If someone or something causes **inconvenience**, they cause problems or difficulties. EG *I'm very sorry to have caused so much inconvenience... You have to put up with these inconveniences as best you can.*

2 If you **inconvenience** someone, you cause prob- V+O lems or difficulties for them. EG *All the residents have been inconvenienced by the road works.*

inconvenient /ɪŋ1kənvi:njənt, -vi:nɪənt/. Some- ADJ QUALIT thing that is **inconvenient** causes problems or difficulties for you. EG *You live quite a long way out. Don't you find it a bit inconvenient?... I seem to have come at an inconvenient time.*

incorporate /ɪŋ1kɔ:pəreɪt/, **incorporates, incorporating, incorporated. 1** If something **is incor-** V+O+*into/in* **porated** into another thing, it becomes a part of that thing. EG *They were incorporated into the Zulu Empire... ...legislation compelling manufacturers to incorporate safety features in all new cars.*
◊ **incorporation** /ɪŋ1kɔ:pəreɪʃə0n/. ◊ N UNCOUNT EG *...the incorporation of Austria into the German Empire.*

2 If something **incorporates** another thing, it V+O includes that thing as one of its parts. EG *These houses usually incorporated a long gallery.*

incorrect /ɪŋ1kərekt/. Something that is **incor-** ADJ CLASSIF **rect** is wrong or untrue. EG *Sonny dismissed the information as incorrect... ...spelling mistakes and incorrect English.* ◊ **incorrectly.** ◊ ADV EG *The problem has been incorrectly defined.*

incorrigible /ɪŋ1kɒrɪdʒə1bə0l/. Someone who is ADJ CLASSIF **incorrigible** has faults or bad habits that will never change. EG *...incorrigible criminals... 'Oh, James, you are incorrigible!' she said.*

incorruptible /ɪŋ1kərʌptə1bə0l/. Someone who is ADJ CLASSIF **incorruptible** cannot be bribed or persuaded to do things that they should not do. EG *They were both wise and incorruptible men.*

increase, increases, increasing, increased; pronounced /ɪŋ1kri:s/ when it is a noun and /ɪŋ1kri:s/ when it is a verb.

1 If something **increases** or if you **increase** it, it V-ERG becomes larger in amount. EG *Crime has increased by three per cent in the past year... ...men seeking to increase their knowledge.* ◊ **increased.** ◊ ADJ CLASSIF EG *...increased productivity.* ◊ **increasing.** ◊ ADJ CLASSIF EG *Japanese industry is making increasing use of robots.*

2 An **increase** is a rise in the number, level, or N COUNT amount of something. EG *At the meeting they demanded a sharp increase in wages.*

3 If something is **on the increase**, it is becoming PHRASE more frequent. EG *Crime is on the increase.*

increasingly /ɪŋ1kri:sɪŋli1/. You use **increasing-** SUBMOD OR ADV **ly** to indicate that a situation or quality is becoming greater in intensity or more common. EG *It was becoming increasingly difficult to find jobs... The cases he dealt with increasingly repelled him... Men increasingly find that they need more training.*

incredible /ɪŋ1kredə1bə0l/. **1** Something that is **incredible** is **1.1** amazing or very unusual. ADJ CLASSIF EG *They were wearing incredible uniforms... It was an incredible experience.* ◊ **incredibly.** ◊ ADV SEN EG *Upstairs, incredibly, the beds were already made.* **1.2** very ADJ CLASSIF great in amount or degree. EG *They get an incredible amount of money.* ◊ **incredibly.** ◊ SUBMOD EG *The water was incredibly hot... I'm in an incredibly privileged position.*

2 You can use **incredible** to say that you think that ADJ CLASSIF something cannot possibly be true. EG *You've no basis for this incredible suggestion.*

incredulous /ɪŋ1kredjə4ləs/. If someone is **in-** ADJ QUALIT **credulous**, they are unable to believe what they have just heard because it is very surprising or shocking. EG *'You left her all alone?' He sounded incredulous.* ◊ **incredulously.** ◊ ADV EG *I stared at him incredulously.* ◊ **incredulity** /ɪŋ1krɪ2dju:lɪ1ti1/. ◊ N UNCOUNT EG *I read the document with incredulity.*

increment /ɪŋ1krəmə2nt/, **increments.** An **in-** N COUNT **crement** is an addition to something, especially a regular addition to someone's salary.

incriminate /ɪŋ1krɪmɪneɪt/, **incriminates, in-** V+O **criminating, incriminated.** If something **incriminates** you, it provides evidence that you are the person responsible for a crime. EG *They raided his laboratory to seize any papers that might incriminate them.* ◊ **incriminating.** ◊ ADJ QUALIT EG *They began a search for incriminating evidence.*

incubate /ɪŋ1kjə4beɪt/, **incubates, incubating, incubated. 1** When a bird **incubates** its eggs or V-ERG Technical when they **incubate**, it keeps them warm until they hatch.

2 The time that an infection or virus takes to **incubate** is the time that it takes to affect people and make them ill. V Technical

incubator /ɪŋ[1]kjə[4]beɪtə/, **incubators.** An **incubator** is a piece of hospital equipment in which an ill or very weak baby is kept for a time after it is born. N COUNT

inculcate /ɪŋ[1]kʌlkeɪt, ɪŋ[1]kʌlkeɪt/, **inculcates, inculcating, inculcated.** If you **inculcate** an idea or an opinion in someone, you teach it to them so that it becomes fixed in their mind. EG *We want to inculcate the values of marriage and family life into our children.* V+O: USU+*in/into* Formal

incumbent /ɪŋ[1]kʌmbənt/, **incumbents. 1** If it is **incumbent** on you to do something, it is your duty or responsibility to do it. EG *It was incumbent on editors to exercise discretion.* ADJ PRED Formal

2 An **incumbent** is the person who is holding a particular post. EG *...the new incumbent.* N COUNT Formal

incur /ɪŋ[1]kɜː/, **incurs, incurring, incurred.** If you **incur** something unpleasant, it happens because of something you do. EG *...the risk of incurring her displeasure... ...business expenses incurred outside the office.* V+O Formal

incurable /ɪŋ[1]kjʊərəbə[0]l/. **1** If someone has an **incurable** disease, they cannot be cured of it. EG *...incurable cancer.* ADJ CLASSIF

2 You can use **incurable** to describe people who will never change their attitudes or habits. EG *...incurable optimists.* ◇ **incurably.** EG *...the incurably servile housekeeper.* ADJ CLASSIF: ATTRIB ◇ ADV+ADJ

incursion /ɪŋ[1]kɜːʃə[0]n/, **incursion.** An **incursion** is a small military invasion into another country. EG *...their incursion into Yugoslavia.* N COUNT+SUPP

indebted /ɪndɛtɪ[2]d/. If you are **indebted** to someone, **1** you are grateful to them for something. EG *I am indebted to Bob Waller for many of the ideas expressed here.* ◇ **indebtedness.** EG *I readily acknowledge my indebtedness to my friends.* **2** you owe them money. EG *His company became indebted to the bank.* ◇ **indebtedness.** EG *Home ownership involves higher indebtedness than renting.* ADJ PRED+*to* ◇ N UNCOUNT ADJ PRED American ◇ N UNCOUNT

indecency /ɪndiːsənsi[1]/. The **indecency** of something or someone is the fact that they are morally or sexually offensive. N UNCOUNT

indecent /ɪndiːsənt/. Something that is **indecent 1** is shocking because it relates to naked people or sexual acts. EG *...indecent jokes.* **2** breaks rules of good behaviour or morality. EG *The rush to become a White House correspondent was indecent.* ADJ QUALIT ADJ QUALIT

indecipherable /ɪndɪsaɪfə[0]rəbə[0]l/. **1** If writing is **indecipherable**, you cannot read it. ADJ QUALIT Formal

2 If the expression on a person's face or a gesture is **indecipherable**, you cannot understand it. EG *An indecipherable glance passed between them.* ADJ QUALIT Formal

indecision /ɪndɪsɪʒə[0]n/ is uncertainty about what you should do. EG *She felt ill with anxiety and indecision.* N UNCOUNT

indecisive /ɪndɪsaɪsɪv/. If you are **indecisive**, you do not find it easy to make decisions. EG *There was nothing dithering or indecisive about him.* ADJ QUALIT

indeed /ɪndiːd/. **1** You use **indeed 1.1** to confirm or agree with something that has just been said. EG *'I think you knew him.' – 'I did indeed.'* **1.2** to add a comment or statement which strengthens the point you have already made. EG *This act has failed to bring women's earnings up to the same level. Indeed the gulf is widening.* ADV SEN

2 You also use **indeed** at the end of a clause to give extra force to the word 'very', or to emphasize a particular word. EG *We have very little information indeed... Thank you very much indeed... The possibility of rescue now seemed remote indeed.*

3 You can also use **indeed** to express anger, indignation, or scorn about something. EG *'She wants to go too.' – 'Does she indeed!'* EXCLAM Spoken

indefatigable /ɪndi[1]fætɪgəbə[0]l/. You use **indefatigable** to describe people who do something a lot and never get tired of doing it. EG *All through her life she was an indefatigable traveller.* ADJ CLASSIF Formal

indefensible /ɪndi[1]fɛnsəbə[0]l/. Statements, actions, or ideas that are **indefensible** cannot be justified because they are completely wrong or unacceptable. EG *He denounced the judge's savage attack as totally indefensible.* ADJ QUALIT Formal

indefinable /ɪndi[1]faɪnəbə[0]l/. A quality or feeling that is **indefinable** cannot easily be described. EG *...the indefinable quality of leadership.* ◇ **indefinably.** EG *Terry had somehow indefinably altered.* ADJ CLASSIF ◇ ADV

indefinite /ɪndɛfɪnɪ[1]t/. **1** If something is **indefinite**, people have not decided when it will end. EG *I was going to have to leave for an indefinite period... Members of the union began an indefinite strike this morning.* ADJ CLASSIF

2 Actions, events, or situations that are **indefinite** are not exact or clear. EG *Milner advised him not to answer so indefinite a proposal.* ADJ QUALIT

indefinite article, indefinite articles. The **indefinite article** is a term used in grammar for the words 'a' and 'an'. In this dictionary 'a' and 'an' are described as DET. See the entry headed DETERMINERS for more information. N COUNT: USU *the*+N

indefinitely /ɪndɛfɪnɪ[1]tli[1]/. If something will continue **indefinitely**, it will continue until there is a reason for it to change or end. EG *The Regency Hotel was closed indefinitely.* ADV

indelible /ɪndɛlɪbə[0]l/. **1** If a mark or stain is **indelible**, it cannot be removed or washed out. EG *His fingertips had turned an indelible black.* ADJ CLASSIF

2 **Indelible** pens and pencils make marks that cannot be removed or washed out. ADJ CLASSIF

3 Memories, impressions, or details that are **indelible** will never be forgotten. EG *...all the indelible memories of childhood.* ◇ **indelibly.** EG *The number was indelibly printed on her brain.* ADJ CLASSIF ◇ ADV

indelicate /ɪndɛlɪkɪ[1]t/. Behaviour that is **indelicate** is rude or offensive. EG *Simon was hungry, but felt it would be indelicate to make too much fuss about it.* ADJ QUALIT Formal

indentation /ɪndɛnteɪʃə[0]n/, **indentations.** An **indentation** is a dent or groove in the surface or edge of something. EG *The high heels of her boots made little indentations in the carpet.* N COUNT

independence /ɪndɪpɛndəns/. **1** If a country has **independence**, it is not ruled by any other country. EG *The country has had 24 years of independence.* N UNCOUNT

2 If you refer to someone's **independence**, you are referring to the fact that they are independent. EG *She shows great independence of mind.* N UNCOUNT

independent /ɪndɪpɛndənt/. **1** Something that is **independent** exists, happens, or acts separately from other people, groups, or things. EG *Two independent studies came to the same conclusions... ...20 clinics which are independent of the National Health Service.* ◇ **independently.** EG *Agriculture developed independently in many different parts of the globe... This decision was taken quite independently of any other organization.* ADJ CLASSIF: OFT+*of* ◇ ADV

2 If you are **independent**, **2.1** you form your own opinions and arrange your own life, rather than relying on other people or copying them. EG *They wanted to encourage independent thought.* **2.2** you can support yourself financially. EG *I became financially independent.* ADJ QUALIT

3 An **independent** school, broadcasting company, or other organization does not receive money from the government. ADJ CLASSIF

4 **Independent** countries and states are not ruled ADJ CLASSIF

by other countries and have their own government.

5 An **independent** inquiry or opinion is held by people who are not involved in a situation and so are able to make a fair judgement. EG *He backs the need for an independent inquiry into charity law.* ADJ CLASSIF : ATTRIB

indescribable /ɪndɪ^{2}skraɪbəbə^{0}l/. Something that is **indescribable** is too intense or extreme to be described properly. EG *...the indescribable sadness of those final pages... The smell was indescribable.* ADJ CLASSIF
◊ **indescribably.** EG *The air was getting indescribably foul... ...an indescribably sad cry.* ◊ SUBMOD

indestructible /ɪndɪ^{2}strʌktə^{1}bə^{0}l/. Something that is **indestructible** cannot be destroyed. EG *Our friendship is indestructible.* ADJ CLASSIF

indeterminate /ɪndi^{1}tɜːmɪnət/. If something is **indeterminate**, you are not able to say exactly what it is. EG *...a figure of indeterminate sex, encased in a quilted body suit.* ADJ QUALIT

index /ɪndeks/, **indexes, indexing, indexed; indices** /ɪndɪsiːz/. The plural form of the noun is usually **indexes** for paragraph 1 and **indices** for paragraph 2.
1 An **index** is **1.1** an alphabetical list that is sometimes printed at the back of a book to tell you where to find information about particular things or people in the book. **1.2** a collection of cards with information on them, arranged in alphabetical order. N COUNT
2 An **index** is also a system by which changes in the value of something can be compared or measured. EG *...a 0.3 per cent rise in the wholesale prices index.* N COUNT
3 If you **index** a book or collection of information, you provide an index for it. V+O

index finger, index fingers. Your **index finger** is the finger that is next to your thumb. N COUNT

indicate /ɪndɪkeɪt/, **indicates, indicating, indicated.** **1** If something **indicates** that something is true, it gives you information which makes you decide that it is true. EG *These studies indicate that it's best to change your car every two years... This absurd action indicated the level of their intelligence.* V+REPORT OR V+O
2 If you **indicate** something to someone, you show them where it is, especially by pointing to it. EG *She sat down in the armchair that Mrs Jones indicated.* V+O
3 If you **indicate** a particular fact, you mention it in a brief, often general, way. EG *As I have already indicated, there is now more competition for jobs than there used to be... I indicated that I had not seen enough of his work to be able to judge it.* V+O OR V+REPORT
4 If something **indicates** something else, it is a sign of that thing. EG *An erect tail on a cat indicates aggression... The lights above the lift doors indicated that the lift was ascending.* V+O OR V+REPORT
5 When someone who is driving a car **indicates**, they show which way they are going to turn by making lights on the car flash or by signalling with their hand. V+O OR V+REPORT

indication /ɪndɪkeɪʃə^{0}n/, **indications.** An **indication** is a sign which gives you an idea of what someone feels, what is happening, or what is likely to happen. EG *The President gave a clear indication yesterday of his willingness to meet the visitors... All the indications are that both sides will soon reach an agreement... There was no indication that he ever noticed my absence.* N COUNT OR N UNCOUNT

indicative /ɪndɪkətɪv/. **1** If something is **indicative** of something else, it is a sign of that thing. EG *He regarded their action as indicative of their lack of courage.* ADJ PRED+*of*
2 If a verb is in the **indicative**, it is in the form used for making statements. N SING : *the*+N

indicator /ɪndɪkeɪtə/, **indicators.** **1** An **indicator** is something which tells you what something is like, what is happening, or what is likely to happen. EG *Price is not always an indicator of quality.* N COUNT Formal
2 A car's **indicators** are the lights at the front and back which are used to show when it is turning left or right. See picture at CAR. N COUNT

indices /ɪndɪsiːz/ is a plural of **index**.

indict /ɪndaɪt/, **indicts, indicting, indicted.** When someone **is indicted** for a crime, they are officially charged with it. EG *The General was indicted for treason.* V+O : USU PASS Formal

indictment /ɪndaɪtmənt/, **indictments.** **1** If you say that something is an **indictment** of something else, you mean that it shows how bad that thing is. EG *It is a striking indictment of our educational system that so many children cannot read or write.* N COUNT+SUPP
2 An **indictment** is an official charge of a crime made against a person. EG *Robbins is under indictment for fraud.* N COUNT OR N UNCOUNT Formal

indifferent /ɪndɪfə^{0}rənt/. **1** If you are **indifferent** to something, you have no interest in it. EG *Children fail to progress if their parents seem indifferent to their success.* ADJ QUALIT : OFT+*to*
◊ **indifferently.** EG *Mark smiled at me briefly, indifferently, and hurried away.* ◊ ADV
◊ **indifference** /ɪndɪfə^{0}rəns/. EG *...Aitken's indifference to criticism.* ◊ N UNCOUNT
2 If you describe things or people as **indifferent**, you mean that they are not of a very good standard. EG *He was a gifted painter but an indifferent actor.* ADJ QUALIT

indigenous /ɪndɪdʒɪnəs/. Something that is **indigenous** is originally from the country in which it is found, rather than having come there from another country. EG *...the indigenous population... The elephant is indigenous to India.* ADJ CLASSIF Formal

indigestible /ɪndɪdʒestəbə^{0}l/. Food that is **indigestible** cannot be digested easily. ADJ QUALIT

indigestion /ɪndɪdʒestʃə^{0}n/ is pain that you get in your abdomen when you find it difficult to digest food. EG *Food that is too fatty may cause indigestion.* N UNCOUNT

indignant /ɪndɪgnənt/. If you are **indignant**, you are shocked and angry. EG *Many taxpayers are indignant at what they regard as an illegal use of public funds.* ADJ QUALIT
◊ **indignantly.** EG *'Why not?' cried Judy indignantly.* ◊ ADV

indignation /ɪndɪgneɪʃə^{0}n/ is the feeling of shock and anger which you have when you think that what someone has done is unjust or unfair. EG *She seethed with indignation.* N UNCOUNT

indignity /ɪndɪgnɪ^{1}ti^1/, **indignities.** An **indignity** is something that makes you feel embarrassed or humiliated. EG *He hated the rules and the petty indignities of prison life... ...the indignity of slavery.* N COUNT OR N UNCOUNT

indigo /ɪndɪgəʊ/. Something that is **indigo** is a dark purplish-blue in colour. EG *...an indigo sky.* ADJ COLOUR

indirect /ɪndaɪrekt/. **1** Something that is **indirect** is not done or caused directly, but by means of something or someone else. EG *A sudden increase in oil prices would have serious indirect effects.* ADJ CLASSIF
◊ **indirectly.** EG *I suppose I was indirectly responsible for the whole thing.* ◊ ADV
2 An **indirect** route or journey does not use the shortest way between two places. ADJ CLASSIF
3 An **indirect** answer or reference does not directly mention the thing that is actually being talked about. ADJ QUALIT

indirect object. See **object**.

indiscreet /ɪndɪskriːt/. If you are **indiscreet**, you talk about or do things openly when you should have kept them secret. EG *...an indiscreet comment.* ADJ QUALIT

indiscretion /ɪndɪskreʃə^{0}n/, **indiscretions.** **Indiscretion** is behaviour that is unacceptable by being incautious, tactless, or by revealing secrets. EG *How could she commit such an indiscretion?* N UNCOUNT OR N COUNT

indiscriminate /ɪndɪskrɪmɪnɪ^{1}t/. An **indiscriminate** action does not involve any careful thought or choice. EG *...indiscriminate slaughter... Television watchers tend to be indiscriminate in their viewing habits.* ADJ QUALIT
◊ **indiscriminately.** EG *He reads widely and indiscriminately.* ◊ ADV

indispensable /ɪndɪspensəbə^{0}l/. If something is **indispensable**, it is absolutely essential. EG *In my* ADJ CLASSIF : OFT+*to* *job, a telephone is indispensable... Energy is indispensable to modern industrial societies.*

indisputable /ɪndɪspjuːtəbəl/. If a fact is **indisputable**, it is obviously and definitely true. EG *We're going to have a very hard time. That's indisputable... This is a work of indisputable genius.* — ADJ CLASSIF
◇ **indisputably.** EG *The book is indisputably a masterpiece.* — ◇ ADV

indissoluble /ɪndɪsɒljəbəl/. A relationship or link that is **indissoluble** can never be ended. EG *...the indissoluble ties of mother to child.* — ADJ CLASSIF Formal

indistinct /ɪndɪstɪŋkt/. Something that is **indistinct** is unclear and difficult to see or hear. EG *His words were faint and often indistinct... ...an indistinct footpath.* — ADJ QUALIT ◇ **indistinctly.** EG *I mumbled indistinctly through a mouthful of food.* — ◇ ADV

indistinguishable /ɪndɪstɪŋgwɪʃəbəl/. If two things are **indistinguishable**, they are so similar that it is impossible to tell them apart. EG *Some synthetic meat is indistinguishable from the natural product in taste.* — ADJ CLASSIF: OFT+*from*

individual /ɪndɪvɪdjʊəl/, **individuals. 1 Individual** means relating to one particular person or to each person separately, rather than to a large group. EG *...the preservation of individual liberty... ...individual tuition... We can identify each individual whale by its song.* — ADJ CLASSIF: ATTRIB ◇ **individually.** EG *The children can work individually or in small groups... Each fruit should be wrapped individually in paper.* — ◇ ADV
2 An **individual** is a person. EG *...the freedom of the individual... Fourier seems to be a somewhat eccentric individual.* — N COUNT

individualist /ɪndɪvɪdjəlɪst/, **individualists.** If you are an **individualist**, you like to do things in your own way. EG *Academics are such individualists.* — N COUNT

individualistic /ɪndɪvɪdjəlɪstɪk/. If you are **individualistic**, you like to do things in your own way. EG *Lions are highly individualistic animals.* — ADJ CLASSIF

individuality /ɪndɪvɪdjuːælɪti/. If something has **individuality**, it is different from all other things and is therefore more noticeable and interesting. EG *The advertisement lacks any individuality.* — N UNCOUNT

indivisible /ɪndɪvɪzɪbəl/. If something is **indivisible**, it cannot be divided into different parts. EG *...the ancient Greek belief that the atom is indivisible.* — ADJ CLASSIF

indoctrinate /ɪndɒktrɪneɪt/, **indoctrinates, indoctrinating, indoctrinated.** If you **indoctrinate** someone, you teach them a particular belief with the aim that they will only accept that belief and will not accept any other; used showing disapproval. — V+O ◇ **indoctrination** /ɪndɒktrɪneɪʃən/. EG *It is difficult to overcome the early indoctrination of children.* — ◇ N UNCOUNT

indolent /ɪndələnt/. Someone who is **indolent** is lazy. EG *...an indolent girl with a moody mouth... ...an indolent smile.* — ADJ QUALIT Formal ◇ **indolence** /ɪndələns/. EG *...the indolence of his movements.* — ◇ N UNCOUNT

indomitable /ɪndɒmɪtəbəl/. Someone who is **indomitable** never admits that they have been defeated. EG *The boy had been kept alive by his indomitable spirit.* — ADJ QUALIT Formal

indoor /ɪndɔː/. You use **indoor** to describe things which are situated or happen inside a building rather than outside. EG *...indoor games such as table tennis. ...indoor swimming pools.* — ADJ CLASSIF: ATTRIB

indoors /ɪndɔːz/. If something happens **indoors**, it happens inside a building. EG *The concert is held indoors when it rains... We'd better go indoors.* — ADV AFTER VB

indubitable /ɪndjuːbɪtəbəl/. Something that is **indubitable** is definite and cannot be doubted. — ADJ CLASSIF Formal ◇ **indubitably.** EG *There was Thomas, dirty and muddy but indubitably alive.* — ◇ ADV

induce /ɪndjuːs/, **induces, inducing, induced. 1** To **induce** a particular state or condition means to cause it. EG *...pills guaranteed to induce sleep... Failure induces a total sense of inferiority.* — V+O
2 To **induce** someone to do something means to persuade or influence them to do it. EG *What on earth had induced her to marry a man like that?* — V+O+*to*-INF

inducement /ɪndjuːsmənt/, **inducements.** An **inducement** is something that is offered to someone in order to persuade them to do something. EG *These tax advantages provide the main inducement to become a home-owner.* — N COUNT

indulge /ɪndʌldʒ/, **indulges, indulging, indulged. 1** If you **indulge** in something or **indulge** a hobby or interest, for example, you allow yourself to have or do something that you enjoy. EG *Let us indulge in a little daydreaming... Jack had spent the previous three weeks indulging his passion for climbing... He indulged himself by smoking another cigarette.* — V+*in*, V+O, OR V-REFL
2 If you **indulge** someone or their wishes, you let them have or do whatever they want. EG *He was usually prepared to indulge his sister if it did not mean a great deal of trouble.* — V+O

indulgence /ɪndʌldʒəns/, **indulgences. 1** An **indulgence** is something that you allow yourself to do or have because it gives you pleasure. EG *Smoking was his one indulgence.* — N COUNT
2 Indulgence is the act of indulging yourself or another person. EG *Simon listened to her with indulgence.* — N UNCOUNT

indulgent /ɪndʌldʒənt/. If you are **indulgent**, you treat a person with special kindness. EG *He was an indulgent father, ever ready to provide new clothes.* — ADJ QUALIT ◇ **indulgently.** EG *He smiled indulgently at her.* — ◇ ADV

industrial /ɪndʌstrɪəl/. **1** You use **industrial** to describe things which relate to industry or are used in it. EG *...industrial robots... ...industrial and technical change.* — ADJ CLASSIF: ATTRIB
2 An **industrial** city or country is one in which industry is important or highly developed. — ADJ CLASSIF: USU ATTRIB

industrial action. When a group of workers take **industrial action**, they go on strike or take other action as a way of protesting about their pay or working conditions. — N UNCOUNT

industrial estate, industrial estates. An **industrial estate** is an area which has been specially planned for a lot of factories. — N COUNT

industrialise /ɪndʌstrɪəlaɪz/. See **industrialize.**

industrialism /ɪndʌstrɪəlɪzəm/ is the state of having an economy based on industry. EG *...as men were enslaved by developing industrialism.* — N UNCOUNT

industrialist /ɪndʌstrɪəlɪst/, **industrialists.** An **industrialist** is a person who owns or controls large amounts of money or property in industry. — N COUNT

industrialize /ɪndʌstrɪəlaɪz/, **industrializes, industrializing, industrialized;** also spelled **industrialise.** — V-ERG
When a country **industrializes** or when it **is industrialized**, it develops a lot of industries.
◇ **industrialized.** EG *...the industrialized world... ...those societies which became industrialized during the last century.* — ◇ ADJ CLASSIF: ATTRIB ◇ **industrialization** /ɪndʌstrɪəlaɪzeɪʃən/. EG *...the rising cost of industrialization.* — ◇ N UNCOUNT

industrial relations. When you refer to **industrial relations**, you are referring to the relationship between employers, workers, and trade unions in industry. EG *...the future of industrial relations in Britain.* — N PLURAL

industrious /ɪndʌstrɪəs/. Someone who is **industrious** works very hard. EG *...an industrious student.* — ADJ QUALIT

industry /ɪndəstri/, **industries. 1 Industry** is the work and processes involved in manufacturing things in factories. EG *Japanese industry is making increasing use of robots.* — N UNCOUNT
2 An **industry** consists of all the people and the processes that are involved in manufacturing or producing a particular thing. EG *...the oil industry.* — N COUNT

Is everyone in an industry industrious?

3 **Industry** is also the quality of working very hard. EG *...the old virtues of self-reliance, industry, and frugality.* N UNCOUNT Formal

inedible /ɪnɛdɪbə⁰l/. Something that is **inedible** is too nasty or poisonous to eat. ADJ CLASSIF

ineffective /ɪnɪfɛktɪv/. Something that is **ineffective** has no effect. EG *The therapy was obviously ineffective.* ◊ **ineffectiveness.** EG *He was disgusted by the ineffectiveness of the government.* ADJ QUALIT ◊ N UNCOUNT

ineffectual /ɪnɪfɛktʃʊ⁰əl/. Something that is **ineffectual** fails to do what it is supposed to do. EG *...ineffectual policies.* ◊ **ineffectually.** EG *...trying ineffectually to brush the mud off his jacket.* ADJ QUALIT ◊ ADV

inefficient /ɪnɪfɪʃənt/. 1 A person, organization, or system that is **inefficient** achieves results slowly and not in the most economical way. EG *...inefficient farming.* ◊ **inefficiently.** EG *She works slowly and inefficiently.* ◊ **inefficiency** /ɪnɪfɪʃənsi¹/. EG *He criticised the inefficiency of public authorities.* ADJ QUALIT ◊ ADV ◊ N UNCOUNT

2 An **inefficient** machine or piece of equipment does not work effectively and wastes energy. ADJ QUALIT

inelegant /ɪnɛlɪgənt/. Something that is **inelegant** is not attractive or graceful. EG *Glass chandeliers have been replaced by inelegant plastic ones... ...his inelegant dressing gown.* ADJ QUALIT

ineligible /ɪnɛlɪdʒə¹bə⁰l/. If you are **ineligible** for something, you are not qualified for it or entitled to it. EG *I am ineligible for unemployment benefit.* ADJ CLASSIF: OFT+*for* Formal

inept /ɪnɛpt/. Someone who is **inept** does something with a complete lack of skill. EG *...the government's inept handling of the crisis.* ADJ QUALIT

ineptitude /ɪnɛptɪtju:d/ is a complete lack of skill. EG *...his record of political ineptitude.* N UNCOUNT Formal

inequality /ɪnɪkwɒlɪ¹ti¹/, **inequalities.** 1 **Inequality** is a difference in social status, wealth, or opportunity between groups in a society. EG *...but inequality is the great problem here... We found great inequalities of opportunity.* N UNCOUNT OR N COUNT

2 An **inequality** is also a difference in the size or amount of two or more things. N COUNT OR N UNCOUNT

ineradicable /ɪnɪ²rædɪkəbə⁰l/. Something that is **ineradicable** cannot be removed. EG *...an ineradicable tendency to be frivolous.* ADJ CLASSIF Formal

inert /ɪnɜ:t/. Someone or something that is **inert** does not move at all and appears to be lifeless. EG *I carried her, still inert, up the stairs to her room.* ADJ CLASSIF

inertia /ɪnɜ:ʃɪ⁰ə/. If you have a feeling of **inertia**, you feel very lazy and unwilling to do anything. EG *Though I wanted to go, I stayed from sheer inertia.* N UNCOUNT

inescapable /ɪnɪ²skeɪpəbə⁰l/. If something, especially a fact, is **inescapable**, it cannot be avoided. EG *...an inescapable conclusion.* ADJ CLASSIF

inestimable /ɪnɛstɪməbə⁰l/. Something that is **inestimable** is extremely great or good. EG *Maria's advice proved of inestimable value.* ADJ CLASSIF Formal

inevitable /ɪnɛvɪtəbə⁰l/. 1 If something is **inevitable**, it is certain to happen and cannot be prevented or avoided. EG *If this policy continues, then violence is inevitable... It's inevitable that you should feel indignant.* ◊ **inevitability** /ɪnɛvɪtəbɪlɪ¹ti¹/. EG *You must recognize the inevitability of change.* ADJ CLASSIF ◊ N UNCOUNT

2 The **inevitable** is something that is certain to happen and cannot be prevented or avoided. EG *I suddenly became fatalistic, resigning myself to the inevitable.* N SING: *the*+N

3 You can also use **inevitable** humorously to describe something that happens so regularly that you are able to predict it. EG *We went inside for the inevitable cup of tea.* ADJ CLASSIF: ATTRIB

inevitably /ɪnɛvɪtəbli¹/. If something **inevitably** happens or will happen, it is the only possible result. EG *Inevitably, a shouting match ensued between us... A household of this size inevitably has problems.* ADV OR ADV SEN

inexcusable /ɪnɪ²kskju:zəbə⁰l/. Something that is **inexcusable** is too bad to be justified or tolerated. EG *The local paper declared such waste inexcusable.* ADJ QUALIT

inexhaustible /ɪnɪ²gzɔ:stəbə⁰l/. If something is **inexhaustible**, there is so much of it that it cannot be used up. EG *The sun is an inexhaustible source of energy... His patience must be inexhaustible.* ADJ CLASSIF

inexorable /ɪnɛksə⁰rəbə⁰l/. Something that is **inexorable** cannot be prevented from continuing. EG *...the inexorable rise in the cost of living.* ◊ **inexorably.** EG *These facts led inexorably to one conclusion.* ADJ CLASSIF Formal ◊ ADV

inexpensive /ɪnɪ²kspɛnsɪv/. Something that is **inexpensive** does not cost much. EG *...an inexpensive wine.* ADJ QUALIT

inexperience /ɪnɪ²kspɪərɪəns/. If you refer to someone's **inexperience**, you are referring to the fact that they are inexperienced. EG *You're bound to make a few mistakes through inexperience.* N UNCOUNT

inexperienced /ɪnɪ²kspɪərɪənst/. If you are **inexperienced**, you have little or no experience of a particular situation or activity. EG *...an inexperienced swimmer.* ADJ QUALIT

inexplicable /ɪnɪ²ksplɪkəbə⁰l/. If something is **inexplicable**, you cannot explain why it happened or why it is true. EG *I still find this incident inexplicable.* ◊ **inexplicably.** EG *Anita had inexplicably disappeared.* ADJ QUALIT ◊ ADV

inextricably /ɪnɪ²kstrɪkəbə⁰li¹/. If two or more things are **inextricably** linked, they cannot be separated. EG *Social and economic factors are inextricably linked.* ADV

INF stands for **infinitive**

Verbs in English have two infinitive forms. One is the simple form of the verb, for example 'understand'. And the other is the simple form with 'to', for example 'to understand'.

When +INF is used in the Extra Column, it means that the word is followed by a verb in the infinitive without 'to'. So the label for **make 8** says V+O+INF. This means that this meaning of 'make' is followed by the infinitive, as in *They made me* ***feel*** *guilty* and *I couldn't make her* ***change*** *her mind.*

When +*to*-INF is used in the Extra Column, it means that the word is followed by a verb in the infinitive with 'to'. So the label for **got 3** says V+*to*-INF. This means that this meaning of 'got' is usually followed by the infinitive with 'to', as in *We've got* ***to go*** *now* and *They'd got* ***to catch*** *a bus at 6.*

And the label for **glad 3** says ADJ PRED+*to*-INF. This means that this meaning of 'glad' is usually followed by the infinitive with 'to', as in *I'd be glad* ***to help*** and *She was glad* ***to see*** *us.*

infallible /ɪnfælɪbə⁰l/. Someone or something that is **infallible** is never wrong. EG *Doctors aren't infallible... ...an infallible cure for rheumatism.* ADJ CLASSIF

infamous /ɪnfəməs/. **Infamous** people or things are well-known because they are evil or connected with something evil. EG *How well I remember that infamous night.* ADJ CLASSIF

infancy /ɪnfənsi¹/. 1 Your **infancy** is the period in your life when you are a very young child. EG *The child died in infancy... He came to England in his infancy.* N UNCOUNT

2 If something is **in** its **infancy**, it has only just started. EG *This research is only in its infancy.* PHRASE

infant /ɪnfənt/, **infants.** An **infant** is a very young child or baby. EG *...a newborn infant.* N COUNT Formal

infantile /ɪnfəntaɪl/. 1 You use **infantile** to describe behaviour or disease which very young children have. EG *...infantile paralysis.* ADJ QUALIT Formal

2 Someone who is **infantile** behaves in a foolish and childish way. EG *You're so horribly infantile!* ADJ QUALIT

infantry /ɪnfəntri[1]/. The **infantry** are the soldiers in an army who fight on foot rather than in tanks or on horses. — N COLL

infant school, infant schools. An **infant school** is a school for children between the ages of five and seven. — N COUNT British

infatuated /ɪnfætjʊeɪtɪ[2]d/. If you are **infatuated** with someone, you have a strong feeling of love or passion for them that other people think is ridiculous. EG *He was for several years infatuated with her.* — ADJ PRED : USU+*with*

infatuation /ɪnfætjʊeɪʃən/. An **infatuation** for someone is a strong feeling of love or passion for them that other people think is ridiculous. EG *This is not love but a foolish infatuation.* — N SING

infect /ɪnfɛkt/, **infects, infecting, infected. 1** To **infect** people, animals, plants, or food means to cause them to suffer from germs or to carry germs. EG *Imported birds can infect their owners with an unpleasant illness.* ◊ **infected.** EG *...infected milk... ...a man limping on a badly infected leg.* — V+O : OFT+*with*; ◊ ADJ CLASSIF

2 When a feeling or influence **infects** people, places, or things, it spreads to them. EG *Pessimism had a way of infecting everyone.* — V+O

infection /ɪnfɛkʃən/, **infections. 1** An **infection** is a disease caused by germs. EG *I had an ear infection... ...chest infections... Radiation lessened bodily resistance to infection.* — N COUNT OR N UNCOUNT

2 Infection is the state of becoming infected. EG *There is little risk of infection.* — N UNCOUNT

infectious /ɪnfɛkʃəs/. **1** If you have an **infectious** disease, other people can catch it from you, even if they do not touch you. — ADJ QUALIT

2 If a feeling is **infectious**, it spreads to other people. EG *Don't you find her enthusiasm infectious?... What an infectious laugh he has!* — ADJ QUALIT

infer /ɪnfɜː/, **infers, inferring, inferred.** If you **infer** that something is the case, **1** you decide that it is true, on the basis of information you have. EG *He can infer that if the battery is dead then the horn will not sound... As a result of this simple statement, I could infer a lot about his former wives.* **2** you say something to suggest that it is the case without actually saying so directly. Many people consider that this use is wrong, and that the right word to use is 'imply'. EG *I do not want to infer by this criticism that there is something fundamentally wrong with the system.* — 1: V+REPORT OR V+O+*from*; 2: V+REPORT

inference /ɪnfərəns/, **inferences. 1** An **inference** is a conclusion that you draw about something. EG *The inferences drawn from data have led to some major changes in our policy.* — N COUNT

2 Inference is the act of drawing conclusions about something. EG *We should understand the importance of the industrial revolution and, by inference, the coming computer revolution.* — N UNCOUNT

inferior /ɪnfɪərɪə/, **inferiors. 1** Someone who is **inferior** is less important than other people or has a lower position in society. EG *Charlie, aged sixteen, felt inferior to lads of his own age... Mary does not rebel against her inferior status.* ◊ **inferiority** /ɪnfɪərɪɒrɪti[1]/. EG *...feelings of inferiority... ...an inferiority complex.* — ADJ QUALIT : OFT+*to*; ◊ N UNCOUNT

2 Your **inferiors** are people who have a lower position or status than you. EG *He complained of the slackness and stupidity of his inferiors.* — N COUNT : USU+POSS

3 Something that is **inferior** is of worse quality than something else of a similar type. EG *It was a cheap and inferior product.* — ADJ QUALIT : OFT+*to*

infernal /ɪnfɜːnəl/. You use **infernal** to describe something that is very unpleasant, especially when you are angry about it. EG *Will you stop that infernal noise?* — ADJ CLASSIF : ATTRIB Outdated

inferno /ɪnfɜːnəʊ/, **infernos.** You can refer to a very large dangerous fire as an **inferno**. — N COUNT Literary

infertile /ɪnfɜːtaɪl/. **1** Someone who is **infertile** is unable to have or produce babies. EG *She learned she was infertile.* ◊ **infertility** /ɪnfɜːtɪlɪ[1]ti[1]/. EG *...an infertility clinic.* — ADJ CLASSIF; ◊ N UNCOUNT

2 Infertile soil is of poor quality, and so plants cannot grow in it. EG *...infertile tropical soils.* ◊ **infertility.** EG *There were few farms there because of the infertility of the soil.* — ADJ QUALIT; ◊ N UNCOUNT

infested /ɪnfɛstɪ[2]d/. If a plant or area is **infested** with insects, rats, or other pests, many of them are on it or in it, usually causing damage. EG *...broad beans infested with blackfly.* — ADJ PRED

infidelity /ɪnfɪdɛlɪ[1]ti[1]/, **infidelities.** When **infidelity** occurs, a person who is married or who has a steady relationship with someone has sex with another person. EG *...a widow who discovers her late husband's infidelity.* — N UNCOUNT OR N COUNT

in-fighting is rivalry or quarrelling between members of the same organization. — N UNCOUNT

infiltrate /ɪnfɪltreɪt/, **infiltrates, infiltrating, infiltrated.** If people **infiltrate** an organization, they join it secretly in order to spy on its activities or to influence its decisions. EG *The organization was infiltrated by the police... Some of them infiltrated into its highest councils.* ◊ **infiltration** /ɪnfɪltreɪʃən/. EG *...the infiltration of the party by extreme left-wing groups.* — V+O OR V+*into*; ◊ N UNCOUNT

infinite /ɪnfɪnə[1]t/. Something that is **infinite 1** is extremely large in amount or degree. EG *Qualified doctors are found in an infinite variety of careers.* ◊ **infinitely.** EG *The process of unloading had been infinitely easier than putting the stuff on.* **2** has no limit, end, or edge. EG *...that desert land of infinite blue air.* — ADJ CLASSIF; ◊ SUBMOD; 2: ADJ CLASSIF

infinitesimal /ɪnfɪnɪtɛsɪməl/. Something that is **infinitesimal** is extremely small. EG *The chances that the company will have any problems are infinitesimal.* — ADJ CLASSIF Formal

infinitive /ɪnfɪnɪ[1]tɪv/, **infinitives.** The **infinitive** or the **infinitive** form of a verb is the form which does not have inflections, such as *do, take,* and *eat.* The infinitive can either be used on its own or with *to* in front of it. The infinitive is abbreviated to INF in the Extra Column in this dictionary. See the entry headed INF for more information. — N COUNT

infinity /ɪnfɪnɪ[1]ti[1]/ is **1** a number that is larger than any other number and can never be given an exact value. EG *...an infinity of possible combinations.* **2** a point that is further away than any other point and can never be reached. EG *There was nothing but darkness stretching away to infinity.* — N UNCOUNT

infirm /ɪnfɜːm/. **1** A person who is **infirm** is weak or ill. EG *His grandfather was over eighty years of age, infirm and totally blind.* ◊ **infirmity** /ɪnfɜːmɪ[1]ti[1]/, **infirmities.** EG *...physical infirmity or weakness... ...the infirmities of old age.* — ADJ QUALIT Formal; ◊ N COUNT OR N UNCOUNT

2 The **infirm** are people who are infirm. EG *...the needs of the old and infirm.* — N PLURAL : the+N

infirmary /ɪnfɜːməri[1]/, **infirmaries.** Some hospitals are called **infirmaries**. EG *...Manchester Royal Infirmary.* — N COUNT Outdated

inflame /ɪnfleɪm/, **inflames, inflaming, inflamed.** Something that **inflames** someone makes them very angry or excited. EG *Her question seemed to inflame him all the more.* — V+O

inflamed /ɪnfleɪmd/. If part of your body is **inflamed**, it is red and often hot and swollen, because of an infection or an injury. — ADJ QUALIT Formal

inflammable /ɪnflæməbəl/. An **inflammable** material or chemical burns easily. — ADJ QUALIT

inflammation /ɪnfləmeɪʃən/. An **inflammation** is a painful redness or swelling of part of the body. EG *Some children have inflammation of the ears when they have colds.* — N UNCOUNT OR N SING

inflammatory /ɪnflæmətəri[1]/. An **inflammatory** speech or action is likely to make people very angry or hostile. EG *...an inflammatory speech about terrorists.* — ADJ QUALIT

If you are informative, are you an informer?

inflatable /ɪnfleɪtəbə^{0}l/. An **inflatable** object can be filled with air. EG *...inflatable lifejackets.* ADJ CLASSIF

inflate /ɪnfleɪt/, **inflates, inflating, inflated.** When you **inflate** something or when it **inflates**, it becomes bigger as it is filled with air or another gas. EG *...a rubber dinghy that took half a hour to inflate.* V-ERG

inflated /ɪnfleɪtɪ^{2}d/ **1** An **inflated** object has been filled with air until it is firm. EG *...the large inflated tyre they used as a raft.* ADJ CLASSIF

2 If you have an **inflated** opinion of yourself, you think you are much more important than you really are. EG *...his inflated self-image.* ADJ QUALIT

3 An **inflated** price or salary is higher than is considered reasonable. EG *...food and clothing which had to be bought at inflated prices.* ADJ QUALIT

inflation /ɪnfleɪʃə^{0}n/ is a general increase in the prices of goods and services in a country. EG *Chile has reduced its inflation in the past year from a hundred per cent to fifty.* N UNCOUNT

inflationary /ɪnfleɪʃənə^{0}ri^1/. An **inflationary** action or event causes inflation. EG *...inflationary wage demands... ...inflationary economic policies.* ADJ QUALIT Formal

inflect /ɪnflɛkt/, **inflects, inflecting, inflected.** If a word **inflects**, its ending or form changes in order to show its grammatical function. If a language **inflects**, it has words in it that change their endings or forms in order to show their grammatical functions. V ◇ **inflected.** EG *German is an inflected language.* ◇ ADJ CLASSIF

inflection /ɪnflɛkʃə^{0}n/, **inflections;** also spelled **inflexion.** An **inflection** is **1** the way that you change the sound of your voice when you speak. EG *She spoke in a low voice, always without inflection.* N COUNT OR N UNCOUNT
2 a change in the form of a word that shows its grammatical function, for example a change that makes a noun plural or makes a verb into the past tense.

inflexible /ɪnflɛksɪbə^{0}l/. Something that is **inflexible** cannot be altered. EG *Nursery schools have inflexible hours.* ADJ QUALIT ◇ **inflexibility** /ɪnflɛksɪ^{1}bɪlɪ^{1}ti^1/. EG *...dogmatic inflexibility in the face of change.* ◇ N UNCOUNT

inflexion /ɪnflɛkʃə^{0}n/. See **inflection**.

inflict /ɪnflɪkt/, **inflicts, inflicting, inflicted.** If you **inflict** something unpleasant on someone, you make them suffer it. EG *...the suffering that would be inflicted upon innocent people. ...the dreadful way she had inflicted her problems on him.* V+O : OFT+*on/upon*

influence /ɪnfluəns/, **influences, influencing, influenced. 1 Influence** is power that you have which makes it likely that other people will agree with you or do what you want. EG *The government would use its influence to try to make the negotiations successful... Moscow retains some influence over their affairs.* N UNCOUNT ● If you are **under the influence** of someone or something, you are being affected or controlled by them. EG *He was under the influence of friends who were highly conservative... They were deeply under the influence of alcohol.* ● PHRASE

2 The **influence** that someone or something has on people or situations is the effect that they have on them. EG *His teachings still exert a strong influence... ...the influence of religion on society.* N COUNT

3 Someone or something that is an **influence** on people or things has an effect on them. EG *He was a bad influence on the children... ...influences in drama and literature.* N COUNT+SUPP

4 If you **influence** a person, thing, or situation, you have an effect on the way that person acts or on what happens. EG *I didn't want him to influence me in my choice... Is British art influenced at all by American painting?* V+O

influential /ɪnfluɛnʃə^{0}l/. Someone who is **influential** has a lot of influence over people. EG *...a powerful and influential politician.* ADJ QUALIT

influenza /ɪnfluɛnzə/ is the same as flu. EG *She died in the great influenza epidemic.* N UNCOUNT Formal

influx /ɪnflʌks/. An **influx** of people or things into a place is their steady arrival there in large numbers. EG *...a massive influx of refugees from neighbouring countries.* N SING+SUPP

info /ɪnfəʊ/ is the same as information. EG *...the info on where the meeting was.* N UNCOUNT Informal

inform /ɪnfɔːm/, **informs, informing, informed.** If you **inform** someone of something, you tell them about it. EG *He intended to see Barbara to inform her of his objections... I informed her that I was unwell... 'They are late,' he informed her.* ● See also **informed**. V+O : USU+*of*, REPORT, OR QUOTE

informal /ɪnfɔːmə^{0}l/. **1** You use **informal** to describe behaviour or speech that is relaxed and casual rather than correct and serious. In this dictionary, language of this kind is indicated by the word 'Informal' in the Extra Column. EG *...a relaxed and quite informal discussion.* ADJ QUALIT ◇ **informally.** EG *...people talking informally together.* ◇ ADV
◇ **informality** /ɪnfɔːmælɪ^{1}ti^1/. EG *...an atmosphere of informality.* ◇ N UNCOUNT

2 You also use **informal** to describe **2.1** relaxed social occasions, where you do not have to wear smart clothes or behave correctly. EG *...an informal party.* ADJ QUALIT **2.2** clothes that are suitable for wearing when you are relaxing, but not for formal occasions. ADJ QUALIT ◇ **informally.** EG *The producer was informally dressed in a blue silk shirt open at the neck.* ◇ ADV
2.3 something that is done unofficially. EG *We have informal contacts with over 500 firms.* ADJ CLASSIF
◇ **informally.** EG *Germany and Russia agreed informally to abide by the agreement.* ◇ ADV

informant /ɪnfɔːmənt/, **informants.** An **informant** is **1** someone who gives another person a piece of information. **2** the same as an informer. N COUNT

information /ɪnfəmeɪʃə^{0}n/. If you have **information** about something, you know something about it. EG *I'm afraid I have no information on that... She provided me with a very interesting piece of information about his past.* N UNCOUNT

informative /ɪnfɔːmətɪv/. Something that is **informative** gives you useful information. EG *...an informative guidebook... Nothing that she said was very informative.* ADJ QUALIT

informed /ɪnfɔːmd/. If you make an **informed** guess about something, you use your knowledge to decide what you think the answer should be. ADJ CLASSIF : ATTRIB

informer /ɪnfɔːmə/, **informers.** An **informer** is someone who tells the police that another person has done something illegal. N COUNT

infra-red /ɪnfrə rɛd/. **Infra-red** light is below the colour red in the spectrum and cannot be seen. EG *...infra-red photography.* ADJ CLASSIF

infrequent /ɪnfriːkwənt/. If something is **infrequent**, it does not happen often. EG *...her sister's infrequent letters.* ADJ QUALIT ◇ **infrequently.** EG *My parents were only able to visit us infrequently.* ◇ ADV

infringe /ɪnfrɪndʒ/, **infringes, infringing, infringed. 1** If you **infringe** a law or an agreement, you break it. EG *They occasionally infringe the law by parking near a junction.* V+O Formal

2 If you **infringe** people's rights or **infringe** on them, you do not allow the people the rights or freedom that they are entitled to. EG *They were citizens with legal rights, which were being infringed... We must fight them when they infringe on our children's right to freedom.* V+O OR V+*on/upon*

infringement /ɪnfrɪnd^{0}ʒmə^{2}nt/, **infringements.**
1 If an action is an **infringement** on your rights, it restricts you unfairly. EG *The new law is an infringement on free speech.* N COUNT OR N UNCOUNT : USU+*of/on*

2 An **infringement** of a law, rule, or agreement is the breaking of it. EG *...small infringements of prison discipline.* N COUNT OR N UNCOUNT : USU+*of*

infuriate /ɪnfjʊəri^{1}eɪt/, **infuriates, infuriating, infuriated.** If something or someone **infuriates** you, they make you extremely angry. EG *Is he trying to infuriate me? He's succeeding... Old jeans* V+O *and T-shirts infuriated him.* ◊ **infuriated.** EG *...a small group of infuriated little boys.* ◊ ADJ QUALIT

infuriating /ɪnfjʊəri¹eɪtɪŋ/. Something that is **infuriating** annoys you very much. EG *...her infuriating habit of criticizing people all the time.* ADJ QUALIT

-ing is added to verbs **1** to form present participles. EG *I was walking along the road... She sat by the window, drinking coffee.* **2** to form uncountable nouns that refer to activities. Nouns like these are often not defined in this dictionary, but are treated with the related verbs. EG *Farming was something I really enjoyed... We need to spend more money on advertising.* SUFFIX

> **-ING** stands for **present participle**
> When a verb is followed by another verb, sometimes the second verb must be in the form that ends in '-ing'. In these cases the label in the Extra Column will include + -ING. An example is **enjoy 1**, where the Extra Column says V+O OR V+ -ING, showing that the verb can be followed either by an object or by a form ending in '-ing', as in *You're interesting and I enjoy talking to you* and *They enjoyed reading novels when they were young.*
> ING is also used as part of the label for some nouns. See the entry headed NOUNS for information about this.

ingenious /ɪndʒiːnjəs, -nɪəs/. An **ingenious** idea, plan, or device is very clever. EG *...an ingenious method of forecasting economic trends.* ADJ QUALIT
◊ **ingeniously.** EG *The hangers were ingeniously fixed to the wardrobe by pieces of wire.* ◊ ADV

ingenuity /ɪndʒɪnjuːɪ¹ti¹/ is cleverness and skill at inventing things or working out plans. EG *With a bit of ingenuity you can do almost anything.* N UNCOUNT

ingenuous /ɪndʒenjuːəs/. Someone who is **ingenuous** is innocent, trusting, and not capable of deceiving people. EG *His expression was frank, ingenuous, and engaging.* ADJ QUALIT

ingrained /ɪŋ¹greɪnd/. If habits and beliefs are **ingrained**, they are difficult to change or destroy. EG *The belief that one should work hard is ingrained in our culture.* ADJ QUALIT : OFT+*in*

ingratiate /ɪŋ¹greɪʃi¹eɪt/, **ingratiates, ingratiating, ingratiated.** If you try to **ingratiate** yourself with other people, you try to make them like you; used showing disapproval. EG *They resented his knack for ingratiating himself with officers.* V-REFL : USU+*with*
◊ **ingratiating** /ɪŋ¹greɪʃi¹eɪtɪŋ/. EG *...an ingratiating smile.* ◊ ADJ QUALIT

ingratitude /ɪŋ¹grætɪtjuːd/ is the lack of gratitude for something that has been done for you. EG *I was shocked and enraged at such ingratitude.* N UNCOUNT

ingredient /ɪŋ¹griːdɪənt/, **ingredients. 1** The **ingredients** of something that you cook or prepare are the different foods that you use. EG *Mix the ingredients to a soft dough.* N COUNT
2 An **ingredient** of a situation is one of the essential parts of it. EG *The most essential ingredient in economic progress is investment.* N COUNT+SUPP

inhabit /ɪnhæbɪt/, **inhabits, inhabiting, inhabited.** If a place or region **is inhabited**, people live there. EG *The town was a seaside resort, inhabited by fishermen and hoteliers.* V+O : USU PASS

inhabitant /ɪnhæbɪtənt/, **inhabitants.** The **inhabitants** of a place are the people who live there. N COUNT

inhale /ɪnheɪl/, **inhales, inhaling, inhaled.** When you **inhale** or when you **inhale** smoke, fumes, or a smell, you breathe in. EG *She put the cigarette between her lips and inhaled deeply.* V OR V+O

inherent /ɪnhɪərənt, -her-/. Qualities or characteristics that are **inherent** in something are a necessary and natural part of it. EG *...the dangers inherent in this kind of political system... ...my inherent laziness.* ◊ **inherently.** EG *Power stations are themselves inherently inefficient.* ADJ CLASSIF : OFT+*in* ◊ ADV

inherit /ɪnherɪt/, **inherits, inheriting, inherited. 1** If you **inherit** something such as a position, situation, or attitude, you take it over from people who came before you. EG *They inherited a weak economy... ...traditions inherited from the past.* V+O : OFT+*from*
2 If you **inherit** money or property, you receive it from someone who has died. V+O
3 If you **inherit** a characteristic or quality, you are born with it, because your parents or ancestors had it. EG *This kind of brain damage may be inherited.* V+O

inheritance /ɪnherɪtə⁰ns/, **inheritances. 1** An **inheritance** is **1.1** money or property which you receive from someone who is dead. EG *He had no motive for depriving his son of the inheritance... ...the customs of inheritance in Asia.* **1.2** a situation or thing which you have taken over from people who came before you. EG *...our alphabet, an inheritance from the Greeks.* N COUNT OR N UNCOUNT; N SING+SUPP Formal
2 Inheritance is also the fact of being born with characteristics or qualities which your parents or ancestors had. EG *To what extent does human nature depend on genetic inheritance?* N UNCOUNT +SUPP

inheritor /ɪnherɪtə/, **inheritors.** Someone who is an **inheritor** of something inherited it from people who came before them. EG *...the inheritors of a literary tradition.* N COUNT+SUPP

inhibit /ɪnhɪbɪt/, **inhibits, inhibiting, inhibited.** If something **inhibits** an action or the development of something, it prevents it or slows it down. EG *The drugs with which the animals are fed inhibit their development.* V+O

inhibited /ɪnhɪbɪtɪ¹d/. If you are **inhibited**, you find it difficult to behave naturally and to show your real feelings. EG *Her severe upbringing had left her inhibited.* ADJ QUALIT

inhibition /ɪnh⁰ɪbɪʃə⁰n/, **inhibitions. Inhibitions** are feelings of fear or embarrassment that make it difficult for you to behave naturally. EG *...a child who is free from inhibitions... She's prepared to argue without inhibition.* N COUNT OR N UNCOUNT

inhospitable /ɪnhɒspɪtəbə⁰l/. **1** If a place is **inhospitable**, it is unpleasant for people to live in. EG *...inhospitable deserts.* ADJ QUALIT
2 If you are **inhospitable**, you do not like having guests and do not make people feel welcome when they visit you. EG *I don't like to be inhospitable, but I've got an awful lot to do.* ADJ QUALIT

inhuman /ɪnhjuːmən/. **1** Behaviour that is **inhuman** is extremely cruel or brutal. EG *...barbarous and inhuman atrocities.* ADJ QUALIT
2 Something that is **inhuman** is not human, and is therefore strange or frightening. EG *Their faces looked inhuman, covered with scarlet and black paint.* ADJ CLASSIF

inhumane /ɪnhjuːmeɪn/. A way of treating people or animals that is **inhumane** is extremely cruel. ADJ QUALIT

inhumanity /ɪnhjuːmænɪ¹ti¹/ is extreme cruelty or the lack of kind feelings towards people. EG *...man's inhumanity to man.* N UNCOUNT

inimical /ɪnɪmɪkə⁰l/. Conditions that are **inimical** to something make it hard for it to survive. EG *The very nature of society is inimical to freedom.* ADJ CLASSIF : USU PRED+*to* Formal

inimitable /ɪnɪmɪtəbə⁰l/. If someone has an **inimitable** quality or characteristic, that quality is very good or is very typical of that person. EG *The Welsh Rugby team have their own inimitable style.* ADJ CLASSIF Formal

iniquitous /ɪnɪkwɪtəs/. If you describe something as **iniquitous**, you mean that it is very bad and unfair. EG *...this iniquitous policy.* ADJ QUALIT Formal

iniquity /ɪnɪkwɪ¹ti¹/, **iniquities.** An **iniquity** is something that is very wicked or unjust. EG *We fought a revolution to put an end to such iniquities... ...Rose's iniquity and selfishness.* N COUNT OR N UNCOUNT Formal

How is someone related to their in-laws?

initial /ɪnɪʃə^0l/, **initials, initialling, initialled;** spelled **initialed** and **initialing** in American English.

1 You use **initial** to describe something that happens at the beginning of a process, in contrast to what happens later. EG *...the initial stages of learning English... My initial reaction was one of great relief.* — ADJ CLASSIF: ATTRIB

2 Your **initials** are the set of capital letters which begin each of your names, or begin your first names. For example, if your full name is Karen Anne Fox, your initials are K.A.F. — N PLURAL

3 When you **initial** a document, you write your initials on it in order to show that you have seen it or have officially approved it. *He picked up his pen and initialed the papers.* — V+O

initially /ɪnɪʃə^0li^1/ means in the early or original stages of a process. EG *I don't remember who initially conceived the idea.* — ADV

initiate, initiates, initiating, initiated; pronounced /ɪnɪʃi^1eɪt/ when it is a verb, and /ɪnɪʃi^1ət/ when it is a noun.

1 If you **initiate** something, you cause it to start. EG *We should initiate direct talks with the trades unions.* ◊ **initiation** /ɪnɪʃieɪʃə^0n/. EG *...the initiation of a new revolutionary practice.* — V+O; ◊ N UNCOUNT +*of*

2 If you **initiate** someone into a type of knowledge or into a group, you conduct a ceremony or teach them special things so that they become a member of a group. EG *To understand, one must be initiated into great mysteries.* ◊ **initiation.** EG *...an initiation ceremony.* — V+O+*into*; ◊ N UNCOUNT

3 An **initiate** is a person who has recently been allowed to join a particular group and who has been taught special things. EG *...an initiate into the world of politics.* — N COUNT

initiative /ɪnɪʃɪ^0ətɪv/, **initiatives. 1** An **initiative** is an important act, which is an attempt to solve a problem. EG *...launching various initiatives to tackle real or imagined problems.* — N COUNT: USU PLURAL

2 If you have the **initiative**, you are in a stronger position than the people you are competing with or fighting against. EG *They had lost the initiative.* — N SING: *the*+N

3 If you **take the initiative** in a situation, you are the first person to do something. EG *In Sweden employers have taken the initiative in promoting health insurance schemes.* — PHRASE

4 If you have **initiative**, you are able to decide what to do, and to take action, without needing other people to tell you what to do. — N UNCOUNT

5 If you **use** your **initiative**, or if you do something **on** your **own initiative**, you make decisions or take action using your own judgement rather than being told what to do. EG *In special circumstances we have to use our initiative... In 1912 he had gone to Berlin on his own initiative.* — PHRASE

inject /ɪndʒɛkt/, **injects, injecting, injected. 1** If you **inject** someone with a liquid, you use a syringe to get it into their blood. EG *She injected a sleeping drug into my arm... Animals were injected with various doses.* — V+O: OFT +*into/with*

2 If you **inject** something such as excitement or interest into a situation, you add it. EG *She was trying to inject some fun into the grim proceedings.* — V+O: OFT+*into*

3 If you **inject** money into a business or organization, you provide more money for it. EG *Enormous sums of money are injected each year into teaching.* — V+O: OFT+*into*

injection /ɪndʒɛkʃə^0n/, **injections. 1** If you have an **injection**, someone puts a liquid into your blood using a syringe, especially in order to prevent you getting an illness. EG *You had a smallpox injection when you were five.* — N COUNT

2 An **injection** of money into a business or organization is the putting of extra money into it. EG *They only survived because of massive injections of commercial funds.* — N COUNT+*of*

injunction /ɪndʒʌŋkʃə^0n/, **injunctions.** An **injunction** is a formal order, especially one issued by a court of law in order to stop someone doing something. EG *We will apply to the courts for an injunction against the march.* — N COUNT

injure /ɪndʒə/, **injures, injuring, injured.** If you **injure** someone, you damage a part of their body. EG *I feared they might injure themselves... Peter injured his right hand in an accident... She was not badly injured.* — V+O OR V-REFL

injury /ɪndʒəri^1/, **injuries.** An **injury** is damage done to a person's body. EG *The earthquake caused many deaths and severe injuries... Louis received an injury to his head... He was weakened by illness and injury.* — N COUNT OR N UNCOUNT

injustice /ɪndʒʌstɪs/, **injustices. 1 Injustice** is unfairness and lack of justice in a situation. EG *There's social injustice everywhere... He contemplated the injustices of life.* — N UNCOUNT OR N COUNT

2 If you say that you have **done** someone **an injustice**, you mean that your opinion about them was too severe or harsh. EG *I feel I've done him rather an injustice.* — PHRASE

ink /ɪŋk/, **inks. Ink** is the coloured liquid used for writing or printing. EG *Please write in ink.* — N MASS

inkling /ɪŋklɪŋ/. If you **have an inkling** of something, you suspect what it is or suspect that it is the case. EG *He had an inkling of what was going on... I had no inkling that she was interested in me.* — PHRASE

inky /ɪŋki^1/ means **1** very black, like ink. EG *...inky forests of evergreens on the mountains... ...an inky sky.* **2** covered in ink. EG *...an inky handkerchief.* — ADJ COLOUR Literary; ADJ QUALIT

inland /ɪnlə^3nd/ means away from the coast, towards the middle of a country. EG *The Sahara was once an inland sea... Donkeys bear goods inland to the towns and villages.* — ADJ CLASSIF: ATTRIB OR ADV

in-laws. Your **in-laws** are the parents of your husband or wife, and possibly his or her other close relatives too. — N PLURAL

inlet /ɪnlə^2t/, **inlets.** An **inlet** is a narrow strip of water which goes from a sea or lake into the land. — N COUNT

inmate /ɪnmeɪt/, **inmates.** The **inmates** of an institution such as a prison or a psychiatric hospital are the people living there. EG *In prison you learned about other inmates and their crimes.* — N COUNT

inmost /ɪnməʊst/ means the same as innermost. EG *You read my inmost thoughts.* — ADJ CLASSIF: ATTRIB

inn /ɪn/, **inns.** An **inn** is a small hotel or a pub, usually an old one. EG *...the Pilgrim's Inn.* — N COUNT Outdated

innate /ɪneɪt/. An **innate** quality or ability is one which a person is born with. EG *They believed intelligence was innate, and unlikely to change... ...an innate talent for music.* ◊ **innately.** EG *I don't think that anybody is innately good.* — ADJ CLASSIF; ◊ ADV

inner /ɪnə/. **1** You use **inner** to describe a part of something which is contained or enclosed inside the outer part. EG *There were several flats overlooking the inner courtyard.* — ADJ CLASSIF: ATTRIB

2 Inner feelings are feelings which you have but do not show to other people. EG *...his inner feelings of failure... ...inner doubts.* — ADJ CLASSIF: ATTRIB

inner city, inner cities. You use **inner city** to refer to the centre of a large city where people live and where there are often social and economic problems. EG *This is one of the most serious problems in the inner cities... ...the problems for inner-city children.* — N SING: *the*+N, OR N PLURAL

innermost /ɪnəməʊst/. Your **innermost** thoughts and feelings are your most personal and secret ones. EG *...her innermost wishes.* — ADJ CLASSIF: ATTRIB Literary

innings /ɪnɪŋz/. **Innings** is both the singular and the plural form. — N COUNT

An **innings** is a period in a game of cricket during which a particular player or team is batting.

innocent /ɪnəsənt/, **innocents. 1** If someone is **innocent**, **1.1** they are not guilty of a crime. EG *He was accused of a crime of violence of which he was innocent... ...the suffering that would be inflicted upon innocent people.* ◊ **innocence** /ɪnəsəns/. EG *He desperately protested his innocence.* **1.2** they have no experience or knowledge of the more — ADJ CLASSIF; ◊ N UNCOUNT; ADJ QUALIT complex or unpleasant aspects of life. EG *I was very young, and very innocent.* ◇ **innocence.** EG *He had a peculiar air of childlike innocence.* ◇ N UNCOUNT

2 An **innocent** is a person who has no experience or knowledge of the more complex or unpleasant aspects of life. EG *He was a financial genius but a political innocent.* N COUNT Literary

3 An **innocent** remark or action is not intended to offend or upset people, although it may do so. EG *It was an innocent question.* ◇ **innocently.** EG *'What did I do wrong?' asked Howard, innocently.* ADJ QUALIT ◇ ADV

innocuous /ɪnɒkju:əs/. Something that is **innocuous** is not at all harmful. EG *Most of these substances are relatively innocuous.* ADJ QUALIT

innovate /ɪnə^{6}veɪt/, **innovates, innovating, innovated.** To **innovate** means to introduce changes and new ideas. EG *...the industry's capacity to respond swiftly to market changes and to innovate.* ◇ **innovator** /ɪnə^{6}veɪtə/, **innovators.** EG *The Pope thought of himself as an innovator.* V ◇ N COUNT

innovation /ɪnə^{6}veɪʃə^{0}n/, **innovations. 1** An **innovation** is a new thing or a new way of doing something. EG *...a series of remarkable innovations in textile manufacturing.* N COUNT

2 **Innovation** is the introduction of new things or new ways of doing things. EG *...a period of technological innovation.* N UNCOUNT

innovative /ɪnəvətɪv/. **1** Something that is **innovative** is new and original. EG *...their innovative campaign style... ...innovative ideas.* ADJ QUALIT

2 Someone who is **innovative** introduces changes and new ideas. EG *...a pioneering and innovative banker.* ADJ QUALIT

innovatory /ɪnəvətə^{0}ri^{1}, ɪnəveɪtə^{0}ri^{1}/ means the same as innovative. EG *His music was innovatory in its time.* ADJ QUALIT

innuendo /ɪnju:ɛndəʊ/, **innuendoes** or **innuendos. Innuendo** is indirect reference to something rude or unpleasant. EG *...a campaign of innuendo and gossip... He became a target for sexual innuendoes.* N UNCOUNT OR N COUNT

innumerable /ɪnju:mə^{0}rəbə^{0}l/ means too many to be counted. EG *The industrial age has brought innumerable benefits.* ADJ CLASSIF

inoculate /ɪnɒkjə^{4}leɪt/, **inoculates, inoculating, inoculated.** If you **are inoculated** against a disease, you are injected with a weak form of the disease as a way of protecting you against it. ◇ **inoculation** /ɪnɒkjə^{4}leɪʃə^{0}n/, **inoculations.** EG *...prevention of disease by inoculation... ...inoculations against tetanus.* V+O : OFT +*against/with* ◇ N COUNT OR N UNCOUNT

inoffensive /ɪnəfɛnsɪv/. Someone or something that is **inoffensive** is harmless or not unpleasant. EG *...a nice, quiet, inoffensive little fellow.* ADJ QUALIT

inordinate /ɪnɔ:dɪnɪ^{1}t/ means much greater than you would expect. EG *The idea of this gave me inordinate pleasure... Colin always spent an inordinate length of time in the bathroom.* ◇ **inordinately.** EG *...an achievement of which I was inordinately proud.* ADJ CLASSIF : USU ATTRIB Formal ◇ ADV+ADJ

inorganic /ɪnɔ:gænɪk/. **Inorganic** substances are substances such as stone and metal that do not come from living things. EG *...inorganic materials... ...inorganic fertilizers.* ADJ CLASSIF

input /ɪnpʊt/, **inputs. Input** consists of **1** information or resources that a group or project receives. EG *The project requires the input of more labour.* **2** information that is put into a computer. N UNCOUNT OR N COUNT / N UNCOUNT

inquest /ɪŋ^{1}kwɛst/, **inquests.** An **inquest** is an official inquiry to find out what caused someone's death. EG *There have been demands from his family for an inquest.* N COUNT

inquire /ɪn^{1}kwaɪə/, **inquires, inquiring, inquired;** also spelled **enquire** /ɪ^{2}n^{1}kwaɪə/. If you **inquire** about something, you ask for information about it. EG *'What will it cost?' inquired Miss Musson... He inquired whether it was possible to leave his case at the station... He went to enquire about the times of trains to Edinburgh.* V+A, OR V-SPEECH : ONLY WH Formal

inquire after. If you **inquire after** someone, you ask for information about them, for example about their health. EG *She enquired after Mrs Carstair's daughter, who had just had a baby.* PHRASAL VB : V+PREP, HAS PASS

inquire into. If you **inquire into** something, you investigate it carefully. EG *The police inquired into the deaths of two young girls.* PHRASAL VB : V+PREP, HAS PASS

inquiring /ɪŋ^{1}kwaɪərɪŋ/. **1** If you have an **inquiring** mind, you have a great interest in learning new things. ADJ QUALIT : ATTRIB

2 An **inquiring** expression shows that you want to know something. EG *...the people's inquiring faces.* ◇ **inquiringly.** EG *I looked at her inquiringly.* ADJ QUALIT ◇ ADV

inquiry /ɪ^{1}nkwaɪəri^{1}/, **inquiries;** also spelled **enquiry** /ɪ^{2}n^{1}kwaɪəri^{1}/, especially for paragraph 1.1.

1 An **inquiry** is **1.1** a question which you ask someone in order to get some information. EG *This is what I have been able to learn in my enquiries... I shall make some enquiries.* **1.2** an official investigation into something. EG *Opposition MPs have called for an inquiry... ...a public enquiry.* N COUNT

2 Inquiry is the process of asking about something in order to find out information about it. EG *On further enquiry, however, I discovered that there had been nobody at home that evening.* N UNCOUNT

inquisitive /ɪŋ^{1}kwɪzɪ^{1}tɪv/. If you are **inquisitive**, you like finding out about things. EG *He tried not to sound inquisitive.* ◇ **inquisitively.** EG *I glanced inquisitively through the open doorway.* ADJ QUALIT ◇ ADV

inroads /ɪnrəʊdz/. If something **makes inroads** into something else, it starts affecting it or destroying it. EG *Our party hasn't made great inroads in Scotland... They are highly sensitive to any inroads upon their independence.* PHRASE

insane /ɪnseɪn/. **1** Someone who is **insane** is mad. EG *Some went insane.* ◇ **insanity** /ɪnsænɪ^{1}ti^{1}/. EG *He saw the beginnings of insanity in her.* ADJ CLASSIF ◇ N UNCOUNT

2 If you describe something or someone as **insane**, you mean that they are very foolish. EG *This idea is totally insane... You'd be insane to do that.* ◇ **insanely.** EG *I must admit that I was insanely jealous.* ◇ **insanity.** EG *I laughed at the insanity of it all.* ADJ QUALIT Informal ◇ ADV ◇ N UNCOUNT

insatiable /ɪnseɪʃɪ^{0}əbə^{0}l/. A desire or greed that is **insatiable** is very great. EG *...an insatiable curiosity... ...an insatiable appetite for power.* ◇ **insatiably.** EG *She was insatiably curious.* ADJ CLASSIF ◇ ADV

inscribe /ɪnskraɪb/, **inscribes, inscribing, inscribed.** If some words **are inscribed** on an object or if an object **is inscribed** with some words, the words are written or carved on the object. EG *The names of the dead were inscribed on the wall... ...a ring inscribed 'To My Darling'.* V+O+A OR V+O+C : USU PASS Formal

inscription /ɪnskrɪpʃə^{0}n/, **inscriptions.** An **inscription** is words that are written or carved on something. EG *The inscription above the door was in English.* N COUNT

inscrutable /ɪnskru:təbə^{0}l/. Someone who is **inscrutable** does not show by their words or behaviour what they are really thinking. EG *The candidates are pretty inscrutable.* ADJ QUALIT

insect /ɪnsɛkt/, **insects.** An **insect** is a small animal that has six legs. Most insects have wings. Ants, flies, butterflies, and beetles are all insects. N COUNT

insecticide /ɪnsɛktɪsaɪd/, **insecticides. Insecticide** is a chemical that is used to kill insects. N MASS

insecure /ɪnsɪkjʊə/. **1** If you feel **insecure**, you feel that you are not good enough in some way, or are not loved. EG *What had I done to make you so insecure and frightened?* ◇ **insecurity** /ɪnsɪ^{2}kjʊərɪ^{1}ti^{1}/. EG *...feelings of insecurity.* ADJ QUALIT ◇ N UNCOUNT

2 Something that is **insecure** is not safe or well-protected. EG *Their place in society is insecure.* ◇ **insecurity.** EG *...financial insecurity.* ADJ QUALIT ◇ N UNCOUNT

What will kill an insect?

insensitive /ɪnsɛnsɪtɪv/. Someone who is **insensitive** is not aware of other people's feelings, and does not realize when they have upset or annoyed people. EG *...bad-mannered, loud, insensitive oafs... ...the insensitive attitude of the government.* ADJ QUALIT
◊ **insensitivity** /ɪnsɛnsɪtɪvɪ[1]ti[1]/. EG *There were times when he showed a curious insensitivity.* ◊ N UNCOUNT

inseparable /ɪnsɛpə[0]rəbə[0]l/. **1** If two things are **inseparable**, they are so closely connected that they cannot be considered separately. EG *Culture is inseparable from class... The social and ecological costs are inseparable.* ADJ CLASSIF: OFT+*from* Formal
2 Friends who are **inseparable** are always together. EG *Soon they were inseparable.* ADJ QUALIT Formal

insert /ɪnsɜːt/, **inserts, inserting, inserted. 1** If you **insert** an object into something, you put the object inside it. EG *He inserted the wooden peg into the hole.* V+O : USU+A
2 If you **insert** a comment in a piece of writing or a speech, you include it. EG *The President inserted one unscripted item in his speech.* V+O

inshore /ɪnʃɔː/ means in the sea but quite close to the land. EG *...inshore fishermen... These fish are not found inshore.* ADJ CLASSIF: ATTRIB OR ADV

inside /ɪnsaɪd/, **insides. 1** Something or someone that is **inside** a place, container, or object is surrounded by its sides. EG *Two minutes later we were inside the taxi... You left your lighter inside... It is a fruit with a seed inside.* ▸ used as an adjective. EG *The door had no inside bolt.* PREP OR ADV ▸ ADJ CLASSIF: ATTRIB
2 The **inside** of something is the part or area that its sides surround or contain. EG *The inside of my mouth was dry... ...the inside of the castle.* N COUNT
3 You can also say that someone is **inside** when they are in prison. ADV Informal
4 On a wide road, the **inside** lanes are the ones which are closest to the edge of the road. ADJ CLASSIF: ATTRIB
5 Inside information is obtained from someone who is involved in a situation and therefore knows a lot about it. ADJ CLASSIF: ATTRIB
6 If you are **inside** an organization, you belong to it. EG *Nobody inside the company will be surprised.* PREP
7 If you say that someone has a feeling **inside** them, you mean that they have not expressed this feeling. EG *His true feelings keep surging up inside him... I always felt inside that I wanted to write.* PREP OR ADV
8 If something such as a piece of clothing is **inside out**, the inside part has been turned so that it faces outwards. PHRASE
9 Your **insides** are your internal organs, especially your stomach. EG *What we all need is a bit of food in our insides.* N PLURAL: USU+POSS Informal

insider /ɪnsaɪdə/, **insiders.** An **insider** is someone who is involved in a situation and who knows more about it than other people. EG *According to one insider, the government is getting worried.* N COUNT

insidious /ɪnsɪdi[1]əs/. Something that is **insidious** is unpleasant and develops gradually without being noticed. EG *The leaflets were a more insidious form of propaganda.* ADJ QUALIT

insight /ɪnsaɪt/, **insights.** If you gain **insight** into a complex situation or problem, you gain an understanding of it. EG *...a number of interesting psychological insights.* N UNCOUNT OR N COUNT

insignia /ɪnsɪgnɪə/. **Insignia** is both the singular and the plural form. N COUNT
An **insignia** is a badge or sign which shows that a person or object belongs to a particular organization. EG *...military insignia... ...a plane bearing the insignia of the Condor Legion.*

insignificant /ɪnsɪgnɪfɪkənt/. Something that is **insignificant** is not at all important. EG *Whatever I write seems so insignificant... ...an insignificant minority.* ADJ QUALIT
◊ **insignificance** /ɪnsɪgnɪfɪkəns/. EG *This emergency plunges all her other problems into insignificance.* ◊ N UNCOUNT

insincere /ɪnsɪnsɪə/. Someone who is **insincere** is not sincere. EG *...people whose admiration is extravagant and often insincere.* ADJ QUALIT
◊ **insincerity** /ɪnsɪnsɛrɪ[1]ti[1]/. EG *The young are quick to recognize insincerity.* ◊ N UNCOUNT

insinuate /ɪnsɪnjuːeɪt/, **insinuates, insinuating, insinuated. 1** If you **insinuate** that something is true, you hint in an unpleasant way that it is true. EG *He insinuated that my wife had betrayed my trust in her.* V+REPORT: ONLY *that*
2 If you **insinuate** yourself into a particular position, you manage slowly and cleverly to get yourself into that position; used showing disapproval. EG *He eventually insinuated himself into a key position in the Party.* V-REFL+*into*

insipid /ɪnsɪpɪd/. **1** If you describe someone or something as **insipid**, you mean that they are dull and boring. EG *I used to find him insipid.* ADJ QUALIT
2 Food or drink that is **insipid** has very little taste. EG *...gigantic insipid tomatoes, huge flavourless lettuces.* ADJ QUALIT

insist /ɪnsɪst/, **insists, insisting, insisted. 1** If you **insist** that something is true, you say it very firmly and refuse to change your mind. EG *She insisted that Jim must leave... 'But you know that she's innocent,' the girl insisted.* V+REPORT: ONLY *that*, OR V+QUOTE
2 If you **insist** on something, you say that you must do it or have it, and refuse to give in. EG *He insisted on paying for the meal... We were right to insist on reform.* V+*on*

insistence /ɪnsɪstəns/ Someone's **insistence** on something is the fact that they keep saying firmly that it must be done. EG *...my insistence on secrecy.* N UNCOUNT: OFT+*on*

insistent /ɪnsɪstənt/. **1** Someone who is **insistent** keeps saying firmly that something must be done. EG *There have been insistent demands that more should be done to provide for poor families.* ADJ QUALIT
◊ **insistently.** EG *No-one has spoken more insistently on the subject of education than her.* ◊ ADV
2 If you describe a noise or action as **insistent**, you mean that it continues for a long time and gets your attention. EG *...the insistent ringing of the telephone.* ADJ QUALIT ◊ **insistently.** EG *I tugged insistently at his jacket.* ◊ ADV

in situ /ɪn sɪtjuː/. If something remains **in situ**, especially while something is done to it, it remains where it is. EG *They will carry out further analysis in situ.* ADV Formal

insofar as /ɪnsə[6]fɑːr ə[3]z/. You use **insofar as** when giving the reason for something or when showing the extent of something. EG *...contemptuous of the traditional culture, except insofar as it provided precious metals.* CONJ Formal

insolent /ɪnsələnt/. Someone who is **insolent** is very rude or impolite. EG *...an insolent remark.* ADJ QUALIT
◊ **insolence** /ɪnsələns/. EG *I was taken to the headmistress for my insolence.* ◊ N UNCOUNT

insoluble /ɪnsɒljə[4]bə[0]l/. An **insoluble** problem is so difficult that it is impossible to solve. EG *The problems confronting this country are insoluble.* ADJ CLASSIF

insolvent /ɪnsɒlvənt/. Someone who is **insolvent** does not have enough money to pay their debts. EG *He revealed that he was insolvent by 1.2m pounds.* ADJ CLASSIF Formal

insomnia /ɪnsɒmnɪə/. Someone who suffers from **insomnia** finds it difficult to sleep. N UNCOUNT

insomniac /ɪnsɒmni[1]æk/, **insomniacs.** An **insomniac** is a person who finds it difficult to sleep. N COUNT

inspect /ɪnspɛkt/, **inspects, inspecting, inspected. 1** If you **inspect** something, you look at every part of it carefully. EG *She inspected his scalp for lice.* V+O ◊ **inspection** /ɪnspɛkʃə[0]n/, **inspections.** EG *Closer inspection revealed crabs among the rocks.* ◊ N UNCOUNT OR N COUNT
2 When officials **inspect** a place, they visit it in order to find out whether regulations are being obeyed. EG *The fire prevention branch inspects factories and all sorts of public buildings.* V+O
◊ **inspection.** EG *...carrying out an inspection of the kitchen.* ◊ N COUNT OR N UNCOUNT

inspector /ɪnspɛktə/, **inspectors.** An **inspector** is **1** an official whose job is to find out whether organizations are obeying official regulations. EG N COUNT

...*the factory inspector... The inspector's report was released to the public.* **2** an officer in the police force. EG ...*Inspector Flint.*

inspiration /ɪnspɪreɪʃəⁿn/, **inspirations. 1** If you get **inspiration** from someone or something, you get new ideas from them which make you enthusiastic and encourage you to do something. EG *I have derived inspiration from Freud.* N UNCOUNT

2 The **inspiration** for something such as a piece of work or a theory is the thing that provides the basic idea or example for it. EG *He was later to become the inspiration for the comic strip character, Superman... The British Civil Service provided the inspiration for the system in India.* N SING+SUPP

3 If you get **inspiration**, you suddenly think of a good idea. EG *I had an inspiration... He paused, searching for inspiration.* N UNCOUNT OR N COUNT

inspire /ɪnspaɪə/, **inspires, inspiring, inspired. 1** If someone or something **inspires** you to do something, they make you want to do it by giving you new ideas and enthusiasm. EG *Not even Churchill could inspire the Party to reform... They were too gloomy to be inspired by his enthusiasm... The strikes appear to be politically inspired.* V+O: OFT+*to*-INF

2 Someone or something that **inspires** a particular emotion in people makes them feel this emotion. EG ...*a man who inspired confidence in women.* V+O: OFT+*in*

inspired /ɪnspaɪəd/. **1** Someone who is **inspired** is brilliant and very creative in their work. EG *As an architect, he was an inspired amateur... ...works of inspired beauty.* ADJ QUALIT

2 An **inspired** guess is very clever and accurate. EG *It was just an inspired guess.* ADJ QUALIT

inspiring /ɪnspaɪərɪŋ/. Something or someone that is **inspiring** is exciting and makes you enthusiastic and interested. EG *It was an inspiring occasion... I'm afraid it may not be inspiring to watch.* ADJ QUALIT

instability /ɪnstəbɪlɪ¹ti¹/, **instabilities. Instability** is a lack of stability in a place, situation, or person. EG *Various signs of political instability began to appear.* N UNCOUNT OR N COUNT

install /ɪnstɔːl/, **installs, installing, installed. 1** If you **install** a piece of equipment in a place, you put it there so that it is ready to be used. EG *We have just installed central heating.* V+O OR V+O+A

2 If you **install** someone in an important job or position, you officially give them the job or position. EG *He installed a man named Briceland as head of the advertisement department.* V+O OR V+O+A

3 If you **install** yourself in a place, you settle there and make yourself comfortable. EG *By now he was installed at number 7 New King Street.* V-REFL+A

installation /ɪnstəleɪʃəⁿn/, **installations. 1** An **installation** is a place that contains equipment and machinery which are being used for a particular purpose. EG ...*North Sea oil and gas installations... ...missile installations.* N COUNT

2 The **installation** of a piece of equipment involves putting it into place and making it ready for use. EG ...*the installation of the colour TV.* N UNCOUNT

instalment /ɪnstɔːlməⁿnt/, **instalments;** spelled **installment** in American English. **1** If you pay for something in **instalments**, you pay small sums of money at regular intervals over a period of time. EG *I paid one hundred dollars in four monthly instalments.* N COUNT

2 If a story is published in **instalments**, part of it is published each day, week, or month. EG ...*the first instalment of the story.* N COUNT

instance /ɪnstəns/, **instances. 1** You use **for instance** when mentioning a particular event, situation, or person that is an example of what you are talking about. EG *I mean, for instance, a man like Tom... For instance, an electric fire is a relatively expensive method of heating a room.* ADV SEN

2 An **instance** is a particular example of an event, situation, or person. EG *I do not think that in this instance the doctor was right... ...instances of government injustice.* N COUNT

3 You say **in the first instance** when mentioning something that should be done first before anything else. EG *The library will supply a list of addresses to which you should apply in the first instance.* PHRASE Formal

instant /ɪnstənt/, **instants. 1** An **instant** is an extremely short period of time. EG *Bal hesitated for an instant... It was all gone in a single instant.* N COUNT: USU SING

2 If you say that something happened at a particular **instant**, you are referring to the actual moment at which it happened. EG *At that instant, an angry buzzing began.* N SING+SUPP

3 If you do something **the instant** something else happens, you do it as soon as it happens. EG *She must have dashed out the instant I grabbed the phone.* CONJ

4 If you say that something must be done **this instant**, you mean that it must be done immediately. PHRASE

5 You use **instant** to describe something that happens immediately without any delay. EG *Herschel did not have instant success.* ADJ CLASSIF

◊ **instantly.** EG *He was killed instantly.* ◊ ADV

6 Instant food is food that has been specially made so that you can prepare it with very little time and effort. EG ...*instant coffee.* ADJ CLASSIF

instantaneous /ɪnstənteɪnɪəs/. Something that is **instantaneous** happens immediately and very quickly. EG ...*an instantaneous look of happiness... Death was instantaneous.* ◊ **instantaneously.** EG *The pain passed instantaneously.* ADJ CLASSIF ◊ ADV

instead /ɪnstɛd/. If you do one thing **instead of** another or if you do it **instead**, you do the first thing rather than the second thing. EG *If you want to have your meal at seven o'clock instead of five o'clock, you can... Instead of going straight to work, he took a bus into town... Robert had a great desire to turn away from her but instead he took her and led her towards the house.* PREP OR ADV SEN

instep /ɪnstɛp/, **insteps.** Your **instep** is the middle part of your foot, where it curves upwards. N COUNT

instigate /ɪnstɪgeɪt/, **instigates, instigating, instigated.** If you **instigate** an event or situation, you cause it to happen by your own effort or work. EG *Sir Ernest Cassel instigated the Anglo-German talks of 1912.* ◊ **instigation** /ɪnstɪgeɪʃəⁿn/. EG *One husband, at the instigation of his wife, called the police.* ◊ **instigator** /ɪnstɪgeɪtə/, **instigators.** EG *The instigator of the plot was Colonel Fletcher.* V+O Formal ◊ N UNCOUNT ◊ N COUNT

instil /ɪnstɪl/, **instils, instilling, instilled;** spelled **instill, instills** in American English. If you **instil** an idea or feeling into someone, you make them think it or feel it. EG *The presence of the guard was supposed to instil awe and fear in us.* V+O: OFT+*in/into*

instinct /ɪnstɪŋkt/, **instincts. 1** An **instinct** is the natural tendency that a person has to behave or react in a particular way without thinking about it or planning it. EG ...*a fundamental instinct for survival... She knew, by instinct, that he wouldn't come back... ...the maternal instinct.* N COUNT OR N UNCOUNT

2 If it is your **instinct** to do something in a particular situation, you want to do it or feel that it is right. EG *My first instinct was to resign... She really ought to trust Nick's instincts in these matters.* N COUNT: USU+*to*-INF

instinctive /ɪnstɪŋkᵒtɪv/. An **instinctive** feeling, idea, or action is one that you have or do without thinking logically about it. EG *Brody took an instinctive dislike to the man... My instinctive reaction was to take a couple of rapid steps backwards.* ADJ CLASSIF

◊ **instinctively.** EG *Charles instinctively understood I wanted to be alone.* ◊ ADV

institute /ɪnstɪtjuːt/, **institutes, instituting, instituted. 1** An **institute** is an organization set up to do a particular type of work, especially research N COUNT

If something is installed, is it an instalment?

or teaching. EG *I visited a number of research institutes in Asia... ...the Massachusetts Institute of Technology.*

2 If you **institute** a system, rule, or course of action, you start it. EG *Mr Wilson was in Opposition when the scheme was instituted.* [V+O Formal]

institution /ɪnstɪtjuːʃə[0]n/, **institutions.** 1 An **institution** is a custom or a system that is considered an important or typical feature of a society, usually because it has existed for a long time. EG *...the institution of marriage.* [N COUNT]

2 An **institution** is also 2.1 a large organization, for example a university, bank, or church. EG *These universities accept lower grades than the more prestigious institutions... ...financial institutions.* 2.2 a building where certain people are kept or looked after, for example people who are mentally ill or children who have no parents. EG *He may end up in a mental institution.* [N COUNT]

institutional /ɪnstɪtjuːʃə[0]nəl, -ʃənə[0]l/ means 1 relating to a large organization, for example a university, bank, or church. EG *...institutional reform.* 2 relating to a building where people are kept or looked after. EG *The child has been in institutional care for many years.* [ADJ CLASSIF : ATTRIB]

institutionalized /ɪnstɪtjuːʃə[0]nəlaɪzd/; also spelled **institutionalised.** 1 If someone is **institutionalized**, they have been living in an institution for a long time and so they find it hard to look after themselves. EG *...institutionalized children.* [ADJ CLASSIF]

2 If a custom or a system is **institutionalized**, it is part of the social system of a society. EG *...institutionalized religion.* [ADJ CLASSIF]

instruct /ɪnstrʌkt/, **instructs, instructing, instructed.** 1 If you **instruct** someone to do something, you tell them to do it. EG *'Breathe in,' he instructed her... I've been instructed to take you to London.* [V+O+to-INF, QUOTE, OR REPORT Formal]

2 Someone who **instructs** people in a subject or skill teaches it to them. [V+O]

instruction /ɪnstrʌkʃə[0]n/, **instructions.** 1 An **instruction** is something that someone tells you to do. EG *She was only following the instructions of her supervisor.* [N COUNT]

2 **Instructions** are clear and detailed information on how to do something, especially written information. EG *Read the instructions before you switch on the engine.* [N PLURAL]

3 **Instruction** in a subject or skill is teaching that someone gives you about it. [N UNCOUNT]

instructive /ɪnstrʌktɪv/. Something that is **instructive** gives you useful information. EG *His seminars were instructive and illuminating occasions.* [ADJ QUALIT]

instructor /ɪnstrʌktə/, **instructors.** An **instructor** is a person who teaches you something, especially a skill such as driving or skiing. EG *...a Swiss ski instructor.* [N COUNT]

instrument /ɪnstrə[4]mə[2]nt/, **instruments.** 1 An **instrument** is 1.1 a tool or device that is used to do a particular task. EG *...surgical instruments... ...instruments of torture.* 1.2 a device that is used for making measurements of something such as speed, height, or sound. EG *The co-pilot was watching a panel of instruments.* [N COUNT]

2 A musical **instrument** is an object such as a piano, guitar, or violin, which you play in order to produce music. EG *...stringed instruments.* [N COUNT]

3 Something that is an **instrument** for achieving a particular aim is used by people to achieve that aim. EG *Incomes policy is a weak instrument for reducing inflation... The Labour Party is the only instrument of change open to them.* [N COUNT+SUPP Formal]

instrumental /ɪnstrə[4]mentə[0]l/. 1 Someone or something that is **instrumental** in a process or event helps to make it happen. EG *The organization was instrumental in getting a ban on certain furs.* [ADJ QUALIT]

2 **Instrumental** music is performed by instruments and not by voices. [ADJ CLASSIF]

insubordination /ɪnsəbɔːdɪneɪʃə[0]n/ is disobedient behaviour. EG *...charges of insubordination.* [N UNCOUNT Formal]

insubstantial /ɪnsəbstænʃə[0]l/. Something that is **insubstantial** is not very large, solid, or strong. EG *...a feathery, insubstantial plant... ...slender and insubstantial structures.* [ADJ QUALIT]

insufferable /ɪnsʌfə[0]rəbə[0]l/. If you find someone or something **insufferable**, you find them very unpleasant or annoying. EG *He was becoming an insufferable pest with his stealing.* [ADJ CLASSIF]

insufficient /ɪnsəfɪʃənt/. Something that is **insufficient** is not enough for a particular purpose. EG *Insufficient research has been done... These steps will be insufficient to change our economic decline.* [ADJ CLASSIF : OFT+for OR to-INF]
◇ **insufficiently.** EG *My hand had proved insufficiently strong to open the door.* [◇ ADV]

insular /ɪnsjə[4]lə/. People who are **insular** are unwilling to meet new people or to consider new ideas. EG *He lived a rather insular life.* [ADJ QUALIT]

insulate /ɪnsjə[4]leɪt/, **insulates, insulating, insulated.** 1 If you **insulate** a person from harmful things, you protect them from those things. EG *The leaders were able to insulate the local population from these dangerous influences... ...in a sheltered, womb-like world, insulated against the events of life outside.* [V+O: OFT+from/against Formal]

2 If a material or substance **insulates** something, it keeps the thing warm by covering it in a thick layer. EG *The function of a mammal's hair is to insulate the body.* [V+O]

3 If you **insulate** a tool or electrical device, you cover it with rubber or plastic in order to prevent electricity passing through it and giving the person using it an electric shock. EG *...two small electrical screwdrivers with insulated handles.* [V+O]

insulation /ɪnsjə[4]leɪʃə[0]n/ is a thick layer of a material or substance, which keeps something warm. EG *...a long roll of roof insulation.* [N UNCOUNT]

insult, insults, insulting, insulted; pronounced /ɪnsʌlt/ when it is a verb and /ɪnsʌlt/ when it is a noun.

1 If you **insult** someone, you say something rude about them, or offend them by doing something that shows you have a low opinion of them. EG *You don't have to apologize to me. You didn't insult me... He feels deeply insulted.* ◇ **insulting.** EG *He did use insulting language.* [V+O] [◇ ADJ QUALIT]

2 An **insult** is a rude remark about someone or an action that offends them. EG *The older boys yelled out insults... I would take it as an insult if you left.* [N COUNT]

● You say **'to add insult to injury'** when mentioning an action or fact that makes a situation you are involved in even more unfair or unpleasant. EG *To add insult to injury, the penalty was awarded to the other side.* [● PHRASE]

insuperable /ɪnsj[0]uːpə[0]rəbə[0]l/. A problem that is **insuperable** cannot be solved. EG *It would be an insuperable barrier to unity.* [ADJ CLASSIF Formal]

insupportable /ɪnsəpɔːtəbə[0]l/. If you find something **insupportable**, you find it so unpleasant that you cannot accept it. EG *Accusations of that kind are quite insupportable... The strain would be insupportable.* [ADJ CLASSIF Formal]

insurance /ɪnʃʊərəns, -ʃɔː-/. 1 **Insurance** is an agreement in which you pay a fixed sum of money to a special company, usually each year. Then, if you become ill or if your property is damaged or stolen, the company pays you a sum of money. EG *...private health insurance... ...insurance companies.* ● See also **national insurance**. [N UNCOUNT]

2 If you do something as an **insurance** against something unpleasant, you do it in order to protect yourself in case the unpleasant thing happens, or in order to prevent it from happening. EG *They build up supplies as an insurance against drought.* [N SING : USU+against]

insure /ɪnʃʊə, -ʃɔː/, **insures, insuring, insured.** 1 If you **insure** yourself or your property, you pay money to an insurance company so that, if you become ill or if your property is damaged or stolen, [V+O OR V-REFL]

the company will pay you a sum of money. EG *Insure your baggage before you leave home.*
◇ **insured.** EG *The house is not insured against fire.* ◇ ADJ PRED

2 If you do something to **insure** against something unpleasant happening, you do it in order to protect yourself in case it happens, or in order to prevent it from happening. EG *In years of good rainfall they expand their stocks to insure against drought.* V+*against*

3 See also **ensure**.

insurgent /ɪnsɜːdʒənt/, **insurgents. Insurgents** are people who are fighting against the government or army of their own country. EG *Insurgents partially damaged the embassy.* N COUNT: USU PLURAL

insurmountable /ɪnsəmaʊntəbəºl/. A problem that is **insurmountable** cannot be solved. EG *The bureaucratic obstacles to this proved insurmountable.* ADJ CLASSIF Formal

insurrection /ɪnsərɛkʃəºn/, **insurrections.** An **insurrection** is violent action that is taken by a large group of people against the rulers of their country. EG *We are not prepared for an armed insurrection... Such policies were intended to prevent insurrection.* N COUNT OR N UNCOUNT

intact /ɪntækt/. Something that is **intact** is complete and has not been damaged or changed in any way. EG *...the only window that remained intact... They are fighting to keep village life intact.* ADJ QUALIT: USU PRED

intake /ɪnteɪk/, **intakes. 1** Your **intake** of food, drink, or air is the amount that you eat, drink, or breathe in, or the process of taking it into your body. EG *Nurses kept measuring her fluid intake.* N UNCOUNT +SUPP

2 The people who are accepted into an institution or organization at a particular time are referred to as a particular **intake**. EG *...the army's huge emergency intake of soldiers.* N COUNT: USU+SUPP

intangible /ɪntændʒɪbəºl/. A quality or idea that is **intangible** is hard to define or explain. EG *...a vast and intangible subject.* ADJ QUALIT

integral /ɪntɪ²grəl/. Something that is an **integral** part of something else is an essential part of it. EG *The Young Socialists were an integral feature of the Labour movement... The concept of loyalty is integral to the story.* ADJ CLASSIF: OFT+*to*

integrate /ɪntɪ²greɪt/, **integrates, integrating, integrated. 1** If people **integrate** into a social group, they mix with people in that group. EG *...helping the individual integrate quickly into the community... ...ways of integrating handicapped children into ordinary schools.* ◇ **integration** /ɪntɪ²greɪʃəºn/. EG *He campaigned for the integration of immigrants into British society.* V-ERG+*into*; ALSO V OR V+*with*: RECIP; ◇ N UNCOUNT

2 If you **integrate** things, you combine them so that they are closely linked or so that they form one thing. EG *The two regional railway systems were integrated.* V+O

integrated /ɪntɪ²greɪtɪ²d/. An **integrated** institution is intended for use by people of all races or groups. EG *...an integrated school for Protestants and Catholics.* ADJ CLASSIF: ATTRIB

integrity /ɪntɛgrɪ¹ti¹/. **1 Integrity** is the quality of being honest and firm in your moral principles. EG *He was particularly respected for his integrity... My husband was a man of the highest integrity.* N UNCOUNT

2 The **integrity** of something such as a group of people is its quality of being one united or connected thing. EG *They were totally committed to the survival and integrity of the nation.* N UNCOUNT +POSS Formal

intellect /ɪntə²lɛkt/, **intellects. Intellect** is **1** the ability to think and to understand ideas and information. EG *...the intellect of modern man... ...the idea of computers with intellects.* **2** the quality of being very intelligent or clever. EG *He was born into a family noted for its intellect.* N UNCOUNT OR N COUNT; N UNCOUNT

intellectual /ɪntə²lɛktʃʊºəl/, **intellectuals. 1 Intellectual** means involving a person's ability to think and to understand ideas and information. EG *...children in need of extra emotional or intellectual stimulation... ...his tremendous intellectual powers.* ◇ **intellectually.** EG *...an intellectually challenging occupation.* ADJ CLASSIF: ATTRIB; ◇ ADV

2 An **intellectual** is someone who spends a lot of time studying and thinking about complicated ideas. EG *...scholars and intellectuals.* ▸ used as an adjective. EG *...all the intellectual Oxford people... ...an intellectual conversation.* N COUNT; ▸ ADJ QUALIT

intelligence /ɪntɛlɪdʒəns/. **1** Someone's **intelligence** is their ability to understand and learn things. EG *...a person of average intelligence... She prided herself on her intelligence.* N UNCOUNT

2 Intelligence is the ability to think and understand instead of doing things by instinct or automatically. EG *Do hedgehogs have intelligence?... ...computer intelligence.* N UNCOUNT

3 Intelligence is also information that is gathered by the government or the army about their country's enemies. EG *...American intelligence services.* N UNCOUNT

intelligent /ɪntɛlɪdʒənt/. **1** Someone who is **intelligent** has the ability to understand and learn things well. EG *Jo is an intelligent student... ...a very intelligent question.* ◇ **intelligently.** EG *They dealt with that problem intelligently.* ADJ QUALIT; ◇ ADV

2 An animal or computer that is **intelligent** has the ability to think and understand instead of doing things by instinct or automatically. EG *We have shown that computers can be intelligent.* ADJ CLASSIF

intelligentsia /ɪntɛlɪdʒɛntsɪə/. The **intelligentsia** in a community are the most educated people in it. N COLL: *the*+ Formal

intelligible /ɪntɛlɪdʒəbəºl/. Something that is **intelligible** can be understood. EG *Make sure that your letters are intelligible... Describe it in a way that would be intelligible to an outsider.* ADJ QUALIT

intend /ɪntɛnd/, **intends, intending, intended. 1** If you **intend** to do something, you have decided to do it or have planned to do it. EG *This is my job and I intend to do it... He had intended staying longer... He woke later than he had intended.* V+*to*-INF OR -ING

2 If you **intend** something to happen or to have a particular effect or function, you have planned that it should happen or should have this effect or function. EG *We never intended the scheme to be permanent... It is intended as a handbook, for frequent reference... It had been intended that a second group should be assembled.* V+O+*to*-INF, *as*, OR REPORT: ONLY *that*

3 Something that **is intended** for a particular person or purpose has been planned or made for that person or purpose. EG *The man had drunk what had been intended for me... They are not yet intended for use.* V+O: USU PASS+*for*

intended /ɪntɛndɪ²d/. You use **intended** to describe the thing that you are trying or planning to achieve, do, or affect. EG *What is the intended result?... ...your intended trip abroad... ...his intended victim.* ADJ CLASSIF: ATTRIB

intense /ɪntɛns/. **1** Something that is **intense** is very great in strength or degree. EG *The effects of the drug are intense and brief... ...the intense heat... The row caused her intense unhappiness.* ADJ QUALIT
◇ **intensely.** EG *She had suffered intensely.* ◇ ADV
◇ **intensity** /ɪntɛnsɪ¹ti¹/. EG *The debates are renewed with great intensity.* ◇ N UNCOUNT

2 If you describe a person as **intense**, you mean that they seem very serious all the time. EG *It was like Jane to be so intense and dramatic about the future.* ADJ QUALIT

intensify /ɪntɛnsɪfaɪ/, **intensifies, intensifying, intensified.** If you **intensify** something or if it **intensifies**, it becomes greater in strength or degree. EG *In the late 1960s the pressures suddenly intensified.* ◇ **intensified.** EG *...intensified international competition.* V-ERG; ◇ ADJ CLASSIF: ATTRIB

intensive /ɪntɛnsɪv/. An **intensive** activity involves the concentration of energy or people on ADJ QUALIT

If you intercede with someone, are they arguing with you or with someone else?

one particular task in order to try to achieve a great deal in a short time. EG *...the last intensive preparation for my exams... ...an intensive struggle against racism.* ◊ **intensively.** EG *The land was developed very intensively in the mid 1930s.* ◊ ADV

intensive care is extremely thorough care provided by hospitals for people who are so ill that they would die if they were not being looked after. N UNCOUNT

intent /ɪntɛnt/, **intents.** **1** A person's **intent** is their intention to do something. EG *The conference declared its intent to organize a national movement... They signed a declaration of intent.* N UNCOUNT Formal

2 When you look **intent**, you show that you are paying great attention to someone or something. EG *He gazed at their intent faces... She was brushing her hair, intent on her face in the mirror.* ADJ QUALIT
◊ **intently.** EG *I stood behind a parked van, watching intently.* ◊ ADV

3 If you are **intent** on doing something, you are determined to do it. EG *They were intent on keeping what they had.* ADJ PRED +*on/upon*

4 You use the phrase **to all intents and purposes** to suggest that a situation is not exactly as you describe it but the effect is the same as if it were. EG *She was to all intents and purposes the infant's mother.* ADV SEN

intention /ɪntɛnʃə^{0}n/, **intentions.** An **intention** that you have is an idea or plan of what you are going to do. EG *He confirmed his intention to leave next April... He was suspicious of the government's intentions... She had no intention of spending the rest of her life working as a waitress.* N COUNT OR N UNCOUNT

intentional /ɪntɛnʃə^{0}nəl, -ʃənə^{0}l/. Something that is **intentional** is deliberate. EG *...intentional misrepresentation.* ◊ **intentionally.** EG *I banged the door. Not intentionally.* ADJ CLASSIF ◊ ADV

inter- is used to form adjectives that describe something as moving, existing, or happening between similar things or groups of people. For example, inter-governmental relations are relations between governments. EG *...intercontinental missiles... ...inter-state roads... ...inter-racial marriages.* PREFIX

interact /ɪntəræ̱kt/, **interacts, interacting, interacted.** **1** When people **interact** with each other, they communicate or work together. EG *Mothers and babies interact in a very complex way.* ◊ **interaction** /ɪntəræ̱kʃə^{0}n/, **interactions.** EG *There is a need for more interaction between staff and children.* V OR V+*with*: RECIP ◊ N UNCOUNT OR N COUNT

2 When one thing **interacts** with another, the two things react together and affect each other's development or nature. EG *The bacteria's genes interact with those of many plants.* ◊ **interaction.** EG *...a method of encouraging the interaction of ideas.* V OR V+*with*: RECIP ◊ N UNCOUNT OR N COUNT

interactive /ɪntəræ̱ktɪv/. **Interactive** use of a computer is use in which the user and the computer communicate directly with each other via a keyboard and a screen. EG *...interactive graphic systems... ...interactive computer games.* ADJ CLASSIF Technical

intercede /ɪntəsi̱ːd/, **intercedes, interceding, interceded.** If you **intercede** with a person, you talk to them in order to try to end a disagreement that they have with another person. EG *Ten years before, I had interceded for him with his employer.* V: OFT+*with* Formal

intercept /ɪntəsɛ̱pt/, **intercepts, intercepting, intercepted.** If you **intercept** someone or something that is travelling from one place to another, you stop them. EG *The car was intercepted and stopped by a policeman.* V+O

intercession /ɪntəsɛ̱ʃə^{0}n/, **intercessions.** **Intercession** is an act of trying to end a disagreement between two people, usually by talking to one of them. EG *Through the intercession of a friend, my request was granted.* N UNCOUNT OR N COUNT Formal

interchange /ɪntətʃeɪnd^{0}ʒ/, **interchanges.** **1** The **interchange** of things, people, or ideas is the exchange of things, people, or ideas. EG *...a regular forum for the interchange of information and ideas... ...interchange between the classes.* N UNCOUNT OR N COUNT +SUPP

2 An **interchange** on a motorway is a junction where it meets a main road or another motorway. N COUNT

interchangeable /ɪntətʃe̱ɪnd^{0}ʒəbə^{0}l/. Things that are **interchangeable** can be exchanged with each other without making any difference to a situation. EG *We tend to use these terms as if they were freely interchangeable... ...interchangeable forms of energy.* ◊ **interchangeably.** EG *In many of the speeches, the word 'fascist' was used interchangeably with the word 'racist'.* ADJ CLASSIF ◊ ADV

intercom /ɪ̱ntəkɒm/, **intercoms.** An **intercom** is a device which people use to communicate with each other when they are in different rooms. It is usually like a box with a microphone for talking into and a loudspeaker to hear the reply. EG *A voice on the intercom said, 'It's Mr Vaughan.'* N COUNT

interconnect /ɪntəkənɛ̱kt/, **interconnects, interconnecting, interconnected.** Things that **interconnect** or that **are interconnected** are connected to each other or with each other. EG *The nervous system is a complicated network of interconnecting parts... Monarch, court and government were all interconnected.* V OR V+*with*: RECIP; ALSO V-PASS

intercontinental /ɪntəkɒntɪnɛ̱ntə^{0}l/ is used to describe something that exists or happens between continents. EG *...an intercontinental flight.* ADJ CLASSIF

intercourse /ɪ̱ntəkɔːs/ is the act of having sex. EG *He had had sexual intercourse with her.* N UNCOUNT Formal

interdependent /ɪntədɪ^{1}pɛ̱ndənt/. People or things that are **interdependent** all depend on each other. EG *Plants and animals are strongly interdependent.* ◊ **interdependence** /ɪntədɪ^{1}pɛ̱ndəns/. EG *...the interdependence of economies.* ADJ CLASSIF ◊ N UNCOUNT Formal

interest /ɪ̱ntə^{0}rə^{2}st/, **interests, interesting, interested.** **1** If you have an **interest** in something, you want to learn or hear more about it. EG *None of them had the slightest interest in music... Brody was beginning to lose interest.* N SING OR N UNCOUNT

2 Your **interests** are the things that you spend time on because you enjoy them. EG *He had two consuming interests: rowing and polo.* N COUNT

3 Something that is of **interest** attracts your attention because it is exciting or unusual. EG *There was nothing of any great interest in the paper today.* N UNCOUNT

4 If something **interests** you, you want to learn more about it or to continue doing it. EG *Young men should always look for work which interests them.* V+O

5 If you **interest** someone in something, you persuade them to do it or to buy it. EG *Can I interest you in yet another horror movie?* V+O: OFT+*in*

6 If you have an **interest** in something being done, you want it to be done because you will benefit from it. EG *They had no interest in the overthrow of the established order... They would protect the interests of their members.* ● Something that is **in the interests** of a person or group will benefit them in some way. EG *It is not in the interests of any of us to have a weak government.* ● See also **vested interest**. N COUNT: OFT+*in* ● PHRASE

7 If you do something **in the interests** of a particular thing, you do it in order to achieve or preserve this thing. EG *She was prepared to sacrifice this principle in the interests of domestic harmony.* PHRASE

8 Someone who has **interests** in a particular type of business owns companies or shares of this type. EG *...an industrialist with business interests in Germany.* N PLURAL

9 **Interest** is money that you receive if you have invested a sum of money, or money that you pay if you have borrowed money. EG *...the interest you pay on your mortgage... ...high interest rates.* N UNCOUNT

interested /ɪ̱ntə^{0}rə^{2}stɪ^{2}d/. **1** Someone who is **interested** in something **1.1** wants to know more about it. EG *I'm very interested in birds... She was* ADJ QUALIT: USU PRED+*in* genuinely interested in everyone she met... He looked interested.* **1.2** thinks that it is important and worth giving attention to. EG *We are interested only in the efficiency of the company as a whole.* ADJ PRED+*in*

2 Someone who is **interested** in doing something wants to do it. EG *My sister is interested in becoming a nurse... No. I'm not interested.* ADJ PRED: USU+*in*

3 An **interested** party or group of people is affected by or involved in a particular event or situation. EG *We talked to a group of scientists who know about this work, and other interested parties.* ADJ CLASSIF: ATTRIB

interesting /ɪntə^{0}rə^{2}stɪŋ/. If you find something **interesting**, it attracts or holds your attention, for example because you think it is exciting or unusual. EG *That's a very interesting question... He was not very interesting to talk to... It must be quite interesting for you.* ADJ QUALIT

interestingly /ɪntə^{0}rə^{2}stɪŋli^1/. You use **interestingly** to introduce a piece of information that you think is interesting and unexpected. EG *Interestingly enough, America is now dependent on Africa for 40% of its oil imports.* ADV SEN

interfere /ɪntəfɪə/, **interferes, interfering, interfered. 1** If you **interfere** in a situation, you try to influence it or become involved in it although it does not really concern you; used showing disapproval. EG *My mother interferes in things... They didn't interfere with us and we didn't interfere with them... Don't interfere.* V: USU+A

2 Something that **interferes** with a situation, process, or activity has a damaging effect on it. EG *Child-bearing will not interfere with a career.* V: OFT+*with*

interference /ɪntəfɪərəns/. **1 Interference** is the act of interfering in something. EG *I wanted to do the thing on my own without outside interference or help... They didn't want any interference from their national government.* N UNCOUNT

2 When there is **interference**, a radio signal is affected by other radio waves so that it cannot be received properly. N UNCOUNT

interfering /ɪntəfɪərɪŋ/. An **interfering** person tries to get involved in other people's affairs, especially when their advice is not wanted. EG *...an interfering old woman.* ADJ QUALIT

interim /ɪntərɪm/ is used to describe things that are intended to be used only until something more permanent is arranged or produced. EG *...a temporary or interim arrangement... ...an interim loan... ...an interim report.* ADJ CLASSIF: ATTRIB

interior /ɪntɪərɪə/, **interiors. 1** The **interior** of something is the inside part of it. EG *Very little is known about the deep interior of the earth... The castle has its interior well preserved.* N COUNT

2 You use **interior** to describe something that is inside a building or vehicle. EG *...an interior room without windows.* ADJ CLASSIF: ATTRIB

3 The **interior** of a country or continent is the central area of it. EG *The interior of the island consists largely of swamps.* N SING: *the*+N

4 An **interior** minister or political department deals with affairs in their own country. EG *The Interior Department framed a criminal code forbidding church services.* ADJ CLASSIF: ATTRIB

interject /ɪntədʒɛkt/, **interjects, interjecting, interjected.** If you **interject**, you say something and interrupt someone else who is speaking. EG *'No, no,' interjected Schmidt... If I may interject a word here.* V, V+QUOTE, OR V+O Formal

interjection /ɪntədʒɛkʃə^{0}n/, **interjections. 1** An **interjection** is something you say which interrupts someone else who is speaking. EG *The bishop was prepared for this interjection.* N COUNT Formal

2 In grammar, an **interjection** is a word or expression which you use to express a strong feeling such as surprise, pain, or horror, and which you often say loudly and emphatically. In this dictionary words like this are described as EXCLAM in the Extra Column. N COUNT

interlock /ɪntəlɒk/, **interlocks, interlocking, interlocked.** Things that **interlock** with each other fit into each other so that they are firmly joined together. EG *All the units interlock with one another rigidly... He interlocked his fingers.* V-ERG: ALSO V OR V+*with*: RECIP

interloper /ɪntələupə/, **interlopers.** An **interloper** is a person who interferes in something or who is in a place where they are not supposed to be. EG *Any interloper who heckled would be removed from the meeting.* N COUNT

interlude /ɪntəlu:d/, **interludes.** An **interlude** is a short period of time when an activity or event stops for a break. EG *After this interlude, the band started up again.* N COUNT

intermarry /ɪntəmæri^1/, **intermarries, intermarrying, intermarried.** When people from different social, racial, or religious groups **intermarry**, they marry each other. V OR V+*with*: RECIP

intermediary /ɪntəmi:djəri^1/, **intermediaries.** An **intermediary** is a person who passes messages or proposals between two people or groups. EG *He dealt through an intermediary with Beaverbrook himself... This spirit serves as an intermediary between men and the gods.* N COUNT

intermediate /ɪntəmi:dɪət/, **intermediates. 1** An **intermediate** stage or position is one that occurs between two other stages or positions. EG *One group of animals developed into another by way of intermediate forms.* ADJ CLASSIF: ATTRIB

2 Intermediate students are no longer beginners, but are not yet advanced. EG *...an English course, intermediate level, for adult students.* ADJ CLASSIF

interminable /ɪntɜ:mɪnəbə^{0}l/. Something that seems **interminable** seems to continue for a very long time. EG *I was glad of company for this interminable flight.* ADJ CLASSIF ◇ **interminably.** EG *MPs argued each point interminably.* ◇ ADV

intermingle /ɪntəmɪŋgə^{0}l/, **intermingles, intermingling, intermingled.** When people or things **intermingle**, they mix with each other. EG *The police intermingled with the crowds.* V OR V+*with*: RECIP Formal

intermission /ɪntəmɪʃə^{0}n/, **intermissions.** An **intermission** is an interval between two parts of a play. N COUNT American

intermittent /ɪntəmɪtənt/. Something that is **intermittent** happens occasionally rather than continuously. EG *I became aware of a faint, intermittent noise, somewhere outside.* ADJ QUALIT

◇ **intermittently.** EG *The magazine had been published intermittently since the war.* ◇ ADV

intern /ɪntɜ:n/, **interns, interning, interned.** To **intern** someone means to put them in prison, for political reasons. EG *They were interned for subversive activities.* V+O Formal

internal /ɪntɜ:nə^{0}l/. **1** You use **internal 1.1** to describe things that exist or happen inside a place, person, or object. EG *You should lag internal pipes to prevent them from freezing.* ADJ CLASSIF: ATTRIB ◇ **internally.** EG *The house has been rebuilt internally.* ◇ ADV **1.2** to describe the political and commercial activities inside a country. EG *...the internal politics of France.* ADJ CLASSIF: ATTRIB **1.3** to describe something that exists or happens within a particular organization. EG *...an internal bank memorandum.* ADJ CLASSIF: ATTRIB

2 Internal ideas or images exist in your thoughts or in your mind. EG *We have both external and internal values.* ADJ CLASSIF Formal

international /ɪntənæʃənə^{0}l/, **internationals. 1 International** means involving different countries. EG *...international affairs... They signed an international agreement on nuclear waste.* ADJ CLASSIF

◇ **internationally.** EG *She's an internationally famous historian.* ◇ ADV

2 An **international** is a sports match between teams from two countries. N COUNT

If something happens at intervals, does it happen in an interval?

internment /ɪntɜːnmə²nt/ is imprisonment for political reasons. EG *...the internment of human-rights activists... ...two years of internment.* N UNCOUNT Formal

interpersonal /ɪntəpɜːsə⁰nəl/ means relating to relationships between people. EG *...interpersonal relationships... ...interpersonal skills.* ADJ CLASSIF : ATTRIB

interplay /ɪntəpleɪ/. The **interplay** between two or more things is the way that they react with each other and have an effect on each other. EG *...the interplay between practical and theoretical constraints... ...the interplay of market forces.* N UNCOUNT : USU+*of/between* Formal

interpose /ɪntəpəʊz/, **interposes, interposing, interposed.** If you **interpose**, you interrupt with a comment or question. EG *'Enough of this!' interposed Miss Musson.* V OR V+QUOTE Formal

interpret /ɪntɜːprɪt/, **interprets, interpreting, interpreted.** 1 If you **interpret** something in a particular way, you decide that this is its meaning or significance. EG *I'm not quite sure how to interpret that question... The election result is being interpreted as a serious setback for the government.* V+O : OFT+*as*

2 If you **interpret** what someone is saying, you translate it immediately into another language. EG *Paul had to interpret for us.* V+O OR V

interpretation /ɪntɜːprɪteɪʃə⁰n/, **interpretations.** 1 An **interpretation** of something is an explanation of what it means. EG *This passage is open to a variety of interpretations.* N COUNT OR N UNCOUNT

2 A performer's **interpretation** of a piece of music or a dance is the particular way in which they choose to perform it. EG *Do you find his interpretation of Chopin satisfactory?* N COUNT OR N UNCOUNT

interpreter /ɪntɜːprɪtə/, **interpreters.** An **interpreter** is a person whose job is to listen to what someone is saying and translate it immediately into another language. EG *I talked to him through an interpreter.* N COUNT

interrelate /ɪntəri¹leɪt/, **interrelates, interrelating, interrelated.** If two or more things **interrelate** or **are interrelated**, there is some kind of connection between them, so that they have an effect on one another. EG *These courses interrelate in a variety of ways... All three factors are interrelated.* V-ERG : USU PASS Formal

interrogate /ɪntɛrəgeɪt/, **interrogates, interrogating, interrogated.** If someone, especially a police officer or an army officer, **interrogates** you, they question you thoroughly for a long time, in order to get information from you. EG *They had been interrogated for 20 hours about political demonstrations.* ◇ **interrogation** /ɪntɛrəgeɪʃə⁰n/, **interrogations.** EG *Waddell had undergone a lengthy interrogation... We've had him under interrogation for 36 hours.* V+O; ◇ N COUNT OR N UNCOUNT

interrogative /ɪntərɒgətɪv/, **interrogatives.** 1 An **interrogative** sentence is one that has the form of a question. ADJ CLASSIF

2 An **interrogative** is a word such as 'who', 'how', or 'why', which can be used to ask a question. N COUNT

interrogator /ɪntɛrəgeɪtə/, **interrogators.** An **interrogator** is a person who questions someone thoroughly for a long time. N COUNT

interrupt /ɪntərʌpt/, **interrupts, interrupting, interrupted.** 1 If you **interrupt** someone who is speaking, you say or do something that causes them to pause or stop. EG *Sorry to interrupt you... 'Mother!' interrupted Delia.* V+O, V+QUOTE, OR V

2 If you **interrupt** an activity, you temporarily prevent it from continuing. EG *Bain had interrupted his holiday to go to Hamburg.* V+O

interruption /ɪntərʌpʃə⁰n/, **interruptions.** 1 An **interruption** is something which temporarily prevents an activity from continuing. EG *She hates interruptions when she's working.* N COUNT

2 **Interruption** is the act of interrupting someone or something. EG *We should be safe from interruption.* N UNCOUNT

intersect /ɪntəsɛkt/, **intersects, intersecting, intersected.** 1 When roads **intersect**, they cross each other. EG *The highway intersected Main Street in a busy crossing.* V OR V+O : RECIP

2 If an area **is intersected** by roads or railways, they cross it and divide it into smaller areas. EG *The marshes were intersected by a maze of ditches.* V+O : USU PASS

intersection /ɪntəsɛkʃə⁰n/, **intersections.** An **intersection** is a place where roads cross each other. EG *...a city at the intersection of three motorways.* N COUNT : OFT+*of/with*

interspersed /ɪntəspɜːst/. If something is **interspersed** with other things, these things occur at various points in it. EG *...shabby shops and houses interspersed with modern offices and banks... ...a story interspersed with long silences.* ADJ PRED +*with/by*

intertwine /ɪntətwaɪn/, **intertwines, intertwining, intertwined.** If two things **intertwine** or **are intertwined**, they are joined together in a very close or complicated way. EG *Their tails intertwine... Reality and art are intertwined.* V-ERG; ALSO V OR V+*with* : RECIP

interval /ɪntəvəl/, **intervals.** 1 An **interval** is the period of time between two events or dates. EG *...the interval between supper and bedtime... ...after an interval of ten years.* N COUNT : OFT +*between/of*

2 At a play or concert, an **interval** is a break between two of the parts. EG *The audience were going out for the interval... ...the tea interval.* N COUNT

3 If something happens **at intervals**, it happens several times, with gaps or pauses in between. EG *At intervals, the carriage was halted... They kept coming back at six-month intervals.* PHRASE

4 If things are placed **at** particular **intervals**, there are spaces between them. EG *They were scattered through the forest, at varying intervals.* PHRASE

5 In music, an **interval** is the difference in pitch between two notes. N COUNT Technical

intervene /ɪntəviːn/, **intervenes, intervening, intervened.** 1 If you **intervene**, you take action in a situation that you were not originally involved in. EG *Two officers intervened to stop their recording... The State may intervene in disputes between employers and workers.* ◇ **intervention** /ɪntəvɛnʃə⁰n/, **interventions.** EG *He was against American intervention in the war.* V : OFT+*in*; ◇ N UNCOUNT OR N COUNT

2 If you **intervene** when someone is talking, you interrupt them by saying something. EG *'Yes,' intervened Grant, 'but you had it.'* ◇ **intervention, interventions.** *...the angry interventions of Lord Grant.* V OR V+QUOTE; ◇ N UNCOUNT OR N COUNT

3 You can say that an event **intervenes** when it delays something or prevents it from happening. EG *This will produce a result unless the weather intervenes.* V

4 If an event happens a particular number of days or years after another event, you can say that that number of days or years **intervenes** between the two events. EG *Ten years had intervened since she had last seen Joe.* V

intervening /ɪntəviːnɪŋ/. 1 An **intervening** period of time is one which separates two events or points in time. EG *What happened in the intervening years?* ADJ CLASSIF : ATTRIB

2 An **intervening** object or area exists between two others. EG *The intervening space consists of empty windows.* ADJ CLASSIF : ATTRIB

interview /ɪntəvjuː/, **interviews, interviewing, interviewed.** 1 An **interview** is 1.1 a formal meeting at which someone is asked questions in order to find out if they are suitable for a job or for a course of study. EG *I had an interview for a job on a newspaper... He was invited for interview at three universities.* N COUNT OR N UNCOUNT 1.2 a conversation in which a journalist asks a famous person questions. EG *...my interview with the Duke... ...a television interview.* N COUNT

2 If an employer **interviews** you, he or she asks you questions in order to find out whether you are suitable for a job. EG *I was once interviewed for a part in a film.* V+O

3 When a famous person **is interviewed**, a journalist asks this person a series of questions. EG *Hopkins was interviewed by Wyndham for Queen magazine.* ◇ **interviewer** /ɪntəvjuːə/, **interviewers.** EG *Television interviewers were being too aggressive.* V+O : USU PASS ◇ N COUNT

interwoven /ɪntəwəʊvə^{0}n/. If things are **interwoven**, they are joined together in a very close and complicated way. EG *Social and international unity have become interwoven.* ADJ CLASSIF

intestine /ɪntɛstɪn/, **intestines.** Your **intestines** are the tubes in your body through which food from your stomach passes. EG *...pains in the intestine.* ◇ **intestinal** /ɪntɛstɪnə^{0}l/. EG *...the cause of serious intestinal infections... ...an enzyme which exists in the intestinal lining.* N COUNT : USU PLURAL ◇ ADJ CLASSIF : ATTRIB

intimacy /ɪntɪ^{1}məsi^{1}/, **intimacies. 1** When there is **intimacy** between people, they have a close relationship. EG *...the intimacy between mother and child... Never before had he known such intimacy with another person.* N UNCOUNT : OFT+ *between/with*

2 Intimacies are things that are said or done by people in a close relationship. EG *I like sharing these little intimacies.* N COUNT : USU PLURAL

intimate, intimates, intimating, intimated; pronounced /ɪntɪ^{1}mət/ when it is an adjective or noun, and /ɪntɪmeɪt/ when it is a verb. **1** If two people have an **intimate** relationship, they are very good friends. EG *...her best and most intimate friend.* ◇ **intimately.** EG *I don't know any girls intimately.* ADJ QUALIT ◇ ADV

2 Your **intimates** are your close friends. EG *He let one or two intimates know his good news.* N COUNT Literary

3 If you are **intimate** with someone, you have a sexual relationship with them. EG *He had been intimate with a number of women.* ADJ CLASSIF Formal

4 **Intimate** things are very personal and private. EG *...the most intimate details of their personal lives.* ◇ **intimately.** EG *...women talking intimately to other women.* ADJ QUALIT ◇ ADV

5 An **intimate** place or occasion has a pleasant and friendly atmosphere. EG *...small and intimate night clubs... ...an intimate meal with the family.* ADJ QUALIT

6 An **intimate** connection between ideas or organizations is very strong or close. EG *...its intimate bonds with government.* ◇ **intimately.** EG *These two questions are intimately linked.* ADJ QUALIT : USU ATTRIB ◇ ADV

7 If you have an **intimate** knowledge of something, you know it in great detail. EG *...someone with an intimate knowledge of the station.* ◇ **intimately.** EG *He knew the contents of the files intimately.* ADJ QUALIT : ATTRIB ◇ ADV

8 If you **intimate** something, you tell it to someone, often in an indirect way. EG *Forbes intimated that he would prefer to do this later.* V+O OR V+REPORT : ONLY *that* Formal

intimation /ɪntɪmeɪʃə^{0}n/, **intimations.** An **intimation** of something is an indication or feeling that it is likely to exist, happen, or be true. EG *For the first time I felt some intimation of danger... ...the first intimations of a new idea.* N COUNT+SUPP Formal

intimidate /ɪntɪmɪdeɪt/, **intimidates, intimidating, intimidated.** If you **intimidate** someone, you frighten them, sometimes as a deliberate way of making them do something. EG *In 1972 his neighbours intimidated his family into leaving.* ◇ **intimidation** /ɪntɪmɪdeɪʃə^{0}n/. EG *Young suffered imprisonment and intimidation.* V+O ◇ N UNCOUNT

intimidated /ɪntɪmɪdeɪtɪ^{2}d/. If people are **intimidated**, they feel afraid and have no confidence in themselves. EG *Theo was intimidated by so many strangers.* ADJ QUALIT

intimidating /ɪntɪmɪdeɪtɪŋ/. If something is **intimidating**, it causes you to feel afraid and to lose confidence in yourself. EG *The rooms were huge and intimidating.* ADJ QUALIT

into /ɪntuː/. **1** If you put one thing **into** another thing, you put it inside the other thing, so that it is enclosed or surrounded. EG *Pour some water into a glass... He slipped the note into his pocket.* PREP

2 If you go **into** a place or vehicle, you move from being outside it to being inside it. EG *He walked into a police station... They got into the car.* PREP

3 If one thing gets **into** another thing, it enters it and becomes part of it. EG *Drugs may get into the milk... ...Britain's entry into the Common Market.* PREP

4 If you are walking or driving a vehicle and you bump **into** something or crash **into** something, you hit it accidentally. EG *I bumped into a chair.* PREP

5 When you get **into** a piece of clothing, you put it on. EG *She changed into her best dress.* PREP

6 If someone or something gets **into** a particular state, they start being in that state. EG *The Labour Government came into power in 1974... The assembly was shocked into silence.* PREP

7 If something changes **into** a new form or shape, it then has this new form or shape. EG *The bud develops into a flower... The play was made into a movie... He folded his newspaper into a neat rectangle... I tore her letter into eight pieces.* PREP

8 An investigation **into** a subject or event is concerned with that subject or event. EG *...research into emotional problems... Some MPs demanded a full enquiry into the incident.* PREP

9 If you are very interested in something and like it very much, you can say that you are **into** it. EG *Teenagers are into those romantic novels.* PREP Informal

intolerable /ɪntɒlərəbə^{0}l/. If something is **intolerable**, it is so bad or so severe that people can no longer accept it. EG *All my employees found it intolerable... ...the things that made his life intolerable... ...an intolerable dullness.* ◇ **intolerably.** EG *The days were still intolerably hot.* ADJ QUALIT ◇ ADV

intolerant /ɪntɒlərənt/. If you are **intolerant**, you disapprove of behaviour and opinions which are different from your own. EG *He was intolerant of other people's weakness... We are giving support to intolerant regimes.* ◇ **intolerance** /ɪntɒlərəns/. EG *She accused the men of ignorance and intolerance... ...religious intolerance.* ADJ QUALIT ◇ N UNCOUNT

intonation /ɪntə^{6}neɪʃə^{0}n/, **intonations. Intonation** is the way that your voice rises and falls when you speak. EG *...their accents and intonations... ...a Northern intonation.* N UNCOUNT OR N COUNT

intone /ɪntəʊn/, **intones, intoning, intoned.** If you **intone** something, you say it in a slow and serious way, not allowing your voice to rise and fall very much. EG *He was intoning, '...and so it is my privilege and pleasure'... They intoned the afternoon prayers.* V+O OR V+QUOTE Literary

intoxicated /ɪntɒksɪkeɪtɪ^{2}d/. **1** If someone is **intoxicated**, they are drunk. EG *Thompson went into town and got very intoxicated.* ADJ QUALIT Formal

2 If you are **intoxicated** by an event, idea, or feeling, it makes you very excited so that you behave in an extreme way. EG *Intoxicated by victory, he was dancing... They became intoxicated with pride.* ADJ PRED +*by/with*

intoxicating /ɪntɒksɪkeɪtɪŋ/. **1** An **intoxicating** drink contains alcohol and can make you drunk. EG *...the intoxicating wine.* ADJ QUALIT Formal

2 Something that is **intoxicating** causes you to be very excited and to behave in an uncontrolled or foolish way. EG *...her intoxicating beauty.* ADJ QUALIT

intoxication /ɪntɒksɪkeɪʃə^{0}n/ is **1** the state of being drunk. EG *They were in an advanced state of intoxication.* **2** the state of being so excited that you behave in an uncontrolled or foolish way. EG *...the intoxication of success.* N UNCOUNT Formal; Formal

intractable /ɪntræktəbə^{0}l/. **1 Intractable** people are stubborn and difficult to influence or control. EG *On one issue Luce was intractable.* ADJ QUALIT Formal

2 Intractable problems seem impossible to deal with. EG *Labour problems can be more intractable.* ADJ QUALIT

intransigent /ɪntrænsɪdʒənt/. If someone is **intransigent**, they refuse to change their behaviour ADJ QUALIT Formal

Are there any intransitive verbs on these pages?

or opinions; used showing disapproval. EG *...their intransigent attitude over our debts.*
◊ **intransigence** /ɪntrænsɪdʒəns/. EG *The party is forced into violence by the intransigence of its opponents.* ◊ N UNCOUNT +POSS

intransitive /ɪntrænsɪtɪv/. An **intransitive** verb does not have an object. In this dictionary V is used in the Extra Column to show that a verb is intransitive. See the entry headed VERBS for more information. ADJ CLASSIF

intrepid /ɪntrepɪd/. An **intrepid** person acts bravely, ignoring difficulties and danger. EG *This intrepid woman was unlikely to hand over her money... ...the route of those intrepid explorers.* ADJ QUALIT Literary

intricacy /ɪntrɪkəsi^{1}/, **intricacies. 1** The **intricacies** of a situation are its complicated or subtle details. EG *...the intricacies of American politics.* N PLURAL : USU+*of*

2 When you talk about the **intricacy** of something, you are referring to the fact that it has many parts or details. EG *...the technical intricacy of modern industry.* N UNCOUNT

intricate /ɪntrɪkə^{1}t/. Something that is **intricate** has many small parts or details. EG *They were painted in intricate patterns... ...long, intricate discussions.* ◊ **intricately.** EG *...intricately patterned necklaces... ...an intricately carved door.* ADJ QUALIT ◊ ADV

intrigue, intrigues, intriguing, intrigued; pronounced /ɪntri:g/ when it is a noun and /ɪntri:g/ when it is a verb.

1 Intrigue is the making of secret plans that are intended to harm other people. EG *...a great deal of political intrigue... ...financial intrigues.* N UNCOUNT OR N COUNT

2 If someone or something **intrigues** you, you are fascinated by them and curious about them. EG *The idea seemed to intrigue him... I was intrigued by the small brown paper packet.* ◊ **intrigued.** EG *Intrigued, I followed the instructions.* V+O ◊ ADJ PRED
◊ **intriguing.** EG *This intriguing woman was an exceptional mathematician... That sounds most intriguing.* ◊ ADJ QUALIT

intrinsic /ɪntrɪnsɪk/. The **intrinsic** qualities of something are the important and basic qualities of it. EG *...the intrinsic idiocy of the plan... ...objects which have no intrinsic value.* ◊ **intrinsically.** EG *His material was intrinsically interesting.* ADJ CLASSIF : ATTRIB Formal ◊ ADV

introduce /ɪntrə^{6}dju:s/, **introduces, introducing, introduced. 1** If you **introduce** someone to a person they do not know, you tell them each other's name, so that they can get to know each other. EG *Hogan introduced him to Karl... At a party in Hollywood, I was introduced to Charlie Chaplin.* V+O : OFT+*to*

2 If you **introduce** yourself to someone you do not know, you tell them your name, so that you can get to know them. EG *I had better introduce myself. I am Mark Rodin... A man came up and introduced himself as the Bishop.* V-REFL

3 If you **introduce** a speaker to an audience, you tell the audience who the speaker is and what they are going to talk about. V+O

4 When someone **introduces** a television or radio programme, they say a few words at the beginning of it to tell you what it will be about. V+O

5 If you **introduce** something to a place, situation, or system, you take it there or use it there for the first time. EG *Rabbits had been introduced into Australia by Europeans... Banks will soon introduce new savings plans.* V+O

6 If you **introduce** someone to something, you cause them to learn about it or experience it for the first time. EG *We introduced them to the new methods... He was first introduced to politics as a child.* V+O+*to*

introduction /ɪntrə^{6}dʌkʃə^{0}n/, **introductions. 1** The **introduction** of something into a place or system is the act of taking it there or using it there for the first time. EG *The Government saw the introduction of new technology as vital.* N UNCOUNT +SUPP

2 Your **introduction** to something is the occasion when you experience it for the first time. EG *This was my first real introduction to agriculture.* N SING : USU+*to*

3 The **introduction** to a book or talk is the first part, which tells you what the rest of the book or talk is about. EG *Johnston contributes a delightful introduction to Smith's book.* N COUNT

4 Books which explain the basic facts about a subject often have **Introduction** as part of their title. EG *An Introduction to English Literature.*

5 An **introduction** is also the act of telling two people each other's names so that they can get to know each other. EG *Sam got to his feet and I made the introductions.* N COUNT

introductory /ɪntrə^{6}dʌktə^{0}ri^{1}/. **Introductory** remarks, books, or courses are intended to give you a general idea of a particular subject, often before more detailed information is given. EG *After the introductory speeches Hughes began his talk... ...a good introductory chapter on forests.* ADJ CLASSIF : ATTRIB

introspection /ɪntrə^{6}spekʃə^{0}n/ is the act of examining your own thoughts, ideas, and feelings. EG *I simply hadn't time for introspection.* N UNCOUNT Formal

introspective /ɪntrə^{6}spektɪv/. **Introspective** people spend a lot of time examining their own thoughts, ideas, and feelings. EG *The boy was downcast and introspective.* ADJ QUALIT Formal

introvert /ɪntrə^{6}vɜ:t/, **introverts.** An **introvert** is a quiet, shy person who spends a lot of time alone. EG *...a bashful introvert.* N COUNT Formal

introverted /ɪntrə^{6}vɜ:tɪ^{2}d/. **Introverted** people are quiet, shy, and spend a lot of time alone. EG *He was without doubt the most introverted boy in my school... During pregnancy, a woman often becomes introverted.* ADJ QUALIT Formal

intrude /ɪntru:d/, **intrudes, intruding, intruded.**

1 If you **intrude** on someone, you disturb them when they are in a private place or having a private conversation. EG *He felt that he couldn't intrude... I don't want to intrude on your family.* V : OFT +*on/upon*

2 If something **intrudes** on your mood or your life, it disturbs it or has an unpleasant effect on it. EG *I shall not intrude on your grief.* V+*on*

3 You can say that someone **is intruding** when they enter a place without permission. EG *I heard peals of laughter from the intruding children.* V : OFT +*on/upon*

intruder /ɪntru:də/, **intruders.** An **intruder** is a person who enters a place without permission. EG *An intruder had come into his home.* N COUNT

intrusion /ɪntru:ʒə^{0}n/, **intrusions. 1** If someone disturbs you when you are in a private place or having a private conversation, you can describe their behaviour as an **intrusion**. EG *I must ask your pardon for this intrusion.* N COUNT OR N UNCOUNT

2 An **intrusion** is also something that affects your mood or your life in an unwelcome way. EG *I resent the intrusion of the outside world.* N COUNT OR N UNCOUNT

intrusive /ɪntru:sɪv/. If someone or something is **intrusive**, they disturb your mood or life in an unwelcome way. EG *...this intrusive insect... ...Gordon's intrusive interest in our religious activities.* ADJ QUALIT

intuit /ɪntju:ɪt/, **intuits, intuiting, intuited.** If you **intuit** something, you guess it by using your feelings, rather than your knowledge. EG *She intuited that Peter would be glad to see her.* V+O OR V+REPORT Formal

intuition /ɪntju:ɪʃə^{0}n/, **intuitions.** Your **intuition** is a feeling that something is true or exists although you have no evidence or proof of it. EG *My intuition told me to stay away... ...arguments based on intuition... I've got an intuition that something is wrong.* N UNCOUNT OR N COUNT

intuitive /ɪntju:ɪtɪv/. **Intuitive** ideas or feelings tell you that something is true or exists although you have no evidence or proof of it. EG *I got a strong intuitive feeling that he was lying... ...his intuitive understanding of nature.* ◊ **intuitively.** EG *I felt intuitively that they would not return.* ADJ QUALIT Formal ◊ ADV

inundate /ɪnʌndeɪt/, **inundates, inundating, inundated. 1** If you **are inundated** with things, you receive so many of them that you cannot deal with V+O : USU PASS +*with* them all. EG *She was inundated with telephone calls... They had been inundated with applications.*

2 If an area of land **is inundated**, it becomes covered with water. EG *...inundated areas... ...the floods that inundate northern India every year.* V+O : USU PASS Formal

inure /ɪnjʊə/, **inures, inuring, inured.** If you **inure** yourself to something unpleasant, you experience it so often that you learn to accept it. EG *...people who inure themselves to tragedy... ...a man who was inured to disappointment.* V-REFL+*to* Formal

invade /ɪnveɪd/, **invades, invading, invaded. 1** To **invade** a country means to enter it by force with an army. EG *...Kennedy's secret plan to invade Cuba... ...the invading forces.* ◊ **invader** /ɪnveɪdə/, **invaders.** EG *The invaders had been defeated.* V+O; ◊ N COUNT : USU PLURAL

2 If people or animals **invade** a place, they enter it in large numbers. EG *The town was invaded by reporters... ...pests that invade the home.* V+O

3 If someone or something **invades** your privacy, they disturb you when you want to be alone. V+O

invalid, invalids; pronounced /ɪnvəlɪd/ in paragraph 1 and /ɪnvælɪd/ in paragraphs 2 and 3.

1 An **invalid** is someone who is very ill or disabled and who needs to be cared for by someone else. EG *The family treated her like an invalid... ...her invalid mother.* ◊ **invalidity** /ɪnvəlɪdɪ^{1}ti^1/. EG *...an invalidity pension.* N COUNT; ◊ N MOD

2 If an argument, conclusion or result is **invalid**, it is not correct or not reasonable. EG *The comparison is invalid.* ◊ **invalidity.** EG *My experiments show the invalidity of his argument.* ADJ CLASSIF; ◊ N UNCOUNT

3 If an official process, contract, or document is **invalid**, it has not followed the laws or regulations and is not legally acceptable. EG *The marriage was invalid... The court ruled his election invalid.* ADJ CLASSIF

invalidate /ɪnvælɪdeɪt/, **invalidates, invalidating, invalidated. 1** If something **invalidates** an argument, conclusion, or result, it proves that it is wrong. EG *Such exceptions do not invalidate the rule.* V+O Formal

2 If something **invalidates** an official process, contract, or document, it causes it to be legally unacceptable. EG *The marriage would invalidate any earlier will.* V+O Formal

invaluable /ɪnvæljʊ^{0}əbə^{0}l/. If someone or something is **invaluable**, they are extremely useful. EG *This experience proved invaluable later on... He was an invaluable source of information.* ADJ CLASSIF

invariable /ɪnveərɪəbə^{0}l/. Something that is **invariable** always happens or never changes. EG *They followed an invariable routine.* ◊ **invariably** /ɪnveərɪəbli^1/. EG *The conversation invariably returns to politics... Our receptionists are almost invariably female.* ADJ CLASSIF; ◊ ADV

invasion /ɪnveɪʒə^{0}n/, **invasions. 1** When there is an **invasion** of a country, an army enters it by force. EG *...the invasion of Europe by the Allies in 1944... It enabled us to remain free from invasion.* N COUNT OR N UNCOUNT

2 You can describe the arrival of large numbers of things or people in a place as an **invasion.** EG *...the invasion of Italian movies in the fifties.* N UNCOUNT +SUPP

invective /ɪnvektɪv/. **Invective** consists of rude and unpleasant things that people say when they are very angry or annoyed with someone. EG *...women hurling invective at us... A torrent of invective awaited them.* N UNCOUNT Formal

invent /ɪnvent/, **invents, inventing, invented. 1** If you **invent** something, you are the first person to think of it or make it. EG *...the men who invented the sewing machine... ...a game he had invented... He invented this phrase himself.* V+O

2 If you **invent** a story or excuse, you try to persuade people that it is true when it is not, often for dishonest reasons. EG *...lies invented for a political purpose.* V+O

invention /ɪnvenʃə^{0}n/, **inventions. 1** An **invention** is a machine or system that has been invented by someone. EG *He was working on his invention... Writing was the most revolutionary of all human inventions.* N COUNT

2 If you refer to someone's account of something as an **invention**, you mean that it is not true and that they have made it up. EG *The account was a deliberate and malicious invention.* N COUNT

3 When someone creates something that has never existed before, you can refer to this event as the **invention** of the thing. EG *...the invention of printing.* N UNCOUNT +SUPP

4 Invention is also the ability to invent things or to have clever and original ideas. EG *...his powers of invention.* N UNCOUNT

inventive /ɪnventɪv/. An **inventive** person is good at inventing things or has clever and original ideas. EG *He is inventive in dealing with physical problems.* ◊ **inventiveness.** EG *The musicians can play, even if they do lack inventiveness.* ADJ QUALIT; ◊ N UNCOUNT

inventor /ɪnventə/, **inventors.** An **inventor** is a person who has invented something, or whose job is to invent things. EG *...Cockerell, the inventor of the hovercraft... ...inventors and engineers.* N COUNT

inventory /ɪnvə^{2}ntri^1/, **inventories.** An **inventory** is a written list of all the objects in a particular place. EG *...compiling an inventory of the treasures that lay hidden in the ship.* N COUNT Formal

inverse /ɪnvɜːs/. **1** If there is an **inverse** relationship between two things, one of them decreases as the other increases. EG *The time spent varies in inverse proportion to the amount of work done.* ADJ CLASSIF Formal

2 The **inverse** of something is its exact opposite. EG *It represents the inverse of everything I find worth preserving.* ▸ used as an adjective. EG *The inverse case is also worth considering.* N SING Formal; ▸ ADJ CLASSIF : ATTRIB

inversion /ɪnvɜːʃə^{0}n/, **inversions.** When there is an **inversion** of something, it is changed into its opposite. EG *...this curious inversion of facts... ...an inversion of the expected order.* N UNCOUNT OR N COUNT : USU+SUPP Formal

invert /ɪnvɜːt/, **inverts, inverting, inverted.** If you **invert** something, you turn it upside down or back to front. EG *The chairs are inverted on the tables.* ◊ **inverted.** EG *It was shaped like an inverted cone.* ● See also **inverted commas.** V+O Formal; ◊ ADJ CLASSIF

invertebrate /ɪnvɜːtɪbreɪt, -brə^{1}t/, **invertebrates.** An **invertebrate** is a creature that does not have a spine, for example an insect, a worm, or an octopus. EG *...other floating invertebrates.* N COUNT Technical

inverted commas are the punctuation marks (' and ' or " and ") that are used in writing to indicate where speech or a quotation begins and ends. N PLURAL

invest /ɪnvest/, **invests, investing, invested. 1** If you **invest** an amount of money, you pay it into a bank or buy shares with it, so that you will receive a profit. EG *...investing in stocks and shares... £20 million of public money had been invested.* ◊ **investor** /ɪnvestə/, **investors.** EG *The investor is entitled to a reasonable return on his money.* V+O OR V : OFT+*in*; ◊ N COUNT

2 If you **invest** money, time, or energy in something, you use it to try and make the thing successful. EG *They are willing to invest energy in a European disarmament campaign... They have failed to invest in job creation in the cities.* V+O OR V : OFT+*in* Formal

3 If you **invest** in something useful, you buy it because it will be more efficient or cheaper over a period of time. EG *Good shoes are worth investing in even though they are expensive.* V+*in* OR V+O+*in*

4 To **invest** someone with rights or responsibilities means to give them to them legally or officially. EG *The law invests the shareholders alone with legal rights.* V+O+*with* Formal

investigate /ɪnvestɪgeɪt/, **investigates, investigating, investigated.** If you **investigate** an event, situation, or person, you try to find out all the facts about them. EG *He had come to investigate* V+O OR V

If something is invaluable, is it also valuable?

a murder... I sent my men to investigate.
◊ **investigation** /ɪnvɛ̱stɪgeɪ̱ʃə°n/, **investigations.** EG *Sherman ordered an investigation into her death... ...the results of their investigations.* ◊ N COUNT OR N UNCOUNT

investigative /ɪnvɛ̱stɪgətɪv/. **Investigative** activities involve trying to find out all the facts about events, situations, or people. EG *He was doing investigative work on Kennedy... ...investigative reporters.* ADJ CLASSIF : ATTRIB Formal

investigator /ɪnvɛ̱stɪgeɪtə/, **investigators.** An **investigator** is someone whose job is to investigate events, situations, or people. EG *Aircraft accident investigators got to the scene quickly.* N COUNT

investment /ɪnvɛ̱stmənt/, **investments. 1 Investment** is the activity of buying shares or of putting money into a bank account in order to obtain a profit. EG *We aim to encourage investment.* N UNCOUNT

2 An **investment** is **2.1** the amount of money you put into a bank account or buy shares with. EG *...a better return on the investment.* N COUNT **2.2** something that you buy. EG *The tractors proved a superb investment.* Informal

3 If you make an **investment** of time or effort in something, you spend time or effort in order to achieve something. EG *It might be a better investment of time to teach the children to cook.* N UNCOUNT +SUPP

inveterate /ɪnvɛ̱tərə't/. You use **inveterate** to say that someone has been doing something for a long time and that they are not likely to stop doing it. For example, an inveterate liar is someone who has always told lies and who will probably continue to tell lies. EG *Hubert had been an inveterate hunter... ...their inveterate distrust of others.* ADJ CLASSIF : ATTRIB Formal

invidious /ɪnvɪ̱dɪəs/. **1** An **invidious** task or job is unpleasant to do, because it is likely to make you unpopular. EG *The role of a critic can be an invidious one.* ADJ QUALIT

2 An **invidious** comparison or decision is an unfair one because the things involved are not similar or are almost equal in value or quality. EG *He defended American police against invidious comparisons with Scotland Yard... This involves an invidious choice.* ADJ CLASSIF

invigilator /ɪnvɪ̱dʒɪleɪtə/, **invigilators.** An **invigilator** is someone who supervises the people taking an examination. The invigilator makes sure that the examination starts and finishes at the correct time and that nobody cheats. N COUNT

invigorating /ɪnvɪ̱gəreɪtɪŋ/. Something that is **invigorating** makes you feel more energetic. EG *The air here is invigorating... ...an invigorating bath... You will find it an invigorating experience.* ADJ QUALIT

invincible /ɪnvɪ̱nsə'bə°l/. **1** An **invincible** army or sports team is very powerful and difficult to defeat. EG *They are invincible in battle... ...an army of invincible strength.* ADJ CLASSIF

2 If someone has an **invincible** belief or attitude, it cannot be changed. EG *...their invincible contempt for foreigners.* ADJ CLASSIF : ATTRIB

inviolable /ɪnvaɪ̱ələbə°l/. If a law or principle is **inviolable**, you cannot or must not break it. EG *Tradition was considered inviolable.* ADJ CLASSIF Formal

inviolate /ɪnvaɪ̱ələ't/. If something is **inviolate**, it cannot be harmed or affected. EG *...leaving the truth inviolate... ...its walls inviolate as a fortress.* ADJ CLASSIF Formal

invisible /ɪnvɪ̱zə'bə°l/. **1** If something is **invisible**, you cannot see it, because it is hidden or because it is very small or faint. EG *Her legs were invisible beneath the table... ...hairs invisible to the naked eye.* ADJ CLASSIF ◊ **invisibly.** EG *...draw the lines almost invisibly pale.* ◊ ADV ◊ **invisibility** /ɪnvɪzə'bɪ̱lɪ'ti'/. EG *The main advantage is the submarine's invisibility.* ◊ N UNCOUNT

2 In stories, **invisible** people or things cannot be seen by anybody. EG *He waves his magic wand and turns himself invisible.* ADJ CLASSIF

invitation /ɪnvɪteɪ̱ʃə°n/, **invitations. 1** An **invitation** is a written or spoken request to come to an event such as a party, a meal, or a meeting. EG *Cindy accepted invitations to cocktail parties and private dinners... I had an invitation to go and talk to the cadets.* N COUNT

2 The card or paper on which an invitation is written is also called an **invitation.** EG *...engraved invitations... Jenny was waving the invitation.* N COUNT

3 Behaviour that encourages you to do something is sometimes referred to as an **invitation.** EG *She declined the invitation to address him as 'Charles'... Houses left unlocked are an open invitation to burglary.* N SING+*to*-INF OR *to*

invite /ɪnvaɪ̱t/, **invites, inviting, invited. 1** If you **invite** someone to something such as a party or meal, you ask them to come to it. EG *Invite her to the party... Leggett invited me for lunch at the hotel.* V+O : OFT+*to*

2 If someone **invites** you to do something, they formally ask you to do it. EG *I was invited to attend future meetings... He was invited for interview.* V+O : OFT+*to*-INF OR *for*

3 If someone **invites** discussion or criticism, they encourage you to discuss or criticize what they have said or done. EG *He stopped speaking and invited discussion.* V+O Formal

4 If someone or something **invites** confidence or disbelief, they cause you to feel confident in them, or to disbelieve them. EG *This kind of statement invites disbelief.* V+O Formal

5 If something **invites** danger or trouble, it makes danger or trouble more likely. EG *To speak of it to others would invite danger.* V+O Formal

inviting /ɪnvaɪ̱tɪŋ/. If you say that something is **inviting**, you mean that it is attractive and desirable. EG *The place was green and inviting... ...large dark eyes, shy but inviting.* ADJ QUALIT ◊ **invitingly.** EG *The packet of cigarettes lay invitingly open.* ◊ ADV

invocation /ɪ̱nvə'keɪ̱ʃə°n/, **invocations.** An **invocation** is a spoken request to a god for help or forgiveness. EG *They murmured invocations to the gods.* N COUNT OR N UNCOUNT

invoice /ɪ̱nvɔɪs/, **invoices.** An **invoice** is an official document that lists the goods or services that you have received from a person or company and says how much money you owe for them. EG *His firm sent you an invoice for it six months ago.* N COUNT

invoke /ɪnvəʊ̱k/, **invokes, invoking, invoked. 1** If you **invoke** a law, you use it to justify what you are doing. EG *The Government invoked the Emergency Powers Act.* V+O Formal

2 If you **invoke** a principle, proverb, famous person, or book, you quote them or use them as examples to support your argument. EG *They invoke Lenin and Trotsky... The phrase invoked was 'the country is going to the dogs'.* V+O Formal

3 If you **invoke** feelings of a particular kind, you cause someone to feel them. EG *They tried to invoke popular enthusiasm for the war.* V+O Formal

involuntary /ɪnvɒ̱ləntə°ri'/. **Involuntary** actions are done suddenly and without intention because people are unable to control themselves. EG *There were one or two involuntary exclamations.* ADJ CLASSIF ◊ **involuntarily.** EG *I shivered involuntarily.* ◊ ADV

involve /ɪnvɒ̱lv/, **involves, involving, involved.** **1** If a situation or activity **involves** someone or something, **1.1** it includes or uses them as a necessary part. EG *Caring for a one-year-old involves changing nappies... Some of the experiments involve the equipment you've seen.* V+O OR V+-ING **1.2** it concerns or affects them. EG *Workers are never told about things which involve them.* V+O

2 If you **involve** yourself in something, you take part in it. EG *They involve themselves deeply in community affairs.* V-REFL : OFT+*in*/*with*

3 If you **involve** someone else in something, you get them to take part in it. EG *Did you have to involve me in this?* V+O : OFT+*in*

4 If a book, play, or film **involves** you, it makes you feel that you are taking part in the events it describes or shows. EG *...the ability of the film to involve you imaginatively.* V+O

involved /ɪnvɒlvd/. **1** If someone or something is **involved** in or with a situation or activity, they are taking part in it. EG *Should religious leaders get involved in politics?... ...companies involved in producing the aircraft... He is involved with editing... ...the large number of people involved.* ADJ PRED: OFT+*in/with*

2 If you are deeply or intensely **involved** in something, you feel very strongly or enthusiastically about it. EG *I was deeply involved in my work... She became terribly involved with writing.* ADJ PRED: OFT+*with/in*

3 The things **involved** in a task, situation, or system are the things that are required in order to achieve it or understand it, or the problems that it causes. EG *There is quite a lot of work involved... What is involved in making a television programme?... Explain the principles involved.* ADJ PRED: OFT+*in*

4 If you describe a situation or activity as **involved**, you mean that it is very complicated;. EG *We had long, involved discussions.* ADJ QUALIT

5 If you are **involved** with another person, you are having a close relationship with them. EG *He had become involved with her in Brussels.* ADJ PRED: OFT+*with*

involvement /ɪnvɒlvmənt/. **1** Your **involvement** in something is the fact that you are taking part in it. EG *...parental involvement in schools... ...the active involvement of workers.* N UNCOUNT: OFT+*in/of/with*

2 Involvement is also the concern and enthusiasm that you feel about something. EG *...his deep involvement with socialism.* N UNCOUNT: OFT+*with/in*

invulnerable /ɪnvʌlnə[0]rəbə[0]l/. If someone or something is **invulnerable**, they cannot be harmed or damaged. EG *The nuclear submarine is almost invulnerable to attack.* ◇ **invulnerability** /ɪnvʌlnə[0]rəbɪlɪ[1]ti[1]/. EG *Parents have a feeling of invulnerability.* ADJ CLASSIF; ◇ N UNCOUNT

inward /ɪnwəd/, **inwards. 1** Your **inward** thoughts or feelings are the ones that you do not express or show to other people. EG *...my inward happiness... She hid an inward amusement.* ADJ CLASSIF: ATTRIB

◇ **inwardly.** EG *I remained inwardly unconvinced.* ◇ ADV

2 If something moves or faces **inward** or **inwards**, it moves or faces towards the inside or centre of something. EG *The door swung inward... His cell faced inwards.* ADV AFTER VB

3 An **inward** movement is one towards the inside or centre of something. EG *...the inward flow of air.* ADJ CLASSIF: ATTRIB

iodine /aɪədi:n/ is a dark-coloured substance used in medicine and photography. N UNCOUNT

ion /aɪən/, **ions. Ions** are electrically charged atoms. EG *...calcium ions... ...ions of nitrogen.* N COUNT Technical

-ion, -ions. See **-ation**.

iota /aɪəʊtə/. You can refer to an extremely small amount of something as an **iota** . EG *I don't feel one iota of guilt... I don't think you've changed an iota.* N PART

IOU /aɪ əʊ ju:/, **IOUs.** An **IOU** is a written promise to pay back money that you have borrowed. **IOU** is an abbreviation for 'I owe you'. EG *He wrote out an IOU for five thousand dollars.* N COUNT

IQ /aɪ kju:/, **IQs.** Your **IQ** is your level of intelligence, which is measured by a special test. **IQ** is an abbreviation for 'intelligence quotient'. EG *He had an IQ of 50... The IQ of our students is quite low.* N UNCOUNT +SUPP

irascible /ɪræsɪ[1]bə[0]l/. An **irascible** person becomes angry very easily. EG *He is irascible and violent... ...Jeff's irascible outbursts.* ADJ QUALIT Formal

irate /aɪreɪt/. If you are **irate**, you are very angry about something. EG *The Bishop looked irate... ...calming down irate customers... ...an irate letter.* ADJ QUALIT Formal

ire /aɪə/ is anger. EG *He incurred the ire of the authorities.* N UNCOUNT Literary

iridescent /ɪrɪdɛsənt/. Something that is **iridescent** has bright colours that seem to keep changing. EG *...the iridescent blue and orange glow... ...iridescent feathers.* ADJ CLASSIF Literary

iris /aɪrɪs/, **irises. 1** The **iris** in your eye is the round coloured part. EG *...eyelids dropping over blue irises.* N COUNT

2 An **iris** is also a tall plant with long leaves and large purple, yellow, or white flowers. N COUNT

Irish /aɪrɪʃ/. **1** Something that is **Irish 1.1** belongs or relates to the whole of Ireland, to its people, or to its language. EG *She spoke with an Irish accent.* ADJ CLASSIF

1.2 belongs or relates to the Republic of Ireland. EG *...the Irish Prime Minister.*

2 The **Irish** are the people who come from Ireland. EG *The majority of the Irish accept these proposals.* N PLURAL: *the*+N

Irishman /aɪrɪʃmə[3]n/, **Irishmen.** An **Irishman** is a man who comes from Ireland. N COUNT

Irishwoman /aɪrɪʃwʊmən/, **Irishwomen.** An **Irishwoman** is a woman who comes from Ireland. N COUNT

irk /ɜ:k/, **irks, irking, irked.** If something **irks** you, it irritates or annoys you. EG *...twisting his shoulders as if his jacket irked him... Such tactics clearly irked Gordon.* V+O: NO IMPER

irksome /ɜ:ksəm/. If something is **irksome**, it irritates or annoys you. EG *I found Clare's methods rather irksome... ...an irksome responsibility.* ADJ QUALIT

iron /aɪən/, **irons, ironing, ironed. 1 Iron** is a hard, dark metal found in rocks. It is used to make objects such as gates and fences, and also to make other metals such as steel. Small amounts of iron occur in your blood and in food. EG *...a lump of iron... ...an iron bar... ...the iron and steel industries... Seaweed has a high iron content.* N UNCOUNT

2 An **iron** is an electrical device with a handle and a heated flat metal base. You rub an iron over clothes to remove creases. EG *If it's cotton or linen, use a hot iron.* N COUNT

3 If you **iron** clothes, you remove the creases from them using an iron. EG *I can't iron shirts.* ● See also **ironing, ironing board**. V+O

4 You can use **iron** to describe the character or behaviour of someone who is very firm in their decisions and actions, and who can control their feelings. EG *He was able to enforce his iron will... ...her iron composure... ...iron discipline.* ADJ CLASSIF: ATTRIB

iron out. If you **iron out** difficulties, you get rid of them successfully. EG *I thought most of our problems were ironed out.* PHRASAL VB: V+O+ADV

Iron Curtain. 1 The **Iron Curtain** refers to the border between the Soviet Union and its East European allies and the Western European countries. EG *...the Soviet side of the Iron Curtain.* ● If something happens **behind the Iron Curtain**, it happens in the Soviet Union or in one of the East European countries that are allied to it. EG *Sales of his novels were most brisk behind the Iron Curtain.* N PROPER: *the*+N; ● PHRASE

2 The **Iron Curtain** countries are the Soviet Union and its East European allies. N MOD

ironic /aɪrɒnɪk/. **1** If someone makes **ironic** remarks or gestures, they are joking or really mean the opposite of what they say. EG *It was possible that his thanks were ironic... ...an ironic smile.* ADJ QUALIT

2 An **ironic** situation is strange or amusing because it is very unusual or is the opposite of what was expected. EG *It is ironic that the people who complain most loudly are the ones who do least to help.* ADJ QUALIT

ironical /aɪrɒnɪkə[0]l/ means the same as ironic. ADJ QUALIT

ironically /aɪrɒnɪkə[0]li[1]/. **1** You say **ironically** to draw attention to an unusual or amusing aspect of a situation. EG *Ironically, the intelligence chief was the last person to hear the news.* ADV SEN

2 If you say something **ironically**, you are joking or you really mean the opposite of what you say. EG *'Do you want to search the apartment?' she enquired ironically.* ADV

ironing /aɪənɪŋ/ is the activity of using a hot iron to remove creases from clothes. EG *She's doing the ironing.* N UNCOUNT

ironing board, ironing boards. An **ironing board** is a long, narrow board covered with cloth, on which you iron clothes. N COUNT

If you are irascible, are you easily irked?

ironwork /aɪənwɜːk/ refers to objects or parts of buildings that are made of iron. EG *...brick houses with painted ironwork... ...ironwork gates.* N UNCOUNT

irony /aɪrəni[1]/, **ironies. 1 Irony** is a way of speaking which indicates that you are joking or that you really mean the opposite of what you say. EG *She said with slight irony, 'Bravo'... She spoke simply, without irony.* N UNCOUNT

2 The **irony** of a situation is an unusual or unexpected aspect of it. EG *The irony is that many politicians agree with him... History has many ironies.* N COUNT OR N UNCOUNT

irrational /ɪræʃə[0]nəl, -ʃənə[0]l/. **Irrational** feelings or behaviour are not based on logical reasons or clear thinking. EG *His anxiety was irrational... ...an irrational child.* ADJ QUALIT ◇ **irrationally.** EG *They were accused of acting irrationally.* ◇ ADV ◇ **irrationality** /ɪræʃə[0]nælɪ[1]ti[1]/. EG *...the irrationality of contemporary economics.* ◇ N UNCOUNT

irreconcilable /ɪrekənsaɪləbə[0]l/. **1** If two ideas or actions are **irreconcilable**, they are so different from each other that it is not possible or reasonable to believe, accept, or do both of them. EG *Their views had been irreconcilable from the beginning.* ADJ CLASSIF Formal

2 An **irreconcilable** disagreement is so serious that it cannot be settled. EG *...an irreconcilable clash of loyalties.* ADJ CLASSIF

irreducible /ɪrɪdjuːsɪ[1]bə[0]l/. Something that is **irreducible** cannot be reduced in amount or cannot be made simpler. EG *...the irreducible essence of art.* ADJ CLASSIF Formal

irrefutable /ɪrɪfjuːtəbə[0]l/. A statement that is **irrefutable** cannot be denied or cannot be shown to be incorrect. EG *That is an opinion, not an irrefutable fact... His argument is virtually irrefutable.* ADJ CLASSIF Formal

irregular /ɪregjə[4]lə/, **irregulars. 1** Something that is **irregular** is not smooth or straight, or does not form a regular pattern. EG *...its rough, irregular surface... ...dark, irregular markings on the photos.* ADJ QUALIT

◇ **irregularly.** EG *...irregularly shaped fields.* ◇ ADV

◇ **irregularity** /ɪregjə[4]lærɪti[1]/, **irregularities.** EG *The whole building was full of holes and irregularities.* ◇ N COUNT OR N UNCOUNT

2 Irregular actions happen with different periods of time between them. EG *...feeding them at irregular intervals... The newspaper's appearance became increasingly irregular.* ADJ QUALIT ◇ **irregularly.** EG *He went home, irregularly, at weekends.* ◇ ADV

◇ **irregularity.** EG *These illnesses can be caused by irregularity in feeding... This is more likely to produce irregularities of heart rate.* ◇ N COUNT OR N UNCOUNT

3 Irregular behaviour is considered to be unusual or not acceptable. EG *It isn't signed. This is irregular... ...his irregular working hours.* ADJ QUALIT

◇ **irregularity.** EG *The report revealed a large number of irregularities.* ◇ N COUNT OR N UNCOUNT

4 An **irregular** verb, noun, or adjective does not inflect in the same way as most other verbs, nouns, or adjectives in the language. ADJ CLASSIF

irrelevance /ɪreləvəns/. The **irrelevance** of something is the fact that it is not connected with what you are talking about or dealing with. EG *'By the way,' he added with apparent irrelevance, 'will you be locking it?'* N UNCOUNT +SUPP

irrelevancy /ɪreləvənsi[1]/, **irrelevancies.** You can refer to something that you think has no useful purpose as an **irrelevancy.** EG *School is an irrelevancy... He should not waste his time with irrelevancies.* N COUNT Formal

irrelevant /ɪreləvənt/. If you say that something is **irrelevant**, you mean that it is not connected with what you are talking about or dealing with, and is therefore not important. EG *The book was full of irrelevant information... He felt that right and wrong were irrelevant to the situation.* ADJ QUALIT

irreligious /ɪrɪlɪdʒəs/. An **irreligious** person does not have a religion. EG *My family were completely irreligious... ...an irreligious society... ...irreligious attitudes.* ADJ QUALIT

irremediable /ɪrə[1]miːdjəbə[0]l/. If a situation or state is **irremediable**, it is very bad and cannot be made better. EG *Irremediable damage has been done.* ADJ CLASSIF Formal

irreparable /ɪrepə[0]rəbə[0]l/. **Irreparable** damage is so severe that it cannot be repaired or put right again. EG *She has done irreparable harm to her reputation... I had made an irreparable mistake.* ADJ CLASSIF Formal

irreplaceable /ɪrɪpleɪsəbə[0]l/. If things are **irreplaceable**, they are so special that they cannot be replaced if they are lost or destroyed. EG *My jewellery is totally irreplaceable.* ADJ CLASSIF

irrepressible /ɪrɪpresɪ[1]bə[0]l/. **Irrepressible** people are lively, energetic, and cheerful. EG *Basil is irrepressible, funny, and affectionate.* ADJ QUALIT

irreproachable /ɪrɪprəʊtʃəbə[0]l/. If someone's behaviour or character is **irreproachable**, it is so good or correct that it cannot be criticized. EG *...McKinley's irreproachable character... He had done an irreproachable job of presiding over the tribunal.* ADJ CLASSIF

irresistible /ɪrɪzɪstəbə[0]l/. **1** If your wish to do something is **irresistible**, it is so strong that you cannot prevent yourself doing it. EG *The urge to laugh was irresistible... ...an irresistible desire to sing.* ADJ QUALIT

2 If you describe someone or something as **irresistible**, you mean that you find them very attractive or interesting. EG *He found her irresistible... His charm was irresistible to them.* ADJ QUALIT ◇ **irresistibly.** EG *The songs are irresistibly catchy.* ◇ SUBMOD

3 An **irresistible** force cannot be stopped or controlled. EG *...an irresistible attack... They put irresistible pressure upon the government.* ADJ CLASSIF

◇ **irresistibly.** EG *The waves take you irresistibly onwards.* ◇ ADV

irresolute /ɪrezəluːt/. If you are **irresolute**, you cannot decide what to do. EG *He stood irresolute at the top of the stairs.* ADJ QUALIT Formal

irrespective /ɪrɪspektɪv/. If something is true or if it happens **irrespective of** other things, those things do not affect it or are not considered to be important. EG *They demanded equal pay irrespective of age or sex... ...available to all students, irrespective of where they live.* PREP Formal

irresponsible /ɪrɪspɒnsɪ[1]bə[0]l/. People who are **irresponsible** do things without properly considering their possible consequences; used showing disapproval. EG *You've behaved like an irresponsible idiot... It would be irresponsible of me to encourage you... ...the irresponsible application of technology.* ADJ QUALIT

◇ **irresponsibly.** EG *...acting unfairly and irresponsibly.* ◇ ADV ◇ **irresponsibility** /ɪrɪspɒnsɪbɪlɪ[1]ti[1]/. EG *...youthful irresponsibility.* ◇ N UNCOUNT

irretrievable /ɪrɪtriːvəbə[0]l/. **Irretrievable** harm is so severe that it cannot be put right again. EG *...the irretrievable damage done to the Earth.* ADJ CLASSIF Formal

◇ **irretrievably.** EG *The war was irretrievably lost.* ◇ ADV

irreverent /ɪrevə[0]rənt/. If you are **irreverent**, you do not show the respect for someone or something that other people expect you to show. EG *...rude and irreverent comments.* ADJ QUALIT ◇ **irreverence** /ɪrevə[0]rəns/ EG *His irreverence has frequently landed him in trouble.* ◇ N UNCOUNT

irreversible /ɪrɪvɜːsɪ[1]bə[0]l/. Situations that are **irreversible** cannot be changed, stopped, or improved. EG *We've done something irreversible... The damage may be irreversible... ...irreversible changes to the climate... ...an irreversible decision.* ADJ CLASSIF

irrevocable /ɪrevəkəbə[0]l/. Actions or decisions that are **irrevocable** cannot be stopped or changed. EG *The US has given its irrevocable commitment to the Russians.* ADJ CLASSIF Formal ◇ **irrevocably.** EG *The world had changed irrevocably.* ◇ ADV

irrigate /ɪrɪgeɪt/, **irrigates, irrigating, irrigated.** To **irrigate** land means to supply it with water in order to help crops to grow. EG *A small* V+O

pump will irrigate about an acre of land... You had to work hard to irrigate the fields. ◇ **irrigated.** EG *...the irrigated areas of the Ganges plain.* ◇ ADJ CLASSIF
◇ **irrigation** /ɪrɪgeɪʃə^{0}n/. EG *...a complex irrigation system... ...the area under irrigation.* ◇ N UNCOUNT

irritable /ɪrɪtəbə^{0}l/. If you are **irritable**, you easily become annoyed. EG *Judy was feeling hot, tired, and irritable.* ADJ QUALIT ◇ **irritably.** EG *'What do you want me to do?' she said irritably.* ◇ ADV ◇ **irritability** /ɪrɪtəbɪlɪ^{1}ti^{1}/. EG *...periods of irritability.* ◇ N UNCOUNT

irritant /ɪrɪtənt/, **irritants. 1** If something continually annoys you, you can refer to it as an **irritant.** EG *Lack of national independence was a strong irritant.* N COUNT Formal

2 An **irritant** is also a substance which causes a part of your body to become itchy or sore. EG *Its juice is a serious irritant... ...irritant gases.* N COUNT Formal

irritate /ɪrɪteɪt/, **irritates, irritating, irritated.**
1 If something **irritates** you, it gradually makes you slightly angry, because you do not like it but cannot stop it continuing. EG *His style irritated some officials.* V+O ◇ **irritated.** EG *Dixon, irritated by this question, said nothing... ...an irritated gesture.* ◇ ADJ QUALIT ◇ **irritating.** EG *I found it irritating to be with the men... ...an irritating noise.* ◇ ADJ QUALIT ◇ **irritatingly.** EG *She was irritatingly slow.* ◇ SUBMOD OR ADV

2 If something **irritates** a part of your body, it causes it to be itchy or sore. EG *The detergent can irritate sensitive feet.* V+O ◇ **irritating.** EG *Their irritating bites leave large red patches.* ◇ ADJ QUALIT

irritation /ɪrɪteɪʃə^{0}n/, **irritations. 1 Irritation** is a feeling of slight anger because something that you do not like continues to happen. EG *I began to feel the same irritation with all of them... ...showing no irritation at her behaviour.* N UNCOUNT

2 If you have **irritation** in a part of your body, you have an itchy, sore, or painful feeling there. EG *...eye irritation.* N UNCOUNT

3 An **irritation** is something that causes you to be slightly angry because you do not like it but cannot stop it continuing. EG *The weather was a slight irritation... ...the irritations of everyday existence.* N COUNT

is /ɪz/ is the third person singular of the present tense of **be.**

-ise, -ises, -ising, -ised. See **-ize.**

-ish is used to form adjectives. You use it **1** to indicate that something has a quality to a limited extent. For example, 'reddish' means slightly red. EG *He had a yellowish complexion... He was a biggish fellow.* **2** to indicate that someone or something has the qualities of a particular kind of thing or person. For example, someone who is childish behaves like a child. EG *She was a beautiful kittenish creature.* SUFFIX

Islam /ɪzlɑːm/ is the religion of the Muslims, which teaches that there is only one God and that Mohammed is His prophet. N UNCOUNT

Islamic /ɪzlæmɪk/ means belonging or relating to Islam. EG *...Islamic laws... ...Islamic countries.* ADJ CLASSIF: ATTRIB

island /aɪlənd/, **islands.** An **island** is a piece of land that is completely surrounded by water. EG *There are pigs on the island... ...the island of Cyprus... ...the Channel Islands.* N COUNT

islander /aɪləndə/, **islanders. Islanders** are people who live on an island. EG *The islanders had never seen a car... ...the Falkland Islanders.* N COUNT

isle /aɪl/, **isles.** An **isle** is an island. EG *...a desert isle... ...the Isle of Wight... ...the British Isles.* N COUNT Literary

-ism, -isms. -ism is used to form nouns that refer to **1** political or religious movements and beliefs. EG *...the emergence of nationalism... ...the importance of Hinduism as a unifying force.* **2** attitudes and behaviour. EG *Clem's eyes gleamed with fanaticism... ...an opportunity for heroism... He had begun to regret his criticisms.* SUFFIX

isn't /ɪzə^{0}nt/ is the usual spoken form of 'is not'. EG *It isn't dark... That's right, isn't it?*

isolate /aɪsəleɪt/, **isolates, isolating, isolated. 1** If something **isolates** you or if you **isolate** yourself, you are physically or socially set apart from other people. EG *His wealth isolated him... They isolated themselves in order to build a new society.* V+O OR V-REFL

2 If you **isolate** an idea or word, you consider it separately from the other ideas or words that are connected with it or close to it. EG *I isolated that sentence from the rest of the text.* V+O: OFT+*from*

3 If you **isolate** a substance, you separate it from other substances so that you can examine it in detail. EG *You can isolate genes and study how they work.* V+O: OFT+*from*

4 If you **isolate** a sick person or animal, you keep them apart from other people or animals, so that their illness does not spread. EG *David had to be isolated for whooping cough.* V+O

5 If you **isolate** people, **5.1** you cause them to lose their friends or supporters because you are opposed to them and want to weaken them. EG *Could we isolate the administration, and thus force it to accept our demands?* **5.2** you cause them to stop liking you or supporting you because you do things that they do not approve of. EG *One by one, the chairman isolated all the good people in the firm.* V+O

isolated /aɪsəleɪtɪ^{2}d/. **1** An **isolated** place is a long way away from any town or village. EG *...an isolated farmhouse.* ADJ QUALIT

2 If you feel **isolated**, you feel lonely and without friends or help. EG *I had become isolated, defensive, and humourless.* ADJ PRED

3 An **isolated** example or incident is one that is rare and that is not part of a general pattern. EG *...a few isolated acts of violence.* ADJ CLASSIF: ATTRIB

isolation /aɪsəleɪʃə^{0}n/. **1 Isolation** is a state in which you feel separate from other people, because you live far away from them or because you do not have any friends. EG *...the isolation of city life... ...mothers living in isolation and poverty.* N UNCOUNT

2 If something exists or happens **in isolation**, it exists or happens separately from other things of the same kind. EG *A single country acting in isolation is vulnerable to competition... These questions can't be answered in isolation from each other.* PHRASE

issue /ɪʃuː/, **issues, issuing, issued. 1** An **issue** is an important problem or subject that people are discussing or arguing about. EG *I raised the issue with him... ...the issue of immigration.* N COUNT: USU+SUPP

2 If something is the **issue**, it is the thing you consider to be the most important part of a situation or discussion. EG *That's just not the issue... You cannot go on evading the issue.* N SING: *the*+N

3 The thing **at issue** is the thing that is being argued about. EG *The point at issue is this.* PHRASE

4 If you **make an issue of** something, you make a fuss about it. EG *She didn't want to make an issue of it... Some people make such an issue of adoption.* PHRASE

5 An **issue** of a magazine or newspaper is a particular edition of it. EG *The article had appeared in the previous day's issue.* N COUNT

6 If someone **issues** a statement, they make it formally or publicly. EG *They issued a serious warning... The rebels issued a proclamation.* V+O

7 If someone **issues** something to you or **issues** you with it, they officially give it to you. EG *Radios were issued to the troops... She was issued with travel documents.* V+O: OFT+*to/with*

8 When something **issues** from a place, it comes out of it. EG *...the smells issuing from the kitchen.* V+*from* Literary

-ist, -ists. -ist is added to nouns, often in place of '-ism', to form nouns and adjectives. The nouns refer to people who have particular beliefs, jobs, or interests. For example, a pacifist believes in pacifism and a journalist works in journalism. These count nouns and adjectives are often not defined in this dictionary, but are treated with the nouns from SUFFIX

What do you find in italics in this dictionary?

which they are derived. EG *She was a committed fatalist... ...imperialist sentiments... ...a nuclear physicist... ...a professional pianist.*

isthmus /ɪsθ^{0}məs/, **isthmuses.** An **isthmus** is a narrow area of land connecting two larger areas. EG *...the Isthmus of Panama.* N COUNT Formal

it /ɪt/ is used as the subject of a verb or as the object of a verb or preposition.

1 You use **it** **1.1** to refer to an object, animal, or other thing that has already been mentioned or whose identity is known. **It** can also be used to refer to a child. EG *...a tray with glasses on it... The man went up to the cat and started stroking it... The strike went on for a year before it was settled.* PRON : SING **1.2** to refer to a situation or fact, or to say something about a situation or fact. EG *She was frightened, but tried not to show it... It was very pleasant at the Hochstadts... It took Simon some time to work out what she meant... He found it hard to make friends... It was a pity that her spelling was so bad... It doesn't matter.*

2 You also use **it**, mainly as the subject of the verb 'be', **2.1** when you are making statements about the weather, the time, the date, or the day of the week. EG *It's hot... It's raining here... It is nearly one o'clock... It's the 6th of April today.* PRON : SING **2.2** when you are stating or asking who is speaking on the telephone or who is present. EG *It's me – Mary... Who is it?* **2.3** when you are emphasizing or drawing attention to something. EG *It's my mother I'm worried about.*

italics /ɪtælɪks/ are letters which have been printed so that they slope to the right. Italics are often used to emphasize a word or sentence. The examples in this dictionary are printed in italics. N PLURAL

itch /ɪtʃ/, **itches, itching, itched. 1** When you **itch** or when a part of your body **itches**, you have an unpleasant feeling on your skin that makes you want to scratch. EG *At first, you will itch... My toes are itching like mad.* V ▸ used as a noun. EG *...an itch that must be scratched.* ▸ N COUNT

2 If you **itch** to do something, you are very eager or impatient to do it. EG *I was itching to get away.* V+*to*-INF Informal ▸ used as a noun. EG *....the itch to travel... I've had an itch to go there.* ▸ N SING : OFT+*to*-INF

itchy /ɪtʃi^1/. If you are **itchy** or if a part of your body is **itchy**, you have an unpleasant feeling on your skin that makes you want to scratch. EG *Don't you feel all itchy?... My skin became dry and itchy.* ADJ QUALIT

it'd /ɪtə^{0}d/ is **1** a spoken form of 'it would'. EG *If I went on the train, it'd be cheaper.* **2** a spoken form of 'it had', especially when 'had' is an auxiliary verb. EG *It'd just been killed.*

item /aɪtəm/, **items. 1** An **item** is **1.1** one of a collection or list of objects. EG *The first item he bought was a clock... ...a list of household items.* N COUNT **1.2** one of a number of matters that you are dealing with. EG *I had two items of business to attend to before lunch.*

2 An **item** in a newspaper or magazine is a report or article. EG *...an item in the Sacramento Times.* N COUNT

itemize /aɪtəmaɪz/, **itemizes, itemizing, itemized;** also spelled **itemise.** If you **itemize** a number of things, you make a list of them. EG *The contents of his pockets were itemized and confiscated.* V+O

itinerant /ɪ^{5}tɪnərənt/. **Itinerant** workers travel around a region, working for short periods in different places. EG *...itinerant vegetable sellers... ...itinerant preachers.* ADJ CLASSIF : ATTRIB Formal

itinerary /ɪ^{5}tɪnərəri^1/, **itineraries.** An **itinerary** is a plan of a journey, including the route and the places that will be visited. EG *A detailed itinerary is supplied.* N COUNT

it'll /ɪtə^{0}l/ is a spoken form of 'it will'. EG *It'll be quite interesting.*

its /ɪts/. You use **its** to indicate that something belongs or relates to a thing, place, animal, or child that has just been mentioned or whose identity is known. See **it**. EG *The creature lifted its head... The group held its first meeting last week.* DET POSS

it's /ɪts/ is **1** the usual spoken form of 'it is'. EG *It's very important... It's snowing.* **2** a spoken form of 'it has', especially when 'has' is an auxiliary verb. EG *It's been nice talking to you.*

itself /ɪtsɛlf/. **1** You use **itself** as the object of a verb or preposition when the same thing, animal, or child is also the subject of the clause. See **it**. EG *Britain must bring itself up to date... It wraps its furry tail around itself.* PRON REFL : SING

2 You can use **itself** to emphasize the subject or object of a clause and to make it clear what you are referring to. EG *The town itself was very small... Growing up in London was itself exciting.* PRON REFL : SING

3 If you say that something has a particular quality **in itself**, you are emphasizing that it has this quality because of its own nature, regardless of any other factors. EG *The process is, in itself, an act of worship.* PHRASE

-ity, -ities. -ity is added to adjectives, sometimes in place of '-ous', to form nouns. These nouns usually refer to a state or quality. For example, 'tranquillity' refers to the state of being tranquil. Nouns of this kind are not usually defined in this dictionary, but are treated with the related adjectives. EG *The function of their bones is to give rigidity... ...a tradition of political neutrality... About this there is unanimity among sociologists.* SUFFIX

I've /aɪv/ is the usual spoken form of 'I have', especially when 'have' is an auxiliary verb. EG *I've never met her... I've only been there once.*

ivory /aɪvə^{0}ri^1/. **1 Ivory** is the hard white bone which forms the tusks of elephants. It is valuable, and is often used to make ornaments. EG *Gold, slaves and ivory were sent north... ...an ivory dealer... ...ivory chess sets.* N UNCOUNT

2 Ivory is also a creamy-white colour. EG *...ivory teeth... ...her ivory legs.* ADJ COLOUR

ivy /aɪvi^1/ is a plant that grows up walls and trees and has small, shiny leaves with several pointed edges. EG *...a broken ivy branch.* N UNCOUNT

-ize, -izes, -izing, -ized; also spelled **-ise, -ises, -ising, -ised.** Verbs that can end in either '-ize' or '-ise' are dealt with in this dictionary as ending in '-ize'. SUFFIX

Some verbs ending in **-ize** are derived from adjectives. These verbs describe the processes by which things or people are changed to a particular state or condition. For example, when something is popularized, it becomes popular. EG *Parliament finally legalized trade unions... Most of the country had been industrialized.*

J j

J, j /dʒeɪ/, **Js, j's. J** is the tenth letter of the English alphabet. N COUNT

jab /dʒæb/, **jabs, jabbing, jabbed. 1** If you **jab** something somewhere, you push it there with a quick, sudden movement. EG *She jabbed her knitting needles into a ball of wool... He jabbed his finger at me... ...jabbing the knife into the fruit.* V+O+A

2 A **jab** is an injection of a substance into your blood to prevent illness. EG *Everyone was queueing up to have their jabs.* N COUNT Informal British

jabber /dʒæbə/, **jabbers, jabbering, jabbered.** Someone who **is jabbering** is talking very quickly and excitedly. EG *She was jabbering in Italian to her husband.* V: OFT+A OR V+O Informal

jack /dʒæk/, **jacks.** A **jack** is **1** a mechanical device that is used to lift a heavy object off the ground. **2** a playing card with a picture of a young man on it. Jacks are higher than the ten and lower than the queen. EG *...the jack of clubs.* N COUNT

jacket /dʒækɪt/, **jackets. 1** A **jacket** is a short coat with long sleeves and an opening at the front. See picture at CLOTHES. EG *He wore a tweed sports jacket... From his jacket pocket he took out a small screwdriver.* • See also **dinner jacket, lifejacket.** N COUNT

2 The **jacket** of a baked potato is its skin. EG *...potatoes in their jackets.* N COUNT

3 The **jacket** of a book is the paper cover that protects the book. EG *...colourful book jackets.* N COUNT

jack-knife /dʒæknaɪf/, **jack-knifes, jack-knifing, jack-knifed; jack-knives. Jack-knives** is the plural of the noun.

1 If an articulated lorry **jack-knifes**, the trailer swings round at a sharp angle to the cab in an uncontrolled way. EG *Traffic was stopped after an articulated truck jack-knifed in heavy rain.* V

2 A **jack-knife** is a large knife with a blade that can be folded into the handle. N COUNT

jackpot /dʒækpɒt/, **jackpots.** A **jackpot** is the most valuable prize in a game or lottery. N COUNT

jade /dʒeɪd/ is a hard green stone that is used for making jewellery and ornaments. N UNCOUNT

jaded /dʒeɪdɪ^{2}d/. If you are **jaded**, you have no enthusiasm because you are tired and bored. EG *...jaded housewives who'd like to try something different... They are getting a little jaded.* ADJ QUALIT

jagged /dʒægɪ^{2}d/. Something that is **jagged** has a rough, uneven shape with lots of sharp points. EG *...the jagged outline of the crags... ...small pieces of jagged metal.* ADJ QUALIT

jaguar /dʒægju^{4}ə/, **jaguars.** A **jaguar** is a large animal which is a member of the cat family and has dark spots on its back. N COUNT

jail /dʒeɪl/, **jails, jailing, jailed;** also spelled **gaol** in British English. **1** A **jail** is a place where people are kept locked up, usually because they have been found guilty of a crime. EG *...women who spent years in jail... He went to jail for attempted robbery... ...a heavy jail sentence.* N COUNT OR N UNCOUNT

2 If someone **is jailed**, they are put into jail. EG *He was jailed for five years.* V+O: USU PASS

jailer /dʒeɪlə/, **jailers;** also spelled **gaoler** in British English. A **jailer** is a person who is in charge of a jail. N COUNT Outdated

jam /dʒæm/, **jams, jamming, jammed. 1 Jam** is a food that is made by cooking fruit with sugar. Usually you spread jam on bread. EG *...pots of raspberry and blackcurrant jam.* N MASS

2 If you **jam** something somewhere, you push it there roughly. EG *Then he jammed his hat back on... Reporters jammed microphones in our faces.* V+O+A

3 If something **jams** or if you **jam** it, it becomes fixed in position and cannot move freely or work properly. EG *The machines jammed and broke down... I jammed the window shut.* V-ERG: OFT+A

4 If a road **is jammed** with vehicles, it is filled completely with them, so that the traffic cannot move. EG *The town was jammed with traffic.* V+O: USU PASS

5 If you **jam** a lot of things into a place, they are pressed tightly together so that they can hardly move. EG *The fridge won't work properly if you jam in too much food.* V+O

6 A **jam** is a situation where there are so many vehicles on a road that none of them can move. EG *There were traffic jams, and police clearing people away.* N COUNT

7 If you are in a **jam**, you are in a very difficult situation. EG *He finds himself in exactly the same jam as his brother was in ten years before.* N COUNT Informal

8 To **jam** a radio, radar, or electronic signal means to prevent it from being received or heard clearly. This happens because other signals are being transmitted on the same wavelength. V+O

jamboree /dʒæmbəriː/, **jamborees.** A **jamboree** is a party or celebration which a large number of people go to. EG *...an open-air jamboree that attracted 250,000 people.* N COUNT

jam-packed. A place that is **jam-packed** is so full of people or things that there is no room for any more. EG *The streets were jam-packed that day.* ADJ CLASSIF Informal

jangle /dʒæŋgə^{0}l/, **jangles, jangling, jangled.** If metal objects **jangle**, they make a ringing noise by hitting against each other. EG *I ran upstairs, the keys jangling in my pockets.* ▸ used as a noun. EG *...the jangle of armour.* V-ERG ▸ N SING

janitor /dʒænɪtə/, **janitors.** A **janitor** is a person whose job is to look after a building. N COUNT

January /dʒænjʊ^{0}əri^{1}/ is the first month of the year in the Western calendar. EG *On 24 January Harold left for Constantinople.* N UNCOUNT

jar /dʒɑː/, **jars, jarring, jarred. 1** A **jar** is a glass container with a lid that is used for storing food such as jam. EG *I was having trouble unscrewing the tops of fruit jars, jam jars and so on.* N COUNT

2 If something **jars** on you, you find it unpleasant or annoying. EG *The harsh, metallic sound jarred on her.... He had a way of speaking that jarred.* ◊ **jarring.** EG *...a jarring office block.* V: OFT+*on* ◊ ADJ QUALIT

3 If something **jars** you, it gives you an unpleasant shock. EG *This thought jarred me... He was evidently jarred by my appearance.* ◊ **jarring.** EG *...a jarring experience.* V+O ◊ ADJ QUALIT

4 If things **jar** or if something **jars** them, they strike against each other with quite a lot of force. EG *The house shook and his bones were jarred.* ▸ used as a noun. EG *Knocks and jars can cause weakness in the spine.* V-ERG ▸ N COUNT

jargon /dʒɑːgə^{0}n/ is language containing words that are used in special or technical ways. Jargon is used to talk about particular subjects. EG *...complex legal jargon... They use so much professional jargon.* N UNCOUNT: USU+SUPP

jaundice /dʒɔːndɪs/ is an illness that makes your skin and eyes yellow. N UNCOUNT

jaundiced /dʒɔːndɪst/. A **jaundiced** attitude or view is unenthusiastic or pessimistic. EG *He takes a rather jaundiced view of societies and clubs.* ADJ QUALIT Literary

jaunt /dʒɔːnt/, **jaunts.** A **jaunt** is a short journey which you go on for pleasure. EG *We went on a motor jaunt to Marrakesh.* N COUNT

jaunty /dʒɔːnti^{1}/ means cheerful, full of confidence, and energetic. EG *She adjusted her hat to a jaunty angle... He spoke suddenly in a jaunty tone.* ADJ QUALIT

javelin /dʒævə^{0}lɪn/, **javelins.** A **javelin** is a long spear that is used in sports competitions. N COUNT

jaw /dʒɔː/, **jaws.** 1 Your **jaw** is 1.1 the lower part of your face below your mouth. Your jaw moves up and down when you eat. See picture at THE HUMAN BODY. EG *His jaw dropped in surprise.* 1.2 one of the two bones in your head which your teeth are attached to. EG *...the upper jaw... The panther held a snake in its jaws.* N COUNT

2 If you talk about the **jaws** of something unpleasant such as death or hell, you are referring to a dangerous or unpleasant situation. EG *The nation has been snatched out of the jaws of war.* N PLURAL +SUPP Literary

jazz /dʒæz/, **jazzes, jazzing, jazzed. Jazz** is a style of music that has an exciting rhythm and is usually played with drums, saxophones, and trumpets. EG *...a jazz concert.* N UNCOUNT

jazz up. If you **jazz** something **up**, you make it look more interesting, colourful, or exciting. EG *They've certainly jazzed this place up since the last time I was here.* PHRASAL VB : V+O+ADV Informal

jazzy /dʒæzi¹/, **jazzier, jazziest.** 1 If you describe something as **jazzy**, you mean that it is colourful and modern. EG *He was dressed in a jazzy suit and a large yellow cravat.* ADJ QUALIT

2 Music that is **jazzy** is in the style of jazz. EG *...a large orchestra playing jazzy rhythms.* ADJ CLASSIF

jealous /dʒɛləs/. If you are **jealous**, 1 you feel anger or bitterness towards someone who has something that you would like to have. EG *I often felt jealous because David could go out when he wished... They may feel jealous of your success.* ADJ QUALIT 2 you feel that you must try to keep something that you have, because you think someone else might take it away from you. EG *She was a very jealous woman... He was jealous of his wife and suspected her of adultery.* ADJ QUALIT ◇ **jealously.** EG *They were jealously guarding their independence.* ◇ ADV

jealousy /dʒɛləsi¹/, **jealousies. Jealousy** is 1 the feeling of resentment and bitterness that you have when you think someone is trying to take away something that you feel belongs to you. EG *Hate, jealousy, the desire to kill all rose to the surface... He was good at talking me out of my suspicions and jealousies.* 2 the feeling you have when you wish that you could have the qualities or possessions that someone else has. EG *We often feel jealousy of our brothers and sisters.* N UNCOUNT OR N COUNT

jeans /dʒiːnz/ are casual trousers that are made of strong blue denim. EG *Three young men came out, all in jeans... ...a pair of jeans.* N PLURAL

jeep /dʒiːp/, **jeeps.** A **jeep** is a small four-wheeled vehicle that can travel over rough ground. EG *A jeep pulled up and a marine jumped out.* N COUNT

jeer /dʒɪə/, **jeers, jeering, jeered.** If you **jeer** at someone, you say rude and insulting things to them. EG *Boys had jeered at him at school... He was jeered and booed as a traitor.* V : OFT+*at* OR V+O ▸ used as a plural noun. EG *...the taunts and jeers of passers-by.* ▸ N PLURAL ◇ **jeering.** EG *...the jeering crowd.* ◇ ADJ CLASSIF

jell /dʒɛl/. See **gel.**

jelly /dʒɛli¹/, **jellies.** 1 **Jelly** is 1.1 a clear food made from gelatine, which is usually sweetened, flavoured with fruit juices, and eaten as a dessert. 1.2 a kind of jam made by boiling fruit juice and sugar. EG *...slices of bread, smeared with butter and jelly.* N MASS

2 If your legs or arms feel like **jelly**, they feel very weak, often because you are ill or afraid. N UNCOUNT

jellyfish /dʒɛli¹fɪʃ/. **Jellyfish** is both the singular and the plural form. N COUNT

A **jellyfish** is a creature that lives in the sea and has a body that looks like clear jelly. Some jellyfish can sting you.

jeopardize /dʒɛpədaɪz/, **jeopardizes, jeopardizing, jeopardized;** also spelled **jeopardise.** If you **jeopardize** something, you do something that may destroy or damage it. EG *This judgment may jeopardize his job... I didn't want to jeopardize my relationship with my new friend.* V+O

jeopardy /dʒɛpədi¹/. If someone or something is **in jeopardy**, they are in a dangerous situation. EG *She had placed herself in jeopardy in order to save my life... Their future is in jeopardy.* PHRASE

jerk /dʒɜːk/, **jerks, jerking, jerked.** 1 If you **jerk** something, you pull it or move it suddenly and forcefully. EG *He jerked the boy savagely to his feet... The door of the van was jerked open... He jerked his head around to stare at me.* V-ERG : USU+A ▸ used as a noun. EG *The man pulled the girl back with a jerk.* ▸ N COUNT

2 If you **jerk** in a particular direction or in a particular way, you move with a very sudden and quick movement. EG *She jerked away from him... Jerking suddenly awake, he lay very still and listened.* V+A

3 If you call someone a **jerk**, you mean that they are very stupid; an offensive use. N COUNT

jerky /dʒɜːki¹/, **jerkier, jerkiest.** Movements that are **jerky** are very sudden and abrupt. EG *She lit a cigarette with quick, jerky movements.* ADJ QUALIT

jersey /dʒɜːzi¹/, **jerseys.** 1 A **jersey** is a piece of clothing made of knitted wool, that covers the upper part of your body and your arms and does not open at the front. EG *She pulled on her striped jersey and her jeans.* N COUNT

2 **Jersey** is a knitted woollen fabric used especially to make women's clothing. N UNCOUNT

jest /dʒɛst/, **jests.** A **jest** is an amusing comment or a joke. EG *His Lordship hoped that a jest would be excused.* N COUNT Outdated ● If you say something **in jest**, you do not mean it seriously, but want to be amusing. EG *It was said half in jest.* ● PHRASE

jet /dʒɛt/, **jets, jetting, jetted.** 1 A **jet** is a very fast modern aeroplane. EG *She woke just as the big jet from Hong Kong touched down.* N COUNT OR *by*+N

2 If you **jet** somewhere, you travel there in a fast aeroplane. EG *A Pennsylvania teenager jets regularly to a doctor in Frankfurt, Germany.* V+A

3 A **jet** of water or gas is a strong, fast, thin stream of it. EG *He blew a jet of water into the air.* N COUNT

4 **Jet** is a hard black stone that is used in jewellery. N UNCOUNT

jet-black. Something that is **jet-black** is very dark black in colour. EG *His hair was jet black.* ADJ COLOUR

jet engine, jet engines. A **jet engine** is an engine in which hot air and gases are pushed out at the back. Jet engines are used for most modern aeroplanes. N COUNT

jetlag /dʒɛtlæg/ is a feeling of confusion and tiredness that people experience after a long journey in an aeroplane. EG *With jet-lag still a problem, I almost fell asleep during the meeting.* N UNCOUNT

jet set. The **jet set** are rich and successful people, especially young people, who live in a luxurious way. EG *...the whole French and Italian jet set.* N SING : *the*+N

jettison /dʒɛtɪsə⁰n, -zə⁰n/, **jettisons, jettisoning, jettisoned.** If you **jettison** something, you deliberately reject it or throw it away. EG *...ideas too valuable, too sacred, to jettison... I also thought it was time to jettison the blue overcoat.* V+O Formal

jetty /dʒɛti¹/, **jetties.** A **jetty** is a wide stone wall or wooden platform at the edge of the sea or a river, where boats can wait while people get on and off. EG *The boat was tied up alongside a crumbling limestone jetty.* N COUNT

Jew /dʒuː/, **Jews.** A **Jew** is a person who believes in and practises the religion of Judaism. N COUNT

jewel /dʒuːə⁰l/, **jewels.** A **jewel** is a precious stone such as a diamond or ruby that is used to decorate valuable things that you wear, such as rings or necklaces. EG *She was wearing even more jewels than the Queen Mother!... ...a jewel box.* N COUNT

jewelled /dʒuːə⁰ld/; spelled **jeweled** in American English. **Jewelled** items and ornaments are decorated with precious stones. EG *...a jewelled brooch.* ADJ CLASSIF : ATTRIB

jeweller /dʒuːə⁰lə/, **jewellers;** spelled **jeweler** in American English. A **jeweller** is a person who buys, sells, and repairs jewellery and watches. N COUNT

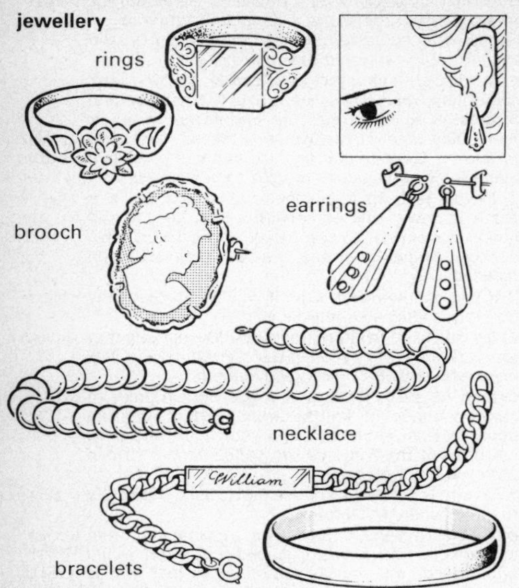

jewellery /dʒu:ə⁰lri¹/; spelled **jewelry** in American English. **Jewellery** consists of ornaments such as rings, bracelets, and necklaces which are often made of valuable metal such as gold, and which are sometimes decorated with precious stones. EG *She thought some of her jewellery was missing... ...a jewellery box.* N UNCOUNT

Jewess /dʒu:ɪ²s/, **Jewesses.** A **Jewess** is a woman or girl who is Jewish. N COUNT Formal

Jewish /dʒu:ɪʃ/. A person or thing that is **Jewish** belongs or relates to the religion of Judaism or to people who follow this religion. EG *Jewish scholars... ...a beautiful Jewish woman... ...a Jewish wedding... ...Jewish teaching.* ADJ CLASSIF

jibe /dʒaɪb/, **jibes;** also spelled **gibe.** A **jibe** is a rude or insulting remark about someone. EG *He swallowed and tried to smile at the jibe.* N COUNT

jiffy /dʒɪfi¹/. If you say that you will do something **in a jiffy**, you mean that you will do it quickly and very soon. EG *I'll be back in a jiffy.* PHRASE Informal

jig /dʒɪg/, **jigs, jigging, jigged. 1** A **jig** is a lively folk dance, popular in the past among country people. N COUNT

2 To **jig** means to dance or move in an uneven way, especially bouncing up and down. EG *Others began to jig and stamp and shuffle.* V: OFT+A

jiggle /dʒɪgə⁰l/, **jiggles, jiggling, jiggled.** If you **jiggle** something, you move it quickly from side to side. EG *She jiggled the front door handle.* V+O Informal

jigsaw /dʒɪgsɔ:/, **jigsaws.** A **jigsaw** or **jigsaw puzzle** is a game using a picture on cardboard or wood that has been cut up into odd shapes. You have to make the picture again by putting the pieces together correctly. N COUNT

jilt /dʒɪlt/, **jilts, jilting, jilted.** If you **jilt** someone who you have promised to marry, you end your relationship with them suddenly; used showing disapproval. EG *He had jilted her to marry a maidservant.* V+O Outdated

jingle /dʒɪŋgə⁰l/, **jingles, jingling, jingled. 1** When something **jingles** or when you **jingle** it, it makes a gentle ringing noise, like small bells. EG *...waving her arms in the air so that her charm bracelet jingled.* ▸ used as a noun. EG *I can hear the jingle of bracelets coming up behind me in the dark.* V-ERG ▸ N SING

2 A **jingle** is a short and simple tune, often with words, used to advertise a product on radio or television. N COUNT

jinx /dʒɪŋks/, **jinxes.** A **jinx** is bad luck, or a thing or person that is thought to bring bad luck. EG *...Muck Hall: the farm with the jinx on it.* N COUNT: USU SING

jittery /dʒɪtə⁰ri¹/. Someone who is **jittery** feels extremely nervous. EG *The postponement had made them jittery.* ADJ QUALIT Informal

job /dʒɒb/, **jobs. 1** A **job** is **1.1** the work that a person does regularly in order to earn money. EG *Gladys finally got a good job as a secretary.* N COUNT **1.2** a particular task. EG *There are always plenty of jobs to be done round here... ...a repair job.* N COUNT

2 The **job** of a particular person or thing is their duty or function. EG *It's not their job to decide what ought to be the law.* N COUNT+POSS

3 If you say that you had a **job** doing something, you are emphasizing how difficult it was to do. EG *I had a job sneaking into the house unnoticed.* N SING Informal

4 If you say that someone **is doing** a good job or **is making a good job of** something, you mean that they are doing something well. EG *Daddy thought we'd made a very good job of the bathroom.* • **it's a good job**: see **good.** PHRASE

5 If you say that something is **just the job**, you mean that it is exactly what you wanted or needed. PHRASE Informal

jobless /dʒɒblɪ²s/. **1** Someone who is **jobless** does not have a job, even though they would like one. EG *During the depression millions were jobless and homeless.* ADJ CLASSIF

2 The **jobless** are people who are jobless. EG *We have to do more for the poor and the jobless.* N PLURAL: *the*+N

job lot, job lots. A **job lot** is a number of cheap things of poor quality which are sold together, for example in an auction. EG *He bought a job lot of 50 books for £3.* N COUNT

job sharing is the arrangement by which two people work part-time at the same job, for example one person working in the morning and the other in the afternoon. N UNCOUNT

jockey /dʒɒki¹/, **jockeys, jockeying, jockeyed. 1** A **jockey** is someone who rides a horse in a horse race. N COUNT

2 If people **jockey for position**, they try to get into a better position than their rivals. EG *Rival trade union organizations continuously jockey for position.* PHRASE

jocular /dʒɒkjə⁴lə/. **1** Someone who is **jocular** is cheerful and often makes jokes. EG *The resemblance was noted by a jocular English visitor.* ADJ QUALIT

2 Something that is **jocular** is intended to make people laugh. EG *...a jocular remark.* ADJ QUALIT

jodhpurs /dʒɒdpəz/ are special trousers that you wear when you are riding a horse. N PLURAL

jog /dʒɒg/, **jogs, jogging, jogged. 1** If you **jog**, you run slowly, often as a form of exercise. EG *...people who jog or play squash... He jogged off down the lane.* ▸ used as a noun. EG *I speeded up to a jog and moved up the road briskly.* ◇ **jogger** /dʒɒgə/, **joggers.** EG *...a couple of track-suited joggers.* ◇ **jogging** /dʒɒgɪŋ/. EG *...the current enthusiasm for jogging.* V: OFT+A ▸ N SING ◇ N COUNT ◇ N UNCOUNT

2 If you **jog** something, you push or bump it slightly so that it shakes or moves. EG *She jogged her cup of chocolate... Be careful not to jog the table.* V+O

3 If someone or something **jogs** your **memory**, they remind you of something. EG *He had demonstrated the sound to jog my memory.* PHRASE

join /dʒɔɪn/, **joins, joining, joined. 1** If one person or thing **joins** another, the two people or things come together. EG *He went for a walk before joining his brother for tea... The helicopter was quickly joined by a second... The Missouri joins the Mississippi at St Louis.* V OR V+O: RECIP

2 If you **join** a queue, you go and stand at the end of V+O

If you think that something is beyond a joke, do you think that it is funny?

it. EG *They went off to join the queue for coffee... The van joined the row of cars.*

3 If you **join** a club, society, or organization, you become a member of it. EG *We both joined the Labour Party... He's joined the army.* V+O

4 If you **join** an activity, you become involved with it. EG *They were invited to join the feasting.* ● to **join forces**: see **force**. V+O

5 If you **join** two things, you fasten or fix them together. EG *Cut them down the middle and join the two outside edges together.* V+O : USU+A

6 If a line, a path, or a bridge **joins** two things, it connects them. EG *Draw a straight line joining these two points... The cities are joined by telecommunication links.* V+O : USU+A

7 A **join** is a place where two things are fastened or fixed together. EG *The repair was done so well, you could hardly see the join.* N COUNT

join in. If you **join in** an activity, you become involved in it. EG *He took his coat off and joined in the work... Parents should join in these discussions.* PHRASAL VB : V+ADV/PREP

join up. 1 If someone **joins up**, they become a member of the army, the navy, or the air force. EG *At eighteen, just before joining up and going abroad, I met Elizabeth.* PHRASAL VB : V+ADV British **2** If you **join up** two things, you fasten or fix them together. EG *I used to join up all his paper clips in a long chain.* V+O+ADV

joiner /dʒɔɪnə/, **joiners.** A **joiner** is a person who makes wooden window frames, door frames, and doors. N COUNT British

joint /dʒɔɪnt/, **joints. 1 Joint** means shared by or belonging to two or more people. EG *We have opened a joint account at the bank... The presentation was a joint effort.* ◊ **jointly.** EG *It was built jointly by France and Germany.* ADJ CLASSIF : ATTRIB ◊ ADV

2 A **joint** is **2.1** a part of your body such as your elbow or knee where two bones meet and are able to move together. EG *He can feel the rheumatism in his joints... ...the joints of the fingers.* **2.2** the place where two things are fastened or fixed together. EG *Cracks appeared at the joints between the new plaster and the old.* N COUNT

3 A **joint** of meat is a fairly large piece of meat which is suitable for roasting. EG *...a joint of roast beef.* N COUNT

4 You can refer to a night club or other place where people go for entertainment as a **joint**. EG *He was employed in a poky little jazz joint in San Francisco.* N COUNT Informal

5 Some people refer to a cigarette which contains cannabis as a **joint**. N COUNT Informal

jointed /dʒɔɪntɪ^{2}d/. Something that is **jointed** has joints that move. EG *The doll had jointed legs and arms.* ADJ CLASSIF

joke /dʒəʊk/, **jokes, joking, joked. 1** A **joke** is something that is said or done to make you laugh, for example a funny story. EG *Dave was telling me this joke about a penguin.* N COUNT

2 If you **joke**, you tell funny stories or say things that are amusing and not serious. EG *They never joked about sex... Don't worry, I was only joking.* V : OFT +*about/with*

3 If you say that someone or something is a **joke**, you mean that they are ridiculous and not worthy of respect. EG *His colleagues regard him as a joke.* N SING : *a*+N Informal

4 If you say that a situation has gone **beyond a joke**, you mean that it has become annoying or worrying. EG *The whole thing is getting beyond a joke.* PHRASE

5 If you say that something is **no joke**, you mean that it is very difficult and unpleasant. EG *It's no joke running up mountains at the age of forty six!* PHRASE Informal

6 You say **'You're joking'** or **'You must be joking'** when someone has just said something very surprising. CONVENTION

joker /dʒəʊkə/, **jokers. 1** Someone who is a **joker** likes making jokes or doing amusing things. EG *I enjoyed working with Hitchcock. He was a great joker.* N COUNT

2 The **joker** in a pack of cards is a card which does not belong to any of the four suits. In many card games it can be used instead of any card. N COUNT

jokey /dʒəʊki^1/. Something that is **jokey** is amusing and does not have any serious meaning. EG *They all had jokey nicknames.* ADJ QUALIT Informal

jokingly /dʒəʊkɪŋli^1/. If you say or do something **jokingly**, you do it to amuse someone or without seriously meaning it. EG *My friend said jokingly that George had lost around two hundred pounds.* ADV

jollity /dʒɒlɪti^1/ is cheerful behaviour. EG *He admired her high spirits and her jollity.* N UNCOUNT Outdated

jolly /dʒɒli^1/, **jollier, jolliest. 1** Someone who is **jolly** is happy and cheerful. EG *Buddy's mother was a jolly, easy-going woman.* ADJ QUALIT

2 An event that is **jolly** is lively and enjoyable. EG *At Christmas we have an awfully jolly time: tree, carols and all that stuff.* ADJ QUALIT Outdated

3 You can use **jolly** to emphasize something. EG *We provide a jolly good service, I think... It was jolly decent of him to think of me, I must say.* SUBMOD Informal British

4 You can use **jolly well** to emphasize what you are saying, especially when you are annoyed or upset. EG *I'm jolly well not going to ring her up!* ADV Informal British

jolt /dʒəʊlt/, **jolts, jolting, jolted. 1** If something **jolts** or if you **jolt** it, it moves suddenly and violently. EG *She jolted his arm... ...enormous loads that jolted and swayed.* ▸ used as a noun. EG *I came down slowly at first, but then with a jolt.* V-ERG ▸ N COUNT

2 If you **are jolted** by something, it gives you an unpleasant surprise or shock. EG *I was jolted awake by a bright light.* ▸ used as a noun. EG *The aim of Detention Centres is to give kids a jolt.* V+O : USU PASS ▸ N SING

jostle /dʒɒsə^{0}l/, **jostles, jostling, jostled.** If people **jostle** or **jostle** each other, **1** they bump against each other or push each other in a crowd. EG *Pedestrians jostled them on the pavement.* **2** they compete with each other for attention or for a reward. EG *Photographers, models, and singers, all jostled for money and fame.* V+O OR V

jot /dʒɒt/, **jots, jotting, jotted.** If you **jot** something down, you write it down in the form of a short informal note. EG *I asked you to jot down a few ideas... I jot odd notes in the back of the diary.* V+O+A

journal /dʒɜːnə^{0}l/, **journals.** A **journal** is **1** a magazine for people with a particular interest. EG *...a trade journal.* **2** an account which you write of your daily activities. EG *For nearly three months he had been keeping a journal.* N COUNT

journalism /dʒɜːnə^{0}lɪzə^{0}m/ is the job of collecting, writing, and publishing news in newspapers and magazines and on television and radio. EG *Have you ever thought of going into journalism?* N UNCOUNT

journalist /dʒɜːnə^{0}lɪst/, **journalists.** A **journalist** is a person who works on a newspaper or magazine and writes articles for it. EG *She worked as a journalist on The Times.* N COUNT

journalistic /dʒɜːnə^{0}lɪstɪk/ means relating to the work of a journalist. EG *I had no journalistic experience in Britain... ...journalistic investigations.* ADJ CLASSIF : ATTRIB

journey /dʒɜːni^1/, **journeys, journeying, journeyed. 1** When you make a **journey**, you travel from one place to another. EG *He went on a journey to London... She'll want her supper straightaway after that long journey.* ● If you **break** your **journey** somewhere, you stop there for a short time so that you can have a rest. EG *He is staying in Singapore, where he is breaking his journey home to Australia.* N COUNT ● PHRASE

2 If you **journey** somewhere, you travel there. EG *The nights became colder as they journeyed north.* V+A Literary

jovial /dʒəʊvɪəl/. Someone who is **jovial** behaves in a cheerful and happy way. EG *He was a big, heavy, jovial man... ...a jovial smile.* ADJ QUALIT

jowl /dʒaʊl/, **jowls.** Your **jowls** are the lower parts of your cheeks, covering your jawbones. EG *...an old woman with heavy jowls and a double chin.* N COUNT : USU PLURAL

joy /dʒɔɪ/, **joys. 1 Joy** is a feeling of great happiness. EG *She shouted with joy when I told her she* N UNCOUNT *was free... His face showed his joy the moment he saw me... Her look of joy gave way to one of misery.*

2 Something that is a **joy** makes you feel happy or gives you great pleasure. EG *She discovered the joy of writing... His one joy is playing squash.* N COUNT+SUPP

joyful /dʒɔɪfʊl/. 1 Something that is **joyful** causes happiness and pleasure. EG *I still felt sad even after you'd announced the joyful tidings.* ADJ QUALIT

2 Someone who is **joyful** is extremely happy. EG *The joyful parents named him Lexington.* ADJ QUALIT

◇ **joyfully.** EG *We welcomed him joyfully to the club.* ◇ ADV

joyless /dʒɔɪlɪ²s/. Something or someone that is **joyless** produces or experiences no pleasure. EG *...years and years of joyless married life... I hope I never become as joyless as they have become.* ADJ QUALIT

joyous /dʒɔɪəs/ means extremely happy and enthusiastic. EG *I spread my arms wide and felt joyous and exalted and free.* ◇ **joyously.** EG *He flung back the curtains joyously and let the sunlight pour in.* ADJ QUALIT Literary ◇ ADV

joyride /dʒɔɪraɪd/, **joyrides.** If someone goes for a **joyride**, they drive around for pleasure in a car that they have just stolen. EG *That joyride was a silly stunt.* N COUNT

JP, JPs. A **JP** is a local magistrate in Britain. **JP** is an abbreviation for 'Justice of the Peace'. N COUNT

jubilant /dʒuːbɪlənt/. If you are **jubilant**, you feel extremely happy and successful. EG *...a jubilant Labour Party Conference.* ADJ QUALIT

jubilation /dʒuːbɪleɪʃə⁰n/ is a feeling of great happiness and success. EG *There was a general air of jubilation.* N UNCOUNT Formal

jubilee /dʒuːbɪliː, dʒuːbɪli¹/, **jubilees.** A **jubilee** is a special anniversary of an event, especially the 25th or 50th anniversary. EG *...the college's silver jubilee year.* N COUNT

Judaism /dʒuːdeɪɪzə⁰m/ is the religion of the Jewish people, which is based on the Old Testament of the Bible and on the Jewish book of laws and traditions. N UNCOUNT

judge /dʒʌdʒ/, **judges, judging, judged.** 1 A **judge** is 1.1 the person in a court of law who decides how the law should be applied to people, for example how criminals should be punished. EG *Last week she appeared before a judge... Judge Arnason set Miss Davis free on bail.* 1.2 a person who decides who will be the winner of a competition. EG *The panel of judges consisted of a variety of famous people.* N COUNT

2 If someone is a good **judge** of something, they can understand it and make decisions about it. If they are a bad **judge** of something, they cannot understand it or make decisions about it. EG *He was a good judge of character... Nick, a perfect judge of such matters, had ordered a light French wine.* N COUNT+SUPP

3 If you **judge** a competition, you decide who the winner is. EG *The competition was judged by the local mayor.* V+O

4 If you **judge** something, you form an opinion about it by thinking carefully about it. EG *It's impossible to judge her age... The operation must be judged a failure... He judged it wiser to put a stop to this quarrel... I'm not in a position to judge.* V+O, V+O+C, OR V

5 If you **judge** someone, you decide whether they are good or bad after you have thought about their character, behaviour, and life style. EG *She seemed to be watching him, judging him... Social workers declare that they are not out to judge people, but simply want to help.* V+O

6 You use **judging from** or **judging by** to mention the reasons that cause you to believe something. EG *There was some great national celebration in town, judging by the firework displays everywhere... He was extremely attractive, to judge from the newspaper photographs.* PREP

judgement /dʒʌdʒmə²nt/, **judgements;** also spelled **judgment.** 1 A **judgement** is 1.1 an opinion that you have or give after thinking carefully about something. EG *I shall make my own judgement on this matter when I see the results... In our judgment, her plan has definitely succeeded.* 1.2 a decision made by a judge or by a court of law. EG *The final judgment will probably be made in court... Mr Justice Dillon gave his judgement the week before.* N COUNT: OFT+SUPP; N COUNT OR N UNCOUNT

2 **Judgement** is 2.1 the ability to make sensible guesses about a situation or sensible decisions about what to do. EG *This is a case that calls for judgement rather than expert knowledge... My father did not permit me to question his judgement... ...an error of judgement.* 2.2 the process of deciding how good something or someone is. EG *I have a great fear of judgment... During her career a scientist must survive many judgments.* N UNCOUNT; N UNCOUNT OR N COUNT

3 If you **pass judgement** on something, you give your opinion about it, especially if you are making a criticism. EG *I can't pass judgement until I know all the facts.* PHRASE

4 If you **reserve judgement** about something, you do not give an opinion about it until you know more about it. EG *Jenny was still reserving judgment until she could check out the details.* PHRASE

5 If something is **against** your **better judgement**, you believe that it would be more sensible not to do it. PHRASE

6 A **judgement** is also something unpleasant that happens to you and that is considered to be a punishment from God. EG *War is a judgement on us all for our sins.* N COUNT

judicial /dʒuːdɪʃə⁰l/ means 1 relating to judgement in a court of law. EG *The two territories had differing political, judicial, and educational systems.* 2 showing or using judgement in thinking about something. EG *...the young man's calm judicial gaze... ...examined with judicial care.* ADJ CLASSIF: ATTRIB Formal; Literary

judiciary /dʒuːdɪʃəri¹/. The **judiciary** is the branch of authority in a country which is concerned with justice and the legal system. N SING: *the*+N Formal

judicious /dʒuːdɪʃəs/. An action or decision that is **judicious** shows good judgement and sense. EG *They made judicious use of government incentives... ...surveying them with a judicious eye.* ADJ QUALIT Formal

◇ **judiciously.** EG *You put your case most judiciously.* ◇ ADV

judo /dʒuːdəʊ/ is a sport in which two people fight each other and each tries to throw the other one to the ground. N UNCOUNT

jug /dʒʌg/, **jugs.** 1 A **jug** is a container which is used for holding and pouring liquids. EG *...a big white jug full of beer... ...the milk jug.* N COUNT

jug

2 You can use **jug** to refer to the contents of a jug, as in a **jug** of water or a **jug** of milk. N PART

juggernaut /dʒʌgənɔːt/, **juggernauts.** A **juggernaut** is a very large lorry. N COUNT British

juggle /dʒʌgə⁰l/, **juggles, juggling, juggled.** 1 If you **juggle**, you throw things into the air, catching each one and throwing it up again so that there are several of them in the air at the same time. V OR V+O

2 If you **juggle** numbers or ideas, or **juggle** with them, you rearrange them repeatedly in order to V+O OR V+*with*

What months of the year are on these pages?

make them fit the pattern that you want them to fit. EG *Both of them juggle their working hours to be with the children... He was still juggling with figures and possibilities.*

juggler /dʒʌglə/, **jugglers.** A **juggler** is someone who juggles in order to entertain people. N COUNT

jugular /dʒʌgjə^{4}lə/, **jugulars.** Your **jugular** or **jugular vein** is a large vein in your neck that carries blood from your head back to your heart. N COUNT

juice /dʒuːs/, **juices. 1 Juice** is the liquid that can be obtained from a fruit or a plant. EG *Try squeezing a little lemon juice and garlic into it... ...two glasses of pineapple juice.* N MASS

2 The **juices** of a joint of meat are the liquid that comes out of it when you cook it. EG *...spooning the juices over the top of a leg of lamb.* N COUNT OR N UNCOUNT

3 The **juices** in your stomach are the fluids that help you to digest food. EG *...digestive juices.* N PLURAL

juicy /dʒuːsi^1/, **juicier, juiciest. 1** A fruit or other food that is **juicy** has a lot of juice in it. EG *...juicy, ripe tomatoes.* ADJ QUALIT

2 Something that is described as **juicy 2.1** is very interesting and enjoyable. EG *The title part of the play is the juiciest for an actor.* **2.2** describes or represents sexual behaviour in a way that people consider to be pleasing or exciting. EG *He describes some juicy scenes in the 'Priest of Love'.* ADJ QUALIT Informal; Informal

jukebox /dʒuːkbɒks/, **jukeboxes.** A **jukebox** is a large record player in pubs and bars. You put a coin in and choose the record that you want to hear. EG *...the noise of reggae music from the jukebox.* N COUNT

July /dʒə^{4}laɪ/ is the seventh month of the year in the Western calendar. EG *On leaving school in July 1942, Tony very much wanted to join the RAF.* N UNCOUNT

jumble /dʒʌmbə^{0}l/, **jumbles, jumbling, jumbled.**
1 A **jumble** is a lot of different things that are all mixed together in a confused or untidy way. EG *...a chaotic jumble of motor vehicles of every description... ...a jumble of colours and patterns and noises and smells.* N PART OR N SING

2 If you **jumble** things, or **jumble** them **up**, you mix them together so that they are not in the correct order. EG *The bits and pieces were jumbled up with a lot of stuff that would never be needed again.* V+O: OFT+*up*, USU PASS

jumble sale, jumble sales. A **jumble sale** is an event that is held to raise money, usually for a charity. People bring old things that they do not want any more, and other people buy them for small amounts of money. N COUNT

jumbo /dʒʌmbəʊ/, **jumbos. 1 Jumbo** means very large; used especially in advertising. EG *...jumbo steaks... ...a jumbo vacuum cleaner.* ADJ CLASSIF: ATTRIB

2 A **jumbo** or a **jumbo jet** is a very large jet aeroplane. N COUNT

jump /dʒʌmp/, **jumps, jumping, jumped. 1** If you **jump** somewhere, **1.1** you push your feet against the ground and go into the air. EG *He jumped down from the terrace... The horse jumps over a small stream.* ▸ used as a noun. EG *It was a spectacular jump.* **1.2** you move there quickly and suddenly. EG *Ralph jumped to his feet... He jumped up and went across to the large bookcase.* V: USU+A; ▸ N COUNT; V+A

2 If you **jump** something such as a fence, you jump over it or across it. V+O

3 If you **jump**, your body makes a sudden movement because you have just been badly frightened or surprised by something. EG *A sudden noise made me jump... I spoke so loudly that they jumped.* V

4 If an amount or level **jumps**, it increases by a large amount in a short time. EG *The population jumped to nearly 10,000.* ▸ used as a noun. EG *...a massive jump in expenditure.* V: USU+A; ▸ N COUNT: USU+SUPP

5 If someone **jumps** a queue, they move to the front of it before it is their turn to do so; used showing disapproval. V+O

6 If you **keep one jump ahead** of an opponent or rival, you manage always to be in a better position than they are. PHRASE

7 to **jump to a conclusion**: see **conclusion.** • to **jump the gun**: see **gun.** • to **jump out of** your **skin**: see **skin.**

jump at. If you **jump at** an offer or opportunity, you accept it eagerly as soon as it is offered to you. EG *I suggested it to him, and he jumped at the idea.* PHRASAL VB: V+PREP, HAS PASS

jumper /dʒʌmpə/, **jumpers.** A **jumper** is **1** a piece of clothing made of knitted wool, that covers the upper part of your body and your arms and does not open at the front. **2** a pinafore dress. N COUNT British; American

jumpy /dʒʌmpi^1/, **jumpier, jumpiest.** If you are **jumpy**, you are nervous or worried about something. EG *The very thought of it makes me feel slightly jumpy.* ADJ QUALIT Informal

junction /dʒʌŋkʃə^{0}n/, **junctions.** A **junction** is a place where roads or railway lines join. EG *She began walking towards the junction of Cortez Avenue and Main Street.* N COUNT

juncture /dʒʌŋktʃə/, **junctures. At** a particular **juncture** means at a particular point in time, especially when it is a very important time in a series of events. EG *She knew that any move on her part at this juncture would be interpreted as a sign of weakness.* PHRASE Formal

June /dʒuːn/ is the sixth month of the year in the Western calendar. EG *Labour was defeated in the General Election of 19 June 1970.* N UNCOUNT

jungle /dʒʌŋgə^{0}l/, **jungles. 1** A **jungle** is a forest in a hot country where tall trees and other plants grow very closely together. EG *...the Amazon jungle... ...immense tracts of impenetrable jungle.* N COUNT OR N UNCOUNT

2 You can refer to a situation where everything is very complicated as a **jungle**. EG *He'd never have got anywhere in the jungle of real politics.* N SING+SUPP

junior /dʒuːnjə/, **juniors. 1** Someone who is **junior** holds an unimportant position in an organization or profession. EG *She's a junior minister at the Home Office... We could give the job to somebody more junior.* ▸ used as a noun. EG *Police officers later blamed their juniors for not spotting these clues.* ADJ QUALIT; ▸ N COUNT

2 If you are someone's **junior**, you are younger than they are. EG *She was married at the age of seventy-seven to a man seventeen years her junior.* N SING+POSS

junior school, junior schools. A **junior school** in England or Wales is a school for children between the ages of about seven and eleven. N COUNT OR N UNCOUNT

junk /dʒʌŋk/ is **1** an amount of old or useless things. EG *Look, get that junk off the table, will you!* **2** second-hand goods that are being sold cheaply. EG *We got most of our furniture from junk shops and jumble sales.* N UNCOUNT Informal; N MOD Informal

junk food is food that is not very good for your health but is easy and quick to prepare. N MASS

junkie /dʒʌŋki^1/, **junkies.** A **junkie** is someone who is addicted to a drug that they inject into their body. EG *Of course I'm worried. You're turning into a junkie.* N COUNT Informal

jurisdiction /dʒʊə^{0}rɪsdɪkʃə^{0}n/ is the power that a court of law or someone in authority has to carry out legal judgements or enforce laws. EG *The Governor had no jurisdiction over prices.* N UNCOUNT

juror /dʒʊərə/, **jurors.** A **juror** is a member of a jury. EG *The jurors gave their verdict.* N COUNT

jury /dʒʊəri^1/, **juries.** A **jury** is **1** a group of people in a court of law who listen to the facts about a crime and decide whether the person accused is guilty or not. EG *A jury would never convict on that evidence... ...trial by jury.* **2** a group of people who decide who the winner of a competition is. EG *We'd like to test the opinion of our jury in Broadcasting House.* N COLL

just /dʒʌst/. **1** If you say that something has **just** happened, you mean that it happened a very short time ago. EG *I've just sold my car... She had only just moved in.* ADV

2 If you say that you are **just** doing something, you mean that you will finish doing it very soon. If you ADV say that you are **just** going to do something, you mean that you will do it very soon. EG *I'm just making us some coffee, Chris... They were just about to leave when there was a knock on the door.*

3 You can also use **just** to emphasize that something happens or happened at exactly the moment you are talking about. EG *The telephone rang just as I was about to serve up the dinner... Judy didn't like to tell him just then.* ADV

4 Just now means **4.1** a very short time ago. EG *She was here just now.* **4.2** at the present time. EG *Nasty weather we're having just now.* PHRASE

5 You say **just a minute**, **just a moment**, or **just a second** when you are asking someone to wait for a short time. EG *'Have you got John's address?' – 'Just a minute. I'll have a look.'* CONVENTION

6 You also use **just** **6.1** to indicate that something is no more important, interesting, difficult, or great than you say it is. EG *It's just a story... It is not just a children's film... Just add boiling water.* **6.2** to indicate that you are talking about a small part or sample, not the whole of an amount. EG *These are just a few of the enquiries.* **6.3** to indicate that what you are saying is the case, but only by a very small degree or amount. EG *The heat was just bearable... He could only just hear them... It might just help.* **6.4** to give emphasis to what you are saying. EG *I just know there's something wrong... Just listen to that noise.* ADV

7 Just also means exactly or precisely. EG *That's just what I wanted to hear... Rattlesnake is just like chicken, only tougher... She was as fat as he was and just as unattractive... The real debate is about just how much money you should spend.* ADV

8 If you say that someone is **just** the person, you mean that they are the right person. If something is **just** the thing, it is the right thing. EG *He knew just the place... Sam would be just the person!* ADV

9 If you say that you can **just** imagine something, you mean that it is easy for you to imagine it. EG *Ah yes, I can just see him as a dentist.* ADV

10 You also use **just** when you are politely making a request, interrupting someone, or changing the subject. EG *Can I just use your lighter please?* ADV

11 You use **just about** to say that something is so close to a particular level or state that it can be regarded as having reached it. EG *She was just about his age... Everything is just about ready.* PHRASE

12 Someone or something that is **just** is reasonable and fair. EG *...a just punishment... ...a just and civilised society.* ◊ **justly.** EG *I believe that I have acted justly.* ADJ QUALIT ◊ ADV

justice /dʒʌstɪs/, **justices. 1 Justice** is **1.1** fairness in the way that people are treated. EG *The concept of justice is very basic in human thought... ...economic justice.* **1.2** the system that a country uses in order to make sure that people obey the law. EG *The courts are a very important part of our British system of justice.* N UNCOUNT

2 The **justice** of a claim, argument, or cause is its quality of being reasonable and right. EG *They believe in the justice of their cause.* N UNCOUNT +SUPP

3 If a criminal **is brought to justice**, he or she is tried in a court of law and punished. EG *The murderer will in time be brought to justice.* PHRASE

4 If you **do justice to** something, you deal with it properly and completely. EG *I am the only man in Europe capable of doing it justice, of making a perfect job of it.* PHRASE

5 A **justice** is a judge. EG *...justices of the Supreme Court.* N COUNT American

Justice of the Peace, Justices of the Peace. A **Justice of the Peace** is a local magistrate in Britain. N COUNT

justifiable /dʒʌstɪfaɪəbəl/. An opinion, action, or fact that is **justifiable** is acceptable or correct because there is a good reason for it. EG *I hope this is a justifiable interpretation.* ◊ **justifiably.** EG *The Government is justifiably unpopular.* ADJ QUALIT ◊ ADV

justification /dʒʌstɪfɪkeɪʃən/, **justifications.** A **justification** for something is a good reason or explanation for it. EG *We all have justifications for what we do... There was no justification for higher interest rates.* N COUNT OR N UNCOUNT

justified /dʒʌstɪfaɪd/. **1** If you think that someone is **justified** in doing something, you think that they have good reasons for doing it. EG *I think he was quite justified in refusing to help her.* ADJ PRED

2 An action that is **justified** is reasonable and acceptable. EG *In these circumstances, massive industrial action is justified and necessary.* ADJ QUALIT

justify /dʒʌstɪfaɪ/, **justifies, justifying, justified.** If someone **justifies** a particular action or idea, they give a good reason why it is sensible or necessary. EG *The decision has been fully justified... I'm not going to try and justify myself... How did they justify putting that thing on a gallery wall?* V+O, V-REFL, OR V+-ING

jut /dʒʌt/, **juts, jutting, jutted.** If something **juts** out, it sticks out above or beyond a surface. EG *The living room window juts out... A line of rocks jutted into the sea.* V+A

juvenile /dʒuːvəˈnaɪl/, **juveniles. 1 Juvenile** activity or behaviour involves young people who are not adults. EG *...the increase in juvenile crime... ...juvenile offenders.* ADJ CLASSIF : ATTRIB

2 You can say that someone is **juvenile** when they are behaving in a silly way. EG *Mike has a somewhat juvenile sense of humour.* ADJ QUALIT

3 A **juvenile** is a child or young person who is not yet old enough to be regarded as an adult. EG *17% of all crime in 1983 was committed by juveniles.* N COUNT Legal

juvenile delinquent, juvenile delinquents. A **juvenile delinquent** is a young person who is guilty of committing crimes, especially vandalism or violence. N COUNT

juxtapose /dʒʌkstəpəʊz/, **juxtaposes, juxtaposing, juxtaposed.** If you **juxtapose** two things or ideas, you put them next to each other, often in order to emphasize the difference between them. EG *She juxtaposes her photographs with illustrations of flowers.* ◊ **juxtaposition** /dʒʌkstəpəzɪʃən/, **juxtapositions.** EG *...the juxtaposition of extreme wealth and poverty.* V+O OR V+O+*with* : RECIP Formal ◊ N COUNT OR N UNCOUNT

K k

K, k /keɪ/, **Ks, k's. K** is the eleventh letter of the English alphabet. N COUNT

kaleidoscope /kəlaɪdəskəʊp/, **kaleidoscopes. 1** A **kaleidoscope** is a tube that you hold in your hand. When you look through one end and turn the tube, you see a pattern of colours which keeps changing. N COUNT

2 You can refer to any pattern of colours that keeps changing as a **kaleidoscope**. EG *Alongside the railway line, in a kaleidoscope of colours, cars and lorries swept by.* N SING+SUPP Literary

kangaroo /kæŋgəruː/, **kangaroos.** A **kangaroo** is a large Australian animal which moves by jumping N COUNT on its back legs. Female kangaroos carry their babies in a pouch on their stomachs.

karate /kəˈrɑːti¹/ is a sport in which people fight using their hands, elbows, feet, and legs. N UNCOUNT

kebab /kəˈbæb/, **kebabs.** A **kebab** consists of small pieces of meat and sometimes vegetables that have been put on a thin metal rod and grilled. N COUNT

keel /kiːl/, **keels, keeling, keeled.** If you say that something is **on an even keel**, you mean that it is working or proceeding smoothly and satisfactorily. EG *Most governments are able to keep their economies on an even keel.* PHRASE

keel over. If something **keels over**, it falls over sideways. EG *The pillar was liable to keel over at any moment... One of the athletes suddenly keeled over.* PHRASAL VB : V+ADV

keen /kiːn/, **keener, keenest. 1** If you are **keen** to do something, you want to do it very much. EG *Her solicitor was keener to talk than she was... He didn't seem all that keen on having it... He's not keen for Charlotte to know.* ADJ PRED : OFT+*to*-INF OR *on*

2 You use **keen** to show that someone enjoys a particular sport or activity and does it a lot. For example, if someone is a **keen** golfer, they enjoy playing golf very much. EG *He was not a keen gardener... Boys are as keen on cooking as girls are.* ADJ QUALIT : ATTRIB OR ADJ PRED+*on*

3 Keen people are enthusiastic and are interested in everything they do. EG *They were highly-motivated students, very keen.* ADJ QUALIT

4 If you have a **keen** interest or a **keen** desire, your interest or desire is very strong. EG *He took a keen interest in domestic affairs... She had a keen desire to see the union brought under the rule of law.* ◇ **keenly.** EG *I was keenly interested in outdoor activities.* ADJ QUALIT : USU ATTRIB ◇ ADV

5 If you are **keen** on someone, you find them very attractive. EG *Molly was very keen on the music master.* ADJ PRED+*on* Informal

6 If you have **keen** sight or hearing, for example, you can see or hear very well. EG *It takes a keen eye to spot them... ...people with keen powers of observation.* ADJ QUALIT

7 You say that a contest is **keen** when the competitors are trying very hard and it is not clear who will win. EG *The competition for the first prize was keen.* ◇ **keenly.** EG *...a keenly contested football match.* ADJ QUALIT ◇ ADV

keenly /kiːnlɪ¹/. If you watch or listen **keenly**, you watch or listen with great concentration. EG *He was watching Tortyev keenly.* ● See also **keen.** ADV

keep /kiːp/, **keeps, keeping, kept** /kɛpt/. **1** To **keep** someone or something in a particular state or place means to cause them to remain in that state or place. EG *They had been kept awake by nightingales... She kept her arm around her husband as she spoke... He bought a guard dog to keep out intruders... Sorry to keep you waiting.* V+O+A, V+O+C, OR V+O+-ING

2 If you **keep** in a particular state or place, you remain in that state or place. EG *They've got to hunt for food to keep alive... Keep in touch... They kept away from the forest.* V+C OR V+A

3 If you **keep** doing something, **3.1** you do it repeatedly. EG *I keep making the same mistake.* **3.2** you continue doing it without stopping. EG *The men just kept walking... Keep searching.* V+-ING

4 If you **keep** something, you continue to have it. EG *Why didn't Daddy let me keep the ten dollars?... She would not be able to keep her job.* V+O

5 If you **keep** something in a particular place, you have it there so that you can use it whenever you need it. EG *...the shelf where the butter and cheese were kept... Keep a spare key in your bag.* V+O : USU+A

6 Keep is used with some nouns to indicate that someone does something or continues to do it. For example, if you **keep** a grip on something, you continue to hold it or control it. EG *They would keep a look-out for him.* V+O : NO PASS

7 To **keep** someone or something from doing a particular thing means to prevent them from doing it. EG *She had to hold the boy tight, to keep him from falling.* V+O+*from*

8 If something **keeps** you, it makes you arrive somewhere later than expected. EG *Am I keeping you from your party?... What kept you?* V+O : OFT+*from*

9 When you **keep** something such as a promise or an appointment, you do what you said you would do. EG *Hearst kept his word.* V+O

10 If you **keep** something from someone, you do not tell them about it. EG *Why did you keep it from me?* ● If you **keep** something **to yourself**, you do not tell anyone about it. EG *They keep their discoveries to themselves.* V+O+*from* ● PHRASE

11 If you **keep yourself to yourself**, you do not talk much to other people. PHRASE

12 If you **keep** a record of a series of events, you make a written record of it. EG *We keep a record of the noise levels... I did not keep any notes.* V+O

13 People who **keep** animals own them and take care of them. EG *My dad kept chickens.* V+O

14 Your **keep** is the cost of food and other things that you need in your daily life. EG *The grant includes £19 for your keep during the vacation.* N SING+POSS

15 If food **keeps**, it stays in good condition. V : NO CONT

16 If you ask someone how they **are keeping**, you are asking if they are well. V+A : ONLY CONT

17 If you **keep at it**, you continue doing something that you have started. EG *You've just got to keep at it.* PHRASE

18 If a sign on a piece of land says **'Keep Out'**, it is warning you not to go onto the land.

19 If you say that something is **in keeping** with something else, you mean that it seems right or suitable with it. If it is **out of keeping**, it does not seem right or suitable. EG *Her white socks and brown shoes were not quite in keeping with her beautiful satin evening dress... In keeping with the government policy of non-interference, they refused to take any action.* PHRASE

keep back. If you **keep** some information **back**, you do not tell everything that you know about something. EG *You can't write an autobiography without keeping something back.* PHRASAL VB : V+O+ADV

keep down. If you **keep** the number or size of something **down**, you do not allow it to get bigger. EG *The French are very concerned to keep costs down.* PHRASAL VB : V+O+ADV

keep off. If you **keep** something **off**, you prevent it from reaching you and harming you. EG *They built a bamboo shelter to keep the rain off.* PHRASAL VB : V+O+ADV/PREP

keep on. 1 If you **keep on** doing something, **1.1** you continue doing it without stopping. EG *They kept on walking for a while in silence.* **1.2** you do it repeatedly. EG *I kept on getting up and staring out of the window.* **2** If someone **keeps on** about something, they talk about it often or for a long time, in an irritating way. EG *She kept on about the car.* PHRASAL VB : V+ADV+-ING; V+ADV, OFT+*about*

keep on at. If someone **keeps on at** you, they repeatedly ask or tell you to do something, in an irritating way. PHRASAL VB : V+ADV+PREP

keep to. 1 If you **keep to** a rule, plan, or agreement, you do exactly what you are expected or supposed to do. EG *We must keep to the deadlines.* **2** If you **keep** something **to** a particular number or quantity, you limit it to that number or quantity. EG *Keep it to a minimum.* PHRASAL VB : V+PREP, HAS PASS; V+O+PREP

keep up. 1 If one person or thing **keeps up** with another, the first one moves, progresses, or increases as fast as the second. EG *I started to run, so that she had to hurry to keep up with me... Pensions were increased to keep up with the rise in prices.* **2** If you **keep up** with what is happening, you make sure that you know about it. EG *Even friends have trouble keeping up with each other's whereabouts.* **3** If you **keep** something **up**, **3.1** you continue to do it or provide it. EG *She kept up a steady moaning... He was unable to keep up the* PHRASAL VB : V+ADV, OFT+*with*; V+ADV, OFT+*with*; V+O+ADV

payments. **3.2** you prevent it from becoming less. EG *It's important to keep up the standard.*

keeper /kiːpə/, **keepers. 1** A **keeper** is a person who takes care of the animals in a zoo. N COUNT

2 If you say that you **are not** someone's **keeper**, you mean that you are not responsible for what they do or for what happens to them. EG *She was not her sister's keeper.* PHRASE

keep-fit is the activity of keeping your body in good condition by doing special exercises. N UNCOUNT

ken /kɛn/. If something is **beyond** your **ken**, you do not have enough knowledge to be able to understand it. PHRASE Formal

kennel /kɛnəl/, **kennels. 1** A **kennel** is a small hut made for a dog to sleep in. N COUNT

2 A **kennels** is a place where people can leave their pet dogs when they go on holiday, or where dogs are bred. EG *He had arranged to leave Towser at a kennels.* N SING

kept /kɛpt/ is the past tense and past participle of **keep.**

kerb /kɜːb/, **kerbs;** spelled **curb** in American English. The **kerb** is the raised edge between a pavement and a road. EG *The taxi pulled into the kerb... She was standing on the kerb.* N COUNT

kernel /kɜːnəl/, **kernels. 1** The **kernel** of a nut is the part that is inside the shell. N COUNT

2 You can refer to the most basic part of something as its **kernel**. EG *...the men who form the kernel of this army... There is a kernel of truth in what you say.* N COUNT+*of* Formal

kerosene /kɛrəsiːn/ is a liquid that is used as a fuel in some heaters and lamps. N UNCOUNT American

kestrel /kɛstrəl/, **kestrels.** A **kestrel** is a small falcon. N COUNT

ketchup /kɛtʃəp/ is a thick, cold sauce made from tomatoes. N UNCOUNT

kettle /kɛtəl/, **kettles.** A **kettle** is a covered round container that you use for boiling water. It has a handle on top and a spout. EG *They put the kettle on to make a cup of tea.* N COUNT

key /kiː/, **keys. 1** A **key** is **1.1** a specially shaped piece of metal which you place in a lock and turn in order to open or lock a door, a drawer, or a suitcase. EG *He locked the bag and put the key in his pocket... I've lost the key to the filing cabinet.* **1.2** a specially shaped piece of metal or plastic which you turn, for example in order to wind up a clock. N COUNT

2 The **keys** of a typewriter, computer keyboard, or cash register are the buttons that you press in order to operate it. See picture at TYPEWRITER. N COUNT

3 The **keys** of a piano or organ are the black and white bars that you press in order to play it. N COUNT

4 In music, a **key** is a scale of musical notes that starts at one particular note. EG *...the key of D.* N UNCOUNT OR N COUNT

5 The **key** to a map, diagram, or technical book is a list of the symbols and abbreviations used in it, with explanations of what they mean. N COUNT

6 The **key** things or people in a group are the most important ones. EG *The country's key industries are coal, engineering, and transport... Unemployment was a key issue during the election campaign.* ADJ CLASSIF : ATTRIB

7 The **key** to a desirable situation or result is the way in which it can be achieved. EG *Education became the key to progress.* N COUNT : USU *the*+N

keyboard /kiːbɔːd/, **keyboards. 1** The **keyboard** of a typewriter or a computer terminal is the set of keys that you press in order to operate it. N COUNT

2 The **keyboard** of a piano or organ is the set of black and white keys that you press in order to play it. EG *She reached out her hands to the keyboard and began to play.* N COUNT

keyhole /kiːhəʊl/, **keyholes.** A **keyhole** is the hole in a lock that you put a key in. N COUNT

keynote /kiːnəʊt/, **keynotes.** The **keynote** of an activity or policy is the most important part of it. EG *The keynote for Labour policy, he saw, was planning.* N COUNT : USU SING

key-ring, key-rings. A **key-ring** is a ring which you use to keep your keys together. N COUNT

kg is an abbreviation for 'kilogram'. EG *It weighs only 20 kg.*

khaki /kɑːki/. Something that is **khaki** is yellowish-brown in colour. EG *...khaki shorts... The boys looked smart in khaki and polished brass.* ADJ COLOUR

kibbutz /kɪbʊts/, **kibbutzes** or **kibbutzim** /kɪbʊtsim/. A **kibbutz** is a place of work in Israel, for example a farm or factory, where the workers live together and share all the duties and income. EG *He wrote to the Jewish agency asking to visit a kibbutz.* N COUNT

kick /kɪk/, **kicks, kicking, kicked. 1** If you **kick** someone or something, you hit them with your foot. EG *He protested violently, and threatened to kick me... We caught sight of Christopher, kicking a tin can down the High Street.* ▸ used as a noun. EG *He gave him a good kick.* V+O ▸ N COUNT

2 If you **kick**, you move your feet violently or suddenly, for example when you are dancing or swimming. EG *Simon was floating in the water and kicking with his feet.* V : OFT+A

3 If someone **gets a kick** from something, they get a feeling of intense pleasure or excitement from it. EG *They loved debate, and got a kick out of court proceedings.* PHRASE Informal

4 If someone does something **for kicks**, they do it because they find it exciting. PHRASE Informal

5 If you say that you **kicked** yourself or **could have kicked** yourself, you mean that you were very annoyed with yourself because you did something wrong. EG *I kicked myself for not having thought of it earlier.* V-REFL Informal

6 If you **kick** a habit, such as smoking, you give it up. V+O Informal

7 See also **free kick**.

kick about or **kick around.** If something **is kicking about** or **is kicking around**, it is lying somewhere and has been forgotten. EG *His old bike has been kicking about among the bushes for days.* PHRASAL VB : V+ADV, ONLY CONT Informal

kick off. 1 When you **kick off** an event or a discussion, you start it. EG *They kicked off a two-month tour of the U.S. with a party in Washington.* PHRASAL VB : V+ADV OR V+O+ADV Informal

2 See also **kick-off**.

kick out. If you **kick** someone **out** of a place, you force them to leave. EG *He kicked me out... She kicked me out of the room.* PHRASAL VB : V+O+ADV Informal

kick up. If you **kick up** a fuss or a row, you get very annoyed or upset about something. EG *When I told him, he kicked up a fuss.* PHRASAL VB : V+ADV+O Informal

kick-off, kick-offs. Kick-off or the **kick-off** is the time at which a game of football officially starts. EG *Kick-off is at 2.30.* N COUNT OR N UNCOUNT

kid /kɪd/, **kids, kidding, kidded. 1** You can refer to a child as a **kid**. EG *...five-year-old kids... I can remember the feelings I had when I was a kid... ...his wife and kids.* N COUNT Informal

2 Young people who are no longer children are sometimes referred to as **kids**. EG *GM's college kids pay only $1,200 tuition.* N COUNT Informal American

3 You can refer to your younger brother or sister as your **kid** brother or **kid** sister. EG *Are you going to bring your kid brother along?* ADJ CLASSIF : ATTRIB Informal

4 If you **are kidding**, you are saying something that is not really true, as a joke. EG *They're not sure whether I'm kidding or not... I'm not kidding, Jill. He could have taken it if he'd wanted.* ● You can say **'No kidding'** to emphasize that what you are saying is true, or that you mean it. EG *No kidding, Ginny, you look good.* V : ONLY CONT Informal ● PHRASE

5 If you **kid** someone, you tease them. EG *Tim's friends kidded him about his odd clothes.* V+O

6 If people **kid** themselves, they allow themselves to believe something that is not true because they V-REFL : OFT+REPORT

What do you think 'kilo-' means in 'kilogram' and 'kilometre'?

wish that it was true. EG *They like to kid themselves they're keeping fit.*

7 A **kid** is also a young goat. N COUNT

kidnap /kɪdnæp/, **kidnaps, kidnapping, kidnapped. 1** If someone **kidnaps** you, they take you away by force, usually in order to demand money from your family, employers, or government. EG *He was kidnapped by terrorists just over a month ago.* V+O

◊ **kidnapping, kidnappings.** EG *...the kidnapping of a royal child... They charged me with murder and kidnapping.* ◊ N UNCOUNT OR N COUNT ◊ **kidnapper** /kɪdnæpə/, **kidnappers.** EG *I had given up all hope of tracing her kidnapper.* ◊ N COUNT

2 Kidnap is the crime of kidnapping someone. EG *...the threat of kidnap or assassination... ...a kidnap victim.* N UNCOUNT

kidney /kɪdni^1/, **kidneys.** Your **kidneys** are the two organs in your body that produce urine. EG *He had kidney trouble.* N COUNT

kill /kɪl/, **kills, killing, killed. 1** When someone or something **kills** a person, animal or plant, they cause the person, animal, or plant to die. EG *She killed him with a hammer... He had tried to kill himself five times... Her mother was killed in a car crash... The sun had killed most of the plants... ...a desire to kill.* V+O, V-REFL, OR V

2 The act of killing an animal after hunting it is referred to as the **kill**. EG *The hunters move in for the kill... The female lions make the majority of kills.* N COUNT

3 If you say that something **is killing** you, you mean that it is causing you great pain. EG *These shoes are killing me.* V+O : USU CONT Informal

4 If something **kills** an activity, process, or feeling, it prevents it from continuing. EG *His behaviour outraged me and killed our friendship... These latest measures killed all hope of any relaxation of the system.* V+O

5 When you **kill time**, you occupy yourself by doing something unimportant or uninteresting while you are waiting for something. EG *He spent long hours keeping out of the way, killing time.* PHRASE

6 to kill two birds with one stone: see **bird**. ● See also **killing**.

kill off. If you **kill** something **off**, you completely destroy it. EG *This discovery killed off one of the last surviving romances about the place... The bacteria had been killed off.* PHRASAL VB : V+O+ADV

killer /kɪlə/, **killers. 1** A **killer** is a person who has killed someone. EG *He became a ruthless killer.* N COUNT

2 You can refer to anything that causes death as a **killer**. EG *The lion is one of the most efficient killers in the animal world... Heart disease is the major killer of our time.* N COUNT

killing /kɪlɪŋ/, **killings. 1** A **killing** is an act in which one person deliberately kills another. EG *...a brutal killing which had occurred in the neighbourhood... The killings were random, gruesome, and baffling.* N COUNT

2 If you **make a killing**, you make a large profit very quickly and easily. PHRASE Informal

kiln /kɪln/, **kilns.** A **kiln** is an oven in which you bake things such as pottery and bricks. N COUNT

kilo /ki:ləʊ/, **kilos.** A **kilo** is the same as a kilogram. EG *...a kilo of fresh strawberries.* N COUNT OR N PART

kilogram /kɪlə^{6}græm/, **kilograms;** also spelled **kilogramme.** A **kilogram** is a metric unit of weight that is a thousand grams and is equal to 2.2 pounds. Its abbreviation is 'kg'. N COUNT OR N PART

kilometre /kɪlə^{6}mi:tə, kɪlɒmɪtə/, **kilometres;** spelled **kilometer** in American English. A **kilometre** is a metric unit of distance that is a thousand metres. Its abbreviation is 'km'. EG *We could see rain falling about a kilometre away.* N COUNT

kilt /kɪlt/, **kilts.** A **kilt** is a short pleated skirt that is sometimes worn by Scotsmen. Kilts can also be worn by women and girls. N COUNT

kin /kɪn/. Your **kin** are your relatives. See also **next of kin**. N UNCOUNT Outdated

kind /kaɪnd/, **kinds; kinder, kindest. 1** If you talk about a particular **kind** of thing, you are talking about one of the classes or sorts of that thing. EG *Was he carrying a weapon and, if so, what kind of weapon?... ...processes of an entirely new kind... He had a seizure of some kind... These thoughts weren't the kind he could share with anyone.* N COUNT OR N UNCOUNT +SUPP

2 You use **kind of** when you want to say that something can be roughly described in a particular way. EG *He spoke in a kind of sad whisper.* PHRASE Informal

3 In American English, **kind of** is used to say that something is partly true or partly the case. EG *I felt kind of sorry for him.* PHRASE Informal

4 You use **of a kind** to say that something belongs to a particular class of things but that it is not really satisfactory. EG *A solution of a kind has been found to this problem.* PHRASE

5 Payment **in kind** is payment in the form of goods or services, rather than money. PHRASE

6 Someone who is **kind** is gentle, caring, and helpful. EG *We were much kinder to one another after that night... It was kind of you to come.* ADJ QUALIT

◊ **kindly.** EG *'You're not to blame yourself, Smithy,' Rick said kindly.* ◊ ADV ◊ **kindness.** EG *He treated his labourers with kindness and understanding.* ◊ N UNCOUNT

7 If someone asks you if you would **be kind enough** to do something or **be so kind as** to do it, they are asking you politely but rather firmly to do it. EG *Before you go to bed, would you be kind enough to close the window.* PHRASE

8 See also **kindly, kindness**.

kindergarten /kɪndəgɑ:tə^{0}n/, **kindergartens.** A **kindergarten** is a school for young children who are not old enough to go to a primary school. N COUNT OR N UNCOUNT

kind-hearted. Someone who is **kind-hearted** is kind, loving, and gentle. ADJ QUALIT

kindle /kɪndə^{0}l/, **kindles, kindling, kindled. 1** If something **kindles** an idea or feeling in you, it makes you begin to have that idea or feeling. EG *...the aspirations kindled in us in early childhood.* V+O Literary

2 If you **kindle** a fire, you light wood, coal, or paper in order to start it. V+O

kindling /kɪndlɪŋ/ is small pieces of dry wood that you use to start a fire. EG *They would pull up the blackened stalks for kindling.* N UNCOUNT

kindly /kaɪndli^1/. **1** Someone who is **kindly** is kind, caring, and sympathetic. EG *Being a kindly and reasonable man, he at once apologized... The students were watching her with kindly interest.* ADJ QUALIT : ATTRIB

◊ **kindliness.** EG *...the great virtues of humility and kindliness.* ◊ N UNCOUNT

2 If you ask someone to **kindly** do something, you are asking them to do it in a way that shows that you are angry or annoyed with them. EG *Kindly take your hand off my knee.* ADV+INF

3 If someone **looks kindly** on something, they approve of it. EG *The White House will look more kindly on a robust economy.* PHRASE

4 If someone **does not take kindly to** something, they do not like it. EG *They are unlikely to take kindly to this suggestion.* PHRASE

5 See also **kind**.

kindness /kaɪndnɪ^{2}s/, **kindnesses.** A **kindness** is a helpful or considerate act. EG *She thanked them both many times for all their kindnesses.* ● See also **kind**. N COUNT

kindred /kɪndrɪ^{2}d/. Someone that you describe as a **kindred** spirit has the same view of life or the same interests that you have. EG *When I saw his work I recognized him as a kindred spirit... They must have recognised each other as kindred souls.* ADJ CLASSIF : ATTRIB

king /kɪŋ/, **kings. 1** A **king** is a man who is the head of his country. He is a member of the royal family. EG *...King Arthur... Three Saxon kings are buried here... ...the King of Spain.* N COUNT

2 In chess, the **king** is the most important piece. When you are in a position to capture your opponent's king, you win the game. N COUNT

3 A **king** is also a playing card with a picture of a king on it. N COUNT

kingdom /kɪŋdəm/, **kingdoms. 1** A **kingdom** is a country or region that is ruled by a king or queen. EG *...the United Kingdom.* N COUNT

2 All the animals in the world, including the birds, fish, and insects, can be referred to together as the animal **kingdom**. All the plants can be referred to as the plant **kingdom**. EG *This creature has the largest eyes in the whole animal kingdom.* N SING+SUPP

kingfisher /kɪŋfɪʃə/, **kingfishers.** A **kingfisher** is a brightly-coloured bird which lives near rivers and lakes and catches fish. N COUNT

king-size. King-size things or **king-sized** things are of the largest size that you can get. EG *...his king-size bed... ...king-size cigarettes.* ADJ CLASSIF : ATTRIB

kinky /kɪŋki[1]/. If you describe someone's behaviour as **kinky**, you mean that it is strange, and probably connected with unusual sexual practices. EG *There must be something very kinky going on.* ADJ QUALIT Informal

kinship /kɪnʃɪp/. **1 Kinship** is the relationship between members of the same family. EG *Their ties of kinship mean a lot to them.* N UNCOUNT Formal

2 If you feel **kinship** with someone, you feel close to them, because you have a similar background or similar feelings or ideas. EG *He felt a deep kinship with the other students.* N UNCOUNT +SUPP Literary

kiosk /kiːɒsk/, **kiosks.** A **kiosk** is a small shop where you can buy things such as sandwiches or newspapers through an open window. EG *We were eating hamburgers at an all-night kiosk.* N COUNT

kipper /kɪpə/, **kippers.** A **kipper** is a herring which has been preserved by being hung in smoke. N COUNT

kiss /kɪs/, **kisses, kissing, kissed. 1** If you **kiss** someone, you touch them with your lips to show affection or to greet them. EG *He bent down and kissed his wife on the cheek... I kissed her goodbye and drove away... They stopped and kissed.* ▸ used as a noun. EG *Give me a kiss... They long for a mother's goodnight kiss.* V+O OR V : RECIP ▸ N COUNT

2 If you **kiss** an object, you touch it lightly with your lips, usually as a sign of reverence. EG *She had always wanted to kiss the Pope's ring.* V+O

kit /kɪt/, **kits. 1** A **kit** is a group of items that are kept together because they are used for similar purposes. EG *...my first-aid kit... ...a tool kit.* N COUNT+SUPP

2 Your **kit** is the special clothing that you use when you take part in a sport. EG *Have you brought your squash kit?* N UNCOUNT : USU+SUPP

3 A **kit** is also a set of parts that can be put together in order to make something. EG *...a do-it-yourself radio kit... ...people who build their cars from kits.* N COUNT

kitchen /kɪtʃɪn/, **kitchens.** A **kitchen** is a room that you use for cooking and for household jobs such as washing dishes. See picture at HOUSE. EG *Brody went into the kitchen and opened the refrigerator... She left the cheese on the kitchen table.* N COUNT

kite /kaɪt/, **kites.** A **kite** is an object consisting of a light frame covered with paper or cloth. It has a long string attached to it. You hold the string and the kite flies in the air. N COUNT

kitten /kɪtə[0]n/, **kittens.** A **kitten** is a very young cat. N COUNT

kitty /kɪti[1]/, **kitties.** A **kitty** is an amount of money consisting of contributions from several people, which is spent on things that they will share or use together. EG *After we paid the phone bill there was nothing left in the kitty.* N COUNT : USU SING

kiwi /kiːwi[1]/, **kiwis.** A **kiwi** is a type of bird that lives in New Zealand. Kiwis cannot fly. N COUNT

kiwi fruit, kiwi fruits. Kiwi fruit is often also used as the plural form. N COUNT

A **kiwi fruit** is a fruit with a brown hairy skin and green flesh.

Kleenex /kliːnɛks/, **Kleenexes. Kleenex** can also be used as the plural form. N UNCOUNT OR N COUNT Trademark

Kleenex is soft tissue paper that is used as a handkerchief. EG *...a packet of Kleenex... Have you got a Kleenex?*

km is a written abbreviation for 'kilometres' or 'kilometre'. EG *My older sister lives about 10km from our village.*

knack /næk/. If you have the **knack** of doing something, you are able to do it, although other people find it difficult. EG *He had the knack of balancing his pile of objects perfectly... Others seem to have a knack for combining colours and patterns.* N SING : USU+*of/for*

knackered /nækəd/. If you are **knackered**, you are exhausted. ADJ PRED Informal

knead /niːd/, **kneads, kneading, kneaded.** When you **knead** dough, you press and squeeze it with your hands so that it becomes smooth and ready to cook. V+O

knee /niː/, **knees. 1** Your **knee** is the place where your leg bends. See picture at THE HUMAN BODY. EG *Your knee's bleeding... Kindly take your hand off my knee.* N COUNT

2 The **knee** of a piece of clothing is the part that covers your knee. EG *There was a triangular tear at the knee of his trousers.* N COUNT

3 If you have something on your **knee**, it is resting on the upper part of your legs when you are sitting down. EG *She sat with Marcus by her side and Maria on her knee.* N COUNT

4 If you are on your **knees**, you are kneeling. EG *Kurt threw himself on his knees... The woman got up off her knees.* N PLURAL

5 If something **brings** a country **to** its **knees**, it weakens and almost destroys it. EG *The cost of the war would have brought the kingdom to its knees.* PHRASE

kneecap /niːkæp/, **kneecaps.** Your **kneecaps** are the bones at the front of your knees. N COUNT

knee-deep. If you are **knee-deep** in something, it is as high as your knees. EG *He stood there knee-deep in the grass.* ADJ PRED+*in*

knee-high. If something is **knee-high**, it is as high as your knees. EG *I crept through a mass of knee-high nettles.* ADJ CLASSIF

kneel /niːl/, **kneels, kneeling, knelt** /nɛlt/, **kneeled. Knelt** and **kneeled** can both be used as the past tense and past participle.

1 If you **are kneeling**, your legs are bent under you and your knees are touching the ground and supporting the rest of your body. EG *Ralph was kneeling by the fire.* ◇ **kneeling.** EG *The kneeling figure was Mary Darling.* V ◇ ADJ CLASSIF : ATTRIB

2 If you **kneel** or **kneel** down, you bend your legs and lower your body until your knees are touching the ground. EG *I knelt down beside her... Together they kneeled in prayer.* V : OFT+*down*

knew /njuː/ is the past tense of **know.**

knickers /nɪkəz/ are a piece of underwear worn by women and girls. Knickers have holes for your legs and elastic around the top. EG *...a pair of knickers.* N PLURAL

knick-knacks /nɪk næks/ are small ornaments. EG *Their house was full of plants and attractive knick-knacks.* N PLURAL

knife /naɪf/, **knives** /naɪvz/; **knifes, knifing, knifed. Knives** is the plural form of the noun and **knifes** is the third person singular of the present tense of the verb.

1 A **knife** is an object that you hold in your hand and use to cut things. A knife consists of a sharp, flat piece of metal attached to a handle. EG *...knives and forks... ...men armed with knives... ...a knife blade.* See picture at WEAPONS. N COUNT

2 To **knife** someone means to attack and injure them with a knife. EG *Rausenberger had been knifed and robbed near his home.* ◇ **knifing, knifings.** EG *There were often knifings or brawls.* V+O ◇ N COUNT

What title is a knight given?

3 See also **carving knife**, **jack-knife**, **penknife**, **pocket knife**.

knight /naɪt/, **knights, knighting, knighted. 1** In medieval times, a **knight** was a man of noble birth, who served his king or lord in battle, riding a horse. EG *...knights in armour.* N COUNT

2 In modern times, a **knight** is a man who has been given a knighthood. N COUNT

3 In chess, a **knight** is a piece that is shaped like a horse's head. N COUNT

4 If a man **is knighted**, he is given a knighthood. EG *He was knighted by Queen Anne in 1705.* V+O : USU PASS

knighthood /naɪthʊd/, **knighthoods.** A **knighthood** is a title that is given to a man by a British king or queen for his outstanding achievements or for service to his country. A man who has been given a knighthood puts 'Sir' in front of his name. N COUNT

knit /nɪt/, **knits, knitting, knitted. 1** When someone **knits** something, they make it from wool or a similar thread using knitting needles or a machine. EG *She wore a scarf that she had knitted... I had just finished knitting her a cardigan... The old lady sat in her doorway and knitted.* ◇ **knitted.** EG *...a knitted shawl.* V+O, V+O+O, V+O+*for*, OR V ◇ ADJ CLASSIF

2 If you **knit** your **brows**, you frown because you are angry or worried. EG *He sat there knitting his brows and twisting his napkin.* PHRASE Literary

3 A group of people who are close-**knit**, closely **knit**, or tightly **knit** feel closely linked to each other. EG *It's a very close-knit community... They live in tightly knit families.* ADJ QUALIT

knitting /nɪtɪŋ/ is **1** something that is being knitted. EG *She picked up her knitting.* **2** the action or process of knitting. N UNCOUNT

knitting needle, knitting needles. A **knitting needle** is a long thin stick made of plastic or metal, with a point at one end. You use two knitting needles when you are knitting. See picture at NEEDLES. N COUNT

knitwear /nɪtwɛə/ is clothing that has been knitted. EG *...the family knitwear business.* N UNCOUNT

knives /naɪvz/ is the plural of **knife.**

knob /nɒb/, **knobs.** A **knob** is **1** a round handle on a door or drawer. EG *He turned the knob and the door burst open... ...mahogany cabinets with polished brass knobs.* **2** a rounded lump on a flat surface or on top of a stick or post. EG *Her umbrella is elegantly capped with a glass knob... The bed had one gilt knob missing.* **3** a round switch, for example on a television or radio. EG *...the knobs on his tape recorder.* N COUNT

knobbly /nɒbli¹/. Something that is **knobbly** has large lumps on it, making it uneven rather than smooth. EG *...her knobbly old hand.* ADJ QUALIT

knock /nɒk/, **knocks, knocking, knocked. 1** If you **knock** at a door or window, you hit it, usually several times, in order to attract someone's attention. EG *He knocked softly on the door.* ▸ used as a noun. EG *There was a knock at the door.* V : OFT+*at/on* ▸ N COUNT

2 If you **knock** something, you hit it roughly, so that it moves or falls over. EG *In the excitement he knocked over his chair... The glass had been knocked out from windows.* ▸ used as a noun. EG *Knocks can cause weaknesses in the spine.* V+O : USU+A ▸ N COUNT

3 If you **knock** someone down or **knock** them unconscious, you hit them very hard, so that they fall or become unconscious. EG *Dad knocked him to the floor... Rudolph had seen him knock Thomas unconscious with one blow of his fist.* V+O+A OR V+O+C

4 If you **knock** an attitude or kind of behaviour out of someone, you cause them to lose it or stop it, by treating them roughly. EG *All this training might knock the enthusiasm out of him a bit... He was to knock the foolishness out of me eventually.* V+O+*out of* Informal

5 If you **knock** someone or something, you criticize them. EG *He was always knocking the performance of fellow-actors.* V+O Informal

6 If someone receives a **knock**, they have an unpleasant experience which seriously affects their plans or their way of life. EG *She has suffered some hard knocks.* N COUNT

knock about or **knock around. 1** If someone **is knocked about** or **is knocked around**, they are hit several times. EG *He did not like the thought of a woman being knocked about.* **2** Someone who **has knocked about** or **has knocked around** has had experience in a lot of different places or situations. EG *I'm a bachelor, I've knocked about the world a bit, known a few women.* **3** If you **knock about** or **knock around** with someone, you spend your spare time with them. EG *Who's she knocking around with now?* PHRASAL VB : V+O+ADV, USU PASS Informal; V+ADV/PREP Informal; V+ADV, OFT+*with* Informal

knock back. If you **knock back** a drink, you drink it quickly. EG *He won't be too happy if he finds me knocking back his whisky.* PHRASAL VB : V+O+ADV Informal

knock down. 1 If a vehicle **knocks** someone **down**, it hits them so that they fall and are injured or killed. EG *He was knocked down by a bus.* **2** If you **knock down** a building or part of a building, you deliberately destroy it or remove it. EG *I'd knock the wall down between the two rooms.* PHRASAL VB : V+O+ADV

knock off. 1 If someone **knocks** an amount **off** the price of something, they reduce the price by that amount. EG *He knocked £50 off the price, because it was slightly scratched.* **2** If someone **knocks** something **off**, they steal it. EG *He was planning to knock off a few videos that weekend.* **3** When people **knock off**, they finish work at the end of the day or before a break. EG *We knock off at 5.* PHRASAL VB : V+O+ADV/PREP; V+O+ADV Informal; V+ADV Informal

knock out. 1 If someone **knocks** you **out**, they make you unconscious by hitting you. EG *He hit me so hard he knocked me out.* **2** If a drug **knocks** you **out**, you become unconscious after taking it. EG *The tablet had knocked her out for four hours.* **3** If a person or team **is knocked out** of a competition, they are defeated in a game, so that they do not play any more games. **4** See also **knockout.** PHRASAL VB : V+O+ADV; V+O+ADV; V+O+ADV : OFT+*of*

knocker /nɒkə/, **knockers.** A **knocker** is a piece of metal attached to the door of a building, which you use to hit the door in order to attract the attention of the people inside. N COUNT

knock-on. If something has a **knock-on** effect, it causes a series of events to happen, one after another. EG *We need to find a solution that doesn't have so many knock-on effects.* ADJ CLASSIF : ATTRIB

knockout /nɒkaʊt/, **knockouts. 1** In boxing, a **knockout** is a blow that makes one of the boxers fall to the floor and not be able to stand up before the referee has counted to ten. EG *Davies won by a knockout.* N COUNT

2 A **knockout** competition is one in which the winner of each match goes on to the next round, until one competitor or team is the winner. ADJ CLASSIF : ATTRIB

knoll /nəʊl/, **knolls.** A **knoll** is a small hill. EG *...a grassy knoll on the outskirts of Waltham.* N COUNT Literary

knot /nɒt/, **knots, knotting, knotted. 1** A **knot** is a place in a piece of string, rope, or cloth where one end has been passed through a loop and pulled tight. You tie a knot in order to join two things together or to keep something firmly in place. EG *He had tied a crude knot... The knot of her headscarf hung beneath her chin.* N COUNT

2 If you **knot** a piece of string, rope, or cloth, you pass one end of it through a loop and pull it tight. ◇ **knotted.** EG *...a knotted handkerchief.* V+O ◇ ADJ CLASSIF

3 If you **knot** something around something else, you fasten it to it by tying a knot. EG *He knotted a towel about his neck... I set off with the rope knotted round my waist.* V+O+A

4 A **knot** of people is a group of them standing very close together. EG *...watched by a knot of sightseers.* N PART

5 If you say that you have a **knot** in your stomach, you mean that your stomach feels uncomfortable because you are anxious or afraid. EG *Gant felt the knot of tension harden in his stomach.* N COUNT+SUPP

6 A **knot** in a piece of wood is a small hard area where a branch used to grow. N COUNT

7 A **knot** is also a unit of speed. The speed of ships and aircraft is measured in knots. EG *...an underwater object moving at over 150 knots.* N COUNT

knotty /nɒti¹/. A **knotty** problem is difficult to solve. EG *He and Don had solved many a knotty problem in this room... ...a knotty question.* ADJ QUALIT : ATTRIB Informal

know /nəʊ/, **knows, knowing, knew** /nju:/, **known. 1** If you **know** something, you have it correctly in your mind. EG *I don't know her address... I knew that she had recently graduated from law school... We knew what to expect... No one knew how to repair it... 'Will they come back?' – 'I don't know.'* V+O; ALSO V : USU+REPORT, NO CONT, NO IMPER

2 If you **know** of something or **know** about it, you have heard about it. EG *Many people did not even know of their existence... Claud knew about the killing.* V+*of/about* : NO CONT, NO IMPER

3 If you **let** someone **know** about something, you tell them about it. EG *I'll find out about the car and let you know what happened.* PHRASE

4 If you **know** a language, you can understand it and speak it. EG *Shanti knew a few words of English.* V+O : NO CONT, NO IMPER

5 If you **know** about a subject, you have studied it and have some knowledge of it. EG *He knew about pictures... They knew a lot about films... I don't know much about physics, I'm afraid.* V OR V+O+*about* : NO CONT, NO IMPER

6 If you **know** someone, you have met them and talked to them. EG *Do you know David?* V+O : NO CONT

7 If you **know** a place or a thing, you are familiar with it. EG *He knew London well.* V+O : NO CONT

8 If you **get to know** a person or place, you find out what they are like. EG *I'd like the chance to get to know him.* PHRASE

9 You use **know** in the passive to say what people call someone or something. For example, if a forest **is known** as the Big Thicket, people call it the Big Thicket. V-PASS+*as*

10 If you **know better** than someone else, your ideas are more sensible or more correct than theirs. EG *The experts, who knew better, laughed at the idea.* PHRASE

11 If you say that someone ought to **know better**, you mean that they ought to behave in a more sensible and acceptable way. EG *Brian is old enough to know better.* PHRASE

12 If you say that a particular person **knows best**, you mean that they are always right about what should be done. EG *Parents always know best.* PHRASE

13 You say **'you know' 13.1** to emphasize or draw attention to what you are saying. EG *You were very naughty, you know... You know, most of the time he seems like a fool.* **13.2** to fill a gap in a conversation, for example when you are uncertain about what you are going to say next. EG *She thought a lot about her appearance, you know, and spent a lot of her money on clothes.* **13.3** to try to explain more clearly what you mean. EG *...the old desk. You know, the one that's broken.*

14 You say **'I know' 14.1** to indicate that you agree with what has just been said. EG *'It's quite extraordinary.' – 'I know.'* **14.2** to indicate that you realize or accept that something is true. EG *I get frightened in the night sometimes – it's silly, I know.* CONVENTION

15 You say **'You never know'** to indicate that, although it is uncertain what will happen, there is some hope that things might turn out well. EG *Well, I can't promise anything, but you never know.* CONVENTION

16 Some people say **'God knows'** or **'Heaven knows'** to emphasize that they do not know something. EG *God knows why they did it... What would he do with them? Heaven only knows.* CONVENTION OR PHRASE Informal

17 Someone who is **in the know** has information about something that only a few people have. PHRASE

18 See also **knowing, known.**

know-how. Someone who has **know-how** knows methods of doing something, especially something scientific or technical. EG *They now had the facilities and knowhow to produce advanced weapons.* N UNCOUNT Informal

knowing /nəʊɪŋ/. A **knowing** gesture or remark shows that you understand something, for example why someone has done something, even though it has not actually been mentioned directly. EG *This is usually greeted with deep sighs and knowing looks... ...a knowing smile.* ADJ CLASSIF : ATTRIB

knowingly /nəʊɪŋli¹/. **1** If you do something wrong **knowingly**, you do it knowing that it is wrong. EG *They knowingly broke laws that ban trade in rare reptiles.* ADV

2 If you look, smile, or wink **knowingly**, you do it in a way that shows that you understand something, even though it has not actually been mentioned directly. EG *The girls looked knowingly at each other.* ADV

knowledge /nɒlɪdʒ/. **1 Knowledge** is information and understanding about a subject, which someone has in their mind. EG *...advances in scientific knowledge... All knowledge comes to us through our senses... He is the only person I know with a real knowledge of income-tax legislation.* N UNCOUNT : USU+SUPP

2 If you say that something is true **to your knowledge**, you mean that you know that it is true. EG *Of these thirty-seven couples, thirty-five, to my knowledge, are still married.* ADV SEN

3 If you say that something is true **to the best of your knowledge**, you mean that you think that it is true, but you do not know definitely that it is true. EG *This is a play which to the best of my knowledge has never been performed in Britain.* ADV SEN

knowledgeable /nɒlɪdʒəbə⁰l/. You describe someone as **knowledgeable** when they know a lot about many different things or a lot about a particular subject. EG *He was surprisingly knowledgeable about what was going on in the theatre.* ADJ QUALIT

known /nəʊn/. **1 Known** is the past participle of **know.**

2 If something is **known** to people, they are aware of it and have information about it. EG *There's no known cure for a cold... ...the most dangerous substance known to man.* ADJ CLASSIF

3 If you **let it be known** that something is the case, you make sure that people know it, without telling them directly. EG *She let it be known that she wanted to leave China.* PHRASE Formal

4 See also **well-known.**

knuckle /nʌkə⁰l/, **knuckles.** Your **knuckles** are the rounded pieces of bone where your fingers join your hands, and where your fingers bend. EG *As he fell, he scraped the skin off his knuckles... Her hands were clasped so violently that the knuckles showed white.* N COUNT : USU PLURAL

Koran /kɔ:rɑ:n/. The **Koran** is the sacred book on which the religion of Islam is based. N PROPER : *the*+N

kosher /kəʊʃə/. **Kosher** food is approved of by the laws of Judaism. EG *They all buy kosher meat.* ADJ CLASSIF

kow-tow /kaʊ taʊ/, **kow-tows, kow-towing, kow-towed.** If you **kow-tow** to someone, you behave very humbly and respectfully towards them, especially because you hope to get something from them. EG *He rather resents having to kow-tow to anyone.* V : OFT+*to* Informal

L l

L, l /ɛl/, **Ls, l's. 1 L** is the twelfth letter of the English alphabet. N COUNT

2 L is the symbol for 'learner driver'. In Britain, a large red 'L' on a white background is attached to cars in which people are learning to drive.

3 L or **l** is also an abbreviation for 'litre'.

lab /læb/, **labs.** A **lab** is the same as a laboratory. EG *Your X-rays have just come back from the lab.* N COUNT Informal

label /leɪbə^{0}l/, **labels, labelling, labelled;** spelled **labeling** and **labeled in American English.**

1 A **label** is a piece of paper or plastic that is attached to an object to give information about it, for example to say what it is, who owns it, or how you should use it. EG *The bottles got wet and all the labels came off.* N COUNT

2 If you **label** something, you attach a label to it. EG *...the brown pot labelled 'Salt'.* V+O OR V+O+C

3 If people **label** you as something, they describe you or think of you in that way, even though you do not agree with their opinion; used showing disapproval. EG *I wasn't going to be labelled mad... Once you are labelled as a secretary you will never become anything else... His behaviour is labelled deviant.* ▸ used as a noun. EG *He was not willing to accept the label of anarchist.* V+O : OFT+*as* OR V+O+C ▸ N COUNT +SUPP

labor /leɪbə/. See **labour**.

laboratory /lə^{3}bɒrətə^{0}ri^1/, laboratories. A **laboratory** is **1** a building or a room that contains special scientific equipment. Scientists use laboratories to do experiments or for research. EG *The geologists took the samples back to the laboratory.* **2** a room in a school or university which contains scientific equipment, and where students are taught about science subjects such as chemistry. ● See also **language laboratory**. N COUNT

laborious /lə^{3}bɔːriəs/. Something that is **laborious** takes a lot of effort. EG *Clearing the forest is a laborious business.* ◊ **laboriously.** EG *...laboriously hand-written books.* ADJ QUALIT ◊ ADV

labour /leɪbə/, **labours, labouring, laboured;** spelled **labor** in American English.

1 Labour is very hard work, especially work that does not need a lot of skill. EG *I really enjoy manual labour... ...a pleasant distraction from his political labours.* ● If you do something as a **labour of love,** you do it because you really want to, even though it involves hard work and you will get no reward for it. N UNCOUNT OR N COUNT ● PHRASE

2 People who **labour** work hard using their hands. EG *He was sent to labour as a peasant in a commune.* V : USU+A Formal

3 If you **labour** at something, you do it with difficulty. EG *Tim had laboured over a letter to Gertrude.* ◊ **laboured.** EG *McKellen's breathing was laboured.* V+A ◊ ADJ QUALIT

4 Labour is used to refer to **4.1** the workers of a country or industry, considered as a group. EG *...a shortage of skilled labour.* **4.2** the work done by a group of workers. EG *They are threatening a withdrawal of labour in support of their claims.* N UNCOUNT

5 If you **labour** under a delusion or misapprehension, you continue to believe something which is not true. EG *He laboured under the misapprehension that nobody liked him.* V+*under*

6 If you **labour** a point or an argument, you talk about it in great and unnecessary detail. EG *There is no need to labour the point.* V+O

7 Labour is also the last stage of pregnancy, in which the baby is gradually pushed out of the womb by the mother. EG *She was in labour for seven hours.* N UNCOUNT

labourer /leɪbə^{0}rə/, **labourers.** A **labourer** is a person who does a job which involves a lot of hard physical work. EG *...a farm labourer.* N COUNT

labyrinth /læbə^{1}rɪnθ/, **labyrinths.** A **labyrinth** is a complicated series of narrow corridors or streets, through which it is difficult to find your way. EG *He wandered through the labyrinths of the Old Town.* N COUNT

lace /leɪs/, **laces, lacing, laced. 1 Lace** is very delicate cloth which is made with a lot of holes in it. EG *...a white lace handkerchief.* N UNCOUNT

2 Laces are pieces of cord or string that are put through holes along the two edges of something and tied in order to fasten the two edges together. EG *He spent ten minutes tying the laces of his shoes.* N COUNT : USU PLURAL

3 If you **lace** food or drink with alcohol or a drug, you put a small amount of it into the food or drink. EG *...coffee laced with brandy.* V+O : OFT+*with*

lace up. If you **lace** something **up**, you fasten it by pulling two ends of a lace tight and tying them together. EG *He bent and laced up his shoes.* PHRASAL VB : V+O+ADV

lacerate /læsəreɪt/, **lacerates, lacerating, lacerated.** If something **lacerates** your skin, it cuts it deeply. ◊ **lacerated.** EG *I could not shave my lacerated face.* ◊ **laceration** /læsə^{0}reɪʃə^{0}n/, **lacerations.** EG *The pain of my lacerations had become less.* V+O ◊ ADJ CLASSIF ◊ N COUNT

lace-up, lace-ups. Lace-ups or **lace-up** shoes are shoes which are fastened with laces. N COUNT : USU PLURAL

lack /læk/, **lacks, lacking, lacked. 1** If there is a **lack** of something, there is not enough of it, or there is none at all. EG *I hated the lack of privacy in the dormitory... Lack of proper funding is making our job more difficult.* N SING OR N UNCOUNT : USU+*of*

2 If something happens **for** or **through lack of** something, it happens because there is not enough of it. EG *His department was shut down for lack of funds.* PHRASE

3 If you say that there is **no lack of** something, you mean that there is a great deal of it, and perhaps more than you need. EG *There was no lack of schools to choose from.* PHRASE

4 If you **lack** something, you do not have it. EG *They lack the confidence to make friends... The advertisement lacks any individuality.* V+O

5 If you say that something **is lacking**, you mean that it does not exist, or there is not enough of it. EG *'What is lacking in this case,' he concluded, 'is a corpse.'* V : ONLY CONT

6 If someone or something is **lacking** in a particular quality, they do not have it or do not have enough of it. EG *Philip was not lacking in intelligence or ability.* ADJ PRED+*in*

lackey /læki^1/, **lackeys.** If you call someone a **lackey**, you mean that they follow someone's orders completely, without ever questioning them; used showing disapproval. EG *They said that the police were lackeys of the Establishment.* N COUNT

laconic /lə^{3}kɒnɪk/. Someone who is **laconic** uses very few words to say something, so that they seem very casual. EG *...the laconic entries in his diary.* ◊ **laconically.** EG *Sam was laconically directed to an office in a nearby street.* ADJ QUALIT ◊ ADV

lacquer /lækə/, **lacquers, lacquering, lacquered. 1 Lacquer** is **1.1** a special type of paint which is put on wood or metal in order to protect it and make it shiny. EG *The red lacquer work on the upper walls was badly chipped.* **1.2** a liquid which some women put on their hair to hold their hairstyle neatly in place. N MASS

2 If you **lacquer** wood or metal, you cover it with V+O

lacquer in order to protect it and make it shiny.
◊ **lacquered.** EG *...a lacquered box.* ◊ ADJ CLASSIF

lacy /leɪsi[1]/. Something that is **lacy** is made from lace or has pieces of lace attached to it. EG *...a lacy dress... She was propped up against lacy pillows.* ADJ CLASSIF

lad /læd/, **lads.** A **lad** is a boy or young man. EG *He used to collect stamps when he was a lad.* N COUNT

ladder /lædə/, **ladders. 1** A **ladder** is a piece of equipment used for climbing up something such as a wall or a tree. It consists of two long pieces of wood, metal, or rope with steps fixed between them. N COUNT

2 When someone keeps moving to higher levels in a society or an organization, you can refer to their progress as a **ladder**. EG *Joining the golf club takes you up the social ladder a little bit more.* N SING : the+N

3 A **ladder** in a pair of tights or stockings is a torn part where some of the vertical threads have broken, leaving only the horizontal threads. N COUNT

laden /leɪdə[0]n/. If someone is holding or carrying a lot of heavy things, you can say that they are **laden** with them. EG *Ken arrived laden with presents... The trees were laden with fruit.* ADJ CLASSIF : USU PRED+*with* Literary

ladle /leɪdə[0]l/, **ladles, ladling, ladled. 1** A **ladle** is a large, round, deep spoon with a long handle, used for putting food such as soup or stew into bowls. N COUNT

2 If you **ladle** food such as soup or stew, you serve it using a large spoon such as a ladle. EG *'Plenty here,' said the man, ladling the soup into bowls.* V+O : USU+A

lady /leɪdi[1]/, **ladies. 1** You can use **lady** as a polite way of referring to a woman. EG *...a rich American lady... ...a little old lady... ...a lady novelist... ...elderly ladies living on their own.* N COUNT

2 You can say **'ladies'** when you are addressing a group of women. EG *'Ladies,' George appealed, 'Could I have your attention, please?'... Good evening, ladies and gentlemen.* VOCATIVE

3 If you say that a woman is a **lady**, you mean that she behaves in a polite, dignified, and graceful way. EG *Many of the farmers' wives were trying to be ladies.* N COUNT Outdated

4 A **lady** is a woman from the upper classes. EG *I rode in her carriage like a lady... The lords and ladies are all gathered at the palace.* N COUNT

5 Lady is a title used in front of the names of some women from the upper classes. EG *...Lady Diana Cooper.*

6 A **ladies** is a public toilet for women. EG *Where's the ladies, please?* N SING : USU the+N

7 Ladies' or **lady's** is used to describe something that belongs to girls or women, or something that is done or used by them. EG *She sang in a ladies' choir... ...Mellifont Ladies' College.* ADJ CLASSIF : ATTRIB

ladylike /leɪdi[1]laɪk/. If you say that a woman or girl is **ladylike**, you mean that she behaves in a polite, dignified, and graceful way. EG *She took little ladylike sips of the cold drink.* ADJ QUALIT

lag /læg/, **lags, lagging, lagged. 1** If you **lag** behind someone or something, you move or progress more slowly than they do. EG *He set off at a brisk walk, Kate lagging behind... Britain's economic development must lag behind that of almost every other industrial nation.* V : OFT *behind*

2 When something such as trade or investment **lags**, there is less of it than there was before. EG *Production lagged and unemployment rose.* V : OFT *behind*

3 A time **lag** is a period of time between two related events. EG *There will be a one-year lag between the time I write this book and its publication... ...a small time lag.* N COUNT+SUPP

4 If you **lag** a pipe, a hot water tank, or the inside of a roof, you cover it with a special material to prevent heat escaping from it. V+O

lager /lɑːgə/, **lagers. Lager** is a kind of light beer. EG *...a bottle of ice-cold lager.* N MASS

lagoon /lə[3]guːn/, **lagoons.** A **lagoon** is an area of calm sea water that is separated from the ocean by reefs or sand. N COUNT

laid /leɪd/ is the past tense and past participle of **lay.**

laid up. If you are **laid up**, you have to stay in bed because you are ill. EG *He had been laid up for five days with a bad cold.* ADJ CLASSIF

lain /leɪn/ is the past participle of **lie** in some of its meanings.

lair /lɛə/, **lairs.** A **lair** is a place where a wild animal lives, usually a place which is underground or well-hidden. EG *...animals that refuse to come out of their lairs.* N COUNT

lake /leɪk/, **lakes.** A **lake** is a large area of fresh water, surrounded by land. N COUNT

lamb /læm/, **lambs. 1** A **lamb** is a young sheep. N COUNT

2 Lamb is the flesh of a sheep or lamb eaten as food. EG *...roast lamb.* N UNCOUNT

lame /leɪm/. **1** If you are **lame**, you are unable to walk properly because an injury or illness has damaged one or both of your legs. EG *The illness left her permanently lame... ...a lame horse.* ADJ QUALIT

2 If you describe an excuse, argument, or remark as **lame**, you mean that it is poor or weak. EG *My lame excuse was that I had too much else to do.* ADJ QUALIT

◊ **lamely.** EG *'I didn't recognize you,' Claude said lamely.* ◊ ADV

lament /ləment/, **laments, lamenting, lamented.** If you **lament** something, you express your sadness or regret about it. EG *He laments the changing pattern of life in the countryside.* ▸ used as a noun. EG *'It's a dying industry,' is his lament.* V-SPEECH OR V Literary ▸ N COUNT

lamentable /ləmentəbə[0]l, læməntəbə[0]l/. If you describe something as **lamentable**, you mean that it is very unfortunate or disappointing. EG *...the lamentable state of the industry in the Sixties.* ADJ CLASSIF : USU ATTRIB Formal

◊ **lamentably.** EG *...the lamentably inadequate plans for retraining officers.* ◊ SUBMOD OR ADV SEN

lamp /læmp/, **lamps.** A **lamp** is a device which produces light by using electricity or by burning oil or gas. EG *She turned on the bedside lamp... ...the street lamp outside Mrs Flanagan's house.* N COUNT

lamp-post, lamp-posts. A **lamp-post** is a tall metal or concrete pole beside a road with a light at the top. N COUNT

lampshade /læmpʃeɪd/, **lampshades.** A **lampshade** is a covering that is fitted round an electric light bulb in order to decorate it and make the light less harsh. N COUNT

land /lænd/, **lands, landing, landed. 1 Land** is an area of ground with few or no buildings on it. EG *It's good agricultural land... ...a piece of land.* N UNCOUNT

2 If you refer to someone's **land** or **lands**, you mean an area of land which they own. N COUNT+POSS

3 Land or the **land** refers to the part of the world that is solid ground rather than sea or air. EG *We turned away from land and headed out to sea.* N UNCOUNT, OR N SING : the+N

4 A particular **land** is a particular country. EG *...a land where there is never any rain... Australia is the land of opportunities.* N COUNT : USU+SUPP Literary

5 If someone or something **lands** somewhere, **5.1** they come down to the ground or in water after moving through the air. EG *The last man slipped and landed in the water.* **5.2** they arrive there after a journey by air. EG *His plane lands at six-thirty.* V : USU+A

6 To **land** people or goods somewhere means to unload them there at the end of a journey, especially a journey by ship. V+O : USU+A

7 If you **land** in an unpleasant situation or if something **lands** you in it, you come to be in it. EG *That would have landed him in jail.* V-ERG+A Informal

8 If you **land** someone with something that causes difficulties, you cause them to have to deal with it. EG *...when a clergyman is landed with a huge rectory... You landed us with that awful man.* V+O+*with* Informal

land up. If you **land up** in a particular place or situation, you arrive in it after a long journey or at PHRASAL VB : V+ADV, OFT+A

Is your country landlocked?

the end of a long series of events. EG *She landed up in Rome.*

landed /lændɪ[2]d/. **Landed** people own a lot of land. EG *...landed gentry.* ADJ CLASSIF : ATTRIB

landing /lændɪŋ/, **landings. 1** In a house or other building, a **landing** is an area at the top of a staircase, with rooms leading off it. N COUNT

2 A **landing** is also a place with a wooden platform where boats stop to let people get on or off. N COUNT

3 When the pilot of an aircraft makes a **landing**, he brings the aircraft down to the ground. EG *We had to make an emergency landing.* N COUNT OR N UNCOUNT

landlady /lændleɪdi[1]/, **landladies.** A **landlady** is **1** a woman who owns a house, flat, or room that other people live in, in return for payment of rent. **2** a woman who owns or runs a pub. N COUNT

landlocked /lændlɒkt/. A country that is **landlocked** is surrounded by other countries and does not have its own sea coast. ADJ CLASSIF

landlord /lændlɔːd/, **landlords.** A **landlord** is **1** a man who owns a house, flat, or room that other people live in, in return for payment of rent. **2** a man who owns or runs a pub. N COUNT

landmark /lændmɑːk/, **landmarks. 1** A **landmark** is a building or feature of the land which is easily noticed and which you can use to judge your position. EG *The Chamberlain tower is a landmark visible for miles.* N COUNT

2 You can also refer to an important stage in the development of something as a **landmark**. EG *The discovery of penicillin was a landmark in medicine.* N COUNT : USU+SUPP

landscape /lændskeɪp/, **landscapes, landscaping, landscaped. 1** The **landscape** is everything that you can see when you look across an area of land, including hills, rivers, buildings, and trees. EG *...the beauty of the Welsh landscape.* N COUNT

2 A **landscape** is a painting which shows a scene in the countryside. EG *She painted landscapes and portraits.* N COUNT

3 If you **landscape** an area of land, you alter it by planting trees and bushes there to produce a pleasing effect. EG *...landscaped grounds.* V+O

landslide /lændslaɪd/, **landslides. 1** In an election, a **landslide** is a victory in which a person or political party gets far more votes or seats than their opponents. EG *Taylor should win by a landslide... ...a landslide victory.* N COUNT

2 A **landslide** is also a large amount of earth and rocks falling down a cliff or down the side of a mountain. EG *The slightest noise might set off a landslide.* N COUNT

lane /leɪn/, **lanes. 1** A **lane** is a narrow road in the country. EG *She turned and went back down the lane... ...Park Lane.* N COUNT

2 Roads, race courses, and swimming pools are sometimes divided into **lanes**. These are parallel strips separated from each other by lines or ropes. EG *He changed lanes to make a left turn.* N COUNT

language /læŋgwɪdʒ/, **languages. 1** A **language** is a system of communication which consists of a set of sounds and written symbols which are used by the people of a particular country for talking or writing. EG *...the English language... ...a foreign language... I can speak six languages.* N COUNT

2 Language is the ability to use words in order to communicate. Human beings have this ability but animals do not. EG *This research helps teachers to understand how children acquire language.* N UNCOUNT

3 You can refer to the words used in connection with a particular subject as the **language** of that subject. EG *...the language of sociology.* N UNCOUNT +SUPP

4 When you talk about the **language** of a piece of writing or a speech, you are referring to the style in which it is written or spoken. EG *I admire the directness of the language.* N UNCOUNT

5 Language is also used to refer to other means of communication such as sign language, computer languages, and animal language. N UNCOUNT OR N COUNT

language laboratory, language laboratories. A **language laboratory** is a room in a college or school in which people can learn to improve their knowledge of languages by listening to tape recordings, recording their own voices, and having their mistakes corrected. N COUNT

languid /læŋgwɪd/. Someone who is **languid** shows little energy or interest and is slow and casual in their movements. EG *...a languid wave of the hand.* ◇ **languidly.** EG *He looked up languidly.* ADJ QUALIT Literary ◇ ADV

languish /læŋgwɪʃ/, **languishes, languishing, languished.** You say that people **languish** when they are forced to remain and suffer in an unpleasant situation. EG *A few people enjoyed rich lifestyles while the majority languished in poverty.* V : USU+A Literary

languor /læŋgə/ is a feeling of not having any energy or interest in anything. EG *...the languor of the summer afternoon.* N UNCOUNT Literary

lanky /læŋki[1]/. Someone who is **lanky** is tall and thin and moves rather awkwardly. EG *Quentin was a lanky boy with long skinny legs.* ADJ QUALIT

lantern /læntən/, **lanterns.** A **lantern** is a lamp consisting of a metal frame with glass sides and an oil lamp or candle inside. Lanterns were used in former times. N COUNT

lap /læp/, **laps, lapping, lapped. 1** Your **lap** is the flat area formed by your thighs when you are sitting down. EG *Her youngest child was asleep in her lap... He placed the baby on the woman's lap.* N COUNT+POSS

2 In a race, you say that a competitor has completed a **lap** when he or she has gone round the course once. N COUNT

3 If you **lap** another competitor in a race, you pass them while they are still on the previous lap. V+O

4 When water **laps** against something, it touches it gently and makes a soft sound. EG *Waves lapped against the side of the boat.* V+A OR V+O

5 When an animal **laps**, it drinks. EG *The cat was lapping at a saucer of milk.* V+O OR V+A

lap up. 1 When an animal **laps up** a drink, it drinks it up very eagerly. EG *The cat was lapping up the milk as if it had not fed for days.* **2** If someone **laps up** information or attention, they accept it eagerly, often when it is not really true or sincere. EG *It was a lie, but millions of newspaper readers lapped it up.* PHRASAL VB : V+O+ADV V+O+ADV

lapel /lə[3]pel/, **lapels.** The **lapels** of a jacket or coat are the two parts at the front that are folded back on each side and join on to the collar. N COUNT

lapse /læps/, **lapses, lapsing, lapsed. 1** A **lapse** is an unexpected piece of bad behaviour by someone who usually behaves well. EG *I intended to make up for this lapse in manners at the next party.* N COUNT

2 If you have a **lapse** of memory or a **lapse** of concentration, you forget to do something or fail to concentrate on something. N COUNT+SUPP

3 If you **lapse** into a particular kind of behaviour, you start behaving that way. EG *He lapsed into an unhappy silence... She keeps lapsing into jargon.* V+*into*

4 A **lapse** of time is a period of time that is long enough for a situation to change. EG *After a certain lapse of time it would be safe for Daisy to return... He was not conscious of the time lapse.* ▸ used as a verb. EG *Hours lapsed between each phone call.* N SING+SUPP ▸ V

5 If a situation, relationship, or legal contract **lapses**, it is allowed to end or to become invalid rather than being continued. EG *...traditions which had never lapsed... He allowed his membership of the union to lapse.* V

larch /lɑːtʃ/, **larches.** A **larch** is a tree with needle-shaped leaves. N COUNT

lard /lɑːd/ is soft white fat obtained from pigs. It is used in cooking. N UNCOUNT

larder /lɑːdə/, **larders.** A **larder** is a room or cupboard in which food is kept. EG *...a well-stocked larder... Some cheese had vanished from the larder.* N COUNT

large /lɑːdʒ/, **larger, largest. 1** Something that is **large** is greater in size or amount than is usual or average. EG *...a large house... ...a large and well equipped army... She made a very large amount of money.* ADJ QUALIT

2 You use **by and large** to indicate that a statement is mostly true but is not completely true. EG *By and large, they were free to do as they wished.* ADV SEN

3 You use **at large** to indicate that you are talking about most of the people mentioned. EG *There has been unrest in the country at large.* PHRASE

4 If you say that a dangerous person or animal is **at large**, you mean that they have escaped and have not yet been captured. PHRASE

largely /lɑːdʒli¹/. **1** You use **largely** to say that a statement is mostly true but is not completely true. EG *The evidence shows them to be largely correct... Her work is largely confined to the cinema.* ADV

2 You also use **largely** to introduce the main reason for an event or situation. EG *We were there largely because of the girls... He was acquitted, largely on the evidence of a tape recording.* ADV OR ADV SEN

large-scale. 1 A **large-scale** action or event happens over a wide area or involves a lot of people or things. EG *...large-scale forest fires... ...a large-scale farming operation.* ADJ QUALIT : ATTRIB

2 A **large-scale** map or diagram represents a small area of land or a building or a machine on a scale that is large enough for small details to be shown. ADJ QUALIT : ATTRIB

lark /lɑːk/, **larks, larking, larked. 1** A **lark** is a small brown bird that has a pleasant song. N COUNT

2 If you do something for a **lark**, you do it because you think it is amusing, rather than for any serious purpose. EG *For a lark, she walked in and asked his name... To me the whole thing was just a lark.* N COUNT Informal British

lark about. If you **lark about**, you enjoy yourself doing silly things. PHRASAL VB : V+ADV

larva /lɑːvə/, **larvae** /lɑːviː/. A **larva** is an insect at the stage of its life when it looks like a short, fat worm. This is the stage after it has developed from an egg and before it changes into an adult. N COUNT

lascivious /ləsɪvɪəs/. **Lascivious** people have a strong desire for sex. EG *He wanted to protect Frances from unscrupulous or lascivious men.* ADJ QUALIT

laser /leɪzə/, **lasers.** A **laser** is a narrow beam of concentrated light that is used especially for cutting very hard materials and in surgery. Lasers are produced by special machines which are also called **lasers**. EG *A laser beam would cut into it... ...experiments with laser weapons.* N COUNT

lash /læʃ/, **lashes, lashing, lashed. 1** Your **lashes** are the hairs that grow on the edge of your eyelids. N PLURAL

2 A **lash** is **2.1** the thin strip of leather at the end of a whip. EG *He gasped as the lash hit him.* **2.2** a blow with a whip on someone's back as a punishment. EG *...a public flogging of thirty-nine lashes.* N COUNT

3 If someone **lashes** you, they hit you with a whip. V+O

4 If the wind or rain **lashes** something, it hits it violently. EG *High winds lashed the branches of the elm.* V+O OR V+A Literary

5 If you **lash** one thing to another, you tie them firmly together. EG *We lashed our boats together.* V+O+*to/together*

lash out. 1 If you **lash out**, you try to hit someone with your hands or feet or with a weapon. EG *When cornered, they lash out with savage kicks.* PHRASAL VB : V+ADV

2 You can also say that someone **lashes out** when they criticize or scold people in an angry way. EG *Harris lashed out against the Committee.* V+ADV, USU+*at/against*

lass /læs/, **lasses.** In some parts of Britain, a young woman or girl is referred to as a **lass**. EG *She'd worked on the farm as a lass.* N COUNT

last /lɑːst/, **lasts, lasting, lasted. 1** You use **last** to describe the most recent period of time, event, or thing. EG *I went to a party last night... ...the last four years... Thanks for your last letter.* ORDINAL

2 The **last** thing or part is **2.1** the one that comes at the end. EG *He missed the last bus... I saw the last five minutes of it... Hooper was the last to leave.* **2.2** the one at the end of a row of things. EG *...the last classroom along that passage... ...the last of a string of islands.* **2.3** the only one that remains. EG *She removed the last traces of make-up... Otto drank the last of the brandy.* ORDINAL

3 You can use **last** to emphasize that you do not want to do something or that something is unlikely to happen or be true. EG *The last thing I want to do is offend you... I would be the last to suggest that.* ORDINAL

4 If something **last** happened on a particular occasion, it has not happened since then. EG *They last saw their homeland nine years ago.* ADV

5 If something happens **last**, it happens after everything else. EG *He added the milk last.* ADV

6 If something **lasts**, **6.1** it continues to exist or happen. EG *His speech lasted for exactly fourteen minutes... Profits are as high as ever. It won't last.* **6.2** it continues to be in good condition. EG *A fresh pepper lasts about three weeks.* V : USU+A

7 If a quantity of something **lasts** for a period of time, there is enough of it for someone to use during that period. EG *A cheap box of toothpowder lasts two years... He had only £8 left to last him till he reached Bury.* V+A OR V+O+A

8 Last is also used in these phrases. **8.1** You use **before last** to refer to the thing, event, or person immediately before the most recent one. For example, the year **before last** was the one before the most recent one. **8.2** You use **last but** with a number when referring to a thing that comes before the final one in a series. For example, there are two things after the **last** thing **but** two. EG *...during the last day but one of the trial.* **8.3** You use **the last** to indicate that something did not happen or exist again after a particular time, or that it will never happen or exist again. EG *That was the last I ever saw of Northcliffe.* **8.4** If something happens **last thing**, it happens at the end of a period of time. EG *...the sink where we all had to wash last thing at night.* **8.5** If you **leave** something **till last**, you deal with it after everything else. **8.6** You use expressions such as **to the last detail** or **to the last man** to emphasize that you are including every single thing or person. EG *The robbery was planned down to the last detail... State the actual amount down to the last 10p.* PHRASES

9 At last is used in these ways. **9.1** If you say that something has happened **at last** or **at long last**, you mean it has happened after you have been waiting for it for a long time. EG *I'm free at last... At long last I've found a girl that really loves me.* **9.2 At last** also means at the end of a long period of time. EG *At last Ralph stopped work and stood up.* PHRASE Literary

last-ditch. You can refer to your final attempt to do something that you have previously failed to do as a **last-ditch** attempt. EG *The Treasury made a last-ditch attempt to intervene.* ADJ CLASSIF : ATTRIB

lasting /lɑːstɪŋ/. Something that is **lasting** continues to exist or to have an effect for a very long time. EG *This may provide a lasting solution to our problems... ...lasting friendships.* ADJ CLASSIF : ATTRIB

lastly /lɑːstli¹/. You use **lastly 1** when you want to make a final point that is connected with the other ones you have already mentioned. EG *Lastly, I would like to ask you about your future plans.* **2** when you are saying what happens after everything else in a series of actions or events. EG *Lastly he jabbed the knife into the trunk of the tree.* ADV SEN / ADV

last-minute. A **last-minute** action is done just before something else happens, usually before something important which is planned to happen at a fixed time. EG *...a last-minute attempt to stop the school being closed... We have some last-minute details to talk over.* ADJ CLASSIF : ATTRIB

Do Latin Americans speak Latin?

latch /lætʃ/, **latches, latching, latched.** 1 A **latch** is a fastening on a door or gate. It consists of a metal bar which is held in place to lock the door and which you lift in order to open the door. N COUNT

2 If you **latch** a door or gate, you fasten it by means of a latch. ◇ **latched.** EG *Both doors were open and latched in position.* V+O ◇ ADJ CLASSIF

3 If a door with a lock that locks automatically is **on the latch**, the lock has been set so that it does not lock automatically when you shut the door. EG *He closed the door and left it on the latch in case Tom had forgotten his key.* PHRASE

latch onto. If you **latch onto** someone or something, you become very involved with them, because you are interested in them or find them useful. EG *She latched onto someone with a family business.* PHRASAL VB : V+PREP, HAS PASS Informal

late /leɪt/, **later, latest.** 1 **Late** means near the end of a period of time, a process, or a piece of work. EG *Very late at night, I got a phone call... Decker arrived in late September... ...Picasso's late work... ...in the late afternoon... ...late in 1952.* ADV OR ADJ QUALIT : ATTRIB

2 If you are **late** for something or if you arrive **late**, you arrive after the time that was arranged. EG *I was ten minutes late for my appointment... I apologise for my late arrival.* ADJ QUALIT : OFT ATTRIB, OR ADV

3 If it is **too late** for something, that thing is no longer possible or useful. If something happens **too late**, the right time for it has passed. EG *It's too late to change that now... I realized my mistake too late.* PHRASE

4 You use **late** to describe things that happen after the normal time. EG *We had a late lunch at the hotel... ...if you get up late.* ADJ QUALIT OR ADV

5 **As late as** means at a particular time or period that is surprisingly late. EG *Even as late as 1950 coal provided over 90% of our energy.* PREP

6 You use **late** when you are talking about someone who is dead, especially someone who has died recently. EG *...the late Harry Truman.* ADJ CLASSIF : ATTRIB

7 Something that has been happening **of late** has been happening recently. EG *My wife has been rather tired of late.* PHRASE Formal

8 See also **later, latest.**

latecomer /leɪtkʌmə/, **latecomers.** A **latecomer** is someone who arrives after the time that they should have arrived. N COUNT

lately /leɪtli¹/. If something has happened **lately**, it has happened recently. EG *John has seemed worried lately.* ADV

latent /leɪtənt/ is used to describe something which is hidden and not obvious at the moment, but which may develop further in the future. EG *I believe that everyone has a latent mathematical ability.* ADJ CLASSIF

later /leɪtə/. 1 **Later** is the comparative of **late**.

2 You use **later** or **later on** to refer to a time or situation that is after the one that you have been talking about or after the present one. EG *I returned four weeks later... Later on this evening, we shall have some music... See you later... We will discuss this in more detail in a later chapter.* ADV OR ADJ CLASSIF : ATTRIB

3 You also use **later** to refer to the last part of someone's life or to the last part of a period of time. EG *This may cause illness in later life... ...the later eighteenth century.* ADJ CLASSIF : ATTRIB

lateral /lætə⁰rəl/ is used to describe something which relates to the sides of something, or to describe a sideways movement. EG *All of these primitive sea creatures had well developed lateral fins.* ADJ CLASSIF : ATTRIB

latest /leɪtɪ²st/. 1 **Latest** is the superlative of **late**.

2 You use **latest** to describe something that is the most recent thing of its kind. EG *...the latest news... ...her latest book... ...the latest fashions from Paris.* ADJ QUALIT : SUPERL

3 You use **at the latest** to emphasize that something must happen at or before a particular time and not after that time. EG *Changes will become necessary by the autumn at the latest.* PHRASE

lathe /leɪð/, **lathes.** A **lathe** is a machine which is used for shaping wood or metal. It works by turning the wood or metal continually against a tool which cuts it. N COUNT

lather /lɑːðə/, **lathers, lathering, lathered.** 1 **Lather** is a white mass of bubbles which is produced by mixing soap or washing powder with water. EG *It is important when washing clothes to maintain a good lather throughout the wash.* N SING OR N UNCOUNT

2 If you **lather** something, you rub soap or washing powder into it or on it until a lather is produced, in order to clean it. EG *Lather the carpet with a sponge and rub gently until the stain has gone.* V+O

Latin /lætɪn/. 1 **Latin** is the language which the ancient Romans used to speak. N UNCOUNT

2 **Latin** is used to refer to people who come from the countries where French, Italian, Spanish, and Portuguese are spoken. EG *He had Latin blood... ...the Latin nations.* ADJ CLASSIF

Latin American, Latin Americans. 1 **Latin American** means relating or belonging to the countries of South and Central America. EG *...Latin American countries.* ADJ CLASSIF

2 A **Latin American** is someone who lives in or comes from South or Central America. N COUNT

latitude /lætɪtjuːd/, **latitudes.** 1 The **latitude** of a place is its distance to the north or south of the Equator: compare **longitude**. EG *We are at the precise latitude of Corfu.* N COUNT OR N UNCOUNT

2 **Latitude** is freedom to choose the way in which you do something. EG *She was given considerable latitude in how she spent the money.* N UNCOUNT Formal

latrine /lətriːn/, **latrines.** A **latrine** is a hole in the ground which is used as a toilet, for example when you are camping. N COUNT

latter /lætə/. 1 When two people, things, or groups have just been mentioned, you refer to the one that was mentioned second as the **latter**. EG *They were eating sandwiches and little iced cakes, (the latter obtained from Mrs Kaul's bakery).* ▸ used as an adjective. EG *The novel was made into a film in 1943 and again in 1967: I prefer the latter version to the former.* N SING OR N PLURAL : the+N ▸ ADJ CLASSIF

2 You use **latter** to describe the second part of a period of time. EG *By the latter half of July the total was well over two million.* ADJ CLASSIF

3 **Latter** also means recent. EG *He was the sort of admirer she had been having in these latter years.* ◇ **latterly.** EG *I have found that latterly this rapport is getting less and less.* ADJ CLASSIF : ATTRIB ◇ ADV Formal

latter-day is used to describe something or someone that is a modern equivalent of something or someone in the past. EG *...the latter-day martyr, Edith Cavell.* ADJ CLASSIF : ATTRIB

lattice /lætɪs/, **lattices.** A **lattice** is a pattern or structure made of strips which cross over each other diagonally leaving holes in between. A lattice can be used as a framework or as a decoration. EG *Their houses are in traditional style of clay over a lattice of bamboo.* N COUNT

laudable /lɔːdəbə⁰l/. If you describe something as **laudable**, you mean that it deserves to be praised or admired. EG *The programme was inspired by laudable motives of improving housing conditions.* ADJ QUALIT Formal

laugh /lɑːf/, **laughs, laughing, laughed.** 1 When you **laugh**, you make the sound by which people show that they are happy or amused. EG *He grinned, then started to laugh... The young men laughed at his jokes.* ▸ used as a noun. EG *'Hurry up,' said Tony with a laugh... It was a terrible laugh, very quiet and intense.* V ▸ N COUNT

2 **Laugh** is used in these expressions. **2.1** If you **laugh** your **head off**, you laugh very loudly for a long time. **2.2** If you **laugh out loud** or **laugh aloud**, you laugh loudly at something, especially when this is an unusual thing to do, for example when you are on your own. EG *It's rare to come across any book which makes you laugh out loud.* **2.3** When comedians **get** or **raise a laugh**, they PHRASES Informal

succeed in making their audience laugh. EG *His act would always get a huge laugh.* **2.4** If you do something **for a laugh** or **for laughs**, you do it as a joke or for fun. EG *I gave him the wrong address just for a laugh.* **2.5** If someone **has the last laugh**, they succeed after appearing to have been defeated. EG *Henry had outlived all the others to have the last laugh.* — Informal

laugh at. If you **laugh at** someone or something, you mock them or make jokes about them. EG *I don't think it's nice to laugh at people's disabilities.* — PHRASAL VB : V+PREP, HAS PASS

laugh off. If you **laugh off** a serious situation, you try to suggest that it is amusing and unimportant, for example by making a joke about it. EG *Despite being in trouble with the Government, Northcliffe attempted to laugh the matter off.* — PHRASAL VB : V+O+ADV

laughable /lɑːfəbə⁰l/. You say that something is **laughable** when it seems amusing because it is so obviously unsuccessful, foolish, or poor in quality. EG *It's almost laughable to talk about a 'policy'.* — ADJ QUALIT
◇ **laughably.** EG *They appear almost laughably pompous.* — ◇ ADV

laughing stock. If someone is a **laughing stock**, they have been made to seem ridiculous. EG *Arthur was the laughing stock of the neighbourhood.* — N SING

laughter /lɑːftə/ is the act of laughing, or the sound of people laughing. EG *Mr Evans heard laughter and applause as the speaker ceased... We roared with laughter.* — N UNCOUNT

launch /lɔːntʃ/, **launches, launching, launched.**
1 When a ship **is launched**, it is put into water for the first time. — V+O : OFT PASS
2 To **launch** a rocket, missile, or satellite means to send it into the air or into space. EG *Soviet rockets launched more satellites into orbit.* ▸ used as a noun. EG *They gave only a few minutes' warning of the missile launch.* — V+O; ▸ N COUNT
3 To **launch** a large and important activity, for example a political movement or a military attack, means to start it. EG *The government has launched a massive literacy campaign... Guerrilla attacks were launched against the police.* — V+O
4 If a company **launches** a new product, it starts to make it available to the public. EG *A magazine called 'The Week' was launched in January 1964.* ▸ used as a noun. EG *We are already selling millions of copies just one year after the launch.* — V+O; ▸ N COUNT
5 A **launch** is a large motor-boat. — N COUNT

launch into. If you **launch into** a speech, fight, or other activity, you start it enthusiastically. EG *He launched into a long speech about the dangers of taking drugs.* — PHRASAL VB : V+PREP, HAS PASS

launder /lɔːndə/, **launders, laundering, laundered.** When you **launder** clothes, sheets, and towels, you wash and iron them. — V+O, Outdated

launderette /lɔːndə⁰rɛt/, **launderettes.** A **launderette** is a shop in which there are washing machines and dryers which people can pay to use to wash and dry their clothes. — N COUNT

laundry /lɔːndri¹/, **laundries. 1 Laundry** is **1.1** dirty clothes, sheets, and towels that are being washed or are about to be washed. EG *The washing machine takes about two hours to do my laundry.* **1.2** clean clothes, sheets, and towels that have been washed. EG *...laundry hung out to dry in the sun.* — N UNCOUNT, OR N SING : the+N
2 A **laundry** is **2.1** a firm that washes and irons clothes, sheets, and towels for people. **2.2** a room in a house or hotel where clothes, sheets, and towels are washed. — N COUNT

laurel /lɒrə⁰l/, **laurels. 1** A **laurel** is a small evergreen tree with shiny leaves. — N COUNT
2 If you say that someone **is resting on** their **laurels**, you mean that they feel so satisfied with what they have already achieved that they are not bothering to make any more effort. EG *We have no cause to rest on our laurels.* — PHRASE

lava /lɑːvə/ is a kind of rock which comes out of a volcano in the form of a very hot liquid, and gradually cools and becomes solid. — N UNCOUNT

lavatory /lævətə⁰ri¹/, **lavatories.** A **lavatory** is a toilet. — N COUNT

lavender /lævɪ¹ndə/ is a garden plant that has sweet-smelling, bluish-purple flowers on long stalks. — N UNCOUNT

lavish /lævɪʃ/, **lavishes, lavishing, lavished. 1** If you are **lavish** with your money or time, you are very generous in the way that you spend it for other people's benefit. EG *...the lavish hospitality of Indian princes.* ◇ **lavishly.** EG *Rich merchants lavishly entertained travelling tradesmen.* — ADJ QUALIT; ◇ ADV
2 If you **lavish** money, affection, or time on someone or something, you spend a lot of money on them or give them a lot of affection or attention. EG *Everything was lavished on her one and only child... He lavished presents on her.* — V+O+on/upon
3 Something that is **lavish 3.1** is very large in amount. EG *The meal, he said, would be nothing fancy, but the portions would be lavish.* ◇ **lavishly.** EG *They were lavishly paid.* **3.2** has an appearance of great wealth and extravagance. EG *...lavish funeral parlours.* ◇ **lavishly.** EG *The building has been lavishly restored to a fresh brilliance.* — ADJ QUALIT; ADJ QUALIT; ◇ ADV

law /lɔː/, **laws. 1** The **law** is a system of rules that a society or government develops in order to deal with business agreements, social relationships, and crime. EG *It's against the law to demonstrate here... She was caught breaking the law... Every company must by law submit accounts annually.* — N SING : the+N, OR N UNCOUNT
2 A particular type of **law**, for example company **law** or criminal **law**, is the group of rules in a system of law which deals with a particular set of agreements, relationships, or crimes. EG *She's the Senate's expert on constitutional law... The soldiers faced charges under military law.* — N UNCOUNT +SUPP
3 A **law** is **3.1** one of the rules in a system of law which deals with a particular type of agreement, relationship, or crime. EG *Many of the laws passed by Parliament are never enforced... ...immigration laws.* **3.2** a rule or set of rules for good behaviour which seems right and important for moral, religious, or emotional reasons. EG *Children soon accept social laws.* — N COUNT
4 Law or **the law** is all the professions which deal with advising people about the law, representing people in court, or giving decisions and punishments. EG *I was planning a career in law... There are curious parallels between medicine and the law... ...a New York law firm.* — N UNCOUNT, OR N SING : the+N
5 Law is the study of systems of law and how laws work. EG *A degree in law would be an advantage in the job market.* — N UNCOUNT
6 Some people refer to government authorities, especially the police, as the **law**. EG *He found himself in trouble with the law again.* — N SING : the+N, Informal
7 When someone **lays down the law**, they give other people orders because they think that they are right and the other people are wrong; used showing disapproval. — PHRASE
8 A **law** is also **8.1** a natural process or pattern in which a particular cause always leads to a particular effect and nothing can stop it happening. EG *...the laws of nature... The laws that govern the behaviour of light are universal.* **8.2** a scientific rule that people have invented to describe and explain the way that nature works. EG *...the second law of heat distribution.* — N COUNT+SUPP

law-abiding. Someone who is **law-abiding** always obeys the law. EG *...respectable, law-abiding citizens.* — ADJ QUALIT : USU ATTRIB

law and order. When people talk about **law and order**, they are referring to **1** the acceptance and obeying of the laws of a country by the people who live there. EG *There were periods of unrest and a* — N UNCOUNT

Do lawyers lay down the law?

breakdown of law and order. **2** the use of strict laws as a way of controlling a society, especially when the police or the army are used. EG *Are they not prepared to enforce law and order among their own people?*

law court, law courts. A **law court** is a place where legal matters are decided by a judge and jury or by a magistrate. N COUNT

lawful /lɔ:fʊl/. **Lawful** activities, organizations, and products are allowed by law. EG *...lawful publications... Use all lawful means to persuade employers.* ◇ **lawfully.** EG *The tenant cannot be lawfully evicted.* ADJ CLASSIF Formal ◇ ADV

lawless /lɔ:lɪ²s/. **Lawless** actions break the laws of a country or state. EG *...the lawless activities of these gangs.* ◇ **lawlessness.** EG *...our disapproval of lawlessness and violence.* ADJ CLASSIF Formal ◇ N UNCOUNT

lawn /lɔ:n/, **lawns.** A **lawn** is an area of grass that is kept cut short. A lawn is usually part of a garden or park. EG *I'm going to mow the lawn.* N COUNT OR N UNCOUNT

lawnmower /lɔ:nməʊə/, **lawnmowers.** A **lawnmower** is a machine for cutting grass on lawns. N COUNT

lawsuit /lɔ:su:t/, **lawsuits.** A **lawsuit** is a case in a court of law which concerns a dispute between two people, rather than the prosecution of a criminal by the police. EG *He had sought to bring a lawsuit against the airline.* N COUNT Formal

lawyer /lɔ:jə, lɔɪə/, **lawyers.** A **lawyer** is a person who is qualified to advise people about the law and represent them in court. EG *I sought the advice of a lawyer.* N COUNT

lax /læks/. If you say that someone's behaviour or a system is **lax**, you mean that rules are not being obeyed or standards are not being maintained. EG *Standards are regarded by some experts as being far too lax... Procedures are lax, discipline is weak.* ADJ QUALIT

laxative /læksətɪv/, **laxatives.** A **laxative** is something that you eat or drink which stops you being constipated. N COUNT

lay /leɪ/, **lays, laying, laid** /leɪd/. **Lay** is also the past tense of the verb **lie** in some meanings.

1 If you **lay** something somewhere, you place it there so that it rests there. EG *She laid the baby gently down on its bed... She laid a hand on his shoulder.* V+O+A

2 When you **lay** the table, you arrange the knives, forks, plates, and other things on a table before a meal. EG *I'm not laying a place at table for him.* V+O

3 If you **lay** something such as a carpet or a cable, you put it on or in the ground in its proper position. EG *They're laying water pipes and electricity cables.* V+O

4 When a female bird or animal **lays** an egg, the egg comes out of its body. V+O OR V

5 If you **lay** a trap, **5.1** you hide a trap and set it in order to catch an animal. **5.2** you deceive someone in order to catch them or get them to do what you want. EG *He walked right into the trap I had laid for him.* V+O

6 If you **lay hold of** someone or something, you grab them and hold them tight. PHRASE

7 If you **lay** the basis for something, you make preparations for it in order to make sure that it will happen in the way you want it to. EG *Her new policy helped to lay the foundations of electoral success.* V+O

8 If you **lay** something on someone, you cause them to be affected by it. EG *Women lay most of the blame on men... A curse has been laid on those who violated the tomb of the King.* V+O+*on/upon*

9 If you **lay emphasis on** something, you emphasize it. EG *His lawyer will lay great emphasis on his state of mind at the time.* PHRASE

10 If you **lay** someone **open to** criticism or attack, you do something which is likely to make people criticize or attack them. EG *That kind of behaviour can lay you open to the charge of wasting the company's time.* PHRASE

11 You use **lay** to describe people who are **11.1** involved with a Christian church but are not members of the clergy, monks, or nuns. EG *...a lay preacher.* **11.2** not trained or qualified in a particular subject or activity. EG *The computer has become much more accessible to the lay person.* ADJ CLASSIF: ATTRIB

12 to **lay claim to**: see **claim**.

lay before. If you **lay** an idea or problem **before** someone, you present it to them, for example in order to obtain their approval or advice. EG *What exactly was the scheme he intended to lay before them?* PHRASAL VB: V+O+PREP Formal

lay down. 1 If rules or people in authority **lay down** what people must do, they tell people what they must do. EG *...the conditions laid down by the Department of Health.* ● to **lay down the law**: see **law**. **2** If someone **lays down** their **life** in a war or struggle, they are killed while fighting for something. PHRASAL VB: V+O+ADV PHRASE Literary

lay into. If you **lay into** someone, you start attacking them physically or criticizing them severely. PHRASAL VB: V+PREP, HAS PASS

lay off. 1 If workers **are laid off** by their employers, they are told to leave their jobs, usually because there is no more work for them to do. **2** If you tell someone to **lay off**, you are telling them to leave you alone. **3** See also **layoff**. PHRASAL VB: V+O+ADV V+ADV/PREP, USU IMPER

lay on. If you **lay on** food, entertainment, or a service, you provide it, especially in a generous way. EG *We laid on a great show for them.* PHRASAL VB: V+O+ADV

lay out. 1 If you **lay out** a group of things, you spread them out and arrange them. EG *Clothes, jewels, and ornaments were laid out on the ground.* PHRASAL VB: V+O+ADV

2 You can describe the design of a garden, building, or town by saying how it **is laid out**. EG *Their settlement is laid out traditionally as a small village.* **3** See also **layout**. V-PASS+ADV

layabout /leɪəbaʊt/, **layabouts.** If you say that someone is a **layabout**, you mean that they are idle and lazy. EG *He's just a drunken layabout.* N COUNT Informal

lay-by, lay-bys. A **lay-by** is a short strip of road by the side of a main road, where cars can stop for a while. EG *Pull into the next lay-by.* N COUNT

layer /leɪə/, **layers.** A **layer** is a flat piece of something or a quantity of something that covers a surface or that is between two other things. EG *A fine layer of dust covered everything... He wrapped each component in several layers of foam rubber.* N COUNT: USU+SUPP

layman /leɪmə³n/, **laymen.** A **layman** is a person who is not qualified or experienced in a particular subject or activity. EG *...a task for industrial experts rather than for laymen.* N COUNT

layoff /leɪj⁰ɒf/, **layoffs.** When there are **layoffs** in a company, people are told to leave their jobs, usually because there is no more work for them to do. EG *Textile companies announced 2,000 fresh layoffs last week.* N COUNT

layout /leɪj⁰aʊt/, **layouts.** The **layout** of a garden, building, or piece of writing is the way in which the parts of it are arranged. EG *He knew the airport layout intimately.* N COUNT+SUPP

laze /leɪz/, **lazes, lazing, lazed.** If you **laze** somewhere or **laze** about, you relax and do nothing. EG *...lazing by the hotel pool.* V: OFT+A

lazy /leɪzi¹/, **lazier, laziest. 1** Someone who is **lazy** tries to avoid doing any work or making any effort to do something. EG *His maths teacher thought he was bright but lazy.* ◇ **laziness.** EG *Only laziness prevented him from doing it.* ADJ QUALIT ◇ N UNCOUNT

2 Lazy actions are done slowly without making very much effort. EG *She gave a lazy smile.* ◇ **lazily.** EG *Philip was lazily combing his hair.* ADJ QUALIT: ATTRIB ◇ ADV

lb, lbs. You use **lb** as a written abbreviation for 'pound' when you are describing the weight of something. The plural can be either 'lb' or 'lbs'. EG *...a 2lb bag of sugar... ...a fish weighing about 10 lbs.*

lead, leads, leading, led /lɛd/; pronounced /li:d/ except in paragraphs 19 and 20, where it is pronounced /lɛd/.

1 If you **lead** a group of moving people, you walk V+O: USU+A; ALSO V or ride in front of them. EG *He led a demonstration through the City.*

2 If you **lead** someone somewhere, you take them there. EG *My mother takes me by the hand and leads me downstairs.* V+O+A ● If you **lead the way**, you go in front of someone in order to show them where to go. EG *I led the way to Andrew's cabin.* ● PHRASE

3 If something such as a road, pipe, or wire **leads** somewhere, it goes there. EG *The steps lead down to his basement. ...the main street leading to the centre of the city.* V+A

4 If a door or gate **leads** to a place, you can get to the place by going through it. EG *There was a gate on our left leading into a field.* V+*to/into*

5 If you **are leading** in a race or competition, you are winning. EG *Becker leads by five games to four.* V

6 In a race or competition, if you have the **lead** or are in the **lead**, you are winning. EG *This win gave him the overall lead... The USSR was well in the lead.* N SING

7 If you **lead** a group of people or an organization, you are officially in charge of it. EG *The Labour Party was led by Wilson.* V+O OR V

8 If you **lead** an activity, you start it or guide it. EG *The rioting was led by students.* V+O

9 If you **take the lead**, you start doing something before other people do. EG *It was France who took the lead in the development of the airbus.* PHRASE

10 If you give a **lead**, you do something which is considered to be a good example to follow. EG *The European Community should give a lead... Other firms are now following the company's lead.* N COUNT

11 You can use **lead** when saying what sort of life someone has. For example, if you **lead** an exciting life, your life is exciting. V+O

12 If something **leads** to an unpleasant situation, it causes that situation to happen. EG *...a drinking spree which had led to his court appearance.* V+*to*

13 If something **leads** you to do something, it influences or affects you so that you do that thing. EG *Recent evidence is leading historians to reassess that event... This led him to an obsession with art.* V+O+*to*-INF OR V+O+A

14 A dog's **lead** is a long, thin chain or piece of leather which you attach to the dog's collar so that you can keep the dog under control. N COUNT

15 A **lead** in a piece of electrical equipment is a piece of wire which supplies electricity to the equipment. N COUNT

16 The **lead** in a play or film is the most important role in it. EG *Richard was signed up to play the lead.* N SING : *the*+N

17 The **lead** singer in a pop group is the one who sings the main tunes. ADJ CLASSIF : ATTRIB

18 A **lead** is also a piece of information which may help the police to find out who committed a crime. N COUNT

19 **Lead** is a soft, grey, heavy metal. N UNCOUNT

20 The **lead** in a pencil is the centre part of it which makes a mark on paper. N COUNT

21 See also **leading**.

lead off. **1** If a road or corridor **leads off** from a place, it starts at that place and goes away from it. EG *...a side street leading off from a road of shops.* PHRASAL VB : V+ADV+A **2** If a room **leads off** a place, there is an entrance to it in that place. EG *...rooms leading off the courtyard.* V+PREP

lead up to. **1** Events that **lead up to** a situation happen one after the other until that situation is reached. EG *...the chain of events that led up to her death.* PHRASAL VB : V+ADV+PREP **2** If you **lead up to** a particular subject in a conversation, you gradually guide the conversation to a point where you can introduce that subject. EG *Ever since you came in you've been leading up to this one question.*

leaden /lɛd^{ə}n/. **1** A **leaden** sky or sea is dark grey and has no movement of clouds or waves. ADJ CLASSIF Literary

2 If your movements are **leaden**, you are moving slowly and heavily, because you are tired. EG *He took two leaden steps forward.* ADJ QUALIT Literary

3 You can describe a conversation as **leaden** when it is very dull. ADJ QUALIT Literary

leader /liːdə/, **leaders.** **1** The **leader** of an organization or a group of people is the person who is in charge of it. EG *...the leader of the Labour Party... He didn't know how to be a decisive leader.* N COUNT

2 The **leader** in a race or competition is the person who is winning at a particular time. N COUNT

leadership /liːdəʃɪp/. **1** You can refer to the people who are in charge of a group or organization as the **leadership**. EG *...the gap between the leadership and the men they represent.* N SING : *the*+N

2 If a group of people is under your **leadership**, you are their leader. EG *...an independent group under the leadership of Jones... ...the election of Wilson to the leadership of the Labour Party.* N SING

3 Someone who shows **leadership** shows that they have the qualities of a good leader. EG *...a task calling for energy and firm leadership.* N UNCOUNT

leading /liːdɪŋ/. **1** The **leading** people or things in a group are the most important ones. EG *A demand for change came from leading politicians.* ADJ CLASSIF : ATTRIB

2 The **leading** role in a play or film is the main one. EG *She played the leading role in The Winter's Tale... ...their leading lady, Yvonne Printemps.* ADJ CLASSIF : ATTRIB

3 The **leading** person or thing in a line of moving people or things is the one at the front of the line. EG *The leading car was full of security men.* ADJ CLASSIF : ATTRIB

leaf /liːf/, **leaves** /liːvz/; **leafs, leafing, leafed.** **Leaves** is the plural of the noun. **Leafs** is the third person singular, present tense, of the phrasal verb.

1 The **leaves** of a tree or plant are the parts that are flat, thin, and usually green. Many trees and plants lose their leaves in the autumn and grow new leaves in the spring. N COUNT

2 When trees are **in leaf**, they have leaves on their branches. PHRASE

leaf through. If you **leaf through** a book or newspaper, you turn the pages quickly without looking at them carefully. EG *While he is waiting he leafs through a magazine.* PHRASAL VB : V+PREP

leaflet /liːflɪ^{2}t/, **leaflets, leafleting, leafleted.** **1** A **leaflet** is a little book or a piece of paper containing information about a particular subject. EG *The company produces a little leaflet called 'Protect your Pipes from Frost'.* N COUNT

2 If you **leaflet** a place, you distribute leaflets there, especially as part of a campaign. EG *All the local houses and shops had been leafleted.* V+O

leafy /liːfi^{1}/, **leafier, leafiest.** **1** **Leafy** trees and plants have a lot of leaves. EG *...leafy green vegetables.* ADJ QUALIT

2 You say that a place is **leafy** when there are a lot of trees and plants there. EG *...a leafy suburb.* ADJ QUALIT

league /liːg/, **leagues.** **1** A **league** is a group of people, clubs, or countries that have joined together for a particular purpose or because they share a common interest. EG *...the National Book League... ...the football league.* N COLL

2 If you are **in league with** someone, you are working with them for a particular purpose, often secretly. EG *They are in league with the police.* PHRASE

leak /liːk/, **leaks, leaking, leaked.** **1** If a container or other object **leaks**, there is a hole or crack in it which liquid or gas can pass through. EG *The roof leaks... ...leaking drain pipes.* V ▸ used as a noun. EG *I fixed a small leak in the roof of her shed.* ▸ N COUNT

2 When liquid or gas **leaks** through an object or **leaks** out of it, it passes through a hole or crack in it. EG *The water was still slowly leaking out.* V : USU+A ▸ used as a noun. EG *There's been a gas leak.* ▸ N COUNT

3 If someone **leaks** a piece of secret information, they let the public know about it. EG *He made sure the story was leaked to the media.* V+O : OFT+*to* ▸ used as a noun. EG *...the possibility of a security leak.* ▸ N COUNT

leak out. If information that you want to keep secret **leaks out**, it becomes known to other PHRASAL VB : V+ADV

When is the next leap year?

people. EG *News of their engagement leaked out just before Christmas.*

leakage /li:kɪdʒ/, **leakages.** If there is a **leakage** of liquid or gas, an amount of it comes out of an object through a crack or hole. EG *A leakage in the hydraulic system was diagnosed.* N COUNT

leaky /li:ki¹/, **leakier, leakiest.** Something that is **leaky** has holes or cracks in it which liquids or gases can pass through. EG *...a leaky roof.* ADJ QUALIT

lean /li:n/, **leans, leaning, leaned, leant** /lent/. **Leaned** and **leant** are both used as the past tense and past participle of the verb.

1 When you **lean** in a particular direction, you bend your body in that direction. EG *He was sitting on the edge of his chair and leaning eagerly forwards... I leaned out of the window.* V+A

2 If you **lean** on something, you rest against it so that it partly supports your weight. If you **lean** an object on something, you place the object so that its weight is partly supported by the thing it is resting against. EG *He leaned against a tree... He leaned the bike against a railing.* V+A OR V+O+A

3 If you **lean** towards a particular idea or action, you approve of it and behave in accordance with it. EG *...parents who naturally lean towards strictness.* V+*towards*

4 If you **lean** on someone, **4.1** you try to influence them by threatening them. EG *They can lean on the administration by threatening to withhold their subscriptions.* **4.2** you depend on them for support and encouragement. EG *They lean heavily upon each other for support.* V+*on/upon*

5 Someone who is **lean** is thin but looks strong and fit. EG *...a lean, handsome man.* ADJ QUALIT

6 **Lean** meat does not have very much fat. ADJ QUALIT

7 A **lean** period of time is one in which people do not have very much food, money, or success. EG *In the lean years, crop failures are common.* ADJ QUALIT

leaning /li:nɪŋ/, **leanings.** If you have a **leaning** towards a particular belief or type of behaviour, you tend to have that belief or to behave in that way. EG *...their different political leanings.* N COUNT+SUPP

leant /lent/ is one of the forms of the past tense and past participle of **lean.**

leap /li:p/, **leaps, leaping, leaped** /li:pt/ or /lept/, **leapt** /lept/. **Leaped** and **leapt** are both used as the past tense and past participle of the verb.

1 If you **leap** somewhere, **1.1** you jump high in the air or jump a long distance. EG *Some monkeys can leap five metres from one tree to another... They leaped into the water.* ▸ used as a noun. EG *She took a flying leap at the fence.* **1.2** you move there suddenly and quickly. EG *She leapt into a taxi and headed for the Bronx.* V+O OR V: USU+A; ▸ N COUNT; V+A

2 You can say that things **leap** when they suddenly advance or increase by a large amount. EG *The number of computers in the world is leaping upwards daily.* ▸ used as a noun. EG *...an economic leap forward... ...a leap in oil prices.* V+A; ▸ N COUNT: USU+SUPP

3 You can say that your **heart leaps** when you experience a sudden strong feeling of surprise, fear, or happiness. EG *My heart leapt at the thought of seeing her again.* PHRASE Literary

leap at. If you **leap at** a chance or opportunity, you accept it quickly and eagerly. EG *David would have leaped at the chance to go.* PHRASAL VB: V+PREP

leapt /lept/ is one of the forms of the past tense and past participle of **leap.**

leap year, leap years. A **leap year** is a year in which there are 366 days instead of 365. There is a leap year every four years. N COUNT

learn /lɜ:n/, **learns, learning, learned, learnt.** **Learned** and **learnt** are both used as the past tense and past participle of the verb.

1 If you **learn** facts or **learn** a skill, you obtain knowledge of the facts or gain the skill as a result of studying or training. EG *Children learn foreign languages very easily... He had never learnt to read and write... The best way to learn is by practical experience.* ◊ **learner, learners.** EG *She is a very slow learner.* V+O, V+*to*-INF, OR V; ◊ N COUNT

2 If you **learn** something such as a poem or the script of a play, you study or repeat the words so much that you can remember them without looking at them. EG *We have to learn the whole poem.* V+O

3 You say that people **learn** to behave in a particular way when they gradually start behaving that way as a result of a change in their attitudes. EG *Women must learn to value themselves as individuals... If only these people could learn to live together.* V+*to*-INF

4 If you **learn** of something, you find out about it, usually by being told about it. EG *They offered help as soon as they learnt of the accident... She was extremely upset to learn that he had died... ...the night when he learned the truth about Sam.* V+*of*, V+REPORT, OR V+O

5 See also **learning**.

learned /lɜ:nɪ²d/. **1** Someone who is **learned** has gained a lot of knowledge by studying, and is respected for this. EG *...the learned professions.* ADJ QUALIT

2 **Learned** books or papers have been written by someone with a lot of academic knowledge. EG *...new ideas announced in learned journals.* ADJ QUALIT: ATTRIB

learning /lɜ:nɪŋ/ is knowledge that has been gained through studying. EG *...a man of learning.* N UNCOUNT

learnt /lɜ:nt/ is one of the forms of the past tense and past participle of **learn.**

lease /li:s/, **leases, leasing, leased.** **1** A **lease** is a legal agreement by which the owner of a building or piece of land allows someone else to use it for a period of time in return for money. EG *The house was let on a 99-year lease.* N COUNT

2 If you **lease** property from someone or if they **lease** it to you, they allow you to use it in return for money. EG *They leased a house at Cospoli... He had persuaded the local council to lease him a house.* V+O, V+O+O, OR V+O+*to*

3 If you say that someone who seemed to be failing or becoming weaker has been given **a new lease of life**, you mean that they are now more lively or successful. EG *After her marriage it was as though she'd got a new lease of life.* PHRASE

least /li:st/. **1** You use **at least** **1.1** to say that the number or amount mentioned is the smallest that is likely, and that the actual number or amount may be greater. EG *He drank at least half a bottle of whisky a day... I must have slept twelve hours at least.* **1.2** to say that something is the minimum which should be done, although in fact you think that more than this ought to be done. EG *Go to see the administrator or at least write a letter.* **1.3** to indicate an advantage that exists in spite of the disadvantage or bad situation that has just been mentioned. EG *The process looks rather laborious but at least it is not dangerous.* ADV SEN

2 You can also use **at least** when you want to correct something that you have just said. EG *A couple of days ago I spotted my ex-wife; at least I thought I did, I wasn't sure.* ADV SEN

3 You use **least** **3.1** to say that an amount of something is as small as it can be. EG *...the thinner animals, who had the least muscle over their bones.* **3.2** to say that something is true to as small a degree or extent as is possible. EG *He came out when I least expected it... They're the ones who need it the least.* **3.3** to say that something has less of a particular quality than most other things of its kind. EG *...one of the smallest and least powerful of the African states.* **3.4** to emphasize that a particular situation or thing is much less important or serious than other ones. EG *That was the least of her worries.* QUANTIF; ADV SUPERL; SUBMOD; ADJ QUALIT: SUPERL

4 **Least** is also used in these phrases. **4.1** You can use **in the least** and **the least bit** to emphasize a negative. EG *I don't mind in the least, I really don't... She wasn't the least bit jealous.* **4.2** If you say that something is **the least that** someone **can do**, you mean that they should do that even if they cannot do anything more. EG *And if I can't protect them* PHRASES *from something, the least I can do is warn them that there is a danger.* **4.3** You can use **to say the least** to suggest that a situation is actually much more extreme or serious than you say it is. EG *...a development which will have, to say the least, intriguing effects.* **4.4** You can use **not least** when giving an important example or reason. EG *...all western countries, not least the USA.* **4.5** You can use **least of all** after a negative statement to emphasize that it applies especially to a particular person or thing. EG *Nobody seemed amused, least of all Jenny.*

leather /lɛðə/ is the specially treated skin of animals. It is used for making shoes, clothes, bags, and furniture. EG *...leather jackets.* N UNCOUNT

leathery /lɛðəri^{1}/. If the texture of something is **leathery**, it is tough, like leather. EG *The wrinkled, leathery face broke into a smile.* ADJ QUALIT

leave /li:v/, **leaves, leaving, left** /lɛft/. **1** When you **leave** a place, you go away from it. EG *They left the house to go for a walk after tea... My train leaves at 11.30.* V+O OR V

2 If you **leave** a person or thing somewhere, they remain there when you go away. EG *Leaving Rita in a bar, I made for the town library... Leave your phone number with the secretary... I had left my raincoat in the restaurant.* V+O : USU+A

3 If you **leave** a place or institution, you go away permanently from it. EG *What do you want to do when you leave school?... She told him she was going to leave her job... She wanted to leave China altogether.* V+O OR V

4 If someone **leaves** their husband or wife, they stop living with him or her and finish the relationship. EG *My husband had left me for another woman.* V+O OR V

5 If you **leave** a particular amount of something, you do not use it, and so it remains available to be used later. EG *Leave some of the stew for the boys... I meant to leave myself with fifteen pounds a week.* ● See also **left 2**. V+O : OFT+A

6 If something **leaves** a mark, effect, or impression, it causes that mark, effect, or impression to remain as a result. EG *I didn't want him to leave a trail of wet footprints... Does it leave a stain?* V+O

7 To **leave** someone or something in a particular state or position means to cause them to remain or be in that state or position. EG *Who left the gates open?... The result has left everybody dissatisfied... You are left with two alternatives.* V+O+A, V+O+C, OR V+O+O

8 If you **leave** a space or gap in something, you deliberately make that space or gap. EG *Remember to leave a space between the fridge and the wall.* V+O

9 If you **leave** something to someone, you give them the responsibility for dealing with it. EG *He said the whole business should be left to the courts... Leave it with me, I'll fix it... He left it to us to try and sort it out.* V+O+*to/with*

10 If you **leave** something until a particular time, you delay dealing with it. EG *Why do you always leave things to the last minute?* V+O : OFT+A

11 If you **leave** a particular subject, you stop talking about it and start discussing something else. EG *Let's leave the budget and go on to another question. I want to leave that for the moment.* V+O

12 If you **leave** property or money to someone, you arrange for it to be given to them after you have died. EG *She did not leave a very large legacy.* V+O, V+O+O, OR V+O+*to*

13 Leave is **13.1** a period of time when you do not have to do your usual job, but which is not a holiday. EG *She was granted a year's maternity leave... ...sick leave.* **13.2** a period of time when you are on holiday from your job. EG *He'd come over on leave from Northern Ireland... He asked for forty-eight hours' leave.* N UNCOUNT +SUPP

14 Leaves is also the plural form of **leaf**.

leave behind. 1 If you **leave** someone or something **behind**, you go away permanently from them. EG *I hated having to leave behind all my friends.* PHRASAL VB : V+O+ADV **2** If you **leave** an object or a situation **behind**, it remains after you have left a place. EG *Millie had left her watch behind... ...leaving behind an unsolved mystery.* V+O+ADV

leave off. 1 If you **leave** someone or something **off** a list, you do not include them in that list. EG *Hopper was too important to be left off the guest list.* PHRASAL VB : V+O+PREP **2** If you continue doing something **from where** you **left off**, you start doing it again at the point where you had previously stopped doing it. EG *He sat down at the piano again and started playing from where he left off.* PHRASE

leave out. 1 If you **leave** someone or something **out**, you do not include them in something. EG *One or two scenes in the play were left out.* PHRASAL VB : V+O+ADV **2** If you **feel left out**, you feel unhappy because you have not been included in a group or activity. PHRASE

lecherous /lɛtʃərəs/. A man who is **lecherous** behaves towards women in a way which shows that he is thinking of them in a sexual way; used showing disapproval. ADJ QUALIT

lectern /lɛktə^{5}n/, **lecterns.** A **lectern** is a high sloping desk on which someone puts their notes or a book when they are standing up and talking or reading to an audience. N COUNT

lecture /lɛktʃə/, **lectures, lecturing, lectured. 1** A **lecture** is a talk that someone gives in order to teach people about a particular subject. EG *...a series of lectures on literature... I went to a lecture he gave at the African Institute.* ▸ used as a verb. EG *He lectured on Economic History at the University.* N COUNT ▸ V

2 If someone **lectures** you about something, they criticize you or tell you how you should behave. EG *I had always been lectured about not talking with my mouth full.* ▸ used as a noun. EG *He'll give her a lecture on accepting her responsibilities.* V+O+A ▸ N COUNT

lecturer /lɛktʃərə/, **lecturers.** A **lecturer** is a person who teaches at a university or college. EG *...a lecturer in sociology.* N COUNT

lectureship /lɛktʃəʃɪp/, **lectureships.** A **lectureship** is the position of lecturer at a university or college. EG *She was offered a lectureship at Birmingham University.* N COUNT

led /lɛd/ is the past tense and past participle of **lead.**

ledge /lɛdʒ/, **ledges.** A **ledge** is **1** a narrow, flat place in the side of a cliff or mountain. EG *Only a bird could get to that ledge.* **2** a narrow shelf along the bottom edge of a window. EG *...students sitting on the window ledges.* N COUNT

ledger /lɛdʒə/, **ledgers.** A **ledger** is a book in which a company or organization writes down the amounts of money it spends and receives. N COUNT

leek /li:k/, **leeks.** A **leek** is a long thin vegetable which is white at one end and has long green leaves. N COUNT

leer /lɪə/, **leers, leering, leered.** If someone **leers** at you, they smile in an unpleasant way, usually because they are sexually interested in you. EG *He leaned over and leered at them, saying, 'Good morning, little girls.'* ▸ used as a noun. EG *He was staring down with a leer on his face.* V : OFT+*at* ▸ N COUNT

left /lɛft/. **1 Left** is the past tense and past participle of **leave**.

2 If there is a certain amount of something **left** or **left over**, it remains after the rest has gone or been used. EG *I only had two pounds left... He drained what was left of his drink... We had a bit of time left over.* ADJ PRED

3 Left is one of two opposite directions, sides, or positions. If you are facing north and you turn to the left, you will be facing west. In the word 'to', the 't' is to the left of the 'o'. EG *There was a gate on our left leading into a field... His was the third door to* N UNCOUNT OR N SING

Which word on these pages is used in Britain but not in America?

the left. ▸ used as an adverb or an adjective. EG *He turned left and began strolling down the street... She came forward looking neither right nor left... In his left hand he clutched a book.* ▸ ADV OR ADJ CLASSIF: ATTRIB

4 The **Left** is used to refer to the people or groups who support socialism rather than capitalism. EG *This fear is by no means confined to the extreme left.* N COLL: SING, *the*+N

left-hand is used to describe something which is on the left side. EG *She noted it down on the left-hand side of the page.* ADJ CLASSIF: ATTRIB

left-handed. Someone who is **left-handed** uses their left hand rather than their right hand for activities such as writing or throwing a ball. EG *...left-handed batsmen... They both play golf left-handed.* ADJ CLASSIF OR ADV

leftist /lɛftɪst/, **leftists. 1** Socialists and communists are sometimes referred to as **leftists**. N COUNT

2 People and organizations connected with socialism and communism are sometimes described as **leftist**. ADJ CLASSIF: ATTRIB

left-luggage office, left-luggage offices. A **left-luggage office** is a place in a railway station or airport where you can pay to leave your luggage for a short period of time. N COUNT British

leftover/lɛftəʊvə/, **leftovers. 1** You can refer to food that remains uneaten after a meal as the **leftovers**. EG *The dogs eat the leftovers.* N PLURAL

2 You use **leftover** to describe an amount of something that remains after the rest of it has been used. EG *...a bottle of left-over perfume.* ADJ CLASSIF: ATTRIB

left-wing. 1 Left-wing people have political ideas that are close to socialism or communism. EG *...left-wing journalists.* ADJ QUALIT

2 The **left wing** of a political party consists of the members of it whose beliefs are closer to socialism or communism than those of its other members. EG *...the left wing of the Labour Party.* N SING: *the*+N

left-winger, left-wingers. A **left-winger** is a person whose political beliefs are close to socialism or communism, or closer to them than most of the other people in the same group or party. N COUNT

leg /lɛg/, **legs. 1** Your **legs** are the two long parts of your body that are connected to your hips and have your feet at the end of them. See picture at THE HUMAN BODY. N COUNT

2 The **legs** of an animal, bird, or insect are the thin parts of its body that it uses to stand on or to move across the ground. EG *...creatures with short legs and long tails.* N COUNT

3 The **legs** of a pair of trousers are the parts that cover your legs. N COUNT

4 A **leg** of lamb or pork is a piece of meat that consists of the thigh of a sheep, lamb, or pig. N COUNT+SUPP

5 The **legs** of a piece of furniture such as a table or chair are the thin vertical parts that touch the floor and support the furniture's weight. N COUNT+SUPP

6 A **leg** of a long journey is one part of it. EG *They set off on the first leg of their 12,000 mile journey.* N COUNT

7 Leg is also used in these phrases. **7.1** If you **pull** someone's **leg**, you tell them something untrue as a joke. EG *'You're pulling my leg.' – 'No, it's true.'* **7.2** If you say that someone **does not have a leg to stand on**, you mean that what they have done or said cannot be justified or proved. **7.3** If you say that something is **on** its **last legs**, you mean that it is in a very bad condition and will soon fall to pieces or stop working. EG *Most of the houses were on their last legs.* PHRASES Informal

legacy /lɛgəsiˈ/, **legacies. 1** A **legacy** is money or property which you receive after someone has died because they said in their will that you should have it. EG *All I've got is that little legacy my aunt left me. ...a legacy of five thousand pounds.* N COUNT

2 A **legacy** of an event or period of history is something that exists after it and as a result of it. EG *These characteristics of British industry are a legacy of pre-war unemployment.* N COUNT+SUPP

legal /liːgə°l/. **1 Legal** is used to describe things that relate to the law. EG *...the British legal system... ...legal obligations... ...a legal dispute.* ADJ CLASSIF: ATTRIB

2 An action or situation that is **legal** is allowed by a law. EG *Capital punishment is legal in many countries.* ◇ **legally.** EG *We are not legally married.* ADJ CLASSIF; ◇ ADV

legality /lɪˈgælɪˈtiˈ/. If you talk about the **legality** of an action or situation, you are talking about whether it is legal or not. EG *He disputed the legality of the invasion.* N UNCOUNT +SUPP

legalize /liːgəlaɪz/, **legalizes, legalizing, legalized;** also spelled **legalise.**
If an action or situation **is legalized**, a law is passed that makes it legal. EG *The government had finally legalized trade unions.* V+O

legend /lɛdʒənd/, **legends. 1** A **legend** is a very old story that may be based on real events. EG *The original inhabitants, according to legend, were blacksmiths.* N COUNT OR N UNCOUNT

2 If you refer to someone as a **legend**, you mean that they are very famous and admired. EG *Brook has become something of a legend.* N COUNT

legendary /lɛdʒəndə°riˈ/. A **legendary** person or thing is **1** very famous. EG *...one of his many legendary acts of courage.* **2** described in an old legend. EG *...the legendary king.* ADJ CLASSIF

legible /lɛdʒəˈbə°l/. If a piece of writing is **legible**, it is written or printed clearly enough to be read. EG *...a crumpled but still legible document.* ADJ QUALIT

legion /liːdʒə°n/, **legions. 1** A **legion** of people is a large number of them. EG *...legions of foreign visitors.* N COUNT OR N PART

2 If you say that things of a particular kind are **legion**, you mean that there are a great number of them. EG *Stories about him are legion.* ADJ PRED Formal

legislate /lɛdʒɪsleɪt/, **legislates, legislating, legislated.** When a government or state **legislates**, it passes a new law. EG *Parliament must eventually legislate against fox-hunting.* V Formal

legislation /lɛdʒɪsleɪʃə°n/ consists of a law or laws passed by a government or state. EG *...tax legislation... ...the introduction of legislation to govern industrial relations.* N UNCOUNT +SUPP

legislative /lɛdʒɪslətɪv/ means involving or relating to the process of making and passing laws. EG *The Government should consider further legislative reforms... ...a legislative assembly.* ADJ CLASSIF: ATTRIB Formal

legislator /lɛdʒɪsleɪtə/, **legislators.** A **legislator** is a person who is involved in making or passing laws. EG *Many of the legislators who drafted the bill are landowners.* N COUNT Formal

legislature /lɛdʒɪslətʃə/, **legislatures.** The **legislature** of a state or country is the group of people there who have the power to make and pass laws. N COUNT: USU *the*+N Formal

legitimate /lɪ²dʒɪtɪməˈt/. Something that is **legitimate** is **1** reasonable and acceptable. EG *Religious leaders have a legitimate reason to be concerned.* ADJ CLASSIF
◇ **legitimacy** /lɪ²dʒɪtɪmɪˈsiˈ/. EG *...the legitimacy of our complaint.* ◇ N UNCOUNT **2** allowed or justified by law. EG *...a legitimate business transaction.* ADJ CLASSIF ◇ **legitimacy.** EG *They challenge the very legitimacy of the government.* ◇ N UNCOUNT

leisure /lɛʒə/. **1 Leisure** is time when you are not working and can do things that you enjoy doing. EG *Not everybody wants more leisure.* N UNCOUNT

2 If someone does something **at leisure** or **at** their **leisure**, they do it slowly, taking as much time as they want. EG *Now I can read at leisure.* PHRASE

leisurely /lɛʒəliˈ/. A **leisurely** action is done in a relaxed way without hurrying. EG *My wife went off for a leisurely walk round the gardens.* ADJ QUALIT ▸ used as an adverb. EG *He strolled leisurely away from the bar.* ▸ ADV

lemon /lɛmə°n/, **lemons. 1** A **lemon** is a bright yellow fruit with sour juice. EG *...slices of lemon.* N COUNT OR N UNCOUNT

2 Lemon is a drink that tastes of lemons. EG *...a glass of lemon.* N UNCOUNT

lemonade /lɛmənеɪd/ is a colourless, sweet, fizzy drink. N UNCOUNT

lend /lɛnd/, **lends, lending, lent** /lɛnt/. **1** If you **lend** someone money or **lend** them something that you own, you allow them to have it or use it for a period of time. EG *I had to lend him a pound... She was reading a book I had lent her... ...lending money to Poland.* V+O+O OR V+O+*to*

2 If you **lend** your support to a person or group, you support them. EG *He was there lending advice and support.* V+O+*to*, V+O+O, OR V+O

3 If something **lends** a particular quality to something else, it gives it that quality. EG *Tradition lends order to the world... It would lend credibility to her arguments.* V+O+*to* OR V+O+O

4 If something **lends** itself to being dealt with or considered in a particular way, it is easy to deal with it or consider it in that way. EG *...problems which do not lend themselves to simple solutions... This model lends itself to the process of duplication.* V-REFL+*to*

5 If you **lend** someone **a hand**, you help them. EG *You may have to lend a hand with the training.* PHRASE

length /lɛŋkᶿθ/, **lengths. 1** The **length** of something is the amount that it measures from one end to the other. EG *It grows to a length of three or four metres... The snake was a metre and a half in length.* N UNCOUNT OR N COUNT +SUPP

2 If something happens or exists along the **length** of something, it happens or exists for the whole way along it. EG *They travelled the length of the island... ...looking down the length of the boulevard.* N SING : *the*+N+*of*

3 If you say that something happens throughout **the length and breadth** of a country, you are emphasizing that it happens everywhere in it. PHRASE Literary

4 If you swim a **length** in a swimming pool, you swim from one end to the other. N COUNT

5 A **length** of wood, string, cloth, or other material is a long piece of it. EG *...a length of rope... ...a short length of steel chain.* N COUNT+SUPP

6 The **length** of an event, activity, or situation is the amount of time for which it lasts. EG *The length of the visit depends on you... It is foolish to expect to be happy for any length of time.* N UNCOUNT OR N COUNT +SUPP

7 The **length** of something is also its quality of being long. EG *I hope the length of this letter will make up for my not having written earlier.* N UNCOUNT

8 If someone does something **at length**, **8.1** they do it after a long interval or period of time. EG *There was another silence. At length Claire said, 'You mean you're not going?'* **8.2** they do it for a long time. EG *He spoke at some length about the press... He studied the pictures at length.* PHRASE Written

9 If someone **goes to great lengths** to achieve something, they try very hard and perhaps do extreme things in order to achieve it. EG *He was willing to go to great lengths to avoid admitting his error... They will go to considerable lengths to buy petrol.* PHRASE

lengthen /lɛŋkᶿθən/, **lengthens, lengthening, lengthened.** When something **lengthens** or **is lengthened**, it becomes longer. EG *The waiting lists are lengthening... The money has been spent on lengthening the runway.* V-ERG

lengthy /lɛŋkᶿθiˡ/, **lengthier, lengthiest.** Something that is **lengthy** lasts for a long time. EG *This is a lengthy process for the patient... ...lengthy explanations... ...a lengthy wait at the airport.* ADJ QUALIT

lenient /liːnɪənt/. When someone in authority is **lenient**, they are not as strict or as severe as expected. EG *Fines were low and magistrates often too lenient.* ◇ **leniently.** EG *Offenders had been treated leniently by the judge.* ADJ QUALIT ◇ ADV

lens /lɛnz/, **lenses.** A **lens** is a thin, curved piece of glass or plastic which is part of something such as a camera, telescope, or pair of glasses. When you look through a lens, things appear clearer, larger, or smaller. See picture at CAMERAS. ● See also **contact lens**. N COUNT

lent /lɛnt/. **1 Lent** is the past tense and past participle of **lend**.

2 In the Christian calendar, **Lent** is the period of forty days before Easter, during which some Christians give up something that they enjoy. N UNCOUNT

lentil /lɛntɪˡl/, **lentils. Lentils** are dried seeds taken from a lentil plant which are cooked and eaten. N COUNT : USU PLURAL

leopard /lɛpəd/, **leopards.** A **leopard** is an animal that looks like a large cat with yellow fur and black spots. Leopards live in Africa and Asia. N COUNT

leotard /lɪətɑːd/, **leotards.** A **leotard** is a tight-fitting piece of clothing that some people wear when they practise dancing or do exercises. N COUNT

leper /lɛpə/, **lepers.** A **leper** is a person who has leprosy. EG *...a leper hospital.* N COUNT

leprosy /lɛprəsiˡ/ is a serious infectious disease that damages people's skin and flesh. N UNCOUNT

lesbian /lɛzbɪən/, **lesbians.** A **lesbian** is a homosexual woman. ▸ used as an adjective. EG *...lesbian activities.* N COUNT ▸ ADJ CLASSIF

less /lɛs/. **1 Less** means **1.1** not as much in amount or degree as before or as something else. EG *A shower uses less water than a bath... We had less than three miles to go... Sixty per cent of them are aged 20 or less... With practice it becomes less of an effort.* **1.2** not having as much of a quality as before or as something else. EG *From this time on, I felt less guilty... Fires occurred less frequently outside this area... ...the less developed countries.* QUANTIF SUBMOD

2 If you do something **less** than before or **less** than someone else, you do it to a smaller extent or not as often. EG *You probably use them less than I do... The more I hear about him, the less I like him.* ADV : COMPAR

3 You use **less and less** to say that something is becoming smaller all the time in degree or amount. EG *He found them less and less interesting... There is less and less freedom for children... They had less and less to talk about.* PHRASE

4 You use **less than** to say that something does not have a particular quality. For example, if you say that something is **less than** perfect, you are emphasizing that it is not perfect. EG *It would have been less than fair.* PHRASE

5 You can use **no less** as an emphatic way of expressing surprise or admiration at the importance of someone or something. EG *...the President of the United States, no less.* ADV SEN

6 You can use **no less than** before an amount to indicate that you think the amount is surprisingly large. Some people consider that it is incorrect to use 'no less than' when referring to a number of things rather than to an amount of something. EG *By 1880, there were no less than fifty-six coal mines... ...no less than 40 per cent of the material.* PHRASE

7 Less also means the same as minus. EG *He earns £200 a week, less tax.*

8 more or less: see **more**. ● See also **lesser**.

-less is added to nouns in order to form adjectives that describe something or someone as not having the thing that the noun refers to. EG *...meaningless sounds... ...landless peasants.* SUFFIX

lessen /lɛsən/, **lessens, lessening, lessened.** If something **lessens** or **is lessened**, it becomes smaller in amount or degree. EG *Separating the sick from the healthy lessens the risk of infection... Their financial hardship has lessened.* ◇ **lessening.** EG *...a lessening of his power... ...lessening of taxation.* V-ERG ◇ N UNCOUNT +SUPP

lesser /lɛsə/ is used to indicate that something is smaller in degree, importance, or amount than something else that is mentioned. EG *These customs are common in Czechoslovakia and to a lesser extent in Hungary and Romania... ...charges of attempted murder and lesser crimes.* ADJ CLASSIF : COMPAR

If the rain lets up, does it lessen?

lesson /lɛsən/, **lessons. 1** A **lesson** is a short period of time during which people are taught about a particular subject or taught how to do something. EG *...tennis lessons... ...a history lesson.* N COUNT

2 If an experience teaches you a **lesson**, it makes you realize the truth or realize what should be done. EG *The lesson of that bizarre episode is that Mr Smith is not to be trusted... This is a lesson that every generation has to learn.* N COUNT

3 If you **teach** someone **a lesson**, you punish them for something that they have done in order to make sure that they do not do it again. PHRASE

lest /lɛst/. If you do something **lest** something unpleasant should happen, you do it to try to prevent the unpleasant thing from happening. EG *I had to grab the iron rail at my side lest I slipped off.* CONJ Formal

let /lɛt/, **lets, letting.** The form **let** is used in the present tense and is the past tense and past participle of the verb.

1 If you **let** something happen, you allow it to happen without doing anything to stop it. EG *People here sit back and let everyone else do the work... She kept lifting handfuls of sand and letting it pour through her fingers.* V+O : USU+INF, NO PASS

2 If you **let** someone do something, you give them your permission to do it. EG *My parents wouldn't let me go out with boys.* V+O : USU+INF, NO PASS

3 If you **let** someone in, out, or through, you allow them to go there, for example by opening a door or moving out of the way. EG *'I rang the bell,' Rudolph said, 'and your friend let me in.'... I asked him to stop the car and let me out.* V+O+A

4 You can use **let me** in discussions before saying something. EG *Richard, let me start by asking you, what is the Institute's main aim?* PHRASE

5 You use **let's** or **let us** when you are making a suggestion about what you and the people you are talking to should do. EG *Let's go... Let's wait for Guy... Let us give her one more chance.* PHRASE

6 If you say **let** someone do something, **6.1** you are saying that you think they should do it. EG *If she insists on going so early, let her take a taxi.* **6.2** you mean that you do not care if they do it. EG *Let them think what they want.* V+O+INF : ONLY IMPER

7 If you **let go** of someone or something, you stop holding them. EG *Let go of me... They let go of the chains and stumbled to their feet.* PHRASE

8 If you **let** a person or animal **go**, you allow them to leave or to escape. PHRASE

9 If you say that something is not the case, **let alone** something else, you mean that since the first thing is not the case, the second thing cannot be, because it is more difficult or unusual. EG *I had never seen him, let alone spoken to him... The story was not worth reading, let alone filming.* PHRASE

10 If you **let** your house or land to someone, you allow them to use it in exchange for regular payments. EG *The cottage was let to an actress.* V+O

let down. 1 If you **let** someone **down**, you disappoint them, usually by not doing something that you said you would do. EG *They felt strongly that the school system had let them down.* ● See also **letdown**. **2** If you **let down** something filled with air, such as a tyre, you allow air to escape from it. PHRASAL VB : V+O+ADV; V+O+ADV

let in. If something **lets in** water or air, it has a hole or crack which allows the water or air to get into it. EG *My old boots had been letting in water.* PHRASAL VB : V+O+ADV

let in for. If you wonder what you have **let** yourself **in for**, you think that you may be getting involved in something difficult or unpleasant. EG *What have we let ourselves in for?* PHRASAL VB : V+O+ADV+PREP Informal

let in on or **let into.** If you **let** someone **in on** a secret or **let** someone **into** a secret, you tell it to them. EG *He didn't want to let Uncle Harold in on the news just yet.* PHRASAL VB : V+O+ADV+PREP, OR V+O+PREP

let off. 1 If you **let** someone **off** a duty or task, you say that they do not have to do it. EG *We have been let off our homework because of the concert.* PHRASAL VB : V+O+ADV/PREP

2 If you **let** someone **off**, you give them no punishment, or a less severe punishment than they expect. EG *He let me off with a reprimand.* **3** If you **let off** a gun or a bomb, you fire the gun or cause the bomb to explode. V+O+ADV; V+O+ADV

let on. If you do not **let on** about something secret, you do not tell anyone about it. EG *Don't let on we went to that dance.* PHRASAL VB : V+ADV, WITH BROAD NEG

let out. 1 If you **let** water, air, or breath **out**, you allow it to come out freely. EG *He let the water out and refilled the bath... Piggy let out his breath with a gasp.* **2** If you **let out** a sound, you make that sound. EG *She let out a terrible shriek.* PHRASAL VB : V+O+ADV

let up. If something **lets up**, it stops or becomes less. EG *Day followed day and still the heat did not let up.* ● See also **let-up**. PHRASAL VB : V+ADV

letdown /lɛtdaʊn/, **letdowns.** If you say that something is a **letdown**, you mean that it is disappointing. EG *For the visitor expecting something special, this is rather a let-down.* N COUNT : USU a+N Informal

lethal /liːθəºl/. Something that is **lethal** can kill people or animals. EG *The chemical is lethal to rats but safe for cattle... ...a lethal weapon.* ADJ QUALIT

lethargic /lɪ²θɑːdʒɪk/. Someone who is **lethargic** has no energy or enthusiasm. EG *I often feel tired and lethargic.* ◇ **lethargy** /lɛθədʒi¹/. EG *He was determined to shake them out of their lethargy.* ADJ QUALIT Formal ◇ N UNCOUNT

let's /lɛts/ is the usual spoken form of 'let us'.

letter /lɛtə/, **letters. 1** When you write a **letter**, you write a message on paper and then send it to someone. EG *She wrote a letter to Harold... Peter received a letter from his wife... They informed Victor by letter.* N COUNT OR by+N

2 Letters are written symbols which represent the sounds of a language. N COUNT

letterbox /lɛtəbɒks/, **letterboxes.** A **letterbox** is **1** a rectangular hole in a door through which letters are delivered. **2** a large metal container in the street into which you post letters. N COUNT

lettering /lɛtəºrɪŋ/ is writing in which the letters are not joined to each other. EG *Underneath it, in smaller lettering, was a name.* N UNCOUNT +SUPP

lettuce /lɛtɪs/, **lettuces.** A **lettuce** is a plant with large green leaves that you eat in salads. N COUNT OR N UNCOUNT

let-up, let-ups. If there is a **let-up** of something, there is less of it. EG *There was a noticeable let-up of violence.* N UNCOUNT OR N COUNT

leukaemia /luːkiːmɪə/; also spelled **leukemia. Leukaemia** is a disease of the blood, which can kill people. N UNCOUNT

level /lɛvəºl/, **levels, levelling, levelled;** spelled **leveling** and **leveled** in American English.

1 A **level** is a point on a scale, for example a scale of amount, importance, or difficulty. EG *Mammals maintain their body temperature at a constant level... ...a high level of unemployment... ...an intermediate level English course.* N COUNT+SUPP

2 The **level** of a lake or river, or the **level** of a liquid in a container, is the height of its surface. EG *The level of the lake continues to rise... Check the oil level and tyre pressure of your car regularly.* ● See also **sea level**. N SING : the+N

3 If one thing is at the **level** of another thing, it is at the same height as the other thing. EG *He had a pile of books which reached to the level of his chin.* N SING+SUPP

4 If one thing is **level** with another thing, it is at the same height as the other thing. EG *He had his hands in front of him, level with his chest.* ADJ PRED : OFT+with

5 If something such as trade stays **level** with something else, it gets larger or smaller at the same rate as the other thing. EG *Food production is going to keep level with population growth.* ADJ PRED : OFT+with

6 If you are going somewhere and you draw **level** with someone, you get closer to them until you are at their side. EG *Coming towards me was a man and when we drew level, I smiled.* ADV AFTER VB

7 Something that is **level** is completely flat, with no ADJ QUALIT part higher than any other. EG *The floor is quite level.*

8 If you **level** an area of land, you make it flat. EG *...gardeners digging and levelling the ground.* V+O

9 If people **level** something such as a building or a wood, they knock it down completely so that there is nothing left. EG *Specially built tractors levelled more than 1,000 acres of forest.* V+O

10 If you **level** a criticism or accusation at or against someone, you criticize or accuse them. EG *...criticisms he has levelled against gangsters... Serious charges were levelled at television during the sixties.* V+O+*at/against*

level off or **level out. 1** If something **levels off** or **levels out**, it stops increasing or decreasing. EG *Economic growth was starting to level off.* **2** When an aircraft **levels off** or **levels out**, it travels horizontally after it has been travelling upwards or downwards. EG *The plane levelled off at 35,000 feet.* PHRASAL VB: V+ADV

level crossing, level crossings. A **level crossing** is a place where a railway line crosses a road at the same level. N COUNT British

level-headed. Someone who is **level-headed** can act calmly in difficult situations. ADJ QUALIT

lever /liːvə/, **levers. 1** A **lever** is **1.1** a handle or bar that you pull or push in order to operate a piece of machinery. EG *Howard pushes the gear lever in.* **1.2** a bar, one end of which is placed under a heavy object so that when you press down on the other end you can move the object. EG *There was nothing rigid to serve as a lever.* N COUNT

2 A **lever** is also something that you can use as a means of getting someone to do something. EG *Industrial action may be threatened as a political lever.* N COUNT: USU+SUPP

leverage /liːvəʳrɪdʒ/ is **1** the ability to influence people. EG *Relatively small groups can exert immense political leverage.* **2** the force that is applied to an object when a lever is used. N UNCOUNT: USU+SUPP

levity /lɛvɪˡtiˡ/ is behaviour in which someone treats serious matters in a light-hearted way. EG *I've been appalled by the levity with which some politicians discuss this issue.* N UNCOUNT Formal

levy /lɛviˡ/, **levies, levying, levied. 1** A **levy** is a sum of money that you have to pay, for example as a tax to the government. N COUNT

2 When a government or organization **levies** a tax or other sum of money, it demands it from people. V+O

liability /laɪəbɪlɪˡtiˡ/, **liabilities. 1** If you say that someone or something is a **liability**, you mean that they cause a lot of problems or embarrassment. EG *Colley was an asset in the drawing room but a liability on any battlefield.* N COUNT

2 A company's **liabilities** are the sums of money which it owes. EG *The company has had to undertake heavy liabilities.* N COUNT: USU PLURAL Technical

3 If you have **liability** for something such as a debt or an accident, you are legally responsible for it. N UNCOUNT Legal

liable /laɪəbəˡl/. **1** Something that is **liable** to happen is very likely to happen. EG *I feel that the play is liable to give offence to many people.* ADJ PRED +*to*-INF

2 If people or things are **liable** to something, they are likely to experience it or do it. EG *I was liable to sea-sickness... ...an improved design which is less liable to error.* ADJ PRED+*to* Formal

3 If you are **liable** for something such as a debt, you are legally responsible for it. ADJ PRED: OFT+*for*

liaise /liˡeɪz/, **liaises, liaising, liaised.** When organizations or people **liaise** with each other, they work together and keep each other fully informed. EG *Members can help by liaising with the press.* V+*with/between*

liaison /liˡeɪzɒn/, **liaisons. 1 Liaison** is cooperation and the exchange of information between different organizations or between different sections of an organization. EG *...liaison between the army and the government... ...a need to maintain liaison with local organizations with similar objectives.* N UNCOUNT

2 A **liaison** is a sexual relationship which is regarded as immoral. EG *The security services had discovered his liaison with Miss Keeler.* N COUNT Formal

liar /laɪə/, **liars.** A **liar** is someone who tells lies. EG *You're a liar... He called me a liar.* N COUNT

libel /laɪbəˡl/, **libels. Libel** or a **libel** is something written which wrongly accuses someone of something, and which is therefore against the law. EG *Hinds brought an action for libel against him... This was a gigantic libel.* N UNCOUNT OR N COUNT

libellous /laɪbəˡləs/; spelled **libelous** in American English. If something written is **libellous**, it wrongly accuses someone of something, and is therefore against the law. EG *...libellous comments... We must be careful not to say anything libellous.* ADJ QUALIT

liberal /lɪbəʳrəl/, **liberals. 1** Someone who is **liberal** is tolerant of different kinds of behaviour or opinions. EG *My school was traditional, but more liberal than other public schools... ...a liberal democracy.* ▸ used as a noun. EG *...a pair of enlightened liberals.* ADJ QUALIT ▸ N COUNT

2 Liberal also means giving, using, or taking a lot of something. EG *Could any man make a more liberal offer?... ...a liberal provision of guns.* ADJ QUALIT

◊ **liberally.** EG *Tim helped himself liberally to some more wine.* ◊ ADV

liberalism /lɪbəʳrəlɪzəʳm/ is the belief that people should have a lot of political freedom. N UNCOUNT

liberalize /lɪbəʳrəlaɪz/, **liberalizes, liberalizing, liberalized;** also spelled **liberalise.** When a country or government **liberalizes** its laws or its attitudes, it makes them less strict and allows people more freedom. EG *There was a move to liberalize the state abortion laws.* ◊ **liberalization** /lɪbəʳrəlaɪzeɪʃəʳn/. EG *He called for the liberalization of the laws relating to immigration.* V+O OR V ◊ N UNCOUNT

liberate /lɪbəreɪt/, **liberates, liberating, liberated. 1** To **liberate** someone means to help them to achieve a freer and happier way of life. EG *He claimed that socialism alone could liberate black people... ...liberating people from poverty.* V+O: OFT+*from* Formal

◊ **liberation** /lɪbəreɪʃəʳn/. EG *...the women's liberation movement.* ◊ N UNCOUNT

2 If prisoners **are liberated**, they are released from prison. V+O Formal

3 To **liberate** a place means to free it from the political or military control of another country. EG *...the hero who liberated Cuba.* ◊ **liberation.** EG *...wars of national liberation.* V+O Formal ◊ N UNCOUNT

liberated /lɪbəreɪtɪ²d/. You say that people are **liberated** when they do not accept all the ideas and ways of behaviour which are traditional in their society. EG *...a liberated couple.* ADJ QUALIT

libertarian /lɪbətɛərɪən/, **libertarians.** Someone who is **libertarian** believes in the idea of people being free to think and behave in the way that they want. ▸ used as a noun. EG *Education is a topic in which libertarians have taken a close interest.* ADJ CLASSIF Formal ▸ N COUNT

liberty /lɪbətiˡ/, **liberties. 1 Liberty** is **1.1** the freedom to live your life in the way that you want, especially without a lot of interference from the government. EG *...respect for individual liberty... ...increasing attacks on their liberties.* **1.2** the freedom to go wherever you want, which you lose when you are a prisoner. EG *...that fundamental aspect of imprisonment, the loss of liberty.* N UNCOUNT OR N PLURAL Formal; N UNCOUNT Formal

2 A criminal who is **at liberty** has not yet been caught, or has escaped from prison. EG *Only one important figure remains at liberty.* PHRASE Formal

3 If you are not **at liberty** to do something, you have not been given permission to do it. PHRASE Formal

4 You say that someone **is taking a liberty** when they do or say something that involves another person without asking the person's permission first. EG *I took the liberty of looking you up in the* PHRASE

Which word on these pages has two different plurals?

phone book... He was not the sort of man with whom one took liberties.

librarian /laɪbrɛərɪən/, **librarians.** A **librarian** is a person who is in charge of a library or who has been trained to do responsible work in a library. N COUNT

library /laɪbrəri[1]/, **libraries. 1** A **library** is an institution or a part of an institution that keeps books and newspapers for people to read. Most libraries allow their members to borrow books for certain periods of time. EG *... public libraries... ...a library book... ...a new extension to the library.* N COUNT

2 A **library** is also a private collection of books or gramophone records. N COUNT : USU+SUPP

libretto /lɪbrɛtəʊ/, **librettos** or **libretti.** The **libretto** of an opera or musical play is the words that are sung and spoken in it. N COUNT

lice /laɪs/ is the plural of **louse.**

licence /laɪsəns/, **licences;** spelled **license** in American English. **1** A **licence** is an official document which gives you permission to do, use, or own something. EG *...a driving licence... The first page carried the licence number and the full name of the holder.* N COUNT

2 If someone does something **under licence**, they do it by special permission from a government or other authority. EG *Badgers can be killed under licence in those areas.* PHRASE

3 See also **off-licence.**

license /laɪsəns/, **licenses, licensing, licensed.** If a government or other authority **licenses** a person, organization, or activity, they officially give permission for the person or organization to do something, or for the activity to take place. EG *The Royal College examines and licenses surgeons.* V+O

◇ **licensing.** EG *...a licensing authority... ...licensing controls.* ◇ ADJ CLASSIF : ATTRIB

licensed /laɪsənst/. **1** If you are **licensed** to do something, you have official permission from a government or other authority to do it. EG *These men are licensed to carry firearms... You must be licensed to drive... ...a licensed pilot.* ADJ CLASSIF

2 If something that you own or use is **licensed**, you have official permission to own it or use it. EG *The car is licensed and insured.* ADJ CLASSIF

3 If a restaurant or hotel is **licensed**, it has a licence to sell alcoholic drinks. ADJ CLASSIF

licensing hours are the times of the day when a pub is allowed to sell alcoholic drinks. N PLURAL British

licensing laws are the laws which control the selling of alcoholic drinks. N PLURAL British

licentious /laɪsɛntʊəs/. If you describe a person as **licentious**, you mean that they are very immoral, especially in their sexual behaviour. ADJ QUALIT Formal

lick /lɪk/, **licks, licking, licked. 1** When you **lick** something, you move your tongue across its surface. EG *He licked the last of the egg off his knife... The cat was licking its paw... All I do is lick stamps and address envelopes.* ▸ used as a noun. EG *...a few licks and nibbles.* V+O ▸ N COUNT

2 If you **lick** your **lips**, you move your tongue across your lips, often when you see food that attracts you. EG *She looked at the plate and licked her lips.* PHRASE

3 If you **lick** someone, you easily defeat them in a fight or competition. EG *I'm sure you could lick both of them.* V+O Informal

4 If you say that someone is **licking** their **wounds**, you mean that they are recovering after being defeated or humiliated. EG *She'd rather be left alone to lick her wounds in solitude.* PHRASE

5 If you **lick** something **into shape**, you improve it so that it is ready to be used. PHRASE

licorice /lɪkərɪs, -ɪʃ/. See **liquorice.**

lid /lɪd/, **lids. 1** A **lid** is the top of a box or other container which can be removed or raised when you want to open the container. EG *I lifted the lid... She was opening and closing the lid of her tin.* N COUNT

2 Your **lids** are the same as your eyelids. EG *She looked round from under half-closed lids.* N COUNT : USU PLURAL

lie /laɪ/. The forms **lie, lies, lying, lay** /leɪ/, **lain** /leɪn/ are used for the verb in paragraphs 1 to 6 and for the phrasal verbs. The forms **lie, lies, lying, lied** are used for the verb in paragraph 8. **Lies** is also the plural form of the noun in paragraph 7.

1 If you **are lying** somewhere, you are in a horizontal position and are not standing or sitting. EG *Judy was lying flat on the bed... I lay there trying to remember what he looked like... She lay ill for days... Lie on your side.* V+A OR V+C

2 If an object **lies** in a particular place, it is in a flat position in that place. EG *The weapon was found lying in a ditch... ...the folder lying open before him... The coffin lay undisturbed for centuries.* V+A OR V+C

3 If you say that a place **lies** in a particular position, you mean that it is situated there. EG *The bridge lies beyond the docks... This town lies at the southernmost tip of the island.* V+A

4 If you say that the cause of something or the solution to a problem **lies** somewhere, you are indicating what you think the cause or solution is. EG *The causes of this lie deep in the history of society... Its attraction lay in its simplicity.* V+A Formal

5 If something **lies** ahead or **lies** before you, it is going to happen in the future. EG *Endless hours of pleasure lie before you... ...an unwelcome foretaste of what lay in store.* V+A

6 You can use **lie** to say what position someone is in during a competition. For example, if they **are lying** third, they are third. V+C

7 A **lie** is something that someone says which they know is untrue. EG *You're telling lies now.* • See also **white lie.** N COUNT

8 If someone **is lying**, they are saying something which they know is untrue. EG *You lied to me... 'Certainly not,' I lied.* V OR V+QUOTE

9 See also **lying.**

lie about or **lie around. 1** If you **lie about** or **lie around**, you spend your time relaxing and being lazy. EG *We lay around smoking... ...lying about in their rooms.* **2** If things are left **lying about** or **lying around**, they are left somewhere in an untidy way. EG *The bottles were left lying around overnight.* PHRASAL VB : V+ADV Informal; V+ADV

lie down. 1 When you **lie down**, you move into a horizontal position, usually in order to rest or sleep. EG *He lay down on the couch.* • See also **lie-down.** PHRASAL VB : V+ADV

2 If you **take** unfair treatment **lying down**, you accept it without complaining or resisting. EG *She was never one to take bullying lying down.* PHRASE Informal

lie with. If the responsibility for something **lies with** you, it is your responsibility. EG *Are you saying that the fault generally lies with the management?* PHRASAL VB : V+PREP Formal

lie-down. If you have a **lie-down**, you lie down on a bed and rest. N SING : a+N Informal

lie-in. If you have a **lie-in**, you stay in bed later than usual in the morning. EG *The meeting's not until ten o'clock, so I can have a lie-in.* N SING : a+N Informal

lieutenant, lieutenants; pronounced /lɛftɛnənt/ in British English and /luːtɛnənt/ in American English.

A **lieutenant** is a junior officer in the army or navy. EG *...Lieutenant Lawton.* N COUNT

life /laɪf/, **lives** /laɪvz/. The form **lives** is also the third person singular of the present tense of the verb 'live' and is then pronounced /lɪvz/.

1 Life is **1.1** the quality which people, animals, and plants have when they are not dead and which objects and substances do not have. EG *...her last hours of life... How far do we allow a doctor to have power over life and death?* **1.2** things which are alive. EG *Is there life on Jupiter?... ...plant life.* N UNCOUNT; N UNCOUNT : OFT+SUPP

2 Someone's **life** is **2.1** their state of being alive. EG *She had risked her life to save mine... He nearly lost his life.* **2.2** the period of time during which they are alive. EG *People spend their lives worrying* N COUNT : USU+POSS *about money... I've never boiled a potato in my life... I've had such a fascinating life.*

3 Life is also the events and experiences that happen to people, either generally or in a particular place. EG *Life is probably harder for women... I don't know what you want out of life... Sport has always been a part of university life.* — N UNCOUNT

4 If you say that an activity or interest is someone's **life**, you mean that they spend most of their time on it. EG *Fishing was their entire life.* — N UNCOUNT +POSS

5 A person or place that is full of **life** is full of activity and excitement. — N UNCOUNT

6 The **life** of a machine, object, or substance is the period of time that it lasts for. EG *Underlays double the life of a carpet.* — N SING

7 Life is also used in these phrases. **7.1** If someone or something that has been inactive **comes to life**, they become active. EG *Their political movement came to life again.* **7.2** If you **hold on** to something **for dear life**, you hold on very tightly because it is important that you do not let go. EG *I held on to the ledge for dear life.* **7.3 For life** means for the rest of a person's life. EG *If you help me, I'll be your friend for life.* **7.4** If you say that you cannot understand or remember something **for the life of** you, you mean that you cannot understand or remember it, however hard you try. EG *I can't for the life of me see why you want them.* **7.5** If you **live** your **own life**, you live in the way that you want to, without other people's advice or interference. EG *She was 18 after all, entitled to live her own life.* **7.6** If you describe a situation as **a matter of life and death**, you mean that someone may die if people do not act immediately. EG *Phone an ambulance. It's a matter of life and death.* **7.7** If someone **takes** a person's **life**, they kill that person. EG *On the eve of his conviction, he took his own life.* **7.8** to **risk life and limb**: see **limb**. • See also **way of life**. — PHRASES; Informal (7.2); Informal (7.4); Formal (7.7)

lifebelt /laɪfbɛlt/, **lifebelts.** A **lifebelt** is a large ring used to keep a person afloat and prevent them from drowning when they fall into the sea or other deep water. — N COUNT

lifeboat /laɪfbəʊt/, **lifeboats.** A **lifeboat** is **1** a large boat which is sent out from a port or harbour in order to rescue people who are in danger at sea. **2** a small boat which is carried on a ship and which people on the ship use to escape when the ship is in danger of sinking. — N COUNT

lifebuoy /laɪfbɔɪ/, **lifebuoys.** A **lifebuoy** is the same as a lifebelt. — N COUNT

life-cycle, life-cycles. The **life-cycle** of an animal or plant is the series of changes and developments that it passes through from the beginning of its life until its death. EG *...the life-cycle of the salmon... They complete their life-cycle in a single growing season.* — N COUNT: USU+POSS

life expectancy, life expectancies. The **life expectancy** of a person, animal, or plant is the length of time that they are normally likely to live. EG *Women have a longer life expectancy than men.* — N COUNT OR N UNCOUNT

life form, life forms. A **life form** is any living thing such as an animal or plant. EG *Many of the deep-sea life forms feed directly on bacteria.* — N COUNT+SUPP

lifeguard /laɪfgɑːd/, **lifeguards.** A **lifeguard** is a person at a beach or swimming pool whose job is to rescue people when they are in danger of drowning. — N COUNT

life imprisonment. When criminals are sentenced to **life imprisonment**, they are sentenced to stay in prison for the rest of their lives, although they are usually released after several years. — N UNCOUNT

lifejacket /laɪfdʒækə't/, **lifejackets.** A **lifejacket** is a sleeveless jacket which you wear in order to stay afloat in the water when you are in danger of drowning. — N COUNT

lifeless /laɪflɪ²s/. **1** A person or animal that is **lifeless** is dead. EG *...the lifeless body of Lieutenant Dowling.* — ADJ CLASSIF; Literary

2 You can use **lifeless** to describe machines and objects when you want to emphasize that they are not living things. EG *...a lifeless chunk of rock.* — ADJ CLASSIF

3 A **lifeless** place or area does not have anything living or growing there. EG *...a time when the earth was completely lifeless.* — ADJ CLASSIF

4 You can also say that people or things are **lifeless** when you find them dull and not lively or exciting. EG *The characters in the novel are lifeless... ...a lifeless voice.* — ADJ QUALIT

lifelike /laɪflaɪk/. **1** Something that is **lifelike** has the appearance of being alive. EG *...extremely lifelike computer-controlled robots.* — ADJ QUALIT

2 A **lifelike** painting or acting performance is very realistic. — ADJ QUALIT

lifeline /laɪflaɪn/, **lifelines. 1** You refer to something as a **lifeline** when it is very important in helping people to survive, or in helping an activity to continue. EG *The household became my lifeline, my only link with the outside world... ...the oil lifeline of Western Europe.* — N COUNT: USU+SUPP

2 A **lifeline** is also a rope which you throw to someone when they are in danger of drowning. — N COUNT

lifelong /laɪflɒŋ/ means existing or happening for the whole of a person's life. EG *...her friend and lifelong companion.* — ADJ CLASSIF: ATTRIB

life science, life sciences. The **life sciences** are sciences such as zoology, botany, and anthropology, which are concerned with human beings, animals, and plants. — N COUNT: USU PLURAL

life sentence, life sentences. When criminals receive a **life sentence**, they are sentenced to stay in prison for the rest of their lives, although they are usually released after several years. — N COUNT

life-size. Life-size or **life-sized** paintings, sculptures, or models are the same size as the person or thing that they represent. EG *...a life-size inflatable whale... ...a life-size statue.* — ADJ CLASSIF

lifespan /laɪfspæn/, **lifespans. 1** The **lifespan** of a person, animal, or plant is the period of time during which they are alive. EG *...the human lifespan... In our brief life-span we normally experience only a few of these problems.* — N COUNT+SUPP

2 The **lifespan** of a product, organization, or idea is the period of time during which it exists or is used. EG *This job had a planned life-span of five years.* — N COUNT+SUPP

life style, life styles. Your **life style** is the way you live, for example the conditions you live in and the things you normally do. EG *...this highly urban lifestyle... This will affect the life-styles of many people.* — N COUNT+SUPP

lifetime /laɪftaɪm/, **lifetimes. 1** A **lifetime** is the length of time that someone is alive. EG *I have spent a lifetime in politics... I've seen a lot of changes in my lifetime.* — N COUNT

2 The **lifetime** of something is the period of time that it lasts. EG *...during the lifetime of this parliament.* — N SING+POSS

lift /lɪft/, **lifts, lifting, lifted. 1** If you **lift** something, you move it to another position, usually upwards. EG *He lifted the glass to his mouth... She lifted down the wooden boxes.* — V+O: USU+A

2 If you **lift** a part of your body, you move it to a higher position. EG *He lifted his hand to ring the doorbell... She lifted her feet on to the settee.* — V+O

3 If you **lift** your eyes or your head, you look up. EG *She lifted her eyes from the ground and fixed them on me.* — V+O; Literary

4 A **lift** is a device like a large box that moves up and down inside a tall building and carries people from one floor to another. EG *I took the lift to the eighth floor.* — N COUNT; British

5 If you give someone a **lift**, you take them in your car from one place to another in order to help — N COUNT: USU a+N

> Find two words on these pages which refer to the same thing.

them. EG *He gave her a lift back to London that night... She offered me a lift home.*
6 When fog or mist **lifts**, it disappears or moves upwards. EG *Around midday, the fog lifted.* V
7 If people in authority **lift** a law or rule that prevents people from doing something, they end it. EG *He lifted the ban on the People's Party.* V+O
8 If you **lift** a piece of writing or music that has been written by someone else, you copy it and use it in your own work. EG *Most of the article was lifted from a woman's magazine.* V+O: OFT+*from*

lift-off, lift-offs. Lift-off or a **lift-off** is the launching of a rocket into space. N UNCOUNT OR N COUNT

ligament /lɪgəmə²nt/, **ligaments.** A **ligament** is a band of strong tissue in your body, which connects bones. EG *He had torn a ligament in his knee playing squash.* N COUNT

light /laɪt/, **lights, lighting, lighted, lit** /lɪt/; **lighter, lightest.** The forms **lighted** and **lit** are both used as the past tense and past participle of the verb, although **lit** is more usual.
1 Light is the brightness that lets you see things, and that comes from the sun, the moon, lamps, or fire. EG *We are dependent on the sun for heat and light... By the light of a torch, she began to read.* N UNCOUNT
2 A **light** is anything that produces light, especially an electric bulb. EG *She went into her daughter's room and turned on the light.* N COUNT
3 A place or object that **is lit** by something has light shining in it or on it. EG *...a room lit by candles.* V+O
◊ **lighted.** EG *He looked up thoughtfully at the lighted windows.* ◊ ADJ CLASSIF: ATTRIB
4 If a building or room is **light**, it has a lot of natural light in it, for example because it has large windows. ADJ QUALIT
5 If it is **light**, it is daytime. ADJ PRED
6 If there is a particular **light** in someone's eyes, their eyes show a particular emotion. EG *I could see a questioning and reproachful light in Jane's eyes.* N SING+SUPP Literary
7 If you **light** something, you make it start burning. EG *She stopped and lit a match... Light the gas fire if you feel chilly.* ◊ **lighted.** EG *...a lighted candle.* V+O ◊ ADJ CLASSIF
8 If someone asks you for a **light**, they want some matches or a cigarette lighter in order to start their cigarette burning. N SING: *a*+N
9 If you **set light to** something, you make it start burning. PHRASE
10 Light is also used in these phrases. **10.1** If someone **sees the light**, they finally realise or understand something they ought to. **10.2** If a new event or piece of information **throws** or **casts light on** something, it makes it easier to understand. EG *His diaries throw a new light upon certain incidents.* **10.3** If something **comes to light** or **is brought to light**, it becomes known. EG *It has come to light that he was lying.* **10.4** When you talk about **the light at the end of the tunnel**, you are referring to the end of an unpleasant situation, which you are looking forward to. EG *There was no victory in sight, no light at the end of the tunnel.* **10.5 First light** is the time in the early morning when the sun begins to rise. EG *They attacked at first light.* **10.6** If someone **goes out like a light**, they fall asleep or become unconscious very quickly. **10.7 green light**: see **green**. PHRASES; Formal; Informal
11 If you see something in a particular **light**, you think about it in that way. EG *We were now seeing things in a different light... He appeared that day in the worst possible light.* N SING+SUPP
12 In the light of something means considering it or taking it into account. EG *This development is significant in the light of what happened later.* PHRASE
13 Something that is **light 13.1** does not weigh very much. EG *The bag was very light, as though there were nothing in it.* ◊ **lightness.** EG *...the extreme lightness of this particular shoe.* **13.2** is not very great in amount, degree, or intensity. EG *A light rain was falling... The traffic on the highway was light that day.* ADJ QUALIT; ◊ N UNCOUNT; ADJ QUALIT
14 Light colours are very pale. EG *...light blue eyes.* ADJ QUALIT
15 Light work does not involve much physical effort. EG *He has grown much weaker and is now capable of only light work.* ADJ QUALIT
16 Movements and actions that are **light** are graceful or gentle and are done with very little force or effort. EG *She runs up the stairs two at a time with her light graceful step.* ◊ **lightly.** EG *He kissed his wife lightly on the cheek.* ◊ **lightness.** EG *For a heavy man he moves with surprising lightness and speed.* ADJ QUALIT; ◊ ADV; ◊ N UNCOUNT
17 Light books, plays, or pieces of music entertain you without making you think very deeply. EG *...light entertainment and comedy.* ADJ QUALIT
18 If you speak in a **light** way, you sound as if you do not think that what you are saying is important or serious. EG *...a cool, light, insolent voice.* ◊ **lightly.** EG *He said sorry as lightly as possible.* ADJ QUALIT; ◊ ADV
19 See also **lighting**, **lightly**.
light up. 1 If something **lights up** something else, it shines light on all of it. EG *The fire was still blazing, lighting up the sky.* **2** If your face or eyes **light up**, you suddenly look very happy. EG *His face lit up at the sight of Cynthia.* **3** If you **light up** a cigarette or pipe, you start smoking. EG *George lit up and puffed away for a while.* PHRASAL VB: V+O+ADV; V+ADV; V+O+ADV OR V+ADV

light bulb, light bulbs. A **light bulb** is the round glass part of an electric light or lamp which light shines from. N COUNT

lighten /laɪtə⁰n/, **lightens, lightening, lightened. 1** When something **lightens** or when you **lighten** it, it becomes less dark in colour. EG *After the rain stops, the sky lightens a little... Constant exposure to the sun had lightened my hair.* V-ERG
2 You also say that you **lighten** something when you make it less heavy. EG *They began to lighten their products in an effort to increase sales.* V+O
3 If someone's face or expression **lightens**, it becomes more cheerful, happy, and relaxed. EG *Her whole expression lightened.* V-ERG

lighter /laɪtə/, **lighters. 1** A **lighter** or a **cigarette lighter** is a small device which produces a flame that you can light a cigarette or pipe with. EG *Can I use your lighter?* N COUNT
2 Lighter is the comparative of **light**.

light-fingered. If you say that someone is **light-fingered**, you mean that they steal things. ADJ CLASSIF Informal

light-headed. If you are **light-headed**, you feel rather dizzy and faint. ADJ QUALIT

light-hearted. 1 Someone who is **light-hearted** is cheerful and happy. EG *He was in a light-hearted mood.* ◊ **light-heartedly.** EG *She flirted with them light-heartedly and enjoyed herself enormously.* ADJ QUALIT; ◊ ADV
2 Something that is **light-hearted** is entertaining or amusing, and not serious. EG *Let me finish with a slightly more light-hearted question.* ADJ QUALIT

lighthouse /laɪthaʊs/, **lighthouses.** A **lighthouse** is a tower in or near to the sea which contains a powerful flashing lamp. Lighthouses are used to guide ships or to warn them of danger. N COUNT

light industry, light industries. Light industry is industry in which only small items are made, for example household goods and clothes. N COUNT OR N UNCOUNT

lighting /laɪtɪŋ/. The **lighting** in a place is the way that it is lit, for example by electric lights or candles, or the quality of the light in it. EG *...artificial lighting... ...poorly designed street lighting.* N UNCOUNT

lightly /laɪtli¹/. If you say that something is not done **lightly**, you mean that it is not done without serious thought. EG *This is not a charge to make lightly against the government... He knew it was not being said lightly.* • See also **light**. ADV

lightning /laɪtnɪŋ/. **1 Lightning** is the very bright flashes of light in the sky that you see during a thunderstorm. EG *...a flash of lightning... He was struck by lightning, and nearly died.* N UNCOUNT
2 Lightning describes things that happen very quickly or last for only a short time. EG *He drew his gun with lightning speed.* ADJ CLASSIF: ATTRIB

lightning conductor, lightning conductors. A **lightning conductor** is a long, thin piece of metal that is placed on top of a building and that goes as far as the ground. It allows lightning to reach the ground safely without damaging the building. N COUNT British

lightning rod, lightning rods. A **lightning rod** is the same as a lightning conductor. N COUNT American

lightweight /laɪtweɪt/. Something that is **lightweight** weighs less than most other things of the same type. EG *...a grey lightweight suit... ...lightweight cameras.* ADJ QUALIT

light-year, light-years. 1 A **light-year** is the distance that light travels in a year. N COUNT Technical

2 You can use **light-years** to mean a very long time. EG *Last Tuesday seemed light-years away already.* N COUNT: USU PLURAL Informal

likable /laɪkəbə⁰l/. See **likeable**.

like /laɪk/, **likes, liking, liked. 1** If you say that one person or thing is **like** another, you mean that they have similar characteristics. EG *He looked like Clark Gable... She's very like her younger sister... She's nothing like I imagined... 'I'm glad you came.' – 'Yes. It was like old times.'... The lake was like a bright blue mirror.* PREP

2 If you ask someone what something is **like**, you are asking them to describe it or to give their opinion of it. EG *What was Essex like?... What did they taste like?... I don't remember what she was like.* PREP

3 You can use **like** to introduce an example of the thing that you have just mentioned. EG *You only get them in big countries, like Africa or India... They knew very little about home activities like cooking.* PREP

4 You can use **like** to say that something is true of a particular thing because it is true of all things of that kind. EG *There's no point in stirring up a lot of publicity about a foolish thing like this.* PREP

5 You can use **like** to say that someone or something is in the same situation as another person or thing. EG *He, like everybody else, had worried about it... She died in childbirth, like Sir Thomas More's wife Jane.* PREP

6 If you say that someone is behaving **like** a particular person or thing, you mean that what they are doing is what that person or thing typically does. EG *You're behaving like a perfect idiot... She began to shake like a jelly.* PREP

7 If you say **and the like** after mentioning some things or people, you are indicating that there are other similar things or people that can be included in what you are saying. EG *...the activities of ruthless mine owners and the like.* PHRASE

8 You say **'like this'**, **'like that'**, or **'like so'** when you are showing someone how something is done. EG *Twist it round and put it on here, like that.* PHRASE

9 You also use **'like this'** or **'like that'** when you are drawing attention to something that you are doing or that someone else is doing. EG *Stop laughing like that!... Does he often talk like this?* PHRASE

10 If you say that something is **like** you remembered it or **like** you imagined it, you mean that it is the way you remembered or imagined it. EG *Is it like you remembered it?... It didn't work out quite like I intended it to.* CONJ Informal

11 You can sometimes use **nothing like** instead of 'not' when you want to emphasize a negative statement. EG *The cast is nothing like as numerous as one might suppose... There is nothing like enough practice given in solving problems.* PHRASE

12 You use **something like** to indicate that a number or quantity is an estimate, not an exact figure. EG *Something like ninety per cent of the crop was destroyed.* PHRASE

13 If you **like** something, you find it pleasant or attractive, or you approve of it. EG *I like reading... She's a nice girl, I like her... They didn't like what they saw... What is it you like about them?... A strike is going to take place whether we like it or not... Her folks like her to get in early.* V+O: OFT+-ING OR to-INF; ALSO V+-ING OR to-INF

14 If you say that you would **like** something or would **like** to do something, you are expressing a wish or desire. EG *I'd like to marry him... Would you like some coffee?... He would have liked a pint of beer before he started... Do what you like... He can stay here if he likes... I'd like you to come.* V+O, V+to-INF, OR V+O+to-INF

15 You say **if you like** when you are offering to do something for someone. EG *I'll drive, if you like.* ADV SEN

16 See also **liking**.

-like. You can add **-like** to a noun when you want to describe something as similar to the thing referred to by the noun. EG *The landscape has a dream-like air... ...a rock-like hump.*

likeable /laɪkəbə⁰l/; also spelled **likable.** If you describe someone or something as **likeable**, you mean that they are pleasant and therefore easy to like. EG *...a very attractive and likeable young man.* ADJ QUALIT

likelihood /laɪkli¹hʊd/. The **likelihood** of something happening is the fact that it is likely to happen. EG *There is every likelihood that she will succeed... This increases the likelihood of an attack.* N SING: USU+of OR REPORT

likely /laɪkli¹/, **likelier, likeliest. 1** If something is **likely**, it is probably true or will probably happen. EG *What kind of change is likely?... It seemed hardly likely that they would agree.* ADJ QUALIT

2 If you are **likely** to do something, you will probably do it. EG *They were not likely to forget it.* ADJ PRED +to-INF

3 Very likely or **most likely** means probably. EG *Very likely none of them would know the name.* ADV SEN

4 You use **likely** to describe people or things who will probably be suitable for a particular purpose. EG *The local committee is always looking out for likely recruits... ...likely candidates for appeal.* ADJ CLASSIF: ATTRIB

5 If you say to someone that what they have just told you is **a likely story**, you are saying in a humorous way that you don't believe it. PHRASE

like-minded. People who are **like-minded** have similar opinions, ideas, or interests to each other. EG *...Hubbard and his like-minded colleagues.* ADJ CLASSIF

liken /laɪkən/, **likens, likening, likened.** If you **liken** something **to** something else, you say that it is similar to it in some way. EG *It has a mildly nutty taste which has been likened to new potatoes.* PHRASAL VB: V+O+PREP

likeness /laɪknɪ²s/, **likenesses. 1** If one thing has a **likeness** to another, it is similar to it in appearance. EG *...a china dog that bore a likeness to his aunt... The boy's likeness to her son was startling.* N SING: OFT+to

2 If you say that a picture of someone is a good **likeness** of them, you mean that it looks very much like them. EG *The portrait shows a lot of talent. A very good likeness.* N COUNT: OFT+of

likewise /laɪkwaɪz/. **1** You use **likewise** when you are comparing two things and saying that they are similar. EG *In Yugoslavia there was a special local way of doing it, likewise in Italy.* ADV SEN

2 If you do one thing, and someone else **does likewise**, they do the same thing. EG *He is relaxing and invites them to do likewise.* PHRASE

liking /laɪkɪŋ/. **1** If you have a **liking** for someone or something, you like them. EG *I took an enormous liking to Davies the moment I met him... She was developing a liking for Scotch.* N SING+SUPP

2 If something is **to** your **liking**, you like it. EG *Organising Christmas relief funds was more to his liking than the routine work on Capitol Hill... Did they find the temperature to their liking?* PHRASE

3 If something is too big or too fast **for** your **liking**, you would prefer it to be smaller or slower. EG *You are progressing too fast for his liking.* PHRASE

lilac /laɪlək/, **lilacs. 1** A **lilac** is a small tree. It has pleasant-smelling flowers, which are also called **lilac**. EG *...lilac bushes in the garden.* N COUNT OR N UNCOUNT

2 Something that is **lilac** is pale pinkish-purple in colour. EG *...her plain lilac dress.* ADJ COLOUR

> If something is likely to happen, do you think it will happen?

Lilo /laɪləʊ/, **Lilos.** A **Lilo** is a long, flat plastic mattress that you fill with air and use for lying on, for example when you are camping or at the seaside. N COUNT Trademark

lilt /lɪlt/, **lilts.** If you say that someone speaks with a **lilt**, you mean that the pitch of their voice rises and falls in a pleasant way, as if they were singing. EG *There was something familiar in the lilt of her voice... ...his Irish lilt.* N COUNT

lilting /lɪltɪŋ/. A **lilting** voice or song rises and falls in pitch in a pleasant way. EG *The lark sings its lilting song... She spoke to him in her lilting Arabic.* ADJ CLASSIF

lily /lɪli¹/, **lilies.** A **lily** is a plant with large flowers that are often white. The flowers are also called **lilies**. EG *She added a wild lily to her bouquet.* N COUNT

limb /lɪm/, **limbs.** 1 Your **limbs** are your arms and legs. EG *He was very tall with long limbs... We cough, yawn, and stretch our limbs.* N COUNT

2 The **limbs** of a tree are its branches. EG *Thick smoke rose into the tree's upper limbs.* N COUNT Literary

3 If you say that someone has gone **out on a limb**, you mean that they have done or said something that is risky or extreme. EG *I never heard him go out on a limb like that before.* PHRASE

4 If someone **risks life and limb**, they do something very dangerous that may cause them to die or be seriously injured. PHRASE

-limbed is used after an adjective to indicate that a person or animal has limbs of a particular type or appearance. EG *The female athlete tends to be longer limbed... ...loose-limbed, well-built kids.*

limber /lɪmbə/, **limbers, limbering, limbered.** If you **limber up**, you prepare for a sport by practising or doing exercises. EG *We had no time to limber up on the practice range.* PHRASAL VB : V+ADV

limbo /lɪmbəʊ/. 1 If you are in **limbo**, you are in a situation where you do not know what will happen next and you have no control over things. EG *Refugees may remain in limbo for years.* N UNCOUNT

2 The **limbo** is a West Indian dance in which you have to pass under a low bar while leaning backwards. The bar is moved nearer to the floor each time you go under it. N SING : *the*+N

lime /laɪm/, **limes.** 1 A **lime** is 1.1 a small round fruit that has a dark green skin and tastes like a lemon. 1.2 a large tree with pale green leaves which is often planted in parks in towns and cities. EG *...the long avenue of limes.* N COUNT

2 **Lime** or **lime juice** is a non-alcoholic drink that is made from the juice of limes. N UNCOUNT

3 **Lime** is also 3.1 a chemical substance which you spread onto soil in order to improve its quality. 3.2 a white-coloured rock used for building or for making cement. EG *...a lime quarry.* 3.3 a white substance used for painting walls. N UNCOUNT

limelight /laɪmlaɪt/. If someone is in the **limelight**, a lot of attention is being paid to them, because they are famous or because they have done something very unusual or exciting. EG *He was only happy when he was in the limelight.* N SING : *the*+N

limerick /lɪmərɪk/, **limericks.** A **limerick** is a humorous poem which has five lines and a special rhythm and way of rhyming. N COUNT

limestone /laɪmstəʊn/ is a white-coloured rock which is used for building and making cement. N UNCOUNT

limit /lɪmɪt/, **limits, limiting, limited.** 1 A **limit** is the greatest amount, extent, or degree of something that is possible or allowed. EG *There is no limit to the risks they are prepared to take... The powers of the human brain are stretched to the limit... ...a motorist exceeding the speed limit.* N COUNT : USU+SUPP

2 The **limits** of a situation are the facts involved in it which make only some actions or results possible. EG *...the problems of applying that system within the limits of a weekly, two-hour meeting.* N PLURAL

3 If you **limit** something, you do something to ensure that it will not become greater than a particular amount or degree. EG *The government plans to limit military expenditure... Japanese exports would be limited to 1.68m vehicles.* V+O

4 If someone or something **limits** you, they reduce the number of things that you can have or do. EG *Why should the people of this country limit me that way?* ◊ **limiting.** EG *Many of these customs were narrow and limiting.* V+O ◊ ADJ QUALIT

5 If you **limit** yourself or **limit** your actions, you deal only with particular things or people. EG *Will he limit himself to seeing that the enterprise is approved?... I am limiting my observations to the Christian faith.* V+O OR V-REFL : USU+*to*

6 If something **is limited** to a particular place or group of people, it exists only in that place, or is had or done only by that group. EG *This problem is not limited to Sweden.* V+O : USU PASS+*to*

7 If you add **within limits** to a statement, you mean that it applies only to reasonable or normal situations. EG *Within limits, the higher the temperature, the quicker the chemical reaction.* ADV SEN

8 If a place is **off limits**, you are not allowed to go there. PHRASE

9 You say that someone **is the limit** when you are very annoyed with them. PHRASE Informal

limitation /lɪmɪteɪʃə⁰n/, **limitations.** 1 **Limitation** is the control or reduction of something. EG *...the limitation of trade union power... ...arms limitation talks.* N UNCOUNT

2 If you talk about the **limitations** of someone or something, you mean that they can only do some things and not others, or that they can only achieve a fairly low degree of success or excellence. EG *It's important to know your own limitations... The technique has its limitations.* N PLURAL : USU+POSS

3 When there are **limitations** on something, it is not allowed to grow or extend beyond certain limits. EG *All limitations on earnings must cease... I am willing to accept certain limitations on my freedom.* N COUNT : USU PLURAL

limited /lɪmɪtɪ²d/. 1 Something that is **limited** is not very large in amount or degree, or not large enough. EG *The choice was very limited... ...a painter of limited abilities.* ADJ QUALIT

2 A **limited** company is one in which the shareholders are legally responsible for only a part of any money that it may owe to other people or companies, for example if it goes bankrupt. EG *The Foundation had become a limited company... ...Hourmont Travel Limited.* ADJ CLASSIF British

limitless /lɪmɪtlɪ²s/. You say that something is **limitless** when it is extremely large in amount or number. EG *...the computer's limitless memory... ...our limitless fascination with toys and games.* ADJ CLASSIF Literary

limp /lɪmp/, **limps, limping, limped; limper, limpest.** 1 If you **limp**, you walk with difficulty or in an uneven way because one of your legs or feet is hurt. EG *He picked up his bag and limped back to the road... Two of the dogs were limping badly.* V : OFT+A

▸ used as a noun. EG *He walks with a limp... She had a slight limp.* ▸ N COUNT : USU SING

2 If someone is **limp**, they have no strength or energy in their body, so that they can be moved easily. EG *Her hand felt limp and damp.* ◊ **limply.** EG *The tiny baby lay limply on her arm.* ADJ QUALIT ◊ ADV

3 Something that is **limp** is soft and not stiff or firm. EG *...a dressing-gown of limp, shiny fabric.* ◊ **limply.** EG *The rope fell limply to the ground.* ADJ QUALIT ◊ ADV

line /laɪn/, **lines, lining, lined.** 1 A **line** is a long, thin mark on a surface, or something that looks long and thin. EG *...a diagonal red line on the label... ...a straight line joining those two points... ...the hard thin line of Lynn's mouth.* N COUNT

2 If there are **lines** on someone's face, their face has wrinkles or creases in it. N COUNT : USU PLURAL

3 A **line** of people or things is a number of them positioned one behind another or side by side in a row. EG *...long lines of poplar trees... The men formed themselves into a line.* ● See also **picket line**. N COUNT OR N PART

4 A **line** is also **4.1** one of the rows of words or symbols in a piece of writing. EG *I have read every line... They sang the next line of the song.* N COUNT **4.2** a sentence or remark that is said by an actor in a play or film. EG *She found it impossible to remember her lines.*

5 You can refer to a long piece of string or wire as a **line** when it is being used for a particular purpose. EG *...washing hanging on a line... The fish was heavy at the end of my line... ...a fallen power line... ...a telephone line.* N COUNT: USU+SUPP

6 Line is also used to refer to a route, for example: **6.1** a particular route along which something moves. EG *Wireless waves travel in straight lines.* N COUNT **6.2** a route along which people move or send messages or supplies. EG *All lines of communication had been cut... ...the supply lines to enemy formations.* N COUNT: USU PLURAL +SUPP **6.3** a railway track. EG *...repairs to the line beyond Tring.* N COUNT **6.4** a particular route along which a train, coach, or bus service regularly operates. EG *They took the wrong line on the London Tube.* N COUNT

7 You can use **line** to refer to **7.1** the edge, outline, or shape of something. EG *...the firm, delicate lines of Paxton's buildings... ...a superb line from nose to brow, a real conqueror's face.* N COUNT+SUPP **7.2** the boundary between areas occupied by enemy armies during a war. EG *They were dropped by parachute behind enemy lines.* ● See also **front line**.

8 The **line** between two classes or types of people or things is the point at which they are divided or considered different. EG *The traditional social dividing lines are becoming blurred... She will be living below the poverty line.* N COUNT+SUPP

9 A particular **line** of research or argument, for example, is a particular series of things or type of thing that is done or said. EG *...his particular line of research... ...future lines of development.* N COUNT+SUPP

10 The **line** that someone takes on a problem or topic is their attitude or policy towards it. EG *...the official line of the Labour Party... The President takes a much harder line.* N COUNT+SUPP

11 Your **line** of business or work is the kind of work that you do. EG *A man in my line of business has to take precautions... Well, it's not my line, really, is it?* N SING+POSS

12 A particular **line** is also a particular type of product that a company makes or sells. EG *Unprofitable lines will be discontinued.* N COUNT

13 A particular **line** of people or things is a series of similar people or things that existed one after another. EG *...the long line of American Presidents.* N SING+SUPP

14 If people or things **line** a road or room, they are present in large numbers along its edges or sides. EG *The streets were lined with cars... Trophies lined the walls of her bedroom.* V+O

15 If you **line** a container or a piece of clothing, you put a layer of something such as paper or cloth on the inside surface of it. EG *Line the cupboards and drawers with paper... ...a coffin lined with velvet... ...a pair of thick fur-lined boots.* V+O: OFT+*with*

16 If something **lines** a container or an area inside a person, animal, or plant, it forms a layer on the inside surface. EG *...tiny hairs lining the nose.* V+O

17 Line is used after 'in' in these phrases. PHRASES **17.1** When people or cars are **in line**, they are in a row one behind another, waiting for something. EG *We had to wait in line at the counter.* **17.2** If you are **in line for** something, you are likely to get it. EG *You are next in line for promotion.* **17.3** If one thing is **in line** with another, the two things are next to each other or form part of a straight row. EG *She shifted her chair to bring it in line with her neighbours.* **17.4** If one person or group is **in line** with others, it is doing the same thing as the others. EG *Africa may bring itself in line with the rest of the world on this matter.* **17.5** If something is done **in line** with a policy, guideline, or standard, it is done following that policy, guideline, or standard. **17.6** If you keep someone **in line**, you make them behave in the way that they are supposed to. **17.7** You can use **line** to say what sort of thing you are referring to. For example, something **in the** sports **line** means something connected with sports. EG *Call me if anything in the electrical line has to be done.*

18 Line is used after 'on' in these phrases. PHRASES **18.1** If you are **on line** when using a large computer, you type on a keyboard with a screen directly into the computer. **18.2** If your job, career, or reputation is **on the line**, you may lose it or harm it as a result of doing something brave or foolish. EG *I didn't dare fight and put my job on the line, so I went along with them.*

19 Line is also used in these phrases. PHRASES **19.1** If you **draw the line** at a particular activity, you refuse to do it, because it is more than you are prepared to do. EG *There is a point at which they will have to draw the line.* **19.2** If something happens somewhere **along the line**, it happens during a process or activity. EG *We slipped up somewhere along the line... He had fought us all along the line.* **19.3** If something happens **on** or **along** particular **lines**, it happens in that way. EG *The population is split along religious lines... He thinks along the same lines as you.* **19.4** You use the phrases **on the lines of** and **along the lines of** when you are giving a general description of what someone has said or of what you want. EG *Driberg opened with a question on the lines of: 'What do you think about the present political situation?'* **19.5** If someone is **on the right lines**, they are thinking or acting in a way that is sensible or likely to produce useful results. EG *Do his policies strike you as being on the right lines?* **19.6** If someone is **out of line** or **steps out of line**, they do not behave in the way that they are supposed to. **19.7** to **drop** someone **a line**: see **drop**. ● to **read between the lines**: see **read**. ● See also **lined**, **lining**, **hard line**, **hot line**, **party line**.

line up. 1 If people **line up** or if you **line** them **up**, they stand in a row or form a queue. EG *They lined us up and marched us off.* PHRASAL VB: V-ERG+ADV **2** If something **is lined up** for someone, it is arranged for them. EG *A formal farewell party was lined up.* V+ADV+O: OFT PASS **3** See also **line-up**.

linear /lɪnɪ^{1}ə/. **1** A **linear** process is one in which something progresses straight from one stage to another. EG *...linear thinking... ...events occurring simultaneously rather than in a linear sequence.* ADJ CLASSIF Formal

2 A **linear** shape or form consists of lines, especially straight lines. ADJ CLASSIF Formal

3 Linear movement is movement in a straight line. EG *...turning linear motion into rotary motion.* ADJ CLASSIF Formal

lined /laɪnd/. **1** If someone's face or skin is **lined**, it has wrinkles or lines on it. EG *Their faces are lined, immeasurably sad.* ADJ QUALIT

2 Lined paper has lines printed across it. EG *He was writing on a lined pad.* ADJ CLASSIF

linen /lɪnɪn/. **1 Linen** is a kind of cloth that is used for making tea-towels, tablecloths, sheets, and clothes. EG *...a white linen suit.* N UNCOUNT

2 You can refer to tablecloths, sheets, and similar things that are used in a house as **linen**. EG *...bed linen... ...the linen cupboard.* N UNCOUNT

liner /laɪnə/, **liners. 1** A **liner** is a large ship in which people travel long distances. N COUNT

2 A bin **liner** or a dustbin **liner** is a plastic bag that you put inside a waste-bin or dustbin so that the rubbish can be easily taken out. EG *...black polythene bin liners.* N COUNT+SUPP

linesman /laɪnzmə^{3}n/, **linesmen.** A **linesman** is an official who assists the referee or umpire in games such as football and tennis by watching the boundary line of the field or court and indicating when the ball goes outside it. N COUNT

Can you be a linguist if you speak only one language?

line-up, line-ups. The **line-up** for a sports event or other public activity is the people who are going to take part in it. EG *...the line-up for the next game.* N COUNT Informal

linger /lɪŋgə/, **lingers, lingering, lingered. 1** When ideas, practices, or feelings **linger**, they continue to exist for a long time. EG *The resentment and the longings lingered... This tradition apparently manages to linger on.* V: OFT+*on* ◊ **lingering.** EG *There was no lingering sense of guilt.* ◊ ADJ CLASSIF: ATTRIB

2 If you **linger** somewhere, you stay there for a longer time than is necessary, for example because you are enjoying yourself. EG *Davis lingered for a moment in the bar... ...lingering over their meals.* V+A

lingerie /lɒnʒəri^{1}/ is women's underwear and night-clothes. N UNCOUNT Formal

linguist /lɪŋgwɪst/, **linguists.** A **linguist** is **1** someone who can speak several languages. **2** someone who studies or teaches linguistics. N COUNT

linguistic /lɪŋgwɪstɪk/, **linguistics. 1 Linguistics** is the study of the way in which language works. EG *...a broad introduction to linguistics.* N UNCOUNT

2 Linguistic studies, developments, or ideas relate to language or linguistics. EG *...linguistic development between the ages of nought and four.* ADJ CLASSIF ◊ **linguistically.** EG *...conversations which are linguistically perfect.* ◊ ADV

lining /laɪnɪŋ/, **linings. 1** A **lining** is a layer of cloth attached to the inside of something in order to make it thicker or more slippery, or to protect it. EG *...a white cloak with a scarlet lining... ...the lining of the case.* N COUNT OR N UNCOUNT

2 The **lining** of your stomach or nose, for example, is the layer of flesh on the inside. N COUNT

link /lɪŋk/, **links, linking, linked. 1** You say that two things **are linked** when there is a relationship between them, for example because one causes the other. EG *Evidence has been offered linking the group to a series of bomb attacks.* V+O: OFT+ *with/to* ▸ used as a noun. EG *There seems to be a link between the rising rate of unemployment and the rise in crime... We have very close links with industry.* ▸ N COUNT: OFT+ *between/with*

2 You say that two places or objects **are linked** when there is a physical connection between them so that you can travel or communicate between them. EG *...a canal linking the Pacific and Atlantic oceans... The television camera had been linked to a computer.* V+O: OFT+*to* ▸ used as a noun. EG *They opened a rail link between the two towns... A telephone link between Washington and Moscow was established.* ▸ N COUNT: USU+*between*

3 If you **link** two things, you join them by putting part of one through the other one, or by knotting them together. EG *She linked her hand through the crook of his elbow.* V+O: OFT+A ◊ **linked.** EG *They walked along, arms linked.* ◊ ADJ CLASSIF

4 A **link** is also one of the rings in a chain. N COUNT

link up. If you **link up** two items or places, you connect them to each other in some way. EG *This computer can be linked up to other computers.* PHRASAL VB: V+O+ADV

linkage /lɪŋkɪdʒ/, **linkages.** The **linkage** between two things is the connection between them. EG *...the linkage between causes and effects.* N UNCOUNT OR N COUNT

lino /laɪnəʊ/ is the same as linoleum. EG *...a landing with cracked lino on the floor.* N UNCOUNT

linoleum /lɪnəʊlɪəm/ is a floor covering which is made of cloth covered with a hard shiny substance. EG *...shiny linoleum floors.* N UNCOUNT Formal

lion /laɪən/, **lions. 1** A **lion** is a large, wild member of the cat family which is found in Africa. Lions have yellowish fur, and male lions have long hair on their head and neck. N COUNT

2 If someone gets the **lion's share** of something, they get the largest part of it, leaving very little for other people. EG *The lion's share of investment has gone to a few favoured companies.* N PART

lioness /laɪənɪ^{2}s/, **lionesses.** A **lioness** is a female lion. N COUNT

lip /lɪp/, **lips. 1** Your **lips** are the top and bottom edges of your mouth. See picture at THE HUMAN BODY. EG *He had a freshly lit cigarette between his lips.* N COUNT: USU PLURAL

2 Lip is used in these phrases. **2.1** If you say that something is **on everyone's lips**, you mean that many people are talking about it. PHRASE **2.2** If you say to someone **'my lips are sealed'**, you mean that you will keep a secret that they have just told you. CONVENTION **2.3** If you **keep a stiff upper lip**, you do not show any emotion, even though it is difficult not to. PHRASE

lip-read, lip-reads, lip-reading. If someone can **lip-read**, they can understand what you are saying by watching the way your lips move. Deaf people sometimes do this. V

lip-service. If you say that someone pays **lip-service** to an idea, you mean that they pretend to be in favour of it, but they do not do anything to support it; used showing disapproval. EG *Our major political parties pay lip-service to the ideal of community participation.* N UNCOUNT

lipstick /lɪpstɪk/, **lipsticks. Lipstick** is a coloured substance which women put on their lips. EG *She was wearing lipstick and mascara.* N MASS

liqueur /lɪkjʊə/, **liqueurs.** A **liqueur** is a strong alcoholic drink with a sweet taste, which is often drunk after a meal. N MASS

liquid /lɪkwɪd/, **liquids. 1** A **liquid** is a substance such as water which is not solid and which flows and can be poured. N MASS

2 Something that is **liquid** is in the form of a liquid rather than being solid or a gas. EG *...liquid polish.* ADJ CLASSIF

liquidate /lɪkwɪdeɪt/, **liquidates, liquidating, liquidated. 1** When someone **liquidates** people who are causing problems, they get rid of them by killing them. EG *All his supporters were expelled, exiled, or liquidated.* V+O

2 When a company **is liquidated**, it is closed down, usually because it has large debts and cannot repay them. V+O Technical ◊ **liquidation** /lɪkwɪdeɪʃə^{0}n/. EG *By April 1969, the group faced liquidation.* ◊ N UNCOUNT

liquidizer /lɪkwɪdaɪzə/, **liquidizers.** A **liquidizer** is an electrical machine that you use to crush food and make it liquid. N COUNT

liquor /lɪkə/, **liquors. Liquor** is strong alcoholic drink. EG *Drinking cheap liquor made their heads ache... I never touch hard liquor.* N MASS American

liquorice /lɪkərɪs, -ɪʃ/; also spelled **licorice. Liquorice** is a firm black substance with a strong taste, which is used for making sweets. N UNCOUNT

lisp /lɪsp/, **lisps, lisping, lisped. 1** If someone has a **lisp**, they pronounce the sounds 's' and 'z' as if they were 'th'. For example, they say 'thing' instead of 'sing'. N COUNT: USU SING

2 When someone **lisps**, they speak with a lisp. EG *'Thay yeth,' she lisped.* V OR V+QUOTE

list /lɪst/, **lists, listing, listed. 1** A **list** is a set of things which are written down one below the other. EG *Look at your list of things to be mended... Find out all their names and make a list.* ● See also **short-list**. N COUNT: OFT+*of*

2 To **list** a set of things means to mention them all one after the other. EG *There was a label on each case listing its contents.* V+O

3 If something **is listed**, it is included as an item on a list. EG *He is still listed in the files by his code name, the Jackal.* V+O: USU PASS

listed /lɪstɪ^{2}d/. **Listed** buildings are protected by law from being demolished or altered, because they are old or important. ADJ CLASSIF British

listen /lɪsə^{0}n/, **listens, listening, listened. 1** If you **listen** to someone who is talking or **listen** to a sound, you give your attention to the person or the sound. EG *Paul, are you listening?... Listen carefully to what he says... They listen to some music or read until I put them to bed... 'Listen,' Claude whispered, 'I've got something to tell you.'* V: OFT+*to*

2 If you **listen** for a sound, you keep alert and are ready to hear it if it occurs. EG *She sat quite still, listening for her baby's cry.* V+*for*

3 To **listen** to someone also means to believe them V: OFT+*to* or accept their advice. EG *No one here will listen to you, not without proof... He refused to listen to reason.*

listen in. If you **listen in** to a private conversation, you secretly listen to it. PHRASAL VB : V+ADV

listener /lɪs(ə)nə/, **listeners. 1** Your **listeners** are the people who are listening to you when you are explaining or describing something. EG *She told the tale so well that both her listeners were enchanted.* N COUNT

2 People who listen to the radio are often referred to as **listeners**. EG *We've had a number of letters from listeners about the future of British industry.* N COUNT

listless /lɪstlɪ²s/. If you are **listless**, you have no energy or enthusiasm. EG *She became listless and bored.* ◇ **listlessly.** EG *Rose watched him listlessly.* ADJ QUALIT; ◇ ADV

lit /lɪt/ is a past tense and past participle of **light.**

liter /liːtə/. See **litre**.

literacy /lɪt(ə)rəsi¹/ is the ability to read and write. EG *Mass literacy was only possible after the invention of printing.* N UNCOUNT

literal /lɪt(ə)rəl/. **1** If you use a word or expression in its **literal** sense, you use it with its most basic meaning or with its main meaning. EG *She was older than I was, and not only in the literal sense.* ADJ CLASSIF : USU ATTRIB

2 If you make a **literal** translation of something written or spoken in a foreign language, you translate each word, rather than trying to give the general meaning using words that sound natural. EG *...a literal translation from the German.* ADJ CLASSIF : ATTRIB

3 If you say that something is a **literal** fact or the **literal** truth, you are emphasizing that it is true. ADJ CLASSIF : USU ATTRIB

literally /lɪt(ə)rəli¹/. **1** You use **literally** **1.1** to emphasize that what you are saying is actually true, even though it seems surprising or exaggerated. EG *I have literally begged my son for help... They were literally starving to death.* **1.2** to indicate that a word or expression which has more than one meaning is being used in its most basic sense, rather than in a more abstract, metaphorical sense. EG *They are people who have literally and spiritually left home.* ADV

2 People sometimes add **literally** to an exaggerated statement to make it even more exaggerated. EG *They are literally willing to sell you the shirt off their backs.* ADV Informal

3 If you translate a word or expression **literally**, you translate it giving its most simple or basic meaning. EG *...a wati-pulka (literally 'big man').* ADV

4 If you **take** something **literally**, you think that a word or expression is being used with its most simple or basic meaning. EG *Don't misunderstand or take that too literally.* PHRASE

literary /lɪt(ə)rəri¹/. **1 Literary** means concerned with or connected with the writing, study, or appreciation of literature. EG *...his genuine pleasure at her literary success... The text has some literary merit... ...literary critics.* ADJ CLASSIF : ATTRIB

2 Literary words and expressions are rather unusual ones which are used to create a special effect in a poem, speech, or novel. In this dictionary, words and expressions of this kind are indicated by the use of the word 'Literary' in the Extra Column. ADJ QUALIT

literate /lɪt(ə)rə¹t/. **1** Someone who is **literate** is able to read and write. EG *Only half the children in this class are literate.* ADJ CLASSIF

2 If you say that someone is highly **literate**, you mean that they are well educated and intelligent. EG *...the children of highly literate parents.* ADJ QUALIT

literature /lɪt(ə)rətʃə/. **1** Novels, plays, and poetry are referred to as **literature**. EG *I envy you having a friend with whom you can discuss art and literature... ...a degree in English Literature.* N UNCOUNT

2 Books and articles about a particular subject are referred to as the **literature** on this subject. EG *The recent literature on animal behaviour is extensive.* N UNCOUNT +SUPP

3 Literature is also printed information that is produced by people who are trying to sell you something or to give you advice. EG *All major political parties print literature for hopeful candidates.* N UNCOUNT : USU+SUPP

litigation /lɪtɪgeɪʃ(ə)n/ is the process of fighting or defending a case in a civil court of law. EG *It was not unusual for the bank to be involved in litigation over failed companies.* N UNCOUNT Formal

litre /liːtə/, **litres;** spelled **liter** in American English. **1** A **litre** is a metric unit of volume that is equal to a thousand cubic centimetres or 1.76 pints. EG *...a litre of wine.* N PART

2 You use **litre** when talking about the capacity of a car engine. For example, if a car has a 2 **litre** engine, its engine's cylinders have a capacity of 2 litres. EG *...a 1.3 litre Vauxhall Astra.* N COUNT+SUPP

litter /lɪtə/, **litters, littering, littered. 1 Litter** is rubbish, such as bits of paper and old bottles, which is left lying around outside. EG *There were piles of litter in the streets.* N UNCOUNT

2 If a number of things **litter** a place or if the place **is littered** with them, they are scattered around in it, in an untidy way. EG *Papers littered every surface... The floor was littered with ashtrays.* V+O

3 A **litter** is a group of animals born to the same mother at the same time. EG *It was the finest puppy in a litter of six.* N COUNT

litter bin, litter bins. A **litter bin** is a container, usually outside or in a public building, into which people can put rubbish. N COUNT British

little /lɪt(ə)l/. For paragraphs 6 and 8, the comparative is **less** and the superlative is **least**. See separate entries for **less** and **least**.

1 Little things are small in size. EG *...a little table with a glass top... ...those little dark villages... ...little groups of people.* ADJ QUALIT : USU ATTRIB

2 A **little** child is very young. EG *...two little girls... I often heard him do that when I was little.* ADJ QUALIT

3 Your **little** sister or brother is younger than you are. EG *My little brother loves school.* ADJ QUALIT : ATTRIB

4 A **little** distance, period of time, or event is short in length. EG *...after he had walked for a little way... She lay awake a little while longer... ...a little chat.* ADJ QUALIT : ATTRIB

5 You use **little** to indicate that something is not serious or important. EG *Don't bother me with little things like that... ...annoying little mishaps.* ADJ CLASSIF : ATTRIB

6 You also use **little** to emphasize that there is only a very small amount of something. EG *John and I had very little money left... Little of the equipment was standardized... There is little to worry about... She ate little.* QUANTIF

7 If something happens **little by little**, it happens very gradually. EG *Then I learnt, little by little, the early history of her family.* PHRASE

8 Little means not very often or to only a small extent. EG *Richardson interrupted very little... She seemed little changed.* ADV BRD NEG

9 A little of something is a small amount of it. EG *He spoke a little French... The waiter poured a little of the wine into a glass.* QUANTIF

10 A little or **a little bit** means to a small extent or degree. EG *He frowned a little and then closed his eyes... I felt a little uncomfortable... I thought he was a little bit afraid.* PHRASE

11 If you do something **a little**, you do it for a short time. EG *He walked about a little.* PHRASE

little finger, little fingers. Your **little finger** is the smallest finger on your hand. N COUNT

live, lives, living, lived. The word **live** is pronounced /lɪv/ when it is a verb and /laɪv/ when it is an adjective or adverb. The word **lives** is pronounced /lɪvz/ when it is a verb and /laɪvz/ when it is the plural of **life**.

1 If someone **lives** in a particular place, their home is there. EG *Where do you live?... I used to live in Grange Road... My grandmother lived with us for 15 years.* V+A

How many little fingers do you have?

2 If you **live** in particular circumstances or **live** a particular kind of life, you are in those circumstances or your life is of that kind. EG *We lived very simply... They are forced to live entirely artificial lives... We live in a technological society... Many people do not live by these standards.* V+A OR V+O

3 To **live** means to be alive. EG *Women seem to live longer than men... She lost her will to live... I hope I shall live to see peace.* V : NO CONT

4 **Live** animals or plants are alive, rather than being dead or artificial. EG *They grasp live snakes while dancing to bring rain.* ADJ CLASSIF : ATTRIB

5 A **live** television or radio programme is one in which an event is broadcast at the time that it happens, rather than being recorded first. EG *...live pictures of a man walking on the moon... The concert will be broadcast live on Radio Three.* ADJ CLASSIF OR ADV

6 A **live** performance is one that is done in front of an audience, rather than being a recorded one. EG *...live theatre... I would like to perform live as much as possible.* ADJ CLASSIF OR ADV

7 A **live** wire or piece of electrical equipment is directly connected to a source of electricity. ADJ CLASSIF

8 **Live** bullets, bombs, or missiles have not yet exploded or been fired. ADJ CLASSIF

9 If you **live it up**, you have a very enjoyable and exciting time, for example by going to lots of parties. EG *They were living it up in Amsterdam.* PHRASE Informal

10 **Lives** is the plural of **life**.

11 See also **living**.

live down. If you are unable to **live down** a mistake or failure, you are unable to make people forget that you did it. EG *If you were beaten by Jack, you'd never live it down.* PHRASAL VB : V+O+ADV

live for. If you **live for** a particular thing, it is the most important thing in your life. EG *...a man who lived for pleasure.* PHRASAL VB : V+PREP

live in. If someone **lives in**, they live in the place where they work or study. EG *The rest of the students tend to live in.* ● See also **live-in**. PHRASAL VB : V+ADV

live off. If you **live off** a particular source of money, you get from it the money that you need. EG *They were living off welfare.* PHRASAL VB : V+PREP

live on. **1** If you **live on** a particular amount of money, you have that amount of money to buy things. EG *I don't have enough to live on.* PHRASAL VB : V+PREP **2** If you **live on** a particular kind of food, it is the only kind of food you eat. EG *She lived on berries and wild herbs.* V+PREP **3** If something **lives on**, it is remembered for a long time or it continues to exist in some form. EG *The Marilyn Monroe legend lives on in Hollywood.* V+ADV, OFT+A

live out. **1** If you **live out** your life in a particular place or in particular circumstances, you stay in that place or remain in those circumstances until the end of your life. EG *He lived out the remaining years of his life in London.* PHRASAL VB : V+O+ADV, USU+A **2** If someone **lives out**, they do not live in the place where they work or study. V+ADV

live together. If two people **live together**, they live in the same house and have a sexual relationship but are not married to one another. PHRASAL VB : V+ADV

live up to. If someone or something **lives up to** people's expectations, they are as good as they were expected to be. EG *She succeeded in living up to her extraordinary reputation.* PHRASAL VB : V+ADV+PREP

live with. **1** If you **live with** someone, you live in the same house as them and have a sexual relationship with them but are not married to them. PHRASAL VB : V+PREP **2** If you have to **live with** an unpleasant situation, you have to accept it and carry on with your life or work. EG *They have to live with the consequences of their decision.* V+PREP, HAS PASS

live-in. **Live-in** boyfriends or girlfriends live in the same house as the person they are having a sexual relationship with. ADJ CLASSIF : ATTRIB Informal

livelihood /laɪvlɪhʊd/, **livelihoods.** Your **livelihood** is the job or other source of income which gives you the money to buy the things that you need. EG *...their fear of losing their livelihood... Their principal livelihood was in the sea.* N COUNT OR N UNCOUNT

lively /laɪvli[1]/, **livelier, liveliest.** **1** You describe people as **lively** when they behave in an enthusiastic and cheerful way. EG *Her parents were lively, eccentric, and attractive individuals... Four lively youngsters suddenly burst into the room.* ADJ QUALIT

2 You say that a place, event, or book is **lively** when there are lots of interesting and exciting things happening in it. EG *...a lively debate... It should be a lively evening.* ADJ QUALIT

3 Someone who has a **lively** mind is intelligent and interested in a lot of different things. ADJ QUALIT

4 You use **lively** to describe a feeling when it is a strong and enthusiastic one. EG *She took a lively interest in everything... ...an institution for which I have a lively admiration.* ADJ QUALIT : ATTRIB

liven /laɪvə[0]n/, **livens, livening, livened.** **1** If a place or event **livens up** or if you **liven** it **up**, it becomes more interesting and exciting. EG *There are lots of new shops and things. The place is really livening up.* PHRASAL VB : V-ERG+ADV

2 If people **liven up** or if something **livens** them **up**, they become more cheerful and energetic. EG *At least the incident livened her up.* V-ERG+ADV

liver /lɪvə/, **livers.** **1** Your **liver** is a large organ in your body which processes your blood and helps to clean unwanted substances out of it. N COUNT

2 **Liver** is the liver of some animals, especially lambs, pigs, and cows, which is cooked and eaten. N UNCOUNT

livestock /laɪvstɒk/. Animals such as cattle and sheep which are kept on a farm are referred to as **livestock**. EG *They encourage farmers to keep more livestock.* N UNCOUNT OR N PLURAL

livid /lɪvɪd/. **1** Someone who is **livid** is extremely angry. EG *He said, 'No, you won't.' I was absolutely livid.* ADJ QUALIT Informal

2 Something that is **livid** is an unpleasant dark purple or greyish blue colour. EG *...livid bruises.* ADJ QUALIT Literary

living /lɪvɪŋ/. **1** A **living** person or animal is alive. EG *I have no living relatives... She had been in Amity for as long as anyone living could remember.* ADJ CLASSIF

2 The work that you do for a **living** or to earn your **living** is the work that you do to earn the money that you need in your daily life. EG *I never expected to earn my living as an artist... He made a modest living by painting... What do you do for a living?* N SING

3 You use **living** **3.1** when you are talking about the quality of people's daily lives. EG *The quality of urban living has been damaged by excessive noise levels... ...the demand for better living standards.* N UNCOUNT +SUPP **3.2** when you are talking about places where people sleep, eat, and relax when they are not working. EG *...the living quarters of the hotel staff... We are trying to improve living conditions at sea.* ADJ CLASSIF : ATTRIB

4 **within living memory**: see **memory**. ● See also **cost of living**, **standard of living**.

living-room, living-rooms. The **living-room** in a house is the room where people sit and relax. N COUNT

lizard /lɪzəd/, **lizards.** A **lizard** is a small animal with short legs, a long tail, and a rough, dry skin. N COUNT

-'ll is a short form of 'will' or 'shall' used in spoken English and informal written English. EG *He'll come back... They'll spoil our picnic... That'll be all right.*

load /ləʊd/, **loads, loading, loaded.** **1** If you **load** a vehicle or container or **load** things into it, you put things into it. EG *...when they came to load the van with their things... They were ordered to begin loading the lorries... We started loading the pheasants into the sacks.* V+O OR V+O+A

2 A **load** is something which is being carried somewhere. EG *We took up our heavy load and trudged back... Its load of minerals was dumped at sea.* N COUNT

3 When someone **loads** a gun, they put a bullet in it so that it is ready to use. V+O

4 When someone **loads** a camera, computer, or V+O

tape recorder or **loads** film or tape into it, they put film or tape into it so that it is ready to use.

5 If people talk about **loads** of something or a **load** of something, they mean a lot of it. EG *We talked about loads of things.* — N PART, Informal

6 People say that something is **a load of rubbish** or **a load of junk** as a way of expressing their disapproval of it. EG *You paid twenty pounds for a load of junk like this?* — PHRASE, Informal

7 See also **workload**.

loaded /ləʊdɪd/. **1** If something is **loaded** with things, it has a large number of them in it or on it. EG *...a truck loaded with bricks... ...waitresses with loaded trays.* — ADJ QUALIT : OFT+*with*

2 If you are **loaded** with things or **loaded down** with them, you are carrying a lot of them. EG *A man precedes him up the stairs, loaded with bundles... She was loaded down with parcels.* — ADJ PRED : OFT+*with*

3 If you say that someone is **loaded**, you mean that they have a lot of money. — ADJ PRED, Informal

4 A **loaded** remark or question has more significance, meaning, or purpose than it appears to have. — ADJ QUALIT

loaf /ləʊf/, **loaves** /ləʊvz/. A **loaf** of bread is bread in a shape that can be cut into slices. — N COUNT OR N PART

loan /ləʊn/, **loans, loaning, loaned. 1** A **loan** is a sum of money that you borrow. EG *They found it impossible to get a bank loan... The government had to make a further loan of 3.3m pounds to save the industry.* — N COUNT

2 If someone gives you a **loan** of something or if you have the **loan** of it, you borrow it from them. EG *He asked for the loan of twelve dozen glasses.* — N SING+*of*

3 If something is **on loan**, it has been borrowed. EG *Most of his books are on loan from the library.* — PHRASE

4 If you **loan** something to someone, you lend it to them. EG *He never loaned his car to anybody... I'll loan you fifty dollars.* — V+O+*to* OR V+O+O

loath /ləʊθ/; also spelled **loth.** If you are **loath** to do something, you are unwilling to do it. EG *Governments have been loath to impose any sanctions.* — ADJ PRED +*to*-INF

loathe /ləʊð/, **loathes, loathing, loathed.** If you **loathe** something or someone, you dislike them very much. EG *I particularly loathed team games at school.* — V+O

loathing /ləʊðɪŋ/ is a feeling of great dislike and disgust. EG *He remembered his school days with loathing... She had a loathing for the smell of cooking.* — N UNCOUNT

loathsome /ləʊðsəm/. If you say that someone or something is **loathsome**, you mean that they are horrible and you dislike them very much. EG *I hate the loathsome way you use other people.* — ADJ QUALIT

loaves /ləʊvz/ is the plural of **loaf.**

lob /lɒb/, **lobs, lobbing, lobbed. 1** If you **lob** something, you throw it so that it goes quite high in the air. EG *She wrapped a piece of paper round a stone and lobbed it into the next garden.* — V+O : USU+A

2 If you **lob** the ball in a game of tennis, you hit it high into the air so that it lands behind your opponent. EG *Miss Evert reached to lob a return of Miss Wade's.* ▸ used as a noun. EG *...high lobs to the backhand corner.* — V+O OR V; ▸ N COUNT

lobby /lɒbi^1/, **lobbies, lobbying, lobbied. 1** The **lobby** of a hotel or other large building is the area behind the main door which has corridors and staircases leading off it. EG *I rushed into the hotel lobby.* — N COUNT

2 A **lobby** is also a group of people who try to persuade a government or council that a particular thing should be done. EG *...an increasingly strong and well organized lobby for the abolition of film censorship... ...the anti-nuclear lobby.* — N COLL+SUPP

3 If you **lobby** a member of a government or council, you try to persuade them that a particular thing should be done. EG *He lobbied the Home Secretary, ministers, and other members of parliament... We should all be lobbying for stricter controls on guns.* — V+O OR V+A

lobe /ləʊb/, **lobes.** The **lobe** of your ear is the soft part at the bottom. — N COUNT

lobster /lɒbstə/, **lobsters.** A **lobster** is a sea creature that has a hard shell, two large claws, and eight legs. — N COUNT

local /ləʊkə^{0}l/, **locals. 1** A **local** council is responsible for the government of a small part of a country, for example a town or a county. EG *Some local councils give grants to parents with low incomes... ...local government.* ◇ **locally.** EG *Should housing policy be decided nationally or locally?* — ADJ CLASSIF : ATTRIB; ◇ ADV

2 Local means existing in or belonging to the area where you live or work. EG *Members are drawn from all sections of the local community... ...a picture in the local paper... Telephone your local police station.* ◇ **locally.** EG *Everything we used was bought locally.* — ADJ CLASSIF : USU ATTRIB; ◇ ADV

3 You can refer to the people who live in a particular district as the **locals.** EG *The locals view these road improvements with alarm.* — N COUNT : USU PLURAL, Informal

4 A **local** anaesthetic affects only one part of your body. — ADJ CLASSIF, Medical

locality /ləʊkælɪ^{1}ti^1/, **localities.** A particular **locality** is a small area of a country or city. EG *...the anxiety of people living in the same locality.* — N COUNT

localized /ləʊkəlaɪzd/; also spelled **localised.** Something that is **localized** exists or occurs only in one place or in one part of your body. EG *...localized problems of erosion... ...a localized pain in the back of her head.* — ADJ CLASSIF

locate /ləʊkeɪt/, **locates, locating, located. 1** If you **locate** something or someone, you find them. EG *He located a better restaurant in the next street... If you do locate him, call me.* — V+O, Formal

2 If something **is located** in a particular place, it is in that place. EG *The house was located in the heart of the city.* — V-PASS+A, Formal

location /ləʊkeɪʃə^{0}n/, **locations. 1** A particular **location** is a particular place, especially the place where something happens or where something is situated. EG *Election officials ran out of ballot papers at six locations... The new job involves a new employer, a new location, and a new set of colleagues... ...the size and location of your office.* — N COUNT+SUPP

2 If a film is made **on location**, it is made away from a studio. — PHRASE

loch /lɒx/, **lochs.** A **loch** is a large area of water in Scotland that is completely or almost completely surrounded by land. EG *...Loch Lomond.* — N COUNT

lock /lɒk/, **locks, locking, locked. 1** When you **lock** a door, a drawer, or a suitcase, you fasten it by means of a key. EG *Lock the door after you leave.* ◇ **locked.** EG *I tried the front door, and found that it was locked... ...the locked cupboard.* — V+O; ◇ ADJ CLASSIF

2 If you **lock** something in a cupboard, a room, or a drawer, you put it inside and lock the door of the cupboard or room, or lock the drawer. EG *He had locked all his papers in the safe... He locked them away in a drawer.* — V+O : USU+A

3 You say that something **locks** or **is locked** in a position or place when it moves into that position or place and is held firmly there. EG *Smoothly the rod locked into place.* — V-ERG : USU+A

4 You say that people **are locked** in a fight or argument when they are fighting or arguing and cannot stop. EG *Rebel groups and government forces are locked in a fierce battle for control of the country.* — V-PASS+A

5 The **lock** on a door, a drawer, or a suitcase is the part which you use to keep it shut and to prevent other people from opening it. To open it, you must first turn a key in the lock. EG *The key rattling in the lock startled me.* — N COUNT ● If something is **under lock and key**, it is in a room or container which has — ● PHRASE

Where does a lodger lodge?

been locked. EG *She would keep any sensitive documents under lock and key.*

6 A **lock** is also a place on a canal or river where walls have been built with gates at each end so that boats can move to a higher or lower section of the canal or river, by gradually changing the water level inside the gates. N COUNT

7 A **lock** of hair is a small bunch of hairs on someone's head. EG *A lock of hair had fallen down over her eyes... He shook his black locks.* N COUNT

8 If you gain or lose something **lock, stock, and barrel**, you gain or lose every single part of it. EG *I got it for £5000, lock, stock and barrel, a sixty-five-acre Suffolk farm.* PHRASE

lock in. If you **lock** someone **in**, you put them in a place and lock the door so that they cannot get out. PHRASAL VB : V+O+ADV

lock out. If you **lock** someone **out**, you prevent them from getting into a place by locking the doors. EG *She had been locked out of the house.* PHRASAL VB : V+O+ADV : OFT+*of*

lock up. **1** You can say that someone **is locked up** when they are put in prison or in a special psychiatric hospital. EG *The idea of being locked up in jail filled her with horror... They locked him up as a madman.* PHRASAL VB : V+O+ADV **2** When you **lock up**, you make sure that all the doors and windows of a building are properly closed or locked so that burglars cannot get in. V+ADV OR V+O+ADV

3 See also **lockup**.

locker /lɒkə/, **lockers.** A **locker** is a small cupboard in which you can keep your personal belongings and which you lock with a key. Lockers are often provided in schools and railway stations. N COUNT

locket /lɒkɪ²t/, **lockets.** A **locket** is a piece of jewellery containing something such as a picture which a woman wears on a chain round her neck. N COUNT

lockup /lɒkʌp/, **lockups.** A **lockup** is a jail or cell. EG *They hustled him off and put him in the lockup.* N COUNT American

locomotive /ləʊkəməʊtɪv/, **locomotives.** A **locomotive** is a railway engine. N COUNT Formal

locust /ləʊkəst/, **locusts. Locusts** are insects that live in hot countries and fly in large groups. They eat crops and can cause a lot of damage. N COUNT

lodge /lɒdʒ/, **lodges, lodging, lodged. 1** A **lodge** is **1.1** a small house at the entrance to the grounds of a large house. N COUNT **1.2** a hut in the country or in the mountains where people stay when they go to shoot animals for sport. EG *They went to a shooting lodge in Scotland for the weekend.* N COUNT : USU+SUPP

2 If you **lodge** in someone else's house, you live there, often for only a short period of time. EG *He had arranged for me to lodge with his daughter.* V+A

3 If something **lodges** somewhere or **is lodged** there, it becomes stuck there. EG *The bullet had lodged a quarter of an inch from his spine... I had somehow got the bone lodged in my throat.* V-ERG+A

4 If something **lodges** in your mind or heart or **is lodged** there, you remember it for a long time afterwards. EG *Facts don't lodge easily in my mind.* V-ERG+A

5 If you **lodge** a complaint, protest, or accusation, you formally make it. EG *I was going to ring you to lodge a formal complaint... ...the charges that had been lodged against them.* V+O Formal

lodger /lɒdʒə/, **lodgers.** A **lodger** is a person who you allow to live in a part of your house in return for money. EG *She allowed her student lodgers a lot of freedom.* N COUNT

lodging /lɒdʒɪŋ/, **lodgings. 1** If you are provided with **lodging**, you are provided with a place to stay for a period of time. EG *They were offered free lodging in first-class hotels.* N UNCOUNT

2 If you live in **lodgings**, you live in a room or rooms in someone's house and you pay them money to live there. EG *They have to find lodgings in the village.* N COUNT : USU PLURAL

loft /lɒft/, **lofts.** A **loft** is the space inside the sloping roof of a house or other building. People sometimes keep things in lofts. N COUNT

lofty /lɒfti¹/, **loftier, loftiest. 1** Something that is **lofty** is very high. EG *We explored lofty corridors... ...a lofty platform.* ADJ QUALIT Literary

2 A **lofty** idea or aim is noble, important, and admirable. EG *...trying to maintain a lofty principle... Such lofty goals justify any means.* ADJ QUALIT Literary

3 Someone who behaves in a **lofty** way behaves in a proud and rather unpleasant way, as if they are very important. EG *She hated his lofty manner.* ADJ QUALIT Formal
◊ **loftily.** EG *'I can't permit that,' Otto said loftily.* ◊ ADV

log /lɒg/, **logs, logging, logged. 1** A **log** is a piece of a thick branch or a piece of the trunk of a tree which has fallen or been cut down. EG *He threw another log on the fire.* N COUNT

2 A **log** is also an official written account which describes the important events that happen each day, for example on board a ship. EG *The Controller entered this in his log.* N COUNT

3 If you **log** an event or fact, you record it officially in writing. EG *The death must be logged.* V+O

log in or **log into;** also **log on.** When someone **logs into** a computer system or **logs in**, they gain access to the system, usually by giving a special word or name that it will accept. PHRASAL VB : V+PREP OR V+ADV Technical

log out. When someone who is using a computer system **logs out**, they finish using the system, by giving a special word. PHRASAL VB : V+ADV Technical

loggerheads /lɒgəhɛdz/. If people are **at loggerheads**, they disagree strongly with each other. EG *He and Thomas were continually at loggerheads.* PHRASE

logic /lɒdʒɪk/. **1 Logic** is a method of reasoning that involves a series of statements, each of which must be true if the statement before it is true. N UNCOUNT

2 If you refer to the **logic** of a conclusion, you are referring to the fact that it has been correctly worked out according to the laws of logic. EG *It is difficult to believe, and yet the logic of the deduction is undeniable.* N UNCOUNT

3 Different kinds of **logic** are different ways of thinking about things that are characteristic of particular people, groups, or activities. EG *Economic logic dictated the policy of centralization.* N UNCOUNT +SUPP

logical /lɒdʒɪkə⁰l/. **1** In a **logical** argument or analysis, each statement is true if the statement before it is true. EG *I made little attempt at logical argument... This is a masterly, logical analysis of the procedure.* ADJ CLASSIF ◊ **logically.** EG *Everything has to be logically analysed.* ◊ ADV

2 A **logical** conclusion or result is the only one that can reasonably result from a particular set of facts or from a particular event. EG *There is only one logical conclusion... To him violence was a logical inevitability.* ADJ CLASSIF ◊ **logically.** EG *It follows logically that one of them is lying.* ◊ ADV

3 You can say that a course of action is **logical** when it seems reasonable or sensible in the circumstances. EG *Wouldn't it have been more logical for them to make the arrest downstairs?... It seemed a logical idea to everyone but my mother.* ADJ QUALIT
◊ **logically.** EG *Therefore, logically, he had to go.* ◊ ADV SEN

logistic /lə⁷dʒɪstɪk/, **logistics. 1** You can refer to the skilful organization of something that involves a lot of people or equipment as the **logistics** of it. EG *...the tiresome logistics of modern broadcasting... Logistics and transport remained a problem.* N PLURAL Formal

2 Logistic or **logistical** means relating to the organization of something complicated. EG *...faced with daunting logistic and administrative problems.* ADJ CLASSIF : ATTRIB Formal

logo /ləʊgəʊ/, **logos.** The **logo** of a company or organization is the special design or way of writing its name that it puts on all its products and possessions. EG *You will be welcome at all hotels displaying our logo.* N COUNT

loincloth /lɔɪnklɒθ/, **loincloths.** A **loincloth** is a piece of cloth that covers a man's sexual parts. It is sometimes worn by men in very hot countries. N COUNT

loins /lɔɪnz/. Someone's **loins** are the front part of their body between their waist and thighs, especially their sexual parts. N PLURAL Literary

loiter /lɔɪtə/, **loiters, loitering, loitered.** If you **loiter** somewhere, you remain there or walk up and down without any real purpose. EG *Remember not to loiter on the way.* V: OFT+A

loll /lɒl/, **lolls, lolling, lolled. 1** If you **loll** somewhere, you sit or lie in a very relaxed position. EG *The students lolled in the grass... ...lolling about in the summer sun.* V+A

2 If your head or tongue **lolls**, it hangs down loosely. EG *...feeling so sleepy, head lolling, eyes closing... Her tongue lolled out, her eyes were rolled back.* V: OFT+A

lollipop /lɒlɪpɒp/, **lollipops.** A **lollipop** is a sweet consisting of a hard disc or ball of a sugary substance on the end of a stick. EG *She was sitting on the front step sucking a lollipop.* N COUNT

lolly /lɒli[1]/, **lollies. 1** A **lolly** is **1.1** a piece of flavoured ice or ice cream on a stick. **1.2** a lollipop. N COUNT Informal

2 You can also refer to money as **lolly**. EG *They took all his lolly and his clothes.* N UNCOUNT Informal

lone /ləʊn/. A **lone** person or thing is alone or is the only one in a particular place or group. EG *They saw ahead a lone figure walking towards them... They made an attack on the area's lone hospital.* ADJ CLASSIF: ATTRIB

lonely /ləʊnli[1]/, **lonelier, loneliest. 1** Someone who is **lonely** is unhappy because they are alone or do not have any friends. EG *I didn't feel lonely at all... ...lonely widows.* ◇ **loneliness.** EG *They suffer from isolation, poverty and loneliness.* ADJ QUALIT ◇ N UNCOUNT

2 A **lonely** situation or period of time is one in which you feel alone and unhappy. EG *...that lonely night in Dakota.* ADJ QUALIT

3 A **lonely** place is one where very few people come and which is a long way from places where people live. EG *...lonely country roads.* ADJ QUALIT

loner /ləʊnə/, **loners.** A **loner** is a person who prefers to be alone rather than be with other people. N COUNT

lonesome /ləʊnsə[0]m/. **1** Someone who is **lonesome** is unhappy because they are alone or do not have any friends. EG *I get lonesome sometimes.* ADJ QUALIT American Informal

2 A **lonesome** place is one where very few people come and which is a long way from places where people live. EG *...a lonesome valley.* ADJ QUALIT American Informal

long /lɒŋ/, **longer** /lɒŋgə/, **longest** /lɒŋgɪ[2]st/; **longs, longing, longed. 1** You use **long** to say that a great amount of time passes while something is happening or is in existence. EG *I haven't known her long... Sorry it took so long... Our oil won't last much longer... I had guessed long ago... Not long after our arrival a curious thing happened.* ADV

2 A **long** event or period of time lasts or takes a great amount of time. EG *There was a long pause... They are demanding longer holidays.* ADJ QUALIT: USU ATTRIB

3 You use **for long** when you are saying that something happens or is the case for a great amount of time. EG *Men have been indoctrinated for too long... It didn't stay there for long.* PHRASE

4 You use **long** when asking questions or giving information about amounts of time. EG *'How long have you been married?' – 'Five years.'... His speeches are never less than two hours long.* ADV, OR ADJ AFTER N

5 Something that **no longer** happens used to happen in the past but does not happen now. EG *We can no longer afford to live there... I couldn't stand it any longer.* PHRASE

6 If you say that something will happen **before long**, you mean that it will happen soon. EG *They're bound to catch him before long.* PHRASE

7 You use **long** to emphasize that something happens for the whole of a particular time. For example, if something happens all day **long**, it happens throughout the day. EG *We row all day long.*

8 Something that is **long** measures a great distance from one end to the other. EG *She had long dark hair... ...a long line of cars... ...long tables... It may look a long way on the map but it isn't.* ADJ QUALIT

9 You use **long** when giving information or asking questions about how much something measures from one end to the other. EG *...an area 3,000 feet long and 900 feet wide... How long is that side?* ADJ AFTER N

10 A **long** book or other piece of writing contains a lot of words. EG *...an enormously long novel.* ADJ QUALIT: USU ATTRIB

11 If you say that one thing is true **as long as** or **so long as** another thing is true, you mean that it is true if or when the other thing is true. EG *We were all right as long as we kept our heads down.* CONJ

12 You can say **'So long'** as a way of saying goodbye. CONVENTION Informal

13 If you **long** for something, you want it very much. EG *They longed for green trees and open spaces... They're longing to see you.* V+*for* OR *to*-INF

14 See also **longing**.

long-distance. Long-distance travel or communication is travel or communication between places that are far apart. EG *...long-distance motor coaches... ...long-distance phone calls.* ADJ CLASSIF: ATTRIB

long-drawn-out. A **long-drawn-out** process or conflict lasts an unnecessarily long time. EG *...a long-drawn-out struggle.* ADJ CLASSIF: ATTRIB

longevity /lɒndʒɛvɪ[1]ti[1]/ is long life. EG *...improved health care resulting in increased longevity.* N UNCOUNT Formal

longing /lɒŋɪŋ/, **longings.** A **longing** is a rather sad feeling of wanting something very much, especially something that you are unlikely to get. EG *People have a longing for normality... He gazed with longing and apprehension into the future.* N COUNT OR N UNCOUNT

longingly /lɒŋɪŋli[1]/. If you think **longingly** about something you want, you think about it with a feeling of desire. EG *I began to think longingly of bed... I eyed the cold drinks longingly.* ADV

longitude /lɒŋɪtju:d/, **longitudes.** The **longitude** of a place is its distance to the west or east of a line passing through Greenwich in England: compare **latitude**. N COUNT OR N UNCOUNT

long-lasting, longer-lasting. Something that is **long-lasting** lasts for a long time. EG *The failure of the dam is unlikely to have long-lasting environmental consequences... Solid rubber is longer-lasting.* ADJ QUALIT

long-life. Long-life milk, fruit juice, and batteries last longer than ordinary kinds. ADJ CLASSIF: ATTRIB

long-lived. Something that is **long-lived** lives or lasts for a long time. EG *Bats are surprisingly long-lived creatures... ...a long-lived rebellion.* ADJ QUALIT

long-lost is used to describe someone or something that has not been seen for a long time. EG *She greeted me like a long-lost daughter... These pictures were based on a long-lost mosaic.* ADJ CLASSIF: ATTRIB

long-range. 1 A **long-range** piece of military equipment is able to hit a target a long way away, or to travel a long way. EG *...a modern long-range strategic missile... ...long-range bombers.* ADJ CLASSIF: ATTRIB

2 A **long-range** plan or prediction relates to a period extending a long time into the future. EG *...the necessity for long-range planning.* ADJ CLASSIF: ATTRIB

long-sighted. If you are **long-sighted**, you cannot see things near you clearly, but you can see things a long way away. ADJ QUALIT

long-standing. Something that is **long-standing** has existed for a long time. EG *...his long-standing reputation as a scholar... ...a long-standing feud.* ADJ QUALIT

long-suffering. Someone who is **long-suffering** patiently bears continual trouble or bad treatment. EG *...his noble, long-suffering wife.* ADJ QUALIT

long-term. 1 Long-term things are intended to continue or to be effective for a long time in the future. EG *...hopes for a long-term solution to the problem... I hesitated before making a long-term commitment of this importance.* ADJ QUALIT: USU ATTRIB

If you are a loner, are you lonesome?

2 When you talk about what happens in the **long term**, you are talking about what happens over a long period of time. EG *The results, in the long term, were successful.* N SING : *the*+N

long wave is a range of radio waves which are used for broadcasting. N UNCOUNT

long-winded. If you describe something that has been written or said as **long-winded**, you mean that it contains many more words than are necessary and is therefore boring. EG *...long-winded prayers.* ADJ QUALIT

loo /lu:/, **loos.** People sometimes refer to a toilet as the **loo**. EG *I think she's in the loo... He wanted to go to the loo.* N COUNT Informal

look /lʊk/, **looks, looking, looked. 1** If you **look** in a particular direction, you turn your eyes in that direction so that you can see what is there. EG *She turned to look out of the window... They looked at each other... He blushed and looked away.* ▸ used as a noun. EG *Take a good look... Did you have a look at the shop?* V : USU+A ▸ N SING

2 To **look** at something also means to read or examine it, usually not thoroughly. EG *'I'd like to look at his medical history,' Percival said.* ▸ used as a noun. EG *Tony, I've had a look at that book you wrote... You should let a doctor have a look at her.* V+*at* ▸ N SING

3 If you give someone a **look**, you look at them with an expression on your face that shows what you are thinking. EG *Don't give me such severe looks. What have I done?* N COUNT : USU+SUPP

4 If you **look** for someone or something, you try to find them. EG *I've been looking for you... She looked around for some paper... ...people looking for work.* V : OFT+*for*

5 If you **look** at a subject, problem, or situation, you think about it or study it. EG *Let's look at the implications of these changes.* ▸ used as a noun. EG *We have to take a hard look at the whole situation.* V+*at* ▸ N SING

6 If you **look** at a situation from a particular point of view, you judge it or consider it from that point of view. EG *If you're a Democrat, you look at things one way, and if you're a Republican you look at them very differently.* V+*at*

7 You say **'look'** or **'look here'** when you want someone to pay attention to what you are saying, often when you are angry or upset. EG *Look, Mrs Kintner, you've got it wrong.* CONVENTION

8 You also use **look** to draw attention to something, when you are surprised or angry, or when you are giving an example of something. EG *Goodness, look at the time. I promised I'd be home at six... Now look what you've done... I mean, look at fortune tellers.* V+*at* OR WH : ONLY IMPER

9 If a window, room, or building **looks** out onto a particular thing, it has a view of that thing. EG *The kitchen window looks out onto a yard.* V+A

10 You use **look** when describing something's appearance or someone's appearance or expression. For example, if something **looks** nice, its appearance is nice. EG *You look very pale... He looked as if he hadn't slept very much... 'What does he look like?' - 'Pale, thin, dark-haired.'* V+C OR V+*as if/like*

11 If someone or something has a particular **look**, they have that appearance or expression. EG *He didn't have the look of a man who was thinking... There is a nervous look in their eyes.* ● You say **by the look of** or **by the looks of** something or someone when you are giving an opinion about them which is based on their appearance. EG *It's been there all summer by the look of it.* N SING+SUPP ● PHRASE

12 When you refer to someone's **looks**, you are referring to how beautiful or handsome they are. EG *She had lost her looks... I didn't marry him for his looks... ...his good looks and charm.* N PLURAL

13 You use **look** to say how something seems to you. For example, if a situation **looks** bad, it seems bad. If it **looks** as if something is the case, it seems as if it is the case. EG *The plan looks impressive enough on paper... Looks like we're going to be late... It looks like a good book.* V+C OR V+*as if/like*

look after. 1 If you **look after** someone or something, you do what is necessary in order to keep them safe, well, or in good condition. EG *Your husband ought to be looking after the baby.* **2** If you **look after** something, you are responsible for it and deal with it. EG *The duty of the local authority is to look after the interests of local people.* PHRASAL VB : V+PREP, HAS PASS; V+PREP, HAS PASS

look back. 1 If you **look back**, you think about things that happened in the past. EG *People can often look back and reflect on happy childhood memories.* **2** If you say that someone did something and **never looked back**, you mean that they then became very successful. EG *He borrowed $10,000 to start his Hollywood restaurant and never looked back.* PHRASAL VB : V+ADV; PHRASE

look down on. If you **look down on** someone or something, you think that they are inferior or unimportant. EG *Farm labourers used to be looked down on.* PHRASAL VB : V+ADV+PREP

look forward to. If you **are looking forward to** something, you want it to happen because you think you will enjoy it. EG *I'm quite looking forward to it... I look forward to seeing you in Washington.* PHRASAL VB : V+ADV+PREP

look into. If you **look into** something, you find out about it and examine the facts. EG *A working party was set up to look into the problem.* PHRASAL VB : V+PREP, HAS PASS

look on. 1 If you **look on** while something happens, you watch it. EG *His parents looked on with a triumphant smile.* **2** If you **look on** something as a particular thing, you think of it as that thing. EG *She looked on us as idiots.* PHRASAL VB : V+ADV; V+PREP+A, HAS PASS

look out. You say **'look out'** to warn someone that they are in danger. EG *'Look out,' I said. 'There's something coming.'* ● See also **lookout**. CONVENTION

look out for. If you **look out for** a particular thing, you make sure that you notice it when it is there. EG *It's a film we shall look out for in the next couple of months.* PHRASAL VB : V+ADV+PREP

look round. If you **look round** a building or place, you walk round it and look at the different parts of it. PHRASAL VB : V+PREP

look through. If you **look through** something, you examine all of it in order to find what you are looking for. EG *He looked through the clothing on the bed.* PHRASAL VB : V+PREP

look to. 1 If you **look to** someone for something such as help or advice, you expect or hope that they will provide it. EG *Many people in the community will be looking to us for leadership.* **2** If you **look to** the future, you think about it, often with a particular emotion. EG *Some New Englanders look to the future with a certain anxiety.* PHRASAL VB : V+PREP, OFT+*to*-INF OR *for*; V+PREP

look up. 1 If you **look up** a piece of information, you find it out by looking in a book. EG *He consulted his dictionary to look up the meaning of 'apotheosis'.* **2** If you **look** someone **up**, you visit them after you have not seen them for a long time. EG *It was such a fine day he thought he'd look me up.* **3** If a situation **is looking up**, it is improving. EG *Things are looking up.* PHRASAL VB : V+O+ADV; V+O+ADV Informal; V+ADV, USU CONT Informal

look upon. If you **look upon** something as a particular thing, you think of it as that thing. EG *Houses are looked upon as investments.* PHRASAL VB : V+PREP+A, HAS PASS

look up to. If you **look up to** someone, you respect and admire them. EG *His younger brothers look up to him.* PHRASAL VB : V+ADV+PREP

look-alike, look-alikes. A person's **look-alike** is someone who looks very like them. EG *It was only the Minister's look-alike.* N COUNT

look-in. If you fail to do something because too many other people are doing it, you can say that you did not get a **look-in**. EG *James talks so much that all the others barely get a look-in.* N SING : *a*+N, WITH BROAD NEG Informal

lookout /lʊkaʊt/, **lookouts. 1** A **lookout** is **1.1** a place from which you can see clearly in all directions. EG *...a lookout platform.* **1.2** someone who is watching for danger. EG *Two of the burglars were tipped off by a lookout and escaped.* N COUNT

2 If you are **on the lookout** or are **keeping a** PHRASE

lookout for something, you are paying attention so that you will notice it when it appears or happens. EG *I'm on the lookout for a second-hand car... She sat a little distance away keeping a lookout for danger.*

loom /lu:m/, **looms, looming, loomed. 1** You say that something **looms** when it appears as a tall, unclear shape, often in a frightening way. EG *As you get closer they loom above you like icebergs.* V: USU+A

2 You can say that an event or situation **looms** when it will soon happen and it will bring you problems. EG *The next general election loomed.* V

● You say that a problem or situation **looms large** when you are worrying about it a lot. EG *The meeting loomed large.* ● PHRASE

3 A **loom** is a machine that is used for weaving thread into cloth. N COUNT

loom up. You say that something **looms up** when it appears as a tall, unclear shape, often in a frightening way. EG *...a huge Victorian edifice that loomed up in front of us.* PHRASAL VB: V+ADV

loony /lu:ni[1]/, **loonies. 1** You describe behaviour or ideas as **loony** when they seem mad or eccentric. EG *There seems to be this loony idea that you have to be passionately in love to get married.* ADJ QUALIT Informal

2 You call someone a **loony** when they behave in a way that seems mad or eccentric. EG *He's probably a loony, poor old soul... They sent me to this loony doctor.* N COUNT Informal

loop /lu:p/, **loops, looping, looped. 1** A **loop** is a curved or circular shape in something long, for example in a piece of string. EG *...loops of blue and pink ribbon.* N COUNT

2 If you **loop** something such as rope around an object, you tie a length of it in a loop around the object. EG *The king had pearls looped round his neck.* V+O: USU+A

3 If something **loops**, it goes in a circular direction that makes the shape of a loop. EG *Birds loop and weave through the tall trees.* V: OFT+A

loophole /lu:phəʊl/, **loopholes.** A **loophole** in the law is a small mistake or omission which allows you to avoid doing something that the law intends you to do. EG *A number of obvious loopholes exist for tax avoidance.* N COUNT

loose /lu:s/, **looser, loosest. 1** Something that is **loose** is **1.1** not firmly held or fixed in place. EG *The doorknob is loose and rattles... ...loose strands of copper wire.* ◇ **loosely.** EG *Willie held the phone loosely.* **1.2** not attached to anything else. EG *...a few loose sheets of paper.* ADJ QUALIT ◇ ADV ADJ CLASSIF

2 Loose clothes are rather large and do not fit closely to your body. EG *...a loose cotton shirt.* ◇ **loosely.** EG *His black garments hung loosely from his powerful shoulders.* ADJ QUALIT ◇ ADV

3 When a woman's hair is **loose**, it is hanging freely round her shoulders rather than being tied back. EG *She shook her hair loose.* ADJ CLASSIF

4 If you set animals **loose**, you release them when they have been tied up or kept in a box or cage. EG *He had taken some white rats into church and let them loose on the floor.* ADJ CLASSIF

5 You say that people cut **loose** or are set **loose** when they become free from the influence or authority of other people. EG *The younger generation have tended to cut loose from the influence of class background.* ADJ PRED

6 If a dangerous person is **on the loose**, they are free and there is a possibility that you might meet them and be harmed by them. EG *A bandit leader was on the loose in the hills.* PHRASE

7 People refer to a woman as a **loose** woman when they consider that she is sexually promiscuous; used showing disapproval. ADJ QUALIT: ATTRIB Outdated

8 A **loose** organization or administration is not strictly controlled. EG *A loose grouping of 'radicals' was formed which met once a week... The country has a loose federal structure.* ADJ QUALIT

9 If you are **at a loose end**, you have nothing to do and are bored. PHRASE

loosen /lu:sən/, **loosens, loosening, loosened. 1** If you **loosen** something or if it **loosens**, it becomes less firm or less tightly held in place. EG *The tyre on one of his wheels had loosened... The wind had loosened some leaves.* V-ERG

2 If you **loosen** your clothing or **loosen** something that is tied or fastened, you undo it slightly. EG *He loosened his seat-belt... He took off his jacket and loosened his tie.* V+O

loosen up. If you **loosen up** or if something **loosens** you **up**, you become calmer and less worried than you were. EG *Her second drink loosened her up... As the day wore on he loosened up and became more chatty.* PHRASAL VB: V-ERG+ADV Informal

loot /lu:t/, **loots, looting, looted. 1** When people **loot** shops or houses, they steal things from them during a battle or a riot. EG *Shops were looted and wrecked in London.* ◇ **looting.** EG *There was widespread looting of stores and shops.* V+O OR V ◇ N UNCOUNT

2 Stolen money or goods can be referred to as **loot**. EG *He told his wife where the loot was hidden.* N UNCOUNT Informal

lop /lɒp/, **lops, lopping, lopped.** If you **lop** a tree, you cut off some of its branches. V+O

lop off. If you **lop** something **off**, you cut it away from what it was attached to, usually with a quick, strong stroke. PHRASAL VB: V+O+ADV

lope /ləʊp/, **lopes, loping, loped.** When people or animals **lope**, they run in an easy and relaxed way, taking long steps. EG *The dog started to lope alongside my car.* V+A

lopsided /lɒpsaɪdı[2]d/. Something that is **lopsided** is uneven because its two sides are different from each other. EG *...a lopsided smile.* ADJ QUALIT

loquacious /lə[6]kweɪʃəs/. People who are **loquacious** talk a lot. EG *He is an easy, loquacious man.* ADJ QUALIT Formal

lord /lɔ:d/, **lords. 1 Lord** is the title used in front of the name of some British peers. EG *...Lord Harewood... ...Lord Alfred Douglas.*

2 In Britain, judges, bishops, and some members of the nobility are addressed as 'my **Lord**'.

3 Lord is also used in the title of officials of very high rank in Britain. EG *...The Lord Mayor of London... ...the Lord Chief Justice.*

4 A **lord** is a man who has a high rank in the British nobility. EG *...lords and ladies.* N COUNT

5 The word **lord** is often used in expressions such as 'lord and master' and 'lord of the manor' to refer to men who are in positions of authority. N COUNT

6 In the Christian church, people refer to God and to Jesus Christ as **Lord**. N PROPER

7 You can say **'good Lord!'** or **'oh Lord!'** when you are surprised, amused, shocked, or worried about something. EG *'Good Lord!' I said. 'You still here?'* EXCLAM

Lordship /lɔ:dʃɪp/, **Lordships.** Your **Lordship** or his **Lordship** is a respectful way of addressing or talking about a judge, bishop, or lord. EG *I'm sorry, sir, his Lordship is in his bath... Their Lordships were late for dinner.*

Lord's Prayer. The **Lord's Prayer** is a very important Christian prayer that was originally taught by Jesus Christ to his disciples. N SING: *the*+N

lore /lɔ:/. The **lore** of a particular country or culture is the traditional stories and history of it. EG *...Jewish mystical lore.* ● See also **folklore**. N UNCOUNT +SUPP

lorry /lɒri[1]/, **lorries.** A **lorry** is a large vehicle that is used to transport goods by road. N COUNT British

lose /lu:z/, **loses, losing, lost** /lɒst/. **1** If you **lose** something, **1.1** you do not know where it is, for example because you have forgotten where you put it. EG *You haven't lost the ticket, have you?* **1.2** you no longer have it, although you would like to have it, often because it has been taken away from you or destroyed. EG *I might lose my job... ...a* V+O

If you lopped a leg off a chair, would it be lopsided?

complete list of all the goods lost in the fire... He lost the use of his legs. **1.3** you have less of it than you used to have. EG *He has lost a lot of weight... Brody was beginning to lose interest.*

2 If you **lose** a close relative or friend, he or she dies. EG *I lost my father when I was nine.* V+O : NO CONT

3 If you **lose** an opportunity or **lose** time, you waste it. EG *Bill lost no time in telling everyone about his idea... He will lose his chances of promotion.* V+O

4 If a business **loses** money, it earns less money than it spends. V+O

5 If you **have** something **to lose**, you are in a position where you may suffer if you do something unsuccessfully. EG *The price was too high and he had too much to lose... They had absolutely nothing to lose.* PHRASE

6 If you **lose sight of** something, you can no longer see it. PHRASE

7 If you **lose sight of** an aim, argument, or idea, you gradually forget about it. EG *We've lost sight of moral values.* PHRASE

8 If a clock or watch **loses** time, it shows a time that is earlier than the real time. V+O

9 If you **lose** a competition or argument, someone does better than you and defeats you. EG *They expected to lose the election.* ◊ **losing.** EG *He'd never played on a losing side.* V+O OR V; ◊ ADJ CLASSIF : ATTRIB

10 If you **lose** your way, you get lost when you are trying to go somewhere. V+O

11 See also **lost.** ● to **lose face**: see **face.** ● to **lose** your **head**: see **head.** ● to **lose** your **nerve**: see **nerve.** ● to **lose** your **temper**: see **temper.** ● to **lose touch**: see **touch.**

lose out. If you **lose out**, you suffer a loss or disadvantage. EG *They did not lose out in the struggle to keep up with inflation.* PHRASAL VB : V+ADV

loser /luːzə/, **losers. 1** The **loser** of a game, contest, or struggle is the person who is defeated. N COUNT

● Someone who is **a good loser** accepts the fact that they have lost a game or contest and does not complain. Someone who is **a bad loser** hates losing and complains a lot when they do. ● PHRASE

2 You say that someone or something is a **loser** when they are always unsuccessful or when they seem likely to be unsuccessful. EG *You're a loser, Bill... He avoided losers.* N COUNT Informal

3 If someone is the **loser** as the result of an action or event, they are in a worse situation because of it. EG *She will be the loser if she fails to respond to your friendly overtures.* N COUNT : *the*+N

loss /lɒs/, **losses. 1 Loss** is the fact of no longer having something or of having less of it than you had before. EG *...temporary loss of vision... ...the loss of liberty... ...heat loss.* N UNCOUNT : OFT+*of*

2 Loss of life occurs when many people die, for example in a battle or a disaster. EG *The loss of life was appalling... Artillery fire caused heavy losses.* N UNCOUNT OR N COUNT

3 The **loss** of a close relative or friend is his or her death. EG *...the loss of my daughter and husband.* N UNCOUNT +SUPP

4 If a business makes a **loss**, it earns less money than it spends. EG *The company announced a huge loss for the first half of the year.* N COUNT OR N UNCOUNT

5 If you are **at a loss**, you do not know what to do. EG *I was at a complete loss as to how I could lay my hands on the money.* PHRASE

6 If you **cut** your **losses**, you stop trying to do something, in order to prevent the bad situation you are in from becoming worse. EG *You ought to cut your losses and start again.* PHRASE

7 If you say that someone or something is a **dead loss**, you mean that they are completely useless or unsuccessful. PHRASE Informal

lost /lɒst/. **1 Lost** is the past tense and past participle of **lose.**

2 If you are **lost**, you do not know where you are or you are unable to find your way. EG *There was that time when we got lost out in Dennington.* ADJ CLASSIF : USU PRED

3 If you say that you would be **lost** without someone or something, you mean that you would be unhappy or unable to work properly without them. EG *I am lost without him.* ADJ PRED +*without*

4 If something is **lost**, you cannot find it. EG *Shopping lists on old envelopes tend to get lost.* ADJ CLASSIF

5 If advice or a comment is **lost** on someone, they do not understand it, or they pay no attention to it. EG *The lesson was not lost on the committee.* ADJ PRED+*on*

6 If you tell someone to **get lost**, you are rudely telling them to go away. PHRASE Informal

lost property consists of things that people have lost or accidentally left in a public place, for example at a railway station. Lost property is kept safe in a special office so that people can collect it. EG *...a lost property office.* N UNCOUNT

lot /lɒt/, **lots. 1** A **lot** of something or **lots** of something is a large amount of it. EG *We owed a lot of money... This is a subject that worries a lot of people... I feel that we have a lot to offer... ...a big house with lots of windows.* N PART

2 A lot means to a great extent or degree. EG *The man in the photograph looked a lot like Mr Williams... The weather's a lot warmer there... Thanks a lot.* PHRASE

3 If you do something **a lot**, you do it often or for a long time. EG *He laughs a lot.* PHRASE

4 When you refer to the **lot**, you are referring to the whole of a particular amount of something. EG *Wilks bet his last ten pounds and lost the lot.* N SING : *the*+N Informal

5 You can refer to a particular group of people as a particular **lot.** EG *They were a rather arrogant boring lot.* N SING+SUPP Informal

6 You can refer to a set or group of things as a particular **lot.** EG *...two sets of cards, one lot written in blue, the other in red... I get two lots of everything.* N COUNT OR N PART

7 Your **lot** is the kind of life you have. EG *She was quite content with her lot.* N COUNT+POSS

8 A **lot** in an auction is one of the objects or groups of objects that are being sold. EG *Lot No 359 was a folder of 11 original sketches.* N COUNT

9 If people **draw lots** or **cast lots** to decide who will do something, each of them takes a stick or piece of paper from a container. The person who takes the stick or piece of paper that is different from the others is chosen. PHRASE

10 See also **parking lot.**

loth /ləʊθ/. See **loath.**

lotion /ləʊʃ^{ə}n/, **lotions.** A **lotion** is a liquid that you use on your skin or hair. EG *...a bottle of suntan lotion... ...a tube of hand lotion.* N MASS

lottery /lɒt^{ə}ri^{1}/, **lotteries. 1** When a **lottery** is held, people buy tickets with different numbers on them. Several numbers are chosen and the people whose tickets have these numbers on them win prizes. EG *...a lottery ticket.* N COUNT

2 If you describe a contest as a **lottery**, you mean that the result depends entirely on luck or chance, rather than being decided in a fairer way; used showing disapproval. EG *The British election system will become a lottery.* N SING : *a*+N

loud /laʊd/, **louder, loudest. 1** You say that a noise is **loud** when the level of sound is very high. For example, thunder is loud and your voice is loud when you shout. EG *His voice was loud and savage... There was a loud explosion... He spoke louder.* ADJ QUALIT OR ADV

◊ **loudly.** EG *The audience laughed loudly.* ◊ ADV

2 If someone is **loud** in their support or condemnation of something, they express their opinion often and in a strong way. EG *Northcliffe's newspapers were loud in their condemnation of British sentimentality.* ◊ **loudly.** EG *Most people loudly allege that all this is just another excuse.* ADJ QUALIT : OFT+*in*; ◊ ADV

3 If you say something **loud and clear**, what you say can be easily understood. EG *The message goes out loud and clear.* PHRASE

4 If you say something **out loud**, you say it, rather than just thinking it. EG *She was praying out loud... I laughed out loud at the thought.* PHRASE

5 You say that a piece of clothing is **loud** when it has very bright colours or a large, bold pattern; used showing disapproval. EG *...young men in loud shirts and jackets.* ADJ QUALIT

loud-mouthed /laʊdmaʊðd/. Someone who is **loud-mouthed** talks a lot, especially in an unpleasant, offensive, or stupid way. EG *...a loud-mouthed, hard-drinking actor.* ADJ QUALIT

loudspeaker /laʊdspiːkə/, **loudspeakers.** A **loudspeaker** is a piece of equipment that makes your voice sound louder. EG *He made an announcement over the loudspeaker.* N COUNT

lounge /laʊnd[o]ʒ/, **lounges, lounging, lounged. 1** A **lounge** is a room in a house, hotel, or club where people sit and relax. N COUNT

2 A **lounge** at an airport is a very large room for passengers to wait in. EG *...the arrivals lounge.* N COUNT

3 The **lounge** or **lounge bar** in a pub or hotel is a comfortably furnished bar where the drinks are more expensive than in the other bars. N COUNT British

4 If you **lounge** somewhere, you lean against something or lie on something in a comfortable and lazy way. EG *She lounged on the rug.* V: USU+A

lounge about or **lounge around.** If you **lounge about** or **lounge around**, you spend your time in a relaxed and lazy way; usually used showing disapproval. EG *...people who were lounging about, apparently with nothing to do.* PHRASAL VB: V+ADV/PREP

louse /laʊs/, **lice** /laɪs/. **Lice** are small insects that live on the bodies of people or animals. N COUNT

lousy /laʊzi[1]/. **1** If you describe something as **lousy**, you mean that it is of very bad quality or that you do not like it at all. EG *The hotels are lousy... ...a lousy hockey game.* ADJ QUALIT Informal

2 If you feel **lousy**, you feel ill. EG *I feel really lousy tonight.* ADJ PRED Informal

lout /laʊt/, **louts.** If you call a young man a **lout**, you mean that he behaves in an impolite or aggressive way. EG *...gangs of drunken louts.* N COUNT

lovable /lʌvəbə[o]l/. Someone who is **lovable** has attractive qualities, and it is easy to like them very much. EG *...a mischievous but lovable child.* ADJ QUALIT

love /lʌv/, **loves, loving, loved. 1** If you **love** someone, **1.1** you feel romantically or sexually attracted to them, and they are very important to you. EG *I do not think I love him enough to marry him... 'I love you, Albert.' – 'I love you too, Mabel.'* **1.2** you feel that their happiness is very important to you, and so you behave in a kind and caring way towards them. EG *He gave us a little baby. A little baby to love... They make us feel safe and secure, loved and wanted.* V+O

2 If you **love** something, **2.1** you feel that it is important and want to protect it. EG *They don't love their village in the way that their parents did.* **2.2** you like it very much. EG *We both love dancing... I love Haydn and Schubert.* V+O

3 Love is **3.1** a very strong feeling of affection towards someone who you are romantically or sexually attracted to. EG *Her love for him never wavered... You are not marrying for love... ...a Russian love song.* N UNCOUNT: OFT+*for* **3.2** the feeling that a person's happiness is very important to you, and the way you show this feeling in your behaviour towards them. EG *...maternal love... Children need love and understanding.* N UNCOUNT **3.3** a strong liking for something or enjoyment of it. EG *...a man with a genuine love of literature... It was designed and built with love.* N UNCOUNT: OFT+*of*

4 If you would **love** to have or to do something, you very much want to have it or to do it. EG *I would love a photograph of Edith Evans... Posy said she'd love to stay.* V+O OR V+*to*-INF

5 Some people use **love** as an affectionate way of addressing someone. Men usually address only women and children as **love**. EG *Thanks a lot, love.* VOCATIVE Informal

6 In tennis, **love** is a score of zero. NUMBER

7 You can write **love** or **love from**, followed by your name, as an informal way of ending a letter to a friend or relation. EG *Hope you are all well at home. Love, Dan.* CONVENTION

8 If you **send** someone your **love** or say **'give them my love'**, you ask another person to tell them that you are thinking about them with affection. EG *They send you their love.* PHRASE

9 If you are **in love** with someone, you feel romantically or sexually attracted to them, and they are very important to you. EG *They are in love with each other and wish to marry.* PHRASE

10 If you **fall in love** with someone, you start to be in love with them. EG *I fell madly in love with Ellen the first time I saw her.* PHRASE

11 When two people **make love**, they have sex. PHRASE

12 If you have **a love-hate relationship** with someone or something, you have strong feelings of both love and hate towards them. PHRASE

13 a **labour of love**: see **labour**. • See also **loving**.

love affair, love affairs. A **love affair** is a romantic and often sexual relationship between two people who love each other but who are not married to each other. N COUNT

loveless /lʌvlɪ[2]s/. In a **loveless** relationship or situation, there is no love. EG *...a loveless marriage.* ADJ CLASSIF: ATTRIB

love letter, love letters. A **love letter** is a letter that you write to someone in order to tell them that you love them. N COUNT

love life, love lives. Someone's **love life** is the part of their life that consists of their romantic and sexual relationships. EG *He had a very emotional lovelife and was always changing partners.* N COUNT

lovely /lʌvli[1]/, **lovelier, loveliest. 1** Someone or something that is **lovely** is very beautiful and therefore pleasing to look at or listen to. EG *'Doesn't she look lovely, Albert?' she whispered... To me Hong Kong was one of the loveliest places in the world.* ADJ QUALIT ◊ **loveliness.** EG *Coffee was being handed out by a girl of film-star loveliness.* ◊ N UNCOUNT

2 If you describe something as **lovely**, you are saying how much you like it. EG *'What a lovely surprise!' she said... Lovely day, isn't it?... It was lovely to hear from you again.* ADJ QUALIT

3 You can describe someone as **lovely** when you like them very much because they are friendly, kind, and generous. EG *We've got lovely neighbours... She's the sweetest, loveliest person.* ADJ QUALIT

love-making refers to romantic activities, especially sexual activities, that take place between two people. EG *...ardent love-making.* N UNCOUNT

lover /lʌvə/, **lovers. 1** Your **lover** is someone who you are having a sexual relationship with but are not married to. EG *Jenny and I were lovers.* N COUNT

2 You can refer to people as **lovers** when they are in love with each other. EG *...young lovers.* N COUNT Outdated

3 You can also use **lover** to refer to someone who enjoys something very much. For example, an art **lover** is someone who enjoys art. EG *...a music lover.* N COUNT+SUPP

loving /lʌvɪŋ/. **1** Someone who is **loving** feels or shows love to other people. EG *...a loving, beautiful wife.* ADJ QUALIT ◊ **lovingly.** EG *For a moment she looked at her grandson lovingly.* ◊ ADV

2 Loving actions are done with great enjoyment and care, especially by someone with special knowledge or understanding. EG *...tending the gardens with loving care.* ADJ CLASSIF: ATTRIB ◊ **lovingly.** EG *The Society of Antiquaries have lovingly restored the building.* ◊ ADV

low /ləʊ/, **lower, lowest; lows. 1** Something that is **low** **1.1** measures a short distance from the bottom to the top, or from the ground to the top. EG *...a low brick wall... ...a low table... ...low hills.* ADJ QUALIT **1.2** is close to the ground. EG *She made a low curtsey... I asked him to fly low over the beach... He bent lower and lower.* ADJ QUALIT OR ADV **1.3** is close to the bottom of something. EG *She saw the scar low on his spine.* ADJ QUALIT OR ADV

Should you always try to write lucidly?

2 A dress or blouse that is described as **low** leaves a woman's neck and the top part of her chest bare. EG *...a low neckline... Her dress was cut low in front.* ADJ QUALIT OR ADV

3 **Low** means small in amount, value, or degree. EG *...workers on low incomes... Temperatures are lower on the continent in winter than in Britain... ...low expectations... ...a low tar cigarette.* ADJ QUALIT

4 You can use **low** with numbers. For example, if a number or level is **in the low** twenties, it is more than twenty, but not as much as twenty-five. EG *The temperature is in the low eighties.* PHRASE

5 If a supply of something is **low** or if you are **low** on a particular type of thing, you do not have much of it left. EG *We're a bit low on claret.* ADJ PRED

6 If the quality or standard of something is **low**, it is bad. EG *...a low standard of living... ...low-grade material.* ADJ QUALIT

7 **Low** is used to describe people who are near the bottom of a particular scale or system. EG *...a junior executive of a fairly low grade... ...the lowest 85 per cent of the working population.* ADJ QUALIT

8 If you have a **low** opinion of someone, you disapprove of them or dislike them. ADJ QUALIT

9 You also use **low** to describe people and actions which are not respectable and which you disapprove of. EG *...mixing with low company... Well I'm not doing that. I haven't sunk that low.* ADJ QUALIT OR ADV

10 If a sound is **low**, 10.1 it is deep. EG *...a long low note on the horn.* ADJ QUALIT 10.2 it is quiet or soft. EG *Smithy spoke to him in a low and urgent voice... He turned the radio on low.* ADJ QUALIT OR ADV

11 A light that is **low** is dim rather than bright. ADJ QUALIT

12 Someone who is feeling **low** is depressed. ADJ QUALIT

13 A **low** is the worst or smallest level that something has ever reached. EG *Output was at a record low.* N COUNT+SUPP

14 If you **are lying low**, you are avoiding being seen in public. EG *She'll have to lie low for a couple of years.* PHRASE Informal

low-cut dresses and blouses leave a woman's neck, shoulders, and the top part of her chest bare. ADJ QUALIT

lower /ləʊə/, **lowers, lowering, lowered.** 1 **Lower** is the comparative of **low**.

2 **Lower** is used to describe 2.1 the bottom one of a pair of things. EG *Thomas was lying in the lower bunk... Jane sucked at her lower lip.* 2.2 the less important one of two organizations or systems that work together. EG *He could argue his case in the lower court.* 2.3 the bottom part of something. EG *The bullet had penetrated the lower left corner of his back.* ADJ CLASSIF : ATTRIB

3 **Lower** also describes people or things that are less important than other people or things. EG *...the lower levels of the organization.* ADJ CLASSIF : ATTRIB

4 If you **lower** something, 4.1 you move it slowly downwards. EG *He lowered his glass... Lynn lowered herself into the water.* V+O 4.2 you make it less in amount, value, or quality. EG *The voting age was lowered to eighteen... Mexican hotels are lowering their rates sharply.* V+O ◇ **lowering.** EG *...the lowering of examination standards.* ◇ N SING +SUPP

5 If you **lower** your eyes, you look downwards. EG *She lowered her eyes and remained silent.* V+O

6 If you **lower** your voice, you speak more quietly. V+O

lower class, lower classes. The **lower class** or **lower classes** are the social class that is below the middle class. EG *I'm one of the lower classes and I'm proud of it... ...lower-class families.* N COUNT : USU PLURAL

low-key. Something that is **low-key** or **low-keyed** is not obvious or intense. EG *The organization lent us support in its own low-key way.* ADJ QUALIT

lowlands /ləʊlə³ndz/. A flat area of land that is approximately at sea level is sometimes referred to as the **lowlands**. EG *...the Scottish Lowlands... The cattle are brought down to the lowlands.* N PLURAL

lowly /ləʊli¹/, **lowlier, lowliest.** Something that is **lowly** is low in rank, status, or importance. EG *...a lowly employee... ...his lowly social origins.* ADJ QUALIT

low-paid. When workers earn only a small amount of money, you can say that they are **low-paid** or that their jobs are **low-paid**. EG *...low-paid workers... ...women in low paid jobs.* ADJ QUALIT

low tide is the time at which the sea is at its lowest level at the coast each day before it starts to rise again. EG *The rocks are exposed at low tide.* N UNCOUNT

loyal /lɔɪəl/. Someone who is **loyal** remains firm in their friendship or support for someone or something. EG *Most Tories remained loyal to the Government... ...a loyal friend.* ADJ QUALIT : OFT+*to* ◇ **loyally.** EG *For thirty years she had served him loyally.* ◇ ADV

loyalty /lɔɪəlti¹/, **loyalties.** 1 **Loyalty** is behaviour in which you stay firm in your friendship or support for someone or something. EG *I am convinced of your loyalty to the cause.* N UNCOUNT

2 **Loyalties** are feelings of friendship, support, or duty towards someone or something. EG *...an issue that transcended party loyalties... ...their loyalties to the church.* N COUNT : USU PLURAL

lozenge /lɒzɪ²ndʒ/, **lozenges.** 1 A **lozenge** is a tablet which you can suck when you have a cough or sore throat. EG *...throat lozenges.* N COUNT

2 A **lozenge** is also a shape like a square which usually has two corners pointing up and down that are further apart than the corners that point sideways. N COUNT

LP /ɛl piː/, **LPs.** An **LP** is a record which has about 25 minutes of music or speech on each side. N COUNT

L-plate /ɛl pleɪt/, **L-plates. L-plates** are square white pieces of plastic or metal with a red 'L' on them which you attach to the front and back of a car when you are learning to drive. N COUNT

LSD /ɛl ɛs diː/ is a very powerful drug which causes strong hallucinations. N UNCOUNT

Ltd is written after the name of a company. **Ltd** is an abbreviation for 'limited'. EG *...Cobuild Ltd.*

lubricate /luːbrɪkeɪt/, **lubricates, lubricating, lubricated.** If you **lubricate** part of a machine, you put a substance such as oil onto it so that it moves smoothly. EG *The chain might need lubricating.* V+O ◇ **lubrication** /luːbrɪkeɪʃə⁰n/. EG *...the lubrication system of the engine.* ◇ N UNCOUNT

lucid /luːsɪd/. 1 Writing or speech that is **lucid** is clear and easy to understand. EG *...a brief and lucid account.* ADJ QUALIT Formal ◇ **lucidly.** EG *Her ideas are very lucidly set out in his book.* ◇ ADV ◇ **lucidity** /luːsɪdɪ¹ti¹/. EG *He expresses himself with quiet lucidity.* ◇ N UNCOUNT

2 When someone who has been ill or confused is **lucid**, they are able to think clearly again. EG *There was a ringing in my head, yet I was lucid.* ADJ QUALIT Formal ◇ **lucidity.** EG *In one of his moments of lucidity, he came upstairs to talk.* ◇ N UNCOUNT

3 Things that are **lucid** are very bright and clear. EG *...a lucid light.* ADJ QUALIT Literary

luck /lʌk/. 1 **Luck** or good **luck** is success that does not come from your own abilities or efforts. EG *I had some wonderful luck... He wished me luck.* N UNCOUNT

2 **Bad luck** is lack of success or bad things that happen to you, that have not been caused by yourself or other people. EG *One spring we had a lot of bad luck.* PHRASE

3 **Luck** is used in these phrases. 3.1 If you say **'Bad luck'** or **'Hard luck'** to someone, you are expressing sympathy when they have failed to do something or failed to get something. EG *Tough luck, Barrett. You played a great game.* CONVENTION 3.2 If you say **'Good luck'** or **'Best of luck'** to someone, you are saying that you hope that they will be successful. EG *Good luck to you, my boy... Best of luck with the exams.* CONVENTION 3.3 If you say that someone is **in luck**, you mean that they are lucky on a particular occasion. PHRASE

3.4 If you say that someone **is pushing** their **luck**, you mean that they are taking a risk and may get into trouble. PHRASE 3.5 When someone **tries** their **luck** at something, they try to succeed at it. EG *He came to England to try his luck at a musical career.* PHRASE 3.6 You can add **with luck** or **with any luck** to a statement to indicate that you hope that a particu- ADV SEN Informal lar thing will happen. EG *This one should work with a bit of luck... With any luck they might forget all about it.*

luckily /lʌkɪli¹/. You can add **luckily** to what you are saying to indicate that you are glad that something happened. EG *Luckily, Saturday was a fine day... Luckily, Joe came to my rescue... Luckily for you, I happen to have the key.* ADV SEN

luckless /lʌklɪ²s/. If someone is **luckless** or if something that they do is **luckless**, they are unsuccessful or unfortunate. EG *This trip of ours has been singularly luckless.* ADJ QUALIT Literary

lucky /lʌki¹/, **luckier, luckiest. 1** You say that someone is **lucky** **1.1** when they have something that is very desirable, or when they are in a very desirable situation. EG *I'm lucky in having an excellent teacher... He was the luckiest man in the world.* **1.2** when they always seem to have good luck. EG *Are you lucky at cards?* ADJ QUALIT

2 If you describe an event or situation as **lucky**, you mean that it had good effects or consequences, although it happened by chance and not as a result of planning or preparation. EG *It's lucky I'm here... It was lucky that I had cooked a big joint... ...a lucky guess.* ADJ QUALIT

3 People describe something that they wear or have with them as **lucky** when they believe that it helps them to be successful. EG *...his lucky sweater.* ADJ CLASSIF

4 If you say that someone **will be lucky** to do something, you mean it is very unlikely that they will be able to do it. EG *We will be lucky to get five pounds for it.* PHRASE Informal

lucrative /lu:krətɪv/. Something that is **lucrative** earns you a lot of money. EG *It had been an exciting and lucrative business... ...the lucrative trade in tea and porcelain.* ADJ QUALIT Formal

ludicrous /lu:dɪkrəs/. If you describe something as **ludicrous**, you mean that it is extremely foolish, unreasonable, or unsuitable. EG *I had a ludicrous feeling of pride in him... ...one teacher for every 100 pupils, it was ludicrous.* ◇ **ludicrously.** EG *...a ludicrously low price.* ADJ QUALIT ◇ ADV

lug /lʌg/, **lugs, lugging, lugged.** If you **lug** a heavy object from one place to another, you carry it there with difficulty. EG *She lugged the suitcase out into the hallway.* V+O : USU+A Informal

luggage /lʌgɪdʒ/ consists of the suitcases and bags that you have with you when you are travelling. EG *They did not have much luggage.* ● See also **left-luggage office**. N UNCOUNT

lugubrious /lə⁴gu:brɪəs/. You describe someone or something as **lugubrious** when they are sad and dull, and not lively or cheerful. EG *...a lugubrious face... ...lugubrious hymns.* ADJ QUALIT Formal

lukewarm /lu:kwɔ:m/. **1** Something that is **lukewarm** is only slightly warm. EG *...lukewarm water.* ADJ QUALIT

2 If you describe someone as **lukewarm**, you mean that they do not show much enthusiasm or interest. EG *...her parents' lukewarm response... He was lukewarm about the committee.* ADJ QUALIT

lull /lʌl/, **lulls, lulling, lulled. 1** A **lull** is a period of quiet or of little activity. EG *...a lull in the conversation... After a lull of several weeks, there has been a resumption of bombing.* N COUNT : USU+SUPP

2 If you describe a situation as the **lull before the storm**, you mean that you think something very unpleasant is going to happen soon. PHRASE

3 If something **lulls** you, **3.1** it causes you to feel calm or sleepy. EG *...lulling us into slumber.* **3.2** it causes you to feel safe and secure. EG *He had lulled me into thinking that I had won.* V+O : USU+*into*

lullaby /lʌləbaɪ/, **lullabies.** A **lullaby** is a quiet song which you sing to help a child go to sleep. N COUNT

lumber /lʌmbə/, **lumbers, lumbering, lumbered. 1 Lumber** consists of **1.1** tree trunks, logs, or planks of wood that have been roughly cut up. EG *...piles of lumber... ...a lumber company.* **1.2** old and unwanted things, especially old pieces of furniture. EG *...the lumber room.* N UNCOUNT American British

2 If someone **lumbers** from one place to another, they move there very slowly and clumsily. EG *He lumbered upstairs looking for the bathroom... Donkeys lumbered by.* V+A

lumber with. If you **are lumbered with** something such as a duty, you have to deal with it even though you do not want to. EG *Women are still lumbered with the cooking and cleaning.* PHRASAL VB : V+O+PREP, OFT PASS

luminous /lu:mɪnəs/. Something that is **luminous** shines or glows, especially in the dark. EG *...the luminous hands of my watch.* ADJ QUALIT

lump /lʌmp/, **lumps, lumping, lumped. 1** A **lump** is a piece of a solid substance, of any shape or size. EG *...lumps of clay... ...a lump of butter.* N COUNT OR N PART

2 A **lump** on or in someone's body is a small, hard piece of flesh that is formed as a result of an injury or an illness. EG *...a small lump, a little growth just above the right eye.* N COUNT

3 A **lump** of sugar is a small amount of sugar shaped like a cube. EG *Black coffee, two lumps, please.* N PART

4 If you **lump** different people or things together, you consider them in the same way or combine them into one large group. EG *'Don't lump me and Dave together,' he interrupted... The old rural counties were lumped together into new units.* V+O+*with/together*

5 If you say that someone will **have to lump it**, you mean that they must accept a situation or decision whether they like it or not. EG *'He won't like that.' – 'Then he'll lump it.'* PHRASE Informal

lump sum, lump sums. A **lump sum** is an amount of money that is paid as a large amount on a single occasion rather than as smaller amounts on several separate occasions. EG *He has been offered a tax-free lump sum of $4,000.* N COUNT

lumpy /lʌmpi¹/. Something that is **lumpy** contains lumps or is covered with lumps. EG *...sitting on his lumpy mattress... ...a big bowl of lumpy porridge.* ADJ QUALIT

lunacy /lu:nəsi¹/ is **1** very strange or foolish behaviour. EG *This comment would have seemed sheer lunacy to his ancestors... It would be lunacy to marry.* **2** severe mental illness. N UNCOUNT Outdated

lunar /lu:nə/ means concerning the moon or travel to the moon. EG *...the lunar surface... ...the lunar spacecraft.* ADJ CLASSIF : ATTRIB Formal

lunatic /lu:nətɪk/, **lunatics. 1** If you describe someone as a **lunatic**, you mean that they behave in a stupid and annoying way. EG *The man's a bloody lunatic.* N COUNT Informal

2 A **lunatic** is also someone who is mad. EG *Out of a dozen patients, three or four were lunatics.* N COUNT Outdated

3 If you say that a proposal or an action is **lunatic**, you mean that it is foolish and likely to be dangerous. EG *This Government's policies are lunatic.* ADJ QUALIT

lunatic asylum, lunatic asylums. A **lunatic asylum** is a place where people were locked up in former times when they were considered to be mad. N COUNT

lunatic fringe. If you refer to a group of people as the **lunatic fringe**, you mean that they are very extreme in their opinions or behaviour. EG *...the lunatic fringe of the movement.* N SING : *the*+N

lunch /lʌnt⁰ʃ/, **lunches, lunching, lunched. 1 Lunch** is a meal that you have in the middle of the day. EG *What did you have for lunch?... We had a late lunch... After lunch I went to see our doctor.* N UNCOUNT OR N COUNT

2 When you **lunch**, you eat lunch, especially at a restaurant. EG *Why don't you two lunch with me tomorrow?... She was lunching off beer and cheese rolls in a pub.* V : USU+A Formal

luncheon /lʌnt⁰ʃə⁰n/, **luncheons. 1** A **luncheon** is a formal meal in the middle of the day. EG *I had met him at a civic luncheon... ...a luncheon party.* N COUNT

2 Luncheon is the meal that you eat in the middle N UNCOUNT

Is it fun to be with someone who is lugubrious?

of the day. EG *I was planning something hot for luncheon.*

lunch hour, lunch hours. Your **lunch hour** is the period in the middle of the day when you stop work in order to have a meal. EG *The secretaries were just back from their lunch hour.* N COUNT

lunchtime /lʌntᵒʃtaɪm/, **lunchtimes. Lunchtime** is the time in the middle of the day when people have lunch. EG *She's going to see him at lunchtime.* N COUNT OR N UNCOUNT

lung /lʌŋ/, **lungs.** Your **lungs** are the two parts of your body inside your chest which fill with air when you breathe. EG *She filled her lungs with smoke... ...lung cancer.* N COUNT: USU PLURAL

lunge /lʌndᵒʒ/, **lunges, lunging, lunged.** If you **lunge** in a particular direction, you move there suddenly and clumsily. EG *He lunged toward me.* V: USU+A
▸ used as a noun. EG *When he makes a lunge at you, run.* ▸ N COUNT: USU SING

lurch /lɜːtʃ/, **lurches, lurching, lurched. 1** To **lurch** means to make a sudden, jerky movement. EG *He lurched and fell... The boat lurched ahead.* V: USU+A
▸ used as a noun. EG *With a tremendous lurch he fell over me.* ▸ N COUNT
2 If you **lurch** from one thing to another, you suddenly change your opinions, attitude, or behaviour. EG *After lurching away from Socialism in 1976, they now seem to be lurching back.* V+A
3 If someone **leaves** you **in the lurch**, they go away or stop helping you at a very difficult or dangerous time. EG *It's the whole theatre group he's leaving in the lurch.* PHRASE Informal

lure /lʊə/, **lures, luring, lured. 1** To **lure** someone means to attract them and cause them to do something or go somewhere. EG *The price also lures students... Why else had Halliday come up, if not to lure me away?* V+O: USU+A
2 A **lure** is an attractive quality that something has. EG *Many economists have succumbed to the fatal lure of mathematics.* N COUNT+SUPP

lurid /lʊərɪd/. Something that is **lurid 1** involves a lot of violence or sex; used showing disapproval. EG *...lurid stories about the war... ...lurid novels.* ADJ QUALIT **2** is very brightly coloured. EG *...lurid polyester skirts.* ADJ QUALIT
◊ **luridly.** EG *...a luridly coloured advertisement.* ◊ ADV

lurk /lɜːk/, **lurks, lurking, lurked. 1** To **lurk** somewhere means to wait there secretly so that you cannot be seen. EG *Wild boars and wolves lurked near the isolated camp.* V: USU+A
2 If something such as a memory, suspicion, or danger **lurks**, it exists, but you are only slightly aware of it. EG *...outdated prejudices lurking in the minds of individuals.* V: USU+A

luscious /lʌʃəs/. **1** If you describe something as **luscious**, you mean that you find it extremely attractive. EG *...a luscious car... She was looking luscious in faded overalls and a flannel shirt.* ADJ QUALIT
2 Luscious food is juicy and delicious. EG *...a basket of luscious figs.* ADJ QUALIT

lush /lʌʃ/, **lusher, lushest. 1** You describe fields or gardens as **lush** when the grass or plants there are very healthy and are growing well and thickly. EG *...a landscape of lush green meadows.* ADJ QUALIT
2 You can describe places or ways of life as **lush** when they are very rich and full of luxury. EG *...lush restaurants in London and Paris.* ADJ QUALIT

lust /lʌst/, **lusts, lusting, lusted. 1 Lust** is a feeling of strong sexual desire for someone; used showing disapproval. N UNCOUNT
2 A **lust** for something is a very strong and eager desire to possess or gain it; used showing disapproval. EG *...the lust for power.* N COUNT: OFT+*for*

lust after or **lust for. 1** If you **lust after** something or **lust for** it, you have a very strong desire to possess it. EG *They lusted after the gold of El Dorado.* PHRASAL VB: V+PREP, HAS PASS
2 If you **lust after** someone or **lust for** them, you feel a very strong sexual desire for them. EG *How I lusted for that girl!* V+PREP, HAS PASS

lustful /lʌstfʊl/ means feeling or expressing strong sexual desire. EG *...lustful thoughts.* ADJ CLASSIF

lustre /lʌstə/; spelled **luster** in American English.
1 Lustre is gentle shining light that is reflected from a surface, for example from polished metal. EG *...the lustre of encrusted gold.* N UNCOUNT Literary
2 You can refer to the qualities of something that make it interesting and exciting as its **lustre**. EG *...the tarnished lustre of his name.* N UNCOUNT Literary

lusty /lʌstiˡ/, **lustier, lustiest. Lusty** means healthy and full of strength and energy. EG *...a strong and lusty boy of whom any father could be proud.* ◊ **lustily.** EG *They stood waving their Union Jacks and singing lustily.* ADJ QUALIT ◊ ADV

luxuriant /lʌgzjʊərɪənt, lʌgʒ-/. **1** You can describe plants, trees, and gardens which are large, healthy, and growing well as **luxuriant**. EG *...luxuriant forests.* ADJ QUALIT
2 You can also use **luxuriant** to describe someone's hair when it is very thick and healthy. EG *...his pale lined face and luxuriant, flowing hair.* ADJ QUALIT

luxuriate /lʌgzjʊərɪeɪt, lʌgʒ-/, **luxuriates, luxuriating, luxuriated.** If you **luxuriate** in something, you relax in it and enjoy it very much. EG *...bath tubs in which you could lie back and luxuriate... I luxuriated in my retirement.* V: USU+*in*

luxurious /lʌgzjʊərɪəs, lʌgʒ-/. **1** Something that is **luxurious** is very comfortable and expensive. EG *...big, luxurious cars.* ◊ **luxuriously.** EG *We lived luxuriously.* ADJ QUALIT ◊ ADV
2 Luxurious actions express great pleasure and comfort. EG *She took a deep luxurious breath.* ADJ QUALIT
◊ **luxuriously.** EG *She stretched luxuriously.* ◊ ADV

luxury /lʌkʃəᵒriˡ/, **luxuries. 1 Luxury** is very great comfort, especially among beautiful and expensive surroundings and possessions. EG *We lived in great luxury... ...a life of ease and luxury.* N UNCOUNT
2 A **luxury** is **2.1** something expensive which is not necessary but which gives you pleasure. EG *Her mother provided her with clothes and little luxuries.* N COUNT **2.2** a pleasure which you do not often have the opportunity to enjoy. EG *Privacy was an unknown luxury.* N SING+SUPP
3 Luxury is used, especially in advertising, to describe expensive things which are very comfortable or of a special design. EG *...luxury hotels... ...a luxury car.* ADJ CLASSIF: ATTRIB

-ly is added to adjectives to form adverbs. For example 'loudly' means in a loud way, and 'rudely' means in a rude way. Adverbs like these are often not defined in this dictionary but are treated with the related adjectives. EG *He walked slowly down the street... 'I was hoping you would,' Morris said mischievously.* SUFFIX

lying /laɪɪŋ/. **1 Lying** is the present participle of **lie**.
2 A **lying** person is dishonest or deceitful. EG *...those lying journalists.* ADJ CLASSIF: ATTRIB
3 Lying is the act of telling lies. EG *She's incapable of lying.* N UNCOUNT

lynch /lɪntᵒʃ/, **lynchs, lynching, lynched.** If an angry crowd of people **lynch** someone, they kill them because they believe that they have committed a crime. EG *At one point he was in danger of being lynched.* V+O

lyric /lɪrɪk/, **lyrics. 1 Lyric** poetry is written in a simple and direct style, and is usually about love. ADJ CLASSIF: ATTRIB
2 The **lyrics** of a modern song are its words. EG *The lyrics are maddeningly memorable.* N PLURAL

lyrical /lɪrɪkəᵒl/. **1** Something that is **lyrical** is **1.1** poetic and musical. EG *He tries to bring into his plays a special lyrical quality.* ADJ CLASSIF **1.2** very romantic. EG *...a dreamy, lyrical study of the Covent Garden flower market.* ADJ QUALIT
2 If you are **lyrical** about something, you are very enthusiastic and eager about it. EG *Ned was growing lyrical.* ◊ **lyrically.** EG *It was Johnson, I remembered, who had written so lyrically about Woolley.* ADJ PRED ◊ ADV

M m

M, m /ɛm/, **Ms, m's. 1 M** is the thirteenth letter of the English alphabet. N COUNT

2 m is a written abbreviation for 'metres' or 'metre'.

M.A. /ɛm eɪ/, **M.A.s.** An **M.A.** is a higher degree in the arts or social sciences. **M.A.** is an abbreviation for 'Master of Arts'. EG *...an M.A. in Applied Linguistics.* N COUNT

ma'am /mɑːm/ is a spoken abbreviation for 'madam'. EG *A gentleman has called, ma'am.* VOCATIVE Outdated

mac /mæk/, **macs.** A **mac** is the same as a mackintosh. EG *They wore their plastic macs... She was pulling on her old mac.* N COUNT Informal British

macabre /məkɑːbrə^{0}/ events or stories are very strange and horrible, and usually involve death or injury. EG *...macabre sacrifices... ...a macabre story.* ADJ QUALIT

macaroni /mækərəʊni^{1}/ is a kind of pasta made in the shape of short hollow tubes. N UNCOUNT

machete /məʃɛti^{1}/, **machetes.** A **machete** is a large knife with a broad blade. N COUNT

machine /məʃiːn/, **machines, machining, machined. 1** A **machine** is a piece of equipment which uses electricity or power from an engine. EG *She took the paper out of the roller and shut the machine... The machine is beyond repair.* N COUNT

2 If you **machine** something, you make it, cut it, or change its shape using a machine. ◊ **machining.** EG *The work of machining a part is very slow.* V+O ◊ N UNCOUNT

3 You also use **machine** to refer to a well-controlled system or organization. EG *...the might of the enemy war machine... They had perfected their own propaganda machine.* N COUNT+SUPP

machine gun, machine guns. A **machine gun** is a gun which works automatically and which fires a lot of bullets very quickly one after the other. EG *...bursts of machine-gun fire.* N COUNT

machinery /məʃiːnə^{0}ri^{1}/. **1** If you talk about **machinery**, you are referring to machines in general, or to machines that are used in a factory. EG *Machinery is being introduced to save labour... ...the export of textile machinery to India.* N UNCOUNT

2 The **machinery** of a government or organization is the system that it uses in order to deal with things. EG *The party controls the state machinery... We need to discuss ways of improving the machinery of government.* N UNCOUNT +SUPP

machismo /mætʃɪzməʊ, -kɪz-/ is aggressively masculine behaviour or attitudes; used showing disapproval. EG *...the powerful machismo of the hero.* N UNCOUNT

macho /mætʃəʊ/. You describe a man as **macho** when you think that he behaves or dresses in an aggressively masculine way; used showing disapproval. EG *He emerged with a macho swagger... They were dressed in macho leather.* ADJ QUALIT Informal

macintosh /mækɪntɒʃ/. See **mackintosh.**

mackerel /mækə^{0}rəl/, **mackerels.** A **mackerel** is a kind of fish. The plural form of 'mackerel' is either 'mackerel' or 'mackerels'. EG *...shoals of mackerel.* N COUNT OR N UNCOUNT

mackintosh /mækɪntɒʃ/, **mackintoshes;** also spelled **macintosh.** A **mackintosh** is a raincoat, especially one made from a particular kind of waterproof cloth. EG *He took off his black mackintosh.* N COUNT

mad /mæd/, **madder, maddest. 1** Someone who is **mad** has a mind that does not work in a normal way, so that their behaviour is very strange and sometimes frightening. EG *Rose was mad, there was no doubt about it... She was married to a man who'd gone mad.* ◊ **madness.** EG *...the terrible madness that overtook the king.* ADJ CLASSIF ◊ N UNCOUNT

2 You can also say that someone is **mad 2.1** when they do or say things that you think are very foolish. EG *You must be mad!... They think I am mad to live in such a place.* ◊ **madness.** EG *It is madness for them to remain unarmed.* **2.2** when they are very angry. EG *He got pretty mad... They're mad at me for getting them up so early.* ADJ QUALIT ◊ N UNCOUNT ADJ PRED

3 You use **mad** to describe behaviour that is wild and uncontrolled. EG *I was dashing around in the usual mad panic... ...the mad whirl of pleasure.* ADJ CLASSIF: ATTRIB

4 If you say that someone **is driving** you **mad** or that they **will drive** you **mad**, you mean that they are annoying you very much by their behaviour. EG *These blinking kids will drive me mad.* PHRASE

5 If you are **mad** about something or someone, you like them very much indeed. EG *For years he's been mad about opera... I'm mad about you.* ADJ PRED +about Informal

6 If you do something **like mad**, you do it very energetically or enthusiastically. EG *They were still arguing like mad at six in the evening.* PHRASE Informal

7 When an audience **goes mad**, they cheer and clap very enthusiastically. EG *Thousands of people are ready to go mad at the mere sight of him.* PHRASE Informal

madam /mædə^{0}m/. People sometimes address a woman as **Madam** when they are being very formal and polite. 'Dear Madam' is often used at the beginning of letters. EG *Dear Madam, Thank you for your letter replying to our advertisement... 'Yes, madam,' Harry Standish said.* VOCATIVE

madden /mædə^{0}n/, **maddens, maddening, maddened.** If something **maddens** you, it makes you feel very angry or annoyed. EG *The colonel's calmness maddened Pluskat.* ◊ **maddening.** EG *It makes a maddening clicking noise... Lady Sackville was a maddening person to live with.* V+O ◊ ADJ QUALIT Outdated

made /meɪd/ is the past tense and past participle of **make.**

-made combines with words such as 'factory' to indicate that something has been made or produced in a particular way or at a particular place. EG *It's factory-made... Locally-made goods had to pay internal customs duties.* ● See also **handmade, home-made, man-made, self-made.**

made-to-measure. A **made-to-measure** suit or shirt is one that is made by a tailor to fit you exactly, rather than one that you buy in a shop. ADJ CLASSIF

madhouse /mædh^{0}aʊs/, **madhouses.** If you say that a place is a **madhouse**, you mean that it is full of noise and confusion. EG *This place will be a madhouse when all the kids arrive.* N COUNT: USU SING

madly /mædli^{1}/. **1** If you do something **madly**, you do it very quickly, because you are eager, excited, or afraid. EG *We began rushing around madly in the dark.* ADV

2 If you are **madly in love** with someone, you are very much in love with them. EG *I fell madly in love with Ellen the first time I ever saw her.* PHRASE

madman /mædmə^{3}n/, **madmen. 1** A **madman** is a man who is mad. EG *They locked him up as a madman.* N COUNT

2 You can refer to someone who behaves in a very foolish or irresponsible way as a **madman.** EG *I have had enough trouble with that madman Smith.* N COUNT

magazine /mægəziːn/, **magazines. 1** A **magazine** is a publication with a paper cover which is issued regularly, usually weekly or monthly, and which contains articles, stories, photographs and advertisements. EG *I got the recipe from a woman's magazine... ...a magazine article.* N COUNT

2 On radio or television, a **magazine** is a programme with interesting stories about people and N COUNT events. EG *Newsbeat is the popular news magazine on Radio 1.*

maggot /mægət/, **maggots.** A **maggot** is a tiny creature that looks like a very small worm. Maggots turn into flies. N COUNT

magic /mædʒɪk/. **1** In fairy stories, **magic** is a special power that can make apparently impossible things happen. For example, it can control events in nature or make people disappear. EG *He could see the magic beginning to do its work... She was accused of inflicting bad fortune on them through evil magic.* ▸ used as an adjective. EG *...the magic forest... How fast the magic potion worked!* N UNCOUNT ▸ ADJ CLASSIF : ATTRIB

2 Magic is also the art and skill of performing tricks to entertain people, for example by seeming to make things appear and disappear. EG *He was in his bedroom practising magic tricks.* N UNCOUNT

3 The **magic** of something is a special quality that makes it seem wonderful and exciting. EG *...the magic of theatre... They need a bit of magic in their lives.* ▸ used as an adjective. EG *That was a truly magic moment.* N UNCOUNT ▸ ADJ QUALIT

magical /mædʒɪkəᵒl/. **1** Something that is **magical** uses magic or is able to produce magic. EG *I used to believe my mother had magical powers... ...a stream of magical water.* ADJ CLASSIF

2 You can also say that something is **magical** when it has a special mysterious quality that makes it seem wonderful and exciting. EG *The journey had lost all its magical quality.* ADJ QUALIT

◇ **magically.** EG *The horizon was magically filling with ships.* ◇ ADV

magician /mədʒɪʃəᵒn/, **magicians.** A **magician** is **1** a person who performs tricks as a form of entertainment. EG *This process is very effectively used by stage magicians.* **2** a man in a fairy story who has magic powers. N COUNT

magistrate /mædʒɪstreɪt/, **magistrates.** A **magistrate** is an official who acts as a judge in a law court which deals with less serious crimes or disputes. EG *You'll have to appear before the magistrate... ...the magistrates' court.* N COUNT

magnanimous /mægnænɪməs/. If you are **magnanimous**, you are generous towards someone, especially after you have beaten them in a fight or contest. EG *We must encourage new regimes to be magnanimous towards their former oppressors.* ADJ QUALIT

magnate /mægneɪt/, **magnates.** A **magnate** is someone who has become very powerful in a business or industry because they have earned a lot of money from it. EG *...a rich shipping magnate... ...a press magnate.* N COUNT+SUPP

magnet /mægnɪ¹t/, **magnets.** A **magnet** is a piece of iron or other material which attracts iron or steel towards it. EG *The pin was extracted with a magnet.* N COUNT

magnetic /mægnetɪk/. **1** Something that is **magnetic** has the power of a magnet to attract iron or steel towards it. EG *He took a carving knife from a magnetic board on the wall.* ADJ CLASSIF

2 If you say that someone is **magnetic** or has **magnetic** qualities, you mean that they have unusual and exciting qualities that people find attractive. EG *Without magnetic appeal, the politician is unlikely to succeed.* ADJ QUALIT : ATTRIB

magnetic tape, magnetic tapes. Magnetic tape is narrow plastic tape covered with a magnetic substance. It is used for recording sounds, film, or computer information. N UNCOUNT OR N COUNT

magnetism /mægnɪ¹tɪzəᵒm/. **1 Magnetism** is a power that attracts some substances towards others. EG *...the forces of electricity and magnetism.* N UNCOUNT

2 If someone has **magnetism**, they have unusual and exciting qualities which people find very attractive. EG *He had immense personal magnetism.* N UNCOUNT

magnification /mægnɪfɪkeɪʃəᵒn/, **magnifications. 1 Magnification** is the process by which something is made to appear bigger than it actually is, as, for example, when you use a microscope. N UNCOUNT

2 The **magnification** of a microscope, telescope, or pair of binoculars is the degree to which it can magnify things. EG *All the images, even under the highest magnification, were simply points of light.* N UNCOUNT OR N COUNT

magnificent /mægnɪfɪsənt/. Something that is **magnificent** is extremely good, beautiful, or impressive. EG *It's a magnificent book... Her dress is magnificent.* ◇ **magnificently.** EG *They performed magnificently... He was magnificently dressed.* ADJ QUALIT ◇ ADV

magnify /mægnɪfaɪ/, **magnifies, magnifying, magnified. 1** When a microscope or magnifying glass **magnifies** an object, it makes it appear bigger than it actually is. EG *The lenses magnified his eyes to the size of dinner plates.* V+O

2 To **magnify** something also means to make it seem more important than it actually is. EG *His fears have greatly magnified the true dangers... Minor advances were magnified into victories.* V+O

magnifying glass, magnifying glasses. A **magnifying glass** is a piece of glass which makes objects appear bigger than they actually are. N COUNT

magnitude /mægnɪtju:d/ is the great size or great importance of something. EG *They do not recognize the magnitude of the problem.* N UNCOUNT

magpie /mægpaɪ/, **magpies.** A **magpie** is a bird with black and white markings and a long tail. N COUNT

mahogany /məhɒgəni¹/is a dark reddish-brown wood that is used to make furniture. EG *...a tall mahogany bookcase.* N UNCOUNT

maid /meɪd/, **maids.** A **maid** is a woman who works as a servant in a hotel or private house. EG *The maid will bring you your wine in a moment.* N COUNT

maiden /meɪdəᵒn/, **maidens. 1** A **maiden** is a young girl or woman, especially a beautiful one. EG *Maidens performed graceful dances.* N COUNT Literary

2 The **maiden** voyage or flight of a ship or aeroplane is the first official journey that it makes with passengers. ADJ CLASSIF : ATTRIB

maiden aunt, maiden aunts. A **maiden aunt** is an aunt who is quite old but is not married. N COUNT Outdated

maiden name, maiden names. A woman's **maiden name** is the surname she had before she got married and took her husband's surname. EG *My maiden name was Byers.* N COUNT

mail /meɪl/, **mails, mailing, mailed. 1 Mail** is the letters and parcels that the post office delivers to you. EG *If there's anything urgent in the mail, I'll deal with it... Minnie was alone in the post office, sorting mail.* N UNCOUNT

2 The **mail** is the system used by the post office for collecting and delivering letters and parcels. EG *Send it to me by mail.* N SING : *the*+N, OR *by*+N

3 If you **mail** something, you post it. EG *The books had to be mailed directly from the publisher.* V+O

mailbag /meɪlbæg/, **mailbags.** A **mailbag** is a large bag that is used by the post office for carrying letters and parcels. N COUNT

mailbox /meɪlbɒks/, **mailboxes.** A **mailbox** is **1** a box outside your house where the postman delivers letters. **2** a large container in the street where people can post letters. N COUNT American American

mailing list, mailing lists. A **mailing list** is a list of names and addresses that an organization has so that it can send people information. EG *Does anyone wish to be put on the mailing list?* N COUNT

mailman /meɪlməᵌn/, **mailmen.** A **mailman** is a man whose job is to deliver letters and parcels that are sent by post. N COUNT American

mail order is a system of buying goods in which you choose what you want from a firm's catalogue and the firm sends you what you have ordered by post. EG *The record is available by mail order... ...a mail-order firm.* N UNCOUNT

maim /meɪm/, **maims, maiming, maimed.** If someone **maims** another person, they injure them so badly that they cannot use part of their body properly for the rest of their life. EG *These people kill and maim innocent civilians.* V+O

main /meɪn/, **mains.** 1 The **main** thing is the most important thing in a particular situation. EG *What are the main reasons for going to university?... Mrs Foster hurried through the main entrance.* ADJ CLASSIF : ATTRIB

2 If you say that something is true **in the main**, you mean that it is generally true, although there may be exceptions. EG *The Worthingtons are in the main decent, friendly folk... In the main, overseas students want to be on campus.* ADV SEN Formal

3 The **mains** are the pipes or wires which supply gas, water, or electricity to buildings, or which take sewage from them. EG *The radio we have at home plugs into the mains... You needn't turn off the mains water.* N PLURAL : the+N

4 A **main** is a large pipe which carries gas, water, or sewage, and is connected to smaller pipes which link it to buildings. EG *A bulldozer had cut a gas main.* N COUNT

main clause, main clauses. In grammar, a **main clause** is a clause that can stand alone as a complete sentence. N COUNT

mainframe /meɪnfreɪm/, **mainframes.** A **mainframe** is a large computer which can be used by many people at the same time, and which can do very large or complicated tasks. N COUNT

mainland /meɪnlə³nd/. The **mainland** is the large main part of a country or continent, in contrast to the islands that form smaller parts of the country or continent. EG *The motorboat was waiting to ferry him back to the mainland.* ▸ used as an adjective. EG *...the coast of mainland Greece.* N SING : the+N ▸ ADJ CLASSIF : ATTRIB

mainly /meɪnli¹/. You use **mainly** to say that a statement is true in most cases or to a large extent. EG *The political groups have more power, mainly because of their larger numbers... I'll be concentrating mainly on French and German... ...a queue of people, mainly children and old men.* ADV

main road, main roads. A **main road** is a large important road that leads from one town or city to another. EG *We turned off the main road shortly after Alcester.* N COUNT

mainspring /meɪnsprɪŋ/. The **mainspring** of something is the most important reason for it or the thing that is essential to it. EG *Technology was the mainspring of economic growth.* N SING+SUPP Formal

mainstay /meɪnsteɪ/, **mainstays.** The **mainstay** of something is the part of it which is the most important source of its strength or effectiveness. EG *Homemade chocolate cookies were the mainstay of my diet.* N COUNT+SUPP Formal

mainstream /meɪnstri:m/. The **mainstream** is the group of people or ideas that most people agree with, and which is therefore regarded as being normal and conventional. EG *We feel isolated from the mainstream of social life in the community.* ▸ used as an adjective. EG *...mainstream political parties... ...mainstream education.* N SING : USU+SUPP ▸ ADJ CLASSIF : ATTRIB

maintain /meɪnteɪn/, **maintains, maintaining, maintained.** 1 If you **maintain** something, you continue to have it, and do not let it stop or grow weaker. EG *I wanted to maintain my friendship with her... For twenty-five years they had failed to maintain law and order.* V+O

2 If you **maintain** something at a particular rate or level, you keep it at that rate or level, and do not let it become less. EG *One has to maintain the temperature at a very high level.* V+O+A

3 If you **maintain** someone, you provide them with money and the things that they need. EG *I need the money to maintain me until I start a job.* V+O

4 If you **maintain** something such as a building, vehicle, road, or machine, you keep it in good condition by regularly checking it and doing necessary repairs. EG *...the rising cost of maintaining the equipment.* V+O

5 If you **maintain** that something is true, you state your opinion or belief very strongly. EG *Mrs Camish always maintained that he had been a brilliant thinker.* V+REPORT : ONLY that

maintenance /meɪntɪ⁰nəns/. 1 The **maintenance** of something such as a building, road, vehicle, or machine is the process of keeping it in good condition by regularly checking it and doing necessary repairs. EG *He learnt tractor maintenance... Who's responsible for the maintenance and care of the buildings?* N UNCOUNT

2 **Maintenance** is also money that someone gives to a person who they are legally responsible for but are not living with, in order to pay for necessary things such as food and clothes. For example, a man may have to pay maintenance to his ex-wife after a divorce. N UNCOUNT British

3 The **maintenance** of a state or process consists of making sure that it continues and does not stop or become weaker. EG *...the maintenance of law and order... ...the maintenance of an effective incomes policy.* N SING : the+N+of

maisonette /meɪzənet/, **maisonettes.** A **maisonette** is a small flat on two floors of a larger building. EG *She shared an upper maisonette with two other girls.* N COUNT British

maize /meɪz/ is a tall plant which produces sweet corn. EG *...a field planted with maize.* N UNCOUNT

majestic /mədʒestɪk/. Something or someone that is **majestic** is very beautiful, dignified, and impressive. EG *...the majestic proportions of the great Pyramid... She looked majestic in her large, soft hat.* ◇ **majestically.** EG *Wet clouds, heavy with rain, moved majestically overhead.* ADJ QUALIT ◇ ADV

Majesty /mædʒɪ²sti¹/, **Majesties.** You use expressions such as **Your Majesty**, **Her Majesty**, or **Their Majesties** when you are addressing or referring to Kings or Queens; compare **Royal Highness.** EG *...Her Majesty the Queen... Thank you, Your Majesty.*

major /meɪdʒə/, **majors, majoring, majored.** 1 You use **major** to describe something which is more important, serious, or significant than other things. EG *Jones was to play a major part in the improvement of the paper... One major factor was the revolution in communications... Finding a solicitor had been a major problem.* ADJ QUALIT : ATTRIB

2 A **major** is an army officer of medium rank. EG *...Major Burton-Cox.* N COUNT

3 A **major** key is one of the two types of key in which most European music is written. It is based on a scale of notes in which the third note is two tones higher than the first note. EG *They're both in D major.* ADJ CLASSIF

4 If you **major** in a particular subject, you study it as your main subject at university. EG *I decided to major in French.* V+in American

majority /mədʒɒrɪ¹ti¹/, **majorities.** 1 The **majority** of people or things in a group is a number of them that form more than half of the group. EG *...mass movements involving the overwhelming majority of the people... ...the principle of government by the majority.* ● If a group is **in a majority** or **in the majority**, they form more than half of a larger group. N SING : USU+of ● PHRASE

2 A **majority** is the difference between the number of votes that the winner gets in an election and the number of votes that the next person or party gets. EG *I was beaten by a large majority... Benn was returned by a majority of 15,479.* N COUNT : USU SING+SUPP

make /meɪk/, **makes, making, made** /meɪd/. 1 You can use **make** to say that someone performs an action. For example, if you say that someone **makes** a suggestion, you mean that they suggest something. EG *You've got to make a start somewhere... He made the shortest speech I've ever heard... He had two phone calls to make... We have* V+O

If someone is maintained by you, do they give you money?

got to make a really serious effort... I made the wrong decision... He felt I was making a terrible mistake.

2 If something **makes** you do something, it causes you to do it. EG *What makes you ask that?... A sudden noise made Brody jump.* — V+O+INF: IF PASS THEN +to-INF

3 If someone **makes** you do something, they force you to do it. EG *Make him listen!... They were made to sit and wait.* — V+O+INF: IF PASS THEN +to-INF

4 You use **make** to say that someone or something is caused to be a particular thing or to have a particular quality. For example, if something **makes** someone a star, it causes them to become a star. If something **makes** someone happy, it causes them to be happy. EG *I'd like to do something to make the world a better place... The cold was making Posy irritable... He feared the story had made things worse... Jack was the first to make himself heard... The army made a man of me... They're making the old kitchen into a little bedroom.* — V+O+C, V+O+*of*, OR V+O+*into*

5 You use **make** to say how well or how badly someone does something. For example, if you **make** a success of something, you do it well. EG *Let's not make a mess of this.* — V+O+*of*

6 If you **make** something, you produce it or construct it. EG *I like making cakes... ...the greatest film ever made... You can make petroleum out of coal... Martin, can you make us a drink?* — V+O: OFT+A, OR V+O+O

7 If something **is made** of a particular substance, that substance was used to form or construct it. EG *The houses were made of brick... ...a rug made of scraps of old clothes... What is it made of?* — V-PASS+*of*

8 If someone or something **makes** a sound, they produce it or cause it to happen. EG *Try not to make so much noise.* — V+O

9 You use **make** to say what two numbers add up to. For example, if two numbers **make** 12, they add up to 12. — V+C

10 You can use **make** to say what the result of a calculation is. For example, if you **make** the answer to a calculation 144, you calculate it to be 144. EG *I make it thirty-five.* — V+O+C

11 You can use **make** to say what time your watch says it is. For example, if you **make** it 4 o'clock, your watch says it is 4 o'clock. — V+O+C

12 If you **make** money, you get it by working for it or by investing money. EG *He was making ninety dollars a week... She made a £200 profit.* — V+O

13 You can use **make** to say that someone or something has the right qualities for a particular task or role. For example, if you say that someone would **make** a good secretary, you mean that they have the right qualities to be a good secretary. EG *Do garden tools make good gifts?* — V+C OR V+O+C

14 If one part or aspect of something **makes** that thing, it is responsible for the success of that thing. EG *Nicholson's acting really makes the film.* — V+O

15 If you **make** a place, you manage to get there. EG *I made Ramsdale by dawn.* — V+O: USU+A

16 To **make it** means to succeed in getting somewhere in time to do something. EG *We only just made it.* — PHRASE Informal

17 You can also say that someone **makes it** when they are successful in doing something. EG *Blake failed to make it as a commercial airline pilot.* — PHRASE Informal

18 If you are invited to an event and you can **make it**, you are able to attend. EG *The Baxters couldn't make it, I'm afraid.* — PHRASE Informal

19 If you **have got it made**, you are certain to be successful. — PHRASE Informal

20 If you **make** friends or enemies, you cause people to become your friends or enemies. EG *Roger made a number of enemies... Karen made friends with several children.* — V+O

21 The **make** of a product is the name of the company that manufactured it. EG *She couldn't tell what make of car it was.* — N COUNT+SUPP

22 If you **make do** with something, you use it only because you do not have anything better. EG *We had to make do with cheap lodgings.* — PHRASE

23 to **make good**: see **good**. ● to **make way**: see **way**. ● See also **making**.

make for. **1** If you **make for** a place, you move towards it. EG *We joined the crowd making for the exit.* — PHRASAL VB: V+PREP **2** If something **makes for** a particular situation, that situation is likely to result from it. EG *What are the values that make for happy family life?* — Informal

make of. If you ask someone what they **make of** something, you want to know **1** what their impression or opinion of it is. EG *He didn't know what to make of his new boss.* **2** if tney understand what it means. EG *Can you make anything of it?* — PHRASAL VB: V+O+PREP

make off. If you **make off**, you leave somewhere as quickly as possible, often in order to escape. EG *The vehicle made off at once.* — PHRASAL VB: V+ADV

make off with. If you **make off with** something, you steal it. EG *Otto made off with the last of the brandy.* — PHRASAL VB: V+ADV+PREP

make out. **1** If you can **make** something **out**, you can see it, hear it, or understand it. EG *He could just make out the number plate of the car... She tried to make out what was being said... I can't make out if Nell likes him or not.* — PHRASAL VB: V+O+ADV, OR V+ADV+REPORT: ONLY WH **2** If you **make out** that something is the case, you try to cause people to believe that it is the case. EG *People tried to make out that the play was about Britain... He's not really as hard as people make out.* — V+ADV+REPORT, ONLY *that* **3** When you **make out** a form or cheque, you write on it all the necessary information. EG *Did you make out a receipt?* — V+O+ADV

make up. **1** The people or things that **make up** something form that thing. EG *...the various groups which make up society... All substances are made up of molecules.* — PHRASAL VB: V+ADV+O **2** If you **make up** something such as a story, you invent it, sometimes in order to deceive people. — V+O+ADV **3** If you **make** yourself **up**, you put cosmetics such as powder or lipstick on your face. — V-REFL+ADV ◇ **made up.** EG *She had magnificent eyes, heavily made up.* — ◇ ADJ CLASSIF ● See also **make-up**. **4** If you **make up** something, you prepare it by putting different things together. EG *...making up a package large enough for a month.* — V+O+ADV **5** If you **make up** an amount, you add something to it so that it is as large as it should be. EG *Government would have to make up the difference out of its welfare budget.* — V+O+ADV **6** If two people **make up** or **make** it **up**, they become friends again after they have had a quarrel. EG *He and Frank made it up.* — V+ADV OR V+O+ADV **7** To **make up** for something that is lost or missing means to replace it or to compensate for it. EG *If babies put on very little weight at first, eventually they will gain rapidly to make up for it.* — V+ADV: USU+*for* **8** If you **make it up to** someone for disappointing them, you do something for them to show how sorry you are. — PHRASE

make-believe. You refer to someone's behaviour as **make-believe** when they pretend that things are better or more exciting than they really are. EG *His whole life these days was a game of make-believe.* — N UNCOUNT

maker /meɪkə/, **makers.** The **maker** of something is the person or company that makes it. EG *In the studio with me is film maker and critic, Iain Johnstone... The makers of the programme seemed to lose confidence in it... The maker's label was carefully removed.* — N COUNT+SUPP

makeshift /meɪkʃɪft/. Something that is **makeshift** is temporary and of poor quality, but you use it because nothing better is available. EG *Youths erected makeshift barricades... The accommodation was makeshift.* — ADJ QUALIT

make-up. **1** **Make-up** is substances such as lipstick, eye-shadow, and mascara, which women use to make themselves look more attractive, or which actors use when they are acting. EG *...eye make-up... She had a lot of make-up on.* — N UNCOUNT

2 Someone's **make-up** is their character. EG *There* — N UNCOUNT +SUPP

are things in my make-up which do not bear close examination.
3 The **make-up** of something is the different parts that it consists of, and the way these parts are arranged. EG *...the psychological make-up of primitive man.* N UNCOUNT +SUPP

making /meɪkɪŋ/, **makings. 1 Making** is the act or process of producing something. EG *At the end of his life he turned to the making of beautiful books... People should be involved in all decision-making which affects them.* N UNCOUNT +SUPP
2 If a problem is **of** your **own making**, it has been caused by you alone and not by anyone else. EG *The trouble here is of the President's own making.* PHRASE
3 When you describe someone as something **in the making**, you mean that they are gradually becoming that thing. EG *...an economist in the making.* PHRASE
4 If something **is the making of** a person or thing, it is the reason that they are successful. EG *The description of Belfast is the making of the book.* PHRASE
5 If you say that a person or thing has **the makings of** something, you mean that they seem likely to develop in that way. EG *She perceived that here might be the makings of the friendship that had so eluded her in the past.* PHRASE

maladjusted /mæləd͟ʒʌstɪ²d/. **Maladjusted** children have psychological problems and behave in ways which are not acceptable to society. ADJ CLASSIF

malady /mælədi¹/, **maladies.** A **malady** is an illness. EG *Was she affected by the same malady?* N COUNT Outdated

malaise /mə³leɪz/ is a state in which people feel dissatisfied or unhappy but do not know exactly what is wrong. EG *Malaise had set in with the coming of the twentieth century.* N UNCOUNT Formal

malaria /məlɛərɪə/ is a disease which people get from mosquitoes and which causes periods of fever and shivering. N UNCOUNT

male /meɪl/, **males. 1** A **male** is an animal that belongs to the sex that cannot have babies or lay eggs. EG *The males establish a breeding territory.* N COUNT
▸ used as an adjective. EG *...male hamsters.* ▸ ADJ CLASSIF
2 You can refer to a man or a boy as a **male**. EG *...the average American male.* N COUNT ▸ used as an adjective. EG *Your boss is almost certainly there because he is male.* ▸ ADJ CLASSIF
3 Something that is **male** concerns or affects men rather than women. EG *...the production of male hormones... ...male unemployment.* ADJ CLASSIF : ATTRIB

male chauvinism is the belief which some men have that men are naturally better and more important than women. N UNCOUNT

male chauvinist, male chauvinists. A **male chauvinist** is a man who believes that men are naturally better and more important than women. EG *The men in my office are all blatant male chauvinists.* N COUNT ▸ used as an adjective. EG *I hope this won't be taken as a male chauvinist remark.* ▸ ADJ CLASSIF : ATTRIB

malevolent /mə³lɛvələnt/. If someone is **malevolent**, they want to cause harm. EG *These people seemed hard and malevolent... His face was malevolent.* ADJ QUALIT Formal ◊ **malevolence** /mə³lɛvələns/. EG *...the victims of his malevolence.* ◊ N UNCOUNT

malformed /mælfɔːmd/. If something is **malformed**, it does not have the shape that it is supposed to have. EG *...his hideously malformed legs.* ADJ QUALIT Formal

malfunction /mælfʌŋkʃə⁰n/, **malfunctions, malfunctioning, malfunctioned.** If a machine or a computer **malfunctions**, it fails to work properly. V ▸ used as a noun. EG *...a malfunction of the generator.* ▸ N COUNT

malice /mælɪs/ is a desire to cause harm to people. EG *He chuckled with malice... 'So I notice,' he added with a touch of malice.* N UNCOUNT

malicious /məlɪʃəs/. If talk or behaviour is **malicious**, it is intended to harm someone or their reputation. EG *Their talk was slightly malicious and gossipy... ...cold-blooded malicious cruelty.* ADJ QUALIT

malign /məlaɪn/, **maligns, maligning, maligned. 1** If you **malign** someone, you say unpleasant and untrue things about them. EG *He had maligned both women... ...the countries maligned by his newspapers.* V+O Formal
2 Malign behaviour is intended to harm someone. EG *His speeches are open to all sorts of malign interpretation.* ADJ QUALIT Formal

malignant /məlɪgnənt/. **1** If behaviour is **malignant**, it is harmful and cruel. EG *...the consequence of a malignant plot.* ADJ QUALIT
2 If a disease is **malignant**, it is uncontrollable and likely to cause death. EG *I was certain that you had a malignant growth in your larynx.* ADJ CLASSIF

malinger /məlɪŋgə/, **malingers, malingering, malingered.** If you **malinger**, you pretend to be ill in order to avoid working. EG *I'm not malingering, really I'm not.* V : USU CONT

mallet /mælɪ¹t/, **mallets.** A **mallet** is a wooden hammer with a square head. See picture at TOOLS. N COUNT

malnourished /mælnʌrɪʃt/. If someone is **malnourished**, they are physically weak because they have not eaten enough food. EG *The majority of the population is malnourished.* ADJ QUALIT Formal

malnutrition /mælnjuːtrɪʃə⁰n/ is physical weakness caused by not eating enough food. EG *He is showing the first signs of malnutrition.* N UNCOUNT Formal

malpractice /mælpræktɪs/, **malpractices. Malpractice** is behaviour in which someone breaks the law or the rules of their profession in order to gain some personal advantage. EG *A doctor who refused to give treatment is on trial for medical malpractice.* N UNCOUNT OR N COUNT Legal

malt /mɒlt/ is a substance made from grain that has been put in water and then dried in a hot oven. Malt is used in the making of whisky, beer, and other alcoholic drinks. EG *...a bottle of malt whisky.* N UNCOUNT

maltreat /mæltriːt/, **maltreats, maltreating, maltreated.** If people or animals are **maltreated**, they are treated unkindly or violently. EG *We do not intervene unless the children are being physically maltreated.* V+O : USU PASS

mammal /mæmə⁰l/, **mammals. Mammals** are particular types of animals. Female mammals give birth to babies rather than laying eggs, and feed their young with milk from their bodies. Human beings, dogs, lions, and whales are all mammals. N COUNT

mammoth /mæməθ/, **mammoths. 1 Mammoth** means very large indeed. EG *...the immense foyer with its mammoth mirrors... ...a mammoth task.* ADJ CLASSIF : ATTRIB
2 Mammoths were animals like elephants with very long tusks and long hair. Mammoths no longer exist. N COUNT

man /mæn/, **men** /mɛn/; **mans, manning, manned. Men** is the plural of the noun. **Mans** is the 3rd person singular, present tense, of the verb. N COUNT
1 A **man** is **1.1** an adult male human being. EG *Larry was a handsome man in his early fifties... Every man, woman, and child will be taken care of.* **1.2** a human being of either sex. EG *All men are born equal... ...a deserted island where no man could live.*
2 You can refer to human beings in general as **man**. EG *Why does man seem to have more diseases than animals?... ...the most dangerous substance known to man.* N UNCOUNT
3 A woman's **man** is her husband, lover, or boyfriend. EG *Can I bring my man?* N COUNT+POSS Informal
4 The **men** in an army are the ordinary soldiers as opposed to the officers. EG *In all, some 70,000 officers and men died.* N PLURAL
5 People sometimes address a man as **'man'**, especially when they are angry or impatient with him. EG *For heaven's sake, man, can't you see she's had enough?* VOCATIVE

Name three mammals that are *not* mentioned on these pages.

6 If someone **mans** a machine, they operate it. EG *They manned the phones all through the night.* V+O

7 If people talk to each other **man to man**, they talk honestly and openly, treating each other as equals. EG *...a man-to-man discussion.* PHRASE

8 If you **are man enough** to do something, you have the necessary courage to do it; used showing approval. EG *He's not man enough for the job.* PHRASE

9 the man in the street: see **street**. See also **manned, right-hand man**.

-man combines with numbers to indicate that something involves or is designed for the number of people mentioned. EG *The delegates voted to select a new, 20-man Central Committee first... ...one-man shows and exhibitions.*

manage /mænɪdʒ/, **manages, managing, managed. 1** If you **manage** to do something, you succeed in doing it. EG *How he managed to find us is beyond me... Did you manage to get anything to eat?... We'll manage it somehow, I'm sure.* V+*to*-INF, V+O, OR V

2 If someone **manages** an organization, business, or system, they are responsible for controlling it. EG *She manages a chain of pet shops.* V+O

3 If you say that you can **manage** a period of time, you mean that you can spend that time doing something. EG *I wish you could manage the time to come and talk to us... I could manage from about half-past seven till nine.* V+O OR V+A

4 When people **manage**, they are able to continue with an acceptable way of life, although they do not have much money. EG *I don't want charity. I can manage... I've always managed on a teacher's salary.* V

manageable /mænɪdʒəb^{ə}l/. You say that something is **manageable** when you can deal with it because it is not too big or complicated. EG *It is a perfectly manageable task.* ADJ QUALIT

management /mænɪdʒmənt/, **managements. 1** The **management** of a business or other organization is the controlling and organizing of it. EG *She began to take over the management of the estate... It's a question of good management.* N UNCOUNT

2 The people who control an organization can also be referred to as the **management**. EG *...a failure of communication between management and the workforce... They are part of my management team.* N UNCOUNT OR N COUNT

3 Your **management** of something is the way that you control or organize it. EG *The author's management of the plot is admirable... ...the management of money.* N UNCOUNT Formal

manager /mænɪdʒə/, **managers. 1** The **manager** of an organization or of part of an organization is the person who is responsible for running it. EG *What you need is advice from your bank manager... ...the general manager of Philips Ltd in Singapore.* N COUNT

2 The **manager** of a pop star or other entertainer is the person who looks after the star's business interests. N COUNT

3 The **manager** of a sports team is the person who is responsible for organizing and training it. EG *...Don Revie, England's soccer team manager.* N COUNT

manageress /mænɪdʒəres/, **manageresses.** A **manageress** is a woman who is responsible for running a shop or office. EG *The manageress was tall and terrifying... ...the manageress of a bookshop.* N COUNT

managerial /mænɪdʒɪərɪəl/ means relating to the work of a manager or manageress. EG *...technical and managerial skills... She was promoted into some kind of managerial job.* ADJ CLASSIF : ATTRIB

managing director, managing directors. The **managing director** of a company is a director who is also responsible for the way that the company is managed. EG *He's now managing director of English National Opera.* N COUNT

mandarin /mændərɪn/, **mandarins.** A **mandarin** is a small orange which is easy to peel. N COUNT

mandate /mændeɪt/, **mandates. 1** A government's **mandate** is the authority that it has to carry out particular policies as a result of winning an election. EG *The President, strengthened by a powerful conservative mandate, has called for increases in defence spending.* N COUNT Formal

2 A **mandate** is also a task that you are instructed to carry out. EG *Peter's mandate was to find the best available investment.* N COUNT Formal

mandatory /mændətə^{ə}ri^{1}/. If something is **mandatory**, there is a law stating that it must be done. EG *The testing of cosmetics is not mandatory here.* ADJ CLASSIF

mane /meɪn/, **manes.** A horse's or lion's **mane** is the long thick hair that grows from its neck. N COUNT

man-eating. A **man-eating** animal is an animal which has eaten human beings and is very dangerous. EG *...man-eating lions.* ADJ CLASSIF : ATTRIB

maneuver /mənuːvə/. See **manoeuvre**.

manfully /mænfʊli^{1}/. If you do something **manfully**, you do it in a very determined way; often used humorously. EG *I could see Simon manfully wielding a shovel.* ADV

mangle /mæŋgə^{ə}l/, **mangles, mangling, mangled.** If something **is mangled**, it is so crushed or twisted that you cannot see what its original shape was. EG *...the mangled cabs of overturned lorries.* V+O : USU PASS

mango /mæŋgəʊ/, **mangoes** or **mangos.** A **mango** is a large, sweet yellowish fruit which grows in hot countries. N COUNT

mangy /meɪndʒi^{1}/. A **mangy** animal has lost a lot of its hair through disease, or has not been properly looked after by its owner. EG *Rose was sitting in her rocking chair with a mangy cat upon her knee.* ADJ QUALIT

manhandle /mænhændə^{ə}l/, **manhandles, manhandling, manhandled.** If you **manhandle** someone, you treat them very roughly, for example when you are taking them somewhere. EG *He had been manhandled on the street by police.* V+O

manhole /mænhəʊl/, **manholes.** A **manhole** is a covered hole in the ground that leads to a drain or sewer. EG *...an open manhole... ...manhole covers.* N COUNT

manhood /mænhʊd/ is **1** the state of being a man rather than a boy. EG *...the dubious rewards of manhood.* **2** the period of a man's life during which he is a man rather than a boy. EG *He had millions of dollars to play with in his early manhood.* N UNCOUNT

man-hour, man-hours. You use **man-hour** to refer to the amount of time that a piece of work will take. For example, if a job takes 15 man-hours, it takes one person 15 hours to do it or three people five hours to do it. EG *One firm spent a total of 370,000 man-hours on the job.* N COUNT : USU PLURAL

manhunt /mænhʌnt/, **manhunts.** A **manhunt** is a search for someone who has escaped or disappeared. EG *...the biggest manhunt the country had known.* N COUNT

mania /meɪnɪə/, **manias. 1** A **mania** for something is a strong liking for it. EG *...the British mania for television... She had a mania for cleanliness.* N COUNT OR N UNCOUNT : OFT+*for*

2 A **mania** is also a mental illness. EG *...persecution mania... ...the symptoms of religious mania.* N UNCOUNT

maniac /meɪnɪæk/, **maniacs.** A **maniac** is a mad person who is violent and dangerous. EG *She was attacked by a maniac.* N COUNT

manic /mænɪk/. You use **manic** to describe someone's behaviour when they do something extremely quickly or energetically, often because they are very excited or anxious. EG *Weston finished his manic typing.* ADJ QUALIT

manicure /mænɪkjʊə/, **manicures, manicuring, manicured.** If you **manicure** your hands or nails, you care for them by softening the skin and cutting and polishing the nails. EG *She was sitting manicuring her nails.* V+O ▸ used as a noun. EG *His sister gave him a manicure once a month.* ▸ N COUNT OR N UNCOUNT

manifest /mænɪfest/, **manifests, manifesting, manifested. 1** If something is **manifest**, people can easily see that it exists or that it is true. EG *...his manifest disapproval... ..an intense patriotism* ADJ QUALIT Formal *which is made manifest in the teaching in their schools.* ◇ **manifestly.** EG *Hopper was manifestly too important to be left off the guest list.* ◇ ADV

2 If you **manifest** something or if it **manifests** itself, people are made aware of it. EG *It was a question of how we should manifest our resistance... His inventiveness most often manifested itself as a skill in lying.* V+O OR V-REFL Formal

manifestation /mænɪfɛsteɪʃəⁿn/, **manifestations.** A **manifestation** is a sign that something is happening or that something exists. EG *...the first manifestations of the Computer Revolution.* N COUNT+SUPP Formal

manifesto /mænɪfɛstəʊ/, **manifestos** or **manifestoes.** A **manifesto** is a written statement published by a group of people, especially a political party, in which they say what their aims and policies are. EG *...Shirley Williams' election manifesto.* N COUNT

manifold /mænɪfəʊld/. Things that are **manifold** are of many different kinds. EG *Her good works were manifold... His manifold absurdities might have been forgotten.* ADJ CLASSIF Literary

manila /mənɪlə/; also spelled **manilla.** A **manila** envelope or folder is made from a strong brown paper. EG *...a stack of manila envelopes.* ADJ CLASSIF: ATTRIB

manipulate /mə³nɪpjə⁴leɪt/, **manipulates, manipulating, manipulated. 1** If you **manipulate** people, you skilfully cause them to behave in the way that you want them to; used showing disapproval. EG *Small children sometimes manipulate grown-ups.* ◇ **manipulation** /mə³nɪpjə⁴leɪʃəⁿn/, **manipulations.** EG *...his unscrupulous manipulation of people.* V+O; ◇ N UNCOUNT OR N COUNT

2 If you **manipulate** a situation or system, you cause it to develop or operate in the way that you want it to. EG *The job of a manager is to manipulate and control a complex system.* ◇ **manipulation.** EG *...the careful manipulation of circumstances.* V+O; ◇ N UNCOUNT OR N COUNT

3 If you **manipulate** a piece of equipment, you control it in a skilful way. EG *Lawrence manipulated the knobs on his tape recorder.* ◇ **manipulation.** EG *I had bent to watch the mechanic's manipulations.* V+O; ◇ N COUNT OR N UNCOUNT

manipulative /mə³nɪpjə⁴lətɪv/ is used to describe behaviour in which someone skilfully causes people to behave in the way that he or she wants them to; used showing disapproval. EG *...the manipulative powers of the ruler.* ADJ QUALIT Formal

manipulator /mə³nɪpjə⁴leɪtə/, **manipulators.** A **manipulator** is a person who skilfully controls events, systems, or people. EG *...the expert financial manipulator.* N COUNT

mankind /mænkaɪnd/. You can refer to all human beings as **mankind** when you are considering them as a group. EG *You have performed a valuable service to mankind.* N UNCOUNT

manly /mænli¹/. People describe a man's behaviour or character as **manly** when they think that it is typical of a man rather than a woman or boy; used showing approval. EG *He laughed a deep, manly laugh.* ADJ QUALIT

man-made. Something that is **man-made** is made by people, rather than formed naturally. EG *We live in an entirely man-made environment... ...man-made fibres.* ADJ CLASSIF

manned /mænd/. A **manned** vehicle is controlled by people travelling in it. EG *They released special underwater manned vehicles.* ADJ CLASSIF

manner /mænə/, **manners. 1** The **manner** in which you do something is the way that you do it. EG *They filed the report in a routine manner... Their manner of rearing their young is extremely unusual.* N SING+SUPP

2 Your **manner** is the way in which you behave and talk. EG *The judge had been impressed by his manner... He was fat, with a lazy manner.* N SING

3 If you have good **manners**, you behave and speak very politely. EG *She had beautiful manners... His manners were charming.* • See also **table manners**. N PLURAL

4 The **manner** of person you are is the kind of person that you are. EG *What manner of man is he?* N SING+*of* Literary

5 **All manner of** objects or people means objects or people of many different kinds. EG *There were four canvas bags filled with all manner of tools.* PHRASE

6 You say **in a manner of speaking** to indicate that what you have just said is not absolutely or literally true, but is nevertheless true in a general way. EG *If he hadn't been her boss, in a manner of speaking, she would have reported him to the police.* ADV SEN

mannered /mænəd/. If someone's speech or behaviour is **mannered**, it is very artificial, as if they were trying to impress people; used showing disapproval. EG *His conversation is a trifle mannered.* ADJ QUALIT Formal

mannerism /mænərɪzəⁿm/, **mannerisms.** A **mannerism** is a gesture or way of speaking which is very characteristic of a person and which they often use. EG *As she grew older, her mannerisms became more pronounced.* N COUNT

mannish /mænɪʃ/. People describe a woman as **mannish** when they think that she looks or behaves more like a man than a woman; often used showing disapproval. EG *Her voice was low and almost mannish... ...her mannish shirt and tie.* ADJ QUALIT

manoeuvre /mənu:və/, **manoeuvres, manoeuvring, manoeuvred;** spelled **maneuver** in American English. **1** If you **manoeuvre** something into or out of a place, you skilfully move it into or out of the place. EG *Hooper started the car and manoeuvred it out of the parking space.* ▸ used as a noun. EG *Most people seem to manage this manoeuvre without causing havoc.* V OR V+O: USU+A; ▸ N COUNT

2 A **manoeuvre** is also something clever which you do in order to change a situation and make things happen the way that you want them to. EG *These results have been achieved by a series of political manoeuvres.* N COUNT

3 If you have **room for manoeuvre**, you have the opportunity to change your plans if it becomes necessary or desirable. EG *That doesn't leave you much room for manoeuvre.* PHRASE

4 When military **manoeuvres** take place, soldiers and equipment are moved around in a large area of countryside in order to train the soldiers to fight battles. N PLURAL

manor /mænə/, **manors.** A **manor** is a large private house and land in the country, especially one which was built in the Middle Ages. EG *...the restoration of their ancient halls and manors.* N COUNT

manpower /mænpaʊə/. People refer to workers as **manpower** when considering them as a means of producing goods. EG *The country is in need of skilled manpower... We've not got the manpower to do a regular check.* N UNCOUNT

mansion /mænʃəⁿn/, **mansions.** A **mansion** is a large house. EG *...a late eighteenth-century mansion... ...a few old wooden mansions.* N COUNT

manslaughter /mænslɔ:tə/ is the killing of a person by someone who may intend to hurt or injure them but who does not intend to kill them: compare **murder.** EG *He was sentenced to two years for manslaughter.* N UNCOUNT Legal

mantelpiece /mæntəⁿlpi:s/, **mantelpieces;** also spelled **mantlepiece.** A **mantelpiece** is a wood or stone shelf over a fireplace. EG *There was a Chinese clay horse on the mantelpiece.* N COUNT

manual /mænjʊⁿəl/, **manuals. 1 Manual** work is work in which you use your hands or your physical strength rather than your mind. ADJ CLASSIF

2 **Manual** also means operated by hand, rather than by electricity or by a motor. EG *...a manual* ADJ CLASSIF: ATTRIB

Find two words on these pages which are pronounced the same.

system. ◊ **manually.** EG *Such pumps can be operated manually.* ◊ ADV

3 A **manual** is a book which tells you how to do something or how a machine works. EG *The instruction manuals are printed in German.* N COUNT

manufacture /mænjə⁴fæktʃə/, **manufactures, manufacturing, manufactured. 1** When people **manufacture** things, they make them in a factory. EG *Many companies were manufacturing desk calculators... ...manufactured goods.* ▸ used as a noun. EG *...the manufacture and maintenance of vehicles.* V+O ▸ N UNCOUNT

◊ **manufacturing.** EG *India and China had built up important manufacturing industries.* ◊ N UNCOUNT

2 If you **manufacture** information, you invent it. EG *She had manufactured the terrorist story to put everyone off.* V+O

manufacturer /mænjə⁴fæktʃə⁰rə/, **manufacturers.** A **manufacturer** is a person or organization that owns a business that makes goods in large quantities. EG *I'm a manufacturer of farm machinery... ...a furniture manufacturer.* N COUNT

manure /mənjʊə/ is animal faeces, sometimes mixed with chemicals, that is spread on the ground in order to make plants grow healthy and strong. EG *...the powerful odour of horse manure.* N UNCOUNT

manuscript /mænjə⁴skrɪpt/, **manuscripts.** A **manuscript** is 1 a handwritten or typed document, especially the typed version of a book before it is printed. EG *I suggest that you offer your manuscript to a publisher at a later date.* **2** an old document that was written by hand before printing was invented. EG *...a medieval manuscript.* N COUNT

many /meni¹/. The comparative of **many** is **more**, and the superlative is **most**. These words are dealt with separately in this dictionary.

1 If there are **many** people or **many** things, there are a lot of them. EG *Many people have been killed... ...the many brilliant speeches that had been made... Many of the old people were blind.* QUANTIF

2 You use **a good many** or **a great many** to emphasize that you are referring to a very large number of things or people. EG *The information has proved useful to a great many people.* PHRASE

3 You also use **many** to ask how great a quantity is, or to give information about it. EG *How many children has she got?... I used to get a lot of sweets. As many as I liked.* QUANTIF

4 many happy returns: see **return.** ● **in so many words**: see **word.**

map

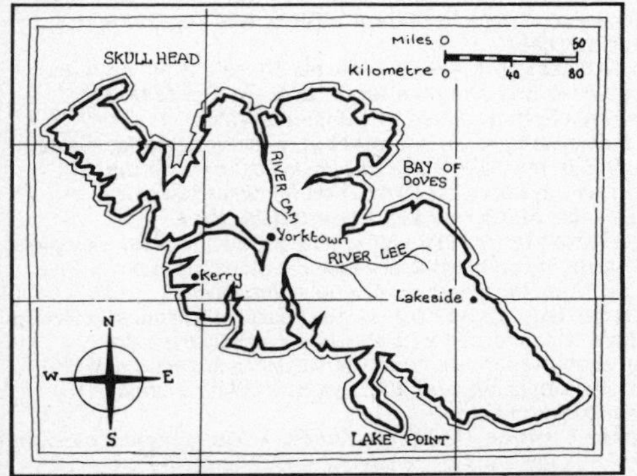

map /mæp/, **maps, mapping, mapped.** A **map** is a drawing of an area as it would appear if you saw it from above. Maps show an area's main features, or give special information about it. EG *Maps can be obtained from the Tourist Office... On the map it is quite a brief strip of road... Look at the rainfall maps on page nineteen.* N COUNT

map out. If you **map out** a plan or task, you work out in detail how you will do it. EG *They met and mapped out their task.* PHRASAL VB : V+O+ADV

maple /meɪpə⁰l/, **maples.** A **maple** is a kind of tree with five-pointed leaves. N COUNT

mar /mɑː/, **mars, marring, marred.** To **mar** something means to spoil its appearance. EG *Graffiti marred the sides of buildings.* V+O

marathon /mærəθə⁰n/, **marathons. 1** A **marathon** is a race in which people run about 26 miles (about 42 km) along roads. EG *...the London Marathon.* N COUNT

2 A **marathon** job or task takes a long time to do and is very tiring. EG *You need stamina to get through such a marathon production.* ADJ CLASSIF : ATTRIB

marauder /mərɔːdə/, **marauders. Marauders** are people who go around looking for something to steal or kill. EG *We were safe from marauders.* N COUNT

marauding /mərɔːdɪŋ/. A **marauding** person or animal is one that roams around looking for something to steal or kill. EG *The countryside was being ravaged by marauding bands.* ADJ CLASSIF : ATTRIB

marble /mɑːbə⁰l/, **marbles. 1 Marble** is a very hard rock which is used to make statues and parts of houses. EG *...a monument in black marble.* N UNCOUNT

2 Marbles is a children's game played with small balls made of coloured glass. You roll a ball along the ground and try to hit an opponent's ball with it. N UNCOUNT

3 A **marble** is one of the small balls used by children in the game of marbles. N COUNT

march /mɑːtʃ/, **marches, marching, marched. 1 March** is the third month of the year in the western calendar. EG *He was assassinated in March 1978.* N UNCOUNT

2 When soldiers **march**, they walk with quick regular steps, as a group. EG *They marched through Norway.* ▸ used as a noun. EG *We were woken in the middle of the night for a long march.* V : USU+A ▸ N COUNT

3 When a large group of people **march**, they walk somewhere together in order to protest about something. EG *The crowds of demonstrators marched down the main street.* ▸ used as a noun. EG *A million people took part in last year's march.* V : USU+A ▸ N COUNT

4 If you **march** somewhere, you walk there quickly, for example because you are angry. EG *He marched out of the store.* V+A

5 If you **march** someone somewhere, you force them to walk there with you by grasping their arm tightly. EG *He took me by the arm and marched me out of the door.* V+O+A

6 The **march** of something is its steady development or progress. EG *...the march of science... ...the slow march to socialism.* N SING+SUPP

mare /meə/, **mares.** A **mare** is an adult female horse. EG *Pa was harnessing his mare.* N COUNT

margarine /mɑːdʒəriːn/ is a yellow substance that looks like butter but is made from vegetable oil and animal fats. You can spread it on bread or use it for cooking. N UNCOUNT

margin /mɑːdʒɪn/, **margins. 1 Margin** is used to refer to the amount by which someone wins a contest. For example, if there are two candidates in an election, and one receives 8765 votes and the other 6789 votes, the winner wins by a margin of 1976 votes. EG *They won by the small margin of five seats.* N COUNT : USU+SUPP

2 If there is a **margin** of something, there is more than you need, and this extra amount allows you more freedom. EG *What is the margin of safety?* N COUNT : USU SING+SUPP

3 The **margins** on a written or printed page are the blank spaces at each side. EG *They get a red tick in the margin to show that it's right.* N COUNT

4 The **margin** of an area is the edge of it. EG *...the east margin of the river... We came to the margin of the wood.* N COUNT : USU+*of* Formal

5 The **margin** of a group, activity, or situation is the part that is least typical of it. EG *There were multitudes of people living on the margin of society.* N COUNT : OFT+*of* Formal

marginal /mɑ:dʒɪnə[0]l/. 1 Something that is **marginal** is small and not very important. EG *The effect will be marginal... ...making marginal adjustments.* ADJ QUALIT

2 A **marginal** seat or constituency is a political constituency where elections are usually won by a very small majority, so that control often changes from one party to another. ADJ QUALIT British

marginally /mɑ:dʒɪnə[0]li[1]/ means to only a small extent. EG *The prices of new houses are marginally higher than old houses.* SUBMOD

marigold /mæri[1]gəʊld/, **marigolds.** A **marigold** is a type of yellow flower. N COUNT

marijuana /mærɪh[0]ʊɑ:nə/ is a type of drug which is is smoked in cigarettes. Marijuana is illegal in Britain. EG *The room reeked of marijuana.* N UNCOUNT

marina /məri:nə/, **marinas.** A **marina** is a small harbour where people keep boats. N COUNT

marinate /mærɪneɪt/, **marinates, marinating, marinated.** If you **marinate** meat or fish or if it **marinates**, you keep it in a mixture of vinegar, oil, and spices before cooking it, so that it develops a special flavour. V-ERG

marine /məri:n/, **marines. 1** A **marine** is **1.1** a soldier in the American Marine Corps. **1.2** a British soldier who serves with the navy. N COUNT

2 Marine is used to describe things relating to the sea. EG *...marine life... ...marine biology.* ADJ CLASSIF : ATTRIB

marital /mærɪtə[0]l/ means relating to marriage. EG *...marital problems.* ADJ CLASSIF : ATTRIB

marital status. If someone asks what your **marital status** is, they want to know whether you are married, single, or divorced. N UNCOUNT Formal

maritime /mærɪtaɪm/ is used to describe things relating to the sea and to ships. EG *...the National Maritime Museum.* ADJ CLASSIF : ATTRIB

marjoram /mɑ:dʒə[0]rəm/ is a kind of herb. N UNCOUNT

mark /mɑ:k/, **marks, marking, marked. 1** A **mark** is a small part of a surface which has changed its colour, for example because something has been spilled on it. EG *...grease marks... Does it leave a mark?... I'm sorry, there seems to be a dirty mark on it.* N COUNT

2 If a substance **marks** a surface, it damages it in some way. EG *Vinegar, lemon juice, egg and salt can mark cutlery.* V-ERG

3 A **mark** is also a written or printed symbol, for example a letter of the alphabet. EG *McNicoll made a few marks on the page with his pen.* N COUNT

4 When a teacher gives you a **mark**, **4.1** he or she gives you a point for a correct answer in a test or examination. EG *You need 120 marks out of 200 to pass.* **4.2** he or she gives you a number or letter to indicate how good or bad your work is. N COUNT

5 When something reaches a particular **mark**, it reaches that stage. EG *Unemployment is well over the three million mark... Once past the halfway mark he found that he was running more easily.* N COUNT+SUPP

6 If something has the **marks** of a particular kind of thing, it has that thing's most typical features. EG *The scene bore all the marks of a country wedding.* N PLURAL +SUPP

7 You can use **mark** to say what an action is intended to express. For example, if you do something as a mark of friendship, you do it to show that you feel friendly towards someone. EG *I took this smile as a mark of recognition.* N COUNT+*of*

8 If you **mark** something, you put a written symbol on it. EG *...reports marked Top Secret... See that everything is marked with your initials.* V+O : USU PASS

9 When a teacher **marks** a student's work, he or she decides how good it is and writes a number or letter on it to indicate this opinion. V+O

10 If something **marks** a place or position, it shows where something else is or where it used to be. EG *The area of burned clay marks the position of several Roman furnaces.* V+O

11 An event that **marks** a particular stage or time is a sign that something different is about to happen. EG *The film marks a turning point in Allen's career... Her resignation marks the end of an era.* V+O

12 If you do something to **mark** an important event, you do it to commemorate this event. EG *The concert is to mark the 75th Anniversary year of the composer's death.* V+O

13 If a particular quality **marks** a person's life or career, the person often shows this quality during their life or career. EG *His cricket has always been marked by courage and determination.* V+O

14 Something that **marks** you as a particular type of person indicates that you are that type of person. EG *These signs marked him as a bachelor eager to wed.* V+O+*as*

15 Mark is used in these phrases. **15.1** If you are **slow off the mark**, you respond to a situation slowly. If you are **quick off the mark**, you respond to a situation quickly. EG *Neighbours were always quick off the mark to ask him round when his wife was away.* **15.2** If you **make** or **leave** your **mark** on something, you have an important influence on it. EG *...a scholar who has made his mark in history... These policies have left indelible marks on British society.* **15.3** If something is **wide of the mark**, it is a long way from being correct. EG *His assessment of the situation might be rather wide of the mark.* **15.4** If you **are marking time**, you are doing something uninteresting or unimportant while you wait for something else to happen. EG *I've been marking time reading books.* PHRASES

16 See also **marked, marking**.

mark off. If you **mark off** an item on a list, you put a line through it or next to it, to show that it has been dealt with. EG *Each day was marked off with a neat X.* PHRASAL VB : V+O+ADV

marked /mɑ:kt/. If you describe something as **marked**, you mean that it is very obvious and easily noticed. EG *He has shown marked improvements in spelling and writing.* ◇ **markedly** /mɑ:kɪ[2]dlɪ[1]/. EG *Business in Nigeria is markedly different from that in Europe.* ADJ QUALIT ◇ SUBMOD OR ADV

marker /mɑ:kə/, **markers.** A **marker** is an object which is used to show the position of something. EG *The post served as a boundary marker.* N COUNT

market /mɑ:kɪt/, **markets, marketing, marketed. 1** A **market** is a place, usually in the open air, where lots of different goods are bought and sold. EG *These women sell fish in the markets... ...a cattle market... ...a market stall.* N COUNT

2 The **market** for a product is the number of people who want to buy it. EG *...the declining commercial vehicle market... There is a vast overseas market.* N COUNT : USU SING+SUPP

3 To **market** a product means to sell it in an organized way and on a large scale. EG *The felt-tip pen was first marketed by a Japanese firm.* V+O

4 If something is **on the market**, it is available for people to buy. EG *It's one of the slowest cars on the market... It's been on the market for three years.* PHRASE

5 See also **black market, Common Market**.

marketable /mɑ:kɪtəbə[0]l/. If a product is **marketable**, it can be sold, because people want to buy it. EG *It was their only marketable commodity.* ADJ QUALIT

marketing /mɑ:kɪtɪŋ/ is the part of business which is concerned with the way a product is sold, for example its price and the way it is advertised. EG *...the importance of effective marketing... ...marketing directors.* N UNCOUNT

market place, market places. 1 The **market place** is the activity of buying and selling, and the places where this occurs. EG *Its products must compete in the international market place.* N SING : *the*+N

2 A **market place** is a small open area in a town where lots of goods are bought and sold. EG *Beggars crowded in every market-place.* N COUNT

What is your marital status?

market research is the activity of collecting and studying information about what people want, need, and buy. N UNCOUNT

marking /mɑːkɪŋ/, **markings. 1 Markings** are coloured shapes or designs on the surface of something. EG *Look at the markings on the petals.* N COUNT: USU PLURAL

2 Marking is the work a teacher does when he or she reads a student's work and gives it a grade. N UNCOUNT

marksman /mɑːksmən/, **marksmen.** A **marksman** is a person who can shoot very accurately with a gun. N COUNT

marmalade /mɑːməleɪd/ is a food like jam made from oranges, lemons, or grapefruit and usually eaten on bread or toast at breakfast. N MASS

maroon /mərуːn/. Something that is **maroon** is dark reddish-purple in colour. EG *...a maroon jacket.* ADJ COLOUR

marooned /məruːnd/. If you are **marooned** in a place, you cannot leave it, for example because it is surrounded by water. EG *...a story about a group of young boys marooned on a desert island.* ADJ CLASSIF

marquee /mɑːkiː/, **marquees.** A **marquee** is a large tent which is used at a fair, garden party, or other outdoor event, usually for eating and drinking in. N COUNT

marquis /mɑːkwɪs/, **marquises;** also spelled **marquess.** A **marquis** is a male member of the nobility. EG *...the Marquis of Stafford.* N COUNT

marriage /mærɪdʒ/, **marriages. 1** A **marriage** is **1.1** the relationship between a husband and wife. EG *It has been a happy marriage... Her fifth marriage lasted only a month.* **1.2** the act of marrying someone. EG *Victoria's marriage to her cousin was not welcomed by her family.* N COUNT; N COUNT OR N UNCOUNT

2 Marriage is the state of being married. EG *I never wanted marriage.* N UNCOUNT

married /mærɪd/. **1** If you are **married**, you have a husband or wife. EG *She's married to an Englishman... He was thirty-five, married with two children... ...a young married woman.* ADJ CLASSIF: OFT+to

2 If you **get married**, you marry someone. EG *I'm getting married... We decided to get married.* PHRASE

3 You use **married** to describe things that involve marriage. EG *...their early married life.* ADJ CLASSIF: ATTRIB

marrow /mærəʊ/, **marrows. 1** A **marrow** is a long, thick, green vegetable with soft white flesh, which you can cook and eat. N COUNT OR N UNCOUNT British

2 Marrow is the soft, fatty substance which fills the space at the centre of the bones of humans and animals. EG *...a bone marrow transplant.* N UNCOUNT

marry /mæri[1]/, **marries, marrying, married. 1** When a man and a woman **marry**, they become each other's husband and wife during a special ceremony. EG *They are in love with each other and wish to marry... I want to marry you.* V OR V+O: RECIP

2 When a clergyman or registrar **marries** two people, he or she is in charge of the ceremony during which the two people become husband and wife. V+O

3 If you **marry** two things together, you succeed in joining them together. EG *...the marrying together of a number of different scientific disciplines.* V+O: OFT+A Formal

4 See also **married**.

marsh /mɑːʃ/, **marshes.** A **marsh** is an area of land which is very wet and muddy. EG *I went off into the marsh... ...a dense plantation bounded by marsh.* N COUNT OR N UNCOUNT

marshal /mɑːʃə[0]l/, **marshals, marshalling, marshalled;** spelled **marshaling** and **marshaled** in American English. **1** If you **marshal** things or people, you gather them together and organize them. EG *He hesitated, marshalling his thoughts... Shipping was being marshalled into convoys... He tried to marshal support.* V+O

2 A **marshal** is an official who helps to organize a public event. EG *If you undergo difficulties, please contact the nearest marshal.* N COUNT

3 In the United States, a **marshal** is a police officer who controls and organizes a particular district. N COUNT

4 See also **field marshal**.

marshmallow /mɑːʃmæləʊ/, **marshmallows. 1 Marshmallow** is a soft, spongy, sweet food. N UNCOUNT

2 Marshmallows are sweets made from marshmallow. N COUNT

marshy /mɑːʃi[1]/. **Marshy** land is covered in marshes. EG *...a stretch of marshy coastline.* ADJ QUALIT

martial /mɑːʃəl/ is used to describe things that relate to soldiers, war, or military matters. EG *...martial music.* ● See also **court-martial**. ADJ CLASSIF: ATTRIB Formal

martial arts. The **martial arts** are the techniques of self-defence that come from the Far East, for example karate and judo. N PLURAL

martyr /mɑːtə/, **martyrs, martyring, martyred.** A **martyr** is someone who was killed because of his or her religious beliefs. EG *St Sebastian was a Christian martyr.* ▸ used as a verb. EG *This is where St Peter was supposed to have been martyred.* N COUNT; ▸ V+O: USU PASS

martyrdom /mɑːtədəm/ is the murder of someone because of his or her religious beliefs. EG *...the martyrdom of St Thomas.* N UNCOUNT

marvel /mɑːvə[0]l/, **marvels, marvelling, marvelled;** spelled **marveling** and **marveled** in American English. **1** If you **marvel** at something, it fills you with surprise or admiration. EG *Early travellers marvelled at the riches of Mali... We marvelled that so much could happen in such a short time.* V: OFT+at OR REPORT, ONLY that

2 A **marvel** is something that makes you feel great surprise or admiration. EG *Paestum is one of the marvels of Greek architecture... It's a marvel that I'm still alive.* N COUNT

marvellous /mɑːvə[0]ləs/; spelled **marvelous** in American English. If you say that people or things are **marvellous**, you mean that they are wonderful and that you are very pleased indeed with them. EG *Two ounces! Oh, Robin, that's marvellous!... Flora, you're marvellous.* ◇ **marvellously.** EG *I slept marvellously well.* ADJ QUALIT; ◇ SUBMOD

Marxism /mɑːksɪzə[0]m/ is a political philosophy based on the writings of Karl Marx. Marxism states that the struggle between people of different social classes is the most important part of history. N UNCOUNT

Marxist /mɑːksɪst/, **Marxists. 1** Something that is **Marxist** is based on or relates to Marxism. EG *...Marxist theory... ...the Marxist Workers' League.* ADJ CLASSIF

2 A **Marxist** is a person who believes in Marxism. EG *The Marxists were forced to revise their plans.* N COUNT

marzipan /mɑːzɪpæn/ is a paste made of almonds, sugar, and egg. It is sometimes put on top of cakes, or used to make small sweets. N UNCOUNT

mascara /mæskɑːrə/ is a substance which women put on their eyelashes in order to make them look thicker or a different colour. N UNCOUNT

mascot /mæskə[7]t/, **mascots.** A **mascot** is an animal, toy, or doll which is thought to bring good luck. EG *Many of them have dolls as mascots... The regimental mascot is a goat called Winston.* N COUNT

masculine /mæskjə[4]lɪn/. **1** Something that is **masculine** relates to or is considered typical of men, in contrast to women. EG *I think it must have something to do with masculine pride.* ADJ QUALIT

2 If you describe a woman as **masculine**, you mean that she has a lot of qualities which make her seem more like a man. EG *...a rather masculine-looking lady.* ADJ QUALIT

masculinity /mæskjə[4]lɪnɪ[1]ti[1]/. **1 Masculinity** is the fact of being a man. EG *In society we assume that masculinity has certain characteristics.* N UNCOUNT

2 A man's **masculinity** consists of the qualities, especially sexual qualities, which are considered to be typical of men. EG *Some men measure their masculinity by anything from their jobs to their drinking habits.* N UNCOUNT: USU+POSS

mash /mæʃ/, **mashes, mashing, mashed.** If you **mash** vegetables, you crush them after they have been cooked. EG *Mash the lentils well.* ◇ **mashed.** EG *...mashed potatoes.* V+O; ◇ ADJ CLASSIF

mask /mɑːsk/, **masks, masking, masked. 1** A **mask** is something which you wear over your face in order to hide or protect it or to make yourself look different. EG *The thieves were wearing masks... ...a surgical mask.* ● See also **gas mask**. N COUNT

2 If you **mask** something, you cover it so that it is difficult to see. EG *Her eyes were masked by huge, round sunglasses.* V+O

3 If you **mask** your feelings, you behave in a way which hides them. EG *Our opponents mask their antagonism behind sweet words.* ▸ used as a noun. EG *He may learn to conceal his annoyance with a mask of politeness.* V+O ▸ N COUNT: USU+SUPP

masked /mɑːskt/. Someone who is **masked** is wearing a mask. EG *Three armed and masked men suddenly burst in.* ADJ CLASSIF

masochism /mæsəᵒkɪzəᵒm/ is behaviour in which someone gets pleasure and satisfaction from suffering physically or mentally. ◇ **masochist, masochists.** EG *Unless you are a complete masochist, you are unlikely to derive much pleasure from the show.* N UNCOUNT ◇ N COUNT

masochistic /mæsəᵒkɪstɪk/. **Masochistic** behaviour is behaviour in which a person suffers physical or mental pain in order to feel pleasure or satisfaction. EG *There are some actors with strong masochistic streaks who wish to hear only criticisms.* ADJ QUALIT

mason /meɪsəᵒn/, **masons.** A **mason** is a person who is skilled at making things out of stone. EG *He carved marble faster than any mason.* N COUNT

masonry /meɪsənri¹/ is bricks or pieces of stone which form part of a wall or building. EG *Large chunks of masonry were beginning to fall.* N UNCOUNT

masquerade /mæskəreɪd/, **masquerades, masquerading, masqueraded.** If you **masquerade** as something, you pretend to be that thing. EG *He might try to masquerade as a policeman... He might be masquerading under an assumed name.* V+AS/UNDER

mass /mæs/, **masses, massing, massed. 1** A **mass** of something is a large amount of it. EG *Bruce stuffed a mass of papers into his briefcase... ...a mass of long grey hair.* N PART: SING

2 When people talk about **masses** of something, they mean a great deal of it. EG *They ate masses and masses of food... They've got simply masses of money.* N PART: PLURAL Informal

3 A **mass** is **3.1** an amount of a solid substance, a liquid, or a gas. EG *The base of the rock cracked and the whole mass toppled into the sea... ...a mass of warm air laden with water vapour.* **3.2** a large area of land. EG *...the great land mass of Asia.* N COUNT Formal

4 You use **mass** to describe something which involves or affects a very large number of people. EG *...the power of mass communication... ...mass unemployment.* ADJ CLASSIF: ATTRIB

5 The **masses** are the ordinary people in society considered as a group. EG *We want to produce opera for the masses.* N PLURAL: the+N

6 When people or things **mass** or when you **mass** them, they gather together into a large crowd or group. EG *The students massed in Paris... The general was massing his troops.* V-ERG

7 The **mass** of an object is the amount of physical matter that it has. EG *The velocity depends on the mass of the object.* N UNCOUNT OR N COUNT Technical

8 Mass is a ceremony in some Christian churches during which people eat bread and drink wine in order to remember the last meal of Jesus Christ. N UNCOUNT OR N COUNT

9 See also **massed**.

massacre /mæsəkə/, **massacres, massacring, massacred.** A **massacre** is the killing of a very large number of people in a violent and cruel way. EG *...the massacre of a village.* ▸ used as a verb. EG *Their tanks massacred more than 32,000 people.* N COUNT OR N UNCOUNT ▸ V+O

massage /mæsɑːdᵒʒ/, **massages, massaging, massaged.** If you **massage** someone, you rub a part of their body in order to make them relax or to stop their muscles from being painful. EG *Could you massage the back of my neck?* ▸ used as a noun. EG *We can relax our muscles by massage.* V+O ▸ N UNCOUNT OR N COUNT

masse. See **en masse**.

massed /mæst/. You use **massed** to describe large groups of people or things that have been collected or brought together. EG *...the massed groups of rival supporters... ...massed brass bands.* ADJ CLASSIF: ATTRIB

massive /mæsɪv/. Something that is **massive** is extremely large in size, quantity, or extent. EG *He opened the massive oak front doors... ...a massive increase in oil prices.* ◇ **massively.** EG *We invested massively in West German machinery.* ADJ CLASSIF ◇ ADV

mass media. The **mass media** are television, radio, and newspapers. EG *The mass media now play an increasing role in shaping our opinions.* N COLL: the+N

mass noun, mass nouns. In grammar, a **mass noun** is a noun which usually has no plural, but which can have a plural in certain circumstances, for example when you mean measures or brands of the thing that the word stands for. Nouns of this type are described as N MASS in this dictionary. See the entry headed NOUNS for more information. N COUNT

mass-produce, mass-produces, mass-producing, mass-produced. When people **mass-produce** something, they make it in large quantities by repeating the same process many times. EG *...a contract for mass-producing cheap computers... ...a vaccine which can be mass-produced cheaply.* ◇ **mass-produced.** EG *...cheap mass-produced exports.* ◇ **mass-production.** EG *Soon the car will go into mass-production.* V OR V+O ◇ ADJ CLASSIF ◇ N UNCOUNT

mast /mɑːst/, **masts. 1** The **masts** of a sailing ship or yacht are the tall upright poles that are used to support its sails. See picture at YACHT. N COUNT

2 A radio or television **mast** is a very tall pole that is used as an aerial to transmit sound or television pictures. N COUNT

master /mɑːstə/, **masters, mastering, mastered. 1** A **master** is a man who has authority over a servant. EG *Sometimes there was no dispute between a master and his slave.* N COUNT Outdated

2 If you are **master** of a situation, you have complete control over it. EG *This was before man was total master of his environment.* N UNCOUNT+of

3 If you **master** a difficult situation, you succeed in controlling it. EG *Confrontations must be mastered as they arise.* V+O

4 If you **master** something, you learn how to do it properly or manage to understand it completely. EG *Slowly, one begins to master the complex skills involved... I mastered the local dialect.* V+O

5 You use **master** to describe someone who is extremely skilled in a job or activity. EG *...master bakers... ...a master plumber.* ADJ CLASSIF: ATTRIB

6 A **master** is also a male teacher at a school. EG *...the science master... ...a master at the Agricultural Training Centre.* ● See also **headmaster**. N COUNT: OFT+SUPP British

masterful /mɑːstəfʊl/. Someone who is **masterful** behaves in a way which shows that they can control people or situations. EG *His voice had become more masterful.* ADJ QUALIT

masterly /mɑːstəli¹/. If you describe an action as **masterly**, you mean that it is done extremely well. EG *It was a masterly performance.* ADJ QUALIT

mastermind /mɑːstəmaɪnd/, **masterminds, masterminding, masterminded. 1** If you **mastermind** a complicated activity, you plan it in detail and make sure that it happens successfully. EG *A young accountant masterminded the take-over of the company.* V+O

2 The **mastermind** of a complicated activity is the person who is responsible for planning and organizing it. EG *The mastermind of the expedition was a Frenchman.* N COUNT

Do people mass-produce masterpieces?

Master of Arts, Masters of Arts. A **Master of Arts** is a person with an M.A. degree. N COUNT

Master of Science, Masters of Science. A **Master of Science** is a person with an M.Sc. degree. EG *He's a Master of Science now.* N COUNT

masterpiece /mɑːstəpiːs/, **masterpieces.** 1 A **masterpiece** is an extremely good painting, novel, film, or other work of art. EG *It is one of the great masterpieces of European art.* N COUNT

2 An artist's, writer's, or composer's **masterpiece** is the best work that they have ever produced. EG *'Gulliver's Travels' is Swift's masterpiece.* N COUNT+POSS

3 If an action is especially clever, you can describe it as a **masterpiece** of that kind of action. EG *...a speech which was a masterpiece of ambiguity.* N COUNT: OFT+of

mastery /mɑːstəºriˡ/. 1 **Mastery** of a skill or art is excellence in it. EG *...his mastery of the language.* N UNCOUNT: OFT+of/over

2 **Mastery** is also complete power or control over something. EG *His sons were struggling to obtain mastery of the country.* N UNCOUNT: OFT+of/over

mat /mæt/, **mats.** 1 A **mat** is a small piece of cloth, card, or plastic which you put on a table, usually in order to protect it. EG *She set his food on the mat before him... ...beer mats.* N COUNT

2 A **mat** is also a small piece of carpet or other thick material which you put on the floor for protection, decoration, or comfort. N COUNT

3 See also **matt, matted, matting.**

match /mætʃ/, **matches, matching, matched.** 1 A **match** is an organized game of football, cricket, chess, or other sport. EG *...a football match.* N COUNT

matches

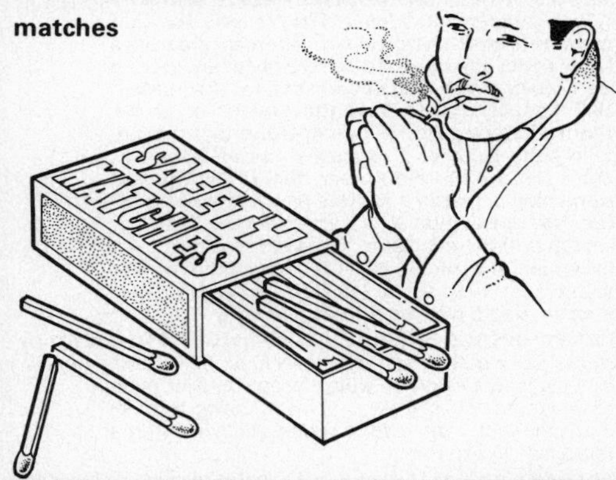

2 A **match** is also one of the small, thin sticks of wood that produce a flame when you strike them against the side of a matchbox. EG *Don't strike a match if you smell gas... ...a box of matches.* N COUNT

3 If one thing **matches** another, the two things are the same as one another, or have similar qualities. EG *The captain's feelings clearly matched my own... Sometimes his inner thoughts and his outer actions do not match.* V OR V+O: RECIP

4 If you **match** one thing with another, you decide that one is suitable for the other, or that there is a connection between them. EG *All you have to do is correctly match the famous personalities with the towns they come from.* V+O OR V+O+with: RECIP; ALSO V+O+up

5 If one thing **matches** another thing or if the two things **match**, they have the same colour or design. EG *All her towels match... She was dressed in a yellow sari with yellow ribbons to match.* V OR V+O: RECIP

6 If you **match** something, you are as good as it, or equal to it in speed, size, or quality. EG *They are trying to upgrade their cars to match the foreign competition... She walked at a pace that Morris's short legs could hardly match.* V+O

7 If you say that something **is no match for** another thing, you mean that it is inferior to it. EG *A machine gun is no match for a tank.* PHRASE

8 See also **matched, matching.**

matchbox /mætʃbɒks/, **matchboxes.** A **matchbox** is a small box that you buy that contains matches. N COUNT

matched /mætʃt/. 1 If you say that two people are well **matched**, you mean that they are suited to one another and are likely to have a happy and successful relationship. EG *I thought we were perfectly matched.* ADJ CLASSIF: ADV+ADJ

2 If two people or groups are well **matched**, they have the same strength or ability. EG *Government and rebel soldiers are evenly matched.* ADJ CLASSIF: ADV+ADJ

matching /mætʃɪŋ/. You use **matching** to describe something which is the same colour or design as something else. EG *...a blue jacket with matching shirt.* ADJ CLASSIF: ATTRIB

matchless /mætʃlɪˀs/. You use **matchless** to describe something that is so good that you think nothing else could be as good. EG *...men and women of matchless honesty.* ADJ CLASSIF Formal

mate /meɪt/, **mates, mating, mated.** 1 Someone's **mate** is their friend; used mainly by men. EG *He supposed his old mate Kowalski would be with them... He went off with his mate.* N COUNT: OFT+POSS Informal

2 An animal's **mate** is its sexual partner. EG *The females are about half the size of their mates.* N COUNT: OFT+POSS

3 When a male animal and a female animal **mate**, they have sex. EG *The majority of amphibians mate in water.* ◊ **mating.** EG *...the mating season... Mosquitoes use sound as a mating call.* V OR V+with: RECIP ◊ ADJ CLASSIF: ATTRIB

4 The **mate** or **first mate** on a ship is the officer who is next in importance to the captain. N SING

material /mətɪərɪəl/, **materials.** 1 A **material** is a solid substance, especially one which can be used in making things. EG *We need a cheap abundant material to make the electrodes... ...synthetic substitutes for natural materials.* N COUNT OR N UNCOUNT

2 **Material** is cloth. EG *The sleeping bags are made of quilted or acrylic material.* N UNCOUNT OR N COUNT

3 Ideas or information that can be used as a basis for a book, play, or film can be referred to as **material**. EG *She hoped to find material for some articles... They researched a lot of background material.* N UNCOUNT

4 You use **material** to describe something which is concerned with possessions, money, and conditions in which people live, rather than with their emotional or spiritual life. EG *...the material comforts of life... ...material possessions.* ◊ **materially.** EG *...conditions which they found materially adequate but spiritually impoverished.* ADJ CLASSIF: ATTRIB ◊ ADV

5 **Materials** are the equipment or things that you need for a particular activity. EG *I packed all my books and writing materials... ...cleaning materials.* N PLURAL: USU+SUPP

materialise /mətɪərɪəlaɪz/. See **materialize.**

materialism /mətɪərɪəlɪzəºm/ is the attitude that someone has when they think that money and possessions are the most important things in life. EG *They were determined to renounce the materialism of the society they had been brought up in.* ◊ **materialist** /mətɪərɪəlɪst/, **materialists.** EG *He was an atheist and a materialist... ...the materialist way of life.* N UNCOUNT ◊ N COUNT

materialistic /mətɪərɪəlɪstɪk/. A **materialistic** person or society thinks that money and possessions are the most important things in life. EG *This society has made people greedy and materialistic.* ADJ QUALIT

materialize /mətɪərɪəlaɪz/, **materializes, materializing, materialized;** also spelled **materialise.** If a possible event **materializes**, it actually happens. EG *Fortunately, the attack did not materialize.* V

maternal /məˀtɜːnəºl/ is used to describe things relating to a mother. EG *...maternal feelings... When the baby arrived, she slipped into the maternal role with ease... ...my maternal grandmother.* ADJ CLASSIF: ATTRIB

maternity /məˀtɜːnɪˡtiˡ/ is used to describe things relating to the help and medical care given to a woman when she is pregnant and when she gives ADJ CLASSIF: ATTRIB birth. EG ...*maternity hospitals... ...increases in maternity allowances... Until now women have been granted a year's maternity leave after giving birth.*

math /mæθ/ is the same as mathematics. EG ...*methods for teaching English or math.* N UNCOUNT American

mathematical /mæθəmætɪkə⁰l/. 1 Something that is **mathematical** involves numbers and calculations. EG ...*mathematical calculations... ...a mathematical formula.* ADJ CLASSIF : ATTRIB

2 If you have a **mathematical** mind, you are clever at doing calculations or understanding problems that involve numbers. ◇ **mathematically.** EG *Here's a problem for those of you who are mathematically inclined.* ADJ QUALIT : ATTRIB ◇ ADV

mathematician /mæθəmətɪʃə⁰n/, **mathematicians.** A **mathematician** is a person who studies problems involving numbers and calculations. N COUNT

mathematics /mæθəmætɪks/ is a subject which involves the study of numbers, quantities, or shapes. EG ...*professor of mathematics at Cambridge.* N UNCOUNT

maths /mæθs/ is the same as mathematics. EG ...*a maths teacher.* N UNCOUNT British

matinee /mætɪneɪ/, **matinees;** also spelled **matinée.** A **matinee** is a play or film which is performed or shown in the afternoon. N COUNT

matrices /meɪtrɪsi:z/ is the plural of **matrix.**

matriculate /mə³trɪkjə⁴leɪt/, **matriculates, matriculating, matriculated.** If you **matriculate**, you register as a student at a university. ◇ **matriculation** /mə³trikjə⁴leɪʃə⁰n/. EG *Work for a degree counts only from the date of matriculation.* V Formal ◇ N UNCOUNT

matrimony /mætrɪməni¹/ means the same as marriage. EG ...*a proposal of matrimony.* ◇ **matrimonial** /mætrɪməʊnɪəl/. EG ...*matrimonial difficulties... ...the matrimonial home... ...family and matrimonial law.* N UNCOUNT Formal ◇ ADJ CLASSIF : ATTRIB

matrix /meɪtrɪks/, **matrices** /meɪtrɪsi:z/. A **matrix** is the environment or context in which something such as a society develops and grows. EG *Attitudes are formed in a matrix of psychological and social complications.* N COUNT+SUPP Formal

matron /meɪtrən/, **matrons.** 1 In a hospital, the **matron** is a senior nurse who is usually in charge of all the nursing staff. N COUNT

2 At a boarding school, the **matron** is a woman who looks after the health and hygiene of the children. N COUNT

matt /mæt/; also spelled **mat.** A **matt** colour, paint, or surface is dull rather than shiny. EG ...*matt black... Raspberries have a matt, spongy surface.* ADJ CLASSIF

matted /mætəd/. Something that is **matted** is twisted together untidily. EG *Their hair was matted and dirt caked their faces.* ADJ QUALIT

matter /mætə/, **matters, mattering, mattered.**
1 A **matter** is an event or situation which you have to deal with, especially one that involves problems. EG *It was a purely personal matter... She's very honest in money matters... This is a matter for the police.* ● **a matter of life and death**: see **life.** N COUNT+SUPP

2 You use **matters** to refer to the situation that you are talking about or that you are involved in. EG *The absence of electricity made matters worse.* N PLURAL

3 You can use **matter** to refer in a general way to all substances or to any substance. EG *An atom is the smallest indivisible particle of matter... The termites feed on vegetable matter.* N UNCOUNT Formal

4 You can refer to books and other things that people read as reading **matter**. EG *He came into contact with a great variety of reading matter.* N UNCOUNT +SUPP Formal

5 You say 'What's **the matter**?' or 'Is anything **the matter**?' when you think that someone has a problem and you want to know what it is. EG *What's the matter, Cynthia? You sound odd... What's the matter with your hand?... We told them that there was nothing the matter.* PHRASE

6 If something **matters** to you, it is important to you. EG *My family were all that mattered to me... Your happiness, that's the only thing that matters.* V : NO CONT

7 If something does not **matter**, it is not important because it does not have an effect on the situation. EG *It does not matter which method you choose.* V WITH BROAD NEG : NO CONT

8 You use **no matter** in expressions such as 'no matter how' and 'no matter what' to indicate that something is true or happens in all circumstances. EG *I told him to report to me after the job was completed, no matter how late it was... They smiled continuously, no matter what was said.* PHRASE

9 You say **no matter what** to indicate that something is definitely going to happen. EG *They're going to win no matter what.* PHRASE

10 **Matter** is also used in these phrases. **10.1** If you do something **as a matter of** principle or policy, you do it for that reason or purpose. EG *Men were prepared to go to prison as a matter of principle, rather than pay this tax... Merchant banks recruit women as a matter of policy.* **10.2** You use **matter** in expressions such as 'a matter of days' when you are drawing attention to how short a period of time is. EG *Within a matter of weeks she was crossing the Atlantic.* **10.3** If you say that something is just **a matter of time**, you mean that it is certain to happen at some time in the future. EG *It appeared to be only a matter of time before they were caught.* **10.4** If you say that something is just **a matter of** doing something, you mean it is easy and can be done just by doing that thing. EG *Skating's just a matter of practice.* **10.5** If you say that a statement is **a matter of opinion**, you mean that people disagree about it or that you do not accept it. EG *'City are as good a team as United.' – 'That's a matter of opinion.'* **10.6** You say **for that matter** to emphasize that a statement you have made about one thing is also true about another. EG *He's shaking with the cold. So am I, for that matter.* **10.7** You say **the fact of the matter is** or **the truth of the matter is** to emphasize that you are telling the truth. EG *I exhausted myself too early, that's the truth of the matter.* **10.8** If you say that something is **another matter** or **a different matter**, you mean that it is very different from the situation that you have just discussed or is an exception to a rule. EG *But Asia was another matter altogether.* **10.9 as a matter of course**: see **course.** ● **as a matter of fact**: see **fact.** PHRASES

matter-of-fact. Someone who is **matter-of-fact** shows no emotion in their speech or behaviour, especially in a situation where people expect them to be emotional. EG *'I see,' she said, trying to seem matter-of-fact... She said it calmly and firmly in a matter-of-fact voice.* ADJ QUALIT

matting /mætɪŋ/ is strong thick material, usually made from a material like rope or straw, which is used as a floor covering. EG *There was rush matting on the floor... ...coconut matting.* N UNCOUNT

mattress /mætrə¹s/, **mattresses.** A **mattress** is a large, flat cushion the same size as a bed, which is put on a bed to make it soft to lie on. N COUNT

mature /mətjʊə/, **matures, maturing, matured; maturer, maturest.** 1 When a child or young animal **matures**, it becomes an adult. EG *She had matured into a self-possessed and articulate young woman.* V

2 When something **matures**, it reaches a state of complete development. EG *The new seeds matured in 120 days.* V

3 If someone **matures**, they become more fully developed in their personality and emotional behaviour. EG *He had matured and quietened down considerably.* V

4 If you describe someone as **mature**, you mean that they are fully developed and balanced in their personality and emotional behaviour. EG *She's in* ADJ QUALIT

If something is matted, is it made of matting?

some ways mature and in some ways rather a child.

5 If something such as wine or cheese **matures** or **is matured**, it is left for a time to allow its full flavour or strength to develop. EG *This whisky achieves its taste and colour by being matured in old wood.* — V-ERG

6 Cheese or wine that is **mature** has been left to allow its full flavour or strength to develop. — ADJ QUALIT

mature student, mature students. In a British college or university, a **mature student** is a student who is over 25 years old. — N COUNT

maturity /mətjʊərɪ¹ti¹, -tʃʊə-/. **1 Maturity** is the state of being fully developed or adult. EG *Only half of the young birds may live to reach maturity.* — N UNCOUNT

2 If someone has **maturity**, they are fully adult in their personality and emotional behaviour. EG *I have long felt that you lacked maturity.* — N UNCOUNT

maul /mɔːl/, **mauls, mauling, mauled.** If someone **is mauled** by an animal, they are savagely attacked and badly injured by it. — V+O : USU PASS

mausoleum /mɔːsəlɪəm/, **mausoleums.** A **mausoleum** is a building which contains the grave of a famous person or the graves of a rich family. — N COUNT

mauve /məʊv/, **mauves.** Something that is **mauve** is of a pale purple colour. EG *...mauve writing paper.* — ADJ COLOUR

maverick /mævəʳrɪk/, **mavericks.** If you say that someone is a **maverick,** you mean that they think and act independently, and do not always do the same as the group that they belong to. ▸ used as an adjective. EG *He is a self-confessed maverick Marxist.* — N COUNT Literary; ▸ ADJ CLASSIF : ATTRIB

max. is a written abbreviation for 'maximum'. EG *...max. 17°C... The cost will be £90 max.*

maxim /mæksɪm/, **maxims.** A **maxim** is a rule for good or sensible behaviour, which is often in the form of a proverb or short saying. EG *Instant action: that's my maxim.* — N COUNT

maximize /mæksɪmaɪz/, **maximizes, maximizing, maximized;** also spelled **maximise.** If you **maximize** something, you make it as great in amount or importance as you can. EG *The company's main objective is to maximize profits.* — V+O

maximum /mæksɪməm/. The **maximum** amount of something is the largest amount that is possible or allowed. EG *The plan must be carried out with maximum speed... They held the prisoner under maximum security conditions... Never exceed the maximum daily dosage of 150 mg.* ▸ used as a noun. EG *Conscription should be limited to a maximum of six months' service.* — ADJ CLASSIF : ATTRIB; ▸ N SING

may /meɪ/. **1** If you say that something **may** happen, you mean that it is possible that it will happen. EG *We may be here a long time... You may be right... We may never know the truth.* — MODAL

2 If you say that something **may** be true, you mean that there is a possibility that it is true, but you are not certain. If you say that something **may** have happened, you mean that it is possible that it happened. EG *This may or may not be true... You may think it's silly, Edward, but it's what I did... A gigantic meteorite may have wiped out the dinosaurs 65 million years ago.* — MODAL

3 If something **may** be done, it is possible to do it. EG *The fat in our diet may be reduced by buying low-fat milk.* — MODAL

4 If someone **may** do something, they are allowed to do it. EG *If the verdict is unacceptable, the defendant may appeal... May I have a word with you, please?... I'll take a seat, if I may.* — MODAL

5 You can use **may** when saying that, although something is true, something else which contrasts with it is also true. EG *They may be seven thousand miles away but they know what's going on over here... Ingenious though these techniques may be, they can hardly be regarded as practical.* — MODAL

6 If you do something so that a particular thing **may** happen, you do it so that it becomes possible for that thing to happen. EG *They struggle to cure diseases so that people may live longer.* — MODAL

7 You use **may** to express a wish that something will happen. For example, if you say 'May you always be happy', you are expressing a wish that someone will always be happy. EG *Long may it continue.* — MODAL Formal

8 May is the fifth month of the year in the Western calendar. EG *The meeting is on the 5th of May.* — N UNCOUNT

maybe /meɪbiː/. You use **maybe 1** to indicate that something is possible or may be true, but you are not certain. EG *Maybe he'll be prime minister one day... Well, maybe you're right... Maybe I ought to grow a moustache.* **2** to indicate that you are making a rough guess at a number or quantity, rather than stating it exactly. EG *There were maybe half a dozen men there... He's in his fifties, I'd say. Fifty-five, maybe.* — ADV SEN

mayhem /meɪhɛm/ is a situation in which there is no order, and a lot of people behave in an uncontrolled way. EG *The kids began to create mayhem in the washrooms.* — N UNCOUNT

mayonnaise /meɪəneɪz/ is a pale, thick sauce which is often eaten with salads. It is made from egg yolks and oil. — N UNCOUNT

mayor /mɛə/, **mayors.** The **mayor** of a town or city is the person who has been elected to be its head for one year and to represent it at some official occasions. — N COUNT

mayoress /mɛərɪ²s/, **mayoresses.** A **mayoress** is the wife of a mayor. — N COUNT

maze

maze /meɪz/, **mazes. 1** A **maze** is a system of complicated passages which it is difficult to find your way through. EG *Some mice were trained to find their way through a simple maze.* — N COUNT

2 A **maze** of ideas or subjects is a large number of them connected with each other in a complicated way. EG *He lost himself in a maze of thoughts.* — N COUNT+*of*

me /mi¹/ is used as the object of a verb or preposition. A speaker or writer uses **me** to refer to himself or herself. EG *He told me about it... He looked at me reproachfully.* — PRON : SING

meadow /mɛdəʊ/, **meadows.** A **meadow** is a field which has grass and flowers growing in it. — N COUNT

meagre /miːgə/; spelled **meager** in American English. If you describe something as **meagre**, you mean that it is very small. EG *...a meagre crop of potatoes... ...his meagre wages.* — ADJ QUALIT

meal /miːl/, **meals. 1** A **meal** is an occasion when people eat or the quantity of food that they eat on that occasion. EG *We always had three good meals a day... ...a simple meal of bread and cheese... When the meal was over, Thomas went out... ...the evening meal.* — N COUNT

2 If you say that someone is **making a meal of** something, you mean that they are using more time and energy to do it than is necessary. — PHRASE Outdated

mealtime /miːltaɪm/, **mealtimes.** A **mealtime** is an occasion when you eat breakfast, lunch, or — N COUNT OR N UNCOUNT dinner. EG *I had a glass of juice three times a day at mealtimes... She looked forward to mealtimes.*

mean /mi̲:n/, **means, meaning, meant** /mɛ̲nt/; **meaner, meanest. 1** If you ask what a word, expression, or gesture **means**, you want it to be explained to you. EG *What does 'imperialism' mean?... What is meant by the term 'mental activity'?* V+O : NO CONT

2 If you ask someone what they **mean**, you are asking them to explain exactly what they are referring to or intending to say. EG *But what do we mean by 'education'?... I know the guy you mean... I thought you meant you wanted to take your own car... You mean that she disliked Celia?* V+O : OFT+*by*, OR V+REPORT : ONLY *that*

3 You say **'I mean' 3.1** when you are explaining something more clearly or justifying something that you have said. EG *Does she drink? Heavily, I mean... If you haven't any climbing boots, you can borrow them. I mean dozens of people have got boots.* **3.2** when you are correcting something that you have just said. EG *This is Herbert, I mean Humbert.* ADV SEN

4 If something **means** a lot to you, it is important to you. EG *These were the friends who had meant most to her since childhood.* V+O : OFT+*to*, NO CONT

5 If one thing **means** another, it shows that the second thing exists, is true, or will happen. EG *A cut in taxes will mean a cut in government spending... Water running down the outside of a wall may mean that the gutters are blocked.* V+O OR V+REPORT : ONLY *that*, NO CONT

6 If you **mean** what you say, you are serious about it and are not joking, exaggerating, or just being polite. EG *I'm going. I mean it... Anyone can programme a computer. And I do mean anyone.* V+O

7 If you **mean** to do something, you intend to do it. EG *I meant to ring you but I'm afraid I forgot... I'm sorry, I didn't mean to be rude.* V+*to*-INF : NO IMPER

8 If something **is meant** to happen, **8.1** it is intended to happen. EG *Sorry, I'm not very good at drawing, but that's meant to be a cube... 'That hurts!' – 'It's meant to!'... His smile was meant for me.* V+O+*to*-INF OR *for* : USU PASS, NO IMPER **8.2** it is strongly expected to happen or exist. EG *Are parents meant to love all their children equally?... I found a road that wasn't meant to be there.* V-PASS+*to*-INF

9 You can use **mean** when you are talking about the reputation of a person or thing. For example, if something **is meant** to be good, it has a reputation for being good. If it **is meant** to be reliable, it has a reputation for being reliable. EG *They're meant to be excellent cars.* V-PASS+*to*-INF

10 A **means** of doing something is a method or object which makes it possible. **Means** is both the singular and the plural form. EG *Scientists are working to devise a means of storing this type of power... We have the means to kill people on a massive scale... An attempt was made to sabotage the ceremony by violent means.* N COUNT+SUPP ● If something is **a means to an end**, you do it only because it will enable you to achieve what you want. EG *I never enjoyed college, it was just a means to an end.* ● PHRASE

11 If you do something **by means of** a particular method or object, you do it using that method or object. EG *The rig is anchored in place by means of steel cables.* PREP

12 You say **'by all means'** as a way of telling someone that you are willing to allow them to do something. EG *'May I go now?' – 'Yes, yes, by all means.'... By all means take a day's holiday.* CONVENTION Formal

13 By no means is used to emphasize that something is not true. EG *It is by no means certain that this is what he did.* PHRASE

14 You can refer to the money that someone has as their **means**. EG *Sutcliffe has a house in Mayfair so he obviously has means.* N PLURAL Formal

15 Someone who is **mean 15.1** is unwilling to spend much money or to use very much of a particular thing. EG *I used to be very mean about hot water.* ADJ QUALIT ◇ **meanness.** EG *These employers were famous for their meanness.* ◇ N UNCOUNT **15.2** is unkind to someone. EG *She had apologized for being so mean to Rudolph.* ADJ QUALIT : OFT+*to* ◇ **meanness.** EG *...his meanness to his sisters.* ◇ N UNCOUNT

16 No mean is used to indicate **16.1** that a person is good at something. EG *Sir George Gilbert Scott, himself no mean architect, approved the plans.* PHRASE Formal **16.2** that an achievement is a great one. EG *Persuading John to come was no mean feat.* Formal

meander /mi'ændə/, **meanders, meandering, meandered. 1** If a river or road **meanders** somewhere, it has a lot of bends in it. EG *A stream meandered towards the sea.* V : USU+A

2 If you **meander** somewhere, you travel or move there slowly. EG *We meandered along eating nuts and blackberries.* V+A

meaning /mi̲:nɪŋ/, **meanings. 1** The **meaning** of a word, expression, or gesture is the thing that it refers to or expresses. EG *The word 'guide' is used with various meanings... Do you know the meaning of the phrase 'cock-and-bull story'?* N COUNT OR N UNCOUNT

2 The **meaning** of what someone says or of something such as a book or film is the thought or idea that it is intended to express. EG *The meaning of the remark was clear... I don't understand the meaning of Pollock's paintings.* N UNCOUNT OR N COUNT

3 If something has **meaning**, it seems to be worthwhile and to have a real purpose. EG *We yearn for beauty, truth, and meaning in our lives... My prayers had real meaning for me at a very early age.* N UNCOUNT

meaningful /mi̲:nɪŋfʊl/. **1** A **meaningful** sentence or event has a meaning that you can understand. EG *Nobody has ever explained electricity to me in a meaningful way... ...the difficulties of achieving meaningful results from scientific surveys.* ADJ QUALIT

2 A **meaningful** look, expression, or remark is intended to express an attitude or opinion. EG *They exchanged meaningful glances.* ADJ QUALIT ◇ **meaningfully.** EG *'Goodnight, and call again. Anytime,' Boon added meaningfully.* ◇ ADV

3 A **meaningful** relationship, experience, or action is serious and important in some way. EG *He felt the need to establish a more meaningful relationship with people... ...meaningful discussions.* ADJ QUALIT ◇ **meaningfully.** EG *At least you'd be filling your time meaningfully.* ◇ ADV

meaningless /mi̲:nɪŋlɪ²s/. **1** Something that is **meaningless 1.1** has no meaning. EG *These songs are largely meaningless.* **1.2** has no importance or relevance. EG *Taxes made the bonus meaningless.* ADJ QUALIT

2 If you feel that your work or life is **meaningless**, you feel that it has no purpose and is not worthwhile. EG *People arrive at a factory and perform a totally meaningless task from eight to five.* ADJ QUALIT

meant /mɛ̲nt/ is the past tense and past participle of **mean.**

meantime /mi̲:ntaɪm/. **In the meantime** means in the period of time between two events. EG *At long last we were released. In the meantime, our friends had informed the newspapers... I will call Doctor Ford. In the meantime you must sleep.* ADV SEN

meanwhile /mi̲:nwaɪl/ means **1** while something else is happening. EG *She ate an olive. Nick, meanwhile, was talking about Rose.* **2** in the period of time between two events. EG *But meanwhile a number of steps will have to be taken.* ADV SEN

measles /mi̲:zə⁰lz/ is an infectious illness that gives you red spots on your skin. ● See also **German measles**. N UNCOUNT

measly /mi̲:zli¹/. A **measly** amount of something is very small or inadequate. EG *One measly tomato, that's all we've had from this plant!* ADJ QUALIT Informal

measurable /mɛ̲ʒə⁰rəbə⁰l/. If something is **measurable**, it is large enough to be noticed or to ADJ CLASSIF Formal

If someone's friendship means a lot to you, is it meaningful?

be significant. EG *Some measurable progress had been made.*

measure /mɛʒə/, **measures, measuring, measured.** 1 When you **measure** something, you find out how big or great it is by using an instrument or device. You can measure the length of something by using a ruler, for example. EG *He measured the diameter of the artery... The explosive force is measured in tons.* V+O

2 If something **measures** a particular distance, its length, width, or depth is that distance. EG *...small slivers of glass measuring a few millimetres across... ...a square area measuring 900 metres on each side.* V+C

3 A **measure** of something is a certain amount of it. EG *Everyone is entitled to some measure of protection.* N PART : SING Formal

4 A **measure** of a strong alcoholic drink such as brandy or whisky is an amount of it in a glass. EG *He poured himself a generous measure of cognac.* N PART

5 Something that is a **measure** of something else shows how great it is. EG *It is a measure of their achievement that the system has lasted so long.* N SING+*of*

6 A **measure** is also an action carried out by a government or other authority in order to achieve a particular result. EG *Measures had been taken to limit the economic decline.* N COUNT : USU PLURAL Formal

7 If something is done **for good measure**, it is done in addition to a number of other actions, in order to make a situation more complete or satisfactory. EG *The waiter had taken away the plates, and, for good measure, had removed his glass.* ADV SEN

8 See also **measuring, tape measure.**

measure up. If someone or something **measures up** to a standard or to someone's expectations, they are good as is required or expected. EG *The state of repair failed to measure up to their exacting standards.* PHRASAL VB : V+ADV, USU+*to*

measured /mɛʒəd/. A **measured** way of speaking or moving is careful and deliberate. EG *...walking at the same measured pace.* ADJ CLASSIF Literary

measurement /mɛʒəmə²nt/, **measurements.** 1 A **measurement** is a result that you obtain by measuring something. EG *Check the measurements first... ...the exact measurements of the office.* N COUNT

2 **Measurement** is the activity of measuring something. EG *...the first actual measurement of the speed of sound.* N UNCOUNT : OFT+*of*

3 Your **measurements** are the size of your chest, waist, hips, and other parts of your body. N PLURAL

MEASUREMENT

This entry shows some ways of expressing measurements such as sizes, distances, weights, and temperatures.

In speech, the actual words that refer to the unit of measurement, for example 'metres', 'miles', 'kilos', 'litres', or 'degrees', are often left out when it is obvious what you are measuring and what units of measurement you are using. When measurements are used like adjectives in front of a noun, you never use the plural form, so that you say 'a two-litre bottle' and 'a twenty-mile walk'.

Here are some ways of saying how big something is. EG *It was ten feet in height... The visitor was six feet tall... ...people who are over six foot... ...heavy planks of wood about three inches thick... ...a tiny cell four feet wide and seven long... ...a block of ice one cubic foot in size.*

Here are some ways of saying how heavy something is. EG *The largest brain possessed by any dinosaur weighed about a kilogram... ...14,000 tons of potatoes... ...a sixteen-ounce bar of soap.*

Here are some ways of saying how hot something is. EG *...a temperature of four hundred degrees centigrade... The temperature touched 100° Fahrenheit in Los Angeles that day... It had been fourteen below zero when they woke up... The temperature was well above freezing point.*

In the following examples, the speaker is referring to clothing sizes or shoe sizes. EG *'What size do you take?' – 'Ten.'... ...a size 9 shoe.*

measuring /mɛʒə⁰rɪŋ/. A **measuring** jug or spoon is one that is specially designed for measuring quantities, especially in cooking. ADJ CLASSIF : ATTRIB

meat /miːt/, **meats. Meat** is the flesh of a dead animal that people cook and eat. N MASS

mecca /mɛkə/, **meccas.** If you say that a place is a **mecca** for people of a particular kind, you mean that many of them go there because there is something there that interests or attracts them. EG *The United States is still a mecca for film-makers.* N COUNT +SUPP : USU SING

mechanic /mɪ²kænɪk/, **mechanics.** 1 A **mechanic** is someone whose job is to repair and maintain machines and engines. N COUNT

2 The **mechanics** of something are the way in which it works or the way in which it is done. EG *...the mechanics of reading.* N PLURAL : *the*+N

mechanical /mɪ²kænɪkə⁰l/. 1 A **mechanical** device has moving parts and uses power in order to do a particular task. EG *They were using a mechanical shovel to clear up the streets.* ADJ CLASSIF

◊ **mechanically.** EG *The glass doors slid open mechanically as she approached them.* ◊ ADV

2 Someone who has a **mechanical** mind understands how machines work and knows how to repair them. EG *...a given level of mechanical ability.* ADJ CLASSIF : ATTRIB

3 If someone's behaviour is **mechanical**, they are doing something without thinking about it, because they have done it many times before. EG *When invention is left out, dancing becomes mechanical and dull.* ◊ **mechanically.** EG *'How are you?' – 'Oh, fine, thanks,' said Philip mechanically.* ADJ QUALIT ◊ ADV

mechanism /mɛkənɪzə⁰m/, **mechanisms.** A **mechanism** is 1 a part of a device or machine that does a particular task. EG *...a locking mechanism... ...steering mechanisms in cars.* N COUNT : USU+SUPP 2 a way of getting something done within a system. EG *There's no mechanism for changing the decision.* N COUNT+SUPP 3 a part of your behaviour that is automatic and that helps you to survive or to cope with a difficult situation. EG *During this regime, the defence mechanism of disbelief operated.* N COUNT+SUPP

mechanize /mɛkənaɪz/, **mechanizes, mechanizing, mechanized;** also spelled **mechanise.** If a type of work **is mechanized**, it is organized so that it is done by machines. ◊ **mechanized.** EG *Housework has become highly mechanised.* V+O OR V ◊ ADJ QUALIT

◊ **mechanization** /mɛkənaɪzeɪʃə⁰n/. EG *...the mechanisation of the postal service.* ◊ N UNCOUNT

medal /mɛdə⁰l/, **medals.** A **medal** is a small piece of metal with a design on it. Medals are given as awards for bravery or as prizes in sporting events. EG *He won six gold medals.* N COUNT

medallion /mɪ²dæljən/, **medallions.** A **medallion** is a round piece of metal which is worn as an ornament on a chain round a person's neck. N COUNT

medallist /mɛdə⁰lɪst/, **medallists.** A **medallist** is a person who has won a medal in sport. EG *She's an Olympic medallist.* N COUNT

meddle /mɛdə⁰l/, **meddles, meddling, meddled.** If you **meddle** in something, you try to influence or change it without being asked to; used showing disapproval. EG *I dared not meddle with my wife's plans.* V : OFT+*in/with*

media /miːdɪə/. You can refer to television, radio, and newspapers as the **media**. EG *These problems have been exaggerated by the media.* N COLL : *the*+N

mediaeval /mɛdɪi:və^{0}l/. See **medieval**.

mediate /mi:di^{1}eɪt/, **mediates, mediating, mediated.** If you **mediate** between two groups who are involved in a dispute, you try to settle the dispute by finding things that they can both agree to. EG *I mediated for him in a quarrel with his brother... He called on the Red Cross to try to mediate the dispute.* ◇ **mediator, mediators.** EG *Tom Hagen was busy trying to find a mediator satisfactory to both parties.*
V: OFT+*between*; ALSO V+O
◇ N COUNT

medic /mɛdɪk/, **medics.** A **medic** is a doctor or medical student. EG *Navy medics operated on the foot... We had more law students than medics.*
N COUNT Informal

medical /mɛdɪkə^{0}l/, **medicals. 1 Medical** means relating to the treatment of illness and injuries and to the prevention of illness. EG *She had to undergo medical treatment... The medical profession was baffled... ...the medical care of babies.*
ADJ CLASSIF: ATTRIB

2 A **medical** is a thorough examination of your body by a doctor. EG *They were all set to give him a medical.*
N COUNT

medication /mɛdɪkeɪʃə^{0}n/, **medications. Medication** is medicine that is used to cure an illness. EG *The doctor can prescribe medication to relieve the symptoms... Don't forget your medication.*
N UNCOUNT OR N COUNT

medicinal /mɛdɪsɪnə^{0}l/. A **medicinal** substance is used to treat and cure illness. EG *...a medicinal herb... ...the medicinal qualities of a plant.*
ADJ CLASSIF

medicine /mɛdɪ^{0}sɪn/, **medicines. 1 Medicine** is the treatment of illness and injuries by doctors and nurses. EG *...the professions of medicine and dentistry... ...the importance of preventative medicine.*
N UNCOUNT

2 A **medicine** is a substance that you drink or swallow in order to cure an illness. EG *...a medicine for his cold... ...cough medicines... ...the cupboard where the medicines were kept.*
N MASS

medieval /mɛdɪi:və^{0}l/; also spelled **mediaeval. Medieval** means belonging or relating to the period between about 1100 AD and about 1500 AD, especially in Europe. EG *...a medieval church... ...medieval German literature.*
ADJ CLASSIF

mediocre /mi:dɪəʊkə/. Something that is **mediocre** is of poor quality. EG *He spent much of his time reading mediocre paperbacks.* ◇ **mediocrity** /mi:dɪɒkrɪ^{1}ti^{1}, mɛd-/. EG *He was dismayed by the mediocrity of the people working with him.*
ADJ QUALIT
◇ N UNCOUNT

meditate /mɛdɪteɪt/, **meditates, meditating, meditated. 1** If you **meditate** on something, you think about it very carefully and deeply for a long time. EG *He was left alone to meditate on his sins.* ◇ **meditation** /mɛdɪteɪʃə^{0}n/, **meditations.** EG *I hope we will not disturb your meditations.*
V: OFT+*on/upon*
◇ N UNCOUNT OR N COUNT

2 If you **meditate**, you remain in a calm, silent state for a period of time, often as part of a religious training or so that you are better able to deal with the problems and difficulties of everyday life. ◇ **meditation.** EG *He was deeply interested in meditation and yoga.*
V
◇ N UNCOUNT

meditative /mɛdɪtətɪv/. A **meditative** action shows that you are thinking carefully about something. EG *Daniel took a meditative sip of tea... We were both quiet and meditative.* ◇ **meditatively.** EG *He was leaning meditatively on his elbow.*
ADJ CLASSIF
◇ ADV

medium /mi:dɪəm/, **mediums. 1** Something that is of **medium** size, degree, or intensity is at the middle point on a scale; for example, it is neither large nor small, or neither light nor dark. EG *...a medium screwdriver... He was of medium height... ...medium brown.*
ADJ CLASSIF: USU ATTRIB

2 A **medium** is something that you can use to communicate or express things. EG *...sending messages through the medium of paper and printed word... ...the major broadcasting medium.*
N COUNT Formal

3 A **medium** is also a person who claims to be able to speak to people who are dead and to receive messages from them.
N COUNT

medium wave is a range of radio waves which are used for broadcasting.
N UNCOUNT

meek /mi:k/. Someone who is **meek** is timid and does what other people say. EG *...a meek suggestion.* ◇ **meekly.** EG *'I'm sorry dear,' Gretchen said meekly.*
ADJ QUALIT
◇ ADV

meet /mi:t/, **meets, meeting, met** /mɛt/. **1** If you **meet** someone, **1.1** you happen to be in the same place as them and start talking to them. EG *I met a Swedish girl on the train... They met each other at a party in London.* **1.2** you both go separately to the same place at the same time, so that you can talk or do something together. EG *They met every day... Meet me under the clock.* **1.3** you are introduced to them and begin talking to them. EG *Come and meet Tony and Rick.*
V OR V+O: RECIP, NO PASS
V OR V+O: RECIP, NO PASS
V+O: NO PASS

2 If you **meet** someone who is coming to see you or if you **meet** their train, plane, or bus, you go to the station, airport, or bus-stop in order to be with them when they arrive there.
V+O

3 When a group of people **meet**, they gather together for a purpose. EG *Teachers in Tokyo met to discuss our methods.*
V

4 If you **meet** with someone, you have a meeting with them. EG *We can meet with the professor Monday night.*
V+*with* American

5 If something **meets** a need, requirement, or condition, it is large enough or good enough to fulfil it. EG *His income is inadequate to meet his basic needs.*
V+O

6 If you **meet** a problem or challenge, you deal satisfactorily with it.
V+O

7 If you **meet** the cost of something, you provide the money for it.
V+O

8 If you **meet** a situation, attitude, or problem, you experience it. EG *Where had I met this kind of ignorance before?*
V+O

9 If something **meets** with a particular reaction or **is met** with that reaction, it gets that reaction from people. EG *All appeals for aid meet with refusal... His approaches had been met with ill-concealed disdain.*
V-ERG+*with*

10 If you **meet** with success, you are successful. If you **meet** with failure, you are unsuccessful.
V+*with*

11 When a moving object **meets** another object, it hits it or touches it. EG *The heavy club met his head with a crack.*
V OR V+O: RECIP

12 If your eyes **meet** someone else's, you both look at each other at the same time. EG *Their eyes meet, and they smile.*
V OR V+O: RECIP

13 The place where two areas or lines **meet** is the place where they are next to one another or join together. EG *...where this road meets the one from Lairg.*
V OR V+O: RECIP

14 to **make ends meet**: see **end**. • to **meet** someone **halfway**: see **halfway**. • See also **meeting**.

meet up. If you **meet up** with someone, you both go separately to the same place at the same time, so that you can talk or do something together. EG *We planned to meet up with them in Florence.*
PHRASAL VB: V+ADV: OFT+*with*

meeting /mi:tɪŋ/, **meetings. 1** A **meeting** is an event in which a group of people discuss proposals and make decisions together. EG *The committee will consider the proposal at its next meeting... A meeting of physicists had been called.*
N COUNT

2 You can refer to the people attending a meeting as the **meeting**. EG *The meeting agreed with him.*
N SING: *the*+N

3 A **meeting** is also an event in which you meet someone. EG *Christopher Milne vividly remembers his first meeting with Alice.*
N COUNT

megalomaniac /mɛgələ^{6}meɪnɪæk/, **megalomaniacs.** A **megalomaniac** is someone who enjoys being powerful, or who believes that they are more powerful or important than they really are.
N COUNT

Find a word on these pages which has two different plurals.

megaphone

megaphone /mɛgəfəʊn/, **megaphones.** A **megaphone** is a cone-shaped device for making your voice sound louder in the open air. You speak into the small end. N COUNT

melancholy /mɛlənkɒli¹/. **1** If you feel **melancholy**, you feel sad. EG *...a deep, melancholy voice.* ▸ used as a noun. EG *When he left, she sank into melancholy.* ADJ QUALIT Literary ▸ N UNCOUNT

2 You describe something as **melancholy** when it makes you feel sad. EG *We acquainted him with the melancholy truth.* ADJ QUALIT Literary

mellow /mɛləʊ/, **mellows, mellowing, mellowed. 1 Mellow** light is soft and golden. EG *...the mellow sunlight.* ADJ QUALIT

2 Mellow stone or brick has a pleasant soft colour because it is old. EG *...a strange Tudor building in mellow brick.* ADJ QUALIT : ATTRIB

3 A **mellow** sound is smooth and pleasant to listen to. EG *...sophisticated rhythms and a mellow sound.* ADJ QUALIT

4 If someone **mellows** or **is mellowed** by something such as age or alcohol, they become more pleasant or relaxed. EG *He mellowed considerably as he got older... He says that age should have mellowed me.* V-ERG

melodious /mɪ²ləʊdɪəs/. A **melodious** sound is pleasant to listen to. EG *...a low melodious laugh.* ADJ QUALIT Formal

melodrama /mɛlə⁶drɑːmə/, **melodramas.** A **melodrama** is a story or play in which a lot of exciting or sad things happen and in which people's emotions are very exaggerated. EG *...a wildly old-fashioned melodrama about a female spy.* N COUNT OR N UNCOUNT

melodramatic /mɛlə⁶drəmætɪk/. **Melodramatic** behaviour is behaviour in which someone treats a situation as much more serious than it really is. EG *'I've called the police.' – 'Must you be so melodramatic?'* ADJ QUALIT

melody /mɛlədi¹/, **melodies.** A **melody** is a tune. EG *...a simple melody composed by Ronnie Bond.* N COUNT Literary

melon /mɛlən/, **melons.** A **melon** is a large juicy fruit which has a thick green or yellow skin. N COUNT OR N UNCOUNT

melt /mɛlt/, **melts, melting, melted. 1** When something **melts** or when you **melt** it, it changes from a solid to a liquid because it has been heated. EG *The snow and ice had melted... Melt the margarine in a saucepan.* V-ERG

2 When something **melts** or **melts** away, it gradually disappears. EG *Lynn's inhibitions melted... Their differences melted away.* V : OFT+*away*

3 If you **melt** into a crowd of people or into your surroundings, you become not at all noticeable. EG *They often wanted to melt into the teeming millions.* V+*into*

melt down. If you **melt down** an object made of metal or glass, you heat it until it melts. EG *Railings were melted down for cannon.* PHRASAL VB : V+O+ADV

melting pot, melting pots. If you describe a place or situation as a **melting pot**, you mean that lots of people of different kinds get mixed together in it. EG *The city is a melting pot of races.* N COUNT : USU SING

member /mɛmbə/, **members. 1** A **member** of a group is one of the people, animals, or things belonging to the group. EG *Babies usually have milder colds than older members of the family... ...junior members of staff... The weaver bird is a member of the sparrow family.* N COUNT+SUPP

2 A **member** of an organization is a person who has joined the organization. EG *...members of trade unions... He shared the disillusionment of many Party members.* N COUNT : USU+SUPP

3 A **member** country or **member** state is one of the countries that has joined an international organization. EG *All the member countries are under pressure to conform.* ADJ CLASSIF : ATTRIB

4 A **member** is also a Member of Parliament. EG *...John Parker, the Labour member for Dagenham.* N COUNT

Member of Parliament, Members of Parliament. A **Member of Parliament** is a person who has been elected to represent people in a country's parliament. N COUNT

membership /mɛmbəʃɪp/, **memberships. 1 Membership** of an organization is the state of being a member of it. EG *Deacon was questioned about his membership of the Nationalist Party... ...membership fees.* N UNCOUNT

2 The **membership** of an organization is the people who belong to it. EG *Membership declined to half a million.* N COUNT OR N UNCOUNT

membrane /mɛmbreɪn/, **membranes.** A **membrane** is a thin piece of skin which connects or covers parts of a person's or animal's body. EG *...the delicate membranes of the throat.* N COUNT Formal

memento /mɪ²mɛntəʊ/, **mementos** or **mementoes.** A **memento** is an object which you keep because it reminds you of a person or a special occasion. EG *...the Presley badge, a memento of the singer's farewell concert.* N COUNT : OFT+*of*

memo /mɛməʊ/, **memos.** A **memo** is an official note from one person to another within the same organization. EG *He wrote a memo to the War Department asking for more soldiers.* N COUNT

memoirs /mɛmwɑːz/. The book which someone writes about their experiences is called their **memoirs**. EG *He was writing his memoirs of his career abroad.* N PLURAL : USU+POSS

memorable /mɛmə⁰rəbə⁰l/. Something that is **memorable** is likely to be remembered because it is special or unusual. EG *...a memorable train journey.* ADJ QUALIT

memorandum /mɛmərændəm/, **memoranda** or **memorandums.** A **memorandum** is an official note or report from one person to another within the same organization. EG *He received a disturbing memorandum from the chief agent of the Party... ...an office memorandum.* N COUNT Formal

memorial /mɪ²mɔːrɪəl/, **memorials. 1** A **memorial** is a structure built in order to remind people of a famous person or event. EG *...a memorial to Queen Alexandra... ...a war memorial.* N COUNT

2 A **memorial** event, object, or prize is in honour of someone who has died, so that they will be remembered. EG *The book won the 1981 George Orwell Memorial Prize... ...funerals and memorial services.* ADJ CLASSIF : ATTRIB

memorize /mɛməraɪz/, **memorizes, memorizing, memorized;** also spelled **memorise.** If you **memorize** something, you learn it thoroughly so that you can remember it exactly. EG *I was able to read a whole page and memorise it in under three minutes.* V+O

memory /mɛmə⁰ri¹/, **memories. 1** Your **memory** is **1.1** your ability to remember things. EG *...people who have good memories.* N COUNT **1.2** the things that you can remember. EG *A few things stand out in my memory... 'Gregory Temple?' he said aloud, searching his memory.* N SING+POSS

2 A **memory** is something that you remember N COUNT+SUPP

about the past. EG *My memories of a London childhood are happy ones.*
3 You can refer to the **memory** of a dead person as a way of referring to that person. EG *It is an insult to the memory of the brave men who died for their country.* N SING: USU+POSS
4 A computer's **memory** is the part of the computer where information is stored. N COUNT
5 Memory is also used in these phrases. **5.1** If you **lose** your **memory**, you can no longer remember things that you used to know. EG *...a story about somebody who's lost his memory.* **5.2** If you **commit** something **to memory**, you learn it thoroughly so that you can remember it exactly. **5.3** If you do something **from memory**, for example recite a poem or play a piece of music, you do it without looking at anything written or printed. EG *The next day he received the following letter (I quote from memory).* **5.4** If something has happened **within living memory**, there are people alive who can remember it happening. EG *The earthquake in San Francisco is well within living memory.* **5.5** If you do something **in memory of** someone who has died, you do it so that people will remember that person. EG *A fund was launched to set up a monument in memory of the dead men.* PHRASES

men /mɛn/ is the plural of **man.**

menace /mɛnɪ¹s/, **menaces, menacing, menaced. 1** Something or someone that is a **menace** is likely to cause serious harm to a person or thing. EG *These riots are a menace to democracy... ...the menace of totalitarianism.* N COUNT
2 Menace is the quality of being or appearing threatening. EG *There was anger and menace in his eyes.* N UNCOUNT
3 If something **menaces** something else, it is likely to harm it. EG *...the formidable threat that menaces Europe.* V+O
4 If someone **menaces** you, they threaten to harm you. EG *We were menaced by drunks.* V+O

menacing /mɛnɪ¹sɪŋ/. If someone's behaviour is **menacing**, they seem to be intending to harm you. EG *He advanced on me in a menacing fashion.* ADJ QUALIT
◇ **menacingly.** EG *Joy scowled at him and waved her knife menacingly.* ◇ ADV

mend /mɛnd/, **mends, mending, mended. 1** If you **mend** something that is damaged or not working, you do something to it so that it works again or is like it was before. EG *I mended some toys for her... He spent the evening mending socks.* V+O
2 If you are **on the mend**, you are recovering from an illness or an injury. EG *He had some colour in his cheeks and was plainly on the mend.* PHRASE Informal
3 If someone **mends** their **ways**, they begin to behave well after they have been behaving badly. EG *You've got to mend your ways or, next time, you will be sent to prison.* PHRASE

mending /mɛndɪŋ/ is **1** the repairing of clothes that have got holes in them. **2** clothes that you have collected together to be mended. EG *...his mother's basket of mending.* N UNCOUNT

menfolk /mɛnfəʊk/. When women refer to their **menfolk**, they mean the men in their family or community. EG *The wives and mothers would do anything to protect their menfolk.* N PLURAL +POSS

menial /miːnɪəl/. **Menial** work is boring and tiring, and the people who do it have a low status. EG *...menial tasks.* ADJ QUALIT

meningitis /mɛnɪndʒaɪtɪs/ is a serious infectious illness which affects your brain and spinal cord. N UNCOUNT

menopause /mɛnə⁶pɔːz/. The **menopause** is the time during which a woman stops menstruating, usually when she is about fifty years old. N SING OR N UNCOUNT

men's room, men's rooms. The **men's room** is a toilet for men in a public building such as a restaurant. N COUNT American

menstrual /mɛnstrʊ⁰əl/ means relating to menstruation. EG *...the menstrual cycle.* ADJ CLASSIF: ATTRIB

menstruate /mɛnstrʊeɪt/, **menstruates, menstruating, menstruated.** When a woman **menstruates**, blood comes from her womb. Women who are fertile menstruate regularly once a month. ◇ **menstruation** /mɛnstrʊeɪʃə⁰n/. EG *...the onset of menstruation.* V Technical ◇ N UNCOUNT

menswear /mɛnzwɛə/ is clothing for men. N UNCOUNT

-ment, -ments. -ment is used to form nouns that refer to actions or states. For example, 'bombardment' refers to the bombarding of a place, and 'disenchantment' refers to the state of being disenchanted. When these nouns are formed from verbs, they are often not defined in this dictionary, but are treated with the related verb. EG *...the commencement of the flight... ...disillusionment with politics... Tree diseases are largely a result of mismanagement.* SUFFIX

mental /mɛntə⁰l/. **1 Mental** means **1.1** relating to the process of thinking or to intelligence. EG *...mental effort... ...one's mental ability.* ◇ **mentally.** EG *She looked at the bouquets, mentally pricing the blooms.* **1.2** relating to the health of a person's mind. EG *...mental illness... ...the mental health of children.* ◇ **mentally.** EG *He was a sick man, mentally and physically.* ADJ CLASSIF: ATTRIB ◇ ADV ADJ CLASSIF: ATTRIB ◇ ADV
2 A **mental** act is one that involves only thinking and not physical action. EG *...mental arithmetic.* ◇ **mentally.** EG *I have kicked myself mentally a hundred times for that stupidity.* ADJ CLASSIF: ATTRIB ◇ ADV

mental hospital, mental hospitals. A **mental hospital** is a hospital for people who are suffering from mental illness. N COUNT

mentality /mɛntælɪ¹ti¹/, **mentalities.** Your **mentality** is your attitudes or ways of thinking; often used showing disapproval. EG *She says I have a slave mentality.* N COUNT+SUPP

mention /mɛnʃə⁰n/, **mentions, mentioning, mentioned. 1** If you **mention** something, you say something about it, usually briefly. EG *Penny decided not to mention her cold... I mentioned to Tom that I was thinking of going back to work.* V+O OR V+REPORT: OFT+*to*
2 A **mention** is a reference to something or someone. EG *My brother used to go purple in the face at the very mention of my name... Mention was made earlier of the new university course in Japanese.* N COUNT OR N UNCOUNT: OFT+*of*
3 You say **'don't mention it'** as a polite reply to someone who has just thanked you for doing something. CONVENTION
4 You use **not to mention** when adding something to a list in an emphatic way. EG *He's always travelling to Buenos Aires and Delhi, not to mention London and Paris.* PHRASE

mentor /mɛntɔː/, **mentors.** Someone's **mentor** is a person who teaches them and gives them advice. EG *...Harold, my mentor from my student days.* N COUNT Formal

menu /mɛnjuː/, **menus.** A **menu** is a list of the kinds of food that you can eat in a particular restaurant. EG *He ordered the most expensive items on the menu.* N COUNT

MEP /ɛm iː piː/, **MEPs.** An **MEP** is a person who has been elected to the European Parliament. **MEP** is an abbreviation for 'Member of the European Parliament'. N COUNT

mercenary /mɜːsɪnə⁰ri¹/, **mercenaries. 1** A **mercenary** is someone who is paid to fight for countries or groups that they do not belong to. N COUNT
2 Someone who is **mercenary** is interested only in the money they can get; used showing disapproval. ADJ QUALIT

merchandise /mɜːtʃəndaɪz/ is goods that are sold. EG *I'd like to examine the merchandise.* N UNCOUNT

merchant /mɜːtʃənt/, **merchants. 1** A **merchant** is a person who buys or sells goods in large quantities, especially one who imports and exports them. EG *...a textile merchant.* N COUNT: USU+SUPP

Do men refer to other men as 'menfolk'?

2 Merchant seamen or ships are involved in carrying goods for trade. EG *He served for many years in the British Merchant Navy.* ADJ CLASSIF : ATTRIB

merchant bank, merchant banks. A **merchant bank** is a bank that deals mainly with businesses and investment. N COUNT

merciful /mɜːsi¹fʊl/. **1** You describe an event or situation as **merciful** when you think it is fortunate or lucky, especially because it stops someone suffering. EG *Death came as a merciful release.* ADJ QUALIT
◇ **mercifully.** EG *He lay down and soon fell into a mercifully dreamless sleep... Mercifully, I hadn't yet had a puncture.* ◇ ADV OR ADV SEN
2 Someone who is **merciful** shows kindness and forgiveness to people who are in their power. EG *I begged him to be merciful.* ADJ QUALIT

merciless /mɜːsi¹lɪ²s/. Someone who is **merciless** is very strict or cruel and does not show any forgiveness towards people. EG *He had a reputation as a merciless foe of gambling.* ◇ **mercilessly.** EG *Unarmed peasants were beaten mercilessly.* ADJ QUALIT ◇ ADV

mercury /mɜːkjə⁴ri¹/ is a silver-coloured metal that exists as a liquid. It is used, for example, in thermometers. N UNCOUNT

mercy /mɜːsi¹/, **mercies. 1** If you show **mercy** to someone, you do not punish them or treat them as severely as you could. EG *He pleaded for mercy.* N UNCOUNT
2 If you describe an event or situation as a **mercy**, you mean that it is fortunate. EG *What a mercy it was that Maisie had given up drinking... Be thankful for small mercies.* N COUNT
3 If you are **at the mercy of** someone or something, they have complete power over you. EG *This action would leave them at the mercy of industrialised countries.* PHRASE

mere /mɪə/, **merest.** The superlative form **merest** is used to give emphasis, rather than in comparisons.
Mere is **1** used to emphasize how unimportant or minor something or someone is. EG *They were mere puppets manipulated by men in search of power... He had found out only by the merest accident.* **2** used when a quality or action that is usually unimportant has a very strong effect. EG *They feared the impact the mere presence of a political prisoner would have... The merest suggestion of marital infidelity enrages him.* **3** used to emphasize how small a particular amount or quantity is. EG *In Tanganyika, a mere 2 per cent of the population lived in towns.* ADJ CLASSIF : ATTRIB

merely /mɪəli¹/. **1** You use **merely 1.1** to emphasize that something is only the thing you say it is and not something better or more important. EG *This is not genuine. It's merely a reproduction... We accept ideas like this merely because they have never been challenged... 'I killed him,' said Stevens, as casually as if they were merely discussing the weather.* **1.2** to emphasize that a particular amount or quantity is very small. EG *January was merely a month away.* ADV
2 You use **not merely** before the less important of two statements, as a way of emphasizing the more important statement. EG *Much of this new industry was not merely in India; it was Indian-owned... The saints have known God – not merely believed in him.* ADV

merge /mɜːdʒ/, **merges, merging, merged. 1** If one thing **merges** with another or if you **merge** them, they combine together to make one whole thing. EG *They advised their clients to merge with another company... The borough of Holborn was merged with St Pancras and Hampstead... The voices merged with one another.* V-ERG; ALSO V OR V+*with* : RECIP
2 If something **merges** into the darkness or the background, you can no longer see it clearly as a separate object. EG *They were painted so that they would merge into the landscape.* V+*into*

merger /mɜːdʒə/, **mergers.** When a **merger** takes place, two companies or organizations join together. EG *...a merger between the two organizations.* N COUNT

meringue /mə²ræŋ/, **meringues.** A **meringue** is a type of crisp, sweet, white cake made by baking a mixture of sugar and egg white. N COUNT

merit /mɛrɪt/, **merits, meriting, merited. 1** If something has **merit**, it is good or worthwhile. EG *...a work of high literary merit... There is undoubtedly some merit in this argument.* N UNCOUNT Formal
2 The **merits** of something are its advantages or good qualities. EG *...the relative merits of cinema and drama... The first version certainly has the merit of being clear.* N COUNT : USU+POSS
3 If you judge something **on** its **merits**, you base your decision about it on how good or worthwhile it is, rather than on your personal feelings. EG *We endeavour to assess any case on its merits.* PHRASE
4 If something **merits** a particular treatment, it is good enough or important enough to be treated in this way. EG *This experiment merits closer examination... It was not important enough to merit a special discussion.* V+O Formal ◇ ADV

mermaid /mɜːmeɪd/, **mermaids.** In stories, a **mermaid** is a woman with a fish's tail instead of legs, who lives in the sea. N COUNT

merrily /mɛrɪli¹/. If you do something **merrily**, you do it without realizing that there are a lot of problems that you have not thought about. EG *Before you skip merrily on to the next page, pause.* ● See also **merry**. ADV

merriment /mɛrɪmə²nt/ is laughter. EG *She put a hand to her mouth to stifle her merriment.* N UNCOUNT Formal

merry /mɛri¹/. **1** If you are **merry**, you are **1.1** happy and cheerful. EG *My in-laws, a merry band from Bath, had joined us... ...his merry blue eyes.* ADJ QUALIT
◇ **merrily.** EG *Dr Mason laughed merrily.* **1.2** slightly drunk. EG *Harvey was getting quite merry.* ADJ PRED Informal
2 A **merry** sound or sight makes you feel cheerful. EG *...merry music.* ◇ **merrily.** EG *The fire was burning merrily.* ADJ QUALIT ◇ ADV
3 People say **Merry Christmas** to each other at Christmas time. CONVENTION
4 See also **merrily**.

merry-go-round, merry-go-rounds. A **merry-go-round** is a large circular platform with wooden or plastic animals and vehicles on it which children ride on as it turns round. N COUNT

mesh /mɛʃ/, **meshes, meshing, meshed. 1 Mesh** is material like a net made from wire, thread, or plastic. EG *...a fence made of stout wire mesh.* N UNCOUNT
2 If two things **mesh** or **mesh** together, they fit together closely. V OR V+*with* : RECIP

mesmerize /mɛzmərαɪz/, **mesmerizes, mesmerizing, mesmerized;** also spelled **mesmerise.** If you **are mesmerized** by something, you are so interested in it or so attracted to it that you cannot think about anything else. EG *Blanche was mesmerized by his voice.* V+O : USU PASS

mess /mɛs/, **messes, messing, messed. 1** If you say that something is a **mess**, you mean that it is in a very untidy state. EG *I know the place is a mess, but make yourself at home... They went back to see how much mess they'd left behind... We cleared up the mess.* N SING OR N UNCOUNT
2 If you describe a situation as a **mess**, you mean that it is full of problems and trouble. EG *My life is such a mess... It seemed a way out from the mess I'd got myself into.* N COUNT : USU SING
3 If something is **in a mess**, it is untidy or disorganized. EG *Her hair was in a terrible mess... The US economy is now in a mess.* PHRASE
4 A **mess** is also a room or building in which members of the armed forces eat. EG *...a bomb attack on an officers' mess.* N COUNT

mess about or **mess around. 1** If you **mess about** or **mess around**, **1.1** you do things without any particular purpose and do not achieve anything. EG *Some of the lads had been messing around when they should have been working at the other* PHRASAL VB : V+ADV Informal *house.* **1.2** you interfere with things and make them worse or untidy. EG *She didn't want you coming and messing about with things.* **2** If you **mess** someone **about** or **mess** them **around,** you are not honest with them or continually change plans which affect them. V+ADV, USU+*with* V+O+ADV Informal

mess up. 1 If you **mess up** something that has been carefully made or done, you spoil it. EG *That will mess up the whole analysis.* **2** If you **mess up** a room, you make it untidy or dirty. EG *I was used to him messing up the kitchen.* PHRASAL VB: V+O+ADV Informal

mess with. If you **mess with** someone or something dangerous, you become involved with them. EG *We don't mess with heroin or any of that stuff.* PHRASAL VB: V+PREP, HAS PASS Informal

message /mɛsɪdʒ/, **messages. 1** A **message** is **1.1** a piece of information or a request that you send to someone or leave for them when you cannot speak to them directly. EG *Oh, there was a message. Professor Marvin rang. He'd like to meet you on Tuesday... He sent a message to Sir Ian Hamilton saying he was returning.* **1.2** an idea that someone tries to communicate to people, for example in a play or a speech. EG *The play's message is that in the end good and right always triumph.* N COUNT

2 If you say that someone **has got the message,** you mean that they have understood what you have been trying to tell them. EG *If we keep complaining, hospitals, doctors and nurses will eventually get the message.* PHRASE Informal

messenger /mɛsɪndʒə/, **messengers.** A **messenger** is someone who takes a message to someone else or who takes messages regularly as their job. EG *By the time the messenger reached him, the damage had been done.* ● If you send something **by messenger,** a messenger delivers it for you. EG *...a note which had just arrived by messenger.* N COUNT ● PHRASE

Messrs /mɛsəz/ is the plural of 'Mr'. **Messrs** is used especially in the names of businesses. EG *Messrs Brant and Prout are dealers in hats.*

messy /mɛsi[1]/. **1 Messy** activities make people or places dirty or untidy. EG *I hate picnics; they're so messy.* ADJ QUALIT

2 Someone who is **messy** leaves things in a dirty or untidy state. EG *Sometimes I'm neat, sometimes I'm messy.* ADJ QUALIT

3 Something that is **messy** looks unpleasant because it is dirty, untidy, or sticky. EG *...messy bits of food... I disliked the messy farmyard.* ADJ QUALIT

4 A **messy** situation is confused or complicated, and involves trouble for people. EG *Brown had been caught in a messy diplomatic dispute.* ADJ QUALIT Informal

met /mɛt/ is the past tense and past participle of **meet.**

metabolism /mɪ[2]tæbəlɪzə[0]m/, **metabolisms.** Your **metabolism** is the chemical process in your body that causes food to be used for growth and energy. EG *Some people's metabolism is more efficient than others.* N UNCOUNT OR N COUNT Technical

metal /mɛtə[0]l/, **metals. Metal** is a hard substance such as iron, steel, copper, or lead. EG *...a metal spoon... It was made of glass and metal.* N MASS

metallic /mɪ[2]tælɪk/. **1** A **metallic** sound is like one piece of metal hitting another. EG *I heard the metallic click of a door handle.* ADJ QUALIT

2 Metallic things or colours shine like metal. EG *Her hair was a metallic gold.* ADJ CLASSIF

3 Metallic things consist of metal. EG *...metallic ores.* ADJ CLASSIF Technical

metalwork /mɛtə[0]lwɜːk/ is the activity of making objects out of metal. EG *She's good at woodwork and metalwork.* N UNCOUNT

metamorphose /mɛtəmɔːfəʊz/, **metamorphoses, metamorphosing, metamorphosed.** When someone or something **metamorphoses** or **is metamorphosed,** they change into something completely different. EG *The headstrong girl metamorphoses into the loving wife and mother.* V-ERG: OFT+*into* Formal

metamorphosis /mɛtəmɔːfəsɪs/, **metamorphoses** /mɛtəmɔːfəsiːz/. When a **metamorphosis** occurs, a person or thing changes into something completely different. EG *Science fiction may be undergoing a metamorphosis.* N COUNT OR N UNCOUNT Formal

metaphor /mɛtəfə[8]/, **metaphors. 1** A **metaphor** is an imaginative way of describing something by saying that it is something else which has the qualities that you are trying to describe. For example, if you want to say that someone is very shy and timid, you might say that they are a mouse. N COUNT OR N UNCOUNT

2 If you consider one thing to be a **metaphor** for another, you consider it to be a symbol of the other thing. EG *She sees the play as a metaphor for the prisons we create for ourselves.* N COUNT OR N UNCOUNT Literary

metaphorical /mɛtəfɒrɪkə[0]l/. You use the word **metaphorical** to indicate that you are not using words with their ordinary meaning, but are trying to describe something by using an image or symbol. EG *I had sprouted metaphorical wings.* ◊ **metaphorically.** EG *I was literally as well as metaphorically wrapped in cotton wool... I was speaking metaphorically.* ADJ CLASSIF ◊ ADV

mete /miːt/, **metes, meting, meted.** If you **mete out** a particular punishment, you officially order that someone shall be punished that way. EG *Magistrates meted out fines of as much as £1,000.* PHRASAL VB: V+ADV, OFT+*to* Formal

meteor /miːtɪə[8]/, **meteors.** A **meteor** is a piece of rock or metal that burns very brightly when it enters the earth's atmosphere from space. N COUNT

meteoric /miːtɪɒrɪk/. A **meteoric** rise to power or success happens very quickly. EG *He enjoyed a meteoric rise to power in Callaghan's government.* ADJ CLASSIF

meteorite /miːtɪəraɪt/, **meteorites.** A **meteorite** is a large piece of rock or metal from space that has landed on the earth. N COUNT

meteorological /miːtɪərəlɒdʒɪkə[0]l/ means relating to the weather or to weather forecasting. EG *Meteorological conditions were reasonably good.* ADJ CLASSIF: ATTRIB Technical

meter /miːtə/, **meters, metering, metered. 1** A **meter** is a device that measures and records something such as the amount of gas or electricity that you have used. EG *Someone comes to read the gas and electricity meters.* N COUNT

2 If the gas, electricity, or water supplied to your house **is metered,** the amount you use is measured and recorded by a meter. V+O

3 See also **metre, parking meter.**

method /mɛθəd/, **methods.** A **method** is a particular way of doing something. EG *...a change in the method of electing the party's leader... No one knows why they use this method.* N COUNT: OFT+SUPP; ALSO N UNCOUNT

methodical /mɪ[2]θɒdɪkə[0]l/. Someone who is **methodical** does things carefully and in a particular order. EG *With methodical thoroughness they demolished the prison.* ◊ **methodically.** EG *He worked quickly and methodically.* ADJ QUALIT ◊ ADV

meticulous /mɪ[2]tɪkjə[4]ləs/. A **meticulous** person does things very carefully and with great attention to detail. EG *He had prepared himself with meticulous care.* ◊ **meticulously.** EG *...meticulously folded newspapers.* ADJ QUALIT ◊ ADV

metre /miːtə/, **metres;** spelled **meter** in American English. A **metre** is a unit of length equal to 100 centimetres. EG *The blue whale grows to over 30 metres long.* N COUNT

metric /mɛtrɪk/ means relating to the system of measurement that uses metres, grammes, and litres. EG *...the new metric sizes for clothes.* ADJ CLASSIF

metro /mɛtrəʊ/, **metros.** The **metro** is the underground railway system in some cities, for example in Paris. N COUNT: USU *the*+N

metropolis /mɪ[2]trɒpəlɪs/, **metropolises.** A **metropolis** is a very large city. N COUNT

metropolitan /mɛtrəpɒlɪtə[0]n/ means belonging to or typical of a large busy city. EG *...seven* ADJ CLASSIF: ATTRIB

Can you eat microchips?

metropolitan districts in the Midlands... ...the metropolitan delights of cinemas and theatres.

mew /mju:/, **mews, mewing, mewed. 1** When a cat **mews**, it makes a soft high-pitched noise. EG *The cat was mewing for its supper.* V

2 A **mews** is a quiet, old yard or street surrounded by houses. EG *...a rear exit into a quiet mews... ...a tiny mews flat.* N COUNT

mg is a written abbreviation for 'milligram' or 'milligrams'. EG *It contained 65mg of Vitamin C.*

miaow /mi'aʊ/, **miaows, miaowing, miaowed.** When a cat goes **'miaow'**, it makes a short high-pitched sound. EG *That sounds like the miaow of a cat.* N COUNT ▸ used as a verb. EG *There was a cat miaowing outside the front door.* V

mice /maɪs/ is the plural of **mouse.**

mickey /mɪki'/. If you **take the mickey** out of someone, you make fun of them. EG *You're always taking the mickey.* PHRASE Informal

micro /maɪkrəʊ/, **micros.** A **micro** is a small computer. N COUNT

micro- is used to form nouns that refer to a very small example of a particular type of thing. For example, a microcomputer is a very small computer. EG *...the invention of the microcassette... ...diseases caused by micro-organisms.* PREFIX

microbe /maɪkrəʊb/, **microbes.** A **microbe** is a very small living thing, which you can see only if you use a microscope. EG *...the microbes in the human gut.* N COUNT

microchip /maɪkrə⁶tʃɪp/, **microchips.** A **microchip** is a small piece of silicon, for example inside a computer, on which electronic circuits are printed. N COUNT

micro-computer, micro-computers. A **micro-computer** is a small computer. N COUNT

microcosm /maɪkrə⁶kɒzə⁰m/, **microcosms.** A place or event that is a **microcosm** of a larger one has all the main features of the larger one and seems like a smaller version of it. EG *Bristol was a microcosm of urban England in the 1970s... Man was regarded as a microcosm of the universe.* N COUNT: OFT+*of*

microfiche /maɪkrə⁶fi:ʃ/, **microfiches.** A **microfiche** is a small sheet of film on which information is stored in very small print. You read the information by putting the microfiche into a machine which magnifies it and projects it. EG *The Periodicals Catalogue is now on microfiche.* N COUNT OR N UNCOUNT

microphone

microphone /maɪkrə⁶fəʊn/, **microphones.** A **microphone** is a device that is used to make sounds louder or to record them on a tape recorder. N COUNT

microprocessor /maɪkrə⁶prəʊsɛsə/, **microprocessors.** A **microprocessor** is a microchip which can be programmed to do a large number of tasks or calculations. N COUNT

microscope

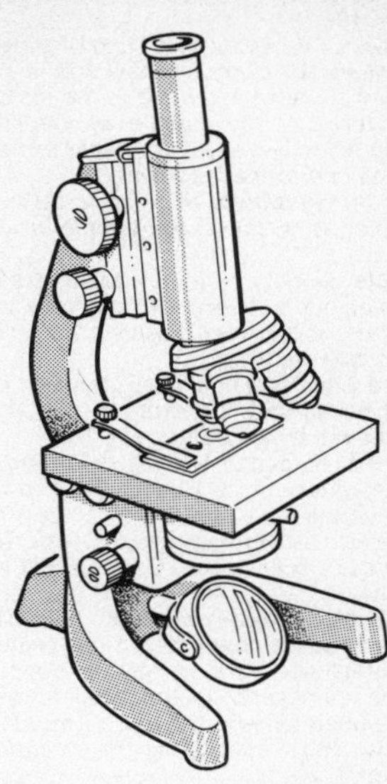

microscope /maɪkrə⁶skəʊp/, **microscopes.** A **microscope** is an instrument which magnifies very small objects so that you can study them. EG *The slides are carefully prepared and examined under the microscope.* N COUNT

microscopic /maɪkrə⁶skɒpɪk/. **1** Something that is **microscopic** is very small. EG *...microscopic forms of life... No-one could decipher my microscopic script.* ADJ CLASSIF

2 A **microscopic** examination of something is very detailed. EG *...a microscopic study of medieval customs.* ADJ CLASSIF

microwave /maɪkrə⁶weɪv/, **microwaves.** A **microwave** or a **microwave oven** is a cooker which cooks food very quickly by short-wave radiation rather than by heat. N COUNT

mid-. 1 mid- is used to form nouns or expressions that refer to the middle part of a period of time. For example the mid-eighteenth century was the middle part of the eighteenth century. EG *It was mid-winter... ...studies published in the mid-1970s... ...the mid-morning sun.* PREFIX

2 mid- is also used to form nouns or adjectives that refer to the middle part of a place. For example, the mid-Atlantic is the middle of the Atlantic. EG *...the Dyfi Valley in mid-Wales... ...mid-ocean ridges.* PREFIX

mid-air. If something happens in **mid-air**, it happens in the air rather than on the ground. EG *The bird turned in mid-air and darted away... ...a mid-air collision.* N UNCOUNT

midday /mɪddeɪ/ is twelve o'clock in the middle of the day. EG *Just before midday the telephone rang... ...a midday meal.* N UNCOUNT

middle /mɪdə⁰l/, **middles. 1** The **middle** of something is the part of it that is furthest from its edges, ends, or outside surface. EG *In the middle of the lawn was a great cedar tree... He sat down in the middle of the front row... ...the white lines painted along the middle of the highway.* N COUNT: USU SING+SUPP

2 The **middle** thing or person in a row or series is the one that has an equal number of things or people on each side, or before it and after it. EG *...the middle button of her black leather coat... She was the middle child of the three.* ADJ CLASSIF: ATTRIB

3 Your **middle** is the front part of your body at N COUNT: USU+POSS your waist. EG *He had a large green towel wrapped round his middle.*

4 The **middle** of an event or period of time is the part that comes after the first part and before the last part. EG *We landed at Canton in the middle of a torrential storm... ...the middle of December.* N SING : *the*+N+*of*

▸ used as an adjective. EG *...the middle fortnight of July... He was in his middle thirties.* ▸ ADJ CLASSIF : ATTRIB

5 If you are **in the middle of** doing something, you are busy doing it. EG *I'm in the middle of washing up.* PHRASE

6 The **middle** course or way is a moderate course of action that lies between two opposite and extreme courses. EG *Between Fascism or revolution there is a middle course.* ADJ CLASSIF : ATTRIB

middle age is the period in your life when you are between about 40 and 60 years old. EG *...a grave, courteous man in late middle age.* N UNCOUNT

middle-aged. Someone who is **middle-aged** is between the ages of about 40 and 60. EG *...a middle-aged businessman.* ADJ CLASSIF

Middle Ages. In European history, the **Middle Ages** were the period between about 1100 AD and about 1500 AD. N PLURAL : *the*+N

middle class, middle classes. The **middle class** or the **middle classes** are the people in a society who are not working class or upper class, for example managers, doctors, and lawyers. EG *...the new Indian middle classes... ...middle class families... Watson's upbringing was comfortably middle-class.* N COUNT : OFT PLURAL

middle distance. The **middle distance** is the area or space between the foreground and the distance in a view or in a painting. EG *He stood at the gate, gazing into the middle distance.* N SING : *the*+N

Middle East. The **Middle East** is a part of Asia. It includes Iran and all the countries in Asia that are to the west and south-west of Iran. N PROPER : *the*+N

Middle Eastern means coming from or relating to the Middle East. EG *...Middle Eastern oil.* ADJ CLASSIF : ATTRIB

middleman /mɪdəˀlmæn/, **middlemen.** A **middleman** is someone who buys things from the people who produce them and sells them to other people at a profit; often used showing disapproval. N COUNT

middle name, middle names. A person's **middle name** is a name that they have which comes between their first name and their surname. N COUNT

middle-of-the-road politicians or opinions are moderate, and usually between two political extremes. EG *...middle-of-the-road Labour MPs.* ADJ QUALIT

middle school, middle schools. A **middle school** is a state school in Britain that children go to between the ages of 8 or 9 and 12 or 13. N COUNT

middling /mɪdlɪŋ/ means of average quality. EG *...a woman of middling intellectual attainments.* ADJ CLASSIF : ATTRIB

midge /mɪdʒ/, **midges. Midges** are very small flying insects which can bite people. N COUNT

midget /mɪdʒɪt/, **midgets.** A **midget** is a very small person. N COUNT

midnight /mɪdnaɪt/. **1 Midnight** is twelve o'clock in the middle of the night. EG *It was nearly midnight.* N UNCOUNT

2 Midnight events happen at midnight or in the middle of the night. EG *We were always having midnight parties on beaches.* N MOD

midriff /mɪdrɪf/, **midriffs.** Your **midriff** is the middle of your body, between your waist and your chest. EG *He was up to his midriff in hot water.* N COUNT

midst /mɪdst/. **1** If you are **in the midst of** a group of people or things, you are in the middle of them. EG *I found him in the midst of a group of his friends... ...sitting in the midst of a pile of presents.* PREP

2 If one event happens **in the midst of** another event, it happens while that event is taking place. If you are **in the midst of** doing something, you are doing it at the moment. EG *In the midst of this humiliating scandal, news arrived of Mr Hodge's resignation... Brody was in the midst of swallowing a bite of egg salad sandwich.* PREP

3 You say that someone is **in** your **midst** in order to draw attention to the fact that they are in your group. EG *We have in our midst two Nobel prize-winners.* PHRASE Formal

midsummer /mɪdsʌmə/ is the period in the middle of the summer. EG *...a hot midsummer day in July.* N UNCOUNT

midway /mɪdweɪ/ means in the middle of a place, distance, or period of time. EG *St Germain is midway between Cherbourg and Granville... She arrived midway through the afternoon.* ADV : USU+PREP

midweek /mɪdwiːk/. If you do something **midweek**, you do it in the middle of the week. EG *The Councils meet midweek... ...a midweek film.* ADV OR ADJ CLASSIF : ATTRIB

midwife /mɪdwaɪf/, **midwives.** A **midwife** is a nurse who advises pregnant women and helps them to give birth. N COUNT

might /maɪt/. **Might** is sometimes considered to be the past form of **may**, but in this dictionary the two words are dealt with separately.

1 If you say that something **might** happen, you mean that it is possible that it will happen. EG *I might even lose my job... I might go to a concert tonight... I thought I might find you here.* MODAL

2 If you say that something **might** be true, you mean that there is a possibility that it is true, but you are not certain. If you say that something **might** have happened, you mean that it is possible that it happened. EG *Don't eat it. It might be a toadstool... He might well have said that. I just don't remember.* MODAL

3 If you say that something **might** have happened, you mean that it was possible for it to have happened although it did not in fact happen. EG *A lot of men died who might have been saved.* MODAL

4 If you ask if you **might** do something, you are asking very politely if someone will allow you to do it. EG *Might I suggest that you offer your manuscript to another publisher?... She asked the man's wife if she might borrow a pen.* MODAL Formal

5 If you say to someone that they **might** do something, **5.1** you are suggesting that they do it. EG *The other thing you might find out is who owns the land.* **5.2** you are telling them in an angry way that they ought to do it. If you tell someone that they **might** have done something, you are telling them in an angry way that they ought to have done it. EG *You might do the washing up for a change!... You might have told me.* MODAL

6 You can use **might** when saying that, although something is true, something else which contradicts it or contrasts with it is also true. EG *They might preach liberty, equality, and fraternity, but their record on human rights is pretty awful.* MODAL

7 You use **might** in expressions such as 'I might have known' and 'I might have guessed' to indicate that you are not surprised at a disappointing event or fact. EG *I might have known he wouldn't come.* MODAL

8 Might is the power or strength that someone has. EG *I tied the rope around the tree and heaved with all my might.* N UNCOUNT +SUPP Literary

mightily /maɪtɪli¹/ means to a great extent or degree. EG *Things have changed mightily since then... He's going to complain mightily.* ADV Outdated

mightn't /maɪtəˀnt/ is a spoken form of 'might not'. EG *It mightn't be true at all.*

might've /maɪtəv/ is an informal form of 'might have', especially when 'have' is an auxiliary verb. EG *Someone might've written you a cheque.*

mighty /maɪti¹/, **mightier, mightiest. 1** Something that is **mighty** is **1.1** very powerful or strong. EG *...this mighty nation... We're dealing with forces that are mightier than ourselves.* **1.2** very large and impressive. EG *...a mighty ship... ...two of Asia's mightiest rivers, the Ganges and the Brahmaputra.* ADJ QUALIT Literary Literary

Is a middle-of-the-road politician likely to be militant?

2 Mighty also means the same as very. EG *It's going to be mighty embarrassing... It was mighty generous of you.* SUBMOD American

migraine /mi:greɪn, maɪ-/, **migraines. Migraine** is an extremely painful headache that makes you feel very ill. EG *Do you suffer from migraine?... The experience had brought on one of her migraines.* N UNCOUNT OR N COUNT

migrant /maɪgrənt/, **migrants.** A **migrant** is a person who moves from one place to another, especially in order to find work. EG *...migrants looking for a place to live... ...migrant workers.* N COUNT

migrate /maɪgreɪt/, **migrates, migrating, migrated. 1** If people **migrate**, they move from one place to another, especially in order to find work. EG *Millions have migrated to the cities.* V : USU+A
◇ **migration** /maɪgreɪʃᵊn/, **migrations.** EG *Migration for work is accelerating in the Third World.* ◇ N UNCOUNT OR N COUNT
2 When animals **migrate**, they go and live in a different area for part of the year, usually in order to breed or to find new feeding grounds. EG *Every spring they migrate towards the coast.* V
◇ **migration.** EG *Swallows begin their migration south in early autumn.* ◇ N UNCOUNT OR N COUNT

mike /maɪk/, **mikes.** A **mike** is a microphone. EG *Is the mike turned on?* N COUNT Informal

mild /maɪld/, **milder, mildest. 1** Something that is **mild** is not strong and does not have any powerful or harmful effects. EG *...a mild detergent... ...mild bleach... A slight fever often accompanies a mild infection.* ◇ **mildly.** EG *Judy mildly protested... The skin may become mildly infected.* ADJ QUALIT; ◇ ADV
2 If someone is **mild**, they are gentle and kind. EG *...my wife's mild nature... His eyes were no longer mild but glittered with fury.* ◇ **mildly.** EG *'No need to shout,' he said mildly.* ◇ **mildness.** EG *The Colonel spoke with great mildness.* ADJ QUALIT; ◇ ADV; ◇ N UNCOUNT
3 Mild weather is warmer than usual, especially in the winter or autumn. EG *The weather was comparatively mild through December.* ADJ QUALIT
4 Mild qualities, attitudes, or emotions are not very great or extreme. EG *It was of mild academic interest only... We looked at each other in mild astonishment.* ◇ **mildly.** EG *It was mildly amusing.* ADJ QUALIT; ◇ SUBMOD

mildew /mɪldju:/ is a soft white fungus that grows on things when they are warm and damp. EG *The hall smelt of mildew.* N UNCOUNT

mildly /maɪldli¹/. **1** See **mild**.
2 You say **to put it mildly** when you are describing something less strongly or less critically than it deserves. EG *He and Connally are, to put it mildly, furious.* PHRASE

mile /maɪl/, **miles. 1** A **mile** is a unit of distance that is 1760 yards. A mile is equal to 1.6 kilometres. EG *The island is 16 miles wide... It'll be a thirty mile drive from here.* N COUNT
2 You can refer to a long distance as **miles**. EG *'Frogstone Road? Where's that?' – 'Miles away.'... I had walked for miles and miles.* N PLURAL
3 If you say that you **are miles away**, you mean that you are not concentrating on what is happening around you, but are thinking about something else. PHRASE Informal

mileage /maɪlɪdʒ/, **mileages. 1** Your **mileage** is the distance that you have travelled, measured in miles. EG *The approximate mileage for the complete journey is 200 miles.* N COUNT OR N UNCOUNT
2 The amount of **mileage** that you get out of a particular course of action is how useful it is to you. EG *There is more mileage in this policy.* N UNCOUNT +SUPP

milestone /maɪlstəʊn/, **milestones. 1** If you refer to an event as a **milestone**, you mean that is is an important event in the history or development of something. EG *The conference in 1913 was a milestone in the history of the party.* N COUNT+SUPP
2 A **milestone** is also a stone by the side of a road showing the distances to particular places.

milieu /mi:ljɜ:/, **milieux** or **milieus.** The **milieu** in which you live or work is the group of people that you live among or work among. EG *I was born in a social milieu where education was a luxury.* N COUNT : USU+SUPP Formal

militant /mɪlɪtənt/, **militants.** Someone who is **militant** is very active in trying to bring about extreme political or social change. EG *...militant trade unionists.* ▸ used as a noun. EG *...a number of well-known militants.* ◇ **militantly.** EG *They became militantly nationalistic.* ◇ **militancy** /mɪlɪtənsi¹/. EG *The League is well known for its militancy.* ADJ QUALIT; ▸ N COUNT; ◇ ADV; ◇ N UNCOUNT

military /mɪlɪtəᵒri¹/. **1 Military** means relating to the armed forces of a country. EG *...military leaders... ...direct military action.* ◇ **militarily.** EG *Britain was no longer a militarily powerful nation.* ADJ CLASSIF : ATTRIB; ◇ ADV
2 The **military** are the armed forces of a country, especially the officers of high rank. EG *The politicians and the military will do nothing.* N COLL : *the*+N

militate /mɪlɪteɪt/, **militates, militating, militated.** If something **militates** against something else, it makes it less likely to happen or succeed. EG *Family tensions can militate against learning for many youngsters.* V+*against* Formal

militia /mɪlɪʃə/, **militias.** A **militia** is an organization that operates like an army but whose members are not professional soldiers. EG *...a building guarded by the local police and militia.* N COUNT OR N UNCOUNT

milk /mɪlk/, **milks, milking, milked. 1 Milk** is the white liquid produced by cows, goats, and some other animals. People drink milk, and use it to make butter, cheese, and yoghurt. EG *He only drinks milk in tea or coffee... ...a glass of milk.* ● See also **skimmed milk**. N UNCOUNT
2 When someone **milks** a cow or goat, they get milk from it by pulling its udders. ◇ **milking.** EG *I had to install milking equipment.* V+O OR V; ◇ N UNCOUNT
3 Milk is also **3.1** the white liquid from a woman's breasts which babies drink. EG *A mother's milk takes care of the baby for many months.* **3.2** a white liquid produced inside coconuts. N UNCOUNT
4 If you **milk** a situation or place, you get as much benefit or profit as you can from it, without caring about the effects on other people. EG *The island was milked by the invaders for five centuries.* V+O

milkman /mɪlkməᵌn/, **milkmen.** A **milkman** is a person who delivers milk to people's homes. N COUNT

milk-shake, milk-shakes. A **milk-shake** is a cold drink made by mixing milk with ice cream and a flavouring. EG *We had a strawberry milkshake.* N MASS

milky /mɪlki¹/. **1** Something that is **milky** is a pale white colour. EG *...clouds of milky smoke.* ADJ COLOUR
2 A drink or food that is **milky** contains a lot of milk. EG *We always had milky coffee at lunchtime.* ADJ QUALIT

mill /mɪl/, **mills, milling, milled. 1** A **mill** is **1.1** a building in which grain is crushed to make flour. EG *He sends his crop to a large mill instead of grinding it himself.* ● See also **windmill**. **1.2** a factory used for making materials such as steel, wool, or cotton. EG *He had worked in a steel mill.* N COUNT; N COUNT+SUPP
2 A **mill** is also a small device used for grinding coffee beans or spices into powder. EG *...a pepper mill.* N COUNT+SUPP
3 If you **mill** something such as wheat, you crush and grind it in a mill. EG *Flour is made by milling grain until a fine powder is formed.* V+O
4 grist to the mill: see **grist**. ● See also **milling**, **run-of-the-mill**.
mill about or **mill around.** When a crowd of people **mill about** or **mill around**, they move around in a disorganized way. EG *Students and staff were milling about.* PHRASAL VB : V+ADV/PREP

millennium /mɪlenɪəm/, **millennia** or **millenniums.** A **millennium** is a period of a thousand years. EG *...a landscape that had remained unchanged for millennia.* N COUNT Formal

milligram /mɪlɪgræm/, **milligrams;** also spelled **milligramme.** A **milligram** is a metric unit of weight that is equal to one thousandth of a gramme. EG *...0.3 milligrams of mercury.* N COUNT OR N PART

millilitre /mɪlɪli:tə/, **millilitres;** spelled **milliliter** in American English. A **millilitre** is a metric unit of volume for liquids and gases that is equal to one thousandth of a litre. EG *...45 millilitres of alcohol.* N COUNT OR N PART

millimetre /mɪlɪmi:tə/, **millimetres;** spelled **millimeter** in American English. A **millimetre** is a metric unit of length that is equal to one tenth of a centimetre. EG *...a silicon chip less than a millimetre thick.* N COUNT OR N PART

milling /mɪlɪŋ/. The people in a **milling** crowd move around in a disorganized way. EG *She escaped unnoticed into the milling crowds.* ADJ CLASSIF : ATTRIB

million /mɪljən/, **millions. 1** A **million** or one **million** is the number 1,000,000. See the entry headed NUMBER. EG *...30 million dollars... ...£980 millions... 'How much?' – 'Half a million.'* NUMBER

2 A **million** or **millions** is often used to mean an extremely large number. EG *...millions of mosquitoes... Her books still give pleasure to millions.* N PART : USU PLURAL

millionaire /mɪljəneə/, **millionaires.** A **millionaire** is a very rich person, especially one who has property worth millions of pounds or dollars. N COUNT

millionth /mɪljənθ/, **millionths. 1** The **millionth** item in a series is the one you count as number one million. See the entry headed NUMBER. EG *Six years later the one-millionth Ford rolled off an assembly line.* ORDINAL

2 A **millionth** is one of a million equal parts of something. EG *...a millionth of a second... ...one ten millionth of an inch.* N COUNT : USU+of

millstone /mɪlstəʊn/, **millstones.** If you describe something as **a millstone round** your **neck**, you mean that it is a very unpleasant problem or responsibility that you cannot escape from. EG *The debt becomes an even bigger millstone round the poor man's neck.* PHRASE

mime /maɪm/, **mimes, miming, mimed. 1 Mime** is the use of movements and gestures to express something or tell a story without using speech. EG *...the re-telling of legends in mime and song... In a brilliant mime, he showed how he managed to support the tray.* N UNCOUNT OR N COUNT

2 If you **mime** something, you describe or express it using mime rather than speech. EG *'Dinner,' I said, and mimed cutting meat... They all vigorously mimed that I should speak quietly.* V+O; ALSO V : OFT+-ING OR REPORT

mimic /mɪmɪk/, **mimics, mimicking, mimicked. 1** If you **mimic** someone's actions or voice, you imitate them in an amusing or entertaining way. EG *I can mimic Cockney speech reasonably well... He mimicked the President cruelly.* V+O

2 A **mimic** is a person who is able to mimic people. EG *One of my brothers is a wonderful mimic.* N COUNT

mimicry /mɪmɪkri[1]/ is the action of mimicking someone or something. EG *...his fine talent for mimicry... ...adolescent mimicry of adult behaviour.* N UNCOUNT

min. is **1** a written abbreviation for 'minimum'. **2** a written abbreviation for 'minute' or 'minutes'.

minaret /mɪnəret/, **minarets.** A **minaret** is a tall, thin tower which is part of a mosque. N COUNT

mince /mɪns/, **minces, mincing, minced. 1 Mince** is meat which has been cut into very small pieces. N UNCOUNT British

2 If you **mince** meat, you cut it into very small pieces. EG *Mince the lean meat finely.* ◊ **minced.** EG *...minced beef.* V+O ◊ ADJ CLASSIF : ATTRIB

3 If you **do not mince** your **words**, you tell someone something unpleasant in a very forceful and direct way. EG *They certainly don't mince their words, do they?* PHRASE

4 If you **mince** your way somewhere, you walk with quick small steps in a very affected or effeminate way. EG *Off he goes, mincing his way across the department store.* V OR V+O

mincemeat /mɪnsmi:t/. **1 Mincemeat** is a sticky mixture of small pieces of dried fruit. It is usually cooked in pastry to make mince pies. N UNCOUNT

2 Mincemeat is also meat such as lamb or beef which has been minced. N UNCOUNT American

mincer /mɪnsə/, **mincers.** A **mincer** is a machine which cuts meat into very small pieces. N COUNT

mind /maɪnd/, **minds, minding, minded. 1** Your **mind** is your ability to think, including all the thoughts that you have. EG *All this confusion in the minds of young people was bound to lead to violence... Somewhere at the back of my mind, I had the feeling I'd seen him before... Anne's got a scientific mind.* N COUNT : OFT+SUPP

2 Mind is used in these phrases about thoughts and memory. **2.1** If your **mind is on** something, you are thinking about it. EG *Her mind was not on the announcements she was making.* **2.2** If something **takes** your **mind off** a problem, it helps you to forget about it for a while. **2.3** If something **comes to mind** or **crosses** or **enters** your **mind**, you think of it suddenly and without making any effort. EG *I just pick up whatever groceries come to mind... Scotland springs to mind as an example... The thought never crossed my mind.* **2.4** If you tell someone to **bear** something **in mind** or to **keep** it **in mind**, you are telling them that they should remember it because it is important or relevant. EG *Bear in mind that these are sixty-five-year-old men.* PHRASES

3 Mind is used in these phrases about worrying. **3.1** If something is **on** your **mind**, you are worried or concerned about it and think about it a lot. EG *Let's hear what's on your mind.* **3.2** If something happens which causes you to stop worrying about something, you can say it is **a load off your mind**, or **a weight off your mind.** PHRASES

4 Mind is used in these phrases about people's intentions. **4.1** If you **have** something **in mind**, you intend or want to have it or to do it. EG *It will be up to her to tell you what she has in mind.* **4.2** If you say you **have a mind to** do something, you mean that you would quite like to do it, although you will probably not do it. EG *If they had a mind to, they could easily get it published... I've a good mind to punish you for behaving so badly... I had half a mind to walk out there and then.* **4.3** If you **put** your **mind to** something, you devote a lot of your energy, effort, and attention to it. EG *You could get a job in London, if you put your mind to it.* PHRASES

5 Mind is used in these phrases about opinions and decisions. **5.1** You use **to my mind** to indicate that you are giving your own opinion. EG *The worst part of air travel to my mind is the hanging around in airport lounges.* **5.2** If you have **an open mind**, you do not form an opinion about something or make a decision about it until you know all the facts. EG *The committee tried to keep an open mind.* **5.3** If you have **a closed mind**, you are unwilling to consider or accept new ideas. **5.4** When you **make** your **mind up**, you decide which of a number of possible things you will have or will do. EG *We have to make up our minds quickly, or they'll go without us... My mind's made up.* **5.5** If you **change** your **mind**, you change a decision you have made or an opinion that you had. EG *All of a sudden I changed my mind and decided not to go anywhere.* **5.6** If you are **in two minds** about something, you are uncertain whether or not to do it. EG *I was very much in two minds whether to apply for the Cambridge job.* PHRASES

6 Mind is also used in these phrases. **6.1** If you say that nobody **in** their **right mind** would do something, you mean that you would be very surprised if anyone did it because you think it is foolish or unreasonable. EG *What woman in her right mind would marry a man like that?* **6.2** If you see something in your **mind's eye**, you imagine it and have a clear picture of it in your mind. EG *In her mind's eye, she had pictured herself in the new* PHRASES

If you wouldn't mind some mineral water, would you be very thirsty?

house. **6.3** Your **state of mind** is your mental state at a particular time. EG *She was in a fairly disturbed state of mind.*

7 If you say that you do not **mind** something, you mean that you are not annoyed or bothered by it. EG *I don't mind personal questions at all... You probably do mind, but you're too polite to say so... I don't mind walking... I hope you don't mind, I came early... Do you mind if I stay here?* V+O; ALSO V : OFT+-ING OR REPORT : USU WITH BROAD NEG

8 If you are offered a choice and you say **'I don't mind'**, you mean that you will be happy with any of the things offered. EG *'Tea or coffee?' – 'I don't mind.'* CONVENTION

9 If you say that you **wouldn't mind** something, you mean that you would quite like it. EG *I wouldn't mind a Renault myself.* PHRASE

10 You say **never mind** **10.1** to try and make someone feel better when they have failed to do something or when something unpleasant has happened to them. **10.2** to indicate that something is not important, especially when someone is apologizing to you. EG *Some of their towels are soaking wet, but never mind.* **10.3** to tell someone that they need not do something, because it is not important or because you will do it yourself. EG *What's it like? Oh, never mind, I'll go and see for myself... Never mind about those, Sam!* PHRASE Spoken

11 If you tell someone to **mind** something, you are warning them to be careful so that they do not get hurt or do not damage something. EG *Mind the ice on the step as you go... Mind my specs!* V+O : ONLY IMPER ● You say **'mind out'** as an urgent warning to someone that they are about to get hurt or to damage something. ● EXCLAM Informal British

12 You use **mind** when you are reminding someone of something they must do. EG *Mind you watch that programme tonight.* V+REPORT : ONLY IMPER

13 If you **mind** a child or something such as a shop or luggage, you look after it for someone else for a while. EG *She can get a neighbour to come in and mind the child... My mother is minding the office.* V+O

14 You use **mind you** to emphasize the piece of information that you are adding or the point that you are making, especially when it contrasts with what you have just said. EG *Charles is fit and well. Not happy, mind you, just fit and well.* ADV SEN

15 to **mind** your **own business**: see **business**.

minded /maɪndɪd/. If someone is **minded** to do something, they want or intend to do it. EG *...a country which seems minded to offer total resistance... He can stop here if he is so minded.* ADJ PRED : USU+*to*-INF Formal

minder /maɪndə/, **minders.** A **minder** is **1** a person whose job is to look after someone, for example a child or an old person. EG *...a babyminder.* N COUNT+SUPP **2** a person whose job is to protect someone such as a businessman. N COUNT Informal

mindful /maɪndfʊl/. If you are **mindful** of something, you think about it and consider it when taking action. EG *Be mindful of the needs of others.* ADJ PRED+*of* OR REPORT

mindless /maɪndlɪ²s/. **1 Mindless** actions are regarded as stupid and destructive. EG *...mindless violence... ...the mindless pollution of our cities.* ADJ CLASSIF : ATTRIB

2 A **mindless** job or activity is one that is so simple or is repeated so often that you do not need to think about it. EG *...mindless routine tasks.* ADJ CLASSIF

mine /maɪn/, **mines, mining, mined. 1** A speaker or writer uses **mine** to indicate that something belongs or relates to himself or herself. EG *Margaret was a very old friend of mine... I took her hands in mine... He gave it to me, it's mine.* PRON POSS

2 A **mine** is a place where people dig deep holes and tunnels under the ground in order to get out coal, diamonds, or gold. EG *...a coal mine.* N COUNT

3 If you **mine** coal, diamonds, or gold, you obtain that substance from the ground by digging deep holes and tunnels. EG *They mine their own coal and ore... ...mining for gold.* V+O; ALSO V : OFT+*for*

4 A **mine** is also a bomb which is hidden in the ground or in water and which explodes when people or things touch it. N COUNT

5 If you **mine** an area of land or water, you place mines there. EG *Eight miles of ground had been heavily mined.* V+O

6 If you say that someone is a **mine of information**, you mean that they know a great deal. PHRASE

7 See also **mining**.

minefield /maɪnfi:ld/, **minefields. 1** A **minefield** is an area of land or water where explosive mines have been hidden. N COUNT

2 If you describe a situation as a **minefield**, you mean that it is full of hidden dangers or problems. EG *This could be a political minefield.* N COUNT : USU+SUPP

miner /maɪnə/, **miners.** A **miner** is a person who works underground in mines in order to obtain coal, diamonds, or gold. EG *My grandfather was a coal miner.* N COUNT

mineral /mɪnə⁰rəl/, **minerals.** A **mineral** is a substance such as tin, salt, uranium, or coal that is formed naturally in rocks and in the earth. EG *...a continent exceptionally wealthy in minerals... ...rich mineral deposits.* N COUNT

mineral water is water that comes out of the ground naturally and is often considered healthy to drink. N UNCOUNT

mingle /mɪŋgə⁰l/, **mingles, mingling, mingled.**
1 If things such as sounds, feelings, or smells **mingle** or **are mingled**, they become mixed together. EG *His cries mingled with theirs... Sand and dust mingled with the blood.* V OR V+*with* : RECIP ◇ **mingled.** EG *He loved the mingled smell of jasmine and food in the air... John watched her with mingled dismay and pleasure.* ◇ ADJ CLASSIF

2 If you **mingle**, you move around within a group of people and chat to people you do not know. EG *Get out and mingle a bit... She invited me to drop in and mingle with the guests.* V : OFT+*with*

mini- is used to form nouns that refer to something which is a smaller or less important version of something else. For example, a mini-computer is a computer which is much smaller than a normal computer. EG *He was taken to school by minibus... ...the Chancellor's mini-budget.* PREFIX

miniature /mɪnɪtʃə/, **miniatures. 1** A **miniature** thing is a small copy of something that is usually much larger. EG *...tiny squares and miniature archways... They look like miniature sharks.* ADJ CLASSIF : ATTRIB

2 If you describe one thing as another thing **in miniature**, you mean that it is smaller than the other thing, but otherwise exactly the same. EG *It was an Austrian chalet in miniature.* PHRASE

3 A **miniature** is a very small, detailed painting, often of a person. EG *I collect early English miniatures.* N COUNT

miniaturize /mɪnɪtʃəraɪz/, **miniaturizes, miniaturizing, miniaturized;** also spelled **miniaturise.** If you **miniaturize** a machine, you produce a very small version of it. EG *We miniaturize spacecraft components.* V+O ◇ **miniaturized.** EG *...a miniaturized video recorder... ...miniaturized telescoping systems.* ◇ ADJ CLASSIF : ATTRIB ◇ **miniaturization** /mɪnɪtʃəraɪzeɪʃə⁰n/. EG *...the miniaturization of electronic components.* ◇ N UNCOUNT

minibus /mɪni¹bʌs/, **minibuses.** A **minibus** is a van with seats in the back, which is used as a small bus. EG *We went to school by minibus.* N COUNT, OR *by*+N

minimal /mɪnɪmə⁰l/. Something that is **minimal** is very small in quantity or degree. EG *My knowledge of German was minimal.* ADJ CLASSIF ◇ **minimally.** EG *At that stage the welfare state was only minimally developed.* ◇ ADV Formal

minimize /mɪnɪmaɪz/, **minimizes, minimizing, minimized;** also spelled **minimise.** If you **minimize** something, **1** you reduce it to the smallest amount or degree possible, or prevent it increasing beyond that amount or degree. EG *Our aim must be to minimize the risks... Crop rotations will help to minimise disease.* **2** you make it seem smaller or less important than it really is. EG *He was careful to minimise his role in these proceedings.* V+O

minimum /mɪnɪməᵊm/. **1** The **minimum** amount of something is the smallest that is possible, allowed, or required. EG *...the minimum level of taxation... You need a minimum deposit of $20,000... He only aims to study for the minimum time.* — ADJ CLASSIF: ATTRIB

2 The **minimum** is the smallest amount of something that is possible, allowed, or required. EG *Two hundred pounds is the bare minimum... Practise each day for a minimum of twenty minutes.* — N SING: USU+SUPP

mining /maɪnɪŋ/ is the industry and activities connected with getting coal, diamonds, or other minerals from the ground. EG *...coal mining... ...mining areas... ...a mining engineer.* — N UNCOUNT

minister /mɪnɪstə/, **ministers, ministering, ministered. 1** A **minister** is a person who is in charge of a particular government department. EG *...the minister for Scottish affairs.* • See also **Prime Minister**. — N COUNT

2 A **minister** in a church, especially a Protestant church, is a member of the clergy. — N COUNT

minister to. If you **minister to** people or to their needs, you make sure that they have everything they need or want. EG *Anne had spent her life ministering to the needs of her husband.* — PHRASAL VB: V+PREP, HAS PASS Formal

ministerial /mɪnɪstɪərɪəl/ means relating to a government minister or government ministry. EG *We cannot afford a ministerial crisis.* — ADJ CLASSIF: ATTRIB

ministrations /mɪnɪstreɪʃəᵊnz/. A person's **ministrations** are the things that they do to help or care for someone in a particular situation. EG *I thanked him for his spiritual ministrations.* — N PLURAL: USU+POSS Formal

ministry /mɪnɪstrɪᶦ/, **ministries. 1** A **ministry** is a government department that deals with a particular area of administration within a country. EG *...the Ministry of Energy... The ministry will have no alternative but to cut its expenditure.* — N COUNT: USU+SUPP

2 The **ministry** of a member of the clergy or of a religious person is the work that they do according to their religious beliefs. EG *The central message of Christ's ministry was the concept of grace.* — N COUNT

3 The **ministry** consists of members of the clergy, usually Protestant ones. EG *Michael had intended to join the ministry.* — N SING: *the*+N

mink /mɪŋk/, **minks. 1 Mink** is a very expensive fur that is used to make coats or hats. — N UNCOUNT

2 A **mink** is a small furry animal. — N COUNT

minor /maɪnə/, **minors. 1** You use **minor** to describe something that is not as important, serious, or significant as other things of the same sort. EG *The police were called to quell a minor disturbance... ...minor injuries... ...a rather minor artist.* — ADJ QUALIT: USU ATTRIB

2 A **minor** key is one of the two types of key in which most European music is written. It is based on a scale of notes in which the third note is one and a half tones higher than the first note. EG *...Chopin's Scherzo in B flat minor.* — ADJ CLASSIF

3 A **minor** is a person who is still legally a child. In Britain, people are minors until they reach the age of eighteen. — N COUNT

minority /mɪ[5]nɒrɪᶦtiᶦ/, **minorities. 1** The **minority** of people or things in a group is a number of them that form less than half of the whole group. EG *Only a small minority of children get a chance to benefit from this system... They are a minority group.* — N SING: USU+*of* • If a group is **in a minority** or **in the minority**, they form less than half of a larger group. EG *Artistic people are in a tiny minority in this country.* — • PHRASE

2 A **minority** is a group of people of a particular race or religion who live in a place where most of the people around them are of a different race or religion. EG *Our aim is to improve relations between police and the ethnic minorities.* — N COUNT

mint /mɪnt/, **mints, minting, minted. 1 Mint** is a type of herb that is used in cooking. EG *...a sprig of mint... ...mint tea.* — N UNCOUNT

2 A **mint** is a sweet with a peppermint flavour. EG *...a packet of mints.* — N COUNT

3 The place where the official coins of a country are made is called the **mint**. EG *The Mint has decided to issue the new coins next year.* — N SING: *the*+N

4 When coins or medals **are minted**, they are made in a mint. EG *One of the coins, dated 1693, was minted in Portuguese Africa.* — V+O: USU PASS

5 If something is **in mint condition**, it is in very good condition, as if it was new. — PHRASE

minus /maɪnəs/, **minusses** or **minuses. 1** You use **minus** to show that one number is being subtracted from another. For example, 'five minus three' means the same as 'three subtracted from five'. You represent this in figures as '5 – 3'. EG *Twenty-eight minus two is twenty-six.*

2 A **minus** is a minus sign. EG *There should be a minus there.* — N COUNT

3 Minus is used when you talk about temperatures. For example, **minus** four means four degrees less than zero. EG *Temperatures there are colder than minus 20°C.* — ADJ CLASSIF: ATTRIB

4 Minus is also used in grading work in schools and colleges. An A minus is a better grade than a B plus, but it is not as good as an A. — ADJ AFTER N

minuscule /mɪnəskjuːl/. Something that is **minuscule** is very small indeed. EG *He had to live in this minuscule room.* — ADJ QUALIT

minus sign, minus signs. A **minus sign** is the sign (–) which is put between two numbers in order to show that the second number is being subtracted from the first one. — N COUNT

minute, minutes; pronounced /mɪnɪt/ when it is a noun and /maɪnjuːt/ when it is an adjective.

1 A **minute** is one of the sixty equal parts of an hour. EG *Davis was ten minutes late... An accident had taken place only a few minutes before... This will take about twenty minutes to do.* — N COUNT

2 You can use **a minute** to mean a short time. EG *Will you excuse me if I sit down for a minute?... Wait there a minute... Can I just finish doing this? I won't be a minute.* — N SING: USU *a/one*+N Spoken

3 Minute is also used in these phrases. **3.1** If you do something **the minute** that something else happens, you do it as soon as the other thing happens. EG *Ask for help the minute you're stuck.* **3.2** If you do something **at the last minute**, you do it at the last possible time that it can be done. EG *They were only rescued at the last minute... Why do you always leave things to the last minute?* • See also **last-minute**. **3.3** If you say that something must be done **this minute**, you mean that it must be done immediately. EG *She doesn't have to make a decision this minute.* **3.4** If you say that something will happen at **any minute**, you mean that it is likely to happen very soon. EG *Mrs Curry was going to cry any minute.* **3.5** See also **up-to-the-minute**. — PHRASES

4 The **minutes** of a meeting are the written records of what is said or decided there. EG *You must learn how to take minutes.* — N PLURAL

5 Something that is **minute** is extremely small. EG *...minute amounts of fluoride... I had remembered in minute detail everything that had happened.* — ADJ QUALIT

minutely /maɪnjuːtlɪᶦ//. **1** If you examine something **minutely**, you examine it very carefully, paying attention to small details. EG *She began examining it minutely from all angles.* — ADV

2 Minutely also means very slightly. EG *His fingers trembled minutely.* — ADV

minutiae /maɪnjuːʃiiː, -ʃɪaɪ/ are small, unimportant details. EG *He has little time for the minutiae of the game.* — N PLURAL Formal

miracle /mɪrəkəᵊl/, **miracles. 1** A **miracle** is a wonderful and surprising event, often one which people believe was caused by God. EG *People said that it was a miracle of God... ...a miracle cure.* — N COUNT

2 You can refer to a very surprising and fortunate — N COUNT

If someone is mischievous, are they misbehaving?

event as a **miracle**. EG *My father got a job. It was a miracle.*

miraculous /mɪræ̲kjə⁴ləs/. **1** Something that is **miraculous** has been caused by a miracle. EG *...the miraculous powers of the saint.* ADJ CLASSIF

2 You can describe something that is very surprising and fortunate as **miraculous**. EG *I had been expecting some miraculous change to occur.* ADJ QUALIT

◊ **miraculously.** EG *This time, the door miraculously opened... It seemed, miraculously, that everyone was satisfied.* ◊ ADV OR ADV SEN

3 You can also use **miraculous** to describe something that is extremely beautiful. EG *...fossils of a near miraculous perfection.* ADJ QUALIT

mirage /mɪ̲rɑːʒ/, **mirages.** A **mirage** is **1** an image which you see in the distance or in the air in very hot weather, but which does not actually exist. N COUNT

2 something in the future that you look forward to, but that never actually happens. EG *The promised land turns out to be a mirage.*

mirror /mɪ̲rə/, **mirrors, mirroring, mirrored. 1** A **mirror** is a flat piece of glass which reflects light, so that when you look at it you can see yourself reflected in it. EG *She stared at herself in the mirror.* N COUNT

2 If water **mirrors** something, it reflects it, like a mirror. EG *The clear water mirrored the blue sky.* V+O Literary

3 If one thing **mirrors** another thing, it has similar features to it, and therefore seems like a copy of it. EG *In the country political allegiances mirrored existing divisions in society.* V+O : IF PASS THEN+*in/by* Formal

mirth /mɜ̲ːθ/ is amusement which you express by laughing. EG *His anger gave place to mirth.* N UNCOUNT Literary

mis- is used at the beginning of words to indicate that something is done badly or wrongly. For example, if you mismanage something, you manage it badly. EG *He had misjudged the situation... ...the risks of miscalculation... ...the misuse of psychiatry.* PREFIX

misadventure /mɪsədve̲ntʃə/, **misadventures.** A **misadventure** is an unfortunate incident. EG *...a funny story about a friend's misadventure... ...a verdict of death by misadventure.* N COUNT OR N UNCOUNT Formal

misapprehension /mɪsæpri¹he̲nʃə⁰n/, **misapprehensions.** A **misapprehension** is a wrong idea or impression that you have about something. EG *I was still under a misapprehension as to the threat contained in the letter.* N COUNT OR N UNCOUNT

misappropriate /mɪsəprə̲ʊpri¹eɪt/, **misappropriates, misappropriating, misappropriated.** If you **misappropriate** money, you take it and use it for your own purposes, although it does not belong to you. ◊ **misappropriation** /mɪsəprəupri¹e̲ɪʃə⁰n/. EG *He had been held responsible for the misappropriation of certain funds.* V+O Formal ◊ N UNCOUNT

misbehave /mɪsbi¹he̲ɪv/, **misbehaves, misbehaving, misbehaved.** If someone, especially a child, **misbehaves**, they behave in a way that is not acceptable to other people. EG *When children misbehave, their parents shouldn't become angry.* V

misbehaviour /mɪsbi¹he̲ɪvjə/; spelled **misbehavior** in American English. **Misbehaviour** is behaviour that is not acceptable to other people. N UNCOUNT

miscalculate /mɪskæ̲lkjə⁴leɪt/, **miscalculates, miscalculating, miscalculated.** If you **miscalculate**, you make a mistake in judging a situation or in making a calculation. EG *He badly miscalculated the response to his proposal.* V OR V+O

◊ **miscalculation** /mɪskælkjə⁴le̲ɪʃə⁰n/, **miscalculations.** EG *These miscalculations had serious consequences.* ◊ N COUNT OR N UNCOUNT

miscarriage /mɪskæ̲rɪdʒ/, **miscarriages.** If a woman has a **miscarriage**, she gives birth to a foetus before it is properly formed, with the result that it cannot live. N COUNT OR N UNCOUNT

miscarry /mɪskæ̲ri¹/, **miscarries, miscarrying, miscarried. 1** If a woman **miscarries**, she has a miscarriage. EG *Emma miscarried and nearly died.* V

2 If a plan **miscarries**, it goes wrong and fails. EG *Our scheme had miscarried.* V

miscellaneous /mɪsəle̲ɪnɪəs/. **Miscellaneous** groups of things or people are very different from each other. EG *...a miscellaneous collection of tools... ...miscellaneous enemies of authority.* ADJ QUALIT

mischief /mɪ̲stʃɪf/ is **1** eagerness to have fun, especially by embarrassing people or by playing tricks. EG *Her face was kind, her eyes full of mischief... There was about him an air of mischief.* N UNCOUNT

2 naughty behaviour by children. EG *He was old enough to get into mischief and get beaten.*

mischievous /mɪ̲stʃɪvəs/. **1** A **mischievous** person is eager to have fun, especially by embarrassing people or by playing tricks. EG *He was saucy and mischievous... ...a mischievous smile.* ADJ QUALIT

◊ **mischievously.** EG *Kitty winked mischievously.* ◊ ADV

2 A **mischievous** child is often naughty but does not do any real harm. ADJ QUALIT

misconceived /mɪskə⁷nsi̲ːvd/. A plan or method that is **misconceived** is not the right one for a particular situation and is therefore not likely to succeed. EG *Their whole approach was misconceived.* ADJ QUALIT : USU PRED

misconception /mɪskənse̲pʃə⁰n/, **misconceptions.** A **misconception** is a wrong idea that you have about something. EG *Another misconception is that cancer is infectious... People have the oddest misconceptions about doctors.* N COUNT

misconduct /mɪskɒ̲ndʌkt/ is bad or unacceptable behaviour, especially by a professional person. EG *They were victims of government misconduct.* N UNCOUNT

misdemeanour /mɪsdə¹mi̲ːnə/, **misdemeanours;** spelled **misdemeanor** in American English. A **misdemeanour** is an act that people consider to be shocking or unacceptable. EG *They listened to accounts of his misdemeanours.* N COUNT OR N UNCOUNT Formal

misdirect /mɪsdɪre̲kt/, **misdirects, misdirecting, misdirected. 1** If someone's energy or qualities **are misdirected**, they are used wrongly or inappropriately. EG *Those qualities of leadership could be misdirected.* ◊ **misdirected.** EG *...a misdirected economic system.* V+O : USU PASS Formal ◊ ADJ CLASSIF

2 If you **misdirect** someone, you send them to the wrong place. EG *Passengers for half a dozen flights had been misdirected to the same gate.* V+O

miser /ma̲ɪzə/, **misers.** A **miser** is a person who enjoys saving money and hates spending it; used showing disapproval. EG *Soon she discovered she had married a miser.* N COUNT

miserable /mɪ̲zə⁰rəbə⁰l/. **1** If you are **miserable**, you are very unhappy. EG *Rudolph felt depressed and miserable... They all had miserable faces.* ADJ QUALIT

◊ **miserably.** EG *He looked up miserably.* ◊ ADV

2 If you describe a place or situation as **miserable**, you mean that it makes you feel depressed. EG *Being without a grant is really miserable.* ADJ QUALIT

3 You can describe the weather as **miserable** when it is raining or cold. EG *...a miserable Monday morning.* ADJ QUALIT

4 You can describe something as **miserable** when you think that it is too small. EG *He was given a miserable little room.* ◊ **miserably.** EG *There was one miserably small piece left.* ADJ CLASSIF ◊ SUBMOD

5 A **miserable** failure is very disappointing or humiliating. EG *The play was a miserable failure.* ADJ CLASSIF : ATTRIB

◊ **miserably.** EG *I failed miserably.* ◊ ADV

miserly /ma̲ɪzəli¹/. Someone who is **miserly** is very mean and hates spending money. EG *...a miserly old lady.* ADJ QUALIT

misery /mɪ̲zə⁰ri¹/, **miseries. 1 Misery** is **1.1** great unhappiness. EG *I am ill with misery... ...the miseries of unemployment.* N UNCOUNT OR N COUNT **1.2** the unpleasant living conditions of people who are very poor. EG *They argued for a law to insure people against poverty and misery.* N UNCOUNT

2 If someone **makes** your **life a misery**, they make you unhappy by behaving in an unpleasant way towards you. PHRASE

misfire /mɪsfaɪə/, **misfires, misfiring, misfired.** If a plan **misfires**, it goes wrong. EG *The use of force in support of their demands had misfired.* — V

misfit /mɪsfɪt/, **misfits.** A **misfit** is a person who is not easily accepted by other people, often because their behaviour is very different from everyone else's. EG *In such societies there have always been misfits.* — N COUNT

misfortune /mɪsfɔːtʃən/, **misfortunes.** A **misfortune** is something very undesirable that happens to you. EG *The violinist had the misfortune to turn over two pages at once... They had suffered their share of misfortune.* — N COUNT OR N UNCOUNT

misgiving /mɪsgɪvɪŋ/, **misgivings.** If you have **misgivings** about something, you are worried or unhappy about it. EG *The firm's collapse seemed to confirm their misgivings... I was filled with misgiving about the whole venture.* — N PLURAL OR N UNCOUNT

misguided /mɪsgaɪdɪ[2]d/. **Misguided** opinions and attitudes are wrong, because they are based on wrong information or beliefs. EG *...Sir Terence's view was misguided... ...misguided idealism... ...a misguided genius.* — ADJ QUALIT

mishap /mɪshæp/, **mishaps.** A **mishap** is an unfortunate but not very serious event that happens to you. EG *Tell your mother you have arrived here without mishap... Loss of your property and other mishaps can spoil your stay.* — N COUNT OR N UNCOUNT

misinform /mɪsɪnfɔːm/, **misinforms, misinforming, misinformed.** If you **are misinformed**, you are told something that is wrong or inaccurate. EG *Unfortunately we were misinformed about the purpose of the fund.* — V+O : USU PASS +*about*

misinformation /mɪsɪnfə[8]meɪʃə[0]n/ is deliberately incorrect information. EG *...a piece of blatant misinformation.* — N UNCOUNT

misinterpret /mɪsɪntɜːprɪt/, **misinterprets, misinterpreting, misinterpreted.** If you **misinterpret** something, you understand it wrongly. EG *He saw the smile and misinterpreted it as friendliness.* ◊ **misinterpretation** /mɪsɪntɜːprɪ[2]teɪʃə[0]n/, **misinterpretations.** EG *The new version was less open to misinterpretation... ...their misinterpretation of Scripture.* — V+O; ◊ N UNCOUNT OR N COUNT

misjudge /mɪsdʒʌdʒ/, **misjudges, misjudging, misjudged.** If you **misjudge** someone or something, you form an incorrect idea or opinion about them. EG *I had rather misjudged the timing of the operation.* — V+O

misjudgement /mɪsdʒʌdʒmə[2]nt/, **misjudgements;** also spelled **misjudgment.** A **misjudgement** is the forming of an incorrect idea or opinion about someone or something. EG *They were guilty of a serious misjudgement.* — N COUNT OR N UNCOUNT

mislay /mɪsleɪ/, **mislays, mislaying, mislaid.** If you **mislay** something, you lose it, because you put it somewhere and then forget where it is. EG *I fear I have mislaid my bus ticket.* — V+O

mislead /mɪsliːd/, **misleads, misleading, misled** /mɪsled/. If you **mislead** someone, you make them believe something which is not true. EG *The public has been misled by the optimism surrounding the agreement... They were misled into buying a car.* — V+O

misleading /mɪsliːdɪŋ/. Something that is **misleading** gives you a wrong idea or impression. EG *...misleading information.* — ADJ QUALIT

misled /mɪsled/ is the past tense and past participle of **mislead.**

mismanage /mɪsmænɪdʒ/, **mismanages, mismanaging, mismanaged.** If you **mismanage** something, you organize or deal with it badly. EG *The local people thought that education was being mismanaged.* ◊ **mismanagement** /mɪsmænɪdʒmə[2]nt/. EG *...economic mismanagement.* — V+O; ◊ N UNCOUNT

misnomer /mɪsnəʊmə/, **misnomers.** A **misnomer** is a word or expression that describes something wrongly or inaccurately. EG *The very term 'positive discrimination' is a misnomer.* — N COUNT Formal

misplaced /mɪspleɪst/. A **misplaced** feeling or action is inappropriate, or is directed towards the wrong thing or person. EG *Her fears had been ludicrously misplaced... ...misplaced loyalties.* — ADJ QUALIT

misprint /mɪsprɪnt/, **misprints.** A **misprint** is a mistake in the way something is printed, for example a spelling mistake. EG *There was a misprint in her name.* — N COUNT

misread, misreads, misreading. Misread is used in the present tense, when it is pronounced /mɪsriːd/, and is also the past tense and past participle, when it is pronounced /mɪsred/.

1 If you **misread** a situation or someone's behaviour, you do not understand it properly. EG *Their behaviour was usually misread as indifference... He was unconsciously misreading their actions.* — V+O

2 If you **misread** something that has been written or printed, you read it wrongly, so that you think it says something that it does not say. EG *She had misread a date in the Tour Book.* — V+O

misrepresent /mɪsreprə[1]zent/, **misrepresents, misrepresenting, misrepresented.** If you **misrepresent** someone, you give a wrong account of what they have said or written. EG *Witnesses claim to have been seriously misrepresented... He says that I have misrepresented his views.* ◊ **misrepresentation** /mɪsreprɪ[2]zenteɪʃə[0]n/, **misrepresentations.** EG *All political policies are open to misrepresentation.* — V+O; ◊ N UNCOUNT OR N COUNT

miss /mɪs/, **misses, missing, missed.** 1 You use **Miss** before the name of a girl or unmarried woman when you are speaking to her or referring to her. EG *Good morning, Miss Haynes... I do not know very much about Miss Ravenscroft.*

2 If you **miss** something, **2.1** you do not notice it. EG *He doesn't miss much... You can't miss it, it's on the first floor.* — V+O **2.2** you fail to hit it when you have aimed something at it. EG *She had thrown her plate at his head and missed.* — V+O OR V ▸ used as a noun. EG *We had a few near misses in the first raid.* — ▸ N COUNT

3 If you **miss** someone, you feel sad that they are no longer with you. If you **miss** something, you feel sad that you no longer have it or experience it. EG *The two boys miss their father a great deal... I knew I should miss living in the Transkei.* — V+O OR V+-ING

4 If you **miss** a chance or opportunity, you fail to take advantage of it. EG *It was a good opportunity which it would be a pity to miss.* — V+O

5 If you **miss** something such as a bus, plane, or train, you arrive too late to catch it. EG *She was going to miss her plane if her husband didn't hurry.* — V+O

6 If you **miss** something such as a meeting or an activity, you do not go to it or do not experience it. EG *I couldn't miss a departmental meeting... I tried to cheer her up, telling her she wasn't missing much.* — V+O

7 If you **give** something **a miss**, you decide not to do it or not to go to it. EG *I know you want to go, but I'd advise you to give it a miss.* — PHRASE Informal

8 See also **missing, hit and miss.**

miss out. 1 If you **miss out** something or someone, you do not include them in something. EG *You can miss out a surprising number of words and still be understood.* — PHRASAL VB : V+O+ADV **2** If you **miss out** on something interesting or useful, you do not become involved in it or get it, when other people do. EG *I miss out on all these kind of opportunities.* — V+ADV, OFT+*on*

misshapen /mɪsʃeɪpə[0]n/. Something that is **misshapen** does not have a normal or natural shape. EG *Her misshapen old fingers twitched at her beads.* — ADJ QUALIT

missile /mɪsaɪl/, **missiles.** A **missile** is **1** a weapon that moves long distances through the air and explodes when it reaches its target. EG *...nuclear missiles.* • See also **cruise missile. 2** any object that you throw at someone as a weapon. EG — N COUNT

Name five words on these pages that are still words if you take 'mis-' away.

Demonstrators attacked police using sticks and assorted missiles.

missing /mɪsɪŋ/. 1 If someone or something is **missing**, they are not in the place where you expect them to be, and you cannot find them. EG *She thought some of her jewellery was missing... I want to report a missing person... ...Larry Burrows, missing since 1971.* ADJ CLASSIF

2 If a part of something is **missing**, it has been removed and has not been replaced. EG *The car was a wreck, with all its wheels missing.* ADJ CLASSIF

mission /mɪʃəⁿn/, **missions.** 1 A **mission** is **1.1** an important task that you are given to do, especially one that involves travelling to another country. EG *He has been on confidential missions to Berlin.* N COUNT **1.2** a group of people who have been sent to a foreign country to carry out an official task. EG *He became head of the Ugandan mission there.* N COUNT: USU+SUPP **1.3** a special journey made by a military aeroplane or by a space rocket. EG *...a bombing mission.* N COUNT

2 If you have a **mission**, there is something that you believe it is your duty to try to achieve. EG *...one of those girls who had a mission in life.* N UNCOUNT: USU+SUPP

3 A **mission** is also **3.1** the activity of a group of Christians who have been sent to a place to teach people about Christianity. EG *They conducted five-day evangelistic missions around Britain.* N COUNT **3.2** a building or group of buildings in which missionary work is carried out.

missionary /mɪʃənəⁿri¹/, **missionaries.** A **missionary** is a Christian who has been sent to a foreign country to teach people about Christianity. EG *One of the college girls became a missionary and went out to Africa.* N COUNT

misspend /mɪsspend/, **misspends, misspending, misspent.** If you say that someone has **misspent** time or **misspent** money, you mean that they have wasted it, and could have used it in better ways. EG *I'll tell him about my misspent life... They have misspent their scarce funds on facilities that nobody needs.* V+O

mist /mɪst/, **mists, misting, misted. 1 Mist** consists of a large number of tiny drops of water in the air. When there is a mist, you cannot see very far. EG *Everything was shrouded in mist... ...the mists of early morning.* N UNCOUNT OR N COUNT

2 If your eyes **mist**, you cannot see easily, because there are tears in your eyes. EG *Grandpa's eyes still misted over when he told the tale.* V: OFT+*over*

mist over or **mist up.** When a piece of glass **mists over** or **mists up**, it becomes covered with tiny drops of moisture, so that you cannot see through it easily. EG *His spectacles misted over.* PHRASAL VB: V+ADV

mistake /mɪsteɪk/, **mistakes, mistaking, mistook** /mɪstʊk/, **mistaken** /mɪsteɪkən/. 1 A **mistake** is an action or opinion that is wrong, or that is not what you intended to do. EG *He had made a terrible mistake... We made the mistake of leaving our bedroom window open... I said there must be some mistake because it wasn't my birthday... ...a spelling mistake.* N COUNT ● If you accidentally do something that you did not intend to do, you can say that you did it **by mistake**. EG *I opened the door into the library by mistake.* ● PHRASE

2 If you **mistake** something, you are wrong about it. EG *At first he thought he had mistaken the address... I think you're mistaking how far the responsibility goes.* V+O OR V+REPORT: ONLY WH Formal

3 If you **mistake** someone or something for another person or thing, you wrongly think that they are the other person or thing. EG *You mustn't mistake lack of formal education for lack of wisdom.* V+O+*for*

4 If you say **there's no mistaking** someone or something, you mean that they can be easily recognized or understood. EG *There was no mistaking her... There can be no mistaking his meaning.* PHRASE

mistaken /mɪsteɪkən/. 1 If you are **mistaken** about something, you are wrong about it. EG *I told her she must be mistaken... How could she have been mistaken about a thing like this?... I had been mistaken in believing Nick was mad.* ADJ PRED: OFT+*about/in*

2 If you have a **mistaken** belief or opinion, you believe something which is not true. EG *The discovery of adrenalin came about through a mistaken impression.* ADJ QUALIT ◇ **mistakenly.** EG *The parents may mistakenly believe that they are to blame for their child's illness.* ◇ ADV

mister /mɪstə/. See **Mr.**

mistletoe /mɪsəⁿltəʊ/ is a plant with white berries on it, which grows on trees. Mistletoe is used in Britain as a Christmas decoration. N UNCOUNT

mistook /mɪstʊk/ is the past tense of **mistake.**

mistress /mɪstrɪ²s/, **mistresses.** 1 A man's **mistress** is a woman he is having a sexual relationship with, but who is not married to him. EG *He keeps a mistress.* N COUNT

2 A **mistress** in a school is a female schoolteacher. EG *...the French mistress.* N COUNT: USU+SUPP

3 A servant's **mistress** is the woman who has authority over the servant. EG *She was only carrying out her mistress's orders.* N COUNT

4 If a woman is the **mistress** of a situation, she has complete control over it. EG *Etta was now the acknowledged mistress of the situation.* N COUNT+*of*

mistrust /mɪstrʌst/, **mistrusts, mistrusting, mistrusted. Mistrust** is the feeling that you have towards someone who you do not trust. EG *She gazed on me with a sudden fear and mistrust.* N UNCOUNT ▸ used as a verb. EG *The child soon learns to mistrust offers of affection.* ▸ V+O

misty /mɪsti¹/. If it is **misty**, there is a lot of mist in the air. EG *...a misty autumn morning... The night was cold and misty... We drove through the misty streets.* ADJ QUALIT

misunderstand /mɪsʌndəstænd/, **misunderstands, misunderstanding, misunderstood** /mɪsʌndəstʊd/. If you **misunderstand** someone, you do not understand properly what they say or write. EG *Don't misunderstand me; we're not making any promises... She misunderstood my question.* V+O OR V

misunderstanding /mɪsʌndəstændɪŋ/, **misunderstandings. 1** A **misunderstanding** is a failure to understand something such as a situation or a person's remarks. EG *This was a minor misunderstanding which could be instantly cleared up... ...a source of suspicion and misunderstanding.* N COUNT OR N UNCOUNT

2 If two people have a **misunderstanding**, they have a disagreement or a slight quarrel. EG *They usually sort out their misunderstandings.* N COUNT

misuse, misuses, misusing, misused; pronounced /mɪsjuːs/ when it is a noun and /mɪsjuːz/ when it is a verb.

The **misuse** of something is the use of it in an incorrect, improper, or careless way or for a wrong or dishonest purpose. EG *...the misuse of company funds... She cared deeply about words, and hated their misuse.* N UNCOUNT OR N COUNT ▸ used as a verb. EG *In some cases, pesticides are deliberately misused.* ▸ V+O

mitigate /mɪtɪgeɪt/, **mitigates, mitigating, mitigated.** To **mitigate** something means to make it less unpleasant, serious, or painful. EG *They should endeavour to mitigate distress... ...an attempt to mitigate the unfavourable reaction.* V+O Formal

mitigating /mɪtɪgeɪtɪŋ/. **Mitigating** circumstances make a crime easier to understand, and may result in the person responsible being punished less severely. EG *They may deny the offence or plead mitigating circumstances.* ADJ CLASSIF: ATTRIB Formal Legal

mitten /mɪtəⁿn/, **mittens. Mittens** are gloves which have one section that covers your thumb and another section for your four fingers together. See picture at CLOTHES. N COUNT: OFT PLURAL

mix /mɪks/, **mixes, mixing, mixed. 1** If you **mix** two substances, you stir or shake them together. EG *The mug had been used for mixing flour and water... They drink whisky mixed with beer.* V-ERG; ALSO V OR V+*with*: RECIP

2 If you **mix** something, you make it by stirring or V+O, V+O+O, OR V+O+*for*

shaking other things together. EG *She mixed Clara a drink... He carefully mixed the cement.*

3 A **mix** is a powder containing the correct amounts of all the substances that you need in order to make something. You buy the mix in a packet and add water or another liquid to the powder. EG *...cake mixes... She bought a packet of cement mix.* N MASS+SUPP

4 A **mix** is also two or more things combined together. EG *We should try and keep a broad mix of subjects in our schools... I find the mix of politics and literature very interesting.* N COUNT: USU SING+SUPP

5 If you **mix** two activities or **mix** one activity with another, you do them both at the same time. EG *...the concern for mixing study with work.* V+O OR V+*with*: RECIP

6 If you **mix** with other people, you meet them and talk to them at a social event such as a party. EG *He was making no effort to mix.* V: OFT+*with*

7 See also **mixed**.

mix up. 1 If you **mix up** two things or people, you confuse them, so that you think that one of them is the other one. EG *People even mix us up and greet us by each other's names.* 2 If you **mix up** a number of things that are in a special order or arrangement, you change the order or arrangement. EG *The letters had got too mixed up to be sorted out easily.* 3 See also **mixed up**, **mix-up**. PHRASAL VB: V+O+ADV

mixed /mɪkst/. 1 You use **mixed** to describe something which 1.1 consists of different things of the same general kind. EG *...a mixed salad... ...mixed nuts.* ADJ CLASSIF: ATTRIB 1.2 involves people from two or more different races. EG *...a mixed marriage... He is of mixed parentage: half English, half Dutch.* ADJ CLASSIF

2 **Mixed** education or accommodation is intended for both males and females. EG *...a mixed school.* ADJ CLASSIF

3 Feelings or reactions that are **mixed** consist of some good and some bad things. EG *He has mixed feelings towards his wife.* ADJ QUALIT

mixed bag. If you describe a situation or a group of things or people as a **mixed bag**, you mean that it contains some good things and some bad ones. EG *...a mixed bag of amateurs and old professionals... It's very much a mixed bag of activities and interests.* N SING

mixed doubles is a match in some sports, especially tennis and badminton, in which a man and a woman play as partners against another man and woman. N UNCOUNT

mixed up. 1 If you are **mixed up**, you are confused, often because of emotional or social problems. EG *I got mixed up and forgot which one I'd gone to first... Tim was in a strange mixed-up frame of mind.* ADJ QUALIT

2 If you are **mixed up** in a crime or a scandal, you are involved in it. EG *I wasn't mixed up in it myself.* ADJ PRED: OFT+*in*

mixer /mɪksə/, **mixers.** A **mixer** is a machine used for mixing things together. EG *...a food mixer... ...the big cement mixers.* N COUNT+SUPP

mixing bowl, mixing bowls. A **mixing bowl** is a large bowl used for mixing ingredients when cooking. N COUNT

mixture /mɪkstʃə/, **mixtures.** 1 A **mixture** of things consists of several different things together. EG *I swallowed a mixture of pills... At the conference you could hear an amazing mixture of languages... She stared at the cold green soup in a mixture of disgust and hunger.* N SING+*of*

2 A **mixture** is a substance that consists of other substances which have been stirred or shaken together. EG *...a mixture of water and household bleach... Take care not to spill the mixture.* N COUNT

mix-up, mix-ups. A **mix-up** is a mistake in something that was planned. EG *Due to some administrative mix-up the letters had not been sent.* N COUNT Informal

ml is an abbreviation for 1 'millilitre' or 'millilitres'. EG *...180ml of water.* 2 'mile' or 'miles'.

mm is an abbreviation for 'millimetre' or 'millimetres'. EG *...35mm film... ...standard mirror sizes: 760 x 460mm.*

Mm is used to represent a sound that you make when someone is talking, to indicate that you are listening to them, that you agree with them, or that you are preparing to say something. EG *'That's what you said, isn't it?' – 'Mm, yes. I suppose so.'*

moan /məʊn/, **moans, moaning, moaned.** 1 If you **moan**, 1.1 you make a low and miserable cry because you are in pain or suffering. EG *Otto moaned from the pain.* V ▸ used as a noun. EG *Each time she moved her leg she let out a moan.* ▸ N COUNT 1.2 you speak in a way which indicates that you are very unhappy or anxious. EG *'What am I going to do?' she moaned.* V+QUOTE OR REPORT: ONLY *that*

2 If you **moan** about something, you complain about it. EG *My brother's moaning about money again.* V: OFT+*about* Informal ▸ used as a noun. EG *There are the usual moans if tea is late on the table.* ▸ N COUNT

moat /məʊt/, **moats.** A **moat** is a deep, wide ditch which people used to dig round a hill or castle and fill with water, in order to protect the place. N COUNT

mob /mɒb/, **mobs, mobbing, mobbed.** 1 A **mob** is a large, disorganized, and often violent crowd of people. EG *The police faced a mob throwing bricks and petrol bombs.* N COUNT

2 If people **mob** a person, they gather round the person in a large crowd, in order to express feelings of anger or admiration. EG *Pop stars are always moaning about being mobbed by their fans.* V+O

mobile /məʊbaɪl/, **mobiles.** 1 Something that is **mobile** is able to move freely or to be moved easily. EG *Most antelopes are fully mobile as soon as they are born... The squadron was protected by a highly mobile air defence.* ADJ QUALIT ◇ **mobility** /məʊbɪlɪ¹ti¹/. EG *With the aeroplane, people achieved a physical mobility never before dreamed of.* ◇ N UNCOUNT

2 If you are **mobile**, 2.1 you can move or travel easily from place to place. EG *Many seventy-year-olds are mobile: my mother runs her own car.* ADJ PRED 2.2 you are able to move to a different job or social class. EG *...socially mobile business leaders.* ADJ PRED ◇ **mobility.** EG *...growing affluence, opportunity, and social mobility.* ◇ N UNCOUNT

3 A **mobile** is a light structure which hangs from a ceiling as a decoration. It usually consists of several small objects which move as the air around them moves. N COUNT

mobilize /məʊbɪlaɪz/, **mobilizes, mobilizing, mobilized;** also spelled **mobilise.** 1 If you **mobilize** a group of people, you encourage them all to do something. EG *The Trade Union Congress is prepared to mobilize the whole movement to defeat the bill.* V+O ◇ **mobilization** /məʊbɪlaɪzeɪʃəⁿn/. EG *The building of the canal required the mobilization of large masses of labour.* ◇ N UNCOUNT

2 If a country **mobilizes** or **mobilizes** its armed forces, its armed forces are given orders to prepare to fight a war. V OR V+O Formal ◇ **mobilization.** EG *Defence chiefs urged mobilization at once.* ◇ N UNCOUNT

moccasin /mɒkəsɪn/, **moccasins. Moccasins** are soft leather shoes which have a low heel and a raised seam at the front above the toe. See picture at SHOES. N COUNT

mock /mɒk/, **mocks, mocking, mocked.** 1 If you **mock** someone, you make them appear foolish, for example by saying something funny about them, or by imitating their behaviour. EG *He felt that Mrs Mount was mocking him a little... ...an unsympathetic teacher who had mocked her domestic ambitions.* V+O OR V+QUOTE ◇ **mocking.** EG *She stared at him in her mocking way.* ◇ ADJ QUALIT

2 You use **mock** to describe something which is deliberately not genuine. EG *He shook his head with mock disapproval... Robert squealed in mock terror... ...mock Tudor houses.* ADJ CLASSIF: ATTRIB

If you are mixed up, has there been a mix-up?

MODAL VERBS

A small group of words in English are often called modal verbs or modal auxiliaries (MODAL). They are: **can, could, may, might, must, ought, shall, should, will,** and **would. Be to** and **have to** are also often called modals, but we do not label them as modals in this dictionary. See the entries for **be** and **have.**

The verbs **dare, need,** and **used to,** which some grammars call modals, are called semi-modals in this dictionary. See the entry headed SEMI-MODALS for information about them.

Modals behave rather differently from ordinary verbs:

Followed by an infinitive

Apart from **ought**, modals are followed only by a verb in the infinitive form without **to**. For example: *I must go . . .* *He will come . . .* *They should arrive soon.*

Ought is followed by a verb in the infinitive form with **to**, as in: *She ought to get there by 6.*

No inflections

Modals do not inflect – that is, they do not change their form for the third person singular. So: *I can swim . . .* *He can swim.*
Compare: *I swim . . .* *He swims.*

In questions

Modals come before the subject in questions. So: *Will you meet me at 6 o'clock? . . . What time will you meet me?*

With ordinary verbs the auxiliary **do** is used. For example: *Do you swim?*

In negative clauses

Modals come before the word **not** in negative clauses. Often **not** is abbreviated to **n't** and is added to the modal: *She wouldn't tell me where she had been.*

The forms **can't, won't,** and **shan't** are often used instead of **cannot, will not,** and **shall not**. For example: *I can't remember her name . . .* *They won't be here on time . . .* *I shan't give you a present this year.*

Used on their own

Modals can be used as a verbal group on their own following a full verbal group in order to make a contrast. For example: *I haven't strangled him yet, but I might . . . I'd love to have lunch with you but I can't.*

Used in question tags

Modals are used in question tags. For example: *You will come, won't you? . . . You won't be late, will you?*

3 A **mock** examination or battle is not real but is intended to be like the real event so that people can practise and prepare for the real event. ADJ CLASSIF: ATTRIB

mockery /mɒkə^{0}ri^1/. 1 **Mockery** is the scornful attitude that you express in your speech or behaviour when you think someone is foolish, stupid, or inferior. EG *There was a tone of mockery in his voice... He had ignored Helen's mockery.* N UNCOUNT

2 If something **makes a mockery of** something, it makes it appear foolish and worthless. EG *The strikers were making a mockery of our efforts to build up employment.* PHRASE

3 If you describe an event or situation as a **mockery**, you mean that it is very unsuccessful. EG *The examination was a mockery.* N SING: a+N

mock-up, mock-ups. A **mock-up** of something such as a machine or building is a model of it which is made to do tests on or to show people what it will look like. EG *Here's a mock-up of the central section of the submarine.* N COUNT

modal /məʊdə^{0}l/, **modals.** In grammar, a **modal** or a **modal verb** is a word such as *can* or *would* which is used in a verbal group and which expresses ideas such as possibility, intention, and necessity. See the entry headed MODAL VERBS for grammatical information about them. N COUNT

> **MODAL** stands for **modal verb**
> The verbs *can, could, may, might, must, ought to, shall, should, will,* and *would* are labelled MODAL in the Extra Column.
> See the entry headed MODAL VERBS for information about them.

mod cons /mɒd kɒnz/. If a house has all **mod cons**, it has all the modern facilities such as hot water and heating that make it pleasant to live in. N PLURAL Informal British

mode /məʊd/, **modes.** A **mode** of life or behaviour is a particular way of living or behaving. EG *...conventionally acceptable modes of life... ...the mode of action which protesters adopt today... She always chose this mode of transport.* N COUNT +SUPP: OFT+*of*

model /mɒdə^{0}l/, **models, modelling, modelled;** spelled **modeling, modeled** in American English.

1 A **model** is 1.1 a physical representation that shows what an object looks like or how it works. EG *...scale models of well known Navy ships... I had a model theatre, for which I used to design scenery.* N COUNT

1.2 a system that is being used and that people might want to copy in order to achieve similar results. EG *This system seemed a relevant model for the new Africa.* N COUNT+SUPP Formal

2 Something that is a **model** of clarity or a **model** of fairness is extremely clear or extremely fair. EG *She's a model of discretion.* N COUNT+*of*

3 A **model** wife or a **model** teacher is an excellent wife or an excellent teacher. EG *Jane has turned into a model mother... They are model students.* ADJ CLASSIF: ATTRIB

4 If you **model** yourself on someone, you copy the way that they do things, because you admire them and want to be like them. EG *The children have their parents on which to model themselves.* V-REFL+*on*

5 A **model** is also a particular type of machine, for example a car or washing machine. EG *The Granada is the most popular model.* N COUNT

6 A person who is a **model** 6.1 poses for a painter or photographer as a job. EG *She was one of Rossetti's favourite models.* 6.2 displays clothes by wearing them, especially in a fashion show. EG *She's a fashion model.* N COUNT

7 If you **model** clothes, you display them by wearing them. EG *He models cardigans in knitting books.* ◇ **modelling.** EG *Tom says she's not to do modelling while she's still at school.* V+O OR V; ◇ N UNCOUNT

8 If you **model** shapes or figures, you make them out of a substance such as clay or wood. EG *The children were asked to model an aeroplane out of balsa wood.* V+O

moderate, moderates, moderating, moderated; pronounced /mɒdərə^{1}t/ when it is an adjective or noun, and /mɒdəreɪt/ when it is a verb. 1 Political opinions or policies that are **moderate** are not extreme and are concerned with slow or small changes in the system. EG *...a woman with moderate views... The movement drew its support from moderate conservatives.* ADJ QUALIT

2 A **moderate** is a person whose political opinions and activities are not extreme. EG *The moderates have plenty to be anxious about.* N COUNT

3 A **moderate** amount of something is neither large nor small. EG *The sun's rays, in moderate quantities, are important for health... There's a big dining room and a moderate sized kitchen.* ADJ QUALIT: USU ATTRIB

4 If you **moderate** something or if it **moderates**, it becomes less extreme or violent and more acceptable. EG *She had been given instructions to moderate her tone... The bad weather had moderated.* V-ERG

moderately /mɒdərətli^1/. Something that is **moderately** good or that happens **moderately** fast, for example, is fairly good or happens fairly fast. EG *Her handwriting was moderately good... ...a moderately long beard.* SUBMOD

moderation /mɒdəreɪʃə^{0}n/ is control of your behaviour that stops you acting in an extreme way. EG *He has not displayed the same moderation in his political behaviour as in his private life.* N UNCOUNT ● If you drink alcohol or smoke **in moderation**, you do not drink or smoke too much. ● PHRASE

modern /mɒdə^{5}n/. 1 **Modern** means relating to the present time. EG *Marx still has much to say to the modern world... The social problems in modern society are mounting.* ADJ CLASSIF: ATTRIB

2 Something that is **modern** is new and involves the latest ideas and latest equipment. EG *Japan successfully built up a modern capitalist economy... 'Did you like Stockholm?' – 'Yes, it's very modern, isn't it?'* ◇ **modernity** /mə^{7}dɜːnɪ^{1}ti^1/. EG *...industries half way between tradition and modernity.* ADJ QUALIT; ◇ N UNCOUNT

modern-day. You use **modern-day** to describe something in the present that is very similar to something that happened in the past. EG *He was convinced that he was a modern-day Messiah.* ADJ CLASSIF: ATTRIB

modernize /mɒdənaɪz/, **modernizes, modernizing, modernized;** also spelled **modernise.** If you **modernize** something such as a system or a factory, you change it by replacing old methods or equipment with new ones. EG *...a twenty year programme to modernise Britain's transport system.* ◇ **modernization** /mɒdənaɪzeɪʃə^{0}n/. EG *...plans for modernisation of the Post Office.* V+O; ◇ N UNCOUNT

modern languages. If you study **modern languages**, you study the modern European languages such as French, German, and Russian. N PLURAL

modest /mɒdɪ^{2}st/. 1 A **modest** house or flat is not large or expensive. EG *He moved from his hotel suite into a modest flat.* ADJ QUALIT

2 Something that is **modest** is quite small in amount. EG *...a small theatre with a modest budget.* ◇ **modestly.** EG *He still gambled modestly.* ADJ QUALIT; ◇ ADV

3 Someone who is **modest** 3.1 does not talk much about their abilities, qualities, or possessions; used showing approval. EG *He's got a drawer full of medals but he's too modest to wear them.* ◇ **modestly.** EG *He talks quietly and modestly about his farm.* ◇ **modesty** /mɒdɪ^{2}sti^1/. EG *The real secret of his power was his modesty and his total lack of vanity.* 3.2 is shy and easily embarrassed, especially by nudity or things relating to sex. EG *That such a modest man should be unclothed seems highly improbable.* ◇ **modestly.** EG *They slipped out of their garments modestly.* ADJ QUALIT; ◇ ADV; ◇ N UNCOUNT; ADJ QUALIT; ◇ ADV

Is Britain a monarchy?

◊ **modesty.** EG *She covered herself with a sheet, respecting my modesty.* ◊ N UNCOUNT

modicum /mɒdɪkəm/. A **modicum** of something is a small amount of it. EG *...a designer with a modicum of good taste.* N PART : SING Formal

modification /mɒdɪfɪkeɪʃə[0]n/, **modifications.** A **modification** to something is a small change which you make to it in order to improve it. EG *The engine was pulled apart for modifications... I said I thought the idea might need modification.* N COUNT OR N UNCOUNT

modify /mɒdɪfaɪ/, **modifies, modifying, modified.** If you **modify** something, you change it slightly, often in order to improve it. EG *The present Government has modified this approach... The aircraft were extensively modified and improved.* V+O

module /mɒdju:l/, **modules.** A **module** is a part of a spacecraft which can do certain things independently, often away from the main part of the spacecraft. N COUNT Technical

mohair /məʊheə/ is a kind of very soft wool. EG *...a mohair coat.* N UNCOUNT

moist /mɔɪst/, **moister, moistest.** Something that is **moist** is slightly wet. EG *...moist black earth... His eyes grew moist.* ADJ QUALIT

moisten /mɔɪsə[0]n/, **moistens, moistening, moistened.** If you **moisten** something, you make it slightly wet. EG *The girl moistened her lips.* V+O

moisture /mɔɪstʃə/ is tiny drops of water in the air, on a surface, or in the ground. EG *The kitchen's stone floor was shiny with moisture... Trees have enormous roots that can reach out for moisture far below the surface.* N UNCOUNT

molar /məʊlə/, **molars.** Your **molars** are the large teeth at the side of your mouth. N COUNT

mold /məʊld/. See **mould.**

moldy /məʊldi[1]/. See **mouldy.**

mole /məʊl/, **moles. 1** A **mole** is a dark spot or small, dark lump on someone's skin which is permanent. EG *She had a tiny mole on her cheek.* N COUNT

2 A **mole** is also a small animal with black fur that lives in tunnels in the ground. N COUNT

3 If you refer to someone as a **mole**, you mean that they are secretly working against the government or some other organization of which they are a member. EG *There is some gossip in Westminster that there is a mole in the Thatcher cabinet.* N COUNT

molecule /mɒlɪkju:l/, **molecules.** A **molecule** is the smallest amount of a chemical substance which can exist by itself without changing or breaking apart. EG *The haemoglobin molecule contains only four atoms of iron.* ◊ **molecular** /mə[6]lɛkjə[4]lə/. EG *...molecular biology.* N COUNT Technical ◊ ADJ CLASSIF : ATTRIB

molehill /məʊlhɪl/, **molehills. 1** A **molehill** is a small pile of earth on the ground that has been left by a mole that has been digging there. N COUNT

2 If you say that someone is **making a mountain out of a molehill**, you mean that they are making an unimportant fact or difficulty seem very serious. PHRASE

molest /mə[7]lɛst/, **molests, molesting, molested.**

1 Someone who **molests** children touches them in a sexual way against their will and can be arrested by the police for this. ◊ **molestation** /mɒlɛsteɪʃə[0]n/. EG *...child molestation.* ◊ **molester** /mə[7]lɛstə/, **molesters.** EG *...child molesters.* V+O Formal ◊ N UNCOUNT ◊ N COUNT

2 If someone **molests** you, they annoy you and prevent you from doing something, often by using physical violence. EG *They feared they would be molested by the angry crowd.* V+O Formal

mollify /mɒlɪfaɪ/, **mollifies, mollifying, mollified.** If you **mollify** someone, you do something to make them less upset or angry. EG *Mrs Pringle allowed herself to be mollified.* ◊ **mollified.** EG *She appeared slightly mollified.* V+O Formal ◊ ADJ PRED

molt /məʊlt/. See **moult.**

molten /məʊltə[0]n/. **Molten** rock or metal has been heated to a very high temperature and has become a hot, thick, sticky liquid. EG *...a great mass of molten rock.* ADJ QUALIT

mom /mɒm/, **moms.** Some people refer to their mother as **mom.** EG *When I was born, Mom was forty and Dad forty-six... 'Hey, mom,' said Billy, 'what's that around your neck?'* VOCATIVE OR N COUNT Informal American

moment /məʊmə[2]nt/, **moments. 1** A **moment** is **1.1** a very short period of time. EG *She hesitated for only a moment... A few moments later he heard footsteps... I'll come back to that in a moment... It causes me moments of acute embarrassment.* N COUNT **1.2** the point in time at which something happens. EG *At that precise moment, Miss Pulteney came into the office... ...the moment of death... ...at such a critical moment in his career.* N SING+SUPP

2 Moment is used in these phrases. **2.1** If you say that something is true or is happening **at the moment**, you mean that it is true or is happening now. EG *The biggest problem at the moment is unemployment... I'm sorry, but she's not in at the moment.* **2.2** If you do something at **the last moment**, you do it at the last possible time that it can be done. EG *We escaped from Saigon at the last moment.* **2.3** If you say that you do not believe something **for one moment**, you are emphasizing that you do not believe it at all. EG *I didn't believe for a moment that he was an actor.* **2.4** If you say that you cannot do something **for the moment**, you mean that you cannot do it now, but you will probably be able to do it later. EG *I don't want to discuss this for the moment.* **2.5** If one thing happens **the moment** something else happens, the two things happen at exactly the same time. EG *The moment I saw this, it appealed to me.* **2.6** If you say that someone or something **has** their **moments**, you mean that they are occasionally successful or interesting, although not very often. EG *The film had its moments.* PHRASES

momentary /məʊməntə[0]ri[1]/. Something that is **momentary** lasts for only a few seconds. EG *There was a momentary pause.* ◊ **momentarily** /məʊməntɛərɪ[1]li[1]/. EG *I had momentarily forgotten.* ADJ CLASSIF ◊ ADV

momentous /mə[6]mɛntəs/. Something that is **momentous** is very important, often because of the effect that it will have in the future. EG *There was no doubt it would be a momentous occasion.* ADJ CLASSIF Formal

momentum /mə[6]mɛntəm/ is **1** the ability that something has to keep developing. EG *It was necessary to crush the rebel movement before it had a chance to gather momentum.* **2** the ability that an object has to continue moving as a result of the speed it already has. EG *...the momentum of the rocket.* N UNCOUNT

monarch /mɒnək/, **monarchs.** A **monarch** is a king, queen, or other royal person who reigns over a country. N COUNT

monarchist /mɒnəkɪst/, **monarchists.** A **monarchist** is a person who believes that their country should have a monarch. N COUNT Formal

monarchy /mɒnəki[1]/, **monarchies.** A **monarchy** is a system in which a monarch reigns over a country and in which the next monarch will be another member of the same family. EG *We want to abolish the monarchy... I have never been an opponent of monarchy... ...the English monarchy.* N COUNT : USU *the*+N, OR N UNCOUNT

monastery /mɒnəstri[1]/, **monasteries.** A **monastery** is a building or collection of buildings in which a group of monks live. N COUNT

Monday /mʌndi[1]/, **Mondays. Monday** is one of the seven days of the week. It is the day after Sunday and before Tuesday. Most people start their week's work on a Monday. EG *It was cold last Monday... ...a plan for reducing ticket prices on Mondays.* N UNCOUNT OR N COUNT

monetary /mʌnɪ[2]tə[0]ri[1]/ means relating to money, especially the total amount of money in a country. EG *...Washington's tight monetary policy... ...monetary value... ...the monetary system.* ADJ CLASSIF : ATTRIB Formal

money /mʌni[1]/. **1 Money** consists of the coins or bank notes that you use when you buy something. N UNCOUNT

EG *I spent all my money on sweets... I had very little money left... They may not accept English money.*
2 If you **make money**, you obtain money by earning it or by making a profit. EG *To make money you've got to take chances.* PHRASE
3 If you **get** your **money's worth**, you get good value for the money that you spend. EG *I always insist on getting my money's worth.* PHRASE Informal

> **MONEY**
> This entry shows some of the ways in which you can refer to money.
> When you express amounts of money in writing, the main unit of currency that you are using is usually shown by a symbol or letter in front of the figures. For example, £100 means one hundred pounds, $100 means one hundred dollars, and $2.50 means two dollars and fifty cents. If an amount of money consists of only a smaller unit, for example only pence or cents, then the symbol or letter usually follows the figures. For example, 50p means fifty pence.
> When you express amounts of money in speech, you sometimes leave out the words that refer to the unit of currency, although you can say them after the numbers. For example, you write £10 but you say 'ten pounds'.
> The following examples show a few ways of expressing amounts of money. EG *He was making ninety dollars a week... It costs 35 pounds a kilo... ...a million and a half dollars... ...the ten-cent packet of balloons... The machine wouldn't take 10p pieces... Total British losses were close to a quarter of a million pounds.*

mongrel /mʌŋgrəl/, **mongrels.** A **mongrel** is a dog with parents of different breeds. EG *If you want a dog, you can get a mongrel from a pet store.* N COUNT

monitor /mɒnɪtə/, **monitors, monitoring, monitored. 1** If you **monitor** something, you check regularly how it is changing or developing over a period of time. EG *The child's progress is being monitored.* V+O
2 If you **monitor** sounds, especially radio broadcasts, you record them or listen carefully to them in order to obtain information. EG *They were getting news by monitoring BBC broadcasts.* V+O
3 A **monitor** is a machine that is used to check or record things. EG *The patient was connected to the monitor.* N COUNT

monk /mʌŋk/, **monks.** A **monk** is a member of a male religious community. N COUNT

monkey /mʌŋki¹/, **monkeys.** A **monkey** is an animal which has a long tail and lives in hot countries. Monkeys climb trees. N COUNT

mono /mɒnəʊ/ is used to describe a record or a system of playing music in which all the sound is directed through one speaker only. ADJ CLASSIF OR N UNCOUNT

monogamy /mə⁷nɒgəmi¹/ is the custom of being married to only one person at a particular time. EG *Lifelong monogamy has other drawbacks.* N UNCOUNT Formal
◇ **monogamous** /mə⁷nɒgəməs/. EG *...monogamous marriage.* ◇ ADJ CLASSIF

monogrammed /mɒnəgræmd/. Something that is **monogrammed** is marked with a design that includes a person's initials. EG *...his monogrammed hair brushes.* ADJ CLASSIF

monolithic /mɒnə⁶lɪθɪk/. **1** An organization or system that is **monolithic** is very large and gives the impression that it will never change. EG *...the monolithic character of the main political parties.* ADJ QUALIT
2 Something that is **monolithic** is very large and impressive. EG *...the great monolithic rock.* ADJ QUALIT

monologue /mɒnəlɒg/, **monologues.** A **monologue** is a long speech by one person, for example in a play. EG *He went into a long monologue, only part of which I understood.* N COUNT OR N UNCOUNT

monopolize /mə⁷nɒpəlaɪz/, **monopolizes, monopolizing, monopolized;** also spelled **monopolise.** If you **monopolize** something, you control it completely and prevent other people having a share in it. EG *The Dutch wanted to monopolize the profitable spice trade from the East.* V+O

monopoly /mə⁷nɒpəli¹/, **monopolies. 1** A **monopoly** on a particular subject or activity is complete control of it by one person or a group of people. EG *I don't believe the medical profession has a monopoly on morality.* N COUNT: OFT+*on/of*
2 A **monopoly** of an industry is control of most of the industry by only one or a few large firms. N COUNT OR N UNCOUNT

monosyllable /mɒnə⁶sɪləbə⁰l/, **monosyllables.** If someone speaks in **monosyllables**, they speak using only very short words, for example 'yes' or 'no'. EG *He was answering only in monosyllables.* N COUNT: OFT PLURAL

monotone /mɒnətəʊn/, **monotones.** A **monotone** is a sound which does not vary at all in tone or loudness and is very boring to listen to. EG *He droned on in a steady monotone.* N COUNT

monotonous /mə⁷nɒtənəs/. Something that is **monotonous** has a dull and regular pattern which never changes and is very boring. EG *...people who have monotonous jobs... Barrack life is shown to be squalid and monotonous.* ADJ QUALIT ◇ **monotony** /mə⁷nɒtəni¹/. EG *...the monotony of work on the assembly line.* ◇ N UNCOUNT: OFT+*of*

monsoon /mɒnsuːn/, **monsoons.** The **monsoon** is the season in Southern Asia when there is a lot of very heavy rain. EG *Even during the monsoons the afternoons were warm and clear.* N COUNT

monster /mɒnstə/, **monsters. 1** A **monster** is a large imaginary creature that looks very frightening. EG *...Dracula, Frankenstein, and every horrible monster you could think of.* N COUNT
2 Monster means extremely large. EG *...the monster Piccadilly Hotel.* ADJ CLASSIF: ATTRIB
3 If you describe someone as a **monster**, you mean that they are cruel, frightening, or evil. EG *You're a monster. A detestable, abominable monster.* N COUNT OR VOCATIVE

monstrosity /mɒnstrɒsɪ¹ti¹/, **monstrosities.** A **monstrosity** is something that is large and extremely ugly. EG *...a monstrosity of a house he bought near Leatherhead.* N COUNT

monstrous /mɒnstrəs/. **1** If you describe a situation or event as **monstrous**, you mean that it is extremely shocking or unfair. EG *The court's judgement was absolutely monstrous.* ADJ QUALIT
2 Something that is **monstrous** is **2.1** extremely ugly and frightening. EG *...this dense and monstrous urban wilderness.* **2.2** extremely large. EG *They went from one building to another in a fleet of monstrous vehicles.* ADJ QUALIT

month /mʌnθ/, **months.** A **month** is **1** one of the twelve periods of time that a year is divided into, for example January or February. EG *It's happened three times this month... I'm going away later in the month... The pay will be five hundred pounds a month... ...the month of March.* **2** a period of about four weeks. EG *He was kidnapped just over a month ago... Four months later she died.* N COUNT

monthly /mʌnθli¹/. You use **monthly** to describe something that happens, is done, or appears once a month or every month. EG *...a monthly meeting... My monthly income was two hundred pounds... Most of our staff are paid monthly.* ADJ CLASSIF: ATTRIB OR ADV

monument /mɒnjə⁴mə²nt/, **monuments.** A **monument** is **1** a large structure, usually made of stone, which is built to remind people of an event in history or of a famous person. EG *Across the* N COUNT

> Give four examples of monosyllables on these pages.

north side of the grass is the monument to F D Roosevelt. **2** a very old building, castle or bridge which is regarded as an important part of a country's history. EG *...an ancient monument.*

monumental /mɒnjə4mentə0l/. **1** A **monumental** building or sculpture is very large and historically or artistically important. EG *...the monumental facade of the Royal School.* ADJ CLASSIF : ATTRIB

2 A **monumental** book or musical work is very impressive and likely to be important for a long time. EG *...Wedderburn's monumental work, 'The Worker and the Law'.* ADJ CLASSIF : USU ATTRIB

3 You can also use **monumental** to describe something that you think is very extreme. EG *That night there was a monumental hailstorm... It was a case of monumental bad manners.* ADJ CLASSIF : USU ATTRIB

moo /mu:/, **moos, mooing, mooed.** If a cow **moos**, it makes the noise that cows typically make. V
▸ used as a noun. EG *The cow gave a low moo.* ▸ N COUNT

mooch /mu:tʃ/, **mooches, mooching, mooched.** If you **mooch** about, you walk about slowly with no particular purpose. EG *He mooched about the house in his pyjamas... Jack and I, hands in pockets, mooched silently up the lane.* V+A Informal

mood /mu:d/, **moods. 1** Your **mood** is the way you are feeling about things at a particular time, especially how cheerful or how angry you are. EG *He was always in a good mood... She was in one of her bad moods... I wasn't in the mood for helping.* N COUNT

2 If you are in a **mood**, you are angry and impatient. EG *When Chris was in one of his moods, he was unpleasant to everyone.* N COUNT

3 The **mood** of a group of people is the way that they think and feel about something. EG *The debate took place amid a mood of growing political despair... The mood of this week's meeting has been one of cautious optimism.* N SING : USU+SUPP

moody /mu:di1/, **moodier, moodiest.** Someone who is **moody 1** is depressed or unhappy, so that they do not talk very much or are impatient with other people. EG *He's only moody because things aren't working out at home.* ◊ **moodily.** EG *She drank her coffee moodily.* **2** often changes in their feelings, for example from being cheerful to being angry, within a short period of time. EG *He was generally moody and unpredictable.* ADJ QUALIT ◊ ADV ADJ QUALIT

moon /mu:n/, **moons. 1** The **moon** is **1.1** the round object in the sky that you can often see at night. EG *...television pictures of a man walking on the moon.* N SING : *the*+N

1.2 the particular shape or appearance of the moon. EG *The sky was a brilliant silver from the full moon... ...a crescent moon.* N SING

2 A **moon** is an object like a small planet that travels round a planet. EG *...Jupiter's four moons.* N COUNT

3 If you are **over the moon**, you are very pleased about something. EG *I was over the moon to get your letter.* PHRASE Informal

4 If you say that something happens **once in a blue moon**, you mean that it happens very rarely. PHRASE

moonbeam /mu:nbi:m/, **moonbeams.** A **moonbeam** is a ray of light from the moon. N COUNT

moonless /mu:nlɪ2s/. A **moonless** sky or night is dark because there is no moon in the sky. ADJ CLASSIF

moonlight /mu:nlaɪt/, **moonlights, moonlighting, moonlighted. 1 Moonlight** is the light that comes from the moon at night. EG *The field looked like water in the moonlight... Our meeting took place by moonlight.* N UNCOUNT

2 If you **moonlight**, you have a second job in addition to your main job, often without informing your main employers or the tax office. EG *She moonlighted as a waitress.* V Informal

moonlit /mu:nlɪt/. Something that is **moonlit** is lit up or made bright by moonlight. EG *I've spent many a moonlit night here.* ADJ CLASSIF

moor /mʊə, mɔ:/, **moors, mooring, moored. 1** A **moor** is a high area of open and uncultivated land that is covered mainly with grass and heather. EG *The mists had vanished from the moor... He used to go for long walks on the moors.* N COUNT

2 If a boat **is moored**, it is attached to the land with a rope. EG *Boats were moored on both sides of the river.* V+O : USU PASS

mooring /mʊərɪŋ, mɔ:-/, **moorings.** A **mooring** is the place on land where a boat can be tied. EG *During the storm, boats were torn from their moorings.* N COUNT

moorland /mʊələ3nd, mɔ:-/, **moorlands. Moorland** is land which consists of moors. EG *...the beauty of Britain's moorlands.* N UNCOUNT OR N PLURAL

moose /mu:s/. **Moose** is both the singular and the plural form. A **moose** is a large North American deer that has very flat antlers. N COUNT

mop /mɒp/, **mops, mopping, mopped. 1** A **mop** is a tool for washing floors. It consists of a sponge or a cluster of pieces of string attached to a long handle. N COUNT

2 If you **mop** a floor, you clean it with a mop. V+O

3 If you **mop** a liquid from a surface or if you **mop** the surface, you wipe the surface with a dry cloth in order to remove the liquid. EG *He mopped the sweat from his face... Mop it with a tissue... He mopped his sweating brow.* V+O : OFT+A

4 A **mop** of hair is a large amount of loose or untidy hair. EG *...a coarse mop of black hair.* N PART

mop up. If you **mop up** a liquid, you wipe it with a cloth or sponge so that the liquid is absorbed. EG *Mother started mopping up the oil.* PHRASAL VB : V+O+ADV OR V+ADV

mope /məʊp/, **mopes, moping, moped.** If you **mope**, you feel miserable and are not interested in anything. EG *He just sits about, moping in an armchair.* V

moped /məʊpɛd/, **mopeds.** A **moped** is a type of small motorcycle. N COUNT

moral /mɒrə0l/, **morals. 1 Morals** are principles and values based on what a person or society believes are the right or acceptable ways of behaving. EG *Business morals nowadays are very low... Films like this are a danger to public morals.* N PLURAL

2 Moral means concerned with whether people's behaviour is right or acceptable. EG *I'm in a moral dilemma... I have noticed a fall in moral standards... He feels responsible for her moral welfare.* ADJ CLASSIF : ATTRIB

3 Moral courage or duty is based on what you believe is right or acceptable, rather than on what the law says should be done. EG *He had that moral courage which enables a man to stand alone... It is our moral duty to stay.* ADJ CLASSIF : ATTRIB

4 Someone who is **moral** behaves in a way that they know is right or acceptable. ADJ QUALIT

5 If you give **moral support** to someone, you encourage them in what they are doing by expressing approval and enthusiasm. EG *I looked across to give moral support to my colleagues.* PHRASE

6 The **moral** of a particular situation, story, or event is what you learn from it about how you should or should not behave. EG *The moral is clear: you must never marry for money.* N SING

morale /mɒrɑ:l/ is the amount of confidence and optimism that you have in a difficult, dangerous, or important situation. EG *The morale of the men was good... The past 15 months have destroyed morale.* N UNCOUNT

moralise /mɒrəlaɪz/. See **moralize.**

moralist /mɒrəlɪst/, **moralists.** A **moralist** is someone who has strong ideas about right and wrong behaviour. EG *My grandfather was a stern moralist.* N COUNT

moralistic /mɒrəlɪstɪk/. If you are **moralistic**, you make strong or harsh judgements about people on the basis of your own beliefs about what is right; used showing disapproval. EG *She had rebuked David for his moralistic attitude to his clients.* ADJ QUALIT

morality /mə7rælɪ1ti1/, **moralities. 1 Morality** is the idea that some behaviour is right and acceptable and that other behaviour is wrong. EG *...the decline in traditional morality.* N UNCOUNT

2 A **morality** is a system of principles and values N COUNT concerning people's behaviour, which is generally accepted by a society or by a particular group of people. EG *Conflicts must arise between the two moralities.*

3 When you talk about the **morality** of something, you are talking about how right or acceptable it is. EG *...arguments concerning the morality of taking part in a war.* N UNCOUNT

moralize /mɒrəlaɪz/, **moralizes, moralizing, moralized;** also spelled **moralise.** If someone **moralizes**, they tell people what they think is right or wrong, especially in a particular situation; used showing disapproval. EG *...moralizing about the dangers of drink.* V : USU+A

morally /mɒrəli[1]/. 1 You use **morally** when you are talking about whether people's behaviour is right or acceptable. EG *It is morally wrong not to do more to help the poor.* ADV+ADJ

2 If you behave **morally**, you behave in a way that you believe is right or acceptable. EG *I try to live morally.* ADV

morass /mər<u>æ</u>s/, **morasses.** If you describe a situation as a **morass**, you mean that it is extremely complicated and confused. EG *These men are usually bogged down in a morass of paperwork.* N COUNT : USU SING+SUPP

moratorium /mɒrət<u>ɔː</u>rɪəm/, **moratoriums.** A **moratorium** on a particular activity is the stopping of it for a fixed period of time as a result of an official agreement. EG *The meeting did agree to extend the moratorium on the building of new warships.* N COUNT : OFT+*on* Formal

morbid /m<u>ɔː</u>bɪd/. If you say that someone or something is **morbid**, you mean that they have too great an interest in unpleasant things, especially in death. EG *It's morbid to dwell on cemeteries and suchlike... ...morbid imaginations.* ADJ QUALIT

more /m<u>ɔː</u>/. 1 **More** means a greater number or amount than before or than something else. EG *Do you spend more time teaching, or doing research?... Better management may enable one man to milk more cows... Most men still earn much more than their wives... He saw more than 800 children dying of starvation.* QUANTIF

2 If something happens **more**, **2.1** it happens to a greater extent. EG *The books that are true to life will attract them more.* **2.2** it continues to happen. EG *They talked a bit more... I apologized and thought no more about it... The employers don't want quality work any more.* ADV : COMPAR ● If you do something **once more** or **twice more**, you do it again once or twice. EG *She wanted to perform it once more before she died.* ● PHRASE

3 **More** is also used to refer to an additional thing or amount of something. EG *In the next hour he found two more diamonds... Have some more coffee, Vicar... I wanted to find out more about her.* QUANTIF

4 You can use **more** in front of adjectives or adverbs to form comparatives. EG *Your child's health is more important than the doctor's feelings... Next time, I will choose more carefully.* SUBMOD

5 You use **more and more** to indicate that something is becoming greater in amount, extent, or degree all the time. EG *More and more people grew ill... They began to dance, slowly at first, then more and more quickly.* PHRASE

6 If you say that something is **more** one thing **than** another, you mean that it is like the first thing rather than the second. EG *He always seemed old to me, more like a grandfather than a father... They were more amused than concerned.* PHRASE

7 If something is true **more or less**, it is true in a general way, but is not completely true. EG *Brian more or less implied that we were lying.* ADV SEN

8 If something is **more than** a particular thing, it has greater value or importance than this thing. EG *It wasn't much more than a formality... This is more than a hunter's job... At the moment our tree looks like nothing more than a branch.* PHRASE

9 You can also use **more than** to emphasize that something is true to a greater degree than is necessary or than is said. EG *You'll have more than enough money for any equipment you need... This was a more than generous arrangement.* PHRASE

10 You use **what is more** to introduce an additional piece of information which supports or emphasizes the point you are making. EG *What's more, he adds, there are no signs of a change.* ADV SEN

moreover /mɔːr<u>əʊ</u>və/ is used to introduce a piece of information or an opinion that adds to or supports the previous statement. EG *They have accused the Government of corruption. Moreover, they have named names.* ADV SEN Formal

morgue /m<u>ɔː</u>g/, **morgues.** A **morgue** is a building where dead bodies are kept before being cremated or buried. EG *...the city morgue.* N COUNT

morning /m<u>ɔː</u>nɪŋ/, **mornings.** 1 The **morning** is **1.1** the part of each day between the time that people usually wake up and noon or lunchtime. EG *She left after breakfast on Saturday morning... I was reading the morning paper.* N COUNT OR N UNCOUNT **1.2** the part of a day between midnight and noon. EG *She died in the very early hours of this morning... It was five o'clock in the morning.* N COUNT

2 If you say that something will happen **in the morning**, you mean that it will happen during the morning of the following day. EG *You'll feel awful in the morning if you drink so much.* PHRASE

morning sickness is a feeling of sickness that some women have in the morning in the first few months of pregnancy. N UNCOUNT

moron /m<u>ɔː</u>rɒn/, **morons.** If you describe someone as a **moron**, you mean that they are very stupid. EG *Louise is in love with that moron.* N COUNT Informal

moronic /mə[8]r<u>ɒ</u>nɪk/. If you say that someone is **moronic**, you mean that they are very stupid. ADJ QUALIT Informal

morose /mər<u>əʊ</u>s/. Someone who is **morose** is miserable, bad-tempered, and not willing to talk much to other people. EG *He was morose and silent.* ADJ QUALIT ◇ **morosely.** EG *The man followed me morosely round the museum.* ◇ ADV

morphine /m<u>ɔː</u>fiːn/ is a drug which is used to relieve pain. N UNCOUNT

morsel /m<u>ɔː</u>sə[0]l/, **morsels.** A **morsel** of something, especially food, is a very small piece or amount of it. EG *He had a morsel of food caught between one tooth and another.* N PART

mortal /m<u>ɔː</u>tə[0]l/, **mortals.** 1 When you describe people as **mortal**, you are referring to the fact that they have to die and cannot live forever. EG *Remember that you are mortal... There was no mortal man who could hurt them now.* ADJ CLASSIF

2 You can refer to a **mortal** to emphasize that you are talking about an ordinary person, rather than someone who has power or has achieved something. EG *He passed first time, something which we mortals couldn't manage.* N COUNT

3 If someone receives a **mortal** wound or blow, they die as a result of it. ADJ CLASSIF ◇ **mortally.** EG *Blake was mortally wounded.* ◇ ADV

4 If two people are in **mortal** combat, they are trying to kill each other. EG *They were locked in mortal combat.* ADJ CLASSIF : ATTRIB

5 A **mortal** enemy or threat is extremely serious and causes you to feel strong fear or hatred. EG *They regard the police as their mortal enemies... We are all in mortal danger.* ADJ CLASSIF : ATTRIB

mortality /mɔːt<u>æ</u>lɪ[1]ti[1]/ is **1** the fact that all people must die. EG *...man contemplating his own mortality.* N UNCOUNT **2** the number of people who die within a particular period of time or on a particular occasion. EG *Infant mortality on the island has been reported at 200 per 1,000 births.*

mortar /m<u>ɔː</u>tə/, **mortars.** 1 A **mortar** is a short cannon which fires missiles high into the air for a N COUNT

What is your mother-tongue?

short distance. EG *We returned fire with mortars and machine-guns.*

2 Mortar is a mixture of sand, water, and cement, which is put between bricks to make them stay firmly together. EG *The new buildings were solid brick and mortar.* N UNCOUNT

mortgage /mɔːgɪdʒ/, **mortgages, mortgaging, mortgaged. 1** A **mortgage** is a loan of money which you get from a bank or building society in order to buy a house. EG *We can't get a mortgage... ...mortgage repayments.* N COUNT

2 If you **mortgage** your house or land, you use it as a guarantee to a company in order to borrow money from them. EG *He will have to mortgage his land for a loan.* V+O Technical

mortify /mɔːtɪfaɪ/, **mortifies, mortifying, mortified.** If you **are mortified**, you feel very offended, ashamed, or embarrassed. EG *She was deeply mortified at this rebuff.* ◇ **mortifying.** EG *There were some mortifying setbacks.* ◇ **mortification** /mɔːtɪfɪkeɪʃəⁿn/. EG *Davie was hiding his head in his hands with mortification.* V+O : USU PASS ◇ ADJ QUALIT ◇ N UNCOUNT

mortuary /mɔːtʃʊ⁰əri¹/, **mortuaries.** A **mortuary** is a special room in a hospital where dead bodies are kept before being buried or cremated. N COUNT

mosaic /məʊzeɪɪk/, **mosaics.** A **mosaic** is a design made of small coloured pebbles or pieces of coloured glass set in concrete or plaster. EG *...a Roman mosaic... ...walls covered with mosaics.* N COUNT OR N UNCOUNT

Moslem /mɒzləⁿm/. See **Muslim.**

mosque /mɒsk/, **mosques.** A **mosque** is a building where Muslims go to worship. N COUNT

mosquito /mə⁷skiːtəʊ/, **mosquitoes** or **mosquitos. Mosquitoes** are small insects which live in damp places and bite people in order to suck their blood. EG *...hands covered with mosquito bites.* N COUNT

moss /mɒs/, **mosses. Moss** is a very small soft green plant which grows on damp soil, or on wood or stone. EG *The bark was covered with moss.* N MASS

mossy /mɒsi¹/, **mossier, mossiest.** Something that is **mossy** is covered with moss. EG *...a flight of mossy stone steps... ...a long mossy path.* ADJ QUALIT

most /məʊst/. **1 Most** of a group of things or people means nearly all of them, or the majority of them. **Most** of something means nearly all of it. EG *Most Arabic speakers understand Egyptian... I saw most of the early Shirley Temple films... He used to spend most of his time in the library.* QUANTIF

2 The **most** means **2.1** a larger amount than anyone or anything else. EG *This is the area that attracts the most attention.* **2.2** the largest amount that is possible. EG *The most I could learn was that Lithgow had been sacked.* QUANTIF

3 You can use **most** in front of adjectives or adverbs to form superlatives. EG *It was one of the most important discoveries ever made... These are the works I respond to most strongly.* SUBMOD

4 Most means to a greater degree or extent than anything else. EG *What he most feared was being left alone... I liked him the most... Which do you value most – wealth or health?* ADV SUPERL

5 You can use **most** to emphasize an adjective or adverb. For example, if you say that something is **most** interesting, you mean that it is very interesting. EG *The trading results show a most encouraging trend... I would most certainly love a drink... He always acted most graciously.* SUBMOD Formal

6 You use **at most** when stating the maximum number that is possible or likely. EG *I only have fifteen minutes or twenty minutes at the most... There would be at most a hundred people listening.* PHRASE

7 If you **make the most of** something, you get the maximum use, help, or advantage from it. EG *Governments should face up to the situation and make the most of it.* PHRASE

-most is used to form adjectives that describe something as being further in a particular direction than other things of the same kind. For example, the northernmost part of a country is the part that is furthest to the north. EG *...the southernmost tip of the island... ...the innermost room of the castle... ...the topmost branches of a tree.* SUFFIX

mostly /məʊstli¹/ is used to indicate that a statement is generally true, for example true about the majority of a group of things or people, or true most of the time. EG *The men at the party were mostly fairly young... A rattlesnake hunts mostly at night... They were mostly women.* ADV OR ADV SEN

MOT /ɛm əʊ tiː/, **MOTs.** An **MOT** is a British test which is made each year on all road vehicles that are more than 3 years old, in order to check that they are safe to drive. EG *Our ageing minibus failed its MOT.* N COUNT

motel /məʊtɛl/, **motels.** A **motel** is a hotel intended for people who are travelling by car, which has space to park cars near the rooms. N COUNT

moth /mɒθ/, **moths.** A **moth** is an insect like a butterfly, which usually flies about at night. N COUNT

mothball /mɒθbɔːl/, **mothballs. Mothballs** are small white balls made of a special chemical, which you can put amongst clothes or blankets in order to keep moths away. N COUNT

moth-eaten. Clothes that are **moth-eaten** look very old and ragged with holes in. EG *...moth-eaten sweaters and worn-out shoes.* ADJ QUALIT

mother /mʌðə/, **mothers, mothering, mothered. 1** Your **mother** is the woman who gave birth to you. EG *I always did everything my mother told me... You are looking wonderful, Mother.* N COUNT OR VOCATIVE

2 If you **mother** someone, **2.1** you look after them and bring them up, usually when you are their mother. EG *Female monkeys who were badly mothered became bad mothers themselves.* **2.2** you treat them with great care and affection, and often spoil them. EG *Both the other senior typists tended to mother me.* V+O : USU PASS; V+O

motherhood /mʌðəhʊd/ is the state of being a mother. EG *...girls preparing for motherhood.* N UNCOUNT

mother-in-law, mothers-in-law. Someone's **mother-in-law** is the mother of their husband or wife. N COUNT

motherless /mʌðələ²s/. If someone is **motherless**, their mother has died, or has left them and gone away. EG *What a bad thing it is to leave a child motherless.* ADJ CLASSIF

motherly /mʌðəli¹/. A **motherly** person shows warm, kind, and protective feelings like those of a mother. EG *...a plump, motherly woman... Motherly hands touched him lightly, lovingly.* ADJ QUALIT

mother-of-pearl is the hard, smooth substance which forms a layer on the inside of the shells of some shellfish. It is often used to make buttons or to decorate things. N UNCOUNT

mother-to-be, mothers-to-be. A **mother-to-be** is a woman who is pregnant, especially for the first time. N COUNT

mother-tongue, mother-tongues. Your **mother-tongue** is the language that you learnt from your parents when you were a child. N COUNT

motif /məʊtiːf/, **motifs.** A **motif** is a design which is used as a decoration. EG *There were white curtains with black and red motifs on them.* N COUNT : USU+SUPP

motion /məʊʃəⁿn/, **motions, motioning, motioned. 1 Motion** is the process of continually changing position or moving from one place to another. EG *The bed swayed with the motion of the ship... Just keep moving, stay in motion.* ● See also **slow motion.** N UNCOUNT

2 A **motion** is an action, gesture, or movement. EG *He made stabbing motions with his spear... With a quick motion of her hands, she did her hair up in a knot.... He made chewing motions with his jaws.* N COUNT : USU+SUPP

3 A **motion** in a meeting or debate is a formal proposal which the people present discuss and then vote on. EG *He proposed the motion that 'the Public Schools of England should be abolished.'* N COUNT

4 If you **motion** to someone, you make a movement with your hand in order to show them what V+*to* OR V+O+*to*

they should do. EG *He motioned Tom to follow him... He shook hands and motioned him to a seat.*

5 If you **go through the motions**, **5.1** you say or do something that is expected of you, without being very sincere or serious about it. EG *Major Hawks went through the motions of advising me to quit.* PHRASE

5.2 you pretend to do something by making the movements associated with a particular action. EG *He laughed and went through the motions of aiming a slow punch at my jaw.*

6 A process or event that is **in motion** is happening already. EG *The changes are already in motion... ...helping to set the programmes in motion.* PHRASE

motionless /məʊʃə[0]nlɪ[2]s/. Someone or something that is **motionless** is not moving at all. EG *Rudolph sat motionless... ...queues of motionless cars.* ADJ CLASSIF

motivate /məʊtɪveɪt/, **motivates, motivating, motivated.** 1 If you **are motivated** by something, especially an emotion, it causes you to behave in a particular way. EG *...people motivated by envy and the lust for power... My decision to make this trip was motivated by a desire to leave the country.* V+O : USU PASS

◊ **motivation** /məʊtɪveɪʃə[0]n/, **motivations.** EG *There's a political motivation for these actions... What was the motivation to stay at school?* ◊ N COUNT OR N UNCOUNT

2 If you **motivate** someone, you make them feel determined to do something. EG *You have first got to motivate the children and then to teach them.* V+O

◊ **motivated.** EG *...highly motivated and enthusiastic people.* ◊ ADJ QUALIT ◊ **motivation.** EG *She insists her success is due to motivation rather than brilliance.* ◊ N UNCOUNT

motive /məʊtɪv/, **motives.** Your **motive** for doing something is your aim or purpose in doing it. EG *Was there some sinister motive for their action?... I urge you to question his motives.* N COUNT

motley /mɒtli[1]/. A **motley** collection of people or things is one in which the people or things are all very different from each other. EG *...a motley collection of hats and coats.* ADJ QUALIT : ATTRIB

motor /məʊtə/, **motors, motoring, motored.** 1 A **motor** is a part of a machine or vehicle that uses electricity or fuel to produce movement, so that the machine or vehicle can work. EG *He got into the car and started the motor... ...an electric motor.* N COUNT

2 **Motor** means relating to vehicles with a petrol engine or diesel engine. EG *...the decline of the motor industry... ...a motor mechanic.* ADJ CLASSIF : ATTRIB

3 If you **are motoring** somewhere, you are travelling there in a car. EG *They spent a week motoring through Italy.* ● See also **motoring**. V : USU+A Outdated

motorbike /məʊtəbaɪk/, **motorbikes.** A **motorbike** is the same as a motorcycle. EG *...youths riding up and down on powerful motorbikes.* N COUNT British Informal

motor car, motor cars. A **motor car** is the same as a car. N COUNT Formal

motorcycle /məʊtəsaɪkə[0]l/, **motorcycles.** A **motorcycle** is a two-wheeled vehicle that has an engine. EG *...cars and motorcycles for hire.* N COUNT

motorcyclist /məʊtəsaɪklɪst/, **motorcyclists.** A **motorcyclist** is a person who rides a motorcycle. EG *...police motorcyclists.* N COUNT

motoring /məʊtə[0]rɪŋ/ means relating to cars and to driving. EG *...motoring offences.* ADJ CLASSIF : ATTRIB

motorist /məʊtə[0]rɪst/, **motorists.** A **motorist** is a person who drives a car. N COUNT

motorized /məʊtə[0]raɪzd/; also spelled **motorised. Motorized** vehicles have engines. EG *...motorized transport.* ADJ CLASSIF

motorway /məʊtəweɪ/, **motorways.** A **motorway** is a big road that has been specially built for fast travel over long distances. N COUNT British

mottled /mɒtə[0]ld/. Something that is **mottled** is covered with areas or spots of a different colour. EG *...a mottled camouflage jacket.* ADJ QUALIT

motto /mɒtəʊ/, **mottoes** or **mottos.** A **motto** is a short sentence or phrase that expresses a rule for good or sensible behaviour. EG *...the school motto, 'To strive, to seek, to find.'* N COUNT

mould /məʊld/, **moulds, moulding, moulded;** spelled **mold** in American English.

1 If you **mould** someone, you influence them over a long period of time so that their character develops in a particular way. EG *...the desire to mould the child into a disciplined creature.* V+O

2 If you **mould** something, you create it or change it over a long period of time. EG *We have spent the past year creating and moulding this industry... Television plays a dominant role in moulding public opinion.* V+O Formal

3 If you **mould** a substance such as plastic or clay, you make it into a particular shape. EG *...clay moulded into pots.* V+O

4 A **mould** is a container that you use to make something into a particular shape. You pour a liquid substance into the mould, and when the substance becomes solid you take it out and it has the same shape as the mould. N COUNT

5 If a person fits into or is cast in a **mould** of a particular kind, they are of a particular type, usually a common type. EG *He doesn't fit into the mould of the typical retired army officer... She won't have the guts to break out of the mould and move to another firm.* N COUNT : USU+SUPP

6 **Mould** is a soft grey, green, or blue substance that sometimes forms on old food or on damp walls or clothes. EG *...nasty green mould... Peanuts, when they go bad, produce a mould.* N MASS

mouldy /məʊldi[1]/; spelled **moldy** in American English. Something that is **mouldy** is covered with mould. EG *...mouldy fruit.* ADJ QUALIT

moult /məʊlt/, **moults, moulting, moulted;** spelled **molt** in American English. When an animal or bird **moults**, it loses its fur, hair, or feathers so that new fur, hair, or feathers can grow. V

mound /maʊnd/, **mounds.** A **mound** is **1** a pile of earth which is like a very small hill. EG *...a large circular mound of earth... ...a few grass mounds.* N COUNT **2** a large and rather untidy pile of things. EG *He lay in his bunk under a mound of blankets... ...mounds of tasteless rice.* N PART

mount /maʊnt/, **mounts, mounting, mounted. 1** If you **mount** a campaign or a particular course of action, you prepare it and carry it out. EG *We mounted a sustained attack on the government... No rescue operations could be mounted.* V+O

2 If you **mount** an exhibition or display, you organize and present it. EG *We mounted an exhibition of recent books.* V+O

3 If something **is mounting**, it is increasing. EG *Social problems in modern society are mounting... The temperature mounted rapidly.* V ◊ **mounting.** EG *Everywhere there is mounting unemployment.* ◊ ADJ CLASSIF : ATTRIB

4 If you **mount** something such as a staircase or a platform, you go up to the top of it. EG *Walter mounted the steps and pressed the bell.* V+O Formal

5 When someone **mounts** a horse, they climb on to its back so that they can ride it. EG *The brothers watched as she mounted the mare.* ● See also **mounted**. V+O OR V

6 If you **mount** an object in a particular place, you fix it there firmly. EG *The sword was mounted in a mahogany case.* V+O : USU+A

7 **Mount** is used as part of the name of a mountain. EG *...Mount Erebus.*

8 If you **mount a guard** over something, you get someone to guard it. If you **mount guard** over something, you guard it yourself. EG *Strong police guards were mounted at all hospitals... She had been asked to mount guard over a number of dogs.* PHRASE

mount up. If something **mounts up**, it increases. EG *The soil becomes more and more acidic as pollution mounts up.* PHRASAL VB : V+ADV

Should you eat mousse if it is mouldy?

mountain /maʊntɪn/, **mountains. 1** A **mountain** is a very high piece of land with steep sides which are difficult to climb. EG *...a pleasant hotel in the mountains... ...a mountain road... ...the Rocky Mountains.* N COUNT

2 You can refer to a very large amount of something as a **mountain** of it. EG *...a mountain of rubble... ...mountains of letters and memoranda.* N PART

3 to **make a mountain out of a molehill**: see **molehill**.

mountaineer /maʊntɪnɪə/, **mountaineers.** A **mountaineer** is a person who climbs mountains. N COUNT

mountaineering /maʊntɪnɪərɪŋ/ is the activity of climbing mountains as a hobby or sport. N UNCOUNT

mountainous /maʊntɪnəs/. **1** A **mountainous** area has a lot of mountains. EG *I was walking through mountainous country.* ADJ QUALIT

2 A **mountainous** thing or person is unusually large or high. EG *...ranks of mountainous females.* ADJ CLASSIF : ATTRIB

mountainside /maʊntɪnsaɪd/, **mountainsides.** A **mountainside** is one of the steep sides of a mountain. EG *...hurtling down the mountainside.* N COUNT

mounted /maʊntɪ²d/. **Mounted** police or soldiers ride horses when they are on duty. ADJ CLASSIF : ATTRIB

mourn /mɔːn/, **mourns, mourning, mourned. 1** If you **mourn** someone who has died or **mourn** for them, you are very sad and think about them a lot. EG *I remained to mourn him in Chicago... I shall always love Guy and mourn for him.* • See also **mourning**. V+O OR V+*for*

2 If you **mourn** something or **mourn** for it, you are very sad because you no longer have it. EG *I mourned for the loss of my beauty.* V+O OR V+*for*

mourner /mɔːnə/, **mourners.** A **mourner** is a person who attends a funeral. EG *I went out into the garden to join the mourners.* N COUNT

mournful /mɔːnfʊl/. **1** If you are **mournful**, you are very sad. EG *Jefferson looked mournful... He addressed Thomas in a mournful voice.* ADJ QUALIT Literary

◊ **mournfully.** EG *He shook his head mournfully.* ◊ ADV

2 A **mournful** sound seems very sad. EG *The little train kept up its mournful howl.* ADJ QUALIT Literary

mourning /mɔːnɪŋ/. **1 Mourning** is behaviour in which you show sadness about a person's death. EG *Beards were shaved off as a sign of mourning.* N UNCOUNT

2 If you are **in mourning**, you are wearing special clothes or behaving in a special way because a member of your family has died. EG *He was in mourning for his wife.* PHRASE

mouse /maʊs/, **mice** /maɪs/. A **mouse** is a very small furry animal with a long tail. EG *The cat was there to keep the mice out of the kitchen.* N COUNT

moussaka /mʊsɑːkə/, **moussakas. Moussaka** is a cooked dish consisting of layers of meat and aubergines. N MASS

mousse /muːs/, **mousses. Mousse** is a sweet, light food made from eggs and cream. EG *...chocolate mousse.* N MASS

moustache /məstɑːʃ/, **moustaches;** spelled **mustache** /mʌstæʃ/ in American English. A man's **moustache** is the hair that grows on his upper lip. EG *...a tall man with a moustache.* N COUNT

mousy /maʊsi¹/. **Mousy** hair is a dull, light brown colour. ADJ QUALIT

mouth, mouths, mouthing, mouthed. The noun is pronounced /maʊθ/ in the singular and /maʊðz/ in the plural. The verb is pronounced /maʊð/.

1 Your **mouth** is your lips, or the space behind your lips where your teeth and tongue are. You use your mouth for eating and speaking. See picture at THE HUMAN BODY. EG *She opened her mouth to say something, then closed it... Mr Geard had his mouth full of sponge cake.* N COUNT

2 The **mouth** of a cave or hole is the entrance to it. EG *There was a vicious snarling in the mouth of the shelter.* N COUNT : USU+*of*

3 The **mouth** of a river is the place where it flows into the sea. EG *We lived near the mouth of the Bashee River.* N COUNT : USU+*of*

4 If you **mouth** something, you form words with your lips without making any sound. EG *She mouthed the word no... Jane mouthed 'Water?'* V+O OR V+QUOTE

5 shut your **mouth**: see **shut**. • **by word of mouth**: see **word**. • See also **hand-to-mouth, loud-mouthed, open-mouthed, mouth-watering**.

mouthful /maʊθfʊl/, **mouthfuls. 1** A **mouthful** of food or drink is an amount that you put or have in your mouth. EG *He took another mouthful of whisky... 'Don't you like me?' she asked between mouthfuls.* N COUNT OR N PART

2 If you say that a name or phrase is a bit of a **mouthful**, you mean that it is long or difficult to say. N COUNT Informal

mouth organ, mouth organs. A **mouth organ** is a small musical instrument. You play it by moving it across your lips and blowing and sucking air through it. N COUNT

mouthpiece /maʊθpiːs/, **mouthpieces. 1** The **mouthpiece** of a telephone is the part that you speak into. EG *She had her hand over the mouthpiece.* N COUNT

2 The **mouthpiece** of something such as a musical instrument is the part that you put into your mouth. N COUNT

3 The **mouthpiece** of a person or organization is the person who publicly states their opinions and policies. EG *He became the official mouthpiece of the leadership.* N COUNT : USU+SUPP

mouthwash /maʊθwɒʃ/, **mouthwashes. Mouthwash** is a liquid that you rinse your mouth with, in order to clean and freshen it. N MASS

mouth-watering. Mouth-watering food looks or smells extremely delicious. EG *...mouth-watering ingredients like raisins.* ADJ QUALIT

movable /muːvəbə⁰l/; also spelled **moveable.** Something that is **movable** can be moved from one place to another. EG *The room is divided by movable screens.* ADJ CLASSIF

move /muːv/, **moves, moving, moved. 1** When you **move** something or when it **moves**, its position changes or keeps changing. EG *Workmen were moving a heavy wardrobe in a bedroom... I'll have to move the car... The curtains behind began to move.* V-ERG

2 When you **move, 2.1** you change your position or go to a different place. EG *I was so scared I couldn't move... He moved eagerly towards the door to welcome his visitors... He could hear Felicity moving about upstairs.* V : USU+A ▸ used as a noun. EG *They had been watching his every move... For a good half hour neither she nor any of the others made a move.* ▸ N SING **2.2** you act or begin to do something. EG *If we are going to go ahead, let's move fast.* V

3 If you **move** or if you **move** house, you go and live in a different house, taking your possessions with you. EG *My parents moved from Hyde to Stepney... They had decided to retire from farming and move away.* V : USU+A; ALSO V+O ▸ used as a noun. EG *I wrecked a good stereo on my last move.* ▸ N COUNT ◊ **moving.** EG *Moving costs have risen considerably.* ◊ N UNCOUNT

4 If you **move** or **are moved** from one place or job to another, you go from one place or job to another. EG *Executives are being moved around from one company to another... He'd moved to the BBC from publishing.* V-ERG : OFT+A ▸ used as a noun. EG *Regular moves for junior executives are a company policy.* ▸ N COUNT

5 If you are **on the move**, you are going from one place to another. EG *Billie Jean is constantly on the move.* PHRASE

6 If you **move** towards a particular state, activity or opinion, you start to be in that state, do that activity, or have that opinion. EG *We are moving rapidly into the nuclear age... Public opinion was moving strongly in favour of disarmament.* V+A ▸ used as a noun. EG *This was the first step in his move away from the Labour party.* ▸ N COUNT

7 If a situation **is moving**, it is developing or progressing. EG *Events now moved swiftly... A writer must keep the story moving.* V

8 If something **moves** you to do something, it influences you and causes you to do it. EG *What has moved the President to take this step?* V+O+*to*-INF Formal

9 If something **moves** you, it causes you to feel a deep emotion, usually sadness or sympathy. EG *The whole incident had moved her profoundly.* V+O
◇ **moved.** EG *He was too moved to speak.* ◇ ADJ QUALIT

10 If you **move** a motion or amendment at a meeting, you formally propose it so that everyone present can vote for or against it. V+O

11 A **move** is also 11.1 an action that you take in order to achieve something. EG *Accepting this job was a very good move... For six days neither side made a move.* 11.2 an act of putting a counter or chess piece in a different position on the board when it is your turn to do so in a game. EG *Whose move is it?* N COUNT

12 If you tell someone to **get a move on**, you are telling them to hurry. PHRASE Informal

13 See also **moving**.

move down. If you **move down**, you go to a lower level, grade, or class. EG *When they fail their mathematics exams they move down a year.* PHRASAL VB : V+ADV, USU+A

move in. 1 If you **move in** somewhere, you begin to live in a different house or place. EG *He moved in with Mrs Camish.* 2 If soldiers or police **move in**, they go towards a place or person in order to attack them or deal with them. EG *They were under orders to move in from France.* PHRASAL VB : V+ADV

move off. When vehicles or people **move off**, they start moving away from a place. EG *The gleaming fleet of cars prepared to move off.* PHRASAL VB : V+ADV

move on. When you **move on**, 1 you leave a place and go somewhere else. EG *After three weeks in Hong Kong, we moved on to Japan.* 2 you finish one thing and start doing something else. EG *Can we move on to the second question?* PHRASAL VB : V+ADV

move out. If you **move out**, you leave the house or place where you have been living, and go and live somewhere else. PHRASAL VB : V+ADV

move up. If you **move up**, you go to a higher level, grade, or class. EG *The Vice-President should move up into the Presidency... ...moving up the scale.* PHRASAL VB : V+ADV/PREP

moveable /mu:vəbə^{0}l/. See **movable**.

movement /mu:vmə^{2}nt/, **movements.** 1 **Movement** involves 1.1 changing position or going from one place to another. EG *He heard movement in the hut... ...the soft movement of the flags... Tom lit a cigarette with quick, jerky movements.* 1.2 transporting goods from one place to another. EG *...the movement of oil cargoes.* 1.3 a gradual development or change in an attitude, opinion, or policy. EG *...the party's general leftward movement... There was a movement towards a revival of conscription.* N UNCOUNT OR N COUNT

2 Your **movements** are everything which you do or plan to do during a period of time. EG *I don't know why you have any interest in my movements.* N PLURAL

3 A **movement** is also a group of people who share the same beliefs, ideas, or aims. EG *...the Trade Union Movement... ...the successful movement to abolish child labour.* N COUNT : USU+SUPP

4 A **movement** of a piece of classical music is one of its major sections. EG *There is an immensely long first movement.* N COUNT

movie /mu:vi^1/, **movies.** 1 A **movie** is a cinema film. EG *...a war movie... I went to a movie.* N COUNT

2 The cinema is sometimes called the **movies**. EG *We decided to spend the afternoon at the movies... ...going to the movies.* N PLURAL : *the*+N American

moving /mu:vɪŋ/. 1 Something that is **moving** causes you to feel a deep emotion, usually sadness or sympathy. EG *There is a moving account of his father's death.* ◇ **movingly.** EG *Her childhood is movingly described.* ADJ QUALIT ◇ ADV

2 A **moving** model or part of a machine is able to move. EG *These devices have no moving parts.* ADJ CLASSIF : ATTRIB

3 See also **move**.

mow /məʊ/, **mows, mowing, mowed, mown** /məʊn/. **Mowed** and **mown** are both used as the past participle.

1 If you **mow** an area of grass, you cut it using a lawnmower. EG *Everyone was mowing their lawns.* V+O OR V

2 If you **mow** corn or wheat, you cut it. V+O OR V

mow down. To **mow down** a large number of people means to kill them all violently at one time. EG *Several children had strayed onto an airport runway and been mown down by a jet.* PHRASAL VB : V+O+ADV

mower /məʊə/, **mowers.** A **mower** is a machine for cutting grass, corn, or wheat. N COUNT

MP /ɛm pi:/, **MPs.** An **MP** is a person who has been elected to represent people in a country's parliament. **MP** is an abbreviation for 'Member of Parliament'. EG *...the MP for South East Bristol.* N COUNT

mph is an abbreviation for 'miles per hour'. **mph** is used after a number to indicate the speed of something. EG *These cars are reasonably economical at a steady 56 mph.*

Mr /mɪstə/. 1 **Mr** is used before a man's name when you are speaking or referring to him. EG *...Mr Jenkins... ...Mr John Watson.*

2 **Mr** is sometimes used before words like 'president' and 'chairman' when you are addressing the person who holds that position. EG *Yes, Mr President.*

Mrs /mɪsɪz/ is used before the name of a married woman when you are speaking or referring to her. EG *...Mrs Carstairs.*

Ms /məz/ is used before a woman's name when you are speaking or referring to her, especially in written English. If you use **Ms**, you are not specifying whether the woman is married or not.

M.Sc. /ɛm ɛs si:/, **M.Scs.** An **M.Sc.** is a higher degree in a scientific subject. **M.Sc.** is an abbreviation for 'Master of Science'. N COUNT

much /mʌtʃ/. For paragraphs 1, 2, and 4, the comparative is **more** and the superlative is **most**. See separate entries for **more** and **most**.

1 You use **much** to emphasize that something is true to a great extent. EG *Myra and I are looking forward very much to the party... He is very much at ease in life... In Vienna, the travellers stopped for a much-needed rest... Now I feel much more confident.* ADV

2 If something does not happen **much**, it does not happen very often. EG *She doesn't talk about them much.* ADV

3 If one thing is **much** the same as another thing, it is very similar to it. EG *The landscape was then much as it is today... The two poems convey much the same emotional tone.* ADV

4 You also use **much** to refer to a large amount or proportion of something. EG *We hadn't got much money... Much of the recent trouble has come from outside... There wasn't much to do... She had endured so much.* QUANTIF

5 You also use **much** when you ask questions or give information about the size of an amount. EG *How much money have you got left?... How much did he tell you?... He's done as much as I have.* QUANTIF

6 **Much** is also used in these phrases. 6.1 If you say that something is **not so much** one thing as another, you mean that it is more like the second thing than the first. EG *It was not so much an argument as a monologue.* PHRASE 6.2 If you say **so much for** a particular thing, you mean that it has not been successful or helpful. EG *So much for the experts and their learning.* PHRASE 6.3 If you say that **much as** one thing is true, another thing is not true, you mean that although the first thing is true, the second thing is not true. EG *Much as she likes him she would never consider marrying him.* CONJ 6.4 **Nothing much** means an amount that is so small PHRASE

How many abbreviations are there on these pages?

that it is not important. EG *There's nothing much left.* **6.5** If a situation or action is **too much** for you, it is so difficult, tiring, or upsetting that you cannot cope with it. EG *The long journey each day might prove too much for him.* **6.6** If you describe something as **not much of a** particular type of thing, you mean that it is small or of poor quality. EG *It wasn't much of a garden.* **6.7** If you do not **so much as** do a particular thing, you do not even do that, when you were expected to do more. EG *John strolled by without so much as a glance of recognition.* **6.8** You say **'I thought as much'** after you have just been told something that you had expected or guessed. **6.9 a bit much**: see **bit**. • **not up to much**: see **up**. — PHRASE; PHRASE; PHRASE; CONVENTION

muchness /mʌtʃnɪ²s/. If two or more things are **much of a muchness**, they are very similar. EG *In general appearance the men were all much of a muchness.* — PHRASE, Informal

muck /mʌk/, **mucks, mucking, mucked. Muck** is **1** dirt or some other unpleasant substance. EG *There was muck everywhere.* **2** manure. EG *...a muck heap.* — N UNCOUNT, Informal, Informal

muck about or **muck around.** If you **muck about** or **muck around**, you behave in a stupid way and waste time. EG *She was mucking about with a jug of flowers on the table.* — PHRASAL VB : V+ADV, Informal

muck out. If you **muck out** a stable, pigsty, or cow shed, you clean it. — PHRASAL VB : V+O+ADV

muck up. If you **muck** something **up**, you do it very badly or fail when you try to do it. EG *'How was the exam?' – 'I mucked it up.'* — PHRASAL VB : V+O+ADV, Informal

mucky /mʌki¹/. **1** Something that is **mucky** is very dirty. EG *...mucky fields.* — ADJ QUALIT, Informal

2 A **mucky** book or film describes or shows a lot of sex; used showing disapproval. — ADJ QUALIT, Informal

mucus /mju:kəs/ is a liquid that is produced in some parts of your body, for example your nose. — N UNCOUNT, Formal

mud /mʌd/ is a wet, sticky mixture of earth and water. EG *She was covered in mud.* — N UNCOUNT

muddle /mʌdə⁰l/, **muddles, muddling, muddled.**

1 A **muddle** is a state of disorder or untidiness. EG *With the right government, the country wouldn't be in such a muddle... ...the worsening muddle of her finances.* — N COUNT OR N UNCOUNT

2 If you **muddle** things, you cause them to become mixed up or in the wrong order. EG *I wish you wouldn't muddle my books and drawings.* — V+O

3 If you **muddle** someone, you cause them to become confused. EG *Don't muddle her with too many suggestions.* ◊ **muddled.** EG *I'm sorry. I thought I had. I'm getting muddled.* — V+O; ◊ ADJ QUALIT

4 A **muddle** is also a state of confusion in the mind. EG *I have got into a muddle.* — N COUNT OR N UNCOUNT

muddle along. If you **muddle along**, you live or exist without a proper plan or purpose in your life. EG *The church has lost its way, muddling along from Sunday to Sunday.* — PHRASAL VB : V+ADV

muddle through. If you **muddle through**, you manage to do something even though you do not really know how to do it properly. EG *The children are left to muddle through on their own.* — PHRASAL VB : V+ADV

muddle up. If you **muddle** things **up**, you cause them to become mixed up or in the wrong order. EG *Later they may muddle up your names with those of your cousins.* ◊ **muddled up.** EG *You've got the story muddled up.* — PHRASAL VB : V+O+ADV; ◊ ADJ QUALIT

muddy /mʌdi¹/, **muddier, muddiest; muddies, muddying, muddied. 1** Something that is **muddy** contains mud or is covered in mud. EG *...a muddy ditch... ...the muddy floor.* — ADJ QUALIT

2 A **muddy** colour is dull and brownish. EG *The landscape turns a mottled, muddy brown.* — ADJ QUALIT

3 If you **muddy** a situation or issue, you make it less clear and less easy to understand. EG *The issue has been muddied by allegations of bribery.* — V+O

mudguard /mʌdgɑ:d/, **mudguards.** The **mudguards** on a bicycle or other vehicle are the metal or plastic parts above the tyres, which prevent mud from the road from being splashed up onto the rider or the vehicle. EG *...a racing model with no mudguards and special tyres.* See picture at BICYCLE. — N COUNT

muesli /mju:zli¹/ is a mixture of chopped nuts, dried fruit, and grains that you eat for breakfast with milk or yoghurt. — N UNCOUNT

muffin /mʌfɪn/, **muffins.** A **muffin** is a kind of small, round bread roll which you eat hot. — N COUNT

muffle /mʌfə⁰l/, **muffles, muffling, muffled.** If something **muffles** a sound, it makes the sound quieter and more difficult to hear. EG *The snow muffled the sound of our footsteps.* — V+O

muffled /mʌfə⁰ld/. **1** A **muffled** sound is quiet, dull, or difficult to hear, rather than being clear and sharp. EG *'I don't know,' he said in a muffled voice... ...a muffled explosion.* — ADJ QUALIT

2 If you are **muffled** or **muffled up**, you are wearing thick, warm clothes, and very little of your body or face can be seen. EG *He was heavily muffled in a black overcoat... ...a boy muffled up in a blue scarf.* — ADJ PRED

muffler /mʌflə/, **mufflers.** A **muffler** is a scarf. EG *...with a long, knitted muffler around her neck.* — N COUNT, Outdated

mug /mʌg/, **mugs, mugging, mugged. 1** A **mug** is a large, deep cup with straight sides. EG *...a chipped mug.* — N COUNT

2 You can also use **mug** to refer to a mug and its contents, or to the contents only. EG *He sipped at his mug of coffee.* — N PART

3 If someone **mugs** you, they attack you in order to steal your money. EG *They lurk in dark side streets and mug passers-by.* ◊ **mugging, muggings.** EG *There has been a great increase in vandalism and muggings.* ◊ **mugger, muggers.** EG *Gangs of teenage muggers roam the streets.* — V+O, Informal; ◊ N UNCOUNT OR N COUNT; ◊ N COUNT

4 If you say that someone is a **mug**, you mean that they are stupid and easily deceived by other people. EG *'All right,' he said, like the mug he was, 'I won't say anything.'* — N COUNT, Informal

muggy /mʌgi¹/. If the weather is **muggy**, it is unpleasantly warm and damp. EG *...the muggy, perfumed air of West Africa.* — ADJ QUALIT

mule /mju:l/, **mules.** A **mule** is an animal produced by a horse and a donkey. — N COUNT

mull /mʌl/, **mulls, mulling, mulled.** If you **mull** something **over**, you think about it for a long time, often before deciding what to do. EG *I sat there and tried to mull things over in my mind.* — PHRASAL VB : V+O+ADV

multi- means 'many'. It is added to the beginning of nouns and adjectives. EG *...multilateral... ... multi-storey.* — PREFIX

multifarious /mʌltɪfɛərɪəs/. **Multifarious** things are of many different kinds. EG *...pursuing their multifarious hobbies and interests.* — ADJ CLASSIF, Formal

multilateral /mʌltɪlætə⁰rəl/. Something that is **multilateral** involves at least three different countries or groups of people. EG *...multilateral nuclear disarmament.* — ADJ CLASSIF

multinational /mʌltɪnæʃə⁰nəl/, **multinationals.**

1 A **multinational** company has branches in many different countries. EG *Many of the West's large multinational companies have operations in Africa.* ▸ used as a noun. EG *Trade in bananas is dominated by three huge food multinationals.* — ADJ CLASSIF; ▸ N COUNT

2 You use **multinational** to describe something that involves several different countries. EG *...the multinational forces deployed under the treaty.* — ADJ CLASSIF

multiple /mʌltɪpə⁰l/. You use **multiple** to describe things that consist of many parts, involve many people, or have many uses. EG *There have been several multiple collisions in fog this winter... ...multiple locks on the doors.* — ADJ CLASSIF : ATTRIB

multiple-choice. When you do a **multiple-choice** test or question, you have to choose the correct answer from several possible answers that are listed on the question paper. — ADJ CLASSIF

multiple sclerosis /mʌltɪpə^{0}l sklərəʊsɪs/ is a serious disease of the nervous system, which affects your ability to move. N UNCOUNT

multiplication /mʌltɪplɪkeɪʃə^{0}n/. **1 Multiplication** is the process of calculating the total of one number multiplied by another number. EG *...multiplication and division.* N UNCOUNT

2 The **multiplication** of things of a particular kind is a large increase in the number or amount of them. EG *...the multiplication of universities.* N UNCOUNT +SUPP

multiplication sign, multiplication signs. A **multiplication sign** is the sign (x) which is put between two numbers to show that they are being multiplied. N COUNT

multiplicity /mʌltɪplɪsɪ^{1}ti^1/. A **multiplicity** of things is a large number or a large variety of them. EG *...the multiplicity of languages spoken in Africa.* N SING+*of* Formal

multiply /mʌltɪplaɪ/, **multiplies, multiplying, multiplied. 1** When something **multiplies** or **is multiplied**, it increases greatly in number or amount. EG *The shops began to multiply, eventually springing up in almost every town in the area.* V-ERG

2 When animals **multiply**, they increase in number by giving birth to large numbers of young. EG *The creatures began to multiply very rapidly.* V

3 If you **multiply** one number by another, you calculate the total which you get when you add the number to itself a particular number of times. For example, 2 multiplied by 3 is equal to 2 plus 2 plus 2, which equals 6. EG *Multiply this figure by the number of years you have worked.* V+O : OFT+*by*

multitude /mʌltɪtju:d/, **multitudes.** A **multitude** of things or people is a very large number of them. EG *It didn't work out quite like I intended it to, for a multitude of reasons... 'We are keeping our options open,' he had told the assembled multitude.* N PART OR N COUNT Formal

mum /mʌm/, **mums. 1** Your **mum** is your mother. EG *My mum used to live here... I've been put in the special class, Mum.* N COUNT OR VOCATIVE Informal

2 If you **keep mum** about something, you don't tell anyone about it. PHRASE Informal

mumble /mʌmbə^{0}l/, **mumbles, mumbling, mumbled.** If you **mumble**, you speak very quietly and indistinctly so that the words are difficult to understand. EG *Stop mumbling, for goodness sake... He took my hand and mumbled, 'Don't worry.'... I mumbled something about having an appointment.* V OR V-SPEECH : ONLY *that*

mummified /mʌmɪfaɪd/. A **mummified** dead body has stayed preserved for a long time, especially because special oils were rubbed into it. ADJ CLASSIF

mummy /mʌmi^1/, **mummies. 1 Mummy** means mother; used especially by children. EG *Mummy put me on the train at Victoria.* N COUNT OR VOCATIVE Informal

2 A **mummy** is a dead body which was preserved long ago by being rubbed with special oils and wrapped in cloth. EG *...a gilded Egyptian mummy case.* N COUNT

mumps /mʌmps/ is a disease that causes a painful swelling of the glands in the neck. N UNCOUNT

munch /mʌntʃ/, **munches, munching, munched.** If you **munch** something, you chew it steadily and thoroughly. EG *The father and son sat there, munching bread and butter.* V+O OR V

mundane /mʌndeɪn/. Something that is **mundane** is very ordinary, and not interesting or unusual. EG *...mundane tasks such as washing up.* ADJ QUALIT

municipal /mju:nɪsɪpə^{0}l/ means associated with or belonging to a city or town which has its own local government. EG *...a big municipal housing scheme... ...the municipal gardens.* ADJ CLASSIF : ATTRIB

munificent /mju:nɪfɪsənt/. Someone who is **munificent** is very generous. ADJ QUALIT Formal

munitions /mju:nɪʃə^{0}nz/ are bombs, guns, and other military supplies. EG *...munitions factories.* N PLURAL

mural /mjʊərəl/, **murals.** A **mural** is a picture which is painted on the wall of a room or building. N COUNT

murder /mɜ:də/, **murders, murdering, murdered. 1 Murder** is the deliberate and unlawful killing of a person. EG *...attempted murder... ...the rising number of murders in San Francisco.* N UNCOUNT OR N COUNT

2 To **murder** someone means to kill them deliberately and unlawfully. EG *His father, mother, and sister were all murdered by the terrorists.* V+O OR V

◇ **murderer, murderers.** EG *I want to track down the murderers of my son.* ◇ N COUNT

3 If you say that someone **gets away with murder**, you mean that they do whatever they like and nobody punishes them. PHRASE Informal

murderous /mɜ:də^{0}rəs/. **1** Someone who is **murderous** is likely to murder someone or wants to murder someone. EG *...murderous savages... The girl might have murderous tendencies.* ADJ CLASSIF

2 A **murderous** attack or other action results in the death of many people. EG *...murderous guerrilla raids.* ADJ CLASSIF

murk /mɜ:k/. You can refer to the darkness or the thick mist somewhere as the **murk**. EG *Through the murk the dull red sun was visible.* N SING : *the*+N

murky /mɜ:ki^1/. **1** Places that are **murky** are dark and rather unpleasant. EG *We looked out into the murky streets.* ADJ QUALIT

2 Water that is **murky** is dark in colour and has a lot of mud or leaves in it. EG *...murky ponds.* ADJ QUALIT

3 You also use **murky** to describe something that you suspect is dishonest or morally wrong. EG *...murky goings-on in a local picture gallery.* ADJ QUALIT Literary

murmur /mɜ:mə/, **murmurs, murmuring, murmured. 1** If you **murmur** or if you **murmur** something, you say it very quietly. EG *'Darling,' she murmured... 'I suggest we climb Ben Nevis tomorrow.' They murmured agreement.* V, V+O, OR V+QUOTE

2 A **murmur** is **2.1** something that someone says which can hardly be heard. EG *There were murmurs of sympathy.* N COUNT **2.2** a continuous, quiet, indistinct sound. EG *...the murmur of waves on a beach.* N SING+SUPP

muscle /mʌsə^{0}l/, **muscles, muscling, muscled.**
1 A **muscle** is a piece of flesh inside your body which is able to become smaller and to get bigger again. Your muscles enable you to make movements. EG *The boys couldn't help admiring their bulging muscles.* N COUNT OR N UNCOUNT

2 If someone has **muscle**, they have power, which enables them to do something difficult. EG *The campaign was valueless without the muscle of an organisation behind it.* N UNCOUNT Informal

muscle in. If you **muscle in** on something or **muscle** your way **in**, you force your way into a situation when you have no right to and when you are not welcome. EG *They are jealous of your success and resent the way you are muscling in on their territory.* PHRASAL VB : V+ADV+*on* OR V+O+ADV

muscular /mʌskjə^{4}lə/. **1 Muscular** means involving or affecting your muscles. EG *Great muscular effort is needed... ...muscular pains.* ADJ CLASSIF : ATTRIB

2 Someone who is **muscular** has strong, firm muscles. EG *...a short but muscular man of 35... ...his muscular arms.* ADJ QUALIT

muscular dystrophy /mʌskjə^{4}lə dɪstrəfi^1/ is a serious disease in which your muscles become gradually weaker. N UNCOUNT

muse /mju:z/, **muses, musing, mused. 1** If you **muse**, you think about something slowly or without a serious purpose. EG *She lay musing for a while... 'I can't see him as a family man,' she mused.* V : USU+A, OR V+QUOTE Literary

2 A **muse** is an imaginary force which is believed to give people inspiration and creative ideas, especially for poetry or music. EG *...the muse of music.* N COUNT Formal

museum /mju:zɪəm/, **museums.** A **museum** is a building where large numbers of interesting and valuable objects are kept and displayed to the public. EG *...classical sculpture in the British Museum.* N COUNT

Are all mummies mummified?

musical instruments

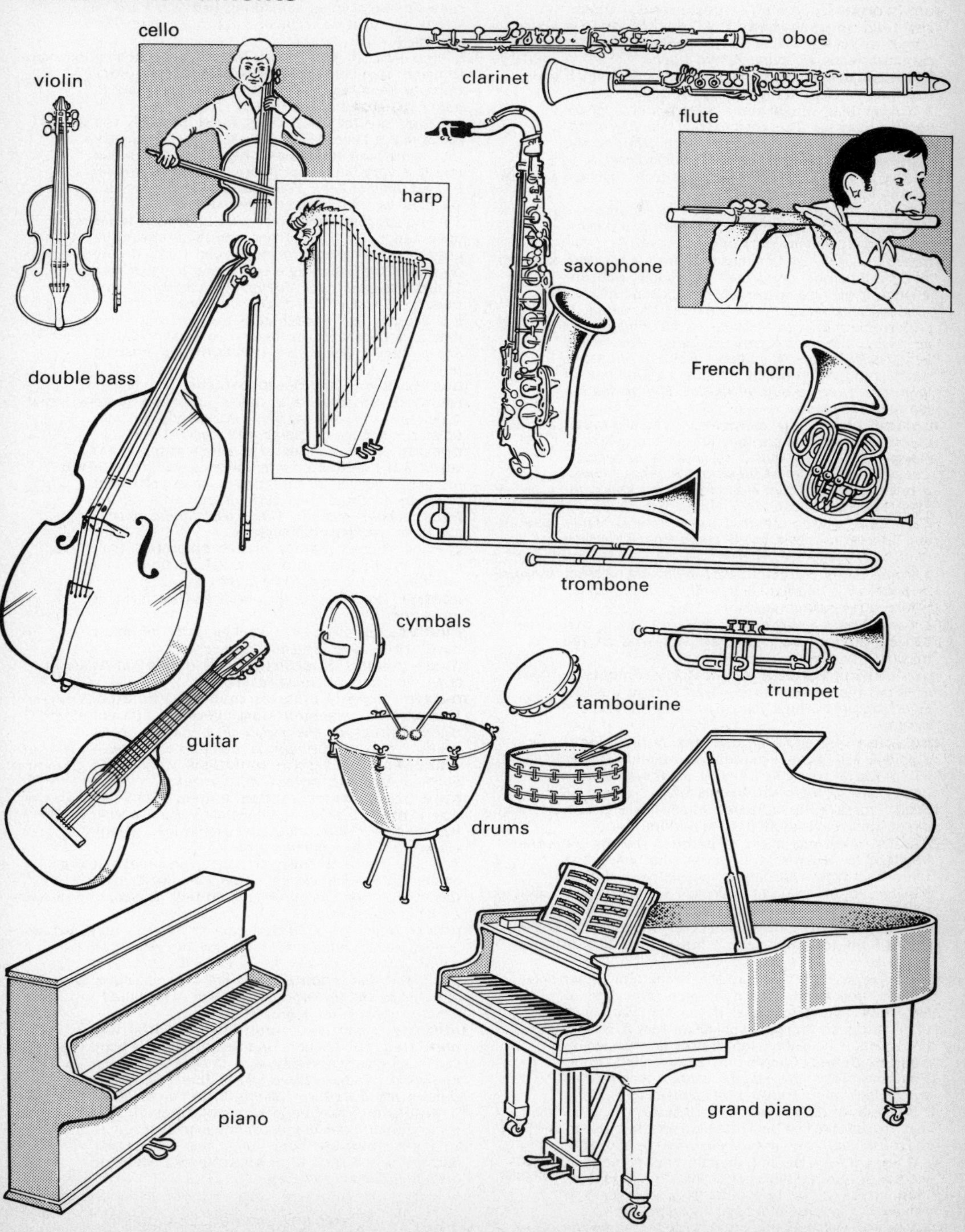

mush /mʌʃ/. If you refer to a substance as **mush**, you mean that it is in the form of a thick soft paste. EG *He gulped down the tasteless mush.* — N UNCOUNT OR N SING, Informal

mushroom /mʌʃru^{4}m/, **mushrooms, mushrooming, mushroomed. 1** A **mushroom** is a fungus with a short stem and a round top. You can eat mushrooms. EG *...a mushroom quiche.* — N COUNT

2 A **mushroom** cloud is a large cloud of dust which rises into the sky after a nuclear explosion. — N MOD

3 If something **mushrooms**, it grows or appears very quickly. EG *The organization quickly mushroomed into a mass movement of the middle classes... Factories mushroomed everywhere.* — V

mushy /mʌʃi^1/. **1** Vegetables and fruit that are **mushy** have become too soft. — ADJ QUALIT

2 Stories that are **mushy** are very sentimental; used showing disapproval. EG *The film is a mushy, but strangely moving story of young love.* — ADJ QUALIT

music /mju:zɪk/ is **1** sounds that are put together in a pattern and performed by people who are singing or playing instruments. EG *...dance music... ...the music of Irving Berlin.* **2** the art of creating or performing music. EG *He plans to make his career in music... One of his granddaughters was having her music lesson.* **3** symbols written on paper which represent musical sounds. EG *Not one of them could read a note of music... She placed the music on the piano.* — N UNCOUNT

musical /mju:zɪkə^{0}l/, **musicals. 1** You use **musical** to describe things that are concerned with playing or studying music. EG *...a musical career... ...one of London's most important musical events.* — ADJ CLASSIF : ATTRIB

◊ **musically.** EG *There is a lot going on musically every night in London.* — ◊ ADV

2 Someone who is **musical** has a natural ability and interest in music. EG *He came from a musical family.* — ADJ QUALIT

3 Sounds that are **musical** are tuneful and pleasant to hear. EG *A musical bell softly sounded somewhere in the passageway.* — ADJ QUALIT

4 A **musical** is a play or film that uses singing and dancing in the story. EG *She appeared in the musical 'Oklahoma'.* — N COUNT

musical instrument, musical instruments. A **musical instrument** is an object such as a piano, guitar, or violin which you play in order to produce music. — N COUNT

musician /mju:zɪʃə^{0}n/, **musicians.** A **musician** is a person who plays a musical instrument as their job, or plays it well as a hobby. EG *The musicians began packing their instruments away.* — N COUNT

musk /mʌsk/ is a substance which has a strong, sweet smell and is used to make perfume. — N UNCOUNT

Muslim /mʊzlɪm, mʌz-/, **Muslims;** also spelled **Moslem.** A **Muslim** is a person who believes in Islam and lives according to its rules. EG *...a pious Muslim on his way to Mecca.* ▸ used as an adjective. EG *...the medieval Muslim philosophers.* — N COUNT; ▸ ADJ CLASSIF

muslin /mʌzlɪn/ is a very thin cotton material. — N UNCOUNT

mussel /mʌsə^{0}l/, **mussels.** A **mussel** is a kind of shellfish. — N COUNT

must /mʌst/. **1** If you say that something **must** happen, you mean that it is very important or necessary that it happens. If you say that something **must** not happen, you mean that it is very important or necessary that it does not happen. EG *Your family and children must always come first... You must learn to remain calm... You mustn't worry about me... Things must change.* — MODAL

2 If you say that you **must** do something, you mean that you want to do it and intend to do it fairly soon. EG *I must come over and see you when he's away.* — MODAL, Informal

3 If you tell someone that they **must** do something, you are suggesting that they should do it or inviting them to do it. EG *You must play at the ship's concert... You must come and visit me.* — MODAL, Informal

4 You ask why someone **must** do something when you are angry or upset about it and do not understand why they are doing it. EG *Why must she be so nasty to me?* — MODAL

5 You say **'if you must'** when you cannot stop someone from doing something that you think is wrong or stupid. EG *Write and ask them yourself if you must.* — CONVENTION

6 You say **'if you must know'** when telling someone something that you did not really want them to know. EG *If you must know, I'm going to help him look for an apartment.* — CONVENTION

7 If you say that something **must** be true, you mean that it is very likely that it is true. If you say that something **must** have happened, you mean that it is very likely that it happened. EG *You must be very fond of her... You must be Florrie Brown... We must have taken the wrong road.* — MODAL

8 If you say that something **must** be true or **must** have happened in order for something else to be possible, you mean that the second thing is only possible if the first thing is true or has happened. EG *In order to qualify for Unemployment Benefit, you must have paid at least 26 contributions.* — MODAL

9 If you say that something is a **must**, you mean that it is absolutely necessary. EG *Rubber gloves are a must if your skin is sensitive to washing powders.* — N SING : a+N, Informal

mustache /mʌstæʃ/. See **moustache**.

mustard /mʌstəd/ is a yellow or brown paste which tastes hot and spicy and is usually eaten with meat. EG *...hot dogs dripping with mustard.* — N UNCOUNT

muster /mʌstə/, **musters, mustering, mustered. 1** If you **muster** something such as strength or energy, you use or gather as much as you can in order to do something. EG *I hit him with all the force I could muster... The group cannot muster sufficient working class support.* — V+O; ◊ ADJ CLASSIF

2 When soldiers **muster** or **are mustered**, they gather in one place in order to take action. EG *An enormous convoy mustered in the city.* — V-ERG

mustn't /mʌsə^{0}nt/ is the usual spoken form of 'must not'.

must've /mʌstə^{0}v/ is a spoken form of 'must have', when 'have' is an auxiliary verb.

musty /mʌsti^1/. Something that is **musty** smells stale and damp. EG *...musty old books.* — ADJ QUALIT

mutate /mju:teɪt/, **mutates, mutating, mutated.** If an animal or plant **mutates**, it develops different characteristics as the result of a change in its genes. ◊ **mutated.** EG *...a mutated flu virus.* — V : OFT+*into*, Technical

◊ **mutation** /mju:teɪʃə^{0}n/, **mutations.** EG *The rate at which mutations occur is fairly regular.* — ◊ N COUNT OR N UNCOUNT

mute /mju:t/, **mutes, muting, muted. 1** Someone who is **mute** is silent and does not speak. EG *Sally was staring at him, mute and awestruck... Fanny clasped her hands in mute protest.* — ADJ CLASSIF, Formal

2 If you **mute** a noise or sound, you make it quieter. EG *She had closed all the windows to mute the sounds from the town.* ◊ **muted.** EG *People spoke in muted voices.* — V+O, Formal; ◊ ADJ CLASSIF

muted /mju:tɪ^{2}d/. **1 Muted** colours are soft and gentle. EG *...a muted colour scheme of cream and white.* — ADJ CLASSIF

2 If a reaction is **muted**, it is not very strong or intense. EG *On the whole, criticism was muted... ...muted enthusiasm.* • See also **mute**. — ADJ QUALIT

mutilate /mju:tɪleɪt/, **mutilates, mutilating, mutilated. 1** If someone **is mutilated**, their body is damaged very severely. EG *Both bodies had been mutilated... They tortured and mutilated their victims.* ◊ **mutilated.** EG *...photos of mutilated bodies.* — V+O : USU PASS; ◊ ADJ CLASSIF

◊ **mutilation** /mju:tɪleɪʃə^{0}n/, **mutilations.** EG *...the death or mutilation of innocent men and women.* — ◊ N COUNT OR N UNCOUNT

2 If you **mutilate** something, you deliberately damage it and spoil it. EG *Almost every book had been mutilated in some way.* — V+O : USU PASS

If criticism is muted, is it mute?

mutinous /mju:tınəs/. A person who is **mutinous** is likely to disobey or rebel against the people in authority. EG *The crew were restive and mutinous.* ADJ CLASSIF Formal

mutiny /mju:tıni[1]/, **mutinies, mutinying, mutinied.** A **mutiny** is a rebellion by a group of people against a person in authority. EG *It's like a slave ship after a successful mutiny... Mutiny can lead to riot.* ▸ used as a verb. EG *He shot himself when his regiment mutinied.* N COUNT OR N UNCOUNT ▸ V

mutter /mʌtə/, **mutters, muttering, muttered.** If you **mutter**, you speak very quietly so that you cannot easily be heard, often in a cross or unfriendly way. EG *Denis could be heard muttering to himself about my stupidity... He refused her invitation with a muttered excuse... 'Sorry,' he muttered.* ▸ used as a noun. EG *...a quick low mutter.* V: OFT+*to*; ALSO V-SPEECH: ONLY *that* ▸ N COUNT

mutton /mʌtə[0]n/. **1 Mutton** is meat from an adult sheep. EG *...a leg of mutton.* N UNCOUNT

2 If you describe a woman as **mutton dressed as lamb**, you mean that she is trying to look younger than she really is. PHRASE Informal

mutual /mju:tʃʊ[0]əl/. You use **mutual** **1** to describe something that two or more people do to each other or for each other, or a feeling that they have towards each other. EG *They are in danger of mutual destruction... I didn't like him and I was sure the feeling was mutual.* **2** to describe something which two or more people share. EG *They had discovered a mutual interest in rugby football... He sent a mutual friend to ask me to reconsider my decision.* ADJ CLASSIF: USU ATTRIB

mutually /mju:tʃʊ[0]əli[1]/. **1** You use **mutually** when describing a situation in which two or more people feel the same way about each other. EG *He enjoyed a mutually respectful relationship with them.* ADV+ADJ

2 If two things are **mutually exclusive** or **mutually contradictory**, they cannot both be true or both exist somewhere at the same time. EG *The principles on which it is based are mutually contradictory.* PHRASE

muzzle /mʌzə[0]l/, **muzzles, muzzling, muzzled. 1** The **muzzle** of an animal such as a dog or a wolf is its nose and mouth. N COUNT

2 A **muzzle** is a wire cover or a strap that is put over a dog's nose and mouth so that it cannot bite people or bark. N COUNT

3 If you **muzzle** a dog, you put a muzzle over its nose and mouth. V+O

4 The **muzzle** of a gun is the open end where the bullets come out when it is fired. N COUNT

muzzy /mʌzi[1]/. Someone who feels **muzzy** is unable to think clearly, because they are ill or have drunk a lot of alcohol. ADJ QUALIT

my /maı/. **1** A speaker or writer uses **my** to indicate that something belongs or relates to himself or herself. EG *My name is Alan Jones... I closed my eyes... My mother died in 1945.* DET POSS

2 You use **my** in some titles when you are talking to someone with that title. EG *I can, my Lord.*

myopic /maıɒpık/. Someone who is **myopic** is unable to see things which are far away from them. EG *She thinks Dolly is myopic and should see a good optician.* ADJ CLASSIF Formal

myriad /mırıəd/, **myriads.** A **myriad** of people or things is a very large number of them. EG *...a myriad of political action groups... ...myriads of tiny yellow flowers.* ▸ used as an adjective. EG *...myriad pots of paint... ...embroidered with a myriad pearls.* N PART Literary ▸ ADJ CLASSIF

myself /maıself/. A speaker or writer uses **myself** **1** as the object of a verb or preposition in a clause where 'I' is the subject or 'me' is a previous object. EG *If you do not help me, I will kill myself... I was thoroughly ashamed of myself... I poured myself a small drink.* **2** to emphasize the subject or object of a clause. EG *I myself feel that Muriel Spark is very underrated... I find it a bit odd myself... My first pupil today is a Pole like myself.* **3** in expressions such as 'I did it myself' in order to say that he or she did something without any help or interference from anyone else. EG *I dealt with it myself.* PRON REFL: SING

mysterious /mıstıərıəs/. **1** Something that is **mysterious** is strange and is not known about or understood. EG *Their grandson died of a mysterious illness... ...mysterious black boxes covered with wires.* ◇ **mysteriously.** EG *The American had mysteriously disappeared.* ADJ QUALIT ◇ ADV

2 If you are **mysterious** about something, you deliberately do not talk about it, especially when you want people to be curious about it. EG *Stop being so mysterious.* ◇ **mysteriously.** EG *They smiled mysteriously and said nothing.* ADJ QUALIT ◇ ADV

mystery /mıstə[0]ri[1]/, **mysteries. 1** A **mystery** is something that is not understood or known about. EG *These two deaths have remained a mystery... ...to probe the mysteries of the universe.* N COUNT

2 If you talk about the **mystery** of someone or something, you are talking about how difficult they are to understand or to know about. EG *The place continues to fascinate visitors, cloaked in its mystery... ...the mystery of God.* N UNCOUNT +SUPP

3 A **mystery** person or thing is one whose identity or nature is not known. EG *...the mystery voice... ...a mystery tour... ...a mystery package.* ADJ CLASSIF: ATTRIB

mystic /mıstık/, **mystics. 1** A **mystic** is a religious person who spends a lot of time praying and meditating. N COUNT

2 Mystic means the same as mystical. EG *...a performer in a mystic rite.* ADJ QUALIT: ATTRIB

mystical /mıstıkə[0]l/. Something that is **mystical** involves spiritual powers and influences that most people do not understand. EG *...religious and mystical experiences.* ADJ QUALIT: ATTRIB

mysticism /mıstısızə[0]m/ is religious belief which cannot be explained very easily and is very profound and personal. N UNCOUNT

mystify /mıstıfaı/, **mystifies, mystifying, mystified.** If something **mystifies** you, you find it impossible to explain or understand. EG *They say that they are mystified by the decision.* ◇ **mystified.** EG *I felt a bit mystified.* V+O ◇ ADJ QUALIT

mystique /mısti:k/ is an atmosphere of mystery and importance or difficulty which is associated with a particular person or thing. EG *...the mystique surrounding doctors.* N UNCOUNT Formal

myth /mıθ/, **myths.** A **myth** is **1** an untrue belief or explanation. EG *...myths about the causes of cancer... ...the myth of love at first sight.* **2** a story which has been made up to explain how the world began or to justify religious beliefs. EG *...Greek myths... ...queens in history, legend, and myth.* N COUNT; N COUNT OR N UNCOUNT

mythic /mıθık/. Something that is **mythic** exists in a myth or is like something in a myth. EG *My husband has none of the attributes of a mythic lover.* ADJ CLASSIF: ATTRIB Formal

mythical /mıθıkə[0]l/. Something that is **mythical** **1** is imaginary and only exists in myths. EG *...mythical monsters.* **2** is untrue or does not exist. EG *They trekked out to the west coast in search of the mythical opportunities there.* ADJ CLASSIF: USU ATTRIB

mythology /mıθɒlədʒi[1]/. **1 Mythology** refers to stories that have been made up in the past to explain how the world began or to justify religious beliefs. EG *Prometheus in Greek mythology brought fire to man.* ◇ **mythological.** EG *Jupiter was the Roman mythological king of the heavens.* N UNCOUNT ◇ ADJ CLASSIF: ATTRIB

2 You can also use **mythology** to refer to beliefs that a lot of people have about something which are not true. EG *...the whole mythology of national greatness.* N UNCOUNT

N n

N, n /ɛn/, **Ns, n's. 1 N** is the fourteenth letter of the English alphabet. N COUNT
2 N is also a written abbreviation for 'north'.

> **N** stands for **noun**
> Words which are labelled N in the Extra Column are nouns.
> See the entry headed NOUNS for information about them.

nadir /neɪdɪə, næ-/. The **nadir** of something is its worst time. EG *The fortunes of Trotskyism reached their nadir... The government was at the nadir of its unpopularity.* N SING : USU+POSS Literary

nag /næg/, **nags, nagging, nagged. 1** If someone **nags** you, they keep complaining to you in an irritating way. EG *He used to nag me endlessly about money... Daddy, you don't have to nag at me.* V+O OR V
2 If a doubt or suspicion **nags** at you, you keep thinking and worrying about it. EG *Something that she had said had been nagging at him.* V+*at* ◇ **nagging.** EG *I have a nagging suspicion that one of the wheels is loose... She had a nagging sense of inadequacy.* ◇ ADJ CLASSIF : ATTRIB

nail /neɪl/, **nails, nailing, nailed. 1** A **nail** is a small piece of metal with a sharp end. You hit the nail with a hammer in order to push it into something. See picture at TOOLS. EG *...the mirror that hung from a nail on the wall.* N COUNT ● If you say that someone has **hit the nail on the head**, you mean that what they have said is exactly right. ● PHRASE ● a **nail in** another thing's **coffin**: see **coffin**.
2 If you **nail** something somewhere, you attach it there using a nail or nails. EG *They nail plastic sheets over their windows... There were signs nailed to the trees.* V+O+A
3 Your **nails** are the thin hard areas that cover the ends of your fingers and toes. EG *He keeps biting his nails... ...her long red nails.* N COUNT
nail down. If you **nail** something **down**, you fix it firmly to the floor with nails. PHRASAL VB : V+O+ADV
nail up. If you **nail** something **up**, you fix it to a vertical surface using nails. EG *...the warning notice that he had nailed up on the pole.* PHRASAL VB : V+O+ADV

nail brush, nail brushes. A **nail brush** is a small brush that you use for cleaning your nails. N COUNT

nail file, nail files. A **nail file** is a small strip of metal that you rub on the end of your nails to make them smooth and give them a rounded shape. N COUNT

nail polish is the same as nail varnish. N UNCOUNT

nail varnish is a thick liquid that women paint on their nails. N UNCOUNT

naive /naɪiːv/; also spelled **naïve.** Someone who is **naive** believes that things are much less complicated or difficult than they really are. EG *You're surely not so naive as to think that this will change anything.* ADJ QUALIT ◇ **naively.** EG *They naively assume that things can only get better.* ◇ ADV ◇ **naivety** /naɪiːvə[ə]ti[1]/; also spelled **naïvety** or **naïveté.** EG *In this he showed political naivety.* ◇ N UNCOUNT

naked /neɪkɪ[2]d/. **1** Someone who is **naked** is not wearing any clothes. EG *He was naked except for a pair of underpants... ...the men's naked bodies.* ADJ CLASSIF ◇ **nakedness.** EG *They seized towels to hide their nakedness.* ◇ N UNCOUNT
2 You describe objects as **naked** when they are not covered, especially when you would expect them to be covered. EG *...naked light bulbs... Never look for a gas leak with a naked flame.* ADJ CLASSIF : ATTRIB
3 Naked emotions are easily noticed, because they are strongly felt. EG *His face broke into an expression of naked anxiety.* ADJ CLASSIF : ATTRIB
4 If someone shows **naked** aggression, hostility, or greed, they do not try to hide their aggressive, hostile, or greedy behaviour. EG *The home employment offered to housewives is naked exploitation... ...naked dictatorship.* ADJ CLASSIF : ATTRIB
5 If you can see something with the **naked** eye, you can see it without using a microscope, binoculars, or a telescope. EG *...microscopic hairs, invisible to the naked eye.* ADJ CLASSIF : ATTRIB

name /neɪm/, **names, naming, named. 1** The **name** of a person, thing, or place is the word or group of words that you use to identify them. EG *His name is Richard Arnason.* N COUNT : USU+POSS
2 If you **name** someone or something, **2.1** you give them a name. EG *She wanted to name the baby Colleen.* V+O+C **2.2** you identify them by saying their name. EG *...a Minister, whom he did not name... ...various flowers: roses, tulips and snapdragons, to name only a few.* V+O OR V+O+*as* ● See also **named**.
3 If you **name** someone or something after a person or thing, you give them the same name as that person or thing. EG *The College in Holborn is named after her.* V+O+*after/for*
4 If you **name** something, for example a date for a meeting or the price of some goods, you say what you want it to be. EG *He named a price he thought would scare me off.* V+O
5 You can refer to someone's reputation as their **name**. EG *Grey spoke out in public to clear Haldane's name... They were giving the country a bad name.* N COUNT
6 You can say that someone is a **name** or a big **name** when they have become famous. N COUNT : USU+SUPP
7 Name is also used in these phrases. PHRASES **7.1** If you mention someone **by name**, you say their name rather than referring to them in a more indirect way. **7.2** You can use **by name** or **by the name of** when you are saying what someone is called. EG *...the grocer, Jackson by name... ...a Swedish engineer by the name of George Scheutz.* Formal **7.3** If you **call** someone **names**, you insult or offend them by using unpleasant words to describe them. **7.4** Something that exists **in name only** does not have the status or position that it is officially supposed to have. EG *Many of these branches are inactive, existing in name only.* **7.5** If something is registered or recorded **in** your **name**, it officially belongs to you or has been reserved for you. **7.6** If you do something **in the name of** an ideal or a group of people, you do it because you believe in the ideal or represent the people. EG *The group claims to speak in the name of 'the simple people of the country'.* **7.7** If you **make a name for yourself**, you do something very well and become well-known and admired for it. EG *George Eliot had already made a name for herself as a writer.*
8 See also **brand name, Christian name, maiden name.**

named /neɪmd/. When you say what a person, thing, or place is **named**, you give their name. EG *...a lecturer named Harold Levy.* ADJ PRED

name-dropping is the habit of referring to famous people as though they were your friends, in order to impress people. EG *There was a good deal of academic name-dropping.* N UNCOUNT

nameless /neɪmlɪ[2]s/. **1** You describe people and things as **nameless** when you do not know their name or when they have not been given a name. EG *...the nameless ones who built the village... ...a new and nameless disease.* ADJ CLASSIF : ATTRIB

2 If you say that someone or something will remain **nameless**, you mean that you will not say their name, because you do not want to cause embarrassment. EG *We spend half our time cleaning up after others, who shall be nameless... I remember one movie, which shall remain nameless, that was described as 'two hours of boredom'.* ADJ PRED

3 A **nameless** emotion is one that you cannot describe or explain. EG *He felt a nameless terror and sensed that death was near.* ADJ CLASSIF : ATTRIB Literary

namely /neɪmli¹/. You use **namely** to introduce detailed information about what you have just said. EG *...three famous physicists, namely Simon, Kurte and Mendelsohn... He could not do anything more than what he had promised – namely, to look after Charlotte's estate.* ADV SEN

namesake /neɪmseɪk/, **namesakes.** Your **namesake** is someone who has the same name as you. EG *Remember what happened to your namesake.* N COUNT+POSS

nanny /næni¹/, **nannies.** A **nanny** is a woman who is paid by parents to look after their children. N COUNT

nanny goat, nanny goats. A **nanny goat** is a female goat. N COUNT

nap /næp/, **naps, napping, napped. 1** A **nap** is a short sleep that you have during the day. EG *It was time for her to take a nap.* ▸ used as a verb. EG *That afternoon while Wendy was napping, I went to the cellar.* N COUNT ▸ V

2 If you **are caught napping**, something happens to you when you are not prepared for it. PHRASE Informal

nape /neɪp/, **napes.** The **nape** of your neck is the back of it. N COUNT : USU SING+*of*

napkin /næpkɪn/, **napkins.** A **napkin** is a small piece of cloth or paper that you use when you are eating to protect your clothes, or to wipe your mouth or hands. N COUNT

nappy /næpi¹/, **nappies.** A **nappy** is a piece of soft thick cloth or paper which is fastened round a baby's bottom in order to soak up its urine and faeces. EG *I seem to spend all day changing nappies.* N COUNT British

narcissus /nɑːsɪsəs/, **narcissi** /nɑːsɪsɪ⁵/. A **narcissus** is a yellow, white, or orange flower that looks like a daffodil. The plural form is either 'narcissus' or 'narcissi'. N COUNT

narcotic /nɑːkɒtɪk/, **narcotics. Narcotics** are drugs which make you sleepy and unable to feel pain. Some people become addicted to narcotics. N COUNT

narrate /nəreɪt/, **narrates, narrating, narrated.** If you **narrate** a story, you tell it. EG *He narrated this tale with great effect.* ◇ **narration** /nəreɪʃə⁰n/. EG *The richness of the novel comes from his narration.* V+O ◇ N UNCOUNT Formal

narrative /nærətɪv/, **narratives.** A **narrative** is a story or an account of events or experiences. EG *...the narrative of her battle against depression.* N COUNT

narrator /nə³reɪtə/, **narrators.** The **narrator** of a story is the person who is telling it. N COUNT

narrow /nærəʊ/, **narrower, narrowest; narrows, narrowing, narrowed. 1** Something that is **narrow** has a very small distance from one side to the other. EG *We turned into a narrow lane... The stream became narrower.* ◇ **narrowness.** EG *...the narrowness of the tunnels.* ADJ QUALIT ◇ N UNCOUNT

2 If something **narrows**, it becomes less wide. EG *The river narrowed and curved sharply to the left.* V

3 If you **narrow** your eyes or if they **narrow**, you almost close them. EG *'I want you back here in five minutes,' he growled, narrowing his eyes.* V-ERG

4 If you describe someone's ideas, attitudes, or beliefs as **narrow**, you mean that they are concerned with only a few aspects of something and ignore the more important aspects. EG *I think you are taking too narrow a view.* ◇ **narrowness.** EG *He criticized the narrowness of the range of opinion represented.* ADJ QUALIT ◇ N UNCOUNT

5 If the difference between two things **narrows** or if the range of something **narrows**, it becomes smaller. EG *The gap between the rich and the poor is narrowing.* ◇ **narrowing.** EG *...the narrowing of the individual's field of choice.* V-ERG ◇ N UNCOUNT +SUPP

6 If you have a **narrow** victory, you just succeed in winning. If you have a **narrow** defeat, someone just beats you. EG *It was a narrow victory, by only five votes.* ◇ **narrowly.** *The motion was narrowly defeated.* ADJ QUALIT : ATTRIB ◇ ADV

7 If you have a **narrow** escape, something very unpleasant nearly happens to you. EG *...narrow misses.* ◇ **narrowly.** EG *He narrowly escaped being run over.* ADJ QUALIT : ATTRIB ◇ ADV

narrow down. If you **narrow** something **down**, you reduce it to a small number of things. EG *They had narrowed the choice down to a dozen sites.* PHRASAL VB : V+O+ADV

narrow-minded. If you say that someone is **narrow-minded**, you mean that they are unwilling to consider new ideas or other people's opinions. EG *How narrow-minded he had become... ...a narrow-minded approach to broadcasting.* ADJ QUALIT

nasal /neɪzə⁰l/. **1** You produce **nasal** sounds when air passes through your nose as well as your mouth when you are speaking. EG *He spoke in a nasal voice... ...singing in a nasal tone.* ADJ QUALIT

2 **Nasal** also means relating to your nose. EG *...the nasal passages... ...nasal discharge.* ADJ CLASSIF : ATTRIB

nasturtium /nə³stɜːʃə⁰m/, **nasturtiums.** A **nasturtium** is a brightly-coloured garden flower. N COUNT

nasty /nɑːsti¹/, **nastier, nastiest. 1** Something that is **nasty** is very unpleasant to see, experience, or feel. EG *This place has a nasty smell... I got a nasty feeling that I was being followed.* ADJ QUALIT : USU ATTRIB

2 You can also describe things as **nasty** when you think that they are unattractive or in bad taste. EG *It's a tacky, nasty little movie.* ADJ QUALIT : USU ATTRIB

3 A **nasty** problem or question is a difficult and worrying one. EG *This presented a nasty problem to Mayor Lindsay.* ADJ QUALIT : USU ATTRIB

4 You describe a disease or injury as **nasty** when it is serious or looks very unpleasant. EG *Rats carry very nasty diseases... A nasty bruise rose where the handbag had landed.* ADJ QUALIT : USU ATTRIB

5 You describe someone's behaviour as **nasty** when they behave in an unkind and unpleasant way. EG *Why must she be so nasty to me?* ◇ **nastily.** EG *He was staring at them nastily.* ADJ QUALIT : USU ATTRIB ◇ ADV

nation /neɪʃə⁰n/, **nations. 1** A **nation** is a country, together with its social and political structures. EG *...a powerful nation... ...the great accomplishments of their nation.* N COUNT

2 The people who live in a country are sometimes referred to as the **nation**. EG *He appealed to the nation for self-restraint... ...the whole British nation.* N SING : *the*+N

national /næʃə⁰nəl, -ʃənə⁰l/, **nationals. 1 National** means relating to the whole of a country, rather than to part of it or to several countries. EG *It made the headlines in the national newspapers... ...special stamps to mark national and international events.* ◇ **nationally.** EG *Should housing policy be decided nationally or locally?* ADJ CLASSIF : USU ATTRIB ◇ ADV

2 **National** is also used to describe things that are typical of the people of a particular country. EG *Common sense is certainly a national characteristic... ...national dress.* ADJ CLASSIF : ATTRIB

3 You refer to someone as a **national** of a country when they are a citizen of that country and are staying in a different country. EG *Much of the workforce was made up of foreign nationals... ...a German national.* N COUNT+SUPP

national anthem, national anthems. A country's **national anthem** is its official song. National anthems are often played on public occasions. N COUNT

National Health Service. In Britain, the **National Health Service** is a system which provides free or cheap medical care for everybody. It is paid for by taxes. N PROPER : *the*+N

national insurance is the system by which a government collects money regularly from em- N UNCOUNT ployers and employees so that money can be paid to people who are ill, unemployed, or retired.

nationalise /næʃə°nəlaɪz/. See **nationalize.**

nationalism /næʃə°nəlɪzə°m/ is **1** a desire for the political independence of a group of people who have the same religion, language, or culture. EG *...nineteenth-century Czech nationalism.* **2** a great love for your country which may make you believe that it is better or more important than other countries. — N UNCOUNT

nationalist /næʃə°nəlɪst/, **nationalists. 1 Nationalist** ideas or movements are connected with attempts to obtain political independence for a particular group of people. EG *...the nationalist movements of French West Africa.* — ADJ CLASSIF : ATTRIB

2 A **nationalist** is a person with nationalist beliefs. EG *...a great Indonesian nationalist.* — N COUNT

nationalistic /næʃə°nəlɪstɪk/. Someone who is **nationalistic** is very proud of their country and believes that it is better or more important than other countries. EG *...an attempt to arouse nationalistic passions against the foreigner.* — ADJ QUALIT

nationality /næʃə°nælɪ'ti'/, **nationalities.** You use **nationality** to refer to the country that people belong to. For example, someone who has British **nationality** is legally a British citizen. EG *...an identity card proving Belgian nationality... ...scientists of different nationalities.* — N UNCOUNT OR N COUNT

nationalize /næʃə°nəlaɪz/, **nationalizes, nationalizing, nationalized;** also spelled **nationalise.** If a government **nationalizes** a private company or industry, that company or industry becomes owned by the state and controlled by the government. EG *The revolutionary government has nationalized the mines.* — V+O ◇ **nationalized.** EG *Gas and coal are nationalized industries.* — ◇ ADJ CLASSIF ◇ **nationalization** /næʃə°nəlaɪzeɪʃə°n/. EG *He argued for nationalisation on grounds of efficiency.* — ◇ N UNCOUNT

national park, national parks. A **national park** is a large area of land which is protected by the government of a country because of its natural beauty, its plants, or its animals. — N COUNT

national service is a period of service in a country's armed forces, which young people in many countries have to do by law. — N UNCOUNT

nationwide /neɪʃə°nwaɪd/. A **nationwide** activity happens in all parts of a country. EG *...a nationwide campaign to recruit women into trade unions.* — ADJ CLASSIF : ATTRIB
▸ used as an adverb. EG *She had lectured nationwide to various organizations.* — ▸ ADV

native /neɪtɪv/, **natives. 1** Your **native** country is the country where you were born. EG *She made her way home to her native Russia.* — ADJ CLASSIF : ATTRIB

2 A **native** of a country or region is someone who was born there. EG *...John Magee, a native of Northern Ireland.* — N COUNT+SUPP ▸ used as an adjective. EG *They took on low paid work that native Britons would not touch.* — ▸ ADJ CLASSIF : ATTRIB

3 Your **native** language is the first language that you learned to speak when you were a child. EG *She had spoken in her native language... He read a poem in his native Hungarian.* — ADJ CLASSIF : ATTRIB

4 A **native** speaker of a language is someone who has spoken that language since childhood, rather than learning it later. — ADJ CLASSIF : ATTRIB

5 Animals or plants that are **native** to a region live or grow there naturally and have not been brought there by people. EG *These are the only lilies native to Great Britain.* — ADJ CLASSIF : OFT+*to* Formal

natter /nætə/, **natters, nattering, nattered.** When people **natter**, they talk casually for a long time about unimportant things. EG *We just want to natter together about old times.* — V Informal ▸ used as a noun. EG *They like to have a bit of a natter.* — ▸ N SING : a+N

natural /nætʃə°rə°l/, **naturals. 1** If you say that someone's behaviour is **natural** in particular circumstances, you mean that it is the way people normally behave in those circumstances. EG *She's upset. It's natural, isn't it? Today's the funeral... It is natural for trade unions to adopt an aggressive posture.* — ADJ QUALIT : USU PRED

2 You also say that someone's behaviour is **natural** when they are not trying to hide anything or pretend in any way. EG *...walking in a relaxed, natural manner... There was something not quite natural about her behaviour.* — ADJ QUALIT ◇ **naturalness.** EG *I was impressed by their ease and naturalness.* — ◇ N UNCOUNT

3 A **natural** ability or way of behaving is one that you were born with and have not learned. You can also use **natural** to describe a person with a particular natural ability. EG *He had a natural gift for making things work... Follow your own natural inclinations... She was a natural organizer.* — ADJ CLASSIF : ATTRIB

4 If you say that someone is a **natural**, you mean that they seem to have been born with the ability to do something well. EG *He is a great craftsman, a natural.* — N COUNT : USU a+N Informal

5 Natural is used to describe things that exist in nature and that were not made or caused by people. EG *...protection from natural disasters such as earthquakes.* — ADJ CLASSIF : ATTRIB

6 If someone died of **natural causes**, they died because they were ill and not because they committed suicide, were murdered, or were killed in an accident. EG *The post-mortem showed that death was due to natural causes.* — PHRASE

7 Someone's **natural** mother or father is their real mother or father, rather than someone who has adopted or fostered them. EG *She claimed Prince Yousoupoff as her natural father.* — ADJ CLASSIF : ATTRIB

8 A **natural** note in music is not a sharp or a flat. EG *...B natural.* — ADJ AFTER N

natural gas is gas which is found underground or under the sea. It is collected and stored, and piped into people's houses to be used for cooking and heating. — N UNCOUNT

natural history is the study of animals, plants, and other living things. — N UNCOUNT

naturalised /nætʃrəlaɪzd/. See **naturalized.**

naturalist /nætʃrəlɪst/, **naturalists.** A **naturalist** is a person who studies plants, animals, and other living things. — N COUNT

naturalized /nætʃrəlaɪzd/; also spelled **naturalised.** If you are a **naturalized** citizen of a country, you have legally become a citizen of a country that you were not born in. EG *...a naturalized British subject.* — ADJ CLASSIF : ATTRIB

naturally /nætʃrəli'/. **1** You use **naturally** to indicate that you think that something is very obvious and not at all surprising. EG *Dena was crying, so naturally Hannah was upset... 'Do you propose to take account of that?' – 'Naturally.'* — ADV SEN

2 If one thing develops **naturally** from another, it develops as a normal result of it. EG *This leads us fairly naturally into what career advisers call careers counselling.* — ADV

3 If something happens or exists **naturally**, it happens or exists in nature and was not made or caused by people. EG *He found some rock that does not occur naturally within 30 kilometres... They tried to reproduce artificially what they had observed to happen naturally.* — ADV

4 You say that someone is behaving **naturally** when they are not trying to hide anything or to pretend in any way. EG *The children were too frightened to behave naturally.* — ADV

5 You can also use **naturally** to talk about qualities that people were born with, rather than qualities that they have learned or acquired later in their life. EG *...people who are naturally brilliant... She had a naturally cheerful and serene expression.* — ADV+ADJ

6 If something **comes naturally** to you, you find — PHRASE

Find a word on these pages which means 'dark blue'.

that you can do it easily. EG *Politics came naturally to Tony.*

natural resources are all the land, forests, minerals, and sources of energy that occur naturally in a country or in the world, and that can be used by people. EG *They plan to open up the region with its wealth of natural resources.* N PLURAL

nature /neɪtʃə/, **natures. 1 Nature** is all the animals, plants, and other things in the world that are not made by people, and all the events and processes that are not caused by people. EG *...the diversity of nature... A sunset is one of the most beautiful sights in nature... It's Nature's way of being sure that life will continue.* N UNCOUNT

2 The **nature** of something is its basic quality or character. EG *...the unique nature of Elizabethan painting... Such a situation is by nature painful... These problems are political in nature.* N UNCOUNT +SUPP

3 If you say that something is of a particular **nature**, you are saying what characteristic or quality it has. EG *They suffered injuries of a very serious nature... The music he played was of a romantic nature.* N SING+SUPP

4 Someone's **nature** is their character, which they show by their behaviour. EG *Rob had a very sweet nature... ...a woman with a wildly passionate nature... He eventually revealed his real nature.* N SING+SUPP

5 Nature is used in these phrases. **5.1** If you say that something has a particular characteristic **by** its **nature** or **by** its **very nature**, you mean that things of that type always have that characteristic. EG *Trade unions are by their nature conservative bodies.* **5.2** If a way of behaving is **in** someone's **nature**, they behave like that because it is a part of their character. EG *It was not in her nature to tell lies.* **5.3** If someone has a particular characteristic or quality **by nature**, it is a part of their character. EG *I am an optimist by nature... He was polite by nature.* **5.4** If you talk about someone's **better nature**, you are referring to their feelings of kindness and their desire to help other people. **5.5** If a way of behaving is **second nature** to you, you behave like that almost without thinking about it, because you have done it so many times before. PHRASES

● See also **human nature**.

naughty /nɔːti¹/. **1** You say that small children are **naughty** when they behave badly or are disobedient. EG *Don't be a naughty boy.* ADJ QUALIT

2 You describe books, pictures, or words as **naughty** when they are slightly rude or indecent. EG *...little boys who use naughty words... It's rather a naughty play.* ADJ QUALIT

nausea /nɔːzɪə, -sɪə/. If you have a feeling of **nausea**, you feel as if you are going to vomit. N UNCOUNT

nauseate /nɔːzɪeɪt, -sɪ-/, **nauseates, nauseating, nauseated.** If something **nauseates** you, **1** it makes you feel as if you are going to vomit. EG *The thought of food nauseated him.* V+O ◊ **nauseating.** EG *...an incredibly nauseating candy bar.* ◊ ADJ QUALIT **2** it makes you feel strong disgust or dislike. EG *This type of newspaper nauseated her.* V+O ◊ **nauseating.** EG *...his utterly nauseating hypocrisy.* ◊ ADJ QUALIT

nautical /nɔːtɪkə^{0}l/. **Nautical** people and things are involved with ships. EG *...an elderly man in a nautical uniform.* ADJ CLASSIF : ATTRIB

naval /neɪvə^{0}l/. **Naval** people and things belong to a country's navy. EG *...a French naval officer... ...US naval forces.* ADJ CLASSIF : ATTRIB

navel /neɪvə^{0}l/, **navels.** Your **navel** is the small hollow in the middle of the front of your body. See picture at THE HUMAN BODY. N COUNT

navigate /nævɪgeɪt/, **navigates, navigating, navigated. 1** When someone **navigates**, they work out which direction a ship, plane, or car should go, using maps and instruments. EG *Sailors used to navigate by the stars... Distances like that cannot be navigated unless you have a good map.* V OR V+O

◊ **navigation** /nævɪgeɪʃə^{0}n/. EG *You can't teach navigation in the middle of a storm.* ◊ N UNCOUNT

2 If you **navigate** a difficult or dangerous place, you travel through it carefully in order to be safe. EG *Until then no ship had been large enough to navigate the Atlantic.* V+O

navigator /nævɪgeɪtə/, **navigators.** A **navigator** is someone who works out the direction in which a ship or plane should go. EG *He had many years experience as a navigator.* N COUNT

navy /neɪvi¹/, **navies. 1** A country's **navy** is the part of its armed forces that fights at sea. EG *My father's in the Navy... ...Captain Jensen of the US Navy.* N COLL : USU the+N

2 Something that is **navy** or **navy-blue** is dark blue in colour. EG *...a navy-blue jumper.* ADJ COLOUR

NB. You write **NB** to draw someone's attention to what you are going to write next. EG *Total cost: £500. NB. The following items are not included.*

> **N COLL** stands for **collective noun**
> Nouns which have the label N COLL in the Extra Column are words like 'navy', 'audience', and 'committee' which refer to groups of people or things. Words such as 'herd' and 'flock' are called collective nouns in some grammars, but we call them partitive nouns (N PART) in this dictionary.
> See the entry headed NOUNS for more information.

> **N COUNT** stands for **countable noun**
> Nouns which have the label N COUNT in the Extra Column are nouns which regularly use both a singular form and a plural form.
> See the entry headed NOUNS for more information.

-nd. You add **-nd** to most numbers written in figures and ending in 2 in order to form ordinal numbers. 2nd is pronounced the same as 'second'. EG *...2nd October 1957... ...42nd Street...* ...the 132nd Psalm. SUFFIX

NE is an abbreviation for 'north-east'.

near /nɪə/, **nearer, nearest; nears, nearing, neared. 1** If something is **near** a place or thing or **near to** it, it is only a short distance from it. EG *He stood near the door... I wish I lived nearer London... He pulled her nearer to him.* PREP, ADV AFTER VB, OR ADJ QUALIT ◊ **nearness.** EG *All the while I was acutely aware of her nearness... Her heart leapt with terror at the nearness of her enemy.* ◊ N UNCOUNT +SUPP Literary

2 If you are **near** a particular situation or state or **near to** it, you have almost reached it. EG *Her father was angry, her mother near tears... I was very near to giving in to their demands.* PREP

3 If something is similar to something else, you can say that it is **near** it or **near to** it. EG *Most views were fairly near the truth... He is the nearest we have to an English Leonardo da Vinci.* PREP, OR ADV AFTER VB ● If you say that something is **the nearest thing** to a particular type of thing, you mean that it is almost that thing, and there is nothing else more similar. EG *He is the nearest thing we have to a genius.* ● PHRASE

4 Your **near** relatives are the people who are most closely related to you, for example your parents and grandparents. ADJ QUALIT : ATTRIB

5 If something happens **near** a particular time or **near to** it, it happens just before or just after that time. EG *...near the beginning of the play.* PREP

6 If a time or event is **near**, it will happen very soon. EG *...as her wedding day drew near.* ADV AFTER VB ● If you say that something will happen **in the near future**, you mean that it will happen quite soon. EG *These things will be available to us all in the very near future.* ● PHRASE

7 You can also use **near** to say that something almost has a particular quality or almost happens. ADJ CLASSIF : ATTRIB OR ADV +ADJ

EG *...a state of near chaos... ...our near catastrophic economic troubles.*

8 You use **near** in expressions such as **near enough** and **as near as makes no difference** in order to say that something is almost true. EG *He paid £100, or as near as makes no difference.* PHRASE Informal

9 If you say that something was **a near thing**, you mean that it was almost an accident or a disaster. PHRASE

10 You can use **nowhere near** to emphasize that something is not the case. For example, if you say that something is **nowhere near** ready, you mean that it will not be ready for a long time. EG *Lions are nowhere near as fast as the cheetah.* PHRASE Informal

11 If you **are nearing** a place, you are approaching it. EG *As they neared the harbour, it began to rain.* V+O

12 If someone or something **is nearing** a particular stage or point in time, they will soon reach it. EG *...anybody nearing the age of retirement.* V+O

nearby /nɪəbaɪ/. **Nearby** things and places are only a short distance away. EG *...Nottingham and nearby towns... There was a river nearby... Nearby a tractor was pulling a plough.* ADJ CLASSIF OR ADV

nearly /nɪəli1/. **1 Nearly** means not completely or not exactly. EG *Brody had been there for nearly an hour... It was nearly dark... I can nearly swim a mile... They seem to be nearly always male... Nearly everybody went out of business... She was nearly as tall as he was.* ADV

2 You use **not nearly** to emphasize that something is not the case. For example, if you say that something is 'not nearly big enough', you are emphasizing that it is much too small. EG *I haven't spent nearly long enough here... They don't have nearly so many foods to choose from as we do.* PHRASE

nearside /nɪəsaɪd/. The **nearside** of a vehicle is the side that is nearest to the edge of the road when the vehicle is being driven normally. N SING

neat /niːt/, **neater, neatest. 1** Something that is **neat** is tidy and smart. EG *His clothes were neat... This is not a neat household... She had small, neat writing.* ◊ **neatly.** EG *Mother's clothes hung neatly in a row.* ◊ **neatness.** EG *Their desks are models of neatness... I was pleased at the neatness of the stitches.* ADJ QUALIT; ◊ ADV; ◊ N UNCOUNT

2 Someone who is **neat** is careful and tidy in their appearance and behaviour. EG *Ethel was clean and neat and politely spoken.* ADJ QUALIT

3 If you drink an alcoholic drink **neat**, you drink it without anything else added to it. EG *She takes her whisky neat... He gulped the neat brandy down in one draught.* ADJ CLASSIF

nebulous /nɛbjə4ləs/. **Nebulous** ideas are vague and not precise. EG *It's a very nebulous concept... I had a nebulous notion of a life after death.* ADJ QUALIT Formal

necessarily /nɛsɪ2sə0rɪ1li1, nɛsɪ2sɛrɪ1li1/. **1** If you say that something is not **necessarily** the case, you mean that it is not always the case. If you say that something is **necessarily** the case, you are emphasizing that it is always the case. EG *Fleas are not necessarily associated with dirt... Documentaries don't necessarily need interviewers... The secular historian is necessarily concerned only with externals.* ADV : OFT WITH BROAD NEG

2 If something **necessarily** happens in particular circumstances, it must happen in those circumstances. EG *Growth has necessarily levelled off.* ADV Formal

necessary /nɛsə2sə0ri1/. **1** Something that is **necessary** is needed in order to get the result or effect that you want. EG *Are we teaching undergraduates the necessary skills?... Make a soft dough, using a little more water if necessary... ...the colours and patterns necessary for perfect camouflage... I don't want to stay longer than necessary... It is necessary to examine this claim before we proceed any further.* ADJ CLASSIF

2 You can also say that something is **necessary** when it must happen or exist in particular circumstances and cannot be any different. EG *There is no necessary connection between industrial democracy and productivity.* ADJ CLASSIF Formal

necessitate /nɪ2sɛsɪ1teɪt/, **necessitates, necessitating, necessitated.** If something **necessitates** a particular course of action, it makes it necessary. EG *The Government's action had necessitated a by-election... This job would necessitate working with his hands.* V+O OR V+-ING Formal

necessity /nɪ2sɛsɪ1ti1/, **necessities. 1 Necessity** is the need to do something. EG *...the necessity of keeping water uncontaminated... She went to work not out of choice but necessity.* N UNCOUNT

2 Necessities are things that you must have, such as food and clothing. EG *They were supplied with all the necessities of life.* N COUNT

3 You say **of necessity** to emphasize that something must happen or must be the case. EG *The account given here is of necessity extremely brief... Since my French was so poor our conversation was, of necessity, limited.* PHRASE Formal

neck /nɛk/, **necks, necking, necked. 1** Your **neck** is the part of your body which joins your head to the rest of your body. See picture at THE HUMAN BODY. EG *She threw her arms around his neck... The cat had a blue collar round its neck.* ● If something goes **down** your **neck**, it goes inside your collar and down your back. EG *The rain was dripping down our necks.* N COUNT: OFT+POSS; ● PHRASE

2 The **neck** of a dress or shirt is the part which is round your neck or just below it. EG *...a dress with a lace neck... His shirt was open at the neck.* N COUNT

3 The **neck** of a bottle is the long narrow part at one end. N COUNT: USU+SUPP

4 Neck is used in these phrases. **4.1** If you say that you are **up to** your **neck** in problems, you mean that you are deeply involved in them and cannot get away from them. EG *You were up to your neck in trouble with the press.* **4.2** If you say that someone is **breathing down** your **neck**, you mean that they are watching you very closely and checking everything that you do. EG *They should not have their parents breathing down their necks all the time.* **4.3** If you **risk** your **neck**, you do something very dangerous in order to achieve something or to help someone. EG *I thanked him for risking his neck for me.* **4.4** If you **stick** your **neck out**, you do or say something that makes you likely to be criticized or harmed. EG *He was pleased to let someone else stick their neck out and take responsibility.* **4.5 by the scruff of** your **neck**: see **scruff**. ● **a millstone round** your **neck**: see **millstone**. PHRASES Informal; Informal; Informal

5 If two people **are necking**, they are kissing each other passionately. V : USU CONT Outdated

necklace /nɛklɪ1s/, **necklaces.** A **necklace** is a piece of jewellery, such as a chain or string of beads, which a woman wears round her neck. See picture at JEWELLERY. N COUNT

neckline /nɛklaɪn/, **necklines.** The **neckline** of a dress or blouse is the top edge at the front. EG *...a mini-dress with a plunging neckline.* N COUNT

necktie /nɛktaɪ/, **neckties.** A **necktie** is the same as a tie. N COUNT American

née /neɪ/ is used before a name to indicate that it was a woman's surname before she got married. EG *...Jane Carmichael, née Byers.* Formal

need /niːd/, **needs, needing, needed. 1** If you **need** something, it is necessary for you to have it. EG *These animals need food throughout the winter... If you need any help, just give me a ring... Children need to feel they matter to someone... You don't need a degree in mathematics to run a computer.* V+O OR V+*to*-INF

2 If you **need** to do something, you must do it. EG *Before we answer this question, we need to look briefly at the world environment... You might need to visit a specialist.* V+*to*-INF

If someone needles you, do they stick a needle into you?

3 If you tell someone that they **need not** do something, you are saying that there is no good reason why they should do it. EG *You needn't worry.* SEMI-MODAL: WITH BROAD NEG

4 If you say that something **need not** happen or be the case, you mean that it might happen or be the case, but it is not definite or unavoidable. EG *It needn't cost very much.* SEMI-MODAL: WITH BROAD NEG

5 If you say that something that has happened **need not** have happened, you mean that it could have been avoided or prevented. EG *People died of diseases that need not have proved fatal.* SEMI-MODAL: WITH BROAD NEG

6 If you say that something **needs** a particular action or that an action **needs** doing, you mean that this action is necessary. EG *The shed needs a good clean out... Keep a list of all the jobs that need doing... The top rim needs to be cut off.* V+O, V+-ING, OR V+*to*-INF

7 Your **needs** are the things that you need to have in order to have a satisfactory way of life. EG *She learned how to provide for her own needs.* N COUNT: USU PLURAL

8 A **need** is also a strong feeling that you must have something or must do something. EG *I began to feel the need of somewhere to retreat... Their need for money is rising fast... She felt no need to speak.* N SING: OFT+*of*/*for* OR *to*-INF

9 You use the expression **if need be** to say that an action will be carried out if it is considered to be necessary. EG *She said she would stay with me for months and years if need be.* PHRASE

10 If someone or something is **in need of** something, they need it. EG *I am badly in need of advice... The hospital was in need of decorating.* PREP

11 People **in need** do not have enough money, or need help of some kind. PHRASE

12 If you have **no need** of something, it is not necessary for you to have it. If there is **no need** for you to do something or if you have **no need** to do it, it is not necessary for you to do it. EG *The country had no need of Western weapons... There is no need to go into details.* PHRASE

13 If you tell someone that there is **no need** to do something, you are telling them to stop doing it because it annoys you. EG *There's no need to get so worked up about it.* PHRASE Informal

needle /niːdə⁰l/, **needles, needling, needled. 1** A **needle** is a small, very thin piece of polished metal which is used for sewing. It has a sharp point at one end and a hole in the other end for a thread to go through. N COUNT

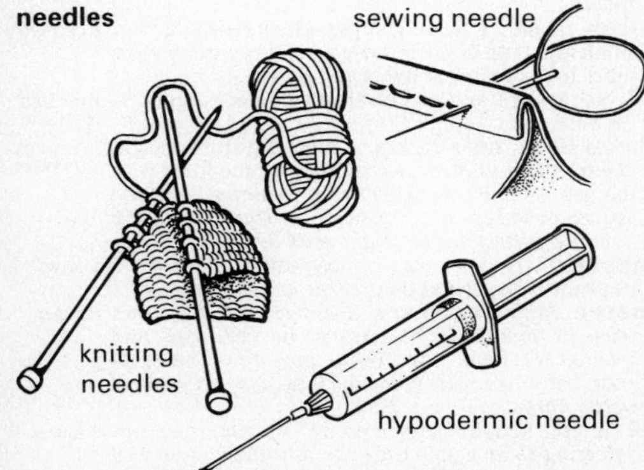

2 You can refer to knitting needles as **needles.** N COUNT

3 The **needle** in a record player is the small pointed instrument that touches the record and picks up the sound signals. N COUNT

4 A **needle** is also the part of a syringe which a doctor or nurse sticks into your body. N COUNT

5 On an instrument that measures something such as speed, weight, or electricity, the **needle** is the thin piece of metal or plastic which moves backwards and forwards on the dial and shows the measurement. N COUNT

6 The **needles** of a pine tree are its very thin pointed leaves. EG *There was nothing on the ground except a thick layer of pine needles.* N COUNT

7 If someone **needles** you, they annoy you by criticizing you repeatedly. EG *She was needling me about Doris.* V+O Informal

8 **a needle in a haystack**: see **haystack**. • See also **pins and needles**.

needless /niːdlɪ²s/. **1** Something that is **needless** is completely unnecessary. EG *The result was needless slaughter... It was a needless risk to run.* ADJ CLASSIF
◊ **needlessly.** EG *This may upset a mother needlessly.* ◊ ADV

2 You say **needless to say** to emphasize that what you are saying is obvious. EG *I left college in disgrace (needless to say without my Diploma)... This new social awareness will, needless to say, bring big changes.* ADV SEN

needlework /niːdə⁰lwɜːk/ is **1** sewing or embroidery that is done by hand. EG *...the basket in which she kept her needlework.* N UNCOUNT **2** the activity of sewing or embroidering. EG *The girls spend much time doing needlework.* N UNCOUNT

needn't /niːdə⁰nt/ is the usual spoken form of 'need not'.

needy /niːdi¹/, **needier, neediest. 1** Someone who is **needy** is very poor and does not have proper housing or enough food or clothing. EG *...helping needy old people throughout the world... They are among the neediest children in Britain.* ADJ QUALIT

2 Needy people are sometimes referred to as **the needy**. EG *It is important to serve everybody, not just the needy.* N PLURAL: the+N

NEG stands for negative

1. NEG is used in the Extra Column beside words such as 'nothing', 'nobody' and 'never' to tell you that the word makes the clause negative and that no other negative word is used in the same clause. So you say *There was **nobody** in the room.* You do not say 'There wasn't nobody in the room'.
2. See the entry at **not** for more information about how we make clauses and phrases negative.
3. NEG is also used in the labels ADV BRD NEG and BROAD NEG. See the entries for ADVERBS and for BROAD NEG for more information.

negate /nɪ²geɪt/, **negates, negating, negated.** If you **negate** something that someone has done, you cause it to have no value or effect. EG *The denial of the importance of minorities negates all our efforts on their behalf.* V+O Formal

negative /negətɪv/, **negatives. 1 Negative** is used to describe something that gives or suggests the answer 'no'. EG *We expected to receive a negative answer.* ◊ **negatively.** EG *The public responded negatively.* ADJ CLASSIF ◊ ADV

2 If an answer is **in the negative**, it is 'no'. EG *This question had been answered in the negative.* PHRASE

3 If you say that someone is **negative** or that they have a **negative** attitude, you mean that they consider only the disadvantages and bad aspects of a situation, rather than the advantages and good aspects. EG *No one else I met ever had such a negative view of Alice Springs... He was especially negative about my written work.* ADJ QUALIT

4 If a medical or other scientific test is **negative**, it shows that something has not happened or is not present. EG *...a negative pregnancy test.* ADJ CLASSIF

5 A **negative** is the image that is first produced when you take a photograph. The negative of a black-and-white photograph is dark in the places where the final photograph is light. N COUNT

6 A **negative** number is less than zero. ADJ CLASSIF

neglect /nɪ²glɛkt/, **neglects, neglecting, neglected.** **1** If you **neglect** someone or something, you do not look after them or give them the attention they deserve. EG *...the farmer who neglects his crops.* ◊ **neglected.** EG *The child looked neglected, scruffy and unloved.* V+O ◊ ADJ QUALIT

2 If you **neglect** to do something, you fail to do it. EG *I neglected to bring a gift... I feel I'm neglecting my duty.* V+*to*-INF OR V+O

3 Neglect is failure to look after someone or something properly. EG *It was the mother's neglect of her infant that caused its death... ...estates suffering from vandalism and neglect.* N UNCOUNT

neglectful /nɪ²glɛktfʊl/. **1** You describe someone as **neglectful** when they do not look after someone or something properly. EG *...a neglectful father.* ADJ QUALIT

2 If you are **neglectful** of something, you do not give it the attention that it should be given. EG *He had been neglectful of his duties.* ADJ QUALIT: OFT+*of*

negligee /nɛglɪʒeɪ/, **negligees;** also spelled **négligée.** A woman's **negligee** is a dressing gown made of very thin material. N COUNT

negligent /nɛglɪdʒənt/. When someone is **negligent**, they do not do something that they ought to do, or do not show care for something that they are responsible for. EG *He has to prove that he has not been negligent.* ◊ **negligently.** EG *They may act foolishly or negligently.* ◊ **negligence** /nɛglɪdʒəns/. EG *The chairman of the Party had been dismissed for negligence.* ADJ QUALIT: USU PRED ◊ ADV ◊ N UNCOUNT

negligible /nɛglɪdʒəbə⁰l/. Something that is **negligible** is so small or unimportant that it is not worth considering or worrying about. EG *The cost in human life had been negligible.... This would have a negligible effect on the temperature.* ADJ CLASSIF

negotiable /nɪ²gəʊʃəbə⁰l/. Something that is **negotiable** can be changed or agreed by means of discussion. EG *The price is negotiable.* ADJ CLASSIF

negotiate /nɪ²gəʊʃieɪt/, **negotiates, negotiating, negotiated.** **1** If you **negotiate** an agreement or a deal, you obtain it by having discussions with other people. EG *He negotiated a trade agreement with Brazil.* V+O: OFT+*with*

2 If you **negotiate** for something, you try to obtain it by having discussions with other people. EG *Paul is negotiating for a job worth £18,000... The National Council negotiates directly with the British Gas Corporation.* V: OFT+*for*/*with*

3 If you **negotiate** an obstacle or difficult piece of ground, you succeed in moving around it or over it. EG *Patrick is not sure whether he can negotiate the turn at the bottom.* V+O

negotiation /nɪ²gəʊʃieɪʃə⁰n/, **negotiations. Negotiations** are discussions that take place between people with different interests, in which they try to reach an agreement. EG *The early stages of their negotiations with the Government were unsuccessful.* ▸ used as an uncount noun. EG *We need to allow more time for negotiation.* N COUNT: USU PLURAL ▸ N UNCOUNT

negotiator /nɪ²gəʊʃieɪtə/, **negotiators. Negotiators** are people who take part in negotiations in business, politics, or international affairs. EG *They acted as negotiators in all dealings with other villages... ...trade union negotiators.* N COUNT

Negro /niːgrəʊ/, **Negroes.** A **Negro** is someone with black skin who comes from Africa or whose ancestors came from Africa. Some people find this word offensive. N COUNT

neigh /neɪ/, **neighs, neighing, neighed.** When a horse **neighs**, it utters a loud sound. V

neighbour /neɪbə/, **neighbours;** also spelled **neighbor** in American English. **1** Your **neighbours** are the people who live near you, especially the people who live next door to you. EG *Don't be afraid of what the neighbours will think.* N COUNT

2 Your **neighbour** is also the person who is standing or sitting next to you. EG *Rudolph turned his head towards his neighbour.* N COUNT+POSS

3 You can refer to something which stands next to something else of the same kind as its **neighbour**. *The young plant risks being overshadowed by its neighbours.* N COUNT+POSS

4 A country's **neighbours** are the countries that are next to it. EG *...battles between Angola and her neighbours.* N COUNT+POSS

neighbourhood /neɪbəhʊd/, **neighbourhoods;** also spelled **neighborhood** in American English.

1 A **neighbourhood** is a part of a town where people live. EG *She'd just moved into the neighbourhood... ...a wealthy neighbourhood... ...my neighbourhood grocery.* N COUNT

2 If something is **in the neighbourhood** of a place, it is near to it. EG *We were heading for a destination in the neighbourhood of the Lofoten Islands.* PHRASE

neighbouring /neɪbə⁰rɪŋ/; also spelled **neighboring** in American English. You use **neighbouring** to describe places and things that are near to the place or thing that you are talking about. EG *Families came from neighbouring villages to look at her.* ADJ CLASSIF: ATTRIB

neighbourly /neɪbəli¹/; also spelled **neighborly** in American English. If people who live near you are **neighbourly**, they are kind, friendly, and helpful to you. EG *That's a neighbourly thing to do.* ADJ QUALIT

neither /naɪðə, niːðə/. **1** You use **neither** in front of the first of two or more words or expressions when you are saying that two or more things are not true or do not happen. The other things are introduced by 'nor'. EG *He spoke neither English nor French... She neither drinks, smokes, nor eats meat... The Englishman was neither gratified nor displeased.* CONJ: NEG

2 You also use **neither** to refer to both of two things or people, when you are making a negative statement about both of them. EG *Neither of us was having any luck... Neither was suffering pain.* PRON SING: NEG, OFT+*of*; ALSO DET

3 If you say that one thing is not the case and **neither** is another, you mean that the second thing is also not the case. EG *'I don't normally drink at lunch.' – 'Neither do I.'* CONJ: NEG

4 If you say that a fact is **neither here nor there**, you mean that it does not matter, because it is not relevant. PHRASE

neolithic /niːəlɪθɪk/ means relating to the period long ago when people first started farming but still used stone weapons and tools. EG *...in neolithic times... ...neolithic weapons... ...neolithic settlements.* ADJ CLASSIF

neon /niːɒn/. **1 Neon** is a gas which exists in very small amounts in the atmosphere. It is used in glass tubes to make bright lights and signs. N UNCOUNT

2 Neon signs and places are lit by neon lights. EG *...a neon city.* N UNCOUNT: OFT N MOD

neon light, neon lights. A **neon light** is a bright electric light that consists of a glass tube filled with the gas neon. Neon lights are sometimes bent into shapes or letters to form signs. EG *The front of the building glittered with bright neon lights.* N COUNT OR N UNCOUNT

nephew /nɛvjuː, nɛf-/, **nephews.** Someone's **nephew** is the son of their sister or brother. N COUNT

nerve /nɜːv/, **nerves.** **1** A **nerve** is a long, thin fibre in your body that transmits messages and feelings between your brain and other parts of your body. EG *...the optic nerves... ...a network of nerve fibres.* N COUNT

2 If you talk about someone's **nerves**, you are referring to how able they are to remain calm and not become worried or tense in a dangerous or stressful situation. EG *Hoping to calm our nerves, we decided to spend the afternoon at the lake... She had strong nerves... All during lunch he had been in a state of nerves.* N PLURAL

3 Nerve is the courage and determination that you N UNCOUNT

Can you think of six nouns which end in '-ness'?

need in order to be able to do something, especially something difficult or dangerous. EG *Nobody had the nerve to remind him that he was several hours late... His nerve began to crack.*

4 **Nerve** is also used in these phrases. **4.1** If someone or something **gets on** your **nerves**, they annoy or irritate you very much. EG *He got on my nerves tonight with his fishing stories.* **4.2** If you **lose** your **nerve**, you suddenly panic and become afraid about something that you are doing. EG *The men inside the building lost their nerve and opened fire on the crowd.* **4.3** If you say that someone **had a nerve** or **had the nerve** to do something, you mean that they have made you angry or shocked by doing something rude or disrespectful. EG *He had the nerve to say Fleet Street was corrupting me... She has a nerve to ask.* PHRASES Informal

nerve-racking. Something that is **nerve-racking** makes you feel very tense and worried. EG *It was a nerve-racking period for us all.* ADJ QUALIT

nervous /nɜːvəs/. 1 If you are **nervous**, you are worried and frightened, and show this in your behaviour. EG *Both actors were exceedingly nervous on the day of the performance.* ◊ **nervously.** EG *He laughed nervously and asked me what I meant.* ◊ **nervousness.** EG *'Pa,' Rudolph began, trying to conquer his nervousness.* ADJ QUALIT ◊ ADV ◊ N UNCOUNT

2 A **nervous** person is very tense and easily upset. EG *She was a particularly nervous woman.* ADJ QUALIT : ATTRIB

3 If you are **nervous** about something, you feel rather afraid or worried about it. EG *People are so nervous about believing anything to be right... He's nervous of thieves in that little shop of his.* ADJ PRED +about/of

4 A **nervous** illness or condition affects your emotions and your mental state. EG *She had suffered a lot of nervous strain.* ADJ CLASSIF : ATTRIB

nervous breakdown, nervous breakdowns. A **nervous breakdown** is an illness in which someone suffers from deep depression, worry, and tiredness, and so has psychiatric treatment. EG *You'll give yourself a nervous breakdown going on working like this.* N COUNT

nervous system, nervous systems. Your **nervous system** is all the nerves in your body together with your brain and spinal cord, which control your movement and reflexes as well as your feelings. N COUNT

nervous wreck, nervous wrecks. If you say that someone is a **nervous wreck**, you mean that they are extremely nervous or worried. EG *I waited so long that by the time my turn came I was a nervous wreck.* N COUNT Informal

-ness, -nesses. -ness is added to adjectives to form nouns. These nouns usually refer to a state or quality. For example 'sadness' is the state of being sad and 'kindness' is the quality of being kind. Nouns formed in this way are often not defined in this dictionary but are treated with the related adjectives. EG *The aim of life is happiness... ...the smallness of the school... He was aware of his weaknesses.* SUFFIX

nest /nest/, **nests, nesting, nested.** 1 A **nest** is **1.1** a place that a bird makes to lay its eggs in, using things like twigs, leaves, moss, and mud. **1.2** the place that groups of insects or other animals make, in which they live and give birth to their young. EG *We had a wasp's nest in the roof.* N COUNT

2 When a bird **nests** somewhere, it builds a nest and settles there to lay its eggs. EG *Hornbills nest in holes in trees.* V : USU+A

nestle /nesəˡl/, **nestles, nestling, nestled.** 1 If you **nestle** somewhere, you move into a comfortable position, often by pressing against someone or something soft. EG *They nestled together on the sofa... ...nestling against his body.* V+A OR V+O+A

2 If something **nestles** somewhere, it is in that place or position and seems safe or sheltered. EG *...a house with other houses nestling against it on both sides... A village nestled in the hills to their right.* V+A

net /net/, **nets, netting, netted;** also spelled **nett** in British English for paragraphs 5 and 6.

1 **Net** is a kind of cloth made of very fine threads that are woven together so that there are small equal spaces between them and you can see through the cloth. EG *All the windows have net curtains.* • See also **netting**. N UNCOUNT

2 A **net** is a piece of netting which is in a particular shape and is used for a particular purpose, for example to keep something in place, or across the centre of a tennis court. EG *...a net to cover the plants... ...a butterfly trapped in a net.* N COUNT

3 If you **net** something, you manage to get it, often by using skill. EG *He was netting his largest fortune.* V+O

4 If you **net** a particular amount of money, you gain it as profit when all expenses have been paid. EG *The plastics began netting £1 billion a year for the company.* V+O : OFT+for, OR V+O+O

5 A **net** result or amount is one that is final, when everything necessary has been considered or included. EG *That gave him a net profit of just over 23%... The net result is a massive labour surplus.* ADJ CLASSIF : ATTRIB OR ADJ AFTER N

6 The **net** weight of something is its weight without its container or wrapping. EG *If you look at the label, you'll see it says 450 g net.* ADJ CLASSIF : ATTRIB OR ADJ AFTER N

netball /netbɔːl/ is a game played by two teams of seven players, usually women. Each team tries to score goals by throwing a ball through a net which is at the top of a pole at each end of the court. N UNCOUNT

nett /net/. See **net**.

netting /netɪŋ/ is material made of pieces of thread or string, or metal wires, that are woven or knotted together so that there are equal spaces between them. EG *The dog scratched impatiently at the netting... ...wire netting on the windows.* N UNCOUNT

nettle /netəˡl/, **nettles.** A **nettle** is a wild plant with spiky leaves covered with little hairs, usually ones that sting. EG *...fields covered with stinging nettles.* N COUNT

network /netwɜːk/, **networks.** 1 A **network** is **1.1** a large number of lines or things such as roads or veins that look like lines, which cross each other or meet at many points. EG *...a network of tiny red veins running over her white skin... ...the network of back streets in the Latin Quarter.* **1.2** a large number of people or organizations that have a connection with each other and work together as a system. EG *...a network of clinics... ...the public telephone network.* N COUNT : USU+SUPP

2 A radio or television **network** is a company or group of companies that usually broadcasts the same programmes at the same time in different parts of the country. EG *She gave an informal interview on a national television network.* N COUNT : OFT MOD+N

neurological /njʊərəˡlɒdʒɪkəˡl/ is used to describe things relating to the nervous system. EG *...a progressive neurological disease.* ADJ CLASSIF : ATTRIB Medical

neurosis /njʊərəʊsɪs/, **neuroses** /njʊərəʊsiːz/. **Neurosis** is a mental illness which causes people to have continual and unreasonable fears and worries. EG *Such problems can distort personality and lead to neurosis.* N UNCOUNT OR N COUNT

neurotic /njʊərɒtɪk/. If you say that someone is **neurotic**, you mean that they continually show a lot of unreasonable anxiety about something. EG *They are becoming neurotic about their careers.* ADJ QUALIT

neutral /njuːtrəˡl/, **neutrals.** 1 A country or person that is **neutral** does not officially support anyone in a disagreement or war. EG *Throughout the hostilities this group remained neutral... Because I was neutral in the conflict I was a welcome visitor.* ▸ used as a noun. EG *The neutrals can give useful advice.* ◊ **neutrality** /njuːtrælɪtiˡ/. EG *We have a tradition of political neutrality for our civil servants.* ADJ CLASSIF ▸ N COUNT ◊ N UNCOUNT

2 If someone is **neutral** or if something that they do is **neutral**, they do not show any emotions or opinions. EG *I waited, but her eyes were neutral...* ADJ CLASSIF

Their decision was neutral on this question... 'Look,' she said in a neutral voice.

3 Neutral is the position between the gears of a car or other vehicle, in which the gears are not connected to the engine. EG *I pushed the handle into neutral.* N UNCOUNT

4 The **neutral** wire in an electric plug is the wire that is not earth or live and that is needed to complete the circuit so that the electric current can flow. ADJ CLASSIF

5 Neutral is used **5.1** to describe things that are pale grey or brown in colour. EG *The water was of a pale, neutral colour, a sort of ashen grey.* ADJ QUALIT **5.2** to describe things that contain no colour at all or that are suitable to be used for any colour. EG *...a neutral shoe cream.* ADJ CLASSIF

neutralize /nju:trəlaɪz/, **neutralizes, neutralizing, neutralized**; also spelled **neutralise.** To **neutralize** something means to prevent it from having any effect or from working properly. EG *Their aim is to neutralize the Council's campaign... All aircraft were neutralized until repairs could be effected.* V+O

neutron /nju:trɒn/, **neutrons.** A **neutron** is an atomic particle that has no electrical charge. N COUNT Technical

neutron bomb, neutron bombs. A **neutron bomb** is a nuclear weapon that is designed to kill people and animals without a large explosion and without destroying buildings. N COUNT

never /nɛvə/. **1 Never** means **1.1** at no time in the past or at no time in the future. EG *I've never been to Europe... I shall never forget this day... I never eat breakfast on Sundays.* **1.2** not in any circumstances at all. EG *What is morally wrong can never be politically right.* ADV : NEG

2 Never ever is an emphatic expression for 'never'. EG *She never ever wears a hat.* PHRASE Informal

3 You use **never** with the simple past tense to mean 'did not'. EG *My bus never arrived... Good gracious! I never knew that.* ADV : NEG Informal

4 If you say **'Well I never'**, you are indicating that you are surprised. EG *Well, I never. It's Mrs Oliver.* EXCLAM Informal

5 never mind: see **mind**.

never-ending. If you describe something as **never-ending**, you are emphasizing that it lasts a very long time, often when you find it depressing or boring. EG *It was a drab, never-ending afternoon... ...the never-ending flow of refugees.* ADJ CLASSIF

nevertheless /nɛvəðəlɛs/ means in spite of what has just been said. EG *She saw Clarissa immediately, but nevertheless pretended to look around for her.* ADV SEN

new /nju:/ **newer, newest; news.** The form **news** is used for the noun in paragraphs 7 to 10.

1 Something that is **new 1.1** has been recently made or created, or is in the process of being made or created. EG *...smart new houses... I haven't really had a new idea in years... ...a new type of bandage that stops minor bleeding almost immediately.* ADJ QUALIT **1.2** has not been used or owned by anyone else. EG *There was another sign advertising new and used tractors... They cost over twenty dollars new.* ADJ CLASSIF **1.3** is different from what you had, used, or experienced before. EG *Not long after that, he got a new job... The villagers were suspicious of anything new.* ADJ CLASSIF : ATTRIB

◇ **newness.** EG *...the newness and strangeness of her surroundings.* ◇ N UNCOUNT **1.4** has only recently been discovered. EG *In 1781 an astronomer named William Herschel discovered a new planet.* ADJ CLASSIF : ATTRIB

2 When you refer to the beginning of a **new** day or period of time, you are referring to the beginning of the next day or period of time. EG *...on the eve of a new era... A new phase was about to start.* ADJ CLASSIF : ATTRIB

3 New is also used to show that something has only just happened. For example, a **new** parent has only recently become a parent. EG *...from the new mother's point of view... Thousands were there to hear the new party leader.* ADJ CLASSIF : ATTRIB

4 If you are **new** to a situation or place or if the situation or place is **new** to you, you have not experienced it or seen it before. EG *...a person who's new to the job of teaching... I'm new here... ...a part of England completely new to him.* ADJ PRED : USU+*to*

5 If you say that something is **as good as new**, you mean that it is now in very good condition, after it has been damaged and then repaired. PHRASE

6 See also **newly**.

7 News is **7.1** information about a recent event or a recently changed situation. EG *I've got some good news for you... ...after receiving the news of my acceptance.* **7.2** information that is given in newspapers and on radio and television about recent events in the country or the world. EG *...a half hour of world and domestic news... It was on the news at 9.30... He's recently been in the news again.* N UNCOUNT, OR N SING : *the*+N

8 If you say **'That's news to me'** when someone tells you something, you mean that you did not know it and you are rather surprised by it. CONVENTION

newborn /nju:bɔ:n/. A **newborn** baby is one that has been born recently. ADJ CLASSIF

newcomer /nju:kʌmə/, **newcomers.** A **newcomer** is a person who has recently arrived to live in a place, joined an organization, or started a job. EG *...newcomers to the neighbourhood.* N COUNT

new-fangled. You can describe an idea or piece of machinery that has been recently created or invented as **new-fangled**, often when you think it is unnecessary or too complicated. EG *...a new-fangled Japanese camera... No doubt they'll produce some new-fangled gadget to dispose of it.* ADJ CLASSIF : ATTRIB Informal

new-found. A **new-found** quality, ability, or person is one that you have discovered recently. EG *...this new-found confidence... ...new-found friends.* ADJ CLASSIF : ATTRIB

newly /nju:li[1]/ is used before past participles to indicate that an action is very recent. EG *...the newly-married couple... ...newly discovered evidence... ...her newly acquired food mixer.* ADV

new moon, new moons. The moon is a **new moon** when it is a thin crescent shape at the start of its four-week cycle of appearing to become larger and then smaller. N COUNT : USU SING

news agency, news agencies. A **news agency** is an organization which collects news stories from all over the world and sells them to newspapers, magazines, and television and radio stations. N COUNT

newsagent /nju:zeɪdʒənt/, **newsagents.** A **newsagent** or **newsagent's** is a shop which sells newspapers and magazines, and often cigarettes, sweets, and stationery. N COUNT

newscaster /nju:zkɑ:stə/, **newscasters.** A **newscaster** is a person who reads the news on a television or radio broadcast. N COUNT

newsflash /nju:zflæʃ/, **newsflashes.** A **newsflash** is an interruption that is made to a radio or television programme to announce an important piece of news. N COUNT

newsletter /nju:zlɛtə/, **newsletters.** A **newsletter** is a printed sheet or several sheets of paper containing information about an organization that is sent regularly to its members. EG *Members receive a newsletter three times a year.* N COUNT

newsmen /nju:zmɛn/ are reporters who work for newspapers, television, or radio. EG *Newsmen had been barred from the trial.* N PLURAL

newspaper /nju:speɪpə/, **newspapers. 1** A **newspaper** is **1.1** a number of large sheets of folded paper on which news, advertisements, and other information is printed. Some newspapers are produced every day from Monday to Saturday, and others once a week. EG *...a weekly newspaper... ...a newspaper article... ...copies of France's leading daily newspaper Le Figaro.* **1.2** an organization that produces a newspaper. EG *I work for a newspaper.* N COUNT

2 Newspaper consists of pieces of old newspapers, N UNCOUNT

Is a newsagent the same as a news agency?

especially when they are being used for another purpose such as wrapping things up. EG *Wedge it with a wad of newspaper.*

newsprint /nju:zprɪnt/ is the cheap, fairly rough paper on which newspapers are printed. EG *...reading through stacks of newsprint.* N UNCOUNT

newt /nju:t/, **newts.** A **newt** is a small animal with a moist skin, short legs, and a long tail. Newts live partly on land and partly in water. N COUNT

New Testament. The **New Testament** is the part of the Bible that deals with the life of Jesus Christ and with Christianity in the early Church. N PROPER : the+N

new wave, new waves. A **new wave** is a movement in art, music, or film, which introduces new ideas instead of following traditional ideas. EG *...one of the young producers from the new wave of British music.* N COUNT

New Year is the time when people celebrate the start of a year. EG *We had a marvellous time over New Year... Happy New Year!* N UNCOUNT, OR N SING : the+N

New Year's Day is the first day of a year. In Western countries this is January 1st. N UNCOUNT

New Year's Eve is the last day of the year, the day that comes before New Year's Day. N UNCOUNT

next /nekst/. **1** The **next** period of time, event, person, or thing is the one that happens or comes immediately after the present one or after the previous one. EG *The next five years are of vital importance... The next day, I left better prepared... I'm getting married next month... My pulse was 40 one minute and 100 the next... I may vote for her at the next election... My next question is, 'What is art?'... What's next on the agenda?* ORDINAL

2 The **next** place or person is the one that is nearest to you or the first one that you come to. EG *The telephone was ringing in the next room... Pull into the next lay-by.* ORDINAL : the+ORDINAL

3 The thing that happens **next** is the thing that happens immediately after something else. EG *The audience does not know what is going to happen next... It's your turn next.* ADV

4 When you **next** do something, you do it for the first time since you last did it. EG *It was some years later when I next saw her.* ADV

5 You use **next** to say that something has more of a particular quality than all other things except one. For example, the thing that is **next** best is the one that is best except for one other thing. EG *The best kind of story is the one with a happy ending; the next best is the one with an unhappy ending.* ADV+SUPERL

6 You use **after next** in expressions such as 'the week after next' or 'the month after next' which refer to the period of time after the next one. For example, when it is May, the month after next is July. EG *He had to go there the week after next.* PHRASE

7 If one thing is **next to** another thing, it is at the side of it. EG *She went and sat next to him... There was a bowl of goldfish next to the bed.* PREP

8 You can also use **next to** to mean almost. EG *I knew next to nothing about him... The photographs were next to useless but they were all we had.* PHRASE

next door. A house that is **next door** to your house is on one side of it. EG *She lived next door to the Wilsons... I'm going next door to tell them to be quiet... ...our next-door neighbour, Joan.* ADV OR ADJ CLASSIF : ATTRIB

next of kin. Your **next of kin** is the person who is your closest relative. EG *The only next of kin seems to be a cousin in Droitwich.* N SING OR N UNCOUNT Formal

NHS /en eɪtʃ es/ is an abbreviation for 'National Health Service'. EG *...free NHS dental treatment.*

nib /nɪb/, **nibs.** The **nib** on a fountain pen is the small pointed piece of metal at the end, where the ink comes out as you write. N COUNT

nibble /nɪbəºl/, **nibbles, nibbling, nibbled. 1** If you **nibble** something, or **nibble** at it, **1.1** you eat it slowly by taking small bites out of it. EG *Just nibble a piece of bread... She nibbled at her food.* V+O; ALSO V : USU+at/on **1.2** you bite it very gently. EG *She nibbled my ear lobe playfully.* V+O OR V+at

2 When a mouse or other small animal **nibbles** something, it takes small bites out of it quickly and repeatedly. EG *It was nibbling the end of a leaf.* V+O OR V+at/on

3 A **nibble** is a gentle or quick bite of something. EG *A few licks and nibbles quickly put him off.* N COUNT

nice /naɪs/, **nicer, nicest. 1** If you say that something is **nice**, you mean that you find it enjoyable, pleasant, or attractive. EG *It would be nice to see you... Did you have a nice time at the party?... How nice you look... It doesn't taste very nice... We had a nice long chat... It's so nice and peaceful here.* ◊ **nicely.** EG *I always think Bessie dresses very nicely.* ADJ QUALIT; ◊ ADV

2 If you say that someone does or says something **nice**, you mean that they are being kind and thoughtful. EG *It's nice of you to say that... How nice of you to come.* ADJ QUALIT

3 If you say that someone is **nice**, you mean that they are friendly and pleasant and that you like them. EG *He was a terribly nice man.* ADJ QUALIT

4 If you are **nice** to someone, you behave in a friendly and pleasant or polite way towards them. EG *Promise me you'll be nice to her when she comes back... I wish I'd been nicer to him.* ◊ **nicely.** EG *You may go if you ask nicely.* ADJ PRED : USU+to; ◊ ADV

nicely /naɪsli¹/. Something that is happening or working **nicely** is working in a satisfactory way or in the way that you want it to happen. EG *You need some form of identification. Your driver's licence will do nicely... He thought he could manage quite nicely without them.* ADV AFTER VB

nicety /naɪsɪ¹ti¹/, **niceties.** A **nicety** is a small detail, especially concerning polite behaviour. EG *Here the niceties of etiquette must be observed.* N COUNT : USU PLURAL +SUPP

niche /ni:ʃ/, **niches. 1** A **niche** is a hollow area in a wall which can be used to hold a statue, or a natural hollow part in a cliff. EG *...the little statue of the saint in his niche near the pulpit.* N COUNT

2 If you say that you have found your **niche** in life, you mean that you have a job or position which is exactly suitable for you. EG *You can then find your own niche in public life.* N COUNT

nick /nɪk/, **nicks, nicking, nicked. 1** If you **nick** something, you make a small cut into the surface of it. EG *He shaved badly, nicking himself in a couple of places.* V+O OR V-REFL

2 A **nick** is a small cut made in the surface of something. EG *I felt with my fingers for nicks in the metal.* N COUNT

3 If someone **nicks** something, they steal it. EG *My typewriter had been nicked.* V+O Informal

4 If something happens **in the nick of time**, it happens successfully, but at the last possible moment. EG *We got there in the nick of time.* PHRASE Informal

5 If you say that something is **in good nick**, you mean that it is in good condition. If it is **in bad nick**, it is in bad condition. PHRASE Informal

nickel /nɪkəºl/, **nickels. 1 Nickel** is a silver-coloured metal that can be mixed with other metals to form an alloy. N UNCOUNT

2 A **nickel** is an American or Canadian coin that is worth five cents. N COUNT

nickname /nɪkneɪm/, **nicknames, nicknaming, nicknamed. 1** A **nickname** is an informal name for someone, especially one that is used by their friends or relations. EG *...Graham Rathbone, whose nickname was Raffy.* N COUNT

2 If you **nickname** someone or something, you give them an informal name. EG *For a brief while, Mrs Thatcher was nicknamed 'Tina'.* V+O+C

nicotine /nɪkəti:n/ is an addictive substance that is contained in tobacco. EG *...teeth browned by nicotine.* N UNCOUNT

niece /ni:s/, **nieces.** Someone's **niece** is the daughter of their sister or brother. N COUNT

niggle /nɪgəºl/, **niggles, niggling, niggled. 1** If something **niggles** you, it makes you worry slightly over a long time. EG *The question niggled at the* V+O OR V back of his mind. ◇ **niggling.** EG *...little niggling doubts.* ◇ ADJ CLASSIF : ATTRIB

2 If you **niggle** or if you **niggle** a person, you criticize the person or fuss about small things. EG *Critics niggled that the rapid production of planes was dangerous.* V, V+O, OR V+REPORT : ONLY *that*

3 A **niggle** is a small worry or doubt that you keep thinking about. EG *There is not the slightest niggle at the back of your mind that you should be spending your time more usefully?* N COUNT

night /naɪt/, **nights. 1** The **night** is **1.1** the part of each period of twenty-four hours when it is dark outside, especially the time when most people are sleeping. EG *He went out late at night when the streets were empty... We walked for six days and six nights... The storm lasted all night long... He woke in the night with a dreadful pain... I cannot sleep at nights.* **1.2** the period of time between the end of the afternoon and midnight, or between the end of the afternoon and the time when you go to bed. EG *I was out that night... I went on Saturday night.* N COUNT OR N UNCOUNT

2 Night is used in these phrases. **2.1** If it is a particular time **at night**, it is between the time when it gets dark and midnight. EG *...eleven o'clock at night.* **2.2** If something happens **day and night** or **night and day**, it happens all the time without stopping. EG *They were being guarded night and day.* **2.3** If you **have an early night**, you go to bed early. If you **have a late night**, you go to bed late. PHRASES

nightcap /naɪtkæp/, **nightcaps.** A **nightcap** is a drink that you have just before you go to bed. N COUNT

nightclub /naɪtklʌb/, **nightclubs.** A **nightclub** is a place where people go in the evening or late at night to drink and to dance or see a show. N COUNT

nightdress /naɪtdrɛs/, **nightdresses.** A **nightdress** is a sort of dress that women or girls wear in bed. N COUNT

nightfall /naɪtfɔːl/ is the time of day when it starts to get dark. EG *By nightfall I was feeling sleepy... We wanted to get out before nightfall.* N UNCOUNT

nightgown /naɪtgaʊn/, **nightgowns.** A **nightgown** is the same as a nightdress. N COUNT American

nightie /naɪti¹/, **nighties.** A **nightie** is a nightdress. N COUNT Informal

nightingale /naɪtɪŋgeɪl/, **nightingales.** A **nightingale** is a small brown European bird. The male nightingale is considered to sing very beautifully. N COUNT

nightlife /naɪtlaɪf/ is the entertainment and social activities that are available at night in towns and cities, such as nightclubs, theatres, and bars. EG *...the exotic nightlife of Montmartre.* N UNCOUNT

nightly /naɪtli¹/. A **nightly** event happens every night. EG *I was watching the nightly television news... My mother prayed nightly.* ADJ CLASSIF : ATTRIB OR ADV

nightmare /naɪtmɛə/, **nightmares.** A **nightmare** is **1** a very frightening dream. EG *He rushed to her room when she had nightmares and comforted her.* **2** a very frightening or unpleasant situation or time. EG *The first day was a nightmare.* N COUNT

nightmarish /naɪtmɛərɪʃ/. If you describe a situation or event as **nightmarish**, you mean that it is extremely frightening. EG *I had nightmarish visions of what could go wrong.* ADJ QUALIT : USU ATTRIB

night school, night schools. Night school is a school where adults can go to educational courses in the evenings. N UNCOUNT OR N COUNT

night shift, night shifts. A **night shift** is a period of work that is done regularly at night as part of a job, for example in a hospital or factory. N COUNT OR N UNCOUNT

night-time is the part of the day between the time when it gets dark and the time when it gets light again. EG *Who would see smoke at night-time?* N UNCOUNT

night-watchman /naɪt wɒtʃmə³n/, **night-watchmen.** A **night-watchman** is a person whose job is to guard buildings at night. N COUNT

nil /nɪl/. **1** If you say that something is **nil**, you mean that it does not exist at all. EG *You can reduce the danger to almost nil.* N UNCOUNT

2 Nil also means the same as nought; often used in scores of sports games. EG *Wales beat England three nil... The number rose from nil to 120 in four years.* N UNCOUNT

nimble /nɪmbə⁰l/, **nimbler, nimblest. 1** Someone who is **nimble** is able to move their fingers, hands, or legs quickly and easily. EG *By now, he was quite nimble on his wooden leg.* ◇ **nimbly.** EG *Nimbly, he swung himself out of the car.* ADJ QUALIT ◇ ADV

2 Someone who has a **nimble** mind is very quick and clever in the way that they think. ADJ QUALIT

nine /naɪn/, **nines. Nine** is the number 9: see the entry headed NUMBER. EG *It had been nine years since she had seen her brother.* NUMBER

nineteen /naɪntiːn/, **nineteens. Nineteen** is the number 19. See the entry headed NUMBER. EG *The ceremony was performed at the same time in nineteen other countries.* NUMBER

nineteenth /naɪntiːnθ/, **nineteenths.** The **nineteenth** item in a series is the one that you count as number nineteen. See the entry headed NUMBER. EG *...the industrialism of the nineteenth century.* ORDINAL

ninetieth /naɪntɪɪ²θ/, **ninetieths.** The **ninetieth** item in a series is the one that you count as number ninety. See the entry headed NUMBER. EG *In his ninetieth year he had lost the ability to speak.* ORDINAL

ninety /naɪnti¹/, **nineties. Ninety** is the number 90. See the entry headed NUMBER. EG *He was making ninety dollars a week... 'Eighty nine and I'll never live to be ninety,' he wheezed.* NUMBER

> **N ING**
> Nouns which have the label N ING in the Extra Column are the names of activities such as 'caravanning' and 'windsurfing', where no verb 'to caravan' or 'to windsurf' is given in the dictionary.
> See the entry headed NOUNS for more information.

ninth /naɪnθ/, **ninths. 1** The **ninth** item in a series is the one that you count as number nine. See the entry headed NUMBER. EG *...the ninth floor of the Hotel.* ORDINAL

2 A **ninth** is one of nine equal parts of something. EG *In exchange for this work they get one ninth of the crop.* N COUNT : USU+*of*

nip /nɪp/, **nips, nipping, nipped. 1** If you **nip** somewhere, usually somewhere nearby, you go there quickly or for a short time. EG *I'll just nip out and post these letters.* V+A Informal

2 If you **nip** someone or something, you pinch them or bite them lightly. EG *The horse nipped me on the back of the head.* ▸ used as a noun. EG *He gave her a nip on the lips.* V+O : OFT+A ▸ N COUNT

nipple /nɪpə⁰l/, **nipples. 1** The **nipples** on your body are the two small pieces of slightly hard flesh on your chest. Babies suck milk through the nipples on their mothers' breasts. EG *Infection can enter the breast through the nipple.* N COUNT

2 A **nipple** is also a piece of rubber or plastic in the shape of a nipple which is fitted to the top of a baby's bottle. N COUNT

nit /nɪt/, **nits. 1** If you call someone a **nit**, you mean that they are stupid or silly. EG *You're choking her, you nit!* N COUNT OR VOCATIVE Informal British

2 Nits are the eggs of a kind of louse that sometimes lives in people's hair. EG *The school doctor looks to see if you have nits in your hair.* N COUNT : USU PLURAL

nitrogen /naɪtrədʒə¹n/ is a colourless element that has no smell and is usually found as a gas. It forms about 78% of the earth's atmosphere, and is found in all living things. N UNCOUNT

Do people go out at night in their nightdresses?

N MASS stands for **mass noun**
Nouns which have the label **N MASS** in the Extra Column are usually found in the singular form, and are not countable. But when you are talking about types of them or measures of them, you can use the plural. So you normally say *I drink **coffee** in the mornings and **tea** in the afternoons.* But you can also say *They stock **teas** and **coffees** from all over the world.*
See the entry headed NOUNS for more information.

N MOD stands for **noun modifier**
Some nouns have the label N MOD in the Extra Column. These are nouns which usually come just in front of other nouns, and are therefore used rather like adjectives.
See the entry headed NOUNS for more information.

no /nəʊ/. 1 You use **no** 1.1 to say that something is not true, to refuse an offer, or to refuse permission. EG *'Did you see that programme last night?' - 'No, I didn't.'... 'They go round kissing one another when they meet.' - 'No they don't.' - 'Yes they do. I've seen them doing it.'... 'Do you want a biscuit?' - 'No thanks.'... 'Can I come too?' - 'No.'* 1.2 to indicate that you do not want someone to do something. EG *'No!' I shrieked. 'Don't!'* CONVENTION: NEG

2 If you say that someone **will not take no for an answer**, you mean that they go on trying to make you agree to something even after you have refused. PHRASE

3 You also use **no** 3.1 to say that you agree with a negative statement that someone else has made. EG *'It's not difficult, you see.' - 'No, it must be quite easy when you know how.'* 3.2 as a way of introducing a correction to what you have just said. EG *...500 grams, no, a little less than that.* 3.3 to express shock or disappointment at something. EG *'Michael's fallen off his bike.' - 'Oh no, not again.'* CONVENTION: NEG

4 You use **no** to indicate that there is not even one thing of a particular kind or not even a small amount of a particular thing. For example, if someone has **no** job or **no** money, they do not have a job or do not have any money. EG *He has given no reason for his decision... I do it all on my own. I have no help at all.* DET: NEG

5 You use **no** to emphasize that someone or something is not a particular kind of person or thing. For example, if you say that someone is **no** fool, you mean that they are definitely not a fool. EG *She is no friend of mine.* DET: NEG

6 You use **no** when emphasizing that something does not exceed a particular amount or number, or does not have more of a particular quality than something else. For example, something that is **no** bigger than a fingernail is not bigger than a fingernail. EG *The whole gun was no longer than eighteen inches... Winners will be notified by post no later than 31st August... ...a job that was no better than a common labourer's.* SUBMOD +COMPAR: NEG

7 **No** is also used, especially on notices, to say that a particular thing is forbidden. EG *No smoking... No talking once we're inside.* DET: NEG Formal

8 If you say **there is no** doing a particular thing, you mean that it is impossible to do that thing. EG *There's no arguing with my father.* PHRASE

No., Nos. No. is a written abbreviation for 'number'. EG *He lives at No. 14 Sumatra Road.*

nobility /nəʊbɪlɪ¹ti¹/. 1 **Nobility** is 1.1 the quality of being noble and admirable in behaviour. EG *He had nobility in defeat... He followed his principles with nobility.* 1.2 the condition of belonging to the nobility of a society. EG *...the silken rope which was the privilege of nobility.* N UNCOUNT

2 The **nobility** of a society are all the people who have titles and high social rank. N COLL: the+N

noble /nəʊbə⁰l/, **nobler, noblest; nobles.** 1 Someone who is **noble** 1.1 is honest, brave, and unselfish, and deserves admiration and respect. EG *Among them were some of the greatest and noblest men in our history... ...a man of noble character.* ◊ **nobly.** EG *She had nobly served the cause of Christianity.* 1.2 belongs to a high social class and has a title. EG *...young men of noble birth.* ▸ used as a noun. EG *Every noble in the land wanted to marry the king's daughter.* ADJ QUALIT; ◊ ADV; ADJ CLASSIF; ▸ N COUNT

2 Something that is **noble** is very impressive in quality or appearance. EG *...an old man with a noble head and a bristling moustache... ...one of the noblest collections of art in England.* ADJ QUALIT

nobody /nəʊbə⁷di¹/, **nobodies.** 1 **Nobody** means not a single person. See also **no-one**. EG *Nobody seems to notice... There was nobody on the bridge at all.* PRON INDEF: NEG

2 Someone who is a **nobody** is not at all important. EG *Miss Watkins was a nobody; no family, no close friends.* N COUNT: OFT a+N

nocturnal /nɒktɜːnə⁰l/. 1 **Nocturnal** events happen during the night. EG *...your nocturnal sightseeing tour of our city.* ADJ CLASSIF: USU ATTRIB

2 An animal that is **nocturnal** is active mostly at night. EG *Their nocturnal habits make long-eared owls hard to see.* ADJ CLASSIF

nod /nɒd/, **nods, nodding, nodded.** 1 If you **nod**, 1.1 you move your head quickly down and up to show that you are answering 'yes' to a question, or to show agreement, understanding, or approval. EG *'Is it true?' She nodded... He nodded his head... I nod in agreement.* 1.2 you bend your head once in a particular direction in order to indicate something or to give someone a signal to do something. EG *'Ask him,' said Ringbaum, nodding towards Philip.* 1.3 you bend your head once to someone as a way of saying hello or goodbye. EG *They all nodded a final goodnight... I nodded to the ladies and sat down.* V OR V+O; V+A; V OR V+O

2 If something **nods**, it bends or moves gently up and down. EG *There was not even a little breeze to make the poppies nod.* V

3 A **nod** is a quick movement of your head down and up. EG *From time to time, he gave him an encouraging nod.* N COUNT: OFT a+N

nod off. If you **nod off**, you fall asleep while you are sitting down, especially when you had not intended to fall asleep. EG *His remarks left delegates nodding off.* PHRASAL VB: V+ADV Informal

nodule /nɒdju⁴l/, **nodules.** A **nodule** is a small round lump on something, often on the root of a plant. EG *...bacteria in the root nodules of beans.* N COUNT

no-go area, no-go areas. A **no-go area** is a place which is controlled by a group of people who use force to prevent other people from entering it. EG *90 per cent of the country had become no-go areas.* N COUNT

noise /nɔɪz/, **noises.** 1 A **noise** is a sound that someone or something makes. EG *A sudden noise made Brody jump... The branches snapped with a dry cracking noise... Dolphins produce a great variety of noises.* N COUNT

2 **Noise** is a loud or unpleasant sound. EG *Try not to make so much noise... ...the noise of the radio next door... Our washing machine is making a terrible noise.* N UNCOUNT OR N COUNT

noiseless /nɔɪzlɪ²s/. Something that is **noiseless** does not make any sound. EG *...a totally noiseless fan.* ADJ QUALIT

noisy /nɔɪzi¹/, **noisier, noisiest.** 1 Someone or something that is **noisy** makes a lot of noise, especially loud or unpleasant noise. EG *The audience was large and noisy.* ◊ **noisily.** EG *My sister was crying noisily.* ADJ QUALIT; ◊ ADV

2 A place that is **noisy** is full of a lot of noise, especially loud or unpleasant noise. EG *They complained that Canton was hot and noisy and they wanted to leave.* ADJ QUALIT

nomad /nəʊmæd/, **nomads.** A **nomad** is a person who belongs to a tribe which travels from place to place rather than living in one place all the time. N COUNT

nomadic /nəʊmædɪk/. People who are **nomadic** travel from place to place rather than living in one place all the time. EG *These tribes have a nomadic way of life.* ADJ CLASSIF

no-man's land is land that is not owned or controlled by anyone, for example the land between two boundaries. N UNCOUNT

nominal /nɒmɪnə⁰l/. 1 You use **nominal** to describe a position or characteristic which something is supposed to have but which it does not have in reality. EG *We were directing the operation, though under the nominal leadership of a guerrilla general.* ADJ CLASSIF ◇ **nominally.** EG *Dad, nominally a Methodist, entered churches only for weddings and funerals.* ◇ ADV

2 A **nominal** price or sum of money is very small in comparison with the real cost or value of the thing you are buying or selling. EG *At a nominal price, the settlers got the rest of the land.* ADJ CLASSIF : ATTRIB

nominate /nɒmɪneɪt/, **nominates, nominating, nominated.** If you **nominate** someone for a job or to a position, you formally choose them to hold that job or position or suggest them as a candidate. EG *Trade unions nominate representatives to public bodies... I've been nominated for a Senior Lectureship.* V+O : USU+*for/to*

nomination /nɒmɪneɪʃə⁰n/, **nominations.** 1 A **nomination** is an official suggestion of someone as a candidate in an election or for a job. EG *...a list of nominations for senior lectureships.* N COUNT

2 The **nomination** of someone to a job or position is their appointment to the job or position. EG *...Judge O'Connor's nomination to the Supreme Court.* N UNCOUNT OR N COUNT

nominee /nɒmɪniː/, **nominees.** A **nominee** is someone who is nominated for something. EG *Dave is this year's nominee for the Exchange scheme.* N COUNT

non-. 1 **non-** is used to form adjectives that describe something as not having a particular quality or feature. For example, a non-nuclear war is a war fought without nuclear weapons. EG *...non-violent demonstrations... ...non-industrial societies.* PREFIX

2 **non-** is also used to form nouns. These nouns refer 2.1 to situations in which a particular kind of action is not taken. *...a non-aggression pact... ...non-payment of fines.* 2.2 to people who do not belong to a particular group. EG *...non-car-owners... ...non-Christians... To the non-angler this can be very puzzling.* PREFIX

non-alcoholic. A **non-alcoholic** drink does not contain alcohol. ADJ CLASSIF

nonchalant /nɒnʃələnt/. Someone who is **nonchalant** behaves calmly and in a way which suggests that they do not care much about things. EG *He tried to sound cheerful and nonchalant.* ADJ QUALIT ◇ **nonchalantly.** EG *The officer waved a hand nonchalantly.* ◇ ADV ◇ **nonchalance** /nɒnʃələns/. EG *The answers are given with so much confidence and such nonchalance.* ◇ N UNCOUNT

noncommittal /nɒnkəmɪtə⁰l/. If someone is **noncommittal**, they do not express their opinion or decision firmly. EG *On planning the government is studiously noncommittal... I received a noncommittal letter in return.* ADJ QUALIT

nonconformist /nɒnkənfɔːmɪst/, **nonconformists.** A **nonconformist** is someone who behaves in an unusual or rebellious way. EG *...the persecution of non-conformists and minorities.* N COUNT ▸ used as an adjective. EG *I've got rather nonconformist ideas on this.* ▸ ADJ QUALIT

nondescript /nɒndɪ²skrɪpt/. Something that is **nondescript** is fairly dull and uninteresting in appearance or design. EG *...a complex of nondescript buildings... The women were dressed in nondescript clothes.* ADJ QUALIT

none /nʌn/. 1 **None** means not a single thing or person, or not even a small amount of a particular thing. EG *None of these suggestions is very helpful... None of us were allowed to go... I have answered every single question. My opponent has answered none... 'You had no difficulty in finding it?' – 'None at all.'* PRON : NEG, OFT+*of*

2 If you say that you will **have none of** something, you mean that you refuse to tolerate it. EG *I'll have none of this nonsense.* PHRASE Informal

3 You use **none too** to mean 'not at all'. For example, **none too** sure means not at all sure. EG *We're none too sure what we're arguing about... He hauled her none too gently to her feet.* PHRASE Formal

nonentity /nɒnentɪ¹tɪ¹/, **nonentities.** If you refer to someone as a **nonentity**, you mean that they are not special or important in any way. EG *Grant came from a family of nonentities.* N COUNT

nonetheless /nʌnðəles/ means in spite of what has just been said. EG *She couldn't act at all. Nonetheless she was a big box office attraction... It was not an impossible task, but they failed nonetheless.* ADV SEN Formal

non-event, non-events. If you describe something that happens as a **non-event**, you mean that it is not at all interesting or exciting. N COUNT

non-existent. Something that is **non-existent** does not exist in a particular place or does not exist at all. EG *Medical facilities are poor or non-existent in most rural areas.* ADJ CLASSIF

non-fiction is writing that gives information or describes real events, rather than telling an invented story. EG *...works of non-fiction... ...non-fiction books.* N UNCOUNT

non-nuclear means not using or involving nuclear weapons or nuclear power. EG *...the deployment of non-nuclear weapons.* ADJ CLASSIF : ATTRIB

no-nonsense. A **no-nonsense** person is firm and efficient. EG *I liked his no-nonsense approach to the whole matter.* ADJ CLASSIF : ATTRIB

nonplussed /nɒnplʌst/. If you are **nonplussed** when something happens, you feel confused and unsure how to react. EG *'I've heard nothing about this,' he said, nonplussed.* ADJ QUALIT

nonsense /nɒnsəns/. 1 You use **nonsense** to refer to 1.1 words that do not mean anything. EG *You can confuse the computer program by typing in nonsense.* N UNCOUNT 1.2 something spoken or written that you think is untrue or stupid. EG *A lot of nonsense is talked about the temperature of wine... 'I am her father.' – 'Nonsense,' he said. 'You are not.'* N UNCOUNT OR EXCLAM 1.3 something that you think is foolish or that you disapprove of. EG *Stop this nonsense, Louisa, for God's sake... We were warned not to get involved in any sort of publicity nonsense.* N UNCOUNT

2 To **make nonsense of** something or to **make a nonsense of** it means to cause it to become ridiculous or pointless. EG *The rest of his policies made nonsense of his call for moderation.* PHRASE

nonsensical /nɒnsensɪkə⁰l/. Something that is **nonsensical** is stupid or ridiculous. EG *This attitude seemed nonsensical to the general public.* ADJ QUALIT

non-smoker, non-smokers. A **non-smoker** is someone who does not smoke. N COUNT

non-starter, non-starters. If a plan or idea is a **non-starter**, it has no chance of success. EG *Such a policy is really a complete non-starter.* N COUNT

non-stick. A **non-stick** saucepan, frying-pan, or baking tin has a layer of a special substance on its inside which prevents food from sticking to it. ADJ CLASSIF

non-stop. A **non-stop** activity continues without any pauses or breaks. EG *They keep up a non-stop* ADJ CLASSIF OR ADV

If something is a non-event, does it happen?

conversation... ...taking the non-stop flight to London... Carter laughed non-stop for several minutes.

non-violent. Non-violent actions, especially actions intended to bring about political change, do not involve hurting people or damaging things. EG *It is to be a peaceful, non-violent protest.* ◇ **non-violence.** EG *...my commitment to the principles of non-violence.* ADJ CLASSIF ◇ N UNCOUNT

non-white, non-whites. Someone who is **non-white** belongs to a race of people who are not of European origin. ▸ used as a noun. EG *Such economic policies are hurting non-whites badly.* ADJ CLASSIF ▸ N COUNT

noodles /nuːdəºlz/ are long thin pieces of pasta. N PLURAL

nook /nʊk/, **nooks.** If you talk about **every nook and cranny** of a place, you are emphasizing that you mean every part of it or every space in it. EG *Toddlers are real explorers. They poke into every nook and cranny.* PHRASE

noon /nuːn/ is twelve o'clock in the middle of the day. EG *The visitor turned up at noon.* N UNCOUNT

noonday /nuːndeɪ/ means happening in the middle part of the day. EG *...a flash brighter than the noonday sun.* N MOD Literary

no-one /nəʊ wʌn/ means not a single person. See also **nobody.** EG *They had seen no-one else all afternoon... Sorry, there's no-one here called Nikki.* PRON INDEF : NEG

noose /nuːs/, **nooses.** A **noose** is a loop at the end of a piece of rope, especially one used to hang someone. N COUNT

nor /nɔː/. You use **nor** 1 after 'neither' in order to introduce the second thing that a negative statement applies to. EG *Neither Margaret nor John was there... My father could neither read nor write.* 2 after a negative statement in order to add something else that the negative statement applies to. EG *Melanie was not to be found – not that day, nor the next day, nor the day after that... I could not afford to eat in restaurants and nor could anyone I knew.* CONJ : NEG

norm /nɔːm/, **norms. 1 Norms** are ways of behaving that are considered normal in a particular society or place. EG *...the conventional norms of polite European society.* N COUNT : USU PLURAL

2 If you say that a situation is the **norm**, you mean that it is usual and expected. EG *In Russia, working wives have been the norm for many years.* N SING : *the*+N

normal /nɔːməºl/. Something that is **normal** is usual and ordinary, and what people expect. EG *Can she lead a normal life?... This is a perfectly normal baby... I've got used to it, it seems normal now.* ADJ QUALIT

normality /nɔːmælɪ¹ti¹/ is a situation in which everything is normal and as people expect. EG *People have a longing for normality.* N UNCOUNT

normally /nɔːməli¹/. 1 If you say that a particular thing **normally** happens, you mean that it is what usually happens. EG *I don't normally drink at lunch... Meetings are normally held three or four times a year... Normally, I keep these at home.* ADV OR ADV SEN

2 If something happens **normally,** it happens in a way that is usual and that people expect. EG *The important thing is that she's eating normally.* ADV

north /nɔːθ/; often spelled with a capital letter. 1 The **north** is 1.1 the direction which is on your left when you are looking towards the direction where the sun rises. EG *The land to the north and east was low-lying... ...Norwegian airfields in the far north.* 1.2 the part of a place or country which is towards the north. EG *...a man from somewhere in the north of England.* N SING : *the*+N

2 **North** means towards the north or to the north of a place or thing. EG *They were heading north... It's 150 miles north of Salisbury.* ADV

3 The **north** part of a place or country is the part which is towards the north. EG *...a flat in north London... ...the mountains of North Arizona.* ADJ CLASSIF : ATTRIB

4 A **north** wind blows from the north. ADJ CLASSIF

north-east; often spelled with a capital letter or capital letters. 1 The **north-east** is 1.1 the direction which is halfway between north and east. EG *Our route lay somewhere to the north-east... We attack from the north-east.* 1.2 the part of a place or country which is towards the north-east. EG *...the north-east of England... ...kids in the North-East.* N SING : *the*+N

2 **North-east** means towards the north-east or to the north-east of a place or thing. EG *Turn left and go north-east towards the station... It's a small town about fifteen kilometers northeast of Uppsala.* ADV

3 The **north-east** part of a place or country is the part which is towards the north-east. EG *The oldest part is close to the north-east entrance... ...in north-east Brazil.* ADJ CLASSIF : ATTRIB

4 A **north-east** wind blows from the north-east. ADJ CLASSIF

north-eastern means in or from the north-east of a region or country. EG *...floods in north-eastern India.* ADJ CLASSIF : ATTRIB

northerly /nɔːðəli¹/. 1 A **northerly** point, area, or direction is to the north or towards the north. EG *...the wet, northerly slopes... We proceeded along a more northerly route.* ADJ QUALIT

2 A **northerly** wind blows from the north. ADJ CLASSIF

northern /nɔːðə⁵n/ means in or from the north of a region or country. EG *...the high mountains of northern Japan... ...the Northern Hemisphere.* ADJ CLASSIF : ATTRIB

North Pole. The **North Pole** is the place on the surface of the earth which is farthest towards the north. N PROPER : *the*+N

northward /nɔːθwəd/ or **northwards** means towards the north. EG *They had fled northwards towards Kurnal.* ▸ **Northward** is also used as an adjective. EG *...the northward drift of the massive Himalayan chain.* ADV AFTER VB ▸ ADJ CLASSIF

north-west; often spelled with a capital letter or capital letters. 1 The **north-west** is 1.1 the direction which is halfway between north and west. EG *At the bridge the lake curves to the north-west.* 1.2 the part of a place or country which is towards the north-west. EG *...a hilly area in the north-west.* N SING : *the*+N

2 **North-west** means towards the north-west or to the north-west of a place or thing. EG *Some 300 miles north-west of Kampala, there is an abandoned village.* ADV

3 The **north-west** part of a place or country is the part which is towards the north-west. EG *...a Roman settlement in north-west England... ...the north-west frontier of India.* ADJ CLASSIF : ATTRIB

4 A **north-west** wind blows from the north-west. ADJ CLASSIF

north-western means in or from the north-west of a region or country. EG *...a cattle station in Northwestern Australia.* ADJ CLASSIF

nose /nəʊz/, **noses, nosing, nosed.** 1 Your **nose** is the part of your face which sticks out above your mouth. You use it for smelling and breathing. See picture at THE HUMAN BODY. EG *Johnny punched me in the nose.* N COUNT

2 The **nose** of a car or plane is the front part of it. EG *He thrust the nose of his plane upward.* N COUNT+SUPP

3 **Nose** is also used in these phrases. 3.1 If you say that someone **has a nose for** something, you mean that they have a natural ability to find it or recognize it. EG *The young have a sensitive nose for insincerity.* 3.2 If you **keep** your **nose out** of something, you do not interfere in it. 3.3 If someone **pokes** or **sticks** their **nose into** something, they try to interfere in it or to find out what is happening, when it does not concern them. EG *He shouldn't poke his nose into their business.* 3.4 If you say that something **gets up** your **nose,** you mean that it annoys you. 3.5 If you **pay through the nose** for something, you pay a very high price for it. EG *Country people have to pay through the nose for their goods.* 3.6 If something is happening **under** your **nose,** it is happening in front of you and it should be obvious to you. EG *Cheating was going on under the teacher's nose.* 3.7 If you **look down** your **nose at** someone or something, you think that they are inferior; used showing disapproval. 3.8 If someone **turns up** their **nose at** something, they reject it because they think that it PHRASES Informal

is not good enough for them; used showing disapproval.

nose about or **nose around.** If you **nose about** or **nose around**, you look around a place that belongs to someone else to see if you can find something interesting. EG *Stay outside the door and see that no one comes nosing around.* PHRASAL VB : V+ADV/PREP Informal

nosebleed /nəʊzbli:d/, **nosebleeds.** If you have a **nosebleed**, blood comes out from inside your nose, usually because it has been hit. N COUNT

nosedive /nəʊzdaɪv/, **nosedives, nosediving, nosedived.** If a plane does a **nosedive**, it flies very fast towards the ground, pointing downwards. EG *The plane went into a deliberate nose-dive.* ▸ used as a verb. EG *Suddenly, it nosedived towards the roof of a school.* N COUNT ▸ V

nosey /nəʊzi[1]/. See **nosy.**

nostalgia /nɒstældʒɪ[0]ə/ is an affectionate and slightly sad feeling that you have for the past. EG *...nostalgia for the good old days.* N UNCOUNT : OFT+*for*

nostalgic /nɒstældʒɪk/. If you feel **nostalgic**, you are thinking affectionately and rather sadly about a happier time in the past. EG *He was full of memories, nostalgic for the past... She knew some of the tunes they were playing, nostalgic reminders of her youth.* ◇ **nostalgically.** EG *...talking nostalgically of the good old days.* ADJ QUALIT ◇ ADV

nostril /nɒstrɪl/, **nostrils.** Your **nostrils** are the two openings at the end of your nose, which you breathe through. EG *...with the smell of smoke in my nostrils.* N COUNT

nosy /nəʊzi[1]/, **nosier, nosiest;** also spelled **nosey.** Someone who is **nosy** tries to find out about things which do not concern them; used showing disapproval. EG *'Who was it?' – 'Don't be so nosy.'* ADJ QUALIT

not /nɒt/. **1** You use **not** to make clauses or sentences negative. **Not** is often shortened to **n't** in informal English. When the verb has an auxiliary or modal auxiliary, you add **not** between the auxiliary and the main verb. EG *I haven't tried to telephone him... She couldn't hear the orchestra properly.* NEG

If the verb does not already have an auxiliary, you need to add 'do'. EG *I don't agree with everything he says... She did not answer.*

When the main verb is 'be', you use **not** without an auxiliary. EG *There wasn't enough room for everybody... It's not unusual.*

2 When **not** is used with verbs such as 'want', 'think', and 'seem', the negative effect of **not** belongs to the clause or infinitive that follows the verb. For example, 'I don't think she's here' means 'I think she's not here'. NEG

3 You use **not**, usually in the form **n't**, in question tags after a positive statement. EG *That's a new one, isn't it?... You've seen this, haven't you?* NEG : AFTER MODAL OR AFTER AUX

4 You can use **not** to make questions **4.1** expressing surprise or annoyance. EG *Don't they realize it's against the law?* **4.2** politely suggesting something. EG *Shouldn't you go and see him?* NEG

5 You can use **not** to represent the negative of a word, group, or clause that has just been used. EG *'Do you know how much it is?' – 'I'm afraid not.'... They'd know if it was all right or not.* NEG

6 You can use **not** before 'all', 'every', or 'always' when you are referring to only some members of a group or some occasions. EG *Not all scientists are honest... Not everyone agrees with me.* NEG

7 You can use **not** or **not even** in front of 'a' or 'one' as emphatic ways of saying that there is none at all of what is being mentioned. EG *The day was very still. There was not even a little breeze... Not one part was missing.* NEG

8 You can use **not** when you are contrasting something that is untrue with something that is true. EG *We wept, not because we were frightened but because we were ashamed.* NEG

9 You use **not that** to introduce a negative clause that decreases the importance of the previous statement. EG *Bob helped him. Not that it was difficult.* CONJ : NEG

10 Not at all is **10.1** an emphatic way of saying 'No'. EG *'Does that seem nonsense to you?' – 'Not at all.'... 'Would you mind?' – 'Not at all.'* **10.2** a polite way of acknowledging a person's thanks. EG *'Thanks.' – 'Not at all.'* CONVENTION : NEG Formal

11 if not: see **if.** • **nothing if not:** see **nothing.**

notable /nəʊtəbə[0]l/. Something or someone that is **notable** is important or interesting. EG *With a few notable exceptions this trend has continued... Watermouth is notable for experimental forms of teaching.* ADJ QUALIT

notably /nəʊtəbli[1]/. You use **notably 1** before giving an important or typical example of something that you are talking about. EG *Some people, notably his business associates, had begun to distrust him.* **2** to emphasize the degree of a quality or action. EG *So far, Wall Street has been notably unimpressed.* ADV / SUBMOD

notch /nɒtʃ/, **notches, notching, notched. 1** A **notch** is a small V-shaped cut in the surface or edge of something. EG *Carve notches at either end of a stick and wind the thread round them.* N COUNT

2 You can refer to a particular level on a scale, for example a scale of achievement, as a **notch.** EG *My regard for Smithy went up another notch.* N COUNT

notch up. If you **notch up** a particular score or total, you achieve it. EG *The Tory candidate had notched up eleven hundred votes.* PHRASAL VB : V+O+ADV

note /nəʊt/, **notes, noting, noted. 1** A **note** is **1.1** a short letter, usually an informal one. EG *She left a note saying she would see us again... She wrote a note to the chief of police.* **1.2** something that you write down to remind you about something, for example what someone said or what you intend to do. EG *I'll make a note of that... I took notes at the lecture.* **1.3** a short piece of additional information that is given in a book or article. EG *Yugoslavia is a different matter (see note on the Yugoslav situation, below).* **1.4** a piece of printed paper that is used as money. EG *...a five pound note.* N COUNT

2 If you **make** or **keep a mental note** of something, you make an effort to remember it. EG *He made a mental note to tell Lamin later who these men were.* PHRASE

3 If you **compare notes** with someone, you talk to them about something and find out whether they have the same opinion, information, or experiences of it as you. EG *There are a few things we might compare notes on.* PHRASE

4 If you **note** a fact, **4.1** you become aware of it. EG *It is important for us to note three basic facts... Note that the report does not carry any form of official recommendation... His audience, I noted with regret, were looking bored.* **4.2** you mention it in order to draw people's attention to it. EG *A government report released last week noted an alarming rise in racial harassment.* V+O OR V+REPORT

5 If you **take note** of something, you pay attention to it because you think that it is important. EG *I had to start taking some note of political developments.* PHRASE

6 A **note** is also **6.1** a sound of a particular pitch, especially one made by a musical instrument or a singer. EG *The slow music rang out, note by solemn note.* **6.2** a written symbol that represents a sound of a particular pitch and length. EG *Not one of them could read a note of music.* N COUNT

7 A **note** of a particular kind is **7.1** a quality in someone's voice that shows how they are feeling. EG *There was a note of triumph in her voice.* **7.2** an atmosphere or mood. EG *Sensing this would be a good note on which to end the interview, I got up... On a more serious note, I must warn you of the risks involved in this project.* N SING+SUPP

Which meaning of 'notice' will you find on a noticeboard?

note down. If you **note** something **down**, you write it down so that you have a record of it. EG *I'll give you time to note down where to send them.* PHRASAL VB: V+O+ADV

notebook /nəʊtbʊk/, **notebooks.** A **notebook** is a small book for writing notes in. N COUNT

noted /nəʊtɪ²d/. Someone or something that is **noted** is well-known and admired for something that they do or have. EG *...a Scottish family noted for its intellect... ...a noted American writer.* ADJ CLASSIF: OFT+for Formal

notepad /nəʊtpæd/, **notepads.** A **notepad** is a pad of paper that you write notes or letters on. N COUNT

notepaper /nəʊtpeɪpə/ is paper that you write letters on. N UNCOUNT

noteworthy /nəʊtwɜːðɪ¹/. A **noteworthy** fact or event is interesting or significant. EG *It was noteworthy that the Count was the only person there.* ADJ QUALIT

nothing /nʌθɪŋ/. **1** You use **nothing** when you are referring to no things, for example no objects, no events, or no ideas. EG *She shook the bottle over the glass; nothing came out... The man nodded but said nothing... There's nothing to worry about.* PRON INDEF: NEG

2 If you say that someone or something is **nothing,** you mean that they are very unimportant. EG *In those days time was nothing. Now it is everything... 'What's the matter with you?' Claud asked. 'It's nothing,' he gasped. 'I'll be all right in a minute.'* PRON INDEF: NEG Informal

3 Nothing is also used in these phrases. **3.1** If you say that an action was done **for nothing**, you mean that it was done either without a good reason or without achieving any worthwhile results. EG *Now they're killing our soldiers. For nothing.* **3.2** If you say about a story or rumour that there is **nothing in it**, you mean that it is untrue. **3.3** If you say about something that you have done that there was **nothing to it**, you mean that it was very easy. **3.4** You use **nothing of the sort** to emphasize a refusal or a negative statement. EG *You will do nothing of the sort... Although we think we are progressing, we may be doing nothing of the sort.* **3.5** You use **nothing if not** to emphasize that someone or something has a particular quality. For example, if you say that someone is **nothing if not** considerate, you mean that they are very considerate. **3.6 Nothing but** a particular thing means only that thing. EG *She could see nothing but his head... ...thirty years of nothing but war.* **3.7** If you say that **there is nothing for it** but to take a particular action, you mean that it is the only possible action that you can take, even though you would prefer not to. EG *There was nothing for it now except to go straight ahead with the plan.* PHRASES British

notice /nəʊtɪs/, **notices, noticing, noticed. 1** If you **notice** something, you become aware of it. EG *I suddenly noticed a friend in the front row... She noticed him scratching his head... She noticed that he was staring at her.* V+O: OFT+-ING OR INF; ALSO V OR V+REPORT

2 Notice is used in these phrases relating to awareness. **2.1** If you **take no notice** of someone or something, you do not allow them to affect what you think or do. EG *Take no notice of him. He's always rude to people.* **2.2** If you **take notice** of something, you behave in a way that shows you are aware of it. EG *I hope the heads of schools will take notice of my comments.* **2.3** If something **comes to** your **notice** or **is brought to** your **notice**, you become aware of it, for example because someone points it out to you. EG *Many cases have come to my notice... We bring to the notice of the committee things that ought to be done.* **2.4** If something **escapes** your **notice**, you do not recognize it or realize it. EG *It did not escape her notice that he kept glancing at her.* PHRASES

3 If someone gets **notice** from other people, they receive attention and are admired or respected. EG *He achieved some public notice in later life.* N UNCOUNT

4 A **notice** is a written announcement which is put in a place where it can be read by everyone. EG *At the main entrance, there was a large notice which said 'Visitors welcome at any time.'* N COUNT

5 If you give **notice** about something that is going to happen, you give a warning in advance that it is going to happen. EG *The union was to give 28 days' notice of strikes... She could have done it if she'd had a bit more notice... They will eject without notice any undesirable person.* N UNCOUNT: USU+SUPP

6 Notice is also used in these phrases relating to advance warnings or information. **6.1** If something can or must be done **at short notice** or **at a moment's notice**, it can or must be done with very little advance warning. EG *It's going to be difficult to fix things at such short notice... It is there ready to be switched on at a moment's notice.* **6.2** If a situation will exist **until further notice**, it will continue until someone changes it and informs people. EG *The beaches are closed until further notice.* **6.3** If an employer **gives** a worker **notice**, the employer tells the worker that he or she must leave within a fixed period of time. EG *She had been given two weeks' notice at the Works.* **6.4** If you **hand in** your **notice,** you tell your employer that you intend to leave your job soon, after a fixed period of time. PHRASES

noticeable /nəʊtɪsəbə⁰l/. Something that is **noticeable** is very obvious, so that it is easy to see or recognize. EG *It did not have any noticeable effect upon the rate of economic growth.* ◊ **noticeably.** EG *As they climbed higher, the air became noticeably cooler.* ADJ QUALIT ◊ ADV

noticeboard /nəʊtɪsbɔːd/, **noticeboards.** A **noticeboard** is a board on a wall, which people pin notices to. N COUNT British

notification /nəʊtɪfɪkeɪʃə⁰n/. If you are given **notification** of something, you are officially informed of it. EG *You will be sent notification of the results of your interview by post.* N UNCOUNT

notify /nəʊtɪfaɪ/, **notifies, notifying, notified.** If you **notify** someone of something, you officially inform them of it. EG *The Housing Department is notified of all planning applications... He wrote to notify me that the cheque had arrived.* V+O: OFT+of OR REPORT

notion /nəʊʃə⁰n/, **notions.** A **notion** is a belief or idea. EG *...the notion that the earth was flat... He had only the vaguest notion of what it was about.* N COUNT: USU+REPORT OR of

notoriety /nəʊtəraɪɪ¹tɪ¹/ is the fact of being well known for something that is bad or undesirable. EG *...terrorists who acquired international notoriety for the kidnapping of government figures.* N UNCOUNT

notorious /nə⁶tɔːrɪəs/. Someone or something that is **notorious** is well known for something that is bad or undesirable. EG *The area was notorious for murders... ...his notorious arrogance.* ADJ QUALIT: OFT+for

◊ **notoriously.** EG *Here, rainfall is notoriously variable and unreliable.* ◊ SUBMOD

notwithstanding /nɒtwɪθstændɪŋ, -wɪð-/. If something is true **notwithstanding** a particular thing, it is true in spite of that thing. EG *Computing remains a growth area in which, notwithstanding economic recessions, the outlook looks bright.* PREP Formal

nought /nɔːt/, **noughts. Nought** is the number 0. See the entry headed NUMBER. EG *...nought point two.* NUMBER

noun /naʊn/, **nouns.** In grammar, a **noun** is a word which is used to refer to a person, a thing, or an abstract idea such as a feeling or quality. In this dictionary, the abbreviation N is used in the grammar notes to mean 'noun'. See the entry headed NOUNS for information about nouns. N COUNT

nourish /nʌrɪʃ/, **nourishes, nourishing, nourished. 1** To **nourish** people or animals means to provide them with food. EG *They had grown stronger now that they were better nourished... ...nourishing their young on small insects.* V+O

2 If you **nourish** a feeling or belief, you encourage it to grow or survive. EG *She had nourished dreams of escape.* V+O Literary

nourishing /nʌrɪʃɪŋ/. Food that is **nourishing** makes you strong and healthy. EG *Ham sandwiches are nourishing and filling... ...a nourishing diet.* ADJ QUALIT

NOUNS

Nouns are the words that you use when you are referring to people, things, and abstract ideas such as feelings and qualities.

A lot of the grammar of nouns is in the way we measure and count them. There are three types of choice:

1 at word level: does the noun have singular and plural forms, or just one form?

2 at noun group level: does the noun go with 'a' or 'some'? Can it occur on its own?

3 at clause level: does the noun go with a singular or a plural verb? (Only the present tense of verbs shows this choice.)

Countable nouns

The most common nouns in English are countable nouns (N COUNT). These are nouns that have both a singular and a plural form. The plural is usually made by adding **-s** to the singular, but if you look at the first line of each entry, you will see exactly how to spell the plural.

When countable nouns are used in the singular, they must have a determiner, such as **a**, **the**, or **my** in front of them. So you say: *... the house ...* *... a friend ...* *... his dog.*

When you want to use an adjective to tell you more about the noun, you put the determiner before the adjective: *... a clean shirt ...* *... that little boy ...* *... her pretty green dress.*

When a countable noun is used in the plural, it can have a determiner, but only when you want to pick out some rather than all of the particular item. So you can say: *... tables ...* *... the tables ...* *... those tables ...* *... her tables.*

Countable nouns go with the same number choice in verbs. For example: *The house is on fire ...* *The table is dirty ...* *Those flowers are lovely.*

Uncountable nouns

Many nouns are uncountable nouns (N UNCOUNT). These are nouns which have only one form. Examples are: *hatred, rice, information, news, furniture.*

You cannot put numbers in front of an uncountable noun, so you cannot say 'one furniture'. You have to say 'one piece of furniture' or 'two items of news', and so on. See the section which follows on partitive nouns.

Uncountable nouns are not usually used with the determiners **a** and **the**, unless extra information about the noun is being given. So you would normally say: *They sell furniture.* But you can also say: *... the furniture I want for my bedroom.*

In the same way you would normally say: *She felt hatred towards his sister.* But you can also say: *I have a hatred of all examinations.*

Uncountable nouns take a verb in the singular. For example: *The furniture is needed urgently.*

Mass nouns

There is a large group of nouns which are very similar to uncountable nouns, but which can also be used occasionally as countable nouns. These are called mass nouns (N MASS). 'Cheese' is a typical example of a mass noun. There are two forms, 'cheese' and 'cheeses'. You usually say: *I like cheese,* and in this case you are referring to cheese in general. Here the noun is like an uncountable noun because it is used without a determiner. However, when you want to refer to different types of cheese, you can say: *There's a shop in Harborne that sells more than a hundred cheeses.* Here it is used like a countable noun in the plural.

Again, you usually say: *I take sugar in tea.* However, when you want to say how much sugar you take, you can say: *I take three sugars in tea,* meaning that you take three spoonfuls or three lumps of sugar.

'Cheese' goes with a singular verb, and 'cheeses' goes with a plural.

Singular nouns

A few nouns are used in the singular form only (N SING). They must have a determiner An example is 'jumble', where you can say: *. . . the jumble which covers my desk . . .   . . . a chaotic jumble of papers.*

For some nouns it is important which determiner you use, and in that case we say so in the Extra Column. For example, the Extra Column label for **harvest 1** says N SING: *the*+N, as in: *Our rice won't last until the harvest.*

And the Extra Column label for **bother 4** says N SING: *a*+N, as in: *It's a bit of a bother . . . Sorry to be a bother, but could you help me?*

These nouns go with singular verbs.

Collective nouns

There is a small group of nouns, such as 'committee' and 'audience', which vary from the usual pattern of countable nouns. They have both singular and plural forms. They need a determiner in the singular.

Their singular form can occur with either a singular or a plural verb. This is because you can think of 'a committee' or 'an audience' as either a complete group or as a number of individual members. Nouns like this are often called 'collective nouns' in grammars; they are given the label N COLL in this dictionary. You can say: *The committee is meeting at the moment,* or: *The committee are meeting at the moment.*

In the same way you can say: *The audience was very enthusiastic, or: The audience were very enthusiastic.*

These nouns also have the normal pattern of countable nouns. So you say: *Their local committees are held every month.*

Turn over for more information about nouns.

MORE ABOUT NOUNS

Plural nouns

Some nouns are only used as plurals (N PLURAL).

They usually end in **-s**, as in: *clothes, scissors.*

They take determiners, just like countable plurals. However, when they modify other nouns they usually drop the **-s**, as in: . . . *trouser pocket* . . . . . . *spectacle case.*

But a few do not, as in: *a clothes shop.*

Some plural nouns, such as **trousers**, **glasses**, and **scissors**, refer to a single object which has two main parts. With these, you often use the phrase **a pair of**, as in: *a pair of scissors* . . . . . . *a pair of jeans* . . . . . . *a pair of knickers.*

Similar to these nouns are a few words like **police** which do not end in **-s** but which behave like plural nouns.

Noun modifiers

A small group of nouns are not used very often on their own, but are more frequently used in front of another noun as if they were adjectives (N MOD). An example of a noun which is used in this way is **capacity**, as in: *a capacity audience* . . . . . . *a capacity crowd.*

Another example is **steel 1**, where the Extra Column says N UNCOUNT: USU N MOD. This means that 'steel' is often used like an adjective in phrases such as: *steel rods* . . . . . . *a steel bar* . . . . . . *a steel works.*

It is also occasionally used as a straightforward noun, as in: *He works in a factory that makes steel.*

Proper nouns

A few nouns in this dictionary are proper nouns (N PROPER), which refer to a particular person, place, or institution. Proper nouns have a capital letter as their first letter. They each have a unique form.

Most proper nouns are used on their own, with no **a** or **the** in front of them: *Father Christmas, Heaven, Hell.*

A few proper nouns, however, always have **the** in front of them, because it is part of their name. So you say: *The Bible, The Continent, The Channel.*

Proper nouns usually take a singular verb, unless their form is clearly plural.

Partitive nouns

A number of nouns are partitive nouns (N PART). They are countable nouns.

They allow us to measure and count things that are normally expressed by uncountable nouns, and to group countable things together. The partitive construction uses the preposition **of** after the partitive noun.

Some partitive nouns allow you to measure things: . . . *two pints of beer* . . . . . . *five tons of coal* . . . . . . *three spoons of sugar.*

Other partitive nouns allow you to refer to individual items of something that is usually expressed by an uncountable noun: *... a bit of paper ... ... a small piece of string ... ... an interesting bit of news.*

Some partitive nouns are followed by countable nouns in the plural, and refer to people, things, or animals which are together in a group: *... a crowd of tourists ... ... a bunch of flowers ... ... a herd of cows ... ... a huge flock of sheep.*

When it is obvious what is being counted or measured, the 'of' phrase can be omitted. For example: *Two pints, please ... Those roses are lovely, I'll have a bunch.*

Nouns with supporting words

Many nouns, of different types, are typically used not by themselves but with supporting words or phrases in the language round about them. These nouns have +SUPP in the Extra Column.

The supporting language can come before or after the noun. If it comes before, it is usually in the form of an adjective or another noun. For example, **album 2** usually has a noun before it which tells you what type of album it is: *stamp album ... ... photograph album.*

If the supporting words come after the noun, they are usually in the form of a relative clause or a prepositional group, often one that starts with **of**. For example, **torrent 2** is usually followed by a phrase starting with **of**: *a torrent of oaths ... ... a torrent of bitter invective.*

Some nouns can have the supporting words either before or after them. For example, as in **way 2**: *He smiled in a superior way ... ... a strange way of grinning ... I don't like the way doctors talk to you.*

The examples which are given for each word give the most typical supporting structures, showing how the word is most frequently used.

'-ing' nouns

The **-ing** form of verbs is often used to describe activities. For example, if you ski, you can say that you 'like skiing' or that you 'go skiing every year'. This is a normal use of the **-ing** form of a verb: it behaves like an uncountable noun, but it can also be used with 'go'.

Some words are most frequently used in the **-ing** form. For example, the verb 'to caravan' is rare, yet the form 'caravanning' is quite common, as in: *I like caravanning ... They go caravanning every summer.*

Words of this type, where no verb is given but where the **-ing** form can be used with **be**, **like**, or **go**, are given in the dictionary with the label N ING in the Extra Column.

nourishment /nʌrɪʃmə²nt/ is the food that people and animals need to grow and remain healthy. EG *She had recovered sufficiently to take some nourishment... The seeds are full of nourishment.* N UNCOUNT

novel /nɒvə⁰l/, **novels. 1** A **novel** is a book that tells an invented story. EG *...reading a novel by Henry James.* N COUNT

2 Something that is **novel** is unlike anything that has been done or created before. EG *...a novel experience... ...novel teaching methods.* ADJ QUALIT

novelist /nɒvə⁰lɪst/, **novelists.** A **novelist** is a person who writes novels. N COUNT

novelty /nɒvə⁰lti¹/, **novelties. 1 Novelty** is the quality of being different, new, and unusual. EG *He became interested because of the novelty of the problem... After twenty years, and hundreds of talks, the novelty had definitely worn off.* N UNCOUNT

2 A **novelty** is **2.1** something that is unusual. EG *The car was still a novelty at that time.* **2.2** a cheap, unusual object that is sold as a gift or souvenir. N COUNT

November /nəʊvɛmbə/ is the eleventh month of the year in the Western calendar. EG *The agreement ends on November 24.* N UNCOUNT

novice /nɒvɪs/, **novices. 1** A **novice** is someone who is not experienced at the job or activity that they are doing. EG *He's still a novice as far as film acting is concerned... ...novice riders.* N COUNT

2 A **novice** in a monastery or convent is a person who is preparing to become a monk or nun. N COUNT

now /naʊ/. **1** You use **now** to refer to the present time, often in contrast to a time in the past or the future. EG *It is now just after one o'clock... I'm going home now... She has three children now... It's two weeks now since I wrote to you... Now is the time to find out... From now on, you are free to do what you like.* ADV

2 You can also use **now** when telling a story or giving an account to refer to a particular time in the past. EG *They were walking more slowly now.* ADV

3 If you say that something will happen **any day now** or **any time now**, you mean that it will happen very soon. EG *Any day now, the local authority is going to close it down.* PHRASE

4 If you say that something happens **now and then**, **every now and then**, or **now and again**, you mean that it happens sometimes but not very often or not regularly. EG *Every now and then there is a confrontation.* PHRASE

5 Now also means as a result of what has recently happened. EG *I was hoping to see you tomorrow. That won't be possible now.* ADV

6 You can use **now that** or **now** when you are talking about the effect of an event or change. EG *Now that she's found him, she'll never let him go... I like him a lot now he's older.* CONJ

7 You can also use **now 7.1** to add emphasis to a statement, remark, request, or command. EG *I ran downstairs. Now this was something the intruder had not expected... They call themselves men! Now, in my day, men were men!... 'I gave it back.' – 'Did you now?'... I must get back to work. Run along, now... Now, come on. Be sensible.* **7.2** when you are searching for something or thinking what to say next. EG *I've got her address somewhere. Now let me see.* Spoken; Spoken Informal

8 You can say **now, now** when you are trying to calm someone or are warning them not to behave in a particular way. EG *'Now, now,' the doctor said, taking her gently by the hand. 'You mustn't get so upset.'* CONVENTION Spoken Outdated

9 You say **now then** to attract people's attention. EG *Now then, who's for a cup of tea?* Spoken

nowadays /naʊədeɪz/ means at the present time, in contrast with what happened in the past. EG *Nowadays most babies in this country are born in a hospital... Why don't we ever see Jim nowadays?* ADV

nowhere /nəʊwɛə/. **1** You use **nowhere** to say that a suitable or relevant place does not exist. EG *There was nowhere to hide... She had nowhere else to go... Nowhere have I seen any mention of this.* ADV : NEG

2 If you say that someone or something appears **from nowhere** or **out of nowhere**, you mean that they appear suddenly and unexpectedly. PHRASE

3 If you say that a place is **in the middle of nowhere**, you mean that it is a long way from other places. EG *I spent hours waiting for a bus in the middle of nowhere.* PHRASE Informal

4 If you say that you **are getting nowhere** or that something **is getting** you **nowhere**, you mean that you are not achieving anything or having any success. EG *Without them I would be nowhere... Calling me names will get you nowhere.* PHRASE

5 If you say that something is **nowhere near** the case, you are emphasizing that it is not the case at all. EG *Lions are nowhere near as fast as the cheetah... One visit is nowhere near enough.* PHRASE

noxious /nɒkʃəs/. A **noxious** gas or substance is harmful or poisonous. EG *...a cloud of noxious paraffin vapour.* ADJ CLASSIF : USU ATTRIB Formal

nozzle /nɒzə⁰l/, **nozzles.** A **nozzle** is a narrow end piece fitted to a hose or pipe to control the flow of a liquid coming out of it. EG *The water shoots out of the nozzle in a powerful jet.* N COUNT

N PART stands for **partitive noun**
1 Nouns which have the label N PART in the Extra Column refer to a part or portion of something. For example, *...a **slice** of cake...* and *...a **piece** of advice.*
2 N PART is also used for words that group countable things together. For example, *...**masses** of people...* and *...**flocks** of sheep.*
See the entry headed NOUNS for more information.

N PLURAL stands for **plural noun**
Nouns which have the label N PLURAL in the Extra Column always have a plural verb when they are the subject of a clause.
See the entry headed NOUNS for more information.

N PROPER stands for **proper noun**
Nouns which have the label **N PROPER** in the Extra Column are the names of particular people, places, or organizations.
See the entry headed NOUNS for more information.

N SING stands for **singular noun**
Nouns which have the label **N SING** in the Extra Column are normally only used in the singular. They always have a determiner such as 'a', 'the', and 'her' in front of them.
See the entry headed NOUNS for more information.

nuance /nju:ɑ:ns/, **nuances.** A **nuance** is a slight difference in sound, appearance, feeling, or meaning. EG *He practised until he could imitate every nuance of Hall's speech.* N COUNT OR N UNCOUNT

nuclear /nju:klɪə/ means relating to the energy that is produced when the nuclei of atoms are split ADJ CLASSIF : ATTRIB

Does a novelist write about novelties?

NUMBERS

Numbers have the label NUMBER in the Extra Column. Most numbers behave in the following ways:

1 They occur in noun groups, coming before any adjectives in the group but after a determiner such as **the** or **these**. For example: *the two old chairs . . . . . . his five older sisters.*

2 Numbers can be the head of a noun group when the context makes it clear what the number refers to: *There were three in the room.*

3 Numbers can be used in front of prepositional phrases beginning with **of**: *There are eleven of us in the team . . . They are two of the nicest people I know.*

How to say numbers aloud:

For numbers greater than a hundred, it is usual to say 'and' before the part of the number which is less than a hundred. For example, 351 is said as 'three hundred and fifty-one' and 49,280 is said as 'forty-nine thousand two hundred and eighty'.

There are different ways of saying numbers greater than a hundred. For example, 250 can be said as 'two hundred and fifty', 'two fifty', or 'two five oh'. For longer numbers such as telephone numbers, it is usual to say the figures individually. For example, you would say the number 131274 as 'one three one two seven four'.

The number 0 is usually said as 'oh', although 'zero', 'nought', and 'nothing' are sometimes used instead.

NUMBERS		ORDINALS		FRACTIONS	
0	zero, nought, nothing				
1	one	1st	first		
2	two	2nd	second	1/2	a half
3	three	3rd	third	1/3	a third
4	four	4th	fourth	1/4	a quarter
5	five	5th	fifth	1/5	a fifth
6	six	6th	sixth	1/6	a sixth
7	seven	7th	seventh	1/7	a seventh
8	eight	8th	eighth	1/8	an eighth
9	nine	9th	ninth	1/9	a ninth
10	ten	10th	tenth	1/10	a tenth
11	eleven	11th	eleventh	etc	etc
12	twelve	12th	twelfth		
13	thirteen	13th	thirteenth		
14	fourteen	14th	fourteenth		
15	fifteen	15th	fifteenth		
16	sixteen	16th	sixteenth		
17	seventeen	17th	seventeenth		
18	eighteen	18th	eighteenth		
19	nineteen	19th	nineteenth		
20	twenty	20th	twentieth		
21	twenty-one	21st	twenty-first		
22	twenty-two	22nd	twenty-second		
30	thirty	30th	thirtieth		
40	forty	40th	fortieth		
50	fifty	50th	fiftieth		
60	sixty	60th	sixtieth		
70	seventy	70th	seventieth		
80	eighty	80th	eightieth		
90	ninety	90th	ninetieth		
100	a hundred	100th	hundredth		
101	a hundred and one	101st	hundred and first		
200	two hundred	200th	two hundredth		
1,000	a thousand	1,000th	thousandth		
1,001	a thousand and one	etc	etc		
10,000	ten thousand				
100,000	a hundred thousand				
1,000,000	a million				
1,000,000,000	a billion				

or combined. EG *...nuclear energy... ...nuclear weapons... ...nuclear war... ...nuclear physics.*

nuclear-free. A **nuclear-free** place is a place where nuclear weapons or nuclear energy are forbidden. EG *...if Europe becomes a nuclear-free zone.* ADJ CLASSIF : ATTRIB

nuclear reactor, nuclear reactors. A **nuclear reactor** is a machine which is used to produce nuclear energy. N COUNT

nucleus /njuːklɪəs/, **nuclei** /njuːklɪaɪ/. **1** The **nucleus** of an atom or cell is the central part of it. EG *...hydrogen nuclei.* N COUNT

2 The **nucleus** of a group of people or things is a small number of people or things which form the most important part of the group. EG *These people formed the nucleus of the American Vegetarian Movement.* N COUNT : OFT+*of*

nude /njuːd/, **nudes. 1** Someone who is **nude** or **in the nude** is not wearing any clothes. EG *They lay nude on the beach.* ADJ CLASSIF OR PHRASE

2 A **nude** is a picture or statue of a person who is not wearing any clothes. N COUNT

nudge /nʌdʒ/, **nudges, nudging, nudged. 1** If you **nudge** someone, you push them gently, usually with your elbow, in order to draw their attention to something or to make them move. EG *The girls grinned and nudged each other.* ▸ used as a noun. EG *Neil, give your companion a nudge.* V+O ▸ N COUNT

2 If you **nudge** someone into doing something, you gently persuade them to do it. EG *People began to nudge the couple into going away.* ▸ used as a noun. EG *I just gave Stroud a nudge in the right direction.* V+O+A ▸ N COUNT

nudity /njuːdɪ[1]ti[1]/ is the state of wearing no clothes. EG *The boys treated nudity as a natural thing.* N UNCOUNT

nugget /nʌgɪ[2]t/, **nuggets.** A **nugget** of information is an interesting or useful piece of information. EG *Where had he picked up that little nugget?* N COUNT

nuisance /njuːsəns/, **nuisances.** If you say that someone or something is a **nuisance**, you mean that they annoy you or cause you problems. EG *It was a nuisance for them to have all these visitors sitting around... I'm sorry to be such a nuisance.* N COUNT : USU SING

● If you **make a nuisance of** yourself, you behave in a way that annoys other people. EG *...teenagers who make nuisances of themselves.* ● PHRASE

numb /nʌm/, **numbs, numbing, numbed. 1** If a part of your body is **numb**, it cannot feel anything. EG *My shoulder no longer hurt – it was completely numb.* ADJ CLASSIF

2 If you are **numb** with shock or fear, you are so shocked or frightened that you cannot think clearly or feel any emotion. EG *Numb with shock, Kunta stood watching blankly.* ADJ QUALIT : OFT+*with*

3 If something such as a blow or cold weather **numbs** a part of your body, it makes it unable to feel anything. EG *Her fingers were numbed by the frost... A stone numbed his shoulder.* V+O

4 If an experience **numbs** you, you can no longer think clearly or feel any emotion. EG *We are numbed by repeated disappointments.* ◊ **numbed.** EG *He stood there in a numbed daze.* V+O ◊ ADJ QUALIT

number /nʌmbə/, **numbers, numbering, numbered. 1** A **number** is any of the words such as 'two', 'nine', or 'eleven', or the symbols such as 1, 3, or 47. You use numbers to say how many things you are referring to or where something comes in a series. EG *...a two-figure number... Your licence number is here... He lives at number 19 New King Street.* N COUNT

2 Someone's **number** is the series of digits that you dial when you telephone them. EG *Ring me tomorrow. Here's my number... He did not know the man's telephone number.* N COUNT : OFT+POSS

3 If you refer to the **number** of things or people in a situation, you are referring to how many things or people there are. EG *A surprising number of men never marry... ...cities with large numbers of children in care... They were produced in vast numbers.* ● **A number** of things means several things. EG *A number of people disagreed.* ● **Any number** of things means a large quantity of them. EG *The work can be done in any number of ways.* N PART OR N COUNT +SUPP ● PHRASE ● PHRASE

4 If a group of people or things **numbers** a particular amount, there are that many of them. EG *The force numbered almost a quarter of a million men.* V+C

5 If you **number** something, you give it a number in a series and write that number on it. EG *I haven't numbered the pages yet.* V+O

6 If someone or something **is numbered** among a particular group, they are considered to belong in that group. EG *She can be numbered among the great musicians of our time.* V+O+*among* USU PASS

7 If you say that someone's **days are numbered,** you mean that they will not survive or be successful for much longer. PHRASE

8 A **number** is also a short piece of music or a song. N COUNT Informal

number one means better, more important, or more popular than anything else of its kind. EG *They regard unemployment as their number one priority.* ADJ CLASSIF Informal

number plate, number plates. The **number plates** of a vehicle are the signs on the front and back that show its registration number. See picture at CAR. N COUNT British

numeracy /njuːmə[0]rəsi[1]/ is the ability to do arithmetic. N UNCOUNT

numeral /njuːmə[0]rəl/, **numerals.** A **numeral** is a symbol used to represent a number. EG *My clock has Roman numerals.* N COUNT Formal

numerate /njuːmə[0]rə[1]t/. Someone who is **numerate** is able to do arithmetic. ADJ CLASSIF

numerical /njuːmɛrɪkə[0]l/ means expressed in numbers or relating to numbers. EG *...numerical data.* ◊ **numerically.** EG *...a numerically small group.* ADJ CLASSIF ◊ ADV

numerous /njuːmə[0]rəs/. **1** If you refer to **numerous** things or people, you mean a lot of things or people. EG *We had numerous discussions on the meaning of communism... George was the only survivor of her numerous children.* QUANTIF

2 If people or things are **numerous**, there are a lot of them. EG *Small enterprises have become more numerous.* ADJ QUALIT

nun /nʌn/, **nuns.** A **nun** is a member of a female religious community. N COUNT

> **N UNCOUNT** stands for **uncountable noun**
> Nouns which have the label N UNCOUNT in the Extra Column do not have plural forms. They are not usually used with determiners such as 'a' or 'this' unless they have a supporting word or phrase.
> See the entry headed NOUNS for more information.

nurse /nɜːs/, **nurses, nursing, nursed. 1** A **nurse** is a person whose job is to care for people who are ill. EG *She's a trained nurse... Nurse Lore was on the telephone.* N COUNT

2 If you **nurse** someone, you care for them while they are ill. EG *She nursed him devotedly.* V+O

3 If you **nurse** an emotion or desire, you feel it strongly for a long time. EG *Wilson had long nursed a desire to build his own yacht.* V+O

4 See also **nursing**.

nursery /nɜːsə[0]ri[1]/, **nurseries. 1** A **nursery** is a place where very young children can be looked N COUNT

> If you are training to be a nurse, do you go to a nursery school?

after while their parents are at work or doing something else.
2 Nursery education is the education of children who are between three and five years old. N MOD
3 A plant **nursery** is a place where plants are grown in order to be sold. N COUNT

nursery rhyme, nursery rhymes. A **nursery rhyme** is a poem or song for young children, especially one that is old or well-known. N COUNT

nursery school, nursery schools. A **nursery school** is a school for children who are between three and five years old. N COUNT OR N UNCOUNT

nursing /nɜːsɪŋ/. **1 Nursing** is the profession of looking after people who are ill. N UNCOUNT
2 A **nursing** mother feeds her baby with milk from her breasts. ADJ CLASSIF : ATTRIB

nursing home, nursing homes. A **nursing home** is a private hospital, especially one for old people. N COUNT

nurture /nɜːtʃə/, **nurtures, nurturing, nurtured. 1** If you **nurture** a young child or a young plant, you care for it while it is growing and developing. EG *...a mother's duty to nurture her children.* V+O Formal
2 If you **nurture** plans, ideas, or people, you encourage their development and success. EG *After spending two years nurturing this project, Bains came to England.* V+O Formal

nut /nʌt/, **nuts. 1 Nuts** grow on trees. They have hard shells and firm insides that can be eaten. EG *...cashew nuts... ...gathering berries, nuts and fruit... The cake has chopped nuts in it.* N COUNT : USU PLURAL
2 A **nut** is also a small piece of metal with a hole in it which a bolt screws into. Nuts and bolts are used to fasten things together. See picture at TOOLS. EG *Take your spanner and tighten the nut.* N COUNT
3 If you say that someone is a **nut**, or that they are **nuts** or **off** their **nut**, you mean that they are mad or very foolish. EG *You must have been nuts to leave this place... I think he's off his nut.* N COUNT, ADJ PRED, OR PHRASE Informal

nutcase /nʌtkeɪs/, **nutcases.** If you say that someone is a **nutcase**, you mean that they behave in a mad or foolish way. N COUNT Informal Outdated

nutmeg /nʌtmɛg/ is a spice. N UNCOUNT

nutrient /njuːtrɪənt/, **nutrients. Nutrients** are substances that help plants and animals to grow. EG *Excessive rainfall washes out valuable minerals and nutrients from the soil.* N COUNT

nutrition /njuːtrɪʃəⁿn/ is the healthiness of the food that you eat. EG *Children need education in good nutrition... ...improvements in nutrition.* N UNCOUNT

nutritious /njuːtrɪʃəs/. Food that is **nutritious** contains substances which help your body to be healthy. EG *The seeds are tasty and nutritious.* ADJ QUALIT

nutshell /nʌtʃɛl/. You use **in a nutshell** to indicate that you are saying something in the briefest way possible. EG *That, in a nutshell, is what we're trying to do here.* ADV SEN

nutter /nʌtə/, **nutters.** If you call someone a **nutter**, you mean that they are mad or very foolish. N COUNT Informal

nutty /nʌti¹/, **nuttier, nuttiest. 1** If you describe someone or something as **nutty**, you mean that they are very foolish. EG *...this nutty idea he has.* ADJ QUALIT Informal
2 Food that is **nutty** tastes of nuts. EG *...rice with a pleasantly nutty taste.* ADJ QUALIT

nuzzle /nʌzəⁿl/, **nuzzles, nuzzling, nuzzled.** If you **nuzzle** someone, you gently rub your nose and mouth against them, often to show affection. EG *'Ellen,' he said, nuzzling her neck... The dog began to nuzzle at his coat.* V+O OR V+A

NW is an abbreviation for 'north-west'.

nylon /naɪlɒn/ is a strong type of artificial cloth. EG *...a dress made of nylon... ...nylon stockings.* N UNCOUNT

O o

O, o /əʊ/, **O's, o's. 1 O** is the fifteenth letter of the English alphabet. N COUNT
2 O is used in exclamations, especially when you are expressing strong feelings. EG *O God, I want to go home... O the joy of those Saturday afternoons... 'He's not the Chancellor now.' – 'O yes, he is.'* EXCLAM

> **O** stands for **object**
> Objects are the words in a sentence which represent the people or things affected by the verb. Many verbs have an object, as in *I like **Italy**... All children like **Italian ice cream**.* Some verbs can have two objects, one of which refers to the person or thing that something is done to and the other refers to the person who is concerned with the result of the action. EG *She gave **me some good advice**... Can you give **me a few examples**?*
> All prepositions are followed by objects, as in *They went into **the room**... I saw her car coming down **the High Street** towards **me**.*
> See the entry headed VERBS for more information about verbs that have objects.

oaf /əʊf/, **oafs.** If you call someone an **oaf**, you mean that they are clumsy and stupid. EG *Paul, you are a big oaf!* N COUNT OR VOCATIVE

oak /əʊk/, **oaks. 1** An **oak** or an **oak tree** is a large tree that often grows in woods and forests. N COUNT
2 Oak is the wood from oak trees, which is strong and hard. EG *...a square oak table.* N UNCOUNT

OAP /əʊ eɪ piː/, **OAPs.** An **OAP** is a man over the age of 65 or a woman over the age of 60. **OAP** is an abbreviation for 'old-age pensioner'. N COUNT British

oar /ɔː/, **oars.** An **oar** is a long pole that is used for rowing a boat. The oar is fixed across the side of the boat, and when you pull one end of it, the other end moves in the opposite direction through the water, causing the boat to move. N COUNT

oasis /əʊeɪsɪs/, **oases** /əʊeɪsiːz/. **1** In a desert, an **oasis** is a small area where water and plants are found. N COUNT
2 You can refer to any pleasant place or situation as an **oasis** when it is surrounded by unpleasant ones. EG *The town was an oasis of prosperity in a desert of poverty.* N COUNT

oat /əʊt/, **oats. Oats** are the grains of a cereal. You use oats for making porridge or for feeding animals. N COUNT : USU PLURAL

oath /əʊθ/, **oaths** /əʊðz/. **1** An **oath** is a formal promise. EG *...an oath of allegiance.* N COUNT ● If someone is **on oath** or **under oath**, they have made a promise, especially a promise to tell the truth in a court of law. EG *...witnesses under oath.* ● PHRASE
2 An **oath** is also an offensive expression or a swear-word. EG *He was answered with a torrent of French oaths.* N COUNT Outdated

oatmeal /əʊtmi:l/. **1 Oatmeal** is a coarse flour made by crushing oats. EG *...oatmeal biscuits.* N UNCOUNT

2 Something that is **oatmeal** is a very pale, creamy brown colour. EG *...an oatmeal coat and brown trousers.* ADJ COLOUR

obedient /ə6bi:dɪənt/. Someone who is **obedient** does the things that they are told to do. EG *She was an obedient little girl.* ADJ QUALIT ◇ **obediently.** EG *'Try it,' Clem ordered. Obediently I picked up the cup.* ◇ ADV ◇ **obedience** /ə6bi:dɪəns/. EG *She failed to show proper obedience and respect to the elders.* ◇ N UNCOUNT

obese /əʊbi:s/. Someone who is **obese** is very fat. EG *If they overeat, they are very likely to become obese.* ADJ QUALIT Formal ◇ **obesity** /ə6bi:sɪ1ti1/. EG *Obesity is a health hazard.* ◇ N UNCOUNT

obey /ə6beɪ/, **obeys, obeying, obeyed.** If you **obey** a person, a command, or an instruction, you do what you are told to do. EG *The troops were reluctant to obey orders... They obeyed me without question... Don't question anything, just obey!* V+O OR V

obituary /ə6bɪtjʊ0əri1/, **obituaries.** An **obituary** is a piece of writing about the character and achievements of someone who has just died. EG *I read Sewell's obituary in the Daily News.* N COUNT

object, objects, objecting, objected; pronounced /ɒbdʒɪ2kt/ when it is a noun and /ə7bdʒɛkt/ when it is a verb. **1** An **object** is anything that has a fixed shape or form, that you can touch or see, and that is not alive. EG *...the shabby, black object he was carrying... ...mats, bowls, and other objects.* N COUNT

2 Someone's **object** or the **object** of what they are doing is their aim or purpose. EG *The minder's object is to keep the child asleep... She would journey for months with the sole object of filming a rare creature.* N COUNT: USU+POSS

3 The **object** of a feeling, a wish, or a kind of behaviour is the thing or person that it is directed towards. EG *...young Eileen, the object of his desires... This did not prevent him being the object of ridicule... She became an object of worship.* N COUNT: USU+*of*

4 In grammar, the object of a verb or a preposition is the word or phrase which completes the structure begun by the verb or preposition. See the entry headed VERBS for more information. N COUNT

5 If you **object** to something, **5.1** you do not like it or do not approve of it. EG *This was exactly what he objected to in Christine... He would never object to sharing whatever he had.* V+*to* **5.2** you say that you do not like it or do not approve of it. EG *We object to the selection of Haldane... You may object that the system makes boys effeminate... The men objected and the women supported them.* V: OFT+*to* OR REPORT: ONLY *that* ◇ **objector** /ə7bdʒɛktə/, **objectors.** EG *...her refusal to listen to objectors.* ◇ N COUNT

objection /ə7bdʒɛkʃə0n/, **objections. 1** If you make or raise an **objection** to something, you say that you do not like it or do not approve of it. EG *They raised objections to Seagram's bid... The objection that he had no experience was ignored.* N COUNT

2 If you **have no objection to** something, you do not dislike it or do not disapprove of it. EG *He had no real objection to drinking.* PHRASE

objectionable /ə7bdʒɛkʃə0nəbə0l/. If you describe someone or something as **objectionable**, you mean that you think they are offensive and unacceptable. EG *...politicians whose views he found objectionable... ...a vulgar and objectionable person.* ADJ QUALIT Formal

objective /ə7bdʒɛktɪv/, **objectives. 1** Your **objective** is what you are trying to achieve. EG *Mobil's primary objective is to win... We shall never achieve our objectives.* N COUNT

2 Information that is **objective** is based on facts. EG *There is no objective evidence... ...a search for objective data.* ADJ CLASSIF

3 If you describe a person as **objective**, you mean that they are trying to be fair and to base their opinions on facts, rather than on personal feelings. EG *...a book on communism written by an astonishingly objective author.* ADJ QUALIT ◇ **objectively.** EG *It was desirable to view these things objectively.* ◇ ADV ◇ **objectivity.** EG *Historians strive after objectivity.* ◇ N UNCOUNT

obligation /ɒblɪgeɪʃə0n/, **obligations.** An **obligation** is something that you must do because you have promised to do it or because it is your duty to do it. EG *He had to go home because of family obligations... We are under no obligation to give him what he wants.* N COUNT OR N UNCOUNT

obligatory /ə7blɪgətə0ri1/. If something is **obligatory**, you must do it, because there is a rule or a law about it. EG *It is not obligatory to answer.* ADJ CLASSIF

oblige /ə6blaɪdʒ/, **obliges, obliging, obliged. 1** If something **obliges** you to do something, it makes you feel that you must do it. EG *Politeness obliged me to go on with the conversation... ...if your business obliges you to stay until tomorrow.* V+O+*to*-INF ◇ **obliged.** EG *I felt obliged to invite him into the parlour.* ◇ ADJ PRED +*to*-INF

2 If you **oblige** someone, you are helpful to them by doing what they have asked you to do. EG *'Who did you ask?' – 'Jim. He's only too glad to oblige.'* V+O OR V

obliging /ə6blaɪdʒɪŋ/. Someone who is **obliging** is willing and eager to be helpful. EG *Mr Carston is a very obliging gentleman.* ADJ QUALIT

oblique /ə7bli:k/. **1** If you describe a statement or comment as **oblique**, you mean that it is indirect and therefore difficult to understand. EG *...an oblique compliment... Alexander took this as an oblique reference to his own affairs.* ADJ QUALIT

2 An **oblique** line is one that slopes at an angle, rather than being vertical or horizontal. EG *...a script which had oblique strokes after every phrase.* ADJ CLASSIF

obliterate /ə7blɪtəreɪt/, **obliterates, obliterating, obliterated.** If something **obliterates** an object or place, it destroys it completely. EG *I watched bombs obliterate the villages.* V+O

oblivion /ə7blɪvɪən/ is **1** the state of not being aware or conscious of what is happening around you. EG *I sank back into oblivion.* **2** the state of having been forgotten or of no longer being considered important. EG *This art faded into oblivion years ago.* N UNCOUNT

oblivious /ə7blɪvɪəs/. If you are **oblivious** of something, you are not aware of it. EG *She seemed oblivious of the attention she was drawing to herself... He was totally oblivious to the fact that he had almost been killed.* ADJ PRED: USU+*to/of*

oblong /ɒblɒŋ/, **oblongs.** An **oblong** is a shape which has two long sides and two short sides and in which all the angles are right angles. See picture at SHAPES. ▸ used as an adjective. EG *...an oblong table.* N COUNT ▸ ADJ CLASSIF

obnoxious /ə7bnɒkʃəs/. If you describe someone as **obnoxious**, you mean that you think they are very unpleasant. EG *He has some obnoxious qualities, but he is reliable.* ADJ QUALIT

oboe /əʊbəʊ/, **oboes.** An **oboe** is a wooden musical instrument that is shaped like a tube. You play it by blowing through a reed inserted at its top. See picture at MUSICAL INSTRUMENTS. N COUNT

obscene /ə7bsi:n/. Something that is **obscene** shocks and offends people, because it involves sex in a way that people find unpleasant. EG *The Herald had been prosecuted for printing obscene advertising... ...huge paintings, many of them obscene.* ADJ QUALIT

obscenity /ə7bsɛnɪ1ti1/, **obscenities. 1 Obscenity** is behaviour that shocks and offends people because it involves sex in a way that people find unpleasant. EG *Existing laws on obscenity are to be tightened.* N UNCOUNT

2 An **obscenity** is a word or expression that is rude and offensive because it relates to sex or bodily functions. EG *They started yelling obscenities.* N COUNT: USU PLURAL

If you have no objection to someone, do you think they are obnoxious?

obscure /əbskjʊə/, **obscurer, obscurest; obscures, obscuring, obscured. 1** Something that is **obscure 1.1** is known by only a few people. EG ...*obscure operas... ...experts in obscure subjects... ...some obscure country.* ADJ QUALIT ◇ **obscurity** /əbskjʊərɪti/. EG *He has risen from obscurity to international fame.* ◇ N UNCOUNT **1.2** is complex and difficult to understand. EG ...*obscure points of theology... France's relationship to the new organization is extremely obscure.* ADJ QUALIT ◇ **obscurity.** EG *Dixon didn't mind the obscurity of the reference.* ◇ N UNCOUNT **1.3** is difficult to see. EG *He saw the hideous, obscure shape rise slowly to the surface.* ADJ QUALIT ◇ **obscurity.** EG *He peered into the obscurity beneath the trees.* ◇ N UNCOUNT

2 To **obscure** something means **2.1** to make it difficult to understand. EG *Words that obscure the truth must be discarded.* V+O **2.2** to prevent it from being seen or heard properly. EG *Some areas were obscured by patches of fog.*

obsequious /əbsiːkwɪəs/. People who are **obsequious** are too eager to help you, to listen to what you say, or to agree with you; used showing disapproval. EG ...*obsequious shop assistants.* ADJ QUALIT

observable /əbzɜːvəbəl/. Something that is **observable** can be seen. EG *It is an action that is observable in almost all countries in the world.* ADJ CLASSIF

observance /əbzɜːvəns/. The **observance** of a law or custom is the practice of obeying or following it. EG ...*observance of speed limits and traffic lights.* N UNCOUNT +SUPP

observant /əbzɜːvənt/. Someone who is **observant** has the ability to notice things that are not usually noticed. EG *You're very observant, Cathy.* ADJ QUALIT

observation /ɒbzəveɪʃən/, **observations. 1 Observation** is the action or process of carefully watching someone or something, especially in order to learn something about them. EG ...*information gathered by observation or experiment... She was put under observation in a nursing home.* N UNCOUNT

2 An **observation** is **2.1** something that you have learned by seeing or watching something and thinking about it. EG ...*clinical observations.* N COUNT **2.2** a comment or remark. EG *We listened to Mama's tearful observations on the subject.*

3 Observation is also the ability to notice things that are not usually noticed. EG ...*keen powers of observation... ...a talent for observation.* N UNCOUNT

observatory /əbzɜːvətəri/, **observatories.** An **observatory** is a special building with telescopes that scientists use to study the sun, the moon, the planets, and the stars. N COUNT

observe /əbzɜːv/, **observes, observing, observed. 1** If you **observe** someone or something, **1.1** you watch them carefully. EG *By observing your boss's moods, you will soon discover when to talk and when to keep quiet.* V+O **1.2** you see them or notice them. EG *He looked out through the window and observed me walking along the boat deck.* Formal

2 You can use **observe** when you are quoting a remark or comment that someone has made. EG *'People aren't interested in spiritual things,' observed the actress.* V+QUOTE OR REPORT Formal

3 If you **observe** something such as a law or custom, you obey it or follow it. EG *I didn't enjoy the party, but the conventions had been observed.* V+O

observer /əbzɜːvə/, **observers.** An **observer** is **1** someone who spends time studying the latest news about a subject or an area of activity. EG ...*political observers.* **2** someone who sees or notices something. EG *A casual observer may get the wrong impression.* N COUNT

obsess /əbsɛs/, **obsesses, obsessing, obsessed.** If something **obsesses** you or if you **are obsessed** with it, you keep thinking about it and find it difficult to think about anything else. EG *He became obsessed with a girl reporter... The image of Madeleine obsessed him.* V+O: OFT PASS +with

obsession /əbsɛʃən/, **obsessions.** When someone cannot stop thinking about something, you can say that they have an **obsession** about it. EG *Taylor's fascination with bees developed into an obsession.* N COUNT

obsessional /əbsɛʃənəl, -ʃənəl/ means the same as obsessive. EG ...*an obsessional need to win.* ADJ QUALIT

obsessive /əbsɛsɪv/. You say that an attitude or kind of behaviour is **obsessive** when someone keeps thinking or behaving in a particular way and seems unable to stop it. EG *Obsessive tidiness in the office is a bad sign.* ADJ QUALIT ◇ **obsessively.** EG *He was obsessively interested in every single detail about my early life.* ◇ ADV

obsolete /ɒbsəliːt/. Something that is **obsolete** is no longer needed because something newer or more efficient has been invented. EG *The Falcon missile was now obsolete... ...obsolete systems.* ADJ CLASSIF

obstacle /ɒbstəkəl/, **obstacles. 1** An **obstacle** is an object that makes it difficult for you to go where you want to go, because it is in your way. EG *Bats can sense obstacles in their path.* N COUNT

2 You can refer to anything that makes it difficult for you to do something as an **obstacle**. EG ...*the bureaucratic obstacles to getting her son over from Jamaica.* N COUNT: USU+SUPP

obstetrician /ɒbstɛtrɪʃən/, **obstetricians.** An **obstetrician** is a doctor who is specially trained to deal with pregnant women and childbirth. N COUNT

obstinate /ɒbstɪnət/. If you describe someone as **obstinate**, you mean that they are very determined to do what they want, and will not change their mind or be persuaded to do something else; used showing disapproval. EG ...*an obstinate, rebellious child with a violent temper.* ADJ QUALIT ◇ **obstinacy** /ɒbstɪnəsi/. EG ...*the obstinacy of the Transport Minister.* ◇ N UNCOUNT

obstruct /əbstrʌkt/, **obstructs, obstructing, obstructed. 1** If something **obstructs** a road or path, it blocks it, so that people or vehicles cannot get past. EG *The crash obstructed the road for several hours.* V+O

2 If someone **obstructs** something such as justice or progress, they prevent it from happening or developing. EG *It is a crime for the President to obstruct justice.* V+O

obstruction /əbstrʌkʃən/, **obstructions. 1** An **obstruction** is something that blocks a road or path. EG *The obstructions could take weeks to clear.* N COUNT

2 Obstruction is the act of deliberately delaying something or preventing something from happening. EG *The unions faced legal obstruction.* N UNCOUNT

obstructive /əbstrʌktɪv/. Someone who is **obstructive** deliberately causes difficulties for other people. EG *He behaved in a very obstructive fashion... ...the obstructive tactics of the authorities.* ADJ QUALIT

obtain /əbteɪn/, **obtains, obtaining, obtained.** If you **obtain** something, you get it or achieve it. EG *She obtained her degree in 1951... These books can be obtained from the Public Library.* V+O Formal

obtainable /əbteɪnəbəl/. Something that is **obtainable** can be obtained. EG *Savings up to 65% are obtainable under this scheme.* ADJ CLASSIF: USU PRED

obtrusive /əbtruːsɪv/. Something that is **obtrusive** is noticeable in an unpleasant way. EG *Equally obtrusive was the graffiti that had started to appear.* ADJ QUALIT ◇ **obtrusively.** EG *Hawke got up and walked obtrusively out of the building.* ◇ ADV

obvious /ɒbvɪəs/. **1** If something is **obvious**, you can easily see it or understand it. EG *It was painfully obvious that I knew very little about it... There's no obvious answer... ...obvious similarities.* ADJ QUALIT

2 If you describe something that someone says as **obvious**, you mean that it is unnecessary and shows lack of imagination. EG *Tove made such an obvious remark... You shouldn't tell such obvious lies.* ADJ QUALIT ● If you say that someone **is stating the obvious**, you mean that they are saying something that everyone knows already. ● PHRASE

obviously /ɒbvɪəsli/. **1** You say **obviously** when you are stating something that you expect people ADV SEN to know already. EG *Obviously I don't need to say how important this project is.*

2 You can also use **obviously** to indicate that something is easily seen, noticed, or recognized. EG *The soldier was obviously badly hurt.* — ADV

occasion /əkeɪʒə^{0}n/, **occasions, occasioning, occasioned. 1** The **occasion** when something happens is the time when it happens. EG *I met him only on one occasion.* — N COUNT

2 An **occasion** is also an important event, ceremony, or celebration. EG *They have the date fixed for the big occasion... ...an important social occasion.* — N COUNT

3 An **occasion** for doing something is an opportunity for doing it. EG *For the girls, nature study was an occasion for lazy walks and idle picnics... He had never had occasion to use his gun.* — N SING+SUPP OR N UNCOUNT +*to*-INF; Formal

4 If something happens **on occasion** or **on occasions**, it happens sometimes, but not very often. EG *You have on occasions surprised people.* — PHRASE; Formal

5 When someone does what is necessary to deal with a difficult situation, you say that they **rise to the occasion**. EG *Dekker had risen to the occasion with an insight that surprised us all.* — PHRASE

6 To **occasion** something means to cause it. EG *...deaths occasioned by police activity... The discovery occasioned me no surprise... ...the frustration they occasioned in the lessons.* — V+O, V+O+O, OR V+O+A; Formal

occasional /əkeɪʒə^{0}nəl, -ʒənə^{0}l/ means happening or being present sometimes, but not regularly or often. EG *...an occasional trip as far as Aberdeen... Apart from the occasional article, he hadn't published anything.* — ADJ CLASSIF : ATTRIB
◊ **occasionally.** EG *Friends visit them occasionally... He was arrogant and occasionally callous.* — ◊ ADV

occult /ɒkʌlt/. Someone who is interested in the **occult** is interested in supernatural or magical forces. EG *...enthusiasm for astrology and the occult.* — N SING : *the*+N
▸ used as an adjective. EG *...the fantastic occult powers that he was said to possess.* — ▸ ADJ CLASSIF : ATTRIB

occupant /ɒkjə^{4}pənt/, **occupants. 1** The **occupants** of a building or room are the people who live or work there. EG *A tidy office means that the occupant doesn't want things disturbed.* — N COUNT

2 You can also refer to someone who is in a room or chair at a particular time as its **occupant**. EG *The room's sole occupants were the boy and a dog.* — N COUNT

occupation /ɒkjə^{4}peɪʃə^{0}n/, **occupations. 1** Your **occupation** is your job or profession. EG *...a poorly paid occupation.* — N COUNT OR N UNCOUNT

2 An **occupation** is also something that you do for pleasure. EG *Riding was her favourite occupation.* — N COUNT

3 When a foreign army moves into a country and takes control of it, you can refer to this as the **occupation** of that country. EG *...the French occupation of North Africa... Holland came under German occupation.* — N UNCOUNT +SUPP

occupational /ɒkjə^{4}peɪʃə^{0}nəl, -ʃənə^{0}l/ means relating to a person's job or profession. EG *...occupational hazards... ...an occupational pension scheme.* — ADJ CLASSIF : ATTRIB

occupier /ɒkjə^{4}paɪə/, **occupiers.** The **occupier** of a house, flat, or piece of land is the person who lives or works there. EG *The occupier of the premises has applied for planning permission.* — N COUNT; Formal

occupy /ɒkjə^{4}paɪ/, **occupies, occupying, occupied. 1** The people who **occupy** a building are the people who live there or work there. EG *Houses occupied by the aged must be centrally heated.* — V+O

2 If something such as a seat **is occupied**, someone is using it, so that it is not available for anyone else to use. EG *At the pub, his usual corner seat was occupied.* — V-PASS

3 When people **occupy** a place or a country, they move into it and gain control of it. EG *The students occupied the Administration Block.* — V+O

4 If you say that something **occupies** a particular place in a system, process, or plan, you mean that it has that place. EG *The demonstration occupies a central place in their political campaign.* — V+O

5 If you **occupy** yourself in doing something, you are busy doing it. EG *They were occupying themselves in growing their own food... It was just a matter of keeping her occupied.* — V-REFL OR V+O

6 If something **occupies** you, it requires your efforts, attention, or time. EG *That work was to occupy him for the rest of his life... His attention was occupied with other matters.* — V+O : IF PASS THEN+*with/in*

7 If something **occupies** a particular period of time, it happens while that amount of time passes. EG *The episode occupied many millions of years.* — V+O

occur /ə^{7}kɜː/, **occurs, occurring, occurred. 1** When an event **occurs**, it happens. EG *The attack occurred about six days ago... ...the changes which have occurred in the past fifty years.* — V : USU+A

2 You can also say that something **occurs** when it exists or is present in a particular place. EG *...two other commonly occurring weeds... Racism and sexism occur in all institutions.* — V : USU+A

3 If a thought or idea **occurs** to you, you suddenly think of it or realize it. EG *As soon as that thought occurred to him, he felt worse... It had never occurred to her that he might insist on paying.* — V+*to* : NO CONT

occurrence /ə^{7}kʌrəns/, **occurrences. 1** An **occurrence** is something that happens. EG *...weeks before the tragic occurrence.* — N COUNT; Formal

2 The **occurrence** of something is the fact that it happens, or the fact that it is present in a particular situation. EG *We may reduce the occurrence of cancer by fifty per cent.* — N UNCOUNT +SUPP

ocean /əʊʃə^{0}n/, **oceans. 1** The **ocean** is the sea. EG *...in the depths of the ocean.* — N SING : *the*+N; Literary

2 Ocean is part of the name of five very large areas of sea. EG *...the Atlantic Ocean.* — N COUNT

o'clock /əklɒk/. You use **o'clock** after numbers from one to twelve to say what time it is. For example, if you say that it is three o'clock, you mean that it is three hours after midday or three hours after midnight; see the entry headed TIME. EG *At two o'clock in the morning Castle was still awake... It was 11 o'clock at night.* — ADV AFTER NUMBER

octagon /ɒktəgən/, **octagons.** An **octagon** is a flat geometrical shape that has eight straight sides. — N COUNT

octagonal /ɒktægənə^{0}l/. Something that is **octagonal** has eight sides. EG *...the octagonal tower.* — ADJ CLASSIF

octave /ɒktɪv/, **octaves.** An **octave** is the musical interval between the first note and the eighth note of a scale. — N COUNT

October /ɒktəʊbə/ is the tenth month of the year in the Western calendar. EG *They will be on show at the Museum until October.* — N UNCOUNT

octopus /ɒktəpəs/, **octopuses.** An **octopus** is a sea creature with eight tentacles which it uses to catch food. — N COUNT

oculist /ɒkjə^{4}lɪst/, **oculists.** An **oculist** is an optician. — N COUNT; American

odd /ɒd/, **odder, oddest; odds. 1** If you say that someone or something is **odd**, you mean that they are strange or unusual. EG *We thought she was rather odd... There's something odd about its shape... It was odd that she still lived at home.* — ADJ QUALIT
◊ **oddly.** EG *The drug made him behave quite oddly... Marsha found the play oddly disappointing.* — ◊ ADV
◊ **oddness.** EG *...the slight oddness in her voice.* — ◊ N UNCOUNT

2 You say **'oddly enough'** before adding a surprising piece of information to what you have been talking about. EG *Oddly enough, it was through him that I met Carson.* — ADV SEN

3 You use **odd** before a noun to indicate that you are not mentioning the type, size, or quality of something, because it is not important. EG *You can add bones, the odd vegetable, and herbs... ...odd bits of glass... He did odd jobs about the place to earn a bit of money.* ● See also **odds and ends.** — ADJ CLASSIF : ATTRIB; Informal

4 You say that two things are **odd** when they do not belong to the same set or pair. EG *...odd socks.* — ADJ CLASSIF : ATTRIB

What does 'oct-' mean in words like 'octagon', 'octave', and 'octopus'?

5 In a group of people or things, the **odd** one **out** is the one that is different from all the others. EG *I was the odd one out; all my friends were in couples.* PHRASE

6 Odd numbers, such as 3, 17, and 129, cannot be divided exactly by the number two. ADJ CLASSIF : ATTRIB

7 You use **odd** after a number to indicate that it is only approximate. EG *We first met twenty odd years ago... Thirty odd pounds, isn't it?* ADV AFTER NUMBER Informal

8 You refer to the probability of something happening as the **odds** that it will happen. In gambling, if you bet one pound on a horse whose odds are '10 to 1', you will receive ten pounds if the horse wins. EG *Nobody will put money on a horse at those odds.* N PLURAL : *the*+N

9 If you say that the **odds are** that something will happen, or that the **odds are in favour of** it happening, you mean that it is likely to happen. If you say that the **odds are against** it, you mean that it is unlikely to happen. EG *The odds are that they will succeed... The odds are against children learning in this environment.* • See also **odds-on.** PHRASE

10 When something happens **against** the **odds**, it happens although it had seemed impossible or extremely unlikely. EG *She managed to do it against all the odds... ...working against appalling odds.* PHRASE

11 If you are **at odds** with someone, you are disagreeing or quarrelling with them. EG *She is at odds with her boss... The allies are at odds over how to respond to the threat.* PHRASE

oddity /ɒdɪti[1]/, **oddities. 1** An **oddity** is someone or something that is very strange. EG *A career woman is still regarded as something of an oddity... ...the oddities and absurdities of the language.* N COUNT

2 The **oddity** of something is the fact that it is very strange. EG *...the oddity of her behaviour.* N UNCOUNT

oddment /ɒdmə[2]nt/, **oddments. Oddments** are things that remain after other things have been used. EG *...old postcards and scraps, all sorts of oddments... ...oddments of furniture.* N COUNT : USU PLURAL

odds and ends. You refer to a group of things as **odds and ends** when you are not saying exactly what they are, because it is not important or necessary to do so. EG *I had a trunk filled with various odds and ends that I would need for camping.* N PLURAL Informal

odds-on. If there is an **odds-on** chance that something will happen, it is very likely that it will happen. EG *It was odds-on that there was no killer... Calderwood is the odds-on favourite to win.* ADJ CLASSIF Informal

odious /əʊdɪəs/. You describe people or things as **odious** when you find them extremely unpleasant. EG *I shouldn't dream of telling the odious woman anything of the sort.* ADJ QUALIT

odour /əʊdə/, **odours;** spelled **odor** in American English. An **odour** is a smell, especially a strong one. EG *...the warm odour of freshly-baked scones... The noise was as appalling as the odour.* N COUNT : USU+SUPP Formal

of /ə[7]v/. **1** You use **of** after nouns referring to quantities, groups, or amounts. EG *...a collection of essays... ...jewellery worth millions of pounds... ...25 gallons of hot water... ...a big piece of apple pie.* PREP

2 You use **of** after a noun referring to a container to form an expression referring to the container and its contents. EG *...a cup of tea.* PREP

3 You use **of** to specify an amount, value, or age. EG *...a price increase of 2%... ...a town of 13,000 people... ...at the age of five... ...a boy of nineteen.* PREP

4 You use **of** to say that something consists of a particular thing. EG *...strong feelings of jealousy... ...an atmosphere of co-operation... ...gifts of olive oil.* PREP

5 You use **of** to say that someone or something has a particular characteristic or quality. EG *...men of matchless honesty... She helped him to a gin and tonic of giant proportions.* PREP

6 You use **of** to say that something is made from a particular substance. EG *They are usually made of cotton... ...a disc of steel.* PREP

7 You use **of** when you are talking about one or more things among a number of similar ones. EG *This is the first of a series of programmes... Many of the students come from other countries.* PREP

8 You use **of** to say that something represents or describes something. EG *...a map of Sweden... ...Mrs Jarrow's account of what happened.* PREP

9 You use **of** when giving your opinion about someone's action. For example, if you say 'That was nasty of him', you mean that what he did was nasty. EG *It was kind of her to take me in.* PREP

10 You use **of 10.1** to say who has the belief, attitude, or characteristic mentioned. EG *...the religious beliefs of the peasant communities... ...the disapproving stares of Rummidge students... ...the average age of commercial farmers... ...the size of the crowd.* **10.2** to say who something belongs to or is controlled by. EG *Imagine a child of yours doing that... ...the Conservative government of Mr Heath.* **10.3** to say what something is a part or a feature of. EG *She clutched the sleeve of his robe... ...the corners of a triangle... ...Act V of Macbeth.* **10.4** to say what group or organization someone belongs to. EG *...the General Secretary of the Tobacco Workers' Union... He was a member of a famous golf club.* **10.5** to say what place a person or organization is connected with. EG *...the Mayor of Moscow... ...the University of California.* PREP

11 You can use **of** after words such as 'town' and 'village' to introduce the name of a place. EG *...the village of Fairwater Green.* PREP

12 You use **of** to say what something relates to or is concerned with. EG *...the whole concept of economic growth... ...the Department of Employment... ...their hopes of a reconciliation... ...the cause of the infection... ...cancer of the stomach.* PREP

13 You use **of** after nouns that have been formed from verbs. The noun group following 'of' is either the object or the subject of the verb. For example, 'the kidnapping of a royal child' refers to a royal child being kidnapped; 'the arrival of the next train' refers to the next train arriving. PREP

14 You use **of** when saying who did or made something. For example, you can refer to the people who organize a meeting as 'the organizers of the meeting'. PREP

15 You use **of** to say that something resembles the thing that is mentioned after 'of'. For example, something that is the colour **of** blood is the same colour as blood. EG *...a boil the size of a golf ball.* PREP

16 You can also use **of** to say that something is like the thing that is mentioned before 'of'. For example, 'a giant of a man' means 'a man like a giant.' PREP

17 You use **of 17.1** to say that something happened at a particular time. EG *...the recession of 1974-75... ...the great conflicts of the past ten years.* **17.2** to say that something is the best or worst thing to happen during a particular time. EG *That was the highlight of the morning.* **17.3** after words like 'day' and 'time' to say when something happened. EG *...on the day of his inauguration... ...at the time of the earthquake.* **17.4** to say what date it is. EG *...the 17th of June.* PREP

18 You also use **of** to say what illness someone died from. EG *She died of pneumonia.* PREP

off /ɒf/. **1** When something is taken **off** something else or when it moves or comes **off** it, it is taken away or it moves away so that it is no longer on the other thing or attached to it. EG *He took his hand off her arm... He was wiping sweat off his face... Miss Archer fell off her chair... The paint was peeling off... Get the car off the road.* PREP OR ADV

2 When you take **off** a piece of clothing, you remove it from your body. EG *He took off his jacket... Let me help you off with your coat.* ADV

3 When you go **off**, you leave a place. EG *He started the motor and drove off abruptly... When are you off to America?... I had to send Matthew off to bed.* ADV AFTER VB

4 You can say that someone is **off** somewhere or **off** doing something when they are in a different ADV+A OR -ING place from yourself. EG *She's off in Florida at some labour conference... A lot of men were off fighting.*

5 When you get **off** a bus, train, or plane, you get out of it. EG *The train stopped and people got off.* PREP, OR ADV AFTER VB

6 If you keep **off** a street or piece of land, you do not go onto it. EG *I kept off the main roads... You have no right to keep people off your land.* PREP

7 If an area of land is walled **off** or fenced **off**, it has a wall or fence around it or in front of it. ADV AFTER VB

8 If something is **off** a coast, it is in the sea and close to the coast. EG *...submarines off the Norwegian coast... ...two islands off the mainland of China.* PREP

9 If a building is **off** a road, it is near it but not next to it. EG *...a hotel just off the Via Condotti.* PREP

10 You can use **off** in these ways when you are talking about not working. **10.1** If you have some time **off**, you do not go to work for a period of time. EG *I would love to have a year off.* ADV **10.2** If it is your day **off**, it is the day when you do not normally work. EG *Tonight is his night off.* ADV **10.3** If you are **off** work, you are not working because you are ill. PREP

11 If you keep **off** a subject, you do not talk about it. EG *She kept off the subject of marriage.* PREP

12 If something such as a machine or an electric light is **off**, it is not functioning. EG *Boylan switched off the headlights. He turned the radio off.* ADJ PRED OR ADV AFTER VB

13 If an agreement or an arranged event is **off**, it has been cancelled. EG *I presume the deal is off.* ADJ PRED OR ADV AFTER VB

14 If food or drink is **off**, it tastes and smells unpleasant because it is going bad. EG *The wine was off.* ADJ PRED

15 If something is a long time **off**, it will not happen for a long time. EG *Control over the mind is not as far off as we think.* ADV OR PREP

16 If you are **off** something, you have stopped using it or liking it. EG *My father was off alcohol... He's gone off liberty.* PREP Informal

17 If you say that someone's behaviour is **a bit off**, you mean that you find it unacceptable and rude. PHRASE Informal

18 If an amount of money is taken **off** the price of something, it costs that amount less than it did before. EG *I knocked 100 pounds off the price.* PREP OR ADV

19 If you obtain something **off** someone, you obtain it from them. EG *I'd never buy anything off him.* PREP Informal

20 If you say that something happens **off and on**, you mean that it happens occasionally. PHRASE

offal /ɒfəl/ refers to the heart, liver, and other internal organs of animals, which people cook and eat. EG *...offal mixed with onions and oatmeal.* N UNCOUNT

off-chance. If you do something **on the off-chance**, you do it because you hope that it will succeed or be useful, although you think that this is unlikely. EG *He collected an enormous amount of information on the off-chance that he might later have a use for it.* PHRASE

off-colour. If you are **off-colour**, you are slightly ill. EG *He's been a bit off-colour for two days.* ADJ PRED

off-day, off-days. If you have an **off-day**, you do not work or perform as well as usual. EG *We all have our off-days, of course.* N COUNT Informal

offence /əˈfɛns/, **offences;** spelled **offense** in American English. **1** An **offence** is a crime. EG *They were arrested for drug offences... Thirteen people were charged with offences including obstruction and resisting arrest.* N COUNT Formal

2 If you give **offence**, you upset or embarrass someone. EG *The play is liable to give offence to many people... His calmly rational voice robbed his words of all offence.* N UNCOUNT: USU+SUPP

3 If you **take offence**, you are upset by something that someone says or does. EG *He was always so quick to take offence.* PHRASE

offend /əˈfɛnd/, **offends, offending, offended. 1** If you **offend** someone, you upset or embarrass them. EG *They took care never to offend their visitors.* ◊ **offended.** EG *Clarissa looked offended.* V+O ◊ ADJ PRED

2 If something **offends** a law, rule, or principle, it breaks it. EG *This process offends every known natural law... It would offend against her conventions.* V+O OR V+*against* Formal

3 To **offend** also means to commit a crime. EG *Criminals who offend again when they're released.* V Formal

offender /əˈfɛndə/, **offenders. 1** An **offender** is someone who has committed a crime. EG *In 1965, 42% of convicted offenders ended up in prison... ...the treatment of young offenders.* N COUNT Formal

2 You can refer to something that causes a particular kind of harm as an **offender**. EG *Television is the worst offender of the lot.* N COUNT+SUPP

offending /əˈfɛndɪŋ/. You use **offending** to describe something that is causing a problem. EG *Smear the juice on the offending areas... He tapped the offending bulge with a pencil.* ADJ CLASSIF: ATTRIB

offense /əˈfɛns/. See **offence**.

offensive /əˈfɛnsɪv/, **offensives. 1** Something that is **offensive** upsets or embarrasses people because it is rude or insulting. EG *That was an extremely offensive remark... Some of the advertisements were highly offensive.* ◊ **offensively.** EG *The examiners were often offensively rude to candidates.* ADJ QUALIT ◊ ADV

2 An **offensive** is a strong attack against someone. EG *...the enemy's air offensive... ...a propaganda offensive against the government.* ▸ used as an adjective. EG *We took immediate offensive action.* N COUNT ▸ ADJ CLASSIF: OFT ATTRIB

3 If you **go on the offensive** or **take the offensive**, you attack or criticize someone before they have the chance to do it to you. EG *He went on the offensive, giving details of blacks being victimized.* PHRASE

offer /ɒfə/, **offers, offering, offered. 1** If you **offer** something to someone, you ask them if they would like to have it or to use it. EG *...an apple which he offered to his friend... I was offered a place at Harvard University... Meadows stood up and offered her his chair.* V+O: USU+*to*; ALSO V+O+O

2 If you **offer** to do something, you say that you are willing to do it. EG *Gopal offered to take us to Mysore... 'We could take it for you,' offered Dolly.* V+*to*-INF OR QUOTE

3 An **offer** is something that someone says they will give you or do for you if you want them to. EG *She accepted the offer of a cigarette... ...Kirk's offer to take me to the clinic.* N COUNT: OFT+SUPP

4 If you **offer** someone information, advice, or praise, you give it to them. EG *...offering him advice about accommodation... They didn't ask Liebermann's name and Liebermann didn't offer it.* V+O+O; ALSO V+O: OFT+*to*

5 If you **offer** someone love or friendship, you show them that you love them or feel friendly towards them. EG *If you tell me the facts, I might be able to offer you more sympathy... Her blue eyes seemed to offer friendship.* V+O+O; ALSO V+O: OFT+*to*

6 If something **offers** a service, opportunity, or product, it provides it. EG *The new car plant offers the prospect of 5,000 jobs... ...the facilities and equipment offered by the playgroup.* V+O+O; ALSO V+O: OFT+*to*

7 An **offer** in a shop is a specially low price for a product, or something extra that you get by buying the product. EG *...cut price offers... ...special offers.* N COUNT+SUPP

8 If something is **on offer**, **8.1** it is available to be used or bought. EG *...the weird and wonderful range of gear on offer.* **8.2** its price is specially reduced for a period of time. EG *This item is on offer for a limited period.* PHRASE

9 If you **offer** an amount of money for something, you say that you will pay that much to buy it. EG *I'll offer you nine pounds for it.* V+O OR V+O+O: USU+*for*

10 An **offer** is also the amount of money that you say that you will pay to buy something. EG *Murgatroyd's offer was the most attractive.* N COUNT

offering /ɒfərɪŋ/, **offerings. 1** You can refer to something that has been specially produced as an **offering**. EG *...last week's offerings of caviar and* N COUNT

If you are off-colour, do you have an off-day?

smoked salmon... ...the latest offering from Wilko Johnson.
2 An **offering** is also something that is offered to a god as a sacrifice. EG *...sacred offerings on the altar.* N COUNT

off-hand. **1** If someone behaves in an **off-hand** way, they are not friendly or polite, and show little interest in what other people are doing or saying. EG *He became increasingly off-hand with Victoria... ...the off-hand contempt with which she treated most men.* ADJ QUALIT
2 If you say something **off-hand**, you say it without needing to think very hard. EG *Off-hand, I can think of three examples.* ADV OR ADV SEN

office /ɒfɪs/, **offices.** **1** An **office** is a room or a part of a building where people work sitting at desks. EG *He called me into his office... You didn't go to the office today?* N COUNT
2 You can refer to the people who work in your office as the **office**. EG *The whole office knows that.* N COLL
3 An **office** is also **3.1** a department of an organization, especially the government, where people deal with a particular kind of administrative work. EG *...your local education office... ...the tax office.* **3.2** a small building or room where people can go for information, tickets, or a service of some kind. EG *...the ticket office... ...the enquiry office.* N COUNT: USU+SUPP
4 Someone who holds **office** has an important job or a position of authority in government or in an organization. EG *The President of the BMA holds office for one year... ...Baldwin's second term of office as Premier.* ● When someone is **in office**, they are in a position of authority to which they were elected or appointed. If they are **out of office**, they are no longer in such a position of authority. EG *...during his first year in office.* ● When someone **takes office**, they are elected or appointed to a position of authority and begin to do their duties. EG *The new Conservative Government took office.* N UNCOUNT; ● PHRASE; ● PHRASE

officer /ɒfɪsə/, **officers.** **1** In the armed forces, an **officer** is a person in a position of authority. EG *...a retired army officer.* N COUNT
2 People with responsible positions in organizations, especially government organizations, are also referred to as **officers**. EG *...a Careers Officer... ...prison officers.* N COUNT: USU+SUPP
3 Members of the police force are sometimes referred to as **officers**. EG *Inspector Darroway was the officer in charge of the investigation... Listen, Officer, why do you need all this information?* N COUNT OR VOCATIVE

official /əfɪʃə⁰l/, **officials.** **1** Something that is **official** is approved by the government or by someone else in authority. EG *The official figures for the year were published in January... Arabic is the official language of Morocco.* ADJ CLASSIF
2 **Official** is used to describe **2.1** things which are used by people in authority as part of their job or position. EG *...the Prime Minister's official residence.* **2.2** activities which people in authority perform as part of their job or position. EG *...an official visit to Tanzania.* ADJ CLASSIF: ATTRIB
3 The **official** time when something happens is the time when it is formally recognized as happening, for example at a public ceremony. EG *...the official opening of the new bridge.* ◊ **officially.** EG *The war officially ended the following year.* ADJ CLASSIF: ATTRIB; ◊ ADV
4 The **official** reason or explanation for something is something incorrect that people are told in the hope that they will believe it, because the truth is embarrassing. EG *Visiting his aunt was only the official motive.* ◊ **officially.** EG *Officially she shares a flat with some girlfriend.* ADJ CLASSIF: ATTRIB; ◊ ADV SEN
5 An **official** is a person who holds a position of authority in an organization. EG *...government officials... ...trade union officials.* N COUNT

officialdom /əfɪʃəldə⁰m/. You use **officialdom** to refer to officials in government and other organizations, especially when you disapprove of their rules and regulations, their slowness, or their unhelpfulness. EG *This leaves the individual at the mercy of officialdom.* N UNCOUNT

officious /əfɪʃəs/. Someone who is **officious** is too eager to tell people what to do; used showing disapproval. EG *...officious interference by managers.* ADJ QUALIT

offing /ɒfɪŋ/. If you say that something is **in the offing**, you mean that it is likely to happen soon. EG *War was already in the offing.* PHRASE

off-licence, off-licences. An **off-licence** is a shop which sells beer, wine, and other alcoholic drinks. N COUNT British

offload /ɒfləʊd/, **offloads, offloading, offloaded.** If you **offload** something that you do not want, you get rid of it, especially by giving it to someone else. V+O: OFT+*onto* Informal

off-peak. **Off-peak** things are available at a time when there is little demand for them, so that they are cheaper than usual. EG *...off-peak electricity.* ADJ CLASSIF: ATTRIB

off-putting. You describe someone as **off-putting** when you find them rather unpleasant and do not want to know them better. EG *She has a rather off-putting manner.* ADJ QUALIT

offset /ɒfsɛt/, **offsets, offsetting.** The form **offset** is used in the present tense and is also the past tense and past participle. V+O: OFT PASS
If one thing **is offset** by another, its effect is reduced by the other thing, so there is no great advantage or disadvantage as a result. EG *They argued that their wage increases would be offset by higher prices.*

offshoot /ɒfʃu:t/, **offshoots.** If one thing is an **offshoot** of another thing, it has developed from the other thing. EG *Afrikaans is an offshoot of Dutch.* N COUNT+SUPP

offshore /ɒfʃɔ:/. Something that is **offshore** is situated in the sea near to the coast. EG *...offshore oil terminals... The boats waited offshore.* ADJ CLASSIF OR ADV

offside /ɒfsaɪd/. **1** The **offside** of a vehicle is the side of it that is furthest from the pavement when you are driving. EG *The mini had touched the offside of the truck with its nearside wing.* N SING British
2 If a player in a game of football or hockey is **offside**, they have broken the rules by moving too far forward. ADJ CLASSIF OR ADV

offspring /ɒfsprɪŋ/. Your **offspring** are your children. 'Offspring' is both the singular and the plural form. EG *How do parents pass genes on to their offspring?* N COUNT: USU+POSS Formal

off-white. Something that is **off-white** is not pure white, but slightly grey or yellow. EG *...a tatty off-white dress... ...bits of paper, some white, some off-white.* ADJ COLOUR

often /ɒfə⁰n/. **1** If something happens **often**, it happens many times or much of the time. EG *We often get very wet cold winters here... It's not often you meet someone who's really interested... She didn't write very often.* ADV
2 You use **often** when you are asking or talking about how frequently something happens. EG *How often do you need to weigh the baby?... John came as often as he could.* ADV
3 **Often** is also used in these phrases. **3.1** If you say that something happens **more often than not**, you mean that it usually happens. EG *More often than not the patient recovers.* **3.2** If you say that something happens **as often as not**, you mean that it happens fairly often. EG *These paintings, as often as not, ended up in America.* **3.3** If you say that something happens **every so often**, you mean that it happens occasionally. EG *Every so often, she spends a weekend in London.* PHRASE

ogle /əʊgə⁰l/, **ogles, ogling, ogled.** If someone **ogles** someone else, they stare at them, especially in a way that indicates a sexual interest; used showing disapproval. EG *The men ogled her lasciviously... ...the ladies ogling their hero.* V+O

ogre /əʊgə/, **ogres.** An **ogre** is a character in fairy stories who is large, cruel, and frightening. N COUNT

oh /əʊ/. You use **oh** 1 to introduce a response or a comment on something that has just been said. EG *'I'll give it to you now.' - 'Oh thanks.'... 'I have a flat in London.' - 'Oh yes, whereabouts?'... 'How's your brother then?' - 'Oh he's fine.'* 2 when you are hesitating while speaking. EG *It was about, oh, half past five when I got home.* 3 to express a feeling such as surprise, pain, annoyance, or joy. EG *She covered her face with her hands and cried, 'Oh! Oh!'... 'He wants to see you immediately,' I said. 'Oh!' she said. Her smile vanished.* EXCLAM

oil /ɔɪl/, **oils, oiling, oiled. 1 Oil** is **1.1** a smooth, thick, sticky liquid that is used as a fuel and for lubricating machines. Oil is found underground, and it can also be manufactured. EG *...alternatives to coal and oil.* N UNCOUNT **1.2** a smooth, thick, sticky liquid that is made from plants or animals. Some oils are used for cooking. EG *...cooking oil... ...olive oil.* N UNCOUNT : USU+SUPP **1.3** a smooth, thick liquid that is often scented and that you rub into your skin or add to your bath. EG *...some sort of delicious bath oil.* N UNCOUNT +SUPP

2 If you **oil** a machine, you put oil into it in order to make it work smoothly. EG *He has to oil and wind the clock... The gun was kept well oiled.* V+O

3 If you **oil** your skin or your hair, you rub oil onto it. EG *He had wavy, oiled hair.* V+O

4 Oils are **4.1** oil paintings. EG *...an exhibition of watercolours and oils by Turner... ...small oils of an early period.* N COUNT : USU PLURAL **4.2** oil paints. EG *...trying to capture the scene in oils.* N PLURAL

oilfield /ɔɪlfiːld/, **oilfields.** An **oilfield** is an area of land or part of the seabed where oil is found and from which it is removed. N COUNT

oil paint, oil paints. Oil paint is a thick paint used by artists. It is made from a coloured powder and linseed oil. N MASS

oil painting, oil paintings. An **oil painting** is a painting that has been painted using oil paint. EG *...really valuable oil paintings.* N COUNT

oil slick, oil slicks. An **oil slick** is a layer of oil that is floating on top of the sea or a lake as the result of an accident, usually one involving an oil tanker. N COUNT

oil well, oil wells. An **oil well** is a hole which is drilled into the ground or the seabed in order to remove the oil which lies underground. N COUNT

oily /ɔɪli¹/. **1** Something that is **oily 1.1** is covered with oil. EG *...oily rags... ...oily fried potatoes.* ADJ QUALIT **1.2** looks or feels like oil. EG *...an oily substance.* ADJ CLASSIF

2 You describe someone as **oily** when you find them unpleasant because they flatter people or behave in an excessively polite way. ADJ QUALIT

ointment /ɔɪntmə²nt/, **ointments. 1** An **ointment** is a smooth thick substance that is put on sore skin or a wound to help it heal. EG *...zinc ointment... ...a tube of sunburn ointment.* N MASS

2 You describe something as a **fly in the ointment** when it spoils a situation and prevents it from being as successful as you had hoped. EG *The only fly in the ointment was that his own son refused to co-operate.* PHRASE

OK /əʊ keɪ/. See **okay**.

okay /əʊkeɪ/, **okays, okaying, okayed;** also spelled **OK. 1** If you say that something is **okay**, you mean that it is acceptable. EG *I asked Jenny how she thought it all went. 'Okay,' she said... I'll have another coffee and then I'll be going, if that's okay... She wanted to know if the trip was OK with the government.* ADJ CLASSIF : USU PRED, OR ADV Informal

2 If you say that someone is **okay**, you mean that they are safe and well. EG *'Where's Jane?' - 'Just back there. She's okay. Just shocked.'* ADJ CLASSIF : USU PRED Informal

3 You can say **okay 3.1** when you are agreeing to something. EG *'I'll be back at a quarter past one.' - 'OK. I'll see you then.'... 'I must go and make a phone call.' - 'Yeah OK.'* CONVENTION Informal **3.2** to check whether the person you are talking to understands what you have just said and accepts it. EG *I'll be back in fifteen minutes. OK?* **3.3** as a way of stopping people from arguing with you or criticizing you by showing that you accept their point, so that you can go on and say something more. EG *'You said you didn't look at it!' - 'Okay, so I did glance at it.'*

4 You can also use **okay** to indicate to someone that you want to start talking about something else or doing something else. EG *Okay, do you mind if we speak a bit of German now?* CONVENTION Informal

5 If someone in authority **okays** something, they officially agree to it or allow it to happen. EG *I'm blowed if I know why, but I'll okay this overdraft.* V+O Informal

▸ used as a noun. EG *I don't want to go on before he's given the OK.* ▸ N SING : the+N

old /əʊld/, **older, oldest. 1** Someone who is **old** has lived for many years and is no longer young. EG *...his old mother... I'm too old, Mr Gerran.* ADJ QUALIT

2 You can refer to people who are old as the **old**. EG *...the particular needs of the old and infirm.* N PLURAL : the+N

3 Something that is **old 3.1** has existed for a long time and is no longer new. EG *...a massive old building of crumbling red brick... ...an old joke.* ADJ QUALIT **3.2** is no longer in a good condition because of its age or because it has been used a lot. EG *...wardrobes full of old clothes.* ADJ QUALIT **3.3** is now no longer used or has been replaced by something else. EG *I was directed into the old dining room... ...his old job at the publishing company.* ADJ CLASSIF : ATTRIB

4 If you say that someone or something is a particular number of years **old**, you mean that they have lived or existed for that length of time. EG *She's about 50 years old... How old are you?... She was a couple of years older than me.* ADJ QUALIT

5 If someone is an **old** friend of yours, they have been your friend for a long time. ADJ QUALIT : ATTRIB

6 In the old days means many years ago, before things changed. EG *Hong Kong was a shopper's paradise in the old days.* PHRASE

7 You can use **old** to express affection or familiarity when you are talking to or about someone you know. EG *I got a letter from good old Lewis.* ADJ CLASSIF : ATTRIB Informal

8 You use **any old** to emphasize that the quality or type of something is not important. EG *Any old board will do.* PHRASE Informal

old-age pensioner, old-age pensioners. An **old-age pensioner** is the same as an OAP. N COUNT

olden /əʊldə⁰n/. **In the olden days** means long ago in the past. PHRASE Informal

old-fashioned. 1 Something that is **old-fashioned** is no longer considered appropriate in style or design, because it has been replaced by something that is more modern. EG *He was wearing old-fashioned plastic-rimmed glasses.* ADJ QUALIT

2 If you are **old-fashioned**, you believe in and behave according to the values and standards of the past. EG *I am very old-fashioned... ...old-fashioned ideas.* ADJ QUALIT

old hand, old hands. An **old hand** is a person who is very skilled at something because they have a lot of experience. EG *...a few old hands in the press corps.* N COUNT

old maid, old maids. People sometimes refer to an old or middle-aged woman as an **old maid** when she has never been married and they think that she will never get married; an offensive expression. N COUNT

old man. Someone's **old man** is their father or their husband. EG *The first letter I got from my old man told me how proud he was of me.* N SING Informal

old master, old masters. An **old master** is **1** a famous painter of the past. **2** a painting by a famous painter of the past. EG *...reproductions of old masters.* N COUNT

Old Testament. The **Old Testament** is the first part of the Bible. It contains Jewish writings, mostly about the history of the Jewish people. N PROPER : the+N

If someone is an old hand at something, are they omniscient?

old wives' tale, old wives' tales. An **old wives' tale** is a common belief that is based on traditional ideas and that is often considered to be foolish or superstitious. N COUNT

old woman, old women. If you call someone, especially a man, an **old woman**, you mean that they are very fussy. EG *He's a bit of an old woman.* N COUNT Informal Outdated

O level, O levels. An **O level** is an educational qualification in a particular subject. O levels are awarded in England, Wales, and Northern Ireland. Schoolchildren usually take O level examinations at the age of 15 or 16, after studying for them for 2 or 3 years. O level examinations are being replaced by GCSE examinations. EG *...minimum qualifications of five O levels... ...O-level Maths.* N COUNT

olive /ɒlɪv/, **olives.** 1 An **olive** is a small green or black fruit that has a bitter taste. Olives are often eaten as a snack or with a meal. N COUNT

2 Something that is **olive** or **olive green** is yellowish-green in colour. EG *...olive green towels.* ADJ COLOUR

olive oil is oil that is obtained by pressing olives. It is used for putting on salads or for cooking. N UNCOUNT

-ological is used to replace '-ology' at the end of nouns in order to form adjectives. These adjectives describe something as relating to a particular science or subject. For example, 'geological' means relating to geology. Adjectives formed in this way are not usually defined in this dictionary, but are treated with the related nouns. EG *...bacteriological research... ...the Zoological Society.* SUFFIX

-ologist, -ologists. -ologist is used to replace '-ology' at the end of nouns in order to form other nouns that refer to people who are concerned with a particular science or subject. For example, a 'biologist' is concerned with biology. Nouns formed in this way are not usually defined in this dictionary, but are treated with the nouns ending in '-ology'. EG *...a well known anthropologist... ...amateur geologists.* SUFFIX

Olympic /əlɪmpɪk/, **Olympics. 1 Olympic** means relating to the Olympic Games. EG *...fencing to Olympic standard... ...an Olympic finalist.* ADJ CLASSIF : ATTRIB

2 The **Olympics** are the Olympic Games. EG *Didn't she win a gold medal at the Olympics?* N PLURAL

Olympic Games. The **Olympic Games** are a set of international sports competitions which take place every four years, each time in a different country. N PLURAL : *the*+N

omelette /ɒmlɪ²t/, **omelettes;** also spelled **omelet** in American English. An **omelette** is a food made by beating eggs and cooking them in a flat pan. N COUNT

omen /əʊmə²n/, **omens.** An **omen** is something that is thought to indicate what is going to happen in the future. EG *An eclipse of the sun is the worst of bad omens... It was a good omen for the trip.* N COUNT

ominous /ɒmɪnəs/. Something that is **ominous** is worrying or frightening because it makes you think that something unpleasant is going to happen. EG *There was an ominous silence.* ◇ **ominously.** EG *Black clouds were piling up ominously.* ADJ QUALIT ◇ ADV

omission /ə⁶mɪʃə⁰n/, **omissions. 1** An **omission** is something that has not been included or not been done, either deliberately or accidentally. EG *The reports were full of errors and omissions.* N COUNT

2 **Omission** is the act of not including someone or something or of not doing something. EG *...the omission of women from these studies.* N UNCOUNT

omit /ə⁶mɪt/, **omits, omitting, omitted.** 1 If you **omit** something, you do not include it, either deliberately or accidentally. EG *Two groups were omitted from the survey – the old and women.* V+O

2 If you **omit** to do something, you do not do it. EG *He omitted to say whether the men were armed.* V+*to*-INF Formal

omnibus /ɒmnɪbə⁹s/, **omnibuses.** An **omnibus** is 1 a book which contains a large collection of stories or articles, often by the same person or about the same subject. 2 a radio or television broadcast which contains two or more similar programmes that were originally broadcast separately. N COUNT

omnipotent /ɒmnɪpətənt/. Someone or something that is **omnipotent** has complete power over things or people. EG *...an omnipotent central committee... ...an omnipotent and perfect deity.* ADJ CLASSIF Formal

omniscient /ɒmnɪsɪənt/. Someone who is **omniscient** knows or seems to know everything. EG *The woman goes as a patient to an omniscient professional... ...faith in an omniscient God.* ADJ CLASSIF Formal

omnivorous /ɒmnɪvərəs/. An **omnivorous** person or animal eats all kinds of food, including both meat and plants. EG *...the change from a vegetarian to an omnivorous diet.* ADJ CLASSIF Technical

on /ɒn/. **1** If you are standing or resting **on** something, it is underneath you and is supporting your weight. EG *They were sitting on chairs... Large, soft cushions lay on the floor... ...a cow grazing on a hill.* PREP

2 If something is **on** a surface or object, it is stuck to it or attached to it. EG *...the posters on the walls... ...the light on the ceiling... ...the buttons on a shirt.* PREP

3 If there is something **on** a piece of paper, it has been written or printed there. EG *...the table on the back page of the book... ...a card with his name on... She wrote it down on a piece of paper.* PREP

4 You use **on** to say what part of your body is supporting your weight. For example, you can lie **on** your back or stand **on** one leg. PREP

5 If someone has a particular expression **on** their face, they have that expression. EG *She had a puzzled expression on her face.* PREP

6 If a building is **on** a road, it is next to it. EG *The house is on Pacific Avenue.* PREP

7 If you get **on** a bus, train, or plane, you get into it in order to travel somewhere. If you are **on** it, you are travelling in it. PREP

8 You can use **on** when mentioning the area of land where someone works or lives. For example, someone can work **on** a farm or a building site, or live **on** a housing estate. PREP

9 If you put, drop, or throw something **on** a surface, you move it or drop it so that it is then supported by the surface. EG *Put the tray on the bed, please... He dropped it on the floor.* PREP

10 When you put **on** a piece of clothing, you place it over a part of your body in order to wear it. If you have it **on**, you are wearing it. EG *She put her shoes on... She had her coat on.* ADV

11 You can say that you have something **on** you if you are carrying it in your pocket or in a bag. PREP

12 If you hurt yourself **on** something, you hurt yourself by accidentally hitting it with a part of your body. EG *He cut himself on the gatepost.* PREP

13 Books, discussions, or ideas **on** a particular subject are concerned with that subject. EG *...books on philosophy, art, and religion.* PREP

14 If information is **on** tape or **on** computer, that is the way that it is stored. PREP

15 If something operates **on** a particular system or principle, that is how it operates. EG *They work on a rota system.* PREP

16 When you watch television or listen to the radio, you see things **on** television or hear things **on** the radio. EG *His first film was shown on television yesterday.* PREP

17 When a musical instrument is played, you say that music is played **on** it. EG *...waltzes played on the violin.* PREP

18 When an activity involving a lot of people is taking place, you can say that it is **on**. EG *The war was on then.* ADV AFTER VB

19 When a play or film is being shown, you can say that it is **on**. EG *What's on at the Odeon?* ADV AFTER VB

20 If something such as a machine or an electric light is **on**, it is functioning. EG *A tap had been left on.* ADV AFTER VB

21 If something happens **on** a particular day or date, that is when it happens. EG *...on the first day of* PREP *term... ...on Thursday night... Caro was born on April 10th.*

22 You use **on** when mentioning an event that was followed by another one. For example, if something happened **on** someone's return, it happened just after they returned. EG *'It's so unfair,' Clarissa said on her return... On being called 'young lady', she laughed.* PREP

23 If you say, for example, that someone worked **on** or chattered **on**, you mean that they continued working or chattering. ADV AFTER VB

24 If you say that something goes **on and on**, you mean that it continues for a very long time. EG *The list goes on and on.* PHRASE

25 If you say that something happens **on and off**, you mean that it happens occasionally. PHRASE

26 If something happens **from** a particular time **on**, it starts to happen at that time, and continues afterwards. EG *From now on, you are free to do what you like.* PHRASE

27 If something affects you, you can say that it has an effect **on** you. EG *The effect on the environment could be considerable.* PREP

28 If you are **on** a council or committee, you are a member of it. PREP

29 Someone who is taking a medicine or drug regularly is **on** that medicine or drug. PREP

30 If you are **on** a particular kind of income, that is the kind of income that you have. EG *...people on a low income.* PREP

31 Taxes or profits that are obtained from something are referred to as taxes or profits **on** it. EG *...a new sales tax on luxury goods... Profits on books will be down... You pay interest on your mortgage.* PREP

32 When you buy something, you spend money **on** it. EG *...the amount of money he spent on clothes... Why waste money on them?* PREP

33 When you pay for something that someone else receives, you can say that it is **on** you. EG *The drinks were always on him.* PREP Informal

34 When you spend time **on** something, you spend time doing it or making it. EG *I spent a lot of time on this picture.* PREP

35 If you say that someone's eyes are **on** something, you mean that they are looking at it. PREP

36 If you are very busy, you can say that you **have a lot on**. If you are not busy, you can say that you **do not have much on**. PHRASE Informal

37 If you say that someone goes **on** at you, you mean that they keep criticizing you, complaining to you, or asking you to do something. EG *I went on at my father to have seat belts fitted... He's always on at me about the way I dress.* ADV AFTER VB *+at* Informal

38 If you say that someone is **on** about something, you mean that they are talking about it. EG *He's always on about yoga... What are you on about?* ADV AFTER VB *+about* Informal

39 If you say that something **is not on**, you mean that it is unacceptable or impossible. EG *That sort of writing just isn't on.* PHRASE Informal

40 and so on: see **so**.

once /wʌns/. **1** If something happens **once**, it happens one time only, or one time within a particular period of time. EG *I've been out with him once, that's all... Some trees only bear fruit once every twenty-five years.* ADV

2 If something was **once** true, it was true at some time in the past, but is no longer true. EG *Texas was once ruled by Mexico.* ADV

3 If something happens **once** another thing has happened, it happens immediately afterwards. EG *Once inside her flat, she glanced at the clock.* CONJ

4 Once is also used in these phrases. **4.1** If you do something **at once**, you do it immediately. EG *They set to work at once... I knew at once that something was wrong.* **4.2** If several things happen **at once** or **all at once**, they all happen at the same time. EG *Everybody is talking at once.* **4.3** If something happens **once again** or **once more**, it happens again. EG *She wanted to see him once more before she died.* **4.4** If a situation exists **once again** or **once more**, it exists again, after not existing for a while. EG *But now companies are once again queueing to join the scheme.* **4.5** If you have done something **once or twice**, you have done it a few times, but not very often. EG *She had been to London once or twice before.* **4.6** If something happens **once in a while**, it happens occasionally but not very often. EG *Once in a while she'd give me some lilacs to take home.* **4.7** If you say that something happened **for once**, you are emphasizing that it does not usually happen. EG *For once Castle went without his lunch.* **4.8** If something happens **once and for all**, it happens completely or finally. EG *They had to be defeated once and for all.* **4.9 Once upon a time** is used at the beginning of a children's story to indicate that the events in it are supposed to have taken place a long time ago. PHRASES

oncoming /ɒnkʌmɪŋ/ means moving towards you. EG *...the oncoming waves... ...oncoming traffic.* ADJ CLASSIF : ATTRIB

one /wʌn/, **ones. 1 One** is the number 1: see the entry headed NUMBER. EG *...one hundred miles... Of these four suggestions, only one is correct... The two friends share one job... The road goes from one side of the town to the other.* NUMBER

2 If you refer to the **one** person or thing of a particular kind, you mean the only person or thing of that kind. EG *Their one aim in life is to go to University... She is the one person with enough medical knowledge to make it possible.* NUMBER

3 You can use **one** **3.1** instead of 'a' to emphasize the adjective or expression that follows it. EG *There was one hell of a row when they came on.* **3.2** in front of someone's name to indicate that you have not met them or heard of them before. EG *The big man is one Bert Lance, a friend of the President.* NUMBER Informal Formal

4 You can also use **one** to refer to a thing or person of a particular kind, especially when you want to describe them or to give new information about them. EG *These trousers aren't as tight as the other ones... ...buying old houses and building new ones... Oh, that's a difficult one to answer, isn't it.* PRON : HAS PLURAL

5 You can use **one** when referring to a time in the past or the future. For example, if you say that you did something **one** day, you mean that you did it on a day in the past. If you say that you will do something **one** day, you mean that you will do it on a day in the future. EG *One day, she went for a swim in the ocean... One evening, I had a visit from Henry Cox... One day you and I must have a long talk together.* NUMBER

6 You can also use **one** after an adjective as a way of addressing or referring to someone you are fond of or admire. EG *Come along now, little ones, off to bed.* PRON+SUPP : HAS PLURAL Outdated

7 You can use **one** after a verb that means 'hit', to indicate that one blow is given. EG *Go on, thump him one.* PRON : SING Informal

8 One is also a personal pronoun and can be used as a subject or an object. A speaker or writer uses **one** to refer to people in general, for example in statements about what usually happens in a particular situation. EG *One can eat well here... The law should guard one against this sort of thing.* PRON : SING Formal

9 One is also used in these phrases. **9.1** If you say that someone is **not one** to do something, you mean that they are not likely to do it, because of their character or habits. EG *Uncle Harold was not one to underestimate the problem.* **9.2 One or two** means a very few. EG *One or two of the girls help in the kitchen.* **9.3** If you are or have **one up on** someone, you have an advantage over them. **9.4 A hundred and one** or **a thousand and one** means a great many. EG *There must be a thousand and one books of this sort on the market.* **9.5** When people PHRASES Informal Formal

What phrase can you use at the beginning of a children's story?

are **at one**, they are in agreement with each other.
9.6 You can use **for one** to emphasize that a particular person is definitely behaving or reacting in a particular way, whatever other people are doing. EG *But I for one feel very grateful and very satisfied.* **9.7 one** thing **after another**: see **another**. • **one another**: see **another**. • **one after the other**: see **other**. • See also **number one**.

one-man. A **one-man** performance is given by one man, rather than by several people. EG *...a one-man show.* ADJ CLASSIF: ATTRIB

one-off, one-offs. A **one-off** is something that happens or is made only once. EG *'A one-off,' he said delightedly. 'A tailor-made gun.'* ▸ used as an adjective. EG *...one-off projects.* N COUNT Informal ▸ ADJ CLASSIF: ATTRIB

one-parent family, one-parent families. A **one-parent family** consists of a child or children living with only one of their parents. N COUNT

onerous /ɒnərəs, əʊ-/. Work that is **onerous** is difficult and unpleasant. EG *...the onerous duties of postal delivery.* ADJ QUALIT Formal

one's /wʌnz/. **1** A speaker or writer uses **one's** to indicate that something belongs or relates to people in general. See paragraph 8 of the entry for **one**. EG *Naturally, one wanted only the best for one's children.* DET POSS Formal

2 One's is also a spoken form of 'one is' or 'one has', especially when 'has' is an auxiliary verb. EG *One's never quite sure exactly how things are going to turn out... One's got to pay for it.* Formal

oneself /wə⁹nsɛlf/. **1** A speaker or writer uses **oneself** as the object of a verb or preposition in a clause where 'one' is the subject or a previous object. See paragraph 8 of the entry for **one**. EG *One must keep such interests to oneself.* PRON REFL: SING

2 Oneself is also used to emphasize the subject or object of a clause. EG *Others might find odd what one finds perfectly normal oneself.* PRON REFL: SING

one-sided. 1 In a **one-sided** activity or relationship, one of the people involved does much more than the other. EG *...a one-sided correspondence... ...one-sided conversations.* ADJ QUALIT

2 A **one-sided** argument or report considers only some of the facts involved in a situation or problem, and is therefore not acceptable. EG *The report is one-sided in its interpretation of the evidence.* ADJ QUALIT

one-time. You use **one-time** to indicate that someone used to have a particular job, position, or role. EG *...Fred Dunn, a onetime farm worker.* ADJ CLASSIF: ATTRIB

one-to-one. In a **one-to-one** relationship, you deal with only one other person. EG *...one-to-one tuition.* ADJ CLASSIF: ATTRIB

one-way. 1 One-way streets are streets along which vehicles can drive in only one direction. ADJ CLASSIF: ATTRIB

2 If you buy a **one-way** ticket, you can use it to travel to a place, but not to travel back again. EG *...a one-way ticket to Jersey.* ADJ CLASSIF: ATTRIB

one-woman. A **one-woman** performance is given by one woman, rather than by several people. ADJ CLASSIF: ATTRIB

ongoing /ɒngəʊɪŋ/. An **ongoing** situation has been happening for quite a long time and is continuing to happen. EG *...an ongoing economic crisis... ...ongoing projects.* ADJ CLASSIF: ATTRIB

onion /ʌnjən/, **onions.** An **onion** is a small, round vegetable. It is white with a brown, papery skin, and has a strong smell and taste. N COUNT OR N UNCOUNT

onlooker /ɒnlʊkə/, **onlookers.** An **onlooker** is someone who watches an event without taking part in it. EG *She blew a kiss to the shivering onlookers.* N COUNT

only /əʊnli¹/. In written English, 'only' is usually placed immediately before the word it qualifies. In spoken English, you can use stress to indicate what 'only' qualifies, so its position is not so important.

1 You use **only** to indicate the one thing that is involved or that happens in a particular situation. EG *He read only paperbacks... I'm only interested in facts... Only Mother knows... The video is to be used for teaching purposes only... She could only obey.* ADV

2 You say that one thing will happen **only if** another thing happens when you want to indicate that it will not happen unless the other thing happens. EG *I will come only if nothing is said to the press... These snakes only attack if they feel cornered or threatened.* CONJ

3 If you talk about the **only** thing involved in a particular situation, you mean that there are no others. EG *I was the only one smoking... It was the only way out.* ADJ CLASSIF: ATTRIB

4 Someone who is an **only** child has no brothers or sisters. ADJ CLASSIF: ATTRIB

5 You can use **only** to emphasize that something is unimportant or small. EG *It was only a squirrel... I was only joking... We only paid £26... It only took half an hour.* ADV

6 You can use **only** to emphasize how recently something happened. EG *This beetle has only recently been discovered... I've only just arrived.* ADV

7 You say that something is **only just** the case to emphasize that it is very nearly not the case. EG *He could only just hear them... The heat was only just bearable.* PHRASE

8 You use **not only** to introduce the first of two linked statements when the second is even more surprising or extreme than the first. EG *Chimpanzees not only use tools but make them.* PHRASE

9 If you say that someone **has only** to do one thing in order to achieve or prove something, you are emphasizing how easily or quickly it can be done. EG *You've only got to read the newspapers to see what can happen to hitch-hikers.* PHRASE

10 You can use **only** to emphasize a wish or hope. EG *I only wish I had the money.* • **if only**: see **if**. ADV

11 You can use **only** to add a comment which slightly changes or corrects what you have just said. EG *Snake is just like chicken, only tougher.* CONJ Informal

12 You can use **only** to introduce the reason why something is not done. EG *'That's what I'm trying to do,' said Mrs Oliver, 'only I can't get near enough.'* CONJ Informal

13 You can use **only** before an infinitive to introduce an event which happens immediately after the previous one, and which is rather surprising or unfortunate. EG *He broke off, only to resume almost at once... I had tried this years before, only to receive a polite refusal.* ADV + *to*-INF

14 You can use **only** to emphasize that you think a course of action or type of behaviour is reasonable in a particular situation. EG *It is only natural that she will have mixed feelings about your promotion.* ADV + ADJ

15 You use **only too** to emphasize that something happens to a greater extent than is expected or wanted. EG *He is normally only too pleased to help... She remembered that night only too clearly.* PHRASE

onrush /ɒnrʌʃ/. You say that there is an **onrush** of a feeling or emotion when it develops suddenly and quickly. EG *...the onrush of her tears... ...an onrush of pain.* N SING + *of* Formal

onset /ɒnsɛt/. The **onset** of something unpleasant is the beginning of it. EG *...the onset of war... ...his brave response to the onset of blindness.* N SING: *the*+N+*of*

onslaught /ɒnslɔːt/, **onslaughts.** An **onslaught** is a violent attack. EG *...a co-ordinated onslaught on enemy airfields.* N COUNT+SUPP

onto /ɒntʊ/; also spelled **on to. 1** If someone or something moves **onto** an object or is put **onto** it, the object is then underneath them and supporting them. EG *I got onto the bed... She spooned a portion of potato onto his plate... I ran out onto the porch.* PREP

2 When you get **onto** a bus, train, or plane, you get into it in order to travel somewhere. PREP

3 If you fasten something **onto** something else, you fasten it to it. EG *I bent a pin and tied it onto a piece of string.* PREP

4 If you hold **onto** something, you hold it firmly. EG *I was still holding onto her shoulders... ...clinging onto his shirt.* PREP

5 If someone who is speaking gets **onto** or moves **onto** a different subject, they begin talking about it. EG *Let's move onto another question.* PREP

onus /əʊnəs/. If you say that the **onus** is on someone to do something, you mean that it is their duty or responsibility to do it. EG *The onus was on me to earn enough to support the family.* [N SING Formal]

onward /ɒnwəd/, **onwards.** When it is an adverb, the form **onwards** is normally used in British English, and **onward** in American English or formal British English.

1 If something happens from a particular time **onwards** or **onward**, it begins to happen at that time and continues happening afterwards. EG *From 1968 onwards the situation began to change... From that time onward he had never spoken to her again.* [ADV]

2 If someone or something moves **onwards** or **onward**, they continue travelling or moving forward. EG *We travelled from China to India, and onwards to East Africa... ...as she ploughed inexorably onward... ...the onward motion of the boat.* [ADV OR ADJ CLASSIF : ATTRIB]

3 You can say that things move **onwards** or **onward** when they continue to develop or progress. EG *...this onward march of the Labour movement.* [ADV OR ADJ CLASSIF : ATTRIB]

ooh /uː/. People say **ooh** when they are surprised or when something pleasant or unpleasant suddenly happens. EG *Ooh, you are awful... Ooh, that feels nice.* [EXCLAM Informal]

oops /ʊps, uːps/. You say **oops** to indicate that there has been a slight accident or mistake. EG *Oops, sorry... Oops! He's fallen down.* [EXCLAM Informal]

ooze /uːz/, **oozes, oozing, oozed. 1** When a thick, sticky liquid **oozes** from an object or when the object **oozes** it, the liquid flows slowly from the object. EG *...blood oozing from his wounds... His sandals oozed black slime.* [V-ERG]

2 You can refer to mud or any similar sticky substance as **ooze**. [N UNCOUNT]

3 If someone **oozes** a quality or feeling, they show it very strongly, often when they do not really feel it. EG *His letter, oozing remorse, appeared in all the newspapers... Her voice oozed with politeness.* [V+O OR V+*with*]

opal /əʊpəl/, **opals.** An **opal** is a precious stone. Opals are mainly whitish or colourless, but colours can be seen in them. [N COUNT OR N UNCOUNT]

opaque /əʊpeɪk/. **1** If an object or substance is **opaque**, you cannot see through it. EG *...the opaque windows of the jail... ...the opaque water.* [ADJ QUALIT]

2 You can say that something is **opaque** when it is difficult to understand. EG *Their intentions remained opaque... Jimmy was opaque to her.* [ADJ CLASSIF Formal]

open /əʊpən/, **opens, opening, opened. 1** When you **open** something such as a door or the lid of a box, or when it **opens**, you move it so that it no longer covers a hole or gap. EG *Elizabeth opened the door and went in... The door opened almost before Brody had finished knocking.* ▸ used as an adjective. EG *...the open window.* [V-ERG; ▸ ADJ CLASSIF]

2 When you **open** a cupboard, container, or letter, you move, remove, or cut part of it so that you can take out what is inside. EG *Open the tool-box... I opened a can of beans.* ▸ used as an adjective. EG *Boylan couldn't get the bottle open... He tore open the envelope.* [V+O; ▸ ADJ CLASSIF]

3 When you **open** a book, you move its covers apart in order to read or write on the pages inside. EG *He opened the book at random.* ▸ used as an adjective. EG *...the open Bible.* [V+O; ▸ ADJ CLASSIF]

4 When you **open** your mouth, you move your lips and teeth apart. EG *She opened her mouth to say something, then closed it.* ▸ used as an adjective. EG *Angelica looked at me with her mouth open.* [V+O; ▸ ADJ CLASSIF]

5 When you **open** your eyes, you move your eyelids upwards so that you can see. EG *She opened her eyes and looked at me.* ▸ used as an adjective. EG *...lying with his eyes wide open.* [V+O; ▸ ADJ CLASSIF]

6 If you have an **open** mind or are **open** to ideas or suggestions, you are prepared to consider any ideas or suggestions. [ADJ QUALIT]

7 If you describe someone as **open**, you mean that they are honest and do not try to hide anything. EG *They looked at her with open curiosity.* ◊ **openness.** EG *...their relaxed openness.* [ADJ QUALIT; ◊ N UNCOUNT]

8 If you say that a person, idea, or system is **open** to something such as criticism or blame, you mean they could be treated in the way indicated. EG *The proposals were certainly open to criticism... Such a description is open to misunderstanding.* [ADJ PRED+*to*]

9 When a shop, office, or public building **opens** or **is opened, 9.1** its doors are unlocked, the people in it start working, and customers can use it. EG *When does the library open?* ▸ used as an adjective. EG *The Tate Gallery is open 10 a.m. - 6 p.m.* [V-ERG; ▸ ADJ CLASSIF] **9.2** it starts operating for the first time. EG *They're opening an office in Birmingham.* [V-ERG]

10 When someone important **opens** a building or a public area, they declare officially in a public ceremony that it is ready to be used or to start operating. ▸ used as an adjective. EG *Lord Shawcross declared the hotel open.* ◊ **opening.** EG *...the opening of the new theatre.* [V+O; ▸ ADJ PRED; ◊ N UNCOUNT +SUPP]

11 When a public event such as a conference or a play **opens**, it begins to take place or to be performed. EG *The UN General Assembly opens in New York later this month.* ◊ **opening.** EG *...the opening of 'Nicholas Nickleby' on Broadway.* [V; ◊ N UNCOUNT]

12 The person who **opens** an event is the first one to speak or do something. EG *Senator Denton opened the hearing by reminding us of our duty.* [V+O]

13 If you **open** an account with a bank, you begin to use their services by giving them some of your money to look after or invest. [V+O]

14 If you **open** something that is blocked, you remove the thing that is blocking it. EG *It took three days to clear the snow and open the road to traffic.* ▸ used as an adjective. EG *Route Nine is now open.* [V+O; ▸ ADJ CLASSIF]

15 If a room or door **opens** into or onto a place, you can go straight to that place from the room or through the door. EG *These rooms have doors opening directly onto the garden.* [V+A]

16 When flowers **open**, they change from being buds and their petals spread out. [V]

17 If something that you are wearing is **open**, it is not fastened. EG *...an open black raincoat... ...an open-necked shirt.* [ADJ CLASSIF]

18 An **open** area of land or sea is a large area that has few things such as buildings or islands in it. EG *The road stretched across open country.* ◊ **openness.** EG *...the openness of Vincent Square.* [ADJ CLASSIF : ATTRIB; ◊ N UNCOUNT]

19 You can use **open** to describe something that is not covered or enclosed. EG *...an open car... Never dry clothes in front of an open fire.* [ADJ CLASSIF : ATTRIB]

20 If you do something **in the open**, you do it out of doors rather than in a building. EG *The children enjoyed sleeping out in the open.* [PHRASE]

21 If an attitude or situation is brought out **into the open**, people are told about it and it is no longer kept secret. [PHRASE]

22 If a course of action is **open** to you, it is possible for you to do it. EG *We should use the opportunities now open to us.* [ADJ PRED+*to*]

23 If a meeting, competition, or invitation is an **open** one, anyone is allowed to take part in it or accept it. EG *Most Council meetings are open to the public... ...the Women's Open Golf Championship.* [ADJ CLASSIF]

24 If you describe a situation or topic as **open**, you mean that it is still being considered and no decision has been made about it yet. EG *I let joining the Party remain an open question... They had left their options open.* [ADJ CLASSIF]

25 See also **opening**, **openly**.

open out. If a road or passage **opens out**, it gradually becomes larger or wider. [PHRASAL VB : V+ADV]

open up. 1 When an opportunity **opens up** or when a situation **opens up** an opportunity, that [PHRASAL VB : V-ERG+ADV]

If someone is opinionated, are they open-minded?

opportunity is given to you. EG *All sorts of possibilities began to open up.* **2** If a place **opens up** or if someone **opens** it **up**, people can then get to it or trade with it more easily. EG *Brunel opened up the West.* **3** When someone **opens up** a building or **opens up**, they unlock the door and open it so that people can get in. V-ERG+ADV; V+O+ADV OR V+ADV

open air. If you are in the **open air**, you are outside rather than in a building. EG *Dry clothes in the open air, if possible... ...open-air swimming pools.* N SING : *the*+N

open day, open days. An **open day** is a special day when the public are allowed to visit a particular school or other institution. EG *You can meet the teacher on open days.* N COUNT

open-ended. An **open-ended** discussion or activity is started without the intention of achieving a particular decision or result. ADJ CLASSIF

opening /əʊpə⁰nɪŋ/, **openings. 1** The **opening** item or part of something is the item or part that comes first. EG *...his opening remarks... ...the opening scene of the play.* ADJ CLASSIF : ATTRIB

2 The **opening** of a book or film is the first part of it. EG *The main characters are established in the opening of the book.* N SING

3 An **opening** is a hole or empty space through which things can pass. EG *We slid through the opening into the field.* N COUNT

4 An **opening** is also **4.1** an opportunity to do something. EG *Charlotte herself provided me with an opening.* **4.2** a job that you can apply for. EG *There were openings in the police force.* N COUNT

5 See also **open**.

opening hours. The **opening hours** of a shop, bank, library, or pub are the times when it is open for business. EG *Banks often have very short opening hours.* N PLURAL

openly /əʊpə⁰nli¹/. If you do something **openly**, you do it without trying to hide anything. EG *His mother wept openly... Margaret was openly angry at the other women.* ADV

open-minded. Someone who is **open-minded** is willing to listen to other people's ideas and consider them. EG *...an intelligent, open-minded man... ...an open-minded approach to new techniques.* ADJ QUALIT

open-mouthed. If someone is looking **open-mouthed** at something, their mouth is open because they are very surprised. EG *She was staring open-mouthed at a picture of her father.* ADJ CLASSIF

open-plan. An **open-plan** building has just one large area on each storey, rather than several separate rooms. EG *...an open-plan office.* ADJ CLASSIF

opera /ɒpə⁰rə/, **operas.** An **opera** is a musical entertainment that is like a play except that most of the words are sung. EG *...choruses from Verdi's operas... ...a book on Italian opera.* N COUNT OR N UNCOUNT

operate /ɒpəreɪt/, **operates, operating, operated. 1** If a business or organization **operates** in a place, it carries out its work there. EG *...the multinational companies which operate in their country... He operates an Afghan news service here.* V-ERG
◊ **operation.** EG *...our first year of operation.* ◊ N UNCOUNT

2 The way that something **operates** is the way that it works or has an effect. EG *We discussed how language operates... ...the way calculators operated... Laws of the same kind operate in nature.* V

3 When you **operate** a machine or device, you make it work. EG *...how to operate the safety equipment.* ◊ **operation.** EG *...instructions for the operation of machinery.* V-ERG; ◊ N UNCOUNT

4 When surgeons **operate**, they cut open a patient's body in order to remove, replace, or repair a diseased or damaged part of it. EG *They operated but it was too late... His knees have been operated on three times.* V

operatic /ɒpərætɪk/ means relating to opera. EG *...operatic roles... ...the local operatic society.* ADJ CLASSIF : OFT ATTRIB

operating theatre, operating theatres. An **operating theatre** is a room in a hospital where surgeons carry out operations. N COUNT

operation /ɒpəreɪʃə⁰n/, **operations. 1** An **operation** is a planned activity that involves many complicated actions. EG *...the biggest police operation in French history... ...military operations in Europe... ...a rescue operation.* N COUNT : USU+SUPP

2 Businesses or companies are sometimes referred to as **operations**. EG *...Multiponics, a large-scale farming operation.* N COUNT : USU+SUPP

3 In a hospital, an **operation** is a form of treatment in which a surgeon cuts open a patient's body in order to remove, replace, or repair a diseased or damaged part. EG *Her mother was about to undergo a major operation... ...heart operations.* N COUNT

4 If something is **in operation**, it is working or being used. EG *...gas drilling rigs in operation in the USA... The plans were put into operation at once.* PHRASE

5 See also **operate**.

operational /ɒpəreɪʃə⁰nəl, -ʃənə⁰l/. **1** A machine or piece of equipment that is **operational** is working or able to be used. EG *...fifty operational warships... The system is not yet operational.* ADJ CLASSIF

2 Operational actions or difficulties occur while a plan or system is being carried out. ADJ CLASSIF : ATTRIB

operative /ɒpə⁰rətɪv/, **operatives. 1** Something that is **operative** is working or having an effect. EG *The scheme was fully operative by 1975.* ADJ CLASSIF

2 An **operative** is a worker. EG *...each operative on a production line.* N COUNT Formal

operator /ɒpəreɪtə/, **operators. 1** An **operator** is a person who works at a telephone exchange or at the switchboard of an office or hotel. EG *He dialled the operator... ...telephone operators.* N COUNT

2 An **operator** is also **2.1** someone who is employed to operate or control a machine. EG *...computer operators.* **2.2** someone who runs a business. EG *...tour operators... ...casino operators.* N COUNT+SUPP

operetta /ɒpərɛtə/, **operettas.** An **operetta** is a type of opera which is light-hearted and often comic and has some of the words spoken rather than sung. N COUNT OR N UNCOUNT

ophthalmic /ɒfθælmɪk/ means relating to or concerned with the medical care of your eyes. EG *...an ophthalmic optician.* ADJ CLASSIF : ATTRIB Formal

opinion /əpɪnjən/, **opinions. 1** Your **opinion** on something is what you think about it. EG *The students were eager to express their opinions... Information of this nature was valuable, in his opinion... We have a high opinion of you.* N COUNT : OFT+POSS

2 If someone **is of the opinion** that something is the case, they think that it is the case. EG *He is of the opinion that money is not important.* PHRASE Formal

3 You can refer to the beliefs or views that people have as **opinion**. EG *...changes in public opinion... Difficulties arise where there's a difference of opinion.* N UNCOUNT

opinionated /əpɪnjəneɪtɪ²d/. You say that someone is **opinionated** when they have firm opinions and refuse to accept that they may be wrong; used showing disapproval. EG *...this inexperienced but opinionated newcomer.* ADJ QUALIT

opinion poll, opinion polls. An **opinion poll** involves asking people for their opinion on a particular subject, especially one concerning politics. N COUNT

opium /əʊpɪəm/ is a drug made from the seeds of a type of poppy. It is used in medicines, and for pleasure. Opium is illegal in many countries. N UNCOUNT

opponent /əpəʊnənt/, **opponents. 1** A politician's **opponents** are other politicians who belong to a different party or have different aims or policies. EG *...their political opponents.* N COUNT : USU+POSS

2 In a game, your **opponent** is the person who is playing against you. EG *He beat his opponent three sets to love.* N COUNT : USU+POSS

3 The **opponents** of an idea or policy do not agree N COUNT : OFT+*of*

with it and do not want it to be carried out. EG *...a leading opponent of the budget cuts.*

opportune /ɒpətju:n/ means happening at a convenient time. EG *It was most opportune that Mrs Davenport should arrive... The call came at an opportune moment.* [ADJ QUALIT; Formal]

opportunism /ɒpətju:nɪzə^{0}m/. If you describe someone's behaviour as **opportunism**, you mean that they take advantage of any opportunity that occurs in order to gain money or power; used showing disapproval. EG *...a piece of cheap, cynical opportunism.* ◊ **opportunist** /ɒpətju:nɪst/, **opportunists.** EG *...the intrigues of a business opportunist.* [N UNCOUNT; Formal] [◊ N COUNT]

opportunistic /ɒpətju:nɪstɪk/. If you describe someone's behaviour as **opportunistic**, you mean that they take advantage of any opportunity that occurs in order to gain money or power; used showing disapproval. EG *...an opportunistic foreign policy.* [ADJ QUALIT; Formal]

opportunity /ɒpətju:nɪ^{1}ti^1/, **opportunities.** An **opportunity** is a situation in which it is possible for you to do something that you want to do. EG *It will give you an opportunity to meet all kinds of people... They would return to power at the first opportunity... ...equality of opportunity.* [N COUNT OR N UNCOUNT]

oppose /əpəʊz/, **opposes, opposing, opposed.** If you **oppose** someone or **oppose** what they want to do, you disagree with what they want to do and try to prevent them from doing it. EG *My father opposed my wish to become a sculptor... He opposed the founding of the Gallery.* [V+O]

opposed /əpəʊzd/. **1** If you are **opposed** to something, you disagree with it or disapprove of it. EG *I am opposed to capital punishment... They were violently opposed to the idea.* [ADJ PRED: USU+*to*]

2 You say that two ideas or systems are **opposed** when they are opposite to each other or very different from each other. EG *...two bitterly opposed schools of socialist thought... ...a strategy which is diametrically opposed to that of the previous government.* [ADJ CLASSIF: OFT+*to*]

3 You use **as opposed to** when you want to make it clear that you are talking about a particular thing and not something else. EG *There's a need for technical colleges as opposed to universities.* [PREP]

opposing /əpəʊzɪŋ/. **Opposing** ideas or tendencies are totally different from each other. EG *We held opposing points of view... I feel there are two opposing tendencies in your work.* [ADJ CLASSIF: ATTRIB]

opposite /ɒpəzɪt, -sɪt/, **opposites. 1** If one thing is **opposite** another, it is on the other side of a space from it. EG *The hotel is opposite a railway station... Lynn was sitting opposite him... The man opposite lifted down her case.* [PREP OR ADV]

2 The **opposite** side or part of something is the side or part that is farthest away from you. EG *...on the opposite side of the street... She burst in through the opposite door.* [ADJ CLASSIF: USU ATTRIB]

3 Opposite is used to describe things of the same kind which are as different as possible in a particular way. For example, north and south are opposite directions, and winning and losing are opposite results in a game. EG *I wanted to impress them but probably had the opposite effect... Paul turned and walked in the opposite direction... Holmes took the opposite point of view.* [ADJ CLASSIF: ATTRIB]

4 If two things of the same kind are completely different in a particular way, you can say that one is the **opposite** of the other. EG *My interpretation was the absolute opposite of Olivier's... My brother is just the opposite. He loves sport.* [N COUNT: USU *the*+N]

5 The opposite sex refers to men if you are talking about women. It refers to women if you are talking about men. EG *The teenage period is crucial in learning about the opposite sex.* [PHRASE]

opposite number, opposite numbers. Your **opposite number** is a person who does the same job as you, but works in a different department, firm, or organization. EG *My opposite numbers in industry don't have this problem.* [N COUNT+POSS]

opposition /ɒpəzɪʃə^{0}n/. **1** When there is **opposition** to a plan or proposal, people disapprove of it and try to prevent it being carried out. EG *It was only built after much opposition from the planners.* [N UNCOUNT]

2 The **opposition** refers to **2.1** the politicians or political parties that form part of a country's parliament but are not in the government. EG *...the leader of the Opposition... ...two new opposition parties.* **2.2** all the people who disagree strongly with a person or an idea. EG *The opposition consisted of chiefs and elders.* **2.3** the person or team you are competing against in a sports event. EG *One player broke through the opposition's defence.* [N COLL: SING]

oppress /ə^{6}prɛs/, **oppresses, oppressing, oppressed. 1** To **oppress** someone means to treat them cruelly or unfairly. EG *...institutions that oppress women.* ◊ **oppressed.** EG *...the sufferings of oppressed people everywhere.* ◊ **oppressor, oppressors.** EG *They didn't have the will to stand up against their foreign oppressors.* [V+O] [◊ ADJ CLASSIF] [◊ N COUNT]

2 If something **oppresses** you, it makes you feel depressed and uncomfortable. EG *Somehow the room oppressed him.* [V+O]

oppression /ə^{6}prɛʃə^{0}n/. **1 Oppression** is the cruel or unfair treatment of a group of people. EG *...the oppression of the weak and defenceless.* [N UNCOUNT]

2 Oppression is also a feeling of depression, especially one caused by a place or situation. EG *Passing the place, my sense of oppression increased.* [N UNCOUNT]

oppressive /ə^{6}prɛsɪv/. **1** You say that the weather is **oppressive** when it is hot and humid. EG *...the oppressive heat of the plains.* ◊ **oppressively.** EG *The room was oppressively hot.* [ADJ QUALIT] [◊ SUBMOD]

2 An **oppressive** situation makes you feel depressed or uncomfortable. EG *The silence became oppressive.* [ADJ QUALIT]

3 Laws, societies, and customs that are **oppressive** treat people cruelly and unfairly. EG *...an oppressive bureaucracy... ...the present oppressive system.* [ADJ QUALIT]

opt /ɒpt/, **opts, opting, opted.** If you **opt** for something, you choose it. If you **opt** to do something, you choose to do it. EG *My father left the choice of career to me, and I opted for law... ...those who opt to cooperate with the regime.* [V+*for* OR *to*-INF]

opt out. If you **opt out** of something, you choose to be no longer involved in it. EG *He tried to opt out of political decision-making.* [PHRASAL VB: V+ADV, OFT+*of*]

optical /ɒptɪkə^{0}l/. **1 Optical** instruments, devices, or processes involve or relate to vision or light. EG *...an optical microscope.* [ADJ CLASSIF: ATTRIB]

2 Optical means relating to the way that things appear to people. EG *...an optical illusion.* [ADJ CLASSIF: ATTRIB]

optician /ɒptɪʃə^{0}n/, **opticians.** An **optician** is someone whose job involves testing people's eyesight or providing glasses and contact lenses. [N COUNT]

optimism /ɒptɪmɪzə^{0}m/ is the feeling of being hopeful about the future. EG *I felt cheerful and full of optimism... There was a definite air of optimism at the headquarters.* ◊ **optimist,** /ɒptɪmɪst/ **optimists.** EG *I'm an optimist by nature.* [N UNCOUNT] [◊ N COUNT]

optimistic /ɒptɪmɪstɪk/. Someone who is **optimistic** is hopeful about the future. EG *...an optimistic estimate.* ◊ **optimistically.** EG *It might work, she thought optimistically.* [ADJ QUALIT] [◊ ADV]

optimum /ɒptɪməm/ means the best that is possible. EG *The optimum feeding time is around dawn... ...in optimum conditions.* [ADJ CLASSIF: ATTRIB; Formal]

option /ɒpʃə^{0}n/, **options. 1** An **option** is something that you can choose to do in preference to one or more alternatives. EG *He had, I would say, two options... ...the option of another referendum.* [N COUNT]

2 If you have the **option** to do something, you can [N SING]

If you have the option to do something, do you do it?

choose whether to do it or not. EG *He was given the option: give them up or lose your job... ...mothers who have no option but to work.*

optional /ɒpʃə^{0}nəl, -ʃənə^{0}l/. If something is **optional**, you can choose whether or not you do it or have it. EG *Games are optional at this school.* ADJ CLASSIF

opulent /ɒpjə^{4}lənt/. **1** Someone who is **opulent** is very wealthy. EG *...all the advantages of an opulent society.* ◇ **opulence** /ɒpjə^{4}ləns/. EG *His eyes had never beheld such opulence.* ADJ QUALIT Formal ◇ N UNCOUNT

2 If you describe an object as **opulent**, you mean that it looks grand and expensive. EG *...the magnificently opulent marble altar.* ADJ QUALIT Formal

or /ɔː, ə/. **1** You use **or** **1.1** to link a number of alternatives. EG *Do you want your drink up there or do you want to come down for it?... Have you any brothers or sisters?* **1.2** to give another alternative, when the first alternative is introduced by 'either' or 'whether'. EG *Most aircraft accidents occur at either take-off or landing... He didn't know whether to laugh or cry... We'd better wait and see whether or not the operation was successful.* **1.3** between two numbers to indicate that you are giving an approximate amount. EG *You are supposed to polish your car three or four times a year.* CONJ

2 You also use **or** to introduce a comment which corrects or modifies what you have just said. EG *The company is paying the rent or at least contributing to it... ...Margaret. Or Molly as she was called.* CONJ

3 If you say that someone should do something **or** something unpleasant will happen, you are warning them that if they do not do it, the unpleasant thing will happen. EG *Don't put anything plastic in the oven or it will probably start melting.* CONJ

4 You can also use **or** to introduce something which is an explanation or justification for a statement you have just made. EG *He can't be that bad, can he, or they wouldn't have allowed him home.* CONJ

5 or else: see **else**. • **or other**: see **other**. • **or so**: see **so**. • **or something**: see **something**.

-or, -ors. **-or** is added to some verbs to form nouns. These nouns refer to people who do a particular kind of work or take a particular kind of action. For example, a supervisor is someone whose job is to supervise people, and a demonstrator is someone who takes part in a demonstration. Nouns like these are sometimes not defined in this dictionary, but are treated with the related verbs. EG *He worked as a translator... ...the instigator of the plot... ...the conquerors of Peru.* SUFFIX

oral /ɔːrəl/, **orals. 1 Oral** is used to describe things that involve speaking rather than writing. EG *...an oral test in German... ...oral reports.* ◇ **orally.** EG *The candidate will be examined orally.* ADJ CLASSIF : ATTRIB ◇ ADV

2 An **oral** is an oral test or examination. EG *In some examinations the oral follows a written paper.* N COUNT

3 Oral medicines are ones that you swallow. EG *...an oral vaccine.* ◇ **orally.** EG *...a pill taken orally.* ADJ CLASSIF ◇ ADV

orange /ɒrɪndʒ/, **oranges. 1** Something that is **orange** is of a colour between red and yellow. EG *...an orange silk scarf.* ADJ COLOUR

2 An **orange** is a round fruit that is juicy and sweet. It has a thick orange skin and is divided into sections inside. N COUNT OR N UNCOUNT

3 Orange is a drink made from oranges or tasting of oranges. EG *...gin and orange.* N UNCOUNT

oration /ɔːreɪʃən/, **orations.** An **oration** is a formal public speech. EG *...a funeral oration.* N COUNT Formal

orator /ɒrətə/, **orators.** An **orator** is someone who is skilled at making speeches. EG *He is a marvellous orator.* N COUNT

oratory /ɒrətə^{0}ri^1/ is the art of making formal speeches. EG *He roused the troops with his oratory.* N UNCOUNT Formal

orbit /ɔːbɪt/, **orbits, orbiting, orbited. 1** An **orbit** is the curved path in space that is followed by an object that is going round a planet, a moon, or the sun. EG *...the orbit of Mercury... How much does it cost to put a satellite into orbit?* N COUNT OR N UNCOUNT

2 If something such as a satellite **orbits** a planet, a moon, or the sun, it goes round and round it. V+O OR V

orbital /ɔːbɪtə^{0}l/. An **orbital** road goes all the way round a large city. ADJ CLASSIF : ATTRIB

orchard /ɔːtʃəd/, **orchards.** An **orchard** is an area of land on which fruit trees are grown. EG *...an apple orchard.* N COUNT

orchestra /ɔːkɪ^{2}strə/, **orchestras.** An **orchestra** is a large group of musicians who play a variety of different instruments together. An orchestra usually plays classical music. EG *The orchestra played the Russian national anthem.* N COUNT

orchestral /ɔːkestrə^{0}l/ means consisting of or relating to the music played by an orchestra. EG *...Mozart's orchestral pieces.* ADJ CLASSIF : ATTRIB

orchestrate /ɔːkɪ^{2}streɪt/, **orchestrates, orchestrating, orchestrated. 1** If you **orchestrate** something, you organize it very carefully in order to produce a particular result or situation. EG *He personally orchestrated that entire evening.* ◇ **orchestrated.** EG *...a brilliantly orchestrated campaign of persuasion and protest.* V+O ◇ ADJ QUALIT : ATTRIB

2 If you **orchestrate** a piece of music, you rewrite it so that it can be played by an orchestra. V+O

orchid /ɔːkɪd/, **orchids.** An **orchid** is a plant with beautiful and unusual flowers. N COUNT

ordain /ɔːdeɪn/, **ordains, ordaining, ordained. 1** When someone **is ordained**, they are made a member of the clergy in a religious ceremony. EG *When I was first ordained, I served as a hospital chaplain.* V+O : USU PASS

2 If someone in authority **ordains** something, they order that it shall happen. EG *Lady Sackville ordained complete discretion... The law ordained that she should be executed.* V+O OR V+REPORT : ONLY *that* Formal

ordeal /ɔːdiːl/, **ordeals.** An **ordeal** is a difficult and extremely unpleasant experience. EG *He described the rest of his terrible ordeal.* N COUNT

order /ɔːdə/, **orders, ordering, ordered. 1** If you do something **in order to** achieve a particular thing, you do it because you want to achieve that thing. EG *He had to hurry in order to reach the next place on his schedule... Rose trod with care, in order not to spread the dirt... They are learning English in order that they can study engineering.* CONJ

2 If someone in authority gives you an **order**, they tell you to do something. EG *George went away to carry out this order... An official inquiry was set up on the orders of the Minister of Health.* • If you are **under orders** to do something, you have been told to do it by someone in authority. N COUNT • PHRASE

3 If someone in authority **orders** people to do something or **orders** something to be done, they tell people to do it. EG *He ordered me to fetch the books... The Captain ordered the ship's masts to be cut down... Sherman ordered an investigation into her husband's death... He ordered me out of the building... 'Sit down!' he ordered... The prime minister ordered that they be taken to women's prisons.* V+O : OFT+*to*-INF OR A; ALSO V+QUOTE OR REPORT : ONLY *that*

4 When you **order** something that you are going to pay for, you ask for it to be brought to you or sent to you. EG *Davis had ordered a second whisky... I'll order now... She ordered an extra delivery of coal.* V+O OR V

5 Something that is **on order** at a shop has been asked for but has not yet been supplied. PHRASE

6 An **order** is something that you ask to be brought to you or sent to you, and that you are going to pay for. EG *A waiter came to take their order... We will continue to deal with overseas orders.* N COUNT

7 If a set of things are arranged or done in a particular **order**, one thing is put first or done first, another thing second, another thing third, and so on. EG *The names are not in alphabetical order.* • If a set of things are done, arranged, or dealt with **in order**, they are done, arranged, or dealt with according to the correct sequence. N UNCOUNT • PHRASE

8 Order is **8.1** the situation that exists when everything is in the correct place or is done at the correct time. EG *I felt it would create some order in* N UNCOUNT *our lives... Gretchen combed her hair into some sort of order.* **8.2** the situation that exists when people live together peacefully rather than fighting or causing trouble. EG *...the task of restoring order.* • If you **keep order** or **keep** people **in order**, you prevent people from behaving in an excited or violent way. • PHRASE

9 A machine or device that is **in working order** is functioning properly and is not broken. EG *He was always finding cars in good working order.* PHRASE

10 A machine or device that is **out of order** is broken and does not work. PHRASE

11 At a meeting, if you describe someone or their behaviour as being **out of order**, you mean that they are doing something incorrect according to the rules of the meeting. EG *The resolution was ruled out of order.* PHRASE Formal

12 When people talk about a particular **order**, they mean the way society is organized at a particular time. EG *They don't accept the existing order.* N SING+SUPP

13 An **order** is also a group of monks or nuns who live according to rules laid down by the person who started the group. N COUNT

14 If you refer to something of a particular **order**, you mean something of a particular quality, amount, or degree. EG *...a thinker of the highest order.* • You use **in the order of** or **of the order of** when giving an approximate figure. EG *Britain's contribution is something in the order of 5 per cent.* N SING+SUPP Formal • PREP

15 a tall order: see **tall**. • See also **law and order**, **mail order**, **postal order**, **standing order**.

order about or **order around.** If you **order** someone **about** or **order** them **around**, you always tell them what to do, in an unsympathetic way. PHRASAL VB : V+O+ADV

ordered /ɔ:dəd/. An **ordered** society or system is well organized or arranged. EG *In Mrs Kaul's house everything was well ordered.* ADJ QUALIT

orderly /ɔ:dəli¹/, **orderlies. 1** Something that is **orderly** is well organized or arranged. EG *...a system of orderly government.* ◇ **orderliness.** EG *We pride ourselves on the orderliness of our way of life.* ADJ QUALIT ◇ N UNCOUNT

2 An **orderly** is an untrained male hospital attendant. EG *I sat at the end of the ward with the orderly.* N COUNT

> **ORDINAL** stands for **ordinal number**
> Numbers such as 'first', 'third', 'fifth', and 'tenth' are called ordinal numbers. They usually come after a determiner such as 'the' and 'my' and before a noun, as in *...the **fifth** house on the right* and *...my **second** child.*
> Ordinals can also behave like pronouns, and so can be used without a following noun, especially when it is obvious what you are talking about. For example, Beethoven's Ninth Symphony is often referred to simply as *Beethoven's **Ninth**.*
> See the entry headed NUMBER for more information.

ordinarily /ɔ:dɪ¹nɛrɪli¹/. If something **ordinarily** happens or is **ordinarily** the case, it usually happens or is usually the case. EG *This room was ordinarily used by the doctor... Ordinarily, of course, we would use the telephone.* ADV OR ADV SEN

ordinary /ɔ:dɪ¹nri¹/. **1** Something that is **ordinary** is not special or different in any way. EG *...ordinary everyday objects... What do ordinary people really think about universities?... She is likeable enough, but very ordinary.* ADJ QUALIT

2 Something that is **out of the ordinary** is unusual or different. EG *I'd like to bring her something a little out of the ordinary.* PHRASE

3 An **ordinary** degree is an undergraduate degree that is lower than an honours degree. ADJ CLASSIF : ATTRIB

ordination /ɔ:dɪneɪʃə⁰n/, **ordinations.** When someone's **ordination** takes place, they are made a member of the Christian clergy in a special ceremony. EG *...the ordination of women.* N COUNT OR N UNCOUNT

ore /ɔ:/, **ores. Ore** is rock or earth from which metal can be obtained. EG *...iron ore.* N MASS

organ /ɔ:gən/, **organs. 1** An **organ** is a part of your body that has a particular purpose or function, for example your heart or your lungs. EG *Children's bones and organs are very sensitive to radiation.* N COUNT

2 An **organ** is also a large musical instrument with pipes of different lengths through which air is forced. You play the organ rather like a piano, using keys and pedals. N COUNT

3 You refer to a newspaper as an **organ** of a particular organization when the organization uses it as a means of giving information or influencing people. EG *They decided to close the newspaper and launch it again as a government organ.* N COUNT : USU+SUPP

organic /ɔ:gænɪk/. **1** Something that is **organic** is produced by or found in plants or animals. EG *The rocks were carefully searched for organic remains.* ADJ CLASSIF

2 Organic gardening or farming uses only natural animal and plant products and does not use fertilizers or pesticides containing artificial chemicals. ◇ **organically.** EG *Buy organically grown vegetables if possible.* ADJ CLASSIF : ATTRIB ◇ ADV

3 Change or development that is **organic** happens gradually and naturally rather than suddenly. EG *Instead of organic growth, there have been abrupt changes.* ADJ CLASSIF Formal

4 If you describe a structure or society as **organic**, you mean that it consists of many parts which all contribute to the way the whole structure or society works. ADJ CLASSIF Formal

organisation /ɔ:gənaɪzeɪʃə⁰n/. See **organization**.

organisational /ɔ:gənaɪzeɪʃə⁰nəl, -ʃənə⁰l/. See **organizational**.

organise /ɔ:gənaɪz/. See **organize**.

organism /ɔ:gənɪzə⁰m/, **organisms.** An **organism** is an animal or plant, especially one that is so small that you cannot see it without a microscope. EG *These creatures are descended from simpler organisms like corals.* N COUNT

organist /ɔ:gənɪst/, **organists.** An **organist** is someone who plays the organ. N COUNT

organization /ɔ:gənaɪzeɪʃə⁰n/, **organizations;** also spelled **organisation. 1** An **organization** is a group of people who do something together regularly in an organized way. Businesses and clubs are organizations. EG *...student organizations... ...the World Health Organisation.* N COUNT

2 The **organization** of a system is the way in which its different parts are related and how they work together. EG *There has been a total change in the organization of society.* N UNCOUNT : USU+SUPP

3 The **organization** of an activity or public event involves making all the arrangements for it. EG *I don't want to get involved in the actual organisation of things.* N UNCOUNT : USU+SUPP

organizational /ɔ:gənaɪzeɪʃə⁰nəl, -ʃənə⁰l/; also spelled **organisational. Organizational** means **1** relating to the way that things are planned and arranged. EG *...an organizational genius named Alfred P. Sloan.* **2** relating to organizations. EG *The group has no political or organisational links with the terrorists.* ADJ CLASSIF : ATTRIB

organize /ɔ:gənaɪz/, **organizes, organizing, organized;** also spelled **organise. 1** If you **organize** an activity or public event, you make all the arrangements for it. EG *We organized a concert in the village hall... I thought that meeting was badly* V+O

> What is the difference between 'ornamental' and 'ornate'?

organized. ◊ **organizer, organizers.** EG *...the organizers of the conference.* ◊ N COUNT

2 If you **organize** things, you arrange them so that they are in a sensible order or in sensible places. EG *He's better able now to organise his thoughts.* V+O

3 When workers or employees **organize**, they form themselves into a group such as a trade union in order to have more power to get things they want. EG *Their poverty prevents them from organizing effectively to improve their wages.* V

organized /ɔːgənaɪzd/; also spelled **organised. 1 Organized** activities are planned and controlled. EG *...an organized holiday... ...organized crime... ...organized games.* ADJ CLASSIF : ATTRIB

2 You say that people or things are **organized** when you admire them because they work in an efficient and effective way. EG *How organised you are!* ADJ QUALIT

orgasm /ɔːgæzə^{0}m/, **orgasms.** An **orgasm** is the moment of greatest pleasure and excitement during sexual activity. N COUNT

orgy /ɔːdʒi^1/, **orgies. 1** An **orgy** is a party in which people behave in a very uncontrolled way. EG *...sexual orgies... ...a drunken orgy.* N COUNT

2 You can refer to a period of intense and extreme activity as an **orgy** of that activity. EG *...an orgy of destruction.* N COUNT+SUPP

orient /ɔːrɪənt/, **orients, orienting, oriented.** If you **orient** yourself to a new situation, you learn about it and prepare to deal with it. EG *The raw newcomer has to orient himself.* • See also **oriented**. V-REFL Formal

oriental /ɔːrɪɛntə^{0}l/. Something that is **oriental** comes from or is associated with eastern and south-eastern Asia, especially China and Japan. EG *...Oriental philosophy... ...her oriental features.* ADJ CLASSIF

orientate /ɔːrɪɛnteɪt/, **orientates, orientating, orientated.** When you **orientate** yourself, you discover where you are by looking at a map, or by searching for familiar places or objects. V-REFL

orientated /ɔːrɪɛnteɪtɪ^{2}d/ means the same as oriented. EG *...a commercially orientated theory... ...career-orientated women... ...an industry orientated towards quick, easy profits.* ADJ CLASSIF : OFT+*towards*/*to*

orientation /ɔːrɪɛnteɪʃə^{0}n/. The **orientation** of an organization or system is the activities that it is concerned with and the aims that it has. EG *...the party's revolutionary orientation.* N UNCOUNT +SUPP

oriented /ɔːrɪɛntɪ^{2}d/. You use **oriented** to indicate what someone or something is interested in or concerned with. For example, if someone is politically **oriented**, they are interested in politics. EG *...export-oriented industries... ...a society oriented towards information.* ADJ CLASSIF : OFT+*towards*/*to*

origin /ɒrɪdʒɪn/, **origins. 1** You can refer to the beginning or cause of something as its **origin** or its **origins**. EG *The unrest has its origins in economic problems... ...the origin of the universe... ...a word of recent origin.* N COUNT OR N UNCOUNT : USU+POSS

2 When you talk about a person's **origin** or **origins**, you are referring to the country, race, or social class of their parents or ancestors. EG *...a woman of Pakistani origin... ...your working-class origins... His origins were humble.* N COUNT OR N UNCOUNT : USU+SUPP

original /ərɪdʒɪnə^{0}l/, **originals. 1** You use **original** to describe the form or use that something had when it first existed, or something that existed at the beginning of a process. EG *They will restore the house to its original state... The original idea came from Dr Ball.* ◊ **originally.** EG *It was originally a toy factory.* ADJ CLASSIF : ATTRIB ◊ ADV

2 You refer to a work of art or a document as an **original** when it is genuine and not a copy. EG *The original is in the British Museum.* ▸ used as an adjective. EG *...working on original documents.* N COUNT ▸ ADJ CLASSIF

3 An **original** piece of writing or music was written recently and has not been published or performed before. EG *...her first collection of short stories, some original, some reprinted.* ADJ CLASSIF

4 If you describe someone, their ideas, or their work as **original**, you mean that they are very imaginative and clever. EG *...a daring and original idea.* ◊ **originality** /ərɪdʒɪ^{1}nælɪti^1/. EG *...a sculptor of genius and great originality.* ADJ QUALIT ◊ N UNCOUNT

originate /ərɪdʒɪneɪt/, **originates, originating, originated.** If something **originated** at a particular time or in a particular place, it began to happen or exist at that time or in that place. EG *These beliefs originated in the 19th century.* V : USU+A

originator /ərɪdʒɪneɪtə/, **originators.** The **originator** of something such as an idea or scheme is the person who first thought of it or began it. EG *The originator of the idea was a young professor.* N COUNT

ornament /ɔːnəmə^{2}nt/, **ornaments. 1** An **ornament** is **1.1** a small object that you display in your home because it is attractive. EG *...painted china ornaments.* **1.2** an object such as a piece of jewellery that someone wears in order to look attractive. N COUNT

2 Ornament refers to decorations and designs on a building or piece of furniture which make it more elaborate. EG *...different styles of ornament.* N UNCOUNT

ornamental /ɔːnəmɛntə^{0}l/. Something that is **ornamental** is intended to be attractive rather than useful. EG *...an ornamental pond.* ADJ CLASSIF

ornamented /ɔːnəmə^{2}ntɪd/. If something is **ornamented** with attractive objects or patterns, it is decorated with them. EG *The sand was ornamented with shells and seaweed.* ADJ CLASSIF : USU+*with*

ornate /ɔːneɪt/. Something that is **ornate** has a lot of decoration on it. EG *...ornate necklaces.* ADJ QUALIT

ornithology /ɔːnɪθɒlədʒi^1/ is the study of birds. EG *I've taken up ornithology.* N UNCOUNT Formal

orphan /ɔːfən/, **orphans, orphaned. 1** An **orphan** is a child whose parents are dead. EG *She became an orphan at twelve.* N COUNT

2 If a child **is orphaned**. its parents die. EG *We adopted the twins when they were orphaned.* V-PASS

orphanage /ɔːfə^{0}nɪdʒ/, **orphanages.** An **orphanage** is a place where orphans are looked after. N COUNT

orthodox /ɔːθədɒks/. **1 Orthodox** beliefs, methods, or systems are the ones that most people have or use. EG *...orthodox medicine.* ADJ QUALIT : ATTRIB

2 People who are **orthodox** believe in the older and more traditional ideas of their religion or political party. EG *...Orthodox Jews... ...a fairly orthodox socialist.* ADJ QUALIT

orthodoxy /ɔːθədɒksi^1/, **orthodoxies. 1** An **orthodoxy** is an accepted view about something. EG *...the prevailing orthodoxy on this problem.* N COUNT

2 Orthodoxy is **2.1** traditional and accepted beliefs. EG *...Islamic orthodoxy... ...Marxist orthodoxy.* N UNCOUNT +SUPP **2.2** the degree to which a person believes in and supports the ideas of their religion or political party. EG *...the rigid orthodoxy of Mr Mzali.* N UNCOUNT : USU+POSS

oscillate /ɒsɪleɪt/, **oscillates, oscillating, oscillated. 1** If something **oscillates**, it moves repeatedly from one position to another and back again. EG *Its wings oscillate up and down.* V : USU+A Formal

2 If you **oscillate** between two moods, attitudes, or types of behaviour, you keep changing from one to the other and back again. EG *His mood oscillated between co-operation and aggression.* V+*between* Formal

ostensible /ɒstɛnsɪbə^{0}l/. If you refer to the **ostensible** purpose, cause, or nature of something, you are referring to the one that it seems or is said to have, which you think may not be the real one. EG *...the ostensible purpose of his excursion.* ◊ **ostensibly.** EG *Rose left the room, ostensibly to explain about dinner to the cook.* ADJ CLASSIF : ATTRIB Formal ◊ ADV OR ADV SEN

ostentation /ɒstɛnteɪʃə^{0}n/. You say that someone's behaviour is **ostentation** when they do things in order to impress other people with their wealth or importance. EG *More than two telephones is pure ostentation.* N UNCOUNT Formal

ostentatious /ɒstɛnteɪʃəs/. **1** You say that something is **ostentatious** when it costs a lot of money ADJ QUALIT Formal

and is intended to impress people. EG *...a magnificent and ostentatious palace.*
2 People who are **ostentatious** try to impress other people with their wealth or importance. ◇ **ostentatiously.** EG *They were never ostentatiously dressed.* — ADJ QUALIT Formal; ◇ ADV
3 You can describe an action as **ostentatious** when it is done in an exaggerated way in order to attract people's attention. EG *...an ostentatious gesture.* ◇ **ostentatiously.** EG *I started ostentatiously clearing the table.* — ADJ QUALIT Formal; ◇ ADV

ostracize /ɒstrəsaɪz/, **ostracizes, ostracizing, ostracized;** also spelled **ostracise.** If you **are ostracized**, people deliberately behave in an unfriendly way towards you and do not allow you to take part in their social activities. EG *Their children were ostracized by teachers and pupils alike.* — V+O : USU PASS Formal

ostrich /ɒstrɪtʃ/, **ostriches.** An **ostrich** is a large African bird that cannot fly. — N COUNT

other /ʌðə/, **others. Other** cannot be used after the determiner 'an'. See **another**.
1 Other people or **other** things are not the people or things that you have just mentioned or have just been talking about. EG *There were some other people in the compartment... There was no other way to do it... ...toys, paints, books and other equipment... Results in other countries are impressive... Some projects are shorter than others.* — ADJ CLASSIF : ATTRIB, OR PRON : HAS PLURAL
2 When you have mentioned the first of two things, you refer to the second one as the **other** one. EG *He had his papers in one hand, his hat in the other... They have two daughters, one a baby, the other a girl of twelve.* — ADJ CLASSIF : ATTRIB, OR PRON : HAS PLURAL
3 The **other** people or things in a group are the rest of them. EG *...the other members of the class... I shall wait until the others come back.* — ADJ CLASSIF : ATTRIB OR N PLURAL
4 You refer to **other** people or **others** when you are talking about people in general, as opposed to yourself. EG *One ought not to inflict one's problems on other people... Working for others can be most fulfilling.* — ADJ CLASSIF : ATTRIB OR N PLURAL
5 If you say that you did something the **other** day or the **other** week, you mean that you did it recently. EG *I saw Davis the other day.* — ADJ CLASSIF : ATTRIB
6 Nothing **other than** a particular thing means only that thing. No one **other than** a particular person means only that person. EG *She never discussed it with anyone other than Derek... I don't have a thing with me other than this coat... There's no choice other than to reopen his case.* — PHRASE : WITH BROAD NEG
7 You say **none other than** a particular person when you want to emphasize how surprising it is that this person is present or involved. EG *It was none other than the famous Mr Victor Hazel.* — PHRASE
8 You use **every other** when talking about the intervals at which something occurs. For example, if something happens **every other** day, it could happen on the 1st, 3rd, 5th, etc of a particular month. EG *Their local committees are usually held every other month.* — PHRASE
9 Other is also used in these phrases. **9.1** You use **one after the other** to emphasize that actions or events happen with very little time between them. EG *Stone, Prattley and Unwin came forward one after the other... We saw the three plays one after the other.* **9.2** You say **or other** after words such as 'some', 'something', or 'somehow' to emphasize that you cannot or do not want to be more precise about the information that you are giving. EG *For some reason or other your name was omitted... Somehow or other, he reached the Alps.* **9.3** You use **one or other** to refer to one or more things or people in a group, when it does not matter which one is thought of or chosen. EG *One or other current must be altered.* **9.4 each other**: see **each**. ● **in other words**: see **word**. — PHRASES

otherwise /ʌðəwaɪz/. **1** You use **otherwise** after stating a situation or fact, in order to say what the result or consequence would be if this situation or fact was not the case. EG *It's perfectly harmless, Mabel, otherwise I wouldn't have done it... Wash five times a day. You're not properly clean otherwise.* — ADV SEN
2 You use **otherwise** when stating the general condition or quality of something after you have mentioned an exception to this general condition or quality. EG *The cement is slightly cracked but otherwise in good condition... That was a sudden outbreak in an otherwise blameless career.* — ADV SEN OR SUBMOD
3 Otherwise also means in a different way. EG *Stiff and formal, the man was incapable of acting otherwise.* — ADV Formal
4 You use **or otherwise** as a way of referring to things of a different sort in addition to the sort you have just mentioned. EG *It had no effect on its users, beneficial or otherwise... Both sides understand, consciously or otherwise, the limitations of the treaty.* — PHRASE

otter /ɒtə/, **otters.** An **otter** is a small animal with a long tail. Otters swim well and catch and eat fish. — N COUNT

ouch /aʊtʃ/. People say **'Ouch!'** when they suddenly feel pain. — EXCLAM

ought /ɔːt/. **1** If you say that someone **ought** to do something, you mean that it would be a good idea or the right thing to do. EG *She ought to see the doctor... Oughtn't we to phone for the police?... 'I don't care,' he said. 'Well, you ought to,' she said... It's getting late; I think I ought to go.* — MODAL
2 If you say that someone **ought** to have done something, you mean that it would have been a good idea or the right thing to do. EG *I ought to have said yes... I ought not to have come here.* — MODAL
3 If you say that something **ought** to be true, you mean that you expect it to be true. EG *It ought to be quite easy... He ought to be out of jail by now.* — MODAL

oughtn't /ɔːtəᵒnt/ is a spoken form of 'ought not'.

ounce /aʊns/, **ounces. 1** An **ounce** is a unit of weight used in Britain and the USA. There are sixteen ounces in a pound, and one ounce is equal to 28.35 grams. See the entry headed MEASUREMENT. EG *...an ounce of tobacco... The baby gains 6 to 8 ounces a week.* ● See also **fluid ounce**. — N COUNT OR N PART
2 You can also refer to a very small amount of something as an **ounce**. EG *...using every ounce of strength he possessed... ...anyone with an ounce of intelligence.* — N PART : USU SING Informal

our /aʊə/. A speaker or writer uses **our** to describe something that belongs or relates both to himself or herself and to one or more other people. EG *...our children... This could change our lives.* — DET POSS

ours /aʊəz/. A speaker or writer uses **ours** to refer to something that belongs or relates both to himself or herself and to one or more other people. EG *It is a very different country from ours.* — PRON POSS

ourselves /aʊəselvz/. **1** A speaker or writer uses **ourselves** as the object of a verb or preposition in a clause where 'we' is the subject or 'us' is a previous object. See **we**. EG *We almost made ourselves ill... In 1968 we built ourselves a new surgery.* — PRON REFL : PLURAL
2 Ourselves is also used to emphasize the subject or object of a clause. EG *In teaching, we ourselves have to do a lot of learning.* — PRON REFL : PLURAL
3 A speaker or writer also uses **ourselves** in expressions such as 'we did it ourselves' in order to say that he or she, together with one or more other people, did something without any help or interference from anyone else. — PRON REFL : PLURAL

-ous is added to some nouns to form adjectives that describe qualities. For example, someone who is courageous shows courage and someone who is envious feels envy. EG *...scandalous stories... ...a mountainous region... ...a hazardous journey.* — SUFFIX

In what country do you find the outback?

oust /aʊst/, **ousts, ousting, ousted.** If you **oust** someone from a job or a place, you force them to leave it. EG *...the coup which ousted the President... ...ousting peasants from their lands.*
V+O Formal

out /aʊt/. **1** When you go **out** of a place or get **out** of something such as a vehicle, you leave it, so that you are no longer inside it. EG *She rushed out of the house... The lift doors opened and they stepped out into the foyer... She's just got out of bed.*
ADV: OFT+*of*

2 If you are **out**, you are not at home or not at your usual place of work. EG *He came when I was out... Joe is out looking for her.*
ADV AFTER VB

3 If you are in a building and you look **out** of the window, you look through the window at things that are outside the building. EG *She stared out at the rain... I was standing looking out over the view.*
ADV AFTER VB: OFT+PREP

4 You can use **out** to indicate that something is happening outside a building rather than inside it. EG *Many people were sleeping out... It's hot out.*
ADV AFTER VB

5 If you take something **out** of a container or place, you remove it from the container or place. EG *She opened a box and took out a cigarette... He got out a book and read.*
ADV AFTER VB: OFT+*of*

6 If someone or something is kept **out** of a place, they are prevented from going into it. EG *It's designed to keep out intruders.*
ADV AFTER VB: OFT+*of*

7 If a light is **out**, it is no longer shining. EG *The lights went out.*
ADV AFTER VB

8 If a fire or cigarette is **out**, it is no longer burning. EG *He helped to put the fire out.*
ADV AFTER VB

9 If flowers are **out**, their petals have opened. EG *The daffodils were out.*
ADJ PRED

10 If workers are **out**, they are on strike. EG *The men stayed out for nearly a month.*
ADJ PRED Informal

11 If you say that a proposal or suggestion is **out**, you mean that it is unacceptable. EG *That's right out, I'm afraid.*
ADJ PRED

12 If you say that something such as a type of clothing is **out**, you mean that it is unfashionable. EG *Romance is making a comeback. Reality is out.*
ADJ PRED

13 When the sea or tide goes **out**, the sea moves away from the shore rather than towards it.
ADV AFTER VB

14 If you say that a calculation or measurement is **out**, you mean that it is incorrect. EG *It's only a couple of degrees out.*
ADJ PRED

15 If someone is **out** to do something, they intend to do it. EG *They're out to use your house as a free hotel.*
ADJ PRED+*for* OR TO-INF Informal

16 Out of is used in these ways. **16.1** You use **out of** to say what emotion or motive causes someone to do something. For example, if you do something **out of** pity, you do it because you pity someone. EG *He wrote that review out of pure spite.* **16.2** If you get something such as pleasure or an advantage **out of** something, you get it as a result of being involved in that thing. **16.3** If you are **out of** something, you no longer have any of it. EG *We're out of paper.* **16.4** If something is made **out of** a particular material, it is made from it. EG *You can make petroleum out of coal.* **16.5** If you pay for something **out of** a particular sum of money, you pay for it using some of that money. EG *Is he paying for your trip out of parish funds?* **16.6** If you get some information **out of** someone, you persuade or force them to tell it to you. EG *You're not going to get anything out of her.* **16.7** If you are **out of** the rain, the sun, or the wind, you are sheltered from it. **16.8** You use **out of** to indicate what proportion of a group of things something is true of. For example, if something is true of one **out of** five things, it is true of one fifth of all things of that kind.
PREP

out-. You can use **out-** to form verbs that describe an action as being done better by one person than by another. For example, if you can outswim someone, you can swim further or faster than they can. EG *Surely you can outfight him... She managed to outrun them.*
PREFIX

out-and-out. You use **out-and-out** to emphasize that someone or something has all the characteristics of a particular type of person or thing. EG *He's an out-and-out villain... ...an out-and-out triumph.*
ADJ CLASSIF: ATTRIB

outback /aʊtbæk/. The parts of Australia where very few people live are referred to as the **outback**.
N SING: *the*+N

outboard motor, outboard motors. An **outboard motor** is a motor with a propeller that you can fix to the back of a small boat.
N COUNT

outbreak /aʊtbreɪk/, **outbreaks.** An **outbreak** of something unpleasant is a sudden occurrence of it. EG *...the outbreak of war... ...outbreaks of disease.*
N COUNT+SUPP

outbuilding /aʊtbɪldɪŋ/, **outbuildings. Outbuildings** are small buildings such as barns or stables that are part of a larger property.
N COUNT: USU PLURAL

outburst /aʊtbɜːst/, **outbursts. 1** An **outburst** is a sudden and strong expression of emotion, especially anger. EG *I apologize for my outburst just now.*
N COUNT

2 An **outburst** of violent activity is a sudden period of this activity. EG *There followed an outburst of shooting.*
N COUNT+SUPP

outcast /aʊtkɑːst/, **outcasts.** An **outcast** is someone who is rejected by a group of people. EG *They are treated as outcasts.*
N COUNT

outcome /aʊtkʌm/, **outcomes.** The **outcome** of an action or process is the result of it. EG *Nobody dared predict the outcome of the election.*
N COUNT: USU SING+*of*

outcrop /aʊtkrɒp/, **outcrops.** An **outcrop** is a large area of rock that sticks out of the ground. EG *...a massive outcrop of granite.*
N COUNT: USU+SUPP

outcry /aʊtkraɪ/, **outcries.** An **outcry** is a strong reaction of disapproval or anger by many people. EG *The experiments continued, despite the public outcry against them.*
N COUNT

outdated /aʊtdeɪtɪ²d/. If you say that a word, idea, or way of behaving is **outdated**, you mean that it is old-fashioned and no longer useful. In this dictionary, language of this kind is indicated by the use of the word 'Outdated' in the Extra Column. EG *...outdated methods of management.*
ADJ QUALIT

outdo /aʊtduː/, **outdoes, outdoing, outdid, outdone.** If you **outdo** someone, you are more successful than they are at a particular activity. EG *A heavy person can outdo a lighter one in such jobs.*
V+O

outdoor /aʊtdɔː/. **Outdoor** activities or clothes take place or are used in the open air, rather than in a building. EG *...outdoor work... He was fully dressed in his outdoor clothes.*
ADJ CLASSIF: ATTRIB

outdoors /aʊtdɔːz/. If something exists or happens **outdoors**, it exists or happens in the open air, rather than in a building. EG *School classes were held outdoors... Let them go outdoors and play.*
ADV AFTER VB

outer /aʊtə/. The **outer** parts of something are the parts which contain or enclose the other parts, and which are furthest from the centre. EG *Peel off the outer plastic cover of the flex... ...the building's outer walls.*
ADJ CLASSIF: ATTRIB

outermost /aʊtəməʊst/. The **outermost** thing in a group of things is the one that is furthest from the centre. EG *The outermost wall is 150 metres away.*
ADJ CLASSIF: ATTRIB

outer space refers to the area outside the Earth's atmosphere where the other planets and the stars are situated. EG *...radiation in outer space.*
N UNCOUNT

outfit /aʊtfɪt/, **outfits. 1** An **outfit** is a set of clothes. EG *She wore a black ski outfit... I can't afford a new evening outfit.*
N COUNT: USU+SUPP

2 You can refer to an organization as an **outfit**. EG *I joined this outfit hoping to go abroad... ...a couple of guys from a security outfit.*
N COUNT Informal

outgoing /aʊtgəʊɪŋ/, **outgoings. 1** You use **outgoing** to describe **1.1** someone who is leaving an important job. EG *...the outgoing president in his last days of office.* **1.2** something that is leaving a place. EG *...outgoing mail... ...incoming and outgoing passengers.*
ADJ CLASSIF: ATTRIB

2 Someone who is **outgoing** is very friendly and eager to meet and talk to people. EG *Adler was an outgoing, sociable kind of man.*
ADJ QUALIT

3 Your **outgoings** are the amounts of money
N PLURAL

which you spend. EG *Try to reduce as many outgoings as possible.*

outgrow /aʊtgrəʊ/, **outgrows, outgrowing, outgrew, outgrown. 1** If you **outgrow** a piece of clothing, you get bigger and can no longer wear it. EG *Small children outgrow their shoes at a fast rate.* V+O

2 If you **outgrow** a way of behaving, you stop behaving in that way because you are older and more mature. EG *She had now outgrown her juvenile sense of humour.* V+O

outhouse /aʊthaʊs/, **outhouses.** An **outhouse** is a small building or shed attached to a house or in its garden. N COUNT

outing /aʊtɪŋ/, **outings.** An **outing** is an occasion on which you leave your house, school, or place of work, usually for an enjoyable activity. EG *...family outings on the River Thames... We went on a theatre outing.* N COUNT

outlandish /aʊtlændɪʃ/. If you describe something as **outlandish**, you mean that it very unusual or strange. EG *He was ashamed of his father's outlandish looks... ...an outlandish idea.* ADJ QUALIT

outlast /aʊtlɑːst/, **outlasts, outlasting, outlasted.** If one thing **outlasts** another, it lives or exists longer than the other thing. EG *Even those trees would outlast him... She had not yet outlasted her usefulness to the party.* V+O

outlaw /aʊtlɔː/, **outlaws, outlawing, outlawed. 1** When something **is outlawed**, it is made illegal. EG *...legislation which will outlaw this system... The use of poison gas was outlawed.* V+O

2 An **outlaw** is a criminal who is hiding from the authorities. EG *...a band of outlaws.* N COUNT Outdated

outlay /aʊtleɪ/, **outlays.** An **outlay** is an amount of money that is invested in a project or business. EG *...an initial outlay for clothing and books... ...a total outlay of £72,550.* N COUNT : USU+SUPP Formal

outlet /aʊtlɪ²t/, **outlets. 1** An **outlet** is an activity which allows you to express your feelings or ideas. EG *They can find no outlet for their grievances... Competitiveness can find an outlet in sport.* N COUNT

2 An **outlet** is also a hole or pipe through which water or air can flow away. EG *...the sewage outlet... ...an outlet pipe.* N COUNT

outline /aʊtlaɪn/, **outlines, outlining, outlined. 1** If you **outline** an idea or plan, you explain it in a very general way. EG *I outlined my reasons.* ▸ used as a noun. EG *...a brief outline of European art.* ● If you describe something **in outline**, you describe it in a very general way. V+O ▸ N SING ● PHRASE

2 You say that an object **is outlined** when you can see its general shape because there is a light behind it. EG *He was clearly outlined in the light of a lamp.* ▸ used as a noun. EG *He saw the outline of a house against the sky.* V+O : USU PASS ▸ N SING

outlive /aʊtlɪv/, **outlives, outliving, outlived. 1** If you **outlive** someone, you are still alive after they have died. EG *Olivia outlived Pepita by eighteen years.* V+O

2 If something **outlives** something else, it still exists when the other thing no longer exists. EG *The organization had outlived its usefulness.* V+O

outlook /aʊtlʊk/. **1** Your **outlook** is your general attitude towards life. EG *My whole outlook on life had changed... They are European in outlook.* N UNCOUNT +SUPP

2 The **outlook** of a situation is the way it is likely to develop. EG *The economic outlook is bright.* N SING+SUPP

outlying /aʊtlaɪɪŋ/. **Outlying** places are far away from the main cities of a country. EG *...teachers from outlying villages.* ADJ CLASSIF : ATTRIB

outmoded /aʊtməʊdɪ²d/. Something that is **outmoded** is old-fashioned and no longer useful. EG *...outmoded techniques.* ADJ QUALIT

outnumber /aʊtnʌmbə/, **outnumbers, outnumbering, outnumbered.** If one group of people or things **outnumbers** another, it has more people or things in it than the other group. EG *The men outnumbered the women by four to one... They are outnumbered by the Democrats.* V+O

out of date. Something that is **out of date** is old-fashioned and no longer useful. EG *It wasn't published until 1972, by which time it was out of date... This is rather an out-of-date concept.* ADJ QUALIT

out of doors means outside a building rather than inside it. EG *Hunting dogs should be kept out of doors... We sat out-of-doors beneath the trees.* ADV

out-of-the-way. Out-of-the-way places are not often visited. EG *Our expeditions have been to some out-of-the-way places.* ADJ QUALIT

out of work. Someone who is **out of work** does not have a job. EG *...out-of-work actors.* ADJ CLASSIF

out-patient, out-patients. An **out-patient** is someone who receives treatment at a hospital but does not stay there overnight. EG *The psychiatrists dealt with her as an out-patient... ...an out-patient clinic.* N COUNT

outpost /aʊtpəʊst/, **outposts.** An **outpost** is a small settlement in a foreign country or a distant area. EG *...a trading outpost.* N COUNT

outpouring /aʊtpɔːrɪŋ/, **outpourings. 1** An **outpouring** of something is a large amount of it that is produced very rapidly. EG *...a prolific outpouring of ideas and energy... ...an outpouring of wild rumours.* N COUNT+SUPP

2 Someone's **outpourings** are strong feelings that they express in speech or writing in an uncontrolled way. EG *...the hysterical outpourings of fanatics... ...John's sentimental outpourings.* N PLURAL +SUPP

output /aʊtpʊt/, **outputs. 1** You use **output** to refer to the amount of something that a person or thing produces. EG *The party maintains a constant output of pamphlets... Their total industrial output grew at an annual rate of 7%.* N UNCOUNT OR N COUNT

2 The **output** of a computer is the information that it displays on a screen or prints on paper as a result of a particular program. N UNCOUNT OR N COUNT

outrage /aʊtreɪdʒ/, **outrages, outraging, outraged. 1** If something **outrages** you, it makes you extremely shocked and angry. EG *The idea outraged me... One woman was outraged by this response.* ◇ **outraged.** EG *...the expression of outraged dignity on his face.* V+O ◇ ADJ QUALIT

2 Outrage is a strong feeling of anger and shock. EG *Benn shared this sense of outrage.* N UNCOUNT

3 An **outrage** is an act or event which people find very shocking, especially one that involves violence. EG *There have been more reports of bomb outrages in Falmouth... 'It's an outrage!' says Howard. 'Who invited him?'* N COUNT

outrageous /aʊtreɪdʒəs/. If you describe something as **outrageous**, you mean that you find it very shocking. EG *She used to say some outrageous things... ...outrageous crimes.* ◇ **outrageously.** EG *He was behaving outrageously.* ADJ QUALIT ◇ ADV OR SUBMOD

outright /aʊtraɪt/. **1** You use **outright** to describe actions and behaviour that are open and direct, rather than indirect. EG *...an outright refusal... ...outright hostility... If I ask outright I get nowhere.* ADJ CLASSIF : ATTRIB OR ADV

2 Outright also means complete and total. EG *...an outright victory... The government has banned it outright.* ● If someone **is killed outright**, they die immediately rather than being injured and dying slowly. ADJ CLASSIF : ATTRIB OR ADV ● PHRASE

outset /aʊtset/. If something happens **at the outset** of an event, process, or period of time, it happens at the very beginning of it. If something happens **from the outset**, it happens from the beginning onwards. EG *You should explain this to him at the outset... The police had participated from the outset.* PHRASE

outside /aʊtsaɪd/. **1** The **outside** of a container or building is the part which surrounds or encloses the rest of it. EG *...the outside of the bottle...* N COUNT OR ADJ CLASSIF : ATTRIB

Is an outsider out of doors?

Examine the property closely from the outside... ...a wooden shed that stood against the outside wall.

2 If you are **outside**, you are not inside a building but are quite close to it. EG *Let's go outside... It was dark outside... There was a demonstration outside the Social Security office... ...an outside lavatory.* ADV, PREP, OR ADJ CLASSIF : ATTRIB

3 If you are **outside** a room, you are not in it but are in the hall or corridor next to it. EG *He's on the landing outside.* ADV OR PREP

4 When you talk about the **outside** world, you are referring to things that happen or exist in places other than your own home or community. EG *They don't want to go out into the outside world.* ADJ CLASSIF

5 People or things **outside** a country, town, or region are not in it. EG *Nobody outside California knew much about him... ...a small village just outside Birmingham... We live outside of London.* PREP, OR ADV+*of*

6 On a wide road, the **outside** lanes are the ones which are closest to its centre. ADJ CLASSIF : ATTRIB

7 People who are **outside** a group or organization are not members of it. EG *The bill was supported by a mass movement outside Parliament... Since 1974, no outside body has questioned the advice.* PREP OR ADJ CLASSIF : ATTRIB

8 Something that is **outside** a particular range of things is not included within it. EG *The pipeline was outside his range of responsibility.* PREP

9 Something that happens **outside** a particular period of time does not happen during that time. EG *You'll have to do it outside office hours.* PREP

outsider /aʊtsaɪdə/, **outsiders.** An **outsider** is **1** someone who is not involved with a particular group or organization. EG *...an independent committee of seven outsiders.* **2** someone who is not accepted by a group, or who feels that they do not belong in it. EG *...the sense of being out of place, of being an outsider.* N COUNT

outsize /aʊtsaɪz/. **1 Outsize** or **outsized** things are much larger than usual. EG *...a blonde with outsize spectacles... ...an outsized envelope.* ADJ CLASSIF : ATTRIB

2 Outsize clothes are specially made for very large people. ADJ CLASSIF : ATTRIB

outskirts /aʊtskɜːts/. The **outskirts** of a city or town are the parts that are furthest from its centre. EG *The garage was on the outskirts of town... They should reach the outskirts of London on May 27th.* N PLURAL : USU *the*+N+*of*

outsmart /aʊtsmɑːt/, **outsmarts, outsmarting, outsmarted.** If you **outsmart** someone, you cleverly defeat them or gain an advantage over them. EG *The council outsmarted us by releasing their own press statement.* V+O

outspoken /aʊtspəʊkən/. If you are **outspoken**, you give your opinions about things openly, even if they shock people. EG *You are younger and more outspoken than they are... ...clear, outspoken statements.* ADJ QUALIT

outstanding /aʊtstændɪŋ/. **1** If you describe a person or their work as **outstanding**, you mean that they are very good, especially when compared to others. EG *She would never be an outstanding actress... His war record was outstanding.* ADJ QUALIT

◇ **outstandingly.** EG *...an outstandingly successful director.* ◇ SUBMOD

2 Outstanding also means very obvious or important. EG *There are significant exceptions, of which oil is the outstanding example.* ADJ CLASSIF : ATTRIB

3 Money that is **outstanding** has not yet been paid and is still owed to someone. EG *There is fifty pounds outstanding... ...£280 in outstanding fines.* ADJ CLASSIF

outstretched /aʊtstrɛtʃt/. If your arms or hands are **outstretched**, they are stretched out as far as possible. EG *...balancing himself with outstretched arms... He sat there, hand outstretched in greeting.* ADJ CLASSIF

outstrip /aʊtstrɪp/, **outstrips, outstripping, outstripped.** If one thing **outstrips** another thing, it becomes larger in amount or more successful than the other thing. EG *His wealth far outstripped Northcliffe's... His newspaper outstripped its rivals in circulation.* V+O

outward /aʊtwəd/, **outwards. 1** If something moves or faces **outwards** or **outward**, it moves or faces away from the place you are in or the place you are talking about. EG *He swam outwards into the bay... The door opened outwards.* ADV AFTER VB

2 An **outward** journey is a journey that you make away from a place that you are intending to return to later. EG *It was time to begin the outward trek... Our journey outwards was delayed at the airport.* ADJ CLASSIF : ATTRIB OR ADV

3 The **outward** feelings or qualities of someone or something are the ones they appear to have, rather than the ones they actually have. EG *I said it with what I hoped was outward calm.* ◇ **outwardly.** EG *He is seething, but outwardly he remains composed... Outwardly they have much in common.* ADJ CLASSIF : ATTRIB ◇ ADV

4 The **outward** features of something are the ones that you can see from the outside. EG *...the outward and visible signs of the disease.* ADJ CLASSIF : ATTRIB

outweigh /aʊtweɪ/, **outweighs, outweighing, outweighed.** If you say that the advantages of an action **outweigh** the disadvantages, you mean that the advantages are more important than the disadvantages, and that the action is worth doing. EG *The benefits from the medicine outweigh the risks of treatment.* V+O Formal

outwit /aʊtwɪt/, **outwits, outwitting, outwitted.** If you **outwit** someone, you cleverly defeat them or gain an advantage over them. EG *They managed to outwit Bill and get inside.* V+O

outworn /aʊtwɔːn/. An **outworn** idea or method is old-fashioned and no longer useful. EG *...an outworn superstition.* ADJ CLASSIF Formal

oval /əʊvəºl/, **ovals.** An **oval** is a shape that is like a circle, but is wider in one direction than the other. See picture at SHAPES. EG *...an oval mirror.* N COUNT : OFT N MOD

ovary /əʊvəºri¹/, **ovaries.** A woman's **ovaries** are the two organs in her body that produce eggs. N COUNT Technical

ovation /ə⁶veɪʃəºn/, **ovations.** An **ovation** is a long burst of applause. EG *The crowd broke into a thunderous ovation.* ● If you receive a **standing ovation**, the audience stand up and applaud you. EG *Joan got the loudest and longest standing ovation I have heard.* N COUNT Formal ● PHRASE

oven /ʌvəºn/, **ovens.** An **oven** is a cooker or part of a cooker that is like a box with a door. You put food inside the oven in order to cook it. EG *She took the pie out of the oven.* N COUNT

over /əʊvə/. **1** If one thing is **over** another thing, **1.1** it is directly above it, with a space between them. EG *I had reached the little bridge over the stream... ...the monument over the west door.* **1.2** it is supported by it and its ends are hanging down on each side of it. EG *Leave it to dry over the back of the sofa.* **1.3** it covers it. EG *Her hair hung down over her eyes... Place a piece of blotting paper over the stain... She was wearing a short robe over her bathing suit... Students were spraying paint over each other.* PREP

2 If you look **over** or talk **over** an object, you look or talk across the top of it. EG *The ponies would come and look over the wall... She was watching him over the rim of her cup.* PREP

3 If you look **over** a piece of writing or a collection of things, you quickly look at all the writing or all the things. EG *He ran his eye over one particular paragraph.* PREP

4 If a window has a view **over** a piece of land, you can see the land through the window. EG *The windows look out over a park.* PREP

5 All over a place means in every part of it. EG *I've been all over Austria... They come from all over the world.* PREP

6 If you go **over** to a place, you go to it. EG *The doctor walked over to the door... I've got some friends coming over tonight... Liz, come over here.* ADV AFTER VB

7 If someone or something moves **over** an area or surface, they move across it. EG *She ran back, skipping over the grass... His pen moved rapidly over the paper.* PREP

8 If you go **over** something such as a river, bridge, or boundary, you cross it. EG *...on the way back over the Channel... We crossed over into Tennessee very late that night.* PREP, OR ADV+PREP

9 If something is on the opposite side of a road or river, you can say that it is **over** the road or river. EG *Eastwards over the Severn lie the hills.* PREP

10 If something is **over** in a particular position, it is a short distance away from you. EG *Mr Stryker was standing over by the window.* ADV+PREP

11 Over there means in a place a short distance away from you, or in another country. **Over here** means near you, or in the country you are in. EG *Who's the woman over there?... Are you over here on a trip?* PHRASE

12 If someone or something gets **over** a barrier, they get to the other side of it by going across the top of it. EG *Castle stepped over the dog... They throw their rubbish over the fence into the neighbour's garden.* PREP

13 If you lean **over**, you bend your body in a particular direction. If you are leaning **over** an object, you have bent your body and the top part of it is above the object. EG *Pat leaned over and picked it up... He crouched over a typewriter.* ADV AFTER VB, OR PREP

14 If something rolls **over** or is turned **over**, its position changes so that the part that was facing upwards is now facing downwards. EG *He flicked over the page... She tipped the pan over.* ADV AFTER VB

15 If something is **over** a particular amount, measurement, or age, it is more than that amount, measurement, or age. EG *They paid out over 3 million pounds... ...people aged 80 or over... She did it for over a week.* PREP OR ADV

16 Over and above something means in addition to it. EG *They have difficulties over and above the usual disadvantages suffered by poor children.* PREP

17 If you say that an activity is **over** or **all over**, you mean that it is completely finished. EG *Rodin's search was over... Why worry her when it's all over?* ADV

18 If someone has control or influence **over** other people, they are able to control them or influence them. EG *...his authority over them.* PREP

19 You also use **over** to indicate what a disagreement or feeling relates to or is caused by. EG *...disagreements over administrative policies... They were always quarrelling over women... ...the anxiety which the Commander suffered over it... I found him still chuckling over a telephone call he had received.* PREP

20 If something happens **over** a period of time or **over** a meal or a drink, it happens during that time or during that meal or drink. EG *He'd had flu over Christmas... ...a process developed over many decades... I was going to read it over lunch.* PREP

21 If you say that something is happening **all over again**, you mean that it is happening again, and you are implying that it is tiring, boring, or unpleasant. EG *The whole thing began all over again.* PHRASE

22 If you say that something happened **over and over** or **over and over again**, you mean that it happened many times. EG *I read it over and over again... Over and over, the same stories kept cropping up.* PHRASE

over-. You can add **over-** to an adjective or verb to indicate that a quality exists or an action is done to too great an extent. For example, if you say that someone is being over-cautious, you mean that they are being too cautious. EG *...an over-confident young man... ...over-ripe fruit... My mother had always over-protected me.* PREFIX

overall, overalls; pronounced /əʊvərºɔ:l/ when it is an adjective or an adverb and /əʊvərºɔ:l/ when it is a noun.

1 You use **overall** to indicate that you are talking about a situation in general or about the whole of something. EG *...the overall pattern of his life... The overall impression was of a smoky industrial city.* ADJ CLASSIF : ATTRIB

▸ used as an adverb. EG *Overall, imports account for half of our stock.* ▸ ADV SEN

2 Overalls consist of a single piece of clothing that combines trousers and a jacket. You wear overalls over your clothes in order to protect them from dirt while you are working. N PLURAL

3 An **overall** is a piece of clothing shaped like a coat that you wear over your clothes in order to protect them from dirt while you are working. N COUNT

overawe /əʊvərɔ:/, **overawes, overawing, overawed.** If you **are overawed** by something, you are very impressed by it and a little afraid of it. EG *Don't be overawed by what the experts say.* V+O : USU PASS

overbalance /əʊvəbæləns/, **overbalances, overbalancing, overbalanced.** If you **overbalance**, you fall over or nearly fall over, because you are not in a steady position. V

overbearing /əʊvəbɛərɪŋ/. Someone who is **overbearing** tries to make other people do what he or she wants in an unpleasant and forceful way. EG *...her jealous, overbearing mother-in-law.* ADJ QUALIT

overboard /əʊvəbɔ:d/. **1** If you fall **overboard**, you fall over the side of a ship into the water. EG *He had to hang on to avoid being washed overboard.* ADV AFTER VB

2 If you **throw** a plan or idea **overboard**, you abandon it because you think that it is no longer useful. EG *They threw Baldwin's policy overboard.* PHRASE Informal

overcame /əʊvəkeɪm/ is the past tense of **overcome.**

overcast /əʊvəkɑ:st/. If it is **overcast**, there are a lot of clouds in the sky and the light is poor. EG *It was a warm day, but overcast... ...the grey, overcast sky.* ADJ QUALIT

overcoat /əʊvəkəʊt/, **overcoats.** An **overcoat** is a thick, warm coat that you wear in winter. N COUNT

overcome /əʊvəkʌm/, **overcomes, overcoming, overcame** /əʊvəkeɪm/. The form **overcome** is used in the present tense and is also the past participle.

1 If you **overcome** a problem or a feeling, you successfully deal with it or control it. EG *I was still trying to overcome my fear of the dark... We tried to overcome their objections to the plan.* V+O

2 If you **are overcome** by a feeling, you feel it very strongly. EG *I was overcome by a sense of failure... He was overcome with astonishment.* V+O : USU PASS

overcrowded /əʊvəkraʊdɪ^{2}d/. If a place is **overcrowded**, there are too many things or people in it. EG *...overcrowded cities... ...the overcrowded sitting-room.* ADJ QUALIT

overcrowding /əʊvəkraʊdɪŋ/. You say that there is **overcrowding** when more people are living in a place than it was designed for. EG *There is serious overcrowding in our prisons.* N UNCOUNT

overdo /əʊvədu:/, **overdoes** /əʊvədʌz/, **overdoing, overdid** /əʊvədɪd/, **overdone** /əʊvədʌn/. **1** If someone **overdoes** something, they behave in an exaggerated way. EG *Wish them luck, but don't overdo it or they may become suspicious.* V+O

2 If you **overdo** an activity, you try to do more than you can physically manage. EG *Don't overdo it. It's very hot in the sun.* V+O

overdone /əʊvədʌn/. If you say that food is **overdone**, you mean that it has been cooked for too long. ADJ PRED

overdose /əʊvədəʊs/, **overdoses.** If someone takes an **overdose** of a drug, they take more of it than is safe. EG *Alice took an overdose after a row with her mother... ...an overdose of sleeping pills.* N COUNT

overdraft /əʊvədrɑ:ft/, **overdrafts.** An **overdraft** is an arrangement with a bank that allows you to spend more money than you have in your account. EG *She asked for a fifty-pound overdraft.* N COUNT

overdue /əʊvədju:/. **1** If a person, bus, or train is **overdue**, they have not arrived and it is after the ADJ QUALIT

If it is overcast, do you wear an overcoat?

time when they were expected to arrive. EG *They're half an hour overdue. I wish they'd come.*

2 If you say that a change or an event is **overdue**, you mean that it should have happened before now. EG *Reform in all these areas is long overdue.* ADJ QUALIT

3 If something borrowed or due to be paid is **overdue**, it is now later than the date when it should have been returned or paid. EG *The rent on his apartment was three weeks overdue... ...overdue library books.* ADJ QUALIT

overestimate /əʊvər^{0}ɛstɪmeɪt/, **overestimates, overestimating, overestimated. 1** If you **overestimate** something, you think that it is greater in amount or importance than it really is. EG *We greatly overestimated the time this would take... It is possible to overestimate the problem.* V+O

2 If you **overestimate** someone, you think that they have more of a skill or quality than they really have. EG *Her confidence drained away and he knew he had overestimated her.* V+O

overflow, overflows, overflowing, overflowed; pronounced /əʊvəfləʊ/ when it is a verb and /əʊvəfləʊ/ when it is a noun.

1 If a liquid or a river **overflows**, it flows over the edges of the container it is in or the place where it is. EG *He was careful to see that the jar did not overflow... Rivers often overflow their banks.* V OR V-ERG

2 When people **overflow** a place, there are too many of them in it and some of them have to go outside. EG *The crowd overflowed the auditorium.* V OR V-ERG

3 If something **is overflowing** with things, it is too full of them. EG *The table was overflowing with clothes.* V+*with* : USU CONT ● If you say that something is filled **to overflowing** or full **to overflowing**, you mean that it is extremely full. EG *The ashtrays were full to overflowing.* ● PHRASE

4 If someone **is overflowing** with a feeling, they are experiencing it very strongly and show this in their behaviour. EG *...a nurse overflowing with love.* V : OFT+*with*

5 An **overflow** is a hole or pipe through which liquid can flow out of a container when it gets too full. EG *...the sink overflow... ...overflow pipes.* N COUNT

overgrown /əʊvəgrəʊn/. If a place is **overgrown**, it is thickly covered with plants because it has not been looked after. EG *...a large house, overgrown with brambles... ...the overgrown path.* ADJ QUALIT

overhang /əʊvəhæŋ/, **overhangs, overhanging, overhung** /əʊvəhʌŋ/. If one thing **overhangs** another, **1** it sticks out sideways above it. EG *...a tree which overhung the lake... ...the shadow of an overhanging rock.* **2** it is supported by it and hangs down its sides. EG *...wet clothes overhang the tub.* V+O OR V

overhaul /əʊvəhɔːl/, **overhauls, overhauling, overhauled. 1** If you **overhaul** a piece of equipment, you clean it, check it thoroughly, and repair any faults. EG *The engines were overhauled before our departure.* V+O

2 If you **overhaul** a system or method, you examine it carefully and change it in order to improve it. EG *The company needs to overhaul its techniques and methods.* ▸ used as a noun. EG *...a major overhaul of the country's educational system.* V+O ▸ N COUNT

overhead, overheads; pronounced /əʊvəhɛd/ when it is an adverb and /əʊvəhɛd/ when it is an adjective or a noun. **1** If something is **overhead**, it is above you or above the place that you are talking about. EG *Seagulls were circling overhead... The guard switched on an overhead light.* ADV OR ADJ CLASSIF : ATTRIB

2 The **overheads** of a business are its regular and essential expenses. EG *...reducing expenditure on overheads.* N PLURAL

overhear /əʊvəhɪə/, **overhears, overhearing, overheard** /əʊvəhɜːd/. If you **overhear** someone, you hear what they are saying when they are not talking to you and they do not know that you are listening. EG *Judy overheard him telling the children about it... I was too far away to overhear their conversation.* V+O

overheat /əʊvəhiːt/, **overheats, overheating, overheated.** If a piece of equipment **overheats**, it becomes hotter than it should, usually because there is a fault in it. EG *The appliances might overheat and catch fire.* V-ERG

overhung /əʊvəhʌŋ/ is the past tense and past participle of **overhang.**

overjoyed /əʊvədʒɔɪd/. If you are **overjoyed**, you are extremely pleased about something. EG *Francis was overjoyed to see him... They were overjoyed at this treatment.* ADJ PRED

overland /əʊvəlænd/. An **overland** journey is made across land rather than by ship or aeroplane. EG *...an overland march across the desert... You travelled overland to India?* ADJ CLASSIF OR ADV AFTER VB

overlap; overlaps, overlapping, overlapped; pronounced /əʊvəlæp/ when it is a verb and /əʊvəlæp/ when it is a noun.

1 If one thing **overlaps** another, one part of it covers a part of the other thing. EG *The circles overlap... A quilt must overlap the sides of the bed.* V OR V+O : RECIP

2 If two ideas or activities **overlap**, they involve some of the same subjects, people, or periods of time. EG *We worked overlapping shifts so there were always two of us on duty.* ▸ used as a noun. EG *There is no overlap between our material and that of Lipset.* V, V+O, OR V+*with* : RECIP ▸ N UNCOUNT OR N COUNT

overload /əʊvələʊd/, **overloads, overloading, overloaded. 1** If you **overload** a vehicle, you put more things or people into it than it was designed to carry. EG *...little boats overloaded with desperate people.* V+O : USU PASS

2 If you **overload** an electrical system, you connect too many appliances to it and damage it. EG *Your fuse has blown because you have overloaded the circuit.* V+O

3 If you **overload** someone with work or problems, you give them more work or problems than they can cope with. EG *Medical services were overloaded with casualties.* V+O : USU PASS +*with*

overlook /əʊvəlʊk/, **overlooks, overlooking, overlooked. 1** If a building or window **overlooks** a place, you can see the place clearly from the building or window. EG *Elegant buildings overlooked the square... ...a room which overlooked the garden.* V+O

2 If you **overlook** a fact or problem, you ignore it, do not notice it, or do not realize its importance. EG *They overlook the enormous risks involved.* V+O

3 If you **overlook** someone's faults or bad behaviour, you forgive them and do not criticize them. EG *I decided to overlook his unkindness.* V+O

overnight /əʊvənaɪt/. **1 Overnight** means during all of the night. EG *If you leave your bike here overnight, it's likely to disappear... Soak the raisins overnight in water... ...an overnight stay.* ADV OR ADJ CLASSIF : ATTRIB

2 Overnight cases or clothes are ones that you take when you go and stay somewhere for one or two nights. EG *He packed a little overnight bag.* ADJ CLASSIF : ATTRIB

3 You can say that something happened **overnight** when it happened very quickly and unexpectedly. EG *The colonel became a hero overnight... You can't expect these problems to be solved overnight.* ADV

overpass /əʊvəpɑːs/, **overpasses.** An **overpass** is a structure which carries one road over the top of another one. N COUNT American

overpopulated /əʊvəpɒpjə^{4}leɪtɪ^{2}d/. A city or country that is **overpopulated** has too many people living in it. ADJ CLASSIF

overpopulation /əʊvəpɒpjə^{4}leɪʃə^{0}n/. If there is **overpopulation** in a place, there are too many people living there. EG *Many problems are caused by poverty and overpopulation.* N UNCOUNT

overpower /əʊvəpaʊə/, **overpowers, overpowering, overpowered. 1** If you **overpower** someone, you seize them despite their struggles because you are stronger than they are. EG *They easily overpowered her and dragged her inside.* V+O

2 If an emotion or sensation **overpowers** you, it V+O

affects you very strongly. EG *Occasionally this desire overpowers me and leads me to be cruel.*
◇ **overpowering.** EG *...an overpowering feeling of failure... ...an overpowering anger.* ◇ ADJ QUALIT

overran /əʊvəræn/ is the past tense of **overrun.**

overrate /əʊvəreɪt/, **overrates, overrating, overrated.** If you **overrate** something, you think it is better or more important than it really is. EG *They overrate the extent of political freedom in England.* ◇ **overrated.** EG *They feel that maths is somewhat overrated as a school subject.* V+O; ◇ ADJ QUALIT

override /əʊvəraɪd/, **overrides, overriding, overrode** /əʊvərəʊd/, **overridden** /əʊvərɪdəⁿn/. **1** You say that something **overrides** other things when people decide that it is more important than these things. EG *The day-to-day struggle for survival overrode all other things... These common interests override the divisions between them.* V+O

2 If you **override** a person or their decisions, you cancel their decisions because you have more authority than they have. EG *Will they dare override what the people decide?* V+O

overriding /əʊvəraɪdɪŋ/ means more important than anything else in a particular situation. EG *The overriding need in the world is to promote peace.* ADJ CLASSIF : ATTRIB

overrule /əʊvəruːl/, **overrules, overruling, overruled.** If someone in authority **overrules** a person or **overrules** their decisions, they officially decide that their decisions are incorrect or not valid. EG *The judgement was overruled by the Supreme Court... Frank was overruled by the planners in Berlin.* V+O

overrun /əʊvərʌn/, **overruns, overrunning, overran** /əʊvəræn/, **overrun. 1** If an army **overruns** a country, it succeeds in occupying it very quickly. EG *The north was overrun by the advancing troops.* V+O

2 If animals or plants **overrun** a place, they spread quickly all over it. EG *The city is overrun by rodents.* V+O

3 If an event or meeting **overruns**, it continues for a longer time than it was intended to. EG *I think we've overrun our time, haven't we?* V OR V+O

overseas /əʊvəsiːz/. **1** You use **overseas** to describe things that happen or exist in foreign countries that you must cross the sea to get to. EG *There is a vast overseas market for our goods... Roughly 4 million Americans travel overseas each year.* ADJ CLASSIF : ATTRIB OR ADV

2 An **overseas** student or visitor comes from a foreign country that you must cross the sea to get to. ADJ CLASSIF : ATTRIB

oversee /əʊvəsiː/, **oversees, overseeing, oversaw** /əʊvəsɔː/, **overseen.** If someone in authority **oversees** a job or an activity, they make sure that it is done properly. EG *We need a guy to oversee our operations in Guyana.* V+O

overseer /əʊvəsiːə/, **overseers.** An **overseer** is someone whose job is to make sure that employees are working properly. N COUNT

overshadow /əʊvəʃædəʊ/, **overshadows, overshadowing, overshadowed. 1** You say that one thing **overshadows** another when it is much taller than the other thing and is close to it. EG *...the elm trees overshadowing the school.* V+O

2 If someone or something **is overshadowed** by another person or thing, they are less successful, important, or impressive than the other person or thing. EG *She was sometimes overshadowed by the more talkative members... This incident was soon overshadowed by a greater drama.* V+O : USU PASS

3 If an unpleasant event or feeling **overshadows** something, it affects it and makes it less happy or enjoyable. EG *The closing entry of the diary is overshadowed by Pepys's fear of his failing eyesight.* V+O : USU PASS

overshoot /əʊvəʃuːt/, **overshoots, overshooting, overshot** /əʊvəʃɒt/. If you **overshoot** a place that you want to get to, you go too far or too fast and pass the place by mistake. EG *Natalie's glider overshot the landing zone and crashed into a field.* V+O OR V

oversight /əʊvəsaɪt/, **oversights.** An **oversight** is something which you do not do and which you should have done. EG *My oversight was in not remembering to inform the authorities... Through some administrative oversight, he was released.* N COUNT OR N UNCOUNT

oversimplify /əʊvəsɪmplɪfaɪ/, **oversimplifies, oversimplifying, oversimplified.** If you **oversimplify** something, you describe or explain it so simply that what you say is no longer true or reasonable. EG *We may have oversimplified the discussion by ignoring this.* ◇ **oversimplified.** EG *...an oversimplified view of the world.* V+O OR V; ◇ ADJ QUALIT

oversize /əʊvəsaɪz/. You say that things are **oversize** or **oversized** when they are too big, or much bigger than usual. EG *...a girl in an oversize pair of slacks... ...an oversized tent.* ADJ CLASSIF

oversleep /əʊvəsliːp/, **oversleeps, oversleeping, overslept** /əʊvəslept/. If you **oversleep**, you sleep longer than you intended to. EG *Some mornings I oversleep and miss breakfast.* V

overstate /əʊvəsteɪt/, **overstates, overstating, overstated.** If you **overstate** something, you describe or explain it in a way that exaggerates its importance or a quality that it has. EG *Its effect on history cannot be overstated... She may be overstating the case.* V+O

overstep /əʊvəstep/, **oversteps, overstepping, overstepped.** If you **overstep the mark**, you behave in an unacceptable way. EG *Last week he overstepped the mark and there will be trouble.* PHRASE

overt /əʊvɜːt/. An action or attitude that is **overt** is done or shown in an open and obvious way. EG *...overt hostility... ...overt acts of violence.* ◇ **overtly.** EG *His jokes got more overtly malicious.* ADJ QUALIT; ◇ ADV

overtake /əʊvəteɪk/, **overtakes, overtaking, overtook** /əʊvətʊk/, **overtaken. 1** If you **overtake** a moving vehicle or person, you pass them because you are moving faster than they are. EG *The truck had overtaken us... I was overtaken by a car.* V+O OR V

2 If an event **overtakes** you, it happens unexpectedly or suddenly. EG *...all the changes that have overtaken Shetland recently.* V+O

3 If a feeling **overtakes** you, it affects you very strongly. EG *Utter weariness overtook me.* V+O Literary

overthrow, overthrows, overthrowing, overthrew /əʊvəθruː/, **overthrown. Overthrow** is pronounced /əʊvəθrəʊ/ when it is a verb and /əʊvəθrəʊ/ when it is a noun. **1** When a government or a leader **is overthrown**, they are removed by force. EG *He was arrested for attempting to overthrow the regime.* ▸ used as a noun. EG *...the overthrow of the dictator.* V+O; ▸ N COUNT

2 If an idea, value or standard **is overthrown**, it is replaced by another one. EG *Laws are openly violated, standards of behaviour are overthrown.* V+O : USU PASS

overtime /əʊvətaɪm/ is time that you spend at your job in addition to your normal working hours. EG *He had been putting in overtime whenever he could.* ▸ used as an adverb. *They often worked overtime.* N UNCOUNT; ▸ ADV

overtone /əʊvətəʊn/, **overtones.** If something has **overtones** of an idea or quality, it suggests that idea or quality but does not openly express it. EG *The play has heavy political overtones... ...a pleasure that carried no overtones of fear.* N COUNT : USU PLURAL +SUPP

overtook /əʊvətʊk/ is the past tense of **overtake.**

overture /əʊvətjʊə/, **overtures. 1** An **overture** is a piece of music, often one that is the introduction to an opera or play. EG *...Elgar's 'Cockaigne' Overture.* N COUNT

2 If you make **overtures** to someone, you behave in a friendly or romantic way towards them. EG *Mrs* N PLURAL : USU+SUPP

If you make overtures to someone, do you play them a piece of music?

Thorne had made overtures of friendship... He feared they would reject his overtures.

overturn /əʊvətɜːn/, **overturns, overturning, overturned. 1** If something **overturns** or if you **overturn** it, it turns upside down or on its side. EG *She overturned the chairs and hurled the cushions about... His car crashed into a tree and overturned.* V-ERG

2 If someone who has more authority or power than you **overturns** your decision, they change it. EG *If they persist in their attitude he can't overturn their decision.* V+O

3 To **overturn** a government or system means to remove it or destroy it. EG *The unrest might have overturned the military rulers.* V+O

overview /əʊvəvjuː/, **overviews.** An **overview** of a situation is a a general understanding or description of it as a whole. EG *...a short report giving a useful overview of recent developments.* N COUNT: USU SING+*of*

overweight /əʊvəweɪt/. If someone is **overweight**, they are too fat, and therefore unhealthy. EG *Nearly half the people in this country are overweight... ...an overweight schoolgirl.* ADJ QUALIT

overwhelm /əʊvəwɛlm/, **overwhelms, overwhelming, overwhelmed. 1** If you **are overwhelmed** by a feeling or event, it affects you very strongly and suddenly. EG *He was overwhelmed by the intensity of her love... The horror of it all had overwhelmed me.* V+O: USU PASS

2 If a group of people **overwhelm** a place or another group, they gain complete control or victory over them. EG *Their mission was to seize the bridges and overwhelm the garrison.* V+O

overwhelming /əʊvəwɛlmɪŋ/. **1** Something that is **overwhelming** affects you very strongly. EG *...an overwhelming sense of powerlessness... The city is overwhelming and a little frightening.* ADJ QUALIT

◇ **overwhelmingly.** EG *They had been overwhelmingly appreciative.* ◇ ADV

2 You can use **overwhelming** to say that one part of something is much greater than the rest of it. EG *An overwhelming majority of people are in favour of this plan.* ◇ **overwhelmingly.** EG *It is still an overwhelmingly rural country.* ADJ CLASSIF ◇ ADV+ADJ

overwork /əʊvəwɜːk/, **overworks, overworking, overworked. 1** If you **are overworking** or **are overworked**, you are working too hard. EG *You look tired. Have you been overworking?... They were overworked and poorly paid.* ▸ used as a noun. EG *...a body made weak through undernourishment and overwork.* V-ERG ▸ N UNCOUNT

2 If you **overwork** something, you use it too much. EG *Farmers have overworked the soil.* V+O

◇ **overworked.** EG *'Crisis' has become one of the most overworked words of modern politics.* ◇ ADJ QUALIT

overwrought /əʊvərɔːt/. Someone who is **overwrought** is very upset and uncontrolled in their behaviour. EG *I am very tired and overwrought... Don't let people see you in this overwrought state.* ADJ QUALIT

ow /aʊ/. People say **'Ow!'** when they suddenly feel pain. EG *Ow! You're hurting me!* EXCLAM

owe /əʊ/, **owes, owing, owed. 1** If you **owe** money to someone, they have lent it to you and you have not yet paid it back. EG *I still owe you seven pounds... I paid Gower what I owed him.* V+O: OFT+*to*; ALSO V+O+O

2 If you **owe** a quality or ability to someone or something, they are responsible for giving it to you. EG *She owed her technique entirely to his teaching... The plains owe their fertility to the minerals deposited there by the river.* V+O+*to*

3 If you say that you **owe** someone gratitude, respect, or loyalty, you mean that they deserve it from you. EG *We owe you our thanks, Dr Marlowe... Neither he nor Melanie owe me any explanation.* V+O+O OR V+O+*to* Formal

4 You use **owing to** when you are introducing the reason for something. EG *I missed my flight owing to a traffic hold-up... There was some difficulty, owing to Baldwin's precarious position.* PREP

owl /aʊl/, **owls.** An **owl** is a bird with a flat face and large eyes, which hunts small animals at night. N COUNT

own /əʊn/, **owns, owning, owned. 1** You use **own 1.1** to emphasize that something belongs to a particular person. EG *She'd killed her own children... His background was similar to my own.* **1.2** to emphasize that something is typical of a particular person or thing. EG *Each city has its own peculiarities... His style is distinctive, very much his own.* **1.3** to emphasize that someone does something without any help from other people. EG *They are expected to make their own beds... I said 'What about lunch?' and he said, 'Oh, get your own.'* ADJ CLASSIF: ATTRIB, ONLY AFTER POSS

2 When you are **on** your **own**, you are alone. EG *She lived on her own... ...sitting on his own.* PHRASE

3 If you do something **on** your **own**, you do it without any help from other people. EG *We want to write a book on our own.* PHRASE

4 If you say that you have a particular thing **of** your **own**, you are emphasizing that you have it, rather than someone else. EG *She has troubles of her own... This type of glass has a colour and character all of its own.* PHRASE

5 If you **get** your **own back** on someone who has harmed you or tricked you, you harm them or trick them in return. PHRASE Informal

6 If you **own** something, it is your property, because you bought it or someone gave it to you. EG *...a huge old house owned by an Irish doctor... Who owns the land here?* V+O

7 to **hold** your **own**: see **hold**.

own up. If you **own up** to something wrong that you have done, you admit that you did it. EG *They don't want to own up to this... Was Bert owning up to Mrs Welch?* PHRASAL VB: V+ADV, OFT+*to*

owner /əʊnə/, **owners.** The **owner** of something is the person to whom it belongs. EG *The owner of the store was at his desk... The average car owner drives 10,000 miles per year.* N COUNT: USU+SUPP

ownership /əʊnəʃɪp/ is the state of owning something. EG *...public ownership of land... ...the desire for home ownership.* N UNCOUNT

ox /ɒks/, **oxen.** An **ox** is a bull that has been castrated. Oxen are used for pulling vehicles or carrying things. EG *...a plough pulled by two oxen.* N COUNT

oxygen /ɒksɪdʒəⁿn/ is a colourless gas that exists in large quantities in the air. All plants and animals need oxygen in order to live. Without oxygen, nothing can burn. N UNCOUNT

oyster /ɔɪstə/, **oysters.** An **oyster** is a large, flat shellfish. Some oysters can be eaten, others produce pearls. N COUNT

oz is a written abbreviation for 'ounce' or 'ounces'. EG *...3 oz of butter.*

P p

P, p /piː/, **Ps, p's. 1 P** is the sixteenth letter of the English alphabet. N COUNT
2 p is an abbreviation for 'pence' or 'penny'. EG *It's only 10p... ...a 50p piece.*
3 You write **p.** before a number as an abbreviation for 'page'. The plural form is 'pp.'. EG *See p. 72... ...Tables I and II on pp. 40-43.*

pace /peɪs/, **paces, pacing, paced. 1** The **pace** of something is the speed at which it happens or is done. EG *...the pace of change... The sale resumed at a brisk pace... He sets the pace.* N UNCOUNT: USU+SUPP
2 Your **pace** is the speed at which you walk. EG *He proceeds at a leisurely pace... He quickened his pace.* N SING: USU+SUPP
3 If something **keeps pace** with something else that is changing, it changes quickly in response to it. EG *Earnings have not kept pace with inflation... Any country which fails to keep pace with these developments will soon be in trouble.* PHRASE
4 If you **keep pace** with someone who is walking or running, you succeed in going as fast as them, so that you remain close to them. PHRASE
5 If you do something **at** your **own pace**, you do it at a speed that is comfortable for you. EG *It's best to let him do the job at his own pace.* PHRASE
6 If you take a number of **paces**, you walk that number of steps. EG *He took two quick paces forward.* N COUNT
7 A **pace** is also the distance that you move when you take one step. EG *He stopped when he was a few paces away.* N COUNT
8 If you **pace** a small area, you keep walking up and down it, because you are anxious or impatient. EG *She paced the room angrily... Harold paced nervously up and down the platform.* V+O OR V+A

pacifism /pæsɪfɪzəᵒm/ is the belief that war and violence are always wrong. ◇ **pacifist** /pæsɪfɪst/, **pacifists.** EG *I was accused of being a pacifist.* N UNCOUNT ◇ N COUNT

pacify /pæsɪfaɪ/, **pacifies, pacifying, pacified.** If you **pacify** someone who is angry or upset, you succeed in making them become calm. EG *The manager was trying hard to pacify our clients.* V+O

pack /pæk/, **packs, packing, packed. 1** When you **pack** a bag or when you **pack**, you put your belongings into a bag, because you are leaving a place or going on holiday. EG *He packed his bags and left.* ◇ **packing.** EG *Have you started your packing?* V+O OR V ◇ N UNCOUNT
2 When people **pack** things, for example in a factory, they put them into containers or parcels so that they can be transported and sold. V+O
3 If people or things **are packed** into a place or **pack** a place, there are so many of them that the place is full. EG *About 300 of us were packed into a half-built mansion... Thirty thousand people packed into the stadium to hear him.* V-ERG+A OR V+O
4 A **pack** is a bag containing your belongings that you carry on your back when you are travelling. N COUNT
5 A **pack** of things is a packet of them. EG *...a pack of cigarettes.* N COUNT American
6 A **pack** of playing cards is a complete set of playing cards. N COUNT
7 A **pack** of wolves or dogs is a group of them that hunt together. EG *They hunt in packs.* N COUNT OR N PART
8 You can refer to a group of people who go around together as a **pack**. EG *The boys always went about as a pack... They're like a pack of kids.* N COUNT OR N PART
9 See also **packed, packing**.

pack in. If you say that someone **has packed** something **in**, you mean that they have stopped doing it. EG *It's a good job. I don't think he'd pack it in.* PHRASAL VB: V+O+ADV Informal British

pack off. If you **pack** someone **off** somewhere, you send them there to stay for a period of time. EG *They pack their sons off to boarding school... I packed her off to bed.* PHRASAL VB: V+O+ADV Informal

pack up. If you **pack up** your belongings or if you **pack up**, you put all your belongings in a case or bag, because you are leaving. EG *Once term finishes we all pack up and go home.* PHRASAL VB: V+O+ADV OR V+ADV

package /pækɪdʒ/, **packages, packaging, packaged. 1** A **package** is a small parcel. EG *...a small package wrapped in tissue paper.* N COUNT
2 Some Americans refer to a packet as a **package**. EG *...a package of cigarettes.* N COUNT American
3 When something **is packaged**, it is put into packets to be sold. EG *The cereal is packaged in plain boxes.* V+O: USU PASS
4 A **package** is also a set of suggestions that are presented together and must be accepted or rejected as a group. EG *...the announcement of a fresh package of spending cuts... They offered a package worth sixty million dollars.* N COUNT

package holiday, package holidays. A **package holiday** or a **package tour** is a holiday arranged by a travel company in which your travel and your accommodation are booked for you. N COUNT

packaging /pækɪdʒɪŋ/ is the container that something is sold in. EG *...disposable packaging.* N UNCOUNT

packed /pækt/. **1** A place that is **packed** is very crowded. EG *The theatre was packed... ...a vast room packed with excited people... ...a packed courtroom.* ADJ QUALIT
2 Something that is **packed** with things contains a very large number of them. EG *The book is packed full of information.* ADJ PRED: OFT+with

packed lunch, packed lunches. A **packed lunch** is food, for example sandwiches, which you take to work, to school, or on an outing and eat as your lunch. N COUNT

packet /pækɪt/, **packets. 1** A **packet** is a small container in which a quantity of something is sold. Packets are either small boxes made of thin cardboard, or bags or envelopes made of paper or plastic. EG *The room was littered with cups and cigarette packets... Check the washing instructions on the packet.* N COUNT
2 When you refer to a **packet** of something, you are referring to a packet and its contents, or to the contents only. EG *...a packet of cigarettes... ...a packet of crisps... ...a packet of carrot seed.* N PART
3 A **packet** is also a small flat parcel. N COUNT

packing /pækɪŋ/ is the paper, plastic, or other material which is put round things that are being sent somewhere. ● See also **pack**. N UNCOUNT

packing case, packing cases. A **packing case** is a large wooden box in which things are put so that they can be stored or taken somewhere. N COUNT

pact /pækt/, **pacts.** A **pact** is a formal agreement between two or more people or governments to do a particular thing or to help each other. EG *A pact was signed banning all military activity... ...a non-aggression pact between the two countries.* N COUNT

pad /pæd/, **pads, padding, padded. 1** A **pad** is a fairly thick, flat piece of a material such as cloth or foam rubber. Pads are used, for example, to clean things or protect things. EG *Dab the wound with a cotton wool pad soaked in antiseptic... Elbow pads and knee pads are essential on a skateboard.* N COUNT
2 A **pad** of paper is a number of pieces of paper which are fixed together along the top or the side, so that each piece can be torn off when it has been used. EG *He took a pad and pencil from his pocket.* N COUNT
3 A helicopter **pad** or a launch **pad** is an area of N COUNT

flat, hard ground from which helicopters take off or rockets are launched. EG *The helicopter was in the air, hovering about a metre above the pad.*

4 You can refer to the place where you live as your **pad**, especially if it is a flat. EG *...his bachelor pad in Davies Street.* N COUNT Informal

5 When someone **pads** somewhere, they walk there with steps that are fairly quick and heavy but not very loud. EG *Harold padded out of the room.* V+A

6 A cat's or dog's **pads** are the soft, fleshy parts on the bottom of its paws. N COUNT: USU PLURAL

padded /pædɪ²d/. Something that is **padded** has soft material on it or inside it which makes it less hard, protects it, or gives it a different shape. EG *The steering wheel is padded with real leather... ...a padded bra... ...a padded sofa.* ADJ CLASSIF

padding /pædɪŋ/ is soft material which is put on something or inside it in order to make it less hard, to protect it, or to give it a different shape. EG *...a jacket with padding at the shoulders.* N UNCOUNT

paddle /pædə⁰l/, **paddles, paddling, paddled. 1** A **paddle** is a short pole with a wide, flat part at one end or at both ends, which you hold in your hands and use as an oar to move a small boat through water. N COUNT

2 If you **paddle** a boat, you move it through water using a paddle. EG *The people paddle from place to place in canoes.* V+O OR V+A

3 If you **paddle,** you walk or stand in shallow water at the edge of the sea, for pleasure. EG *It was too cold for paddling.* ▸ used as a noun. EG *We had a bit of a paddle.* V ▸ N SING

paddock /pædək/, **paddocks. 1** A **paddock** is a small field where horses are kept. N COUNT

2 At a race course, the **paddock** is the place where the horses are kept just before each race. N COUNT

paddy /pædi¹/, **paddies.** A **paddy** or a **paddy field** is a field that is kept flooded with water and is used for growing rice. N COUNT

padlock

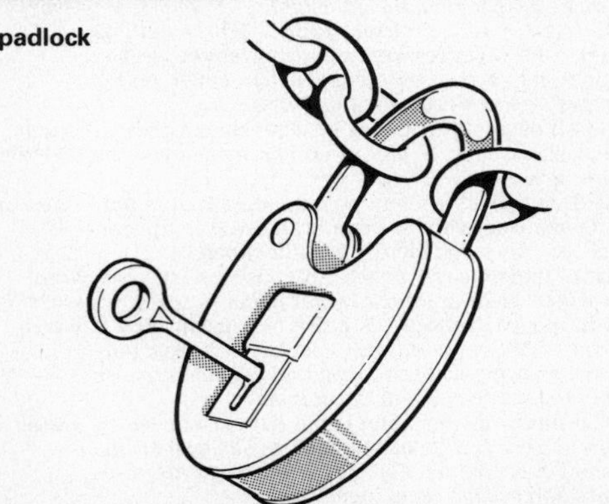

padlock /pædlɒk/, **padlocks.** A **padlock** is a lock which is used for fastening two things or two parts of something together. It consists of a block of metal with a U-shaped bar attached to it. One end of the bar is released when the padlock is unlocked with a key. N COUNT

paediatrician /piːdɪətrɪʃə⁰n/, **paediatricians;** also spelled **pediatrician.** A **paediatrician** is a doctor who specializes in treating sick children. N COUNT

pagan /peɪgə⁰n/, **pagans. 1** Some people use **pagan** to describe religious beliefs and practices that do not belong to any of the main religions of the world. EG *...an ancient pagan festival... ...pagan gods.* ADJ CLASSIF

2 A **pagan** is a person who has pagan beliefs or takes part in pagan practices. EG *They burnt thousands of pagans and heretics.* N COUNT

page /peɪdʒ/, **pages. 1** A **page** is one side of one of the pieces of paper in a book, magazine, or newspaper. Each page usually has a number printed at the top or bottom. EG *The story appeared on the front page of the Daily Mail... For details of pensions, see page 16.* N COUNT

2 The **pages** of a book, magazine, or newspaper are the pieces of paper it consists of. EG *Ellen aimlessly turned the pages of her magazine.* N COUNT

pageant /pædʒənt/, **pageants. 1** A **pageant** is a show, often performed out of doors, which is made up of historical or literary scenes. N COUNT

2 You can refer to any grand and colourful ceremony as a **pageant**. EG *...the pageant of the Duke's immense, sumptuous funeral.* N COUNT Literary

pageantry /pædʒəntri¹/. You can refer to grand and colourful ceremonies as **pageantry**. EG *The week was crammed with festivities and pageantry.* N UNCOUNT

paid /peɪd/. **1 Paid** is the past tense and past participle of **pay**.

2 If you do **paid** work or if you are a **paid** worker, you receive money for the work that you do. EG *You may be doing some paid work after retirement... Most of the work is done by paid staff.* ADJ CLASSIF: USU ATTRIB

3 If you are well **paid**, you receive a lot of money for the work that you do. If you are badly **paid**, you do not receive much money for it. EG *Secretaries are pretty well paid these days... ...women in low paid jobs.* ADJ CLASSIF

4 If you have **paid** holiday or **paid** leave, you are given your wages or salary even though you are not at work. ADJ CLASSIF: ATTRIB

paid-up. If you are a **paid-up** member of a group, you have paid the money required to be a member. EG *Over three million people in Britain are paid-up members of conservation groups.* ADJ CLASSIF: ATTRIB

pail /peɪl/, **pails.** A **pail** is a bucket, usually made of metal or wood. EG *...metal pails filled with milk.* N COUNT Outdated

pain /peɪn/, **pains, paining, pained. 1** If you have **pain** or a **pain**, you have an unpleasant feeling in a part of your body because you are ill or have been hurt. EG *He was in pain... She complained of severe pains in her chest... ...acute abdominal pain.* N UNCOUNT OR N COUNT

2 **Pain** is also the feeling of unhappiness that you have when something unpleasant or upsetting happens. EG *How well I understood the confusion and pain of her parents... ...the pain of realizing that she had failed.* N UNCOUNT

3 If something **pains** you, it makes you feel upset or unhappy. EG *It pained him that his father talked like that... Such remarks always pained him.* V+O: NO CONT

4 **Pains** is used in these phrases. **4.1** If you **take pains** to do something, you try hard to do it successfully or well. EG *She took great pains to conceal this from her parents... She always took great pains with her make-up.* **4.2** Someone who **is at pains** to do something is very eager and anxious to do it. EG *She was at pains to show that she cared nothing for them.* **4.3** If you say that you got a particular thing **for** your **pains**, you mean that you got it as a reward for something you did, and you think that you deserved a much better reward. EG *A cup of tea was all I got for my pains.* PHRASES Formal

5 If you say that someone is **a pain** or **a pain in the neck**, you mean that you find them very annoying or irritating. PHRASE Informal

pained /peɪnd/. Someone who looks or sounds **pained** seems rather upset or offended. EG *She raised her eyebrows and looked pained... ...a pained expression.* ADJ QUALIT

painful /peɪnfʊl/. **1** If a part of your body is **painful**, it hurts. EG *My back is so painful that I cannot stand upright any more.* ADJ QUALIT

2 You say that things are **painful 2.1** when they cause you physical pain. EG *My boots are still painful... ...a long and painful illness.* ◇ **painfully.** EG *She struck him, quite painfully, with the ruler.* ADJ QUALIT ◇ ADV

2.2 when they are upsetting, unpleasant, or difficult. EG *...the painful process of growing up... It was* ADJ QUALIT *painful to admit that I was wrong... Progress had been slow and painful.* ◊ **painfully.** EG *I was always painfully aware of my shortcomings.* ◊ ADV+ADJ

painless /peɪnlɪ²s/. Something that is **painless 1** causes or involves no physical pain. EG *...painless childbirth.* ◊ **painlessly.** EG *My tooth came out quite painlessly.* **2** does not involve much effort or unhappiness. EG *...the painless way to learn German... There is no painless transition to socialism.* ◊ **painlessly.** EG *Industrialization in western countries was achieved painlessly.* ADJ QUALIT; ◊ ADV; ADJ QUALIT; ◊ ADV

painstaking /peɪnsteɪkɪŋ/. Someone who is **painstaking** carries out tasks extremely carefully and thoroughly. EG *He had been an efficient and painstaking worker... The picture had been cleaned with painstaking care.* ◊ **painstakingly.** EG *He painstakingly records details of every race.* ADJ QUALIT; ◊ ADV

paint /peɪnt/, **paints, painting, painted. 1 Paint** is a coloured liquid that you put onto a surface using a brush in order to protect the surface or to make it look nice. EG *...a tin of pink paint... ...non-drip paints.* N MASS

2 Paint is also a coloured liquid or thick paste, or a coloured substance that can be mixed with a liquid, which you use to make a picture or a design. EG *...tubes of oil paint... In the art room, the brushes and paints had been set out.* N MASS

3 A covering of dried paint on an object is often referred to as the **paint**. EG *The paint was flaking off the walls.* N SING : *the*+N

4 When you **paint** something or **paint** a picture of it, you make a picture of it on paper or canvas using paint. EG *Whistler painted his mother in a rocking chair... I tried to paint a picture of a pigeon... He painted a little.* V+O OR V

5 When you **paint** a wall or an object, you cover it with paint. EG *The rooms were painted green.* ◊ **painted.** EG *...painted furniture... ...white-painted passages.* V+O OR V+O+C; ◊ ADJ CLASSIF : ATTRIB

6 When you **paint** a design or message on a surface, you put it on the surface using paint. EG *...white lines painted along the middle of the road.* ◊ **painted.** EG *...the wastebasket with the painted roses.* V+O+A; ◊ ADJ CLASSIF

7 If a woman **paints** her lips or nails, she puts lipstick or nail varnish on them. EG *Taking out her lipstick, she began to paint her lips.* V+O

8 See also **painting**.

paintbrush /peɪntbrʌʃ/, **paintbrushes.** A **paintbrush** is a brush which you use for putting paint onto something. See picture at BRUSHES. N COUNT

painter /peɪntə/, **painters.** A **painter** is **1** an artist who paints pictures. EG *...a landscape painter.* **2** someone whose job is painting the walls, doors, and other parts of buildings. N COUNT

painting /peɪntɪŋ/, **paintings. 1** A **painting** is a picture which someone has produced using paint. EG *...a large painting by Rossetti... ...a painting of a horse... ...oil paintings.* N COUNT

2 Painting is **2.1** the activity of painting pictures. **2.2** the activity of painting parts of buildings. N UNCOUNT

paintwork /peɪntwɜːk/. The **paintwork** of a building or vehicle is the covering of paint on it or the parts that are painted. EG *Use warm water and detergent to wash paintwork... The paintwork was chipped.* N UNCOUNT

pair /pɛə/, **pairs, pairing, paired. 1** You refer to two things as a **pair** when they are the same size and shape and they are intended to be used together. EG *He bought a pair of boots... Dragonflies have two pairs of wings.* N PART

2 You also use **pair** when you are referring to certain objects which have two main parts of the same size and shape. EG *...a pair of trousers... ...a pair of scissors... ...a pair of sunglasses.* N COUNT : USU+*of*

3 You can refer to two people as a **pair** when they are standing or walking together or when they have some kind of relationship with each other. EG *They were a sinister pair... They'd always been a devoted pair.* N COLL

4 See also **au pair**.

pair off. When people **pair off** or **are paired off**, they become grouped in pairs. EG *They'll probably pair off for company... People are paired off according to their level of competence.* PHRASAL VB : V-ERG+ADV

pajamas /pədʒɑːməz/. See **pyjamas**.

pal /pæl/, **pals.** Your **pal** is your friend. EG *Where's your pal tonight?... I had a pal with me... Is he a pal of yours?* N COUNT Informal Outdated

palace /pælɪs/, **palaces.** A **palace** is a very large, grand house, especially one which is the home of a king, queen, or president. EG *The palace ceased to be a royal residence in 1960... The Queen appeared on the balcony of Buckingham Palace.* N COUNT

palatable /pælətəbə⁰l/. **1** If you describe food or drink as **palatable**, you mean that it tastes quite pleasant. EG *The food looked quite palatable.* ADJ QUALIT Formal

2 If you describe something such as an idea as **palatable**, you mean that you are willing to accept it. EG *The truth is not always palatable.* ADJ QUALIT Formal

palate /pælə¹t/, **palates. 1** Your **palate** is the top part of the inside of your mouth. N COUNT

2 You can also refer to someone's ability to judge good food and wine as their **palate**. EG *All that junk food must have ruined my palate.* N COUNT

palatial /pəleɪʃə⁰l/. If a house is **palatial**, it is large and splendid like a palace. ADJ QUALIT

pale /peɪl/, **paler, palest. 1** Something that is **pale** is whitish, or not strong or bright in colour. EG *He had on a pale blue shirt... The house is built of pale stone.* ADJ QUALIT

2 If someone looks **pale,** their face looks a lighter colour than usual, because they are ill, frightened, or shocked. EG *You look awfully pale: are you all right?... Joan collapsed, pale and trembling.* ◊ **paleness.** EG *Symptoms are unusual paleness and tiredness.* ADJ QUALIT; ◊ N UNCOUNT

3 A **pale** light is very weak and dim. EG *I looked down at the beach in the pale light.* ADJ CLASSIF Literary

pall /pɔːl/, **palls, palling, palled. 1** If something **palls**, it becomes less interesting or less enjoyable. EG *It's one of the few delights that never palls... George's jokes were beginning to pall.* V

2 A **pall** of smoke is a thick cloud of smoke above a place or in it. EG *A pall of smoke hung over the entire area.* N COUNT : USU SING+*of*

pallid /pælɪd/. Someone or something that is **pallid** is unattractively or unnaturally pale in appearance. EG *...his pallid face... ...a pallid moon.* ADJ QUALIT Literary

pallor /pælə/ is an unhealthy paleness in someone's face. EG *I was struck by her pallor.* N SING Literary

palm /pɑːm/, **palms. 1** A **palm** or a **palm tree** is a tree that grows in hot countries. It has long leaves growing at the top, and no branches. EG *He sat in the shade beneath the palms.* N COUNT

2 The **palm** of your hand is the flat surface which your fingers can bend towards. EG *She placed the money in his palm... Claud spat on the palms of his hands and rubbed them together.* N COUNT+POSS

palpable /pælpəbə⁰l/. Something that is **palpable** is so obvious or intense that it is easily noticed. EG *The president's scepticism was palpable... ...a palpable lie.* ◊ **palpably.** EG *It was palpably unjust.* ADJ QUALIT Formal; ◊ ADV+ADJ

paltry /pɔːltri¹/. A **paltry** sum of money is one that you consider to be very small. EG *...a paltry wage... The deal cost him a paltry £100.* ADJ QUALIT : ATTRIB

pamper /pæmpə/, **pampers, pampering, pampered.** If you **pamper** someone, you treat them too kindly and do too much for them in order to make them comfortable. V+O

pamphlet /pæmflɪ²t/, **pamphlets.** A **pamphlet** is a very thin book, with a paper cover, which gives information about something. N COUNT

If a house is palatial, is it a palace?

pan /pæn/, **pans.** A **pan** is a round metal container with a long handle, which is used for cooking things in, usually on top of a cooker. EG *He started tipping beans into a pan... ...pots and pans.* — N COUNT

panacea /pænəsɪə/, **panaceas.** A **panacea** is something that is supposed to be a cure for any problem or illness. EG *...an obsession with technology as a panacea for life's ills... There are no easy solutions and certainly no political panaceas.* — N COUNT

panache /pənæʃ, -nɑːʃ/. If you do something with **panache**, you do it in a confident, stylish, and elegant way. EG *He made his final speech with more panache than he had ever shown before... The boy danced with equal energy but less panache.* — N UNCOUNT

pancake /pænkeɪk/, **pancakes.** A **pancake** is a thin, flat, circular piece of cooked batter. Pancakes are usually folded and eaten hot with a sweet or savoury filling. — N COUNT

panda /pændə/, **pandas.** A **panda** or a **giant panda** is a large animal rather like a bear, which has black and white fur and lives in China. — N COUNT

pandemonium /pændə[1]məʊnɪəm/. If there is **pandemonium** in a place, the people there are behaving in a very confused and noisy way. EG *When the spectators heard about this, pandemonium broke loose... Pandemonium followed. The cavalry were called out.* — N UNCOUNT

pander /pændə/, **panders, pandering, pandered.** If you **pander** to someone or to their wishes, you do everything that they want; used showing disapproval. EG *Big business firms pander to the teenagers of today... They pander to their children's slightest whim.* — V+*to*

pane /peɪn/, **panes.** A **pane** of glass is a flat sheet of glass in a window or door. EG *Smash a pane in the window and climb in... ...small square panes of green glass.* — N COUNT

panel /pænə[0]l/, **panels. 1** A **panel** is a small group of people who are chosen to do something, for example to discuss something in public or to make a decision about something. EG *...questions answered by a panel of experts... ...an interviewing panel for a new teacher.* — N COLL

2 A **panel** is also a flat, rectangular piece of wood or other material that forms part of a larger object such as a door. EG *There were glass panels in the front door... ...a ceiling with painted panels.* — N COUNT

3 A control **panel** or instrument **panel** is a board or surface which contains switches and controls to operate a machine or piece of equipment. EG *The instrument panel is just forward of the wheel.* — N COUNT: USU+SUPP

panelled /pænə[0]ld/; spelled **paneled** in American English. **1** A **panelled** room has decorative wooden panels covering its walls. EG *His office was panelled in dark wood.* — ADJ CLASSIF

2 A **panelled** door does not have a flat surface but has square or rectangular areas set into its surface. — ADJ CLASSIF: USU ATTRIB

panelling /pænə[0]lɪŋ/; spelled **paneling** in American English. **Panelling** consists of boards or strips of wood covering a wall inside a building. EG *...the hall, with its panelling and its splendid carved oak screen.* — N UNCOUNT

pang /pæŋ/, **pangs.** A **pang** is a sudden, strong feeling, for example of sadness or pain. EG *She felt a sudden pang of regret... He was conscious of a sharp pang of guilt... ...hunger pangs.* — N COUNT: USU+*of*

panic /pænɪk/, **panics, panicking, panicked. 1** **Panic** is a very strong feeling of anxiety or fear, especially one that makes you act without thinking carefully. EG *Sandy was close to panic... These rumours spread panic... Some of them got into their cars and took off in a panic.* — N UNCOUNT OR N COUNT

2 If you **panic**, you suddenly become very anxious or afraid, and often act quickly and without thinking carefully. EG *She panicked as his hand closed on her wrist... Don't panic. Sit still and keep calm.* — V

panic-stricken. Someone who is **panic-stricken** is very anxious or afraid, and is often acting without thinking carefully. EG *...a panic-stricken crowd... She heard a rustle behind her and turned, panic-stricken.* — ADJ CLASSIF

panorama /pænərɑːmə/, **panoramas.** A **panorama** is a view in which you can see a long way over a wide area of land. EG *...a vast panorama of windswept mountain tops... ...every bend in the road revealing fresh panoramas of empty beaches.* — N COUNT: OFT+*of*

panoramic /pænəræmɪk/. If you have a **panoramic** view, you can see a long way over a wide area. EG *...a panoramic view of the valley.* — ADJ CLASSIF

pansy /pænzi[1]/, **pansies.** A **pansy** is a small garden flower with large, round petals. — N COUNT

pant /pænt/, **pants, panting, panted. 1** **Pants** are a piece of underwear which have two holes to put your legs through and elastic around the top. EG *...a pair of pants.* — N PLURAL

2 In America, trousers are referred to as **pants**. EG *He fumbled in his pants pocket for his whistle.* — N PLURAL American

3 If you **pant**, you breathe quickly and loudly with your mouth open, because you have been doing something energetic. EG *We lugged the branch along, panting and puffing... 'Let me go,' she panted.* — V OR V+QUOTE

panther /pænθə/, **panthers.** A **panther** is a large wild animal that belongs to the cat family. Panthers are usually black. — N COUNT

panties /pæntɪz/ are pants worn by women or girls. EG *Gretchen was pulling on her panties.* — N PLURAL

pantomime /pæntə[6]maɪm/, **pantomimes.** A **pantomime** is a funny musical play for children. Pantomimes are based on fairy stories and are usually performed at Christmas. — N COUNT

pantry /pæntri[1]/, **pantries.** A **pantry** is a small room where food is kept, in a house. EG *A pint of milk had disappeared from the pantry.* — N COUNT

papal /peɪpə[0]l/ is used to describe things relating to the Pope. EG *...a papal election.* — ADJ CLASSIF: ATTRIB

paper /peɪpə/, **papers, papering, papered. 1** **Paper** is a material that you write on or wrap things with. The pages of this book are made of paper. EG *Rudolph picked up the piece of paper and gave it to her... ...a paper bag.* — N UNCOUNT

2 A **paper** is a newspaper. EG *I read about the riots in the papers... Where do you get your daily paper?* — N COUNT

3 **Papers** are sheets of paper with information on them. EG *He consulted the papers on his knee.* — N PLURAL

4 Your **papers** are official documents, for example your passport or identity card, which prove who you are or give you official permission to do something. EG *One of the men in the car had no papers... ...false papers.* — N PLURAL

5 A **paper** is also **5.1** a part of a written examination in which you answer a number of questions in a particular period of time. EG *He failed the history paper... You have two hours for each paper.* **5.2** a long essay written on an academic subject. EG *...a paper on linguistics and literary criticism.* — N COUNT

6 **Paper** agreements, qualifications, or profits are ones that are stated by official documents to exist, although they have no real effectiveness or existence. EG *My paper qualifications declared me to be a doctor.* — N MOD

7 If you put your thoughts down **on paper**, you write them down. EG *He had put his suggestions down on paper.* — PHRASE

8 If something seems to be the case **on paper**, it seems to be the case from what you read or hear about it, but it may not really be the case. EG *The project looks impressive enough on paper.* — PHRASE

9 If you **paper** a wall, you put wallpaper on it. EG *The lounge was papered and painted first.* — V+O

paper over. If you **paper over** a difficulty, you try to hide it by giving the impression that things are going well. EG *There is no papering over the fact that basic disputes exist.* — PHRASAL VB: V+ADV+O

paperback /peɪpəbæk/, **paperbacks.** A **paperback** is a book with a paper cover. EG *'The Honorary Consul' is now available in paperback.* — N COUNT OR *in*+N

paper boy, paper boys. A **paper boy** is a boy who delivers newspapers to people's homes. N COUNT

paperclip

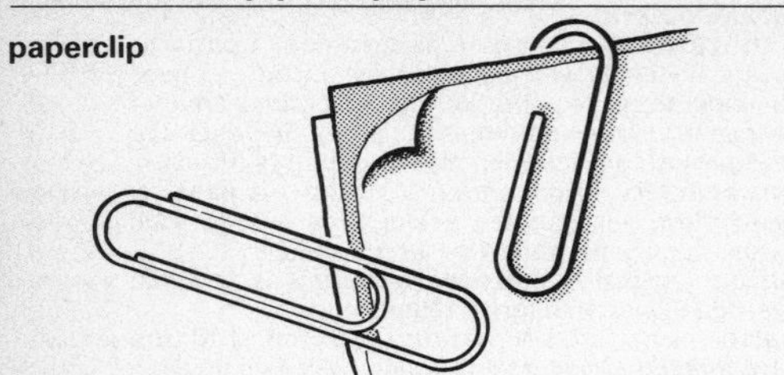

paper clip, paper clips. A **paper clip** is a small piece of bent wire that is used to fasten papers together. N COUNT

paper shop, paper shops. A **paper shop** is the same as a newsagent's. N COUNT

paperweight /peɪpəweɪt/, **paperweights.** A **paperweight** is a small, heavy object which you place on papers to prevent them from being disturbed or blown away. N COUNT

paperwork /peɪpəwɜːk/ is the routine part of a job which involves writing or dealing with letters, reports, and records. EG *There was a single desk where all the paperwork seemed to be done.* N UNCOUNT

papier-mâché /pæpjeɪmæʃeɪ/ is a mixture of pieces of paper and glue, which is used to make objects such as bowls, ornaments, and models. EG *...papier-mâché boxes lacquered with flowers.* N UNCOUNT

paprika /pæprɪkə/ is a red powder that is used for flavouring food. N UNCOUNT

par /pɑː/. If you say that something is **on a par** with something else, you mean that the two things are equally good or equally bad. EG *He put Warhol on a par with Titian... Forcing a child to learn is on a par with forcing a man to adopt a religion.* PHRASE

parable /pærəbə⁰l/, **parables.** A **parable** is a short story which is told in order to make a moral or religious point. N COUNT

parachute /pærəʃuːt/, **parachutes.** A **parachute** is a device which enables you to jump from an aircraft and float to the ground. It consists of a large circle of thin cloth attached to your body by strings. N COUNT

parade /pəreɪd/, **parades, parading, paraded. 1** A **parade** is **1.1** a line of people or vehicles moving somewhere together, for example through the streets of a town, to celebrate a special day or event. EG *When the war was over there was a parade in London.* **1.2** an occasion on which soldiers march together in front of important people or the public. ● When soldiers are **on parade**, they are standing or marching together on a formal occasion. N COUNT; ● PHRASE

2 When people **parade** or **are paraded**, they walk together in a formal group, so that other people can see them. EG *The army paraded round the square... The captured criminals were paraded in chains through the streets.* V-ERG+A

3 If you **parade** something, you show it to people in order to impress them. EG *She seldom or never paraded this knowledge.* V+O

paradise /pærədaɪs/, **paradises. 1** According to some religions, **Paradise** is a wonderful place where people go after they die, if they have led good lives. N PROPER

2 You can refer to a place or situation that seems perfect as **paradise** or a **paradise**. EG *...the palm-fringed paradise of Mauritius... 'That must have been interesting.' – 'For me it was paradise.'* N UNCOUNT OR N SING

3 You can also use **paradise** to indicate that a place is very attractive to a particular kind of person. For example, you can say that a river where there is a lot of fish is an 'angler's paradise'. EG *Hong Kong was a shopper's paradise then.* N COUNT+SUPP

paradox /pærədɒks/, **paradoxes. 1** You describe something as a **paradox** when it involves two facts which you would not expect to be both true or two qualities which you would not expect to exist together. EG *It was crowded and yet at the same time peaceful. This was a paradox she often remarked on.* N COUNT

2 A **paradox** is also a statement which contradicts itself. N COUNT OR N UNCOUNT

paradoxical /pærədɒksɪkə⁰l/. You say that something is **paradoxical** when it involves two facts which you would not expect to be both true or two qualities which you would not expect to exist together. EG *It's paradoxical that the loneliest people live in the most crowded places.* ADJ QUALIT

◊ **paradoxically** /pærədɒksɪkə⁰li¹/. EG *Paradoxically, he represented both escape and safety.* ◊ ADV SEN

paraffin /pærəfɪn/ is a strong-smelling liquid which is used as a fuel in heaters and lamps. N UNCOUNT

paragon /pærəgə⁰n/, **paragons.** If you describe someone as a **paragon**, you mean that they are perfect or that they have as much of a particular quality as anyone can have. EG *He was a paragon of honesty.* N COUNT: USU+SUPP

paragraph /pærəgrɑːf/, **paragraphs.** A **paragraph** is a section of a piece of writing. A paragraph always begins on a new line. In this dictionary, a **paragraph** is one of the sections of an entry numbered 1, 2, 3, and so on. N COUNT

parallel /pærəlɛl/, **parallels, paralleling, paralleled;** also spelled **parallelling** and **parallelled** in British English. **1** A **parallel** is something that is very similar to something else, but that exists or happens in a different place or at a different time. EG *It is not difficult to find a living parallel for these prehistoric creatures... We must search many past centuries for a parallel.* ● If you say that something has **no parallel**, you mean that there is nothing else like it or nothing else as good. EG *...a book which has no parallel in the English language.* N COUNT; ● PHRASE

2 If you show that there are **parallels** between two things, you show that they are similar in some ways. EG *There are curious parallels between medicine and law... His career and attitudes have interesting parallels with Potter's... We can draw parallels here with the Antarctic.* N COUNT: USU PLURAL +*between/with*

3 If something **parallels** something else, it is as good as that thing or similar to it. EG *...computers with intellects paralleling Man's... His career has almost exactly paralleled that of Hopper.* V+O

4 If you refer to a **parallel** event or situation, you are referring to one that happens at the same time as another, or one that is similar to another. EG *...an endless process of destruction and a parallel process of re-creation.* ADJ CLASSIF: OFT+*with/to*

5 If two lines or two long objects are **parallel**, they are the same distance apart all along their length. EG *The boys were marching in two parallel lines... Vanderhoff Street ran parallel to Broadway.* ADJ CLASSIF: OFT+*to/with*

paralyse /pærəlaɪz/, **paralyses, paralysing, paralysed;** spelled **paralyze** in American English. **1** If something **paralyses** you, it causes you to have no feeling in your body or in part of it, and to be unable to move. EG *A stroke paralysed half his face... Wasps catch spiders and paralyse them with a sting.* ◊ **paralysed.** EG *...a person paralysed from the neck down.* V+O; ◊ ADJ CLASSIF

2 You can say that people, places, or organizations **are paralysed** by something when it makes them unable to act or function properly. EG *She was paralysed by uncertainty... Great cities are paralysed by strikes and power failures.* ◊ **paralysed.** EG *What he saw left him paralysed with fright.* V+O: USU PASS; ◊ ADJ PRED +*with*

paralysis /pəræləˡsɪs/ is the loss of feeling in your body or in part of it, and the inability to move. EG N UNCOUNT

Where do parishioners live?

One drop of this poison would be enough to induce paralysis and blindness.

parameter /pəræmə¹tə/, **parameters.** **Parameters** are factors or limits which affect the way that something can be done or made. EG *It is necessary to be aware of all the parameters that have a bearing on the design process... ...a solution that falls within certain parameters.* N COUNT: USU PLURAL Formal

paramilitary /pærəmɪlɪtə⁰ri¹/. A **paramilitary** organization behaves like an army but is not the official army of a country. EG *...a paramilitary terrorist group.* ADJ CLASSIF: ATTRIB

paramount /pærəmaʊnt/. Something that is **paramount** or of **paramount** importance is more important than anything else. EG *The interests of the child are paramount.* ADJ CLASSIF

paranoia /pærənɔɪə/. Someone who suffers from **paranoia** wrongly believes that other people are trying to harm them. N UNCOUNT

paranoid /pærənɔɪd/. If you say that someone is **paranoid**, you mean that they are extremely suspicious, distrustful, and afraid of other people. EG *You're getting paranoid... ...a paranoid terror of young people.* ADJ QUALIT

parapet /pærəpɪ²t/, **parapets.** A **parapet** is a low wall along the edge of a bridge, roof, or balcony. EG *They leaned over the low stone parapet and stared into the pool.* N COUNT

paraphernalia /pærəfəneɪlɪə/. You can refer to a large number of objects that someone has with them or that are connected with a particular activity as **paraphernalia.** EG *The girls gathered together their hockey sticks, satchels, and other paraphernalia.* N UNCOUNT: USU+SUPP

paraphrase /pærəfreɪz/, **paraphrases, paraphrasing, paraphrased.** **1** A **paraphrase** of something written or spoken is the same thing expressed in a different way. EG *This article was a close paraphrase of Dixon's own original article.* N COUNT

2 If you **paraphrase** someone or **paraphrase** something that they have said or written, you express what they have said or written in a different way. EG *We must, to paraphrase Socrates, bring out the knowledge that people have inside them... ...paraphrasing a poem.* V+O OR V

parasite /pærəsaɪt/, **parasites.** **1** A **parasite** is a small animal or plant that lives on or inside a larger animal or plant and gets its food from it. N COUNT

◇ **parasitic** /pærəsɪtɪk/. EG *...tiny parasitic insects.* ◇ ADJ CLASSIF

2 If you call someone a **parasite**, you mean that they get money or other things from other people without doing anything in return; used showing disapproval. ◇ **parasitic.** EG *...their parasitic exploitation of the masses.* N COUNT ◇ ADJ QUALIT

parasol /pærəsɒl/, **parasols.** A **parasol** is an object like an umbrella that provides shade from the sun. Large parasols are often placed over tables out of doors. N COUNT

paratroops /pærətru:ps/. The form **paratroop** is used before a noun. N PLURAL

Paratroops are soldiers who are trained to be dropped by parachute into battle or into enemy territory. EG *...paratroop attacks.*

parcel /pɑ:sə⁰l/, **parcels.** A **parcel** is something wrapped in paper. EG *He started undoing a little parcel tied with string... Charities sent parcels of clothes.* ● **part and parcel**: see **part.** N COUNT: OFT+*of*

parched /pɑ:tʃt/. **1** If the ground or plants are **parched**, they are very dry, because there has been no rain. EG *...the parched plains of India.* ADJ QUALIT

2 If your mouth, throat, or lips are **parched**, they are unpleasantly dry. EG *She touched her wet fingertips to her parched lips.* ADJ QUALIT

3 If you say that you are **parched**, you mean that you are very thirsty. ADJ PRED Informal

parchment /pɑ:tʃmə²nt/. **1** In former times, **parchment** was the skin of a sheep or goat that was used for writing on. N UNCOUNT

2 Parchment is a kind of thick yellowish paper. N UNCOUNT

pardon /pɑ:də⁰n/, **pardons, pardoning, pardoned.** **1** You say **'Pardon?'** or **'I beg your pardon?'** when you have not heard or understood what someone has just said and you want them to repeat it. EG *'How old is she?' – 'Pardon?' – 'I said how old is she?'* CONVENTION

2 People also say **'I beg your pardon?'** when they are surprised or offended by something that someone has just said. EG *'Where the devil did you get her?' – 'I beg your pardon?'* CONVENTION

3 You say **'I beg your pardon'** or **'I do beg your pardon'** as a way of apologizing for accidentally doing something wrong, for example disturbing someone or making a mistake. EG *It is treated in the sentence as a noun – I beg your pardon – as an adjective.* CONVENTION

4 Some people say **'Pardon me'** instead of 'Excuse me'. EG *Pardon me, Sergeant, I wonder if you'd do me a favour?* CONVENTION

5 If you **pardon** someone, you forgive them or do not punish them for doing something bad or wrong. EG *I hope that poor fellow may be pardoned for whatever crime he has committed.* ▸ used as a noun. EG *I had to beg her pardon.* V+O ▸ N UNCOUNT OR N COUNT

pardonable /pɑ:də⁰nəbə⁰l/. You describe someone's bad behaviour as **pardonable** when you can understand why they behaved like that and think that they should be forgiven in the circumstances. EG *It was an exaggeration, but a pardonable one.* ADJ QUALIT

pare /pɛə/, **pares, paring, pared.** When you **pare** something, you cut off its skin or its outer layer. EG *Mother was paring apples.* V+O

pare down. If you **pare** something **down**, **1** you make it smaller by cutting thin pieces off it. EG *...pared-down fingernails.* **2** you reduce it. EG *I had pared my possessions down to almost nothing.* PHRASAL VB: V+O+ADV; V+O+ADV

parent /pɛərənt/, **parents.** **1** Your **parents** are your father and mother. EG *Her parents are well-off... ...the bond between parents and children.* N COUNT

◇ **parental** /pərɛntə⁰l/. EG *...lack of parental control... ...parental love.* ◇ ADJ CLASSIF: ATTRIB

2 The **parent** organization of a particular organization created it and usually still controls it. EG *Subsidiaries are represented on the board of directors of the parent company.* N MOD

parenthood /pɛərənthʊd/ is the state of being a parent. EG *...the responsibility of parenthood.* N UNCOUNT

par excellence /pɑ:r⁰ ɛksəlɑ:ns/. You say that something is a particular kind of thing **par excellence** in order to emphasize that it is the best possible example of that kind of thing. EG *She was strongly committed to her job, a policewoman par excellence.* ADJ AFTER N

parish /pærɪʃ/, **parishes.** **1** A **parish** is a village or part of a town which has its own church and clergyman. EG *...the parish of St Mark's, Sambourne Fishley... ...the parish church.* N COUNT

2 A **parish** is also a small country area which has its own elected council. EG *Stroud parish has a population of 20,000... ...a parish councillor.* N COUNT

parishioner /pərɪʃənə/, **parishioners.** A clergyman's **parishioners** are the people who live in his parish, especially the ones who go to his church. EG *She had been one of his parishioners in Shropshire.* N COUNT

parity /pærɪ¹ti¹/. If there is **parity** between two things, they are equal. EG *...the theoretical parity in powers between the two Houses of Parliament... Women workers at the factory went on strike for parity with men.* N UNCOUNT: OFT+ between/with Formal

park /pɑ:k/, **parks, parking, parked.** **1** A **park** is a public area of land with grass and trees, usually in a town, where people go in order to relax and enjoy themselves. EG *She took her children for a walk in the park... ...Hyde Park.* N COUNT

2 A private area of grass and trees around a large country house can also be referred to as a **park.** N COUNT British

3 When you **park** a vehicle or **park** somewhere, you drive the vehicle into a position where it can stay for a period of time, and leave it there. EG *She* V+O; ALSO V: USU+A *parked in front of the library.* ◇ **parked.** EG *We could see the lights of a parked car.* ◇ ADJ CLASSIF ◇ **parking.** EG *...a 'No parking' sign.* ◇ N UNCOUNT

4 See also **car park**, **national park**.

parka /pɑːkə/, **parkas.** A **parka** is a jacket or coat which has a quilted lining and a hood with fur round the edge. N COUNT

parking lot, parking lots. A **parking lot** is an area of ground where people can leave their cars. N COUNT American

parking meter, parking meters. A **parking meter** is a device next to a parking space which you have to put money into when you park there. N COUNT

parking ticket, parking tickets. A **parking ticket** is a piece of paper with instructions to pay a fine, which a traffic warden puts on your car when you have parked it somewhere illegally. N COUNT

parkland /pɑːklə^{3}nd/ is land with grass and trees on it. EG *...twenty-five acres of parkland.* N UNCOUNT

parlance /pɑːləns/. You use **parlance** in phrases such as **'in common parlance'** or **'in medical parlance'** when you want to indicate what kind of people normally use an expression that you are using. EG *In common parlance that's known as having your cake and eating it... ...the National Economic Development Council ('Neddy' in popular parlance).* PHRASE Formal

parliament /pɑːlə^{1}mə^{2}nt/, **parliaments. 1** The **parliament** of a country is the group of people who make or change its laws. EG *...the creation of Welsh and Scottish parliaments... He was the second farm-worker to get into Parliament.* ● See also **Member of Parliament**. N COUNT OR N UNCOUNT

2 If something happens in a particular **parliament**, it happens during the time when a parliament is doing its work. EG *They discussed the policies that they would like to see implemented in the next parliament.* N COUNT+SUPP

parliamentary /pɑːlə^{1}mentə^{0}ri^1/ is used to describe things that are connected with a parliament or with Members of Parliament. EG *...the start of each parliamentary session... He was a Liberal parliamentary candidate.* ADJ CLASSIF: ATTRIB

parlour /pɑːlə/, **parlours;** spelled **parlor** in American English. A **parlour** is a sitting-room. N COUNT Outdated

parochial /pə^{3}rəʊkɪəl/. If you describe someone as **parochial**, you mean that they are too concerned with their own local affairs and interests when they should be thinking about more important things. EG *This is a narrow and parochial view.* ADJ QUALIT

parody /pærədi^1/, **parodies. 1** A **parody** is a humorous piece of writing, drama, or music which copies the style of a well-known person or represents a familiar situation in an exaggerated way. EG *...a parody of American life... ...real modern verse, not parody.* N COUNT OR N UNCOUNT

2 You can describe something as a **parody** of a particular kind of thing when it is a very poor example of it. EG *...a scruffy parody of a wig... Her face was twisted into the parody of a smile.* N COUNT: USU+*of*

parole /pərəʊl/. When prisoners are given **parole**, they are released before their prison sentence is due to end, on condition that they behave well. EG *Prisoners are entitled to apply for parole.* N UNCOUNT

● Prisoners who are **on parole** have been given parole. ● PHRASE

paroxysm /pærəksɪzə^{0}m/, **paroxysms. 1** A **paroxysm** of rage or jealousy is a sudden, very strong feeling of rage or jealousy. EG *In a sudden paroxysm of rage, Wilt hurled the vase across the room.* N COUNT+*of*

2 A **paroxysm** is also a series of violent, uncontrollable movements that your body makes because you are coughing, laughing, or in great pain. EG *...a painful paroxysm of coughing... ...three men in paroxysms of laughter.* N COUNT: OFT+*of*

parquet /pɑːkeɪ/ is a floor covering made of small rectangular blocks of wood fitted together in a pattern. EG *...the highly polished parquet floor.* N UNCOUNT: USU N MOD

parrot /pærət/, **parrots, parroting, parroted. 1** A **parrot** is a tropical bird with a curved beak and brightly-coloured or grey feathers. Parrots can be kept as pets and sometimes copy what people say. N COUNT

2 If you **parrot** what someone else has said, you repeat it, often without really understanding what it means. V+O

3 If you learn or repeat something **parrot fashion**, you learn or repeat it accurately but without really understanding what it means. PHRASE

parry /pæri^1/, **parries, parrying, parried. 1** If you **parry** a question or argument, you cleverly avoid answering it or dealing with it. EG *Instead of answering he parried with another question.* V+O OR V+*with*

2 If you **parry** a blow from someone who is attacking you, you push aside their arm or weapon so that you are not hurt. V+O OR V

parsimonious /pɑːsɪməʊnɪəs/. Someone who is **parsimonious** is very unwilling to spend money. ADJ QUALIT Formal

parsley /pɑːsli^1/ is a small plant with curly leaves that are used for flavouring or decorating savoury food. N UNCOUNT

parsnip /pɑːsnɪp/, **parsnips.** A **parsnip** is a long, thick, pale cream vegetable that grows under the ground. N COUNT OR N UNCOUNT

parson /pɑːsə^{0}n/, **parsons.** A **parson** is a vicar or other clergyman. N COUNT Outdated

part /pɑːt/, **parts, parting, parted. 1** If something is **part** of something else or is a **part** of it, **1.1** it is one of the pieces or areas that the other thing consists of. EG *The bridge is part of the main road... The head is the most sensitive part of the body... I don't know this part of London very well... Unscrew the plug. It is now in two parts.* **1.2** it is one of the aspects, things, or sections that the other thing consists of. EG *Economic measures must form part of any solution to this crisis... Finding the money would be the hard part... The first part of that statement is a lie.* N PART OR N UNCOUNT

2 A particular **part** of a period of time is one of the shorter periods that it consists of. EG *...the latter part of the twentieth century.* N PART

3 A **part** for a machine or vehicle is one of the pieces that is used to make it or to replace a broken piece. EG *...a group of workers who make parts for generators.* N COUNT

4 **Part** of something is some of it. EG *Part of the ceiling collapsed... My brothers went to school for part of the day and to work for the rest of it... A sizeable part of the labour force now live in the cities.* N UNCOUNT OR N PART

5 If you say that something is **part** one thing, **part** another, you mean that it is to some extent the first thing and to some extent the second thing. EG *This extraordinary document is part fiction and part fact.* ADV

6 You can use **part** when you are talking about the proportions of substances in a mixture. For example, if some instructions say that you should use two **parts** disinfectant to three **parts** water, you can mix two cups of disinfectant with three cups of water, or two pints of disinfectant with three pints of water. EG *Mix together equal parts of salt and soda crystals.* N PART Technical

7 A **part** in a play or film is one of the roles in it which an actor or actress can perform. EG *She plays the part of the witch.* N COUNT

8 Your **part** in something that happens is your involvement in it. EG *He was arrested for his part in the demonstrations.* N SING: USU+POSS

9 If you **play** a large or important **part** in something, you are very involved in it and have an important effect on what happens. EG *Men should play a bigger part in children's upbringing.* PHRASE

10 If you **take part** in an activity, you do it together with other people. EG *I asked her if she'd take part in a discussion about the uprising... They* PHRASE

Do you get a parking ticket from a parking meter?

want to take an active part in their country's affairs.

11 If you say that you **want no part of** something, you mean that you do not want to be involved in it at all. PHRASE

12 When you are describing people's thoughts or actions, you can say **for** her **part** or **for** my **part**, for example, to introduce what a particular person thinks or does. EG *Christopher's family despised my family, and my family, for their part, hated Christopher's.* PHRASE Formal

13 If you talk about a feeling or action **on** someone's **part**, you are referring to something that they feel or do. EG *I consider this a gross oversight on your part.* PHRASE Formal

14 **For the most part** means mostly or usually. EG *The forest is, for the most part, dark and wet.* PHRASE

15 **In part** means to some extent but not completely. EG *The improvement was brought about in part by the Trade Union Movement.* PHRASE

16 If you say that something is **part and parcel** of something else, you are emphasizing that it is involved or included in it. EG *These things are part and parcel of my everyday life.* PHRASE

17 If you say that something happened for **the best part** or **the better part** of a period of time, you mean that it happened for most of that time. EG *The men stayed for the best part of a year.* PHRASE

18 If things that are next to each other **part** or if you **part** them, they move in opposite directions, so that there is a space between them. EG *Ralph's lips parted in a delighted smile... Rudolph went to the window and parted the curtains.* V-ERG

19 If your hair **is parted** in the middle or at one side, it is combed in two different directions so that there is a straight line running from the front of your head to the back. V+O : USU PASS

20 When two people **part**, they leave each other. EG *A year ago they had parted for ever... I parted from them on excellent terms.* • to **part company**: see **company**. V OR V+*from* : RECIP Formal

21 If you **are parted** from someone you love, you are prevented from being with them. V+O : USU PASS

22 See also **parting**, **partly**.

part with. If you **part with** something that is valuable or that you would prefer to keep, you give it or sell it to someone else. EG *She didn't want to part with the money.* PHRASAL VB : V+PREP

partial /pɑːʃə^{0}l/. 1 A **partial** thing, state, or quality is not complete or whole. EG *I could give it only partial support... ...a partial solution... ...partial victory.* ADJ CLASSIF : USU ATTRIB

2 If you are **partial** to something, you like it very much. EG *The vicar is very partial to roast pheasant... George is not partial to the married state.* ADJ PRED+*to* Formal

3 Someone who is **partial** supports a particular person or thing, for example in a competition or dispute, when they should be completely fair and unbiased. EG *Children feel insecure with parents who are partial.* ADJ QUALIT

partially /pɑːʃə^{0}li^1/ means to some extent, but not completely. EG *...a horse partially hidden by the trees... Dolly might have been partially responsible for it... He refused, partially because he was too tired.* ADV

participant /pɑːtɪsɪpənt/, **participants.** Someone who is a **participant** in an activity takes part in it. EG *She was a willing participant in these campaigns... The participants were mainly teenagers.* N COUNT : OFT+*in*

participate /pɑːtɪsɪpeɪt/, **participates, participating, participated.** If you **participate** in an activity, you take part in it. EG *We asked high school students to participate in an anti-drugs campaign.* V : USU+*in*

◊ **participation** /pɑːtɪsɪpeɪʃə^{0}n/. EG *The success of the festival depended upon the participation of the whole community.* ◊ N UNCOUNT

participle /pɑːtɪsɪpə^{0}l/, **participles.** In grammar, a **participle** is a form of a verb that can be used in compound tenses of the verb. There are two participles in English: the past participle, which usually ends in '-ed', and the present participle, which usually ends in '-ing'. N COUNT

particle /pɑːtɪkə^{0}l/, **particles.** A **particle** of something is a very small piece or amount of it. EG *...particles of metal... ...food particles.* N PART OR N COUNT

particular /pətɪkjə^{4}lə/, **particulars.** 1 If you refer to a **particular** thing, you are emphasizing that you are talking about only one thing in a group of similar things, and not about the others. EG *Let me ask you about one particular artist... She wasn't, at that particular moment, watching the cat at all.* ADJ CLASSIF : ATTRIB

2 If a person or thing has a **particular** quality or possession, it is distinct and belongs only to them. EG *It is important to discuss a child's particular problems and interests... Each species has its own particular place on the reef.* ADJ CLASSIF : ATTRIB

3 You use **in particular** to indicate that what you are saying applies especially to one thing or person. EG *Joan Greenwood in particular I thought was wonderful... This gesture is found in particular in Brazil... ...Africans, and in particular African women.* ADV SEN

4 You can use **particular** to emphasize that something is greater or more intense than usual. EG *The shortage of airfields gave particular concern.* ADJ QUALIT : ATTRIB

5 **Particulars** are facts or details about something or someone. EG *Renshaw jotted down a few particulars in his notebook.* N PLURAL Formal

6 If you say that someone is **particular**, you mean that they choose things and do things very carefully, and are not easily satisfied. EG *They're quite particular about their personnel.* ADJ PRED : OFT+*about*

particularly /pətɪkjə^{4}ləli^1/. 1 You use **particularly** to indicate that what you are saying applies especially to one thing or situation. EG *It was hard for children, particularly when they were ill... He was challenged by the workers, particularly Gibson... He particularly dislikes quiz shows.* ADV

2 **Particularly** also means more than usually or normally. EG *She was looking particularly attractive today... This is not particularly difficult to do.* SUBMOD

parting /pɑːtɪŋ/, **partings.** 1 **Parting** is an occasion when one person leaves another. EG *She felt unable to bear the strain of parting... George said no more until their final parting.* N UNCOUNT OR N COUNT

2 The **parting** in someone's hair is the line running from the front to the back of their head where their hair has been combed in opposite directions. N COUNT

partisan /pɑːtɪzæn/, **partisans.** 1 Someone who is **partisan** strongly supports a particular person or cause. EG *There are real dangers in a partisan Civil Service... ...partisan political passions.* ▸ used as a noun. EG *He was a partisan of General Jackson.* ADJ QUALIT ▸ N COUNT

2 A **partisan** is also a member of an unofficial armed force that is formed in a country to fight enemy soldiers who are occupying it. EG *...those who fought in the hills as partisans.* N COUNT

partition /pɑːtɪʃə^{0}n/, **partitions, partitioning, partitioned.** 1 A **partition** is a wall or screen that separates one part of a room or vehicle from another. EG *In one corner behind a partition was a lavatory... David tapped on the glass partition and the car stopped.* N COUNT

2 If you **partition** a room, you separate one part of it from another by means of a partition. EG *They had partitioned the inside into offices.* V+O

3 **Partition** is the dividing of a country into parts so that each part becomes an independent country. EG *...the partition of India in 1947.* ▸ used as a verb. EG *One plan involved partitioning the country.* N UNCOUNT ▸ V+O

partitive /pɑːtɪtɪv/, **partitives.** In grammar, a **partitive** is a word or expression that comes before a noun and indicates that part of a thing is being referred to rather than the whole of it. See the entry headed NOUNS for more information. N COUNT OR ADJ CLASSIF : ATTRIB

partly /pɑːtli^1/ means to some extent, but not completely. EG *The brass handles are partly obscured by white paint... The actors were not happy,* ADV *partly because of the scenery... This is partly a political and partly a legal question.*

partner /pɑːtnə/, **partners, partnering, partnered.** 1 Your **partner** is 1.1 the person you are married to or are having a romantic or sexual relationship with. EG *A marriage is likely to last if you and your partner are similar in personality.* 1.2 the person you are doing something with, for example dancing with or playing with in a game against two other people. EG *May I be your partner?... ...dance partners.* N COUNT

2 The **partners** in a business are the people who share the ownership of it. EG *She was a partner in a firm of solicitors... ...the senior partner.* N COUNT

3 The **partner** of a country or organization is another country or organization with which they have an alliance or agreement. EG *This move will not please Britain's EEC partners.* N COUNT

4 If you **partner** someone, you are their partner in a game or at a social occasion. EG *He found himself partnering Mrs Keppel at bridge.* V+O

partnership /pɑːtnəʃɪp/, **partnerships. Partnership** is a relationship in which two or more people, organizations, or countries work together as partners. EG *...new forms of partnership between management and workers... We are going into partnership... Our aim is to establish a working partnership with the teachers.* N UNCOUNT OR N COUNT

part of speech, parts of speech. A **part of speech** is a particular grammatical class of word, for example noun, adjective, or verb. N COUNT

partridge /pɑːtrɪdʒ/, **partridges.** A **partridge** is a wild bird with brown feathers, a round body, and a short tail. N COUNT

part-time. If someone is a **part-time** worker or has a **part-time** job, they work for only a part of each day or week. EG *We employ five part-time receptionists.* ▸ used as an adverb. EG *40 per cent of women work part-time.* ADJ CLASSIF : USU ATTRIB ▸ ADV

party /pɑːti¹/, **parties.** 1 A **party** is a political organization whose members have similar aims and beliefs, usually an organization that tries to get its members elected to the government of a country. EG *He's a member of the Labour Party... The PDG is not a political party... ...party leaders... The party does well in local elections.* N COUNT

2 A **party** is also a social event, often in someone's home, at which people enjoy themselves doing things such as eating, drinking, dancing, talking, or playing games. EG *...a birthday party... They gave a farewell party for her.* ● See also **garden party**. N COUNT

3 A **party** of people is a group of people who are doing something together, for example travelling together. EG *He took a party of Americans on a tour... ...rescue parties.* N PART OR N COUNT

4 One of the people involved in a legal agreement or dispute can be referred to as a particular **party**. EG *He is obviously within his rights in expecting the guilty party to pay up.* ● See also **third party**. N COUNT+SUPP Formal

5 Someone who **is a party to** an action or agreement is involved in it, and therefore partly responsible for it. EG *They simply wouldn't be a party to such a ridiculous enterprise.* PHRASE

party line, party lines. 1 The **party line** on a particular issue is the official view taken by a political party, which its members are expected to support. EG *They could be guaranteed to trot out the party line on all issues.* N SING : *the*+N

2 A **party line** is a telephone line shared by two or more houses or offices. N COUNT

pass /pɑːs/, **passes, passing, passed.** 1 To **pass** someone or something means to go past them without stopping. EG *We passed the New Hotel... ...a passing car... Please let us pass.* V+O OR V

2 When someone or something **passes** in a particular direction, they move in that direction. EG *They passed through an arched gateway... Slabs of toffee pass along a conveyor belt.* V+A

3 If something such as a road or pipe **passes** along a particular route, it goes along that route. EG *The stream and road pass through green fields... The pipe passed under the city sewer.* V+A

4 If you **pass** something to someone, you take it in your hand and give it to them. EG *She passed me her glass... Pass the sugar, please.* V+O : OFT+*to*, OR V+O+O

5 If you **pass** something such as a rope through, over, or round something, you put one end of it through, over, or round that thing. EG *Pass the string under the hook.* V+O+A

6 If something **passes** from one person to another, the second person then has it instead of the first. EG *Her property passes to her next of kin.* V+*to*

7 If you **pass** the ball to someone in your team in a game such as football, hockey, or rugby, you kick, hit, or throw it to them. V+O : USU+A, OR V+A

8 When a period of time **passes**, it happens and finishes. EG *The time seems to have passed so quickly... The crisis passed.* ◇ **passing.** EG *The passing of time brought news of them.* V ◇ N UNCOUNT +SUPP

9 If you **pass** a period of time in a particular way, you spend it in that way. EG *Men pass their lives farming their small plots of land.* V+O+-ING OR V+O+A

10 If you **pass** through a stage of development or a period of time, you experience it. EG *Mrs Yule had to pass through a few years of bitterness... This area has not passed through the agricultural revolution.* V+*through*

11 If someone or something **passes** a test or **is passed** by someone, they are considered to be of an acceptable standard. EG *I passed my driving test in Holland... You have to get 120 marks out of 200 to pass... This drug has been passed by the US Food and Drug Administration.* V+O OR V-ERG

12 If an amount **passes** a particular total or level, it becomes greater than that total or level. EG *...when unemployment passed 2 million.* V+O

13 When people in authority **pass** a new law or a proposal, they formally agree to it or approve it. EG *Many of the laws passed by Parliament are never enforced.* V+O

14 When a judge **passes** sentence on someone, he or she says what their punishment will be. V+O

15 If someone or something **passes** for a particular thing or **passes** as it, they are accepted to be that thing, even though they do not have all the right qualities. EG *...that brief period that passes for summer in those regions... A strip of space 4 feet wide passed as a kitchen.* V+*for/as*

16 If something **passes** without comment or reaction or **passes** unnoticed, nobody comments on it, reacts to it, or notices it. EG *Social change was so slow that it passed unnoticed.* V+A OR V+C

17 A **pass** in a game such as football, hockey, or rugby is the act of kicking, hitting, or throwing the ball to someone in your team. N COUNT

18 A **pass** in an examination or test is a successful result in it. EG *She got a grade A pass in physics.* N COUNT

19 A **pass** is also a document that allows you to do something. EG *I have a pass to go from New York to East Hampton.* N COUNT

20 A **pass** in a mountainous area is a narrow way between two mountains. EG *...the Khyber Pass.* N COUNT

21 **to pass judgement**: see **judgement**. ● **to pass the time**: see **time**. ● **to pass water**: see **water**. ● See also **passing**.

pass around. See **pass round**.

pass away. If you say that someone **passed away**, you mean that they died. EG *Your husband sent it to us shortly before he passed away.* PHRASAL VB : V+ADV Outdated

pass by. If you **pass by** something, you go past it. EG *We pass by another marker... I was just passing by and I saw your car.* PHRASAL VB : V+ADV/PREP

pass off. If you **pass** something **off** as another thing, you convince people that it is that other PHRASAL VB : V+O+ADV+*as*

If you have a part-time job, do you work all the time?

thing. EG *The man who made the cabinet passed it off as an antique.*

pass on. If you **pass** something **on** to someone, you give it to them after you have used it or been given it. EG *He handed a sheet to Lee to pass on to me... Philip assured her that he had passed on the invitation.* PHRASAL VB : V+O+ADV, OFT+*to*

pass out. If you **pass out**, you faint or collapse. EG *I thought I was going to pass out.* PHRASAL VB : V+ADV

pass over. If you **pass over** a topic in a conversation, you do not discuss it. EG *He passed over the events of that week.* PHRASAL VB : V+PREP

pass round or **pass around.** If a group of people **pass** something **round** or **pass** it **around**, they each take it and then give it to the next person. EG *Pass the matches round.* PHRASAL VB : V+O+ADV/ PREP

pass up. If you **pass up** a chance or an opportunity, you do not také advantage of it. EG *I wouldn't have passed up the chance for a million dollars.* PHRASAL VB : V+O+ADV

passable /pɑ:səbə⁰l/. **1** If you say that something is **passable**, you mean that its quality is satisfactory. EG *...some passable small restaurants... They make a passable imitation of the Spanish drink.* ADJ QUALIT

2 If a road or path is **passable**, it is not completely blocked, and people can still use it. EG *Many of these roads are not passable in bad weather.* ADJ PRED

passage /pæsɪdʒ/, **passages. 1** A **passage** is **1.1** a long, narrow space with walls or fences on both sides, which connects one place or room with another. EG *At the end of the narrow passage was a bathroom... We went along a little passage to the garden.* N COUNT **1.2** an empty space that allows you to move through a crowd of people or things. EG *Her aides had to go on ahead of her to clear a passage.* N SING **1.3** a long, narrow hole or tube in your body, which air or liquid can pass along. EG *...the nasal passages... ...the passages into the lungs.* N COUNT : USU+SUPP

2 A **passage** in a book, speech, or piece of music is a section of it that you are considering separately from the rest. EG *There's one brilliant passage in the book, where the Italian finds the money... The flute and oboe have long solo passages.* N COUNT

3 The **passage** of someone or something is **3.1** their movement from one place to another. EG *The wind of the train's passage ruffled his hair.* **3.2** their progress from one stage in their development or situation to another. EG *...his rapid passage into senior philosophical circles.* N UNCOUNT +POSS

4 A **passage** is also a journey by ship. EG *The passage across to Belfast was very rough.* N COUNT

5 The **passage** of a period of time is its passing. EG *...despite the passage of two thousand years.* N SING : *the*+N+*of*

passageway /pæsɪdʒweɪ/, **passageways.** A **passageway** is a long, narrow space with walls or fences on both sides, which connects one place or room with another. N COUNT

passenger /pæsɪndʒə/, **passengers.** A **passenger** in a vehicle such as a bus, boat, or plane is a person who is travelling in it, but who is not the driver or a member of the crew. EG *The ferry service handles 400 passengers a week.* N COUNT

passer-by /pɑ:sə baɪ/, **passers-by.** A **passer-by** is a person who is walking past someone or something. EG *One of the boys stopped a passer-by and asked him to phone an ambulance.* N COUNT

passing /pɑ:sɪŋ/. **1 Passing** feelings, activities, or fashions last for only a short period of time. EG *...the passing whims of her mother.* ADJ CLASSIF : ATTRIB

2 If you mention something **in passing**, you mention it briefly while you are talking or writing about something else. EG *We can note, in passing, the rapid expansion of private security organisations.* PHRASE

3 See also **pass**.

passion /pæʃə⁰n/, **passions. 1 Passion** is **1.1** a feeling of very strong sexual attraction for someone. EG *I felt such extraordinary passion for this girl.* **1.2** a very strong feeling about something or a strong belief in something. EG *Anna hated them with passion... ...their attempt to arouse nationalistic passions against the foreigner.* N UNCOUNT OR N PLURAL

2 If you have a **passion** for something, you have a very strong interest in it and like it very much. EG *She had developed a passion for gardens... Biology is their great passion at the moment.* N COUNT+SUPP

passionate /pæʃənə¹t/. A **passionate** person **1** has very strong feelings about something or a strong belief in something. EG *...a passionate social reformer... ...a passionate speech.* ◊ **passionately.** EG *People care deeply and passionately about this issue.* ADJ QUALIT ◊ ADV **2** has strong romantic or sexual feelings and expresses them in their behaviour. EG *...a passionate and lonely woman... ...passionate love.* ◊ **passionately.** EG *They were kissing passionately.* ADJ QUALIT ◊ ADV

passive /pæsɪv/. **1** Someone who is **passive** does not react or show their feelings when things are said to them or done to them. EG *She was so enraged that she could remain passive no longer.* ◊ **passively.** EG *They accept passively every law that is passed.* ADJ QUALIT ◊ ADV

2 In grammar, the **passive** is the form of the verb which is made up of the auxiliary verb 'be' and the past participle of a main verb. See the entry headed VERBS for more information. N UNCOUNT

passport /pɑ:spɔ:t/, **passports. 1** A **passport** is an official document containing your name, photograph, and personal details, which you need to show when you enter or leave a country. EG *My husband has a British passport.* N COUNT

2 If you say that a thing is a **passport** to an achievement, you mean that this thing makes it possible. EG *The right contacts were the only passports to success.* N COUNT+*to*

password /pɑ:swɜ:d/, **passwords.** A **password** is a secret word or phrase that you must know in order to be allowed to enter a place such as a military base, or allowed to use a computer system. N COUNT

past /pɑ:st/. **1** The **past** is the period of time before the present, and the things that happened in that period. EG *He was highly praised in the past as head of the National Security Agency... ...the great Sanskrit dramas of the past.* N SING : *the*+N

2 Your **past** consists of all the things that happened to you before the present time. EG *He never discussed his past... ...Britain's imperial past.* N SING : USU+POSS

3 Past things are things that happened or existed before the present time. EG *He refused to answer questions about his past business dealings... They criticised past Governments for spending £3,500m on military aid... ...in past centuries.* ADJ CLASSIF : ATTRIB

4 You use **past** to talk about an amount of time that has finished. If you talk about the **past** week or the **past** five years, for example, you mean the week or five years before the present week or year. EG *I've spent the past eight years at sea... He'd been through such a lot in the past hour.* ADJ CLASSIF : ATTRIB

5 You use **past** when you are telling the time. For example, if it is twenty **past** six, it is twenty minutes after six o'clock. EG *It's ten past eleven... ...half past eight... It's quarter past.* PREP OR ADV

6 If something such as a situation or feeling is **past**, it no longer exists. EG *All danger was now past... ...things one remembers, although they are past and gone.* ADJ PRED

7 If you go **past** something, you go near it and then continue moving until you are on the other side of it. EG *He walked past Lock's hat shop... He drove straight past me... People ran past laughing.* PREP OR ADV

8 If something is **past** a place, it is situated on the other side of it. EG *Past Doctor Ford's surgery was the grocer's.* PREP

9 If you say that someone is **past it**, you mean that they no longer have the skill or energy to do something because they are too old. PHRASE Informal

10 If you say that you **would not put it past** someone to do something, you mean that you PHRASE would not be surprised if they did it, because of their character or previous actions. EG *I wouldn't put it past him to shoot the husband and the wife.*

pasta /pæstə/ is a type of food made from a mixture of flour, eggs, and water that is formed into different shapes. Spaghetti, macaroni, and noodles are types of pasta.
N UNCOUNT

paste /peɪst/, **pastes, pasting, pasted. 1 Paste** is **1.1** a soft, wet, often sticky mixture of a substance and a liquid, which can be spread easily. EG *Mix together the flour and the water to form a paste.*
N UNCOUNT OR N COUNT

1.2 a soft, smooth, sticky mixture of food that you spread onto bread or toast. EG *...sandwiches filled with duck paste.*
N UNCOUNT

2 If you **paste** something on a surface or if you **paste** a surface with it, you put glue or paste on it and stick it on the surface. EG *Labels were pasted to some of the clippings... The children were busy pasting gold stars on a chart.*
V+O+A

3 Paste is also a hard shiny glass that is used for making imitation jewellery. EG *...sparkling like a paste brooch.*
N UNCOUNT

pastel /pæstə^{0}l/, **pastels. 1 Pastel** colours are pale rather than dark or bright. EG *...pastel shades of pink, blue, and brown.* ▸ used as a noun. EG *Our new range of paints includes some new subtle pastels.*
ADJ CLASSIF : ATTRIB; ▸ N COUNT : USU PLURAL

2 Pastels are also small sticks of different coloured chalks that are used for drawing pictures.
N COUNT : USU PLURAL

pasteurized /pɑːstjəraɪzd/. **Pasteurized** milk or cream has had bacteria removed from it by means of a special heating process.
ADJ CLASSIF

pastime /pɑːstaɪm/, **pastimes.** A **pastime** is something that you do because you enjoy it or are interested in it, rather than as part of your job. EG *...leisurely pastimes, like gardening, woodwork, music and toy-making.*
N COUNT

pastoral /pɑːstə^{0}rəl/. The **pastoral** duties and activities of clergy in the Christian churches relate to the general needs of people, rather than just their religious needs. EG *...a pastoral visit.*
ADJ CLASSIF : ATTRIB

past participle, past participles. In grammar, the **past participle** of a verb is a form which usually ends in '-ed' or '-en'. It is used to form some tenses and the passive voice, and can also be used like an adjective in front of nouns.
N COUNT

pastry /peɪstri^{1}/, **pastries. 1 Pastry** is a food made of flour, fat, and water that is mixed into a dough and then rolled flat. It is used for making pies and flans.
N MASS

2 A **pastry** is a small cake made with sweet pastry. EG *...pastries filled with custard or whipped cream.*
N COUNT

past tense. In grammar, the **past tense** is used to refer mainly to things that happened or existed before the time when you are speaking or writing.
N SING : *the*+N

pasture /pɑːstʃə/, **pastures. Pasture** is land that has grass growing on it and that is used for farm animals to graze on. EG *...five acres of pasture... ...the lush green pastures of Ireland.*
N UNCOUNT OR N COUNT

pasty, pasties; pronounced /peɪsti^{1}/ when it is an adjective and /pæsti^{1}/ when it is a noun.

1 If you are **pasty** or if you have a **pasty** face, you look pale and unhealthy. EG *They looked pasty and red-eyed because they'd been up all night.*
ADJ QUALIT

2 A **pasty** is a small pie which consists of pastry folded around meat, vegetables, or cheese.
N COUNT

pat /pæt/, **pats, patting, patted. 1** If you **pat** something, you tap it or hit it lightly, usually with your fingers. EG *He patted the tree trunk softly.* ▸ used as a noun. EG *...a friendly pat on the shoulder.*
V+O; ▸ N COUNT

2 A **pat** of butter or something else soft is a small lump of it.
N PART

3 A **pat** answer or remark is something you say that sounds prepared, for example an answer to a question that you are expecting to be asked. EG *I unfailingly gave my pat reply.*
ADJ CLASSIF : ATTRIB

patch /pætʃ/, **patches, patching, patched. 1** A **patch** is **1.1** a piece of material which you use to cover a hole in something. EG *I mended holes in the sheets by sewing on square patches.* **1.2** a small piece of material which you wear to cover an injured eye. EG *...an eye patch.*
N COUNT

2 If you **patch** something that has a hole in it, you mend it by fastening a patch over the hole. EG *They patched the leaking roof... Anne sat by the fire, patching a pair of jeans.*
V+O

3 A **patch** on a surface is a part of it which is different in appearance from the area around it. EG *...the damp patch at the corner of the ceiling... ...patches of snow... He had a bald patch.*
N COUNT+SUPP

4 You can refer to a part of something which you are considering separately from the rest as a **patch**. EG *There are some wonderful patches in this poem... ...the difficult patches in their relationship.*
N COUNT+SUPP

5 If you say that someone or something **is not a patch on** someone or something else, you mean that they are not nearly as good as the other person or thing. EG *Joe's not a patch on his father.*
PHRASE Informal

patch together. If you **patch** something **together**, you form it from a number of parts in a quick or careless way. EG *A new government was patched together with the help of the military.*
PHRASAL VB : V+O+ADV

patch up. 1 If you **patch up** something which is damaged, you mend it or patch it so that it can be used. EG *They have to patch up the mud walls that the rains have battered.* **2** If you **patch up** a quarrel or relationship with someone, you try to be friends again and not to quarrel any more. EG *They tried to patch things up.*
PHRASAL VB : V+O+ADV; V+O+ADV

patchwork /pætʃwɜːk/. **1** A **patchwork** quilt or dress has been made by sewing together small pieces of material of different colours. EG *...a patchwork skirt... ...patchwork cushions.*
ADJ CLASSIF : ATTRIB

2 If you refer to something as a **patchwork**, you mean that it is made up of different parts or pieces. EG *...this marvellous patchwork of meadows and marsh.*
N SING+SUPP

patchy /pætʃi^{1}/. **1** Something that is **patchy** is not spread evenly, but is scattered around in small quantities. EG *If you dye clothes in too small a pan, the colour will be patchy.*
ADJ QUALIT

2 If you describe information or knowledge as **patchy**, you mean that it is incomplete or unsatisfactory, for example because it is not correct in all parts. EG *The evidence is a bit patchy... He has a rather patchy grasp of history.*
ADJ QUALIT

pâté /pæteɪ/ is a mixture of meat, fish, or vegetables with various flavourings, which is blended into a paste and eaten cold. EG *...chicken liver pâté.*
N MASS

patent /peɪtə^{0}nt/, **patents, patenting, patented;** also pronounced /pætə^{0}nt/ in paragraphs 1 and 2.

1 A **patent** is an official right to be the only person or company allowed to make or sell a new product for a certain period of time. EG *The first English patent for a typewriter was issued in 1714... To protect his new invention he took out a patent on it... ...drugs whose patents had expired.*
N COUNT

2 If you **patent** something, you obtain a patent for it. EG *In the early 1870s he patented the sugar cube... I never attempted to patent the idea.*
V+O

3 You can use **patent** to say that something is obvious. EG *...a patent impossibility in such a small room... This is patent nonsense... ...the patent honesty of Butler.* ◊ **patently.** EG *Anne was patently annoyed.*
ADJ CLASSIF : ATTRIB Formal; ◊ ADV

4 Patent or **patent leather** is leather or plastic which has a shiny surface and is used especially to make shoes and handbags. EG *...a pair of black patent leather shoes.*
N UNCOUNT : USU N MOD

paternal /pətɜːnə^{0}l/ is used to describe things relating to a father. EG *...lack of paternal love... ...a paternal duty... ...our paternal grandmother.*
ADJ CLASSIF : ATTRIB

path /pɑːθ/, **paths. 1** A **path** is **1.1** a long, thin line of ground that has been marked by people walking,
N COUNT

What food is mentioned on these pages?

for example through a forest or up a mountain. EG *The path was easy to follow, then it just stopped.* **1.2** a strip of ground for people to walk on. Paths are often covered with concrete or gravel and made in gardens, parks, or along the sides of roads. EG *He went up the path to his front door.*

2 Your **path** is the space ahead of you which you are moving towards. EG *On arrival he found his path barred... It moves forward killing anything in its path.* ● If you **cross** someone's **path** or if your **paths cross**, you meet them by chance. EG *Our paths had crossed many years before.* N COUNT+POSS ● PHRASE

3 The **path** of something is the line which it moves along in a particular direction. EG *The bullet had scored its path across the skin of the fruit... The flight path of the 747 carried it directly overhead.* N COUNT+POSS

4 A **path** that you take is a particular course of action or way of doing something. EG *I criticized the path the government was taking... He saw public ownership as one of many paths to achieving a socialist society.* N COUNT+SUPP

pathetic /pəθetɪk/. If you describe someone or something as **pathetic**, **1** you mean that they are sad and weak or helpless, and that they make you feel pity and sadness. EG *It was pathetic to see a man to whom reading meant so much become almost totally blind... The kitten was so tiny and pathetic.* ◇ **pathetically.** EG *He looked pathetically defenceless.* **2** you mean that they are so bad or weak that they make you feel impatient or angry. EG *Our efforts so far have been rather pathetic... It was a stupid pathetic joke.* ADJ QUALIT ◇ ADV ADJ QUALIT

pathological /pæθəlɒdʒɪkəºl/. **1** You use **pathological** to describe people who behave in an extreme way and cannot control themselves easily. EG *...a pathological liar... He has a pathological urge to succeed... ...a pathological fear of being late.* ADJ CLASSIF

2 Pathological also means relating to pathology. EG *...pathological changes in the nervous system... ...a pathological deviation from normal sexual development.* ADJ CLASSIF : ATTRIB Medical

pathology /pəᶾθɒlədʒiˡ/ is the branch of medicine that is concerned with the study of the way diseases and illnesses develop. N UNCOUNT Medical

pathos /peɪθɒs/ is a quality in a situation, film, or play that makes people feel sadness and pity. EG *...the pathos of his situation... They have eyes full of sadness and pathos... ...a scene of real pathos.* N UNCOUNT Formal

pathway /pɑːθweɪ/, **pathways.** A **pathway** is a path which you can walk along or a route which you can take. EG *Marsha could make out a possible pathway through the wire.* N COUNT

patience /peɪʃəns/. **1** If you have **patience**, you are able to stay calm and not get annoyed, for example when you are waiting for something. EG *It took a vast amount of patience not to shout at him... Paul was waiting his turn with patience... I've lost all patience with him and his excuses.* N UNCOUNT

2 If you **try** someone's **patience**, you annoy them so much that it is very difficult for them to stay calm. EG *I tried her patience to the limit.* PHRASE

3 Patience is also a card game for only one player. N UNCOUNT

patient /peɪʃənt/, **patients. 1** If you are **patient**, you are able to stay calm and not get annoyed, for example when you are waiting for something. EG *He was very patient with me... Just be patient.* ◇ **patiently.** EG *He answered my questions patiently... James waited patiently for her to finish.* ADJ QUALIT ◇ ADV

2 A **patient** is a person who is receiving medical treatment from a doctor or hospital, or who is registered with a particular doctor. EG *...a consultant who treats kidney patients at the Manchester Royal Infirmary.* N COUNT

patio /pætɪəʊ/, **patios.** A **patio** is an area of paving or concrete in a garden close to a house, where people can sit in chairs. EG *She was sitting in a deck chair on the patio.* N COUNT

patriot /pætrɪət, peɪt-/, **patriots.** Someone who is a **patriot** loves their country and feels very loyal towards it. EG *...Swiss patriots.* N COUNT

patriotic /pætrɪɒtɪk, peɪt-/. Someone who is **patriotic** loves their country and feels very loyal towards it. EG *...a patriotic song... ...patriotic fervour... Perhaps I'm old-fashioned and patriotic.* ADJ QUALIT

patriotism /pætrɪətɪzəºm, peɪt-/ is love for your country and loyalty towards it. EG *Her patriotism would not permit her to buy a foreign car.* N UNCOUNT

patrol /pətrəʊl/, **patrols, patrolling, patrolled. 1** When soldiers, police, or guards **patrol** an area or building, they move around it in order to make sure that there is no trouble there. EG *I saw men patrolling the streets with rifles on their backs... ...the policeman who is patrolling in a dangerous area.* ▸ used as a noun. EG *An entire platoon was ambushed during a patrol... The police came in a black patrol car.* V+O OR V+A ▸ N COUNT

2 People who are **on patrol** are patrolling an area. EG *Two policemen on patrol saw the boy running away.* PHRASE

3 A **patrol** is also a group of soldiers or vehicles that are patrolling an area. N COUNT

patron /peɪtrən/, **patrons.** A **patron** is **1** a person who supports and gives money to artists, writers, or musicians. EG *His portraits did not always please his patrons... ...an entrepreneur and patron of the arts.* **2** an important person who is interested in a particular charity, group, or campaign and who allows his or her name to be used for publicity. EG *Our Chamber Music Society has the Lord Mayor as its patron.* **3** a person who uses a particular shop or hotel, especially one who uses it frequently. EG *Patrons are requested to wear neat attire.* N COUNT : USU+POSS Formal

patronage /pætrənɪdʒ/ is the support and money given by someone to a person or a group such as a charity. EG *...public patronage of the arts... Dalton the physicist received lavish patronage.* N UNCOUNT

patronize /pætrənaɪz/, **patronizes, patronizing, patronized;** also spelled **patronise. 1** If someone **patronizes** you, they speak or behave towards you in a way which seems friendly, but which shows that they think they are superior to you in some way; used showing disapproval. EG *She seemed to think that experience gave her the right to patronise... Don't patronize me!* ◇ **patronizing** /pætrənaɪzɪŋ/. EG *Their smile was rather patronizing... ...a patronizing attitude.* V+O OR V ◇ ADJ QUALIT

2 Someone who **patronizes** artists, writers, or musicians supports them and gives them money. EG *Henry VII patronized a Flemish artist, Mabuse.* V+O Formal

patron saint, patron saints. The **patron saint** of a place, an activity, or a group of people is someone, usually a saint, who is believed to give them special help and protection. EG *...the patron saint of the abbey... ...St Hubert, patron saint of hunters.* N COUNT+SUPP

patter /pætə/, **patters, pattering, pattered. 1** If something **patters** on a surface, it hits it quickly several times, making quiet, tapping sounds. EG *Spots of rain pattered on the window... Dead leaves pattered against the walls... I heard her feet pattering about upstairs.* V+A

2 A **patter** is a series of quick, quiet, tapping sounds. EG *They heard a patter of paws on matting as the dog came to meet them... They fell with a soft patter, like raindrops on dry leaves.* N SING

3 An entertainer's **patter** or a salesperson's **patter** is a speech or talk that he or she has learned and says quickly in order to entertain or influence people. EG *He gave the usual patter about watertight boxes... Bill kept up a steady patter.* N COUNT : USU+SUPP

pattern /pætəºn/, **patterns, patterned. 1** A **pattern** is a particular way in which something is usually done or organized. EG *Over the next few months their work pattern changed... ...behaviour patterns... It fits in with the pattern of her family life.* N COUNT : OFT+SUPP

2 A **pattern** is also **2.1** an arrangement of lines or shapes, especially a design in which the same shape is repeated at regular intervals over a surface. EG *Jack was drawing a pattern in the sand with his forefinger... ...a frock with a pattern of little red apples.* **2.2** a diagram or shape that you can use as a guide when you are making something such as a model or a piece of clothing. EG *...sewing patterns.* N COUNT

3 If something new **is patterned** on something else that already exists, it is deliberately made so that it has similar features to it. EG *The 'Daily Dispatch' was patterned on the British press.* V-PASS+*on*

patterned /pætəⁿnd/. Something that is **patterned** is covered with a pattern or design. EG *...patterned carpets... ...ties patterned with flowers.* ADJ CLASSIF

paunch /pɔːntʃ/, **paunches.** If a man has a **paunch**, he has a fat stomach. N COUNT

pauper /pɔːpə/, **paupers.** A **pauper** is a very poor person. EG *Jefferson died a pauper.* N COUNT Outdated

pause /pɔːz/, **pauses, pausing, paused. 1** If you **pause** while you are speaking, you stop speaking for a short time, often in order to think before you continue. EG *He paused and then went on in a low voice.* V

2 If you **pause** while you are moving or doing something, you stop for a moment. EG *He paused with a hand on the doorknob... He does not pause for breath until he reaches the top floor... He can do this without pausing in his work.* V

3 A **pause** is **3.1** a moment of silence when a sound, for example speech or music, stops before beginning again. EG *She continued after a pause... My signal will be three knocks, a pause, then two more.* **3.2** a short period when you stop doing what you are doing, for example to have a rest, before continuing again. EG *He went on for 35 minutes without a pause... The insect moves slowly, with frequent pauses to gather strength.* N COUNT

pave /peɪv/, **paves, paving, paved. 1** When a road or an area of ground **is paved**, it is covered with blocks of stone or concrete, so that it is suitable for walking or driving on. ◊ **paved.** EG *...a steep causeway paved with slabs of granite.* V+O : OFT PASS ◊ ADJ CLASSIF

2 If one thing **paves the way** for another, it creates a situation in which the other thing is more likely to happen or more able to happen. EG *His work paved the way for Burkitt's theories.* PHRASE

pavement /peɪvməˀnt/, **pavements.** A **pavement** is a path with a hard surface, usually by the side of a street. EG *He was standing on the pavement outside the bank.* N COUNT

pavilion /pəvɪljən/, **pavilions.** A **pavilion** is a building on the edge of a sports field where players can change their clothes and wash. N COUNT British

paving stone, paving stones. Paving stones are flat pieces of stone, usually square in shape, that are used for making pavements. N COUNT : USU PLURAL

paw /pɔː/, **paws, pawing, pawed. 1** The **paws** of an animal such as a cat, dog, or bear are its feet, which have claws for gripping things and soft pads for walking on. EG *...a black cat with white paws.* N COUNT

2 If an animal **paws** something, it draws its paw or hoof over it or hits at it. EG *...bulls pawing the earth... The dog pawed at the door again.* V+O OR V+*at*

pawn /pɔːn/, **pawns, pawning, pawned. 1** If you **pawn** something that you own, you leave it with a pawnbroker, who gives you money for it and who can sell it if you do not pay back the money before a certain time. EG *Brian didn't have a watch – he had pawned it some years ago.* V+O

2 In chess, a **pawn** is the smallest and least valuable playing piece. Each player has eight pawns at the start of the game. N COUNT

3 If you refer to someone as a **pawn**, you mean that another person is using them for his or her own advantage. EG *We are simply pawns in the hands of larger powers... Their players were being used as pawns to gain international support.* N COUNT

pawnbroker /pɔːnbrəʊkə/, **pawnbrokers.** A **pawnbroker** is a person who will lend you money if you give them something that you own. The pawnbroker can sell that thing if you do not pay back the money before a certain time. N COUNT

pay /peɪ/, **pays, paying, paid** /peɪd/. **1** When you **pay** an amount of money to someone, you give it to them because you are buying something from them or because you owe it to them. When you **pay** a bill or a debt, you pay the amount that is required or owed. EG *He had paid £5,000 for the boat... ...money to pay the window cleaner... He paid his bill and left... Pay me five pounds... Willie paid for the drinks... I'll pay by cheque.* • to **pay through the nose**: see **nose**. V+O OR V+O+O; ALSO V : OFT+A

2 When your employers **pay** you, they give you your wages or salary. EG *She was being paid sixty dollars a week... The company pays well.* V+O, V+O+O, OR V+A

3 Someone's **pay** is the money that they receive as their wages or salary. EG *The pay is dreadful... She lost three weeks' pay... ...a pay rise of £20 a week.* N UNCOUNT

4 If a job, deal, or investment **pays** a particular amount, it brings you that amount of money. EG *She complained about her job and how poorly it paid... A day's work pays £2,500.* V+O OR V+A

5 If a course of action **pays**, it results in some advantage or benefit for you. EG *It pays to keep on the right side of your boss.* V : OFT+*to*-INF

6 If you **pay** for something that you do or have, you suffer as a result. EG *He paid dearly for his mistake... The men paid with their lives... You failed, and you must pay the penalty.* V+*for/with* OR V+O

7 You use **pay** with some nouns to indicate that something is given or done. EG *It would be nice if you paid me a visit... I paid little attention to what I heard... It was probably the greatest compliment I could have paid her.* V+O OR V+O+O

8 If you **pay** your **way**, you pay for things that you need rather than letting other people pay for them. PHRASE

9 See also **paid**.

pay back. 1 If you **pay back** some money that you have borrowed from someone, you return it to them. EG *I'll pay you back next week.* **2** If you **pay** someone **back** for doing something unpleasant to you, you make them suffer for what they did. PHRASAL VB : V+O+ADV; V+O+ADV

pay off. 1 If you **pay off** a debt, you give someone all the money that you owe them. EG *He had used the firm's money to pay off gambling debts.* **2** If an action **pays off**, it is successful. EG *It was a risk and it paid off.* **3** See also **payoff**. PHRASAL VB : V+O+ADV; V+ADV

pay out. If you **pay out** money, usually a large amount, you spend it on a particular thing or activity. EG *He had paid out good money to educate Julie at a boarding school.* PHRASAL VB : V+O+ADV

pay up. If you **pay up**, you give someone the money that you owe them. EG *Pay up, son, and come along quietly.* PHRASAL VB : V+ADV

payable /peɪəbəⁿl/. **1** If an amount of money is **payable**, it has to be paid or it can be paid. EG *The interest payable on these loans was vast... This allowance is payable whether she lives with the man or not.* ADJ PRED

2 If a cheque is made **payable** to you, it has your name written on it to indicate that you are the person who will receive the money. EG *Cheques should be made payable to Trans Euro Travel Ltd.* ADJ PRED+*to*

payment /peɪməˀnt/, **payments. 1 Payment** is the act of paying money to someone or of being paid. EG *Was the payment of rent optional?... When can I expect payment?* N UNCOUNT

2 A **payment** is an amount of money that is paid to someone. EG *Some said that social security payments were too high.* N COUNT

payoff /peɪɒf/, **payoffs. 1** A **payoff** is a result of a particular action, usually a good one. EG *Some carry* N COUNT

If you pay off a debt, do you pay up?

out research and hope that there could be a practical pay-off.

2 A **payoff** is also a payment made to someone when they have been dismissed from their job. EG *The casualties received generous redundancy pay-offs.* N COUNT

payroll /peɪrəʊl/, **payrolls.** If you are on an organization's **payroll**, you are employed and paid by that organization. N COUNT

PC /piː siː/, **PCs.** A **PC** is a male police officer of the lowest rank in Britain. **PC** is an abbreviation for 'police constable'. EG *...PC Cooper.* N COUNT

pea /piː/, **peas. Peas** are small, round, green seeds which are eaten as a vegetable. EG *...a packet of frozen peas.* N COUNT: USU PLURAL

peace /piːs/. 1 If you have **peace**, you are not being disturbed, and you are in calm, quiet surroundings. EG *I shall need some peace and quiet in which to practise... Go away and leave us in peace... He returned to the peace of his village.* N UNCOUNT

2 If you have a feeling of **peace** or if you are at **peace**, you feel contented and calm and not at all worried. EG *...the search for inner peace... For your own peace of mind you should find out what happened... ...a child at peace with her surroundings.* N UNCOUNT

3 When a country is at **peace**, it is not involved in a war. EG *Their activities threaten world peace... ...peace negotiations... ...in times of peace.* N UNCOUNT

4 If there is **peace** among a group of people or if they live at **peace** with each other, they live or work together in a friendly way and do not quarrel. EG *She had done it for the sake of peace in the family... ...the peace and good order of society.* N UNCOUNT

5 If you **make peace** with someone or **make** your **peace** with them, you put an end to your quarrel with them, often by apologizing. EG *He went to her room to make peace.* PHRASE

peaceable /piːsəbəᵒl/. Someone who is **peaceable** tries to avoid quarrelling or fighting with other people. EG *...peaceable citizens.* ADJ QUALIT

peaceful /piːsfʊl/. 1 A **peaceful** place or time is quiet, calm, and undisturbed. EG *It's so nice and peaceful here... ...peaceful parks and gardens... It was a peaceful Christmas.* ◊ **peacefully.** EG *They lived there peacefully, happily.* ADJ QUALIT ◊ ADV

2 Someone who feels or looks **peaceful** is calm and not at all worried. EG *He looked peaceful as he lay there.* ◊ **peacefully.** EG *That night he slept peacefully.* ADJ QUALIT ◊ ADV

3 **Peaceful** people are not violent and try to avoid quarrelling or fighting with other people. EG *...the most peaceful nation on earth... ...peaceful demonstrations in Bonn.* ADJ QUALIT

peach /piːtʃ/, **peaches.** 1 A **peach** is a soft, round, juicy fruit with sweet yellow flesh and pinky-orange skin. Peaches grow in warm countries. EG *...the best peaches I ever tasted.* N COUNT

2 Something that is **peach** is pale pinky-orange in colour. EG *...soft peach chiffon.* ADJ COLOUR

peacock /piːkɒk/, **peacocks.** A **peacock** is a large bird. The male has a very long tail which it can spread out like a fan and which is marked with beautiful blue and green spots. N COUNT

peak /piːk/, **peaks, peaking, peaked.** 1 The **peak** of a process or an activity is the point at which it is at its strongest, most successful, or most fully developed. EG *They were trained to a peak of physical fitness... Computer technology has not yet reached its peak.* N COUNT: USU SING

2 When someone or something **peaks**, they reach the highest value or the highest level of success. EG *The annual workload peaks at harvest time.* V

3 The **peak** level or value of something is its highest level or value. EG *...the peak voltage... ...a peak output of 165 cars per day.* ADJ CLASSIF: ATTRIB

4 The **peak** of a mountain is the pointed top of it; also sometimes used of the mountain itself. EG *It is one of the highest peaks in the Alps.* N COUNT

5 The **peak** of a cap is the part at the front that sticks out above your eyes. EG *He wore a brown cloth cap with the peak pulled down over his eyes.* N COUNT

peaked /piːkt/. A **peaked** cap has a pointed or rounded part that sticks out above your eyes. ADJ CLASSIF: ATTRIB

peal /piːl/, **peals, pealing, pealed.** 1 When bells **peal**, they ring one after the other, making a musical sound. EG *Nearby church bells pealed across the quiet city.* ▸ used as a noun. EG *...a peal of bells.* V ▸ N COUNT

2 A **peal** of laughter or thunder consists of a long, loud series of sounds. EG *...bursting into peals of laughter... I was woken up by that peal of thunder.* N COUNT+SUPP

peanut /piːnʌt/, **peanuts. Peanuts** are small oval-shaped nuts that grow under the ground. Peanuts are often eaten as a snack, especially roasted and salted. N COUNT: USU PLURAL

pear

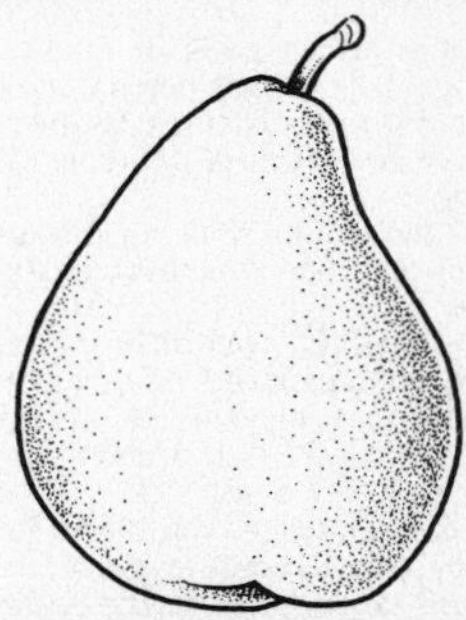

pear /pɛə/, **pears.** A **pear** is a sweet, juicy fruit which is narrow near its stalk, and wider and rounded at the bottom. Pears have white flesh and thin green or yellow skin. N COUNT

pearl /pɜːl/, **pearls.** A **pearl** is a hard, round object which is shiny and creamy white in colour. Pearls grow inside the shell of an oyster and are used for making expensive jewellery. EG *She was wearing a string of pearls.* • See also **mother-of-pearl**. N COUNT

pearly /pɜːliˡ/. Something that is **pearly** has the appearance of pearls. EG *...pearly teeth... ...pearly pink light... ...pearly water... ...pearly skies.* ADJ CLASSIF

peasant /pɛzəᵒnt/, **peasants.** A **peasant** is a person who works on the land, especially one who owns a small piece of land in a poor country. N COUNT

peasantry /pɛzəᵒntriˡ/. All the peasants in a country are referred to as the **peasantry**. EG *The middle classes were no friends of the peasantry.* N COLL Outdated

peat /piːt/ is black or brown decaying plant material which is found under the ground in some cool, wet regions. Peat can be added to soil to help plants grow, or can be burnt on fires instead of coal. N UNCOUNT

pebble /pɛbəᵒl/, **pebbles.** A **pebble** is a smooth, round stone which is found on seashores and river beds. EG *...the pebbles on the beach.* N COUNT

peck /pɛk/, **pecks, pecking, pecked.** 1 If a bird **pecks** something, it moves its beak forward quickly and bites at it. EG *...a plump brown hen, pecking around for grains of corn... Larger birds may peck holes in their eggs.* ▸ used as a noun. EG *It hopped over and made a quick peck at the ground.* V+O OR V: USU+A ▸ N COUNT

2 If you **peck** someone on the cheek, you give them a quick, light kiss. ▸ used as a noun. EG *She gave him a peck on the cheek.* V+O: USU+A ▸ N COUNT

peckish /pɛkɪʃ/. If you say that you are feeling **peckish**, you mean that you are fairly hungry. EG *Well, children, I expect you're feeling rather peckish.* ADJ PRED Informal British

peculiar /pɪ²kjuːlɪə/. 1 If you describe someone or something as **peculiar**, you mean that they are strange, often in an unpleasant way. EG *That lemon is a very peculiar shape... He was wearing a* ADJ QUALIT *peculiar suit... She gave him a peculiar look.* ◇ **peculiarly.** EG *Molly is behaving rather peculiarly these days.* ◇ ADV

2 If you say that you feel **peculiar**, you mean that you feel slightly ill or dizzy. EG *Seeing blood makes me feel a bit peculiar inside.* ADJ PRED

3 If something is **peculiar** to a particular thing, person, or situation, it belongs or relates only to that thing, person, or situation. EG *...the style of decoration peculiar to the late 1920s.* ADJ CLASSIF : OFT+*to*
◇ **peculiarly.** EG *It's an idiom that people recognise as peculiarly English... ...that peculiarly feminine form of love.* ◇ ADV

peculiarity /pɪ²kjuːlɪærɪ¹ti¹/, **peculiarities. 1** A **peculiarity** that someone or something has is a strange or unusual habit or characteristic. EG *It was one of Boylan's peculiarities that he wanted to humiliate her.* N COUNT : USU+POSS

2 A **peculiarity** is also a thing or quality which belongs or relates only to that person or thing. EG *Each city has its own peculiarities, its own history and character... Is this form of politeness really a British peculiarity?* N COUNT : USU+POSS

3 **Peculiarity** is the quality of being strange, often in an unpleasant way. EG *...the peculiarity of the colonial situation.* N UNCOUNT

pedal /pɛdə⁰l/, **pedals, pedalling, pedalled;** spelled **pedaling** and **pedaled** in American English. **1** The **pedals** on a bicycle are the two parts that you push with your feet in order to make the bicycle move. See picture at BICYCLE. N COUNT

2 When you **pedal** a bicycle, you push the pedals around with your feet to make it move. EG *It was time to pedal the three miles to the restaurant... His legs were aching from pedalling too fast.* V+O OR V

3 A **pedal** in a car or on a machine is a lever that you press with your foot in order to control the car or machine. N COUNT

pedant /pɛdənt/, **pedants.** If you say that someone is a **pedant**, you mean that they are too concerned with unimportant details or traditional rules, especially in connection with academic subjects. EG *...some pedant muttering something about 'only canvas would be used by real artists.'* N COUNT

pedantic /pɪ²dæntɪk/. If you describe someone as **pedantic**, you mean that they are too concerned with unimportant details or traditional rules, especially in connection with academic subjects. EG *...a fussy and pedantic middle-aged clerk.* ADJ QUALIT

peddle /pɛdə⁰l/, **peddles, peddling, peddled. 1** Someone who **peddles** drugs sells illegal drugs. V+O

2 If someone **peddles** an idea or piece of information, they try hard to get people to accept it. EG *...the unreliable gossip that had been peddled for so long... ...those who peddled this solution.* V+O

peddler /pɛdlə/, **peddlers.** A drug **peddler** is a person who sells illegal drugs. N COUNT : USU+SUPP

pedestal /pɛdɪ²stə⁰l/, **pedestals. 1** A **pedestal** is the base on which a statue or a column stands. EG *At the top of the steps was a bust of Shakespeare on a pedestal.* N COUNT

2 If you **put** someone **on a pedestal**, you admire them too much and do not think that they have any bad qualities at all. EG *I put you on a pedestal: I would have died for you.* PHRASE

pedestrian /pɪ²dɛstrɪən/, **pedestrians. 1** A **pedestrian** is a person who is walking rather than travelling in a vehicle, especially in a town. EG *Pedestrians jostled them on the pavement.* N COUNT

2 If you describe something as **pedestrian**, you mean that it is ordinary and not at all interesting. EG *He brings a touch of style to a government whose members are pretty pedestrian.* ADJ QUALIT

pedestrian crossing, pedestrian crossings. A **pedestrian crossing** is a place where pedestrians can cross a street and where motorists must stop to let them cross. N COUNT

pediatrician /piːdɪətrɪʃə⁰n/. See **paediatrician**.

pedigree /pɛdɪgriː/, **pedigrees. 1** If a dog, cat, or other animal has a **pedigree**, its ancestors are known and recorded. An animal is considered to have a good pedigree when all its known ancestors are of the same type. EG *...fine dogs with pedigrees.* N COUNT

2 A **pedigree** animal is descended from animals which have all been of a particular type, and is therefore considered to be of good quality. ADJ CLASSIF : ATTRIB

3 Someone's **pedigree** is their background or ancestry. EG *He had a criminal pedigree... ...party activists with middle class pedigrees.* N COUNT : USU+SUPP

pee /piː/, **pees, peeing, peed.** Some speakers think that this word is rude. Informal
When someone **pees**, they urinate. *The little boys looked anxiously around for somewhere to pee.* V
▸ used as a noun. EG *I need a pee.* ▸ N SING : *a*+N

peek /piːk/, **peeks, peeking, peeked.** If you **peek** at something or someone, you have a quick look at them, often secretly. EG *He peeked through the bedroom door.* ▸ used as a noun. EG *I took a peek at the list.* V : USU+A Informal ▸ N COUNT : USU *a*+N

peel /piːl/, **peels, peeling, peeled. 1** The **peel** of a fruit such as a lemon or an apple is its skin. EG *...grated lemon peel.* N UNCOUNT : USU+SUPP

2 When you **peel** fruit or vegetables, you remove their skins. EG *I found Jane peeling potatoes.* V+O

3 If a painted surface **is peeling** or if the paint **is peeling** off it, the paint is coming off it in patches. EG *The paint was peeling off the woodwork... ...peeling yellow walls.* V : OFT+*off*, USU CONT

4 If you **are peeling** or if your skin **is peeling**, small pieces of skin are coming off your body, usually because you are sunburnt. EG *Her nose was peeling.* V : USU CONT

peel off. 1 If you **peel** something **off** a surface, you pull it off gently in one piece. EG *I peeled some moss off the wood... Peel off the outer plastic cover.* **2** If you **peel off** a tight piece of clothing, you take it off, especially by turning it inside out. EG *She peeled off her sweater.* PHRASAL VB : V+O+ADV/PREP; PHRASAL VB : V+O+ADV

peelings /piːlɪŋz/. Potato **peelings** are pieces of skin peeled from potatoes. N PLURAL +SUPP

peep /piːp/, **peeps, peeping, peeped. 1** If you **peep** at something, you have a quick look at it, often secretly. EG *They crept up to the glass doors and peeped inside.* ▸ used as a noun. EG *I was allowed in to have a peep at the painting.* V : USU+A ▸ N COUNT

2 If something **peeps** out from behind or under something, a small part of it is visible or becomes visible. EG *The sun was just peeping over the horizon... ...a paper peeping out from under his arm.* V+A Literary

3 If you say that you haven't heard a **peep** out of someone, you mean that they have not said anything or made any noise. N SING : *a*+N Informal

peer /pɪə/, **peers, peering, peered. 1** If you **peer** at something, you look at it very hard, usually because it is difficult to see very clearly. EG *Howard sat peering through the windscreen.* V+A

2 A **peer** is a member of the nobility. N COUNT

3 Your **peers** are the people who are the same age as you or who have the same status as you. EG *...comparing students with their peers outside university.* N COUNT : USU PLURAL Formal

peerage /pɪərɪdʒ/, **peerages. 1** A **peerage** is the rank of being a peer. EG *...an heir to a peerage.* N COUNT

2 The peers of a country are referred to as the **peerage**. EG *...his elevation to the peerage.* N SING : *the*+N

peer group, peer groups. Your **peer group** is the group of people you know who are the same age as you or who have the same social status as you. N COUNT Technical

peeved /piːvd/. If you are **peeved** about something, you are annoyed about it. EG *He was rather peeved to discover that they had gone.* ADJ QUALIT Informal

> If you put someone on a pedestal, are they a statue?

peevish /piːvɪʃ/. Someone who is **peevish** is bad-tempered. EG *Patty was peevish because the cousins took little notice of her.* ◊ **peevishly.** EG *'Where have you been?' she asked peevishly.* ADJ QUALIT; ◊ ADV

peg /pɛg/, **pegs, pegging, pegged.** 1 A **peg** is 1.1 a small hook or knob that is attached to a wall or door and is used for hanging things on. EG *He takes his coat from the peg.* **1.2** a wooden or plastic object used for attaching washing to a clothes line. N COUNT

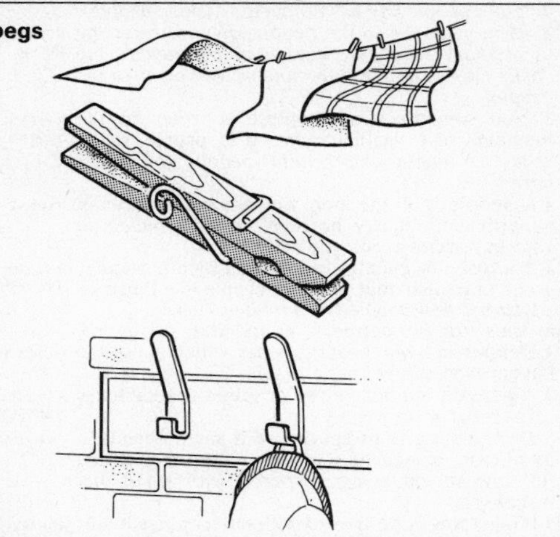

pegs

2 If you **peg** something somewhere, you fix it there with pegs. EG *Mamma came out and pegged wet clothes on the line.* V+O+A

3 If the price or amount of something **is pegged** at a particular level, it is fixed at that level. EG *Its cost was pegged at $750 million.* V+O : USU PASS +*at/to*

pejorative /pədʒɒrətɪv/. A **pejorative** word or expression is one that expresses criticism. EG ...*the pejorative term 'junk food'.* ADJ QUALIT Formal

pelican /pɛlɪkən/, **pelicans.** A **pelican** is a large water bird. It catches fish and keeps them in the bag-like bottom part of its beak. N COUNT

pelican crossing, pelican crossings. A **pelican crossing** is a place where pedestrians can cross a road by pressing a button which operates traffic lights to stop the traffic. N COUNT

pellet /pɛlɪ²t/, **pellets.** A **pellet** is a small ball of paper, mud, lead, or other material. EG ...*a pellet of mud*... ...*shotgun pellets.* N COUNT : USU+SUPP

pelt /pɛlt/, **pelts, pelting, pelted.** 1 If you **pelt** someone with things, you throw things at them. EG *He was pelted with eggs.* V+O+*with*

2 If it **is pelting** with rain or if the rain **is pelting down**, it is raining very hard. V : OFT+*down* Informal

3 If you **pelt** somewhere, you run there very fast. EG *I pelted up the stairs.* V+A Informal

4 Something that is moving **at full pelt** is moving very fast indeed. EG *He drove away at full pelt.* PHRASE Informal

pelvis /pɛlvɪs/, **pelvises.** Your **pelvis** is the wide, curved group of bones at the level of your hips. N COUNT

pen /pɛn/, **pens, penning, penned.** 1 A **pen** is a long thin object which you use to write in ink. N COUNT

2 If someone **pens** a letter, article, or book, they write it. EG *Infuriated, he penned a blistering reply.* V+O Literary

3 A **pen** is also a small area with a fence round it in which farm animals are kept for a short time. N COUNT

4 If people or animals **are penned** somewhere or **are penned up**, they are forced to remain in a very small area. EG ...*the boredom of endless hours penned up in a hot and dusty railway carriage.* V+O : OFT+*up*, USU PASS

penal /piːnə⁰l/. 1 **Penal** means relating to the punishment of criminals. EG ...*the British penal system*... ...*Howard's book on penal reform.* ADJ CLASSIF : ATTRIB

2 A **penal** institution or colony is one where criminals are imprisoned or kept. ADJ CLASSIF : ATTRIB

penalize /piːnəlaɪz/, **penalizes, penalizing, penalized;** also spelled **penalise.** If someone **is penalized** for something, they are made to suffer some disadvantage because of it. EG *It would be unfair to penalise those without a job... You will be penalized if you touch the ball with your hand.* V+O : USU PASS

penalty /pɛnə⁰lti¹/, **penalties.** 1 A **penalty** is a punishment that someone is given for doing something which is against a law or rule. EG *There are now stiffer penalties for drunken drivers.* N COUNT

2 In games such as football, rugby, and hockey, a **penalty** is a chance to score a goal without being prevented by other players. A penalty is given when a member of the other team commits a foul. N COUNT

3 The **penalty** that you pay for something you have done is something unpleasant that you experience as a result. EG *I had to pay the penalty for the wrong decisions I made.* N COUNT

penance /pɛnəns/. If you do **penance** for something wrong that you have done, you do something that you find unpleasant to show that you are sorry. EG *As penance for his condescension, he forced himself to be pleasant to them.* N UNCOUNT

pence /pɛns/ is a plural form of **penny.**

pencil /pɛnsə⁰l/, **pencils, pencilling, pencilled.**
1 A **pencil** is an object that you write or draw with. It consists of a thin piece of wood with a rod of graphite in the middle. ● If you write or draw something **in pencil**, you do it using a pencil. N COUNT; ● PHRASE

2 If you **pencil** something, you write it using a pencil. EG *He pencilled his initials at the end.* ◊ **pencilled.** EG ...*a pencilled note.* V+O; ◊ ADJ CLASSIF

pendant /pɛndənt/, **pendants.** A **pendant** is an ornament on a chain that you wear round your neck. EG ...*an amethyst pendant.* N COUNT

pending /pɛndɪŋ/. 1 Something that is **pending** 1.1 is going to happen soon. EG *He knew my examination was pending.* **1.2** is waiting to be dealt with or settled. EG ...*a pending lawsuit.* ADJ CLASSIF Formal; Formal

2 If something is done **pending** a future event, it is done until that event happens. EG *An interim government is to be set up, pending elections.* PREP Formal

pendulum /pɛndjə⁴ləm/, **pendulums.** 1 The **pendulum** of a clock is a rod with a weight at the end which swings from side to side in order to make the clock work. N COUNT

2 You can use the idea of a **pendulum** and the way it swings regularly as a way of talking about regular changes in a situation or in people's opinions. EG ...*the pendulum of fashion... Now the pendulum is swinging in the other direction.* N SING : *the*+N +SUPP

penetrate /pɛnɪtreɪt/, **penetrates, penetrating, penetrated.** 1 If someone or something **penetrates** an area that is difficult to get into, they succeed in getting into it or through it. EG *They penetrated into territory where no man had ever gone before... The sun was not high enough yet to penetrate the thick foliage overhead.* ◊ **penetration** /pɛnɪtreɪʃə⁰n/. EG ...*the penetration of hostile defences.* V+O OR V+A; ◊ N UNCOUNT

2 If someone **penetrates** an enemy group or a rival organization, they succeed in joining it in order to get information or cause trouble. V+O

penetrating /pɛnɪtreɪtɪŋ/. 1 A **penetrating** sound is loud and usually high-pitched. EG ...*his penetrating voice.* ADJ QUALIT

2 If someone gives you a **penetrating** look, it makes you think that they know what you are thinking. EG ...*his penetrating gaze*... ...*those gentle but penetrating brown eyes.* ADJ QUALIT

3 Someone who has a **penetrating** mind understands and recognizes things quickly and thoroughly. EG ...*a penetrating question.* ADJ QUALIT

pen-friend, pen-friends. A **pen-friend** is someone, especially a foreigner, who you write letters to and receive letters from, although the two of you may never have met. N COUNT

penguin /pɛŋgwɪn/, **penguins.** A **penguin** is a black and white bird found mainly in the Antarctic. Penguins cannot fly. N COUNT

penicillin /pɛnɪsɪlɪn/ is an antibiotic. N UNCOUNT

peninsula /pɪ²nɪnsjə⁴lə/, **peninsulas.** A **peninsula** is an area of land that is almost surrounded by water. N COUNT

penis /piːnɪs/, **penises.** A man's **penis** is the part of his body that he uses when urinating and when having sex. N COUNT

penitent /pɛnɪtənt/. Someone who is **penitent** is very sorry for something wrong that they have done. EG *We sat silent, penitent for having missed his point.* ADJ QUALIT Literary

penitentiary /pɛnɪtɛnʃə⁰ri¹/, **penitentiaries.** A **penitentiary** is a prison. N COUNT American

penknife /pɛnnaɪf/, **penknives.** A **penknife** is a small knife with a blade that folds back into the handle. N COUNT

pen name, pen names. A writer's **pen name** is the name that he or she uses on books and articles instead of his or her real name. N COUNT

penniless /pɛnɪlɪ²s/. Someone who is **penniless** has hardly any money at all. ADJ QUALIT

penny /pɛni¹/, **pennies** or **pence** /pɛns/. The plural form is **pennies** except for sense 1.2 where it is **pence**.

1 A **penny** is **1.1** a British coin which is worth one hundredth of a pound. **1.2** the amount of money which a penny is worth. EG *...a ten pence coin... They only cost a few pence.* **1.3** a British coin used before 1971 that was worth one twelfth of a shilling. **1.4** a coin that is worth one cent. N COUNT; American

2 **Penny** is also used in these phrases. **2.1** If you say **the penny dropped**, you mean that someone suddenly understood or realized something. EG *I detected a sweetish, acrid odour and the penny dropped. Chloroform.* **2.2** If you say to someone who has been quiet and thoughtful **'a penny for your thoughts'**, you are asking them to tell you what they are thinking about. **2.3** If you say that you are going to **spend a penny**, you mean that you are going to the toilet. **2.4** Things that are said to be **two a penny** or **ten a penny** are very common and easy to get. EG *We have fifty men like that – drivers are two a penny.* PHRASES; Outdated British

penny-pinching is the practice of spending very little money. EG *Good preventive health care means we cannot allow penny-pinching.* ▸ used as an adjective. EG *...penny-pinching miserly old men.* N UNCOUNT; ▸ ADJ QUALIT

pension /pɛnʃə⁰n/, **pensions, pensioning, pensioned.** Someone who has a **pension** regularly receives a sum of money from the state or from a former employer because they have retired or because they are widowed or disabled. EG *...an old age pension... ...a retired judge living on a state pension.* N COUNT

pension off. If someone **is pensioned off**, they are made to retire from work and are given a pension. EG *We were pensioned off at the age of fifty.* PHRASAL VB: V+O+ADV, USU PASS

pensioner /pɛnʃənə/, **pensioners.** A **pensioner** is someone who receives a pension, especially a pension paid by the state to retired people. N COUNT

pensive /pɛnsɪv/. Someone who is **pensive** is thinking deeply about something. EG *Jefferson looked pensive. 'What's wrong?' asked Tyler.* ADJ QUALIT

◊ **pensively.** EG *He gazed pensively at the water.* ◊ ADV

pentathlon /pɛntæθlə⁷n/, **pentathlons.** A **pentathlon** is a sports competition in which each person must compete in five different athletic events. N COUNT

penthouse /pɛnthaʊs/, **penthouses.** A **penthouse** or a **penthouse** apartment or suite is a luxurious flat or set of rooms at the top of a tall building. N COUNT OR N MOD

pent-up /pɛnt ʌp/. **Pent-up** emotions or energies have been held back and not expressed or released. EG *...pent-up frustrations... ...sports in which they can get rid of some of their pent-up energy.* ADJ CLASSIF: USU ATTRIB

penultimate /pɪ²nʌltə¹mə¹t/. The **penultimate** thing in a series of things is the last but one. EG *...the penultimate paragraph of the letter.* ADJ CLASSIF Formal

people /piːpə⁰l/, **peoples, peopling, peopled.** 1 **People** are men, women, and children. EG *There were 120 people at the lecture... Talk to the people concerned and see how they feel... The amount of potatoes people buy has dropped... ...young people.* N PLURAL

2 When you refer to the **people**, you are referring to ordinary men and women in contrast to the upper classes or the government. EG *Power to the people!* N PLURAL: the+N

3 You sometimes use **people** to refer to the members of a particular group of people. EG *He spoke at length and I think people got rather bored.* N PLURAL Spoken

4 A **people** is all the men, women, and children of a particular country or race. EG *...the beliefs of various peoples across the world.* N COUNT

5 If a place or country **is peopled** by a particular group of people, that group of people live there. EG *...Istanbul, now peopled by 4 million Turks.* V+O: USU PASS +by/with

pepper /pɛpə/, **peppers, peppering, peppered.**

1 **Pepper** is a hot-tasting powder which is used to flavour food. EG *...pepper and salt.* N UNCOUNT

2 A **pepper** is a hollow red or green vegetable. EG *...a salad of green peppers.* N COUNT OR N UNCOUNT

3 If something **is peppered** with small objects, a lot of those objects hit it or are scattered on it. EG *I felt my fingers being peppered with small, hot fragments.* V+O: USU PASS +with

4 If one thing is **peppered** with other things, it has a lot of those other things in it. EG *His French is heavily peppered with Americanisms.* ADJ PRED +with

peppermint /pɛpəmɪnt/, **peppermints.** 1 **Peppermint** is a strong flavouring that makes your mouth feel cold. EG *...peppermint candy.* N UNCOUNT

2 A **peppermint** is a peppermint-flavoured sweet. N COUNT

pep talk /pɛp tɔːk/, **pep talks.** A **pep talk** is a speech which is intended to encourage a group of people to make more effort or to feel more confident. N COUNT Informal

per /pɜː/. You use **per** to express rates and ratios. For example, if something costs £50 **per** year, you must pay £50 each year for it. If a vehicle is travelling at 40 miles **per** hour, it travels 40 miles each hour. EG *The dwellings have more than six people per room... ...an income of less than £1000 per person.* PREP

per annum /pɜː ænəm/. A particular amount **per annum** means that amount each year. EG *It costs £125 per annum.* ADV

perceive /pəsiːv/, **perceives, perceiving, perceived.** 1 If you **perceive** something, you see, notice, or realize it, especially when it is not obvious. EG *Many insects can perceive colours that are invisible to us... They failed to perceive that this was what I objected to.* V+O OR V+REPORT

2 If you **perceive** someone or something as doing a particular thing, it is your opinion that they do this thing. EG *It is important that the president be perceived as moving the country forward... This theory expresses the truth as I perceive it.* V+O: OFT+as

per cent /pəsɛnt/. You use **per cent** to talk about amounts. For example, if an amount is 10 **per cent** of a larger amount, it is equal to 10 hundredths of the larger amount. EG *45 per cent of Americans were against it... A good tumbler drier can reduce ironing by 80 per cent.* PHRASE

percentage /pəsɛntɪdʒ/, **percentages.** A **percentage** is a fraction of an amount expressed as a particular number of hundredths of that amount. EG *...areas with a high percentage of immigrants.* N COUNT: OFT+of

What is the penultimate headword on these pages?

perceptible /pəsɛptɪbə^{0}l/. Something that is **perceptible** can only just be seen or noticed. EG *There was a barely perceptible flicker of light.* — ADJ QUALIT

perception /pəsɛpʃə^{0}n/, **perceptions. 1** Someone who has **perception** realizes or notices things that are not obvious. EG *...a person of extraordinary perception... This requires a good deal of perception.* — N UNCOUNT

2 A **perception** is an opinion that you have formed as a result of noticing something. EG *...representing his perceptions through his painting... My perception of her had changed.* — N COUNT

3 Perception is the recognition of things using your senses, especially the sense of sight. EG *...visual perception... ...the perception of movement.* — N UNCOUNT

perceptive /pəsɛptɪv/. Someone who is **perceptive** is good at noticing or realizing things, especially things that are not obvious. EG *...a perceptive critic... She made a very perceptive comment.* — ADJ QUALIT

perch /pɜːtʃ/, **perches, perching, perched. 1** If you **perch** on a wall or table, you sit on the very edge of it. EG *Dr Quilty perched on the corner of his desk... They gathered round the tables or perched at the bar.* ◊ **perched.** EG *Flora, perched on the side of the bath, laughed.* — V+A; ◊ ADJ PRED +A

2 If you **perch** one thing on another, you put it on the top or edge of the other thing, so that it looks as if it might fall off. EG *He would take out his spectacles and perch them on the end of his nose... The building perches precariously within a few feet of a sudden drop.* ◊ **perched.** EG *...a little village perched above the lake.* — V-ERG+A; ◊ ADJ PRED +A

3 When a bird **perches** on a branch or a wall, it stands there. — V: USU+A

4 A **perch** is **4.1** a short rod for a bird to stand on. EG *...a large cage with perches.* **4.2** a high place where someone is sitting. EG *He climbed all the way to his favourite perch near the top.* — N COUNT

percolator /pɜːkəleɪtə/, **percolators.** A **percolator** is a special piece of equipment for making and serving coffee. — N COUNT

percussion /pəkʌʃə^{0}n/. The **percussion** in an orchestra or band consists of the instruments that are hit, for example drums and cymbals. EG *We had Dailey on percussion, and Flannery on the clarinet.* See picture at MUSICAL INSTRUMENTS. — N SING: *the*+N, OR N UNCOUNT

peremptory /pərɛmptə^{0}ri^{1}/. Someone who does something in a **peremptory** way does it in a way that shows that they expect to be obeyed immediately; used showing disapproval. EG *Our conversation was interrupted by a peremptory thudding at the door.* ◊ **peremptorily.** EG *'Come!' he said peremptorily.* — ADJ QUALIT Formal; ◊ ADV

perennial /pɪ^{2}rɛnɪəl/, **perennials. 1** A **perennial** situation is one that keeps occurring or that never ends. EG *...the perennial problems of isolation in old age... ...a perennial feature of British politics.* — ADJ CLASSIF

2 A **perennial** is a plant that lives for several years. EG *Garlic is a hardy perennial.* — N COUNT

perfect, perfects, perfecting, perfected; pronounced /pɜːfɪ^{2}kt/ when it is an adjective or a noun, and /pəfɛkt/ when it is a verb.

1 Something that is **perfect** is as good as it can possibly be. EG *She speaks perfect English... This was the perfect moment to move in... I've got the perfect solution... ...a perfect example of fair play.* — ADJ CLASSIF

2 You can use **perfect** to give emphasis to the noun following it. EG *They may be perfect strangers... I have a perfect right to be here... It makes perfect sense... 'Never,' I said with perfect calm.* — ADJ CLASSIF: ATTRIB

3 If you **perfect** something, you improve it so that it becomes as good as it can possibly be. EG *She hoped to perfect her technique.* — V+O

4 In grammar, the **perfect** tense of a verb in English is the tense that is formed with the present tense of the auxiliary 'have' and the past participle of the main verb. — ADJ CLASSIF: ATTRIB

perfection /pəfɛkʃə^{0}n/ is the quality of being perfect. EG *...gardens of incredible perfection... ...the perfection of its shimmering colours.* — N UNCOUNT ● If something is done **to perfection**, it is done so well that it could not be done any better. EG *The dress fitted her to perfection.* — ● PHRASE

perfectionist /pəfɛkʃənɪst/, **perfectionists.** Someone who is a **perfectionist** refuses to do or accept anything that is not perfect. — N COUNT

perfectly /pɜːfɪ^{2}kt^{0}li^{1}/. **1** You can use **perfectly** to emphasize an adjective or adverb. EG *It's a perfectly reasonable question... I'll be perfectly frank with you... I knew perfectly well it was a trap.* — SUBMOD

2 If something is done **perfectly**, it is done so well that it could not possibly be done better. EG *The plan worked perfectly... The climate suited Len perfectly... She understood him perfectly.* — ADV

perforated /pɜːfəreɪtɪd/. Something that is **perforated** has had a number of small holes made in it. EG *...a perforated steel plate.* — ADJ CLASSIF

perforation /pɜːfəreɪʃə^{0}n/, **perforations. Perforations** are small holes that are made in something, especially in paper. — N COUNT: USU PLURAL

perform /pəfɔːm/, **performs, performing, performed. 1** When you **perform** a task or action, especially a complicated one, you do it. EG *About 200 heart operations a year are performed at the Brook Hospital... The ceremony was performed in nineteen other countries.* — V+O

2 If something **performs** a particular service or function, it does it. EG *Their organization performs a vital service.* — V+O

3 If you **perform** a play, a piece of music, or a dance, you do it in front of an audience. EG *He performed for them a dance of his native Samoa... We had to perform on stage.* — V+O OR V

4 If someone or something **performs** well, they work or function well. If they **perform** badly, they work or function badly. EG *...the difficulty of finding a rifle which will perform satisfactorily under those conditions.* — V+A

performance /pəfɔːməns/, **performances. 1** A **performance** consists of entertaining an audience by doing something such as singing, dancing, acting a play, or acting a role in a play. EG *I think Roger Rees gives a remarkable performance... ...an amateur performance of 'Macbeth'... ...excellent performances from both actresses... ...with two performances on Wednesdays.* — N COUNT

2 Someone's or something's **performance** is how successful they are. EG *...Britain's poor economic performance in the 1970's... ...after a disappointing performance in the 220-yards semi-final.* — N UNCOUNT: USU+SUPP

3 A car's **performance** is its ability to go fast and accelerate quickly. EG *...high performance cars.* — N UNCOUNT

4 The **performance** of a task or action is the doing of it. EG *...the performance of his Presidential duties... ...another machine will then repeat the performance.* — N SING: USU+*of*

performer /pəfɔːmə/, **performers.** A **performer** is a person who acts, sings, or does other entertainment in front of audiences. — N COUNT

perfume /pɜːfju^{4}m/, **perfumes.** A **perfume** is **1** a pleasant-smelling liquid which you put on your body to make yourself smell nice. EG *...a bottle of perfume... ...an expensive perfume.* ◊ **perfumed** /pɜːfju^{4}md/. EG *...a perfumed towel.* — N MASS; ◊ ADJ QUALIT **2** a pleasant smell. EG *The familiar perfumes of wild flowers filled her nostrils.* ◊ **perfumed.** EG *...the perfumed air.* — N COUNT; ◊ ADJ QUALIT Literary

perfunctory /pəfʌŋktə^{0}ri^{1}/. A **perfunctory** action is done quickly and carelessly. EG *Max gave his wife a perfunctory kiss.* — ADJ QUALIT Formal

perhaps /pəhæps/. **1** You use **perhaps** to indicate that you are not sure whether something is true, correct, possible, or likely to happen. EG *Perhaps Andrew is right after all... Perhaps I'll come. Perhaps not... Not many people used to go there, perhaps because it was on the edge of town... There are perhaps fifty women here.* — ADV SEN

2 You also use **perhaps** to add politeness to a — ADV SEN request, an offer, or an opinion. EG *Perhaps I might keep these, for a day or two?... Perhaps I had better explain what we try to do here... I think that's perhaps her finest picture.*

peril /pɛrɪl/, **perils. 1** A **peril** is a great danger. EG *...the perils of being a fugitive... The arms race is the greatest single peril now facing the world... They placed themselves in great peril by openly opposing him.* N COUNT OR N UNCOUNT Literary

2 If you say that someone does something **at** their **peril**, you are warning them that they will probably suffer as a result of doing it. EG *You become neglectful at your peril.* PHRASE Literary

perilous /pɛrɪləs/. Something that is **perilous** is very dangerous. EG *The perilous journey was over.* ADJ QUALIT Literary

◇ **perilously** . EG *It came perilously close to destruction... ...stepping perilously near the crate.* ◇ ADV

perimeter /pərɪmɪtə/, **perimeters.** The **perimeter** of an area of land is the whole of its outer edge or boundary. EG *...the perimeter of the clearing... ...dog patrols around the perimeter fence.* N COUNT

period /pɪərɪəd/, **periods. 1** A particular **period** is a particular length of time. EG *...over a period of several months... ...long periods of rain... ...a short period of time... ...in the Edwardian period.* N COUNT: USU+SUPP

2 At a school or college, a **period** is one of the parts that the day is divided into. EG *There were five periods of French a week.* N COUNT

3 Period costumes, objects, and houses were made at an earlier time in history, or look as if they were made then. EG *...period furniture.* ADJ CLASSIF: ATTRIB

4 A woman's **period** is the bleeding from her womb that happens each month. N COUNT

5 A **period** is also a full stop. N COUNT

periodic /pɪəri¹ɒdɪk/. A **periodic** event or situation happens occasionally, at fairly regular intervals. EG *...periodic droughts.* ADJ CLASSIF: ATTRIB

periodical /pɪəri¹ɒdɪkə^{0}l/, **periodicals. 1** A **periodical** is a magazine, especially a serious or academic one. N COUNT

2 Periodical means the same as periodic. EG *These mood shifts are periodical and recurring.* ADJ CLASSIF: ATTRIB

◇ **periodically** /pɪəri¹ɒdɪkə^{0}li¹/. EG *We met them periodically during the summer break.* ◇ ADV

peripheral /pərɪfə^{0}rəl/. **1** A **peripheral** thing or part of something is of little importance compared with other things or parts. EG *...the peripheral features of religion.* ADJ QUALIT Formal

2 Peripheral also means on or relating to the edge of an area. EG *This gives greater peripheral vision... ...Russia's peripheral provinces.* ADJ CLASSIF Formal

periphery /pərɪfəri¹/, **peripheries. 1** The **periphery** of an area is the edge of it. EG *The cost of land on the periphery of Calcutta went up.* N COUNT: USU *the*+N Formal

2 The **periphery** of a field of activity is the part of it that is not as important or basic as the main part. EG *...people working on the periphery of education.* N COUNT: USU *the*+N

periscope /pɛrɪskəʊp/, **periscopes.** A **periscope** is a vertical tube through which people in a submarine can see above the surface of the water. N COUNT

perish /pɛrɪʃ/, **perishes, perishing, perished. 1** If people or animals **perish**, they die as a result of an accident or as a result of very hard conditions. EG *All the passengers and crew members perished.* V Literary

2 If something **perishes**, it comes to an end or is destroyed for ever. EG *The old religion is perishing.* V Literary

3 If rubber **perishes**, it starts to fall to pieces. V

perishable /pɛrɪʃəbə^{0}l/. **Perishable** types of food go bad quite quickly. EG *In the Third World, all perishable food has to be eaten within twenty-four hours.* ADJ QUALIT

perjury /pɜːdʒəri¹/. If someone who is giving evidence in a court of law commits **perjury**, they lie. EG *She was charged with perjury.* N UNCOUNT Legal

perk /pɜːk/, **perks, perking, perked.** A **perk** is something extra, such as a car, that your employers give you in addition to your salary. EG *There are nice perks too, such as help with your mortgage.* N COUNT Informal

perk up. When someone **perks up**, they become more cheerful. EG *John was being a misery. He perked up when we got there, though.* PHRASAL VB: V-ERG+ADV

perky /pɜːki¹/, **perkier, perkiest.** If someone is **perky**, they are cheerful and lively. ADJ QUALIT

perm /pɜːm/, **perms, perming, permed.** If you have a **perm**, your hair is treated with chemicals and then curled so that the curls last for several months. ▸ used as a verb. EG *She had her hair permed.* N COUNT ▸ V+O: USU PASS

permanent /pɜːmənənt/. **1** Something that is **permanent** lasts for ever or for a very long time. EG *Some drugs taken in large quantities cause permanent brain damage.* ◇ **permanently.** EG *My imprisonment was likely to scar me permanently.* ADJ QUALIT ◇ ADV

◇ **permanence** /pɜːmənəns/. EG *People have a need for permanence.* ◇ N UNCOUNT

2 A **permanent** feature of a situation or place is present all the time. EG *...the only permanent water supply... I began to live in an almost permanent state of fear.* ◇ **permanently.** EG *The doors were kept permanently locked.* ADJ CLASSIF ◇ ADV

permeate /pɜːmɪeɪt/, **permeates, permeating, permeated. 1** If an idea, feeling, or attitude **permeates** something, it affects every part of it or is present throughout it. EG *...the extent to which secrecy permeates every part of our society.* V+O OR V+*through* Formal

2 If a liquid, smell, or flavour **permeates** something, it spreads through it. EG *Damp can easily permeate the wood... Dangerous chemicals may permeate through the soil into rivers.* V+O OR V+*through* Formal

permissible /pəmɪsəbə^{0}l/. If something is **permissible**, it is allowed by the rules. EG *...the maximum permissible levels of radiation... It was permissible to ask a question.* ADJ CLASSIF Formal

permission /pəmɪʃə^{0}n/. If you are given **permission** to do something, someone says that they will allow you to do it. EG *I have permission to tell you... He refused permission for Biddle to enter Britain... You can't go without permission.* N UNCOUNT

permissive /pəmɪsɪv/. A **permissive** society allows things which other people disapprove of, especially freedom in sexual behaviour. EG *...the frequency of divorce within the permissive society.* ADJ QUALIT

◇ **permissiveness.** EG *...sexual permissiveness.* ◇ N UNCOUNT

permit, permits, permitting, permitted; pronounced /pəmɪt/ when it is a verb, and /pɜːmɪt/ when it is a noun.

1 If you **permit** something, you allow it. EG *Her father would not permit her to eat sweets... He permitted himself a slight smile... The doctor has permitted him only two meals a day.* V+O: OFT+*to*-INF; ALSO V+O+O Formal

2 If something **permits** a particular thing to happen, it makes it possible for it to happen. EG *Our regulations permit us to get rid of him... Had time permitted, we would have stayed longer... The timetable permits teams only a few weeks for preparation.* V+O: OFT+*to*-INF; ALSO V OR V+O+O Formal

3 A **permit** is an official document which says that you may do something, for example work in a foreign country. EG *She could not get in without a permit... ...work permits.* N COUNT

permutation /pɜːmjuːteɪʃə^{0}n/, **permutations.** A **permutation** is one of the ways in which a number of things can be arranged. EG *You can form any number of permutations out of these symbols.* N COUNT Formal

pernicious /pənɪʃəs/. If you describe something as **pernicious**, you mean that it is very harmful. EG *This had a pernicious influence on countless generations... ...pernicious institutions and teachings.* ADJ QUALIT Literary

pernickety /pənɪkɪ¹ti¹/. Someone who is **pernickety** worries too much about small, unimportant details. EG *You can't be so pernickety about everything!* ADJ QUALIT Informal

perpendicular /pɜːpə²ndɪkjə⁴lə/. Something that is **perpendicular** is tall and points straight up, ADJ CLASSIF Formal

If you commit perjury, do you perpetrate a crime?

rather than being sloping. EG *...the perpendicular cliff-face... ...the supporting perpendicular stones.*

perpetrate /pɜːpɪ^{2}treɪt/, **perpetrates, perpetrating, perpetrated.** If someone **perpetrates** a crime, they do it. EG *...a fraud perpetrated by lawyers.* ◊ **perpetrator** /pɜːpɪ^{2}treɪtə/, perpetrators. EG *...the perpetrator of the crime.*
V+O : USU PASS Formal; ◊ N COUNT

perpetual /pəpɛtjʊ^{0}əl/. A **perpetual** situation or quality never ends or changes. EG *These bats live in deep caves in perpetual darkness... She had me in perpetual fear.* ◊ **perpetually.** EG *The younger children seemed to be perpetually hungry... She was perpetually answering the doorbell.*
ADJ CLASSIF : ATTRIB Formal; ◊ ADV

perpetuate /pəpɛtjuːeɪt/, **perpetuates, perpetuating, perpetuated.** If someone or something **perpetuates** a situation or belief, they cause it to continue. EG *...an education system that perpetuates inequality.*
V+O Formal

perplexed /pəplɛkst/. If you are **perplexed**, you do not understand something or you do not know what to do. EG *For a moment Mr Adams looked perplexed... He said in a perplexed voice: 'Sir?'.*
ADJ QUALIT

perplexing /pəplɛksɪŋ/. If something is **perplexing**, you do not understand it or do not know how to deal with it. EG *...a perplexing and difficult problem.*
ADJ QUALIT

perplexity /pəplɛksɪ^{1}ti^1/ is the feeling of being perplexed. EG *She looked at us in some perplexity.*
N UNCOUNT

persecute /pɜːsɪkjuːt/, **persecutes, persecuting, persecuted.** If someone **persecutes** you, they treat you cruelly and unfairly, usually because they do not approve of your beliefs. EG *Members of these sects are ruthlessly persecuted and suppressed.*
V+O

persecution /pɜːsɪkjuːʃə^{0}n/, **persecutions. Persecution** is cruel and unfair treatment of a person or group, usually because other people do not approve of their beliefs. EG *...the persecution of minorities.*
N UNCOUNT OR N COUNT

persevere /pɜːsɪvɪə/, **perseveres, persevering, persevered.** If you **persevere** with something, you keep trying to do it and do not give up. EG *Don't give up – just persevere. You'll win in the end.* ◊ **perseverance** /pɜːsɪvɪərəns/. EG *I underestimated his perseverance.*
V : OFT+*with*; ◊ N UNCOUNT

persist /pəsɪst/, **persists, persisting, persisted.**
1 If something **persists**, especially something undesirable, it continues to exist. EG *Political differences still persist... The pain persisted until the morning.*
V
2 If you **persist** in doing something, you continue to do it, even though it is difficult or other people are against it. EG *People still persist in thinking that standards are going down... He persisted with his policy of conciliation... 'And what,' persisted Casson, 'is to prevent us?'*
V : USU+A; ALSO V+QUOTE

persistent /pəsɪstənt/. **1** Something that is **persistent** continues to exist or happen for a long time. EG *How do you get rid of a persistent nasty smell?* ◊ **persistently.** EG *...persistently rattling window frames.* ◊ **persistence** /pəsɪstəns/. EG *Because of the persistence of the depression, I saw my doctor.*
ADJ QUALIT; ◊ ADV; ◊ N UNCOUNT
2 Someone who is **persistent** continues trying to do something, even though it is difficult or other people are against it. EG *I think you have to be persistent if people say no to you.* ◊ **persistently.** EG *...policemen who tried persistently to force their way into his house.* ◊ **persistence.** EG *In the end our persistence was rewarded.*
ADJ QUALIT; ◊ ADV; ◊ N UNCOUNT

person /pɜːsə^{0}n/, **persons.** The form **persons** is only used in very formal or legal language, and the word 'people' is normally used instead to refer to more than one person: see **people**.
1 A **person** is a man or a woman. EG *There was far too much meat for one person... I want to see the person responsible for accounts... She was a charming person.*
N COUNT
2 You can use **person** in expressions such as 'I'm an outdoors person' or 'I'm not a coffee person' when you are saying whether or not you like a particular activity or thing.
N COUNT+SUPP Informal
3 If you do something **in person**, you do it yourself rather than letting someone else do it for you. EG *He wished he had gone to the house in person.*
PHRASE
4 If you hear or see someone **in person**, you are present to hear or see them, rather than hearing them on the radio or seeing them on television. EG *Now I had the chance to hear her speak in person.*
PHRASE
5 You use **in the person of** in front of someone's name when you want to say that they are the thing you are referring to. EG *We had, in the person of Susan Smith, an outstanding leader.*
PREP
6 In grammar, a **person** is a person in a conversation. The first **person** is the speaker, the second **person** is the person being spoken to, and the third **person** is anyone else listening but not taking part in the conversation.

-person, -persons. -person is used instead of '-man' or '-woman' in words such as 'spokesman' or 'chairwoman' when you want to refer to a person who does a particular job or activity but you do not want to indicate their sex. EG *He spoke to CND chairperson Joan Ruddock.*
SUFFIX

personage /pɜːsə^{0}nɪdʒ/, **personages.** A **personage** is a famous or important person. EG *...a distinguished personage.*
N COUNT Formal

personal /pɜːsə^{0}nəl/. **1** A **personal** opinion, quality, or thing belongs or relates to a particular person rather than to other people. EG *My personal view is that he should resign... It's a matter of personal preference... ...his personal belongings.*
ADJ CLASSIF : ATTRIB
2 If you give something your **personal** care or attention, you deal with it yourself rather than letting someone else deal with it. EG *The book was translated from the German under the personal supervision of the author.*
ADJ CLASSIF : ATTRIB
3 Personal matters relate to your feelings, relationships, and health, which you may find embarrassing. EG *...the most intimate details of their personal lives... ...personal problems.*
ADJ QUALIT
4 Personal comments refer to someone's appearance or character in an offensive way. EG *I think we're getting too personal.*
ADJ QUALIT
5 Personal hygiene involves keeping your body clean.
ADJ CLASSIF : ATTRIB

personal assistant, personal assistants. A **personal assistant** is a person who does secretarial and administrative work for someone.
N COUNT

personality /pɜːsənælɪ^{1}ti^1/, **personalities. 1** Your **personality** is your whole character and nature. EG *He has a wonderful personality... He never began to understand her complicated personality.*
N COUNT +SUPP OR N UNCOUNT
2 You can refer to a famous person, especially in entertainment, broadcasting, or sport, as a **personality**. EG *...a television personality.*
N COUNT

personalized /pɜːsə^{0}nəlaɪzd/; also spelled **personalised.** Something that is **personalized** **1** has its owner's initials or name on it. EG *...personalized pens.* **2** has been designed specially for one person. EG *...a personalized service.*
ADJ CLASSIF

personally /pɜːsə^{0}nəli^1/. **1** You use **personally** to emphasize that you are giving your own opinion. EG *Well, personally, I feel that this is very difficult.*
ADV SEN
2 If you do something **personally**, you do it yourself rather than letting someone else do it. EG *Since then I have undertaken all the enquiries personally.*
ADV
3 Something that affects you or that applies to you **personally** affects you or applies to you rather than to other people. EG *I wasn't referring to you personally... It would be unjust for him to bear personally the great expenses involved.*
ADV
4 If you **take** something that someone says **personally**, you are upset because you think that they are criticizing you in particular.
ADV

personal pronoun, personal pronouns. In grammar, **personal pronouns** refer to people and
N COUNT

things. Personal pronouns are labelled PRON in the Extra Column. See the entry headed PRONOUNS for more information.

personify /pə⁵sɒnɪfaɪ/, **personifies, personifying, personified.** If you say that someone **personifies** a particular quality, you mean that they seem to have that quality to a very large degree. EG *He seemed to personify the evil that was in the world.* V+O

personnel /pɜːsənɛl/. The **personnel** of an organization are the people who work for it. EG *We've advertised for extra security personnel... ...military personnel... I hadn't got the personnel to cope with it.* N PLURAL Formal

perspective /pəspɛktɪv/, **perspectives. 1** A **perspective** is a particular way of thinking about something, especially one that is influenced by your beliefs or experiences. EG *He wanted to leave the country in order to get a better perspective on things... It was impossible for me to identify with his religious perspective.* N COUNT: USU+SUPP

2 If you get something **into perspective**, you judge its real importance by considering it in relation to everything else. EG *It will help to put in perspective the vast gulf that separates existing groups.* PHRASE

3 Perspective is a method by which things in the background of a picture are made to look further away than things in the foreground. N UNCOUNT

perspiration /pɜːspə¹reɪʃə⁰n/ is the liquid which comes out in drops on the surface of your skin when you are hot or frightened. EG *There were beads of perspiration on his upper lip.* N UNCOUNT Formal

perspire /pəspaɪə/, **perspires, perspiring, perspired.** When you **perspire**, a liquid comes out in drops on the surface of your skin. EG *Hot and perspiring, John toiled up the dusty ascent.* V Formal

persuade /pəsweɪd/, **persuades, persuading, persuaded. 1** If someone or something **persuades** you to do something, they cause you to do it by giving you a good reason for doing it. EG *Marsha was trying to persuade Posy to change her mind... ...as the threat of unemployment persuades workers to moderate their pay demands... He is the sort of man that could be persuaded into anything.* V+O: USU+*to*-INF; ALSO V+O+A

2 If someone **persuades** you that something is true, they cause you to believe that it is true, usually by talking to you. EG *We worked hard to persuade them that we were genuinely interested... I had persuaded myself that I could continue like this.* ◇ **persuaded.** EG *Few of them are persuaded of the benefits of the shop.* V+O OR V-REFL: OFT+REPORT OR *of* ◇ ADJ PRED

persuasion /pəsweɪʒə⁰n/, **persuasions. 1 Persuasion** is the act of persuading someone to do something or to believe that something is true. EG *They didn't need much persuasion... I had to adopt other methods of persuasion.* N UNCOUNT

2 If you are of a particular **persuasion**, you have a particular set of beliefs. EG *...people of different political persuasions... ...those who were not of the Roman Catholic persuasion.* N COUNT+SUPP Formal

persuasive /pəsweɪsɪv/. Someone or something that is **persuasive** is likely to persuade someone to believe or do a particular thing. EG *...a very persuasive argument... You were very useful, Jimmie, very persuasive.* ADJ QUALIT

pertain /pəteɪn/, **pertains, pertaining, pertained.** Something that **pertains** to something else belongs or relates to it. EG *...documents pertaining to the suspects.* V+*to* Formal

pertinent /pɜːtɪnənt/. Something that is **pertinent** is relevant to a particular subject. EG *I asked him a lot of pertinent questions about the original production.* ADJ QUALIT Formal

perturbed /pətɜːbd/. Someone who is **perturbed** is worried. EG *She was perturbed about a rash which had come out on her face.* ADJ PRED Formal

peruse /pəruːz/, **peruses, perusing, perused.** If you **peruse** a piece of writing, you read it to find out what it says. EG *He took the letter and perused it... Having perused its contents, he flung down the paper.* V+O Formal

pervade /pə⁵veɪd/, **pervades, pervading, pervaded.** Something that **pervades** a place or thing is a noticeable feature throughout it. EG *An atmosphere of contentment pervades the school... A strong smell of fish pervaded the coach.* V+O Formal

pervasive /pə⁵veɪsɪv/. Something that is **pervasive** is present or felt throughout a place or thing. EG *...a pervasive atmosphere of fear... ...the Church's all-pervasive influence.* ADJ QUALIT Formal

perverse /pəvɜːs/. Someone who is **perverse** deliberately does things that are unreasonable or that will result in harm. EG *It would be perverse to refuse... He takes a perverse delight in irritating people.* ◇ **perversely.** EG *They persisted, perversely, in trying to grow grain.* ADJ QUALIT ◇ ADV

perversion /pəvɜːʃə⁰n/, **perversions. 1** A **perversion** is a sexual desire or action that is considered abnormal and unacceptable. N COUNT OR N UNCOUNT

2 The **perversion** of something is the changing of it so that it is no longer what it should be. EG *...the systematic perversion of the truth.* N COUNT OR N UNCOUNT

perversity /pəvɜːsɪ¹ti¹/. Someone who shows **perversity** deliberately does things that are unreasonable or that other people do not want them to do. EG *...her perversity as a child... Some perversity in my nature caused me to refuse.* N UNCOUNT

pervert, perverts, perverting, perverted; pronounced /pəvɜːt/ when it is a verb, and /pɜːvɜːt/ when it is a noun.

1 If you **pervert** something, for example a process or society, you interfere with it so that it is not what it used to be or should be. EG *Traditional ceremonies were perverted into meaningless rituals.* V+O Formal

2 A **pervert** is a person whose behaviour, especially sexual behaviour, is harmful or disgusting. N COUNT

perverted /pəvɜːtɪ²d/. **1** Someone who is **perverted** has disgusting behaviour or ideas, especially sexual ones. ADJ QUALIT

2 Something that is **perverted** is wrong, unnatural, or harmful. EG *...the inventions of a perverted imagination... ...a perverted form of love.* ADJ QUALIT

pessimism /pɛsɪmɪzə⁰m/ is the belief that bad things are going to happen. EG *His pessimism was unjustified.* ◇ **pessimist** /pɛsɪmɪst/, **pessimists.** EG *Pessimists tell us that the family is doomed.* N UNCOUNT ◇ N COUNT

pessimistic /pɛsɪmɪstɪk/. Someone who is **pessimistic** thinks that bad things are going to happen. EG *Success now seemed very remote and Bernard felt pessimistic... This is too pessimistic a view.* ◇ **pessimistically.** EG *'Well, let's get it over with,' he said pessimistically.* ADJ QUALIT ◇ ADV

pest /pɛst/, **pests. 1** A **pest** is an insect or small animal which damages crops or food supplies. EG *Cold kills off lots of diseases and pests in the soil.* N COUNT

2 You refer to someone, especially a child, as a **pest** when they keep bothering you. N COUNT Informal

pester /pɛstə/, **pesters, pestering, pestered.** If you **pester** someone, you keep asking them to do something, or you keep bothering them. EG *Everyone pestered me so much that I gave it up... For years Desiree had been pestering him to take her to Europe.* V+O: OFT+A

pesticide /pɛstɪsaɪd/, **pesticides. Pesticides** are chemicals which farmers put on their crops to kill harmful animals, especially insects. N MASS

pet /pɛt/, **pets, petting, petted. 1** A **pet** is a tame animal that you keep in your home to give you company and pleasure. EG *It is against the rules to keep pets... ...his pet dog.* N COUNT

2 Someone's **pet** theory, project, or subject is one that they particularly support or like. EG *We were listening to a gardener with his pet theories.* ADJ CLASSIF: ATTRIB

What is the connection between 'pharmaceuticals' and a 'pharmacist'?

3 If you **pet** a person or animal, you pat or stroke them affectionately. V+O

4 If two people, especially a teenage couple, **are petting**, they are kissing and stroking each other. V Informal

petal /pɛtə[0]l/, **petals.** The **petals** of a flower are the thin coloured or white parts which together form the flower. EG *...rose petals.* N COUNT

peter /piːtə/, **peters, petering, petered.** If something **peters out**, it gradually comes to an end. EG *The tracks petered out a mile or two later... The meeting petered out after two hours.* PHRASAL VB : V+ADV

petite /pətiːt/. A woman who is **petite** is small and slim. EG *...his petite bride.* ADJ QUALIT

petition /pɪ[2]tɪʃə[0]n/, **petitions, petitioning, petitioned. 1** A **petition** is **1.1** a document signed by a lot of people which asks a government or other official group to do something. EG *He presented a petition signed by 10,357 electors.* **1.2** an application to a court of law for some legal action to be taken. EG *She has filed a petition for divorce... The court ordered him to pay the costs of the petition.* N COUNT Formal

2 If you **petition** someone in authority, you make a formal request to them. EG *It is my duty to petition the court to declare this action illegal.* V+O OR V Formal

petrified /pɛtrɪfaɪd/. If you are **petrified**, you are extremely frightened. EG *If I hadn't been alone I wouldn't have been nearly so petrified.* ADJ QUALIT Informal

petrol /pɛtrəl/ is a liquid which is used as a fuel for motor vehicles. EG *...a petrol pump.* N UNCOUNT British

petroleum /pə[2]trəʊlɪəm/ is oil which is found under the surface of the earth or under the sea bed. Petrol and paraffin are obtained from petroleum. N UNCOUNT

petrol station, petrol stations. A **petrol station** is a garage by the side of the road where petrol is sold and put into vehicles. N COUNT British

petticoat /pɛti[1]kəʊt/, **petticoats.** A **petticoat** is a piece of clothing like a thin skirt, which is worn under a skirt or dress. N COUNT

petty /pɛti[1]/, **pettier, pettiest. 1 Petty** things are small and unimportant. EG *But these were petty details... ...petty problems.* ADJ QUALIT

2 If you describe someone's behaviour as **petty**, you mean that they care too much about unimportant things and perhaps that they are unnecessarily unkind. EG *...petty jealousies.* ADJ QUALIT

petty cash is money that is kept in the office of a company, ready to be used for making small payments when necessary. N UNCOUNT

petulant /pɛtjə[4]lənt/. Someone who is **petulant** is unreasonably angry and upset in a childish way. EG *With a petulant snarl, I pushed the door.* ADJ QUALIT
◇ **petulantly.** EG *'Oh, why do you say that?' I cried petulantly.* ◇ ADV

pew /pjuː/, **pews.** A **pew** is a long wooden seat with a back, which people sit on in church. N COUNT

pewter /pjuːtə/ is a grey metal made by mixing tin and lead. EG *...pewter plates.* N UNCOUNT

phantom /fæntə[0]m/, **phantoms. 1** A **phantom** is a ghost. EG *He was staring at her as if she were a phantom.* N COUNT Literary

2 You use **phantom** to describe something which you think you see or hear but which is not real. EG *...a phantom presence.* ADJ CLASSIF : ATTRIB Literary

pharmaceutical /fɑːməsjuːtɪkə[0]l/, **pharmaceuticals. 1 Pharmaceutical** means connected with the industrial production of medicines. EG *...the world's largest pharmaceutical company.* ADJ CLASSIF : ATTRIB Formal

2 Pharmaceuticals are medicines. EG *...the sale of pharmaceuticals.* N PLURAL Formal

pharmacist /fɑːməsɪst/, **pharmacists.** A **pharmacist** is a person who is qualified to prepare and sell medicines. N COUNT

pharmacy /fɑːməsi[1]/, **pharmacies.** A **pharmacy** is a shop where medicines are sold. N COUNT

phase /feɪz/, **phases, phasing, phased. 1** A **phase** is a particular stage in a process or in the gradual development of something. EG *When this happens, society enters a dangerous phase... ...the second phase of the Revolution.* N COUNT : USU+SUPP

2 If you **phase** an action or change over a period of time, you cause it to happen in stages. EG *The reduction in nuclear weapons would be phased over approximately ten years... ...the phased introduction of new technology.* V+O

phase in. If you **phase in** something, for example a new way of doing something, you introduce it gradually. EG *...in the 1970's, when Britain phased in the EEC system.* PHRASAL VB : V+O+ADV, HAS PASS

phase out. If you **phase** something **out**, you gradually stop using it. EG *This type of weapon was now being finally phased out.* PHRASAL VB : V+O+ADV, HAS PASS

Ph.D. /piː eɪtʃ diː/, **Ph.D.s.** A **Ph.D.** is a degree awarded to people who have done advanced research into a particular subject. **Ph.D.** is an abbreviation for 'Doctor of Philosophy'. EG *He's got a Ph.D. in psychology... ...Jenny Remfrey, Ph.D.* N COUNT

pheasant /fɛzə[0]nt/, **pheasants. Pheasant** can also be used as the plural form. N COUNT
A **pheasant** is a long-tailed bird. Pheasants are often shot as a sport or for eating.

phenomena /fɪ[2]nɒmɪnə/ is the plural of **phenomenon.**

phenomenal /fɪ[2]nɒmɪnə[0]l/. Something that is **phenomenal** is so great or good that it is very unusual indeed. EG *It was a phenomenal success... ...the phenomenal growth of international trade.* ADJ QUALIT
◇ **phenomenally.** EG *It's phenomenally expensive.* ◇ SUBMOD

phenomenon /fɪ[2]nɒmɪnən/, **phenomena** /fɪ[2]nɒmɪnə/. A **phenomenon** is something that is observed to happen or exist. EG *...animals and plants and other natural phenomena... Is this concern about energy a recent phenomenon?* N COUNT : USU+SUPP

phew /fjuː/ is used to represent the soft whistling sound that you make when you breathe out quickly, for example when you are very hot or when you are relieved. EG *'Phew,' she said, 'it's hot out.'* EXCLAM

philanthropist /fɪlænθrəpɪst/, **philanthropists.** A **philanthropist** is someone who freely gives money to people who need it. EG *...wealthy philanthropists... ...the great philanthropists of the past.* N COUNT

philanthropy /fɪlænθrəpi[1]/ is the giving of money to people who need it, without wanting anything in return. EG *...an organization noted for its philanthropy... ...acts of philanthropy or affection.* N UNCOUNT

philistine /fɪlɪstaɪn/, **philistines.** If you call someone a **philistine**, you mean that they do not admire or recognize good art, music, or literature. EG *What does a lousy little philistine like you know about it?* ▸ used as an adjective. EG *From Chelsea he raged at a philistine public.* N COUNT ▸ ADJ QUALIT

philosopher /fɪlɒsəfə/, **philosophers. 1** A **philosopher** is a person who creates or studies theories about basic things such as the nature of existence or how people should live. EG *...the Greek philosopher Thales.* N COUNT

2 If you refer to someone as a **philosopher**, you mean that they think deeply and seriously about life and other basic matters. N COUNT

philosophic /fɪləsɒfɪk/ means the same as philosophical. ADJ CLASSIF

philosophical /fɪləsɒfɪkə[0]l/. **1 Philosophical** means concerned with or relating to philosophy. EG *They used to have long philosophical conversations... ...philosophical and religious ideas.* ADJ CLASSIF : ATTRIB

2 Someone who is **philosophical** does not get upset when disappointing or disturbing things happen; used showing approval. EG *He was a placid boy with a philosophical approach to life.* ADJ QUALIT
◇ **philosophically.** EG *He accepted their conclusion philosophically.* ◇ ADV

philosophy /fɪlɒsəfi[1]/, **philosophies. 1 Philosophy** is the study or creation of theories about basic things such as the nature of existence or how people should live. EG *...an expert on Eastern philosophy... ...a series of philosophy lectures.* N UNCOUNT

2 A **philosophy** is **2.1** a particular set of ideas that a philosopher has. EG *...the political philosophies of the West.* **2.2** a particular theory that someone has N COUNT+SUPP

PHRASAL VERBS

A phrasal verb (PHRASAL VB) is a combination of two words which has a single meaning. One word is a verb, and the other word is either a preposition or an adverb, such as **in**, **back**, and **down**. So you have phrasal verbs such as **take in**, **take back**, and **take down**. In some cases, you can have both an adverb and a preposition, as in **look forward to** and **get in on**. You will find phrasal verbs at the end of the entries which deal with the verb. So phrasal verbs starting with **take**, such as **take back**, **take down**, **take in**, and so on are explained at the end of the entry for **take**.

Types of phrasal verb

There are a number of common types of phrasal verb:

+ADV means that there is an adverb.

+PREP means that there is a preposition, which of course will always have an object.

+ADV/PREP means that the particle can be used either as an adverb or as a preposition.

V used on its own means that the verb is intransitive.

+O means that the verb is transitive.

These combine to give the following patterns:

V+ADV

The verb is intransitive and is followed by an adverb. For example: *The plane took off two hours late.*

V+PREP

The verb is intransitive and is followed by a prepositional group, as in: *They looked round the Cathedral.*

V+PREP, HAS PASS

The prepositional object can become the subject of a passive clause. For example: *She's looking after her sister's children . . .   The children were always well looked after.*

V+ADV+PREP

The verb is intransitive and is followed by both an adverb and a prepositional group. The preposition always comes after the adverb: *I began to look forward to their visits.*

V+ADV/PREP

The verb is intransitive and is followed by a word that can be either an adverb or a preposition. For example: *The road to Lutterworth branches off here.* ('off' is an adverb) . . . *It branches off the main road.* ('off' is a preposition)

V+O+ADV

The verb is transitive and is followed by an adverb: *Some women choose to stay at home and bring up their children . . . The children were brought up by their mother.*

The object can normally come before or after the adverb, unless it is a pronoun, in which case it must come before the adverb. So: *They took him on.*

V+ADV+O

In a small group of verbs, the object always comes after the adverb, except when it is a pronoun. For example: *I am trying to give up smoking.*

V+O+PREP

The verb is transitive and is followed by a prepositional group: *We talked Donald into agreement.*

V+O+ADV+PREP

The verb is transitive and is followed by both an adverb and a prepositional group. The preposition always comes after the adverb, but the object can come before or after the adverb. For example: *She took her unhappiness out on her husband. / She took out her unhappiness on her husband.*

V+O+ADV/PREP

The verb is transitive and is followed by a word that can be either an adverb or a preposition. For example: *I crossed my name off the list . . . She crossed her name off.*

V−ERG+ADV

The verb is ergative and is followed by an adverb. So: *The rioters burned down five shops . . . The house burned down in a few minutes.*

V−ERG+PREP

The verb is ergative and is followed by a preposition: *The workers' demands centred around pay and conditions . . . Much of her teaching is centred around the family situation.*

about how to live or how to deal with a particular situation. EG *...new philosophies of child rearing.*

phlegm /flɛm/ is the thick yellowish substance that develops in your throat and at the back of your nose when you have a cold. N UNCOUNT

phlegmatic /flɛgmætɪk/. Someone who is **phlegmatic** stays calm even when upsetting or exciting things happen. EG *He was a phlegmatic, rather unemotional man.* ADJ QUALIT Formal

phobia /fəʊbɪə/, **phobias.** A **phobia** is an irrational fear or hatred of something. EG *I've got a phobia about spiders.* N COUNT

phone /fəʊn/, **phones, phoning, phoned. 1** The **phone** is an electrical system that you use to talk to someone else in another place, by dialling a number on a piece of equipment and speaking into it. EG *Most of the work is carried out over the phone... We have heard from her by phone a couple of times... I must go and make a phone call... Could you give me Frau Doring's phone number?* N SING : *the*+N OR *by*+N

2 A **phone** is the piece of equipment that you use when you talk to someone by phone. EG *I'm scared to answer the phone... The phone rang... She picked up the phone and dialled a number.* N COUNT : USU *the*+N

3 When you **phone** someone, you dial their phone number and speak to them by phone. EG *I went back to the motel to phone Jenny... Harland phoned to tell me what time the bus was due.* V+O OR V

4 If you are **on the phone**, **4.1** you are speaking to someone by phone. EG *I spent an hour on the phone trying to sort things out.* **4.2** you have a phone in your home or place of work, so that you can be contacted by phone. EG *Are you on the phone?* PHRASE

phone up. When you **phone** someone **up**, you dial their phone number and speak to them by phone. EG *I must phone her up tonight.* PHRASAL VB : V+O+ADV OR V+ADV

phone book, phone books. A **phone book** is a book that contains an alphabetical list of the names, addresses, and telephone numbers of the people in a town or area. N COUNT

phone booth, phone booths. A **phone booth** is **1** a place in a station, hotel, or other public building where there is a public telephone. **2** a small shelter in the street in which there is a public telephone. N COUNT American

phone box, phone boxes. A **phone box** is a small shelter in the street in which there is a public telephone. EG *Every phone box in Selly Oak had been vandalized.* N COUNT British

phone-in, phone-ins. A **phone-in** is a programme on radio or television in which people telephone with questions or opinions and their calls are broadcast. EG *...a late-night phone-in programme.* N COUNT

phonetic /fə^{6}nɛtɪk/, **phonetics. 1 Phonetics** is the study of speech sounds. N UNCOUNT Technical

2 Phonetic means relating to the sound of a word or to the sounds that are used in languages. EG *...phonetic spelling.* ADJ CLASSIF : ATTRIB Technical

phoney, phoneys; phonier, phoniest; also spelled **phony. 1** Something that is **phoney** is false rather than genuine. EG *He gave a phony name and address... She put on a phoney English accent.* ADJ CLASSIF Informal

2 Someone who is **phoney** is insincere or pretentious. EG *He thought all grown-ups were phony... ...your phoney manners.* ▸ used as a noun. EG *I suddenly realized what a phoney he is.* ADJ QUALIT Informal ▸ N COUNT

phosphorescent /fɒsfərɛsənt/. Something that is **phosphorescent** glows with a soft light but gives out little or no heat. EG *...a phosphorescent gas.* ADJ CLASSIF Formal

photo /fəʊtəʊ/, **photos.** A **photo** is the same as a photograph. EG *I took a magnificent photo of him.* N COUNT Informal

photocopier /fəʊtə^{6}kɒpɪə/, **photocopiers.** A **photocopier** is a machine which quickly copies documents onto paper by photographing them. N COUNT

photocopy /fəʊtə^{6}kɒpi^1/, **photocopies, photocopying, photocopied. 1** A **photocopy** is a copy of a document made using a photocopier. EG *We need to make a photocopy to send to staff members.* N COUNT

2 If you **photocopy** a document, you make a copy of it using a photocopier. V+O

photogenic /fəʊtədʒɛnɪk/. Someone who is **photogenic** looks nice in photographs. EG *Photogenic girls were sought for a series of adverts.* ADJ QUALIT

photograph /fəʊtəgrɑːf, -græf/, **photographs, photographing, photographed. 1** A **photograph** is a picture that is made using a camera. EG *I take photographs of things that interest me... They contacted the police after seeing his photograph in a newspaper.* N COUNT

2 When you **photograph** someone or something, you use a camera to obtain a picture of them. EG *She photographed the pigeons in Trafalgar Square.* V+O

photographer /fətɒgrəfə/, **photographers.** A **photographer** is someone who takes photographs, especially as a job. EG *...Robert L. Beck, photographer for Life magazine.* N COUNT

photographic /fəʊtəgræfɪk/. **1 Photographic** means connected with photographs or photography. EG *...expensive photographic equipment.* ADJ CLASSIF : ATTRIB

2 If you have a **photographic** memory, you are able to remember things in great detail after you have seen them. ADJ CLASSIF : ATTRIB

photography /fətɒgrəfi^1/ is the skill, job, or process of producing photographs. EG *Fox-Talbot was a pioneer of photography.* N UNCOUNT

Photostat /fəʊtə^{6}stæt/, **Photostats.** A **Photostat** is a particular type of photocopy. EG *...a photostat of the report.* N COUNT Trademark

phrasal verb /freɪzəl vɜːb/, **phrasal verbs.** A **phrasal verb** is a combination of a verb and an adverb or preposition, used together to have a particular meaning. In this dictionary, phrasal verbs have the label PHRASAL VB in the Extra Column. See the entry headed PHRASAL VERBS for more information. N COUNT

phrase /freɪz/, **phrases, phrasing, phrased. 1** A **phrase** is **1.1** a short group of words that people often use as a way of referring to something or saying something, especially a group of words that is memorable or whose meaning is not obvious from the words contained in it. Phrases are labelled PHRASE in the Extra Column. See the entry headed PHRASES for more information. EG *People still use the phrase 'doctor's orders'... It was Asa Briggs who originally coined the phrase 'redrawing the map of learning'.* **1.2** a small group of words which forms a unit, either on its own or within a sentence. EG *My German was practically nil – a few phrases here and there.* N COUNT

2 If you **phrase** something in a particular way, you express it in words in that way. EG *The moment I'd said it, I could see that I'd phrased it wrong.* V+O+A

3 A **turn of phrase** is a particular way of expressing something in words. EG *You have a nice turn of phrase.* • **to coin a phrase**: see **coin**. PHRASE

phrase book, phrase books. A **phrase book** is a book used by people travelling abroad which has lists of useful words and expressions in a foreign language, together with the translation of each word or expression. EG *...a French phrase book.* N COUNT

phraseology /freɪzɪɒlədʒi^1/. If something is expressed using a particular type of **phraseology**, it is expressed in words and expressions of that style and type. EG *...the sort of phraseology used by some journalists.* N UNCOUNT +SUPP Formal

physical /fɪzɪkə^{0}l/. **1 Physical** qualities, actions, or things are connected with a person's body, rather than with their mind. EG *All his physical and emotional needs would be attended to... He never used physical punishment on me.* ◇ **physically.** EG *He looked physically fit... She didn't attract me physically.* ADJ CLASSIF : USU ATTRIB ◇ ADV

2 Physical also means **2.1** relating to the struc- ADJ CLASSIF

Would you like to take photos of someone who is photogenic?

PHRASES

A phrase is a group of words that you use together. The meaning of the whole phrase is often difficult to guess from the usual meanings of the words. Phrases in the dictionary have the label PHRASE in the Extra Column. The best way to find a phrase in the dictionary is to guess which is the least common word in it, and to look up that word. When all the words seem to be equally common, the phrase will usually be found at either a verb or a noun.

1 Some phrases normally occur at a particular place in the structure of a clause. For example, the phrase **for life** is usually an adjunct. So you say: *He'll be a friend for life.* Whenever possible, the explanation shows you where the phrase is typically used in a clause, and the examples always show this.

2 In many phrases, one or more of the words can inflect, so that the verb can change from present to past or the noun from singular to plural. So that in the phrase **to break your heart**, you can say: *She said that I had broken her heart* or *Their hearts were broken by the news.*

3 Phrases are often followed by a particular grammatical structure. So that you usually '**take delight in** doing something' rather than just 'take delight' or even 'take delight in something'. For example: *She takes a positive delight in being criticized.* The dictionary entry shows the phrase in its typical structure. For example, the dictionary entry for the phrase **turn a deaf ear** says 'If you **turn a deaf ear** to something that someone says, you refuse to pay attention to it'.

ture, size, or shape of something that can be touched and seen. EG *...the physical characteristics of the earth... ...the physical size of a computer.* **2.2** connected with physics or the laws of physics. EG *...basic physical laws.*

3 Physical things can be touched and seen. EG *...a step towards the replacement of physical money by electronic money... ...an opportunity for children to look at the nature of the physical world around them.* ◇ **physically.** EG *Some religions suppose that there is a Heaven physically above the earth.* — ADJ CLASSIF : ATTRIB; ◇ ADV

physician /fɪzɪʃəⁿn/, **physicians.** A **physician** is a doctor. EG *...consultant physicians in geriatric medicine.* — N COUNT American

physicist /fɪzɪsɪst/, **physicists.** A **physicist** is a person who studies physics. EG *...a well-known nuclear physicist.* — N COUNT

physics /fɪzɪks/ is the scientific study of forces and qualities such as heat, light, sound, pressure, gravity, and electricity, and the way that they affect objects. EG *According to our present ideas of physics, nothing can travel faster than light... ...nuclear physics.* — N UNCOUNT

physiology /fɪzɪɒlədʒiˈ/. **1 Physiology** is the scientific study of how people's and animals' bodies function, and of how plants function. — N UNCOUNT

2 The **physiology** of an animal or plant is the way that it functions. EG *He was interested in the physiology of bulls.* ◇ **physiological** /fɪzɪəlɒdʒɪkəⁿl/. EG *...physiological changes.* — N SING+POSS; ◇ ADJ CLASSIF

physiotherapist /fɪzɪəʊθɛrəpɪst/, **physiotherapists.** A **physiotherapist** is a person whose job is doing physiotherapy. — N COUNT

physiotherapy /fɪzɪəʊθɛrəpiˈ/ is medical treatment which involves doing exercises or having part of your body massaged or warmed. — N UNCOUNT

physique /fɪziːk/, **physiques.** Someone's **physique** is the shape and size of their body; used especially of a man's body. EG *...a good-looking lad with a fine physique, powerful and attractive.* — N COUNT OR N UNCOUNT

pi /paɪ/ is a number, approximately 3.142, which is equal to the circumference of a circle divided by its diameter. It is usually represented by the Greek letter π.

pianist /pɪənɪst/, **pianists.** A **pianist** is a person who plays the piano. — N COUNT

piano /piˈænəʊ/, **pianos.** A **piano** is a large musical instrument with a row of black and white keys. When these keys are pressed down by the player's fingers, little hammers hit wire strings and different notes are played. See picture at MUSICAL INSTRUMENTS. EG *I play the piano.* • See also **grand piano.** — N COUNT

pick /pɪk/, **picks, picking, picked. 1** If you **pick** a particular person or thing, you choose that one. EG *Next time let's pick somebody else... I could not have picked a better way to travel.* • If you **pick and choose**, you carefully choose only things that you really want and reject the others. EG *A good secretary can pick and choose her job.* — V+O; • PHRASE

2 If you are told to **take** your **pick**, you can choose any one that you like from a group of things. EG *Take your pick. Choose whichever one of the three methods you fancy.* — PHRASE

3 When you **pick** flowers, fruit, or leaves, you break them off the plant or tree and collect them. EG *...the woods where we picked blackberries... How nice of the children to pick her some flowers.* — V+O, V+O+O, OR V+O+*for*

4 If you **pick** something from a place, you remove it from there with your fingers or your hand. EG *He picked his blazer off a chair... She picked a cigarette from her box and lit it.* — V+O+A

5 If you **pick** your nose or teeth, you remove dirt from your nostrils or food from your teeth. EG *He had just had a meal and was picking his teeth.* — V+O

6 If you **pick** a fight or quarrel with someone, you deliberately cause one. EG *He had ceased to pick quarrels with her.* — V+O : OFT+*with*

7 If someone such as a thief **picks** a lock, they — V+O open it without a key, for example by using a piece of wire.

8 If you **pick** your **way** across an area, you walk across it very carefully in order to avoid obstacles or dangerous things. EG *He began to pick his way over the rocks.* PHRASE

9 A **pick** is the same as a pickaxe. N COUNT

10 to **pick** someone's **brains**: see **brain**. • to **pick holes in** something: see **hole**. • to **pick** someone's **pocket**: see **pocket**. • See also **hand-picked**.

pick at. If you **pick at** the food that you are eating, you eat only very small amounts of it. EG *Laing was picking morosely at his salad.* PHRASAL VB : V+PREP

pick on. If you **pick on** someone, you criticize them unfairly or treat them unkindly. EG *Why are you always picking on me?* PHRASAL VB : V+PREP, HAS PASS Informal

pick out. If you **pick out** someone or something, 1 you recognize them when it is difficult to see them, for example because they are among a large group. EG *Ralph picked out Jack easily, even at that distance.* PHRASAL VB : V+O+ADV **2** you choose them from a group of people or things. EG *This is the job they picked out for me.* V+O+ADV

pick up. **1** When you **pick** something **up**, you lift it up. EG *He stooped down to pick up the two pebbles... The telephone rang and Judy picked it up.* PHRASAL VB : V+O+ADV **2** When you **pick up** something or someone that is waiting to be collected, you go to the place where they are and take them away, often in a car. EG *I might get my brother to come and pick me up.* V+O+ADV **3** If someone **is picked up** by the police, they are arrested and taken to a police station. EG *I don't want you to be picked up for drunkenness.* V+O+ADV, USU PASS **4** If you **pick up** something such as a skill or an idea, you acquire it without effort. EG *Did you pick up any Swedish?... I may pick up a couple of useful ideas for my book.* V+ADV+O Informal **5** If you **pick up** someone you do not know, you talk to them and try to start a sexual relationship with them. EG *I doubt whether Tony ever picked up a woman in his life.* V+O+ADV Informal **6** If a piece of equipment, for example a radio or a microphone, **picks up** a signal or sound, it receives it or detects it. EG *It was easier to pick up Radio Luxembourg than the Light Programme.* V+ADV+O **7** If trade or the economy of a country **picks up**, it improves. EG *The economy is picking up.* V+ADV **8** When you **pick up the pieces** after a disaster, you do what you can to get the situation back to normal again. EG *When the confusion dies down, we can try to pick up the pieces.* PHRASE **9** When a vehicle **picks up speed**, it begins to move more quickly. PHRASE **10** See also **pick-up**.

pickaxe /pɪkæks/, **pickaxes**; spelled **pickax** in American English. A **pickaxe** is a tool consisting of a curved, pointed piece of metal with a long handle joined to the middle. Pickaxes are used for breaking up rocks or the ground. N COUNT

picker /pɪkə/, **pickers.** A fruit **picker** or cotton **picker** is a person who picks fruit or cotton, usually for money. EG *...strawberry pickers.* N COUNT+SUPP

picket /pɪkɪt/, **pickets, picketing, picketed. 1** When a group of people, usually trade union members, **picket** a place of work, they stand outside it in order to protest about something, to prevent people from going in, or to persuade the workers to join a strike. EG *The plan was to picket docks and power stations.* V+O OR V ◊ **picketing.** EG *...before the mass picketing and its consequent mass arrests began.* ◊ N UNCOUNT ▸ used as a noun. EG *...the historic picket at Saltley coke depot.* ▸ N COUNT

2 Pickets are people who are picketing a place of work. EG *We could hear the chanting of the pickets.* N COUNT

picket line, picket lines. A **picket line** is a group of pickets outside a place of work. EG *The engineering union have joined them on the picket line.* N COUNT

pickle /pɪkəᵊl/, **pickles, pickling, pickled. 1 Pickles** are vegetables or fruit, sometimes cut into pieces, which have been kept in vinegar or salt water for a long time so that they have a strong, sharp taste. EG *...a jar of pickles.* N COUNT OR N UNCOUNT

2 When you **pickle** food, you keep it in vinegar or salt water so that it does not go bad and it develops a strong, sharp taste. EG *...pickled herring.* V+O

3 If you are in a **pickle**, you are in a difficult and awkward situation. EG *So how did you get yourself in this pickle?* N SING Informal

pickpocket /pɪkpɒkɪt/, **pickpockets.** A **pickpocket** is a person who steals things from people's pockets or handbags in public places. N COUNT

pick-up, pick-ups. A **pick-up** or a **pick-up truck** is a small truck with low sides that can be easily loaded and unloaded. N COUNT

picnic /pɪknɪk/, **picnics, picnicking, picnicked.** When people have a **picnic**, they eat a meal out of doors, usually in a field or wood or at the beach. EG *They often went on picnics... We used to take a picnic lunch and eat it on the beach.* N COUNT ▸ used as a verb. EG *The woods might be full of people picnicking.* ▸ V : USU+A

picnicker /pɪknɪkə/, **picnickers.** A **picnicker** is someone who is having a picnic. N COUNT

picture /pɪktʃə/, **pictures, picturing, pictured. 1** A **picture** consists of lines and shapes that are drawn, painted, or printed on a surface and that show a person, thing, or scene. EG *It is the single most important picture Picasso ever painted... Most of my pictures are engravings or screen prints... He picked up a book to look at the pictures.* N COUNT

2 A **picture** is also **2.1** a photograph. EG *We all had our pictures taken.* **2.2** an image which you see on a television screen. EG *We have all seen television news pictures of their forces in action.* N COUNT

3 If someone or something **is pictured** in a newspaper or magazine, they appear in a photograph in it. EG *Murray was pictured in The Times sharing a platform with Mostyn.* V+O : USU PASS+A

4 You can also refer to a film as a **picture**. EG *We worked together in the last picture I made.* N COUNT

5 If you go to the **pictures**, you go to see a film at a cinema. EG *She met him at the pictures... Will you take me to the pictures?* N PLURAL : *the*+N British

6 If you have a **picture** of something in your mind, **6.1** you have an idea or memory of it in your mind as if you were actually seeing it. EG *A picture flashed through Kunta's mind of the panther springing at him.* **6.2** you have an impression or belief about it. EG *They can get quite a distorted picture of what's going on.* N COUNT

7 If you **picture** something in your mind, you think of it so that you have a clear idea of what it is like. EG *He could picture all too easily the consequences of being caught.* V+O

8 If you give a **picture** of what something is like, you describe it in words or represent it in a film. EG *Mr Hamilton gives a most interesting picture of Monty's family background... You paint a rather bleak picture.* N COUNT : USU SING+SUPP

9 When you refer to the **picture** in a particular place, you are referring to the situation there. EG *In Nigeria, the picture appears to be different.* N SING : USU *the*+N

10 Picture is also used in these phrases. **10.1** If you **get the picture**, you understand the situation, especially one which someone is describing to you. EG *I get the picture. You want to keep the whole thing quiet.* PHRASES Informal **10.2** If you **put** someone **in the picture**, you tell them about a situation which they need to know about. EG *Let me put you in the picture about the situation there.* **10.3** If you say that someone is **in the picture**, you mean that they are involved in the situation that you are talking about. If you say that they are **out of the picture**, you mean that they are not involved in the situation. EG *She hated being out of the picture.*

If you get the picture, do you buy it?

10.4 You use **picture** to describe what someone looks like. For example, if you say that someone is **a picture of** health or **the picture of** misery, you mean that they look extremely healthy or extremely miserable. EG *Vidal was a picture of sophisticated detachment.*

picture rail, picture rails. A **picture rail** is a narrow piece of wood which is fixed to the walls of some rooms just below the ceiling. Pictures can be hung from it using string and hooks. N COUNT

picturesque /pɪktʃərɛsk/. A place that is **picturesque** is attractive and interesting to look at, usually because it is old and unspoiled. EG *...a small hotel overlooking the picturesque fishing harbour of Zeebrugge.* ADJ QUALIT

piddling /pɪdlɪŋ/ means small or unimportant. EG *...piddling little jobs... They gave her a piddling sum by way of compensation.* ADJ CLASSIF : USU ATTRIB Informal

pie /paɪ/, **pies. 1** A **pie** consists of meat, vegetables, or fruit, which is baked in pastry. EG *...chicken pie... ...a piece of apple pie.* N COUNT OR N UNCOUNT

2 If you describe an idea, plan, or promise as **pie in the sky**, you mean that you think that it is very unlikely to happen. EG *Can society really believe in the pie-in-the-sky promises of Professor Grant?* PHRASE

piece /piːs/, **pieces, piecing, pieced. 1** A **piece** of something is **1.1** a bit or part of it that has been broken off, torn off, or cut off. EG *He came back dragging a great big piece of a tree... ...folded pieces of cloth... She cut the cake and gave me a piece... He tore both letters into small pieces.* **1.2** one of the individual parts or sections which it is made of, especially a part that can be removed. EG *Piece by piece he assembled the rifle... ...like pieces fitting into a jigsaw puzzle.* N PART

2 You use **piece** to refer to an individual object of a particular type. EG *The only piece of clothing she bought was a jumper... ...each piece of furniture... ...the most important piece of apparatus.* N PART

3 You use **piece** to refer to an individual group of facts or an individual action or product. EG *...a valuable piece of information... ...a thoughtful piece of research... ...this piece of advice... ...a piece of music... Meeting Mrs Hooke was a piece of good fortune.* N PART

4 A **piece** is also **4.1** something that is written or created, for example an article, play, or short musical composition. EG *...a thoughtful piece about President Roosevelt... It was a classic piece called Forever Is For Us.* **4.2** an object, for example a vase or a table, that is considered valuable or interesting. EG *...a piece from Chippendale's Chinese period.* N COUNT

5 You can refer to specific coins as **pieces**. For example, a 10p **piece** is a coin that is worth 10p. EG *The machine wouldn't take 10p pieces... ...a lighter that was no bigger than a 50p piece.* N COUNT+SUPP

6 The **pieces** which you use when you play a board game such as chess or backgammon are the specially shaped objects which you move around on the board. N COUNT

7 Piece is also used in these phrases. **7.1** If someone or something is still **in one piece** after a dangerous journey or experience, they are safe and not damaged or hurt. **7.2** If something is smashed **to pieces**, is taken **to pieces**, or falls **to pieces**, it is broken or comes apart so that it is in separate pieces. EG *The poster had been ripped to pieces... He took to pieces and reassembled an entire engine.* **7.3** If you **go to pieces**, you are so upset or nervous that you lose control of yourself and cannot do what you should do. EG *He did not go to pieces as I feared he might.* **7.4** If someone **tears** you **to pieces** or **pulls** your work **to pieces**, they criticize you or your work very severely. **7.5 bits and pieces**: see **bit**. • **a piece of cake**: see **cake**. • to **pick up the pieces**: see **pick up**. PHRASES Informal Informal

piece together. 1 If you **piece together** the truth about something, you gradually discover it. EG *She had not yet been able to piece together exactly what had happened.* **2** If you **piece** something **together**, you gradually make it by joining several things or parts together. EG *She pieced together the torn-up drawing.* PHRASAL VB : V+O+ADV V+O+ADV

piecemeal /piːsmiːl/. A **piecemeal** change or process happens gradually, usually at irregular intervals. EG *...the piecemeal accumulation of land... Films are financed piecemeal; the distributor doles out money little by little.* ADJ CLASSIF OR ADV AFTER VB

piecework /piːswɔːk/. If you do **piecework**, you are paid according to the amount of work that you do rather than the length of time that you work. N UNCOUNT

pier /pɪə/, **piers.** A **pier** is a large structure which sticks out into the sea at a seaside town and which people can walk along. N COUNT

pierce /pɪəs/, **pierces, piercing, pierced.** If a sharp object **pierces** something or if you **pierce** something with a sharp object, the object goes into it and makes a hole in it. EG *When the snake's fangs pierce its victim's flesh, the venom is injected... The pointed end of the stick pierced through its throat into its mouth.* V+O OR V+A

pierced /pɪəst/. A **pierced** object has had holes made in it deliberately. EG *...pierced wooden screens... ...pierced ears.* ADJ CLASSIF

piercing /pɪəsɪŋ/. **1** A **piercing** sound or voice is high-pitched and very sharp and clear in an unpleasant way. EG *I was jolted out of my exhaustion by piercing screams.* ADJ QUALIT

2 If someone's eyes are **piercing**, they are bright and seem to look at you very intensely. EG *He had piercing blue eyes.* ADJ QUALIT

3 A **piercing** wind makes you feel very cold. ADJ QUALIT

piety /paɪɪti/ is strong religious belief, or religious behaviour. EG *...men of true piety.* N UNCOUNT

piffling /pɪflɪŋ/. Something that is **piffling** is small or unimportant, and ridiculous. EG *The steps taken are so piffling in the face of the enormity of the problem.* ADJ QUALIT Informal

pig /pɪg/, **pigs. 1** A **pig** is a pink or black animal with short legs and not much hair on its skin. Pigs are often kept on farms for their meat. N COUNT

2 If you call someone a **pig**, you mean that you think they are unpleasant in some way, especially that they are greedy or unkind; an offensive use. N COUNT Informal

3 If you **make a pig of** yourself, you eat a great deal; used showing disapproval. PHRASE Informal

pigeon /pɪdʒɪn/, **pigeons.** A **pigeon** is a bird, usually grey in colour, which has a fat body. Pigeons often live in towns. N COUNT

pigeon-hole, pigeon-holes. A **pigeon-hole** is one of the sections in a frame on a wall where letters and messages can be left for someone. EG *Howard strolled over to the rows of pigeon-holes to collect his mail.* N COUNT

piggyback /pɪgibæk/, **piggybacks.** If you give someone a **piggyback**, you carry them high on your back, supporting them under their knees. N COUNT

piggybank /pɪgibæŋk/, **piggybanks.** A **piggybank** is a small container shaped like a pig, with a slot in it to put coins in. Children use piggybanks to save money in. N COUNT

pig-headed. Someone who is **pig-headed** refuses to change their mind about things; used showing disapproval. EG *...sheer pig-headed determination.* ADJ QUALIT

piglet /pɪglɪt/, **piglets.** A **piglet** is a young pig. N COUNT

pigment /pɪgmənt/, **pigments.** A **pigment** is a substance that gives something a particular colour. EG *It forms part of the red pigment of blood.* N COUNT OR N UNCOUNT Formal

pigsty /pɪgstaɪ/, **pigsties. 1** A **pigsty** is a hut with a yard where pigs are kept on a farm. N COUNT

2 If you describe a room or a house as a **pigsty**, you mean that it is very dirty and untidy. N COUNT Informal

pigtail /pɪgteɪl/, **pigtails.** A **pigtail** is a length of hair that has been divided into three and then plaited. EG *...a girl with a blonde pigtail down her back.* N COUNT

pilchard /pɪltʃəd/, **pilchards.** A **pilchard** is a small fish that lives in the sea. EG *...tins of pilchards.* N COUNT

pile /paɪl/, **piles, piling, piled. 1** A **pile** of things is **1.1** a quantity of them which form a mass that is high in the middle and has sloping sides. EG *There in front of me was a great pile of old tin cans... ...a pile of sand.* **1.2** a quantity of them which have been put neatly somewhere so that each thing is on top of the one below. EG *He lifted a pile of books from the bedside table.* N PART

2 If you **pile** a quantity of things somewhere, you put them there so that they form a pile. EG *Brody picked up the heap of papers and piled them on top of a radiator... Her hair was piled high on her head.* V+O+A

3 If a surface **is piled** with a quantity of things, it is covered with piles of them. EG *His desk was piled with papers.* V+O : USU PASS +*with*

4 If you talk about **piles** of something or a **pile** of something, you mean a large amount of it. EG *He's got an enormous pile of money stashed away.* N PART Informal

5 If a group of people **pile** into or out of a vehicle, they all get into it or out of it in a rather disorganized way. EG *The troops piled into the coaches.* V+A

6 Piles are painful swellings that appear in the veins inside a person's anus. N PLURAL

7 The **pile** of a carpet or of a fabric such as velvet is its soft surface, which consists of lots of little threads standing on end. EG *...a luxurious deep pile carpet.* N UNCOUNT

pile up. 1 If you **pile up** a quantity of things or if they **pile up**, you put them somewhere or they collect somewhere, forming a pile. EG *All her possessions were piled up there... The papers she was meant to be reading piled up untouched on her desk.* **2** If things **pile up** or if someone **piles** them **up**, more and more of them happen or are acquired. EG *All these disasters piled up on the unfortunate villagers... Last year the company piled up losses totalling £4 billion.* PHRASAL VB : V-ERG+ADV; V-ERG+ADV

pile-up, pile-ups. A **pile-up** is a road accident in which several vehicles crash into each other. EG *There had been a twenty-car pile-up on the M1.* N COUNT

pilgrim /pɪlgrɪm/, **pilgrims.** A **pilgrim** is a person who makes a journey to a holy place for a religious reason. N COUNT

pilgrimage /pɪlgrɪmɪdʒ/, **pilgrimages.** A **pilgrimage** is a journey that someone makes to a holy place for a religious reason. EG *She made the pilgrimage to Lourdes... ...a place of pilgrimage.* N COUNT OR N UNCOUNT

pill /pɪl/, **pills. 1** A **pill** is a small, round mass of medicine that you swallow without chewing. EG *I took a sleeping pill.* N COUNT

2 The **pill** is a type of pill that some women take regularly so that they do not become pregnant. EG *I'm not on the pill.* N SING : *the*+N

pillage /pɪlɪdʒ/, **pillages, pillaging, pillaged. Pillage** is the stealing of property in a violent way, usually by a group of people. ▸ used as a verb. EG *They pillaged and looted every house in the village.* N UNCOUNT Outdated ▸ V+O

pillar /pɪlə/, **pillars. 1** A **pillar** is a tall, narrow, solid structure, which is usually used to support part of a building. EG *I fell asleep leaning against a pillar on someone's porch.* N COUNT

2 If you describe someone as a **pillar** of a group that they belong to, you mean that they are an active and important member of it. EG *I thought you had to be a pillar of the community to foster children... ...pillars of society.* N COUNT : USU+*of*

pillar box, pillar boxes. A **pillar box** is a tall red cylinder with a narrow hole in it where you can put letters to be collected by a postman. Pillar boxes are found in streets. N COUNT British

pillion /pɪljən/. When you ride **pillion** on a motorcycle, you sit behind the person who is controlling it. ADV AFTER VB

pilloried /pɪləri^{1}d/. If someone **is pilloried**, they are criticized severely, especially in newspapers or on radio and television. EG *He was pilloried and his resignation demanded.* V-PASS Formal

pillow /pɪləʊ/, **pillows.** A **pillow** is a rectangular cushion which you rest your head on when you are in bed. N COUNT

pillowcase /pɪlə^{6}keɪs/, **pillowcases.** A **pillowcase** is a cover for a pillow, which can be removed and washed. N COUNT

pillowslip /pɪlə^{6}slɪp/, **pillowslips.** A **pillowslip** is the same as a pillowcase. N COUNT

pilot /paɪlət/, **pilots, piloting, piloted. 1** A **pilot** is a person who is trained to fly an aircraft. EG *...an experienced pilot.* N COUNT

2 When someone **pilots** an aircraft, they act as its pilot. EG *...a jolly man who piloted his own airplane.* V+O

3 If you **pilot** a new law or scheme, you try to introduce it. EG *He was keen to see through the Bill which John Silkin was piloting.* V+O

4 A **pilot** scheme or study is used to test whether a particular scheme or product will be successful, before it is introduced on a large scale. EG *This year we are trying a pilot scheme whereby the university leases one or two houses for students.* ADJ CLASSIF : ATTRIB

pilot light, pilot lights. A **pilot light** is a small gas flame in a cooker, boiler, or fire which burns all the time and which lights the main large flame when the gas is turned fully on. N COUNT

pimp /pɪmp/, **pimps.** A **pimp** is a man who controls prostitutes, gets clients for them, and takes a large part of their earnings. N COUNT Informal

pimple /pɪmpə^{0}l/, **pimples.** A **pimple** is a small red spot, especially one on your face. N COUNT

pimply /pɪmpli^{1}/. Someone who is **pimply** has a lot of pimples, especially on their face. EG *He was an ugly, pimply little boy.* ADJ QUALIT

pin /pɪn/, **pins, pinning, pinned. 1** A **pin** is a very small, thin rod of metal with a point at one end. Pins can be stuck through things, for example through two pieces of cloth, in order to fasten them together. ● See also **drawing pin**, **safety pin**. N COUNT

pins

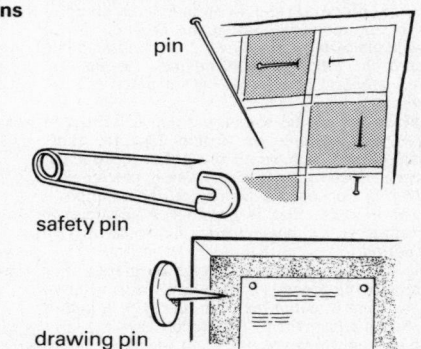

pin

safety pin

drawing pin

2 If you **pin** something somewhere, you fasten it there with a pin, a drawing pin, or a safety pin. EG *She wore a white rose pinned to her blouse.* V+O+A

3 If someone **pins** you in a particular position, they hold you or press down on you firmly so that you cannot move. EG *His strong arms were around me, pinning me down.* V+O+A

4 If someone **pins** the blame for something on you, they say, often unfairly, that you did it or caused it. EG *You can't pin that on me.* V+O+*on/upon* Informal

5 If you **pin** your hopes on something, you hope very much that it will produce the result you want, because it is the only thing that is likely to. EG *He pinned his hopes on the prospect of a split in the opposition party.* V+O+*on/upon*

pin down. 1 If you try to **pin down** something PHRASAL VB :

If someone's face is pinched, has someone else pinched it?

which is hard to describe, you try to say exactly what it is or what it is like. EG *The courts have found obscenity impossible to pin down as a punishable offence.* 2 If you **pin** someone **down**, you force them to make a definite statement, which they have been trying to avoid doing. EG *He was anxious to pin the Minister down to some definite commitment.* V+O+ADV / V+O+ADV

pin up. 1 If you **pin up** a poster or a notice, you pin it to a wall so that it can be seen easily. EG *The map was pinned up and became the centre of attention.* 2 If you **pin up** part of a piece of clothing, you pin the bottom of it to a higher part of it. EG *The hem was pinned up.* 3 See also **pin-up**. PHRASAL VB : V+O+ADV / V+O+ADV

pinafore /pɪnəfɔː/, **pinafores.** A **pinafore** or a **pinafore dress** is a dress with no sleeves, which a woman or girl wears over a blouse or sweater. N COUNT

pincer /pɪnsə/, **pincers.** 1 **Pincers** are a tool consisting of two pieces of metal that are hinged in the middle. Pincers are used for gripping things or for pulling things out. See picture at TOOLS. EG *...a pair of pincers.* N PLURAL

2 The **pincers** of a crab or a lobster are its front claws. N COUNT : USU PLURAL

pinch /pɪntʃ/, **pinches, pinching, pinched.** 1 If you **pinch** someone, you squeeze a part of their body between your thumb and first finger. EG *Dr. Hochstadt pinched Judy's cheek as she passed.* V+O

▸ used as a noun. EG *She gave my wrist a little pinch.* ▸ N COUNT

2 A **pinch** of something is the amount of it that you can hold between your thumb and your first finger. EG *Season with salt and a pinch of cinnamon.* ● to **take** something **with a pinch of salt**: see **salt**. N PART

3 If someone **pinches** something, they steal it. EG *I pinched fourpence from the box.* V+O Informal

4 **At a pinch** means if absolutely necessary and if there is no alternative. EG *At a pinch the new doctor would do.* PHRASE Informal

5 If you **are feeling the pinch**, you do not have as much money as you used to, and so you cannot buy things you would like to buy. EG *The big fashion establishments have been feeling the pinch lately.* PHRASE

pinched /pɪntʃt/. If someone's face is **pinched**, it looks thin and pale, usually because they are ill or cold. EG *He lay on his bed, looking pinched and worn.* ADJ QUALIT

pincushion /pɪnkʊʃəⁿn/, **pincushions.** A **pincushion** is a very small cushion that you stick pins and needles into so that you can get them easily when you need them. N COUNT

pine /paɪn/, **pines, pining, pined.** 1 A **pine** or a **pine tree** is a tall evergreen tree which has long, thin, sharp leaves and a fresh smell. N COUNT

2 **Pine** is the pale-coloured wood of pine trees, which is often used for making furniture. EG *...sitting at the pine table.* N UNCOUNT

3 If you **are pining** for something, you want it very much and feel sad because you cannot have it. EG *Most of them were pining to be recognized and admitted as citizens... Helen pines for you.* V+*for* OR *to*-INF : USU CONT

pine away. If someone **pines away**, they gradually become weaker and die because they are very unhappy. EG *I believe she actually pined away – lost her will to live.* PHRASAL VB : V+ADV

pineapple /paɪnæpəⁿl/, **pineapples.** A **pineapple** is a large oval fruit that grows in hot countries. It is sweet, juicy, and yellow inside and has a thick, brownish skin. EG *...a slice of pineapple.* N COUNT OR N UNCOUNT

ping /pɪŋ/, **pings, pinging, pinged.** If a bell or a piece of metal **pings**, it makes a short, high-pitched noise. EG *The bell pings; the lift doors open.* V

▸ used as a noun. EG *There is a loud ping from the alarm clock.* ▸ N COUNT

ping-pong /pɪŋ pɒŋ/ is the game of table tennis. N UNCOUNT

pink /pɪŋk/, **pinker, pinkest; pinks.** 1 Something that is **pink** is of a colour between red and white. EG *...the white and pink blossom of orchard apples... ...brilliant reds and pinks and oranges... The bathroom was decorated in pink.* ADJ COLOUR

2 If you go **pink**, your face turns a slightly redder colour than usual because you are embarrassed or angry, or because you are doing something energetic. EG *He went very pink, and looked away.* ADJ COLOUR

3 **Pinks** are small plants that people grow in their gardens. Pinks have sweet-smelling pink, white, or red flowers. N COUNT

pinkish /pɪŋkɪʃ/ means slightly pink in colour. EG *...a faint pinkish glow.* ADJ COLOUR

pinnacle /pɪnəkəⁿl/, **pinnacles.** 1 A **pinnacle** is a pointed cone-shaped piece of stone or rock. EG *...the pinnacles of St John's Church... ...the white pinnacles of the distant mountains.* N COUNT

2 The **pinnacle** of something is the best or highest level of it. EG *These newspapers were regarded as the pinnacle of journalism... The civil service was the pinnacle of his employment hopes.* N COUNT : USU SING+*of*

pinpoint /pɪnpɔɪnt/, **pinpoints, pinpointing, pinpointed.** 1 If you **pinpoint** something, you discover or explain exactly what it is. EG *You can pinpoint any danger and we can deal with it... In their book, Jackson and Marsden pinpointed the difference.* V+O

2 If you **pinpoint** the position of something, you discover or show its exact position. EG *'Just here,' he said, pinpointing it on the map.* V+O

pins and needles. If you get **pins and needles** in part of your body, you feel sharp tingling pains there for a while because it has been in an awkward or uncomfortable position. N PLURAL

pin-stripe. Pin-stripe cloth or **pin-striped** cloth has very narrow vertical stripes. EG *He wore a pin-stripe suit... ...a black jacket and pin-striped trousers.* ADJ CLASSIF : ATTRIB

pint /paɪnt/, **pints.** 1 A **pint** is **1.1** in Britain, a unit of measurement for liquids that is equal to one-eighth of an imperial gallon or 568 cubic centimetres. EG *...one pint of milk.* **1.2** in America, a unit of measurement for liquids that is equal to one-eighth of an American gallon or 473 cubic centimetres. N PART

2 If you have a **pint** in a pub, you have a pint of beer. EG *He likes having a couple of pints with his lunch.* N COUNT

pin-up, pin-ups. A **pin-up** is a picture of an attractive woman or man. EG *The bathroom wall was plastered with pin-ups of film stars.* ▸ used as an adjective. EG *...pin-up girls.* N COUNT / ▸ ADJ CLASSIF : ATTRIB

pioneer /paɪənɪə/, **pioneers, pioneering, pioneered.** 1 Someone who is referred to as a **pioneer** in a particular area of activity is one of the first people to be involved in it and develop it. EG *He was a pioneer of photography.* N COUNT

2 Someone who **pioneers** a new activity, invention, or process is one of the first people to do it. EG *...a hospital which pioneered open heart surgery in this country.* ◇ **pioneering.** EG *...a pioneering and innovative banker.* V+O / ◇ ADJ CLASSIF : ATTRIB

3 A **pioneer** is also one of the first people to live or farm in a particular place. EG *They all went out as pioneers, with little or nothing.* N COUNT

pious /paɪəs/. Someone who is **pious** is very religious and moral. EG *Mrs Smith was a very pious woman who attended Church services regularly.* ADJ QUALIT

pip /pɪp/, **pips, pipping, pipped.** 1 A **pip** is one of the small hard seeds in a fruit such as an apple, orange, or pear. N COUNT

2 The **pips** on the radio are a series of short, high-pitched sounds that are used as a time signal. N COUNT

3 If you **pip** someone **at the post**, you just beat them in a competition or in a race to achieve something. PHRASE Informal

pipe /paɪp/, **pipes, piping, piped.** 1 A **pipe** is a long, round, hollow object, usually made of metal or plastic, through which a liquid or gas can flow. EG *...hot water pipes.* N COUNT

2 To **pipe** a liquid or gas somewhere means to transfer it from one place to another through a pipe. EG *Hot water is piped to all the rooms.* V+O : USU+A

pipe

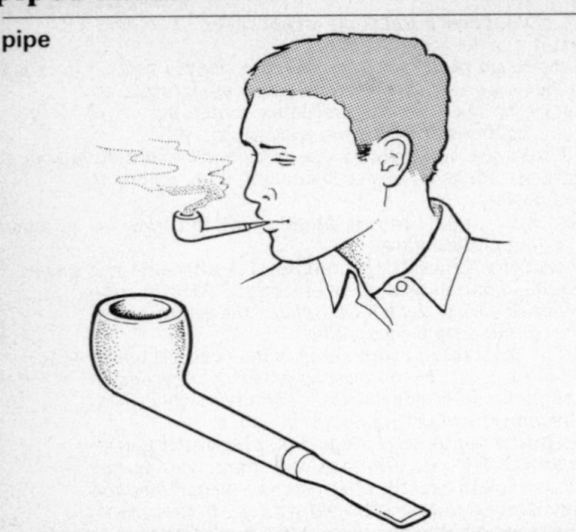

3 A **pipe** is also an object which is used for smoking tobacco. You put the tobacco into the cup-shaped part at the end of the pipe, light it, and breathe in the smoke through a narrow tube. EG *He was sitting in his armchair, smoking a pipe and reading the paper.* N COUNT

4 Pipes are the same as bagpipes. N PLURAL

5 If someone **pipes** something, they say it in a high-pitched voice. EG *'It's for you,' he piped, waving a purple envelope.* V+O OR V+QUOTE Written

6 See also **piping**, **piping hot**.

piped music is music which is played through loudspeakers in some supermarkets, restaurants, and other public places. N UNCOUNT

pipe dream, pipe dreams. A **pipe dream** is a hope or plan that you have which you know will never really happen. EG *He considered such hopes to be pipe dreams.* N COUNT

pipeline /paɪplaɪn/, **pipelines. 1** A **pipeline** is a large pipe which is used for carrying oil or gas over a long distance, often underground. N COUNT

2 If you say that something is **in the pipeline**, you mean that it is already planned or begun and will be completed soon. EG *More improvements were in the pipeline.* PHRASE

piper /paɪpə/, **pipers.** A **piper** is a musician who plays the bagpipes. N COUNT

piping /paɪpɪŋ/. **1 Piping** is metal, plastic, or another substance made in the shape of a pipe or tube. EG *...a length of steel piping.* N UNCOUNT

2 If someone speaks in a **piping** voice, they speak in a high-pitched voice. EG *In a piping voice she ordered me to sit down.* ADJ CLASSIF : ATTRIB Written

piping hot. Food or water that is **piping hot** is very hot. EG *...mugs of piping hot coffee.* ADJ CLASSIF

piquant /piːkənt, -kɑːnt/. **1** Food that is **piquant** has a pleasantly spicy taste. EG *...piquant crab soup with chilli.* ADJ QUALIT Formal ◇ **piquancy** /piːkənsi¹/. EG *...using herbs or spices to give variety and piquancy.* ◇ N UNCOUNT

2 Something that is **piquant** is interesting and exciting. EG *...a piquant face with large appealing dark-blue eyes.* ADJ QUALIT Formal ◇ **piquancy.** EG *Argument adds piquancy to the contest.* ◇ N UNCOUNT

pique /piːk/ is the feeling of anger and resentment that you have when your pride is hurt. EG *He withdrew from the contest in a fit of pique.* N UNCOUNT

piqued /piːkt/. If someone is **piqued**, they are angry and resentful because their pride has been hurt. ADJ QUALIT

piracy /paɪrə¹sɪ/. **1 Piracy** was robbery carried out by pirates. N UNCOUNT

2 You can also refer to the illegal copying of things such as video tapes and computer programs as **piracy**. EG *...software piracy.* N UNCOUNT : USU+SUPP

piranha /pɪrɑːnə/, **piranhas.** A **piranha** is a small, fierce fish from South America. N COUNT

pirate /paɪrə¹t/, **pirates, pirating, pirated. 1 Pirates** were sailors who attacked other ships and stole property from them. N COUNT

2 Someone who **pirates** video tapes, cassettes, books, or computer programs copies and sells them when they have no right to do so. V+O ◇ **pirated.** EG *There were a lot of pirated editions.* ◇ ADJ CLASSIF

3 Pirate is used to describe illegal copies of things. EG *...pirate videos.* ADJ CLASSIF : ATTRIB

pirouette /pɪruet/, **pirouettes.** In ballet, a **pirouette** is a fast turn of the dancer's body which is done on the toes or on the ball of the foot. N COUNT

piss /pɪs/, **pisses, pissing, pissed**; a very informal, rude word which many speakers avoid using. Informal

1 To **piss** means to urinate. V

2 If someone has a **piss**, they urinate. N SING : *a*+N

3 Piss is urine. N UNCOUNT

piss down. If it **is pissing down**, it is raining hard. PHRASAL VB : V+ADV

piss off. If someone tells a person to **piss off**, they are telling the person in a rude way to go away. PHRASAL VB : V+ADV, USU IMPER

pissed /pɪst/; a very informal, rude word. Someone who is **pissed** is drunk. ADJ PRED Informal

pissed off; a very informal, rude word. If someone is **pissed off** with something, they feel bored and irritated by it. ADJ PRED Informal

pistol /pɪstə⁰l/, **pistols.** A **pistol** is a small gun that you hold in your hand. N COUNT

piston /pɪstə⁰n/, **pistons.** A **piston** is a cylinder or metal disc that is part of an engine. Pistons slide up and down inside tubes and cause various parts of the engine to move. N COUNT

pit /pɪt/, **pits, pitting, pitted. 1** A **pit** is **1.1** a large hole that is dug in the ground. EG *The pit was stacked with ammunition.* **1.2** a small, shallow hole in the surface of something. EG *...scratches and pits on the enamel.* N COUNT

2 A **pit** is also a coal mine. EG *...the men coming home from the pit.* N COUNT

3 A gravel **pit** or clay **pit** is a very large hole that is left where gravel or clay has been dug from the ground. N COUNT+SUPP

4 If you have a feeling in **the pit of your stomach**, you have a physical feeling inside your body at the front, usually because you are afraid or anxious. EG *...the ache in the pit of her stomach.* PHRASE

5 In motor racing, the **pits** are the areas at the side of the track where drivers stop for refuelling and repairs during races. N PLURAL : *the*+N

6 If you describe someone or something as **the pits**, you mean that they are the worst of their kind. EG *That first week is the pits, isn't it?* PHRASE Informal

7 If you **pit** your **wits against** someone, you compete with them in a test of knowledge or intelligence. PHRASE

8 See also **pitted**.

pitch /pɪtʃ/, **pitches, pitching, pitched. 1** A football **pitch**, hockey **pitch**, or cricket **pitch** is an area of ground that is marked out and used for playing that particular game. N COUNT : USU+SUPP

2 If you **pitch** something somewhere, you throw it with quite a lot of force, usually aiming it carefully. EG *He was pitching a penny at a crack in the sidewalk.* V+O : USU+A

3 If someone or something **pitches** somewhere, they fall forwards suddenly and with a lot of force. EG *He suddenly pitched headlong to the ground.* V+A

4 If someone **is pitched** into a new situation, they are suddenly forced into it. EG *This pitched him into the political arena.* V+O : USU+A

5 The **pitch** of a sound is its degree of highness or lowness. EG *Her voice dropped to a lower pitch.* N UNCOUNT

Is 'pitiless' the opposite of 'pitiful'?

6 If something reaches a high **pitch**, it reaches a high level or degree. EG *Excitement about the wedding is now at fever pitch... Her frustration mounted to such a pitch of anger that she could no longer keep silent.* N SING: USU+SUPP

7 If you **pitch** something at a particular level or degree of difficulty, you set it at that level. EG *Her lectures are pitched directly at the level of the students.* V+O+A

8 When you **pitch** a tent, you put it into an upright position using the poles and fix it securely to the ground. EG *They pitched their tents at the edge of the field.* V+O

pitch in. If you **pitch in**, you join in an activity. EG *They will be expected to pitch in and make their own beds.* PHRASAL VB: V+ADV Informal

pitch-black. If a place or the night is **pitch-black** or **pitch-dark**, it is completely dark. EG *We started off through the pitch-black woods.* ADJ CLASSIF

pitched battle, pitched battles. A **pitched battle** is a very fierce and violent fight. EG *Police fought a pitched battle with about 40 youths.* N COUNT

pitcher /pɪtʃə/, **pitchers. 1** A **pitcher** is a jug. EG *...a pitcher of water.* N COUNT American

2 In baseball, the **pitcher** is the person who throws the ball to the person who is batting. N COUNT

pitchfork /pɪtʃfɔːk/, **pitchforks.** A **pitchfork** is a large fork with a long handle and two prongs that is used for lifting hay or grass. N COUNT

piteous /pɪtɪəs/. Something that is **piteous** is so sad that you feel great pity for the person involved. EG *There were piteous sounds of suffering and pain.* ADJ QUALIT Literary

pitfall /pɪtfɔːl/, **pitfalls.** The **pitfalls** involved in doing something are the ways in which you might fail or be harmed, or the things you might do wrong. EG *...the pitfalls of pursuing such a drastic policy... We must bear in mind the pitfalls and try to avoid them.* N COUNT: USU PLURAL

pith /pɪθ/. The **pith** of an orange, lemon, or other citrus fruit is the white substance between the peel and the inside of the fruit. N UNCOUNT

pithy /pɪθi[1]/. A **pithy** comment or piece of writing is short, direct, sensible, and memorable. EG *...her brisk, pithy, ironic observations... ...pithy working-class humour.* ADJ QUALIT

pitiable /pɪtɪəbə[0]l/. Someone who is **pitiable** is in such a sad or weak situation that you feel pity for them. EG *She was in a pitiable plight.* ADJ QUALIT

pitiful /pɪtɪfʊl/. Someone or something that is **pitiful** is so sad, weak, or small that you feel pity for the person involved. EG *...his thin, bony legs and his pitiful arms... ...the pitiful sound of a human being in pain.* ◊ **pitifully.** EG *He looks pitifully thin.* ADJ QUALIT ◊ ADV

pitiless /pɪtɪlɪ[2]s/. Someone or something that is **pitiless** shows no feelings of pity or mercy. EG *His face was cool and pitiless... ...enduring the pitiless rain upon their bare backs.* ADJ CLASSIF

pittance /pɪtə[0]ns/. If you receive a **pittance**, you receive only a very small amount of money. EG *They are tired of working for a pittance.* N SING: a+N

pitted /pɪtɪ[2]d/. If the surface of something is **pitted**, it is covered with a lot of small, shallow holes. EG *The walls were pitted with bullet holes... His face was pitted and unshaven.* ADJ CLASSIF

pity /pɪti[1]/, **pities, pitying, pitied. 1** If you feel **pity** for someone, you feel very sorry for them. N UNCOUNT

2 If you **pity** someone, you feel very sorry for them. EG *She pitied him with her whole heart... I know how horrible it is to be pitied.* V+O

3 If you say that it is a **pity** that something is the case, you mean that you feel disappointed about it. EG *It will be a terrible pity if this should happen... Pity you missed that film last night.* N SING: a+N

4 If you add **more's the pity** to a comment, you are expressing your disappointment or regret about something. EG *'I didn't write that letter.' – 'More's the pity. If you had, you might have a job now.'* ADV SEN

5 If you **take pity on** someone, you feel sorry for them and help them. EG *A man who spoke English took pity on us and it was all sorted out.* PHRASE

pivot /pɪvət/, **pivots, pivoting, pivoted. 1** A **pivot** is the pin or the central point on which something balances or turns. EG *The compass needle swung round on its pivot.* N COUNT

2 If something **pivots**, it balances or turns on a central point. EG *Michael stopped, pivoted and walked back in.* V

3 The **pivot** in a situation is the most important thing which everything else is based on or arranged around. EG *We were important, essential, the pivot of their lives.* N COUNT

pizza /piːtsə/, **pizzas.** A **pizza** is a flat, round piece of dough covered with tomatoes, cheese, and other kinds of food, and then baked in an oven. N COUNT OR N UNCOUNT

placard /plækɑːd/, **placards.** A **placard** is a large notice that is carried in a march or demonstration or is displayed in a public place. EG *...placards which declared 'Troops off Campus Now!'* N COUNT

placate /plə[3]keɪt/, **placates, placating, placated.** If you **placate** someone, you try to stop them feeling angry or resentful by doing or saying things that will please them. EG *...the desire of politicians to placate the public.* V+O

place /pleɪs/, **places, placing, placed. 1** A **place** is any point, building, area, town, or country. EG *The cellar was a very dark place... ...photographs of places taken during his travels abroad... Do you know a place called The Farmer's Inn?... ...a meeting place... Please give your name, address, age, place of birth, and religion... We were looking for a good place to camp... Of course it was no place to raise a child... The saloon, I decided, was the place for me.* N COUNT: OFT+SUPP

2 You can refer to the position where something was, or where it should be, as its **place**. EG *She put the book back in its place on the shelf... Don't park your car in the wrong place.* N COUNT+SUPP

3 If something is **in place**, it is in its correct or usual position. If it is **out of place**, it is not in its correct or usual position. EG *He held the handle in place while the glue set... Jane screwed the grille back into place... She was slightly out of breath but not one hair was out of place.* PHRASE

4 If things are **all over the place**, they are in many different places. EG *We have shops in Paris, New York and all over the place... There were clothes and old shoes all over the place.* PHRASE

5 Place can be used after 'any', 'no', 'some', or 'every' to mean 'anywhere', 'nowhere', 'somewhere', or 'everywhere'. EG *You are not going any place... He had no place else to go.* N SING American Informal

6 Your **place** is the house, flat, or room where you live. EG *Could I stay at your place for a bit, Rob?... What sort of place do they have?* N COUNT: USU+POSS Informal

7 Your **place** at a table, in a classroom, or in a hotel, for example, is a space, seat, or room that is intended for you to use or that you normally use. EG *I had a place reserved at the Youth Hostel in Stockholm... I took my place in class... Mrs Kaul had to leave her place and go to the back of the room.* N COUNT: USU+POSS

8 A **place** at a table is also a space with a knife, fork, and other things arranged on it, so that one person can sit down and eat. EG *Every day 12 places are laid for dinner.* N COUNT

9 If you have a **place** on a committee or at a college, for example, you are a member of the committee or are accepted by the college as a student. EG *I got a place at a teachers' training college... ...university places.* N COUNT

10 Someone's or something's **place** in a society, system, or situation, is their position or role in relation to other people or things. EG *...Britain's place in the world... Frank felt it was not his place to raise any objection... The demonstration occupies a central place in their political campaign...* N COUNT+SUPP

One day we shall change places, and you will stay at home and I shall go to work.

11 Your **place** in a competition or on a scale is your position at the end of the competition or on the scale. First place is the winning or top position. EG *She took first place in the Crafts Fair... The US leapt from sixth place to second.* — N COUNT

12 A good **place** to do something in a situation or activity is a good time or stage at which to do it. EG *This could be a very good place to start... This is not the place for a detailed description of his problems.* — N COUNT: USU SING+SUPP

13 Your **place** in a book or speech is the point that you have reached in reading or speaking it. EG *Her finger was pressed to the page as if marking her place... He lost his place in his notes.* — N COUNT+POSS

14 If you cannot understand something complicated and then everything **falls into place**, you suddenly understand how the different parts of it are connected and it becomes clearer. EG *...the incident on the bus, the police searches – it all fell into place.* — PHRASE

15 You say **in the first place** when you are talking about the beginning of a situation or about the situation as it was before a series of events. EG *Nobody can remember what was agreed in the first place... How did she become interested in the French Revolution in the first place?* — PHRASE

16 You say **in the first place** and **in the second place** to introduce the first and second in a series of points or reasons. EG *...information that, in the first place, would have been very difficult for me to obtain and, in the second place, would have been useless anyhow.* — ADV SEN

17 When something **takes place**, it happens. EG *The next attack took place four hours later... The talks will take place in Vienna... Profound political changes have been taking place in the country.* — PHRASE

18 If you **place** something somewhere, you put it there neatly or carefully. EG *She placed the music on the piano and sat down... Chairs had been placed in rows all down the room.* — V+O+A

19 If you **place** a person or thing in a particular state, you cause them to be in it. EG *The agreement was not placed at risk... Chamberlain placed the Cabinet in a difficult situation.* — V+O+A

20 If you **place** responsibility, pressure, blame, or a restriction on someone, you make them have it or be affected by it. EG *The responsibility placed upon us is too heavy to bear... Renewed pressure will be placed on the Government this week... Vita is placing most of the blame on her mother.* — V+O+*on/upon*

21 If you **place** emphasis on something, you emphasize it. EG *The New Left placed much emphasis on the role of culture.* — V+O+*on/upon*

22 If you **place** an order for goods or an advert in a newspaper, for example, you ask a company to send you the goods or you ask the newspaper to publish the advert. — V+O

23 If you recognize someone but you cannot **place** them, you cannot remember exactly who they are or where you have met them before. EG *She was looking at me as if she could not quite place me.* — V+O

24 If you say how many decimal **places** there are in a number, you are saying how many numbers there are to the right of the decimal point. — N COUNT

25 **Place** is also used in these phrases. **25.1** If one thing is used **in place of** another, or if it **takes the place of** the other thing, it replaces the other thing. EG *This task is carried out by robots in place of human workers... Armed soldiers were soon to take the place of diplomats.* **25.2** If you **put** someone **in** their **place**, you show them that they are less important or clever than they think they are. EG *I decided to put this upstart politely in his place.* **25.3** If someone or something is **out of place** in a situation, they are unsuitable or do not fit easily into it. EG *I never overcame the sense of being out of place, of being an outsider... The degree of detail seems out of place in a book so limited on scope.* — PHRASES

placed /pleɪst/. If someone is well **placed**, they have more advantages or resources than other people. EG *How well are we placed with regard to America?... As for finance, we're better placed than people think.* — ADJ PRED

placement /pleɪsmə[2]nt/, **placements.** 1 The **placement** of something is the act of putting it in a particular place. EG *I spent a week directing the placement of the boulders.* — N UNCOUNT +SUPP

2 If someone gets a **placement**, they get a job for a period of time which will give them experience in the work they are training for. EG *Amongst other placements, he spent some months at the Children's Hospital.* — N COUNT

placid /plæsɪd/. 1 Someone who is **placid** is calm and does not easily become excited, angry, or upset. EG *He was a placid boy with a philosophical approach to life.* — ADJ QUALIT

2 A **placid** place is calm and peaceful. EG *...the placid harbour waters.* — ADJ QUALIT

plagiarism /pleɪdʒərɪzə[0]m/ is the practice of using or copying someone else's idea or work and pretending that you thought of it or created it. EG *It was a shameless piece of plagiarism.* — N UNCOUNT

plague /pleɪg/, **plagues, plaguing, plagued.** 1 A **plague** is a very infectious disease that spreads quickly and kills large numbers of people. — N COUNT OR N UNCOUNT

2 A **plague** of unpleasant things is a large number of them that arrive or happen at the same time. EG *...a plague of locusts.* — N COUNT+*of*

3 If unpleasant things **plague** you, they keep happening and cause you a lot of trouble or suffering. EG *The system is plagued by technical faults... He suffered severe back injuries, which plague him to this day.* — V+O

4 If you **plague** someone, you keep bothering them or asking them for something. EG *The readers were urged to plague their MP with letters of protest.* — V+O: OFT+*with*

5 If you say that you **avoid** someone or something **like the plague**, you are emphasizing that you deliberately avoid them completely. — PHRASE

plaice /pleɪs/. **Plaice** is both the singular and the plural form. A **plaice** is a kind of flat fish. EG *Cod, haddock, and plaice are excellent all-purpose fish.* — N COUNT OR N UNCOUNT

plain /pleɪn/, **plains; plainer, plainest.** 1 A **plain** is a large, flat area of land with very few trees on it. EG *...vast plains covered in yellow grasses.* — N COUNT

2 A **plain** object or surface is entirely in one colour and has no pattern, design, or writing on it. EG *Put it in a plain envelope.* — ADJ CLASSIF: ATTRIB

3 **Plain** things are very simple in style. EG *She felt ashamed of her plain dress... I enjoy good plain food; nothing fancy.* — ADJ QUALIT

4 If a fact or situation is **plain**, it is easy to recognize or understand. EG *It was plain that Eddie wanted to get back to sleep... Their difficulty is plain.* — ADJ QUALIT: USU PRED

5 **Plain** statements are direct and easy to understand. EG *...a plain statement of fact.* — ADJ QUALIT

6 You can use **plain** before a noun or an adjective in order to emphasize it. EG *Petty is the wrong word. It's plain meanness... Logical judgment can also be just plain wrong.* — ADJ CLASSIF: ATTRIB OR SUBMOD

7 A woman or girl who is **plain** is not at all beautiful. EG *...a plain plump girl with pigtails.* — ADJ QUALIT

8 **plain sailing**: see **sailing**.

plain-clothes. **Plain-clothes** police officers are wearing ordinary clothes instead of a uniform. EG *Lebel ordered a plain-clothes detective to check into the hotel.* — ADJ CLASSIF: ATTRIB

plainly /pleɪnli[1]/. 1 If you say that something is **plainly** the case, you mean that it is obviously the case. EG *He was plainly angry.* — ADV SEN

Find two words on these pages which are pronounced in the same way.

2 If you can see, hear, or smell something **plainly**, you can see, hear, or smell it easily. EG *You could see the oysters quite plainly, lying all over the sea-bed.* ADV

3 If you say something **plainly**, you say it in a way that is easy to understand and cannot be mistaken. ADV

plaintiff /pleɪntɪf/, **plaintiffs.** A **plaintiff** is a person who brings a legal case against someone in a court of law. N COUNT Legal

plaintive /pleɪntɪv/. A **plaintive** sound or voice is sad and high-pitched. EG *...a plaintive wail.* ADJ QUALIT

plait /plæt/, **plaits, plaiting, plaited. 1** If you **plait** three or more lengths of hair or rope together, you twist them over and under each other to make one thick length. EG *Her thick brown hair was plaited in a single braid down her back... ...long ropes of plaited rushes.* V+O : USU PASS

2 A **plait** is a length of hair or rope that has been plaited. EG *...her long gold plaits, each tied with a red ribbon.* N COUNT

plan /plæn/, **plans, planning, planned. 1** A **plan** is a method of achieving something that you have worked out in detail beforehand. EG *I told them of my plan... ...a plan to give women more power... ...her plan for union reform.* N COUNT

2 If you **plan** what you are going to do, you decide in detail what you are going to do. EG *At breakfast I planned my day... We must plan for the future.* V+O OR V+*for*

3 If you **plan** to do something, you intend to do it. EG *What do you plan to do after college?... I was planning a career in law.* ◇ **planned.** EG *...news of the planned sale of 50,000 acres of state forests.* V+*to*-INF OR V+O ◇ ADJ CLASSIF

4 If you have **plans**, you are intending to do a particular thing. EG *The gales forced him to change his plans... He was making plans to sell his house.* N PLURAL

5 When you **plan** something that you are going to make, build, or create, you decide what the main parts of it will be and how they will be arranged. EG *How do you plan a book?... ...the art of planning gardens.* V+O

6 A **plan** is also **6.1** a list or diagram of the main parts that are going to be included in something, for example in a piece of writing. EG *...a plan of a story.* **6.2** the shape and design of a garden, building, or group of buildings. EG *...the plan and overall design of the building.* **6.3** a detailed drawing that shows what each floor of a building looks like from above. EG *Make a neat plan of your new home.* N COUNT

7 A **plan of action** or a **plan of campaign** is a series of actions that you have decided to take in order to achieve something. EG *His plan of campaign is to cycle into town and collect the money personally.* PHRASE

8 If something happens **according to plan**, it happens in the way that it was intended to happen. EG *The whole thing was going according to plan.* PHRASE

9 See also **planning**.

plan on. If you **plan on** doing something, you intend to do it. EG *I plan on staying in London for the foreseeable future.* PHRASAL VB : V+PREP, HAS PASS

plan out. If you **plan out** what you are going to do, you decide in detail what you are going to do. EG *I hadn't even planned out the route yet.* PHRASAL VB : V+O+ADV

plane /pleɪn/, **planes, planing, planed. 1** A **plane** is a vehicle with wings and one or more engines, which can fly through the air. EG *We went by plane... We bought the cigarettes on the plane.* N COUNT OR *by*+N

2 A **plane** is also a flat surface. EG *...an elaborate structure of coloured planes.* N COUNT Technical

3 You can refer to a particular level of something as a particular **plane**. EG *She tried to lift the conversation onto a more elevated plane... Such poetry belongs to another class, another plane of sensitivity.* N COUNT+SUPP Literary

4 A **plane** is also a tool that has a flat bottom with a sharp blade in it. You move the plane over a piece of wood in order to remove thin pieces of its surface. N COUNT

5 If you **plane** a piece of wood, you make it smaller or smoother by using a plane. V+O

planet /plænɪ[1]t/, **planets.** A **planet** is a large, round object in space that moves around a star. The Earth is a planet. EG *They have the capacity to kill every human being on the planet... ...the orbit of the planet Mars.* N COUNT

planetarium /plænɪ[1]tɛərɪəm/, **planetariums.** A **planetarium** is a building where lights are shone on the ceiling to represent the planets and the stars and to show how they appear to move. N COUNT

planetary /plænɪ[1]tə[0]ri[1]/ means relating to or belonging to planets. EG *...the planetary exploration programme.* ADJ CLASSIF : ATTRIB

plank /plæŋk/, **planks.** A **plank** is a long rectangular piece of wood. N COUNT

planner /plænə/, **planners. 1** The **planners** in local government are the people who decide how land should be used and what new buildings should be built. EG *...architects and planners.* N COUNT : USU PLURAL

2 A **planner** is a person who works out in detail what is going to be done in the future. EG *...TV programme planners.* N COUNT

planning /plænɪŋ/. **1 Planning** is the process of deciding in detail how to do something before you actually start to do it. EG *The project is still in the planning stage.* • See also **family planning**. N UNCOUNT

2 Planning is also control by the local government of the way that land is used in an area and of what new buildings are built there. EG *...the concrete deserts created by modern planning at its worst.* N UNCOUNT

plant /plɑːnt/, **plants, planting, planted. 1** A **plant** is a living thing that grows in the earth and has a stem, leaves, and roots. EG *...alpine herbs and plants... ...a tall banana plant... ...plant pots.* N COUNT

2 When you **plant** a seed, plant, or young tree, you put it into the ground so that it will grow there. EG *I spent weeks planting potatoes one spring... Each autumn we planted primroses in the garden.* V+O

3 When someone **plants** land with a particular type of plant or crop, they put plants or seeds into the land to grow them there. EG *...small front gardens planted with rose trees.* V+O : USU+*with*

4 A **plant** is also a factory or a place where power is generated. EG *...the re-opening of a nuclear plant after an accident.* N COUNT

5 Plant is large machinery that is used in industrial processes. EG *The company plans to spend nearly £1 billion on new plant and equipment.* N UNCOUNT Technical

6 If you **plant** something somewhere, you put it there firmly. EG *I planted my deckchair beside hers... 'Hello,' he said, planting a kiss on her cheek.* V+O+A

7 If someone **plants** something such as a bomb somewhere, they hide it in the place where they want it to function. EG *They had planted the bomb beneath the house... I haven't planted a microphone in your desk.* V+O : USU+A

8 If you **plant** something such as a weapon or drugs on someone, you put it amongst their belongings or in their house or office so that they will be wrongly accused of a crime. EG *I'm convinced the evidence was planted in John's flat.* V+O : USU+A

9 If an organization **plants** an informer or a spy somewhere, they send that person there so that they can do something secretly. EG *The CIA had planted its agents in all the strategic areas.* V+O : USU+A

plant out. When you **plant out** young plants, you plant them in the ground in the place where they are to be left to grow. EG *We had to rear it in a nursery and plant it out.* PHRASAL VB : V+O+ADV

plantation /plɑːnteɪʃə[0]n/, **plantations.** A **plantation** is **1** a large piece of land, especially in a tropical country, where crops such as cotton, tea, or sugar are grown. EG *...rubber plantations.* **2** a large number of trees that have been planted together. EG *...conifer plantations.* N COUNT

planter /plɑːntə/, **planters.** A **planter** is a person who owns or manages a plantation in a tropical country. EG *...Indian tea planters.* N COUNT+SUPP

plaque /plæk, plɑːk/, **plaques.** **1** A **plaque** is a flat piece of metal, wood, or stone, which is fixed to a wall or monument in memory of a famous person or event. EG *...a memorial plaque at the crematorium... A plaque marks the site of Chippendale's workshops.* N COUNT

2 Plaque is a substance that forms on the surface of your teeth. It consists of saliva, bacteria, and food. N UNCOUNT

plasma /plæzmə/ is the clear fluid part of blood which contains the corpuscles and cells. N UNCOUNT

plaster /plɑːstə/, **plasters, plastering, plastered.** **1 Plaster** is a smooth paste made of sand, lime, and water which dries and forms a hard layer. Plaster is used to cover walls and ceilings inside buildings. EG *The walls were in a dreadful condition – the plaster was peeling off.* N UNCOUNT

2 If you **plaster** a wall or ceiling, you cover it with a layer of plaster. EG *...a wall that was poorly plastered.* V+O

3 A **plaster** is a strip of sticky material used for covering small cuts or sores on your body. EG *I dabbed the cut and applied a plaster.* N COUNT

4 If you have a leg or arm **in plaster**, you have a cast made of plaster of Paris around your leg or arm, in order to protect a broken bone and allow it to mend. EG *...a fractured ankle encased in plaster.* PHRASE

5 See also **plastered**.

plaster cast, plaster casts. A **plaster cast** is a case made of plaster of Paris, which is used for protecting broken bones by keeping part of the body stiff and rigid. N COUNT

plastered /plɑːstəd/. **1** If something is **plastered** to a surface, it is sticking to the surface. EG *His wet hair was plastered to his forehead.* ADJ PRED+*to*

2 If something is **plastered** with a sticky substance, it is covered with the substance. EG *Her back was thickly plastered with suntan oil.* ADJ PRED +*with*

3 If a surface is **plastered** with posters or notices, it is covered with them. EG *The walls of his tiny shop were plastered with pictures of actors and actresses.* ADJ PRED +*with*

4 If someone is **plastered**, they are very drunk. EG *You can't go and get plastered before church!* ADJ PRED Informal

plaster of Paris /plɑːstər əv pærɪs/ is a type of plaster made from white powder and water which dries quickly and is used to make plaster casts. N UNCOUNT

plastic /plæstɪk/, **plastics. Plastic** is a material which is produced by a chemical process and which is used to make many objects. It is light in weight and does not break easily. EG *The roofs are covered in winter by sheets of plastic... What's special about this new type of plastic?* ▸ used as an adjective. EG *Village potters become redundant as cheap plastic bowls and buckets flood the market... ...a plastic bag... The plastic seating was uncomfortable.* N UNCOUNT OR N COUNT ▸ ADJ CLASSIF

Plasticine /plæstɪsiːn/ is a soft coloured substance like clay which children use for making little models. N UNCOUNT Trademark

plastic surgery is the practice of performing operations to repair or replace skin which has been damaged, or to improve people's appearance by changing features of their body. EG *One of the survivors needed plastic surgery.* N UNCOUNT

plate /pleɪt/, **plates, plating, plated.** **1** A **plate** is **1.1** a round or oval flat dish that is used to hold food. EG *The dirty plates have been stacked in a pile on the kitchen table... He looked at the food on his plate... ...plates of sandwiches.* **1.2** a flat sheet of metal, especially on machinery or a building. EG *We got into the cellar through a round hole covered by a metal plate.* **1.3** a small flat piece of metal with someone's name written on it, which you usually find beside the front door of an office or house. EG *I read her name on the polished brass plate.* ● See also **number plate**. N COUNT

2 Plate is dishes, bowls, and cups that are made of precious metal, especially silver, gold, or pewter. EG *We would prefer church plate and other treasures to be stored in bank vaults.* N UNCOUNT

3 Metal that **is plated** is covered with a thin layer of a precious metal such as gold or silver. ▸ used as an adjective. EG *...gold-plated brooches.* V+O : USU PASS ▸ ADJ CLASSIF

4 A **plate** in a book is a picture or photograph which takes up a whole page and is usually printed on better quality paper than the rest of the book. N COUNT

5 A dental **plate** is a piece of plastic which is shaped to fit inside a person's mouth and which a set of false teeth is attached to. N COUNT

6 If you **have a lot on** your **plate**, you have a lot of work to do or a lot of things to deal with. EG *I know you've got a lot on your plate – so take it easy.* PHRASE Informal

7 If something **is handed** to you **on a plate**, you get it very easily. EG *She got handed the job on a plate.* PHRASE

plateau /plætəʊ/, **plateaus** or **plateaux.** **1** A **plateau** is a large area of high and fairly flat land. N COUNT

2 If you say that an activity or process has reached a **plateau**, you mean that it has reached a stage where there is no further change or development. EG *In the seventies the US space programme seemed to have reached a plateau of development.* N COUNT

plate glass is thick glass made in large, flat pieces, which is used especially to make large windows and doors. EG *...a new plate-glass window.* N UNCOUNT

platform /plætfɔːm/, **platforms.** **1** A **platform** is **1.1** a flat structure, usually made of wood, which people stand on when they make speeches or give a performance. EG *The speaker mounted the platform.* **1.2** a flat raised structure or area, usually one which something can stand on or land on. EG *...helicopter landing platforms... ...loading platforms.* N COUNT

2 A **platform** in a railway station is the area beside the rails where you wait for or get off a train. EG *Jordache paced nervously up and down the platform.* N COUNT

3 You can say that someone has a **platform** when they have an opportunity to tell people what they think or want. EG *It provides a platform for the consumer's viewpoint.* N COUNT : USU+SUPP

4 The **platform** of a political party is what they say they will do if they are elected. EG *He campaigned on a socialist platform.* N COUNT+SUPP

5 In a bus, the **platform** is the area of floor at the front or back where you get on and off. N SING : *the*+N

platinum /plætɪnəm/. **1 Platinum** is a very valuable, silvery-grey metal. It is often used for making jewellery. N UNCOUNT

2 Platinum hair is very fair, almost white. EG *...a platinum blonde.* ADJ COLOUR

platitude /plætɪtjuːd/, **platitudes.** A **platitude** is a statement which is considered boring and meaningless because it has been made many times before in similar situations. EG *...empty platitudes about democracy.* N COUNT Formal

platonic /plətɒnɪk/. **Platonic** relationships or feelings of affection do not involve sex. EG *Her interest in him was entirely platonic.* ADJ CLASSIF

platoon /plətuːn/, **platoons.** A **platoon** is a small group of soldiers which is commanded by a lieutenant. EG *In his platoon he had thirty-two men.* N COLL

platter /plætə/, **platters.** A **platter** is a large, flat plate used for serving food. EG *There were five kinds of cheese on a wooden platter.* N COUNT Outdated

plausible /plɔːzəˈbəᵒl/. An explanation or statement that is **plausible** seems likely to be true or valid. EG *Such a theory seems very plausible... ...a plausible answer.* ADJ QUALIT

play /pleɪ/, **plays, playing, played.** **1** When children **play**, they spend time with their toys or taking part in games. EG *The kids went off to play* V : USU+A

Is a playboy playful?

on the swings... I played with the children all day... Her grandchildren enjoy playing with her old toys.

2 When you **play** a sport, game, or match, you take part in it. EG *I played squash three times a week... Do you play chess?... I used to play for the village cricket team.* V+O OR V

3 When one person or team **plays** another, they compete against them in a sport or game. EG *Did you see McEnroe playing Connors the other day?* V+O OR V+*against*

4 If you **play** a joke or a trick on someone, you deceive them or give them a surprise in a way that you think is funny, but that often causes problems for them or annoys them. EG *I presumed someone was playing a rather silly joke.* V+O

5 You can use **play** to say how someone behaves, when they are deliberately behaving in a certain way. For example, if someone **plays** safe, they do not take any risks. If they **play** the innocent, they pretend to be innocent. EG *They would play it cool if they saw the boys again... Don't you play the wise old professor with me, Franz... This year we're playing host to the New Sussex Opera.* V+O+C OR V+C Informal

6 A **play** is a piece of writing which is performed in a theatre, on the radio, or on television. EG *Wesker has written four major plays since then... I saw the play a couple of years ago.* N COUNT

7 If an actor **plays** a role or character in a play or film, he or she performs the part of that character. EG *Brutus was played by James Mason... I was asked to play in a revival of 'Ghosts'.* V+O OR V+A

8 If you **play** a musical instrument or **play** a tune on it, you produce music from it. EG *Out on the balcony, a man stood playing a trombone... Doesn't he play beautifully?... The child played him a tune.* V+O, V+A, OR V+O+O

9 If you **play** a record or tape, you listen to it on a record player, tape recorder, or cassette player. EG *I'll play you the tape in a minute.* V+O OR V+O+O

10 When light **plays** somewhere, it moves about on a surface in an unsteady way. EG *The glossy patches of sunshine played over their bodies.* V+A Literary

11 When something **comes into play** or **is brought into play**, it begins to be used or to have an effect. EG *Computer systems were brought into play to draw up attack strategies.* PHRASE Formal

12 If something or someone **plays a part** or **plays a role** in a situation, they are involved in it and have an effect on it. EG *Examinations seem to play a large part in education... Television plays a dominant role in moulding public opinion.* PHRASE

13 If you **play for time**, you try to delay something happening, so that you can prepare for it or prevent it from happening. EG *She was playing for time, half hoping that he would forget all about it.* PHRASE

play along. If you **play along** with a person or with their plans, you agree with them and do what they want, even though you are not sure whether they are right. EG *I'll play along with them for the moment.* PHRASAL VB : V+ADV, USU+*with*

play at. 1 If you **play at** an activity, you do it without effort or seriousness. EG *They played at being huntsmen.* PHRASAL VB : V+PREP **2** If you ask **what** someone **is playing at**, you are angry because you think that they are doing something stupid or wrong. EG *What do you think you're playing at?... I don't know what the police are playing at.* CONVENTION Informal

play back. When you **play back** a tape or film, you listen to the sounds or watch the pictures after recording them. PHRASAL VB : V+O+ADV

play down. If you **play down** something, you try to make people think that it is less important than it really is. EG *He played down his recent promotion.* PHRASAL VB : V+O+ADV

play off against. If you **play** people **off against** each other, you make them compete or argue, so that you gain some advantage. EG *Annie played one parent off against the other.* PHRASAL VB : V+O+ADV +PREP

play on. If you **play on** people's weaknesses or faults, you deliberately use them in order to achieve what you want. EG *He used to play on their prejudices and their fears.* PHRASAL VB : V+PREP, HAS PASS

play up. 1 If something such as a machine or a part of your body **is playing up** or **is playing** you **up**, it is not working properly. EG *Our phone is playing up again... Is your leg still playing you up?* PHRASAL VB : V+ADV OR V+O+ADV

2 When children **are playing up**, they are being naughty and are difficult to control. PHRASE Informal

play upon. To **play upon** something means the same as to play on it. EG *He found himself in a position to play upon the fears of his colleagues.* PHRASAL VB : V+PREP, HAS PASS Formal

playboy /pleɪbɔɪ/, **playboys.** A **playboy** is a rich man who spends most of his time enjoying himself in expensive ways. N COUNT

player /pleɪə/, **players. 1** In sports, a **player** is a person who takes part in a sport or game. EG *...Gerald Davies, the former Welsh rugby player.* N COUNT

2 You can use **player** to refer to a musician. For example, a piano **player** is someone who plays the piano. EG *He's one of the most original guitar players in jazz.* N COUNT

3 A **player** is also an actor. EG *The players came on stage with their backs to the audience.* N COUNT Outdated

4 See also **record player**.

playful /pleɪfʊl/. **1** Someone who is **playful** is friendly and jokes a lot. EG *He was just being playful... She gave Philip's hand a little playful squeeze.* ◇ **playfully.** EG *Elaine kissed Harold playfully on the cheek.* ADJ QUALIT ◇ ADV

2 An animal that is **playful** is lively and cheerful. EG *...a playful kitten.* ADJ QUALIT

playground /pleɪgraʊnd/, **playgrounds.** A **playground** is a piece of land where children can play. EG *He could hear the children in the playground nearby... ...a school playground.* N COUNT

playgroup /pleɪgru:p/, **playgroups.** A **playgroup** is an informal kind of school for very young children where they learn things by playing. N COUNT OR N UNCOUNT

playhouse /pleɪhaʊs/, **playhouses.** A **playhouse** is a theatre. EG *...London playhouses.* N COUNT Outdated

playing card, playing cards. Playing cards are thin pieces of cardboard with numbers or pictures printed on them, which are used to play various games. EG *...a pack of playing cards.* N COUNT

playing field, playing fields. A **playing field** is a large area of grass where people play sports. N COUNT

playmate /pleɪmeɪt/, **playmates.** A child's **playmate** is another child who often plays with him or her. EG *Over the summer my playmates were my cousins.* N COUNT

playoff /pleɪɒf/, **playoffs.** A **playoff** is an extra game which is played to decide the winner of a sports competition when two or more people have got the same score. N COUNT

play on words. A **play on words** is a clever and amusing use of a word with more than one meaning, or a word that sounds like another word, so that what you say has two different meanings. N SING

playpen /pleɪpɛn/, **playpens.** A **playpen** is a small structure which is designed for a baby or young child to play safely in. It has bars or a net round the sides and is open at the top. N COUNT

plaything /pleɪθɪŋ/, **playthings.** A **plaything** is a toy or other object that a child plays with. EG *I used to get them new playthings to keep them quiet.* N COUNT Formal

playtime /pleɪtaɪm/ is a period of time between lessons at school when children can play outside. N UNCOUNT

playwright /pleɪraɪt/, **playwrights.** A **playwright** is a person who writes plays. N COUNT

plc /pi: ɛl si:/. is an abbreviation for 'public limited company'. It is used after the name of a company whose shares can be bought by the public. EG *...National Westminster Bank plc.*

plea /pli:/, **pleas. 1** A **plea** is an intense, emotional request for something. EG *She at last responded to his pleas for help.* N COUNT

2 In a court of law, a **plea** is the answer which someone gives when they have been charged with a crime, in which they say whether they are guilty N COUNT Legal or not. EG *I agreed to enter a plea of guilty if the Crown would drop the charge against my friend.*

plead /pliːd/, **pleads, pleading, pleaded.** 1 If you **plead** with someone to do something, you ask them in an intense, emotional way to do it. EG *He was pleading with her to control herself... She wrote to the Prime Minister pleading for restraint... 'Take me with you,' he pleaded.*
V+A OR V+QUOTE

2 If someone, especially a lawyer, **pleads** someone else's case or cause, they speak in support or defence of that person. EG *Of course his mother does her best to plead his case... Who will plead for us?*
V+O OR V+A Formal

3 If you **plead** a particular thing as the reason for doing or not doing something, you give it as your excuse. EG *The Government might find it convenient to plead ignorance... I pleaded that I felt ill.*
V+O OR V+REPORT: ONLY *that*

4 When someone charged with a crime **pleads** guilty or not guilty in a court of law, they officially state that they are guilty or not guilty of the crime. EG *'How do you plead?' – 'Not guilty.'*
V+C OR V

pleading /pliːdɪŋ/, **pleadings.** 1 A **pleading** expression or gesture shows that you want something very much. EG *Then he saw his brother's pleading expression and his heart softened.*
ADJ CLASSIF: ATTRIB

2 **Pleading** is asking someone in an intense, emotional way to do something. EG *After days of tearful pleading and sulking, she stayed... It was hard to resist his daughter's pleadings.*
N UNCOUNT OR N PLURAL

pleasant /plɛzə^{0}nt/, **pleasanter, pleasantest.** 1 Something that is **pleasant** is nice and enjoyable or attractive. EG *...a pleasant chat... It was pleasant to sit under the apple tree.* ◊ **pleasantly.** EG *I was pleasantly surprised... ...a pleasantly nutty taste.*
ADJ QUALIT · ◊ ADV

2 Someone who is **pleasant** is friendly and likeable. EG *They were pleasant lads... Dr Lake wrote a very pleasant letter to my father.* ◊ **pleasantly.** EG *'Please come in,' she said pleasantly.*
ADJ QUALIT · ◊ ADV

pleasantry /plɛzə^{0}ntri^{1}/, **pleasantries. Pleasantries** are casual, friendly remarks which you say in order to be polite. EG *We stood exchanging a few pleasantries.*
N COUNT Formal

please /pliːz/, **pleases, pleasing, pleased.** 1 You say **please** 1.1 when you are politely asking someone to do something. EG *'Follow me, please,' the guide said... Please don't interfere, Boris.* **1.2** when you are politely asking for something. EG *Hello. Could I speak to Sue, please?* **1.3** when you are accepting something politely. EG *'Do you want some milk?' – 'Yes please.'* **1.4** to attract someone's attention; used especially by children to attract the attention of a teacher or other adult. EG *Please, miss, why is that wrong?*
ADV SEN · ADV SEN · CONVENTION · CONVENTION

2 If someone or something **pleases** you, they make you feel happy and satisfied. EG *You're an impossible man to please, Emmanuel... Neither idea pleased me... Rose was anxious to please.*
V+O OR V

3 You use **please** in expressions such as 'as she pleases' and 'whatever you please' to indicate that someone can do or have whatever they want. EG *Judy had a right to come and go as she pleased... He can get anyone he pleases to work with him.*
V OR V+O

4 You say **if you please** as a very polite and formal way of attracting someone's attention. EG *Captain Imrie stopped me at the door. 'If you please, Dr Marlowe, a word with you.'*
CONVENTION Formal

5 You say **'please yourself'** to indicate that you do not mind or care whether the person you are talking to does a particular thing or not. EG *'Do you mind if I wait?' I asked. Melanie shrugged: 'Please yourself.'*
CONVENTION Informal

pleased /pliːzd/. 1 If you are **pleased**, you are happy about something or satisfied with something. EG *She seemed very pleased that he had come... He was pleased with my progress... She did not look at all pleased.*
ADJ PRED

2 You say **'Pleased to meet you'** as a polite way of greeting someone who you are meeting for the first time.
CONVENTION

pleasing /pliːzɪŋ/. Something that is **pleasing** gives you pleasure and satisfaction. EG *...a pleasing piece of news... It has a pleasing smell.*
ADJ QUALIT Formal

pleasurable /plɛʒə^{0}rəbə^{0}l/. Something that is **pleasurable** is pleasant and enjoyable. EG *...a pleasurable sensation... Not every child expects reading to be pleasurable.*
ADJ QUALIT Formal

pleasure /plɛʒə/, **pleasures. 1 Pleasure** is **1.1** a feeling of happiness, satisfaction, or enjoyment. EG *McPherson could scarcely conceal his pleasure at my resignation... I can't understand how people can kill for pleasure.* **1.2** the activity of enjoying yourself rather than working. EG *She is a disciplined creature who will put duty before pleasure... He set off on another of his European pleasure tours.*
N UNCOUNT

2 A **pleasure** is an activity or experience that you find very enjoyable and satisfying. EG *What a pleasure it would be to hunt in these forests!... Will you do me the pleasure of joining me in a drink?... ...the pleasures of choral singing.*
N COUNT: USU+SUPP

3 You can say **'It's a pleasure'** or **'My pleasure'** as a polite way of replying to someone who has just thanked you for doing something. EG *'Thank you for talking to us about your research.' – 'It's a pleasure.'*
CONVENTION

4 You can say **'With pleasure'** as a polite way of saying that you are very willing to do something. EG *'Could you help?' – 'With pleasure.'*
CONVENTION Formal

pleat /pliːt/, **pleats.** A **pleat** in a piece of clothing is a permanent fold that is made in the cloth.
N COUNT

pleated /pliːtɪd/. A **pleated** piece of clothing has pleats in it. EG *...a brown pleated skirt.*
ADJ CLASSIF

pledge /plɛdʒ/, **pledges, pledging, pledged.** 1 A **pledge** is a solemn promise to do something. EG *The Government should fulfil its 1979 Manifesto pledge... He gave a pledge to handle the affair in a friendly manner.*
N COUNT: OFT+REPORT

2 If you **pledge** something, you promise solemnly that you will do it or give it. EG *They will pledge $1 million to fund the project... The government pledged to reduce the level of imports... He has pledged that the ban will be lifted after two years.*
V+O, V+*to*-INF, OR V+REPORT: ONLY *that*

3 If you **pledge** yourself to something, you commit yourself to following a particular course of action or to supporting a particular person, group, or idea. EG *The new organization pledged itself to the revolutionary overthrow of the dictator.*
V-REFL+*to* OR *to*-INF

plentiful /plɛntɪful/. Something that is **plentiful** exists in large amounts or numbers. EG *Food became more plentiful each day.*
ADJ QUALIT

plenty /plɛnti^{1}/. If there is **plenty** of something, there is a large amount of it. If there are **plenty** of things, there is a large number of them. EG *We've got plenty of time... There are always plenty of jobs to be done... They would have plenty to eat.*
QUANTIF

pleurisy /plʊərɪ^{1}si^{1}/ is a serious illness in which a person's lungs are inflamed and breathing is difficult.
N UNCOUNT

pliable /plaɪəbə^{0}l/. 1 If something is **pliable**, you can bend it easily without breaking it. EG *...a soft and pliable material.*
ADJ QUALIT

2 Someone who is **pliable** can be easily influenced and controlled by other people. EG *I am too passive and pliable.*
ADJ QUALIT

pliant /plaɪənt/. 1 Someone who is **pliant** can be easily influenced and controlled by other people. EG *The Democrats may not be as pliant as they appear... She was pliant and docile.*
ADJ QUALIT

2 If something is **pliant**, you can bend it easily without breaking it.
ADJ QUALIT

pliers /plaɪəz/ are a tool used for holding or pulling out things such as nails, or for bending or cutting wire. See picture at TOOLS. EG *Use a pair of pliers.*
N PLURAL

If a lawyer pleads a case, is he pleading?

plight /plaɪt/. If you refer to someone's **plight**, you mean that they are in a difficult situation that is full of problems. EG *...the plight of the mentally handicapped... He had heard of my plight through an acquaintance.* N SING+POSS Formal

plimsoll /plɪmsəl/, **plimsolls.** **Plimsolls** are shoes made of canvas with flat rubber soles, which people wear for sports and leisure. N COUNT

plod /plɒd/, **plods, plodding, plodded.** **1** If someone **plods** along, they walk slowly and heavily. EG *He plodded along the road.* V: USU+A

2 If you say that someone **plods** on or **plods** along with a job, you mean that they work slowly and without enthusiasm. EG *He plodded on in the Board of Trade.* V+A

plonk /plɒŋk/, **plonks, plonking, plonked.** **1** If you **plonk** something somewhere, you put it or drop it there heavily and carelessly. EG *Bottles of beer were plonked on the wooden table... ...plonking himself down in the middle of the room.* V+O+A Informal

2 **Plonk** is cheap or poor quality wine. EG *Shall we get a bottle of plonk?* N UNCOUNT Informal

plop /plɒp/, **plops, plopping, plopped.** **1** A **plop** is a soft gentle sound, like the sound made by something light dropping into water. EG *My hat landed with a plop in the bucket.* N COUNT

2 If something **plops** into a liquid, it drops into it with a soft gentle sound. EG *Great big tears plopped into her soup.* V+A

plot /plɒt/, **plots, plotting, plotted.** **1** A **plot** is a secret plan by a group of people to do something that is illegal or wrong. EG *Another plot to assassinate the General was uncovered.* N COUNT

2 If people **plot** something or **plot** to do something, they plan secretly to do it. EG *They were accused of plotting to assassinate the President... Anyone convicted of plotting against the king will be executed.* V+O, V+to-INF, OR V+*against*

3 The **plot** of a film, novel, or play is the story and the way in which it develops. EG *They were having some difficulty in following the plot.* N COUNT

4 A **plot** of land is a small piece of land. EG *His land is split up into several widely scattered plots.* N COUNT

5 When someone **plots** the position or course of a plane or ship, they mark it on a map or chart in order to see what course or direction it is taking. EG *They plotted the new positions of each vessel.* V+O

6 When you are drawing a graph, you **plot** the points on it by marking them at the correct places to form the graph. EG *These figures can be plotted on a graph.* V+O

plough /plaʊ/, **ploughs, ploughing, ploughed;** also spelled **plow** in American English.

1 A **plough** is a large farming tool with sharp blades which is attached to a tractor or an animal such as a horse. A plough is pulled across the soil to turn it over, usually before seeds are planted. N COUNT

2 When someone **ploughs** an area of land, they turn over the soil using a plough. EG *A small tractor can plough an acre in six to nine hours.* V+O OR V

3 If you **plough** on, you continue moving or trying to complete something, although it needs a lot of effort. EG *The fighters ploughed on to their destination airfields... My mother ploughed her way through the list of recipes.* V+A

4 If one thing **ploughs** into another, it crashes into it. EG *The car wavered crazily before ploughing into the bank.* V+*into*

5 If someone **ploughs** money into a business or company, they invest large sums of money in it. EG *...the huge sums of money which were ploughed into computing.* V+O: USU+*into*

plough up. If an area of land **is ploughed up**, the soil is turned over using a plough. EG *Nearly half of his grassland was ploughed up to grow corn.* PHRASAL VB: V+ADV, USU PASS

ploughman's lunch /plaʊmənz lʌntʃ/, **ploughman's lunches.** A **ploughman's lunch** or a **ploughman's** is a snack consisting of bread, cheese and pickles. It is usually bought and eaten in a pub. N COUNT British

plow /plaʊ/. See **plough**.

ploy /plɔɪ/, **ploys.** A **ploy** is a way of behaving that you have planned carefully in order to get something you want. EG *This was a tactful ploy to get Thomas to mention his present salary... This headache was clearly a delaying ploy.* N COUNT

pluck /plʌk/, **plucks, plucking, plucked.** **1** If you **pluck** a fruit, flower, or leaf, you take it in your hand and pull it in order to remove it from its stalk where it is growing. EG *He plucked a tomato and offered it to Hilda.* V+O Literary

2 If you **pluck** something from somewhere, you take hold of it and pull it with a sharp movement. EG *He laughed and plucked the paper from my hand... Rough hands plucked at my jacket.* V+O OR V: USU+A Written

3 If you **pluck** a chicken or other dead bird, you pull its feathers out to prepare it for cooking. V+O

4 If someone **plucks** their eyebrows, they pull out some of the hairs using tweezers, in order to look more attractive. V+O

5 If you **pluck** a guitar or other stringed musical instrument, you use your fingers to pull the strings and let them go, so that they make a sound. V+O OR V+A

6 **Pluck** is courage. EG *Why don't you ask her? You've got no pluck.* N UNCOUNT

7 If you **pluck up the courage** to do something frightening, you make an effort to be brave enough to do it. EG *I eventually plucked up enough courage to go in.* PHRASE

plucky /plʌki[1]/. Someone who is **plucky** has courage. EG *This schoolgirl story featured a plucky heroine.* ADJ QUALIT Outdated

plug /plʌg/, **plugs, plugging, plugged.** **1** A **plug** is **1.1** a small plastic object with metal pieces which fit into the holes in a socket and connect the wire from a piece of electrical equipment to the electricity supply. EG *This lamp doesn't have a plug... Do you know how to change a plug?* **1.2** a socket that is a source of electricity, usually in the wall of a room. EG *...electricity from a plug in the garage.* N COUNT; Informal

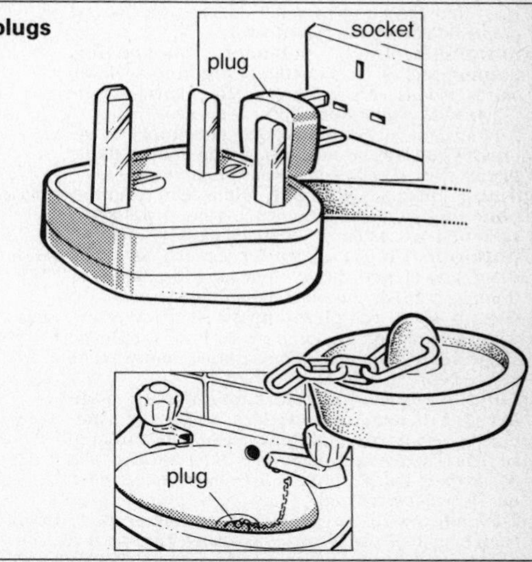

2 A **plug** is also a thick, circular piece of rubber or plastic that you use to block the hole in a bath or sink when it is filled with water. N COUNT

3 If you **plug** a hole, you block it with something. EG *He plugged the cracks with paper... Have you plugged all the leaks?* V+O

4 If someone **plugs** a book or film, they praise it in order to encourage people to buy it or see it. EG *The radio stations are plugging the record like mad.* V+O Informal

▸ used as a noun. EG *Can I quickly give our new show a plug?*

plug in. If you **plug in** a piece of electrical equipment, you push its plug into an electric socket so that it can work. EG *I plugged in the kettle... She plugged the lamp into a wall-socket.* PHRASAL VB: V+O+ADV OR V+O+PREP

plughole /plʌghəʊl/, **plugholes.** A **plughole** is a small hole in a bath or sink which allows the water to flow away. N COUNT

plum /plʌm/, **plums. 1** A **plum** is a small, sweet fruit with a smooth red or yellow skin and a stone in the middle. EG *...a basket of plums... ...plum jam.* N COUNT

2 A **plum** job is a very good job that a lot of people would like. EG *They held most of the plum jobs... She was given a plum part: the lead in a £3m film.* N MOD

plumage /plu:mɪdʒ/. A bird's **plumage** is all the feathers on its body. EG *...a bird of brilliant plumage... Its plumage had turned grey.* N UNCOUNT

plumb /plʌm/, **plumbs, plumbing, plumbed.** If someone **plumbs the depths** of an unpleasant emotion, they experience it to an extreme degree. EG *The story shows how she plumbs the depths of humiliation.* PHRASE

plumber /plʌmə/, **plumbers.** A **plumber** is a person whose job is to connect and repair things such as water and drainage pipes, baths, and toilets. EG *The plumbers came to mend the pipes.* N COUNT

plumbing /plʌmɪŋ/. **1** The **plumbing** in a building consists of the water and drainage pipes, baths, and toilets in the building. EG *Will it need new wiring and plumbing?* N UNCOUNT

2 Plumbing is the work of connecting and repairing things such as water and drainage pipes, baths, and toilets. EG *...minor plumbing repairs.* N UNCOUNT

plume /plu:m/, **plumes. 1** A **plume** is **1.1** a large, often brightly coloured bird's feather. EG *...an ostrich plume.* **1.2** a bunch of long, thin strands of material, tied at one end and flowing loosely at the other. Plumes are usually attached to soldiers' helmets and horses' heads as decoration. EG *...four horses with black plumes.* N COUNT Formal

2 A **plume** of smoke is a large quantity of it that rises into the air in a small column. EG *The last plume of blue smoke curled away.* N COUNT+*of*

plummet /plʌmɪt/, **plummets, plummeting, plummeted. 1** If something **plummets** downwards, it falls very quickly. EG *The explosion sent the aircraft plummeting towards the sea.* V+A

2 If an amount, rate, or price **plummets**, it decreases quickly and suddenly. EG *The price of paper plummeted... His popularity has plummeted.* V

plump /plʌmp/, **plumper, plumpest; plumps, plumping, plumped.** Someone who is **plump** is rather fat. EG *...a plump, red-faced man.* ADJ QUALIT

plump for. If you **plump for** someone or something, you choose them, often after hesitating or thinking carefully. EG *She plumped for the eclair.* PHRASAL VB: V+PREP

plump up. If you **plump up** a cushion or pillow, you squeeze and shake it back into a rounded shape. EG *He plumped up the cushions and switched on the lamp.* PHRASAL VB: V+O+ADV

plunder /plʌndə/, **plunders, plundering, plundered. 1** If someone **plunders** a place or **plunders** things from a place, they steal things from it. EG *The conquerors plundered their wealth and burnt their cities... Imperialist governments plunder the weaker nations.* V+O OR V Literary

2 Plunder is **2.1** the activity of stealing property from people or places. EG *...the savage burning and plunder of the commercial centre of town.* N UNCOUNT **2.2** the property that is stolen. EG *He escaped with his plunder.* N SING

plunge /plʌndʒ/, **plunges, plunging, plunged. 1** If something **plunges** in a particular direction, it falls in that direction. EG *They plunged into the pool together... The car plunged into the river.* V+A ▸ used as a noun. EG *They were relying on the plunge into icy waters to kill me.* ▸ N COUNT

2 If you **plunge** an object into something, you push it quickly or violently into it. EG *She plunged her hands into her coat pockets... He plunged the knife into her breast.* V+O+A ▸ N COUNT

3 To **plunge** someone or something into a state means to cause them suddenly to be in that state. EG *The hall was plunged into darkness... ...the danger of plunging society into chaos and anarchy.* V-ERG+A

4 If you **plunge** into an activity, you suddenly get very involved in it. EG *She plunged bravely into the debate.* V+*into*

5 If an amount or rate **plunges**, it decreases quickly and suddenly. EG *Sales have plunged by 24%.* V ▸ used as a noun. EG *Prices started a downward plunge.* ▸ N COUNT

6 If you **take the plunge**, you decide to do something that you consider difficult or risky. EG *Take the plunge and start your own firm... We took the plunge and got married.* PHRASE

plunger /plʌndʒə/, **plungers.** A **plunger** is a device for unblocking pipes and sinks. It consists of a rubber cup on the end of a stick. You press it up and down over the pipe or the hole in the sink, and the suction moves the blockage. EG *...a sink plunger.* N COUNT

pluperfect /plu:pɜ:fɪ²kt/ is the term used in grammar for the tense of a verb describing actions that were completed before another event in the past happened. The pluperfect in English is formed using 'had' followed by the past participle of the verb, as in the sentences 'I had gone by then' and 'She'd eaten them before I arrived'. N SING : *the*+N

plural /plʊərəl/, **plurals. 1** In grammar, **plural** is the term used for a noun, pronoun, determiner, adjective, or verb when it refers to two or more people, things, or groups. EG *Use the first person plural... The singular is 'louse' and the plural is 'lice'.* ADJ CLASSIF OR N COUNT

2 Plural also means **2.1** consisting of more than one person or thing. EG *The only plural occupancy of the throne was during the reign of William and Mary.* ADJ CLASSIF: ATTRIB Formal **2.2** consisting of different kinds of people or things. EG *A democratic society is a plural society... We need a plural system of education, with different kinds of institutions.* Formal

plus /plʌs/. **1** You say **plus** or write a **plus** sign (+) to show that one number or quantity is being added to another. EG *That's seventy-two plus ninety-six... ...5 + 3.*

2 You use **plus** after a number to show that the actual number or quantity is greater than the one mentioned. EG *...my 25 years plus as a police officer... They take the exams at 13 plus.* ADJ AFTER N

3 Teachers use **plus** in grading work in schools and colleges. 'B plus' is a better grade than 'B', but it is not as good as 'A'.

4 You can also use **plus** to add an item to one or more that you have already mentioned. EG *Now five people, plus Val, are missing... He wore strange scarves and beads, plus he was English.* PREP OR CONJ

plush /plʌʃ/. Something that is **plush** is very smart, comfortable, and expensive. EG *...his plush car with reclining seats.* ADJ QUALIT

plus sign, plus signs. A **plus sign** is the sign (+) which is put between two numbers in order to show that the second number is being added to the first one. N COUNT

plutonium /plu:təʊnɪəm/ is a radioactive element used especially as a fuel in nuclear power stations. N UNCOUNT

ply /plaɪ/, **plies, plying, plied. 1** If you **ply** someone with food or drink, you keep giving them more of it. EG *Dolly plied me with sweets.* V+O+*with*

2 If you **ply** someone with questions, you keep asking them questions. EG *I plied him with questions about his novel.* V+O+*with*

3 If a ship or boat **plies** somewhere, it makes regular journeys there. EG *...a new passenger liner* V+O OR V+A

If you take the plunge, do you fall?

to ply the North Atlantic route... ...the ferry that plies between Dover and Boulogne.
4 If you **ply** a trade, you do a particular kind of work regularly as your job. EG *They received a warning not to ply their trade in the town.* V+O
5 Ply is the thickness of wool, thread, or rope, which is measured by the number of strands it is made from. EG *...four-ply wool.*

plywood /plaɪwʊd/ is wood that consists of thin layers of wood stuck together. EG *...the flimsy plywood door.* N UNCOUNT

p.m. /piː ɛm/ after a number refers to a particular time between noon and midnight. EG *Some of the shops stay open until 7 p.m.* ADV

pneumatic /njuːmætɪk/. **1** A **pneumatic** drill is operated by compressed air and is very powerful. ADJ CLASSIF : ATTRIB
2 Pneumatic means filled with air. EG *...a pneumatic chair.* ADJ CLASSIF : ATTRIB

pneumonia /njuːməʊnɪə/ is a serious disease which affects your lungs and makes it difficult for you to breathe. EG *She nearly died of pneumonia.* N UNCOUNT

PO /piː əʊ/is an abbreviation for 'Post Office'.

poach /pəʊtʃ/, **poaches, poaching, poached. 1** If someone **poaches** fish, animals, or birds, they illegally catch them on someone else's property. EG *He had been poaching deer.* V+O OR V
2 If someone **poaches** an idea or a book, they dishonestly or illegally use the idea or publish the book. EG *Meanwhile, their company implacably poach the masterpieces.* V+O
3 When you **poach** an egg, you remove its shell and cook the egg gently in boiling water. EG *...poached eggs and beans.* V+O
4 If you **poach** food such as fish, you cook it gently in boiling water or milk. EG *...poached salmon.* V+O

poacher /pəʊtʃə/, **poachers.** A **poacher** is someone who illegally catches fish, birds, or animals on someone else's property. N COUNT

PO Box is used before a number to refer to an address to which you can send letters or money, which the Post Office keeps until they are collected by the person who has paid for the service. EG *...PO Box 48.*

pocket /pɒkɪt/, **pockets, pocketing, pocketed. 1** A **pocket** is **1.1** a small bag that is sewn into a piece of clothing, and that is used for carrying small things such as money or a handkerchief. EG *She put her hand in her coat pocket.* **1.2** a pouch or bag which is attached to a suitcase or car door, for example, and which is used for putting things in. N COUNT
2 If someone **pockets** something, they put it in their pocket. EG *I locked the door and pocketed the key.* V+O
3 You can say that someone who steals something **pockets** it. EG *...servants who pocketed household funds for their own use.* V+O
4 You use **pocket** to describe something that is small enough to fit into a pocket. EG *...a pocket calculator... ...a pocket torch.* N MOD
5 A **pocket** of something is a small area of it. EG *We sat in the pocket of warmth by the fire.* N PART
6 Pocket is also used in these phrases. **6.1** If you say that people **live in each other's pockets**, you mean that they are always together and depend on each other too much. **6.2** If someone **picks** your **pocket**, they steal something from your pocket. **6.3** If you are **out of pocket**, you have less money than you should have, usually because you have paid for something for someone else. EG *I don't want you to end up out of pocket.* PHRASES Informal

pocketbook /pɒkɪtbʊk/, **pocketbooks.** A **pocketbook** is **1** a small book or notebook. **2** a wallet or small case which is used for carrying money and papers. N COUNT American

pocket knife, pocket knives. A **pocket knife** is the same as a penknife. N COUNT

pocket money is money which a child is given by his or her parents every week. EG *When he was ten, his pocket money was 50p a week.* N UNCOUNT

pod /pɒd/, **pods.** A **pod** is a seed container that grows on some plants such as peas or beans. N COUNT

podgy /pɒdʒi¹/. Someone who is **podgy** is fairly fat. EG *...a small, podgy girl.* ADJ QUALIT Informal

poem /pəʊɪm/, **poems.** A **poem** is a piece of writing in which the words are arranged in short lines which often rhyme. EG *...a selection of Robert Browning's poems.* N COUNT

poet /pəʊɪt/, **poets.** A **poet** is a person who writes poems. EG *...the Soviet poet, Yevtushenko.* N COUNT

poetic /pəʊɛtɪk/. **1** Something that is **poetic** is very beautiful, expressive, and sensitive. EG *...a poetic and beautiful picture of the landscape... ...great poetic speeches.* ◊ **poetically.** EG *...a poetically true vision of Australia.* ADJ QUALIT ◊ ADV
2 Poetic also means relating to poetry. EG *...a poetic tradition older than writing.* ADJ CLASSIF : ATTRIB

poetical /pəʊɛtɪkəl/ means the same as poetic. ADJ

poetry /pəʊɪtri¹/. **1 Poetry** is poems, considered as a form of literature. EG *...a book of poetry... ...poetry recitals.* N UNCOUNT
2 You can also refer to a quality of beauty or greatness that people see or experience in something as **poetry**. EG *...the poetry of human existence.* N UNCOUNT +SUPP

poignant /pɔɪnjənt/. Something that is **poignant** makes you feel very sad. EG *His cry of protest is still poignant today.* ◊ **poignantly.** EG *He poignantly describes poverty as it existed in his own childhood.* ◊ **poignancy** /pɔɪnjənsi¹/. EG *It was a moment of extraordinary poignancy.* ADJ QUALIT ◊ ADV ◊ N UNCOUNT Formal

point /pɔɪnt/, **points, pointing, pointed. 1** A **point** is something that you say which expresses a particular fact, idea, or opinion. EG *That's a very good point... We had a long argument on this point... I want to make several quick points... Let me tell you a little story to illustrate my point... I see your point... I take your point about needing new recordings... To prove his point, Mr Higgerson gave me the letter.* N COUNT : USU+SUPP
2 If you say that someone has a **point**, you mean that you accept that what they have said is important or should be considered. EG *You've got a point there.* N COUNT : USU a+N
3 The **point** is the most important part of what you are saying or discussing. EG *The point was that Dick could not walk... You've all missed the point... Philip, I may as well come straight to the point. I'm pregnant.* N SING : the+N
4 If you say that something is **beside the point**, you mean that it is not relevant to the subject that you are discussing. If it is **to the point**, it is relevant. EG *In art as a whole the notion of taste is beside the point... His letters are intelligible and to the point.* PHRASE
5 A **point** is also a detail, aspect, or quality of something or someone. EG *The two books have some interesting points in common... This is just a minor point of criticism... The court dismissed the charges on a technical point... That's his best point, I think... Your strong points are your speed and accuracy... The main point on the agenda was left till the end of the meeting... Experts are still arguing over the finer points of how it operates.* N COUNT+SUPP
6 If you **make a point of** doing something, you do it in a very deliberate or obvious way. EG *You make a point of forgetting everything I have said... I made a special point of being sociable.* PHRASE
7 If you ask what the **point** of something is, or say that there is no **point** in it, you are talking about what its purpose is or how useful it is. EG *I didn't see the point of boring you with all this... There was not much point in thinking about it.* N SING : USU+SUPP
8 A **point** is also a particular place or position where something happens, often marked on a drawing or map by a dot or other symbol. EG *We were nearing the point where the lane curved round to the right... Her gaze shifted to a point over my left shoulder... The missile can strike at almost* N COUNT+SUPP

any point on the globe... The circle passes through those two points.

9 The **points** of a compass are the 32 marks on it that show the directions, especially North, South, East, and West. N COUNT+SUPP

10 The **point** of something such as a pin, needle, or knife is the thin, sharp end of it. EG *His moustache had been rolled into two tight points... It just has a short point.* N COUNT

11 On a railway track, the **points** are the levers and rails at a place where two tracks join or separate. N COUNT: USU PLURAL

12 The decimal **point** in a number is the dot that separates the whole numbers from the fractions. EG *...four point eight.*

13 You also use **point** to refer to a particular time or moment, or a particular stage in the development of something. EG *At one point, I was dreadfully rude... At the point of death, the woman suddenly clutched his hand... Do you ever reach a point where you just can't agree with her?... The strikers brought the economy to crisis point... His dinner had been the high point of his evening... I could not fall asleep unless I exercised to the point of exhaustion.* N SING+SUPP

14 If you are **on the point of** doing something, you are just going to do it. EG *As they were on the point of setting out, a light rain began to fall... Capitalism was on the point of collapse.* PHRASE

15 If you say that something is true **up to a point**, you mean that it is true to a certain extent but not completely. EG *He is right, but only up to a point.* PHRASE

16 In some sports, competitions, and games, a **point** is one of the single marks that are added together to give the total score. EG *The panel of judges gave him the highest points.* N COUNT

17 A **point** is also an electric socket. EG *The room has a wash-basin and an electric-shaver point.* N COUNT

18 If you **point** at something, you hold out your finger or an object such as a stick towards the thing, in order to show someone where it is or to make them notice it. EG *'Over there,' she said and pointed to the door... He pointed a finger at my friend and hissed with rage.* • to **point the finger at** someone: see **finger**. V: USU+*at/to*; ALSO V+O: USU+*at*

19 If you **point** something at someone, you aim the tip or end of it towards them. EG *They were horrified when I told them I had actually pointed a gun at someone.* V+O+A

20 If something **points** to a place or **points** in a particular direction, it shows where that place is or faces in that direction. EG *There was a street sign that pointed down towards the cemetery... One of its toes pointed backwards.* V+A

21 If something **points** to a particular situation, it suggests that the situation exists or is likely to occur. EG *Her questions point to a desire to know some vital truth... This activity points to the likelihood that an armed revolution is imminent.* V+*to*

22 to **be a case in point**: see **case**. • **in point of fact**: see **fact**. • **a sore point**: see **sore**. • See also **focal point**, **pointed**, **vantage point**.

point out. 1 If you **point out** an object or place, you make people look at it or show them where it is. EG *On car journeys we all used to shout and point out lovely places along the way... I can always recognize plants after they have been pointed out to me.* PHRASAL VB: V+O+ADV **2** If you **point out** a fact or mistake, you inform someone about it or draw their attention to it. EG *Mr Merritt pointed this problem out to you the other day... She pointed out that he was wrong.* V+O+ADV OR V+ADV

point-blank. 1 If you say something **point-blank**, you say it very directly or rudely, without explaining or apologizing. EG *She asked him point-blank if I was with him on Saturday... ...a point-blank refusal to discuss the matter.* ADV OR ADJ CLASSIF: ATTRIB

2 If you shoot someone or something **point-blank**, you shoot them when the gun is touching them or extremely close to them. EG *He shot him in the brain, point-blank... ...shooting at point-blank range.* ADV OR ADJ CLASSIF: ATTRIB

pointed /pɔɪntɪ^{2}d/. **1** Something that is **pointed** has a point at one end. EG *His daughter has a pointed nose... ...pointed trees.* ADJ CLASSIF

2 Pointed comments or behaviour express criticism, warning, or unpleasantness in a very obvious way. EG *Etta gave a pointed look in their direction... She made two pointed comments.* ◇ **pointedly.** EG *'How old is he?' Freya asked pointedly.* ADJ QUALIT ◇ ADV

pointer /pɔɪntə/, **pointers. 1** A **pointer** is a piece of advice or information which helps you to understand a situation or to find a way of making progress. EG *She gave him a few more pointers... ...a list of things that seemed to be pointers to the truth of what happened.* N COUNT

2 A **pointer** is also a long, thin piece of wood or metal that is used to point at something such as a chart on a wall or a dial on a machine. EG *The pointer on the weighing machine is not accurate.* N COUNT

pointless /pɔɪntlɪ^{2}s/. Something that is **pointless** has no use, sense, or purpose. EG *...pointless violence... It was pointless to protest.* ◇ **pointlessly.** EG *He had pointlessly hurt her.* ADJ QUALIT ◇ ADV

point of view, points of view. 1 You can refer to the opinions or attitudes that someone has about something as their **point of view**. EG *We understand your point of view... An outsider who can offer a fresh point of view may stimulate new ideas.* N COUNT

2 If you consider something **from a** particular **point of view**, you are using one aspect of a situation in order to judge the situation. EG *From the commercial point of view, they have little to lose... We'll consider the problem from the point of view of the way it was handled.* PHRASE

poise /pɔɪz/ is a calm, dignified, self-controlled manner. EG *She received me with incredible poise for one so young.* N UNCOUNT

poised /pɔɪzd/. **1** If a part of your body is **poised**, it is completely still but ready to move at any moment. EG *He waited with fingers poised over the keys... I saw her hand poised to strike.* ADJ PRED

2 If you are **poised** to do something, you are ready to take action at any moment. EG *...powerful military forces, poised for invasion... His party seems poised to return to power.* ADJ PRED: USU+*to*-INF OR *for*

3 If you are **poised**, you are calm, dignified, and self-controlled. EG *She was poised and diplomatic on the telephone.* ADJ PRED

poison /pɔɪzə^{0}n/, **poisons, poisoning, poisoned.**
1 Poison is a substance that harms or kills people or animals if they swallow it or absorb it. EG *It was deadly poison and if he drank it he'd die.* N MASS

2 If someone **poisons** another person, they kill the person or make them ill by means of poison. EG *He had been poisoned with strychnine.* ◇ **poisoning.** EG *The poisoning had not been accidental.* V+O ◇ N UNCOUNT

3 If you **are poisoned** by a substance, it makes you very ill. EG *You can be poisoned by agricultural and industrial wastes.* ◇ **poisoning.** EG *These swans died of lead poisoning... ...food poisoning.* V+O: USU PASS ◇ N UNCOUNT

4 If food, drink, or a weapon **is poisoned**, it has poison added to it. EG *...a poisoned whisky bottle.* V+O: USU PASS

5 If water, air, or land **is poisoned**, it is damaged by harmful substances such as chemicals. EG *...our poisoned air and polluted streams and lakes.* V+O: USU PASS

6 Something that **poisons** a good situation or relationship spoils it or destroys it. EG *...the despair that poisoned the Romantic movement.* V+O Literary

poisonous /pɔɪzə^{0}nəs/. **1** Something that is **poisonous** will kill you or make you ill if you swallow or absorb it. EG *...a poisonous plant.* ADJ QUALIT

2 An animal that is **poisonous** produces a poison that will kill you or make you ill if you are bitten by ADJ QUALIT

If people are poles apart, are they a long way from each other?

the animal. EG *...one of the most poisonous snakes in the world... ...poisonous spiders.*

3 If you describe something as **poisonous**, you mean that it is extremely unpleasant and likely to spoil or destroy a good relationship or situation. EG *The article contained some poisonous allegations about his social behaviour.* ADJ QUALIT Formal

poke /pəʊk/, **pokes, poking, poked. 1** If you **poke** someone or something, you quickly push them with your finger or with a sharp object. EG *People poked the students with their umbrellas... You almost poked my eye out... Ralph began to poke little holes in the sand.* ▸ used as a noun. EG *Len gave him an affectionate poke.* V+O : USU+A ▸ N COUNT

2 If you **poke** one thing into another, you push the first thing into the second thing. EG *Never poke scissors into an electric socket.* V+O+A

3 If something **pokes** out of or through another thing, you can see part of it appearing from behind or underneath the other thing. EG *...cotton wool poking out of his ear... ...a shoot poking through the earth... Blades of grass poked up between the paving stones.* V+A

4 If you **poke** your head through an opening or if it **pokes** through an opening, you push it through, often so that you can see something more easily. EG *The driver slowed down and poked his head out of the window... His secretary poked her head through the door.* V-ERG+A

5 to **poke fun at** someone: see **fun**.

poke about or **poke around.** If you **poke about** or **poke around** for something, you search for it, usually by moving lots of objects around. EG *He was lying flat on his stomach, poking around under the bed with his arm.* PHRASAL VB : V+ADV, USU+A Informal

poke at. If you **poke at** something, you make lots of little pushing movements at it with a sharp object. EG *The chef poked at his little pile of ashes.* PHRASAL VB : V+PREP

poker /pəʊkə/, **pokers. 1 Poker** is a card game that people usually play in order to win money. N UNCOUNT

2 A **poker** is a metal bar which you use to move coal or wood in a fire. EG *She prodded the fire gently with the poker.* N COUNT

poky /pəʊki^1/, **pokier, pokiest.** A room or house that is **poky** is uncomfortably small. EG *Her flat has three poky little rooms.* ADJ QUALIT Informal

polar /pəʊlə/. **1 Polar** describes the area around the North and South Poles. EG *...the melting of the polar ice caps.* ADJ CLASSIF : ATTRIB

2 Polar is also used to describe things which are completely opposite in character, quality, or type. EG *...the polar extremes of 'totalitarianism' and 'democracy.'* ADJ CLASSIF : ATTRIB Formal

polar bear, polar bears. A **polar bear** is a large white bear which lives near the North Pole. N COUNT

polarize /pəʊləraɪz/, **polarizes, polarizing, polarized;** also spelled **polarise.** If people **polarize** or if something **polarizes** them, they form into two separate groups with opposite opinions or positions. EG *In Britain the political debate is polarized between two major parties... Media coverage helps to polarize the public's views on the subject.* V-ERG

◇ **polarization** /pəʊləraɪzeɪʃə^{0}n/. EG *...a growing polarisation between rich and poor countries.* ◇ N UNCOUNT

pole /pəʊl/, **poles. 1** A **pole** is a long, thin piece of wood or metal, used especially for supporting things. EG *...tent poles... ...telegraph poles.* N COUNT

2 The earth's **poles** are the two opposite ends of its axis. N COUNT+SUPP

3 If you say that two people are **poles apart**, you mean that they have completely different beliefs and opinions. EG *Politically they were poles apart.* PHRASE

police /pə^{0}liːs/, **polices, policing, policed. 1** The **police** are **1.1** the official organization that is responsible for making sure that people obey the law. EG *The police were called... Three police cars arrived.* **1.2** the men and women who are members of this organization. EG *280 people were arrested and 117 police injured.* N PLURAL : the+N; N PLURAL

2 To **police** a place means to preserve law and order in it by means of the police or the army. EG *It is impossible to police such a vast area.* V+O

police force, police forces. A **police force** is the police organization in a particular country or area. EG *We have the finest police force in the world.* N COUNT

policeman /pə^{0}liːsmə^{3}n/, **policemen** /pə^{0}liːsmə^{2}n/. A **policeman** is a man who is a member of the police force. EG *He had been a policeman for six years.* N COUNT

police officer, police officers. A **police officer** is a policeman or policewoman. N COUNT

police station, police stations. A **police station** is the local office of a police force in a particular area. EG *A youth was being questioned at Cannon Row police station.* N COUNT

policewoman /pə^{0}liːswʊmən/, **policewomen** /pə^{0}liːswɪmɪn/. A **policewoman** is a woman who is a member of the police force. N COUNT

policy /pɒlɪsi^1/, **policies. 1** A **policy** is a set of ideas or plans that is used as a basis for making decisions, especially in politics, economics, or business. EG *There is no change in our policy... ...a policy of reconciliation... ...economic and foreign policy... They oppose Conservative policies.* N COUNT OR N UNCOUNT

2 An insurance **policy** is a document which shows the agreement that you have made with an insurance company. EG *...a life assurance policy... This service is free to policy holders.* N COUNT Technical

polio /pəʊlɪəʊ/ is a serious infectious disease caused by a virus. It often causes paralysis. EG *She had been crippled by polio.* N UNCOUNT

polish /pɒlɪʃ/, **polishes, polishing, polished. 1 Polish** is a substance that you put on the surface of an object in order to clean it, protect it, and make it shine. EG *Use wax polish on wooden furniture... ...shoe polish.* N UNCOUNT

2 If you **polish** something, **2.1** you put polish on it. EG *Leather needs polishing with good quality cream.* ◇ **polished.** EG *She slipped on the polished wooden floor.* **2.2** you rub it with a cloth to make it shine. EG *I polished my glasses with a handkerchief.* V+O ◇ ADJ QUALIT V+O

3 If you say that something has **polish**, you mean that it is elegant and of good quality. EG *It's an honest book but it hasn't got polish.* N UNCOUNT

polish off. If you **polish** something **off**, you finish it completely and quickly. EG *Last year's papers were polished off in half an hour... I had no trouble polishing off the pudding.* PHRASAL VB : V+O+ADV Informal

polished /pɒlɪʃt/. **1** Someone who is **polished** shows confidence and sophistication. EG *He had the most polished, sophisticated manner.* ADJ QUALIT

2 If you describe an ability or skill as **polished**, you mean that it is of a very high standard. EG *My German was not very polished... ...polished actors.* ADJ QUALIT

polite /pəlaɪt/, **politer, politest. 1** Someone who is **polite** has good manners and is not rude to other people. EG *He was very polite to his superiors... It's polite to ask before you help yourself... ...a polite refusal.* ◇ **politely.** EG *He thanked me politely.* ◇ **politeness.** EG *I do expect reasonable politeness and consideration.* ADJ QUALIT ◇ ADV ◇ N UNCOUNT

2 You refer to people who consider themselves to be socially superior as **polite** society and **polite** company. EG *...the conventional norms of polite European society.* ADJ CLASSIF : ATTRIB

politic /pɒlɪtɪk/, **politics. Politic** is an adjective and **politics** is a plural noun or an uncount noun.

1 Politics are the actions or activities which people use to achieve power in a country, society, or organization. EG *Emily has never had the slightest interest in politics... He was active in Liberal politics... ...local politics... ...office politics.* N PLURAL OR N UNCOUNT

2 Your **politics** are your beliefs about how a country ought to be governed. EG *I have no politics... Her politics could be described as radical.* N PLURAL

3 Politics is the study of the ways in which a country is governed. EG *...a lecturer in politics.* N UNCOUNT

4 If you say that something is **politic**, you mean that it seems to be the most sensible thing to do in the circumstances. EG *It might be more politic to tell him yourself than let him find out from someone else.* ADJ QUALIT Formal

political /pəlɪtɪkə^{0}l/. **1 Political** means relating to politics. EG *...the major political parties... ...political developments... He was sent to jail for his political views... ...demands for political and religious freedom.* ◇ **politically.** EG *...a country which is politically stable and prosperous.* ADJ CLASSIF : USU ATTRIB; ◇ ADV

2 Someone who is **political** is interested in politics and holds strong beliefs about it. EG *He was always very political.* ADJ QUALIT

political prisoner, political prisoners. A **political prisoner** is someone who has been imprisoned because they have expressed views that criticize or disagree with their own government. N COUNT

politician /pɒlɪtɪʃə^{0}n/, **politicians.** A **politician** is a person whose job is in politics, especially a member of parliament. EG *...Labour and Tory politicians.* N COUNT

politicize /pəlɪtɪsaɪz/, **politicizes, politicizing, politicized;** also spelled **politicise.** If you **politicize** someone or something, you make them more political. EG *The British people were politicized by their wartime experiences.* ◇ **politicization** /pəlɪtɪsaɪzeɪʃə^{0}n/. EG *...the increasing politicization of the country.* V+O; ◇ N UNCOUNT Formal

poll /pəʊl/, **polls, polling, polled. 1** A **poll** is a survey in which people are asked their opinions about something, usually in order to find out how popular something is or to predict what will happen in the future. EG *Last year the polls gave the President a 10 to 15 point lead.* ● See also **opinion poll**. N COUNT

2 If you **are polled** on something, you are asked what you think about it as part of a survey. EG *A majority of those polled wanted 'stricter law enforcement'.* V+O : USU PASS

3 The **polls** means a political election. EG *The party won a convincing victory at the polls with an overall majority of ninety-seven seats.* N PLURAL : the+N

4 If a political party or a candidate **polls** a particular number of votes, they get that number of votes in an election. EG *In 1959 they only polled 43.7% of the votes.* V+O

pollen /pɒlən/ is a fine powder produced by flowers. It fertilizes other flowers of the same species so that they produce seeds. N UNCOUNT

pollinate /pɒlɪneɪt/, **pollinates, pollinating, pollinated.** To **pollinate** a plant or tree means to fertilize it with pollen. EG *The plant may pollinate itself.* ◇ **pollination** /pɒlɪneɪʃə^{0}n/. EG *Planting trees in groups helps pollination.* V+O; ◇ N UNCOUNT

polling day is the day on which people vote in an election. N UNCOUNT

pollutant /pəluːtənt/, **pollutants.** A **pollutant** is a substance that pollutes the environment, especially a poisonous chemical. EG *The main pollutants in this country are sulphur dioxide and smoke.* N COUNT

pollute /pəluːt/, **pollutes, polluting, polluted.** To **pollute** the water, air, or atmosphere means to make it dirty and dangerous to live in or to use. EG *Our water supply is becoming polluted with nitrates.* V+O

pollution /pəluːʃə^{0}n/ is **1** the process of polluting the water, air, or atmosphere. EG *...changes in the climate due to pollution of the atmosphere by industrial waste.* **2** the unpleasant substances that pollute the water, air, or atmosphere. EG *They didn't seem to notice the pollution and the noise.* N UNCOUNT

polo /pəʊləʊ/ is a game played between two teams of players. The players ride horses and use wooden hammers with long handles to hit a ball. N UNCOUNT

polo-necked /pəʊləʊ nɛkt/. A **polo-necked** sweater has a thick fold of material at the top which covers most of a person's neck. ADJ CLASSIF : ATTRIB

poltergeist /pɒltəgaɪst/, **poltergeists.** A **poltergeist** is an invisible force which is believed to move furniture or throw objects around, and which is often thought of as a type of ghost. N COUNT

poly /pɒli^{1}/, **polys.** A **poly** is the same as a polytechnic. EG *...a poly student.* N COUNT Informal

polyester /pɒli^{1}ɛstə/ is a type of cloth used especially to make clothes. EG *...polyester skirts.* N UNCOUNT

polystyrene /pɒli^{1}staɪriːn/ is a very light, plastic substance used especially to make containers or as an insulating material. EG *...white polystyrene ceiling tiles... ...foam polystyrene.* N UNCOUNT

polytechnic /pɒli^{1}tɛknɪk/, **polytechnics.** A **polytechnic** is a college in Britain where you can go to study after leaving school. EG *...a course in drama at Manchester Polytechnic.* N COUNT

polythene /pɒli^{1}θiːn/ is a type of plastic made into thin sheets or bags and used especially to keep food fresh. EG *...a polythene bag.* N UNCOUNT

polyunsaturated /pɒli^{1}ʌnsætjə^{4}reɪtɪ^{2}d/. **Polyunsaturated** oils and margarines are made mainly from vegetable fats and are considered healthier than those made from animal fats. ADJ CLASSIF

pomegranate /pɒmi^{1}grænɪt/, **pomegranates.** A **pomegranate** is a round fruit with a thick, reddish skin. It contains lots of small seeds with juicy flesh around them. N COUNT

pomp /pɒmp/ is the use of a lot of ceremony, fine clothes, and decorations, especially on a special occasion. EG *...coming ashore with pomp and ceremony... ...the pomp of Queen Elizabeth's court.* N UNCOUNT

pompous /pɒmpəs/. **1** Someone who is **pompous** behaves in a very serious way because they think they are more important than they really are; used showing disapproval. EG *Anything I say about it is bound to sound pompous... ...a pompous document of over 500 pages.* ◇ **pompously.** EG *They puffed pompously at fat German cigars.* ◇ **pomposity** /pɒmpɒsɪ^{1}ti^{1}/. EG *They were annoyed by my pomposity, my insistence on taking the blame for the whole affair.* ADJ QUALIT; ◇ ADV; ◇ N UNCOUNT Formal

2 A **pompous** building or ceremony is very grand and elaborate. EG *...the pompous splendour of Hyde Park Hotel... ...a pompous celebration.* ADJ QUALIT

pond /pɒnd/, **ponds.** A **pond** is a small area of water that is smaller than a lake. EG *...an ornamental pond in the garden.* N COUNT

ponder /pɒndə/, **ponders, pondering, pondered.** If you **ponder**, you think about something carefully. EG *Hooper seemed to ponder for a moment, then he nodded... Mary pondered upon the meaning of life... I pondered the ethics of the situation.* V : USU+A; ALSO V+O Literary

ponderous /pɒndə^{0}rəs/. **1** Speech or writing that is **ponderous** is very dull and serious. EG *He spoke in a slow, ponderous way.* ◇ **ponderously.** EG *She nodded ponderously.* ADJ QUALIT Literary; ◇ ADV

2 An object that is **ponderous** is large and heavy. EG *...ponderous royal tombs.* ADJ QUALIT Literary

3 A **ponderous** action is very slow or clumsy. EG *...taking a ponderous swing at the ball.* ◇ **ponderously.** EG *Slowly, ponderously, the vehicle shifted a few inches.* ADJ QUALIT Literary; ◇ ADV

pong /pɒŋ/, **pongs, ponging, ponged. 1** A **pong** is an unpleasant smell. EG *There was a pong in the room.* N COUNT British Informal

2 If you say that something **pongs**, you mean that it has an unpleasant smell. EG *Take that thing away! It pongs!* V British Informal

pontoon /pɒntuːn/, **pontoons.** A **pontoon** is a floating platform, often one used to support a bridge. EG *...pontoon bridges.* N COUNT

pony /pəʊni^{1}/, **ponies.** A **pony** is a type of small horse. EG *Two girls rode up on small ponies.* N COUNT

ponytail /pəʊni^{1}teɪl/, **ponytails.** A **ponytail** is a hairstyle in which someone's hair is tied up at the N COUNT

What is an informal word for a polytechnic?

back of the head and hangs down like a tail. EG *She had her hair tied back in a ponytail.*

poodle /pu:dəl/, **poodles.** A **poodle** is a type of dog with thick curly hair. N COUNT

pooh /pu:/. You say **'Pooh'** to express your disgust at an unpleasant smell. EG *Pooh! It really stinks in here!* EXCLAM Informal

pool /pu:l/, **pools, pooling, pooled. 1** A **pool** is **1.1** a small area of still or slow-moving water. EG *...long stretches of sand with rocks and pools.* **1.2** a swimming pool. EG *She went swimming in the hotel pool.* N COUNT

2 A **pool** of liquid or light is a small area of it. EG *He was lying dead in a pool of blood... A spotlight threw a pool of violet light onto the stage.* N COUNT+*of*

3 A **pool** of people, money, or things is a number of them that are collected together to be used or shared by several people or organizations. EG *...car pools... ...a pool of agricultural workers.* N COUNT+SUPP

4 If people **pool** their money, knowledge, or equipment, they allow it to be collected and used or shared by all of them. EG *We pooled our money, bought a van, and travelled... Families pooled their food resources in a common kitchen.* V+O

5 Pool is a game. Players use long, thin sticks to hit coloured balls with numbers on them into six holes around the edges of a table. EG *...a pool table.* N UNCOUNT

6 If you do the **pools**, you take part in a gambling competition in which people try to win money by guessing correctly the results of football matches. EG *...pools coupons... They won £300,000 on the Pools.* N PLURAL: *the*+N British

poor /pʊə, pɔ:/, **poorer, poorest. 1** Someone who is **poor** has very little money and few possessions. EG *I was a student then, and very poor... ...a poor family... He was now one thousand pounds poorer.* ADJ QUALIT

2 The **poor** are people who are poor. EG *The children of the poor are more likely to get diseases.* N PLURAL: *the*+N

3 A **poor** country or place is inhabited by people with very little money and few possessions. EG *...a shop in a poor part of Stratford... ...aid to the poorer countries.* ADJ QUALIT

4 You can use **poor** to describe someone who you are expressing sympathy for. EG *Poor old Dennis, he can't do a thing right.* ADJ CLASSIF: ATTRIB

5 If you describe something as **poor**, you mean that it is of a low quality or standard or that it is in bad condition. EG *...books in a very poor condition... In spite of poor health, I was able to continue working... The pay was poor... ...poor weather conditions.* ◇ **poorly.** EG *...poorly designed equipment.* ADJ QUALIT ◇ ADV

6 You also use **poor** to describe someone who is not very skilful in a particular activity. For example, a **poor** cook cooks badly. EG *She was a very poor swimmer... I am a poor businessman.* ◇ **poorly.** EG *I spoke Spanish so poorly.* ADJ QUALIT: ATTRIB ◇ ADV

7 If something is **poor** in a particular quality or substance, it contains very little of the quality or substance. EG *The water was poor in oxygen... Their food was poor in nutritive value.* ADJ PRED+*in*

poorly /pʊəli^1, pɔ:-/. If someone is **poorly**, they are ill. EG *Your brother's had an operation and he's quite poorly.* ADJ PRED Informal British

pop /pɒp/, **pops, popping, popped. 1 Pop** is modern music that usually has a strong rhythm and uses electronic equipment. EG *...pop music... ...pop concerts... ...a pop group.* N UNCOUNT

2 You can refer to fizzy drinks such as lemonade as **pop**. EG *...soda pop.* N MASS Informal

3 Some people call their father **Pop**. EG *Pop and I went for walks.* N PROPER OR VOCATIVE

4 Pop is used to represent a short sharp sound, for example the sound made by bursting a balloon or by pulling a cork out of a bottle. EG *The cork came out with a loud pop.* ▸ used as a verb. EG *The engine began coughing and popping... The cork popped and flew out of the bottle.* ▸ V

5 If your eyes **pop**, you look very surprised or excited. EG *His mouth hung open and his eyes popped.* V Informal

6 If you **pop** something somewhere, you put it there quickly. EG *He popped a piece of gum into his mouth... I popped a note through her letter box.* V+O+A Informal

7 If you **pop** into or out of a place, you quickly go in or out. EG *Suddenly she popped out from behind a bush... Why don't you pop in for a coffee... I'm just popping out for a haircut.* V+A

pop up. If someone or something **pops up**, they appear in a place or situation unexpectedly. EG *He's one of those rare types who pops up every so often.* PHRASAL VB: V+ADV

popcorn /pɒpkɔ:n/ is a snack which consists of grains of maize that are heated until they burst and become large and light. EG *...a bag of popcorn.* N UNCOUNT

Pope /pəʊp/, **Popes.** The **Pope** is the head of the Roman Catholic Church. EG *...Pope John Paul II.* N COUNT OR N PROPER

poplar /pɒplə/, **poplars.** A **poplar** is a type of tall, thin tree. N COUNT

popper

popper /pɒpə/, **poppers.** A **popper** is a device for fastening clothes. It consists of two pieces of plastic or metal, one with a small lump on it and the other with a small hole in it. You press the two bits together in order to fasten the popper. N COUNT British

poppy /pɒpi^1/, **poppies.** A **poppy** is a plant with a large, delicate, red flower. N COUNT

populace /pɒpjə^{4}lə^{1}s/. The **populace** of a country is its people. EG *They represented only a fraction of the general populace... The populace went wild.* N SING: *the*+N Formal

popular /pɒpjə^{4}lə/. **1** Something that is **popular** is enjoyed or liked by a lot of people. EG *The Tower of London is the most popular tourist attraction in Britain... Swimming is very popular with all ages.* ◇ **popularity** /pɒpjə^{4}lærɪ^{1}ti^1/. EG *...the popularity of science fiction films.* ADJ QUALIT ◇ N UNCOUNT

2 Popular ideas or attitudes are approved of or held by most people. EG *Contrary to popular belief, science does not offer us certainties... ...the popular image of feminism.* ADJ CLASSIF: ATTRIB

3 Popular newspapers and television programmes are aimed at ordinary people and not at specialists in a particular subject. EG *The popular press is obsessed with the Royal Family... ...a series of popular talks on medicine.* ADJ CLASSIF: ATTRIB

4 Someone who is **popular** is liked by most people. EG *He became a popular Governor... He has always been popular among Conservatives.* ◇ **popularity.** EG *...his immense popularity with radio audiences.* ADJ QUALIT ◇ N UNCOUNT

5 Popular is used to describe political activities which involve all people, and not just members of political parties. EG *This is not a mere party issue, but deserves wider popular debate... ...their advocacy of popular democracy.* ADJ CLASSIF: ATTRIB Formal

popularize /pɒpjə^{4}ləraɪz/, **popularizes, popularizing, popularized;** also spelled **popularise. 1** To **popularize** something means to make a lot of people interested in it and able to enjoy it. EG *Television has done a great deal to popularize snooker.* V+O

2 To **popularize** an academic subject or scientific idea means to make it more easily understandable to ordinary people. EG *Scientific notions soon become inaccurate when they are popularized.*
V+O Formal

popularly /pɒpjə^{4}ləli^1/. You use **popularly** to indicate **1** that a name or title is used by most people, although it is not the official name or title. EG *This theory was popularly called the Big Bang.* **2** that an idea is believed by most people, although it may not be true. EG *It is popularly believed that eating carrots makes you see better in the dark.*
ADV

populate /pɒpjə^{4}leɪt/, **populates, populating, populated. 1** If an area **is populated** by people or animals, those people or animals live there, often in large numbers. EG *The town is heavily populated by immigrants... ...the rabbits that thickly populated the area.* ◊ **populated.** EG *...the densely populated countryside.*
V+O : USU PASS; ◊ ADJ QUALIT

2 To **populate** an area means to cause plants, animals, or people to live there. EG *Convicts from France were sent to populate the islands.*
V+O

population /pɒpjə^{4}leɪʃə^{0}n/, **populations.** The **population** of a country or area is **1** all the people who live in it. EG *The country is unable to feed its population... Kandahar has a population of 230,000... ...the increase in population.* **2** all the people or animals of a particular type in it. EG *...a prison population of 44,000... In these areas, populations of mosquitoes are greatly reduced.*
N COUNT OR N UNCOUNT; N COUNT : USU+SUPP

populous /pɒpjə^{4}ləs/. A **populous** country or area has a lot of people living in it. EG *...the less populous areas of London.*
ADJ QUALIT Formal

porcelain /pɔːsə^{0}lɪ^{3}n/ is a hard, shiny substance made by heating clay. It is used to make cups, plates, and ornaments. EG *...antique pottery and porcelain... ...a porcelain statue.*
N UNCOUNT

porch /pɔːtʃ/, **porches.** A **porch** is **1** a sheltered area at the entrance to a building. It has a roof and sometimes has walls. EG *...a big house with a glass porch.* **2** a raised platform built along the outside wall of a house and often covered with a roof. EG *She sat beside me on the back porch.*
N COUNT; American

porcupine /pɔːkjə^{4}paɪn/, **porcupines.** A **porcupine** is an animal with many long, thin, sharp spikes on its back.
N COUNT

pore /pɔː/, **pores, poring, pored. 1** Your **pores** are the small holes in your skin. EG *...the pores round his nose.*
N COUNT

2 The **pores** of a plant are the small holes on its surface. EG *...mushrooms with minute yellow pores.*
N COUNT

3 Pores in rocks or soil are the tiny gaps or cracks in them. EG *...water trapped in pores in rocks.*
N COUNT

pore over. If you **pore over** information, you look at it and study it very carefully. EG *Monks pored over ancient texts... We pored over our maps.*
PHRASAL VB : V+PREP, HAS PASS

pork /pɔːk/ is meat from a pig, usually fresh and not smoked or salted. EG *...pork chops.*
N UNCOUNT

porn /pɔːn/ means the same as pornography. EG *...porn shops... ...porn movies.*
N UNCOUNT Informal

pornography /pɔːnɒgrəfi^1/ refers to books, magazines, and films that are designed to cause sexual excitement by showing naked people or referring to sexual acts. EG *...pornography in the cinema.* ◊ **pornographic** /pɔːnəgræfɪk/. EG *...pornographic films and magazines.*
N UNCOUNT; ◊ ADJ QUALIT

porous /pɔːrəs/. Something that is **porous** has many small holes in it, which water and air can pass through. EG *The volcanic rocks are porous.*
ADJ QUALIT

porpoise /pɔːpəs/, **porpoises.** A **porpoise** is a sea animal that looks similar to a dolphin.
N COUNT

porridge /pɒrɪdʒ/ is a thick, sticky food made from oats cooked in water or milk.
N UNCOUNT

port /pɔːt/, **ports. 1** A **port** is **1.1** a town by the sea or on a river, which has a harbour. EG *...a fishing port... It is the major port on this coastline.* **1.2** a harbour area with docks and warehouses, where ships load or unload goods or passengers.
N COUNT

2 The **port** side of a ship is the left side when you are facing towards the front of it. EG *A wave caught the trawler on her port bow.* ▸ used as a noun. EG *...a hundred yards to port.*
ADJ CLASSIF : ATTRIB; ▸ N UNCOUNT

3 Port is a type of strong, sweet red wine. EG *...a glass of port.*
N MASS

portable /pɔːtəbə^{0}l/. A machine or device that is **portable** is designed to be easily carried or moved. EG *...a little portable TV... ...portable typewriters... ...a portable radio.*
ADJ CLASSIF

portal /pɔːtə^{0}l/, **portals.** A **portal** is a large, impressive doorway at the entrance to a building. EG *...villas with huge marble portals.*
N COUNT Literary

portent /pɔːtɛnt/, **portents.** A **portent** is something that indicates what is likely to happen in the future. EG *Are dreams a portent of things to come?.. ...a hopeful portent.*
N COUNT Formal

portentous /pɔːtɛntəs/. Something that is **portentous** is important in indicating or affecting future events. EG *Its consequences were historically portentous.*
ADJ QUALIT Formal

porter /pɔːtə/, **porters.** A **porter** is **1** a person whose job is to be in charge of the entrance of a building such as a hotel. EG *...throwing open doors like a hotel porter.* **2** a person whose job is to carry things, for example to carry people's luggage at a railway station. EG *...railway porters.*
N COUNT

portfolio /pɔːtfəʊlɪəʊ/, **portfolios.** A **portfolio** is **1** a thin, flat case for carrying papers or drawings in. **2** a set of drawings or paintings that represent an artist's work. EG *...a portfolio of photographs.*
N COUNT

porthole /pɔːthəʊl/, **portholes.** A **porthole** is a small round window on the side of a ship or aircraft. EG *...the portholes of the cabin.*
N COUNT

portico /pɔːtɪkəʊ/, **porticos** or **porticoes.** A **portico** is a large, covered area at the entrance to a building, with pillars supporting the roof. EG *...a palace with a huge marble portico.*
N COUNT Formal

portion /pɔːʃə^{0}n/, **portions, portioning, portioned. 1** A **portion** of something is a part of it. EG *...the lower portion of the counter... Divide the cake into eight portions... A large portion of this money would come to her.*
N PART

2 A **portion** is the amount of food that is given to one person at a meal. EG *He held out his plate for a second portion... ...a small portion.*
N PART

portion out. If you **portion out** something, you share it out among a group of people. EG *...the food that Tim was carefully portioning out.*
PHRASAL VB : V+O+ADV

portly /pɔːtli^1/, **portlier, portliest.** Someone who is **portly**, especially a man, is rather fat. EG *...portly middle-aged gentlemen.*
ADJ QUALIT Outdated

portrait /pɔːtrɪ^{3}t/, **portraits.** A **portrait** is a painting, drawing, or photograph of someone. EG *...a famous portrait of the musician... She painted landscapes and portraits.*
N COUNT

portray /pɔːtreɪ/, **portrays, portraying, portrayed. 1** When an actor or actress **portrays** someone, he or she plays that person in a play or film. EG *In her final sketch she portrayed a temperamental countess... The animals were portrayed by actors in masks.*
V+O

2 When a writer or artist **portrays** something, he or she writes a description or produces a painting of it. EG *...writers who tried to portray London in words.*
V+O

3 If you **portray** someone or something in a certain way, you give a particular impression of them by emphasizing some of their features. EG *Advertising tends to portray women in a very traditional role... Minor mishaps were portrayed as major tragedies.*
V+O+A

portrayal /pɔːtreɪəl/, **portrayals. 1** An actor's **portrayal** of a character in a play or film is the way that he or she portrays the character. EG *He*
N COUNT : USU+*of*

Find an outdated word on these pages to describe someone who is fat.

got the award for his portrayal of Willy Loman in 'Death of a Salesman'.

2 An artist's **portrayal** of something is a drawing, painting, or photograph of it. *...an eye-catching portrayal of the beautiful Madame Chiang.* N COUNT: USU+*of*

3 The **portrayal** of something in a book or film is **3.1** the act of describing it or showing it. EG *...portrayals of sexual behaviour.* **3.2** the way that it is made to appear. EG *...his portrayal by the media as an enemy of democracy.* N COUNT: USU+*of*

pose /pəʊz/, **poses, posing, posed. 1** If you **pose** for a photograph or painting, you stay in a particular position so that someone can photograph you or paint you. EG *The bride and groom posed for the photograph.* V: USU+A

2 You can say that people **are posing** when they behave in an exaggerated way because they want other people to admire them. ◇ **poser, posers.** EG *You're always posing. How I hate posers.* V ◇ N COUNT

3 If you **pose** as someone, you pretend to be that person in order to deceive people. EG *...an agent posing as a telephone engineer.* V+*as*

4 If something **poses** a problem or a danger, it is the cause of the problem or danger. EG *The ship's length must pose considerable steering problems... He posed a serious threat to their authority.* V+O

5 If you **pose** a question, you ask it. EG *This brings me back to the question you posed earlier.* V+O Formal

6 Your **pose** is the way that you stand, sit, or lie, especially when you are being photographed. EG *...hundreds of photographs in various poses.* N COUNT+SUPP

7 A **pose** is also a way of behaving that is intended to impress or deceive people. EG *...his pose as the champion of the proletariat.* N COUNT: USU+SUPP

posh /pɒʃ/. **1** If you describe something as **posh**, you mean that it is smart, fashionable, and expensive. EG *She had stayed in posh hotels.* ADJ QUALIT Informal

2 If you describe a person as **posh**, you mean that they belong to the upper classes. EG *...your posh friends... ...putting on her posh voice.* ADJ QUALIT Informal

position /pəzɪʃəⁿn/, **positions, positioning, positioned. 1** The **position** of someone or something is **1.1** the place where they are. EG *They tell the time by the position of the sun... The house is in a very exposed position... He had shifted position from the front to the back of the room.* **1.2** the way in which they are sitting or lying, or the direction in which they are facing. EG *I helped her to a sitting position... Hold it in an upright position... He pushed the catch down into the ready position.* N COUNT OR N UNCOUNT; N COUNT+SUPP

2 If someone or something is **in position**, they are in their correct or usual place. EG *By 8.05 the groups were in position... Keep it in position with a rubber band.* PHRASE

3 If you **position** something somewhere, you put it there. EG *Mel positioned his car alongside the foreman's... The boy positioned himself near the door.* V+O OR V-REFL: USU+A

4 Your **position** in society is the importance that you have in it. EG *Women hold a strong position in Aboriginal society... ...people in positions of power and influence.* N COUNT+SUPP

5 A **position** in a company or organization is a job or post in it. EG *...top management positions... Thorn lost his position as steward.* N COUNT Formal

6 Your **position** in a race or competition is your place among the winners at the end, or your place at some time during the event. EG *She sprinted hard to hold third position.* N COUNT+SUPP

7 Your **position** at a particular time is the situation that you are in. EG *It puts me in a rather difficult position... You are in the fortunate position of having no responsibilities.* N COUNT+SUPP

8 If you are **in a position** to do something, you are able to do it. If you are **in no position** to do it, you are unable to do it. EG *I would then be in a position to do that for her... He's in a good position to predict the election results... They were in no position to help.* PHRASE

9 If you say that you are **in no position** to criticize someone, you mean that you do not want to, because you are equally guilty or wrong. EG *...nor are we in any position to reproach them.* PHRASE

10 Your **position** on a particular subject or situation is your attitude towards it or your opinion of it. EG *...if you take a multilateralist position... What is their position on the proposed sale of aircraft?* N COUNT+SUPP Formal

positive /pɒzɪtɪv/. **1** If you are **positive** about something, you are completely sure about it. EG *He was positive that he had seen it in the newspaper... 'Are you sure you don't want her address?' – 'Positive.'* ADJ PRED: OFT+REPORT OR *about*

2 If you have a **positive** attitude to things, you are hopeful and confident. EG *I began to feel more positive... ...positive feelings about life.* ADJ QUALIT

3 If you make a **positive** decision or take **positive** action, you do something definite in order to deal with a task or problem. EG *They have a positive policy of preventative dental care.* ADJ QUALIT

4 Feelings or actions that are considered morally good or socially useful are sometimes described as **positive**. EG *...positive feelings like tenderness and joy... Being creative and productive are seen as positive values.* ADJ QUALIT

5 If the response to something is **positive**, it shows agreement, approval, or encouragement. EG *Public response was positive.* ◇ **positively.** EG *Thomson replied positively: 'There will be no change in policy.'* ADJ QUALIT ◇ ADV

6 **Positive** evidence gives definite proof of the truth or identity of something. EG *I was looking for some positive evidence that Barney came to the flat.* ◇ **positively.** EG *The body has been positively identified.* ADJ CLASSIF: ATTRIB ◇ ADV

7 If a medical or scientific test is **positive**, it shows that something has happened or is present. EG *...a positive pregnancy test.* ADJ CLASSIF

8 A **positive** number is greater than zero. ADJ CLASSIF

9 You can use **positive** to describe a surprising or unexpected pleasant quality that something has. EG *I find cooking a positive pleasure... Life in a town brings positive advantages to children.* ADJ CLASSIF: ATTRIB

positively /pɒzɪtɪvli¹/. You use **positively 1** to emphasize that you really mean what you are saying. EG *It's quite positively the last time that you'll see me.* **2** to emphasize that something really is the case, although it may sound surprising or extreme. EG *Her friends had been positively abusive... I didn't object. I positively approved her initiative.* ADV SEN; ADV

POSS stands for **possessive**

Some nouns have the label +POSS in the Extra Column. This means that there is either a possessive form before it or a prepositional group immediately after it.

1 The possessive form can be a possessive determiner (DET POSS), such as *my, your, her, his, its, our, their.* For example, *...**her** relatives... ...**our** house.*

2 The possessive form can be a noun or a name with an apostrophe '**'s**', such as *the **writer's, someone's, John's**,* and *Professor **Smith's**.* If the noun is plural, or if it already ends in 's', the possessive is formed by adding only an apostrophe, as in *I've read all **Dickens'** books... ...the **teachers'** strike.*

3 The prepositional group following the noun must begin with 'of', as in *They said a prayer for the souls **of the men who had drowned**.*

possess /pəzɛs/, **possesses, possessing, possessed. 1** If you **possess** something, you have it or V+O: NO CONT, NO IMPER own it. EG *How I longed to possess a suit like that... They were found guilty of possessing petrol bombs.*

2 If something **possesses** a particular feature or quality, it has that feature or quality. EG *For hundreds of years London possessed only one bridge... Television possesses a superficial magic.* V+O : NO CONT, NO IMPER Formal

3 If you **possess** a quality or ability, you have that quality or ability. EG *He possessed the qualities of a war leader... ...skills they do not possess.* V+O : NO CONT, NO IMPER

4 If a feeling or belief **possesses** you, it strongly influences your behaviour or thinking. EG *A violent rage possessed him... I was possessed with the notion that I was not alone.* V+O : NO CONT, NO IMPER Literary

possession /pəzɛʃəⁿn/, **possessions. 1 Possession** is the state of having or owning something. EG *Freedom depended on the possession of land... The possession of a degree does not guarantee you a job... They took possession of the island.* N UNCOUNT : USU+POSS

2 If something is **in** your **possession** or if you are **in possession** of it, you have it or have obtained it. EG *I had in my possession a portion of the money... The document came into the possession of the Daily Mail... MacDonald has been in possession of the letter for some weeks.* PHRASE Formal

3 Your **possessions** are the things that you own or have with you at a particular time. EG *He had few possessions... Check your possessions on arrival.* N COUNT : USU PLURAL

possessive /pəzɛsɪv/. **1** Someone who is **possessive** about another person wants all that person's love and attention. EG *She was very possessive about Rod.* ◊ **possessiveness.** EG *...a child's possessiveness towards its mother.* ADJ QUALIT ◊ N UNCOUNT

2 When people are **possessive** about things that they own, they do not like other people to use them. EG *I am possessive about my car.* ADJ QUALIT

3 Possessive is a grammatical term used to describe words that indicate the person or thing that an object, feature, or quality belongs to. ADJ CLASSIF OR N COUNT

possessor /pəzɛsə/, **possessors.** The **possessor** of something is the person who has it or owns it. EG *I was the proud possessor of two tickets to the opera.* N COUNT : USU+POSS Formal

possibility /pɒsɪbɪlɪ¹ti¹/, **possibilities. 1** If you say there is a **possibility** that something is true, you mean that it might be true. EG *We must accept the possibility that we might be wrong.* N COUNT : OFT+REPORT OR SUPP

2 If there is a **possibility** of something happening, it might happen. EG *There was now no possibility of success.* N COUNT : OFT+*of* OR REPORT

3 If there is a **possibility** of someone doing something, they could do it and might do it. EG *I considered the possibility of joining the Communist Party... That was one of the possibilities that was suggested.* N COUNT+SUPP

possible /pɒsɪbəⁿl/, **possibles. 1** If it is **possible** to do something, it can be done. EG *It is possible for us to measure his progress... They are doing everything possible to take care of you... They wished, where possible, to avoid new conflicts... Whenever possible, loads were flown in... 'When do you want to go?' – 'This weekend, if possible.'* ADJ CLASSIF

2 A **possible** event is one that might happen. EG *His staff warned him of the possible consequences.* ADJ CLASSIF

3 If you describe someone as, for example, a **possible** Prime Minister, you mean that he or she may become the Prime Minister. EG *America and Russia were both possible financiers of the dam.* ADJ CLASSIF : ATTRIB

4 If you say that it is **possible** that something is true or correct, you mean that although you do not know whether it is true or correct, you accept that it might be. EG *It is possible that he said these things... That's one possible answer.* ADJ CLASSIF

5 If you do something **as soon as possible**, you do it as soon as you can. If you get **as much as possible** of something, you get as much of it as you can. EG *Go as soon as possible... I like to know as much as possible about my patients... He sat as far away from the others as possible.* PHRASE

6 If you describe something as **the best possible** or **the worst possible** thing, you mean that no other thing of that kind could be better or worse. EG *We provide the best possible accommodation for our students... ...the harshest possible conditions.* PHRASE

7 If you describe someone or something as a **possible**, you mean that they are one of several people or things that could be chosen for a particular job or purpose. EG *He sounds like a possible... The first three houses were all possibles.* N COUNT

possibly /pɒsɪbli¹/. **1** You use **possibly** to indicate that you are not sure whether something is true or might happen. EG *Television is possibly to blame for this... The threat was possibly not very great... This must have been a little reading-room, possibly Leo's study.* ADV SEN

2 You use **possibly** to emphasize that you are surprised, puzzled, or shocked by something that you have seen or heard. EG *How could it possibly accomplish anything?... I wondered what he could possibly be doing it for.* ADV+INF

3 You use **possibly** to emphasize that someone has tried their hardest to do something, or has done it as well as they can. EG *He planned to come back as soon as he possibly could... I have made myself as comfortable as I possibly can... He will do everything he possibly can to aid you.* ADV+MODAL

4 You use **possibly** with a negative modal, to emphasize that something definitely cannot happen or definitely cannot be done. EG *I can't possibly stay in all the weekend... Nobody could possibly tell the difference.* ADV

post /pəʊst/, **posts, posting, posted. 1** The **post** is the public service or system by which letters and parcels are collected and delivered. EG *You'll get these through the post... There is a cheque for you in the post... Winners will be notified by post.* N SING : *the*+N OR *by*+N British

2 You can refer to letters and parcels that are delivered to you as your **post**. EG *There is some post for you... Rose was reluctant to answer her post.* N UNCOUNT

3 If you **post** a letter or parcel, you send it to someone by putting it in a post-box or by taking it to a post office. EG *I'm going to post a letter... I'll be glad to post you details... Post it to the social security office.* V+O, V+O+O, OR V+O+*to*

4 If you **keep** someone **posted**, you keep giving them the latest information about a situation that they are interested in. EG *David promised to keep them posted.* PHRASE

5 A **post** is a strong, upright pole made of wood or metal that is fixed into the ground. EG *A dog sat chained to a post outside.* • See also **lamp-post**. N COUNT

6 A **post** in a company or organization is a job or official position in it. EG *...a post at the High School... She is well qualified for the post.* N COUNT Formal

7 In a battle, a soldier's or sailor's **post** is the place where he or she has been told to remain and to do his or her job. EG *Every man was at his post... He had to leave his post and flee.* N COUNT+POSS

8 If you **are posted** somewhere, you are sent there by the organization that you work for. EG *I have been posted to Paris.* V+O+A : USU PASS

post- is used to form words that describe something as taking place after a particular date, event, or period. For example, post-school education is education that you receive after you have left school. EG *...the post-1918 period... ...a post-election survey.* PREFIX

postage /pəʊstɪdʒ/ is the money that you pay for sending letters and parcels by post. EG *Send 25p extra for postage and packing.* N UNCOUNT

postage stamp, postage stamps. A **postage stamp** is a small piece of gummed paper that you buy from the post office and stick on an envelope or parcel before you post it. N COUNT

Where would you put a postcode?

postal /pəʊstəˈl/ is used to describe things connected with the public service of carrying letters and parcels from one place to another. EG *...increases in postal charges... ...the postal service.* ADJ CLASSIF : ATTRIB

postal order, postal orders. A **postal order** is a piece of paper representing a sum of money which you can buy at a post office and send to someone as a way of sending them money by post. N COUNT British

post-box, post-boxes. A **post-box** is a metal box with a hole in it, which you put letters into to be collected by a postman. N COUNT

postcard /pəʊstkɑ:d/, **postcards.** A **postcard** is a piece of thin card, often with a picture on one side, which you can write on and send to people without using an envelope. EG *I sent her a postcard from Eastbourne.* N COUNT

postcode /pəʊstkəʊd/, **postcodes.** Your **postcode** is a short sequence of numbers and letters at the end of your address, which helps the post office to sort the mail. N COUNT British

poster /pəʊstə/, **posters.** A **poster** is a large notice or picture that you stick on a wall or noticeboard, often in order to advertise something. EG *...cinema posters... ...colourful posters of Paris and Venice.* N COUNT

posterity /pɒstɛrɪˈtiˈ/. You can refer to everyone who will be alive in the future as **posterity**. EG *This fine building should be preserved for posterity.* N UNCOUNT Formal

postgraduate /pəʊstgrædju:ət/, **postgraduates.** A **postgraduate** is a student with a first degree from a university who is studying or doing research at a more advanced level. ▸ used as an adjective. EG *...postgraduate students... Many students go on and do postgraduate work.* N COUNT ▸ ADJ CLASSIF : ATTRIB

posthumous /pɒstjəˈməs/ is used to describe something that happens after someone's death but that relates to something that they did before they died. EG *...a posthumous award for bravery... ...a posthumous publication.* ◇ **posthumously.** EG *...a posthumously published article.* ADJ CLASSIF ◇ ADV

posting /pəʊstɪŋ/, **postings.** A **posting** is a job that you are given by your employers, which involves going to a different town or country. EG *I've been given an overseas posting to Japan.* N COUNT

postman /pəʊstməˈn/, **postmen.** A **postman** is a man whose job is to collect and deliver letters and parcels that are sent by post. N COUNT

postmark /pəʊstmɑ:k/, **postmarks.** A **postmark** is a mark which is printed on letters and parcels at a post office. It shows the time and place at which something is posted. N COUNT

postmaster /pəʊstmɑ:stə/, **postmasters.** A **postmaster** is a man who is in charge of a post office. N COUNT Outdated

postmistress /pəʊstmɪstrɪˈs/, **postmistresses.** A **postmistress** is a woman who is in charge of a post office. N COUNT Outdated

post-mortem /pəʊst mɔ:təm/, **post-mortems.** A **post-mortem** is a medical examination of a dead person's body in order to find out how they died. N COUNT

post office, post offices. 1 The **Post Office** is the national organization that is responsible for postal services. N SING : *the*+N

2 A **post office** is a building where you can buy stamps, post letters and parcels, and use other services provided by the national postal service. N COUNT

postpone /pəˈstˈpəʊn/, **postpones, postponing, postponed.** If you **postpone** an event, you arrange for it to take place at a later time than was originally planned. EG *Could you postpone your departure for five minutes?... The flight had been postponed until eleven o'clock.* ◇ **postponement** /pəˈstˈpəʊnməˈnt/, **postponements.** EG *...the postponement of the wedding.* V+O : OFT+A ◇ N COUNT OR N UNCOUNT

postscript /pəʊstskrɪpt/, **postscripts.** A **postscript** is a message written at the end of a letter after you have signed your name. You usually write 'PS' in front of it. N COUNT

posture /pɒstʃə/, **postures, posturing, postured.**
1 Your **posture** is the position or manner in which you stand or sit. EG *...his stiff, upright posture... ...hands held out in the imploring posture of a beggar.* N UNCOUNT : USU+SUPP

2 A **posture** is also an attitude that you have towards something. EG *They are trying to adopt a more co-operative posture.* N COUNT+SUPP

3 You say that someone **is posturing** when they are trying to give a particular impression in order to deceive people. EG *...posturing to project an air of knowledge.* V : USU CONT Formal

post-war is used to describe things that happen, exist, or are made in the period immediately after a war, especially the 1939-45 war. EG *...a postwar building... ...a relic of the postwar era.* ADJ CLASSIF : ATTRIB

posy /pəʊziˈ/, **posies.** A **posy** is a small bunch of flowers. EG *...posies of wild flowers.* N COUNT

pot /pɒt/, **pots, potting, potted.** 1 A **pot** is a deep round container used for cooking, especially one used for cooking stews and soups. EG *...clay pots.* N COUNT OR N PART

2 You can refer to a teapot or coffee pot as a **pot**. You can also refer to the tea or coffee inside it as a **pot**. EG *I'll go and make a fresh pot of tea.* N COUNT OR N PART

3 A **pot** is also a deep bowl or cylindrical container for paint or some other thick liquid. EG *There were old paint pots stacked on the shelves.* N COUNT OR N PART

4 You can refer to a flowerpot as a **pot**. EG *Pots of geraniums stood on the window-sill.* N COUNT

5 If you **pot** a plant, you put it into a flowerpot filled with earth, so that it can grow there. ◇ **potted.** EG *...watering the potted plants.* V+O ◇ ADJ CLASSIF

6 Cannabis is sometimes referred to as **pot**. EG *He was said to have smoked pot occasionally.* N UNCOUNT Informal

7 See also **chimney pot**, **melting pot**, **potted**.

potato /pəteɪtəʊ/, **potatoes.** A **potato** is a round white vegetable with a brown or red skin. Potatoes grow underground. EG *...baked potatoes.* N COUNT OR N UNCOUNT

potent /pəʊtəˈnt/. 1 Something that is **potent** is very effective and powerful. EG *Potent new weapons will shortly be available... ...a potent argument.* ◇ **potency** /pəʊtəˈnsiˈ/. EG *Princess Ida's spell lost its potency... ...the potency of history.* ADJ QUALIT ◇ N UNCOUNT : USU+POSS

2 A man who is **potent** is capable of having sex. EG *In early adulthood you are at your most potent.* ◇ **potency.** EG *...sexual potency.* ADJ QUALIT ◇ N UNCOUNT

potentate /pəʊtəˈnteɪt/, **potentates.** A **potentate** is a ruler who has direct power over his people. N COUNT Formal

potential /pətɛnʃəˈl/. 1 You use **potential** to describe something as capable of becoming a particular kind of thing. EG *All 92 countries are customers or potential customers of the United States... ...potential sources of food production.* ◇ **potentially.** EG *Electricity is potentially dangerous, so treat it with respect.* ADJ CLASSIF : ATTRIB ◇ SUBMOD

2 Your **potential** is the range of abilities and talents that you have, although these abilities and talents may not be in full use yet. EG *Many children do not achieve their potential.* N UNCOUNT +SUPP

3 If you say that someone or something has **potential**, you mean that they have the necessary ability or quality to be successful or to develop in a particular way. EG *Has this woman got executive potential?... The land has great strategic potential.* N UNCOUNT +SUPP

potentiality /pətɛnʃɪælɪˈtiˈ/, **potentialities.** If something has **potentiality** or **potentialities**, it is capable of being used or developed in particular ways. EG *...the realization of human potentiality... He was swift to publicise the potentialities of motoring and flight.* N COUNT OR N UNCOUNT +SUPP Formal

pothole /pɒthəʊl/, **potholes.** A **pothole** is a large hole in the surface of a road, caused by traffic and bad weather. EG *...ground that is riddled with potholes.* N COUNT

potion /pəʊʃəˈn/, **potions.** A **potion** is a drink that contains medicine, poison, or something that is supposed to have magic powers. EG *...a medicine chest stuffed with potions and ointments... ...love potions.* N COUNT

potted /pɒtɪ[2]d/. **1 Potted** meat or fish has been cooked and put into a small sealed container. EG *...potted shrimps.* ADJ CLASSIF : ATTRIB

2 A **potted** biography or history contains the main facts about someone or something in a short and simplified form. EG *...potted character studies of famous authors.* ADJ CLASSIF : ATTRIB

potter /pɒtə/, **potters, pottering, pottered.** A **potter** is someone who makes pottery. N COUNT

potter about. If you **potter about** or **potter around**, you pass the time in a gentle, unhurried way, doing pleasant but unimportant things. EG *He loved to potter around in the garden.* PHRASAL VB : V+ADV/PREP British

pottery /pɒtə[0]ri[1]/, **potteries. 1 Pottery** is **1.1** pots, dishes, and other objects which are made from clay and then baked in an oven until they are hard. EG *...a sale of antique pottery and porcelain.* **1.2** the craft or activity of making pottery. EG *My hobbies are pottery and basket-weaving.* N UNCOUNT

2 A **pottery** is a factory or workshop where pottery is made. N COUNT

potty /pɒti[1]/, **potties. 1** A **potty** is a deep bowl which a small child uses instead of a toilet. N COUNT

2 If you say that someone is **potty**, you mean that they are crazy or foolish. EG *They thought she was potty... I think it's a potty idea.* ADJ QUALIT Informal

pouch /paʊtʃ/, **pouches. 1** A **pouch** is a flexible container like a small bag. EG *He took the cards and put them in the leather pouch on his belt... ...a tobacco pouch.* N COUNT

2 A **pouch** is also a pocket of skin on some animals. Female kangaroos have pouches on their stomachs in which their babies grow. N COUNT

poultry /pəʊltri[1]/. **Poultry** is both the singular and the plural form.

1 You can refer to chickens, ducks, and other birds that are kept for their eggs and meat as **poultry**. EG *They keep poultry.* N PLURAL

2 You can also refer to the meat of these birds as **poultry**. EG *They sell a wide range of cooked, frozen and fresh poultry.* N UNCOUNT

pounce /paʊns/, **pounces, pouncing, pounced. 1** When an animal or bird **pounces** on something, it leaps on it and grabs it. EG *He had seen leopards pouncing on young baboons.* V : OFT +*on/upon*

2 If someone **pounces** on you, they come towards you suddenly and take hold of you. EG *The police were about to pounce upon us.* V : OFT +*on/upon*

3 If you **pounce** on something such as a mistake, you draw attention to it. EG *Local politicians are quick to pounce on any trouble.* V : OFT +*on/upon*

pound /paʊnd/, **pounds, pounding, pounded. 1** A **pound** is a unit of money which is used in Britain. One British pound is divided into a hundred pence. Many other countries have a unit of money called a **pound**. EG *I was paid fifty pounds a week... ...his thirty-five thousand pound house.* N COUNT

2 The British currency system is sometimes referred to as the **pound**. EG *...a 13% fall in the pound against the dollar.* N SING : *the*+N

3 A **pound** is also a unit of weight used mainly in Britain, America, and other countries where English is spoken. One pound is equivalent to 0.454 kilograms. EG *...one pound of rice... He weighs about 140 pounds.* N COUNT OR N PART

4 If you **pound** something or **pound** on it, you hit it loudly and repeatedly. EG *In frustration she would pound the dining-room table... They began pounding on the walls.* ◇ **pounding.** EG *The pounding of the drums grew louder.* V+O OR V+A; ◇ N UNCOUNT

5 If you **pound** something, you crush it into a paste or a powder or into very small pieces. EG *The women of the village pounded grain in their mortars.* V+O

6 If your heart **is pounding**, it is beating with an unusually strong and fast rhythm. EG *My heart pounded with joy.* ◇ **pounding.** EG *I felt only the pounding of my heart.* V; ◇ N UNCOUNT

pour /pɔː/, **pours, pouring, poured. 1** If you **pour** a liquid or other substance, you make it flow steadily out of a container by holding the container at an angle. EG *The waiter poured the wine into her glass... ...a machine that poured grain into sacks.* V+O : USU+A

2 If you **pour** someone a drink, you fill a cup or glass with the drink so that they can drink it. EG *He poured Ellen a glass of wine... Lally poured herself another cup of tea... She poured a drink for herself.* V+O+O, V+O, OR V+O+*for*

3 When a liquid or other substance **pours** somewhere, for example through a hole, it flows there quickly and in large quantities. EG *The rain poured through a hole in the roof... The sweat began to pour down his face.* V+A

4 When it rains very heavily, you can say that it **is pouring**. EG *In London it poured all the time... It was absolutely pouring with rain.* ◇ **pouring.** EG *Don't go out in the pouring rain.* V OR V+A; ◇ ADJ CLASSIF : ATTRIB

5 If people or animals **pour** into or out of a place, they go there quickly and in large numbers. EG *Refugees are now pouring into this country.* V+A

6 If information **pours** into or out of a place, a lot of it is obtained or given. EG *Messages of encouragement poured in from people of all kinds... ...the lies that poured from headquarters.* V+A

7 If you **pour** money or energy into an activity or organization, you use a lot of money or energy in order to do the activity or help the organization. EG *The state is pouring money into further education... They poured their energies into religious reform.* V+O+*into*

pour out. 1 If you **pour out** a drink, you fill a cup or glass with it. EG *Castle poured out two glasses of whisky.* **2** If you **pour out** your thoughts, feelings, or experiences, you tell someone all about them. EG *I was on the verge of pouring out all my feelings.* PHRASAL VB : V+O+ADV; V+O+ADV

pout /paʊt/, **pouts, pouting, pouted.** If you **pout**, you stick out your lips as a way of showing that you are annoyed. EG *She tossed back her hair and pouted.* ◇ **pouting.** EG *...girls with pouting mouths... ...a pouting blonde.* V; ◇ ADJ CLASSIF

poverty /pɒvəti[1]/ is the state of being extremely poor. EG *There are thousands living in poverty.* N UNCOUNT

poverty-stricken. Poverty-stricken people or places are extremely poor. EG *...this small poverty-stricken town.* ADJ CLASSIF

powder /paʊdə/, **powders, powdering, powdered. 1 Powder** consists of many tiny particles of a solid substance. EG *Their bones turn to powder... ...washing powders.* N MASS

2 A **powdered** substance is one which is in the form of a powder. EG *...powdered milk.* ADJ CLASSIF : ATTRIB

3 If you **powder** yourself, you cover parts of your body with scented powder. EG *She lightly powdered her face.* ◇ **powdered.** EG *You could see each wrinkle on her powdered face.* V+O OR V-REFL; ◇ ADJ CLASSIF

power /paʊə/, **powers, powering, powered. 1** If someone has **power**, they have a lot of control over people and activities. EG *...his yearning for power... It gave the President too much power.* N UNCOUNT

2 If you have the ability or opportunity to do something, you can refer to this as a **power**. EG *They did not have the power of speech... They lose the power to walk... They were equals except in earning power.* ● If it is **in** or **within** your **power** to do something, you are able to do it. EG *It may not be within their power to help... I did everything in my power to console her.* N UNCOUNT +SUPP; ● PHRASE

3 If someone in authority has the **power** to do something, they have the legal right to do it. EG *...the court's power to punish young offenders... The Government curbed the Lords' powers.* N COUNT OR N UNCOUNT +SUPP

4 When people take **power** or come to **power**, they take charge of a country's affairs. EG *The Wilson Government came to power in 1964... The Tories were restored to power for more than four* N UNCOUNT

Are the 'powers that be' powerful?

years. • If a group of people are **in power**, they are in charge of a country's affairs. EG *The Tories were in power at the time.* • PHRASE

5 If you talk about **the powers that be**, you are referring to the people in authority. EG *He was commissioned to write this report by the powers that be.* PHRASE

6 The **power** of something is the physical strength that it has to move or damage things. EG *I underestimated the power of the explosion.* N UNCOUNT +SUPP

7 **Power** is the energy that is obtained, for example, by burning a fuel or by using the wind or the sun. EG *...steam power... ...a cheap source of power.* N UNCOUNT

8 Electricity is often referred to as **power**. EG *Water and power have still not reached some rural areas... ...a power failure.* N UNCOUNT

9 The device that **powers** a machine provides the energy that the machine needs in order to work. EG *Its radar equipment was powered by a nuclear reactor.* V+O

powerful /paʊəfʊl/. **1** A **powerful** person or organization is able to control or influence people and events. EG *They organize themselves into powerful and effective trade unions... ...the most powerful government in western Europe.* • See also **all-powerful**. ADJ QUALIT

2 You say that someone's body is **powerful** when it is physically strong. EG *He had broad shoulders and powerful arms.* ◇ **powerfully.** EG *They were young, powerfully built men.* ADJ QUALIT ◇ ADV

3 If a person or animal gives you a **powerful** blow or kick, they hit you or kick you with great force. EG *The stallion will attack with powerful kicks and bites.* ADJ QUALIT

4 You can say that a machine or a substance is **powerful** when it is effective because it is very strong. EG *...a powerful engine... ...a powerful and quick-acting medicine.* ADJ QUALIT

5 A **powerful** smell is strong and unpleasant. ◇ **powerfully.** EG *...a room smelling powerfully of cats.* ADJ QUALIT ◇ ADV

6 A **powerful** voice is loud and can be heard from a long way away. ADJ QUALIT

7 You describe a piece of writing, speech, or work of art as **powerful** when it has a strong effect on people's feelings or beliefs. EG *I find his argument very powerful... He produced a series of extraordinarily powerful paintings.* ADJ QUALIT

powerless /paʊəlɪ[2]s/. **1** Someone who is **powerless** is unable to control or influence events. EG *Without the support of the party, the Cabinet is powerless.* ◇ **powerlessness.** EG *She experienced an overwhelming sense of powerlessness.* ADJ CLASSIF ◇ N UNCOUNT

2 If you are **powerless** to do something, you are completely unable to do it. EG *I stood there watching, feeling powerless to help.* ADJ PRED +to-INF

power station, power stations. A **power station** is a place where electricity is generated. N COUNT

pp. is the plural of **p.** and means 'pages'.

practicable /præktɪkəbə[0]l/. If a task, plan, or idea is **practicable**, people are able to carry it out successfully. EG *The noise will be reduced as far as is practicable.* ADJ CLASSIF Formal

practical /præktɪkə[0]l/, **practicals. 1** The **practical** aspects of something involve real situations and events, rather than just ideas and theories. EG *The SDP faces practical difficulties of organization and finance... Much of the information was of no practical use... Practical experience of broadcasting would be valuable.* ADJ CLASSIF : ATTRIB

2 You describe people as **practical** when they make sensible decisions and deal effectively with problems. EG *Try to be as methodical and practical about it as you can... What a practical mind you have.* ADJ QUALIT

3 You can also describe someone as **practical** when they are good at doing jobs with their hands. ADJ QUALIT

4 **Practical** ideas and methods are likely to be effective or successful in a real situation. EG *Their ideas are too opposed to our way of thinking to be considered practical... How long will it be before nuclear fusion becomes practical?* ADJ QUALIT

5 You can describe clothes and things in your house as **practical** when they are suitable for a particular purpose rather than fashionable or attractive. EG *Ceramic tiles are very hard on the feet, though practical.* ADJ QUALIT

6 A **practical** is an examination or a lesson in which you make things or do experiments rather than simply write. N COUNT

practicality /præktɪkælɪti[1]/, **practicalities.** The **practicalities** of a situation are the practical aspects of it, as opposed to its theoretical aspects. EG *He turned out to know very little about the practicalities of teaching... That idea is impractical, but practicality isn't everything.* N COUNT OR N UNCOUNT

practical joke, practical jokes. A **practical joke** is a trick that is intended to embarrass someone or make them look ridiculous. N COUNT

practically /præktɪkə[0]li[1]/ means almost, but not completely or exactly. EG *The town was practically deserted... He knew practically no English... She practically forced him into joining the army.* ADV

practice /præktɪs/, **practices. 1** You can refer to something that people do regularly as a **practice**. EG *Benn began the practice of holding regular meetings... ...the ancient Japanese practice of binding the feet from birth.* N COUNT

2 The work done by doctors is referred to as the **practice** of medicine. People's religious activities are referred to as the **practice** of a religion. EG *...the practice of the Christian religion... They lived on their earnings from private medical practice.* N UNCOUNT +SUPP

3 **Practice** is regular training or exercise in something, or a lot of experience in it. EG *I help them with their music practice... Skating's just a matter of practice... With practice it becomes less of an effort.* N UNCOUNT

4 A doctor's or lawyer's **practice** is his or her business, often shared with other doctors or lawyers. EG *...a medical practice... ...a doctor with a private practice.* N COUNT

5 **Practice** is used in these phrases. **5.1** If you **put** a belief or method **into practice**, you behave or act in accordance with it. EG *He had not yet attempted to put his principles into practice... I'm not sure how effective these methods will be when put into practice.* PHRASE **5.2** What happens **in practice** is what actually happens, in contrast to what is supposed to happen. EG *In practice, he exerted little influence over the others... What it means in practice is that he does twice the work for half the money.* ADV SEN **5.3** If you are **out of practice** at doing something, you have not had much experience of it recently. PHRASE

6 See also **practise**.

practise /præktɪs/, **practises, practising, practised;** also spelled **practice, practices, practicing, practiced** in American English.

1 If you **practise** something, you keep doing it regularly in order to be able to do it better. EG *I played the piece I had been practising for months... These are quite hard to do until you've practised a bit.* V+O OR V

2 You say that an activity **is practised** when people do it regularly, for example as a custom. EG *These crafts were practised by many early cultures... ...a charming custom still practised in the suburbs.* V+O : USU PASS

3 Someone who is **practised** at doing something is good at it because they have had a lot of experience of it. EG *A practised burglar rarely leaves any trace of his presence... His was a practised performance.* ADJ CLASSIF

4 When people **practise** something such as a religion, they take part in the activities associated with it. EG *They have managed to practise their religion for years... We have never been allowed to* V+O *practise democracy.* • to **practise what** you **preach**: see **preach**.

5 If something cruel is regularly done to people, you can say that it **is practised** on them. EG *I am horrified at the cruelty practised on these helpless victims... Torture was certainly practised in these countries.* [V+O+A: USU PASS]

6 Someone who **practises** medicine or law works as a doctor or a lawyer. EG *He went on to study law and practise it... He's in Hull practising medicine now.* ◊ **practising.** EG *He is now a practising doctor in Essex.* [V+O; ◊ ADJ CLASSIF: ATTRIB]

practitioner /præktɪʃənə/, **practitioners.** Doctors are sometimes referred to as **practitioners** or medical **practitioners**. [N COUNT: USU+SUPP Formal]

pragmatic /prægmætɪk/. A **pragmatic** way of dealing with something is based on practical considerations, rather than theoretical ones. EG *He argued the case for increased state intervention on wholly pragmatic grounds... ...pragmatic reasons for their behaviour.* ◊ **pragmatically.** EG *We have to be ready to tackle situations pragmatically.* [ADJ QUALIT; ◊ ADV]

pragmatism /prægmətɪzəm/ is a way of thinking or of dealing with problems in a practical way, rather than by using theory or abstract principles. [N UNCOUNT Formal]

prairie /prɛəri/, **prairies.** A **prairie** is a very large area of flat, grassy land in North America. EG *...days of travel across the prairies.* [N COUNT OR N UNCOUNT]

praise /preɪz/, **praises, praising, praised. 1** If you **praise** someone or something, you express approval for their achievements or qualities. EG *Sylvia had a stern father who never praised her... They praised his speech for its clarity and humour.* [V+O]

2 Praise is what you say or write about someone when you are praising them. EG *Three entrants were singled out for special praise... She finds it hard to give praise.* [N UNCOUNT]

3 If you **sing** someone's **praises**, you praise them in an enthusiastic way. EG *Liz is forever singing your praises.* [PHRASE]

praiseworthy /preɪzwɜːði/. If you say that something is **praiseworthy**, you mean that it is very good and deserves to be praised. EG *...a praiseworthy action.* [ADJ QUALIT Formal]

pram /præm/, **prams.** A **pram** is a baby's cot on wheels. EG *...a young mother pushing a pram.* [N COUNT]

prance /prɑːns/, **prances, prancing, pranced. 1** If someone **prances**, they walk or move around with exaggerated movements because they want people to look at them and admire them. EG *...young girls who pranced around town.* [V+A]

2 When a horse **prances**, it moves with quick, high steps. [V: USU+A]

prank /præŋk/, **pranks.** A **prank** is a childish trick. EG *...a boyish prank.* [N COUNT Outdated]

prawn /prɔːn/, **prawns.** A **prawn** is a small shellfish, similar to a shrimp. [N COUNT]

pray /preɪ/, **prays, praying, prayed. 1** When people **pray**, they speak to God in order to give thanks or to ask for his help. EG *He kneeled down and prayed to Allah... The men prayed for forgiveness... She prayed that God would send her the necessary strength.* [V: USU+A OR REPORT: ONLY *that*]

2 When someone wants something very much, you can say that they **pray** for it. EG *He got what he had prayed for, the command of a division... Praying she would not see me, I hurried inside.* [V+*for* OR REPORT: ONLY *that*]

prayer /prɛə/, **prayers. 1 Prayer** is the activity of praying to God. EG *Her eyes were shut and her lips were moving in prayer.* [N UNCOUNT]

2 If you **say** your **prayers**, you pray. [PHRASE]

3 A **prayer** is **3.1** the words that you say when you pray on a particular occasion. EG *I made a brief prayer for her recovery.* **3.2** a set form of words which is used during a religious service. EG *He repeated his favourite passage of the Passover Prayer.* [N COUNT]

4 You can refer to a strong hope that you have as a **prayer**. EG *My one prayer is that I don't live to be really old.* [N COUNT]

5 A short religious service can be referred to as **prayers**. EG *There were family prayers every morning.* [N PLURAL]

pre- is used to form words that describe something as taking place before a particular date, event, or period. For example, a pre-lunch meeting is a meeting that you have before your lunch. EG *...pre-1914 Europe... ...the pre-Christmas period... ...pre-trial interviews.* [PREFIX]

preach /priːtʃ/, **preaches, preaching, preached.**

1 When a member of the clergy **preaches** a sermon or **preaches**, he or she gives a talk on a religious or moral subject during a church service. EG *The chaplain preached to a packed church.* [V+O OR V]

2 When people **preach** a belief or a course of action, they try to persuade other people to accept the belief or to take the course of action. EG *They preach peace while preparing for war... He used to go round the villages preaching Socialism.* [V+O]

3 If someone gives you advice in a boring, moralizing way, you can say that they **are preaching** at you. [V: OFT+*at*]

4 If you say that someone **practises what** they **preach**, you mean that they behave in the way that they encourage other people to behave in; used showing approval. [PHRASE]

preacher /priːtʃə/, **preachers.** A **preacher** is a person, usually a member of the clergy, who preaches sermons as part of a church service. [N COUNT]

preamble /priːæmbəl/, **preambles.** A **preamble** is an introduction that comes before something you say or write. EG *...an intensely long preamble... Philip said quickly without preamble, 'Somebody shot your father.'* [N COUNT OR N UNCOUNT]

precarious /priˈkɛərɪəs/. **1** Something that is **precarious** is in a dangerous position because it is not securely held in place and seems likely to fall. EG *The streams have to be crossed by precarious rows of bricks... The monkeys cling to their mother's fur in a most precarious fashion.* ◊ **precariously.** EG *For the rest of the journey I sat precariously on the roof of the cabin.* [ADJ QUALIT; ◊ ADV]

2 If your situation is **precarious**, you are not in complete control of events and might fail in what you are doing. EG *The management was in a precarious position... Life will be more precarious in the year 2000 than it is now.* ◊ **precariously.** EG *I found myself living, somewhat precariously, from one assignment to another.* [ADJ QUALIT; ◊ ADV]

precaution /priˈkɔːʃən/, **precautions.** A **precaution** is an action that is intended to prevent something dangerous or unpleasant from happening. EG *I had taken the precaution of swallowing two sea sickness tablets... ...fire precautions... As a precaution he had put his wallet in his briefcase... These precautions proved unnecessary.* [N COUNT: USU+SUPP]

precautionary /priˈkɔːʃənəri/. **Precautionary** actions are taken in order to prevent something dangerous or unpleasant from happening. EG *I would have to take precautionary steps to keep him out... Precautionary measures were unnecessary.* [ADJ CLASSIF Formal]

precede /priˈsiːd/, **precedes, preceding, preceded. 1** If one event or period of time **precedes** another, it happens before it. EG *...the drop in temperature that precedes a heavy thunderstorm... The children's dinner was preceded by games.* [V+O Formal]

2 If you **precede** someone somewhere, you go in front of them. EG *She preceded him across the hallway... We were preceded by a huge man called Teddy Brown.* [V+O Formal]

3 A sentence, paragraph, or chapter that **precedes** another one is written or printed just before it. [V+O]

Where would you put a preamble?

◇ **preceding.** EG *...the activities we discussed in the preceding chapter.* ◇ ADJ CLASSIF : ATTRIB

precedence /prɛsɪdəns/. If one thing **takes precedence** over another, it is regarded as more important than the other thing. EG *The peaceful ordering of society takes precedence over every other consideration.* PHRASE Formal

precedent /prɛsɪdənt/, **precedents. 1** A **precedent** is an action or official decision that can be referred to in order to justify taking a similar action or decision. EG *The Supreme Court had already set a precedent... This case was something of a precedent.* N COUNT Formal

2 If there is a **precedent** for something, that thing has happened before, or something similar to it has happened before. EG *There was no precedent for the riots... She set a precedent for women runners... He broke with precedent by making his maiden speech on a controversial subject.* N COUNT OR N UNCOUNT Formal

precept /priːsɛpt/, **precepts.** A **precept** is a general rule that helps you to decide how you should behave in particular circumstances. EG *...precepts of tolerance and forgiveness.* N COUNT Formal

precinct /priːsɪŋkt/, **precincts. 1** A shopping **precinct** is a specially built shopping area in the centre of a town, in which cars are not allowed. N COUNT British

2 In the United States, a **precinct** is a part of a city which has its own police force and fire service. EG *...police at work patrolling the 12th precinct.* N COUNT American

3 The **precincts** of an institution are its buildings and land. EG *Gambling is prohibited within the precincts of the University.* N PLURAL Formal

precious /prɛʃəs/. **1** If you describe something as **precious**, you mean that it is valuable and useful and should not be wasted or used badly. EG *The one resource more precious than any other was land... They have lost precious working time.* ADJ QUALIT

2 Precious objects and materials are worth a lot of money because they are rare. EG *Salt is nearly as precious as gold in many places.* ADJ QUALIT

3 You say that things are **precious** when they are very important to you, often because you associate them with special events or people. EG *I imagine he treasures that letter as one of the precious mementoes of his Presidency.* ADJ QUALIT

4 People sometimes use **precious** to express their dislike for things which other people think are important. EG *I'm sick and tired of your precious brother-in-law... How sentimental you are about your precious ideas.* ADJ CLASSIF : ATTRIB Informal

5 If you describe someone as **precious**, you mean that they behave in a formal and unnatural way. EG *...that rather precious but oddly likeable young man... He has a slightly precious prose style.* ADJ QUALIT

6 If you say that there is **precious little** of something, you mean that there is very little of it. EG *There's precious little they can learn from us... He was a man with no charm and precious few virtues.* PHRASE

precious metal, precious metals. A **precious metal** is a valuable metal such as gold or silver. N COUNT OR N UNCOUNT

precious stone, precious stones. A **precious stone** is a valuable stone that is used for making jewellery. Diamonds, rubies, and sapphires are precious stones. N COUNT

precipice /prɛsɪpɪs/, **precipices.** A **precipice** is a very steep cliff on a mountain. EG *I looked over the precipice.* N COUNT

precipitate /prɪˈsɪpɪteɪt/, **precipitates, precipitating, precipitated.** If something **precipitates** a new event or situation, it causes it to happen, usually suddenly and unexpectedly. EG *This would precipitate an economic crisis... The explosion was precipitated by the start of police enquiries.* V+O Formal

precipitous /prɪˈsɪpɪtəs/. A **precipitous** area of land is high and has very steep sides. EG *...precipitous hillsides... We bumped over the precipitous road to the ferry.* ADJ CLASSIF

précis /preɪsiː/. **Précis** is both the singular and the plural form. It is pronounced /preɪsiːz/ in the plural.
A **précis** is a short piece of writing which contains the main points of a book or report, but not the details. EG *...a comprehensive précis of the main points of the case.* N COUNT

precise /priˈsaɪs/. **1** You use **precise** to emphasize that you are describing something correctly and exactly. EG *At that precise moment we were interrupted by the telephone... The precise nature of the disease has not yet been established.* ADJ CLASSIF : ATTRIB

2 Something that is **precise** is exact and accurate in all its details. EG *Mr Jones gave him precise instructions... The timing had to be very precise... Try to be reasonably precise.* ADJ QUALIT

3 You say **'to be precise'** to indicate that you are giving more detailed or accurate information about what you have just said. EG *I have to be up early – 4 a.m. to be precise.* PHRASE

precisely /priˈsaɪsliˈ/. **1 Precisely** means accurately and exactly. EG *He made the knots precisely, losing no time... Let me explain to you precisely what I am going to do.* ADV

2 You can use **precisely 2.1** to emphasize that you are giving a complete and correct explanation of something. EG *He was furious, precisely because he had not been consulted.* ADV **2.2** to confirm that what someone has just said is true. EG *'So he's a professional assassin?' – 'Precisely.'* CONVENTION

precision /priˈsɪʒəⁿn/. If you do something with **precision**, you do it exactly as it should be done. EG *The attack was carried out with clockwork precision... He had established a reputation for unfailing precision in his job.* N UNCOUNT

preclude /priˈkluːd/, **precludes, precluding, precluded.** If something **precludes** an event or action, it prevents the event or action from happening. EG *This should not preclude a search for a better hypothesis... It sets limits on the powers of the Government, and precludes it from acting unconstitutionally.* V+O : OFT+*from* Formal

precocious /priˈkəʊʃəs/. **Precocious** children behave in a way that makes them seem older than they really are. EG *I have a brilliant, precocious pupil in my class.* ◇ **precociously.** EG *...his precociously articulate children.* ADJ QUALIT ◇ ADV

preconceived /priːkənsiːvd/. If you have **preconceived** ideas about something, you have already decided about it before you have had enough information or experience to form a fair opinion. EG *The development of the idea depended on getting away from preconceived notions.* ADJ CLASSIF : ATTRIB

preconception /priːkəˀnsɛpʃəⁿn/, **preconceptions.** Your **preconceptions** about something are beliefs that you have about it before you have had enough information or experience to form a fair opinion. EG *He tries to deny information that challenges his preconceptions.* N COUNT

precondition /priːkəˀndɪʃəⁿn/, **preconditions.** If one thing is a **precondition** for another thing, it must happen or be done before the second thing can happen or exist. EG *Economic growth was regarded as the precondition for greater equality... Protection of the environment is a precondition of a healthy society.* N COUNT : USU+*for/of* Formal

precursor /priˈkɜːsə/, **precursors.** If something is a **precursor** of something more important, it is similar to it and happens or exists before it. EG *Railways were the precursors of modern transport.* N COUNT : OFT+*of/to* Formal

predator /prɛdətə/, **predators.** A **predator** is an animal that kills and eats other animals. EG *The whiting is a major predator on smaller fish.* N COUNT

predatory /prɛdətəⁿriˈ/. **1 Predatory** animals live by killing other animals for food. ADJ CLASSIF : ATTRIB

2 Predatory people are eager to gain something out of someone else's weakness or suffering. EG *Her sharp dark eyes held a somewhat predatory expression.* ADJ CLASSIF : ATTRIB

predecessor /pri:dɪsɛsə/, **predecessors. 1** Your **predecessor** is the person who had your job before you. EG *She wasn't being paid the same wage as her predecessor.* N COUNT+POSS

2 The **predecessor** of an object or machine is the object or machine that it replaced. N COUNT+POSS

predestination /pri:dɛstɪneɪʃən/ is the belief that people have no control over events because they have already been decided by God or by fate. N UNCOUNT

predestined /pri:dɛstɪnd/. If you say that a situation was **predestined**, you mean that it could not have been prevented or altered because it had already been decided by God or by fate. EG *I was predestined to be a slave.* ADJ CLASSIF

> **PREDET** stands for **predeterminer**
> Words which have the label PREDET in the Extra Column are words which come before a determiner in a noun group. In this dictionary the words 'all, both, half, double, treble, twice, such,' and 'what' are called predeterminers.
> See the entry headed DETERMINERS for more information.

predetermined /pri:dɪtɜ:mɪnd/. If you say that something is **predetermined**, you mean that its form or nature was decided by previous events or by people rather than by chance. EG *He believes that we're all genetically predetermined... The energy industries expanded at their own predetermined rate.* ADJ CLASSIF Formal

predicament /pri'dɪkəmə²nt/, **predicaments.** If you are in a **predicament**, you are in an unpleasant difficult situation. EG *He hasn't realized his predicament... We are in a worse predicament than ever.* N COUNT+SUPP

predicative /pri'dɪkətɪv/. In grammar, if an adjective is in **predicative** position, it comes after a verb. ADJ CLASSIF: ATTRIB

predict /pri'dɪkt/, **predicts, predicting, predicted.** If you **predict** an event, you say that it will happen. EG *He predicted a brilliant future for the child... The government predicts that the region will draw 500,000 tourists a year... You can't predict what they are going to do.* V-SPEECH

predictable /pri'dɪktəbə⁰l/. Something that is **predictable** happens in a way that you can know about in advance. EG *The outcome is not always predictable... Certain conditions have led to fairly predictable kinds of behaviour.* ADJ QUALIT
◊ **predictably.** EG *Predictably, the affair went hopelessly wrong... ...situations where everyone behaves predictably.* ◊ ADV SEN OR ADV
◊ **predictability** /prə'dɪktəbɪlɪ'ti'/. EG *It happened month by month, with boring predictability.* ◊ N UNCOUNT

prediction /pri'dɪkʃə⁰n/, **predictions.** If you make a **prediction** about something, you say what you think will happen. EG *...a prediction of the likely outcome of the next election... That's a very confident prediction... ...methods of prediction.* N COUNT OR N UNCOUNT

predilection /pri:dɪlɛkʃə⁰n/, **predilections.** If you have a **predilection** for something, you have a strong liking for it. EG *...the American predilection for salads with every meal.* N COUNT Formal

predispose /pri:dɪspəʊz/, **predisposes, predisposing, predisposed.** If something **predisposes** you to think or behave in a particular way, it is one of the reasons why you think or behave in that way. ◊ **predisposed.** EG *She was predisposed to be critical.* V+O+to-INF OR to; ◊ ADJ PRED Formal

predisposition /pri:dɪspəzɪʃə⁰n/, **predispositions.** If you have a **predisposition** to behave in a particular way, you tend to behave like that because of the kind of person that you are. EG *She may have inherited a predisposition to murder the man she marries.* N COUNT: USU+SUPP Formal

predominance /pri'dɒmɪnəns/. **1** If there is a **predominance** of one type of person or thing, there are many more of that type than of any other type. EG *...the predominance of traders and businessmen in the party's ranks.* N UNCOUNT: USU+of Formal

2 If someone or something has **predominance**, they have the most power or importance among a group of people or things. EG *We now have total predominance in the European market.* N UNCOUNT Formal

predominant /pri'dɒmɪnənt/. If something is **predominant**, it is more important or noticeable than other things of the same kind. EG *Italian opera became predominant at the end of the 17th century... The predominant mood among policy-makers is one of despair.* ADJ CLASSIF Formal

predominantly /pri'dɒmɪnəntli'/. You use **predominantly** to indicate which feature or quality is most noticeable in a situation. EG *The debates were predominantly about international affairs... Their first reaction was predominantly one of dismay.* ADV

predominate /pri'dɒmɪneɪt/, **predominates, predominating, predominated. 1** If one type of person or thing **predominates** in a group, there are more of that type in the group than any other type. EG *In most churches, women predominate in the congregations.* V Formal

2 When a feature or quality **predominates**, it is the most noticeable one in a situation. EG *Feelings rather than facts predominate.* V Formal

pre-eminent /pri:ɛmɪnə²nt/. If someone or something is **pre-eminent** in a group, they are more important, powerful, or capable than other people or things in the group. EG *For the next thirty years Bryce was the pre-eminent figure in Canadian economic policy.* ADJ CLASSIF
◊ **pre-eminence** /pri: ɛmɪnəns/. EG *No one doubted his pre-eminence in financial matters.* ◊ N UNCOUNT Formal

preen /pri:n/, **preens, preening, preened. 1** When people **preen** themselves, they spend time making themselves look neat and attractive. EG *He preened himself in front of the mirror.* V-REFL

2 When birds **preen** their feathers, they clean them and arrange them neatly using their beaks. EG *A peacock pecked and preened on the lawn.* V+O OR V

prefab /pri:fæb/, **prefabs.** A **prefab** is a house built with parts which have been made in a factory and then quickly put together. N COUNT British

prefabricated /pri'fæbrɪkeɪtɪ²d/. **Prefabricated** buildings are built with parts which have been made in a factory so that they can be easily carried and put together. ADJ CLASSIF: ATTRIB

preface /prɛfɪ's/, **prefaces, prefacing, prefaced. 1** A **preface** is an introduction at the beginning of a book, which explains what the book is about or why it was written. EG *Granville-Barker had written a fine preface to the play.* N COUNT: OFT+to

2 If you **preface** an action or speech with something else, you do or say this other thing first. EG *Each girl prefaced her remarks with 'sorry'.* V+O+with/by Formal

prefect /pri:fɛkt/, **prefects.** A **prefect** is an older pupil at a British school who does special duties and helps the teachers to control the younger pupils. N COUNT

prefer /pri'fɜ:/, **prefers, preferring, preferred.** If you **prefer** one thing to another, you like the first thing better, so you are more likely to choose it if there is a choice. EG *I prefer Barber to his deputy... A glass of sherry? Or would you prefer a cocktail?... The Head Master prefers them to act plays they have written themselves... They prefer to suffer deprivation rather than claim legal aid... I'd prefer that he remain forgotten.* V+O: USU+to OR to-INF; ALSO V+to-INF OR REPORT: ONLY that

preferable /prɛfə⁰rəbə⁰l/. If you say that one thing is **preferable** to another, you mean that it is more desirable or suitable. EG *Gradual change is* ADJ CLASSIF: USU PRED+to

> If one person in a group predominates, is he or she pre-eminent?

preferable to sudden, large-scale change... Many people find this method immensely preferable.
◊ **preferably.** EG *Clean the car from the top, preferably with a hose and warm water.* ◊ ADV SEN

preference /prɛfəʳrəns/, **preferences. 1** If you have a **preference** for something, you would like to have it or do it rather than something else. EG *Employers may show a preference for those with the same outlook... I continue to live in this country by preference... I took the non-stop flight to London, in preference to the two-stage journey via New York... Each of us has personal preferences for certain types of entertainment.* N COUNT OR N UNCOUNT

2 If you give **preference** to someone, you choose them rather than choosing someone else. EG *Preference was given to those who had overseas experience.* N UNCOUNT

preferential /prɛfərɛnʃəl/. If you get **preferential** treatment, you are treated better than other people and therefore have an advantage over them. EG *Disabled people at work should have preferential treatment.* ADJ CLASSIF : ATTRIB

prefix /priːfɪks/, **prefixes.** A **prefix** is a letter or group of letters which is added to the beginning of a word in order to make a new word. See below. N COUNT

> **PREFIX**
> Some letters or groups of letters are labelled PREFIX in the Extra Column. This means that they are not usually used by themselves as words, but they are put immediately in front of a word to form a new word. Sometimes the new word is written as one word, and sometimes the two parts are joined by a hyphen. An example of a group of letters which is labelled **PREFIX** is 'pre-', which forms words that describe something as happening or belonging before a certain time or event. So, for example, 'pre-war' means 'before the war' and 'pre-1960' means 'before 1960'.

pregnancy /prɛgnənsi¹/, **pregnancies. Pregnancy** is the condition of being pregnant or the period of time during which a female is pregnant. EG *The breasts enlarge during pregnancy... She has had fifteen pregnancies.* N UNCOUNT OR N COUNT

pregnant /prɛgnənt/. If a woman or female animal is **pregnant**, she has a baby or babies developing in her body. EG *She married and immediately got pregnant... She was three months pregnant... My mother was pregnant with me at the time.* ADJ CLASSIF

prehistoric /priːhɪstɒrɪk/. **Prehistoric** people and things existed at a time before information was written down. EG *...prehistoric hunters... ...prehistoric cooking pots.* ADJ CLASSIF : ATTRIB

prejudice /prɛdʒʊdɪs/, **prejudices. 1 Prejudice** is an unreasonable dislike of someone or something, for example of a particular group of people. EG *Prejudice against women is becoming less severe... ...racial prejudice... Barber was a man of strong prejudices.* N UNCOUNT OR N COUNT

2 If people show **prejudice** in favour of someone or something, they prefer them, often unreasonably, to other people or other things of the same kind. EG *There was some regrettable prejudice in favour of middle class children.* N UNCOUNT

prejudiced /prɛdʒʊdɪst/. A person who is **prejudiced** against someone has an unreasonable dislike of them. A person who is **prejudiced** in favour of someone has an unreasonable preference for them. EG *People were prejudiced against her... She had been prejudiced in his favour from the start... We all know how difficult it is to reason with a prejudiced person.* ADJ QUALIT

preliminary /pri¹lɪmɪnəʳri¹/, **preliminaries.** **Preliminary** activities or discussions take place in preparation for an event before it starts. EG *...preliminary arrangements... Preliminary discussions on Stage III had already begun.* ▸ used as a noun. EG *He spent a long time on polite preliminaries... Secondary education is a necessary preliminary for university education.* ADJ QUALIT : ATTRIB ▸ N COUNT : USU PLURAL

prelude /prɛljuːd/, **preludes.** You can describe an event as a **prelude** to a more important event when it happens before it and acts as an introduction to it. EG *This speech has been hailed by his friends as the prelude to his return to office.* N COUNT : USU+*to*

premature /prɛmətjʊə/. **1** Something that is **premature** happens earlier than usual or earlier than people expect. EG *This disease produces premature aging... ...the premature departure of the visitors.* ◊ **prematurely.** EG *The warden retired prematurely with a nervous disorder.* ADJ CLASSIF ◊ ADV

2 You can say that something is **premature** when it happens too early and is therefore inappropriate. EG *The final word 'goodbye' had been premature... It's a bit premature to be thinking about having one's biography written.* ADJ QUALIT

3 A **premature** baby is born before the date when it was due to be born. ADJ CLASSIF

premeditated /pri¹mɛdɪteɪtɪ²d/. An action that is **premeditated** is planned or thought about before it is done. EG *...a premeditated act of murder.* ADJ CLASSIF

premier /prɛmjə/, **premiers. 1** The leader of the government of a country is sometimes referred to as the country's **premier**. EG *...the French premier... ...Premier Francisco Pinto Balsemao.* N COUNT

2 Premier is used to describe something that is considered to be the best or most important thing of a particular type. EG *The article referred to Hull as Europe's premier port.* ADJ CLASSIF : ATTRIB

premiere /prɛmɪɛə, prɛmɪə/, **premieres.** The **premiere** of a new play or film is the first public performance of it. EG *The film had its world premiere at San Sebastian.* N COUNT

premiership /prɛmjəʃɪp/. The **premiership** is the position of being the leader of a government. EG *He should never have been considered for the premiership... ...in the later years of his premiership.* N UNCOUNT

premise /prɛmɪs/, **premises. 1** The **premises** of a business or an institution are all the buildings and land that it occupies on one site. EG *Some of the food was grown on the premises... In 1971 the firm moved to new premises in Bethnal Green.* N PLURAL

2 A **premise** is something that you suppose is true and that you use as a basis for developing an idea. EG *...if one accepts the premise that all knowledge comes to us through our senses... I'm questioning whether the whole premise is correct.* N COUNT : USU+SUPP Formal

premium /priːmɪəm/, **premiums. 1** A **premium** is **1.1** an extra sum of money that you have to pay for something in addition to the normal cost. EG *Investors were willing to pay a premium for companies that offered such a potential for growth.* **1.2** a sum of money that you pay regularly to an insurance company for an insurance policy. EG *...tax relief on life insurance premiums.* N COUNT

2 If something is **at a premium**, **2.1** it is being sold at a higher price than usual, for example because it is in short supply. EG *Fertilizer is sold at a premium by government officials.* **2.2** it is wanted or needed, but is difficult to get or achieve. EG *Student flats are at a premium.* PHRASE

3 To **put** or **place a high premium** on a quality or characteristic means to make it especially important or to regard it as especially important. EG *This system places an enormous premium on learning efficiency.* PHRASE

premium bond, premium bonds. Premium bonds are numbered tickets that are sold by the government in Britain. Each month, a computer randomly selects several numbers, and the people whose tickets have those numbers win money. N COUNT

premonition /premənɪʃə°n/, **premonitions.** If you have a **premonition**, you have a feeling that something is going to happen, often something unpleasant. EG *...a premonition of failure... He had a sudden terrible premonition that she had run away.*
N COUNT: USU+SUPP

prenatal /priːneɪtə°l/ is used to describe things relating to the medical care of women during pregnancy. EG *...prenatal classes for expectant mothers.*
ADJ CLASSIF: ATTRIB

preoccupation /priːɒkjə4peɪʃə°n/, **preoccupations.** If you have a **preoccupation** with something, you keep thinking about it because it is important to you. EG *...Alexander's preoccupation with the past... Keeping warm was Morris's main preoccupation in his first few days there.*
N COUNT OR N UNCOUNT

preoccupied /priːɒkjə4paɪd/. Someone who is **preoccupied** is thinking a lot about something, and so hardly notices other things. EG *His wife becomes more and more preoccupied with the children... She seemed rather preoccupied and distant.*
ADJ QUALIT: OFT+*with*

preoccupy /priːɒkjə4paɪ/, **preoccupies, preoccupying, preoccupied.** If something **preoccupies** you, you think about it a lot. EG *This is a question which increasingly preoccupies me.*
V+O

> **PREP** stands for **preposition**
> Words that are labelled PREP in the Extra Column are prepositions such as 'for', 'with', and 'from'. Prepositions always have an object.
> **1** The object can be a noun, noun group, or pronoun, as in *...the search* ***for*** *truth...helping learners* ***with*** *real English ...I've never thought* ***about*** *it.*
> **2** The object can be a clause with a verb in the '-ing' form, as in ***By*** *doing this, he achieved his aim.*

preparation /prepəreɪʃə°n/, **preparations. 1** The **preparation** of something is the activity of getting it ready. EG *Benn was involved in the preparation of Labour's manifesto... ...food preparation... Education should be a preparation for life.*
N UNCOUNT: USU+SUPP

2 Preparations are all the arrangements that are made for a future event. EG *He'll have to make preparations for the funeral... Elaborate preparations were being made to get me out.*
N PLURAL

3 A **preparation** is a mixture that has been prepared for use as food, medicine, or a cosmetic. EG *...beauty preparations.*
N COUNT Formal

preparatory /prə2pærətə°ri1/. **Preparatory** actions are done before doing something else, as a preparation for it. EG *...a preparatory report... ...preparatory language courses.*
ADJ CLASSIF: ATTRIB Formal

preparatory school, preparatory schools. A **preparatory school** is the same as a prep school.
N COUNT OR N UNCOUNT Formal

prepare /priˈpeə/, **prepares, preparing, prepared. 1** If you **prepare** something, you make it ready for something that is going to happen. EG *A room has been prepared for you... He had spent days preparing the site of the statue... Schools have to prepare children for life in the community.*
V+O

2 If you **prepare** for an event or action that will happen soon, you get yourself ready for it. EG *The guests prepared for their departure... I jumped up and prepared to defend myself... Prepare yourself for a shock.*
V: OFT+*for* OR *to*-INF; ALSO V-REFL+*for*

3 When you **prepare** food, you get it ready to be eaten, for example by cooking it. EG *He had spent all morning preparing the meal... She had prepared a thermos of hot onion soup.*
V+O

prepared /priˈpeəd/. **1** If you are **prepared** to do something, you are willing to do it if necessary. EG *What sort of risks are you prepared to take?... I'm prepared to say I was wrong... Many countries seem prepared to consider nuclear energy.*
ADJ PRED +*to*-INF

2 If you are **prepared** for something, you are ready for it because you think that it might happen. EG *I was not really prepared for her fits of boredom... Be prepared for power cuts by buying lots of candles.*
ADJ PRED: OFT+*for*

3 Something that is **prepared** has been done or made beforehand, so that it is ready when it is needed. EG *He read out a prepared statement... ...a specially prepared fluorescent screen.*
ADJ CLASSIF

preponderance /priˈpɒndə°rəns/. If there is a **preponderance** of one type of person or thing in a group, there are more of that type than of any other. EG *There is a definite preponderance of women among those who study English Literature.*
N UNCOUNT: USU+*of* Formal

preposition /prepəzɪʃə°n/, **prepositions.** A **preposition** is a word such as 'by', 'for', 'into', or 'with', which usually has a noun group as its object. Words which are prepositions have PREP in the Extra Column. See the entry headed PREP for more information.
N COUNT

preposterous /priˈpɒstə°rəs/. If you describe something as **preposterous**, you mean that it is extremely unreasonable and foolish. EG *The situation was preposterous... ...a preposterous idea.*
ADJ QUALIT

prep school, prep schools. A **prep school** is a private school in Britain where children are educated until the age of 11 or 13.
N COUNT OR N UNCOUNT

prerequisite /priːrekwɪzɪt/, **prerequisites.** If one thing is a **prerequisite** for another, it must happen or exist before the other thing is possible. EG *Confidence is a prerequisite for mastering other more formal skills... Ownership of great estates was a prerequisite of power.*
N COUNT: USU+SUPP Formal

prerogative /priˈrɒgətɪv/, **prerogatives.** If something is the **prerogative** of a particular person or group, it is a privilege or a power that only they have. EG *...luxuries which were considered the prerogative of the rich.*
N COUNT: USU+*of* Formal

prescribe /priˈskraɪb/, **prescribes, prescribing, prescribed. 1** If a doctor **prescribes** medicine or treatment for you, he or she tells you what medicine or treatment to have. EG *Her doctor prescribed a sedative.*
V+O

2 If someone **prescribes** an action or duty, they state formally that it must be carried out. EG *The factory laws prescribed a heavy fine for contravention of this rule.* ◇ **prescribed.** EG *The list of prescribed duties has been drawn up by the federation.*
V+O Formal; ◇ ADJ CLASSIF: ATTRIB

prescription /priˈskrɪpʃə°n/, **prescriptions. 1** A **prescription** is **1.1** a piece of paper on which a doctor has written the name of a medicine you need. You give it to a chemist in exchange for the medicine. EG *...a prescription for sleeping tablets.* **1.2** medicine which a doctor has told you to take. EG *I'm not sleeping even with the prescription Ackerman gave me.*
N COUNT

2 If a medicine is available **on prescription**, you can get it from a chemist if a doctor gives you a prescription for it. EG *...a drug which used to be available only on prescription.*
PHRASE

presence /prezəns/, **presences. 1** If you talk about someone's **presence** in a place, you are referring to the fact that they are there. EG *He tried to justify his presence in Belfast... He was aware of her presence... He had to cope with the presence of her family.*
N UNCOUNT +POSS

2 If you are **in** someone's **presence**, you are in the same place as they are. EG *I felt comfortable in her presence... Haldane repeated his statement in the presence of the chairman.*
PHRASE

3 If you say that someone has **presence**, you mean that they impress people by their appearance and manner. EG *He had tremendous physical presence.*
N UNCOUNT

4 A **presence** is a person or creature that you
N COUNT

Who do you give a prescription to?

cannot see, but that you are aware of. EG *...a mysterious winged presence, felt rather than seen.*

presence of mind is the ability to act quickly and sensibly in a difficult situation. EG *Richard had the presence of mind to step forward and pick it up.* N UNCOUNT

present, presents, presenting, presented; pronounced /prɛzənt/ when it is an adjective or noun, and /pri[1]zɛnt/ when it is a verb.
1 You use **present** to describe people and things that exist now, rather than those that existed in the past or those that may exist in the future. EG *The present system has many failings... The present chairperson is a woman... Economic planning cannot succeed in present conditions.* ADJ CLASSIF : ATTRIB ● **The present day** is the period of history that is taking place now. EG *This tradition has continued till the present day.* ● PHRASE ● See also **present-day**.
2 The **present** is the period of time that is taking place now and the things that are happening now. EG *We have to come to terms with the present.* N SING : *the*+N
3 If something is happening **at present**, it is happening now. EG *He is at present serving a life sentence... I don't want to get married at present.* PHRASE
4 If a situation exists **for the present**, it exists now but is likely to change. EG *For the present she continues with the antibiotics... That's all for the present, Miss Livingstone.* PHRASE
5 If someone is **present** at an event, they are there. EG *He had been present at the dance... There was a photographer present.* ADJ PRED
6 A **present** is something that you give to someone, for example at Christmas or when you visit them. EG *I gave him an atlas as a birthday present... He had brought home a present for her.* N COUNT
7 If you **present** someone with something such as a prize, or if you **present** it to them, you formally give it to them. EG *He presented her with a signed copy of his book... One of his constituents presented a petition to Parliament.* V+O+*with*, OR V+O : OFT+*to*
8 If something **presents** a difficulty or a challenge, it causes it or provides it. EG *The tornado presented the island with severe problems... Everest presented a challenge to Hillary.* V+O : OFT+*to*, OR V+O+*with*
9 When you **present** information, you give it to people in a formal way. EG *...a way of presenting new material... Our teachers were trying to present us with an accurate picture of history.* V+O : OFT+*to*, OR V+O+*with*
10 If you **present** someone or something in a particular way, you describe them in that way. EG *Her lawyer wanted to present her in the most favourable light... They present the British as the colonialist oppressor.* V+O+A
11 If you **present** yourself somewhere, you officially arrive there, for example for an appointment. EG *The next morning I presented myself at their offices.* V-REFL+A
12 If an opportunity **presents** itself, it occurs, often when you do not expect it. EG *Was he going to do it again if the opportunity presented itself?* V-REFL
13 If someone **presents** a programme on television or radio, they introduce each part of it or each person on it. EG *...'University Link', compiled and presented by Dr Brian Smith.* V+O
14 If you **present** someone to an important person, you officially introduce them. EG *May I present Mr Rudolph Wallace.* V+O Formal

presentable /pri[1]zɛntəbə[0]l/. If you say that someone or something is **presentable**, you mean that they are quite attractive or quite good, and are suitable for other people to see. EG *She looked quite presentable... ...some of his more presentable pictures.* ADJ QUALIT

presentation /prɛzənteɪʃə[0]n/, **presentations. 1** The **presentation** of information is the process of making it available to people, for example by broadcasting it or printing it. EG *...the collection and presentation of statistical data.* N UNCOUNT : OFT+*of*
2 Presentation is the appearance of something and the impression that it gives to people. EG *Presentation is very important in cooking.* N UNCOUNT
3 A **presentation** is **3.1** a formal event in which someone is given something such as a prize. EG *I said I would not be able to attend the presentation.* N COUNT
3.2 a lecture or a talk about something. EG *Darwin was urged to deliver a presentation on the subject to the Linnean Society.* N COUNT Formal **3.3** something that is performed before an audience, for example a play or a ballet. EG *He directed a theatrical presentation of 'Danton's Death'.* N COUNT+SUPP Formal

present-day. You use **present-day** to describe people and things that exist now. EG *...present-day Japanese children... ...social conditions in present-day India.* ADJ CLASSIF : ATTRIB

presenter /pri[1]zɛntə/, **presenters.** A **presenter** is a person who introduces a television or radio programme, especially a programme that gives news or information. N COUNT

presently /prɛzəntli[1]/. **1** You use **presently** to indicate that something happened quite a short time after the time or event that you have just mentioned. EG *Presently I got the whole story.* ADV SEN OR ADV
2 If you say that something will happen **presently**, you mean that it will happen quite soon. EG *He will be here presently.* ADV
3 If you say that something is **presently** happening, you mean that it is happening now. EG *...the oil rigs that are presently in operation.* ADV

present participle, present participles. The **present participle** of an English verb is the form that ends in '-ing'. It is used to form some tenses, and to form adjectives and nouns from a verb. N COUNT

present tense. The **present tense** of a verb is used mainly when you want to talk about things that happen or exist at the time of speaking or writing. N SING : *the*+N

preservative /pri[1]zɜːvətɪv/, **preservatives.** A **preservative** is a chemical that prevents things from decaying. Some preservatives are added to food, and others are used to treat wood or metal. N MASS

preserve /pri[1]zɜːv/, **preserves, preserving, preserved. 1** If you **preserve** a situation or condition, you make sure that it remains as it is, and is not changed or ended. EG *We are interested in preserving world peace... I stood there, determined to preserve my dignity.* V+O ◊ **preservation** /prɛzəveɪʃə[0]n/. EG *...the preservation of democracy.* ◊ N UNCOUNT
2 If you **preserve** something, you take action to save it or protect it from damage. EG *...a big house which had been preserved as a museum... ...a paint spray which would preserve it from corrosion.* V+O
3 If you **preserve** food, you prevent it from decaying so that you can store it for a long time. EG *Deep freezing is the simplest way of preserving food.* V+O
4 Preserves are foods such as jam and marmalade that are made by cooking fruit with a large amount of sugar and that can be stored for a long time. N MASS

preserved /pri[1]zɜːvd/. Something that is well **preserved** is in good condition or is unchanged even though it is very old. EG *There are some excellently preserved fossilized tree stumps.* ADJ QUALIT

preside /pri[1]zaɪd/, **presides, presiding, presided.** If you **preside** over a formal meeting or event, you are in charge or act as the chairperson. EG *He had presided over a seminar for theoretical physicists.* V : USU +*over/at* Formal

presidency /prɛzɪdənsi[1]/. The **presidency** is the position of being the president of a country. EG *He is to be nominated for the presidency.* N SING : *the*+N, OR N UNCOUNT

president /prɛzɪdənt/, **presidents. 1** The **president** of a country that has no king or queen is the person who has the highest political position and is the leader of the country. EG *The French president arrived in the United States this week... ...the assassination of President Kennedy.* N COUNT
2 The **president** of an organization is the person N COUNT

who has the highest position in it. EG *...the former President of the Royal Academy.*

presidential /prɛzɪdɛnʃəºl/. **Presidential** activities or things relate or belong to a president. EG *...the next presidential election... ...John Kennedy's presidential airplane.* — ADJ CLASSIF : ATTRIB

press /prɛs/, **presses, pressing, pressed. 1** If you **press** one thing against another, you hold it or push it firmly against the other thing. EG *Stroganov pressed his hand to his heart... She pressed her palms together... The animal presses itself against a tree trunk.* — V+O+A

2 If you **press** a button or switch, you push it with your finger in order to make a machine or device work. EG *He could press the buzzer and wake her... Mrs Carstairs pressed an electric bell.* ▸ used as a noun. EG *All this can be called up at the press of the right button.* — V+O; ▸ N COUNT

3 If you **press** on something or **press** it, you push hard against it with your hand or your foot. EG *The driver may press harder on the accelerator... She pressed down upon the velvet cloth... ...pressing the mattress with his fingers.* — V : USU+A, OR V+O

4 If you **press** clothes, you iron them in order to get rid of the creases. EG *He always pressed his trousers before wearing them.* — V+O

5 If you **press** for something, you try hard to persuade someone to give it to you or to agree to it. EG *He pressed for full public ownership... The labourers formed a union to press for higher wages.* — V+*for*

6 If you **press** someone, you try hard to persuade them to do something or to tell you something. EG *He pressed me to have a cup of coffee with him... Don't press me on this point.* — V+O : USU+A

7 If you **press** something on someone, you give it to them and insist that they take it. EG *His aunt was pressing upon him cups of tea and cookies.* — V+O+*on/upon*

8 If you **press** charges against someone, you make an official accusation against them which has to be decided in a court of law. EG *They decided against pressing charges.* — V+O

9 The **Press** refers to **9.1** newspapers. EG *...the British press... ...an amusing story in the press... Press comments could be merciless.* **9.2** journalists. EG *I got to know a lot of the American press... Granville-Barker would never meet the press.* — N COLL : SING, *the*+N

10 If someone **gets a good press**, they are praised in the newspapers, or on television or radio. If they **get a bad press**, they are criticized in the newspapers, or on television or radio. EG *Civil servants tend to get rather a poor press... I hope he'll get a fairer press in his own country.* — PHRASE

11 A printing **press** is a machine used for printing books, newspapers, and leaflets. EG *Since then the presses have scarcely stopped turning.* — N COUNT

12 See also **pressed**, **pressing**.

press on. If you **press on**, you continue doing something in spite of difficulties. EG *They courageously pressed on with their vital repair work.* — PHRASAL VB : V+ADV

press conference, press conferences. When a famous person such as a politician or film star gives a **press conference**, he or she holds a meeting in order to answer questions put by newspaper and television reporters. — N COUNT

pressed /prɛst/. If you say that you are **pressed** for money or **pressed** for time, you mean that you do not have enough money or time at the moment. EG *He was always pressed for money.* — ADJ PRED : OFT+*for*

pressing /prɛsɪŋ/. Something that is **pressing** needs to be dealt with immediately. EG *I remembered a pressing appointment with the doctor.* — ADJ QUALIT

pressure /prɛʃə/, **pressures, pressuring, pressured. 1 Pressure** is **1.1** force that you produce when you press hard on something. EG *It took a bit of pressure to make the lid close... He disliked the pressure of her hand... It bent when pressure was put upon it.* **1.2** the force that a quantity of gas or liquid has on a surface that it touches. EG *I'll just check the tyre pressure... The water pressure may need adjusting.* ● See also **blood pressure**. — N UNCOUNT; N UNCOUNT +SUPP

2 If someone puts **pressure** on you, they try to persuade you to do something. EG *For a long time he's been trying to put pressure on us to go... The main pressure for change is coming from the unions... ...under pressure from feminists.* — N UNCOUNT : USU+SUPP

3 If you feel **pressure**, you feel that you must do a lot of tasks or make a lot of decisions, especially when you have very little time. EG *Parents can suffer from too much pressure... We do our best work under pressure... ...the pressures of public life.* — N UNCOUNT OR N PLURAL

4 If you **pressure** someone to do something, you try forcefully to persuade them to do it. EG *The children are not pressured to eat... Some young people are pressured into staying on at school.* — V+O : USU+*to*-INF OR *into*

pressure cooker, pressure cookers. A **pressure cooker** is a large saucepan with a lid that fits tightly, in which you can cook food quickly using steam at high pressure. — N COUNT

pressure group, pressure groups. A **pressure group** is an organized group of people who are trying to persuade a government or other authority to do something, for example to change a law. EG *There followed six years of campaigning by pressure groups.* — N COUNT

pressurize /prɛʃəraɪz/, **pressurizes, pressurizing, pressurized;** also spelled **pressurise.** If you **pressurize** someone to do something, you try forcefully to persuade them to do it. EG *It was a move designed to pressurise workers to return earlier.* — V+O : USU+*to*-INF OR *into*

pressurized /prɛʃəraɪzd/; also spelled **pressurised.** The pressure inside a **pressurized** container or area is different from the pressure outside it. EG *...the pressurized cabin of a Boeing 707.* — ADJ CLASSIF

prestige /prɛstiːʒ/. If you have **prestige,** other people admire you because of your position in society or the high quality of your work. EG *He is looking for a job with some prestige attached to it.* — N UNCOUNT

prestigious /prɛstɪdʒɪºəs/. Something that is **prestigious** is important, influential, and admired by people. EG *...one of the most prestigious universities in the country.* — ADJ QUALIT

presumably /priˈzjuːməbliˈ/. If you say that something is **presumably** the case, you mean that you think it is the case, although you are not certain. EG *Presumably they're a bit more expensive... The bomb was presumably intended to go off while the meeting was in progress.* — ADV SEN

presume /priˈzjuːm/, **presumes, presuming, presumed. 1** If you **presume** that something is the case, you think that it is the case, although you are not certain. EG *I presume you know why I am here... If you do not come, I shall presume the deal is off... You are married, I presume?* — V : USU+REPORT : ONLY *that*

2 If something **is presumed** to be the case, people believe that it is the case, although they are not certain. EG *...Larry Burrows, missing and presumed dead since 1971... He got away and is presumed to be living in Spain.* — V+O+*to*-INF OR C : USU PASS

presumption /priˈzʌmpʃəºn/, **presumptions.** A **presumption** is something that is presumed by someone to be true. EG *...based on the presumption that heaven has four walls.* — N COUNT : USU+SUPP

presumptuous /priˈzʌmptjʊəs/. If you describe someone's behaviour as **presumptuous**, you mean that they are doing things that they have no right or authority to do. EG *It is dangerous and presumptuous to interfere between parents and children.* — ADJ QUALIT

presuppose /priːsəpəʊz/, **presupposes, presupposing, presupposed.** If one thing **presupposes** another, the first thing cannot be true or exist unless the second is true or exists. EG *The whole* — V+O OR V+REPORT : ONLY *that* Formal

If you presume that something is the case, are you presumptuous?

myth of the Ascension presupposes there is a Heaven physically above the Earth... All arguments must presuppose logic.

pretence /pri'tens/, **pretences;** spelled **pretense** in American English. **1** A **pretence** is an action or way of behaving that is intended to make people believe something that is not true. EG *She leapt up with a pretence of eagerness... Work is not available to them even though we make a pretence that it is.* N COUNT OR N UNCOUNT

2 If you do something **under false pretences**, you do it when people do not know the truth about you and your intentions. EG *I felt that I was taking money under false pretences.* PHRASE

pretend /pri'tend/, **pretends, pretending, pretended.** If you **pretend** that something is the case, you act in a way that is intended to make people believe that it is the case, although in fact it is not. EG *Her father tried to pretend that nothing unusual had happened... Philip politely pretended not to have heard this remark... He pretended to fall over.* V+REPORT: ONLY *that*, OR V+*to*-INF

pretension /pri'tenʃᵊn/, **pretensions.** Someone with **pretensions** claims or pretends that they are more important than they really are. EG *He has pretensions to greatness... He is evidently a person of some social pretension.* N UNCOUNT OR N COUNT

pretentious /pri'tenʃəs/. If you say that someone or something is **pretentious**, you mean that they try to seem important or significant, but you do not think that they are. EG *...one of the most pretentious films of all time.* ADJ QUALIT

pretext /pri:tekst/, **pretexts.** A **pretext** is a reason which you pretend has caused you to do something. EG *The Government invented a 'plot' as a pretext for arresting opposition leaders... They withdrew their support on an ideological pretext.* N COUNT

pretty /prɪti'/, **prettier, prettiest. 1** If you describe someone, especially a girl, as **pretty**, you mean that they are nice to look at and attractive in a delicate way. EG *Who's that pretty little girl?... She looked pretty in her long white dress.* ◇ **prettily.** EG *She smiled prettily.* ADJ QUALIT ◇ ADV

2 A place or a thing that is **pretty** is nice to look at in a rather conventional way. EG *...a very pretty garden... The wallpaper was very pretty, covered in roses.* ◇ **prettiness.** EG *...the fairy-tale prettiness of the town.* ADJ QUALIT ◇ N UNCOUNT

3 You can use **pretty** before an adjective or adverb to mean 'quite' or 'rather'. EG *I thought it was pretty good... I'm pretty certain she enjoys it.* SUBMOD Informal

4 Pretty much or **pretty well** means 'almost'. EG *I felt pretty much the same... She hated pretty well all of them.* PHRASE Informal

prevail /pri'veɪl/, **prevails, prevailing, prevailed. 1** If a custom or belief **prevails** in a particular place at a particular time, it is normal or most common in that place at that time. EG *...the traditions that have prevailed in Britain since the 17th century.* ◇ **prevailing.** EG *The prevailing view shifted still further.* V+A ◇ ADJ CLASSIF: ATTRIB

2 If a proposal or a principle **prevails**, it gains influence or is accepted, often after an argument. EG *In the end, common sense prevailed... Political arguments had prevailed over economic sense.* V: OFT+*over*

prevalent /prevələnt/. A condition or belief that is **prevalent** is very common. EG *...the liberal atmosphere prevalent in the late 1960s... ...one theory prevalent among scientists.* ◇ **prevalence** /prevələns/. EG *...the prevalence of snobbery in Britain.* ADJ QUALIT ◇ N SING: *the*+N+*of* Formal

prevaricate /pri'værɪkeɪt/, **prevaricates, prevaricating, prevaricated.** If you **prevaricate**, you do not give a direct, truthful answer or a firm decision when people want one. EG *The doctors prevaricated, arguing the need for additional tests.* V

prevent /pri'vent/, **prevents, preventing, prevented. 1** If you **prevent** someone from doing something, you do not allow them to start doing it. EG *My only idea was to prevent him from speaking... Have you been instructed to prevent me entering?* V+O+*from* OR -ING

2 If people or things **prevent** something from happening, they ensure that it does not happen. EG *It was not enough to prevent war... ...a layer of fat beneath the skin that prevents their body heat from escaping.* V+O: OFT+*from* OR -ING

preventative /pri'ventətɪv/ means the same as preventive. EG *...preventative medicine.* ADJ CLASSIF: ATTRIB

prevention /pri'venʃᵊn/ is action that prevents something from happening. EG *...the prevention of cruelty to animals... ...fire prevention.* N UNCOUNT: OFT+*of*

preventive /pri'ventɪv/. **Preventive** actions are intended to help prevent things such as disease or crime. EG *Preventive measures are essential... ...preventive medicine.* ADJ CLASSIF: ATTRIB

preview /pri:vju:/, **previews.** A **preview** is an opportunity to see something such as a film or an art exhibition before it is officially shown to the public. EG *Welcome to the press preview of the Seyer Street exhibition.* N COUNT

previous /pri:vɪəs/. **1** A **previous** event or thing is one that happened or came before the one that you are talking about. EG *He had children from a previous marriage... We were always told how valuable our previous career experience would be.* ADJ CLASSIF: ATTRIB

2 You refer to the period of time or the thing immediately before the one that you are talking about as the **previous** one. EG *They had arrived the previous night... The previous Government had decided to build it.* ADJ CLASSIF: ATTRIB

previously /pri:vjəsli'/. **1 Previously** means at some time before the period that you are talking about. EG *I had previously lived the life of a miser... He was previously British consul in Atlanta.* ADV

2 You can use **previously** to say how much earlier one event was than another event. EG *This load had been dispatched three months previously... They had retired ten years previously.* ADV

pre-war /pri: wɔ:/. **Pre-war** things existed before a war, especially the 1939-45 war. EG *...the prewar telephone network.* ADJ CLASSIF: ATTRIB

prey /preɪ/, **preys, preying, preyed. 1** The creatures that an animal hunts and eats in order to live are its **prey**. EG *The mole seeks its prey entirely underground.* • See also **bird of prey**. N UNCOUNT +POSS

2 If someone or something **falls prey to** a person or their action, they are taken control of by that person. EG *...to help prevent the company falling prey to a Stock Exchange raid.* PHRASE

prey on. 1 An animal that **preys on** another kind of animal lives by catching and eating this kind of animal. EG *The amphibians were hunters, preying on worms and insects.* **2** If something **preys on** your **mind,** you cannot stop thinking and worrying about it. EG *Barton reluctantly agreed, but the decision preyed on his mind.* PHRASAL VB: V+PREP, HAS PASS; V+PREP

price /praɪs/, **prices, pricing, priced. 1** The **price** of something is the amount of money that you must pay in order to buy it. EG *The price of firewood has risen steeply... The price is still only £1.05... Petrol will continue to drop in price.* • See also **cut-price**. N COUNT: USU+SUPP, OR N UNCOUNT

2 The **price** that you pay for something that you want is an unpleasant thing that you have to do or suffer in order to get it. EG *This was the price that had to be paid for progress... This is a small price to pay for freedom... The price of such protection was an inevitable dependence.* N SING+SUPP

3 If you want something **at any price**, you are determined to get it, even if unpleasant things happen as a result. EG *...the desire to win at any price... His slogan is peace at any price.* PHRASE

4 If you get something that you want **at a price**, you get it but something unpleasant happens as a result. EG *Ford's grip on the market is one obtained at a price.* PHRASE

5 If something **is priced** at a particular amount, it costs that amount to buy. EG *The least expensive* V+O: USU PASS *will be priced at £7,000... ...reasonably priced accommodation.*

priceless /praɪslɪ[2]s/. Something that is **priceless** 1 is worth a very large amount of money. EG *...a beautiful priceless sapphire.* 2 is extremely useful. EG *This priceless asset has enabled him to win innumerable tournaments.* ADJ CLASSIF

pricey /praɪsi[1]/. If you say that something is **pricey**, you mean that it is expensive. EG *The book was a bit pricey.* ADJ QUALIT Informal

prick /prɪk/, **pricks, pricking, pricked. 1** If you **prick** something or **prick** holes in it, you make small holes in it with a sharp object such as a pin. EG *Prick the apples all over, using the prongs of a fork... I pricked little holes in the wrapping... He pricked himself with the needle.* V+O : USU+A

2 If something sharp **pricks** you, it sticks into you or presses your skin and causes you pain. EG *Sharp thorns pricked his knees.* V+O

3 If tears **prick** your eyes, you feel small, sharp pains in your eyes because you are about to cry. V+O Literary

4 A **prick** is a small, sharp pain that you get when something pricks you. EG *...the sharp pricks as the pellets struck his hands.* N COUNT

prick up. 1 If an animal **pricks up** its **ears**, its ears suddenly point straight up. PHRASE **2** If you **prick up** your **ears**, you suddenly listen eagerly when you hear something interesting or important. EG *He pricked up his ears at the sound of his father's voice.* PHRASE

prickle /prɪkə[0]l/, **prickles, prickling, prickled.**
1 Prickles are small, sharp points that stick out from leaves or from the stalks of plants. N COUNT : OFT PLURAL

2 If your skin **prickles**, it feels as if a lot of small, sharp points are being stuck into it, either because of something touching it or because you feel a strong emotion. EG *The shirt I was wearing made my skin prickle... My skin prickled with fear.* V : OFT+*with*
▸ used as a noun. EG *I felt a prickle of pleasure.* ▸ N COUNT

prickly /prɪkli[1]/. **1** Something such as a plant that is **prickly** has a lot of sharp points sticking out from it. EG *...prickly thorn bushes.* ADJ QUALIT

2 Someone who is **prickly** loses their temper very easily. EG *...a prickly and tiresome man.* ADJ QUALIT

pride /praɪd/, **prides, priding, prided. 1 Pride** is a feeling of satisfaction which you have because you or people close to you have done something good or possess something good. EG *His mother looked at him with affection and pride... She pointed with pride to the fine horses she had trained.* N UNCOUNT

2 If you **take pride** in something that you have or do, you feel pleased and happy because of it. EG *I take great pride in the success of my children.* PHRASE

3 If you **pride** yourself on a quality or skill that you have, you are very proud of it. EG *Mrs Hochstadt prided herself on her intelligence... They prided themselves on being patient.* V-REFL+*on*

4 Someone or something that is your **pride and joy** is very important to you and makes you feel very happy. EG *Their baby daughter was their pride and joy.* PHRASE

5 Pride is also **5.1** a sense of dignity and self-respect. EG *My pride did not allow me to complain too often... Pride alone prevented her from giving up.* **5.2** a feeling of being superior to other people. EG *There is a lot of pride in the phrase 'no one can fool me'.* N UNCOUNT

6 If you **swallow** your **pride**, you decide that you have to do something that you are rather ashamed to do. EG *He swallowed his pride and accepted the money.* PHRASE

7 If something has **pride of place**, it is the most important thing in a group of things. EG *Musical compositions take pride of place in the festivities.* PHRASE

priest /priːst/, **priests.** A **priest** is **1** a member of the Christian clergy in the Catholic, Anglican, or Orthodox church. **2** a man in many non-Christian religions who has particular duties and responsibilities in the place where people worship. EG *...a Buddhist priest.* N COUNT

priestess /priːstɛs/, **priestesses.** A **priestess** is a woman in a non-Christian religion who has particular duties and responsibilities in the place where people worship. N COUNT

priesthood /priːsthʊd/. The **priesthood** is the position of being a priest. EG *...the responsibilities of the priesthood.* N SING : *the*+N

priestly /priːstli[1]/ is used to describe things that belong or relate to a priest. EG *...priestly duties... ...a priestly blessing.* ADJ CLASSIF : ATTRIB

prig /prɪg/, **prigs.** If you call someone a **prig**, you mean that they are irritating because they behave in a very moral way and disapprove of other people's behaviour. EG *Jason was a self-righteous prig.* N COUNT

priggish /prɪgɪʃ/. If you describe someone as **priggish**, you mean that they are irritating because they are very moral and disapproving. ADJ QUALIT

prim /prɪm/. If you describe someone as **prim**, you mean that they behave very correctly and are easily shocked by anything rude or improper; often used showing disapproval. EG *...a prim, severe woman.* ADJ QUALIT ◊ **primly.** EG *His sister sat primly with her legs together.* ◊ ADV

prima donna /priːmə dɒnə/, **prima donnas. 1** A **prima donna** is the main female singer in an opera. N COUNT

2 If you describe someone as a **prima donna**, you mean that they are difficult to deal with because their moods change suddenly. EG *Bob was a prima donna who played heartily at office politics.* N COUNT

primaeval /praɪmiːvə[0]l/. See **primeval.**

primarily /praɪmərəli[1]/. You use **primarily** to indicate the most important feature of something or reason for something. EG *These linguists were concerned primarily with the structure of languages... The issue was primarily a political one.* ADV

primary /praɪməri[1]/, **primaries. 1** You use **primary** to describe something that is extremely important or most important for someone or something. EG *One of Europe's primary requirements was minerals... She gets her primary satisfaction from her career.* ADJ CLASSIF : USU ATTRIB

2 Primary education is given to pupils between the ages of 5 and 11 in Britain. ADJ CLASSIF : ATTRIB

3 A **primary** is an election in an American state in which people vote for someone to become a candidate for a political office. N COUNT

primary colour, primary colours. The **primary colours** are red, yellow, and blue. They can be mixed together in different ways to make all other colours. N COUNT

primary school, primary schools. A **primary school** is a school in Britain for children between the ages of 5 and 11. N COUNT OR N UNCOUNT

primate /praɪmeɪt, -mə[1]t/, **primates.** A **primate** is a member of the group of mammals which includes humans, monkeys, and apes. N COUNT

prime /praɪm/, **primes, priming, primed. 1** You use **prime** to describe **1.1** something that is most important in a situation. EG *What was said was of prime importance... Maths is no longer a prime requirement for a career in accountancy.* **1.2** something that is of the best possible quality. EG *He wants his herd delivered in prime condition.* **1.3** an example of a particular kind of thing that is absolutely typical. EG *We had, a few years ago, a prime example of the power of the press to embarrass.* ADJ CLASSIF : ATTRIB

2 Someone's or something's **prime** is the stage in their existence when they are at their strongest, most active, or most successful. EG *I had been a* N SING+POSS

Should a Prime Minister be principled?

good player in my prime... ...machines past their prime.

3 If you **prime** someone about something, you give them information about it beforehand, so that they are prepared for it. EG *I had primed him for this meeting... He is well primed to enter the profession.* V+O : USU+A

4 If you **prime** wood, you cover it with special paint to prepare it for the main layer of paint. V+O

Prime Minister, Prime Ministers. . The leader of the government in some countries is called the **Prime Minister**. EG *The Prime Minister publicly deplored the affair... ...the Prime Minister of France.* N PROPER OR N COUNT

primeval /praɪmiːvəºl/; also spelled **primaeval.** You use **primeval** to describe things that belong to a very early period in the history of the world. EG *...primeval forests... ...our primeval ancestors.* ADJ CLASSIF : ATTRIB

primitive /prɪmɪtɪv/. **1 Primitive** means **1.1** belonging to a society of people who live in a very simple way, usually without industries or a writing system. EG *...anthropologists who have studied primitive tribes... The most commonly cited example of a primitive device is the abacus.* **1.2** of an early type. EG *...primitive insect-eating mammals... ...primitive microprocessors.* ADJ CLASSIF : USU ATTRIB

2 If you describe something as **primitive**, you mean that it is very simple in style or very old-fashioned. EG *The sleeping accommodation is somewhat primitive.* ADJ QUALIT

primrose /prɪmrəʊz/, **primroses.** A **primrose** is a wild plant which has pale yellow flowers in spring. N COUNT

prince /prɪns/, **princes.** A **prince** is **1** a male member of a royal family, especially the son of the king or queen of a country. EG *...Prince Charles.* **2** the male royal ruler of a small country or state. N COUNT

princely /prɪnsli¹/. **1** Something that is **princely** belongs to a prince or is suitable for a prince. EG *...the princely courts of Asia.* ADJ CLASSIF

2 A **princely** sum of money is a large sum of money. EG *We're managing to sell them at a princely £25 a time.* ADJ QUALIT : ATTRIB

princess /prɪnsɛs/, **princesses.** A **princess** is a female member of a royal family, usually the daughter of a king or queen or the wife of a prince. EG *...Princess Mary, only daughter of King George V... ...the Prince and Princess of Wales.* N COUNT

principal /prɪnsɪpəºl/, **principals. 1 Principal** means main or most important. EG *Political domination was rarely their principal aim... ...the principal character in James Bernard Fagan's play.* ADJ CLASSIF : ATTRIB

2 The **principal** of a school or college is the person in charge of it. N COUNT

principality /prɪnsɪpælɪ¹ti¹/, **principalities.** A **principality** is a country that is ruled by a prince. EG *...the principality of Monaco.* N COUNT

principally /prɪnsɪpəºli¹/ means more than anything else. EG *He dealt principally with Ethiopia... ...a protein which occurs principally in wheat.* ADV

principle /prɪnsɪpəºl/, **principles. 1** A **principle** is a general belief that you have about the way you should behave, which influences your behaviour. EG *...a man of high principles... She abandoned her principles... Our party remains a party of principle.* N COUNT OR N UNCOUNT

● If you do something **on principle**, you do it because of a particular belief that you have. EG *I had to vote for him, of course, on principle.* ● PHRASE

2 A **principle** is also **2.1** a general rule about how something should be done. EG *...the principles of formal logic... ...a party organized on Leninist principles.* **2.2** a general scientific law which explains how something happens or works. EG *...the principle of acceleration.* N COUNT+SUPP

3 If you agree with something **in principle**, you generally agree to the idea of it but may be unable or unwilling to support it in practice. EG *We are willing, in principle, to look afresh at the 1921 constitution.* PHRASE

principled /prɪnsɪpəºld/. **Principled** behaviour is based on moral principles. EG *...the principled stand we have taken on matters of contemporary concern... I forgot you were so high principled.* ADJ QUALIT

print /prɪnt/, **prints, printing, printed. 1** If someone **prints** a book, newspaper, or leaflet, they produce it in large quantities by a mechanical process. EG *I asked him for an estimate to print a weekly paper for me.* ◇ **printing.** EG *Universal literacy was only possible after the invention of printing... ...a printing press.* V+O ◇ N UNCOUNT

2 If someone **prints** a speech or a piece of writing, they include it in a newspaper or magazine. EG *The paper printed a big exclusive story about Margaret Thatcher... This interview was not printed in the national press.* V+O

3 The letters and numbers on a page of a book or newspaper are referred to as the **print**. EG *The print is rather poor... ...paragraphs in bold print.* N UNCOUNT

4 If something appears **in print**, it appears in a book or newspaper. EG *He admitted it in print.* PHRASE

5 If a book is **out of print**, it is no longer available from a publisher. PHRASE

6 A **print** is **6.1** a picture that is copied from a painting by photography or made mechanically from specially prepared surfaces. **6.2** one of the photographs from a film that has been developed. EG *...simple black and white prints.* N COUNT

7 If you **print** a pattern on cloth, you reproduce it many times on the cloth, usually by using dye and special machinery. EG *...a pattern which is printed onto the fabric by hand.* V+O

8 A **print** is also a footprint or a fingerprint. EG *His feet left prints in the soft soil.* N COUNT : OFT PLURAL

9 If you **print** when you write something, you write in letters that are not joined together. EG *There was an envelope on her desk with her name printed on it... As long as you print clearly, you don't have to type.* V OR V+O

print out. When information from a computer **is printed out**, it is reproduced on paper. ● See also **printout**. PHRASAL VB : V+O+ADV

printer /prɪntə/, **printers.** A **printer** is **1** a person or firm that prints books, newspapers, or leaflets. **2** a machine that is connected to a computer and that prints out information from the computer on paper. N COUNT

printout /prɪntaʊt/, **printouts.** A **printout** is a piece of paper on which information from a computer has been printed. EG *...a printout of the result.* N COUNT OR N UNCOUNT

prior /praɪə/. **1** If something happens **prior to** a particular time or event, it happens before that time or event. EG *It occurred in Dallas, just prior to President Kennedy's assassination.* PREP Formal

2 You use **prior** to describe something that has happened or been planned earlier. EG *No prior knowledge should be required... I have a prior engagement... ...without prior warning.* ADJ CLASSIF : ATTRIB

3 A **prior** claim or duty is more important than other claims or duties. EG *There are many others who have a prior claim... He feels a prior obligation to his job as a journalist.* ADJ CLASSIF : ATTRIB

priority /praɪɒrɪ¹ti¹/, **priorities. 1** Something that is a **priority** must be done or dealt with as soon as possible. EG *Getting food was the main priority... Factories seemed to be China's highest priority.* N COUNT+SUPP

▸ used as an adjective. EG *The waiting list contains a thousand priority cases.* ▸ ADJ CLASSIF : ATTRIB

2 When you talk about someone's **priorities**, you are talking about which tasks or things they consider most important and which they consider less important. EG *We must find out the priorities of the public... I have a different order of priorities... He had his priorities right.* N PLURAL

3 If someone or something has **priority** or is given **priority** over other things, they are considered more important than other things and are therefore dealt with first. EG *These children are given priority when day nursery places are allocated.* N UNCOUNT

prise /praɪz/, **prises, prising, prised;** also spelled **prize.** If you **prise** something open or **prise** it away from a surface, you force it to open or force it to come away from the surface. EG *He prised the lids off both tins of paint... I prised her arms free.* V+O+A

prism /prɪzə^{0}m/, **prisms.** A **prism** is an object made of clear glass or plastic which has many straight sides. It separates the light which passes through it into the colours of the rainbow. N COUNT

prison /prɪzə^{0}n/, **prisons. 1** A **prison** is a building where criminals are kept in order to punish them and to protect other people from them. EG *I had never before been inside a prison... He died in prison... He was sent to prison for two years.* N COUNT OR N UNCOUNT

2 You can describe your situation as a **prison** when it makes you feel unhappy and you cannot easily escape from it. EG *The Kirks' marriage had become a prison.* N SING Literary

prisoner /prɪzə^{0}nə/, **prisoners. 1** A **prisoner** is **1.1** a person who is kept in a prison as a punishment. EG *He was the only prisoner permitted to enter my cell.* **1.2** a person who has been captured by an enemy, for example in war. N COUNT

2 If someone **is taken prisoner**, they are captured. PHRASE

prisoner of war, prisoners of war. A **prisoner of war** is a soldier who is captured by the enemy during a war and is kept as a prisoner until the end of the war. N COUNT

pristine /prɪstiːn/. Something that is **pristine** is extremely clean or new. EG *He wiped his fingers on his pristine handkerchief.* ADJ CLASSIF Formal

privacy /praɪvəsi[1], prɪvəsi[1]/. If you have **privacy**, you are alone or you can be alone, so that you can do things without other people seeing you or disturbing you. EG *I hated the lack of privacy in the dormitory... ...the privacy of your own home... Take it home and read it in privacy.* N UNCOUNT

private /praɪvə[1]t/, **privates. 1** Something that is **private** is for the use of one person or group only, rather than for the general public. EG *All rooms have got private bath and WC... The fields were private property.* ADJ CLASSIF: USU ATTRIB

2 Private is used to describe services that you pay for or industries that are owned by an individual person or group, rather than services and industries that are controlled by the state. EG *...private education... ...private health insurance.* ADJ CLASSIF: ATTRIB

◇ **privately.** EG *...privately owned firms.* ◇ ADV

3 Private discussions take place between a small group of people and are kept secret from other people. EG *I have asked the editors to apply to the Prime Minister for a private interview.* ADJ CLASSIF: ATTRIB

◇ **privately.** EG *The notion was discussed privately between the two men at lunch.* ◇ ADV

4 If you do something **in private**, you do it without other people being present, usually because it is something that you want to keep secret. EG *Could we talk to you in private?* PHRASE

5 Private activities and belongings are connected with your personal life rather than with your work or business. EG *She never spoke about her private life... I have an official diary and a private diary.* ADJ CLASSIF: ATTRIB

6 Your **private** thoughts or plans are things that are personal and that you do not talk about to other people. EG *He was deep in his own private thoughts... He was engaged in a private quest of his own.* ◇ **privately.** EG *Privately Ben felt close to despair.* ADJ CLASSIF: ATTRIB ◇ ADV

7 If you describe a place as **private**, you mean that it is quiet and you can be alone there without being disturbed. EG *...a private place of meditation.* ADJ QUALIT

8 Someone who is a **private** person is very quiet by nature and does not share their thoughts and feelings with other people. EG *Away from the glare of publicity he becomes an intensely private man.* ADJ QUALIT

9 A **private** is a soldier who has the lowest rank in an army. N COUNT

private school, private schools. A **private school** is a school which is not supported financially by the government and which parents have to pay for their children to go to. N COUNT

privation /praɪveɪʃə^{0}n/, **privations.** If you suffer **privation** or **privations**, you are deprived of things that you need in life. EG *Life was riddled with privation... ...the privations of frontier life.* N UNCOUNT OR N COUNT Formal

privatize /praɪvətaɪz/, **privatizes, privatizing, privatized;** also spelled **privatise.** If a government **privatizes** a company, industry, or service that is owned and controlled by the state, it changes its ownership so that it is then owned by an individual or group. EG *Now the company is being privatised.* ◇ **privatization** /praɪvətaɪzeɪʃə^{0}n/. EG *...the privatisation of the telephone service.* V+O ◇ N UNCOUNT

privet /prɪvɪt/ is a type of bush with small leaves that stay green all year round. It is often grown in gardens to form hedges. EG *...houses separated by privet hedges.* N UNCOUNT

privilege /prɪvɪ^{0}lɪdʒ/, **privileges. 1** A **privilege** is a special right or advantage that only one person or group has, so that they are in a better position than other people. EG *The privileges of these prisoners included being allowed daily visits... The children would resent any special privileges given to the staff... ...the power and privilege which they had once enjoyed.* N COUNT OR N UNCOUNT

2 If you describe something that you have the opportunity to do as a **privilege**, you mean that you are very pleased to have the opportunity to do it, because most people never have it. EG *Some years ago I had the privilege of meeting the world's oldest man... It was a privilege to work with such a great actress.* N SING: USU+SUPP

privileged /prɪvɪ^{0}lɪdʒd/. Someone who is **privileged** has an advantage or opportunity that most other people do not have. EG *I am privileged to have worked with her so often... It was expensive and available only to the privileged few.* ADJ QUALIT

privy /prɪvi[1]/. If you are **privy** to something secret, you have been allowed to know about it. EG *Very few of them were privy to the details of the conspiracy.* ADJ PRED+*to* Formal

prize /praɪz/, **prizes, prizing, prized. 1** A **prize** is something of value, for example money or a trophy, that is given to someone who has the best results in a competition or game, or as a reward for doing good work. EG *I entered two competitions and won prizes... My pig won first prize at Skipton Fair... ...Nobel Prize winners.* N COUNT

2 You use **prize** to describe things that are of such good quality that they win prizes or deserve to win prizes. EG *...prize carnations.* ADJ CLASSIF: ATTRIB

3 Something that **is prized** is wanted and admired because it is considered to be very valuable or good in quality. EG *These fish are highly prized for their excellent flavour.* V+O: USU PASS

4 See also **prise**.

pro /prəʊ/, **pros. 1** A **pro** is a professional. EG *He's a pro and I'm only an amateur.* N COUNT Informal

2 The pros and cons of something are its advantages and disadvantages, which you consider so that you can make a sensible decision. EG *The pros and cons of strike action were discussed.* PHRASE

pro- is used to form adjectives that describe people as supporting something such as a country, person, or idea. For example, a pro-government newspaper is one that supports the government of its country. EG *...the Government's pro-American policy... ...the pro-nuclear lobby.* PREFIX

probability /prɒbəbɪlɪ[1]ti[1]/, **probabilities. 1** The **probability** of something happening is how likely it is to happen, which is sometimes expressed as a N COUNT OR N UNCOUNT

If you are in the process of doing something, have you finished it?

fraction or a percentage. EG *He must calculate the probability of failure... It had a high probability of succeeding.*

2 The **probability** that something will happen is the fact that it is likely to happen. EG *The real source of his gloom was the probability that Kathy would not come... The probability is that they will find themselves in debt.* N COUNT OR N UNCOUNT

3 If you say that something is true **in all probability**, you mean that you think it is very likely to be true. EG *They could, in all probability, perform any kind of calculation.* ADV SEN

probable /prɒbəbə^{0}l/. If you say that something is **probable**, you mean that it is likely to be true or likely to happen. EG *It seems very probable that they are descended from a single ancestor... This is the most probable interpretation of the situation... The Belgians face a probable general election this autumn.* ADJ QUALIT

probably /prɒbəbli^{1}/. If you say that something is **probably** the case, you mean that you think it is likely to be the case, although you are not sure. EG *He probably kept your examination papers... Next year I shall probably be looking for a job... The owner is probably a salesman.* ADV SEN

probation /prə^{6}beɪʃə^{0}n/ is **1** a period of time during which a person who has committed a crime has to obey the law and be supervised by a probation officer, rather than being sent to prison. EG *I wondered whether Daniel would be let off on probation.* **2** a period of time during which someone is judging your character and ability while you work, in order to see if you are suitable for that type of work. EG *He was a mechanic who was on probation.* N UNCOUNT

probation officer, probation officers. A **probation officer** is a person whose job is to supervise and help people who have committed crimes and been put on probation. N COUNT

probe /prəʊb/, **probes, probing, probed. 1** If you **probe**, you ask questions or make enquiries in order to discover facts about something. EG *She had learnt not to probe too far... We were probing for information relevant to our needs... ...to probe the mysteries of the universe.* V: OFT+A, OR V+O ▸ used as a noun. EG *...a probe into suspected drug dealing in Florida.* ▸ N COUNT

2 A **probe** is a long thin metal instrument that doctors and dentists use to examine very delicate parts of the body. N COUNT

3 If you **probe** something, you poke it with something long and thin in order to examine it. EG *The bird was probing the mound with its bill... I probed through his hair with my fingertips.* V+O OR V+A

problem /prɒbləm/, **problems. 1** A **problem** is **1.1** a situation that is unsatisfactory and causes difficulties for people. EG *They have financial problems... ...to help solve the problem of racism... The problem is that she can't cook.* **1.2** a puzzle that requires logical thought or mathematics to solve it. EG *...the development of problem-solving programs.* N COUNT

2 Problem children are difficult for people to deal with. EG *...the destructive behaviour of problem children.* ADJ CLASSIF: ATTRIB

3 You can say **'No problem'** as a way of telling someone that you can easily do something for them and will do it. CONVENTION Informal Spoken

problematic /prɒbləmætɪk/. Something that is **problematic** involves problems and difficulties. EG *...the problematic nature of the relationship.* ADJ QUALIT Formal

problematical /prɒbləmætɪkə^{0}l/ means the same as problematic. ADJ QUALIT Formal

procedure /prə^{6}siːdʒə/, **procedures.** A **procedure** is a way of doing something, especially the usual or correct way. EG *...the proper procedure to be followed in decision-making... ...a procedure for recording drugs administered... This was not standard procedure.* N COUNT OR N UNCOUNT

proceed, proceeds, proceeding, proceeded. The verb is pronounced /prə^{6}siːd/; the plural noun in paragraph 5 is pronounced /prəʊsiːdz/.

1 If you **proceed** to do something, you do it after doing something else. EG *He proceeded to explain... ...and then proceeds to throw stones through the windows.* V+to-INF

2 If you **proceed** with a course of action, you continue with it. EG *It is necessary to examine this claim before we proceed any further.* V: OFT+A Formal

3 If an activity, process, or event **proceeds**, it goes on and does not stop. EG *Preparations were proceeding on schedule.* V

4 If you **proceed** in a particular direction, you go in that direction. EG *...as we were proceeding along Chiswick High Street.* V: USU+A Formal

5 The **proceeds** of an event or activity are the money that has been obtained from it. EG *The proceeds will be given away to a deserving charity.* N PLURAL

proceeding /prə^{6}siːdɪŋ/, **proceedings. 1** You can refer to an organized series of events that happen in a place as the **proceedings**. EG *Millions of people watched the proceedings on television.* N COUNT: USU PLURAL Formal

2 Legal **proceedings** are legal action taken against someone. EG *I shall institute proceedings against you for unfair dismissal.* N PLURAL Formal

process /prəʊsɛs/, **processes, processing, processed. 1** A **process** is **1.1** a series of actions which are carried out in order to achieve a particular result. EG *It has been a long process getting this information... ...industrial processes... The best solution can only be found by a process of trial and error.* **1.2** a series of things which happen naturally and result in a biological or chemical change. EG *...the digestive processes.* N COUNT: USU+SUPP

2 If you **are in the process of** doing something, you have started to do it and are still doing it. EG *She is still in the painful process of growing up.* PHRASE

3 If you are doing something and you do something else **in the process**, you do the second thing as a result of doing the first thing. EG *I got him out, but overbalanced in the process and fell.* PHRASE

4 When raw materials or foods **are processed**, they are treated chemically or industrially before they are used or sold. EG *...chemically processed food.* V+O ◇ **processing.** EG *...the processing and storing of radioactive materials.* ◇ N UNCOUNT

5 When people **process** information, they put it through a system or into a computer in order to deal with it. EG *Your application will take a few weeks to process... Ten computers are processing the data.* ● See also **word processing**. V+O

procession /prə^{6}sɛʃə^{0}n/, **processions.** A **procession** is a group of people who are walking, riding, or driving in a line as part of a public event. EG *Lady Branwell led the procession through the main street of the village.* N COUNT

proclaim /prə^{6}kleɪm/, **proclaims, proclaiming, proclaimed.** If people **proclaim** something, they formally make it known to the public. EG *The Government proclaimed a state of emergency.* V-SPEECH Formal

proclamation /prɒkləmeɪʃə^{0}n/, **proclamations.** A **proclamation** is a public announcement about something important. EG *The king issued a proclamation outlawing the rebels.* N COUNT

procreate /prəʊkrieɪt/, **procreates, procreating, procreated.** When animals or people **procreate**, they produce young animals or babies. V OR V+O ◇ **procreation** /prəʊkrieɪʃə^{0}n/. EG *...the natural process of procreation.* ◇ N UNCOUNT Formal

procure /prəkjʊə/, **procures, procuring, procured.** If you **procure** something, you obtain it. EG *It would be necessary to procure more grain.* V+O Formal

prod /prɒd/, **prods, prodding, prodded. 1** If you **prod** someone or something, you give them a quick push with your finger or with a pointed object. EG *She prodded a bean with her fork... He prodded Kunta roughly towards the raised platform.* V+O: USU+A ▸ used as a noun. EG *Mrs Travers gave her a prod.* ▸ N COUNT

2 If you **prod** someone who has not yet done V+O+A

something that they should do, you remind them to do it. EG ...*companies who prod the ministry into action every now and again.* ▸ used as a noun. EG *The Home Office took their time replying, despite numerous prods from Mr Harper.* ▸ N COUNT

prodigal /prɒdɪgəºl/. If you describe someone as a **prodigal** son or daughter, you mean that they left their family but have now returned. ADJ CLASSIF Literary

prodigious /prədɪdʒəs/. Something that is **prodigious** is amazingly great. EG ...*a prodigious store of information... ...prodigious amounts of food.* ADJ QUALIT Formal

produce, produces, producing, produced; pronounced /prədjuːs/ when it is a verb, and /prɒdjuːs/ when it is a noun.

1 To **produce** something means to cause it to happen. EG *All our efforts have not produced an agreement... This drug has produced terrible effects on children.* V+O

2 If you **produce** something, you make or create it. EG ...*factories producing electrical goods... These artists produce works of great beauty.* V+O

3 When things or people **produce** something, it comes from them or slowly forms from them, especially as the result of a biological or chemical process. EG *The sun produces light and heat... Parents are responsible for the offspring they produce.* V+O

4 If you **produce** evidence or an argument, you show it or explain it to people in order to make them agree with you. EG *He produces no evidence for his belief.* V+O : OFT +*for/against*

5 If you **produce** an object from somewhere, you bring it out so that it can be seen. EG *Poirot produced the letter from his pocket.* V+O : USU+A

6 If someone **produces** a play, film, programme, or record, they organize it and decide how it should be done. EG *The film was directed, written and produced by Mel Brooks.* V+O

7 **Produce** is food or other things that are grown in large quantities to be sold. EG *They go to market to buy supplies and sell their produce.* N UNCOUNT

producer /prədjuːsə/, **producers. 1** A **producer** is a person whose job is organizing plays, films, programmes, or records. EG ...*a TV producer.* N COUNT

2 A **producer** of a food or material is a company or country that provides or grows a large amount of it. EG *The Soviet Union is the world's leading crude oil producer... ...producers of consumer goods.* N COUNT : USU+SUPP

product /prɒdʌkt/, **products. 1** A **product** is something that a company makes. EG *There are masses of car-cleaning products available.* N COUNT : USU PLURAL

2 Something or someone that is a **product** of a particular situation or process exists or has particular qualities as a result of that situation or process. EG *The uniformity of the dancers was the product of hours of training... She is a product of the 1970s... ...a product of the party's weakness.* N COUNT+*of*

production /prədʌkʃəºn/, **productions. 1 Production** is **1.1** the process of manufacturing or growing something in large quantities. EG ...*more efficient methods of production.* **1.2** the amount of goods manufactured or grown by a company or country. EG *Industrial production has fallen by 20% over two years.* **1.3** the making of plays, films, programmes, or records. EG ...*members of the production crew and the cast.* N UNCOUNT

2 The **production** of something is its creation as the result of a natural process. EG ...*the production of electricity.* N UNCOUNT +SUPP

3 A **production** is a play, opera, or other show that is performed. EG ...*Peter Hall's production of The Tempest at the Old Vic.* N COUNT

production line, production lines. A **production line** is an arrangement of machines in a factory where the products pass from machine to machine until they are finished. EG ...*cars coming off the production line at British Leyland.* N COUNT

productive /prədʌktɪv/. **1** Something or someone that is **productive** manufactures or grows a large amount of goods. EG *Agriculture and industry both grew more productive.* ADJ QUALIT

2 If a meeting or a relationship is **productive**, good or useful things happen as a result of it. EG ...*a productive friendship.* ADJ QUALIT

productivity /prɒdəºktɪvɪ¹ti¹/ is the rate at which goods are produced. EG *There have been enormous increases in agricultural productivity.* N UNCOUNT

Prof. is an abbreviation for 'professor'. You write it in front of a professor's name. EG ...*Prof. Brewer.*

profess /prəºfɛs/, **professes, professing, professed. 1** If you **profess** to do or have something, you claim that you do it or have it. EG *Nell didn't like her, or professed not to... ...his professed commitment to the school.* V+*to*-INF OR V+O Formal

2 If you **profess** a feeling or opinion, you openly express it. EG *Many have professed disgust at this use of weapons.* V+O Formal

profession /prəºfɛʃəºn/, **professions. 1** A **profession** is a type of job that requires special training and that has a fairly high status, for example the job of doctor or lawyer. EG *She decided on law or journalism as her profession.* ● If you are, for example, a teacher or a lawyer, you can say that you are a teacher **by profession** or a lawyer **by profession**. N COUNT ● PHRASE

2 You can use **profession** to refer to all the people who have the same profession. EG *The medical profession are doing a very difficult job.* N COLL

professional /prəºfɛʃəºnəl, -ʃənəºl/, **professionals. 1 Professional** means relating to a person's work, especially work that requires special training. EG *I sought professional advice.* ADJ CLASSIF : ATTRIB

◇ **professionally.** EG *They are professionally qualified.* ◇ ADV

2 You use **professional** to describe things that people do to earn money rather than as a hobby. For example, a **professional** actor does acting as a job. EG ...*a professional painter.* ADJ CLASSIF : ATTRIB

◇ **professionally.** EG *He played the oboe professionally.* ◇ ADV

3 **Professional** people have jobs that require special training and that have a fairly high status. EG *The flat is ideal for the professional single person... ...two busy professional people.* ADJ CLASSIF : ATTRIB

4 If something that someone does or produces is **professional**, it is of a very high standard. EG *He had typed the whole scheme out in a very professional manner.* ADJ QUALIT

5 A **professional** is **5.1** someone who has a job that requires special training and has a fairly high status. EG ...*nurses, doctors, social workers, and other professionals.* **5.2** someone who plays a sport to earn money rather than as a hobby. EG *He has 17 championship victories as a professional plus two amateur titles.* **5.3** someone who does their work very skilfully. N COUNT

professionalism /prəºfɛʃəºnəlɪzəºm/. Someone's **professionalism** is the skilful way in which they do a job. EG *The paper was produced with incredible speed and professionalism by the students.* N UNCOUNT

professor /prəfɛsə/, **professors. 1** A **professor** in a British university has the highest rank of the teachers in a department. EG ...*the Professor of English at Strathclyde University... ...Professor Cole.* N COUNT

2 A **professor** in an American or Canadian university or college is a teacher there. N COUNT

proffer /prɒfə/, **proffers, proffering, proffered.**

1 If you **proffer** something to someone, you hold it towards them so that they can take it or touch it. EG *He put down his luggage and proffered his passport... ...before he could proffer her one of them.* V+O OR V+O+O Formal

Does a professor profess to do something?

2 If you **proffer** something to someone, you offer it to them. EG *The solution he proffered to the banks was a novel one... She had already proffered her resignation... Society proffers him no reward.* V+O: OFT+*to*, OR V+O+O Formal

proficient /prəfɪʃənt/. If you are **proficient** in something, you can do it quite well. EG *They were all proficient in needlework... ...a proficient swimmer.* ADJ QUALIT: OFT+*in/at* ◊ **proficiency** /prəfɪʃənsi¹/. EG *...your proficiency in English... Technical proficiency is essential.* ◊ N UNCOUNT: OFT+*in*

profile /prəʊfaɪl/, **profiles. 1** Your **profile** is the outline of your face as it is seen when someone is looking at you from the side. EG *She glanced at his haughty profile.* N COUNT ● If you see someone **in profile**, you see them from the side. EG *She sat observing his face in profile.* ● PHRASE

2 A **profile** of someone is a short article or programme in which their life and character are described. EG *She wanted to write profiles of the founders of the Party.* N COUNT

3 If you **keep a low profile**, you avoid doing things that will make people notice you. EG *Keep a low profile until you have had time to settle in.* PHRASE

profit /prɒfɪt/, **profits, profiting, profited. 1** A **profit** is an amount of money that you gain when you are paid more for something than it cost you to make it, get it, or do it. EG *The company made a profit of 113 per cent... The profits are used to buy more equipment... ...to make as much profit as he can.* N COUNT OR N UNCOUNT

2 If you **profit** from something, you benefit or gain something from it. EG *I profited from his advice... They had profited by their experience.* V+*from/by* Formal

profitable /prɒfɪtəbə⁰l/. Something that is **profitable 1** makes a profit. EG *The farm is a highly profitable business... It was more profitable to export the crops.* ADJ QUALIT ◊ **profitably.** EG *Can the motor vehicle industry operate profitably?* ◊ ADV **2** is useful and results in some benefit for you. EG *He certainly made profitable use of the lessons he had learnt.* ADJ QUALIT ◊ **profitably.** EG *There was little I could profitably do sitting at my desk.* ◊ ADV

profound /prə⁶faʊnd/. **1** You use **profound** to emphasize the great degree or intensity of something. EG *...in a state of profound shock... The war was to have a profound effect on all our lives.* ADJ QUALIT ◊ **profoundly.** EG *I found the film profoundly moving.* ◊ ADV Formal

2 A **profound** idea or work is serious and shows great intellectual understanding. EG *It's a profound book... ...a very profound question.* ADJ QUALIT

profuse /prə⁶fjuːs/ is used to indicate that a quantity of something is very large. EG *There were profuse apologies for its absence.* ADJ QUALIT Formal ◊ **profusely.** EG *He was bleeding profusely.* ◊ ADV

profusion /prə⁶fjuːʒə⁰n/. If there is a **profusion** of something or if it occurs in **profusion**, there is a very large quantity of it. EG *...a profusion of new words... Daffodils grow in enormous profusion under the trees... ...the profusion of colour.* N PART: SING OR N UNCOUNT Formal

prognosis /prɒgnəʊsɪs/, **prognoses** /prɒgnəʊsiːz/. A **prognosis** is a prediction about the future of someone or something, especially about whether a patient will recover from an illness. EG *It was a serious heart defect; the prognosis was poor, even with treatment.* N COUNT Formal

program /prəʊgræm/, **programs, programming, programmed. 1** A **program** is a set of instructions that a computer follows in order to perform a particular task. N COUNT

2 When you **program** a computer, you give it a set of instructions to make it able to perform a particular task. EG *Can computers be programmed to hold intelligent conversations?* V+O ◊ **programming.** EG *...computer programming.* ◊ N UNCOUNT

3 See also **programme**.

programme /prəʊgræm/, **programmes, programming, programmed;** also spelled **program** in American English. **1** A **programme** of actions or events is a series of actions or events that are planned to be done. EG *...a programme of modernization... They have embarked on an ambitious energy programme... ...their programme of meetings, talks and exhibitions.* N COUNT: USU+SUPP

2 A television **programme** or radio **programme** is something that is broadcast on television or radio. EG *...the last programme in our series on education... ...gardening programmes.* N COUNT

3 A theatre **programme** or concert **programme** is a booklet or sheet of paper which gives information about the play or concert you are attending. N COUNT

4 When you **programme** a machine or system, you set its controls so that it will work in a particular way. EG *The radiators are programmed to come on at six every morning.* V+O: USU+*to*-INF

programmer /prəʊgræmə/, **programmers.** A computer **programmer** is a person whose job involves writing programs for computers. N COUNT

progress, progresses, progressing, progressed; pronounced /prəʊgrɛs/ when it is a noun, and /prə⁶grɛs/ when it is a verb.

1 **Progress** is **1.1** the process of gradually getting nearer to achieving something or completing something. EG *She is making good progress with her German... They came in from time to time to check on my progress.* N UNCOUNT **1.2** changes and advances in a society that make life better or more civilized. EG *...technological progress... ...the progress in transportation.*

2 The **progress** of a situation or action is the way in which it develops. EG *He followed the progress of hostilities with impatience.* N SING: *the*+N+*of*

3 If something is **in progress**, it is happening. EG *The battle was still in progress.* PHRASE

4 To **progress** means **4.1** to become more advanced, skilful, or higher in rank over a period of time. EG *You're not progressing quickly enough... Technology did not progress any further for centuries.* V: USU+A **4.2** to continue. EG *My impressions changed as the trip progressed.* V

5 If you **progress** to something which naturally comes after what you previously did or had, you start doing it or having it. EG *From there we progressed to a discussion on politics.* V+*to*

progression /prə⁶grɛʃə⁰n/, **progressions. 1** A **progression** is a gradual development from one state to another. EG *The progression from one extreme to the other is gradual.* N COUNT+SUPP Formal

2 A **progression** of things is a number of things which come one after the other. EG *It is part of a connected progression of events.* N COUNT+*of* Formal

progressive /prə⁶grɛsɪv/. **1** Someone who is **progressive** or has **progressive** ideas has modern ideas about how things should be done. EG *Some young parents are eager to be progressive.* ADJ QUALIT

2 A **progressive** change happens gradually over a period of time. EG *...the progressive industrialization of our society.* ADJ CLASSIF ◊ **progressively.** EG *It became progressively easier to see.* ◊ ADV

prohibit /prə⁶hɪbɪt/, **prohibits, prohibiting, prohibited.** If someone **prohibits** something, they forbid it or make it illegal. EG *The country has a law prohibiting employees from striking... She believes that nuclear weapons should be totally prohibited... ...to prohibit the use of lead in petrol.* V+O: OFT+*from*

prohibition /prəʊɪbɪʃə⁰n/, **prohibitions. 1** A **prohibition** is a law or rule forbidding something. EG *Of course, some of these prohibitions have social value... ...a prohibition on nuclear weapons.* N COUNT Formal

2 The **prohibition** of something is the forbidding of it. EG *...the prohibition of strikes.* N UNCOUNT

prohibitive /prə⁶hɪbɪtɪv/. If the cost of something is **prohibitive**, it is so high that you cannot afford it. EG *The cost of making them by hand is prohibitive... ...the prohibitive price of domestic labour.* ADJ QUALIT

project, projects, projecting, projected; pronounced /prɒdʒɛkt/ when it is a noun, and /prə⁶dʒɛkt/ when it is a verb.

1 A **project** is 1.1 a large-scale attempt to do or achieve something, which is carefully planned and will take some time. EG *...the cancellation of the Blue Streak Missile project.* 1.2 a detailed study of a subject by a pupil or student. EG *He's doing a project on Scottish oil.*
N COUNT

2 If something **is projected**, it is planned to happen in the future. EG *There were demonstrations against the projected visit.*
V+O : USU PASS

3 If a future amount **is projected**, it is estimated. EG *The population of Calcutta is projected to rise to seventy million people.*
V+O : USU PASS

4 If you **project** a light, film, or picture onto a screen or wall, you make it appear there. EG *The images were projected on a screen.*
V+O

5 If someone **projects** you as a particular thing, they try to make people believe that you are that thing. EG *He had projected himself as a reformer.*
V+O OR V-REFL : USU+*as*

6 If something **projects**, it sticks out above or beyond a surface or edge. EG *He could see the end of a spear projecting over the rock.*
V : USU+A Formal

projection /prədʒɛkʃə^{0}n/, **projections.** 1 A **projection** is an estimate of a future amount. EG *The company made projections of sales of 3000 aircraft.*
N COUNT

2 A **projection** is also a part of something that sticks out. EG *...the projection on the mantelpiece.*
N COUNT Formal

3 The **projection** of a film or picture is the act of projecting it onto a screen or wall. EG *...a projection room... ...arranges the hire and projection of films.*
N UNCOUNT

projector /prədʒɛktə/, **projectors.** A **projector** is a machine that projects films or slides onto a screen or wall.
N COUNT

proletarian /prəʊlɪtɛərɪən/ means relating to the proletariat. EG *...establishing a new proletarian party... ...proletarian violence... ...the proletarian masses.*
ADJ CLASSIF : ATTRIB Technical

proletariat /prəʊlɪtɛərɪət/. You can refer to working-class people, especially industrial workers, as the **proletariat**. EG *He identified himself with the proletariat and their struggles.*
N COLL : SING Technical

proliferate /prə^{6}lɪfəreɪt/, **proliferates, proliferating, proliferated.** If things **proliferate**, they increase in number very quickly. EG *Polytechnics proliferated all over the country.* ◇ **proliferation** /prə^{6}lɪfəreɪʃə^{0}n/. EG *We can prevent the proliferation of nuclear weaponry.*
V Formal
◇ N UNCOUNT : OFT+*of*

prolific /prə^{6}lɪfɪk/. A **prolific** writer, artist, or composer produces a large number of works.
ADJ QUALIT

prologue /prəʊlɒg/, **prologues.** A **prologue** is a speech or section that introduces a play or book.
N COUNT

prolong /prə^{6}lɒŋ/, **prolongs, prolonging, prolonged.** To **prolong** something means to make it last longer. EG *All the time people are seeking to prolong life.*
V+O

prolonged /prə^{6}lɒŋd/. A **prolonged** event or situation continues for a long time, or for longer than expected. EG *...a prolonged and bitter struggle... ...a prolonged period of uncertainty.*
ADJ QUALIT

promenade /prɒmənɑːd/, **promenades.** At a seaside town, the **promenade** is a raised road or path next to the beach.
N COUNT : USU *the*+N

prominent /prɒmɪnənt/. 1 Someone who is **prominent** is important. EG *...US Senators and other prominent American personalities.* ◇ **prominence** /prɒmɪnəns/. EG *Alan Travers had risen to prominence in his wife's organisation.*
ADJ QUALIT
◇ N UNCOUNT

2 Something that is **prominent** is very noticeable or is an important part of something else. EG *There were two prominent landmarks.* ◇ **prominently.** EG *...a large photograph prominently displayed in her front room... In the labour market before 1974, women figured prominently.*
ADJ QUALIT
◇ ADV

promiscuous /prəmɪskjʊəs/. Someone who is **promiscuous** has sex with many different people; used showing disapproval. EG *...when young people engage in promiscuous behaviour.* ◇ **promiscuity** /prɒmɪskjuːɪ^{1}ti^{1}/. EG *Parents often worry about sexual promiscuity when their children reach adolescence.*
ADJ QUALIT
◇ N UNCOUNT

promise /prɒmɪs/, **promises, promising, promised.** 1 If you **promise** that you will do something, you say to someone that you will definitely do it. EG *Promise me you'll go... I'll be back at one, I promise... 'I won't fail you', he promised... I promised to take the children to the fair.*
V : OFT +REPORT, QUOTE, OR *to*-INF; ALSO V+O+REPORT OR QUOTE

2 If you **promise** someone something, you tell them that you will definitely give it to them or make sure that they have it. EG *I promised him a canary for his birthday... The government promise better homes for all who need them.*
V+O+O OR V+O+A

3 If a situation or event **promises** to have a particular quality or to be a particular thing, it shows signs that it will have that quality or be that thing. EG *The debate promises to be lively... Early mist had promised a clear day.*
V+*to*-INF OR V+O

4 A **promise** is a statement which you make to someone in which you say that you will definitely do something or give them something. EG *They tried to break the promises made in negotiations... They fulfilled their promise to revive trade.*
N COUNT

5 If someone or something shows **promise**, they seem likely to be very good or successful. EG *She showed considerable promise as a tennis player... The relationship held little promise of happiness.*
N UNCOUNT

promising /prɒmɪsɪŋ/. Someone or something that is **promising** seems likely to be very good or successful. EG *I consulted the menu. It looked promising... ...a most promising new actress.*
ADJ QUALIT

promote /prəməʊt/, **promotes, promoting, promoted.** 1 If people **promote** something, 1.1 they help it to happen, increase, or spread. EG *The government could do more to promote economic growth.* 1.2 they try to make it popular or successful. EG *The new town was vigorously promoted as an ideal place to settle.*
V+O

2 If someone **is promoted**, they are given a more important job in the organization they work for. EG *He had recently been promoted to captain.*
V+O : OFT+*to*

promoter /prəməʊtə/, **promoters.** 1 A **promoter** is a person who helps organize and finance an event, especially a sports event. EG *...a bullfight promoter... ...concert promoters.*
N COUNT

2 The **promoter** of a cause or idea tries to make it become popular. EG *She was a tireless promoter of new causes.*
N COUNT

promotion /prəməʊʃə^{0}n/, **promotions.** 1 If you are given **promotion**, you are given a more important job in the organization you work for. EG *What, if any, are your chances of promotion?*
N UNCOUNT OR N COUNT

2 The **promotion** of a product, event, or idea is an attempt to make it popular or successful, especially by advertising. EG *There are government controls on the promotion of cigarettes.*
N UNCOUNT

3 A **promotion** is a publicity campaign that is intended to increase the sales of a product.
N COUNT

prompt /prɒmp^{0}t/, **prompts, prompting, prompted.** 1 If something **prompts** someone to do something, it causes them to decide to do it and then to do it. EG *The Times article prompted him to call a meeting of the staff... My choice was prompted by a number of considerations.*
V+O : OFT+*to*-INF OR A

2 If you **prompt** someone who has just stopped talking, you say something to indicate that you wish them to continue talking. EG *'Yes?' Morris prompted, after a pause.*
V+O OR V+QUOTE

3 A **prompt** reaction or action comes or is done without any delay. EG *Professor Hamburg got a prompt reply... She requires prompt medical attention.*
ADJ QUALIT : USU ATTRIB

4 You use **prompt** to talk about exact times. For example, if you say that something will happen at 8 o'clock **prompt**, you mean that it will happen at exactly 8 o'clock.
ADV

Where would you find a promenade?

PRONOUNS

A pronoun is a word that is used to refer to people or things without naming or describing them. Pronouns are used in similar ways to noun groups, and so a pronoun can be the subject, object, or complement of a clause, or the object of a preposition. Most pronouns are used in place of complete noun groups, and so they are not normally used with determiners or adjectives. The pronouns **one** and **ones** are different, however, because they are used in place of a noun rather than a complete noun group. See the dictionary entry for **one** for an explanation of its uses.

1 Personal pronouns (PRON) refer to people and things. When the pronoun is the subject of a clause, the words **I**, **you**, **he**, **she**, **it**, **we**, and **they** are used. When the pronoun is the object of a clause, or when it comes after a preposition, the words **me**, **you**, **him**, **her**, **it**, **us**, and **them** are used. For example: *I gave him a record for Christmas and he gave me a book.*

2 The possessive form (PRON POSS) is used to show who something belongs to. The possessive pronouns are **mine**, **yours**, **his**, **hers**, **its**, **ours**, and **theirs**. Possessive pronouns stand as full noun groups: *Although yours is new, I still prefer mine.*
See also the entry headed DETERMINERS for information about the words **my**, **your**, **his**, **her**, **its**, **our**, and **their**, which are labelled DET POSS in this dictionary.

3 Relative pronouns (PRON REL) introduce relative clauses. The pronouns **who**, **whose**, and **whom** refer back to people, **which** refers back to things, and **that** refers back to either people or things. At the same time these words introduce subordinate clauses in a sentence, giving extra information about the people or things they refer to. For example: *You are the only person who knows anything about me . . . There's one question which I'd like to ask you . . . . . . ice cream that Mum had made.*

4 Reflexive pronouns (PRON REFL) are formed by adding 'self' or 'selves' to other pronouns: **myself**, **yourself**, **himself**, **herself**, **itself**, **ourselves**, **yourselves**, and **themselves.** They are used as the objects of clauses or prepositions when they refer to the same person or thing as the subject of the clause. For example: *He bought himself a tie . . . She poured herself a drink . . . They treated themselves to a good meal.* Reflexive pronouns can also be used to add emphasis when you are saying that a particular person or thing did something: *He baked the bread himself . . . I myself saw the accident . . . You yourself said it's only a routine check.*

5 The words **this**, **that**, **these**, and **those** can be used as pronouns (also PRON) to refer to things that have already been mentioned in the conversation, or to things that are around you in the real world. They can be used as the subject or object of a clause. For example: *She gave me this for my birthday . . . These are for you.*

6 There is a group of words, also labelled PRON, which are usually used in front of nouns but which can, when it is obvious what they refer to, be used on their own. Examples are **all**, **both**, **few**, and **none**, as in: ***All** were waiting silently . . . He got angry with **both** of them . . . Many of us tried but **few** succeeded . . . **None** could afford to buy books.*

7 There is a small class of indefinite pronouns (PRON INDEF) which you use when you cannot or do not want to refer to any particular person or thing by name. These are: **anybody**, **anyone**, **anything**, **everybody**, **everyone**, **everything**, **nobody**, **no-one**, **nothing**, **somebody**, **someone**, and **something**. If you want to modify an indefinite pronoun with an adjective, you have to put the adjective after the pronoun, and not before it. So you say: *It's nothing serious, I hope?*

prompting /prɒmpᵒtɪŋ/, **promptings.** If you respond to **prompting**, you do what someone encourages or reminds you to do. EG *She did it without any prompting.* N UNCOUNT OR N COUNT

promptly /prɒmpᵒtli¹/. If you do something **promptly**, 1 you do it immediately. EG *He slapped her and she promptly burst into tears... When you receive orders you must obey them promptly without question.* ADV 2 you do it at exactly the time that has been arranged. EG *I arrived at the gates promptly at six o'clock.* ADV

> **PRON** stands for **pronoun**
> Words which are labelled PRON in the Extra Column are pronouns.
> See the entry headed PRONOUNS for more information.

prone /prəʊn/. 1 If someone or something is **prone** to something, they have a tendency to be affected by it or to do it. EG *He was prone to indigestion... A computer was fairer and less prone to error... They were prone to argue.* ADJ PRED+*to* TO-INF
2 If you are lying **prone**, you are lying flat with the front of your body facing downwards. EG *She was lying prone on the floor.* ADJ CLASSIF Formal

prong /prɒŋ/, **prongs.** The **prongs** of a fork are the long, thin pointed parts. N COUNT

> **PRON INDEF** stands for **indefinite pronoun**
> There are 12 words labelled PRON INDEF in the Extra Column - 'anybody, anyone, anything, everybody, everyone, everything, nobody, no-one, nothing, somebody, someone, something'.
> See the entry headed PRONOUNS for more information.

pronoun /prəʊnaʊn/, **pronouns.** In grammar, a **pronoun** is a word that is used to replace a noun or a noun group that has already been mentioned or that will be mentioned later. 'He', 'she', and 'them' are all pronouns. Words that are pronouns have the label PRON in the Extra Column. See the entry headed PRONOUNS for more information. N COUNT

pronounce /prənaʊns/, **pronounces, pronouncing, pronounced.** 1 To **pronounce** a word means to say it in the way it is usually said or in a particular way. EG *I can't pronounce his name... ...the town of Ixtlan, pronounced East-lon.* V+O
2 If you **pronounce** something to be true, you formally state that it is true. EG *The victim was pronounced dead on arrival at the hospital.* V+O+C Formal
3 If someone **pronounces** a verdict or opinion on something, they formally give their verdict or opinion. EG *'Are the people ready to pronounce their verdict?' - 'Guilty.'... She was asked to pronounce on the merits of an antique vase.* V+O, V+QUOTE, OR V+*on* Formal

pronounced /prənaʊnst/. Something that is **pronounced** is very noticeable. EG *He spoke with a pronounced English accent.* ADJ QUALIT

pronouncement /prənaʊnsmə²nt/, **pronouncements.** A **pronouncement** is a formal or official statement. EG *...official pronouncements made by politicians.* N COUNT

> **PRON POSS** stands for **possessive pronoun**
> There are seven words labelled PRON POSS in the Extra Column - 'mine, yours, hers, his, its, ours, theirs'.
> See the entry headed PRONOUNS for more information.

> **PRON REFL** stands for **reflexive pronoun**
> There are nine words labelled PRON REFL in the Extra Column - 'myself, yourself, herself, himself, itself, oneself, ourselves, themselves, yourselves'.
> See the entry headed PRONOUNS for more information.

> **PRON REL** stands for **relative pronoun**
> There are ten words labelled PRON REL in the Extra Column - 'that, when, where, whereby, wherein, which, who, whom, whose, why'.
> See the entry headed PRONOUNS for more information.

pronunciation /prənʌnsɪeɪʃəᵒn/, **pronunciations.** 1 The **pronunciation** of a word or language is the way in which it is usually pronounced. EG *...the recommended American pronunciation.* N UNCOUNT OR N COUNT
2 Someone's **pronunciation** of a word is the way in which they pronounce it. EG *He tried to correct Francois's pronunciation.* N COUNT: USU SING+POSS

proof /pru:f/, **proofs.** 1 **Proof** is a fact or a piece of evidence which shows that something is true or exists. EG *Do you have any proof of that allegation?... He hadn't any proof that Davis had not died.* N UNCOUNT OR N COUNT
2 The **proofs** of a printed publication are a first copy of it that is printed so that mistakes can be corrected before more copies are printed. N COUNT

-proof combines with nouns to form adjectives which indicate that something cannot be damaged by a particular thing or person. EG *This building's supposed to be earthquake-proof... Can these containers be made vandal-proof?* • See also **fireproof**, **waterproof**.

prop /prɒp/, **props, propping, propped.** 1 If you **prop** an object on or against something, you support it by putting something underneath it or by resting it against something. EG *She propped her chin on her hand and gazed at him... His gun lay propped against the wall.* V+O+A
2 Someone or something that is a **prop** for a system, institution, or person is the main thing that makes it able to survive. EG *They ceased to be the prop of the imperial administration... Discussing everything was the prop of their marriage.* N COUNT+SUPP
3 A **prop** is also a stick or other object that you use to support something. EG *We need a clothes prop for the washing line.* N COUNT
4 The **props** in a play or film are all the objects and pieces of furniture that are used in it. EG *The sets, props, and costumes were all ready.* N COUNT: USU PLURAL

prop up. 1 If you **prop** an object **up**, you support it in a particular position by putting something underneath it or by resting it against something. EG *His feet were propped up on the coffee table.* PHRASAL VB: V+O+ADV, USU+A
2 If one organization or group of people **props up** another, it helps the other one to survive. EG *The Government does not intend to prop up declining industries.* V+O+ADV

propaganda /prɒpəgændə/ is information, often exaggerated or false information, which an organization publishes or broadcasts in order to influence people. EG *...a campaign of anti-British propaganda.* N UNCOUNT

> If you have a propensity to do something, are you prone to do it?

propagandist /prɒpəgændɪst/, **propagandists.** A **propagandist** is a person who tries to persuade people to support a particular idea or group; often used showing disapproval. EG *...dedicated revolutionary activists and propagandists.* N COUNT

propagate /prɒpəgeɪt/, **propagates, propagating, propagated.** 1 If people **propagate** an idea or piece of information, they spread it and try to make people believe it or support it. EG *The group is doing what it can to propagate the rumour... They toured the principal cities to propagate her cause.* V+O Formal

2 If you **propagate** plants, you grow more of them from the original ones. V-ERG Technical

propel /prə^{6}pɛl/, **propels, propelling, propelled.** 1 To **propel** something in a particular direction means to cause it to move in that direction. EG *The bullet is propelled out of the chamber.* V+O : USU+A

2 If something **propels** you into a particular action, it causes you to do it. EG *...a sense of guilt strong enough to propel him into action.* V+O+A

propeller /prə^{6}pɛlə/, **propellers.** A **propeller** is a device with blades which is attached to a boat or aircraft. The engine makes the propeller spin round and causes the boat or aircraft to move. N COUNT

propensity /prəpɛnsɪ^{1}ti^1/, **propensities.** If you have a **propensity** to behave in a particular way, you have a natural tendency to do this. EG *...our propensity to evil... ...their propensity for mass gatherings... There was no evidence of any propensity to act violently towards others.* N COUNT : USU+*for/to* OR *to*-INF Formal

proper /prɒpə/. 1 You use **proper** to describe things that you consider to be real and satisfactory rather than inadequate in some way. EG *He's never had a proper job... Lack of proper funding is making our job more difficult.* ADJ CLASSIF : ATTRIB

2 The **proper** thing is the one that is correct or most suitable. EG *Everything was in its proper place... What's the proper word for those things?* ADJ CLASSIF : ATTRIB

3 If you say that a way of behaving is **proper**, you mean that it is considered socially acceptable and right. EG *It wasn't proper for a man to cry.* ADJ CLASSIF

4 You can add **proper** after a word or name that refers to a place to emphasize that you are referring to the main or central part of the place and not to its edges or outer parts. EG *By the time I got to the village proper everyone was out to meet me.* ADJ AFTER N

properly /prɒpəli^1/. 1 If something is done **properly**, it is done correctly and satisfactorily. EG *We must see that the children are properly fed... The reviewers aren't doing their job properly.* ADV

2 If someone behaves **properly**, they behave in a way that is considered acceptable and not rude. ADV

proper noun, proper nouns. In grammar, a **proper noun** is a noun which is the name of a person, place, or institution. Proper nouns are usually spelled with a capital letter at the beginning. Words that are proper nouns have N PROP in the Extra Column. See the entry headed NOUNS for more information. N COUNT

property /prɒpəti^1/, **properties.** 1 Someone's **property** is all the things that belong to them or something that belongs to them. EG *Their job is to protect private property... Her property passes to her nephew.* N UNCOUNT

2 A **property** is a building and the land belonging to it. EG *He arranged to rent the property.* N COUNT Formal

3 The **properties** of a substance or object are the ways in which it behaves in particular conditions. EG *...the physical properties of substances.* N COUNT : OFT PLURAL

prophecy /prɒfɪsi^1/, **prophecies.** A **prophecy** is a statement in which someone says something that they believe will happen. EG *The prophecy was fulfilled... ...a prophecy which was greeted with ridicule.* N COUNT OR N UNCOUNT

prophesy /prɒfɪsaɪ/, **prophesies, prophesying, prophesied.** If you **prophesy** that something will happen, you say that you strongly believe that it will happen. EG *He has prophesied that the State will be destroyed... He prophesied a violent uprising.* V-SPEECH

prophet /prɒfɪt/, **prophets.** A **prophet** is 1 a person who is believed to be chosen by God to say the things that God wants to tell people. 2 someone who predicts that something will happen in the future. EG *The prophets of doom have been proved wrong before.* N COUNT Literary

prophetic /prə^{6}fɛtɪk/. If something was **prophetic**, it described or suggested something that did happen later. EG *...now, more than fifty years after she wrote those prophetic words.* ADJ QUALIT

propitious /prə^{6}pɪʃəs/. If something is **propitious**, it is likely to lead to success. EG *It was hardly a propitious time to join one of those newspapers.* ADJ QUALIT Formal

proponent /prə^{6}pəʊnənt/, **proponents.** If you are a **proponent** of a particular idea or course of action, you actively support it. EG *...the proponents of conservation.* N COUNT : USU+POSS Formal

proportion /prəpɔːʃə^{0}n/, **proportions.** 1 A **proportion** of an amount or group is a part of it. EG *Courts are now sending a smaller proportion of offenders to prison... There is always a proportion of the crowd which wants to make trouble.* N PART

2 The **proportion** of one kind of thing in a group is the number of things of that kind compared to the total number of things in the group. EG *The proportion of women in the total work-force has risen.* N PART

3 The **proportion** of one amount to another is how much greater one is than the other. EG *The proportion of workers to employers was large... Usually men outnumber women, but we have about equal proportions at Sussex.* N COUNT

4 You can refer to the size of something as its **proportions**. EG *...a gin and tonic of giant proportions... We are trying to reduce the problem to manageable proportions.* N PLURAL : USU+SUPP

5 If one thing increases or decreases **in proportion to** another thing, it increases or decreases to the same degree as that thing. EG *Reliability has increased in proportion to the number of switching units.* PHRASE

6 If one thing is small **in proportion** to another thing, it is small when you compare it with the other thing. EG *Babies have big heads in proportion to their bodies.* PHRASE

7 If you say that something is **out of all proportion** to something else, you mean that it is far greater or more serious than it should be. EG *These buildings were built out of all proportion to any human scale.* PHRASE

8 If you say that someone has **got** something **out of proportion**, you mean that they think it is more important or worrying than it really is. EG *Haven't you got things just a little bit out of proportion, Captain?* PHRASE

9 If someone has a **sense of proportion**, they know what is really important and what is not. EG *Remember where you are and who you are, keep a sense of proportion.* PHRASE

proportional /prəpɔːʃə^{0}nəl, -ʃənə^{0}l/. If one amount is **proportional** to another, it always remains the same fraction of the other. EG *As a rule the suicide rates are proportional to the size of the city.* ADJ CLASSIF : OFT+*to*

◇ **proportionally.** EG *Males have proportionally longer legs and larger feet than females.* ◇ ADV

proportionate /prəpɔːʃə^{0}nə^{1}t/ means the same as proportional. EG *After a run, your recovery time is proportionate to your fitness.* ADJ CLASSIF : OFT+*to* ◇ **proportionately.** EG *Britain spent proportionately more on research than its competitors... Poorer people are losing proportionately more through these tax changes.* ◇ ADV

proposal /prəpəʊzə^{0}l/, **proposals.** A **proposal** is 1 a plan which is suggested for people to think about and decide upon. EG *There is controversy about a proposal to build a new nuclear power station... ...proposals for cheaper flights to the United States.* 2 a request that someone makes to a person to marry them. EG *She told me that the* N COUNT *second proposal of marriage which she received came from an Italian prince.*

propose /prəpəuz/, **proposes, proposing, proposed.** 1 If you **propose** a plan or idea, you suggest it for people to think about and decide upon. EG *He proposed a bargain... I proposed that the culprits should be fined.* ◇ **proposed.** EG *...the proposed alliance.* V+O OR V+REPORT : ONLY *that* ◇ ADJ CLASSIF : ATTRIB

2 If you **propose** to do something, you intend to do it. EG *I do not propose to discuss this matter.* ◇ **proposed.** EG *...my proposed trip to America... The proposed tests should be interesting.* V+*to*-INF ◇ ADJ CLASSIF : ATTRIB

3 If someone **proposes** a motion in a debate, they introduce it and speak about why they agree with it. EG *Webb proposed the motion 'That this House has no confidence in the Government'.* V+O

4 If you **propose** a toast to someone or something, you ask people to drink a toast to them. V+O

5 If you **propose** to someone, you ask them to marry you. EG *He had known her for two years before he proposed... Was he proposing marriage?* V : OFT+*to*; ALSO V+O

proposition /prɒpəzɪʃə⁰n/, **propositions, propositioning, propositioned.** 1 A **proposition** is 1.1 a statement expressing a theory or opinion. EG *I had plenty of evidence to support the proposition that man was basically selfish.* 1.2 an offer or arrangement that someone suggests. EG *He came to me one day with an extraordinary proposition.* N COUNT

2 If someone **propositions** you, they ask you to have sex with them. V+O Formal

proprietary /prə⁶praɪətə⁰ri¹/. **Proprietary** substances are ones that are sold under a trade name. EG *For grease marks try a proprietary dry cleaner.* ADJ CLASSIF : ATTRIB Formal

proprietor /prə⁶praɪətə/, **proprietors.** The **proprietor** of a hotel, shop, or newspaper is the person who owns it. N COUNT

proprietress /prə⁶praɪətrɪ²s/, **proprietresses.** The **proprietress** of a hotel, shop, or newspaper is the woman who owns it. N COUNT

propriety /prə⁶praɪəti¹/ is the quality of being socially or morally acceptable. EG *I doubt the propriety of receiving a lady this late at night.* N UNCOUNT Formal

prosaic /prəuzeɪɪk/. Something that is **prosaic** is dull and uninteresting. EG *...a prosaic building... ...a prosaic existence... His methods were so prosaic.* ADJ QUALIT

prose /prəuz/ is ordinary written language, in contrast to poetry. EG *...descriptive prose... ...a fancy prose style... ...a piece of continuous prose.* N UNCOUNT

prosecute /prɒsɪkju:t/, **prosecutes, prosecuting, prosecuted.** 1 If someone **is prosecuted,** they are charged with a crime and put on trial. EG *He was prosecuted for drunken driving.* V+O OR V

2 The **prosecuting** lawyer in a trial tries to prove that the person who is on trial is guilty. ADJ CLASSIF : ATTRIB

prosecution /prɒsɪkju:ʃə⁰n/, **prosecutions.** 1 **Prosecution** is the action of charging someone with a crime and putting them on trial. EG *He could face criminal prosecution... The Smiths brought a prosecution against the organizers.* N UNCOUNT OR N COUNT

2 The lawyers who try to prove that a person on trial is guilty are called the **prosecution.** EG *Today he will be questioned by the prosecution.* N SING : *the*+N

prosecutor /prɒsɪkju:tə/, **prosecutors.** A **prosecutor** is a lawyer or official who brings charges against someone or tries to prove in a trial that they are guilty. N COUNT American

prospect, prospects, prospecting, prospected; pronounced /prɒspekt/ when it is a noun, and /prə⁷spekt/ when it is a verb.

1 If there is some **prospect** of something happening, there is a possibility that it will happen. EG *There was little prospect of significant military aid... ...the prospects for peace... ...the prospect that the skills learnt might have to be unlearnt.* N UNCOUNT : OFT+*of/for* OR REPORT

2 A particular **prospect** is something that you expect or know is going to happen. EG *She did not relish the prospect of climbing another flight of stairs... You may be daunted by this bleak prospect.* N COUNT OR N UNCOUNT : USU+*of*

3 Someone's **prospects** are their chances of being successful in their career, especially by being promoted quickly. EG *Success or failure here would be crucial to his future prospects.* N PLURAL : USU+POSS

4 If people **prospect** for oil, gold, or some other valuable substance, they look for it in the rock or under the sea. V : OFT+*for*

prospective /prə⁷spektɪv/. You use **prospective** to refer to something that someone wants to do or be. For example, a **prospective** tenant wants to be a tenant somewhere. EG *Godalming College has been forced to turn away 300 prospective students... ...prospective buyers.* ADJ CLASSIF : ATTRIB

prospectus /prə⁷spektəs/, **prospectuses.** A **prospectus** is a document produced by a college, school, or company, which gives details about it. N COUNT

prosper /prɒspə/, **prospers, prospering, prospered.** If people or businesses **prosper**, they are successful and do well financially. EG *The farmers prospered.* V

prosperity /prɒsperɪ¹ti¹/ is a condition in which a person or community is doing well financially. EG *...a period of wealth and prosperity.* N UNCOUNT

prosperous /prɒspə⁰rəs/. Someone who is **prosperous** is wealthy and successful. ADJ QUALIT

prostitute /prɒstɪtju:t/, **prostitutes, prostituting, prostituted.** 1 A **prostitute** is a person, usually a woman, who has sex with men in exchange for money. N COUNT

2 If you **prostitute** yourself or your talents, you use your talents for unworthy purposes, usually for money. V-REFL OR V+O

prostitution /prɒstɪtju:ʃə⁰n/ is the work of people who have sex with men in exchange for money. N UNCOUNT

prostrate, prostrates, prostrating, prostrated; pronounced /prɒstreɪt/ when it is a verb, and /prɒstreɪt/ when it is an adjective.

1 If you **prostrate** yourself, you lie flat on the ground with your face downwards. EG *I wanted to throw my arms about him, prostrate myself before him.* V-REFL

2 If you are **prostrate**, you are lying flat on the ground with your face downwards. EG *...the prostrate figure of Mr Green.* ADJ CLASSIF

protagonist /prə⁶tægənɪst/, **protagonists.** 1 Someone who is a **protagonist** of an idea or movement is a supporter of it. EG *She was a vehement protagonist of sexual equality.* N COUNT : USU+SUPP Formal

2 A **protagonist** in a play or event is one of the main people in it. N COUNT Formal

protect /prə⁶tekt/, **protects, protecting, protected.** To **protect** someone or something means to prevent them from being harmed or damaged. EG *She had his umbrella to protect her from the rain... Babies are protected against diseases like measles by their mothers' milk... The Common Law has always protected individual rights.* ◇ **protector** /prə⁶tektə/, **protectors.** EG *...ecologists and protectors of wildlife.* V+O : USU+A ◇ N COUNT

protection /prə⁶tekʃə⁰n/. If something gives **protection** against something unpleasant, it prevents people or things from being harmed or damaged by it. EG *The mud walls of these huts offer little protection against rats... We need protection from the sun's rays... She put on dark glasses as a protection against the strong light.* N UNCOUNT

protective /prə⁶tektɪv/. 1 A **protective** object or action is intended to protect something or someone from harm. EG *...protective clothing and equipment.* ADJ CLASSIF : ATTRIB

2 If someone is **protective** towards you, they show a strong desire to keep you safe. EG *She felt very protective towards her sister.* ◇ **protectively.** EG *Rudolph sat up, an arm tightening protectively around Julie's shoulder.* ADJ QUALIT : OFT+*towards* ◇ ADV

protégé /prɒtɪʒeɪ/, **protégés;** also spelled **protégée** when referring to a woman. N COUNT+POSS

If there is a prospect of rain, will it definitely rain?

If you are the **protégé** of an older and more experienced person, that person helps you and guides you over a period of time. EG *She was a painter and a protégée of Duncan Grant.* ◇ ADJ CLASSIF: ATTRIB

protein /prəʊti:n/, **proteins. Protein** is a substance found, for example, in meat, eggs, and milk. You need protein in order to grow and be healthy. N COUNT OR N UNCOUNT

protest, protests, protesting, protested; pronounced /prətɛst/ when it is a verb, and /prəʊtɛst/ when it is a noun.

1 If you **protest** about something or against something, you say or show publicly that you object to it. EG *Labour MPs took to the streets to protest against government economic policy... ...a group protesting at official inaction... I was shoved, protesting, into a side room.* ◇ **protester, protesters.** EG *The protesters surrendered to the police after about an hour.* V: USU +about/against/at ◇ N COUNT

2 If you **protest** something, you protest about it. EG *He protested the action in a phone call to the mayor.* V+O American

3 If you **protest** that something is the case, you insist that it is the case, when other people think that it may not be. EG *They protested that they had never heard of him... 'You're wrong,' I protested... The mother protested her innocence.* V-SPEECH: ONLY *that*

4 A **protest** is the act of saying or showing publicly that you object to something. EG *They joined in the protests against the government's proposals... There was a wave of student riots, in protest at university conditions.* N COUNT OR N UNCOUNT

Protestant /prɒtɪ²stənt/, **Protestants.** A **Protestant** is someone who belongs to the branch of the Christian church which separated from the Catholic church in the sixteenth century. EG *Most of them were Protestants... ...Protestant groups.* N COUNT

protestation /prɒtɛsteɪʃə⁰n, prɒ/, **protestations.** A **protestation** is a strong declaration that something is true or not true. EG *...Meehan's vehement protestations of innocence.* N COUNT Formal

protocol /prəʊtəkɒl/ is a system of rules about the correct way to act in formal situations. EG *She was ignorant of protocol... Beaton had to face a tricky problem of protocol.* N UNCOUNT

proton /prəʊtɒn/, **protons.** A **proton** is an atomic particle that has an electrical charge. N COUNT Technical

prototype /prəʊtə⁶taɪp/, **prototypes.** A **prototype** is the first model that is made of something new. EG *Funds for testing of the prototypes ran out... ...a prototype plane.* N COUNT

protracted /prə⁶trækɪ²d/. Something that is **protracted** lasts a long time, especially longer than usual. EG *She was late returning to the office after a protracted lunch... ...Tim's protracted absence.* ADJ QUALIT

protrude /prə⁶tru:d/, **protrudes, protruding, protruded.** If something **protrudes** from somewhere, it sticks out. EG *He tripped over a pair of boots protruding from under the table... ...his protruding ribs... A steel stud protruded upwards.* V: USU+A Formal

proud /praʊd/, **prouder, proudest. 1** If you feel **proud**, you feel glad about something good that you or someone close to you owns or has done. EG *They seemed proud of what they had accomplished... Their country should be proud of them... It makes me proud to be an American.* ◇ **proudly.** EG *He was grinning proudly, delighted with his achievement.... 'I was a cop,' said Mac proudly.* ADJ QUALIT: OFT+*of* OR *to*-INF ◇ ADV

2 Someone who is **proud 2.1** has dignity and self-respect. EG *He was a poor but very proud old man.* **2.2** feels that they are superior to other people. EG *She was too proud to apologize.* ADJ QUALIT

prove /pru:v/, **proves, proving, proved, proven** /pru:və⁰n/. **Proved** and **proven** are both used as the past participle.

1 To **prove** that something is true means to show definitely that it is true. EG *He was able to prove that he was an American... He is going to have to prove his innocence... She has to be proved wrong.* V+REPORT, V+O, OR V+C

◇ **proven.** EG *This man is a proven liar... ...based on proven fact.*

2 If someone or something **proves** to have a particular quality, they are found to have that quality. EG *I proved to be hopeless as a teacher... This information has proved useful to many people.* V+*to*-INF OR V+C

proverb /prɒvɜ:b/, **proverbs.** A **proverb** is a short sentence that people often quote, which gives advice or tells you something about life. EG *...the old Jewish proverb 'A man is not a man until he has a son.'* N COUNT

proverbial /prəvɜ:bɪəl/. You use **proverbial** when you want to emphasize that what you are saying is part of a well-known proverb or expression. EG *It is rather like looking for the needle in the proverbial haystack.* ADJ CLASSIF: ATTRIB

provide /prəvaɪd/, **provides, providing, provided.** If you **provide** something that someone needs or wants, you give it to them or make it available to them. EG *Most animals provide food for their young... The government cannot provide all young people with a job... A victory next Sunday could provide the opportunity he needs.* ◇ **provider, providers.** EG *...her duties as a provider of food.* V+O: OFT +*for/with* ◇ N COUNT

• See also **provided, providing.**

provide for. 1 If you **provide for** someone, you support them and give them the things that they need. EG *Parents are expected to provide for their children... Each of us would be provided for.* PHRASAL VB: V+PREP, HAS PASS

2 If you **provide for** a possible future event, you make arrangements to deal with it. EG *Should the law provide for these cases?* V+PREP, HAS PASS Formal

provided /prəvaɪdɪ²d/. If you say that something will happen **provided** or **provided that** something else happens, you mean that the first thing will happen only if the second thing also happens. EG *Children were permitted into the hall, provided they sat at the back... She was prepared to come, provided that she might bring her daughter.* CONJ

providence /prɒvɪdəns/ is God or a force which is believed by some people to arrange the things that happen to us. EG *The money lender proposed that they let providence decide the matter.* N UNCOUNT Literary

providential /prɒvɪdɛnʃə⁰l/. An event that is **providential** is lucky. EG *...his providential deliverance from danger.* ADJ CLASSIF Formal

providing /prəvaɪdɪŋ/. If you say that something will happen **providing** or **providing that** something else happens, you mean that the first thing will happen only if the second thing also happens. EG *It would be pleasant living in Glasgow providing you were living in a nice flat.* CONJ

province /prɒvɪns/, **provinces. 1** A **province** is a large section of a country, which has its own administration. EG *...rallies in Zimbabwe's five provinces... ...the authorities in Guangdong province.* N COUNT

2 The **provinces** are all the parts of a country except the part where the capital is situated. EG *...teenage life in the provinces.* N PLURAL: *the*+N

3 If you say that a subject or activity is a particular person's **province**, you mean that this person has special knowledge about it or special responsibility for it. EG *Dating fossils will always remain the province of the specialist.* N SING+POSS Formal

provincial /prəvɪnʃə⁰l/. **1 Provincial** means connected with the parts of a country outside the capital. EG *...provincial newspapers... ...provincial towns... ...the provincial police.* ADJ CLASSIF: ATTRIB

2 Someone or something that is **provincial** is narrow-minded and unsophisticated. EG *His art is primitive and provincial.* ADJ QUALIT

provision /prəvɪʒə⁰n/, **provisions. 1** The **provision** of something is the act of giving it or making it available to people who need it. EG *...helping needy people by the provision of food, clothing, and shelter... ...the provision of credit.* N UNCOUNT: OFT+*of*

2 If you make **provision** for a future need, you make arrangements to ensure that it is dealt with. EG *She did not make any provision for her chil-* N UNCOUNT: OFT+*for* *dren... They made provision for the defence of Britain... He failed to make provision for this threat.*

3 A **provision** in an agreement or law is an arrangement which is included in it. EG *The Act excluded from its provisions death by murder.* N COUNT

4 **Provisions** are supplies of food. EG *We set out with enough provisions for the long trip.* N PLURAL

provisional /prəvɪʒəⁿnəl, -ʒənəⁿl/. Something that is **provisional** may be changed in the future. EG *...a provisional government... ...a provisional diagnosis of schizophrenia... ...the provisional cost.* ADJ CLASSIF

proviso /prəvaɪzəʊ/, **provisos.** A **proviso** is a condition in an agreement. You agree to do something if this condition is fulfilled. EG *At last she consented, with the proviso that he should repay her as soon as he could.* N COUNT: OFT+REPORT

provocation /prɒvəkeɪʃəⁿn/, **provocations.** If you describe something that someone does as **provocation**, you mean that they did it deliberately in order to make someone react angrily or violently. EG *They must not react to this provocation... She has a tantrum at the least provocation.* N UNCOUNT OR N COUNT

provocative /prəvɒkətɪv/. Something that is **provocative** is 1 intended to make people react angrily or argue against it. EG *He wrote a provocative article on 'Anti-racialism'.* 2 intended to make someone feel sexual desire. EG *...a provocative dance... ...exposing her leg in a provocative way.* ADJ QUALIT

provoke /prəvəʊk/, **provokes, provoking, provoked.** 1 If you **provoke** someone, you deliberately annoy them and try to make them behave aggressively. EG *Ray was trying to provoke them into fighting... They are armed and ready to shoot if provoked in the slightest way.* V+O

2 If something **provokes** a violent or unpleasant reaction, it causes it. EG *The petition provoked a storm of criticism.* V+O

prow /praʊ/, **prows.** The **prow** of a ship or boat is the front part of it. N COUNT

prowess /praʊɪ²s/. Someone's **prowess** is their outstanding ability at doing a particular thing. EG *There are legends about his prowess as a jockey... ...her conversational prowess.* N UNCOUNT Formal

prowl /praʊl/, **prowls, prowling, prowled.** 1 When animals or people **prowl** around, they move around quietly, for example when they are hunting. EG *I found four foxes prowling round my flock one night... Gangs of youths prowl the streets.* V: OFT+A, OR V+O

2 An animal or person that is **on the prowl** is prowling around. PHRASE

proximity /prɒksɪmɪ¹ti¹/. **Proximity** to a place is nearness to that place. EG *...the town's proximity to the northern cape of Japan.* N UNCOUNT +SUPP Formal

proxy /prɒksi¹/. If you do something **by proxy**, you arrange for someone else to do it for you. EG *Soviet support, direct or by proxy, ended any further threats.* PHRASE

prude /pruːd/, **prudes.** If you call someone a **prude**, you mean that they are easily shocked by things relating to nudity or sex; used showing disapproval. EG *Don't be such a prude.* N COUNT

prudent /pruːdənt/. Someone who is **prudent** is sensible and careful. EG *He now considered it prudent to carry a revolver.* ◇ **prudently.** EG *Fanny prudently resolved to keep silent.* ◇ **prudence** /pruːdəns/. EG *I consider that I have acted with proper diligence and prudence.* ADJ QUALIT ◇ ADV ◇ N UNCOUNT Formal

prudish /pruːdɪʃ/. If you describe someone as **prudish**, you mean that they are easily shocked by things relating to nudity or sex; used showing disapproval. EG *...four aunts, religious and prudish.* ADJ QUALIT

prune /pruːn/, **prunes, pruning, pruned.** 1 A **prune** is a dried plum. N COUNT

2 When you **prune** a tree or bush, you cut off some of the branches. EG *He went to prune the roses.* V+O

pry /praɪ/, **pries, prying, pried.** When someone **pries**, they try to find out about someone else's private affairs, often secretly. EG *Look, I'm not trying to pry... So don't go prying into my affairs or you'll get hurt.* V: OFT+*into*

PS /piː ɛs/. You write **PS** to introduce a further message at the end of a letter after you have signed it. EG *With love from us both, Dad. PS Mum asks me to remind you to bring back her duvet.*

psalm /sɑːm/, **psalms.** The **Psalms** are the 150 songs, poems, and prayers which together form the Book of Psalms in the Bible. EG *The reading of the Psalm was ended... ...the 24th Psalm.* N COUNT

pseud /sjuːd/, **pseuds.** If you say that someone is a **pseud**, you mean that they are trying to appear very well-educated or artistic, in a pretentious way. N COUNT Informal

pseudo- is used to form adjectives and nouns that describe something as not being the thing that it is claimed to be. For example, if you describe a country as a pseudo-democracy, you mean that it is not really a democracy, although its government claims that it is. EG *...pseudo-scientific ideas... ...pseudo-liberals.* PREFIX

pseudonym /sjuːdənɪm/, **pseudonyms.** A **pseudonym** is a name which a writer uses instead of his or her real name. EG *Many journalists wrote under pseudonyms.* N COUNT

psych /saɪk/, **psychs, psyching, psyched.** The spellings **psyche, psyches** are also used. If you **psych** yourself **up** before a contest or a difficult task, you prepare yourself for it mentally, especially by telling yourself that you can win or succeed. EG *He had to psych himself into writing the book.* PHRASAL VB: V-REFL+ADV Informal

psyche /saɪki¹/, **psyches.** 1 Your **psyche** is your mind and your deepest feelings and attitudes. EG *It is easy to understand how a person's psyche can be damaged by such experiences.* N COUNT: USU+SUPP

2 See also **psych**.

psychedelic /saɪkədɛlɪk/. 1 **Psychedelic** drugs are drugs such as LSD, which affect your mind and make you imagine that you are seeing strange things. EG *...the use of drugs in the pursuit of psychedelic experience.* ADJ CLASSIF: ATTRIB

2 **Psychedelic** art has bright colours and strange patterns. EG *...psychedelic posters.* ADJ CLASSIF

psychiatric /saɪkɪætrɪk/ means 1 relating to psychiatry. EG *...a psychiatric hospital... ...the psychiatric profession.* 2 involving mental illness. EG *...psychiatric disorders... ...a mother with psychiatric problems.* ADJ CLASSIF: ATTRIB

psychiatrist /saɪkaɪətrɪst/, **psychiatrists.** A **psychiatrist** is a doctor who treats people suffering from mental illness. EG *It was arranged that I should see a psychiatrist.* N COUNT

psychiatry /saɪkaɪətri¹/ is the branch of medicine concerned with the treatment of mental illness. EG *...a Professor of Psychiatry.* N UNCOUNT

psychic /saɪkɪk/. 1 Someone who is **psychic** or who has **psychic** powers has strange mental powers, such as being able to read the minds of other people or to see into the future. ADJ CLASSIF

2 **Psychic** means relating to the mind rather than the body. EG *Most of the psychic damage to a child is done in the first five years of its life.* ADJ CLASSIF Formal

psychical /saɪkɪkəⁿl/ means the same as psychic. EG *...the Society for Psychical Research.* ADJ CLASSIF Formal

psycho /saɪkəʊ/, **psychos.** A **psycho** is someone who is mad and who does violent things, such as killing people. EG *...a raving psycho who kills just for kicks.* ▸ used as an adjective. EG *He was practically psycho.* N COUNT Informal ▸ ADJ PRED

psychoanalyse /saɪkəʊænəlaɪz/, **psychoanalyses, psychoanalysing, psychoanalysed;** also spelled **psychoanalyze** in American English. When a psychotherapist or psychiatrist **psychoanalyses** someone who is mentally ill, he or she V+O

Name four jobs on these pages.

examines or treats them using the method of psychoanalysis.

psychoanalysis /saɪkəʊənælɪsɪs/ is the examination or treatment of someone who is mentally ill by asking them about their feelings and their past in order to try to discover what may be causing their condition. EG *He sought help through psychoanalysis.* N UNCOUNT

psychoanalyst /saɪkəʊænəlɪst/, **psychoanalysts.** A **psychoanalyst** is someone who treats people who are mentally ill using the method of psychoanalysis. N COUNT

psychoanalyze /saɪkəʊænəlaɪz/. See **psychoanalyse**.

psychological /saɪkə^{6}lɒdʒɪkəl/. **1 Psychological** means concerned with a person's mind and thoughts. EG *Are there important psychological differences between the two sexes?* ADJ CLASSIF
◊ **psychologically.** EG *She was tough, both physically and psychologically.* ◊ ADV

2 Psychological also means relating to psychology. EG *...psychological tests.* ADJ CLASSIF : ATTRIB

psychologist /saɪkɒlədʒɪst/, **psychologists.** A **psychologist** is a person who studies the human mind and tries to explain why people behave in the way that they do. N COUNT

psychology /saɪkɒlədʒi^1/. **1 Psychology** is the scientific study of the human mind and the reasons for people's behaviour. N UNCOUNT

2 The **psychology** of a person is the kind of mind that they have, which makes them think or behave in the way that they do. EG *...the psychology of the travelling salesman.* N UNCOUNT +SUPP

psychopath /saɪkə^{6}pæθ/, **psychopaths.** A **psychopath** is someone who is mad and does violent things, such as killing people. N COUNT
◊ **psychopathic** /saɪkə^{6}pæθɪk/. EG *...a film about a psychopathic murderer.* ◊ ADJ CLASSIF : ATTRIB

psychosis /saɪkəʊsɪs/ is a kind of severe mental illness. EG *...acute psychosis following the birth of her first child.* N UNCOUNT Medical

psychosomatic /saɪkə^{6}sə^{6}mætɪk/. A **psychosomatic** illness is a physical illness which someone has because they are very worried or unhappy. ADJ CLASSIF

psychotherapist /saɪkəʊθerəpɪst/, **psychotherapists.** A **psychotherapist** is a person who treats people who are mentally ill using psychotherapy. N COUNT

psychotherapy /saɪkəʊθerəpi^1/ is the use of psychological methods to treat people who are mentally ill, rather than using physical methods such as drugs or surgery. EG *Psychotherapy has helped me enormously... ...psychotherapy sessions.* N UNCOUNT

psychotic /saɪkɒtɪk/, **psychotics.** Someone who is **psychotic** has a type of severe mental illness. EG *...a psychotic patient... ...the treatment of psychotic conditions.* ▸ used as a noun. EG *Do you want to turn the children into a bunch of psychotics?* ADJ CLASSIF Medical ▸ N COUNT

pt, pts. pt is a written abbreviation for 'pint'. The plural is either 'pt' or 'pts'. EG *...1 pt warm water.*

PTO /piː tiː əʊ/ is a written abbreviation for 'please turn over'. You write it at the bottom of a page to indicate that there is more writing on the other side.

pub /pʌb/, **pubs.** A **pub** is a building where people can have drinks, especially alcoholic drinks, and talk to their friends. EG *We used to go drinking in a pub called the Soldier's Arms.* N COUNT

puberty /pjuːbəti^1/ is the stage in someone's life when they start to become physically like an adult. EG *...a boy who has reached the age of puberty.* N UNCOUNT

public /pʌblɪk/. **1** You can refer to people in general, or to all the people in a particular country or community, as the **public**. EG *...appeals to the public... All members of the public are welcome... The gardens are open to the public.* N COLL : SING, *the*+N

2 You can refer to a set of people in a country who share a common interest, activity, or characteristic as a particular kind of **public**. EG *...literature available to the general reading public.* N COLL : SING, *the*+N

3 Public means relating to all the people in a country or community. EG *The campaigners have attracted significant public support... The politicians have to respond to public opinion... The problem was how to sustain public interest... These fumes are a hazard to public health.* ADJ CLASSIF : ATTRIB

4 Public spending is money spent by the government of a country to provide services for its people. EG *The government is reducing public spending.* ADJ CLASSIF : ATTRIB

5 Public buildings and services are provided for everyone to use. EG *Both of these books can be obtained from the Public Library... ...public transport... ...public telephones.* ADJ CLASSIF : ATTRIB

6 If someone is a **public** figure or in **public** life, they are known about by many people because they are often mentioned in newspapers and on television. EG *...famous and highly respected public figures... Well-known people from all sections of public life gave the scheme their support.* ADJ CLASSIF : ATTRIB

7 Public is used to describe statements, actions, and events that are made or done in such a way that any member of the public can see them or be aware of them. EG *No public announcement had yet been made... We hold weekly public meetings... ...public speakers addressing large groups of people.* ADJ CLASSIF : ATTRIB
◊ **publicly.** EG *I am going to say what I think of him openly and publicly.* ◊ ADV
● If you say or do something **in public**, you say or do it when a group of other people are present. EG *He repeated in public what he had said in private.* ● PHRASE

8 If a fact is made **public**, it becomes known to everyone rather than being kept secret. EG *The cause of death was not made public.* ADJ PRED

9 A **public** place is one where people can go about freely and where you can easily be seen and heard. EG *This is a very public place. Can we talk somewhere else?* ADJ QUALIT

publican /pʌblɪkən/, **publicans.** A **publican** is a person who owns or manages a pub. EG *He was born in 1871, the son of a publican.* N COUNT British Formal

publication /pʌblɪkeɪʃə^{0}n/, **publications. 1** The **publication** of a book or magazine is the act of printing it and sending it to shops to be sold. EG *Several of her articles have already been accepted for publication.* N UNCOUNT

2 A **publication** is a book or magazine that has been published. EG *...a respected scholar with a long list of publications to his name.* N COUNT

public bar, public bars. A **public bar** is a room in a British pub where the furniture is plain and the drinks are cheaper than in the other bars. N COUNT

public company, public companies. A **public company** is a company whose shares can be bought by the general public. N COUNT

public convenience, public conveniences. A **public convenience** is a toilet that is provided in a public place for everyone to use. N COUNT British

public house, public houses. A **public house** is the same as a pub. EG *...the customers of a local public house... The best place to talk was the public house.* N COUNT British

publicise /pʌblɪsaɪz/. See **publicize**.

publicist /pʌblɪsɪst/, **publicists.** A **publicist** is a person who publicizes things, especially as part of a job in advertising or journalism. N COUNT

publicity /pʌblɪsɪ^{1}ti^1/. **1 Publicity** is information or actions intended to attract the public's attention to someone or something. EG *There was some advance publicity for the book.* N UNCOUNT

2 When newspapers and television pay a lot of attention to something, you can say that it is receiving **publicity**. EG *Feminism has attracted a lot of publicity... She sought out publicity.* N UNCOUNT

publicize /pʌblɪsaɪz/, **publicizes, publicizing, publicized;** also spelled **publicise.** If you **publicize** a fact or event, you make it widely known to V+O the public. EG *His programme for reform was well publicised in his newspapers.*

public relations is 1 the part of an organization's work that is concerned with obtaining the public's approval for what it does. EG *...running a large public relations department.* N UNCOUNT 2 the state of the relationship between an organization and the public. EG *It's good for public relations.* N PLURAL

public school, public schools. 1 In Britain, a **public school** is a private school that provides secondary education which parents have to pay special fees for. The pupils often live at the school during the school term. EG *...a public school education.* N COUNT OR N UNCOUNT

2 In the USA, Australia, and some other parts of the world, a **public school** is a school that is supported financially by the government from the taxes that all working people pay. N COUNT OR N UNCOUNT

public-spirited. Someone who is **public-spirited** tries to help the community that they belong to. EG *She's a public-spirited woman who takes part in politics.* ADJ QUALIT

publish /pʌblɪʃ/, **publishes, publishing, published.** 1 When a company **publishes** a book or magazine, it prints copies of it, which are sent to shops and sold. EG *The Collins Cobuild dictionary was published in 1987.* V+O

2 When the people in charge of a newspaper or magazine **publish** a piece of writing, they print it in their newspaper or magazine. EG *The Times would never publish any letter I sent in.* V+O

3 If someone **publishes** a book or an article that they have written, they arrange to have it published. EG *He has published quite a lot of articles.* V+O

4 If you **publish** information or an opinion, you make it known to the public by having it printed in a newspaper or magazine. EG *He received a long prison term for publishing his views.* V+O

publisher /pʌblɪʃə/, **publishers.** A **publisher** is a person or a company that publishes books. EG *The publishers of the book are Collins.* N COUNT

publishing /pʌblɪʃɪŋ/ is the profession of publishing books. EG *I'd like a career in publishing.* N UNCOUNT

puce /pjuːs/. Something that is **puce** is a dark purple colour. EG *...his puce complexion.* ADJ COLOUR

pucker /pʌkə/, **puckers, puckering, puckered.**
1 When a part of your face **puckers** or when you **pucker** it, it becomes wrinkled because you are frowning or trying not to cry. EG *His face puckered, the tears leapt from his eyes.* V-ERG

2 If fabric or other material **puckers**, it becomes wrinkled or creased. V-ERG

pudding /pʊdɪŋ/, **puddings.** 1 A **pudding** is a cooked sweet food made with flour, fat, and eggs, and usually served hot. EG *They want vanilla pudding... ...steamed puddings.* N COUNT OR N UNCOUNT

2 Some people refer to the sweet course of a meal as the **pudding**. EG *Can they have second helpings of pudding?* N UNCOUNT Informal British

3 See also **Yorkshire pudding**.

puddle /pʌdəˡl/, **puddles.** A **puddle** is a small, shallow pool of liquid that has spread on the ground. EG *The road was filled with puddles from the rain... ...a puddle of blood.* N COUNT

puff /pʌf/, **puffs, puffing, puffed.** 1 If someone **puffs** a cigarette or pipe or if they **puff** at it, they smoke it. EG *He puffed his pipe for several moments... He sat at the desk and puffed at his cigar... She puffed on the cigarette and sipped her drink.* V+O OR V+*at*/*on*
▸ used as a noun. EG *She raised the cigarette to her lips, intending to take a puff.* ▸ N COUNT : IF SING OFT *a*+N

2 If you **are puffing**, you are breathing loudly and quickly with your mouth open because you are out of breath after a lot of physical effort. EG *We lugged the branch underneath, panting and puffing.* V : USU CONT ▸ used as a noun. EG *Her breath came in puffs and gasps.* ▸ N COUNT

3 A **puff** of air or smoke is a small amount of it that is blown out from somewhere. EG *The stove let out a puff of smoke.* N PART

4 See also **puffed**.

puff out. To **puff** something **out** means to make it larger and rounder, usually by filling it with air. EG *Their chests were puffed out like angry swans... They puffed out their cheeks.* PHRASAL VB : V-ERG+ADV

puff up. If part of your body **puffs up** as a result of an injury, it becomes swollen. EG *Small areas on their arms or legs would puff up.* PHRASAL VB : V+ADV

puffed /pʌft/. 1 If a part of your body is **puffed** or **puffed up**, it is swollen because of an injury. EG *Her left eye is all puffed up.* ADJ PRED

2 If you are **puffed** or **puffed out**, you are breathing with difficulty because you have been using a lot of energy. EG *By the time I got to the top I was pretty well puffed out.* ADJ PRED Informal

puffin /pʌfɪn/, **puffins.** A **puffin** is a black and white bird with a large, brightly-coloured beak. Puffins live by the sea. N COUNT

puff pastry is a type of pastry which is very light and flaky. N UNCOUNT

puffy /pʌfi¹/. Something that is **puffy** has a round, swollen appearance. EG *One eye was a slit in his puffy cheek.* ADJ QUALIT

pugnacious /pʌgneɪʃəs/. Someone who is **pugnacious** is always ready to quarrel or start a fight. EG *I got punched in the face by a pugnacious apprentice.* ADJ QUALIT Formal

puke /pjuːk/, **pukes, puking, puked.** When someone **pukes**, they vomit. EG *The baby puked a couple more times.* V Informal

pull /pʊl/, **pulls, pulling, pulled.** 1 When you **pull** something, you hold it firmly and use force in order to move it towards you. EG *The women's job was to pull the grass and weeds out of the corn... She pulled Paul's hair so hard that he yelled... He hoisted the rope over the branch and pulled with all his strength... He got back into bed and pulled the blankets around him... He pulled forward a chair... They started pulling up the floorboards... I shut my eyes when I pulled the trigger.* V+O : USU+A; ALSO V

2 When a vehicle, animal, or person **pulls** a cart or piece of machinery, they are attached to it or hold it, so that it moves along behind them when they move forward. EG *Farmers were driving open carts pulled by donkeys.* V+O

3 If you **pull** a part of your body in a particular direction, or if you **pull** away, you move a part of your body with force. EG *'Let go of me,' she said, and pulled her arm savagely out of his grasp... He tried to kiss her, but she pulled away fiercely.* V+O+A OR V+A

4 If you **pull** yourself out of a place, you hold onto something and use effort to move your body out of the place. EG *Ralph pulled himself out of the water.* V-REFL+A

5 If you **pull** at something, you hold it and move it towards you and then let it go again. EG *'Come home now, Jim,' she said, pulling at his sleeve.* V+*at*

6 When you **pull** a curtain or blind, you move it across a window in order to cover or uncover it. EG *She closed the window and pulled the blind.* V+O

7 If you **pull** something apart or **pull** it to pieces, you break it or take it apart without much care. EG *If you pull apart one of the calculators, you won't get it back together again... Try and stop the cat pulling the Christmas tree to bits.* V+O+A

8 To **pull** people means to attract their support or interest. EG *He was interested in the number of voters she would pull.* V+O Informal

9 If you **pull** a muscle, you injure it by stretching it. EG *Despite pulling a muscle, he managed to finish third in the race.* V+O

10 to **pull** your **socks up**: see **sock**.

pull apart. If you **pull** fighting people or animals **apart**, you separate them using force. EG *I rushed in and tried to pull the dogs apart.* PHRASAL VB : V+O+ADV

pull away. When a vehicle **pulls away**, it starts PHRASAL VB :

When a bus pulls up, does it pull in?

moving forward. EG *The bus pulled away... As the lights changed, I pulled away and drove past him.* V+ADV

pull down. If a building **is pulled down**, it is deliberately destroyed, often in order to build a new one. EG *Why did they pull those houses down?* PHRASAL VB : V+O+ADV

pull in. When a vehicle **pulls in** somewhere, it stops there. EG *I pulled in for petrol... The London train pulled in to the station.* PHRASAL VB : V+ADV, OFT+A

pull off. 1 If you **pull** clothes **off**, you take them off quickly. EG *He pulled off his shirt... She pulled off her shoes and stockings.* PHRASAL VB : V+O+ADV 2 If someone has succeeded in doing something very difficult, you can say that they **have pulled** it **off**. EG *She had succeeded, triumphantly: she had pulled it off.* V+O+ADV Informal

pull on. If you **pull** clothes **on**, you put them on quickly. EG *He started to pull on his tattered shorts.* PHRASAL VB : V+O+ADV

pull out. 1 When a vehicle **pulls out** from a place, it moves out of the place. EG *The train pulled out of the station.* PHRASAL VB : V+ADV 2 If you **pull out** of a difficult situation, you succeed in getting out of it. EG *It's going to take us even longer to pull out of this recession.* V-ERG+ADV 3 If you **pull out** of an agreement or business deal, you withdraw from it. EG *You pay a 10% deposit which you lose if you pull out before completion... He pulled his party out of the coalition.* V-ERG+ADV 4 If an army **pulls out** of a place, it leaves it. EG *Troops had begun to pull out of the area... The Prime Minister intended to pull them out soon.* V-ERG+ADV

pull over. 1 When a vehicle **pulls over**, it moves closer to the side of the road. EG *Pull over, Oliver. Stop the car.* PHRASAL VB : V+ADV 2 See also **pullover**.

pull through. If you **pull through** a serious illness or if the doctor **pulls** you **through**, you recover from it. EG *I think she'll pull through.* PHRASAL VB : V-ERG+ADV/PREP

pull together. 1 If people **pull together**, they co-operate with each other. EG *We all pulled together during the war.* PHRASAL VB : V+ADV 2 If you are upset or excited and someone tells you to **pull** yourself **together**, they are telling you to control your feelings and behave calmly again. EG *That's quite enough of that. Pull yourself together now.* PHRASE

pull up. 1 When a vehicle **pulls up**, it slows down and stops. EG *The rain stopped as we pulled up at the hotel.* PHRASAL VB : V+ADV 2 If you **pull up** a chair, you move it closer to something or someone. EG *I pulled up a chair and sat down to watch the news.* V+O+ADV 3 If something **pulls** you **up short**, it makes you stop what you are doing. EG *The man's evident surprise pulled him up short.* PHRASE

pulley /pʊli¹/, **pulleys.** A **pulley** is a device which is used for lifting or lowering heavy weights. It consists of a wheel with a hollow rim which is fixed above the ground. You pass a rope over the rim, attach one end of the rope to the weight, and pull or gradually release the other end. N COUNT

pullover /pʊləʊvə/, **pullovers.** A **pullover** is a woollen piece of clothing that covers the upper part of your body and your arms. You put it on by pulling it over your head. See picture at CLOTHES. N COUNT

pulp /pʌlp/, **pulps, pulping, pulped.** 1 If an object is turned into a **pulp**, it is crushed or beaten until it is soft, smooth, and wet. EG *We squashed the berries into a pulp.* N UNCOUNT OR N SING

2 The **pulp** of a fruit or vegetable is the soft inner part. EG *Fill the bowl with the fruit pulp.* N UNCOUNT

3 Wood **pulp** is material made from crushed wood. It is used to make paper. EG *...supplies of wood pulp needed for the newsprint.* N UNCOUNT

4 People sometimes refer to books or magazines as **pulp** when they consider them to be of poor quality. EG *They seem satisfied with cheap tabloids, trite films, and the pulp library of crime.* N UNCOUNT : USU N MOD

5 To **pulp** something means to crush it. EG *Once gnawed, ground, and pulped, the food has to be digested.* V+O

pulpit /pʊlpɪt/, **pulpits.** A **pulpit** is a small raised platform in a church with a rail or barrier around it, where a member of the clergy stands to preach. EG *The vicar descended from the pulpit.* N COUNT

pulpy /pʌlpi¹/. Something that is **pulpy** is soft, smooth, and wet, often because it has been crushed or beaten. EG *Her lips felt pulpy and tender.* ADJ QUALIT

pulsate /pʌlseɪt/, **pulsates, pulsating, pulsated.** If something **pulsates**, it moves or shakes with strong, regular movements. EG *The creature has no heart, only a number of pulsating arteries... Her final top note pulsated with triumph.* V

pulse /pʌls/, **pulses, pulsing, pulsed.** 1 Your **pulse** is the regular beating of blood through your body, which you can feel when you touch particular parts of your body, especially your wrist. EG *Her pulse started to race.* N COUNT : USU SING • When a doctor or nurse **takes** your **pulse**, he or she finds out the speed of your heartbeat by feeling the pulse in your wrist. EG *He was busy taking her pulse.* • PHRASE

2 A **pulse** is also a regular beat in music, which is often produced by a drum. EG *...a rhythm which contains a basic pulse.* N SING

3 Some seeds which can be cooked and eaten are called **pulses**, for example the seeds of peas, beans, and lentils. EG *...protein foods such as fish, pulses, and wholemeal bread... ...a range of cereals, pulses and vegetables.* N COUNT : USU PLURAL

4 If something **pulses**, it moves or shakes with strong, regular movements. EG *...a soft rhythmic pulsing sound.* V

pulverize /pʌlvəraɪz/, **pulverizes, pulverizing, pulverized;** also spelled **pulverise.** 1 To **pulverize** something means to make it into a powder by crushing it. EG *The processes involved pulverising the nuts.* V+O

2 When guns or bombs **pulverize** a place, they destroy it completely. EG *Vast areas were pulverized by enemy tanks.* V+O

pumice /pʌmɪs/ or **pumice stone** is a kind of grey stone that is very light in weight. You can use it to clean surfaces, or you can rub it on your skin in order to soften it. N UNCOUNT

pummel /pʌmə⁰l/, **pummels, pummelling, pummelled;** spelled **pummeling, pummeled** in American English. V+O

If you **pummel** someone or something, you beat them again and again using your fists. EG *She tipped some water into the bowl of flour and fat, and pummelled it fiercely.*

pump /pʌmp/, **pumps, pumping, pumped.** 1 A **pump** is a machine which is used to force a liquid or gas to flow in strong, regular movements in a particular direction. N COUNT

2 A **pump** is also 2.1 a device for bringing water to the surface from below the ground. Pumps often have a handle that you push in order to force the water upwards. EG *...the village pump... We scrubbed ourselves under the pump.* N COUNT 2.2 a device that you use in order to force air into something, especially into the tyre of a vehicle. EG *...a bicycle pump.*

3 A petrol **pump** is a machine with a hose attached to it from which you can fill a car with petrol. N COUNT

4 **Pumps** are canvas shoes with flat rubber soles which people wear for sports and leisure. N COUNT : USU PLURAL

5 To **pump** a liquid or gas in a particular direction means to force it to flow in that direction, using a pump. EG *We can use the electricity to pump water back into a dam or a reservoir.* V+O+A

6 To **pump** water, oil, or gas means to get a supply of it from below the surface of the ground, using a pump. EG *John went to a cast-iron pump and started pumping water to drink.* V+O

7 If you **pump** money or energy into something, you put a lot of money or energy into it. EG *Most governments have pumped all available funds into large-scale modern technological projects.* V+O+*into* Informal

8 If you **pump** someone about something, you keep asking them questions in order to get information. EG *I pumped him discreetly about his past.* V+O Informal

pumpkin /pʌmpᵊkɪn/, **pumpkins.** A **pumpkin** is a large, round, orange-coloured vegetable with a thick skin. EG ...*pumpkin pie.* N COUNT OR N UNCOUNT

pun /pʌn/, **puns.** A **pun** is a clever and amusing use of words that have more than one meaning, or words that have the same sound, so that what you say has two different meanings. For example, if you say 'Schmidt copied out scores of symphonies', this could mean either that Schmidt copied out the written versions of symphonies or that he copied out a very large number of symphonies, because 'scores of' has these two different meanings. N COUNT

punch /pʌntʃ/, **punches, punching, punched. 1** If you **punch** someone, you hit them hard with your fist. EG *Boylan punched him hard on the nose... I was punched in the stomach.* V+O

2 A **punch** is a hard blow with your fist. EG *I landed a number of punches... Ringbaum, swaying with the punch, kept his balance.* N COUNT

3 A **punch** is also a tool that you use for pushing holes in something. EG *He made a small hole in the belt with a leather punch.* N COUNT

4 If you **punch** holes in something, you make holes in it by pushing or pressing it with something sharp. EG *Edward was punching holes in a can.* V+O

5 Punch is a drink usually made from wine or spirits mixed with sugar, lemons, and spices. EG ...*hot rum punch.* N MASS

punch-line, punch-lines. The **punch-line** of a joke or funny story is its last sentence or phrase, which gives it its humour. N COUNT

punch-up, punch-ups. A **punch-up** is a fight in which people hit each other. EG *'Looks as though you've been in a real punch-up,' says the barmaid.* N COUNT Informal British

punchy /pʌntʃiˡ/, **punchier, punchiest.** If you describe a piece of writing as **punchy**, you mean that it is effective and forceful, because points are made clearly, briefly, and decisively. EG ...*a punchy little leaflet.* ADJ QUALIT

punctual /pʌŋktjuᵊəl/. Someone who is **punctual** arrives somewhere or does something at the right time and is not late. EG *I expect my guests to be punctual for breakfast.* ◇ **punctually.** EG *Mary arrived at the New Inn punctually at ten o'clock.* ADJ PRED ◇ ADV

punctuate /pʌŋktjueɪt/, **punctuates, punctuating, punctuated. 1** If an activity **is punctuated** by things, it is interrupted by them at intervals. EG *The old lady's words were punctuated by noise from outside... They had a jolly conversation, punctuated with bursts of laughter.* V+O : USU PASS +*by/with* Formal

2 When you **punctuate** a piece of writing, you put punctuation in it. V+O Formal

punctuation /pʌŋktjueɪʃᵊn/ is the marks such as full stops, commas, and question marks that you use in writing to divide words into sentences and clauses. EG *The punctuation needs putting right.* N UNCOUNT

punctuation mark, punctuation marks. A **punctuation mark** is a sign such as a full stop, comma, or question mark that you use in writing to divide words into sentences and clauses. N COUNT

puncture /pʌŋktʃə/, **punctures, puncturing, punctured. 1** A **puncture** is a small hole in a car tyre or bicycle tyre that has been made by a sharp object. EG *One of the wheels has a puncture.* N COUNT

2 To **puncture** something means to make a small hole in it. EG *The shrapnel may puncture tyres, fuel tanks and radiators.* V+O

pundit /pʌndɪt/, **pundits.** A **pundit** is a person who knows a lot about a subject and is often asked to give information or opinions about it. EG *John Lowerson is one of our pundits on local history.* N COUNT Informal

pungent /pʌndʒənt/. **1** Something that is **pungent** has a strong, unpleasant smell or taste. EG *The pungent, choking smell of sulphur filled the air.* ADJ QUALIT

2 Speech or writing that is **pungent** has a direct, powerful effect and often cleverly criticizes something. EG *This is the pungent and original argument.* ADJ QUALIT Formal

punish /pʌnɪʃ/, **punishes, punishing, punished. 1** To **punish** someone means to make them suffer in some way because they have done something wrong. EG *They discovered his crime and punished him for it.* V+O : OFT+*for*

2 To **punish** a crime means to punish anyone who commits that crime. EG *They punished adultery with death.* V+O

punishable /pʌnɪʃəbəᵊl/. If a crime is **punishable** in a particular way, anyone who commits it is punished in that way. EG *Possession of drugs is punishable by prison.* ADJ CLASSIF : OFT+*by*

punishing /pʌnɪʃɪŋ/. A **punishing** experience makes you very weak or helpless. EG *The purpose was to inflict a punishing defeat on the enemy.* ADJ QUALIT : ATTRIB

punishment /pʌnɪʃməˀnt/, **punishments. 1 Punishment** is the act of punishing someone. EG *Punishment and prison sentences cannot reform the hardened criminal.* N UNCOUNT

2 A **punishment** is a particular way of punishing someone. *He maintained that the only true punishment for murder was death.* N COUNT

3 Punishment is also severe physical treatment of any kind. EG *The crew were in no condition to withstand any further punishment from the sea.* N UNCOUNT

4 See also **capital punishment, corporal punishment.**

punitive /pjuːnɪˡtɪv/. **Punitive** actions are intended to punish people and are therefore harsh. EG *We will take no punitive action against those who have broken the rules.* ADJ CLASSIF : USU ATTRIB

punk /pʌŋk/, **punks. 1 Punk** or **punk rock** is rock music that is played in a fast, loud, and aggressive way and is often a protest against conventional attitudes and behaviour. EG ...*a punk rock concert.* N UNCOUNT

2 Punk clothes or styles are associated with punk music and are very noticeable and unconventional. EG ...*punk haircuts.* ADJ CLASSIF : ATTRIB

3 A **punk** or a **punk rocker** is a young person who likes punk music and dresses in a very noticeable and unconventional way, for example by having brightly coloured hair and wearing metal chains. EG ...*punk rockers with safety pins in their ears.* N COUNT

punnet /pʌnɪt/, **punnets.** A **punnet** is a small, light, square box in which soft fruits such as strawberries or raspberries are often sold. EG ...*punnets of strawberries.* N COUNT OR N PART

punt /pʌnt/, **punts, punting, punted. 1** A **punt** is a long boat with a flat bottom. You move the boat along by standing at one end and pushing a long pole down against the bottom of the river. N COUNT

2 When you **punt**, you travel along a river in a punt. EG *I punted slowly on.* V : OFT+A

punter /pʌntə/, **punters. 1** A **punter** is a person who bets money on horse races. EG *Favourites, as any punter will tell you, do not always win.* N COUNT Informal British

2 People sometimes refer to their customers or clients as the **punters.** EG *What was the punters' reaction to it?* N COUNT : USU PLURAL Informal British

puny /pjuːniˡ/, **punier, puniest.** Someone or something that is **puny** is very small or weak. EG ...*a puny old man... ...her puny efforts.* ADJ QUALIT

pup /pʌp/, **pups. 1** A **pup** is a young dog. EG ...*a cocker spaniel pup.* N COUNT

2 Some other young animals are also called **pups.** EG ...*a seal pup.* N COUNT

pupil /pjuːpɪᵊl/, **pupils. 1** The **pupils** of a school are the children who go to it. EG ...*a school with more than 1300 pupils.* N COUNT

2 A **pupil** of a painter, musician, or other expert is someone who studies under that expert and learns his or her skills. EG *Auerbach and Kossoff were pupils of David Bomberg.* N COUNT+POSS

3 The **pupils** of your eyes are the small, round, black holes in the centre of them. N COUNT

puppet /pʌpɪt/, **puppets. 1** A **puppet** is a doll that you can move, either by pulling strings which are N COUNT

Does a punter punt?

attached to it or by putting your hand inside its body and moving your fingers.

2 You can refer to people or countries as **puppets** when their actions are controlled by more powerful people or countries, although they may appear to be independent. EG *...puppet governments.* N COUNT

puppy /pʌpi[1]/, **puppies.** A **puppy** is a young dog. EG *Don't buy a puppy less than seven weeks old.* N COUNT

purchase /pɜːtʃə[i]s/, **purchases, purchasing, purchased.** 1 When you **purchase** something, you buy it. EG *He sold the house he had purchased only two years before.* V+O Formal

2 **Purchase** is the buying of something. EG *We need to know the exact day of purchase.* N UNCOUNT Formal

3 A **purchase** is something that you buy. EG *Among his purchases were several books.* N COUNT Formal

purchaser /pɜːtʃə[i]sə/, **purchasers.** The **purchaser** of something is the person who buys it. EG *The house becomes the permanent property of the purchaser... ...purchasers of paintings.* N COUNT Formal

pure /pjʊə/, **purer, purest.** 1 **Pure** means not mixed with anything else. EG *...a dress of pure silk... ...pure white... ...pure happiness.* ADJ CLASSIF: ATTRIB

2 Something that is **pure** is clean, healthy, and does not contain any harmful substances. EG *An advantage of breast feeding is that the milk is always pure... ...the pure, dry desert air.* ◊ **purity** /pjʊərɪti[1]/. EG *...the importance of purity in the water supply.* ADJ QUALIT ◊ N UNCOUNT

3 If people describe a woman or girl as **pure**, they mean that she does not do the things that they consider to be sinful, such as having sex. EG *Teddy Boylan's not fit for your pure, beautiful little sister to marry... ...pure in mind and body.* ◊ **purity.** EG *...secret thoughts which defiled her purity.* ADJ QUALIT Literary ◊ N UNCOUNT

4 A **pure** sound is very clear and pleasant to hear. EG *The singer's voice remained pure and clear throughout the evening.* ◊ **purity.** EG *...a tonal purity that no human soprano could challenge.* ADJ CLASSIF ◊ N UNCOUNT

5 **Pure** science or **pure** research is concerned only with theory and not with how this theory can be used in practical ways. EG *...chemistry, both pure and applied... ...pure maths.* ADJ CLASSIF: ATTRIB

6 **Pure** also means complete and total. EG *I came on the idea by pure chance... He shut his eyes in pure bliss.* ADJ CLASSIF: ATTRIB

puree /pjʊreɪ/, **purees, pureeing, pureed.** 1 A **puree** is food which has been mashed or blended so that it forms a thick, smooth sauce. EG *...tomato puree... ...chestnut puree.* N MASS

2 If you **puree** food, you make it into a puree. EG *I use a blender to puree cooked vegetables.* V+O

purely /pjʊəli[1]/. 1 **Purely** means involving only one feature or characteristic and not including anything else. EG *...something purely practical like mending a washing machine... There's nothing personal in this. Purely a routine check.* ADV

2 You use **purely and simply** to emphasize that a particular thing is the only thing involved and no others are considered. EG *It is done through ignorance purely and simply.* ADV SEN

purgatory /pɜːgətə[0]ri[1]/. 1 **Purgatory** is the place where Roman Catholics believe the spirits of dead people are sent to suffer for their sins before they go to heaven. N PROPER

2 You can refer to a very unpleasant experience as **purgatory**. EG *It was a sort of purgatory that had to be endured.* N UNCOUNT

purge /pɜːdʒ/, **purges, purging, purged.** 1 When people **purge** an organization, they remove from it all the members who are no longer thought to be acceptable. EG *...to purge the government of Latimer's supporters... They had done their best to purge extremists from the party.* ▸ used as a noun. EG *They discovered that there were infiltrators inside the party. A purge began.* V+O: OFT+*of/from* ▸ N COUNT

2 If you **purge** your mind of an undesirable feeling such as envy, you stop yourself from having this feeling. EG *I tried desperately to purge myself of these dangerous desires.* V+O OR V-REFL: OFT+*of*

purify /pjʊərɪfaɪ/, **purifies, purifying, purified.** If you **purify** a substance, you make it pure by removing any harmful, dirty, or inferior substances from it. EG *...specially purified water.* V+O

purist /pjʊərɪst/, **purists.** A **purist** is a person who believes in absolute correctness, especially concerning a particular subject which they know a lot about. EG *Musical purists were outraged at this innovation.* N COUNT

puritan /pjʊərɪtə[0]n/, **puritans.** You refer to someone as a **puritan** when they live according to strict moral or religious principles, especially by avoiding physical pleasures. EG *...an austere old puritan.* ▸ used as an adjective. EG *...puritan morality... Their attitude is puritan in such matters.* N COUNT ▸ ADJ QUALIT

puritanical /pjʊərɪtænɪkə[0]l/. Someone who is **puritanical** behaves according to strict moral or religious principles, especially by avoiding physical pleasures. EG *...a puritanical distaste for alcohol.* ADJ QUALIT

purple /pɜːpə[0]l/, **purples.** Something that is **purple** is of a reddish-blue colour. ADJ COLOUR

purplish /pɜːplɪʃ/ means slightly purple in colour. EG *What's that purplish spot on your neck?* ADJ COLOUR

purport /pə[s]pɔːt/, **purports, purporting, purported.** If you say that something **purports** to do or be a particular thing, you mean that it is claimed to do or be that thing. EG *...advertisements for cosmetics purporting to delay the development of wrinkles.* V+*to*-INF Formal

purpose /pɜːpəs/, **purposes.** 1 The **purpose** of something is the reason for which it is made or done. EG *The purpose of the meeting was to discuss the committee's report... The prisoners did not know what the purpose of the robberies was... The buildings are now used as a prison, but they weren't built for that purpose.* N COUNT

2 Your **purpose** is the thing that you want to achieve. EG *Her only purpose in life was to get rich.* N COUNT

3 **Purpose** is the feeling of having a definite aim and of being determined to achieve it. EG *She has given them a sense of purpose.* N UNCOUNT

4 **Purpose** is used in these phrases. **4.1** If you do something **on purpose**, you do it deliberately. EG *He had gone there on purpose, to see what happened.* **4.2** You use the phrase **for all practical purposes** to suggest that a situation is not exactly as you describe it but the effect is the same as if it were. EG *The rest are now, for all practical purposes, useless.* **4.3** If something **serves a purpose**, it is useful. EG *I knew it would serve no purpose to argue with her.* **4.4** If you say that something was **to no purpose**, you mean that no good result came from it. If you say that it was **to good purpose**, you mean that it was useful. EG *He used his past experience to good purpose.* **4.5 to all intents and purposes**: see **intent**. PHRASES

purpose-built. A **purpose-built** building has been specially designed and built for a particular use. EG *...a purpose-built nursery school.* ADJ CLASSIF: USU ATTRIB

purposeful /pɜːpəsfʊl/. If someone is **purposeful**, they show that they have a definite aim and a strong desire to achieve it. EG *They were striving to bring about change in a purposeful way.* ◊ **purposefully.** EG *She began walking slowly but purposefully towards the bridge.* ADJ QUALIT ◊ ADV

purposeless /pɜːpəslɪ[2]s/. If an action is **purposeless**, it does not seem to have a sensible purpose. EG *...casual, unprovoked and purposeless violence.* ADJ QUALIT

purposely /pɜːpəsli[1]/. If you do something **purposely**, you do it deliberately. EG *She purposely sat in the outside seat.* ADV

purr /pɜː/, **purrs, purring, purred.** 1 When a cat **purrs**, it makes a low vibrating sound with its throat because it is contented. V

2 When an engine or machine **purrs**, it makes a quiet, continuous, vibrating sound. EG *I heard cars* V

purr in the distance. ▸ used as a noun. EG *I could hear the gentle purr of a movie projector.* ▸ N SING

3 When someone **purrs**, they speak in a soft, gentle voice because they are pleased about something. EG *'It's wonderful,' she purred delightedly.* V+QUOTE

purse /pɜːs/, **purses, pursing, pursed.** 1 A **purse** is a very small bag that people, especially women, keep their money in. EG *She began hunting in her purse for some coins.* N COUNT British

2 A **purse** is also the same as a handbag. EG *She strolled along, swinging her old white purse.* N COUNT American

3 If you **purse** your lips, you move them into a small, rounded shape. EG *He pursed his lips in distaste.* V+O

purser /pɜːsə/, **pursers.** The **purser** on a ship is an officer who deals with the accounts and official papers. On a passenger ship, the purser is also responsible for the welfare of the passengers. N COUNT

pursue /pəsjºuː/, **pursues, pursuing, pursued.** 1 If you **pursue** an activity, interest, or plan, you do it or carry it out. EG *Lyttleton pursued a policy of peace and order... His wealth enabled him to pursue his passionate interest in art.* V+O Formal

2 If you **pursue** a particular aim or result, you make efforts to achieve it, often over a long period of time. EG *Economic growth must not be pursued at the expense of environmental pollution.* V+O Formal

3 If you **pursue** a particular topic, you try to find out more about it. EG *I don't want to pursue that question now.* V+O Formal

4 If you **pursue** someone or something, you follow them, usually in order to catch them. EG *Weasels pursue rats and mice as well as birds... The police pursued the wrong car.* ◇ **pursuer, pursuers.** EG *He managed to give his pursuers the slip.* V+O Formal ◇ N COUNT

pursuit /pəsjºuːt/, **pursuits.** 1 Your **pursuit** of something that you want consists of your attempts at achieving it. EG *...the pursuit of happiness... How far should any of us go in pursuit of what we want?* N UNCOUNT+*of* Formal

2 The **pursuit** of an activity, interest, or plan consists of all the things that you do when you are carrying it out. EG *He spent the summer in the vigorous pursuit of sport.* N UNCOUNT+*of* Formal

3 The **pursuit** of someone or something is the act of chasing them. EG *...a gamekeeper in pursuit of a poacher.* ● If you are **in hot pursuit** of someone, you are chasing after them with great determination. EG *He started running – with all the others in hot pursuit.* N UNCOUNT Formal ● PHRASE

4 **Pursuits** are activities, especially activities that you enjoy doing when you are not working. EG *Games like chess are rather intellectual pursuits.* N COUNT: USU+SUPP Formal

pus /pʌs/ is a thick yellowish liquid that forms in wounds when they are infected. N UNCOUNT

push /pʊʃ/, **pushes, pushing, pushed.** 1 When you **push** something, you press it using force, often in order to move it. EG *She pushed the button that locked the door... She pushed the drawing across the desk... I pushed open the door... Castle pushed his bicycle up King's Road.* ▸ used as a noun. EG *The gate slid open at the push of a button... My car's broken down – would you give me a push?* V+O: OFT+A; ALSO V ▸ N COUNT: USU SING

2 If you **push** through things that are blocking your way or **push** your **way** through them, you use force in order to be able to move past them. EG *Ralph pushed between them to get a better view... I pushed my way through the people.* V+A, OR PHRASE

3 To **push** a value or amount up or down means to cause it to increase or decrease. EG *The oil boom will push the inflation rate up to higher levels.* V+O+A

4 If you **push** someone into doing something, you urge or force them to do it. EG *No one pushed me into this; I decided to do it of my own accord... The government was pushed to desperate extremes.* V+O: OFT+A Informal

5 If you **push** for something, you try very hard to achieve it. EG *He is pushing for secret balloting in Party elections.* ▸ used as a noun. EG *India led the non-aligned nations in a push for sanctions.* V+*for* ▸ N SING+*for*

6 To **push** something also means to try to increase its popularity or to attract people to it. EG *...huge adverts pushing slimming drugs.* V+O Informal

7 When someone **pushes** drugs, they sell them illegally. V+O Informal

8 If someone **gives** you **the push**, they end their relationship with you. EG *He gave me the push last week.* PHRASE Informal British

9 If your employer **gives** you **the push**, he or she dismisses you from your job. EG *Another forty workers have been given the push.* PHRASE Informal British

10 to **push** your **luck**: see **luck**. ● See also **pushed**, **pushing**.

push ahead. If you **push ahead** with something, you make progress with it. EG *They have pushed ahead with an optimistic development strategy.* PHRASAL VB: V+ADV

push around. If someone **pushes** you **around**, they give you orders in a rude and insulting way. EG *We're not going to let them push us around.* PHRASAL VB: V+O+ADV Informal

push in. When someone **pushes in**, they come into a queue in front of other people; used showing disapproval. EG *Felicity pushed in next to Howard.* PHRASAL VB: V+ADV

push off. When you **push off**, you leave a place. EG *It's time I was pushing off... Push off. You're not wanted.* PHRASAL VB: V+ADV Informal

push on. When you **push on**, you continue travelling somewhere. EG *I wanted to push on.* PHRASAL VB: V+ADV

push over. If you **push** someone or something **over**, you push them so that they fall onto the ground. EG *The children were pushing each other over on the sand.* ● See also **pushover**. PHRASAL VB: V+O+ADV

push through. If you **push** something **through**, you succeed in getting it accepted, often with difficulty. EG *I'll see that the scheme is pushed through at the earliest date.* PHRASAL VB: V+O+ADV

push bike, push bikes. People sometimes refer to a bicycle as a **push bike**. EG *She used to do her rounds on an old push bike.* N COUNT Informal

push-button. A **push-button** machine or process is controlled by means of buttons or switches. EG *...push-button telephones.* ADJ CLASSIF: ATTRIB

pushchair /pʊʃtʃɛə/, **pushchairs.** A **pushchair** is a small chair on wheels, in which a baby or small child can sit and be wheeled around. N COUNT British

pushed /pʊʃt/. 1 If you are **pushed** for something such as time or money, you do not have enough of it. EG *Sorry – can't stop – I'm a bit pushed for time.* ADJ PRED: USU+*for* Informal

2 If you **are hard pushed** to do something, you find it very difficult to do it. EG *Most of us are hard pushed to understand where all the money goes.* PHRASE Informal

pusher /pʊʃə/, **pushers.** A **pusher** is a person who sells illegal drugs. EG *...professional dope pushers... Most of the pushers were addicts themselves.* N COUNT Informal

pushing /pʊʃɪŋ/. If you say that someone is **pushing** a particular age, you mean that they are nearly that age. EG *Until a man is pushing sixty-five, he doesn't usually think about retirement.* PREP Informal

pushover /pʊʃəʊvə/, **pushovers.** You say that something is a **pushover** when it is easy to do or easy to get. EG *From a British point of view, it sounds like a pushover.* N SING: a+N Informal

pushy /pʊʃi¹/, **pushier, pushiest.** Someone who is **pushy** behaves in a forceful way to get things done, often because they want to do better or get more than anyone else. EG *I have to be pushy in my job or I get nowhere at all.* ADJ QUALIT Informal

puss /pʊs/. People sometimes call a cat by saying **'Puss'**. EG *'Puss! Puss!' he called.* VOCATIVE

pussy /pʊsi¹/, **pussies.** You can refer to a cat as a **pussy** or a **pussy cat**. EG *I'll show you the pussy cats... How are the pussies getting on?* N COUNT Informal

put /pʊt/, **puts, putting.** The form **put** is used in the present tense and is the past tense and past participle of the verb.

1 When you **put** something in a particular place or position, you move it into that place or position. EG V+O+A

What is an American word for a handbag?

She put her hand on his arm... I put her suitcase on the table... Marsha put her cup down... The women put a garland round her neck.

2 If you **put** someone somewhere, you cause them to go there and to stay there for a period of time. EG *They had to put him into an asylum... I have to put the kids to bed.* V+O+A

3 When you **put** an idea or remark in a particular way, you express it in that way. EG *He didn't put it quite as crudely as that... They cannot put their feelings into words... To put it briefly, the man is mad and may become dangerous.* V+O : USU+A

4 When you **put** a question to someone, you ask them the question. EG *I put this question to Dr Leslie Cook.* V+O : OFT+*to*

5 If you **put it to** someone that something is true, you suggest that it is true, especially when you think that they will be unwilling to admit this. EG *I put it to him that, in fact, he was losing a good worker.* PHRASE

6 To **put** someone or something in a particular state or situation means to cause them to be in that state or situation. EG *It puts me in a rather difficult position... The company closed several months ago, putting 120 people out of a job... This would put the party into power.* V+O+A

7 You can use **put** when you are expressing someone's estimate of the size or importance of something. EG *The pipeline's cost is now put at 2.7 billion pounds... He always put duty before pleasure... I wouldn't put him in the same class as Verdi.* V+O+A

8 If you **put** time, strength, or energy into an activity, you use it in doing that activity. EG *She put all her energy into tidying the place up.* V+O+*into*

9 If you **put** money into a business or project, you invest the money in it. EG *Capitalists are encouraged to put their wealth into productive enterprises.* V+O+*into*

10 To **put** something on people or things means to cause them to have it, or to cause them to be affected by it. EG *It puts a tremendous responsibility on us... We put pressure on our children to learn to read... ...a plan to put a tax on children's clothes.* V+O+*on/upon*

11 If you **put** written information somewhere, you write or type it there. EG *Put all the details on the card... He couldn't read what Ken had put for his address... For profession he put down simply 'business man'.* V+O : USU+A

12 to be **hard put** to do something: see **hard**. • to **stay put**: see **stay**.

put across or **put over.** When you **put** something **across** or **put** it **over**, you succeed in describing or explaining it to someone. EG *You need the skill to put your ideas across... It is difficult for her to put over her own thoughts.* PHRASAL VB : V+O+ADV

put aside. If you **put** something **aside**, you keep it to be dealt with or used at a later time. EG *My aunt put aside her sewing and chatted to me... Your best plan is to put aside funds to cover these bills.* PHRASAL VB : V+O+ADV

put away. 1 If you **put** something **away**, you put it into the place where it is normally kept, for example in a cupboard or a drawer. EG *Right – put your books away.* PHRASAL VB : V+O+ADV **2** If someone **is put away**, they are sent to prison or to a mental hospital for a long time. EG *The doctor wanted to have him put away.* V+O+ADV Informal

put back. To **put** something **back** means to delay it or postpone it. EG *The meeting's been put back till Monday... This will put production back at least a month.* PHRASAL VB : V+O+ADV, USU+A

put by. If you **put by** a sum of money, you keep it so that you can use it at a later time. EG *I've got a bit put by.* PHRASAL VB : V+O+ADV

put down. 1 When soldiers, police, or the government **put down** a riot or rebellion, they stop it by using force. EG *These riots were put down by the local police.* PHRASAL VB : V+O+ADV **2** If you **put** someone **down**, you criticize them or make them appear foolish. EG *...her infuriating habit of putting people down in small ways.* • See also **put-down**. V+O+ADV Informal **3** When an animal **is put down**, it is killed because it is dangerous or very ill. EG *We had to have the cat put down.* V+O+ADV, USU PASS

put down to. If you **put** something **down to** a particular thing, you believe that it is caused by that thing. EG *I put it down to arthritis.* PHRASAL VB : V+O+ADV +PREP

put forward. If you **put forward** something or someone, you suggest that they should be considered or chosen for a particular purpose or job. EG *They rejected every proposal put forward... Too few women's names are put forward.* PHRASAL VB : V+O+ADV

put in. 1 If you **put in** an amount of time or effort doing something, you spend that time or effort doing it. EG *I put in fifteen hours of work daily... You've put in a lot of work.* PHRASAL VB : V+O+ADV **2** If you **put in** a request or **put in** for something, you make a formal request or application. EG *I put in a request for an interview... After the gamekeeper died, Father put in for his job.* V+O+ADV OR V+ADV+*for* **3** to **put in a good word** for someone: see **word**.

put off. 1 If you **put** something **off**, you delay doing it. EG *Don't put it off till tomorrow.* PHRASAL VB : V+O+ADV **2** If you **put** someone **off**, **2.1** you make them wait for something that they want. EG *I'm sorry, but I can't put him off any longer.* V+O+ADV **2.2** you make them give up trying to get or do something. EG *Nothing would put her off once she had made up her mind.* V+O+ADV **3** To **put** someone **off** something means to cause them to dislike it. EG *I had seen enough to put me off farm work.* V+O+ADV/ PREP

put on. 1 When you **put on** a piece of clothing, you place it on your body in order to wear it. EG *I put on my jacket.* PHRASAL VB : V+O+ADV **2** When people **put on** a show, exhibition, or service, they perform it, arrange it, or organize it. EG *A French company has put on 'Peter Grimes'... They're putting on a special train service.* V+O+ADV **3** If someone **puts on** weight, they become heavier. EG *She had put on over a stone since I last saw her.* V+O+ADV **4** If you **put on** a piece of equipment or a device, you make it start working. EG *He put on the light... She put the radio on... Put the brake on and leave the car in gear.* V+O+ADV **5** If you **put on** a record or tape, you place it on a record player or in a tape machine and listen to it. V+O+ADV **6** If you **put** food **on**, you begin to cook it. EG *She often forgets to put the dinner on before she goes to collect the children.* V+O+ADV **7** If you **put** a sum of money **on** something, you make a bet about it. For example, if you put £10 on a racehorse, you bet £10 that it will win. V+O+ADV/ PREP **8** To **put** a particular amount **on** the cost or value of something means to add that amount to it. EG *This will put another 5p a gallon on petrol.* V+O+PREP **9** If you **put on** a way of behaving, you behave in a way that is not natural to you or that does not express your real feelings. EG *She put on that look of not caring... I don't see why you have to put on a phoney English accent.* V+O+ADV **10** If someone is putting you **on**, they are teasing you by trying to make you believe something that is not true. EG *'You're putting me on,' said Deirdre.* V+O+ADV, ONLY CONT Informal

put onto. If you **put** someone **onto** something useful, you tell them about it. EG *One of his friends put him on to Voluntary Service Overseas.* PHRASAL VB : V+O+PREP

put out. 1 If you **put out** an announcement or story, you make it known to a lot of people. EG *He put out a statement denouncing the commission's conclusions.* PHRASAL VB : V+O+ADV **2** If you **put out** a fire, a candle, or a cigarette, you make it stop burning. EG *He helped to put the fire out... Sheldon put out his cigar.* V+O+ADV **3** If you **put out** an electric light, you make it stop shining by pressing a switch. EG *She put out the light.* V+O+ADV **4** If you **put out** things that will be needed, you place them somewhere ready to be used. EG *I put clean clothes out for you on the bed.* V+O+ADV **5** If you **put out** your hand, you move it forward, away from your body. EG *I walked over to one young woman and put out my hand.* V+O+ADV **6** If you **put** your back, hip, or shoulder **out**, you injure yourself so that one of your bones is no longer in its normal position. V+O+ADV Informal **7** If V-PASS+ADV you **are put out**, you are rather annoyed or upset by something. EG *I was somewhat put out when the audience laughed loudly.* **8** If you **put** yourself **out**, you do something for someone even though it requires a lot of effort or causes you problems. EG *He was putting himself out to please her.* V-REFL+ADV

put over. See **put across**.

put through. 1 When someone **puts through** a telephone call or a caller, they make the connection that allows the caller to speak to the person they are phoning. EG *'Data Room, please.' – 'I'll put you through.'* PHRASAL VB: V+O+ADV **2** If someone **puts** you **through** an unpleasant experience, they make you experience it. EG *I'm sorry to put you through this again.* V+O+PREP

put together. 1 If you **put** something **together**, you join its different parts to each other so that it can be used. EG *He started to put his fishing rod together.* PHRASAL VB: V+O+ADV **2** If you **put** an event **together**, you organize or arrange it. EG *The agency has put together the biggest ever campaign for a new car.* V+O+ADV
3 If you say that something is bigger or better than several things **put together**, you mean that it is bigger or has more good qualities than all of these things together. EG *He is smarter than all your colonels put together.* PHRASE

put up. 1 If people **put up** a wall or a building, they construct it. EG *We shall have to put up a fence.* PHRASAL VB: V+O+ADV **2** If you **put up** an umbrella or a hood, you unfold it or raise it so that it covers you. EG *I should put your umbrella up.* V+O+ADV **3** If you **put up** a poster or notice, you fix it to a wall or board. EG *These posters were put up all over the place.* V+O+ADV **4** If you **put up** resistance to something, you resist it. EG *America has put up so much resistance to Concorde... We had put up a fierce struggle.* V+ADV+O **5** If you **put up** money for something, you provide the money that is needed to pay for it. EG *The National Council for the Arts put up half the cost.* V+ADV+O **6** To **put up** the price of something means to cause it to increase. EG *This is what happens when they put up prices too far.* V+O+ADV **7** If someone **puts** you **up**, you stay at their home for one or more nights. EG *I offered to put him up for the night.* V-ERG+ADV **8** to **put up a fight**: see **fight**. ● a **put-up job**: see **put-up**.

put up to. If you **put** someone **up to** something wrong or foolish, you suggest that they do it and you encourage them to do it. EG *Julie herself had probably put them up to it.* PHRASAL VB: V+O+ADV+PREP

put up with. If you **put up with** something, you tolerate or accept it, even though you find it unpleasant or unsatisfactory. EG *The natives have to put up with gaping tourists... I can't think why I put up with it.* PHRASAL VB: V+ADV+PREP

put-down, put-downs. A **put-down** is something that you say or do which criticizes someone or makes them appear foolish. EG *The ultimate put-down is to be given a pat on the head.* N COUNT Informal

putrefy /pjuːtrɪfaɪ/, **putrefies, putrefying, putrefied.** When something **putrefies**, it rots and produces a disgusting smell. EG *Thousands of bodies were decomposing and putrefying.* V Formal

putrid /pjuːtrɪd/. Something that is **putrid** is rotten and beginning to smell disgusting. EG *...a rotted and putrid mess.* ADJ CLASSIF Formal

putty /pʌti^1/ is a stiff paste used to fix glass panes into frames and to fill cracks or holes in woodwork. N UNCOUNT

put-up. If something is a **put-up job**, it has been arranged beforehand in order to deceive someone. PHRASE Informal

put-upon. If you are **put-upon**, you have been treated badly by someone who has taken advantage of your willingness to help them. EG *I felt cheated and put-upon.* ADJ QUALIT Informal

puzzle /pʌzə^{0}l/, **puzzles, puzzling, puzzled. 1** If something **puzzles** you, it makes you feel confused because you do not understand it. EG *There was one sentence which puzzled me deeply.* V+O ◊ **puzzling.** EG *I find this rather puzzling.* ◊ ADJ QUALIT
2 If you **puzzle** over something, you try hard to think of the answer to it or the explanation for it. EG *Astronomers had puzzled over these white ovals for some time.* V+A
3 A **puzzle** is a question, game, or toy which you have to think about carefully in order to answer it correctly or put it together properly. N COUNT
4 You can describe anything that is hard to understand as a **puzzle**. EG *The motives of the film-makers remain a puzzle.* N SING

puzzle out. If you **puzzle out** a problem, you find the answer to it by thinking hard about it. EG *She sat down and tried to puzzle out the reports.* PHRASAL VB: V+O+ADV

puzzled /pʌzə^{0}ld/. Someone who is **puzzled** is confused because they do not understand something. EG *Madeleine looked puzzled.* ADJ QUALIT

puzzlement /pʌzə^{0}lmənt/ is confusion that you feel when you do not understand something. EG *I looked at him in puzzlement.* N UNCOUNT

pyjamas /pədʒɑːməz/; spelled **pajamas** in American English. The forms **pyjama** and **pajama** are used before another noun. N PLURAL
A pair of **pyjamas** consists of loose trousers and a loose jacket that people, especially men, wear in bed. EG *...pyjama trousers.*

pylon /paɪlə^{7}n/, **pylons. Pylons** are very tall metal structures which hold electric cables high above the ground so that electricity can be transmitted over long distances. EG *...electricity pylons.* N COUNT

pyramid /pɪrəmɪd/, **pyramids. 1** The **Pyramids** are ancient stone buildings built over the tombs of dead kings and queens in Egypt. They have triangular walls that slope upwards and inwards to a single point. N COUNT
2 A **pyramid** is a shape, object, or pile of things with a flat base and flat triangular sides that slope upwards and inwards to a point. EG *She made a pyramid of cans... ...pyramids of skulls.* See picture at SHAPES. N COUNT

Pyrex /paɪrɛks/ is a type of strong glass which is used for making bowls and dishes that do not break when you cook things in them. EG *...Pyrex dishes.* N UNCOUNT Trademark

python /paɪθə^{7}n/, **pythons.** A **python** is a large, long snake that kills animals by squeezing them with its body. N COUNT

Q q

Q, q /kjuː/, **Qs, q's.** Q is the seventeenth letter of the English alphabet. N COUNT

quack /kwæk/, **quacks, quacking, quacked. 1** If a duck **quacks**, it makes the noise that ducks typically make. V ▸ used as a noun. EG *A feeble quack was heard from beyond the pond.* ▸ N COUNT

2 If you call a doctor or an unqualified person a **quack**, you mean that they claim to be skilled in medicine but they are not. N COUNT

quad /kwɒd/, **quads. Quads** are the same as quadruplets. N COUNT

quadrangle /kwɒdræŋgəºl/, **quadrangles.** A **quadrangle** is an open square area with buildings round it. N COUNT

quadruped /kwɒdrʊpɛd/, **quadrupeds.** Any four-legged animal can be referred to as a **quadruped**. N COUNT Formal

quadruple /kwɒdrʊpəºl/, **quadruples, quadrupling, quadrupled.** When an amount or number **quadruples**, it becomes four times as large. EG *In the last twenty years wheat production has almost quadrupled... We could quadruple output to around 10 million tons.* V-ERG

quadruplet /kwɒdrʊplɪ²t, kwɒdruːplɪ²t/, **quadruplets. Quadruplets** are four children who are born to the same mother at the same time. N COUNT

quail /kweɪl/, **quails, quailing, quailed. 1** A **quail** is a small bird which is often shot and eaten. The plural is either 'quail' or 'quails'. N COUNT OR N UNCOUNT

2 If you **quail**, you feel very afraid. EG *She quailed before his angry bitterness.* V Formal

quaint /kweɪnt/, **quainter, quaintest.** Something that is **quaint** is attractive because it is strange and rather old-fashioned. EG *...quaint little houses... ...a quaint fishing village... ...quaint ideas.* ADJ QUALIT

quake /kweɪk/, **quakes, quaking, quaked. 1** If you **quake**, you tremble or shake because you are very afraid. EG *I stood there quaking with fear.* V

2 A **quake** is the same as an earthquake. EG *On average, there are four major quakes in a century.* N COUNT Informal

qualification /kwɒlɪfɪkeɪʃəºn/, **qualifications. 1** Your **qualifications** are the examinations that you have passed. EG *I haven't got any qualifications in English Literature.* ● See also **qualify**. N COUNT

2 The **qualifications** needed for a particular activity or task are the qualities and skills that you need in order to do it. EG *One of the qualifications you need in advertising is a fertile mind.* N COUNT

3 A **qualification** is also a detail or explanation that you add to a statement to make it less strong or less generalized. EG *Two qualifications need to be made... Few people praised him without qualification.* N COUNT OR N UNCOUNT

qualified /kwɒlɪfaɪd/. **1** Someone who is **qualified** has passed the examinations that they need to pass in order to work in a particular profession. EG *These tests have to be carried out by a qualified doctor... She is qualified to teach.* ADJ CLASSIF

2 If you are **qualified** to do something, you have the qualities or skills necessary to do it. EG *She did not feel qualified to discuss it... They were better qualified to suggest improvements.* ADJ PRED: OFT+*to*-INF

3 Qualified agreement or praise is not total and suggests that you have doubts. EG *The reaction was one of qualified praise.* ADJ QUALIT

qualify /kwɒlɪfaɪ/, **qualifies, qualifying, qualified. 1** When someone **qualifies**, they pass the examinations that they need to pass in order to work in a particular profession. EG *I was thirty-three before I qualified as a doctor.* V

◊ **qualification.** EG *Even after qualification, jobs were hard to find.* ◊ N UNCOUNT

2 If you **qualify** a statement, you add a detail or explanation to it to make it less strong or less generalized. EG *If I said that Warsaw was grim and grey, that statement has to be qualified.* V+O

3 If someone **qualifies** for something, they have the right to have it or to do it. EG *By working all their lives, people qualify automatically for their pensions.* V+*for*

4 If you **qualify** in a competition, you are successful in one part of it and go on to the next stage. EG *He worked all season to qualify for the match.* V

qualitative /kwɒlɪtətɪv, -teɪt-/ means relating to the quality of something. EG *...qualitative improvements... ...a qualitative change.* ADJ CLASSIF: ATTRIB

quality /kwɒlɪ¹ti¹/, **qualities. 1** The **quality** of something is how good or bad it is. EG *The quality of the photograph was poor... I've got some good quality paper.* N UNCOUNT: USU+SUPP

2 Something of **quality** is of a high standard. EG *...a programme of quality... The employers don't want quality work any more.* N UNCOUNT

3 A person's **qualities** are their good characteristics, such as kindness or honesty. EG *Asquith paid tribute to his personal qualities... ...the qualities they look for in a teacher.* N COUNT+SUPP

4 The **qualities** of a substance or an object are its physical characteristics. EG *...the abstract qualities of the painting... The skin on the baby's face had a pearly translucent quality.* N COUNT+SUPP

qualm /kwɑːm/, **qualms.** If you have **qualms** about something that you are doing, you are worried that it may not be right. EG *I sometimes have qualms about our teaching methods.* N COUNT: USU PLURAL

quandary /kwɒndəºri¹/, **quandaries.** If you are in a **quandary**, you cannot decide what to do. EG *He found himself in a quandary... I couldn't offer any resolutions of this quandary.* N COUNT

> **QUANTIF stands for quantifier**
> Words which have the label QUANTIF in the Extra Column are words such as 'most', 'least', and 'several' which tell you about the amount or quantity of something.
> See the entry headed QUANTIFIERS for more information.

quantitative /kwɒntɪtətɪv, -teɪt-/ means relating to the size or amount of something. EG *It is not yet possible to make a quantitative assessment of the effectiveness of our investment.* ADJ CLASSIF: USU ATTRIB

quantity /kwɒntɪ¹ti¹/, **quantities. 1** A **quantity** is an amount that you can measure or count. EG *You only need a very small quantity... Natural gas was discovered in large quantities beneath the North Sea... ...a quantity of leaves.* N COUNT OR N PART

2 Things that are produced **in quantity** are produced in large amounts. EG *The meat is produced in quantity and sold in Eastern Europe.* PHRASE

3 Quantity is the amount of something that there is; often used in contrast to its quality and how good it is. EG *Materials are being seen in terms simply of quantity rather than quality... The food supply has grown less, in quantity and quality.* N UNCOUNT

4 If you say that someone or something is an **unknown quantity**, you mean that you do not know anything about them. EG *To Shanti the outside world was a totally unknown quantity.* PHRASE

quantum /kwɒntəºm/. **1 Quantum** is used to describe various theories in physics and mathematics which are concerned with the properties and N MOD Technical

QUANTIFIERS

Quantifiers (labelled QUANTIF in the Extra Column) are used to say how much of something there is. The main quantifiers are: **both**, **few**, **least**, **less**, **little**, **many**, **more**, **most**, **much**, **plenty**, **several**, **some**, and **a little**.

1 Quantifiers come in front of a noun: ***many*** *miles away . . .* *. . . **less** sugar.*

2 Some quantifiers are used with countable nouns in the plural: ***few*** *books . . . . . . **several** girls.* Others are used with uncountable nouns: ***much*** *money.*

3 They can be used in front of the preposition **of**: ***Most*** *of my work is political.*

4 They can be used as a complete group in the same way as pronouns: ***Little*** *can be seen of the Roman remains . . .* *There is **little** to say about him.*

behaviour of atomic particles. EG *...quantum mechanics... ...quantum physics.*

2 A **quantum** leap or jump is a very great change, increase, or advance. EG *...a quantum leap in growth... ...sudden quantum jumps in values.* — ADJ CLASSIF : ATTRIB Formal

quarantine /kwɒrəntiːn/, **quarantines, quarantining, quarantined.** If a person or animal is in **quarantine**, they may have a disease and they are being kept separate from other people or animals to prevent the disease from spreading. EG *Her dog was in quarantine.* — N SING : *the*+N, OR N UNCOUNT
▸ used as a verb. EG *He was quarantined in the hope of containing the infection.* — ▸ V+O

quarrel /kwɒrəºl/, **quarrels, quarrelling, quarrelled**; spelled **quarreling, quarreled** in American English.

1 A **quarrel** is an angry argument between two or more people. EG *I don't think we should enter into a family quarrel... There wasn't any evidence of quarrels between them.* — N COUNT
▸ used as a verb. EG *They quarrelled quite often... I don't want to quarrel with you... It was not worth quarrelling about.* — ▸ V OR V+*with* : RECIP

2 If you say that you have no **quarrel** with something, you mean that you do not object to it. EG *I wouldn't have any quarrel with this proposal myself.* — N COUNT+*with*

3 If you say that you would **quarrel** with something that someone has said, you mean that you disagree with it. EG *One thing I would quarrel with in your introduction is the suggestion that people do not care.* — V+*with* Formal

quarrelsome /kwɒrəlsəm/. People who are **quarrelsome** are always having angry arguments. EG *His brothers were greedy and quarrelsome.* — ADJ QUALIT

quarry /kwɒriˡ/, **quarries, quarrying, quarried. 1** A **quarry** is a place that is dug out in order to extract stone, slate, or minerals. EG *...sandstone quarries.* — N COUNT

2 To **quarry** a stone or mineral means to remove it from a quarry by digging, drilling, or blasting. EG *These limestones have been quarried for centuries.* — V+O OR V

3 A person's or animal's **quarry** is the animal that they are hunting. The plural form is also 'quarry'. EG *Move slowly, or you will startle your quarry.* — N COUNT : USU+POSS

quart /kwɔːt/, **quarts.** A **quart** is a unit of volume that is equal to two pints. EG *...a quart of milk.* — N PART

quarter /kwɔːtə/, **quarters. 1** A **quarter** is one of four equal parts of something. EG *...a quarter of a century... It took me an hour and a quarter to make a phone call.* — N COUNT
▸ used as an adjective. EG *...the quarter century following the Second World War.* — ▸ ADJ CLASSIF : ATTRIB
● See also **three-quarters**.

2 If it is a **quarter** to a particular hour, it is fifteen minutes before that hour. In American English, you say that it is a **quarter** of a particular hour. See the entry headed TIME. EG *It's quarter to five... They allowed you to go at a quarter to eight.*

3 If it is a **quarter** past a particular hour, it is fifteen minutes past that hour. See the entry headed TIME. EG *We're due at Janet's at quarter past eleven... ...a quarter past three in the afternoon.*

4 A **quarter** is also **4.1** a period of three months. EG *In the last quarter of 1980 inflation rose by 1%.* — N COUNT **4.2** an American or Canadian coin that is worth 25 cents. — N COUNT **4.3** four ounces of something. EG *A quarter of walnuts, please.* — N PART : USU SING

5 You can refer to an area in a town or city where a particular group of people live or work as a particular **quarter**. EG *...the Black quarters of New York, Detroit or Washington.* — N COUNT : USU+SUPP

6 If you refer to the feeling or reaction in certain **quarters** or from a particular **quarter**, you are referring rather vaguely to the feeling or reaction of a particular person or group of people. EG *Male prejudice still exists in certain quarters.* — N COUNT +SUPP : USU PLURAL

7 You can refer to the room or rooms provided for a person such as a soldier to live in as that person's **quarters**. EG *...servants' quarters.* — N PLURAL

8 If you see someone **at close quarters**, you see them from a place that is very close to them. EG *It was a privilege to observe her at such close quarters.* — PHRASE

quarter-final /kwɔːtəfaɪnəºl/, **quarter-finals.** A **quarter-final** is one of the four matches in a competition which decides which four players or teams will compete in the semi-final. EG *A win by Leicestershire would give them a chance of qualifying for the quarter-finals.* — N COUNT

quarterly /kwɔːtəliˡ/, **quarterlies. 1** If something happens **quarterly**, it happens regularly four times a year, at intervals of three months. EG *...an annual salary paid monthly or quarterly... We meet quarterly... ...a quarterly conference.* — ADV AFTER VB OR ADJ CLASSIF : ATTRIB

2 A **quarterly** or a **quarterly** publication is a magazine or journal that is published regularly four times a year, at intervals of three months. — N COUNT OR ADJ CLASSIF : ATTRIB

quartet /kwɔːtet/, **quartets.** A **quartet** is **1** a group of four people who play musical instruments or sing together. EG *...the Amadeus String Quartet.* **2** a piece of music for four instruments or four singers. EG *...a Beethoven quartet.* — N COUNT

quartz /kwɔːts/ is a kind of hard, shiny crystal. It is used in making electronic equipment and very accurate watches and clocks. EG *...a quartz clock.* — N UNCOUNT

If you do something without question, do you quibble about it?

quash /kwɒʃ/, **quashes, quashing, quashed.** If someone in authority **quashes** a decision or judgement, they officially reject it and make it no longer legally valid. EG *Their prison sentences were quashed on appeal.* V+O

quasi- /kweɪzaɪ/ is used to form adjectives and nouns that describe something as being in many ways like something else, without actually being that thing. EG *...a quasi-religious experience... They have turned their countries into quasi-republics.* PREFIX

quaver /kweɪvə/, **quavers, quavering, quavered.** If someone's voice **quavers**, it sounds unsteady, for example because they are nervous or uncertain. EG *Ginny's voice was quavering... 'Am I safe?' he quavered.* V OR V+QUOTE

quay /kiː/, **quays.** A **quay** is a long platform beside the sea or a river where boats can be tied up and loaded or unloaded. N COUNT

quayside /kiːsaɪd/. The **quayside** is the area at the edge of a quay. N SING

queasy /kwiːzi[1]/, **queasier, queasiest.** If you feel **queasy**, you feel rather ill, as if you are going to be sick. EG *She felt a little queasy on the boat.* ADJ QUALIT

queen /kwiːn/, **queens. 1** A **queen** is **1.1** a woman who rules a country as its monarch. EG *...Queen Victoria.* **1.2** a woman who is married to a king. EG *Henry VIII married his first Queen in the Tower of London.* N COUNT

2 A **queen** or a **queen bee** is a large female bee which can lay eggs. N COUNT

3 In chess, the **queen** is the most powerful piece. It can be moved backwards, forwards, sideways, or diagonally. N COUNT

4 A **queen** is also a playing card with a picture of a queen on it. EG *...the queen of spades.* N COUNT

queer /kwɪə/, **queerer, queerest; queers. 1** Something that is **queer** is strange. EG *He's a queer character, my friend Evans... It gave her a queer sensation to shake hands with a murderer.* ADJ QUALIT

2 People sometimes call a homosexual man a **queer**; a very offensive use. N COUNT

quell /kwɛl/, **quells, quelling, quelled. 1** To **quell** opposition or violent behaviour means to put an end to it using persuasion or force. EG *The police had been called in to quell a minor disturbance.* V+O

2 If you **quell** unpleasant feelings such as fear or grief, you stop yourself having these feelings. EG *I was trying to quell a growing unease.* V+O

quench /kwɛntʃ/, **quenches, quenching, quenched.** When you are thirsty, you can **quench** your thirst by having a drink. V+O

querulous /kwɛrj[0]ʊləs/. Someone who is **querulous** often complains about things; used showing disapproval. EG *...querulous children... Otto spoke in a weakly querulous voice.* ADJ QUALIT Formal

query /kwɪəri[1]/, **queries. querying, queried. 1** A **query** is a question. EG *If you have any queries, please don't hesitate to write... The assistant accepted my cheque without query.* ▸ used as a verb. EG *'How much do I owe you?' I queried.* N COUNT OR N UNCOUNT ▸ V+QUOTE

2 If you **query** something, you check it by asking about it because you are not sure if it is correct. EG *Your expenses have been queried by someone in the finance department.* V+O

quest /kwɛst/, **quests.** A **quest** is a long and difficult search for something. EG *Little did I know when I embarked on this quest how futile it would be... ...the quest for truth.* N COUNT: OFT+*for* Literary

question /kwɛstʃə[0]n/, **questions, questioning, questioned. 1** A **question** is something which you say or write in order to ask someone about something. EG *Jill began to ask Fred a lot of questions about his childhood... A panel of experts will answer questions on education.* N COUNT

2 If you **question** someone, you ask them a lot of questions about something. EG *I started questioning her about Jane and Anthony.* ◇ **questioning.** EG *The three men were taken to the police station for questioning.* V+O: OFT+*about* ◇ N UNCOUNT

3 If you **question** something, you express your doubts about whether it is true, reasonable, or worthwhile. EG *Women are questioning their traditional role in society... No one ever questioned the necessity of the visit.* V+O

4 If you say that there is some **question** about something, you mean that there is doubt or uncertainty about it. EG *There has been some question as to whether or not the President will resign.* N UNCOUNT +SUPP

5 A **question** is also **5.1** a problem or a point which needs to be discussed. EG *His resignation raised the question of his successor... It is difficult for them to admit there is another side to the missile question.* N COUNT+SUPP **5.2** a problem which is set in an examination in order to test your knowledge or ability. EG *You have to answer four questions in two hours.* N COUNT

6 Question is also used in these phrases. **6.1** If something is **beyond question**, there is no doubt at all about it. EG *She knew beyond question that I was a person who could be trusted.* **6.2** To **bring** something **into question** means to make people think more seriously about it. EG *Unemployment has brought into question the right of married women to work.* **6.3** If you **call** something **into question**, you express serious doubts about it. EG *Are you calling my professional competence into question?* **6.4** If you say that something is **open to question**, you mean that it is not yet certain and people might disagree about it. **6.5** If you say that something is **out of the question**, you mean that it is impossible. EG *She knew that a holiday this year was out of the question.* **6.6** If you say **there is no question of** doing something, you mean that it is impossible to do it. EG *With so much happening there was no question of getting a full night's sleep.* **6.7** If you do something **without question**, you do it without arguing or asking why it is necessary. EG *They obeyed me without question.* **6.8** The time **in question** or the place **in question** is the time or place which you have just been talking about. EG *Did James have dinner with you on the night in question?... He was surprised to see the woman in question enter the shop.* PHRASES

questionable /kwɛstʃənəbə[0]l/. If you say that something is **questionable**, you mean that it may be wrong or not suitable. EG *It is questionable whether the rat is a suitable test model... ...questionable projects like convention centres.* ADJ QUALIT

question mark, question marks. 1 A **question mark** is the punctuation mark (?) which is used in writing at the end of a question. N COUNT

2 If there is doubt or uncertainty about something, you can say that there is a **question mark** over it. EG *A question mark hangs over the Party's recent success.* N COUNT

questionnaire /kw[0]ɛstʃənɛə/, **questionnaires.** A **questionnaire** is a written list of questions which are answered by a lot of people in order to provide information for a report or a survey. N COUNT

question tag, question tags. A **question tag** is a very short clause at the end of a statement which changes the statement into a question. In *'She said half price, didn't she?'*, the words *'didn't she'* are a question tag. N COUNT

queue /kjuː/, **queues, queueing, queued.** The present participle is also spelled **queuing**.

1 A **queue** is a line of people or vehicles that are waiting for something. EG *She was in the queue for coffee... I had to wait in a long, slow queue.* N COUNT

2 When people **queue** or **queue up**, they stand in a line waiting for something. EG *People were queueing up for his autograph... They had queued for hours to get in.* V: OFT+*up*

quibble /kwɪbə[0]l/, **quibbles, quibbling, quibbled. 1** When people **quibble**, they argue about a small matter which is not important. EG *He had become more difficult, quibbling about minor points.* V: USU+A

2 A **quibble** is a minor objection to something. N COUNT

quiche /kiːʃ/, **quiches.** A **quiche** is a tart filled with a savoury mixture of eggs, cheese, and other things. Quiches can be eaten either hot or cold. N COUNT

quick /kwɪk/, **quicker, quickest.** 1 Someone or something that is **quick** moves or does things with great speed. EG *She was precise and quick in her movements... Her hands were quick and strong.* ADJ QUALIT
◊ **quickly.** EG *I walked quickly up the passage.* ◊ ADV
2 Something that is **quick** 2.1 takes or lasts only a short time. EG *Let's just have a quick look at that... ...a quick visit.* ◊ **quickly.** EG *They embraced quickly.* 2.2 happens without any delay or with very little delay. EG *You're likely to get a quicker reply if you telephone... John was quick to help him.* ◊ **quickly.** EG *She wants to get the whole thing over with as quickly as possible.* ADJ QUALIT ◊ ADV ADJ QUALIT ◊ ADV
3 **quick as a flash**: see **flash**. • **quick off the mark**: see **mark**. • **quick on the uptake**: see **uptake**.

quicken /kwɪkəºn/, **quickens, quickening, quickened.** If something **quickens** or if you **quicken** it, it moves at a greater speed. EG *This thought made him quicken his pace... His voice quickened.* V-ERG

quicksand /kwɪksænd/, **quicksands. Quicksand** is deep, wet sand that you sink into when you try to walk on it. N UNCOUNT OR N COUNT

quickstep /kwɪkstɛp/. The **quickstep** is a ballroom dance with a lot of quick steps. N SING : *the*+N

quid /kwɪd/. A **quid** is the same amount of money as a pound. The plural form is also 'quid'. EG *It cost 45 quid.* N COUNT Informal British

quiet /kwaɪət/, **quieter, quietest; quiets, quieting, quieted.** 1 Something or someone that is **quiet** makes only a small amount of noise. EG *Bal said in a quiet voice, 'I have resigned.'... The music had gone very quiet.* ◊ **quietly.** EG *'I'm going to do it,' I said quietly.* ADJ QUALIT ◊ ADV
2 If a place is **quiet**, there is very little noise there. EG *It was very quiet in there; you could just hear the wind moving the trees.* ADJ QUALIT
3 You also say that a place is **quiet** when nothing very exciting or important happens there. EG *The village is so quiet now.* ADJ QUALIT
4 **Quiet** is silence. EG *Ralph was on his feet too, shouting for quiet.* N UNCOUNT
5 If you are **quiet**, you do not say anything. EG *There was nothing to say so she kept quiet... Be quiet and listen.* ◊ **quietly.** EG *We lay quietly.* ADJ PRED ◊ ADV
6 A **quiet** person behaves in a calm way and is not easily made angry or upset. EG *She is thoughtful, quiet and controlled.* ADJ QUALIT
7 You describe activities as **quiet** when they happen in secret or in such a way that people do not notice. EG *He conducted some quiet diplomacy during his world tour... The funeral was as quiet as the marriage had been.* ◊ **quietly.** EG *She quietly took a flat in a suburb of Paris.* • If something is done **on the quiet**, it is done secretly or in such a way that people do not notice. • If you **keep quiet** about something, you do not say anything about it. EG *You must keep quiet about what you saw.* ADJ QUALIT ◊ ADV • PHRASE • PHRASE
8 You describe colours or clothes as **quiet** when they are not bright or not too noticeable. ADJ QUALIT

quiet down. If someone **quiets down** or if you **quiet** them **down**, they become less noisy or less active. EG *When he quieted down, I began to tell him the truth.* PHRASAL VB : V-ERG+ADV American

quieten /kwaɪətəºn/, **quietens, quietening, quietened.** If you **quieten** a person or an animal, you make them become less noisy. EG *To quieten her I had to tie her to a tree.* V+O

quieten down. If someone or something **quietens down**, they become less noisy, less active, and more calm. EG *We quietened down to think.* PHRASAL VB : V+ADV British

quill /kwɪl/, **quills.** 1 A **quill** is a pen made from a bird's feather. N COUNT
2 A bird's **quills** are large, stiff feathers on its wings and tail. N COUNT
3 The **quills** of an animal such as a porcupine are the stiff, sharp points on its body. N COUNT

quilt /kwɪlt/, **quilts.** A **quilt** is a cover filled with feathers or some other warm, soft material, which you put over yourself when you are in bed. N COUNT

quilted /kwɪltɪ²d/. Something that is **quilted** consists of two layers of fabric with a layer of soft thick material between them. EG *She was wearing a pink quilted jacket.* ADJ CLASSIF

quinine /kwɪniːn/ is a drug that is used to treat fevers such as malaria. N UNCOUNT

quintet /kwɪntɛt/, **quintets.** A **quintet** is 1 a group of five singers or musicians singing or playing together. 2 a piece of music written for five instruments or five singers. EG *...Schubert's 'Trout' quintet.* N COUNT

quip /kwɪp/, **quips, quipping, quipped.** A **quip** is an amusing or clever remark. EG *I remember your quips and jokes.* ▸ used as a verb. EG *'I've read so much about him', Philip quipped.* N COUNT Outdated ▸ V+QUOTE

quirk /kwɜːk/, **quirks.** A **quirk** is 1 a habit or aspect of a person's character which is odd or unusual. EG *Everyone has his little quirks.* 2 a strange occurrence that is difficult to explain. EG *By one of those strange quirks of fate, both had died within a few days of each other.* N COUNT : USU+SUPP

quit /kwɪt/, **quits, quitting.** The form **quit** is used in the present tense and past tense, and is also the past participle.
1 If you **quit** doing something, you stop doing it. EG *Jack wants to quit smoking... I had never quit feeling that way about him.* V : OFT+-ING, OR V+O American
2 If you **quit**, or **quit** a job, you resign from it. EG *I'm going to quit psychiatry... A week later he quit and went home to America.* V OR V+O
3 If you say to someone 'We **are quits**', you mean that neither of you owes the other one anything. PHRASE Informal
4 If people **call it quits**, they agree that an argument or fight should be ended. EG *We decided to call it quits.* PHRASE Informal

quite /kwaɪt/. 1 You use **quite** 1.1 to indicate that something is the case to a fairly great extent but not to a very great extent. EG *He was quite young... It seemed quite a long time... I could save quite a lot of money... He calls quite often... I quite enjoy looking round museums.* 1.2 to emphasize that something is completely the case or very much the case. EG *I stood quite still... You're quite sure you don't mind?... Oh I quite agree... Quite frankly, I'm too miserable to care... The matter is quite simple.* SUBMOD OR ADV
2 You use **quite** after a negative 2.1 to indicate that something is almost true. EG *It's not quite big enough... I didn't quite understand what it was all about.* 2.2 to indicate that you do not know something exactly. EG *I don't know quite where to go.* ADV : WITH BROAD NEG
3 You use **quite a** to emphasize that something is very unusual, impressive, or significant. EG *It was quite a sight... They have quite a problem.* PHRASE
4 You can say **'quite'** or **'quite so'** to express your agreement with someone. EG *'It does a lot for public relations.'-'Quite.'* CONVENTION Formal

quiver /kwɪvə/, **quivers, quivering, quivered.** If something **quivers**, it shakes or trembles. EG *His fingers quivered uncontrollably.* ▸ used as a noun. EG *Her whole body gave a slight quiver.* V ▸ N SING : a+N

quiz /kwɪz/, **quizzes, quizzing, quizzed.** 1 A **quiz** is a game or competition in which someone tests your knowledge by asking you questions. EG *...musical quizzes on TV... ...a quiz programme.* N COUNT
2 If you **quiz** someone, you ask them questions because you want to obtain information from them. EG *She couldn't be sure why he was quizzing her.* V+O

quizzical /kwɪzɪkəºl/. If you give someone a **quizzical** look, you look at them with a slight smile, because you know them well and are suspicious of ADJ QUALIT

If you were losing a race, would you quit?

their behaviour or are amused by it. EG *I could see from Clare's quizzical glance that she knew that.*

quota /kwəʊtə/, **quotas.** A **quota** is a limited number or quantity of something which is officially allowed. EG *...an import quota of 1.6m cars... ...a daily food quota.* N COUNT

quotation /kwəʊteɪʃə^{0}n/, **quotations. 1** A **quotation** is a sentence or phrase from a book, poem, or play. EG *...a quotation from a novel by Somerset Maugham... He recited a long bible quotation.* N COUNT: OFT+*from*

2 When someone gives you a **quotation**, they tell you how much they will charge to do a particular piece of work. EG *They submitted quotations and agreed prices... Get a free quotation for the job.* N COUNT

quotation mark, quotation marks. Quotation marks are punctuation marks that are used in writing to show where speech or a quotation begins and ends. They are usually written or printed as ' and '. N COUNT: USU PLURAL

quote /kwəʊt/, **quotes, quoting, quoted. 1** If you **quote** someone or something, you repeat the exact words that they have written or said. EG *He was quoted in the paper as saying: 'This strike is evil.'... She quoted the Chinese proverb about lighting candles... 'Change and decay in all around I see,' Castle quoted... ...quoting from a film he'd seen.* V+O, V+QUOTE, OR V+A

2 If you **quote** something such as a law or a fact, you state it because it supports what you are saying. EG *They quote figures to compare the costs of adult education in different countries... I will quote only one or two examples.* V+O

3 If you **quote** a price, you suggest a price for which you are willing to do a particular piece of work. EG *Ask the refuse department to come and quote for removing the stuff... They quoted a price of twenty thousand dollars.* V+O, V+O+O, OR V+*for*

4 A **quote** from a book, poem, or play is a sentence or phrase from it. EG *...a short quote from the Oration.* N COUNT: OFT+*from*

5 A **quote** for a piece of work is the price that someone says they will charge you to do the work. EG *Try getting a quote from a caterer for a really big party.* N COUNT

6 Quotes are the same as quotation marks. EG *Her comments are placed in quotes.* N PLURAL Informal

> **QUOTE** stands for **direct speech**
> +QUOTE is used in the Extra Column after verbs which can be used to describe direct speech, as in *'Your father was a good friend to me,' he **remarked**.*
> See the entry headed VERBS for more information.

R r

R, r /ɑː/, **Rs, r's. R** is the eighteenth letter of the English alphabet. N COUNT

rabbi /ræbaɪ/, **rabbis.** A **rabbi** is a Jewish religious leader, usually one who is in charge of a synagogue, one who is qualified to teach Judaism, or one who is an expert on Jewish law. N COUNT

rabbit /ræbɪt/, **rabbits.** A **rabbit** is a small furry animal with long ears. Rabbits live in holes in the ground. N COUNT

rabble /ræbə^{0}l/. A **rabble** is a crowd of noisy, disorderly people. EG *...a rabble of boys and girls of all ages.* N SING

rabid /ræbɪd, reɪ-/. **1** You use **rabid** to describe someone who has very strong and unreasonable opinions on a subject, especially in politics. EG *...a rabid feminist... ...rabid Republicans who worshipped Genet.* ADJ QUALIT: ATTRIB

2 A dog or other animal that is **rabid** is infected with rabies. EG *...a rabid dog.* ADJ CLASSIF

rabies /reɪbi^{1}z/ is a serious disease which causes people and animals, especially dogs, to go mad and die. N UNCOUNT

race /reɪs/, **races, racing, raced. 1** A **race** is a competition to see who is the fastest, for example in running, swimming, or driving. EG *She came second in the race... The race is run through the streets of London... ...a horse race.* N COUNT

2 A **race** for power or control is a situation in which people or organizations compete with each other for power or control. EG *The race for the White House is now on.... ...the arms race.* ● See also **rat race**. N SING+SUPP

3 If you **race** someone or **race** against them, you compete with them in a race. EG *They would often race one another to the bus stop... She has raced against some of the best runners in the country.* V+O OR V+A

3 If you **race** an animal or vehicle, you prepare it for races and make it take part in races. EG *The Australians race camels... He races pigeons... They race vintage cars.* V+O: NO PASS

4 If you **race** somewhere, you go there as quickly as possible. EG *He turned and raced after the others... She raced down the stairs... We had to race across London to get the train.* V+A

5 If your heart **races**, it beats very quickly because you are excited or afraid. EG *His heart raced as he saw the plane coming in to land.* V

6 You describe a situation as a **race against time** when you have to work very fast in order to do something before a particular time. PHRASE

7 A **race** is also one of the major groups which human beings can be divided into according to their physical features, such as the colour of their skin. EG *The law prohibits discrimination on the grounds of colour or race.* ● See also **human race**. N COUNT OR N UNCOUNT

8 See also **racing**.

racecourse /reɪskɔːs/, **racecourses.** A **racecourse** is a track on which horses race. N COUNT British

racehorse /reɪshɔːs/, **racehorses.** A **racehorse** is a horse that is trained to run in races. N COUNT

race relations are the ways in which people of different races behave towards each other. EG *...efforts to improve race relations.* N PLURAL

racial /reɪʃə^{0}l/ describes things relating to people's race. EG *...racial discrimination... ...racial prejudice... ...racial equality... ...racial harmony.* ADJ CLASSIF: USU ATTRIB
◊ **racially.** EG *...children of racially mixed parentage.* ◊ ADV

racialism /reɪʃəlɪzə^{0}m/ is the same as racism. N UNCOUNT
◊ **racialist** /reɪʃəlɪst/, **racialists.** EG *...racialist brutality... ...racialist attitudes.* ◊ ADJ QUALIT OR N COUNT

racing /reɪsɪŋ/ refers to races between animals, especially horses, or between vehicles. EG *...racing stables... ...motor racing... ...a racing car.* N UNCOUNT

racism /reɪsɪzə^{0}m/ is the belief that some races are inferior to others. It also refers to the treatment of certain people as inferior because they belong to a particular race; used showing disapproval. EG *...subtle forms of racism... ...a struggle against racism.* N UNCOUNT ◊ **racist** /reɪsɪst/, **racists.** EG *...racist posters... He's a racist and a sexist.* ◊ ADJ QUALIT OR N COUNT

rack /ræk/, **racks, racking, racked.** The verb is also spelled **wrack** in American English.
1 A **rack** is a piece of equipment that is used for holding things or for hanging things on. EG *He rinsed the plates and put them on the rack to drain... He counted the bits of luggage on the racks.* N COUNT
2 If someone **is racked** by something, it causes them great suffering or pain. EG *She stood there, racked by indecision, and began to cry.* V+O : USU PASS +by/with Literary
3 If you **rack** your **brains**, you try very hard to think of something. EG *Even racking his brains he couldn't think of a single example.* PHRASE Informal

racket /rækɪt/, **rackets;** also spelled **racquet** in paragraph 3. 1 If someone is making a **racket**, they are making a loud unpleasant noise. EG *...the non-stop racket that a healthy baby makes.* N SING
2 A **racket** is an illegal activity that is used to make money. EG *He was involved in an insurance racket.* N COUNT
3 A **racket** is also an oval-shaped bat with strings across it. Rackets are used in tennis, squash, and badminton. EG *...a tennis racket.* N COUNT

racy /reɪsi¹/, **racier, raciest. Racy** writing or behaviour is lively, amusing, and slightly shocking. EG *...a racy, romantic historical novel.* ADJ QUALIT

radar /reɪdɑː/ is a way of discovering the position or speed of things that cannot be seen, by using radio signals. EG *His speed was checked by radar.* N UNCOUNT

radiant /reɪdɪənt/. 1 Someone who is **radiant** is so happy that their joy shows in their face. EG *Charlotte, you look radiant... ...Haig's radiant optimism.* ADJ QUALIT ◇ **radiantly.** EG *Jane smiled radiantly.* ◇ ADV
◇ **radiance** /reɪdɪəns/. EG *...the radiance of her features... Hilary lost a little of her radiance.* ◇ N UNCOUNT
2 Something that is **radiant** glows brightly. EG *...a morning of radiant light.* ADJ QUALIT ◇ **radiance.** EG *The candle's light threw a faint radiance on the sleeping girl.* ◇ N UNCOUNT Literary

radiate /reɪdi¹eɪt/, **radiates, radiating, radiated.** 1 If things **radiate** out from a place, they form a pattern that is like lines drawn from the centre of a circle to various points on its edge. EG *...roads that radiated before us... Rods radiate outwards from the centre.* V : USU+A
2 If you **radiate** an emotion or quality or if it **radiates** from you, people can see it very clearly in your face and in your behaviour. EG *In the evening Val was back, radiating confidence... There was a tenderness that radiated from her.* V+O OR V+*from*

radiation /reɪdi¹eɪʃəⁿn/ is 1 very small particles of a radioactive substance that can cause illness and death. EG *Those exposed to a very large amount of radiation experience internal bleeding.* N UNCOUNT
2 energy that comes from a particular source, for example the sun. EG *...heat radiation.*

radiator /reɪdɪeɪtə/, **radiators.** 1 A **radiator** is a hollow metal device, usually connected by pipes to a central heating system, that is used to heat a room. N COUNT
2 The **radiator** in a car is the part of the engine which is filled with water in order to cool the engine. N COUNT

radical /rædɪkəⁿl/, **radicals.** 1 A **radical** is someone who believes that there should be great changes in society and tries to bring about these changes. EG *...a new group of radicals who turned against the established social order.* N COUNT ▸ used as an adjective. EG *...a radical barrister... The League had become too radical.* ▸ ADJ QUALIT
2 You use **radical** to describe things that relate to the basic nature of something. EG *...a radical disagreement over fundamentals... ...radical advances in computer design.* ADJ QUALIT : USU ATTRIB ◇ **radically.** EG *Attitudes towards education will have to change radically.* ◇ ADV

radii /reɪdɪaɪ/ is the plural of **radius.**

radio /reɪdɪəʊ/, **radios, radioing, radioed.** 1 **Radio** is 1.1 a system of sending sound over a distance by transmitting electrical signals. EG *...radio waves... We managed to establish radio communication with them.* N UNCOUNT 1.2 the broadcasting of programmes for the public to listen to, by sending out signals from a transmitter. EG *...a song that had been on the radio a lot... ...a local radio station.* N SING : *the*+N, OR N UNCOUNT
2 A **radio** or a **radio set** is the piece of equipment that you use when you listen to radio programmes. EG *She switched on the radio... ...advertisements on radio and television.* N COUNT, OR *on*+N
3 If you **radio** someone, you send a message to them by radio. EG *I had radioed Rick and arranged to have a car waiting for me.* V+O OR V

radioactive /reɪdɪəʊæktɪv/. Something that is **radioactive** contains a substance that produces energy in the form of powerful and harmful rays. EG *...radioactive waste.* ADJ QUALIT

radioactivity /reɪdɪəʊæktɪvɪ¹ti¹/ is radioactive energy. EG *...a serious leak of radioactivity.* N UNCOUNT

radiographer /reɪdɪɒgrəfə/, **radiographers.** A **radiographer** is a person who is trained to take X-rays. N COUNT

radiography /reɪdɪɒgrəfi¹/ is the process of taking X-rays, usually for medical examinations. N UNCOUNT

radiologist /reɪdɪɒlədʒɪst/, **radiologists.** A **radiologist** is a doctor who is trained in radiology. N COUNT

radiology /reɪdɪɒlədʒi¹/ is the branch of medical science that uses radioactivity. N UNCOUNT

radiotherapy /reɪdɪəʊθɛrəpi¹/ is the treatment of diseases such as cancer by using radiation. N UNCOUNT

radish /rædɪʃ/, **radishes.** A **radish** is a small red or white root vegetable with a fairly strong taste, which you can eat raw in salads. N COUNT

radius /reɪdɪəs/, **radii** /reɪdɪaɪ/. 1 The **radius** of a circle is the distance from its centre to its outside edge. N COUNT
2 You use **radius** to refer to the distance from a particular place that something happens or exists. EG *The missile landed within a half-mile radius of its target.* N SING+SUPP

raffle /ræfəⁿl/, **raffles.** A **raffle** is a competition in which you buy tickets with numbers on them. Afterwards some numbers are chosen, and if your ticket has one of these numbers on it, you win a prize. EG *...organizing a raffle... ...raffle tickets.* N COUNT

raft /rɑːft/, **rafts.** A **raft** is 1 a floating platform made from large pieces of wood tied together. 2 an inflatable rubber or plastic mattress that floats on water. N COUNT

rafter /rɑːftə/, **rafters. Rafters** are the sloping pieces of wood that support a roof. N COUNT

rag /ræg/, **rags.** 1 A **rag** is a piece of old cloth which you can use to clean or wipe things. EG *Wiping his hands on a rag, he went out to the car... ...a crumpled piece of rag.* N COUNT OR N UNCOUNT
2 **Rags** are old, torn clothes. EG *They were thin and hungry, dressed in rags... ...beggars in dirty rags.* N PLURAL
3 People refer to a newspaper as a **rag** when they do not have a high opinion of it. EG *...the local rag.* N COUNT Informal
4 You use **rags to riches** to describe the way in which someone quickly becomes very rich after they have been quite poor. EG *...his kind of overnight rags-to-riches story.* PHRASE Informal
5 If you describe something as **a red rag to a bull,** you mean that it is certain to make someone very angry. EG *...a retired colonel to whom anything modern was a red rag to a bull.* PHRASE Informal
6 See also **ragged.**

rage /reɪdʒ/, **rages, raging, raged.** 1 **Rage** is strong anger that is difficult to control. EG *She was trembling with rage... I stormed out of the room in a rage.* N UNCOUNT OR N COUNT
2 If you **rage** about something, you speak or think very angrily about it. EG *'How do you mean, you can't tell me?' he raged... ...raging at his own weakness.* V : USU+A, OR V+QUOTE
3 You say that something powerful or unpleasant V : USU+A

If you are making a racket, are you intending to play tennis?

rages when it continues with great force or violence. EG *There was a monsoon raging outside... The debate raged throughout the whole day.*
◊ **raging**. EG *...the season of bitter cold and raging blizzards.* ◊ ADJ CLASSIF : ATTRIB

4 **Raging** feelings or desires are very intense and severe. EG *...a raging thirst.* ADJ CLASSIF : ATTRIB

5 When something is popular and fashionable, you can say that it is the **rage**. EG *Jogging and aerobics were all the rage that year.* N SING Informal

ragged /rægɪd/. 1 Someone who is **ragged** is wearing clothes that are old and torn. EG *...a ragged, skinny man of about fifty.* ADJ QUALIT

2 **Ragged** clothes are old and torn. ADJ QUALIT

3 You can say that something is **ragged** when it is untidy and uneven. EG *They were herded into a ragged line... ...ragged allotments.* ADJ QUALIT

ragtime /rægtaɪm/ is a kind of jazz music that became popular in America in the early 1900s. N UNCOUNT

raid /reɪd/, **raids, raiding, raided.** 1 When soldiers **raid** a place, they make a sudden armed attack against it. EG *Blanco's supporters are still raiding villages along the border.* ▸ used as a noun. EG *Both the bridges were destroyed in bombing raids.* ◊ **raider, raiders**. EG *...a band of raiders.* V+O ▸ N COUNT ◊ N COUNT

2 If people **raid** a building, they enter it by force, usually in order to steal something. The police might raid a place to look for dangerous criminals or illegal drugs. EG *They shot him and raided his laboratory to seize his papers... Their headquarters in London were raided by the police.* ▸ used as a noun. EG *...police raids... The gang had carried out a series of bank raids.* ◊ **raider**. EG *It was clear that the raiders had been in the house much longer.* V+O ▸ N COUNT ◊ N COUNT

rail /reɪl/, **rails.** 1 A **rail** is 1.1 a horizontal bar attached to posts or fixed round the edge of something and used as a fence or support. EG *Holding on to the rail with one hand, he pulled himself up.* **1.2** a horizontal bar that you hang things on. EG *...picture rails... ...a towel rail.* N COUNT

2 The steel bars which trains run on are called **rails**. N COUNT

3 If you travel somewhere by **rail**, you travel there in a train. If you send something by **rail**, you send it in a train. EG *I usually go by rail... ...rail travel.* N UNCOUNT

railcard /reɪlkɑːd/, **railcards.** A **railcard** is an identity card that allows people to buy train tickets cheaply. EG *...a Senior Citizens Railcard.* N COUNT

railing /reɪlɪŋ/, **railings.** A **railing** is a fence made from metal bars. EG *I peered through the railings into the courtyard.* N COUNT

railroad /reɪlrəʊd/, **railroads.** A **railroad** is the same as a railway. EG *...railroad tracks.* N COUNT American

railway /reɪlweɪ/, **railways.** A **railway** is 1 a route between two places along which trains travel on steel rails. EG *...the railway to Addis Ababa... ...the early days of railways... ...a railway station.* 2 a company or organization that operates railway routes. EG *...the Western Australian Government Railways.* N COUNT British; British

railway line, railway lines. A **railway line** is a route between two places along which trains travel on steel rails. EG *...the railway line from London to Brighton.* N COUNT

rain /reɪn/, **rains, raining, rained.** 1 **Rain** is water that falls from the clouds in small drops. EG *You can't go home in this rain... A light rain had begun to fall.* N UNCOUNT

2 When rain falls, you can say that it **is raining**. EG *It had started to rain... Is it raining?* V

3 If something **rains** from above, it falls rapidly and in large quantities. EG *Ash rained from the sky.* V+A

rain down. If something **rains down**, it falls rapidly and in large quantities. EG *Mortar shells rained down... ...raining down arrows from both sides.* PHRASAL VB : V-ERG+ADV

rain off. If a sports match **is rained off**, it has to stop, or it is not able to start, because of rain. PHRASAL VB : V-PASS+ADV

rainbow /reɪnbəʊ/, **rainbows.** A **rainbow** is an arch of different colours that you can sometimes see in the sky when it is raining. N COUNT

raincoat /reɪnkəʊt/, **raincoats.** A **raincoat** is a waterproof coat that you wear when it is raining. N COUNT

raindrop /reɪndrɒp/, **raindrops.** A **raindrop** is a single drop of rain. N COUNT

rainfall /reɪnfɔːl/ is the amount of rain that falls in a place during a particular period. EG *...the average monthly rainfall of London.* N UNCOUNT

rainforest /reɪnfɒrɪst/, **rainforests.** A **rainforest** is a thick forest of tall trees which is found in tropical areas where there is a lot of rain. N COUNT OR N UNCOUNT

rainstorm /reɪnstɔːm/, **rainstorms.** A **rainstorm** is a fall of very heavy rain. N COUNT

rainwater /reɪnwɔːtə/ is rain that has been stored in a tank or bucket. N UNCOUNT

rainy /reɪni[1]/. 1 If it is **rainy**, it is raining a lot. EG *Most tropical areas have rainy and dry seasons... ...a rainy Sunday afternoon.* ADJ QUALIT

2 If you say that you are saving something **for a rainy day**, you mean that you are saving it until a time in the future when you might need it. EG *They put part of the money in the bank for a rainy day.* PHRASE

raise /reɪz/, **raises, raising, raised.** 1 If you **raise** something, you move it so that it is in a higher position. EG *He tried to raise the window, but the sash cord was broken... Ralph raised a hand for silence.* ● If you **raise** your **eyebrows**, you show surprise by moving your eyebrows upwards. V+O ● PHRASE

2 If you **raise** yourself, you stretch your body so that you are standing up straight, or so that you are no longer lying flat. EG *Slowly she raised herself to her full height.* V-REFL Literary

3 If you **raise** the rate or level of something, you increase it. EG *The maximum speed was raised to seventy miles per hour.* V+O

4 To **raise** the standard of something means to improve it. EG *Putting teachers in day nurseries would raise standards.* V+O

5 If you **raise** your voice, you speak more loudly, usually because you are angry. V+O

6 A **raise** is an increase in your wages or salary. EG *He thought about asking his boss for a raise.* N COUNT American

7 If you **raise** money for a charity or an institution, you get people to give you money for it. V+O

8 If you **raise** money that you need, you manage to get it, for example by selling your property or by borrowing. EG *He raised £300 to finance it.* V+O

9 If someone or something **raises** a particular emotion or memory in you, they cause you to feel it or remember it. EG *For me it always raises fond memories of broad main streets.* V+O

10 Someone who **raises** a child looks after it until it is grown up. EG *It was no place to raise a child.* V+O

11 If someone **raises** a particular type of animal or crop, they breed that type of animal or grow that type of crop. EG *He moved to Petaluma to raise chickens.* V+O

12 If you **raise** a subject, an objection, or a question, you mention it or bring it to someone's attention. EG *You would have to raise that with Mr Gerran personally... The Foreign Office raised no objection... ...questions raised by Senators.* V+O

13 to **raise a finger**: see **finger**.

raised /reɪzd/. A **raised** object or area is higher than the area that surrounds it. EG *He stood on a raised platform.* ADJ CLASSIF

raisin /reɪzə⁰n/, **raisins. Raisins** are dried grapes. N COUNT

rake /reɪk/, **rakes, raking, raked.** 1 A **rake** is a garden tool consisting of a row of metal teeth attached to a long handle. See picture at TOOLS. N COUNT

2 If you **rake** a surface, you move a rake across it in order to make it smooth and level. EG *The field had been raked.* V+O OR V

3 If you **rake** leaves or weeds, you move them somewhere using a rake. EG *Jeremy had raked the fallen leaves into a pile.* V+O+A

4 If you call a man a **rake**, you mean that he is rather immoral, because he has sexual relationships with many women.
N COUNT Outdated Literary

rake in. If you say that someone **is raking in** money, you mean that they are earning a lot of it fairly easily. EG *They're raking it in!*
PHRASAL VB : V+O+ADV, USU CONT Informal

rake up. If you **rake up** something unpleasant or embarrassing that happened in the past, you talk about it or remind someone about it. EG *Don't go raking up what happened thirteen years ago.*
PHRASAL VB : V+O+ADV

rally /ræli[1]/, **rallies, rallying, rallied. 1** A **rally** is **1.1** a large public meeting that is held in order to show support for something such as a political party. EG *...a big anti-government rally in Hyde Park.* **1.2** a competition in which vehicles are driven over public roads. EG *...the Monte Carlo Rally.*
N COUNT

2 A **rally** in tennis, badminton, or squash is a continuous series of shots that the players exchange without stopping.
N COUNT

3 When people **rally** to something, they unite to support it. EG *She believed that the voters would rally to the Conservatives... They made a final effort to rally their supporters.*
V-ERG : IF V THEN+A

4 When a sick person **rallies**, he or she begins to become stronger again.
V

rally round. When people **rally round**, they work as a group in order to support someone or something at a difficult time. EG *I'm very lucky. Everyone has rallied round... The party rallied round him after his election defeat.*
PHRASAL VB : V+ADV/PREP

ram /ræm/, **rams, ramming, rammed. 1** If one vehicle **rams** another, it crashes into it with a lot of force. EG *The ship had been rammed by a British destroyer.*
V+O

2 If you **ram** something somewhere, you push it there with great force. EG *I rammed the bolt back across the door... He rammed the tobacco into his pipe.*
V+O+A

3 A **ram** is an adult male sheep.
N COUNT

4 If something **rams home** a fact or idea, it makes you fully understand it or accept it. EG *The First World War rammed home the same lesson.*
PHRASE

ramble /ræmbə[0]l/, **rambles, rambling, rambled. 1** A **ramble** is a long walk in the countryside. EG *We were out on a country ramble.* ▸ used as a verb. EG *...rambling over the Yorkshire hills.*
N COUNT
▸ V+A

2 When someone **rambles**, they talk in a confused way. EG *He often rambled and said strange things.*
V : NO IMPER

ramble on. You say that someone **rambles on** when they talk for a long time in a confused way. EG *...listening to Miriam as she rambled on.*
PHRASAL VB : V+ADV

rambling /ræmblɪŋ/. **1** A **rambling** building has no regular shape and spreads out in many directions. EG *We bought a rambling old house near the village.*
ADJ QUALIT

2 Rambling speech or writing is very confused. EG *She wrote me a long rambling letter.*
ADJ QUALIT

ramification /ræmɪfɪkeɪʃə[0]n/, **ramifications.** The **ramifications** of a decision, idea, or plan are all the aspects of it that make it more complicated, especially when they are not obvious at first. EG *Not many people actually understand the ramifications of these guidelines.*
N COUNT : USU PLURAL+SUPP Formal

ramp /ræmp/, **ramps.** A **ramp** is a sloping surface between two places that are at different levels. EG *It was driven up a ramp and straight on to the train.*
N COUNT

rampage /ræmpeɪdʒ/, **rampages, rampaging, rampaged. 1** When people or animals **rampage**, they rush about in a wild or violent way, usually causing damage or destruction. EG *...elephants rampaging through the bush.*
V : OFT+A

2 If people **go on the rampage**, they rush about in a wild or violent way. EG *A section of the crowd broke loose and went on the rampage.*
PHRASE

rampant /ræmpənt/. If you describe something such as a crime or disease as **rampant**, you mean that it is growing or spreading in an uncontrolled way. EG *Political apathy is rampant.*
ADJ QUALIT

rampart /ræmpɑːt/, **ramparts.** A **rampart** is an earth bank, often with a wall on it, that is built to protect a fort, castle, or city.
N COUNT : USU PLURAL Outdated

ramshackle /ræmʃækə[0]l/. A **ramshackle** building is badly made or in bad condition, and likely to fall down. EG *...a ramshackle cottage.*
ADJ QUALIT : ATTRIB

ran /ræn/ is the past tense of **run.**

ranch /rɑːntʃ/, **ranches.** A **ranch** is a large farm in the United States, especially one used for raising cattle, sheep, or horses. EG *...cattle ranches.*
N COUNT

rancher /rɑːntʃə/, **ranchers.** A **rancher** is someone who owns or manages a ranch.
N COUNT

rancid /rænsɪd/. If butter, bacon, or other fatty foods are **rancid**, they have gone bad and taste stale and unpleasant.
ADJ QUALIT

rancour /ræŋkə/; spelled **rancor** in American English. **Rancour** is a feeling of deep and bitter hatred. EG *He was shaken by rage and rancour.*
N UNCOUNT Formal

random /rændə[0]m/. **1** If you do something in a **random** way, you do it without a definite plan or pattern. EG *The way the books were arranged seemed completely random... This is just a random selection of the complaints we have received.*
ADJ QUALIT : USU ATTRIB

◇ **randomly.** EG *Ink had been randomly squirted on the floor and the walls.*
◇ ADV

2 If something is done **at random**, it is done without a definite plan or pattern. EG *He opened the book at random... I let my thoughts come at random.*
PHRASE

randy /rændi[1]/, **randier, randiest.** Someone who is **randy** is eager to have sexual intercourse. EG *The heat made them both randy.*
ADJ QUALIT Informal

rang /ræŋ/ is the past tense of **ring.**

range /reɪnʒ/, **ranges, ranging, ranged. 1** The **range** of something is the maximum area within which it can reach things or detect things. EG *What is the range of their transmitters?... Their tanks stayed just beyond the range of our big guns... ...medium range ballistic missiles.* ● If something is **within range**, it is near enough to be reached or detected. If it is **out of range**, it is too far away to be reached or detected. EG *We managed to keep out of range.*
N COUNT+SUPP
● PHRASE

2 If you shoot something **at** close **range**, you are very close to it when you shoot it. If you shoot something **at** a **range** of, for example, half a mile, you are half a mile away from it when you shoot it.
PHRASE

3 A **range** of things is a number of different things of the same general kind. EG *They were questioned on a range of subjects from politics to astrology... ...a wide range of electrical goods... ...the range of research activities in the university.*
N SING+SUPP

4 A **range** is the complete group that is included between two points on a scale of measurement or quality. EG *There are three price ranges... The age range is from six months to forty-seven years.*
N COUNT+SUPP

5 When things **range** between two points or **range** from one point to another, they vary within these points on a scale of measurement or quality. EG *Their politics ranged from liberal to radical... They were offered increases ranging from £6.71 to £16.31 a week.*
V+A

6 If a piece of writing or speech **ranges** over a group of topics, it includes all those topics. EG *The book ranges historically as far back as the Renaissance... The conversation ranged widely.*
V+A

7 If you **range** people or things somewhere, you arrange them in a line or in lines. EG *Books were ranged on shelves on the walls.*
V+O+A Formal

8 A **range** of mountains or hills is a line of mountains or hills. EG *...a splendid mountain range.*
N COUNT+SUPP

9 A rifle **range** or a firing **range** is a place where people can practise shooting at targets.
N COUNT : USU+SUPP

Would you like to live in a ramshackle building?

ranger /reɪndʒə/, **rangers.** A **ranger** is a person whose job is to look after a forest or park. EG *...the head ranger of a vast national park.* N COUNT

rank /ræŋk/, **ranks, ranking, ranked. 1** Someone's **rank** is the position or grade that they have in an organization. EG *A prisoner of war must only reveal his name, rank, and number... She achieved the rank of professor at the age of 31... He wasn't getting the salary to which he was entitled by rank.* N COUNT OR N UNCOUNT

● If someone **pulls rank**, they make unfair use of the authority that they have in an organization. EG *She usually gets her way without needing to pull rank.* ● PHRASE

2 When you say what something **ranks**, you say what position it has on a scale. EG *The island ranks as one of the poorest of the whole region... Philips was ranked third in size among the industrial corporations.* V-ERG+A : NO CONT

3 The **ranks** are the ordinary members of an organization, especially of the armed forces. EG *...a senior officer who had risen from the ranks.* N PLURAL : *the*+N

4 When you become a member of a large group of people, you can say that you are joining its **ranks**. EG *...the growing ranks of the unemployed.* N PLURAL +SUPP

5 When the members of a group **close ranks**, they support each other in a united way and oppose any attack or criticism. PHRASE

6 Your **rank** is the social class that you belong to. EG *...people from the upper and middle ranks of society... We cater for everyone, regardless of age or social rank.* N COUNT OR N UNCOUNT Outdated

7 A **rank** is also a row of people or things. EG *Ralph examined the ranks of boys.* N COUNT : USU PLURAL

8 You use **rank** to describe a bad or undesirable quality that exists in an extreme form. EG *...rank corruption... ...rank favouritism.* ADJ CLASSIF : ATTRIB

9 You can describe something as **rank** when it has a strong and unpleasant smell. ADJ QUALIT Formal

rank and file. The **rank and file** are the ordinary members of an organization as opposed to the leaders or officers. EG *There are now considerable political differences between the leadership and the rank and file.* N COLL : SING, *the*+N

rankle /ræŋkə^{0}l/, **rankles, rankling, rankled.** Something that **rankles** makes you feel angry or bitter. EG *The argument with Sam earlier on still rankled.* V

ransack /rænsæk/, **ransacks, ransacking, ransacked.** If you **ransack** a building or a room, you disturb everything in it and leave it in a mess, because you are looking for something. EG *Detectives ransacked the house.* V+O

ransom /rænsə^{0}m/, **ransoms, ransoming, ransomed. 1** A **ransom** is an amount of money that you must pay in order to set free a person who has been kidnapped. EG *The family paid a ransom of £50,000 for the child's release.* N COUNT

2 If someone **holds** you **to ransom**, **2.1** they keep you as a prisoner until money is paid for you to be set free. EG *The minister's daughter was held to ransom.* **2.2** they put you in a position in which you are forced to agree to unreasonable demands. EG *She accused them of holding the nation to ransom.* PHRASE

rant /rænt/, **rants, ranting, ranted.** You say that someone **rants** when they talk in a loud, excited, and angry way. EG *He would rant like this till she could not bear it any more.* V : USU+A ◇ **ranting, rantings.** EG *...the rantings and ravings of these lunatics.* ◇ N COUNT

rap /ræp/, **raps, rapping, rapped. 1** If you **rap** on something or if you **rap** it, you hit it with a series of quick blows. EG *He rapped on the table and called for silence.* V+A OR V+O+A

2 A **rap** is a quick hit or knock against something. EG *A light rap sounded at the door.* N COUNT

3 If you receive **a rap over the knuckles**, you receive a warning or criticism. PHRASE

4 If you **take the rap**, you are blamed or punished for something, even if it is not your fault. EG *Lloyd will have to take the rap.* PHRASE Informal

rap out. If you **rap out** an order or a question, you say it quickly and sharply. EG *'Is that the truth?' he suddenly rapped out.* PHRASAL VB : V+ADV+O OR V+ADV+QUOTE

rapacious /rəpeɪʃəs/. Someone who is **rapacious** is extremely greedy for money. EG *...rapacious businessmen.* ADJ QUALIT Formal

rape /reɪp/, **rapes, raping, raped. 1** When a man **rapes** a woman, he violently forces her to have sex with him when she does not want to. EG *...an organization to help women who have been raped.* V+O

▸ used as a noun. EG *She had to testify to his attempts at rape... ...a rape victim.* ▸ N UNCOUNT OR N COUNT

2 The **rape** of the countryside or the earth is the destruction or spoiling of it. EG *...the rape of their beautiful landscape by developers.* N SING+*of* Formal

rapid /ræpɪd/, **rapids. 1** Something that is **rapid** **1.1** happens very fast. EG *...a time of rapid economic growth... ...the rapid development of British industry.* ADJ QUALIT ◇ **rapidly.** EG *The situation had rapidly deteriorated.* ◇ ADV ◇ **rapidity** /rəpɪdɪ^{1}ti^{1}/. EG *The film shows the rapidity of the changes in this area of medicine.* ◇ N UNCOUNT **1.2** moves with great speed. EG *He took a few rapid steps towards the beach.* ADJ QUALIT ◇ **rapidly.** EG *They walked rapidly past the churchyard.* ◇ ADV

2 Rapids are parts of a river where the water moves very fast, often over rocks. EG *Further down the river there is another stretch of rapids.* N PLURAL

rapist /reɪpɪst/, **rapists.** A **rapist** is a man who has raped a woman. N COUNT

rapport /ræpɔː/. If people have a **rapport** with each other, they have a relationship in which they are able to understand each other very well. EG *There is insufficient rapport between hospitals and family doctors.* N UNCOUNT

rapt /ræpt/. Someone who is **rapt** is so interested or fascinated by something that they cannot stop looking at it or cannot think about anything else. EG *Claud was staring at me, rapt... My audience listened in rapt silence.* ADJ QUALIT

rapture /ræptʃə/, **raptures. 1 Rapture** is is an overpowering feeling of delight. EG *...his face shining with rapture... ...the first raptures of their honeymoon.* N UNCOUNT OR N PLURAL Literary

2 If you **go into raptures** about something, you express strong enthusiasm for it. EG *I had gone into raptures over the country I had been through.* PHRASE

rapturous /ræptʃərəs/. A **rapturous** feeling or reaction is one which in which you feel very great happiness or enthusiasm. EG *They went out to a rapturous reception from their supporters.* ADJ QUALIT Literary

rare /rɛə/, **rarer, rarest. 1** Something that is **rare** **1.1** is not common and is therefore interesting or valuable. EG *These wild flowers are so rare that I want to do whatever I can to save them... Diane's hobby is collecting rare books.* **1.2** does not happen very often. EG *Cases of smallpox are extremely rare... It's rare to come across any book which makes you laugh out loud.* ADJ QUALIT

2 You use **rare** to describe an extremely good or remarkable quality. EG *...her rare gift for comedy.* ADJ QUALIT : ATTRIB

3 Meat that is **rare** is cooked very lightly so that the inside is still red. ADJ QUALIT

4 See also **rarely, rarity.**

rarefied /rɛərɪfaɪd/; also spelled **rarified.** You use **rarefied** to describe people or things that seem not to be connected with ordinary life, because of their high social or academic standards; used showing disapproval. EG *...the rather rarefied atmosphere of university life... ...the rarefied world of the very rich.* ADJ QUALIT : USU ATTRIB

rarely /rɛəli^{1}/ means not very often. EG *We very rarely quarrel... I'd rarely seen a man look so unhappy... Rarely has so much time been wasted by so many people.* ADV BRD NEG

rarity /rɛərɪ^{1}ti^{1}/, **rarities. 1** A **rarity** is something that is interesting or valuable because it is so unusual. EG *Bat twins are a rarity... ...six bags of gold coins, many of which were rarities.* N COUNT

2 The **rarity** of something is the fact that it is very N UNCOUNT uncommon. EG *Many animals are endangered by their rarity and beauty.*

rascal /rɑːskəⁿl/, **rascals.** If you refer to a man or a child as a **rascal**, you mean that he or she does bad or dishonest things. N COUNT Outdated

rash /ræʃ/, **rashes. 1** Someone who is **rash** does foolish things, because they act without thinking carefully first. EG *Don't be rash... Don't do anything rash... Some rash promises were made.* ◇ **rashly.** EG *I'm not a man who does things rashly.* ADJ QUALIT ◇ ADV

2 A **rash** is an area of red spots that appear on your skin when you are ill or have an allergy. EG *...a man with a rash on one side of his neck.* N COUNT

3 A **rash** of events is a large number of them that all happen in a short period of time. EG *A rash of robberies had suddenly struck the country.* N PART

rasher /ræʃə/, **rashers.** A **rasher** of bacon is a thin slice of it. N COUNT

rasp /rɑːsp/, **rasps, rasping, rasped.** To **rasp** means to make a harsh unpleasant sound. EG *Crickets rasped loudly... 'It's frightful,' she rasped.* ▸ used as a noun. EG *...the rasp of sandpaper on wood.* ◇ **rasping.** EG *...a dry rasping voice.* V OR V+QUOTE ▸ N SING ◇ ADJ QUALIT

raspberry /rɑːzbəⁿri¹/, **raspberries. 1** A **raspberry** is a small, soft, red fruit that grows on bushes. EG *...raspberry jam.* N COUNT

2 If you blow a **raspberry**, you make an insulting sound by putting your tongue out and blowing. EG *He blew a loud and lengthy raspberry.* N COUNT

rat /ræt/, **rats. 1** A **rat** is an animal with a long tail which looks like a large mouse. N COUNT

2 If you call someone a **rat**, you mean that you are angry with them or dislike them because they have deceived you or done something unpleasant. EG *Oh, you rat... They're all rats in our business.* N COUNT Informal

rate /reɪt/, **rates, rating, rated. 1** The **rate** at which something happens is **1.1** the speed at which it happens over a period of time. EG *...the rapid rate of change which the industrial world is facing... ...an 8% inflation rate.* **1.2** the number of times that it happens during a period of time. EG *The divorce rate is fantastically high... ...a rising rate of unemployment.* N COUNT+SUPP N COUNT+SUPP

2 The **rate** of taxation or interest is its level, expressed as a percentage. EG *This money is taxed at the rate of 59%... ...a good rate of interest.* N COUNT : USU+SUPP

3 If you say that **at this rate** something will happen, you mean that it will happen if things continue to develop as they have been developing. EG *At this rate we'll be millionaires by Christmas!* PHRASE

4 You use **at any rate 4.1** to indicate that what you have just said might be exaggerated or too general, and that you want to be more precise. EG *They felt, or at any rate Dan felt, both relieved and frightened.* **4.2** to indicate that the important thing is what you are going to say now and not what has just been said. EG *I don't think there's been an edition since 1977; at any rate that's the one I'll be referring to.* ADV SEN

5 Rates are a local tax in Britain which has to be paid by people who own buildings or rent unfurnished buildings. EG *They find it hard to pay their rates... For a while fares in London were subsidised by the rates.* N PLURAL

6 You use **rate** to talk about people's opinion of someone or something. For example, if someone **is rated** as brilliant, people consider them to be brilliant. If you **rate** something as good, you consider it to be good. EG *She was a self-taught geologist, rated as one of the best... Leontiev rated socialism highly... He was rated a successful man... She rated herself below average.* V+O+A, V+A, V+O+C, OR V+C : NO CONT

7 If you **rate** something, you deserve it. EG *Who was this man who rated such a long obituary in the Times?* V+O : NO CONT

8 See also **rating.**

ratepayer /reɪtpeɪə/, **ratepayers.** In Britain, a **ratepayer** is a person who has to pay rates. N COUNT

rather /rɑːðə/. **1** You use **rather** to say that something is the case to a slight extent or to quite a large extent. EG *I'm rather puzzled by this question... He looked rather pathetic standing in the rain outside... The company thought I did rather well... I rather think it was fifty pounds... I'm in rather a hurry. I've got to go.* ADV OR SUBMOD

2 If you say that you **would rather** do a particular thing, you mean that you would prefer to do that thing. If you **would rather** someone did a particular thing, you would prefer them to do that thing. EG *He'd rather be out playing golf... 'What was all that about?' – 'I'm sorry, I'd rather not say.'... Would you rather she came to see me?* PHRASE

3 You use **rather than** to say what someone does not do, in contrast to what they actually do. EG *I have used familiar English names rather than scientific Latin ones... She likes to keep things rather than throw them away.* PREP OR CONJ

4 You also use **rather 4.1** to introduce a correction to something that you have said. EG *Suddenly there stood before him, or rather above him, a gigantic woman.* **4.2** when stating what you think is true, after you have stated what you think is not true. EG *This was no matter for congratulation, but rather a matter for vengeance.* ADV SEN

ratify /rætɪfaɪ/, **ratifies, ratifying, ratified.** When people **ratify** a written agreement or document, they give their formal approval to it, usually by signing it. EG *Over 90 countries ratified an agreement to ban the use of these chemicals.* ◇ **ratification** /rætɪfɪkeɪʃəⁿn/. EG *Opposition objections prevented ratification of the proposals.* V+O Formal ◇ N UNCOUNT

rating /reɪtɪŋ/, **ratings. 1** A **rating** is a score or assessment based on how much of a particular quality something has. EG *...jobs which are assigned a low rating on the economic scale.* N COUNT : USU+SUPP

2 The **ratings** are the statistics published each week which show how popular each television programme is. EG *The ratings are a disaster and the reviews are worse.* N PLURAL

ratio /reɪʃɪəʊ/, **ratios.** A **ratio** is a relationship between two numbers, amounts, or measurements, which shows how much greater one is than the other. For example, if there are two boys and six girls in a room, the ratio of boys to girls is one to three. EG *...a high teacher/pupil ratio... ...a ratio of one tutor to five students.* N COUNT : USU+SUPP

ration /ræʃəⁿn/, **rations, rationing, rationed. 1** When something is scarce, your **ration** of it is the amount that you are allowed to have. EG *...a 20 percent reduction in monthly meat rations.* N COUNT

2 When something **is rationed**, you are only allowed to have a limited amount of it, usually because there is a shortage. EG *Meat, flour and sugar were all rationed.* ◇ **rationing.** EG *...food and petrol rationing during the war.* V+O : USU PASS ◇ N UNCOUNT

3 Rations are the food which is supplied to a soldier or a member of an expedition each day. EG *They had two days' rations and a couple of tents.* N PLURAL

rational /ræʃəⁿnəl, -ʃənəⁿl/. Someone who is **rational** is able to make decisions and judgements that are based on reason rather than on emotion. EG *Let's talk about this like two rational people... Panic destroys rational thought.* ◇ **rationally.** EG *Let's discuss this rationally.* ◇ **rationality** /ræʃənælɪ¹ti¹/. EG *The debate soon lost all semblance of rationality.* ADJ QUALIT ◇ ADV ◇ N UNCOUNT

rationale /ræʃənɑːl/. The **rationale** for a course of action, practice, or belief is the set of reasons on which it is based. EG *We discussed the rationale for taking city kids into the country.* N SING : OFT+*for/of*

rationalism /ræʃəⁿnəlɪzəⁿm/ is the belief that your life should be based on reason and not on emotions or religious beliefs. ◇ **rationalist** N UNCOUNT ◇ N COUNT

Is the rat race a race between rats?

/ræʃə^{0}nəlɪst/, **rationalists**. EG *Lavrov was a thorough rationalist.*

rationalize /ræʃə^{0}nəlaɪz/, **rationalizes, rationalizing, rationalized;** also spelled **rationalise. 1** If you **rationalize** something that you are unhappy or unsure about, you think of reasons to justify it or explain it. EG *I rationalise my decision by saying that I need the money.* ◇ **rationalization** /ræʃə^{0}nəlaɪzeɪʃə^{0}n/, **rationalizations**. EG *They devise elaborate rationalizations for their behaviour.* — V+O; ◇ N COUNT OR N UNCOUNT

2 When a company, system, or industry **is rationalized**, it is made more efficient, especially by getting rid of staff and equipment that are not needed. EG *Society and industry had been rationalized and modernized.* ◇ **rationalization**. EG *...the continuing rationalization of the armed forces.* — V+O; ◇ N UNCOUNT

rat race. If you refer to a type of work or way of life as a **rat race**, you mean that the people in it are all competing fiercely with each other. EG *I was determined to get out of the rat race.* — N SING: USU *the*+N

rattle /rætə^{0}l/, **rattles, rattling, rattled. 1** When something **rattles** or when you **rattle** it, it makes a series of short, regular knocking sounds because it is being shaken or it is hitting against something hard. EG *A cold November wind rattled the windows... The chains of playground swings rattled in the dark.* ▸ used as a noun. EG *The rattle of the engine became louder.* — V-ERG; ▸ N COUNT

2 A **rattle** is a baby's toy with loose bits inside which make a noise when the baby shakes it. — N COUNT

3 If something **rattles** you, it makes you worried or annoyed. EG *It was an attempt to get him rattled... His questions obviously rattled her.* — V+O

rattle off. If you **rattle** something **off**, you say it or do it very quickly and without much effort. EG *She rattled off a few names that I tried to write down... ...a machine capable of rattling off thousands of calculations in a few minutes.* — PHRASAL VB: V+O+ADV

rattle on. When someone **rattles on** about something, they talk about it for a long time in a way that annoys you. EG *Some of the women would rattle on about sex.* — PHRASAL VB: V+ADV, OFT+*about*

rattle through. If you **rattle through** something, you deal with it quickly in order to finish it. EG *They rattled through the rest of the meeting.* — PHRASAL VB: V+PREP, HAS PASS

rattlesnake /rætə^{0}lsneɪk/, **rattlesnakes.** A **rattlesnake** is a poisonous American snake. — N COUNT

ratty /ræti^{1}/, **rattier, rattiest.** If someone is **ratty**, they are very irritable. EG *All right, don't get ratty... The pain makes you ratty.* — ADJ QUALIT; British Informal

raucous /rɔːkəs/. You describe someone's voice as **raucous** when it is loud and rough. EG *...the sound of her raucous voice... ...raucous laughter.* — ADJ QUALIT

ravage /rævɪdʒ/, **ravages, ravaging, ravaged. 1** To **ravage** something means to harm it or damage it so much that it is almost destroyed. EG *...the diseases which ravage Aboriginal populations... ...a country ravaged by war.* — V+O

2 The **ravages** of the weather, time, or war are the damaging effects that it has. EG *...the ravages of rain and sun.* — N PLURAL: USU+*of*

rave /reɪv/, **raves, raving, raved. 1** If someone **raves**, they talk in an excited and uncontrolled way because they are very angry. EG *He sat and raved at me for half an hour... He started raving about the horror and brutality of war.* — V: OFT+A

2 If you **rave** about something, you speak or write about it with great enthusiasm. EG *One newspaper raved: 'the most exciting play I have ever seen.'... People were raving about his fantastic course.* — V+*about* OR V+QUOTE; Informal

3 When someone writes a **rave** notice or review, they praise something such as a play or book in a very enthusiastic way. EG *Stoppard's new play has received rave reviews.* — N COUNT; Informal

4 When people **rave it up**, they enjoy themselves in a lively way, for example by drinking and dancing a lot at a party. EG *...a huge crowd raving it up in Trafalgar Square.* ● See also **rave-up**. — PHRASE; Informal

5 See also **raving**.

raven /reɪvə^{0}n/, **ravens. 1** A **raven** is a large bird with shiny black feathers and a deep harsh call. — N COUNT

2 Raven hair is a shiny black colour. EG *...a raven-haired girl.* — ADJ COLOUR: ATTRIB

ravenous /rævənəs/. If you are **ravenous**, you are very hungry indeed. EG *By that time I was ravenous... Most infants have a ravenous appetite.* ◇ **ravenously**. EG *I was ravenously hungry.* — ADJ QUALIT; ◇ ADV

rave-up, rave-ups. A **rave-up** is a very lively party. EG *We are looking for more friends to have a rave-up with tonight.* — N COUNT; British Informal

ravine /rəviːn/, **ravines.** A **ravine** is a very deep narrow valley with steep sides. — N COUNT

raving /reɪvɪŋ/, **ravings. 1** If you say that someone is **raving**, you mean that they are mad. EG *You're all raving lunatics... He went raving mad.* — ADJ CLASSIF: ATTRIB, OR ADV+ADJ; Informal

2 If you refer to the things that someone says or writes as their **ravings**, you mean that they are talking or writing like a mad person. EG *...the ravings of an obsessed anarchist.* — N PLURAL

ravish /rævɪʃ/, **ravishes, ravishing, ravished.** If you **are ravished** by something, it gives you great pleasure and delight, because it is very beautiful. EG *He was ravished by the beauty of the language.* — V+O: OFT PASS; Literary

ravishing /rævɪʃɪŋ/. Someone or something that is **ravishing** is very beautiful. EG *I'd forgotten how ravishing you looked... ...a ravishing blonde.* — ADJ QUALIT

raw /rɔː/. **1** Food that is **raw** is not cooked. EG *...a piece of raw meat... ...a raw carrot.* — ADJ CLASSIF

2 A **raw** substance is in its natural state before being used in a manufacturing process. EG *...exports of raw cotton... ...raw rubber from Malaysia.* — ADJ CLASSIF: ATTRIB

3 If a part of your body is **raw**, the skin has come off or been burnt, so it is sore. EG *Every boy's feet had big raw blisters on them.* — ADJ QUALIT

4 If you describe someone as **raw**, you mean that they are too young or too new in a job to know how to behave properly. EG *He's just a raw kid... ...raw newcomers.* — ADJ QUALIT

5 Raw weather is unpleasantly cold and wet. EG *...a raw day in Sunderland.* — ADJ QUALIT

6 If you say that you have been given **a raw deal**, you mean that you have been treated unfairly. EG *He thinks he's got a raw deal from life.* — PHRASE; Informal

raw material, raw materials. 1 Raw materials are the natural substances that are used in making something, for example in an industrial process. EG *...coal, oil, gas, and other raw materials.* — N COUNT OR N UNCOUNT

2 If you describe something as **raw material** for a particular thing, you mean that you can make this thing from it. EG *She makes use of people she meets as raw material for her fiction.* — N UNCOUNT: USU+SUPP

ray /reɪ/, **rays. 1** A **ray** is a beam of heat or light. EG *...the rays of the sun... ...ultraviolet rays.* — N COUNT: USU PLURAL+SUPP

2 A **ray** of hope or comfort is a small amount of it that makes a bad situation seem less bad. EG *She let a ray of originality into his life.* — N PART

rayon /reɪɒn/ is a smooth fabric made from cotton, wool, or synthetic fibres. — N UNCOUNT

raze /reɪz/, **razes, razing, razed.** If people **raze** a building, town, or forest, they completely destroy it. EG *Many villages were razed to the ground.* — V+O

razor /reɪzə/, **razors.** A **razor** is a tool that people use for shaving. EG *...an electric razor.* — N COUNT

razor blade, razor blades. A **razor blade** is a small, thin, flat piece of metal with a very sharp edge, that you fasten to a razor and use for shaving. — N COUNT

Rd is a written abbreviation for 'road'. EG *...49 St Johns Rd.*

-rd. You add **-rd** to most numbers written in figures and ending in 3 in order to form ordinal numbers. 3rd is pronounced the same as 'third'. EG *...3rd November 1972... ...23rd Street... ...the 143rd Psalm.* — SUFFIX

re- is used to form verbs and nouns that refer to the repeating of an action or process. For example, to re-read something means to read it again, and to re-marry means to marry again. EG *He re-lit his* — PREFIX *pipe... ...the re-introduction of an incomes policy by the government.*

-'re is a shortened form of 'are'. In spoken English it is added to the end of the pronoun or noun which is the subject of the verb. For example, 'we are' can be shortened to 'we're'. EG *You're quite right... They're lovely... What're you waiting for?*

reach /riːtʃ/, **reaches, reaching, reached. 1** When you **reach** a place, you arrive there. EG *It was dark by the time I reached their house... It took three days for the letter to reach me.* V+O

2 If you **reach** in a particular direction, you stretch out your arm in order to do something or to get something. EG *He reached into his inside pocket and produced a pen... She reached across the desk and shook my hand... I reached out my hand to touch him.* V+A OR V+O+A

3 If you say that you can **reach** something, you mean that you can touch it by stretching out your arm and hand. EG *I can't reach that shelf unless I stand on a chair.* V+O

4 You can say that you **reach** someone when you succeed in contacting them by telephone. EG *I tried to reach you at home several times... Where can I reach you?* V+O

5 If something **reaches** a place, point or level, it extends as far as that place, point, or level. EG *When the water reached his waist, he had to start swimming... She wore a long blue skirt reaching down to the ground... Rumours of an enemy invasion began to reach the capital.* V+O OR V+A

6 If someone or something **reaches** a particular stage, condition, or level, they get to it. EG *Unemployment has reached a very high level... Kangaroos can reach speeds of 60 kph... Most children stay at home until they reach school age.* V+O

7 When people **reach** an agreement, decision, or result, they succeed in achieving it. EG *They managed to reach an agreement on rates of pay.* V+O

8 If something is within **reach**, you can touch it by stretching out your arm and hand. If it is **beyond** your **reach** or **out of reach**, you cannot touch it. EG *Keep all medicines out of reach of children.* N UNCOUNT +SUPP

9 If a place is within **reach**, you can get there. EG *The flat is within easy reach of the shops.* N UNCOUNT +SUPP

10 If you refer to the upper or lower **reaches** of a place, you are referring to the upper or lower parts of it. EG *...the upper reaches of the Amazon... ...the most inaccessible reaches of the jungle.* N PLURAL +SUPP

react /riˈækt/, **reacts, reacting, reacted. 1** When you **react** to something that has happened to you, you behave in a particular way because of it. EG *She tends to react strongly if he lights a cigarette... I wondered how he'd react to such a blunt question.* V: OFT+*to*

2 If you **react** against the way other people behave, you deliberately behave in a different way. EG *They reacted against the formality of their predecessors.* V+*against*

3 When someone **reacts** to a drug, they are made ill by it. V: OFT+*to*

4 When one chemical substance **reacts** with another, it combines with it chemically to form another substance. V OR V+*with*: RECIP

reaction /riˈækʃən/, **reactions. 1** Your **reaction** to something is what you feel, say, or do because of it. EG *My immediate reaction was one of revulsion... What was the reaction to these proposals?* N COUNT OR N UNCOUNT +SUPP

2 A **reaction** against something is a way of behaving or doing something that is deliberately different from what has been done before. EG *My work has never been a reaction against Abstract Expressionism.* N COUNT+ *against*

3 A **reaction** against something that is popular or accepted is a change of public opinion in which it becomes unpopular. EG *This led to a reaction against public expenditure.* N COUNT+ *against*

4 You refer to your ability to move quickly in response to something, for example when you are in danger, as your **reactions**. EG *...a computer game designed to time their reactions.* N PLURAL

5 Reaction is the belief that the political or social system of your country should not change; used showing disapproval. EG *Once again the forces of reaction prevailed.* N UNCOUNT Formal

6 A chemical **reaction** is a process in which two substances combine together chemically to form another substance. N COUNT

reactionary /riˈækʃənəri/, **reactionaries.** Someone who is **reactionary** tries to prevent changes in the political or social system of their country; used showing disapproval. EG *...reactionary forces.* ▸ used as a noun. EG *...political reactionaries.* ADJ QUALIT ▸ N COUNT

reactor /riˈæktə/, **reactors.** A **reactor** is the same as a nuclear reactor. EG *They are making the reactors as safe as they possibly can.* N COUNT

read, reads, reading. Read is used in the present tense, when it is pronounced /riːd/, and is also the past tense and past participle, when it is pronounced /rɛd/.

1 When you **read** or when you **read** something written, **1.1** you look at written words or symbols on a page and understand them. EG *Have you read that article?... I remember reading about it in the paper... I have never been able to read music.* V+O OR V: USU+A **1.2** you say aloud the words that are written. EG *Shall I read to you?* V+O OR V+*to*

2 If you **read between the lines**, you understand what someone really means, even though they do not say it openly. EG *Reading between the lines it is easy to see that she was desperately unhappy.* PHRASE

3 If you say that a book or magazine is **a good read**, you mean that it is very enjoyable to read. PHRASE

4 If you refer to how a piece of writing **reads**, you are referring to its style. EG *It read like a translation from the Latin.* V+A

5 You can use **read** when saying what is written on something or in something. For example, if a notice **reads** 'Exit', the word 'Exit' is written on it. V+C

6 If you can **read** someone's moods or mind, you can judge how they are feeling or what they are thinking. EG *He so often reads my thoughts.* V+O

7 When you **read** a meter or gauge, you look at it and record the figure on it. V+O

8 If a measuring device **reads** a particular amount, it shows that amount. EG *The thermometers are reading 108 degrees in the shade.* V+C

9 If you **read** a subject at university, you study it. EG *He went up to Oxford to read history.* V+O

10 See also **reading**.

read into. If you **read** a meaning **into** something, you think it is there although it may not actually be there. EG *Some people read sex into the most innocent story.* PHRASAL VB: V+O+PREP

read out. If you **read** a piece of writing **out**, you say it aloud. EG *Could you just read out this next paragraph?* PHRASAL VB: V+O+ADV

read up on. If you **read up on** a subject, you read a lot about it so that you become informed on it. EG *You can read up on the theory later.* PHRASAL VB: V+ADV+PREP

readable /riːdəbəl/. If you say that a book or article is **readable**, you mean that it is interesting and worth reading. EG *It's a very readable book.* ADJ QUALIT

reader /riːdə/, **readers.** A **reader** of a book, newspaper, or magazine is a person who reads it. EG *All of them were keen readers of detective stories... The paper is gathering one thousand new readers a week.* N COUNT: OFT+SUPP

readership /riːdəʃɪp/. The **readership** of a book, newspaper, or magazine is all the people who read it. EG *...a readership of about ten million people.* N SING+SUPP

readily /rɛdɪli/. **1** If you do something **readily**, you do it in a way which shows that you are very ADV

What two ways can 'read' be pronounced?

willing to do it. EG *He readily accepted an invitation to dinner.*

2 You also use **readily** to say that something can be done or obtained quickly and easily. For example, if you say that something can be readily understood, you mean that people can understand it quickly and easily. EG *Personal computers are readily available these days.*
ADV

readiness /rɛdɪnɪ^{2}s/. **1 Readiness** is the state of being prepared for something. EG *He faces it with calm readiness and resolute determination.*
N UNCOUNT

2 Your **readiness** to do something is your willingness or eagerness to do it. EG *I restated our readiness to resume negotiations.*
N UNCOUNT +to-INF

reading /riːdɪŋ/, **readings. 1 Reading** is the activity of reading books. EG *I don't do a lot of reading.*
N UNCOUNT

2 A **reading** is a text that is read aloud to an audience, for example in church. EG *We all said 'Amen!' when the readings were done.*
N COUNT

3 A poetry **reading** is an entertainment in which poetry is read to an audience.
N COUNT+SUPP

4 The **reading** on a meter or gauge is the figure or measurement that it shows.
N COUNT

readjust /riːədʒʌst/, **readjusts, readjusting, readjusted. 1** If you **readjust** or **readjust** yourself, you adapt to a new situation. EG *It is difficult to readjust to changing environments.*
V OR V-REFL : OFT+to

◊ **readjustment** /riːədʒʌstmə^{2}nt/, **readjustments.** EG *...a period of readjustment.*
◊ N UNCOUNT OR N COUNT

2 If you **readjust** something, you alter it so that it is in a better position. EG *He readjusted the saddle before getting on... ...peering through a microscope, continually readjusting the focus.*
V+O

ready /rɛdi^1/, **readies, readying, readied. 1** If someone or something is **ready**, they have prepared themselves or have been prepared for something, or they now have the right qualities for something. EG *We were getting ready for bed... By eight she was ready to leave... You're nowhere near ready for such a job... Lunch is ready... Their crops would soon be ready for harvesting.*
ADJ PRED : OFT+for OR to-INF

2 If you are **ready** to do something, you are willing to do it. EG *...couples who are ready to move house in order to get work.*
ADJ PRED +to-INF

3 If you are **ready** for something, you need it or want it. EG *We were all ready for sleep.*
ADJ PRED+for

4 If something is **ready** to do something, it is about to do it or likely to do it. EG *...an over-ripe plum, ready to fall... I was ready to cry.*
ADJ PRED +to-INF

5 You use **ready** to describe things that are able to appear or be used very quickly and easily. EG *He had a ready, engaging smile... ...ready cash.*
ADJ CLASSIF : ATTRIB

6 When you **ready** something, you prepare it for a particular purpose. EG *The satellite would be readied with all possible haste... Standard Oil are readying themselves for a monumental struggle.*
V+O OR V-REFL Formal

7 See also **readily, readiness.**

ready-made. 1 If something that you buy is **ready-made**, you can use it immediately. EG *...ready-made products such as baked beans... You can buy your greenhouse ready-made.*
ADJ CLASSIF : ATTRIB OR ADV

2 If you have a **ready-made** reply to a question, you can answer it immediately. EG *He had no ready-made answers.*
ADJ CLASSIF

reaffirm /riːəfɜːm/, **reaffirms, reaffirming, reaffirmed.** If you **reaffirm** something, you state it again. EG *The ministers reaffirmed their intention not to surrender.*
V+O OR V+REPORT Formal

real /rɪəl/. **1** Something that is **real 1.1** actually exists and is not imagined, invented, or theoretical. EG *You must know the difference between what's real and make-believe... ...real or imagined feelings of inferiority.* **1.2** is natural or traditional, and not artificial or an imitation. EG *...real leather... ...fancy chocolates, with real liqueurs inside.*
ADJ CLASSIF

2 You also use **real** to say that something **2.1** has all the characteristics or qualities that such a thing typically has. EG *...the only real accident that I've ever had... I used to tell him he wasn't a real Christian.* **2.2** is the true or original thing of its kind, in contrast to one that people may wrongly believe to be true. EG *That is the real reason for the muddle... My real home is in Tshabo.*
ADJ CLASSIF : ATTRIB

3 If you say that a thing or event is **the real thing**, you mean that it is the actual thing or event, and not an imitation or rehearsal. EG *'You're being recorded now.' – 'Is this the real thing?'*
PHRASE

4 You can use **real** to emphasize that something exists, especially something unpleasant. EG *The threat of attack was a very real one... Everyone knew that Ray had no real chance of winning.*
ADJ QUALIT

5 If you say that something is **for real**, you mean that it is actually happening or being done. EG *It was done. I was on my own. For real.*
PHRASE Informal

6 You use **in real terms** when you are talking about the actual value or cost of something. For example, if your salary rises by 5% but prices rise by 10% in the same period, you can say that **in real terms** your salary has fallen. EG *Government spending this year is 12% up in real terms.*
PHRASE

7 Real is sometimes used instead of 'very'. EG *I was getting some real good stories... You and I must have lunch together real soon.*
SUBMOD American

8 See also **really.**

real estate is property in the form of buildings and land. EG *He acquired a bit of real estate... ...real estate agents.*
N UNCOUNT American

realise /rɪəlaɪz/. See **realize.**

realism /rɪəlɪzə^{0}m/. **1** When people show **realism** in their behaviour, they recognize and accept the true nature of a situation and try to deal with it in a practical way. EG *He marvelled at his father's lack of realism... There is a new mood of realism in Britain... ...economic realism.*
N UNCOUNT

2 In painting, novels, and films, **realism** is the representing of things and people in a way that is like real life. EG *...the awesome realism of Aztec sculptures... Extraordinary degrees of realism are reached in the film.*
N UNCOUNT

realist /rɪəlɪst/, **realists.** A **realist** is someone who recognizes and accepts the true nature of a situation and tries to deal with it in a practical way. EG *I am a realist and know that all this cannot last.*
N COUNT

realistic /rɪəlɪstɪk/. **1** If you are **realistic** about a situation, you recognize and accept its true nature and try to deal with it in a practical way. EG *They were more realistic about its long term commercial prospects... ...a realistic attempt to solve problems.* ◊ **realistically.** EG *She accepted the position realistically... ...looking at it realistically.*
ADJ QUALIT
◊ ADV

2 You say that a painting, story, or film is **realistic** when the people and things in it are like people and things in real life. EG *...a 19th century realistic novel... ...would make any new film surprisingly realistic.*
ADJ QUALIT

reality /riˈælɪ^{1}ti^1/, **realities. 1 Reality** is the real nature of everything, rather than the way someone imagines it to be. EG *He is out of touch with reality... She had never seemed able to face reality... He cannot change reality.*
N UNCOUNT

2 The **reality** of a situation is the truth about it, especially when it is unpleasant or unwelcome. EG *...the harsh reality of daily life... ...the realities of politics and diplomacy.*
N COUNT+SUPP

3 You say that something has become a **reality** when it actually exists or is actually happening. EG *The Popular Front was already a reality... Daydreams had become realities.*
N COUNT OR N UNCOUNT

4 You can use **in reality 4.1** to introduce a statement about the real nature of something, when it contrasts with something incorrect that has just been described. EG *They imagined that they made the rules but, in reality, they were mere puppets.* **4.2** to say that something exists or happens in real life rather than in stories or films. EG *The sound was far more menacing in reality than in the movies.*
ADV SEN

realize /rɪəlaɪz/, **realizes, realizing, realized;** also spelled **realise. 1** If you **realize** something, you become aware of it. EG *She realized the significance of what he was trying to do... I realized that this man wasn't going to hurt me... He is much more remarkable than many people realized.* — V+O OR V+REPORT
◇ **realization** /rɪəlaɪzeɪʃᵊn/. EG *This realization was shattering for all of us.* — ◇ N UNCOUNT
2 When someone **realizes** a design or an idea, they put it into a physical form, for example by painting a picture or building a machine. EG *No design is too sophisticated for him to realize.* — V+O Formal
3 If your hopes, desires, or fears **are realized**, the things that you hope for, desire, or fear actually happen. EG *Our national aspirations could be realised... My worst fears were realized.* — V+O : USU PASS Formal
◇ **realization**. EG *...the realization of a lifelong dream.* — ◇ N UNCOUNT

really /rɪəli¹/. **1** You can use **really** to emphasize what you are saying. EG *It is really very difficult... I really ought to go... I really think I've had enough.* — ADV Spoken
2 You can also use **really** to give emphasis to an adjective or adverb. EG *It was really good... These fires produce really obnoxious fumes... We're doing really well.* — SUBMOD Spoken
3 You use **really** when you are talking about the real facts about something, as opposed to something incorrect which has just been said. EG *I want to know what really happened... What I'm really saying is, I'm delighted... He's not really going for a bath; he's going to sit in the garden.* — ADV
4 People use **really** in questions when they want you to answer 'no'. EG *Do you really think they bother to listen to us?... Is there really anything new to say about him?* — ADV Spoken
5 People sometimes add **really** to negative statements to avoid seeming impolite. EG *I'm not really in favour of that... 'Any more problems?' – 'Not really, no.'* — ADV : WITH BROAD NEG
6 You can say **'Really?' 6.1** to indicate that you are listening with interest to what someone is telling you. EG *'It was quite close to the airport.' – 'Really?'* **6.2** to express surprise or disbelief at what someone has said, or to check that you have understood them properly. EG *'Nobody was allowed inside unless he'd been injected by Doc Murray.' – 'Really?'... 'Inflation's dropped faster than it did under Labour.' – 'Has it really?'* — CONVENTION
7 Some people say **'Really!'** or **'Well, really!'** when they are very annoyed. — EXCLAM

realm /relm/, **realms. 1** You can refer to any area of activity or thought as a **realm**. EG *Changes would not be confined to the technical realm... Clearly, we are in the realm of imagination rather than historical fact.* — N COUNT+SUPP Formal
2 A **realm** is also a country that has a king or queen. EG *...the established church of the realm.* — N COUNT Formal

reap /ri:p/, **reaps, reaping, reaped. 1** When people **reap** a crop such as corn, they cut it down and gather it. — V+O
2 When people **reap** benefits or rewards, they obtain them as a result of hard work or careful planning. EG *One day we will reap the full benefits of North Sea oil.* — V+O

reappear /ri:əpɪə/, **reappears, reappearing, reappeared.** When people or things **reappear**, you can see them again, because they have returned from another place or because they are being used again. EG *The waiter reappeared with a loaded tray... From time to time 'Gypsy' clothes reappear as a fashion.* — V : USU+A
◇ **reappearance** /ri:əpɪərəns/, **reappearances.** EG *He wanted to know the reason for my sudden reappearance.* — ◇ N UNCOUNT OR N COUNT

reappraisal /ri:əpreɪzᵊl/, **reappraisals.** If there is a **reappraisal** of something such as a policy, people think about it carefully and decide whether they want to change it. EG *...a reappraisal of U.S. policy toward South Asia.* — N COUNT OR N UNCOUNT Formal

rear /rɪə/, **rears, rearing, reared. 1** The **rear** of something such as a building or vehicle is the part that is at the back of it. EG *He walked toward the rear of the house.* — N SING : *the*+N, USU+*of*
▸ used as an adjective. EG *I got out and examined the right rear wheel.* — ▸ ADJ CLASSIF : ATTRIB
2 If you are at the **rear** of a queue or of a moving line of people, you are the last person in it. EG *The motorcycles dropped back to a position at the rear of the convoy.* — N SING : *the*+N, USU+*of*
● If you **bring up the rear**, you are the last person in a moving line of people. — ● PHRASE
3 Your **rear** is the part of your body that you sit on. EG *She slapped him on the rear.* — N COUNT Informal
4 If you **rear** children, you bring them up until they are old enough to look after themselves. If you say that someone **was reared** in a particular way or in a particular place, you are describing how or where they were brought up. EG *Geraldo has adopted and reared four children... ...girls reared in country houses... ...a child reared without love.* — V+O
5 When a horse **rears** or **rears up**, it moves the front part of its body upwards, so that its front legs are high in the air and it is standing on its back legs. EG *...rearing up on his hind legs.* — V : OFT+*up*
6 When something unpleasant happens, you can say that it **rears** its **ugly head**. EG *Dissension might so easily have reared its ugly head.* — PHRASE

rearrange /ri:əreɪndʒ/, **rearranges, rearranging, rearranged.** If you **rearrange** something, you organize or arrange it in a different way. EG *She rearranged the furniture.* — V+O

rearrangement /ri:əreɪndʒmə²nt/, **rearrangements.** A **rearrangement** is a change in the way that something is arranged or organized. EG *...the rearrangement of the examination system.* — N COUNT OR N UNCOUNT

reason /ri:zᵊn/, **reasons, reasoning, reasoned.**
1 The **reason** for something is the fact or situation which explains why it happens or exists. EG *I asked the reason for the decision... There is a good reason why these committees are secret... Public pressure is towards more street lighting: the reason is that people feel safer in well-lit streets.* — N COUNT : USU+SUPP
2 If you say that you have **reason** to believe something or **reason** to feel something, you mean that there are definite reasons why you believe it or feel it. EG *I have reason to believe that you are concealing something... You had good reason to be distressed... I'm getting annoyed, and with reason.* — N UNCOUNT : USU+*to*-INF
3 Reason is also the ability that people have to think and make judgements. EG *He had to rely less on reason than on the rousing of emotion.* — N UNCOUNT
4 Reason is used in these phrases. **4.1** If something happens **by reason of** something else, it happens because of it. EG *I enjoyed a measure of protection by reason of my age.* — PREP Formal
4.2 If you say that **for some reason** a particular thing happened, you mean that it happened and you do not know why. EG *For some reason we talked about death.* — PHRASE
4.3 If you get someone to **listen to reason**, you persuade them to listen to sensible arguments and be influenced by them. EG *The man refused to listen to reason.* — PHRASE
5 If you **reason** that something is the case, you decide that it is the case after thinking carefully about all the facts. EG *Copernicus reasoned that the earth revolved around the sun... 'Very few Americans,' I reasoned, 'would know that.'* ● See also **reasoned, reasoning**. — V+REPORT : ONLY *that*, OR V+QUOTE
reason with. If you **reason with** someone, you argue with them in order to try to persuade them to do something or to accept something. EG *We all know how difficult it is to reason with a prejudiced person.* — PHRASAL VB : V+PREP, HAS PASS

reasonable /ri:zᵊnəbᵊl/. **1** If you say that someone is being **reasonable**, you mean that they are behaving in a fair and sensible way. EG *Our mother was always very reasonable... I can't do that,* — ADJ QUALIT

Would you rebuff someone who made a reasonable suggestion?

Morris. Be reasonable. ◇ **reasonableness**. EG *The landlords responded with great reasonableness.* ◇ N UNCOUNT

2 You describe a decision or explanation as **reasonable** when there are good reasons for thinking that it is correct. EG *There was no reasonable explanation for her decision... It was quite reasonable to suppose that he wanted the money too.* ADJ QUALIT

3 A **reasonable** amount of something is a fairly large amount. EG *...a reasonable amount of luck... A reasonable number of students are involved.* ADJ QUALIT

4 If the price of something is **reasonable**, it is fair and not too high. EG *...a good range of wines at reasonable prices... The tickets cost a very reasonable £30.* ADJ QUALIT

reasonably /ri:zənəbli/. **1** If you say that something is **reasonably** large or **reasonably** good, you mean that it is fairly large or fairly good. EG *I'm reasonably broad across the shoulders... ...a reasonably well-known writer.* SUBMOD

2 If you say that someone is behaving **reasonably**, you mean that they are behaving in a fair and sensible way. ADV

reasoned /ri:zənd/. A **reasoned** argument or explanation is based on sensible reasons, rather than on an appeal to people's emotions. EG *We must counter their propaganda with reasoned argument... They had been offered a reasoned explanation of the phenomena.* ADJ CLASSIF : ATTRIB

reasoning /ri:zənɪŋ/is the process by which you reach a conclusion after thinking about all the facts. EG *I'm puzzled by his reasoning... What is the reasoning behind that decision?* N UNCOUNT

reassemble /ri:əsɛmbəl/, **reassembles, reassembling, reassembled.** If you **reassemble** something, you put it back together after it has been taken apart. EG *He reassembled an entire engine.* V+O

reassert /ri:əsɜ:t/, **reasserts, reasserting, reasserted. 1** If you **reassert** something such as power or authority, you make it clear that you have it again. EG *He made efforts to reassert his authority over them.* V+O

2 If something such as an idea or habit **reasserts** itself, it becomes noticeable again. EG *The urge to survive reasserted itself.* V-REFL

reassess /ri:əsɛs/, **reassesses, reassessing, reassessed.** If you **reassess** something, you think about it and decide whether it still has the same value or importance. EG *He was reassessing his political position.* V+O

reassessment /ri:əsɛsmənt/, **reassessments.** If you make a **reassessment** of something, you think about it and decide whether it still has the same value or importance. EG *...a reassessment of the effect of family and schooling.* N COUNT OR N UNCOUNT

reassurance /ri:əʃʊərəns/, **reassurances. 1** If you give someone **reassurance**, you say things to them that help them to stop worrying. EG *She wants reassurance, that is all... Men came to her for comfort and reassurance.* N UNCOUNT

2 Reassurances are things that you say to help people stop worrying. EG *Reassurances were given that investigations would proceed.* N COUNT

reassure /ri:əʃʊə/, **reassures, reassuring, reassured.** If you **reassure** someone, you say or do things that help them to stop worrying. EG *I was trying to reassure her that things weren't as bad as she thought.* ◇ **reassuring**. EG *The woman smiled at him in a reassuring manner.* ◇ **reassuringly**. EG *She looked at me reassuringly.* V+O : OFT+REPORT : ONLY *that*; ◇ ADJ QUALIT; ◇ ADV

rebate /ri:beɪt/, **rebates.** A **rebate** is an amount of money which is paid back to you because you have paid more tax, rent, or rates than you needed to. EG *You should get a tax rebate.* N COUNT

rebel, rebels, rebelling, rebelled; pronounced /rɛbəl/ when it is a noun, and /rɪbɛl/ when it is a verb. **1 Rebels** are people who are fighting against their own country's army in order to change the political system there. EG *The rebels made regular attacks on the railways... Rebel groups controlled the centre of the city.* N COUNT

2 You also describe someone as a **rebel** when they behave differently from other people because they have rejected their society's values. N COUNT

3 When people **rebel**, **3.1** they fight against their own country's army in order to change the political system there. EG *The Duke of Monmouth rebelled against James II in 1685.* **3.2** they behave differently from other people because they have rejected their society's or parents' values. EG *...adolescents who rebel and demand freedom and independence.* V : OFT+ *against*

rebellion /rɪbɛljən/, **rebellions. 1** A **rebellion** is a violent, organized action by a large group of people who are trying to change their country's political system. N COUNT OR N UNCOUNT

2 Opposition to the leaders of an organization can also be referred to as a **rebellion**. EG *He faces a growing rebellion from the left wing of his party.* N UNCOUNT OR N COUNT

rebellious /rɪbɛljəs/. Someone who is **rebellious** does not do what someone in authority wants them to do. EG *...an obstinate, rebellious child with a violent temper.* ◇ **rebelliously**. EG *'Nonsense,' said my assistant rebelliously.* ADJ QUALIT; ◇ ADV

rebuff /rɪbʌf/, **rebuffs, rebuffing, rebuffed.** If you **rebuff** someone, you refuse to cooperate with them or to agree to what they are suggesting. EG *He tried to question the girl and got rebuffed.* ▸ used as a noun. EG *She didn't understand that her rebuff had hurt him.* V+O : USU PASS; ▸ N COUNT

rebuild /ri:bɪld/, **rebuilds, rebuilding, rebuilt** /ri:bɪlt/. **1** When a town or building **is rebuilt**, it is built again after it has been damaged or destroyed. EG *They will be allowed to rebuild the bridges.* V+O

2 When an organization **is rebuilt**, it is developed again after it has stopped or become ineffective. EG *...help him to rebuild his nation's shattered economy.* V+O

rebuke /rɪbju:k/, **rebukes, rebuking, rebuked.** If you **rebuke** someone, you speak severely to them because they have said or done something that you do not approve of. EG *She often rebuked David for his authoritarian attitude.* ▸ used as a noun. EG *He received a stern rebuke from his superiors.* V+O : OFT+*for*; ▸ N COUNT OR N UNCOUNT

recall /rɪkɔ:l/, **recalls, recalling, recalled. 1** When you **recall** something, you remember it. EG *I started to recall the years after the War... Deirdre recalled seeing a poster on his wall... 'I ran outside to look for my children,' recalled Miriam... I recalled that my blankets had been taken away.* ▸ used as a noun. EG *Why are some memories more available for recall than others?* V+O; ALSO V+-ING, QUOTE, OR REPORT; ▸ N UNCOUNT

2 If you **are recalled** to a place, you are ordered to return there. EG *Eighteen months ago they recalled him to Mozambique... Parliament was hastily recalled from recess.* V+O : USU+A

recapture /ri:kæptʃə/, **recaptures, recapturing, recaptured. 1** When you **recapture** a pleasant feeling, you feel it again. EG *She failed to recapture her earlier mood.* V+O

2 When soldiers **recapture** a place, they capture it from the people who had taken it from them. EG *The Turks had returned and recaptured their trench.* ▸ used as a noun. EG *...the recapture of the lost territories.* V+O; ▸ N SING

3 When animals or prisoners **are recaptured**, they are caught after they have escaped. V+O

recede /rɪsi:d/, **recedes, receding, receded. 1** If something **recedes**, it moves away into the distance. EG *Now and then cars passed me, their tail-lights receding.* V

2 You also say that something **recedes** when it becomes less clear or less bright. EG *Already the memory was receding.* V

3 If you say that a man's hair **is receding**, you mean that he is starting to go bald by losing hair at the front of his head. V

receipt /rɪˈsiːt/, **receipts.** 1 A **receipt** is a piece of paper that you give or send to someone to confirm that you have received money or goods from them. EG *Give students a written receipt for each payment.* N COUNT

2 Money received in a shop or a theatre is often referred to as the **receipts**. EG *The receipts from admission fees fell sharply.* N PLURAL

3 The **receipt** of something is the act of receiving it. EG *You have to sign here and acknowledge receipt... We are awaiting the receipt of further information.* N UNCOUNT Formal

receive /rɪˈsiːv/, **receives, receiving, received.** V+O
1 When you **receive** something, **1.1** someone gives it to you. EG *Did they receive money for their work?* **1.2** you get it after it has been sent to you. EG *Northcliffe received a letter from his brother.*

2 You can use **receive** to say that certain kinds of thing happen to you. For example if you are injured, you can say that you **received** an injury. EG *...the criticism he received in England... She received a tremendous ovation.* V+O • If you **are on the receiving end** of something unpleasant, you are the person that it happens to. EG *You may find yourself on the receiving end of my father's temper.* • PHRASE

3 When you **receive** a visitor or a guest, you welcome them. EG *Tell her I shall be delighted to receive her... Fass received Lieber in his office.* V+O

4 If you say that something **is received** in a particular way, you mean that people react to it in that way. EG *Her latest novel has been very well received... This news was received with contempt.* V+O+A: USU PASS

received /rɪˈsiːvd/. The **received** opinion about something or the **received** way of doing something is the one that is generally accepted as correct. EG *...received ideas... ...received religion.* ADJ CLASSIF: ATTRIB Formal

receiver /rɪˈsiːvə/, **receivers.** A **receiver** is 1 the part of a telephone that you hold near to your ear and speak into. EG *He replaced the receiver.* 2 a radio or television set. 3 a person who receives something. EG *...receivers of stolen goods.* N COUNT

recent /riːsənt/. A **recent** event or period of time happened only a short while ago. EG *They talked about their recent trip to Africa... Few sights have become more familiar in recent times.* ADJ QUALIT: USU ATTRIB

recently /riːsəntli[1]/. If something happened **recently**, it happened only a short time ago. EG *Recently, I lectured to seven hundred Swedes... The problem has been ignored until very recently... This flower was discovered as recently as 1903.* ADV

receptacle /rɪˈsɛptəkə[0]l/, **receptacles.** A **receptacle** is an object which you use to put or keep things in. EG *Please put your cigarette ends into the receptacle provided... ...receptacles for ink.* N COUNT Formal

reception /rɪˈsɛpʃə[0]n/, **receptions.** 1 In a hotel, office, or hospital, **reception** is the place where reservations, appointments, and enquiries are dealt with. EG *...the young man at the reception desk.* N UNCOUNT

2 A **reception** is a formal party which is given to welcome someone or to celebrate a special event. EG *The reception was held in the Albany.* N COUNT

3 If something or someone has a particular kind of **reception**, that is the way people react to them. EG *I wrote to George about the enthusiastic reception of his book... Butler received a hostile reception in Bristol.* N COUNT+SUPP

4 The **reception** of guests is the act of formally welcoming them. EG *...a room which was kept for the reception of visitors.* N SING Formal

5 If you get good **reception** from your radio or television, the sound or picture is clear. EG *I'm getting perfect reception now... Radio reception kept fading.* N UNCOUNT

receptionist /rɪˈsɛpʃənɪst/, **receptionists.** The **receptionist** in a hotel, office, or doctor's surgery is the person whose job is to deal with guests or clients when they first arrive, answer the telephone, and arrange reservations or appointments. EG *He handed back his key to the receptionist.* N COUNT

receptive /rɪˈsɛptɪv/. Someone who is **receptive** to new ideas or suggestions is willing to consider and accept them. EG *We need people who are receptive to new ideas... The public began to develop a more receptive attitude.* ADJ QUALIT: OFT+*to*

recess, recesses; pronounced /rɪˈsɛs/ in paragraph 1 and /riːsɛs/ in paragraphs 2 and 3.
1 A **recess** is a period of holiday between the sessions of work of a committee or parliament. EG *The committee is going into recess for a couple of weeks.* N UNCOUNT OR N COUNT

2 In a room, a **recess** is a small extra area that is created when one part of a wall is built further back than the rest. EG *...the arched window recess.* N COUNT

3 The **recesses** of something are its deep or hidden parts. EG *I pushed the problem down into the dim recesses of my mind.* N COUNT +SUPP: USU PLURAL

recession /rɪˈsɛʃə[0]n/, **recessions.** A **recession** is a period when the economy of a country is less successful, for example because industry is producing less and more people are becoming unemployed. N COUNT OR N UNCOUNT

RECIP stands for **reciprocal**
A number of verbs have the additional label RECIP in the Extra Column. This is used to indicate a particular pattern that the verb makes with two noun groups. A typical example is **meet**. If we know that 'John met Mary', then we also know that 'Mary met John', that 'John and Mary met', and that 'John and Mary met each other'. EG *When he was at university he* ***met*** *Barbara... Barbara* ***met*** *him in London... The couple* ***met*** *a week before the wedding... They* ***met*** *each other at a party.*
From this it can be seen that either of the two noun groups can be the subject or the object of the verb without changing the meaning of the sentence. 'He met Barbara' means that 'Barbara met him'.
Also, the two noun groups can be joined by 'and' to make the subject of the verb. In that case there is no object, except for the phrase 'each other', which is sometimes used. So that 'Barbara and Howard met at university' means the same as 'Barbara and Howard met each other at university'.
Many verbs use the preposition 'with' to make a reciprocal pattern. For example, the verb **argue**, as in EG *I was arguing with him about the miners' strike... He was arguing with me... Why do we always argue about money?*
Here, too, either of the noun groups can be the subject or the prepositional object without changing the meaning of the sentence. When they are both the subject, there is no prepositional object, except for the phrase 'with each other', which is sometimes used.

recipe /rɛsɪpi[1]/, **recipes.** 1 A **recipe** is a list of ingredients and a set of instructions that tell you how to cook something. EG *...a recipe for beetroot soup... It's one of Aunt Jane's recipes.* N COUNT

2 If you say that something is a **recipe** for disaster or a **recipe** for success, you mean that it is likely N SING+*for*

Is a recluse happy to receive visitors?

to result in disaster or success. EG *This policy appeared to be a recipe for disaster.*

recipient /rɪ²sɪpɪənt/, **recipients.** The **recipient** of something is the person who receives it. EG *...letters kept by the recipients.* N COUNT Formal

reciprocal /rɪ²sɪprəkə⁰l/ A **reciprocal** arrangement or agreement is one in which two people or two groups of people agree to help each another in a similar way. EG *Their social security system is linked to Britain's by a reciprocal agreement.* ADJ CLASSIF Formal

reciprocate /rɪ²sɪprəkeɪt/, **reciprocates, reciprocating, reciprocated.** If you **reciprocate** someone's feelings or behaviour towards you, you have the same feelings about them or behave the same way towards them. EG *This hostile attitude is reciprocated by potential employers... Invitations to the home of a subordinate may be accepted, but not reciprocated.* V+O OR V Formal

recital /rɪ¹saɪtə⁰l/, **recitals.** A **recital** is a performance of music or poetry, usually given by one person. EG *She had been asked to give a piano recital.* N COUNT

recitation /rɛsɪteɪʃə⁰n/, **recitations.** When someone does a **recitation**, they say aloud a piece of poetry or other writing that they have learned. N UNCOUNT OR N COUNT

recite /rɪ¹saɪt/, **recites, reciting, recited. 1** When someone **recites** a poem or other piece of writing, they say it aloud after they have learned it. EG *She recited a speech from 'As You Like It'.* V+O OR V+QUOTE

2 If you **recite** a list of things, you say it aloud. EG *Mrs Zapp recited a catalogue of her husband's sins.* V+O

reckless /rɛklɪ²s/. Someone who is **reckless** shows a lack of care about danger or about the results of their actions. EG *I don't like the way he drives. He's reckless... They denounced the government for its reckless squandering of public funds.* ADJ QUALIT

◇ **recklessly.** EG *He accelerated recklessly round a blind corner.* ◇ ADV ◇ **recklessness.** EG *...the recklessness of the attack.* ◇ N UNCOUNT

reckon /rɛkə⁰n/, **reckons, reckoning, reckoned.**

1 If you say that you **reckon** that something is true, you mean that you think that it is true. EG *She reckoned that there was a risk... I reckon he's stupid... What do you reckon?* V+REPORT: ONLY *that* Informal

2 If you say that something **is reckoned** to be true, you mean that people think that it is true. EG *About 40 per cent of the country is reckoned to be illiterate... It was reckoned a fine job but the money wasn't great.* V+O+*to*-INF OR V+O+C: USU PASS

3 If you say that someone **reckons** to do something, you mean that they claim or expect to do it. EG *They reckon to sell the same amount each year.* V+*to*-INF

4 When you **reckon** an amount, you calculate it. EG *The number of days lost through unemployment in 1968 can be reckoned at 146 million.* V+O OR V

reckon on. If you **reckon on** something, you feel certain that it will happen and therefore make your plans believing that it will happen. EG *He reckoned on a large reward if he succeeded.* PHRASAL VB: V+PREP, HAS PASS

reckon with. 1 If you say that you had not **reckoned with** something, you mean that you had not expected it and so were not prepared for it. EG *She had not reckoned with a surprise of this sort.* PHRASAL VB: V+PREP, HAS PASS

2 If you say that someone or something is **to be reckoned with**, you mean that they must be dealt with and it will be difficult. EG *There was also Gertrude to be reckoned with... The Union has always been a force to be reckoned with.* PHRASE

reckon without. If you say that you had **reckoned without** something, you mean that you had not expected it and so were not prepared for it. EG *They reckoned without Margaret's determination.* PHRASAL VB: V+PREP

reckoning /rɛkə⁰nɪŋ/, **reckonings. 1** A **reckoning** is a calculation. EG *It's only a rough reckoning... By his own reckoning, he had taken five hours to get there.* N COUNT OR N UNCOUNT

2 The **day of reckoning** for someone is the time when they are eventually punished for things that they have done wrong. EG *The day of reckoning had not yet come for Harold.* PHRASE

reclaim /rɪ¹kleɪm/, **reclaims, reclaiming, reclaimed. 1** If you **reclaim** something that you have lost or something that has been taken away from you, you succeed in getting it back. EG *You must present this ticket when you reclaim your luggage.* V+O

2 When people **reclaim** land, they make it suitable for use, for example by draining it or irrigating it. EG *Lowland bogs have been reclaimed.* V+O

◇ **reclaimed.** EG *...reclaimed land.* ◇ ADJ CLASSIF

recline /rɪ¹klaɪn/, **reclines, reclining, reclined.** If you **recline**, you sit or lie with the upper part of your body supported at an angle. EG *She was reclining comfortably in her chair.* V: USU+A

reclining /rɪ¹klaɪnɪŋ/. A **reclining** chair or seat has a back which can be adjusted so that you can lie down or sit with the upper part of your body supported at an angle. ADJ CLASSIF: ATTRIB

recluse /rɪ¹klu:s/, **recluses.** A **recluse** is a person who lives alone and deliberately avoids other people. N COUNT

recognise /rɛkəg⁰naɪz/. See **recognize**.

recognition /rɛkəg⁰nɪʃə⁰n/. **1 Recognition** is the experience of recognizing someone or something. EG *She walked past me without so much as a glance of recognition.* N UNCOUNT

2 If something has changed **beyond recognition** or **out of all recognition**, it has changed so much that you can no longer recognize it. EG *The social structure has changed beyond recognition.* PHRASE

3 When there is **recognition** of something, people realize or accept that it exists or that it is true. EG *There has been insufficient recognition of the magnitude of the problem... This might lead to a recognition by both the superpowers that arms talks must continue.* N UNCOUNT +SUPP

4 If something is done **in recognition of** someone's achievements, it is done as a way of showing official appreciation of them. EG *He was awarded a knighthood in recognition of his great contribution to the British cinema.* PHRASE

recognizable /rɛkəg⁰naɪzəbə⁰l/; also spelled **recognisable.** Something that is **recognizable** is easy to recognize or identify. EG *...a recognizable voice... There was an old statue barely recognisable as Charles II.* ADJ QUALIT ◇ **recognizably.** EG *Its arrangement is recognizably based on what existed before.* ◇ ADV

recognize /rɛkəg⁰naɪz/, **recognizes, recognizing, recognized;** also spelled **recognise. 1** If you **recognize** someone or something, you know who or what they are, because you have seen or heard them before or because someone has described them to you. EG *She didn't recognise me at first... The postmistress recognised her as Mrs Pennington's daughter... They are trained to recognize the symptoms of radiation-sickness.* V+O OR V+O+*as*: NO CONT

2 You also say that you **recognize** something when you realize or accept that it exists or that it is true. EG *Governments are beginning to recognize the problem... We recognise this as a genuine need... They refused to recognise that a wrong decision had been made.* V+O, V+O+*as*, OR V+REPORT

3 You say that something **is recognized** when it is accepted or approved. EG *Are qualifications gained in Britain recognized in other European countries?* V+O

◇ **recognized.** EG *There are several recognized techniques for dealing with this.* ◇ ADJ CLASSIF

4 When a new government **is recognized**, it is accepted as the legal government of a country. EG *The new regime was at once recognized by China.* V+O

5 When an achievement **is recognized**, people officially show their appreciation of it. EG *The nation recognized her efforts by making her home a historical monument.* V+O

recoil /rɪ¹kɔɪl/, **recoils, recoiling, recoiled. 1** You say that someone **recoils** from something when it gives them an immediate feeling of fear, V: OFT+*from*/*at* dislike, or horror. EG *He recoiled in horror from the savagery which he witnessed... Parents may recoil at this kind of behaviour.*

2 You also say that someone **recoils** from something when they move their body, or part of their body, quickly away from it because it gives them a painful or unpleasant feeling. EG *When he touched the man's arm, he recoiled in horror, for it was cold and rigid.* V : USU+A

recollect /rɛkəlɛkt/, **recollects, recollecting, recollected.** If you **recollect** something, you remember it. EG *He was unable to recollect the names... He does not recollect how long they were in the house.* V+O OR V+REPORT

recollection /rɛkəlɛkʃəⁿn/, **recollections. 1** If you have a **recollection** of something, you remember it. EG *I have a vivid recollection of the house where I was born... ...my recollections of Australia.* N COUNT

2 Recollection is the experience of remembering something. EG *She had a flash of recollection.* N UNCOUNT

recommend /rɛkəmɛnd/, **recommends, recommending, recommended. 1** If someone **recommends** something to you, they suggest that you should have it or use it, because it is good or useful. EG *...a fine novel which I'd strongly recommend... ...the 70° recommended for old people... Perhaps you could recommend me a solicitor.* V+O : OFT+*for*, OR V+O+O

2 If you **recommend** an action, you suggest that it should be done. EG *They recommended a merger of the two biggest supermarket groups... The Harveys do not recommend other couples to have families of this size... He would strongly recommend that I had it next year... Mr Tebbit recommends cycling as a good form of exercise.* V+O : OFT+*to*-INF; ALSO V+REPORT OR -ING

recommendation /rɛkəmɛndeɪʃəⁿn/, **recommendations.** If you make a **recommendation, 1** you suggest that someone should have something or use something, because it is good or useful. EG *The best way to find a gardener is through personal recommendation.* N COUNT OR N UNCOUNT **2** you advise someone what is the best thing to do. EG *The final choice will depend largely on what recommendation they make to the Prime Minister... ...recommendations for training.* N COUNT

reconcile /rɛkəⁿnsaɪl/, **reconciles, reconciling, reconciled. 1** If you **reconcile** two beliefs that seem to be opposed to each other, you find a way in which both of them can be held by the same person at the same time. EG *I cannot reconcile the two points of view... I asked how he would reconcile apartheid with Christianity.* V+O : OFT+*to*/*with*

2 If you **are reconciled** with someone, you become friendly with them again after a quarrel or disagreement. EG *They had been reconciled with their families.* V+O : OFT+*with*/*to*, USU PASS ◇ **reconciliation** /rɛkəⁿnsɪlɪˈeɪʃəⁿn/. EG *...hopes of reconciliation in Western Europe.* ◇ N UNCOUNT

3 If you **reconcile** yourself to an unpleasant situation, you accept it. EG *He told them to reconcile themselves to their misery on earth.* V-REFL+*to* ◇ **reconciled.** EG *After a while he grew reconciled to the situation.* ◇ ADJ PRED +*to*

reconnaissance /rɪˀkɒnɪˈsəns/ is the process of obtaining military information about a place by sending soldiers, planes, or satellites there. EG *They decided to step up reconnaissance of enemy naval movements... ...reconnaissance planes.* N UNCOUNT

reconsider /riːkəⁿnsɪdə/, **reconsiders, reconsidering, reconsidered.** If you **reconsider** a decision or a way of doing something, you think about it and try to decide whether it should be changed. EG *He asked me to reconsider my decision... They have had to reconsider how modern warfare should be waged.* V+O OR V : OFT+REPORT, ONLY WH ◇ **reconsideration** /riːkəⁿnsɪdəreɪʃəⁿn/. EG *This would allow time for reconsideration.* ◇ N UNCOUNT

reconstruct /riːkəⁿnstrʌkt/, **reconstructs, reconstructing, reconstructed. 1** If you **reconstruct** a building that has been destroyed or badly damaged, you build it again. V+O

2 When a system or policy **is reconstructed**, it is replaced with one that works in a different way. EG *...an attempt to reconstruct race relations policy.* V+O

3 If you **reconstruct** an event that happened in the past, you obtain a complete description of it by combining a lot of small pieces of information. V+O

reconstruction /riːkəⁿnstrʌkʃəⁿn/, **reconstructions. 1 Reconstruction** is the process of making a country normal again after a war, for example by replacing buildings that have been damaged or destroyed. EG *They played an active role in the reconstruction of post-war Britain.* N UNCOUNT

2 When the **reconstruction** of a building takes place, it is built again after it has been damaged or destroyed. N UNCOUNT

record, records, recording, recorded; pronounced /rɛkɔːd/ when it is a noun or adjective and /rɪˈkɔːd/ when it is a verb.

1 If you keep a **record** of something, you keep a written account of it or store information about it in a computer so that it can be referred to later. EG *Keep a record of any repair bills... ...medical records.* N COUNT

2 If you **record** something, you write it down, film it, or put it into a computer so that it can be referred to later. EG *All personnel details could be recorded on a computer... Their every action was recorded by concealed cameras.* V+O

3 A **record** is a round, flat piece of black plastic on which sound, especially music, is stored. You listen to the sound by playing the record on a record player. EG *...jazz records.* N COUNT

4 When music or speech **is recorded**, it is put onto a tape or a record, so that it can be heard again later. EG *We had better be careful what we say since it's being recorded.* V+O

5 A **record** is also the shortest time or the longest distance that has ever been achieved in a particular sport. EG *He held the record for the mile... ...world records.* N COUNT

6 You use **record** to say that something is higher, lower, or better than has ever been achieved before. EG *Unemployment was at a record high.* ADJ CLASSIF : ATTRIB

7 Your **record** is all the facts that are known about your achievements or character. EG *Mr Gerran has a very distinguished record.* N COUNT+SUPP

8 If someone has a **record** of behaviour of a particular kind, they are known to have behaved in that way. EG *...a man with a record of instability.* N COUNT+SUPP

9 **Record** is also used in these phrases. **9.1** If something that you say is **off the record**, it is not official and not intended to be published or made known. EG *Now that remark was off the record, understand?* **9.2** If you are **on record** as saying something, you have said it publicly and it has been written down. EG *You're on record as saying that you will retire at the end of the year.* **9.3** If you keep information **on record**, you write it down or store it in a computer so that it can be referred to later. **9.4** You use **on record** to say that something is, for example, the best or largest thing of its kind that has been noticed and recorded in writing. EG *...the highest monthly figures on record.* **9.5** If you **set** or **put the record straight**, you show that something which has been regarded as true is in fact not true. EG *Harold Begbie wrote a book to put the record straight.* PHRASES

10 See also **recording, track record**.

recorded delivery. If you send a letter or parcel by **recorded delivery**, you receive an official note telling you that it has been received. N UNCOUNT British

recorder /rɪˈkɔːdə/, **recorders. 1** You can refer to a cassette recorder, a tape recorder, or a video recorder as a **recorder**. EG *He switched off the recorder.* N COUNT

Where does a rector live?

2 A **recorder** is also a hollow musical instrument that you play by blowing down one end and putting your fingers over a series of holes. See picture at MUSICAL INSTRUMENTS. N COUNT

recording /rɪ1kɔ:dɪŋ/, **recordings.** 1 A **recording** of something is a record, tape, or video of it. EG *...a new recording of the Second Symphony... Very few recordings of Picasso's voice exist.* N COUNT

2 **Recording** is the process of making records, tapes, or videos. EG *...a recording engineer... ...recording equipment.* N UNCOUNT: USU N MOD

record player, record players. A **record player** is a machine on which you play records. N COUNT

recount, recounts, recounting, recounted; pronounced /rɪ1kaʊnt/ in paragraphs 1 and 2 and /ri:kaʊnt/ in paragraph 3.

1 If you **recount** a story, you tell it. EG *I'll just recount one anecdote.* V+O Formal

2 If you **recount** an event, you describe what happened. EG *I let Henry recount the incident in his own words.* V+O Formal

3 A **recount** is a second count of votes in an election when the result is very close. EG *I'm demanding a recount.* N COUNT

recourse /rɪ1kɔ:s/. If you have **recourse** to something, you use it in order to help you in a difficult situation. EG *We need never have recourse to violence... Industrial action is the only recourse we have.* N UNCOUNT: USU+*to* Formal

recover /rɪ1kʌvə/, **recovers, recovering, recovered.** 1 When you **recover** from an illness or an injury, you become well again. EG *It was weeks before he fully recovered... ...a wound from which he did not recover.* V: OFT+*from* ◇ **recovered.** EG *Stay at home until you are fully recovered.* ◇ ADJ PRED

2 If you **recover** from an unhappy or unpleasant experience, you stop being upset by it. EG *They took a long time to recover from this shock.* V: OFT+*from*

3 If you **recover** something that has been lost or stolen, you get it back. EG *I would do my best to recover these documents... They recovered her body from the old mine-shaft.* V+O: OFT+*from*

4 If you **recover** your former mental or physical state or **recover** the ability to do something, you get it back again. EG *She quickly recovered her composure... He died without recovering consciousness... He was beginning to recover the use of his voice.* V+O

5 If you **recover** money that you have spent or invested, you get the same amount back. EG *We recovered our purchase price in the first year.* V+O

recovery /rɪ1kʌvə0ri1/, **recoveries.** 1 If a sick person makes a **recovery**, he or she becomes well again. EG *He made a good recovery from his stroke... The shock of the operation delayed his recovery.* N UNCOUNT OR N COUNT

2 When there is a **recovery** in a country's economy, it improves after it has been in a bad state. EG *His advisers insisted that economic recovery was in sight.* N UNCOUNT OR N COUNT

3 You talk about the **recovery** of something when you get it back after it has been lost or stolen. EG *...the recovery of the treasure.* N UNCOUNT: USU+SUPP Formal

4 You talk about the **recovery** of someone's physical or mental state when they return to this state. EG *The news was sufficient to bring about the recovery of his equanimity.* N UNCOUNT: USU+SUPP Formal

recreate /ri:kri1eɪt/, **recreates, recreating, recreated.** If you **recreate** something, you succeed in making it happen or exist again. EG *This country can no longer hope to recreate its past... The opportunity could not be recreated.* V+O

recreation /rɛkri1eɪʃə0n/, **recreations. Recreation** consists of things that you do to exercise your body or mind when you are not working or studying. EG *Sport and recreation have always been part of university life... The library was reserved for quieter recreations.* N UNCOUNT OR N COUNT ◇ **recreational** /rɛkri1eɪʃənə0l/. EG *...the recreational use of forests... ...recreational facilities.* ◇ ADJ CLASSIF: USU ATTRIB

recreation ground, recreation grounds. A **recreation ground** is a piece of public land, usually in a town, where people can go to play sport and games. N COUNT

recrimination /rɪ2krɪmɪneɪʃə0n/, **recriminations. Recriminations** are accusations that two people or two groups of people make about each other. EG *There will be recriminations, no doubt.* N PLURAL ▸ used as an uncount noun. EG *...prolonged bouts of recrimination.* ▸ N UNCOUNT

recruit /rɪ1kru:t/, **recruits, recruiting, recruited.** 1 If you **recruit** people for an organization, you get them to join it or work for it. EG *It is becoming harder to recruit youngsters for the farms... I am recruiting for the Union.* V+O OR V: OFT+A ◇ **recruiting.** EG *Other organizations reported sharp rises in recruiting... ...a recruiting centre.* ◇ N UNCOUNT

2 A **recruit** is a person who has recently joined an organization or an army. EG *He joined the firm as a young recruit more than thirty years ago... ...the army, with its ranks swollen by these new recruits.* N COUNT

3 If you **recruit** someone for a particular purpose, you get them to do something for you. EG *Men from the villages were recruited to carry stores... Mothers and fathers could be recruited to help.* V+O: OFT+*for* OR *to*-INF

recruitment /rɪ1kru:tmə2nt/. When **recruitment** takes place, people are persuaded to join an organization or an army. EG *...the mass recruitment of volunteer teachers... ...a recruitment scheme.* N UNCOUNT

rectangle /rɛktæŋgə0l/, **rectangles.** A **rectangle** is a four-sided shape whose angles are all right angles. Each side of a rectangle is the same length as the one opposite to it. See picture at SHAPES. N COUNT ◇ **rectangular** /rɛktæŋgjə4lə/. EG *...a rectangular flower-bed.* ◇ ADJ CLASSIF

rectify /rɛktɪfaɪ/, **rectifies, rectifying, rectified.** If you **rectify** something which is wrong, you change it so that it becomes correct or satisfactory. EG *Armed forces were sent in to rectify the situation... The tenant will be held responsible for rectifying any damage.* V+O

rector /rɛktə/, **rectors.** A **rector** is a Church of England priest who is in charge of a parish. N COUNT

rectory /rɛktə0ri1/, **rectories.** A **rectory** is a house in which a rector and his family live. N COUNT

recuperate /ri1kj0u:pəreɪt/, **recuperates, recuperating, recuperated.** When you **recuperate**, you recover your health or strength after you have been ill or injured. EG *I was recuperating from an accident in the gym.* V: OFT+*from* Formal ◇ **recuperation** /ri1kj0u:pəreɪʃə0n/. EG *My mother has gone to Bath for rest and recuperation.* ◇ N UNCOUNT

recur /rɪ1kɜ:/, **recurs, recurring, recurred.** If something **recurs**, it happens again, either once or many times. EG *It was probable that the same circumstances would now recur... It was a phrase that was to recur again and again.* V: USU+A

recurrence /rɪ1kʌrəns/, **recurrences.** If there is a **recurrence** of something, it happens again. EG *There were minor recurrences of her eye trouble.* N COUNT OR N UNCOUNT Formal

recurrent /rɪ1kʌrənt/ means the same as recurring. EG *...a recurrent feeling of illness... ...his recurrent successes... ...recurrent dreams.* ADJ CLASSIF: ATTRIB Formal

recurring /rɪ1kɜ:rɪŋ/. **Recurring** things happen many times. EG *Food scarcity will be a recurring problem in the future.* ADJ CLASSIF: ATTRIB

recycle /ri:saɪkə0l/, **recycles, recycling, recycled.** If you **recycle** things that have already been used, such as bottles or sheets of paper, you process them so that they can be used again. V+O ◇ **recycled.** EG *...recycled paper.* ◇ ADJ CLASSIF

red /rɛd/, **redder, reddest; reds.** 1 Something that is **red** is the colour of blood or of a ripe tomato. EG *...a bunch of red roses... ...brilliant paintings in reds and greens.* ADJ COLOUR

2 If you say that someone's face is **red**, you mean that it is redder than its normal colour, because ADJ COLOUR

they are embarrassed or angry. EG *Jack turned, red in the face... Ralph clenched his fist and went very red.*

3 You describe someone's hair as **red** when it is between red and brown in colour. ADJ COLOUR

4 If you are **in the red** or if your bank account is **in the red**, you have spent more money than you have in your account and therefore you owe money to the bank. PHRASE Informal

5 If you **see red**, you become very angry. PHRASE

6 If you call someone a **red**, you mean that they support communism, socialism, or left-wing ideas in general; used showing disapproval. N COUNT

reddish /rɛdɪʃ/. Something that is **reddish** is slightly red in colour. ADJ COLOUR

redeem /rɪ'diːm/, **redeems, redeeming, redeemed. 1** When something **redeems** an unpleasant thing or situation, it prevents it from being completely bad. V+O ◇ **redeeming.** EG *...a book with no redeeming qualities.* ◇ ADJ CLASSIF : ATTRIB

2 If you **redeem** yourself, you do something that makes people have a good opinion of you again after you have behaved badly. EG *He was trying to redeem himself for his earlier failure.* V-REFL

3 If you **redeem** something, you get it back from someone by repaying them money that you have borrowed from them. EG *They came to redeem their jewellery.* V+O Technical

redemption /rɪ'dɛmp⁰ʃə⁰n/ is freedom from the consequences of sin and evil which Christians believe was made possible by Jesus Christ's death on the cross. N UNCOUNT Formal

redevelopment /riːdi'vɛləpmə²nt/. When **redevelopment** takes place, the buildings in a part of a town are knocked down and new buildings are built in their place. EG *The area is undergoing redevelopment.* N UNCOUNT

red herring, red herrings. If you say that something is a **red herring**, you mean that it is irrelevant and takes people's attention away from what is important. EG *They were using the issue as a red herring.* N COUNT

red-hot. 1 You say that metal is **red-hot** when it has been heated to such a high temperature that it has turned red. ADJ CLASSIF

2 You also use **red-hot** to describe people or situations that are full of very strong feelings. EG *...a red-hot revolutionary... ...red-hot patriotism.* Informal

redistribute /riːdɪstrɪbjuːt/, **redistributes, redistributing, redistributed.** When something such as money **is redistributed**, it is shared among people or organizations in a different way from the way that it was previously shared. EG *Money would be redistributed from the traditional arts institutions.* V+O ◇ **redistribution** /riːdɪstrɪbjuːʃə⁰n/. EG *We do not envisage any redistribution of wealth and power.* ◇ N UNCOUNT

redouble /riːdʌbə⁰l/, **redoubles, redoubling, redoubled.** If you **redouble** your efforts, you try much harder to achieve something. EG *She redoubled her efforts to attract his curiosity.* V+O

redress, redresses, redressing, redressed; pronounced /rɪ'drɛs/ when it is a verb and either /rɪ'drɛs/ or /riːdrɛs/ when it is a noun.

1 If you **redress** something such as a wrong or a grievance, you do something to correct it or to improve things for the person who has been badly treated. EG *He did all that he could to redress these wrongs.* V+O Formal ● If you **redress the balance** between two things that have become unequal, you make them equal again. EG *We were refused the pay increase needed to redress the balance.* ● PHRASE Formal

2 Redress is compensation for something wrong that has been done. EG *Your claims for redress may yet succeed.* N UNCOUNT Formal

red tape. You refer to official rules and procedures as **red tape** when they seem unnecessary and cause delay. EG *Applying for the grant involves a great deal of red tape.* N UNCOUNT

reduce /rɪ'djuːs/, **reduces, reducing, reduced. 1** If you **reduce** something, you make it smaller. EG *They have promised to reduce public expenditure... The work-force would have to be reduced from 13,000 to 7,500.* V+O : OFT+from/to ◇ **reduced.** EG *...a reduced rate of production.* ◇ ADJ CLASSIF

2 If you say that someone **is reduced** to a weaker or inferior state, you mean that they change to this state as a result of something that happens to them. EG *He was reduced to tears... Her mother was reduced to infantile dependence.* V+O+to : USU PASS

3 If you say that someone **is reduced** to doing something, you mean that they have to do it, although it is unpleasant or humiliating. EG *They are reduced to begging in the streets... We were reduced to desperate measures to get an interview with her.* V+O+to : USU PASS

reduction /rɪ'dʌkʃə⁰n/, **reductions.** When there is a **reduction** in something, it is made smaller. EG *The unions will be demanding a reduction in working hours... ...a 6 per cent reduction in industrial investment.* N UNCOUNT OR N COUNT : OFT+in/of

redundancy /rɪ'dʌndənsi¹/, **redundancies. 1** When there are **redundancies**, an organization dismisses some of its employees because their jobs are no longer necessary or because the organization can no longer afford to pay them. EG *The trade unions accepted 3500 redundancies.* N COUNT : USU PLURAL

2 Redundancy is the state of no longer having a job because you have been made redundant. EG *The possibility of redundancy was present in their minds... You should get a redundancy payment.* N UNCOUNT

redundant /rɪ'dʌndənt/. **1** If you are made **redundant**, you are dismissed by your employer because your job is no longer necessary or because your employer cannot afford to keep paying you. EG *Alumetal Ltd will be making 250 workers redundant next year.* ADJ CLASSIF

2 Something that is **redundant** is no longer needed because it has been replaced by something else. EG *...skills which have been made redundant by technological advance... ...a large warehouse which faces onto three redundant docks.* ADJ QUALIT

reed /riːd/, **reeds. Reeds** are tall plants that grow in large groups in shallow water or marshy ground. They have strong, hollow stems that can be used for making things such as baskets. N COUNT : USU PLURAL, OR N UNCOUNT

reef /riːf/, **reefs.** A **reef** is a long line of rocks or sand that is just above or just below the surface of the sea. N COUNT

reek /riːk/, **reeks, reeking, reeked. 1** If something **reeks** of a particular thing, it smells very strongly of it. EG *Thomas appeared, reeking powerfully of brandy.* V : OFT+of/with

2 If there is a **reek** of something, there is a very strong, unpleasant smell of it. EG *...the sickening reek of blood.* N SING+SUPP

reel /riːl/, **reels, reeling, reeled. 1** A **reel** is a cylindrical object around which you wrap something such as thread or cinema film. EG *...a reel of white string.* N COUNT OR N PART

2 The **reel** on a fishing-rod is a round device that you use to control the length of the fishing line. For example, when you have caught a fish, you shorten the line by turning the handle on the reel, and so pull the fish towards you. N COUNT

3 When someone **reels** somewhere, they move there unsteadily as if they were going to fall. EG *I reeled back into the room.* V : USU+A

4 If you say that your brain or your mind **is reeling**, you mean that you are very confused because you have too many things to think about. EG *His mind was reeling with all that he had seen and heard.* V

5 A **reel** is also a type of fast Scottish dance. N COUNT

If people are made redundant, is there a reduction in the number of jobs?

reel in. If you **reel in** a fish, you pull it towards you by turning the handle on the reel and shortening the line. PHRASAL VB : V+O+ADV

reel off. If you **reel off** information, you repeat it from memory quickly and easily. EG *He could reel off the names of all the capitals of Europe.* PHRASAL VB : V+O+ADV

re-elect, re-elects, re-electing, re-elected. When someone such as an MP or a trade union official **is re-elected**, they win a new election and are therefore able to continue in their position as MP or union official. EG *I was re-elected with a majority of over 4,300... The Council re-elected him President.* ◊ **re-election.** EG *He stood for re-election.* V+O : OFT PASS, OR V+O+C ◊ N UNCOUNT

re-examine, re-examines, re-examining, re-examined. If you **re-examine** your ideas or beliefs, you think about them carefully because you are no longer sure if they are correct. EG *This forced researchers to re-examine their assumptions about man's early evolution.* ◊ **re-examination.** EG *This has prompted a re-examination of the purposes of education in modern Britain.* V+O ◊ N COUNT OR N UNCOUNT

ref. is written in front of a code at the top of business letters. The code refers to a file in which correspondence is kept. EG *Ref. ESB/33593/64.*

refectory /rɪfɛktəᵒriᴵ/, **refectories.** In a university or a monastery, the **refectory** is the dining hall. N COUNT

refer /rɪ¹fɜː/, **refers, referring, referred. 1** If you **refer to** a particular subject or person, you talk about them or mention them. EG *In his letters he rarely referred to political events... I am not allowed to describe the officers or refer to them by name.* V+*to* : HAS PASS

2 If you **refer** to someone or something by a particular expression, you use it as their name when you are talking about them. EG *This kind of art is often referred to as 'minimal art'... ...the decline of what I refer to as the industrial working class.* V+*to*+*as* : HAS PASS

3 If a word or expression **refers** to something, it is used as a name for it. EG *In the 18th century, 'antique' referred specifically to Greek and Roman antiquities.* V+*to* : HAS PASS

4 If you **refer to** a source of information such as a reference book, you look at it in order to find something out. EG *She could make a new dish without referring to a cookery book.* V+*to* : HAS PASS

5 If you **refer** someone to a source of information, you tell them to look for something there. EG *I refer you to a paper by Sutherland.* V+O+*to*

6 If you **refer** a task or problem to a person or an organization, you formally tell them about it, so that they can deal with it. EG *She referred the matter to the European Court of Justice.* V+O+*to*

referee /rɛfəriː/, **referees.** The **referee** is the official who controls a football or hockey game or a boxing or wrestling match. N COUNT

reference /rɛfəᵒrəns/, **references. 1** If you make **reference** to someone or something or make a **reference** to them, you talk about them or mention them. EG *...the person to whom Philip had made such contemptuous reference... There is no further reference to him in her diary.* N UNCOUNT OR N COUNT : USU+*to* Formal

2 Reference is also the act of referring to someone or something for information or advice. EG *They acted without reference to the police committee... ...a wrist-size computer for quick reference and portability.* ● If you keep information **for future reference**, you keep it because it might be useful in the future. N UNCOUNT : OFT+*to* ● PHRASE

3 You use **'with reference to'** to indicate who or what you are talking or writing about. EG *Dear Sir, With reference to your recent communication, the matter is being dealt with as speedily as possible.* PREP Formal

4 A **reference** is also something such as a number or a name that tells you where you can obtain information. EG *...the two page references that I gave you.* N COUNT

5 If someone gives you a **reference** when you are applying for a job, they write a letter to the employer describing your character and abilities. EG *I've got to get a reference from the University... I've given you a marvellous reference.* N COUNT

6 You look at **reference** books or visit a **reference** library in order to obtain information. EG *...a valuable reference document... He returned to the Reference Room and put the volume back.* N MOD

referendum /rɛfərɛndəm/, **referenda** /rɛfərɛndə/ or **referendums.** A **referendum** is a vote in which all the people in a country or region are asked whether they agree or disagree with a particular policy. N COUNT

refill /riːfɪl/, **refills, refilling, refilled.** If you **refill** something, you fill it again after it has been emptied. EG *Sue refilled Jennifer's glass... He went off to refill the aquarium.* ▸ used as a noun. EG *I handed her my cup for a refill.* V+O ▸ N COUNT Informal

refine /rɪ¹faɪn/, **refines, refining, refined. 1** When a substance **is refined**, it is made pure by having all other substances removed from it. EG *...men who tested and refined gold.* ◊ **refining.** EG *...the refining of petroleum.* V+O ◊ N UNCOUNT

2 If you **refine** something such as a theory or an idea, you improve it by making small alterations to it. EG *I used these meetings to refine my ideas.* V+O

refined /rɪ¹faɪnd/. **1 Refined** people are very polite and well-mannered. EG *...a thin, refined man in a bow tie.* ADJ QUALIT

2 If you describe a machine or process as **refined**, you mean that it has been carefully developed and is therefore very efficient. EG *The new model was larger, faster, and more refined than its predecessor.* ADJ QUALIT

3 A **refined** substance has been made pure by having other substances removed from it. EG *...refined oil.* ADJ CLASSIF

refinement /rɪ¹faɪnmə²nt/, **refinements. 1 Refinements** are small alterations that you make to something in order to improve it. EG *...refinements of the system.* N COUNT OR N UNCOUNT

2 Refinement in someone's behaviour is politeness and good manners and a dislike of anything vulgar. EG *Mr Willet's tone changed to one of genteel refinement.* N UNCOUNT

refinery /rɪ¹faɪnəᵒriᴵ/, **refineries.** A **refinery** is a factory where substances such as oil or sugar are refined. EG *...oil refineries.* N COUNT

reflect /rɪ¹flɛkt/, **reflects, reflecting, reflected.**
1 If you say that something **reflects** a person's attitude or **reflects** a situation, you mean that it is a consequence of this attitude or situation. EG *The choice of school reflected Dad's hopes for us... Relative profits reflected relative efficiency in performance.* V+O

2 When something **reflects** light or heat, the light or heat is sent back from it and does not pass through it. EG *Although it feels like a normal fabric it reflects heat back into the room.* V+O

3 When something **is reflected** in a mirror or in water, you can see its image in the mirror or water. EG *I saw street lamps mistily reflected in black water.* V+O

4 When you **reflect** on something or **reflect** over it, you think deeply about it. EG *Rodin reflected long over Casson's argument.* V : OFT+*on/over*

5 If you **reflect** that something is the case, you are aware that it is the case and think about it. EG *Well, I reflected, I couldn't say I hadn't been warned.* V+REPORT : ONLY *that*, OR V+QUOTE

reflection /rɪ¹flɛkʃəᵒn/, **reflections. 1** If you say, for example, that something is a **reflection** of a person's attitude or a situation, you mean that it is a consequence of it. EG *Their behaviour was a reflection of their very different personalities.* N COUNT+*of*

2 If you say that something is a **reflection** or a sad **reflection** on something else, you mean that it N SING+*on/upon* gives a bad impression of it. EG *This is a very sad reflection on the state of the Labour Party.*

3 A **reflection** is an image that you can see in a mirror or in water. EG *She was standing there looking at her reflection in the mirror... The reflections from the fireworks twinkled in the river.* N COUNT

4 **Reflection** is the process by which light and heat are sent back from a surface and do not pass through it. N UNCOUNT Technical

5 **Reflection** is thought. You can refer to your thoughts about something as your **reflections**. EG *'You ought to take it,' she said, after a moment's reflection... Furious flashes of light jolted me out of my reflections.* • You say **on reflection** to indicate that you have thought very carefully about something. EG *I suppose, on reflection, there is something immoral about it.* N UNCOUNT OR N COUNT; • ADV SEN

reflective /rɪˈflɛktɪv/. If you are **reflective**, you are thinking deeply about something. EG *He studied the statement in the same reflective way he always studied things... There was a long reflective silence.* ◊ **reflectively**. EG *Barney scratched his chin reflectively.* ADJ QUALIT; ◊ ADV

reflex /riːflɛks/, **reflexes.** 1 A **reflex** or a **reflex** action is a sudden, uncontrollable movement made by a part of your body as a result of pressure or a blow. EG *...the reflex that makes the baby kick.* N COUNT

2 If you have good **reflexes**, you have the ability to act quickly when something unexpected happens, for example while you are driving a car. EG *She had incredible reflexes.* N PLURAL

reflexive pronoun /rɪˈflɛksɪv prəʊnaʊn/, **reflexive pronouns.** In grammar, a **reflexive pronoun** is one which refers back to the subject of a sentence or clause. For example, in the sentence 'you'll just have to do it yourself', the reflexive pronoun 'yourself' refers back to 'you'. N COUNT

reflexive verb /rɪˈflɛksɪv vɜːb/, **reflexive verbs.** In grammar, a **reflexive verb** is a transitive verb in which the subject and object refer to the same person or thing. The object is always a reflexive pronoun. For example in the sentence 'He introduced himself', the object of the verb, 'himself', refers to the subject of the verb, 'he'. N COUNT

reform /rɪˈfɔːm/, **reforms, reforming, reformed.** 1 **Reform** consists of changes and improvements to a law, social system, or institution. EG *He called for the reform of the divorce laws... ...the task of carrying through the necessary reforms.* ▸ used as a verb. EG *...proposals to reform the Labour Party.* N UNCOUNT OR N COUNT; ▸ V+O

2 When someone **reforms** or **is reformed**, they stop doing something that society does not approve of, such as stealing things or drinking too much alcohol. EG *You have had every chance to reform... Prison sentences cannot reform the criminal.* ◊ **reformed**. EG *...a reformed alcoholic.* V-ERG; ◊ ADJ CLASSIF

reformer /rɪˈfɔːmə/, **reformers.** A **reformer** is someone who tries to improve something such as a law or a social system. EG *His early experiences turned him into a passionate social reformer.* N COUNT

refrain /rɪˈfreɪn/, **refrains, refraining, refrained.** 1 If you **refrain** from doing something, you deliberately do not do it. EG *I carefully refrained from looking at him.* V: OFT+*from* Formal

2 A **refrain** is a short, simple part of a song, which you repeat many times. N COUNT

refresh /rɪˈfrɛʃ/, **refreshes, refreshing, refreshed.** 1 If something **refreshes** you when you have become hot or tired, it makes you feel cooler or more energetic. EG *I hoped that sleep would refresh me enough to remain civil.* ◊ **refreshed**. EG *These trains are so luxurious that you can end a long journey feeling positively refreshed.* V+O; ◊ ADJ QUALIT: USU PRED

2 If someone **refreshes** your **memory**, they tell you something that you have forgotten. PHRASE

refreshing /rɪˈfrɛʃɪŋ/. 1 You say that something is **refreshing** when it is pleasantly different from what you are used to. EG *It was a refreshing change for her to meet a woman executive... I found a refreshing absence of industrial sprawl.* ◊ **refreshingly**. EG *The plot is refreshingly intelligent and original.* ADJ QUALIT; ◊ ADV

2 A **refreshing** bath or drink makes you feel energetic or cool again after you have been uncomfortably tired or hot. EG *He enjoyed the refreshing swims in the nearby creek.* ADJ QUALIT

refreshment /rɪˈfrɛʃməˈnt/, **refreshments.** 1 **Refreshments** are drinks and small amounts of food that are provided, for example, during a meeting or a journey. EG *There was a stop for refreshments between Coalmont and Ramsdale.* N PLURAL

2 You can refer to food and drink as **refreshment**. EG *Come into the house for some refreshment.* N UNCOUNT Formal

refrigerator /rɪˈfrɪdʒəreɪtə/, **refrigerators.** A **refrigerator** is a large container which is kept cool inside, usually by electricity, so that the food and drink in it stays fresh. N COUNT

refuge /rɛfjuːdʒ/, **refuges.** 1 When you take **refuge**, 1.1 you try to protect yourself from unhappiness or unpleasantness by behaving or thinking in a particular way. EG *He seeks refuge in silence... One must be careful not to take refuge in delusion.* 1.2 you try to protect yourself from physical harm by going to a particular place. EG *Whole families had taken refuge down the tunnels.* N UNCOUNT

2 A **refuge** is a place where you go for safety and protection. EG *A small cave was the only refuge from the cold.* N COUNT

refugee /rɛfjuˈdʒiː/, **refugees. Refugees** are people who have been forced to leave their country because there is a war there or because of their political or religious beliefs. EG *...a massive influx of refugees... ...a refugee camp.* N COUNT

refund, refunds, refunding, refunded; pronounced /riːfʌnd/ when it is a noun and /rɪfʌnd/ when it is a verb.
A **refund** is a sum of money which is returned to you, for example because you have paid someone too much money or because you have returned goods to a shop. ▸ used as a verb. EG *I used to refund people their money.* N COUNT; ▸ V+O OR V+O+O

refusal /rɪˈfjuːzəˈl/, **refusals.** 1 You describe someone's behaviour as a **refusal** to do something 1.1 when they deliberately do not do it. EG *In all his films we see his refusal to create outright villains.* 1.2 when they say firmly that they will not do it. EG *...the refusal of the workers to use forklift trucks.* N UNCOUNT +*to*-INF; N COUNT OR N UNCOUNT

2 You also talk about someone's behaviour as a **refusal** 2.1 when they do not give you something, or do not allow you to have it. EG *All appeals met with bureaucratic refusal... I made many applications and had many refusals.* 2.2 when they do not accept something that has been offered to them. EG *...this refusal of a gift offered to us.* N COUNT OR N UNCOUNT; N UNCOUNT: OFT+*of*

refuse, refuses, refusing, refused; pronounced /rɪfjuːz/ when it is a verb, and /rɛfjuːs/ or /rɛfjuːz/ when it is a noun.
1 If you **refuse** to do something, 1.1 you deliberately do not do it. EG *He refused to accept this advice... Their bosses refuse to allow them any responsibility.* 1.2 you say firmly that you will not do it. EG *I refuse to believe that it can't be done... He was dismissed for refusing to join a union.* V: OFT+*to*-INF

2 If someone **refuses** you something, they do not give it to you or do not allow you to have it. EG *Only the president could refuse him a loan... The Council refused permission for them to live together.* V+O+O OR V+O+A

3 If you **refuse** something that is offered to you, you do not accept it. EG *I offered him wine but he refused it.* V+O

4 **Refuse** consists of the rubbish and all the things that are not wanted in a house, shop, or factory, N UNCOUNT Formal

What kind of register does a registrar keep?

and that are regularly thrown away. EG ...*a dump for refuse... ...refuse collection.*

regain /rɪˈgeɪn/, **regains, regaining, regained.** V+O If you **regain** something that you have lost, you get it back again. EG *He might be able to regain his old job... He never regained political power.*

regal /riːgəˡl/. If you describe something as **regal**, ADJ QUALIT you mean that it is suitable for a king or queen, because it is very splendid. EG ...*a regal staircase leading into a vast reception hall.*

regale /rɪˈgeɪl/, **regales, regaling, regaled.** If V+O+*with* someone **regales** you with stories or jokes, they tell you a lot of them, whether you want to hear them or not. EG *I used to have a dentist who regaled me with extraordinary stories.*

regard /rɪˈgɑːd/, **regards, regarding, regarded.**

1 If you **regard** someone or something as being a V+O+*as* OR V-REFL+*as* particular thing or as having a particular quality, you believe that they are that thing or have that quality. EG *I regard it as one of my masterpieces... Parents were still regarded as being responsible for the control of their children... She now regarded herself as a woman.*

2 If you **regard** something or someone with a V+O: OFT+*with* feeling such as dislike or respect, you have that feeling about them. EG *He is regarded with some suspicion by the country's leaders... His visitors regarded him with envy.*

3 If someone is highly **regarded**, people have a lot ADJ QUALIT: AFTER ADV of respect for them. EG *The more highly regarded cameramen were kept very busy.*

4 If you have a high **regard** for someone, you have N UNCOUNT: USU+*for* a lot of respect for them. EG *I have a high regard for Mike... My regard for him grew day by day.*

5 **Regards** is used in expressions like 'best re- N PLURAL gards' and 'with warm regards' as a way of expressing friendly feelings towards someone. EG *Give my regards to your daughter.*

6 Some people say **as regards, with regard to**, or PREP Formal **in regard to** when indicating what they are talking or writing about. EG *As regards the car, I put an advertisement in the paper... With regard to the gas fire, we hardly use it... My upbringing was fairly strict in regard to obedience and truthfulness.*

7 Some people say **in this regard** or **in that** PHRASE Formal **regard** to indicate that what they are about to say is connected with what they have just said. EG *In this regard, the child may be thought of as having two homes.*

regarding /rɪˈgɑːdɪŋ/. You can use **regarding** to PREP indicate what you are talking or writing about. EG *There was always some question regarding education.*

regardless /rɪˈgɑːdlɪˀs/. 1 If something happens PREP **regardless of** something else, it happens in spite of it. EG *If they are determined to strike, they will do so regardless of what the law says.*

2 If you say that someone did something **regard-** ADV AFTER VB **less**, you mean that they did it even though there were problems or factors that could have stopped them. EG *Mrs Hochstadt walked on regardless.*

regatta /rɪgætə/, **regattas.** A **regatta** is a sports N COUNT event consisting of races between yachts or rowing boats.

reggae /regeɪ/ is a kind of West Indian popular N UNCOUNT music with a very strong beat.

regime /reɪʒiːm/, **regimes;** also spelled **régime.** N COUNT: USU+SUPP A **regime** is 1 a system or method of government. EG ...*a socialist regime... ...a regime where decision making is shared by all.* 2 a group of people who rule a country. EG ...*the corrupt regime that had ruled since 1921.*

regiment /redʒɪməˀnt/, **regiments.** A **regiment** N COUNT is a large group of soldiers that is commanded by a colonel.

regimental /redʒɪmentəˡl/ means belonging to a ADJ CLASSIF: ATTRIB particular regiment. EG *They took their orders from the regimental commander.*

regimentation /redʒɪmenteɪʃəⁿn/ is very strict N UNCOUNT Formal control over a group of people. EG *He detested every aspect of public school: the regimentation, the monotony, and the lack of privacy.*

regimented /redʒɪmentɪˀd/. Something that is ADJ QUALIT Formal **regimented** is very strictly controlled; used showing disapproval. EG ...*the tightly regimented life of the prison.*

region /riːdʒən/, **regions.** 1 A **region** is a large N COUNT area of land that is different from other areas of land, for example because it is one of the different parts of a country or because it has a particular geographical feature. EG *The country has nine autonomous regions... ...fighting in the Central Region... ...desert regions.*

2 You can refer to a part of your body as a **region.** N COUNT+SUPP EG *He was complaining of pains in the shoulder region.*

3 You say **in the region of** to indicate that an PREP amount that you are stating is only approximate. EG *Temperatures would be in the region of 500 degrees centigrade.*

regional /riːdʒəⁿnəl, -dʒənəˡl/. **Regional** organiza- ADJ CLASSIF tions and activities relate to a particular area of a country. EG *Most regional committees meet four times a year... Apply to your local Regional Hospital Board for details.*

register /redʒɪstə/, **registers, registering, registered.** 1 A **register** is an official list or record of N COUNT things. EG ...*the electoral register... ...the register of births, marriages, and deaths.*

2 If you **register** for something, you put your name V: USU+A on an official list, for example to enable you to receive a service. EG *You must register for work at the employment agency... They're coming to register as students on the English course.*

◇ **registered.** EG *They are registered with the* ◇ ADJ CLASSIF *University Health Service... ...a registered drug addict.*

3 If you **register** something, such as the name of V+O: USU+A someone who has just died, or the details of ownership of your car, you have these facts recorded on an official list. EG *One of the cars was registered in my name.*

4 When an amount **registers** or **is registered**, it V-ERG is shown on a scale or measuring instrument. EG *The inflation index registered a modest 7.8% annual rate.*

5 If you **register** your feelings or opinions about V+O something, you make them clear to other people, often by the expression on your face. EG *He stared at me for a moment, his face registering disbelief... Thousands joined the march to register their opposition to cuts in education.*

registered /redʒɪstəd/. A **registered** letter or ADJ CLASSIF: ATTRIB parcel is sent by a special postal service, for which you have to pay extra money to insure it in case it is lost. EG ...*a registered letter.*

registrar /redʒɪstrɑː/, **registrars.** A **registrar** is N COUNT 1 a person whose job is to keep official records, especially of births, marriages, and deaths. 2 a senior administrative official in a college or university.

registration /redʒɪstreɪʃəⁿn/. The **registration** N UNCOUNT of something such as a person's name or the details of an event is the recording of it in an official list. EG ...*a certificate of registration of death.*

registration number, registration numbers. N COUNT The **registration number** of a car or other road vehicle is the series of letters and numbers that are shown at the front and back of it.

registry /redʒɪstriˡ/, **registries.** A **registry** is a N COUNT place where official records are kept.

registry office, registry offices. A **registry** N COUNT **office** is a place where births, marriages, and deaths are officially recorded, and where people can get married without a religious ceremony.

regress /riˈgres/, **regresses, regressing, re-** V: OFT+*to* Formal **gressed.** When people or things **regress**, they return to a worse condition or way of life. EG *Since 1976 many rivers have regressed from being clean to being grossly polluted.* ◇ **regression** /ri^{1}grɛʃə^{0}n/. EG *...technological progress combined with moral and social regression.* ◇ N UNCOUNT: OFT+*to*

regressive /ri^{1}grɛsɪv/. Behaviour, activities, or processes that are **regressive** involve a return to a worse condition or way of life. EG *This fee has been criticized as a regressive tax.* ADJ QUALIT Formal

regret /rɪ^{1}grɛt/, **regrets, regretting, regretted.** **1** If you **regret** something that you have done, you wish that you had not done it. EG *I immediately regretted my decision... It made me regret that I had left home... Afterwards he regretted having spoken to them.* ▸ used as a noun. EG *Linda has no regrets at having become a banker.* V+O; ALSO V+REPORT OR -ING ▸ N UNCOUNT OR N COUNT

2 You can say that you **regret** something as a polite way of saying that you are sorry about it. EG *London Transport regrets any inconvenience caused by these delays... The Prime Minister regrets that he is unable to reconsider your case.* ▸ used as a noun. EG *We informed them with regret of our decision.* V+O; ALSO V+REPORT OR *to*-INF: NO CONT Formal ▸ N UNCOUNT

regretful /rɪ^{1}grɛtfʊl/. If you are **regretful**, you feel sorry about something. EG *Michael gave me a sad regretful smile.* ◇ **regretfully**. EG *He shook his head regretfully.* ADJ QUALIT ◇ ADV

regrettable /rɪ^{1}grɛtəbə^{0}l/. You describe something as **regrettable** when you think that it is unfortunate and that it should not happen. EG *...the regrettable manifestations of cruelty to children... His tiredness caused him to make a regrettable error.* ◇ **regrettably** /rɪ^{1}grɛtəbli^1/. EG *Regrettably few of them have gone to university... Regrettably, it is not an easy plant to grow in this country.* ADJ QUALIT ◇ SUBMOD OR ADV SEN

regroup /ri:gru:p/, **regroups, regrouping, regrouped.** When soldiers **regroup**, they form an organized group again, in order to continue fighting. EG *They regrouped and were ordered to open fire.* V

regular /rɛgjə^{4}lə/, **regulars. 1** You say that things are **regular** when they have equal amounts of time or space between them. EG *He could hear her deep, regular breathing... The doctor examined the baby at regular intervals... There were regular lines of holes between the windows.* ◇ **regularly**. EG *...regularly spaced cabbages.* ADJ QUALIT ◇ ADV

2 You also say that something is **regular** when it has a well-balanced appearance. EG *His face was sun-tanned, with regular features... It's easy to draw because it's such a regular shape.* ADJ QUALIT

3 Regular events or activities continue to happen according to a definite arrangement or plan, so that they happen, for example, at the same time each day or each week. EG *They give regular Sunday afternoon concerts... You need to take regular exercise.* ◇ **regularly**. EG *The members meet regularly in one another's homes.* ADJ QUALIT ◇ ADV

4 A **regular** event is also one that happens often. EG *...one of the regular bombings.* ◇ **regularly**. EG *Children are regularly abandoned.* ADJ QUALIT ◇ ADV

5 If you are a **regular** customer at a shop or a **regular** visitor to a place, you go there often. EG *...our regular customers... Gerald and I are regular churchgoers.* ▸ used as a noun. EG *He's one of the regulars at the village pub.* ADJ QUALIT: ATTRIB ▸ N COUNT

6 Your **regular** way of doing something is the way that you normally do it. Your **regular** time for doing something is the time when you normally do it. EG *It's past his regular bedtime... You can get in touch with a psychiatrist through your regular doctor.* ADJ CLASSIF: ATTRIB

7 A **regular** verb, noun, or adjective inflects in the same way as most verbs, nouns, or adjectives in the language. ADJ CLASSIF

regularity /rɛgjə^{4}lærɪ^{1}ti^1/. If something happens with **regularity**, it happens often. EG *The same exam questions cropped up with unfailing regularity.* N UNCOUNT

regulate /rɛgjə^{4}leɪt/, **regulates, regulating, regulated. 1** To **regulate** an activity or process means to control it, usually by means of rules. EG *Economic activity was regulated by the supply of money... ...rigid rules regulating all aspects of life.* ◇ **regulated**. EG *His life was too well regulated to be affected by affairs of the heart.* V+O ◇ ADJ QUALIT

2 If you **regulate** a machine or device, you adjust it to control the way it operates. EG *Do you know how to regulate the boiler?* V+O

regulation /rɛgjə^{4}leɪʃə^{0}n/, **regulations. 1 Regulations** are rules made by a government or other authority in order to control the way something is done or the way people behave. EG *There are specific regulations governing these types of machines... You can't do that. It's against the regulations.* ▸ used as an adjective. EG *He had the short regulation haircut of a policeman.* N COUNT: USU PLURAL ▸ ADJ CLASSIF: ATTRIB

2 Regulation is the controlling of an activity or process, usually by means of rules. EG *...strict regulation over toxic waste disposal.* N UNCOUNT

regurgitate /ri^{1}gɜ:dʒɪteɪt/, **regurgitates, regurgitating, regurgitated. 1** If you **regurgitate** food, you bring it back up from your stomach before it is digested. EG *The young feed on regurgitated food from the parent birds.* V+O Technical

2 If you **regurgitate** ideas or facts, you repeat them without understanding them properly. EG *The student is expected to regurgitate an answer to the teacher.* V+O Formal

rehabilitate /ri:h^{0}əbɪlɪteɪt/, **rehabilitates, rehabilitating, rehabilitated.** To **rehabilitate** someone who has been ill or in prison means to help them to live a normal life again. EG *He used exercise programmes to rehabilitate heart-attack victims.* ◇ **rehabilitation** /ri:h^{0}əbɪlɪteɪʃə^{0}n/. EG *...the rehabilitation of drug addicts.* V+O ◇ N UNCOUNT

rehearsal /rɪ^{1}hɜ:sə^{0}l/, **rehearsals.** A **rehearsal** of a play, dance, or piece of music is a practice, in which it is prepared for a performance. N COUNT OR N UNCOUNT

rehearse /rɪ^{1}hɜ:s/, **rehearses, rehearsing, rehearsed. 1** If people **rehearse** a play, dance, or piece of music, they practise it in order to prepare for a performance. EG *The actors began to rehearse a few scenes... Stay and hear the orchestra rehearse.* V+O OR V

2 If you **rehearse** something that you are going to say, you silently practise it by imagining that you are saying it. EG *She was secretly rehearsing various amusing ways of telling what had happened.* V+O Formal

rehouse /ri:hauz/, **rehouses, rehousing, rehoused.** If someone **is rehoused**, they are provided with a different house to live in, usually a better one than their previous one. EG *Young families are being rehoused in New Towns.* V+O: USU PASS

reign /reɪn/, **reigns, reigning, reigned. 1** You can say that something **reigns** when it is the strongest or most noticeable feature of a situation or period of time. EG *Peace has reigned in Europe... ...the sense of comfort which reigned over the town.* ▸ used as a noun. EG *...a reign of terror... The reign of love has begun.* V: USU+A Literary ▸ N SING+*of*

2 When a king or queen **reigns**, he or she rules a country. EG *The emperor Chia Ching reigned from 1522 to 1566... ...the reigning monarch.* V: USU+A

3 The **reign** of a king or queen is the period during which he or she rules. EG *...George III's long reign.* N COUNT+POSS

reimburse /ri:ɪmbɜ:s/, **reimburses, reimbursing, reimbursed.** If you **reimburse** someone for something, you pay them back the money that they have spent or lost. EG *I promised to reimburse her for the damage to her car.* V+O: OFT+*for*, OR V+O+O Formal

rein /reɪn/, **reins. 1 Reins** are the thin leather straps attached to a horse's bridle, which you hold and use for controlling the horse when you are N PLURAL

What two words on these pages are pronounced in the same way?

riding it or when it is pulling a vehicle. EG *He pulled at the reins.*

2 If you **give a free rein to** someone, you give them a lot of freedom to do what they want. If you **keep a tight rein on** them, you control them firmly. EG *He has given a free rein to the Security Service in their investigations.* PHRASE

reincarnate /riːɪŋ'kɑːneɪt/, **reincarnates, reincarnating, reincarnated.** If people believe that they will be **reincarnated** when they die, they believe that their spirit will be born again and will live in the body of another person or animal. V+O : USU PASS

reincarnation /riːɪŋkɑːneɪʃə⁰n/, **reincarnations. 1 Reincarnation** is supposed to happen when someone is born again after death and lives again in the body of another creature. EG *I believe in reincarnation.* N UNCOUNT

2 A **reincarnation** is a person or animal in whose body a dead person is believed to have been born again. EG *They all regarded us as reincarnations of their ancestors.* N COUNT

reindeer /reɪndɪə/. A **reindeer** is a deer with large antlers that lives in northern areas of Europe, Asia, and America. The plural form is also **reindeer**. N COUNT

reinforce /riːɪnfɔːs/, **reinforces, reinforcing, reinforced. 1** If something **reinforces** a feeling, situation, or process, it strengthens it. EG *This sort of experience reinforces their feelings of worthlessness... They hope to reinforce their domination in these countries.* V+O

2 If something **reinforces** an idea or point of view, it provides more evidence or support for it. EG *This report reinforces practically everything that has been said.* V+O

3 To **reinforce** an object means to make it stronger or harder. EG *I had not thought of reinforcing the handles with leather.* ◊ **reinforced**. *...reinforced helmets.* V+O : OFT+*with* ◊ ADJ CLASSIF

reinforcement /riːɪnfɔːsmə²nt/, **reinforcements. 1 Reinforcements** are soldiers who are sent to join an army in order to make it stronger. EG *News reached them of the safe arrival of reinforcements.* N PLURAL

2 Reinforcement is **2.1** the strengthening of something. EG *...the reinforcement of existing systems.* N UNCOUNT

2.2 something that is added to a material or an object in order to make it harder or stronger. EG *...barges with fibreglass reinforcement.* N UNCOUNT OR N COUNT

reinstate /riːɪnsteɪt/, **reinstates, reinstating, reinstated. 1** If you **reinstate** someone, you give them back a job or position which had been taken from them. EG *He was four times sacked and four times reinstated.* V+O

2 To **reinstate** something means to make it exist again. EG *...threats to reinstate this tax... The trip reinstated my faith in myself.* V+O

reiterate /riːɪtəreɪt/, **reiterates, reiterating, reiterated.** If you **reiterate** something, you say it again. EG *He reiterated this advice several more times during the meeting.* V-SPEECH Formal

reject, rejects, rejecting, rejected; pronounced /rɪ'dʒɛkt/ when it is a verb and /riːdʒɛkt/ when it is a noun.

1 If you **reject** something such as a proposal or request, you do not accept it or you do not agree to it. EG *The Labour Party rejected offers to discuss the reform of the House of Lords... The amendment was rejected by 207 votes to 143.* ◊ **rejection** /riːdʒɛkʃə⁰n/, **rejections**. EG *...his rejection of repeated requests for military action.* V+O ◊ N UNCOUNT OR N COUNT

2 If you **reject** a belief or a political system, you decide that you do not believe in it and do not want to live by its rules. EG *It was hard for me to reject my family's religious beliefs... Some people reject the idea of a mixed economy.* ◊ **rejection**. EG *There had been a widespread rejection of many of the traditional processes of political participation.* V+O ◊ N UNCOUNT

3 If an employer **rejects** a person who has applied for a job, he or she does not offer that person the job. EG *Many candidates were rejected.* ◊ **rejection**. EG *After a week he received his rejection letter.* V+O ◊ N UNCOUNT OR N COUNT

4 If a machine **rejects** a coin that you put in it, the coin comes out and the machine does not work. EG *The phone-box often jammed, or rejected perfectly good coins.* V+O

5 A **reject** is a product that has not been accepted for use, because something is wrong with it. EG *We got the rejects half price.* N COUNT

rejoice /rɪ'dʒɔɪs/, **rejoices, rejoicing, rejoiced.** If you **rejoice**, you are very pleased about something. EG *All his friends gathered to rejoice in his freedom... I rejoice to hear it.* V : OFT+*in* OR *to*-INF Literary

rejuvenate /ri'dʒuːvɪneɪt/, **rejuvenates, rejuvenating, rejuvenated. 1** If something **rejuvenates** you, it makes you feel or look young again. EG *I think we were rejuvenated by the experience.* ◊ **rejuvenating**. EG *...rejuvenating cosmetics.* V+O ◊ ADJ QUALIT

2 If you **rejuvenate** an organization or system, you make it more lively and more efficient, for example by introducing new ideas. EG *He resolved to rejuvenate the party.* V+O

relaid /riːleɪd/ is a past tense and past participle of **relay.**

relapse, relapses, relapsing, relapsed; pronounced /rɪ'læps/ when it is a verb and either /rɪlæps/ or /riːlæps/ when it is a noun.

1 You say that someone **relapses** into an undesirable way of behaving when they start to behave that way again. EG *She relapsed into depression... Cameron relapsed into silence again.* ▸ used as a noun. EG *...her relapses into alcoholism.* V : USU+*into* ▸ N COUNT : OFT+*into*

2 If a sick person has a **relapse**, their health suddenly gets worse after it had been improving. N COUNT

relate /rɪ'leɪt/, **relates, relating, related. 1** If you say that one thing **relates** to another or if you **relate** one thing to another, you are saying that there is a connection between the two things. EG *Let us examine the way that the words in a sentence relate to each other... They were very religious and related everything to a dependence on God.* ◊ **related**. EG *...two important and closely related questions.* V-ERG OR V-ERG+*to* : RECIP ◊ ADJ CLASSIF

2 If you say that something **relates** to a particular subject, you mean that it concerns that subject. EG *I want to ask you a question that relates to electricity... ...discussion on matters relating to home-making in all its aspects.* V+*to*

3 If you can **relate** to someone, you can understand how they feel or behave and so are able to communicate with them or deal with them easily. EG *Children need to learn to relate to other children.* V OR V+*to* : RECIP

4 If you **relate** a story, you tell it. EG *Davis related the experience of three Cuban girls.* V+O Literary

related /rɪ'leɪtɪ²d/. **1** People who are **related** belong to the same family. EG *...four people closely related to each other.* ADJ CLASSIF : OFT+*to*

2 If you say that different types of animal or different languages are **related**, you mean that they have developed from the same type of animal or language. EG *Termites are closely related to cockroaches... French and Spanish are related languages.* ADJ CLASSIF : OFT+*to*

relation /rɪ'leɪʃə⁰n/, **relations. 1** You use **in relation to 1.1** when you are talking about the state or size of something compared to other things. EG *Wages are very low in relation to the cost of living.* PREP

1.2 when you are talking about where something is compared to other things. EG *Using this portable communications system, everybody knows exactly where they are in relation to everybody else.*

2 If you talk about the **relation** of one thing to another, you are talking about the connection or similarity between them. EG *She argued that literature has no relation to reality.* N UNCOUNT : USU+*of/to*

3 Your **relations** are the members of your family. EG *I was a distant relation of her husband.* N COUNT: OFT+POSS

4 **Relations** between people or groups are contacts between them and the way in which they behave towards each other. EG *This fear is causing East-West relations to deteriorate... The unions should have close relations with management.* N PLURAL: USU+SUPP

relationship /rɪˈleɪʃəⁿʃɪp/, **relationships. 1** The **relationship** between two people or groups is the way in which they feel and behave towards each other. EG *Pakistan's relationship with India has changed dramatically.* N COUNT: OFT +*between/with*

2 A **relationship** is also a close friendship between two people, especially one involving romantic or sexual feelings. EG *When the relationship ended two months ago he said he wanted to die... ...a sexual relationship.* N COUNT: OFT +*between/with*

3 The **relationship** between two things is the way in which they are connected. EG *What is the relationship between language and thought?* N COUNT

relative /rɛlətɪv/, **relatives. 1** You use **relative** 1.1 to say that something is true to a certain degree or extent, especially when compared with other things of the same kind. EG *The head of the department is a relative newcomer... He chose to return to the relative peace of his childhood village.* **1.2** when you are comparing the size or quality of two things. EG *There was a discussion on the relative naval strengths of the two countries.* ADJ CLASSIF: ATTRIB

2 **Relative to** something means with reference to it or in comparison with it. EG *There is a shortage of labour relative to the demand for it.* PREP Formal

3 Your **relatives** are the members of your family. EG *His wife had gone to visit some of her relatives for a few days.* N COUNT: USU+POSS

4 If you say that something is **relative**, you mean that it needs to be considered and judged in relation to other things. EG *All human values are relative.* ADJ CLASSIF Formal

relative clause, relative clauses. In grammar, a **relative clause** is a subordinate clause that is introduced by a relative conjunction or a relative pronoun, such as 'where' or 'who'. N COUNT

relatively /rɛlətɪvli¹/ means to a fairly large extent or degree. EG *It was relatively easy to find her house... A relatively small number of people disagreed.* SUBMOD

relative pronoun, relative pronouns. In grammar, a **relative pronoun** is a pronoun such as 'who' that is used to introduce a relative clause. N COUNT

relax /rɪˈlæks/, **relaxes, relaxing, relaxed. 1** If you **relax** or if something **relaxes** you, you feel more calm and less worried or tense. EG *He saw that nothing was wrong, and relaxed... Just lie back and relax... Running relaxes you.* V-ERG

2 When a part of your body **relaxes**, it becomes less stiff or firm. EG *She watched the muscles of his arms hardening and relaxing.* V-ERG

3 If you **relax** your grip or hold on something, you hold it less tightly than before. V-ERG

4 If you **relax** a rule or **relax** your control over something, you make it less strict. EG *He had no intention of relaxing his policies.* V+O

relaxation /riːlækseɪʃəⁿn/. **1 Relaxation** refers to ways of spending time that are pleasant and restful. EG *It is so necessary for the mother to have some rest and relaxation.* N UNCOUNT

2 If there is **relaxation** of a rule or control, it is made less strict. EG *The authorities encouraged a general relaxation in child discipline.* N UNCOUNT: OFT+*of/in*

relaxed /rɪˈlækst/. If you are **relaxed**, you are calm and not worried or tense. EG *It was a relaxed and informal discussion... The children benefit from the relaxed atmosphere.* ADJ QUALIT

relaxing /rɪˈlæksɪŋ/. Something that is **relaxing** is pleasant and helps you to relax. EG *It is a delightful, relaxing place for a holiday.* ADJ QUALIT

relay, relays, relaying, relayed, relaid; pronounced /riːleɪ/ in paragraphs 1, 2, and 3, /riˈleɪ/ in paragraph 4, and /riːleɪ/ in paragraph 5. The past tense and past participle of the verb are **relayed** in paragraphs 3 and 4, and **relaid** in paragraph 5.

1 A **relay** or a **relay race** is a race between two or more teams, for example teams of runners or swimmers. Each member of the team runs or swims one section of the race. N COUNT ● If people do something **in relays**, they do it in small groups at different times. EG *The children at our school have to be fed in two relays.* ● PHRASE

2 A **relay** is a piece of equipment that receives television or radio signals from one place and sends them on to another place. EG *...relay stations in space.* N COUNT

3 To **relay** television or radio signals means to send them or broadcast them. EG *The Sunday Concert will be relayed live on Radio Three.* V+O

4 If you **relay** something that has been said to you, you repeat it to another person. EG *McKenzie relayed the question to me.* V+O: OFT+*to*

5 If you **relay** something such as a carpet or a road surface, you lay it again. EG *She wanted to relay the carpet in her new home.* V+O

release /rɪˈliːs/, **releases, releasing, released. 1** If you **release** a person or animal that has been in captivity, you set them free. EG *They had just been released from prison.* ▸ used as a noun. EG *Nearly a year after his release he was still unable to sleep properly.* V+O: OFT+*from* ▸ N UNCOUNT

2 If something **releases** you from an unpleasant situation or feeling, it frees you from it. EG *This releases them from personal responsibility... This failure released him from any obligation to take further exams.* ▸ used as a noun. EG *...a feeling of release... ...a release from tension.* V+O: OFT+*from* Formal ▸ N UNCOUNT OR N SING

3 If someone in authority **releases** something, they make it available or issue it. EG *Their aim was to release money for the schools... ...in a statement released at 8 a.m.* V+O Formal

4 A press **release** or a publicity **release is** an official written statement that is given to reporters. N COUNT+SUPP

5 If you **release** something, you stop holding it. EG *He quickly released her hand.* V+O Formal

6 If you **release** a device, you move it so that it stops holding something. EG *I ran to the door and released the catch.* V+O

7 If something such as gas or water **is released**, it is let out of an enclosed space. EG *...releasing radioactivity into the environment.* ▸ used as a noun. EG *...the controlled release of water from reservoirs.* V+O ▸ N UNCOUNT: USU+SUPP

8 When a new film, record, or video **is released**, people can see it or buy it. V+O

9 A new **release** is a new record or video that has just become available for people to buy. N COUNT

10 If a film is **on release**, it is available for showing in public cinemas. PHRASE

relegate /rɛlɪ²geɪt/, **relegates, relegating, relegated.** If you **relegate** someone or something, you give them a less important position or status. EG *These old bits of furniture were relegated to the attics... The management had relegated Mr Pelker to the role of part-time consultant.* V+O: USU+A

relent /rɪˈlɛnt/, **relents, relenting, relented.** If you **relent**, you allow someone to do something that you did not allow them to do before. EG *Sometimes our parents would relent and permit us to meet... He relented somewhat and smiled at her.* V

relentless /rɪˈlɛntlɪ²s/. **1** Something that is **relentless** never stops or never becomes less intense. EG *...the relentless beating of the sun on the roofs... ...the relentless population increase... You get tired of relentless cynicism.* ◇ **relentlessly.** EG *The chase relentlessly continues.* ADJ CLASSIF ◇ ADV Literary

2 Someone who is **relentless** is determined to do ADJ QUALIT

What grammatical words are explained on these pages?

something and refuses to give up. ◇ **relentlessly**. EG ...*a relentlessly ambitious politician.* ◇ ADV Literary

relevant /rɛləvənt/. 1 If something is **relevant**, it is connected with what is being talked or written about. EG ...*highly relevant information... This is not strictly relevant to what I'll be saying.* ADJ QUALIT: OFT+*to*
◇ **relevance** /rɛləvəns/. EG *She did not understand the relevance of his remarks.* ◇ N UNCOUNT: OFT+*to*
2 Something that is **relevant** to people is important to them. EG *They accept that what you are doing is relevant to their problems.* ADJ QUALIT: OFT+*to* ◇ **relevance**. EG *He spoke about the religion of Islam and its relevance to people there.* ◇ N UNCOUNT: OFT+*to*
3 The **relevant** thing of a particular kind is the one that is appropriate. EG *They are made to conform with the relevant British Standards... Members are drawn from people living in the relevant area.* ADJ CLASSIF: ATTRIB

reliable /rɪˈlaɪəbəˀl/. 1 People or things that are **reliable** can be trusted to work well or to behave in the way that you want them to. EG *She is a charming and reliable person... The diesel engine is long-lasting and extremely reliable.* ADJ QUALIT ◇ **reliably**. EG *They worked reliably under battle conditions.* ◇ ADV
◇ **reliability** /rɪˈlaɪəbɪlɪˈtiˈ/. EG *These machines have always been noted for reliability.* ◇ N UNCOUNT
2 Information that is **reliable** is very likely to be correct. EG *The telegram was based on information from a reliable source.* ADJ QUALIT ◇ **reliably**. EG *We are reliably informed that her new record will be released in the autumn.* ◇ ADV

reliant /rɪˈlaɪənt/. Someone who is **reliant** on something needs it and often cannot live or work without it. EG *They are reliant on government funds... We have become reliant on mechanical equipment.* ADJ PRED+*on/upon* ◇ **reliance** /rɪˈlaɪəns/. EG ...*the student's reliance on the teacher... ...complete reliance on drugs.* ◇ N UNCOUNT: USU+*on/upon*

relic /rɛlɪk/, **relics.** 1 When very old things or customs are still used or practised, you can refer to them as **relics** of an earlier time. EG *These ideas are relics of Victorian discipline.* N COUNT: USU+SUPP
2 A **relic** is also something which was made or used a long time ago but is no longer used. EG *We visited a museum with relics of great explorers.* N COUNT: USU+SUPP
3 In a church, a **relic** is the body of a saint or something else associated with a saint, which some people regard as holy. N COUNT

relief /rɪˈliːf/. 1 If you feel **relief**, you feel glad because something unpleasant has not happened or is no longer happening. EG *I breathed a sigh of relief... To my relief, he found the suggestion acceptable.* N UNCOUNT OR N SING
2 **Relief** is also money, food, or clothing that is provided for people who are very poor or hungry. EG *She outlined what was being done to provide relief... ...Christmas relief funds.* N UNCOUNT

relieve /rɪˈliːv/, **relieves, relieving, relieved. 1** If something **relieves** an unpleasant feeling, it makes it less unpleasant. EG *Anxiety may be relieved by talking to a friend... The passengers in the plane swallow to relieve the pressure on their eardrums.* V+O
2 If someone or something **relieves** you of an unpleasant feeling or difficulty, they cause you to no longer have it. EG *The news relieved him of some of his embarrassment.* V+O+*of*

relieved /rɪˈliːvd/. If you are **relieved**, you feel glad because something unpleasant has not happened or is no longer happening. EG *I am relieved to hear that this isn't true... He felt enormously relieved that they had taken the matter so calmly.* ADJ QUALIT: USU PRED

religion /rɪˈlɪdʒən/, **religions. 1 Religion** is the belief in a god or gods and the activities that are connected with this belief, such as prayer or worship in a church or temple. EG *Politics and religion were daily topics of conversation... The school placed strong emphasis on religion.* N UNCOUNT
2 A **religion** is a particular system of belief in a god or gods and the activities that are connected with this system. EG ...*the Christian religion... What is your religion?* N COUNT

religious /rɪˈlɪdʒəs/. 1 You use **religious** to describe things connected with religion or with one particular religion. EG *All religious activities were suppressed... ...people who have no religious faith.* ADJ CLASSIF: ATTRIB
2 Someone who is **religious** has a strong belief in a god or gods. EG *Our parents were very religious.* ADJ QUALIT

religiously /rɪˈlɪdʒəsliˈ/. If you do something **religiously**, you do it very regularly because you regard it as a duty. EG *The ornaments were all religiously dusted by Gertrude.* ADV

relinquish /rɪˈlɪŋkwɪʃ/, **relinquishes, relinquishing, relinquished.** If you **relinquish** something such as authority or responsibility, you give it up. EG *She relinquished the editorship of the newspaper.* V+O Formal

relish /rɛlɪʃ/, **relishes, relishing, relished. 1** If you **relish** something, you get a lot of enjoyment from it. EG *He relishes the challenge of competition.* V+O
▸ used as a noun. EG *In his book he exposed with relish all the evils of our present day.* ▸ N UNCOUNT
2 If you **relish** the idea, thought, or prospect of something, you are looking forward to it very much. EG ...*rebels who relish the prospect of conflict and violence... She didn't relish the idea of going on her own.* V+O
3 **Relish** is a sauce or a pickle that you add to food in order to give it more flavour. N MASS

relive /riːlɪv/, **relives, reliving, relived.** If you **relive** something that has happened to you in the past, you remember it and imagine that you are experiencing it again. EG *You spend too much time reliving old joys.* V+O

relocate /riːləʊkeɪt/, **relocates, relocating, relocated.** If people or businesses **relocate** or **are relocated**, they move to a different place. EG *Semi-skilled workers find themselves compelled to relocate... They relocated me in another building.* V-ERG
◇ **relocation** /riːləʊkeɪʃəˀn/. EG *Priority must be given to the relocation of industry.* ◇ N UNCOUNT

reluctant /rɪˈlʌktənt/. If you are **reluctant** to do something, you are unwilling to do it. EG *He is reluctant to be photographed... The reluctant bridegroom smiled for the first time.* ADJ QUALIT: OFT+*to*-INF ◇ **reluctantly**. EG *A wage increase of 21% was reluctantly conceded.* ◇ ADV
◇ **reluctance** /rɪˈlʌktəns/. EG *They showed reluctance to support these measures... They released her with reluctance.* ◇ N UNCOUNT

rely /rɪˈlaɪ/, **relies, relying, relied. 1** If you **rely** on someone or something, you need them and depend on them in order to live or work properly. EG *He's relying on me completely... She is forced to rely on social security money... Hong Kong's prosperity relies heavily on foreign businesses.* V+*on/upon*
2 If you can **rely** on someone to work well or to behave as you want them to, you can trust them to do this. EG *One could always rely on him to be polite and do the right thing... They cannot be relied upon to offer much support.* V+*on/upon*

remain /rɪˈmeɪn/, **remains, remaining, remained. 1** To **remain** in a particular state or condition means to stay in that state or condition and not change. EG *Oliver remained silent... He remained standing... The results of these experiments remain a secret.* V+C
2 If you **remain** in a place, you stay there and do not move away. EG *I was allowed to remain at home... Otto was having difficulty in remaining in his seat.* V: USU+A
3 You can say that something **remains** when it still exists. EG *Even today remnants of this practice remain... He was cut off from what remained of his family... The fact remains that they mean to destroy us.* V ◇ **remaining**. EG ...*the demise of her last remaining relatives.* ◇ ADJ CLASSIF: ATTRIB
4 If something **remains** to be done, it has not yet been done and still needs to be done. EG *One hazard remained to be overcome.* V+*to*-INF

5 If you say that something **remains to be seen**, you mean that nobody is certain what will happen. EG *It remains to be seen what the long term effects will be.* PHRASE

6 The **remains** of something are the parts of it that are left after most of it has been taken away or destroyed. EG *I searched through the bombed remains of the house... The remains of the meat sat on the kitchen table.* N PLURAL: USU+*of*

7 The **remains** of a person or animal are the parts of their body that are left after they have died, sometimes when they have been dead for a long time. EG *They discovered the remains of a huge dinosaur.* N PLURAL +POSS

8 **Remains** are things that have been found from an earlier period of history, usually buried in the ground, for example parts of buildings and pieces of pottery. EG *...Roman remains.* N PLURAL

remainder /rɪˈmeɪndə/. The **remainder** of something is the part of it that remains after the other parts have gone or been dealt with. EG *She went to Brighton where she lived for the remainder of her life... I will pay you a hundred pounds deposit and the remainder on delivery.* N SING: *the*+N

remake, remakes, remaking, remade /riːmeɪd/. **Remake** is pronounced /riːmeɪk/ when it is a verb, and /riːmeɪk/ when it is a noun.

1 If you **remake** something, you make it again, especially in a way that is better than before. EG *Ask what the price is for remaking old mattresses.* V+O

2 A **remake** is a film that has the same story, and often the same title, as a film that was made earlier. EG *...the 1934 remake of 'Young Men in Spats'.* N COUNT

remand /rɪˈmɑːnd/, **remands, remanding, remanded.** 1 If a judge **remands** a person who is accused of a crime, the trial does not take place immediately, and the person is ordered to come back to court at a later date. EG *He was remanded for trial at the central criminal court.* V+O: OFT PASS

2 If someone accused of a crime is **on remand**, they have appeared in court and are waiting for their trial to begin. PHRASE

remark /rɪˈmɑːk/, **remarks, remarking, remarked.** 1 If you **remark** that something is the case, you say that it is the case. EG *'Your father was a good friend to me,' he remarked... Mary's friends remarked that she could hate as passionately as she could love... His friends remarked on his failure to arrive.* V+QUOTE OR REPORT: ONLY *that*; ALSO V+*on*

2 A **remark** is something that you say, often in a casual way. EG *At school some of the children used to make unkind remarks about my clothes... He closed the discussion with the remark that 'the economy shows signs of improving'.* N COUNT: OFT+REPORT

remarkable /rɪˈmɑːkəbəˀl/. When you are very impressed by something that someone does, you can say that they are **remarkable** or that what they do is **remarkable**. EG *She was a remarkable woman... He prepared the dinner with remarkable speed and efficiency.* ◊ **remarkably**. EG *He has recovered from the accident remarkably well.* ADJ QUALIT ◊ SUBMOD OR ADV SEN

remedial /rɪˈmiːdɪəl/. **Remedial** activities 1 are intended to improve someone's health when they are ill. EG *...remedial exercises for handicapped children.* 2 are intended to improve someone's ability to read, write, or do maths. EG *...a remedial English course.* ADJ CLASSIF: ATTRIB Formal

remedy /rɛmɪˈdiˈ/, **remedies, remedying, remedied.** 1 A **remedy** is 1.1 a successful way of dealing with a problem. EG *...a drastic remedy for lawlessness and disorder.* N COUNT: OFT+*for* 1.2 something that is intended to cure you when you are ill or in pain. EG *...a remedy for skin and ear trouble... ...home-made remedies can often lessen the pain.* N COUNT

2 If you **remedy** something that is wrong or harmful, you correct it or improve it. EG *Technicians laboriously tried to find and remedy faults... Can we remedy this at a later stage?* V+O

remember /rɪˈmɛmbə/, **remembers, remembering, remembered.** 1 If you **remember** people or events from the past, your mind still has an impression of them and you are able to think about them. EG *He remembered the man well... I remember him falling down the steps... I remembered that the shop was on the way to Muswell Hill... I fell silent, remembering what I had heard.* V+O OR V: OFT +-ING; ALSO V+REPORT

2 If you can **remember** something, you are able to bring it back into your mind by making an effort to do so. EG *I'm trying to remember the things I have to do... There was something else, but she could not remember what it was.* V+O OR V: OFT+-ING; ALSO V+REPORT

3 If you **remember** to do something, you do it when you intend to. EG *Remember to go to the bank.* V: USU+*to*-INF

4 You say **remember** when you are reminding someone of something. EG *Remember that women did not gain the vote until 1918.* V OR V+REPORT: ONLY *that*

5 If you ask someone to **remember** you to a person who you have not seen for a long time, you are asking them to pass your greetings to that person. EG *Remember me to your Grandma.* V+O+*to*: NO CONT

remembrance /rɪˈmɛmbrəns/. If you do something in **remembrance** of a dead person, you do it as a way of showing that you remember them and respect them. EG *We stood in silence for two minutes in remembrance of the dead.* N UNCOUNT Formal

remind /rɪˈmaɪnd/, **reminds, reminding, reminded.** 1 If someone **reminds** you of a fact or event that you already know about, they deliberately say something which makes you think about it. EG *She had to remind him that he had a wife... Remind me to speak to you about Davis... Miss Lemon reminded him of two appointments.* V+O +*of/about*, REPORT, OR *to*-INF

2 If you say that someone or something **reminds** you of another person or thing, you mean that they are similar to the other person or thing and that they make you think about them. EG *Your son reminds me of you at his age... What does that remind you of?* V+O+*of*

reminder /rɪˈmaɪndə/, **reminders.** 1 You say that one thing is a **reminder** of another when the first thing makes you think about the second thing. EG *Seeing her again was a painful reminder of how different things had been five years ago.* N COUNT: USU+SUPP

2 A **reminder** is also a letter or note that is sent to tell you that you have not done something such as pay a bill or return library books. EG *I've had another reminder from the library.* N COUNT

reminisce /rɛmɪnɪs/, **reminisces, reminiscing, reminisced.** If you **reminisce** about something from your past, you write or talk about it, often with pleasure. EG *He reminisced about the 'old days' and how times had changed.* V: OFT+*about* Formal

reminiscence /rɛmɪnɪsəns/, **reminiscences.** Someone's **reminiscences** are things that they remember from the past, and which they talk or write about. EG *She continued with fascinating reminiscences of their marriage.* N COUNT: USU PLURAL

reminiscent /rɛmɪnɪsənt/. If you say that something is **reminiscent** of something else, you mean that it reminds you of it. EG *The atmosphere was reminiscent of spy movies... There was a sweet smell, vaguely reminiscent of coffee.* ADJ PRED+*of* Formal

remission /rɪˈmɪʃəˀn/. If someone in prison gets **remission**, their prison sentence is reduced, usually because they have behaved well. EG *I got four months' remission for good conduct.* N UNCOUNT

remnant /rɛmnənt/, **remnants.** A **remnant** of something is a small part of it that is left over when the main part has disappeared or been destroyed. EG *Even today remnants of this practice remain.* N COUNT: USU+*of*

What is the difference between 'remind' and 'remember'?

remorse /rɪˈmɔːs/ is a strong feeling of guilt about something that you have done. EG *I had been filled with remorse over hurting her.* — N UNCOUNT Formal

remote /rɪˈməʊt/, **remoter, remotest. 1 Remote** areas are far away from places where people live, and are therefore difficult to get to. EG *Television has begun to penetrate even the remote areas of Java... Many children living in remote places cannot get to the playgroup.* — ADJ QUALIT

2 If something happened in the **remote** past, it happened a very long time ago. EG *...research into the remote past.* — ADJ QUALIT

3 If something is **remote** from a particular subject or area of experience, it is not relevant to it because it is very different. EG *Much new knowledge is remote from the immediate interests of the ordinary person... His stories are too remote from everyday life.* — ADJ QUALIT : USU PRED+*from*

4 If you describe someone as **remote**, you mean that they behave as if they do not want to be friendly or closely involved with other people. EG *She was a silent girl, cool and remote... The union leaders have to beware of getting too remote from their members.* ◊ **remoteness**. EG *He criticised the remoteness of public authorities.* — ADJ QUALIT; ◊ N UNCOUNT

5 If the possibility of something happening is **remote**, it is very unlikely that it will happen. EG *Winning is only a remote possibility at the moment.* — ADJ QUALIT

remote control is a system of controlling a machine or a vehicle from a distance by using radio or electronic signals. EG *The missile is guided by remote control.* — N UNCOUNT

remotely /rɪˈməʊtli¹/. **1** You use **remotely** with a negative statement to emphasize the statement. EG *Agreement did not seem remotely possible at the time... I've never seen anything remotely like it.* — SUBMOD : USU WITH BROAD NEG

2 If someone or something is **remotely** placed or situated, they are a long way from other people or places. EG *Living as remotely situated as she did, it was very difficult to get to see her.* — ADV

removal /rɪˈmuːvəᵊl/. **1** The **removal** of something is the act of removing it. EG *He consented to the removal of the flags... ...a stain removal kit... ...the removal of the threat of intervention.* — N UNCOUNT : USU+SUPP

2 A **removal** company transports furniture from one building to another, for example when people move house. EG *...removal men.* — N MOD

remove /rɪˈmuːv/, **removes, removing, removed. 1** If you **remove** something from a place, you take it away. EG *The servants came in to remove the cups... He removed his hand from the man's collar.* — V+O : OFT+*from*

2 If you **remove** clothing, you take it off. EG *Will you remove your shoes before you go in, please?* — V+O

3 If you **remove** a stain from something, you treat it with a chemical or wash it and make the stain disappear. EG *This mixture can remove stains from metal and china.* — V+O : OFT+*from*

4 If you **are removed** from something such as a committee, you are not allowed to continue as a member of it. EG *They made an attempt to remove her from the General Council.* — V+O : OFT+*from*

5 If you **remove** an undesirable situation or attitude, you get rid of it. EG *The situation can be helped by removing those inequalities... Instant publication would have removed suspicion.* — V+O

removed /rɪˈmuːvd/. If you say that an idea or situation is far **removed** from something, you mean that it is very different from it. EG *His ideas on foreign policy were far removed from those of the Government.* — ADJ PRED +*from*

rename /riːˈneɪm/, **renames, renaming, renamed.** If you **rename** something, you give it a new name instead of the name it had before. EG *Mr Haq has taken over the Carousel Cafe and renamed it The Pearl of India.* — V+O : OFT+C

render /rɛndə/, **renders, rendering, rendered. 1** You can use **render** to say that someone or something is changed into a particular state. For example, if you **render** something harmless, you do something to it that makes it harmless. EG *...equipment which has been rendered obsolete... It rendered him unconscious for a considerable period... Frank was rendered speechless by her reply.* — V+O+C Formal

2 If you **render** someone help or assistance, you help them. EG *Dr Lister Smith rendered vital first aid to Commander Bond.* — V+O, V+O+O, OR V+O+*to* Formal

rendering /rɛndəᵊrɪŋ/, **renderings.** A **rendering** of a play, poem, or piece of music is a performance of it. EG *They began with a loud rendering of the hymn 'Onward Christian Soldiers'.* — N COUNT : USU+*of* Formal

rendezvous /rɒndeɪvuː/. **Rendezvous** is both the singular and the plural form. It is pronounced /rɒndeɪvuːz/ when it is the plural.

A **rendezvous** is **1** a meeting, often a secret one, that you have arranged with someone for a particular time and place. EG *We made a dawn rendezvous.* **2** a place where you have arranged to meet someone, often secretly. EG *I met him at a secret rendezvous outside the city.* — N COUNT

rendition /rɛndɪʃəᵊn/, **renditions.** A **rendition** of a play, poem, or piece of music is a performance of it. EG *...a rendition of 'The Four Seasons'.* — N COUNT : USU+*of* Formal

renegade /rɛnɪgeɪd/, **renegades.** A **renegade** is a person who abandons the religious, political, or philosophical beliefs that he or she used to have, and accepts opposing or different beliefs. EG *He was a traitor and renegade... Renegade supporters of the deposed King are still raiding villages.* — N COUNT Formal

renew /rɪˈnjuː/, **renews, renewing, renewed. 1** If you **renew** an activity, you begin it again. EG *He renewed his threat to resign... She at once renewed her attack on Judy.* ◊ **renewed**. EG *We must prepare for renewed efforts to recruit more members.* — V+O; ◊ ADJ CLASSIF : ATTRIB

2 If you **renew** a relationship with someone, you start it again after you have not seen them for some time. EG *I hoped that we might renew our friendship.* — V+O : OFT+*with*

3 When you **renew** something such as a licence or a contract, you extend the period of time for which it is valid. EG *The studio did not renew his contract.* — V+O

4 You can say that something **is renewed** when it grows again or is replaced after it has been destroyed or lost. ◊ **renewed**. EG *He looked at me with renewed interest.* — V+O : USU PASS; ◊ ADJ CLASSIF : ATTRIB

renewal /rɪˈnjuːəl/, **renewals. 1** If there is a **renewal** of an activity or situation, it starts again. EG *Renewal of hostility with neighbouring countries seemed likely... ...a renewal of civil disorder in U.S. cities.* — N UNCOUNT : USU+*of*

2 The **renewal** of a document such as a licence or a contract is an official extension of the time for which it remains valid. EG *Some licences need yearly renewal... ...visa renewals.* — N UNCOUNT OR N COUNT

renounce /rɪˈnaʊns/, **renounces, renouncing, renounced. 1** If you **renounce** a belief or a way of behaving, you decide to stop believing in it or behaving in that way. EG *...their determination to renounce the materialism of society... We have renounced the use of force to settle our disputes.* — V+O Formal

2 If you **renounce** an official post, rank, or title, you formally give it up. EG *The Earl wanted to renounce his peerage.* — V+O Formal

renovate /rɛnəveɪt/, **renovates, renovating, renovated.** If someone **renovates** an old building or a machine, they repair and improve it and get it back into good condition. EG *The house had been renovated three years earlier.* ◊ **renovation** /rɛnəveɪʃəᵊn/, **renovations**. EG *...the renovation of old buildings.* — V+O; ◊ N UNCOUNT OR N COUNT

renown /rɪˈnaʊn/. A person of **renown** is well known, usually for something good. EG *His renown as a soldier spread throughout the country.* — N UNCOUNT Literary

renowned /rɪˈnaʊnd/. A person who is **renowned** for something, usually something good, is well — ADJ QUALIT : OFT+*for* known because of it. EG *The locals are renowned for their hospitality.*

rent /rɛnt/, **rents, renting, rented. 1** If you **rent** something, you pay its owner a sum of money every week or every month in order to be able to have it and use it yourself. EG *They rented a villa not far from Rome... He rented a colour TV soon after moving in.* ◊ **rented**. EG *...a rented flat.* — V+O; ◊ ADJ CLASSIF

2 Rent is the amount of money that you pay regularly to rent a house, flat, or piece of land. EG *He made enough money to pay the monthly rent punctually.* — N SING OR N UNCOUNT

rent out. If you **rent out** something such as a room or a car, you allow it to be used in return for payment. EG *They had to rent out the upstairs room for years.* — PHRASAL VB: V+O+ADV

rental /rɛntᵊl/, **rentals. 1** You use **rental** to describe things that are connected with the renting out of goods and services. EG *...a computer rental service.* — ADJ CLASSIF: ATTRIB

2 The **rental** is the amount of money that you have to pay when you rent something such as a television or a car. EG *The quarterly rental will be £35.* — N COUNT: USU SING

reorganize /riˈɔːgənaɪz/, **reorganizes, reorganizing, reorganized;** also spelled **reorganise.** If you **reorganize** something, you organize it in a new way that is intended to make it more efficient or acceptable. EG *The manufacturers were reorganising the soap industry.* ◊ **reorganization** /riːɔːgənaɪzeɪʃᵊn/, **reorganizations**. EG *Recently there has been a reorganisation of the Health Service.* — V+O OR V; ◊ N UNCOUNT OR N COUNT

rep /rɛp/, **reps.** A **rep** is a person whose job is to sell a company's products or services, especially by travelling round and visiting other companies. EG *I've been working as a sales rep.* — N COUNT: USU+SUPP Informal

repaid /riˈpeɪd/ is the past tense and past participle of **repay.**

repair /rɪˈpɛə/, **repairs, repairing, repaired. 1** A **repair** is something that you do to mend a machine, piece of clothing, or other thing that has been damaged or is not working properly. EG *He had left his car for repairs in the garage.* — N COUNT OR N UNCOUNT

2 If something such as a building is **in good repair**, it is in good condition. If it is **in bad repair**, it is in bad condition. EG *...a small wooden shed in poor repair.* — PHRASE Formal

3 If you **repair** something that has been damaged or is not working properly, you mend it. EG *No one knew how to repair the engine.* — V+O

4 If you **repair** something wrong or harmful that someone has done, you do something to correct it or make it less serious. EG *Can you see any way in which we can repair these two very major omissions?* — V+O Formal

repartee /rɛpɑːtiː/ is conversation that consists of quick, witty comments and replies. EG *...his constant chatter and repartee with the spectators.* — N UNCOUNT

repay /riˈpeɪ/, **repays, repaying, repaid** /riˈpeɪd/. **1** If you **repay** money, you give it back to the person who you borrowed or took it from. EG *He plans to repay most of that debt... He ordered the President to repay the money to the State.* — V+O, V+O+O, OR V+O+*to*

2 If you **repay** a favour that someone did for you, you do something or give them something in return. EG *We hope we can repay you for the pleasure you have given us.* — V+O: OFT+*for*

repayment /riˈpeɪməᵊnt/, **repayments. 1 Repayments** are amounts of money which you pay at regular intervals to a person or organization in order to repay a debt over a period of time. EG *They faced the burden of loan repayments.* — N COUNT: USU PLURAL

2 The **repayment** of money is the process of paying it back to the person you owe it to. EG *...repayment of international debts.* — N UNCOUNT: USU+SUPP

repeal /rɪˈpiːl/, **repeals, repealing, repealed.** If the government **repeals** a law, it officially ends it, so that it is no longer valid. EG *Nine countries repealed their anti-discrimination laws last year.* — V+O Legal

▸ used as a noun. EG *...a campaign for the repeal of incomes legislation.* — ▸ N UNCOUNT: USU+*of*

repeat /rɪˈpiːt/, **repeats, repeating, repeated. 1** If you **repeat** something, you say or write it again. EG *Haldane repeated his statement in the presence of the Prime Minister... 'We need half a million dollars,' Monty kept repeating. 'Half a million dollars.'* — V-SPEECH

2 If you **repeat** something that someone else has said or written, you say or write the same thing. EG *Ballin repeated what he had been told by Haldane.* — V+O OR V+QUOTE

3 If you **repeat** an action, you do it again. EG *I decided not to repeat the mistake of my first marriage.* — V+O

4 If you **repeat** yourself, you say or do something which you have said or done before. EG *People tend to repeat themselves a lot in conversation... History often repeats itself.* — V-REFL

5 If a television or radio programme **is repeated**, it is broadcast again. EG *'How Many Miles to Babylon' is being repeated on Radio 4 next Sunday afternoon.* — V+O: USU PASS

6 A **repeat** is something which is done again or which happens again. EG *'Any Answers' can first be heard tomorrow night at 8, with a repeat on Monday afternoon... ...a repeat performance of the play.* — N COUNT

repeated /rɪˈpiːtɪᵊd/. **Repeated** actions or events are ones which happen many times. EG *After repeated attempts, the manager finally managed to call the police... Anxious patients require repeated reassurance that they are getting better.* — ADJ CLASSIF: ATTRIB

repeatedly /rɪˈpiːtɪdliˈ/. If you do something **repeatedly**, you do it many times. EG *The child learns to read by seeing the words repeatedly.* — ADV

repel /rɪˈpɛl/, **repels, repelling, repelled.** If something **repels** you, you find it horrible and disgusting. EG *Any deformity frightened and repelled her.* — V+O

repellent /rɪˈpɛlənt/, **repellents. 1** If you find something **repellent**, you find it horrible and disgusting. EG *The idea of eating meat has become repellent to me.* — ADJ QUALIT: OFT+*to* Formal

2 Repellent is a chemical which is used to keep insects or other creatures away from an area. EG *...a bottle of insect repellent.* — N MASS

repent /rɪˈpɛnt/, **repents, repenting, repented.** If you **repent**, you feel sorry for something bad that you have done in the past. EG *He may repent of his sins... He lived to repent his early love.* — V: OFT+*of/for*, OR V+O Formal

repentance /rɪˈpɛntəns/ is sorrow and regret that you feel for something bad that you have done in the past. EG *...prayers of repentance.* — N UNCOUNT Formal

repentant /rɪˈpɛntənt/. Someone who is **repentant** feels sorrow and regret for something bad that they have done in the past. EG *...repentant sinners.* — ADJ QUALIT Formal

repercussion /riːpəkʌʃᵊn/, **repercussions.** The **repercussions** of an event or action are the effects that it has at a later time. EG *They cannot foresee the complex repercussions of these changes... What happened had enormous repercussions on my family.* — N COUNT: USU PLURAL Formal

repertoire /rɛpətwɑː/. A musician's **repertoire** consists of all the music that he or she has learned and can perform. Similarly, an actor's or actress's **repertoire** consists of all the parts he or she has learned and can perform. EG *It was wonderful to be able to extend my song repertoire.* — N SING+SUPP

repertory /rɛpətᵊriˈ/ is the practice of performing a small number of plays in a theatre for a fairly short time, using the same actors in every play. EG *After leaving drama school I joined a repertory company.* — N UNCOUNT Formal

repetition /rɛpɪtɪʃᵊn/, **repetitions.** When there is a **repetition** of something that has happened — N COUNT OR N UNCOUNT

Why might you rephrase a question?

before, it happens again. EG *He didn't want a repetition of the scene with his mother.*

repetitious /rɛpɪtɪʃəs/ means the same as repetitive. EG *...endlessly repetitious jobs.* [ADJ QUALIT]

repetitive /rɪˈpɛtɪtɪv/. Something that is **repetitive** contains unnecessary repetition, and is therefore boring. EG *His job consists of dull, repetitive work... ...a shrill, repetitive sound.* [ADJ QUALIT]

rephrase /riːfreɪz/, **rephrases, rephrasing, rephrased.** If you **rephrase** a question or statement, you ask it or say it again in a different way. [V+O]

replace /riˈpleɪs/, **replaces, replacing, replaced. 1** When one thing **replaces** another, the first thing takes the place of the second thing. EG *Thomas bought a new sweater to replace the one he lost... Arabic script was replaced with the Roman alphabet.* [V+O: OFT+*with*]

2 If you **replace** one thing with another, you use the second thing in place of the first one. EG *The airline is currently replacing its DC10s with Boeing 747s.* [V+O: OFT+*with*]

3 If you **replace** something that is damaged or lost, you get a new thing which will perform the same function. EG *The books that have been stolen will have to be replaced.* [V+O]

4 To **replace** something also means to put it back in the place where it was before. EG *She replaced the receiver.* [V+O]

replacement /riˈpleɪsməˀnt/, **replacements. 1** The **replacement** of someone or something happens when they are replaced by another person or thing. EG *...the resignation of Jo Grimond and his replacement by Jeremy Thorpe... ...the replacement of steam by diesel.* [N UNCOUNT]

2 A **replacement** for someone or something is another person or thing that takes their place. EG *The Colonel's replacement was due any day now.* [N COUNT]

replay, replays, replaying, replayed; pronounced /riːpleɪ/ when it is a verb and /riːpleɪ/ when it is a noun.

1 If two sports teams **replay** a match in a competition, they play it again because the previous match between them was a draw. ▸ used as a noun. EG *Who won the replay?* [V+O; ▸ N COUNT]

2 If you **replay** something that you have recorded on tape or film, you play it again in order to listen to it or look at it. EG *He rewound the tape and replayed a few bits and pieces.* [V+O]

replenish /riˈplɛnɪʃ/, **replenishes, replenishing, replenished.** To **replenish** something means to make it full or complete again by adding a quantity of the substance or material that has been lost or removed. EG *We have to import an extra 4 million tons of wheat to replenish our reserves... Mr Jones replenished his glass.* [V+O Formal]

replica /rɛplɪkə/, **replicas.** A **replica** of a statue, machine, or building is an accurate copy of it. EG *...a plaster replica of the Venus di Milo.* [N COUNT]

reply /rɪˈplaɪ/, **replies, replying, replied. 1** When you **reply** to something that someone has said or written to you, you say or write something as an answer. EG *'Did you have a nice journey?' – 'Yes,' Jenny replied, 'nice and quick.'... He gave me no chance to reply to his question... I sent you a letter, and you never replied.* [V: USU +QUOTE OR REPORT: ONLY *that*; ALSO V+*to*]

2 A **reply** is something that you say or write when you reply to someone. EG *He called 'Sarah', but there was no reply... I received about a dozen replies to my enquiry.* [N COUNT: OFT+*to*]

3 If you say or do something **in reply** to something that someone else has said or done, you say or do it as an answer to them. EG *I have nothing to say in reply to your question.* [PHRASE]

report /rɪˈpɔːt/, **reports, reporting, reported. 1** If you **report** something that has happened, you tell people about it. EG *The papers reported that Southern England was 'paralysed' by snow... Accidents must be reported to the police within twenty-four hours.* ◇ **reported.** *...the last reported position of the hurricane.* [V-SPEECH: ONLY *that*; ALSO V+O: OFT+*to*-INF OR *to*; ◇ ADJ CLASSIF: ATTRIB]

2 If you **report** on an event or subject, you tell people about it, because it is your job or duty to do so. EG *He was summoned to report on the accident to his supervisor... On his return from the Summit the Prime Minister reported to the Cabinet.* [V: OFT+*on* OR *to*]

3 If someone **reports** you to a person in authority, they tell the person about something wrong that you have done. EG *You should have reported them to the police.* [V+O: OFT+*to*]

4 If you **report** to a person or place, you go to that person or place and say that you are ready to start work. EG *The next morning he reported for duty at Jack Starke's office... I told him to report to me after the job was completed.* [V: OFT+*to/for*]

5 A **report** is a written or spoken account of an event or situation. EG *Write a report on the visit... There have been no reports of bomb attacks... ...a newspaper report that he had been killed.* [N COUNT: OFT +REPORT]

6 A school **report** is an official written account of how well or how badly a pupil has done during the term that has just finished. [N COUNT British]

7 See also **reporting.**

report back. If you **report back** to someone, you tell them about something that it was your job to find out about. EG *She was sent to attend the meeting and then to report back on its discussions.* [PHRASAL VB: V+ADV]

REPORT stands for **report clause**

REPORT is used in the Extra Column to say that the word being described is followed by a report clause. Verbs, nouns, and adjectives can be followed by report clauses. Report clauses tell you what someone has said or what they have thought, and they come after words which refer to speaking or thinking.

The most typical report clauses come after verbs and begin with 'that', as in EG *He thought **that he had missed the train**.* It is, however, usually possible to omit the 'that', so you can say EG *He thought **he had missed the train**.*

Report clauses can also begin with a WH word such as 'why, where', or 'how', as in EG *They asked me **why I changed my mind**.*

When the label in the Extra Column says V+REPORT or V+O+REPORT, it means that the report clause can begin with 'that', with no 'that', or with a WH word.

When there are restrictions on the kind of report clause that is possible, the labels in the Extra Column say what they are. For example, the Extra Column label for **think 1** says V+REPORT: ONLY *that*; and for **wonder 1** and **describe** it says V+REPORT: ONLY WH. EG *I think **that you should go**... I think **a woman has as much right to work as a man**... I'm beginning to wonder **why we ever invited them**... He described **how he was kidnapped**.*

Verbs with +REPORT can usually have the report clause, without 'that', in front of them, as in EG ***You should go**, I think.*

When nouns or adjectives have the label +REPORT, they can be followed by a report clause with 'that'. The 'that' cannot usually be omitted, and it is not usually possible to have a report clause that begins with a WH word. EG *He felt certain **that she would disapprove**... I was conscious **that he had changed his tactics**... ...his conviction **that he could run a newspaper**.*

reportedly /rɪˈpɔːtɪdliˈ/. If something is **reportedly** true, someone has said that it is true. EG *He has reportedly instructed his family not to interfere if he tries to kill himself... Tests reportedly showed that the substance was harmless.* ADV Formal

reported speech is speech that gives an account of something that someone has said, but without quoting the actual words that are used. **Reported speech** is usually introduced by a verb such as 'say' or 'tell' followed by the word 'that'. See entry headed REPORT. N UNCOUNT

reporter /rɪˈpɔːtə/, **reporters.** A **reporter** is someone who writes news articles or who broadcasts news reports. EG *He told his story to a reporter from a Chicago newspaper... ...a television reporter.* N COUNT

reporting /rɪˈpɔːtɪŋ/ is the presenting of news in newspapers or on radio or television. EG *The magazine was asked to be much less selective in its reporting.* N UNCOUNT

repose /rɪˈpəʊz/ is a state in which you are resting and feel calm. EG *He thought her face was lovely in repose.* N UNCOUNT Literary

repository /rɪˈpɒzɪtəriˈ/, **repositories.** A **repository** is a place where something is kept safely. EG *The Foreign Office was regarded as the repository of all relevant information.* N COUNT+SUPP Formal

reprehensible /rɛprɪhɛnsəˈbəl/. If you describe behaviour as **reprehensible**, you mean that it is very bad and morally wrong. EG *It is reprehensible to cheat other people.* ADJ QUALIT Formal

represent /rɛprɪˌzɛnt/, **represents, representing, represented. 1** If you **represent** someone or their views, you act on their behalf, for example by expressing their views in a parliament or meeting. EG *Thirty one nations are now represented at the Disarmament Conference... ...lawyers representing relatives of the victims.* V+O

2 If a group of people is **well represented** or **strongly represented** at a particular place, there are a lot of them there, or a lot of examples of their work. EG *All these artists are well represented at the exhibition.* PHRASE

3 If a sign or symbol **represents** something, it is accepted as meaning that thing, in the same way that a word is accepted as meaning something. EG *The word 'love' was represented by a small red heart.* V+O

4 If an object **represents** an idea to people, they think of it as a symbol or expression of that idea. EG *To many of the local people these castles represent a hundred years of domination by the aristocracy.* V+O : NO PASS, NO CONT

5 You can say that something **represents** a particular thing when it is an example of that type of thing. EG *Does the budget represent a departure from stated government policy?... Universities represent a very sizeable resource.* V+C : NO CONT Formal

6 If you **represent** something in a particular way, you describe it in that way. EG *The evacuation of our forces was represented as a triumphant success.* V+O : USU+A

representation /rɛprɪˌzɛnteɪʃən/, **representations. 1 Representation** is the state of being represented by someone in a parliament or on a committee. EG *They're campaigning for student representation on the university's governing bodies.* N UNCOUNT

2 You can describe a picture or statue of someone as a **representation** of them. EG *...crude representations of angels.* N COUNT : OFT+*of* Formal

3 Representations are formal requests, complaints, or statements made to a government or another official group. EG *The committee's enquiry arose from representations made by a group of local residents.* N PLURAL Formal

representative /rɛprɪˌzɛntətɪv/, **representatives. 1** A **representative** is a person who has been chosen to act on behalf of another person or a group of people. EG *The Consumer Congress is made up of representatives of a wide range of organizations... ...representatives from the police... ...union representatives.* N COUNT

2 A **representative** group consists of a small number of people who have been chosen to make decisions on behalf of a larger group. EG *The government consists of two representative assemblies.* ADJ CLASSIF : ATTRIB

3 Something that is **representative** is typical of the group to which it belongs. EG *We questioned a representative cross-section of the public... Are these incidents representative of the way things have gone?* ADJ QUALIT : OFT+*of*

repress /riˈprɛs/, **represses, repressing, repressed. 1** If you **repress** a feeling, you succeed in not showing it or not feeling it. EG *It was all I could do to repress my laughter.* V+O

2 If a group of people **repress** the people they have authority over, they restrict their freedom and control them by force. EG *The military officers would help to exploit and repress their own people.* V+O

repressed /riˈprɛst/. You use **repressed** to describe **1** people who do not allow themselves to have natural feelings and desires, especially sexual ones. ADJ QUALIT **2** feelings that people do not allow themselves to have. *...the child's repressed hate of his mother.* ADJ QUALIT

repression /riˈprɛʃən/. **1 Repression** is the use of force to restrict and control a group of people, especially the people of a country. EG *They wanted to fight all forms of injustice and repression.* N UNCOUNT

2 Repression also refers to the way that people do not allow themselves to have natural feelings and desires, especially sexual ones. N UNCOUNT

repressive /riˈprɛsɪv/. **Repressive** governments use force and unjust laws to restrict and control their people. EG *...a repressive society.* ADJ QUALIT

reprieve /rɪˈpriːv/, **reprieves, reprieving, reprieved. 1** If someone who has been sentenced to death **is reprieved**, their sentence is changed and they are not executed. V+O : USU PASS

2 A **reprieve** is **2.1** a delay before something very unpleasant happens. EG *The finding of oil represents a colossal reprieve for the islanders.* **2.2** an official order cancelling a death sentence. N COUNT

reprimand /rɛprɪmɑːnd/, **reprimands, reprimanding, reprimanded.** If you **reprimand** someone, you officially tell them that they should not have done a particular thing. EG *He was called to the office of a superior to be reprimanded.* V+O ▸ used as a noun. EG *...a gentle reprimand.* ▸ N COUNT

reprint, reprints, reprinting, reprinted; pronounced /riːprɪnt/ when it is a verb and /riːprɪnt/ when it is a noun.

1 If a book **is reprinted**, further copies of it are printed when all the other ones have been sold. V+O : USU PASS

2 A **reprint** is a copy of a book which has been reprinted. EG *...the 1959 reprint of his book.* N COUNT

reprisal /rɪˈpraɪzəl/, **reprisals. 1 Reprisals** are violent actions that are taken by a group of people against another group who have harmed them. EG *They engaged in brutal reprisals against those who had fought them.* N COUNT : USU PLURAL

2 Reprisal is the act of carrying out reprisals. EG *There have been threats of reprisal.* N UNCOUNT Formal

reproach /rɪˈprəʊtʃ/, **reproaches, reproaching, reproached. 1** If you express **reproach**, you show that you feel sad and rather angry about something that someone has done. EG *She was still staring at him in shocked and silent reproach... ...a long letter of reproach.* N UNCOUNT Formal

2 If you **reproach** someone, you tell them, rather sadly, that they have done something wrong. EG *He used to reproach her mother for not being nice* V+O OR V-REFL : OFT+*for/with* Formal *enough to her... He had bitterly reproached himself for his complacency.* ▸ used as a noun. EG *She responded submissively to his reproaches.* ▸ N COUNT

reproachful /rɪ1prəʊtʃfʊl/. **Reproachful** looks or remarks show that you feel sad and rather angry about something that someone has done. EG *She was looking at me with rather reproachful brown eyes.* ◇ **reproachfully**. EG *Morris looked at her reproachfully.* ADJ QUALIT; ◇ ADV

reproduce /ri:prədju:s/, **reproduces, reproducing, reproduced. 1** If you **reproduce** something, you produce a copy of it. EG *This painting has never been reproduced anywhere... She tried to reproduce his accent.* V+O

2 When people, animals, or plants **reproduce**, they produce more of their own kind. EG *Bacteria reproduce by splitting into two.* V OR V-REFL

reproduction /ri:prədʌkʃə0n/, **reproductions. 1** A **reproduction** is a modern copy of a painting or piece of furniture. EG *...reproductions of Impressionist paintings... ...reproduction Colonial furniture.* N COUNT

2 The **reproduction** of sound, art, or writing is the copying of it. EG *The Controller has no objection to the reproduction of the Report.* N UNCOUNT

3 Reproduction is the process by which a living thing produces more of its own kind. EG *Today's lesson is about plant reproduction.* N UNCOUNT

reproductive /ri:prədʌktɪv/ means relating to the reproduction of living things. EG *...a worm's digestive and reproductive systems.* ADJ CLASSIF : ATTRIB

reproof /rɪ1pru:f/, **reproofs. 1** A **reproof** is something that you say to someone to show that you disapprove of what they have done. EG *This reproof was ignored.* N COUNT Formal

2 If you say or do something as **reproof**, you say or do it to show that you disapprove of what someone has done. EG *Discipline and reproof are out of fashion.* N UNCOUNT Formal

reprove /rɪ1pru:v/, **reproves, reproving, reproved.** If you **reprove** someone, you tell them that they have behaved wrongly or foolishly. ◇ **reproving**. EG *She received a reproving look from her Aunt Agnes.* V+O : OFT+*for* Formal; ◇ ADJ CLASSIF

reptile /rɛptaɪl/, **reptiles.** A **reptile** is an animal which has a scaly skin and lays eggs. Snakes and lizards are reptiles. N COUNT

republic /rɪ1pʌblɪk/, **republics.** A **republic** is a country which has a president rather than a king or queen and is governed by elected representatives. EG *Cuba became an independent republic... ...the Republic of Ireland.* N COUNT

repudiate /rɪ1pju:dɪeɪt/, **repudiates, repudiating, repudiated.** If you **repudiate** something, you say that you will not accept it or have anything to do with it. EG *He repudiated the authority of the Church.* ◇ **repudiation** /rɪ1pju:dɪeɪʃə0n/. EG *...his repudiation of the evidence.* V+O Formal; ◇ N UNCOUNT : OFT+*of*

repugnant /rɪ1pʌgnənt/. If something is **repugnant** to you, you think it is horrible and disgusting. EG *The majority of British people find this sort of souvenir repugnant... The idea was repugnant to him.* ADJ QUALIT : OFT+*to* Formal

repulsion /rɪ1pʌlʃə0n/ is a strong feeling of dislike and disgust. EG *She shivered with repulsion... I can't help feeling repulsion.* N UNCOUNT Formal

repulsive /rɪ1pʌlsɪv/. Something that is **repulsive** is horrible and disgusting. EG *...his repulsive appearance... It's a repulsive idea... His behaviour was absolutely repulsive.* ADJ QUALIT

reputable /rɛpjə4təbə0l/. A **reputable** company or person is known to be good and reliable. EG *All reputable companies give a guarantee.* ADJ QUALIT

reputation /rɛpjə4teɪʃə0n/, **reputations.** The **reputation** of someone or something is the opinion that people have about what they are like, especially about how good they are. EG *She had a reputation as a very good writer... ...his reputation for integrity... He had earned the reputation of being a formidable opponent.* N COUNT : USU+SUPP

reputed /rɪ1pju:tɪ2d/. If something is **reputed** to be true or to exist, some people say that it is true or that it exists. EG *The buildings were reputed to be haunted... ...their reputed beauty.* ADJ PRED +*to*-INF OR ADJ CLASSIF : ATTRIB

reputedly /rɪ1pju:tɪdli1/. If something is **reputedly** true, it is said to be true. EG *...events that reputedly took place thousands of years ago.* ADV

request /rɪ1kwɛst/, **requests, requesting, requested. 1** If you **request** something, you ask for it politely or formally. EG *The President requested an emergency session of the United Nations... Visitors are requested not to pick the flowers.* V+O : OFT+*to*-INF, OR V+REPORT, ONLY *that* Formal

2 If you make a **request** for something, you ask for it politely. EG *I made repeated requests for money... ...an urgent request to devise some games.* N COUNT

3 If something is given or done **on request**, it is given or done whenever you ask for it. EG *A booklet on this subject will be sent on request.* PHRASE

4 If you do something **at** someone's **request**, you do it because they have asked you to. EG *We went into Afghanistan at the request of the Afghan government.* PHRASE

require /rɪ1kwaɪə/, **requires, requiring, required. 1** If you **require** something or if something **is required**, you need it or it is necessary. EG *Is there anything you require, Mr Heissman?... Parliamentary approval would be required for it.* V+O : OFT+*for* Formal

2 If you **are required** to do something, you have to do it because someone says you must do it. EG *All the boys were required to study religion... He was doing what was required of him... The course requires you to be bilingual.* ◇ **required**. EG *Check that the machines meet required standards.* V+O : USU PASS +*to*-INF, *of*, OR REPORT, ONLY *that* Formal; ◇ ADJ CLASSIF OR ADJ AFTER N

requirement /rɪ1kwaɪəmə2nt/, **requirements. 1** A **requirement** is something that you must have or do in order to do something that you want to do. EG *Maths is no longer the most important requirement for a career in accounting... The applicant meets our general entrance requirements.* N COUNT : USU+SUPP

2 Your **requirements** are things that you need. EG *Mexico imported half her grain requirements in 1940.* N COUNT : USU+SUPP Formal

requisite /rɛkwɪzɪt/ means necessary for a particular purpose. EG *They needed time to establish the requisite number of prisons.* ADJ CLASSIF : ATTRIB Formal

requisition /rɛkwɪzɪʃə0n/, **requisitions, requisitioning, requisitioned.** If people, especially soldiers, **requisition** something, they formally demand it and take it for their own use. EG *Transport was being requisitioned by the army.* V+O Formal

re-route /ri:ru:t/, **re-routes, re-routing, re-routed.** If traffic **is re-routed**, it is directed along different roads, for example because a road is blocked. V+O : USU+A

rescue /rɛskju:/, **rescues, rescuing, rescued. 1** If you **rescue** someone, you get them out of a dangerous or unpleasant situation. EG *He was rescued from the sinking aircraft by a passing ship... The Cabinet decided not to rescue the company.* ◇ **rescuer, rescuers**. EG *The man's shouts could not be heard by the rescuers.* V+O; ◇ N COUNT

2 Rescue is help which gets someone out of a dangerous or unpleasant situation. EG *Rescue was at hand... ...the size of the rescue operation.* N UNCOUNT

3 If you **go** or **come to** someone's **rescue**, you help them when they are in danger or difficulty. EG *Toby came to my rescue... It was William who came to the rescue.* PHRASE

4 A **rescue** is a successful attempt to save someone from a dangerous or unpleasant situation. EG *The coastguard may be working on as many as 20 rescues at any one time.* N COUNT

research /rɪ1sɜ:tʃ/, **researches, researching, researched. 1 Research** is work that involves studying something and trying to discover facts about it. EG *...scientific research... I was doing some research on Indian literature... Soon after, Faraday began his researches into electricity.* N UNCOUNT OR N PLURAL

2 If you **research** something, you try to discover V+O OR V facts about it. EG *The historical background to the play had been very carefully researched... I spent some time researching abroad.* ◇ **researcher, researchers.** EG *...a team of researchers.* ◇ N COUNT

resemblance /rɪ^{1}zɛmbləns/. If there is a **resemblance** between two people or things, they are similar to each other. EG *She bore a striking resemblance to his wife.* N SING OR N UNCOUNT

resemble /rɪ^{1}zɛmbə^{0}l/, **resembles, resembling, resembled.** If one thing or person **resembles** another, they are similar to each other. EG *You resemble him very much physically... The situation closely resembles that of Europe in 1940.* V+O : NO CONT, NO IMPER

resent /rɪ^{1}zɛnt/, **resents, resenting, resented.** If you **resent** something, you feel bitter and angry about it. EG *I resented his attitude... They resent being treated as common criminals.* V+O

resentful /rɪ^{1}zɛntfʊl/. If you are **resentful**, you feel resentment. EG *He was resentful at the way he had been treated... I felt resentful about having to see him again.* ADJ QUALIT

resentment /rɪ^{1}zɛntmə^{2}nt/ is bitterness and anger. EG *He was filled with resentment... I felt no resentment against Keith.* N UNCOUNT

reservation /rɛzəveɪʃə^{0}n/, **reservations. 1** If you have **reservations** about something, you are not sure that it is entirely good or right. EG *I have reservations about the desirability of such a change... He shared his assistant's reservations.* N COUNT

2 If you do something without **reservation**, you do it without any doubts at all. EG *They accepted the plan without reservation... With a little more reservation, I would recommend the second film.* N UNCOUNT

3 If you make a **reservation**, you arrange for something such as a table in a restaurant or a room in a hotel to be kept for you. EG *I will make the reservation for seven thirty.* N COUNT

reserve /rɪ^{1}zɜːv/, **reserves, reserving, reserved. 1** If something **is reserved** for a particular person or purpose, it is kept specially for that person or purpose. EG *The garden is reserved for those who work in the museum... I had a place reserved at the Youth Hostel... He gave me a look of the sort usually reserved for naughty schoolchildren.* V+O : USU PASS

2 If you say that you **reserve the right** to do something, you mean that you will do it if you feel that it is necessary. EG *The French reserved the right to decide their own agricultural policy.* PHRASE Formal

3 A **reserve** is a supply of something that is available for use when it is needed. EG *We have large coal reserves... ...the mobilization of reserve forces... He was able to draw on vast reserves of talent and enthusiasm.* N COUNT : USU+SUPP

4 If you have something **in reserve**, you have it available for use when it is needed. EG *I kept some tranquillizers in reserve in case I became agitated.* PHRASE

5 In sport, a **reserve** is someone who is available to play as part of a team if one of the members cannot play on a particular occasion. N COUNT

6 A nature **reserve** is an area of land where the animals, birds, and plants are officially protected. N COUNT : USU+SUPP

7 If someone shows **reserve**, they keep their feelings hidden. EG *His tone had lost the cautious reserve it had previously had.* N UNCOUNT

reserved /rɪ^{1}zɜːvd/. Someone who is **reserved** keeps their feelings hidden. *He is reserved and cautious, never making a swift decision.* ADJ QUALIT

reservoir /rɛzəvwɑː/, **reservoirs. 1** A **reservoir** is a lake that is used for storing water before it is supplied to people. N COUNT

2 A **reservoir** of something is a large quantity of it that is available to be used. EG *Industry must have a reservoir of cheap labour.* N PART

reside /rɪ^{1}zaɪd/, **resides, residing, resided.** If a quality **resides** in something, it is in that thing. EG *Real power now resides in the workshop... The value of his sculptures resides in their simplicity.* V : USU+*in*, NO CONT, NO IMPER Formal

residence /rɛzɪdəns/, **residences. 1** A **residence** is a house where people live. EG *...the Prime Minister's official residence.* N COUNT Formal

2 Your place of **residence** is the place where you live. EG *What is your place of residence?... ...lifelong residence in one place.* N UNCOUNT Formal

3 If you **take up residence** somewhere, you go and live there. EG *They had taken up residence on the top floor of a hotel.* PHRASE Formal

4 If an important person is **in residence** in a particular place, they are living there. EG *None of the royal family are in residence at the palace at the moment.* PHRASE Formal

5 See also **hall of residence**.

resident /rɛzɪdənt/, **residents. 1** The **residents** of a house or area are the people who live there. EG *The local residents complained... She became a permanent resident of California.* N COUNT

2 Someone who is **resident** in a country or a town lives there. EG *...students resident in England... Since 1947 she has been resident abroad.* ADJ CLASSIF : USU PRED+*in* Formal

3 A **resident** doctor or tutor lives in the place where he or she works. ADJ CLASSIF

residential /rɛzɪdɛnʃə^{0}l/. **1** A **residential** area contains mainly houses rather than offices or factories. EG *...fashionable residential suburbs.* ADJ CLASSIF : ATTRIB

2 A **residential** institution is an institution in which you can live while you are studying there or being cared for there. EG *...residential colleges... ...residential courses... ...children living in residential care.* ADJ CLASSIF : ATTRIB

residual /rɪ^{2}zɪdjʊ^{0}əl/ is used to describe what remains of something when most of it has gone. EG *...a prehistoric fish with residual limbs... ...the residual prejudices of the past.* ADJ CLASSIF : ATTRIB Formal

residue /rɛzɪdjuː/, **residues.** A **residue** of something is a small amount that remains after most of it has gone. EG *Residues of pesticides can build up in the soil.* N COUNT : USU+SUPP Formal

resign /rɪ^{1}zaɪn/, **resigns, resigning, resigned. 1** If you **resign** from a job or position, you formally announce that you are leaving it, usually because of something that has happened. EG *She resigned from the Government... Lloyd George was threatening to resign.* V : OFT+FROM, OR V+O

2 If you **resign** yourself to an unpleasant situation or fact, you accept it because you realize that you cannot change it. EG *You're a widow now, Mrs Pearl. I think you must resign yourself to that fact.* V-REFL+*to*

3 See also **resigned**.

resignation /rɛzɪgneɪʃə^{0}n/, **resignations. 1** Your **resignation** is a formal statement of your intention to leave a job or position. EG *Mr McPherson has accepted my resignation... ...her letter of resignation.* N COUNT OR N UNCOUNT

2 Resignation is the acceptance of an unpleasant situation or fact because you realize that you cannot change it. EG *She spoke with quiet resignation.* N UNCOUNT

resigned /rɪ^{1}zaɪnd/. If you are **resigned** to an unpleasant situation or fact, you accept it without complaining because you realize that you cannot change it. EG *They feel resigned to losing their money.* ◇ **resignedly** /rɪ^{1}zaɪnədli^1/. EG *'He will come,' said Joe resignedly.* ADJ CLASSIF : OFT+*to* ◇ ADV

resilient /rɪ^{1}zɪljənt/. People and things that are **resilient** are able to recover quickly from unpleasant or damaging events. EG *He's bright, resilient, and ambitious.* ◇ **resilience** /rɪ^{1}zɪljəns/. EG *The chairman has shown remarkable resilience.* ADJ QUALIT ◇ N UNCOUNT

resin /rɛzɪn/, **resins. Resin** is **1** a sticky substance that is produced by some trees. **2** a substance that is produced chemically and used to make plastics. N MASS

> If you resign from your job, are you resigned to it?

resist /rɪˈzɪst/, **resists, resisting, resisted. 1** If you **resist** something such as a change, you refuse to accept it and try to prevent it. EG *Our trade union has resisted the introduction of automation... He resisted demands for a public enquiry.* V+O

2 If you **resist** someone or **resist** an attack by them, you fight back against them. EG *Any attack will be resisted with force if necessary.* V+O

3 If you **resist** the temptation to do something, you stop yourself from doing it although you would like to do it. EG *I can't resist teasing him... I resisted the temptation to get very drunk.* V+O OR V+-ING

resistance /rɪˈzɪstəns/, **resistances. 1 Resistance** to something such as a change or a new idea is a refusal to accept it. EG *There will be fierce resistance if this is attempted... ...resistance to bureaucratic controls.* N UNCOUNT: OFT+*to*

2 Resistance to an attack consists of fighting back against the people who have attacked you. EG *The advancing army met with no resistance... ...a group of resistance fighters.* N UNCOUNT

3 The **resistance** of your body to germs or diseases is its power to remain unharmed or unaffected by them. EG *...resistance to infection.* N UNCOUNT: OFT+*to*

resistant /rɪˈzɪstənt/. **1** Someone who is **resistant** to something is opposed to it and wants to prevent it. EG *They are extremely resistant to change.* ADJ PRED: OFT+*to* Formal

2 If something is **resistant** to a particular thing, it is not harmed by it. EG *This type of plastic is highly resistant to steam... Many pests are now resistant to the commoner insecticides.* ADJ QUALIT: OFT+*to*

-resistant is used to form adjectives that describe something as not harmed or not affected by a particular substance. EG *...penicillin-resistant strains of bacteria... ...water-resistant make-up.*

resolute /rɛzəljuːt/. Someone who is **resolute** shows great determination not to change their mind or not to give up a course of action. EG *We urged him to be resolute... ...their resolute refusal to make any real concessions.* ◊ **resolutely**. EG *She resolutely refused to speak to me.* ADJ QUALIT Formal ◊ ADV

resolution /rɛzəljuːʃən/, **resolutions. 1** A **resolution** is a formal decision taken at a meeting by means of a vote. EG *Congress passed a resolution accepting his services.* N COUNT

2 If you make a **resolution**, you decide to try very hard to do something. EG *I'm always making resolutions, like giving up smoking.* N COUNT

3 Resolution is determination to do something or not do something. EG *A note of resolution entered his voice.* N UNCOUNT

4 The **resolution** of a problem or difficulty is the final solving of it. EG *I longed for the resolution of the agonizing dilemma.* N UNCOUNT: USU+SUPP Formal

resolve /rɪˈzɒlv/, **resolves, resolving, resolved. 1** If you **resolve** to do something, you make a firm decision to do it. EG *I resolved to tell the truth... He had already resolved that Kitchener should be appointed.* V+*to*-INF OR REPORT: ONLY *that* Formal

2 Resolve is absolute determination to do what you have decided to do. EG *We must be firm in our resolve to oppose them.* N UNCOUNT Formal

3 To **resolve** a problem, argument, or difficulty means to find or provide a solution to it. EG *There are a number of ways of resolving the problem... The Cabinet met to resolve the crisis.* V+O Formal

resonant /rɛzənənt/. A sound that is **resonant** is deep and strong. EG *She could hear her father's resonant voice.* ◊ **resonance** /rɛzənəns/. EG *His voice suddenly took on a new resonance.* ADJ QUALIT ◊ N UNCOUNT

resonate /rɛzəneɪt/, **resonates, resonating, resonated.** If something **resonates**, it vibrates and produces a deep, strong sound. EG *His laughter resonated among the rocks.* V Formal

resort /rɪˈzɔːt/, **resorts, resorting, resorted. 1** If you **resort** to a course of action that you do not really approve of, you adopt it because you cannot see any other way of achieving what you want to achieve. EG *They had not so far chosen to resort to violence... Some groups have resorted to terrorism.* V+*to*

2 If you do something **as a last resort**, you do it because you can find no other way of getting out of a difficult situation or of solving a problem. EG *As a last resort he went to the British Library.* PHRASE

3 You use **in the last resort** when giving the basic truth or the most important fact about something. EG *We must have prisons in the last resort to contain people who break the law frequently... The difference was in the last resort no more than a matter of emphasis.* PHRASE Formal

4 A **resort** is a place where a lot of people spend their holidays. EG *...a seaside resort.* N COUNT: USU+SUPP

resound /rɪˈzaʊnd/, **resounds, resounding, resounded. 1** When a noise **resounds**, it is heard very loudly and clearly. EG *His steps resounded in the courtyard.* V Literary

2 If a place **resounds** with noise, it is filled with it. EG *The room began to resound with that powerful voice.* V: OFT+*with* Literary

resounding /rɪˈzaʊndɪŋ/. **1** A **resounding** sound is loud and echoing. EG *The tile sprang from the wall with a resounding crack.* ADJ CLASSIF: ATTRIB

2 You can refer to a very great success as a **resounding** success. EG *It was a resounding victory for the party.* ADJ CLASSIF: ATTRIB

resource /rɪˈzɔːs, -sɔːs/, **resources.** The **resources** of a country, organization, or person are the things that they have and can use. EG *...Britain's energy resources... Julius had invested all his resources in an unsuccessful restaurant.* N COUNT: USU PLURAL

resourceful /rɪˈzɔːsfʊl, -sɔːs-/. Someone who is **resourceful** is good at finding ways of dealing with problems. EG *...an able, resourceful politician.* ◊ **resourcefulness**. EG *They faced misfortune with resourcefulness and courage.* ADJ QUALIT ◊ N UNCOUNT

respect /rɪspɛkt/, **respects, respecting, respected. 1** If you **respect** someone, you have a good opinion of their character or ideas. EG *He was particularly respected for his integrity.* ◊ **respected**. EG *...a highly respected scholar.* V+O ◊ ADJ QUALIT

2 If you have **respect** for someone, you have a good opinion of them. EG *I had an enormous respect and admiration for him... It is up to you to gain her respect.* • See also **self-respect**. N UNCOUNT: OFT+*for*

3 You can say **with respect** when you are politely disagreeing with someone or criticizing them. EG *But Mr Hume, with respect, that wouldn't work.* PHRASE Formal

4 If you **respect** someone's wishes, rights, or customs, you do not do anything that they would dislike or regard as wrong. EG *She respected his need for peace and quiet... We must respect the practices of cultures different from our own.* ▸ used as a noun. EG *...respect for the rights of the minority.* V+O ▸ N UNCOUNT: OFT+*for*

5 If you **pay** your **last respects** to someone who has just died, you express your respect or affection for them by coming to see their body or their grave. EG *His family came to pay their last respects.* PHRASE

6 You use expressions like **in this respect** and **in many respects** to indicate that what you are saying applies to the feature you have just mentioned or to many features of something. EG *We are lagging behind in this respect... He is different from the people around him in many respects.* PHRASE

7 You use **with respect to** to say what something relates to. EG *He informed me about my rights with respect to the forthcoming extradition.* PREP Formal

respectable /rɪˈspɛktəbəl/. **1** Someone or something that is **respectable** is approved of by society and considered to be morally correct. EG *He looked like a respectable American businessman... ...young people from respectable homes... This change had made it respectable to be on the Left.* ◊ **respectability** /rɪˈspɛktəbɪlɪˈti/. EG *...a statesman of great eminence and respectability.* ADJ QUALIT ◊ N UNCOUNT

2 You can also say that something is **respectable** ADJ QUALIT when you mean that it is adequate or acceptable. EG *He had begun to earn a very respectable income... He came a respectable fourth in the race.*

respectful /rɪˈspɛkt°fʊl/. If you are **respectful** or if your behaviour is **respectful**, you show respect for someone. EG *The woman kept a respectful silence.* ◊ **respectfully**. EG *He expected them to stand respectfully when he entered the room.* — ADJ QUALIT; ◊ ADV

respective /rɪˈspɛktɪv/ means relating separately or belonging separately to the people you have just mentioned. EG *He drove them both to their respective homes.* — ADJ CLASSIF : ATTRIB

respectively /rɪˈspɛktɪvlɪˈ/ means in the same order as the items that have just been mentioned. EG *Harvard University and MIT are respectively the fourth and fifth largest employers in the area.* — ADV

respiration /rɛspəreɪʃ°n/. Your **respiration** is your breathing. EG *His respiration was quick and shallow.* — N UNCOUNT, Technical

respiratory /rɛspə°rɔtrɪˈ/ means relating to your breathing or to the parts of your body involved in breathing. EG *...respiratory infections.* — ADJ CLASSIF : ATTRIB, Technical

respite /rɛspɪ°t/. A **respite** is a short period of rest from something unpleasant. EG *She had got a job in town primarily as a respite from her husband... She was interrogated without respite for twenty-four hours.* — N UNCOUNT, OR N SING : a+N, Formal

resplendent /rɪˈsplɛndənt/. If you describe someone as **resplendent**, you mean that their appearance is very impressive. EG *Miss Jackson, resplendent in a new red suit, watched the ceremony.* — ADJ QUALIT : OFT+in, Formal

respond /rɪˈspɒnd/, **responds, responding, responded.** When you **respond** to something that is done or said, you react to it by doing or saying something yourself. EG *The crowd waved and the liner responded with a blast on its siren... The government has responded to pressure by moving towards reform... The council responded by calling the raid 'deplorable'.* — V : OFT+to/with, V+by+-ING, OR V+QUOTE

response /rɪˈspɒns/, **responses. 1** Your **response** to an event or to something that is said is what you do or say as a reaction or reply to it. EG *The Government response to the riots was firm... As an immediate response the university has cut admissions by 20 per cent... The proposal has produced a united response from the French people.* — N COUNT

2 If you do or say something **in response** to an event, action, or question, you do it or say it as a reaction or reply to it. EG *Clearly, they did it in response to external pressures... Will waved his hand in response.* — PHRASE

responsibility /rɪˈspɒnsəbɪlɪˈtɪˈ/, **responsibilities. 1** If you have **responsibility** for something or if something is your **responsibility**, it is your duty to deal with it and make decisions relating to it. EG *She took over the responsibility for the project... The handling of the vessel remained his responsibility.* — N UNCOUNT : OFT+for

2 If you accept **responsibility** for something that has happened, you agree that you were to blame for it or caused it. EG *I made a mistake and I will assume responsibility for it.* — N UNCOUNT : OFT+for

3 Your **responsibilities** are duties that you have because of your job or position. EG *...the responsibilities of citizenship.* — N COUNT : USU PLURAL

4 If you have a **responsibility** to someone, you have a duty to help them or to look after them. EG *I presume you take your responsibility to your students seriously?* — N COUNT

responsible /rɪˈspɒnsəb°l/. **1** If you are **responsible** for something, it is your job or duty to deal with it and make decisions relating to it. EG *...the minister responsible for civil defence... The children were responsible for cleaning their own rooms.* — ADJ PRED : OFT+for

2 If you are **responsible** for something bad that has happened, you caused it or could have prevented it. EG *I hold you personally responsible for all this.* — ADJ PRED : OFT+for

3 If you are **responsible** to a person or group, you are controlled by them and have to report to them about what you have done. EG *We're responsible to a development committee.* — ADJ PRED : OFT+to

4 You describe someone as **responsible** when they behave properly without needing to be controlled by anyone else. EG *...responsible members of the local community.* ◊ **responsibly**. EG *You are doing your job conscientiously and responsibly.* — ADJ QUALIT; ◊ ADV

5 **Responsible** jobs involve making important decisions or carrying out important actions. EG *A lot of women didn't want responsible jobs.* — ADJ QUALIT : ATTRIB

responsive /rɪˈspɒnsɪv/. **1** Someone who is **responsive** is quick to show emotions such as pleasure and affection. EG *The children were the most responsive members of the audience.* — ADJ QUALIT

2 If you are **responsive** to things that happen, you take notice of them and react to them in an appropriate way. EG *Broadcasters should be responsive to public opinion... Industry is highly responsive to consumer demand.* — ADJ PRED : OFT+to

rest /rɛst/, **rests, resting, rested. 1** You refer to all the remaining parts of something or to all the other parts of something as the **rest** of it. EG *He spent the rest of his life in prison... It was happening not only in America but also throughout the rest of the world... It was just another grave like all the rest... The rest of us were allowed to go home.* — N SING : the+N OFT+of

2 If you **rest** or if you **rest** your body, you do not do anything active for a period of time. EG *Go back to bed and rest... The boy stopped for a moment to rest... Stop to relax and rest your muscles.* — V OR V+O

3 If you get some **rest** or have a **rest**, you sit or lie quietly, not doing anything active, and relax. EG *It was weeks before I got a decent night's rest... They wanted a rest.* — N UNCOUNT OR N COUNT : USU SING

4 If something such as an idea **rests** on a particular thing, it depends on that thing. EG *I believe that the future of civilisation rests on that decision.* — V+on/upon

5 If a responsibility or duty **rests** with you, you have that responsibility or duty. — V+with, Formal

6 If something **rests** somewhere or if you **rest** it there, its weight is supported by something. EG *He let her shoulders rest against his knees... ...a tub with a wide edge to rest your arm on.* — V-ERG+A

7 If your eyes **rest** on a particular object or person, you stop looking round you and look at that object or person. EG *Her eyes travelled slowly upward and rested on his hands.* — V+on/upon, Literary

8 A **rest** is also an object that is used to support something, especially your head or feet. EG *...a foot rest... ...a head rest.* — N COUNT : USU+SUPP

9 When an object that has been moving **comes to rest**, it finally stops. EG *It would drop thousands of feet before coming to rest.* — PHRASE, Formal

10 If you **put** or **set** someone's **mind at rest**, you say something to them that stops them worrying about something. EG *Let me set your mind at rest. There is nothing to worry about.* — PHRASE

11 If someone **lays** or **puts** an idea **to rest**, they succeed in proving that it is not true. EG *Mr Casey vowed to lay to rest allegations of improper business dealings.* — PHRASE, Formal

12 If you tell someone to **rest** assured that something is the case, you are reassuring them that it is the case. EG *Rest assured that everything's under control.* — V+C : OFT+REPORT, ONLY that

restaurant /rɛstə°rɒnt, -rɒŋ/, **restaurants.** A **restaurant** is a place where you can buy and eat a meal. EG *...a splendid Hungarian restaurant.* — N COUNT

rested /rɛstɪ²d/. If you feel **rested**, you feel more energetic because you have just had a rest. — ADJ QUALIT

If you are restrained, are you responsive?

restful /rɛstfʊl/. Something that is **restful** helps you to feel calm and relaxed. EG *The lighting is restful... ...a restful town.* ADJ QUALIT

restive /rɛstɪv/. If you are **restive**, you are impatient, bored, or dissatisfied. EG *The crew were restive and mutinous.* ADJ QUALIT Formal

restless /rɛstlɪ²s/. If you are **restless**, **1** you are bored, impatient, or dissatisfied, and you want to do something else. EG *I knew that within a fortnight I should feel restless again.* ◇ **restlessness**. EG *They are showing some signs of restlessness.* **2** you are always moving, because you find it difficult to stay still. EG *She was restless and fidgety.* ◇ **restlessly**. EG *He walked restlessly around the room.* ADJ QUALIT ◇ N UNCOUNT ADJ QUALIT ◇ ADV

restore /rɪ¹stɔː/, **restores, restoring, restored. 1** To **restore** something means to cause it to exist again. EG *...the task of restoring order... This generous action restored my faith in human beings.* V+O
◇ **restoration** /rɛstəreɪʃə⁰n/. EG *...the restoration of law and order.* ◇ N UNCOUNT
2 To **restore** someone or something to a previous state or condition means to cause them to return to that state or condition. EG *...a Charter which will restore pensioners to a position of equality... The Tories were restored to power.* V+O+*to*
3 When someone **restores** an old building, painting, or piece of furniture, they repair it and clean it, so that it returns to its original condition. V+O
◇ **restoration**. EG *...the restoration of ancient halls and manors.* ◇ N UNCOUNT
4 If you **restore** something that was lost or stolen to someone, you return it to them. EG *The territories were restored to their former owners.* V+O : OFT+*to* Formal

restrain /rɪ¹streɪn/, **restrains, restraining, restrained. 1** If someone or something **restrains** you, they stop you from doing what you were going to do. EG *She raised a finger as if to restrain Morris from speaking... He had been unable to restrain himself from telling Gertrude.* V+O OR V-REFL : OFT+*from*
2 If you **restrain** something that is growing or increasing, you prevent it from getting too large. EG *...the efforts of governments to restrain inflation.* V+O

restrained /rɪ¹streɪnd/. Someone or something that is **restrained** is very calm and unemotional. EG *He was polite and restrained... It is written in restrained and formal language.* ADJ QUALIT

restraint /rɪ¹streɪnt/, **restraints. 1 Restraints** are rules or conditions that limit or restrict someone or something. EG *The king suffered few restraints on his freedom of action... ...an agreed policy of income and price restraint.* N COUNT OR N UNCOUNT
2 Restraint is calm, controlled, and unemotional behaviour. EG *'Dear me,' he said with splendid restraint.* N UNCOUNT

restrict /rɪ¹strɪkt/, **restricts, restricting, restricted. 1** If you **restrict** something, you put a limit on it in order to prevent it becoming too large. EG *They restricted the number of students joining these faculties... A third possibility would be to restrict wage increases.* ◇ **restricted**. EG *...the restricted field of vision provided by the camera.* V+O ◇ ADJ QUALIT
2 To **restrict** people or animals means to limit their movements or actions. EG *Some manufacturers were not prepared to restrict themselves voluntarily.* V+O OR V-REFL
3 If you **restrict** someone or their activities to one thing, they can only do or deal with that thing. EG *The State should restrict its activities to the maintenance of law and order... I will restrict myself to countries where English is the main language.* V+O+*to* OR V-REFL+*to*
4 If something **is restricted** to a particular group, only that group can have it or do it. EG *Membership is restricted to men.* V+O+*to*

restricted /rɪ¹strɪktɪ²d/. **1** Something that is **restricted** is quite small or limited. EG *Many of these are of restricted importance... The range of choices, fortunately, is not as restricted as this.* ADJ QUALIT
2 A **restricted** document is one that only people with special permission can read. ADJ CLASSIF
3 A **restricted** area is one that only people with special permission can enter. ADJ CLASSIF

restriction /rɪ¹strɪkʃə⁰n/, **restrictions. 1** A **restriction** is an official rule that limits what you can do or that limits the amount or size of something. EG *The government placed restrictions on sales of weapons... ...traffic restrictions.* N COUNT : OFT+*on/of*
2 You can refer to anything that limits what you can do as a **restriction**. EG *...small salaries which placed restrictions on our social life... ...the restrictions of ageing.* N COUNT : OFT +*on/of*
3 When there is **restriction** of something that might grow, it is prevented from becoming too large. EG *...profit restriction.* N UNCOUNT
4 When there is **restriction** of people or **restriction** of their movements or actions, they are limited in their movements or actions. EG *Tight clothing causes restriction of free movement... There is no restriction on filming in the area.* N UNCOUNT

restrictive /rɪ¹strɪktɪv/. Something that is **restrictive** prevents you from doing what you want to. EG *...teenagers eager to escape restrictive home environments.* ADJ QUALIT

restructure /riːstrʌktʃə/, **restructures, restructuring, restructured.** To **restructure** an organization or system means to change the way it is organized, usually in order to make it work more effectively. EG *...proposals for restructuring the industry.* V+O

result /rɪzʌlt/, **results, resulting, resulted. 1** A **result** is something that happens or exists because of something else that has happened. EG *I nearly missed the flight as a result of going to Havana... The result was further victimisation... Twice he followed his own advice, with disastrous results.* N COUNT
2 If something **results** in a particular situation or event, it causes that situation or event to happen. EG *The use of such techniques could result in disastrous ecological changes... This will result in consumers paying higher prices.* V+*in*
3 If something **results** from a particular event or action, it is caused by that event or action. EG *Four-fifths of the damage resulted from bombing... A saving in cost would result.* V : OFT+*from*
4 A **result** is also **4.1** the final situation that exists at the end of a contest. EG *...the result of the Warrington by-election... ...the football results.* **4.2** the number that you get when you do a calculation. EG *The result should be calculated to three decimal places.* N COUNT
5 Your **results** are the marks or grades that you get for examinations you have taken. EG *You need good A-level results.* N COUNT : USU PLURAL

resultant /rɪzʌltənt/. When you refer to the **resultant** situation or thing, you are referring to the situation or thing that was caused by the event you have just mentioned. EG *The resultant improvement in health totally justified the treatment.* ADJ CLASSIF : ATTRIB Formal

resume /rɪ¹zj⁰uːm/, **resumes, resuming, resumed. 1** If you **resume** an activity or if it **resumes**, it begins again. EG *She was ready to resume her duties... He resumed reading... The music would stop at intervals, then resume after a while.* V-ERG
2 If you **resume** your former place or position, you return to it. EG *He resumed his seat.* V+O

resumption /rɪ¹zʌmp⁰ʃə⁰n/. When there is a **resumption** of an activity, it begins again after it has stopped for a while. EG *They are pressing for a quick resumption of arms negotiations.* N UNCOUNT Formal

resurgence /rɪ¹sɜːdʒəns/. If there is a **resurgence** of an attitude or activity, it reappears and grows. EG *There has been a resurgence of small scale guerrilla activity.* N UNCOUNT : OFT+*of*

resurrect /rɛzərɛkt/, **resurrects, resurrecting, resurrected.** When you **resurrect** something, you cause it to exist again after it had disappeared or ended. EG *There is not the remotest possibility of the government ever resurrecting the Maplin proj-* V+O *ect.* ◊ **resurrection** /rɛzərɛkʃəⁿn/. EG *...the resurrection of the Jazz Festival.* ◊ N UNCOUNT

resuscitate /rɪˈsʌsɪteɪt/, **resuscitates, resuscitating, resuscitated.** If you **resuscitate** someone who has lost consciousness, you cause them to become conscious again. V+O Formal

retail /riːteɪl/ is the activity of selling goods to the public. EG *We have opened a retail department... The original retail price was $80.* N UNCOUNT: USU N MOD

retailer /riːteɪlə/, **retailers.** A **retailer** is a person or business that sells goods to the public. N COUNT

retain /rɪˈteɪn/, **retains, retaining, retained. 1** If you **retain** something, you keep it. EG *We are fighting to retain some independence.* V+O Formal

2 If an object or substance **retains** heat or a liquid, it continues to contain it. EG *Water retains heat much longer than air.* V+O

retaliate /rɪˈtælieɪt/, **retaliates, retaliating, retaliated.** If you **retaliate** when someone harms or annoys you, you do something which harms or annoys them in return. EG *...the ability to retaliate during an attack... They retaliated by changing the venue for the meeting.* ◊ **retaliation** /rɪˈtælieɪʃəⁿn/. EG *It was agreed that immediate retaliation was necessary... They staged these attacks in retaliation for attacks on their own civilians.* V: USU+A ◊ N UNCOUNT

retaliatory /rɪˈtæljətəⁿtriˈ/. If you take **retaliatory** action, you try to harm someone who has harmed you. EG *...a retaliatory attack against an opponent's cities.* ADJ CLASSIF Formal

retarded /rɪˈtɑːdɪᵈd/. If someone is **retarded**, their mental development is much less advanced than that of most people of their age. EG *Her younger daughter was mentally retarded.* ADJ CLASSIF

retch /rɛtʃ/, **retches, retching, retched.** If you **retch**, your stomach moves as if you are vomiting. EG *The stench almost made him retch.* V

retention /rɪˈtɛnʃəⁿn/. The **retention** of something is the keeping of it. EG *They voted in favour of the retention of capital punishment.* N UNCOUNT Formal

rethink /riːθɪŋk/, **rethinks, rethinking, rethought.** If you **rethink** something such as a plan or a policy, you think about it and change it. EG *This forced us to rethink all of our plans.* V+O OR V

reticent /rɛtɪsənt/. Someone who is **reticent** does not tell people about things. EG *She was always extremely reticent about her colleagues.* ◊ **reticence** /rɛtɪsəns/. EG *...her reticence about her personal life.* ADJ QUALIT: OFT+*about* ◊ N UNCOUNT

retire /rɪˈtaɪə/, **retires, retiring, retired. 1** When older people **retire**, they leave their job and usually stop working altogether. EG *Women, unlike men, retire at sixty... They had decided to retire from farming.* V: OFT+A

2 If you **retire** to another room or place, you leave the people you are with so that you can be on your own. EG *I retired to my study upstairs.* V: USU+A Formal

3 When you **retire**, you go to bed. EG *She retired early with a good book.* V Formal

retired /rɪˈtaɪəd/. A **retired** person is an older person who has left his or her job and has usually stopped working altogether. EG *...a retired Army officer.* ADJ CLASSIF

retirement /rɪˈtaɪəməⁿnt/ is **1** the time when a worker retires. EG *Since my retirement, I have felt more energetic.* **2** the period in a person's life after they have retired. EG *...the house that his father had bought for his retirement.* N UNCOUNT

retiring /rɪˈtaɪərɪŋ/. **1** Someone who is **retiring** is shy and avoids meeting other people. EG *She was a shy, retiring girl.* ADJ QUALIT

2 A **retiring** official or employee is one who is going to retire very soon. EG *...Jim Dacre, the retiring Labour MP.* ADJ CLASSIF: ATTRIB

retort /rɪˈtɔːt/, **retorts, retorting, retorted.** To **retort** means to reply angrily to someone. EG *'I wish no such thing,' retorted Sarah... Lady Sackville retorted that if they came, she would leave.* ▸ used as a noun. EG *...a sharp retort.* V+QUOTE OR REPORT: ONLY *that* Written ▸ N COUNT

retrace /riːtreɪs/, **retraces, retracing, retraced.** If you **retrace** your steps or **retrace** your way, you return to where you started from by going back along the same route. EG *Stella retraced her steps toward the entrance.* V+O: USU+A

retract /rɪˈtrækt/, **retracts, retracting, retracted. 1** If you **retract** something that you have said or written, you say that you did not mean it. EG *At his trial, he retracted his confession.* V+O Formal

2 When a part of a machine or animal **retracts** or **is retracted**, it moves inwards or back. EG *The frog's eyes retract when its tongue shoots out.* V-ERG Formal

retreat /rɪˈtriːt/, **retreats, retreating, retreated. 1** If you **retreat**, you move away from something or someone. EG *Betsy and I retreated to the edge of the field... She retreated from him, pressing her back against the door.* V: USU+A

2 When an army **retreats**, it moves away from enemy forces in order to avoid fighting them. EG *They retreated a few kilometres.* ▸ used as a noun. EG *...the retreat of Napoleon's army... They can be starved into retreat.* V ▸ N COUNT OR N UNCOUNT

3 If you **retreat** from something such as a plan or a way of life, you give it up and do something safer or less extreme. EG *The Government was retreating from its commitments... The country retreated into neutrality.* ▸ used as a noun. EG *There has been a gradual retreat from the original principles.* V: OFT+*from/into* ▸ N COUNT OR N UNCOUNT

4 A **retreat** is a quiet, secluded place that you go to in order to rest or to do things in private. EG *They met at a woodland retreat near the Canadian capital... ...a weekend retreat.* N COUNT Written

5 If you **beat a retreat**, you run away from something. EG *He beat a hasty retreat.* PHRASE

retribution /rɛtrɪbjuːʃəⁿn/ is punishment for a crime. EG *...the fear of retribution.* N UNCOUNT Literary

retrieval /rɪˈtriːvəⁿl/. The **retrieval** of information from a computer is the process of getting it back. EG *...data retrieval.* N UNCOUNT

retrieve /rɪˈtriːv/, **retrieves, retrieving, retrieved. 1** If you **retrieve** something, you get it back from the place where you left it. EG *I ran back to my room and retrieved my bag.* V+O Formal

2 If you **retrieve** a situation, you bring it back into a more acceptable state. EG *Henry did his best to retrieve the situation.* V+O Formal

retrograde /rɛtrəᵍgreɪd/. You describe an action as **retrograde** when you think that it makes a situation worse rather than better. EG *The move was held to be an economically retrograde step.* ADJ CLASSIF Formal

retrospect /rɛtrəᵍspɛkt/. When you consider something **in retrospect**, you think about it afterwards, and often have a different opinion about it from the one that you had at the time. EG *There are some things that you only become totally conscious of in retrospect... In retrospect, what I had done was clearly unjustifiable.* PHRASE OR ADV SEN

retrospective /rɛtrəᵍspɛktɪv/. **1 Retrospective** feelings or opinions concern things that happened in the past. EG *...his retrospective embarrassment over the incident.* ◊ **retrospectively**. EG *Her father was described retrospectively as 'reserved and taciturn'.* ADJ CLASSIF Formal ◊ ADV OR ADV SEN

2 Retrospective laws or legal actions take effect from a date before the date when they are officially approved. ◊ **retrospectively**. EG *They are going to retrospectively validate unlawful actions.* ADJ CLASSIF Formal ◊ ADV

return /rɪˈtɜːn/, **returns, returning, returned. 1** When you **return** to a place, you go back there after you have been away. EG *I returned from the Middle East in 1956... He returned home several hours later... Her husband left for work one morning and did not return.* V: USU+A

When would you say 'Many happy returns'?

2 Your **return** is your arrival back at a place where you had been before. EG *On his return Haldane reported to the Cabinet... Julie had been tired since her return from New York.* N UNCOUNT +POSS

3 If you **return** something that you have borrowed or taken from someone else, you give it back to them. EG *He borrowed my best suit and didn't return it.* ▸ used as a noun. EG *Greece will be offered the return of these treasures as a goodwill gift.* V+O : OFT+*to* ▸ N UNCOUNT

4 If you **return** something to its previous place, you put it back there. EG *We returned the books to the shelf.* V+O+*to* Formal

5 When you **return** the ball during a game, you hit it back to your opponent. ▸ used as a noun. EG *Miss Evert reached to lob a return of Miss Wade's.* V+O ▸ N COUNT

6 If you **return** someone's action, you do the same thing to them that they have just done to you. If you **return** someone's feeling, you feel the same way towards them as they feel towards you. EG *He didn't return their greetings... She was looking for somebody to return her affection.* V+O

7 If you do something **in return** for what someone else has done for you, you do it because they did that thing for you. EG *They had nothing to give in return.* PHRASE

8 If a feeling or situation **returns**, it comes back or happens again after a period of absence. EG *If the pain returns, the treatment is repeated... After nine months, the rains returned.* ▸ used as a noun. EG *...the return of better times.* V ▸ N SING+SUPP

9 If you **return** to a subject that you have mentioned before, you begin talking about it again. EG *We shall return to this theme in Chapter 7.* V+*to*

10 If you **return** to an activity that you were doing before, you start doing it again. EG *After lunch, Edward returned to his gardening.* ▸ used as a noun. EG *There seems to be a return to the use of wood in furniture-making.* V+*to* ▸ N SING+*to*

11 If you **return** to a state that you were formerly in, you are in that state again. EG *...the groans of wounded men returning to consciousness.* ▸ used as a noun. EG *He referred to the Party's hopes for a return to power.* V+*to* ▸ N SING+*to*

12 When a judge or jury **returns** a verdict, they announce whether they think the person on trial is guilty or not. V+O Legal

13 A **return** or a **return ticket** is a ticket for a train, bus, or aeroplane that allows you to travel to a particular place and then back again. EG *...a return ticket to Vienna.* N COUNT

14 The **return** on an investment is the profit that you get from it. EG *Companies seek higher returns by investing in other corporations.* N COUNT OR N UNCOUNT

15 You say **many happy returns** or **many happy returns of the day** as a way of wishing someone a happy birthday. CONVENTION

16 If you say that you have reached **the point of no return**, you mean that you now have to continue with what you are doing and it is too late to stop. PHRASE

reunion /riˈjuːnjəⁿn/, **reunions.** A **reunion** is **1** a party attended by members of the same family, school, or other group who have not seen each other for a long time. EG *...a family reunion.* N COUNT **2** a meeting between two people who have been separated for some time. EG *...her hope of reunion with her father.* N COUNT OR N UNCOUNT

reunite /riːjuːnaɪt/, **reunites, reuniting, reunited.** **1** If two people **are reunited**, they meet each other again after they have been separated for some time. EG *It won't be long before you are reunited with your family.* V+O : USU PASS

2 If someone **reunites** a divided organization or country, they bring its parts together to make it united again. EG *During 1979-80 he worked to reunite the Labour movement.* V+O

rev /rɛv/, **revs, revving, revved.** When you **rev** the engine of a vehicle or **rev** it **up**, you increase the engine speed by pressing the accelerator. EG *He revved the motor and then roared off... I heard the sound of an engine revving up.* V-ERG : OFT+*up*

Rev. Rev and **Revd** are written abbreviations for 'Reverend'. EG *...the Rev David Drew.*

reveal /rɪˈviːl/, **reveals, revealing, revealed.** **1** To **reveal** something means to make people aware of it. EG *They were not ready to reveal any details of the arrest... A newspaper had once revealed that he'd wanted to marry his cousin... Howard now revealed a certain talent for fixing things.* V+O, V+REPORT, OR V+A

2 If you **reveal** something that has been out of sight, you uncover it so that people can see it. EG *She drew the curtains aside to reveal beautiful gardens.* V+O

revealing /rɪˈviːlɪŋ/. **1** An action or statement that is **revealing** tells you something that you did not know, especially about the person doing it or making it. EG *He had nothing very revealing to say.* ADJ QUALIT

2 Women's clothes that are **revealing** allow more of their body to be seen than is usual. EG *...revealing black nightdresses.* ADJ QUALIT

revel /rɛvəⁿl/, **revels, revelling, revelled;** spelled **reveling** and **reveled** in American English. If you **revel** in a situation or experience, you enjoy it very much. EG *She seemed to revel in her success.* V : USU+*in*

revelation /rɛvəleɪʃəⁿn/, **revelations.** **1** A **revelation** is a fact that is made known to people, especially a surprising or interesting one. EG *His book offers no illuminating personal revelations.* N COUNT : USU PLURAL

2 If you say that an experience was a **revelation**, you mean that it made you realize something very surprising. EG *The whole episode was a revelation to him of how poor the family had been.* N SING : *a*+N, OFT+*to*

revelry /rɛvəⁿlriˈ/ is noisy and often drunken enjoyment. EG *The sound of good-natured revelry filled the hotel.* N UNCOUNT Outdated

revenge /rɪˈvɛndʒ/, **revenges, revenging, revenged.** **1** **Revenge** involves hurting someone who has hurt you. EG *They were eager for revenge... They had taken their revenge by blowing up his house.* N UNCOUNT

2 If you **revenge** yourself on someone who has hurt you, you hurt them in return. EG *She will revenge herself on those who helped him to escape.* V-REFL : OFT+*on* Formal

revenue /rɛvɪ²njuː/, **revenues. Revenue** is money that a company, organization, or government receives from people. EG *The editor was concerned at the drop in advertising revenue... A recession would reduce government tax revenues.* N UNCOUNT OR N PLURAL

reverberate /rɪˈvɜːbəreɪt/, **reverberates, reverberating, reverberated.** **1** When a loud sound **reverberates** through a place, it echoes and seems to shake the place. EG *A clap of thunder reverberated throughout the house.* V : USU+A Literary

2 You can say that an event or idea **reverberates** when it has a powerful effect which lasts a long time. EG *This was a shock which was to reverberate through the whole of his married life.* V : USU+A Literary

revere /rɪˈvɪə/, **reveres, revering, revered.** If you **revere** someone, you respect and admire them greatly. EG *...her dead mother, whose memory she revered.* ◇ **revered**. EG *He was a revered figure with a national reputation.* V+O Formal ◇ ADJ QUALIT

reverence /rɛvəⁿrəns/ is a feeling of great respect for someone or something. EG *The sect teaches reverence for all life.* N UNCOUNT

Reverend /rɛvəⁿrənd/ is a title used before the name or rank of a member of the clergy. EG *...the Reverend John Lamb.*

reverent /rɛvəⁿrənt/. If your behaviour is **reverent**, you show great respect for someone or something. EG *We filed past the tomb in a reverent manner.* ◇ **reverently**. EG *She laid the book reverently on the desk.* ADJ QUALIT ◇ ADV

reversal /rɪˈvɜːsəⁿl/, **reversals.** **1** When there is a **reversal** of a process or policy, it is changed to the N COUNT : USU SING+SUPP opposite process or policy. EG *Fortunately there was a reversal of this suicidal tendency... They were pressing for a reversal of British policy.*

2 When there is a **reversal** of two things, each one acquires the position or function that the other one had. EG *Events in this present century have produced a complete reversal of roles.* N COUNT: USU SING+SUPP

reverse /rɪˈvɜːs/, **reverses, reversing, reversed.** 1 When someone **reverses** a process, decision, or policy, they change it to the opposite process, decision, or policy. EG *The farmers want to see this trend reversed... On January 31, the party reversed its decision and agreed to the change.* V+O

2 If you **reverse** the order of a set of things, you arrange them in the opposite order, so that the first thing comes last. V+O

3 If you **reverse** the positions or functions of two things, you change them so that each thing has the position or function that the other one had. EG *In this play the traditional sex roles are reversed... The next stage was to reverse the positions of the two pictures.* V+O

4 When a car **reverses** or when you **reverse** it, you drive it backwards. EG *The street was so narrow that cars which entered it had to reverse out again.* V-ERG

5 If your car is in **reverse**, you have changed gear so that you can drive it backwards. EG *I threw the truck into reverse.* N UNCOUNT

6 **Reverse** means opposite to what is usual or to what has just been described. EG *In the past ten years I think we've seen the reverse process.* ADJ CLASSIF: ATTRIB

7 The **reverse** is the exact opposite of what has just been mentioned. EG *You may think we have been making a profit. In fact the reverse is true.* N SING: *the*+N

8 If a process happens **in reverse** or goes **into reverse**, things happen in the opposite way to what usually happens or to what has been happening. EG *At this point the Party's fortunes went into reverse.* PHRASE

9 If you **reverse the charges** when you make a telephone call, the person who you are calling receives the bill and not you. PHRASE British

reversion /rɪˈvɜːʃəⁿn/. **Reversion** to a former state, system, or kind of behaviour is a change back to it. EG *...this reversion to pre-scientific attitudes.* N UNCOUNT+*to* Formal

revert /rɪˈvɜːt/, **reverts, reverting, reverted.** When people or things **revert** to a former state, system, or type of behaviour, they go back to it. EG *He was reverting rapidly to adolescence... Areas that are cleared for farming sometimes revert to forest later.* V+*to* Formal

review /rɪˈvjuː/, **reviews, reviewing, reviewed.**

1 A **review** is an article in a newspaper or magazine, or an item on television or radio, in which someone gives their opinion of something such as a new book or play. EG *...a review of Lord Harewood's autobiography... ...book reviews.* N COUNT

2 When there is a **review** of a situation or system, it is formally examined in order to decide whether changes are needed. EG *A review of public expenditure began immediately.* N COUNT OR N UNCOUNT ▸ used as a verb. EG *By law, state pensions must be reviewed once a year.* ▸ V+O

3 When something **comes up for review**, the time arrives for it to be formally examined to see whether changes are needed. When it is **under review**, it is being examined in this way. EG *They had the situation under review.* PHRASE

4 If you **review** a situation, you consider it carefully. EG *Dawdling over a cup of coffee, he reviewed his situation once more.* V+O

5 If you **review** something such as a new book or play, you write an article or give a talk on television or radio in which you express your opinion of it. V+O ◇ **reviewer, reviewers.** EG *Reviewers loved the book.* ◇ N COUNT

revise /rɪˈvaɪz/, **revises, revising, revised.** 1 If you **revise** something, you alter it in order to make it better or more correct. EG *The judges may revise their selection process... This book has sold a half-million copies since it was revised last year.* V+O ◇ **revised.** EG *...a revised estimate of $9,000,000.* ◇ ADJ CLASSIF

2 When you **revise** for an examination, you read things again in order to learn them thoroughly. EG *I've been revising for the last three days... I was revising Dickens last night.* V OR V+O

revision /rɪˈvɪʒəⁿn/, **revisions.** 1 A **revision** of something is an alteration that is made to it in order to improve it. EG *They're discussing a complete revision of the timetable... The Shops Act is in need of revision.* N COUNT OR N UNCOUNT: OFT+*of*

2 When you do **revision**, you read things again in order to learn them for an examination. EG *I've got to do some revision.* N UNCOUNT

revitalize /riːˈvaɪtəlaɪz/, **revitalizes, revitalizing, revitalized;** also spelled **revitalise.** V+O
To **revitalize** something means to make it more active or lively. EG *...its plan to revitalise the American economy... ...the Liverpool poets who revitalized poetry in England in the 1960s.*

revival /rɪˈvaɪvəⁿl/, **revivals.** When there is a **revival** of something, it becomes active again. EG *Inflation may start to rise with the revival of trade... Why is there such a revival of interest in the supernatural?* N UNCOUNT OR N COUNT: USU+SUPP

revive /rɪˈvaɪv/, **revives, reviving, revived.** 1 When something such as a feeling or a practice **revives** or **is revived**, it becomes active, popular, or successful again. EG *My spirits revived as we drove out into the countryside... They failed to fulfil their promises to revive the economy.* V-ERG

2 When you **revive** someone who has fainted or when they **revive**, they become conscious again. EG *They had difficulty in reviving him... He slowly began to revive.* V-ERG

revoke /rɪˈvəʊk/, **revokes, revoking, revoked.** When someone in authority **revokes** something such as a licence or an order, they cancel it. EG *The permission was revoked.* V+O Formal

revolt /rɪˈvəʊlt/, **revolts, revolting, revolted.** A **revolt** is a violent attempt by a group of people to change their country's political system. EG *...the Peasants' Revolt of 1381... The settlers rose in revolt.* N COUNT OR N UNCOUNT ▸ used as a verb. EG *Large sections of the army revolted against the civil government.* ▸ V: OFT +*against*

revolting /rɪˈvəʊltɪŋ/. You say that something is **revolting** when you think that it is horrible and disgusting. EG *The smell was quite revolting.* ADJ QUALIT

revolution /rɛvəljᵒuːʃəⁿn/, **revolutions.** 1 A **revolution** is a successful attempt by a large group of people to change the political system of their country by force. EG *...the fiftieth anniversary of the Russian revolution... France seemed to be on the verge of revolution.* N COUNT OR N UNCOUNT

2 A **revolution** is also an important change in a particular area of human activity. EG *...the Industrial Revolution... ...the Computer Revolution... ...the revolution in communications.* N COUNT

revolutionary /rɛvəljᵒuːʃənəⁿriˈ/, **revolutionaries.** 1 **Revolutionary** activities are intended to cause a political revolution. EG *They had fled as a result of their revolutionary activities.* ADJ CLASSIF

2 A **revolutionary** is a person who tries to cause a revolution or who takes part in one. N COUNT ▸ used as an adjective. *...a revolutionary leader.* ▸ ADJ CLASSIF

3 **Revolutionary** ideas and developments involve great changes in the way that something is done or made. EG *...a revolutionary change in the way cars are manufactured.* ADJ QUALIT

revolutionize /rɛvəljᵒuːʃənaɪz/, **revolutionizes, revolutionizing, revolutionized;** also spelled **revolutionise.** When something **revolutionizes** an activity, it causes great changes in the way that V+O

What is ambiguous about 'The peasants are revolting'?

it is done. EG *Our ideas will revolutionize the film industry.*

revolve /rɪ¹vɒlv/, **revolves, revolving, revolved. 1** If you say that someone's life **revolves** around something, you mean that it is the main feature of their life. EG *Rural life revolved around agriculture.* V+*around*/*round*

2 If a discussion **revolves** around a particular topic, it is mainly about that topic. EG *The discussion revolved round three topics.* V+*around*/*round*

3 When something **revolves**, it moves or turns in a circle around a central point or line. EG *...the discovery that the earth revolved around the sun.* V: OFT+*around*/*round*
◇ **revolving**. EG *They were watering the ground with big revolving sprinklers.* ◇ ADJ CLASSIF: ATTRIB

revolver /rɪ¹vɒlvə/, **revolvers.** A **revolver** is a kind of gun that you hold in your hand. See picture at WEAPONS. N COUNT

revolving door

revolving door, revolving doors. A **revolving door** consists of four glass doors which turn together around a vertical post. N COUNT

revulsion /rɪ¹vʌlʃə⁰n/ is a strong feeling of disgust or disapproval. EG *Germ warfare has always been regarded with revulsion.* N UNCOUNT

reward /rɪ¹wɔːd/, **rewards, rewarding, rewarded. 1** A **reward** is something that you get or are given because you have done something useful or good. EG *...a reward for outstanding service... ...the emotional rewards of parenthood... They work with no thought of reward.* N COUNT OR N UNCOUNT

2 To **reward** someone means to give them something because they have done something useful or good. EG *People should be rewarded for special effort... They rewarded the winners with gifts of fruit and flowers.* V+O

rewarding /rɪ¹wɔːdɪŋ/. Something that is **rewarding** gives you a lot of satisfaction. EG *...rewarding jobs... ...a rewarding novel.* ADJ QUALIT

rewind /riːwaɪnd/, **rewinds, rewinding, rewound** /riːwaʊnd/. When you **rewind** the tape on a tape recorder, you make the tape go backwards so that you can play it again. V+O OR V

rewrite /riːraɪt/, **rewrites, rewriting, rewrote** /riːrəʊt/, **rewritten** /riːrɪtə⁰n/. If you **rewrite** a piece of writing, you write it in a different way in order to improve it. EG *Scenes 9 and 10 need rewriting.* V+O

rhetoric /rɛtərɪk/ is fine-sounding speech or writing that is meant to convince and impress people; often used showing disapproval. EG *I was expecting the usual fiery rhetoric from the Chairman... ...political rhetoric.* N UNCOUNT

rhetorical /rɪ²tɒrɪkə⁰l/. **1** A **rhetorical** question is one which is asked in order to make a statement rather than to get an answer. ADJ CLASSIF

2 Rhetorical language is intended to be grand and impressive. EG *...their rhetorical threats to 'crush the oppressors'.* ADJ CLASSIF

rheumatic /ruːmætɪk/. **1 Rheumatic** pains are caused by rheumatism. ADJ CLASSIF

2 Someone who is **rheumatic** suffers from rheumatism. ADJ CLASSIF

rheumatism /ruːmətɪzə⁰m/ is an illness that makes your joints or muscles stiff and painful. EG *They were crippled with rheumatism.* N UNCOUNT

rhino /raɪnəʊ/, **rhinos.** A **rhino** is the same as a rhinoceros. N COUNT

rhinoceros /raɪnɒsə⁰rəs/, **rhinoceroses.** A **rhinoceros** is a large animal with one or two horns on its nose. Rhinoceroses live in Africa and Asia and eat plants. N COUNT

rhododendron /rəʊdədɛndrən/, **rhododendrons.** A **rhododendron** is a bush with large pink or purple flowers. N COUNT

rhubarb /ruːbɑːb/ is a plant with long red stems which people eat after cooking them with sugar. N UNCOUNT

rhyme /raɪm/, **rhymes, rhyming, rhymed. 1** If one word **rhymes** with another or if two words **rhyme**, they have a very similar sound. Words that rhyme with each other are often used in poems. EG *She called him Guppy, to rhyme with puppy.* V OR V+*with*: RECIP

2 A **rhyme** is **2.1** a word which rhymes with another word. EG *...two words he could not find a rhyme for.* **2.2** a short poem which has rhyming words at the ends of its lines. EG *...children's games and rhymes.* ● See also **nursery rhyme**. N COUNT

3 Rhyme is the use of rhyming words as a technique in poetry. EG *She had a gift for rhythm and rhyme.* ● If something is written **in rhyme**, it is written as a poem in which the lines rhyme. EG *Tennyson's work was mostly in rhyme.* N UNCOUNT ● PHRASE

rhythm /rɪðə⁰m/, **rhythms.** A **rhythm** is **1** a regular movement or beat. EG *...the rhythm of the drums... J J Cale uses rhythm for the opposite effect in his music.* **2** a regular pattern of changes, for example changes in your body, in the seasons, or in the tides. EG *...the rhythms of the sea.* N COUNT OR N UNCOUNT; N COUNT

rhythmic /rɪðmɪk/. If a movement or sound is **rhythmic**, it is repeated at regular intervals, forming a regular pattern or beat. EG *The machine made a soft rhythmic sound.* ◇ **rhythmically**. EG *The cradle rocked rhythmically to and fro.* ADJ QUALIT ◇ ADV

rib /rɪb/, **ribs.** Your **ribs** are the curved bones that go from your backbone to your chest. EG *He had a broken rib.* N COUNT

ribald /rɪbə⁰ld/. **Ribald** remarks are rather rude and refer to sex in a humorous way. EG *...exclamations of ribald encouragement... ...ribald laughter.* ADJ QUALIT Outdated

ribbon /rɪbə⁰n/, **ribbons. 1** A **ribbon** is a long, narrow piece of cloth that you use for tying things together or as a decoration. EG *There was a white ribbon in her hair... ...a length of silk ribbon.* N COUNT OR N UNCOUNT

2 A typewriter **ribbon** is a long, narrow piece of cloth containing a special ink that you put into a typewriter to make it work. N COUNT OR N UNCOUNT

rib-cage, rib-cages. Your **rib-cage** is the structure of ribs in your chest. N COUNT

rice /raɪs/ is a food consisting of white grains which you cook and eat, usually with meat or vegetables. The plant from which rice is taken is also called **rice**. EG *She cooked a dish of rice and chicken... ...a rice field.* N UNCOUNT

rich /rɪtʃ/, **richer, richest; riches. 1** Someone who is **rich** has a lot of money or valuable possessions. EG *She was extremely rich... Our father was a very rich man.* ADJ QUALIT

2 Riches are valuable possessions or large amounts of money. EG *...young men in search of adventure and riches.* N PLURAL

3 If you talk about the earth's **riches**, you are referring to things that exist naturally in large quantities and that are useful to people, for example minerals, wood, and oil. EG *...the exploitation of the earth's riches.* N PLURAL

4 If something is **rich** in a desirable substance or quality, it contains a lot of it. EG *The sea bed is rich in buried minerals... The story is rich in comic and dramatic detail.* ADJ PRED+*in*

5 A **rich** deposit of a mineral or other substance ADJ QUALIT: ATTRIB consists of a large amount of it. EG ...*the world's richest vein of copper.*

6 Rich soil contains large amounts of substances that make it good for growing crops or flowers in. ADJ QUALIT

7 Rich food contains a lot of fat or oil. EG *He was prone to indigestion after rich restaurant meals.* ADJ QUALIT

8 Rich colours, smells, and sounds are strong and pleasant. EG *The sea was a deep rich blue... ...the rich sound of the brass instruments.* ADJ QUALIT

9 If you say that a place has a **rich** history, you mean that its history is very interesting. EG *The town has a rich social history.* ADJ QUALIT

richly /rɪtʃli¹/. **1** If someone is **richly** rewarded for something, they are rewarded well by being given something very valuable. ADV

2 If you feel strongly that someone deserves something or has earned it, you can say that it is **richly** deserved or **richly** earned. EG *It was a richly deserved honour.* ADV

3 If a place is **richly** provided with something, it has a lot of it. EG *These libraries are richly equipped with games and books.* ADV

4 If something is **richly** decorated, it has a lot of elaborate and beautiful decoration on it. EG ...*the richly carved wooden screen.* ADV

rickety /rɪkɪ¹ti¹/. A **rickety** building or piece of furniture has not been made strongly, and is therefore likely to collapse or break. EG *She started off down the rickety stairs.* ADJ QUALIT

rickshaw /rɪkʃɔː/, **rickshaws.** A **rickshaw** is a simple vehicle that is used in Asia for carrying passengers. Some rickshaws are pulled by a man who walks or runs in front. N COUNT

ricochet /rɪkəʃeɪ, rɪkəʃɛt/, **ricochets, ricocheting, ricocheted;** also spelled **ricochetting, ricochetted.** When a bullet **ricochets**, it hits a surface and bounces away from it. EG *The bullet ricochetted off the ceiling.* V : USU+A

rid /rɪd/, **rids, ridding.** The form **rid** is used in the present tense and is the past tense and past participle of the verb.

1 When you **get rid of** something that you do not want, you take action so that you no longer have it. EG *She bathed thoroughly to get rid of the last traces of make-up... How do they get rid of rats and mice?... We had to get rid of the director.* PHRASE

2 If you **rid** a place of something unpleasant or annoying, you succeed in removing it completely. EG *We must rid the country of this wickedness.* V+O+*of* Formal

3 If you **rid** yourself of something undesirable, you take action so that you no longer have it or are no longer affected by it. EG *He had rid himself of his illusions.* V-REFL+*of* Formal

4 If you are **rid** of someone or something that had been worrying or annoying you, they are no longer with you or affecting you. EG *Eric was glad to be rid of him.* ADJ PRED+*of*

riddance /rɪdə⁰ns/. You say **good riddance** to indicate that you are glad that someone has left. CONVENTION Informal

ridden /rɪdə⁰n/ is the past participle of **ride.**

riddle /rɪdə⁰l/, **riddles. 1** A **riddle** is a puzzle in which you ask a question that seems to be nonsense but which has a clever or amusing answer, for example 'When is a door not a door? When it's ajar.' N COUNT

2 If you describe something as a **riddle**, you mean that you are unable to understand it or find an answer to it. EG *I was trying to solve the perplexing riddle of how to help my people.* N COUNT

riddled /rɪdə⁰ld/. **1** If something is **riddled** with holes, it is full of them. EG *They had left the whole building riddled with holes.* ADJ PRED +*with*

2 If something is **riddled** with undesirable qualities or features, it is full of them. EG ...*cities riddled with corruption.* ADJ PRED +*with*

ride /raɪd/, **rides, riding, rode** /rəʊd/, **ridden** /rɪdə⁰n/. **1** When you **ride** a horse, you sit on it and control its movements. EG *Every morning he used to ride his mare across the fields... He arrived later, riding on his large white horse.* V+O OR V

2 When you **ride** a bicycle or a motorcycle, you sit on it, control it, and travel along on it. EG *He rode round the campus on a bicycle.* V+O OR V+A

3 When you **ride** in a vehicle such as a car, you travel in it. EG *That afternoon he rode in a jeep to the village.* V+A

4 A **ride** is a journey on a horse or bicycle, or in a vehicle. EG *I'd like to go for a ride... ...the bus ride to Worcester... Like a ride to the village?* N COUNT

5 If you say that someone **has taken** you **for a ride**, you mean that they have deceived you or cheated you. PHRASE Informal

ride up. If a skirt or dress **rides up**, it moves upwards, out of its proper position. PHRASAL VB : V+ADV

rider /raɪdə/, **riders.** A **rider** is someone who is riding a horse, a bicycle, or a motorcycle. EG *The rider was thrown off... ...a motorcycle rider.* N COUNT

ridge /rɪdʒ/, **ridges.** A **ridge** is **1** a long, narrow piece of raised land. EG *We drove up a hillside and finally stopped on a high ridge.* **2** a raised line on a flat surface. EG *He was counting the ridges in the wet sand.* N COUNT

ridicule /rɪdɪkjuːl/, **ridicules, ridiculing, ridiculed.** If you **ridicule** someone or **ridicule** what they say or do, you make fun of them in an unkind way. EG *He is liable to be teased and ridiculed.* V+O

▸ used as a noun. EG *His prophecy was greeted with a good deal of ridicule.* ▸ N UNCOUNT

ridiculous /rɪdɪkjə⁴ləs/. If you say that something is **ridiculous**, you mean that it is very foolish. EG *It would be ridiculous to pretend that there were no difficulties... Don't be so ridiculous... They charge you a ridiculous price.* ◇ **ridiculously**. EG *He let out his house at a ridiculously low rent.* ADJ QUALIT ◇ SUBMOD

rife /raɪf/. If you say that something bad or unpleasant is **rife**, you mean that it is very common. EG *Bribery and corruption in the government service were rife.* ADJ PRED Formal

rifle /raɪfə⁰l/, **rifles, rifling, rifled. 1** A **rifle** is a gun with a long barrel. See picture at WEAPONS. N COUNT

2 When someone **rifles** something, they steal everything they want from it. EG *He rifled the dead man's wallet... She found him rifling her fridge.* V+O

3 If you **rifle** through things, you make a quick search among them. EG *The doctor rifled through the papers.* V+*through*

rift /rɪft/, **rifts. 1** A **rift** between people is a serious quarrel that makes them stop being friends. EG *It had been nine years since she had seen her brother, as a result of a rift between them.* N COUNT : OFT +*between/in*

2 A **rift** is also a split that appears in something solid, especially in the ground. EG *The Jemez Mountains face Santa Fe across the rift.* N COUNT

rig /rɪg/, **rigs, rigging, rigged. 1** If someone **rigs** an election, a job appointment, or a game, they dishonestly arrange it so that they achieve the result that they want. V+O

2 A **rig** is a large structure that is used for looking for oil or gas and for taking it out of the ground or the sea bed. EG ...*an oil rig... ...a drilling rig.* N COUNT

rig up. If you **rig up** a device or structure, you make it and fix it in place using any materials that are available. EG *He had rigged up a listening device.* PHRASAL VB : V+O+ADV

rigging /rɪgɪŋ/. The ropes which support a ship's masts and sails are referred to as the **rigging**. N UNCOUNT

right /raɪt/, **rights, righting, righted. 1** If something is **right**, it is correct and in accordance with the facts. EG *You get full marks for getting the right answer... You are French, is that right?... I hope I'm pronouncing the name right.* ADJ CLASSIF OR ADV

2 If someone is **right** about something, they are ADJ PRED

Does a right-hand man have to be right-handed?

correct in what they say or think about it. EG *Lally was right about the repairs which the cottage needed... You're absolutely right.* ◊ **rightly**. EG *The arts are, as Geoffrey rightly said, underfinanced.* ◊ ADV

3 If something such as a choice, action, or decision is the **right** one, it is the best or most suitable one. EG *Are you sure that was the right decision?... I thought it was the right thing to do... Clare is obviously the right person to talk to about it.* ◊ **rightly**. EG *He can be very good at acting when he is rightly cast.* ADJ CLASSIF; ◊ ADV

4 If something isn't **right**, there is something unsatisfactory about the situation or thing that you are talking about. EG *She sensed that things weren't right between us.* ADJ PRED: WITH BROAD NEG

5 If you say that someone is **right** to do something, you mean that you think that they are morally justified in doing it. EG *We were right to insist on certain reforms... I don't think it's right to leave children alone in a house.* ◊ **rightly**. EG *Many people are rightly indignant.* ADJ PRED: USU+*to*-INF; ◊ ADV

6 **Right** is used to refer to actions that are considered to be morally good and acceptable. EG *One must have some principles, some sense of right and wrong.* N UNCOUNT

7 If you refer to the **right** people or the **right** places, you are referring to people and places that are socially admired. EG *He knew all the right people.* ADJ CLASSIF: ATTRIB

8 The **right** side of a piece of material is the side that is intended to be seen and that faces outwards when it is made into clothes. ADJ CLASSIF: ATTRIB

9 You say **'Right'** in order to attract someone's attention, especially when you want to begin something. EG *Right, open your mouth, let's have a look.* ADV SEN

10 If you have a **right** to do or have something, you are morally or legally entitled to do it or have it. EG *...the right to strike... They will fight for their rights... ...basic civil and political rights.* N COUNT

11 **Right** is one of two opposite directions, sides, or positions. If you are facing north and you turn to the right, you will be facing east. In the word 'to', the 'o' is to the right of the 't'. EG *On my left was Tony Heard and on my right Allister Sparks... They turned their heads from left to right.* ▸ used as an adverb or an adjective. EG *Turn right off Broadway into Caxton Street... Her right hand was covered in blood.* N UNCOUNT OR N SING; ▸ ADV OR ADJ CLASSIF: ATTRIB

12 The **Right** is used to refer to the people or groups who support the political ideals of capitalism and conservatism rather than socialism. N COLL: SING

13 **Right** is used **13.1** to emphasize the precise place that you are talking about. EG *Our hotel was right on the beach... Stay right here.* **13.2** to emphasize how far something moves or extends, or how long something continues. EG *We took the lift right down to the basement... This went on right up until 1975.* **13.3** to emphasize a noun referring to something bad. EG *They've made a right mess of that, haven't they?* ADV+A; ADV+A; ADJ CLASSIF: ATTRIB Informal

14 **Right** also means immediately and without delay. EG *I'll be right back... The Music Hall is going to close down right after Easter.* ADV+A

15 If you **right** something that has fallen or rolled over or if it **rights** itself, it returns to its normal upright position. EG *The ship righted itself.* V+O OR V-REFL

16 To **right** a wrong means to correct it or compensate for it. V+O

17 **Right** is also used in these phrases. **17.1** If you **get** something **right**, you do it correctly. EG *Get the spelling right this time.* **17.2** If you **put right** or **set right** a mistake or an unsatisfactory situation, you do something to make things satisfactory. EG *The only way we can put things right is by borrowing even more money.* **17.3** **Right now** means at this moment. EG *I have no time right now to discuss your problems.* **17.4** **Right away** means immediately and without any delay. EG *He had written down a list of things to do right away.* **17.5** If you are **in the right**, what you are doing is morally or legally correct. **17.6** If you say that something should be true **by rights**, you are emphasizing that it should be true, although it isn't. EG *I should by rights speak German – my mother's German – but I only know a few words.* **17.7** If you have a position, title, or claim to something **in** your **own right**, you have it because of what you are yourself rather than because of other people. EG *He had emerged as a leader in his own right.* **17.8** to **reserve the right to** do something: see **reserve**. ● to **serve** someone **right**: see **serve**. ● **on the right side of** someone: see **side**. ● See also **all right**. PHRASES; Informal; Formal

right angle, right angles. 1 A **right angle** is an angle of 90°. A square has four right angles. N COUNT

2 If one thing is **at right angles** to another, or if two things are **at right angles**, they are situated so that they form an angle of 90° where they touch each other. EG *...four corridors at right angles to each other.* PHRASE

righteous /raɪtʃəs/. **Righteous** people behave in a way that is morally good, religious, and praiseworthy. EG *...a righteous and wise man... ...righteous anger.* ◊ **righteousness**. EG *Some of us strive for righteousness.* ADJ QUALIT Formal; ◊ N UNCOUNT

rightful /raɪtfʊl/. Someone's **rightful** possession, place, or role is one which they have a legal or moral right to have. EG *They had been deprived of their rightful share of the property... He can now take his rightful place as president.* ADJ CLASSIF: ATTRIB Formal

right-hand is used to describe something which is on the right side. EG *...a biggish house on the right-hand side of the road.* ADJ CLASSIF: ATTRIB

right-handed. Someone who is **right-handed** uses their right hand rather than their left hand for activities such as writing and painting. ADJ CLASSIF

right-hand man, right-hand men. If you refer to a man as your **right-hand man**, you mean that he is the person who helps you most in your work. EG *I'm counting on you being my right-hand man.* N COUNT: USU+POSS

right of way, rights of way. 1 When a car or other vehicle has **right of way**, it has the right to cross a road or continue round a roundabout, and other traffic must stop for it. N UNCOUNT

2 A **right of way** is a public path across private land. N COUNT

right-wing. 1 Right-wing people support conservatism and capitalism. EG *...the election of a right-wing government... They are very right-wing.* ADJ QUALIT

2 The **right wing** of a political party consists of the members who are most in favour of conservatism and capitalism. EG *If he started to introduce reforms, his right wing would challenge him.* N SING

right-winger, right-wingers. A **right-winger** is a person who supports conservatism and capitalism or whose political beliefs are closer to conservatism than those of most of the other people in the same party. N COUNT

rigid /rɪdʒɪd/. **1** Laws or systems that are **rigid** cannot be changed or varied, and are therefore considered to be rather severe. EG *Some mothers resented the rigid controls.* ◊ **rigidity** /rɪdʒɪdɪ'ti'/. EG *...the rigidity of Victorian marriage.* ADJ QUALIT; ◊ N UNCOUNT

2 You say that people are **rigid** when they are not able or not willing to change their way of thinking or behaving; used showing disapproval. EG *...the rigid attitude of the Foreign Secretary.* ADJ QUALIT

3 A **rigid** substance or object is stiff and does not bend easily. EG *...with permed hair in rigid waves... I sat upright, rigid with nervousness.* ◊ **rigidity**. EG *The function of bones is largely to give rigidity.* ADJ QUALIT; ◊ N UNCOUNT

rigidly /rɪdʒɪdli'/. **1** If you stay **rigidly** in one position, you do not move. EG *I looked rigidly ahead... My features stayed rigidly fixed in the same expression.* ADV

2 If you deal with something **rigidly**, you do it in a very strict way with no possibility of variation or ADV

change. EG *These suggestions must not be interpreted too rigidly.*

rigorous /rɪgə°rəs/. **Rigorous** is used to describe things that are done or carried out in a very thorough and strict way. EG *...rigorous controls... ...a rigorous training schedule.* ◊ **rigorously.** EG *These methods have been rigorously tested over many years.* ADJ QUALIT ◊ ADV

rigours /rɪgəz/; spelled **rigors** in American English. The **rigours** of a situation or way of life are the features that make it unpleasant and hard to bear. EG *...the rigours of a city winter.* N PLURAL: *the*+N+*of* Formal

rim /rɪm/, **rims.** 1 The **rim** of a container such as a cup or glass is the edge that goes all the way round the top. EG *Whisky splashed over the rim of his glass... ...the rim of the bath.* N COUNT

2 The **rim** of a circular object such as a wheel is its outside edge. EG *Muller's glasses had gold rims.* N COUNT

rind /raɪnd/, **rinds.** 1 The **rind** of a fruit such as a lemon is its thick outer skin. N COUNT OR N UNCOUNT

2 The **rind** of cheese or bacon is the hard outer edge which you do not usually eat. N COUNT OR N UNCOUNT

ring /rɪŋ/, **rings, ringing, rang** /ræŋ/, **rung** /rʌŋ/. For paragraphs 13 and 14, the past tense and past participle is **ringed**.

1 If you **ring** someone, you phone them. EG *You must ring the hospital at once... He may ring again.* V+O OR V

2 If you **give** someone **a ring**, you phone them. EG *Give me a ring if you need me.* PHRASE Informal

3 When you **ring** a bell or when a bell **rings**, it makes a sound. EG *In the distance a church bell was ringing... I waited for the phone to ring... He had to ring the bell several times before the door was opened.* • to **ring a bell**: see **bell**. V-ERG

4 If you **ring** for someone or something, you ring a bell to call them or to have them brought. EG *He rang for Tracy and asked, 'What's wrong with Davis?'* V: OFT+*for*

5 A **ring** is the sound made by a bell. EG *There was a ring at the door.* N COUNT

6 If a place **rings** with a sound, the sound there is very loud. EG *We went into a barn that rang with the cries of geese and turkeys.* V: OFT+*with* Literary

7 If a sound or statement **rings in** your **head** or **rings in** your **ears**, you remember it vividly. EG *He left with the cheers still ringing in his ears.* PHRASE Literary

8 If you say that a statement **rings true**, you mean that it seems likely to be true. EG *The bishop's answers so often ring true.* PHRASE

9 You can use **ring** to say what quality something seems to have. For example, if an argument has a plausible **ring**, it seems quite plausible. EG *The books he mentioned had a familiar ring about them... The name had an unpleasant ring to it.* N SING: *a*+N+SUPP

10 A **ring** is also **10.1** a small circle of metal that you wear on your finger as an ornament or to show that you are engaged or married. See picture at JEWELLERY. EG *...a diamond ring.* **10.2** an object or group of things which has the shape of a circle. EG *I like to blow smoke rings... They formed a ring round him... ...a ring of excited faces.* N COUNT

11 At a boxing match, show jumping contest, or circus, the **ring** is the enclosed space with seats round it where the contest or performance takes place. N COUNT

12 A **ring** is also a group of people who do something illegal together over a period of time. EG *The police exposed a large drug ring operating in the area.* N COUNT

13 If you **ring** something, you draw a circle round it. EG *I got a map and ringed all the likely villages.* V+O

14 If something **is ringed** with something else, it has that thing all the way around it. EG *...a valley ringed with mountains.* V-PASS: USU+*with*

ring back. If you **ring** someone **back**, you phone them, either because they phoned you earlier when you were not there, or because you did not finish an earlier conversation on the phone. EG *He asked if you'd ring him back when you got in.* PHRASAL VB: V+O+ADV OR V+ADV

ring off. When you **ring off** at the end of a telephone call, you put down your receiver. PHRASAL VB: V+ADV

ring out. If sounds **ring out**, they are heard loudly and clearly. EG *Her voice rang out.* PHRASAL VB: V+ADV

ring up. If you **ring** someone **up**, you phone them. EG *He rang me up to tell me that he had found the letter.* PHRASAL VB: V+O+ADV OR V+ADV

ringing /rɪŋɪŋ/. A **ringing** sound can be heard very clearly. EG *...clear ringing tones.* ADJ CLASSIF: ATTRIB

ringleader /rɪŋli:də/, **ringleaders.** The **ringleader** of a group of people who are causing trouble is the person who is leading them. EG *The six ringleaders were arrested and charged.* N COUNT

ring road, ring roads. A **ring road** is a road that goes all the way round the edge of a town so that traffic does not have to go through the town centre. N COUNT

rink /rɪŋk/, **rinks.** A **rink** is a large area, usually indoors, where people go to ice-skate or roller-skate. EG *There's a good ice rink in Leeds... ...a skating rink.* N COUNT

rinse /rɪns/, **rinses, rinsing, rinsed.** 1 When you **rinse** something, you wash it without using soap. EG *He rinsed his hands under the tap.* ▸ used as a noun. EG *Just give these a quick rinse.* V+O ▸ N COUNT

2 If you **rinse** your mouth or **rinse** it **out**, you wash it by holding a mouthful of liquid in it, for example to get rid of an unpleasant taste. V+O: OFT+*out*

riot /raɪət/, **riots, rioting, rioted.** 1 When there is a **riot**, a crowd of people behave violently in a public place. EG *In May 1968 there was a wave of student riots.* N COUNT

2 When people **riot**, they behave violently in a public place. EG *If food prices are put up too far, the people will riot.* ◊ **rioter, rioters.** EG *Courts dealt with rioters quickly and harshly.* V ◊ N COUNT

3 If people **run riot**, they behave in a wild and uncontrolled manner. EG *You shouldn't allow the children to run riot.* PHRASE

riotous /raɪətəs/. 1 **Riotous** behaviour is violent and uncontrolled behaviour, for example damaging vehicles and buildings and fighting in public. EG *...a riotous mob... He was found guilty of riotous behaviour.* ADJ CLASSIF: ATTRIB Formal

2 You can also describe people's behaviour as **riotous** when they do things in an enthusiastic and rather wild way. EG *Both children would come rushing out in a riotous welcome.* ADJ QUALIT

rip /rɪp/, **rips, ripping, ripped.** 1 When you **rip** something or when it **rips**, it is torn violently. EG *The poster had been ripped to pieces... Two of the canvas bags had ripped.* V-ERG

2 If you **rip** something away, you remove it quickly and violently. EG *I ripped the phone from her hand... He ripped his shirt off.* V+O+A

3 A **rip** is a long cut or split in something made of cloth or paper. EG *He had seen the rip in the book.* N COUNT

rip off. If someone **rips** you **off**, they cheat you by charging you too much money for something. EG *The local shopkeepers were all trying to rip off the tourists.* • See also **rip-off**. PHRASAL VB: V+O+ADV Informal

rip up. If you **rip** something **up**, you tear it into small pieces. EG *I wanted to rip up my schedule and fill out a new one.* PHRASAL VB: V+O+ADV

ripe /raɪp/, **riper, ripest.** 1 When fruit or grain is **ripe**, it is fully grown and ready to be eaten. EG *The pears are heavy and ripe.* ADJ QUALIT

2 If you say that something is **ripe** for a change of some kind, you mean that it is ready for it or likely to experience it. EG *Our people are ripe for freedom... The nation was ripe for collapse.* ADJ PRED+*for*

3 If you say **the time is ripe**, you mean that a suitable time has arrived for something to be done. EG *The time was ripe to break his silence.* PHRASE

4 If someone lives to a **ripe old age**, they live to be very old. PHRASE

If you rise at 8 o'clock, do you stand up?

ripen /raɪpə^{0}n/, **ripens, ripening, ripened.** When crops **ripen** or when the sun **ripens** them, they become ripe. EG *...fields of ripening wheat.* V-ERG

rip-off, rip-offs. If you say that something that you bought was a **rip-off**, you mean that you were charged too much for it. N COUNT Informal

ripple /rɪpə^{0}l/, **ripples, rippling, rippled. 1 Ripples** are little waves on the surface of water caused by the wind or by an object dropping into the water. EG *A twig made tiny ripples on the water... ...sending out patterns of ripples.* N COUNT: USU PLURAL

2 When the surface of an area of water **ripples** or when something **ripples** it, a number of little waves appear on it. EG *A gentle breeze rippled the surface of the sea.* V-ERG

3 If there is a **ripple** of laughter or applause, people laugh or applaud quietly for a short time. EG *There was a ripple of amused applause from the newsmen.* N SING+*of*

rise /raɪz/, **rises, rising, rose** /rəʊz/, **risen** /rɪzə^{0}n/. **1** If something **rises**, it moves upwards. EG *Clouds of birds rose from the tree-tops... He could see the smoke from his bonfire rising up in a white column.* V: OFT+A

2 When you **rise**, **2.1** you stand up. EG *Dr Willoughby rose to greet him.* **2.2** you get out of bed. EG *They had risen at dawn.* V: OFT+A Formal

3 When the sun or moon **rises**, it appears from below the horizon. V

4 You can also say that something **rises** when it appears as a large, tall shape. EG *St Paul's rose majestically from the trees.* V: USU+A Literary

5 If land **rises**, it slopes upwards. EG *He followed Jack towards the castle where the ground rose slightly.* V ◇ **rising**. EG *The house was built on rising ground.* ◇ ADJ CLASSIF: ATTRIB

6 If a sound **rises**, it becomes louder or higher. EG *His voice rose to a shriek.* V: USU+A

7 If a sound **rises** from a group of people, it comes from them. EG *A loud gasp rose from the boys.* V: USU+*from*

8 If an amount **rises**, it increases. EG *Prices rose by more than 10%... The temperature began to rise.* V ◇ **rising**. EG *...the rising rate of inflation.* ◇ ADJ CLASSIF

9 A **rise** in the amount of something is an increase in it. EG *...the rise in crime... ...price rises.* N COUNT+SUPP

10 A **rise** is an increase in wages or salary. EG *...a pay rise of about £20 a week... I asked for a rise.* N COUNT

11 If you **rise** to a challenge or remark, you respond to it in some way, rather than ignoring it. V+*to*

12 When the people in a country **rise** up, they start fighting the people in authority there. EG *The settlers rose in revolt.* V: OFT+*up* ◇ **rising, risings**. EG *...a big peasant rising in the West of France.* ◇ N COUNT

13 If someone **rises** to a higher position or status, they become more important, successful, or powerful. EG *Bergson rose rapidly to fame.* V+A

14 Someone's **rise** is the process by which they become more important, successful, or powerful. EG *...the decline of the Liberal Party and the rise of Labour... ...his rise to fame.* N SING

15 If something **gives rise to** an event or situation, it causes the event or situation to happen. EG *This breakthrough could give rise to ethical problems.* PHRASE

16 to **rise to the occasion**: see **occasion**.

rise above. If you **rise above** a difficulty or problem, you manage not to let it affect you. EG *She was in continual pain, but rose above it.* PHRASAL VB: V+PREP

risk /rɪsk/, **risks, risking, risked. 1** If there is a **risk** of something unpleasant, there is a possibility that it will happen. EG *There is very little risk of infection... ...the risk that their men might disappear without trace.* N COUNT OR N UNCOUNT

2 If something that you do is a **risk**, it might have unpleasant or undesirable results. EG *Such a response would be an irrational risk.* N SING

3 You say that an object is a **risk** when it is likely to cause danger. EG *Your television is a fire risk if left plugged in overnight.* N SING

4 Risk is also used in these phrases. **4.1** If someone or something is **at risk**, they are in a situation where something unpleasant might happen to them. EG *The sick and lonely are most at risk... You're putting my career at risk.* **4.2** If you do something **at the risk of** something unpleasant happening, you do it although you know that the unpleasant thing might happen as a result. EG *...ensuring short-term survival at the risk of long-term ruin.* **4.3** If you tell someone that they are doing something **at** their **own risk**, you are warning them that, if they are harmed, it will be their own responsibility. **4.4** If you **run** the **risk** of doing or experiencing something undesirable, you do something knowing that the undesirable thing might happen as a result. EG *We run the risk of confusing the voters.* **4.5** If you **take a risk**, you do something which you know might be dangerous or have unpleasant consequences. EG *I am taking a tremendous risk.* PHRASES

5 If you **risk** something unpleasant, you do something knowing that the unpleasant thing might happen as a result. EG *They were willing to risk losing their jobs.* V+O OR V+-ING

6 If you **risk** an action, you do it, even though you know that it might have undesirable consequences. EG *If you have an expensive rug, don't risk washing it yourself.* V+O OR V+-ING

7 If you **risk** someone's life, you put them in a dangerous position where they might be killed. EG *She had risked her life to help save mine.* V+O

risky /rɪski^1/, **riskier, riskiest.** If you say that an activity or action is **risky**, you mean that it is dangerous or likely to fail. EG *The whole thing has become too risky.* ADJ QUALIT

risqué /rɪskeɪ, rɪskeɪ/. Jokes or stories that are **risqué** are considered to be slightly rude or offensive because they refer to sex. ADJ QUALIT

rite /raɪt/, **rites.** A **rite** is a traditional ceremony that is carried out by a particular group or within a particular society. EG *...the rite of circumcision... ...fertility rites.* N COUNT: USU+SUPP

ritual /rɪtjʊ^{0}əl/, **rituals. 1** A **ritual** is a series of actions which people regularly carry out in a particular situation, because it is the custom to do so. EG *Our society has many rituals of greeting, farewell, and celebration.* N COUNT OR N UNCOUNT

2 Ritual activities happen as part of a ritual or tradition. EG *...the practice of ritual murder.* ADJ CLASSIF: ATTRIB

rival /raɪvə^{0}l/, **rivals, rivalling, rivalled;** spelled **rivaling, rivaled** in American English. **1** Your **rival** is someone who you are competing with. EG *His newspaper outstripped its rivals in circulation.* N COUNT ▸ used as an adjective. EG *Fighting broke out between rival groups.* ▸ ADJ CLASSIF: ATTRIB

2 If you say that something **rivals** something else, you mean that it is of the same standard or quality as the other thing. EG *Of all the flowers in the garden few can rival the lily.* V+O

rivalry /raɪvəlri^1/, **rivalries. Rivalry** is active competition between people. EG *Burr's rivalry with Hamilton began in those days... ...the intense rivalries between groups and personalities.* N COUNT OR N UNCOUNT

river /rɪvə/, **rivers.** A **river** is a large amount of fresh water flowing continuously in a long line across land. EG *We fished in the river after lunch... ...the River Thames.* N COUNT

riverside /rɪvəsaɪd/. The **riverside** is the area of land by the banks of a river. EG *They had reached the rocks by the riverside.* N SING: *the*+N

rivet /rɪvɪt/, **rivets, riveting, riveted. 1** If you **are riveted** by something, it fascinates you and holds your interest completely. EG *I was riveted by his presentation.* V+O: USU PASS

2 A **rivet** is a short, thin bolt with a flat head which is used to fasten flat pieces of metal together. N COUNT

riveting /rɪvɪtɪŋ/. Something that is **riveting** is extremely interesting and exciting. EG *...a riveting television documentary.* ADJ QUALIT

RN /ɑː ɛn/ is a written abbreviation for 'Royal Navy', the navy of the United Kingdom. EG *...Captain Andrew Waugh, RN.*

road /rəʊd/, **roads. 1** A **road** is a long piece of hard ground which is built between two places so that people can drive or ride easily from one place to the other. EG *...the road from Belfast to Londonderry... The ruins were accessible by road... ...Tottenham Court Road.* N COUNT OR by+N

2 If you are **on the road**, you are travelling in a vehicle or going on a journey by road. EG *I did meet some lovely people on the road.* PHRASE

3 If you say that someone is **on the road** to something, you mean that they are likely to achieve it. EG *She was well on the road to recovery... This is the first step on the road to victory.* PHRASE

roadblock /rəʊdblɒk/, **roadblocks.** When the police or the army put a **roadblock** across a road, they stop all the traffic going through, for example because they are looking for a criminal. N COUNT

roadside /rəʊdsaɪd/, **roadsides.** The **roadside** is the area at the edge of a road. EG *I sat down by the roadside and cried... ...a roadside cafe.* N COUNT: USU SING

roadway /rəʊdweɪ/, **roadways.** A **roadway** is the same as a road. EG *He began to cross the roadway towards me.* N COUNT Formal

roam /rəʊm/, **roams, roaming, roamed.** If you **roam** an area or **roam** around it, you wander or travel around it without having a particular purpose. EG *He roamed the streets at night... They roam over the hills and plains.* V+O OR V+A

roar /rɔː/, **roars, roaring, roared. 1** If something **roars**, it makes a very loud noise. EG *The wind roared in the forest.* ▸ used as a noun. EG *I could hear the roar of traffic outside.* V ▸ N COUNT

2 If someone **roars with laughter**, they laugh in a very noisy way. EG *He put back his head and roared with laughter.* PHRASE

3 If someone **roars**, they shout something in a very loud voice. EG *'Forward with the Revolution,' the crowd roared back.* V OR V+QUOTE

4 When a lion **roars**, it makes the loud sound that lions typically make. ▸ used as a noun. EG *The lion let out one of its roars.* V ▸ N COUNT

roaring /rɔːrɪŋ/. **1 Roaring** means making a very loud noise. EG *He sat on the terrace a few feet from the roaring traffic.* ADJ CLASSIF: ATTRIB

2 A **roaring** fire is one which is burning with large flames and sending out a lot of heat. ADJ CLASSIF: ATTRIB

3 If someone **does a roaring trade** in a type of goods, they sell a lot of them. EG *He was doing a roaring trade in T-shirts.* PHRASE Informal

4 If something is a **roaring** success, it is very successful indeed. ADJ CLASSIF: ATTRIB

roast /rəʊst/, **roasts, roasting, roasted. 1** When you **roast** meat or when it **roasts**, you cook it by dry heat in an oven or over a fire. EG *We got ourselves two fine chickens and roasted them.* V-ERG

2 If you **roast** things such as nuts or coffee beans, you heat them. EG *He was roasting chestnuts.* V+O

3 Roast meat is meat that has been cooked by roasting. EG *I ordered roast beef.* ADJ CLASSIF: ATTRIB

4 A **roast** is a piece of meat that has been cooked by roasting. EG *...taking the roast out of the oven.* N COUNT OR N UNCOUNT

rob /rɒb/, **robs, robbing, robbed. 1** If someone **robs** you, they steal money or property from you. EG *The only way I can get the money is to rob a few banks... He tried to rob her of her share.* V+O: OFT+*of*

2 If you **rob** someone of something that they deserve, have, or need, you take it away from them. EG *You robbed me of my moment of glory... The joy of battle had robbed him of his discretion... As these trees grow tall, they rob the grass of light.* V+O+*of*

robber /rɒbə/, **robbers. Robbers** are people who steal a lot of money or property from a bank, a shop, or a vehicle, often by using force or threats. EG *...bank robbers... Did they ever catch the robbers?* N COUNT

robbery /rɒbəºri¹/, **robberies. 1 Robbery** is the crime of stealing a lot of money or property from a bank, a shop, or a vehicle, often by using force or threats. EG *He was arrested on charges of armed robbery.* N UNCOUNT

2 When there is a **robbery**, someone steals a lot of money or property from a bank, a shop, or a vehicle. EG *...if he had committed the robbery.* N COUNT

robe /rəʊb/, **robes.** A **robe** is a loose piece of clothing which covers all of your body and reaches the ground. EG *...priests and archbishops in their ceremonial robes.* N COUNT Formal

robin /rɒbɪn/, **robins.** A **robin** is a small brown bird with a red neck and breast. N COUNT

robot /rəʊbɒt/, **robots.** A **robot** is a machine which is programmed to move and perform certain tasks automatically. EG *Japanese industry is making increasing use of robots.* N COUNT

robust /rə⁶bʌst, rəʊbə⁹st/. Someone or something that is **robust** is very strong and healthy. EG *She has four robust daughters... The once robust economy now lies in ruins.* ADJ QUALIT

rock /rɒk/, **rocks, rocking, rocked. 1 Rock** is the hard substance which the earth is made of. EG *Large masses of rock are constantly falling into the sea.* N UNCOUNT

2 A **rock** is **2.1** a piece of rock that sticks up out of the ground or the sea, or that has broken away from a mountain or a cliff. EG *I sat down on a rock.* N COUNT
2.2 a small stone that you can pick up. EG *She started putting the rocks in his shirt pocket.* American

3 When something **rocks** or when you **rock** it, it moves slowly and regularly backwards and forwards or from side to side. EG *She sat there, rocking gently backwards and forwards... Our parents cuddle and hug us, and rock us gently back and forth.* V-ERG
● to **rock the boat**: see **boat**.

4 If something **rocks** people, it shocks and horrifies them. EG *France was rocked by an outbreak of violent crime.* V+O Written

5 Rock or **rock music** is music with simple tunes and a very strong beat that is played and sung, usually loudly, by a small group of people with electric guitars and drums. EG *...a rock concert... ...rock groups.* N UNCOUNT

6 Rock is also a sweet made in long, hard sticks which are sold at tourist places. EG *...a stick of rock.* N UNCOUNT

7 If you have an alcoholic drink such as whisky **on the rocks**, you have it with lumps of ice. PHRASE

8 If someone's marriage or relationship is **on the rocks**, it is unsuccessful and is about to end. PHRASE

rock and roll is a kind of music with a strong beat sung and played by small groups, especially in the 1950s. N UNCOUNT

rocker /rɒkə/, **rockers. 1** A **rocker** is the same as a rocking-chair. N COUNT American

2 If you say that someone is **off** their **rocker**, you mean that they are mad. EG *His landlady appeared to be slightly off her rocker.* PHRASE Informal

rockery /rɒkəºri¹/, **rockeries.** A **rockery** is a raised part of a garden which is built of stones and soil and on which small plants are grown. N COUNT

rocket /rɒkɪt/, **rockets, rocketing, rocketed. 1** A **rocket** is **1.1** a space vehicle that is shaped like a long tube. EG *...a space rocket.* **1.2** a missile containing explosive that drives itself through the air by sending out burning gas. EG *Rebels fired anti-tank rockets for three consecutive nights.* **1.3** a firework that quickly goes high into the air and then explodes. N COUNT

2 If things such as prices and profits **rocket**, they increase very quickly and suddenly. EG *His profits rocketed... Land sales rocketed.* V Informal

rock-hard. Something that is **rock-hard** is very hard indeed. EG *...the rock-hard earth.* ADJ CLASSIF

If something is a roaring success, does it make a noise?

rocking-chair, rocking-chairs. A **rocking-chair** is a chair that is built on two curved pieces of wood so that you can rock yourself backwards and forwards when you are sitting in it. N COUNT

rocking-horse, rocking-horses. A **rocking-horse** is a toy horse which a child can sit on and rock backwards and forwards. N COUNT

rock pool, rock pools. A **rock pool** is a small pool between rocks on the seashore. N COUNT

rocky /rɒki[1]/. A place that is **rocky** is covered with rocks. EG *She drives carefully up the rocky lane.* ADJ QUALIT

rod /rɒd/, **rods.** A **rod** is a long, thin pole or bar, usually one made of metal or wood. EG *The aluminium rod that held the seats broke.* N COUNT

rode /rəʊd/ is the past tense of **ride.**

rodent /rəʊdənt/, **rodents.** A **rodent** is a small mammal which has sharp front teeth. Rats, mice, rabbits, and squirrels are rodents. EG *Some of the crop may be eaten up by insects or rodents.* N COUNT

roe /rəʊ/ is the eggs or sperm of a fish, which is eaten as food. EG *...fried cod's roe.* N UNCOUNT

rogue /rəʊg/, **rogues.** A **rogue** is a man who behaves in a dishonest or criminal way. EG *You're all cheats and rogues.* N COUNT Outdated

role /rəʊl/, **roles. 1** Someone's or something's **role** is their position and function in a situation or society. EG *What is the role of the University in modern society?... He had played a major role in the formation of the United Nations.* N COUNT+SUPP

2 A **role** is one of the characters that an actor or singer can play in a film, play, or opera. EG *She played the leading role in The Winter's Tale.* N COUNT: USU+SUPP

roll /rəʊl/, **rolls, rolling, rolled. 1** When something **rolls** or when you **roll** it, it moves along a surface, turning over and over many times. EG *The bucket rolled and clattered down the path... He rolled a boulder down the slope... She rolled off the sofa.* V-ERG: USU+A

2 When vehicles **roll** along, they move along. EG *Trucks with loudspeakers rolled through the streets... The bus rolled to a stop.* V+A

3 If drops of liquid **roll** down a surface, they move quickly down it. EG *He stood in a corner with tears rolling down his face.* V+A

4 If you **roll** your eyes or if your eyes **roll**, they turn up or turn from one side to another, for example because you are very frightened. V-ERG Written

5 If you **roll** something flexible into a cylinder or a ball, you form it into a cylinder or a ball by wrapping it several times around itself or by shaping it between your hands. EG *She went on sorting the socks, rolling them into neat little bundles.* ◊ **rolled.** EG *...a rolled newspaper... ...a rolled umbrella.* V+O+A; ◊ ADJ CLASSIF: ATTRIB

6 A **roll** of paper or cloth is a long piece of it that has been wrapped many times around itself or around a tube. EG *...a roll of film.* N COUNT: OFT+*of*

7 A **roll** is a small loaf of bread that is eaten by one person. N COUNT

8 A **roll** is also an official list of people's names. EG *...the roll of members... He is on the parish roll.* N COUNT+SUPP

9 A **roll** of drums is a long, rumbling sound made by drums. N COUNT

10 You say that something is several things **rolled into one** to emphasize that it combines the best qualities of all those things. EG *A good musical is a new play, a new opera and a new ballet all rolled into one.* PHRASE

11 to **start the ball rolling**: see **ball.** • See also **rock and roll, sausage roll, toilet roll.** • See also **rolling.**

roll in. If something **is rolling in**, it is being received in large quantities. EG *Once we get there the money will just start rolling in.* PHRASAL VB: V+ADV Informal

roll over. If someone who is lying down **rolls over**, they move so that a different part of them is facing upwards. PHRASAL VB: V+ADV

roll up. 1 If you **roll up** something flexible, you wrap it several times around itself until it is shaped like a cylinder or a ball. EG *The mattress was rolled up... The map kept rolling up.* PHRASAL VB: V-ERG+ADV

2 If you **roll up** your sleeves or trouser legs, you fold the edges over several times, making them shorter. EG *His father had his sleeves rolled up.* V+O+ADV

roll-call, roll-calls. If you take a **roll-call**, you check which of the members of a group are present by reading their names out. Each member has to answer when his or her name is read out. N COUNT

roller /rəʊlə/, **rollers. 1** A **roller** is a cylinder that turns round in a machine or device. EG *She pulled the sheet of paper out of the roller.* N COUNT

2 Rollers are hollow tubes that women roll their hair round in order to make it curly. N COUNT: USU PLURAL

roller-coaster /rəʊlə kəʊstə/, **roller-coasters.** A **roller-coaster** is a small railway that goes up and down steep slopes and that people ride on for pleasure at fairs. N COUNT

roller-skate, roller-skates, roller-skating, roller-skated. 1 Roller-skates are shoes with four small wheels on the bottom. N COUNT: USU PLURAL

2 If you **roller-skate**, you move over a flat surface wearing roller-skates. EG *Christopher taught the children to roller skate.* V

rolling /rəʊlɪŋ/. **1 Rolling** hills are small hills with gentle slopes that extend a long way into the distance. EG *...the rolling countryside west of Detroit.* ADJ CLASSIF: ATTRIB

2 A **rolling** walk is slow and swaying, usually because the person is drunk or very fat. ADJ CLASSIF: ATTRIB

3 If you say that someone is **rolling in it**, you mean that they are very rich. PHRASE Informal

rolling pin, rolling pins. A **rolling pin** is a cylinder that you roll several times over uncooked pastry in order to spread it. N COUNT

Roman Catholic /rəʊmən kæθə[0]lɪk/, **Roman Catholics.** A **Roman Catholic** is the same as a Catholic. N COUNT

Roman Catholicism /rəʊmən kəθɒlɪsɪzə[0]m/ is the same as Catholicism. N UNCOUNT

romance /rəʊmæns, rəmæns/, **romances. 1** A **romance** is a relationship between two people who are in love with each other but who are not married to each other. EG *...a wartime romance... Young people are re-discovering romance and passion.* N COUNT OR N UNCOUNT

2 Romance is the pleasure and excitement of doing something new or exciting. EG *There is romance to be found in life on the river.* N UNCOUNT

3 A **romance** is also a novel about a love affair. EG *...historical romances.* N COUNT

Roman numeral /rəʊmən nju:mə[0]rəl/, **Roman numerals. Roman numerals** are the letters used by Romans in ancient times to write numbers, for example I(=1), IV(=4), VIII(=8), XL(=40). Roman numerals are still used sometimes. N COUNT: USU PLURAL

romantic /rə[6]mæntɪk/, **romantics. 1** Someone who is **romantic** has a lot of ideas that are not based on real life, for example about love or about ways of changing society. EG *She's as romantic as a child of sixteen.* ▸ used as a noun. EG *Cedric's a great romantic.* ADJ QUALIT; ▸ N COUNT

2 Romantic means connected with sexual love. EG *A woman needs a romantic attachment.* ADJ CLASSIF: ATTRIB

3 A **romantic** play, film, or story describes or represents a love affair. EG *...a charming romantic comedy starring Audrey Hepburn.* ADJ CLASSIF: ATTRIB

4 Something that is **romantic** is beautiful in a way that strongly affects your feelings. EG *...a romantic moonlight ride.* ◊ **romantically.** EG *Her long hair was spread romantically over the pillow.* ADJ QUALIT; ◊ ADV

romanticism /rə[6]mæntɪsɪzə[0]m/ refers to thoughts and feelings which are idealistic and romantic, rather than realistic. EG *...the romanticism of the women's magazines.* N UNCOUNT

romanticize /rə[6]mæntɪsaɪz/, **romanticizes, romanticizing, romanticized;** also spelled **romanticise.** If you **romanticize** someone or something, V+O you think or talk about them in a way that is not at all realistic and makes them seem better than they really are. ◊ **romanticized**. EG *...romanticized notions about marriage.* ◊ ADJ QUALIT

romp /rɒmp/, **romps, romping, romped.** When children **romp** around, they play and move around in a noisy, happy way. EG *They romped with their dogs.* ▸ used as a noun. EG *It's an excuse for a great romp.* V: USU+A ▸ N SING: a+N

rompers /rɒmpəz/ are a piece of clothing worn by babies or young children. Rompers consist of loose trousers and a top that are joined together. N PLURAL

roof /ruːf/, **roofs** /ruːvz, ruːfs/. **1** The **roof** of a building is the covering on top of it. See picture at HOUSE. EG *...a yellow brick house with a slate roof... I fixed a leak in the roof of her shed.* N COUNT

2 The **roof** of a car or other vehicle is the covering on top of it. See picture at CAR. N COUNT

3 The **roof** of your mouth or of a cave is the highest part of it. N COUNT

4 Roof is also used in these phrases. **4.1** If you have a **roof over your head**, you have somewhere to live. EG *She was without money and with no real roof over her head.* **4.2** If you say that something happens **under** someone's **roof**, you mean that it happens in their home. EG *Are we prepared to let this happen under our own roofs?* **4.3** If you say that someone **hit the roof** or **went through the roof**, you mean that they were very angry indeed. PHRASES Informal

roofed /ruːft/. You can use **roofed** to say what kind of roof a building has. EG *...houses roofed with reddish-brown tiles... ...red-roofed farmhouses.* ADJ CLASSIF

roofing /ruːfɪŋ/ is material used for making or covering roofs. EG *He sells bundles of rushes for roofing... Slate is the very best roofing material.* N UNCOUNT

roof-rack, roof-racks. A **roof-rack** is a metal frame that is fixed on top of a car and used for carrying large objects. N COUNT

rooftop /ruːftɒp/, **rooftops. Rooftops** are the outside parts of roofs. EG *...a bedroom with a view over the roof-tops.* N COUNT: USU PLURAL

rook /rʊk/, **rooks. 1** A **rook** is a large black bird. N COUNT

2 In chess, a **rook** is a piece which can move forwards, backwards, or sideways. N COUNT

room /ruːm/, **rooms. 1** A **room** is one of the separate sections in a house or other building, which has its own walls, ceiling, floor, and door. EG *The room contained a couch and a glass cabinet... Boylan came back into the room... She's in the music room.* N COUNT

2 If there is **room** for something, there is enough space for it. EG *There wasn't enough room for everybody... Just keep the crowd back so I have room to move.* N UNCOUNT: OFT+SUPP

3 If there is **room** for a particular kind of behaviour or action, people are able to behave in that way or to take that action. EG *There ought to be room for differences of opinion... There is room for much more research.* N UNCOUNT: USU+*for*

roommate /ruːmmeɪt/, **roommates.** Your **roommate** is the person who you share a rented room with. N COUNT

roomy /ruːmi1/, **roomier, roomiest.** A place that is **roomy** is large inside, so that you can move around freely and comfortably. EG *...a ground floor apartment which was roomy but sparsely furnished.* ADJ QUALIT

roost /ruːst/, **roosts, roosting, roosted. 1** A **roost** is a place where birds rest or build their nests. EG *The gulls were returning to their roosts among the rocks.* N COUNT

2 When birds **roost**, they settle in a particular place for the night. EG *The chickens roost there all winter.* V: OFT+A

3 If you talk about someone's **chickens coming home to roost**, you are talking about the fact that they are now experiencing the consequences of their past actions. PHRASE

4 Someone who **rules the roost** in a particular place has control and authority over the people there. PHRASE

rooster /ruːstə/, **roosters.** A **rooster** is an adult male chicken. N COUNT American

root /ruːt/, **roots, rooting, rooted. 1** The **roots** of a plant are the parts that grow under the ground. EG *These trees have large, spreading roots.* N COUNT

2 The **root** of a hair or tooth is the part beneath the skin. EG *They pulled her hair out by the roots.* N COUNT

3 Your **roots** are the place or culture that you or your family grew up in, which you have now left. EG *People are searching again for their roots... They are now utterly cut off from their peasant roots.* N PLURAL

● If you **put down roots** in a particular place, you become connected with it, for example by taking part in activities there or by making a lot of friends. ● PHRASE

4 If you talk about the **root** or the **roots** of something, you mean its original cause or its basis. EG *Perhaps the root of the tragedy was here... Unemployment and inflation were at the root of the community's frustration.* N COUNT: USU+POSS

5 The **root** cause of something is its basic cause. EG *...the root causes of poverty.* ADJ CLASSIF: ATTRIB

6 If things **take root**, they start to grow or develop. EG *The seedlings of bushes and trees might take root there... ...the ideas that were to take root in a new land.* PHRASE

7 If people or animals **root** through things, they search through them, pushing them aside. EG *Meadows rooted around in his bag and pulled out a map.* V+A

8 See also **grass roots, square root.**

root out. If you **root** someone or something **out**, you find them and force them from the place they are in. EG *He's in there somewhere. Let's go and root him out.* PHRASAL VB: V+O+ADV

rooted /ruːtɪ1d/. **1** If you say that something is **rooted** in something else, you mean that it is strongly influenced by it or has developed from it. EG *His methods are rooted in years of experience... ...attitudes deeply rooted in history.* ADJ PRED+*in*

2 If you say that someone's feelings or opinions are **rooted**, you mean that they are not likely to change, because the person feels them or believes in them very strongly. EG *...deeply rooted impulses... He has no rooted objections to it.* ● See also **deep-rooted**. ADJ QUALIT

3 If you are **rooted to the spot**, you are unable to move, for example because you are very afraid. PHRASE

rootless /ruːtlɪ2s/. Someone who is **rootless** does not belong to any particular place or country. EG *...a rootless vagabond.* ADJ CLASSIF

rope /rəʊp/, **ropes, roping, roped. 1** A **rope** is a piece of very thick string, made by twisting together several thinner pieces. EG *They should be tied together with a rope... ...a piece of rope.* N COUNT OR N UNCOUNT

2 If you **rope** one thing to another, you tie them together with a rope. EG *The wagons were roped together.* V+O: OFT+*to*/*together*

3 If you say that someone **knows the ropes**, you mean that they know how something should be done. EG *My friend knows the ropes, she can show them around... I know the ropes. Let me handle this.* PHRASE Informal

rope in. If you **rope** someone **in** to do something, you persuade them to help you to do it. EG *Some amazing people were roped in to work on these projects... How did he get roped into that?* PHRASAL VB: V+O+ADV

rope off. If you **rope off** an area, you tie ropes between posts all around its edges, to keep people away from it. EG *The quay was roped off and the spectators were pushed back.* PHRASAL VB: V+O+ADV

rosary /rəʊzəri1/, **rosaries.** A **rosary** is a string of beads that Catholics and Hindus use for counting N COUNT

Is there any difference between a roster and a rota?

prayers. A series of prayers counted in this way is also called a **rosary**.

rose /rəʊz/, **roses. 1** A **rose** is a garden flower with a pleasant smell that grows on a bush with thorny stems. EG *The soil here is so good for roses... Eleanor was holding an armful of red roses.* N COUNT

2 If you tell someone that a situation is **not a bed of roses**, you are warning them that it is not as pleasant or as easy as they might think. EG *Your life is unlikely to be a bed of roses.* PHRASE

3 Something that is **rose** is reddish-pink in colour. ADJ COLOUR

4 Rose is also the past tense of **rise**.

rosé /rəʊzeɪ/ is wine which is pink in colour. N UNCOUNT

rosette /rəʊzɛt/, **rosettes.** A **rosette** is a large, circular badge made from coloured ribbons, which is worn as a prize in a competition or to show support for a sports team or political party. N COUNT

roster /rɒstə/, **rosters.** A **roster** is a list of people who each take it in turn to do a particular job. EG *...the committee's roster of officials.* N COUNT

rostrum /rɒstrəm/, **rostrums** or **rostra** /rɒstrə/. A **rostrum** is a raised platform on which someone stands when they are speaking to an audience or conducting an orchestra. N COUNT

rosy /rəʊzi[1]/, **rosier, rosiest. 1** Something that is **rosy** is reddish-pink in colour. EG *...rosy clouds... ...the dim, rosy light.* ADJ COLOUR

2 If you describe someone as **rosy**, you mean that their face is pink and that they look healthy. EG *He had five children, all rosy and handsome... ...her bright eyes and rosy cheeks.* ADJ QUALIT

3 If you say that a situation seems **rosy**, you mean that it seems likely to be pleasing or successful. EG *Bal tried to give a rosy picture of his prospects... He had not made things seem too rosy.* ADJ QUALIT

rot /rɒt/, **rots, rotting, rotted. 1** When food, wood, or other substances **rot**, they decay and can no longer be used. EG *Her teeth were rotting... ...the smell of rotting vegetables.* ▸ used as a noun. EG *Destroy any bulbs with rot and buy healthy ones.* V; ▸ N UNCOUNT

2 When something **rots** an object or a substance, it causes it to decay. EG *Bleach might rot the fibres.* V+O

3 If you say that someone **is rotting**, you mean that their physical or mental condition is getting worse, because they have been in a bad situation for a long time. EG *You will rot in jail... You must leave him and get out. You're just rotting here.* V : USU+A

4 If you say that **the rot is setting in**, you mean that a situation is beginning to get worse and that nothing can prevent this from happening. PHRASE

5 If you say that what someone is saying is **rot**, you mean that they are saying very silly things. EG *You're talking absolute rot.* N UNCOUNT Outdated Informal

rot away. When something **rots away**, it decays until it falls to pieces or none of it remains. EG *His body is rotting away... The shack rotted away.* PHRASAL VB : V+ADV

rota /rəʊtə/, **rotas.** A **rota** is a list of people who take turns to do a particular job. EG *We have a cooking rota... The office work was shared on a rota system.* N COUNT

rotary /rəʊtə⁰ri[1]/ means moving in a circular direction. EG *...the rotary motion of the racket.* ADJ CLASSIF : ATTRIB

rotate /rəʊteɪt/, **rotates, rotating, rotated. 1** When something **rotates** or when you **rotate** it, it turns with a circular movement. EG *...two drums rotating in opposite directions.* V-ERG : USU+A

2 If you **rotate** a group of things or people, or if they **rotate**, you use each of them in turn, and, when you have used all of them, you begin with the first one again. EG *Weeds and diseases are controlled by rotating the crops... They rotate the jobs so that everyone gets a turn.* V-ERG

rotation /rəʊteɪʃə⁰n/, **rotations. 1 Rotation** is circular movement. EG *...the earth's rotation... ...the rotations of the ceiling fan.* N UNCOUNT OR N COUNT

2 When there is **rotation** of a group of things or people, you use each of them in turn and, when you have used all of them, you begin with the first one again. EG *Crop rotations will help to minimize disease... She did everything in strict rotation.* N UNCOUNT OR N COUNT

rotor /rəʊtə/, **rotors.** The **rotors** or **rotor** blades of a helicopter are the four long, flat, thin pieces of metal on top of it which go round and lift it off the ground. EG *The rotors turned more slowly.* N COUNT

rotten /rɒtə⁰n/. **1** When food, wood, or other substances are **rotten**, they have decayed and can no longer be used. EG *...rotten eggs... The wood was so rotten that when they pulled, it broke.* ADJ QUALIT

2 If you describe something as **rotten**, you mean that it is of very poor quality. EG *...a rotten novel... It was a rotten school.* ADJ QUALIT Informal

3 If you say that a situation is **rotten**, you mean that it is very unfair or unpleasant. EG *They're having a rotten deal... Must be rotten, having your every movement watched.* ADJ QUALIT Informal

4 If you describe someone as **rotten**, you mean that they are very unpleasant or unkind. EG *He was a rotten bastard, like all men.* ADJ QUALIT Informal

5 If you feel **rotten**, you feel very ill. EG *I asked him how he was. 'Rotten,' said the Duke.* ADJ PRED Informal

6 You use **rotten** to emphasize your dislike for something or your anger or frustration about it. EG *She was mumbling away about her rotten old sugar.* ADJ CLASSIF : ATTRIB Informal

rouge /ruːʒ/ is a red powder which women and actors put on their cheeks in order to give them more colour. EG *They wore lipstick and rouge.* N UNCOUNT

rouged /ruːʒd/. If a woman's or actor's cheeks are **rouged**, they look red because they are covered in rouge. EG *...an elderly lady with rouged cheeks.* ADJ QUALIT

rough /rʌf/, **rougher, roughest; roughs, roughing, roughed. 1** If a surface is **rough**, it is uneven and not smooth. EG *They journeyed for several weeks over rough roads... ...the rough surface of the stone.* ◊ **roughness.** EG *Roughness of the skin can be caused by bad diet.* ADJ QUALIT; ◊ N UNCOUNT

2 You say that people are **rough** when they use too much force and not enough care or gentleness. EG *There were complaints of rough handling, especially by younger policemen... I grabbed her by the shoulders. Maybe I was too rough.* ◊ **roughly.** EG *He shoved the boy roughly aside.* ADJ QUALIT; ◊ ADV

3 If you say that someone is having a **rough** time, you mean that they are experiencing something difficult or unpleasant. EG *I knew they were having a rough time and I felt sorry for them.* ADJ QUALIT

4 A **rough** calculation or guess is approximately correct. EG *Multiply the weekly amount by fifty two to get the rough annual cost.* ◊ **roughly.** EG *...a woman of roughly her own age.* ADJ QUALIT; ◊ ADV

5 A **rough** description or drawing indicates only the most important features of something, without much detail. EG *Mr Boggis drew a rough sketch... ...a rough outline of the proposals.* ◊ **roughly.** EG *Could you tell us roughly what is required?* ADJ QUALIT; ◊ ADV

6 You can say that something is **rough** when it is not well made. EG *They built a rough shelter of branches and leaves.* ◊ **roughly.** EG *The pieces were then roughly cobbled together.* ADJ QUALIT; ◊ ADV

7 If the sea or a sea journey is **rough**, the weather is windy or stormy and there are very big waves. EG *By now the sea was really rough... ...ninety rough minutes on a cross-Channel trip.* ADJ QUALIT

8 You can say that a town or district is **rough** when there is a lot of crime or violence there. EG *Abilene was one of the roughest towns in America.* ADJ QUALIT

9 When people **sleep rough**, they sleep in unusual places, often out of doors, usually because they have no home. EG *We had great fun sleeping rough on the beach.* PHRASE

10 If you have to **rough it**, you have to live without the possessions and comforts that you normally have. EG *You may have to rough it for a while.*

rough out. If you **rough out** a drawing or an idea, you draw or write the main features of it before you do it in detail. EG *I've roughed out a scene for my new play.* PHRASAL VB : V+O+ADV

rough up. If someone **roughs** you **up**, they attack you and hit or beat you. EG *They roughed me up a bit and then left me.* PHRASAL VB: V+O+ADV Informal

rough and ready. If you describe something as **rough and ready**, you mean that it has been made, done, or arranged in a hurry and may not be totally satisfactory. EG *...a rough-and-ready calculation... ...rough and ready treatments... The accommodation was a bit rough and ready.* ADJ QUALIT

rough and tumble. If you refer to the **rough and tumble** of a situation, you mean that the people involved try hard to get what they want, and do not worry about upsetting or harming others. EG *...the rough and tumble of world politics.* N UNCOUNT

roulette /ruːlɛt/ is a gambling game in which a ball is dropped onto a revolving wheel with numbered holes in it. The players bet on which hole the ball will be in when the wheel stops spinning. N UNCOUNT

round /raʊnd/, **rounder, roundest; rounds, rounding, rounded.** The form **around** can be used instead of **round** when it is a preposition or an adverb. ADJ QUALIT

1 Something that is **round** is **1.1** shaped like a ball. EG *...heavy round stones.* **1.2** shaped like a circle. EG *Shanti had a round face.* **1.3** curved, like the letter 'c'. EG *...the round bulge of the girl's belly.*

2 If something or a group of things is **round** or **around** something else, it surrounds it. EG *She was wearing a scarf round her head... We were sitting round a table eating and drinking... There was a wall all the way round.* PREP OR ADV

3 The distance **round** or **around** something is the length of its boundary or circumference. EG *It measures fifteen feet round the trunk.* PREP OR ADV

4 You can refer to the area near a place as the area **round** or **around** it. EG *We were the first farmers round here to use the new fertilizers.* PREP OR ADV

5 If something happens or exists in many parts of a place, you can say that it happens or exists **round** or **around** that place. EG *Think of what's happening politically round the world... He now has five shops scattered around the town.* PREP

6 If something moves **round** or **around** you, it keeps moving in a circle and you are at the centre of the circle. EG *The earth moves round the sun... The youth danced around her in his pyjamas.* PREP, OR ADV AFTER VB

7 If something is going **round and round**, it is spinning or moving in small circles. EG *He twirled round and round... A swallow flew frantically round and round.* PHRASE

8 When someone goes to the other side of something, you can say that they have gone **round** it or **around** it. EG *They sailed round the Cape... The boys had disappeared around a corner.* PREP, OR ADV AFTER VB

9 If you turn or look **round** or **around**, you turn so that you are facing in a different direction. EG *He swung round and faced the window.* ADV AFTER VB

10 If you go **round** or **around** a place, you go to several different parts of it. EG *I wandered around the orchard.* PREP, OR ADV AFTER VB

11 When someone comes **round** or comes **around**, they visit you. EG *Her friend Emily came round... I'd like to ask him round for dinner.* ADV AFTER VB

12 If there is a way **round** or **around** a problem or difficulty, there is a solution to it. PREP

13 Round about means **13.1** very near a place. EG *...the shepherds who live round about here... She knew all the people in the houses round about.* PREP OR ADV **13.2** approximately. EG *I've been here for round about ten years... The lads were round about eighteen.* PREP

14 When you **round** something, you move in a curve past the edge or corner of it. EG *...as he rounded the corner at the top of the stairs.* V+O

15 A **round** of events is a series of events that is part of a larger series. EG *Turkey is eager for a further round of talks... We were on our final round of visits.* N COUNT+SUPP

16 When people such as doctors go on their **rounds** or make their **rounds**, they make a series of visits as part of their job. N COUNT

17 A competition usually consists of a series of **rounds**. Each round is a set of games. The winners of these games go on to play in the next round. N COUNT

18 A **round** of golf is one game. EG *She's playing a round of golf.* N COUNT

19 In a boxing or wrestling match, a **round** is one of the periods during which the boxers or wrestlers fight. N COUNT

20 If you buy a **round** of drinks, you buy a drink for each member of the group of people that you are with. EG *He would have liked to pay for a round himself... It's my round.* N COUNT

21 A **round** of ammunition is the bullet or bullets that are released when a gun is fired. N COUNT

round up. If you **round up** animals or people, you gather them together. EG *They had rounded up people at gunpoint.* ● See also **roundup**. PHRASAL VB: V+O+ADV

roundabout /raʊndəbaʊt/, **roundabouts. 1** At a funfair, a **roundabout** is a large, circular mechanical device with seats, often in the shape of animals or cars, on which children sit and go round and round. N COUNT British

2 In a playground, a **roundabout** is a circular platform that children sit or stand on. The platform is made to rotate by being pushed. N COUNT British

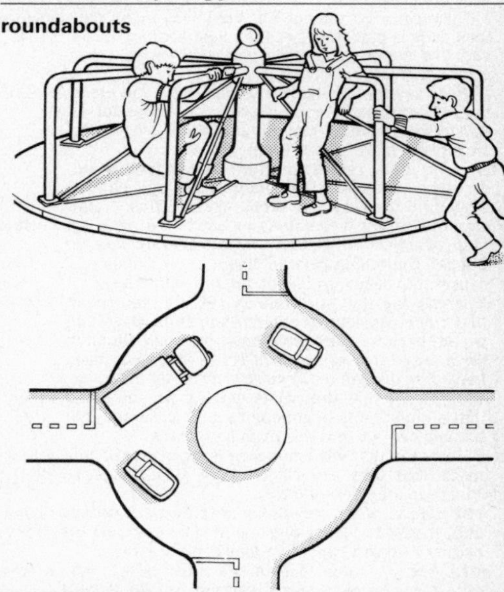

3 A **roundabout** is also a circle at a place where several roads meet. You drive round it until you come to the road that you want. EG *He got stuck in a traffic jam at the roundabout.* N COUNT British

4 If you do something in a **roundabout** way, you do not do it in the simplest or most direct way. EG *They drove back to Glasgow by a long roundabout route... He told me this in a rather gentle, roundabout way.* ADJ QUALIT: USU ATTRIB

rounded /raʊndɪ²d/. Something that is **rounded** is curved in shape, without any points or sharp edges. EG *...rounded hills... Its teeth are small and rounded.* ADJ CLASSIF

rounders /raʊndəz/ is a game played by two teams, in which a player scores points by hitting a ball thrown by a member of the other team and running round all four sides of a square. N UNCOUNT British

Who gets royalties?

roundly /raʊndli¹/. If you say something **roundly**, you say it very forcefully. EG *Britain was roundly condemned for selling arms to the rebels... 'What utter rubbish!' declared Miss Clare roundly.* ADV

round-the-clock activities happen all day and all night. EG *...keeping the hotel under round-the-clock surveillance... They are offering free round the clock legal advice.* ▸ used as an adverb. EG *Factories are working round the clock to keep pace with the demand.* ADJ CLASSIF : ATTRIB ▸ ADV

round trip, round trips. If you make a **round trip**, you travel to a place and then back again. EG *He made the eighty mile round trip and was back in time for dinner.* N COUNT

roundup /raʊndʌp/, **roundups. 1** On television or radio, a **roundup** of news is a summary of it. EG *...the news followed by the sports roundup.* N COUNT : USU SING

2 When there is a **roundup** of people or animals, they are collected from different places and brought to one place. EG *In a massive roundup, they arrested several hundred leaders.* N COUNT : USU SING

rouse /raʊz/, **rouses, rousing, roused. 1** If you **rouse** or if someone **rouses** you, you wake up. EG *I was worried when I couldn't rouse her.* V-ERG Formal

2 If you **rouse** yourself to do something, you make yourself get up and do it. EG *After a moment he roused himself to talk to Christine.* V-REFL

3 If something **rouses** you, it makes you very emotional or excited. EG *He roused the troops with his oratory... He could move quickly when roused to anger.* ◊ **rousing.** EG *...a rousing cheer.* V+O ◊ ADJ QUALIT

4 If something **rouses** an emotion in you, it causes you to feel it. EG *The proposal roused fears among the public.* V+O : USU+A

rout /raʊt/, **routs, routing, routed.** If an army or a sports team **routs** its opponents, it defeats them completely and easily. EG *Spain could not muster sufficient resources to rout the Cubans.* ▸ used as a noun. EG *The retreat turned into a rout... The terrified army fled in rout.* V+O ▸ N COUNT OR N UNCOUNT

route /ru:t/, **routes, routing, routed. 1** A **route** is a way from one place to another. EG *I took the route through Beechwood... ...the main route out of London to the west.* ● See also **en route**. N COUNT : USU+SUPP

2 A bus **route** or train **route** is a way between two places which buses or trains travel along regularly. EG *...shipping routes through the North Sea... ...bus routes into the city centre.* N COUNT : USU+SUPP

3 The **route** of a procession or a race is the way that it is planned to go. EG *...the wedding procession route... A million people were lining the route.* N SING : *the*+N

4 You can refer to a way of achieving something as a **route**. EG *Another route is by active participation in a trade union.* N COUNT+SUPP

5 When vehicles **are routed** past a place or through it, they are made to travel past it or through it. EG *Flights were being routed around the trouble area.* V+O : USU PASS+A

routine /ru:ti:n/, **routines. 1** You describe activities as **routine** when you do them as a normal part of your job, rather than for a special reason. EG *They made a routine check on the whole section.* ◊ **routinely.** EG *This information is routinely collected and published.* ADJ CLASSIF ◊ ADV

2 You can also describe activities as **routine** when you do them so often that they have become uninteresting. EG *We spend a lot of time performing mindless routine tasks.* ADJ QUALIT

3 A **routine** is **3.1** the usual way or order in which you do something. EG *...his daily routine... Davis's death has upset our routine.* N COUNT OR N UNCOUNT **3.2** the boring repetition of a series of tasks. EG *...the dreary office routine... The routine was unbelievably tedious.* N UNCOUNT +SUPP

rove /rəʊv/, **roves, roving, roved.** Someone who **roves** an area or **roves** around it wanders around in it. EG *...the thugs who rove the streets at night... We lived a roving life.* V+A OR V+O Literary Outdated

row, rows, rowing, rowed; pronounced /rəʊ/ for paragraphs 1 to 5, and /raʊ/ for paragraphs 6 to 8.

1 A **row** of things or people is a number of them arranged in a line. EG *...a large hall filled with rows of desks... They were standing neatly in a row.* N PART

2 In a theatre or cinema, each line of seats is called a **row**. EG *...the young woman in the second row.* N COUNT

3 If the same thing happens several times **in a row**, it happens that number of times without interruption. EG *...three bad summers in a row... He was elected president three times in a row.* PHRASE

4 When you **row**, you sit in a boat and make it move through the water by using oars. EG *We rowed slowly towards the centre of the river.* ▸ used as a noun. EG *...a row on the lake.* V : USU+A, OR V+O ▸ N SING

5 If you **row** people or goods somewhere, you take them there in a boat, using oars. EG *I rowed them there and set them ashore.* V+O : USU+A

6 A **row** is a serious disagreement between politicians or public institutions. EG *This row broke out on the eve of the Congress.* N COUNT Informal

7 If two people have a **row**, they have a noisy argument or quarrel. EG *They were always having terrible rows.* ▸ used as a verb. EG *He never rowed with her mother.* N COUNT Informal ▸ V OR V+*with* : RECIP

8 If you say that someone is making a **row**, you mean that they are making a loud, unpleasant noise. EG *'Little beasts!' said Anne. 'What a row they make!'* N COUNT : USU SING Informal

rowboat /rəʊbəʊt/, **rowboats.** A **rowboat** is the same as a rowing boat. N COUNT American

rowdy /raʊdi¹/, **rowdier, rowdiest.** When people are **rowdy**, they are noisy, rough, and likely to cause trouble. EG *Not all teenage boys are rowdy.* ADJ QUALIT

rowing /rəʊɪŋ/ is a sport in which people or teams race against each other in specially built rowing boats. EG *...a rowing club.* N UNCOUNT

rowing boat, rowing boats. A **rowing boat** is a small boat that you move through the water by using oars. EG *He set off to sea alone in a rowing boat.* N COUNT British

royal /rɔɪəl/, **royals. 1 Royal** describes something that belongs to or involves a king, a queen, or members of their family. EG *...the royal wedding... ...a royal palace... ...the royal family.* ADJ CLASSIF : ATTRIB

2 Royal also describes someone who is a king or queen or a member of their family. EG *...a royal child.* ADJ CLASSIF : ATTRIB

3 Royal is used in the names of institutions or organizations that are officially appointed or supported by a member of a royal family. EG *...the Royal Navy... ...the Royal Opera House.*

4 Members of the royal family are sometimes referred to as the **royals**. EG *The royals hadn't put in an appearance yet.* N COUNT : USU PLURAL Informal

royal blue. Something that is **royal blue** is deep blue in colour. ADJ COLOUR

Royal Highness, Royal Highnesses. You use expressions such as **Your Royal Highness** and **Their Royal Highnesses** when you are addressing or referring to members of royal families who are not Kings or Queens; compare **Majesty**. EG *...Her Royal Highness Princess Alexandra.*

royalist /rɔɪəlɪst/, **royalists.** A **royalist** is someone who supports their country's royal family or who believes that their country should have a king or queen. EG *They were both fervent royalists... He belonged to a royalist family.* N COUNT

royalty /rɔɪəlti¹/, **royalties. 1** The members of a royal family are sometimes referred to as **royalty**. EG *...an official visit by royalty... ...generations of English royalty.* N UNCOUNT

2 Royalties are payments made to authors and musicians which are linked to the sales of their books or records, or to performance of their works. EG *...all the royalties from my next play... There should be a substantial income from royalties.* N COUNT : USU PLURAL

RSVP /ɑ:r ɛs vi: pi:/ means 'please reply'. It is written at the end of invitations. CONVENTION

rub /rʌb/, **rubs, rubbing, rubbed. 1** If you **rub** something, you move your hand or a cloth back- V+O OR V+A wards and forwards over it while pressing firmly. EG *He groaned and rubbed his eyes... He rubbed at his throat... Peter rubbed his glasses slowly.*

2 If you **rub** a part of your body against a surface, you move it backwards and forwards while pressing it against the surface. EG *She rubbed her cheek against my temple.* V+O+A

3 If you **rub** a substance onto a surface, you spread it over the surface using your hand. EG *The ointment he rubbed into the wound made it feel better.* V+O+A

4 If two things **rub** together or if you **rub** them together, they move backwards and forwards, pressing against each other. EG *He rubbed his hands and laughed... His massive thighs rubbed together as he walked.* V-ERG : OFT + *together*

5 If someone draws attention to something that involves you and that you find embarrassing, you can say that they **are rubbing it in**. EG *'How old are you? Forty?' – 'All right, no need to rub it in.'* PHRASE Informal

6 If you **rub** someone **up the wrong way**, you unintentionally offend them or annoy them. PHRASE Informal

7 to **rub salt into** someone's **wounds**: see **salt**. • to **rub shoulders with** someone: see **shoulder**.

rub off on. If someone's habits or characteristics **rub off on** you, you develop the same habits or characteristics after spending time with them. EG *They hoped that some of his prowess might rub off on them.* PHRASAL VB : V+ADV+PREP Informal

rub out. If you **rub out** something that someone has written on paper or on a blackboard, you remove it by rubbing it with a rubber or a cloth. PHRASAL VB : V+O+ADV

rubber /rʌbə/, **rubbers.** 1 **Rubber** is a strong, waterproof, elastic substance made from the sap of a tropical tree or produced chemically. N UNCOUNT

2 **Rubber** things are made of rubber. EG *...a rubber ball... ...rubber gloves.* ADJ CLASSIF

3 A **rubber** is a small piece of rubber that you use to rub out mistakes that you have made while writing, drawing, or typing. N COUNT

4 A **rubber** is also a series of games played between the same two people or teams, especially in cricket or bridge. N COUNT

rubber band, rubber bands. A **rubber band** is a thin circle of rubber that you put around things in order to hold them together. N COUNT

rubber stamp, rubber stamps, rubber-stamping, rubber-stamped. 1 A **rubber stamp** is a small device with something such as a name or a date on it. You press it on to an ink pad and then on to a document in order to show that the document has been officially dealt with. N COUNT

2 When someone in authority **rubber-stamps** something, they agree to it without thinking about it or discussing it; used showing disapproval. EG *The Council merely rubber-stamp decisions taken by him and his office.* V+O

rubbery /rʌbəᵒriˡ/. Something that is **rubbery** looks or feels soft or elastic like rubber. EG *...a long, rubbery piece of seaweed.* ADJ QUALIT

rubbish /rʌbɪʃ/. 1 **Rubbish** consists of unwanted things or waste material. EG *That old shed is full of rubbish... ...a local rubbish dump.* N UNCOUNT

2 You can refer to something as **rubbish** when you think that it is of very poor quality. EG *There is so much rubbish on TV.* N UNCOUNT

3 You can refer to an idea or a statement as **rubbish** if you think that it is foolish or wrong. EG *Don't talk rubbish... How can you believe such rubbish?* N UNCOUNT OR CONVENTION Informal

rubble /rʌbəᵒl/. 1 When a building is destroyed, the bits of brick, stone, or other materials that remain are referred to as **rubble**. EG *Every building was reduced to rubble... Injured people lay amongst the rubble.* N UNCOUNT

2 **Rubble** is also the small pieces of stone that are used to build the foundations for roads and houses.

rubric /ruːbrɪk/, **rubrics.** A **rubric** is a set of rules or instructions, for example the instructions at the beginning of an examination paper. N COUNT Formal

ruby /ruːbiˡ/, **rubies.** A **ruby** is a dark red jewel. EG *...a gift of rubies and diamonds.* N COUNT

rucksack

rucksack /rʌksæk/, **rucksacks.** A **rucksack** is a bag with straps that go over your shoulders, so that you can carry things on your back, for example when you are walking or climbing. N COUNT

rudder /rʌdə/, **rudders.** 1 A **rudder** is a device for steering a boat. It consists of a vertical piece of wood or metal at the back of the boat. See picture at YACHT. N COUNT

2 An aeroplane's **rudder** is a vertical piece of metal at the back which is used to make the plane turn to the right or to the left.

ruddy /rʌdiˡ/, **ruddier, ruddiest.** 1 Something that is **ruddy** is reddish in colour. EG *His cheeks were ruddy... The craft still burned, throwing a ruddy glare into the night sky.* ADJ COLOUR Literary

2 **Ruddy** is used as a mild swear word to add emphasis or to express anger. EG *It's the biggest ruddy miracle of them all... Get on with the ruddy film!* ADJ CLASSIF OR ADV Outdated

rude /ruːd/, **ruder, rudest.** 1 When people are **rude**, they behave in a way that is not polite. EG *I was rather rude to a young nurse... It's rude to stare... ...rude remarks.* ◊ **rudely**. EG *The President cannot rudely ignore a head of state.* ◊ **rudeness**. EG *He seemed not to notice their rudeness.* ADJ QUALIT ◊ ADV ◊ N UNCOUNT

2 **Rude** is used to describe words and behaviour that are likely to embarrass or offend people, because they relate to sex or other bodily functions. EG *...a rude gesture... ...a rude joke.* ADJ QUALIT : USU ATTRIB

3 You use **rude** to describe events that are unexpected and unpleasant. EG *...a rude awakening to the realization that he had been robbed.* ◊ **rudely**. EG *My belief in the future was rudely shattered.* ADJ QUALIT : ATTRIB ◊ ADV

4 Objects can be described as **rude** when they are very simply and roughly made. EG *I sat on the edge of one of the rude tables.* ADJ QUALIT : ATTRIB Literary

rudimentary /ruːdɪmentəᵒriˡ/. 1 Something that is **rudimentary** is very basic or undeveloped and therefore unsatisfactory. EG *...a rather rudimentary planning system... ...rudimentary equipment.* ADJ QUALIT Formal

2 Knowledge that is **rudimentary** includes only the simplest and most important facts. EG *I had gathered only the most rudimentary information... ...rudimentary mathematics.* ADJ QUALIT Formal

rudiments /ruːdɪməⁿnts/. When you learn the **rudiments** of something, you learn only the simplest and most important things about it. EG *I had time to pick up the rudiments of driving... He was teaching them the rudiments of Christianity.* N PLURAL : *the*+N, USU+*of*

rue /ruː/, **rues, ruing, rued.** If you **rue** something that you have done, you are sorry that you did it, because it has had unpleasant results. EG *I had ample cause to rue that decision.* V+O Literary Outdated

rueful /ruːfʊl/. If someone is **rueful**, they feel or express regret or sorrow in a quiet and gentle way. ADJ QUALIT Literary

On these pages, find two words that refer to the same game.

EG *She managed a rueful little smile.* ◊ **ruefully**. EG *Rita said ruefully, 'You're too old for that.'* ◊ ADV

ruffian /rʌfɪən/, **ruffians.** A **ruffian** is a man who behaves violently and is involved in crime. EG *Some local ruffians are responsible for this.* N COUNT Outdated

ruffle /rʌfə⁰l/, **ruffles, ruffling, ruffled.** 1 If you **ruffle** someone's hair, you move your hand quickly and fairly roughly over their head as a way of showing affection. V+O

2 **Ruffles** are small folds made in a piece of material or sewn onto it in order to decorate it. EG *...a dress adorned with ruffles and ribbons.* N COUNT: USU PLURAL

ruffled /rʌfə⁰ld/. 1 Something that is **ruffled** is no longer smooth or neat. EG *...the ruffled bedclothes... She emerged, her hair ruffled and her face red.* ADJ QUALIT

2 **Ruffled** clothes are decorated with small folds of material. EG *...a ruffled white blouse.* ADJ CLASSIF

3 You say that someone is **ruffled** when they are surprised, confused, or annoyed. EG *He was not easily ruffled... 'Why don't you come back later?' said Alex, mildly ruffled.* ADJ QUALIT

rug /rʌg/, **rugs.** 1 A **rug** is a piece of thick material like a carpet but covering only a small area. EG *The floor was covered with rugs.* N COUNT

2 A **rug** is also a small blanket which you use to cover your shoulders or your knees. EG *She took a tartan rug out of her case.* N COUNT

rugby /rʌgbi¹/ is a game played by two teams, who try to score points by carrying an oval ball to their opponents' end of the pitch, or by kicking the ball over a bar fixed between two goalposts. N UNCOUNT

rugged /rʌgɪ²d/. 1 A **rugged** area of land is rocky, uneven, and with few trees or plants. EG *The coastline is wild and rugged.* ADJ QUALIT Literary

2 If you describe a man as **rugged**, you mean that he has strong, rough features. EG *He was rugged and handsome.* ADJ QUALIT Literary

rugger /rʌgə/ is the same as rugby. EG *I got badly hurt at rugger once... ...a rugger player... ...a rugger ball.* N UNCOUNT Informal

ruin /ruːɪn/, **ruins, ruining, ruined.** 1 To **ruin** something means to severely harm, damage, or spoil it. EG *You are ruining your health... India's textile industry was ruined... Villages had been burned and ruined.* ◊ **ruined**. EG *...the ruined patch of garden... ...my ruined career.* V+O ◊ ADJ CLASSIF

2 To **ruin** someone means to cause them to no longer have any money. EG *The contract would certainly have ruined him... We are all ruining ourselves.* ◊ **ruined**. EG *...a ruined man.* V+O ◊ ADJ CLASSIF

3 **Ruin** is the state of no longer having any money. EG *Crow was heading for ruin.* N UNCOUNT

4 The **ruins** of something are the parts of it that remain after it has been severely damaged or weakened. EG *The Progressive Party was founded on the ruins of our Federal Party.* N COUNT: USU PLURAL

5 The **ruins** of a building are the parts of it that remain after the rest has been destroyed. EG *...the ruins of a castle... I walked around the ruins... It was splendid once, but it is a ruin now.* N COUNT: USU PLURAL

6 If something is **in ruin** or **in ruins**, it is completely spoiled. EG *Their once robust economy lies in ruins... The regime collapsed in total ruin.* PHRASE

7 If a building or place is **in ruin** or **in ruins**, most of it has been destroyed and only parts of it remain. EG *The castle, partly in ruins, stands on a crag... The villages are crumbling into ruin.* PHRASE

ruined /ruːɪnd/. A **ruined** building or place has been very badly damaged and is no longer used. EG *...a ruined castle... ...the ruined city of Tiahuanaco.* ADJ CLASSIF: ATTRIB

ruinous /ruːɪnəs/. If something that you are paying for is **ruinous**, it costs far more money than you can afford. EG *The effects would be ruinous... ...the ruinous expense of a funeral.* ADJ CLASSIF

rule /ruːl/, **rules, ruling, ruled.** 1 **Rules** are instructions that tell you what you are allowed to do and what you are not allowed to do. EG *...the rules of chess... It is against the rules to keep pets... This is forbidden under rule 7(c)... If she breaks the rules, she will be punished.* N COUNT: OFT PLURAL

2 The **rules** of something such as a language are statements that describe the way that things usually happen in it. EG *There are rules for English spelling and pronunciation.* N COUNT: OFT PLURAL

3 If something is the **rule**, it is the normal state of affairs. EG *Short haircuts became the rule.* N SING: *the*+N

4 If you say that something happens **as a rule**, you mean that it usually happens. EG *Doctors are not as a rule trained in child rearing.* PHRASE

5 If someone in authority **bends the rules** or **stretches the rules**, they allow you to do something, even though it is against the rules. PHRASE

6 When someone **rules** a country, they have the power to control its affairs, and they use this power. EG *...states ruled by kings... The military government went on ruling the country.* ▸ used as a noun. EG *...the dangers of one-party rule... ...the days of British rule.* V+O OR V+*over* ▸ N UNCOUNT +SUPP

7 When someone in authority **rules** on a particular matter, they give an official decision about it. EG *I was asked to rule on the case of a British seaman... The Supreme Court ruled that there was no federal offence involved.* V+A OR V+REPORT: ONLY *that* Formal

8 See also **ground rules**, **ruling**, **work-to-rule**.

rule out. 1 If you **rule out** an idea, solution, or course of action, you reject it, because it is impossible or unsuitable. EG *Washington need not rule out military aid.* 2 If one thing **rules out** another, it prevents it from happening or from being possible. EG *The radio was on, effectively ruling out conversation... A search had ruled out that possibility.* PHRASAL VB: V+O+ADV; V+O+ADV

ruler /ruːlə/, **rulers.** 1 A **ruler** is a person who rules a country. EG *Caesar was then ruler of Persia... ...the world's rulers.* N COUNT

2 A **ruler** is also a long, narrow, flat piece of wood, metal, or plastic with straight edges marked in inches or centimetres, which you use to measure things or to draw straight lines. EG *Measure the holes with a ruler.* N COUNT

ruling /ruːlɪŋ/. 1 The **ruling** group of people in an organization or country is the group that controls its affairs. EG *...the Church's ruling body... The ruling class will not surrender its power.* ADJ CLASSIF: ATTRIB

2 A **ruling** is an official decision made by a judge or court. EG *The judge gave his ruling... The Supreme Court ruling still stands.* N COUNT

rum /rʌm/, **rums.** 1 **Rum** is an alcoholic drink made from sugar cane juice. EG *He sipped his rum... ...a bottle of rum.* N MASS

2 If you describe people or things as **rum**, you mean that they are rather strange. EG *They were rum old boys... ...rum ideas... In a rum sort of way, Charles had helped enormously.* ADJ QUALIT Informal Outdated British

rumble /rʌmbə⁰l/, **rumbles, rumbling, rumbled.** 1 If something **rumbles**, it makes a low, continuous noise, often while moving slowly. EG *...the rumbling noise of barrels being rolled down the ramp.* ▸ used as a noun. EG *...a menacing rumble of distant thunder... ...the rumble of a passing truck.* V: OFT+A ▸ N COUNT: USU+*of*

2 If you **rumble** someone or something, you find out the truth about them, which was being concealed. EG *You've rumbled that already, surely.* V+O Informal

rumbling /rʌmblɪŋ/, **rumblings.** 1 A **rumbling** is a low, continuous noise. EG *There was a distant rumbling and the air-conditioning came on... ...the rumbling of thunder.* N COUNT

2 **Rumblings** are signs that a bad situation is developing. EG *There were rumblings of discontent... ...the first rumblings of World War II.* N COUNT: USU PLURAL

ruminate /ruːmɪneɪt/, **ruminates, ruminating, ruminated.** If you **ruminate** about something, you think about it very carefully. EG *George is now ruminating about the possibility... She ruminated a bit longer and then said, 'Older, I think.'* V: USU+A Formal

rummage /rʌmɪdʒ/, **rummages, rummaging, rummaged.** If you **rummage** somewhere, you V+A search for something there by moving things in a careless way. EG *He rummaged around in his drawer... She was rummaging among the books and magazines.*

rummy /rʌmi¹/ is a card game in which players try to collect cards of the same value or cards in a sequence. EG *I had to play rummy with Dr Lutz.* N UNCOUNT

rumour /ru:mə/, **rumours, rumoured;** spelled **rumor** in American English. **1** A **rumour** is a story or piece of information that may or may not be true, but that people are talking about. EG *There's a rumour that Mangel is coming here to speak... ...rumours of street fighting and violence... Rumour has it that she's pregnant.* N COUNT

2 If something **is rumoured**, people are suggesting that it is true, but they do not know for certain. EG *It was rumoured that the body had been removed... He was rumored to be living in Detroit.* V-PASS +REPORT OR *to*-INF

rump /rʌmp/, **rumps. 1** The **rump** of a group, organization, or political party consists of the members who remain in it after the rest have left it. EG *The party has dwindled to a disorganized rump.* N COUNT

2 An animal's **rump** is its rear end. EG *He sent the horse forward with a slap on its rump.* N COUNT

3 Rump or **rump steak** is meat cut from the rear end of a cow. N UNCOUNT

4 A person's **rump** is his or her buttocks. EG *He rubbed his rump.* N COUNT Informal

rumple /rʌmpə⁰l/, **rumples, rumpling, rumpled.** If you **rumple** something, you cause it to be untidy or creased. EG *...rumpling the papers on her desk... He rumpled her hair.* V+O ◇ **rumpled.** EG *...a rumpled grey suit.* ◇ ADJ QUALIT

rumpus /rʌmpəs/. A **rumpus** is a lot of noise or argument. EG *They caused a rumpus in the House of Commons... I never heard such a rumpus.* N SING

run /rʌn/, **runs, running, ran** /ræn/. The form **run** is used in the present tense of the verb and is also the past participle.

1 When you **run**, you move quickly, leaving the ground during each stride, because you are in a hurry to get somewhere or because you are taking part in a race. EG *I ran downstairs to open the door... She ran after me and coaxed me to come back... He ran the mile in just over four minutes.* V: OFT+A OR V+O ▸ used as a noun. EG *He found himself breaking into a run... We had to go for a cross-country run every weekend.* ▸ N COUNT: USU SING

2 If you say that something long, such as a road, **runs** in a particular direction, you are describing its course or position. EG *The reef runs parallel to the coast... ...a tunnel running from the Mediterranean into the Dead Sea.* V+A

3 If you **run** an object or your hand over something, you move the object or your hand over it. EG *He ran his hand over her hair... She ran her finger down a list of names.* V+O+A

4 If someone **runs** in an election, they take part as a candidate. EG *He ran for Governor.* V+A American

5 If you **run** something such as a business or an activity, you are in charge of it or you organize it. EG *She ran the office as a captain runs a ship... We run a course for local teachers.* V+O

6 If you **run** an experiment, computer program, or tape, you start it and let it continue. EG *Check everything and run the whole test again.* V+O

7 You can use **run** to say how something develops or progresses. EG *We tried to keep the business running smoothly.* V+A

8 If you **run** a car or piece of equipment, you have it and use it. EG *A freezer doesn't cost much to run... Its running costs were low.* V+O

9 When a machine **is running**, it is switched on and operating. EG *The engine was running.* V

10 If you **run** a machine on or off a particular source of energy, you use that source to make it work. EG *You can run the entire system off a mains plug... The heater ran on half-price electricity.* V-ERG+A

11 If a train or bus **runs** somewhere, it travels on a regular route at set times. EG *No buses have been running in the town for the past week.* V-ERG+A

12 If you **run** someone somewhere in a car, you drive them there. EG *Would you mind running me to the station?* V+O+A

13 If a liquid **runs** in a particular direction, it flows in that direction. EG *Tears were running down his face... The river ran past our house.* V+A OR V+C

14 If you **run** water or if you **run** a tap, you cause water to flow from the tap. EG *She was running hot water into the tub... Run my bath now!* V+O: USU+A

15 If a tap **is running**, water is coming out of it. V: USU CONT

16 If your nose **is running**, mucus is flowing out of it, usually because you have a cold. V: USU CONT

17 If the colour in something such as a piece of clothing **runs**, it comes out when the piece of clothing is washed. V

18 If a feeling **runs** through your body, it passes through it quickly and strongly. EG *A sharp tingling sensation ran through her.* V+A

19 If newspapers or magazines **run** a particular item or story, they publish it. EG *The local newspaper ran a feature on Liverpool.* V+O

20 You use **run** to indicate that you are quoting someone else's words or ideas. EG *'Attack on mother-to-be' ran the Evening News headline.* V+QUOTE

21 If an amount **is running** at a particular level, it is at that level. EG *Unemployment is running at 20 per cent.* V+O+*at*: USU CONT

22 If a play, event, or legal contract **runs** for a particular period of time, it lasts for that period of time. EG *'Chu-Chin-Chow' ran for years... The monsoons had six weeks more to run.* V+A

23 If someone or something **is running** late, they have taken more time than had been planned. EG *I'm running a bit over time, I'm afraid.* V+A

24 A **run** is also a journey somewhere. EG *It's a fair run up to Glasgow... ...planes which unload their bombs, on the home run, on innocent villages.* N COUNT: USU+SUPP

25 In the theatre, a **run** is the period of time during which performances of a play are given. EG *The play ended its six-week run at the Regent.* N COUNT+SUPP

26 A **run** of success or failure is a series of successes or failures. EG *Leeds United had a run of wins in December.* N COUNT+SUPP

27 In cricket or baseball, a **run** is a score of one, which is made by players running between marked places on the pitch after hitting the ball. EG *They had beaten England by seventeen runs.* N COUNT

28 If you say that someone is different from the average **run** or common **run** of people, you mean that they are different from ordinary people. EG *Politicians seem to be more fallible than the average run of mankind.* N SING: *the*+N +SUPP Literary

29 If someone is **on the run**, **29.1** they are trying to escape or hide from someone such as the police or an enemy. **29.2** they are being severely defeated in a contest or competition. EG *The Conservatives are on the run throughout Wales.* PHRASE

30 If you **make a run for it** or if you **run for it**, you go somewhere quickly in order to escape from something. EG *It was still raining hard, but we made a run for it... We'll just have to run for it.* PHRASE

31 If you talk about what will happen **in the long run**, you are saying what you think will happen over a long period of time in the future. If you talk about what will happen **in the short run**, you are saying what you think will happen in the near future. EG *Their policy would prove very costly in the long run.* PHRASE

32 If a river or well **runs dry**, it ceases to have any water in it. PHRASE

33 If people's feelings **are running high**, they are PHRASE

Has a runner-up been running?

very angry, concerned, or excited. EG *Public indignation was running high.*

34 to make your **blood run cold**: see **blood**. • to **run its course**: see **course**. • to **run** someone or something **to ground**: see **ground**. • to **run riot**: see **riot**. • to **run** the **risk**: see **risk**. • to **run short**: see **short**. • to **run wild**: see **wild**. • See also **running, trial run**.

run across. If you **run across** someone, you meet them unexpectedly. EG *He ran across Tom and asked him what was happening.* PHRASAL VB : V+PREP

run along. If you tell a child to **run along**, you mean that you want them to go away. EG *Run along up to bed now, Sam.* PHRASAL VB : V+ADV Informal

run away. 1 If you **run away** from a place, you leave it because you are unhappy there. EG *He had run away from home at the age of thirteen... I ran away to Brighton.* PHRASAL VB : V+ADV, OFT+*from* **2** If you **run away** from something unpleasant or new, you try to avoid dealing with it or thinking about it. EG *I can't run away from the horrors of the war.* V+ADV, OFT+*from* **3** See also **runaway**.

run away with. If you let your emotions **run away with** you, you fail to control them and cannot think sensibly. EG *They did not allow their enthusiasm to run away with them.* PHRASAL VB : V+ADV+PREP

run down. 1 If you **run down** people or things, you criticize them strongly. EG *She was not used to people running down their own families.* PHRASAL VB : V+O+ADV **2** If people **run down** an industry or an organization, they deliberately reduce its size or activity. EG *The air force had been run down.* V+O+ADV **3** See also **run-down**.

run into. 1 If you **run into** problems or difficulties, you unexpectedly begin to experience them. EG *The firm ran into foreign exchange problems.* PHRASAL VB : V+PREP **2** If you **run into** someone, you meet them unexpectedly. EG *You might run into him one of these days.* V+PREP

3 If a vehicle **runs into** something, it accidentally hits it. EG *She did not notice the driver's signal and ran into the back of his bus... Taxis swerve round rickshaws, buses run into handcarts.* V+PREP, HAS PASS **4** You use **run into** to say that something costs a lot of money. EG *...exports running into billions of dollars.* V+PREP

5 If one thing **runs into** another, it is difficult to see or hear the division between them. EG *The words run into each other.* V+PREP

run off. 1 If you **run off** with someone, you secretly go away with them in order to live with them or marry them. EG *His wife ran off with another man.* PHRASAL VB : V+ADV OR V+ADV+*with* : RECIP **2** If you **run off** copies of a piece of writing, you produce them using a machine. V+O+ADV

run on. If something **runs on**, it continues for longer than expected. EG *Donleavy tends to let his jokes run on too long.* PHRASAL VB : V+ADV

run out. 1 If you **run out** of something, you have no more of it left. EG *We were rapidly running out of money.* • to **run out of steam**: see **steam**. PHRASAL VB : V+ADV,OFT+*of* **2** If something **runs out**, it becomes used up so that there is no more left. EG *Time is running out fast... My luck seemed to have run out.* V+ADV **3** When a legal document **runs out**, it becomes no longer valid. EG *My passport's run out.* V+ADV

run over. If a vehicle **runs over** someone or something, it knocks them down. EG *Rosamund nearly got run over last night.* PHRASAL VB : V+PREP, HAS PASS

run through. 1 If something **runs through** a group of people or things, it is present in all of them, or spreads through all of them. EG *...the deep-rooted prejudice that runs through our society... A kind of shock-wave ran through the room.* PHRASAL VB : V+PREP **2** If you **run through** something, you rehearse it or practise it. EG *You could hear the performers running through the whole programme in the background.* V+PREP, HAS PASS

3 If you **run through** a list of items, you read or mention all the items quickly. V+PREP **4** See also **run-through**.

run to. 1 If you **run to** someone, you go to them for help or to tell them something. EG *I didn't think he'd run to you with the story.* PHRASAL VB : V+PREP **2** If something **runs to** a particular amount or size, it is that amount or size. EG *The transcript runs to 1,200 pages.* V+PREP Formal

run up. 1 If someone **runs up** bills or debts, they acquire them by buying a lot of things or borrowing money. V+ADV+O **2** See also **run-up**.

run up against. If you **run up against** problems, you suddenly begin to experience them. EG *Sooner or later we would run up against major problems... You never know what you're liable to run up against.* PHRASAL VB : V+ADV+PREP

runaway /rʌnəweɪ/, **runaways. 1** A **runaway** is a child who leaves home without telling anyone where he or she is going. EG *They failed to find any trace of the runaways.* N COUNT

2 A **runaway** vehicle is moving and its driver has lost control of it. EG *...a runaway bulldozer.* ADJ CLASSIF : ATTRIB

3 A **runaway** situation happens unexpectedly and cannot be controlled. EG *...the runaway success of 'Nicholas Nickleby'... ...the runaway inflation after the war.* ADJ CLASSIF : ATTRIB

run-down, run-downs. 1 If someone is **run-down**, they are tired or ill. EG *'You're probably run down,' Clarissa said. 'You need a holiday.'* ADJ PRED Informal

2 A **run-down** building or area is in very poor condition. EG *...two small rooms in a run-down building.* ADJ QUALIT

3 When the **run-down** of an industry or organization takes place, it is reduced in size or activity. EG *...the run-down of the coal industry.* ▸ used as an adjective. EG *...run-down public services.* N SING+SUPP ▸ ADJ QUALIT

4 If you give someone the **run-down** on a situation or subject, you tell them the important facts about it. EG *Let me give you the rundown on the Ritz Hotel situation.* N COUNT : USU SING+*on* Informal

rung /rʌŋ/, **rungs. 1 Rung** is the past participle of **ring**.

2 The **rungs** on a ladder are the wooden or metal bars that form the steps. EG *I had my foot on the first rung when she grabbed my arm.* N COUNT

3 If you reach a particular **rung** in an organization, you reach that level in it. EG *...the lower rungs of management.* N COUNT+SUPP

runner /rʌnə/, **runners. 1** A **runner** is a person who runs, especially for sport or pleasure. EG *...a long-distance runner... Not being a fast runner, I was glad I was close to the hall.* N COUNT

2 A drugs **runner** or gun **runner** is someone who illegally takes drugs or guns into a country. N COUNT+SUPP

3 Runners are thin strips of wood or metal underneath something which help it to move smoothly. EG *Push the driving seat back on its runners... ...sledge runners.* N COUNT

runner bean, runner beans. Runner beans are the long green pods of a climbing plant. You eat these pods as a vegetable. N COUNT

runner-up, runners-up. A **runner-up** is someone who finishes in second place in a race or competition. EG *...runner-up in the British Open.* N COUNT

running /rʌnɪŋ/. **1 Running** is the activity of running, especially as a sport. EG *He started professional running only eight years ago... ...running tracks... ...running techniques.* N UNCOUNT

2 The **running** of something such as a business is the managing or organizing of it. EG *...the day-to-day running of the school.* N UNCOUNT +SUPP

3 You use **running** to describe things that continue without stopping over a period of time. EG *...a running battle between architects and planners... ...a running commentary.* ADJ CLASSIF : ATTRIB

4 You also use **running** to describe things that keep happening regularly. For example, if something has happened every day for three days, you can say that it has happened for three days **running** or that it has happened for the third day **running**. EG *For three days running he had left the sandwiches at home... For the fourth year running, the weather was awful.* ADJ AFTER N

5 Running water is **5.1** water that is flowing rather than standing still. EG *...the sound of running* ADJ CLASSIF : ATTRIB *water.* **5.2** water that is supplied to a house through pipes and taps.

6 If someone **makes the running** in a situation, they are more active than the other people involved. EG *Women made all the running in demands for change.* PHRASE

7 If someone is **in the running** for something, they have a good chance of winning or obtaining it. If they are **out of the running**, they have no chance of winning or obtaining it. EG *He's still in the running for the leadership of the Labour Party.* PHRASE

runny /rʌni[1]/, **runnier, runniest. 1** Something that is **runny** is more liquid than usual or than was intended. EG *They had runny eggs for breakfast.* ADJ QUALIT

2 If someone's nose or eyes are **runny**, liquid is flowing from them. ADJ QUALIT

run-of-the-mill. A **run-of-the-mill** person or thing is very ordinary, with no special or interesting features. EG *...a run-of-the-mill customer.* ADJ QUALIT

runt /rʌnt/, **runts.** If you call a small person a **runt**, you are expressing your dislike for them. EG *Pegler was a skinny little runt.* N COUNT

run-through, run-throughs. A **run-through** for an event is a rehearsal or practice for it. EG *He agreed to come to a run-through.* N COUNT

run-up. The **run-up** to an event is the period of time just before it. EG *...to reduce taxation in the run-up to the election.* N SING : *the*+N

runway /rʌnweɪ/, **runways.** A **runway** is a long strip of ground with a hard surface which is used by aeroplanes when they are taking off or landing. EG *...the main runways at Heathrow Airport.* N COUNT

rupee /ruːpiː/, **rupees.** A **rupee** is a unit of money that is used in India, Pakistan, and some other countries. N COUNT

rupture /rʌptʃə/, **ruptures, rupturing, ruptured. 1** A **rupture** is a severe injury in which a part of your body tears or bursts open. EG *See if you can open it without suffering a rupture.* ▸ used as a verb. EG *He ruptured himself playing football... ...the Mayor's ruptured appendix.* N COUNT; ▸ V+O, V-REFL, OR V

2 When there is a **rupture** between people, their relationship ends. EG *There has been a fundamental rupture between us.* ▸ used as a verb. EG *...at the risk of rupturing relations with the British.* N COUNT Formal; ▸ V+O

rural /rʊərəl/ means **1** existing far away from large towns or cities. EG *...a rural postmaster... ...poverty in the rural areas.* **2** typical of areas that are far away from large towns or cities. EG *India is still an overwhelmingly rural country... She spoke in a very rural accent.* ADJ CLASSIF : ATTRIB; ADJ QUALIT

ruse /ruːz/, **ruses.** A **ruse** is an action which is intended to deceive someone. EG *The offer was just a ruse to gain time... His ruse had failed.* N COUNT Formal

rush /rʌʃ/, **rushes, rushing, rushed. 1** If you **rush** somewhere, you go there quickly. EG *Please don't rush off... I'll rush over on Monday morning... When they saw us, they rushed forward.* V : USU+A

2 When people **rush** to do something, they do it without delay, because they are very eager to do it. EG *People were rushing to buy the newspaper... Her friends rushed to her aid.* V+*to*-INF OR *to*

3 If you **rush** something, you do it in a hurry. EG *I rushed my lunch.* ◊ **rushed**. EG *It'll be a bit of a rushed job, I'm afraid.* V+O OR V+*at*; ◊ ADJ CLASSIF : ATTRIB

4 If you **rush** someone or something to a place, you take them there quickly. EG *Barnett was rushed to hospital with a broken back.* V+O+A

5 If you **rush** someone into doing something, you make them do it without allowing them enough time to think about it. EG *Do not be rushed into parting with goods before taking legal advice.* V+O : USU+*into*

6 If you are **rushed off** your **feet**, you are very busy. EG *I've been rushed off my feet all day.* PHRASE Informal

7 If there is **no rush** to do something, there is no need to do it quickly. EG *There is no rush to fill the vacancy... I'm not in any rush.* PHRASE

8 You can refer to a part of the day that is usually busy as the **rush**. EG *...the five o'clock rush.* N SING : *the*+N

9 If there is a **rush** for something or a **rush** to do something, there is a sudden increase in people's attempts to get it or do it. EG *There had been a rush for tickets... ...a rush to find the treasure.* N SING+SUPP

10 If air or liquid **rushes** somewhere, it flows there suddenly and quickly. EG *The water rushed in over the top of his boots.* ▸ used as a noun. EG *There was a little rush of air... She shouted above the rush of water.* ◊ **rushing**. EG *They were carried along in the rushing stream... The rushing waters will carry them away.* V : USU+A; ▸ N SING : USU+SUPP; ◊ ADJ CLASSIF : ATTRIB

11 If you experience a **rush** of a feeling, you suddenly experience it very strongly. EG *She felt a rush of pity for the boy... The memory came back with a painful rush.* N SING : USU+SUPP

12 Rushes are plants that grow near water and have long, thin stems. EG *I hid in the rushes... ...baskets made from rushes.* N COUNT : USU PLURAL

rush in or **rush into.** If you **rush in** or if you **rush into** a situation, you get involved in it without thinking about it carefully. EG *You wanted to rush in and protect him... Don't rush into marriage.* PHRASAL VB : V+ADV/PREP

rush-hour. The **rush-hour** is one of the periods of the day when most people are travelling to or from work. EG *I had to start in the morning rush-hour... ...rush-hour traffic.* N SING : *the*+N

Russian /rʌʃə[0]n/, **Russians. 1** Someone or something that is **Russian** belongs or relates to the Soviet Union. EG *...Russian dancers... ...the Russian Embassy.* ADJ CLASSIF

2 A **Russian** is a person who comes from the Soviet Union. EG *His father is a Russian.* N COUNT

3 Russian is the official language of the Soviet Union. EG *He had learnt to speak some Russian.* N UNCOUNT

rust /rʌst/, **rusts, rusting, rusted. 1 Rust** is a brown substance that forms on iron or steel when it comes into contact with water. EG *The car looked free of rust.* N UNCOUNT

2 When a metal object **rusts**, it becomes covered in rust. EG *The fittings had rusted.* ◊ **rusted**. EG *...kicking some rusted tins.* V; ◊ ADJ CLASSIF

rustic /rʌstɪk/. You use **rustic** to describe things that are simple in a way that is typical of places far away from large cities. EG *...rustic comfort and good food... ...rustic benches.* ADJ CLASSIF : ATTRIB Formal

rustle /rʌsə[0]l/, **rustles, rustling, rustled. 1** When something **rustles** or when you **rustle** it, it makes soft sounds as it moves. EG *...mice rustling about... He rustled his papers.* ◊ **rustling, rustlings**. EG *Jim heard some furtive rustlings among the bushes.* V-ERG; ◊ N COUNT OR N UNCOUNT

2 A **rustle** is a soft sound made by something moving gently. EG *She heard a rustle behind her and turned... ...the rustle of chocolate wrappers.* N COUNT OR N UNCOUNT

rustle up. If you **rustle up** a meal, you cook it quickly, using whatever food you have available. EG *I'll rustle something up... We could rustle up an omelette.* PHRASAL VB : V+O+ADV

rusty /rʌsti[1]/, **rustier, rustiest. 1** Something that is **rusty** is affected by rust. EG *...a heap of rusty tins... ...a rusty old truck.* ADJ QUALIT

2 If someone's skill or knowledge is **rusty**, it is not as good as it was before, because they have not used it for a long time. EG *My German's pretty rusty... Dilley looked rusty through lack of bowling.* ADJ QUALIT

rut /rʌt/, **ruts. 1** A **rut** is a deep, narrow mark made in the ground by the wheels of vehicles. EG *We bumped over the ruts.* N COUNT

2 If someone is in a **rut**, they have become fixed in their way of thinking and doing things, and find it difficult to change. EG *He is in a real rut... Some people never get out of their ruts.* N COUNT

ruthless /ruːθlɪ[2]s/. **1** Someone who is **ruthless** is very harsh or cruel, and will do anything that is necessary to achieve what they want. EG *His adver-* ADJ QUALIT

If you get the sack, are you given a large bag?

sary was ruthless... Political power was in the hands of a few ruthless men. ◊ **ruthlessly**. EG *Napoleon acted swiftly and ruthlessly.* ◊ ADV
◊ **ruthlessness**. EG *He often operated with extreme ruthlessness.* ◊ N UNCOUNT
2 A **ruthless** action is done forcefully and thoroughly. EG *...a ruthless investigation... ...the ruthless suppression of the revolt.* ADJ QUALIT

rye /raɪ/ is a type of grass that is grown in cold countries for animals to eat. Bread and whisky are made from rye. EG *...rye bread.* N UNCOUNT

S s

S, s /ɛs/, **S's, s's** /ɛsɪz/. **1 S** is the nineteenth letter of the English alphabet. N COUNT
2 s was a written form of 'shilling' or 'shillings' in Britain before decimal currency was introduced in 1971.
3 S is a written abbreviation for 'south'.

-s; also spelled **-es. 1 -s** and **-es** are added to nouns to form plurals. EG *...dogs, cats, and rabbits... ...ancient palaces... ...profits and losses... ...a sack of potatoes.*
2 -s and **-es** are added to verbs to form the third person singular present tense. EG *The lift stops at the fifth floor... He realizes what he has done... He pushes the button.*

-'s. 1 -'s is added to singular nouns to form possessives. With a plural noun ending in '-s', you form the possessive by adding **-'**. EG *...Ralph's voice... ...the President's conduct... ...friends of the wife's... ...one's self-esteem... ...my colleagues' offices.*
2 -'s is added to plural nouns that do not end in 's' to form possessives. EG *...women's rights... ...children's games.*
3 -'s is the shortened form of 'is' in spoken English. For example, 'he is' can be shortened to 'he's'. EG *He's a novelist... She's charming... It's fantastic... There's no hurry... Mary's going to look after you.*
4 -'s is the shortened form of 'has' in spoken English, especially where 'has' is an auxiliary verb. For example, 'It has gone' can be shortened to 'It's gone'. EG *He's got a problem... She's gone home... It's got to be done... Anne's got a scientific mind.*
5 -'s is added to letters, numbers, abbreviations, and acronyms to form plurals. EG *...a row of q's... ...the 1870's.*

Sabbath /sæbəθ/. The **Sabbath** is the day of the week when members of some religious groups, especially Jews and Christians, do not work. EG *No amount of arguing could make them break the Sabbath.* N PROPER : the+N

sabotage /sæbətɑːʒ/, **sabotages, sabotaging, sabotaged. 1** If a machine, railway line, or bridge **is sabotaged**, it is deliberately damaged or destroyed, for example in a war or as a protest. EG *The power station had been sabotaged by anti-government guerrillas.* ▸ used as a noun. EG *...widespread sabotage and the disruption of rail communications.* V+O : USU PASS ▸ N UNCOUNT
2 If someone **sabotages** a plan or a meeting, they deliberately prevent it from being successful. EG *I don't wish to be accused of sabotaging the President's programme.* V+O

saccharine /sækəraɪn, -riːn/; also spelled **saccharin**. **Saccharine** is a very sweet chemical substance that some people use instead of sugar. N UNCOUNT

sachet /sæʃeɪ/, **sachets.** A **sachet** is a small closed plastic or paper packet, containing a very small quantity of something. N COUNT OR N PART

sack /sæk/, **sacks, sacking, sacked. 1** A **sack** is a large bag made of rough woven material. Sacks are used to carry or store goods. EG *...a large sack containing oranges... ...sacks of flour.* N COUNT OR N PART
2 If your employers **sack** you, they say that you can no longer work for them, often because your work is not good enough. EG *Three railwaymen were sacked because they would not join a union.* V+O
● If you **get the sack** or **are given the sack**, your employer sacks you. EG *Years ago he would have got the sack for something like that.* ● PHRASE

sacking /sækɪŋ/ is rough woven material that is used to make sacks. EG *...a piece of old sacking.* N UNCOUNT

sacrament /sækrəmə²nt/, **sacraments.** A **sacrament** is an important Christian religious ceremony such as communion, baptism, or marriage. N COUNT

sacred /seɪkrɪ²d/. **1** Something that is **sacred** is **1.1** believed to be holy and to have a special connection with God. EG *They entered the sacred mosque.... ...a group of sacred elephants.* ADJ QUALIT
◊ **sacredness**. EG *...the sacredness of the shrine had been violated.* ◊ N UNCOUNT **1.2** connected with religion or used in religious ceremonies. EG *...sacred music.* ADJ CLASSIF
2 You can describe something as **sacred** when it is regarded as too important to be changed or interfered with. EG *She saw motherhood as woman's sacred calling... In their search for a good news story, nothing was sacred.* ◊ **sacredness**. EG *...the sacredness of private property.* ADJ QUALIT ◊ N UNCOUNT

sacrifice /sækrɪfaɪs/, **sacrifices, sacrificing, sacrificed. 1** To **sacrifice** an animal means to kill it in a special religious ceremony as an offering to God. EG *White animals were sacrificed by white-robed priests.* ▸ used as a noun. EG *...a ritual sacrifice.* V+O ▸ N UNCOUNT OR N COUNT
2 If you **sacrifice** something that is valuable or important, you give it up, often in order to be able to do something else. EG *...women who have sacrificed career and marriage to care for elderly relatives.* ▸ used as a noun. EG *...a mother's sacrifices for her children.* V+O ▸ N COUNT OR N UNCOUNT

sacrificial /sækrɪfɪʃə⁰l/ means connected with or used in a religious sacrifice. EG *...sacrificial victims.* ADJ CLASSIF : ATTRIB

sacrilege /sækrɪlɪdʒ/. **1 Sacrilege** is behaviour that shows great disrespect for a holy place or object. EG *He might have to be punished for his sacrilege.* N UNCOUNT
2 You can use **sacrilege** to refer to disrespect that is shown for someone who is widely admired or for a belief that is widely accepted. EG *Criticism of Woolley is sacrilege.* N UNCOUNT

sacrilegious /sækrɪlɪdʒəs/. If your behaviour is **sacrilegious**, you show great disrespect towards something holy or towards something that people think should be respected. EG *It would have been sacrilegious to speak.* ADJ QUALIT

sacrosanct /sækrə⁶sæŋkt/. If you describe something as **sacrosanct**, you mean that people consider it to be special and are unwilling to criticize or change it. EG *...the ruthlessness of leaders when their power was sacrosanct... He seems to think there's something sacrosanct about his annual fishing trip.* ADJ CLASSIF : USU PRED

sad /sæd/, **sadder, saddest. 1** If you are **sad**, you are not happy, usually because something has happened that you do not like. EG *She looked sad... He was sad to see her go... The more he thought about it, the sadder he became... ...a sad face.* ADJ QUALIT
◊ **sadly**. EG *He shook his head sadly... 'Not a cent,'* ◊ ADV

she said sadly. ◇ **sadness.** EG *The news filled him with sadness.* ◇ N UNCOUNT

2 Sad stories and **sad** news make you feel sad. EG *She told Susan there was some sad news for her... It seems rather sad that this should happen to you.* ADJ QUALIT
◇ **sadness.** EG *...the indescribable sadness of those final pages.* ◇ N UNCOUNT

3 You use **sad** to describe an unfortunate situation. EG *The sad fact is that full employment may never be regained... This is a very sad comment on what is happening to our cities.* ADJ QUALIT : ATTRIB ◇ **sadly.** EG *One aspect of education today has been sadly neglected... Sadly, we don't appear to have much chance of getting the contract.* ◇ ADV OR ADV SEN

sadden /sædə^{0}n/, **saddens, saddening, saddened.** If something **saddens** you, it makes you feel sad. EG *I'm saddened by the fact that so many people died for nothing... This is one of the things that saddens me most.* V+O

saddle /sædə^{0}l/, **saddles, saddling, saddled. 1** A **saddle** is **1.1** a leather seat that you put on the back of an animal so that you can ride the animal. EG *Jennifer swung herself into the saddle.* ● See also **side-saddle. 1.2** a seat on a bicycle or motorcycle. See picture at BICYCLE. N COUNT

2 If you **saddle** a horse or pony, you put a saddle on it. EG *He saddled his horse and rode off.* V+O

3 If you **saddle** someone with a problem or with responsibility, you put them in the position where they have to deal with it. EG *The last thing I want is to saddle myself with a second mortgage.* V+O+*with* OR V-REFL+*with*

saddle up. If you **saddle up**, you put a saddle on a horse or pony. EG *I saddled up and rode off... He went out to saddle up his horse.* PHRASAL VB : V+ADV OR V+O+ADV

saddlebag /sædə^{0}lbæg/, **saddlebags.** A **saddlebag** is a bag fastened to the saddle of a horse, bicycle, or motorcycle. N COUNT

sadism /seɪdɪzə^{0}m, sæ-/ is a type of behaviour in which a person obtains pleasure from hurting other people and making them suffer. EG *He teased her with malicious sadism.* ◇ **sadist, sadists.** EG *...sadists and bullies.* N UNCOUNT ◇ N COUNT

sadistic /sədɪstɪk/. Someone who is **sadistic** obtains pleasure from hurting other people and making them suffer. EG *He was nothing but a sadistic drunkard... ...scenes of sadistic cruelty.* ADJ QUALIT
◇ **sadistically.** EG *He was sadistically cruel in his interrogations.* ◇ ADV

s.a.e. /ɛs eɪ iː/, **s.a.e.s.** An **s.a.e.** is an envelope on which you have stuck a stamp and written your own name and address. You send it to someone so that they can send you something such as information in it. **s.a.e.** is an abbreviation for 'stamped addressed envelope'. EG *Please include s.a.e. for return of material.* N COUNT

safari /səfɑːri^{1}/, **safaris.** A **safari** is an expedition for hunting or observing wild animals, especially in East Africa. EG *...a safari arranged by a travel agency... We're going on safari.* N COUNT, OR *on*+N

safe /seɪf/, **safer, safest; safes. 1** Something that is **safe** does not cause physical harm or danger. EG *This powder is not safe for babies... He asked me if it was safe to let my friend go out alone... Keep your passport in a safe place.* ◇ **safely.** EG *Most food can safely be frozen for months.* ADJ QUALIT ◇ ADV

2 You are **safe** from something when you cannot be harmed by it. EG *We're safe now. They've gone... They were safe from attack.* ● You say that someone is **safe and sound** when they are still alive or unharmed after being in danger. EG *I'm glad to see you home safe and sound.* ADJ PRED : OFT+*from* ● PHRASE

3 A **safe** journey or arrival is one in which people or things reach their destination without being harmed. EG *We are relying on the safe delivery of essential equipment.* ◇ **safely.** EG *I sent a telegram to my mother saying I had arrived safely.* ADJ CLASSIF : ATTRIB ◇ ADV

4 If it is **safe** to say something, you can say it with very little risk of being wrong. EG *These practices, it is safe to say, are no longer common.* ◇ **safely.** EG *These creatures, we can safely say, have been dead a long time.* ADJ QUALIT ◇ ADV

5 If a secret is **safe** with you, you will not tell it to anyone. EG *They knew their secrets would be safe with him.* ADJ PRED : OFT+*with*

6 Safe is also used in these phrases. **6.1** If you **play safe**, you do not take unnecessary risks. EG *Play safe and always wear goggles.* **6.2** If you are doing something **to be on the safe side**, you are doing it as a precaution, in case something unexpected happens. EG *I'll take a few extra groceries, just to be on the safe side.* **6.3** If someone or something is **in safe hands**, they are being looked after by a reliable person and will not be harmed. EG *Don't worry, she's in safe hands at the hospital.* PHRASES Informal

7 A **safe** is a strong metal cupboard with special locks, in which you keep money, jewellery, and other valuable things. N COUNT

safeguard /seɪfgɑːd/, **safeguards, safeguarding, safeguarded. 1** To **safeguard** something means to prevent it from being harmed or destroyed. EG *The Bureau's purpose was to safeguard human life... They have to fight to safeguard their future.* V+O Formal

2 A **safeguard** is a law or rule intended to prevent someone or something from being harmed. EG *This clause was inserted as a safeguard against possible exploitation.* N COUNT : OFT+*against* Formal

safekeeping /seɪfkiːpɪŋ/. If something is given to you for **safekeeping**, it is given to you so that you will make sure that it is not harmed or stolen. EG *It had been placed in a Paris museum for safekeeping.* N UNCOUNT Formal

safety /seɪfti^{1}/. **1 Safety** is **1.1** the state of being safe from harm or danger. EG *He was assured of his daughter's safety.* **1.2** a place where you are safe from danger. EG *They swam to the safety of a small, rocky island.* N UNCOUNT

2 If you are concerned about the **safety** of something, you are concerned that it might be harmful or dangerous. EG *People worry about the safety of nuclear energy.* N UNCOUNT

3 Safety features or measures are intended to make something less dangerous. EG *Every car will come with built-in safety features.* N MOD

safety belt, safety belts. A **safety belt** is a strap attached to a seat in a car or aeroplane. You fasten it round your body when you are travelling in the car or aeroplane. N COUNT

safety catch, safety catches. The **safety catch** on a gun is a catch that stops you firing the gun accidentally. N COUNT

safety net, safety nets. 1 In a circus, a **safety net** is a large net that is placed below performers on a high wire or trapeze in order to catch them and prevent them being injured if they fall off. N COUNT

2 A **safety net** is also something that you can rely on to help you if you get into a difficult situation. EG *The Fund is our safety net if anything should go wrong.* N COUNT

safety pin, safety pins. A **safety pin** is a bent metal pin used for fastening things together. The point of the pin has a cover so that it cannot hurt anyone. See picture at PINS. N COUNT

safety-valve, safety-valves. 1 A **safety-valve** is a piece of equipment in a machine that allows liquids or gases to escape when the pressure inside the machine becomes too great. N COUNT

2 You can use **safety-valve** to refer to anything that allows you to express strong feelings without harming other people. EG *...a safety-valve for the harmless release of rebellious feelings.* N COUNT

sag /sæg/, **sags, sagging, sagged.** When something **sags**, it hangs down loosely or sinks downwards in the middle. EG *The bed sagged in the* V

Find two words on these pages with the same pronunciation.

middle... His pocket sagged with the weight of the coins.

saga /sɑːgə/, **sagas.** A **saga** is a long story, account, or sequence of events. EG *I related some of the episodes of my domestic saga... ...a saga of financial mismanagement.* N COUNT: USU+SUPP

sage /seɪdʒ/, **sages. 1** A **sage** is a person who is regarded as being very wise. EG *...the great sages buried in the city.* N COUNT Literary

2 A **sage** person is wise and knowledgeable, usually because they are old and have had a lot of experience. EG *...sage parents anxious to dispense their wisdom.* ◇ **sagely.** EG *He nodded his head sagely.* ADJ QUALIT Literary ◇ ADV

3 Sage is a herb used in cooking. N UNCOUNT

said /sed/ is the past tense and past participle of **say.**

sail /seɪl/, **sails, sailing, sailed. 1** A **sail** is a large piece of material attached to the mast of a ship. The wind blows against the sail and pushes the ship along. See picture at YACHT. EG *...the white sails of the yacht.* N COUNT

2 When a ship moves over the sea, it **sails.** EG *The ship sailed down the east coast of South America... We were shortly to sail for New York.* V+A

3 To **sail** a boat means to make it move across water using its sails. EG *I spent two weeks swimming and sailing in New Hampshire.* V+O OR V

4 When a ship **sets sail,** it leaves a port. EG *The Beagle set sail on 27 December 1831.* PHRASE

5 If someone or something **sails** somewhere, they move there steadily and fairly quickly. EG *I watched the ball as it went sailing over the bushes.* V+A

sail through. If you **sail through** a difficult situation or experience, you deal with it very easily and successfully. EG *She was expecting to sail through her exams.* PHRASAL VB: V+ADV/PREP

sailing /seɪlɪŋ/, **sailings. 1** A **sailing** is a voyage made by a ship carrying passengers. EG *...regular sailings from Portsmouth.* N COUNT

2 Sailing is the activity or sport of sailing boats. EG *...the traditional Royal sailing week in August.* N UNCOUNT

3 If you describe a task as **plain sailing,** you mean that it is very easy. EG *Once we've fixed the computer, it will be plain sailing.* PHRASE

sailor /seɪlə/, **sailors.** A **sailor** is a man who works on a ship as a member of its crew. EG *He had been a sailor in the Italian navy.* ● If you are **a good sailor,** you are able to travel on a boat in rough weather without being seasick. N COUNT ● PHRASE

saint /seɪnt/, **saints.** A **saint** is a dead person who is officially recognized and honoured by the Christian church because his or her life was a perfect example of the way Christians should live. EG *...the church of Saint Francis.* N COUNT

saintly /seɪntli¹/. A **saintly** person behaves in a very good or very holy way. EG *He was not at all a religious or saintly man... ...saintly virtues.* ADJ QUALIT

sake /seɪk/, **sakes. 1** If you do something **for the sake of** something, you do it for a particular purpose or in order to achieve a particular result. EG *I usually check from time to time, just for safety's sake... Let us assume, for the sake of argument, that the level of unemployment does not fall.* PHRASE

2 If you do something **for** its **own sake,** you do it because you enjoy it, and not for any other reason. EG *I'm studying the subject for its own sake.* PHRASE

3 When you do something **for** someone's **sake,** you do it in order to help them. EG *We moved out to the country for the children's sake... I must break the bonds for both our sakes... It is better for all our sakes that the trail should be lost.* PHRASE

4 Some people say **for God's sake** or **for heaven's sake** in order to express annoyance or impatience, or to add force to a question or request. EG *What are you staring at for heaven's sake?... For God's sake don't tell anyone.* CONVENTION

salad /sæləd/, **salads.** A **salad** is a mixture of uncooked vegetables. It is usually eaten with other foods as part of a meal. EG *I am not fond of salad... ...chicken salad.* ● See also **fruit salad.** N MASS

salami /səlɑːmi¹/, **salamis. Salami** is a type of sausage made from chopped meat and spices. N MASS

salaried /sælərɪd/. **Salaried** people receive a salary from their job. EG *The report listed the names of all salaried employees.* ADJ CLASSIF: USU ATTRIB

salary /sæləri¹/, **salaries.** A **salary** is the money that someone is paid for their job each month, especially when they have a professional job. EG *She earns a high salary as an accountant... ...the difference in salary between an instructor and a lecturer.* N COUNT OR N UNCOUNT

sale /seɪl/, **sales. 1** The **sale** of goods is the selling of them for money. EG *...new laws to control the sale of guns... We've just made our first sale.* N COUNT: USU+SUPP

2 If something such as a house or a car is **for sale** or **up for sale,** its owner is trying to sell it. EG *Their house is up for sale.* PHRASE

3 Products that are **on sale** can be bought in shops. EG *The only English newspaper on sale was the Morning Star.* PHRASE

4 The **sales** of a product are the quantity that is sold. EG *Data General's sales grew by 140% a year... Car sales are 5 per cent down... Sales of the magazine are declining.* N PLURAL

5 The part of a company that deals with **sales** deals with selling the company's products. EG *...a sales executive.* N PLURAL

6 A **sale** is **6.1** an occasion when a shop sells things at less than their normal price. EG *They're having a clearance sale.* **6.2** an event when goods are sold to the person who offers the highest price. EG *...the quarterly cattle sale.* ● See also **jumble sale.** N COUNT

salesman /seɪlzmə³n/, **salesmen.** A **salesman** is a man whose job is selling things, especially directly to shops or other businesses. EG *...a shoe salesman... ...chief salesman of Vickers... ...a travelling salesman.* N COUNT

salient /seɪlɪənt/. The **salient** points or facts of a situation are the most important ones. EG *...the salient points of the prime minister's speech.* ADJ QUALIT: USU ATTRIB Formal

saline /seɪlaɪn/. A **saline** substance or liquid contains salt. EG *She broke the crystals off into this water and made a saline solution.* ADJ CLASSIF: ATTRIB Formal

saliva /səlaɪvə/ is the watery liquid that forms in your mouth and helps you to chew and digest food. N UNCOUNT

sallow /sæləʊ/. If a person's skin is **sallow,** it has a pale yellowish colour and looks unhealthy. EG *...her sallow face.* ADJ QUALIT

sally /sæli¹/, **sallies, sallying, sallied. Sallies** are clever and amusing remarks. EG *The laughter with which his sallies were greeted excited him.* N COUNT: USU PLURAL Literary

sally forth or **sally out.** If someone **sallies forth** or **sallies out** somewhere, they go there quickly or energetically. EG *He sallied out into the raw London night... The animals sallied forth to meet them.* PHRASAL VB: V+ADV Literary

salmon /sæmən/. **Salmon** is both the singular and the plural form. A **salmon** is a large silver-coloured fish. EG *...smoked salmon.* N COUNT OR N UNCOUNT

salmonella /sælmənelə/ is a kind of bacteria which can cause severe food poisoning. N UNCOUNT

salon /sælɒn/, **salons.** A **salon** is **1** a place where hairdressers or beauticians work. EG *...a hairdressing salon.* **2** a shop where smart, expensive clothes are sold. EG *She is dressed by Dior, whose salon is located across the street.* N COUNT

saloon /səluːn/, **saloons. 1** A **saloon** is a car with seats for four or more people, a fixed roof, and a boot that is separated from the rear seats. EG *...Ford Cortina saloons.* N COUNT

2 In the United States, a **saloon** is a place where alcoholic drinks are sold and drunk. EG *There were nine saloons in those days, and they stayed open all the time.* N COUNT

3 In Britain, the **saloon** or **saloon bar** in a pub or N COUNT hotel is a comfortable bar where the drinks are more expensive than in the other bars.

salt /sɒlt/, **salts, salting, salted. 1 Salt** is a strong-tasting substance, in the form of white powder or crystals, which is used to improve the flavour of food or to preserve it. Salt occurs naturally in sea water. N UNCOUNT

2 When you **salt** food, you add salt to it. EG *The potatoes should be lightly salted.* ◊ **salted.** EG *...salted peanuts.* V+O ◊ ADJ CLASSIF

3 Salt is used in these phrases. **3.1** If you describe someone as **the salt of the earth**, you mean that you like and respect them very much because they always do what is required, deal with any problems, and never make a fuss. EG *Rodin worshipped soldiers as the true salt of the earth.* **3.2** If something **rubs salt into** your **wounds,** it makes the unpleasant situation that you are in even worse, often by reminding you of your failures or faults. EG *The proposed ten per cent cut in wages is really rubbing salt into the wound.* **3.3** If you **take** something **with a pinch of salt**, you do not believe that it is completely accurate or true. EG *This calculation has to be taken with a pinch of salt.* PHRASES Informal

salt cellar, salt cellars. A **salt cellar** is a small container for salt which is used at mealtimes. N COUNT

salty /sɒlti¹/, **saltier, saltiest.** Something that is **salty** contains salt or tastes of salt. EG *We washed them in salty water.* ADJ QUALIT

salubrious /səlu:brɪəs/. A place that is **salubrious** is pleasant and healthy. EG *...one of the less salubrious suburbs of London.* ADJ QUALIT Formal

salutary /sæljəⁱtəⁱri¹/. A **salutary** experience is good for you, even though it may seem difficult or unpleasant. EG *It is salutary to consider that in future we will not have such easy access to coal... The defeat was a deserved punishment, but also a salutary shock.* ADJ QUALIT Formal

salute /səlu:t/, **salutes, saluting, saluted. 1** If you **salute** someone, you greet them or show your respect with a formal sign. Soldiers salute officers by raising their right hand so that their fingers touch their forehead. EG *He stood as if he were saluting the flag.* ▸ used as a noun. EG *He greeted King Edward VIII with the customary salute.* V+O OR V ▸ N COUNT

2 To **salute** a person or an achievement means to publicly show or state your admiration for them. EG *...festivals in Spain that salute the independence of the Spanish character.* ▸ used as a noun. EG *...a salute to America.* V+O ▸ N COUNT

salvage /sælvɪdʒ/, **salvages, salvaging, salvaged. 1** When you **salvage** things, you manage to save them, for example from a ship that has sunk, or from a building that has been destroyed. EG *...a finely decorated window salvaged from an old chemist's shop.* V+O : OFT+*from*

2 The **salvage** from wrecked ships or destroyed buildings consists of the things that are saved from them. EG *The insurers are entitled to take the wreck as salvage... ...a salvage operation.* N UNCOUNT

3 If you **salvage** something from a difficult situation, you manage to get something useful from it so that it is not a complete failure. EG *They were salvaging what they could from the present unhappy state of affairs.* V+O : OFT+*from*

salvation /sælveɪʃəⁿn/. **1** In Christianity, the **salvation** of a person is the fact that Christ has saved them from evil. N UNCOUNT

2 The **salvation** of someone or something is the act of saving them from harm. EG *The country's salvation was of immense importance to the British.* N UNCOUNT

3 If someone or something is your **salvation**, they are responsible for saving you from harm or from an unpleasant situation. EG *Small industries will be the salvation of many areas now in decline... Their children were their only salvation.* N SING+POSS

salve /sælv/, **salves, salving, salved.** If you **salve** your **conscience** by doing something, it makes you feel less guilty or worried. EG *We give money to charities, and thus salve our consciences.* PHRASE

same /seɪm/. **1** If two things are the **same** or if one thing is the **same** as another, the two are exactly like each other in some way. EG *They both wore the same overcoats... Look! They're exactly the same... He did exactly the same as John did.* ADJ CLASSIF : ATTRIB, OR PRON : *the* +ADJ/PRON

2 If two things have the **same** quality or if one thing has the **same** quality as another, they both have that quality. EG *He and Tom were exactly the same age... It was the same colour as the wall.* ADJ CLASSIF : ATTRIB, *the*+ADJ

3 You use **same 3.1** to indicate that you are referring to only one thing, and not to different ones. EG *We come from the same place... It was possible to work while watching TV at the same time.* **3.2** to refer to something that has already been mentioned. EG *For the same reason, the United States lodged a formal protest... The same is true of the arts... It's the same with teenage fashions.* ADJ CLASSIF : ATTRIB, *the*+ADJ · ADJ CLASSIF : ATTRIB, OR PRON : *the* +ADJ/PRON

4 Something that is still the **same** has not changed in any way. EG *The village stayed the same... He will never be the same again.* ADJ CLASSIF : ATTRIB, OR PRON : *the*+ ADJ/PRON

5 Same is also used in these phrases. **5.1** You say **all the same** or **just the same** to indicate that a situation or your opinion has not changed, in spite of something that has happened or been said. EG *She knew he wasn't listening, but she went on all the same... All the same, the courses are very popular.* **5.2** If you say **'It's all the same to me'**, you mean that you do not care which of several things happens or is chosen. **5.3** You say **'Thanks all the same'** when you are thanking someone for an offer that you are refusing. EG *'Do you want a lift?' – 'No, but thanks all the same.'* **5.4** If something **is not the same**, it is not as pleasant or as good as something that you would prefer. EG *We started out again by car. But it wasn't the same.* ADV SEN · CONVENTION · CONVENTION · PHRASE

sameness /seɪmnɪ²s/. The **sameness** of something is its lack of variety. EG *I was struck by the sameness of clothing among the villagers.* N UNCOUNT : USU+SUPP

sample /sɑ:mpəⁿl/, **samples, sampling, sampled. 1** A **sample** of a substance or product is **1.1** a small quantity of it that shows you what it is like. EG *...free samples of shampoo.* **1.2** a small amount of it that is examined and analysed scientifically. EG *I'll take water samples here and in East Hampton... She took a sample of her urine to a clinic.* N COUNT

2 A **sample** of people or things is a number of them chosen out of a larger group and then used in tests or used to provide information about the whole group. EG *...a random sample of 10,000 adult civilians... ...a representative sample of viewers.* N COUNT

3 If you **sample** food or drink, you taste a small amount of it in order to find out if you like it. EG *Next he sampled the roast beef.* V+O

4 If you **sample** a place or situation, you experience it for a short time in order to find out about it. EG *They can learn the language and sample the British way of life.* V+O

sanatorium /sænətɔ:rɪəm/, **sanatoriums** or **sanatoria** /sænətɔ:rɪə/; spelled **sanitarium** /sænɪtɛərɪəm/ in American English. A **sanatorium** is an institution that provides medical treatment and rest for people who have been ill for a long time. EG *A dreadful breakdown sent me to a sanatorium for more than a year.* N COUNT

sanctify /sæŋktɪfaɪ/, **sanctifies, sanctifying, sanctified. 1** If the Church or a holy person **sanctifies** something, they officially bless it or approve it and declare that it should be treated or considered as holy. EG *St Francis wanted to sanctify poverty, not to abolish it... ...the silver of the sanctified coffin.* V+O

2 If something **is sanctified** by someone or some- V+O : USU PASS

Is a sandwich course part of a meal?

thing, they approve of it, support it, and want it to remain exactly as it is. EG *...the assumption, sanctified by the famous words of the Constitution... Teachers helped to protect and sanctify the power that was so ruthlessly being used.*

sanctimonious /sæŋktɪməʊnɪəs/. Someone who is **sanctimonious** tries to appear deeply religious and virtuous; used showing disapproval. EG *...a sanctimonious hypocrite.* ADJ QUALIT

sanction /sæŋk⁰ʃə⁰n/, **sanctions, sanctioning, sanctioned. 1** If someone in authority **sanctions** an action or practice, they officially approve of it and allow it to be done. EG *...the law of 1856 which sanctioned the remarriage of widows.* ▸ used as a noun. EG *Some months later our proposal was given official sanction.* V+O ▸ N UNCOUNT +SUPP

2 A **sanction** is a severe course of action which is intended to make people obey the law. EG *The ultimate sanction of the government is the withdrawal of funds.* N COUNT

3 Sanctions are measures taken by countries to restrict trade and official contact with a country that has broken international law. EG *The UN would impose economic sanctions against the offending nation.* N PLURAL : OFT +*against*

sanctity /sæŋk⁰tɪ¹ti¹/. If you talk about the **sanctity** of something, you mean that it is very important and should always be respected. EG *...the sanctity of marriage... ...the sanctity of human life.* N UNCOUNT : USU+*of*

sanctuary /sæŋk⁰tj⁰ʊəri¹/, **sanctuaries.** A **sanctuary** is **1** a place of safety for someone. EG *It was Clement's island and his sanctuary... I was glad to climb into the sanctuary of my bed.* **2** a place where birds or animals are protected and allowed to live freely. EG *She wants to turn her orchard into a bird sanctuary.* N COUNT OR N UNCOUNT; N COUNT : USU+SUPP

sand /sænd/, **sands, sanding, sanded. 1 Sand** is a powdery substance that consists of extremely small pieces of stone. Most deserts and beaches are made of sand. EG *The children played in the sand at the water's edge... ...grains of sand.* N UNCOUNT

2 Sands are a large area of sand, for example a beach or a desert. EG *...miles of empty sands.* N PLURAL

3 If you **sand** something, you rub sandpaper over it in order to make it smooth or clean. EG *A scratched item of furniture can be professionally sanded.* V+O

sandal /sændəl/, **sandals. Sandals** are light shoes that you wear in warm weather, which have straps instead of a solid part over the top of your foot. See picture at SHOES. N COUNT

sand castle, sand castles. A **sand castle** is a heap of sand which children make when they are playing on the beach. N COUNT

sandpaper /sændpeɪpə/ is strong paper that has a coating of sand on it. It is used for rubbing wooden or metal surfaces to make them smoother. N UNCOUNT

sandstone /sændstəʊn/ is a type of rock. EG *...a long sandstone cliff.* N UNCOUNT

sandstorm /sændstɔːm/, **sandstorms.** A **sandstorm** is a strong wind in a desert area, which creates large moving clouds of sand. N COUNT

sandwich /sænwɪdʒ, -wɪtʃ/, **sandwiches, sandwiched. 1** A **sandwich** consists of two slices of bread with a layer of food such as cheese or meat between them. EG *...eating sandwiches in the office for lunch... ...a bacon, lettuce, and tomato sandwich.* N COUNT

2 When one thing **is sandwiched** between two other things, it is in a very narrow space between them. EG *Wooden shacks are sandwiched between modern blocks of flats.* V-PASS+A

sandwich course, sandwich courses. A **sandwich course** is an educational course in which you have periods of study in between periods of work in industry or business. EG *...a sandwich course in civil engineering.* N COUNT British

sandy /sændi¹/. **1** A **sandy** area is covered with sand. EG *...the long sandy beach.* ADJ QUALIT

2 Sandy hair is light orange-brown in colour. ADJ COLOUR

sane /seɪn/, **saner, sanest. 1** Someone who is **sane** is able to think and behave normally and reasonably, and is not mentally ill. EG *She appeared to be completely sane.* ADJ QUALIT

2 If you refer to a **sane** action or system, you mean one that you think is reasonable and sensible. EG *It is the only sane thing to do... ...a sane educational system.* ADJ QUALIT

sang /sæŋ/ is the past tense of **sing.**

sanguine /sæŋgwɪn/. If you are **sanguine** about something, you are cheerful and confident that things will happen as you want them to. EG *He was not sanguine about Bill's probable reactions.* ADJ QUALIT

sanitarium /sænɪtɛəriəm/. See **sanatorium.**

sanitary /sænɪtə⁰ri¹/. **1** If you say that a place is not **sanitary**, you mean that it is not very clean. EG *I sat in a small and not very sanitary café in Soho.* ADJ QUALIT

2 Sanitary also means concerned with keeping things clean and hygienic. EG *Sanitary conditions in the hospitals had deteriorated rapidly... ...a sanitary inspector.* ADJ CLASSIF : ATTRIB

sanitary napkin, sanitary napkins. A **sanitary napkin** is the same as a sanitary towel. N COUNT American

sanitary towel, sanitary towels. A **sanitary towel** is a pad of thick soft material which women wear during their periods. N COUNT

sanitation /sænɪteɪʃə⁰n/ is the process of keeping places clean and hygienic, especially by providing a sewage system and a clean water supply. EG *They live in conditions of appalling sanitation... ...the lack of sanitation and adequate health care.* N UNCOUNT

sanity /sænɪ¹ti¹/. **1** A person's **sanity** is their ability to think and behave normally and reasonably. EG *...the doubts he had about Wilt's sanity... On this occasion they lost their sanity.* N UNCOUNT

2 Sanity is also the quality of having a purpose and a regular pattern, rather than being confusing and worrying. EG *They give some point and sanity to daily life.* N UNCOUNT

sank /sæŋk/ is the past tense of **sink.**

Santa Claus /sæntə klɔːz/ is another name for Father Christmas. N PROPER

sap /sæp/, **saps, sapping, sapped. 1** If something **saps** your strength or confidence, it gradually weakens or destroys it over a period of time. EG *The constant tension at work was sapping my energy.* V+O

2 Sap is the watery liquid in plants and trees. EG *The sap was rising in the maples.* N UNCOUNT

sapling /sæplɪŋ/, **saplings.** A **sapling** is a young tree. EG *...a row of saplings.* N COUNT

sapphire /sæfaɪə/, **sapphires.** A **sapphire** is a precious stone which is blue in colour. EG *...a sapphire and diamond ring.* N COUNT

sarcasm /sɑːkæzə⁰m/ is speech or writing which actually means the opposite of what it seems to say. Sarcasm is usually intended to mock or insult someone. EG *'Oh yeah,' said Jenny with broad sarcasm, 'I notice how you hate getting paid.'* N UNCOUNT

sarcastic /sɑːkæstɪk/. Someone who is **sarcastic** says or does the opposite of what they really mean in order to mock or insult someone. EG *She seemed her usual sarcastic self at dinner... He turned to me with a sarcastic smile.* ◊ **sarcastically.** EG *'Do you mind if I take notes?' said Stuart sarcastically.* ADJ QUALIT; ◊ ADV

sardine /sɑːdiːn/, **sardines.** A **sardine** is a kind of small sea fish. EG *...tins of sardines.* N COUNT

sardonic /sɑːdɒnɪk/. Someone who is **sardonic** is mocking or scornful in their behaviour. EG *...a sardonic young man who never joined in the fun... ...a sardonic chuckle.* ◊ **sardonically.** EG *She smiled sardonically.* ADJ QUALIT; ◊ ADV

sari /sɑːri¹/, **saris.** A **sari** is a piece of clothing worn especially by Indian women. It consists of a long piece of thin material that is wrapped around the body. N COUNT

sartorial /sɑːtɔːrɪəl/ means relating to clothes and to the way they are made or worn. EG *People's sartorial habits have changed.* ADJ CLASSIF : ATTRIB Formal

sash /sæʃ/, **sashes.** A **sash** is a long piece of cloth which people wear round their waist or over one shoulder, especially with formal or official clothes.
N COUNT

sash window, sash windows. A **sash window** is a window which consists of two frames placed one above the other. The window can be opened by sliding one frame over the other.
N COUNT

sat /sæt/ is the past tense and past participle of **sit.**

Satan /seɪtə^{0}n/. **Satan** is the Devil, considered to be the chief opponent of God.
N PROPER

satanic /sətænɪk/. Something that is **satanic** is considered to be caused by or influenced by Satan. EG *...a satanic cult.*
ADJ QUALIT

satchel /sætʃə^{0}l/, **satchels.** A **satchel** is a bag with a long strap that schoolchildren use for carrying books.
N COUNT

sated /seɪtɪ^{2}d/. If you are **sated** with something, you have had more of it than you can enjoy at one time. EG *They were sated with fresh air and hard exercise.*
ADJ CLASSIF : USU PRED Formal

satellite /sætəlaɪt/, **satellites. 1** A **satellite** is **1.1** an object which has been sent into space in order to collect information or to be part of a communications system. Satellites move continually round the earth or around another planet. EG *...communications satellites... The pictures were transmitted by satellite.*
N COUNT OR *by*+N

1.2 a natural object in space that moves round a planet or star. EG *Astronomers were excited to discover a small, oddly shaped satellite, Jupiter's 14th moon.*
N COUNT

2 You can also use **satellite** to refer to a country or organization which has no real power of its own, but which is dependent on a larger and more powerful country or organization. EG *The party consolidates its power by building up satellite organizations.*
N COUNT

satin /sætɪn/ is a smooth and shiny kind of cloth, usually made from silk. EG *The bride was dressed in white satin.*
N UNCOUNT

satire /sætaɪə/, **satires. 1 Satire** is humour and exaggeration that is used to show how foolish or wicked some people's behaviour or ideas are. EG *...exquisite touches of irony and satire.*
N UNCOUNT

2 A **satire** is a play or novel that uses satire to criticize something. EG *...a brilliant political satire... ...a satire on existing society.*
N COUNT

satirical /sətɪrɪkə^{0}l/. A drawing or piece of writing that is **satirical** uses satire to criticize something. EG *...a satirical fortnightly magazine... He attacked the stupidity of women's trailing skirts in satirical cartoons.*
ADJ QUALIT

satisfaction /sætɪsfækʃə^{0}n/. **1 Satisfaction** is the pleasure that you feel when you do something that you wanted or needed to do. EG *She read what she had written with satisfaction... ...a sigh which expressed her satisfaction at being there... ...a sense of satisfaction.*
N UNCOUNT

2 If you get **satisfaction** from someone, you get money or an apology from them because of some harm or injustice which has been done to you. EG *Consumers who have been unable to get satisfaction from their local branch should write direct to the Chairman.*
N UNCOUNT

3 If you do something **to** someone's **satisfaction**, they are happy with the way you have done it. EG *Every detail was worked out to everyone's satisfaction.*
PHRASE

satisfactory /sætɪsfæktə^{0}ri^{1}/. Something that is **satisfactory** is acceptable to you or fulfils a particular need or purpose. EG *His doctor described his general state of health as fairly satisfactory... It will be much more satisfactory if you are given more responsibility.* ◇ **satisfactorily.** EG *She was not recovering satisfactorily from the accident.*
ADJ QUALIT
◇ ADV

satisfied /sætɪsfaɪd/. **1** If you are **satisfied** with something, you are happy because you have got what you wanted. EG *He was well satisfied with the success of the aircraft... ...satisfied customers who had bought the car.*
ADJ QUALIT

2 If you are **satisfied** that something is true or has been done properly, you are convinced about this after checking it. EG *He turned to me and nodded, satisfied... We can be satisfied that we've missed nothing important.*
ADJ PRED

satisfy /sætɪsfaɪ/, **satisfies, satisfying, satisfied. 1** If someone or something **satisfies** you, they give you enough of what you want to make you pleased or contented. EG *More frequent feeding will usually help to satisfy a baby... He had not even been able to satisfy her simple needs... The firm has been unable to satisfy demand for its new small car.*
V+O

2 If someone or something **satisfies** you that something is true or has been done properly, they convince you by giving you more information or by showing you what has been done. EG *He would need to satisfy the authorities that he had paid tax for the previous three years... I glanced around, satisfied myself that the last diner had left, and turned off the lights.*
V+O OR V-REFL : OFT+REPORT, ONLY *that*

3 If you **satisfy** the requirements for something, you are good enough or suitable to fulfil these requirements. EG *There is some doubt whether they can satisfy our entrance requirements.*
V+O

satisfying /sætɪsfaɪɪŋ/. Something that is **satisfying** gives you a feeling of pleasure and fulfilment. EG *There's nothing more satisfying than doing the work you love.*
ADJ QUAL

satsuma /sætsuːmə/, **satsumas.** A **satsuma** is a fruit that looks like a small orange.
N COUNT

saturate /sætʃəreɪt/, **saturates, saturating, saturated. 1** If a place **is saturated** with things, it is so full of those things that no more can be added. EG *The next morning, teams saturated the community with literature about the attack... The area where his brother was killed was saturated with photographs of the wanted man.* ◇ **saturation** /sætʃəreɪʃə^{0}n/. EG *Even when the market reaches saturation, the process doesn't stop.*
V+O : USU PASS +*with/in*
◇ N UNCOUNT

2 If someone or something **is saturated**, they become extremely wet. EG *Philip was totally saturated.*
V+O : USU PASS

Saturday /sætədi^{1}/, **Saturdays. Saturday** is one of the seven days of the week. It is the day after Friday and before Sunday. EG *What did you do on Saturday?... I spent a Saturday being trained... Fridays and Saturdays are more lively.*
N UNCOUNT OR N COUNT

saturnine /sætənaɪn/. Someone who is **saturnine** is gloomy and unfriendly. EG *A saturnine customs officer looked through our baggage.*
ADJ QUALIT Literary

sauce /sɔːs/, **sauces.** A **sauce** is a thick liquid which is served with other food. EG *...tomato sauce... ...chicken in walnut sauce... Make a sauce to go with the fish.*
N MASS

saucepan /sɔːspən/, **saucepans.** A **saucepan** is a deep metal cooking pot, usually with a long handle and a lid.
N COUNT

saucer /sɔːsə/, **saucers.** A **saucer** is a small curved plate on which you stand a cup. EG *She offered me tea in her best cup and saucer... ...a saucer of milk.* ● See also **flying saucer**.
N COUNT OR N PART

saucy /sɔːsi^{1}/, **saucier, sauciest.** Someone who is **saucy** is rather cheeky in a light-hearted, amusing way. EG *Don't be saucy with me.*
ADJ QUALIT Informal

sauna /sɔːnə/, **saunas.** A **sauna** is **1** a hot steam bath, after which you usually have a bath in cold water. **2** the room or building where you have a sauna.
N COUNT

saunter /sɔːntə/, **saunters, sauntering, sauntered.** If you **saunter** somewhere, you walk there in a slow, casual way. EG *He sauntered up and down, looking at the shops and the people.*
V+A

sausage /sɒsɪdʒ/, **sausages. 1 Sausage** is finely minced meat which is mixed with other ingredi-
N UNCOUNT

Does sausage have a savoury flavour?

ents and put into a thin casing like a tube. EG *We lunched on garlic sausage and bread.*

2 A **sausage** is a tube-shaped piece of sausage meat. EG *...bacon, eggs, and sausages for breakfast.* N COUNT

sausage roll, sausage rolls. A **sausage roll** is a small amount of sausage meat which is covered with pastry and cooked. N COUNT

sauté /səʊteɪ/, **sautés, sautéing, sautéed.** When you **sauté** food, you fry it quickly in hot oil or butter. EG *Sauté the chicken breasts until they are golden brown.* ◇ **sautéed.** EG *...sautéed potatoes.* V+O ◇ ADJ CLASSIF

savage /sævɪdʒ/, **savages, savaging, savaged. 1** Something that is **savage** is extremely cruel, violent, and uncontrolled. EG *His voice was loud and savage... ...two weeks of savage rioting... ...one of those savage remarks about the futility of life.* ◇ **savagely.** EG *The dog began to bark savagely.* ADJ QUALIT ◇ ADV

2 If you refer to someone as a **savage**, you mean that they are cruel, violent, or uncivilized. EG *You don't understand what savages these people are.* N COUNT

3 If a dog **savages** you, it attacks you violently. V+O

4 If you **savage** someone or **savage** something they have done, you criticize them severely. EG *An opposition spokesman savaged the Government's housing investment programme.* V+O

savagery /sævɪdʒri[1]/ is extremely cruel and violent behaviour. EG *I was appalled by the savagery of the attack.* N UNCOUNT

save /seɪv/, **saves, saving, saved. 1** If you **save** someone or something, you help them to avoid harm or to escape from a dangerous or unpleasant situation. EG *An artificial heart could save his life... She saved him from drowning... Only love can save the world.* V+O: OFT+*from*

2 If you **save** money, you gradually collect it by not spending it, usually so that you can buy something that you want. EG *They had managed to save enough to buy a house... She told him that she was saving with a building society.* V+O OR V

3 If you **save** time or money, you prevent the loss or waste of it. EG *This measure would save the government £185 million... You could save up to 75 per cent of your heat loss by efficient insulation... The manufacturers save money on promotion... It's an attempt to save on labour costs.* V+O: OFT+*on*, V+*on*, OR V+O+O

4 If you **save** something, you keep it because it will be needed later. EG *Always save business letters, bills, and receipts... Will you save him a place at your table?* V+O OR V+O+O

5 If someone or something **saves** you from doing something or **saves** you the trouble of doing it, they do it for you or change the situation so that you do not have to do it. EG *Well, that saves me from denying it... A vote would save us a lot of trouble... You could save yourself a lot of work if you used a computer... Using electronic circuit boards saves wiring up thousands of individual transistors.* V+O+*from*, V+O+O, V-REFL+O, OR V+-ING

6 If a goalkeeper **saves** or **saves** a shot, he or she succeeds in preventing the ball from going into the goal. EG *The shot was saved by Buller, who returned to Liverpool last week after three seasons with Barcelona.* ▸ used as a noun. EG *He made a brilliant save.* V OR V+O ▸ N COUNT

7 You can use **save** or **save for** to introduce the only things, people, or ideas that your main statement does not apply to. EG *No visitors are allowed save in the most exceptional cases... The curtained stage was empty save for a few pieces of furniture.* PREP Formal

save up. If you **save up** money, you collect it by not spending it, usually so that you can buy something that you want. EG *It took me a year to save up for a new coat.* PHRASAL VB: V+ADV

saving /seɪvɪŋ/, **savings. 1** A **saving** is a reduction in the amount of time or money that is used or needed. EG *...a very great saving in cost as well as in manpower... The new management had achieved even bigger savings.* N COUNT

2 Your **savings** are the money that you have saved, especially in a bank or a building society. EG *She drew out all her savings... ...a savings account.* N PLURAL

-saving combines with words like 'time' and 'labour' to describe something which prevents the wasting of time or labour. EG *...energy-saving gadgets.*

saviour /seɪvɪə/, **saviours. 1** A **saviour** is a person who saves people from danger. EG *Many people regarded Churchill as the saviour of the country.* N COUNT

2 In Christianity, the **Saviour** is Jesus Christ. N PROPER: *the*+N

savour /seɪvə/, **savours, savouring, savoured;** spelled **savor** in American English. **1** If you **savour** food or drink, you eat or drink it slowly in order to taste its full flavour and to enjoy it properly. EG *Meadows took a bite of meat, savoured it, and said, 'Fantastic.'* V+O

2 If you **savour** an experience, you take great pleasure and delight in it, enjoying it as much as you can. EG *He leaned back into his seat, savouring the comfort.* V+O

savoury /seɪvə[0]ri[1]/; spelled **savory** in American English. **1 Savoury** food has a salty or spicy flavour rather than a sweet one. ADJ QUALIT

2 If you describe something as not very **savoury**, you mean that it is not very pleasant, respectable, or morally acceptable. EG *...the less savoury episodes in her past.* ADJ QUALIT: USU WITH BROAD NEG

saw /sɔː/, **saws, sawing, sawed, sawn** /sɔːn/. **1 Saw** is the past tense of **see**.

2 A **saw** is a tool for cutting wood, which has a blade with sharp teeth along one edge. See picture at TOOLS. N COUNT

3 If you **saw** something, you cut it with a saw. EG *I started sawing the branches off the main trunk.* V+O: OFT+A

sawdust /sɔːdʌst/ is very small pieces of wood which are produced when you saw wood. N UNCOUNT

sax /sæks/, **saxes.** A **sax** is the same as a saxophone. EG *...a lovely sax... There was one kid who played sax.* N COUNT OR N UNCOUNT Informal

saxophone /sæksəfəʊn/, **saxophones.** A **saxophone** is a musical wind instrument. It is made of metal in a curved shape, and is often played in jazz bands. See picture at MUSICAL INSTRUMENTS. EG *...Kessler on the bass, Westerman on the saxophone, Dailey on the percussion... He revolutionised jazz saxophone playing.* N COUNT OR N UNCOUNT

say /seɪ/, **says** /sɛz/, **saying** /seɪɪŋ/, **said** /sɛd/. **1** When you **say** something, you speak words. EG *'Please come in,' she said... He said it was an accident... People kept coming up to us to say hello... He had said nothing to me about his meeting... He knelt down and said his prayers.* V-SPEECH

2 You use **say** to introduce what you are actually saying, or to indicate that you are expressing an opinion or admitting a fact. EG *I just want to say how pleased I am to be here... I must say, it's a very sexist play... I think I can safely say that we have all learnt a great deal this evening... One thing you have to say about Americans: they love drama.* V+REPORT OR V+O

3 If you **say** something **to** yourself, you think it. EG *I began to say to myself, 'What about becoming an actor?'* PHRASE

4 If you **say** something in a letter or a book, for example, you express it in writing. EG *She wrote to say she wanted to meet me in London... There were stickers all over the crate saying: 'Glass – Handle with Care'.* V+QUOTE OR REPORT

5 If something such as a clock or map **says** something, it gives you information when you look at it. EG *The clock says that it is six o'clock... The road was not where the map said it should be.* V+O OR V+REPORT: ONLY *that*

6 If something **says** something about a person, situation, or thing, it reveals something about them. EG *The title says it all... Their glances seemed to be saying something about their relationship.* V+O OR V+REPORT: ONLY *that*

7 If you state that you can't **say** something, you are indicating in a polite or indirect way that it is not V: MODAL+V, WITH BROAD NEG

the case or is not true. EG *I can't say I've heard of them... No one could say he was not practical.*

8 You use **say** in expressions such as 'just say' and 'let's say' when you want to discuss something that might possibly happen or be true. EG *Just say you found treasure in your garden. Would you sell it?* V+REPORT: ONLY *that*

9 You also use **say 9.1** when you mention something as an example. EG *Compare, say, a Michelangelo painting with a Van Gogh.* **9.2** when you mention an approximate amount or time. EG *...in the next, say, ten years.*

10 If you have a **say** in something, you have the right to give your opinion and influence decisions. EG *People want a much greater say in how the country should be governed.* ● If you **have** your **say**, you give your opinion. N SING / ● PHRASE

11 Say is also used in these phrases. **11.1** You use **to say the least** to suggest that a situation is actually much more serious, shocking, or extreme than you say it is. EG *She lacked tact (to say the least) in expressing her views.* ADV SEN **11.2** You use **that is to say** to indicate that you are about to express the same idea more clearly. EG *The Romans left Britain in 410 AD – that is to say, England was under Roman rule for nearly 500 years.* ADV SEN Formal **11.3** You use **to say nothing of** when you add something which gives even more strength to the point you are making. EG *The effort required is immense, to say nothing of the cost.* PHRASE **11.4** If something **goes without saying**, it is obvious or is bound to be true. EG *It goes without saying that I am grateful for all your help.* PHRASE **11.5** You use **say** in expressions such as 'What would you say to a cup of tea?' as a way of making a suggestion or an offer. PHRASE Informal **11.6** You use **'I wouldn't say no'** to indicate that you would like something, especially something that has just been offered to you. EG *'Drink, Ted?' – 'I wouldn't say no, Brian.'* CONVENTION Informal **11.7** You use the expression **'I'll say this for** him, her, or them', before you mention a quality that you admire in someone, especially when you have been criticizing them. EG *I will say this for the Suffolk farmers, they're loyal.* PHRASE **11.8** If something **has a lot to be said for it**, it has a lot of good qualities. PHRASE **11.9** If you **don't have much to say for** yourself, you do not speak much. PHRASE Informal

saying /seɪɪŋ/, **sayings.** A **saying** is a traditional sentence that people often say and that gives advice or information about human life and experience. EG *There is a saying that 'man shall not live by bread alone'.* N COUNT

scab /skæb/, **scabs. 1** A **scab** is a hard, dry covering that forms over the surface of a wound. EG *A great scab had formed on his right knee.* N COUNT

2 You can use **scab** to refer to someone who continues to work when the people that he or she works with are on strike; used showing disapproval. N COUNT

scaffold /skæfə^{6}ld/, **scaffolds.** A **scaffold** is a platform on which criminals used to be executed. EG *Guy Fawkes died on the scaffold.* N COUNT

scaffolding /skæfə^{6}ldɪŋ/ is a temporary framework of metal poles and wooden boards that is used by workmen to climb up and stand on while they are constructing, repairing, or painting the outside walls of a tall building. N UNCOUNT

scald /skɔːld/, **scalds, scalding, scalded. 1** If you **scald** yourself, you burn yourself with very hot liquid or steam. EG *When it was cool enough not to scald my lips, I swallowed the coffee and asked for more.* V-REFL OR V+O

2 A **scald** is a burn caused by very hot liquid or steam. N COUNT

scalding /skɔːldɪŋ/. Something that is **scalding** is extremely hot. EG *...scalding coffee.* ADJ CLASSIF

scale /skeɪl/, **scales, scaling, scaled. 1** If you refer to the **scale** of something, you are referring to its size, especially when it is very big. EG *The scale of change is so enormous... ...the sheer scale of the United States.* N SING+SUPP

2 You use **scale** in expressions such as **large scale** and **on a small scale** when you are indicating the size, extent, or degree of one thing when compared to other similar things. EG *The district grew peas on a large scale... The plan was never very grand in scale... ...small scale methods of getting energy.* N UNCOUNT: OFT+SUPP

3 A **scale** is a set of levels or numbers which are used in a particular system of measuring things or are used in comparing things. EG *...the scale by which we measure the severity of earthquakes... ...a temperature scale... ...the pay scale... It happened everywhere, through the social scale.* N COUNT: USU+SUPP

4 The **scale** of a map, plan, or model is the relationship between the measurements of something in the real world and the measurements of it in the map, plan, or model. EG *...a map with a scale of 1:50,000.* N COUNT OR N UNCOUNT ▸ used as an adjective. EG *I used to collect scale models of ships.* ▸ ADJ CLASSIF ● If a map, plan, or model is **to scale**, it is accurately drawn or made according to the scale being used. EG *Draw it out to scale neatly on graph paper.* ● PHRASE

5 A **scale** is also a sequence of musical notes that are played or sung in an upward or downward order. EG *...the scale of C.* N COUNT

6 The **scales** of fish or reptiles are the small, flat pieces of hard skin that cover their bodies. N COUNT: USU PLURAL

7 Scales are a piece of equipment for weighing things, for example for weighing amounts of food that you need in order to make a particular dish. EG *...a pair of scales.* N PLURAL

8 If you **scale** something high or steep, you climb up or over it. EG *She scaled the barrier like a Commando.* V+O

scale down. If something **is scaled down**, it has been made smaller in size or amount than it used to be. EG *The operations were scaled down... ...a scaled-down version.* PHRASAL VB: V+O+ADV, USU PASS

scalloped /skɒləpt, skæl-/. **Scalloped** objects are decorated with a series of small curves along the edges. EG *...a blue and green scalloped design.* ADJ CLASSIF: ATTRIB

scalp /skælp/, **scalps, scalping, scalped. 1** Your **scalp** is the skin under the hair on your head. EG *...rubbing his sore scalp.* N COUNT

2 To **scalp** someone who has just been killed means to remove the skin and hair from the top of their head. EG *The whole family had been scalped.* V+O

3 A **scalp** is also the piece of skin and hair that is removed when someone is scalped. N COUNT

scalpel /skælpə^{0}l/, **scalpels.** A **scalpel** is a knife with a short, thin, sharp blade. Scalpels are used by surgeons during operations. N COUNT

scaly /skeɪli^{1}/. Something that is **scaly** is covered in small, stiff patches of hard skin. EG *...round patches of scaly skin.* ADJ QUALIT

scamper /skæmpə/, **scampers, scampering, scampered.** When people or small animals **scamper** somewhere, they move with small, quick, bouncing steps. EG *The squirrels scamper along the twigs.* V+A

scampi /skæmpi^{1}/ are large prawns that are often fried in batter and eaten. N PLURAL British

scan /skæn/, **scans, scanning, scanned. 1** When you **scan** an area, a group of things, or a piece of writing, you look at it very carefully, usually because you are looking for something in particular. EG *Anxiously Carol scanned their faces to see who she might know... ...lifeguards scanning the sea for shark fins.* V+O

2 If a machine **scans** something, it examines it quickly, for example by moving a beam of light or X-rays over it. EG *The reconnaissance plane's job was to scan the oceans with its radar.* V+O ▸ used as a noun. EG *A liver scan was performed.* ▸ N COUNT

Is a scapegoat an animal?

scandal /skændə^{0}l/, **scandals. 1** A **scandal** is a situation or event that a lot of people think is very shocking and immoral. EG *We can't afford another scandal in the firm... It became known as the Marconi scandal.* N COUNT

2 Scandal is talk about people's shocking and immoral behaviour. EG *Someone must have been spreading scandal.* N UNCOUNT

3 You can refer to something as a **scandal** when you are angry about it. EG *The defences were a scandal.* N SING : *a*+N

scandalize /skændə^{0}laɪz/, **scandalizes, scandalizing, scandalized;** also spelled **scandalise.** If you **are scandalized**, you are shocked and offended. EG *He was uncertain whether to laugh or be scandalized.* V+O : USU PASS

scandalous /skændə^{0}ləs/. **1** Something that is **scandalous** is considered immoral and shocking. EG *There were some scandalous stories about her... ...scandalous scenes of ladies with bare breasts.* ADJ QUALIT

2 You can describe something as **scandalous** when it makes you very angry. EG *It is scandalous that the public should be treated in this way.* ADJ QUALIT

◇ **scandalously**. EG *...schemes offering scandalously large tax advantages.* ◇ SUBMOD

scanner /skænə/, **scanners.** A **scanner** is a machine which is used to examine things, for example by moving a beam of light or X-rays over them. Scanners are used in places such as hospitals, airports, and research laboratories. N COUNT

scant /skænt/. If you say that something receives **scant** attention, you mean that it receives less attention than you think it should receive. EG *The campaign was conducted with scant regard for truth.* ADJ QUALIT : ATTRIB

scanty /skænti^{1}/, **scantier, scantiest.** You describe something as **scanty** when it is smaller in quantity or size than you think it should be. EG *...a rather scanty but enthusiastic audience... ...a waitress in her scanty nightclub costume... ...scanty information about their pupils.* ADJ QUALIT ◇ **scantily**. EG *The bedroom was scantily furnished.* ◇ ADV

scapegoat /skeɪpgəʊt/, **scapegoats.** If someone is made a **scapegoat**, they are blamed for something that has happened, although it may not be their fault, because other people are very angry about it. EG *In their search for a scapegoat, the government found an easy target in the unions.* N COUNT

scar /skɑː/, **scars, scarring, scarred. 1** A **scar** is a mark on the skin which is left after a wound has healed. EG *There was a scar on her arm.* N COUNT

2 If your skin **is scarred**, it is badly marked as a result of a wound. EG *They will be scarred for life.* V+O : USU PASS

3 If an object **is scarred**, it is damaged and there are ugly marks on it. EG *...the scarred tree trunk.* V+O : USU PASS

4 A **scar** is also a permanent effect on someone's mind that results from a very unpleasant physical or emotional experience. EG *The scars of poverty have undoubtedly left their mark.* N COUNT

5 If an unpleasant experience **scars** you, it has a permanent effect on you, and influences the way you think and behave. EG *It wasn't the violence of the attack that scarred my mind.* V+O

scarce /skɛəs/, **scarcer, scarcest. 1** If something is **scarce**, there is not very much of it. EG *...an environment where water is scarce.* ADJ QUALIT

2 If you **make** yourself **scarce**, you quickly leave the place you are in, usually in order to avoid a difficult or embarrassing situation. PHRASE Informal

scarcely /skɛəsli^{1}/. **1** You use **scarcely** to say that something is only just true or is not quite true. EG *I can scarcely remember what we ate... They were scarcely ever apart... ...a very young man, scarcely more than a boy.* ADV BRD NEG

2 You can use **scarcely** in an ironic way to say that something is certainly not true. EG *There could scarcely be a less promising environment for children.* ADV BRD NEG

3 If you say **scarcely** had one thing happened when something else happened, you mean that the first event was followed immediately by the second. EG *Scarcely had the car drawn to a halt when armed police surrounded it.* ADV BRD NEG

scarcity /skɛəsɪ^{1}ti^{1}/. If there is a **scarcity** of something, there is not enough of it. EG *...the scarcity of food.* N UNCOUNT Formal

scare /skɛə/, **scares, scaring, scared. 1** When people or things **scare** you, they frighten you. EG *I didn't mean to scare you.* V+O ● If something **scares the life out of** you or **scares the hell out of** you, it makes you very frightened. ● PHRASE Informal

2 If something gives you a **scare**, it frightens you. EG *The first attack gave me a scare... That night I had an even worse scare.* N COUNT

3 A **scare** is a situation in which many people are afraid because they think that something dangerous is happening. EG *Since none of the fragments picked up was radioactive the scare died down... ...a rabies scare.* N COUNT : USU+SUPP

scare away or **scare off.** If you **scare** animals or people **away** or **scare** them **off**, you frighten them so that they go away. EG *The least shadow or movement would scare the fish away.* PHRASAL VB : V+O+ADV

scarecrow /skɛəkrəʊ/, **scarecrows.** A **scarecrow** is an object in the shape of a person, which is put in a field where crops are growing in order to frighten birds away. N COUNT

scared /skɛəd/. **1** If you are **scared** of someone or something, you are frightened of them. EG *Everybody's scared of him... He was terribly scared... She was too shocked and scared to move.* ADJ PRED ● If you are **scared stiff** or **scared to death**, you are extremely frightened. ● PHRASE Informal

2 If you are **scared** that something unpleasant might happen, you are nervous and worried because you think that it might happen. EG *I'm scared that these will turn out to be the wrong ones... They're scared of making a fool of themselves.* ADJ PRED +REPORT OR +*of*

scarf /skɑːf/, **scarfs** or **scarves** /skɑːvz/. A **scarf** is a piece of cloth that you wear round your neck or head, usually to keep yourself warm. See picture at CLOTHES. EG *The girl wrapped her black woollen scarf tightly round her neck.* N COUNT

scarlet /skɑːlə^{1}t/, **scarlets.** Something that is **scarlet** is bright red. EG *...a scarlet handkerchief... ...silky materials in scarlets, blues, and greens.* ADJ COLOUR

scarlet fever is an infectious disease which causes a painful throat, a high temperature, and a red rash. N UNCOUNT

scarves /skɑːvz/ is a plural of **scarf.**

scary /skɛəri^{1}/. Something that is **scary** is rather frightening. EG *It was a scary moment.* ADJ QUALIT Informal

scathing /skeɪðɪŋ/. If you are **scathing** about something, you criticize it harshly and scornfully. EG *Miss Jackson was scathing about our efforts... ...a rather scathing article about lady novelists.* ADJ QUALIT : OFT+*about*

◇ **scathingly**. EG *He refers scathingly to these superstitions.* ◇ ADV

scatter /skætə/, **scatters, scattering, scattered. 1** If you **scatter** things over an area, you throw or drop them so that they spread all over the area. EG *Parrots scatter their food about and make a mess... The papers had been scattered all over the floor.* V+O : USU+A

2 If a group of people **scatter**, they suddenly separate and move in different directions. EG *The boys scattered, squealing in horror.* V

3 A **scatter** of things is a number of them spread over an area in an irregular way. EG *My eye was drawn to a small scatter of bone fragments.* N PART : SING Literary

scattered /skætəd/. **1** Things that are **scattered** are spread over an area and are a long way from each other. EG *We drove over the debris scattered across the streets... The old people could not visit their scattered families.* ADJ CLASSIF

2 If something is **scattered** with a lot of small things, they are spread all over it. EG *Her hair was scattered with pollen.* ADJ PRED+ *with*

scattering /skætəʳrɪŋ/. A **scattering** of things is a small number of them spread over a large area. EG *...the blue night sky with its scattering of stars.* N PART : SING Literary

scavenge /skævɪndʒ/, **scavenges, scavenging, scavenged.** If someone **scavenges** for food or other things or **scavenges** things, they collect them by searching among waste and unwanted objects. EG *I had no resources at all, except what I could scavenge or beg.* V : OFT+*for* OR V+O ◊ **scavenger, scavengers.** EG *...a scavenger living from the dustbins behind restaurants.* ◊ N COUNT

scenario /sɪnɑːrɪəʊ/, **scenarios. 1** If you talk about a likely or possible **scenario**, you are talking about the way in which a situation may develop. EG *The death of democracy becomes quite a likely scenario.* N COUNT

2 The **scenario** of a film is a piece of writing that gives an outline of the story. N COUNT Technical

scene /siːn/, **scenes. 1** A **scene** is one of the parts of a play, film, or book in which a series of events happen in the same place. EG *...the balcony scene from 'Romeo and Juliet'... It was like some scene from a Victorian novel.* N COUNT

2 Paintings and drawings of places are sometimes called **scenes**. EG *...the harbour scenes that he drew as a teenager.* N COUNT+SUPP

3 You can describe something that you see as a **scene** of a particular kind. EG *The moon rose over a scene of extraordinary destruction... ...a scene of domestic tranquillity.* N COUNT+SUPP

4 The **scene** of an event is the place where it happened. EG *...the scene of the crime.* N COUNT : USU SING

5 If you have a **change of scene**, you go somewhere different after being in a particular place for a long time. EG *She was excited by the thought of a change of scene.* PHRASE

6 You can refer to an area of activity as a particular type of **scene**. EG *...the business scene... ...the German political scene.* N SING : *the*+N +SUPP

7 If you make a **scene**, you embarrass people by publicly showing your anger about something. EG *There was a scene, and Father called Christopher a liar... Clarissa dear, please don't make a nasty scene.* N COUNT

8 Scene is also used in these phrases. **8.1** If something is done **behind the scenes**, it is done secretly. EG *Officials working behind the scenes urged them to avoid further confrontation.* **8.2** When someone appears **on the scene**, they arrive. **8.3** You also say that someone or something appears **on the scene** when they become widely known or used. EG *The computer burst upon the scene around 1950.* **8.4** If you say that a place or activity **is not** your **scene**, you mean that you do not like it. **8.5** If you **set the scene** for someone, you tell them what they need to know in order to understand what is going to happen or be said next. EG *First of all let's set the scene: in 1900 the population of the world was much smaller.* PHRASES Informal

scenery /siːnəʳrɪ¹/. **1** When you are in the countryside, you can refer to everything you see around you as the **scenery**. EG *As we neared the border the scenery became lush and spectacular... We had time to admire the scenery.* N SING OR N UNCOUNT

2 In a theatre, the **scenery** is the painted cloth and boards at the back of the stage. EG *Who designed the scenery?... The production uses a minimum of scenery.* N SING OR N UNCOUNT

scenic /siːnɪk/. A **scenic** place or route is attractive and has nice views. EG *The island has a scenic coastline... ...a scenic railway.* ADJ QUALIT

scent /sɛnt/, **scents, scenting, scented. 1** A **scent** is a pleasant smell. EG *...the overpowering scent of English garden flowers.* N COUNT

2 Scent is a liquid that women put on their skin to make themselves smell nice. EG *She walked in smelling of French scent.* N MASS

3 An animal's **scent** is its smell. EG *The queen bee produces a scent which attracts the other bees.* N UNCOUNT OR N COUNT

4 When an animal **scents** something, it becomes aware of it by smelling it. EG *...when it scents its prey.* V+O

5 If you **scent** something, you feel that it is going to happen. EG *He scented danger.* V+O Literary

scented /sɛntɪ²d/. Something that is **scented** has a pleasant smell. EG *...scented soap... ...a sweet-scented variety of rose.* ADJ CLASSIF

sceptic /skɛptɪk/, **sceptics;** spelled **skeptic** in American English. A **sceptic** is a person who has doubts about things that other people believe. N COUNT

sceptical /skɛptɪkəʳl/; spelled **skeptical** in American English. If you are **sceptical** about something, you have doubts about it. EG *Robert's father was sceptical about hypnotism... Mrs Swallow gave a sceptical grunt.* ADJ QUALIT ◊ **sceptically.** EG *I had listened sceptically to the broadcast.* ◊ ADV

scepticism /skɛptɪsɪzəʳm/; spelled **skepticism** in American English. **Scepticism** is great doubt about something. EG *He listened with growing scepticism... There was widespread scepticism about these proposals.* N UNCOUNT

schedule /ʃɛdjuˀl/, **schedules, scheduling, scheduled;** also pronounced /skɛdjuˀl/, especially in American English.

1 A **schedule** is a plan that gives a list of events or tasks, together with the times at which each thing should happen or be done. EG *...the next place on his busy schedule... ...the daily schedule of classes.* N COUNT

2 If something is done **to schedule** or **according to schedule**, it is done at the times that were planned in advance. EG *The operations have been carried out according to schedule.* PHRASE

3 If something happens **on schedule**, it happens at the time planned. EG *Simon showed up right on schedule.* PHRASE

4 If something happens **ahead of schedule**, it happens earlier than the time planned. EG *We arrived several hours ahead of schedule.* PHRASE

5 If you are **behind schedule**, you are doing things later than the times planned. PHRASE

6 If something **is scheduled** to happen, arrangements have been made for it to happen. EG *He was scheduled to leave Plymouth yesterday... A meeting had been scheduled for that day... ...a department store now scheduled for demolition.* V+O+*to*-INF OR *for* : USU PASS

7 A **schedule** is also a written list of things, for example a list of prices, details, or conditions. N COUNT Formal

scheme /skiːm/, **schemes, scheming, schemed.**

1 A **scheme** is a large-scale plan or arrangement produced by a government or other organization. EG *...the State pension scheme... ...a scheme to build 63 houses.* N COUNT

2 You can also refer to a person's plan for achieving something as a **scheme**. EG *...an ambitious scheme... ...some scheme for perfecting the world.* N COUNT

3 When people **scheme**, they make secret plans; used showing disapproval. EG *He schemed against her... She schemed on her daughter's behalf.* V : OFT+A ◊ **scheming.** EG *...a ruthless, scheming man... ...his scheming old father.* ◊ ADJ CLASSIF : ATTRIB

4 Someone's **scheme of things** is the way in which they want things to be organized. EG *There was an important place for the State in their scheme of things.* PHRASE

5 When people talk about **the scheme of things**, they are referring to the way that everything in the world seems to be organized. EG *Man needed to understand his place in the scheme of things.* PHRASE

schizophrenia /skɪtsəˀfriːnɪə/ is a serious mental illness. People who suffer from it are unable to relate their thoughts and feelings to what is happening around them. N UNCOUNT

schizophrenic /skɪtsəˀfrɛnɪk/, **schizophrenics.** A **schizophrenic** is a person who is suffering from N COUNT

If you scoff at something, are you sceptical about it?

schizophrenia. EG ...*a paranoid schizophrenic.* ▸ *used as an adjective.* EG ...*a schizophrenic patient.* ▸ ADJ CLASSIF

scholar /skɒlə/, **scholars. 1** A **scholar** is a person who studies an academic subject and knows a lot about it. EG ...*Benjamin Jowett, the theologian and Greek scholar.* N COUNT

2 Someone who is a good **scholar** is good at learning things at school or college, and someone who is a bad **scholar** is bad at learning things. EG *Philpott was a poor scholar.* N COUNT+SUPP Outdated

3 A **scholar** is also a pupil or student who has obtained a scholarship. EG ...*an Eton scholar.* N COUNT

scholarly /skɒləli[1]/. A **scholarly** person spends a lot of time studying and knows a lot about academic subjects. ADJ QUALIT

scholarship /skɒləʃɪp/, **scholarships. 1** If you get a **scholarship** to a school or university, your studies are paid for by the school or university or by some other organization. EG *I applied for a scholarship to study philosophy at Oxford.* N COUNT

2 Scholarship is serious academic study and the knowledge that is obtained from it. EG ...*the Islamic tradition of scholarship.* N UNCOUNT

scholastic /skə[7]læstɪk/. Your **scholastic** ability and achievements are your ability to study and your achievements while you are at school. EG *He was more involved in sports than in scholastic achievements.* ADJ CLASSIF : ATTRIB Formal

school /sku:l/, **schools. 1 School** or a **school** is a place where children are educated. EG ...*a school with more than 1300 pupils... I went to school here... He was doing badly at school... What do you want to do when you leave school?... ...the school holidays... ...once their children reach school age.* N UNCOUNT OR N COUNT

2 If something happens before **school** or after **school**, it happens before or after the part of the day when you are at school. EG *We met every day after school.* N UNCOUNT

3 University departments and colleges are sometimes called **schools**. EG *I went to an art school... She had recently graduated from law school... ...medical school.* N COUNT OR N UNCOUNT +SUPP

4 In America, university is often referred to as **school**. N UNCOUNT Informal

5 A particular **school of thought** is a particular theory or opinion that is shared by a group of people. EG *One school of thought argues that the enterprise should be abandoned... There seemed to be two schools of thought.* PHRASE

6 A large group of dolphins or fish can be referred to as a **school**. EG ...*a school of dolphins.* N PART

7 See also **schooling**, **boarding school**, **finishing school**, **first school**, **grammar school**, **high school**, **infant school**, **junior school**, **middle school**, **night school**, **nursery school**, **prep school**, **primary school**, **private school**, **public school**, **secondary school**, **summer school**, **Sunday school**.

schoolboy /sku:lbɔɪ/, **schoolboys.** A **schoolboy** is a boy who goes to school. N COUNT

schoolchild /sku:ltʃaɪld/, **schoolchildren. Schoolchildren** are children who go to school. EG *The hall was rapidly filling with schoolchildren.* N COUNT : OFT PLURAL

schooldays /sku:ldeɪz/. Your **schooldays** are the period of your life when you are at school. EG *I enjoyed my schooldays.* N PLURAL : USU+POSS

schoolgirl /sku:lgɜ:l/, **schoolgirls.** A **schoolgirl** is a girl who goes to school. N COUNT

schooling /sku:lɪŋ/. Your **schooling** is the education that you receive at school. EG *Many of the workers had no schooling at all... Her schooling had been highly irregular.* N UNCOUNT Informal

school-leaver, school-leavers. School-leavers are young people who have just left school and who are looking for a job or are doing their first job. EG ...*the growth of unemployment among school-leavers.* N COUNT : USU PLURAL

schoolmaster /sku:lmɑ:stə/, **schoolmasters.** A **schoolmaster** is a man who teaches children in a school. N COUNT Outdated

schoolmistress /sku:lmɪstrɪ[2]s/, **schoolmistresses.** A **schoolmistress** is a woman who teaches children in a school. EG ...*the village schoolmistress.* N COUNT Outdated

schoolroom /sku:lru[4]m/, **schoolrooms.** A **schoolroom** is a classroom, especially the only classroom in a small school. N COUNT Outdated

schoolteacher /sku:lti:tʃə/, **schoolteachers.** A **schoolteacher** is a teacher in a school. N COUNT

schoolteaching /sku:lti:tʃɪŋ/ is the work that schoolteachers do. EG *I was thinking of going in for schoolteaching.* N UNCOUNT Outdated

schoolwork /sku:lwɜ:k/ is the work that a child does at school or as homework. N UNCOUNT

science /saɪəns/, **sciences. 1 Science** is the study of the nature and behaviour of natural things and the knowledge that we obtain about them. EG ...*the importance of mathematics to science... Why don't many girls go into science?* N UNCOUNT

2 A **science** is **2.1** a particular branch of science, for example physics or biology. **2.2** the study of some aspect of human behaviour, for example psychology or sociology. ● See also **social science**. N COUNT

science fiction consists of stories and films about events that take place in the future or in other parts of the universe. N UNCOUNT

scientific /saɪəntɪfɪk/. **1 Scientific** is used to describe things that relate to science or to a particular science. EG ...*scientific research... ...scientific instruments.* ◇ **scientifically**. EG ...*a scientifically advanced civilization.* ADJ CLASSIF ◇ ADV

2 If you do something in a **scientific** way, you do it systematically, using experiments or tests. EG ...*a scientific study of a language.* ◇ **scientifically**. EG *Our relationship to apes has been confirmed scientifically.* ADJ QUALIT ◇ ADV

scientist /saɪəntɪst/, **scientists.** A **scientist** is an expert who does work in one of the sciences. EG ...*a distinguished medical scientist.* ● See also **social scientist**. N COUNT

scissors

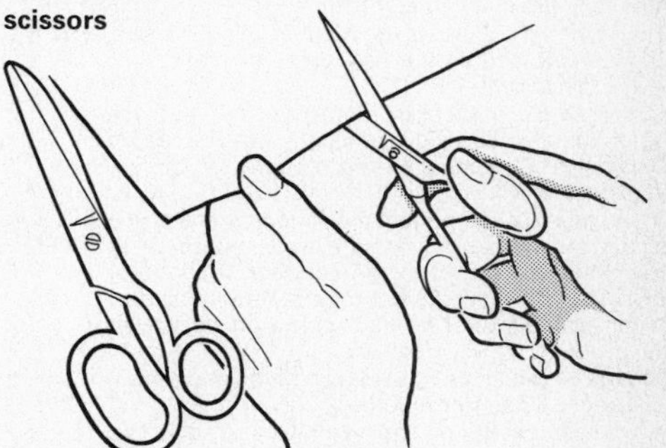

scissors /sɪzəz/ are a small tool with two sharp blades which are screwed together. You use scissors for cutting things such as paper and cloth. EG *She took a pair of scissors and cut his hair... I wish I'd brought some scissors.* N PLURAL

scoff /skɒf/, **scoffs, scoffing, scoffed. 1** If you **scoff**, you speak in a scornful, mocking way about something. EG *They scoff at the idea that he will retire next year... 'Women's movement!' they scoffed. 'There isn't one.'... Let them scoff.* V OR V+QUOTE : OFT+*at*

2 If you **scoff** food, you eat it quickly and greedily. EG *They scoffed the lot.* V+O Informal

scold /skəʊld/, **scolds, scolding, scolded.** If you **scold** someone, you speak angrily to them because they have done something wrong. EG *He scolded his daughter for keeping them waiting.* V+O OR V+QUOTE

scone /skəʊn, skɒn/, **scones. Scones** are small cakes made from flour and fat. They are usually eaten with butter. N COUNT

scoop /sku:p/, **scoops, scooping, scooped. 1** If you **scoop** something up, **1.1** you put your hands under it and lift it in a quick movement. EG *The boys began to scoop up handfuls of water.* **1.2** you pick it up with something such as a spoon. EG *He scooped some instant coffee into a cup.* V+O : USU+A

2 A **scoop** is an object like a large spoon which is used for picking up a quantity of a food such as ice cream or flour. N COUNT

3 A **scoop** is also an exciting news story which is reported in one newspaper before it appears anywhere else. EG *He got all the big scoops for the paper.* N COUNT

scoop out. If you **scoop** part of something **out**, you remove it using a spoon or other tool. EG *Scoop out the flesh of the melon with a teaspoon.* PHRASAL VB : V+O+ADV

scooter /sku:tə/, **scooters.** A **scooter** is a small, lightweight motorcycle with a low seat. N COUNT

scope /skəʊp/. **1** If there is **scope** for a particular kind of behaviour, you have the opportunity to act in this way. EG *There is not much scope for originality.* N UNCOUNT : USU+SUPP

2 The **scope** of an activity, topic, or piece of work is the whole area which it deals with or includes. EG *Lack of time limited the scope of the course... It seemed out of place in a book so limited in scope.* N UNCOUNT : USU+SUPP

scorch /skɔ:tʃ/, **scorches, scorching, scorched.** If something **is scorched**, it is burned slightly or damaged by heat. EG *I once scorched a beautiful pink suit while ironing it... The lawn was scorched and the soil was baked hard... The sun scorched my face.* V+O

scorching /skɔ:tʃɪŋ/. If you use **scorching** to describe the weather, you mean that it is very hot. EG *...a scorching day.* ADJ QUALIT Informal

score /skɔ:/, **scores, scoring, scored. 1** If someone **scores** in a game, they get a goal, a run, or a point. EG *Barnes scored from a distance of twenty feet... Fowler scored 83.* V OR V+O

2 Someone's **score** is the total number of runs or points they get in a game or test. N COUNT

3 The **score** in a game is the number of goals, runs, or points obtained by the two teams or players. EG *'What's the score?' – '2 – 0'.* N COUNT

4 If you **score** a success, victory, or hit, you are successful in what you are doing. EG *The Royal Shakespeare Company scored a runaway success with 'Richard III'.* V+O

5 If you **score** over someone or **score** a point, you gain an advantage over them or defeat them in some way. EG *The Government was anxious to score over the opposition in the education debate... Gareth grinned, as if he had scored an important point.* V+A OR V+O : OFT+*over*

6 Scores of things means a large number of them. EG *We received scores of letters.* N PART : PLURAL

7 A **score** is twenty or approximately twenty. The plural is also 'score'. EG *None of these groups had more than a score of supporters... Even in my two score years the world has changed.* N COUNT OR N PART Outdated

8 If something sharp **scores** a surface, it cuts a line into it. EG *Each stone is scored with very thin grooves.* V+O Formal

9 The **score** of a piece of music is the written version of it. N COUNT

10 On this score or **on that score** means in relation to the thing already mentioned. EG *There was no need for concern on that score.* PHRASE Formal

scorn /skɔ:n/, **scorns, scorning, scorned. 1** If you treat someone or something with **scorn**, you show contempt for them. EG *This suggestion was greeted with scorn... She had nothing but scorn for those who got themselves into debt.* ● If you **heap scorn** on something or **pour scorn on** it, you say that you think it is worthless. EG *Burgin heaped scorn on painting and sculpture... She poured scorn on my ideas.* N UNCOUNT ● PHRASE

2 If you **scorn** someone or something, you feel or show contempt for them. EG *She scorned the girls who worshipped football heroes... What is now admired as art was then scorned as vulgar extravagance.* V+O : OFT+*as*

3 If you **scorn** something, you refuse to have it or accept it because you think it is not good enough or suitable for you. EG *Although his hearing was not good, he scorned a deaf aid.* V+O Formal

scornful /skɔ:nfʊl/. If you are **scornful**, you show contempt for someone or something. EG *She is openly scornful of the idea that girls are weaker than men... ...scornful laughter.* ◇ **scornfully**. EG *She looked at him scornfully.* ADJ QUALIT ◇ ADV

scorpion /skɔ:pɪən/, **scorpions.** A **scorpion** is a small tropical animal which looks like a large insect. It has a long tail with a poisonous sting on the end. N COUNT

Scot /skɒt/, **Scots. 1** A **Scot** is a person who comes from Scotland. N COUNT

2 Scots is a dialect of the English language that is spoken in Scotland. EG *He speaks broad Scots.* N UNCOUNT

3 Scots also means the same as Scottish. EG *He spoke with a Scots accent.* ADJ CLASSIF : ATTRIB

scotch /skɒtʃ/, **scotches. 1 Scotch** or **scotch whisky** is whisky made in Scotland. EG *...a bottle of Scotch.* N UNCOUNT

2 A **scotch** is a glass of scotch. EG *He fixed two more scotches.* N COUNT

3 Scotch is sometimes used to mean Scottish. ADJ CLASSIF

Scotsman /skɒtsmə[3]n/, **Scotsmen.** A **Scotsman** is a man who comes from Scotland. N COUNT

Scotswoman /skɒtswʊmən/, **Scotswomen.** A **Scotswoman** is a woman who comes from Scotland. N COUNT

Scottish /skɒtɪʃ/. Something that is **Scottish** belongs or relates to Scotland, its people, or its language. EG *...the Scottish mountains... ...Scottish football... ...the Scottish legal system.* ADJ CLASSIF

scoundrel /skaʊndrə[0]l/, **scoundrels.** People call a man a **scoundrel** when he behaves very badly towards other people, especially by cheating them or deceiving them. N COUNT Outdated

scour /skaʊə/, **scours, scouring, scoured.** If you **scour** a place for something or someone, you make a thorough search there for them. EG *Traders were scouring the villages for family treasures.* V+O : USU+A

scourge /skɜ:dʒ/. When something causes a lot of trouble or suffering to a group of people, you can refer to it as a **scourge**. EG *Smallpox was the scourge of the Western world.* N SING : OFT+*of*

scout /skaʊt/, **scouts, scouting, scouted. 1** A **scout** or a **boy scout** is a boy who is a member of the Scout Association. Scouts go camping, learn how to look after themselves, and do things to help other people. EG *He joined the boy scouts... He was going away with the local scout troop.* N COUNT

2 A **scout** is also a person who is sent to an area of countryside to find out the position of an enemy army. EG *The scouts reported that the enemy was advancing.* N COUNT

3 If you **scout** for something or **scout** around for it, you search for it in different places. EG *We'll scout around to see if anyone is here.* V+A

scowl /skaʊl/, **scowls, scowling, scowled.** When someone **scowls**, they frown to show that they are angry or displeased. EG *I scowled at him.* ▸ used as a noun. EG *Her grin changed to a scowl.* V : OFT+*at* ▸ N COUNT

scrabble /skræbə[0]l/, **scrabbles, scrabbling, scrabbled. 1** If you **scrabble** at something, you scrape at it with your fingers or feet. EG *The woman scrabbled at the side of the boat... I hung there, scrabbling with my feet to find a foothold.* V+A

Which is the odd one out - Scots, Scotch or Scottish?

2 If you **scrabble** around, you move your hands about in order to find something that you cannot see. EG *I scrabbled around on the floor and eventually found my ring... She scrabbled in her handbag.* V+A
3 Scrabble is a word game played with letters on a board. N PROPER Trademark

scramble /skræmbəl/, **scrambles, scrambling, scrambled. 1** If you **scramble** over rough or difficult ground, you move quickly over it using your hands to help you. EG *John scrambled up the bank.* V : USU+A
2 You also **scramble** when you move to a different position or place in a hurried, undignified way. EG *He scrambled to his feet... The smaller boys were trying to scramble out of the way.* ▸ used as a noun. EG *We had an awful scramble to get to the airport.* V+A ▸ N SING

scrambled egg, scrambled eggs. Scrambled egg or **scrambled eggs** is a food consisting of eggs mixed together and then cooked in a pan. N UNCOUNT OR N PLURAL

scrap /skræp/, **scraps, scrapping, scrapped. 1** A **scrap** of something is a very small piece or amount of it. EG *He found a scrap of paper and a pencil... ...a rug made of scraps of old clothes... ...scraps of information.* N PART
2 Scraps are pieces of unwanted food which are thrown away or given to animals. EG *...a tame puppy, begging for scraps.* N PLURAL
3 If there is **not a scrap** of something, there is none of it at all. EG *There was not a scrap of evidence against him... It never made a scrap of difference to his feelings for her.* PHRASE
4 If you **scrap** something, you get rid of it or cancel it, for example because you no longer think it is suitable. EG *The existing system should be completely scrapped... Plans have now been scrapped for four nuclear power stations.* V+O
5 Scrap or **scrap metal** is metal from old or damaged machinery or cars. EG *All he could do was sell it for scrap.* N UNCOUNT
6 You can refer to a fight or a quarrel as a **scrap**. EG *Mr Roberts loved a scrap.* N COUNT Informal

scrapbook /skræpbʊk/, **scrapbooks.** A **scrapbook** is a book with blank pages. People stick things such as pictures or newspaper articles into scrapbooks in order to make a collection. N COUNT

scrape /skreɪp/, **scrapes, scraping, scraped. 1** If you **scrape** something from a surface or **scrape** it off, you remove it by pulling a knife or other object over it. EG *She scraped the mud off her boots.* V+O+A
2 If you **scrape** something, you remove its skin or surface by pulling a knife over it. EG *The nuts can be eaten raw once they have been scraped.* V+O
3 If you **scrape** one thing against another, you rub the first thing against the second, causing slight damage. EG *He scraped his hand painfully on a rock.* V+O+*against/on*
4 If something **scrapes** something else or **scrapes** against it, it rubs against it and damages it slightly or makes a harsh noise. EG *In winter, the branches tapped and scraped the glass... His beard scraped against her skin.* ▸ used as a noun. EG *...the clink and scrape of knives and forks.* V+O OR V+*against/on* ▸ N SING
5 You say that people **scrape** when they spend as little money as possible, in order to have enough money to buy things that they want or need. EG *People scraped and saved to get their boys into private schools.* V : OFT+*to*-INF
6 If you are in a **scrape**, you are in a difficult situation which you have caused yourself. EG *He got into several scrapes.* N COUNT Outdated
7 to **scrape the barrel**: see **barrel**.

scrape through. If you **scrape through** an examination, you just succeed in passing it. PHRASAL VB : V+ADV/PREP

scrape together or **scrape up.** If you **scrape together** or **scrape up** an amount of money or a number of things, you succeed in obtaining them with difficulty. EG *He scraped up the money to start a restaurant.* PHRASAL VB : V+O+ADV

scratch /skrætʃ/, **scratches, scratching, scratched. 1** If a sharp object **scratches** you, it rubs against your skin, cutting you slightly. EG *I got scratched by a rose bush... His knees were scratched by thorns.* V+O
2 A **scratch** is a small cut on your body. EG *You're not going to die. It's only a scratch.* N COUNT
3 If you **scratch** yourself or **scratch**, you rub your fingernails against your skin because it is itching. EG *Jackson was sleepily scratching himself.* ● If you say that someone **is scratching** their **head**, you mean that they are thinking hard and trying to solve a problem or puzzle. EG *That will make him scratch his head.* V-REFL, V+O, OR V ● PHRASE
4 If you **scratch** an object, you accidentally make small cuts on it which spoil its appearance. V+O
5 Scratches are marks where something has been scratched. EG *White shoe polish can hide scratches on white woodwork.* N COUNT
6 If you say that an article or report only **scratches the surface**, you mean that it deals with a subject in a superficial way. PHRASE
7 If you do something **from scratch**, you do it without making use of anything that has been done before. EG *Now we have to start again from scratch... We're building it from scratch.* PHRASE
8 If you say that something is **up to scratch**, you mean that it is good enough. EG *My Economics isn't likely to be up to scratch.* PHRASE

scrawl /skrɔːl/, **scrawls, scrawling, scrawled. 1** If you **scrawl** something, you write it in a careless and untidy way. EG *Someone had scrawled 'What does it all mean?' across the cover... I tried to read his notes scrawled on a piece of paper.* V+O : OFT+A
2 You can refer to writing that looks careless and untidy as a **scrawl**. EG *I did my best to write neatly instead of with my usual scrawl.* N COUNT

scrawny /skrɔːni¹/, **scrawnier, scrawniest.** A **scrawny** person or animal is unpleasantly thin and bony. EG *...a scrawny youth... ...scrawny cattle.* ADJ QUALIT

scream /skriːm/, **screams, screaming, screamed. 1** When someone **screams**, they make a very loud, high-pitched cry, usually because they are in pain or are very frightened. EG *Kunta screamed as a whip struck his back.* ▸ used as a noun. EG *He was awakened by the sound of screams.* V ▸ N COUNT
2 When anything makes a loud, high-pitched noise, you can say that it **screams**. EG *The jets screamed overhead... The birds screamed in the trees.* ▸ used as a noun. EG *The car roared round the corner with a scream of tyres.* V ▸ N SING
3 If you **scream** something, you shout it in a loud, high-pitched voice. EG *'Get out of there,' I screamed... I screamed that I was all right.* V-SPEECH : ONLY *that*
4 You can say that someone is a **scream** when you think that they are very funny. EG *Do you know Sheila? She's a scream.* N SING : *a*+N Informal

screech /skriːtʃ/, **screeches, screeching, screeched. 1** When a person or an animal **screeches**, they make an unpleasant, loud, high-pitched cry. EG *'You'll be sorry you did that!' she screeched.* ▸ used as a noun. EG *The parrot gave a loud screech.* V : OFT+QUOTE OR REPORT, ONLY *that* ▸ N COUNT
2 If a vehicle **screeches**, its tyres make an unpleasant high-pitched noise on the road. EG *The bus came screeching to a stop.* ▸ used as a noun. EG *I heard a screech of tyres.* V : USU+A ▸ N SING

screen /skriːn/, **screens, screening, screened. 1** A **screen** is a flat, vertical surface on which a picture is shown. Television sets and computer terminals have screens, and films are shown on a screen in cinemas. EG *A picture would flash onto the screen... The television screen remained the centre of attention.* N COUNT
2 The films that are shown in cinemas are sometimes referred to as the **screen**. EG *...Greta Garbo and other stars of the screen.* N SING : *the*+N
3 When a film or a television programme **is** V+O : USU PASS

screened, it is shown in the cinema or broadcast on television. EG *They tried to prevent the programme being screened.* ◊ **screening, screenings.** EG *There was an attempt to stop the screening.* ◊ N UNCOUNT OR N COUNT

4 A **screen** is also a vertical panel which can be moved around. It is used to keep cold air away from part of a room, or to create a smaller area within the room. EG *He got up and walked behind the screen.* N COUNT

5 If you **screen** someone, you stand in front of them or place something in front of them, in order to prevent them from being seen or hurt. EG *I moved in front of her trying to screen her.* V+O

6 When an organization **screens** people, **6.1** they investigate them to make sure that they are not likely to be dangerous or disloyal. EG *The Secret Service screens several hundred people every week.* **6.2** they examine them to make sure that they do not have a particular disease. EG *...a study of women who were screened for breast cancer.* ◊ **screening.** EG *...a screening at a London medical centre.* V+O; ◊ N UNCOUNT OR N COUNT

screen off. If you **screen off** part of a room, you make it into a separate area, using a screen. PHRASAL VB : V+O+ADV

screenplay /skri:npleɪ/, **screenplays.** The **screenplay** of a film is the script. EG *'The French Lieutenant's Woman' has a screenplay by Harold Pinter.* N COUNT

screw /skru:/, **screws, screwing, screwed. 1** A **screw** is a small, sharp piece of metal which you use to fix two things together. When you twist the screw with a screwdriver, it goes through one thing and into the other thing. See picture at TOOLS. N COUNT

2 If you **screw** something to something else, **2.1** you fix it there by means of a screw or screws. EG *Squeaking floorboards should be screwed down... I'm going to screw some handles onto the bathroom cabinet.* **2.2** you fasten it or fix it by twisting it round and round. EG *He screwed the lid tightly onto the top of the jar... ...hollow tubes which screw together.* V-ERG+A

screw up. 1 If you **screw up** your face or something flexible, you twist it or squeeze it so that it no longer has its natural shape. EG *She screwed up her eyes as she faced the sun... She screwed up the paper and tossed it in the bin.* PHRASAL VB : V+O+ADV **2** If you **screw** something **up**, you cause it to fail or be spoiled. EG *He can't do that; that screws up all my arrangements.* V+O+ADV Informal

screwdriver /skru:draɪvə/, **screwdrivers.** A **screwdriver** is a tool that is used for turning screws. It consists of a metal rod with a thin end that fits into the top of the screw. See picture at TOOLS. N COUNT

scribble /skrɪbə[0]l/, **scribbles, scribbling, scribbled. 1** If you **scribble** something, you write it quickly and roughly. EG *She was scribbling a letter to her mother... We were scribbling away furiously.* V+O OR V : OFT+A

2 To **scribble** also means to make meaningless marks or rough drawings using a pencil or pen. EG *Someone's scribbled all over the wall.* V+A

3 You can refer to something that has been written or drawn quickly and roughly as **scribble** or a **scribble**. EG *She was looking at my scribble, trying to work out what it said... There are scribbles on the lift wall.* N UNCOUNT OR N COUNT

scrimp /skrɪmp/, **scrimps, scrimping, scrimped.** If you **scrimp and save**, you live cheaply and spend as little money as possible. EG *I was scrimping and saving to buy necessities.* PHRASE

script /skrɪpt/, **scripts. 1** The **script** of a play, film, or television programme is the written version of it. EG *You can't have good acting without a decent script.* N COUNT

2 You can refer to a particular system of writing as a particular **script**. EG *...the Arabic script.* N COUNT OR N UNCOUNT

3 You can refer to handwriting as **script**. EG *Nobody could decipher my microscopic script.* N UNCOUNT Literary

scripture /skrɪptʃə/, **scriptures.** You use **scripture** or **scriptures** to refer to writings that are regarded as sacred in a particular religion, for example the Bible in Christianity. EG *They invoked Hindu scripture to justify their position... The scripture says, 'Man cannot live on bread alone.'* N UNCOUNT OR N COUNT

scriptwriter /skrɪptraɪtə/, **scriptwriters.** A **scriptwriter** is a person who writes scripts for films or for radio or television programmes. N COUNT

scroll /skrəʊl/, **scrolls.** A **scroll** is a long roll of paper, parchment, or other material with writing on it. EG *...an ancient Chinese scroll.* N COUNT

scrounge /skraʊnd[0]ʒ/, **scrounges, scrounging, scrounged.** If you **scrounge** something such as food or money, you get it by asking someone for it, rather than by buying it or earning it. EG *He had come over to scrounge a few cans of food... She was always scrounging.* V+O OR V Informal

scrounger /skraʊnd[0]ʒə/, **scroungers.** If you call someone a **scrounger**, you mean that they try to get things such as money or food without working for them. N COUNT Informal

scrub /skrʌb/, **scrubs, scrubbing, scrubbed. 1** If you **scrub** something, you rub it hard in order to clean it, using a stiff brush and water. EG *They scrub the kitchen floor every day... He scrubbed his hands at the sink.* ▸ used as a noun. EG *That floor needs a good scrub.* V+O OR V; ▸ N SING

2 If you **scrub** dirt or stains off something, you remove them by rubbing hard. EG *There was a stain on the collar and he tried to scrub it off.* V+O+A

3 Scrub consists of low trees and bushes in an area that has very little rain. EG *The country is flat, grassy, and covered in scrub.* N UNCOUNT

scruff /skrʌf/, **scruffs.** If someone holds you **by the scruff of** your **neck**, they hold the back of your neck or collar. EG *Don't pick up a puppy by the scruff of its neck.* PHRASE

scruffy /skrʌfi[1]/, **scruffier, scruffiest.** Someone or something that is **scruffy** is dirty and untidy. EG *We looked scruffy... ...a scruffy child.* ADJ QUALIT

scrum /skrʌm/, **scrums.** A **scrum** in the game of rugby is a formation in which players from each side form a tight group and push against each other with their heads down in an attempt to get the ball. N COUNT

scruples /skru:pə[0]lz/ are moral principles or beliefs that make you unwilling to do something that seems wrong. EG *He had no scruples about borrowing money... ...religious scruples.* N PLURAL

scrupulous /skru:pjə[4]ləs/. Someone who is **scrupulous 1** takes great care to do what is fair, honest, or morally right. EG *The paper was not entirely scrupulous in setting out its assumptions.* ◊ **scrupulously.** EG *...the pressure on manufacturers to behave scrupulously.* **2** is thorough, exact, and pays careful attention to detail. EG *...a historian with a reputation for scrupulous scholarship... They pay scrupulous attention to style.* ◊ **scrupulously.** EG *Everything was scrupulously clean.* ADJ QUALIT; ◊ ADV; ADJ QUALIT; ◊ ADV

scrutinize /skru:tɪnaɪz/, **scrutinizes, scrutinizing, scrutinized;** also spelled **scrutinise.** If you **scrutinize** something, you look at it or examine it very carefully. EG *Bank examiners scrutinized the books of 600 financial institutions... He began to scrutinize the faces in the compartment.* V+O

scrutiny /skru:tɪni[1]/. If something is under **scrutiny**, it is being studied or observed very carefully. EG *At these visits the whole college comes under scrutiny... ...close scrutiny by explosives experts.* N UNCOUNT

scuff /skʌf/, **scuffs, scuffing, scuffed.** If you **scuff** your feet, you drag them along the ground by walking without lifting them. EG *My sister was scuffing her feet as we walked down the road.* V+O

Does a scruffy child have scuffed shoes?

scuffed /skʌft/. If shoes are **scuffed**, their surface has been damaged by rubbing and knocking against things. EG *...a man in a baggy suit and scuffed shoes.* ADJ QUALIT

scuffle /skʌfəºl/, **scuffles, scuffling, scuffled.** A **scuffle** is a rough fight or struggle. EG *Two policemen were injured in the scuffle that followed.* N COUNT
▸ used as a verb. EG *The girls scuffled for the best seats.* ▸ V

scullery /skʌləri¹/, **sculleries.** A **scullery** is a small room next to a kitchen where washing and other domestic work is done. N COUNT

sculpt /skʌlpt/, **sculpts, sculpting, sculpted.** When a sculpture is made, you can say that it **is sculpted**. EG *...a nude woman, sculpted in marble.* V+O : USU PASS Formal

sculptor /skʌlptə/, **sculptors.** A **sculptor** is someone who makes sculptures. N COUNT

sculpture /skʌlptʃə/, **sculptures. 1** A **sculpture** is a work of art that is produced by carving or shaping stone, wood, or clay. EG *...Aztec sculptures... ...an exhibition of 20th century sculpture.* N COUNT OR N UNCOUNT

2 Sculpture is the art of making sculptures. EG *The college offers classes in sculpture.* N UNCOUNT

sculptured /skʌlptʃəd/. **Sculptured** objects have been carved or shaped from something. EG *...sculptured heads of civic dignitaries.* ADJ CLASSIF

scum /skʌm/. **1 Scum** is a layer of a dirty or unpleasant-looking substance on the surface of a liquid. EG *There was green scum over the pond.* N SING OR N UNCOUNT

2 If you call people **scum**, you are expressing your feelings of dislike and disgust for them. EG *I have to mix with scum.* N PLURAL

scurrilous /skʌrɪləs/. If you say or write something **scurrilous**, you criticize someone unfairly or untruthfully in a way that is likely to damage their reputation. EG *...a scurrilous weekly magazine.* ADJ QUALIT

scurry /skʌri¹/, **scurries, scurrying, scurried.** When people or small animals **scurry** somewhere, they run there quickly and hurriedly. EG *Everyone scurried for cover... A mouse scurried across the floor.* V+A

scuttle /skʌtəºl/, **scuttles, scuttling, scuttled. 1** When people or small animals **scuttle** somewhere, they run there with short, quick steps. EG *A porcupine scuttled across the road.* V+A

2 You can refer to a coal scuttle as a **scuttle**. EG *I began to fill the scuttle with coal.* N COUNT

scythe /saɪð/, **scythes, scything, scythed. 1** A **scythe** is a tool with a long handle and a long curved blade. You use it with a swinging movement to cut long grass or grain. N COUNT

2 If you **scythe** grass or grain, you cut it with a scythe. EG *Jem whistled as he scythed the grass.* V+O OR V

SE is an abbreviation for 'south-east'.

sea /siː/, **seas. 1** The **sea** is the salty water that covers about three-quarters of the earth's surface. EG *I watched the children running into the sea... ...a wrecked ship at the bottom of the sea... ...calm seas... ...sea travel... ...a bit of blue sea.* N COUNT : *the*+N; ALSO N UNCOUNT

2 A **sea** is a large area of salty water that is sometimes part of an ocean and sometimes surrounded by land. EG *...the North Sea... ...the Caspian Sea.* N COUNT

3 Sea is used in these phrases. **3.1 At sea** means on or under the sea, far away from land. EG *...a storm at sea... Submarines can stay at sea for weeks.* **3.2** You can say that someone is **at sea** when they are in a state of confusion or uncertainty. **3.3** If you travel or send something **by sea**, you travel or you send it in a ship. EG *They sent all the heavy equipment by sea.* **3.4** If you spend some time **by the sea**, you spend it at the seaside. EG *...a pleasant weekend by the sea.* **3.5** If something floats **out to sea**, it floats away from the shore. If you look **out to sea**, you look across the sea from the shore. EG *The little boat was swept out to sea... He stared out to sea.* PHRASES

4 A **sea** of people or things is a very large number of them. EG *...a sea of white faces... ...a sea of buttercups... ...a sea of troubles.* N PART : SING

seabed /siːbɛd/. The **seabed** is the ground under the sea. EG *...pipelines on the sea-bed.* N SING : *the*+N

seabird /siːbɜːd/, **seabirds. Seabirds** are birds that live near the sea and get their food from it. N COUNT

seaboard /siːbɔːd/, **seaboards.** A **seaboard** is the part of a country that is next to the sea. EG *...the eastern seaboard of the United States.* N COUNT : USU SING Formal

seafaring /siːfɛərɪŋ/. **Seafaring** people are people who work as sailors. EG *Britain has always been a seafaring nation.* ADJ CLASSIF : ATTRIB

seafood /siːfuːd/ refers to shellfish such as lobsters, mussels, and crabs, and to other sea creatures that you can eat. EG *...fresh local seafood... ...a seafood restaurant.* N UNCOUNT

seafront /siːfrʌnt/, **seafronts.** The **seafront** is the part of a seaside town that is next to the sea. It usually consists of a road with buildings facing the sea. EG *I walked along the seafront.* N COUNT

sea-going. Sea-going boats and ships are designed for travelling on the sea, rather than on lakes, rivers, or canals. ADJ CLASSIF : ATTRIB

seagull /siːgʌl/, **seagulls.** A **seagull** is a common kind of seabird. EG *Our boat was followed by a flock of seagulls.* N COUNT

seal /siːl/, **seals, sealing, sealed. 1** A **seal** is **1.1** an official mark that is fixed to documents to show that they are legal or genuine. **1.2** something fixed to a container or letter that must be broken before the container or letter can be opened. EG *I noticed that the seals of the packet had been broken.* N COUNT

2 If you **seal** an envelope, you stick down the flap so that the envelope cannot be opened without being torn. V+O
◇ **sealed.** EG *He took a sealed envelope from the folder on his desk.* ◇ ADJ CLASSIF

3 If you **seal** an opening, you fill it or cover it with something in order to prevent air, gas, or a liquid getting in or out. EG *...a thin tube sealed at one end... Small cracks can be sealed with this compound.* V+O : USU PASS

4 If something **puts** or **sets the seal on** something, it makes it definite or confirms how it is going to be. EG *The recent floods put the seal on a disappointing summer... The experience set the seal on their friendship.* PHRASE

5 If someone **gives** something their **seal of approval**, they officially say that they approve of it. PHRASE

6 A **seal** is also a large, shiny animal without legs, which eats fish and lives partly on land and partly in the sea. N COUNT

seal off. If you **seal** a place **off**, you prevent people from getting into it or out of it by blocking all the entrances. PHRASAL VB : V+O+ADV

sea level. If you are at **sea level**, you are at the same level as the surface of the sea. EG *...land below sea level.* N UNCOUNT

sea lion, sea lions. A **sea lion** is a type of large seal. N COUNT

seam /siːm/, **seams. 1** A **seam** is a line of stitches which joins two pieces of cloth together. N COUNT

2 When something is very full, you can say that it is **bursting** or **bulging at the seams**. EG *Schools and universities are bulging at the seams.* PHRASE

3 A **seam** is also a long, narrow layer of coal beneath the ground. N COUNT

seaman /siːməᵊn/, **seamen.** A **seaman** is a sailor. EG *...with a crew of experienced seamen.* N COUNT

seamed /siːmd/. If something is **seamed**, it has long, thin lines on its surface. EG *His brown face was seamed and wrinkled.* ADJ QUALIT

séance /seɪɑːns/, **séances;** also spelled **seance.** A **séance** is a meeting in which people try to speak to people who are dead. N COUNT

search /sɜːtʃ/, **searches, searching, searched. 1** If you **search** for something, you look carefully for it. If you **search** a place, you look carefully for something there. EG *He glanced around the room, searching for a place to sit... He searched through* V+A OR V+O : OFT+*for*

a drawer and eventually found the photo... I searched the city for a room.

2 If the police **search** you, they examine your clothing because they think that you may have something hidden in it. EG *We were stopped by the police and searched.* V+O

3 A **search** is an attempt to find something by looking for it. EG *I found the keys after a long search... ...the search for oil.* ● If you go **in search** of something, you try to find it. EG *We went round the town in search of a place to stay.* N COUNT ● PHRASE

4 When you are trying to think of something, you can say that you **are searching** for it or **are searching** your mind for it. EG *She searched her mind for some words of comfort.* V OR V+O: OFT+*for*

search out. If you **search** something **out**, you keep looking for it until you find it. EG *I have been searching out old sewing patterns.* PHRASAL VB: V+O+ADV

searching /sɜ:tʃɪŋ/. A **searching** question or look is intended to discover the truth about something. EG *We had to answer the searching questions of the Social Security officials... He gave the girl a quick, searching look.* ◊ **searchingly**. EG *She was looking at me searchingly.* ADJ QUALIT: USU ATTRIB ◊ ADV

search party, search parties. A **search party** is an organized group of people who are searching for someone who is lost or missing. N COUNT

searing /sɪərɪŋ/. **1** A **searing** pain is very sharp and causes a burning feeling. EG *He felt a searing pain in his left arm.* ADJ QUALIT: ATTRIB

2 A **searing** speech or piece of writing strongly criticizes something or someone. EG *...a searing exposure of modern America.* ADJ QUALIT: ATTRIB

seashell /si:ʃɛl/, **seashells.** A **seashell** is the empty shell of a small sea creature. N COUNT

seashore /si:ʃɔ:/, **seashores.** The **seashore** is the part of a coast where the land slopes down into the sea. EG *...a walk along the seashore.* N COUNT

seasick /si:sɪk/. If someone is **seasick** when they are travelling in a boat, they vomit or feel sick because of the way the boat is moving. EG *He felt seasick.* ◊ **seasickness**. EG *He suffers from seasickness.* ADJ QUALIT ◊ N UNCOUNT

seaside /si:saɪd/. The **seaside** is a place next to the sea, especially one where people go for their holidays. EG *We spent the weekend at the seaside... ...a seaside resort.* N SING: *the*+N

season /si:zə⁰n/, **seasons, seasoning, seasoned.**
1 The **seasons** are the four periods into which a year is divided, because there is different weather in each period. They are called spring, summer, autumn, and winter. EG *...the endless cycle of the seasons.* N COUNT

2 A **season** is also the period during each year when something usually happens. EG *...the breeding season... ...the planting season... When does the football season end?* N COUNT+SUPP

3 The holiday **season** is the time when most people have their holiday. EG *Hotel rooms are available even at the height of the season.* ● If you go to a place **out of season**, you go there when it is not the busy holiday period. EG *We've often been there out of season, and it's much nicer.* N COUNT ● PHRASE

4 If a fruit or vegetable is **in season**, it is the time of year when it is ready for eating and is widely available. If it is **out of season**, it is not widely available. PHRASE

5 A **season** of films is several of them shown as a series because they are connected in some way. EG *...a season of Clint Eastwood movies.* N COUNT+SUPP

6 If you **season** food, you add salt, pepper, or spices to it in order to improve its flavour. EG *...tuna fish seasoned with salt.* V+O: OFT+*with*

7 See also **seasoned, seasoning**.

seasonal /si:zənə⁰l/. Something that is **seasonal** happens during one particular time of the year. EG *People found seasonal work on farms.* ◊ **seasonally**. EG *People there are employed seasonally.* ADJ CLASSIF ◊ ADV

seasoned /si:zə⁰nd/ means having a lot of experience of something. For example, a **seasoned** traveller is someone who has travelled a lot. EG *...a seasoned election campaigner... ...seasoned troops.* ADJ QUALIT: ATTRIB

seasoning /si:zə⁰nɪŋ/ is salt, pepper, or spices that are added to food to improve its flavour. N UNCOUNT

season ticket, season tickets. A **season ticket** is a train or bus ticket that you can use continually during a certain period, without having to pay each time. N COUNT

seat /si:t/, **seats, seating, seated. 1** A **seat** is an object that you can sit on, for example a chair. EG *Come in, take a seat... Roger sat down carefully, using the edge of the crate as a seat... There was some beer on the back seat of the car... I rang the theatre to see if I could get seats for the show.* N COUNT

2 The **seat** of a chair is the part that you sit on. N COUNT

3 If you **seat** yourself somewhere, you sit down. EG *'Thank you,' she said, seating herself on the sofa.* ◊ **seated**. EG *General Tomkins was seated behind his desk.* V-REFL: OFT+A ◊ ADJ PRED

4 A building or vehicle that **seats** a particular number of people has enough seats for that number. EG *The hall seats four hundred.* V+O: NO CONT

5 The **seat** of a piece of clothing is the part that covers your bottom. EG *Her jeans had a gaping hole in the seat.* N SING: *the*+N

6 When someone is elected to parliament, you can say that they or their party have won a **seat**. EG *The Nationalists failed to win a single seat.* N COUNT

7 If you **take a back seat**, you allow other people to have all the power and to make all the decisions. PHRASE

seat-belt, seat-belts. A **seat-belt** is a strap attached to a seat in a car or an aeroplane. You fasten it across your body in order to prevent yourself being thrown out of the seat if there is a sudden movement. See picture at CAR. N COUNT

seating /si:tɪŋ/. **1** You can refer to the seats in a place as the **seating**. EG *The plastic seating was uncomfortable.* N UNCOUNT

2 A **seating** plan indicates how the seats are arranged in a theatre or where people will sit on a formal occasion. EG *Here's a seating plan of the concert hall.* ADJ CLASSIF: ATTRIB

seaweed /si:wi:d/, **seaweeds. Seaweed** is a plant that grows in the sea. N MASS

sec /sɛk/, **secs.** If you ask someone to wait a **sec**, you are asking them to wait for a very short time. EG *Hang on a sec. Let me have a look... I'll join you in a sec.* N COUNT Informal British

secluded /si¹klu:dɪ²d/. A **secluded** place is quiet, private, and undisturbed. EG *...secluded beaches... ...in a secluded corner of the garden.* ADJ QUALIT

seclusion /si¹klu:ʒə⁰n/. If you are living in **seclusion**, you are in a quiet place away from other people. EG *You'd probably feel more at home in the seclusion of Flint Street.* N UNCOUNT

second, seconds, seconding, seconded; pronounced /sɛkənd/ except for paragraph 10, when it is pronounced /sɪ²kɒnd/.

1 A **second** is one of the sixty parts that a minute is divided into. EG *She looked at me for a few seconds... The rocket was rising at the rate of 300 feet per second.* N COUNT

2 A **second** is also used to mean a very short time. EG *Could I see your book for a second?* N COUNT

3 If you say that something happens in **seconds** or within **seconds**, you mean that it happens very quickly and suddenly. EG *In seconds the building had gone up in flames... Seconds later they were outside.* N PLURAL

4 The **second** item in a series is the one that you count as number two: see entry headed NUMBER. EG *...his father's second marriage... ...in the second week of August... ...the second of February.* ORDINAL

Would you choose a secluded place for doing things in secret?

5 You say **second** when you want to make a second point or give a second reason for something. EG *And second, this kind of policy doesn't help to create jobs.* ADV SEN

6 If you experience something **at second hand**, you are told about it by other people rather than experiencing it yourself. EG *I knew nothing about Judith except what I'd heard at second hand.* ● See also **second-hand**. PHRASE

7 If you say that something is **second only to** something else, you mean that the other thing is the only one that is better than it. EG *San Francisco is second only to New York as the tourist city of the States.* PHRASE

8 Seconds are goods that are sold cheaply in shops because they are slightly faulty. N COUNT: USU PLURAL

9 If you **second** a proposal in a meeting or debate, you formally agree with it so that it can then be discussed or voted on. EG *I seconded Gene's nomination.* V+O

10 If you **are seconded** somewhere, you are moved there temporarily in order to do special duties. EG *He was for a time seconded to the army.* V+O: USU PASS

11 second nature: see **nature**.

secondary /sɛkəndə^{0}ri^1/. **1** Something that is **secondary** is less important than something else. EG *Many older people still believe that men's careers come first and women's careers are secondary.* ADJ QUALIT

2 Secondary education is given to pupils between the ages of 11 or 12 and 18. ADJ CLASSIF: ATTRIB

secondary school, secondary schools. A **secondary school** is a school for pupils between the ages of 11 or 12 and 18. N COUNT

second-best. Something that is **second-best** is not as good as the best thing of its kind but is better than all the other things of that kind. EG *...businessmen in their second-best suits... Hiring professionals is impractical, so as a second-best, we will use unpaid amateurs.* ADJ CLASSIF OR N SING

second-class. 1 Second-class things are things which are regarded as less valuable or less important than other things of the same kind. EG *There can be no second-class citizens in a free society.* ADJ CLASSIF: ATTRIB

2 A **second-class** ticket allows you to travel in the ordinary type of accommodation on a train, aircraft, or ship. EG *He sat in a second-class carriage reading a local newspaper.* N UNCOUNT: USU N MOD

3 Second-class postage is a cheaper and slower type of postage. EG *...a second-class stamp... There's no hurry - send it second-class.* ADJ CLASSIF OR ADV

4 A **second-class** degree is a good or average degree obtained from a British university. ADJ CLASSIF: ATTRIB

second cousin, second cousins. Your **second cousins** are the children of your parents' first cousins. N COUNT

second-hand. 1 Something that is **second-hand** is not new and has been owned by someone else. EG *...second-hand clothing... ...second-hand cars... It's a book he bought second-hand, years ago.* ADJ CLASSIF OR ADV

2 A **second-hand** shop sells second-hand goods. EG *He buys his clothes from a second-hand shop.* ADJ CLASSIF: ATTRIB

3 If you hear a story **second-hand**, you hear it from someone who has heard it from someone else. EG *...a second-hand report.* ADV OR ADJ CLASSIF

second language. Someone's **second language** is a language which is not their native language but which they use at work or at school. EG *...learners of English as a second language.* N SING

secondly /sɛkəndli^1/. You say **secondly** when you want to make a second point or give a second reason for something. EG *Firstly, the energy already exists in the ground. Secondly, there's plenty of it.* ADV SEN

second-rate. If you describe something as **second-rate**, you mean that it is of poor quality. EG *...a second-rate department store... ...second-rate ideas... ...second-rate students.* ADJ QUALIT

second thoughts. 1 If you **have second thoughts** about a decision that you have made, you have doubts about it and begin to wonder if it was wise. PHRASE

2 You say **on second thoughts** when you suddenly change your mind about something that you are saying or something that you have decided to do. EG *Tell me more about America. No, on second thoughts, tell me more about your family.* PHRASE

secrecy /siːkrɪsi^1/ involves keeping something secret. EG *She stressed the necessity of absolute secrecy... The operation was conducted in secrecy.* N UNCOUNT

secret /siːkrɪt/, **secrets. 1** Something that is **secret** is known about by only a small number of people, and is not told or shown to anyone else. EG *The letter was marked 'secret'... We came through a secret back entrance... ...secret negotiations.* ADJ QUALIT

◊ **secretly.** EG *Their work had to be done secretly.* ◊ ADV

2 If you do something **in secret**, you do it without anyone else knowing. EG *I arranged to meet him in secret... He'll manufacture it in secret.* PHRASE

3 You use **secret** to describe someone who does something that they do not tell other people about. For example, if someone is your **secret** admirer, they admire you secretly. EG *She had become a secret drinker.* ◊ **secretly.** EG *He secretly hoped I would one day change my mind... Secretly, perhaps, some of them were also a little scared.* ADJ CLASSIF: ATTRIB ◊ ADV OR ADV SEN

4 A **secret** is a fact that is known by only a small number of people, and is not told to anyone else. EG *The results of these experiments remain a secret... I'll tell you a secret... She has made no secret of the fact that she wants a job.* N COUNT

5 If you describe a way of behaving as the **secret** of achieving something, you mean that it is the best way or the only way to achieve it. EG *The secret is not to involve too many other people... Think big! This is the secret of success.* N SING: *the*+N

secret agent, secret agents. A **secret agent** is a person who is employed by a government to find out the secrets of other governments. N COUNT

secretarial /sɛkrətɛəriəl/. **Secretarial** work or training involves the work of a secretary. EG *...a secretarial course... ...secretarial staff.* ADJ CLASSIF: ATTRIB

secretariat /sɛkrətɛəriət/, **secretariats.** A **secretariat** is a department that is responsible for the administration of an international political organization. EG *...a senior member of the U.N. Secretariat.* N COUNT

secretary /sɛkrətə^{0}ri^1/, **secretaries. 1** A **secretary** is a person who is employed to do office work, such as typing letters, answering phone calls, and arranging meetings. N COUNT

2 The **secretary** of a club or other organization is the person whose job involves keeping records and writing letters. EG *If you want to join the cricket club, write to the secretary.* N COUNT

3 Secretary is used in the titles of ministers who are in charge of the main government departments. EG *...the Social Services Secretary... ...one of the best Foreign Secretaries since the war.* N COUNT+SUPP

secrete /si^{1}kriːt/, **secretes, secreting, secreted.**

1 If part of a plant, animal, or human **secretes** a liquid, it produces it. EG *The skin pores enlarge and secrete more oil.* ◊ **secretion** /si^{1}kriːʃə^{0}n/. EG *Hormone secretion is controlled by the pituitary gland.* V+O ◊ N UNCOUNT

2 If you **secrete** something somewhere, you hide it there so that nobody will find it. EG *...clothes that she had secreted in her basket.* V+O: OFT+A Formal

secretive /siːkrɪtɪv, si^{1}kriːtɪv/. If you are **secretive**, you like to keep your knowledge, feelings, or intentions hidden from other people. EG *She's very secretive about money matters.* ADJ QUALIT

secret service, secret services. A country's **secret service** is a secret government department whose job is to find out enemy secrets and to prevent its own government's secrets from being discovered. N COUNT

sect /sɛkt/, **sects.** A **sect** is a group of people that has separated from a larger group and has a N COUNT particular set of religious or political beliefs. EG *Two religious sects came into being, one of which was the Quakers... ...an extremist Protestant sect... ...the dictatorship of a socialist minority sect.*

sectarian /sɛktɛəriən/. **1 Sectarian** means resulting from the differences between sects. EG *The conference had collapsed in sectarian squabbles.* ADJ CLASSIF: ATTRIB Formal

2 Someone who is **sectarian** strongly supports a particular sect. EG *This group is frequently attacked as sectarian and fanatical.* ADJ QUALIT Formal

section /sɛkʃə[0]n/, **sections.** A **section** of something is one of the parts which the thing is divided into or is formed from. EG *I passed the written part but failed the oral section... ...the first-class section of the train... ...well-known people from all sections of public life.* • See also **cross-section**. N COUNT: USU+SUPP

sector /sɛktə/, **sectors. 1** A **sector** of a country's economy is a particular part of it. EG *...the manufacturing sector... ...Government support for the voluntary sector... ...the movement of weak firms from the private sector to the public sector.* N COUNT: USU+SUPP

2 A **sector** of a large group is a smaller group which is part of it. EG *...a very narrow sector of the Labour Party... ...resistance from all sectors of the Black community.* N COUNT+SUPP

secular /sɛkjə[4]lə/. You use **secular** to describe things that have no connection with religion. EG *...secular education... The choir sings both sacred and secular music... ...a new secular morality.* ADJ CLASSIF

secure /sɪ[2]kjʊə/, **secures, securing, secured. 1** If you **secure** something, you get it after a lot of effort. EG *He secured only 526 votes... We spent the morning securing their agreement... I did everything possible to secure him a posting.* V+O OR V+O+O Formal

2 If you **secure** a place, you make it safe from harm or attack. EG *They endeavoured to secure the bridge from the threat of attack.* V+O: OFT+ *from/against* Formal

3 If a building is **secure**, it is tightly locked or well protected, so that people cannot enter it or leave it. EG *Try and make your house as secure as you can.* ADJ QUALIT: USU PRED

4 If you **secure** an object, you fasten it firmly to another object. EG *A plastic box was secured to the wall by screws.* V+O

5 If an object is **secure**, it is fixed firmly in position. EG *Check that the leads to the battery are in good condition and secure.* ◊ **securely**. EG *The chain seemed to be securely fastened.* ADJ QUALIT: USU PRED ◊ ADV

6 If a position or power is **secure**, it is safe and certain not to be lost. EG *You've got a secure job... It was a time when authority was secure and unchallenged.* ◊ **securely**. EG *The strike was securely under the union's control.* ADJ QUALIT ◊ ADV

7 A **secure** base or foundation is strong and reliable. EG *You need a secure base for the business.* ADJ QUALIT

8 If you feel **secure**, you feel safe and happy and are not worried about life. EG *We feel financially secure.* ADJ QUALIT: USU PRED

security /sɪ[2]kjʊərɪ[1]ti[1]/, **securities. 1 Security** refers to all the precautions that are taken to protect a country, for example from war, spying, or violence. EG *...a possible threat to national security... Security forces were patrolling the streets... ...a top security prison.* N UNCOUNT: USU N MOD

2 Security is legal protection against possible harm or loss. EG *He hasn't got security of employment... The tenants are exploited and have no security of tenure.* N UNCOUNT

3 A feeling of **security** is a feeling of being safe and not having worries. EG *Children count on their parents for love and security.* N UNCOUNT

4 Securities are stocks, shares, bonds, or other certificates that you buy as a way of investing money, in order to earn regular interest from them or to sell them later for a profit. N COUNT: USU PLURAL Technical

5 See also **social security**.

sedate /sɪ[2]deɪt/, **sedates, sedating, sedated. 1** Someone who is **sedate** is quiet, calm, and rather dignified. EG *Irene was graver and more sedate, though equally brilliant.* ◊ **sedately**. EG *He walked sedately down the lane.* ADJ QUALIT ◊ ADV

2 If you **are sedated**, you are given a drug to calm you or to make you sleep. V+O: USU PASS

sedation /sɪ[2]deɪʃə[0]n/ is the use of drugs in order to calm someone or to make them sleep. EG *Freddie was still under sedation in his parents' house.* N UNCOUNT

sedative /sɛdətɪv/, **sedatives. 1** A **sedative** is a drug that calms you or makes you sleep. EG *The doctor may prescribe a sedative... Dolly had taken a sedative.* N COUNT

2 Something that is **sedative** has the effect of calming you or making you sleep. EG *This drink has been recognised to have sedative properties.* ADJ CLASSIF

sedentary /sɛdəntə[0]ri[1]/. If you have a **sedentary** occupation or way of life, you sit down a lot of the time and do not have much exercise. EG *I'm bored with sedentary work... ...the sedentary lives we lead.* ADJ QUALIT

sediment /sɛdɪmə[2]nt/, **sediments. Sediment** is **1** solid material that settles at the bottom of a liquid. EG *Most of the sediment has sunk to the bottom.* **2** the material such as earth and rocks that has been carried along and then left somewhere by water, ice, or wind. EG *Rivers are bringing lots of sediment down to the sea... The lake sediments preserved evidence of an unusual hunting accident.* N UNCOUNT OR N COUNT

seduce /sɪ[1]djuːs/, **seduces, seducing, seduced. 1** If something **seduces** you, it is so attractive that it tempts you to do something that you would not normally approve of. EG *He was seduced into saying that he would do it... Both he and his partner had been seduced by the grandeur of the scheme.* V+O: OFT+ *into*

2 If someone **seduces** another person, especially a young inexperienced person, they persuade that person to have sex with them. EG *He used to seduce all the maids up there in his house.* ◊ **seduction** /sɪ[1]dʌkʃə[0]n/, **seductions**. EG *The girl's seduction is an important part of the story.* V+O ◊ N COUNT OR N UNCOUNT

seductive /sɪ[1]dʌktɪv/. **1** Something that is **seductive** is very attractive or tempting. EG *These are seductive arguments.* ◊ **seductively**. EG *...when the music is played more seductively.* ADJ QUALIT ◊ ADV

2 A person, especially a woman, who is **seductive** is very attractive sexually. EG *...the seductive softness of Mary's long limbs.* ◊ **seductively**. EG *Percival was leaning seductively forward and speaking in a low voice.* ADJ QUALIT ◊ ADV

see /siː/, **sees, seeing, saw** /sɔː/, **seen** /siːn/. **1** When you **see** something, you notice it using your eyes, or you look at it. EG *We suddenly saw a boat through a gap in the fog... I saw him glance at his watch... He went to India to see the Taj Mahal... Did you see 'The Doctor's Dilemma' on telly last night?... Some animals have the ability to see in very dim light.* V+O OR V: NO IMPER, NO CONT

2 If you **see** someone, you visit them or meet them. EG *Perhaps she did not wish to come and see me... It would be a good idea for you to see a doctor for a checkup... They still saw quite a lot of Anthony.* V+O

3 If you **see** someone to a particular place, you accompany them to make sure that they get there safely. EG *I went down to see her safely to her car.* V+O+A

4 If you **see** that something is true or exists, you realise that it is true or exists, by carefully observing it or thinking about it. EG *Etta could see that he wasn't listening... She begins to see that she has a choice... I was trying not to let the jailers see my agitation.* V+REPORT OR V+O: NO IMPER, NO CONT

5 If you **see** what someone means or **see** why something happened, you understand what they mean or understand why it happened. EG *'Yes,' she said. 'I see what you mean.'... I can see why Mr Smith is worried... Somebody got killed and I don't see how.* V+O OR V+REPORT: NO CONT, NO IMPER

How many phrases are there with the word 'see' in them?

6 You say '**I see**' to indicate that you understand what someone is telling you. EG *'Humbert is Dolly's real father.' – 'I see.'* CONVENTION

7 You say '**you see**' when you are telling someone something and you are very concerned that they should understand it. EG *That's very nice of you but, you see, Kurt, I have no money.* ADV SEN

8 If you ask what someone **sees** in a particular person or thing, you want to know what they find attractive about that person or thing. EG *'What can she see in him?' asked another friend.* V+O+*in*: NO IMPER, NO CONT

9 If you say that you will **see** what is happening or what the situation is, you mean that you intend to find out what is happening or what the situation is. EG *I'd better go and see what he wants... I must phone her up and see if she can come tonight.* V+REPORT: NO CONT

10 If you say that you will **see if** you can do something, you mean that you will try to do it. EG *See if you can find my birthday book somewhere.* PHRASE

● When someone asks you for help, if you say that you will **see what you can do**, you mean that you will try to help them. ● PHRASE

11 If you **see** that something is done or if you **see to it** that it is done, you make sure that it is done. EG *See that everything is marked with your initials... I'll see to it that there is some action.* V OR PHRASE +REPORT: ONLY *that*

12 If you **see** one thing as another thing, you have the opinion that it is that other thing. EG *I did not see his determination as a defect... The problem, as I see it, is not advice but direct help.* V+O+A

13 If you say that a person or a period of time **sees** a particular change or event, you mean that the change or event takes place while that person is alive or during that period of time. EG *In recent times we have seen a huge split develop between rich and poor nations... How would you like to see education changed?... Last week saw a drop in interest rates.* V+O

14 If you **see** something happening in the future, you imagine it, or predict that it will happen. EG *She saw herself seated behind the cash register, smiling... Can you see women going into combat carrying forty-pound guns?* V+O: USU+A, NO IMPER

15 People say '**I'll see**' or '**We'll see**' to indicate that they do not intend to make a decision immediately, and will decide later. EG *'Will you write to me?' she asked. 'I'll see,' he said.* CONVENTION

16 See is used in books to indicate to readers that they should look at another part of the book, or at another book, because more information is given there. EG *Reference to this problem is made elsewhere (see Chapter 14).* V+O: ONLY IMPER

17 People say '**let me see**' or '**let's see**' when they are trying to remember something, or are trying to find something. EG *I think I've got her name somewhere. Now let me see.* PHRASE

18 You can use '**seeing that**' or '**seeing as**' to introduce the reason for what you are doing or saying. EG *Seeing that you're the guest on this little trip, you can decide where we're going.* CONJ Informal

19 'See you' and '**see you later**' are informal ways of saying goodbye to someone when you expect to meet them again soon. CONVENTION Informal

see about. 1 When you **see about** something, you arrange for it to be done or provided. EG *Rudolph went into the station to see about Thomas's ticket.* PHRASAL VB: V+PREP **2** If someone says that they will do something, and you say '**We'll see about that**', you mean that you intend to prevent them from doing it. EG *'We're not moving.' – 'We'll see about that.'* CONVENTION

see off. When you **see** someone **off**, you go with them to the station, airport, or port that they are leaving from, and say goodbye to them there. PHRASAL VB: V+O+ADV

see through. 1 If you **see through** someone or **see through** what they are doing, you realize what their intentions are, even though they are trying to hide them. EG *She had learned to see through him... The jailers saw through my scheme.* PHRASAL VB: V+PREP, HAS PASS **2** See also **see-through**.

see to. If you **see to** something that needs attention, you deal with it. EG *Don't you worry about that. I'll see to that... He went out to see to the chickens.* PHRASAL VB: V+PREP: HAS PASS

seed /si:d/, **seeds. 1** A **seed** is the small, hard part of a plant from which a new plant grows. EG *...sunflower seeds... ...a packet of seed... There's something so satisfying about planting seeds.* N COUNT OR N UNCOUNT

2 You can use **seeds** to refer to the cause or beginning of a feeling or process that gradually develops and becomes stronger or more important. EG *The seeds of doubt had been sown... It contains the seeds of its own destruction... This protest contains the seeds of workers' control and socialism.* N PLURAL: *the*+N+*of* Literary

seedling /si:dlıŋ/, **seedlings.** A **seedling** is a young plant that has been grown from a seed. N COUNT

seedy /si:di[1]/. If you describe a person or place as **seedy**, you mean that they look untidy or in bad condition. EG *...a seedy character with a cigarette between his lips... ...a seedy and rundown photographer's studio.* ADJ QUALIT

seek /si:k/, **seeks, seeking, sought** /sɔ:t/. **1** If you **are seeking** something such as a job or a place to live, you are trying to find one. EG *Thousands of people were seeking food and shelter... Books are eagerly sought for and sold on the streets.* V+O OR V+*for* Formal

2 When someone **seeks** something such as peace, revenge, or the answer to a problem, they try to obtain it. EG *Both countries are seeking peace... They are seeking a 10 per cent reduction in their work force.* V+O Formal

3 If you **seek** someone's help or advice, you go to them and ask them for it. EG *I was seeking the help of someone who spoke French.* V+O OR V+*for* Formal

4 If you **seek** to do something, you try to do it. EG *Power stations are seeking to reduce their use of oil... ...anybody who seeks to govern this country.* V+*to*-INF Formal

seek out. If you **seek out** someone or something, you keep looking for them until you find them. EG *It was unusual for anyone to seek out her husband.* PHRASAL VB: V+O+ADV

seem /si:m/, **seems, seeming, seemed. 1** If someone or something **seems** to have a particular quality or attitude, they give the impression of having that quality or attitude. EG *Even minor problems seem important... It seemed like a good idea... You seem to be very interested.* V+C OR V+*to*-INF

2 If something **seems** to be the case, you get the impression that it is the case. EG *There don't seem to be many people here today... It seemed as though I had known them for a long time... Berger's thesis seems right... It seemed that everybody smoked cigarettes.* V+*to*-INF, V+A, V+C, OR V+REPORT: ONLY *that*

3 You use **seem 3.1** to indicate that you are not completely certain that what you are saying is correct. EG *The experiments seem to prove that sugar is not good for you... For the time being, Thatcher seems politically secure.* V+*to*-INF OR V+C **3.2** when you are describing something to indicate that you are not sure that you remember it correctly. EG *I seem to remember that he was a fiction writer.* V+*to*-INF **3.3** when you are giving your opinion about something or asking someone else's opinion. EG *Does that seem nonsense to you?... It did seem to me that she was far too romantic... That would seem a sensible thing to do.* V+C, V+*to*, OR V+*to*-INF

4 If you say that you cannot **seem** to do something, you mean that you have tried to do it and are unable to do it. EG *I can't seem to get to sleep.* V: MODAL+ BROAD NEG +V+*to*-INF

seeming /si:mıŋ/. If you talk about someone's **seeming** willingness or **seeming** interest, for example, you mean that they appear to you to be willing or interested, but you are not sure. EG *...his seeming willingness to participate... The old woman's seeming inattention provoked her.* ADJ CLASSIF: ATTRIB Formal

◊ **seemingly.** EG *...their seemingly limitless resources... Seemingly they don't have any problems.* ◊ SUBMOD OR ADV SEN

seen /si:n/ is the past participle of **see.**

seep /siːp/, **seeps, seeping, seeped.** If a liquid or gas **seeps** through something, it flows through it very slowly and in small amounts. EG *I used to lie awake at night watching the rain seep through the cracks... The petrol fumes seeped into the cab.* V+A

seethe /siːð/, **seethes, seething, seethed. 1** When you **are seething**, you are very angry about something but do not express your feelings about it. EG *I seethed with secret rage... By now David was seething.* V

2 If a place **is seething** with people or things, it is very full of them and they are all moving about. EG *The streets of London seethed with a marching, cheering crowd.* ◇ **seething**. EG *...a seething mass of maggots.* V+*with* ◇ ADJ CLASSIF : ATTRIB

see-through. See-through clothes are made of thin cloth, so that you can see a person's body or underclothes through them. EG *...a see-through blouse... ...the beige see-through dress.* ADJ CLASSIF : ATTRIB

segment /sɛgmə²nt/, **segments. 1** A **segment** of something is one part of it, considered separately from the rest. EG *A much larger segment of the population might be affected... I did show her a segment of the eight-page letter.* N PART

2 A **segment** of an orange or grapefruit is one of the sections into which it is easily divided. N COUNT

segregate /sɛgrɪgeɪt/, **segregates, segregating, segregated.** To **segregate** two groups of people or things means to keep them physically apart from each other. EG *They tried to segregate pedestrians and vehicles... Little effort was made to segregate the sexes.* V+O

segregated /sɛgrɪgeɪtɪ²d/. A **segregated** group of people is kept apart from other people belonging to a different sex, race, or religion. EG *He refused to play before segregated audiences.* ADJ CLASSIF

segregation /sɛgrɪgeɪʃə⁰n/ is the practice of officially keeping apart people of different sexes, or different racial or religious groups. EG *...segregation in the schools... ...articles on apartheid and segregation.* N UNCOUNT

seize /siːz/, **seizes, seizing, seized. 1** If you **seize** something, you take hold of it quickly and firmly. EG *Clarissa seized her arm and dragged her into the kitchen... I seized him by the collar... Seizing the bowl, he ran off.* V+O

2 When a group of people **seize** a place or **seize** control of it, they take control of it quickly and suddenly, using force. EG *The airfield had been seized by US troops... ...plots to seize power in Britain... ...seizing complete control of the Gulf.* V+O

3 When someone **is seized**, they are arrested or captured. EG *A university professor was seized on Wednesday by three armed men.* V+O : USU PASS

4 If you **seize** an opportunity, you take advantage of it, and do something that you want to do. EG *Derrick seized the chance and went to Spain.* V+O

seize on or **seize upon.** If you **seize on** something or **seize upon** it, you show great interest in it, often because it is useful to you. EG *This was one of the points that I seized upon with some force... ...seizing on it as an excuse for a rest period.* PHRASAL VB : V+PREP, HAS PASS

seize up. 1 If a part of your body **seizes up**, it suddenly stops working, because you have strained it. EG *Your back may seize up.* **2** If an engine **seizes up**, it stops working, because of overheating or lack of oil. PHRASAL VB : V+ADV; V+ADV

seize upon. See **seize on**.

seizure /siːʒə/, **seizures. 1** If someone has a **seizure**, they have a sudden violent attack of an illness, especially a heart attack or an epileptic fit. N COUNT

2 If there is a **seizure** of power in a place, a group of people suddenly take control of the place, using force. EG *...the seizure of factories by the workers.* N UNCOUNT

seldom /sɛldə⁰m/. If something **seldom** happens, it happens only occasionally. EG *It seldom rains there... The waiting time was seldom less than four hours... He seldom feels confident.* ADV BRD NEG

select /sɪ²lɛkt/, **selects, selecting, selected. 1** If you **select** something, you choose it from a number of things of the same kind. EG *They select books that seem to them important... There was a large number of people from whom she could select friends.* ◇ **selected**. EG *We were shown carefully selected places during our visit.* V+O ◇ ADJ CLASSIF : ATTRIB

2 A **select** group is a small group of some of the best people or things of their kind. EG *They are members of a select band of professional athletes.* ADJ CLASSIF : ATTRIB

3 Something that is **select** has many desirable features, and is available only to people who have a lot of money or who belong to a high social class. EG *He went to a select New England school.* ADJ QUALIT

selection /sɪ²lɛkʃə⁰n/, **selections. 1 Selection** is the selecting of one or more people or things from a group. EG *She stood little chance of selection... ...the judges' selection process.* N UNCOUNT

2 A **selection** of people or things is a set of them that have been selected from a larger group. EG *The orchestra was playing a selection of tunes from the Merry Widow.* N PART

3 The **selection** of goods in a shop is the particular range of goods that it has available and from which you can choose what you want. EG *We have London's largest selection of office furniture.* N PART

selective /sɪ²lɛktɪv/. **1** A **selective** process applies only to a few things or people. EG *...the selective education of the most talented children.* ◇ **selectively**. EG *Trees are felled selectively.* ADJ CLASSIF : ATTRIB ◇ ADV

2 When someone is **selective**, they choose things carefully, for example the things that they buy or do. EG *They are particularly selective in their television watching.* ◇ **selectively**. EG *A film crew was selectively filming broken windows of shops owned by white people.* ADJ QUALIT ◇ ADV

self /sɛlf/, **selves** /sɛlvz/. Your **self** is your basic personality or nature. EG *By evening she was her normal self again... He was his usual imperturbable self... ...when his wife reveals her real self to him.* N COUNT+POSS

self- 1 combines with adjectives and nouns to refer to something that you do by yourself or do to yourself. For example, if you are self-admiring, you admire yourself. EG *...self-induced catastrophes... ...self-improvement... ...self-pity.* **2** combines with adjectives to describe something such as a device that does something automatically by itself. EG *...a self-locking door... ...self-fulfilling prophecies.*

self-assured. Someone who is **self-assured** shows confidence in what they say and do. EG *His comments were firm and self-assured.* ADJ QUALIT

self-centred. Someone who is **self-centred** is only concerned with their own wants and needs and never thinks about other people. EG *He was much too self-centred to notice her.* ADJ QUALIT

self-confessed is used to describe someone who admits openly that they have a particular characteristic which is usually considered to be bad. EG *...a self-confessed racialist.* ADJ CLASSIF : ATTRIB

self-confident. Someone who is **self-confident** behaves confidently because they feel sure of their abilities or worth. EG *She was remarkably self-confident for her age.* ◇ **self-confidence**. EG *He can only develop self-confidence if he is told he is clever.* ADJ QUALIT ◇ N UNCOUNT

self-conscious. Someone who is **self-conscious** is easily embarrassed and nervous because they feel that everyone is looking at them and judging them. EG *I stood there, feeling self-conscious. Was my hair out of place?... Patrick is self-conscious about his baldness.* ADJ QUALIT

self-contained. 1 Something that is **self-contained** is complete and separate and does not need help or resources from outside. EG *...a society* ADJ CLASSIF

If a shop has a good selection, are you likely to find what you want?

SEMI-MODALS

The verbs **need**, **dare**, and **used** are often called semi-modals. This is because they are similar to modals in some ways but not in all. You can also use **need** and **dare** as main verbs, and they then behave like any ordinary verb. See below, and also the entries in the dictionary for **need** and **dare**.

When **need**, **dare**, and **used** are semi-modals:

Followed by an infinitive

Need and **dare** are followed by an infinitive without 'to': *I didn't dare send it ... You needn't worry.*

Used is always followed by **to**: *I used to feel guilty about him.*

With or without inflections

Need and **used** do not inflect, so the form does not change: *He need not do anything ... Things are worse than they used to be.*

Note that the example with **need** could refer to either the present or the past, but the example with **used** refers only to the past.

Dare can inflect, although it does not always do so in the present tense: *She dare not express her feelings ... No one dares disturb him.* The form **dared** is used to express past time: *Nobody dared open his mouth.*

With negatives

Dare and **used** are frequently followed by **not** or **never**, and **need** is nearly always used with a negative. **Not** can be shortened to **n't** and attached to the verb: *You need never worry about money ... I needn't say any more ... She daren't go upstairs ... They used not to bother.*

In questions

Dare and **need** can also be used in questions, coming in front of the subject: *Dare I ask where you have been? ... Need I say more?*

Referring back

Need, **dare**, and **used** can all be used to refer back to a previous verbal group: *I won't go in by myself, I daren't ... "I'll tell you as much as I know" – "You needn't, I'm not interested" ... She still goes dancing, but not as often as she used to.*

As ordinary verbs

When **dare** and **need** are used as ordinary verbs, they have the normal range of auxiliaries and modals in front of them: *He doesn't dare tell her what he did ... They didn't dare go home ... Do you need any help? ... Don't you dare come here again!*

of immense power, self-contained and well organized.
2 A **self-contained** flat has all its own facilities, so that a person living there does not have to share rooms such as a kitchen or bathroom with other people. ADJ CLASSIF

self-control. Your **self-control** is your ability to control your feelings so that you appear calm, even when you feel angry or afraid. EG *He lost his self-control and cried aloud.* N UNCOUNT

self-defence. 1 **Self-defence** is the use of violence or special physical skills and techniques to protect yourself against someone who is trying to hurt you. EG *He had struck her in self-defence... They carry knives as instruments of self-defence.* N UNCOUNT
2 If you say something **in self-defence**, you give reasons for your behaviour to someone who thinks you have behaved wrongly. EG *'I didn't want to go anyway,' he grumbled in self-defence.* PHRASE

self-employed. If you are **self-employed**, you organize your own work, pay, and taxes, rather than being employed by a person or firm and being paid regular wages or a salary. EG *...a self-employed builder and decorator.* ADJ CLASSIF

self-evident. A fact or situation that is **self-evident** is so obvious that there is no need for proof or explanation. EG *The need for reform was self-evident.* ADJ CLASSIF

self-government is government or control of a country or organization by its own people rather than by others. EG *In Parliament he called for the democratic self-government of the colonies.* N UNCOUNT

self-imposed. A **self-imposed** task, condition, or responsibility is one that you have deliberately accepted for yourself. EG *...troubles that were largely self-imposed... ...self-imposed restrictions.* ADJ CLASSIF

self-indulgent. If you are **self-indulgent**, you allow yourself to have or do things that you enjoy very much. ◊ **self-indulgence**. EG *Temptations to self-indulgence should be resisted.* ADJ QUALIT ◊ N UNCOUNT

self-interest is the attitude of always wanting to do what is best for yourself rather than for anyone else. EG *Are they influenced by duty or self-interest?* N UNCOUNT

selfish /sɛlfɪʃ/. If you are **selfish**, you care only about yourself, and not about other people. EG *...a totally selfish attitude... That's a selfish argument... How mean and selfish you are!* ◊ **selfishly**. EG *Why is he acting so selfishly?* ◊ **selfishness**. EG *He felt ashamed of his selfishness.* ADJ QUALIT ◊ ADV ◊ N UNCOUNT

selfless /sɛlflɪ²s/. If you are **selfless**, you care about other people and their needs rather than considering yourself and your own needs. EG *It was impossible to repay years of selfless devotion.* ADJ QUALIT

self-made is used to describe people who have become successful and rich through their own efforts. EG *My father was a self-made man... ...a self-made millionaire.* ADJ CLASSIF: ATTRIB

self-respect is a feeling of confidence and pride that you have in your own ability and worth. EG *Billy needs to have his self-respect restored.* N UNCOUNT

self-righteous. Someone who is **self-righteous** is convinced that they are right in their beliefs, attitudes, and behaviour and that other people are wrong. EG *...self-righteous indignation... ...the self-righteous assumption that this could never happen to him.* ◊ **self-righteousness**. EG *There was a strong note of self-righteousness in his voice.* ADJ QUALIT ◊ N UNCOUNT

self-sacrifice is the giving up of what you want so that other people can have what they need. EG *The children's education demanded effort and self-sacrifice... I admired her self-sacrifice.* N UNCOUNT

self-satisfied. If you describe someone as **self-satisfied**, you mean that they are so pleased about their achievements or their situation that they do not feel there is any need to do anything more; used showing disapproval. ADJ QUALIT

self-service. A **self-service** shop, restaurant, or garage is one where you serve yourself rather than being served by another person. ADJ CLASSIF

self-sufficient. If a country or group is **self-sufficient**, it is able to produce or make everything that it needs. EG *This country is self-sufficient in energy supplies.* ADJ QUALIT: OFT+*in*

sell /sɛl/, **sells, selling, sold** /səʊld/. 1 If you **sell** something, you let someone have it in return for money. EG *He is going to sell me his car... She sold the house to the local council... I hope to sell the house for £30,000.* V+O, V+O+O, OR V+O+*to*
2 If a shop **sells** a particular thing, it has it available for people to buy. EG *Do you sell flowers?* V+O
3 If something **sells** for a particular price, it is offered for sale at that price. EG *These little books sell for 95p each... ...a pocket calculator selling at the same price.* V+*for/at*
4 If something **sells**, it is bought by the public, usually in fairly large quantities. EG *Their revolutionary jet did not sell well... Our product sells in forty-seven countries.* V: USU+A
5 Something that **sells** a product makes people want to buy the product. EG *Scandal and gossip is what sells newspapers.* V+O
6 If you **sell** yourself, you present yourself in a way which makes people have confidence in you and your abilities. EG *You've got to sell yourself at the interview.* V-REFL Informal
sell off. If you **sell** something **off**, you sell it all, usually because you need the money. EG *He was forced to sell off his land.* PHRASAL VB: V+O+ADV
sell out. 1 If a shop **is sold out** of something or **has sold out** of it, it has sold it all and there is none of it left in the shop. EG *They've sold out of bread.* PHRASAL VB: V+ADV, OFT+*of*
2 If a performance of a play, film, or other entertainment **is sold out**, all the tickets have been sold. V+O+ADV, USU PASS
sell up. If you **sell up**, you sell everything you have, such as your house or your business, because you need the money. PHRASAL VB: V+ADV OR V+O+ADV

seller /sɛlə/, **sellers.** A **seller** is a person or a business that sells something. EG *Umbrella sellers went out of business.* ● See also **best-seller**. N COUNT

Sellotape /sɛləteɪp/ is transparent sticky tape that is sold in rolls and is used for sticking together things such as paper and cardboard. EG *I tried to stick the sign back on with Sellotape.* N UNCOUNT Trademark

selves /sɛlvz/ is the plural of **self.**

semblance /sɛmbləns/. If there is a **semblance** of a particular condition or quality, it appears to exist, even though this may be a false impression. EG *By this time some semblance of order had been established... This indifference helped him to regain a semblance of calm.* N SING+*of* Formal

semen /siːmɛn/ is the liquid containing sperm that is produced by the sex organs of men and male animals. N UNCOUNT

semi- is used to form adjectives and nouns that describe someone or something as being partly, but not completely, in a particular state. For example, someone who is semi-conscious is not completely conscious. EG *...semi-skilled workers... He lived in semi-retirement... We sat in the semi-darkness.* PREFIX

semicircle /sɛmiˈsɜːkə⁰l/, **semicircles.** A **semicircle** is one half of a circle. EG *We sat in a big semicircle round Hunter's desk.* N COUNT

semi-colon, semi-colons. A **semi-colon** is a punctuation mark (;) which is used in writing to separate different parts of a sentence or list or to indicate a pause. N COUNT

semi-detached. A **semi-detached** house is a house that is joined to another house on one side by a shared wall. ▸ used as a noun. EG *They have a small semi-detached.* ADJ CLASSIF ▸ N SING British

Does it make sense to stop a competition at the semi-finals?

semi-final, semi-finals. A **semi-final** is one of the two matches in a competition that are played to decide which two players or teams will compete in the final. EG *We reached the semi-final of the World Cup.* N COUNT

seminar /sɛmɪnɑː/, **seminars.** A **seminar** is a class at a college or university in which the teacher and a small group of students discuss a topic. N COUNT

semi-precious. Semi-precious stones are stones such as opals or turquoises that are used in jewellery. They are less valuable than precious stones such as diamonds, rubies, and sapphires. ADJ CLASSIF : ATTRIB

SEN /ɛs iː ɛn/, **SEN's.** An **SEN** is someone who has successfully completed a two-year practical course in nursing in the United Kingdom. **SEN** is an abbreviation for 'State Enrolled Nurse'. N COUNT

Senate /sɛnɪ¹t/. The **Senate** is the smaller and more important of the two councils in the government of some countries, for example in the U.S.A. EG *This proposal was approved by both the House and the Senate.* N PROPER : the+N

senator /sɛnətə/, **senators.** A **senator** is a member of a law-making senate. EG *...Senator Edward Kennedy.* N COUNT

send /sɛnd/, **sends, sending, sent** /sɛnt/. **1** When you **send** something to someone, you arrange for it to be taken and delivered to them, for example by post. EG *I drafted a letter and sent it to the President... You will be sent a timetable of the election... Send it round in the morning.* V+O : OFT+*to* OR V+O+O

2 If you **send** a radio signal or message, you cause it to go to a place by means of radio waves. EG *Marconi succeeded in sending a signal across the Atlantic.* V+O : USU+A

3 If you **send** someone somewhere, **3.1** you tell them to go there. EG *The doctor sent me to a specialist... Could you send someone round to help?* **3.2** you arrange for them to stay there for a period of time. EG *His parents couldn't afford to send him to university.* V+O+A

4 If something **sends** things or people in a particular direction, it causes them to move in that direction. EG *The stubble was burning in the fields, sending wisps of black smoke into the air... The noise sent them racing towards the bush.* V+O+A OR V+O+-ING

send for. 1 If you **send for** someone, you ask them to come and see you, by sending them a message. EG *She sent for a doctor... We'd better send for the police.* PHRASAL VB : V+PREP, HAS PASS

2 If you **send for** something or **send off for** it, you write and ask for it to be sent to you. EG *Send for the nomination forms before it's too late... I'll send off for them next week.* V+PREP OR V+ADV+PREP, HAS PASS

send in. If you **send in** a report or an application, you send it to a place where it will be officially dealt with. EG *Don't forget to send in your entries for the competition... I was expected to send in a written report every two months.* PHRASAL VB : V+O+ADV

send off. If you **send off** a letter or parcel, you send it somewhere by post. EG *You fill in both parts of the form, then send it off.* PHRASAL VB : V+O+ADV

send off for. See paragraph **2** of **send for**.

send up. If you **send** someone or something **up**, you imitate them in a way that makes them appear foolish. EG *Wodehouse sends up the world of Buchan.* PHRASAL VB : V+O+ADV Informal

senile /siːnaɪl/. If old people become **senile**, they become confused, can no longer remember things, and are unable to look after themselves. EG *The old lady was now half blind and nearly senile.* ADJ CLASSIF

◊ **senility** /sənɪlɪ¹ti¹/. EG *Sheila became increasingly affected by senility.* ◊ N UNCOUNT

senior /siːnjə/, **seniors. 1** The **senior** people in an organization or profession have the highest and most important jobs in it. EG *...senior officers... He held a very senior position in the British Foreign Service... ...a senior member of staff.* ADJ QUALIT

2 If someone is **senior** to you in an organization or profession, they have a higher and more important job than you. EG *There are plenty of others senior to me: George and Jock for example.* ADJ QUALIT : OFT+*to*

3 Someone who is your **senior** is older than you are. EG *She was at least fifteen years his senior.* N SING+POSS

4 At a school or college, the **seniors** are the pupils or students who are older and have reached an advanced level in their studies. N COUNT

senior citizen, senior citizens. A **senior citizen** is a person who is old enough to receive an old-age pension. EG *...free bus travel for senior citizens.* N COUNT

seniority /siːni¹ɒrɪ¹ti¹/. A person's **seniority** in an organization is their degree of importance and power compared to other people who work there. EG *The size of office will vary according to your seniority... The report listed their names in order of seniority.* N UNCOUNT

sensation /sɛnseɪʃə⁰n/, **sensations. 1** A **sensation** is a physical feeling. EG *...a sharp tingling sensation that ran through her whole body... It produces a mild burning sensation in the mouth.* N COUNT : USU+SUPP

2 You can use **sensation** to refer to the general feeling or impression caused by a particular experience. EG *It was a strange sensation to return to the school again after so long... She had the sensation that she had done all this before.* N COUNT : USU+SUPP

3 If an event or situation is a **sensation**, it causes great excitement or interest. EG *The film was an overnight sensation... The discovery was hailed as the scientific sensation of the century.* N COUNT

sensational /sɛnseɪʃə⁰nəl, -ʃənə⁰l/. **1** Something that is **sensational** is so remarkable that it causes great excitement and interest. EG *This is the most sensational result of any election since the war... ...sensational discoveries.* ADJ QUALIT

2 You can describe something as **sensational** when you think that it is extremely good. EG *I've discovered a sensational health-food store... That was a sensational evening.* ◊ **sensationally.** EG *Edith Evans was sensationally good.* ADJ QUALIT ◊ SUBMOD Informal

sense /sɛns/, **senses, sensing, sensed. 1** Your **senses** are the physical abilities of sight, smell, hearing, touch, and taste. EG *They all have an excellent sense of smell.* ● See also **sixth sense**. N COUNT

2 If you **sense** something, you become aware of it or you realize it, although it is not very obvious. EG *Doctors often sense uneasiness in people... He sensed that she did not want to talk to him.* V+O OR V+REPORT

3 If you have a **sense** of guilt or shame, for example, you feel guilty or ashamed. EG *I was overcome by a sense of failure.* N SING+*of*

4 If you have a **sense** of something such as duty or justice, you can recognize it and you believe that it is important. EG *She has a strong sense of justice.* N SING+*of*

5 Someone who has a **sense** of timing or style, for example, has a natural ability for timing or style. EG *A good sense of timing is important for an actor... He hasn't got much dress sense.* N SING+SUPP

6 Sense is the ability to make good judgements and to behave sensibly. EG *She had the good sense to realize that the plan would never work... Your friends have more money than sense.* ● See also **common sense**. N UNCOUNT

7 If you say that there is **no sense** or **little sense** in doing something, you mean that nothing useful would be gained by doing it. EG *There's no sense in making people unhappy.* PHRASE

8 The phrase **make sense** is used in these ways. **8.1** If something **makes sense**, you can understand it. EG *I looked at the printed page but the words made no sense.* **8.2** When you **make sense** of something, you succeed in understanding it. EG *You had to read it six times to make any sense of it.* **8.3** If a course of action **makes sense**, it seems sensible. EG *Under these conditions it made sense to adopt labour-saving methods.* PHRASE

9 If you say that someone **talks sense**, you mean that what they say is sensible. EG *On defence matters he talked a great deal of sense.* PHRASE

10 If you say that someone has **come to** their PHRASE

senses or has **been brought to** their **senses**, you mean that they have stopped being foolish and are being sensible again.

11 A **sense** of a word or expression is one of its possible meanings. EG *I don't like the Washington climate – in all senses of the word.* N COUNT

12 If you say that something is true **in a sense**, you mean that it is partly true, or that it is true in one way. EG *In a sense, I still love him.* ADV SEN

senseless /sɛnslɪ^{2}s/. 1 You describe an action as **senseless** when it seems to have no meaning or purpose. EG *It was a senseless thing to do... He made senseless expeditions to India.* ADJ QUALIT

2 If someone is **senseless**, they are unconscious. EG *A heavy blow with a club knocked him senseless.* ADJ CLASSIF

sense of humour. 1 Someone who has a **sense of humour** often finds things amusing, rather than being serious all the time. EG *He lacked any sense of humour.* N SING

2 Someone's **sense of humour** is the way that they are amused by certain things but not by others. EG *I see your sense of humour hasn't changed.* N UNCOUNT

sensibility /sɛnsɪbɪlɪ^{1}ti^{1}/, **sensibilities.** Someone's **sensibility** is their ability to experience deep feelings. EG *...a writer of high sensibility and intelligence... These words touched his sensibilities.* N UNCOUNT OR N COUNT

sensible /sɛnsɪbə^{0}l/. A **sensible** person is able to make good decisions and judgements based on reasons rather than emotions. EG *It seemed sensible to move to a bigger house... ...sensible decisions.* ADJ QUALIT ◇ **sensibly**. EG *They sensibly concluded that this wouldn't be a good idea.* ◇ ADV

sensitive /sɛnsɪtɪv/. 1 If you are **sensitive** to other people's problems and feelings, you show understanding and awareness of them. EG *We're trying to make people more sensitive to the difficulties faced by working mothers... ...a sensitive story about the problems of growing up.* ADJ QUALIT: OFT+to ◇ **sensitively**. EG *...this well acted, sensitively directed play.* ◇ ADV ◇ **sensitivity** /sɛnsɪtɪvɪ^{1}ti^{1}/. EG *Her remarks showed a lack of sensitivity.* ◇ N UNCOUNT

2 If you are **sensitive** about something, it worries you or makes you upset or angry. EG *You really must stop being so sensitive about your accent... He's very sensitive to criticism.* ADJ QUALIT: OFT+about/to

3 A **sensitive** subject or issue needs to be dealt with carefully because it is likely to cause disagreement or make people angry or upset. EG *This is one of the most sensitive issues that the government faces.* ADJ QUALIT

4 Something that is **sensitive** to a physical force, substance, or condition is easily affected by it and often harmed by it. EG *Children's bones are very sensitive to radiation... ...people with sensitive skin.* ADJ QUALIT: OFT+to ◇ **sensitivity**. EG *...the sensitivity of the lining of the nasal cavity.* ◇ N UNCOUNT

5 A **sensitive** piece of scientific equipment is capable of measuring or recording very small changes. EG *...highly sensitive electronic cameras.* ADJ QUALIT

sensory /sɛnsə^{0}ri^{1}/ means relating to the physical senses. EG *With these two highly developed sensory organs it hunts at night for insects.* ADJ CLASSIF: ATTRIB Formal

sensual /sɛnsjʊ^{0}əl/. 1 Someone or something that is **sensual** shows or suggests a great liking for physical pleasures, especially sexual pleasures. EG *...an extravagantly sensual woman... ...plump sensual lips.* ADJ QUALIT ◇ **sensuality** /sɛnsjuælɪ^{1}ti^{1}/. EG *Her body shone through the cloth with sheer sensuality.* ◇ N UNCOUNT

2 Something that is **sensual** gives pleasure to your physical senses rather than to your mind. EG *...the subtle, sensual rhythms of the drums.* ADJ QUALIT ◇ **sensuality**. EG *...the sensuality of English music.* ◇ N UNCOUNT

sensuous /sɛnsjʊ^{0}əs/. Something that is **sensuous** gives pleasure to the mind or body through the senses. EG *Sculpture is a sensuous art... ...a sensuous colour... ...fresh peaches, sweet, cool, and sensuous.* ADJ QUALIT ◇ **sensuously**. EG *Her fingers sensuously stroked his neck.* ◇ ADV

sent /sɛnt/ is the past tense and past participle of **send.**

sentence /sɛntəns/, **sentences, sentencing, sentenced.** 1 A **sentence** is a group of words which, when they are written down, begin with a capital letter and end with a full stop. EG *Most of them could read a simple sentence in English... ...the opening sentence of the report... He put the phone down before she could finish the sentence.* N COUNT

2 In a law court, a **sentence** is the punishment that a person receives after they have been found guilty of a crime. EG *If found guilty they will face a sentence of ten years in prison... He is serving a life sentence for murder.* N COUNT OR N UNCOUNT

3 When a judge **sentences** someone, he or she states in court what their punishment will be. EG *Griffiths was sentenced to four years' imprisonment for robbery.* V+O: OFT+to

sentence adverb, sentence adverbs. In grammar, a **sentence adverb** is an adverb which comments on the whole clause or sentence rather than on a single word. Sentence adverbs usually express the speaker's or writer's personal opinion. In this dictionary the label ADV SEN is used in the Extra Column to mean 'sentence adverb'. See the entry headed ADVERBS for more information. N COUNT

sentiment /sɛntɪmə^{2}nt/, **sentiments.** 1 A **sentiment** that people have is an attitude which is based on their thoughts and feelings. EG *These events led to a vast upsurge of anti-imperialist sentiment.* N UNCOUNT OR N COUNT

2 Someone's **sentiment** is an idea or feeling that they express in words. EG *These sentiments were generally echoed by other speakers at the meeting.* N COUNT

3 **Sentiment** is an emotion such as tenderness, romance, or sadness, which influences a person's behaviour. EG *I'm worried that you might be doing it out of sentiment. Out of affection for me.* N UNCOUNT

sentimental /sɛntɪmɛntə^{0}l/. 1 Someone or something that is **sentimental** feels or arouses emotions such as tenderness, romance, or sadness, sometimes to an extent which is considered exaggerated. EG *...sentimental songs... People have become sentimental about the passing of ways and customs.* ADJ QUALIT ◇ **sentimentally**. EG *Romantic love and motherhood are sentimentally idealized.* ◇ ADV ◇ **sentimentality** /sɛntɪmɛntælɪ^{1}ti^{1}/. EG *...her sentimentality about animals.* ◇ N UNCOUNT

2 You use **sentimental** to describe things relating to a person's emotions. EG *The ring had been her mother's and she wore it for sentimental reasons.* ADJ CLASSIF ◇ **sentimentally**. EG *He had become sentimentally attached to a postgraduate student.* ◇ ADV

sentry /sɛntri^{1}/, **sentries.** A **sentry** is a soldier who guards a camp or a building. EG *...look-out posts where sentries kept watch... Who is on sentry duty tonight?* N COUNT

separate, separates, separating, separated; pronounced /sɛpə^{0}rə^{1}t/ when it is an adjective and /sɛpəreɪt/ when it is a verb. 1 If one thing is **separate** from another, the two things are apart from each other and are not connected. EG *Rosa had remained separate from us, asking for a room by herself... Two masses can be kept separate inside the bomb casing... They left the party in 1963 to form the first separate Maoist group in Britain.* ADJ CLASSIF: OFT+from ◇ **separately**. EG *What we achieve together is more important than what we can do separately.* ◇ ADV

2 **Separate** things are individual and distinct from each other. EG *The sunlight caught each tiny separate hair and made it shine... Babies feed eagerly for two separate reasons.* ADJ CLASSIF ◇ **separately**. EG *Wash each pile separately.* ◇ ADV

3 If you **separate** people or things, you move them or keep them apart so that they are not connected V+O OR V+O+from: RECIP

Make a list of the things that you own that have serial numbers on them.

or cannot communicate. EG *Even at dinner time we were separated; she ate in one place, and I ate in another... In any angry discussion he would separate the opponents and soothe them.*

4 If you **separate** ideas from each other, you consider them individually and show the distinction between them. EG *Faith and God to me are the same thing, I can't separate them.* — V+O OR V+O+*from*: RECIP

5 A detail that **separates** one thing from another thing shows that the two things are different from each other. EG *Higher living standards separate the older generation from their children.* — V+O+*from*

6 If an object, period of time, or distance **separates** two people, groups, or things, it exists between them and prevents them from having contact with each other. EG *A fence at the back of the garden separated us from the neighbours... ...the Great Lakes separating Canada from America.* — V+O: USU+*from*

7 If you **separate** a group of things or if you **separate** them out, you divide them so that each different part becomes separate. EG *Most schools decide to separate out their pupils into different groups according to age.* — V+O: OFT+*out*

8 If a group of people or things **separate**, they move away from each other after being together or connected for a time. EG *They talked by the gate, unwilling to separate... The two pipes separated from each other.* — V OR V+*from*: RECIP

9 If a couple who are married or living together **separate**, they decide to live apart. EG *Her parents separated when she was eleven.* — V: OFT+*from*

separated /sɛpəreɪtɪ2d/. Someone who is **separated** from their wife or husband lives apart from them, but is not divorced. EG *My wife and I are separated.* — ADJ PRED

separation /sɛpəreɪʃə0n/, **separations. 1** The **separation** of two or more people, things, or groups is their movement away from each other or their state of being kept apart from each other. EG *...the separation of infant from mother.* — N UNCOUNT

2 A **separation** between two or more people is a period of time that they spend apart from each other. EG *Children recover remarkably quickly from a brief separation from their parents.* — N COUNT OR N UNCOUNT

3 If a couple who are married or living together have a **separation**, they decide to live apart. EG *Last night we talked about a separation.* — N COUNT OR N UNCOUNT

September /sɛptɛmbə/ is the ninth month of the year in the Western calendar. EG *Gladys died on September 27th, 1976.* — N UNCOUNT

septic /sɛptɪk/. If a wound or a part of your body becomes **septic**, it becomes infected with poison. — ADJ CLASSIF

sequel /siːkwə0l/, **sequels. 1** A book or film which is a **sequel** to an earlier one continues the story of the earlier one. EG *He starred in 'The Godfather' and in its sequel, 'The Godfather II'.* — N COUNT: OFT+*to*

2 The **sequel** to something that happened is an event or situation that happened after it or as a result of it. EG *There was an amusing sequel to this incident.* — N COUNT: OFT+*to*

sequence /siːkwə0ns/, **sequences. 1** A **sequence** of events or things is a number of events or things that come one after another in a particular order. EG *...the strange sequence of events that led up to the murder.* — N COUNT+*of*

2 A particular **sequence** is a particular order in which things happen or are arranged. EG *The paintings are exhibited in a chronological sequence... These recordings are in sequence and continuous.* — N COUNT OR N UNCOUNT

3 A film **sequence** is a part of a film that shows a single set of actions. EG *What did you think of that ghastly sequence at the end?* — N COUNT

sequin /siːkwɪn/, **sequins. Sequins** are small, shiny discs that are sewn on clothes to decorate them. EG *...a dress embroidered with thousands of tiny sequins.* — N COUNT: USU PLURAL

serene /sɪ2riːn/. Someone or something that is **serene** is calm and quiet. EG *She had a naturally cheerful and serene expression... ...a serene mountain landscape.* — ADJ QUALIT ◊ **serenely**. EG *Her blue eyes gazed serenely into space.* — ◊ ADV ◊ **serenity** /sɪ2rɛnɪ1ti1/. EG *I was moved by her serenity and confidence.* — ◊ N UNCOUNT

serf /sɜːf/, **serfs. Serfs** were a class of people in medieval Europe who had to work on their master's land and could not leave without his permission. — N COUNT

sergeant /sɑːdʒənt/, **sergeants.** A **sergeant** is **1** a non-commissioned officer of middle rank in the army or the air force. **2** an officer with the next to lowest rank in the police force. — N COUNT

sergeant major, sergeant majors. A **sergeant major** is a non-commissioned army officer of the highest rank. — N COUNT

serial /sɪərɪəl/, **serials.** A **serial** is a story which is broadcast on television or radio or published in a magazine in a number of parts over a period of time. EG *The novel has recently been dramatized as a television serial.* — N COUNT

serialize /sɪərɪəlaɪz/, **serializes, serializing, serialized;** also spelled **serialise.** If a book **is serialized**, it is broadcast on the radio or television or published in a magazine in a number of parts. EG *His book 'Blood on the Snow' is currently being serialized on 'Woman's Hour'.* — V+O: USU PASS

serial number, serial numbers. The **serial number** of an object is the number on that object which identifies it. EG *...the serial number of the cheque card.* — N COUNT

series /sɪəri1z/. **Series** is both the singular and the plural form.

1 A **series** of things or events is a number of them that come one after the other. EG *He was arrested in connection with a series of armed bank robberies... ...a series of lectures on American politics.* — N COUNT: USU+*of*

2 A radio or television **series** is a set of programmes of a particular kind which have the same title. EG *...the popular television series, 'Yes, Minister'... ...a new 6 week series on Europe.* — N COUNT

serious /sɪərɪəs/. **1** Problems or situations that are **serious** are very bad and cause people to be worried. EG *Bad housing is one of the most serious problems in the inner cities... ...a serious illness... It is in a serious condition.* — ADJ QUALIT ◊ **seriously**. EG *She was seriously ill.* — ◊ ADV ◊ **seriousness**. EG *...the seriousness of the problem.* — ◊ N UNCOUNT

2 Serious matters are important and deserve careful and thoughtful consideration. EG *It's time to get down to the serious business of the meeting... She is a serious candidate for the presidency.* — ADJ QUALIT

3 Serious work or consideration of something involves thinking about things deeply and thoughtfully because they are important. EG *The programme is a forum for serious political discussion... ...a serious newspaper.* — ADJ CLASSIF: ATTRIB

4 If someone is **serious** about something, they are sincere about what they are saying, doing, or intending to do. EG *You can't be serious!... I knew that he was serious about the struggle.* — ADJ QUALIT: OFT+*about*

◊ **seriously**. EG *I'm seriously thinking of retiring.* — ◊ ADV

◊ **seriousness**. EG *I see no reason, in all seriousness, why women should not become priests.* — ◊ N UNCOUNT

5 People who are **serious** are thoughtful, quiet, and slightly humourless. EG *She was a rather serious girl... ...a serious manner.* — ADJ QUALIT ◊ **seriously**. EG *He talked very seriously and solemnly about theoretical matters.* — ◊ ADV

seriously /sɪərɪəsli1/. **1** You say **seriously 1.1** to indicate that you really mean what you say. EG *What I do think is important, quite seriously, is that people should know the facts.* — ADV SEN **1.2** when you are surprised by what someone has said, as a way of asking them if they really mean it. EG *'I've given up my job.' – 'Seriously?'* — CONVENTION

2 If you **take** someone or something **seriously**, you believe that they are important and deserve attention. EG *They take their responsibilities seriously... His work was not taken seriously.* — PHRASE

3 See also **serious**.

sermon /sɜːmən/, **sermons.** A **sermon** is a talk on a religious or moral subject that is given by a member of the clergy as part of a church service. EG *...the church where John Donne preached his first sermon.* N COUNT

serpent /sɜːpənt/, **serpents.** A **serpent** is a snake. N COUNT Literary

serrated /sɪ²reɪtɪ²d/. A **serrated** object has a row of V-shaped points along the edge. EG *...serrated scissors... ...huge serrated leaves.* ADJ CLASSIF : ATTRIB

serum /sɪərə⁰m/, **serums.** A **serum** is a liquid that is injected into someone's blood to protect them against a poison or disease. EG *This serum was most effective against snake poison.* N COUNT OR N UNCOUNT

servant /sɜːvə⁰nt/, **servants.** A **servant** is someone who is employed to work in another person's house, for example as a cleaner or a gardener. EG *She worked all her life as a domestic servant.* ● See also **civil servant**. N COUNT

serve /sɜːv/, **serves, serving, served. 1** If you **serve** your country, an organization, or a person, you do useful work for them. EG *For over thirty years, she has served the company loyally and well... He served with the army in France.* V+O OR V+A

2 If something **serves** as a particular thing or **serves** a particular purpose, it performs a particular function. EG *There was a long, grey building that served as a cafeteria... This will serve as a valuable reminder of the dangers involved... His refusal to answer only serves to increase our suspicions... I failed to see what purpose this could serve.* V+A, V+*to*-INF, OR V+O

3 If something **serves** people or an area, it provides them with something that they need. EG *There were five water taps to serve all thirty camps... ...work which will serve the community.* V+O

4 If you **serve** people or if you **serve** food and drink, you give people food and drink. EG *When everybody had been served, the meal began... A leg of lamb came next, served with new potatoes... I served the children their meal.* V+O

5 Serve is sometimes used in recipes. For example, a recipe that **serves** six provides enough food for six people. V+O : NO CONT

6 Someone who **serves** customers in a shop or a bar helps them and provides them with what they want to buy. EG *The bartender refused to serve us... She spent six months serving in a shop.* V+O OR V

7 When a court **serves** a legal order on someone or **serves** them with it, it sends the legal order to them. EG *The court served her with an enforcement notice.* V+O+*on* OR V+O+*with* Legal

8 If you **serve** something such as a prison sentence or an apprenticeship, you spend a period of time doing it. EG *He is now serving a life sentence in an Italian jail.* V+O

9 When you **serve** in games such as tennis and badminton, you throw up the ball or shuttlecock and hit it to start play. EG *He served an ace.* ▸ used as a noun. EG *Her second serve went into the net.* V OR V+O ▸ N COUNT

10 If you say it **serves** someone **right** when something unpleasant happens to them, you mean that it is their own fault and you have no sympathy for them. EG *'I feel terrible.' – 'Serves you right for drinking so much.'* PHRASE

11 See also **serving**.

serve out or **serve up.** If you **serve out** food or **serve** it **up**, you give it to people as a meal. EG *Army kitchens serve up better fare than some hotels do.* PHRASAL VB : V+O+ADV

service /sɜːvɪs/, **services, servicing, serviced.** N COUNT+SUPP
1 A **service** is **1.1** an organization or system that provides something for the public, for example transport or information. EG *I think the train service is better than it used to be... ...the postal service.* **1.2** an official organization or government department that does a particular job. EG *...the diplomatic service.*

2 A **service** is also a job that an organization can do for you. EG *The post office can forward your letters; the fee for this service is £6... It boosts demand for goods and services... ...taking people out of factories into service industries.* N COUNT+SUPP

3 The **services** are the army, the navy, and the air force. EG *Young people are being encouraged to join the services.* N PLURAL : the+N

4 Your **services** are the work that you can do for people. EG *They will be very happy to give their services free of charge.* N PLURAL +POSS

5 Service is the state or activity of working for a particular person or organization. EG *Conscription would be limited to a maximum of six months' service.* N UNCOUNT

6 Service is also the process of being served in a shop or restaurant. EG *He hammered the table for immediate service.* N UNCOUNT

7 If someone or something is **of service** to you, they help you or are useful to you. EG *In what way may I be of service to you?* PHRASE Formal

8 If a machine or type of vehicle is in **service**, it is being used or is able to be used. EG *Most of the vehicles had been withdrawn from service.* N UNCOUNT : AFTER PREP

9 When a machine **is serviced**, it is examined, adjusted, and cleaned so that it will keep working efficiently and safely. EG *Gas appliances should be serviced regularly.* ▸ used as a noun. EG *The car needs a service.* V+O ▸ N COUNT

10 A religious **service** is a religious ceremony. EG *...the Sunday evening service.* N COUNT

11 A dinner **service** or a tea **service** is a complete set of dishes, plates, and other pieces of china. N COUNT : USU+SUPP

12 A **services** is a place where you can stop on a motorway and where there is a garage, a restaurant, a shop, and toilets. The plural is also **services**. N COUNT

13 See also **Civil Service, community service, National Health Service, national service**.

serviceable /sɜːvɪsəbə⁰l/. Something that is **serviceable** performs its function effectively. EG *I wore serviceable boots.* ADJ QUALIT Formal

service charge. A **service charge** is an amount that is added to your bill in a restaurant to pay for the work of the waiter or waitress who serves you. EG *The service charge is 10 per cent.* N SING

serviceman /sɜːvɪsmə³n/, **servicemen.** A **serviceman** is a man who is in the army, navy, or air force. N COUNT

serviette /sɜːvɪet/, **serviettes.** A **serviette** is a square of cloth or paper that you use to protect your clothes or to wipe your mouth when you are eating. N COUNT

servile /sɜːvaɪl/. Someone who is **servile** is too eager to do things for someone and shows them too much respect. EG *...the incurably servile housekeeper.* ADJ QUALIT Formal

serving /sɜːvɪŋ/, **servings. 1** A **serving** is an amount of food that is given to one person at a meal. EG *His mother was spooning out servings of tuna fish casserole.* N COUNT

2 A **serving** spoon or dish is used for giving out food at a meal. ADJ CLASSIF : ATTRIB

session /seʃə⁰n/, **sessions. 1** A **session** is **1.1** a meeting of an official group. EG *...an emergency session of the United Nations Security Council.* N COUNT **1.2** a period during which the meetings of an official group are regularly held. EG *...the government's programme for the 1966-67 parliamentary session.* N COUNT

2 When an official group is **in session**, it is formally holding a meeting. *The court is still in session.* PHRASE

3 A **session** of a particular activity is a period of that activity. EG *...a tough bargaining session... ...an all-night drinking session.* N COUNT : USU+SUPP

What service do you use when you set the table?

set /sɛt/, **sets, setting.** The form **set** is used in the present tense and is the past tense and past participle of the verb.

1 A **set** of things is a number of things that belong together or that are thought of as a group. EG *...a set of encyclopaedias... We soon encountered a new set of problems... ...a chess set.* N COUNT+SUPP OR N PART

2 If you **set** something somewhere, you put it there, especially in a careful or deliberate way. EG *He filled the kettle and set it on the stove.* V+O+A

3 If something **is set** in a particular place or position, it is in that place or position. EG *The house is set back from the road... His eyes were set close together.* V-PASS+A

4 If something **is set** into a surface, it is fixed there and does not stick out. EG *There was one tiny window set into the stone wall.* V+O+*into/in*: USU PASS

5 You can use **set** to say that a person or thing causes something to be in a particular condition or situation. EG *Let me set your mind at rest... The change was set in motion by President Carter... One prisoner had been set free... A gust of wind set all the candles spluttering.* V+O+A, V+O+C, OR V+-ING

6 When the sun **sets**, it goes below the horizon. V

7 When someone **sets** a trap, they prepare it. V+O

8 When someone **sets** the table, they prepare it for a meal by putting plates and cutlery on it. V+O

9 When someone **sets** a clock or control, they adjust it to a particular point or level. EG *His alarm clock was set for four a.m.* V+O: OFT+A

10 If you **set** a time, price, or level, you decide what it will be. EG *They haven't set a date for the wedding... The government set a minimum price of £1.15.* V+O: OFT+A

11 You use **set** to describe something which is fixed and does not change. EG *We paid a set amount for the course... There are no set rules laid down for dealing with this kind of emergency... Her day usually followed a set pattern.* ADJ CLASSIF: ATTRIB

12 If you **are set in** your **ways**, your habits and ideas are not likely to change. EG *She is too old and set in her ways ever to change.* PHRASE

13 If you **set** something such as a precedent or a standard, you establish it for other people to copy or to try to achieve. EG *Try and set the younger children a good example... They tended to follow the trend set by the other banks.* V+O, V+O+O, OR V+O+*for*

14 If someone **sets** you some work or **sets** you a target, they say that you must do the work or reach the target. EG *She had set a composition for her pupils... The new management set itself three aims.* V+O, V+O+O, OR V+O+*for*

15 A **set** book must be studied by students taking a particular course. ADJ CLASSIF: ATTRIB

16 If you are **set** to do something, you are ready to do it or are likely to do it. EG *The left-wing seem set to do very well in the general election.* ADJ PRED: OFT +*to*-INF OR *for*

17 If you are **set** on doing something, you are strongly determined to do it. EG *She is set on regaining her title.* ADJ PRED+*on*

18 If you **set** your face or jaw, you put on a fixed expression of determination. EG *I set my face into a grimace.* V+O

19 When something such as glue, jelly, or cement **sets**, it becomes firm or hard. EG *The cement had set hard.* V OR V+C

20 If someone **sets** a poem to music, they write music for it. V+O+*to*: USU PASS

21 A television **set** is a television. EG *We have a TV set in the living room.* N COUNT: USU+SUPP

22 The **set** for a play or film is the furniture or scenery on the stage or in the studio. N COUNT

23 If a play, film, or story **is set** at a particular time or in a particular place, the events in it take place at that time or in that place. EG *The play is set in a small Midlands village.* V+O+A: USU PASS

24 In tennis, a **set** is one of the groups of six or more games that form part of a match. N COUNT

25 to **set eyes on** someone: see **eye**. • to **set fire to** something: see **fire**. • to **set foot**: see **foot**. • to **set** your **heart on** something: see **heart**. • to **set sail**: see **sail**. • to **set the stage for**: see **stage**. • to **set to work**: see **work**. • See also **setting**.

set about. If you **set about** doing something, you start doing it. EG *The next morning they set about cleaning the house.* PHRASAL VB: V+PREP, USU+-ING

set against. 1 If you **set** one fact or argument **against** another, you consider the first one in relation to the second one. EG *This slight improvement has to be set against an enormous increase in crime.* PHRASAL VB: V+O+PREP 2 To **set** one person **against** another means to cause them to become enemies or rivals. V+O+PREP

set apart. If a characteristic **sets** you **apart** from other people, it makes you recognizably different from the others. EG *His exceptional height set him apart from the rest of the men.* PHRASAL VB: V+O+ADV, OFT+*from*

set aside. 1 If you **set** something **aside** for a special use or purpose, you keep it available for that use or purpose. EG *Try and set aside time to do some mending jobs.* PHRASAL VB: V+O+ADV 2 If you **set aside** a belief, principle, or feeling, you decide that you will not be influenced by it. EG *We must try and set aside our past hostilities.* V+O+ADV

set back. 1 If something **sets** you **back** or **sets back** a project or scheme, it causes a delay. EG *This has set back the whole programme of nuclear power in America.* PHRASAL VB: V+O+ADV 2 If something **sets** you **back** a large amount of money, it costs you that much money. EG *The legal costs set him back something in the order of £10,000.* V+O+ADV+O Informal 3 See also **setback**.

set down. If you **set down** your thoughts or experiences, you write them all down. EG *They were asked to set down a summary of their views.* PHRASAL VB: V+O+ADV

set in. If something unpleasant **sets in**, it begins and seems likely to continue or develop. EG *A feeling of anti-climax set in... It must be treated quickly before infection sets in.* PHRASAL VB: V+ADV

set off. 1 When you **set off**, you start a journey. EG *Dan set off down the mountain to find help... He set off on a trip to Mexico.* PHRASAL VB: V+ADV 2 If something **sets off** an event or a series of events, it causes it to start happening. EG *Most analysts expected that Mobil's offer would set off a new round of bidding for Conoco.* V+ADV+O

set on. To **set** animals **on** someone means to cause the animals to attack them. EG *We were afraid they might set the dogs on us.* PHRASAL VB: V+O+PREP

set out. 1 When you **set out**, you start a journey. EG *We set out along the beach... They set out for Cuba on a two-day trip.* PHRASAL VB: V+ADV, OFT+A 2 If you **set out** to do something, you start trying to do it. EG *They had failed in what they had set out to do.* V+ADV+*to*-INF 3 If you **set** things **out**, you arrange or display them somewhere. EG *There were plenty of chairs set out for the guests.* PHRASAL VB: V+O+ADV 4 If you **set out** a number of facts, beliefs, or arguments, you give them in writing or speech in a clear, organized way. EG *Darwin set out his theory in detail in 'The Origin of Species'.* V+O+ADV

set up. 1 If you **set** something **up**, you make the preparations that are necessary for it to start. EG *It took a long time to set up the experiment... The government were setting up an inquiry into the affair... An anti-terrorist squad was set up.* PHRASAL VB: V+O+ADV ◊ **setting up**. EG *...the setting up of a Northern Seas Environmental Control Agency.* ◊ N SING 2 If you **set up** a structure, you place it or build it somewhere. EG *A fund was launched to set up a monument in memory of the dead men.* PHRASAL VB: V+O+ADV 3 If you **set up** somewhere, you establish yourself in a new home or business. EG *She left her parents' home and set up on her own... He used the money to set himself up in business.* PHRASAL VB: V+ADV+A, V+O+ADV+A, OR V-REFL +ADV+A • If you **set up home** or **set up house**, you buy a house or flat and start living in it. • PHRASE 4 If something **sets up** a process or series of events, it causes it to begin. EG *It may become possible to set up a nuclear chain reaction.* PHRASAL VB: V+ADV+O 5 If someone **sets** you **up**, they make it seem that you have done something wrong when you have not. EG *Those three women set him up.* PHRASAL VB: V+O+ADV Informal 6 See also **set-up**.

setback /sɛtbæk/, **setbacks.** A **setback** is an event that delays your progress or makes your position worse than it was before. EG *The by-election result is a serious setback for the government... They had to face up to innumerable setbacks before they achieved their goal.* N COUNT

settee /sɛtiː/, **settees.** A **settee** is a long comfortable seat with a back and arms, which two or three people can sit on. N COUNT

setting /sɛtɪŋ/, **settings. 1** A particular **setting** is a particular place or type of surroundings which someone or something is in. EG *The castle provided the perfect setting for a horror story... Children should be cared for in a home setting.* N COUNT+SUPP

2 A **setting** is also one of the positions to which the controls of a machine can be adjusted. EG *Set the control to the coldest setting.* N COUNT

settle /sɛtə^{0}l/, **settles, settling, settled. 1** If someone **settles** an argument, they end it by making a decision about who is right or about what to do. EG *The strike went on for over a year before it was finally settled.* V+O

2 If something **is settled**, it has all been decided and arranged. EG *Good, well, that's settled then.* V+O : USU PASS

3 If you **settle** a bill, you pay the amount that you owe. V+O

4 When people **settle** in a new country or area, or when they **settle** somewhere after moving around a lot, they start living there permanently. EG *He had settled in England.* V+A

5 If you **settle** yourself somewhere or **settle** somewhere, you sit down or make yourself comfortable. EG *He settled himself beside her in the car... Casson took off his raincoat and settled before the fire.* V-REFL OR V : USU+A

6 If something **settles**, it sinks slowly down and becomes still. EG *The dust was settling... The hull of the boat slowly settled in the mud.* V : USU+A

7 When birds or insects **settle** on something, they land on it from above. EG *...flies and other insects that settle on plants growing on the banks.* V+A

8 See also **settled**.

settle down. 1 If you **settle down** to something, you prepare to do it and concentrate on it. EG *...before they settle down to university work... He had settled down to watch a sports programme... He settled down for supper.* PHRASAL VB : V+ADV, USU+*to*, *to*-INF, OR *for* **2** When someone **settles down**, they start living a quiet life in one place, especially when they get married or buy a house. EG *You should get a job and settle down.* V+ADV **3** If people who are upset or noisy **settle down**, they become calm or quiet. EG *Take it easy, she'll be all right, settle down.* V+ADV

settle for. If you **settle for** something, you choose or accept it, especially when it is not what you really want but there is nothing else available. EG *When in doubt he settled for hamburgers.* PHRASAL VB : V+PREP

settle in. If you **are settling in**, you are becoming used to living in a new place or doing a new job. EG *And how are you settling in, Mr Swallow?* PHRASAL VB : V+ADV

settle on. If you **settle on** a particular thing, you choose it after considering other possible choices. EG *Have you settled on a name for him yet?* PHRASAL VB : V+PREP, HAS PASS

settle up. When you **settle up**, you pay a bill. EG *As soon as the money arrived I was able to settle up with him.* PHRASAL VB : V+ADV OR V+ADV+*with* : RECIP

settled /sɛtə^{0}ld/. **1** If you have a **settled** way of life, you stay in one place rather than travelling around. EG *...the advent of settled civilization.* ADJ CLASSIF

2 A **settled** system stays the same all the time. EG *...an easy, rich, peaceful and settled social order.* ADJ QUALIT

3 If you feel **settled**, you have been living or working in a place long enough to feel comfortable there. ADJ QUALIT

settlement /sɛtə^{0}lmə^{2}nt/, **settlements. 1** A **settlement** is an official agreement between two sides who were involved in a conflict or argument. EG *The chance for a peaceful political settlement has disappeared... ...enormous wage settlements.* N COUNT

2 A **settlement** is also a place where people have come to live and have built homes. EG *He lives in the jungle, in a settlement by a river.* N COUNT

settler /sɛtlə/, **settlers.** A **settler** is someone who goes to live in a new country. EG *The first white settlers in South Africa were Dutch.* N COUNT

set-up, set-ups. A particular **set-up** is a particular system or way of organizing something. EG *I've only been here a couple of days and I don't quite know the set-up.* N COUNT : USU SING Informal

seven /sɛvə^{0}n/ **sevens. Seven** is the number 7: see the entry headed NUMBER. EG *I am seven years older than Wendy.* NUMBER

seventeen /sɛvə^{0}ntiːn/ **seventeens. Seventeen** is the number 17: see the entry headed NUMBER. EG *Buxhall is seventeen miles from Akenfield.* NUMBER

seventeenth /sɛvə^{0}ntiːnθ/ **seventeenths.** The **seventeenth** item in a series is the one that you count as number seventeen: see the entry headed NUMBER. EG *It was Rudolph's seventeenth birthday.* ORDINAL

seventh /sɛvə^{0}nθ/, **sevenths. 1** The **seventh** item in a series is the one that you count as number seven: see the entry headed NUMBER. EG *She died giving birth to her seventh child.* ORDINAL

2 A **seventh** is one of seven equal parts of something. N COUNT : USU+*of*

seventieth /sɛvə^{0}ntɪɪθ/ **seventieths.** The **seventieth** item in a series is the one that you count as number seventy: see the entry headed NUMBER. ORDINAL

seventy /sɛvə^{0}nti^1/, **seventies. Seventy** is the number 70: see the entry headed NUMBER. EG *...seventy per cent of the people.* NUMBER

sever /sɛvə/, **severs, severing, severed. 1** To **sever** something means to cut right through it so that one part is completely separated from the rest of it. EG *A bulldozer had severed a gas pipe... The boy's legs were severed at the hip.* V+O

2 If you **sever** a relationship or connection that you have with someone, you end it suddenly and completely. EG *She had to sever all ties with her parents... He severed his connection with the party.* V+O

several /sɛvə^{0}rəl/. **Several** people or things means a fairly small number of people or things. EG *He returned home several hours later... Several hundred people were killed... Several of us are married and have children.* QUANTIF

severe /sɪ^{2}vɪə/, **severer, severest. 1** You use **severe** to describe something that is very bad or undesirable. EG *The blast caused severe damage and heavy loss of life... ...a severe shortage of food.* ADJ QUALIT

◇ **severely.** EG *A fire had severely damaged the school... Bad weather severely hampered the emergency services.* ◇ ADV ◇ **severity** /sɪ^{2}vɛrɪti^1/. EG *...the severity of the world-wide recession.* ◇ N UNCOUNT

2 Someone who is **severe** is stern and treats people rather harshly. EG *I hope the magistrate has not been too severe with him... I was his severest critic... ...her severe upbringing.* ADJ QUALIT ◇ **severely.** EG *'You didn't answer Mr Crow's question,' said the old lady severely.* ◇ ADV ◇ **severity.** EG *...prison sentences of excessive severity.* ◇ N UNCOUNT

sew /səʊ/, **sews, sewing, sewed, sewn** /səʊn/. When someone **sews**, they join pieces of cloth together, or attach things such as buttons to cloth, by passing thread through them with a needle. EG *They teach the children to cook, sew, or knit... ...sewing buttons onto one of my shirts... We sewed military uniforms.* • See also **sewing**. V OR V+O

sew up. 1 If you **sew up** two pieces of cloth, you join them together using a needle and thread. PHRASAL VB : V+O+ADV

2 If something such as a deal **is sewn up**, you have arranged things so that you are certain to be successful. EG *Trask and Bass have it all sewn up.* V+O+ADV, USU PASS Informal

sewage /suːɪdʒ/ is waste matter from homes and factories, which flows away through sewers. N UNCOUNT

If you are shaded by a tree, are you in shadow?

sewer /suːə/, **sewers.** A **sewer** is a large underground channel that carries waste matter and rain water away, usually to a place where it is treated and made harmless. N COUNT

sewing /səʊɪŋ/ is **1** the activity of making or mending clothes or other things using a needle and thread. N UNCOUNT **2** clothes or other things that are being sewn. EG *My aunt put aside her sewing.* N UNCOUNT

sewing machine, sewing machines. A **sewing machine** is a machine that you use for sewing. N COUNT

sewn /səʊn/ is the past participle of **sew.**

sex /sɛks/, **sexes. 1** The two **sexes** are the two groups, male and female, into which people and animals are divided according to the function they have in producing young. EG *...people of both sexes... ...a member of the opposite sex.* N COUNT

2 The **sex** of a person or animal is their characteristic of being either male or female. EG *...tests to ascertain the sex of the baby before it was born... ...to prevent discrimination on the grounds of sex.* N UNCOUNT

3 Sex is the physical activity by which people and animals can produce young, or it is activities connected with this. EG *The film contains no explicit sex or violence.* N UNCOUNT ● If two people **have sex**, they perform the act of sex. ● PHRASE

sexism /sɛksɪzəᵒm/ is the belief that the members of one sex, usually women, are less intelligent or less capable than those of the other sex and should be treated differently; used showing disapproval. EG *Their aims are to fight sexism in the world at large.* N UNCOUNT

sexist /sɛksɪst/, **sexists. 1** Something that is **sexist** involves sexism; used showing disapproval. EG *...sexist attitudes... ...sexist advertising... ...sexist toys like guns and dolls.* ADJ QUALIT

2 If you refer to a person, especially a man, as a **sexist**, you mean that they have sexist attitudes; used showing disapproval. N COUNT

sexless /sɛkslɪ²s/. If you describe a person as **sexless**, you mean that they have no sexual feelings. EG *...nondescript middle-aged sexless couples.* ADJ CLASSIF

sexual /sɛksjʊᵒəl/. **1 Sexual** feelings or activities are connected with the act of sex or with people's desire for sex. EG *...sexual attraction... They were not having a sexual relationship.* ADJ CLASSIF : USU ATTRIB ◇ **sexually.** EG *I find her sexually attractive.* ◇ ADV

2 Sexual also means **2.1** relating to the differences between male and female people or animals. EG *...campaigning for non-discrimination and sexual equality.* ADJ CLASSIF : ATTRIB **2.2** relating to the biological process by which people and animals produce young. EG *...sexual reproduction.* ADJ CLASSIF : ATTRIB

sexual intercourse is the physical act of sex between a man and a woman. N UNCOUNT Formal

sexuality /sɛksjʊælɪ¹ti¹/. A person's **sexuality** is their ability to experience sexual feelings. N UNCOUNT

sexy /sɛksi¹/, **sexier, sexiest.** Someone or something that is **sexy** is sexually exciting or sexually attractive. EG *...her sexy brown eyes.* ADJ QUALIT

sh /ʃ/ is a noise that you make in order to tell someone to be quiet. EG *Sh! The boys are in bed.* EXCLAM

shabby /ʃæbi¹/, **shabbier, shabbiest. 1** Something that is **shabby** looks old and is in bad condition. EG *...his shabby clothes... ...a shabby house with worn carpeting on the stairs.* ADJ QUALIT ◇ **shabbily.** EG *They were shabbily dressed.* ◇ ADV

2 Someone who is **shabby** is wearing old, worn clothes. EG *...shabby children in the streets.* ADJ QUALIT

3 You describe someone's behaviour as **shabby** when they behave in an unfair or unacceptable way. EG *...a series of shabby compromises.* ADJ QUALIT ◇ **shabbily.** EG *Don't you think you've treated me a little shabbily?* ◇ ADV

shack /ʃæk/, **shacks.** A **shack** is a small hut built from bits of wood or metal. N COUNT

shackle /ʃækəᵒl/, **shackles, shackling, shackled. 1** If you **are shackled** by something, it prevents you from doing what you want to do. EG *He is shackled by domestic responsibilities.* V+O : USU PASS Literary

2 You can use **shackles** to refer to circumstances that prevent you from doing what you want to do. EG *There are a few who have managed to throw off the shackles of the past.* N PLURAL : USU+SUPP Literary

3 Shackles are two metal rings joined by a chain which are fastened around someone's wrists or ankles in order to prevent them from moving or escaping. N PLURAL

4 To **shackle** someone means to put shackles on them. EG *The guards shackled his wrists and ankles.* V+O

shade /ʃeɪd/, **shades, shading, shaded. 1 Shade** is an area of darkness under or next to an object such as a tree, where the sun cannot reach. EG *There are no trees or bushes to give shade... Right now the air is cool in the shade... He led the way to the shade of a large oak tree.* N UNCOUNT, OR N SING : *the*+N

2 If a place or person **is shaded** by something, that thing prevents light from falling on the place or person. EG *The broad walks are shaded by chestnut trees.* V+O : USU PASS

3 If you **shade** your **eyes**, you put your hand across your forehead in order to prevent a bright light from shining into your eyes. PHRASE

4 A **shade** is the same as a lampshade. EG *...a lamp with a thick silk shade.* N COUNT

5 The **shades** of a particular colour are its different forms. For example, emerald green and olive green are shades of green. EG *They wore tight-fitting jackets in shades of pink, blue, and brown.* N COUNT

6 The **shades** of something abstract are its different forms. EG *The phrase has many shades of meaning... ...various shades of socialist opinion.* N COUNT+SUPP

7 When something **shades** into something else, there is no clear division between the two things. EG *...reds shading into pinks... ...innocence shading into ignorance.* V+*into*

shadow /ʃædəʊ/, **shadows. 1** A **shadow** is a dark shape on a surface that is made when something stands between a light and the surface. EG *...a car parked in the shadow of a tree... The smoky fires cast dancing shadows upon the wide circle of faces.* N COUNT

2 Shadow is darkness in a place caused by something preventing light from reaching it. EG *The whole canyon is in shadow.* N UNCOUNT

3 If you say that someone or something is **a shadow of** their **former self**, you mean that they are much less strong or vigorous than they used to be. EG *The organization is now no more than a shadow of its former self.* PHRASE

4 If there is no **shadow of a doubt** about something, there is no doubt at all about it. EG *I never had a shadow of a doubt that he was right.* N SING+*of* : WITH BROAD NEG

5 A British Member of Parliament who is a member of the **Shadow** Cabinet or who is a **Shadow** Cabinet minister belongs to the main opposition party and takes a special interest in matters of a particular kind. EG *He is Shadow Secretary for Trade and Industry.* ADJ CLASSIF : ATTRIB British

shadowy /ʃædəʊi¹/. **1** A **shadowy** place is dark or full of shadows. EG *...a shadowy alcove.* ADJ CLASSIF

2 A **shadowy** figure or shape is someone or something that you can hardly see because it is dark or misty. EG *...the shadowy musicians in the background.* ADJ CLASSIF : ATTRIB

3 You describe people and activities as **shadowy** when very little is known about them. EG *...the shadowy world of espionage.* ADJ QUALIT

shady /ʃeɪdi¹/, **shadier, shadiest. 1** A **shady** place is sheltered from bright sunlight by buildings or trees. EG *We found a shady spot in the park to have a rest.* ADJ CLASSIF

2 Shady trees produce a lot of shade. ADJ CLASSIF

3 You describe people and their activities as **shady** when you think that their activities are dishonest or illegal. EG *...shady dealings.* ADJ QUALIT Informal

shaft /ʃɑːft/, **shafts. 1** A **shaft** is a vertical passage, for example one for a lift. EG *...the lift shaft.* N COUNT

2 A **shaft** in a machine is a rod that turns round N COUNT

shapes

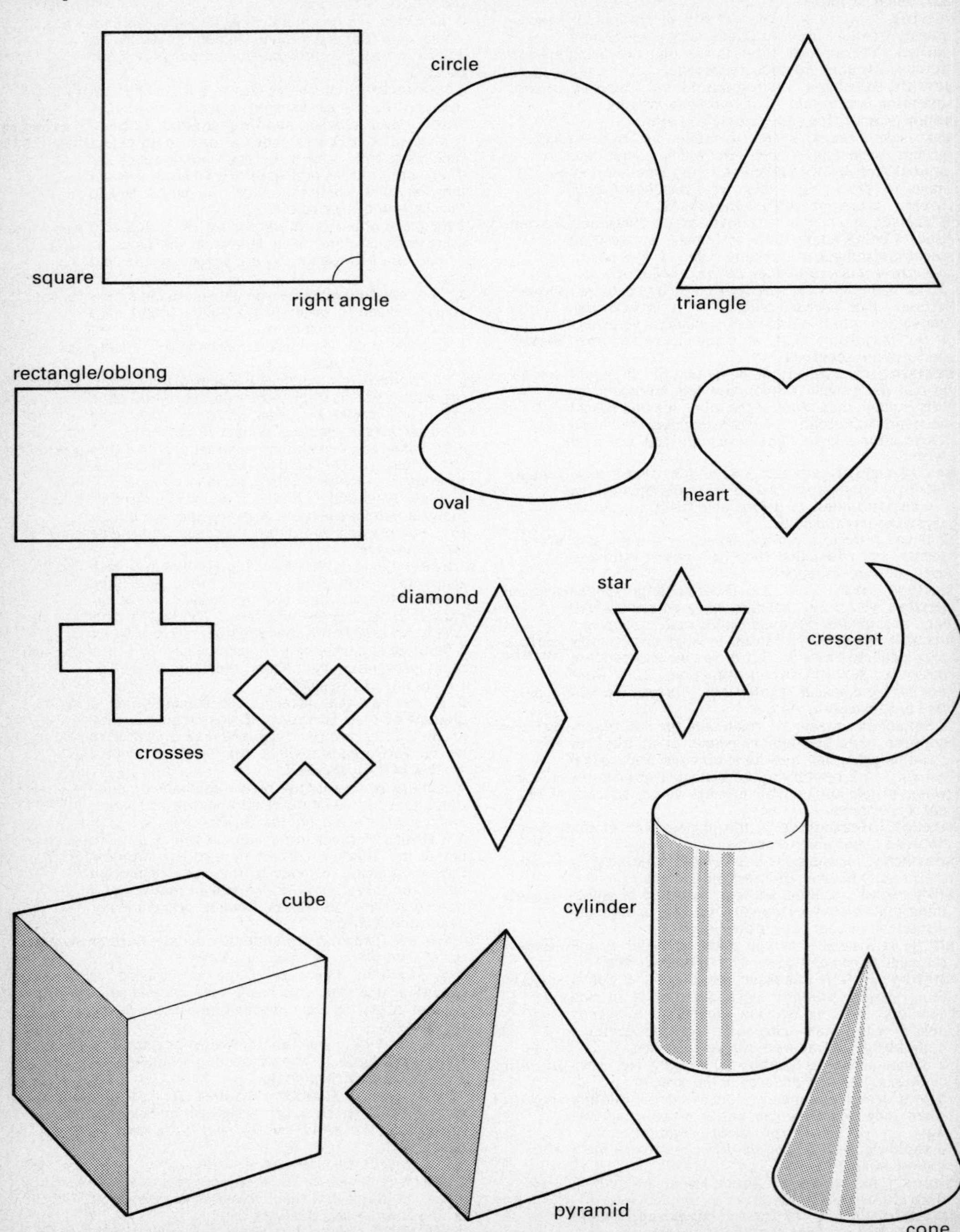
circle
square
right angle
triangle
rectangle/oblong
oval
heart
star
diamond
crescent
crosses
cube
cylinder
pyramid
cone

and round in order to transfer movement in the machine. EG *...the drive shaft.*

3 A **shaft** of light is a beam of light. EG *The hatch was opened, admitting a shaft of daylight.* N COUNT : USU+*of*

shaggy /ʃægi¹/. **Shaggy** hair or fur is long and very untidy. EG *...his shaggy, unkempt beard... Shaggy sheep roamed on the higher slopes.* ADJ QUALIT

shake /ʃeɪk/, **shakes, shaking, shook** /ʃʊk/, **shaken. 1** If you **shake** someone or something, you hold them and move them quickly backwards and forwards or up and down. EG *He awakened to find himself being shaken roughly by his father... He shook from a bag a heap of dried leaves... The wind shook white petals from the tree.* ▸ used as a noun. EG *She gave her skirts a vigorous shake.* V+O : OFT+A ▸ N COUNT

2 If something **shakes**, it moves from side to side or up and down with quick, small movements. EG *The earth shook and the sky darkened... He was shaking with laughter.* V

3 If your voice **is shaking**, you cannot control it properly and it trembles, because you are nervous or angry. EG *His eyes were wild and his voice shook.* V

4 If something **shakes** you, it makes you feel shocked and upset. EG *My mother's death had shaken him dreadfully.* ◊ **shaken**. EG *I was badly shaken. I had never had a crash before.* V+O : NO CONT ◊ ADJ QUALIT

5 If something **shakes** your beliefs or ideas, it makes you feel less certain about them. EG *The lecture did little to shake his convictions.* V+O

6 If you **shake hands** with someone or **shake** their **hand**, you hold their right hand in your own when you are meeting them, saying goodbye to them, or congratulating them. EG *Elijah and I shook hands and said good night.* PHRASE

7 If you **shake** your **head**, you move it from side to side in order to say 'no' or to show disbelief or sadness. EG *He offered her a cigarette. She shook her head. 'No thank you. I don't smoke.'* PHRASE

shake off. If you **shake off** someone or something that you do not want, you manage to get away from them or get rid of them. EG *It had taken Franklin several hours to shake off the police.* PHRASAL VB : V+O+ADV

shake-up, shake-ups. A **shake-up** is a major set of changes in an organization or system. EG *Many were eager for a shake-up in the two-party system.* N COUNT

shaky /ʃeɪki¹/, **shakier, shakiest. 1** If you are **shaky**, you are shaking or feeling weak because you are frightened, shocked, or ill. EG *I was nervous and a bit shaky when he watched me.* ◊ **shakily**. EG *The man stood up shakily.* ADJ QUALIT ◊ ADV

2 You can use **shaky** to describe something that is rather weak or not very good. EG *After a shaky start the orchestra grew more confident... ...a company with very shaky financial prospects.* ADJ QUALIT

shall /ʃə³l/. **1** If someone says that they **shall** do something, they mean that they intend to do it. EG *I shall get angry in a moment... We probably shan't sleep much... I shan't let you go.* MODAL

2 If you say that something **shall** happen, you are emphasizing that it will definitely happen. EG *It must be done and therefore it shall be done.* MODAL Formal

3 If you say to someone that they **shall** do something, you are ordering them to do it. EG *You're here to enjoy yourself, and enjoy yourself you shall... No more drink shall be drunk tonight.* MODAL Formal

4 You use **shall** in questions **4.1** when you are asking someone for advice. EG *Whatever shall I do?... Where shall we go for our drink?* **4.2** when you are asking someone if they would like you to do something. EG *Shall I shut the door?* **4.3** when you are suggesting to someone that you should both do something together. EG *Shall we go and see a film?... We'll go forward a little more, shall we?* MODAL MODAL

shallow /ʃæləʊ/, **shallower, shallowest; shallows. 1** A **shallow** hole, container, or layer of something measures only a short distance from the top to the bottom. EG *When the fish comes into shallow water, grab it by the tail... ...a shallow bowl... ...a shallow valley.* ADJ QUALIT

2 A person, idea, or activity that is **shallow** does not show or involve any serious or careful thought; used showing disapproval. EG *This kind of life is shallow and trivial... I was too young and shallow to understand love.* ◊ **shallowness**. EG *...the shallowness of her social life.* ADJ QUALIT ◊ N UNCOUNT

3 If your breathing is **shallow**, you take only a very small amount of air into your lungs at each breath. ADJ QUALIT

4 The **shallows** are the shallow part of an area of water. EG *Thousands of little fish swim in the shallows.* N PLURAL : the+N

sham /ʃæm/, **shams.** Something that is a **sham** is not real or not really what it seems to be; used showing disapproval. EG *Their independence is a sham.* ▸ used as an adjective. EG *...a sham fight... This is rather a sham enterprise.* N COUNT ▸ ADJ CLASSIF : ATTRIB

shamble /ʃæmbə⁰l/, **shambles, shambling, shambled. 1** If a place, event, or situation is a **shambles**, everything is in disorder. EG *The rehearsal was a shambles.* N SING : a+N

2 If you **shamble** somewhere, you walk clumsily, dragging your feet. EG *They got up and shambled out.* V+A

shame /ʃeɪm/, **shames, shaming, shamed. 1** **Shame** is an uncomfortable feeling that you have when you know that you have done something wrong or embarrassing, or when you know that someone close to you has. EG *The memory fills me with shame... Simon lowered his face in shame.* N UNCOUNT

2 If someone brings **shame** on you, they make other people lose their respect for you. EG *Don't bring shame on the family.* N UNCOUNT

3 If something **shames** you, it causes you to feel shame. EG *It shamed him to know that his father had behaved in such a way.* V+O

4 If you **shame** someone into doing something, you force them to do it by making them feel ashamed not to. EG *Father was shamed into helping them.* V+O+A

5 If you say that it is **a shame** that something happened, you are saying how sorry you are that it happened. EG *It's a shame he didn't come too... What a shame. Never mind... It's a shame to waste all this food.* N SING : a+N

shamefaced /ʃeɪmfeɪst/. If you are **shamefaced**, you feel embarrassed because you have done something that you know you should not have done. ADJ QUALIT

shameful /ʃeɪmfʊl/. If you describe a person's action or attitude as **shameful**, you mean that it is so bad that the person ought to be ashamed. EG *It shows a shameful lack of concern.* ◊ **shamefully**. EG *The government have shamefully neglected this area.* ADJ QUALIT ◊ ADV

shameless /ʃeɪmlɪ²s/. Someone who is **shameless** behaves in a way which is considered unacceptable, but is not at all ashamed of their behaviour. EG *Her husband had run off with a shameless gipsy woman.* ◊ **shamelessly**. EG *Matty flatters me shamelessly.* ADJ CLASSIF ◊ ADV

shampoo /ʃæmpuː/, **shampoos. Shampoo** is a soapy liquid that you use for washing your hair. N MASS

shandy /ʃændi¹/, **shandies. Shandy** is a drink which is made by mixing beer and lemonade. N MASS

shan't /ʃɑːnt/ is the usual spoken form of 'shall not'.

shanty town /ʃænti¹ taʊn/, **shanty towns.** A **shanty town** is a collection of rough huts which poor people live in. N COUNT

shape /ʃeɪp/, **shapes, shaping, shaped. 1** The **shape** of an object or area is the appearance of its outside edges, for example whether it is round, square, curved, or wide. EG *Bear Island is triangular in shape... ...a huge animal the size and shape of a rhinoceros... You can spin-dry this sweater and it will still retain its shape.* N COUNT OR N UNCOUNT

2 A **shape** is **2.1** something which has a definite form, for example a circle, square, or triangle. EG N COUNT

...patterns created from geometric shapes. **2.2** an object or person that you cannot see clearly. EG *One could just distinguish a slim shape in a short white dress.*

3 The **shape** of something such as a plan or an organization is its structure and size. EG *...developments which may alter the future course and shape of industry.* N SING+POSS

4 If you **shape** an object, you give it a particular shape, usually by using your hands. EG *He began to shape the dough into rolls.* V+O: OFT+*into*

5 Something or someone that **shapes** a thing or activity causes it to develop in a particular way. EG *It was the Greeks who shaped the thinking of Western man.* V+O

6 You use **in the shape of** before mentioning exactly what you are referring to, after referring to it in a general way. EG *...large-scale enterprise in the shape of mines or plantations.* PREP

7 Shape is also used in these phrases. **7.1** If someone or something is **in good shape**, they are in a good condition or state of health. If they are **in bad shape**, they are in a bad condition or state of health. EG *He looked in good shape.* **7.2** If you say that you will not accept or tolerate something **in any shape or form**, you are emphasizing that you will not accept or tolerate it at all. EG *I'm strongly opposed to violence in any shape or form.* **7.3** If someone **licks** you **into shape** or **knocks** you **into shape**, they make you work or behave as they want you to. EG *...knocking their children into shape.* **7.4** When something **takes shape**, it develops and starts to have a definite structure or shape. EG *The organization began to take shape.* PHRASES; Informal

shape up. The way that someone or something **is shaping up** is the way that they are developing. EG *This campaign is shaping up as one of the most intensive sales campaigns ever.* PHRASAL VB: V+ADV, USU+A

shaped /ʃeɪpt/. Something that is **shaped** like a particular object or in a particular way has the kind of shape indicated. EG *...a chair shaped like a saddle... ...weirdly shaped trees.* ADJ CLASSIF

-shaped combines with nouns to form adjectives describing the shape of an object. EG *...an egg-shaped face... ...a star-shaped card.*

shapeless /ʃeɪplɪ^{2}s/. Something that is **shapeless** does not have a distinctive or attractive shape. EG *...shapeless pyjamas.* ADJ QUALIT

shapely /ʃeɪpli^{1}/. A **shapely** person, especially a woman, has an attractive shape. EG *She had a slim waist and shapely legs.* ADJ QUALIT

share /ʃɛə/, **shares, sharing, shared. 1** If you **share** something with another person, you both use it or do it. EG *Ralph went upstairs to the room he shared with his brother... We share the washing up... Let's share the petrol costs... Both partners share in rearing their family.* V+O OR V+O+*with*: RECIP; ALSO V+A

2 When you **share** an experience that someone else has, you are with them and so you experience it too. EG *Old age was something they would never be able to share.* V+O OR V+O+*with*: RECIP

3 If you **share** a thought or a piece of news with someone, you tell them about it. EG *He was so excited about his idea that he felt he had to share it with someone.* V+O OR V+O+*with*: RECIP

4 If two people or things **share** a particular quality, characteristic, or idea, they both have it. EG *I share your concern... ...people who share the same interests.* V+O

5 If you have or do a **share** of something, you have or do part of it. EG *An increasing share of the work is handed over to computers... ...a campaign for parents to have a share in discussing school policy.* N SING: OFT+*of/in*

6 If you have or do your **share** of something, you have or do the amount that is fair for you. EG *It does help when a father does his share at home... ...if one man seizes more than his fair share of the food.* N SING+POSS

7 The **shares** of a company are the equal parts into which its ownership is divided. Shares can be bought by people as an investment. EG *A week ago, the firm's shares jumped 10p to 114p... I wonder how many companies he has shares in?* N COUNT: USU PLURAL

share out. If you **share out** an amount of something, you give each person in a group an equal or fair part of it. EG *The fairest way to share things out is to distribute them equally.* PHRASAL VB: V+O+ADV

shareholder /ʃɛəhəʊldə/, **shareholders.** A **shareholder** is a person who owns shares in a company. N COUNT

shark /ʃɑːk/, **sharks.** A **shark** is a very large fish with sharp teeth. Sharks sometimes attack people. N COUNT

sharp /ʃɑːp/, **sharper, sharpest; sharps. 1** A **sharp** object **1.1** has a very thin edge that is good for cutting things. EG *Cut it away with a sharp knife.* **1.2** has a very finely pointed end. EG *...small, sharp teeth... He stepped on a sharp thorn.* ADJ QUALIT

2 A **sharp** picture, outline, or distinction is very clear and easy to see or understand. EG *...sharp, fresh footprints in the snow... We try to draw a sharp dividing line between Civil Service and Government.* ◇ **sharply**. EG *The memory remains sharply engraved on my mind.* ADJ QUALIT; ◇ ADV

3 Someone who is **sharp** is quick to notice, hear, or understand things; used showing approval. EG *You've got to be sharp to get ahead... His sharp eyes would never miss it.* ADJ QUALIT

4 A **sharp** change happens suddenly and is very big. EG *...sharp food-price increases.* ◇ **sharply**. EG *Sales of the car have risen sharply in recent weeks.* ADJ QUALIT; ◇ ADV

5 You also use **sharp** to describe an action that is done quickly and firmly. EG *She received a sharp clout on the head... With his finger and thumb he gave it a sharp turn.* ◇ **sharply**. EG *Both birds turned their heads sharply at the sound.* ADJ QUALIT; ◇ ADV

6 If someone says something in a **sharp** way, they say it suddenly and rather firmly or angrily. EG *A sharp order came through his headphones.* ◇ **sharply**. EG *'Don't talk nonsense,' she said sharply.* ADJ QUALIT; ◇ ADV

7 A **sharp** sound is very short and sudden and quite loud. EG *...the sharp crack of a twig.* ADJ QUALIT

8 Sharp pain or cold hurts a lot when it affects you. EG *His blistered foot at that moment caused him a sharp pang.* ADJ QUALIT

9 Food that has a **sharp** taste is slightly sour but also fresh. EG *...the sharp, pure taste of gooseberries.* ADJ QUALIT

10 You can use **sharp** to indicate that something happens at exactly the time mentioned. EG *His train came in at eight sharp.* ADV

11 A **sharp** in music is a note that is a semitone higher than the note which is described by the same letter. It can be represented by the symbol (♯). EG *...the C sharp minor Prelude.* N COUNT, OR ADJ AFTER N

12 If a musical note is played or sung **sharp**, it is slightly higher in pitch than it should be. ADV OR ADJ QUALIT

sharpen /ʃɑːp^{ə}n/, **sharpens, sharpening, sharpened. 1** If you **sharpen** an object, you make its edge very thin or you make its end pointed. EG *Roger sharpened a stick at both ends.* V+O

2 If your senses or abilities **sharpen** or **are sharpened**, you become quicker at noticing things or at thinking. EG *His eyes and instincts sharpened as he saw the fort in the distance... Generations of urban living had sharpened their wits.* V-ERG

3 If your voice **sharpens**, you speak more angrily and quickly than you did before. EG *'Who told you?' Her voice had sharpened a little... Fear and urgency sharpened Sarah's voice.* V-ERG

4 If something **sharpens** the disagreements or differences between people, it makes them fiercer or greater. EG *This sharpened the conflict between* V-ERG

Would you be upset if someone spoke to you sharply?

them... Tension in society has increased and sharpened.

sharpener /ʃɑːpə^{ə}nə/, **sharpeners.** A pencil **sharpener** is an object or device used for sharpening pencils. N COUNT

shatter /ʃætə/, **shatters, shattering, shattered.**
1 If something **shatters** or if you **shatter** it, it breaks into a lot of small pieces. EG *The vase fell from her hand and shattered on the floor.* V-ERG
2 If something **shatters** your beliefs or hopes, it destroys them. EG *The trip completely shattered my ideas of what schools were supposed to do.* V+O
3 If someone **is shattered** by an event, it shocks and upsets them very much. EG *My father was shattered by the news.* V-PASS

shattered /ʃætəd/. Someone who is **shattered** is **1** very shocked and upset. EG *When Harris died, Dean was shattered.* **2** very tired. EG *I'm shattered after a day's work.* ADJ PRED; Informal

shattering /ʃætə^{ə}rɪŋ/. Something that is **shattering 1** shocks and upsets you very much. EG *...a shattering experience.* **2** makes you very tired. EG *Sunday had been a shattering day.* ADJ QUALIT

shave /ʃeɪv/, **shaves, shaving, shaved. 1** When a man **shaves**, he cuts hair from his face using a razor. EG *When he had shaved and dressed, he went down to the kitchen... He had shaved off his beard.* V, V+O, OR V+O+*off*
▸ used as a noun. EG *He had a shave and a bath.* ▸ N COUNT
2 If someone **shaves** a part of their body, they cut all the hair from it using a razor. EG *She shaved her legs and under her arms.* V+O OR V+O+*off*
3 If you **shave** off part of a piece of wood or other material, you cut very thin pieces from it. EG *...shaving an inch off the inside.* V+O+*off*
4 If you describe something as a **close shave**, you mean that there was nearly an accident or a disaster but it was avoided. PHRASE; Outdated
5 See also **shaving**.

shaven /ʃeɪvə^{ə}n/. If a part of someone's body is **shaven**, it has been shaved. EG *His hair was very short, the back of his neck shaven.* ● See also **clean-shaven**. ADJ CLASSIF

shaver /ʃeɪvə/, **shavers.** A **shaver** is an electric tool, used for shaving hair from the face and body. N COUNT

shaving /ʃeɪvɪŋ/, **shavings. 1** You use **shaving** to describe something that people use when they shave. EG *...a shaving brush.* ADJ CLASSIF : ATTRIB
2 Shavings are small, very thin pieces of something such as wood which have been cut from a larger piece. N COUNT : USU PLURAL

shawl /ʃɔːl/, **shawls.** A **shawl** is a large piece of woollen cloth which a woman wears over her shoulders or head, or which is wrapped around a baby to keep it warm. N COUNT

she /ʃiː/ is used as the subject of a verb. **1** You use **she** to refer to a woman or girl who has already been mentioned, or whose identity is known. EG *'So long,' Mary said as she passed Miss Saunders... Ask her if she can do something with them.* PRON : SING
2 You also use **she 2.1** to refer to a nation. EG *Britain is a poor nation now, and she would do well to remember this.* **2.2** to refer to a ship, car, or other vehicle. EG *She does 0 to 60 in 10 seconds.* PRON : SING

sheaf /ʃiːf/, **sheaves** /ʃiːvz/. **1** A **sheaf** of papers is a bundle of papers. EG *...a thick sheaf of letters.* N PART OR N COUNT
2 A **sheaf** of corn is a bundle of ripe corn plants tied together. N PART OR N COUNT

shear /ʃɪə/, **shears, shearing, sheared, shorn** /ʃɔːn/. The past participle can be either **sheared** or **shorn**.
1 To **shear** a sheep means to cut the wool off it. EG *I sheared 500 ewes.* V+O
2 A pair of **shears** is a tool like a very large pair of scissors, used especially for cutting garden hedges. See picture at TOOLS. N PLURAL
3 See also **shorn**.

shear off. If something such as a piece of metal **shears off**, it breaks. EG *Another bolt has sheared off.* PHRASAL VB : V-ERG+ADV

sheath /ʃiːθ/, **sheaths. 1** A **sheath** is a covering for the blade of a knife. EG *He wiped the knife and put it back in the sheath.* N COUNT
2 A **sheath** is also a rubber covering for a man's penis that is used as a contraceptive. N COUNT

sheathe /ʃiːð/, **sheathes, sheathing, sheathed.** When you **sheathe** a knife, you put it in its sheath. V+O

sheaves /ʃiːvz/ is the plural of **sheaf.**

shed /ʃɛd/, **sheds, shedding.** The form **shed** is used in the present tense and is the past tense and past participle of the verb.
1 A **shed** is a small building that is used for keeping things in. EG *She went to find her wellingtons in the shed... ...the coal shed.* N COUNT
2 When an animal **sheds** hair or skin, some of its hair or skin drops off. When a tree **sheds** its leaves, its leaves fall off in the autumn. EG *...like a snake shedding its skin.* V+O
3 To **shed** something also means to get rid of it. EG *2,600 workers are due to be shed by the company... I shed all my restraint.* V+O; Formal
4 If a lorry **sheds** its load, the goods that it is carrying accidentally fall onto the road. V+O
5 If you **shed** tears, you cry. EG *...a child shedding tears over a broken toy.* V+O
6 To **shed blood** means to kill people in a violent way. EG *They called for an end to the shedding of blood.* PHRASE
7 If something **sheds light on** a problem, it makes it easier to understand by providing more information about it. PHRASE

she'd /ʃiːd/. **1 She'd** is the usual spoken form of 'she had', especially when 'had' is an auxiliary verb. EG *It was too late. She'd done it.*
2 She'd is also a spoken form of 'she would'. EG *She said she'd come by train.*

sheen /ʃiːn/. If something has a **sheen**, it has a smooth and gentle brightness on its surface. EG *...beautiful, long hair with a silky sheen.* N SING+SUPP

sheep /ʃiːp/. **Sheep** is both the singular and the plural form.
1 A **sheep** is a farm animal with a thick woolly coat. Sheep are kept for their wool or for their meat. EG *...a flock of sheep.* ● See also **black sheep**. N COUNT
2 If you say that a group of people are **like sheep**, you mean that if one person does something, all the others copy that person. PHRASE

sheepdog /ʃiːpdɒg/, **sheepdogs.** A **sheepdog** is a breed of dog. Some sheepdogs are used for controlling sheep. N COUNT

sheepish /ʃiːpɪʃ/. If you look **sheepish**, you look slightly embarrassed because you feel foolish or you have done something silly. EG *He gave me a sheepish grin.* ◊ **sheepishly**. EG *Jo looked up at his father sheepishly.* ADJ QUALIT; ◊ ADV

sheepskin /ʃiːpskɪn/ is the skin and wool of a sheep, used especially for coats and rugs. EG *...a sheepskin jacket.* N UNCOUNT : USU N MOD

sheer /ʃɪə/. **1 Sheer** means complete and not involving or mixed with anything else; often used simply to emphasize the word it describes. EG *The eighth floor of the hotel was sheer luxury... Many of the audience walked out through sheer boredom.* ADJ CLASSIF : ATTRIB
2 A **sheer** cliff or drop is a completely vertical one. EG *...a gorge with sheer rock sides.* ADJ QUALIT
3 Sheer is used to describe silk or other material which is very thin, light, and delicate. ADJ QUALIT

sheet /ʃiːt/, **sheets. 1** A **sheet** is a large rectangular piece of cloth, usually made of cotton. Sheets are used with blankets or a duvet to make a bed. EG *It was bliss to sleep in a soft bed with clean sheets again.* ● **as white as a sheet**: see **white**. N COUNT
2 A **sheet** of paper is a rectangular piece of paper. EG *He handed a typewritten sheet to Karen.* N COUNT
3 A **sheet** of glass, metal, or wood is a large, flat, thin piece of it. EG *...a single sheet of glass.* N COUNT

sheikh /ʃeɪk/, **sheikhs;** also spelled **sheik.** A **sheikh** is an Arab chief or ruler. N COUNT

shelf /ʃɛlf/, **shelves** /ʃɛlvz/. A **shelf** is a flat piece of wood, metal, or glass which is attached to a wall or to the sides of a cupboard. Shelves are used for keeping things on. EG *There were a lot of books on the shelves along the walls.* N COUNT

shelf life. The **shelf life** of a product, especially food, is the length of time that it can be kept in a shop before it becomes too old to sell. EG *This process should give butter a longer shelf life.* N SING+SUPP

shell /ʃɛl/, **shells, shelling, shelled. 1** The **shell** of an egg or nut is the hard covering which surrounds it. EG *...the blue shells of sparrows' eggs... ...coconut shells.* N COUNT OR N UNCOUNT

2 The **shell** of a tortoise, snail, or crab is the hard, protective covering that it has on its back. N COUNT OR N UNCOUNT

3 A **shell** is the hard covering which surrounds, or used to surround, a small, soft sea creature. EG *...a handkerchief full of shells which my sister had collected... ...oyster shells.* N COUNT OR N UNCOUNT

4 If you **shell** peas or nuts, you remove the natural covering from them. EG *I sat shelling some peas.* V+O

5 You can refer to the frame of a building, boat, car, or other structure as a **shell**. EG *...the burned-out shell of wood and mud that had once been their home.* N COUNT

6 A **shell** is also a metal container filled with explosives that can be fired from a large gun over long distances. EG *Arnold had his leg smashed when a shell hit the truck he was driving.* N COUNT

7 To **shell** a place means to fire explosive shells at it. EG *They continued to shell towns on the northern coast.* V+O

shell out. If you **shell out** for something, you spend money on it. EG *He will have to shell out another three hundred dollars for the licence.* PHRASAL VB: V+ADV OR V+O+ADV Informal

she'll /ʃiːl/ is the usual spoken form of 'she will'. EG *I hope she'll be all right.*

shellfish /ʃɛlfɪʃ/. **Shellfish** is both the singular and the plural form. N COUNT

A **shellfish** is a small creature that lives in the sea and has a shell. EG *...edible shellfish.*

shelter /ʃɛltə/, **shelters, sheltering, sheltered.**

1 A **shelter** is a small building or covered place which is made to protect people from bad weather or danger. EG *That shelter might fall down if the rain comes back.* N COUNT

2 If a place provides **shelter**, it provides protection from bad weather or danger. EG *He found shelter in caves... We waited in the shelter of the trees.* N UNCOUNT

3 If you **shelter** in a place, you stay there and are protected from bad weather or danger. EG *It is natural to shelter from a storm.* V: USU+A

4 If a place or thing **is sheltered** by something, it is protected by that thing from wind and rain. EG *This wide alley is sheltered by plane trees.* V+O: USU PASS

5 If you **shelter** someone, **5.1** you provide them with a place to stay or live. EG *Can those being sheltered be adequately fed?* **5.2** you help them by hiding them when other people are looking for them. EG *Some villagers are prepared to shelter wanted men.* V+O

6 If you have **shelter**, you have a place where you can stay or live. EG *The basic necessities of life are food, shelter and clothing.* N UNCOUNT

sheltered /ʃɛltəd/. **1** A place that is **sheltered** is protected from wind and rain. EG *I lay down in the warmest and most sheltered spot I could find.* ADJ QUALIT

2 If you have a **sheltered** life, you do not experience things which other people experience, especially unpleasant things. EG *We lived a sheltered life in our Irish village.* ADJ QUALIT

3 Sheltered accommodation is designed for old or handicapped people. It allows them to be independent but also gives them supervision when they need it. EG *...a sheltered housing scheme.* ADJ CLASSIF: ATTRIB

shelve /ʃɛlv/, **shelves, shelving, shelved. 1** If you **shelve** a plan, you decide not to continue with it for a while. EG *The project seems to have been shelved for the moment.* V+O

2 If a seashore **shelves**, it slopes downwards. EG *The beach shelved steeply... ...long, gently shelving sands.* V

3 Shelves is the plural of **shelf**.

shelving /ʃɛlvɪŋ/ is a set of shelves. EG *Thousands of books are stocked on more than 8 miles of shelving in the library.* N UNCOUNT

shepherd /ʃɛpəd/, **shepherds, shepherding, shepherded. 1** A **shepherd** is a person whose job is to look after sheep. N COUNT

2 If you **shepherd** someone somewhere, you accompany them there to make sure that they go to the right place. EG *I shepherded them towards the lobby.* V+O: USU+A

shepherd's pie is a dish consisting of minced meat covered with a layer of mashed potato. N UNCOUNT

sheriff /ʃɛrɪf/, **sheriffs.** A **sheriff** is a person who is elected to make sure that the law is obeyed in a particular county. N COUNT American

sherry /ʃɛri[1]/, **sherries. Sherry** is a strong alcoholic drink made from grapes. It is usually drunk before a meal. N MASS

she's /ʃiːz/. **1 She's** is the usual spoken form of 'she is'. EG *She's Swedish.*

2 She's is also a spoken form of 'she has', especially when 'has' is an auxiliary verb. EG *She's gone back to Montrose.*

shield /ʃiːld/, **shields, shielding, shielded. 1** A **shield** is **1.1** a large piece of metal or leather which soldiers used to carry to protect their bodies while they were fighting. **1.2** a sports trophy or a badge that is shaped like a shield. EG *I shall remove her prefect's shield.* N COUNT

2 Something which is a **shield** against a particular danger provides protection from it. EG *Dark pigment in the skin provides an effective shield against the sun... ...a wind shield.* N COUNT: OFT+*against*

3 Something or someone that **shields** you from a danger protects you from it, by being or putting a barrier between you and it. EG *Her parasol was propped up behind her to shield her from the sun.* V+O OR V-REFL: USU+*from*

shift /ʃɪft/, **shifts, shifting, shifted. 1** If you **shift** something or if it **shifts**, it moves. EG *He shifted the chair closer to the bed... Muller's eyes shifted to the telephone.* V-ERG: OFT+A

2 A **shift** in opinion or in a situation is a slight change in it. EG *...a radical shift in public opinion... You may detect a shift of emphasis.* N COUNT+SUPP

3 If someone's opinion or a situation **shifts** or **is shifted**, it changes slightly. EG *...shifting the balance of financial control... 'I don't know,' Margaret said, shifting from her earlier attitude.* V OR V-ERG: OFT+A

4 If you **shift** responsibility or blame onto someone else, you transfer it to them. V+O: USU+A

5 A **shift** is also a set period of time during which people work in a factory. EG *He had chosen the midnight to 8 shift.* N COUNT

shifty /ʃɪfti[1]/. Someone who looks **shifty** gives the impression of being deceitful and dishonest. EG *...a man with small shifty eyes... He gave me a shifty look.* ADJ QUALIT Informal

shilling /ʃɪlɪŋ/, **shillings.** A **shilling** was a unit of money used in Britain until 1971 which was the equivalent of 5p. There were twenty shillings in an English pound. N COUNT

shimmer /ʃɪmə/, **shimmers, shimmering, shimmered.** If something **shimmers**, it shines with a faint, unsteady light. EG *I sat looking at the sea shimmering in the moonlight.* V

shin /ʃɪn/, **shins, shinning, shinned.** Your **shin** is the front part of your leg between your knee and your ankle. EG *He kicked her shin.* N COUNT

shin up. If you **shin up** a tree or a pole, you climb it quickly and easily, using your hands and PHRASAL VB: V+PREP/ADV

What do you find inside shells?

legs to grip it. EG *I shinned up a lamp post to get a better view.*

shine /ʃaɪn/, **shines, shining, shone** /ʃɒn/. **1** When the sun or a light **shines**, it gives out bright light. EG *The sun shone all day.* V

2 If you **shine** a torch or a lamp somewhere, you point it there, so that you can see something when it is dark. EG *I asked him to shine the headlight on the door.* V+O+A

3 Something that **shines** is very bright, usually because it is reflecting light. EG *His eyes shone like stars.* V

4 Something that has a **shine** is bright because it reflects light. EG *...the shine of the handles on the doors.* N SING

5 Someone who **shines** at a skill or activity does it extremely well. EG *He shines at amateur theatricals.* V : OFT+*at*

shingle /ʃɪŋgə°l/. **Shingle** consists of small rough pieces of stone on the shore by a sea or a river. EG *The beach is a mixture of sand and shingle.* N UNCOUNT

shining /ʃaɪnɪŋ/. **1 Shining** things are very bright, usually because they are reflecting light. EG *...rows of shining glasses... ...its shining feathers.* ADJ CLASSIF

2 A **shining** achievement or quality is a very good one which should be greatly admired. EG *She was a shining example to people everywhere.* ADJ CLASSIF : ATTRIB

shiny /ʃaɪni^1/, **shinier, shiniest.** Something that is **shiny** is bright and reflects light. EG *...shiny black shoes... ...shiny cars.* ADJ QUALIT

ship /ʃɪp/, **ships, shipping, shipped. 1** A **ship** is a large boat which carries passengers or cargo. EG *The ship was due to sail the following morning... They were sent home by ship.* N COUNT OR *by*+N

2 If people or things **are shipped** somewhere, they are sent there on a ship or by some other means of transport. EG *They had their luggage shipped to Nigeria... The cattle were shipped out by rail.* V+O : USU PASS+A

shipping /ʃɪpɪŋ/ is **1** the transport of cargo on ships. EG *It was sent at a cost, including shipping, of only £35.* **2** ships considered as a group. EG *Nearly a fifth of the shipping had been sunk.* N UNCOUNT

shipwreck /ʃɪprɛk/, **shipwrecks, shipwrecked.**

1 If there is a **shipwreck**, a ship is destroyed in an accident at sea. EG *The whole family perished in a shipwreck.* N COUNT OR N UNCOUNT

2 A **shipwreck** is a ship which has been destroyed in an accident at sea. EG *Treasure has sometimes been found in shipwrecks.* N COUNT

3 If someone **is shipwrecked**, their ship is destroyed in an accident at sea but they survive and manage to reach land. EG *He was shipwrecked off the lonely island of Iona.* V-PASS

shipyard /ʃɪpjɑːd/, **shipyards.** A **shipyard** is a place where ships are built and repaired. EG *Many shipyards will have to close.* N COUNT

shirk /ʃɜːk/, **shirks, shirking, shirked.** If someone **shirks** a job or task, they avoid doing it; used showing disapproval. EG *It was a job everyone shirked whenever possible.* V+O OR V

shirt /ʃɜːt/, **shirts.** A **shirt** is a piece of clothing that you wear on the upper part of your body. Shirts have a collar, sleeves, and buttons down the front. See picture at CLOTHES. EG *He was wearing a suit and a shirt and tie.* N COUNT

shirtsleeves /ʃɜːtsliːvz/. If a man is **in shirtsleeves** or **in** his **shirtsleeves**, he is wearing a shirt but not a jacket. EG *I lay on the bed in my shirt-sleeves.* PHRASE

shiver /ʃɪvə/, **shivers, shivering, shivered. 1** When you **shiver**, your body shakes slightly because you are cold or frightened. EG *I stood shivering with cold on the doorstep.* V ▸ used as a noun. EG *I could not repress a shiver whenever I thought of him.* ▸ N COUNT

2 If something **gives** you **the shivers**, it makes you feel very frightened. EG *That place gives me the shivers.* PHRASE Informal

shivery /ʃɪvəri^1/. If you are **shivery**, you cannot stop shivering, because you are cold or frightened. ADJ QUALIT Informal

shoal /ʃəʊl/, **shoals.** A **shoal** of fish is a large group of them swimming together. N PART

shock /ʃɒk/, **shocks, shocking, shocked. 1** If you have a **shock**, you suddenly have an experience which is unpleasant, upsetting, or very surprising. EG *I slapped her hand and she got such a shock that she dropped the milk... It was a shock to discover that they were English... I recovered gradually from the shock of her death.* N COUNT

2 Shock is a person's emotional and physical condition when something very frightening or upsetting has happened to them. EG *Numb with shock, she stood watching as they took his body away.* N UNCOUNT

3 In medicine, **shock** is a serious physical condition in which your blood cannot circulate properly, for example because you have had a bad injury. EG *She was taken to hospital suffering from shock.* N UNCOUNT

4 A **shock** is also **4.1** a slight movement in something when it is hit or jerked by something else. EG *This padding should absorb any sudden shocks.* N COUNT OR N UNCOUNT **4.2** the same as an electric shock. N COUNT Informal

5 If something **shocks** you, **5.1** it makes you feel very upset, because it involves death or suffering and because you had not expected it. EG *She was deeply shocked by her husband's death.* V+O : NO CONT ◊ **shocked.** EG *I was shocked at the damage I had done.* ◊ ADJ QUALIT **5.2** it upsets or offends you because you think it is rude or morally wrong. EG *Are you easily shocked?* V+O OR V ◊ **shocked.** EG *Don't look so shocked.* ◊ ADJ QUALIT

6 A **shock** of hair is a very thick mass of hair on a person's head. EG *He was tall and handsome with a shock of hair falling over his forehead.* N PART Written

shocking /ʃɒkɪŋ/. Something that is **shocking 1** is very bad. EG *The paintwork was really shocking... I'm shocking at spelling.* **2** makes people feel upset or angry, because they think that it is morally wrong. EG *It was shocking how badly paid these young girls were... ...the most shocking book of its time.* ADJ QUALIT

shoddy /ʃɒdi^1/. Something that is **shoddy** has been done or made carelessly or badly. EG *It is up to the teacher not to accept shoddy work... ...tiny shoddy houses... ...shoddy goods.* ADJ QUALIT

shoe /ʃuː/, **shoes, shoeing, shod** /ʃɒd/. **1 Shoes** are objects which you wear on your feet. They cover most of your foot and you wear them over socks or stockings. EG *I took off my shoes... She needs a new pair of shoes.* N COUNT

2 When someone **shoes** a horse, they fix horseshoes onto its hooves. V+O

shoelace /ʃuːleɪs/, **shoelaces. Shoelaces** are long, narrow pieces of material like pieces of string that you use to fasten your shoes. EG *He stopped to tie up his shoelace.* N COUNT : USU PLURAL

shoestring /ʃuːstrɪŋ/. **1** If you do something **on a shoestring**, you do it using very little money. EG *...cookery on a shoestring.* PHRASE Informal

2 A **shoestring** budget is one where you have very little money to spend. EG *She made the film on a shoestring budget.* ADJ CLASSIF : ATTRIB

shone /ʃɒn/ is the past tense and past participle of **shine.**

shoo /ʃuː/, **shoos, shooing, shooed. 1** If you **shoo** an animal or a person somewhere, you make them go there by waving your hands or arms at them. EG *She shooed the birds in the direction of the open window.* V+O+A

2 You say or shout **'Shoo'** at an animal in order to make it go away. EG *'Go away!' we shouted. 'Shoo!'* EXCLAM

shook /ʃʊk/ is the past tense of **shake.**

shoot /ʃuːt/, **shoots, shooting, shot** /ʃɒt/. **1** To **shoot** means to fire a bullet from a gun. EG *We were told to shoot first and ask questions later... ...troops that are being shot at.* V : OFT+*at*

2 If someone **shoots** a person or an animal, they kill them or injure them by firing a gun at them. EG *He shot his wife and then shot himself.* V+O OR V-REFL

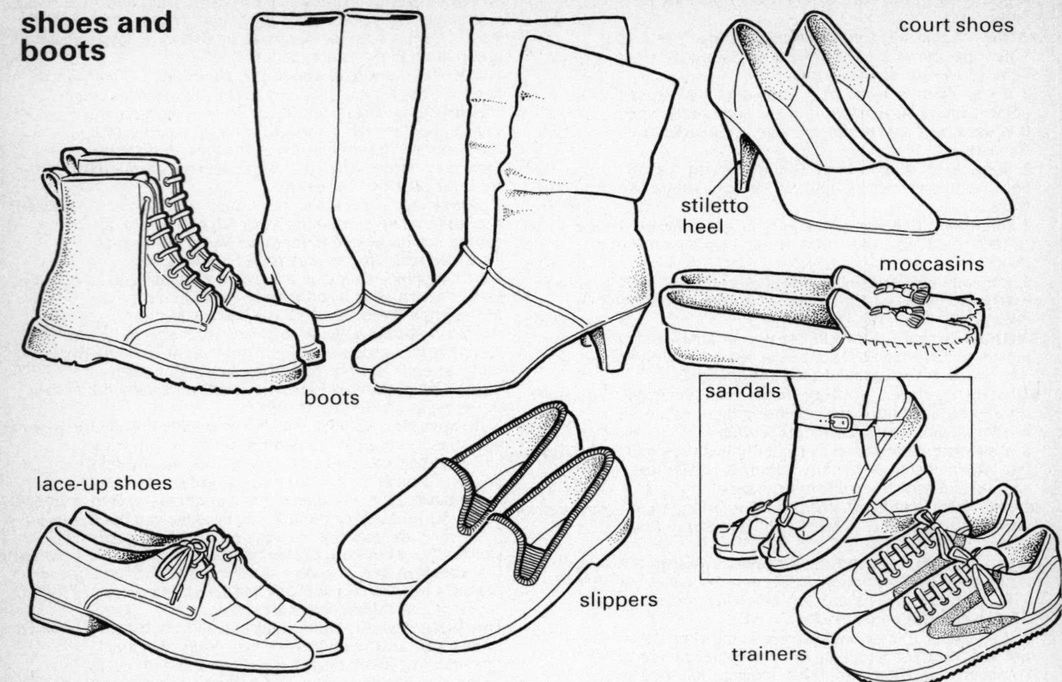

3 If people **shoot**, they hunt birds or animals with a gun as a form of sport. EG *He was too busy to fish or shoot.* V OR V+O British

4 A **shoot** is an occasion when people hunt birds or animals with guns as a form of sport. EG *They often take part in the local shoot.* N COUNT British

5 If you **shoot** an arrow, you fire it from a bow. V+O

6 If someone or something **shoots** in a particular direction, they move in that direction quickly and suddenly. EG *She shot back into the room.* V+A

7 If you **shoot** something somewhere, you send or move it there quickly and suddenly. EG *He shot out his hand and stopped the child from falling.* V+O+A

8 If you **shoot** a glance at someone or something, you look at them quickly and briefly. EG *He shot a suspicious glare at me.* V+O+*at* OR V+O+O

9 When a film **is shot**, it is photographed using film cameras. EG *Most of the film was shot in Spain.* V+O OR V

10 A **shoot** is also a plant that is beginning to grow, or a new part growing from a plant or tree. EG *A few tender shoots of green had started to appear.* N COUNT

11 See also **shot**.

shoot down. 1 If someone **shoots down** an aeroplane or helicopter, they make it fall to the ground by hitting it with a bullet or missile. **2** If someone **shoots down** someone else, they shoot them with a gun. **3** If you **shoot** someone **down** or **shoot down** their ideas, you show that their ideas are wrong or foolish. PHRASAL VB: V+O+ADV; V+O+ADV; V+O+ADV

shoot up. If something **shoots up**, it grows or increases very quickly. EG *The inflation rate shot up from 30% to 48%.* PHRASAL VB: V+ADV

shooting /ʃuːtɪŋ/, **shootings.** A **shooting** is an occasion when someone is killed or injured by being shot with a gun. EG *The police arrived fifteen minutes after the shooting.* N COUNT OR N UNCOUNT

shoot-out, shoot-outs. A **shoot-out** is a fight in which people shoot at each other with guns. EG *He was wounded during a shoot-out with the police.* N COUNT

shop /ʃɒp/, **shops, shopping, shopped. 1** A **shop** is a building or part of a building where things are sold. EG *Two customers came into the shop... ...a shoe shop.* N COUNT

2 When you **shop**, you go to shops and buy things. EG *We allow the older girls to shop in the village without an escort... They went shopping after lunch.* V: USU+A ◇ **shopper, shoppers.** EG *The city centre was crowded with shoppers.* ◇ N COUNT: USU PLURAL

3 You can also refer to a place where things are made as a **shop**. EG *...metalwork shops.* N COUNT+SUPP

4 See also **shopping**.

shop around. If you **shop around**, you go to different shops in order to compare the prices and quality of something before you decide to buy it. PHRASAL VB: V+ADV

shop assistant, shop assistants. A **shop assistant** is a person who works in a shop selling things to customers. N COUNT

shop floor. The **shop floor** is used to refer to all the workers in a factory, especially in contrast to the management. EG *There should be participation in decisions made on the shop floor.* N SING: USU *the*+N

shopkeeper /ʃɒpkiːpə/, **shopkeepers.** A **shopkeeper** is a person who owns a small shop. N COUNT

shoplifting /ʃɒplɪftɪŋ/ is stealing from a shop by walking round the shop and hiding things in a bag or in your clothes. N ING

shopping /ʃɒpɪŋ/. Your **shopping** consists of the things that you have bought from shops, especially food and groceries. EG *She put her shopping away in the kitchen.* N UNCOUNT

shopping centre, shopping centres. A **shopping centre** is an area in a town where a lot of shops have been built close together. N COUNT

shop-soiled. Goods that are **shop-soiled** are slightly dirty or damaged, usually because they have been in a shop for a long time. ADJ QUALIT British

shop steward, shop stewards. A **shop steward** is a trade union member who is elected by the N COUNT other members in a factory or office to speak for them at official meetings.

shore /ʃɔ:/, **shores, shoring, shored. 1** The **shore** of a sea, lake, or wide river is the land along the edge of it. EG *We could see the trees on the other shore... ...swimming close to the shore.* N COUNT

2 Someone who is **on shore** is on the land rather than on a ship. PHRASE

shore up. If you **shore** something **up**, you do something in order to strengthen it. EG *Action is needed to shore up economic links with American suppliers.* PHRASAL VB : V+O+ADV

shoreline /ʃɔ:laɪn/, **shorelines.** A **shoreline** is the edge of a sea, lake, or wide river. N COUNT

shorn /ʃɔ:n/. **1** If grass or hair is **shorn**, it is cut very short. EG *...shorn blades of grass... ...his shorn head.* ADJ CLASSIF

2 Shorn is the past participle of **shear**.

short /ʃɔ:t/, **shorter, shortest; shorts. 1** If something lasts for a **short** time, it does not last very long. EG *...a short holiday... The war was far shorter than they expected... He uttered a short cry of surprise.* ADJ QUALIT

2 When you use **short** to describe a period of time, you mean that it seems to have passed very quickly. EG *In a couple of short years she has destroyed all our hopes.* ADJ CLASSIF : ATTRIB

3 Speeches, letters, or books that are **short** do not have many words or pages in them. EG *She spoke in short sentences.* ADJ QUALIT

4 Someone who is **short** is not as tall as most people are. EG *...a short, fat man.* ADJ QUALIT

5 Something that is **short** measures only a small amount from one end to the other. EG *Her hair was cut short... She led the way down a short flight of steps... She showed us the shortest way home.* ADJ QUALIT

6 If you are **short** with someone, you are rude to them, because you are impatient or angry. EG *He was very short with her.* ADJ PRED +*with*

7 If you have a **short** temper, you get angry very easily. ADJ QUALIT

8 Shorts are trousers with very short legs. See picture at CLOTHES. N PLURAL

9 If you are **short** of something or if it is **short**, you do not have enough of it. EG *We're dreadfully short of staff at present... When money is short, we stick to a very careful budget.* ADJ PRED : OFT+*of*

10 If something **is running short** or if you **are running short of** it, you have almost used up your supply of it. EG *Water was running short... We were running short of food.* PHRASE

11 If you are **short of breath**, you have difficulty in breathing in enough air, for example after running or climbing stairs quickly. PHRASE

12 If someone is **short on** a particular quality, they do not have as much of it as you think they should have. EG *She was intelligent but a bit short on wisdom.* PHRASE Informal

13 If someone or something is **short of** a place or amount, they have not quite reached it. EG *He drove up the hill and stopped the car just short of the summit... He was only a year short of fifty.* PREP

14 Short of a particular thing means except for that thing or without actually doing that thing. EG *Short of dynamiting his door open, how do I attract his attention?* CONJ

15 You use **nothing short of** to emphasize that the thing that you are referring to is very great or extreme. For example, if you say that an action is **nothing short of** heroic, you are emphasizing that it is heroic. PHRASE

16 If something **is cut short**, it is stopped before it has finished. EG *The war cut short his education.* PHRASE

17 If something **brings** you **up short** or **pulls** you **up short**, it makes you suddenly stop what you are doing. EG *We were brought up short by the news.* PHRASE

18 If you **stop short** or if something **stops** you **short**, you suddenly stop what you are doing, for example because something has surprised you. EG *The soldier took a few steps and then stopped short... His disapproval stopped her short.* PHRASE

19 If someone **stops short of** doing something, they come close to doing it but do not actually do it. EG *He just stopped short of calling her a murderer.* PHRASE

20 If a person or thing is called something **for short**, that is the short version of their name. EG *Her name was Madeleine but Celia always called her 'Maddy' for short.* PHRASE

21 If a name **is short for** another name, it is the short version of that name. EG *It's short for 'Madeleine'.* PHRASE

22 You use the expression **in short** when you have been giving a lot of details and you want to give a conclusion or summary. EG *I was packing, arranging the trip, cleaning the house, and saying countless goodbyes. In short, it was a hectic week.* ADV SEN

23 at short notice: see **notice**. • **to cut a long story short**: see **story**. • **in short supply**: see **supply**.

shortage /ʃɔ:tɪdʒ/, **shortages.** If there is a **shortage** of something, there is not enough of it. EG *There's a world shortage of fuel... ...the housing shortage after the last war.* N COUNT : USU+SUPP

shortbread /ʃɔ:tbrɛd/ is a kind of biscuit made from flour, sugar, and butter. N UNCOUNT

shortcake /ʃɔ:tkeɪk/ is the same as shortbread. N UNCOUNT

short-circuit, short-circuits. If there is a **short-circuit** in an electrical system or device, there is a wrong connection or a damaged wire, so that electricity travels along the wrong route and damages the system or device. EG *The lamp-post was heating up from an electrical short-circuit inside.* N COUNT

shortcoming /ʃɔ:tkʌmɪŋ/, **shortcomings. Shortcomings** are faults or weaknesses which a person or thing has. EG *You've got to realize your own shortcomings... ...whatever shortcomings the airport might have.* N COUNT : USU PLURAL

shortcrust /ʃɔ:tkrʌst/. **Shortcrust** pastry is made with a lot of fat and crumbles very easily. ADJ CLASSIF : ATTRIB

short-cut, short-cuts. A **short-cut** is **1** a quicker way of getting somewhere than the usual route. EG *Will you show me that short cut to Wirral Hill?* **2** a method of achieving something more quickly than if you use the usual methods. EG *Parents of twins simply have to find short-cuts in housework.* N COUNT

shorten /ʃɔ:tə⁰n/, **shortens, shortening, shortened. 1** If you **shorten** an event or the length of time that something lasts, or if it **shortens**, it does not last as long as it would otherwise do or as it used to do. EG *The colonel had a plan to shorten the war.* V-ERG

2 If an object **shortens** or if you **shorten** it, it becomes smaller in length. EG *She wondered if she could have the sleeves shortened... The back muscles contract and shorten as your leg lifts.* V-ERG

shortfall /ʃɔ:tfɔ:l/, **shortfalls.** If there is a **shortfall** in something, there is less of it than you need. EG *A shortfall of energy supplies seems inevitable in the near future.* N COUNT : USU SING+SUPP

shorthand /ʃɔ:th⁰ænd/. **1 Shorthand** is a way of writing which uses signs to represent words or syllables. Shorthand is used especially by secretaries to quickly write down what someone is saying. N UNCOUNT

2 You can also use **shorthand** to mean a quick or simple way of referring to something. EG *All slogans are shorthand for something more complex.* N UNCOUNT

short-list, short-lists, short-listing, short-listed. 1 If someone is on a **short-list**, for example for a job or a prize, they are one of a small group of people that have been chosen from a larger group. The small group is judged again and a final decision is made about which of them is the best. EG *He produced a short-list of three MPs for the post.* N COUNT

2 If someone or something **is short-listed** for a job or a prize, they are put on a short-list. EG *Her novel has been short-listed for the Booker Prize.* V+O : USU PASS

short-lived. Something that is **short-lived** does not last very long. EG *His joy and relief were short-lived... He founded the shortlived Nationalist Party.* ADJ QUALIT

shortly /ʃɔːtli[1]/. **1** If something is going to happen **shortly**, it is going to happen soon. If something happened **shortly** after something else, it happened soon after it. EG *She's going to London shortly... She died in an accident shortly afterwards... Shortly before dawn he had an idea.* ADV

2 If you speak to someone **shortly**, you speak to them in a cross or impatient way. EG *'You ought to be in bed,' I said shortly.* ADV

short-sighted. **1** If you are **short-sighted**, you cannot see things properly when they are far away, because there is something wrong with your eyes. EG *He finally realized that he was short-sighted and went to the optician.* ADJ QUALIT

2 If you are **short-sighted** about something, or if your ideas are **short-sighted**, you do not make proper or careful judgements about the future. EG *Until this short-sighted policy is reversed we shall never make any progress.* ADJ QUALIT

short-staffed. A company that is **short-staffed** does not have enough people working for it. EG *They're rather short-staffed at the moment.* ADJ QUALIT: USU PRED

short-tempered. Someone who is **short-tempered** gets angry very quickly. EG *Lebel was short-tempered with him, which was unusual.* ADJ QUALIT

short-term. **1** **Short-term** effects or developments will happen soon, rather than happening more gradually over a longer period of time. EG *The effects of the Computer Revolution will be felt in the short-term future.* ADJ QUALIT

2 A **short-term** problem or a solution lasts for only a short time. EG *The artificial heart is designed only for short-term use.* ADJ QUALIT

short wave is a range of radio waves which are used for broadcasting. EG *The only communication with the mainland was by short-wave radio.* ADJ CLASSIF

shot /ʃɒt/, **shots.** **1** **Shot** is the past tense and past participle of **shoot**.

2 A **shot** is an act of firing a gun. EG *One of them fired several shots at Ward.* N COUNT

3 Someone who is a good **shot** can shoot well. EG *He's an excellent shot.* N COUNT: ADJ+N

4 In sports such as football, golf, or tennis, a **shot** is an act of kicking or hitting the ball, especially in an attempt to score a point. EG *Try to hit the green with your first shot... Oh, good shot.* N COUNT

5 A **shot** is also a photograph or a picture seen in a film. EG *I got some great shots of you... The film also contained some shots of the University.* N COUNT

6 If you have a **shot** at something, you attempt to do it. EG *I'd love to have a shot at hang-gliding.* N COUNT Informal

7 A **shot** of a drug is an injection of it. EG *The doctor gave her a shot of Librium.* N COUNT

8 If you do something **like a shot**, you do it without any delay or hesitation. EG *I told him to bring her at once. He was off like a shot.* PHRASE Informal

shotgun /ʃɒtgʌn/, **shotguns.** A **shotgun** is a gun used for shooting birds and animals which fires a lot of small metal balls at one time. N COUNT

shot put. In athletics, the **shot put** is a competition in which the contestants throw a heavy metal ball as far as possible. N SING: *the*+N

should /ʃə[4]d/. **Should** is sometimes considered to be the past form of **shall**, but in this dictionary the two words are dealt with separately.

1 If you say that something **should** happen, you mean that you think it is right or a good idea. EG *Crimes should be punished... These birds shouldn't be in a cage... Should we remain in the Common Market?* MODAL

2 You use **should** in questions when you are asking someone for advice, permission, or information. EG *Where should I meet you tonight?... Should I turn the light on?* MODAL

3 You use 'I **should**' when you are giving someone advice. EG *If you have anything really confidential I should install a safe... I shouldn't bother to copy these down.* MODAL Informal

4 If you say that something **should** happen or **should** be true, you mean that you think it will probably happen or is probably true. EG *We should be there by dinner time... There shouldn't be any difficulties... She should be alone.* MODAL

5 If you say that something **should have** happened, you mean that it did not happen, but you expected it to happen or you wish that it had happened. EG *Muskie should have won by a huge margin... You should have thought about that before you invited her.* MODAL

6 If you say that something **should have** happened by now, you mean that it has probably happened by now. EG *Dear Mom, you should have heard by now that I'm O.K.* MODAL

7 If you say that you **should** do something in a particular situation, you mean that you would do it if you were in that situation. EG *And the first thing I should do would be to teach you how to cook.* MODAL Formal

8 If you say that you **should** like to do something, you are saying politely that you want to do it. EG *I should be delighted to try it... I should like to give you a little practical advice.* MODAL

9 You can use **should** in conditional sentences when you are talking about things that might happen. EG *If we should be seen arriving together, they would get suspicious... Should you have an accident, synthetic quilts are quite easy to wash.* MODAL

10 You can use **should** in a 'that' clause after some verbs and adjectives. EG *It was arranged that Celia should come to Switzerland... It's strange you should come today.* MODAL

11 If you say that you **should** think something is true, you mean that you think it is true but you are not sure. EG *I should think it was about twelve years ago... He weighs, I should say, about 140 pounds.* MODAL

shoulder /ʃəʊldə/, **shoulders, shouldering, shouldered.** **1** Your **shoulders** are the two parts of your body between your neck and the tops of your arms. See picture at THE HUMAN BODY. EG *Sally patted me on the shoulder.* N COUNT

2 If you look **over** your **shoulder**, you look behind you by turning your neck. EG *He stopped and looked over his shoulder.* PHRASE

3 If someone needs **a shoulder to cry on**, they need a person who will listen sympathetically to all their troubles. PHRASE

4 If you **rub shoulders with** famous people, you meet them and talk to them. EG *...attend the royal wedding, rub shoulders with world leaders.* PHRASE Informal

5 The **shoulders** of a piece of clothing are the parts that cover your shoulders. EG *...dust on the shoulders of his expensive suit.* N COUNT: USU PLURAL

6 If you **shoulder** something heavy, you put it across one of your shoulders so that you can carry it more easily. EG *He shouldered his bundle again and set off.* V+O

7 If you **shoulder** the responsibility or blame for something, you accept it. EG *The government is expected to shoulder the responsibility for financing the project.* V+O

8 You can say that a person's problems or responsibilities are on that person's **shoulders**. EG *The burden of decision is placed on the shoulders of the individual.* N PLURAL

9 A **shoulder** is also a joint of meat from the upper part of the front leg of an animal. EG *...a shoulder of lamb.* N COUNT OR N UNCOUNT

shoulder-bag, shoulder-bags. A **shoulder-bag** is a bag that has a long strap so that it can be carried on a person's shoulder. See picture at BAGS. N COUNT

shoulder blade, shoulder blades. Your **shoulder blades** are the two large, flat, triangular bones N COUNT: USU PLURAL

If you tell someone to shove off, are you speaking to them shortly?

that you have in the upper part of your back, below your shoulders.

shouldn't /ʃʊdənt/ is the usual spoken form of 'should not'.

should've /ʃʊdəv/ is the usual spoken form of 'should have', especially when 'have' is an auxiliary verb.

shout /ʃaʊt/, **shouts, shouting, shouted. 1** A **shout** is a loud call or cry. EG *Excited shouts and laughter could be heard from the garden.* N COUNT

2 If you **shout**, you say words as loudly as you can, so that you can be heard from a long distance away. EG *The children on the sand were shouting with excitement... She shouted at us for spoiling her evening... 'Stop it!' he shouted.* V-SPEECH : ONLY *that*; ALSO V+*at*

shout down. If people **shout** a person **down**, they prevent the person from being heard by shouting at them. EG *Mr Healey was shouted down at a meeting in Birmingham.* PHRASAL VB : V+O+ADV

shout out. If you **shout** something **out**, you suddenly shout it. EG *I just had time to shout out and warn them not to cross the road.* PHRASAL VB : V+ADV OR V-SPEECH+ADV

shove /ʃʌv/, **shoves, shoving, shoved.** If you **shove** someone or something, you push them with a quick, violent movement. EG *He shoved the man through the door... He shoved the letter under her door.* ▸ used as a noun. EG *I gave him a shove in the direction of the street.* V+O+A; ▸ N COUNT : USU SING

shove off. If you tell someone to **shove off**, you are telling them angrily to go away. EG *You shove off, Eric. See?* PHRASAL VB : V+ADV, USU IMPER Informal

shovel /ʃʌvəˈl/, **shovels, shovelling, shovelled;** spelled **shoveling** and **shoveled** in American English.

1 A **shovel** is a tool like a spade, used for lifting and moving earth, coal, or snow. EG *He was working with a pick and shovel... ...a coal shovel.* N COUNT

2 If you **shovel** earth, coal, or snow, you lift and move it with a shovel. EG *She helped us shovel the snow off the front path.* V+O

3 If you **shovel** something somewhere, you push a lot of it quickly into that place. EG *They were shovelling food into their mouths.* V+O+A

show /ʃəʊ/, **shows, showing, showed, shown** /ʃəʊn/. **1** If something **shows** that a state of affairs exists, it gives information that proves it or makes it clear to people. EG *The post-mortem shows that death was due to natural causes... These figures show an 8.5% increase in exports.* V OR V+O : USU+REPORT

2 If a picture or piece of writing **shows** something, it represents it or gives information about it. EG *The painting shows four athletes bathing... A statement showing how much you need to pay is sent each month.* V+O OR V+REPORT

3 If you **show** someone something, you give it to them, take them to it, or point to it, so that they can see it or know what you are referring to. EG *I showed William what I had written... Let me show you the garden... She showed me where to park the car... Fetch that lovely drawing and show it to the vicar.* V+O+O, V+O+REPORT, OR V+O+*to*

4 If you **show** someone to a room or seat, you lead them there. EG *I was shown into a large apartment.* V+O+A

5 If you **show** someone how to do something, you do it yourself so that they can watch you and learn how to do it. EG *The woman took the gun and showed how the cylinder slotted into the barrel... Show us a card game.* V+O+*how*, V+*how*, OR V+O+O

6 If something **shows** or if you **show** it, it is visible or noticeable. EG *The edge of the moon is just showing... The stitching is so fine that it doesn't show at all... He had a strange fierce way of grinning that showed his teeth.* V OR V-ERG

7 If you **show** yourself, you move into a position where you can be seen by other people. EG *Come out from there and show yourself.* V-REFL

8 If something **shows** a quality or characteristic, it has this quality or characteristic in a noticeable way. EG *Prices began to show some signs of decline in 1974... The sketch shows a lot of talent.* V+O

9 If you **show** a particular attitude or quality, you behave in a way that makes this attitude or quality clear to other people. EG *This is a way in which Britain can show a readiness to help... He dared not show that he was pleased... She was feeling sad and didn't want to show it.* V+O OR V+REPORT : ONLY *that*

10 If you **show** someone an emotion or reaction such as affection or mercy, you behave towards them with affection or mercy. EG *She often showed me kindness... I had been taught to show respect towards my elders.* V+O+O, V+O +*to/towards*, OR V+O

11 If you say **it just goes to show** that something is the case, you mean that what you have just said proves that it is the case. EG *It all goes to show that people haven't changed.* PHRASE

12 If you **have** something **to show for** your efforts, you have achieved something as a result of what you have done. EG *Rodin's search was over and what he had to show for it was three slim dossiers.* PHRASE

13 A **show** of a feeling or quality is an attempt that you make to appear to have that feeling or quality. EG *She put on a good show of looking interested... ...those who had made open shows of defiance.* N COUNT : USU+*of*

14 If something is done **for show**, it has no real purpose and is done just to give a good impression. EG *These regulations are just for show.* PHRASE

15 A **show** is a form of entertainment at the theatre or on television that usually consists of several items. EG *Joy Leomine has been appearing in a show in London.* N COUNT

16 To **show** a film or television programme means to make it available for people to watch. EG *One evening the school showed a cowboy film.* V-ERG : IF V ONLY CONT
◇ **showing, showings.** EG *He had just been to a private showing of the film.* ◇ N COUNT

17 A **show** is also an exhibition of things, often things that have been entered in a competition. EG *...a flower show.* N COUNT : USU+SUPP

18 If something is **on show**, it has been put in a place where it can be seen by the public. EG *The photographs are on show at the Museum until October.* PHRASE

19 A **show of hands** is a method of voting in which people raise their hands and the number of hands is counted. PHRASE

show around. See **show round**.

show off. 1 If someone **shows off**, they behave in a way that makes their skills or good qualities very obvious, in order to impress people. EG *...kids showing off on the diving board.* **2** If you **show off** something that you own, you show it to a lot of people because you are proud of it. EG *He was eager to show off the new car.* **3** See also **show-off**. PHRASAL VB : V+ADV; V+O+ADV

show round. If you **show** someone **round** a place or **show** them **around** it, you go round it with them, pointing out all its interesting or important features. PHRASAL VB : V +O+ADV/PREP

show up. 1 If you **show up**, you appear at a place where you are expected by someone. EG *Over a hundred people showed up at the meeting... He showed up at ten o'clock the next morning.* **2** If something **shows up** or **is shown up**, it can be clearly seen. EG *Dark colours will not show up against a similar background.* **3** If someone is with you and they **show** you **up**, they behave in a way that makes you feel embarrassed and ashamed of them. PHRASAL VB : V+ADV Informal; V-ERG+ADV; V+O+ADV

showbiz /ʃəʊbɪz/ is the same as show business. EG *We do get some remarkable glimpses of showbiz here.* N UNCOUNT Informal

show business is the entertainment industry of film, theatre, and television. EG *Then he went into show business.* N UNCOUNT

showcase /ʃəʊkeɪs/, **showcases. 1** A **showcase** is a glass container with valuable objects inside it, for example at an exhibition or in a museum. EG *...showcases of gold artefacts.* N COUNT

2 You use **showcase** to refer to a situation or setting in which something is displayed or presented to its best advantage. EG *This opera is a stunning showcase for the company.* N COUNT+SUPP Formal

showdown /ʃəʊdaʊn/, **showdowns.** A **showdown** is a big argument or conflict which is intended to settle a dispute that has lasted for a long time. EG *It's time for a showdown with your boss.* N COUNT : OFT SING+*with*

shower /ʃaʊə/, **showers, showering, showered.**
1 A **shower** is a device used for washing yourself. It consists of a pipe or hose which ends in a flat piece with a lot of holes in it so that water comes out in a spray. EG *All rooms have got a bath, shower and toilet.* N COUNT

2 If you have a **shower**, you wash yourself by standing under a spray of water from a shower. EG *A hot shower and a change of clothes would be wonderful.* N COUNT ▸ used as a verb. EG *I'll shave and shower and then have some coffee.* ▸ V

3 A **shower** is also a short period of light rain. EG *...a week of scattered showers.* N COUNT

4 You can refer to a lot of light things that are falling as a **shower** of them. EG *...a shower of falling leaves.* N PART

5 If you **are showered** with a lot of small light things, they are scattered onto you from above. EG *Suddenly the lid came off and showered him with flakes of rust.* V+O+A

6 If you **shower** a person with presents or kisses, you give them a lot of presents or kisses in a very generous and extravagant way. EG *They showered each other with gifts at Christmas.* V+O+A

showery /ʃaʊəri[1]/. If the weather is **showery**, there are showers of rain but it does not rain all the time. ADJ QUALIT

show jumping is a sport in which horses are ridden in competitions to demonstrate their skill in jumping over walls and fences. N UNCOUNT

shown /ʃəʊn/ is the past participle of **show.**

show-off, show-offs. If you say that someone is a **show-off**, you mean that they behave in a way that shows their skills or abilities very obviously, in order to impress people; used showing disapproval. N COUNT Informal

showroom /ʃəʊru[4]m/, **showrooms.** A **showroom** is a shop in which goods are displayed for sale, especially goods such as cars or electrical or gas appliances. EG *The new model will be in the showrooms in a fortnight's time.* N COUNT

showy /ʃəʊi[1]/. Something that is **showy** is very noticeable because it is large, colourful, or bright. EG *...a showy bracelet and earrings.* ADJ QUALIT

shrank /ʃræŋk/ is the past tense of **shrink.**

shrapnel /ʃræpnə[0]l/ consists of small pieces of metal which are scattered from exploding bombs and shells. EG *He'd been caught in the knee by a piece of shrapnel.* N UNCOUNT

shred /ʃrɛd/, **shreds, shredding, shredded. 1** If you **shred** something such as food or paper, you cut it or tear it into very small pieces. EG *Carrots taste delicious shredded in salad.* V+O

2 A **shred** of material is a small narrow piece of it. EG *She took the letter and ripped it to shreds.* N COUNT : USU PLURAL

3 If you say that there is no **shred** of something, you mean that there is not even a small amount of it. EG *There is no shred of evidence to support the theory that Emily was murdered.* N PART

shrew /ʃru:/, **shrews.** A **shrew** is a small brown animal like a mouse with a long pointed nose. N COUNT

shrewd /ʃru:d/, **shrewder, shrewdest.** Someone who is **shrewd** is able to understand and judge a situation quickly and to use this understanding to their own advantage. EG *He is a shrewd and sometimes ruthless adversary... It was a shrewd assessment.* ADJ QUALIT ◇ **shrewdly.** EG *She looked at him shrewdly.* ◇ ADV

shriek /ʃri:k/, **shrieks, shrieking, shrieked.** If you **shriek**, you give a sudden loud scream. EG *She shrieked in alarm... Ralph shrieked with laughter.* V : OFT +*with/in* ▸ used as a noun. EG *She let out a shriek of laughter.* ▸ N COUNT : OFT+*of*

shrill /ʃrɪl/, **shriller, shrillest.** A **shrill** sound is high-pitched, piercing, and unpleasant to listen to. EG *The boys broke into shrill, excited cheering... ...the shrill screaming of jet engines.* ADJ QUALIT ◇ **shrilly.** EG *Lewis whistled shrilly.* ◇ ADV

shrimp /ʃrɪmp/, **shrimps.** A **shrimp** is a small shellfish with a long tail and many legs. N COUNT

shrine /ʃraɪn/, **shrines.** A **shrine** is a holy place of worship which is associated with a sacred person or object. EG *He went to the shrine of St Foy.* N COUNT

shrink /ʃrɪŋk/, **shrinks, shrinking, shrank** /ʃræŋk/, **shrunk** /ʃrʌŋk/. **1** If cloth **shrinks** or if you **shrink** it, it becomes smaller in size, usually as a result of being washed. EG *You should dry-clean curtains if possible, as they are less likely to shrink.* V-ERG

2 If something **shrinks**, it becomes smaller. EG *He commented on the amazing way in which computers have recently shrunk in size.* V-ERG

3 If you **shrink** away from something, you move away from it because you are frightened or horrified by it. EG *The boys shrank away in horror... She shrank back, quivering.* V+A

4 If you **shrink** from a task or duty, you are reluctant to do it because you find it unpleasant. EG *He shrank from giving Francis a direct answer.* V+*from*

shrinkage /ʃrɪŋkɪdʒ/ is a decrease in the size or amount of something. EG *...the steady shrinkage of the tropical forests.* N UNCOUNT

shrivel /ʃrɪvə[0]l/, **shrivels, shrivelling, shrivelled;** spelled **shriveling** and **shriveled** in American English. When something **shrivels** or **shrivels up**, it becomes dry and wrinkled, usually because it loses moisture in the heat. EG *The seedlings had shrivelled up a bit in the hot sun... Every year we have a long dry season that shrivels and scorches plants.* V-ERG : OFT+*up*

shroud /ʃraʊd/, **shrouds, shrouding, shrouded.**
1 A **shroud** is a cloth which is used for wrapping a dead body. EG *The doctor wanted to use the sheet for a shroud.* N COUNT

2 If something **is shrouded** in darkness or fog, it is hidden by it. EG *Everything was shrouded in mist and raindrops.* V+O : USU PASS+*in*

3 If something **is shrouded** in mystery, very little is known about it. EG *The precise sequence of events is shrouded in mystery.* V+O : USU PASS+*in*

shrub /ʃrʌb/, **shrubs.** A **shrub** is a low plant like a small tree with several woody stems instead of a trunk. EG *...flowering shrubs.* N COUNT

shrubbery /ʃrʌbə[0]ri[1]/, **shrubberies.** A **shrubbery** is the part of a garden where a lot of shrubs are growing. N COUNT OR N UNCOUNT

shrug /ʃrʌg/, **shrugs, shrugging, shrugged.** If you **shrug** your shoulders, you raise them to show that you are not interested in something or that you do not know or care about it. EG *Don't just shrug your shoulders. Say something!... 'Do you mind if I wait?' I asked. Melanie shrugged. 'Please yourself.'* V+O OR V ▸ used as a noun. EG *The man nodded with a faint shrug of his shoulders.* ▸ N COUNT : USU SING

shrug off. If you **shrug** something **off**, you ignore it or treat it as if it is not really important or serious. EG *The chairman shrugs off any criticism that their methods are not strictly legal.* PHRASAL VB : V+O+ADV

shrunk /ʃrʌŋk/ is the past participle of **shrink.**

shrunken /ʃrʌŋkə[0]n/. Something that is **shrunken** has become smaller than it used to be. EG *...a shrunken old man.* ADJ QUALIT

shudder /ʃʌdə/, **shudders, shuddering, shuddered. 1** If you **shudder**, you tremble with fear, horror, or disgust. EG *Robert shuddered with fear... The smell made her shudder.* V : OFT+A ▸ used as a noun. EG *Max looked round him with a shudder.* ▸ N COUNT : USU SING

2 If you say that you **shudder to think** of something, you mean that you expect it to be so awful or PHRASE

Is a shy person likely to be a show-off?

disastrous that you do not really want to think about it. EG *I shudder to think of the consequences.*

3 If something such as a machine or vehicle **shudders**, it shakes suddenly in a very violent manner. EG *The tank braked and shuddered to a violent halt.* V

shuffle /ʃʌfəºl/, **shuffles, shuffling, shuffled. 1** If you **shuffle**, **1.1** you walk without lifting your feet properly off the ground. EG *He slipped on his shoes and shuffled out of the room.* ▸ used as a noun. EG *We recognized him by his distinctive walk, a kind of shuffle.* V: USU+A ▸ N SING **1.2** you move your feet about while standing or you move your bottom about while sitting, often because you feel uncomfortable or embarrassed. EG *I looked at the ground, shuffled my feet and mumbled something defensive... I was shuffling in my seat.* V+O OR V

2 If you **shuffle** a pack of cards, you mix them up before you begin a game. EG *He took out the cards, shuffled them, and put them down on the table.* V+O OR V

shun /ʃʌn/, **shuns, shunning, shunned.** If you **shun** someone or something, you deliberately avoid them. EG *These people shun publicity.* V+O

shunt /ʃʌnt/, **shunts, shunting, shunted.** If you **shunt** objects or people somewhere, you move them to a different place. EG *...the sound of heavy desks being shunted across the room... He shunted me into a corner and looked over both shoulders before speaking.* V+O: USU+A Informal

shush /ʃʊʃ, ʃʌʃ/. You say **shush** when you are telling someone to be quiet. EXCLAM

shut /ʃʌt/, **shuts, shutting.** The form **shut** is used in the present tense and is the past tense and past participle of the verb.

1 If you **shut** something or if it **shuts**, its position is changed so that it fills a hole or gap. EG *I shut the door quietly... He goes in and the door shuts behind him.* ▸ used as an adjective. EG *The windows were all shut.* V-ERG ▸ ADJ PRED

2 If you **shut** your eyes, you lower your eyelids so that you cannot see anything. EG *Mrs Kaul shut her eyes for a moment.* ▸ used as an adjective. EG *He lay with his eyes shut.* V+O ▸ ADJ PRED

3 If you **shut** your mouth, you place your lips together so that nothing can get into your mouth or out of it. EG *Mr Boggis opened his mouth, then quickly shut it again.* V+O ● If someone tells you to **shut** your **mouth** or **shut** your **face**, they are telling you very rudely to stop talking. ● PHRASE Informal ● If someone asks you to **keep** your **mouth shut** about something, they are asking you not to tell anyone else about it. EG *He warned me to keep my mouth shut about his visit.* ● PHRASE Informal

4 When a shop or pub **shuts** or when someone **shuts** it, it is closed and you cannot go into it until the next time that it is open. EG *'What time do the shops shut?' – 'Half past five.'* ▸ used as an adjective. EG *I'm afraid all the pubs will be shut.* V-ERG ▸ ADJ PRED

shut away. If you **shut** something **away**, you keep it in a special room or cupboard where people cannot see it. EG *We have a small number of books which are shut away.* PHRASAL VB: V+O+ADV

shut down. If a factory or business **shuts down** or if someone **shuts** it **down**, it closes and stops working. EG *His department was shut down for lack of funds... That year my grandfather had to shut down the forge.* ● See also **shutdown**. PHRASAL VB: V-ERG+ADV

shut in. 1 If someone **shuts** you **in** a room, they close the door so that you cannot leave it. EG *He was shut in with an assortment of strangers.* **2** If you **shut** yourself **in** a room, you stay in there and make sure nobody else can get in. EG *She shut herself in the bathroom and wept.* PHRASAL VB: V+O+ADV/PREP V-REFL+ADV/PREP

shut out. 1 If you **shut** something or someone **out**, you prevent them from getting into a place, for example by closing the doors. EG *They had covered the holes to shut out the water.* PHRASAL VB: V+O+ADV **2** If you **shut out** a thought or a feeling, you prevent yourself from thinking or feeling it. EG *She found it impossible to shut out the pain.* V+O+ADV

shut up. 1 If you **shut up**, you stop talking. EG *She was always telling him to shut up... Shut up and listen.* PHRASAL VB: V+ADV **2** If someone **shuts** you **up**, they prevent you from talking. EG *Turn the television on. That usually shuts them up.* V+O+ADV Informal

shutdown /ʃʌtdaʊn/, **shutdowns.** A **shutdown** is the closing of a factory, shop, or other business. EG *Refinery owners have already resorted to temporary shutdowns.* N COUNT

shutter /ʃʌtə/, **shutters. 1 Shutters** are wooden or metal covers fitted on the outside of a window. They can be opened to let in the light, or shut to keep out the sun or the cold or to protect the windows from damage. EG *...an old brick house with green shutters... ...closing the windows, fastening the shutters, and turning off all the lights.* N COUNT: USU PLURAL

2 The **shutter** in a camera is the part which opens to allow light through the lens when a photograph is taken. N COUNT

shuttered /ʃʌtəd/. A **shuttered** window has its shutters closed. EG *All doors were locked and the windows closed and shuttered.* ADJ CLASSIF

shuttle /ʃʌtəºl/, **shuttles, shuttling, shuttled. 1** A **shuttle** service is an air, bus, or train service which makes frequent journeys between two places. ADJ CLASSIF: ATTRIB

2 A **shuttle** is a plane used in a shuttle service. EG *He caught the nine o'clock shuttle to New York.* N COUNT

3 See also **space shuttle**.

shy /ʃaɪ/, **shyer, shyest; shies, shying, shied. 1** A **shy** person is nervous and uncomfortable in the company of other people. EG *I've always been a bit shy... ...a shy smile.* ◊ **shyly**. EG *She smiled shyly at him.* ADJ QUALIT ◊ ADV

2 If you are **shy** of doing something, you are unwilling to do it because you are afraid of what might happen. EG *Don't be shy of telling them what you think.* ADJ PRED+OF

3 When a horse **shies**, it moves away suddenly, because something has frightened it. V

4 See also **work-shy**.

shy away from. If you **shy away from** doing something, you avoid doing it, often because you are afraid or not confident enough. EG *Are you going to grasp these opportunities or shy away from them?* PHRASAL VB: V+ADV+PREP

Siamese twins /saɪəmiːz twɪnz/ are twins who are born joined to each other by a part of their bodies. N PLURAL

sibling /sɪblɪŋ/, **siblings.** Your **siblings** are your brothers and sisters. N COUNT Formal

sick /sɪk/, **sicker, sickest. 1** If you are **sick**, you are ill. EG *Your uncle is very sick.* ADJ QUALIT

2 If you feel **sick**, you feel ill in your stomach, and food that you have eaten is likely to be sent out through your mouth. EG *Flying always makes me feel sick.* ADJ PRED ● If you **are sick**, food that you have eaten is sent out through your mouth. EG *I think I'm going to be sick.* ● PHRASE

3 If you say that something **makes** you **sick**, you mean that you feel angry or disgusted about it. EG *It makes me sick the way they waste our money.* PHRASE

4 If you are **sick** of something, you are very annoyed by it and want it to stop. EG *We're sick of sitting around waiting for something to happen... Europe was sick of war.* ADJ PRED+of

5 You describe acts, stories, or jokes as **sick** when they deal with death, cruelty, or suffering in a frivolous way. EG *She made a rather sick joke.* ADJ QUALIT

6 If you are **worried sick**, you are extremely worried. EG *He was worried sick that the factory might close.* PHRASE Informal

sickbed /sɪkbɛd/, **sickbeds.** Your **sickbed** is the bed that you are lying in while you are ill. EG *I was able to watch television from my sickbed.* N COUNT

sicken /sɪkəºn/, **sickens, sickening, sickened. 1** If something **sickens** you, it makes you feel dis- V+O gusted. EG *The young officers were sickened by the greed of their generals.*

2 If you **sicken**, you become ill. EG *In these conditions a child could sicken and die in a year.* V Outdated

sickening /sɪkə⁰nɪŋ/. You describe something as **sickening** 1 when it gives you feelings of horror or disgust. EG *The car crashed with a sickening crunch into a tree... The food smelled sickening.* 2 when it annoys you very much. EG *Her mother's only concerned about the money. How sickening!* ADJ QUALIT Informal

sickle /sɪkə⁰l/, **sickles.** A **sickle** is a tool that is used for cutting grass and grain crops. It has a short handle and a long, curved blade. N COUNT

sickly /sɪkli¹/, **sicklier, sickliest.** 1 A **sickly** person is weak, unhealthy, and often ill. EG *He was a sickly and ineffective man.* ADJ QUALIT

2 Things that you describe as **sickly** are very unpleasant to smell or look at. EG *There was a musty, sickly smell... ...a sickly brown shirt.* ADJ QUALIT

sickness /sɪknɪ²s/, **sicknesses. 1 Sickness** is **1.1** the state of being ill or unhealthy. EG *...people who are not working because of sickness or unemployment.* **1.2** a condition in which you feel ill in your stomach and in which food that you have eaten is sent out through your mouth. EG *The disease causes sickness and diarrhoea.* • See also **morning sickness.** N UNCOUNT

2 A **sickness** is a particular illness. EG *...the first signs of radiation sickness.* N COUNT OR N UNCOUNT

side /saɪd/, **sides, siding, sided.** 1 The **side** of something is a position to the left or right of it, rather than in front of it or behind it. EG *A taxi bumped into us from the side... Standing on either side of him were two younger men... 'Get out of my way,' she cried, pushing Tom to one side... I sat down by her side.* N COUNT

2 **Side** is used in these phrases referring to position or closeness. **2.1** If something is **on every side** or **on all sides** of you, you are surrounded by it. EG *The sea lay on every side.* **2.2** If you put something **to one side** or **on one side**, you keep it separate from other things, so that you can deal with it later. **2.3** If something moves **from side to side**, it moves repeatedly to the left and to the right. EG *The ship was swaying from side to side.* **2.4** If two people are **side by side**, they are sitting, standing, or walking next to each other. **2.5** If two people or things do something **side by side**, they do it together. EG *Student and tutor learn side by side... Two interdependent communities evolved side by side.* **2.6** If someone stays **at your side** or **by your side**, they stay near you and give you comfort or support. EG *He wanted to live forever by her side.* PHRASES

3 Something that is on one **side** of a boundary or barrier is in one of the two areas that the boundary or barrier separates. EG *We were told of threatening developments on the other side of the border.* N COUNT: USU SING+SUPP

4 Your **sides** are the parts of your body under your arms from your armpits down to your hips. EG *She lay on her side with her back to me.* N COUNT

5 The **sides** of an area or surface are **5.1** its two halves. EG *Blood was streaming from one side of her face... She was driving on the wrong side of the road.* N COUNT: USU+SUPP **5.2** its edges. EG *A hedge surrounds my garden on three sides... Mowbray's practically on the other side of the city.* N COUNT

6 The **sides** of an object are its flat outside surfaces. EG *The box opens on this side.* N COUNT

7 The **sides** of a building or a vehicle are the vertical outer parts which are not its front or its back. EG *Hogan walked round to the driver's side and unlocked the car door.* ▸ used as an adjective. EG *Smithy left the side door open.* N COUNT ▸ ADJ CLASSIF: ATTRIB

8 The **sides** of a rectangular object are its two long edges. EG *She was kneeling by the side of the bed.* N COUNT

9 The **sides** of a hill or valley are the sloping parts between its top and bottom. EG *We were driving up the side of a mountain.* N COUNT

10 The **sides** of something flat, for example a piece of paper, are its two flat surfaces. EG *What does the leaflet say on the other side?* N COUNT

11 A **side** road or **side** street is a less important road or street leading off an important one. EG *I slipped away down a side street.* ADJ CLASSIF: ATTRIB

12 The two **sides** in a war, argument, or game are the two groups of people who are fighting or arguing with each other, or playing against each other. EG *The argument was settled to the satisfaction of both sides.* N COUNT

13 The two **sides** of an argument are the different points of view of the people who are arguing. EG *She only ever hears his side of things.* N COUNT

14 The two **sides** in an agreement or a relationship are the two people or groups who are dealing with each other. EG *Both sides were confident that they would benefit from the partnership.* N COUNT

15 **Side** is used in these phrases referring to supporting someone. **15.1** If you **take sides** or **take** someone's **side**, you support one of the two people who are involved in an argument. EG *I wouldn't want anyone to take my side against Tom.* **15.2** If you are **on** someone's **side**, you are supporting them in an argument or a war. EG *Whose side are you on?... Do everything you can to win people on to your side.* **15.3** If something is **on** your **side**, it helps you when you are trying to achieve something. EG *Luck was on our side.* PHRASES

16 The two **sides** of your family are your mother's family and your father's family. EG *My grandparents on my father's side were both Polish.* N COUNT

17 A particular **side** of something such as a situation or someone's character is one aspect of it. EG *The producers wanted to emphasize the political side of the play... There is something distasteful about this side of her character.* N COUNT: USU+SUPP

18 **Side** is also used in these phrases. **18.1** If you do something **on the side**, you do it in addition to your main work. EG *If the farm prospers, we could start a little business on the side.* **18.2** If you say that something is **on the** large **side** or **on the** small **side**, for example, you mean that it is slightly too large or slightly too small. EG *The food is excellent though on the expensive side.* **18.3** If you keep **on the right side of** someone, you try to please them and avoid annoying them. If you get **on the wrong side of** someone, you annoy them and make them dislike you. **18.4 to be on the safe side**: see **safe.** • to **err on the side of** something: see **err.** PHRASES

side with. If you **side with** someone, you support them in a quarrel or argument. EG *The daughters sided with their mothers.* PHRASAL VB: V+PREP

sideboard /saɪdbɔːd/, **sideboards. 1** A **sideboard** is a long, fairly low cupboard, normally kept in dining rooms to put plates and glasses in. N COUNT

2 If a man has **sideboards**, he has a strip of hair growing down the side of each cheek. N PLURAL British

sideburns /saɪdbɜːnz/ are the same as sideboards. N PLURAL

side-effect, side-effects. 1 The **side-effects** of a drug are the effects that the drug has on you in addition to its function of curing illness or pain. EG *This type of aspirin can have appalling side-effects.* N COUNT: USU PLURAL

2 The **side-effects** of a situation are the unplanned things that happen in addition to the main results or effects. EG *One side-effect of the crisis could be that she loses her job.* N COUNT: USU PLURAL

sidelight /saɪdlaɪt/, **sidelights.** The **sidelights** on a vehicle are the small lights at the front that help other drivers to notice the vehicle and to judge its width. N COUNT

sideline /saɪdlaɪn/, **sidelines. 1** A **sideline** is something that you do in addition to your main job in order to earn extra money. EG *Fishing is both a relaxing hobby and a money-producing sideline.* N COUNT

What is the opposite of keeping on the right side of someone?

2 The **sidelines** are the lines marking the long sides of the playing area, for example on a football pitch or tennis court. N COUNT: USU PLURAL

3 If you are on **the sidelines** in a situation, you are not personally involved in it. EG *I prefer to stand on the sidelines and watch... ...watching the drama from the sidelines.* N PLURAL Literary

sidelong /saɪdlɒŋ/. If you look at someone or something **sidelong** or if you give them **sidelong** looks, you look at them out of the corner of your eyes, because they are to one side of you. EG *Ralph looked at him sidelong and said nothing... Terry and I exchanged sidelong glances.* ADV OR ADJ CLASSIF: ATTRIB

side-saddle. When you ride a horse **side-saddle**, you sit on a special saddle with both your legs on one side rather than one leg on each side of the horse. ADV OR ADJ CLASSIF: ATTRIB

sideshow /saɪdʃəʊ/, **sideshows. Sideshows** are the stalls at a fairground or circus where you can do things such as shooting at moving targets and throwing darts. N COUNT

sidestep /saɪdstɛp/, **sidesteps, sidestepping, sidestepped.** If you **sidestep** a problem, you manage to avoid discussing it or dealing with it. EG *...a book that does not sidestep essential questions.* V+O

sidetracked /saɪdtrækt/. If you **are sidetracked**, you forget what you are supposed to be doing or saying and start doing or talking about something else. EG *I told him how I'd been sidetracked by Mr Starke.* V-PASS

sidewalk /saɪdwɔːk/, **sidewalks.** A **sidewalk** is the same as a pavement. EG *He avoided stepping on a crack in the sidewalk.* N COUNT American

sideways /saɪdweɪz/ means from or to the side of something or someone. EG *Flames blew out sideways from the fire... ...a sideways glance... She sat leaning sideways a little.* ADV OR ADJ CLASSIF: ATTRIB

siding /saɪdɪŋ/, **sidings.** A **siding** is a short railway track beside the main tracks, where engines and carriages are left when they are not being used. N COUNT

sidle /saɪdəˀl/, **sidles, sidling, sidled.** If you **sidle** somewhere, you walk there uncertainly or cautiously, as if you do not want anyone to notice you. EG *She stammered some apology as she sidled towards the door.* V+A

siege /siːdʒ/, **sieges.** A **siege** is **1** a military operation in which an army tries to capture a place by surrounding it and preventing food or help from reaching the people inside. EG *...the siege of Mafeking... Galilee had been under siege for months.* **2** a situation in which a place is surrounded for a long period of time, for example by police, in order to force the people inside to come out. EG *He had been in London to report on the Embassy siege in May 1980.* N COUNT OR N UNCOUNT

siesta /siˈɛstə/, **siestas.** A **siesta** is a short sleep or rest which people have in the early afternoon in hot countries. EG *She hadn't yet emerged from her siesta.* N COUNT OR N UNCOUNT

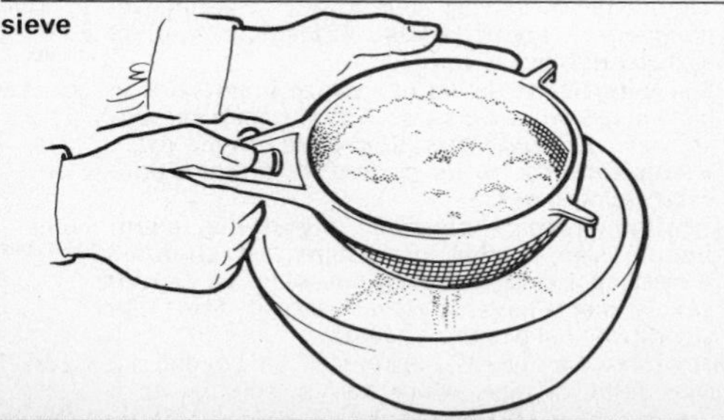

sieve /sɪv/, **sieves, sieving, sieved. 1** A **sieve** is a tool used, especially in the kitchen, for separating liquids from solids or larger pieces of something from smaller pieces of it. It usually consists of a metal ring with a wire net attached underneath, which the liquids or smaller pieces pass through, leaving the solids or larger pieces in the net. N COUNT

2 When you **sieve** a liquid or powdery substance, you put it through a sieve. EG *Sieve the flour into a basin to remove all the lumps.* V+O

3 If you say that someone has **a memory like a sieve**, you mean that they often forget things. PHRASE

sift /sɪft/, **sifts, sifting, sifted. 1** If you **sift** a loose or powdery substance such as flour or sand, you put it through a sieve in order to remove large pieces or lumps. EG *Always sift icing sugar through a fine sieve.* V+O

2 If you **sift** through something such as evidence, you examine it thoroughly. EG *There are archives and documents to be sifted through... He was accustomed to sifting evidence and assessing the difference between fact and fiction.* V+*through*: HAS PASS OR V+O

sigh /saɪ/, **sighs, sighing, sighed. 1** When you **sigh**, you let out a deep breath, as a way of expressing feelings such as disappointment, tiredness, or pleasure. EG *She sighed and shook her head sadly... Sighing with relief, she took the money.* V

2 A **sigh** is the action of sighing or the sound that someone makes when they sigh. EG *With a sigh, he rose and walked slowly away... They had breathed a great sigh of relief at the ending of the war.* • If you **heave a sigh**, you sigh. N COUNT • PHRASE

sight /saɪt/, **sights, sighting, sighted. 1 Sight** is the ability to see. EG *Her sight is failing.* N UNCOUNT

2 The **sight** of something is the act of seeing it or an occasion on which you see it. EG *I had my first sight of home for two years... He was reduced to tears at the sight of the hundreds of dead bodies.* N SING: OFT+*of*

3 A **sight** is something that you see. EG *This was the most encouraging sight I'd seen all day... It was an awe-inspiring sight.* N COUNT+SUPP

4 The **sights** are the places that are interesting to see and that are often visited by tourists. EG *...the sights of London.* N PLURAL

5 If you say that something is **a sight** better or **a sight** worse, you mean that is very much better or very much worse. EG *It's a damn sight better than most of the places we've stayed in.* PHRASE Informal

6 If you **sight** someone or something, you see them, often briefly or suddenly. EG *The missing woman has been sighted in the Birmingham area.* V+O

7 Sight is also used in these phrases. **7.1** If you say that something or someone seems to have certain characteristics **at first sight**, you mean that when you first see them that is how they appear. EG *The problem is not as simple as it might seem at first sight.* **7.2** If something is **in sight**, you can see it. If it is **out of sight**, you cannot see it. EG *As soon as the car was out of sight, we relaxed... At last a bus came into sight.* **7.3** If a result or a decision is **in sight**, it is likely to happen within a short time. EG *It seemed that an end to his agony was in sight.* **7.4** If someone is ordered to do something **on sight**, they have to do it without delay, as soon as a person or thing is seen. EG *They used to shoot on sight in those days.* **7.5** If you **catch sight of** someone, you see them suddenly or briefly. EG *She caught sight of her mother.* **7.6** If you **lose sight of** an important part of a situation, you no longer pay attention to it because you are worrying about less important things. EG *We mustn't get so bogged down by detail that we lose sight of our main objectives.* **7.7** If you **know** someone **by sight**, you can recognize them when you see them, but you have never met them and talked to them. **7.8** If you **set** your **sights on** something, you decide that you want it and try very hard to get it. EG *We have set our sights on a bigger house.* PHRASES

sighted /saɪtɪ²d/. People who are **sighted** are not blind. EG *...if you are blind or poorly sighted... ...partially sighted children.* • See also **clear-** ADJ CLASSIF

sighted, far-sighted, long-sighted, short-sighted.

sighting /saɪtɪŋ/, **sightings.** A **sighting** is an occasion on which something is seen, especially something unusual or unexpected. EG *There had been four reports of shark sightings.* N COUNT: USU+SUPP

sightless /saɪtlɪ^{2}s/. Someone who is **sightless** is blind. EG *He covered his sightless eyes.* ADJ CLASSIF

sight-read, sight-reads, sight-reading. The form **sight-read** is used in the present tense and is also the past tense and past participle. V OR V+O
Someone who can **sight-read** can play or sing music from a printed sheet the first time they see it, without practising it beforehand.

sightseeing /saɪtsiːɪŋ/. If you go **sightseeing**, you travel around in order to see the interesting places that tourists usually visit. EG *Allow some time in all the major cities for sightseeing.* N ING

sightseer /saɪtsiːə/, **sightseers.** A **sightseer** is someone who is travelling around in order to visit places of interest. EG *The Changing of the Guard is normally watched by a large crowd of sightseers.* N COUNT

sign /saɪn/, **signs, signing, signed. 1** A **sign** is **1.1** a mark or shape that always has a particular meaning, for example in mathematics or music. EG *...a minus sign... ...the equals sign.* **1.2** a movement of your arms, hands, or head which is intended to have a particular meaning. EG *Through signs she communicated that she wanted the women to hide.* N COUNT

2 A **sign** is also a piece of wood, metal, or plastic with words or pictures on it. Signs tell you where or what a particular place is, or give you a warning or an instruction. EG *The exit sign is marked with an arrow... A sign saying 'Women's Centre' hung over the door.* N COUNT

3 If there is a **sign** of something, a characteristic feature of it is present, which shows that it exists or is happening. EG *How pleasant to see a sign of summer once again... The Englishman showed no signs of his annoyance... His sores had begun to show signs of healing.* N COUNT+*of*

4 If you say that there is **no sign of** someone, you mean that they have not yet arrived, although you are expecting them to come. PHRASE

5 If you **sign** a document, you write your name on it, usually at the end or in a special space. EG *Sign your name in the book each time you use the photocopier... Sign here to acknowledge receipt.* V+O OR V

sign away. If you **sign** something **away**, you sign official documents that mean that you no longer own it or have a right to it. EG *Chiefs were encouraged to sign away land that appeared to be unoccupied.* PHRASAL VB: V+O+ADV

sign for. If you **sign for** something, **1** you officially state that you have received it, by signing a form or book. EG *When signing for any parcel, always add 'not inspected'.* **2** you officially agree to do a piece of work, by signing a legal contract. EG *He signed for his second film.* PHRASAL VB: V+PREP, HAS PASS; V+PREP, HAS PASS Informal

sign in. If you **sign in**, you officially indicate that you have arrived at a hotel or club, by signing a book or form. EG *They signed in at the reception desk.* PHRASAL VB: V+ADV

sign on. If you **sign on**, **1** you officially agree to work for an organization or do a course of study by signing a contract or form. EG *He signed on the next morning with the RAF... You could sign on for a course in word processing.* **2** you officially state that you are unemployed, so that you can receive money from the government in order to live. PHRASAL VB: V+ADV; ◊ ADV; V+ADV British

sign out. If you **sign out**, you officially state that you have left a hotel or club, by signing a book or form. PHRASAL VB: V+ADV

sign up. 1 If you **sign up**, you officially agree to do a job or course of study, by signing a contract or form. EG *He signed up as a painter on the Federal Art Project.* **2** If someone **signs** you **up**, you sign a contract stating that you will work for them. PHRASAL VB: V+ADV; V+O+ADV

signal /sɪgnə^{0}l/, **signals, signalling, signalled;** spelled **signaling** and **signaled** in American English. **1** A **signal** is a gesture, sound, or action which is intended to give a particular message to the person who sees or hears it. EG *My signal will be three knocks... He sat in the studio and waited for the signal to speak.* N COUNT

2 If you **signal** something or if you **signal** to someone, you make a gesture or sound in order to give a particular message to someone. EG *Don signalled his permission... Signal the driver to move off... ...a parent signalling to a child in the distance... The helpers signalled that all was ready.* V+O: OFT+*to*-INF; ALSO V: OFT+*to* OR REPORT

3 If an event or action is a **signal** of something, it suggests that this thing exists or is going to happen. EG *This was the first signal that an attack was brewing.* N COUNT+SUPP

4 If something **signals** an event, it suggests that the event is happening or likely to happen. EG *This decision seemed to signal a switch in the paper's editorial policy... ...the crisis signalling that the final moment was near.* V+O OR V+REPORT

5 A **signal** is also **5.1** a piece of equipment beside a railway, which indicates to train drivers whether they should stop the train or not. **5.2** a series of radio waves, light waves, or electrical impulses, which carry information. EG *Marconi finally succeeded in sending a signal across the Atlantic.* N COUNT

6 A **signal** triumph or failure is one that is especially important. EG *The year has seen one signal triumph for the Labour Party.* ADJ CLASSIF: ATTRIB Formal

signal box, signal boxes. A **signal box** is a small building near a railway, which contains the switches used to control the signals. N COUNT

signatory /sɪgnətə^{0}ri^{1}/, **signatories.** The **signatories** of an official document are the people who sign it. EG *...a signatory to the North Atlantic Treaty.* N COUNT: OFT+*of/to* Formal

signature /sɪgnə^{1}tʃə/, **signatures.** Your **signature** is your name, when you write it in your own characteristic way. EG *He underlined his signature with a little flourish... ...petitions bearing nearly half a million signatures.* N COUNT

signature tune, signature tunes. A **signature tune** is the tune which is always played at the beginning or end of a particular television or radio programme. N COUNT

significance /sɪgnɪfɪkəns/. The **significance** of something is its importance. EG *The meeting was of no significance... A year later I found out the true significance of the name.* N UNCOUNT

significant /sɪgnɪfɪkənt/. **1** A **significant** amount of something is a large amount of it. EG *Exports reached £232 million, making a significant contribution to the balance of payments... Lack of insulation can result in a significant amount of heat being lost.* ◊ **significantly.** EG *Prices were significantly reduced.* ADJ CLASSIF: ATTRIB; ◊ ADV

2 Something that is **significant** is important. EG *The incident was very significant... ...a significant discovery.* ◊ **significantly.** EG *Significantly, there was no reference to Iran.* ADJ QUALIT; ◊ ADV OR ADV SEN

3 A **significant** action or gesture is intended to have a special meaning. EG *With a significant look at her husband, Mrs Hochstadt went out.* ◊ **significantly.** EG *He cleared his throat significantly a few times.* ADJ QUALIT; ◊ ADV

signify /sɪgnɪfaɪ/, **signifies, signifying, signified.** A sign, symbol, or gesture that **signifies** something has a particular meaning. EG *Leggett gave a long wheeze, to signify disgust... Short pips signify that the phone is engaged.* V+O OR V+REPORT

signpost /saɪnpəust/, **signposts.** A **signpost** is a sign beside a road, which has information on it N COUNT

If something is silvery, is it made of silver?

such as the name of a town and how far away it is. EG ...*a signpost marked 'Fairford 8 miles'.*

signposted /saɪnpəʊstɪ²d/. A road or route that is **signposted** has signposts beside the road to show the way. EG *The route is well signposted.* ADJ PRED

Sikh /siːk/, **Sikhs.** 1 A **Sikh** is a person who believes in the Indian religion of Sikhism. N COUNT

2 Something that is **Sikh** belongs or relates to the Sikhs or to their religious beliefs and customs. EG ...*a Sikh name... ...Sikh cavalry... ...Sikh ideals.* ADJ CLASSIF

Sikhism /siːkɪzm/ is an Indian religion which teaches that there is only one God. N UNCOUNT

silence /saɪləns/, **silences, silencing, silenced.**

1 If there is **silence**, it is quiet because nobody is speaking. EG *We walked on in silence... There was a shocked silence.* N UNCOUNT OR N COUNT

2 The **silence** of a place is the extreme quietness that normally exists there. EG ...*the silence of the mountains.* N SING : the+N

3 Someone's **silence** about something is their failure or refusal to tell people anything about it. EG *Levy's silence on the subject was unnerving.* N UNCOUNT +SUPP

4 If you **silence** someone or something, you stop them speaking or making a noise. EG *Rodin silenced him with a gesture... Butler's firm speech failed to silence opposition.* V+O

silencer /saɪlənsə/, **silencers.** A **silencer** is a device on a car exhaust or a gun which makes it quieter. N COUNT

silent /saɪlənt/. 1 Someone who is **silent 1.1** is not speaking. EG *The woman was silent for a moment.* ◇ **silently.** EG *We finished breakfast silently.* ADJ CLASSIF **1.2** does not talk to people very much. EG *She was a silent girl, cool and aloof.* ADJ QUALIT

2 If you are **silent** about something, you do not tell people anything about it. EG *He remained absolutely silent on his plans for using the money.* ADJ PRED

3 Something that is **silent** makes no sound at all. EG *The guns have fallen silent.* ◇ **silently.** EG *It appeared suddenly and silently out of the dusk.* ADJ CLASSIF ◇ ADV

4 A **silent** film has only pictures and no sound or speech. EG *In 1924 I did my first silent film.* ADJ CLASSIF : ATTRIB

5 A **silent** letter in a word is written but not pronounced. For example, the 'k' in the word 'know' is silent. ADJ CLASSIF

silhouette /sɪluːɛt/, **silhouettes.** A **silhouette** is the outline of a dark shape when it has a bright light or pale background behind it. EG *The figure turned towards the sunrise, a tiny silhouette with uplifted arms.* N COUNT

silhouetted /sɪluːɛtɪ²d/. If something is **silhouetted** against a background, you can see its silhouette. EG ...*hills silhouetted against a pale blue sky.* ADJ PRED : USU+*against*

silicon /sɪlɪkən/ is an element that is used to make parts of computers and other electronic equipment. EG ...*mini-computers on tiny silicon chips.* N UNCOUNT

silk /sɪlk/, **silks. Silk** is a kind of smooth, fine cloth which is made from a substance produced by silkworms. EG ...*a white silk scarf.* N MASS

silken /sɪlkə⁰n/. You use **silken** to describe things that are smooth and soft. EG ...*silken hair.* ADJ CLASSIF Literary

silkworm /sɪlkwɜːm/, **silkworms.** A **silkworm** is a type of caterpillar that produces a substance used to make silk. N COUNT

silky /sɪlki¹/, **silkier, silkiest.** Something that is **silky** is smooth and soft. EG ...*fine silky skin.* ADJ QUALIT

sill /sɪl/, **sills.** A **sill** is a ledge at the bottom of a window, either inside or outside a building. EG *She sat with one elbow resting on the sill of the open window... ...bending over the window sill.* N COUNT

silly /sɪli¹/, **sillier, silliest.** If you say that someone is **silly**, you mean that they are behaving in a foolish or childish way. EG *You're a silly little boy... You silly fool!... It was a silly thing to say... How silly of me. I do apologise.* ADJ QUALIT

silt /sɪlt/, **silts, silting, silted. Silt** is fine sand, soil, or mud which is carried along by a river. EG *The problem is keeping the harbours free of silt.* N UNCOUNT

silt up. If a river or lake **silts up** or **is silted up**, it becomes blocked with silt. PHRASAL VB : V-ERG+ADV

silver /sɪlvə/, **silvers. 1 Silver** is a valuable greyish-white metal that is used for making jewellery and ornaments. EG ...*a little box made of solid silver... ...beautiful silver coffee pots.* N UNCOUNT

2 **Silver** is also coins that are made from silver or that look like silver. EG ...*leaving five pounds in silver in case somebody needed change.* N UNCOUNT

3 In a house, the **silver** is the things there that are made from silver, especially cutlery and dishes. EG *The silver sparkled in the candlelight.* N UNCOUNT

4 You describe something as **silver** when it is greyish-white in colour. EG ...*sparkling silver paint... ...a tall old man with long silver hair.* ADJ COLOUR

5 A **silver** is the same as a silver medal. N COUNT

silver birch, silver birches. A **silver birch** is a tree with a greyish-white trunk and branches. N COUNT

silver jubilee, silver jubilees. A **silver jubilee** is the 25th anniversary of an important event. EG *It's the College's Silver Jubilee year.* N COUNT

silver medal, silver medals. If you win a **silver medal**, you come second in a competition, especially a sports contest, and are given a medal made of silver as a prize. N COUNT

silver-plated. Something that is **silver-plated** is covered with a very thin layer of silver. EG ...*silver-plated forks.* ADJ CLASSIF

silver wedding, silver weddings. A married couple's **silver wedding** is the 25th anniversary of their wedding. N COUNT

silvery /sɪlvə⁰ri¹/. Something that is **silvery** looks like silver. EG ...*a silvery dress... His hair is silvery.* ADJ COLOUR

similar /sɪmɪlə/. If one thing is **similar** to another, or if two things are **similar**, they have features that are the same. EG *My problems are very similar to yours... The four restaurants were all serving similar food at similar prices.* ADJ QUALIT : OFT+*to*

similarity /sɪmɪlærɪ¹ti¹/, **similarities.** If there is a **similarity** between two or more things, they are similar to each other. EG *There were points of similarity between them... ...the similarities and differences between British and American English... Many species have close similarities with one another.* N UNCOUNT OR N COUNT : USU +*between/with*

similarly /sɪmɪləli¹/. You use **similarly** to say that something is similar to something else that you have just mentioned. EG *Other guests sat under similarly striped umbrellas... Similarly, savings certificates should be registered with the Post Office.* ADV OR ADV SEN

simile /sɪmɪli¹/, **similes.** A **simile** is an expression which describes a person or thing as being similar to someone or something else. For example, the sentences 'She runs like a deer' and 'He's as white as a sheet' are similes. N COUNT

simmer /sɪmə/, **simmers, simmering, simmered.** When you **simmer** food or when it **simmers**, you cook it by keeping it at boiling point or just below boiling point. EG *Simmer the beans for four hours until tender.* V-ERG

simmer down. If you **simmer down**, you stop being angry about something. EG *I thought the trip might give me time to simmer down.* PHRASAL VB : V+ADV Informal

simper /sɪmpə/, **simpers, simpering, simpered.** When someone **simpers**, they smile in a rather silly way. EG *The maid lowered her chin and simpered.* ▸ used as a noun. EG *'Thank you, doctor,' said the nurse with a simper.* V ▸ N COUNT

simple /sɪmpə⁰l/, **simpler, simplest. 1** If something is **simple**, **1.1** it is not complicated, and is therefore easy to understand. EG *The point I am making is a very simple one... ...a very simple calculator.* **1.2** it consists only of things that are necessary, without any extra features. EG ...*a tall woman in a simple brown dress.* ADJ QUALIT

2 If a problem is **simple** or if its solution is **simple**, the problem can be solved easily. EG *The solution is very simple.* ADJ QUALIT

3 A **simple** task is easy to do. EG *It's a simple operation, you can do it in a lunch hour.* ADJ QUALIT

4 If you describe people or their way of life as **simple**, you mean that they have an uncomplicated way of life. EG *They are only simple farmers... Nature, the simple life, that's what I need.* ADJ QUALIT

5 A person who is **simple** is mentally retarded. EG *Noreen despised Joyce and said she was simple.* ADJ QUALIT

6 You use **simple** to emphasize that the thing you are mentioning is the only important or relevant one. EG *Simple fear of death is often what turns people to religion.* ADJ CLASSIF : ATTRIB

7 See also **simplicity**, **simply**.

simple-minded. Someone who is **simple-minded** interprets everything in a way that is too simple, because they do not understand how complicated things are. EG *She was regarded by everyone as simple-minded.* ADJ QUALIT

simplicity /sɪmplɪsɪ¹ti¹/. **1** The **simplicity** of something is the fact that it is uncomplicated and can be understood easily. EG *The advantage of the idea was its simplicity... The major considerations were simplicity and effectiveness.* N UNCOUNT

2 If you say that there is **simplicity** in the way that someone behaves or dresses, you mean that they behave or dress in a simple way that is very attractive. EG *He dressed with elegant simplicity.* N UNCOUNT

simplification /sɪmplɪfɪkeɪʃə⁰n/, **simplifications.** A **simplification** is the thing that you produce when you make something simpler. EG *I see this proposal as a long overdue simplification.* N COUNT OR N UNCOUNT

simplify /sɪmplɪfaɪ/, **simplifies, simplifying, simplified.** If you **simplify** something, you make it easier to understand or do. EG *The subject is immensely complex, and hard to simplify.* V+O

◇ **simplified**. EG *The account given so far is a simplified one... ...a simplified version of the model.* ◇ ADJ QUALIT

simplistic /sɪmplɪstɪk/. A **simplistic** view or interpretation of something makes it seem much simpler than it really is. EG *The Department has based its policies on a rather simplistic analysis of the situation... ...a simplistic attitude.* ADJ QUALIT

simply /sɪmpli¹/. **1** You use **simply** to emphasize that something consists of only one thing, happens for only one reason, or is done in only one way. EG *The job of a caterpillar is simply to eat... It's simply a question of hard work... A good deal can be done simply by suggestion.* ADV

2 You also use **simply** to emphasize what you are saying. EG *I simply can't believe it... I was happy, there is simply no other word for it.* ADV

3 If you say or write something **simply**, you do it in a way that makes it easy to understand. EG *'His life is finished,' he said simply.* ADV

simulate /sɪmjə⁴leɪt/, **simulates, simulating, simulated. 1** If you **simulate** a feeling or an action, you pretend that you are feeling it or doing it. EG *We used this trick in the Army to simulate illness... Bomb tests can be simulated on computers.* V+O

2 If you **simulate** an object, a substance, or a noise, you produce something that looks or sounds like it. EG *The wood is carved to simulate hair... The body is simulated by packed straw... ...simulated silver.* V+O

simulation /sɪmjə⁴leɪʃə⁰n/, **simulations. 1 Simulation** or a **simulation** is the process of simulating something or the result of simulating it. EG *Spectators are entertained by the simulation of fighting... The viewer was unable to distinguish reality from simulation.* N UNCOUNT OR N COUNT

2 A **simulation** is also an attempt to solve a problem by representing the problem mathematically, often using a computer. EG *Computer modelling and simulation have been used as an aid to battle tactics.* N COUNT OR N UNCOUNT Technical

simultaneous /sɪmə⁴lteɪnɪəs/. Things which are **simultaneous** happen or exist at the same time. EG *...the simultaneous failure of all the lifts in the building.* ADJ CLASSIF ◇ **simultaneously**. EG *His fear and his hate grew simultaneously.* ◇ ADV

sin /sɪn/, **sins, sinning, sinned. 1 Sin** is behaviour which is considered to be very bad and immoral. EG *They believed they were being punished for their sins.* ● See also **cardinal sin**. N UNCOUNT OR N COUNT

2 If you **sin**, you do something that is believed to be very bad and immoral. EG *You have sinned against the Lord.* V : OFT +*against* ◇ **sinner, sinners**. EG *Christ is inviting sinners to repentance.* ◇ N COUNT

3 If a man and a woman **are living in sin**, they are living together as if they are married although they are not married. PHRASE Outdated

since /sɪns/. **1** If something has happened **since** a particular time or event, it has happened from that time or event until now. EG *Since 1974, Marilyn has lived in Paris... I've been wearing glasses since I was three... For the first time since leaving home, she is without a boyfriend... I came here in 1972 and I have lived here ever since.* PREP, CONJ, OR ADV

2 Since also means at some time after a particular time or event in the past. EG *He used to be an art student. He has since become a lawyer.* ADV

3 If something has **long since** happened, it happened a long time ago. EG *The time for talking has long since passed.* PHRASE Formal

4 You use **since** to introduce the reason for something. EG *Aircraft noise is a problem here since we're close to Heathrow Airport... Since it was Saturday, he stayed in bed an extra hour.* CONJ

sincere /sɪnsɪə/. If you are **sincere**, you say the things that you really mean or believe. EG *He was decent, sincere, a good man... The apology was sincere.* ADJ QUALIT ◇ **sincerity** /sɪnsɛrɪ¹ti¹/. EG *The Head Master is a man of deep conviction and sincerity.* ◇ N UNCOUNT

sincerely /sɪnsɪəli¹/. **1** If you say or feel something **sincerely**, you really mean it or feel it, and are not joking or being dishonest. EG *'I owe you an awful lot,' I said sincerely... He loves you very sincerely... I am sincerely delighted to hear that.* ADV

2 You write **Yours sincerely** before your signature at the end of a formal letter. EG *...Yours sincerely, Winston S. Churchill.* CONVENTION

sinew /sɪnju:/, **sinews.** A **sinew** is a cord in your body that connects a muscle to a bone. EG *The sinews of his arm were tense.* N COUNT OR N UNCOUNT

sinewy /sɪnju:i¹/. Someone who is **sinewy** has a lean body with strong muscles. EG *...his sinewy brown arm... She was a tall, sinewy type.* ADJ QUALIT

sinful /sɪnfʊl/. **1** Someone who is **sinful** has a tendency to commit sins. EG *Good women have always saved sinful men in stories.* ADJ QUALIT

2 Something that is **sinful** is considered to be wicked or immoral. EG *She believed that eyeshadow was sinful... ...a sinful desire... That is a sinful thing to say!* ADJ QUALIT

sing /sɪŋ/, **sings, singing, sang** /sæŋ/, **sung** /sʌŋ/. **1** If you **sing**, or if you **sing** a song, you make musical sounds with your voice, usually producing words that fit a tune. EG *I started to sing... The song is sung by Romy Blakeley.* V, V+O, OR V+QUOTE

2 If you **sing** someone a song, you sing it to them so that they can listen to it. EG *Would you like me to sing you a song?* V+O+O OR V+O+*to*

3 If someone **sings** a particular type of music or a particular musical role, they perform it as a singer, especially as a professional. EG *For five years I didn't sing opera on stage at all.* V+O

4 If you **sing** someone's **praises**, you enthusiastically praise them. EG *I understand that he's now singing the praises of Mcleod.* PHRASE

5 When birds or insects **sing**, they make pleasant sounds. EG *I could hear birds singing in the trees.* V OR V+O

6 See also **singing**.

Could your sister be called a sissy?

singe /sɪndʒ/, **singes, singeing, singed.** **1** If you **singe** something, or if it **singes**, you burn it very slightly so that it changes colour but does not catch fire. EG *She didn't notice that she had singed her gown.* V-ERG

2 A **singe** is a slight burn, especially on cloth or hair. N COUNT

singer /sɪŋə/, **singers.** A **singer** is a person who sings, especially as part of their job. EG *His mother was an actress and a singer.* N COUNT

singing /sɪŋɪŋ/. **1 Singing** is **1.1** the activity of making musical sounds with your voice. EG *The dancing and singing ended at midnight.* **1.2** the art of being a singer. EG *I went to her for singing lessons.* **1.3** the pleasant sounds made by birds or insects. EG *...the singing of the blackbirds.* N UNCOUNT

2 Your **singing** voice is the quality of your voice when you sing. EG *He had a fine singing voice.* ADJ CLASSIF: ATTRIB

single /sɪŋgəºl/, **singles, singling, singled.** **1** If you refer to a **single** thing, you mean only one, and not more. EG *We heard a single shot... I just couldn't think of a single thing to say.* ADJ CLASSIF: ATTRIB

2 You use **single** to indicate that you are considering something on its own and separately from the other things like it. EG *This is the most important single invention since the wheel... We went to the house every single day for six months.* ADJ CLASSIF: ATTRIB

3 If you are **single**, you are not married. ADJ CLASSIF

4 A **single** bed or room is intended to be used by only one person. ADJ CLASSIF

5 A **single** ticket is a ticket for a journey from one place to another but not back again. EG *How much is the single fare to London?* ▸ used as a noun. EG *A single to Edinburgh, please.* ADJ CLASSIF British ▸ N COUNT

6 A **single** is also a small gramophone record which has one short song on each side. N COUNT

7 Singles is a game of tennis or badminton in which one player plays another player. EG *The high serve is used a lot in singles.* N UNCOUNT

8 in single figures: see **figure**. • **in single file**: see **file**.

single out. If you **single** someone **out** from a group, you choose them and give them special attention or treatment. EG *Three other people were singled out for special praise.* PHRASAL VB: V+O+ADV

single cream is thin cream that does not have a lot of fat in it. N UNCOUNT British

single-handed. If you do something **single-handed**, you do it on your own, without help from anyone else. EG *He had rescued the girl single-handed.* ADV

single-minded. Someone who is **single-minded** has only one aim or purpose and is determined to achieve it. EG *...the single-minded pursuit of wealth.* ADJ QUALIT

singly /sɪŋgli¹/. If people do something **singly**, they do it on their own or one by one. EG *The children came out singly or in small groups.* ADV

sing-song. **1** A **sing-song** voice repeatedly rises and falls in pitch. EG *The dialect of the area has a sing-song intonation.* ADJ CLASSIF: ATTRIB

2 A **sing-song** is an occasion when a group of people sing songs together for pleasure. EG *We had a sing-song after the match.* N COUNT

singular /sɪŋgjə⁴lə/. **1** In grammar, the **singular** of a noun is the form of it that refers to one person or thing, and not more. EG *The singular of 'lice' is 'louse'... What is the singular form of 'media'?* N SING

2 Something that is **singular** is unusual and remarkable. EG *...a lady of singular beauty... ...a singular ignorance of human nature.* ADJ QUALIT Formal

singularly /sɪŋgjə⁴ləli¹/ means to a remarkable or extraordinary degree. EG *Then we did some singularly boring experiments.* SUBMOD Formal

sinister /sɪnɪstə/. Something that is **sinister** makes you afraid that something evil or harmful will happen. EG *...a rather sinister figure walking behind the bushes... ...an evil and sinister place.* ADJ QUALIT

sink /sɪŋk/, **sinks, sinking, sank** /sæŋk/, **sunk** /sʌŋk/. **1** A **sink** is **1.1** a large basin in a kitchen, with taps that supply water, used especially for washing dishes. EG *There was a stack of dirty dishes in the sink.* **1.2** the same as a washbasin. N COUNT

2 If something **sinks**, it moves slowly downwards, especially below the surface of water. EG *The boat sank to the bottom of the lake... The sun had just sunk below the horizon.* V: USU+A

3 If people **sink** a ship, they cause it to sink by attacking it with bombs or torpedoes. V+O

4 If you **sink** back or down, you move into a lower position. EG *She sank back in her chair and sipped her drink... She sank to her knees.* V+A

5 If an amount or value **sinks**, it decreases. EG *Wages have sunk so low in relation to the cost of living... ...if the energy input sinks or increases.* V+A

6 If your voice **sinks**, it becomes quieter. EG *His voice had sunk to a whisper.* V Literary

7 If you **sink** into an unpleasant or less active state, you pass gradually into it. EG *My father sank further into debt... I sank into a deep sleep.* V+*into*

8 If your heart **sinks** or your spirits **sink**, you become depressed or lose hope. EG *His heart sank at the thought that the exams were a week away.* V

9 If you **sink** something sharp into something solid, you make it go deeply into it. EG *He sank his teeth into the apple.* V-ERG+*into*

10 See also **sunken**.

sink in. When a statement or fact **sinks in**, it becomes fully understood or realized. EG *It took a moment or two for her words to sink in.* PHRASAL VB: V+ADV

sinuous /sɪnjʊəs/. Something that is **sinuous** **1** moves with smooth twists and turns, like a snake. EG *Women danced sinuous dances in the middle of the room.* **2** has many smooth wavy turns and curves. EG *...a sinuous trail of slime.* ADJ QUALIT Literary Literary

sinus /saɪnəs/, **sinuses.** Your **sinuses** are the spaces in the bones of your skull just behind your nose. EG *...blowing his nose noisily to clear the blocked sinuses... ...a sinus infection.* N COUNT: USU PLURAL

sip /sɪp/, **sips, sipping, sipped.** **1** If you **sip** a drink, you drink by taking just a small amount at a time. EG *The guests were sipping their drinks.* V+O

2 A **sip** is a small amount of drink that you take into your mouth. EG *She took another sip from her glass... Give them a few sips of water.* N COUNT OR N PART

siphon /saɪfəºn/, **siphons, siphoning, siphoned;** also spelled **syphon.** **1** If you **siphon** a liquid or **siphon** it off, you draw it out of a container through a tube by using atmospheric pressure. EG *Claude siphoned off a little petrol from his father's car.* V+O: OFT+*off*

2 A **siphon** is a tube that you use for siphoning liquid. • See also **soda siphon**. N COUNT

3 If you **siphon** money or resources or **siphon** them off, you cause them to be used for a purpose for which they were not intended. EG *This scheme involved siphoning colossal sums of money into public transport.* V+O: OFT+*off*

sir /sɜː/. **1** People sometimes call a man **sir** when they are being formal and polite. 'Dear Sir' is often used at the beginning of official letters. In spoken English, the plural of 'sir' is 'gentlemen'. EG *Dear Sir, I am writing in response to your letter of the 25th... What would you like, sir?... Brigadier Tomlinson wants to see you, sir.*

2 Sir is the title used in front of the name of a knight or baronet. EG *...Sir John Hargreaves.*

siren /saɪərəºn/, **sirens.** A **siren** is a warning device which makes a long, loud, wailing noise. Most fire engines, ambulances, and police cars have sirens. EG *...the distant wail of police sirens.* N COUNT

sissy /sɪsi¹/, **sissies;** also spelled **cissy.** A boy is described as a **sissy**, especially by other boys, if he does not like sport and is afraid to do things that are slightly dangerous. EG *You're a lot of cry-babies and sissies.* N COUNT Informal

sister /sɪstə/, **sisters.** **1** Your **sister** is a girl or woman who has the same parents as you. EG *My sister Jane married a farmer... Have you got any* N COUNT *brothers and sisters?* • See also **half-sister**, **step-sister**.

2 A **sister** is **2.1** a woman who is a member of a religious order. EG *The Sisters taught her a love of religion... ...Sister Catherine.* N COUNT **2.2** a senior nurse who supervises a hospital ward. British

3 A woman sometimes refers to other women as her **sisters** when she feels very close to them because they work for the same organization or have the same aims or beliefs. EG *They would go to Paris and stay with feminist sisters there.* N COUNT

4 The **sister** of something is another thing of the same type that has the same function or that was built at the same time. EG *The city shows every sign of outgrowing its sister.* N COUNT+POSS ▸ used as an adjective. EG *Her sister ship was sunk by a torpedo.* ▸ ADJ CLASSIF : ATTRIB

sister-in-law, sisters-in-law. Your **sister-in-law** is the sister of your husband or wife, or the wife of your brother. Some people also refer to a woman as their **sister-in-law** when she is married to their wife's or husband's brother. N COUNT

sisterly /sɪstəli^{1}/. A woman's **sisterly** feelings are the feelings of warmth and affection that she has towards her sister or brother or towards a man who she likes very much but does not love. ADJ CLASSIF : ATTRIB

sit /sɪt/, **sits, sitting, sat** /sæt/. **1** If you **are sitting** somewhere, for example in a chair or on the floor, your weight is supported by your buttocks rather than your feet, and the upper part of your body is upright. EG *She was sitting on the edge of the bed... I was sitting at my desk reading.* V : USU+A

2 When you **sit** somewhere, you lower your body until you are sitting on something. EG *He came into the room and sat in his usual chair.* V : USU+A

3 If you **sit** an examination, you take it. EG *After the third term, we'll be sitting the exam.* V+O British

4 If you **sit** on a committee, you are a member of it. EG *Representatives of the workers should sit on the board of directors.* V+*on*

5 When a parliament, law court, or other official body **sits**, it officially carries out its work. EG *Visitors are only allowed in on days when the Houses are not sitting.* V Formal

6 If you say that a building or other object **sits** in a particular place, you mean that it is in that place. EG *The little parish church sits cosily in the middle of the village.* V+A Literary

7 If you **sit tight**, you remain in the same place or situation and do not take any action. EG *All they have to do is sit tight until the Republic recognises their claims.* PHRASE

8 See also **sitting**, **baby-sit**. • to **sit on the fence**: see **fence**.

sit about or **sit around.** If you **sit about** or **sit around**, you spend a lot of time doing nothing except sit. EG *We were tired of sitting about waiting for something to happen.* PHRASAL VB : V+ADV, OFT+-ING Informal

sit back. If you **sit back** while something is happening, you relax and do not become involved in it. EG *He believes he has the right to sit back while others do the hard work.* PHRASAL VB : V+ADV Informal

sit down. 1 When you **sit down** or **sit** yourself **down**, you lower your body until you are sitting on something. EG *He sat down on the edge of the bed... Sit down and ask yourself, 'What do I really want?'* PHRASAL VB : V+ADV OR V-REFL+ADV

2 If you **sit** someone **down**, you make them sit down. EG *I sat him down and gave him a drink.* V+O+ADV **3** See also **sit-down**.

sit in on. If you **sit in on** a meeting or discussion, you are present while it is taking place but do not take part in it. EG *I was allowed to sit in on the deliberations of the board.* PHRASAL VB : V+ADV+PREP

sit out. If you **sit** something **out**, you wait patiently for it to finish, without taking any action. EG *They would retire to their caves to sit out the winter.* PHRASAL VB : V+O+ADV

sit through. If you **sit through** something such as a concert or a lecture, you stay until it is finished although you are not enjoying it. PHRASAL VB : V+PREP, HAS PASS

sit up. If you **sit up**, **1** you bring yourself into a sitting position when you have been leaning back or lying down. EG *She sat up in bed when she saw him coming.* PHRASAL VB : V+ADV **2** you do not go to bed although it is very late. EG *Sometimes I sit up reading until three or four in the morning.* V+ADV

sitcom /sɪtkɒm/, **sitcoms.** A **sitcom** is a television comedy series which shows the same set of characters in each episode, in amusing situations that are similar to everyday life. N COUNT

sit-down. 1 If you have a **sit-down**, you sit down and rest for a short time. EG *When we got to the top we had a bit of a sit-down.* N SING : *a*+N Informal

2 A **sit-down** meal is served to people sitting at tables. EG *...sit-down dinners.* ADJ CLASSIF : ATTRIB

site /saɪt/, **sites, siting, sited. 1** A **site** is a piece of ground that is used for a particular purpose or where a particular thing happens. EG *...dusty building sites... ...a caravan site... It is built on the site of the old Lion Tower... ...the site of the murder of the little princes in 1483.* N COUNT : USU+SUPP

2 If something **is sited** in a particular place or position, it is put there or built there. EG *They refused to have cruise missiles sited on their soil.* V+O+A : USU PASS

sit-in, sit-ins. A **sit-in** is a protest in which people go into a public place and stay sitting there for a long time. EG *The students voted to continue the sit-in.* N COUNT

sitting /sɪtɪŋ/, **sittings.** A **sitting** is **1** one of the times when a meal is served, for example in a school, when there is not enough space for everyone to eat at the same time. EG *The first sitting for breakfast is at 7.30.* N COUNT **2** one of the occasions when an official body, such as a parliament or law court, meets in order to carry out its work. EG *It was the first sitting of the Senate since the election.*

sitting-room, sitting-rooms. A **sitting-room** is a room in a house where people sit and relax. EG *Castle went back into the sitting-room.* N COUNT

sitting tenant, sitting tenants. A **sitting tenant** is a person who officially rents a house or flat as their home. EG *If you're a sitting tenant, then you're protected by a number of laws.* N COUNT

situate /sɪtjʊeɪt/, **situates, situating, situated.** If you **situate** something such as an idea or fact, you relate it to a particular context, especially in order to understand it better. EG *The dangers which press upon us must be situated in this context.* V+O+A Formal

situated /sɪtjʊeɪtɪ^{2}d/. If something is **situated** in a particular place or position, it is in that place or position. EG *The control centre is situated many miles away... ...the building in which Morris's office was situated... Their flat was most conveniently situated.* ADJ PRED

situation /sɪtjʊeɪʃə^{0}n/, **situations. 1** You use the word **situation** to refer generally to what is happening in a particular place at a particular time. EG *The situation was beginning to frighten me... It's an impossible situation... The situation in Georgia is radically different... ...the economic situation.* N COUNT : USU SING+SUPP

2 Your **situation** is the things that are happening to you or that are likely to happen to you at a particular time. EG *He knew a lot about my father's situation... ...the seriousness of his situation.* N COUNT : USU+POSS

3 The **situation** of a building or town is the kind of surroundings that it has. EG *The city is in a beautiful situation.* N COUNT : USU+SUPP Formal

4 A **situation** is also a job, especially a professional job, a clerical job, or a job as a servant. EG *It's not so easy to find another situation.* N COUNT Outdated • **Situations Vacant** is the title of a column or page in a newspaper where jobs of all kinds are advertised. EG *She studied the 'Situations Vacant' columns in the newspapers.* • PHRASE

situation comedy, situation comedies. A **situation comedy** is a type of comedy, especially N COUNT OR N UNCOUNT

What can you put on your feet to move around on snow?

on television or radio, which shows the characters in amusing situations that are similar to everyday life.

six /sɪks/, **sixes. 1 Six** is the number 6: see entry headed NUMBER. EG *He was about six feet tall... ...during the past six months.* NUMBER

2 If a place or event is **at sixes and sevens**, it is disorganized. EG *The household is at sixes and sevens at the moment.* PHRASE Informal

sixteen /sɪksti:n/, **sixteens. Sixteen** is the number 16: see entry headed NUMBER. EG *...a young woman of sixteen.* NUMBER

sixteenth /sɪksti:nθ/, **sixteenths. 1** The **sixteenth** item in a series is the one that you count as number sixteen: see entry headed NUMBER. EG *...a furnished room on the sixteenth floor.* ORDINAL

2 A **sixteenth** is one of sixteen equal parts of something. N COUNT: USU+*of*

sixth /sɪksθ/, **sixths. 1** The **sixth** item in a series is the one that you count as number six: see entry headed NUMBER. EG *On the sixth day we went on an excursion... ...the sixth of March.* ORDINAL

2 A **sixth** is one of six equal parts of something. EG *...one sixth of an acre of land.* N COUNT: USU+*of*

sixth form, sixth forms. The **sixth form** in a British school consists of the classes that pupils go into at the age of about sixteen, usually in order to study for 'A' Levels. EG *...a group of sixth-form pupils.* N COUNT

sixth former, sixth formers. A **sixth former** is a pupil who is in the sixth form. N COUNT

sixth sense. You say that someone has a **sixth sense** when they somehow know things although they do not have any direct evidence of them. EG *He had a sort of sixth sense for tracking down burglary suspects.* N SING: USU *a*+N

sixtieth /sɪkstɪə^{2}θ/, **sixtieths.** The **sixtieth** item in a series is the one that you count as number sixty: see entry headed NUMBER. EG *The dinner was in celebration of Mr Barrett's sixtieth birthday.* ORDINAL

sixty /sɪksti^1/, **sixties. Sixty** is the number 60: see entry headed NUMBER. EG *She was being paid sixty dollars a week.* NUMBER

sizable /saɪzəbə^{0}l/. See **sizeable**.

size /saɪz/, **sizes, sizing, sized. 1** The **size** of something is **1.1** how big or small it is. EG *The company doubled its size in nine years... We saw butterflies the size of birds... ...a block of ice one cubic foot in size.* **1.2** the fact that it is very large. EG *The Grand was the only hotel of any size in the town... The world overwhelms us by its sheer size.* N UNCOUNT

2 A **size** is one of a series of graded measurements, especially for things such as clothes or shoes. EG *'What size do you take?' – 'Ten.'... ...a jacket three sizes too big.* N COUNT

3 If you **cut** someone **down to size**, you embarrass or humiliate them in order to make them realize that they are not as important as they think they are. EG *Your boss isn't just trying to cut you down to size, but actually to get rid of you.* PHRASE Informal

size up. If you **size up** a person or situation, you carefully look at the person or think about the situation, so that you can decide how to act. EG *...people sizing each other up as if for a fight.* PHRASAL VB: V+O+ADV Informal

sizeable /saɪzəbə^{0}l/; also spelled **sizable.** Something that is **sizeable** is fairly large. EG *...a sizeable sum of money... ...a sizeable number of students.* ADJ QUALIT

sizzle /sɪzə^{0}l/, **sizzles, sizzling, sizzled.** If something **sizzles**, it makes a hissing sound like the sound made by frying food. EG *The steak and kidney pudding sizzled deliciously on the stove.* V

skate /skeɪt/, **skates, skating, skated. 1** A **skate** is **1.1** an ice-skate. **1.2** a roller-skate. N COUNT

2 If you **skate**, you move about on ice wearing ice-skates. EG *I took her skating last week.* ◇ **skating.** EG *There is skating in the winter.* ◇ **skater, skaters.** EG *...skaters gliding along the frozen Thames.* V; ◇ N UNCOUNT; ◇ N COUNT

3 A **skate** is also a kind of flat sea fish. N COUNT

4 If you **skate** round or over a difficult subject, you avoid discussing it. EG *He skated round the subject once or twice... The book skates over the technicalities of adult life.* V+A, HAS PASS

skateboard /skeɪtbɔ:d/, **skateboards.** A **skateboard** is a narrow board with wheels at each end, which people stand on and ride for pleasure. N COUNT

skateboarding /skeɪtbɔ:dɪŋ/ is the activity of riding on a skateboard. N ING

skein /skeɪn/, **skeins.** A **skein** is a loosely coiled length of thread, especially wool or silk. EG *...a skein of wool.* N COUNT

skeletal /skɛlɪ^{2}tə^{0}l/. **1** You use **skeletal** to describe things that relate to skeletons. EG *...skeletal remains... ...their skeletal structure.* ADJ CLASSIF: ATTRIB

2 A **skeletal** person is extremely thin. EG *...harrowing photographs of skeletal children in the desert.* ADJ CLASSIF

skeleton /skɛlɪ^{2}tə^{0}n/, **skeletons. 1** Your **skeleton** is the framework of bones which supports and protects your organs and muscles. EG *...the skeleton of a gigantic whale.* N COUNT

2 If you say that someone has **a skeleton in the cupboard**, you mean that they are keeping an unpleasant fact about their private life secret. PHRASE

3 A **skeleton** staff is the smallest amount of staff necessary in order to run an organization or service. EG *They only employ a skeleton staff of fulltime workers at weekends.* N MOD

skeptic /skɛptɪk/. See **sceptic**.

skeptical /skɛptɪkə^{0}l/. See **sceptical**.

sketch /skɛtʃ/, **sketches, sketching, sketched. 1** A **sketch** is a drawing that is done quickly without a lot of details. EG *...a rough sketch.* ▸ used as a verb. EG *These little drawings were sketched by a seventeenth century botanist... I sometimes sketched her.* N COUNT; ▸ V+O OR V

2 If you **sketch** a situation or incident, you give a short description of it, including only the most important facts. EG *His rise to power is briefly sketched in the first two chapters.* ▸ used as a noun. EG *...a brief sketch of the school's early history.* V+O; ▸ N COUNT

3 A **sketch** is also a short humorous piece of acting, usually forming part of a comedy show. EG *I loved the sketch about the dead parrot.* N COUNT

sketch in. If you **sketch in** details about something, you tell them to people. EG *In this programme I'm going to sketch in a bit of the background to the current crisis.* PHRASAL VB: V+O+ADV

sketch out. If you **sketch out** a situation or incident, you give a short description of it, including only the most important facts. EG *He sketched out his plan for the new sales campaign.* PHRASAL VB: V+ADV

sketchy /skɛtʃi^1/, **sketchier, sketchiest.** Something that is **sketchy** does not have many details. EG *...his sketchy lecture notes... I had only the sketchiest notion of what it was all about.* ADJ QUALIT

skewer /skju:ə/, **skewers, skewering, skewered. 1** A **skewer** is a long metal pin which is used to hold pieces of food together during cooking. N COUNT

2 If you **skewer** something, you push a long, thin, pointed object through it. EG *They skewered bits of meat on branches and held them in the flames.* V+O

ski /ski:/, **skis, skiing, skied. 1 Skis** are long, flat, narrow pieces of wood, metal, or plastic that are fastened to boots so that you can move easily on snow. EG *...a pair of skis.* N COUNT

2 When people **ski**, they move on snow wearing skis, especially as a sport or a holiday activity. EG *They go skiing every winter.* V

3 You use **ski** to describe things that are concerned with skiing. EG *...ski boots... ...a Swiss ski instructor... ...a ski resort.* ADJ CLASSIF: ATTRIB

skid /skɪd/, **skids, skidding, skidded.** If a vehicle **skids**, it slides sideways or forwards while moving, for example when you are trying to stop it suddenly on a wet road. EG *He slammed on his brakes and skidded into a wall... We skidded to a halt.* ▸ used as a noun. EG *The car went into a skid.* V: USU+A; ▸ N COUNT

skilful /skɪlfʊl/; spelled **skillful** in American English. Someone who is **skilful** at something does it very well. EG *The girl had grown more skilful with the sewing-machine... ...a skilful hunter... ...skilful political manoeuvres.* ◇ **skilfully.** EG *...a skilfully organized campaign.* ADJ QUALIT ◇ ADV

skill /skɪl/, **skills. 1 Skill** is the knowledge and ability that enables you to do something well. EG *Organized games involve skill, competition and teamwork... The carving shows remarkable technical skill.* N UNCOUNT

2 A **skill** is a type of work or craft which requires special training and knowledge. EG *...the skills of painting and drawing... ...learning new skills.* N COUNT

skilled /skɪld/. **1** Someone who is **skilled** has the knowledge and ability to do something well. EG *...hand-made items produced by skilled craftsmen.* ADJ QUALIT

2 **Skilled** work can only be done by people who have had some training; used especially of manual and industrial work. ADJ CLASSIF : ATTRIB

skillful /skɪlfʊl/. See **skilful**.

skim /skɪm/, **skims, skimming, skimmed. 1** If you **skim** something from the surface of a liquid, you remove it. EG *Skim off the cream.* V+O+A

2 If something **skims** a surface, it moves quickly along just above it. EG *The birds swoop in a breathtaking arc to skim the pond.* V+O

3 If you **skim** a piece of writing, you read through it quickly. EG *I thought I would skim through a few of the letters.* V+O OR V+*through*

skimmed milk is milk from which the cream has been removed. N UNCOUNT

skimp /skɪmp/, **skimps, skimping, skimped.** If you **skimp** on something, you use less time, money, or material for it than you really need. EG *Don't skimp on stair carpet... When people get harassed work is skimped or rushed.* V : OFT+*on*, OR V+O

skimpy /skɪmpi[1]/. Something that is **skimpy** is too small in size or quantity. EG *...little girls in skimpy cotton frocks.* ADJ QUALIT

skin /skɪn/, **skins, skinning, skinned. 1** Your **skin** is the natural covering of your body. EG *They had light skin and blue eyes... The poison may be absorbed through the skin... ...skin cancer.* N UNCOUNT OR N COUNT

2 An animal **skin** is skin with fur on it which has been removed from a dead animal. Skins are used to make things such as coats or rugs. EG *There was a polar bear skin on the floor.* N COUNT OR N UNCOUNT

3 The **skin** of a type of food is its outer layer or covering. EG *Cook the potatoes quickly with their skins on... ...sausage skins.* N COUNT OR N UNCOUNT

4 If a **skin** forms on the surface of a liquid, a fairly solid layer forms on it. EG *The custard had a thick skin on it.* N COUNT OR N UNCOUNT

5 If you **skin** a dead animal, you remove its skin. EG *The boys skinned and cleaned the day's game.* V+O

6 If you **skin** part of your body, you injure it by accidentally scraping some of the skin off. EG *She skinned her knee.* V+O

7 **Skin** is also used in these phrases. **7.1** If you do something **by the skin of** your **teeth**, you just manage to do it but very nearly fail. EG *I only passed by the skin of my teeth.* **7.2** If you say that something made you **jump out of** your **skin**, you mean that it surprised or shocked you very much. EG *He nearly jumped out of his skin when he saw her face at the window.* **7.3** If you try to **save** your own **skin** or to **protect** your own **skin**, you try to save yourself from something dangerous or unpleasant. EG *My first thought was to protect my own skin.* PHRASES

skin-deep. If you say that beauty or glamour is only **skin-deep**, you mean that people or things that look attractive may really be bad or worthless. ADJ CLASSIF

skinhead /skɪnhɛd/, **skinheads.** A **skinhead** is a young person whose hair is shaved or cut very short. Skinheads are usually regarded as violent and aggressive. N COUNT

skinny /skɪni[1]/. Someone who is **skinny** is very thin. EG *He's tall and skinny.* ADJ QUALIT Informal

skint /skɪnt/. If you are **skint**, you have no money. EG *I could do with £10, I'm skint.* ADJ PRED Informal

skin-tight. Skin-tight clothes fit very tightly so that they show the shape of a person's body. ADJ CLASSIF

skip /skɪp/, **skips, skipping, skipped. 1** If you **skip** along, you move almost as if you are dancing, with a series of little jumps from one foot to the other. EG *He skipped around the room.* ▸ used as a noun. EG *...taking little skips as they walked.* V : USU+A ▸ N COUNT

2 When someone **skips**, they jump up and down over a rope which they or two other people are holding at each end and turning round and round. EG *Three energetic little girls were skipping in the playground.* V

3 If you **skip** something that you usually do, you deliberately do not do it. EG *I could skip every lecture for a month and still graduate... I decided to skip lunch.* V+O Informal

4 A **skip** is a large metal container for holding rubbish and old bricks. EG *Debris was being loaded into skips.* N COUNT British

skipper /skɪpə/, **skippers.** You can use **skipper** to refer to **1** the captain of a ship or boat. EG *I had to pass the signals to the skipper.* **2** the captain of a sports team. N COUNT Informal Informal

skirmish /skɜːmɪʃ/, **skirmishes, skirmishing, skirmished.** A **skirmish** is **1** a minor battle. EG *...a bitter skirmish in the half light of dawn.* ▸ used as a verb. EG *The expedition spent two years crossing deserts and skirmishing with tribesmen.* **2** a short, sharp argument. EG *She described the early skirmishes in the campaign for equality for women.* N COUNT ▸ V N COUNT

skirt /skɜːt/, **skirts, skirting, skirted. 1** A **skirt** is a piece of clothing worn by women and girls which fastens at the waist and hangs down to above or below the knees. See picture at CLOTHES. EG *...a very short skirt.* N COUNT

2 Something that **skirts** an area is situated around the edge of it. EG *...the path which skirted the house.* V+O

3 If you **skirt** something, you go around the edge of it. EG *As I walked through the lobby, I had to skirt a group of ladies... They skirted round a bus.* V+O OR V+*round/around*

4 If you **skirt** a problem or question, you avoid dealing with it. EG *The President has skirted the issue.* V+O OR V+*round/around*

skittle /skɪtə[0]l/, **skittles. 1** A **skittle** is a wooden object used as a target in the game of skittles. N COUNT

2 **Skittles** is a game in which players try to knock over as many skittles as they can out of a group of nine by throwing a ball at them. N UNCOUNT

skive /skaɪv/, **skives, skiving, skived.** If you **skive**, you avoid working, especially by staying away from a place. EG *Were you skiving or were you really ill?... He's always skiving off.* V : OFT+*off* Informal British

skulk /skʌlk/, **skulks, skulking, skulked.** If you **skulk** somewhere, you stay there because you do not want to be seen or do not want to meet people. EG *There were half a dozen foxes skulking in the undergrowth.* V+A

skull /skʌl/, **skulls.** Your **skull** is the bony part of your head which encloses your brain. EG *He had two broken ribs and a fractured skull.* N COUNT

skunk /skʌŋk/, **skunks.** A **skunk** is a small black and white animal which gives off an unpleasant smell if it is frightened or attacked. N COUNT

sky /skaɪ/, **skies.** The **sky** is the space around the earth which you can see when you stand outside and look upwards, and where you can see the sun, the moon, and the stars. EG *There were little white clouds high in the blue sky... ...the night skies of London.* ● **pie in the sky**: see **pie**. N SING : *the*+N, OR N COUNT +SUPP

Does this dictionary have any slang in it?

sky-high. 1 If prices or wages go **sky-high**, they reach a very high level. EG *Land value has gone sky-high... ...sky-high property prices.* ADV OR ADJ CLASSIF

2 If you **blow** something **sky-high**, you destroy it completely. EG *His argument has just been blown sky-high.* PHRASE

skylight /skaɪlaɪt/, **skylights.** A **skylight** is a window in a roof. N COUNT

skyline /skaɪlaɪn/, **skylines.** The **skyline** is the line where the sky meets buildings or the land. EG *...the impressive Manhattan skyline.* N COUNT: USU SING+SUPP

skyscraper /skaɪskreɪpə/, **skyscrapers.** A **skyscraper** is a very tall building in a city. EG *The view was blocked by new skyscrapers.* N COUNT

skyward /skaɪwəd/, **skywards.** If you look **skyward** or **skywards**, you look up towards the sky. EG *He had a habit of looking skyward each time he made a pronouncement.* ADV AFTER VB Literary

slab /slæb/, **slabs.** A **slab** of something is a thick, flat piece of it. EG *...a great slab of rock... ...a concrete slab... ...a slab of cheese.* N PART OR N COUNT

slack /slæk/, **slacker, slackest; slacks.** 1 Something that is **slack** is loose and not firmly stretched or tightly in position. EG *...a slack rope... ...his slack and wrinkled skin.* ADJ QUALIT

2 The **slack** in a rope, thread, or wire is the part of it that hangs loose. N UNCOUNT

3 A **slack** period is one in which there is not much work or activity. EG *Very few hotels offered work for the slack season.* ADJ QUALIT

4 If you are **slack** in your work, you do not do your work properly. EG *Security's got a bit slack.* ADJ QUALIT
◊ **slackness.** EG *She was dismissed for slackness.* ◊ N UNCOUNT

5 **Slacks** are casual trousers. EG *I put on a pair of golfing slacks and a blazer.* N PLURAL Outdated

slacken /slækə⁰n/, **slackens, slackening, slackened.** 1 If something **slackens** or if you **slacken** it, it becomes slower, less active, or less intense. EG *She slackened her pace... The rain began to slacken.* V-ERG

2 If your grip or your body **slackens** or if you **slacken** it, it becomes looser or more relaxed. EG *The grip on Casson's right wrist did not slacken... Slacken your legs and slowly lie back.* V-ERG

slacken off. If something **slackens off**, it becomes slower, less active, or less intense. EG *The Depression slackened off and prosperity returned.* PHRASAL VB: V+ADV

slag /slæg/, **slags, slagging, slagged.** If you **slag** someone **off**, you criticize them in an unpleasant way. EG *Mark's always slagging off his friends behind their backs.* PHRASAL VB: V+O+ADV Informal

slag heap, slag heaps. A **slag heap** is a hill made of waste materials from mines and factories. N COUNT

slain /sleɪn/ is the past participle of **slay.**

slam /slæm/, **slams, slamming, slammed.** 1 If you **slam** a door or window or if it **slams**, it shuts noisily and with great force. EG *She went out, slamming the door behind her... I waited for the gate behind me to slam shut.* V-ERG: OFT+A

2 If you **slam** something down, you put it there quickly and with great force. EG *He slammed the money on the table.* V+O+A

slander /slɑːndə/, **slanders, slandering, slandered.** A **slander** is an untrue spoken statement about someone which is intended to damage their reputation. EG *I'll sue her for slander.* ▸ used as a verb. EG *She slandered him behind his back.* N COUNT OR N UNCOUNT ▸ V+O

slang /slæŋ/. Words, expressions, and meanings which are very informal are referred to as **slang**. EG *...the Dictionary of American Slang... ...military slang.* ▸ used as an adjective. EG *'Porridge' is a slang term for 'prison'.* N UNCOUNT ▸ ADJ CLASSIF: ATTRIB

slanging match /slæŋɪŋ mætʃ/, **slanging matches.** A **slanging match** is an angry quarrel in which people insult each other. EG *We had a full-scale slanging match.* N COUNT British

slangy /slæŋi¹/. **Slangy** speech or writing has a lot of slang in it. EG *...slangy colloquial passages.* ADJ QUALIT

slant /slɑːnt/, **slants, slanting, slanted.** 1 Something that **slants** is sloping, rather than horizontal or vertical. EG *The old wooden floor slanted a little.* V
◊ **slanting.** EG *...a slanting roof... ...her slanting eyes.* ◊ ADJ CLASSIF: ATTRIB

2 A **slant** is a slanting position. EG *For some reason the shelf was set on a slant.* N SING

3 If news or information **is slanted**, it is presented in a way that shows favour towards a particular group or opinion. EG *Burger's report was obviously slanted.* V+O: USU PASS

4 A particular **slant** on a subject is a particular way of thinking about it, especially one that is unfair, biased, or prejudiced. EG *I was furious at the slant that had been put on the evidence... ...a leftist political slant... I don't know whether it's possible to get a new slant on it these days.* N SING+SUPP

slap /slæp/, **slaps, slapping, slapped.** 1 If you **slap** someone, you hit them with the palm of your hand. EG *He slapped her across the face... I slapped her hand.* ▸ used as a noun. EG *Give him a slap if he is too much of a pest.* V+O ▸ N COUNT

2 If you **slap** someone on the back, you hit them in a friendly manner on their back. EG *I slapped him on the back and wished him the best of luck.* ▸ used as a noun. EG *...a hefty slap on the back.* V+O ▸ N COUNT

3 If you describe something that someone does as **a slap in the face**, you mean that it shocks and upsets you because it shows that they do not support you or respect you. EG *Their refusal was like a slap in the face.* PHRASE

4 If you **slap** something onto a surface, **4.1** you put it there quickly or carelessly. EG *All you have to do is slap a bit of Sellotape across it.* **4.2** you put it there with quite a lot of force. EG *He slapped the report down on the table.* V+O+A

5 If you walk or drive **slap** into something or **slap bang** into something, you walk or drive into it suddenly and with great force. EG *I walked slap into the wall.* ADV+PREP Informal

slapstick /slæpstɪk/ is a simple type of comedy in which the actors behave in a rough and foolish way. EG *...slapstick comics.* N UNCOUNT

slash /slæʃ/, **slashes, slashing, slashed.** 1 If you **slash** something, you make a long, deep cut in it. EG *Jack's face had been slashed with broken glass.* V+O

2 If you **slash** at something, you quickly hit at it with something. EG *...slashing at each other with their swords.* V: OFT+*at*

3 To **slash** something such as money or time means to reduce it by a large amount. EG *...a plan to slash taxes... Disease slashes income.* V+O Informal

4 You say **slash** to refer to a diagonal line that separates letters, words, or numbers. For example, if you are giving the number 340/21/K, you say 'Three four zero, slash two one, slash K.' N COUNT OR N UNCOUNT Spoken

slat /slæt/, **slats. Slats** are the narrow pieces of wood, metal, or plastic in things such as Venetian blinds or cupboard doors. N COUNT: USU PLURAL

slate /sleɪt/, **slates, slating, slated.** 1 **Slate** is a dark grey rock that can be easily split into thin layers. Slate is often used for covering roofs. N UNCOUNT

2 A **slate** is one of the small flat pieces of slate that are used for covering roofs. N COUNT

slatted /slætɪ²d/. Something that is **slatted** is made with slats. EG *...white slatted Venetian blinds.* ADJ CLASSIF

slaughter /slɔːtə/, **slaughters, slaughtering, slaughtered.** 1 To **slaughter** a large number of people means to kill them in a way that is cruel, unjust, or unnecessary. EG *Opponents of the regime were systematically slaughtered.* ▸ used as a noun. EG *Wholesale slaughter was carried out in the name of progress.* V+O ▸ N UNCOUNT

2 To **slaughter** animals such as cows and sheep means to kill them for their meat. EG *...a freshly slaughtered bullock.* ▸ used as a noun. EG *...animals going away to slaughter.* V+O ▸ N UNCOUNT

slaughterhouse /slɔːtəhaʊs/, **slaughterhouses.** N COUNT
A **slaughterhouse** is a place where animals are killed for their meat.

slave /sleɪv/, **slaves, slaving, slaved.** **1** A **slave** is someone who is the property of another person and has to work for that person. EG *...a story about a slave who escapes and becomes a free man.* N COUNT

2 You can also describe someone as a **slave** when they are completely under the control of another person or of a powerful influence. EG *He's just become a slave to possessions and money.* N COUNT+SUPP

3 If you **slave** for someone, you work very hard for them. EG *Why am I slaving away, running a house and family single-handed?* V : USU+A

slave driver, slave drivers. If you call someone a **slave driver**, you mean that they make people work very hard. N COUNT Informal

slavery /sleɪvəʳri[1]/. **1 Slavery** is the system by which people are owned by other people as slaves. EG *...the abolition of slavery.* N UNCOUNT

2 You also use **slavery** to refer to the state of not being free because you have to work very hard or because you are strongly influenced by something. EG *I had at last been freed from the slavery of a 9 to 5 job.* N UNCOUNT +SUPP

slavish /sleɪvɪʃ/. You use **slavish** to describe **1** things that copy or imitate something exactly, without any attempt to be original. EG *...a slavish adherence to things of the past.* ◊ **slavishly**. EG *I don't expect you to slavishly copy this.* **2** someone who always obeys other people; used showing disapproval. EG *...a slavish figure, down on her knees polishing the floor.* ADJ QUALIT; ◊ ADV; ADJ QUALIT

slay /sleɪ/, **slays, slaying, slew** /sljʊuː/, **slain** /sleɪn/. If someone **slays** someone else, they kill them in a violent way. EG *Two visitors were brutally slain yesterday.* V+O Literary

sleazy /sliːzi[1]/. A place that is **sleazy** looks dirty and badly cared for, and not respectable. EG *...a sleazy cafe... ...a sleazy area of town.* ADJ QUALIT

sled /sled/, **sleds.** A **sled** is the same as a sledge. EG *...a sled descending a snowy hill.* N COUNT American

sledge /sledʒ/, **sledges.** A **sledge** is a vehicle which can slide over snow. It consists of a framework which slides on two strips of wood or metal. N COUNT

sledgehammer /sledʒhæmə/, **sledgehammers.** A **sledgehammer** is a large, heavy hammer with a long handle. N COUNT

sleek /sliːk/, **sleeker, sleekest.** **1** Hair or fur that is **sleek** is smooth, shiny, and healthy-looking. EG *...her sleek black hair.* ADJ QUALIT

2 Someone who is **sleek** looks very rich; usually used showing disapproval. EG *They were all too fat and sleek and too pleased with themselves.* ADJ QUALIT

3 A vehicle that is **sleek** has a smooth, graceful shape. EG *...sleek, black cars.* ADJ QUALIT

sleep /sliːp/, **sleeps, sleeping, slept** /slept/. **1 Sleep** is the natural state of rest in which your eyes are closed and your mind and body are inactive and unconscious, usually for several hours every night. EG *I haven't been getting enough sleep recently... She fell into a dreamless sleep... Now go to sleep and stop worrying... I didn't get to sleep until six in the morning.* N UNCOUNT

2 When you **sleep**, you rest in a state of sleep. EG *She slept till ten in the morning... He was so excited he could hardly sleep.* ◊ **sleeping**. EG *I glanced down at the sleeping figure.* V; ◊ ADJ CLASSIF : ATTRIB

3 A **sleep** is a period of sleeping. EG *He hadn't had a proper night's sleep for a month... You'll feel better if you have a little sleep.* N SING : a+N

4 If a house **sleeps** a particular number of people, it has beds for that number. EG *Each apartment sleeps up to five adults.* V+O : NO CONT, NO PASS

5 If a part of your body **goes to sleep**, you lose the sense of feeling in it. EG *His foot had gone to sleep.* PHRASE

6 If a sick or injured animal is **put to sleep**, it is painlessly killed. EG *Sheba had to be put to sleep.* PHRASE

7 See also **sleeping**.

sleep around. If someone **sleeps around**, they have sex with several different people; used showing disapproval. EG *I did everything I could to hurt her, including sleeping around.* PHRASAL VB : V+ADV Informal

sleep off. If you **sleep off** the effects of eating or drinking too much or the effects of a drug, you recover from them by sleeping. EG *We went back to our room to sleep it off.* PHRASAL VB : V+O+ADV

sleep through. If you **sleep through** a noise, it does not wake you up. EG *The girl slept through everything.* PHRASAL VB : V+PREP, HAS PASS

sleep together. If two people **sleep together**, they have a sexual relationship, but are not usually married to each other. PHRASAL VB : V+ADV

sleep with. If you **sleep with** someone, you have sex with them. EG *Willie had slept with Mary Jane.* PHRASAL VB : V+PREP

sleeper /sliːpə/, **sleepers.** **1** You use **sleeper** to say how deeply someone sleeps. For example, someone who is a light **sleeper** is easily woken up. EG *Eva was a sound sleeper.* N COUNT+SUPP

2 A **sleeper** is also **2.1** a bed on a train. EG *I booked a first-class sleeper.* **2.2** a train with beds for passengers on overnight journeys. EG *I usually go up to London on the sleeper.* N COUNT; N COUNT

3 Railway **sleepers** are the large, heavy beams that support the rails of a railway track. N COUNT British

sleeping /sliːpɪŋ/. You use **sleeping** to describe places where people sleep. EG *The sleeping accommodation is somewhat primitive.* • See also **sleep**. ADJ CLASSIF : ATTRIB

sleeping bag, sleeping bags. A **sleeping bag** is a large deep bag with a warm lining which is used for sleeping in, especially when camping. N COUNT

sleeping pill, sleeping pills. A **sleeping pill** or a **sleeping tablet** is a pill that you can take to help you sleep. N COUNT

sleepless /sliːplɪ[2]s/. **1** A **sleepless** night is one during which you do not sleep. EG *He'd had a sleepless night.* ADJ QUALIT

2 Someone who is **sleepless** is unable to sleep. EG *Late in the night, sleepless and troubled, he went for a walk.* ◊ **sleeplessness**. EG *I began to suffer from sleeplessness.* ADJ QUALIT; ◊ N UNCOUNT

sleepwalk /sliːpwɔːk/, **sleepwalks, sleepwalking, sleepwalked.** If someone **is sleepwalking**, they are walking around while they are asleep. EG *She must have been sleepwalking.* V : USU CONT

sleepy /sliːpi[1]/, **sleepier, sleepiest.** **1** If you are **sleepy**, you are very tired and are ready to go to sleep. EG *She suddenly started to feel very sleepy... ...a sleepy yawn.* ◊ **sleepily**. EG *'Where have you been?' Rudolph asked sleepily.* ADJ QUALIT; ◊ ADV

2 A **sleepy** place is very quiet and does not have much activity or excitement. EG *...sleepy villages.* ADJ QUALIT : ATTRIB

sleet /sliːt/, **sleeting.** **1 Sleet** is rain that is partly frozen. EG *An icy sleet was beginning to fall.* N UNCOUNT

2 If it **is sleeting**, sleet is falling from the sky. EG *It started to sleet.* V : ONLY CONT OR INF

sleeve /sliːv/, **sleeves.** **1** The **sleeves** of a piece of clothing are the parts that cover your arms. EG *...a yellow dress with short sleeves.* N COUNT

2 A record **sleeve** is the stiff envelope in which a gramophone record is kept. EG *...the photograph of the conductor on the record sleeve.* N COUNT

3 If you **have** something **up** your **sleeve**, you have an idea or plan which you have not told anyone about. EG *She thought the old man had some clever trick up his sleeve.* PHRASE

sleeveless /sliːvlɪ[2]s/. A **sleeveless** piece of clothing has no sleeves. EG *...a blue sleeveless dress.* ADJ CLASSIF : ATTRIB

sleigh /sleɪ/, **sleighs.** A **sleigh** is a vehicle which can slide over snow. Sleighs are usually pulled by horses. N COUNT

sleight of hand /sleɪt əv hænd, slaɪt əv hænd/. **1** If you do something by **sleight of hand**, you do it using quick skilful movements of your hands which N UNCOUNT

Find two words on these pages that mean the same as 'slim'.

other people cannot see. EG *He switched the watches by sleight of hand.*

2 Sleight of hand is also a skilful piece of deception. EG *With a little statistical sleight of hand we could make things look all right.* N UNCOUNT

slender /slɛndə/. **1** A **slender** person is attractively thin and graceful. EG *...the girl's slender waist... She crossed her slender legs.* ADJ QUALIT

2 You use **slender** to describe something that is small in amount or degree when you would like it to be greater. EG *With such slender resources they cannot hope to achieve their aims... ...slender prospects of promotion.* ADJ QUALIT

slept /slɛpt/ is the past tense and past participle of **sleep.**

sleuth /slu:θ/, **sleuths.** A **sleuth** is a detective. EG *...a series about a lady sleuth.* N COUNT Outdated

slew /slj^u:/ is the past tense of **slay.**

slice /slaɪs/, **slices, slicing, sliced. 1** A **slice** is a piece of food that has been cut from a larger piece. EG *She cut him three large slices of bread... ...slices of chicken pie.* N COUNT OR N PART

2 If you **slice** food, you cut it into thin pieces. EG *I saw her slicing an apple.* V+O

3 A **slice** of something is a part of it. EG *Rents provided a large slice of his income.* N PART

4 If something **slices** a substance or **slices** through it, it cuts or moves through it quickly, like a knife. EG *They sliced the air with their knives... The shark's fin sliced through the water.* V+O OR V+*through*

sliced /slaɪst/. **Sliced** bread is bread that has been cut into slices before being wrapped up and sold. EG *...a large sliced loaf.* ADJ CLASSIF : ATTRIB

slick /slɪk/. **1** Something such as a book or film that is **slick** is well-made and attractive, but has little quality or sincerity; used showing disapproval. EG *Some people thought the broadcasts too slick.* ADJ QUALIT

2 A **slick** action is done quickly and smoothly, and without any obvious effort. EG *...a relay race round London, with slick baton-changing.* ADJ QUALIT

3 Someone who is **slick** speaks easily and persuasively but is not sincere; used showing disapproval. EG *...a slick, evasive answer.* ADJ QUALIT

4 See also **oil slick**.

slide /slaɪd/, **slides, sliding, slid** /slɪd/. **1** When something **slides** or when you **slide** it, it moves smoothly over or against something else. EG *The gate slid open at the push of a button... She slid the key into the keyhole.* V-ERG : USU+A

2 To **slide** somewhere means to move there smoothly and quietly. EG *An elderly lady slid into the seat... The black Mercedes slid away.* V : USU+A

3 If you **slide** into a particular attitude, you change to it smoothly and gradually, and usually unintentionally. EG *He felt himself sliding into obsession.* V+A

4 A **slide** is a small piece of photographic film which can be projected onto a screen so that you can see the picture. EG *...colour slides showing rice fields in Bangkok.* N COUNT

5 A **slide** is also a piece of glass on which you put something that you want to examine through a microscope. N COUNT

6 A **slide** in a playground is a structure that has a steep slope for children to slide down. N COUNT

7 See also **hair slide**.

slight /slaɪt/, **slighter, slightest; slights, slighting, slighted. 1** Something that is **slight** is very small in degree or quantity. EG *He had a slight German accent... ...after a slight hesitation... He'd had a slight stroke... I haven't the slightest idea what you're talking about.* ◊ **slightly**. EG *White wine should be slightly chilled... 'Do you know him?' – 'Slightly.'* ● You use **in the slightest** to emphasize a negative statement. EG *My tennis hadn't improved in the slightest.* ADJ QUALIT : USU ATTRIB; ◊ ADV; ● PHRASE : WITH BROAD NEG

2 Someone who is **slight** has a slim and delicate body. EG *I watched her slight figure cross the street.* ADJ QUALIT

3 If you **slight** someone, you insult them by treating them as if they were unimportant. EG *His fear of being slighted made him avoid people.* ▸ used as a noun. EG *It was a slight on a past award-winner, Stevenson.* V+O; ▸ N COUNT

slim /slɪm/, **slimmer, slimmest; slims, slimming, slimmed. 1** Someone who is **slim** has an attractively thin and well-shaped body. EG *...a tall, slim girl with long, straight hair.* ADJ QUALIT

2 If you **are slimming**, you are trying to make yourself thinner and lighter by eating less food or healthier food, or by taking exercise. EG *I may be slimming but I've no intentions of starving myself.* ◊ **slimmer, slimmers.** EG *...clubs for slimmers.* V; ◊ N COUNT

3 You describe an object as **slim** when it is thinner than usual. EG *...a slim book.* ADJ QUALIT

4 If the chance of something happening is **slim**, it is unlikely to happen. EG *The chance of American intervention is slim.* ADJ QUALIT

slime /slaɪm/ is a thick, slippery substance which covers a surface or comes from the bodies of animals such as snails. EG *There was a green slime around the edges of the tub... ...a trail of slime.* N UNCOUNT

slimy /slaɪmi[1]/. **1** Something that is **slimy** is covered in slime. EG *...a slimy pond... ...crawling, slimy creatures.* ADJ QUALIT

2 You use **slimy** to describe people who are friendly and pleasant in an insincere way; used showing disapproval. EG *...a slimy politician.* ADJ QUALIT Informal

sling /slɪŋ/, **slings, slinging, slung** /slʌŋ/. **1** If you **sling** something somewhere, you throw it there. EG *She slung the book across the room.* V+O+A

2 If you **sling** something over your shoulder or over a chair, for example, you put it there quickly and carelessly so that it hangs down. EG *Patrick gets his camera bag and slings it over his shoulder.* ◊ **slung.** EG *His few bits of clothing were slung over a string on the wall.* V+O+A; ◊ ADJ PRED

3 If you **sling** something such as a rope between two points, you attach it so that it hangs loosely between them. ◊ **slung.** EG *Pieces of meat were hanging to dry over a rope slung on the wall.* V+O+A : USU PASS; ◊ ADJ PRED

4 A **sling** is **4.1** an object made of ropes, straps, or cloth that is used for carrying things. EG *Mothers carry their babies around with them in slings.* **4.2** a piece of cloth which supports someone's broken or injured arm and is tied round their neck. EG *His arm was in a sling.* N COUNT

slink /slɪŋk/, **slinks, slinking, slunk** /slʌŋk/. If you **slink** somewhere, you move there in a slow and secretive way because you do not want to be seen. EG *I slunk away to my room, to brood in front of the fire.* V+A

slip /slɪp/, **slips, slipping, slipped. 1** If you **slip**, you accidentally slide and lose your balance. EG *I slipped on the snow and sprained my ankle.* V

2 If something **slips**, it slides out of place or out of your hands, especially accidentally. EG *It slipped from his fingers and fell with a bump... She pulled up her sock which had slipped down.* V : USU+A

3 If you **slip** somewhere, you go there quickly and quietly. EG *I hope we can slip away before she notices.* V+A

4 If you **slip** something somewhere, you put it there quickly in a way that does not attract attention. EG *He slipped it quickly into his pocket.* V+O+A

5 If something **slips** your **mind**, you forget about it. EG *It must have slipped his mind.* PHRASE

6 If you **let slip** information, you say it without intending to, especially when you had wanted to keep it secret. EG *He carelessly let slip this information in conversation with a journalist.* PHRASE

7 If you **slip** into clothes or **slip** them on, you put them on quickly or easily. If you **slip** out of clothes or **slip** them off, you take them off quickly or easily. EG *I slipped into my pyjamas... He slipped on his shoes and went out... She slipped off her dress.* V+A OR V+O+A

8 If you **give** someone **the slip**, you succeed in escaping from them. EG *I tried to follow her but she gave me the slip.* PHRASE Informal

9 A **slip** is a small mistake. EG *I must have made a slip somewhere.* ● **slip of the tongue**: see **tongue**. N COUNT
10 A **slip** of paper is a small piece of paper. N COUNT
11 A **slip** is also a piece of clothing without sleeves that a woman wears under her dress. EG *...a black nylon slip.* N COUNT
slip up. If you **slip up**, you make a mistake. EG *We must have slipped up somewhere.* ● See also **slip-up**. PHRASAL VB : V+ADV
slipped disc, slipped discs. If you have a **slipped disc**, one of the discs in your spine has moved out of its proper position. N COUNT
slipper /slɪpə/, **slippers. Slippers** are loose, soft shoes that you wear in the house. See picture at SHOES. N COUNT : USU PLURAL
slippery /slɪpə⁰ri¹/. 1 Something that is **slippery** is smooth, wet, or greasy and is therefore difficult to hold or walk on. EG *The soap was smooth and slippery... ...a slippery pavement.* ADJ QUALIT
2 If you say that someone is on **a slippery slope**, you mean that they are becoming worse in a way that is difficult to stop. EG *The economy is steadily sliding down the slippery slope.* PHRASE Formal
slip-up, slip-ups. A **slip-up** is a small or unimportant mistake. N COUNT Informal
slit /slɪt/, **slits, slitting.** The form **slit** is used in the present tense and is the past tense and past participle of the verb.
1 If you **slit** something, you make a long narrow cut in it. EG *She got a knife and slit the envelope... He slit open the packet with his thumb nail... He slit the fawn's throat.* V+O : OFT+A
2 A **slit** is **2.1** a long narrow cut. EG *We make a tiny slit in it with a razor blade.* **2.2** a long narrow opening in something. EG *...neon light came through the slits in the blind.* N COUNT
slither /slɪðə/, **slithers, slithering, slithered.** If you **slither** somewhere, you slide along the ground in an uneven way. EG *We slithered down the steep slope... A huge snake was slithering under my bed.* V : USU+A
sliver /slɪvə/, **slivers.** A **sliver** of something is a small thin piece of it. EG *...a sliver of soap.* N COUNT OR N PART
slob /slɒb/, **slobs.** A **slob** is someone who is very lazy and untidy. EG *You're a slob.* N COUNT Informal
slobber /slɒbə/, **slobbers, slobbering, slobbered.** If someone **slobbers**, they let liquid fall from their mouth, like babies do. EG *Sally was happily slobbering in her pram.* V
slog /slɒg/, **slogs, slogging, slogged.** 1 If you **slog** at something, you work hard and steadily at it. EG *The children are slogging away at revision.* V+A Informal
2 If you **slog** somewhere, you make a long and tiring journey there. EG *...slogging through the snow.* V+A Informal
3 If you describe a task as a **slog**, you mean that it is tiring and requires a lot of effort. EG *...the hard slog of trying to get views changed.* N SING Informal
4 You can also refer to a long and tiring journey as a **slog**. EG *...his long slog home.* N SING Informal
slogan /sləʊgə⁰n/, **slogans.** A **slogan** is a short, easily-remembered phrase. Slogans are used in advertisements and by political parties. EG *Racist slogans were scratched on walls throughout the city.* N COUNT
slop /slɒp/, **slops, slopping, slopped.** If liquid **slops** or if you **slop** it, it spills over the edge of a container in a messy way. EG *We carried the buckets, slopping water, back to the kitchen.* V-ERG : USU+A
slope /sləʊp/, **slopes, sloping, sloped.** 1 A **slope** is a flat surface that is at an angle, so that one end is higher than the other. EG *She rode up a grassy slope.* ● **a slippery slope**: see **slippery**. N COUNT
2 If a surface **slopes**, it is at an angle, so that one end is higher than the other. EG *The roof sloped down at the back.* ◇ **sloping**. EG *...gently sloping hills.* V : USU+A ◇ ADJ CLASSIF : ATTRIB
3 If something **slopes**, it leans to the right or to the left rather than being upright. ◇ **sloping**. EG *...sloping handwriting.* V : USU+A ◇ ADJ CLASSIF : ATTRIB
4 The **slope** of something is the angle at which it slopes. EG *...a slope of ten degrees.* N SING+SUPP
sloppy /slɒpi¹/. Something that is **sloppy** is messy, careless, or muddled. EG *...sloppy workmanship.* ◇ **sloppily**. EG *...a sloppily run hospital.* ADJ QUALIT Informal ◇ ADV
slosh /slɒʃ/, **sloshes, sloshing, sloshed.** If a liquid **sloshes** or if you **slosh** it, it splashes or moves around in a messy way. EG *The whiskey sloshed over from his glass on to his hand... They sat out on the decks laughing and sloshing water everywhere.* V-ERG : USU+A
sloshed /slɒʃt/. Someone who is **sloshed** is drunk. EG *Everyone is totally sloshed.* ADJ PRED Informal
slot /slɒt/, **slots, slotting, slotted.** 1 A **slot** is a narrow opening in a machine or container, for example a hole that you put coins in to make a machine work. EG *He put money in the slot and the music started again.* N COUNT
2 When something **slots** into something else or when you **slot** it in, you put it into a space where it fits. EG *The cylinder just slots into the barrel.* V-ERG+*in/into*
3 A **slot** is also a place in a schedule, scheme, or organization. EG *Students get only two slots in the week for private study.* N COUNT
sloth /sləʊθ/ is laziness. EG *Mrs Humbert would have to overcome her habitual sloth and write to Miss Phalen.* N UNCOUNT Formal
slot machine, slot machines. A **slot machine** is a machine from which you can get food or cigarettes or on which you can gamble. You work it by putting coins into a slot in the machine. N COUNT
slouch /slaʊtʃ/, **slouches, slouching, slouched.** If you **slouch**, you have your shoulders and head drooping down. EG *Many children slouch because of lack of self-confidence.* ▸ used as a noun. EG *Brad straightened out of his usual slouch.* V ▸ N SING
slough /slʌf/, **sloughs, sloughing, sloughed.** 1 When an animal such as a snake **sloughs off** its skin, its skin comes off naturally. 2 If you **slough off** something that you no longer need, you get rid of it. EG *Women are less willing than their husbands to slough off a friendship after a move.* PHRASAL VB : V+O+ADV V+O+ADV Literary
slovenly /slʌvənli¹/. Someone who is **slovenly** is careless, untidy, or inefficient. EG *His appearance was even more slovenly than usual.* ADJ QUALIT
slow /sləʊ/, **slower, slowest; slows, slowing, slowed.** 1 Something or someone that is **slow 1.1** moves, does something, or happens without very much speed. EG *His movements were all deliberate and slow... He is turned down for being too old and slow... ...slow music... ...the slow rate of growth.* ADJ QUALIT
▸ used as an adverb. EG *You're going too slow.* ▸ ADV
◇ **slowly**. EG *He nodded slowly and walked very sadly out of the door* ◇ **slowness**. EG *Time passed with agonizing slowness.* **1.2** takes a long time or is done after a delay. EG *...slow changes in the family structure... They have slow reflexes... I was slow in reacting to her news.* ◇ **slowly**. EG *He slowly began to realize what she meant.* ● **slowly but surely**: see **surely**. ◇ ADV ◇ N UNCOUNT ADJ QUALIT ◇ ADV
2 If something **slows** or if you **slow** it, it starts to move or happen more slowly. EG *He slowed to a walk... ...ways of slowing population growth.* V-ERG
3 Someone who is **slow** is not very clever. ADJ PRED
4 If you describe an activity, place, or story as **slow**, you mean that it is not very busy or exciting. EG *Business will be slow in the shop for another hour.* ADJ PRED
5 If a clock or watch is **slow**, it shows a time that is earlier than the correct time. EG *That clock's half an hour slow.* ADJ PRED
slow down. 1 If something **slows down** or if you **slow** it **down**, it starts to move or happen more slowly. EG *Economic growth has slowed down dramatically... Harold slowed the car down.* 2 If PHRASAL VB : V-ERG+ADV V+ADV

Is a slum a smart place to live in?

someone **slows down**, they become less active. EG *He needs to slow down a little or he'll get an ulcer.*

slow up. If something **slows up** or if you **slow** it **up**, it starts to move or happen more slowly. EG *The extra weight would have slowed me up considerably... She slowed up a little.* PHRASAL VB : V-ERG+ADV

slow motion is movement which is much slower than normal, especially in a film or on television. EG *I dreamt I was falling off a cliff in slow motion.* N UNCOUNT
▸ used as an adjective. EG *...slow-motion film of people talking.* ▸ ADJ CLASSIF

slow-witted. Someone who is **slow-witted** is not very clever. ADJ QUALIT

sludge /slʌdʒ/ is thick mud. EG *I was covered in sludge and weeds.* N UNCOUNT

slug /slʌg/, **slugs, slugging, slugged. 1** A **slug** is a small, slow-moving creature with a long, slimy body, like a snail without a shell. N COUNT
2 A **slug** of an alcoholic drink is a mouthful or a quantity of it. EG *Ken took a long slug of scotch.* N PART Informal
3 If you **slug** someone, you hit them hard. EG *I raised a fist to slug Eddie.* V+O Informal

sluggish /slʌgɪʃ/. Something that is **sluggish** moves or works very slowly, much slower than normal. EG *I feel very sluggish... ...the black sluggish waters of East Canal.* ADJ QUALIT

slum /slʌm/, **slums.** A **slum** is an area of a city where living conditions are very bad. EG *I grew up in a slum... ...children from a slum area.* N COUNT

slumber /slʌmbə/, **slumbers, slumbering, slumbered. Slumber** is sleep. EG *She fell into a heavy slumber... Roused from his slumbers, O'Shea departed.* N UNCOUNT OR N COUNT Literary
▸ used as a verb. EG *One old man slumbered over his newspaper.* ▸ V

slump /slʌmp/, **slumps, slumping, slumped. 1** If something such as the value of something **slumps**, it falls suddenly and by a large amount. EG *Profits last year slumped from $40 million to $26 million.* V
▸ used as a noun. EG *...the continuing slump in oil demand.* ▸ N COUNT
2 A **slump** is also a time when there is a lot of unemployment and poverty in a country. EG *The slump set in during the summer of 1921.* N COUNT
3 If you **slump** somewhere, you fall or sit down there heavily. EG *Sarah slumped against the wall.* V+A

slung /slʌŋ/ is the past tense and past participle of **sling.**

slunk /slʌŋk/ is the past tense and past participle of **slink.**

slur /slɜː/, **slurs, slurring, slurred. 1** A **slur** is an insulting remark which could damage someone's reputation. EG *He got angry whenever anyone cast the slightest slur on the regiment.* N COUNT
2 If you **slur** your speech or if your speech **slurs**, you pronounce words in a way which is not clear or distinct, often because you are drunk. EG *'I'll sing for you,' he said, his voice slurring so that he could barely be understood.* V-ERG
◇ **slurred.** EG *His words were slurred and his breath smelled of wine.* ◇ ADJ QUALIT

slurp /slɜːp/, **slurps, slurping, slurped.** If you **slurp** a liquid, you drink it noisily. EG *He slurped the soup greedily.* V+O OR V

slush /slʌʃ/ is snow which has begun to melt. N UNCOUNT

slushy /slʌʃi¹/. **1** Ground that is **slushy** is covered in wet snow. EG *A thaw had set in and the streets were slushy.* ADJ QUALIT
2 A **slushy** story or idea is extremely romantic and sentimental. EG *...a slushy film.* ADJ QUALIT

sly /slaɪ/, **slyer, slyest.** The forms **slier** and **sliest** are also used.
1 A **sly** look, expression, or remark shows that you know something that other people do not know or that was meant to be a secret. EG *A slow sly smile was creeping around the corners of his mouth.* ADJ QUALIT
◇ **slyly.** EG *She glanced slyly at Madeleine.* ◇ ADV
2 Someone who is **sly** is clever at deceiving people. EG *They are suspicious and wary and sly.* ADJ QUALIT

smack /smæk/, **smacks, smacking, smacked. 1** If you **smack** someone, you hit them with your hand. EG *He smacked her on the bottom.* V+O
▸ used as a noun. EG *I gave him a smack in the face.* ▸ N COUNT
2 If you **smack** something somewhere, you put it or throw it there so that it makes a loud, sharp noise. EG *He laughed, smacking the flat of his hand on the steering wheel.* V+O+A
▸ used as a noun. EG *She gave out the books, dropping them with a satisfying smack on each desk.* ▸ N SING
3 If you **smack** your **lips**, you open and close your mouth noisily, especially before or after eating. EG *He looked at the plate and smacked his lips.* PHRASE
4 If something **smacks** of something else, it reminds you of it or is like it. EG *Any literature other than romantic novels smacked to her of school.* V+*of* Formal
5 Something that is **smack** in a particular place is exactly in that place. EG *The office was right smack in the middle of town.* ADV+PREP Informal
6 If one thing runs **smack** into another thing, it hits it directly with a great deal of force. EG *The bus ran smack into a car.* ADV+PREP Informal

small /smɔːl/, **smaller, smallest. 1** Someone or something that is **small** is not large in physical size. EG *She was rather small in stature... The male is smaller than the female... This is the smallest church in England.* ADJ QUALIT
◇ **smallness.** EG *The smallness of the courtroom exaggerated its height.* ◇ N UNCOUNT
2 A **small** group or amount consists of only a few things or not much of something. EG *...small families... ...a relatively small number of people... ...a small amount of milk.* ADJ QUALIT
3 A **small** child is a very young child. EG *She had two small children.* ADJ QUALIT
4 You also use **small** to describe something that is not significant or great in degree. EG *Certain small changes resulted from my report... Why did he never make the smallest effort to reach my father?... ...a matter of small importance.* ADJ QUALIT
5 If you say that something does something **in a small way**, you mean that it does it to a limited extent. EG *...if, in their own small way, they had been able to help.* PHRASE
6 The **small of** your **back** is the narrow part of your back where it curves inwards slightly. EG *She had a pain in the small of her back.* PHRASE
7 the small hours: see **hour.** • **small wonder**: see **wonder**.

small ad, small ads. A **small ad** in a newspaper is a short advertisement in which you can advertise something such as an object for sale or a room to let. N COUNT : USU PLURAL

small change is coins of low value. EG *I need some small change to make a phone call.* N UNCOUNT

small fry is used to refer to people who are considered to be unimportant. EG *Being small fry they had done what they were told.* N UNCOUNT

smallish /smɔːlɪʃ/. Something that is **smallish** is fairly small. EG *He was a smallish man.* ADJ QUALIT

smallpox /smɔːlpɒks/ is a serious infectious disease that causes a high fever and a rash. N UNCOUNT

small-scale. A **small-scale** activity or organization is limited in extent. EG *...small-scale industry.* ADJ CLASSIF : ATTRIB

small talk is conversation at social occasions about unimportant things. EG *We stood around making small talk.* N UNCOUNT

smarmy /smɑːmi¹/. Someone who is **smarmy** is unpleasantly polite and flattering. EG *...a nasty little man, smarmy and obsequious.* ADJ QUALIT Informal

smart /smɑːt/, **smarter, smartest; smarts, smarting, smarted. 1** Someone who is **smart** is pleasantly neat and clean in appearance. EG *The boys looked smart in their school uniforms.* ADJ QUALIT
◇ **smartly.** EG *...a smartly dressed executive.* ◇ ADV
2 You can also describe someone as **smart** when they are clever. EG *She's one of the smartest students in the whole school... ...a smart idea.* ADJ QUALIT American
3 A **smart** place or event is connected with wealthy and fashionable people. EG *We met at a very smart lunch party.* ADJ QUALIT
4 A **smart** movement or action is sharp and quick. ADJ QUALIT : ATTRIB

EG *...the smart crack of a whip... ...moving along at a smart trot.* ◊ **smartly**. EG *Grabbing the bottle, she hit him smartly on the head.* ◊ ADV Written

5 If a part of your body or a wound **smarts**, you feel a sharp stinging pain in it. EG *His eyes smarted from the smoke of the fire.* V

6 If you **are smarting** from something such as criticism or unkindness, you feel upset about it. EG *Brody smarted under Quint's derision.* V: OFT+A

smarten /smɑːtə⁰n/, **smartens, smartening, smartened.** If you **smarten** yourself **up** or if you **smarten** a place **up**, you make yourself or the place look neater and tidier. EG *The New Electric Cinema has been smartened up.* PHRASAL VB: V-REFL+ADV OR V+O+ADV

smash /smæʃ/, **smashes, smashing, smashed. 1** If you **smash** something, you break it into many pieces by hitting it, throwing it, or dropping it. EG *Some windows have been smashed... I nearly smashed the TV set.* V+O

2 If something **smashes**, it breaks into many pieces when it falls and hits the ground. EG *A plate dropped from his fingers and smashed on the kitchen floor.* V: NO CONT

3 If you **smash** through something such as a wall, you move forwards by hitting it and breaking it. EG *The police smashed their way into eleven homes.* V+A OR V+O+A

4 If something **smashes** or **is smashed** against something solid, it moves very fast and with great force against it. EG *The waves smashed onto the shore... The sea smashed the boat against the rocks.* V-ERG+A

5 If people **smash** something such as a political system or a person's career, they deliberately ruin it. EG *We are interested in transforming the system rather than smashing it.* V+O

6 A play or film that is a **smash** or a **smash** hit is very successful and popular. EG *The show was a smash hit in London and New York.* N SING OR N MOD

7 A **smash** is also a car crash. EG *She had a serious motor smash on the way to Scotland.* N COUNT Informal

8 See also **smashed, smashing**.

smash up. If you **smash** something **up**, you completely destroy it by hitting it and breaking it into many pieces. EG *He started smashing up all the furniture.* PHRASAL VB: V+O+ADV

smashed /smæʃt/. Someone who is **smashed** is extremely drunk. ADJ PRED Informal

smashing /smæʃɪŋ/. If you describe something as **smashing**, you mean that you like it very much. EG *We had a smashing time.* ADJ QUALIT Informal

smattering /smætə⁰rɪŋ/. A **smattering** of knowledge or information is a very small amount of it. EG *Jane spoke Spanish, and a smattering of Greek.* N PART: SING

smear /smɪə/, **smears, smearing, smeared. 1** A **smear** is a dirty or greasy mark caused by something rubbing against a surface. EG *...a smear of blue paint.* N COUNT

2 To **smear** something means to make dirty or greasy marks on it. EG *Soot smeared our faces... The windows were all smeared.* V+O

3 If you **smear** a surface with a greasy or sticky substance or **smear** the substance onto the surface, you spread a layer of the substance over the surface. EG *Smear the baking tin with butter... She smeared this blood onto a slide.* V+O+A

4 A **smear** is also an unpleasant and untrue rumour or accusation that is intended to damage someone's reputation. EG *Party leaders denounced the allegation as a right-wing smear.* N COUNT

smell /smɛl/, **smells, smelling, smelled, smelt** /smɛlt/. The forms **smelled** and **smelt** are both used as the past tense and past participle of the verb.

1 The **smell** of something is the effect that it has on your nose; used especially when the effect is unpleasant. EG *What's that smell?... ...the smell of fresh bread... The air had a sweet smell... ...cooking smells.* N COUNT

2 If something **smells**, it has an effect on your nose. EG *The room smelled of cigars... Our kitchen smelt like a rubber factory... The papers smelt musty and stale... Dinner smells good.* V: OFT+*of/like* OR V+C

3 If you **smell** something, **3.1** you become aware of it because of the effect it has on your nose. EG *Don't strike a match if you smell gas.* **3.2** you put your nose near it and breathe in, in order to discover its smell. EG *She picked up the soap and smelled it.* V+O

4 Smell is the ability that your nose has. EG *They all have an excellent sense of smell.* N UNCOUNT

5 If you **smell** something such as danger or trouble, you feel instinctively that it is likely to happen. EG *He's shrewd and can smell a successful project.* ● If you **smell a rat**, you become suspicious that there is something wrong. EG *I accepted with suspicious gratitude. I could smell a rat.* V+O: NO CONT ● PHRASE

smelly /smɛli¹/. Something that is **smelly** has an unpleasant smell. EG *...some rather smelly cheese.* ADJ QUALIT

smile /smaɪl/, **smiles, smiling, smiled. 1** When you **smile** because you are pleased or amused or are being friendly, the corners of your mouth curve upwards and you sometimes show your teeth. EG *Hooper smiled and leaned back in his chair... The girl was smiling at me.* V

2 A **smile** is the expression that you have on your face when you smile. EG *Barber welcomed me with a smile... ...a mocking, unpleasant smile.* N COUNT

3 If you **smile** something, you say it with a smile or express it by a smile. EG *'That remains to be seen,' smiled Mrs Barrett... She smiled her approval.* V+O OR V+QUOTE

smirk /smɜːk/, **smirks, smirking, smirked.** If you **smirk**, you smile in an unpleasant way. EG *'That's where you're wrong,' Ellen said, smirking.* ▸ used as a noun. EG *Mark detected a smirk on the clerk's face.* V ▸ N COUNT

smock /smɒk/, **smocks.** A **smock** is a loose garment, rather like a long blouse, usually worn by women. N COUNT

smog /smɒg/ is a mixture of fog and smoke which occurs in some busy industrial cities. EG *Black smog reduced visibility to about fifty yards.* N UNCOUNT

smoke /sməʊk/, **smokes, smoking, smoked. 1 Smoke** consists of gas and small bits of solid material that are sent into the air when something burns. EG *The room was full of smoke... ...cigarette smoke.* N UNCOUNT

2 If something **is smoking**, smoke is coming from it. EG *Down below in the valleys the chimneys were smoking.* V

3 When someone **smokes** a cigarette, pipe, or cigar, they have it in their mouth, sucking the smoke into their mouth and blowing it out again. EG *He was sitting quietly in his armchair, smoking a pipe... He sat and smoked and stared out of the window.* V+O OR V

4 If you **smoke**, you have the habit of smoking cigarettes, or perhaps a pipe. EG *Do you smoke?* ◊ **smoker, smokers.** EG *One smoker in 20 will give up the habit permanently... ...a pipe smoker.* V ◊ N COUNT

5 To **smoke** fish or meat means to hang it over burning wood so that the smoke will preserve it and give it a special flavour. ◊ **smoked.** EG *...smoked salmon.* V+O ◊ ADJ CLASSIF: ATTRIB

smokeless /sməʊklɪ²s/. **Smokeless** fuel burns without producing smoke. ADJ CLASSIF: ATTRIB

smoking /sməʊkɪŋ/. **1 Smoking** is the act or habit of smoking cigarettes or other forms of tobacco. EG *Does smoking cause cancer?... I'm trying to give up smoking.* N UNCOUNT

2 A **smoking** section or compartment is intended for people who want to smoke. EG *Do you want to go in the smoking or non-smoking section?* ADJ CLASSIF: ATTRIB

What is the difference between smirk and smile?

smoky /sməʊki¹/. **1** A place that is **smoky** has a lot of smoke in the air. EG *...a smoky industrial scene of the 1930's.* ADJ QUALIT

2 You can also use **smoky** to describe something that looks like smoke, for example because it is slightly blue or grey or because it appears cloudy. EG *...the smoky twilight.* ADJ CLASSIF : ATTRIB

smolder /sməʊldə/. See **smoulder**.

smooth /smu:ð/, **smoother, smoothest; smooths, smoothing, smoothed. 1** A **smooth** surface has no roughness, lumps, or holes. EG *Your skin looks so smooth... The boulders were so smooth and slippery I couldn't get a grip.* ADJ QUALIT

2 A **smooth** liquid or mixture has been mixed well so that it is without lumps. EG *...a smooth paste.* ADJ QUALIT

3 If you **smooth** something, you move your hands over its surface to make it smooth and flat. EG *Don't iron pyjamas. Just smooth and fold them... He turned his head and smoothed back the hair over one temple.* V+O

4 A **smooth** movement or process happens or is done evenly and steadily with no sudden changes or breaks. EG *He walked with a long, smooth stride.* ADJ QUALIT
◇ **smoothly**. EG *The snake glides smoothly towards it.* ◇ ADV

5 A **smooth** ride, flight, or sea crossing is very comfortable because there are no bumps or jolts. ADJ QUALIT

6 You use **smooth** to describe something that is going well and is free of problems or trouble. EG *Cooperation is essential if you are going to lead a smooth existence in the office.* ◇ **smoothly**. EG *Life is running smoothly for them.* ADJ QUALIT ◇ ADV

7 A man who is **smooth** is extremely smart, confident, and polite, especially in a way that you find rather unpleasant. ADJ QUALIT

8 If you **smooth the path** or **smooth the way** of something, you make it easier or more likely to happen. EG *Goodwill and cooperation can go a long way towards smoothing your way to the top.* PHRASE

smooth out. If you **smooth** something **out**, you move your hands over its surface to make it smooth and flat. EG *I started smoothing out the tablecloth.* PHRASAL VB : V+O+ADV

smooth over. If you **smooth over** a problem or difficulty, you make it less serious and easier to deal with, especially by talking to the people concerned. EG *I tried to smooth over the awkwardness of this first meeting.* PHRASAL VB : V+ADV+O

smother /smʌðə/, **smothers, smothering, smothered. 1** If you **smother** a fire, you cover it with something in order to put it out. EG *She grabbed a blanket to smother the flames.* V+O

2 To **smother** someone means to kill them by covering their face with something so that they cannot breathe. V+O

3 Things that **smother** something cover it completely. EG *White roses smothered the apple tree... She smothered him with kisses.* ◇ **smothered.** EG *The pear tree was smothered in ivy... ...bonnets smothered with sequins.* V+O : OFT+*with/in* ◇ ADJ PRED : OFT+*with/in*

4 If you **smother** someone, you show your love for them too much and protect them too much. EG *She should love them without smothering them with attention.* V+O : OFT+*with*

5 If you **smother** an emotion or emotional reaction, you control it so that people do not notice it. EG *I turned away and tried to smother my sobs.* V+O

smoulder /sməʊldə/, **smoulders, smouldering, smouldered;** spelled **smolder** in American English. **1** If something **smoulders**, it burns slowly, producing smoke but not flames. EG *The ruins are still smouldering.* V

2 If anger or hatred **is smouldering** within you, you continue to feel it but rarely show it. EG *Inside me was a smouldering anger at what he had done.* V Literary

smudge /smʌdʒ/, **smudges, smudging, smudged. 1** A **smudge** is a dirty mark caused by rubbing a powder or a wet substance onto something. EG *He had a smudge of flour on his face... The wallpaper had smudges all over it.* N COUNT

2 If you **smudge** something, you make it dirty or messy by touching it or putting a mark on it. EG *I'm not allowed to kiss her in case I smudge her lipstick... Her cheeks were smudged with tears.* V+O : OFT+A

smug /smʌg/. Someone who is **smug** is very pleased with how good or clever they are; used showing disapproval. EG *...looks of smug satisfaction.* ◇ **smugly**. EG *'I know all that,' I said smugly.* ADJ QUALIT ◇ ADV
◇ **smugness**. EG *'That,' I said with pardonable smugness, 'happens to be mine.'* ◇ N UNCOUNT

smuggle /smʌgə⁰l/, **smuggles, smuggling, smuggled.** If someone **smuggles** things or people into a country or place or out of it, they take them there illegally or secretly. EG *She smuggled these diamond bracelets out... ...smuggling refugees into the country.* ◇ **smuggler, smugglers**. EG *...hunting drug smugglers.* V+O : USU+A ◇ N COUNT

snack /snæk/, **snacks.** A **snack** is a small, quick meal, or something which you eat between meals. EG *Sardines can be served on toast as a delicious snack... We ate a snack supper in a pub.* N COUNT

snack bar, snack bars. A **snack bar** is a place where you can buy small meals such as sandwiches, and also drinks. N COUNT

snag /snæg/, **snags, snagging, snagged. 1** A **snag** is a small problem or disadvantage. EG *It cleans very effectively. The only snag is that it dissolves plastics.* N COUNT

2 If you **snag** part of your clothing on a sharp or rough object, it gets caught on the object and tears. EG *I snagged my best skirt on a bramble.* V+O : OFT+*on/with*

snail /sneɪl/, **snails.** A **snail** is a small animal with a long, slimy body and a spiral-shaped shell. Snails move very slowly. N COUNT

snake /sneɪk/, **snakes, snaking, snaked. 1** A **snake** is a long, thin reptile with no legs. EG *He was bitten by a poisonous snake.* N COUNT

2 Something that **snakes** in a particular direction goes in that direction in a line with a lot of bends. EG *The procession snaked round the houses.* V+A Literary

snap /snæp/, **snaps, snapping, snapped. 1** If something **snaps** or if you **snap** it, it breaks suddenly, usually with a sharp cracking noise. EG *The rope snapped... One of those kicks could snap you in half like a dry twig.* ▸ used as a noun. EG *The snap of a twig broke the silence.* V-ERG ▸ N SING

2 If you **snap** something into a particular position or if it **snaps** into that position, it moves quickly into that position, with a sharp sound. EG *She snapped the silver chain around her neck... The jaws snapped shut around her arm.* ▸ used as a noun. EG *The trap closes with a sudden snap.* V-ERG+A ▸ N SING

3 If you **snap** your **fingers**, you make a sharp sound by moving your middle finger quickly across your thumb, for example in order to attract someone's attention. EG *He snapped his fingers in the air and cried, 'Waiter!'* PHRASE

4 If a dog or other animal **snaps** at you, it shuts its jaws quickly near you. EG *The dogs ran snapping and barking at his heels.* V : OFT+*at*

5 If someone **snaps** at you, they speak to you in a sharp, unfriendly way. EG *'Don't do that!' she snapped.* V+*at* OR V+QUOTE

6 A **snap** decision or action is one that you take suddenly, without thinking about it carefully. EG *The snap reaction of the press was to welcome the change... The strike led to a snap election.* ADJ CLASSIF : ATTRIB

7 A **snap** is a photograph that is taken quickly and casually. EG *I had taken dozens of snaps of Daisy.* N COUNT Informal

8 If someone who is depressed **snaps out of it**, they suddenly become more cheerful, especially by making an effort. EG *Come on, snap out of it!* PHRASE

snap up. If you **snap** something **up**, you buy it quickly because it is a bargain or because it is just what you want. EG *All these houses were snapped up as soon as they were offered for sale.* PHRASAL VB : V+O+ADV

snapshot /snæpʃɒt/, **snapshots.** A **snapshot** is a photograph that is taken quickly and casually. EG *...family snapshots.* — N COUNT

snare /snɛə/, **snares.** A **snare** is a trap for catching birds or small animals. It consists of a loop of wire or rope which pulls tight around the animal. EG *...a rabbit snare.* — N COUNT

snarl /snɑːl/, **snarls, snarling, snarled. 1** When an animal **snarls**, it makes a fierce, rough sound in its throat while showing its teeth. EG *...dogs snarling and snapping at the heels of sheep.* ▸ used as a noun. EG *The leopard gave a snarl of fury.* — V; ▸ N COUNT

2 If you **snarl**, you say something in a fierce, angry way. EG *'Let me alone,' I snarled.* — V : OFT+QUOTE

snatch /snætʃ/, **snatches, snatching, snatched.**
1 If you **snatch** something or **snatch** at it, you take it or pull it away quickly. EG *He snatched the letter from the man's hand... He remembered snatching at his gun.* — V+O OR V+*at*

2 If you **snatch** a small amount of time or an opportunity, you quickly make use of it. EG *I packed, then snatched four hours' sleep... She snatched a brief time alone with him... I snatched the opportunity to tell them that I was leaving.* — V+O

3 A **snatch** of a conversation or a song is a very small piece of it. EG *...listening to snatches of overheard conversation.* — N COUNT OR N PART

sneak /sniːk/, **sneaks, sneaking, sneaked. 1** If you **sneak** somewhere, you go there very quietly on foot, trying to avoid being seen or heard. EG *I didn't notice Bob sneaking up behind me.* — V+A

2 If you **sneak** something somewhere, you take it there secretly. EG *Eugene would sneak food down to his room... I tried to sneak a blanket away.* — V+O+A

3 If you **sneak** a look at someone or something, you secretly have a quick look at them. — V+O+A

4 A **sneak** preview of something is an unofficial opportunity to look at it before it is officially shown to the public. EG *We were shown his latest masterpiece in a sneak preview.* — N COUNT

5 A **sneak** is someone who tells people in authority that someone else has done something naughty or wrong; used showing disapproval. EG *He has acquired a reputation as a sneak.* — N COUNT, Informal

sneaker /sniːkə/, **sneakers. Sneakers** are casual shoes with rubber soles. — N COUNT : USU PLURAL

sneaking /sniːkɪŋ/. If you have a **sneaking** feeling about something or someone, you are rather ashamed or unwilling to have this feeling. EG *His book leaves one with a sneaking admiration for his shameless commercialism... I have a sneaking suspicion you're right.* — ADJ CLASSIF : ATTRIB

sneaky /sniːki[1]/. Someone who is **sneaky** does things secretly rather than openly; used showing disapproval. EG *I had a sneaky glimpse at the list.* — ADJ QUALIT, Informal

sneer /snɪə/, **sneers, sneering, sneered.** If you **sneer** at someone or something, you express your contempt for them by the expression on your face or by what you say. EG *She was afraid he would sneer at the idea.* ▸ used as a noun. EG *'Oh yes,' said McFee, a sneer flitting over his face.* — V : OFT+*at* OR QUOTE; ▸ N COUNT

sneeze /sniːz/, **sneezes, sneezing, sneezed. 1** When you **sneeze**, you suddenly take in your breath and then blow it down your nose noisily. People sneeze a lot when they have a cold. ▸ used as a noun. EG *...the sound of coughs and sneezes.* — V; ▸ N COUNT

2 If you say that something **is not to be sneezed at**, you mean that it is worth having. EG *The pension from the university was small but not to be sneezed at.* — PHRASE, Informal

snide /snaɪd/. A **snide** comment or remark is one which criticizes someone nastily, often in an indirect, sarcastic way. EG *There were one or two snide comments about my family.* — ADJ QUALIT

sniff /snɪf/, **sniffs, sniffing, sniffed. 1** When you **sniff**, you breathe in air through your nose hard enough to make a sound, for example when you are trying not to cry, or in order to show disapproval or scorn. EG *Felicity said, sniffing, 'When will you see me again?'* ▸ used as a noun. EG *She gave a bitter sniff... The classroom rang with coughs, sniffs, and sneezes.* — V; ▸ N COUNT

2 If you **sniff** something, you smell it by sniffing. EG *'What a revolting smell,' he said, sniffing the air... The dog sniffed at Marsha's bags.* ▸ used as a noun. EG *He cracked the seal on the bottle and took a cautious sniff.* — V+O OR V+A; ▸ N COUNT

3 If you **sniff** something such as glue, you deliberately breathe it in as a drug. EG *...glue sniffing.* — V+O

sniff out. If you **sniff** something **out**, you discover it after some searching. EG *I ordered the Central Office to sniff out a suitable job for him.* — PHRASAL VB : V+O+ADV, Informal

sniffle /snɪfə[0]l/, **sniffles, sniffling, sniffled.** If you **are sniffling**, you keep sniffing, for example because you have a cold. — V

snigger /snɪgə/, **sniggers, sniggering, sniggered.** If you **snigger**, you laugh quietly and disrespectfully, for example at something rude. EG *What are you sniggering at?* ▸ used as a noun. EG *His sniggers became uncontrollable.* — V; ▸ N COUNT

snip /snɪp/, **snips, snipping, snipped.** If you **snip** off part of something, you cut it off with scissors or shears in a single quick action. EG *Brian snipped energetically at the hedge... He took out a cigar and, after snipping off the end, lit it.* — V : OFT+A, OR V+O

snipe /snaɪp/, **snipes, sniping, sniped. 1** If someone **snipes** at you, they criticize you. EG *The unions are an easy target to snipe at.* — V : OFT+*at*

2 To **snipe** at someone also means to shoot at them from a hidden position. EG *Just then someone started sniping at us.* ◇ **sniper, snipers.** EG *A sniper's bullet tore up a wall two inches above his head.* — V : OFT+*at*; ◇ N COUNT

snippet /snɪpɪt/, **snippets.** A **snippet** of information, news, or gossip is a small piece of it. EG *Occasionally children come out with absolutely fascinating snippets of information.* — N PART OR N COUNT

snivel /snɪvə[0]l/, **snivels, snivelling, snivelled;** spelled **sniveling, sniveled** in American English. If someone **is snivelling**, they are crying and sniffing in a way that irritates you. — V

snob /snɒb/, **snobs.** A **snob** is **1** someone who admires upper-class people and despises lower-class people; used showing disapproval. — N COUNT **2** someone who believes that they are superior to other people because of their intelligence or taste; used showing disapproval. EG *You were always an intellectual snob.* — N COUNT+SUPP

snobbery /snɒbə[0]ri[1]/ is the attitude of a snob; used showing disapproval. EG *Social snobbery reached a peak in the last century... There used to be a kind of snobbery in England about Central European writing.* — N UNCOUNT

snobbish /snɒbɪʃ/. Someone who is **snobbish** is too proud of their social status, intelligence, or taste. EG *She was too snobbish to mix with her neighbours... She had a snobbish attitude towards the theatre.* — ADJ QUALIT

snog /snɒg/, **snogs, snogging, snogged.** When two people **snog**, they kiss and cuddle each other for a period of time. EG *...snogging in the dark.* ▸ used as a noun. EG *They went outside for a quiet snog.* — V OR V+*with* : RECIP, Informal; ▸ N SING

snooker /snuːkə/ is a game involving balls on a large table. The players use a long stick to hit a white ball, and score points by knocking coloured balls into the pockets at the sides of the table. — N UNCOUNT

snoop /snuːp/, **snoops, snooping, snooped.** Someone who **is snooping** is secretly looking round a place in order to find out things. EG *He might have been killed simply for snooping around where he wasn't welcome.* — V : USU+A

snooty /snuːti[1]/. Someone who is **snooty** behaves as if they are superior to other people; used — ADJ QUALIT

Which words on these pages name noises you can make with your nose and mouth?

showing disapproval. EG *She is beautiful but snooty... I got a very snooty letter from them rejecting my application.*

snooze /snuːz/, **snoozes, snoozing, snoozed.** A **snooze** is a short, light sleep, especially during the day. EG *I've just had a nice snooze.* ▸ used as a verb. EG *I lay on the sofa, snoozing.* N SING : a+N Informal ▸ V

snore /snɔː/, **snores, snoring, snored.** When someone who is asleep **snores**, they make a loud noise each time they breathe. EG *He snored loudly on the camp-bed.* ▸ used as a noun. EG *I could hear heavy snores coming from the bedroom.* V ▸ N COUNT

snorkel /snɔːkə^{0}l/, **snorkels.** A **snorkel** is a tube through which a person swimming just under the surface of the sea can breathe. N COUNT

snorkelling /snɔːkə^{0}lɪŋ/; spelled **snorkeling** in American English. If you go **snorkelling**, you swim underwater using a snorkel. N ING

snort /snɔːt/, **snorts, snorting, snorted. 1** When people or animals **snort**, they breathe air noisily out through their noses. People snort in order to express contempt, disapproval, or amusement. EG *The pigs grunted and snorted... My sister snorted with laughter.* ▸ used as a noun. EG *Clarissa gave a snort of disgust.* V ▸ N COUNT

2 If someone **snorts** something, they say it with a snort. EG *'Garbage!' Eddie snorted.* V+QUOTE

snout /snaʊt/, **snouts.** The **snout** of an animal such as a pig is its long nose. N COUNT

snow /snəʊ/, **snows, snowing, snowed. 1 Snow** consists of a lot of soft white bits of frozen water that fall from the sky in cold weather. EG *Outside the snow lay thick on the ground... Two inches of snow fell in London.* ▸ used as a plural noun. EG *...driving down from the snows of the Alps... ...the winter snows.* N UNCOUNT ▸ N PLURAL : the+N Literary

2 When it **snows**, snow falls from the sky. EG *It was snowing quite heavily.* • See also **snowed in, snowed under**. V

snowball /snəʊbɔːl/, **snowballs, snowballing, snowballed. 1** A **snowball** is a ball of snow. Children often throw snowballs at each other. N COUNT

2 If something such as a project or campaign **snowballs**, it rapidly increases and grows. EG *The strike movement snowballed into a nationwide general strike.* V

snowbound /snəʊbaʊnd/. If people or vehicles are **snowbound**, they cannot go anywhere because of heavy snow. ADJ CLASSIF

snowdrift /snəʊdrɪft/, **snowdrifts.** A **snowdrift** is a deep pile of snow formed by the wind. N COUNT

snowdrop /snəʊdrɒp/, **snowdrops.** A **snowdrop** is a small white flower which appears in the early spring. N COUNT

snowed in. If you are **snowed in** or **snowed up**, you cannot go anywhere because of heavy snow. EG *Perhaps we'll be snowed in for a week.* ADJ PRED

snowed under. If you are **snowed under**, you have a large amount of work to deal with, especially paperwork. EG *At present we are snowed under with work.* ADJ PRED

snowflake /snəʊfleɪk/, **snowflakes.** A **snowflake** is one of the soft, white bits of frozen water that fall as snow. EG *...snowflakes melting in her hair.* N COUNT

snowman /snəʊmæn/, **snowmen.** A **snowman** is a large shape made out of snow, especially by children, which is supposed to look like a person. N COUNT

snowplough /snəʊplaʊ/, **snowploughs;** spelled **snowplow** in American English. A **snowplough** is a vehicle which is used to push snow off roads or railway lines. N COUNT

snowy /snəʊi^1/. Something that is **snowy** has a lot of snow. EG *...two high snowy peaks... ...snowy streets... I went to see him one snowy day in London.* ADJ QUALIT

snub /snʌb/, **snubs, snubbing, snubbed.** If you **snub** someone, you deliberately insult them by ignoring them or by behaving rudely towards them. EG *Both she and her husband were snubbed by the intellectuals they knew.* ▸ used as a noun. EG *But George was impervious to snubs.* V+O ▸ N COUNT

snub-nosed. Someone who is **snub-nosed** has a short nose which points slightly upwards. ADJ CLASSIF

snuff /snʌf/ is powdered tobacco which people take by sniffing it up their nose. EG *...a snuff box.* N UNCOUNT

snuffle /snʌfə^{0}l/, **snuffles, snuffling, snuffled.** If people or animals **snuffle**, they make sniffing noises. EG *Brian snuffled into his handkerchief... ...snuffling pigs.* V

snug /snʌg/. **1** If you are **snug**, you feel warm and comfortable. EG *We lit a big fire which made us feel very snug and safe.* ◇ **snugly**. EG *Jamie was snugly wrapped in a white woollen scarf.* ADJ QUALIT ◇ ADV

2 If a place is **snug**, it is warm and comfortable. EG *It was warm and dry in his snug studio.* ADJ QUALIT

3 Something that is **snug** fits very closely or tightly. EG *...snug overcoats.* ◇ **snugly**. EG *The metal box fitted snugly into the bottom.* ADJ QUALIT ◇ ADV

snuggle /snʌgə^{0}l/, **snuggles, snuggling, snuggled.** If you **snuggle** somewhere, you settle yourself into a warm, comfortable position, especially by moving closer to another person. EG *He turned over to snuggle close to her.* V+A

so /səʊ/. **1** You use **so 1.1** when you are referring back to something that has just been mentioned. EG *Do you enjoy romantic films? If so, you should watch the film on ITV tonight... 'Is there anything else you want to tell me about?' – 'I don't think so.'... The issue is unresolved, and will remain so until the next SDP Congress.* **1.2** when you are agreeing with a statement that has just been made. EG *'The phone isn't working.' – 'So I see.'* ADV; ADV SEN

2 If you say that a state of affairs **is so**, you mean that it is the way that it has been described. EG *It is worth knowing just why this is so.* PHRASE

3 If you say that one person or thing does something and **so** does another one, you mean that the second person or thing does it too. EG *Etta laughed heartily and so did he... His shoes are brightly polished; so is his briefcase.* ADV SEN

4 You use **so** and **so that** to introduce something that happens because of the situation you have just mentioned. EG *He speaks very little English, so I talked to him through an interpreter... The door was open, so that anyone passing could look in.* CONJ

5 You use **so that** and **so as** to introduce the reason for doing the thing that you have just mentioned. EG *He has to earn lots of money so that he can buy his children nice food and clothes... They went on foot, so as not to be heard.* CONJ

6 You say **'So?'** and **'So what?'** to indicate that you think that something that someone has said is unimportant. EG *'Someone will see us.' – 'So what?'* CONVENTION Informal

7 You can use **so** in a discussion or talk when you are checking that you have correctly understood something, when you are summarizing something, or when you are moving on to a new stage. EG *So it wasn't just an accident?... And so for now, goodnight... So what are the advantages of nuclear energy?* ADV SEN

8 You can also use **so** when you are saying that something is done or arranged in the way that you describe. EG *They have the eyes so located as to give a wide field of vision... The others are moving right to left, like so.* ADV

9 You use the structures **as...so** and **just as...so** when you want to indicate that two events or situations are alike in some way. EG *Just as one gesture can have many different meanings, so many different gestures can have the same meaning... As with the railways, so with coal.*

10 You use **and so on** or **and so forth** at the end of a list to indicate that there are other items that you could also mention. EG *You can program a computer to paint, play chess and so on.* PHRASE

11 You use **or so** when you are giving an approximate amount. EG *We arrived a month or so ago.* PHRASE

12 You can also use **so** to describe or emphasize the degree or extent of something. EG *I'm so glad you could come... Don't go so fast... The objection is so fundamental and so widely accepted that it needs to be answered in detail... Carrying the weight was not so difficult.* ADV

13 You can use **so** before words such as 'much' and 'many' when you are saying that there is a definite limit to something but you are not saying what this limit is. EG *We will only pay so much, no more... ...an old friend with only so long to live.*

14 You use the structures **not so much** and **not so much...as** to say that something is one kind of thing rather than another kind. EG *...a cry not so much of pain as of amazement.* PHRASE

15 ever so: see **ever**. • **so far, so far as**: see **far**. • **so long, so long as**: see **long**. • **so much for**: see **much**. • **every so often**: see **often**. • **so there**: see **there**.

soak /sə͟ʊk/, **soaks, soaking, soaked. 1** When you **soak** something or leave it to **soak**, you put it into a liquid and leave it there. EG *'Can I help you with the dishes?' – 'Oh, I'll just leave them to soak.'... Soak the material for several hours in cold water... ...breadcrumbs soaked in red wine.* V-ERG

2 When a liquid **soaks** something, it makes it very wet. EG *A stream of water came in and soaked both sleeping bags.* V+O

3 When a liquid **soaks** through something, it passes through it. EG *The blood had soaked through the handkerchief.* V+A

soak up. When a soft or dry substance **soaks up** a liquid, the liquid goes into the substance. EG *The soil soaked up a huge volume of water.* PHRASAL VB : V+O+ADV

soaked /sə͟ʊkt/. If someone or something gets **soaked**, they get extremely wet. EG *It was pouring down and we all got soaked... His beret was soaked.* ADJ PRED

soaking /sə͟ʊkɪŋ/. If something is **soaking** or **soaking wet**, it is very wet. EG *My boots were soaking wet inside.* ADJ CLASSIF

so-and-so, so-and-sos. 1 You use **so-and-so** instead of a name or word when you are indicating the sort of thing that is usually said or done and are not bothering to give a specific name or example. EG *What happens is that somebody will phone me and say, 'Mrs So-and-So would like a visit.'* N UNCOUNT Informal

2 You call someone a **so-and-so** when you are annoyed with them. N COUNT Informal

soap /sə͟ʊp/, **soaps, soaping, soaped. 1 Soap** is a substance that you use with water for washing yourself or sometimes for washing clothes. EG *...a bar of yellow soap... Soap and towels were provided.* N MASS

2 If you **soap** yourself, you rub soap on your body in order to wash yourself. EG *She soaped herself all over.* V-REFL

3 A **soap** is the same as a soap opera. N COUNT

soap opera, soap operas. A **soap opera** is a popular television drama serial about the daily lives and problems of a group of people. N COUNT

soapy /sə͟ʊpi¹/. Something that is **soapy** is full of soap or covered with soap. EG *Wash your brushes in warm soapy water.* ADJ QUALIT

soar /sɔ͟ː/, **soars, soaring, soared. 1** If an amount **soars**, it quickly increases by a great deal. EG *Property prices have soared... Rice production soared from 694,000 tons to 913,000.* V : OFT *+from/to*

2 If something **soars** into the air, it goes quickly up into the air. EG *Flames were soaring into the sky.* V : USU+A

3 Trees or buildings that **soar** upwards are very tall. ◊ **soaring**. EG *...the soaring spire of St Patrick's... ...soaring tree trunks.* V+A ◊ ADJ CLASSIF : ATTRIB

4 If music **soars**, it rises greatly in volume or pitch. EG *Her voice soared into a girlish treble.* ◊ **soaring**. EG *...the soaring, triumphant horn notes.* V ◊ ADJ CLASSIF

sob /sɒb/, **sobs, sobbing, sobbed. 1** When someone **sobs**, they cry in a noisy way, breathing in short breaths. EG *She was sobbing bitterly.* ◊ **sobbing**. EG *The sobbing began again.* V ◊ N UNCOUNT

2 If you **sob** something, you say it at the same time as you are crying. EG *'It hurts!' sobbed Patty.* V+QUOTE

3 A **sob** is one of the noises that you make when you are crying. EG *She began to weep in gasping, choking sobs.* N COUNT

sober /sə͟ʊbə/, **soberer, soberest; sobers, sobering, sobered. 1** When you are **sober**, you are not drunk. EG *Rudolph knew he had to stay sober to drive home.* ADJ QUALIT

2 A **sober** person is serious and thoughtful. EG *...sober and sensible attitudes.* ◊ **soberly**. EG *'That's true,' Andy said soberly.* ADJ QUALIT ◊ ADV

3 Sober colours and clothes are plain and rather dull. EG *...a pair of sober black walking shoes.* ◊ **soberly**. EG *...a soberly dressed office employee.* ADJ QUALIT : ATTRIB ◊ ADV

sober up. When someone **sobers up**, they stop being drunk. EG *When you sober up you may be ashamed of what you've done.* PHRASAL VB : V+ADV

sobering /sə͟ʊbəᵒrɪŋ/. **Sobering** words, actions, or ideas make you become serious. EG *His words had a sobering effect on Freddie... There was a more sobering thought: perhaps we should not succeed.* ADJ QUALIT

sobriety /səᵒbra͟ɪəti¹/ is serious and thoughtful behaviour. EG *...his mood of sobriety.* N UNCOUNT Formal

so-called. You use **so-called 1** to indicate that you think that a particular word is incorrect or misleading. EG *...her so-called friends... ...the so-called 'developed' countries.* **2** to indicate that something is generally referred to by the name that you have used. EG *Why did the so-called Agricultural Revolution occur?* ADJ CLASSIF : USU ATTRIB Formal

soccer /sɒkə/ is the same as football. **Soccer** is not used to refer to American football. N UNCOUNT

sociable /sə͟ʊʃəbəᵒl/. **Sociable** people are friendly and enjoy talking to other people. EG *Adler was an outgoing, sociable kind of man.* ◊ **sociability** /sə͟ʊʃəbɪlɪ¹ti¹/. EG *There was no doubt about his sociability.* ADJ QUALIT ◊ N UNCOUNT

social /sə͟ʊʃəᵒl/. **1 Social** means **1.1** relating to society or to the way society is organized. EG *...a particular culture and social structure... ...government social and economic policy... ...demands for modernisation and social change.* ◊ **socially**. EG *...socially useful activities.* **1.2** relating to the status or rank that someone has in society. EG *...children from different social backgrounds... He is compelled by social pressures to seek advancement.* ◊ **socially**. EG *They must behave in a way which will be socially acceptable.* **1.3** relating to leisure activities that involve meeting other people. EG *We've met at social and business functions... ...their circle of social contacts.* ◊ **socially**. EG *...the only people my father ever visited socially.* ADJ CLASSIF : ATTRIB ◊ ADV ADJ CLASSIF : ATTRIB ◊ ADV ADJ CLASSIF : USU ATTRIB ◊ ADV

2 Social animals live in groups and do things together. EG *...social animals such as hyenas and wolves.* ADJ CLASSIF : ATTRIB

socialise /sə͟ʊʃəlaɪz/. See **socialize**.

socialism /sə͟ʊʃəlɪzəᵒm/ is a set of left-wing political principles based on the belief that the state should own industries on behalf of the people and that everyone should be equal. N UNCOUNT

socialist /sə͟ʊʃəlɪst/, **socialists. 1 Socialist** means based on socialism or relating to socialism. EG *...a Labour government with socialist policies... ...the French Socialist Party.* ADJ CLASSIF

2 A **socialist** is a person who believes in socialism or who is a member of a socialist party. N COUNT

socialize /sə͟ʊʃəlaɪz/, **socializes, socializing, socialized;** also spelled **socialise.** If you **socialize**, you meet other people socially, for example at parties. EG *I socialized with the philosophy students.* ◊ **socializing**. EG *...people who do all their socialising in pubs.* V : OFT+*with* ◊ N UNCOUNT

If you socialize, are you sociable or a socialist?

social life, social lives. Your **social life** consists of the activities in which you meet your friends and acquaintances, for example at parties. EG *...busy, competent people, with active social lives.* N COUNT OR N UNCOUNT

social science, social sciences. 1 Social science is the scientific study of society. N UNCOUNT

2 The **social sciences** are the various branches of social science. EG *Economics is the oldest of the social sciences.* N COUNT: USU PLURAL

social scientist, social scientists. A **social scientist** is a person who studies or teaches social science. N COUNT

social security is a system by which the government pays money regularly to people who have no other income or only a very small income. EG *...social security benefits.* N UNCOUNT

social services. The **social services** in a district are the services provided by the local authority to help people who have social and financial problems or needs. EG *...major cuts in social services... ...the local social services department.* N PLURAL

social work is work which involves giving help and advice to people with serious financial problems or family problems. N UNCOUNT

social worker, social workers. A **social worker** is a person whose job is to do social work. N COUNT

society /səsaɪəti^1/, **societies. 1 Society** is the people in a country, who have a particular way of life. EG *...society's attitude towards the elderly... ...the role of women in Western society... We live in a multi-racial society.* N UNCOUNT OR N COUNT

2 A **society** is also an organization for people who have the same interest or aim. EG *I'm on the committee of the local film society... ...the Royal Horticultural Society.* N COUNT

sociology /səʊsɪɒlədʒi^1/ is the study of human societies. EG *...sociology students.* ◊ **sociological.** EG *...sociological studies of criminals... ...sociological issues.* ◊ **sociologist** /səʊsɪɒlədʒɪst/, **sociologists.** EG *This is what sociologists have been saying for years.* N UNCOUNT ◊ ADJ CLASSIF: ATTRIB ◊ N COUNT

sock /sɒk/, **socks. 1 Socks** are pieces of clothing which cover your foot and ankle and are worn inside shoes. See picture at CLOTHES. EG *...a pair of light-blue wool socks.* N COUNT

2 If you tell someone to **pull** their **socks up**, you mean that they should start working or studying harder, because they have been lazy or careless recently. PHRASE Informal British

socket /sɒkɪt/, **sockets. 1** A **socket** is a place on a wall or on a piece of electrical equipment into which you can put a plug or bulb. EG *I put a bulb in the lamp socket.* N COUNT

2 You can refer to any hollow part or opening in a structure which another part fits into as a **socket.** EG *...deep eye sockets... ...the hip socket.* N COUNT: USU+SUPP

soda /səʊdə/, **sodas. Soda** is the same as soda water. EG *...a whisky and soda.* N MASS

soda siphon, soda siphons; also spelled **soda syphon.** A **soda siphon** is a special bottle from which you can squirt soda water into a drink. N COUNT

soda water is fizzy water used for mixing with alcoholic drinks and fruit juice. N UNCOUNT

sodden /sɒdə^{0}n/. Something that is **sodden** is extremely wet. EG *Her slippers were sodden.* ADJ QUALIT

sofa /səʊfə/, **sofas.** A **sofa** is a long, comfortable seat with a back and usually with arms, which two or three people can sit on. N COUNT

soft /sɒft/, **softer, softest. 1** Something that is **soft 1.1** changes shape or bends easily when you press it. EG *...a soft bed... His feet left prints in the soft soil.* ADJ QUALIT **1.2** is pleasant to touch, and not rough or hard. EG *...soft black fur... Her skin was soft and white.* ◊ **softness.** EG *...the softness of her arms.* ADJ QUALIT

1.3 is very gentle and has no force. EG *...a soft breeze.* ◊ **softly.** EG *Mike softly placed his hand on her shoulder.* ADJ QUALIT ◊ ADV

2 A **soft** sound or voice is quiet and not harsh. EG *She had a soft South German accent.* ◊ **softly.** EG *'Listen,' she said softly.* ADJ QUALIT ◊ ADV

3 A **soft** light or colour is pleasant and restful to look at because it is not bright. EG *...the soft glow of the evening light... ...walls in soft pink stone.* ADJ QUALIT

4 Someone who is **soft 4.1** is kind and cares about other people's feelings. EG *He's got a very soft heart.* **4.2** is not strict enough or severe enough. EG *...the 'soft' approach to juvenile offenders... She's kind to everyone without ever being soft about it.* ADJ QUALIT

5 Soft drugs are illegal drugs, such as marijuana, which are not considered to be very strong or harmful. ADJ CLASSIF

6 Soft is also used in these phrases. **6.1** If you **have a soft spot for** someone, you are especially fond of them. **6.2** If you describe someone as a **soft touch**, you mean that they can easily be persuaded to lend you money or to do things for you. **6.3** If you say that someone is **soft in the head**, you mean that they are silly. PHRASES Informal Informal Informal

soft drink, soft drinks. A **soft drink** is a cold, non-alcoholic drink such as lemonade or fruit juice. N COUNT

soften /sɒfə^{0}n/, **softens, softening, softened. 1** If something **is softened** or **softens**, it becomes less hard, stiff, or firm. EG *Fry the onions for about 10 minutes to soften them... ...the softened leather.* V-ERG

2 If something **softens** a shock or a damaging effect, it makes it seem less severe. EG *He had alcohol to soften the blow... ...the softening effect of music.* V+O

3 If you **soften**, you become more sympathetic and less hostile or critical. EG *'I'm sorry about your mother,' Ira said, softening... She gradually softened towards me... I refused to be softened.* V-ERG

4 If your expression **softens** or if something **softens** it, it becomes much more gentle and friendly. EG *His mother's face softened a little.* V-ERG

soften up. If you **soften** someone **up**, you put them into a good mood before asking them to do something. EG *I wondered if there was any hope of softening him up.* PHRASAL VB: V+O+ADV Informal

soft-hearted. Someone who is **soft-hearted** has a very sympathetic and kind nature. ADJ QUALIT

soft-spoken. Someone who is **soft-spoken** has a quiet, gentle voice. ADJ QUALIT

software /sɒftwɛə/. Computer programs are referred to as **software.** EG *My job is writing the software.* N UNCOUNT

soggy /sɒgi^1/. Something that is **soggy** is unpleasantly wet. EG *...a soggy dishcloth... ...soggy biscuits.* ADJ QUALIT

soil /sɔɪl/, **soils, soiling, soiled. 1 Soil** is the substance on the land surface of the earth in which plants grow. EG *The soil here is very fertile.* N UNCOUNT

2 You use **soil** in expressions like 'British soil' to refer to a country's territory. EG *...if no foreign armies had invaded Russian soil.* N UNCOUNT +SUPP

3 If you **soil** something, you make it dirty. EG *She never soils her dainty fingers with a washing up mop.* ◊ **soiled.** EG *...a soiled handkerchief.* V+O ◊ ADJ QUALIT

solace /sɒlə^{1}s/. **1 Solace** is a feeling of comfort that makes you feel less sad. EG *He began to find solace in the Bible.* N UNCOUNT Formal

2 If something is a **solace** to you, it makes you feel less sad. EG *Her poetry has always been a solace to me in times of stress.* N SING Formal

solar /səʊlə/. **1 Solar** is used to describe things relating to the sun. EG *They accurately predicted solar eclipses.* ADJ CLASSIF: ATTRIB

2 Solar power is obtained from the sun's light and heat. EG *...the potential of solar energy.* ADJ CLASSIF: ATTRIB

solar system. The **solar system** is the sun and all the planets and comets that go round it. N PROPER: *the*+N

sold /səʊld/ is the past tense and past participle of **sell.**

soldier /səʊldʒə/, **soldiers.** A **soldier** is a person in an army. EG *These exits are guarded by soldiers.* N COUNT

sole /səʊl/, **soles. 1** The **sole** thing or person of a particular type is the only one of that type. EG *In some families, the woman is the sole wage earn-* ADJ CLASSIF: ATTRIB *er... They went with the sole purpose of making a nuisance of themselves.*

2 If you have **sole** charge or ownership of something, you are the only person in charge of it or who owns it. EG *She has the sole responsibility for bringing up the child... He acquired sole control of the newspaper in 1914.* ADJ CLASSIF : ATTRIB

3 The **sole** of your foot or of a shoe or sock is the underneath surface of it. EG *...holes in the soles of my shoes.* N COUNT

4 A **sole** is a kind of flat fish that you can eat. The plural can also be **sole**. N COUNT OR N UNCOUNT

solely /səʊlli[1]/. If something involves **solely** one thing, it involves only this thing and no others. EG *This is solely a matter of money... The blame for this situation lies solely with the government.* ADV

solemn /sɒləm/. **1** Someone or something that is **solemn** is very serious rather than cheerful or humorous. EG *The service of burial is done with solemn and mournful music... ...the solemn tones of Winston Churchill.* ◊ **solemnly**. EG *Ralph nodded solemnly.* ◊ **solemnity** /sə[7]lɛmnɪ[1]ti[1]/. EG *...the solemnity of the occasion.* ADJ QUALIT; ◊ ADV; ◊ N UNCOUNT

2 A **solemn** promise or agreement is one that you make in a very formal, sincere way. EG *The government has solemn commitments and must honour them.* ◊ **solemnly**. EG *Jacob solemnly vowed to keep this promise.* ADJ CLASSIF : ATTRIB; ◊ ADV

solicit /səlɪsɪt/, **solicits, soliciting, solicited. 1** If you **solicit** money, help, or an opinion from someone, you ask them for it. EG *We had to solicit contributions to pay off her debts... Roy solicited aid from a number of influential members.* V+O Formal

2 When prostitutes **solicit**, they offer to have sex with people in return for money. ◊ **soliciting**. EG *She's been fined £35 for soliciting.* V; N UNCOUNT

solicitor /səlɪsɪtə/, **solicitors.** A **solicitor** is a lawyer who gives legal advice and prepares legal documents and cases. EG *I was advised to put the matter into the hands of a solicitor.* N COUNT

solicitous /səlɪsɪtəs/. A person who is **solicitous** shows anxious concern for someone. EG *The hotel personnel could not have been more solicitous.* ◊ **solicitously**. EG *'Now, Mr Gerran, you must take it easy,' I said solicitously.* ADJ QUALIT Formal; ◊ ADV

solicitude /səlɪsɪtju:d/. The **solicitude** that someone shows is their anxious concern for someone. EG *I was moved by their genuine kindness and solicitude for Karin.* N UNCOUNT Formal

solid /sɒlɪd/, **solids. 1** A **solid** substance or object stays the same shape whether it is in a container or not, and is hard or firm. EG *The basic choice is gas, electricity, or solid fuel... ...a solid layer of earth... Even the sea around them is frozen solid.* ADJ CLASSIF

2 A **solid** is a substance that stays the same shape whether it is in a container or not. EG *You must at least know whether it's a solid or a liquid or a gas.* N COUNT

3 A **solid** object or mass does not have a space inside it, or holes or gaps in it. EG *...a solid-tyred bus... ...steps carved into the solid rock... The car park was packed solid.* ADJ CLASSIF

4 If an object is made of **solid** gold or **solid** oak, for example, it is made of gold or oak all the way through. EG *Is that bracelet really solid gold?* ADJ CLASSIF : ATTRIB

5 A structure that is **solid** is strong and is not likely to collapse or fall over. EG *...solid Victorian houses.* ◊ **solidly**. EG *...large houses built solidly of wooden planks.* ◊ **solidity** /səlɪdɪ[1]ti[1]/. EG *...their appearance of massive solidity.* ADJ QUALIT; ◊ ADV; ◊ N UNCOUNT

6 If you describe someone as **solid**, you mean that they are very respectable and reliable. EG *She regarded them as solid, good, dull people.* ◊ **solidly**. EG *...a solidly respectable family.* ADJ QUALIT; ◊ ADV

7 If something is **solid**, it is reliable, strong, and large in amount. EG *...a veteran British Council worker, with solid experience in Asia and Africa... Solid evidence is needed... It is important that he has a firm, solid foundation of scientific knowledge on which to build.* ◊ **solidly**. EG *They are solidly behind the proposal.* ◊ **solidity**. EG *...giving an added strength and solidity to the state.* ADJ QUALIT; ◊ ADV; ◊ N UNCOUNT

8 If you do something for a **solid** period of time, you do it without any pause or interruption throughout that time. EG *I waited a solid hour... ...fifteen minutes' solid conversation... I read for two hours solid.* ◊ **solidly**. EG *If you work for ten weeks solidly you might stand more of a chance.* ADJ CLASSIF : ATTRIB OR ADV; ◊ ADV

solidarity /sɒlɪdærɪ[1]ti[1]/. If a group of people show **solidarity**, they show complete unity and support for each other. EG *...working-class solidarity... ...a great international gesture of women's solidarity with women.* N UNCOUNT

solidify /səlɪdɪfaɪ/, **solidifies, solidifying, solidified.** When a liquid **solidifies**, it changes into a solid. EG *Pour the fat into a basin and when it has solidified take it out.* V

solitary /sɒlɪtə[0]ri[1]/. **1** A **solitary** activity is one that you do alone. EG *He formed the habit of taking long solitary walks.* ADJ CLASSIF : ATTRIB

2 A person or animal that is **solitary** spends a lot of time alone. EG *Tigers are solitary creatures.* ADJ QUALIT

3 A **solitary** person or object is alone and has no others nearby. EG *Madeleine walked over to the solitary figure.* ADJ CLASSIF : ATTRIB

solitary confinement. A prisoner who is in **solitary confinement** is being kept alone in a prison cell. N UNCOUNT

solitude /sɒlɪtju:d/ is the state of being alone. EG *He preferred solitude... One can study far better in solitude.* N UNCOUNT

solo /səʊləʊ/, **solos. 1** A **solo** is a piece of music that is played or sung by one person alone. EG *...a clarinet solo by Donizetti.* N COUNT

2 A **solo** performance or activity is done by one person alone. EG *The morning of Will Kent's solo flight was fine and clear.* ▸ used as an adverb. EG *...the boat in which he sailed solo round the world.* ADJ CLASSIF : ATTRIB; ▸ ADV AFTER VB

soloist /səʊləʊɪst/, **soloists.** A **soloist** is a person who plays a musical instrument alone or sings alone. EG *They have professional soloists and an amateur chorus.* N COUNT

soluble /sɒljə[4]bə[0]l/. A substance that is **soluble** will dissolve in a liquid. EG *...soluble tablets... The powder is soluble in water.* ADJ CLASSIF

solution /səlu:ʃə[0]n/, **solutions. 1** A **solution** is a way of dealing with a difficult situation so that the difficulty is removed. EG *It's a very neat little solution to our problem... The only solution is to create an entirely new system.* N COUNT : OFT+*to*

2 The **solution** to a riddle or a puzzle is the answer to it. EG *...the crossword solution.* N COUNT : OFT+*to*

3 A **solution** is also a liquid in which a solid substance has been dissolved. EG *Immerse it in a solution of detergent and water.* N COUNT OR N UNCOUNT Technical

solve /sɒlv/, **solves, solving, solved.** If you **solve** a problem or a question, you find a solution or an answer to it. EG *...the failure of successive Government policies to solve Britain's economic problems... ...solving crossword puzzles.* V+O

solvent /sɒlvənt/, **solvents. 1** If a person or a company is **solvent**, they have enough money to pay all their debts. EG *He behaved as if he alone kept the airport solvent.* ADJ QUALIT Formal

2 A **solvent** is a liquid that can dissolve other substances. EG *...rubber solvents.* N COUNT OR N UNCOUNT Formal

sombre /sɒmbə/; spelled **somber** in American English. **1 Sombre** colours and places are dark and dull. EG *...two women dressed in sombre black... ...the sombre oak-panelled room.* ADJ QUALIT

2 If someone is **sombre**, they are serious, sad, or pessimistic. EG *Her face grew sombre... Mr Morris took a more sombre view.* ◊ **sombrely**. EG *Mercer shook his head sombrely.* ADJ QUALIT; ◊ ADV

How many words are there on these pages that talk about people doing things alone?

some /sʌm/. **1** You use **some** to refer to a quantity of something or to a number of people or things, when you are not stating the quantity or number precisely. EG *She had a piece of pie and some coffee... I've got some friends coming over... 'You'll need graph paper.' – 'Yeah, I've got some at home.'* QUANTIF
2 You also use **some** to emphasize that a quantity or number is fairly large. EG *I did not meet her again for some years... They were having some difficulty in following the plot.* DET
3 If you refer to **some** of the people or things in a group, you mean a few of them but not all of them. If you refer to **some** of a particular thing, you mean a part of it but not all of it. EG *Some sports are very dangerous... She took some of the meat out.* QUANTIF
4 If you refer to **some** person or thing, you are referring to that person or thing vaguely, without stating precisely which one you mean. EG *We found it lying in some ditch in the middle of the desert... At some stage in your career you may need my help.* DET
5 You can also use **some** in front of a number to indicate that it is approximate. EG *...a single layer of stone, some four metres thick.* ADV+NUMBER Formal
6 You can also use **some** to indicate that a word being used to refer to something is not in fact accurate. EG *Some holiday that turned out to be!* DET Informal

somebody /sʌmbəˀdiˡ/. See **someone**.

some day means at a date in the future that is unknown or that has not yet been decided. EG *I'd like to see it some day... I hope someday we'll have enough money to get those pictures.* ADV

somehow /sʌmhaʊ/. **1** You use **somehow** to say that you do not know how something was done or will be done. EG *...a boy who'd somehow broken his thumb... We'll manage somehow.* ADV
2 You also use **somehow** to indicate that you do not know the reason for something you are saying. EG *Somehow it didn't seem important to him any more... To hear her talking this way was somehow shocking.* ADV SEN OR ADV+ADJ

someone /sʌmwəˀn/. You use **someone** or **somebody** to refer to a person without saying exactly who you mean. EG *There's someone coming upstairs... She wrote a book on somebody famous... It belongs to somebody else.* PRON INDEF: SING

someplace /sʌmpleɪs/ means the same as somewhere. EG *Why don't you boys go and sit someplace else?* ADV American Informal

somersault /sʌməsɒːlt/, **somersaults.** A **somersault** is a rolling or turning movement which you do by turning upside down and bringing your legs over your head. EG *My sister turned a somersault.* N COUNT

something /sʌmθɪŋ/. **1** You use **something** to refer in a vague way to anything that is not a person, for example an object, action, or quality. EG *Hendricks saw something ahead of him... I've got something to do tonight... Something terrible has happened... There's something peculiar about him... His name is Victor something.* PRON INDEF: SING
2 If you say that what you have or what has been done is **something**, you mean that it is useful, even if only in a small way. EG *Of course I've got my savings now, that's something.* PRON INDEF: SING
3 You can use **something** to say that the description or amount that you are giving is not exact. EG *I can't remember the details, but it was something like this... Profits have fallen by something over 35%... ...a tax cut at something near 10 per cent.* ADV+PREP
4 If you say that a person or thing is **something of** a particular thing, you mean that they are that thing to a limited extent. EG *Their size does seem to be something of a handicap... It is something of a mystery why the party should continue to support this policy.* PHRASE
5 You use the expression **or something** to indicate that you are uncertain about what you have just said. EG *She had cancer or something.* PHRASE Informal
6 If you say that **there is something in** an idea or suggestion, you mean that it is quite good and should be considered seriously. EG *I believe there is something in having ballots in trade unions.* PHRASE
7 If you say that a person or thing **is really something**, you mean that you are very impressed by them. PHRASE Informal
8 something like: see **like**.

sometime /sʌmtaɪm/. **1 Sometime** means at a time in the future or the past that is unknown or that has not yet been decided. EG *Can I come and see you sometime?... He saw Frieda Maloney sometime last week.* ADV
2 You also use **sometime** to refer to a job or role that a person used to have. EG *...Sir Alfred Munnings, sometime President of the Royal Academy.* ADJ CLASSIF: ATTRIB Formal

sometimes /sʌmtaɪmz/. You use **sometimes** to say that something happens on some occasions. EG *Sometimes I wish I was back in Africa... Sometimes they just come for a term, sometimes six months.* ADV

somewhat /sʌmwɒt/ means to some extent or degree. EG *...a fine, though somewhat daunting, director... Communication has altered things somewhat... I found, somewhat to my surprise, that I enjoyed myself.* ADV Formal

somewhere /sʌmwɛə/. **1** You use **somewhere** **1.1** to refer to a place without saying exactly where you mean. EG *They lived somewhere near Bournemouth... There's an ashtray somewhere.* **1.2** when giving an approximate amount, number, or time. EG *This part of the church was built somewhere around 700 AD... ...somewhere between 55,000 and 60,000 men.* ADV
2 If you say that you **are getting somewhere**, you mean that you are making progress towards achieving something. PHRASE

son /sʌn/, **sons.** Someone's **son** is their male child. EG *Don Culver is the son of an engineer... ...photographs of their sons and daughters.* N COUNT

sonar /səʊnɑː/ is equipment on a ship which can calculate the depth of the sea or the position of an underwater object using sound waves. EG *Sonar has a limited range... ...sonar apparatus.* N UNCOUNT

sonata /sənɑːtə/, **sonatas.** A **sonata** is a piece of classical music written for the piano or for a piano and one other instrument. EG *...Beethoven piano sonatas.* N COUNT

song /sɒŋ/, **songs. 1** A **song** consists of words and music that are sung together. EG *...a love song... I heard somebody singing a song... We all burst into song.* N COUNT OR N UNCOUNT
2 A bird's **song** is the pleasant, musical sounds that it makes. EG *...the sweet song of the skylark.* N COUNT OR N UNCOUNT
3 If you buy something **for a song**, you buy it for much less than its real value. EG *I was wearing a dress that I had bought for a song in India.* PHRASE Informal
4 If you say that someone is making a **song and dance** about something, you mean that they are making an unnecessary fuss about it. PHRASE Informal

son-in-law, sons-in-law. Someone's **son-in-law** is the husband of their daughter. N COUNT

sonnet /sɒnɪt/, **sonnets.** A **sonnet** is a poem with 14 lines, in which some lines rhyme with others according to certain fixed patterns. N COUNT

soon /suːn/, **sooner, soonest. 1** If something is going to happen **soon**, it will happen in a very short time from now. If something happened **soon** after a particular time or event, it happened a short time after it. EG *It will soon be Christmas... I should finish in a few years, perhaps sooner... He rented a TV soon after moving into his apartment... Contact the police as soon as possible.* ADV OR ADV+PREP
2 You say **the sooner the better** when you think something should be done as soon as possible. EG *The sooner we get out the better.* CONVENTION
3 If you say that something will happen **sooner or later**, you mean that it will happen at some time in the future, even though it might take a long time. PHRASE

EG *If you do not look after it carefully, sooner or later your car will fall to bits.*

4 If you say that something will happen **as soon as** something else happens, you mean that it will happen immediately after the other thing happens. EG *As soon as we get the tickets we'll send them to you... As soon as she got out of bed the telephone stopped ringing.* CONJ

5 If you say that **no sooner** has one thing happened **than** another thing happens, you mean that the second thing happens immediately after the first thing. EG *No sooner had he closed his eyes than he fell asleep.* PHRASE

6 If you say that you **would just as soon** do something, you mean that you would be equally willing to do it as to do something else. EG *I'd just as soon turn around and go back.* PHRASE

7 If you say that you **would sooner** do something, you mean that you would prefer to do it. EG *I would sooner read than watch television.* PHRASE

soot /sʊt/ is black powder which rises in the smoke from a fire and collects on the inside of chimneys. N UNCOUNT

soothe /suːð/, **soothes, soothing, soothed.** 1 If you **soothe** someone who is angry or upset, you make them feel calmer. EG *He tried to soothe her by making conversation... She was soothed by his detachment from her troubles.* V+O
◊ **soothing.** EG *...soothing music... ...a soothing voice... ...a few soothing words.* ◊ ADJ QUALIT

2 Something such as ointment that **soothes** pain makes the pain less severe. EG *...cream she put on to soothe her sunburn.* V+O

sooty /sʊti[1]/. Something that is **sooty** is covered with soot. EG *...sooty windows... ...his sooty hands.* ADJ QUALIT

sophisticated /səfɪstɪkeɪtɪ[2]d/. 1 A **sophisticated** person 1.1 shows experience in social situations and knows about culture, fashion, and other matters that are considered socially important. EG *...a glossy magazine for today's sophisticated woman... ...a sophisticated lifestyle.* 1.2 is knowledgeable and able to understand complicated matters. EG *...a politically sophisticated electorate.* ADJ QUALIT

2 A **sophisticated** machine or device is made using advanced and complex methods. EG *These planes are among the most sophisticated aircraft now being manufactured.* ADJ QUALIT

sophistication /səfɪstɪkeɪʃə[0]n/. The **sophistication** of people, methods, or machines, is their quality of being sophisticated. EG *Their elegantly cut suits projected sophistication... The machinery will grow in sophistication and power.* N UNCOUNT

soppy /sɒpi[1]/. If you describe someone or something as **soppy**, you mean that they are silly or foolishly sentimental. EG *...the soppy expressions on their faces... Don't be soppy, Manfred.* ADJ QUALIT Informal

soprano /səprɑːnəʊ/, **sopranos.** A **soprano** is a woman, girl, or boy with a high singing voice. N COUNT

sordid /sɔːdɪd/. Something that is **sordid** 1 involves dishonest or immoral behaviour. EG *...a rather sordid affair.* 2 is dirty, unpleasant, or depressing. EG *...a sordid street.* ADJ QUALIT

sore /sɔː/, **sores.** 1 If part of your body is **sore**, it causes you pain and discomfort. EG *Her throat was so sore she could not talk... I've got sore feet after all that walking.* ADJ QUALIT

2 A **sore** is a painful place on the body where the skin is infected. EG *She had a big sore on her leg.* N COUNT

3 If you are **sore** about something, you are angry and upset about it. EG *Nobody believed him, and this made him sore as hell.* ADJ PRED : OFT+*about* American

4 People sometimes use **sore** to describe something that is causing great difficulty, worry, or suffering. EG *Man is in sore need of new standards.* ADJ CLASSIF : ATTRIB Literary
◊ **sorely.** EG *They were sorely in need of rest.* ◊ ADV

5 If something is **a sore point** with someone, it is likely to make them angry or embarrassed if you try to discuss it. EG *'Have you got any children, Lynn?' – 'Hm. Sore point.' – 'Oh, sorry.'* PHRASE

sorrow /sɒrəʊ/, **sorrows. 1 Sorrow** is a feeling of deep sadness or regret. EG *She wrote to express her sorrow at the tragic death of their son.* N UNCOUNT

2 **Sorrows** are events or situations that cause deep sadness. EG *...suffering the sorrows that life brings.* N COUNT

sorrowful /sɒrə[6]fʊl/. Someone or something that is **sorrowful** shows or causes deep sadness. EG *It was a sorrowful day in that town when the orders came to close down the mine.* ADJ QUALIT Literary

sorry /sɒri[1]/, **sorrier, sorriest.** 1 You say **'Sorry'** or **'I'm sorry'** as a way of apologizing to someone for something that you have done which has upset them or caused them difficulties. EG *I'm sorry I'm late... Sorry about the coffee on your bedspread... 'You're giving me a headache with all that noise.' – 'Sorry,' Thomas said... I'm sorry if I worried you.* ADJ PRED : OFT+REPORT, *about/for,* OR *to*-INF

2 If you are **sorry** about a situation, you feel sadness, regret, or disappointment about it. EG *He was sorry he had agreed to stay... No one seemed very sorry to see me go.* ADJ PRED : OFT +*about/for,* REPORT, OR *to*-INF

3 You use **sorry** as a polite introduction when you are saying that you are unable to help someone or when you are giving someone bad news. EG *I'm sorry but there's no-one here called Nikki... I'm sorry to say that the experiment has failed.* CONVENTION OR ADJ PRED +*to*-INF

4 You also say **'I'm sorry'** to express your regret and sadness when you hear sad or unpleasant news. EG *'Jenny's dead,' I told him. 'I'm sorry,' he said in a stunned whisper.* CONVENTION

5 If you are or feel **sorry** for someone who is unhappy or in an unpleasant situation, you feel sympathy and sadness for them. EG *I knew they were having a rough time and I felt sorry for them.* ADJ PRED+*for*

6 If you are or feel **sorry** for yourself, you are miserable and feel pity for yourself. EG *How dare you feel sorry for yourself? It was your own fault!* ADJ PRED+*for* +REFL

7 You also say **sorry** 7.1 when you haven't heard something that someone has said and you want them to repeat it. EG *'Have you seen the health guide book anywhere?' – 'Sorry?' – 'Seen the health guide book?'* CONVENTION 7.2 as a polite introduction when you are disagreeing with someone or refusing to do something for them. EG *I'm sorry, I wouldn't agree with that at all, Brian.* CONVENTION OR ADJ PRED 7.3 to correct yourself when you have said something incorrect. EG *It's in the southeast, sorry, southwest corner of the USA.* ADV SEN

8 You also use **sorry** to describe people and things that are in a bad physical or mental state. EG *He had never seen such a sorry lot... 'We are in a sorry state,' she lamented.* ADJ QUALIT : ATTRIB

sort /sɔːt/, **sorts, sorting, sorted.** 1 If you talk about a particular **sort** of something, you are talking about one of the different types of that thing. EG *'What sort of iron did she get?' – 'A steam iron.'... ...a rock plant of some sort... There were five different sorts of biscuits... There are all sorts of reasons why this is true.* N COUNT+SUPP

2 You use **sort of** when you want to say that something can roughly be described in a particular way. EG *She was wearing a sort of velvet dress... I heard a strangling sort of noise.* PHRASE Informal

3 If you describe something as a thing **of sorts**, you mean that it belongs to this class of things but is not of very good quality. EG *...cleaning a carpet of sorts... Farlow was a lawyer of sorts.* PHRASE

4 You describe someone as a particular **sort** when you are describing their character. EG *She was a good sort... He's not the marrying sort.* N SING+SUPP

5 If you feel **out of sorts**, you feel slightly unwell, discontented, or annoyed. EG *She complained of being out of sorts... ...when you are out of sorts with the group.* PHRASE

6 If you **sort** things, you separate them into different classes, groups, or places, so that you can arrange them in a useful or sensible order. EG V+O OR V+A

If someone is in a sorry state, are they apologizing?

Minnie was in the office, sorting mail... They had got mixed up and needed to be sorted into three sets... He was sorting through a pile of socks.

sort out. 1 If you **sort out** a group of things, you organize them or tidy them. EG *It took a while to sort out all our luggage.* 2 If you **sort out** a problem, you deal with it and find a solution to it. EG *I need to get my own problems sorted out... We have to sort things out between us.* PHRASAL VB : V+O+ADV; V+O+ADV

SOS /ɛs əʊ ɛs/. An **SOS** is a signal which indicates to other people that you are in danger and need help quickly. EG *...an SOS from a private plane proceeding to Nassau... No SOS messages were received.* N SING

so-so. If you say that something is **so-so**, you mean that it is average in quality, rather than being very good or very bad. EG *Some of the food is very good, some of it's so-so.* ADJ CLASSIF OR ADV Informal

souffle /suːfleɪ/, **souffles;** also spelled **soufflé.** A **souffle** is a light food made from a mixture of beaten egg whites and other ingredients that is baked in the oven. EG *...a cheese souffle.* N COUNT OR N UNCOUNT

sought /sɔːt/ is the past tense and past participle of **seek.**

sought-after. Something that is **sought-after** is in great demand, usually because it is rare or of very good quality. EG *The most sought-after item was an early painting by Picasso.* ADJ QUALIT

soul /səʊl/, **souls.** 1 A person's **soul** is 1.1 the spiritual part of them which is believed to continue existing after their body is dead. EG *They said a prayer for the souls of the men who had been drowned.* 1.2 their mind, character, thoughts, and feelings. EG *Only someone with the soul of a poet can understand this... His soul was in turmoil.* N COUNT : USU+POSS

2 The **soul** of a nation or a political movement is the special quality it has that represents its basic nature. EG *...the soul of the American people.* N SING

3 You can refer to someone as a particular kind of **soul** when you are describing their character or condition. EG *She was a kind soul... Poor soul!* N SING+SUPP

4 You use **soul** in negative statements like 'not a soul' to mean nobody at all. EG *When I first went there I didn't know a single soul... I swear I will never tell a soul.* N SING : a+N, WITH BROAD NEG

5 **Soul** or **soul music** is a type of pop music performed mainly by black American musicians. EG *...a new soul band from Chicago.* N UNCOUNT

6 If you **keep body and soul together**, you have enough money to provide what you need to live. EG *I was earning just enough to keep body and soul together.* PHRASE

soul-destroying. Something that is **soul-destroying** makes you depressed, often because it is so boring. EG *The job has soul-destroying aspects.* ADJ QUALIT

soulful /səʊlfʊl/. Something that is **soulful** expresses deep feelings. EG *...big, soulful eyes.* ADJ QUALIT

soulless /səʊlɪ²s/. Something that is **soulless** lacks human qualities and the ability to feel or produce deep feelings. EG *The place seemed soulless... ...a soulless routine job.* ADJ QUALIT

sound /saʊnd/, **sounds, sounding, sounded; sounder, soundest.** 1 A **sound** is something that you hear. EG *He heard the sound of footsteps in the hall... He opened the door without a sound... The bells were making a gentle, tinkling sound.* N COUNT

2 **Sound** is what you hear. EG *Sound travels better in water than in air.* N UNCOUNT

3 The **sound** on a television is what you hear coming from the television set. Its loudness can be controlled. EG *When the news had finished Morris turned down the sound.* N SING : the+N

4 If something such as a horn **sounds** or if you **sound** it, it makes a noise. EG *A car passed him at top speed, sounding its horn.* • to **sound the alarm**: see **alarm**. V-ERG

5 You can use **sound** 5.1 to say what quality a noise has. EG *The rustling of the woman's dress sounded alarmingly loud... Her footsteps sounded like pistol shots.* 5.2 to say what emotion or quality someone seems to have when they speak. EG *'Ah,' Piper said. He sounded a little discouraged... You know, you sound just like an insurance salesman.* 5.3 to say what quality you think something has, when you have just heard about it or read about it. EG *'They've got a small farm down in Devon.' – 'That sounds nice.'... It all sounded so crazy that I laughed out loud... It sounds to me as though he's just doing it to be awkward.* V+C OR V+as/like

6 The **sound** of something that you have heard about or read about is the impression you have of what it is like. EG *I don't like the sound of linguistics... She had a rather off-putting manner by the sound of it.* N SING : the+N

7 If a structure, part of someone's body, or someone's mind is **sound**, it is in good condition or healthy. EG *My heart is basically sound.* • **safe and sound**: see **safe**. ADJ QUALIT

8 Something or someone that is **sound** is reliable and sensible. EG *Adam met every objection with sound arguments... Is this sound advice?* ADJ QUALIT

9 If you are **sound asleep**, you are sleeping deeply. PHRASE

10 See also **soundly**.

sound out. If you **sound** someone **out**, you question them in order to find out what their opinion is about something. PHRASAL VB : V+O+ADV

sound effect, sound effects. Sound effects are the sounds that are created artificially to make a play more realistic, especially a radio play. N COUNT : USU PLURAL

soundly. 1 If someone is **soundly** defeated or beaten, they are defeated or beaten thoroughly. EG *He was grabbed and soundly whipped.* ADV

2 If you sleep **soundly**, you sleep deeply and do not wake during your sleep. EG *I slept soundly that night.* ADV

soundproof /saʊnd⁰pruːf/. Something such as a room that is **soundproof** is able to stop all sound from getting in or out. EG *The studio was soundproof.* ADJ CLASSIF

soundtrack /saʊnd⁰træk/, **soundtracks.** The **soundtrack** of a film is its sound, speech, and music. N COUNT

soup /suːp/, **soups. Soup** is liquid food made by boiling meat, fish, or vegetables in water. EG *...a bowl of soup... ...chicken soup.* N MASS

sour /saʊə/, **sours, souring, soured.** 1 Something that is **sour** has a sharp taste like the taste of a lemon or an unripe apple. EG *Add enough sugar to keep it from tasting sour.* ADJ QUALIT

2 **Sour** milk has an unpleasant taste because it is no longer fresh. ADJ CLASSIF

3 Someone who is **sour** is bad-tempered and unfriendly. EG *I received a sour look every time I passed her house.* ADJ QUALIT

4 If something **goes sour** or **turns sour**, it becomes less enjoyable or less satisfactory. EG *The evening had turned sour.* PHRASE

5 If a friendship, situation, or attitude **sours** or if something **sours** it, it becomes less friendly, enjoyable, or hopeful. EG *These latest cuts might sour relations between the government and the military.* V-ERG

source /sɔːs/, **sources.** 1 The **source** of something is 1.1 the person, place, or thing which you get it from. EG *...one of the world's main sources of uranium... Candidates are required to publish the sources of their campaign funds... ...the development of new energy sources.* 1.2 the place where it starts from or the thing which causes it. EG *They're trying to trace the source of the trouble... Bad housing is their main source of worry.* N COUNT : USU+SUPP

2 A **source** is a person or book that provides information for a news story or for a piece of research. EG *Western diplomatic sources confirmed reports of fighting in the capital... The story was based on information from a 'reliable source'.* N COUNT

3 The **source** of a river or stream is the place N SING

where it begins. EG *We are following the creek to its source.*

south /saʊθ/; often spelled with a capital letter. **1** The **south** is **1.1** the direction which is on your right when you are looking towards the direction where the sun rises. EG *We want to find a quiet place in the hills to the south of the little town... The island is a mile in length from north to south.* N SING : the+N, OR N UNCOUNT

1.2 the part of a place or country which is towards the south. EG *...the South of France... She's from the South.* N SING : the+N

2 South means towards the south or to the south of a place or thing. EG *I travelled south by bus through Philadelphia... I was living in a house just south of Market Street.* ADV

3 The **south** part of a place or country is the part which is towards the south. EG *...South Wales... She owned a boarding house on the south coast.* ADJ CLASSIF : ATTRIB

4 A **south** wind blows from the south. ADJ CLASSIF

south-east; often spelled with a capital letter or capital letters. **1** The **south-east** is **1.1** the direction which is halfway between south and east. EG *To the south-east there is a dense date plantation.* N SING : the+N, OR N UNCOUNT **1.2** the part of a place or country which is towards the south-east. EG *...the south-east of England.* N SING : the+N, OFT+of

2 South-east means towards the south-east or to the south-east of a place or thing. EG *...a forest somewhere south-east of Berlin.* ADV

3 The **south-east** part of a place or country is the part which is towards the south-east. EG *...a bookshop in south-east London.* ADJ CLASSIF : ATTRIB

4 A **south-east** wind blows from the south-east. ADJ CLASSIF

south-eastern means in or from the south-east of a region or country. EG *We were staying in Beaumont, in southeastern Kansas.* ADJ CLASSIF : ATTRIB

southerly /sʌðəli[1]/. **1** A **southerly** point, area, or direction is to the south or towards the south. EG *They headed in a southerly direction... ...the most southerly tip of Bear Island.* ADJ QUALIT

2 A **southerly** wind blows from the south. ADJ CLASSIF

southern /sʌðə[5]n/ means in or from the south of a region or country. EG *...the southern edge of the Sahara... ...a Southern English accent.* ADJ CLASSIF : ATTRIB

South Pole. The **South Pole** is the place on the surface of the earth which is farthest towards the south. N PROPER : the+N

southward /saʊθwəd/ or **southwards** means towards the south. EG *A level expanse of low-lying country extended southward.* ▸ **Southward** is also used as an adjective. EG *The shore was badly eaten away on its southward side.* ADV ▸ ADJ CLASSIF

south-west; often spelled with a capital letter or capital letters. **1** The **south-west** is **1.1** the direction which is halfway between south and west. EG *To the south-west lay the city.* N SING : the+N, OR N UNCOUNT **1.2** the part of a place or country which is towards the south-west. EG *...the south-west of England... We moved on to Dallas in the South-West.* N SING : the+N

2 South-west means towards the south-west or to the south-west of a place or thing. EG *It flows south-west to the Atlantic Ocean... ...the mountain road southwest of Sappora.* ADV

3 The **south-west** part of a place or country is the part which is towards the south-west. EG *...Conservative Party agent for Southwest Staffordshire.* ADJ CLASSIF : ATTRIB

4 A **south-west** wind blows from the south-west. ADJ CLASSIF

south-western means in or from the south-west of a region or country. EG *...the mountains of the southwestern United States.* ADJ CLASSIF

souvenir /suːvənɪə, suːvənɪə/, **souvenirs.** A **souvenir** is something which you buy or keep to remind you of a holiday, place, or event. EG *He kept a spoon as a souvenir of his journey... ...a souvenir shop.* N COUNT

sovereign /sɒvrɪn/, **sovereigns. 1** A **sovereign** is a king, queen, or other royal ruler of a country. N COUNT

2 A **sovereign** state or country is independent and not under the authority of any other country. EG *The Punjab was the last sovereign independent Indian state.* ADJ CLASSIF : ATTRIB

3 Sovereign is used to describe someone who has the highest power in a country. EG *Parliament is sovereign... He will be given sovereign powers.* ADJ CLASSIF

sovereignty /sɒvrə[1]nti[1]/ is complete political power that a country has to govern itself or another country or state. EG *...a threat to national sovereignty... ...the abandonment of British sovereignty over Africa.* N UNCOUNT

sow, sows, sowing, sowed, sown; pronounced /səʊ/ when it is a verb, and /saʊ/ when it is a noun. **1** If you **sow** seeds or **sow** an area of land with seeds, you plant the seeds in the ground. EG *You can sow winter wheat in October... The land was cleared of weeds and sown with grass.* V+O OR V+O+with

2 If someone **sows** an undesirable feeling or situation, they cause it to begin and develop. EG *She attacked those who sow dismay and division in the party... ...sowing doubt and uncertainty.* V+O Literary

3 A **sow** is an adult female pig. N COUNT

soya /sɔɪj[0]ə/. **Soya** flour, butter, or other food is made from soya beans. N UNCOUNT : USU N MOD

soya bean, soya beans. Soya beans are a type of bean that can be eaten or used to make flour, oil, or soy sauce. N COUNT

soy sauce /sɔɪ sɔːs/ is a dark brown liquid made from soya beans and used as a flavouring, especially in Chinese cooking. N UNCOUNT

spa /spɑː/, **spas.** A **spa** is a place where water with minerals in it bubbles out of the ground. People drink the water or bathe in it in order to improve their health. N COUNT

space /speɪs/, **spaces, spacing, spaced. 1 Space** is **1.1** the area that is empty or available in a place, building, or container. EG *There was just enough space for a bed... Belongings take up space... I did not have the space to store the bricks... ...the luggage space at the back of the car.* **1.2** the vast area that lies beyond the Earth's atmosphere and surrounds the stars and planets. EG *...the first human being to travel in space... ...space research.* N UNCOUNT

2 Space in a talk or piece of writing is the amount of the talk or writing that is available for a particular thing to be discussed. EG *There is no space in this book to argue the alternative viewpoint... I shall devote some space to describing my own experiences.* N UNCOUNT

3 If a place gives a feeling of **space**, it gives an impression of being large and open. EG *The low hills give a feeling of great, intense space... A mirror can add space to a room.* N UNCOUNT

4 If you are looking or staring **into space**, you are looking straight in front of you, without actually looking at anything in particular. PHRASE

5 A **space** is **5.1** a gap or empty place in something solid or crowded. EG *The door had spaces at the top and bottom... ...an open space in the jungle.* **5.2** a place or area that is empty and available for people to use or fill. EG *There were two spaces on the morning plane to Canton... We spent half an hour looking for a parking space... There is no official space for it on the form.* N COUNT

6 A **space** of time is a period of time. EG *It happened three times in the space of five months... He should arrive in a very short space of time.* N SING+of

7 If you **space** a series of things, you arrange them so that they are not all together but have gaps between them. EG *The lines were spaced well apart... I had to space my inquiries carefully.* V+O : OFT PASS+A

8 See also **outer space**.

space out. If you **space** things **out**, you arrange them so that they are not all together but have PHRASAL VB : V+O+ADV

If you are staring into space, are you looking up into the sky?

gaps between them. EG *These books should have large print well spaced out on the page.*

spacecraft /speɪskrɑːft/. **Spacecraft** is both the singular and the plural form. N COUNT
A **spacecraft** is a rocket or other vehicle that can travel in space.

Space Invaders is the name of a computer game in which players use control buttons and levers to try to shoot and destroy spaceships that move and attack them on a computer screen. N UNCOUNT

spaceship /speɪsʃɪp/, **spaceships.** A **spaceship** is a spacecraft that carries people through space. N COUNT

space shuttle, space shuttles. A **space shuttle** is a spacecraft that is designed to travel into space and back to earth many times. N COUNT

spacious /speɪʃəs/. A room or other place that is **spacious** is large in size or area inside. EG *...a spacious dining-room... ...spacious parks.* ADJ QUALIT

spade /speɪd/, **spades. 1** A **spade** is a tool used for digging, with a flat metal blade and a long handle. See picture at TOOLS. EG *...a garden spade.* N COUNT

2 Spades is one of the four suits in a pack of playing cards. Each card in the suit is marked with one or more black symbols in the shape of a heart-shaped leaf with a stem. N UNCOUNT

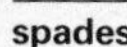
spades

3 A **spade** is also one of the thirteen playing cards in the suit of spades. N COUNT

spaghetti /spəgɛti¹/ is a type of food made from pasta. It looks like long pieces of string and is usually served with a sauce. N UNCOUNT

span /spæn/, **spans, spanning, spanned. 1** A **span** is **1.1** the period of time between two dates or events, or the period during which something exists or functions. EG *...during the forty-year span from 1913 to 1953... ...in the short span that man has been on earth.* N COUNT: USU+SUPP **1.2** the range of things that are included in a subject or task. EG *Each manager has a fixed span of responsibility.* N SING: USU+SUPP

2 If something **spans** a particular length of time, it lasts throughout that time. EG *At 79, Dame Flora can look back at a career spanning more than half a century.* V+O

3 The **span** of something is the total length of it from one end to the other, especially when it is stretched out as far as possible. EG *Some eagles have a wing span of one and a half metres.* N COUNT: OFT+SUPP

4 A bridge that **spans** something such as a river or a valley stretches right across it. EG *...a long lake spanned by a high, arching iron bridge.* V+O

spangle /spæŋgə⁰l/, **spangles. Spangles** are small pieces of metal or plastic which sparkle brightly and are used to decorate clothing or hair. N COUNT

spangled /spæŋgə⁰ld/. Something that is **spangled** with small bright objects is covered with them so that it sparkles. EG *...a crown spangled with glitter... ...the star-spangled night sky.* ADJ CLASSIF: OFT+*with*

spaniel /spænjəl/, **spaniels.** A **spaniel** is a type of dog with long ears that hang down. N COUNT

spank /spæŋk/, **spanks, spanking, spanked.** If you **spank** a child, you punish it by hitting its bottom several times with your hand. V+O

spanner /spænə/, **spanners.** A **spanner** is a metal tool with a specially shaped end that fits round a nut so that you can loosen or tighten the nut. See picture at TOOLS. N COUNT

spare /spɛə/, **spares, sparing, spared. 1** You use **spare 1.1** to describe something that is the same as things that you are already using, but that you do not need yet and are keeping ready. EG *Keep a spare fuse handy by the fuse box... Take a spare shirt and a spare set of underwear.* ADJ CLASSIF ▸ used as a noun. EG *There are some spares at the back if anyone wants more.* ▸ N COUNT **1.2** to describe something that is not being used by anyone, and is therefore available for you to use. EG *We found a spare parking meter... There were no chairs spare.* ADJ CLASSIF

2 Time or money **to spare** is extra time or money that is not needed for a particular purpose. EG *He often had money to spare nowadays... She caught her plane with a few minutes to spare.* PHRASE

3 If you **spare** something for a particular purpose, you make it available for that purpose. EG *I got to my feet, thanking him for sparing time to see me... Nowadays more land is needed to grow food and less can be spared to graze cattle.* V+O: USU+*for* OR *to*-INF

4 If a person or a place **is spared**, they are not harmed, although someone threatened them or harmed other people or places. EG *The great cities of the Rhineland had not been spared... Thank God we were spared.* V+O: OFT PASS

5 If you **spare** someone an unpleasant experience, you prevent them from suffering it. EG *We telephoned, wishing to spare poor Charlotte two or three hours of suspense... At least I am spared the shame of the children knowing.* V+O+O

6 If you **spare no expense** in doing something, you do it as well as possible, without trying to save money. EG *The Agency has spared no expense with the system for storage.* PHRASE

spare part, spare parts. Spare parts are parts that you can buy separately to replace old or broken parts in a piece of equipment, usually parts that are designed to be easily removed or fitted. EG *The tractors are out of order and there are no spare parts to get them working again... The guarantee includes the cost of spare parts and labour.* N COUNT: USU PLURAL

sparing /spɛərɪŋ/. Someone who is **sparing** uses or gives something only in very small quantities. EG *She was sparing with heat and light.* ◇ **sparingly.** EG *Use hot water sparingly.* ADJ QUALIT: USU+*with* ◇ ADV

spark /spɑːk/, **sparks, sparking, sparked. 1** A **spark** is **1.1** a tiny, bright piece of burning material that flies up from something that is burning. EG *The fire sent smoke and sparks over the top of the fence.* N COUNT **1.2** a flash of light that is caused by electricity and often makes a crackling sound. EG *Watch the gap for a blue spark. If there isn't one, check the circuit.*

2 A **spark** of a particular quality is a small but noticeable amount of the quality. EG *A faint spark of pleasure came into his eyes.* N COUNT+*of*

3 If one thing **sparks** another thing or **sparks** it off, it causes the second thing to start happening. EG *The crisis was sparked by the assassination of the duke... The letter sparked off a friendship between the two men.* V+O: OFT+*off*

sparkle /spɑːkə⁰l/, **sparkles, sparkling, sparkled. 1** If something **sparkles**, it is clear and bright and shines with a lot of very small points of light. EG *They looked down to the sea, sparkling in the sun... The lawn was sparkling with frost.* V ▸ used as a noun. EG *Her eyes had lost their sparkle.* ▸ N UNCOUNT

2 Someone who **sparkles** is lively, intelligent, and witty. EG *It was years since he'd tried to sparkle.* V
◇ **sparkling.** EG *She felt electric, sparkling, and irresistible.* ◇ ADJ CLASSIF

spark plug, spark plugs. A **spark plug** is a device in the engine of a motor vehicle, which causes the electric sparks that ignite the fuel. N COUNT

sparrow /spærəʊ/, **sparrows.** A **sparrow** is a very common, small brown bird. N COUNT

sparse /spɑːs/, **sparser, sparsest.** Something that is **sparse** is small in number or amount and spread out over an area. EG *The population was sparse... ...his sparse white hair... ...the sparse rain-* ADJ QUALIT *fall.* ◇ **sparsely**. EG *...a sparsely populated region... ...his sparsely furnished room.* ◇ ADV

spartan /spɑːtən/. A **spartan** way of life is very simple with no luxuries. EG *...the spartan lives of the islanders... ...spartan accommodation.* ADJ QUALIT

spasm /spæzəm/, **spasms.** A **spasm** is **1** a sudden tightening of your muscles. EG *Spasms shook her lungs and chest.* N COUNT OR N UNCOUNT **2** a sudden strong pain or unpleasant emotion which lasts for a short period of time. EG *...a spasm of anger.* N SING+*of*

spasmodic /spæzmɒdɪk/. Something that is **spasmodic** happens suddenly for short periods of time at irregular intervals. EG *As she talked, she kept making spasmodic dashes to the window.* ADJ QUALIT
◇ **spasmodically**. EG *The orchestra continued to play spasmodically.* ◇ ADV

spastic /spæstɪk/, **spastics.** Someone who is **spastic** is born with a disability which makes it difficult for them to control their muscles, especially their arm and leg muscles. ▸ used as a noun. *...the Spastics Society.* ADJ CLASSIF ▸ N COUNT

spat /spæt/ is the past tense and past participle of **spit.**

spate /speɪt/. A **spate** of things is a large number of them that happen or appear within a short period of time. EG *The incident caused another spate of protests... ...a spate of new books about the man.* N PART : SING

spatial /speɪʃəl/ is used to describe things relating to size, area, or position. EG *...spatial and temporal variations... ...spatial perception.* ADJ CLASSIF : ATTRIB Formal

spatter /spætə/, **spatters, spattering, spattered.** If something **spatters** a surface or **spatters** a liquid over it, it covers the surface with drops of the liquid. EG *He picked up his spoon so hurriedly that it spattered milk over his cardigan... Beer spattered the bedspread.* ◇ **spattered**. EG *My goggles were spattered with mud.* V+O : OFT+A ◇ ADJ CLASSIF

spawn /spɔːn/, **spawns, spawning, spawned. 1** **Spawn** is a soft, jelly-like substance containing the eggs of fish, frogs, or other amphibians. N UNCOUNT
2 When fish, frogs, and other amphibians **spawn**, they lay their eggs. V
3 If something **spawns** something else, it causes it to happen or to be created. EG *Poverty had spawned numerous religious movements.* V+O Literary

speak /spiːk/, **speaks, speaking, spoke** /spəʊk/, **spoken** /spəʊkən/. **1** When you **speak**, you use your voice in order to say words. EG *Simon opened his mouth to speak... She spoke with an Irish accent... Mary turned her head to speak to him... He hadn't been able to speak of what had happened.* ◇ **spoken**. EG *...a robot capable of understanding spoken commands.* V ◇ ADJ CLASSIF : ATTRIB
2 If you **speak** a foreign language, you know the language and are able to have a conversation in it. EG *The men at the airport spoke fluent English.* V+O
3 If you **speak** for a group of people, you give their opinion on their behalf. EG *I'm only speaking for myself, not for my colleagues.* V+*for*
4 When someone **speaks** to a group of people, they make a speech. EG *It was announced that the Prime Minister would speak to the nation on television.* V : USU+A
5 Speak is also used in these phrases. **5.1** You say **so to speak** to draw attention to the fact that what you are saying is not literally true, but is a colourful way of describing a situation. EG *He goes to work early; before the office is awake, so to speak.* ADV SEN
5.2 Nobody to speak of or **nothing to speak of** means hardly anyone or anything, or only unimportant people or things. EG *'Did you find anything?' – 'No, nothing to speak of.'* PHRASE **5.3** If you say **'speak for yourself'** when someone has said something, you mean that what they have said is only their opinion or applies only to them. EG *'Posy, we're ridiculous.' – 'Speak for yourself.'* CONVENTION Informal **5.4** If you are **on speaking terms** with someone, you are quite friendly with them and often talk to them. EG *They were rarely on speaking terms.* PHRASE **5.5** If you **speak well** or **speak highly** of someone, you say good things about them. If you **speak ill** of someone, you criticize them. EG *The students spoke highly of their history lecturer.* PHRASE **5.6** If you **speak** your **mind** about something, you say exactly what you think about it. PHRASE **5.7** If you say that something **speaks for itself**, you mean that its meaning or quality is so obvious that it does not need any special explanation. EG *His writing speaks for itself.* PHRASE
6 See also **speaking**.

speak out. If you **speak out** in favour of something or against something, you say publicly that you think it is a good thing or a bad thing. EG *He spoke out against racial discrimination many times... We lose the courage to speak out.* PHRASAL VB : V+ADV, USU+A

speak up. 1 To **speak up** means the same as to speak out. EG *Never be frightened of speaking up for your beliefs... The cricketers themselves should speak up in favour of it.* PHRASAL VB : V+ADV, USU+A **2** If you ask someone to **speak up**, you are asking them to speak more loudly. V+ADV

speaker /spiːkə/, **speakers. 1** A **speaker** is **1.1** a person who is speaking. **1.2** a person who is making a speech to a group of people. EG *The chairman got up to introduce the speaker.* N COUNT
2 A **speaker** of a particular language is a person who can speak that language. EG *Some sounds are very difficult for French speakers of English.* N COUNT : USU+SUPP
3 A **speaker** is also a piece of equipment on a radio or record-player, through which the sound comes out. N COUNT

speaking /spiːkɪŋ/. **1** You use expressions such as **generally speaking** and **technically speaking** to indicate the kind of statement you are making. EG *America is still, generally speaking, the most technologically advanced... Roughly speaking, there are two possibilities.* ADV SEN
2 You can say '**speaking as** a parent' or '**speaking as** a teacher', for example, to indicate that the opinion you are giving is based on your experience as a parent or as a teacher. EG *Speaking as a married woman, I consider it important to provide nursery schools for all children who need them.* ADV SEN
3 You can say **speaking of** a thing that has just been mentioned as a way of introducing a new topic which has some connection with that thing. EG *It's nice to have an admirer who gives nothing away. Speaking of giving away, I have brought you a present.* V+*of*
4 Speaking is the activity of giving speeches and talks. EG *...public speaking.* N UNCOUNT : USU+SUPP

spear /spɪə/, **spears, spearing, speared. 1** A **spear** is a weapon consisting of a long pole with a sharp point. See picture at WEAPONS. N COUNT
2 If you **spear** something, you push or throw a spear or other pointed object into it. EG *Lally took her fork and speared an oyster from its shell.* V+O

spearhead /spɪəhɛd/, **spearheads, spearheading, spearheaded. 1** If someone **spearheads** a campaign, they lead it. EG *In India, Mrs Gandhi's son Sanjay spearheaded a 'moral crusade' against slums.* V+O Literary
2 The **spearhead** of a campaign is the person or group that leads it. EG *...the spearhead of a nationalist movement.* N COUNT Literary

special /spɛʃəl/, **specials. 1** Something that is **special** is more important or better than other things of its kind. EG *...china that was reserved for special occasions... Is there anything special you would like for dinner, dear?* ADJ QUALIT
2 You use **special 2.1** to describe someone who is officially appointed, or something that is needed or intended for a particular purpose. EG *He was a special adviser to Mrs Judith Hart at the Ministry... To marry a foreigner, special permission had to be* ADJ CLASSIF : ATTRIB

If you have specks on your specs, can you see clearly?

obtained... My Hoover has special attachments for upholstery... ...special schools for maladjusted children. **2.2** to describe something that belongs or relates to only one particular person, group, or place. EG *He spoke his own special variety of German... Hospital food seldom caters for the special needs of the aged.* **2.3** to describe something that is not ordinary but is better than usual or of a high quality or standard. EG *She made a special effort to be polite... Some places do special offers in May.*

3 A **special** is a product or programme which is only available or shown at a certain time, or which is made for a special purpose. EG *Monday's special was chicken... I had seen his production of a TV special called 'The Male of the Species.'* N COUNT

4 See also **speciality**, **specially**.

specialise /spɛʃəlaɪz/. See **specialize**.

specialist /spɛʃəlɪst/, **specialists.** A **specialist** is a person who studies a particular subject or skill and knows a lot about it. EG *She is a specialist in Eastern European affairs... ...an eye specialist.* N COUNT
▸ used as an adjective. EG *...a specialist teacher of mathematics... ...specialist committees.* ▸ ADJ CLASSIF : ATTRIB

speciality /spɛʃiælɪ¹ti¹/, **specialities. 1** Someone's **speciality** is a particular type of work that they do or a subject that they know a lot about. EG *Work with children is their speciality... They enjoy talking about their own specialities.* N COUNT

2 A **speciality** of a particular place is a special product that is always very good there. EG *Chocolate gateau was a speciality of the Café de Rome.* N COUNT+SUPP

specialize /spɛʃəlaɪz/, **specializes, specializing, specialized;** also spelled **specialise.** If you **specialize** in a thing, you make this thing your speciality, for example in your work or when you are studying. EG *...a shop specializing in camping equipment.* ◇ **specialization** /spɛʃəlaɪzeɪʃə⁰n/. EG *...the increasing specialisation of working life.* V : OFT+*in* ◇ N UNCOUNT

specialized /spɛʃəlaɪzd/; also spelled **specialised.** Someone or something that is **specialized** is trained or developed for a particular purpose or area of knowledge. EG *...highly specialised staff... ...radar and specialised television systems.* ADJ QUALIT

specially /spɛʃəli¹/. **1** If something has been done **specially** for a particular person or purpose, it has been done only for that person or purpose. EG *...free hotels run by the state specially for tourists... The rules were specially designed to protect travellers.* ADV

2 You also use **specially** to say that something has a particular quality more than average. EG *...a pub where the beer was specially good.* SUBMOD Informal

specialty /spɛʃəlti¹/, **specialties.** A **specialty** is the same as a speciality. EG *...suitable people to practise a specialty in a hospital.* N COUNT American

species /spiːʃiːz/. **Species** is both the singular and the plural form. N COUNT
A **species** is a class of plants or animals whose members have the same main characteristics and are able to breed with each other. EG *There are more than two hundred and fifty species of shark.*

specific /spɪ²sɪfɪk/, **specifics. 1** You use **specific** to refer to a particular fixed area or subject. EG *Education should not be restricted to any one specific age group... On certain specific issues there may be changes of emphasis.* ADJ CLASSIF : ATTRIB

2 If a description is **specific**, it is precise and exact. EG *It was a tooth, a tiger-shark tooth, to be more specific.* ADJ QUALIT

3 Something that is **specific** to a particular thing is connected with that thing only. EG *It's the program that's specific to this problem.* ADJ PRED

4 The **specifics** of a subject are the particular details of it that need to be considered. EG *Let us focus on the specifics of Bengal's life.* N PLURAL

specifically /spɪ²sɪfɪkə⁰li¹/. You use **specifically 1** to emphasize that a particular subject is being considered individually and separately from other things. EG *It is Christianity with which we are specifically concerned.* ADV **2** to indicate that you are stating or describing something precisely and clearly. EG *...the peasant rising in the West of France, in Brittany specifically... The point is specifically made in the following passage.* ADV **3** to emphasize a particular way of describing something. EG *It's a specifically medical problem.* ADV+ADJ

specification /spɛsɪfɪkeɪʃə⁰n/, **specifications.** A **specification** is a requirement which is clearly stated, for example about the necessary features in the design of something. EG *...ships built to merchant ship specifications.* N COUNT

specify /spɛsɪfaɪ/, **specifies, specifying, specified.** If you **specify** something, **1** you state it or describe it precisely. EG *The report specified seven areas where the Government had a responsibility.* V+O

2 you clearly state it as a requirement. EG *The landlord can specify that rent be paid in cash.* V+REPORT OR V+O

specimen /spɛsɪmɪ²n/, **specimens. 1** A **specimen** is a single plant or animal which is an example of a particular species or type and is examined by scientists. EG *The fins of fossil specimens are carefully dissected.* N COUNT

2 A **specimen** of something is an example or small amount of it which gives an idea of what the whole of it is like. EG *...an authentic specimen of the work of Carl Andre.* N COUNT

speck /spɛk/, **specks.** A **speck** is **1** a very small stain, mark, or shape. EG *There was a speck of blood on his collar.* N COUNT **2** a very small piece of a powdery substance. EG *...a tiny speck of dust.* N PART

speckled /spɛkə⁰ld/. A surface that is **speckled** is covered with small marks, spots, or shapes. EG *...a blouse speckled with daisies... ...a speckled thrush.* ADJ CLASSIF : OFT+*with*

specs /spɛks/. Someone's **specs** are their glasses. EG *I've been wearing specs since I was three.* N PLURAL Informal

spectacle /spɛktəkə⁰l/, **spectacles. 1** Someone's **spectacles** are their glasses. N PLURAL Formal

2 A **spectacle** is **2.1** a strange or interesting sight or scene. EG *She stood at the head of the stairs and surveyed the spectacle.* N COUNT **2.2** a grand and impressive event or performance. EG *It was a grand seven-hour spectacle consisting of songs, comedy acts, and acrobatics.* N COUNT OR N UNCOUNT

spectacular /spɛktækjə⁴lə/, **spectaculars. 1** Something that is **spectacular** is very impressive or dramatic. EG *The most spectacular of these extraordinary fossils can be seen in the museum... It was a spectacular jump.* ADJ QUALIT

2 A **spectacular** is a show or a performance which is very grand and impressive. EG *They are to hold a fashion spectacular on Friday with 100 models.* N COUNT+SUPP

spectator /spɛkteɪtə/, **spectators.** A **spectator** is a person who watches something, especially a sporting event. EG *The spectators rose to their feet to pay tribute to an outstanding performance.* N COUNT

spectra /spɛktrə/ is a plural of **spectrum.**

spectre /spɛktə/, **spectres;** spelled **specter** in American English. A **spectre** is **1** a ghost. EG *...dim red spectres with purple eyes.* N COUNT **2** a frightening image or idea which you have in your mind. EG *...the spectre of another world war.* N SING : *the*+N+*of* Literary

spectrum /spɛktrəm/, **spectra** /spɛktrə/ or **spectrums. 1** The **spectrum** is the range of different colours which is produced when light passes through a prism or through a drop of water. A rainbow shows the colours in the spectrum. N SING : *the*+N

2 A **spectrum** is a range of light waves or radio waves within particular frequencies. EG *...the electro-magnetic spectrum... ...the higher energy X-ray spectrum.* N COUNT

3 A **spectrum** of opinions or emotions is a range of different opinions or emotions, especially when one end of the range is considered to be opposite to the other end. EG *They have support at both ends of the political spectrum... We have experienced together the whole spectrum of emotion.* N COUNT : USU SING+SUPP

speculate /spɛkjə^{4}leɪt/, **speculates, speculating, speculated.** 1 If you **speculate** about something, you think about it together with all its possible aspects or effects. EG *It is natural for us to speculate about the reasons for their visits... Industry sources speculated that the least expensive model will be priced at £7000.* ◊ **speculation** /spɛkjə^{4}leɪʃə^{0}n/, **speculations**. EG *The papers are full of speculation about who is likely to be the next prime minister.* [V : USU +about/on OR REPORT; ◊ N UNCOUNT OR N COUNT]

2 If someone **speculates** financially, they buy property, stocks, or shares, in the hope of being able to sell them again at a higher price and make a profit. EG *She speculated successfully on the stock exchange.* [V]

speculative /spɛkjə^{4}lətɪv/. 1 A piece of information that is **speculative** is based on speculation rather than knowledge. EG *Budgets and profit forecasts were equally speculative.* [ADJ QUALIT]

2 Someone who has a **speculative** expression seems to be trying to guess what someone or something is like. EG *He looked at me with an oddly speculative glint in his eyes.* [ADJ QUALIT : ATTRIB]

3 **Speculative** is used to describe activities which involve buying goods or shares in the hope of being able to sell them again at a higher price and make a profit. EG *...speculative aircraft projects... ...speculative builders.* [ADJ CLASSIF : ATTRIB]

speculator /spɛkjə^{4}leɪtə/, **speculators.** A **speculator** is a person who speculates financially. [N COUNT]

sped /spɛd/ is a past tense and past participle of **speed.**

speech /spiːtʃ/, **speeches. 1 Speech** is **1.1** the ability to speak or the act of speaking. EG *She was so shocked that she lost her powers of speech.* **1.2** spoken language. EG *In ordinary speech we often shorten the word 'cannot' to 'can't'. ...communication through writing and speech.* [N UNCOUNT]

2 A **speech** is **2.1** a formal talk which someone gives to an audience. EG *Mr Macmillan presented the prizes and made a speech on the importance of education.* **2.2** a group of lines spoken by a character in a play. EG *She recited a speech from 'As You Like It'.* [N COUNT]

3 Your **speech** is the way in which you speak. EG *I detected a slight Brooklyn accent in her speech.* [N SING+POSS]

4 The **speech** of a particular country or region is the language or dialect spoken in that country or region. EG *He can mimic Cockney speech quite well.* [N UNCOUNT +SUPP]

speechless /spiːtʃlɪ^{2}s/. If you are **speechless**, you are temporarily unable to speak, usually because something has shocked you. EG *She was speechless with astonishment.* [ADJ CLASSIF]

speed /spiːd/, **speeds, speeding, sped** /spɛd/, **speeded.** The past tense and past participle is **sped** in paragraph 3, but **speeded** for the phrasal verb.

1 The **speed** of something is **1.1** the rate at which it moves or travels. EG *I drove at great speed to West Bank... ...capable of reaching speeds of over 110kph.* **1.2** the rate at which it happens or is done. EG *None of us grows at the same speed.* [N UNCOUNT +SUPP OR N COUNT; N UNCOUNT OR N COUNT]

2 **Speed** is **2.1** very fast movement or travel. EG *The train gathered speed... The car is travelling at speed.* **2.2** a very fast rate at which something happens or is done. EG *...a room of busy journalists typing at speed.* [N UNCOUNT]

3 If you **speed** somewhere, you move or travel there quickly, usually in a vehicle. EG *They sped along Main Street towards the highway.* [V+A]

4 Someone who **is speeding** is driving a car or other vehicle faster than the legal speed limit. EG *They said you were speeding.* ◊ **speeding.** EG *His driver's licence was suspended for speeding.* [V : ONLY CONT; ◊ N UNCOUNT]

speed up. 1 When something **speeds up** or when you **speed** it **up**, its speed increases so that it moves or travels faster. EG *They're way ahead of us. Speed up!* **2** When a process or activity **speeds up** or when something **speeds** it **up**, it happens at a faster rate. EG *Africa's population growth speeded up... Warmth speeds up chemical reactions.* [PHRASAL VB : V-ERG+ADV; V-ERG+ADV]

speed limit, speed limits. The **speed limit** on a road is the maximum speed at which you are legally allowed to drive a vehicle on that road. [N COUNT : USU SING]

speedometer /spiˈdɒmɪtə/, **speedometers.** A **speedometer** is an instrument in a vehicle which shows how fast the vehicle is moving. See picture at CAR. [N COUNT]

speedy /spiːdi^{1}/. A **speedy** action happens or is done very quickly. EG *A speedy settlement of the strike is essential.* ◊ **speedily**. EG *Such doubts were now speedily removed.* [ADJ QUALIT; ◊ ADV]

spell /spɛl/, **spells, spelling, spelled, spelt** /spɛlt/. The forms **spelled** and **spelt** are both used as the past tense and past participle of the verb.

1 When you **spell** a word, you write or speak each letter in the word in the correct order. EG *'My name is Khulaifi. Shall I spell that for you?'... Bauxite is spelt B A U X I T E... Ninety per cent of the words were spelt wrong.* [V+O]

2 Someone who can **spell** knows the correct order of letters in most words. [V]

3 If something **spells** a particular result, often an unpleasant one, it suggests that this will be the result. EG *Nuclear conflict would spell the end of life as we know it... Any discussion of politics would spell disaster.* [V+C : NO CONT]

4 A **spell** of a particular activity or type of weather is a short period of time during which this activity or type of weather occurs. EG *...a spell of good summer weather... She had a spell as editor.* [N COUNT : USU+SUPP]

5 A **spell** is also **5.1** a situation in which events are controlled by a magical power. EG *The spell of the wicked fairy was broken.* **5.2** a sequence of words used to perform magic. [N COUNT]

6 If you are **under** someone's **spell**, you are so fascinated by them that you cannot think about anything else. EG *The people on the stage were completely under his spell.* [PHRASE]

7 See also **spelling**.

spell out. 1 If you **spell** something **out**, you explain it in detail or in a very clear way. EG *Let me try and spell out what I mean by that.* **2** If you **spell out** a word, you write or speak each letter in the word in the correct order. EG *We had to spell out the words we heard.* [PHRASAL VB : V+O+ADV; V+O+ADV]

spellbound /spɛlbaʊnd/. If you are **spellbound**, you are so fascinated by something that you cannot think about anything else. EG *We were all spellbound as we listened to her.* [ADJ CLASSIF : USU PRED]

spelling /spɛlɪŋ/, **spellings. 1** A **spelling** is the correct order of the letters in a word. EG *They were given twenty spellings to learn.* [N COUNT]

2 **Spelling** is the ability to spell words in the correct way, or the way that words are spelt. EG *I'm terrible at spelling... In this language the pronunciation has changed over the centuries but the spelling has not.* [N UNCOUNT]

spelt /spɛlt/ is a past tense and past participle of **spell.**

spend /spɛnd/, **spends, spending, spent** /spɛnt/.

1 When you **spend** money, you pay money for things that you want. EG *We always spend a lot of money on parties... The buildings need a lot of money spent on them.* • to **spend a penny**: see **penny**. [V+O : OFT+*on*, OR V]

2 If you **spend** time somewhere or energy doing something, you pass the time there or use your energy doing it. EG *He spent most of his time in the library... She woke early, meaning to spend all day writing.* [V+O+A]

3 See also **spent**.

Where would you find a spine?

spending /spendɪŋ/ is payment of large amounts of money for public services by a government or other organization. EG *City departments must reduce their spending by £35 million before July 1st... ...government spending cuts.* N UNCOUNT

spent /spent/. **1 Spent** is the past tense and past participle of **spend**.

2 Spent is used to describe something that has already been used and cannot be used again. EG *It will take several seconds to extract the spent cartridge and insert a fresh one... ...spent matches.* ADJ CLASSIF : USU ATTRIB

sperm /spɜːm/, **sperms. Sperm** can also be used as the plural form. N COUNT

A **sperm** is a cell which is produced in the sex organs of a male animal and can enter a female animal's egg and fertilize it.

spew /spjuː/, **spews, spewing, spewed.** When things **spew** from something or when it **spews** them out, the things come out of it in large quantities. EG *Its cargo of canned goods had spewed out... Coal-burning factories spewed dense dirty smoke.* V-ERG : OFT+A

sphere /sfɪə/, **spheres. 1** A **sphere** is an object that is perfectly round in shape like a ball. N COUNT

2 A **sphere** of activity or interest is a particular area of activity or interest. EG *Apart from photography, he has several other spheres of interest... He works in the sphere of race relations.* N COUNT+SUPP

3 A **sphere** of people is a group of them who are similar in social status or who have the same interests. EG *...mixing in the academic sphere.* N COUNT

spherical /sferɪkəˀl/. Something that is **spherical** has the shape of a sphere. EG *The world is spherical... ...the red, spherical berries.* ADJ CLASSIF

spice /spaɪs/, **spices, spicing, spiced. 1 Spice** is powder or seeds from a plant, which you put in food to give it flavour. Cinnamon, ginger, and paprika are spices. N COUNT OR N UNCOUNT

2 When you **spice** food, you add spice to it. EG *Take the peas and butter and spice them with nutmeg.* V+O : OFT+*with*
◇ **spiced.** EG *The soup was heavily spiced.* ◇ ADJ CLASSIF

3 If you **spice** something that you do or say, or if you **spice** it **up**, you add excitement or liveliness to it. EG *His speech was spiced with anti-imperialist sentiment.* V+O OR V+O+*up*

4 Spice is something which makes life more exciting. EG *Variety is the spice of life.* N UNCOUNT

spicy /spaɪsiˡ/, **spicier, spiciest. Spicy** food is strongly flavoured with spices. EG *...a spicy sauce.* ADJ QUALIT

spider /spaɪdə/, **spiders.** A **spider** is a small creature with eight legs. Some types of spider make webs. EG *She had a spider on her leg.* N COUNT

spidery /spaɪdəriˡ/. **Spidery** handwriting consists of thin, angular lines and is hard to read. EG *...faded, spidery writing that he could not read.* ADJ QUALIT : ATTRIB

spike /spaɪk/, **spikes. 1** A **spike** is a long piece of metal with a sharp point. EG *Their heads were cut off and impaled on spikes.* ◇ **spiked** /spaɪkt/. EG *...spiked shoes.* N COUNT ◇ ADJ CLASSIF

2 Any long, pointed object can be referred to as a **spike**. EG *The plant bears spikes of greenish flowers.* N COUNT

spiky /spaɪkiˡ/. Something that is **spiky** has sharp points. EG *...a tiny man with spiky hair... The shrub has spiky green leaves.* ADJ QUALIT : ATTRIB

spill /spɪl/, **spills, spilling, spilled, spilt** /spɪlt/. The forms **spilled** and **spilt** are both used as the past participle and past tense of the verb.

1 If you **spill** a liquid or if it **spills**, it accidentally flows over the edge of a container. EG *She carried the bucket without spilling a drop... Make sure the water doesn't spill over the floor.* V-ERG

2 If people or things **spill** out of a place, they come out of it in large numbers. EG *Crowds started spilling out of bars.* V+A

3 to **spill the beans**: see **bean**.

spin /spɪn/, **spins, spinning, spun** /spʌn/. **1** If something **spins** or if you **spin** it, it turns quickly around a central point. EG *The football went spinning into the canal... He spun the chair round to face the desk.* V-ERG : USU+A

2 When you **spin** washing, it is turned round and round quickly in a spin drier or a washing machine to get the water out. V+O

3 If your head **is spinning**, you feel dizzy because you are excited, ill, or drunk. EG *His head was spinning from wine and liqueurs.* V : USU CONT

4 When people **spin**, they make thread by twisting together pieces of fibre using a device or machine. EG *My mother taught me to spin.* V OR V+O

spin out. If you **spin** something **out**, you make it last longer than it otherwise would. EG *I might be able to spin my talk out to three-quarters of an hour.* PHRASAL VB : V+O+ADV

spinach /spɪnɪdʒ, -ɪtʃ/ is a kind of vegetable with large green leaves. N UNCOUNT

spinal /spaɪnəˀl/ means relating to your spine. EG *...the spinal joints... ...a spinal injury.* ADJ CLASSIF : ATTRIB

spinal column, spinal columns. Your **spinal column** is your spine. N COUNT Formal

spinal cord, spinal cords. Your **spinal cord** is a bundle of nerves inside your spine which connects your brain to nerves in all parts of your body. N COUNT

spindly /spɪndliˡ/. Something that is **spindly** is long and thin and looks very weak. EG *...spindly legs... ...spindly trees.* ADJ QUALIT

spin drier, spin driers; also spelled **spin dryer.** A **spin drier** is a machine that is used to spin washing to get the water out. N COUNT

spin-dry, spin-dries, spin-drying, spin-dried. When you **spin-dry** washing, you get the water out of it using a spin drier or a washing machine. V+O

spine /spaɪn/, **spines. 1** Your **spine** is the row of bones down your back. EG *...pressure on the spine... A bullet penetrated his spine.* N COUNT

2 The **spine** of a book is the narrow stiff part which the pages and covers are attached to. N COUNT

3 Spines are also long, sharp points on an animal's body or on a plant. EG *...a cactus with red spines.* N COUNT

spineless /spaɪnlɪ²s/. If you say that someone is **spineless**, you mean that they are cowardly. EG *I think they're a spineless pair... Oh, you're so spineless.* ADJ QUALIT

spin-off, spin-offs. A **spin-off** is something useful that unexpectedly results from an activity that was designed to achieve something else. EG *The search for knowledge frequently has beneficial spin-offs for mankind.* N COUNT OR N UNCOUNT

spinster /spɪnstə/, **spinsters.** A **spinster** is a woman who has never been married, especially an old or middle-aged woman. N COUNT Outdated Formal

spiral /spaɪərəˀl/, **spirals, spiralling, spiralled;** spelled **spiraling** and **spiraled** in American English. **1** A **spiral** is a curved shape which winds round and round, with each curve above the previous one or outside it. ▸ used as an adjective. EG *We followed him up the spiral staircase... ...an antelope with spiral horns.* N COUNT ▸ ADJ CLASSIF : ATTRIB

2 If something **spirals**, it moves up or down in a spiral curve. EG *The swans came spiralling down... A small bird shot up, spiralling into the sky.* V+A

3 If an amount or level **spirals**, it rises quickly and at an increasing rate. EG *Military budgets had continued to spiral.* ▸ used as a noun. EG *...a wage and price spiral.* V ▸ N SING

4 If an amount or level **spirals** downwards, it falls quickly and at an increasing rate. EG *Costs started to spiral downwards.* ▸ used as a noun. EG *Industry entered a spiral of decline.* V+A ▸ N SING+SUPP

spire /spaɪə/, **spires.** The **spire** of a church is the tall cone-shaped structure on the top. N COUNT

spirit /spɪrɪt/, **spirits, spiriting, spirited. 1** Your **spirit** is the part of you that is not physical and that is connected with your deepest thoughts and feelings. EG *Fulfilment must be sought through the spirit, not the body or the mind.* N SING

2 The **spirit** of a dead person is a non-physical part N COUNT of them that is believed to remain alive after their death. EG *We pray to our dead ancestors' spirits.*

3 A **spirit** is also a supernatural being. EG *The charm is worn to ward off evil spirits.* N COUNT

4 **Spirit** is liveliness, energy, and self-confidence. EG *...a performance full of spirit and originality.* N UNCOUNT

5 You can use **spirit** to refer to a particular kind of attitude. EG *...the pioneering spirit... He made the proposal in a spirit of rebellion... Governments must approach this subject in a new spirit.* N SING+SUPP

6 If you **enter into the spirit of** an activity or event, you take part in it in an enthusiastic way. EG *Try to enter into the spirit of the thing.* PHRASE

7 You can refer to your **spirits** when saying how happy or unhappy you are. For example, if your spirits are high, you are happy. EG *The children lifted my spirits with their laughter.* N PLURAL +SUPP

8 The **spirit** of a law or an agreement is the way that it was intended to be interpreted or applied. EG *I think we'd be breaking the spirit of the agreement if we went ahead.* N SING : *the*+N+*of*

9 **Spirits** are strong alcoholic drinks such as whisky and gin. EG *They brought with them several bottles of spirits.* N PLURAL

10 If you **spirit** someone out of a place or **spirit** them into it, you get them out of it or into it quickly and secretly. EG *Somehow the Action Service had spirited him across the frontier.* V+O+A

11 See also **white spirit**.

spirited /spɪrɪtɪ¹d/. A **spirited** action shows great energy and courage. EG *Despite spirited resistance by Republican forces, the town fell to the Nationalists... ...spirited discussions.* ● See also **high-spirited, public-spirited.** ADJ QUALIT

spiritual /spɪrɪtʃuºəl/ means 1 relating to people's deepest thoughts and beliefs, rather than to their bodies and physical surroundings. EG *...people's pursuit of material ends to the neglect of their spiritual needs.* ADJ CLASSIF ◊ **spiritually**. EG *...a spiritually sick society.* ◊ ADV ◊ **spirituality** /spɪrɪtjuælɪ¹ti¹/. EG *...the decline of spirituality in our time.* ◊ N UNCOUNT 2 relating to people's religious beliefs. EG *...the spiritual authority of the Christian Church.* ADJ CLASSIF

spit /spɪt/, **spits, spitting, spat** /spæt/. **Spit** is used as the past tense of the verb in American English.

1 **Spit** is the watery liquid produced in your mouth. You usually use **spit** to refer to an amount of it that has been forced out of someone's mouth. N UNCOUNT

2 When people **spit**, they force an amount of spit out of their mouth, sometimes in order to show hatred or scorn. EG *The driver spat contemptuously.* V

3 If you **spit** liquid or food somewhere, you force a small amount of it out of your mouth. EG *If I don't like it I can always spit it out.* V+O : USU+A

4 When people say something in an angry or hostile way, you can say that they **spit** it **out**. EG *He spat out his answer.* V+O : OFT+QUOTE OR V+O+*out*

5 If it is raining very lightly, you can say that it **is spitting**. EG *'Is it raining?' – 'Only spitting.'* V : ONLY CONT

6 A **spit** is a long rod which is pushed through a piece of meat and hung over an open fire while the meat is roasted. EG *There was still food left on the wooden spits.* N COUNT

7 If you say that someone is **the spitting image of** another person, you mean that they look very like that other person. EG *She was the spitting image of his mother.* PHRASE

spite /spaɪt/. 1 You use **in spite of** to introduce a statement which makes what you have just said seem surprising. EG *The morning air was still clear and fresh, in spite of all the traffic... In spite of poor health, my father was always cheerful.* PREP

2 If you do something **in spite of** yourself, you do it although you did not really intend to or expect to. EG *Jane became edgy in spite of herself.* PREP

3 If you do something nasty because of **spite**, you do it deliberately because you want to hurt or upset someone. EG *He wrote that review out of pure spite.* N UNCOUNT

4 If you do something nasty to **spite** someone, you do it deliberately in order to hurt or annoy them. EG *They are being controversial just to spite us.* V+O : ONLY INF

5 If you **cut off** your **nose to spite** your **face**, you deliberately do something that you think will hurt someone, without realizing or caring that it will hurt you as well. PHRASE

spiteful /spaɪtfʊl/. Someone who is **spiteful** does nasty things to people they dislike. EG *Thomas could be so spiteful to his little brother... They told spiteful stories about her.* ADJ QUALIT

spittle /spɪtəºl/ is the watery liquid which is produced in your mouth. N UNCOUNT Outdated

splash /splæʃ/, **splashes, splashing, splashed. 1** If you **splash** around in water, you hit or disturb the water in a noisy way, causing some of it to fly up into the air. EG *Ralph started to run, splashing through the shallow water... They proceeded to hurl themselves about, splashing everybody within sight.* V+A OR V+O

2 If water **splashes** on something or **splashes** something, it hits it and scatters in a lot of small drops. EG *Drenching spray splashed over the deck... They flinched as the cold rain splashed them.* V+A OR V+O

3 If you **splash** a liquid somewhere, you pour or throw it there rather carelessly. EG *He splashed his face with water... Otto splashed some brandy into a glass.* V+O+A

4 A **splash** is the sound made when something hits water or falls into it. EG *She disappeared into the water with a splash.* N COUNT

5 A **splash** of a liquid is a small quantity of it that has been spilt on something. EG *He wiped away the splash of gasoline on the near fender.* N PART OR N COUNT

6 A **splash** of colour is an area of a bright colour which contrasts strongly with the colours around it. EG *A large bouquet of tulips made a brilliant splash of yellow on the table.* N PART

splash out. If you **splash out** on something, especially on a luxury, you buy it even though it costs a lot of money. EG *We splashed out on a colour television.* PHRASAL VB : V+ADV, OFT+*on* Informal

splatter /splætə/, **splatters, splattering, splattered.** If a thick wet substance **is splattered** on something or **splatters** on it, it is splashed or thrown over it. EG *Food was splattered all over the kitchen walls... She was wearing an apron splattered with blood.* V-ERG : USU+A

splay /spleɪ/, **splays, splaying, splayed.** If two or more things **are splayed** or **splay** out, their ends are spread out away from each other. EG *He pressed the mattress with splayed fingers... The brush's bristles were beginning to splay out.* V-ERG : OFT+*out*

splendid /splɛndɪd/. **1** If you say that something is **splendid**, you mean that it is excellent. EG *She wrote splendid detective novels... I think it's a splendid idea... I thought life was simply splendid.* ADJ QUALIT ◊ **splendidly**. EG *She was caring for him splendidly.* ◊ ADV

2 If you say that a building or work of art is **splendid**, you mean that it is beautiful and impressive. EG *...splendid seventeenth-century paintings... In the middle of Hull stands a splendid Victorian building.* ADJ QUALIT ◊ **splendidly**. EG *...a splendidly furnished room.* ◊ ADV

splendour /splɛndə/, **splendours;** spelled **splendor** in American English. **1** If you talk about the **splendour** of something, you are referring to the fact that it is beautiful and impressive. EG *...the splendour of Urbino... The room was decorated with great splendour.* N UNCOUNT

2 The **splendours** of something are its beautiful N PLURAL

If you splash out on a new coat, do you get it wet?

and impressive features. EG *...the Elizabethan splendours of Watermouth Hall.*

splint /splɪnt/, **splints.** A **splint** is a long piece of wood or metal that is fastened to a broken arm, leg, or back. N COUNT

splinter /splɪntə/, **splinters, splintering, splintered. 1** A **splinter** is a very thin, sharp piece of wood, glass, or other hard substance, which has broken off from a larger piece. EG *...splinters of coloured glass... Sue was worried about splinters in her bare feet.* N COUNT

2 If something **splinters** or **is splintered**, it breaks into thin, sharp pieces. EG *When feeding dogs, avoid chicken, rabbit or fish bones which can splinter... ...the splintered wood of a snapped plank.* V-ERG

3 A **splinter** group or organization is a group of people who break away from a larger group and form a separate organization. ADJ CLASSIF : ATTRIB

split /splɪt/, **splits, splitting.** The form **split** is used in the present tense and is the past tense and past participle of the verb.

1 If something **splits** or if you **split** it, it is divided into two or more parts. EG *Three people died when their car split in two after hitting a tree... Main roads like motorways can split communities in half... The children were split into two groups.* V-ERG

2 If an organization **splits** or **is split**, one group of members disagree strongly with the other members. EG *The council split down the middle over the issue... The government is split on how to deal with the situation.* ▸ used as a noun. EG *The last thing he wanted was a split in the party.* V-ERG; ▸ N COUNT : USU+*in*

3 A **split** between two things is a division or difference between them. EG *He experiences a split between his thoughts and his actions... ...the split between reality and the perception of it.* N COUNT : USU SING+*between*

4 If something such as wood or a piece of clothing **splits** or **is split**, a long crack or tear appears in it. EG *It was a very poor quality wood which had already split in many places.* ▸ used as an adjective. EG *Eric fingered his split lip.* V-ERG; ▸ ADJ CLASSIF

5 A **split** is also a long crack or tear. EG *There's a split down the page of the atlas.* N COUNT

6 If two or more people **split** something, they share it between them. EG *The profits are to be split fifty-fifty between the two of them.* V+O

7 If you **split the difference**, you agree on a figure which is halfway between the two different figures that have been mentioned. EG *Okay, we'll split the difference and call it £10.* PHRASE

8 to **split hairs**: see **hair**. ● See also **splitting**.

split off. If part of something **splits off** or **is split off** from the main part of it, it breaks off or is broken or cut off. EG *A particle splits off from the nucleus... A block had been split off from the rock.* PHRASAL VB : V-ERG+ADV

split up. 1 If two people **split up**, they end their relationship or marriage. EG *Howard and I have split up... They are more likely to split up and less likely to remarry... After he split up with his wife he went to Arizona.* PHRASAL VB : V+ADV OR V+ADV+*with* : RECIP **2** If a group of people **split up**, they go away in different directions. EG *In Hamburg the girls split up.* V+ADV **3** If you **split** something **up**, you divide it so that it is in a number of smaller separate sections. EG *You might achieve more by splitting them up into small groups.* V+O+ADV, USU+*into*

split second. You can refer to a very short period of time as a **split second**. EG *For a split second nothing happened... She has to make split-second decisions.* N SING

splitting /splɪtɪŋ/. A **splitting** headache is a very severe one. ADJ CLASSIF : ATTRIB

splutter /splʌtə/, **splutters, spluttering, spluttered. 1** If someone **splutters**, they make spitting sounds and have difficulty speaking clearly. EG *The fumes make you cough and splutter... 'I know them. They're my friends,' I was spluttering.* ▸ used as a noun. EG *'Of course not,' she said with a splutter of mirth.* V OR V+QUOTE; ▸ N COUNT : USU SING

2 If something **splutters**, it makes a series of short, sharp sounds. EG *...the roaring and spluttering of motorbikes.* V

spoil /spɔɪl/, **spoils, spoiling, spoiled, spoilt** /spɔɪlt/. The past participle can be either **spoiled** or **spoilt**.

1 If you **spoil** something, you prevent it from being successful or satisfactory. EG *She shouted at him for spoiling her lovely evening... The presence of the woman spoiled his enjoyment of the view.* V+O

2 If you **spoil** children, you give them everything they want or ask for, which has a bad effect on their character. EG *You're spoiling him, Frieda.* ◊ **spoilt** or **spoiled.** EG *...a spoilt brat.* V+O; ◊ ADJ QUALIT

3 If you **spoil** yourself or **spoil** someone you love, you give yourself or them something nice as a treat. EG *During the first week of the diet, you can spoil yourself a little.* V-REFL OR V+O

4 Spoils are things that people get as a result of winning a battle or of doing something else successfully. EG *...the spoils of war.* N PLURAL : *the*+N Literary

spoil for. If you **are spoiling for** trouble or a fight, you are very eager for it to happen. EG *The unions are spoiling for a fight about pay and conditions once again.* PHRASAL VB : V+PREP, ONLY CONT

spoke /spəʊk/, **spokes. 1 Spoke** is the past tense of **speak**.

2 The **spokes** of a wheel are the bars that connect the outer ring to the centre. See picture at BICYCLE. EG *Her baby caught his fingers in the spokes of the pram wheel.* N COUNT : USU PLURAL

spoken /spəʊkə⁰n/ is the past participle of **speak.** ● See also **well-spoken**.

spokesman /spəʊksmə³n/, **spokesmen.** A **spokesman** is a person who speaks as the representative of a group or organization. EG *Common Market spokesmen claim that more than 800,000 jobs have been lost recently.* N COUNT

spokesperson /spəʊkspɜːsə⁰n/, **spokespersons.** A **spokesperson** is the same as a spokesman. EG *...the spokesperson for the delegation.* N COUNT

spokeswoman /spəʊkswʊmən/, **spokeswomen.** A **spokeswoman** is a female spokesman. EG *'They are staying here as guests of the Queen,' said a Palace spokeswoman.* N COUNT

sponge /spʌndʒ/, **sponges, sponging, sponged. 1** A **sponge** is a piece of a squashy, absorbent substance with lots of little holes in it that you use for cleaning things or washing your body. EG *Wipe the surface with a clean sponge.* N COUNT OR N UNCOUNT

2 If you **sponge** something, you clean it by wiping it with a wet sponge. EG *Don't immerse it in water; just sponge it lightly.* V+O

3 A **sponge** is also a light cake or pudding made from flour, eggs, sugar, and sometimes fat. EG *...baked apple with a layer of sponge on top.* N COUNT OR N UNCOUNT

sponge off or **sponge on.** Someone who **sponges off** other people or **sponges on** them regularly gets money from them without giving anything in return; used showing disapproval. EG *He sponged on his friends.* PHRASAL VB : V+PREP Informal

spongebag /spʌnd⁰ʒbæg/, **spongebags.** A **spongebag** is a small bag in which you keep things such as soap, a flannel, and a toothbrush when you are travelling. N COUNT British

spongy /spʌndʒi¹/. Something that is **spongy** is soft and squashy, like a sponge. EG *...spongy bread.* ADJ QUALIT

sponsor /spɒnsə/, **sponsors, sponsoring, sponsored. 1** If people or organizations **sponsor** something such as an event or someone's training, they pay some or all of the expenses connected with it, often in order to get publicity for themselves. EG *The Administration is sponsoring a research programme... The conference was sponsored by the Guardian.* V+O

2 If you **sponsor** someone who is doing something to raise money for charity, for example running a marathon, you agree to give them a sum of money for the charity if they succeed in doing it. EG *Would* V+O you mind sponsoring me in this swim for cancer research... A sponsored walk brought in £16000.*

3 If you **sponsor** a proposal or suggestion, you officially put it forward and support it. EG *Two Liberal MPs sponsored the Bill.* V+O

4 A **sponsor** is a person or organization that sponsors something or someone. EG *...the sponsor of the lectures... ...Virginia Slims, sponsors of the first professional women's tennis tour.* N COUNT

sponsorship /spɒnsəʃɪp/ is financial support that is given to someone by a sponsor. EG *...industrial sponsorship of the arts.* N UNCOUNT

spontaneity /spɒntəniːɪ[1]ti[1], -neɪ-/ is spontaneous, natural behaviour. EG *...a child's spontaneity.* N UNCOUNT

spontaneous /spɒnteɪnɪəs/. **1 Spontaneous** acts are not planned or arranged, but are done because someone suddenly wants to do them. EG *...a spontaneous display of friendship and affection.* ADJ QUALIT

◇ **spontaneously**. EG *Flo and I decided spontaneously to board a train for Geneva.* ◇ ADV

2 A **spontaneous** event happens because of processes within something rather than being caused by things outside it. EG *...spontaneous explosions.* ADJ QUALIT

◇ **spontaneously**. EG *The fuel ignites spontaneously from the heat created by the compression.* ◇ ADV

spoof /spuːf/, **spoofs.** A **spoof** is something such as an article or television programme that seems to be about a serious matter but is actually a joke. EG *The weather forecast seemed to be some kind of spoof, predicting every possible combination of weather.* N COUNT

spooky /spuːki[1]/, **spookier, spookiest.** A place that is **spooky** has a frightening atmosphere, and makes you feel that there are ghosts around. EG *The Highlands are unbearably spooky... The whole place had a slightly spooky atmosphere.* ADJ QUALIT Informal

spool /spuːl/, **spools.** A **spool** is a round object onto which thread, tape, or film can be wound, especially before it is put in a sewing machine, tape recorder, or projector. EG *She re-wound the tape back on to the spool.* N COUNT

spoon /spuːn/, **spoons, spooning, spooned. 1** A **spoon** is an object used for eating, stirring, and serving food. It is shaped like a small shallow bowl with a long handle. EG *...a knife, fork, and spoon.* N COUNT

2 You can use **spoon** to refer to the amount of a substance that a spoon can hold, as in a **spoon** of sugar or a **spoon** of salt. EG *He takes six spoons of sugar in his tea.* N PART

3 If you **spoon** food somewhere, you pick the food up in a spoon and put it there. EG *He spooned the vegetables onto the plates.* V+O : USU+A

spoonful /spuːnfʊl/, **spoonfuls.** A **spoonful** of a substance is the amount that a spoon can hold. EG *She put a spoonful of milk in each of the two cups.* N PART

sporadic /spə[7]rædɪk/. **Sporadic** occurrences of something happen at irregular intervals. EG *...sporadic glimpses of truth... Sporadic attacks continued throughout the night.* ◇ **sporadically**. EG *Most families watch television sporadically.* ADJ QUALIT ◇ ADV

spore /spɔː/, **spores. Spores** are cells produced by bacteria and non-flowering plants such as fungi which can develop into new bacteria and plants. N COUNT Technical

sport /spɔːt/, **sports, sporting, sported. 1 Sports** are games such as football and cricket and other enjoyable activities which need physical effort and skill. EG *My favourite sport is football... I was bad at sport... ...a sports reporter.* N UNCOUNT OR N COUNT

2 If you say that someone is a **sport** or a good **sport**, you mean that they accept defeat or teasing in a cheerful way. EG *Be a sport, Madeleine.* N COUNT Outdated

3 If you **sport** something noticeable or unusual, you wear it. EG *He sported a beard... One of them even sported an earring.* V+O

sporting /spɔːtɪŋ/ means relating to sport or used for sport. EG *It was his 29th international sporting event... ...a new sporting gun.* ADJ CLASSIF : ATTRIB

sports car, sports cars. A **sports car** is a low, fast car, usually with room for only two people. N COUNT

sports jacket, sports jackets. A **sports jacket** is a man's jacket, usually made of tweed. N COUNT

sportsman /spɔːtsmə[3]n/, **sportsmen.** A **sportsman** is a man who takes part in sports. N COUNT

sportswoman /spɔːtswʊmən/, **sportswomen.** A **sportswoman** is a woman who takes part in sports. EG *She is an enthusiastic sportswoman.* N COUNT

spot /spɒt/, **spots, spotting, spotted. 1 Spots** are small, round, coloured areas on a surface. EG *She was wearing a white blouse with red spots.* N COUNT

2 Spots on a person's skin are small lumps or marks, caused, for example, by a disease. EG *Their bites leave itching red spots on the skin.* N COUNT

3 A **spot** of a substance is a small amount of it. EG *I think there's a spot of ketchup on the tablecloth... I felt a few spots of rain.* N COUNT OR N PART

4 If you have a **spot** of something, you have a small amount of it. EG *He invited them down for a spot of grouse-shooting... What about a spot of lunch?* N PART Informal

5 You can refer to a particular place as a **spot**. EG *It's a lovely spot for a picnic... Four brass plates in the floor mark the spot where the throne stood.* N COUNT : USU+SUPP

6 A **spot** in a television or radio show is a part of it that is regularly reserved for a particular performer or type of entertainment. EG *She's going to do a guest spot on the Muppet Show.* N COUNT : USU+SUPP

7 If you **spot** something, you notice it. EG *I spotted you standing by your car at the gas station.* V+O

8 On the spot is used in these ways. **8.1** If you are **on the spot**, you are at the actual place where something is happening. EG *Certain decisions had to be taken by the man on the spot.* **8.2** If you do something **on the spot**, you do it immediately. EG *They dismissed him on the spot.* **8.3** If you **put** someone **on the spot**, you cause them to have to answer a difficult question or make a difficult decision. EG *I think you've put him on the spot there.* PHRASES

9 to **have a soft spot for** someone: see **soft**. ● See also **blind spot**, **spotted**.

spot check, spot checks. A **spot check** is a random inspection of one thing among a group of things. N COUNT

spotless /spɒtlɪ[2]s/. Something that is **spotless** is perfectly clean. EG *...a spotless white shirt.* ADJ QUALIT

spotlight /spɒtlaɪt/, **spotlights, spotlighting, spotlighted. 1** A **spotlight** is a powerful light, often in a theatre, which can be directed so that it lights up a small area. EG *A spotlight threw a pool of light onto the stage.* N COUNT

2 Someone or something that is in the **spotlight** is getting a great deal of public attention. EG *I was inevitably the man in the spotlight... This incident turned the spotlight on Trent's discoveries.* N SING : *the*+N

spot-on means exactly correct or accurate. EG *You can use this weapon at 130 metres with spot-on accuracy.* ADJ CLASSIF Informal

spotted /spɒtɪ[2]d/. Something that is **spotted** has a pattern of spots on it. EG *...a red and white spotted handkerchief.* ADJ CLASSIF

spotty /spɒti[1]/. Someone who is **spotty** has spots or pimples on their skin, especially on their face. EG *...spotty adolescents.* ADJ QUALIT

spouse /spaʊs, spaʊz/, **spouses.** Someone's **spouse** is the person they are married to. EG *They receive free membership for themselves and their spouses.* N COUNT Formal

spout /spaʊt/, **spouts, spouting, spouted. 1** When liquid or flame **spouts** out of something, it comes out very fast in a long stream. EG *...jets of water spouting up from the basins below... Their tanks came on in hordes, spouting flames.* V-ERG : USU+A

2 If you say that someone **is spouting** something, you mean that they are saying something that they have learned and that they are saying it in a boring V+O OR V+*about*

What is the difference between spotted and spotty?

way. EG *You were always spouting some theory to us at the table.*

3 The **spout** of a kettle or teapot is the tube that the liquid comes out of when you pour it. N COUNT

sprain /spreɪn/, **sprains, spraining, sprained. 1** If you **sprain** a joint such as your ankle or wrist, you accidentally damage it by twisting it or bending it violently. EG *Rosa fell and sprained her ankle.* V+O

2 A **sprain** is the injury caused by spraining a joint. N COUNT

sprang /spræŋ/ is the past tense of **spring.**

sprawl /sprɔːl/, **sprawls, sprawling, sprawled.**

1 If you **sprawl** somewhere, you sit or lie down with your legs and arms spread out in a careless way. EG *Segal sprawled out on the couch... I tried to pick it up, but I overbalanced and fell sprawling.* V : OFT+*out*

2 If you say that a place **sprawls**, you mean that it covers a large area of land. EG *The village sprawls along the coastline... The university sprawls across the Lenin Hills.* ◇ **sprawling.** EG *...a large, sprawling villa... ...a sprawling city.* V+A; ◇ ADJ QUALIT

3 You can use **sprawl** to refer to an area where a city has expanded in an untidy and uncontrolled way. EG *The new towns were to bring an end to London's urban sprawl.* N UNCOUNT +SUPP

sprawled /sprɔːld/. If you are **sprawled** somewhere, you are sitting or lying with your legs and arms spread out in a careless way. EG *He lay sprawled in the chair with his legs stretched out.* ADJ PRED+A

spray /spreɪ/, **sprays, spraying, sprayed.**

1 Spray is a lot of small drops of water which are being splashed or forced into the air. EG *Drenching spray splashed over the deck... A spray of salt water hit her in the face... ...clouds of spray.* N UNCOUNT OR PART

2 A **spray** is a liquid kept under pressure in a can or other container, which you can force out in very small drops. EG *...chemical sprays... ...hair spray... ...a spray insecticide.* N MASS

3 If you **spray** a liquid over something or if you **spray** something with a liquid, you cover it with drops of the liquid, for example using a hose or an aerosol. EG *He sprayed a little eau-de-cologne over himself... Spray the shelves with insecticide.* V+O : USU+A

4 If a lot of small things **spray** somewhere or if you **spray** something with them, they are scattered with a lot of force. EG *A fine red dust sprayed out from the edge of the saw... He was spraying the street with bullets.* V+A; ALSO V+O : USU+A

5 A **spray** is a piece of equipment for spraying water or another liquid, especially over growing plants. EG *...an ordinary garden spray.* N COUNT

6 A **spray** of flowers or leaves is a number of flowers or leaves on one stem or branch. EG *...great sprays of lilies.* N PART

spray can, spray cans. A **spray can** is a can containing liquid under pressure which can be sprayed out. N COUNT

spread /spred/, **spreads, spreading.** The form **spread** is used in the present tense and is the past tense and past participle of the verb.

1 If you **spread** something, you open it out or arrange it over a place or surface, so that all of it can be seen or used easily. EG *He took the envelope, tipped it open and spread the contents on the table.* V+O : USU+A

2 If you **spread** a part of your body, for example your fingers or arms, you stretch them out until they are far apart. EG *He just shrugged and spread his hands.* V+O

3 If you **spread** a substance on a surface or **spread** the surface with the substance, you put a thin layer of the substance over the surface. EG *Liz was spreading marmalade on a piece of toast... I love biscuits spread with butter.* V+O : USU+A

4 A **spread** is a soft food which is put on bread. EG *...cheese spread.* N MASS

5 If something **spreads** or **is spread** by people, it gradually reaches or affects a larger and larger area or more and more people. EG *A stain was spreading on the bathroom ceiling... News of the wreck spread quickly... Disease might be spread very easily.* ▸ used as a noun. EG *Girls have benefited more than boys from the spread of higher education.* V-ERG : USU+A; ▸ N SING

6 If something **spreads** over a period of time, it takes place regularly or continuously over that period. EG *They had experience spreading over twenty years... The breeding season is spread over five months.* V+*over* OR V+O+*over*

7 If you **spread** something such as wealth or work, you distribute it evenly or equally. EG *You are advised to spread the workload.* V+O

8 A **spread** of ideas, interests, or other things is a wide variety of them. EG *The IBA wants to have a broad spread of opinion represented on its board.* N SING : USU+*of*

spread out. 1 If people, animals, or vehicles **spread out** or **are spread out**, they are far apart. EG *They followed him and spread out, nervously, in the forest... My family were spread out all over the countryside.* **2** If something such as a city or forest **spreads out** or **is spread out**, it covers a large area. EG *Through the window, you can see the town spread out below.* **3** If you **spread** something **out**, you open it out or arrange it over a place or surface, so that all of it can be seen or used easily. EG *I removed the tool kit and spread it out on the seat.* **4** If you **spread out** a part of your body, for example your fingers or arms, you stretch them out until they are far apart. EG *He lifted up a hand and held it there, the fingers spread out.* PHRASAL VB : V-ERG+ADV; V-ERG+ADV; V+O+ADV; V+O+ADV

spread-eagled /spred iːgəºld/. Someone who is **spread-eagled** is lying with their arms and legs spread out. EG *Stephanie found him spreadeagled on the stairs.* ADJ CLASSIF

spree /spriː/, **sprees.** If you spend a long time doing something that you enjoy, you can say that you are going on a particular kind of **spree.** EG *Tim was away on a shopping spree... He went on a drinking spree.* N COUNT : USU+SUPP

sprig /sprɪg/, **sprigs.** A **sprig** of a plant is a small twig or stem with leaves on it which someone has picked. EG *...a sprig of holly.* N COUNT : USU+*of*

sprightly /spraɪtli[1]/. Someone, especially an old person, who is **sprightly** is lively and active. EG *Jimmy McGregor is a sprightly 71-year old.* ADJ QUALIT

spring /sprɪŋ/, **springs, springing, sprang** /spræŋ/, **sprung** /sprʌŋ/. **Sprung** is the past participle of the verb and is sometimes used in American English as the past tense.

1 Spring is the season between winter and summer. In the spring the weather begins to get warmer and leaves and plants start to grow again. EG *It would have been better to have waited until the spring... He left in the spring of 1956.* N UNCOUNT OR N COUNT

2 A **spring** is a coil of wire which returns to its original shape after it is pressed or pulled. EG *One day they would get a real sofa, with springs.* N COUNT

3 A **spring** is also a place where water comes up through the ground. EG *...hot volcanic springs.* N COUNT

4 When a person or animal **springs**, they jump upwards or forwards. EG *She sprang to her feet and faced him... The panther crouched, ready to spring.* V : USU+A

5 If something **springs** in a particular direction, it moves suddenly and quickly. EG *Hands sprang up... The door of the safe had sprung open.* V+A

6 If things or people **spring** into action or **spring** to life, they suddenly start being active or suddenly come into existence. EG *A computer will not spring into action without something powering it... At last factories sprang to life again.* V+A

7 If one thing **springs** from another thing, it is the result of it. EG *These problems spring from different causes... Her hostility to him sprang out of sheer envy.* V+*from/ out of*

8 If a boat or container **springs a leak**, water or some other liquid starts coming in or out through a hole or crack. PHRASE

9 If you **spring** some news or a surprise on someone, you tell them something unexpected, without warning them. EG *It was then that I sprang* V+O : OFT+*on*

my surprise... He wondered why this story should be sprung on him.

spring up. If something **springs up**, it suddenly appears or comes into existence. EG *Computer stores are springing up all over the place.* PHRASAL VB : V+ADV

springboard /sprɪŋbɔːd/, **springboards. 1** If something is a **springboard** for an action or enterprise, it makes it possible for the action or enterprise to begin. EG *The campaign might well be the springboard for the launching of a new party.* N COUNT : USU+*for/to*

2 A **springboard** is also a flexible board which you jump on before performing a dive or a gymnastic movement. N COUNT

spring-clean, spring-cleans, spring-cleaning, spring-cleaned. When you **spring-clean** a house, you thoroughly clean everything in it. ◇ **spring-cleaning.** EG *Mrs Pringle came to give me a hand with the spring-cleaning.* V OR V+O ◇ N UNCOUNT

spring onion, spring onions. A **spring onion** is a small onion with long green leaves that is often eaten raw in salads. N COUNT

springtime /sprɪŋtaɪm/ is the period of time during which spring lasts. EG *In the springtime the mountains take on a purple hue.* N UNCOUNT

springy /sprɪŋi¹/. If something is **springy**, it returns quickly to its original shape after you press it. EG *...a springy mattress... The grass was short and springy.* ADJ QUALIT

sprinkle /sprɪŋkəºl/, **sprinkles, sprinkling, sprinkled.** If you **sprinkle** something such as a liquid or powder over something, you scatter it over it. EG *Sprinkle the oil over the courgettes... She sprinkled the cakes with sugar.* V+O : USU+A

sprinkler /sprɪŋklə/, **sprinklers.** A **sprinkler** is a device used to spray water. Sprinklers are used to water plants or lawns or to put out a fire in a building. N COUNT

sprinkling /sprɪŋklɪŋ/. A **sprinkling** of something is a small quantity of it, especially one that is spread over a large area. EG *There is always a sprinkling of sightseers outside the palace... ...a sprinkling of grey hairs.* N PART : USU SING

sprint /sprɪnt/, **sprints, sprinting, sprinted. 1** A **sprint** is **1.1** a short race in which the runners run very fast. EG *...a 100 metre sprint.* **1.2** a fast run. EG *Bessie had suddenly broken into a sprint.* N COUNT / N SING

2 If you **sprint**, you run as fast as you can over a short distance. EG *She sprinted to her car.* V : USU+A

sprinter /sprɪntə/, **sprinters.** A **sprinter** is a person who takes part in short, fast races. N COUNT

sprout /spraʊt/, **sprouts, sprouting, sprouted. 1** When plants or vegetables **sprout**, they produce new leaves or shoots. V OR V+O

2 When leaves or shoots **sprout** somewhere, they grow there. EG *Greenery sprouted between the white gravestones.* V

3 When hairs, feathers, or horns **sprout** or when a person or animal **sprouts** them, they grow. EG *...the hairs sprouting from a mole on her cheek... Some of the young men sprouted moustaches.* V-ERG

4 If things **sprout** up or if something **sprouts** them, they appear or spread rapidly. EG *Caravans had suddenly sprouted up in the fields... San Francisco has sprouted a rash of little theatres.* V-ERG

5 Sprouts or **Brussels sprouts** are vegetables like very small cabbages. N COUNT : OFT PLURAL

6 A **sprout** is a new shoot on a plant. EG *They produce new sprouts almost immediately.* N COUNT

spruce /spruːs/. **Spruce** is both the singular and the plural form.

1 A **spruce** is a kind of evergreen tree. N COUNT

2 Someone who is **spruce** is very neat and smart in appearance. EG *Miss Jackson arrived looking very spruce in a new linen suit.* ADJ QUALIT

sprung /sprʌŋ/ is the past participle or a past tense of **spring.**

spry /spraɪ/, **spryer, spryest.** Someone, especially an old person, who is **spry** is lively and active. EG *Now, at eighty, he was as spry as ever.* ADJ QUALIT

spud /spʌd/, **spuds. Spuds** are potatoes. EG *Are the spuds cooked yet?* N COUNT Informal

spun /spʌn/ is the past tense and past participle of **spin.**

spur /spɜː/, **spurs, spurring, spurred. 1** If something **spurs** you to do something or **spurs** you on, it encourages you to do it. EG *I am not conceited about my achievement but I am spurred on by it... Martin's job offer spurred the others to do something themselves.* V+O+*to*-INF OR *on*

2 If something **spurs** a change or event, it makes it happen faster or sooner. EG *...a period of extremely rapid growth, spurred by the advent of the microprocessor.* V+O

3 Something that acts as a **spur** encourages a person to do something or makes something happen faster or sooner. EG *International competition was a spur to modernisation.* N SING+*to*

4 If you do something **on the spur of the moment**, you do it suddenly, without planning it beforehand. EG *I just took the bus on the spur of the moment.* ● See also **spur-of-the-moment.** PHRASE

5 Spurs are small metal wheels with sharp points attached to the heels of a rider's boots. The rider uses them to urge a horse to go faster. N COUNT

spurious /spjʊərɪəs/. Something that is **spurious** is not genuine or real. EG *I felt a moment's spurious comfort... ...the spurious attractions of modernity.* ADJ QUALIT

spurn /spɜːn/, **spurns, spurning, spurned.** If you **spurn** something, you refuse to accept it. EG *You spurned my friendship.* V+O Formal

spur-of-the-moment. A **spur-of-the-moment** action or decision is sudden and has not been planned. EG *...spur-of-the-moment impulses.* ADJ CLASSIF : ATTRIB

spurt /spɜːt/, **spurts, spurting, spurted. 1** When a liquid or flame **spurts** out of something, it comes out quickly in a thin, powerful stream. EG *...a blow that sent blood spurting from his mouth... My arm began to spurt blood.* ▸ used as a noun. EG *...a small, clear spurt of flame.* V-ERG : USU+A ▸ N COUNT

2 A **spurt** of activity, effort, or emotion is a sudden, brief period of it. EG *Her feelings varied from tenderness to sudden spurts of genuine love.* N COUNT : USU+SUPP

3 If you **spurt** somewhere, you suddenly increase your speed for a short while. EG *With Claude driving they spurted through back streets.* ▸ used as a noun. EG *He drove past cars in fast spurts.* V : USU+A ▸ N COUNT

sputter /spʌtə/, **sputters, sputtering, sputtered.** If something **sputters**, it makes soft hissing and popping sounds. EG *The engine began coughing and sputtering.* V

spy /spaɪ/, **spies, spying, spied. 1** A **spy** is a person whose job is to find out secret information about another country or organization. EG *A member of his staff was discovered to be a foreign spy.* N COUNT

2 Someone who **spies** for a country or organization tries to find out secret information about another country or organization. EG *He was convicted of spying for Russia.* V

3 If you **spy** on someone, you watch them secretly. EG *...girls spying on their unfaithful lovers.* V+*on*

4 If you **spy** something, you notice it. EG *Suddenly Quint spied the triangular fin of a shark coming towards them.* V+O Written

sq is a written abbreviation for 'square'. You write **sq** when you are giving the measurement of an area. EG *...280,000 sq ft of office space.*

squabble /skwɒbəºl/, **squabbles, squabbling, squabbled.** When people **squabble**, they quarrel noisily, usually about something that is not really important. EG *They're always squabbling over details.* ▸ used as a noun. EG *...squabbles between the children.... The bitter squabble raged on.* V ▸ N COUNT

Which are the noisy words on these pages?

squad /skwɒd/, **squads. 1** A **squad** is a section of a police force that is responsible for dealing with a particular type of crime. EG *...the drugs squad.* N COUNT+SUPP

2 A **squad** of soldiers is a small group of them. N COUNT

squad car, squad cars. A **squad car** is a car used by the police. N COUNT

squadron /skwɒdrə^{n}n/, **squadrons.** A **squadron** is a section of one of the armed forces, especially the air force. EG *...a squadron of fighter planes... ...the commander of C Squadron.* N COUNT

squalid /skwɒlɪd/. **1** A place that is **squalid** is dirty, untidy, and in bad condition. EG *The kitchen was squalid... ...our small, squalid flat.* ADJ QUALIT

2 Squalid activities are unpleasant and often dishonest. EG *They're involved in a rather squalid battle as to who controls the party.* ADJ QUALIT

squall /skwɔ:l/, **squalls.** A **squall** is a brief, violent storm. EG *A sudden squall overturned the boat.* N COUNT

squalor /skwɒlə/. You can refer to squalid conditions or surroundings as **squalor**. EG *...poor people living in conditions of squalor.* N UNCOUNT

squander /skwɒndə/, **squanders, squandering, squandered.** If you **squander** money or resources, you use it all up in a foolish and wasteful way. EG *If we squander our fossil fuels, we threaten civilisation... He squandered large quantities of cash on overpriced clothes.* V+O

square /skwɛə/, **squares, squaring, squared. 1** A **square** is a shape with four sides of the same length and four corners that are all right angles. See picture at SHAPES. EG *I folded the newspaper neatly into a square.* N COUNT

2 In a town or city, a **square** is a flat open place, often in the shape of a square. EG *...the town square... ...Trafalgar Square.* N COUNT

3 Something that is **square** has a shape the same as a square or similar to a square. EG *The post office was a small, square building... He had a square ruddy face.* ADJ QUALIT

4 Square is used before units of length when mentioning the area of something. For example, if a rectangle is three metres long and two metres wide, its area is six square metres. EG *...hundreds of square miles of pine forest.* ADJ CLASSIF : ATTRIB

5 Square is also used after units of length when you are giving the length of each side of something that is square in shape. EG *...a silicon chip less than a centimetre square.* ADJ AFTER N

6 If you **square** a number, you multiply it by itself. For example, 3 squared is 3 x 3, or 9. 3 squared is usually written as 3^2. V+O

7 When two people no longer owe each other any money, you can say that they are **square**. ADJ PRED Informal

8 When you **square** two different situations or ideas with each other or when they **square** with each other, they can be accepted together or they seem compatible. EG *How do you square being a Lord with being a Marxist?* V-ERG OR V-ERG+*with* : RECIP

9 A **square** meal is a meal that is large and satisfying. EG *He had gone without a square meal for nearly three days.* N COUNT

10 If you are **back to square one**, you have to start dealing with something from the beginning again because one course of action has failed. EG *If he says 'No', you are back to square one.* PHRASE Informal

squarely /skwɛəli^{1}/. **1 Squarely** means directly and in the middle, rather than indirectly or at an angle. EG *The television mast fell squarely onto a Methodist chapel.* ADV : USU+PREP

2 If you face something **squarely**, you face it directly, without trying to avoid it. EG *This difficulty will have to be squarely faced.* ADV

square root, square roots. The **square root** of a number is a number which produces that number when it is multiplied by itself. For example, 4 is the square root of 16. N COUNT

squash /skwɒʃ/, **squashes, squashing, squashed. 1** If you **squash** something, you press it, so that it becomes flat or loses its shape. EG *I saw a dead cat. It had been squashed by a bus.* V+O : USU PASS

2 Squash is a game in which two players hit a small rubber ball against the walls of a court using rackets. EG *I spent the afternoon playing squash.* N UNCOUNT

3 Squash is also a drink made from fruit juice, sugar, and water. EG *We gave all the children a glass of lemon squash.* N MASS British

squat /skwɒt/, **squats, squatting, squatted. 1** If you **squat** or **squat** down, you crouch, balancing on your feet with your legs bent. EG *He told the boys to squat in a semicircle around him.* V : OFT+*down*

2 Someone or something that is **squat** is short and thick, often in an unattractive way. EG *...a squat, bald, plump man... ...squat wooden churches.* ADJ QUALIT

3 A person who **squats** in an unused building lives there without having a legal right to do so. EG *We were squatting in an empty house.* V ◊ **squatter, squatters**. EG *...the subject of squatters' rights.* ◊ N COUNT

squawk /skwɔ:k/, **squawks, squawking, squawked.** When a bird **squawks**, it makes a loud sharp noise. V ▸ used as a noun. EG *...the sad squawks of the peacocks.* ▸ N COUNT

squeak /skwi:k/, **squeaks, squeaking, squeaked.** If something **squeaks**, it makes a short, high-pitched sound. EG *A door squeaked open nearby... As the dusk deepened, small black bats began squeaking.* V ▸ used as a noun. EG *She let out a squeak.* ▸ N COUNT

squeaky /skwi:ki^{1}/. Something that is **squeaky** makes squeaking noises. EG *...a squeaky iron gate... ...a high, squeaky voice.* ADJ QUALIT

squeal /skwi:l/, **squeals, squealing, squealed.** When people or things **squeal**, they make long, high-pitched sounds. EG *The boys scattered, squealing in horror.* V ▸ used as a noun. EG *There was a squeal of brakes.* ▸ N COUNT

squeamish /skwi:mɪʃ/. If you are **squeamish**, you are easily upset by unpleasant sights or situations. EG *I'm squeamish about surgery.* ADJ QUALIT

squeeze /skwi:z/, **squeezes, squeezing, squeezed. 1** When you **squeeze** something soft or flexible, you press it firmly from two sides. EG *The children were squeezing the packets to find out what was inside... He was holding her hands and squeezing them between his.* V+O ▸ used as a noun. EG *He gave her hand a squeeze.* ▸ N COUNT

2 When you **squeeze** a liquid or a soft substance out of an object, you get the liquid or substance out by pressing the object. EG *Squeeze all the surplus water out of the cloth.* V+O+A

3 If you **squeeze** through or into a small space, you manage to get through it or into it. EG *We squeezed under the wire and into the garden... The inhabitants have to squeeze into a tiny area of living space.* V+A

4 If you say that getting a number of people into a small space is a **squeeze**, you mean that it is only just possible for them all to get into it. EG *We all got in the lift but it was a bit of a squeeze.* N SING : *a*+N Informal

5 If you **squeeze** something into a small amount of time or space, you manage to fit it in. EG *Do you think you can squeeze in your lunch break between the two meetings?* V+O+A

6 If you **squeeze** something out of someone, you persuade them to give it to you. EG *He's hoping to squeeze the extra cash out of his bank manager.* V+O+A

squelch /skwɛltʃ/, **squelches, squelching, squelched.** To **squelch** means to make a wet, sucking sound, like the sound you make when you are walking on wet, muddy ground. EG *I squelched along by the water's edge.* V : USU+A

squid /skwɪd/, **squids.** A **squid** is a sea creature with a long soft body and many tentacles. The plural of 'squid' is either 'squid' or 'squids'. N COUNT

squiggle /skwɪgə^{n}l/, **squiggles.** A **squiggle** is a line that bends and curls in an irregular way. EG *Her signature was a series of inky squiggles.* N COUNT

squint /skwɪnt/, **squints, squinting, squinted. 1** If you **squint** at something, you look at it with your eyes partly closed. EG *He squinted at the brightly coloured figures.* V: USU+*at*

2 If someone has a **squint**, their eyes look in different directions from each other. N COUNT: USU SING

squire /skwaɪə/, **squires.** In former times, the **squire** of an English village was the man who owned most of the land in it. N COUNT

squirm /skwɜːm/, **squirms, squirming, squirmed. 1** If you **squirm**, you move your body from side to side, because you are nervous or uncomfortable. EG *The girls squirmed in their chairs and began giggling.* V: USU+A

2 You can also say that someone **squirms** when they are very embarrassed or ashamed. EG *He squirmed with embarrassment.* V: OFT+*with*

squirrel /skwɪrə[0]l/, **squirrels.** A **squirrel** is a small furry animal with a long bushy tail. Squirrels live mainly in trees. N COUNT

squirt /skwɜːt/, **squirts, squirting, squirted. 1** If you **squirt** a liquid somewhere, the liquid comes out of a narrow opening in a thin fast stream. EG *Squirt a little oil into the keyhole... Water squirted out of a hole in the pipe.* V-ERG: USU+A

2 If you **squirt** something with a liquid, you squirt the liquid at it. EG *One woman was running ahead squirting windows with water.* V+O: USU+*with*

SRN /ɛs ɑːr ɛn/, **SRNs.** An **SRN** is someone who is fully qualified as a nurse in the United Kingdom. **SRN** is an abbreviation for 'State Registered Nurse'. EG *...Jane Wilson SRN.* N COUNT

SS. See **St.**

St. 1 St is a written abbreviation for 'Street'. EG *...22 Harley St, London W1.*

2 St is also a written abbreviation for 'Saint'. The plural is **SS.** EG *...St Anselm... ...SS Peter and Paul.*

-st You add **-st** to most numbers written in figures and ending in 1 in order to form ordinal numbers. 1st is pronounced the same as 'first'. EG *...1st April 1982... ...21st Street... ...the 101st Psalm.* SUFFIX

stab /stæb/, **stabs, stabbing, stabbed. 1** If someone **stabs** you, they push a knife into your body. EG *A man was stabbed to death as he left a London library.* V+O

2 If you say that someone **has stabbed** you **in the back**, you mean that they have done something very harmful to you when you thought that you could trust them. PHRASE

3 If you **stab** something or **stab** at it, you push at it with your finger or with something pointed that you are holding. EG *He stabbed the air with his index finger... She was typing in a fury, her fingers stabbing at the keys.* V+O OR V+A

4 If you have a **stab** at something, you try to do it. EG *I'd like to have a stab at tap dancing... You've had a pretty good stab at it.* N COUNT: OFT+*at* Informal

5 You can refer to a sudden, unpleasant feeling as a **stab** of that feeling. EG *Kitty felt a stab of dismay.* N COUNT+*of* Literary

stabbing /stæbɪŋ/, **stabbings. 1** A **stabbing** is an incident in which someone stabs someone else. N COUNT

2 A **stabbing** pain is a sudden sharp pain. EG *I felt a stabbing pain behind one of my eyes.* ADJ CLASSIF: ATTRIB

stability /stəbɪlɪ[1]ti[1]/ is the state of being stable. EG *...a period of economic growth and stability.* N UNCOUNT

stabilize /steɪbɪ[1]laɪz/, **stabilizes, stabilizing, stabilized;** also spelled **stabilise.** If something **stabilizes** or **is stabilized**, it becomes stable. EG *Eventually your weight will stabilise... The family is one of the great stabilizing elements in society.* V-ERG

stable /steɪbə[0]l/, **stables. 1** If something is **stable**, it is not likely to change or come to an end suddenly. EG *Oil prices are stable for the first time in years... ...a stable marriage... ...politically stable countries.* ADJ QUALIT

2 If an object is **stable**, it is firmly fixed in position and is not likely to move or fall. EG *Eventually they managed to get a more stable structure.* ADJ QUALIT

3 A **stable** is a building in which horses are kept. EG *He went to the stables to fetch his horse.* N COUNT

staccato /stəkɑːtəʊ/. A **staccato** noise consists of a series of short, sharp, separate sounds. EG *...the man's staccato Berlin accent.* ADJ CLASSIF: ATTRIB Literary

stack /stæk/, **stacks, stacking, stacked. 1** A **stack** of things is a neat pile of them. EG *On the sideboard was a stack of plates.* N PART

2 If you **stack** a number of things or **stack** them up, you arrange them in neat piles. EG *I started stacking the chairs... We stacked up the plates and carried them to the sink.* V+O: OFT+*up*

3 If a place or surface **is stacked** with objects, it is filled with piles of them. EG *The shed was stacked with old boxes.* V+O: USU PASS+*with*

4 If you say that someone has **stacks** of something, you mean that they have a lot of it. EG *They've got stacks of money... I've got stacks of socks.* N PART Informal

stadium /steɪdɪəm/, **stadiums.** A **stadium** is a large sports ground with rows of seats all round it. EG *...football stadiums.* N COUNT

staff /stɑːf/, **staffs, staffed. 1** The **staff** of an organization are the people who work for it. EG *She was invited to join the staff of the BBC... There are two students to every member of staff.* N COLL OR N UNCOUNT

2 If an organization **is staffed** by particular people, they are the people who work for it. EG *It was staffed and run by engineers... ...a sports shop staffed by runners.* ● See also **short-staffed.** V+O: USU PASS

staffing /stɑːfɪŋ/ refers to the number of workers employed to work in a particular organization or building. EG *...inadequate staffing... ...the urgency of securing additional staffing... ...staffing problems.* N UNCOUNT

stag /stæg/, **stags.** A **stag** is an adult male deer. N COUNT

stage /steɪdʒ/, **stages, staging, staged. 1** A **stage** is **1.1** a part of a process. EG *In the early stages of learning to read, a child will usually need a lot of help... Agriculture is the first stage of economic development.* **1.2** a period that is part of a longer period. EG *...at this stage in my life.* N COUNT: USU+SUPP

2 In a theatre, the **stage** is a raised platform where actors or other entertainers perform. EG *She stood alone on the enormous stage.* N COUNT ● When an actor or singer is **on stage**, he or she is performing on the stage. EG *She has been accused of being too flamboyant on stage... I didn't sing opera on stage.* ● PHRASE Technical

3 You can refer to acting and the production of plays in a theatre as the **stage**. EG *She retired from the stage some years ago... He's adapted one of his novels for the stage... ...stage productions.* N SING: *the*+N

4 If someone **stages** a play or other show, they organize and present a performance of it. V+O

5 If you **stage** an event or ceremony, you organize it. EG *The women staged a demonstration.* V+O

6 To **set the stage** for something means to make preparations so that it can happen. EG *The stage was now set for a massive publicity drive.* PHRASE

stagecoach /steɪdʒkəʊtʃ/, **stagecoaches. Stagecoaches** were large carriages pulled by horses which carried passengers and mail. N COUNT

stage-manage, stage-manages, stage-managing, stage-managed. If someone **stage-manages** an event, they organize it, especially secretly. EG *Could we be sure that the attacks were not stage-managed?* V+O

stagger /stægə/, **staggers, staggering, staggered. 1** If you **stagger**, you walk very unsteadily, for example because you are ill or drunk. EG *I staggered to the nearest chair.* V: USU+A

2 If something **staggers** you, it surprises you very much. V+O ◇ **staggered.** EG *She was absolutely staggered... We were staggered to learn they would not be returning... I was staggered at how unpleasant the country had become.* ◇ ADJ QUALIT: USU PRED ◇ **staggering.** EG *Its* ◇ ADJ QUALIT

Is stained glass dirty?

estimated cost has climbed to a staggering £35 billion.

3 If things such as people's holidays or hours of work **are staggered**, they are arranged so that they do not all happen at the same time. V+O : USU PASS

stagnant /stæɡnənt/. **1** If something such as a business or society is **stagnant**, there is little activity or little change; used showing disapproval. EG *...stagnant economies.* ADJ CLASSIF

2 Stagnant water is not flowing, and is often dirty and unhealthy. EG *...stagnant pools.* ADJ CLASSIF

stagnate /stæɡneɪt, stæɡneɪt/, **stagnates, stagnating, stagnated.** If something such as a business or society **stagnates**, it becomes inactive or unchanging; used showing disapproval. EG *The economy stagnated as a result of these tax measures.* V ◇ **stagnation** /stæɡneɪʃə⁰n/. EG *Industrial stagnation inevitably leads to the loss of jobs.* ◇ N UNCOUNT

stag night, stag nights. A **stag night** or a **stag party** is a party for a man who is getting married the next day, to which only men are invited. N COUNT

staid /steɪd/. Someone who is **staid** is serious, dull, and rather old-fashioned. EG *...a staid elderly gentleman... I must have seemed rather staid.* ADJ QUALIT

stain /steɪn/, **stains, staining, stained. 1** A **stain** is a mark on something that is difficult to remove. EG *There was a dark oval stain on the chair where his head had rested... ...grease stains.* N COUNT

2 If a liquid **stains** something, the thing becomes coloured or marked by the liquid. EG *Already the beast's blood was staining the sand.* V+O ◇ **stained.** EG *...a little man with stained teeth... His shirt was stained with blood.* ◇ ADJ CLASSIF

stained glass consists of pieces of glass of different colours which are fixed together to make decorative windows or other objects. EG *St Nicholas's has fine Victorian stained-glass windows.* N UNCOUNT

stainless steel /steɪnlɪ²s stiːl/ is a metal made from steel and chromium which does not rust. EG *...a stainless steel sink.* N UNCOUNT

stair /stɛə/, **stairs. 1 Stairs** are a set of steps inside a building which go from one floor to another. EG *He ran up the stairs... ...another flight of stairs... Bill stood at the foot of the stairs.* N PLURAL

2 A **stair** is one of the steps in a set of stairs. EG *A stair creaked as she made her way downstairs.* N COUNT

staircase /stɛəkeɪs/, **staircases.** A **staircase** is a set of stairs inside a house. See picture at HOUSE. EG *...a white marble staircase.* N COUNT

stairway /stɛəweɪ/, **stairways.** A **stairway** is a set of steps, inside or outside a building. EG *He stood halfway up the wooden stairway.* N COUNT

stake /steɪk/, **stakes, staking, staked. 1** If something is **at stake**, it is being risked and might be lost or damaged if you are not successful. EG *There's a great deal of money at stake... He admits that his political life is at stake.* PHRASE

2 The **stakes** involved in a risky action or a contest are the things that can be gained or lost. EG *I'm playing for high stakes.* N PLURAL

3 If you **stake** something such as your money or your reputation on the result of something, you risk your money or reputation on it. EG *He staked his reputation as a prophet on this assertion.* V+O : OFT+*on/upon*

4 If you have a **stake** in something such as a business, its success matters to you, for example because you own part of it. EG *They soon had a substantial stake in the British textile industry.* N COUNT

5 You can use **stakes** to refer to something that is like a contest. For example, you can refer to the choosing of a leader as the leadership **stakes**. EG *...the Presidential stakes... This gives you an advantage in the promotion stakes.* N PLURAL : *the*+N

6 A **stake** is a pointed wooden post which is pushed into the ground, for example in order to support a young tree. EG *His boat was fastened by a chain to a stake in the ground.* N COUNT

7 If you **stake a claim**, you say that something is yours or that you have a right to it. EG *Each group had staked its claim to its own territory.* PHRASE

stale /steɪl/. **1 Stale** food or air is old and no longer fresh. EG *They had nothing to eat but stale bread... The box smelled of stale tobacco... Inside the flat was a musty smell of stale air.* ADJ QUALIT

2 If you feel **stale**, you are no longer enthusiastic or full of interesting ideas because you are tired or bored. EG *You need a break, a change. You're getting stale here.* ADJ QUALIT

stalemate /steɪlmeɪt/. **1 Stalemate** is a situation in which neither side in an argument or contest can win. EG *He hoped that the nuclear stalemate would lead to disarmament... A stalemate had been reached.* N UNCOUNT

2 In chess, **stalemate** is a position in which a player cannot make any move which is permitted by the rules, so that the game ends and no one wins. N UNCOUNT

stalk /stɔːk/, **stalks, stalking, stalked. 1** The **stalk** of a flower or other plant is its main stem. N COUNT

2 The **stalk** of a fruit or leaf is the thin part that joins it to the plant or tree that it grows on. N COUNT

3 If you **stalk** a person or a wild animal, you follow them quietly in order to kill them, catch them, or observe them. EG *We stalked rabbits... He moved like a tiger stalking its prey.* V+O

4 If you **stalk** somewhere, you walk there in a stiff, proud, or angry way. EG *She stalked into the living room... Florrie stalked out, her head high.* V+A

stall /stɔːl/, **stalls, stalling, stalled. 1** A **stall** is a large table on which you put goods that you want to sell or information that you want to give to people. EG *Never buy a dog from a market stall.* N COUNT

2 The **stalls** in a theatre or concert hall are the seats on the ground floor directly in front of the stage. EG *We got seats in the stalls.* N PLURAL : *the*+N

3 When a vehicle **stalls** or when you accidentally **stall** it, the engine stops suddenly. V-ERG

4 If you **stall**, you try to avoid doing something until a later time. EG *'Well?' she said. Tom grinned at her, stalling for time.* V

5 If you **stall** someone, you prevent them from doing something until a later time. EG *Perhaps I can stall him till Thursday or Friday.* V+O

stallion /stæljən/, **stallions.** A **stallion** is a male horse, especially one kept for breeding. N COUNT

stalwart /stɔːlwət/, **stalwarts.** A **stalwart** worker or supporter of an organization is loyal and hard-working. EG *...the proprietor and his three stalwart sons.* ADJ QUALIT ▸ used as a noun. EG *...a stalwart of the Trades Council... They were all Government stalwarts.* ▸ N COUNT

stamina /stæmɪnə/ is the physical or mental energy needed to do a tiring activity for a long time. EG *I did not have the physical stamina needed for digging.* N UNCOUNT

stammer /stæmə/, **stammers, stammering, stammered. 1** If you **stammer**, you speak with difficulty, hesitating and repeating words or sounds, for example because you are nervous. EG *I used to stammer quite badly... 'But...but...that's impossible,' the youth stammered.* V, V+O, OR V+QUOTE

2 Someone who has a **stammer** tends to stammer when they speak. N COUNT : USU SING

stammer out. If you **stammer** something **out**, you stammer as you say it. EG *Before he could stammer out his thanks, she walked away.* PHRASAL VB : V+O+ADV OR V+ADV+QUOTE

stamp /stæmp/, **stamps, stamping, stamped. 1** A **stamp** or a **postage stamp** is a small piece of gummed paper which you stick on an envelope or parcel before you post it. EG *His interests were drawing and stamp collecting.* N COUNT

2 A **stamp** is also a small block of wood or metal which has a pattern or a group of letters on one side. You press it onto an inky pad and then onto a piece of paper in order to produce a mark on the paper. The mark that you produce is also called a N COUNT

stamp. EG *They had German passports with Brazilian entrance stamps.*
3 If you **stamp** a mark or word on an object, you press the mark or word onto the object using a stamp or other device. EG *Articles that conform with the relevant British Standards are stamped with a kite-shaped mark... Unless they are stamped 'ovenproof' assume they are not.* V+O+A OR V+O+C
4 If you **stamp** your foot, you lift your foot and put it down very hard on the ground, for example because you are angry. EG *'Damn you, Edward!' she shouted, stamping her foot.* V+O
5 If you **stamp** somewhere, you walk there putting your feet down very hard on the ground because you are angry. EG *We reluctantly stamped into the principal's office.* V+A
6 If you **stamp** on something, you put your foot down on it very hard. EG *I stamped heavily on her foot and muttered, 'Shut up.'* V+*on*
7 If something bears the **stamp** of a particular quality or person, it clearly has that quality or was done by that person. EG *His work hardly bore the stamp of maturity... ...a designer who has left his stamp on 20th century industry.* N SING+SUPP
8 A quality, feature, or action that **stamps** someone or something as a particular thing shows clearly that they are this thing. EG *His achievement stamps him as one of the masterminds of our era.* V+O+*as*
stamp out. If you **stamp** something **out**, you put an end to it. EG *They are determined to stamp out political extremism.* PHRASAL VB : V+O+ADV

stamped /stæmpt/. A **stamped** envelope or parcel has a stamp stuck on it. EG *Two letters in stamped envelopes were already laid out on the desk.* ADJ CLASSIF

stampede /stæmpi:d/, **stampedes, stampeding, stampeded. 1** When a group of animals **stampede** or **are stampeded**, they rush away wildly because something has frightened them. EG *Outside the goats stampeded.* V-ERG
2 When there is a **stampede**, a group of animals rush away because something has frightened them. EG *...a stampede of elephants.* N COUNT
3 You can also say that there is a **stampede** when a group of people rush somewhere in an uncontrolled way. EG *Her foot got trodden on in the general stampede to the exit.* N COUNT

stance /stæns, stɑ:ns/, **stances. 1** Your **stance** on a particular matter is your attitude about it. EG *They criticized Martin Luther King for his rigid stance on non-violence.* N COUNT +SUPP : OFT+*on*
2 Your **stance** is also the way that you are standing. EG *He altered his stance slightly and leaned against a tree.* N COUNT : USU+SUPP Formal

stand /stænd/, **stands, standing, stood** /stʊd/. **1** When you **are standing**, your body is upright, your legs are straight, and your weight is supported by your feet. EG *She was standing at the bus stop... Stand quietly behind your desks... I stood very still, hoping they wouldn't see me.* V : USU+A
2 When you **stand**, you change your position so that you are standing, rather than sitting. EG *One by one, he asked each graduate to stand.* V Formal
3 If you **stand** aside or **stand** back, you move a short distance sideways or backwards, so that you are standing in a different place. EG *Miss Darke told the girls to stand aside... He stood back and surveyed his handiwork.* V+A
4 If something **stands** somewhere, it is in an upright position in that place. EG *In the middle of the town stands a splendid Victorian building... The empty wine bottles stand in a neat row against the wall... Only one of the houses is still standing.* V : USU+A
5 If you **stand** something somewhere, you put it there in an upright position. EG *He stood the bottle on the bench beside him.* V+O+A
6 If a decision or offer **stands**, it is still valid. EG *Fifty years later, this Supreme Court ruling still stands.* V : NO CONT
7 If something that can be measured **stands** at a particular level, it is at that level. EG *Unemployment in North Wales now stands at 38 per cent.* V+*at*
8 You can use **stand** instead of 'is' when you are describing the state or condition of something. EG *Their honesty stands in total contrast to the deceitfulness of their opponents... His real intentions now stand revealed... They are dissatisfied with the law as it stands.* V+A OR V+C : NO CONT
9 If you ask someone **how** or **where** they **stand** on a particular issue, you are asking them what their attitude or view is. EG *There was never any doubt about where he stood on the racial issue.* PHRASE
10 If something can **stand** a situation or a test, it is good enough or strong enough to withstand it. EG *In its present state, the economy couldn't stand another rise in interest rates... Her arguments could hardly stand close inspection.* V+O : OFT WITH MODAL +BROAD NEG
11 If you cannot **stand** something, **11.1** you cannot bear it or tolerate it. EG *He kept on nagging until I couldn't stand it any longer.* **11.2** you dislike it very strongly. EG *She can't stand children.* V+O : OFT WITH MODAL +BROAD NEG
12 If you **stand** to gain something, you are likely to gain it. If you **stand** to lose something, you are likely to lose it. EG *Other groups stand to make a profit out of it... Few people are yet aware of how much we stand to lose by this agreement.* V+*to*-INF
13 If you **stand** in an election, you are a candidate. EG *She was invited to stand as the Liberal candidate... He has stood for Parliament 21 times.* V : USU+A
14 If you **stand** someone a meal or a drink, you buy it for them. V+O+O
15 If you say **it stands to reason** that something is true or likely to happen, you mean that it is obvious. EG *If they keep doing that, it stands to reason that the police are going to get suspicious.* PHRASE Informal
16 When someone **stands trial**, they are tried in a court of law. EG *He has come back to stand trial on a murder charge.* PHRASE
17 A **stand** is a small shop or stall, outdoors or in a large public building. EG *...a hamburger stand... ...an information stand.* N COUNT+SUPP
18 A **stand** is also an object or piece of furniture that is designed for holding a particular kind of thing. EG *...an umbrella stand... ...a music stand.* N COUNT
19 If you take a **stand** or make a **stand**, you resist attempts to defeat you or to make you change your mind. EG *...a heroic national stand against the invader... It's an important issue and you must be prepared to take a stand on it.* N SING
20 When a witness **takes the stand** in a court of law, he or she answers questions. EG *Hearne had not yet taken the stand.* PHRASE American
21 to **stand a chance**: see **chance**. • to **stand on your own two feet**: see **foot**. • to **stand your ground**: see **ground**. • See also **standing**.
stand by. 1 If you **stand by**, you are ready to provide help or to take action if it becomes necessary. EG *Stand by with lots of water in case a fire breaks out.* PHRASAL VB : V+ADV **2** If you **stand by** and let something bad happen, you do not do anything to stop it. EG *We cannot stand by and watch while our allies are attacked.* V+ADV **3** If you **stand by** someone, you continue to give them support, especially when they are in trouble. EG *If they try to make you resign, we'll stand by you.* V+PREP **4** If you **stand by** an earlier decision, promise, or agreement, you continue to support it or keep it. EG *I said I would do it and I stand by my promise.* V+PREP **5** See also **standby**.
stand down. If someone **stands down**, they resign, often in order to let someone else take their place. EG *She was asked if she was prepared to stand down in favour of a younger candidate.* PHRASAL VB : V+ADV
stand for. 1 If you say that a letter **stands for** a particular word, you mean that it is an abbrevia- PHRASAL VB : V+PREP

If you cannot stand someone, would you be likely to stand them a meal?

tion for that word. EG *T.E.C. stands for Technical Education Certificate.* **2** The ideas or attitudes that someone or something **stands for** are the ones that they support or represent. EG *I disagreed fundamentally with what the party stood for.* **3** If you will not **stand for** something, you will not allow it to happen or continue. EG *He warned that the Army would not stand for it much longer.* V+PREP / V+PREP WITH BROAD NEG

stand in. If you **stand in** for someone, you take their place or do their job, because they are ill or away. EG *He was standing in for his younger brother... You will stand in for me, John?* ● See also **stand-in**. PHRASAL VB : V+ADV, USU+*for*

stand out. If something **stands out**, **1** it can be seen very clearly. EG *The name on the van stood out clearly.* **2** it is much better or much more important than other things of the same kind. EG *One issue stood out as especially important... One article in this collection stands out from all the others.* PHRASAL VB : V+ADV, NO CONT / V+ADV, NO CONT

stand up. 1 When you **stand up**, you change your position so that you are standing, rather than sitting. EG *I put down my glass and stood up.* **2** If something **stands up** to rough treatment, it remains almost undamaged or unharmed. EG *This carpet stands up to the wear and tear of continual use.* **3** If you **stand up** to someone, especially someone more powerful than you are, you defend yourself against their attacks or demands. EG *Maybe if I stood up to him, he'd back down.* **4** If you **stand up** for someone or something that is being attacked or criticized, you defend them vigorously. EG *...people who stood up for human rights... I'm glad to see that he's standing up for himself.* **5** If something such as a claim or a piece of evidence **stands up**, it is accepted as true or satisfactory after being carefully examined. EG *The prosecution had no evidence which would stand up in a court of law.* **6** If you **are stood up** by a boyfriend or girlfriend, they fail to keep an arrangement to meet you. PHRASAL VB : V+ADV / V+ADV, OFT+*to/under* / V+ADV+A / V+ADV+A / V+ADV / V+O+ADV Informal

standard /stændəd/, **standards. 1** A **standard** is a level of quality or achievement, especially a level that is thought to be acceptable. EG *The acting ability of the pupils is of a high standard... You're way below the standard required... We place emphasis on excellence and high standards.* N COUNT OR N UNCOUNT +SUPP

2 A **standard** is also something that you use in order to judge the quality of something else. EG *These families would be classified as rich by Asian standards... By any standard the work was good.* N COUNT+SUPP

3 Standards are moral principles which affect people's attitudes and behaviour. EG *There has been a corruption of moral standards.* N COUNT : USU PLURAL +SUPP

4 You use **standard** to describe things which are usual and normal, rather than being special or extra. EG *There is a standard procedure for recording drugs given to patients.* ADJ CLASSIF

5 Standard spelling, pronunciation, and grammar are generally regarded as correct or acceptable. ADJ CLASSIF

6 If a book is described as a **standard** work or text, it is the one most widely read and recommended about a particular subject. EG *This is the standard work on British moths.* ADJ CLASSIF : ATTRIB

standardize /stændədaɪz/, **standardizes, standardizing, standardized;** also spelled **standardise.** To **standardize** things means to change them so that they all have the same features. EG *Some people have criticized television for standardizing speech, habits, and tastes.* ◊ **standardized.** EG *Equipment is going to become more standardized.* V+O / ◊ ADJ QUALIT

standard lamp, standard lamps. A **standard lamp** is a tall electric light which stands on the floor in a living-room. N COUNT

standard of living, standards of living. Your **standard of living** is the level of comfort and wealth which you have. EG *There will have to be an adjustment to a lower standard of living.* N COUNT : USU SING+SUPP

standby /stændᵊbaɪ/, **standbys. 1** A **standby** is something that is always ready to be used if it is needed. EG *Eggs are a great standby in the kitchen.* N COUNT

2 If someone or something is **on standby**, they are ready to be used if they are needed. EG *We have a crew on stand-by.* PHRASE

3 A **standby** ticket for something such as the theatre or a plane journey is a cheap ticket that you buy just before the performance starts or the plane takes off, if there are still some seats left. N MOD

stand-in, stand-ins. A **stand-in** is a person who takes someone else's place or does someone else's job, because the other person is ill or away. EG *Make sure that your stand-in is available... He was trying to arrange stand-in lecturers for Wilt's classes.* N COUNT

standing /stændɪŋ/. **1** You use **standing** to describe something which is permanently in existence. EG *...a standing committee... This is a standing joke amongst psychologists.* ADJ CLASSIF : ATTRIB

2 Someone's **standing** is their status or reputation. EG *His success was based on his popular standing... She was an economist of considerable standing.* N UNCOUNT +SUPP Formal

3 You use **standing** to say how long something has existed or how long it has had a particular function. For example, if a place is your home of ten years' standing, it has been your home for ten years. EG *...a member of twenty-five years' standing... The present unrest has its origins in social ills of long standing.* PHRASE Formal

standing order, standing orders. A **standing order** is an instruction to your bank to pay a fixed amount of money to someone at regular times. EG *I pay their allowance by standing order.* N COUNT OR *by*+N

standing room is space in a room or bus, where people can stand when all the seats have been taken. EG *Inside there was standing room only.* N UNCOUNT

stand-offish /stændɒfɪʃ/. If you say that someone is **stand-offish**, you mean that they behave in a formal and rather unfriendly way. ADJ QUALIT

standpipe /stændpaɪp/, **standpipes.** A **standpipe** is a vertical pipe that is connected to a water supply and stands in a street or other public place. N COUNT

standpoint /stændpɔɪnt/, **standpoints.** Your **standpoint** is your attitude or opinion about an event, situation, or idea. EG *Up to now, we have only discussed the issue from a western standpoint.* N COUNT+SUPP

standstill /stændstɪl/. If movement or activity comes to a **standstill**, it stops completely. EG *The traffic had come to a standstill... The negotiations are at a standstill.* N SING : *a*+N

stank /stæŋk/ is the past tense of **stink.**

staple /steɪpᵊl/, **staples, stapling, stapled. 1 Staples** are small pieces of wire that are used for holding sheets of paper together firmly. You push the staples through the paper using a special device called a stapler. N COUNT

2 If you **staple** something, you fasten it to something else or fix it in place using staples. EG *The letter was stapled to the other documents in the file.* V+O+A

3 A **staple** meal or food is one that forms a regular and basic part of your everyday food. EG *...the dry bread which is their staple diet.* ADJ CLASSIF : ATTRIB

stapler /steɪplə/, **staplers.** A **stapler** is a special device used for putting staples into sheets of paper. N COUNT

star /stɑː/, **stars, starring, starred. 1** A **star** is a large ball of burning gas in space. Stars appear to us as small points of light in the sky on clear nights. N COUNT

2 You can refer to a shape or an object as a **star** when it has four, five, or more points sticking out of it in a regular pattern. See picture at SHAPES. EG *...little star-shaped flowers.* N COUNT

3 Stars are star-shaped marks that are printed against the name of something to indicate that it is of high quality. EG *...a four-star hotel.* N COUNT

4 Famous actors, musicians, and sports players are often referred to as **stars**. EG *...a tennis star... ...film stars.* N COUNT

5 If an actor or actress **stars** in a play or film, he or she has one of the most important parts in it. EG *She'll be starring in a new play by Alan Bleasdale.* V : USU+A

6 If a play or film **stars** a famous actor or actress, he or she has one of the most important parts in it. EG *The last version of the movie starred John Garfield and Lana Turner.* V+O

7 The horoscope in a newspaper or magazine is sometimes referred to as the **stars**. EG *What do the stars say for today?* N PLURAL Informal

starboard /stɑ:bə^{r}d/. The **starboard** side of a ship is the right side when you are facing towards the front of it. EG *White, icy-cold water foamed over the starboard side.* ▸ used as a noun. EG *...a few hundred yards to starboard.* ADJ CLASSIF Technical ▸ N UNCOUNT

starch /stɑ:tʃ/, **starches. 1 Starch** is a substance that is used for stiffening cloth, especially cotton and linen. N UNCOUNT

2 Starch is also a white substance in foods such as bread, potatoes, pasta, and rice. EG *Your doctor may recommend limiting the amount of starch in your diet... Cut down on the starches.* N MASS

starched /stɑ:tʃt/. **Starched** cloth has been stiffened using starch. EG *They wore starched caps and white gloves.* ADJ CLASSIF

starchy /stɑ:tʃi^1/. **Starchy** food contains a lot of starch. EG *Avoid starchy vegetables such as potato.* ADJ QUALIT

stare /stɛə/, **stares, staring, stared. 1** If you **stare** at something, you look at it for a long time. EG *He stared at us in disbelief... He sat there quietly, staring out of the window.* ▸ used as a noun. EG *She gave him a dreamy stare.* V : USU+A ▸ N COUNT

2 If an answer or solution **is staring** you **in the face**, it is very obvious. PHRASE

starfish /stɑ:fɪʃ/. A **starfish** is a flat, star-shaped creature with five arms that lives in the sea. The plural form is also 'starfish'. N COUNT

stark /stɑ:k/, **starker, starkest. 1** Something that is **stark** is very bare and plain in appearance. EG *...the stark black rocks and deserted beaches... The names were written in stark black print.* ADJ QUALIT

2 Stark means harsh and unpleasant. EG *Those are the stark facts of the matter... ...grim stark poverty.* ADJ QUALIT : ATTRIB

3 Someone who is **stark naked** is completely naked. EG *He came out of the bathroom stark naked.* PHRASE

starlight /stɑ:laɪt/ is the light that comes from the stars at night. EG *I enjoyed the view of the bay in the starlight.* N UNCOUNT

starling /stɑ:lɪŋ/, **starlings.** A **starling** is a very common European bird with greenish-black feathers. EG *...children chattering like starlings.* N COUNT

starry /stɑ:ri^1/. A **starry** night or sky is full of stars. EG *It was a cold, starry night.* ADJ CLASSIF : ATTRIB

starry-eyed. If you are **starry-eyed**, you are so full of dreams or hopes that you do not see how things really are. EG *We were all starry-eyed about visiting London.* ADJ QUALIT

start /stɑ:t/, **starts, starting, started. 1** If you **start** to do something, you do something that you were not doing before and you continue doing it. EG *Ralph started to run... He started laughing... My father started work when he was ten.* ▸ used as a noun. EG *We must make a start now... We've not made a bad start.* V+*to*-INF, V+-ING, V+O, OR V ▸ N SING

2 When something **starts** or when you **start** it, it takes place from a particular time. EG *The meeting starts at 7... We didn't want to start a panic.* ▸ used as a noun. EG *...the start of negotiations... ...at the start of the tax year... The project was doomed to failure from the start.* V-ERG ▸ N COUNT : USU SING

3 If you **get off to a good start**, you are successful in the early stages of doing something. If you **get off to a bad start**, you are not successful in the early stages. EG *Treatment sometimes gets off to a bad start.* ● to **get off to a flying start**: see **flying**. PHRASE

4 You use **start** to say what someone's first job was. For example, if their first job was that of a porter, you can say that they **started** as a porter. EG *She started as a secretary.* V : USU+A

5 When someone **starts** something such as a new business, they create it or cause it to start. EG *He scraped up the money to start a restaurant.* V+O

6 If you **start** an engine or car, or if it **starts**, it starts to work. EG *He couldn't get his engine started.* V-ERG

7 If you **start**, your body jerks as a result of surprise or fear. EG *I sat down so quietly that she started.* ▸ used as a noun. EG *He awakened with a start.* V ▸ N COUNT : USU SING

8 You use **to start with** or **for a start** to introduce the first of a number of things or reasons that you want to mention or could mention. EG *'Why do you call her a witch?' – 'Well, she looks like a witch to start with.'... We can't afford this house for a start.* ADV SEN

9 To start with also means at the very first stage of an event or process. EG *He was an engineer to start with, then a designer.* ADV SEN

10 See also **head start.** ● **in fits and starts**: see **fit.**

start off. 1 You can use **start off** to say what someone's first job was. For example, if their first job was that of a taxi driver, you can say that they **started off** as a taxi driver. EG *I started off as a bookseller.* PHRASAL VB : V+ADV, OFT+*as* **2** If you **start off** by doing something, you do it as the first part of an activity. EG *I started off by showing a slide of the diseased cell... I started off with a Chopin prelude.* V+ADV, OFT+*by* **3** To **start** someone **off** means to cause them to start doing something. EG *It was doing 'Measure for Measure' with him that started me off on this new work.* V+O+ADV **4** To **start** something **off** means to cause it to start. EG *I know what started it all off.* V+O+ADV

start on. If you **start on** something that needs to be done, you start dealing with it. EG *She put the forks in a neat pile and started on the knives.* PHRASAL VB : V+PREP, HAS PASS

start out. 1 If someone or something **starts out** as a particular thing, they are that thing at the beginning although they change later. EG *These areas started out as the private lands of settlers.* PHRASAL VB : V+ADV **2** If you **start out** doing something, you do it at the beginning of an activity. EG *You started out by saying that this was the weapon they used.* V+ADV

start up. 1 If you **start up** something such as a new business, you create it or cause it to start. EG *She wanted to start up a little country pub.* PHRASAL VB : V+O+ADV **2** If you **start up** an engine or a car, you make it start to work. EG *The driver started up the car.* V+O+ADV

starter /stɑ:tə/, **starters. 1** A **starter** is a small quantity of food that is served as the first part of a meal. EG *Serve noodles tossed in butter or cream as a starter.* N COUNT

2 The **starter** of a car is a device that starts the engine. N COUNT

starting point, starting points. 1 A **starting point** is an idea or statement that can be used to begin a conversation or argument. EG *The starting point of the discussion is inflation.* N COUNT : OFT+*of/for*

2 When you make a journey, your **starting point** is the place from which you start. EG *This is a good starting point for a car tour.* N COUNT : OFT+*of/for*

startle /stɑ:tə^{0}l/, **startles, startling, startled.** If something such as a sudden noise **startles** you, it surprises and frightens you slightly. EG *Goodness, you startled me – I thought you were in the garden... He was startled by the fevered look of his patient.* ◊ **startled.** EG *We laughed at the startled expressions on their faces.* V+O ◊ ADJ QUALIT

startling /stɑ:tlɪŋ/. Something that is **startling** is so different or unexpected that people react with surprise. EG *The results were quite startling – a 77% increase in six months.* ADJ QUALIT

Is a stationer in charge of a railway station? If not, who is?

starvation /sta:veɪʃə⁰n/ is extreme suffering or death, caused by lack of food. EG *Many thousands of people die from starvation every year.* N UNCOUNT

starve /sta:v/, **starves, starving, starved.** 1 When people **starve**, they suffer greatly from lack of food and sometimes die. EG *People are starving because of inefficient farming methods.* V

2 To **starve** someone means to not give them any food. EG *You should starve him for twelve hours... Ten men starved themselves to death in the prison.* V+O OR V-REFL

3 If you say that you **are starving**, you mean that you are very hungry. EG *I've got to have something to eat. I'm starving.* V : ONLY CONT Informal

4 If someone or something **is starved** of something that they need, they are suffering because they are not getting enough of it. EG *They seem to be starved of attention from adults... The plant was starved of light and died.* V+O : USU PASS

stash /stæʃ/, **stashes, stashing, stashed.** If you **stash** something valuable in a secret place, you store it there to keep it safe. EG *They had all that money stashed away in the loft.* V+O+A Informal

state /steɪt/, **states, stating, stated.** 1 When you talk about the **state** of someone or something, you are referring to what they are like or what they are experiencing at a particular time. EG *They are very concerned about the state of the churchyard... His general state of health is fairly satisfactory... She seemed in a very queer and nervous state... People wandered about in a state of shock.* N COUNT : USU SING+SUPP

2 If you are **in a state**, you are very upset or nervous about something. EG *He used to get into an awful state as exams approached.* PHRASE Informal

3 If you say that someone **is not in a fit state** to do something, you mean that they are too upset or ill to do it. EG *The parent is often in no fit state to help the children at the time of crisis.* PHRASE

4 Countries are often referred to as **states**. EG *The Latin American states maintained their independence... Their country is now a one-party state.* • See also **head of state**, **welfare state**. N COUNT

5 Some large countries are divided into regions called **states**. These states can make some of their own laws. EG *Haryana and Punjab were the fastest-developing states in India... ...New York State.* N COUNT

6 You can refer to the government of a country as the **state** when you are contrasting it with the ordinary people of the country. EG *...the conflict between the freedom of the individual and the security of the state.* N SING : *the*+N

7 A **state** ceremony or event is a formal one involving the ruler or head of a country. EG *...the state visit of a European monarch.* N MOD

7 If you **state** something, you make it known by saying or writing it, especially in a formal way. EG *The government have stated quite categorically that we're going to see changes... The police were called, but the man refused to state his business... He stated, 'I have passed the stage where such things matter.'* V-SPEECH

stately /steɪtli¹/. Something that is **stately** is impressive because it looks very graceful and dignified. EG *...strong and stately towers.* ADJ QUALIT

stately home, stately homes. A **stately home** is a large old house which has belonged to an aristocratic family for a long time and which can be visited by the public. N COUNT

statement /steɪtmə²nt/, **statements.** 1 A **statement** is something that you say, especially when you give facts or information in a formal way. EG *I could not deny the truth of this statement... The announcement was made in a statement immediately after the meeting... Soon afterwards he made his first public statement about the affair.* N COUNT

2 The **statement** of a policy or theory is the expression of it in words in a fairly formal and definite way. EG *This isn't a list of complaints, merely a statement of fact.* N SING+*of*

3 A **statement** is also a printed document that your bank sends you, which lists all the money that you have paid in or taken out, and also shows how much money you have in your account. N COUNT

state of affairs. A **state of affairs** is the general situation and circumstances connected with a particular thing, person, or event. EG *What our present state of affairs demands is a firm leader... Any relief to this unjust state of affairs is welcome.* N SING

state of mind, states of mind. Your **state of mind** is your mood at a particular time. EG *My sister was in a happier state of mind... ...words that in no way reflected my state of mind.* N COUNT : USU SING

statesman /steɪtsmə³n/, **statesmen.** A **statesman** is an important and experienced politician who is widely known and respected. EG *Terrorism could threaten any visiting statesman.* N COUNT

static /stætɪk/. 1 Something that is **static** does not move or change at all. EG *...a series of static images... ...the static quality in all village life.* ADJ QUALIT

2 **Static** or **static electricity** is electricity which is caused by friction and which collects in things such as your body or metal objects. N UNCOUNT

3 If there is **static** on the radio or television, you hear a series of loud crackling noises. EG *I switched on and got nothing but static.* N UNCOUNT

station /steɪʃə⁰n/, **stations, stationing, stationed.** 1 A **station** is a building by a railway line where a train stops to pick up passengers and goods. EG *The train stopped at a small station.* N COUNT

2 A bus **station** or coach **station** is a place from which buses or coaches begin a journey. N COUNT+SUPP

3 If you talk about a particular radio **station**, you are referring to the programmes broadcast on a particular frequency by a particular radio company. EG *The radio was tuned permanently to his favourite station.* N COUNT

4 If you refer to someone's **station**, you are referring to their position or rank in society. EG *She had been educated above her station.* N SING+POSS Outdated

5 If people **are stationed** somewhere, they are told to stay there, usually so that they can watch someone or be ready to prevent trouble. EG *Two guards were stationed at the top of the stairs.* V+O+A : USU PASS

6 If soldiers **are stationed** in a place, they are sent there to work for a period of time. EG *...the British forces stationed in Germany.* V+O+A : USU PASS

7 See also **fire station**, **gas station**, **petrol station**, **police station**.

stationary /steɪʃənə⁰ri¹/. Something that is **stationary** is not moving. EG *...a stationary boat... The vehicle remained stationary.* ADJ CLASSIF

stationer /steɪʃənə/, **stationers.** A **stationer** is a person who sells paper, envelopes, pens, and other equipment used for writing. N COUNT

stationery /steɪʃənə⁰ri¹/ is paper, envelopes, pens, and other equipment used for writing. N UNCOUNT

stationmaster /steɪʃə⁰nma:stə/, **stationmasters.** A **stationmaster** is the official who is in charge of a railway station. N COUNT

station wagon, station wagons. A **station wagon** is the same as an estate car. N COUNT American

statistic /stətɪstɪk/, **statistics.** 1 **Statistics** are facts which are obtained from analysing information expressed in numbers, for example information about the number of times that something happens. EG *...divorce statistics... I happen to have the official statistics with me.* N COUNT : USU PLURAL

2 **Statistics** is a branch of mathematics concerned with the study of information that is expressed in numbers. EG *I teach statistics.* N UNCOUNT

statistical /stətɪstɪkə⁰l/ means relating to the use of statistics. EG *Statistical techniques are regularly employed.* ◇ **statistically**. EG *Statistically you have a one in six chance of succeeding.* ADJ CLASSIF ◇ ADV SEN OR ADV

statistician /stætɪstɪʃə⁰n/, **statisticians.** A **statistician** is a person who studies statistics or who works using statistics. EG *...a statistician in the Civil Service.* N COUNT

statue /stætjuː/, **statues.** A **statue** is a large sculpture of a person or an animal, made of stone or metal. EG *...a bronze statue of Charles I.* N COUNT

statuette /stætjuɛt/, **statuettes.** A **statuette** is a very small statue which is often displayed on a shelf. EG *...a statuette of a little girl.* N COUNT

stature /stætʃə/. Someone's **stature** is **1** their height and general size. EG *She was rather small in stature.* **2** the importance and reputation that they have. EG *I can't tell you how pleased we are to have someone of your stature here.* N UNCOUNT: USU+SUPP

status /steɪtəs/. **1** Your **status** is **1.1** your position in society. EG *...the changing status of women.* **1.2** the prestige and importance that you have in the eyes of other people. EG *He came in search of wealth, status, and power.* N UNCOUNT

2 Status is also an official classification that a person, organization, or country receives, which gives them particular rights or advantages. EG *They appeared to have dropped their demand for status as political prisoners.* N UNCOUNT +SUPP

3 The **status** of something such as a dispute or a discussion is how important it is. EG *They are meeting to discuss the status of the dispute with club-owners over free membership.* N UNCOUNT +SUPP

status quo /steɪtəs kwəʊ/. The **status quo** is the situation that exists at a particular time. N SING

status symbol, status symbols. A **status symbol** is something that a person has or owns that shows they have prestige and importance in society. EG *A personal chauffeur is undoubtedly a status symbol.* N COUNT

statute /stætjuːt/, **statutes.** A **statute** is a formal rule or law. EG *There have been more than twenty statutes governing what can be published in newspapers.* N COUNT

statutory /stætjə^{4}tə^{0}ri^1/ means relating to rules or laws which have been formally written down. EG *...the IBA's statutory code of advertising standards.* ADJ CLASSIF: USU ATTRIB Formal

staunch /stɔːnt^{0}ʃ/, **staunchest; staunches, staunching, staunched. 1** A **staunch** supporter of someone or something is very loyal to them. EG *Both are staunch supporters of Manchester United... ...Benny's staunchest ally.* ADJ QUALIT: USU ATTRIB

2 If you **staunch** blood, you stop it from flowing out of someone's body. EG *Sophia staunched the blood with a cloth.* V+O Formal

stave /steɪv/, **staves, staving, staved.** If you **stave** something **off**, you delay it happening. EG *They want to stave off any attempt to intervene.* PHRASAL VB: V+O+ADV

stay /steɪ/, **stays, staying, stayed. 1** If you **stay** somewhere, **1.1** you continue to be there and do not move away. EG *Fewer women these days stay at home to look after their children.* **1.2** you live there for a short time as a guest or a visitor. EG *She was staying in the same hotel as I was.* V+A

2 If someone or something **stays** in a particular condition or situation, they continue to be in it. EG *Last night I stayed awake until the whole house was sleeping... We'll work till eight if it stays light.* V+C OR V+A

3 If you **stay** away from a place, you do not go there. EG *This town is unsafe: stay away from here.* V+A

4 If you **stay** out of something, you do not get involved in it. EG *I stayed out of the social life of the school... We try to stay out of politics.* V+A

5 If you **stay put**, you remain somewhere. EG *Those kinds of people stay put in one job all their lives.* PHRASE

6 A **stay** is a short time that you spend somewhere as a guest or visitor. EG *We were good friends throughout my stay in Germany.* N COUNT: USU+SUPP

stay in. If you **stay in**, you remain at home and do not go out. EG *She had to stay in and do the dishes... We ought to have stayed in tonight.* PHRASAL VB: V+ADV

stay on. If you **stay on** somewhere, you remain there. EG *He had stayed on to have a drink... Pupils have to stay on at school till they are 16.* PHRASAL VB: V+ADV

stay out. 1 If you **stay out**, you remain away from home, especially when you are expected to be there. EG *She stayed out all night.* **2** If workers stay out, they remain on strike. EG *The men stayed out for nearly a year.* PHRASAL VB: V+ADV V+ADV

stay up. If you **stay up**, you remain out of bed at a time when most people have gone to bed or at a time when you are normally in bed yourself. EG *Willie liked to eat out in restaurants and stay up late.* PHRASAL VB: V+ADV

stead /stɛd/. If you say that something will **stand** someone **in good stead**, you mean that it will be very useful to them in the future. EG *My school theatrical performances stood me in good stead in later years.* PHRASE

steadfast /stɛdfəst, -fɑːst/. If you are **steadfast** in something that you do, you are convinced that what you are doing is right and you refuse to change it or to give up; used showing approval. EG *The refugees remained steadfast... ...steadfast loyalty.* ADJ QUALIT ◊ **steadfastly.** EG *Her father has steadfastly refused to take part in such activities.* ◊ ADV

steady /stɛdi^1/, **steadier, steadiest; steadies, steadying, steadied. 1** Something that is **steady 1.1** continues or develops gradually and without any interruptions. EG *This year we've seen a steady rise in prices.* ADJ QUALIT ◊ **steadily.** EG *Unemployment has risen steadily.* ◊ ADV **1.2** stays at about the same level or value with not much change or variation. EG *These vehicles are reasonably economical at a steady 56 mph.* ADJ QUALIT ◊ **steadily.** EG *He could hear Rudolph breathing steadily.* ◊ ADV

2 If an object is **steady**, it is firm and does not shake or move about. EG *His hand was not quite steady... Try to hold the tray steady.* ADJ QUALIT

3 If you look at someone or speak to them in a **steady** way, you look or speak in a calm, controlled way. EG *Her voice was faint but steady.* ADJ QUALIT ◊ **steadily.** EG *Foster looked steadily at me for some moments.* ◊ ADV

4 Work that is **steady** is certain to continue for a long period of time. EG *My son has a steady job.* ADJ CLASSIF

5 If you describe a person as **steady**, you mean that they are sensible and reliable. EG *I like Simon very much – he's a very steady boy.* ADJ QUALIT

6 When you **steady** something or when it **steadies**, you stop it shaking or moving about. EG *His elbows were resting on his knees to steady the binoculars... The boat moved slightly, and he steadied himself with his right hand.* V-ERG OR V-REFL

7 When you **steady** yourself, you control your voice or expression, so that people will think that you are calm and not nervous. EG *He drew a deep breath to steady himself.* V-ERG OR V-REFL

steak /steɪk/, **steaks. 1 Steak** is beef without much fat on it. EG *...steak-and-kidney pie.* N MASS

2 A fish **steak** is a large piece of fish. EG *...four halibut steaks.* N COUNT

steal /stiːl/, **steals, stealing, stole** /stəʊl/, **stolen** /stəʊlə^{0}n/. **1** If you **steal** something from someone, you take it away from them without their permission and without intending to return it. EG *He stole knives and a gun... My first offence was stealing a pair of binoculars.* V+O OR V ◊ **stealing.** EG *He had been expelled from his previous school for stealing.* ◊ N UNCOUNT ◊ **stolen.** EG *...stolen credit cards.* ◊ ADJ CLASSIF

2 If you **steal** somewhere, you move there quietly and cautiously so that nobody notices you. EG *Simon came stealing out of the shadows.* V+A Literary

stealth /stɛlθ/. If you use **stealth** when you do something, you do it in such a slow, quiet, and secretive way that other people do not notice what you are doing. EG *Sometimes tigers rely on stealth, creeping towards their victims.* N UNCOUNT

stealthy /stɛlθi^1/. **Stealthy** actions or movements are performed quietly and secretively, so that no one will notice what you are doing. EG *I managed to get there by a series of stealthy movements.* ADJ QUALIT

What things on these pages might be made of metal?

◊ **stealthily**. EG *I heard my landlady creeping stealthily up to my door.* ◊ ADV

steam /sti:m/, **steams, steaming, steamed. 1 Steam** is the hot mist that water turns into when it boils. EG *The room was filled with steam... Steam hissed between the blocks of lava.* N UNCOUNT

2 Steam vehicles and machines are operated using steam as a means of power. EG *The first steam locomotive was introduced in 1825.* ADJ CLASSIF : ATTRIB

3 If something **steams**, it gives off steam. EG *The kettle was steaming away on the stove... Lynn brought her a steaming cup of tea.* V

4 If a vehicle **steams** somewhere, it moves along, giving out steam. EG *A British ship was steaming into Valetta Harbour.* V+A

5 If you **steam** food, you cook it in steam rather than in water. EG *...steamed rice.* V+A

6 If you **let off steam**, you get rid of your energy, anger, or strong emotions by behaving in a noisy or violent way. EG *They can let off steam in pubs where nobody knows them.* PHRASE Informal

7 If you **run out of steam**, you stop doing something because you have no more energy or enthusiasm left. EG *She would let me ramble on until I ran out of steam.* PHRASE Informal

steam up. 1 If you are **steamed up** about something, you are very annoyed about it. EG *What was she getting so steamed up about?* PHRASE Informal

2 When a window or piece of glass **steams up**, it becomes covered with steam or mist. PHRASAL VB : V+ADV

steamer /sti:mə/, **steamers.** A **steamer** is a ship that has an engine powered by steam. N COUNT

steamroller /sti:mrəulə/, **steamrollers.** A **steamroller** is a large, heavy vehicle with wide solid wheels. Steamrollers are used to flatten the surfaces of roads. N COUNT

steamy /sti:mi^{1}/. A place that is **steamy** is very hot and humid because it is full of steam. EG *The corridor opened into a steamy and noisy kitchen.* ADJ QUALIT

steel /sti:l/, **steels, steeling, steeled. 1 Steel** is a very strong metal which is made mainly from iron. Steel is used for making many things, for example bridges, buildings, vehicles, and cutlery. EG *...a modern tower made of concrete and steel.* ● See also **stainless steel**. N UNCOUNT : USU N MOD

2 If you **steel** yourself, you prepare to deal with something unpleasant. EG *You had better steel yourself for a shock.* V-REFL : USU+*for* OR *to*-INF

steel band, steel bands. A **steel band** is a band of people who play music on special metal drums. N COUNT

steel wool is a mass of fine steel threads twisted together into a small ball and used for cleaning surfaces. N UNCOUNT

steelworker /sti:lwɜ:kə/, **steelworkers.** A **steelworker** is a person who works in a steelworks. EG *Steelworkers formed local committees.* N COUNT

steelworks /sti:lwɜ:ks/. A **steelworks** is a factory where steel is made. The plural form is also 'steelworks'. EG *The flames from the steelworks shot skywards.* N COUNT

steely /sti:li^{1}/. You use **steely 1** to describe something that has a hard, greyish colour like steel. EG *The blue sky had changed to a steely grey.* ADJ QUALIT **2** to emphasize that a person is hard, strong, and determined. EG *There was shy modesty behind that steely determination.* ADJ CLASSIF : ATTRIB

steep /sti:p/, **steeper, steepest. 1** A **steep** slope forms a large angle with the horizontal, and is difficult to go up. EG *...a steep little street... He reached the steepest part of the mountain.* ADJ QUALIT

◊ **steeply**. EG *...mountains rising steeply on three sides.* ◊ ADV

2 A **steep** increase in something is a very big increase. EG *There's likely to be a steep increase in unemployment.* ADJ QUALIT ◊ **steeply**. EG *The costs of public services have risen steeply.* ◊ ADV

3 If you say that the price of something is **steep**, you mean that it is expensive. ADJ PRED Informal

steeped /sti:pt/. If a place or person is **steeped** in a quality or characteristic, they are surrounded by it or deeply influenced by it. EG *The house is centuries old and steeped in history.* ADJ PRED+*in*

steeple /sti:pə^{0}l/, **steeples.** A **steeple** is a tall pointed structure on top of the tower of a church. N COUNT

steer /stɪə/, **steers, steering, steered. 1** When you **steer** a car, boat, or plane, you control it so that it goes in the direction that you want. EG *He steered the car through the broad entrance... The freighter steered out of Santiago Bay that evening.* V-ERG OR V

2 If you **steer** someone in a particular direction, you guide them there. EG *He steered me to a table and sat me down in a chair.* V+O : USU+A

3 If you **steer** people towards a particular way of behaving, you change their behaviour, especially without them noticing, and make them behave in that way. EG *He steers the conversation towards more general topics.* V+O : USU+A

steering wheel, steering wheels. The **steering wheel** in a car or lorry is the wheel which the driver holds when he or she is steering the vehicle. See picture at CAR. N COUNT

stem /stem/, **stems, stemming, stemmed. 1** The **stem** of a plant is the long, thin, central part of it which is above the ground. N COUNT

2 The **stem** of a glass or vase is the long thin part of it which connects the bowl to the base. N COUNT

3 The **stem** of a pipe is the long thin part of it through which smoke is sucked. N COUNT

4 If you **stem** something that is spreading from one place to another, you stop it spreading. EG *...stemming the flow of illegal drugs.* V+O

5 If a condition or problem **stems** from something, it started originally because of it. EG *Their aggressiveness stemmed from fear.* V+*from*

stench /stentʃ/, **stenches.** A **stench** is a strong and very unpleasant smell. EG *...the unmistakable stench of rotting eggs.* N COUNT : USU+*of*

stencil /stensə^{0}l/, **stencils, stencilling, stencilled;** spelled **stenciling, stenciled** in American English. **1** A **stencil** is a piece of paper, plastic, or metal which has a design cut out of it. You place the stencil on a surface and use it to create a design, by allowing ink or paint to go through the holes in the stencil onto the surface below. N COUNT

2 If you **stencil** letters or designs, you print them using a stencil. EG *...large dustbins bearing the stencilled word LITTER.* V OR V+O

step /step/, **steps, stepping, stepped. 1** A **step** is the movement that you make when you lift your foot and put it down in a different place, for example when you are walking. EG *She took a step back... I walked on with quick steps.* N COUNT

2 If you **step** on something or **step** in a particular direction, you put your foot on the thing or move your foot in that direction. EG *He had stepped on a thorn... Step over the wire... Tom stepped back.* V+A

3 If someone tells you to **watch** your **step**, they are telling you to be careful about how you behave or what you say so that you don't get into trouble. EG *I'm cleverer than you are, so watch your step.* PHRASE

4 A **step** is also one of a series of actions that you take in order to achieve something. EG *Today's announcement is a step in the right direction... ...the first step on the road to victory.* N COUNT : USU+SUPP

5 A **step** in a process is one of a series of stages. EG *Simmel carried this idea one step further... Brody was several steps ahead of Cassidy.* N COUNT ● If you do something **step by step**, you do it by progressing gradually from one stage to the next. EG *The proof is set out, step by step, on page 6.* ● PHRASE

6 A **step** is also a raised flat surface, often one of a series of surfaces at different heights, on which you put your feet in order to walk up or down to a different level. EG *She was sitting on the top step... ...a flight of concrete steps.* N COUNT

7 People sometimes refer to a stepladder as **steps.** N PLURAL

8 If a group of people are walking **in step**, they are PHRASE moving their feet forward at exactly the same time as each other. EG *...a party of boys marching in step.*

step aside. To **step aside** means the same as to step down. EG *The committee wanted Mr Casey to step aside.* PHRASAL VB : V+ADV

step back. If you **step back** and think about a situation, you think about it in a fresh way as if you were not involved in it. EG *It is tempting to step back and ask whether it is worth all the trouble.* PHRASAL VB : V+ADV

step down. If you **step down** or **step aside** from an important job or position, you resign from it. EG *He stepped down last month because of illness.* PHRASAL VB : V+ADV

step in. If you **step in**, you get involved in a difficult situation, in order to help to find a solution. EG *She really appreciates the way you stepped in and saw to things.* PHRASAL VB : V+ADV

step up. If you **step up** something, you increase it. EG *The government is stepping up its efforts... The pace of exploration for fossil fuels has been stepped up enormously.* PHRASAL VB : V+O+ADV

stepbrother /stɛpbrʌðə/, **stepbrothers.** Someone's **stepbrother** is the son of their stepfather or stepmother. N COUNT

stepchild /stɛptʃaɪld/, **stepchildren.** Someone's **stepchild** is the child of their husband or wife by an earlier marriage. N COUNT

stepdaughter /stɛpdɔːtə/, **stepdaughters.** Someone's **stepdaughter** is the daughter of their husband or wife by an earlier marriage. N COUNT

stepfather /stɛpfɑːðə/, **stepfathers.** Someone's **stepfather** is the man who has married their mother after the death or divorce of their father. N COUNT

stepladder /stɛplædə/, **stepladders.** A **stepladder** is a ladder which you can carry around, consisting of two sloping parts that are hinged together at the top so that it will stand up on its own. EG *He got down off the stepladder.* N COUNT

stepmother /stɛpmʌðə/, **stepmothers.** Someone's **stepmother** is the woman who has married their father after the death or divorce of their mother. N COUNT

stepping stone, stepping stones. 1 A **stepping stone** is a job or event that helps you to make progress, often in your career. EG *That film was a big stepping-stone in my career.* N COUNT

2 Stepping stones are a line of large stones which you can walk on in order to cross a shallow stream or river. N COUNT : USU PLURAL

stepsister /stɛpsɪstə/, **stepsisters.** Someone's **stepsister** is the daughter of their stepfather or stepmother. N COUNT

stepson /stɛpsʌn/, **stepsons.** Someone's **stepson** is the son of their husband or wife by an earlier marriage. N COUNT

stereo /stɛriˈəʊ/, **stereos. 1 Stereo** is used to describe a record or a system of playing music in which the sound is directed through two different speakers. EG *...buying stereo equipment... It sounds much better in stereo.* ADJ CLASSIF OR N UNCOUNT

2 A **stereo** is a record player with two speakers. EG *He turned on the stereo.* N COUNT Informal

stereotype /stɛriˈəʊtaɪp/, **stereotypes, stereotyping, stereotyped. 1** A **stereotype** is a fixed general image or set of characteristics that a lot of people believe represent a particular type of person or thing. EG *The song perpetuates two racist stereotypes.* N COUNT

2 If you **stereotype** someone, you form a fixed general idea or image of them, so that you assume that they will behave in a particular way. EG *These images confine women to stereotyped roles.* V+O

sterile /stɛraɪl/. **1** Something that is **sterile** is completely clean and free from germs. EG *...rolls of sterile bandage.* ADJ CLASSIF

2 A person or animal that is **sterile** is unable to have or produce babies. EG *He had learnt early in his marriage that he was sterile.* ADJ CLASSIF

3 A situation that is **sterile** is lacking in energy and new ideas. EG *The meeting degenerated into a sterile debate.* ADJ QUALIT

sterilize /stɛrɪˈlaɪz/, **sterilizes, sterilizing, sterilized;** also spelled **sterilise. 1** If you **sterilize** a thing or a place, you make it completely clean and free from germs. EG *All nearby brickwork must be sterilized with a blowlamp, then treated with fungicide.* V+O

2 If a person or an animal **is sterilized**, they have a medical operation that makes it impossible for them to have or produce babies. EG *By 1950, 16 per cent of women over twenty had been sterilized.* V+O : USU PASS

sterling /stɜːlɪŋ/ is the money system of Great Britain. EG *Sterling has once again become one of the stronger currencies... ...a hundred and fifty pounds sterling.* N UNCOUNT OR ADJ AFTER N

stern /stɜːn/, **sterner, sternest; sterns. 1** Someone who is **stern** is very serious and strict. EG *Sylvia had a stern father who never praised her... ...a stern warning.* ◊ **sternly.** EG *He walked over to the boy and said to him sternly, 'Give that to me'.* ADJ QUALIT ◊ ADV

2 The **stern** of a boat is the back part of it. EG *She seated herself in the stern.* N COUNT

stethoscope

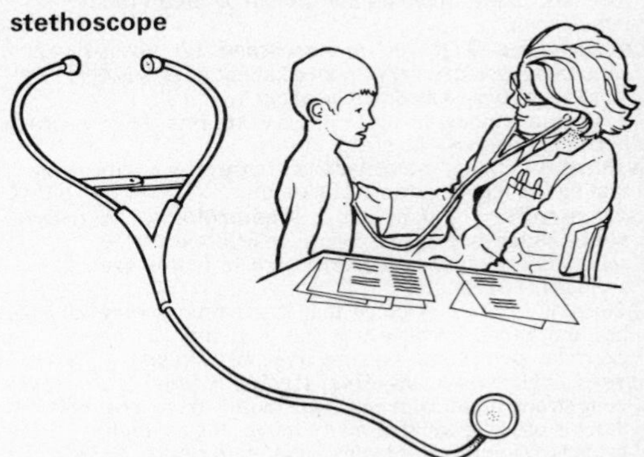

stethoscope /stɛθəskəʊp/, **stethoscopes.** A **stethoscope** is an instrument that a doctor uses to listen to your heart and breathing. It consists of a small disc that the doctor places on your body and a hollow tube that connects the disc to earpieces. N COUNT

stew /stjuː/, **stews, stewing, stewed. 1** A **stew** is a meal which you make by cooking meat and vegetables in liquid at a low temperature. EG *We've got lamb stew tonight.* N MASS

2 When you **stew** meat, vegetables, or fruit, you cook them slowly in liquid in a closed dish. EG *...stewed fruit.* V+O

3 If you **let** someone **stew**, you deliberately leave them to worry about something for a while, rather than telling them something which would make them feel better. EG *Let him stew... He let her stew for a day or two.* PHRASE Informal

steward /stjʊəd/, **stewards. 1** A **steward** is a man who works on a ship, plane, or train, looking after passengers and serving meals to them. N COUNT

2 A **steward** is also a man or woman who helps to organize a race, march, or other public event. ● See also **shop steward**. N COUNT

stewardess /stjʊədɛs/, **stewardesses.** A **stewardess** is a woman who works on a ship, plane, or train, looking after passengers and serving meals to them. EG *The stewardess brought more drinks.* N COUNT

stick /stɪk/, **sticks, sticking, stuck** /stʌk/. **1** A **stick** is a long, thin piece of wood, for example dead wood from a tree. EG *I gathered some sticks to* N COUNT

If you stick your stereo on the table, is it sticky?

start the fire... ...a circle drawn in the dirt with a stick... ...boys armed with sticks... ...hockey sticks.

2 A **stick** of something is a long thin piece of it. EG *...sticks of dynamite.* N PART

3 If you **stick** a pointed object in something, you push it in. EG *He stuck the knife right in... He stuck a cigar in his mouth... The pig had two spears sticking in her side.* V-ERG+A

4 If you **stick** something to something else, you attach it using glue, sticky tape, or another sticky substance. EG *They went round sticking posters on walls... Someone has stuck a label on the crate.* V+O+A

5 If one thing **sticks** to another, it becomes attached to it and is difficult to remove. EG *...sand that sticks to your hair and skin.* V : USU+*to*

6 If something which can usually be moved **sticks**, it becomes fixed in one position and can no longer be moved. EG *If your zip sticks, it might be because a thread has caught in it.* V

7 If something **sticks** in your mind, you remember it for a long time. EG *One lecture stuck in my mind.* V : USU+A

8 If you **stick** something somewhere, you put it there in a rather casual way. EG *She closed the bag and stuck it back on the shelf.* V+O+A Informal

9 If you **stick it** in a difficult situation, you do not leave or give up. EG *I don't know how I've stuck it. It's been hell.* PHRASE Informal

10 If someone **gets the wrong end of the stick**, they completely misunderstand something. PHRASE Informal

11 to **stick** your **neck out**: see **neck**. • to **stick in** your **throat**: see **throat**. • See also **stuck**.

stick around. If you **stick around**, you stay where you are, often because you are waiting for something. EG *I'll stick around and keep an eye on the food.* PHRASAL VB : V+ADV Informal

stick at. If you **stick at** a task or activity, you continue doing it, even if it is difficult. EG *You must stick at it if you want to succeed.* PHRASAL VB : V+PREP

stick by. If you **stick by** someone, you continue to give them help or support. EG *...a good commanding officer who stuck by his men when they got into trouble.* PHRASAL VB : V+PREP

stick out. 1 If you **stick** something **out**, you make it appear from inside or behind something else. EG *Lally stuck her head out of a window... Lynn stuck out her tongue.* 2 If something **sticks out**, 2.1 it extends beyond something else. EG *There was a little chimney sticking out of the roof... A few grey hairs stuck out from under her hat.* 2.2 it is very noticeable because it is unusual. EG *His accent made him stick out... ...a home that would not stick out in an English village.* 3 If someone in a difficult situation **sticks** it **out**, they do not leave or give up. EG *I stuck it out as long as I could.* PHRASAL VB : V+O+ADV; V+ADV, USU+A; V+ADV; V+O+ADV

stick out for. If you **stick out for** something, you keep demanding it and do not accept anything different or less. EG *He stuck out for twice the usual salary, and got it.* PHRASAL VB : V+ADV+PREP

stick to. 1 If you **stick to** someone or something when you are travelling, you stay close to them. EG *I went over the hill instead of sticking to the river.* PHRASAL VB : V+PREP

2 If you **stick to** something, you do not change to something else. EG *They are sticking to their present policy... I think I'll just stick to painting from now on.* 3 If you **stick to** a promise or agreement, you do what you said you would do. EG *They stuck to the bargain.* V+PREP, HAS PASS; V+PREP, HAS PASS

stick together. If people **stick together**, they stay with each other and support each other. EG *The boys learned to stick together.* PHRASAL VB : V+ADV

stick up. 1 If you **stick up** a picture or a notice, you attach it to a wall so that it can be seen. EG *We have a painting stuck up on the wall.* 2 If something long **sticks up**, it points upwards. EG *These plants stick up vertically from the seabed.* PHRASAL VB : V+O+ADV; V+ADV

stick up for. If you **stick up for** a person or a principle, you support or defend them forcefully. EG *He thanked his father for sticking up for him... I was too scared to stick up for my rights.* PHRASAL VB : V+ADV+PREP

stick with. 1 If you **stick with** something, you do not change to something else. EG *I stuck with my staple diet: brown rice.* 2 If you **stick with** someone, you stay close to them. EG *Stick with me and you'll be okay.* PHRASAL VB : V+PREP; V+PREP

sticker /stɪkə/, **stickers.** A **sticker** is a small piece of paper or plastic, with writing or a picture on one side, which you can stick onto a surface. EG *They sell stickers and badges... On the rear window was a sticker saying 'Save the Whales'.* N COUNT

sticking plaster is material that you can stick over a cut or blister in order to protect it. N UNCOUNT

stick-in-the-mud, stick-in-the-muds. If you describe someone as a **stick-in-the-mud**, you mean that they do not like doing anything new. N COUNT : USU SING Informal

stickler /stɪklə/, **sticklers.** If you are a **stickler** for something, you always insist on it. EG *Kitty was a stickler for routine.* N COUNT : USU+*for*

sticky /stɪki[1]/, **stickier, stickiest.** 1 Something that is **sticky** is covered with a substance that can stick to other things and leave unpleasant marks. EG *Her hands were sticky from the ice cream... ...a sticky bottle of fruit juice.* ADJ QUALIT

2 **Sticky** paper has glue on one side so that you can stick it to surfaces. EG *...sticky labels... ...sticky tape.* ADJ CLASSIF : ATTRIB

3 If you describe a situation as **sticky**, you mean that it is difficult or embarrassing. EG *We had a very sticky first day together in London.* ADJ QUALIT Informal

4 **Sticky** weather is unpleasantly hot and damp. EG *...a hot, sticky, July afternoon.* ADJ QUALIT

5 If someone **comes to a sticky end** or **meets a sticky end**, they suffer very badly or die in an unpleasant way. EG *...a disappointed man who had come to an exceptionally sticky end.* PHRASE Informal

stiff /stɪf/, **stiffer, stiffest.** 1 Something that is **stiff** is firm and does not bend easily. EG *Use a stiff brush... ...a new pair of stiff climbing boots... ...stiff brown paper.* ADJ QUALIT

2 Something such as a door or drawer that is **stiff** does not move as easily as it should. EG *The door was rather stiff... ...a stiff latch.* ADJ QUALIT

3 If you are **stiff**, your muscles or joints ache when you move, because of illness or because of too much exercise. EG *My arms were stiff.* ADJ QUALIT

4 **Stiff** behaviour is rather formal and not very friendly or relaxed. EG *...a stiff smile... The letter was stiff and formal.* ◊ **stiffly.** EG *'No, I haven't,' Rudolph said stiffly.* ADJ QUALIT ◊ ADV

5 **Stiff** also means difficult or severe. EG *Competition is so stiff that he'll be lucky to get a place at all... ...a stiff tax... There will be stiffer penalties for drunken drivers.* ADJ QUALIT

6 A **stiff** drink is a large amount of a strong alcoholic drink such as gin or whisky. EG *Morris fixed himself a stiff drink.* ADJ QUALIT : ATTRIB

7 A **stiff** breeze is blowing quite strongly. ADJ QUALIT

8 If you are bored **stiff**, worried **stiff**, or scared **stiff**, you are extremely bored, worried, or scared. EG *We were scared stiff of meeting him... The subject bores them stiff.* ADV AFTER ADJ Informal

stiffen /stɪfə[0]n/, **stiffens, stiffening, stiffened.** 1 If you **stiffen**, you stop moving and stand or sit with muscles that are suddenly tense, for example because you feel afraid or angry. EG *Tom suddenly stiffened with alarm... Her whole body stiffened.* V

2 If your muscles or joints **stiffen**, they become difficult to bend or move. EG *You are unlikely to be troubled with stiffening joints.* V-ERG

3 If attitudes or behaviour **stiffen**, they become stronger or more severe, and less likely to be changed. EG *Resistance stiffened even further last week... You will only stiffen his resolve.* V-ERG

4 When something such as cloth **is stiffened**, it is made firm so that it does not bend easily. ◊ **stiffened.** EG *...a dress of stiffened satin.* V+O : USU PASS ◊ ADJ CLASSIF

stifle /staɪfə[0]l/, **stifles, stifling, stifled.** 1 If someone **stifles** something that is happening, they stop it from continuing. EG *An authoritarian leadership stifled internal debate.* V+O

2 If you **stifle** a cry or a yawn, you prevent yourself from crying out or yawning. EG *She placed a hand over her mouth to stifle a shriek of laughter.* V+O

3 If the air or the atmosphere **stifles** you, it makes you feel as if you cannot breathe properly. EG *She was stifled with its scent.* V+O ◇ **stifling**. EG *...a stifling night... It was stifling inside.* ◇ ADJ QUALIT

stigma /stɪgmə/. If something has a **stigma** attached to it, it has a bad reputation and a lot of people disapprove of it. EG *...the stigma of failure... Some of the stigma attached to mental illness will be removed in future years.* N SING OR N UNCOUNT

stile /staɪl/, **stiles.** A **stile** is an entrance to a field or path that consists of a step on either side of a fence or wall. EG *I set off again along the path, over the stile, and up the lane.* N COUNT

stiletto /stɪletəʊ/, **stilettos. Stilettos** or **stiletto heels** are women's shoes that have high, very narrow heels. See picture at SHOES. N COUNT: USU PLURAL

still /stɪl/, **stiller, stillest; stills. 1** If a situation that used to exist **still** exists, it has continued and exists now. EG *She still lives in London... She was still beautiful... I was still a schoolboy.* ADV

2 If something that has not yet happened could **still** happen, it is possible that it will happen in the future. EG *She could still change her mind... There is still a chance that a few might survive.* ADV

3 If you say that there is **still** an amount of something left, you are emphasizing that there is that amount left. EG *There are ten weeks still to go... I've still got three left.* ADV

4 You use **still 4.1** to emphasize that something is the case in spite of what you have just said. EG *Whatever they have done, they are still your parents.* ADV OR ADV SEN **4.2** when you are dismissing a problem or difficulty as not really worth worrying about. EG *...and that made me miss the last bus. Still, that's life, isn't it?* ADV SEN

5 You also use **still** with 'better' or 'more' to indicate that something has even more of a quality than something else. EG *How about some Bach to begin with? Or, better still, Vivaldi... To the astonishment of his friends, he ran for Governor of New York. More astonishing still, he won.* ADV: WITH COMPAR

6 If you stay **still**, you stay in the same position and do not move. EG *Stand still!... We had to keep still for about four minutes.* ADJ PRED OR ADV AFTER VB

7 When air or water is **still**, it is not moving. EG *...the still water of the lagoon.* ADJ QUALIT

8 If a place is **still**, it is quiet and shows no sign of activity. EG *Around them the forest was very still.* ADJ QUALIT: USU PRED ◇ **stillness**. EG *The stillness of the fields was broken by the sound of a gunshot.* ◇ N UNCOUNT

9 A **still** is a photograph taken from a cinema film which is used for publicity purposes. N COUNT

stillborn /stɪlbɔːn/. A **stillborn** baby is dead when it is born. ADJ CLASSIF

stilt /stɪlt/, **stilts. 1 Stilts** are long upright pieces of wood or metal which are used to support some buildings. EG *Thatched huts were raised high above the paddy fields on stilts.* N COUNT: USU PLURAL

2 Stilts are also two long pieces of wood that circus clowns stand on in order to walk high up above the ground. EG *He is walking on stilts.* N COUNT: USU PLURAL

stilted /stɪltɪ^{2}d/. If someone's behaviour or conversation is **stilted**, they behave or speak in a formal and unnatural way. EG *After some stilted efforts at conversation, he gave up and left.* ADJ QUALIT

stimulant /stɪmjə^{4}lənt/, **stimulants.** A **stimulant** is a drug that makes your body work faster, often increasing your heart rate and making you less likely to sleep. EG *...coffee in which the drug caffeine acts as a stimulant.* N COUNT

stimulate /stɪmjə^{4}leɪt/, **stimulates, stimulating, stimulated. 1** To **stimulate** something means to encourage it to begin or develop further. EG *Rising prices will stimulate demands for higher incomes... An outsider who can offer a fresh point of view may stimulate new ideas.* V+O

2 If something **stimulates** you, it makes you feel full of ideas and enthusiasm. EG *The art course stimulated me.* V+O ◇ **stimulating**. EG *...a conversation which I found both stimulating and exciting.* ◇ ADJ QUALIT ◇ **stimulation** /stɪmjə^{4}leɪʃə^{0}n/. EG *I find great intellectual stimulation in these surroundings.* ◇ N UNCOUNT

3 If something **stimulates** a part of a person's body, it causes it to move or function, usually automatically by a natural reflex. EG *The optical system of the eye stimulates cells in the retina.* V+O Technical

stimulus /stɪmjə^{4}ləs/, **stimuli** /stɪmjə^{4}laɪ/. **1** If something acts as a **stimulus**, it makes a process develop further or more quickly. EG *There would not have been the same stimulus to mechanize production so rapidly.* N COUNT

2 Stimulus is something which causes people to feel energetic and enthusiastic. EG *...all the stimulus and excitement that battle brought.* N UNCOUNT

3 A **stimulus** is something that causes a part of a person's body to move or function, usually automatically by a natural reflex. EG *They change automatically in response to stimuli.* N COUNT Technical

sting /stɪŋ/, **stings, stinging, stung** /stʌŋ/. **1** If an insect, animal, or plant **stings** you, it causes you to feel a sharp pain by pricking your skin, usually with poison. EG *Bees do not normally sting without being provoked.* V+O OR V

2 The **sting** of an insect or animal is the part that stings you. EG *They paralyse their victims with a sting... This is not a worker bee, it has no sting.* N SING

3 If you feel a **sting**, you feel a sharp pain in your skin or in another part of your body. EG *...the sting of ashes in his eyes.* N COUNT

4 If a part of your body **stings** or if something that you put on it **stings**, you feel a sharp pain there. EG *My eyes were stinging.* V-ERG

5 If someone's remarks **sting** you, they make you feel hurt and annoyed. EG *I wondered why I'd said it, knowing it would really sting him.* V+O: NO CONT ◇ **stinging**. EG *He made a stinging attack on Taverne.* ◇ ADJ QUALIT

6 If something **takes the sting out** of a situation, it removes the painful or unpleasant aspect of it. EG *He smiled to take the sting out of his words.* PHRASE

stingy /stɪndʒi^1/. Someone who is **stingy** is very mean. EG *The government was stingy and his salary was miserable.* ADJ QUALIT

stink /stɪŋk/, **stinks, stinking, stank** /stæŋk/, **stunk** /stʌŋk/. **1** Something that **stinks** smells extremely unpleasant. EG *The butcher's shop stank in hot weather... ...a foul, stinking lavatory.* V ▸ used as a noun. EG *The stink of vomit reached Brody almost instantly.* ▸ N SING

2 If you say that a place or situation **stinks**, you mean that you think it is extremely bad or unpleasant. EG *'What do you think of the town?' she asked. 'I think it stinks,' I replied.* V: NO CONT Informal

stinking /stɪŋkɪŋ/. You use **stinking** to describe something that is extremely unpleasant. EG *I've got a stinking cold... You couldn't hide anything in this stinking little town.* ADJ CLASSIF: ATTRIB Informal

stint /stɪnt/, **stints.** A **stint** is a period of time which you spend doing a particular job or activity. EG *I arrived at the University for a three month stint as a lecturer.* N COUNT+SUPP

stipulate /stɪpjə^{4}leɪt/, **stipulates, stipulating, stipulated.** If you **stipulate** that something must be done, you say clearly that it must be done. EG *The document stipulated nine criteria as the basis for any reform... I won't stipulate that it must be a story, just that it should be a written piece.* V+O OR V+REPORT

stir /stɜː/, **stirs, stirring, stirred. 1** When you **stir** a liquid, you mix it inside a container by using V+O

If a shop stocks stockings, what does it sell?

something such as a spoon. EG *The tourist was stirring his coffee and gazing at the buildings.*

2 If you **stir**, you move slightly, for example because you are uncomfortable. EG *The boys stirred uneasily... Etta didn't stir, pretending to be asleep.* (V)

3 If the wind **stirs** an object, it makes it move gently. EG *A stray breath of wind stirred the stillness of the robes.* (V+O)

4 If you **stir** yourself, you move yourself in order to do something. EG *Finally, one of the males stirred himself and took a step forward, hesitantly.* (V-REFL)

5 If something beautiful or terrible **stirs** you, it makes you react with a strong emotion. EG *There was a particular passage which always stirred him profoundly.* (V+O)

6 If an event causes a **stir**, it causes great excitement, shock, or anger among a number of people. EG *Her speech created a huge stir.* (N SING)

7 If a particular mood, feeling, or idea **stirs** in someone, they begin to feel it or think about it. EG *The political debate was reopened and a new mood was stirring... Something seemed to stir within her.* (V: USU+A)

stir up. 1 If something **stirs up** dust or mud, it causes it to rise up and move around. EG *Some gentle winds stirred up the dust.* (PHRASAL VB: V+O+ADV) **2** If you **stir up** trouble or **stir up** a feeling, you cause trouble or cause people to have the feeling. EG *He was prevented from speaking on the grounds that it would 'stir up trouble'... ...a rally called to stir up popular support for nuclear disarmament.* (V+O+ADV)

stirring /stɜːrɪŋ/, **stirrings. 1** You use **stirring** to describe something such as a speech when it makes people very excited or enthusiastic. EG *...one of the most stirring shots of the whole film... They must have been stirring times.* (ADJ QUALIT)

2 When there is a **stirring** of something such as a feeling, people begin to feel it. EG *There was a slight stirring of interest among them... ...the first stirrings of student protest.* (N COUNT: USU+*of*)

stirrup /stɪrəp/, **stirrups. Stirrups** are the two metal loops attached to a horse's saddle, which you place your feet in when you are riding. (N COUNT)

stitch /stɪtʃ/, **stitches, stitching, stitched. 1** When people **stitch** material, they use a needle and thread to join two pieces together or to make a decoration. EG *They were cut out and stitched together... ...finely stitched collars.* (V OR V+O)

2 A **stitch** is one of the short pieces of thread that can be seen on a piece of material when it has been stitched. EG *...the little stitches in the canvas she was embroidering.* (N COUNT)

3 When doctors **stitch** a wound or **stitch** it up, they use a special needle and thread to tie the skin together. EG *The doctor who stitched it should have another look at it tomorrow.* (V+O: OFT+*up*)

4 A **stitch** is also a piece of thread that has been used to tie the skin round a wound. EG *His wound required five stitches.* (N COUNT)

5 If you have a **stitch**, you feel a sharp pain at the side of your stomach, usually after running fast or laughing a lot. EG *I began to have a bad stitch.* (N SING: USU *a*+N)

6 If you are **in stitches**, you are laughing and cannot stop. EG *I then fell down the stairs, which sent everyone into stitches.* (PHRASE Informal)

stock /stɒk/, **stocks, stocking, stocked. 1 Stocks** are shares in the ownership of a company, or investments on which a fixed amount of interest will be paid. EG *Heavy bidding for oil company stocks may be just beginning... ...if they succeed in buying big blocks of stock.* (N COUNT: USU PLURAL OR N UNCOUNT)

2 A shop or factory that **stocks** particular goods keeps a supply of them to sell. EG *Several shops in London stock large fittings.* (V+O: NO CONT)

3 A shop's **stock** is the total amount of goods which it has available to sell. EG *...selling a week's worth of stock in a single day.* (N UNCOUNT) • If particular goods are **in stock** in a shop, they are available to be sold. If they are **out of stock**, they have all been sold and have not yet been replaced. (• PHRASE)

4 If you **stock** a container or shelf, you fill it with food or other things. EG *His locker was always stocked with screws... I found part-time work, stocking shelves in supermarkets.* (V+O)

5 If you have a **stock** of things, you have a supply of them ready to be used. EG *Keep a stock of fuses... They want to conserve coal stocks during the miners' strike.* (N COUNT+SUPP)

6 The **stock** that a person or animal comes from is the original type of people or animals from which they are descended. EG *They were of European stock... He came from sturdy, peasant stock.* (N UNCOUNT)

7 Stock is a liquid that is used to give soups and sauces a stronger flavour. You can make stock by boiling meat, bones, or vegetables in water. (N MASS)

8 A **stock** expression, character, or way of doing something is one that is very commonly used. EG *'Wild and wanton' was a stock phrase of the time.* (ADJ CLASSIF: ATTRIB)

9 If you **take stock**, you pause and think about all the aspects of a situation or event, before deciding what to do next. EG *The emergency committee had a chance to take stock of the situation.* (PHRASE)

10 lock, stock, and barrel: see **lock**. • See also **laughing stock**.

stock up. If you **stock up** with things, you buy a lot of them, in case you cannot get them later. EG *Stock up with groceries and canned foods.* (PHRASAL VB: V+ADV)

stockbroker /stɒkbrəʊkə/, **stockbrokers.** A **stockbroker** is a person whose job is to buy and sell stocks and shares for people who want to invest money. (N COUNT)

stock exchange, stock exchanges. A **stock exchange** is a place where people buy and sell stocks and shares. EG *...the Tokyo Stock Exchange.* (N COUNT: USU *the*+N)

stocking /stɒkɪŋ/, **stockings. Stockings** are pieces of clothing which fit closely over your feet and legs. Stockings are usually made of nylon or silk and worn by women. EG *...a woman in a flowered skirt and black stockings and shoes.* (N COUNT: USU PLURAL)

stockinged /stɒkɪŋd/. If someone is in their **stockinged** feet, they are wearing socks or stockings, but no shoes. (ADJ CLASSIF: ATTRIB)

stock-in-trade. Someone's **stock-in-trade** is a usual part of their behaviour or work. EG *Cynicism was his stock-in-trade.* (N SING+POSS)

stock market, stock markets. The **stock market** is the business organization and activity involved in buying and selling stocks and shares. EG *Prices have risen sharply on the stock market.* (N COUNT: USU *the*+N)

stockpile /stɒkpaɪl/, **stockpiles, stockpiling, stockpiled. 1** If people **stockpile** things, they store large quantities of them for future use. EG *...a nation that stockpiled reserves of food.* (V+O)

2 A **stockpile** of things is a large quantity of them that have been stored for future use. EG *...a stockpile of nuclear weapons.* (N COUNT: USU+SUPP)

stock-still. If someone stands or sits **stock-still**, they do not move at all. EG *She stood stock-still, staring at him.* (ADV AFTER VB)

stocktaking /stɒkteɪkɪŋ/ is the activity of counting and checking all the goods that a shop or business has. (N UNCOUNT)

stocky /stɒki[1]/, **stockier, stockiest. Stocky** people look slightly fat, but strong and solid. EG *...a short, stocky man with dark hair.* (ADJ QUALIT)

stodgy /stɒdʒi[1]/, **stodgier, stodgiest. 1 Stodgy** food is very solid, makes you feel very full, and is difficult to digest. EG *...a stodgy meal.* (ADJ QUALIT)

2 Stodgy people and things are very dull and uninteresting. EG *His friend Beale was stodgy and solemn... Can you imagine anything more stodgy?* (ADJ QUALIT)

stoic /stəʊɪk/ or **stoical** /stəʊɪkə[0]l/. If you behave in a **stoic** or **stoical** way, you accept difficulties and suffering without complaining or getting angry or upset. EG *I admired her stoic patience... He knew how brave and stoical they had to be.* (ADJ QUALIT Formal) ◇ **stoically.** EG *Accept your punishment stoically.* (◇ ADV)

stoicism /stəʊɪsɪzə[0]m/ is stoical behaviour. EG *He endured this treatment with stoicism.* (N UNCOUNT Formal)

stoke /stəʊk/, **stokes, stoking, stoked. 1** If you **stoke** a fire or **stoke** it up, you add coal or wood to it to keep it burning. EG *Willet was stoking up the stove again.* V+O: OFT+*up*

2 If you **stoke** or **stoke** up something such as a feeling, you cause it to be felt more strongly. EG *Similar schemes will only stoke the conflict... He stoked up their disgust.* V+O: OFT+*up*

stole /stəʊl/ is the past tense of **steal.**

stolen /stəʊlə⁰n/ is the past participle of **steal.**

stolid /stɒlɪd/. **Stolid** people do not show much emotion. EG *He was slow to move, stolid, and dependable.* ◇ **stolidly**. EG *He looked thoughtful, puffing stolidly at his pipe.* ADJ QUALIT ◇ ADV

stomach /stʌmək/, **stomachs, stomaching, stomached. 1** Your **stomach** is the organ inside your body where food is digested. EG *Foxes have small stomachs... His stomach was rumbling for breakfast... His stomach knotted with fright.* N COUNT

2 You can also refer to the front part of your body below your waist as your **stomach**. See picture at THE HUMAN BODY. EG *He folded his arms on his rather large stomach... He lay down on his stomach.* N COUNT

3 If you cannot **stomach** something, you cannot accept it because you dislike it or disapprove of it. EG *Rothermere was unable to stomach the idea.* V+O: WITH BROAD NEG

stomach-ache, stomach-aches. If you have a **stomach-ache**, you have a pain in your stomach. N COUNT OR N UNCOUNT

stomp /stɒmp/, **stomps, stomping, stomped.** If you **stomp** somewhere, you walk there with very heavy steps, often because you are angry. EG *I stomped back to the hotel.* V+A

stone /stəʊn/, **stones, stoning, stoned. 1 Stone** is a hard, solid substance found in the ground and often used for building houses. EG *The bits of stone are joined together with cement... ...the little stone bridge... ...a low stone wall.* N UNCOUNT

2 A **stone** is a small piece of rock. EG *Roger picked up a stone and threw it at Henry.* N COUNT

3 You can refer to a jewel as a **stone**. EG *...a ring with a white stone in it.* N COUNT

4 The **stone** in a plum or cherry is the large seed in the middle of it. EG *...plum stones.* N COUNT

5 If you **stone** someone or something, you throw stones at them. EG *Rioters had been stoning the Embassy... They took the man outside and stoned him to death.* V+O

6 A **stone** is also a measurement of weight which is equal to 14 pounds, or 6.35 kilograms. The plural form is 'stone' or 'stones'. EG *She weighed twelve stone.* N COUNT OR N PART

7 If you say that one place is a **stone's throw** from another, you mean that the places are close to each other. EG *They live within a stone's throw of the school.* PHRASE

8 to **kill two birds with one stone**: see **bird.** • See also **stoned**, **cornerstone**, **paving stone**, **precious stone**, **stepping stone**.

Stone Age. The **Stone Age** is the earliest known period of human history, when people used tools and weapons made of stone. N PROPER: *the*+N

stone-cold. Something that is **stone-cold** is very cold indeed. EG *...cups of stone-cold coffee.* ADJ CLASSIF

stoned /stəʊnd/. Someone who is **stoned** is very drunk or is very affected by drugs. ADJ QUALIT Informal

stone deaf. Someone who is **stone deaf** is completely deaf. ADJ CLASSIF

stonework /stəʊnwɜːk/ consists of objects or parts of a building that are made of stone. EG *...figures carved into the stonework.* N UNCOUNT: OFT *the*+N

stony /stəʊni¹/. **1 Stony** ground is rough and contains a lot of stones. EG *...a stony plain between low, barren hills.* ADJ QUALIT

2 If someone's voice, expression, or attitude is **stony**, they do not show any sympathy or friendliness. EG *She turned a stony face on Lucas... Her voice was stony... The announcement was received in stony silence.* ADJ QUALIT

stood /stʊd/ is the past tense and past participle of **stand.**

stooge /stuːdʒ/, **stooges.** A **stooge** is someone who is used by a powerful person to do unpleasant or dishonest tasks. EG *With the help of his stooges, he awarded contracts to favoured firms.* N COUNT Informal

stool

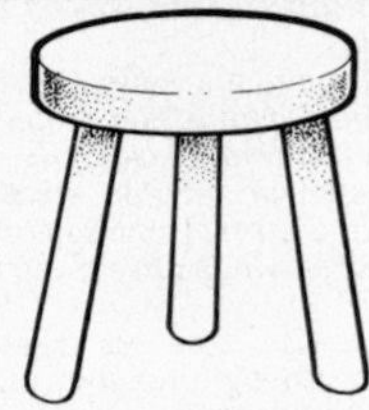

stool /stuːl/, **stools.** A **stool** is a seat with legs but no support for your arms or back. EG *He was sitting on a stool in the kitchen.* N COUNT

stoop /stuːp/, **stoops, stooping, stooped. 1** If you **stoop**, you stand or walk with your shoulders bent forwards. EG *If your ironing board is too low you have to stoop over it.* ▸ used as a noun. EG *He walks with a stoop.* V: OFT+*over* ▸ N COUNT: USU SING

2 If you **stoop** or **stoop** down, you bend your body forwards and downwards. EG *She stooped to feel the carpet... Bert stooped down and arranged them in a row.* V: OFT+*down*

3 When someone does something wrong or immoral that they would not normally do, you can say that they **stoop** to it. EG *They never stooped to spiteful tormenting... Only once did he stoop to the tactics of his opponents.* V+*to*+-ING, V+*to*-INF, OR V+O

stop /stɒp/, **stops, stopping, stopped. 1** If you have been doing something and then you **stop** doing it, you no longer do it. EG *We all stopped talking... He couldn't stop crying... She stopped work to have her baby... Stop it! You're hurting!* V, V+-ING, OR V+O

2 If you **stop** something happening, you prevent it from happening or prevent it from continuing. EG *You're trying to stop my trip to London... How do I stop a tap dripping?... Nothing was going to stop Sandy from being a writer.* V+O: OFT+-ING OR *from*

3 If you **put a stop to** something, you prevent it from happening or continuing. EG *We must put a stop to all this nonsense.* PHRASE

4 If an activity or process **stops**, it comes to an end. EG *The music stopped abruptly... They were waiting for the rain to stop.* V

5 If a machine or device **stops** or if you **stop** it, it no longer works or it is switched off. EG *My watch has stopped... Stop the recording now.* V-ERG

6 When people or things that are moving **stop** or **are stopped**, they no longer move. EG *He followed them for a few yards, and then stopped... Stop people in Oxford Street and ask them to answer these questions... The train stopped at Watford... Stop the car and let me out.* V-ERG

7 A **stop** is **7.1** a place where buses or trains regularly stop so that people can get on and off. EG *We'll get off at the next stop.* **7.2** a time or place at which you stop during a journey. EG *The first stop was a hotel outside Paris.* N COUNT

8 If something that is moving comes to a **stop**, it slows down and no longer moves. EG *The elevator came to a stop on the main floor... Harris brought the plane to a stop.* N SING: *a*+N

9 If you **stop** somewhere on a journey, you stay there for a short while. EG *On my way home I stopped at the shop.* V: USU+A

10 If you **stop** someone's pay or a cheque, you prevent the money from being paid. V+O

11 If you will **stop at nothing** to get or achieve PHRASE

Find two words on these pages that are pronounced the same.

something, you are prepared to do anything, even if it is wrong or dangerous, in order to get it or achieve it.

12 to **stop short**: see **short**.

stop off. If you **stop off** somewhere, you stop there for a short time in the middle of a journey. EG *On the way home I stopped off in London.* PHRASAL VB : V+ADV

stopgap /stɒpgæp/, **stopgaps.** When something acts as a **stopgap**, it serves a purpose for a short time, but is replaced as soon as possible. EG *It can be used as a stopgap with patients who have lost a lot of blood... Pan Am must repay the stopgap loan it received earlier this year.* N COUNT

stopover /stɒpəʊvə/, **stopovers.** A **stopover** is a short stay in a place in between parts of a journey. EG *...a five-week tour abroad with a three-day stopover in the United States.* N COUNT

stoppage /stɒpɪdʒ/, **stoppages.** When there is a **stoppage**, people stop working because of a disagreement with their employers. EG *The stoppage had the full support of both unions.* N COUNT

stopper /stɒpə/, **stoppers.** A **stopper** is a piece of glass, plastic, or cork that fits into the top of a bottle or jar. EG *I put the stopper in the bottle.* N COUNT

stopwatch /stɒpwɒtʃ/, **stopwatches.** A **stopwatch** is a watch with buttons which you press at the beginning and end of an event, so that you can measure exactly how long it takes. N COUNT

storage /stɔːrɪdʒ/ is **1** the keeping of something in a special place until it is needed. EG *A quarter of the crop may be lost in storage... You haven't got much storage space.* **2** the process of storing data in a computer. EG *...computer-based information storage and retrieval systems.* N UNCOUNT

store /stɔː/, **stores, storing, stored. 1** A **store** is a shop. EG *She came out of the store and sat down on the bench... ...smart stores like Harrods... ...a health-food store.* • See also **chain store**. N COUNT

2 When you **store** things, you put them in a container or other place and leave them there until they are needed. EG *The tool kit is stored under the seat... ...storing water for use in the dry season... ...storing and transmitting electricity.* V+O

3 When you **store** information, you keep it in your memory, in a file, or in a computer. EG *...stored as images in the minds of people... ...pocket calculators which can store telephone numbers.* V+O

4 A **store** is also **4.1** a supply of something that you keep somewhere until you need it. EG *...the village's store of grain... ...emergency stores of food and medical equipment.* N COUNT OR N PART **4.2** a place where things are kept while they are not being used. EG *...weapon stores in which nuclear warheads were kept... Goods in store will be insured for loss or damage.* N COUNT OR N UNCOUNT

5 If something is **in store** for you, it is going to happen at some time in the future. EG *Think of all the adventures in store for her... You never know what the next few months have got in store.* PHRASE

6 If you **set great store** on or by something, you think that it is extremely important or necessary. EG *He set the greatest store on carrying out his decision... ...a mother who has set great store by breast-feeding.* PHRASE

store up. If you **store** something **up**, you keep it until you think that the time is right to use it. EG *She had some sausage carefully stored up for the occasion.* PHRASAL VB : V+O+ADV

storehouse /stɔːhaʊs/, **storehouses. 1** A **storehouse** is a warehouse. EG *Food was still plentiful in the storehouses.* N COUNT American

2 When a lot of things can be found together in one place, you can refer to this place as a **storehouse**. EG *...Egypt, the great storehouse of archaeology.* N PART

storekeeper /stɔːkiːpə/, **storekeepers.** A **storekeeper** is a shopkeeper. N COUNT American

storeroom /stɔːru⁴m/, **storerooms.** A **storeroom** is a room in which you keep things until they are needed. EG *...a storeroom for coffins.* N COUNT

storey /stɔːri¹/, **storeys;** spelled **story, stories** in American English. The **storeys** of a building are its different floors or levels. EG *The house was three storeys high... ...a multi-storey car park.* N COUNT

stork /stɔːk/, **storks.** A **stork** is a large bird with a long beak and long legs, which lives near water. N COUNT

storm /stɔːm/, **storms, storming, stormed. 1** A **storm** is very bad weather, with heavy rain, strong winds, and often thunder and lightning. EG *Wait until the storm passes over.* N COUNT

2 A **storm** is also an angry or excited reaction from a large number of people. EG *The decision provoked a storm of criticism from Conservative MPs... ...the storm of applause.* N COUNT : USU+SUPP

3 If you **storm** into or out of a place, you enter or leave it quickly and noisily, because you are angry. EG *I stormed into the room in a rage.* V+A

4 If you **storm**, you say something in a very loud voice, because you are extremely angry. EG *'You misled us,' the professor stormed.* V OR V+QUOTE Literary

5 If people **storm** a place, they attack it. EG *The mob stormed the church.* V+O OR V+A

stormy /stɔːmi¹/, **stormier, stormiest. 1** If the weather is **stormy**, there are strong winds and heavy rain. EG *...that stormy autumn evening.* ADJ QUALIT

2 If a situation is **stormy**, it involves a lot of angry argument or criticism. EG *There was a stormy debate over it... ...the stormy relations between George and his mother.* ADJ QUALIT

story /stɔːri¹/, **stories. 1** A **story** is a description of imaginary people and events, which is written or told in order to entertain people. EG *Tell me a story... ...a story about a foolish hunter... ...ghost stories.* N COUNT

2 The **story** of something is a description of all the important things that have happened to it since it began. EG *The story of the firm begins in 1820... ...her life story.* N COUNT : USU+SUPP

3 A news **story** is a piece of news in a newspaper or in a news broadcast. EG *What is your opinion of the front page story?* N COUNT

4 If someone gives a false explanation or account of something, you can say that they are telling a **story**. EG *I hear that he told you some story about it being a practical joke.* • **tall story**: see **tall**. N COUNT

5 If you say **'It's the same old story'** or **'It's the old story'**, you mean that the same unfortunate situation seems to happen again and again. EG *It's the old story. When I'm happy, Barbara's not.* PHRASE

6 If you say that something is **only part of the story** or is **not the whole story**, you mean that a situation cannot be fully understood because not enough is known about it. EG *One suspects this was only part of the story.* PHRASE

7 You say **to cut a long story short** to indicate that you are going to state the final result of an event and not give any more details. EG *To cut a long story short, you have to go back.* ADV SEN

8 See also **storey**.

stout /staʊt/, **stouter, stoutest. 1** Someone who is **stout** is rather fat. EG *She was becoming stout... With him was a short, stout man.* ADJ QUALIT

2 Something that is **stout** is thick and strong. EG *He broke a stout branch from a bush... ...stout black shoes... A stout cable connected the chains.* ADJ QUALIT

3 Stout actions, attitudes, or beliefs are firm and strong. EG *...the stoutest possible resistance... ...its stoutest Republican allies.* ◊ **stoutly**. EG *Chris stoutly denied Eva's accusations.* ADJ QUALIT : ATTRIB ◊ ADV

stove /stəʊv/, **stoves.** A **stove** is an apparatus which provides heat for heating a room or for cooking. EG *...a gas stove... She left the sausages on the stove.* N COUNT

stow /stəʊ/, **stows, stowing, stowed.** If you **stow** something somewhere or **stow** it **away**, you put it carefully somewhere until it is needed. EG *She stowed the bags in two baskets... His baggage was safely stowed away in the plane.* V+O+A OR V+O+*away*

stowaway /stəʊəweɪ/, **stowaways.** A **stowaway** is a person who hides in a ship, aeroplane, or other vehicle in order to make a journey secretly or without paying the fare. N COUNT

straddle /strædəºl/, **straddles, straddling, straddled.** 1 If you **straddle** someone or something, you sit or stand with one leg on each side of them. EG *He straddled a chair and began fiddling with the keys.* V+O

2 If something **straddles** a place, it crosses it or links different parts of it together. EG *A viaduct straddles the river Wye.* V+O

straggle /strægəºl/, **straggles, straggling, straggled.** 1 If a group of people **straggle** somewhere, they move there slowly and with large, irregular gaps between them. EG *The players straggled across the field.* ◊ **straggler** /stræglə/, **stragglers.** EG *...waiting until the last straggler came in.* V; ◊ N COUNT

2 When things **straggle** over an area, they cover it in an uneven or untidy way. EG *The shacks straggle along the dirt road... ...her hair straggling down over her eyes.* V+A

straggly /strægli¹/. Something that is **straggly** grows or spreads out untidily in different directions. EG *...a straggly beard... ...a few straggly trees.* ADJ QUALIT

straight /streɪt/, **straighter, straightest.** 1 If something such as a line is **straight**, it continues in the same direction and does not bend or curve. EG *...a straight line... ...a long straight road... I saw the car coming straight at me... She was staring straight ahead.* ADJ QUALIT OR ADV

2 If the position of something is **straight**, it is upright or level, rather than sloping or bent. EG *Keep your knees bent and your back straight... Check that all the pictures hang straight.* ADJ CLASSIF OR ADV

3 If someone's hair is **straight**, it has no curls or waves in it. EG *...a tall slim girl with long straight hair.* ADJ QUALIT

4 If you go **straight** to a place, you go there immediately. EG *The doctor told me to go straight to bed... ...youngsters who move straight from school onto the dole queue.* ADV+A

5 If you **get** something **straight**, you make sure that you understand it properly. EG *Let me get this straight – you claim that he hit you first?* PHRASE Informal

6 If you give someone a **straight** answer, you speak honestly and frankly to them. EG *I just want a straight answer to the question.* ADJ CLASSIF

7 A **straight** choice or a **straight** fight involves only two people or things. EG *The voters have a straight choice between the two candidates.* ADJ CLASSIF: ATTRIB

8 If a criminal **is going straight**, he or she is no longer involved in crime and is living an honest life. EG *I'm going straight from now on.* PHRASE

9 If you keep **a straight face**, you manage to look serious, although you want to laugh. EG *I found it hard to keep a straight face.* PHRASE

straight away /streɪt əweɪ/. If you do something **straight away**, you do it immediately and without any delay. EG *You might not recognize it straight away... We went to work straightaway.* ADV

straighten /streɪtəºn/, **straightens, straightening, straightened.** 1 If you **straighten** something, you make it tidy or put it in its proper position. EG *I'll just straighten the bed... Straightening his tie, he knocked on the door.* V+O

2 If you are bending and you then **straighten** or **straighten** up, you make your back or body straight and upright. EG *The man straightened and looked him in the face... He straightens up, combs his hair, and walks into the meeting.* V: OFT+up

straighten out. If you **straighten out** a confused situation, you succeed in getting it organized and tidied up. EG *It'll take six weeks to get things straightened out.* PHRASAL VB: V+O+ADV

straightforward /streɪtfɔːwəd/. 1 Something that is **straightforward** is easy to do or to understand. EG *...a very straightforward set of instructions in simple English.* ADJ QUALIT

2 If your behaviour is **straightforward**, you are honest and frank and do not try to hide your feelings. EG *...the only Senator to speak with straightforward contempt.* ADJ QUALIT

strain /streɪn/, **strains, straining, strained.** 1 If **strain** is put on something, **1.1** it is pulled or stretched in a way that may damage it. EG *You overloaded the floor and put strain on the pipes.* N UNCOUNT

1.2 it has to do more than it is able to do. EG *This policy puts a greater strain on the economic system than it can bear.* N UNCOUNT OR N COUNT

2 Strain is **2.1** a state of worry and tension caused by a difficult situation. EG *...nervous strain... Overcrowding imposes severe mental strains.* **2.2** an injury to a muscle in your body. EG *...back strain.* N UNCOUNT OR N COUNT; N UNCOUNT: OFT+SUPP

3 If you say that a situation is a **strain**, you mean that it causes you to feel worried and tense. EG *I found it a strain being totally responsible for her.* N SING: a+N

4 You can use **strain** to refer to a particular quality in someone's character. EG *It was the romantic strain in me which made me do it.* N SING+SUPP

5 A **strain** of a plant is a particular type of it. EG *...high-yielding strains of wheat.* N COUNT+SUPP

6 When you hear the **strains** of music, you hear music being played. EG *The strains of Chopin drifted in from the music room.* N PLURAL +SUPP Literary

7 To **strain** something means to use it beyond normal or reasonable limits. EG *The oil-price increases have strained the resources of the poorer countries.* V+O

8 If you **strain** to do something, you make a great effort to do it. EG *He was straining to hear what the speaker was saying... He strained his eyes to catch a glimpse of the President.* V+to-INF OR V+O+to-INF

9 If you **strain** a muscle, you injure it by moving suddenly and awkwardly or by doing too much exercise. V+O

10 When you **strain** food, you remove the liquid from it. EG *I'll just strain the potatoes.* V+O

strained /streɪnd/. 1 If you are **strained**, you seem worried and nervous. EG *She looked strained and tired... Her voice was strained.* ADJ QUALIT

2 If relations between people are **strained**, they are unfriendly and do not trust each other. EG *Relations between the two families had become increasingly strained.* ADJ QUALIT

strait /streɪt/, **straits.** 1 You can refer to a narrow strip of sea which joins two large areas of sea as a **strait** or the **straits**. EG *...the Strait of Hormuz... ...the Straits of Gibraltar.* N COUNT

2 You can use **straits** to refer to the situation that someone is in when they do not have enough money. EG *The family was in difficult straits... The company was now in dire financial straits.* N PLURAL

strait jacket, strait jackets. A **strait jacket** is a special piece of clothing which is used to tie the arms of a mental patient or a violent criminal and prevent them from hurting themselves or other people. EG *The cops put me in a strait jacket.* N COUNT

strand /strænd/, **strands, stranding, stranded.** 1 A **strand** of thread, wire, or hair is a single, thin piece of it. EG *...a strand of silk... Make sure that there are no loose strands of wire... A strand of hair fell over her eyes.* N PART

2 A **strand** of a situation or idea is a part of it. EG *...these two strands of industrial policy... Several strands in Kate's life seemed to be pulled together.* N COUNT

3 If a ship, whale, or fish **is stranded**, it is stuck on the shore. EG *The boat was stranded in the mud.* V+O: USU PASS

4 If you **are stranded** in a place, you cannot leave it, for example because you have no money or no transport. EG *He was stranded in Paris.* ◊ **stranded.** EG *...the stranded holidaymakers.* V+O: USU PASS+A; ◊ ADJ CLASSIF

If you go straight home, can you turn any corners?

strange /streɪnd^{0}ʒ/, **stranger, strangest. 1** Something that is **strange** is unusual or unexpected, and may make you feel uneasy or afraid. EG *I had a strange dream last night... It was strange to hear her voice again... The strange thing is that this teacher didn't even know us.* ADJ QUALIT

2 A **strange** place is one that you have never been to before. A **strange** person is one that you have never met before. EG *I don't like strange people coming into my house... Ipswich is really quite strange to me.* ADJ QUALIT

strangely /streɪnd^{0}ʒli^{1}/. **1** If you do something **strangely**, you do it in an unusual or unexpected way. EG *They had acted strangely as he went by... He laughed strangely.* ADV

2 You can use **strangely** to say that something has a particular quality, although you did not expect it to have this quality or cannot explain why it has it. EG *He answered in a strangely calm voice.* SUBMOD

3 You can also use **strangely** or **strangely enough** to emphasize that what you are saying is surprising. EG *'Are students interested in religion these days?' – 'Strangely enough, they are.'* ADV SEN

stranger /streɪnd^{0}ʒə/, **strangers. 1** A **stranger** is someone who you have never met before. EG *A stranger appeared... Antonio was a stranger to all of us.* N COUNT

2 If you are a **stranger** in a place, you do not know the place well. EG *They are strangers in the village and lost their way in the fog.* N COUNT

3 If you are a **stranger** to something, you do not understand it or have not had any experience of it. EG *I was a stranger to this kind of gathering.* N COUNT: OFT+*to*

strangle /stræŋgə^{0}l/, **strangles, strangling, strangled. 1** To **strangle** someone means to kill them by squeezing their throat. EG *He was strangled in his bed.* V+O

2 To **strangle** something means to prevent it from succeeding or developing. EG *Such policies were strangling economic development.* V+O

strangled /stræŋgə^{0}ld/. A **strangled** voice or laugh sounds unclear and muffled. EG *...a strangled cry of amazement.* ADJ CLASSIF: ATTRIB

stranglehold /stræŋgə^{0}lhəuld/, **strangleholds.** If people have a **stranglehold** on something, they have control over it and are preventing it from being free or from developing. EG *The unions have a stranglehold on the country.* N COUNT: USU SING

strap /stræp/, **straps, strapping, strapped. 1** A **strap** is a narrow piece of leather, cloth, or other material. Straps are used to carry things or to fasten things together. EG *I undid the straps, and opened the case... ...high-heeled shoes, with straps above the ankle.* N COUNT

2 If you **strap** something somewhere, you fasten it there with a strap. EG *Children should be strapped into a special car seat... He straps on his watch.* V+O+A

strapping /stræpɪŋ/. You use **strapping** to describe someone who is tall, strong, and healthy-looking. EG *...a strapping boy of eighteen.* ADJ QUALIT

strata /strɑːtə/ is the plural of **stratum.**

stratagem /strætə^{1}dʒəm/, **stratagems.** A **stratagem** is a clever plan that you use to achieve something. EG *...a cunning stratagem to quieten the rebellious peasants.* N COUNT: USU+SUPP

strategic /strətiːdʒɪk/. **1** A **strategic** plan or action is intended to help you to achieve something or gain an advantage. EG *I took up a strategic position near the exit... The police made a strategic withdrawal against overwhelming odds.* ADJ CLASSIF

2 A country's **strategic** weapons and policies are part of the general organization of its defence systems or its organization of a war. EG *His country had made the same strategic error... ...areas occupied for strategic reasons... ...strategic nuclear weapons.* ◇ **strategically.** EG *The islands were strategically important to Venice.* ADJ CLASSIF; ◇ ADV

strategist /strætə^{1}dʒɪst/, **strategists.** A **strategist** is a person who is skilled in planning the best way to gain an advantage or to achieve success, especially in war. EG *...military strategists.* N COUNT

strategy /strætə^{1}dʒi^{1}/, **strategies. 1** A **strategy** is a plan you use in order to achieve something. EG *...Britain's defence strategy... He adopted a strategy of massive deflation.* N COUNT: USU+SUPP

2 Strategy is the art of planning the best way to gain an advantage or to achieve success, especially in war. EG *...a major exercise in military strategy... ...the debate over strategy.* N UNCOUNT

stratum /strɑːtəm/, **strata** /strɑːtə/. **1** A **stratum** of society is a group of people in it who are similar in their education, income, or social class. EG *Our military leaders have always been drawn from the upper strata of society... Let us examine a particular social stratum.* N COUNT: USU+SUPP Formal

2 The **strata** in the earth's surface are the layers of different types of rock or other material. EG *...the underlying rock strata.* N COUNT Technical

straw /strɔː/, **straws. 1 Straw** consists of the dried, yellowish stalks from crops such as wheat or barley. EG *They make the roofs out of straw... ...a straw hat... The eggs were packed in straw.* N UNCOUNT

2 A **straw** is **2.1** a single stalk of straw. **2.2** a thin tube of paper or plastic, which you use to suck a drink into your mouth. EG *Fiona was drinking a milk shake through a straw.* N COUNT

3 If you **are clutching at straws**, you are trying unusual or extreme ideas or methods because other ideas or methods have failed. PHRASE

4 If an event is **the last straw**, it is the latest in a series of unpleasant or unfavourable events, and makes you feel that you cannot tolerate a situation any longer. EG *Colley refused. This was the last straw and a row broke out.* PHRASE

strawberry /strɔːbə^{0}ri^{1}/, **strawberries.** A **strawberry** is a small red fruit which is soft and juicy. It has a thin, slightly rough skin. EG *...strawberry jam... ...strawberries and cream.* N COUNT

stray /streɪ/, **strays, straying, strayed. 1** If someone **strays**, they wander away from where they are supposed to be. EG *Children had strayed on to an airport runway... I hoped my animals wouldn't stray too far.* V: USU+A

2 A **stray** animal has wandered away from its owner's home. EG *...stray cats.* ADJ CLASSIF: ATTRIB

3 If your thoughts **stray**, you do not concentrate on one particular subject, but start thinking or talking about other things. EG *He let his thoughts stray for five minutes... He does not stray from facts.* V

4 Stray things exist separated from other similar things. EG *A hen was pecking around for stray grains of corn.* ADJ CLASSIF: ATTRIB

streak /striːk/, **streaks, streaking, streaked. 1** A **streak** is a long stripe or mark on a surface. EG *The table was smeared with streaks of paint... Her hair had a grey streak in it.* N COUNT: OFT+*of*

2 If something **streaks** a surface, it makes long stripes or marks of a different colour on the surface. EG *His moustache was streaked with grey... The sun is streaking the sea with long lines of gold.* V+O: OFT+*with*

3 If someone has a **streak** of a particular quality, that quality sometimes shows in their behaviour. EG *Children have a streak of cruelty... ...the possessive streak in her.* N COUNT+SUPP

4 If something **streaks** somewhere, it moves there very quickly. EG *The fish streaked away.* V+A

5 A lucky **streak** or a winning **streak** is a continuous series of successes, for example in gambling or sport. An unlucky **streak** is a series of failures or losses. EG *I was on a winning streak tonight.* N COUNT

stream /striːm/, **streams, streaming, streamed. 1** A **stream** is a small, narrow river. EG *He led us along the bank of the stream.* N COUNT

2 You can also refer to a narrow moving mass of liquid, gas, or smoke as a **stream**. EG *Horace blew out a stream of smoke.* ● See also **bloodstream**. N COUNT

3 A **stream** of people or vehicles is a long moving N PART OR N COUNT

line of them. EG *A steady stream of workers left the factory... ...the stream of cars.*
4 A **stream** of things is a large number of them occurring one after another. EG *...a steady stream of questions... The stream of insults continues.* N PART OR N COUNT
5 If a liquid **streams** somewhere, it flows or comes out in large amounts. EG *She stood in the doorway, tears streaming down her face... His back was streaming with sweat.* V-ERG : USU+A
6 If people or vehicles **stream** somewhere, they move there quickly and in large numbers. EG *The doors opened and the audience began to stream out... The cars are streaming by at sixty miles an hour.* V+A
7 When light **streams** somewhere, it shines strongly there after passing through or between things. EG *The sun was streaming in through the windows.* V+A
8 A **stream** in a school is a group of children of the same age and ability who are taught together. EG *...pupils in the top streams.* N COUNT+SUPP
9 To **stream** pupils means to teach them in groups according to their ability. ◊ **streaming**. EG *Our new headmaster says he's going to end streaming.* V+O ◊ N UNCOUNT

streamer /stri:mə/, **streamers.** A **streamer** is a long roll of coloured paper. Streamers are used for decorating rooms that parties are held in. EG *The gym was decorated with maroon streamers.* N COUNT

streamline /stri:mlaɪn/, **streamlines, streamlining, streamlined. 1** To **streamline** an object or a vehicle means to give it a long, narrow shape that allows it to move faster through air or water. ◊ **streamlined.** EG *Their new cars have lighter and more streamlined bodywork.* V+O ◊ ADJ QUALIT
2 To **streamline** an organization or process means to make it more efficient by removing unnecessary parts of it. EG *He aimed to streamline the Post Office... ...an attempt to streamline timber production.* V+O

street /stri:t/, **streets. 1** A **street** is a road in a town or village, usually one with houses along it. EG *The two men walked slowly down the street... ...a street map of Paris... She lives in Seyer Street.* N COUNT
2 You can use **street** when talking about activities that happen out of doors in a town rather than inside a building. EG *We've got to keep youngsters off the streets... We don't usually embrace friends in the street... ...street theatre.* N COUNT : *the*+N
3 If you talk about **the man in the street**, you mean ordinary people in general. EG *The man in the street was unlikely ever to have seen a ghost.* PHRASE
4 If someone is **streets ahead** of you, they have made much more progress than you. EG *They are streets ahead of us in metal designing.* PHRASE Informal
5 If a subject or activity is **right up** your **street**, you are very interested in it or know a lot about it. PHRASE Informal
6 See also **high street**.

streetcar /stri:tkɑ:/, **streetcars.** A **streetcar** is a tram. EG *He caught the next streetcar home.* N COUNT American

strength /strɛŋθ/, **strengths. 1** Your **strength** is the physical energy that you have, which gives you the ability to perform various actions, such as lifting or moving things. EG *I admired his immense physical strength... ...recovering their strength before trying again... He pulled with all his strength.* N UNCOUNT
2 You can use **strength** to refer to someone's confidence or courage in a difficult situation. EG *This gave us the strength to resist further temptation... With unshakable strength of character she stayed on after the crisis.* N UNCOUNT
3 You can refer to the power or influence that someone has as their **strength**. EG *...the enormous strength and influence of the unions... IBM's economic strength is phenomenal... Pacifist movements gathered strength in Norway.* • If a person or organization **goes from strength to strength**, they gradually become more confident or successful. EG *His company went from strength to strength, and in 1911 merged with a number of other companies.* N UNCOUNT • PHRASE
4 Your **strengths** are the qualities and abilities that you have which are an advantage to you. EG *Each firm has its particular strengths and weaknesses.* N COUNT OR N UNCOUNT
5 The **strength** of an object is its ability to be treated roughly, or to support or carry heavy weights, without being damaged or destroyed. EG *It is these rigid struts that give the wing its strength.* N SING
6 The **strength** of a feeling or opinion is the degree to which people have it. EG *The Government had clearly underestimated the strength of popular feeling about this.* N SING : USU+*of*
7 The **strength** of an opinion, argument, or story is the extent to which it influences people or is likely to be true. EG *He continued to deny it, despite the growing strength of the argument... This lent some strength to the complaint.* • If you do one thing **on the strength of** another, the second thing influences you and makes you decide to do the first. EG *The Cabinet agreed to a grant of £4m on the strength of the Company's projections of sales.* N UNCOUNT • PREP
8 The **strength** of a relationship is its degree of closeness. EG *This leads to bonds of deceptive strength being formed with the company.* N UNCOUNT
9 The **strength** of a group of people is the total number of people in it. EG *Their forces in the south were growing in strength.* N UNCOUNT
10 Strength is used in these phrases. **10.1** If a group exists **in strength**, it consists of many people. EG *By Easter, the tourists were arriving in strength.* **10.2** If a group is **at full strength**, it has all its members present. EG *Troops were now up to full strength.* **10.3** If a group is **below strength**, it does not have enough people. PHRASES

strengthen /strɛŋθəⁿn/, **strengthens, strengthening, strengthened. 1** If a number of people **strengthen** a group, they make it more powerful by joining it. EG *The new peers will strengthen the Labour Party in the Upper House.* V+O
2 If something **strengthens** an argument or opinion, it supports it by providing more reasons or evidence for it. EG *The uncertainty about the railways strengthened the argument for planning.* V+O
3 If a feeling or attitude **strengthens** or if someone **strengthens** it, more people feel it or are influenced by it. EG *During the prolonged depression of the seventies, racialism strengthened.* V-ERG
4 If a relationship **strengthens** or if you **strengthen** it, it becomes closer and more successful. EG *We want to strengthen our ties with the United States.* V-ERG
5 If something **strengthens** you, it increases your confidence and determination. EG *It is designed to strengthen you against the hostile world.* V+O
6 If something **strengthens** an object or structure, it makes it able to be treated roughly or able to support heavy weights, without being damaged or destroyed. EG *...struts designed to strengthen the wings of aeroplanes.* V+O

strenuous /strɛnju:əs/. A **strenuous** activity involves a lot of effort or energy. EG *...a strenuous twenty minute walk... Alf made strenuous efforts to improve his reading.* ◊ **strenuously**. EG *He strenuously denied that his airline was in any danger.* ADJ QUALIT ◊ ADV

stress /strɛs/, **stresses, stressing, stressed. 1** If you **stress** a point in a discussion, you put extra emphasis on it because you think it is important. EG *I ought to stress that this was not a trial but an enquiry... He stressed the importance of better public relations.* ▸ used as a noun. EG *...this stress on community values.* V-SPEECH ▸ N UNCOUNT +*on*
2 If you feel or are under **stress**, you feel worried and tense because of difficulties in your life. EG *...parents under stress... ...the stress of examinations... Too many stresses are being placed on the family.* N UNCOUNT OR N COUNT

Find two informal phrases on these pages.

3 Stresses are strong physical pressures applied to an object. EG *Earthquakes can result from stresses in the earth's crust.* N COUNT OR N UNCOUNT

4 Stress is emphasis that you put on a word or on part of a word when you pronounce it, so that it sounds slightly louder. EG *...the importance of stress and intonation.* N UNCOUNT ▸ used as a verb. EG *You should stress the second syllable in 'computer'.* ▸ V+O

stressful /stresful/. If a situation or experience is **stressful**, it causes someone to feel stress. EG *Life with several children is hard and stressful.* ADJ QUALIT

stretch /stretʃ/, **stretches, stretching, stretched. 1** Something that **stretches** over an area or distance extends over this area or distance. EG *...the belt of flat land which stretches from the capital up to York.* V+A

2 A **stretch** of land or water is an area of land or water. EG *...the stretch of water that separates Asia from Europe.* N COUNT+SUPP

3 When you **stretch**, or when you **stretch** yourself, you hold your arms or legs out straight and tighten your muscles. EG *Thomas yawned and stretched.* V, V+O, OR V-REFL

4 A **stretch** of time is a period of time. EG *Any job carries with it daily stretches of boredom.* N COUNT ● If you do an activity for a particular length of time **at a stretch**, you do it for this length of time without stopping. EG *It was impossible to work for more than an hour or so at a stretch.* ● PHRASE

5 When something soft or elastic **stretches** or **is stretched**, it is pulled until it becomes very tight. EG *The skin of her face was stretched very tightly over the bones... Nylon stretches.* V-ERG

6 Stretch material can be stretched. EG *...stretch covers on armchairs.* ADJ CLASSIF : ATTRIB

7 If someone's money or resources **are stretched**, they have hardly enough money or resources for their needs. EG *The nation's resources were already stretched to their limits.* V+O : USU PASS

8 If a job or task **stretches** you, it makes you work hard and use all your energy or skills. V+O

9 If you say that something is not true or possible **by any stretch of the imagination**, you are emphasizing that you think it is completely untrue or absolutely impossible. EG *It could by no stretch of the imagination be seen as a victory.* PHRASE

stretch out. 1 If you **stretch out** or if you **stretch** yourself **out** somewhere, you lie there with your legs and body in a straight line. EG *I just want to stretch out in my own bed.* PHRASAL VB : V+ADV OR V-REFL+ADV **2** If you **stretch out** a part of your body, you hold it out straight. EG *He stretched out a thin arm and took our hands.* V+O+ADV

stretcher /stretʃə/, **stretchers.** A **stretcher** is a long piece of canvas with a pole along each side, which is used to carry an injured or sick person. N COUNT

strew /struː/, **strews, strewing, strewed, strewn** /struːn/. **1** If things **are strewn** somewhere, they are scattered there untidily. EG *His clothes were strewn all over the room... Tourists strew cans and wrappers all across the grass.* V+O : USU PASS+A

2 If things **strew** a place, they lie scattered there. EG *Books and cushions strewed the floor... The carpet is strewn with broken glass.* V+O

stricken /strɪkə^{0}n/. If someone is **stricken** by something unpleasant, they are severely affected by it. EG *Madeleine was stricken by fear... Stricken with arthritis, she lay in bed for many years.* ADJ QUALIT : OFT+*with/by*

strict /strɪkt/, **stricter, strictest. 1** Someone who is **strict** does not tolerate impolite or disobedient behaviour, especially from children. EG *Parents were strict in Victorian times... ...a school with strict discipline.* ADJ QUALIT ◇ **strictly.** EG *The curfew was strictly enforced.* ◇ ADV

2 A **strict** rule or order must be obeyed absolutely. EG *Strict instructions were issued... The Opposition demanded stricter control of prices.* ADJ QUALIT ◇ **strictly.** EG *This is strictly confidential.* ◇ ADV

3 If you talk about the **strict** meaning or truth of something, you mean the precise meaning or the absolute truth. EG *He may not be lying in the strict sense of the word, but he has not told the whole truth.* ADJ CLASSIF : ATTRIB ◇ **strictly.** EG *That's not strictly true.* ◇ SUBMOD

4 You use **strict** to describe someone who never does things that are against their beliefs. For example, a strict vegetarian never eats meat. EG *His family were strict Methodists.* ADJ QUALIT : ATTRIB

strictly /strɪktli^{1}/. **1** If something is **strictly** for a particular thing or person, it is intended to be used or done only by them. EG *The discussion was strictly for members.* ADV+*for*

2 If someone keeps **strictly** to a particular subject or relationship, they do not try to change it. EG *This is a strictly doctor-patient relationship... Everything he said was strictly to the point.* SUBMOD

3 You say **strictly speaking** when you want to correct a statement or add more precise information about it. EG *Paul's a friend of mine. Well, strictly speaking my sister's friend... I think, strictly speaking, you are wrong there.* ADV SEN

stride /straɪd/, **strides, striding, strode** /strəʊd/, **stridden** /strɪdə^{0}n/. **1** If you **stride** somewhere, you walk there with quick, long steps. EG *Louisa watched him striding across the lawn... He was striding out of the entrance.* V : USU+A

2 A **stride** is **2.1** a long step which you take when you are walking or running. EG *...the length of each stride.* N COUNT **2.2** a way of walking with long steps. EG *She walked ahead with her purposeful stride.* N SING

3 If you make **strides** in something that you are doing, you make rapid progress in it. EG *On the question of pay, giant strides have been made.* N COUNT : USU PLURAL

4 If you **take** a problem or difficulty **in** your **stride**, you deal with it calmly and easily. EG *She takes examinations in her stride.* PHRASE

strident /straɪdənt/. **1** A **strident** sound is loud and unpleasant to listen to. EG *His voice was strident and triumphant.* ADJ QUALIT

2 If someone is **strident**, they state their feelings or opinions very strongly; used showing disapproval. EG *...a strident demand for rearmament... ...strident, hostile women.* ADJ QUALIT

strife /straɪf/ is strong disagreement or fighting. EG *...the basis of family strife... The Empire was torn by racial strife.* N UNCOUNT Formal

strike /straɪk/, **strikes, striking, struck** /strʌk/.

1 When there is a **strike**, workers stop doing their work for a period of time, usually to try to get better pay or conditions for themselves. EG *...the miners' strike.* N COUNT ▸ used as a verb. EG *Airline pilots are threatening to strike.* ▸ V ● Workers who are **on strike** are refusing to work. EG *I would never go on strike for more money.* ● PHRASE

2 A hunger **strike** is a refusal to eat anything as a protest about something. A rent **strike** is a refusal to pay your rent. N COUNT+SUPP

3 If you **strike** someone or something, you deliberately hit them. EG *The young man struck his father... He struck the ball beautifully.* V+O Literary

4 If something **strikes** something else or **strikes** against it, it hits it. EG *The house was struck by lightning... The trawler struck against the jetty.* V+O OR V+A

5 If something such as an illness or disaster **strikes**, it suddenly happens. EG *When disaster strikes, you need sympathy and practical advice... ...the earthquake that struck Japan last Tuesday.* V OR V+O

6 To **strike** means to attack someone or something quickly and violently. EG *Raising herself slightly, the snake strikes.* V : OFT+*at* ▸ used as a noun. EG *The Air Force carried out air strikes as a result of the information received.* ▸ N COUNT : OFT+SUPP

7 If an idea or thought **strikes** you, it comes into your mind suddenly. EG *It struck him how foolish his behaviour had been.* V+O : OFT+REPORT : ONLY *that*

8 If something **strikes** you as being a particular thing, it gives you the impression of being that thing. EG *Gertie strikes me as a very silly girl.* V+O : USU+*as*

9 If you **are struck** by something, you are very V+O : USU PASS +*with/by*

impressed by it. EG *He had been struck by what he saw... I was very much struck by London.*
10 When a clock **strikes**, its bells make a sound to indicate what the time is. EG *The church clock struck eleven.* V OR V+O
11 If something that someone says **strikes a** particular **note**, it produces a particular impression or atmosphere. EG *His words struck a slightly false note for me.* PHRASE
12 If something that someone says **strikes a chord**, it makes you feel sympathy or enthusiasm. PHRASE
13 If you **strike** a bargain or a deal with someone, you come to an agreement with them. EG *The council hoped to strike a deal that would give it more power.* V+O
14 If you **strike a balance**, you do something that is halfway between two extremes. EG *It is not easy to strike a balance between too much and too little freedom.* PHRASE
15 If something **strikes fear** or **strikes terror** into people, it causes them to be suddenly very frightened. EG *The tanks struck terror into the hearts of the peasants.* PHRASE
16 If you **are struck dumb** or **are struck blind**, you suddenly become unable to speak or to see. EG *We were struck dumb with horror.* PHRASE
17 If you **strike** a match, you make it produce a flame. EG *He struck a match and put it to his pipe.* V+O
18 If someone **strikes** oil or gold, they discover it in the ground as a result of mining or drilling. V+O
19 If you **strike lucky**, you have good luck. EG *He had struck lucky in having someone who was so sensitive to look after him.* PHRASE
20 See also **striking**.
strike back. If you **strike back**, you attempt to harm someone, because they have harmed you. PHRASAL VB : V+ADV
strike down. If something **strikes** someone **down**, it kills them or severely harms them. EG *Kennedy was struck down by an assassin's bullet.* PHRASAL VB : V+O+ADV
strike off. If someone such as a doctor or lawyer **is struck off**, their name is removed from the official register and they are not allowed to do medical or legal work any more. PHRASAL VB : V+O+ADV, USU PASS
strike out. If you **strike out**, you begin to do something different, often because you want to become more independent. EG *He decided to strike out on his own.* PHRASAL VB : V+ADV, USU+A
strike up. **1** When you **strike up** a conversation or friendship with someone, you begin it. EG *Alice and I struck up a friendship immediately.* **2** When musicians **strike up**, they begin to play music. EG *The band had just struck up Ellington's 'Satin Doll'.* PHRASAL VB : V+ADV+O; V+ADV OR V+ADV+O

striker /straɪkə/, **strikers.** **1 Strikers** are people who refuse to continue working, usually because they want more pay or better conditions. N COUNT
2 In football, a **striker** is a player whose main function is to attack rather than defend. N COUNT

striking /straɪkɪŋ/. **1** Something that is **striking** is so noticeable or unusual that it cannot be ignored. EG *The most striking thing about Piccadilly Circus is the statue of Eros in the centre.* ADJ QUALIT
◊ **strikingly**. EG *The two women appeared strikingly different.* ◊ SUBMOD
2 Someone who is **striking** is very attractive. EG *...a striking redhead... ...his striking good looks.* ADJ QUALIT
◊ **strikingly**. EG *...a strikingly beautiful child.* ◊ SUBMOD

string /strɪŋ/, **strings, stringing, strung** /strʌŋ/.
1 String is thin rope made of twisted threads. EG *She took the parcel and started to undo the string... ...a bunch of balloons on a string.* N UNCOUNT OR N COUNT
2 A **string** of things is a number of them on the same piece of thread or wire. EG *...a string of beads round her neck.* N COUNT OR N PART
3 You can refer to a row of similar things as a **string**. EG *...a string of islands.* N COUNT OR N PART
4 A **string** of similar events is a series of them happening one after the other. EG *It was the latest in a string of hotel disasters.* N COUNT OR N PART
5 The **strings** on a musical instrument such as a violin or guitar are thin pieces of tightly-stretched wire or nylon. You make sounds by plucking the strings or by passing a bow across them. N COUNT
6 The section of an orchestra which consists of stringed instruments played with a bow is called the **strings**. N PLURAL
7 If you **pull strings** to get something done, you use your influence with other people in order to get it done; often used showing disapproval. EG *Derek offered to pull a few strings and get her a place at the university.* PHRASE
8 If something is offered to you with **no strings attached**, it is offered without any special conditions. EG *We will pay you ten per cent with no strings attached.* PHRASE
string out. If things **are strung out** somewhere, they are spread out in a long line. EG *...small towns strung out along the dirt roads.* PHRASAL VB : V-ERG+ADV
string together. If you **string** things **together**, you make them into one thing by adding them to each other, one at a time. EG *I strung together some rhymes to amuse her.* PHRASAL VB : V+O+ADV
string up. To **string** someone **up** means to kill them by hanging them. EG *We will all be strung up from lamp-posts.* PHRASAL VB : V+O+ADV Informal

stringed /strɪŋd[1]/. A **stringed** instrument is a musical instrument which has strings, such as a violin or a guitar. See picture at MUSICAL INSTRUMENTS. ADJ CLASSIF : ATTRIB

stringent /strɪndʒənt/. **Stringent** laws, rules, or conditions are very severe or are strictly controlled. EG *His budget proposal is even more stringent than the President's... These requirements are often very stringent.* ADJ QUALIT Formal

stringy /strɪŋi[1]/, **stringier, stringiest. 1** If food is **stringy**, it is tough and difficult to chew. EG *The meat was grey and stringy.* ADJ QUALIT
2 Stringy hair is thin and rough. ADJ QUALIT

strip /strɪp/, **strips, stripping, stripped. 1** A **strip** of paper, cloth, or other material is a long, narrow piece of it. EG *...a thin strip of paper... The room was bare, apart from a strip of carpet.* N COUNT OR N PART
2 A **strip** of land or water is a long narrow area of it. EG *There was only a narrow strip of beach.* N COUNT OR N PART
3 If you **strip**, you take off your clothes. EG *They told her to strip.* V
4 If someone **strips** you, they take off your clothes, for example in order to search for hidden or illegal things. EG *Before the ship sailed they were stripped and searched.* V+O
5 To **strip** something means to remove everything that is covering its surface. EG *The wind stripped the tree of all its leaves... The paint could easily be stripped off.* V+O : USU+A
6 To **strip** someone of their property, rights, or titles means to take them away from them. EG *She was automatically stripped of all her property and possessions... They were stripping away my remaining pension rights.* V+O+A
7 In a newspaper or magazine, a comic **strip** or a **strip** cartoon is a series of drawings which tell a story. The words spoken by the characters are often written on the drawings. N COUNT
8 If you **tear a strip off** someone or if you **tear** them **off a strip**, you scold them angrily and severely. PHRASE Informal
strip off. 1 If you **strip off** your clothes, you take them off. EG *She hurried into the bathroom, stripping off her clothes... Casson stripped off his raincoat.* **2** If someone **strips off** your clothes, they undress you in order to search you. EG *The other officer stripped off my waistcoat and threw it in the corner.* PHRASAL VB : V+ADV OR V+O+ADV; V+O+ADV

strip club, strip clubs. A **strip club** is a club which people go to in order to see striptease. N COUNT

If someone pulls strings, are they playing a stringed instrument?

stripe /straɪp/, **stripes. 1** A **stripe** is a long line which is usually a different colour or texture from the areas next to it. EG *...a shirt with blue and white stripes.* ◇ **striped** /straɪpt/. EG *...a gentleman in a black coat and striped trousers.* N COUNT ◇ ADJ CLASSIF

2 In the police or the armed forces, **stripes** are narrow bands of material sewn onto a uniform to indicate someone's rank. EG *...a red uniform with sergeant's stripes.* N COUNT

strip lighting is a method of lighting which uses long tubes rather than light bulbs. N UNCOUNT

stripper /strɪpə/, **strippers.** A **stripper** is a person who earns money by doing striptease. N COUNT Informal

striptease /strɪptiːz/ is a form of entertainment in which someone takes off their clothes slowly and in a sexy way to music. N UNCOUNT

strive /straɪv/, **strives, striving, strove** /strəʊv/, **striven** /strɪvəⁿn/. If you **strive** for something or **strive** to do something, you make a great effort to get it or to do it. EG *They strove to give the impression that they were leaving... They have striven for freedom for many years.* V+*for* OR *to*-INF Formal

strode /strəʊd/ is the past tense of **stride.**

stroke /strəʊk/, **strokes, stroking, stroked. 1** If you **stroke** someone or something, you move your hand slowly and gently over them. EG *She put out a hand and stroked the cat... He stroked her hair affectionately.* V+O

2 A **stroke** is a sudden and severe illness which affects your brain, and which often kills people or causes them to be paralysed in one side of their body. EG *Wilson was crippled by a stroke... She had a stroke and was unable to walk again.* N COUNT

3 The **strokes** of a pen or brush are the movements or marks you make with it when you are writing or painting. EG *She began to paint with bold, defiant strokes.* N COUNT

4 When you are swimming or rowing, your **strokes** are the repeated movements you make with your arms or the oars. EG *She swam with steady strokes.* N COUNT

5 A swimming **stroke** is a particular style or method of swimming. See picture at SWIMMING. N COUNT

6 The **strokes** of a clock are the sounds that indicate each hour. EG *At the twelfth stroke, we welcomed in the New Year.* N COUNT

7 If you describe something that happens as a **stroke of luck**, you mean that it is lucky that it happened. EG *We had a real stroke of good luck... Then it came, my stroke of great good fortune.* PHRASE

8 If you describe a thought or idea as a **stroke of genius**, you mean that it is very clever. PHRASE

9 If something happens **at a stroke** or **in one stroke**, it happens suddenly and completely because of one single action. EG *He was determined at a stroke to remove those distinctions.* PHRASE

10 If someone **does not do a stroke** of work, they are very lazy and do no work at all. PHRASE Informal

stroll /strəʊl/, **strolls, strolling, strolled.** If you **stroll** somewhere, you walk in a slow, relaxed way. EG *They strolled along the beach.* ▸ used as a noun. EG *She decided to take a stroll in the garden.* V+A ▸ N COUNT

strong /strɒŋ/, **stronger, strongest. 1** Someone who is **strong 1.1** has powerful muscles and can move or carry heavy things, or hold things very tightly. EG *His strong arms were around me, pinning me down.* **1.2** is very confident and not easily influenced or worried by other people. EG *I felt very strong in the knowledge of my own innocence... ...a strong personality.* ADJ QUALIT

2 Strong objects are not easily broken. EG *...steel cylinders strong enough to survive even a nuclear catastrophe.* ◇ **strongly**. EG *...strongly constructed buildings.* ADJ QUALIT ◇ ADV

3 You use **strong** to describe things that are great in degree or intensity. EG *His teachings still exert a strong influence... ...a strong incentive to buy more machines... ...a strong sense of identity... The strong possibility is that he will be told tomorrow... ...the strong wind... The smell of the gas grew stronger... They still spoke with a strong German accent.* ◇ **strongly**. EG *His mother will strongly influence his choice of a wife.* ADJ QUALIT ◇ ADV

4 If you have **strong** views on something or express your views using **strong** words, you have very definite views or express them in a very definite way. EG *There is strong criticism of certain aspects of the case... He has condemned the present sit-in by students in strong terms... ...a strong Labour supporter.* ◇ **strongly**. EG *I feel very strongly about drugs... I would strongly advise you against such an action... He is remembered for his strongly anti-war attitude.* ADJ QUALIT : USU ATTRIB ◇ ADV

5 If someone in authority takes **strong** action, they act firmly and severely. EG *They introduced a strong anti-inflation programme.* ADJ QUALIT

6 If the arguments for something are **strong**, they are supported by a lot of evidence. EG *There is a strong case for an Act of Parliament.* ADJ QUALIT

7 If a group is **strong**, it has many members or great power. EG *It was essential to build a strong organization.* ADJ QUALIT

8 You can also use **strong** when you are saying how many people there are in a group. For example, if a group is twenty **strong**, there are twenty people in it. ADJ CLASSIF : AFTER NUMBER

9 Your **strong** points or your **strong** subjects are things which you are good at. EG *Maths was always his strong subject.* ADJ QUALIT : ATTRIB

10 A **strong** competitor or candidate is likely to win in a contest. EG *She was a very strong candidate.* ADJ QUALIT : ATTRIB

11 If someone has **strong** nerves or a **strong** stomach, they are not easily frightened or upset. ADJ QUALIT

12 If a relationship is **strong**, it is firm and likely to last for a long time. EG *Links with the trade unions were strong.* ADJ QUALIT

13 Industries, economies, or currencies that are **strong** are financially successful. EG *Sterling has once again become one of the stronger currencies.* ADJ QUALIT

14 Drinks, chemicals, or drugs that are **strong** contain a lot of a particular substance. EG *She made him a cup of tea so strong that he could not drink it... ...a strong household bleach.* ADJ QUALIT

15 If someone or something is still **going strong**, they are still living or still working well after a long time. EG *The society started in 1904 and is still going strong.* PHRASE

stronghold /strɒŋhəʊld/, **strongholds.** If a place is a **stronghold** of an attitude or belief, many people there have this attitude or belief. EG *It is a solid Labour stronghold.* N COUNT+SUPP

stroppy /strɒpi¹/. Someone who is **stroppy** is bad-tempered and obstinate. EG *She threatened to get stroppy.* ADJ QUALIT Informal British

strove /strəʊv/ is the past tense of **strive.**

struck /strʌk/ is the past tense and past participle of **strike.**

structural /strʌktʃəºrəl/ is used to describe an aspect of the structure of something. EG *We plastered over the major structural faults in the walls... I was shocked at the structural damage.* ADJ CLASSIF

structure /strʌktʃə/, **structures, structuring, structured. 1** The **structure** of something is the way in which it is made, built, or organized. EG *She analysed the structure of its skull in great detail... The whole structure of the film was rather simplistic... The class structures of England and America are quite different.* N UNCOUNT : USU+SUPP, OR N COUNT

2 A **structure** is something that has been built or formed in a particular way. EG *We visited the Children's Palace, a great sprawling structure.* N COUNT : USU+SUPP

3 A system or activity that has **structure** is well arranged and organized and is therefore efficient. EG *She loved the sense of structure, organization and enthusiasm.* N UNCOUNT

4 If you **structure** something, you arrange it in a careful, organized pattern or system. EG *They structure their communication to meet the needs of the* V+O *client... They could never achieve anything because they wouldn't structure the group and have effective leadership.*

struggle /strʌgᵊl/, **struggles, struggling, struggled. 1** If you **struggle** to do something, you try very hard to do it, although it is difficult for you. EG *We should give moral support to them as they struggle to build a more democratic society... ...a nationalist movement that has had to struggle for independence.* ▸ used as a noun. EG *...the day-to-day struggle for survival.* V: USU+to-INF OR for ▸ N COUNT: USU SING

2 If you **struggle** when you are being held, you twist, kick, and move violently in order to get free. EG *She struggled in his embrace.* V: OFT+to-INF OR A

3 If two people **struggle** with each other, they fight. EG *We struggled for the gun, until at last it went off.* ▸ used as a noun. EG *There was a moment's struggle and the gun fell to the ground.* V OR V+with: RECIP ▸ N COUNT

4 If you **struggle** to move yourself, you manage to do it with great difficulty. EG *He struggled to his feet... He struggled forward for about half a mile.* V+to-INF OR A

5 An action or activity that is a **struggle** is very difficult for you to do. EG *Reading was a struggle for him.* N SING: a+N

struggle on. If you **struggle on**, you manage with great difficulty to continue doing something. EG *Some struggled on, but those who couldn't were left behind.* PHRASAL VB: V+ADV

strum /strʌm/, **strums, strumming, strummed.** If you **strum** a guitar, you play it by moving your hand quickly up and down across the strings. EG *The guitar player started strumming softly.* V OR V+O

strung /strʌŋ/ is the past tense and past participle of **string.**

strut /strʌt/, **struts, strutting, strutted. 1** Someone who **struts** walks in a proud way, with their head held high and their chest out. EG *Eddie turned around and strutted back to them... ...a peacock strutting on the lawn.* V: USU+A

2 A **strut** is a piece of wood or metal which holds the weight of other pieces in a building. N COUNT

stub /stʌb/, **stubs, stubbing, stubbed. 1** The **stub** of a cigarette or a pencil is the last short piece of it which remains when the rest has been used. EG *...an ashtray full of old cigarette stubs.* N COUNT+SUPP

2 The **stub** of a cheque or ticket is the small part that you keep. N COUNT

3 If you **stub** your toe, you hurt your toe by accidentally kicking something. EG *I stubbed my toe against a stone.* V+O

stub out. When someone **stubs out** a cigarette, they put it out by pressing it against something hard. EG *He stubbed his cigarette out in an ash tray.* PHRASAL VB: V+O+ADV

stubble /stʌbᵊl/. **1** The short stalks which are left standing in fields after corn or wheat has been harvested are referred to as **stubble**. EG *The stubble was burning on the harvested fields.* N UNCOUNT

2 The very short hairs on a man's face when he has not shaved recently are also referred to as **stubble**. EG *There was a hint of stubble round the chin.* N UNCOUNT

stubborn /stʌbᵊn/. **1** Someone who is **stubborn** is determined to do what they want and is very unwilling to change their mind. EG *Our son is stubborn and rebellious... ...his stubborn determination.* ◇ **stubbornly**. EG *'It was an accident,' he said stubbornly, 'and that's that.'* ADJ QUALIT ◇ ADV

2 A **stubborn** stain is difficult to remove. EG *Remove stubborn marks on tiles with a wire brush.* ADJ QUALIT

stubby /stʌbi¹/. A **stubby** object is short and thick. EG *His stubby fingers were strong and mobile.* ADJ QUALIT

stuck /stʌk/. **1 Stuck** is the past tense and past participle of **stick**.

2 If something is **stuck** in a particular position, it is fixed tightly in this position and unable to move. EG *The lift seems to be stuck between the second and third floors.* ADJ PRED: USU+A

3 If you are **stuck** when you are trying to do something, you are unable to continue doing it because it is too difficult. EG *Ask for help the minute you're stuck... They used the dictionary when they got stuck on words.* ADJ PRED

4 If you are **stuck** in a place, you are unable to get away from it. EG *The boss rang to explain that he was stuck in Milan.* ADJ PRED: USU+A

5 If you are **stuck** in an unpleasant situation, you are unable to change it. EG *They are stuck in boring jobs.* ADJ PRED: USU+A

stud /stʌd/, **studs. 1** A **stud** is **1.1** a small piece of metal which is attached to a surface. EG *...black leather with gold studs.* **1.2** a kind of small earring which goes straight through your ear. EG *Some women wore jade studs in their ears.* N COUNT

2 Male horses or other animals that are kept for **stud** are kept to be used for breeding. EG *I'm not going to race him, I'm going to put him to stud... ...stud horses.* N UNCOUNT

3 A **stud** or a **stud farm** is a place where horses are bred. N COUNT

studded /stʌdɪ²d/. Something that is **studded** is decorated with studs or things that look like studs. EG *...enamel bracelets studded with precious stones.* ADJ CLASSIF: OFT+with

student /stju:dᵊnt/, **students. 1** A **student** is **1.1** a person who is studying at a university or college. EG *...a part-time student at King's College, London... ...student nurses.* ● See also **mature student**. **1.2** a person who is studying in a secondary school. N COUNT; American

2 Someone who is a **student** of a particular subject is interested in the subject and is trying to learn about it. EG *It is our treatment of old people which most shocks students of our culture.* N COUNT+of

studied /stʌdɪd/. **1** A **studied** action has been carefully thought about or planned and is not spontaneous or natural. EG *With studied casualness he mentioned his departure to Hilary... ...a studied gesture of impatience.* ADJ CLASSIF: ATTRIB

2 See also **study**.

studio /stju:dɪəʊ/, **studios.** A **studio** is **1** a room where a painter or photographer works. EG *Upstairs he had a studio where he painted a little.* **2** a room where radio or television programmes are recorded, records are produced, or films are made. EG *I went up to the big recording studio in Maida Vale.* N COUNT

studious /stju:dɪəs/. Someone who is **studious** spends a lot of time reading and studying books. ADJ QUALIT

studiously /stju:dɪəsli¹/. If you **studiously** do something, you do it carefully and deliberately. EG *The Colonel studiously examined his folders.* ADV

study /stʌdi¹/, **studies, studying, studied. 1** If you **study** a particular subject, you spend time learning about it. EG *He studied chemistry at university... She's studying for a law degree.* V+O OR V

2 Study is the activity of studying a subject. EG *There are no rooms specifically set aside for quiet study.* N UNCOUNT

3 Studies are subjects which are studied. EG *...the School of European Studies... ...the introduction of new studies into the curriculum.* N PLURAL

4 If you **study** something, you look at it or watch it very carefully. EG *He looked at her hard, studying her face... I studied a map.* V+O

5 A **study** of a subject is a piece of research on it. EG *She has made a close study of male executives and their drinking habits.* N COUNT

6 A **study** by an artist is a drawing which is done in preparation for a larger picture. N COUNT

7 A **study** in a house is a room which you use for reading, writing, and studying. N COUNT

8 See also **studied**.

stuff /stʌf/, **stuffs, stuffing, stuffed. 1** You can refer to a substance, a thing, or a group of things as **stuff**. EG *What's that stuff in the bucket?... Quite a lot of stuff had been stolen... She was reading the travel stuff in the colour supplement.* N UNCOUNT: USU+SUPP

Does a stunt man sometimes work in a studio?

2 If you **stuff** something somewhere, you push it there quickly and roughly. EG *Willie gathered up the bills and stuffed them carelessly into his pocket... Nora stuffed a cigarette into her mouth.* V+O+A

3 If you **stuff** a place or container, you fill it with material or other things until it is full. EG *...stuffing a toy dog.* ◊ **stuffed.** EG *He'd got a big rucksack, stuffed with notes, on his back.* V+O : OFT+*with*; ◊ ADJ CLASSIF

4 If you **stuff** yourself, you eat a lot of food. EG *Karin was stuffing herself with eggs and toast.* V-REFL OR V+O Informal

5 If you **stuff** a bird such as a chicken or a vegetable such as a pepper, you put a mixture of food inside it before cooking it. ◊ **stuffed.** EG *...stuffed olives.* V+O; ◊ ADJ CLASSIF

6 If a dead animal **is stuffed**, it is filled with material so that it can be preserved and displayed. ◊ **stuffed.** EG *...a stuffed parrot.* V+O : USU PASS; ◊ ADJ CLASSIF

7 If you say that someone **knows** their **stuff**, you mean that they are good at doing something because they are experienced at it and know a lot about it. EG *These union negotiators know their stuff.* PHRASE Informal

8 If you are angry with someone for something that they have said or done, you might say **'Get stuffed!'** to them; a rude expression. EXCLAM Informal

stuffing /stʌfɪŋ/ is **1** a mixture of food that is put inside a bird such as a chicken, or a vegetable such as a pepper, before it is cooked. EG *We had chicken with stuffing and new potatoes.* N MASS **2** material that is put inside pillows, cushions, or toys, in order to fill them and make them firm or solid. N UNCOUNT

stuffy /stʌfi[1]/, **stuffier, stuffiest. 1 Stuffy** people or institutions are formal and old-fashioned. ADJ QUALIT

2 If it is **stuffy** in a place, it is unpleasantly warm and there is not enough fresh air. EG *...a stuffy room.* ADJ QUALIT

stultify /stʌltɪfaɪ/, **stultifies, stultifying, stultified.** If something **stultifies** you, it makes you feel dull and stop thinking, because it is so boring or repetitive. EG *The regular use of calculators can stultify a child's capacity to do mental arithmetic.* ◊ **stultifying.** EG *...the stultifying rituals of court procedure.* V+O; ◊ ADJ QUALIT

stumble /stʌmbə[0]l/, **stumbles, stumbling, stumbled. 1** If you **stumble**, you put your foot down awkwardly while you are walking or running and nearly fall over. EG *The man was drunk and he stumbled on the bottom step.* V : NO IMPER

2 If you **stumble** while you are reading aloud or speaking, you make a mistake, and have to pause and read it or say it again. EG *She stumbled over the foreign words.* V : NO IMPER

stumble across or **stumble on.** If you **stumble across** something or **stumble on** it, you find it or discover it unexpectedly. EG *In the course of their search they may stumble across something quite different... Sir Alexander Fleming stumbled on his great discovery of penicillin quite by accident.* PHRASAL VB : V+PREP, HAS PASS

stumbling block, stumbling blocks. A **stumbling block** is something which stops you from doing or getting what you want. EG *Perhaps the biggest stumbling block to disarmament is the deterrent theory.* N COUNT

stump /stʌmp/, **stumps, stumping, stumped. 1** A **stump** is a small part of something that remains when the rest of it has been removed or broken off. EG *We left him sitting on the stump of an old oak tree.* N COUNT

2 The **stumps** in cricket are the three wooden sticks that are placed upright in the ground to form the wicket. N COUNT

3 If a question or problem **stumps** you, you cannot think of any solution or answer to it. EG *...the question that has stumped philosophers since the beginning of time.* V+O

4 If you **stump** somewhere, you walk there with heavy steps. EG *She stumped back into the house.* V+A

stump up. If you **stump up** a sum of money, you pay the money that is required for something, often reluctantly. EG *The government is being asked to stump up the balance.* PHRASAL VB : V+ADV+O

stumpy /stʌmpi[1]/. **Stumpy** things are short and thick. EG *...a short stumpy tail.* ADJ QUALIT

stun /stʌn/, **stuns, stunning, stunned. 1** If you **are stunned** by something, you are very shocked by it. EG *We were all stunned by the news.* ◊ **stunned.** EG *I sat in stunned silence.* V+O : USU PASS; ◊ ADJ QUALIT

2 If something such as a blow on the head **stuns** you, it makes you unconscious or confused and unsteady. EG *He was stunned by a blow from the rifle.* V+O

3 See also **stunning.**

stung /stʌŋ/ is the past tense and past participle of **sting.**

stunk /stʌŋk/ is the past participle of **stink.**

stunning /stʌnɪŋ/. Something that is **stunning** is **1** extremely beautiful or impressive. EG *The film is visually stunning... Her dress was simply stunning.* **2** so unusual or unexpected that people are astonished by it. EG *...a stunning victory in the general election.* ADJ QUALIT

stunt /stʌnt/, **stunts, stunting, stunted. 1** A **stunt** is **1.1** something that someone does in order to get publicity. EG *Climbing up the church tower was a fine publicity stunt.* **1.2** a dangerous and exciting action that someone does in a film. EG *Steve McQueen did most of his own stunts.* N COUNT

2 If one thing **stunts** the growth or development of another, it prevents it from growing or developing as much as it should. EG *These insecticides can stunt plant growth.* ◊ **stunted.** EG *...old, stunted thorn trees.* V+O; ◊ ADJ QUALIT

stunt man, stunt men. A **stunt man** is a man whose job is to do dangerous things in films instead of the actors. N COUNT

stupefied /stjuːpɪfaɪd/. If you are **stupefied**, **1** you feel so tired or bored that you are unable to think clearly. EG *I felt stupefied by the heavy meal.* **2** you are very surprised. EG *He was too stupefied to answer her.* ADJ QUALIT : USU PRED

stupendous /stjuːpɛndəs/. Something that is **stupendous** is extremely large or impressive. EG *The roar of the explosion was stupendous... ...stupendous sums of money.* ADJ QUALIT

stupid /stjuːpɪd/, **stupider, stupidest. 1** Someone who is **stupid** shows a lack of good judgement or intelligence and is not at all sensible. EG *I have been extremely stupid... ...a stupid question.* ◊ **stupidly.** EG *I once stupidly asked him why he smiled so often.* ADJ QUALIT; ◊ ADV

2 You say that something is **stupid** to indicate that you do not like it or that it annoys you. EG *I hate these stupid black shoes.* ADJ CLASSIF Informal

stupidity /stjuːpɪdɪ[1]ti[1]/, **stupidities. Stupidity** is **1** behaviour that is not at all sensible. EG *I used to find her occasional stupidities amusing... He is paying a big price for his stupidity.* N COUNT OR N UNCOUNT **2** the quality of being stupid. EG *...the stupidity of their error.* N UNCOUNT

stupor /stjuːpə/, **stupors.** Someone who is in a **stupor** is almost unconscious. EG *He collapsed in a drunken stupor.* N COUNT

sturdy /stɜːdi[1]/, **sturdier, sturdiest.** Someone or something that is **sturdy** looks strong and is unlikely to be easily damaged or injured. EG *He is short and sturdy... ...sturdy oak tables.* ◊ **sturdily.** EG *...a sturdily built little boy.* ADJ QUALIT; ◊ ADV

stutter /stʌtə/, **stutters, stuttering, stuttered. 1** If someone has a **stutter**, they find it difficult to say the first sound of a word, and so they often hesitate or repeat it two or three times. N COUNT

2 If someone **stutters**, they have difficulty speaking because they find it hard to say the first sound of a word. EG *'I...I want to do it,' she stuttered.* V, V+O, OR V+QUOTE

sty /staɪ/, **sties.** A **sty** is the same as a pigsty. N COUNT

style /staɪl/, **styles, styling, styled. 1** The **style** of something is the general way in which it is done or presented, which often shows the attitudes of the people involved. EG *Some people find our lei-* N COUNT+SUPP *surely style of decision-making rather frustrating... ...western styles of education.*

2 Someone's **style** is all their general attitudes and usual ways of behaving. EG *In characteristic style, he peered over his glasses... Purple is not my style.* N COUNT OR N UNCOUNT: +SUPP

● to **cramp** someone's **style**: see **cramp**.

3 If people or places have **style**, they are smart and elegant. EG *Both were rather short and plump, but they had style... Here you can eat in style.* N UNCOUNT

4 The **style** of a product is its design. EG *These pants come in several styles... The clothes I wore weren't different in style or appearance from those of the other children.* ● See also **hairstyle**. N UNCOUNT OR N COUNT: OFT+SUPP

5 If you **style** a piece of clothing or someone's hair, you design the clothing or do their hair. EG *Her hair was styled in a short cropped pony tail.* V+O: USU PASS

stylish /staɪlɪʃ/. Someone or something that is **stylish** is smart, elegant, and fashionable. EG *...the stylish Swiss resort of Gstaad.* ADJ QUALIT

stylistic /staɪlɪstɪk/ describes things relating to the methods and techniques used in creating a piece of writing, music, or art. EG *Such work lacks any development of stylistic features.* ADJ CLASSIF: ATTRIB

suave /swɑːv/. Someone who is **suave** is charming and polite. EG *...a suave young man... They had suave manners.* ADJ QUALIT

sub-. 1 **sub-** is used at the beginning of words such as 'submerge', 'subway', and 'submarine' that have 'under' as part of their meaning. PREFIX

2 **sub-** is also used to form nouns that refer to the parts or divisions of something. For example, a category may be divided into subcategories, and a species may consist of subspecies. EG *...subsection 1(b) of the report... ...the sub-groups of society.* PREFIX

subconscious /sʌbkɒnʃəs/. 1 Your **subconscious** is the part of your mind that can influence you or affect your behaviour even though you are not aware of it. EG *The knowledge was there somewhere in the depths of his subconscious.* N SING

2 Something that is **subconscious** happens or exists in your subconscious. EG *...a subconscious desire to punish himself.* ADJ CLASSIF

subcontract, subcontracts, subcontracting, subcontracted; pronounced /sʌbkə⁷ntrækt/ when it is a verb, and /sʌbkɒntrækt/ when it is a noun.

1 If one firm **subcontracts** a part of its work to another firm, it pays the other firm to do that part. EG *They had subcontracted some of the work to an electrician.* V+O: OFT+*to*

2 A **subcontract** is a contract between two firms in which one firm agrees to do a part of the other firm's work. EG *We managed to get the subcontract for that job in Edinburgh.* N COUNT

subculture /sʌbkʌltʃə/, **subcultures.** A **subculture** is the ideas, art, and way of life of a group of people within a society, which are different from the ideas, art, and way of life of the rest of the society. EG *...an extremist political subculture.* N COUNT

subdivide /sʌbdɪvaɪd/, **subdivides, subdividing, subdivided.** If something **is subdivided**, it is made into several smaller areas, parts, or sections. EG *Our office was subdivided into departments.* V+O: USU PASS +*into*

subdivision /sʌbdɪvɪʒə⁰n/, **subdivisions.** A **subdivision** is an area or section which is a part of a larger area or section of something. N COUNT

subdue /səbdjuː/, **subdues, subduing, subdued.**

1 If soldiers **subdue** a group of people, they defeat them or bring them under control by using force. EG *Troops were sent to subdue the rebels.* V+O

2 If something **subdues** your feelings, it makes them less strong. EG *This thought subdued my delight at the news.* V+O

3 If something **subdues** a light or a colour, it makes it less bright. V+O

subdued /səbdjuːd/. 1 Someone who is **subdued** is very quiet, often because they are sad. EG *They were subdued and silent.* ADJ QUALIT

2 **Subdued** feelings, sounds, or qualities are not very noticeable. EG *The assembly murmured in subdued agreement.* ADJ QUALIT

3 **Subdued** lights or colours are not very bright. ADJ QUALIT

subhuman /sʌbhjuːmən/. If you describe someone as **subhuman**, you mean that their behaviour is disgusting. ADJ CLASSIF

subject, subjects, subjecting, subjected; pronounced /sʌbdʒɪ²kt/ when it is a noun or adjective, and /səbdʒɛkt/ when it is a verb.

1 The **subject** of a conversation, letter, or book is the thing, person, or idea that is being discussed or written about. EG *I don't have any strong views on the subject... I simply did not know which subjects I could talk about... However much you try to change the subject, the conversation invariably returns to politics.* N COUNT

2 In grammar, the **subject** of a sentence or clause is the word or words that represent the person or thing that is doing the action expressed by the verb. For example, in the sentence 'My cat keeps catching birds', 'my cat' is the subject. N COUNT

3 A **subject** is also something such as maths, chemistry, or English, that you study at school, college, or university. EG *Maths was my best subject at school.* N COUNT

4 The **subjects** of a country are the people who live there. EG *...British subjects.* N COUNT Formal

5 **Subject** peoples and countries are being ruled or controlled by the government of another country. EG *...freedom for the subject peoples of the world.* ADJ CLASSIF: ATTRIB

6 If rulers or governments **subject** their people or their country, they control them strictly and take away their freedom. EG *He began to pass laws to subject every area of the country.* V+O

7 If you are **subject** to something, you are affected by it or likely to be affected by it. EG *Your profit will be subject to tax... He is highly strung and, therefore, subject to heart attacks.* ADJ PRED+*to*

8 If you say that one thing will happen **subject to** another, you mean that it will happen only if the other thing happens. EG *The property will be sold subject to the following conditions.* PREP

9 If you **subject** someone to something unpleasant, you make them experience it. EG *He was subjected to the harshest possible punishment.* V+O+*to*

subjective /səbdʒɛktɪv/. Something that is **subjective** is strongly influenced by personal opinions and feelings. EG *He knew his arguments were subjective, based on intuition.* ADJ QUALIT

subject matter. The **subject matter** of a conversation, book, or film is the thing, person, or idea that is being discussed, written about, or shown. N UNCOUNT

subjugate /sʌbdʒə⁴geɪt/, **subjugates, subjugating, subjugated.** 1 If someone **subjugates** a group of people, they take complete control of them, especially by defeating them in a war. EG *They wondered where Hitler would turn when he had subjugated Europe.* V+O Formal ◇ **subjugation** /sʌbdʒə⁴geɪʃə⁰n/. EG *These people are resisting attempted subjugation by armed minorities.* ◇ N UNCOUNT

2 If your wishes or desires **are subjugated** to something, they are treated as less important than that thing. EG *She has subjugated her own desires to those of her husband.* V+O: USU PASS Formal

subjunctive /səbdʒʌŋktɪv/. The **subjunctive** or **subjunctive mood** is one of the moods that a verb can take in some languages such as French and Latin. In contrast with the indicative and imperative moods, the subjunctive is usually used to express attitudes such as wishing, hoping, and doubting. N SING: *the*+N

sublime /səblaɪm/. 1 If you describe something as **sublime**, you mean that it has a wonderful quality that affects you deeply. EG *She paid me a sublime* ADJ QUALIT Literary

Is it a good idea to use subdued lighting when you are reading?

SUBMODIFIERS

Submodifiers (SUBMOD) are adverbs such as **very**, **quite**, and **surprisingly**. An adjective such as 'happy' can have one of these words in front of it, so that you can vary from being ***exceptionally*** *happy* to ***quite*** *happy*. Submodifiers come in front of adjectives or other adverbs, but are not used with verbs.

Typically, submodifiers are used in front of qualitative adjectives, such as 'ugly', 'big', 'small', 'nice', and so on. For example: *He is rather ugly, but very nice.*

Submodifiers are used to strengthen or weaken the adjective, rather than to add new meaning. So if you want to say that someone has ideas that are more interesting than most people's ideas, you can say: *His ideas are very interesting . . . His ideas are extremely interesting . . . His ideas are terribly interesting.*

There are a number of submodifiers, such as **absolutely**, **utterly**, and **totally**, which can be used with adjectives that are not usually graded: *He became totally blind . . . . . . two totally opposed ideas.*

Submodifiers are often used after **not** to lessen the negative effect of what you are saying. So that instead of using an adjective such as 'boring', 'wrong', or 'stupid' that has a very strong negative feel to it, you can use the corresponding positive adjective, with a negative and with a submodifier, as in: *It wasn't terribly interesting . . . I don't think that's quite right . . . He's not very clever.*

compliment which I shall always cherish... ...the author of this sublime document.

2 You describe something as going **from the sublime to the ridiculous** when it changes from being of high quality to being silly or trivial. EG *The film goes from the sublime to the ridiculous.* PHRASE

subliminal /səblɪmɪnəᵊl/. Something that is **subliminal** affects your mind without you being aware of it. EG *...subliminal advertising.* ADJ CLASSIF

sub-machine gun, sub-machine guns. A **sub-machine gun** is a light, portable type of machine-gun. N COUNT

submarine /sʌbməriːn/, **submarines.** A **submarine** is a type of ship that can travel below the surface of the sea. N COUNT

submerge /səbmɜːdʒ/, **submerges, submerging, submerged. 1** If something **submerges** or if you **submerge** it, it goes below the surface of the water. EG *The alligator showed its snout before submerging.* V-ERG : OFT+A

2 If you **submerge** yourself in an activity, you give all your attention to it and do not think about anything else. EG *I was eager to submerge myself in the feminist movement.* V-REFL+*in*

submerged /səbmɜːdʒd/. If something is **submerged**, it is below the surface of the water. EG *...a line of submerged rocks... The submarine can remain submerged for eight weeks.* ADJ CLASSIF

submission /səbmɪʃəᵊn/. **1 Submission** is a state in which people can no longer do what they want to do because they are under the control of someone else. EG *The trade unions were brought into submission.* N UNCOUNT

2 The **submission** of a proposal or application is the act of sending it to someone, so that they can decide whether to accept it or not. EG *...the submission of these plans to the local authority.* N UNCOUNT Formal

submissive /səbmɪsɪv/. If you are **submissive**, you behave in a quiet, obedient way. EG *She became submissive and subservient.* ADJ QUALIT

submit /səbmɪt/, **submits, submitting, submitted. 1** If you **submit** to something, you accept it, because you are not powerful enough to resist it. EG *They were forced to submit to military discipline... Liang submitted to his beatings... They had to submit to a thorough search at the airport.* V : OFT+*to*

2 If you **submit** a proposal or application to someone, you send it to them so that they can decide whether to accept it or not. EG *I submitted my resignation.* V+O

SUBMOD stands for **submodifier**
Adverbs which have the label SUBMOD in the Extra Column are used in front of adjectives and other adverbs.
See the entry headed SUBMODIFIERS for more information.

subnormal /sʌbnɔːməᵊl/. If someone is **subnormal**, they have less ability or intelligence than a normal person of their age. EG *...a woman who was clearly educationally subnormal... ...homes for subnormal children.* ADJ CLASSIF

subordinate, subordinates, subordinating, subordinated; pronounced /səbɔːdɪnəᶦt/ when it is a noun or adjective, and /səbɔːdɪneɪt/ when it is a verb. **1** If someone is your **subordinate**, they have a less important position than you in the organization that you both work for. EG *He humiliated his senior staff before their subordinates.* N COUNT WITH POSS

2 If one thing is **subordinate** to another, it is less important than the other thing. EG *All other questions are subordinate to this one.* ADJ CLASSIF : OFT+*to* Formal

3 If you **subordinate** one thing to another, you regard it or treat it as less important than the other thing. EG *To keep his job, he subordinated his own interests to the objectives of the company.* V+O+*to* Formal

subordinate clause, subordinate clauses. A **subordinate clause** is a clause which adds some details to the main clause of a sentence. N COUNT

subscribe /səbskraɪb/, **subscribes, subscribing, subscribed.** 1 If you **subscribe** to an opinion or belief, you are one of a number of people who have this opinion or belief. EG *The rest of us do not subscribe to this theory.* V: USU+*to*

2 If you **subscribe** to a magazine or a newspaper, you pay to receive copies of it regularly. EG *I started subscribing to a morning newspaper.* V: USU+*to*

3 If you **subscribe** money to a charity or a campaign, you send money to it regularly. EG *They subscribed to local charities... Substantial sums were subscribed towards the work.* V+O+A

subscriber /səbskraɪbə/, **subscribers.** 1 A magazine's or a newspaper's **subscribers** are the people who pay to receive copies of it regularly. N COUNT

2 **Subscribers** to a service are the people who pay to receive the service. EG *...telephone subscribers.* N COUNT

3 The **subscribers** to a charity or campaign are the people who support it by sending money regularly to it. N COUNT

subscription /səbskrɪpʃəⁿn/, **subscriptions.** A **subscription** is an amount of money that you pay regularly in order to belong to a society, to help a charity or campaign, or to receive copies of a magazine or newspaper. EG *...my first year's subscription to the National Union of Agricultural Workers... He could not afford to renew his magazine subscriptions.* N COUNT

subsequent /sʌbsɪkwənt/. You use **subsequent** to describe something that happens or exists at a later time than something else. EG *Subsequent research has produced even better results.* ADJ CLASSIF: ATTRIB

◊ **subsequently**. EG *Brooke was arrested and subsequently sentenced to five years' imprisonment.* ◊ ADV

subservient /səbsɜːvɪənt/. 1 If you are **subservient**, you do whatever someone wants you to do. EG *She was subservient and eager to please.* ADJ QUALIT: OFT+*to*

◊ **subservience** /səbsɜːvɪəns/. EG *How long would they keep us in subservience?* ◊ N UNCOUNT

2 If you treat one thing as **subservient** to another, you treat it as less important than the other thing. EG *Economic systems became subservient to social objectives.* ADJ PRED+*to*

subside /səbsaɪd/, **subsides, subsiding, subsided.** 1 If a feeling **subsides**, it becomes less violent or intense. EG *She stopped and waited until the pain subsided.* V

2 If a noise **subsides**, it becomes much quieter. EG *His voice subsided to a mutter.* V

3 If water **subsides** or if the ground **subsides**, it sinks to a lower level. EG *The flooded river was subsiding rapidly.* V

subsidence /səbsaɪdəns, sʌbsɪdəns/. When there is **subsidence** in a place, the ground there sinks to a lower level. EG *The cracks in your house are due to subsidence.* N UNCOUNT

subsidiary /səbsɪdjəri¹/, **subsidiaries.** 1 If something is **subsidiary**, it is less important than something else with which it is connected. EG *I tried to discuss this and some subsidiary questions... The Department offers a course in Opera Studies as a subsidiary subject.* ADJ CLASSIF: USU ATTRIB

2 A **subsidiary** or **subsidiary company** is a company which is part of a larger and more important company. EG *The British company is a subsidiary of Racal Electronics.* N COUNT

subsidize /sʌbsɪdaɪz/, **subsidizes, subsidizing, subsidized;** also spelled **subsidise.** 1 If a government or other authority **subsidizes** a public service, they pay part of the cost of it. EG *In this country the State subsidizes education, housing and health care.* V+O

◊ **subsidized**. EG *...subsidized housing.* ◊ ADJ CLASSIF

2 If a government **subsidizes** an industry, they provide money in order to enable the industry to continue. EG *Every government since the last war has subsidized upland farming.* V+O

subsidy /sʌbsɪdi¹/, **subsidies.** A **subsidy** is money that is paid by a government or other authority in order to help a company financially or to pay for a public service. N COUNT OR N UNCOUNT

subsist /səbsɪst/, **subsists, subsisting, subsisted.** If people **subsist**, they are just able to obtain the food that they need in order to stay alive. EG *In some places, the settlers were subsisting on potato peelings.* V: OFT+*on*

subsistence /səbsɪstəns/ is the condition of just having enough food to stay alive. EG *Thousands of pensioners live out their lives at subsistence level.* N UNCOUNT

substance /sʌbstəns/, **substances.** 1 A **substance** is a solid, a powder, or a liquid. EG *He discovered a substance called phosphotase... We try to remove the harmful substances from cigarettes.* N COUNT

2 **Substance** is something that you can touch, rather than something that you can only see, hear, or imagine. EG *They had no more substance than shadows.* N UNCOUNT

3 The **substance** of what someone says or writes is the main thing that they are trying to say. EG *The substance of their talk is condensed into a paragraph.* N SING: the+N+of

4 **Substance** is also the quality of being important or significant. EG *There isn't anything of real substance in her book... There is some substance to this criticism.* N UNCOUNT

substandard /sʌbstændəd/. If something is **substandard**, it is unacceptable because it is below a required standard. EG *...substandard housing.* ADJ CLASSIF

substantial /səbstænʃəⁿl/. 1 **Substantial** means very large in amount or degree. EG *She will receive a substantial amount of money... Many factories suffered substantial damage.* ADJ QUALIT

2 A **substantial** building is large and strongly built. EG *On the site were a number of substantial timber buildings.* ADJ CLASSIF

substantially /səbstænʃəli¹/. 1 If something increases or decreases **substantially**, it increases or decreases by a large amount. EG *The price may go up quite substantially.* ADV

2 If you say that something is **substantially** true, you mean that it is generally true. EG *Steed always maintained that the story was substantially true.* SUBMOD

substantiate /səbstænʃieɪt/, **substantiates, substantiating, substantiated.** To **substantiate** a statement or a story means to supply evidence which proves that it is true. EG *Your report might be difficult to substantiate.* V+O Formal

substitute /sʌbstɪtjuːt/, **substitutes, substituting, substituted.** 1 If you **substitute** one thing for another, you use it instead of the other thing. EG *Force was substituted for argument.* V+O: OFT+*for*

◊ **substitution** /sʌbstɪtjuːʃəⁿn/, **substitutions.** EG *...the substitution of local goods for those previously imported... Some of these substitutions were successful.* ◊ N UNCOUNT OR N COUNT

2 If one thing **substitutes** for another, it takes the place or performs the function of the other thing. EG *In the past, oil has substituted for certain natural materials.* V: OFT+*for*

3 A **substitute** is something that you have or use instead of something else. EG *Their dog was a substitute for the children they never had... She had become attached to her substitute parents.* N COUNT: OFT+*for*

4 If you say that one thing is **no substitute** for another, you mean that it does not have certain desirable features that the other thing has, and is therefore unsatisfactory. EG *The pub was no substitute for a luxury hotel.* PHRASE

Are the definitions in this dictionary succinct?

subsume /səbsju:m/, **subsumes, subsuming, subsumed.** If something **is subsumed** within a larger group or class, it is included within it, rather than being considered as something separate. V+O : USU PASS Formal

subterfuge /sʌbtəfju:d^{ə}ʒ/, **subterfuges.** A **subterfuge** is a trick or a dishonest way of getting what you want. EG *Resistance will be possible only through cheating, subterfuge and sabotage.* N COUNT OR N UNCOUNT

subterranean /sʌbtəreɪnɪən/. A **subterranean** river or tunnel is underground. EG *We wandered through winding subterranean passages.* ADJ CLASSIF : ATTRIB

subtitles /sʌbtaɪtə^{ə}lz/ are the printed translation that you can read at the bottom of the screen when you are watching a foreign film. EG *...an Italian film with English subtitles.* N PLURAL

subtle /sʌtə^{ə}l/, **subtler, subtlest. 1** Something that is **subtle** is not immediately obvious or noticeable, and is therefore a little difficult to explain or describe. EG *His whole attitude had undergone a subtle change... ...subtle forms of racism.* ◇ **subtly.** EG *The tastes are subtly different.* ADJ QUALIT; ◇ ADV

2 Someone who is **subtle** uses indirect and clever methods to achieve something, rather than doing something that is obvious. EG *You must be more subtle... ...the subtlest of our politicians... My plan was subtler.* ◇ **subtly.** EG *He subtly criticized me.* ADJ QUALIT; ◇ ADV

subtlety /sʌtə^{ə}lti^{1}/, **subtleties. 1** A **subtlety** is a very small detail or difference which is difficult to notice. EG *...the subtleties of English intonation... He was aware of the subtleties of Elaine's moods.* N COUNT : USU+*of*

2 Subtlety is **2.1** the quality of being not immediately obvious or noticeable, and therefore difficult to explain or describe. EG *In your cooking remember that subtlety is everything... The subtlety of this process is extraordinary.* **2.2** the ability to notice and recognize things which are not obvious, especially small differences between things. EG *They can sense each other's intentions with great subtlety.* **2.3** the ability to use indirect and clever methods to achieve something, rather than doing something that is obvious. EG *...their subtlety of mind.* N UNCOUNT; Formal

subtract /səbtrækt/, **subtracts, subtracting, subtracted.** If you **subtract** one number from another, you do a calculation in which you take it away from the other number. For example, if you subtract 3 from 5, you get 2. ◇ **subtraction** /səbtrækʃə^{ə}n/, **subtractions.** EG *...simple techniques for handling subtraction and multiplication.* V+O : OFT+*from*; ◇ N UNCOUNT OR N COUNT

subtropical /sʌbtrɒpɪkə^{ə}l/ describes things relating to the areas of the world that lie between the tropical and temperate regions. EG *...sub-tropical forests.* ADJ CLASSIF : ATTRIB

suburb /sʌbɜ:b/, **suburbs.** A **suburb** of a town or city is an area of it which is not close to the centre. People who work in the town or city often live in the **suburbs.** N COUNT

suburban /səbɜ:bə^{ə}n/. **1 Suburban** means relating to a suburb. EG *...suburban areas.* ADJ CLASSIF

2 If you describe something as **suburban,** you mean that it is dull and conventional, and lacks change or excitement. EG *...a suburban lifestyle.* ADJ QUALIT

suburbia /səbɜ:bɪə/ refers to the suburbs of towns and cities considered as a whole. EG *...the gardens of London suburbia.* N UNCOUNT

subversion /səbvɜ:ʃə^{ə}n/ is the attempt to weaken or destroy a political system or a government. EG *She was arrested for subversion.* N UNCOUNT Formal

subversive /səbvɜ:sɪv/, **subversives. 1** Something that is **subversive** is intended to weaken or destroy a political system or government. EG *...subversive literature.* ADJ QUALIT Formal

2 Subversives are people who attempt to weaken or destroy a political system or government. N COUNT Formal

subvert /səbvɜ:t/, **subverts, subverting, subverted.** To **subvert** something means to destroy its power and influence. EG *Conflict and division subvert the foundations of society.* V+O Formal

N COUNT

subway /sʌbweɪ/, **subways.** A **subway** is **1** a passage for pedestrians that goes underneath a busy road. **2** an underground railway. EG *...a subway station.* American

succeed /səksi:d/, **succeeds, succeeding, succeeded. 1** If you **succeed** in doing something, you manage to do it. EG *I succeeded in getting the job... She tried to smile but did not succeed.* V : OFT+*in*

2 If something **succeeds, 2.1** it has the result that is intended. EG *Nobody expected that strike to succeed.* **2.2** it works in a satisfactory way. EG *They had a marriage which succeeded beyond their dreams.* V

3 Someone who **succeeds** gains a high position in what they do, for example in business or politics. EG *She is eager to succeed.* V : OFT+*in*

4 If you **succeed** another person, you are the next person to have their job or position. EG *Somebody's got to succeed Murray as editor.* V+O OR V

5 If one thing **succeeds** another, it comes after it in time. EG *The first demand would be succeeded by others.* ◇ **succeeding.** EG *In the succeeding months, little was heard about him.* V+O; ◇ ADJ CLASSIF ATTRIB

success /səksɛs/, **successes. 1 Success** is **1.1** the achievement of something that you have been trying to do. EG *His attempt to shoot the president came very close to success.* **1.2** the achievement of a high position in a particular field, for example in business or politics. EG *Confidence is the key to success... The firm is assured of success in the coming year.* N UNCOUNT

2 Someone or something that is a **success** achieves a high position, makes a lot of money, or becomes very popular. EG *His next film – 'Jaws' – was a tremendous success.* N COUNT

successful /səksɛsful/. **1** Something that is **successful 1.1** achieves what it was intended to achieve. EG *...a successful attempt to land on the moon.* ◇ **successfully.** EG *The operation had been completed successfully.* **1.2** is popular or makes a lot of money. EG *...a very successful film.* ADJ QUALIT; ◇ ADV; ADJ QUALIT

2 Someone who is **successful** achieves a high position in what they do, for example in business or politics. EG *...a successful writer.* ADJ QUALIT

succession /səksɛʃə^{ə}n/, **successions. 1** A **succession** of things of the same kind is a number of them that exist or happen one after the other. EG *My life is a succession of failures.* N COUNT+*of*

2 Succession is the act or right of being the next person to have an important job or position. EG *...his succession to the peerage.* N UNCOUNT : OFT+*to*

3 If something happens for a number of weeks or years **in succession,** it happens in each of those weeks or years, without a break. EG *Vita went to Florence for the third year in succession.* PHRASE

successive /səksɛsɪv/ means happening or existing one after another without a break. EG *On two successive Saturdays, the car broke down... ...the actions of successive British governments.* ADJ CLASSIF : ATTRIB

successor /səksɛsə/, **successors.** Someone's **successor** is the person who takes their job after they have left. EG *Who will be Brearley's successor?* N COUNT : USU+POSS

success story, success stories. Someone or something that is a **success story** is very successful, often unexpectedly or in spite of unfavourable conditions. EG *One of the greatest success stories in rapid industrialization was Singapore.* N COUNT

succinct /səksɪŋkt/. Something that is **succinct** expresses facts or ideas clearly and in few words. EG *...an accurate and succinct account of their policies.* ADJ QUALIT

succour /sʌkə/; spelled **succor** in American English. **Succour** is help that is given to someone who is suffering or in difficulties. EG *They were busy providing succour to the injured.* N UNCOUNT Formal

succulent /sʌkjə^{4}lənt/. Food that is **succulent** is juicy and delicious. EG *...a succulent mango.* ADJ QUALIT

succumb /səkʌm/, **succumbs, succumbing, succumbed. 1** If you **succumb** to persuasion or V : OFT+*to* desire, you are unable to resist it. EG *He finally succumbed to the temptation to have another drink.*

2 If you **succumb** to an illness, you become affected by it. EG *...those who succumb to ulcers.* V: OFT+*to* Formal

such /sʌtʃ/. **1 Such** a thing or person means the thing or person that you have just mentioned, or a thing or person like the one that you have just mentioned. EG *They lasted for hundreds of thousands of years. On a human time scale, such a period seems an eternity... The nobility held tournaments, but peasants had no time to spare for such frivolity... I don't believe in magic, there is no such thing... It was in Brighton or Bournemouth or some such place.* PREDET, DET, OR PRON

2 You use **such as** or **such...as** to introduce one or more examples of something. EG *...a game of chance such as roulette... ...a prolonged rise in prices such as occurred in the late 1960s... ...such things as pork pies, sausage rolls, and plum cake.*

3 You also use **such** to emphasize the degree or extent of something. EG *It was such a lovely day... It was strange that such elegant creatures made such ugly sounds... There was such a crowd of people.* PREDET OR DET

4 You use **such...that** or **such...as** when saying what the result or consequence of a particular kind of thing is. EG *They have to charge in such a way that they don't make a loss.* PREDET, DET, OR PRON

5 You use **such as it is** or **such as there is** to indicate that something is not very good, important, or useful. EG *Dinner's on the table, such as it is.* PHRASE

6 You use **as such** to indicate that you are considering something by itself and only as an idea, and are not considering any connected things or practical situations. EG *He is not terribly interested in politics as such.* PHRASE

7 You use **such and such** to refer to a thing or person when you do not want to be exact or precise. EG *John always tells me that I have not taken such and such into account.*

suchlike /sʌtʃlaɪk/. You use **suchlike** to refer to things like the ones already mentioned. EG *...artichokes, smoked fish, and suchlike delicacies... ...mills, threshing machines and such like.* DET OR PRON

suck /sʌk/, **sucks, sucking, sucked. 1** If you **suck** something, you hold it in your mouth and pull at it with the muscles in your cheeks and tongue, for example in order to get liquid out of it. EG *The baby went on sucking the bottle... Bite open the fruit and suck out the flesh.* V+O OR V+A

2 If something **sucks** an object or liquid in a particular direction, it draws it there with a powerful force. EG *The water is sucked upwards through the roots.* V+O+A

3 If you **are sucked** into a situation, you are unable to prevent yourself from becoming involved in it. EG *They found themselves sucked into the quarrel.* V+O: USU PASS+*into*

suck up. If you **suck up** to someone in authority, you try to please them; used showing disapproval. EG *He's been sucking up like mad to the boss.* PHRASAL VB: V+ADV, OFT+*to* Informal

sucker /sʌkə/, **suckers. 1** If you call someone a **sucker**, you mean that it is very easy to cheat them. EG *He was no sucker.* N COUNT

2 The **suckers** on some animals and insects are the parts on the outside of their body which they use in order to stick to a surface. N COUNT

suckle /sʌkə°l/, **suckles, suckling, suckled. 1** When a mother **suckles** her baby, she feeds it by letting it suck milk from her breast. V+O

2 When a baby **suckles**, it sucks milk from its mother's breast. V

suction /sʌkʃə°n/ is **1** the process by which liquids, gases, or other substances are drawn from one space to another. EG *The draining process was assisted by suction.* **2** the process by which two surfaces stick together when the air between them is removed. EG *...stuck on to the bath by suction pads.* N UNCOUNT

sudden /sʌdə°n/. **1** Something that is **sudden** happens quickly and unexpectedly. EG *...a sudden drop in the temperature... I felt a sudden twinge of regret.* ◊ **suddenly.** EG *Suddenly, the door opened and in walked the boss.* ADJ QUALIT ◊ ADV OR ADV SEN

2 If something happens **all of a sudden**, it happens so quickly and unexpectedly that you are surprised by it. EG *All of a sudden I noticed that someone was following me.* PHRASE

suds /sʌdz/ are the bubbles that are produced when soap is mixed with water. N PLURAL

sue /su:/, **sues, suing, sued.** If you **sue** someone, you start a legal case against them, usually in order to claim money from them because they have harmed you in some way. EG *He couldn't even sue them for wrongful arrest.* V+O OR V: OFT+*for*

suede /sweɪd/ is thin, soft leather with a slightly rough surface. EG *...boots of light brown suede... ...a suede jacket.* N UNCOUNT

suet /sj°u:ɪt/ is hard animal fat that is used in cooking. N UNCOUNT

suffer /sʌfə/, **suffers, suffering, suffered. 1** If you **suffer** pain, you feel it in your body or in your mind. EG *She was suffering violent abdominal pains... They had suffered a lot of nervous strain.* V+O OR V

2 If you **suffer** from an illness, you are badly affected by it. EG *Seventy-five percent of its population suffers from malnutrition.* V+*from*

3 If you **suffer** something bad, you are in a situation in which something painful, harmful, or very unpleasant happens to you. EG *We were warned to support the government or suffer the consequences.* V+O

4 If you **suffer**, you are badly affected by an unfavourable event or situation. EG *They would be the first to suffer if these proposals were ever carried out.* V

5 If something **suffers**, it becomes worse in quality or condition because it has been neglected or because of an unfavourable situation. EG *I'm not surprised that your studies are suffering.* V

sufferer /sʌfərə/, **sufferers.** A **sufferer** of an illness is a person who is affected by the illness. EG *...sufferers of chronic disease.* N COUNT+SUPP

suffering /sʌfə°rɪŋ/, **sufferings. Suffering** is serious pain which someone feels in their body or their mind. EG *This would cause great hardship and suffering... This might alleviate their sufferings.* N UNCOUNT OR N COUNT

suffice /səfaɪs/, **suffices, sufficing, sufficed.** If something **suffices**, it is enough to achieve a purpose or to fulfil a need. EG *A very few drains will suffice to drain light or sandy soil.* V: NO CONT Formal

sufficiency /səfɪʃənsi[1]/. If there is a **sufficiency** of something, there is enough of it to achieve a purpose or to fulfil a need. EG *We had 600 jet fighters and a sufficiency of airfields to support them.* N SING: USU+*of* Formal

sufficient /səfɪʃənt/. If something is **sufficient** for a particular purpose, there is as much of it as is necessary. EG *Japan had a reserve of oil sufficient for its needs.* ◊ **sufficiently.** EG *He had not insured the house sufficiently.* ADJ CLASSIF ◊ ADV

suffix /sʌfɪks/, **suffixes.** A **suffix** is a letter or group of letters which is added to the end of a word in order to form a new word, often of a different word class. N COUNT

SUFFIX

Some groups of letters have the label SUFFIX in the Extra Column. This means that they are not used by themselves as words, but are added to the end of existing words. By adding a suffix to a word, you create a new word which belongs to a different

Are there any words with suffixes on these pages? If so, what are they?

word class. For example, you can add 'ly' to the adjective 'sad' and create the adverb 'sadly'. To change 'sad' into a noun, you can add 'ness', making the word 'sadness'.

It is worth noting that there are sometimes spelling changes to a word when you add a suffix to it. For example, 'happy' becomes 'happily' and 'happiness', and 'recite' becomes 'recitation'.

You will find many of the words with suffixes *inside* the entry of the same word without a suffix. For example, **sadly** and **sadness** are in the entry for **sad**. This tells you that there is no change in meaning, and that an example is sufficient to show its use. You can always find the words with suffixes by looking for the lozenge (◇) sign.

Here is a list of all the suffixes defined in this dictionary:

-ability, -able, -al, -ance, -ancy, -ation, -ed, -ence, -ency, -er, -est, -ful, -ibility, -ing, -ion, -ise, -ish, -ism, -ist, -ity, -ize, -less, -ly, -ment, -most, -nd, -ness, -ological, -ologist, -or, -ous, -person, -rd, -st, -th, -tion, -ward, -wise.

suffocate /sʌfəkeɪt/, **suffocates, suffocating, suffocated.** If someone **suffocates** or if something **suffocates** them, they die because there is no air for them to breathe. EG *The smoke and fumes almost suffocated me... Sir, we are suffocating. We must surrender.* V-ERG
◇ **suffocation** /sʌfəkeɪʃə^{0}n/. EG *Many slaves died of heat and suffocation.* ◇ N UNCOUNT

suffrage /sʌfrɪdʒ/ is the right that people have to vote for a government or national leader. EG *...the introduction of universal adult suffrage.* N UNCOUNT

sugar /ʃʊgə/, **sugars, sugaring, sugared. 1 Sugar** is a sweet substance, often in the form of white or brown crystals, which is used to sweeten food and drink. EG *Lally poured us all a cup of tea and helped herself to sugar... I take my coffee black with no sugar.* N MASS

2 When you **sugar** food or drink, you add sugar to it. V+O

sugar beet is a plant which is cultivated for the sugar that can be obtained from its root. N UNCOUNT

sugar cane is a tall tropical plant which is cultivated because of the sugar that can be obtained from its thick stems. N UNCOUNT

sugar lump, sugar lumps. A **sugar lump** is a small cube of sugar. N COUNT

suggest /sədʒɛst/, **suggests, suggesting, suggested. 1** If you **suggest** something, you put forward a plan or idea for someone to think about. EG *We have to suggest a list of possible topics for next term's seminars.* V-SPEECH

2 If you **suggest** the name of a person or place, you recommend them to someone. EG *Can you suggest somewhere for a short holiday?* V+O : USU+A

3 If you **suggest** something to someone, you say something to them which puts an idea into their mind. EG *I'm not suggesting that the accident was your fault... It would be foolish to suggest that everyone in Britain is rich.* V+O OR V+REPORT

4 If one thing **suggests** another, it implies it or makes you think that it is the case. EG *His expression suggested some pleasure at the fact that I had come... The forecasts suggest that there will be higher unemployment.* V+O OR V+REPORT

suggestion /sədʒɛstʃə^{0}n/, **suggestions. 1** A **suggestion** is an idea or plan which is put forward for people to think about. EG *I made a few suggestions about how we could spend the afternoon.* N COUNT

2 If there is a **suggestion** of something, there is a slight indication or sign of it. EG *He replied to her question with the merest suggestion of a smile.* N SING+*of*

3 Suggestion is giving people a particular idea by associating it with other ideas. EG *Such is the power of suggestion that within two minutes the patient is asleep.* N UNCOUNT

suggestive /sədʒɛstɪv/. **1** Something that is **suggestive** of something else gives a hint of it or reminds you of it. EG *His behaviour was suggestive of a cultured man.* ADJ PRED+*of*

2 Remarks or looks that are **suggestive** cause people to think about sex. EG *The girls stood around, exchanging gossip and calling out suggestive remarks.* ADJ QUALIT

suicidal /sj^{0}u:ɪsaɪdə^{0}l/. **1** People who are **suicidal** want to kill themselves. EG *What should you do if your friend feels suicidal?* ADJ CLASSIF

2 Behaviour that is **suicidal** leads to great danger or death. EG *They would not risk a suicidal attack on the American fleet.* ADJ CLASSIF

suicide /sj^{0}u:ɪsaɪd/, **suicides. 1** People who commit **suicide** deliberately kill themselves because they do not want to continue living. EG *The founder of British India, Clive, committed suicide in 1774.* N UNCOUNT OR N COUNT

2 You also say that people commit **suicide** when they deliberately do something which ruins their career or position in society. EG *People had told me it was suicide to admit my mistake.* N UNCOUNT

suit /sj^{0}u:t/, **suits, suiting, suited. 1** A man's **suit** consists of a jacket, trousers, and sometimes a waistcoat, all made from the same fabric. EG *He arrived at the office in a suit and tie.* N COUNT

2 A woman's **suit** consists of a jacket and skirt, or sometimes trousers, all made from the same fabric. EG *She wore a black suit and a tiny black hat.* N COUNT

3 A **suit** can also be a piece of clothing that you wear for a particular activity. EG *She was wearing a short robe over her bathing suit.* N COUNT : USU+SUPP

4 If something **suits** you, it is the best thing for you in the circumstances. EG *All this suits my purpose very well.* V+O : NO CONT

5 If a piece of clothing or a particular style or colour **suits** you, it makes you look attractive. EG *That colour will suit you... That coat really suits you.* V+O : NO CONT

6 If you say that something **suits** you, you mean that **6.1** it is convenient for you. EG *Would Monday suit you?... It suits me to be registered here.* **6.2** you like it. EG *A job where I was indoors all day wouldn't suit me.* V+O : NO CONT

7 If you **suit** yourself, you do something just because you want to do it, and do not bother to consider other people. EG *Casual people arrive, at times to suit themselves... If later is more convenient, suit yourself.* V-REFL : USU IMPER

8 If people **follow suit**, they do the same thing that someone else has just done. EG *He bowed his head. Mother and Jenny followed suit.* PHRASE

9 In a court of law, a **suit** is a case in which a person tries to get justice for some wrong that has been done to them. N COUNT

10 A **suit** is also one of the four types of card in a set of playing cards. These are hearts, diamonds, clubs, and spades. N COUNT

suitable /sj^{0}u:təbə^{0}l/. Someone or something that is **suitable** for a particular purpose or occasion is right or acceptable for that purpose or occasion. EG *These flats are not really suitable for families with children... It takes years to turn suitable young men into fighter-pilots.* ADJ QUALIT : OFT+*for*
◇ **suitability** /sj^{0}u:təbɪlɪ^{1}ti^1/. EG *...the candidate's intellectual ability and suitability for admission.* ◇ N UNCOUNT
◇ **suitably**. EG *See that you are suitably dressed for the weather... ...suitably trained teachers.* ◇ ADV

suitcase /sj^{0}u:tkeɪs/, **suitcases.** A **suitcase** is a case in which you carry your clothes when you are travelling. N COUNT

suite /swi:t/, **suites.** A **suite** is **1** a set of rooms in a hotel. EG *They always stayed in a suite at the Ritz.* N COUNT
2 a set of matching furniture for a sitting-room or bathroom. EG *...a three-piece suite for the lounge.*

suited /sj⁰u̱:tɪ²d/. **1** If something is **suited** to a particular purpose or person, it is right or appropriate for that purpose or person. EG *They preferred to join clubs more suited to their tastes... He considered himself ideally suited for the job of Prime Minister.* ADJ PRED: OFT+*to/for*

2 If a man and a woman are well **suited**, they are likely to have a successful relationship because they have similar personalities or interests. ADJ PRED

suitor /sj⁰u̱:tə/, **suitors.** A woman's **suitor** is a man who wants to marry her. EG *She had many suitors.* N COUNT Outdated

sulfur /sʌ̱lfə/. See **sulphur**.

sulk /sʌ̱lk/, **sulks, sulking, sulked.** If you **sulk**, you are silent and bad-tempered for a while because you are annoyed about something. EG *He sulked and behaved badly for weeks after I refused.* V
▸ used as a noun. EG *I thought you were in one of your sulks.* ▸ N COUNT

sulky /sʌ̱lki¹/, **sulkier, sulkiest.** Someone who is **sulky** is sulking about something. EG *Sam glowered at him in sulky silence.* ◊ **sulkily.** EG *'I don't want anything,' the boy answered sulkily.* ADJ QUALIT ◊ ADV

sullen /sʌ̱lən/. Someone who is **sullen** is bad-tempered and does not speak much. EG *...a sullen boy... She looked at the Duke with sullen hatred.* ADJ QUALIT
◊ **sullenly.** EG *'So what?' Thomas said sullenly.* ◊ ADV

sulphur /sʌ̱lfə/; spelled **sulfur** in American English. **Sulphur** is a yellow substance which has a strong unpleasant smell. N UNCOUNT

sultan /sʌ̱ltə⁰n/, **sultans.** A **sultan** is a ruler in some Muslim countries. EG *...the Sultan of Oman.* N COUNT

sultana /sʌltɑ̱:nə/, **sultanas. Sultanas** are dried grapes. N COUNT

sultry /sʌ̱ltri¹/. **1 Sultry** weather is unpleasantly hot and humid. EG *It was hot and sultry.* ADJ QUALIT

2 A **sultry** woman is attractive in a way that suggests hidden passion. ADJ QUALIT

sum /sʌ̱m/, **sums, summing, summed. 1** A **sum** of money is an amount of money. EG *...the staggering sum of 212,000 million pounds... Manufacturers spend huge sums of money on advertising their product.* ● See also **lump sum**. N PART

2 A **sum** is a simple calculation in arithmetic. EG *He couldn't do his sums.* N COUNT

sum up. 1 If you **sum** something **up**, you describe it as briefly as possible. EG *My mood could be summed up by the single word 'boredom'.* **2** If you **sum up** after saying something or **sum up** what has been said, you briefly state the main points again. EG *To sum up: within our society there still exist rampant inequalities.* **3** See also **summing up**. PHRASAL VB: V+O+ADV; V+ADV

summarize /sʌ̱məraɪz/, **summarizes, summarizing, summarized;** also spelled **summarise.** If you **summarize** something, you give a summary of it. EG *The seven categories can be briefly summarized as follows.* V+O OR V

summary /sʌ̱məri¹/, **summaries. 1** A **summary** is a short account of something, which gives the main points but not the details. EG *Here is a summary of the plot.* N COUNT

2 You use **in summary** to indicate that what you are about to say is a summary of what has just been said. EG *In summary, all government departments are administered rather differently.* ADV SEN

3 Summary actions are done without delay, often when something else should have been done first or done instead. EG *...mass arrests and summary executions.* ◊ **summarily.** EG *He summarily dismissed our problem as unimportant... They were summarily evicted.* ADJ CLASSIF: ATTRIB ◊ ADV Formal

summer /sʌ̱mə/, **summers. Summer** is the season between spring and autumn. In the summer the weather is usually warm or hot. EG *I am going to Greece this summer... ...summer holidays.* N COUNT OR N UNCOUNT

summer school, summer schools. A **summer school** is an educational course on a particular subject that is run during the summer. N COUNT OR N UNCOUNT

summertime /sʌ̱mətaɪm/ is the period of time during which summer lasts. EG *The dust from the roads in the summertime was enough to blind you.* N UNCOUNT

summery /sʌ̱məri¹/. Something that is **summery** is suitable for summer or characteristic of summer. EG *...a summery dress... ...a summery fragrance.* ADJ CLASSIF

summing up, summings up. A **summing up** is a summary of something, especially of the evidence presented in a trial. EG *In his summing up, the judge again returned to this point.* N COUNT

summit /sʌ̱mɪt/, **summits. 1** A **summit** is a meeting at which the leaders of two or more countries discuss important matters. EG *Western leaders are gathering for this week's Ottawa summit... ...a summit meeting.* N COUNT

2 The **summit** of a mountain is the top of it. N COUNT

summon /sʌ̱mən/, **summons, summoning, summoned.** If you **summon** someone, you order them to come to you. EG *He summoned his secretary... He was summoned to report on the accident.* V+O

summon up. If you **summon up** your strength, energy, or courage, you make a great effort to be strong, energetic, or brave. EG *...if you can't summon up enough energy to get up early... He eventually summoned up the courage to ask them if Melanie was all right.* PHRASAL VB: V+O+ADV

summons /sʌ̱mənz/, **summonses, summonsing, summonsed. 1** A **summons** is **1.1** an order to come and see someone. EG *I waited in my office for a summons from the boss.* **1.2** an official order to appear in court. N COUNT

2 If someone **is summonsed**, they are officially ordered to appear in court. V+O: USU PASS

sumptuous /sʌ̱mptjʊəs/. Something that is **sumptuous** is magnificent and obviously very expensive. EG *...sumptuous furnishings.* ADJ QUALIT

sum total. The **sum total** of a number of things is all the things added or considered together. N SING: *the*+N

sun /sʌ̱n/, **suns, sunning, sunned. 1** The **sun** is the ball of fire in the sky that the Earth goes round, and that gives us heat and light. N SING: *the*+N

2 You also refer to the light and heat that reach us from the sun as **sun**. EG *You need plenty of sun and fresh air... We all sat in the sun.* N UNCOUNT. OR N SING +SUPP

3 If you **sun** yourself, you sit or lie in a place where the sun shines on you. EG *He spent Saturday sunning himself on the beach.* V-REFL: OFT+A

sunbathe /sʌ̱nbeɪθ/, **sunbathes, sunbathing, sunbathed.** When people **sunbathe**, they sit or lie in a place where the sun shines strongly on them, so that they get a suntan. EG *I spent my afternoons sunbathing instead of doing my work.* V

sunburn /sʌ̱nbɜ:n/. If someone has **sunburn**, their skin is bright pink and sore because they have spent too much time in hot sunshine. N UNCOUNT

sunburnt /sʌ̱nbɜ:nt/; also spelled **sunburned.** Someone who is **sunburnt** **1** has sore, bright pink skin because they have spent too much time in hot sunshine. EG *His neck was badly sunburnt.* **2** has very brown skin because they have spent a lot of time in the sunshine. EG *Carlo was handsomely sunburned.* ADJ QUALIT

sundae /sʌ̱ndi:, -deɪ/, **sundaes.** A **sundae** is a dish of ice cream with cream and nuts or fruit on top. N COUNT

Sunday /sʌ̱ndi¹/, **Sundays. Sunday** is one of the seven days of the week. It is the day after Saturday and before Monday. Christians go to church on Sunday. EG *I never eat breakfast on Sundays.* N UNCOUNT OR N COUNT

Sunday school, Sunday schools. If children go to **Sunday school**, they go to a special class on Sundays in order to learn about Christianity. N UNCOUNT OR N COUNT

sundial /sʌ̱ndaɪəl/, **sundials.** A **sundial** is a device used for telling the time when the sun is shining. The shadow of a pointer falls on a flat N COUNT

Find another word for sunset.

surface that is marked with the hours, and points to the correct hour.

sundown /sʌndaʊn/ is the same as sunset. EG *It was about an hour before sundown.* N UNCOUNT American

sundry /sʌndri¹/. 1 If you refer to **sundry** things or people, you mean several things or people of various sorts. EG *...stools, wicker mats, food bowls, and sundry other objects.* ADJ CLASSIF: ATTRIB Formal

2 **All and sundry** means everyone. EG *She was fondly known to all and sundry as 'Little Madge'.* PHRASE Informal

sunflower /sʌnflaʊə/, **sunflowers.** A **sunflower** is a very tall plant with large yellow flowers. N COUNT

sung /sʌŋ/ is the past participle of **sing.**

sunglasses /sʌnglɑːsɪz/ are spectacles with dark lenses which you wear to protect your eyes from bright sunlight. N PLURAL

sunk /sʌŋk/ is the past participle of **sink.**

sunken /sʌŋkə⁰n/. 1 **Sunken** is used to describe 1.1 things that have sunk to the bottom of the sea or a lake. EG *...the remains of a sunken battleship.* ADJ CLASSIF: ATTRIB

1.2 things that are constructed below the level of the surrounding area. EG *...a sunken garden.*

2 If you have **sunken** cheeks or eyes or a **sunken** chest, they curve inwards and make you look thin and unwell. ADJ CLASSIF

sun lamp, sun lamps. A **sun lamp** is a lamp that produces rays which can make people's skin suntanned. N COUNT

sunlight /sʌnlaɪt/ is the light that comes from the sun. EG *The sea sparkled in the brilliant sunlight.* N UNCOUNT

sunlit /sʌnlɪt/. **Sunlit** places are brightly lit by the sun. EG *...the sunlit slopes of the valley.* ADJ CLASSIF

sunny /sʌni¹/, **sunnier, sunniest.** 1 When it is **sunny**, the sun is shining brightly. ADJ QUALIT

2 **Sunny** places are brightly lit by the sun. EG *...a lovely sunny region of green hills and valleys.* ADJ QUALIT

sunrise /sʌnraɪz/, **sunrises.** 1 **Sunrise** is the time in the morning when the sun first appears in the sky. EG *They left their camp at sunrise.* N UNCOUNT

2 A **sunrise** is the colours and light that you see in the eastern part of the sky when the sun first appears. EG *...the beautiful sunrise over the sea.* N COUNT OR N UNCOUNT

sunset /sʌnsɛt/, **sunsets.** 1 **Sunset** is the time in the evening when the sun disappears out of sight. EG *We'll leave just before sunset.* N UNCOUNT

2 A **sunset** is the colours and light that you see in the western part of the sky when the sun disappears in the evening. EG *You must see some beautiful sunsets here.* N COUNT OR N UNCOUNT

sunshine /sʌnʃaɪn/ is the light that comes from the sun. EG *Families were scattered along the beach enjoying the sunshine.* N UNCOUNT

sunstroke /sʌnstrəʊk/ is an illness caused by spending too much time in hot sunshine. N UNCOUNT

suntan /sʌntæn/, **suntans.** If you have a **suntan**, the sun has turned your skin an attractive brown colour. N COUNT

sun-tanned. Someone who is **sun-tanned** has attractively brown skin because they have been in the sunshine. ADJ QUALIT

super /sj⁰uːpə/. 1 If you say that someone or something is **super**, you mean that they are very nice or good. EG *I've got a super secretary.* ADJ CLASSIF Informal

2 **Super** is also used to describe things that are larger or better than similar things. EG *...a super plastic that is resistant to high temperatures... ...the building of new super warships.* ADJ CLASSIF: ATTRIB

superb /sj⁰ʊpɜːb/. If something is **superb**, its quality is very good indeed. EG *The children's library is superb.* ◊ **superbly.** EG *...a small but superbly equipped workshop.* ADJ CLASSIF ◊ ADV

supercilious /sj⁰uːpəsɪlɪəs/. If you are **supercilious**, you behave in a scornful way towards other people because you think they are inferior to you; used showing disapproval. EG *A slow supercilious smile crossed her face.* ADJ QUALIT

superficial /sj⁰uːpəfɪʃə⁰l/. 1 Something that is **superficial** involves only the most obvious or most easily understood aspects of something. EG *They've only got a superficial knowledge of linguistics... The new scheme has superficial similarities with the old one.* ◊ **superficially.** EG *Superficially it looks rather harmless.* ADJ QUALIT ◊ ADV OR ADV SEN

2 People who are **superficial** do not care very deeply about anything or are not interested in anything serious or important. ADJ QUALIT

3 **Superficial** wounds are not very deep or severe. ADJ QUALIT

superfluous /sj⁰uːpɜːfluəs/. Something that is **superfluous** is unnecessary or is no longer needed. EG *Certain parts of our religion have become superfluous... I had not been using maps at all. They were superfluous with Eddie around.* ADJ CLASSIF

superhuman /sj⁰uːpəhjuːmən/. If you describe a quality that someone has as **superhuman**, you mean that it seems to be much greater than that of ordinary people. EG *You must have superhuman strength... I controlled myself with a superhuman effort.* ADJ CLASSIF

superimpose /sj⁰uːpə⁰rɪmpəʊz/, **superimposes, superimposing, superimposed.** If you **superimpose** one image on another, you put one image on top of another one. EG *Three photos were superimposed one on top of the other.* V+O: OFT +on/with

superintendent /sj⁰uːpə⁰rɪntɛndənt/, **superintendents.** A **superintendent** is 1 a person who has a high rank in the police force. EG *...Superintendent Spence.* 2 a person who is responsible for a particular thing or department. EG *He was attached to the College as Superintendent of Buildings.* N COUNT

superior /sj⁰uːpɪərɪə/, **superiors.** 1 Something or someone that is **superior** to something or someone else is better than them. EG *The computer is vastly superior to the book... I secretly feel superior to him... The school prided itself upon its policy of providing a superior education.* ◊ **superiority** /sj⁰uːpɪərɒrɪ¹ti¹/. EG *...the great superiority of Hoyland over younger abstract painters.* ADJ QUALIT: OFT+to ◊ N UNCOUNT

2 Someone who is **superior** to someone else is more important or has more authority. EG *These matters are better left to someone superior to you.* ADJ CLASSIF: OFT+to

3 Someone who is **superior** behaves in a way which shows that they believe they are better than other people. EG *'You wouldn't understand,' Clarissa said in a superior way.* ADJ QUALIT

4 Your **superior** is a person who has a higher rank in an organization or a higher social position than you. EG *He was called to the office of a superior to be reprimanded... Myra was his social superior.* N COUNT

> **SUPERL** stands for **superlative**
> Some adjectives, and a few adverbs, have the label SUPERL in the Extra Column. This tells you that they are in the superlative form. Therefore, words like *best, worst,* and *most* have this label.
> See the entry headed ADJECTIVES for more information.

superlative /sj⁰uːpɜːlətɪv/, **superlatives.** In grammar, a **superlative** is the form of an adjective which indicates that the person or object being described has more of a particular quality or character than anyone or anything else in a group. N COUNT

supermarket /sj⁰uːpəmɑːkɪt/, **supermarkets.** A **supermarket** is a large shop which sells all kinds of food and household goods. N COUNT

supernatural /sj⁰uːpənætʃrəl/. 1 **Supernatural** creatures, forces, and events are believed by some people to exist or happen, although they are impossible according to scientific laws. EG *...witchcraft, the supernatural power to cure or control.* ADJ CLASSIF

2 Supernatural things and events are referred to as the **supernatural**. EG *Do you believe in the supernatural?* N SING: the+N

superpower /sj⁰uːpəpaʊə/, **superpowers.** A **superpower** is a very powerful country. When N COUNT people talk about 'the superpowers', they usually mean the USA and the USSR.

supersede /sj^{0}uːpəsiːd/, **supersedes, superseding, superseded.** V+O : USU PASS If something **supersedes** something else, it replaces it, often because the other thing has become old-fashioned. EG *Steam locomotives were superseded by diesel... New ways of thinking superseded older ones... This system is already being superseded.*

supersonic /sj^{0}uːpəsɒnɪk/. ADJ CLASSIF **Supersonic** aircraft travel faster than the speed of sound. EG *...the demand for supersonic travel.*

superstar /sj^{0}uːpəstɑː/, **superstars.** N COUNT Informal A **superstar** is a very famous entertainer or sports player. EG *The press built me up into a superstar.*

superstition /sj^{0}uːpəstɪʃə^{0}n/, **superstitions.** N UNCOUNT OR N COUNT **Superstition** is belief in things that are not real or possible, for example magic. EG *They were peasants filled with ignorance and superstition... ...old prejudices and superstitions.*

superstitious /sj^{0}uːpəstɪʃəs/. ADJ QUALIT People who are **superstitious** believe in things that are not real or possible, for example magic. EG *...a superstitious man with an unnatural fear of the dark... ...superstitious practices.*

supervise /sj^{0}uːpəvaɪz/, **supervises, supervising, supervised.** V+O OR V If you **supervise** an activity or a person, you make sure that the activity is done correctly or that the person is behaving correctly. EG *Miss Young had three netball games to supervise... One evening, when there were no staff to supervise her, she walked out of the hospital.*
◇ **supervision** /sj^{0}uːpəvɪʒə^{0}n/. ◇ N UNCOUNT EG *They are under the supervision of qualified social workers.*

supervisor /sj^{0}uːpəvaɪzə/, **supervisors.** N COUNT A **supervisor** is a person who supervises activities or people, especially workers or students. EG *The maintenance supervisor dispatched a crew to repair the damage... My supervisor said he would strongly recommend me for the course.*

> **SUPP** stands for **supporting word or words**
> Many nouns have the label +SUPP in the Extra Column. This means that the noun is not usually used on its own in this sense, but is used with other words, phrases, or clauses which give extra information about it or which add to its meaning in some way.
> See the entry headed NOUNS for more information.

supper /sʌpə/, **suppers.** N UNCOUNT OR N COUNT **Supper** is **1** a meal eaten in the early part of the evening. EG *He insisted on staying for supper.* **2** a small meal eaten just before you go to bed at night.

supplant /səplɑːnt/, **supplants, supplanting, supplanted.** V+O Formal To **supplant** something or someone means to take their place. EG *Electric cars may one day supplant petrol-driven ones... He began his campaign to supplant Gaitskell as party leader.*

supple /sʌpə^{0}l/. **1** ADJ QUALIT Someone who is **supple** moves and bends easily. EG *She had once been slim and supple... He keeps his fingers supple with regular exercises.*
2 ADJ QUALIT If an object or material is **supple**, it is soft and bends easily without cracking or breaking. EG *The leather straps were worn supple with use.*

supplement /sʌplɪmə^{2}nt/, **supplements, supplementing, supplemented.** **1** V+O : OFT +with/by If you **supplement** something, you add something to it, especially in order to make it more adequate. EG *They had to get a job to supplement the family income... I supplemented my diet with vitamin pills.*
2 N COUNT : OFT+to A **supplement** is something that is added to something else, especially in order to make it more adequate. EG *They will sometimes eat fish as a supplement to their natural diet.*
3 N COUNT A magazine or newspaper **supplement** is a separate part of a magazine or newspaper. EG *...the Times Literary Supplement.* ● See also **colour supplement**.

supplementary /sʌplɪmɛntə^{0}ri^1/ ADJ CLASSIF : ATTRIB is used to describe something that is added to another thing in order to make it more adequate. EG *You can claim a supplementary pension.*

supplementary benefit N UNCOUNT is an amount of money that the government in Britain gives regularly to people with no income or very low incomes. EG *They asked if I was on supplementary benefit.*

supplier /sə^{9}plaɪə/, **suppliers.** N COUNT A **supplier** is a person or firm that provides you with something such as goods or equipment. EG *...textile suppliers.*

supply /səplaɪ/, **supplies, supplying, supplied.** **1** V+O : OFT +for/with If you **supply** someone with something, you provide them with it. EG *I can supply you with food and drink... Germany is supplying the steel for the new pipeline... Most large towns there are supplied with electricity.*
2 N COUNT A **supply** of something is an amount of it which someone has or which is available for them to use. EG *Bill had his own supply of whisky... Most houses now have lavatories and a hot water supply.*
3 N PLURAL **Supplies** are food, equipment, and other things needed by a group of people, for example by an army or by people going on an expedition. EG *The plane had been ferrying military supplies over the border.*
4 N UNCOUNT **Supply** is the amount of something that can be produced and made available for people to buy. EG *Economic stability can only be reached if demand and supply are in approximate balance.*
5 PHRASE If something is **in short supply**, there is very little of it available. EG *Petrol is in desperately short supply.*

support /sə^{9}pɔːt/, **supports, supporting, supported.** **1** V+O If you **support** someone or their ideas or aims, you agree with them, want them to succeed, and perhaps help them. EG *A lot of building workers supported the campaign... His work colleagues refused to support him.* ▸ N UNCOUNT used as a noun. EG *The party declared its support for the campaign... The group drew some support from the idealistic young.*
2 V+O If you **support** a sports team, especially a football team, you want them to win and perhaps go regularly to their games.
3 N UNCOUNT If you give **support** to someone during a difficult or unhappy time, you are kind to them and help them. EG *They find it hard to give their children emotional support.*
4 V+O If something **supports** an object, it is underneath the object and holding it up. EG *...the steel girders that supported the walkway... ...a horizontal bar supported by two vertical pillars.*
5 N COUNT A **support** is a bar or other object that supports something. EG *Most large scale buildings now have steel supports.*
6 V-REFL If you **support** yourself, you prevent yourself from falling by holding onto something or by leaning on something. EG *I clung to the outside edge of the door to support myself.* ▸ N UNCOUNT used as a noun. EG *She was standing behind the ladder and holding on to it for support.*
7 N UNCOUNT Financial **support** is money provided to enable a firm or organization to continue, usually by the government. EG *These industries were dependent on state support.*
8 V+O If you **support** someone, you provide them with money or the things that they need. EG *He has a wife and three children to support.*
9 V+O If a fact **supports** a statement or a theory, it helps to show that it is true or correct. EG *There*

> On these pages find an informal way of saying 'yes'.

was simply no visible evidence to support such a theory. ▸ used as a noun. EG *Scholars have found little support for this interpretation... In support of this view, Rose cites Pollock's own evidence.* ▸ N UNCOUNT

supporter /sə[9]pɔːtə/, **supporters.** A **supporter** is a person who supports someone or something, for example a political leader or a sports team. EG *The Minister's supporters did not desert him in his hour of need... He's an Everton supporter.* N COUNT+SUPP

supportive /sə[9]pɔːtɪv/. If you are **supportive**, you are kind and helpful to someone at a difficult or unhappy time in their life. EG *When I became a widow he was supportive.* ADJ QUALIT

suppose /sə[9]pəʊz/, **supposes, supposing, supposed.** 1 If you **suppose** that something is true, you think that it is likely to be true. EG *He supposed that MPs were unaware of the danger... It was quite reasonable to suppose that he wanted the money too... The situation was even worse than was supposed.* V+REPORT: ONLY *that*; ALSO V+O+C

2 You say **I suppose** when you are not entirely certain or enthusiastic about what you are saying. EG *I suppose he wasn't trying hard enough... I don't suppose you would be prepared to stay in Edinburgh?... We could take Davis with us, I suppose... 'So it was worth doing?' – 'I suppose so.'* PHRASE

3 You say **you don't suppose** to introduce a possibility which you want someone else to give their opinion about. EG *You don't suppose he'll get lost out there?* PHRASE

4 You use **suppose** or **supposing** when you are considering a possible situation or action and trying to think what effects it would have. EG *Suppose we don't say a word, and somebody else finds out about it... Supposing something should go wrong, what would you do then?* CONJ

supposed /sə[9]pəʊzd/. 1 The phrase **be supposed** is used in these ways. **1.1** If you say that something **is supposed** to be done, you mean that it should be done because of a rule, instruction, or custom. EG *You are supposed to report it to the police as soon as possible... I'm not supposed to talk to you about this.* **1.2** If you say that something **is supposed** to happen, especially when it does not in fact happen, you mean that it is planned or intended to happen. EG *I was supposed to go last summer... A machine at the entrance is supposed to check the tickets.* **1.3** You say that something **is supposed** to be true when people think that it is true but you do not know for certain that it is true. EG *They are supposed to be the best in London... The hill was supposed to be haunted by the ghost of a leper.* PHRASE

2 You also use **supposed** to express doubt about a way of describing someone or something that is generally believed or stated. EG *...his supposed ancestor, the pirate Henry Morgan... ...the supposed benefits of a progressive welfare state.* ADJ CLASSIF: ATTRIB

◇ **supposedly**. EG *...a robot supposedly capable of understanding spoken commands.* ◇ ADV

supposition /sʌpəzɪʃə[0]n/, **suppositions.** A **supposition** is an idea or statement which is thought or assumed to be true. EG *The supposition is that the infiltrators knew the raids were to take place... That is a most unlikely supposition.* N COUNT Formal

suppress /səprɛs/, **suppresses, suppressing, suppressed.** 1 If an army or government **suppresses** an activity, they prevent it from continuing. EG *The army soon suppressed the revolt.* V+O

◇ **suppression** /səprɛʃə[0]n/. EG *...the suppression of freedom... ...the suppression of rebellions.* ◇ N UNCOUNT: USU+SUPP

2 If someone **suppresses** a piece of information, they prevent it from becoming known to the general public. EG *The committee's report has been suppressed.* ◇ **suppression**. EG *...the deliberate suppression of information.* V+O; ◇ N UNCOUNT: USU+SUPP

3 If you **suppress** your feelings, you prevent yourself from expressing them. EG *Suppressing her annoyance, she smiled at him... She was struggling to suppress her sobs.* ◇ **suppression**. EG *...the polite suppression of a yawn.* V+O; ◇ N UNCOUNT: USU+SUPP

supremacy /sj[0]ʊprɛməsɪ/. If one group of people has **supremacy** over another group, they are more powerful than the other group. EG *...the supremacy of the House of Commons... Their political supremacy continued.* N UNCOUNT

supreme /sjʊpriːm/. 1 **Supreme** is used in the title of a person or an official group to indicate that they are at the highest level in a particular organization or system. EG *The Supreme Commander ordered their release... ...the Supreme Court.* ADJ CLASSIF: ATTRIB

2 You also use **supreme** to emphasize the greatness of something. EG *...one of this century's supreme achievements... ...tasks of supreme importance.* ◇ **supremely**. EG *...a supremely important moment... The only thing he had ever been able to do supremely well was to fly airplanes.* ADJ CLASSIF: USU ATTRIB; ◇ SUBMOD

sure /ʃʊə, ʃɔː/, **surer, surest.** 1 If you are **sure** that something is true, you are certain that it is true. EG *I'm sure she's right... Something had gone wrong, he was sure of it... I'm not quite sure but I think it's half past five.* ADJ PRED: OFT+REPORT OR *of*

2 If you are **sure** about your feelings or wishes, you know exactly what you feel or what you want to do. EG *Jane wasn't sure how she felt about being married... Are you sure you won't have another drink?* ADJ PRED: OFT+REPORT

3 If you are **sure** of yourself, you are very confident about your own abilities or opinions. ADJ PRED+*of*

4 If you say that someone is **sure** of getting something, you mean that they will certainly get it. EG *We can be sure of success... You could not always be sure of winning.* ADJ PRED+*of*

5 If you say that something is **sure** to happen, you mean that it will certainly happen. EG *He was sure to see her again... We're sure to get a place.* ADJ PRED +*to*-INF

6 If you **make sure** that something is the way that you want or expect it to be, you check that it is that way. EG *He glanced over his shoulder to make sure that there was nobody listening... Make sure the brake has been fully released.* PHRASE

7 If you **make sure** that something is done, you take action so that it is done. EG *Ask for a receipt and make sure that you get it... I did it to make sure you noticed.* PHRASE

8 If you tell someone to **be sure** to do something, you mean that they must not forget to do it. EG *Be sure to remind your uncle.* PHRASE

9 You use **sure** to describe something such as a method or a sign when it is reliable or accurate. EG *Going to places is a sure way of getting to know them... Wood dust beneath a piece of furniture is a sure sign of woodworm... She had a sure grasp of the subject.* ADJ QUALIT: USU ATTRIB

10 **Sure** is an informal way of saying 'yes'. EG *'Can I go with you?' – 'Sure.'* CONVENTION Informal

11 You can also use **sure** in order to emphasize what you are saying. EG *He sure is cute... You sure do have an interesting job.* ADV Informal American

12 If you say that something is **for sure** or that you know it **for sure**, you mean that it is definitely true or will definitely happen. EG *One thing was for sure, there was nothing wrong with Allen's eyesight.* PHRASE Informal

13 You say **sure enough** to confirm that something is really true or is actually happening. EG *'The baby's crying,' she said. Sure enough, a yelling noise was coming from upstairs.* ADV SEN

surely /ʃʊəli[1],ʃɔː-/. 1 You use **surely** to emphasize that you think something is true, and often to express surprise that other people do not agree with you. EG *He surely knew the danger... She was surely one of the rarest women of our time... You don't mind that surely?... Good heavens! Surely you are not suggesting she did it on purpose?* ADV SEN

2 If you say that something is happening **slowly but surely**, you mean that it is happening gradually and cannot be stopped. EG *Slowly but surely we're becoming a computer-centred society.* PHRASE

surf /sɜːf/ is the mass of white foam that is formed by waves as they fall upon the shore. EG *We watched the children play in the surf.* N UNCOUNT: OFT the+N

surface /sɜːfɪ¹s/. **surfaces, surfacing, surfaced.**
1 The **surface** of something is the top part of it or the outside of it. EG *...the jumble which covers the surface of my desk... A gentle breeze rippled the surface of the sea... ...the surface of the moon... ...holes in the road surface.* N COUNT: USU+SUPP
2 The **surface** of a situation is what can be seen easily rather than what is hidden or not immediately obvious. EG *His job was not as enviable as it appeared on the surface... This dispute first came to the surface in 1962.* N COUNT ● If a quality or feeling is **below** or **beneath the surface** of something such as a society or a play, it is not obvious when you first consider the thing. EG *You don't have to look far to encounter the tensions beneath the surface.* ● PHRASE
3 If someone or something under water **surfaces**, they come up to the surface of the water. EG *Bobby surfaced twenty feet in front of the boat.* V: OFT+A
4 When a piece of news or a feeling **surfaces**, it becomes known or becomes obvious. EG *Such rumours have surfaced several times over the past ten years... Concern for the children never took long to surface.* V
5 When someone **surfaces** after sleeping, they appear, usually later than expected. EG *He didn't surface today until after eleven.* V: OFT+A Informal

surfboard /sɜːfbɔːd/, **surfboards.** A **surfboard** is a long narrow board that is used in surfing. N COUNT

surfeit /sɜːfɪt/. A **surfeit** of something is an amount which is too large. EG *Recently there has been a surfeit of cricket on the television.* N SING: a+N+of Formal

surfing /sɜːfɪŋ/. When someone goes **surfing**, they ride towards the seashore on the top of a big wave while standing or lying on a surfboard. N ING

surge /sɜːdʒ/, **surges, surging, surged. 1** A **surge** is a sudden great increase in something. EG *A surge of activity spread through the party... There has been a surge in sales of Waugh's novels.* N COUNT: USU SING +in/of
2 A **surge** of an emotion such as pity or anger is a sudden strong feeling of it. EG *She felt a surge of affection for him... ...a surge of jealousy.* N COUNT: USU SING+of
3 If an emotion or sensation **surges** in you, you feel it suddenly and powerfully. EG *Hope surged in Peter... Relief surged through him.* V+A Literary
4 If people or vehicles **surge** forward, they move forward suddenly in a mass. EG *When the doors were flung open, a crowd surged in.* V+A ◊ **surging**. EG *...surging crowds of demonstrators... ...a surging swarm of people.* ◊ ADJ CLASSIF: ATTRIB
5 If water **surges**, it moves forward suddenly and powerfully. EG *...the tides surging over the rocks.* V: USU+A

surgeon /sɜːdʒən/, **surgeons.** A **surgeon** is a doctor who performs surgery. EG *...a brain surgeon.* N COUNT

surgery /sɜːdʒə⁰ri¹/, **surgeries. 1 Surgery** is medical treatment in which someone's body is cut open so that a doctor can repair or remove a diseased or damaged part. EG *He has had major abdominal surgery.* ● See also **plastic surgery**. N UNCOUNT
2 A **surgery** is the room or house where a doctor or dentist works. N COUNT British
3 A doctor's **surgery** is also the period of time each day when he or she sees patients at the surgery. EG *I'll be in for morning surgery at ten.* N COUNT OR N UNCOUNT British

surgical /sɜːdʒɪkə⁰l/. **1 Surgical** equipment and clothing is used in surgery. EG *...surgical instruments... ...a surgical mask.* ADJ CLASSIF: ATTRIB
2 Surgical treatment involves surgery. EG *Some people can have their vision restored by a surgical operation.* ADJ CLASSIF: ATTRIB ◊ **surgically**. EG *The cataract can then be removed surgically.* ◊ ADV

surly /sɜːli¹/. Someone who is **surly** behaves in a rude, bad-tempered way. EG *His voice was surly.* ADJ QUALIT

surmise /səmaɪz/, **surmises, surmising, surmised.** If you **surmise** that something is true, you guess that it is true, although it may not be. EG *The last question, Turing surmised, was the key one... The French, for reasons which could only be surmised, opposed the idea.* V+REPORT, OR V+O Formal

surmount /səmaʊnt/, **surmounts, surmounting, surmounted. 1** If you **surmount** a problem or difficulty, you deal successfully with it. EG *She managed to surmount this obstacle.* V+O
2 If something **is surmounted** by a particular thing, that thing is on top of it. EG *The column is surmounted by a statue.* V+O: USU PASS Formal

surname /sɜːneɪm/, **surnames.** Your **surname** is the name that you share with other members of your family. It is usually your last name. EG *'What's your surname?' – 'Barker.'* N COUNT: USU+POSS

surpass /səpɑːs/, **surpasses, surpassing, surpassed.** To **surpass** someone or something means to be better than them, to do better than them, or to have more of a particular quality than them. EG *The women were able to equal or surpass the men who worked beside them... Your excellent performance surpassed all expectations... In my opinion the jewel is surpassed in beauty by the other ornaments.* V+O Formal

surplus /sɜːpləs/, **surpluses.** A **surplus** is a quantity of something that is extra or more than is needed. EG *...the recent worldwide surplus of crude oil... In this continent there is a vast surplus of workers.* N COUNT OR N UNCOUNT ▸ used as an adjective. EG *...surplus grain.* ▸ ADJ CLASSIF

surprise /səpraɪz/, **surprises, surprising, surprised. 1** A **surprise** is an unexpected event. EG *This ruling came as a surprise to everyone... 'Why don't you tell me?' – 'Because I want it to be a surprise.'* N COUNT ▸ used before a noun. EG *The minister made the surprise announcement in a statement earlier today... ...a surprise attack.* ▸ N MOD
2 Surprise is the feeling that you have when something unexpected happens. EG *Boylan looked at her in surprise... To my surprise, he nodded and agreed.* N UNCOUNT
3 If something **takes** you **by surprise**, it happens to you suddenly or unexpectedly. EG *The storm, when it broke, took them entirely by surprise.* PHRASE
4 If something **surprises** you, it gives you a feeling of surprise. EG *I surprised everyone by gobbling an enormous lunch... It would not surprise me if he ends up in jail.* V+O
5 If you **surprise** someone, you attack them or find them when they are not expecting it. EG *They were surprised by a unit of US marines during the night... She feared her parents would return and surprise them.* V+O

surprised /səpraɪzd/. If you are **surprised** by something, you have a feeling of surprise, because it is unexpected or unusual. EG *The twins were very surprised to see Ralph... I was surprised at the number of bicycles... Gretchen stood up, surprised that Miss Saunders remembered her name.* ADJ QUALIT: USU PRED

surprising /səpraɪzɪŋ/. Something that is **surprising** is unexpected or unusual and makes you feel surprised. EG *He leapt out of the car with surprising agility... It was surprising how much money she managed to earn.* ADJ QUALIT ◊ **surprisingly**. EG *It was surprisingly cheap... Not surprisingly the proposal met with hostile reactions.* ◊ SUBMOD OR ADV SEN

surreal /sərɪəl/ means the same as surrealistic. ADJ QUALIT

surrealist /sərɪəlɪst/. **Surrealist** paintings show strange objects or strange combinations of objects. ADJ CLASSIF: ATTRIB

surrealistic /sərɪəlɪstɪk/. If you describe a situation as **surrealistic**, you mean that it is very strange and like a dream. EG *The search had a kind of mad, surrealistic quality.* ADJ QUALIT

surrender /sərɛndə/, **surrenders, surrendering, surrendered. 1** If you **surrender**, you stop fighting or resisting someone and agree that you have been beaten. EG *All the British forces surrendered... The protesters surrendered to the police* V

If someone is called James Watt, what is his surname?

after about an hour. ▸ used as a noun. EG *They tried to starve us into surrender.* ▸ N UNCOUNT

2 If you **surrender** to a force, temptation, or feeling, you allow it to gain control over you or to influence you. EG *A nation of nature-lovers seemed to have surrendered to technology... ...surrendering to a sense of apathy.* V : OFT+*to*

3 If you **surrender** something, you give it up or let someone else have it. EG *The United States would never surrender this territory.* ▸ used as a noun. EG *The surrender of liberties is irrevocable.* V+O : OFT+*to* ▸ N UNCOUNT

surreptitious /sʌrə²ptɪʃəs/. A **surreptitious** action is done secretly. EG *He began paying surreptitious visits to betting shops.* ◇ **surreptitiously**. EG *Rudolph looked surreptitiously at his watch.* ADJ QUALIT ◇ ADV

surrogate /sʌrəgeɪt, -gə¹t/, **surrogates.** You use **surrogate** to describe a person or thing that acts as a substitute for someone or something else. EG *Uncle Paul has become a surrogate father to me.* ▸ used as a noun. EG *...a surrogate for another person.* ADJ CLASSIF : ATTRIB Formal ▸ N COUNT

surrogate mother, surrogate mothers. A **surrogate mother** is a woman who has agreed to give birth to a baby on behalf of another woman. N COUNT

surround /səraʊnd/, **surrounds, surrounding, surrounded. 1** If something **surrounds** something else, it is situated all around it. EG *Muscles surround blood vessels in the body... The house was surrounded by high walls.* V+O : OFT PASS

2 If people **surround** a person or place, they spread out so that they are positioned all the way round. EG *Don't get near him. Just surround him and keep him there.* V+O

3 If problems or dangers **surround** something, they exist all around it or are closely associated with it. EG *...the dangers which surround us... ...the uncertainty surrounding the future of the railways.* V+O

4 If you **surround** yourself with things, you make sure that you have a lot of them near you all the time. EG *Get involved in social activities and surround yourself with friends.* V-REFL+*with*

surrounding /səraʊndɪŋ/, **surroundings. 1** You use **surrounding** to describe the area which is all around a particular place. EG *Foxes started coming in from the surrounding countryside... They could see into the courtyard from the roofs of the surrounding buildings.* ADJ CLASSIF : ATTRIB

2 You can refer to the place where you live or where you are at the moment as your **surroundings**. EG *We used to live in nice surroundings.* N PLURAL

surveillance /səveɪləns/ is the careful watching of someone, especially by an organization such as the police or the army. EG *Everyone we knew was under surveillance... They intensified their surveillance of her home.* N UNCOUNT Formal

survey, surveys, surveying, surveyed; pronounced /səveɪ/ when it is a verb and /sɜːveɪ/ when it is a noun.

1 If you **survey** something, you look carefully at the whole of it. EG *He drove to a point from which he could survey the beach... She stepped back and surveyed her work.* V+O

2 When people **survey** an area of land, they examine it and measure it, usually in order to make a map of it. EG *He had the land surveyed from a helicopter.* V+O

3 When someone **surveys** a house, they examine it carefully and report on its structure, usually in order to give advice to a person who is buying it. V+O

4 A **survey** is **4.1** a detailed investigation of something, for example people's behaviour or opinions. EG *This book was based on a survey of a thousand male and female graduates... ...a national survey of eye diseases among children.* **4.2** an examination of an area of land. EG *...aerial surveys.* **4.3** a careful examination of a house in order to report on its condition. N COUNT

surveyor /səveɪə/, **surveyors.** A **surveyor** is a person whose job is to survey houses or land. N COUNT

survival /səvaɪvə⁰l/, **survivals. 1 Survival** is continuing to live in spite of nearly dying or being in great difficulty. EG *What are their chances of survival?... ...the day-to-day struggle for survival.* N UNCOUNT

2 Something that is a **survival** from an earlier time has continued to exist from that time. EG *The royal house is full of survivals from many centuries.* N COUNT Formal

survive /səvaɪv/, **survives, surviving, survived.**

1 If someone **survives** or if they **survive** a disaster or illness, they continue to live in spite of coming close to death. EG *Four of his brothers died: the fifth survived... Very few people survived the immediate effects of the explosion... She is Britain's longest surviving transplant patient.* V OR V+O : NO PASS, NO IMPER

2 If you **survive** someone, you continue to live after they have died. EG *She will probably survive me by many years.* V+O : NO IMPER

3 If something **survives**, it continues to exist from an earlier time. EG *I doubt whether the National Health Service will survive to the end of the century... The project survived three changes of government.* V OR V+O : NO PASS, NO IMPER

4 If you **survive** a difficult experience, you manage to cope with it and do not let it affect you too badly. EG *She seems to have survived the divorce pretty well... You have to make difficult decisions to survive in business.* V+O OR V : NO PASS, NO IMPER

survive on. If you **survive on** a particular amount of money or food, you earn just enough money to buy essential things to live, or you have just enough food to live. EG *My salary's only just enough to survive on... They store water to survive on during the drought.* PHRASAL VB : V+PREP

survivor /səvaɪvə/, **survivors. 1** A **survivor** of a disaster or illness is someone who continues to live afterwards in spite of coming close to death. EG *I talked to one of the survivors of the crash.* N COUNT : OFT+SUPP

2 If you describe someone as a **survivor**, you mean that they are able to carry on with their life even though they experience many difficulties. EG *He sounds like one of life's survivors.* N COUNT

susceptible /səseptɪbə⁰l/. **1** If you are **susceptible** to something, you are likely to be influenced by it. EG *We are all susceptible to advertising... These organizations are susceptible to Government pressure.* ADJ PRED : USU+*to*

2 If you are **susceptible** to a disease or injury, you are likely to be affected by it. EG *Many people were lightly dressed and therefore susceptible to burns on their skin.* ◇ **susceptibility** /səseptə¹bɪlɪ¹ti¹/. EG *...his susceptibility to infection.* ADJ QUALIT : USU+*to* ◇ N UNCOUNT : OFT+*to*

suspect, suspects, suspecting, suspected; pronounced /səspekt/ when it is a verb, and /sʌspekt/ when it is a noun or adjective.

1 If you **suspect** something, **1.1** you think that it is likely or is probably true. EG *People suspected that a secret deal had been made... He suspected murder... I suspect the boy is in love.* **1.2** you doubt that it can be trusted or that it is reliable. EG *I had many reasons for suspecting this approach.* V+O OR V+REPORT : ONLY *that* / V+O

2 If you **suspect** someone of a crime, you think that they are guilty of it. EG *He was suspected of treason.* V+O : OFT+*of*

3 A **suspect** is a person who is thought to be guilty of a crime. EG *Last week police finally had a suspect for the murder.* N COUNT

4 If something is **suspect**, it cannot be trusted or regarded as genuine. EG *My friendliness was viewed as suspect by some people... Their military titles were a little suspect.* ADJ QUALIT

suspend /səspend/, **suspends, suspending, suspended. 1** If something **is suspended** from a high place, it is hanging from that place. EG *A model aeroplane was suspended above the stage.* V+O+A : USU PASS

2 If you **suspend** something, you delay it or stop it from happening for a while. EG *There were demands that the trial be temporarily suspended... The builders suspended their work.* V+O

3 If someone **is suspended**, they are prevented from holding a particular job or position for a fixed length of time, usually as a punishment. EG *The people involved in the incident have been suspended from their duties... He was the third member to be suspended from the party.*
V+O : USU PASS

suspender /səspɛndə/, **suspenders. Suspenders** are fastenings hanging down from a belt or girdle which hold a woman's stockings up.
N COUNT : USU PLURAL

suspense /səspɛns/. **1 Suspense** is a state of excitement or anxiety about something that is going to happen very soon, for example when you are waiting for some news. EG *I try to add an element of suspense and mystery to my novels.*
N UNCOUNT

2 If you **keep** someone **in suspense**, you delay telling them something that they are very eager to know about. EG *I did not leave him in suspense, but quickly informed him that he had passed.*
PHRASE

suspension /səspɛnʃ^{ə}n/, **suspensions. 1 Suspension** of something is delaying it or stopping it from happening for a while. EG *...the suspension of all social security payments.*
N UNCOUNT : OFT+*of*

2 Someone's **suspension** is their removal from a job or position for a period of time, usually as a punishment.
N UNCOUNT OR N COUNT

3 A vehicle's **suspension** consists of the springs and shock absorbers attached to the wheels, which give a smooth ride in spite of bumps in the road.
N UNCOUNT

suspension bridge, suspension bridges. A **suspension bridge** is a type of bridge that is supported from above by cables.
N COUNT

suspicion /səspɪʃ^{ə}n/, **suspicions. 1 Suspicion** is the feeling that you do not trust someone or that something is wrong in some way. EG *Derek shared Lynn's suspicion of Michael... I had aroused his suspicions last week... Their friendship is regarded with suspicion by their teachers.*
N UNCOUNT OR N COUNT

2 If someone is **under suspicion**, they are suspected of being guilty of something such as a crime. EG *He felt that he was possibly under suspicion.*
PHRASE

3 A **suspicion** is a feeling that something is probably true or is likely to happen. EG *Investigators have strong suspicions of a clandestine trade.*
N COUNT

4 A **suspicion** of a quality or feeling is a very small amount of it. EG *My dog barks at the slightest suspicion of danger.*
N SING+*of*

suspicious /səspɪʃəs/. **1** If you are **suspicious** of someone, you do not trust them. EG *The policeman on duty became suspicious of the youth and asked him why he was standing there... He shot a suspicious glance at me.* ◊ **suspiciously**. EG *'Why are you laughing?' Rachel asked suspiciously.*
ADJ QUALIT : OFT+*of* ◊ ADV

2 You can use **suspicious** to describe things that make you think that something is wrong with a situation. EG *There were suspicious circumstances about his death... Several suspicious aircraft were spotted.* ◊ **suspiciously**. EG *The lump was suspiciously big.*
ADJ QUALIT ◊ SUBMOD

sustain /səsteɪn/, **sustains, sustaining, sustained. 1** If you **sustain** something, you continue it or maintain it for a period of time. EG *They do not have enough money to sustain a strike... The problem was how to sustain public interest.*
V+O

2 If food or drink **sustains** you, it gives you energy and strength. EG *They had nothing to sustain them all day except two cups of coffee.*
V+O

3 If something **sustains** you, it supports you by giving you help, strength, or encouragement. EG *It is his belief in God that sustains him.*
V+O

sustained /səsteɪnd/. An activity that is **sustained** is continued for a long time. EG *The enemy mounted a sustained attack on the castle.*
ADJ QUALIT

sustenance /sʌstənəns/ is food and drink which helps to keep a person, animal, or plant strong and healthy. EG *We derive our sustenance from the land... Minerals provide sustenance for their roots.*
N UNCOUNT Formal

SW is an abbreviation for 'south-west'.

swab /swɒb/, **swabs.** A **swab** is a small piece of cotton wool used by a doctor or nurse for cleaning a wound or for applying ointment or disinfectant.
N COUNT

swagger /swægə/, **swaggers, swaggering, swaggered.** If you **swagger**, you walk in a proud way, holding your body upright and swinging your hips. EG *She swaggered back to her place by the window.* ▸ used as a noun. EG *Bernard left the room with a swagger.*
V : USU+A ▸ N SING

swallow /swɒləʊ/, **swallows, swallowing, swallowed. 1** If you **swallow** something, you cause it to go from your mouth down into your stomach. EG *He swallowed more pills.* ▸ used as a noun. EG *Brody took a long swallow of his drink.*
V+O ▸ N COUNT

2 If you **swallow**, you make a movement in your throat as if you are swallowing something, often because you are nervous or frightened. EG *He swallowed and closed his eyes.*
V

3 If someone **swallows** a story or a statement, they believe it completely. EG *I sometimes think that crowds will swallow whole any political speech whatsoever.*
V+O

4 If you **swallow** an insult or an unkind remark, you accept it and do not protest. EG *She swallowed the sarcasm and got on with her work.* • to **swallow** your **pride**: see **pride**.
V+O

5 A **swallow** is also a kind of small bird with pointed wings and a forked tail.
N COUNT

swam /swæm/ is the past tense of **swim.**

swamp /swɒmp/, **swamps, swamping, swamped. 1** A **swamp** is an area of very wet land with wild plants growing in it.
N COUNT OR N UNCOUNT

2 If something **swamps** a ship or boat, it fills it with water and causes it to sink. EG *Sudden heavy seas swamped the ship.*
V+O

3 If you **are swamped** by things or people, you have more of them than you can deal with. EG *Pubs were suddenly swamped by a flood of troops... We've been swamped with applicants.*
V+O : USU PASS

swampy /swɒmpi^{1}/. A **swampy** area of land consists mainly of swamps. EG *...swampy river banks.*
ADJ QUALIT

swan /swɒn/, **swans.** A **swan** is a large bird with a very long neck. Swans live on rivers and lakes and are usually white.
N COUNT

swan song. Someone's **swan song** is the last time that they do something for which they are famous, for example the last time that an actor gives a performance in the theatre.
N SING+POSS

swap /swɒp/, **swaps, swapping, swapped;** also spelled **swop. 1** If you **swap** one thing for another, **1.1** you give the first thing to someone and receive the other thing in exchange. EG *He swapped a dozen goats for a female calf... Try swapping homes with a friend.* ▸ used as a noun. EG *Let's do a swap.* **1.2** you remove the first thing and replace it with something else. EG *I swapped my cap for a large black waterproof hat.*
V+O : OFT +*for/with* ▸ N COUNT V+O+*for*

2 If you **swap** stories or opinions with someone, you tell each other stories or give each other your opinions. EG *They swap amusing stories about the place... ...swopping views with the other people.*
V+O : OFT+*with*

swarm /swɔːm/, **swarms, swarming, swarmed.**
1 A **swarm** of bees or other insects is a large group of them flying together. EG *The showers brought swarms of flying insects to torment them.*
N PART

2 When bees or other insects **swarm**, they move or fly in a large group. EG *When the bees swarmed we all rushed out into the garden.*
V

3 When people **swarm** somewhere, they move there quickly in a large group. EG *They swarmed across the bridge and began climbing up the bank.*
V+A

4 A **swarm** of people is a large group of them moving about quickly. EG *She left amid a swarm of photographers.*
N PART

Is a swan song ever a song?

5 If a place **is swarming** with people, it is full of people moving about in a busy way. EG *The White House garden was swarming with security men.*
V+*with*

swarthy /swɔ:ði[1]/. A **swarthy** person has a dark complexion. EG *...his swarthy face.*
ADJ QUALIT

swat /swɒt/, **swats, swatting, swatted.** If you **swat** something such as an insect, you hit it with a quick, swinging movement, using your hand or a flat object.
V+O

swathe /sweɪð/, **swathes. 1** A **swathe** is a long strip of cloth, especially when it is wrapped round someone or something. EG *...balconies strewn with swathes of silk.*
N COUNT

2 A **swathe** of land is a long strip of land that is different from the land on either side of it, for example because it is higher, or has no vegetation. EG *...new roads cutting swathes through our countryside.*
N COUNT Literary

swathed /sweɪðd/. If someone is **swathed** in something, they are completely wrapped in it. EG *She was swathed in bandages from head to foot.*
ADJ PRED+*in*

sway /sweɪ/, **sways, swaying, swayed. 1** When people or things **sway**, they lean or swing slowly from one side to the other. EG *He didn't fall, but swayed a little... She sang and swayed from side to side... ...trees swaying in the wind.*
V : OFT+A

2 If you **are swayed** by something that you hear or read, it influences you. EG *Do not be swayed by glamorous advertisements.*
V+O : USU PASS

3 Sway is the power that someone or something has to influence people. EG *Laing was coming increasingly under the sway of new ideas.* ● If someone or something **holds sway**, they have great power or influence over a particular place or activity. EG *The beliefs which now hold sway may one day be rejected.*
N UNCOUNT Literary ● PHRASE Formal

swear /sweə/, **swears, swearing, swore** /swɔ:/, **sworn** /swɔ:n/. **1** If someone **swears**, they use language that is considered to be rude or blasphemous. Some people often swear when they are angry. EG *Glenys leant out of the car window and swore at the other driver.*
V : OFT+*at*

2 If you **swear** to do something, you solemnly promise that you will do it. EG *I swear I will never tell anyone.*
V+*to*-INF OR REPORT : ONLY *that*

3 If you say that you **swear** that something is true or that you can **swear** to it, you are saying very firmly that it is true. EG *She did not know a thing, she swore... I swear that he never consulted me.*
V+*to* OR REPORT : ONLY *that*

4 See also **sworn**.

swear by. If you say that you **swear by** something, you mean that you believe that it can be relied on to have a particular effect. EG *He swears by my herbal tea to make him sleep.*
PHRASAL VB : V+PREP Informal

swear in. When someone **is sworn in**, they solemnly promise to fulfil the duties of a new job or appointment. EG *The jury was sworn in on May 4.*
PHRASAL VB : V+O+ADV, USU PASS

swear-word, swear-words. A **swear-word** is a word which is considered to be rude or blasphemous, which people use when they are angry.
N COUNT

sweat /swɛt/, **sweats, sweating, sweated. 1 Sweat** is the salty, colourless liquid which comes through your skin when you are hot, ill, or afraid. EG *Jack paused, wiping the sweat from his face.*
N UNCOUNT

2 When you **sweat**, sweat comes through your skin. EG *I lay and sweated in bed... The heat was nearly unbearable, but the sweating people danced.*
V

3 If someone is **in a sweat** or **in a cold sweat**, they are sweating a lot, especially because they are afraid or ill. EG *He awoke trembling and in a cold sweat.*
PHRASE

4 You can refer to hard work or effort as **sweat**. EG *...the money he makes out of the labouring man's sweat.*
N UNCOUNT Literary

sweater /swɛtə/, **sweaters.** A **sweater** is a warm knitted piece of clothing which covers the upper part of your body and your arms. You put it on by pulling it over your head. EG *The girl had come out wearing jeans and a sweater.*
N COUNT

sweatshirt /swɛtʃɜ:t/, **sweatshirts.** A **sweatshirt** is a piece of casual clothing, usually made from thick cotton, which covers the upper part of your body and your arms. You put it on by pulling it over your head.
N COUNT

sweaty /swɛti[1]/. **1** A **sweaty** place or activity makes you sweat because it is hot or tiring. EG *...the sweaty march along the blazing beach.*
ADJ QUALIT

2 If your clothes or parts of your body are **sweaty**, they are soaked or covered with sweat. EG *...students in sweaty sports shirts... ...cold sweaty hands.*
ADJ QUALIT

swede /swi:d/, **swedes.** A **swede** is a round yellow root vegetable with a brown or purple skin.
N COUNT

sweep /swi:p/, **sweeps, sweeping, swept** /swɛpt/. **1** If you **sweep** an area of ground, you push dirt or rubbish off it with a long-handled brush. EG *I must sweep the kitchen floor... ...men sweeping streets... He swept away the broken glass.*
V+O OR V+A

2 If you **sweep** things off something, you push them off with a quick, smooth movement of your arm. EG *He went into the study and swept some books and papers off the couch.*
V+O+A

3 If your hand or arm **sweeps** in a particular direction, it moves in a quick, smooth curve. EG *The dog was flung aside by the panther's sweeping paw.* ▸ used as a noun. EG *With a great sweep of the arm he flung the whole handful high in the air.*
V+A ▸ N COUNT

4 If a strong force **sweeps** you along, it moves you quickly along. EG *She was swept out to sea by the currents.*
V+O+A

5 If something **sweeps** from one place to another, it moves very quickly. EG *Cold winds sweep over the barren, treeless plains... He stared out at the traffic sweeping along the road.*
V+A

6 If ideas, beliefs, or statements **sweep** a place or **sweep** through it, they spread quickly through it. EG *...the camping craze that is currently sweeping America... Change sweeps through the highly industrialized countries.*
V+O OR V+A

7 If something **sweeps** something else away or aside, it removes it quickly and completely. EG *The matter was soon swept from his mind... ...sweeping away restrictions on publication.*
V+O+A

8 If someone's gaze or a light **sweeps** an area, it moves over it. EG *We began rushing around in the dark, sweeping the ground with our flashlights.*
V+O

9 If you **sweep** something **under the carpet**, you try to prevent people from hearing about it, usually because you are rather ashamed of it. EG *This fact has been swept under the carpet for years.*
PHRASE

sweep up. If you **sweep up** dirt or rubbish, you push it together with a brush and then remove it.
PHRASAL VB : V+O+ADV

sweeping /swi:pɪŋ/. **1** A **sweeping** curve is long, wide, and stretched out. EG *...a place where the stream made a sweeping curve.*
ADJ QUALIT : ATTRIB

2 A **sweeping** statement or generalization is a very general one that you assume is true, without considering facts or details carefully; used showing disapproval. EG *It is too easy to make sweeping generalizations about someone else's problems.*
ADJ QUALIT : USU ATTRIB

3 Sweeping effects or consequences are very great. EG *...sweeping public expenditure cuts... They had embarked on a course which might have quite sweeping effects.*
ADJ QUALIT : ATTRIB

sweet /swi:t/, **sweets; sweeter, sweetest. 1** Food or drink that is **sweet** contains a lot of sugar. EG *I had some horribly sweet chocolate gateau... ...a cup of sweet tea.*
ADJ QUALIT

2 Sweets are sweet things such as toffees, chocolates, and mints. EG *She urged her children not to eat too many sweets.*
N COUNT : USU PLURAL British

3 A **sweet** is the same as a dessert. EG *We get a good meal in our canteen; soup and a main meal and a sweet.*
N COUNT British

4 If you describe a feeling as **sweet**, you mean that it gives you great pleasure and satisfaction. EG
ADJ QUALIT

However sweet love is, when it goes there is always bitterness. ◇ **sweetness**. EG *...the sweetness of freedom.* ◇ N UNCOUNT

5 A **sweet** smell is pleasant and fragrant. EG *...the sweet smell of ripe blackberry bushes.* ADJ QUALIT

6 A **sweet** sound is pleasant, smooth, and gentle. EG *...the sweet song of the skylark.* ◇ **sweetly**. EG *...a piper who played sweetly on his pipes.* ADJ QUALIT ◇ ADV

7 If you describe someone as **sweet**, you mean that they are pleasant, kind, and gentle towards other people. EG *My grandparents were very sweet to me... She's a sweet person.* ADJ QUALIT

8 You can also describe someone or something as **sweet** when you think that they are attractive and delightful. EG *Oh! Look at that kitten! How sweet!... She has a really sweet face.* ◇ **sweetly**. EG *She remembered him sitting so sweetly on the cot, looking up at her.* ADJ QUALIT ◇ ADV

9 If someone has a **sweet tooth**, they have a great liking for food that tastes sweet. PHRASE

sweet corn is a vegetable which comes from the maize plant. It is like a long hard stalk covered with small round yellow seeds which taste fairly sweet. N UNCOUNT

sweeten /swiːtə°n/, **sweetens, sweetening, sweetened.** If you **sweeten** food or drink, you add sugar, honey, or another sweet substance to it. EG *...tea sweetened with honey.* V+O

sweetener /swiːtə°nə/, **sweeteners.** A **sweetener** is an artificial substance that can be used in drinks instead of sugar and is usually less fattening. N MASS

sweetheart /swiːthɑːt/, **sweethearts. 1** You call someone **sweetheart** if you are very fond of them. VOCATIVE

2 Your **sweetheart** is your boyfriend or your girlfriend. This word is used especially for young people. EG *He married his childhood sweetheart.* N COUNT

swell /swɛl/, **swells, swelling, swelled, swollen** /swəʊlə°n/. The past participle can be either **swelled** or **swollen**.

1 If part of your body **swells** or **swells** up, it becomes larger and rounder than normal, usually as a result of an injury or an illness. EG *A mosquito had bitten her and her whole arm had swollen up.* V: OFT+*up*

2 When something **swells** or **swells** up, it becomes larger and rounder by being filled with air or liquid. EG *The insect inflates her lungs so that they swell into her abdomen.* V: OFT+*up*

3 If numbers or amounts **swell**, they increase in amount. EG *It took another twenty years for the population to swell to twice its size... The army had its ranks swollen by new recruits.* V-ERG

4 If feelings or sounds **swell**, they suddenly get stronger or louder. EG *His guilt swelled, but he quashed it... The murmur swelled and then died away.* V Literary

5 A **swell** is the regular movement of waves up and down in the open sea. EG *...the gentle, monotonous swell of the ocean.* N COUNT

6 See also **swollen**.

swelling /swɛlɪŋ/, **swellings.** A **swelling** is a raised, curved shape on the surface of your body, that appears as a result of an injury or an illness. EG *He had a painful swelling on his neck.* N COUNT OR N UNCOUNT

sweltering /swɛltə°rɪŋ/. **1** If you describe the weather as **sweltering**, you mean that it is extremely hot and makes you feel uncomfortable. EG *...a good place to go on a sweltering August day.* ADJ CLASSIF

2 If you are **sweltering**, you are so hot that you feel uncomfortable. EG *On the deck everyone was sweltering in the still air.* ADJ CLASSIF

swept /swɛpt/ is the past tense and past participle of **sweep**.

swerve /swɜːv/, **swerves, swerving, swerved.** If a vehicle or other moving thing **swerves**, it suddenly changes direction, often in order to avoid colliding with something else. EG *The car swerved off the road and into the river... I swerved to avoid a lorry that was in my way... A charging shark cannot stop, it can only swerve away to one side.* V: USU+A

swift /swɪft/, **swifter, swiftest; swifts. 1** A **swift** event or process happens very quickly. EG *I made a swift and complete recovery... ...never making a swift decision about anything.* ◇ **swiftly**. EG *No one volunteered very swiftly.* ◇ **swiftness**. EG *...stunned by the swiftness of the assault.* ADJ QUALIT ◇ ADV ◇ N UNCOUNT

2 Something that is **swift** moves very quickly. EG *The president's swift fleet reached Dover around 10 a.m... ...a swift stream... ...a swift glance.* ◇ **swiftly**. EG *He walked swiftly down the dark street.* ◇ **swiftness**. EG *He moved with remarkable swiftness to one side.* ADJ QUALIT ◇ ADV ◇ N UNCOUNT

3 A **swift** is a small bird with crescent-shaped wings. N COUNT

swig /swɪg/, **swigs, swigging, swigged.** If you **swig** a drink, you drink it from a bottle or cup quickly and in large amounts. EG *When her back was turned I swigged two cupfuls from the tub.* ▸ used as a noun. EG *She took a swig of brandy.* V+O OR V+A Informal ▸ N COUNT

swim /swɪm/, **swims, swimming, swam** /swæm/, **swum** /swʌm/. **1** When you **swim**, you move through water by making movements with your arms and legs. EG *The children are learning to swim... We managed to swim ashore... I go swimming twice a week.* ▸ used as a noun. EG *Let's go for a swim.* ◇ **swimmer** /swɪmə/, **swimmers**. EG *He went to the aid of a swimmer in difficulty... Are they good swimmers?* ◇ **swimming**. EG *Her father encouraged her to take up swimming again.* V ▸ N SING ◇ N COUNT ◇ N UNCOUNT

2 If objects seem to you to **swim**, they seem to be moving backwards and forwards, usually because you are ill. EG *The room swam and darkened before his eyes.* V

3 If your head **is swimming**, you feel dizzy. V

swimming bath, swimming baths. A **swimming bath** is a public swimming pool, especially an indoor one. N COUNT British

swimming costume, swimming costumes. A **swimming costume** is the same as a swimsuit. N COUNT British

swimming pool, swimming pools. A **swimming pool** is a place built for people to swim in, usually consisting of a large hole in the ground that has been tiled and filled with water. N COUNT

swimming trunks are the shorts that a man wears when he goes swimming. EG *He put on a pair of swimming trunks and lay out in the sun.* N PLURAL

swimsuit /swɪmsj°uːt/, **swimsuits.** A **swimsuit** is a tight-fitting piece of clothing that a woman wears when she goes swimming. N COUNT

swindle /swɪndə°l/, **swindles, swindling, swindled.** If someone **swindles** you, they deceive you in order to get something valuable from you, especially money. EG *I'm sure they swindled you out of that money.* ▸ used as a noun. EG *I'm afraid we have been the victims of a monumental swindle.* ◇ **swindler** /swɪndlə/, **swindlers**. EG *They are the biggest swindlers on earth.* V+O: OFT+A ▸ N COUNT ◇ N COUNT

swine /swaɪn/, **swines.** If you call someone a **swine**, you mean that you think they are very unpleasant, especially because they have caused you trouble; an offensive word. N COUNT Informal

swing /swɪŋ/, **swings, swinging, swung** /swʌŋ/.

1 If something **swings** or if you **swing** it, it moves repeatedly backwards and forwards or from side to side from a fixed point. EG *The chandelier started to swing... He sat there swinging his legs... Jane walked ahead, swinging the shopping bag.* ▸ used as a noun. EG *She walked with an exaggerated swing of the hips.* V-ERG ▸ N SING

2 If something **swings** in a particular direction or if you **swing** it in that direction, it moves in that direction with a smooth, curving movement. EG *I pushed the door and it swung open... Boylan swung the bag on to the back seat.* ▸ used as a noun. EG *...a grand, impatient swing of his arm.* V-ERG+A ▸ N COUNT

Can a man wear a swimsuit?

swimming

front crawl

butterfly

breaststroke

backstroke

3 If a person or a vehicle **swings** in a particular direction, they turn suddenly in that direction. EG *He swung round and faced the window... The taxi turned left and swung in through the gates.* V-ERG+A

4 If you **swing** at someone or something, you try to hit them with your arm. EG *I swung at him and hit him forcefully... The soldier swung a slow, heavy right hand at Tom.* V+A OR V+O+A

5 A **swing** is a seat hanging by two ropes or chains from a metal frame or from the branch of a tree. You can sit on the seat and move forwards and backwards through the air. N COUNT

6 A **swing** in people's opinions or attitudes is a significant change in them. EG *There was a 16.2% swing to the Social Democrats.* ▸ used as a verb. EG *The balance of power had swung decisively in favour of the moderates.* N COUNT+SUPP ▸ V+A

7 If something is **in full swing**, it is operating fully and is no longer in its early stages. EG *By the 1980's the Computer Revolution was in full swing.* PHRASE

8 If you **get into the swing** of something, you become very involved in it and enjoy what you are doing. EG *Dr Stein had got into the swing of his speech and was enthusiastically quoting authors.* PHRASE Informal

swipe /swaɪp/, **swipes, swiping, swiped. 1** If you **swipe** at something, you try to hit it with a stick or other object, making a swinging movement with your arm. EG *The batsman swiped at the ball and missed it.* ▸ used as a noun. EG *She took a casual swipe at the nettles.* V+*at* ▸ N COUNT : OFT+*at*

2 If you **swipe** something, you steal it quickly. EG *I swiped somebody else's apple.* V+O Informal

swirl /swɜːl/, **swirls, swirling, swirled.** If something **swirls**, it moves round and round quickly. EG *Dust swirled in small circles around me... He swirled his drink round his glass.* ▸ used as a noun. EG *...the slow swirl of the stream.* V-ERG+A ▸ N COUNT

swish /swɪʃ/. **swishes, swishing, swished.** If something **swishes** or if you **swish** it, it moves quickly through the air, making a soft sound. EG *The curtains swished open... ...swishing his long black tail against his sides.* ▸ used as a noun. EG *...the swish of a horse's tail.* V-ERG ▸ N COUNT

switch /swɪtʃ/, **switches, switching, switched. 1** A **switch** is a small control for an electrical device such as a light, a radio, or a heater. You press the switch or move it up or down in order to turn the device on or off. EG *...electric light switches... Somebody pressed the wrong switch.* N COUNT

2 If you **switch** to something different, for example to a different task or a different subject of conversation, you change to it from what you were doing or saying before. EG *I would like now to switch to quite a different topic... He switched his attention back to the magazine.* ▸ used as a noun. EG *...the switch from planned to impromptu tactics... ...a switch in policy.* V OR V+O : OFT+*to/from* ▸ N COUNT

3 If you **switch** something, you remove it and replace it with something else. EG *The plane switched loads and took off.* V+O

switch off. 1 If you **switch off** a light or other electrical device, you stop it working by pressing a switch. EG *He switched the radio off.* PHRASAL VB : V+O+ADV **2** If you **switch off**, you stop paying attention to something, because you are no longer interested in it. EG *I just switched off after the first speech.* V+ADV Informal

switch on. If you **switch on** a light or other electrical device, you make it start working by pressing a switch. EG *He switched on the TV... Would you switch the light on, please?* PHRASAL VB : V+O+ADV

switchboard /swɪtʃbɔːd/, **switchboards.** A **switchboard** is a place in a large office or business where all the telephone calls are connected. EG *The girl on the switchboard told me there was a phone call for me.* N COUNT

swivel /swɪvə^{0}l/, **swivels, swivelling, swivelled;** spelled **swiveling** and **swiveled** in American English. If something **swivels** or if you **swivel** it, it turns around a central point so that it is facing in a different direction. EG *I swivelled right round in my* V-ERG : USU+A *chair... Mellors slowly swivelled his chair round... His head swivelled toward her.*

swollen /swəʊlə⁰n/. **1 Swollen** is the past participle of **swell**.

2 Something that is **swollen** has grown outwards until it is broader or wider than usual. EG *Her fingers were badly swollen with arthritis.* ADJ QUALIT

swoon /swu:n/, **swoons, swooning, swooned.** If you **swoon**, you are strongly affected by your feelings for someone you love or admire very much. EG *We fell in love, and swooned in each other's arms.* V

swoop /swu:p/, **swoops, swooping, swooped. 1** When a bird or aeroplane **swoops**, it suddenly moves downwards through the air in a smooth, curving movement. EG *We saw a distant eagle swoop down from the sky.* V: USU+A ▸ used as a noun. EG *The swallow made a dazzling swoop through the air.* ▸ N COUNT

2 If soldiers or police **swoop** on a place, they move towards it suddenly and quickly, usually in order to attack it or to arrest the people there. EG *British troops swooped down twice in dawn raids.* V+A ▸ used as a noun. EG *The police made a swoop on the headquarters.* ▸ N COUNT

3 If you achieve something **in one fell swoop**, you do it on a single occasion or by a single action. EG *All our problems were solved in one fell swoop.* PHRASE

swop /swɒp/. See **swap**.

sword /sɔ:d/, **swords. 1** A **sword** is a weapon with a handle and a long blade. See picture at WEAPONS. N COUNT

2 If you **cross swords** with someone, you disagree and argue with them about something. EG *It was over this that Clare and Arthur crossed swords.* PHRASE

swore /swɔ:/ is the past tense of **swear.**

sworn /swɔ:n/. **1 Sworn** is the past participle of **swear**.

2 If two people are **sworn enemies**, they dislike each other very much. PHRASE

3 If you make a **sworn** statement or declaration, you swear that everything that you have said in it is true. EG *The American made a sworn statement to the police.* ADJ CLASSIF: ATTRIB

swot /swɒt/, **swots, swotting, swotted. 1** If you **swot**, you study very hard, especially when you are preparing for an examination. EG *How do you find time to swot for exams?* V Informal

2 If you call someone a **swot**, you mean that they study extremely hard and are not interested in other things; used showing disapproval. N COUNT Informal

swot up. If you **swot up** a subject or **swot up** on it, you read as much as you can about it, usually because you are going to be asked questions about it. EG *She swotted up American history.* PHRASAL VB: V+O+ADV OR V+ADV+A Informal

swum /swʌm/ is the past participle of **swim.**

swung /swʌŋ/ is the past tense and past participle of **swing.**

sycamore /sɪkəmɔ:/, **sycamores.** A **sycamore** is a tree that has leaves with five points. N COUNT

syllable /sɪləbə⁰l/, **syllables.** A **syllable** is a part of a word that contains a single vowel-sound and that is pronounced as a unit. So, for example, 'book' has one syllable, and 'reading' has two syllables. N COUNT

syllabus /sɪləbəs/, **syllabuses.** You can refer to the subjects that are studied in a particular course as the **syllabus**. EG *They've got to cover a very wide syllabus... ...the new physics syllabus.* N COUNT

symbol /sɪmbə⁰l/, **symbols. 1** A **symbol** of something such as an idea is a shape or design that is used to represent it. EG *Picasso painted a red circle as a symbol of the Revolution... ...a peace symbol.* N COUNT+SUPP

2 Something that is a **symbol** of a society or aspect of life seems to represent it because it is very typical of it. EG *Perhaps the most glittering symbol of the new Britain was London's Post Office Tower.* N COUNT: USU+*of*

3 A **symbol** for an item in a calculation or formula is a number, letter, or shape that represents the item. EG *I use my own symbol for 'approximately'.* N COUNT

symbolic /sɪmbɒlɪk/. **1** Something that is **symbolic** of someone or something else is regarded or used as a symbol of them. EG *The crescent moon is symbolic of Allah... ...gold, with its rich symbolic significance.* ADJ CLASSIF: USU+*of* ◇ **symbolically**. EG *To put on someone else's clothes is symbolically to take on their personality.* ◇ ADV

2 Symbolic is also used to describe things involving or relating to symbols. EG *Water is full of symbolic associations... ...a symbolic play.* ADJ QUALIT

symbolism /sɪmbəlɪzə⁰m/ is the use of symbols in order to represent something. EG *...messages conveyed by symbolism in the architecture.* N UNCOUNT

symbolize /sɪmbəlaɪz/, **symbolizes, symbolizing, symbolized;** also spelled **symbolise.** If something **symbolizes** something else, it is used or regarded as a symbol of it. EG *...a dancer in a flame-red robe symbolizing the sun.* V+O

symmetrical /sɪmɛtrɪkə⁰l/. If something is **symmetrical**, it has two halves which are exactly the same, except that one half is the mirror image of the other. EG *...pleasingly symmetrical designs.* ADJ CLASSIF ◇ **symmetrically**. EG *Smaller rooms were arranged symmetrically to either side.* ◇ ADV

symmetry /sɪmɪ²tri¹/. Something that has **symmetry** is symmetrical in shape or design. EG *...the symmetry of the Square.* N UNCOUNT

sympathetic /sɪmpəθɛtɪk/. **1** If you are **sympathetic** to someone who has had a misfortune, you are kind to them and show that you understand their feelings. EG *My boyfriend was very sympathetic and it did make me feel better.* ADJ QUALIT ◇ **sympathetically**. EG *She put a hand sympathetically on his arm.* ◇ ADV

2 If you are **sympathetic** to a proposal or action, you approve of it and are willing to support it. EG *He is sympathetic to our cause... The university is not particularly sympathetic to this problem.* ADJ PRED: OFT+*to*

3 You describe someone as **sympathetic** when you like them and approve of the way that they behave. EG *I found him a very sympathetic character.* ADJ QUALIT

sympathize /sɪmpəθaɪz/, **sympathizes, sympathizing, sympathized;** also spelled **sympathise. 1** If you **sympathize** with someone who has had a misfortune, you are sorry for them, and show this in the way you behave towards them. EG *I sympathized with her and tried to help.* V: OFT+*with*

2 If you **sympathize** with someone's feelings, you understand them and are not critical of them, because you think that you would have the same feelings in the same circumstances. EG *I can sympathize with your hesitations... He could neither understand nor sympathize with Isobel's eagerness.* V+*with*

3 If you **sympathize** with a proposal or action, you approve of it and are willing to support it. EG *Everyone sympathised with the anti-colonial cause.* V+*with*

sympathizer /sɪmpəθaɪzə/, **sympathizers;** also spelled **sympathiser.** The **sympathizers** of an organization or cause are the people who approve of it and support it. EG *White was an ardent Communist sympathiser.* N COUNT

sympathy /sɪmpəθi¹/, **sympathies. 1** If you have **sympathy** for someone who has had a misfortune, you are sorry for them, and show this in the way you behave towards them. EG *People feel immediate sympathy for a man left alone with his children.* N UNCOUNT: OFT+*for*

2 If you have **sympathy** with someone's ideas or opinions, you agree with them. EG *On that point I'm in sympathy with Mr McCabe.* N UNCOUNT +*with*

3 Your **sympathies** are your feelings of approval and support for a particular proposal or action. EG *Her sympathies lay with what we were doing... He knows I have strong left-wing sympathies.* N PLURAL

4 If you take some action **in sympathy** with someone else, you do it in order to show that you PHRASE

Find a synonym for 'grammar' on these pages.

support them. EG *They were carrying out a hunger strike in sympathy with mine.*

symphony /sɪmfəni^{1}/, **symphonies.** A **symphony** is a piece of music written to be played by an orchestra, usually in four parts called movements. EG *...Sibelius's Second Symphony.* N COUNT

symptom /sɪmp^{0}təm/, **symptoms. 1** A **symptom** of an illness is something wrong with your body that is a sign of the illness. EG *Most infections are contagious before any symptoms are noticed... The first symptom of a cold is often a sore throat.* N COUNT

2 A **symptom** of a bad condition, for example in a society, is something that happens and that is taken as a sign of this condition. EG *Migration is a symptom of rural poverty.* N COUNT: USU+SUPP

symptomatic /sɪmp^{0}təmætɪk/. If something is **symptomatic** of something else, it is a sign of it. EG *The irritation seems symptomatic of something deeper.* ADJ PRED: USU+*of* Formal

synagogue /sɪnəgɒg/, **synagogues.** A **synagogue** is a building where Jewish people meet to worship or to study their religion. N COUNT

synchronize /sɪŋkrənaɪz/, **synchronizes, synchronizing, synchronized;** also spelled **synchronise. 1** If two people **synchronize** something that they do, they do it at the same time and speed as each other. EG *They frequently synchronize their movements as they talk.* V+O OR V+O+*with*: RECIP

2 If you **synchronize** two watches or clocks, you adjust them so that they say exactly the same time. EG *His watch has been accurately synchronized with the church clock.* V+O OR V+O+*with*: RECIP

syndicate /sɪndɪkə^{1}t/, **syndicates.** A **syndicate** is an association of people or organizations that is formed for business purposes or in order to carry out a project together. EG *...a syndicate of German industrialists.* N COUNT

syndrome /sɪndrəʊm/, **syndromes.** A **syndrome** is **1** a medical condition that is characterized by a particular group of signs and symptoms. EG *...Down's syndrome.* **2** a condition that is characterized by a particular type of activity, behaviour, or feeling. EG *...the capitalist syndrome of growth, profits, competition.* N COUNT+SUPP

synonym /sɪnənɪm/, **synonyms.** A **synonym** is a word or expression which means the same as another word or expression. EG *'Totalitarian' is not a synonym for 'communist'.* N COUNT: OFT+*for/of*

synonymous /sɪnɒnɪməs/. **1** Two words or expressions that are **synonymous** have the same meaning as each other. EG *For these economists 'development' seems to be synonymous with 'growth'.* ADJ CLASSIF: OFT+*with*

2 If you say that one thing is **synonymous** with another, you suggest that the two things are very closely associated with each other so that one implies the other. EG *His name became synonymous with wild fearlessness... Socialism became to him synonymous with peace.* ADJ PRED: OFT+*with*

syntax /sɪntæks/ is the grammatical arrangement of words in a language or the grammatical rules in a language. N UNCOUNT Technical

synthesis /sɪnθə^{1}sɪs/, **syntheses** /sɪnθə^{1}siːz/. **1** A **synthesis** of different ideas or styles is a mixture or combination of these ideas or styles, in which they blend together. EG *...a synthesis of Jewish theology and Greek philosophy.* N COUNT: OFT+*of*

2 The **synthesis** of a substance is the production of it by means of chemical or biological reactions. EG *We need sunlight for the synthesis of vitamin D.* N UNCOUNT +SUPP

synthesize /sɪnθɪsaɪz/, **synthesizes, synthesizing, synthesized;** also spelled **synthesise. 1** If you **synthesize** a substance, you produce it by means of chemical or biological reactions. EG *...proteins which the body is unable to synthesise for itself.* V+O

2 If you **synthesize** different ideas, facts, or experiences, you combine them to develop a single idea or impression. EG *He synthesizes data from a variety of sources... They synthesise their experience into principles and theories.* V+O: OFT+A Formal

synthetic /sɪnθɛtɪk/. **1** A **synthetic** material is made from chemicals or artificial substances rather than from natural ones. EG *...curtains made of synthetic fibres... ...synthetic rubber as a substitute for natural rubber.* ADJ CLASSIF: USU ATTRIB

2 If you describe someone's behaviour as **synthetic**, you mean that it is not sincere or genuine. EG *...a synthetic skin-deep smile.* ADJ QUALIT

3 If you describe food as **synthetic**, you mean that it does not have a natural taste or appearance and is therefore unpleasant. EG *...a frightful synthetic omelette.* ADJ QUALIT

syphilis /sɪfɪlɪs/ is a type of venereal disease. N UNCOUNT

syphon /saɪfə^{0}n/, **syphons.** See **siphon**.

syringe /sɪrɪnd^{0}ʒ, sɪrɪnd^{0}ʒ/, **syringes, syringing, syringed. 1** A **syringe** is a small tube with a plunger and a fine hollow needle or pointed end. Syringes are used for putting liquids into something and for taking liquids out, for example for injecting drugs into a person's body or for taking blood samples from them. EG *I attached the syringe and injected 10cc of the drug.* N COUNT

2 If a doctor **syringes** your ear or a wound, he or she cleans it using a syringe to suck substances out. V+O

syrup /sɪrəp/, **syrups. Syrup** is **1** a sweet liquid made by cooking sugar with water, sometimes with fruit juice as well. EG *...cherry syrup.* **2** a very sweet thick liquid food made from sugar. EG *...bread spread with golden syrup.* N MASS / N UNCOUNT

syrupy /sɪrəpi^{1}/. **1** Liquid that is **syrupy** is sweet or thick like syrup. ADJ QUALIT

2 You can describe behaviour as **syrupy** when it is sentimental in an irritating way. EG *She admired everything she saw in a tone of syrupy earnestness.* ADJ QUALIT

system /sɪstə^{0}m/, **systems. 1** A **system** is **1.1** a way of working, organizing, or doing something in which you follow a fixed plan or set of rules. EG *The new system has been running now for a number of years... They have developed a remarkably efficient system for gathering food.* **1.2** a particular set of rules, especially one in mathematics or science which is used to count or measure things. EG *...Egyptian or Roman number systems.* N COUNT: USU+SUPP

2 A **system** is also the way that a whole institution or aspect of society has been organized and arranged. EG *There's a difference between the Scottish legal system and the English one... ...the need to modernise Britain's transport system.* N COUNT+SUPP

3 People sometimes refer to the government or administration of a country as the **system**. EG *...the revolutionary overthrow of the system.* N SING: *the*+N

4 A **system** of a particular kind is **4.1** a set of equipment or parts such as water pipes or electrical wiring, which is used to supply water, heat, or electricity. EG *Have you thought of installing your own central heating system?* **4.2** a device or set of devices powered by electricity, for example a hi-fi or a computer. EG *They stole the stereo system and the television set.* N COUNT+SUPP

5 A **system** of a particular kind in your body is the set of organs or other parts in your body that together perform a particular function. EG *...a diagram of the digestive system... He has a very delicate nervous system.* N COUNT+SUPP

6 If you **get** something **out of** your **system**, you express the anger or other strong feeling that you have about something, so that you feel better afterwards. EG *Getting it out of my system made me relax a bit.* PHRASE Informal

systematic /sɪstɪmætɪk/. Activity or behaviour that is **systematic** follows a fixed plan, so that things are done in an efficient way. EG *These skills are developed in a formal and systematic way.* ADJ QUALIT

◊ **systematically**. EG *I wish they'd organise themselves more systematically.* ◊ ADV

T t

T, t /tiː/ **Ts, t's.** T is the twentieth letter of the English alphabet. N COUNT

ta /tɑː/ means thank you. EG *He passed it over to Myra, who smiled at him and said 'Ta'.* CONVENTION Informal

tab /tæb/, **tabs. 1** A **tab** is a small piece of cloth or paper that is attached to something. EG *It had the maker's name on a small cloth tab inside.* N COUNT

2 If you **keep tabs on** someone, you make sure that you always know where they are and what they are doing. PHRASE Informal

tabby /tæbi^1/, **tabbies.** A **tabby** is a cat whose fur has grey, brown, or orange stripes. N COUNT ▸ used as an adjective. EG *...a tabby cat.* ▸ ADJ CLASSIF : ATTRIB

table /teɪbə^{0}l/, **tables, tabling, tabled. 1** A **table** is a piece of furniture with a flat top that you put things on. EG *The book is there on the table... ...her bedside table.* N COUNT

2 A **table** is also a set of facts or figures arranged in columns or rows on a piece of paper. N COUNT

3 If you **turn the tables on** someone, you change the situation completely, so that they have the problems that they were trying to cause for you. PHRASE

4 If you **table** something such as a proposal, you say formally that you want it to be discussed at a meeting. EG *...a set of parliamentary questions tabled by Frank Field.* V+O

tableau /tæbləʊ/, **tableaux** or **tableaus.** A **tableau** is a scene from history or a legend, represented by people standing on a stage wearing costumes. N COUNT

tablecloth /teɪbə^{0}lklɒθ/, **tablecloths.** A **tablecloth** is a cloth used to cover a table and keep it clean, especially while you are eating a meal. N COUNT

table manners. Your **table manners** are the way you behave when you are eating a meal. EG *He had to be careful about his table manners.* N PLURAL

tablespoon /teɪbə^{0}lspuːn/, **tablespoons. 1** A **tablespoon** is a large spoon used for serving food. N COUNT

2 You can use **tablespoon** to refer to the amount that a tablespoon contains. EG *Use 1 tablespoon of vinegar to 1 pint of warm water.* N PART

tablespoonful /teɪbə^{0}lspuːnfʊl/, **tablespoonfuls** or **tablespoonsful.** A **tablespoonful** is the amount that a tablespoon contains. EG *...two level tablespoonfuls of sugar.* N PART

tablet /tæblɪ^{2}t/, **tablets. 1** A **tablet** is a small, hard piece of medicine, which you swallow. EG *Take three tablets after each meal... The drug is available in tablet form.* N COUNT

2 A **tablet** is also a flat piece of stone or wood with words cut into it. Tablets are usually fixed to a wall so that a person or event will be remembered for a long time. EG *There is a tablet in memory of those who died.* N COUNT

table tennis is a game played indoors by two or four people. They stand at each end of a long table which has a low net across the middle and hit a small, light ball to each other, using small bats. N UNCOUNT

tabloid /tæblɔɪd/, **tabloids.** A **tabloid** is a newspaper with small pages, short news stories and articles, and a lot of photographs. N COUNT

taboo /təbuː/, **taboos.** A **taboo** is **1** a religious custom that forbids people to do something. EG *...religious taboos against marrying people from another religion.* N COUNT **2** a social custom that some words, subjects, or actions must be avoided because they are considered to be embarrassing or offensive. EG *...the old taboo on kissing in public.* N COUNT ▸ used as an adjective. EG *Birth control is no longer a taboo subject.* ▸ ADJ CLASSIF

tabulate /tæbjə^{4}leɪt/, **tabulates, tabulating, tabulated.** If you **tabulate** information, you arrange it in columns on a page. EG *It took twenty hours to tabulate the results.* V+O

tacit /tæsɪt/ means understood or implied without actually being said or written. EG *They had by tacit agreement not renewed the contract... ...a tacit admission of guilt.* ADJ CLASSIF : USU ATTRIB Formal ◇ **tacitly**. EG *Is she tacitly admitting that her place is in the home?* ◇ ADV

taciturn /tæsɪtɜːn/. Someone who is **taciturn** does not usually talk very much and so sometimes seems unfriendly or depressed. EG *He was a gloomy, taciturn man who never had anything to say.* ADJ QUALIT

tack /tæk/, **tacks, tacking, tacked. 1** A **tack** is a short nail with a broad, flat head, used especially for fixing carpets to the floor. ● to **get down to brass tacks**: see **brass**. N COUNT

2 If you **tack** something to a surface, you nail it there with tacks. EG *Gretchen had tacked some travel posters on the wall.* V+O : OFT+A

3 If you change **tack**, you try to achieve something using a different method from the one you were using before. EG *They didn't seem convinced so I tried another tack.* N UNCOUNT

tack on. If you **tack** something **on** to something else, you add it to it hurriedly and in an unsatisfactory way. EG *They've tacked a couple of new clauses on to the end of the contract.* PHRASAL VB : V+O+ADV

tackle /tækə^{0}l/, **tackles, tackling, tackled. 1** If you **tackle** a difficult task, you start dealing with it in a determined way. EG *...a means of tackling the growing housing problem.* V+O

2 If you **tackle** someone in a game such as football, you try to take the ball away from them. EG *He was tackled before he had a chance to shoot.* V+O ▸ used as a noun. EG *The tackle looked fair but a free kick was awarded.* ▸ N COUNT

3 To **tackle** a person or an animal also means to attack and fight them. EG *Some pythons can tackle creatures as big as goats.* V+O

4 If you **tackle** someone about something that you are not satisfied with, you talk to them about it in order to get something changed or done. EG *He tackled me about several editorials I had written.* V+O : OFT +*about/on*

5 Tackle is the equipment that you need for a sport or activity. EG *...fishing tackle.* N UNCOUNT

tacky /tæki^1/. Something that is **tacky** is badly made and unpleasant. EG *...tacky jewellery... It's a tacky, nasty little movie.* ADJ QUALIT Informal

tact /tækt/ is behaviour in which you are careful to avoid upsetting or offending people. EG *I tried to behave with the utmost tact.* N UNCOUNT

tactful /tæktfʊl/. If you are **tactful**, you are careful not to upset or offend people. EG *Nick was tactful enough not to shatter this illusion... The tactful thing would have been not to say anything.* ADJ QUALIT ◇ **tactfully**. EG *The topic was tactfully dropped.* ◇ ADV

tactic /tæktɪk/, **tactics. Tactics** are **1** the methods that you use to achieve what you want. EG *They use delaying tactics... Different circumstances involve adopting different tactics.* **2** the ways in which troops and equipment are used in order to win a battle. EG *...a general with a sound grasp of tactics.* N COUNT : USU PLURAL

tactical /tæktɪkə^{0}l/. **1** If an action is **tactical**, it is intended to gain an advantage in the future, rather than immediately. EG *This was simply a tactical move by De Gaulle.* ADJ CLASSIF ◇ **tactically**. EG *Tactically, I think we can be faulted for not voting against the strike.* ◇ ADV SEN OR ADV

2 Tactical weapons are used over fairly short distances. EG *...a vast arsenal of tactical nuclear weapons.* ADJ CLASSIF : ATTRIB

3 Anything related to military tactics can be described as **tactical**. EG *...a tactical advance.* ADJ CLASSIF : ATTRIB

tactile /tæktaɪl/ means relating to the feelings that you experience when you touch things. EG *...the tactile qualities of the physical world.* ADJ CLASSIF Formal

tactless /tæktlɪ^{2}s/. If someone is **tactless**, they behave in a way that is likely to upset or offend people. EG *I suppose it was rather tactless of me to ask... Tilly's tactless outburst had really upset her.* ADJ QUALIT
◊ **tactlessly**. EG *She behaved very tactlessly in reminding him of his failure on the Stock Exchange.* ◊ ADV

tadpole /tædpəʊl/, **tadpoles. Tadpoles** are small water creatures which grow into frogs or toads. They have round black heads and long tails. N COUNT

tag /tæg/, **tags, tagging, tagged. 1** A **tag** is a small piece of cloth or paper which is attached to an object and which has information on it about the object or its owner. EG *Have you tied the airline tags on the luggage?... Where's the price tag?* N COUNT
2 Tag is a children's game in which one child chases the others and tries to touch them. N UNCOUNT
tag along. If you **tag along** with someone, you go with them, especially when they have not asked you to. EG *Our younger sisters always wanted to tag along.* PHRASAL VB : V+ADV

tail /teɪl/, **tails, tailing, tailed. 1** The **tail** of an animal, bird, or fish is the part of its body that is at the opposite end to its head. Tails are usually long and thin. EG *The dog was wagging his tail.* N COUNT
2 You can refer to the long thin part at the back of an object as its **tail**. EG *He ran into the street, the tails of his shirt flying... ...the stairway descending from the tail of the plane.* N COUNT : USU+SUPP
3 If a man is wearing **tails**, he is wearing a formal jacket which has two long pieces hanging down at the back. N PLURAL
4 If you **tail** someone, you follow them in order to find out where they go and what they do. EG *All day he was tailed by police cars.* V+O Informal
5 If you toss a coin and it comes down **tails**, the side of it that you can see does not have a person's head on it. ADV AFTER VB
6 If you say that someone has their **tail between** their **legs**, you mean that they are feeling defeated and humiliated. EG *She left the kitchen with her tail between her legs.* PHRASE
7 to not **make head nor tail** of something: see **head**.
tail off. 1 If something **tails off**, it gradually becomes less, and often ends completely. EG *The rains tail off in September... The average figure has tailed off in the last few years.* PHRASAL VB : V+ADV **2** When someone's voice **tails off**, it gradually becomes quieter as they stop speaking. V+ADV

tailor /teɪlə/, **tailors, tailored. 1** A **tailor** is a person who makes clothes, especially for men. EG *In this street there were gentlemen's tailors of the highest quality.* N COUNT
2 Tailored clothes are made to fit close to your body. EG *...a tight-fitting tailored dress.* ADJ CLASSIF : ATTRIB
3 If something **is tailored** for a particular purpose, it is specially designed to be suitable for that purpose. EG *...factories and equipment tailored to meet the needs of the 20th century.* V+O : USU PASS

tailor-made. Something that is **tailor-made** is very suitable for a particular person or purpose or was specially designed for them. EG *Both the play and the role were tailor-made for her.* ADJ CLASSIF : OFT+*for*

taint /teɪnt/, **taints, tainting, tainted. 1** If you **taint** something, you spoil it by adding an undesirable quality to it. EG *He feared that this would taint the scheme with some element of commercialism.* V+O Formal
◊ **tainted**. EG *The report was heavily tainted with racism... ...the tainted profits of conquest in South America.* ◊ ADJ QUALIT : OFT+*with*
2 A **taint** is an undesirable quality in something which spoils it. EG *His career was never free of the taint of corruption.* N SING+SUPP Formal

take /teɪk/, **takes, taking, took** /tʊk/, **taken** /teɪkə^{0}n/. **1** You can use **take** to say that someone performs an action. For example, if you say that someone **takes** a look at something, you mean that they look at it. EG *He took a step towards Jack... I took a magnificent photo of him... She took a shower... Certain decisions had to be taken... He formed the habit of taking long solitary walks... She's not yet taken her driving test.* V+O
2 If someone **takes** office or **takes** power, they start being in control of something. EG *He asked me to take charge... She showed no sign of taking command.* V+O
3 If you **take** a particular attitude or view, you have it. EG *The public was beginning to take a positive interest in defence.* V+O
4 If something **takes** a certain amount of time, you need that amount of time in order to do it. EG *How long will it take?... It may take them several weeks to get back.* V+O OR V+O+O
5 If something **takes** a particular quality or thing, it requires it. EG *It took a lot of courage to admit his mistake... It took three men to hold him down.* V+O
6 If you **take** something, especially when someone is offering it to you, you put your hand round it and hold it. EG *Let me take your coat... She took the menu from him... He took Sam by the hand.* V+O OR V+O+A
7 If you **take** something from one place to another, you carry it there. EG *She gave me some books to take home... He took a cigarette from the box on the table... A maid came to take away the tray... Emma opened her bag and took out her comb.* V+O : USU+A
8 If you **take** someone somewhere, you drive them there in your car or lead them there. EG *It's his turn to take the children to school.* V+O : USU+A
9 If you **take** something that is offered to you, you accept it. EG *She took a job in publishing... We've just had to take a pay cut.* V+O
10 If you **take** the responsibilty or blame for something, you accept the responsibilty or blame for it. EG *She doesn't expect you to take the blame... I would be perfectly willing to take the consequences.* V+O
11 If you are in a shop and you say that you will **take** something, you mean that you will buy it. EG *I'll take a dozen eggs.* V+O
12 If someone **takes** something that belongs to you, they steal it or go away with it without your permission. EG *A pickpocket took Barry's wallet... Someone's taken my pen.* V+O
13 If you **take** pills, medicine, or drugs, you swallow them. EG *I took a couple of aspirins.* V+O
14 If you **take** a house or flat, you start renting it. EG *He had taken a small flat in Brussels.* V+O
15 If soldiers or terrorists **take** people or places, they capture them. EG *We took the village without a shot being fired.* V+O : OFT+A OR C
16 If you can **take** something such as pain or loneliness, you can bear it or endure it. EG *I can't take pain... I can't take any more... Ordinary people find his arrogance hard to take.* V+O : NO CONT
17 If you **take** an event or piece of news well or badly, you react to it well or badly. EG *He would never take her fears seriously.* V+O+A
18 If you **take** students for a subject, you give them lessons in it. EG *She took them for geography.* V+O : USU+A
19 If you **take** a person's temperature or pulse, you measure it. EG *I took her temperature.* V+O
20 If you **take** a particular size in shoes or clothes, you wear that size. EG *She asked what size of shoes he took.* V+O
21 If you **take** a car or train, for example, you use it to go from one place to another. EG *She said she'd take a taxi... I think we ought to take the car.* V+O : USU+A
22 If you **take** a road or route, you travel along it. EG *He took the road southwards into the hills.* V+O : OFT+A
23 If you **take** someone's advice or orders, you do what they say you should do. EG *They have to take* V+O

instructions from her... Take my advice, don't buy a house.
24 To **take** something means to consider it. EG *Let's take one thing at a time... Some men change the world. Take Albert Einstein, for instance.* V+O: OFT IMPER
25 If you **take** someone's meaning, you understand what they are saying. EG *He took my meaning perfectly... They took what I said as a kind of rebuke.* V+O+A
26 Take is also used in these phrases. **26.1** You can say **'I take it'** to check that the person you are talking to knows or understands something, or is giving you correct information. EG *I take it you know what a stethoscope is?... I take it that you've been quite candid with me.* **26.2** If something **takes a lot out of** you or **takes it out of** you, it makes you feel very tired. EG *Talking in a foreign language all day takes a lot out of you.* PHRASES

take aback. If you **are taken aback**, you are surprised or shocked. EG *I was a bit taken aback by this sudden reversal.* PHRASAL VB: V+O+ADV

take after. If you **take after** someone in your family, you look like them or behave like them. EG *You don't take after your sister.* PHRASAL VB: V+PREP

take apart. If you **take** something **apart**, you separate it into the different parts that it is made of. EG *We encouraged them to explore, invent, take things apart, and put them together.* PHRASAL VB: V+O+ADV

take away. If you **take away** one number or amount from another, you subtract it or deduct it. For example, if you take 3 away from 5, you get 2. • See also **takeaway**. PHRASAL VB: V+O+ADV

take back. 1 If you **take** something **back**, **1.1** you return it to the place where you got it from. EG *Don't forget to take your books back to the library.* PHRASAL VB: V+O+ADV
1.2 you agree to accept it again after you have sold it or got rid of it. EG *Shopkeepers are often reluctant to take back unsatisfactory goods.* V+O+ADV **2** If you **take back** something that you said, you admit that it was wrong. EG *I'm going to have to take back all those things I said about you.* V+O+ADV

take down. 1 When people **take down** a temporary structure, they separate it into pieces and remove it. EG *The scaffolding won't be taken down until next year.* PHRASAL VB: V+O+ADV **2** If you **take down** what someone is saying, you write it down. EG *The postmistress began to take down the message.* V+O+ADV

take in. 1 If someone **is taken in**, they are deceived. EG *I wasn't going to be taken in by this kind of sentimentality... I completely took them in by telling them I'd been given a week's holiday.* PHRASAL VB: V+O+ADV, OFT PASS **2** If you **take** something **in**, you understand it when you hear it or read it. EG *People never take in new facts very easily when they're unhappy.* V+O+ADV **3** If something **takes in** something else, the first thing includes the second. EG *The area was stretched to take in some parts of Wales.* V+O+ADV

take off. 1 When an aeroplane **takes off**, it leaves the ground and starts flying. • See also **takeoff**. PHRASAL VB: V+ADV **2** If you **take off** or **take** yourself **off**, you go away suddenly. EG *They took off for a weekend in the country... She took herself off to Amsterdam.* V+ADV OR V-REFL+ADV, USU+A
3 If you **take off** something that you are wearing, you remove it. EG *He took off his glasses and blinked.* V+O+ADV **4** If you **take** time **off**, you do not go to work for one or more days. EG *She's taken the day off.* V+O+ADV

take on. 1 If you **take on** a job or responsibility, you accept it. EG *She takes on more work than is good for her.* PHRASAL VB: V+O+ADV **2** If something **takes on** a new quality, it begins to have that quality. EG *His voice took on a new note of uncertainty... The word 'profession' is taking on a new meaning.* V+ADV+O **3** If you **take** someone **on**, you employ them. EG *They took me on because I was a good mathematician.* V+O+ADV **4** If you **take on** a person or organization that is more powerful than you, you fight them or compete against them. EG *British Leyland plans to take on the competition at home and abroad.* V+O+ADV

take out. If you **take** someone **out**, you invite them to go with you to a restaurant or cinema, for example, and you pay for both of you. EG *He offered to take her out for a meal.* PHRASAL VB: V+O+ADV

take out on. If you **take** your unhappiness or anger **out on** someone, you behave in an unpleasant way towards them, even though it is not their fault that you feel so upset. EG *She took out most of her unhappiness on her husband.* PHRASAL VB: V+O+ADV +PREP

take over. 1 If you **take over** something such as a company or country, you gain control of it. EG *The agency tried to take over another company... Once again the military had taken over.* • See also **takeover**. PHRASAL VB: V+O+ADV OR V+ADV **2** If you **take over** a job or if you **take over**, you start doing the job after someone else has stopped doing it. EG *They want me to take over as editor when Harold leaves.* V+O+ADV OR V+ADV

take to. 1 If you **take to** someone or something, you like them immediately. EG *She immediately took to him... We asked him if the Russians would take to golf.* PHRASAL VB: V+PREP **2** If you **take to** doing something, you begin to do it regularly. EG *He took to wearing black leather jackets.* V+PREP+-ING

take up. 1 If you **take up** an activity or job, you start doing it. EG *I thought I'd take up fishing... My assistant left to take up another post.* PHRASAL VB: V+O+ADV **2** If you **take up** an activity that was interrupted, you continue doing it from the point where it had stopped. EG *Sam took up the story... David was taking up where he had left off.* V+O+ADV OR V+ADV **3** If you **take up** an idea or suggestion, you discuss it further. EG *The committee is expected to take up the question of government grants.* V+O+ADV **4** If something **takes up** an amount of time, space, or effort, it uses that amount. EG *I won't take up any more of your time... Much of the day was taken up with classes or study.* V+ADV+O

take up on. 1 If you **take** someone **up on** an offer that they have made, you accept their offer. EG *I really think you ought to take him up on his offer... I didn't expect her to take me up on my invitation.* PHRASAL VB: V+O+ADV +PREP **2** If you **take** someone **up on** what they have just said, you ask them to explain or justify it. EG *I think I would like to take Tony up on that.* V+O+ADV +PREP

take upon. If you **take** it **upon** yourself to do something, you do it even though it is not your duty or your job. EG *Mrs Kaul took it upon herself to turn round and say 'Sh'.* PHRASAL VB: V+O+PREP

takeaway /teɪkəweɪ/, **takeaways.** A **takeaway** is **1** a shop or restaurant which sells hot cooked food that you eat somewhere else. N COUNT British **2** a hot cooked meal that is sold to be eaten somewhere else. EG *I fancy an Indian takeaway.* British

taken /teɪkəⁿn/. **1 Taken** is the past participle of **take**.
2 If you are **taken** with something, you find it attractive and interesting. EG *Philip had been rather taken with the idea... We were all very taken with Mrs Wilkins.* ADJ PRED +with

takeoff /teɪkɒf/, **takeoffs. Takeoff** is the beginning of a flight, when an aircraft leaves the ground. EG *...fifty minutes after takeoff.* N UNCOUNT OR N COUNT

takeover /teɪkəʊvə/, **takeovers. 1** When someone buys enough shares in a company to gain control of it, you describe this process as a **takeover**. EG *The trend towards takeovers has intensified... ...another oil company ripe for takeover.* N COUNT OR N UNCOUNT
2 When someone takes control of a country by force, this is also described as a **takeover**. EG *He may be ousted by a military takeover.* N COUNT OR N UNCOUNT

taker /teɪkə/, **takers.** If you say that there are no **takers** or few **takers**, you mean that nobody, or hardly anybody, is willing to accept a bet or a challenge. EG *The bookmakers were offering 4 to 1 on, but there were no takers.* N COUNT

If someone talks down to you, are they taller than you?

takings /teɪkɪŋz/. The **takings** are the money that a shop, theatre, or cinema gets from selling its goods or tickets. EG *The manager said that takings were as high as ever.* N PLURAL

talcum powder /tælkəm paʊdə/ is a soft, perfumed powder which people put on their bodies after they have had a bath. N UNCOUNT

tale /teɪl/, **tales. 1** A **tale** is a story, especially one involving adventure or magic. EG *They acted out tales of princes and magic birds.* N COUNT

2 You can refer to an account of a real event as a **tale**, especially when it is interesting or exciting. EG *Everyone had some tale to tell about the very cold winter.* ● See also **old wives' tale**. N COUNT

talent /tælə^{0}nt/, **talents. Talent** is the natural ability to do something well. EG *Does she have talent?... Your work shows a lot of talent... Rudolph had a talent for music... ...my artistic talents.* N UNCOUNT OR N COUNT

talented /tæləntɪ^{2}d/. Someone who is **talented** has a natural ability to do something well. EG *...a young and very talented writer... ...talented children.* ADJ QUALIT

talisman /tælɪzmən/, **talismans.** A **talisman** is an object which you believe has magic powers to protect you or bring you luck. N COUNT Formal

talk /tɔːk/, **talks, talking, talked. 1** When you **talk**, you say things to someone. EG *All the boys were talking at once... They talked about old times... He was the only one in the family she could talk to.* ▸ used as a noun. EG *I must have a long talk with him.* ● See also **small talk**. V: OFT+A ▸ N UNCOUNT OR N COUNT

2 If people **are talking**, they are discussing interesting things that they think are happening, especially other people's private affairs. EG *The neighbours will soon be talking.* ▸ used as a noun. EG *There was a lot of talk about his divorce.* V ▸ N UNCOUNT

3 If you **talk** something such as politics or sport, you discuss it. EG *They won't talk politics in the pub... Let's talk a little business, shall we?* V+O

4 If you **talk** on or about something, you make an informal speech about it. EG *I talked yesterday about the history of the project.* ▸ used as a noun. EG *I used to give the staff a talk on psychology every week.* V+*on/about* ▸ N COUNT

5 If someone **talks**, they give other people secret information. EG *Start talking, Castle. Or I'll shoot.* V

6 You say **talking of** something that has just been mentioned to introduce a new topic which has some connection with that thing. EG *Talking of marriage, isn't it lovely about Claire getting married?* PHRASE

7 Talks are formal discussions, especially between two countries or two sides in a dispute. EG *Talks in London last week produced no hint of a settlement... ...peace talks.* N PLURAL

8 If you say to someone **'You can talk'**, you are telling them that they have the same fault that they have just criticized in someone else. EG *'She's so untidy.' – 'You can talk!'* CONVENTION

talk down to. If someone **talks down to** you, they talk to you in a way that shows that they think they are more important or more clever than you. EG *I think some of the teachers felt they were being talked down to.* PHRASAL VB: V+ADV+PREP

talk into. If you **talk** someone **into** doing something, you persuade them to do it. EG *She talked me into taking a week's holiday.* PHRASAL VB: V+O+PREP

talk out of. If you **talk** someone **out of** doing something, you persuade them not to do it. EG *He tried to talk me out of buying such a big car.* PHRASAL VB: V+O+ADV +PREP

talk over. If you **talk** something **over**, you discuss it with someone. EG *I agreed to go home and talk things over with my father.* PHRASAL VB: V+O+ADV

talkative /tɔːkətɪv/. Someone who is **talkative** talks a lot. EG *She was one of the more talkative members of the class... After the third whisky, he became lively and talkative.* ADJ QUALIT

tall /tɔːl/, **taller, tallest. 1** Someone or something that is **tall** has a greater height than most other people or things. EG *He was a tall, dark man... ...a tall cypress tree.* ADJ QUALIT

2 You use **tall** when you refer to people's height. For example, if you are six feet **tall**, your height is six feet. If you are **taller** than someone else, your height is greater than theirs. EG *How tall is he?... ...a six-foot tall fifteen-year-old... She is starting to grow taller.* ADJ QUALIT OR ADJ AFTER N

3 If you say that a task is **a tall order**, you mean that it will be difficult to do. PHRASE

4 If you describe someone's account of an event as a **tall story**, you mean that it is difficult to believe, because it is so unlikely. EG *He was full of tall stories.* PHRASE

tally /tæli^{1}/, **tallies, tallying, tallied. 1** A **tally** is an informal record of amounts, such as money that you spend or points that you score in a game, which you keep adding to as you go along. EG *Can you keep a tally of your own marks, please?... The tally had now reached thirty-six.* N COUNT

2 If numbers or statements **tally**, they are exactly the same or they give the same results or conclusions. EG *We've checked their stories and they don't quite tally... The amount she mentioned failed to tally with the figure shown in the records.* V OR V+*with*: RECIP

talon /tælən/, **talons.** The **talons** of a bird of prey, such as an eagle, are its hooked claws. N COUNT: USU PLURAL

tambourine /tæmbəriːn/, **tambourines.** A **tambourine** is a musical instrument which you shake or hit with your hand. It consists of a drum skin on a circular frame and small round pieces of metal all around the edge. See picture at MUSICAL INSTRUMENTS. N COUNT

tame /teɪm/, **tamer, tamest; tames, taming, tamed. 1** A **tame** animal or bird is not afraid of people and is not violent towards them. EG *...a tame monkey.* ◇ **tameness.** EG *We were amazed at their tameness.* ADJ QUALIT ◇ N UNCOUNT

2 If you describe people as **tame**, you mean that they do what they are told to do without questioning it; used showing disapproval. EG *...a tame family doctor.* ◇ **tamely.** EG *These measures are unlikely to be accepted as tamely as the government hopes.* ADJ QUALIT ◇ ADV

3 You describe an activity as **tame** when you think that it is uninteresting because it does not involve any excitement or risk. EG *It sounded like a rather tame party.* ADJ QUALIT

4 If you **tame** people or things that are dangerous or likely to cause trouble, you bring them under control. EG *...savages to be tamed and civilized... Governments have found it necessary to tame large concentrations of economic power.* V+O

5 If you **tame** a wild animal or bird, you train it to be obedient and not to be afraid of people. EG *She was a wild owl and I had no intention of taming her.* V+O

tamper /tæmpə/, **tampers, tampering, tampered.** If you **tamper with** something, you interfere with it when you have no right to do so. EG *Someone had tampered with the register and changed the records... He claimed that his briefcase had been tampered with.* PHRASAL VB: V+PREP, HAS PASS

tampon /tæmpɒn/, **tampons.** A **tampon** is a firm, specially shaped piece of cotton wool that a woman puts inside her vagina to absorb the blood when she has a period. N COUNT

tan /tæn/. **1** If you have a **tan**, your skin has become darker than usual because you have spent a lot of time in the sun. EG *She had a beautiful golden tan.* N SING: a+N

2 Something that is **tan** is of a light yellowish-brown colour. EG *...tan shoes.* ADJ COLOUR

tandem /tændə^{0}m/, **tandems. 1** A **tandem** is a bicycle designed for two riders sitting one behind the other. N COUNT

2 If two people do something **in tandem**, they do it working together. EG *...a new play we had written in tandem.* PHRASE

tandoori /tændʊəri¹/ is an Indian method of cooking meat in a clay oven. N UNCOUNT

tang /tæŋ/, **tangs.** A **tang** is a strong, sharp smell or taste. EG *...the tang of an expensive perfume.* N COUNT: USU SING

tangent /tændʒənt/, **tangents. 1** A **tangent** is a straight line that touches a curve at one point but does not cross it. N COUNT
2 If you **go off at a tangent**, you start talking or thinking about something that is not directly connected with what you were talking or thinking about before. EG *His scientific mind immediately went off at a tangent.* PHRASE

tangerine /tændʒəriːn/, **tangerines.** A **tangerine** is a small, sweet orange. N COUNT

tangible /tændʒə¹bə⁰l/. Something that is **tangible** is clear enough or definite enough to be easily seen, felt, or noticed. EG *His rule as Prime Minister brought few tangible benefits to the poor... Politicians always want tangible results.* ADJ QUALIT
◇ **tangibly.** EG *The evidence tangibly supports his claim.* ◇ ADV

tangle /tæŋgə⁰l/, **tangles, tangling, tangled. 1** A **tangle** is a mass of things such as string, wire, or hair twisted together in an untidy way so that they are difficult to separate. EG *...an impenetrable tangle of creepers and trees.* N COUNT: OFT+*of*
2 Something that is **tangled** is twisted together in an untidy way. EG *She pushed the tangled hair back from her face... The wires got all tangled.* ADJ QUALIT
3 If you **are tangled** in wires or ropes or **are tangled** up in them, you are caught or trapped in them so that it is difficult to get free. EG *His leg got tangled in a harpoon line.* V-PASS+A: OFT+*up*
4 You can refer to a state of disorder and confusion as a **tangle**. EG *My tax affairs were in a complete tangle.* N SING
tangle with. If you **tangle with** someone, you get involved in a fight or quarrel with them. EG *I wouldn't tangle with him if I were you.* PHRASAL VB: V+PREP, HAS PASS

tank /tæŋk/, **tanks. 1** A **tank** is a large container, usually made of metal, for holding liquid or gas. EG *The tank will only hold three gallons... ...a petrol tank... ...the cold water tank.* N COUNT
2 A **tank** is also a military vehicle covered with armour and equipped with guns or rockets. N COUNT

tankard /tæŋkəd/, **tankards.** A **tankard** is a large metal mug with a handle that people drink beer from. N COUNT

tanker /tæŋkə/, **tankers.** A **tanker** is a ship, truck, or railway vehicle used for transporting large quantities of gas or liquid. EG *...an oil tanker.* N COUNT

tanned /tænd/. If you are **tanned**, your skin is darker than usual because you have spent a lot of time in the sun. EG *...tanned, slim young men.* ADJ QUALIT

tannery /tænəri¹/, **tanneries.** A **tannery** is a place where animal skins are made into leather. N COUNT

tantalize /tæntəlaɪz/, **tantalizes, tantalizing, tantalized;** also spelled **tantalise.** If something or someone **tantalizes** you, they make you feel hopeful and excited, and then do not allow you to have what you want. ◇ **tantalizing.** EG *This raises the tantalizing possibility that there may be life on other stars.* ◇ **tantalizingly.** EG *Sometimes a new idea may be tantalizingly close.* V+O; ◇ ADJ QUALIT; ◇ ADV

tantamount /tæntəmaʊnt/. If you say that something is **tantamount** to something else, you mean that it is almost the same as it. EG *His statement was tantamount to an admission of responsibility.* ADJ PRED+*to*

tantrum /tæntrəm/, **tantrums.** A **tantrum** is a noisy outburst of bad temper, especially by a child. EG *...a spoiled child who throws tantrums when she doesn't get her own way.* N COUNT

tap /tæp/, **taps, tapping, tapped. 1** A **tap** is a device that you turn in order to control the flow of a liquid or gas from a pipe or container. Sinks and baths have taps attached to them. EG *Someone left the tap running... Turn on the hot tap... ...a gas tap.* N COUNT
2 If you **tap** something or **tap** on it, you hit it lightly with your fingers or with something else. EG *It will come loose if you tap it with a hammer... She tapped on the glass partition.* ▸ used as a noun. EG *I heard a soft tap at the front door.* V+O OR V+A; ▸ N COUNT
3 If you **tap** a resource or situation, you make use of it by getting something that you want from it. EG *...a new way of tapping the sun's energy.* V+O

tape /teɪp/, **tapes, taping, taped. 1 Tape** is plastic made in long strips and covered with a magnetic substance. It is used to record sounds, pictures, and computer information. EG *...a conversation recorded on tape.* ● See also **magnetic tape**, **video tape**. N UNCOUNT
2 A **tape** is a cassette or spool with magnetic tape wound round it. It is used for recording or replaying sounds, pictures, or computer information. EG *Do you want to put on a tape?... His manager persuaded him to make a tape of the song.* N COUNT
3 If you **tape** music, sounds, or television pictures, you record them using a tape recorder or a video recorder. EG *I'm having to tape this talk several days in advance... ...a taped commentary.* V+O
4 A **tape** is also a strip of cloth sewn onto a piece of clothing or other material. Tapes are used to tie things together or to identify who a piece of clothing belongs to. EG *...three metres of white tape... You have to sew name tapes into everything.* N COUNT OR N UNCOUNT
5 In a race, the **tape** is a ribbon stretched across the finishing line. N COUNT
6 Tape is also sticky strips of plastic which you use for sticking things together. EG *...a bit of adhesive tape.* N UNCOUNT
7 If you **tape** one thing to another, you attach them together using sticky tape. V+O+A
8 See also **red tape**.

tape deck, tape decks. A **tape deck** is a machine on which you can play or record tapes. N COUNT

tape measure, tape measures. A **tape measure** is a strip of plastic or cloth with centimetres or inches marked on it. You use it for measuring things. N COUNT

taper /teɪpə/, **tapers, tapering, tapered. 1** You say that something **tapers** when it gradually becomes thinner at one end. EG *Eventually the gallery tapered to a long, narrow corridor.* ◇ **tapered.** EG *The trousers should have tapered legs.* ◇ **tapering.** EG *...long tapering fingers.* V; ◇ ADJ QUALIT; ◇ ADJ QUALIT
2 A **taper** is a long, thin candle. N COUNT
taper off. If something **tapers off**, it gradually becomes much smaller. EG *The economic boom tapered off.* PHRASAL VB: V+ADV

tape recorder, tape recorders. A **tape recorder** is a machine used for recording and playing music, speech, and other sounds. N COUNT

tape recording, tape recordings. A **tape recording** is a recording of speech or other sounds that has been made on a tape. N COUNT

tapestry /tæpɪstri¹/, **tapestries. 1** A **tapestry** is a piece of heavy cloth with a picture or pattern sewn on it. EG *...the Bayeux tapestry.* N COUNT OR N UNCOUNT
2 You can refer to something as a **tapestry** when it is made up of many interesting and different things or people. EG *The book presents a tapestry of teenage life in the provinces.* N COUNT+*of* Literary

tar /tɑː/ is a thick, black, sticky substance that becomes hard when it is cold. It is used in making roads. N UNCOUNT

target /tɑːgɪt/, **targets. 1** A **target** is **1.1** a town, building, or other place at which a weapon such as a missile or bomb is aimed. EG *The missile can land within a half-mile radius of its target... The station was an easy target for an air attack.* **1.2** an object at which you fire arrows or bullets when you are shooting for sport or practice. A target often consists of a large circle with smaller circles inside N COUNT

If you tangle with someone, do you get tangled up?

it, marked on a board or piece of paper. EG *My first two shots missed the target.*

2 When someone or something is being criticized or blamed, you can refer to them as a **target**. EG *In their search for a scapegoat, the Government found an easy target in the unions.* N COUNT: OFT+SUPP

3 A **target** is also a result that you are trying to achieve. EG *It set a target for economic growth in excess of 4% a year.* N COUNT ● If you are **on target**, you are making good progress and are likely to achieve the result you want. EG *The latest sales figures are on target.* ● PHRASE

tariff /tærɪf/, **tariffs.** A **tariff** is a tax that a government collects on goods coming into a country. EG *...a high tariff on all imports.* N COUNT

tarmac /tɑːmæk/. **1 Tarmac** is a material used for making road surfaces. It consists of crushed stones mixed with tar. EG *...a tarmac road.* N UNCOUNT Trademark

2 You can refer to any area with a tarmac surface as the **tarmac**. EG *He went out onto the tarmac where the jet was waiting.* N SING: *the*+N

tarnish /tɑːnɪʃ/, **tarnishes, tarnishing, tarnished. 1** If metal **tarnishes**, it becomes stained and loses its brightness. EG *Chrome doesn't tarnish easily... The damp atmosphere tends to tarnish the brass taps.* V-ERG ◊ **tarnished**. EG *There was a photo in a silver frame, by now rather tarnished.* ◊ ADJ QUALIT

2 If something **tarnishes** your reputation, it damages it and causes people to lose their respect for you. EG *...a trial that tarnished the names of many intellectuals.* V+O ◊ **tarnished**. EG *...an attempt to restore some of their tarnished popularity.* ◊ ADJ QUALIT

tarpaulin /tɑːpɔːlɪn/, **tarpaulins.** A **tarpaulin** is a sheet of heavy, waterproof material that is used to cover things and protect them from rain. N COUNT

tarred /tɑːd/. A **tarred** road has a surface of tar. ADJ CLASSIF

tart /tɑːt/, **tarts; tarter, tartest. 1** A **tart** is a piece of pastry with something sweet, such as jam or cooked fruit, inside. EG *...jam tarts... Have another slice of tart.* N COUNT OR N UNCOUNT

2 A **tart** remark is unpleasant and rather cruel. EG *She spoke with tart contempt.* ADJ QUALIT ◊ **tartly**. EG *She tartly pointed out that he owed her some money.* ◊ ADV

3 Prostitutes are sometimes referred to as **tarts**. EG *Only tarts wore make-up in those days.* N COUNT Informal

tartan /tɑːtəⁿn/, **tartans. Tartan** is woollen cloth from Scotland that has patterns of different coloured stripes crossing each other. EG *...a skirt made of tartan... ...the tartans of the Gordon and Wallace clans... ...a tartan rug.* N UNCOUNT OR N COUNT

task /tɑːsk/, **tasks.** A **task** is a piece of work that must be done. EG *...the endless task of classifying the samples... Computers can be applied to a wide range of tasks.* N COUNT

tassel /tæsəⁿl/, **tassels.** A **tassel** is a bunch of short pieces of material tied together at one end and attached to something as a decoration. EG *...the tassels on their cloaks.* N COUNT

taste /teɪst/, **tastes, tasting, tasted. 1** Your sense of **taste** is your ability to recognize things when you touch them with your tongue. EG *Some animals have a better sense of taste than others.* N UNCOUNT

2 The **taste** of something is the special flavour that it has, for example whether it is sweet or salty. EG *I don't like the taste of fresh fish... The soup was peppered and spiced to improve the taste.* N SING: USU+SUPP

3 If you have a **taste** of food or drink, you try a small amount in order to see what its taste is like. EG *I opened one of the bottles and had a taste of the contents.* N SING

4 When you can **taste** something that you are eating or drinking, you are aware of its flavour. EG *Roger chewed and swallowed so fast that he hardly tasted the meat.* V+O

5 If you **taste** food or drink, you try a small amount in order to decide whether you like it or not. EG *He insisted on pouring the wine for a guest to taste.* V+O

6 If food or drink **tastes** of something, it has a particular flavour, which you notice when you eat or drink it. EG *The tea tasted faintly of bitter almonds.* V+A OR C: NO CONT

7 If you have a **taste** for something, you enjoy it. EG *He had not lost the taste for power... He has little taste for politics... Ben suddenly lost his taste for publicity.* N SING+*for*

8 If you have a **taste** of something such as a way of life or a pleasure, you experience it for a short time. EG *The child may already have had a taste of street life.* N SING+*of*

9 A person's **taste** is their choice in the things that they like or buy. You can show your opinion of their choice by talking about their 'good taste' or their 'bad taste'. EG *She has very good taste in clothes... Her novels are too violent for my taste.* N UNCOUNT: USU+SUPP

10 If you say that something that someone has said or done is **in bad taste**, you mean that it is offensive. If it is **in good taste**, it is not offensive. EG *That remark was in rather poor taste... Her jokes are always in the best possible taste.* PHRASE

tasteful /teɪstfʊl/. If you describe something as **tasteful**, you mean that it is attractive and elegant. EG *The bedroom was simple but tasteful.* ADJ QUALIT ◊ **tastefully** EG *Their house was tastefully furnished.* ◊ ADV

tasteless /teɪstlɪ²s/. **1** If you say that something is **tasteless**, you mean that it is vulgar and unattractive. EG *The room was full of tasteless ornaments.* ADJ QUALIT

2 If you describe a remark or joke as **tasteless**, you mean that it is offensive. EG *Apart from a few tasteless remarks, he was reasonably well-behaved... ...tasteless jokes.* ADJ QUALIT

3 If you describe food as **tasteless**, you mean that it is not enjoyable, because it has very little flavour. EG *The cafeteria serves cold, tasteless pizzas.* ADJ QUALIT

tasty /teɪsti¹/, **tastier, tastiest.** If you describe food as **tasty**, you mean that it is enjoyable, because it has a pleasant flavour. EG *Sunflower seeds are tasty and nutritious.* ADJ QUALIT

tattered /tætəd/. **Tattered** clothing or paper is torn or crumpled. EG *...a man in a tattered shirt... ...paintings tied up in tattered brown paper.* ADJ QUALIT

tatters /tætəz/. **1** Clothes that are **in tatters** are badly torn. EG *He arrived with his garments in tatters.* PHRASE

2 You can say that something is **in tatters** when it has been severely damaged or ruined. EG *Peter was dejected, his confidence in tatters.* PHRASE

tattoo /tætuː/, **tattoos, tattooing, tattooed. 1** If someone **tattoos** you or **tattoos** a picture or design on you, they draw it on your skin by pricking little holes and filling them with coloured dye. EG *He had tattooed the name 'Marlene' on his upper arm.* V+O ◊ **tattooed**. EG *...a tattooed sailor.* ◊ ADJ CLASSIF

2 A **tattoo** is a picture or design tattooed on someone's body. EG *He had a tattoo on the back of his hand.* N COUNT

3 If you beat a **tattoo**, you hit something quickly and repeatedly. EG *He beat a frantic tattoo with his hands on the door.* N COUNT: USU SING

4 A **tattoo** is also a public display of exercises and music given by the army, navy, or air force. N COUNT

tatty /tæti¹/. If you describe something as **tatty**, you mean that it is untidy and rather dirty. EG *...a tatty old skirt... ...this pleasantly tatty seaside resort.* ADJ QUALIT Informal

taught /tɔːt/ is the past tense and past participle of **teach.**

taunt /tɔːnt/, **taunts, taunting, taunted.** If you **taunt** someone, you speak offensively to them about their weaknesses or failures in order to upset or annoy them. EG *...street marchers taunting the police.* V+O ▸ used as a noun. EG *The children had to put up with taunts like 'You haven't got a Dad.'* ▸ N COUNT

taut /tɔːt/. Something that is **taut** is stretched very tight. EG *...a taut wire.* ADJ QUALIT

tavern /tævəⁿn/, **taverns.** A **tavern** is a pub. EG *I opened the door of the Shakespeare Tavern.* N COUNT Outdated

tax /tæks/, **taxes, taxing, taxed. 1 Tax** is an amount of money that you have to pay to the government so that it can pay for public services. EG *...a tax on pensions... The tax cuts take effect on July 1st... ...a reduction in taxes.* N UNCOUNT OR N COUNT

2 If a sum of money **is taxed**, a part of it has to be paid to the government. EG *Any money earned over that level is taxed at the rate of 59%.* V+O : OFT PASS

3 If goods **are taxed**, a part of their price has to be paid to the government. EG *Crops were taxed very heavily.* V+O : OFT PASS

4 If a person or company **is taxed**, they have to pay a part of their income or profits to the government. EG *She was not taxed separately from her husband.* V+O : OFT PASS

5 See also **taxing**.

taxable /tæksəbə^{o}l/. If something is **taxable,** you have to pay tax on it. EG *...taxable income.* ADJ CLASSIF

taxation /tækseɪʃə^{o}n/ is **1** the system by which a government takes some money from the people and spends it on such things as education, health, and defence. **2** the amount of money that people have to pay in taxes. EG *The government is hoping to reduce taxation.* N UNCOUNT

tax-free. When goods or services are **tax-free,** you do not have to pay tax on them. ADJ CLASSIF

taxi /tæksi^{1}/, **taxis, taxiing, taxied. 1** A **taxi** is a car driven by someone whose job is to take you where you want to go in return for money. N COUNT OR *by*+N

2 When an aircraft **taxis**, it moves slowly along the runway before taking off or after landing. EG *The Boeing taxied down the runway.* V : USU+A

taxing /tæksɪŋ/. A **taxing** task requires a lot of mental or physical effort. EG *They faced new and taxing problems.* ADJ QUALIT

taxpayer /tækspeɪə/, **taxpayers. Taxpayers** are people who pay a percentage of their income to the government as tax. N COUNT

TB /tiː biː/is an abbreviation for 'tuberculosis'. N UNCOUNT

tea /tiː/, **teas. 1 Tea** is a drink made with hot water and the chopped, dried leaves of a particular bush. Milk and sugar are often added to the drink. EG *She poured herself another cup of tea... She went into the kitchen to make a fresh pot of tea.* N MASS

2 Tea is also **2.1** the bush whose leaves are used to make tea. EG *He wanted to go to Ceylon and plant tea.* N UNCOUNT **2.2** the chopped, dried leaves of the bush that you use to make tea. EG *...a packet of tea.* N MASS

3 A **tea** is a cup of tea. EG *Two teas, please.* N COUNT

4 Other drinks made with hot water and leaves or flowers are also called **tea**. EG *...mint tea.* N MASS+SUPP

5 Tea is also a light meal that is eaten in the afternoon. Some British people refer to the main meal that they eat in the early evening as **tea**. EG *I always come back from work to find the tea ready... At tea we talked about the day's events... Mr Evans is coming to tea.* N UNCOUNT OR N COUNT

6 If you say that something is **not** your **cup of tea**, you mean that you do not like it and would not choose to do it or to have it. EG *Ballet isn't really my cup of tea.* PHRASE

tea bag, tea bags. A **tea bag** is a small paper bag with tea leaves in it. You put the tea bag into hot water to make tea and then throw the tea bag away. N COUNT

teach /tiːtʃ/, **teaches, teaching, taught** /tɔːt/. **1** If you **teach** someone something, you give them instructions so that they know about it or know how to do it. EG *Mother taught me how to read... Boylan had taught him to drive... Johnny taught me everything I know.* V+O+O; ALSO V+O+REPORT, *to*-INF, OR *to*

2 If you **teach** someone to think or to behave in a particular way, you persuade them to think or to behave in that way. EG *Gandhi taught the world passive resistance... Boys are often taught that they mustn't show their feelings... We've been taught to believe in the wisdom of those who govern us.* V+O+O; ALSO V+O+REPORT, *to*-INF, OR *to*

3 If you **teach** a subject or **teach**, your job is to help students to learn about something at a school, college, or university. EG *I taught history for many years... I found a job teaching English to a group of adults in Paris... Mrs Barton teaches in a secondary modern school.* V+O, V+O+*to*, OR V

teacher /tiːtʃə/, **teachers.** A **teacher** is someone who teaches, especially at a school. EG *...a French teacher... ...a teacher of English Literature.* N COUNT

teaching /tiːtʃɪŋ/, **teachings. 1 Teaching** is the work that a teacher does. EG *Have you done any teaching lately?* N UNCOUNT

2 A person's **teachings** are the principles that they teach to other people. EG *His teachings still exert a strong influence.* N COUNT : USU PLURAL

teacup /tiːkʌp/, **teacups. 1** A **teacup** is a cup that you drink tea from. N COUNT

2 If you describe a situation as a **storm in a teacup**, you mean that a lot of fuss is being made about something that is not important. PHRASE

teak /tiːk/ is a kind of very hard wood. EG *The chairs were of black teak... ...teak furniture.* N UNCOUNT

tea leaf, tea leaves. Tea leaves are the small pieces of dried leaves that are left in a teapot or a cup after you have drunk the tea. N COUNT : USU PLURAL

team /tiːm/, **teams, teaming, teamed. 1** A **team** is a group of people who play together against another group in a sport or game. EG *...the New Zealand rugby team.* N COLL

2 You can refer to any group of people who work together as a **team**. EG *...a team of scientists.* N COLL

team up. If you **team up** with someone, you join them so that you can do something together. EG *He teamed up with a friend and set up a business doing interior decorating.* PHRASAL VB : V+ADV OR V+ADV+*with* : RECIP

teamwork /tiːmwɜːk/ is the ability of a group of people to work well together. EG *Teamwork was even more important in the later stages of the project.* N UNCOUNT

tea party, tea parties. A **tea party** is a social gathering in the afternoon at which you drink tea and eat food such as sandwiches and cakes. N COUNT

teapot /tiːpɒt/, **teapots.** A **teapot** is a container with a lid, a handle, and a spout. You use it for making and serving tea. N COUNT

tear, tears, tearing, tore /tɔː/, **torn** /tɔːn/. **Tear** is pronounced /tɪə/ for paragraph 1, and /tɛə/ for paragraphs 2 to 8 and the phrasal verbs.

1 Tears are the drops of liquid that come out of your eyes when you cry. EG *He was sitting there with tears in his eyes... Tears were streaming down her face... Tears fell from Mother's eyes.* N COUNT : USU PLURAL ● If someone is **in tears**, they are crying. EG *When Curzon heard the news, he burst into tears.* ● PHRASE

2 If you **tear** something made of cloth or paper, you pull it into two pieces or pull it so that a hole appears in it. EG *He tore my coat in the struggle... Regretfully, he tore both letters into small pieces... I tugged at the sleeve to get it free. It tore.* V-ERG : OFT+A ◊ **torn**. EG *...my torn sweater.* ◊ ADJ CLASSIF

3 A **tear** in something such as a piece of clothing is a hole that has been made in it. EG *There was a triangular tear at the knee of his trousers.* ● See also **wear and tear**. N COUNT

4 To **tear** something from somewhere means to remove it roughly and violently. EG *She tore several sheets of paper out of the back of the book... Boats were torn from their moorings by the storm.* V+O+A

5 If you **tear** somewhere, you move very quickly. EG *She came tearing out of the house... He tore off home... They tore down the street after the dog.* V+A

6 If you **are torn** between two or more things, you cannot decide which one to choose, and this makes you feel unhappy. EG *Charles is torn between Susan and his fiancee, Tina.* V+O : USU PASS+A

7 If you **tear loose** or **tear** yourself **loose**, you suddenly and violently escape from someone or PHRASE

What can you buy in a tea shop?

something that is holding you. EG *The piglet tore loose from the creepers.*

8 If you **tear** something **open**, you open it roughly and quickly, by tearing it. EG *He tore open the envelope... I watched her tearing open a packet of sugar.* [PHRASE]

tear apart. 1 If you **tear** something **apart**, you pull it into pieces violently. EG *I tore the parcel apart.* [PHRASAL VB: V+O+ADV] **2** If something **tears** an organization or country **apart**, it causes great quarrels or disturbances. EG *He was fighting against the 'anarchy' which he insisted was tearing the Church apart.* [V+O+ADV] **3** If something **tears** you **apart**, it makes you feel very upset. EG *She is torn apart by conflicting pressures.* [V+O+ADV]

tear at. If you **tear at** something, you violently try to pull pieces off it. EG *The boys tore at the meat like wolves.* [PHRASAL VB: V+PREP]

tear away. If you **tear** someone **away** from a place or activity, you force them to leave the place or stop doing the activity. EG *Mourners often find it difficult to tear themselves away from the grave.* [PHRASAL VB: V+O+ADV, OFT+*from*]

tear down. If you **tear down** a building, you destroy it. EG *It is often cheaper to tear down the buildings than to modify them.* [PHRASAL VB: V+O+ADV]

tear off. If you **tear** your clothes **off**, you take them off quickly in a rough way. EG *I tore off my shirt.* [PHRASAL VB: V+O+ADV]

tear up. If you **tear up** a piece of paper, you pull it into a lot of small pieces. EG *She wrote a suicide note. Then she tore it up.* [PHRASAL VB: V+O+ADV]

tearful /tɪ̲əfʊl/. If you are **tearful**, you are crying. EG *His tearful family came to pay their last respects.* ◊ **tearfully**. EG *He looked at her tearfully.* [ADJ QUALIT; ◊ ADV]

tear gas /tɪ̲ə gæs/ is a gas that causes your eyes to sting and fill with tears. It is sometimes used by the police to control violent crowds. [N UNCOUNT]

tease /ti̲:z/, **teases, teasing, teased. 1** If you **tease** someone, you deliberately embarrass them, trick them, or make fun of them, because this amuses you. EG *She teased him about his girlfriends... 'Ah hah,' the old man teased, 'perhaps you already have a child?'* [V+O, V+O+A, OR V+QUOTE]

2 A **tease** is someone who makes fun of people in a gentle but slightly cruel way. EG *You're a terrible tease. I never know when you're serious.* [N SING: *a*+N]

tea shop, tea shops. A **tea shop** is a small restaurant or café where tea, coffee, cakes, and light meals are served. [N COUNT British]

teaspoon /ti̲:spu:n/, **teaspoons. 1** A **teaspoon** is a small spoon that you use to put sugar into tea or coffee. [N COUNT]

2 A **teaspoon** of food or liquid is the amount that a teaspoon will hold. EG *Add one teaspoon of salt.* [N PART]

teaspoonful /ti̲:spu:nfʊl/, **teaspoonfuls** or **teaspoonsful.** A **teaspoonful** is the amount that a teaspoon will hold. EG *...two teaspoonfuls of sugar.* [N PART]

tea strainer /ti̲: streɪnə/, **tea strainers.** A **tea strainer** is a small metal or plastic object with a lot of small holes in it. It is used to stop tea leaves going into the cup when you are pouring tea. [N COUNT]

teat /ti̲:t/, **teats.** A **teat** is **1** one of the pieces of flesh that stick out on the chest or stomach of a female animal and from which its babies suck milk: compare **nipple**. EG *...tiny naked pink creatures clinging to the teats with their mouths.* **2** a piece of rubber or plastic that is shaped like a teat and is fitted to a bottle so that a baby can suck liquids from it. EG *The baby grabbed the teat and began to suck.* [N COUNT]

teatime /ti̲:taɪm/ is the time in the afternoon when people often have tea. EG *At teatime there was much excited chatter around the table.* [N UNCOUNT British]

tea-towel, tea-towels. A **tea-towel** is a cloth which you use to dry dishes and cutlery after they have been washed. [N COUNT British]

tech /tɛ̲k/, **techs.** A **tech** is the same as a technical college. EG *Actually I teach at the Tech... The woman felt strongly that Techs served a valuable function.* [N COUNT Informal British]

technical /tɛ̲knɪkə⁰l/. **1 Technical** means involving details about machines, processes, and materials that are used, especially in industry, transport, and communications. EG *...scientific and technical knowledge... ...technical advances that improve productivity.* [ADJ QUALIT: USU ATTRIB]

2 You also use **technical** to describe the practical skills and methods a person uses to do an activity such as an art, a craft, or a sport. EG *...wood carving of remarkable technical skill.* [ADJ QUALIT: USU ATTRIB]

3 Technical language involves using special words, or using ordinary words in a special way, in order to describe the details of a subject or activity. In this dictionary, language of this kind is indicated by the word 'Technical' in the Extra Column. [ADJ QUALIT: ATTRIB]

technical college, technical colleges. A **technical college** is a college in Britain where you can study subjects to 'O' or 'A' level, usually as part of the qualifications and training required for a particular job. [N COUNT]

technicality /tɛ̲knɪkæ̲lɪ¹ti¹/, **technicalities. 1** The **technicalities** of a process or activity are the detailed methods used to do it. EG *I was quite interested in the technicalities of the recording.* [N PLURAL]

2 A **technicality** is a point that is based on a strict interpretation of a law or a set of rules. EG *On a technicality, the judge dismissed the case.* [N COUNT]

technically /tɛ̲knɪkə⁰li¹/. **1** If something is **technically** true or correct, it is true or correct when you consider only the facts, laws, or rules but may not be important or relevant in a particular situation. EG *He was technically in breach of contract.* [ADV SEN OR ADV]

2 You use **technically** when discussing details about machines, processes, and materials used, especially in industry, transport, and communications. EG *It's quite clear that the electric car is technically feasible.* [ADV]

3 You also use **technically** when discussing the practical skills and methods a person uses to do an activity such as an art, a craft, or a sport. EG *Pollock was certainly a skilful artist technically.* [ADV]

technician /tɛknɪ̲ʃə⁰n/, **technicians.** A **technician** is someone whose job involves skilled practical work with scientific equipment, for example in a laboratory. [N COUNT]

Technicolor /tɛ̲knɪkʌlə/ is a system of colour photography used in making cinema films. [N UNCOUNT Trademark]

technique /tɛkni̲:k/, **techniques. 1** A **technique** is a particular method of doing something. EG *...the techniques of film-making.* [N COUNT]

2 Technique is skill and ability in an artistic, sporting, or other practical activity that you develop through training and practice. EG *She owed her technique entirely to his teaching.* [N UNCOUNT]

technological /tɛ̲knə⁶lɒ̲dʒɪkə⁰l/ means relating to, resulting from, or associated with technology. EG *...modern scientific and technological knowledge.* ◊ **technologically**. EG *...the world's richest and most technologically advanced nations.* [ADJ CLASSIF: ATTRIB; ◊ ADV]

technology /tɛknɒ̲lədʒi¹/, **technologies. 1 Technology** is the activity or study of using scientific knowledge for practical purposes in industry, farming, medicine, or business. EG *...advances in technology and science.* ◊ **technologist** /tɛknɒ̲lədʒɪst/, **technologists**. EG *...a small group of distinguished scientists and technologists.* [N UNCOUNT; ◊ N COUNT]

2 A **technology** is a particular area of activity that requires scientific methods and knowledge. EG *...computer technology.* [N COUNT OR N UNCOUNT +SUPP]

teddy /tɛ̲di¹/, **teddies.** A **teddy** or a **teddy bear** is a soft toy that looks like a bear. [N COUNT]

tedious /ti̲:dɪəs/. Something that is **tedious** is boring and lasts for a long time. EG *The arguments were tedious and complicated... ...rather tedious lunch parties... ...four weeks of remarkably tedious work.* [ADJ QUALIT]

tedium /tiːdɪəm/. The **tedium** of a situation is its quality of being boring and seeming to last for a long time. EG *...the tedium of being young and poor... ...a cricket match of unspeakable tedium.* N UNCOUNT Formal

teem /tiːm/, **teems, teeming, teemed.** If a place **is teeming** with people, there are a lot of people moving around in it. EG *...a large, busy capital teeming with people.* ◇ **teeming.** EG *She walked home through the teeming streets... ...separating it from the teeming jungle to the east.* V+*with*: USU CONT ◇ ADJ CLASSIF: ATTRIB

teenage /tiːneɪdʒ/. **1 Teenage** people are aged between thirteen and nineteen. EG *...a divorced woman with two teenage children.* ADJ CLASSIF: ATTRIB

2 Teenage fashions and activities are considered to be typical of young people aged between thirteen and nineteen or to be suitable for them. EG *...the teenage culture of pop music and magazines.* ADJ CLASSIF: ATTRIB

teenager /tiːneɪdʒə/, **teenagers.** A **teenager** is someone aged between thirteen and nineteen. EG *...a highly intelligent teenager.* N COUNT

teens /tiːnz/. Your **teens** are the period of your life when you are between thirteen and nineteen years old. EG *She was young, maybe still in her teens... ...her first serious run since her teens.* N PLURAL

teeter /tiːtə/, **teeters, teetering, teetered. 1** If someone or something **teeters,** they move or shake unsteadily and seem about to fall over. EG *My last penny wobbled across the board, teetered about for a second, and then fell over.* V: USU+A

2 If something **teeters** on the brink of disaster, it is very close to disaster. EG *British theatre is in a perilous state, teetering on the brink of ruin.* V+*on*

teeth /tiːθ/ is the plural of **tooth.**

teethe /tiːð/, **teethes, teething, teethed.** When babies **are teething,** their teeth are starting to appear through their gums, usually causing them pain. V: USU CONT

teething troubles are difficulties which arise when a project has just begun or when something is new. EG *They had terrible teething troubles with the steering on the new model.* N PLURAL

teetotal /tiːtəʊtəˀl/. Someone who is **teetotal** never drinks alcohol. ADJ CLASSIF

teetotaller /tiːtəʊtəˀlə/, **teetotallers.** A **teetotaller** is someone who never drinks alcohol. N COUNT

TEFL /tɛfəˀl/ is the teaching of English to students from countries where English is not the main language and where it is not essential for education or jobs. **TEFL** is an abbreviation for 'teaching English as a foreign language'. N UNCOUNT

telecommunications /tɛlɪkəmjuːnɪkeɪʃəˀnz/ is the science and activity of sending signals and messages over long distances using electronic equipment, such as radio or telephone. N UNCOUNT: OFT N MOD

telegram /tɛlɪgræm/, **telegrams.** A **telegram** is a message that is sent by telegraph and then printed and delivered to someone. EG *I sent a telegram to my mother saying I had arrived safely.* N COUNT

telegraph /tɛlɪgræf, -grɑːf/, **telegraphs, telegraphing, telegraphed. 1** The **telegraph is** a system of sending messages over long distances by means of electrical or radio signals, and printing them at the other end. N SING: *the*+N

2 If you **telegraph** someone, you send them a message using the telegraph system. EG *Harold had telegraphed him in France.* V OR V+O: OFT+REPORT OR *to* Outdated

telepathic /tɛlɪpæθɪk/. If someone claims to be **telepathic** or to have **telepathic** powers, they claim to be able to communicate directly with other people using only their minds. ADJ CLASSIF

telepathy /tɪˀlɛpəθiˀ/ is direct communication between people's minds. EG *We are particularly interested in phenomena such as telepathy.* N UNCOUNT

telephone /tɛlɪfəʊn/, **telephones, telephoning, telephoned. 1** The **telephone** is an electrical system that you use to talk to someone in another [place] by dialling a number on a piece of equipment [and] speaking into it. EG *Reports came in by telephone... I have to make a telephone call.* N SING: *the*+N, OR *by*+N

2 A **telephone** is the piece of equipment that you use when you talk to someone by telephone. EG *He put down the telephone.* N COUNT

3 If you **telephone** someone, you dial their telephone number and speak to them by telephone. EG *I'll telephone her this evening... Brody telephoned to thank her.* V OR V+O Formal

4 If you are **on the telephone, 4.1** you are speaking to someone by telephone. **4.2** you have a telephone in your home or place of work, so that you can be contacted by telephone. PHRASE

telephone book, telephone books. A **telephone book** is a book that contains an alphabetical list of names, addresses, and telephone numbers of the people in a town or area. N COUNT

telephone booth, telephone booths. A **telephone booth** is a place in a station, hotel, or other public building where there is a public telephone. N COUNT British

telephone box, telephone boxes. A **telephone box** is a small shelter in the street in which there is a public telephone. N COUNT British

telephone directory, telephone directories. A **telephone directory** is the same as a telephone book. N COUNT

telephone exchange, telephone exchanges. A **telephone exchange** is a building belonging to a telephone company or system, where the telephone lines are connected when someone in the area makes or receives a telephone call. N COUNT

telephone number, telephone numbers. Your **telephone number** is the number that other people dial when they want to talk to you on the telephone. EG *He gave her his telephone number.* N COUNT

telephonist /tɪˀlɛfənɪst/, **telephonists.** A **telephonist** is someone who works in a telephone exchange or whose job is to answer the telephone for a business or other organization. N COUNT British

telephoto lens /tɛlɪfəʊtəʊ lɛnz/, **telephoto lenses.** A **telephoto lens** is a lens which you can attach to a camera and which makes far away things larger and clearer in the photographs. N COUNT

telescope /tɛlɪskəʊp/, **telescopes.** A **telescope** is a long tube-shaped instrument with lenses inside it. You look through a telescope in order to make distant things appear larger and nearer. EG *They peered at the targets through the telescope.* N COUNT

telescopic /tɛlɪskɒpɪk/. **1 Telescopic** instruments and lenses make things seem larger and nearer. EG *The telescopic sight fitted snugly along the top of the gun... ...a 400 mm telescopic lens.* ADJ CLASSIF: ATTRIB

2 A **telescopic** piece of equipment is made of sections that fit or slide into each other so that it can be made shorter when it is not being used. EG *I pulled out the telescopic aerial to its fullest extent.* ADJ CLASSIF: ATTRIB

televise /tɛlɪvaɪz/, **televises, televising, televised.** If an event **is televised,** it is filmed and shown on television. EG *The ceremony would be televised nationally... The BBC agreed to televise the debate.* V+O: USU PASS

television /tɛlɪvɪʒəˀn/, **televisions. 1** A **television** or a **television set** is a piece of electrical equipment consisting of a box with a glass screen. You use a television to watch programmes with pictures and sounds. EG *You don't have a television, do you?... I turned on the television to watch the news.* ● If something is **on television,** you can watch it by using a television set. EG *His first film was shown on television this weekend.* N COUNT ● PHRASE

2 Television 2.1 is the system of sending pictures and sounds by electrical signals over a distance so that people can receive them on a television set. EG *...television pictures transmitted from a camera on the other side of the world.* **2.2** refers to all the programmes, such as plays, films, and news, that are broadcast and that you can watch on a televi- N UNCOUNT

If you have teething troubles, does your mouth hurt?

sion set. EG *The boys were watching television.* **2.3** is the business or industry concerned with making programmes and broadcasting them on television. EG *...the most exciting job in television.*

telex /tɛlɛks/, **telexes, telexing, telexed. 1 Telex** is an international system of sending written messages. The message is typed on a machine in one place and is immediately printed out by a machine in another place. N UNCOUNT

2 A **telex** is **2.1** a machine that sends and receives telex messages. **2.2** a message that is sent by telex. EG *He burst in with an urgent telex.* N COUNT

3 If you **telex** a message, you send it by using a telex machine. EG *The file on this man had been telexed to Paris.* V+O : OFT+*to*

tell /tɛl/, **tells, telling, told** /təʊld/. **1** If you **tell** someone something, you give them information. EG *John refused to tell me her name... He told me that he was a farmer... I told her what the doctor had said... 'Jenny's dead,' I told him... My aunt wrote and told me all about it... She told me the story of her life... 'We told a lot of lies,' said Bill.* V+O+O; ALSO V+O : USU+REPORT, QUOTE, OR A

2 If you **tell** someone to do something, you order, instruct, or advise them to do it. EG *I was furious and told them to get out of my house... Just do as you're told... My uncle smiled and told me not to worry.* V+O+*to*-INF, QUOTE OR REPORT

3 If you can **tell** what is happening or what is true, you are able to judge correctly what is happening or what is true. EG *You can't tell the difference between truth and fiction... I couldn't tell what they were thinking... So far as we can tell, it is still in perfect condition.* V+O OR V+REPORT WITH MODAL : NO CONT

4 If a child can **tell the time**, he or she is able to look at a watch or clock and say what time it is. PHRASE

5 If something **tells** you something, it reveals a fact to you or indicates what you should do. EG *The design of the computer tells us nothing about such things... Every movement they make tells you that they are tired... My intuition told me to stay away.* V+O+O; ALSO V+O : OFT+REPORT OR *to*-INF

6 If an unpleasant or tiring experience begins to **tell**, it begins to have a serious effect. EG *The strain was beginning to tell... All these late nights were beginning to tell on my health.* V : OFT+*on*

7 You say **'I can tell you'**, or **'I can't tell you'** to emphasize what you are saying. EG *Some of your friends have some very funny ideas, I can tell you... I can't tell you how pleased we are to have you here today, Professor.* CONVENTION

8 If someone did not accept something you said or suggested and finds out later that you were right, you can say **'I told you so'** if you want to be slightly cruel and rude. CONVENTION Informal

9 If you say **'Time will tell'**, you mean that the truth about something will not be known until some time in the future. CONVENTION

tell apart. If you can **tell** similar people or things **apart**, you are able to recognize the differences between them and can identify each one. EG *He couldn't tell them apart.* PHRASAL VB : V+O+ADV, WITH MODAL, NO CONT

tell off. If you **tell** someone **off**, you speak to them angrily or seriously because they have done something wrong. EG *We don't want to get told off, do we?... ...and a cop would tell the noisy kids off.* PHRASAL VB : V+O+ADV

telling /tɛlɪŋ/. If something that you say is **telling**, **1** it is very important or relevant. EG *The lawyer made a brief, telling speech to the magistrate.* **2** it reveals thoughts or feelings that you were trying to hide. EG *He let slip a particularly telling remark.* ADJ QUALIT

telling-off, tellings-off. If you give someone a **telling-off**, you speak to them angrily about something foolish or wrong that they have done. EG *When she got back she would give him such a telling-off about that doll.* N COUNT

telltale /tɛlteɪl/. A **telltale** sign reveals information, often about something that is meant to be secret. EG *I was beginning to recognize the first telltale signs of panic.* ADJ CLASSIF : USU ATTRIB

telly /tɛli1/, **tellies.** A **telly** is the same as a television. EG *Dad was half asleep in front of a flickering telly... Did you see it on telly last night?* N COUNT OR N UNCOUNT Informal

temerity /tɪ2mɛrɪ1ti1/. If someone has the **temerity** to do something, they do it boldly and upset people who think that they should not have done it at all. EG *He had the temerity to suggest that a few of us should leave.* N UNCOUNT +SUPP

temp /tɛmp/, **temps.** A **temp** is a secretary who is employed by an agency that sends him or her to work for short periods of time in different offices, replacing secretaries who are ill or on holiday. N COUNT

temper /tɛmpə/, **tempers, tempering, tempered. 1** Your **temper** is **1.1** the tendency you have to become angry or to stay calm. EG *He had a most violent temper.* **1.2** the way you are feeling at a particular time, especially how cheerful or how angry you are. EG *She might come home in a better temper.* N COUNT OR N UNCOUNT; N COUNT OR N UNCOUNT +SUPP

2 If you are in a **temper**, you are extremely angry and cannot control your behaviour. EG *One day the man attacked me in a temper.* N SING : *a*+N, OR N UNCOUNT

3 If you **lose** your **temper**, you become very angry. EG *She suddenly lost her temper and left the room.* PHRASE

4 If someone or something **tempers** something, they make it less extreme or more acceptable. EG *Our delight was tempered by surprise... She tempered her approach to each child... Justice needs to be tempered with efficiency.* V+O Formal

temperament /tɛmpə0rəmə2nt/, **temperaments.** Your **temperament** is your character, which you show in your usual way of behaving or reacting in situations, for example whether you are calm, energetic, or violent. EG *He had a cheerful temperament... She was placid in temperament... They were gamblers by temperament.* N UNCOUNT OR N COUNT

temperamental /tɛmpə0rəmɛntə0l/. **1** Someone who is **temperamental** has moods that change often and suddenly. EG *...a temperamental Polish actress... The old men are pretty temperamental.* ADJ QUALIT

2 Temperamental features relate to the temperament a person has. EG *Many political and temperamental differences exist between them.* ADJ CLASSIF

◊ **temperamentally**. EG *My father wasn't temperamentally suited for business.* ◊ ADV

temperate /tɛmpə0rə1t/. A **temperate** place has weather that is never extremely hot or extremely cold. EG *...the temperate woodlands of Tasmania.* ADJ QUALIT

temperature /tɛmprə1tʃə/, **temperatures. 1** The **temperature** of something or the **temperature** in a place is how hot or cold it is. EG *...a sudden drop in temperature... ...a temperature of 10°C.* N COUNT OR N UNCOUNT

2 Your **temperature** is the temperature of your body. ● If someone **takes** your **temperature**, they use a thermometer to measure your temperature in order to see if you are ill. EG *I took her temperature and it was 40°C.* N COUNT; ● PHRASE

3 If you **have a temperature**, you are ill and your temperature is higher than it usually is. PHRASE

tempestuous /tɛmpɛstjʊəs/. Something or someone that is **tempestuous** is full of very strong emotions. EG *...a tempestuous love affair... He is such a wild and tempestuous character.* ADJ QUALIT

temple /tɛmpə0l/, **temples. 1** A **temple** is a building used for the worship of god in some religions. N COUNT

2 Your **temples** are the flat parts on each side of your forehead. EG *He felt the vein throb in his temple where Thomas had hit him.* N COUNT

tempo /tɛmpəʊ/, **tempos. 1** The **tempo** of an event is the speed at which it happens. EG *Events had been moving at an equally dramatic tempo.* N SING OR N UNCOUNT : USU+SUPP Formal

2 The **tempo** of a piece of music is the speed at which it is played. EG *In fact, considerable fluctuations of tempo are possible in a romantic piece.* N COUNT OR N UNCOUNT Technical

temporary /tɛmpə0rəri1/. Something that is **temporary** lasts for only a short time. EG *...my temporary absence from the saloon... There might be* ADJ CLASSIF

some temporary advantage... ...temporary jobs.
◇ **temporarily**. EG *She is temporarily in charge.* ◇ ADV

tempt /tɛmp[ə]t/, **tempts, tempting, tempted. 1** If you **tempt** someone, you offer them something that they want in order to encourage them to do something that you want them to do. EG *She tried to tempt him into eating some more... The building societies are offering higher rates of interest to tempt new savers.* V+O

2 If you say that you **are tempted** or **feel tempted** to do something, you mean that you want to do it, but you think it might be wrong or harmful. EG *I was tempted to call you last night, but I thought you'd probably be asleep.* PHRASE

3 If you say that someone **is tempting fate**, you mean that they are taking a foolish and unnecessary risk. PHRASE

temptation /tɛmp[ə]teɪʃ[ə]n/, **temptations. 1 Temptation** is the state you are in when you want to do or have something, although you know it might be wrong or harmful. EG *He had the strength to resist further temptation.* N UNCOUNT

2 A **temptation** is something that makes you want to do or have something, although you know it might be wrong or harmful. EG *...the temptations to which he was continually exposed.* N COUNT

tempting /tɛmp[ə]tɪŋ/. Something that is **tempting** makes you want to do or have something, although you know it might be wrong or harmful. EG *...an extremely tempting price... ...spicy vegetable cutlets, the smell of which was so tempting that they became hungry again.* ADJ QUALIT

ten /tɛn/ **tens. Ten** is the number 10: see the entry headed NUMBER. EG *It had been ten years since I left school.* NUMBER

tenacious /tɪ[2]neɪʃəs/. If you are **tenacious**, you are very determined and do not give up easily. EG *They kept a tenacious grip on their possessions... The working classes struggle in the most energetic, most tenacious way.* ◇ **tenacity** /tɪ[2]næsɪ[1]ti[1]/. EG *We respect their tenacity and courage.* ADJ QUALIT ◇ N UNCOUNT

tenancy /tɛnənsi[1]/, **tenancies. Tenancy** is the use of land or property belonging to someone else, for which you pay rent. EG *Once they took up the tenancy they couldn't be evicted... ...a three-year tenancy.* N UNCOUNT OR N COUNT

tenant /tɛnənt/, **tenants.** A **tenant** is someone who pays rent for the place they live in, or for land or buildings that they use. EG *...a tenant who pays rent direct to the landlord.* N COUNT

tend /tɛnd/, **tends, tending, tended. 1** If something **tends** to happen, it happens usually or often. EG *I tend to wake up early in the morning... Shopping lists on old envelopes tend to get lost.* V+*to*-INF

2 If you say that you **tend** to think something, you are giving your opinion in a hesitant or polite way. EG *I tend to think that's not a good solution.* V+*to*-INF

3 If you **tend** someone or something, you look after them very carefully. EG *She'd tended four very sick men... ...a young man who tended his crops well.* V+O Formal

tendency /tɛndənsi[1]/, **tendencies. 1** If there is a **tendency** for something, it starts happening more often or increases in intensity. EG *There is a growing tendency for people to opt out... ...a permanent tendency towards inflation.* N COUNT+SUPP

2 If you have a particular **tendency**, you often behave in a particular way because of your character. EG *I have a tendency to tease... The girl might have murderous tendencies.* N COUNT+SUPP

tender /tɛndə/, **tenderest; tenders, tendering, tendered. 1** Someone who is **tender** expresses gentle and caring feelings. EG *He gave her a tender smile.* ◇ **tenderly**. EG *She cradled the baby tenderly.* ◇ **tenderness**. EG *I have a feeling of great tenderness for you.* ADJ QUALIT ◇ ADV ◇ N UNCOUNT

2 If someone is at a **tender** age, they are young and inexperienced. ADJ QUALIT: ATTRIB

3 Meat that is **tender** is soft and easy to cut or chew. ADJ QUALIT

4 If a part of your body is **tender**, it hurts when you touch it, for example because it is injured. EG *...the tender, swollen side of his jaw.* ADJ QUALIT

5 A **tender** is a formal offer to supply goods or do a job for a particular price. EG *Tenders are to be submitted on 15 December at 10 a.m.* N COUNT Technical

6 If you **tender** a suggestion, an apology, or your resignation, you formally offer it. EG *Dr Mayfield has tendered his resignation.* V+O Formal

tendon /tɛnd[ə]n/, **tendons.** A **tendon** is a strong cord in your body which joins a muscle to a bone. N COUNT

tendril /tɛndrɪ[ə]l/, **tendrils. Tendrils** are short, thin stems which grow on some plants and attach themselves to walls, trees, or other plants. N COUNT: USU PLURAL

tenement /tɛnəmənt/, **tenements.** A **tenement** is a large building that is divided into a lot of small flats. Tenements are situated in a poor area of a city. N COUNT

tenet /tɛnɪ[1]t/, **tenets.** The **tenets** of a theory or belief are the principles on which it is based. EG *...one of the central tenets of capitalism... ...the basic tenets on which this chapter is based.* N COUNT: OFT+*of* Formal

tenner /tɛnə/, **tenners.** A **tenner** is ten pounds or a ten-pound note. EG *He's earning a tenner an hour.* N COUNT Informal

tennis /tɛnɪs/ is a game played by two or four players on a rectangular court. They use rackets to hit a ball over a net which is between them. EG *They've gone to play tennis in the park... ...a tennis court.* N UNCOUNT

tenor /tɛnə/, **tenors. 1** A **tenor** is a male singer whose voice is fairly high. EG *...'Roses of Picardy' sung by an Irish tenor.* ▸ used as an adjective. EG *...his pleasant tenor voice.* N COUNT ▸ ADJ CLASSIF

2 A **tenor** recorder, saxophone, or other musical instrument has a range of notes that are of a fairly low pitch. ADJ CLASSIF: ATTRIB

3 The **tenor** of something is the general meaning or mood that it expresses. EG *I forget the tenor of her reply... The whole tenor of his work was socialist.* N SING+SUPP Formal

tenpin bowling /tɛnpɪn bəʊlɪŋ/ is a game in which you try to knock down ten objects, called tenpins, by rolling a heavy ball towards them. N UNCOUNT

tense /tɛns/, **tenser, tensest; tenses, tensing, tensed. 1** If you are **tense**, you are worried and nervous and cannot relax. EG *They began to grow tense over the likelihood of a long delay.* ADJ QUALIT

2 If your body is **tense**, your muscles are tight and not relaxed. EG *Your neck is tense.* ADJ QUALIT

3 If you **tense**, or if your muscles **tense**, your muscles become tight and stiff. EG *The man on the terrace tensed slightly... 'What are you talking about?' I asked, the skin of my cheek-bones tensing up.* V-ERG: OFT+*up*

4 A **tense** situation or period of time is one that makes people anxious. EG *After a long, tense silence, he asked: 'What is your name?'... The situation was very tense; anything might happen.* ADJ QUALIT

5 The **tense** of a verb is the form which shows whether you are referring to the past, the present, or the future. EG *The present tense is 'I swim' or 'I am swimming'.* N COUNT OR N UNCOUNT

tensed up. If you are **tensed up**, you are nervous and unable to relax. EG *You've been so tensed up, you're ready to explode.* ADJ PRED

tension /tɛnʃ[ə]n/, **tensions. 1 Tension** is the feeling of fear or nervousness that is produced when something difficult, dangerous, or important is happening. EG *...the tension between the two countries... Family tensions are increasing... With tension in his voice he said he wanted to tell me something.* N UNCOUNT OR N PLURAL

2 The **tension** in a rope or wire is how tightly it is stretched, for example between two poles. EG *The loss of tension in the cables is a problem.* N UNCOUNT

Write down the two games that appear on these pages.

tent /tɛnt/, **tents.** A **tent** is a shelter made of canvas or nylon, which you sleep in when you are camping. It is held up by poles and ropes. EG *She pitched her tent in a field.* N COUNT

tentacle /tɛntəkəᵊl/, **tentacles.** The **tentacles** of an animal such as an octopus are the long, thin parts that it uses to feel and hold things, to catch food, and to move. EG *The jellyfish is fringed with stinging tentacles.* N COUNT: USU PLURAL

tentative /tɛntətɪv/. If you are **tentative**, you act or speak slowly and carefully because you are uncertain or afraid. EG *We are tentative about tackling these issues... Each step he took was slightly tentative.* ADJ QUALIT

tenterhooks /tɛntəhʊks/. If you are **on tenterhooks**, you are nervous and excited about something that is going to happen. EG *I was on tenterhooks to see who his passenger was... I will keep him on tenterhooks for just a little longer.* PHRASE

tenth /tɛnθ/, **tenths. 1** The **tenth** item in a series is the one that you count as number ten: see the entry headed NUMBER. EG *...the tenth day of the strike... ...the tenth programme in our series.* ORDINAL

2 A **tenth** is one of ten equal parts of something. EG *...a tenth of a second... The jar was about nine tenths full of leaves... His income is eight tenths of the average wage.* N COUNT: USU+*of*

tenuous /tɛnjuəs/. If an idea, connection, or reason is **tenuous**, it is so slight or weak that it may not really exist or may easily cease to exist. EG *There is only the most tenuous evidence for it... Their links with the school were tenuous... He struggled to maintain his tenuous hold on her.* ADJ QUALIT

tenure /tɛnjuᵊə/ is **1** the legal right to live in a place or to use land or buildings for a period of time. EG *They get tenure under the Rent Act.* N UNCOUNT **2** the period of time during which someone holds an important job in a government or other organization. EG *...the first week of his tenure of the Home Office.* N UNCOUNT: OFT+*of*

tepid /tɛpɪd/. **1** A liquid that is **tepid** is slightly warm. EG *...drinking tepid coffee... They lay their eggs in the shallow tepid pools.* ADJ CLASSIF

2 A feeling or reaction that is **tepid** lacks enthusiasm or liveliness. EG *Tepid applause greeted her efforts.* ADJ QUALIT

term /tɜːm/, **terms, terming, termed. 1** If you talk about something **in** particular **terms**, or **in terms of** a particular thing, you are specifying which aspect of it or whose view of it you are discussing. EG *Life is going to be a little easier in economic terms... He was talking in international terms... In Marxist terms, nationalism of this kind cannot last... In your terms the situation's got worse... A computer is powerful in terms of capacity and speed... These losses are not to be explained in terms of what happened last week.* PHRASE

2 If you are **thinking in terms of** doing something or **talking in terms of** doing it, you are considering doing it. EG *You should be thinking in terms of paying off your debts.* PHRASE

3 If you express something **in** particular **terms**, you express it using a particular type of language or in a way that shows clearly your attitude or feelings. EG *She condemned the decision in strong terms... Try to explain it in terms a small boy might understand.* PHRASE

4 A **term** is a word or expression that is used in relation to a particular subject. EG *He asked them what they understood by the term 'radical'... 'Habeas corpus' is a legal term.* • **contradiction in terms**: see **contradiction.** N COUNT: USU+SUPP

5 You can use **term** to say what someone calls something or what their opinion of it is. EG *...recent breakthroughs in what might be termed 'birth technology'... The press termed the visit a triumph.* V+O+C

6 A **term** is also **6.1** one of the periods of time that each year is divided into at a school or college. EG *...the spring term... It was the first week of term.* N COUNT OR N UNCOUNT **6.2** a period of time during which a particular political party, prime minister, or president is in power. EG *...Baldwin's second term of office as Premier.* N COUNT+SUPP **6.3** a period of time spent doing a particular job or in a particular place. EG *He has just been sentenced to a long prison term.* N COUNT+SUPP

7 If you talk about 'the **long term**' or 'the **short term**', you are talking about what will happen over a long or short period of time in the future. EG *Such a policy would be economically disastrous in the long term... These are only short-term solutions.* PHRASE

8 The **terms** of an agreement or arrangement are the conditions that have been accepted by the people involved in it. EG *We will not accept these terms... They finally agreed to the Bill on the President's terms.* N PLURAL

9 If two people are treated **on the same terms** or **on equal terms**, they are treated in exactly the same way. EG *They decided to let women be conscripted on the same terms as men.* PHRASE

10 If two people are **on** good **terms** or **on** friendly **terms**, they are friendly towards each other. EG *You need to be on friendly terms with him... They were on Christian-name terms.* • **on speaking terms**: see **speak.** PHRASE

11 If you **come to terms with** something difficult or unpleasant, you learn to accept it. EG *He has come to terms with death.* PHRASE

terminal /tɜːmɪnəᵊl/, **terminals. 1** A **terminal** illness or disease causes death gradually and cannot be cured. ADJ CLASSIF

2 A **terminal** patient is dying of a terminal illness or disease. ADJ CLASSIF: ATTRIB

3 A **terminal** is a place where vehicles, passengers, or goods begin or end a journey. EG *...a bus terminal... ...oil terminals.* N COUNT: USU+SUPP

4 A computer **terminal** is a piece of equipment, usually a keyboard and a VDU, that you use to put information into a computer or to obtain information from it. EG *...terminals giving access to larger computers.* N COUNT

terminate /tɜːmɪneɪt/, **terminates, terminating, terminated. 1** When you **terminate** something or when it **terminates**, it ends completely. EG *I thought that he would terminate the discussion then and there... We are confident that the case will terminate with two words: 'Not guilty.'* V-ERG Formal

◇ **termination** /tɜːmɪneɪʃəᵊn/. EG *...the termination of their romance.* ◇ N UNCOUNT

2 When a train or bus **terminates** somewhere, it ends its journey there. V+A Formal

terminology /tɜːmɪnɒlədʒiˡ/, **terminologies.** The **terminology** of a subject is the set of special words and expressions used in connection with it. EG *The author uses Marxist terminology.* N UNCOUNT OR N COUNT

terminus /tɜːmɪnəs/, **terminuses.** A **terminus** is a large railway station or bus station where several routes begin and end. EG *He had waited near the terminus until the last bus had come in.* N COUNT

termite /tɜːmaɪt/, **termites. Termites** are small white insects that eat wood. They live in hot countries in nests made of earth. N COUNT: USU PLURAL

terrace /tɛrəˡs/, **terraces. 1** A **terrace** is a row of similar houses joined together by their side walls. EG *...a house in a fashionable terrace.* N COUNT British

2 A **terrace** is also **2.1** a flat area of stone or grass next to a building, where people can sit or eat meals. EG *He wandered out onto the terrace.* N COUNT **2.2** one of a series of flat areas of ground built like steps on a hillside so that crops can be grown there. EG *...the landscape with its terraces of vines and olives.* N COUNT: USU PLURAL

3 The **terraces** at a football ground are wide steps that people stand on when they are watching a game. EG *...on the terraces of football clubs.* N PLURAL: *the*+N

terraced /tɛrəˡst/. **1** A **terraced** hillside has flat areas of ground like steps built on it so that people can grow crops there. EG *...the forests and terraced vineyards.* ADJ CLASSIF

2 A **terraced** house is one of a row of similar houses that are joined together by their side walls. EG *...an ordinary terraced house in the East End of London.* ADJ CLASSIF British

terrain /tɛreɪn/. The **terrain** in an area is the type of land there, especially the physical features of the land. EG *The commander made a detailed study of the terrain... The terrain was bare and flat... ...hilly terrain.* N UNCOUNT +SUPP

terrapin /tɛrəpɪn/, **terrapins.** A **terrapin** is a small turtle. N COUNT

terrible /tɛrə'bə^{0}l/. **1** A **terrible** experience or situation is very serious and unpleasant. EG *It was a terrible accident, but we did not panic.* ADJ QUALIT

2 If you feel **terrible**, you feel very ill, or feel a very strong and unpleasant emotion. EG *...a terrible sense of guilt.* ADJ QUALIT

3 You describe something as **terrible** when you think that it is very bad or poor quality. EG *I've had a terrible day at the office... ...terrible weather... The food was terrible.* ADJ QUALIT

4 You also use **terrible** to emphasize the great degree or extent of something. EG *I've been a terrible fool... It's a terrible waste of their talents.* ADJ CLASSIF : ATTRIB

terribly /tɛrə'bli^1/. You use **terribly** to emphasize the extent or degree of something. EG *I'm terribly sorry... It's terribly important... It gets terribly cold at night.* SUBMOD Informal

terrier /tɛrɪə/, **terriers.** A **terrier** is a type of small dog. N COUNT

terrific /tərɪfɪk/. **1** If you say that something is **terrific**, you mean that you are very pleased with it or are very impressed by it. EG *Our new carpet looks terrific.* ADJ CLASSIF Informal

2 **Terrific** also means very great in amount, degree, or intensity. EG *...a terrific thunderstorm... ...a terrific amount of money.* ADJ CLASSIF : ATTRIB

terrify /tɛrɪfaɪ/, **terrifies, terrifying, terrified.** If something **terrifies** you, it makes you feel extremely frightened. EG *Rats terrify me.* V+O
◇ **terrifying.** EG *The most terrifying aspect of nuclear bombing is radiation.* ◇ ADJ QUALIT ◇ **terrified.** EG *My sister was too terrified to cry.* ◇ ADJ QUALIT

territorial /tɛrɪtɔːrɪəl/ means concerned with the ownership of a particular area of land or water. EG *...territorial boundaries.* ADJ CLASSIF : ATTRIB

territory /tɛrɪtə^{0}ri^1/, **territories. 1** The **territory** of a country is the land that it controls. EG *This meeting is to be held on neutral territory... ...the French territories on the East coast.* N UNCOUNT OR N COUNT : OFT+SUPP

2 **Territory** is land that has a particular character. EG *We were passing through mountainous territory.* N UNCOUNT +SUPP

3 You can use **territory** to refer to an area of knowledge or experience. EG *All this is familiar territory to readers of her recent novels.* N UNCOUNT +SUPP

terror /tɛrə/, **terrors. 1 Terror** is very great fear. EG *She awakened in terror as the flaming roof came crashing down.* N UNCOUNT

2 A **terror** is something that makes you very frightened. EG *They suffered untold terrors in the dark.* N COUNT

terrorise /tɛrəraɪz/. See **terrorize.**

terrorism /tɛrərɪzə^{0}m/ is the use of violence, especially murder, kidnapping, and bombing, in order to achieve political aims or to influence a government. EG *These measures failed to bring acts of terrorism to an end.* N UNCOUNT ◇ **terrorist** /tɛrərɪst/, **terrorists.** EG *They have given aid to terrorists... She is in prison for terrorist activities.* ◇ N COUNT

terrorize /tɛrəraɪz/, **terrorizes, terrorizing, terrorized;** also spelled **terrorise.** If someone **terrorizes** you, they keep you in a state of fear by using threats or violence. EG *Lee was a bully who terrorized us all.* V+O

terror-stricken. If you are **terror-stricken** or **terror-struck**, you are extremely frightened. EG *...terror-stricken women and children.* ADJ CLASSIF

terse /tɜːs/, **terser, tersest.** A **terse** comment or statement is brief and rather unfriendly. EG *I received a terse and unsympathetic reply... ...the terse message: 'Do not touch'.* ADJ QUALIT

TESL /tɛsə^{0}l/ is the teaching of English to students whose first language is not English, but who live in an English-speaking country or need to use English for their education or job. **TESL** is an abbreviation for 'teaching English as a second language'. N UNCOUNT

test /tɛst/, **tests, testing, tested. 1** When you **test** something, you try it, for example by touching it or using it for a short time, in order to find out what it is, what condition it is in, or how well it works. EG *He tested the water with one toe. 'It's hot!'... The BBC in Scotland wanted to test the range of their transmitters... A number of new techniques were tested.* V+O

2 If you **test** someone, you ask them questions to find out how much they know about something. EG *I will test you on your knowledge of French.* V+O : OFT+on

3 A **test** is a deliberate action or experiment to find out whether something works. EG *They proved it by several tests... ...an underground nuclear test.* N COUNT

4 If an event or situation is a **test** of a person or thing, it reveals their qualities or effectiveness. EG *...the first major test of the President's policies.* N COUNT : OFT+of

5 A **test** is also an examination consisting of a set of questions or tasks, which is intended to measure your knowledge or skill. EG *...a mathematics test... He hadn't passed the test.* N COUNT

6 A medical **test** is an examination of a part of your body in order to make sure that it is healthy or to find out what is making you ill. EG *...a blood test... They rushed her to a hospital for tests.* N COUNT

7 If you **put** something **to the test**, you find out how useful or effective it is by using it. EG *The idea is being put to the test in a theatre in Paris.* PHRASE

8 an acid test: see **acid.**

testament /tɛstəmə^{2}nt/, **testaments.** If one thing is a **testament** to another thing, it shows clearly that the other thing exists or is true. EG *The building is a testament to their success.* • See also **New Testament, Old Testament.** N COUNT : OFT+to Formal

test case, test cases. A **test case** is a legal case in a court of law which establishes an important principle that can then be used in other cases. N COUNT

testicle /tɛstɪkə^{0}l/, **testicles.** A man's **testicles** are the two sex glands that produce sperm. N COUNT

testify /tɛstɪfaɪ/, **testifies, testifying, testified.**
1 When someone **testifies**, they make a formal statement, especially a statement in a court of law. EG *None of the victims would appear in court to testify against him... Witnesses testify to his attempts at rape.* V : OFT+A OR V+REPORT : ONLY that Formal

2 If something **testifies** to an idea, it shows that the idea is likely to be true. EG *All kinds of human experience testify to the close link between love and fear.* V : OFT+to Formal

testimonial /tɛstɪməʊnɪəl/, **testimonials.** A **testimonial** is a statement saying how good someone or something is, usually a statement made by someone in authority. N COUNT

testimony /tɛstɪməni^1/, **testimonies. 1** A person's **testimony** is a formal statement that they make, especially in a court of law. EG *...the angry testimony of injured wives.* N UNCOUNT OR N COUNT

2 If one thing is a **testimony** to another thing, it shows clearly that the other thing exists or is true. EG *This is spectacular testimony to the computer's creative powers.* N UNCOUNT+to Formal

Test match, Test matches. A **Test match** is a cricket or rubgy match that is one of a series played between the same two countries. EG *...the fourth Test match between England and Australia.* N COUNT

If something is terrific, does it terrify you?

test tube

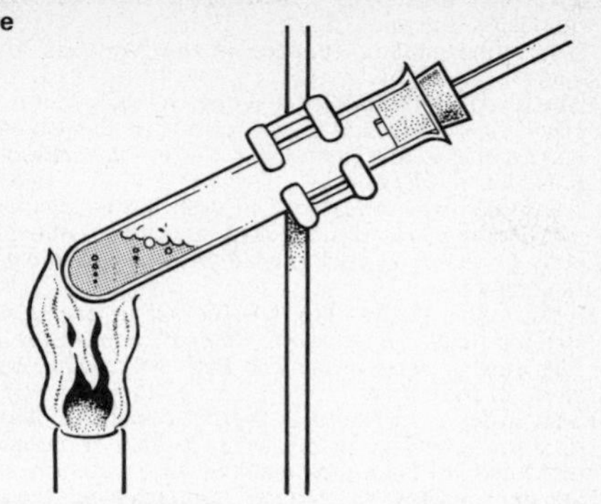

test tube, test tubes. A **test tube** is a small glass container that is used in chemical experiments. N COUNT

test-tube baby, test-tube babies. A **test-tube baby** is a baby that develops from an egg which has been removed from the mother's body, fertilized, and then replaced in her womb. N COUNT

tetanus /tɛtəⁿnəs/ is a serious and painful disease caused by germs getting into wounds. It makes your muscles, especially your jaw muscles, go stiff. N UNCOUNT

tether /tɛðə/, **tethers, tethering, tethered. 1** If you **tether** an animal, you tie it to a post. V+O

2 If you say that you are **at the end of** your **tether**, you mean that you are extremely tired or unhappy and cannot cope with your problems or make any more effort. PHRASE

text /tɛkst/, **texts. 1** The **text** of a book is the main written part of it, rather than the introduction, pictures, or index. EG *The excellent photographs in this book did a lot to amplify the text.* N SING: *the*+N

2 Text is any written material. EG *These machines have the capacity to 'read' printed text.* N UNCOUNT

3 The **text** of a speech or interview is the written version of it. N COUNT: OFT+*of*

4 A **text** is a book or other piece of writing connected with an academic subject or used for a school or college examination. EG *...a text on Oriental philosophy... We're supposed to discuss a text we've been assigned.* N COUNT

textbook /tɛkstbʊk/, **textbooks.** A **textbook** is a book about a particular subject that is intended for students to use. EG *...a history textbook.* N COUNT

textile /tɛkstaɪl/, **textiles. 1** A **textile** is a woven cloth or fabric. EG *The designers have created a new textile... ...a textile factory.* N COUNT

2 Textiles are the industries concerned with making cloth. EG *There are still more people employed in textiles than in computers.* N PLURAL

texture /tɛkstʃə/, **textures.** The **texture** of something is the way that it feels when you touch it, for example how smooth or rough it is. EG *...the slightly rough texture of the cloth.* N UNCOUNT OR N COUNT

-th. You add **-th** to numbers written in figures and ending in 4, 5, 6, 7, 8, 9, 0, 11, 12, or 13 in order to form ordinal numbers. These numbers are pronounced as if they were written as words. For example, 7th is pronounced the same as 'seventh'. EG *...6th June 1982... ...48th Street... ...the 124th Psalm.* SUFFIX

than; usually pronounced /ðən/, but pronounced /ðæn/when you are emphasizing it. **1** You use **than** to link two parts of a comparison. EG *You've got more money than me... She was older than I was... She was fatter than when he last saw her... We talked for more than an hour... ...temperatures lower than 25 degrees.* PREP OR CONJ: AFTER COMPAR

2 You also use **than** in order to link two parts of a contrast. EG *He chose the stairs rather than the lift... She likes to keep things rather than throw them away... I'd rather starve than ask for a penny... I would sooner read than watch television.* PREP OR CONJ

thank /θæŋk/, **thanks, thanking, thanked. 1** You say **thanks** or **thank you** to express your gratitude to someone for something they have done, said, or given you. EG *Thank you very much indeed for coming to see me... Many thanks for your long and interesting letter... 'What'll you have, Castle? A whisky?' – 'A small one, thank you.'... 'Do you want a biscuit?' – 'No thanks.'... 'How are you?' – 'Fine, thanks.'* CONVENTION

2 When you **thank** someone, you express your gratitude to them for something. EG *He thanked me for bringing the books... 'Have a good time,' he said. She smiled at him, thanked him, and drove off.* V+O

3 When you express your **thanks** to someone, you express your gratitude to them for something. EG *He sent a letter of thanks to Haldane.* N PLURAL

4 Thank is used in these phrases. **4.1** You say **thank God, thank goodness** or **thank heavens** when you are very relieved about something. EG *Thank goodness it only lasts an hour.* CONVENTION **4.2** If you say that something happens **thanks to** someone or something, you mean that they caused it to happen. EG *Thanks to him I began to learn to trust my feelings... The building became very well known, thanks to detective films.* PREP

thankful /θæŋkfʊl/. When you are **thankful**, you are very happy and relieved that something has happened. EG *We were thankful that it was all over.* ADJ PRED

thankless /θæŋklɪ²s/. A **thankless** job or task involves doing a lot of hard work that other people do not notice or appreciate. EG *She used to take on thankless jobs like running school dances.* ADJ QUALIT: ATTRIB

Thanksgiving /θæŋksgɪvɪŋ/. **Thanksgiving** or **Thanksgiving Day** is a public holiday in the United States and Canada in the autumn. It was originally a day when people celebrated the end of the harvest and thanked God for it. EG *...the week after Thanksgiving... We always had turkey for our Thanksgiving meal.* N UNCOUNT

that /ðæt, ðə³t/, **those** /ðəʊz/. The pronunciation /ðə³t/ can only be used for paragraphs 3 and 4.

1 You use **that** or **those** to refer to things or people already mentioned or known about. EG *That old woman saved my life... Not all crimes are committed for those reasons... Who are those men?... 'Did you see him?' – 'No.' – 'That's a pity.'... Hello. Is that Mrs Vass? I'm phoning about your car.* DET OR PRON

2 You can use **those** to refer to people or things that you are going to give details about. EG *I want to thank those of you who've offered to help... The scheme was set up to help those concerned with the teaching of reading... Students should write off to those bodies which provide awards.* PRON OR DET

3 You use **that** after some verbs, nouns, and adjectives in order to introduce a clause. EG *She suggested that I telephoned you... He was motivated by the conviction that these tendencies would increase... It is important that you should know precisely what is needed.* CONJ

4 You also use **that** to introduce a relative clause. EG *I reached the gate that opened onto the lake... For dessert there was ice cream that Mum had made herself.* PRON REL

5 If you say that something is not **that** bad or not **that** funny, for example, you mean that it is not as bad or as funny as other people think. EG *It isn't quite that bad.* SUBMOD: WITH BROAD NEG

6 You use **at that** when you are modifying or limiting what you have previously said. EG *There is work for only 250 people, and a very specialized 250 at that.* PHRASE

7 You use **that is** or **that is to say** when you are giving further details about something. EG *It deals with matters of social policy; that is to say, everything from housing to education.* PHRASE

8 You use **that's it** to indicate that nothing more PHRASE

needs to be done or that the end has been reached. EG *They get a direct grant of a sum of money and that's it... 'I quit,' I said. 'That's it. Finish.'*
9 You use **that's that** to say there is nothing more you can do or say about a particular matter. EG *It was an accident, and that's that... The Ravenscrofts refused and that was that.* PHRASE
10 this and that: see **this**.

thatched /θætʃt/. A **thatched** house or one with a **thatched** roof has a roof made of straw or reeds. EG *...a three-hundred-year old thatched cottage... ...mud huts with thatched roofs.* ADJ CLASSIF : ATTRIB

that's /ðæts/ is a spoken form of 'that is'.

thaw /θɔ:/, **thaws, thawing, thawed. 1** When ice or snow **thaws**, it melts. EG *The snow soon thawed and they all went out for a walk... The ice was thawed by the warm wind.* V-ERG
2 A **thaw** is a period of warmer weather, usually at the end of winter, when the snow and ice melts. EG *A thaw had set in and the streets were slushy.* N COUNT : USU SING
3 When you **thaw** frozen food, you take it out of a freezer and leave it in a place where it can warm up so that it is ready for cooking or eating. EG *Unwrap the pastry and then thaw it overnight.* V+O
4 When unfriendly people or unfriendly relationships **thaw**, they start to be more friendly. EG *The Vatican indicated that it might be thawing and accepting the critics' argument.* V-ERG

the; usually pronounced /ðə/ before a consonant and /ði[1]/ before a vowel, but pronounced /ði:/ when you are emphasizing it.
1 You use **the** at the beginning of noun groups to refer to a person or thing that is known about, that has just been mentioned, or that you are going to give details about. EG *The sea was really rough... ...Her Majesty the Queen... He said that she ought to see the doctor... He took Sam by the hand... Do you play the violin?... ...the waiter with the droopy moustache... I think I'll keep the information to myself... They continued walking on the opposite pavement... Another mineral was named by the scientist who first examined it.* DET
2 You can also use **the** in front of a singular noun to refer to all the people or things of that type. EG *The koala bear is a medium-sized creature that lives in trees.* DET
3 You can use **the** in front of a surname in the plural to refer to a married couple or to a whole family who have that surname. EG *...some friends of hers called the Hochstadts.* DET
4 You use **the** in front of an adjective to make it a noun that refers to someone or something that the adjective describes. EG *...institutions for the mentally handicapped... ...the British and the French... The wounded were given first aid... Don't you think that perhaps you're wanting the impossible?* DET
5 You can use **the** in front of ordinal numbers, especially in dates. EG *...Tuesday, May the thirteenth.* DET
6 You use **the** in front of numbers when they refer to decades. EG *...in Stockholm in the thirties.* DET
7 You use **the** in front of two comparative adjectives or adverbs when you are describing how one amount or quality changes in relation to another. EG *The more I hear about him, the less I like him... The longer we look at it the more interesting we find it.* DET
8 You can emphasize **the** to indicate that something or someone is the most famous, most important, or best thing of their kind. EG *It's the club in town.* DET

theatre /θɪətə/, **theatres;** also spelled **theater** in American English. **1** A **theatre** is a building with a stage on which plays and other entertainments are performed. EG *...the new Arnold Wesker play at the National Theatre... Her mother never went to the theatre.* N COUNT
2 You can use the **theatre** to refer to work in the theatre, including acting in, producing, and writing plays. EG *She was only really happy when she was working in the theatre.* N SING : *the*+N
3 In a hospital, a **theatre** is the same as an operating theatre. N COUNT

theatrical /θi[1]ætrɪkə[0]l/. **1** A **theatrical** event or production is one that is performed in a theatre or that relates to the theatre. EG *...posters advertising theatrical productions.* ADJ CLASSIF : ATTRIB
2 You can use **theatrical** to describe behaviour that is exaggerated, unnatural, and done deliberately for effect. EG *Jack moved forward with theatrical caution.* ADJ QUALIT : ATTRIB

theft /θeft/, **thefts. Theft** is the act or crime of stealing. EG *He reported the theft of his passport... The drop in petty crime and theft will mean less work for the police.* N COUNT OR N UNCOUNT

their /ðεə/. **1** You use **their** to indicate that something belongs or relates to people or things that have just been mentioned or whose identity is known. See **they**. EG *...the car companies and their workers... Don't hope to change anyone or their attitudes.* DET POSS
2 You also use **their** with some titles when you are referring to people with that title. EG *Their Lordships were already late for dinner.*

theirs /ðεəz/. You use **theirs** to indicate that something belongs or relates to people or things that have just been mentioned or whose identity is known. EG *It was his fault, not theirs... They were off to visit a friend of theirs.* PRON POSS

them /ðem, ðəm/ is used as the object of a verb or preposition. You use **them** to refer to people or things that have just been mentioned or whose identity is known. EG *He took off his glasses and put them in his pocket... Smith harangued his fellow students and persuaded them that they must support the strike... If I think someone may attempt to take an overdose, I will spend hours talking to them.* PRON

theme /θi:m/, **themes. 1** A **theme** in a discussion or lecture is a main idea or subject in it. EG *...organised public meetings on the theme: 'Law not War'... We shall return to this theme in chapter 7.* N COUNT
2 A **theme** in an artist's work or in a work of literature is an idea in it that an artist or writer develops or repeats. EG *The main theme of the play was clear.* N COUNT
3 In music, a **theme** is a short simple tune on which a piece of music is based. EG *...variations on a theme.* N COUNT
4 A **theme** is also a tune that is played at the beginning and end of a television or radio programme. N COUNT
5 A **theme** song or **theme** tune is a song or tune which is played several times in a film or a musical and which expresses its general mood or is associated with a particular character in it. ADJ CLASSIF : ATTRIB

themselves /ðə[2]mselvz/. **1** You use **themselves** as the object of a verb or preposition when it refers to the same people or things as the subject of the clause or a previous object in the clause. EG *They are trying to educate themselves... They had ceased to think of themselves as rebels.* PRON REFL : PLURAL
2 You also use **themselves** to emphasize the subject or object of a clause, and to make it clear who or what you are referring to. EG *Let's turn to the books themselves... ...a cultural preference on the part of the Chinese themselves.* PRON REFL : PLURAL
3 If people do something **themselves**, they do it without any help from anyone else. EG *They must settle it themselves and get their own solutions.* PRON REFL : PLURAL

then /ðen/. **1 Then** means at a particular time in the past or in the future. EG *I didn't have it then... The situation's changed since then... I'm going to see him at lunchtime. He's busy till then.* ADV

What phrase on these pages means 'approximately'?

2 You use **then** to say that one thing happens after another, or is after another in a list. EG *He went to the village school, then to the grammar school, and then to the university... It didn't hurt at first, but then I realized you could die from a cut like that.* ADV

3 You use **then** in conversation **3.1** to link what you say to something that has just been said. EG *'Have some more cake.' – 'Oh all right then.'.. 'Are you a student?' – 'No, I'm not' – 'What do you do then?'* **3.2** at the end of a topic or at the end of a conversation. EG *Well, that's settled, then... Bye then.* **3.3** after words like 'now', 'well' and 'okay', to draw attention to what you are about to say. EG *Now then, it's time you went to bed.* ADV SEN

4 You use **then** to introduce a summary of what you have said or the conclusion that you are drawing from it. EG *These then are some of the feelings which may occur... Democracy, then, is a form of government.* ADV SEN

5 You can use **then** to introduce the second part of a sentence which begins with 'if'. EG *If any questions do occur to you, then don't hesitate to write.* ADV SEN

6 You use **then** at the beginning of a sentence or after 'and' or 'but' to introduce a comment or an extra piece of information to what you have already said. EG *Then there could be a tax problem... Iron would do the job much better. But then you can't weld iron so easily.* ADV SEN

7 now and then: see **now.** • **there and then:** see **there.**

thence /ðɛns/ means from the place that has just been mentioned. EG *He hitched south towards Italy, and thence into France.* ADV Formal Outdated

theologian /θɪəlәʊdʒɪən/, **theologians.** A **theologian** is someone who studies religion and God. N COUNT

theology /θi^{1}ɒlədʒi^1/ is the study of religion and God. EG *...a diploma in theology.* N UNCOUNT ◇ **theological** /θɪəlɒdʒɪkə^{0}l/. EG *...a theological college.* ◇ ADJ CLASSIF

theorem /θɪərə^{0}m/, **theorems.** A **theorem** is a statement in mathematics that can be proved to be true by reasoning. EG *...the theorem of Pythagoras... ...a book about the attempts to prove Fermat's last theorem.* N COUNT

theoretical /θɪərɛtɪkə^{0}l/ means based on or concerning the ideas and abstract principles of a subject, rather than the practical aspects of it. EG *...theoretical biology... ...theoretical ideas which, in practice, may not work.* ADJ CLASSIF : ATTRIB

theoretically /θɪərɛtɪkə^{0}li^1/. You use **theoretically** to say that although something is supposed to happen or to be the case, it may not in fact happen or be the case. EG *Laws still theoretically controlled the availability of alcohol... It was theoretically possible to get permission from the council.* ADV OR ADV SEN

theorize /θɪəraɪz/, **theorizes, theorizing, theorized;** also spelled **theorise.** If you **theorize** about something, you develop ideas about it in order to try and explain it. EG *...people who theorize about teaching methods... As leisure increases, they theorized, families will spend more time together.* V : USU+*about*

theory /θɪəri^1/, **theories. 1** A **theory** is an idea or set of ideas that is intended to explain something. EG *Darwin spent more than twenty years working on his theory of evolution... Mary is full of fascinating theories about men and women.* N COUNT : OFT+SUPP

2 Theory is **2.1** the set of ideas that relate to a particular subject. EG *...Marxist economic theory.* **2.2** the set of rules and principles that a practical method or skill is based on. EG *...the theory and practice of inoculation.* N UNCOUNT : OFT+SUPP

3 You use **in theory** to say that although something is supposed to happen or to be the case, it may not in fact happen or be the case. EG *In theory all British citizens are eligible for this.* ADV SEN

therapeutic /θɛrəpjuːtɪk/. **1** If something is **therapeutic**, it helps you to feel happier and more relaxed. EG *All that fresh air is very therapeutic.* ADJ QUALIT

2 In medicine, **therapeutic** treatment is designed to treat a disease or to improve a person's health. ADJ CLASSIF

therapist /θɛrəpɪst/, **therapists.** A **therapist** is a person skilled in a particular type of therapy, especially psychotherapy. EG *...a speech therapist.* N COUNT

therapy /θɛrəpi^1/ is the treatment of mental or physical illness, often without the use of drugs or operations. EG *...a short course of heat therapy.* N UNCOUNT

there /ðɛə/. **1** You use **there** as the subject of the verb 'be' to say that something exists or does not exist, or to draw attention to it. EG *There was a new cushion on one of the settees... There must be a reason... There's no inspection service, is there?* PRON

2 You use **there** in front of a verb to emphasize its meaning. The subject of the verb is placed after the verb. EG *Beside them there curls up a twist of blue smoke... There still remains the point about creativity.* PRON Literary Formal

3 If something is **there**, it exists or is available. EG *We talked about reality, about whether things are really there... The problem is still there... The play group is there for the children of staff and students.* ADV : USU AFTER *be*

4 You use **there** to refer to a place that has already been mentioned. EG *I must get home. Bill's there on his own... I walked two miles there and back.* ADV AFTER VB

5 You say **there** to indicate a place that you are pointing to or looking at. EG *'Over there,' she said and pointed to the door... Where's the ball? Oh, there it is.* ADV

6 You use **there** when speaking on the telephone to ask if someone is available to speak to you. EG *Is Jane there, please?* ADV

7 You use **there** to refer to **7.1** a point in a conversation, or an idea that someone has put forward. EG *Could I interrupt you just there?... You're right there Howard.* **7.2** a stage reached in an activity or process. EG *I'll write to the headmaster and then take the matter from there... The man who wants to be president will do anything to get there.* ADV

8 If you say that someone is **not all there**, you mean that they are stupid or not mentally alert. PHRASE Informal

9 If something happens **there and then** or **then and there**, it happens immediately. EG *He terminated the discussion then and there.* PHRASE

10 You say **'There you are'** or **'There you go'** **10.1** when accepting that an unsatisfactory situation cannot be changed. EG *It wasn't a very good reason for refusing, but there you are.* **10.2** when emphasizing that something proves that you were right. EG *There you are, Mabel! What did I tell you?* **10.3** when offering something to someone. EG *'There you are' he said, handing the screws to me.* CONVENTION

11 You can add **'so there'** to what you are saying to show that you have made a firm decision and will not change your mind. EG *Well, I won't apologize, so there.* CONVENTION Informal

12 You can say **'There there'** when comforting a child who is very upset. EG *There, there, it's not your fault.* CONVENTION

thereabouts /ðɛərəbaʊts/. You can add **or thereabouts** after a number to indicate that it is only approximate. EG *Inflation could be down to 8 per cent or thereabouts... It was in 1982 or thereabouts.* PHRASE

thereafter /ðɛərɑːftə/ means after the event or date mentioned. EG *We first met in 1966 and I saw him quite often thereafter.* ADV Formal

thereby /ðɛəbaɪ/ means as an inevitable result of the event or action mentioned. EG *The President had lied and thereby obstructed justice.* ADV SEN Formal

therefore /ðɛəfɔː/. You use **therefore** to introduce a conclusion that you are making. EG *We have a growing population and therefore we need more food... The new car is smaller and therefore cheaper.* ADV SEN

therein /ðɛərɪn/ means in the place or because of the situation just mentioned. EG *...the lakes and the fish therein... He was not a snob, you see. And therein lay his downfall.* ADV Formal

thereupon /ðɛərɔpɒn/ means immediately after an event and usually as a result of it. EG *I flung a few copies of the report in his lap, which thereupon fell to the floor.* ADV Formal

thermal /θɜːməºl/. **1 Thermal** means relating to heat or caused by heat. EG *...the thermal efficiency of an engine... ...thermal energy.* ADJ CLASSIF : ATTRIB

2 Thermal clothes are specially designed to keep you warm in cold weather. EG *...thermal underwear.* ADJ CLASSIF : ATTRIB

thermometer /θəmɒmɪtə/, **thermometers.** A **thermometer** is an instrument for measuring the temperature of a room or of a person's body. It usually consists of a narrow glass tube containing a thin column of mercury which rises and falls as the temperature rises and falls. EG *The thermometer reads 92 degrees... ...a clinical thermometer.* N COUNT

Thermos /θɜːməs/, **Thermoses.** A **Thermos** or a **Thermos flask** is a container which is used to keep hot drinks hot and cold drinks cold. N COUNT Trademark

thermostat /θɜːməstæt/, **thermostats.** A **thermostat** is a device that controls the temperature of a car engine or a house, for example, by switching the cooling or heating system on and off. N COUNT

thesaurus /θɪ²sɔːrəs/, **thesauruses.** A **thesaurus** is a reference book in which words with similar meanings are grouped together. EG *...the new Collins School Thesaurus.* N COUNT

these /ðiːz/ is the plural of **this.**

thesis /θiːsɪs/, **theses** /θiːsiːz/. **1** A **thesis** is an idea or theory that is expressed as a statement and is discussed in a logical way. EG *It is my thesis that Australia underwent fundamental changes in the 1920s.* N COUNT

2 A **thesis** is also a long piece of writing, based on your own research, that you do as part of a university degree, especially a Ph.D. EG *He is writing a thesis on the novels of Jane Austen.* N COUNT

they /ðeɪ/ is used as the subject of a verb. You use **they** **1** to refer to people or things that have just been mentioned or whose identity is known. EG *All universities have chancellors. They are always rather senior people.* **2** to refer to people in general, or to a group of people whose identity is not actually stated. EG *They found the body in a dustbin.* **3** instead of 'he' or 'she' to refer to a person whose sex is not known or not stated. Some people consider this use to be incorrect. EG *Nearly everybody thinks they're middle class... I was going to stay with a friend, but they were ill.* PRON : PLURAL

they'd /ðeɪd/. **1 They'd** is a spoken form of 'they had', especially when 'had' is an auxiliary verb. EG *They said they'd read it all before.*

2 They'd is also a spoken form of 'they would'. EG *I wish they'd publish more books like this.*

they'll /ðeɪəºl/ is the usual spoken form of 'they will'. EG *They'll probably sell it cheaper.*

they're /ðɛə, ðeɪə/ is the usual spoken form of 'they are'. EG *They're not interested.*

they've /ðeɪv/ is the usual spoken form of 'they have', especially when 'have' is an auxiliary verb. EG *They've been studying very hard.*

thick /θɪk/, **thicker, thickest. 1** Something that is **thick** has a large distance between its two opposite surfaces. EG *...thick slices of bread... We were separated by thick concrete walls... ...a thick sweater... Last winter the snow lay thick on the ground.* ADJ QUALIT OR ADV
◊ **thickly.** EG *She buttered my bread thickly.* ◊ ADV

2 If something that consists of several things is **thick**, the things in it are present in large quantities and are grouped very closely together. EG *She had a lot of thick black hair... They were on the edge of the thick forest... She came out of the thickest part of the crowd.* ◊ **thickly.** EG *Plants and trees grew thickly on both sides of the river.* ADJ QUALIT ◊ ADV

3 You use **thick** to say what the width or depth of something is. EG *The tree was one foot thick at the base... Her arms and legs were as thick as trees.* ADJ QUALIT
◊ **thickness.** EG *Insert a new wire of the same thickness and wind it round the screws.* ◊ N UNCOUNT

4 If you say that someone is **thick**, you mean that they are stupid or slow to understand things. EG *He's a bit thick... They were too thick to notice it.* ADJ QUALIT Informal

5 Liquids that are **thick** contain very little water and do not flow easily. EG *The chef has made the sauce too thick... ...thick cream.* ADJ QUALIT

6 Smoke or fog that is **thick** is difficult to see through. EG *The fog seemed to be getting thicker.* ADJ QUALIT

7 If someone's voice is **thick**, they are not speaking clearly, for example because they are ill, upset, or drunk. EG *His voice sounded blurred and thick.* ADJ QUALIT
◊ **thickly.** EG *'Let's get out of here,' Tom said thickly.* ◊ ADV

8 If things happen **thick and fast**, they happen very quickly and in large numbers. EG *More discoveries followed thick and fast.* PHRASE

9 To be **thick with** something means to be full of it or be covered with it. EG *The windows were thick with grime... The air was thick with butterflies.* PHRASE

10 If you are **in the thick of** an activity or situation, you are very involved in it. EG *It won't be long before Amanda is in the thick of O levels.* PHRASE

11 If you continue to do something **through thick and thin**, you do it even though the conditions or circumstances have become very bad. EG *She stayed with her husband through thick and thin.* PHRASE

thicken /θɪkəºn/, **thickens, thickening, thickened. 1** If something **thickens**, it becomes more closely grouped together than it has previously been. EG *Here the vegetation thickens into a jungle.* V

2 If fog or smoke **thickens**, it becomes denser or darker and more difficult to see through. V

3 When you **thicken** a liquid or when it **thickens**, you make it stiffer and more solid. EG *You can use flour to thicken sauces.* V-ERG

4 You say **'The plot thickens'** when a situation or series of events is getting more and more complicated and mysterious. CONVENTION

thicket /θɪkɪt/, **thickets.** A **thicket** is a small group of trees or bushes which are growing closely together. EG *They live in hidden valleys or dense thickets.* N COUNT

thickset /θɪksɛt/. Someone who is **thickset** is broad and heavy, with a solid-looking body. EG *...a big, thickset man with heavy shoulders.* ADJ QUALIT

thick-skinned. Someone who is **thick-skinned** is not easily hurt by what other people say to them or say about them. EG *...a thick-skinned, brutal person.* ADJ QUALIT

thief /θiːf/, **thieves.** A **thief** is a person who steals something from another person, especially without using violence. EG *...jewel thieves.* N COUNT

thieving /θiːvɪŋ/ means involved in stealing things. EG *...those thieving village kids.* ADJ CLASSIF : ATTRIB

thigh /θaɪ/, **thighs.** Your **thighs** are the top parts of your legs, between your knees and your hips. See picture at THE HUMAN BODY. EG *I walked the last six miles in water up to my thighs.* N COUNT

thimble /θɪmbəºl/, **thimbles.** A **thimble** is a small metal or plastic object that you put on the end of your finger to protect it from being pricked by a needle when you are sewing. N COUNT

thin /θɪn/, **thinner, thinnest; thins, thinning, thinned. 1** Something that is **thin** has a small distance between its two opposite surfaces. EG *His nose was long and thin... ...their tall, thin house... ...thin slices of bread... ...thin cotton cloth.* ADJ QUALIT
◊ **thinly.** EG *...fresh, thinly cut bread.* ◊ ADV

2 A person or animal that is **thin** has very little fat on their body. EG *Angela was dreadfully thin.* ADJ QUALIT

3 Liquids that are **thin** contain a lot of water. EG *The liquid was thin and greyish brown.* ADJ QUALIT

4 A crowd or other group of people that is **thin** has very few people in it. EG *The crowd seemed suddenly thinner.* ◊ **thinly.** EG *...a thinly populated region.* ADJ QUALIT ◊ ADV

Is a thesaurus useful for language students?

5 If your hair **is thinning** or if you are getting **thin on top**, you are beginning to go bald. [V : ONLY CONT OR PHRASE]

6 When you say that people or things are **thin on the ground**, you mean that there are not very many of them and so they are hard to find. EG *Good new plays are still rather thin on the ground.* [PHRASE]

7 When a joke or a story **is wearing thin**, it is beginning to lose its interest because it has been repeated too many times. [PHRASE]

8 When your patience or your temper **is wearing thin**, you are beginning to get impatient or angry. [PHRASE]

9 to disappear **into thin air**: see **air**.

thin down. When you **thin** a liquid **down,** you add more water or other liquid to it. EG *The paint has been thinned down too much.* [PHRASAL VB : V+O+ADV]

thing /θɪŋ/, **things. 1** You use **thing** as a substitute for another word when you do not want to be more precise, when you are referring to something that has already been mentioned, or when you are going to give more details about it. EG *He needed a few things so we went to the store to purchase them... It's silly to train a group of people just to do one thing... A terrible thing happened to me on my way to work... Do you know how to drive this thing?... The fourth drawer holds family things such as photographs and letters... I've seen this sort of thing so many times before... Education isn't the same thing as intelligence... The first thing I did when I came back was clean the bathroom... She sobbed last night, a thing she rarely does.* [N COUNT+SUPP]

2 You can use **thing** instead of 'anything' to emphasize what you are saying. EG *I just couldn't think of a thing to say... Don't worry about a thing.* [N SING : a+N]

3 You can say **'The thing is'** to introduce an explanation or opinion relating to something that has just been said. EG *I can't come on Thursday. The thing is, I've already arranged to do something on Thursday.* [PHRASE Spoken]

4 A **thing** is a physical object, rather than plants, animals, or human beings. EG *He's only interested in things and not people.* [N COUNT]

5 Your **things** are your clothes or possessions. EG *She changed into her bathing things... I like my own things around me: my photos and books.* [N PLURAL +POSS]

6 You can use **things** to refer to life in general and the way it is changing or affecting you. EG *Things are going very well for us at the moment... I hope I've not spoiled things... How are things?* [N PLURAL]

7 You can call a person or an animal a **thing** when you are expressing your feelings towards them. EG *She was very cold, poor thing... You lucky thing!* [N COUNT+SUPP]

8 If you say that something is the **thing**, you mean that it is fashionable or popular. EG *Ambivalence is the thing nowadays.* [N SING : *the*+N]

9 You say **with one thing and another** when you mean that there are several reasons for something, but you are not going to explain what they are. EG *He sees a lot of her, you know, with one thing and another.* [PHRASE]

10 You say **for one thing** when you give only one reason for something, but want to indicate that there are other reasons that you are not bothering to give. EG *I prefer badminton to squash. It's not so tiring for one thing.* [PHRASE]

11 Thing is also used in these phrases. **11.1** If you say **it is just one of those things**, you mean that you cannot explain why something happens. **11.2** If you **have a thing** about someone or something, you have very strong feelings about them. EG *I've got a thing about drinking.* **11.3** If you **make a thing** of or out of something, you make it much more important than it really is. EG *He made a big thing of not eating chilli.* [PHRASES; Informal; Informal]

thingamabob /θɪŋəməbɒb/, **thingamabobs.** You can refer to something or someone as **thingamabob** or **thingummy** when you cannot remember or do not know the proper word or name for them. EG *Her phone is out of order. She's getting a new thingamabob.* [N COUNT Informal]

thingummy /θɪŋəmi[1]/, **thingummies.** See **thingamabob**. [N COUNT]

think /θɪŋk/, **thinks, thinking, thought** /θɔːt/. **1** If you **think** that something is the case, you have the opinion that it is the case. EG *I think a woman has as much right to work as a man... You expect everyone to think like you... She thought of Deirdre simply as an old chum... She's cleverer than I thought... He was thought by the Conservatives to be an extreme radical.* [V+REPORT : ONLY *that*, V+A, OR V+*of*+*as*; ALSO V+O+C OR V+O+*to*-INF]

2 If you **think** that something is true, you judge or believe it to be true, but you are not sure. EG *I think it's at six thirty on Sundays... At first I thought he was asleep.* [V+REPORT : ONLY *that*]

3 When you **think** about ideas or problems, you make a mental effort to consider them. EG *That ought to make us think hard about how we can make a safer product... He thought for a moment.* [V : OFT+*about*]

▸ used as a noun. EG *We'll be in touch when we've had a think about what to do.* [▸ N SING : *a*+N, OFT+*about*]

4 If you **think** of something, **4.1** you remember it or it comes into your mind. EG *I can never think of her name... I can think of at least two examples of his stupidity... He can think of no reason for going... I'm trying to think which other companies I can try for you.* **4.2** you create it in your mind using your intelligence and imagination. EG *...a method which had never even been thought of before.* [V : USU+*of*, USU WITH MODAL; ALSO V+REPORT : ONLY WH; V+*of*]

5 If you **are thinking** something at a particular moment, you have ideas in your mind that you do not say out loud. EG *All the while I was thinking, 'What's happening here?'... I lay there thinking how funny it was.* [V+QUOTE OR REPORT]

6 If you **are thinking** of doing something, you are considering doing it in the future. EG *Is he still thinking of going away to Italy for a month?... I thought about being a reporter.* [V+*of/about*]

7 If you **think** of someone, you show consideration for them, their needs, and their problems. EG *It was very kind of you to think of him... You never think about anybody but yourself!* [V+*of/about*]

8 You use **think** in questions and exclamations to express your anger, shock, or surprise at someone's behaviour. EG *Who do you think you are?... Whatever could I have been thinking about?... To think that I trusted him!* [V+REPORT OR V+A]

9 If you **think** a lot of someone or something, you admire them very much or think they are very good. EG *She thinks a lot of you... I didn't think much of his letter... What did you think of her? What did your husband think about it?* [V+QUANTIF +*of/about*]

10 Think is also used in these phrases. **10.1** You say **'I think'** to add politeness to what you are saying, or to make it sound less forceful or rude. EG *I think I ought to go... Thank you, I don't think I will, if you don't mind... I think that you will find my figures are correct.* **10.2** If you **think the best of** people, you expect that they will behave well. If you **think the worst of** people, you expect them to behave badly. EG *You always think the best of everyone... I must say I thought better of you.* **10.3** If you are intending to do something but you **think better of it**, you decide not to do it. EG *She was on the point of waking Ben again, but then thought better of it.* **10.4** If you **think nothing of** doing something that other people consider difficult or strange, you consider it to be easy or normal. EG *We would think nothing of walking six miles just to post a letter.* **10.5** If you **think twice** or **think again** about doing something, you consider it very carefully before you do it and sometimes decide not to do it. EG *You've got to think twice before you spend ten pounds on a book... He may have to think again.* **10.6** If you say **anybody would think** that a particular thing was true, you are expressing your surprise or disapproval at someone's behaviour. EG *Anybody'd think you were our nanny... You would have thought they had never seen a man before.* **10.7** You say **just think** when you feel excited, [PHRASES] fascinated, or shocked by something. EG *Judy, just think, what an opportunity!... Just think how much it's going to cost us.*

11 come to think of it: see **come**. • to **think the world of** someone: see **world**. • See also **thinking**, **thought**.

think back. If you **think back**, you make an effort to remember things that happened to you in the past. EG *I'm thinking back to my own experience as a teacher... ...an opportunity to think back over the year.* PHRASAL VB : V+ADV, OFT+*to/over*

think over. If you **think** something **over**, you consider it carefully before making a decision. EG *I wanted to think over one or two business problems.* PHRASAL VB : V+O+ADV

think through. If you **think** a problem or situation **through**, you consider it thoroughly. EG *I haven't really thought the whole business through in my own mind.* PHRASAL VB : V+O+ADV

think up. If you **think up** something clever or unusual, you create it in your mind. EG *...a new financial agreement he had thought up... ...examples that mathematicians think up.* PHRASAL VB : V+O+ADV

thinker /θɪŋkə/, **thinkers.** A **thinker** is someone who is famous for their ideas on a particular subject, especially someone who is a philosopher. EG *...such thinkers as Plato, Rousseau, and Freud.* N COUNT

thinking /θɪŋkɪŋ/. **1** The general ideas or opinions of a person or group can be referred to as their **thinking**. EG *We are so alike in our thinking... ...a reluctance which dominated the thinking of a whole generation.* N UNCOUNT +SUPP

2 You add **to my way of thinking** to a statement to emphasize that it is your opinion and not a fact. EG *...issues which, to my way of thinking, are some of the fundamental human issues.* ADV SEN

3 Thinking is the activity of using your brain to consider a problem or to create an idea. EG *I've done some thinking... That requires a great deal of serious thinking.* • See also **wishful thinking**. N UNCOUNT

4 You use **thinking** to describe intelligent people who take an interest in important events and issues. EG *...conditions which forced the thinking man to decide that changes must be made.* ADJ CLASSIF : ATTRIB

third /θɜːd/, **thirds. 1** The **third** item in a series is the one that you count as number three: see the entry headed NUMBER. EG *This room was on the third floor.* ORDINAL

2 A **third** is one of three equal parts of something. EG *It covers a third of the world's surface.* N COUNT : USU+*of*

3 A **third** at a British university is the lowest class of honours degree that you can get. N COUNT

thirdly /θɜːdli[1]/. You use **thirdly** when you want to make a third point or give a third reason for something. EG *And thirdly, remember that they have supported you in the past.* ADV SEN

third party, third parties. 1 A **third party** is a person who is not directly involved in a business agreement or legal case, but is affected by it or is asked to take part in a minor way. EG *A third party from outside the village was brought in as a witness.* N COUNT

2 If you have **third-party** insurance and cause an accident, your insurance company will pay money only to other people who are hurt or whose property is damaged, and not to you. ADJ CLASSIF

third person. In grammar, a statement in the **third person** is a statement about another person or thing, and not directly about yourself or about the person you are talking to. The **third person** is expressed as 'he', 'she', 'it', or 'they' with the appropriate form of a verb. N SING : *the*+N

third-rate. Something that is **third-rate** is of a very poor quality or standard. EG *...the seedy world of third-rate theatricals.* ADJ QUALIT

Third World. The poorer countries of Africa, Asia, and South America are sometimes referred to as the **Third World**. EG *I had seen a good deal of the Third World before I visited Calcutta.* N PROPER : *the*+N

thirst /θɜːst/, **thirsts, thirsting, thirsted. 1** If you have a **thirst**, you feel a need to drink something. EG *She had a terrible thirst.* N SING

2 Thirst is the condition of not having enough to drink. EG *She was dying of thirst.* N UNCOUNT

3 A **thirst** for something is a very strong desire for it. EG *...his thirst for knowledge.* N SING+*for* Literary

thirsty /θɜːsti[1]/. **1** If you are **thirsty**, you feel that you need to drink something. EG *Have you got any water? I'm thirsty.* ◊ **thirstily**. EG *Jane drank thirstily.* ADJ QUALIT ◊ ADV

2 Thirsty is also used to describe things that make you feel thirsty. EG *Gardening is really thirsty work.* ADJ QUALIT : ATTRIB

thirteen /θɜːtiːn/ **thirteens. Thirteen** is the number 13: see the entry headed NUMBER. EG *He hadn't appeared in a film for thirteen years.* NUMBER

thirteenth /θɜːtiːnθ/ **thirteenths.** The **thirteenth** item in a series is the one that you count as number thirteen: see the entry headed NUMBER. EG *...my thirteenth birthday.* ORDINAL

thirtieth /θɜːti[1]ə[1]θ/ **thirtieths.** The **thirtieth** item in a series is the one that you count as number thirty: see the entry headed NUMBER. EG *...a parade to celebrate the thirtieth year of Independence.* ORDINAL

thirty /θɜːti[1]/ **thirties. Thirty** is the number 30: see the entry headed NUMBER. EG *...thirty years of marriage.* NUMBER

this /ðɪs/, **these** /ðiːz/. **1** You use **this** to refer to a person or thing that has been mentioned, or to introduce a person or thing that you are going to talk about. EG *The colonel handed him the bag. 'This is for you.'... 'My God,' I said. 'This is awful.'... This is Desiree, my father's second wife... These particular students are extremely bright... So, for all these reasons, my advice is to be very, very careful... Get these kids out of here.* DET OR PRON

2 You also use **this** to introduce a person or thing into a story. EG *I stopped at a junction and this bowler-hatted gent comes up.* DET Spoken Informal

3 You also use **this** when you refer to the present time or place. EG *...the prime minister of this country... Could I make an appointment to see the doctor this morning please?* DET

4 If you say that something will happen **this** Friday or **this** summer, for example, you mean that it will happen on the next Friday or during the next summer. EG *Let's fix a time. This Sunday. Four o'clock.* DET

5 You also use **this** when you are indicating the size or shape of something with your hands. EG *It was about this big.* SUBMOD

6 You say **this is** in order to introduce yourself on the telephone. EG *He looked for her number, and dialled it. 'Sally? This is Martin Brody.'* PHRASE

7 If you say that you are doing or talking about **this and that**, you mean that you are doing or talking about a variety of things that you do not want to specify. EG *'What have you been up to ?' – 'This and that.'* PHRASE

thistle /θɪsə[0]l/, **thistles.** A **thistle** is a wild plant with prickly leaves and purple flowers. N COUNT

thong /θɒŋ/, **thongs.** A **thong** is a long, thin strip of leather, plastic, or rubber. N COUNT

thorn /θɔːn/, **thorns. 1** A **thorn** is **1.1** one of the many sharp points on some plants and trees, for example on rose bushes. EG *He stepped on a sharp thorn.* N COUNT **1.2** a tree or bush such as a hawthorn. EG *...dragging branches of thorn across the entrance.* N COUNT OR N UNCOUNT

2 If you describe someone as a **thorn in** your **flesh** or a **thorn in** your **side**, you mean that they are a constant problem or annoyance to you. EG *Howard is a well-known activist, a thorn in the flesh of the council.* PHRASE

thorny /θɔːni[1]/. **1** A **thorny** plant or tree is covered with thorns. EG *...a long thorny stem.* ADJ QUALIT

How many numbers are there on these pages? Include ordinals.

2 A **thorny** subject or question is difficult to discuss or answer. EG *...the thorny problem of what happens when the boss is absent.* ADJ QUALIT

thorough /θʌrə/. **1** An action that is **thorough** is done very carefully and completely. EG *...a thorough search... These drugs have been subject to very thorough testing.* ◇ **thoroughly**. EG *They had not studied the language thoroughly.* ◇ **thoroughness**. EG *...the thoroughness of the training programme.* ADJ QUALIT ◇ ADV ◇ N UNCOUNT

2 Someone who is **thorough** is very careful and methodical in their work. EG *He is enormously thorough and full of inspiration.* ◇ **thoroughness**. EG *The President was impressed by his speed and thoroughness.* ADJ QUALIT ◇ N UNCOUNT

3 You can use **thorough** to emphasize what you are saying. EG *I'd enjoy giving him a thorough beating.* ◇ **thoroughly**. EG *...a thoroughly unreasonable person... Yes, I thoroughly agree.* ADJ QUALIT : ATTRIB ◇ ADV

thoroughfare /θʌrəfɛə/, **thoroughfares.** A **thoroughfare** is a main road in a town or city. EG *We went back towards the main thoroughfare.* N COUNT Formal

those /ðəʊz/ is the plural of **that.**

though /ðəʊ/. **1** You use **though** to introduce and emphasize a fact or comment which makes another part of the sentence rather surprising. EG *She wore a fur coat, even though it was a very hot day.... Though he hadn't stopped working all day, he wasn't tired.* CONJ

2 You also use **though** to add information that makes a statement less forceful, or points out exceptions to it. EG *It wasn't my decision, though I think I agree with it... She resembled her mother physically, though not mentally... 'It's not very useful.' – 'It's pretty, though, isn't it ?'* CONJ OR ADV SEN

3 as though: see **as.**

thought /θɔːt/, **thoughts. 1 Thought** is the past tense and past participle of **think**.

2 A **thought** is an idea that you have in your mind. EG *The thought never crossed my mind... He couldn't bear the thought of going home... I had vague thoughts of emigrating.* N COUNT : USU SING+SUPP

3 Thought is **3.1** the activity of thinking. EG *She frowned as though deep in thought... After giving our predicament some thought, he said he had a proposal.* **3.2** a particular way of thinking or a particular set of ideas. EG *...two schools of socialist thought.* N UNCOUNT / N UNCOUNT +SUPP

4 Your **thoughts** are **4.1** all the ideas in your mind when you are concentrating on something. EG *They walked back, each deep in his own private thoughts... His mind was empty except for thoughts of her.* **4.2** your opinions on something. EG *Rothermere disclosed his thoughts on Britain.* N PLURAL : USU+POSS

5 You use **thought** to refer to an act of kindness, especially when you are thanking someone. EG *It's a kind thought, sir. I'll tell him you called.* N SING+SUPP

6 a penny for your thoughts: see **penny**. • See also **second thoughts**.

thoughtful /θɔːtfʊl/. **1** If you are **thoughtful**, you are quiet and serious because you are thinking about something. EG *He looked thoughtful for a moment.* ◇ **thoughtfully**. EG *Tom closed the book thoughtfully.* ADJ QUALIT ◇ ADV

2 A **thoughtful** person remembers what other people want or need, and tries to be kind to them. EG *That's very kind of you, Mr Zapp, very thoughtful... I thanked him for his thoughtful gesture.* ◇ **thoughtfully**. EG *The book thoughtfully provides a clue on how to do this.* ADJ QUALIT ◇ ADV

thoughtless /θɔːtlɪ²s/. If you are **thoughtless**, you forget or ignore what other people want, need, or feel. EG *I had to scold Vita severely for being so thoughtless... How thoughtless of you!* ◇ **thoughtlessly**. EG *Traditional sources of employment are thoughtlessly destroyed.* ADJ QUALIT ◇ ADV

thousand /θaʊzənd/, **thousands. 1** A **thousand** or one **thousand** is the number 1,000: see the entry headed NUMBER. EG *...an annual income of twenty thousand dollars.* • **a thousand and one**: see **one**. NUMBER

2 You can say 'a **thousand**' or '**thousands**' when you mean a large number or quantity. EG *I've told him thousands of times.* N PART : USU PLURAL

thousandth /θaʊzənθ/, **thousandths. 1** The **thousandth** item in a series is the one that you count as number one thousand: see the entry headed NUMBER. ORDINAL

2 A **thousandth** is one of a thousand equal parts of something. EG *...a thousandth of a second.* N COUNT : USU+*of*

thrash /θræʃ/, **thrashes, thrashing, thrashed. 1** If someone **thrashes** you, they hit you several times. EG *We were thrashed a lot at school.* ◇ **thrashing, thrashings**. EG *He got a thrashing from his father.* V+O ◇ N COUNT

2 If someone **thrashes** you in a game, contest, or fight, they defeat you completely. EG *They had challenged and thrashed the enemy's navy.* ◇ **thrashing**. EG *...the thrashing our team got at Southampton last week.* V+O ◇ N COUNT

3 If you **thrash** around, you twist and turn your body quickly and violently because you are afraid or are in pain. EG *The boy was thrashing around, trying to get free.* V : OFT+A

thrash out. If you **thrash out** a problem or an idea, you discuss it in detail until you arrive at a solution. EG *...an agreement that we had already thrashed out.* PHRASAL VB : V+O+ADV

thread /θrɛd/, **threads, threading, threaded. 1** A **thread** is a long, very thin piece of cotton, silk, nylon, or wool. Thread is used in sewing. EG *...cotton thread.* N COUNT OR N UNCOUNT

2 The **thread** on something such as a screw or the top of a container is the raised spiral line of metal or plastic around it. N COUNT

3 The **thread** in an argument or story is an idea or theme that connects the different parts of it together. EG *He had lost his thread and didn't know what to say next.* N COUNT

4 When you **thread** a needle, you put a piece of thread through the hole at the end of the needle. V+O

5 If you **thread** your way through people or things, you go forwards slowly, using the spaces between them. EG *We turned and threaded our way through the fairground.* V+O+A OR V+A

threadbare /θrɛdbɛə/. **Threadbare** clothes, carpets, and other pieces of cloth are old and very thin. EG *O'Shea's suit was baggy and threadbare.* ADJ QUALIT

threat /θrɛt/, **threats. 1** A **threat** is a statement that someone will harm you, especially if you do not do what they want. EG *We mustn't give in to threats... Under threat of death, he confessed.* N COUNT OR N UNCOUNT

2 You can refer to anything or anyone that seems likely to harm you as a **threat**. EG *He felt that I was becoming a real threat to his plans.* N COUNT : OFT+*to*

3 If there is a **threat** of something unpleasant happening, it is very possible that it will happen. EG *...the ever-growing threat of flooding.* N COUNT OR N UNCOUNT

threaten /θrɛtəⁿn/, **threatens, threatening, threatened. 1** If you **threaten** to harm someone or **threaten** to do something that will upset them, you say that you will do it. EG *He threatened to resign... They were threatened with imprisonment.* V+*to*-INF; ALSO V+O : OFT+*with*

2 If someone or something **threatens** a person or thing, they are likely to harm that person or thing. EG *He said that the war threatened the peace of the whole world.* ◇ **threatened**. EG *He felt threatened.* V+O ◇ ADJ PRED

3 If something **threatens** to do something unpleasant, it seems likely to do it. EG *The riots threatened to get out of hand.* V+*to*-INF

4 If something unpleasant **threatens** or if someone or something **is threatened** with it, it seems likely to happen. EG *The whole country is threatened with starvation.* V; ALSO V+O : USU PASS+*with*

threatening /θrɛtəⁿnɪŋ/. Something or someone that is **threatening** seems likely to cause harm. EG *...a threatening environment... He became angry* ADJ QUALIT and threatening. ◇ **threateningly**. EG *He advanced threateningly on the boy.* ◇ ADV

three /θriː/ **threes. Three** is the number 3: see the entry headed NUMBER. EG *We agreed to meet three days later.* NUMBER

three-dimensional. 1 A **three-dimensional** picture, film, or image looks as if it is deep or solid rather than flat. ADJ CLASSIF

2 A **three-dimensional** object is solid rather than flat. EG *...a three-dimensional model of the theatre.* ADJ CLASSIF

three-quarters. **Three-quarters** of something is a half of it plus a quarter of it. EG *Three-quarters of the world's surface is covered by water... ...a play lasting one and three-quarter hours.* ▸ used as an adverb or adjective. EG *The tank is three-quarters full... ...a bright three-quarter moon.* QUANTIF ▸ ADV OR ADJ CLASSIF

thresh /θrɛʃ/, **threshes, threshing, threshed.** When people **thresh** corn, wheat, or rice, they beat it in order to separate the grains from the rest of the plant. V+O

threshold /θrɛʃhᵒəʊld/, **thresholds. 1** The **threshold** of a building or room is the floor in the doorway, or the doorway itself. EG *Suddenly the door opened and Madame stood on the threshold... Morris had never crossed the threshold of a public house before.* N COUNT: USU SING Formal

2 A **threshold** is an amount, level, or limit on a scale. When the **threshold** is reached, something else happens or changes. EG *The tax threshold for a single pensioner is £445.* N COUNT+SUPP Formal

3 Someone who is **on the threshold of** an action, activity, or state is about to do it or experience it. EG *He was on the threshold of public life.* PHRASE Formal

threw /θruː/ is the past tense of **throw.**

thrift /θrɪft/ is the quality and practice of being thrifty. EG *...the virtues of thrift, hard work, and punctuality.* N UNCOUNT

thrifty /θrɪftiˡ/, **thriftier, thriftiest.** Someone who is **thrifty** saves money and does not waste things. EG *She was a thrifty housekeeper.* ADJ QUALIT

thrill /θrɪl/, **thrills, thrilling, thrilled. 1** A **thrill** is **1.1** a sudden feeling of great excitement, pleasure, or fear. EG *The sound of the bell sent a thrill of anticipation through her... They get a considerable thrill out of it.* **1.2** an event or experience that gives you a thrill. EG *The thrill for me was finding the rare specimens.* N COUNT

2 If something **thrills** you, or if you **thrill** to it, it gives you a feeling of great pleasure and excitement. EG *It's a sight that never fails to thrill me... ...those who thrill to the taste of smoked salmon.* V-ERG: IF V THEN+*to*

thrilled /θrɪld/. If someone is **thrilled**, they are extremely pleased about something. EG *I was thrilled to be sitting next to such a distinguished author.* ADJ PRED: OFT+*to*-INF

thriller /θrɪlə/, **thrillers.** A **thriller** is a book, film, or play that tells an exciting story about dangerous, frightening, or mysterious events. EG *...a spy thriller... ...a thriller writer.* N COUNT

thrilling /θrɪlɪŋ/. Something that is **thrilling** is very exciting and enjoyable. EG *...a thrilling adventure.. She gave a thrilling performance.* ADJ QUALIT

thrive /θraɪv/, **thrives, thriving, thrived. Throve** /θrəʊv/ is sometimes used for the past tense. When people or things **thrive**, they are healthy, happy, successful, or strong. EG *Are you the type of person who thrives on activity?... My business was thriving.* ◇ **thriving**. EG *...a thriving community.* V: USU+A ◇ ADJ CLASSIF

throat /θrəʊt/, **throats. 1** Your **throat** is **1.1** the back of your mouth and the top part of the tubes inside your neck that go down into your stomach and your lungs. EG *His throat was so dry that he could hardly swallow.* **1.2** the front part of your neck. EG *He grabbed the man by the throat.* N COUNT

2 Throat is used in these phrases. **2.1** If two people are **at each other's throats**, they are quarrelling or fighting violently with each other. EG *When the danger had passed they would again be at each other's throats.* **2.2** If you **ram** or **force** something **down** someone's **throat**, you mention it very often and very emphatically in order to make them accept it, believe it, or learn it. EG *They have this viewpoint rammed down their throats every day.* **2.3** If something **sticks in** your **throat**, you find it unacceptable. EG *It was his arrogance which stuck in my throat.* **2.4** to **clear** your **throat**: see **clear**. PHRASES Informal

throb /θrɒb/, **throbs, throbbing, throbbed. 1** If a part of your body **throbs**, you feel a series of strong beats or dull pains. EG *His head was throbbing.* ▸ used as a noun. EG *She felt her heart give a great throb.* V ▸ N COUNT

2 If something **throbs**, it vibrates and makes a loud, rhythmic noise. EG *The drums seemed to throb in his ears.* ▸ used as a noun. EG *...the throb of the engine.* V ▸ N COUNT

throes /θrəʊz/. If you are **in the throes of** something, you are deeply involved in it. EG *The British Army was in the throes of reorganization.* PHRASE

throne /θrəʊn/, **thrones. 1** A **throne** is a special chair used by a king or queen on important official occasions. EG *...a picture of the Queen seated on a rich throne.* N COUNT

2 The **throne** is a way of referring to the position of being king or queen. EG *...when Queen Victoria was on the throne... ...the heir to the throne.* N SING: *the*+N

throng /θrɒŋ/, **throngs, thronging, thronged. 1** A **throng** is a large crowd of people. EG *A patient throng was waiting in silence.... The throng of guests roared its approval.* N COUNT OR N PART Literary

2 If people **throng** somewhere or **throng** a place, they go there in great numbers. EG *Mourners thronged to the funeral... The lane was thronged with shoppers.* V+A OR V+O Literary

throttle /θrɒtəᵒl/, **throttles, throttling, throttled.** To **throttle** someone means to hold them tightly by the throat so that they cannot breathe, usually in order to kill them. EG *He wanted to put his hands around her throat and throttle her.* V+O

through /θruː/. **1** To move **through** a hole or opening means to move directly from one side or end of it to the other. EG *Go straight through that door and then turn right... The rain poured through a hole in the roof.* PREP, OR ADV AFTER VB

2 If you cut **through** something such as a rope, you cut it into two pieces. EG *The fish must have chewed right through it.* PREP, OR ADV AFTER VB

3 If someone or something travels or moves **through** a place or area, they travel or move across it or in it. EG *We drove through London... We decided to drive straight through to Birmingham... The fish swims through the water... They drove home through the darkness... A chill shot through him.* PREP, OR ADV AFTER VB

4 If you get **through** a barrier or obstruction, you get from one side of it to the other. EG *The traffic couldn't get through.* PREP, OR ADV AFTER VB

5 If an object or hole extends from one side of something to another, you can say that it goes or passes **through** it. EG *The heating pipes pass through tunnels... ...a hat with a feather stuck through it.* PREP, OR ADV AFTER VB

6 If you can see, hear, or feel something **through** an object, the object is between you and the thing you can see, hear, or feel. EG *Lonnie gazed out through a side window... He's looking at them through a magnifying glass... I can hear John snoring right through the partition... She could feel the gravel through the soles of her slippers.* PREP

7 If something happens or exists **through** a period of time, it happens or exists from the beginning until the end. EG *I wished that I could stay through the winter... We had no rain from March right through to October.* PREP, OR ADV+PREP

If you throw your money away, are you thrifty?

8 If you go **through** an experience, it happens to you. EG *He didn't want to go through all that divorce business again.* PREP, OR ADV AFTER VB

9 If you live **through** a historical event, it takes place while you are alive. EG *He lived through the decline of the Liberal Party.* PREP

10 If you are **through** with something, you have finished doing it or using it. EG *He was through with seminars and tutorials.* ADJ PRED : USU+*with*

11 You use **through** in expressions such as 'half-way through' and 'all the way through' to indicate to what extent an action or task is completed. EG *Harris tried to stop the operation halfway through... I do not think she ever saw a play right through.* PREP, OR ADV AFTER VB

12 If something happens because of something else, you can say that it happens **through** it. EG *Many people have difficulty in walking, for example through age or frailty... The discovery of adrenalin came about through a mistake.* PREP

13 If you achieve something **through** particular methods, you use those methods to achieve it. EG *They were opposed to change through violence.* PREP

14 If you go **through** or look **through** a lot of things, you look at them one after another. EG *I wanted to read through as much information as possible... She was sorting through a pile of socks.* PREP, OR ADV AFTER VB

15 Through and through means thoroughly or completely. EG *Those boards are rotten through and through... She knew Mr Evans through and through.* PHRASE

throughout /θru:aʊt/. **1** If something happens **throughout** an event or period of time, it happens during the whole of it. EG *This dream recurred throughout her life... We co-operated throughout with trade unionists.* PREP, OR ADV AFTER VB

2 If something happens or exists **throughout** a place, it happens or exists in all parts of it. EG *The pictures can be transmitted by satellite throughout the world... The house was carpeted throughout.* PREP, OR ADV AFTER VB

throve /θrəʊv/ is a past tense of **thrive.**

throw /θrəʊ/, **throws, throwing, threw** /θru:/, **thrown** /θrəʊn/. **1** When you **throw** an object that you are holding, you move your hand quickly and let go of the object, so that it moves through the air. EG *Roger picked up a stone and threw it at Henry... He threw the book in the air.* V+O : USU+A

2 To **throw** someone or something into a place or position means to put or force them there quickly or carelessly. EG *Tom undressed in the dark, throwing his clothes carelessly over a chair... She threw both letters in the bin... The train braked violently, throwing everyone to the floor.* V+O+A

3 If you **throw** a part of your body in a particular direction, you move it suddenly and with a lot of force. EG *She threw her arms around his neck.* V+O+A

4 If you **throw** yourself somewhere, you move or jump there suddenly and with a lot of force. EG *He threw himself on his bed.* V-REFL+A

5 If a horse **throws** its rider, it makes the rider fall off. V+O

6 If one person or thing **throws** another into an unpleasant situation, it suddenly causes the other person or thing to be in that situation. EG *The thought of being late on occasions like these would throw her into a state of panic... The cop threatened to throw all of us in jail... The Depression had thrown almost everybody out of work.* V+O+A

7 If something **throws** light or shadow on something else, it causes that thing to have light or shadow on it. EG *A spotlight threw a pool of violet light onto the stage.* V+O+A

8 If you **throw** yourself, your energy, or your money into an activity, you become involved in it very actively and enthusiastically. EG *Mrs Kaul threw herself into her work heart and soul... Many women throw all of their energies into a career.* V-REFL+*into* OR V+O+*into*

9 If you **throw** a fit or a tantrum, you suddenly start to behave in an uncontrolled way. EG *She threw a fit of hysterics.* V+O

10 If something such as a remark or an experience **throws** you, it confuses you or surprises you because it is unexpected. EG *It was the fact that she was married that threw me.* V+O Informal

11 a **stone's throw**: see **stone.** • to **throw light on** something: see **light.** • to **throw** your **weight about**: see **weight**.

throw away. 1 When you **throw away** something that you do not want, you get rid of it, for example by putting it in a dustbin. EG *She likes to keep things, even old things, rather than throw them away.* **2** If you **throw away** something good or useful that you have, you waste it rather than using it sensibly. EG *He is evidently prepared to throw his money away... They threw away their advantage.* **3** See also **throwaway**. PHRASAL VB : V+O+ADV; V+O+ADV

throw in. If someone who is selling you one thing **throws in** another, they give you both things but only ask you to pay for the first thing. EG *We only had to pay £9 for bed and breakfast, with lunch thrown in.* PHRASAL VB : V+O+ADV

throw out. 1 If you **throw** something **out, 1.1** you get rid of it, for example by putting it in a dustbin. EG *The broken cooking pots were thrown out.* **1.2** you reject it because it is unsatisfactory. EG *He threw out the scripts for the next six episodes.* **2** If you **throw** someone **out**, you force them to leave a job or a place such as a house or club. EG *Her parents threw her out when they found she was pregnant.* PHRASAL VB : V+O+ADV; V+O+ADV; V+O+ADV

throw up. 1 If someone **throws up**, food or drink from their stomach comes out of their mouth because they are ill. EG *She got out of the car and threw up by the side of the road.* **2** If something **throws up** dust or water, it causes dust or water to rise up into the air. EG *Each passing car threw up a cloud of white dust.* PHRASAL VB : V+ADV OR V+O+ADV Informal; V+O+ADV

throwaway /θrəʊəweɪ/. **1** A **throwaway** product is intended to be used only for a short time, and then to be thrown away. EG *...a throwaway toothbrush.* ADJ CLASSIF : ATTRIB

2 A **throwaway** remark or gesture is made in a casual way, although it is important, in order to have a humorous or strong emotional effect. ADJ CLASSIF : ATTRIB

throwback /θrəʊbæk/, **throwbacks.** Something that is a **throwback** is like something that existed a long time ago. EG *His sentiments were a throwback to the old colonial days.* N COUNT : USU SING+*to*

thrown /θrəʊn/ is the past participle of **throw.**

thrush /θrʌʃ/, **thrushes.** A **thrush** is a type of fairly small bird. N COUNT

thrust /θrʌst/, **thrusts, thrusting.** The form **thrust** is used in the present tense and is the past tense and past participle of the verb.

1 If you **thrust** something somewhere, you push or move it there quickly with a lot of force. EG *The captain thrust his hands into his pockets... He thrust the bag at Buddy.* V+O+A

2 A **thrust** is a sudden forceful movement. EG *...repeated sword thrusts.* N COUNT

3 If you **thrust** your way somewhere, you move along, pushing between people or things. EG *Edward thrust his way towards them.* V+O+A OR V+A

4 The main **thrust** of an activity or idea is the most important part or aspect of it. EG *The main thrust of robot research in the '80s has been towards improving vision techniques.* N SING

thrust upon. If you **thrust** something **upon** someone, you force them to have it. EG *The new religion was thrust upon the population by force.* PHRASAL VB : V+O+PREP, HAS PASS

thud /θʌd/, **thuds, thudding, thudded. 1** A **thud** is a dull sound, usually made by a solid, heavy object hitting something soft. EG *He fell on the floor with a thud.* N COUNT

2 If something **thuds** somewhere, it makes a dull sound, usually by hitting something else. EG *The mail bags thudded onto the platform.* V : USU+A

thug /θʌg/, **thugs.** A **thug** is a very rough and violent person. EG *...a gang of thugs.* N COUNT

thumb /θʌm/, **thumbs, thumbing, thumbed. 1** Your **thumb** is the short, thick finger on the side of your hand. EG *I took her ear between my thumb and forefinger, and tugged it playfully.* N COUNT

2 If you **thumb** a lift, you stand next to a road and stick out your thumb until a driver stops and gives you a lift. EG *Jackie is a confirmed hitch-hiker, thumbing her way all over Europe.* V+O OR V+O+A

thumb through. If you **thumb** through a book or magazine, you turn over the pages quickly rather than reading each page carefully. PHRASAL VB : V+PREP

thumbnail /θʌmneɪl/, **thumbnails. 1** Your **thumbnail** is the nail on your thumb. N COUNT

2 A **thumbnail** sketch or account of something is very brief and gives only the main features of it. ADJ CLASSIF : ATTRIB

thump /θʌmp/, **thumps, thumping, thumped. 1** If you **thump** someone or something, you hit them hard with your fist. EG *I'll thump you, Tommy, if you don't get out of my way... She thumped the table.* V+O

2 If something **thumps** somewhere, it makes a fairly loud, dull sound, usually when it hits something else. EG *The kitchen door opened, feet thumped up the stairs... Two rockets thumped into the ground by the roadside.* V : USU+A

3 When your heart **thumps**, it beats strongly and quickly. EG *My heart was thumping with happiness.* V

4 A **thump** is **4.1** a hard blow that you give with your fist. EG *Ralph pushed between them and got a thump on the chest.* **4.2** a fairly loud but dull sound. EG *He sat down with a thump.* N COUNT

thunder /θʌndə/, **thunders, thundering, thundered. 1 Thunder** is the loud noise that you hear in the sky after a flash of lightning. EG *There's going to be thunder tonight... ...a clap of thunder.* N UNCOUNT

2 When it **thunders**, a loud noise occurs in the sky after a flash of lightning. V

3 If you refer to the **thunder** of something such as traffic or a drum, you are referring to the loud, deep noise it makes. N UNCOUNT+*of*

4 If something **thunders**, it makes a very loud continuous noise. EG *A truck thundered by.* V : USU+A

5 If you **thunder**, you say something loudly and often angrily. EG *'It's not your bed!' thundered Edwin.* V : USU+QUOTE Literary

thunderbolt /θʌndəbəʊlt/, **thunderbolts.** A **thunderbolt** is a flash of lightning, accompanied by thunder, which strikes something such as a building or a tree. N COUNT

thunderous /θʌndəʳrəs/. A **thunderous** noise is very loud and deep. EG *The tree fell with a thunderous crash... ...thunderous applause.* ADJ CLASSIF

thunderstorm /θʌndəstɔːm/, **thunderstorms.** A **thunderstorm** is a storm in which there is thunder and lightning. N COUNT

Thursday /θɜːzdiˡ/, **Thursdays. Thursday** is one of the seven days of the week. It is the day after Wednesday and before Friday. EG *I got your postcard on Thursday... The question was raised at the meeting last Thursday.* N UNCOUNT OR N COUNT

thus /ðʌs/. **1** You use **thus** to introduce the consequence or conclusion of something that you have just said. EG *They are now down to their last 2,000 pounds and thus qualify for social security benefits... Thus, an incomes policy has to be controlled if it is to be effective.* ADV SEN Formal

2 If you say that something is or happens **thus**, you mean that it is or happens in the way you are describing. EG *She lay down. Her eyelids closed. It was thus that Robert saw her... Thus encouraged, Lexington walked through the gate... It has always been thus and will continue to be so.* ADV

thwart /θwɔːt/, **thwarts, thwarting, thwarted.** To **thwart** someone or their plans means to prevent them from doing or getting what they want. EG *The big man's hopes were thwarted by Taylor... She had never tried to thwart him in any way... ...the only factor likely to thwart land reforms.* V+O Formal

thyme /taɪm/ is a type of herb used in cooking. N UNCOUNT

tiara /tiˡɑːrə/, **tiaras.** A **tiara** is a small crown worn by a woman of high social rank on formal occasions. N COUNT

tic /tɪk/, **tics.** If someone has a **tic**, a part of their face or body keeps moving suddenly and they cannot control it. EG *She seemed to have developed a tic in her neck.* N COUNT

tick /tɪk/, **ticks, ticking, ticked. 1** A **tick** is a written mark like a V with the right hand line extended upwards. You use it to show that something is correct or has been dealt with. EG *There was a nice red tick in the margin.* N COUNT

2 If you **tick** something that is written on a piece of paper, you put a tick next to it. V+O

3 When a clock or watch **ticks**, it makes a regular series of short sounds as it works. EG *It was so quiet I could hear my wristwatch ticking away.* V

◇ **ticking**. EG *She could hear a faint ticking.* ◇ N UNCOUNT

4 The **tick** of a clock or watch is the series of short sounds it makes when it is working. EG *The clock in the kitchen had a noisy tick.* N COUNT

5 If you talk about what makes someone **tick**, you are talking about the reasons for their character and behaviour. EG *What makes Patrick tick?* V

tick away or **tick by.** If you say that the seconds, minutes, or hours **tick away** or **tick by**, you are emphasizing the fact that time is passing. EG *The seconds ticked by and still they heard no explosion.* PHRASAL VB : V+ADV

tick off. 1 If you **tick off** an item on a list, you put a tick by it in order to show that it has been dealt with. **2** If you **tick** someone **off**, you speak angrily to them because they have done something wrong. EG *David had ticked her off for being careless.* PHRASAL VB : V+O+ADV; V+O+ADV Informal

tick over. Something that **is ticking over** is working or operating steadily but not as hard or well as it can do. EG *...enough to keep the essential processes ticking over for a few months.* PHRASAL VB : V+ADV, USU CONT

ticket /tɪkɪt/, **tickets. 1** A **ticket** is an official piece of paper or card which shows that you have paid for a journey or have paid to enter a place of entertainment such as a sports ground or cinema. EG *She bought two tickets for the opera... ...bus tickets... I'd like a return ticket to Vienna, please.* N COUNT

● See also **season ticket**.

2 When drivers of road vehicles get a **ticket**, they are given an official piece of paper which says that they have committed a minor driving or parking offence and must pay a fine or appear in court. EG *There was a parking ticket under the windshield wiper.* N COUNT

3 The particular **ticket** on which a candidate fights an election is the set of political policies which he or she supports. EG *He ran as Vice-President on the Republican ticket.* N SING : *the*+N+SUPP

tickle /tɪkəˡl/, **tickles, tickling, tickled. 1** When you **tickle** someone, you move your fingers lightly over their body, often in order to make them laugh. EG *Babies want to be tickled and hugged.* V+O

2 If something **tickles** you or if it **tickles**, it causes an irritating feeling by touching a part of your body lightly. EG *He flicked away a strand of hair that was tickling Ellen's nose.* V+O OR V

3 If a fact or a situation **tickles** you, it amuses you or gives you pleasure. EG *'Yes, sir,' she answered. The Colonel was tickled by that.* V+O

ticklish /tɪklɪʃ/. **1** A **ticklish** problem or situation is difficult and needs to be dealt with carefully. EG *It was a ticklish moment in the discussion.* ADJ QUALIT : USU ATTRIB

2 If someone is **ticklish**, you can make them laugh very easily by tickling them, because they have very sensitive bodies. ADJ QUALIT : USU PRED

tidal /taɪdəˡl/ means relating to or produced by tides. EG *...tidal estuaries... ...tidal energy.* ADJ CLASSIF : ATTRIB

What day comes before Friday?

tidal wave, tidal waves. A **tidal wave** is a very large wave, often caused by an earthquake, that comes over the land and destroys things. N COUNT

tide /taɪd/, **tides, tiding, tided. 1** The **tide** is the regular change in the level of the sea on the shore. When the tide is high, full, or in, it is at its highest level, and when it is low or out, it is at its lowest level. EG *The tide was coming in... The rocks were exposed at low tide.* N SING : *the*+N, OR N UNCOUNT +SUPP

2 The **tide** of opinion or fashion is what the majority of people think or do at a particular time. EG *He's always gone against the tide of fashion.* N SING+*of*

3 A **tide** of things is a large quantity of them. EG *...the tide of highly qualified academics who come looking for work... ...a rising tide of alcoholism.* N PART

tide over. If something will **tide** someone **over**, it will help them through a difficult period of time. EG *I only want to borrow enough to tide me over till Monday.* PHRASAL VB : V+O+ADV/ PREP

tidings /taɪdɪŋz/ are news that someone tells you. EG *He kissed her and told her the good tidings... Pigeons were sent out to spread tidings of the rebellion.* N PLURAL +SUPP Formal

tidy /taɪdi[1]/, **tidier, tidiest; tidies, tidying, tidied. 1** Something that is **tidy** is neat and arranged in an orderly way. EG *It is very difficult to keep a house tidy... ...a tidy desk.* ◇ **tidiness.** EG *...his parents' concern with tidiness and punctuality.* ADJ QUALIT ◇ N UNCOUNT

2 Someone who is **tidy** always keeps their things neat and arranged in an orderly way. EG *I wish you were a little bit tidier!* ADJ QUALIT

3 When you **tidy** a place, you make it neat by putting things in their proper places. EG *You can't tidy a bedroom until you've made the beds.* V+O

4 A **tidy** amount of money is a fairly large amount of it. EG *He managed to make quite a tidy income every year.* ADJ QUALIT : ATTRIB Informal

tidy away. When you **tidy** something **away**, you put it in a cupboard or drawer so that it is not in the way. EG *Someone had tidied my papers away.* PHRASAL VB : V+O+ADV

tidy up. When you **tidy up** or **tidy** a place **up**, you put things back in their proper places so that everything is neat. EG *Then I made the beds and tidied up.* PHRASAL VB : V+ADV OR V+O+ADV

tie /taɪ/, **ties, tying, tied. 1** If you **tie** one thing to another or if you **tie** it in a particular position, you fasten it to the other thing or fasten it in that position, often using string or rope. EG *...one of those labels you tie onto the handle of your suitcase.* V+O+A

2 If you **tie** a piece of string or cloth round something or **tie** something with the string or cloth, you put the string or cloth round it and fasten the ends together in a knot or bow. EG *...a little dog which had a ribbon tied round its neck... ...a parcel tied with string... The children spent the morning tying the straw into small bundles.* V+O+A

3 If you **tie** a knot or a bow in a piece of string or cloth, you fasten the ends together and make a knot or bow. V+O : USU+A

4 When you **tie** your shoelaces, you fasten the ends together in a bow. EG *He was still tying his laces.* V+O

5 A **tie** is a long, narrow piece of cloth that is worn around someone's neck under their shirt collar and tied in a knot at the front. Ties are worn mainly by men. EG *He took off his jacket and loosened his tie.* ● See also **bow tie.** N COUNT

6 Something that **is tied** to or into something else is connected to it or linked closely with it. EG *Canada is more tightly tied into the American economy.* V+O+*to/into* : USU PASS

7 A **tie** is also a connection or feeling that links you with a person, place, or organization. EG *Family ties are often very strong... They want to loosen their ties with Britain.* N COUNT : USU+SUPP

8 If you **tie** with someone in a competition or game, you have the same number of points or the same degree of success. EG *Two actresses tied for the Best Actress award.* ▸ used as a noun. EG *In the event of a tie, the winner will be the contestant who took the shortest time.* V OR V+*with* : RECIP ▸ N COUNT

tie down. A person or thing that **ties** you **down** restricts your freedom, for example by making you live, behave, or act in a particular way. EG *You're not tied down to a date.* PHRASAL VB : V+O+ADV

tie in with. An idea or fact that **ties in with** something else fits in with it or agrees with it. EG *His beliefs didn't seem to tie in at all with reality.* PHRASAL VB : V+ADV+PREP

tie up. 1 If you **tie** something **up**, you put string or rope round it so that it is firm or secure. EG *Clarissa came in, carrying some canvases tied up in brown paper.* PHRASAL VB : V+O+ADV **2** If someone **ties** you **up**, they fasten ropes or chains around you so that you cannot move or escape. V+O+ADV **3** When you **tie up** your shoelaces, you fasten them in a bow. EG *Tie up your laces. Hurry!* V+O+ADV **4** When you **tie up** an animal, you fasten it to a fixed object with a piece of rope or chain so that it cannot run away. V+O+ADV **5** If you **tie up** something such as money or resources, you do something with it, so that it is not available for other people or for other purposes. EG *People don't want to tie their money up for long periods.* V+O+ADV **6** Something that **is tied up** with something else or **ties up** with it is closely linked with it. EG *It tied up with her interest in dance.* V-ERG+ADV, OFT+*with*

tied up. If you are **tied up**, you are busy. EG *I'm tied up right now, can you call me back later?* ADJ PRED Informal

tier /tɪə/, **tiers.** A **tier** is a row or layer of something that has other layers above or below it. EG *The theatre had semicircular tiers of seats.* N COUNT

tiger /taɪgə/, **tigers.** A **tiger** is a large, fierce animal that belongs to the cat family. Tigers are orange-coloured with black stripes. N COUNT

tight /taɪt/, **tighter, tightest; tights. 1** Clothes or shoes that are **tight** fit closely to your body. EG *He was wearing tight cream-coloured trousers.* ◇ **tightly.** EG *...a tightly fitting suit.* ADJ QUALIT ◇ ADV

2 If you hold something or someone **tight**, you hold them firmly and securely. EG *Ann was now clutching the letter tight in her hand.* ▸ used as an adjective. EG *His fingers were tight on Thomas's arm.* ◇ **tightly.** EG *They clung together very tightly.* ADV AFTER VB ▸ ADJ QUALIT ◇ ADV

3 Something that is **tight** is firmly fastened, and difficult to move. EG *...a tight knot.* ◇ **tightly.** EG *He screwed the caps tightly onto the bottles.* ADJ QUALIT ◇ ADV

4 Something that is shut **tight** is shut very firmly. EG *He closed his eyes tight.* ADV AFTER VB

5 Skin, cloth, or string that is stretched **tight** is stretched or pulled so that it is smooth or straight. EG *The skin was stretched tight over her fine facial bones.* ◇ **tightly.** EG *The skin on his face was drawn back tightly like stretched leather.* ADJ QUALIT ◇ ADV

6 You use **tight** to describe things that are very close together. EG *They stood in a tight group... Her hair was arranged in tight curls.* ◇ **tightly.** EG *...houses tightly packed together.* ADJ QUALIT ◇ ADV

7 If your chest or stomach feels **tight**, it feels hard and painful, because you are ill or anxious. ◇ **tightness.** EG *I went to the interview with the familiar tightness in my stomach.* ADJ QUALIT ◇ N UNCOUNT

8 A **tight** plan or arrangement allows only the minimum time or money needed to do something. EG *We have a tight schedule.* ADJ QUALIT

9 A **tight** rule or system of control is very strict. EG *Security has become visibly tighter over the last year.* ◇ **tightly.** EG *...a society which is very tightly controlled.* ADJ QUALIT ◇ ADV

10 Someone who is **tight** is drunk. EG *Some of the village lads tried to get him tight.* ADJ QUALIT Informal

11 Tights are a thin piece of clothing made of stretchy material that fits closely round a person's hips, legs, and feet. They are usually worn by women, and sometimes by male dancers. EG *She had a ladder in her only pair of silk tights.* N PLURAL

12 to **keep a tight rein on** someone: see **rein.** ● to **sit tight**: see **sit.** ● See also **airtight, watertight.**

tighten /taɪtə°n/, **tightens, tightening, tightened. 1** If you **tighten** your hold on something or if your hold **tightens**, you hold the thing more firmly. EG *His fingers tightened around his rifle... He tightened his grip on the spear.* V-ERG : OFT+A

2 If you **tighten** a rope or chain, or if it **tightens**, it is stretched or pulled until it is straight. EG *The chain tightened and the pig's leg was pulled back.* V-ERG

3 When you **tighten** a fastening, you move it so that it is more firmly in place or holds something more firmly. EG *She bent down to tighten the strap of her roller skate.* • to **tighten** your **belt**: see **belt**. V+O

4 If a part of your body **tightens**, it becomes tense and stiff. EG *His face and eyes tightened with hatred.* V

5 If someone **tightens** a rule or system, they make it stricter or more efficient. EG *The authorities tightened security around the embassy.* V+O

tighten up. 1 When you **tighten up** a fastening, you move it so that it is more firmly in place or holds something more firmly. EG *Tighten up the axle nut.* PHRASAL VB : V+O+ADV **2** If someone **tightens up** a rule or system, they make it stricter or more efficient. EG *He said he would take steps to tighten up the administration.* V+O+ADV

tight-fisted /taɪt fɪstɪd/. Someone who is **tight-fisted** is unwilling to spend money. EG *He was unable to squeeze the extra cash out of his tight-fisted employers.* ADJ QUALIT Informal

tightrope /taɪtrəʊp/, **tightropes. 1** A **tightrope** is a tightly-stretched piece of rope on which an acrobat balances and performs tricks. N COUNT

2 If you say that someone is **on a tightrope** or **is walking a tightrope**, you mean that they are in a very difficult or delicate situation and have to be careful about what they say or do. EG *He recognized that he was walking a tightrope: one slip would mean political destruction.* PHRASE

tile /taɪl/, **tiles.** A **tile** is a small, flat, square piece of something such as slate, carpet, or cork. You use tiles to cover surfaces such as floors, walls, or roofs. EG *Polystyrene ceiling tiles help to insulate a room... ...brick houses roofed in reddish-brown tiles.* N COUNT

tiled /taɪld/. A **tiled** surface is covered with tiles. EG *He heard footsteps on the tiled floor... ...stone houses with red tiled roofs.* ADJ CLASSIF

till /tɪl/, **tills. 1 Till** means the same as until. EG *He wrote from morning till night... We didn't get back till 2... Wait till I come back.* PREP OR CONJ

2 A **till** is a drawer or box in a shop where money is kept, usually in a cash register. EG *He put the money into the till.* N COUNT

tilt /tɪlt/, **tilts, tilting, tilted.** If you **tilt** an object or if it **tilts**, it changes position so that one end or side is higher than the other. EG *He tilted the flask and two or three drops trickled out... Let your head gently tilt forwards.* V-ERG : USU+A ▸ used as a noun. EG *He indicated, with a tilt of his head, a girl nearby.* ▸ N COUNT

timber /tɪmbə/, **timbers. 1 Timber** is wood that is used for building houses and making furniture. EG *Most of the region's timber is imported from the south... We live in timber cabins.* N UNCOUNT

2 The **timbers** of a ship or house are the big pieces of wood that have been used to build it. EG *He could hear the ship's timbers creaking.* N COUNT : USU PLURAL

time /taɪm/, **times, timing, timed. 1 Time** is what we measure in hours, days, and years. EG *...a period of time... Time passed, and finally he fell asleep again... You're getting more and more depressed as time goes on.* N UNCOUNT

2 You use **time** to refer to **2.1** a specific point in time, which can be stated in hours and minutes and is shown on clocks. EG *What's the time?... What time did you get back?... Ask the times of planes from Rome to Vienna... I will see you at the same time next week.* N COUNT : USU *the/what* +N SING **2.2** the official system of time that is used in a particular place in the world. EG *It was 1035 hours Greenwich Mean Time... ...at 6 in the evening, local time.* N UNCOUNT +SUPP

3 You also use **time** to refer to **3.1** the period of time that someone spends doing something. EG *How do you find time to write these books?... I didn't have time for tea... She spends most of her time sunbathing... That would take a long time to discuss in detail.* N UNCOUNT OR N SING : USU+SUPP **3.2** a period of time or a point in time, when you are describing what is happening then. EG *It seemed a good time to invite my sister to stay... ...during my time in Toronto... Do you remember that time when Adrian phoned?... He blushed each time she spoke to him... Ask for something different next time... There were times when I didn't know what to do.* N UNCOUNT OR N COUNT

4 A particular **time** in history is a period in it. EG *...the history of modern times... The film begins at the time of the Roman Empire... ...one of the great unsolved mysteries of our time.* N COUNT OR N UNCOUNT +SUPP

5 If you say it is **time** for an action or it is **time** to do it, you mean that it ought to happen or be done now. EG *It is time to go... It was time for tea... The time has come to change things... It is time we realized that we were wrong.* N UNCOUNT +SUPP

6 If something happens for a **time**, it happens for a fairly long period of time. EG *It's nice to be in London for a time... It became clear after a time that he was very ill.* N SING : *a*+N

7 You use **time** after numbers **7.1** to say how often something happens. EG *Ray and I play squash three times a week... The telephone rang a second time.* N COUNT **7.2** when you are saying how much bigger, smaller, better, or worse one thing is compared to another. EG *It would cost me ten times as much... It has become three times as difficult as it used to be.* N PLURAL

8 You use **times** in arithmetic to link numbers or amounts that are multiplied together. EG *5 times 50 – that's 250.*

9 If you **time** something for a particular time, you plan that it should happen at that time. EG *Their disruption was timed for 9.20.* V+O+*for* OR *to*-INF ◇ **timed.** EG *His remarks were badly timed.* ◇ ADJ CLASSIF AFTER ADV • See also **timing**.

10 If you **time** an action or activity, you measure how long it lasts. EG *This was repeated at intervals which he timed on his watch.* V+O

11 You can use **time** when talking about how late or how early you are for an appointment or event. For example, if you are **in time**, you are not late. If you are **in good time** or **ahead of time**, you are earlier than necessary or expected. If you are **on time**, you arrive at the correct time. EG *We're just in time... We got there in plenty of time... She did the exam two years ahead of time... We all got here on time.* PHRASE

12 Time is used with 'at' in these ways. **12.1** You use **at a time** when saying how many things or how much of something is involved in one place, group, or action. EG *He used to abandon his work for many months at a time... There was only room for one person at a time.* PHRASES **12.2** If something happens **at times**, it happens sometimes but not always. EG *She's really rude at times.* **12.3 At one time** or **at any one time** means at a single point in time or during a single period of time. EG *The library has room for six hundred readers at any one time.* **12.4** If you say that something existed or was true **at one time**, you mean that it existed or was true in the past. EG *You worked for them, didn't you, at one time?* **12.5** If you say that something unpleasant is the case **at the best of times**, you are emphasizing that it is the case even when everything else is as pleasant as possible. EG *I find cleaning tedious at the best of times.* **12.6** You use **at the same time** to introduce a statement that contrasts with the previous statement or modifies it. EG *It made us cautious but at the same time it made us willing to take a risk... Such a development would be wel-*

What is two times three?

come. At the same time, it is crucial to recognize the narrowness of the approach.

13 Time is used with other prepositions in these ways. PHRASES **13.1** If you say it is **about time** that something was done, you are emphasizing that you think it should be done. EG *It's about time that Parliament concentrated on unemployment.* **13.2** If someone is **ahead of** their **time**, they have an idea long before other people start thinking in the same way. EG *Diaghilev was ahead of his time.* **13.3** If something was **before** your **time**, it happened or existed before you were born. **13.4** Someone who is **behind the times** is old-fashioned. EG *The law is behind the times on a number of important issues.* **13.5** If you do something **for the time being**, you do it for a short time until something else can be arranged. EG *For the time being, we ought to stay with him.* **13.6** If you do something **from time to time**, you do it occasionally. EG *From time to time she stopped and looked round.* **13.7** If you say that something will happen **in time**, you mean that it will happen eventually. EG *In time the arguments will straighten themselves out.* **13.8** If something will happen **in** a week's **time** or **in** a month's **time**, it will happen after one week or one month has passed. EG *Celia is coming along in about an hour's time... ...in three weeks' time.*

14 Time is also used in these phrases. PHRASES **14.1** When you talk about how well a watch or clock **keeps time**, you are talking about how accurately it measures time. EG *This has kept perfect time since I got it back.* **14.2** If you **have no time for** someone or something, you do not like them or approve of them. Informal EG *I haven't got a lot of time for politicians.* **14.3** If you say that you **made good time** on a journey, you mean that you completed the journey more quickly than you expected. EG *We made pretty good time on the journey up here.* **14.4** If you do something to **pass the time**, you do it because you are bored or are waiting for something else, and not because you really want to do it. EG *They read every page just to pass the time.* **14.5** If you say that something will **take time**, you mean that it will happen slowly or gradually and not immediately. EG *It would take time to get results.* **14.6** If you **take** your **time** doing something, you do it slowly. EG *The steamer took its time.* **14.7** If something happens **time after time** or **time and again**, it happens on many occasions. EG *She had threatened time after time to leave him... Thousands of people have proved it time and time again.*

TIME

This entry shows some of the ways in which you can refer to time in English.

There are a number of ways of asking the time or of saying what time it is. EG *'What time is it, Gordon?' – 'Just after five.'... 'What's the time now?' – 'It's quarter past nine.'... 'Can you tell me the time?' – 'It's twenty-five past twelve.'... 'Have you got the time?' – 'It is nearly one o'clock.'... 'What time does the boat leave from Weymouth?' – 'At a quarter past three in the afternoon.'... The time is six forty-five... My watch says six thirty... It's five to eight and breakfast's at eight o'clock... The time was 10.35 hours Greenwich Mean Time.*

Here are some other ways of talking about time. EG *I'll be back at quarter past one... By eleven o'clock Brody was back in his office... At two o'clock in the morning Castle was still awake... You should be there no later than nine thirty... Office hours are from 9 a.m. to 6 p.m.*

four o'clock four 4 o'clock	four in the morning 4 a.m.	04:00
	four in the afternoon 4 p.m.	16:00
nine o'clock nine 9 o'clock	nine in the morning 9 a.m.	09:00
	nine in the evening nine at night 9 p.m.	21:00
twelve o'clock twelve 12 o'clock	twelve in the morning 12 a.m. midday noon	12:00
	twelve at night 12 p.m. midnight	00:00
a quarter past twelve quarter past twelve twelve fifteen a quarter after twelve		12:15 00:15
twenty-five past two twenty-five minutes past two two twenty-five twenty-five after two		02:25 14:25
half past eleven eleven-thirty half eleven half after eleven		11:30 23:30
a quarter to one quarter to one twelve forty-five a quarter of one		12:45 00:45
ten to eight ten minutes to eight seven-fifty ten of eight		07:50 19:50

time-honoured. A **time-honoured** way of doing something has been used for a very long time. ADJ CLASSIF: ATTRIB EG *...a time-honoured practice.*

timeless /taɪmlɪ^{2}s/. If you describe something as **timeless**, you mean that it is so good, beautiful, or perfect that it cannot be affected by the passing of time or by changes in society or fashion. ADJ CLASSIF Formal EG *His art has something universal, something timeless and enduring from age to age.*

time limit, time limits. A **time limit** is a period of time during which a particular task must be completed. N COUNT EG *I had set myself a time limit of two years.*

timely /taɪmli^{1}/. Something that is **timely** happens at just the right time, so that it is most effective or prevents possible problems or difficulties. ADJ QUALIT EG *...the safe and timely arrival of reinforcements.*

time out. If you take **time out** to do something, you stop your normal activities for a while in order to do it. N UNCOUNT EG *He took time out to chair a meeting of local officials.*

timer /taɪmə/, **timers.** A **timer** is a device that measures time, especially one that is part of a machine. N COUNT EG *The timer on the stove started ringing.* ● See also **egg-timer**.

time scale, time scales. The **time scale** of an event is the length of time during which it happens. N COUNT EG *...the time scale of technological development.*

timetable /taɪmteɪbə^{0}l/, **timetables.** A **timetable** is **1** a plan of the times when particular activities or jobs should be done. N COUNT EG *...a timetable of all events on Wednesday... ...the timetable of a* *second year pupil at a comprehensive school.* **2** a list of the times when particular trains, boats, buses, or aeroplanes arrive and depart. EG *...railway timetables.*

timid /tɪmɪd/. Someone who is **timid** is shy and shows no courage or self-confidence. EG *...a timid young girl... ...a timid smile.* ◇ **timidly**. EG *I left the car and timidly rang the doorbell.* ◇ **timidity** /tɪmɪdɪ^{1}ti^1/. EG *He had a terrible time in overcoming his timidity.* — ADJ QUALIT; ◇ ADV; ◇ N UNCOUNT

timing /taɪmɪŋ/. **1** Someone's **timing** is their skill in judging the right moment at which to do something in a situation or activity. EG *She displayed perfect timing and control.* — N UNCOUNT

2 The **timing** of an event is **2.1** the act of deciding when it should happen. EG *They met to consider the timing of elections.* **2.2** the act of measuring how much time it takes. — N UNCOUNT

tin /tɪn/, **tins. 1 Tin** is a soft silvery-white metal. EG *...a tin can... ...a tin kettle.* — N UNCOUNT

2 A **tin** is **2.1** a metal container which is filled with food and sealed in order to preserve the food. EG *...a tin of sardines... ...a tin of condensed milk... ...the biscuit tin.* **2.2** a small metal container with a lid. EG *...a biscuit tin.* — N COUNT OR N PART British

tinge /tɪndʒ/, **tinges.** A **tinge** of something, especially a colour or a feeling, is a small amount of it. EG *The sky had a greenish tinge... There was a tinge of envy in her voice... Other colonial systems lacked even that tinge of liberalism.* — N COUNT+SUPP

tinged /tɪndʒd/. If something is **tinged** with something else, especially with a colour or a feeling, it has a small amount of that colour or feeling in it. EG *Her eyes were slightly tinged with red... ...joy tinged with bitterness.* — ADJ PRED +*with*

tingle /tɪŋg^{ə}l/, **tingles, tingling, tingled. 1** When a part of your body **tingles**, you feel a slight prickling feeling in it. EG *His fingertips tingled.* ◇ **tingling**. EG *...a sharp tingling in her fingers.* — V; ◇ N UNCOUNT

2 When you **tingle** with excitement or shock, you feel it very strongly. EG *I was tingling with excitement.* — V : USU+*with*

tinker /tɪŋkə/, **tinkers, tinkering, tinkered.** If you **tinker** with something, you make a lot of small adjustments to it in order to repair it or improve it. EG *He's still tinkering with the motor.* — V : USU+*with* Informal

tinkle /tɪŋk^{ə}l/, **tinkles, tinkling, tinkled. 1** If something **tinkles**, it makes a sound like a small bell ringing. EG *I could hear bells tinkling.* ▸ used as a noun. EG *The telephone gave a tinkle.* — V; ▸ N COUNT : OFT+*of*

2 If you **give** someone **a tinkle**, you call them on the telephone. — PHRASE Informal

tinned /tɪnd/. **Tinned** food has been preserved by being sealed in a tin. EG *...tinned peas.* — ADJ CLASSIF

tinny /tɪni^1/, **tinnier, tinniest. 1** A **tinny** sound has an unpleasant high-pitched quality. EG *One hears bursts of tinny pop music from teenagers' handbags.* — ADJ QUALIT

2 If something such as a car is **tinny**, it is made of thin metal and is of poor quality. — ADJ QUALIT

tin-opener /tɪn əʊpə^{0}nə/, **tin-openers.** A **tin-opener** is a tool that you use to open tins of food. — N COUNT

tinsel /tɪnsəl/ consists of small pieces of sparkling, coloured paper attached to long pieces of thread. Tinsel is used to decorate rooms at Christmas. EG *...tinsel on a Christmas tree.* — N UNCOUNT

tint /tɪnt/, **tints, tinted, tinting. 1** A **tint** is a colour. EG *His eyes had a yellow tint.* — N COUNT

2 If you **tint** your hair, you change its colour by adding a weak dye to it. EG *He acquired a preparation for tinting his hair chestnut brown.* — V+O

tinted /tɪntɪ^{1}d/. Something such as glass that is **tinted** is coloured, especially with pale colours. EG *He glanced through the tinted rear window.* — ADJ CLASSIF

tiny /taɪni^1/, **tinier, tiniest.** Something that is **tiny** is extremely small. EG *...tiny shells, the size of your finger nail... ...the tiny little room at the end.* — ADJ QUALIT

-tion, -tions. See **-ation**.

tip /tɪp/, **tips, tipping, tipped. 1** The **tip** of something long and thin is the end of it. EG *He was hanging by his finger tips from a window frame... The animal plucks fruit from the tips of branches.* — N COUNT : OFT+*of*

2 If you **tip** an object, you move it so that it is no longer horizontal or upright. EG *He tipped his soup bowl towards himself... He was sitting with his chair tipped back against the wall.* — V+O+A

3 If you **tip** something somewhere, you pour it there quickly and carelessly. EG *He tipped the contents of the rucksack out on to the floor.* — V+O+A

4 A **tip** is a place where rubbish is dumped. EG *The area was covered with wrecked cars and rubbish tips.* — N COUNT British

5 If you give someone such as a waiter or a taxi driver a **tip**, you give them some money to thank them for their services. EG *The woman gave me a dollar tip.* ▸ used as a verb. EG *I tipped the chauffeur... People aren't tipping very much.* — N COUNT; ▸ V+O OR V

6 A **tip** is also a useful piece of advice or information, often one that is given privately or secretly. EG *He consulted books by well-known tennis players for tips on basic techniques.* — N COUNT

7 If you say that a word or name is **on the tip of** your **tongue**, you mean that you cannot remember it just at the moment, but you are sure you will remember it very soon. — PHRASE

8 If you say that something is **the tip of the iceberg**, you mean that it is only a very small part of a much larger problem. — PHRASE

tip off. If you **tip** someone **off**, you give them information, often privately or secretly, about something that has happened or that is going to happen. EG *The burglars were tipped off by a lookout and escaped.* ● See also **tip-off**. — PHRASAL VB : V+O+ADV

tip over. If you **tip** something **over** or if it **tips over**, it falls over or turns over. EG *She tipped the pan over and a dozen fish flopped out... His chair was tipping over.* — PHRASAL VB : V-ERG+ADV

tip-off, tip-offs. A **tip-off** is a piece of information that you give to someone, often privately or secretly, usually as a warning that something is going to happen. EG *The building was evacuated as the result of a tip-off.* — N COUNT

tipped /tɪpt/. **1** Something that is **tipped** has a tip made of a different substance. EG *They hunted in the woods with spears tipped with stone blades.* — ADJ CLASSIF : OFT+*with*

2 A **tipped** cigarette has a filter at the end which the smoke passes through when you breathe it in. — ADJ CLASSIF

tipsy /tɪpsi^1/. If you are **tipsy**, you are slightly drunk. EG *The wine had made Barton a trifle tipsy.* — ADJ QUALIT Informal

tiptoe /tɪptəʊ/, **tiptoes, tiptoeing, tiptoed. 1** If you **tiptoe** somewhere, you walk there very quietly on your toes. EG *He knocked softly on the door and tiptoed into the room.* — V : USU+A

2 If you do something **on tiptoe**, you do it standing or walking on your toes. EG *They stretched their arms and stood on tiptoe.* — PHRASE

tirade /taɪreɪd/, **tirades.** A **tirade** is a long, angry speech in which you criticize someone or something. EG *He launched into a familiar tirade against the government.* — N COUNT Formal

tire /taɪə/, **tires, tiring, tired. 1** If something **tires** you, it makes you use a lot of energy, with the result that you want to rest or sleep. EG *The run did not seem to tire them at all... The other men began to tire and fall.* — V-ERG

2 If you **tire** of something, you become bored with it. EG *He tired of my questions... The modern businessman never tires of claiming and complaining.* — V+*of*

3 See also **tyre**.

tire out. If something **tires** you **out**, it makes you exhausted. — PHRASAL VB : V+O+ADV

Name some activities that tire you out.

tired /taɪəd/. 1 If you are **tired**, you feel that you want to rest or sleep. EG *I'm sure you must be tired after cycling all that distance.* ◊ **tiredness**. EG *Tiredness overwhelmed me.* • If you are **tired out**, you are exhausted. EG *Have a good trip? I expect you're tired out.* ADJ QUALIT ◊ N UNCOUNT • PHRASE

2 If a person's voice or eyes are **tired**, they show that the person needs rest or sleep. EG *'I'm hungry,' said the little boy in a tired voice.* ADJ QUALIT

3 If you are **tired** of something, you are bored with it. EG *Judy was tired of quarrelling with him.* ADJ PRED+*of*

tireless /taɪələ²s/. Someone who is **tireless** has a lot of energy and never seems to need a rest. EG *Both of them were tireless workers.* ADJ CLASSIF

tiresome /taɪəsəm/. A person or thing that is **tiresome** makes you feel irritated or bored. EG *...a tiresome obstacle to be overcome.* ADJ QUALIT

tiring /taɪərɪŋ/. Something that is **tiring** makes you tired so that you want to rest or sleep. EG *We should have an early night after such a tiring day.* ADJ QUALIT

tissue /tɪsjuː, tɪʃuː/, **tissues.** 1 In animals and plants, **tissue** consists of cells that are similar in appearance and function. EG *...the scar tissue left by a wound.* N MASS Technical

2 **Tissue** or **tissue paper** is thin paper that is used for wrapping things that are easily damaged, such as glass or china. N UNCOUNT

3 A **tissue** is a small, square piece of soft paper that you use as a handkerchief. EG *There was a box of tissues in the back window of the car.* N COUNT

4 You can refer to a totally false story as a **tissue of lies**. EG *Their allegations were a tissue of lies.* PHRASE

titbit /tɪtbɪt/, **titbits.** A **titbit** is a small, tasty piece of food. EG *...a dog begging for titbits.* N COUNT

titillate /tɪtɪleɪt/, **titillates, titillating, titillated.** If something **titillates** someone, it pleases and excites them, especially in a sexual way. EG *...various other bits of scandal designed to titillate.* V+O OR V

title /taɪtə⁰l/, **titles.** 1 The **title** of a book, play, or piece of music is its name. EG *He wrote a book with the title 'The Castle'.* N COUNT

2 Someone's **title** is **2.1** a word such as Lord, Lady, Mr, or Mrs, that is used before their name in order to show their rank or status. **2.2** a word that describes their job or position in an organization. EG *The person in charge usually has a title of some sort like Administration Manager.* N COUNT

3 A **title** in a sports competition is the position of champion. Usually a person or team keeps a title until someone else defeats them. EG *We had beaten Cornell and taken the title.* N COUNT

titled /taɪtə⁰ld/. Someone who is **titled** has a high social rank and has a word such as 'Princess', 'Lord', 'Lady', or 'Sir' before their own name to show this. EG *...titled ladies... ...a titled Englishman.* ADJ CLASSIF

title-holder, title-holders. The **title-holder** is the winner of a competition that takes place regularly. They remain the title-holder until someone else wins it. N COUNT

title role, title roles. If an actor or an actress has the **title role** in a play or film, he or she plays the character referred to in its name. For example, if an actress has the title role in 'Hedda Gabler', she plays Hedda Gabler. EG *...an actor best known for the title role in 'The Eddie Cantor Story'.* N COUNT

titter /tɪtə/, **titters, tittering, tittered.** If you **titter**, you laugh in a way that shows that you are nervous or embarrassed. EG *Someone began to titter. 'What's the matter?' asked the Director.* V

TNT /tiː ɛn tiː/ is a powerful explosive substance. N UNCOUNT

to /tə, tuː/. 1 You use **to** when indicating the place that someone or something is moving towards or pointing at. EG *I'm going with her to Australia... We'll drive to the top of the next hill... The children have gone to school... He thought that he might go to a concert... He was pointing to an oil tanker somewhere on the horizon.* PREP

2 You use **to** when indicating where something is tied or attached, or what it is touching. EG *I was planning to tie him to a tree... He clutched the parcel to his chest.* PREP

3 You use **to** when indicating the position of something. For example, if something is **to** your left, it is on your left. EG *To one side, he could see the block of luxury flats.* PREP

4 You use **to** when indicating who or what an action, a feeling, or your attention is directed towards. EG *He showed the letter to Barbara... She had given German lessons to a leading industrialist... We don't do repairs to farm machines... The answer to your question is unexpectedly simple... They were sympathetic to his ideas... She listened to a flute being played.* PREP

5 You use **to** when indicating someone's reaction to something. For example, if you say that something happens **to** someone's relief, you mean that they are relieved when it happens. EG *To his great surprise he was offered both jobs.* PREP

6 You use **to** when indicating the effect that something has on someone. For example, if something is **to** someone's liking, they are satisfied or pleased with it. EG *It's to your own advantage.* PREP

7 You use **to** when indicating the person whose opinion you are stating, especially when you know that other people may disagree with it. EG *To me it didn't seem necessary.* PREP

8 You use **to** when indicating what something or someone is becoming, or the state or situation that they are progressing towards. EG *It had almost turned to dust over the years... It drove me to distraction and despair... ...her rapid rise to fame... The danger is that a conventional conflict might escalate to a nuclear confrontation.* PREP

9 You use **to** when indicating that something happens until the time or amount mentioned is reached. EG *Breakfast was from 9 to 10 in the morning... The job will take anything from two to five weeks.* PREP

10 You say **from** one thing **to** another when giving two extreme examples of something which emphasize the scope or range of what you are saying. EG *I do everything, from washing up dishes to putting out the cat at night... We have branches in most of the cities of the world, from Yokohama to York.* PHRASE

11 If someone goes **from** place **to** place or **from** job **to** job, they go to several places, or work in several jobs, and spend only a short time in each one. EG *I've spent years going from town to town.* PHRASE

12 If someone moves **to and fro**, they move repeatedly from one place to another and back again, or from side to side. EG *All day, he rushed to and fro between his living quarters and his place of work... She rocked herself to and fro in amusement.* • See also **to-ing and fro-ing**. PHRASE

13 You use **to** in expressions of time that state the number of minutes before a particular hour. For example, 'five **to** eight' means five minutes before eight o'clock: see the entry headed TIME. PREP

14 You use **to** in ratios and rates when saying how many units of one type there are for each unit of another. EG *My car does 35 miles to the gallon... The current exchange rate is $1.78 to the pound.* PREP

15 If you push or shut a door **to**, you close it but do not shut it completely. ADV AFTER VB

16 You use **to** when indicating that two things happen at the same time. For example, if something happens **to** music, it happens at the same time as music is being played. EG *To a chorus of laughter the President left the room.* PREP

17 If you say **'There's nothing to it'**, **'There's not much to it'**, or **'That's all there is to it'**, you are emphasizing how simple or easy you think something is. PHRASE

18 You use **to** with the infinitive of a verb **18.1** when indicating the purpose or intention of an action. EG *People would stroll down the path to admire the garden.* • **in order to**: see **order**. **18.2** when commenting on a statement that you are *to*+INF

making, for example when saying that you are being honest or brief, or that you are summing up or giving an example. EG *To be honest, we knew he was there... To tell you the truth, Phil, I don't want it... To sum up, my contention is that the law must be changed.* **18.3** in various other constructions. EG *She looked up to find Tony standing there... It costs about 150 pounds a week to keep someone in prison... They don't know who to ask... Some of us have got work to do... They were lovely to watch... This is difficult for us to accept... ...the first person to climb Everest... He was too proud to apologize... Sorry to keep you waiting.*

19 To is also used after verbs such as 'refer', 'relate', and 'attend', and in phrasal verbs such as 'see to' and 'come to'. See the individual verb and phrasal verb entries.

toad /təʊd/, **toads.** A **toad** is an animal that looks like a frog but has a drier skin and lives less in the water. EG *I've been sitting here like a toad on a log.* N COUNT

toadstool /təʊdstu:l/, **toadstools.** A **toadstool** is a fungus that looks like a mushroom but is poisonous, so you cannot eat it. N COUNT

toast /təʊst/, **toasts, toasting, toasted. 1 Toast** is bread which has been cut into slices and made brown and crisp by cooking at a high temperature. EG *Lally was spreading marmalade on a piece of toast... I like baked beans on toast.* N UNCOUNT

2 When you **toast** bread, you cook it at a high temperature so that it becomes brown and crisp. V+O

3 If you **toast** yourself or **toast** a part of your body, you sit in front of a fire so that you feel pleasantly warm. EG *He was toasting his toes at the fire.* V-REFL OR V+O

4 When you drink a **toast** to someone, you wish them success or good health, and then drink some wine or other alcoholic drink. EG *It was an old fisherman's custom to drink a toast to the dead... Harold raised his glass in a toast: 'Welcome!'* N COUNT: USU a+N

5 When you **toast** someone, you show your respect for them or wish them success by saying their name, and then drinking some wine or other alcoholic drink. EG *I toasted the young hero and wished him luck.* V+O

6 If someone is the **toast** of a place, they are very popular and are greatly admired there. EG *Joan was the toast of the Senior Common Room.* N SING: *the*+N+*of*

toaster /təʊstə/, **toasters.** A **toaster** is a piece of electric equipment which you use to toast bread. EG *She put her slice of bread in the toaster.* N COUNT

tobacco /təbækəʊ/ is **1** a substance which people smoke in pipes, cigars, and cigarettes. EG *He took out his pipe and filled it with tobacco and lit it.* **2** the plant from which tobacco is obtained. EG *...the cotton and tobacco fields.* N UNCOUNT

tobacconist /təbækənɪst/, **tobacconists.** A **tobacconist** is **1** a person who runs a shop that sells things such as tobacco, cigarettes, and cigars. **2** a shop that sells things such as tobacco, cigarettes, and cigars. N COUNT

toboggan /təbɒgən/, **toboggans, tobogganing, tobogganed. 1** A **toboggan** is a vehicle for travelling on snow. It consists of a flat seat with two narrow pieces of wood or metal underneath that slide easily over the snow. N COUNT

2 If you **toboggan**, you ride on a toboggan. EG *...tobogganing down the long slope.* V: USU+A

today /tədeɪ/. **1 Today** means the day on which you are speaking or writing. EG *I hope you're feeling better today... I had a letter today from my solicitor... Today is Thursday.* ADV OR N UNCOUNT

2 You can refer to the present period of history as **today**. EG *Today we are threatened on all sides by financial and political crises... ...differences between the America of today and the America of thirty years ago.* ADV OR N UNCOUNT

toddle /tɒdəᵒl/, **toddles, toddling, toddled.** When a child **toddles**, it walks unsteadily with short, quick steps. EG *You can see his grandson toddling around in the garden.* V

toddler /tɒdlə/, **toddlers.** A **toddler** is a small child who has just learned to walk. EG *...forty women, many of them with toddlers and young babies.* N COUNT

to-do /tə du:/. When there is a **to-do**, people are very excited, confused, or angry about something. EG *There was an awful to-do about the election result.* N SING+SUPP Informal

toe /təʊ/, **toes, toeing, toed. 1** Your **toes** are the five movable parts at the end of your foot. See picture at THE HUMAN BODY. EG *I stubbed my toe against a stone... I've got sand between my toes.* N COUNT: USU PLURAL

2 The **toe** of a shoe or sock is the part that covers the end of your foot. EG *Maria's shoes had holes in the toes.* N COUNT

3 If you **toe the line**, you behave in the way that people in authority expect you to. EG *She had always tried to toe the line in public.* PHRASE

toenail /təʊneɪl/, **toenails.** Your **toenails** are the thin, hard coverings on the end of your toes. EG *Cut their toenails once a fortnight.* N COUNT: USU PLURAL

toffee /tɒfi¹/, **toffees.** A **toffee** is a chewy sweet that is made by boiling sugar and butter together with water. EG *...a few assorted toffees... ...a chunk of toffee.* N COUNT OR N UNCOUNT

toffee apple, toffee apples. A **toffee apple** is an apple covered with a thin, hard layer of toffee and mounted on a stick. N COUNT

together /təgeðə/. **1** If people do something **together**, they do it with each other. EG *They flew back to London together... You all work together as a team in the office.* ADV

2 If two things happen **together**, they happen at the same time. EG *The reports will have to be seen and judged together before we decide.* ADV AFTER VB

3 If things are joined or fixed **together**, they are joined or fixed to each other. EG *Her hands were clasped tightly together... ...a series of hollow aluminium tubes which screw together.* ADV AFTER VB

4 If things or people are **together**, they are very near to each other. EG *There were two metal plates lying close together on the floor... The fossils are packed densely together in display cases.* ADV AFTER VB

5 Together with something else means as well as that other thing. EG *Lee handed over the key to his room, together with some forms and leaflets.* CONJ

6 If you say that things go **together**, you mean that they fit or suit each other or can both exist or happen without causing any problems. EG *Nell feels marriage and studying don't go together.* ADV AFTER VB

7 You use **together** when you are adding two or more things to each other in order to consider the total as a whole. EG *The two companies together spend more on research than the whole of the rest of the industry.* ADV

toil /tɔɪl/, **toils, toiling, toiled. 1** When people **toil**, they work hard doing unpleasant, difficult, or tiring tasks or jobs. EG *...factories where men toiled all through the night.* V: USU+A Formal

2 Toil is unpleasant, difficult, or tiring work. EG *The wealth of industrial society could only come from the toil of the masses.* N UNCOUNT Formal

toil away. If you **toil away**, you work hard for a long time doing an unpleasant, difficult, or tiring task or job. EG *...the coalminer toiling away in the deepest mines.* PHRASAL VB: V+ADV

toilet /tɔɪlɪ²t/, **toilets. 1** A **toilet** is **1.1** a large bowl with a seat which you use when you want to get rid of urine or faeces from your body. EG *She heard the toilet flush.* **1.2** a small room containing a toilet. EG *He opens the door of the toilet.* N COUNT

2 When you **go to the toilet**, you get rid of urine or faeces from your body in a toilet. EG *He wants to go to the toilet.* PHRASE

Would you call this dictionary a tome?

toilet paper is paper that you use to clean yourself after getting rid of urine or faeces from your body. EG *On the wall was a roll of toilet paper.* N UNCOUNT

toiletries /tɔɪlɪ²trɪz/ are the things that you use when cleaning or taking care of your body, such as soap, deodorant, and toothpaste. EG *Madeleine went across to buy some toiletries.* N PLURAL

toilet roll, toilet rolls. A **toilet roll** is a long strip of toilet paper that is wound around a small cardboard tube. N COUNT OR N UNCOUNT

to-ing and fro-ing /tuːɪŋ ənd frəʊɪŋ/ is a situation in which the same action or the same movement between two places is repeated many times. EG *There was a lot of to-ing and fro-ing between London and Glasgow.* PHRASE

token /təʊkə⁰n/, **tokens. 1** A **token** is a piece of paper or card that is worth a particular amount of money and that can be exchanged for goods. EG *...a record token... I got three book tokens for my birthday.* N COUNT

2 Tokens are also round, flat pieces of metal that are sometimes used instead of money. EG *Some manufacturers minted their own wage tokens.* N COUNT

3 If you give something to someone as a **token** of your feelings for them, you give it to them as a way of expressing those feelings. EG *He gave her a gold brooch as a token of his esteem.* N COUNT

4 Token also means small or unimportant, but intended to show publicly what you think or feel. EG *The union wanted to go beyond one-day token strikes and marches... ...token resistance.* ADJ CLASSIF : ATTRIB

5 You use **by the same token** to introduce a statement that you think is true or correct for the same reasons that were given for a previous statement. EG *We make people mentally old by retiring them, and we may even by the same token make them physically old.* PHRASE

told /təʊld/. **1 Told** is the past tense and past participle of **tell**.

2 You use **all told** when you want to emphasize that everything has been counted. EG *There are only four characters all told in Pinter's new play.* PHRASE

tolerable /tɒlə⁰rəbə⁰l/. If something is **tolerable**, you are able to accept it, although it is not enjoyable or not pleasant. EG *I was given a tolerable meal... They never found the climate tolerable enough to settle there.* ADJ QUALIT

tolerant /tɒlərənt/. If you are **tolerant**, you let other people say and do what they think is right, even if you do not agree with it or approve of it. EG *Michael is a remarkably tolerant person... I think I've become more tolerant of other people's attitudes.* ◇ **tolerance** /tɒlərəns/. EG *He has a sense of humour plus tolerance and patience.* ADJ QUALIT ◇ N UNCOUNT

tolerate /tɒləreɪt/, **tolerates, tolerating, tolerated. 1** If you **tolerate** things that you do not approve of or agree with, you allow them to exist or to happen. EG *They happily tolerated the existence of opinions contrary to their own.* V+O
◇ **toleration** /tɒləreɪʃə⁰n/. EG *...her toleration of religious variety.* ◇ N UNCOUNT

2 If you can **tolerate** something, you are able to accept it, although it is unsatisfactory or unpleasant. EG *I was wondering how much longer I could tolerate isolation... They couldn't tolerate the noise.* V+O

toll /təʊl/, **tolls, tolling, tolled. 1** When someone **tolls** a bell or when it **tolls**, they ring it slowly and repeatedly, often as a sign that someone has died. EG *The bell tolled for him.* V-ERG

2 The death **toll** in an accident is the number of people who have died in it. EG *By Wednesday the death toll had risen to more than 40.* N COUNT+SUPP

3 If something **takes a toll** or **takes its toll**, it has a serious effect and causes a lot of suffering. EG *The walking was beginning to take its toll on all of us.* PHRASE

4 A **toll** is a sum of money that you have to pay in order to use a particular bridge or road. N COUNT

tomato /təmɑːtəʊ/, **tomatoes.** A **tomato** is a small, soft, red fruit that you can eat raw in salads, or cooked as a vegetable or in a sauce. EG *...a lettuce and tomato sandwich.* N COUNT

tomb /tuːm/, **tombs.** A **tomb** is a large grave that is above ground and that usually has a sculpture or other decoration on it. N COUNT

tomboy /tɒmbɔɪ/, **tomboys.** A **tomboy** is a young girl who likes playing rough or noisy games. N COUNT

tombstone /tuːmstəʊn/, **tombstones.** A **tombstone** is a large, flat piece of stone on someone's grave or tomb, on which their name is written. N COUNT

tomcat /tɒmkæt/, **tomcats.** A **tomcat** is a male cat. N COUNT

tome /təʊm/, **tomes.** A **tome** is a large, heavy book. EG *I was attempting to read a weighty tome... ...bookshelves loaded with tomes.* N COUNT Literary

tomorrow /təmɒrəʊ/. **1 Tomorrow** means the day after today. EG *They're coming tomorrow... See you tomorrow... Shall I come tomorrow night?... Tomorrow's concert has been cancelled.* ADV OR N UNCOUNT

2 You can refer to the future, especially the near future, as **tomorrow**. EG *They live today as millions more will live tomorrow... You're always searching after a better tomorrow... ...a citizen of tomorrow's super-industrial world.*

ton /tʌn/, **tons. 1** A **ton** is **1.1** a unit of weight that is equal to 2240 pounds in Britain and to 2000 pounds in the United States. EG *It's made of steel and weighs ten tons... The Japanese extract ten million tons of coal each year from underwater mines.* **1.2** the same as a tonne. N COUNT OR N PART

2 If you say that something **weighs a ton**, you mean that it is very heavy. EG *The batteries alone weighed a ton... It'll need six of us to lift that piano – it weighs a ton!* PHRASE Informal

3 If you **come down on** someone **like a ton of bricks**, you speak very angrily to them or punish them very severely when they do something wrong. EG *The judges will come down on them like a ton of bricks... She came down on me like a ton of bricks when she found out.* PHRASE Informal

4 If you have **tons** of something, you have a lot of it. EG *I've got tons of paper to draw on... He's making tons of money.* N PART : PLURAL Informal British

tone /təʊn/, **tones, toning, toned. 1** Someone's **tone** is a quality in their voice which shows what they are feeling or thinking. EG *'Very good,' he said in an encouraging tone... Her tone was defiant... She was speaking now in cold, sarcastic tones.* N COUNT+SUPP

2 A **tone** is one of the sounds that you hear when you are using a telephone, for example the sound that tells you that a number is engaged. EG *I'm getting the ringing tone, but there doesn't appear to be anyone at home... Don't put your money in until you hear the pay tone.* N COUNT

3 The **tone** of a musical instrument or a singer's voice is the kind of sound it has, for example a rich sound or a thin sound. EG *I wish I had a piano with a better tone.* N COUNT OR N UNCOUNT +SUPP

4 The **tone** of a piece of writing is its style and the opinions or ideas expressed in it. EG *I was greatly offended by the tone of the article.* N UNCOUNT

5 If something **lowers the tone** of a place, it makes it seem less respectable. EG *He said the new people had lowered the tone of the neighbourhood.* PHRASE

6 A **tone** is also one of the lighter, darker, or brighter shades of the same colour. EG *The colours of the pigeons matched the tones of the sky... You need a blue that is darker in tone.* N COUNT OR N UNCOUNT

tone down. If you **tone down** something that you have written, you make it less forceful, severe, or offensive. EG *He advised me to tone down my letter.* PHRASAL VB : V+O+ADV

tone in. If something **tones in** with something else, the two things look nice together because their colours are similar in quality or brightness. EG *The thick velvet toned in with the her dress.* PHRASAL VB : V+ADV, OFT+*with*

tone-deaf. Someone who is **tone-deaf** cannot sing in tune or cannot recognize different tunes. ADJ CLASSIF

tools

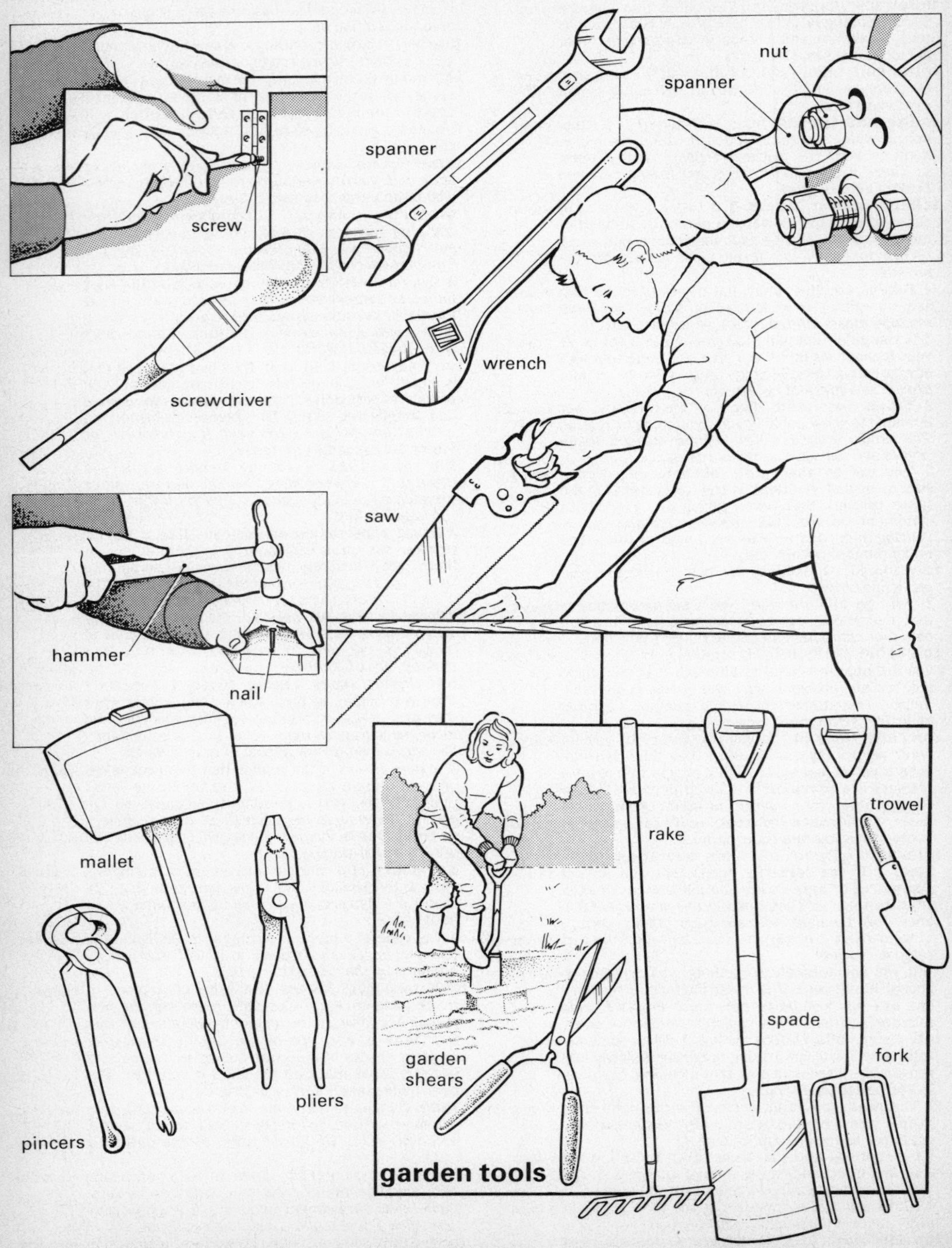
nut
spanner
spanner
screw
wrench
screwdriver
saw
hammer
nail
mallet
trowel
rake
spade
fork
garden shears
pliers
pincers
garden tools

tongs

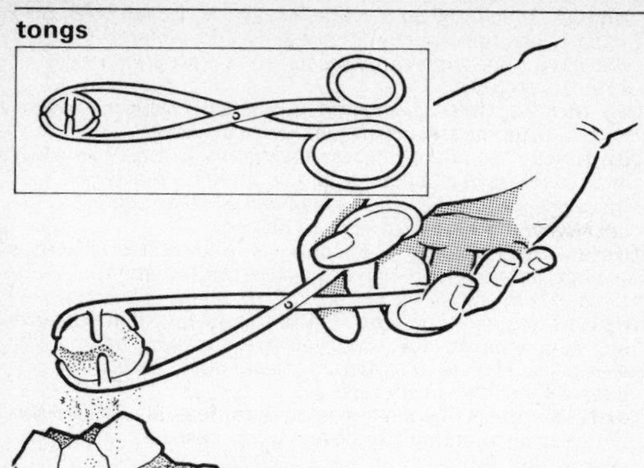

tongs /tɒŋz/. **Tongs** consist of two long narrow pieces of metal joined together at one end. You press the pieces together in order to grip an object and pick it up. EG *She was putting lumps of sugar into her tea with a pair of silver tongs.* N PLURAL

tongue /tʌŋ/, **tongues.** 1 Your **tongue** is the soft part inside your mouth that you can move and use for tasting, licking, and speaking. EG *Lynn stuck out her tongue... He ran his tongue over his lips.* N COUNT

2 You can use **tongue** to refer to the kind of things that a person says. EG *...his eloquent tongue... She had a sharp and hurtful tongue.* N COUNT+SUPP

3 A **tongue** is a language. EG *...an alien tongue... I answered her in her own tongue.* N COUNT Literary

4 **Tongue** is the cooked tongue of an ox. N UNCOUNT

5 The **tongue** of a shoe or boot is the piece of leather which is underneath the laces. N COUNT

6 **Tongue** is used in these phrases. **6.1** If you **hold** your **tongue**, you do not say anything. EG *I just held my tongue and followed them.* **6.2** If you **have** your **tongue in** your **cheek** when you say or do something, you are not being sincere or serious about it, although you may appear to be. EG *I suspect Dr Vidler had his tongue in his cheek when he wrote that.* ● See also **tongue-in-cheek**. **6.3** A **slip of the tongue** is a small mistake that you make when you are speaking, especially a mistake that is humorous or embarrassing. EG *If I did say that, it was just a slip of the tongue.* **6.4 on the tip of** your **tongue**: see **tip**. PHRASES

tongue-in-cheek. A **tongue-in-cheek** remark is made as a joke, and is not serious or sincere. EG *He offered some tongue-in-cheek advice about keeping out of the rain.* ADJ QUALIT

tongue-tied. If you are **tongue-tied**, you are unable to say anything because you feel shy or nervous. EG *He became completely tongue-tied.* ADJ QUALIT

tongue-twister, tongue-twisters. A **tongue-twister** is a sentence or expression which is very difficult to say properly, especially when you try saying it quickly. For example, 'She sells seashells on the seashore' is an English tongue-twister. N COUNT

tonic /tɒnɪk/, **tonics.** 1 **Tonic** or **tonic water** is a colourless, fizzy drink that has a slightly bitter flavour and is often mixed with alcoholic drinks, especially gin. EG *A gin and tonic, please.* N MASS

2 A **tonic** is a medicine that makes you feel stronger, healthier, and less tired. N MASS

3 You can refer to anything that makes you feel stronger or more cheerful as a **tonic**. EG *It was a tonic to talk to her.* N COUNT

4 Skin **tonic** or hair **tonic** is a liquid that you put on your skin or hair in order to improve it. N MASS

tonight /tənaɪt/ means the evening or night that will come at the end of today. EG *I think I'll go to bed early tonight... In tonight's programme we shall be explaining the history of the movement.* ADV OR N UNCOUNT

tonnage /tʌnɪdʒ/. 1 The **tonnage** of a ship is its size or the amount of cargo that it can carry. N UNCOUNT Technical

2 **Tonnage** is also the total number of tons that something weighs, or the total amount that there is of something that is measured in tons. EG *...the total tonnage of TNT used during the last war.* N COUNT: OFT+*of*

tonne /tʌn/, **tonnes.** A **tonne** is a metric unit of weight that is equal to 1000 kilograms. EG *...500 million tonnes of crude oil.* N COUNT OR N PART

tonsil /tɒnsᵊl/, **tonsils.** Your **tonsils** are the two small, soft lumps in your throat at the back of your mouth. N COUNT: USU PLURAL

tonsillitis /tɒnsɪˈlaɪtɪˈs/ is a painful swelling of your tonsils caused by an infection. N UNCOUNT

too /tuː/. 1 You use **too** after adding another person, thing, or aspect that a previous statement applies to or includes. EG *I'm on your side. Seibert is too... There were carrots too... Physically, too, the peoples of the world are incredibly mixed.* ADV SEN

2 You use **too** after adding a piece of information or a comment to a statement, in order to emphasize that it is surprising or important. EG *It was a pretty play, and very sad too... He was always kind and helpful to me. But he could be alarming too... I remember that quite well. It was a Tuesday too... You ought to see a doctor. And quickly, too.* ADV SEN

3 You also use **too** to indicate that there is a greater amount or degree of something than is desirable, necessary, or acceptable. EG *Avoid using too much water... Philip decided it was not too far to walk... Don't leave it in too warm a place.* ADV+QUANTIF OR SUBMOD

4 You use **all too** or **only too** to emphasize that something happens to a greater extent or degree than is pleasant or desirable. EG *I can remember only too well the disasters that followed... The suspicions had proved all too true... All too soon, we had to leave.* PHRASE

5 You can use **too** with a negative when you really mean the opposite, but are being polite, sarcastic, or cautious. EG *That's probably not too far from the truth... He wasn't too keen on it... It's not too bad.* SUBMOD: WITH BROAD NEG

6 **too bad**: see **bad**. ● **too** clever, arrogant, etc **by half**: see **half**. ● **none too**: see **none**.

took /tʊk/ is the past tense of **take**.

tool /tuːl/, **tools.** 1 A **tool** is any instrument or piece of equipment that you hold in your hands in order to help you to do a particular kind of work. Spades, hammers, and knives are tools. N COUNT

2 When workers **down tools**, they stop working suddenly in order to make a protest or to go on strike. EG *Workers downed tools in what soon became a general strike.* PHRASE British

3 **The tools of** your **trade** are the skills, instruments, and other equipment that you need in order to do your job properly. PHRASE

toot /tuːt/, **toots, tooting, tooted.** If you **toot** your car horn, you make it produce a short sound or series of sounds. EG *She tooted the horn... A car horn tooted.* ▸ used as a noun. EG *'Look,' she said and gave a toot on the horn.* V-ERG OR V ▸ N COUNT

tooth /tuːθ/, **teeth** /tiːθ/. 1 Your **teeth** are the hard, white objects in your mouth that you use for biting and chewing food. EG *He had very white, even teeth.* ● See also **wisdom tooth**. N COUNT

2 The **teeth** of a comb, saw, or zip are the parts that stick out in a row on its edge. N COUNT

3 If an official group or a law has **teeth**, it has power and is able to be effective. EG *The code will not have more teeth than the guidelines unless governments support it fully.* N PLURAL

4 **Tooth** and **teeth** are used in these phrases. **4.1** Someone who is **long in the tooth** is old or getting old. EG *She's getting a bit long in the tooth for this sort of thing.* **4.2** If you are **fed up to the back teeth** with something, you are extremely dissatisfied or bored with it. **4.3** If you say that someone **is lying through** their **teeth**, you mean that they are deliberately telling lies. **4.4** to **grit** your **teeth**: see PHRASES Informal

grit. • by the skin of your teeth: see skin. • a sweet tooth: see sweet.

toothache /tu:θeɪk/ is a feeling of pain in one of your teeth. N UNCOUNT

toothbrush /tu:θbrʌʃ/, **toothbrushes.** A **toothbrush** is a small brush with a long handle which you use for cleaning your teeth. See picture at BRUSHES. N COUNT

toothless /tu:θlɪ²s/. If someone is **toothless**, they have no teeth. EG *...a toothless old woman... ...a sly toothless grin.* ADJ CLASSIF

toothpaste /tu:θpeɪst/, **toothpastes. Toothpaste** is a thick substance which you put on your toothbrush and use to clean your teeth. N MASS

toothpick /tu:θpɪk/, **toothpicks.** A **toothpick** is a small wooden, metal, or plastic stick with pointed ends which you use to remove food from between your teeth. EG *...picking his teeth with a gold toothpick.* N COUNT

top /tɒp/, **tops, topping, topped. 1** The **top** of something is its highest point, part, or surface. EG *...at the top of the steps... He filled his glass to the top... ...hill tops... ...the wooden top of the bench.* N COUNT +SUPP : USU *the*+N

2 The **top** thing of a series of things is the highest one. EG *She was sitting on the top step... ...a room on the top floor.* ADJ CLASSIF : ATTRIB

3 The **top** of a street or garden is one end of it, usually the end furthest away from you. EG *...a new building at the top of Victoria Street.* ▸ used as an adjective. EG *The boy waved to her from the top end of the field.* N SING : *the*+N ▸ ADJ CLASSIF : ATTRIB

4 The **top** of a bottle, jar, or tube is a cap or lid that fits onto one end of it and closes it. EG *He unscrewed the top and put the bottle to his mouth.* N COUNT

5 A **top** is a piece of clothing such as a blouse, which a woman wears on the upper half of her body. EG *She wore denim jeans and a denim top.* N COUNT

6 A **top** is also a cone-shaped toy that can spin on its pointed end. N COUNT

7 The **top** of an organization is its highest or most important level. EG *Officials at the top make the decisions.* ▸ used as an adjective. *...top executives... ...top level negotiations.* N SING : *the*+N ▸ ADJ CLASSIF : ATTRIB

8 The **top** of a scale of measurement is the highest point on it. EG *This group is already near the top of the UK income scale.* ▸ used as an adjective. EG *The vehicle's top speed is about 100.* N SING : *the*+N ▸ ADJ CLASSIF : ATTRIB

9 If someone **tops** a poll or popularity chart, they do better than anyone else in it. EG *She topped a nationwide poll for 1981's most outstanding sportswoman.* V+O

10 If something **tops** a particular amount, it becomes greater than that amount. EG *US investments topped fifty million dollars.* V+O

11 If you **top** a remark or action, you follow it with a better or more impressive one. EG *Sudhir topped her story with one about an Indian princess.* V+O : OFT+*with*

12 You use **on top** in these ways. **12.1** If something is **on top** or **over the top** of something else, it is placed over it or on its highest part. EG *She laid her hand on top of his... ...a tower with a little flag on top... Something had been stamped over the top.* **12.2** If something happens **on top** of other things, it happens in addition to them. EG *You don't want to give the poor man ulcers on top of all the problems he's already got.* **12.3** If you are **on top of** what you are doing, you are dealing with it successfully. EG *...jobs that they never really got on top of.* **12.4** When something **gets on top of** you, it makes you feel depressed because you cannot cope with it. EG *You may find the housework is getting on top of you.* PHRASES

13 If you say that something is **over the top**, you mean that it is unacceptable because it is too extreme or exaggerated. EG *Here I think Wenders goes right over the top.* PHRASE

14 off the top of your **head**: see **head.** • **at the top of** your **voice**: see **voice.** • See also **topped, topping.**

top up. If you **top up** a container, you fill it again when it has been partly emptied. EG *The radiator will have to be topped up because of evaporation.* • See also **top-up**. PHRASAL VB : V+O+ADV

top hat, top hats. A **top hat** is a tall hat with a narrow brim that men wear on formal occasions. N COUNT

top-heavy. Something that is **top-heavy** is larger or heavier at the top than at the bottom, and is therefore not stable. EG *...high-heeled shoes and hats top-heavy with feathers and flowers.* ADJ QUALIT

topic /tɒpɪk/, **topics.** A **topic** is a particular subject that you write about or discuss. EG *The main topic of conversation was food.* N COUNT+SUPP

topical /tɒpɪkə⁰l/ means relating to events that are happening at the time you are speaking or writing. EG *They used to discuss topical issues... The question you ask is very topical.* ADJ QUALIT

topless /tɒplɪ²s/. When a woman is **topless**, she is not wearing anything that covers her breasts. EG *...a topless dancer.* ADJ CLASSIF

topmost /tɒpməʊst/. The **topmost** thing in a group of things is the one that is highest or nearest the top. EG *...the topmost branches of the lime trees.* ADJ CLASSIF : ATTRIB

topped /tɒpt/. If something is **topped** by or **topped** with another thing, the other thing covers it or is on top of it. EG *...a heap of stones topped by a wooden cross.* ADJ PRED+A

topping /tɒpɪŋ/, **toppings.** A **topping** is food, such as cream or cheese, that is poured or put on top of other food in order to decorate it or to add to its flavour. EG *...a topping of whipped cream.* N MASS

topple /tɒpə⁰l/, **topples, toppling, toppled. 1** If something **topples**, it becomes unsteady and falls over. EG *He caught the glass just as it began to topple... She toppled from her chair.* V

2 To **topple** a government or leader means to cause them to be no longer in power. EG *This action threatens to topple the government... His regime was toppled in a coup.* V+O

topple over. If something **topples over**, it becomes unsteady and falls over. EG *She looked at the tree nervously, as if expecting it to topple over.* PHRASAL VB : V+ADV

top-secret. Something that is **top-secret** is intended to be kept completely secret. EG *...a top-secret experiment.* ADJ CLASSIF

top-up, top-ups. A **top-up** is another serving of a drink in the same glass that you have just used. EG *Anyone ready for a top-up?* N COUNT Informal

torch /tɔ:tʃ/, **torches.** A **torch** is **1** a small electric light which you can carry in your hand and which gets its power from batteries inside it. EG *He took the torch and disappeared into the dark.* **2** a long stick with burning material at the end that was used in former times to provide light. N COUNT

torchlight /tɔ:tʃlaɪt/ is **1** light that is produced by an electric torch. EG *...the circle of torchlight.* **2** light that is produced by burning torches. EG *...a torchlight procession from the station.* N UNCOUNT

tore /tɔ:/ is the past tense of **tear.**

torment, torments, tormenting, tormented; pronounced /tɔ:mə²nt/ when it is a noun, and /tɔ:ment/ when it is a verb.

1 Torment is extreme pain or unhappiness. EG *...the scream of a man dying in torment.* N UNCOUNT

2 A **torment** is something that causes extreme pain or unhappiness. EG *He was subjected to various torments... His schooldays were a torment.* N COUNT

3 If something **torments** you, it causes you extreme unhappiness. EG *His emotional turmoil continues to torment him.* V+O

4 If someone **torments** you, they annoy you in a playful and rather cruel way. EG *She is forever tormenting and teasing Tom.* V+O

tormentor /tɔ:mentə/, **tormentors.** A **tormentor** is someone who deliberately causes pain or N COUNT : USU+POSS

Name the things on these pages that you can use to clean your teeth.

unhappiness to another person. EG *The child eventually turned on his tormentors.*

torn /tɔːn/ is the past participle of **tear.**

tornado /tɔːneɪdəʊ/, **tornadoes** or **tornados.** A **tornado** is a violent storm with strong circular winds around a funnel-shaped cloud. Tornados move very quickly and cause a lot of damage. N COUNT

torpedo /tɔːpiːdəʊ/, **torpedoes, torpedoing, torpedoed. 1** A **torpedo** is a tube-shaped bomb that travels underwater and explodes when it hits its target. Torpedoes can be fired from ships, submarine, or aircraft. EG *His ship was blown up by a torpedo.* N COUNT

2 If a ship **is torpedoed**, it is hit, and usually sunk, by a torpedo. V+O : USU PASS

torrent /tɒrənt/, **torrents. 1** When a lot of water is falling very rapidly, you can say that it is falling in **torrents**. EG *The rain suddenly burst upon us in torrents... Valerie was now shedding torrents of tears.* N COUNT : USU PLURAL

2 A **torrent** of speech is a lot of it directed continuously at someone. EG *She burst out in a torrent of speech... ...a torrent of questions... He was answered with a torrent of oaths.* N COUNT+SUPP

torrential /tə⁷rɛnʃə⁰l/. **Torrential** rain pours down very rapidly and in great quantities. EG *Before the meeting could end, torrential rain began to pour.* ADJ CLASSIF : ATTRIB

torso /tɔːsəʊ/, **torsos.** Your **torso** is the main part of your body, excluding your head, arms, and legs. EG *...a carving of a woman's torso.* N COUNT

tortoise /tɔːtəs/, **tortoises.** A **tortoise** is a slow-moving animal with a large, hard shell over its body. The tortoise can pull its head and legs into the shell in order to protect them. N COUNT

tortoiseshell /tɔːtəsʃɛl/ is the hard, brown and yellow shell from a sea turtle. It is often polished and used to make jewellery and ornaments. N UNCOUNT

tortuous /tɔːtjʊəs/. **1** A **tortuous** road is full of bends and twists. EG *They walked through the narrow, tortuous streets of the old city.* ADJ QUALIT Formal

2 A **tortuous** piece of writing is long and complicated. EG *I wrote tortuous essays for obscure journals... ...laws framed in tortuous jargon.* ADJ QUALIT Formal

torture /tɔːtʃə/, **tortures, torturing, tortured. 1** **Torture** is great pain that is deliberately caused to someone in order to punish them or to get information from them. EG *...the constant threat of death and torture... Here floggings and tortures were carried out.* N UNCOUNT OR N COUNT

2 If someone **tortures** another person, they deliberately cause that person great pain in order to punish them or get information from them. EG *...prisons where the inmates were tortured and murdered... He saw his relatives being tortured.* V+O

Tory /tɔːri¹/, **Tories.** A **Tory** is a member or supporter of the Conservative Party in Britain. EG *The Tories were restored to power... ...the Tory MP for Hornchurch.* N COUNT Informal

toss /tɒs/, **tosses, tossing, tossed. 1** If you **toss** something somewhere, you throw it there lightly and carelessly. EG *He took the bag and tossed it into some nearby bushes.* V+O : USU+A

2 If you **toss** your head, you move it suddenly backwards. EG *'That's the main thing, isn't it?' said Frederica, tossing her head.* ▸ used as a noun. EG *She gave a toss of her head.* V+O ▸ N COUNT

3 If you **toss** food while preparing it, you gently shake pieces of it in a container with some liquid in order to cover the pieces with the liquid. EG *Serve noodles tossed in cream.* V+O : OFT+*in*

4 If you **toss** a coin or **toss**, you decide something by throwing a coin into the air and guessing which side of it will be facing upwards after it falls. EG *They used the penny to toss for the first round of drinks.* ▸ used as a noun. EG *Business deals were clinched by the toss of a coin.* V OR V+O ▸ N COUNT

5 If something or someone **tosses** or **is tossed**, they move repeatedly from side to side. EG *I tossed and turned all night... Ships were tossed at sea.* V-ERG

toss up. If you **toss up**, you decide something by throwing a coin into the air and guessing which side of the coin will be facing upwards after it falls. PHRASAL VB : V+ADV, OFT+A

toss-up. If you refer to a situation as a **toss-up**, you mean that either of two results seems equally likely. EG *It was a toss-up who would get there first.* N SING : a+N

tot /tɒt/, **tots, totting, totted. 1** A **tot** is a very young child. EG *I've known her since she was a tot.* N COUNT Informal

2 A **tot** of a strong alcoholic drink such as whisky is a small amount of it in a glass. EG *...a tot of whisky.* N PART

tot up. If you **tot up** numbers, you add them together. EG *I was totting up the number of photographs... The machine totted up your score.* PHRASAL VB : V+O+ADV Informal

total /təʊtə⁰l/, **totals, totalling, totalled. 1** A **total** is the number that you get when you add several numbers together. EG *The factory employed a total of forty workers.* ▸ used as an adjective. EG *...the total number of students on campus.* ● See also **sum total.** N COUNT ▸ ADJ CLASSIF : ATTRIB

2 If there are a number of things **in total**, there are that many of them altogether. EG *...a force containing in total over half a million men.* PHRASE

3 When you **total** a set of numbers or objects, you add them all together. EG *Votes cast for each candidate will be totalled to get a result.* V+O

4 If several numbers **total** a certain figure, that is the figure you get when all the numbers are added together. EG *Conoco's 1980 revenues totalled £18.3 billion... They paid fines totalling 16,000 dollars.* V+C

5 You use **total** to say that something is complete. EG *...total secrecy... ...a total failure... ...a total eclipse of the sun.* ◇ **totally.** EG *He became almost totally blind... I totally disagree.* ADJ CLASSIF : USU ATTRIB ◇ SUBMOD OR ADV

totalitarian /təʊtælɪtɛərɪən/. A **totalitarian** political system is one in which one political party controls everything and does not allow any other parties to exist. EG *...the brutalities of the totalitarian regimes.* ADJ CLASSIF

totality /təʊtælɪ¹ti¹/. The **totality** of something is the whole of it. EG *...the totality of life... ...the totality of French culture.* N UNCOUNT : USU+SUPP Formal

totter /tɒtə/, **totters, tottering, tottered. 1** When someone **totters**, they walk in an unsteady way, for example because they are ill or drunk. EG *Thelma tottered from the stage in search of the gin bottle.* V : USU+A

2 If something such as a government **totters**, it becomes weak and is likely to lose control. EG *The wartime Liberal Government was tottering.* V

touch /tʌtʃ/, **touches, touching, touched. 1** If you **touch** something, you gently put your fingers or hand on it. EG *The metal is so hot I can't touch it... Madeleine stretched out her hand to touch his.* ▸ used as a noun. EG *The wood is so rotten that it crumbles at the touch... He remembered the touch of her hand.* V+O ▸ N COUNT : OFT SING

2 If you **are touched** by something, you are emotionally affected by it and feel sad, sympathetic, or grateful. EG *The whole audience was touched... I was very touched by his thoughtfulness... They helped us get the harvest in and I was touched.* V+O : USU PASS

3 When two things **touch**, their surfaces come into contact with one other. EG *Make sure that the wires are not touching... He stood so close to me that our bodies touched... My feet touched the ground.* V OR V+O : RECIP

4 Your sense of **touch** is the sense that tells you what the surface of something is like, for example when you put your fingers on it. EG *The skin was fleshy and slightly waxy to the touch.* N UNCOUNT

5 A **touch** is a detail which is added to something to improve it. EG *The final touches were put to their report.* ● **finishing touches**: see **finish**. N COUNT+SUPP

6 Someone's manner of doing something can be referred to as their **touch**. EG *In the play, religion is handled with quite a light, comic touch... She hasn't got your touch, Flora.* N SING+SUPP

7 A **touch** of something is a very small amount of it. EG *There was a touch of frost this morning.* N SING+SUPP

8 You can use **a touch** to mean slightly or to a small extent. EG *Richard's voice suddenly became important and even a touch official.* PHRASE

9 If you get **in touch** with someone, you contact them by writing to them or telephoning them. If you are, stay, or keep **in touch** with them, you write, phone, or visit each other regularly. EG *A man from the Organization got in touch with me... I'll be in touch with you... Please drop in when you can. I'd like to keep in touch.* PHRASE

10 If you are or keep **in touch** with a subject or situation, you know the latest news or information about it. If you are **out of touch** with it, your knowledge of it is out-of-date. EG *I'm a bit out of touch with new developments.* PHRASE

11 If you **lose touch** with someone, you gradually stop writing, phoning, or visiting each other. PHRASE

12 If you say that something is **touch and go**, you mean that you are uncertain whether it will happen or succeed. EG *It is still touch and go but we managed to get this far.* PHRASE

13 Some people say **'Touch wood'**, and often touch a piece of wood, in order to prevent bad luck. EG *'Has anything gone wrong with your car recently?' - 'No, touch wood.'* PHRASE

14 See also **touching**.

touch down. When an aircraft **touches down**, it lands. EG *He watched the plane as it touched down.* ● See also **touchdown**. PHRASAL VB : V+ADV

touch on. If you **touch on** something, you mention it briefly. EG *...the topic which I touched on at the beginning of this chapter.* PHRASAL VB : V+PREP, HAS PASS

touchdown /tʌtʃdaʊn/, **touchdowns. Touchdown** or a **touchdown** is the landing of an aircraft. EG *Failure of any mechanical system to function after touchdown could destroy human lives.* N UNCOUNT OR N COUNT

touching /tʌtʃɪŋ/. If something is **touching**, it causes feelings of sadness and sympathy. EG *'I've seen the photographs.' - 'Touching, weren't they?'* ADJ QUALIT

touchy /tʌtʃiˡ/, **touchier, touchiest.** 1 If someone is **touchy**, they are easily upset, offended, or irritated. EG *He always was a touchy and bad-tempered man.* ADJ QUALIT

2 A **touchy** subject is one that needs to be dealt with carefully, because it might upset or offend people. EG *I had to face the touchy question: could I really have him arrested?* ADJ QUALIT

tough /tʌf/, **tougher, toughest.** 1 Someone who is **tough** has a strong, independent character and is able to tolerate a lot of pain or hardship. EG *...a tough reporter... He's not hard-hearted but resolute and tough.* ADJ QUALIT

2 A **tough** substance is strong, and difficult to break, cut, or tear. EG *Some plastics are as tough as metal... With a hoe you can tackle tougher weeds.* ADJ QUALIT

3 Meat which is **tough** is difficult to cut and chew. EG *The steak was smelly and a little tough.* ADJ QUALIT

4 A **tough** task, problem, or way of life is difficult or full of hardship. EG *The toughest problem is theft.* ADJ QUALIT

5 **Tough** policies or actions are strict and firm, and show determination. EG *We are convinced that her tough economic policies will succeed.* ADJ QUALIT

toughen /tʌfəᵒn/, **toughens, toughening, toughened.** 1 To **toughen** something means to make it stronger so that it will not break easily. V+O
◊ **toughened**. EG *...the use of toughened glass in windscreens.* ◊ ADJ CLASSIF

2 When someone **toughens** or when a difficult experience **toughens** them, they become stronger and more independent in character. EG *She had been toughened by Guy's death.* V-ERG

toupee /tuːpeɪ/, **toupees.** A **toupee** is a small wig worn by a man to cover a bald patch on his head. N COUNT

tour /tʊə, tɔː/, **tours, touring, toured.** 1 A **tour** is 1.1 a long journey during which you visit several places. EG *I made a five-month tour of India and the Far East.* 1.2 a short trip round a place such as a city or a famous building. EG *Admission to a tour of Parliament is easier in summer... ...guided tours.* N COUNT

2 If you **tour** a place, you go on a journey or trip round it. EG *He spent his vacation touring the highlands of Scotland.* V+O

tourism /tʊərɪzəᵒm, tɔː-/ is the business of providing services for people on holiday, for example hotels, travel arrangements, sightseeing trips, and leisure activities. N UNCOUNT

tourist /tʊərɪst, tɔː-/, **tourists.** A **tourist** is a person who visits places for pleasure and interest. EG *She showed a party of tourists round the museum... You should visit the tourist attractions.* N COUNT

tournament /tʊənəməˀnt, tɔː-/, **tournaments.** A **tournament** is a sports competition in which players who win a match play further matches, until just one person or team is left. EG *...a table tennis tournament.* N COUNT

tousled /taʊzəᵒld/. **Tousled** hair is untidy and looks as if it has not been combed. ADJ QUALIT

tout /taʊt/, **touts, touting, touted.** 1 If someone **touts** something, they try and sell it. EG *...an exporter touting a range of plastic toys.* V+O Informal

2 If someone **touts** for business or custom, they try to obtain it. EG *...porters touting for loads at a railway station.* V+*for*

tow /təʊ/, **tows, towing, towed.** 1 If a vehicle **tows** another vehicle, it pulls it along behind it. EG *...a lorry towing a trailer of hay.* ▸ used as a noun. EG *If you can't get a tow, you'll have to walk.* V+O ▸ N SING : *a*+N

2 If a vehicle is **on tow**, it is being towed by another vehicle. PHRASE

3 If you have someone **in tow**, they are with you because you are looking after them. EG *He arrived on Sunday with his children in tow.* PHRASE Informal

towards /təwɔːdz/; also **toward.** 1 If you move, look, or point **towards** something or someone, you move, look, or point in their direction. EG *He saw his mother running towards him... She turned towards John.* PREP

2 If things develop **towards** a particular situation, that situation becomes nearer in time or more likely to happen. EG *There is a tendency towards inflation... We are drifting towards disaster.* PREP

3 If you have a particular attitude **towards** something or someone, you have that attitude when you think about them or deal with them. EG *He felt very friendly towards them.* PREP

4 If something happens **towards** a particular time or date, it happens just before that time or date. EG *Towards midnight the rain ceased... I went to London towards the end of 1977.* PREP

5 **Towards** a place or area can also mean near to it. EG *He was sitting towards the back of the room.* PREP

6 If you give money **towards** something, you give it to help pay for that thing. EG *British Rail contributed 154,000 pounds towards improving safety... They may give you something towards your housing costs.* PREP

7 You can also use **towards** to indicate the result that you are trying to achieve. EG *The twins did a lot towards making Tom willing to stay.* PREP

towel /taʊəl/, **towels.** A **towel** is a piece of thick, soft cloth that you use to dry yourself with after a wash or bath. ● See also **sanitary towel, tea-towel**. N COUNT

towelling /taʊəlɪŋ/ is thick, soft cloth that is used especially for making towels. EG *...a bit of old towelling... She was dressed in a towelling bathrobe.* N UNCOUNT

tower /taʊə/, **towers, towering, towered.** 1 A **tower** is a tall, narrow building, sometimes attached to a larger building such as a castle or church. EG *...London's Post Office Tower.* N COUNT

2 If you refer to someone as a **tower of strength**, PHRASE

Where would you find a towpath?

you mean that they give you a lot of help, support, and encouragement.

3 Someone or something that **towers** over other people or things is a lot taller than they are. EG *Jane stood up, towering over him.* V+A

tower block, tower blocks. A **tower block** is a tall building divided into flats or offices. N COUNT British

towering /taʊərɪŋ/. A **towering** building or tree is very tall and impressive. EG *...lush green meadows surrounded by towering trees.* ADJ CLASSIF : ATTRIB

town /taʊn/, **towns. 1** A **town** is a place with many streets and buildings where people live and work. EG *...the town of Pangbourne in England.* N COUNT

2 People sometimes refer to the town they live in as **town**. EG *We packed our stuff and left town on a bus.* N UNCOUNT

3 Town is also used to refer to the central part of a city or town. EG *I had lunch in town.* N UNCOUNT ● If you go **out on the town**, you enjoy yourself by visiting some of the places of entertainment in a city or town, especially at night. ● PHRASE

4 If you **go to town** on an activity, you put a lot of effort and enthusiasm into doing it. EG *Once they got permission, they could really go to town on it.* PHRASE

5 See also **ghost town**.

town hall, town halls. The **town hall** is a large building in a town that is owned by the town council and that is often used by them as their headquarters. N COUNT

townspeople /taʊnzpi:pəºl/. The **townspeople** of a town or city are the people who live there. EG *The townspeople refused to buy anything from his shop.* N PLURAL : USU *the*+N Outdated

towpath /təʊpɑ:θ/, **towpaths.** A **towpath** is a path along the side of a canal or river. N COUNT

towrope /təʊrəʊp/, **towropes.** A **towrope** is a strong rope used for towing vehicles. N COUNT

toxic /tɒksɪk/. A **toxic** substance is poisonous. EG *The water became contaminated by toxic chemicals... Aluminium can be highly toxic to fish.* ADJ QUALIT Formal

toy /tɔɪ/, **toys, toying, toyed.** A **toy** is an object that children play with, for example a doll or a model car. EG *The children could bring their own toys... ...a toy soldier... ...a toy theatre.* N COUNT

toy with. 1 If you **toy with** an idea, you consider it casually, without making any decisions about it. EG *I've been toying with the idea for some time.* PHRASAL VB : V+PREP, HAS PASS **2** If you **toy with** an object, you keep moving it about with your fingers, usually while you are thinking about something else. EG *He withdrew the key from his pocket where he had been toying with it.* V+PREP, HAS PASS

trace /treɪs/, **traces, tracing, traced. 1** If you **trace** something, you find it after looking for it. EG *I think I've traced the source of the poison... They were trying to trace her missing husband.* V+O

2 If you **trace** the development of something, you find out or describe how it developed. EG *Throughout the nineteenth century we can trace the gradual progress of this idea.* V+O

3 If you **trace** a drawing or a map, you copy it by covering it with a piece of transparent paper and drawing over the lines underneath. V+O

4 A **trace** is a sign which shows you that someone or something has been in a place. EG *No trace was found of either the bag or its contents.* N COUNT ● If someone disappears **without trace**, they disappear without leaving any signs of where they have gone. EG *Madeleine vanished without trace.* ● PHRASE

5 A **trace** of something is a very small amount of it. EG *I can still see traces of the paint on your hands... There wasn't the slightest trace of fear in my father.* N PART

tracing /treɪsɪŋ/, **tracings.** A **tracing** is a copy that has been made by covering a drawing or map with a piece of transparent paper and drawing over the lines underneath. N COUNT

tracing paper is transparent paper that you use to make tracings. N UNCOUNT

track /træk/, **tracks, tracking, tracked. 1** A **track** is a narrow road or path. EG *I remember riding along a dusty mountain track in Morocco.* N COUNT

2 A **track** is also a piece of ground, often shaped like a ring, which horses, cars, or athletes race around. EG *The recreation ground had a proper cinder track.* N COUNT

3 A railway **track** is a strip of ground with rails on it that a train travels along. EG *The train on the next track was moving.* N COUNT

4 Tracks are marks left on the ground which show that someone or something has been there. EG *The fox didn't leave any tracks.* N PLURAL

5 If you **track** animals or people, you find them by following their footprints or other signs that they have left behind. EG *I lost my camels, tracked them, and found them again.* V+O

6 A **track** on a record or tape is one of the songs or pieces of music on it. EG *That's Sonny Rollins singing on that track.* N COUNT

7 Track is used in these phrases. **7.1** A place that is **off the beaten track** is in a quiet and isolated area. **7.2** If you **hide** your **tracks** or **cover** your **tracks**, you are careful not to leave any signs or clues that might reveal what you have been doing. **7.3** If you **stop dead in** your **tracks** or if someone or something **stops** you **dead in** your **tracks**, you suddenly stop what you are doing, because something has surprised you. EG *He stopped dead in his tracks and gave a gasp of shock.* **7.4** If you **keep track of** things or people, you pay attention to them so that you know where they are or what is happening. If you **lose track of** them, you no longer know where they are or what is happening. EG *We would never be able to keep track of the luggage on such a long journey.* **7.5** If you are **on the right track**, you are thinking in a way that is likely to give you the right answer to a question or problem. If you are **on the wrong track**, you are thinking in a way that is mistaken and that will not give you the right answer. PHRASES

track down. If you **track down** someone or something, you find them by searching for them. EG *They lost all hope of tracking down the submarine.* PHRASAL VB : V+O+ADV

tracker /trækə/, **trackers.** A **tracker** is someone who is skilled at finding people or animals by following their footprints or other signs that they have left behind. EG *Peter was a brilliant tracker.* N COUNT

track record, track records. The **track record** of a person or a company consists of their past achievements or failures in their job or business. EG *They have established a good track record of successful trading.* N COUNT+SUPP

tracksuit /træksjºu:t/, **tracksuits.** A **tracksuit** is a loose, warm suit consisting of trousers and a top. You wear a tracksuit when you are jogging or doing exercises. N COUNT

tract /trækt/, **tracts. 1** A **tract** is a short article expressing a strong opinion on a religious, moral, or political subject. N COUNT

2 A **tract** of land or forest is a large area of it. EG *...immense tracts of impenetrable jungle.* N COUNT

traction engine /trækʃəºn ɛndʒɪn/, **traction engines.** A **traction engine** is a large vehicle that was used in the past for pulling heavy loads. N COUNT

tractor /træktə/, **tractors.** A **tractor** is a farm vehicle with large rear wheels that is used for ploughing fields, sowing crops, and pulling trailers. N COUNT

trade /treɪd/, **trades, trading, traded. 1 Trade** is the activity of buying, selling, or exchanging goods or services. EG *France is heavily dependent on foreign trade... A friend of mine went into the antique trade.* N UNCOUNT

2 When people, firms, or countries **trade**, they buy, sell, or exchange goods or services. EG *They specialized in trading with China.* V : USU+A

3 Someone's **trade** is the kind of work that they do, especially when it requires special training in practical skills. EG *Settle down to learn your trade.* N COUNT

• If you are, for example, a plumber or an electrician, you can say that you are a plumber or electrician **by trade**. EG *By trade he was a dealer in antique furniture.* • PHRASE

4 If you **trade** one thing for another, you exchange it for the other thing. EG *Leah traded a piece of her jewellery for food.* V+O : OFT+*for*

trade in. If you **trade in** something such as your old car or old TV set, you give it to a dealer when you buy a new one so that you get a reduction on the price. EG *You might trade the car in for a smaller one.* PHRASAL VB : V+O+ADV, USU+A

trademark /treɪdmɑːk/, **trademarks. 1** A **trademark** is a name or symbol that a company uses on its products and that cannot legally be used by another company. N COUNT

2 If someone or something has a typical feature, you can refer to this feature as their **trademark**. EG *That's Mr Sedgwick's trademark. He's always got a cigar in his mouth... Long hair had become the trademark of rebellion among the young.* N COUNT+SUPP

trader /treɪdə/, **traders.** A **trader** is a person whose job is to trade in goods. EG *...a whisky trader... ...a wealthy trader in tea.* N COUNT

trade secret, trade secrets. A **trade secret** is information that is known and used by only one firm, for example about the substances required to produce something or about a particular method of producing it. N COUNT

tradesman /treɪdzmə³n/, **tradesmen.** A **tradesman** is a person, for example a shopkeeper, whose job is to sell goods. N COUNT

tradespeople /treɪdzpiːpə⁰l/ are people who sell goods as their job. N PLURAL

trade union, trade unions. The form **trades union** is also used. A **trade union** is an organization of workers that tries to improve the pay and working conditions of its members. EG *...a highly organized trade union... The Secretary of State will meet the trade union leaders tomorrow.* N COUNT

trade unionist, trade unionists. A **trade unionist** is an active member of a trade union. EG *...militant trade unionists.* N COUNT

tradition /trə³dɪʃə⁰n/, **traditions.** A **tradition** is a custom or belief that has existed for a long time without changing. EG *...Britain's long tradition of political independence... I was not going to keep up the family tradition... We must have respect for tradition.* N COUNT OR N UNCOUNT

traditional /trə³dɪʃə⁰nəl, -ʃənə⁰l/. **Traditional** customs or beliefs have existed for a long time without changing. EG *The bride is dressed in traditional costume... Women are questioning their traditional role in society, as wives and mothers.* ADJ CLASSIF

◊ **traditionally**. EG *Traditionally in this culture, there is no figurative art.* ◊ ADV OR ADV SEN

traffic /træfɪk/, **traffics, trafficking, trafficked. 1 Traffic** refers to all the cars and other vehicles that are moving along a road at a particular time. EG *He eased the van out into the line of rush-hour traffic.* N UNCOUNT

2 **Traffic** in something such as drugs is an illegal trade in them. EG *...an operation designed to uncover illegal traffic in protected animals.* N UNCOUNT +SUPP

3 Someone who **traffics** in drugs or other goods buys and sells them even though it is illegal to do so. EG *...rumours that he trafficked in opium.* V+*in*

traffic jam, traffic jams. A **traffic jam** is a long line of cars and other vehicles that cannot move because the road is blocked. N COUNT

traffic light, traffic lights. Traffic lights are the set of red, amber, and green lights at a road junction which control the flow of traffic. The red light means stop, amber means prepare to stop or to move off, and green means go. N COUNT : USU PLURAL

traffic warden, traffic wardens. A **traffic warden** is a person whose job is to make sure that cars are not parked in the wrong place or for longer than is allowed. N COUNT

tragedy /trædʒɪ¹di¹/, **tragedies. 1** A **tragedy** is an event or situation that is very sad and serious. EG *The change of flight plans was the principal cause of the tragedy... I know something of Dolly, the tragedy of her life.* N COUNT OR N UNCOUNT

2 In the theatre, a **tragedy** is a play that has a very sad ending. N COUNT

3 You refer to plays with sad endings as **tragedy**. EG *She acted brilliantly in Greek tragedy.* N UNCOUNT

tragic /trædʒɪk/. **1** Something that is **tragic** is very sad. EG *...the tragic death of his elder brother Michael.* ◊ **tragically**. EG *He was tragically killed in a car crash.* ADJ QUALIT; ◊ ADV OR ADV SEN

2 **Tragic** plays, films, and books have sad endings. EG *...Scott Fitzgerald's tragic novel 'Tender is the Night'... ...the Greek tragic heroes.* ADJ CLASSIF : ATTRIB

trail /treɪl/, **trails, trailing, trailed. 1** A **trail** is a rough path across open country or through forests. EG *...as they trudged along the seemingly endless trail.* N COUNT

2 If someone or something leaves a **trail** behind them, they leave marks or other signs behind them as they move along, which tell you which way they went. EG *Eventually we lost the trail... She didn't want him to leave a trail of wet footprints all over the house.* N COUNT

3 If you are **on the trail of** a person or animal, you are following them or are trying to find them. PHRASE

4 If you **trail** something or if it **trails**, it drags along behind you as you move, or it hangs down loosely. EG *She trails the fingers of her right hand through the water... She went out with her dress trailing behind her on the floor... He had left his horse standing with the reins trailing in the dust.* V-ERG : USU+A

5 If someone **trails** along, they move slowly, without any energy or enthusiasm, often following someone else. EG *I used to trail around after him like a small child.* V+A

6 If you **are trailing** in a game or contest, you have a lower score than your opponents. EG *Public opinion polls showed Giscard trailing Mitterand by as much as 3 points... At half-time, England were trailing 8-5.* V OR V+O : USU CONT

trail away or **trail off.** If a speaker's voice **trails away** or **trails off**, it gradually becomes quieter or more hesitant until it stops completely. EG *'I have an appointment that's very...' His voice trailed off unconvincingly.* PHRASAL VB : V+ADV

trailer /treɪlə/, **trailers. 1** A **trailer** is **1.1** a vehicle like a cart which can be loaded with things and pulled behind a car. **1.2** a vehicle which people use as a home or an office and which can be pulled behind a car. N COUNT; American

2 A **trailer** for a film or a television or radio programme is a set of short extracts from it, which are shown or broadcast in order to advertise it. N COUNT

train /treɪn/, **trains, training, trained. 1** A **train** is a number of carriages or trucks which are pulled by an engine along a railway line. EG *I caught a train to Oxford... We are planning to go by train... ...the long train journey from Leeds.* N COUNT OR *by*+N

2 A **train of thought** is a connected series of thoughts. EG *I felt annoyed with her for interrupting my train of thought.* PHRASE

3 The **train** of a formal dress is a long part at the back of it that rests on the ground. N COUNT

4 If you **train** a person or animal to do something, you teach them how to do it. EG *The police are trained to keep calm.* ◊ **trained**. EG *She's a trained nurse.* V+O : OFT +*to*-INF OR A; ◊ ADJ CLASSIF

5 If you **train** as something, you learn how to do a particular job. EG *She started to train as a nurse... We trained together at art school.* V : OFT+*to*-INF OR A

6 If you **train** for a sports match or a race, you V-ERG

If you start a transatlantic journey in the USA, where are you likely to finish it?

prepare for it by doing exercises and eating a special diet.
7 See also **training**.

trainee /treɪniː/, **trainees.** A **trainee** is someone who is being taught how to do a job. EG *The trainees are shown around each of the departments... ...a trainee chef.* N COUNT

trainer /treɪnə/, **trainers. 1** A **trainer** is a person who trains animals or sports players. N COUNT
2 Trainers are special shoes that people wear for running or jogging. See picture at SHOES. N COUNT: USU PLURAL

training /treɪnɪŋ/. **1 Training** for a particular job involves learning or teaching the skills that are needed for the job. EG *I had a great training as a gardener... ...giving people training in computer programming.* N UNCOUNT
2 Training also involves doing physical exercises and eating a special diet in order to be fit for a sports match or a race. EG *Are you in training for a cross-country run?* N UNCOUNT

traipse /treɪps/, **traipses, traipsing, traipsed.** If you **traipse** somewhere, you go there slowly, because you are tired or because it is a long journey. EG *For eighteen weeks we traipsed around southern England.* V+A Informal

trait /treɪt⁰/, **traits.** A **trait** is a characteristic or tendency that someone has. EG *Certain personality traits had made her unpopular.* N COUNT+SUPP

traitor /treɪtə/, **traitors.** A **traitor** is someone who betrays their country or the group which they belong to, or who stops supporting one group and starts supporting another. EG *He was denounced as a traitor to France.* N COUNT

tram /træm/, **trams.** A **tram** is an electric vehicle for carrying people which travels on rails in the streets of a town. N COUNT OR *by*+N

tramp /træmp/, **tramps, tramping, tramped. 1** A **tramp** is a person who has no home, no job, and very little money. N COUNT
2 If you **tramp** from one place to another, you walk with slow, heavy footsteps. EG *She tramped slowly up the beach... ...if you are tramping the streets all day as a postman.* V+A OR V+O

trample /træmpə⁰l/, **tramples, trampling, trampled. 1** If you **trample** on something, you tread heavily on it so that it is damaged. EG *As soon as I came to, I stood up to avoid being trampled on... They had trampled his lovely rose garden... They led each other back, trampling through the undergrowth.* V+A OR V+O
2 If you **trample** on someone or on their rights or feelings, you behave towards them in a cruel or unjust way. EG *Half the population trample on the rights of the other half... We will not allow ourselves to be trampled on.* V+*on*

trampoline /træmpə⁰li¹n/, **trampolines.** A **trampoline** is an apparatus on which you can do acrobatic jumps. It consists of a large piece of strong cloth held by springs in a frame. N COUNT

trance /trɑːns/, **trances.** A **trance** is a mental state in which your thoughts and actions are controlled by the person who put you in that state. EG *While in a trance a hypnotized person can be instructed to perform a variety of actions.* N COUNT

tranquil /træŋkwɪl/. **1** Something that is **tranquil** is calm and peaceful. EG *...this tranquil island... ...a lake of tranquil blue water.* ◇ **tranquillity** /træŋkwɪlɪti¹/. EG *...a time of political tranquillity.* ADJ QUALIT Literary ◇ N UNCOUNT
2 If you feel **tranquil**, you feel calm and relaxed. EG *...the prospect of a tranquil old age... ...a long, deep, dreamless, tranquil sleep.* ADJ QUALIT Literary

tranquillize /træŋkwɪlaɪz/, **tranquillizes, tranquillizing, tranquillized;** also spelled **tranquillise** and, in American English, **tranquilize.** If people or animals **are tranquillized**, they are given a drug to make them become calm, sleepy, or unconscious. V+O: USU PASS

tranquillizer /træŋkwɪlaɪzə/, **tranquillizers;** also spelled **tranquilliser** and, in American English, **tranquilizer.** A **tranquillizer** is a drug that makes people feel less anxious or nervous. N COUNT

trans- is used to form adjectives that describe something as happening or existing across a place, from one side to the other. For example, a transcontinental journey is a journey across a continent. EG *...the Trans-Alaska pipeline... ...the Trans-Siberian Railway.* PREFIX

transaction /trænzækʃə⁰n/, **transactions.** A **transaction** is a piece of business that involves a deal or arrangement, especially the sale of something. EG *...a business transaction.* N COUNT

transatlantic /trænzə³tlæntɪk/. **1 Transatlantic** journeys or communications involve travelling or communicating across the Atlantic Ocean, especially between Europe and the USA. EG *...a transatlantic phone call... ...regular transatlantic crossings.* ADJ CLASSIF: ATTRIB
2 Transatlantic is also used by Europeans to describe things that happen or exist in the USA, and by Americans to describe things in Europe. EG *...a transatlantic television soap opera.* ADJ CLASSIF: ATTRIB

transcend /trænsend/, **transcends, transcending, transcended.** If one thing **transcends** another, it is not limited by the other thing or it makes the other thing seem unimportant. EG *...a vital national issue that transcended party loyalties... Drama transcends national boundaries.* V+O Formal

transcribe /trænskraɪb/, **transcribes, transcribing, transcribed.** If you **transcribe** something that is spoken or written, you write it down, copy it, or change it into a different form of writing. EG *He transcribed recordings of schoolchildren.* V+O: USU+A

transcript /trænskrɪpt/, **transcripts.** A **transcript** of something that is spoken is a written copy of it. EG *...transcripts of tapes.* N COUNT: OFT+*of*

transfer, transfers, transferring, transferred; pronounced /trænsfɜː/ when it is a verb and /trænsfɜː/ when it is a noun. **1** If you **transfer** something from one place to another, you move it. EG *Perkins transferred the trout to a silver platter... Ten thousand pounds has been transferred into your account.* ▸ used as a noun. EG *...the electronic transfer of money.* V+O: USU+A ▸ N UNCOUNT OR N COUNT
2 If something **is transferred** from one person or group to another, the second one then has it instead of the first. EG *Responsibility is lifted from individual shoulders and transferred to the State... Ravenscroft transferred his affections to his secretary.* ▸ used as a noun. EG *...the transfer of power.* V+O: USU+A ▸ N UNCOUNT
◇ **transference** /trænsfə⁰rəns/. EG *There has been no genuine transference of authority to local level.* ◇ N UNCOUNT: USU+SUPP
3 If you **transfer** to a different place or job, or **are transferred** to it, you move to a different place or job within the same organization. EG *She's been transferred to another department.* ▸ used as a noun. EG *He resisted his transfer to the political section.* V-ERG: OFT+*to* ▸ N COUNT OR N UNCOUNT
4 A **transfer** is also a piece of paper with a design on one side. The design can be ironed or pressed onto cloth, paper, or china. N COUNT

transfixed /trænsfɪkst/. If you are **transfixed** by something, you are so impressed, fascinated, or frightened by it that you do not move. EG *I stood transfixed with terror.* ADJ PRED: USU+*by/with* Literary

transform /trænsfɔːm/, **transforms, transforming, transformed.** If something **is transformed**, it is changed completely. EG *An area of pasture land can be transformed into a barren landscape in two or three years... They claimed to be able to transform the lives of millions of people.* V+O: OFT +*from/into*
◇ **transformation** /trænsfəmeɪʃə⁰n/, **transformations.** EG *...the social and political transformation of society... After a few months, the creature undergoes a transformation.* ◇ N COUNT OR N UNCOUNT

transfusion /trænsfjuːʒə⁰n/, **transfusions.** When a patient is given a blood **transfusion**, blood is put into his or her body. N COUNT

transient /trænzi¹ənt/. Something that is **transient** does not exist or stay in a place very long. EG *In our fast-changing society even failure is transient... ...transient visitors.* ADJ QUALIT Formal

transistor /trænzɪstə/, **transistors.** 1 A **transistor** is a small electronic device in something such as a television or a radio. It is used for amplification and switching. N COUNT

2 A **transistor** or a **transistor radio** is a small portable radio. N COUNT

transit /trænzɪt/. 1 If people or things are **in transit**, they are travelling or being taken from one place to another. EG *The tablets had been lost in transit.* PHRASE

2 A **transit** area or building is where people wait or where goods are kept between different stages of a journey. EG *...the transit lounge.* ADJ CLASSIF : ATTRIB

transition /trænzɪʃə⁰n/, **transitions.** A **transition** is a change from one form or state to another. EG *How do you think this made the transition from book to stage?... The world was in transition from the old-fashioned conflict situation to a new era of co-operation.* N COUNT OR N UNCOUNT : OFT+*from/to*

transitional /trænzɪʃə⁰nəl, -ʃənə⁰l/. A **transitional** period or stage is one during which something changes from one form or state to another. EG *...a transitional period of civil war.* ADJ CLASSIF

transitive /trænzɪtɪv/. In grammar, a **transitive** verb is a verb which has an object. In this dictionary V+O is used in the Extra Column to indicate that the verb is transitive. ADJ CLASSIF

transitory /trænzɪtə⁰ri¹/. If something is **transitory**, it lasts for only a short time. EG *Love is transitory, but art is eternal... ...the transitory nature of human ties in urban society.* ADJ QUALIT

translate /trænsleɪt, trænz-/, **translates, translating, translated.** 1 If you **translate** something that someone has said or written, you say it or write it in a different language. EG *My books have been translated into many languages.* V+O OR V : OFT +*from/into*

2 If you **translate** one thing into another, you change it or convert it into something else. EG *He started to translate into action the dreams of African unity.* V+O+*into*

translation /trænsleɪʃə⁰n, trænz-/, **translations.** A **translation** is a piece of writing or speech that has been translated from a different language. EG *...a new translation of the Bible... It reads like a poor translation from Latin.* N COUNT

translator /trænsleɪtə, trænz-/, **translators.** A **translator** is a person whose job involves translating writing or speech from one language to another. N COUNT

translucent /trænzluːsə⁰nt/. If something is **translucent**, light passes through it, so that it seems to glow. EG *The leaves of the beeches are translucent in the setting sun.* ADJ QUALIT Literary

transmission /trænzmɪʃə⁰n/, **transmissions.** 1 The **transmission** of something involves passing it or sending it to a different place or person. EG *...the transmission of diseases... ...data transmission.* N UNCOUNT

2 The **transmission** of television or radio programmes is the broadcasting of them. EG *...a unique film record that was destroyed after transmission.* N UNCOUNT

3 A **transmission** is a broadcast. EG *Millions would have heard that transmission.* N COUNT

transmit /trænzmɪt/, **transmits, transmitting, transmitted.** 1 When a message or an electronic signal **is transmitted**, it is sent by means of radio waves. EG *The material was transmitted by satellite throughout the world.* V+O : USU PASS

2 To **transmit** something to a different place or person means to pass it or send it to the place or person. EG *...a disease that is sometimes transmitted to humans... ...a superior way of storing and transmitting energy.* V+O : OFT+*to* Formal

transmitter /trænzmɪtə/, **transmitters.** A **transmitter** is a piece of equipment that is used for sending radio signals or for broadcasting programmes. N COUNT

transparency /trænspærənsi¹/, **transparencies.** 1 A **transparency** is a small piece of photographic film in a frame which can be projected onto a screen. N COUNT Technical

2 **Transparency** is the quality that an object or substance has if you can see through it. EG *The crystal lost its transparency.* N UNCOUNT

transparent /trænspærənt/. 1 If an object or substance is **transparent**, you can see through it. EG *...a transparent plastic lid.* ADJ CLASSIF

2 If something such as a feeling is **transparent**, it is easily understood or recognized. EG *We wanted our goals to be transparent.* ◇ **transparently.** EG *...an attitude that was transparently false.* ADJ QUALIT Formal ◇ SUBMOD

transpire /trænspaɪə/, **transpires, transpiring, transpired.** 1 When it **transpires** that something is the case, people discover that it is the case. EG *It finally transpired that he was a special investigator for the CIA.* V Formal

2 When something **transpires**, it happens. EG *Nobody knows what transpired at the meeting.* V Formal

transplant, transplants, transplanting, transplanted; pronounced /trænsplɑːnt/ when it is a noun and /trænsplɑːnt/ when it is a verb.

1 A **transplant** is a surgical operation in which a part of a person's body is replaced because it is diseased. EG *...one of Britain's youngest heart transplant patients.* ▸ used as a verb. EG *Doctors hope to transplant a human heart into the patient within the next few days.* N COUNT OR N UNCOUNT ▸ V+O

2 When something **is transplanted**, it is moved to a different place. EG *...how an established technology can be transplanted to another region... ...transplanting seedlings.* V-ERG : OFT+A

transport, transports, transporting, transported; pronounced /trænspɔːt/ when it is a noun and /trænspɔːt/ when it is a verb.

1 You can refer to things which you travel in such as cars, aircraft, and boats as **transport**. EG *It is easier if you have your own transport... Why can't he use public transport?* N UNCOUNT

2 **Transport** involves moving goods or people from one place to another. EG *The essential means of transport for heavy equipment remained the railway... High transport costs make foreign goods too expensive.* N UNCOUNT

3 When goods or people **are transported** from one place to another, they are moved from one place to another. EG *The goods were transported to East Africa.* V+O : USU+A

transportation /trænspɔːteɪʃə⁰n/ is the same as transport. EG *The food is ready for transportation.* N UNCOUNT American

transvestite /trænzvestaɪt/, **transvestites.** A **transvestite** is a person, usually a man, who enjoys wearing clothes normally worn by people of the opposite sex. N COUNT

trap /træp/, **traps, trapping, trapped.** 1 A **trap** is **1.1** something such as a piece of equipment or a hole that is carefully positioned in order to catch animals or birds. EG *...an otter trap.* **1.2** a trick that is intended to catch or deceive someone. EG *I knew perfectly well it was a trap.* N COUNT

2 Someone who **traps** animals catches them using traps. V+O

3 If you **trap** someone, you trick them so that they do or say something which they did not want to do. EG *This wasn't the first time we had been trapped into a situation like this.* V+O

4 If you **are trapped** somewhere, you cannot move or escape because something is blocking your way or is holding you down. EG *Many people trapped in buildings died before they could be rescued.* V+O : USU PASS

Can you call a bad translation a travesty of the original?

5 If you **are trapped**, you are in an unpleasant situation that you cannot easily change. EG *She felt trapped... Many women are trapped in loveless marriages.* V+O : USU PASS

6 A **trap** is also an unpleasant situation that cannot easily be changed. EG *To break out of the poverty trap they need help from the government.* N COUNT+SUPP

7 When something **traps** gas, water, or energy, it stores it so that it can be used. EG *A building can be designed to trap and store radiation from the sun.* V+O

8 See also **booby-trap**.

trapdoor /træpdɔ:/, **trapdoors.** A **trapdoor** is a small horizontal door in a floor, ceiling, or stage. N COUNT

trapeze /trəpi:z/, **trapezes.** A **trapeze** is a bar of wood or metal hanging from two ropes. Acrobats and gymnasts swing on trapezes and perform skilful movements on them. N COUNT

trappings /træpɪŋz/. The **trappings** of a particular rank, position, or state are the things that you acquire as a result of having it. EG *...the trappings of power that have surrounded him since he took office.* N PLURAL : USU+*of*

trash /træʃ/. **1 Trash** is rubbish. EG *The yards were filled with trash.* N UNCOUNT American

2 If you say that something such as a book, painting, or film is **trash**, you mean that it is not very good. EG *'I've told you not to read that trash,' he said.* N UNCOUNT Informal

trashcan /træʃkæn/, **trashcans.** A **trashcan** is a container you put rubbish in. N COUNT American

trashy /træʃi¹/, **trashier, trashiest. Trashy** books are not very good. ADJ QUALIT Informal

trauma /trɔ:mə/, **traumas. 1** A **trauma** is a very upsetting experience. EG *I look at my daughter and think of what traumas lie in store for her... ...the trauma of having their parents arrested.* N COUNT

2 Trauma is great stress and unhappiness. EG *This would impose unnecessary trauma and suffering.* N UNCOUNT

traumatic /trɔ:mætɪk/. A **traumatic** experience is very upsetting. EG *...the traumatic ordeal of facing a firing squad.* ADJ QUALIT

travel /trævə⁰l/, **travels, travelling, travelled;** spelled **traveling** and **traveled** in American English.

1 When you **travel**, you go from one place to another or you go to several places, especially in a foreign country. EG *I travelled to work by train... Margaret travelled alone around the United States... I travelled sixty miles to buy those books.* V : USU+A OR V+O

▸ used as a noun. EG *...air travel.* ▸ N UNCOUNT

2 Someone's **travels** are the journeys that they make to places a long way from their home. EG *...his extensive travels abroad.* N PLURAL +POSS

3 When something reaches one place from another, you say that it **travels** there. EG *Sound travels better in water than in air... News travels fast.* V+A

travel agency, travel agencies. A **travel agency** is a business which makes arrangements for people's holidays and journeys. N COUNT

travel agent, travel agents. A **travel agent** is a person who works in a travel agency. N COUNT

traveller /trævə⁰lə/, **travellers;** spelled **traveler** in American English. A **traveller** is a person who is making a journey or who travels a lot. N COUNT

traveller's cheque, traveller's cheques; spelled **traveler's check** in American English. **Traveller's cheques** are cheques that you buy at a bank and take abroad with you. You can exchange them for the local currency. N COUNT

traverse /trævɜ:s, trə³vɜ:s/, **traverses, traversing, traversed.** If you **traverse** an area of land or water, you go across it or over it. EG *I traversed the rest of the slope at a run.* V+O Formal

travesty /trævəsti¹/, **travesties.** If you say that something is a **travesty**, you mean that it is a very bad representation or imitation of something. EG *His account of my essay was a travesty... ...the travesties of justice played out in their courts.* N COUNT

trawler /trɔ:lə/, **trawlers.** A **trawler** is a fishing boat on which fish are caught in large nets. N COUNT

tray /treɪ/, **trays.** A **tray** is a flat object with raised edges which is used for carrying food or drinks. EG *There were two champagne glasses on the tray... ...trays of tea and sandwiches.* N COUNT

treacherous /trɛtʃərəs/. **1** A **treacherous** person is likely to betray you. EG *...my treacherous fellow travellers.* ADJ QUALIT

2 You describe the ground or the sea as **treacherous** when it is dangerous and unpredictable. EG *The tides are treacherous and only strong swimmers can make it.* ADJ QUALIT

treachery /trɛtʃəri¹/. If someone betrays their country or betrays a person who trusts them, you describe their action as **treachery**. EG *He could not believe that Clemenza was guilty of treachery.* N UNCOUNT

treacle /tri:kə⁰l/ is a sweet, sticky liquid used in making cakes and puddings. EG *...bread and black treacle... ...treacle tart.* N UNCOUNT

tread /trɛd/, **treads, treading, trod** /trɒd/, **trodden** /trɒdə⁰n/. **1** If you **tread** on something, you step on it. EG *Oh, do be careful, don't tread on the flowers... There is a squeak every time I tread on the pedal.* V+A

2 If you **tread** something into the ground or into a carpet, you crush it into the ground or carpet by stepping on it. EG *Damp chips had been trodden into the carpet.* V+O+A

3 If you **tread** in a particular way, you walk in that way. EG *She trod heavily out of the room.* V+A

4 A person's **tread** is the sound that they make with their feet as they walk. EG *They could hear his heavy limping tread.* N SING+SUPP

5 If you **tread** carefully, you behave carefully or cautiously. EG *The government was treading warily.* V+A

6 If someone who is in deep water **treads water**, they stay afloat in an upright position by moving their legs. PHRASE

7 The **tread** of a tyre or shoe is the pattern of ridges on it that stops it slipping. N COUNT OR N UNCOUNT

8 See also **trodden**.

treason /tri:zə⁰n/ is the crime of betraying your country, for example by helping its enemies. N UNCOUNT Formal

treasure /trɛʒə/, **treasures, treasuring, treasured. 1 Treasure** is a collection of gold or silver objects, or jewels, especially one that has been hidden. EG *...buried treasure.* N UNCOUNT

2 Treasures are valuable works of art. EG *...the sale of art treasures.* N COUNT : USU PLURAL

3 If you **treasure** something, you are very pleased that you have it and you regard it as precious. EG *...one of the memories which they would treasure.* V+O

◇ **treasured.** EG *The letters he wrote me are my most treasured possessions.* ◇ ADJ QUALIT : ATTRIB

4 If you say that someone is a **treasure**, you mean that they are very helpful and useful to you. N COUNT Informal

treasurer /trɛʒərə/, **treasurers.** The **treasurer** of an organization is in charge of its finances and keeps its accounts. N COUNT

treat /tri:t/, **treats, treating, treated. 1** If you **treat** someone in a particular way, you behave that way towards them. EG *We were treated with respect... Their parents continue to treat them as children.* V+O+A

2 If you **treat** something in a particular way, you deal with it that way or you regard it in that way. EG *Electricity is potentially dangerous, so treat it with respect... Does he treat it as some sort of joke?* V+O+A

3 When a doctor **treats** a patient or an illness, he or she tries to make the patient well again. EG *...a way to treat cancer.* V+O

4 If you **treat** something such as wood or cloth, you put a special substance on it in order to protect it or to give it special properties. EG *New timber should be treated with a preservative.* V+O : USU+A

5 If you give someone a **treat**, you buy or arrange something special for them which they will enjoy. N COUNT

EG *Granny took us for tea at Lyons Corner House as a special treat.* ▸ used as a verb. EG *Treat yourself to a new pair of shoes... I was treated to lunch by the vice-president.* ▸ V-REFL OR V+O

treatment /tri:tmə^{2}nt/, **treatments. 1** Medical **treatment** consists of all the things that are done in order to make a sick or injured person well again. EG *...free dental treatment... I tried every treatment the doctor suggested.* N UNCOUNT OR N COUNT

2 Your **treatment** of someone is the way that you behave towards them or the way you deal with them. EG *Their treatment of women is unspeakable... I didn't want special treatment.* N UNCOUNT

treaty /tri:ti^{1}/, **treaties.** A **treaty** is a written agreement between countries. EG *...the Treaty of Versailles... The Government has signed a treaty with Moscow.* N COUNT

treble /trɛbə^{0}l/, **trebles, trebling, trebled.** If something **trebles** or **is trebled**, it becomes three times greater in number or amount than it was. EG *The population has nearly trebled since 1950.* V-ERG

tree /tri:/, **trees.** A **tree** is a tall plant with a hard trunk, branches, and leaves. EG *In the middle of the lawn was a great cedar tree.* ● See also **Christmas tree**, **family tree**. ● to **be barking up the wrong tree**: see **bark**. N COUNT

treetop /tri:tɒp/, **treetops.** The **treetops** are the top part of the trees in a forest. EG *Monkeys were bounding away through the treetops.* N COUNT: USU PLURAL

trek /trɛk/, **treks, trekking, trekked.** If you **trek** somewhere, you go on a long and difficult journey, especially on foot. EG *They trekked for three days along the banks of the Zambezi.* ▸ used as a noun. EG *We set off on a four hour trek through swamps and fields.* V+A ▸ N COUNT

trellis /trɛlɪs/, **trellises.** A **trellis** is a frame which is used to support climbing plants. N COUNT

tremble /trɛmbə^{0}l/, **trembles, trembling, trembled. 1** If you **tremble**, you shake slightly, usually because you are frightened or cold. EG *Claude's hands trembled as he struck a match... 'What is this place?' asked Mother, trembling with fear.* V: OFT+A

2 If something **trembles**, it shakes slightly. EG *The wind made the branches shake and tremble.* V Written

3 If your voice **trembles**, it sounds unsteady, for example because you are upset. EG *'It does concern me.' Fanny's voice trembled a little.* V Written

tremendous /trɪ^{2}mɛndəs/. **1** If you describe something as **tremendous**, you mean that it is very large or impressive. EG *The play became a tremendous hit... They cost a tremendous amount of money.* ◇ **tremendously.** EG *There is a tremendously difficult struggle ahead of us... She envied and admired Judy tremendously.* ADJ QUALIT ◇ ADV

2 You can also describe something as **tremendous** when you think it is very good or pleasing. EG *The view is tremendous... The holiday was tremendous.* ADJ QUALIT

tremor /trɛmə/, **tremors. 1** A **tremor** is **1.1** a shaking movement of your body which you cannot control. EG *Words cannot describe the tremor of pleasure that went through me.* **1.2** an unsteady quality in your voice, for example because you are upset. EG *Burton detected a tremor in the voice of the Controller.* N COUNT

2 A **tremor** is also a small earthquake. EG *These local volcanic tremors are usually not strong.* N COUNT

tremulous /trɛmjə^{4}ləs/. If someone's smile or voice is **tremulous**, it is unsteady because they are nervous, uncertain, or unhappy. EG *Jack's voice went on, tremulous yet determined.* ADJ QUALIT Literary

trench /trɛntʃ/, **trenches.** A **trench** is a long narrow channel dug in the ground, for example for drainage. N COUNT

trend /trɛnd/, **trends.** A **trend** is a change towards doing or being something different. EG *There is a trend towards equal opportunities for men and women... The trend has been to stress the artistic side of education.* N COUNT: USU+SUPP

trendy /trɛndi^{1}/, **trendier, trendiest. Trendy** things or people are fashionable. EG *...trendy clothes... ...trendy intellectuals.* ADJ QUALIT Informal

trepidation /trɛpɪdeɪʃə^{0}n/ is fear or anxiety. EG *'What do you mean?' I asked, with some trepidation... We approached with trepidation.* N UNCOUNT Formal

trespass /trɛspəs/, **trespasses, trespassing, trespassed.** If you **trespass** on someone's land, you go onto it without their permission. EG *...signs saying 'No trespassing'.* ◇ **trespasser, trespassers.** EG *Trespassers will be prosecuted.* V: OFT+*on* ◇ N COUNT

trial /traɪəl/, **trials. 1** A **trial** is the legal process in which a judge and jury decide whether a person is guilty of a particular crime after listening to evidence relating to it. EG *She won't get a fair trial... Huey was awaiting trial for murder.* ● If someone is **on trial**, they are being tried in a court of law. EG *We don't intend to put him on trial.* ● to **stand trial**: see **stand**. N COUNT OR N UNCOUNT ● PHRASE

2 A **trial** is also an experiment in which you test something. EG *We've completed a number of fairly successful trials with laboratory animals.* ● If something is **on trial**, it is being tested or closely examined to see if it is suitable. EG *The Parliamentary system is on trial.* N COUNT OR N UNCOUNT ● PHRASE

3 A **trial** period is a short period of time during which you employ a person or use a thing in order to find out if they are suitable. N MOD

4 If you do something by **trial and error**, you try different methods of doing it until you find one that works well. EG *The best solution can only be found by a process of trial and error.* PHRASE

5 If you talk about the **trials** that someone experiences, you mean the unpleasant things that they experience. EG *...the trials of pregnancy and childbirth.* N COUNT +SUPP: USU PLURAL

trial run, trial runs. A **trial run** is a first attempt at doing something, to make sure that you can do it properly when you need to. N COUNT

triangle /traɪæŋgə^{0}l/, **triangles.** A **triangle** is a flat shape or area which has three straight sides and three angles. See picture at SHAPES. EG *The place of assembly in which he stood was roughly a triangle.* N COUNT

triangular /traɪæŋgjə^{4}lə/. Something that is **triangular** is in the shape of a triangle. EG *I punched two triangular holes in the tin.* ADJ CLASSIF

tribal /traɪbə^{0}l/ describes things relating or belonging to tribes. EG *...tribal leaders... ...a tribal war.* ADJ CLASSIF: ATTRIB

tribe /traɪb/, **tribes.** A **tribe** is a small group of people with the same language and customs. EG *Mr Otunnu is a member of the Acholi tribe... ...primitive tribes in the heart of Africa.* N COUNT

tribesman /traɪbzmə^{3}n/, **tribesmen.** A **tribesman** is a man who belongs to a particular tribe. N COUNT

tribulation /trɪbjə^{4}leɪʃə^{0}n/, **tribulations. Tribulation** is trouble or suffering. EG *Life is uncertain and full of tribulation... ...after many trials and tribulations during the war.* N UNCOUNT OR N PLURAL Formal

tribunal /traɪbju:nə^{0}l/, **tribunals.** A **tribunal** is a special court or committee that is appointed to deal with particular problems. EG *An industrial tribunal was hearing cases of unfair dismissal.* N COLL

tributary /trɪbjə^{4}tə^{0}ri^{1}/, **tributaries.** A **tributary** is a stream or river that flows into a larger river. EG *...the Neander River, a tributary of the Rhine.* N COUNT

tribute /trɪbju:t/, **tributes. 1** A **tribute** is something that you say or do in order to show your admiration and respect for someone. EG *On Johnson's death in 1922, Asquith paid tribute to his personal qualities... She accepted the tribute graciously.* N COUNT OR N UNCOUNT

2 If you say that one thing is a **tribute** to another, you mean that it is the result of the other thing and shows how good the other thing is. EG *The fact that* N SING: *a*+N

Which two words on these pages mean to become three times greater than before?

I survived is a tribute to the indestructibility of the human body.

trick /trɪk/, **tricks, tricking, tricked.** 1 If someone **tricks** you, they deceive you, often in order to make you do something. EG *He realized that the visitors had tricked him... She felt she had been tricked into marriage.* — V+O: OFT+*into*

2 A **trick** is 2.1 a clever or skilful action that someone does in order to entertain people. EG *Mr Poliakin was performing his popular trick of playing the bow with the violin.* 2.2 a clever way of doing something. EG *An old campers' trick is to use three thin blankets instead of one thick one... These are standard tricks of the trade.* — N COUNT

3 A **trick** question is one where the obvious answer is in fact wrong, or one which is intended to make you accidentally reveal something. — ADJ CLASSIF: ATTRIB

4 **Trick** devices and methods are intended to deceive people for a joke or for entertainment. EG *...trick mirrors... ...trick photography.* — ADJ CLASSIF: ATTRIB

5 If you **play a trick** on someone, you do something that is intended to deceive them. EG *They played a dirty trick on us.* — PHRASE

6 If you say that something **does the trick**, you mean that it achieves what you wanted. EG *They thought that just one push would do the trick.* — PHRASE Informal

7 See also **conjuring trick**.

trickery /trɪkəri^1/ is deception. EG *The old man suspected trickery.* — N UNCOUNT

trickle /trɪk^{ə}l/, **trickles, trickling, trickled.** 1 When a liquid **trickles** somewhere, it flows slowly in a thin stream. EG *The tears were beginning to trickle down her cheeks.* — V: USU+A

2 When people or things **trickle** somewhere, they move there slowly in small groups or amounts. EG *The coach parties began trickling back to the car park.* — V+A

3 A **trickle** of liquid is a thin, slow stream of it. EG *...a thin trickle of blood.* — N PART: USU SING

4 A **trickle** of people or things is a small number or quantity of them. EG *A trickle of people were still coming in... Income is down to a trickle.* — N PART: USU SING

tricky /trɪki^1/, **trickier, trickiest.** A **tricky** task or problem is difficult to do or to deal with. EG *Dyeing patterned material is tricky... It had been a slow, tricky job.* — ADJ QUALIT

tricycle /traɪsɪk^{ə}l/, **tricycles.** A **tricycle** is a vehicle similar to a bicycle but with two wheels at the back instead of one. — N COUNT

tried /traɪd/. 1 **Tried** is the past tense and past participle of **try**.

2 A product or method that is **tried and tested** has often been used and has always worked well. — PHRASE

trifle /traɪf^{ə}l/, **trifles, trifling, trifled.** 1 You use **a trifle** to describe a quality or manner that exists to a small extent or degree. EG *She was a trifle breathless... 'They seemed very nice men,' she added, a trifle wistfully.* — PHRASE Formal

2 **Trifles** are things that are considered to be not very important or not very valuable. EG *They worry over trifles.* — N COUNT: USU PLURAL

3 A **trifle** is a cold pudding made of layers of sponge cake, fruit, jelly, and custard. — N COUNT OR N UNCOUNT

trifle with. If you **trifle with** someone or something, you treat them in a disrespectful way, rather than seriously. EG *Mitchell was not someone to be trifled with.* — PHRASAL VB: V+PREP, HAS PASS

trifling /traɪflɪŋ/. Something that is **trifling** is small and unimportant. EG *There was no need for you to come out here on such a trifling matter.* — ADJ QUALIT

trigger /trɪgə/, **triggers, triggering, triggered.** 1 The **trigger** of a gun is the small lever which you pull in order to fire it. See picture at WEAPONS. — N COUNT

2 If something **triggers** an event or **triggers** it **off**, it causes it to happen. EG *There had been disagreements between them, triggered by his work.* — V+O: OFT+*off*

trillion /trɪljən/, **trillions.** 1 A **trillion** is a number representing a million million. EG *...with income now in excess of a trillion dollars.* — NUMBER

2 You can use **trillions** to mean an extremely large number. EG *There are trillions of places where we could go.* — N PART: USU PLURAL Informal

trilogy /trɪlədʒi^1/, **trilogies.** A **trilogy** is a series of three books or plays that have the same characters or the same subject. — N COUNT

trim /trɪm/, **trimmer, trimmest; trims, trimming, trimmed.** 1 Something that is **trim** is neat, tidy, and attractive. EG *...the trim lawns and trees of suburbia... ...a man with a trim beard.* — ADJ QUALIT

2 If someone has a **trim** figure, they are slim. EG *...a trim, balding man in his early sixties.* — ADJ QUALIT

3 If you **trim** your hair or **trim** a hedge, you cut off small amounts of it in order to make it look neater. EG *His beard was freshly trimmed... The grass needed trimming.* — V+O ▸ used as a noun. EG *My hair needs a trim.* — ▸ N SING

4 If a piece of clothing **is trimmed** with things such as ribbons or feathers, these things are added to the edge in order to make it look nice. — V+O: USU PASS +*with* ◊ **trimmed.** EG *Her dress was trimmed with lace at the neck... ...a hat trimmed with ribbons.* — ◊ ADJ PRED +*with*

trim away or **trim off.** If you **trim away** parts of something or **trim** them **off**, you cut them off because they are not needed. EG *Most of the fat should be trimmed off meat.* — PHRASAL VB: V+O+ADV

trimming /trɪmɪŋ/, **trimmings.** 1 The **trimming** or the **trimmings** on a piece of clothing are extra parts added for decoration. EG *...a pink nightdress with nylon lace trimmings.* — N MASS OR N PLURAL

2 **Trimmings** are also nice things that can be added to something or included in something. EG *Tonight it was turkey with all the trimmings.* — N PLURAL

trinket /trɪŋkɪt/, **trinkets.** A **trinket** is a cheap ornament or piece of jewellery. — N COUNT

trio /triːəʊ/, **trios.** A **trio** is a group of three people, especially three musicians or singers who play or sing together. EG *...a trio of journalists... ...the Pump Room Trio.* — N COUNT

trip /trɪp/, **trips, tripping, tripped.** 1 A **trip** is a journey that you make to a place and back again. EG *Morris decided to take a trip to London... ...executives on business trips abroad.* — N COUNT

2 If you **trip**, you knock your foot against something when you are walking, and you fall over or nearly fall over. EG *I tripped and fell... She tripped over a stone.* — V: USU+A

3 If you **trip** someone who is walking along, you put your foot or something else in front of them so that they knock their own foot against it and fall. EG *Somebody thrust out a foot and tripped him.* — V+O

4 You can also refer to a strange or unreal experience that is caused by taking drugs as a **trip**. EG *She had a bad trip.* — N COUNT Informal

5 See also **round trip**.

trip up. If you **trip up** someone who is walking along, you put your foot or something else in front of them so that they knock their own foot against it and fall. — PHRASAL VB: V+O+ADV

tripartite /traɪpɑːtaɪt/ means having three parts or involving three groups of people. EG *...the tripartite system of education... The unions called for tripartite talks.* — ADJ CLASSIF: ATTRIB Formal

tripe /traɪp/. 1 **Tripe** is the stomach of a pig, cow, or ox, which is eaten as food. — N UNCOUNT

2 If you say that something that someone has said or written is **tripe**, you mean that it is silly or not very good. — N UNCOUNT Informal

triple /trɪp^{ə}l/, **triples, tripling, tripled.** 1 **Triple** means consisting of three things or three parts. EG *...a triple alliance... ...a breath-taking triple somersault.* — ADJ CLASSIF: ATTRIB

2 If you **triple** something or if it **triples**, it becomes three times greater in size or number than it was. EG *In three years the company had* — V-ERG

tripled its sales... During this period the Japanese national income has tripled.

triplet /trɪplɪ^{ʔ}t/, **triplets. Triplets** are three children born at the same time to the same mother. N COUNT: USU PLURAL

tripod /traɪpɒd/, **tripods.** A **tripod** is a stand with three legs which you use to support something such as a camera or telescope. N COUNT

trite /traɪt/. Ideas, remarks, and stories that are **trite** are dull and not original. EG *...trite films... ...a trite piece of philosophy.* ADJ QUALIT

triumph /traɪəmf/, **triumphs, triumphing, triumphed. 1** A **triumph** is a great success or achievement. EG *The election result was a personal triumph for the party leader... This machine is a triumph of advanced technology.* N COUNT

2 Triumph is a feeling of great satisfaction when you win or achieve something. EG *He gave a cry of triumph... I saw a gleam of triumph in his eye.* N UNCOUNT

3 If you **triumph**, you win a victory or succeed in overcoming something. EG *They had met the challenge and triumphed... She learned to triumph over her disabilities.* V: OFT+*over*

triumphant /traɪʌmfənt/. Someone who is **triumphant** feels very happy because they have won a victory or have achieved something. EG *...triumphant soldiers... His parents looked on with a triumphant smile.* ◊ **triumphantly**. EG *Robert was looking at me triumphantly.* ADJ QUALIT ◊ ADV

trivia /trɪvɪə/. If you refer to things as **trivia**, you mean that they are unimportant. EG *She takes a childish delight in remembering trivia... ...the trivia of everyday life.* N UNCOUNT

trivial /trɪvɪəl/. Something that is **trivial** is unimportant. EG *All those little details of organization seemed trivial.* ADJ QUALIT

triviality /trɪviæl^{1}ti^1/, **trivialities. 1 Trivialities** are unimportant things. EG *...the daily trivialities which seem so important to men.* N PLURAL

2 The **triviality** of something is the fact that it is unimportant. EG *...conversations of unbelievable triviality.* N UNCOUNT

trivialize /trɪvɪəlaɪz/, **trivializes, trivializing, trivialized;** also spelled **trivialise.** If you **trivialize** something, you make it seem unimportant, although it is actually important. EG *Their political role is often trivialized.* V+O

trod /trɒd/ is the past tense of **tread.**

trodden /trɒdə^{0}n/. **1 Trodden** is the past participle of **tread.**

2 Ground that is **trodden** has been walked over by a lot of people, and is therefore flattened or marked with footprints. EG *The grass was trodden and muddy.* ADJ CLASSIF

trolley /trɒli^1/, **trolleys. 1** A **trolley** is **1.1** a small cart that you use to carry heavy things, for example shopping or luggage. EG *...supermarket trolleys.* **1.2** a small table on wheels on which things, especially food and drinks, can be taken from one part of a building to another. EG *The room-service boy wheeled the trolley in.* N COUNT

2 A **trolley** is also a tram. EG *Cars and trolleys filled the street.* N COUNT American

trombone /trɒmbəʊn/, **trombones.** A **trombone** is a brass musical instrument which you play by blowing into it and sliding part of it backwards and forwards to make different notes. See picture at MUSICAL INSTRUMENTS. N COUNT

troop /tru:p/, **troops, trooping, trooped. 1 Troops** are soldiers, especially ones taking part in military action. EG *They have more than 11,000 troops in Northern Ireland... ...reports on troop movements.* N PLURAL

2 A **troop** of people or animals is a group of them. EG *...a troop of monkeys.* N PART

3 If people **troop** somewhere, they walk there in a group. EG *The twelve men trooped downstairs.* V+A

trophy /trəʊfi^1/, **trophies.** A **trophy** is a prize, for example a silver cup or shield, that is given to the winner of a competition or race. N COUNT

tropical /trɒpɪkə^{0}l/. **Tropical** places or things are in the tropics or come from the tropics. EG *Most tropical areas have rainy and dry seasons... ...tropical rain forests.* ADJ CLASSIF: ATTRIB

tropics /trɒpɪks/. The **tropics** are the hottest parts of the world, near the equator. N PLURAL: *the*+N

trot /trɒt/, **trots, trotting, trotted. 1** When an animal such as a horse **trots**, it moves fairly fast, lifting its feet quite high off the ground. EG *He made the beast turn aside and trot away.* ▸ used as a noun. EG *She urged her pony into an energetic trot.* V: USU+A ▸ N SING

2 If you **trot** somewhere, you move fairly fast, taking small quick steps. EG *We trotted along behind him.* ▸ used as a noun. EG *Hobbs immediately went off at a trot.* V+A ▸ N SING

3 If you say that several things happen **on the trot**, you mean that they happen one after the other, without a break. EG *Try not to miss two lessons on the trot.* PHRASE Informal

trot out. If you **trot out** old ideas or pieces of information, you repeat them in a boring way. EG *They trot out all the old reasons for their failure.* PHRASAL VB: V+O+ADV

trouble /trʌb^{0}əl/, **troubles, troubling, troubled. 1** If you have **trouble** doing something, you have difficulties or problems doing it. EG *You shouldn't have any trouble locating them... This would save everyone a lot of trouble.* N UNCOUNT

2 If you say that one aspect of a situation is the **trouble**, you mean that it is that aspect which is causing problems or making the situation unsatisfactory. EG *It's getting a bit expensive now, that's the trouble... The trouble with you is that you've forgotten what it's like to be young.* N SING: USU *the*+N

3 Your **troubles** are the problems in your life. EG *The old lady next door was telling me all her troubles... She thought that all her troubles were over.* N PLURAL: USU+POSS

4 If you have kidney **trouble** or back **trouble**, for example, there is something wrong with your kidneys or your back. EG *He has heart trouble.* N UNCOUNT +SUPP

5 If you are **in trouble**, **5.1** you have a serious problem. EG *Frank was still in deep financial trouble.* **5.2** someone in authority is angry with you because of something you have done. EG *...if a child is in trouble with the police... I don't want to get you into trouble.* PHRASE

6 If there is **trouble**, people are quarrelling or fighting. EG *He's the sort of person who always makes trouble... The demonstration was cancelled because the police felt that it could lead to trouble.* N UNCOUNT

7 If you say that it is no **trouble** to do something for someone, you mean that you do not mind doing it. EG *'It wouldn't be any trouble.' – 'That's very kind of you.'* N UNCOUNT: WITH BROAD NEG

8 If you **take the trouble** to do something, you do it although it requires some time or effort. EG *Many of them do not even take the trouble to answer letters.* PHRASE

9 If something **troubles** you, it makes you feel rather worried. EG *What's troubling you?... He was deeply troubled by the thought that she might leave him.* ◊ **troubling**. EG *It was a new and troubling thought.* V+O ◊ ADJ QUALIT

10 If you say that you are sorry to **trouble** someone, you are apologizing for disturbing them in order to ask them something. EG *I'm sorry to trouble you, but I wondered if we could have a word some time.* V+O

troubled /trʌbə^{0}ld/. **1** Someone who is **troubled** is worried because they have problems. ADJ QUALIT

2 A **troubled** place, organization, or time has many problems or conflicts. EG *We live in troubled times... ...Britain's troubled car industry.* ADJ QUALIT

troublemaker /trʌbə^{0}lmeɪkə/, **troublemakers.** A **troublemaker** is someone who causes trouble N COUNT

Find two musical instruments on these pages. What are they made of?

or arguments. EG *The trouble-makers are a tiny minority.*

troublesome /trʌbəᵒlsəm/. Someone or something that is **troublesome** causes problems or difficulties. EG *...troublesome tenants.* ADJ QUALIT

trough /trɒf/, **troughs.** **1** A **trough** is a long narrow container from which farm animals drink or eat. N COUNT

2 A **trough** in a system or process is a point at which something is low in amount. EG *The trough in consumption of electricity occurs at night.* N COUNT

troupe /tru:p/, **troupes.** A **troupe** is a group of actors, singers, or dancers who work together. EG *...a troupe of travelling actors.* N COLL

trousers /traʊzəz/. The form **trouser** is usually used before another noun. **Trousers** are a piece of clothing that covers your body from the waist downwards, and covers each leg separately. See picture at CLOTHES. EG *Claud was dressed in a pair of black trousers... He slid it gently into his trouser pocket.* N PLURAL

trout /traʊt/. **Trout** is both the singular and the plural form. A **trout** is a kind of fish that lives in rivers. N COUNT OR N UNCOUNT

trowel /traʊəl/, **trowels.** A **trowel** is **1** a small garden tool with a curved, pointed blade that you use for digging small holes or for removing weeds. See picture at TOOLS. **2** a small tool with a flat, diamond-shaped blade that you use for spreading cement or plaster onto walls. N COUNT

truancy /tru:ənsi¹/ is the practice of children staying away from school without permission. EG *The longer the period of truancy, the harder it becomes to return to school.* N UNCOUNT

truant /tru:ənt/, **truants.** **1** A **truant** is a child who stays away from school without permission. EG *His elder brother had been a habitual truant.* N COUNT

2 If children **play truant**, they stay away from school without permission. EG *In my last year I played truant a lot.* PHRASE

truce /tru:s/, **truces.** A **truce** is an agreement between two people or groups to stop fighting for a short time. EG *The British called a truce.* N COUNT

truck /trʌk/, **trucks.** A **truck** is **1** a lorry. EG *There was a big truck parked on the side of the road... ...a truck driver.* **2** a large motor vehicle which is open at the back and is used for carrying goods, animals, or people, often on rough roads. EG *The farmer drove them out to the orchard in a rusty old truck.* **3** an open vehicle used for carrying goods on a railway. EG *...a long truck loaded with bricks.* N COUNT American; N COUNT

trudge /trʌdʒ/, **trudges, trudging, trudged.** If you **trudge** somewhere, you walk there with slow, heavy steps. EG *Michael trudged up the hill.* ▸ used as a noun. EG *They set off before dawn for the long trudge home.* V+A; ▸ N SING

true /tru:/, **truer, truest.** **1** A story or statement that is **true** is based on facts and on things that really have happened and are not invented. EG *The story about the murder is true... Unfortunately it was true about the illness of little Sylvie.* ADJ QUALIT

2 If a dream, wish, or prediction **comes true**, it actually happens. EG *My wish had come true.* PHRASE

3 You use **true** to describe people or things that have all the characteristics of a particular kind of thing. For example, if you describe someone as a **true** American, you mean that they have all the characteristics of a typical American. EG *I suppose it takes time for true democracy to work.* ADJ QUALIT : ATTRIB

4 **True** feelings are sincere and genuine. EG *We sometimes wish to hide our true feelings... She smiled with true amusement.* ADJ QUALIT : ATTRIB

5 If you are **true to** your **word**, you do what you had promised to do. PHRASE

6 If an object is **true**, it is perfectly straight and level and has a regular and correct shape. EG *The window frame isn't quite true.* ADJ PRED

truffle /trʌfəᵒl/, **truffles.** A **truffle** is **1** a soft round sweet flavoured with chocolate or rum. **2** a round mushroom-like fungus which grows underground and is considered very good to eat. N COUNT

truly /tru:li¹/. **1** **Truly** means completely and genuinely. EG *He was now truly American... He alone truly appreciates it.* ADV

2 If you **truly** feel something, you feel it in a sincere and genuine way. EG *She didn't say what she truly felt.* ADV

3 **Truly** also means to a very great degree. EG *He possessed a truly remarkable talent.* • **well and truly**: see **well**. SUBMOD Formal

4 You also use **truly** to emphasize that you are telling the truth and are not lying. EG *And truly, coming home was the nicest part of the trip.* ADV SEN

5 You can write **yours truly** before your signature at the end of a formal letter. EG *Yours truly, Desmond Burton-Cox.* PHRASE

trump /trʌmp/, **trumps.** **1** **Trumps** is the suit in a game of cards which is chosen to have the highest value in one particular game. N PLURAL

2 Your **trump card** is the most powerful thing that you can use or do in order to gain an advantage over someone. EG *Spain has at last produced her trump card and sent on the field of battle her most deadly weapon.* PHRASE

trumpet /trʌmpɪt/, **trumpets, trumpeting, trumpeted.** **1** A **trumpet** is a brass musical instrument that you play by blowing into it. It has three buttons that you press to get different notes. See picture at MUSICAL INSTRUMENTS. N COUNT

2 When an elephant makes a sound, it **trumpets**. V OR V+O

trumpeter /trʌmpɪtə/, **trumpeters.** A **trumpeter** is someone who plays a trumpet. N COUNT

truncate /trʌŋkeɪt/, **truncates, truncating, truncated.** If something **is truncated**, it is made shorter. EG *The lines were truncated... The truncated corpse was stuffed into a bag.* V+O : USU PASS

truncheon /trʌntᵒʃəᵒn/, **truncheons.** A **truncheon** is a short, thick stick that British policemen carry as a weapon. N COUNT

trundle /trʌndəᵒl/, **trundles, trundling, trundled.** **1** If a vehicle **trundles** somewhere, it moves there slowly. EG *The lorry trundled up the hill.* V+A

2 If you **trundle** something somewhere, you push or pull it along slowly on its wheels. EG *She saw him trundling the push chair along in the nearby park.* V+O+A

trunk /trʌŋk/, **trunks.** **1** The **trunk** of a tree is the large main stem from which the branches grow. N COUNT

2 Your **trunk** is the main central part of your body, but not your neck, head, legs, or arms. N COUNT

3 An elephant's **trunk** is its very long nose that it uses to lift food and water. N COUNT

4 A **trunk** is also a large, strong case or box used for storing things or for taking them on a journey. N COUNT

5 The **trunk** of a car is a covered space at the back or front in which you put luggage or other belongings. N COUNT American

trust /trʌst/, **trusts, trusting, trusted.** **1** If you **trust** someone, you believe that they are honest and will not deliberately do anything to harm you. EG *Everybody liked and trusted him... You can trust me.* ▸ used as a noun. EG *Adam could feel his father's trust in him.* V+O; ▸ N UNCOUNT : OFT+*in*

2 If you **trust** someone to do something, you believe that they will do it successfully or properly. EG *I trust you to find them... She didn't trust anyone to look after her child properly.* V+O+*to*-INF

3 If you **trust** someone with something important or valuable, you give it to them or tell it to them. EG *She's not a person I can trust with this sort of secret... Next year I hope the company will trust me with a bigger budget.* V+O+*with*

4 If you do not **trust** something, you feel that it is not safe or reliable. EG *I don't trust fancy gimmicks in cars... He wanted to get up and walk, but he didn't trust his legs.* V+O : WITH BROAD NEG

5 If you **trust** your judgement or **trust** someone's V+O advice, you believe that it is good or right. EG *Trust your own instincts... She seems to trust his advice about people.*

6 If you say you **trust** that something is true, you mean that you hope and expect that it is true. EG *They will give you a good pension, I trust?... I trust you all like coffee.* — V+REPORT: ONLY *that* Outdated

7 If you say **'trust** someone **to do** something', you mean that it is typical of that person to do that foolish thing. EG *Trust Julia to get the name wrong.* — PHRASE

8 Trust is also responsibility that you are given, for example in your job, to deal with or look after important, valuable, or secret things. EG *The judge took the view that to betray a position of trust in such a manner was disgraceful.* — N UNCOUNT

9 If you **take** something that someone tells you **on trust**, you believe it completely without checking it. — PHRASE

10 A **trust** is a financial arrangement in which an organization keeps and invests money for someone. EG *...a lifetime interest trust.* — N COUNT ● If money is kept **in trust**, it is kept and invested for someone by an organization. EG *His mother's money was left in trust for him to acquire at the age of twenty-five.* — ● PHRASE

11 See also **trusting**.

trustee /trʌstiː/, **trustees.** A **trustee** is someone who has legal control of money or property that they are keeping or investing for another person. EG *Her request for money was turned down by the trustees.* — N COUNT

trusting /trʌstɪŋ/. If you are **trusting**, you tend to believe that people are honest and sincere and do not intend to harm you. EG *Judy had an open and trusting nature.* — ADJ QUALIT

trustworthy /trʌstwɜːði[1]/. Someone who is **trustworthy** is reliable and responsible so that you can trust them completely. EG *He was an experienced and trustworthy travelling companion.* — ADJ QUALIT

trusty /trʌsti[1]/. **Trusty** things and animals are considered to be reliable because they have always worked well in the past. EG *I put on my trusty overcoat... I tied up my trusty horse.* — ADJ QUALIT: ATTRIB

truth /truːθ/, **truths. 1** The **truth** is all the facts about something, rather than things that are imagined or invented. EG *He learned the truth about Sam... He's probably telling the truth... This is not the whole truth.* — N SING: *the*+N

2 If you say that there is **truth** in a statement or story, you mean that it is true, or at least partly true. EG *There is an element of truth in this argument... I could not deny the truth of this statement.* — N UNCOUNT

3 A **truth** is an idea or principle that is generally accepted to be true. EG *It's a book that contains important truths... ...a universal truth.* — N COUNT

4 You say **in truth** or **in all truth** when you are giving your honest opinion about something. EG *In all truth, the British people deserved something better than this.* — PHRASE

5 You say **to tell you the truth** when you are admitting something and emphasizing that you are being honest and not hiding anything. EG *I can't remember his name, to tell you the truth.* — ADV SEN

truthful /truːθfʊl/. **1** Someone who is **truthful** is honest and tells the truth. EG *Many patients are more truthful when they talk to the computer than when they talk to the doctor.* — ADJ QUALIT ◇ **truthfully.** EG *If I ask him a question he will answer it as truthfully as he can.* — ◇ ADV

2 A statement or account that is **truthful** is true rather than invented. EG *He gave a truthful answer.* — ADJ QUALIT

try /traɪ/, **tries, trying, tried. 1** If you **try** to do something, you make an effort to do it because you want to do it. EG *My sister tried to cheer me up... They tried but failed... You can do it if you try... I tried hard not to think about it.* — V: USU+*to*-INF ▸ used as a noun. EG *After a few tries they gave up... It's certainly worth a try.* — ▸ N COUNT

To **try** and do something means to try to do it. EG *We must try and understand... Try and finish that by next Friday.* — V: ONLY INF OR IMPER

3 If you **try** for something, you make an effort to get it or achieve it. EG *The school advised Mr Denby to let his son try for university.* — V+*for*

4 If you **try** something, you use it or do it in order to find out how useful, effective, or enjoyable it is. EG *I tried a different approach to the problem... Have you ever tried painting?... The fourth key he tried opened the lid... He tried his wine.* — V+O OR V+-ING ▸ used as a noun. EG *We can give it a try and see how it looks.* — ▸ N COUNT: USU SING

5 If you **try** a particular place or person, you go to that place or person because you think that they may be able to provide you with something that you want. EG *We tried two or three hotels, but they were full.* — V+O

6 If you **try** a door or window, you try to open it. EG *I tried the handle, but it was locked.* — V+O

7 When a person **is tried**, he or she has to appear in a court of law and the judge and jury listen to the evidence about a crime, and decide if the person is guilty. EG *A youth was tried in the criminal courts for stealing.* — V+O: USU PASS

8 to **try** your **hand** at something: see **hand** ● to **try** your **luck** at something: see **luck**.

try on. If you **try on** a piece of clothing, you put it on to see if it fits you or if it looks nice. EG *She tried on her new party dress.* — PHRASAL VB: V+O+ADV

try out. If you **try** something **out**, you test it in order to find out how useful or effective it is. EG *Oxford is trying out an idea to help working parents... It's best to try this out first on a bit of spare fabric.* — PHRASAL VB: V+O+ADV

trying /traɪɪŋ/. Something or someone that is **trying** is difficult to deal with and makes you feel impatient or annoyed. EG *It had been a most trying experience for them.* — ADJ QUALIT

T-shirt, T-shirts. A **T-shirt** is a piece of clothing that you wear on the top half of your body. It has short sleeves, no collar, and no buttons down the front. See picture at CLOTHES. — N COUNT

tub /tʌb/, **tubs. 1** A **tub** is a wide, circular container of any size. EG *...a tub big enough to hold eighteen gallons... ...tubs of lard.* — N COUNT OR N PART

2 A **tub** is also a bath. EG *I splashed around in the tub.* — N COUNT American

tuba /tjuːbə/, **tubas.** A **tuba** is a very large brass musical instrument that produces very low notes. — N COUNT

tubby /tʌbi[1]/. Someone who is **tubby** is rather fat. EG *She was a short, tubby woman.* — ADJ QUALIT Informal

tube /tjuːb/, **tubes. 1** A **tube** is a round, hollow pipe. Tubes are often used for liquids to move along. EG *...a rubber tube fixed to the tap... He slipped the telescope into the steel tube designed for it.* — N COUNT

2 Some long, thin, hollow parts inside your body are referred to as **tubes**. EG *...a system of breathing tubes.* — N COUNT+SUPP

3 A **tube** of paste is a long, thin container which you squeeze in order to force the paste out through a hole in one end. EG *...a tube of toothpaste... ...tubes of glue... ...antiseptic ointment in a tube or jar.* — N COUNT OR N PART

4 The **tube** is an underground railway, especially the one in London. EG *When I come by tube it takes about an hour.* — N SING: *the*+N, OR *by*+N

tuberculosis /tjʊbɜːkjə[4]ləʊsɪs/ is a serious infectious disease that affects people's lungs and other parts of their body. — N UNCOUNT

tubing /tjuːbɪŋ/ is plastic, rubber, or another material in the shape of a tube. EG *The cooling system runs through 300 feet of copper tubing.* — N UNCOUNT

tuck /tʌk/, **tucks, tucking, tucked. 1** If you **tuck** one piece of clothing into another, you push the loose ends of it inside the other piece so that it is tidy. EG *I sat up and tucked my shirt into my shorts.* — V+O+A

If someone is tubby, how big is their tummy?

2 If you **tuck** something somewhere, you put it there so that it is safe or comfortable. EG *He tucked the shell under his arm... He found the card and tucked it under the phone.* V+O+A

tuck away. 1 If you **tuck away** something such as money, you store it in a safe place. EG *She had a bit of money tucked away.* **2** If something **is tucked away**, it is in a quiet place where very few people go. EG *The parish church is tucked away behind the cathedral.* PHRASAL VB : V+O+ADV; V+O+ADV, OFT PASS

tuck in. 1 If you **tuck** a child or other person **in**, you make them comfortable in bed by straightening their sheets and blankets and pushing the loose ends firmly under the mattress. EG *He was asleep before I tucked him in.* **2** If you **tuck in** your shirt or blouse, you put the loose ends of it inside your trousers or skirt. EG *She buttoned up her shirt and tucked it in.* **3** If you **tuck in**, you eat something with a lot of pleasure. EG *By the end of the holiday she was happily tucking into whatever dishes were put in front of her.* PHRASAL VB : V+O +ADV/PREP; V+O+ADV/ PREP; V+ADV/PREP Informal

tuck up. If you **tuck** a child or other person **up**, you make them comfortable in bed by straightening their sheets and blankets and pushing the loose ends firmly under the mattress. PHRASAL VB : V+O+ADV

Tuesday /tju:zdi¹/, **Tuesdays. Tuesday** is one of the seven days of the week. It is the day after Monday and before Wednesday. EG *Our rugby team goes to Swansea on Tuesday.* N UNCOUNT OR N COUNT

tuft /tʌft/, **tufts.** A **tuft** of something such as hair or grass is a bunch of it that grows closely together. EG *Her tiny head was covered with tufts of fair hair.* N COUNT OR N PART

tug /tʌg/, **tugs, tugging, tugged. 1** If you **tug** something or **tug** at it, you give it a quick pull. EG *He tugged at the handle, and it came off in his hand.* ▸ used as a noun. EG *Tom felt a tug at his sleeve.* V+O OR V+*at*; ▸ N COUNT

2 A **tug** is a small, powerful boat which pulls large ships, usually when they come into a port. N COUNT

tuition /tju:ɪʃə⁰n/ is the teaching of a subject, especially to one person or to a small group. EG *Her father decided she ought to have private tuition.* N UNCOUNT

tulip /tju:lɪp/, **tulips.** A **tulip** is a brightly-coloured garden flower that is shaped like an upside-down bell and that grows in the spring. N COUNT

tumble /tʌmbə⁰l/, **tumbles, tumbling, tumbled.**

1 If you **tumble**, you fall with a rolling or bouncing movement. EG *She pushed him and sent him tumbling downstairs.* ▸ used as a noun. EG *She suffered a tumble running after her kite.* V : USU+A; ▸ N COUNT : USU SING

2 If water **tumbles**, it flows quickly over an uneven surface so that it splashes and swirls a lot. EG *He could hear the water tumbling over the rocks.* V : USU+A

3 If you **tumble** into a situation, you suddenly get into that situation without being able to stop yourself. EG *She tumbled into love... The world tumbled into the atomic age.* V+A

tumble to. If you **tumble to** something, you suddenly understand it or realize what is happening. EG *What if he tumbles to what's going on?* PHRASAL VB : V+PREP, HAS PASS

tumble dryer, tumble dryers; also spelled **tumble drier.** A **tumble dryer** is an electric machine that dries washing quickly. You put the wet clothes inside it and it turns them over slowly while blowing hot air onto them. N COUNT

tumbler /tʌmblə/, **tumblers.** A **tumbler** is a drinking glass with straight sides. N COUNT

tummy /tʌmi¹/, **tummies.** Your **tummy** is **1** the part of the front of your body below your waist. EG *She tickled their tummies.* **2** the parts inside your body where food is digested. EG *...the rumbling of empty tummies... ...tummy upsets.* N COUNT Informal

tumour /tju:mə/, **tumours;** spelled **tumor** in American English. A **tumour** is a mass of diseased or abnormal cells that has grown in a person's or animal's body. EG *He was suffering from a brain tumour.* N COUNT

tumult /tju:mə⁹lt/. A **tumult** is a lot of noise caused by a crowd of people shouting or doing noisy things. EG *A tumult of shots and yells could be heard... Presently the tumult died down.* N COUNT OR N UNCOUNT Formal

tumultuous /tju:mʌltjʊəs/. A **tumultuous** event is very noisy, because people are very happy or excited. EG *When the war was over, there was a tumultuous parade in London.* ADJ CLASSIF : ATTRIB Formal

tuna /tju:nə/. **Tuna** is both the singular and the plural form. **Tuna** or **tuna fish** are large fish that live in warm seas and are caught for food. N UNCOUNT OR N COUNT

tune /tju:n/, **tunes, tuning, tuned. 1** A **tune** is a series of musical notes that occurs repeatedly in a piece of music and forms a main part of it, usually one that is pleasant or memorable. EG *The orchestra was playing a selection of tunes from The Merry Widow.* N COUNT

2 When someone **tunes** a musical instrument, they adjust it so that it produces the right notes. V+O

3 When someone **tunes** an engine or machine, they adjust it so that it works well. EG *I told her the car needed tuning.* V+O

4 If your radio or television **is tuned** to a particular broadcasting station, or if you **tune** to that station, you are listening to or watching the programmes being broadcast by that station. EG *Stay tuned to Radio Desland for a further announcement.* V+O : OFT+*to*; ALSO V+*to*

5 If a musical instrument is **in tune**, it is adjusted so that it produces the right notes exactly. If it is **out of tune**, it does not produce the right notes. If you sing or play an instrument **in tune**, you sing or play the right notes. If you sing or play **out of tune**, you sing or play the wrong notes. PHRASE

6 If you are **in tune** with a group of people, you are in agreement or sympathy with them. If you are **out of tune**, you are not in agreement or sympathy with them. EG *His ideas are in tune with the spirit of his age.* PHRASE

7 If you **change** your **tune**, you say or do something different from what you previously said or did, because your opinion has changed. EG *He soon changed his tune and started working as hard as the others.* PHRASE

8 To the tune of a particular amount means to the extent of that amount. EG *The university subsidises its students to the tune of £100,000 a year.* PHRASE Formal

tune in. If you **tune in** to a particular radio station, you set the controls of your radio, so that you can listen to it. EG *He turned the dial and tuned in to Radio Paris.* PHRASAL VB : V+ADV

tune up. When a group of musicians **tune up**, they adjust their instruments so that they produce the right notes. EG *The orchestra was tuning up for its regular Sunday afternoon broadcast.* PHRASAL VB : V+ADV

tuneful /tju:nfʊl/. A piece of music that is **tuneful** has a pleasant tune. ADJ QUALIT

tunic /tju:nɪk/, **tunics.** A **tunic** is a piece of clothing which covers the top part of your body and reaches to your hips, thighs, or knees. N COUNT

tunnel /tʌnə⁰l/, **tunnels, tunnelling, tunnelled;** spelled **tunneling** and **tunneled** in American English.

1 A **tunnel** is a long passage which has been made under the ground, usually through a hill or under the sea. EG *Suddenly the train roared into a tunnel and everything was black.* • **the light at the end of the tunnel**: see **light**. N COUNT

2 If someone or something **tunnels** somewhere, they make a tunnel. EG *One person suggested tunnelling under the walls.* V+A OR V+O+A

turban /tɜ:bə⁰n/, **turbans.** A **turban** is a head-covering worn by a Hindu, Muslim, or Sikh man. It consists of a long piece of cloth wound round and round his head. N COUNT

turbine /tɜ:bɪ⁵n/, **turbines.** A **turbine** is a machine or engine in which power is produced when a stream of air, gas, water, or steam makes a wheel turn round. N COUNT

turbulent /tɜːbjəˈlənt/. **1** A **turbulent** period of time is one in which there is a lot of confusion and constant change. EG *...a period of fierce and turbulent struggle.* ◊ **turbulence** /tɜːbjəˈləns/. EG *...periods of social turbulence.* — ADJ QUALIT; ◊ N UNCOUNT

2 Turbulent water or air contains currents which suddenly change direction or make violent circular movements. EG *...in the midst of turbulent seas and clashing rocks.* ◊ **turbulence**. EG *The turbulence caused the plane to turn over.* — ADJ QUALIT; ◊ N SING : USU *the*+N

turf /tɜːf/, **turfs, turfing, turfed. 1 Turf** is short, thick, even grass. EG *He was busy levelling the ground and laying turf.* — N UNCOUNT

2 When someone **turfs** an area of ground, they cover it with turf. EG *The hole was padded with earth and turfed with strips of moss.* — V+O

turf out. If you **turf** someone **out**, you force them to leave a place. EG *She was turfed out of her flat... The chief can turf them out at any time.* — PHRASAL VB : V+O+ADV Informal

turkey /tɜːkiˈ/, **turkeys. 1** A **turkey** is a large bird that is kept on a farm for its meat. — N COUNT

2 Turkey is the meat of a turkey. — N UNCOUNT

turmoil /tɜːmɔɪl/ is a state of confusion, disorder, or great anxiety. EG *...his emotional turmoil... The city was in turmoil.* — N UNCOUNT

turn /tɜːn/, **turns, turning, turned. 1** When you **turn** or when you **turn** your head, you move your body or your head so that you are facing in a different direction. EG *He turned to Jan and began to explain... She turned and walked away... They kept turning round to smile at friends... 'You're crying.' – 'Nonsense,' Etta said, turning away.* — V OR V+O : USU+A
▸ used as a noun. EG *He made a smart military turn, clicking his heels.* — ▸ N COUNT

2 When you **turn** something or when it **turns**, it moves and faces in a different direction, or keeps changing the direction it faces in. EG *I have turned the TV to the wall... The wheels started to turn... I turned the saucer over to look at the markings underneath... She idly turned the pages of a magazine... He turned the book upside down.* ▸ used as a noun. EG *...with an agile turn of the wrist.* — V-ERG : USU+A; ▸ N COUNT

3 When you **turn** something such as a knob, key, or switch, you hold it and twist your hand in order to open, start, or adjust something. EG *He turned the handle and pushed open the door... Turn the gas as low as possible.* — V-ERG

4 When you **turn** in a particular direction or **turn** a corner, you change the direction in which you are moving or travelling. EG *You come over a bridge and turn sharply to the right... He turns down a side street... Howard turns the van towards the exit.* ▸ used as a noun. EG *The cars were waiting to make the turn into the campus.* — V OR V-ERG : OFT+A; ▸ N COUNT

5 If you **turn** to a particular page in a book, you find that page. EG *Turn to page 349.* — V+*to*

6 If you **turn** your attention or thoughts to someone or something, you start thinking about them or discussing them. EG *I wonder if we can turn our attention to something you mentioned earlier... His thoughts turned to Calcutta.* — V-ERG+*to*

7 If you **turn** to someone, you ask for their help or advice. EG *She'd turned to him for help.* — V+A

8 When something **turns** into something else or when you **turn** it into something else, it becomes something different. EG *If you apply more heat, the water turns into steam... Soon her glee turned to fear... ...a dramatist turned scriptwriter.* — V-ERG+A

9 You can use **turn** to say that a particular quality in something changes. For example, if something **turns** sour, or if something else **turns** it sour, it changes and becomes sour. EG *My hair has turned completely grey... It will turn the water blue... Things were turning nasty... He had just turned fifteen.* — V-ERG+C

10 A **turn** is also a change in the way that something is happening or being done. EG *In that year things took a sharp turn for the worse... ...every twist and turn in government economic policy... Employers are not happy about this turn of events.* — N COUNT+SUPP

11 If you do someone **a good turn**, you do something that helps or benefits them. — PHRASE

12 If you refer to the **turn** of the century, you mean the period of time including the end of the previous century and the beginning of the century you are talking about. EG *These issues have preoccupied sociology since the turn of the century.* — N SING : *the*+N+*of*

13 If it is your **turn** to do something, you now have the right, chance, or duty to do it, when other people have done it before you or will do it after you. EG *It is his turn to take the children to school... He stood in the queue waiting his turn.* — N COUNT : USU+POSS

14 You use **in turn** to refer to people, things, or actions that are in a sequence one after the other. EG *She went round the ward, talking to each woman in turn... It became in turn a stable, a chapel, and a theatre.* — PHRASE

15 If two or more people **take turns** or **take it in turns** to do something, they do it one after the other. EG *You can take turns paying... They took turns at the same typewriter.* — PHRASE

16 If you **turn** something such as a dress or bag **inside out**, you pull the inside part until it faces outwards. — PHRASE

17 If something such as a system or way of life **is turned upside down** or **turned inside out**, it is changed completely, causing great confusion. EG *All the old theories about child rearing were suddenly turned upside down... Industrial life has been turned inside out by the computer.* — PHRASE

18 See also **turning**.

19 to **turn** your **back on** someone or something: see **back**. • to **turn a blind eye**: see **blind**. • to **turn the tables on** someone: see **table**. • See also **about-turn**.

turn against. If someone **turns against** you or **is turned against** you, they start to dislike you or disapprove of you. EG *They might at any time turn against their masters... You turn everyone against me.* — PHRASAL VB : V-ERG+PREP

turn around. See **turn round**.

turn away. If you **turn** someone **away**, you reject them or send them away. EG *The college has been forced to turn away 300 prospective students.* — PHRASAL VB : V+O+ADV

turn back. 1 If you **turn back** when travelling somewhere, you stop and return to the place you started from. EG *The snow started to fall, so we turned back.* **2** If you **turn** someone **back**, you stop them travelling any farther and make them return in the direction they came from. EG *A lot of the convoys had been turned back at the border.* — PHRASAL VB : V+ADV; V+O+ADV

turn down. 1 If you **turn down** someone's request or offer, you refuse or reject it. EG *I was invited to be foreman but I turned it down... I couldn't turn him down.* **2** If you **turn down** something such as a radio or a heater, you adjust the controls and reduce the amount of sound or heat being produced. EG *If you are hot you can turn the heating down.* — PHRASAL VB : V+O+ADV; V+O+ADV

turn in. When you **turn in**, you go to bed. EG *Before turning in for the night he asked for an early morning call.* — PHRASAL VB : V+ADV Informal

turn off. 1 If you **turn off** the road or path you are going along, you start going along a different road or path which leads away from it. EG *They turned off the main road... Don't turn off, just go straight ahead.* • See also **turn-off**. **2** If you **turn off** something such as a radio, light, or heater, you move the switch or knob that controls it so that it stops working. EG *The switch was sticking and we couldn't turn the heat off... She turned off the tap.* — PHRASAL VB : V+ADV/PREP; V+O+ADV

turn on. 1 If you **turn on** something such as a radio, light, or heater, you move the switch or knob — PHRASAL VB : V+O+ADV

Where would you find turn-ups?

that controls it so that it starts working. EG *Shall I turn the fire on low?... She turned on the shower.* **2** If someone or something **turns** you **on**, they attract you and make you feel sexually excited. EG *...if you meet someone who really turns you on.* **3** If someone **turns on** you, they attack you or speak angrily to you. EG *She turned on the men. 'How can you treat your daughters like this!'* V+O+ADV Informal; V+PREP, HAS PASS

turn out. **1** If something **turns out** a particular way, it happens in that way. EG *Nothing ever turned out right... The transaction turned out badly for them... It turned out to be a sensational evening.* **2** If something **turns out** to be a particular thing, it is discovered to be that thing. EG *The Marvins' house turned out to be an old converted barn... It turned out that the message had been intercepted.* PHRASAL VB: V+ADV+A OR to-INF; V+ADV +to-INF OR REPORT: ONLY *that*

3 If you **turn out** a light or a gas fire, you move the switch or knob that controls it so that it stops giving out light or heat. **4** If a business or other organization **turns out** something, it produces it. EG *Salford was turning out the type of graduate they wanted.* **5** If you **turn** someone **out** or **turn** them **out of** a place, you force them to leave the place. EG *...a woman who had been turned out of the community 20 years before.* **6** If you **turn out** a container, you take all its contents out. EG *Come on everyone, turn out your pockets!* **7** If people **turn out** for an event or activity, they go and take part in it or watch it. EG *Voters turned out in extraordinary numbers for the election.* **8** See also **turned out**, **turnout**. V+O+ADV; V+ADV+O; V+O+ADV OR V+O+ADV+PREP; V+O+ADV; V+ADV

turn over. **1** If you **turn** something **over** in your mind, you think carefully about it. EG *Going home that night, Dr Renshaw turned over the facts of the case.* **2** If you **turn** something **over** to someone, you give it to them because they have a right to it. EG *He had refused to turn over funds that belonged to Potter.* **3** See also **turnover**. PHRASAL VB: V+O+ADV; V+O+ADV

turn round. If you **turn** something **round**, you change the way in which it is expressed. EG *I can turn it round and make it sound funny.* PHRASAL VB: V+O+ADV

turn up. **1** If someone or something **turns up**, they arrive or appear somewhere. EG *He turned up at rehearsal the next day looking awful.* **2** If something **turns up**, it is found or discovered. EG *You must be willing to take a job as soon as one turns up.* **3** If you **turn up** something such as a radio or heater, you adjust the controls and increase the amount of sound or heat being produced. EG *Turn the volume control up.* **4** See also **turn-up**. PHRASAL VB: V+ADV; V-ERG+ADV; V+O+ADV

turned out. You use **turned out** to describe how a person is dressed. For example, someone who is smartly **turned out** is dressed smartly. EG *...attractive girls, well turned out and smart.* ADJ CLASSIF +SUPP

turning /tɜ:nɪŋ/, **turnings.** A **turning** is a road which leads away from the side of another road. EG *It's the next turning on the left.* N COUNT

turning point, turning points. A **turning point** is a time at which an event or change occurs which affects the future of a person or thing. EG *The turning point for the business came in 1974 when I bought the computer... It proved to be a turning point in his life.* N COUNT

turnip /tɜ:nɪp/, **turnips.** A **turnip** is a round vegetable with a greenish-white skin, which grows underneath the ground. N COUNT

turn-off, turn-offs. A **turn-off** is a road which leads away from the side of another road. N COUNT

turnout /tɜ:naʊt/, **turnouts.** The **turnout** at an event is the number of people who go to it. EG *There was a very large turnout at the trial.* N COUNT

turnover /tɜ:nəʊvə/. **1** The **turnover** of people in an organization is the rate at which people leave it and are replaced by others. EG *The group has an extremely high turnover of members.* N UNCOUNT

2 The **turnover** of a company is the value of the goods or services that it has sold during a particular period of time. EG *Annual turnover is about £9,000 million.* N UNCOUNT

turntable /tɜ:nteɪbəˀl/, **turntables.** A **turntable** is the flat, round part of a record player that you put a record on when you play it. N COUNT

turn-up, turn-ups. **1** The **turn-ups** of a pair of trousers are the ends of the trouser legs, which are folded upwards. N COUNT: USU PLURAL

2 If you describe an event as **a turn-up for the books**, you mean that it is very surprising or unexpected. PHRASE Informal

turpentine /tɜ:pəntaɪn/ is a strong-smelling, colourless liquid which is used for cleaning and for making paint thinner. N UNCOUNT

turps /tɜ:ps/ is turpentine. EG *...an awful smell of turps and paint.* N UNCOUNT Informal

turquoise /tɜ:kwɔɪz, -kwɑ:z/, **turquoises.** **1** Something that is **turquoise** has a light bluish-green colour. EG *...the warm turquoise sea.* ADJ COLOUR

2 **Turquoise** is a light bluish-green stone that is quite valuable and is often used in jewellery. N COUNT OR N UNCOUNT

turret /tʌrɪt/, **turrets.** A **turret** is a small, narrow tower on top of a larger tower or other building. N COUNT

turtle /tɜ:təˀl/, **turtles.** A **turtle** is a large reptile which has a thick shell covering its body and which lives in the sea most of the time. N COUNT

tusk /tʌsk/, **tusks.** The **tusks** of an elephant, wild boar, or walrus are the pair of very long, pointed teeth that it has, which are often curved. N COUNT

tussle /tʌsəˀl/, **tussles, tussling, tussled.** A **tussle** is an energetic fight, struggle, or argument between two people, especially about something that they both want. EG *He was still smarting from the tussle over the bottle.* ▸ used as a verb. EG *...directors tussling about levels of authority.* N COUNT; ▸ V OR V+*with*: RECIP

tut or **tut-tut** is used in written English to represent a sound that you make to show that you are annoyed or disapprove of something. You make the sound by putting your tongue behind your teeth and sucking in air. EXCLAM Written

tutor /tju:tə/, **tutors, tutoring, tutored.** **1** A **tutor** is **1.1** a member of staff at a British university or college who teaches small groups of students or gives individual students general help and advice. **1.2** a private teacher who teaches one pupil or a very small group of pupils, usually at the pupil's home. N COUNT

2 If someone **tutors** a person or **tutors** a subject, they teach that person or subject. EG *The majority were tutored by parents... Next year I want to tutor A level maths... I'm tutoring at a local college.* V OR V+O

tutorial /tju:tɔ:rɪəl/, **tutorials.** **1** A **tutorial** is a regular meeting in which a tutor and a small group of students discuss a subject as part of the students' course. N COUNT

2 **Tutorial** means relating to a tutor, especially one at a university or college. EG *All undergraduates attend a tutorial group each week.* ADJ CLASSIF: ATTRIB

tuxedo /tʌksi:dəʊ/, **tuxedos.** A **tuxedo** is a black or white jacket that men wear with a bow tie at formal social events. N COUNT American

TV /ti: vi:/, **TVs.** **TV** is television and a **TV** is a television set. EG *I've just been watching a film on TV... Nicola turned on the TV.* N UNCOUNT OR N COUNT

twaddle /twɒdəˀl/. If you describe something that someone says as **twaddle**, you mean that it is silly or untrue. EG *Beata was talking a load of twaddle.* N UNCOUNT Informal

twang /twæŋ/, **twangs, twanging, twanged.** **1** A **twang** is a sound like the one made by pulling and then releasing a tight wire. EG *...the twang of tennis balls bouncing off tightly-strung rackets.* N COUNT

2 If you **twang** a tight wire or string, or if it **twangs**, it makes a sound as it is pulled and then released. EG *He was sitting twanging a guitar... The bed springs twanged.* V-ERG

tweed /twi:d/ is a thick woollen cloth, often woven from different coloured threads. EG *...seats upholstered in brown tweed... He wore a tweed jacket.* N UNCOUNT

tweet /twi:t/, **tweets, tweeting, tweeted.** When a small bird **tweets**, it makes short, high-pitched sounds. V Informal

tweezers /twi:zəz/ are a small tool consisting of two narrow strips of metal joined at one end. You use tweezers for things like pulling out hairs and picking up small objects. EG *She took the glass out of the back of Farnbach's head with a pair of tweezers.* N PLURAL

twelfth /twɛlf$^{\theta}$θ/, **twelfths. 1** The **twelfth** item in a series is the one that you count as number twelve: see the entry headed NUMBER. EG *...the end of the twelfth century.* ORDINAL

2 A **twelfth** is one of twelve equal parts of something. N COUNT: USU+*of*

twelve /twɛlv/ **twelves. Twelve** is the number 12: see the entry headed NUMBER. EG *They have been married for twelve years.* NUMBER

twentieth /twɛnti^{1}ə^{1}θ/, **twentieths. 1** The **twentieth** item in a series is the one that you count as number twenty: see the entry headed NUMBER. EG *...in the latter half of the twentieth century.* ORDINAL

2 A **twentieth** is one of twenty equal parts of something. EG *He agreed to pay her a twentieth of their value.* N COUNT: USU+*of*

twenty /twɛnti^{1}/, **twenties. Twenty** is the number 20: see the entry headed NUMBER. EG *Twenty minutes later he sighted two helicopters.* NUMBER

twice /twaɪs/. **1** Something that happens **twice** happens two times. EG *I knocked on the door twice... The committee meets twice a year.* ADV

2 If one thing is **twice** as big or old as another thing, or is **twice** the size or age of another thing, it is two times as big or old as the other thing. EG *This is twice as common in France as in England... He's twice my size.* ADV OR PREDET

3 once or twice: see **once**. • to **think twice**: see **think**.

twiddle /twɪdə^{0}l/, **twiddles, twiddling, twiddled. 1** If you **twiddle** something or **twiddle** with it, you twist it or turn it quickly using small movements of your fingers. EG *Ella sat twiddling her long, dark hair... Frank twiddled with the knobs of the radio.* V+O OR V+*with*

2 People who are bored sometimes sit **twiddling** their **thumbs**. This means that they move their thumbs around each other while their fingers are linked together. PHRASE

twig /twɪg/, **twigs.** A **twig** is a very small, thin branch that grows out from a main branch of a tree or bush. EG *He was busy making a little fire from twigs.* N COUNT

twilight /twaɪlaɪt/ is the time after sunset when it is getting dark outside. EG *You'll most likely see these animals at twilight, when they begin the night's hunt.* N UNCOUNT

twin /twɪn/, **twins. 1** If two people are **twins**, they have the same mother and were born on the same day. EG *The two boys looked like twins... She went to stay with her twin sister.* • See also **identical twin**. N COUNT

2 You use **twin** to describe a pair of things that look the same and are close together. EG *...the twin turrets of Tower Bridge... ...a room with twin beds.* N MOD

twine /twaɪn/, **twines, twining, twined. 1 Twine** is strong, smooth string. EG *...a ball of twine.* N UNCOUNT

2 If you **twine** one thing round another, you twist or wind the first thing around the second thing. EG *...twining the rope around his legs. ...a long scarf twined around her neck.* V-ERG+A

twinge /twɪndʒ/, **twinges. 1** If you feel a **twinge** of an unpleasant emotion, you suddenly feel this emotion. EG *Hugh felt a twinge of fear when he saw the officer approaching... ...a twinge of guilt.* N COUNT+SUPP

2 A **twinge** is a sudden, sharp pain. EG *I feel a twinge in my back now and again.* N COUNT

twinkle /twɪŋkə^{0}l/, **twinkles, twinkling, twinkled. 1** If a star or a light **twinkles**, it shines with an unsteady light. EG *He could see the flashing blue lights twinkling through the haze of rain.* V

2 If your eyes **twinkle**, they show that you are amused, excited, or joking. EG *The Englishman's eyes twinkled and he grinned.* ▸ used as a noun. EG *She noticed a twinkle in his eye at the suggestion.* V ▸ N SING

twirl /twɜ:l/, **twirls, twirling, twirled. 1** When you **twirl** something, you make it spin or twist round and round. EG *In a bored way she twirled her parasol... He stood twirling his key on a chain.* V-ERG

2 If you **twirl**, you spin round and round, for example when you are dancing. EG *He twirled round on his toes.* V

twist /twɪst/, **twists, twisting, twisted. 1** When you **twist** something or when it **twists**, you turn one end of it in one direction while holding the other end or turning it in the opposite direction. EG *Never twist or wring woollen garments... Her fingers twisted the handle of her bag.* ▸ used as a noun. EG *He gave one short twist to its neck.* V-ERG ▸ N COUNT

2 When something **twists** or **is twisted**, it moves or bends into a strange shape. EG *Her features twisted into a stare of disgusted incredulity.* ◊ **twisted.** EG *Hundreds of people were trapped under the twisted steel girders.* V-ERG ◊ ADJ CLASSIF

3 If you **twist** part of your body such as your head or shoulders, you turn it while keeping the rest of your body still. EG *Swing your shoulders so that you twist from side to side... She twisted round on the couch to watch him.* V+O OR V

4 If you **twist** part of your body such as your ankle or wrist, you injure it by turning it too sharply or in an unusual direction. EG *I twisted my ankle doing a Mexican hat dance.* V+O

5 If you **twist** someone's **arm**, you persuade them to do something. PHRASE Informal

6 If you **twist** something, you turn it so that it moves around in a circular direction. EG *Brody grabbed the bottle and twisted off the cap.* ▸ used as a noun. EG *She gave a lazy little twist to her parasol.* V+O ▸ N COUNT

7 If you say that you can **twist** someone **round** your **little finger**, you mean that they will do anything that you want them to do. PHRASE Informal

8 If a road or river **twists**, it has a lot of sharp bends. EG *The road began to twist up past the lower slopes of a pine forest.* V: USU+A

9 If you **twist** something that a person has said, you change the meaning slightly. EG *You're twisting my words around.* V+O

10 A **twist** is also the shape that something has when it has been twisted. EG *...a shell with a spiral twist.* N COUNT

11 A **twist** in a story, film, or situation is an unexpected development or event, especially at the end. EG *There was an odd twist to the plot.* N COUNT

twisted /twɪstɪ^{2}d/. If someone's mind or behaviour is **twisted**, it is unpleasantly abnormal. EG *He has become bitter and twisted.* ADJ QUALIT

twit /twɪt/, **twits.** If you call someone a **twit**, you mean that they are silly or thoughtless. EG *Don't be a twit!* N COUNT OR VOCATIVE Informal

twitch /twɪtʃ/, **twitches, twitching, twitched. 1** If you **twitch**, you make little jerky movements which you cannot control. EG *Ralph felt his lips twitch... She trembled and twitched as I touched her... ...their jerking, twitching bodies.* V

2 If you **twitch** something, you give it a little jerk in order to move it. EG *She twitched the curtain into place.* V-ERG

3 A **twitch** is a little jerky movement. EG *...twitches of the muscles.* N COUNT

twitter /twɪtə/, **twitters, twittering, twittered. 1** When birds **twitter**, they make a lot of short, high-pitched sounds. V

If you twist someone's arm, do they need a bandage?

2 If someone **twitters**, they speak very fast in a high-pitched voice. EG *They talked all the time in high, twittering voices.* — V

two /tuː/, **twos. 1 Two** is the number 2: see the entry headed NUMBER. EG *I have been away from London for two weeks... The two boys glared at each other... For a moment or two Simon was happy.* — NUMBER

2 If you cut or divide something **in two**, or if it breaks **in two**, it becomes separated into two pieces or amounts. EG *The twig snapped in two.* — PHRASE

two-dimensional /tuː dəmenʃəⁿnəl, -ʃənəⁿl/. Something that is **two-dimensional** is flat and in two dimensions only. EG *...a two-dimensional sheet of paper.* — ADJ CLASSIF

two-faced. If you describe someone as **two-faced**, you mean that they are not honest in the way that they behave towards other people. EG *He is a two-faced liar and an opportunist... How could she be so two-faced?* — ADJ QUALIT

two-way. 1 Two-way means moving in two opposite directions. EG *...a two-way channel of communication... ...two-way traffic.* — ADJ CLASSIF : ATTRIB

2 Two-way radios and transmitters can both send and receive signals. — ADJ CLASSIF : ATTRIB

tycoon /taɪkuːn/, **tycoons.** A **tycoon** is a person who is successful in business and so has become rich and powerful. EG *...a newspaper tycoon.* — N COUNT

type /taɪp/, **types, typing, typed. 1** A **type** of something is a class of it that has particular features in common and that belongs to a larger group of related things. EG *What type of salt do you prefer?... There are several different types of accounts... They usually test your blood type during pregnancy.* — N COUNT+SUPP

2 If you refer to a particular thing as a **type**, you are thinking of it in relation to other things that have similar qualities. EG *How much longer can you do this type of work?... ...other simple problems of this type... ...a standard type of question.* — N COUNT+SUPP

3 You can refer to someone as a particular **type** when you are describing the appearance or quality that they have. EG *He was good-looking, if you like the strong, dark type... ...an eccentric painter type.* — N COUNT+SUPP

4 If you say that someone is **not** your **type**, you mean that they are not the sort of person who you find interesting or attractive. — PHRASE Informal

5 If you **type** something, you use a typewriter or word processor to write it. EG *I typed the reply.* — V+O OR V

◊ **typing.** EG *I had to do some typing for him... ...typing skills.* — ◊ N UNCOUNT

6 If you **type** information into a computer or word processor, you put it in by pressing keys on the keyboard. EG *The letter was typed into a word processor.* — V+O : USU+A

8 Type is the size or style of printing that is used, for example, in a book or newspaper. EG *The declaration was proclaimed in type four inches deep on the front page.* — N UNCOUNT

type up. If you **type up** your ideas, notes, or handwritten text, you produce a typed form of it. EG *After thinking about it, she typed it up, then we both read it.* — PHRASAL VB : V+O+ADV

typecast /taɪpkɑːst/, **typecasts, typecasting.** The form **typecast** is used in the present tense and is also the past tense and past participle.

If actors or actresses **are typecast**, they play the same type of character in every play or film that they are in. EG *He refused to be typecast as the loser.* — V+O : USU PASS

typewriter

typewriter /taɪpraɪtə/, **typewriters.** A **typewriter** is a machine that you use to write things in print. It has a series of keys that you press in order to write the letters, numbers, or other characters on the paper. — N COUNT

typewritten /taɪprɪtəⁿn/. Something that is **typewritten** has been typed on a typewriter or a word processor. EG *His notes were typewritten.* — ADJ CLASSIF

typhoid /taɪfɔɪd/ is an infectious disease that produces fever and can cause death. — N UNCOUNT

typhoon /taɪfuːn/, **typhoons.** A **typhoon** is a very violent storm in the western Pacific. — N COUNT

typical /tɪpɪkəⁿl/. **1** Something that is **typical** of a particular type of thing shows the most usual characteristics of that type. EG *It was typical tropical weather... Louisa is typical of many young women who attempt suicide.* — ADJ QUALIT : OFT+*of*

2 Behaviour that is **typical** of someone is their most usual behaviour. EG *He crushed the beetle deliberately, which is very typical of him.* — ADJ QUALIT : OFT+*of*

typically /tɪpɪkəⁿli¹/. **1** You use **typically** to say that something usually happens in the way that you are describing. EG *She typically handles less than a dozen accounts at a time.* — ADV OR ADV SEN

2 You also use **typically** to say that something shows all the most usual characteristics or behaviour of a particular type of thing. EG *...this group of typically American students.* — SUBMOD

typify /tɪpɪfaɪ/, **typifies, typifying, typified. 1** If something **typifies** a situation or a thing, it is characteristic of that situation or thing, and shows what it is like. EG *Modern industrial society is typified by these large-scale organizations.* — V+O

2 If someone **typifies** a particular type of person or attitude, they show all the most usual characteristics of that person or attitude. EG *He typified the old Liberalism of Samuel Smiles.* — V+O

typist /taɪpɪst/, **typists.** A **typist** is someone whose job is typing, usually in an office. — N COUNT

tyrannical /tɪrænɪkəⁿl/. A ruler, government, or organization that is **tyrannical** acts cruelly and unjustly towards the people who they control. — ADJ QUALIT

tyranny /tɪrəni¹/ is cruel and unjust rule by a person or small group of people who have absolute power over everyone else in their country or state. EG *They came here to escape political tyranny.* — N UNCOUNT

tyrant /taɪrənt/, **tyrants.** A **tyrant** is a ruler who has absolute power over other people, and who uses this power cruelly and unjustly. — N COUNT

tyre /taɪə/, **tyres;** spelled **tire** in American English. A **tyre** is a thick ring of rubber which is fitted round each wheel of a vehicle such as a car or bicycle, and which is usually filled with air. See pictures at BICYCLE and CAR. EG *When he braked a tyre burst and the car swung off the road.* — N COUNT

U u

U, u /juː/, **U's, u's.** U is the twenty-first letter of the English alphabet. N COUNT

ubiquitous /juːbɪkwɪtəs/. You say that something is **ubiquitous** when it seems to be everywhere. EG *...the ubiquitous white dust of Athens... ...the ubiquitous intelligence service.* ADJ QUALIT Formal

udder /ʌdə/, **udders.** A cow's **udder** is the part of its body that hangs loosely between its legs and produces milk. N COUNT

UFO /juː ɛf əʊ, juːfəʊ/, **UFOs.** A **UFO** is an object seen in the sky or landing on earth which cannot be identified and which some people believe to be a spaceship from another planet. **UFO** is an abbreviation for 'unidentified flying object'. N COUNT

ugh is used in writing to represent the sound that people make when they think that something is unpleasant, horrible, or disgusting. EG *Your clothes are filthy and your hair too – ugh, you're awful.* EXCLAM

ugly /ʌgli[1]/, **uglier, ugliest. 1** Someone or something that is **ugly** is very unattractive and unpleasant to look at. EG *She really was frightfully ugly... This is the ugliest dress I've ever worn.* ADJ QUALIT

2 You describe a situation as **ugly** when it is very unpleasant, usually because it involves violence or aggression. EG *A couple of ugly incidents occurred, and one man was killed.* ADJ QUALIT

uh huh is used in writing to represent a sound that people make when they are agreeing with you, or when they want to show that they understand what you are saying, or when they are answering 'yes'. EG *'Did you know he was rich?' – 'Uh huh. It said so in the paper.'* CONVENTION Informal

UK /juː keɪ/. The **UK** consists of Great Britain and Northern Ireland. **UK** is an abbreviation for 'United Kingdom'. N PROPER : *the+N*

ulcer /ʌlsə/, **ulcers.** An **ulcer** is a sore area on your skin or inside your body. Ulcers are painful and sometimes bleed. EG *...stomach ulcers.* N COUNT

ulterior /ʌltɪərɪə/. If someone has an **ulterior** motive for doing something, they do not show their real reason for doing it, because they think people would not approve of it. EG *I assure you there was no ulterior motive in my suggestion.* ADJ CLASSIF : ATTRIB

ultimate /ʌltɪmə[1]t/. **1** You use **ultimate** to describe **1.1** the final result of a long and complicated series of events. EG *He knew this action was necessary for the ultimate success of the revolution.* **1.2** the most important or powerful thing of a particular kind. EG *Parliament retains the ultimate authority to dismiss the government... We must keep in mind the ultimate goal.* ADJ CLASSIF : ATTRIB

2 You use the expression **the ultimate in** to say that something is the best or most advanced thing of its kind. EG *...the ultimate in luxury.* PHRASE

ultimately /ʌltɪmə[1]tli[1]/. **1 Ultimately** means finally, after a long and complicated series of events. EG *Elections ultimately produced a Communist victory... Ultimately they did get the police to come.* ADV

2 You also use **ultimately** to emphasize that what you are saying is the most important point in a discussion or argument. EG *Ultimately, the problems are not scientific but moral... Isn't it ultimately the fault of the universities?* ADV SEN

ultimatum /ʌltɪmeɪtəm/, **ultimatums.** An **ultimatum** is a warning that you give to someone which states that they must act in a particular way, otherwise you will take action against them. EG *Belgium rejected the ultimatum and war was declared... He gave her an ultimatum to leave.* N COUNT Formal

ultra- is used to form adjectives that describe someone or something as having a quality to an extreme degree. For example, someone who is ultra-intelligent is extremely intelligent. EG *...ultra-sophisticated equipment... ...an ultra-modern building.* PREFIX

ultraviolet /ʌltrəvaɪələ[2]t/. **Ultraviolet** light or radiation causes your skin to become darker in colour after you have been in sunlight. Large amounts of it can be harmful. EG *...the ultraviolet rays of the sun.* ADJ CLASSIF : ATTRIB

um /əm, ʌm/ is used in writing to represent a sound that people make when they are hesitating, usually because they have not decided what to say next. EG *What can be done about it? Well, um, the first thing you can do is colour it.*

umbilical cord /ʌmbɪlɪkə[0]l kɔːd/, **umbilical cords.** The **umbilical cord** is the tube which connects a baby to its mother before it is born and through which the baby receives oxygen and nutrients. N COUNT

umbrella /ʌmbrɛlə/, **umbrellas. 1** An **umbrella** is an object which you carry to protect yourself from the rain. It consists of a long stick with a folding frame covered in cloth. EG *Put your umbrella up. It's going to rain.* N COUNT

2 An **umbrella** is also a device like a large umbrella that protects you from the hot sun when you are sitting or lying outdoors. EG *Other hotel guests sat under striped umbrellas.* N COUNT

3 Umbrella describes a single organization or idea that contains or includes a lot of different organizations or ideas. EG *Corn is an umbrella word for wheat, barley and oats.* ADJ CLASSIF : ATTRIB

umpire /ʌmpaɪə/, **umpires, umpiring, umpired.**
1 In games such as cricket and tennis, the **umpire** is the person whose job is to make sure that the game is played fairly and that the rules are not broken. EG *The umpires declared that play should start.* N COUNT

2 If you **umpire** a game, you are the umpire. V+O OR V

umpteen /ʌmp[0]tiːn/ means very many. EG *They recounted umpteen tales of unfair treatment.* NUMBER Informal

umpteenth /ʌmp[0]tiːnθ/ describes something which has happened many times before. EG *I went to the pictures and saw 'Hello Dolly' for the umpteenth time.* ORDINAL Informal

UN /juː ɛn/. The **UN** is an organization which most countries in the world belong to, and which tries to encourage international peace, co-operation, and friendship. **UN** is an abbreviation for 'United Nations'. N PROPER : *the+N*

un-. 1 un- is added to the beginning of many adjectives, adverbs, and nouns in order to form PREFIX words with the opposite meaning. For example, if something is unavailable, it is not available. EG *...undemocratic regimes... ...an uncomfortable chair... She may unintentionally have caused suffering... He regretted his unkindness.*

2 When a verb describes a process, **2.1** you can add **un-** to the beginning of it in order to form a verb describing the reverse process. EG *He unlocked the door... She untied the rope and rowed back to shore.* **2.2** you can add **un-** to the past participle in order to form an adjective indicating that the process has not been carried out. For example, if your hair is uncombed, it has not been combed. EG *Everywhere hedges remain uncut... ...unconvicted prisoners.* PREFIX

unabashed /ʌnəbæʃt/. If you are **unabashed**, you are not ashamed, embarrassed, or discouraged by something that has been done or said. EG *The little old lady seemed unabashed.* ADJ CLASSIF

unabated /ʌnəbeɪtɪ^{2}d/. If something continues **unabated**, it continues without any reduction in intensity or amount. EG *The war at sea continued unabated... They continued with unabated enthusiasm.* ADV OR ADJ CLASSIF

unable /ʌneɪbə^{0}l/. If you are **unable** to do something, you cannot do it, for example because you do not have the necessary skill or knowledge, or because you do not have enough time or money. EG *Many people were unable to read or write... He was unable to sleep at night because of his anxiety.* ADJ PRED +*to*-INF

unacceptable /ʌnə^{3}ksɛptəbə^{0}l/. If you describe something as **unacceptable**, you mean that you strongly disapprove of it and feel that you cannot allow it to continue. EG *That sort of behaviour was completely unacceptable... ...an unacceptable violation of personal freedom.* ADJ QUALIT ◊ **unacceptably**. EG *Their standard of performance has been unacceptably poor on several recent occasions.* ◊ ADV

unaccompanied /ʌnəkʌmpənɪd/. **1** If you are **unaccompanied**, you are alone. EG *I wouldn't leave him for a moment unaccompanied.* ADJ CLASSIF

2 An **unaccompanied** song is written to be sung by singers alone, without musical instruments. ADJ CLASSIF

unaccountable /ʌnəkaʊntəbə^{0}l/. **1** Something that is **unaccountable** does not seem to have any sensible explanation. EG *For some unaccountable reason, I put the letter in the wrong envelope... I suffer every now and then from unaccountable headaches.* ADJ QUALIT Formal ◊ **unaccountably**. EG *Elaine felt unaccountably shy.* ◊ ADV OR ADV SEN

2 If you are **unaccountable**, you are not responsible to anyone for your actions and you do not have to explain to anyone why you behave in the way you do. EG *Many of our important decision-makers are unaccountable to the public.* ADJ PRED : OFT+*to* Formal

unaccounted /ʌnəkaʊntɪ^{2}d/. If something, especially money, is **unaccounted for**, you do not know where it is or what has happened to it. EG *The remaining 30 per cent were unaccounted for.* PHRASE

unaccustomed /ʌnəkʌstəmd/. **1** If you are **unaccustomed** to something, you are not used to it. EG *They were unaccustomed to wearing suits and ties.* ADJ PRED+*to*

2 If you describe someone's behaviour or experiences as **unaccustomed**, you mean that they do not usually behave like this or have experiences of this kind. EG *Judy cried with unaccustomed vehemence, 'Yes, I know!'... ...his unaccustomed and unwelcome leisure time.* ADJ CLASSIF : ATTRIB

unacquainted /ʌnəkweɪntɪ^{2}d/. If you are **unacquainted** with something, you do not know about it or you have not had much experience of it. EG *...people who are unacquainted with feminist ideas.* ADJ PRED : OFT+*with*

unadulterated /ʌnədʌltəreɪtɪ^{2}d/. **1** Something that is **unadulterated** is completely pure and has had nothing added to it. EG *...unadulterated spring water.* ADJ CLASSIF

2 You can also use **unadulterated** to emphasize a quality, especially a bad quality. EG *It was going to be unadulterated misery from now on.* ADJ CLASSIF : ATTRIB

unaffected /ʌnə^{3}fɛktɪ^{2}d/. **1** Something that is **unaffected** by a particular thing is not changed in any way by it. EG *Jobs have been largely unaffected by automation... This acid is unaffected by heat.* ADJ PRED : OFT+*by*

2 Someone who is **unaffected** is natural and genuine in their behaviour, and not pretentious. EG *He was simple and unaffected and obviously sincere.* ADJ QUALIT

unaided /ʌneɪdɪ^{2}d/. If you do something **unaided**, you do it without help from anyone or anything else. EG *He could not possibly have got through the window unaided... The baby was sitting up unaided.* ADV AFTER VB, OR ADJ CLASSIF

unalterable /ʌnɒltə^{0}rəbə^{0}l, ʌnɔ:l- /. Something that is **unalterable** cannot be changed. EG *She had reached an unalterable decision to marry him.* ADJ CLASSIF

unaltered /ʌnɒltəd, ʌnɔ:l-/. Something that is **unaltered** has not been changed and is therefore still in its original form. EG *The Great Hall survives relatively unaltered... In a few places conditions remain unaltered.* ADJ CLASSIF

unambiguous /ʌnæmbɪgju^{4}əs/. If something spoken or written is **unambiguous**, it can only be interpreted or understood in one way. EG *The rules are quite unambiguous... He made an unambiguous statement of his beliefs.* ADJ QUALIT

unanimous /ju:nænɪməs/. When a group of people are **unanimous**, they all agree about something. EG *The critics have been almost unanimous in their dislike of this film... We reached unanimous agreement.* ADJ CLASSIF ◊ **unanimously**. EG *The union voted unanimously to boycott foreign imports.* ◊ ADV ◊ **unanimity** /ju:nə^{3}nɪmɪ^{1}ti^{1}/. EG *About this there is unanimity among the sociologists.* ◊ N UNCOUNT

unannounced /ʌnənaʊnst/. If an action or event is **unannounced**, it happens unexpectedly and without anyone having being told about it beforehand. EG *Forgive me for this unannounced intrusion... Churchill arrived unannounced.* ADJ CLASSIF, OR ADV AFTER VB

unanswered /ʌnɑ:nsəd/. Something that is **unanswered** has not been answered. EG *Many questions were left unanswered... ...unanswered letters.* ADJ CLASSIF

unarmed /ʌnɑ:md/. If you are **unarmed**, you are not carrying any weapons. EG *They were shooting unarmed peasants... He walked alone and unarmed into the hills... Girls were practising unarmed combat.* ADJ CLASSIF OR ADV

unashamed /ʌnəʃeɪmd/. If someone behaves in an **unashamed** way, they openly do things that other people find rude or shocking. EG *He looked at her with unashamed curiosity... ...their unashamed pursuit of money.* ADJ CLASSIF : ATTRIB

unassuming /ʌnəsj^{0}u:mɪŋ/. An **unassuming** person is modest and quiet and does not wish to be noticed by other people. ADJ QUALIT

unattached /ʌnətætʃt/. **1** If something is **unattached** to something else, it is not formally connected with it. EG *The centre is unattached to any hospital or clinic.* ADJ CLASSIF : USU+*to*

2 An **unattached** person is not married and is not having a steady relationship. EG *A lot of unattached women seem to be very happy.* ADJ CLASSIF

unattended /ʌnətɛndɪ^{2}d/. When people or things are **unattended**, they are not being watched or looked after. EG *Most of the casualties were lying unattended... ...unattended baggage.* ADJ CLASSIF

unattractive /ʌnətræktɪv/. **1** **Unattractive** people and things are unpleasant in their appearance or behaviour and are therefore not liked or wanted. EG *He was physically unattractive... ...unattractive dwellings... ...her unattractive coyness.* ADJ QUALIT

2 If you say that something such as an idea or proposal is **unattractive**, you mean that people do not like it and do not want to be involved with it. EG *Being unemployed is a most unattractive prospect.* ADJ QUALIT

unauthorized /ʌnɔ:θəraɪzd/; also spelled **unauthorised.** If an action is **unauthorized**, it is done without official permission. EG *She made several unauthorized visits to the laboratory.* ADJ CLASSIF

unavoidable /ʌnəvɔɪdəbəˈl/. If something is **unavoidable**, it cannot be avoided or prevented. EG *This delay was unavoidable.* ADJ CLASSIF

unaware /ʌnəwɛə/. If you are **unaware** of something, you do not know about it. EG *I was unaware that he had any complaints... She seemed quite unaware of the other people sitting around her.* ADJ PRED: OFT+of OR REPORT

unawares /ʌnəwɛəz/. If something **catches** you **unawares** or **takes** you **unawares**, it happens when you are not expecting it and are not prepared for it. EG *It's a change like this that catches you unawares.* PHRASE

unbalanced /ʌmˈbælənst/. **1** If someone is **unbalanced**, they are slightly mad. EG *The strain of the past few days has made you mentally unbalanced.* ADJ QUALIT

2 If an account of something is **unbalanced**, it is unfair or inaccurate because it emphasizes some things and ignores others. EG *She complained that the magazine had published an unbalanced report.* ADJ QUALIT

unbearable /ʌmˈbɛərəbəˈl/. If something is **unbearable**, it is so unpleasant, painful, or upsetting that you feel unable to accept it or deal with it. EG *The heat was unbearable... I found it unbearable to be the centre of attention.* ◊ **unbearably**. EG *It was unbearably painful.* ADJ QUALIT ◊ SUBMOD

unbeatable /ʌmˈbiːtəbəˈl/. If you say that something is **unbeatable**, you mean that it is the best thing of its kind. EG *The food here is absolutely unbeatable.* ADJ CLASSIF

unbelievable /ʌmˈbiˈliːvəbəˈl/. **1** If you say that something is **unbelievable**, you mean that it is extremely good, large, or surprising. EG *They work with unbelievable speed... I went to her house in Henley: it was unbelievable.* ADJ QUALIT

2 If you say that an idea or theory is **unbelievable**, you mean that it is so unlikely or so illogical that you cannot believe it. EG *There are many unbelievable aspects to this theory.* ADJ CLASSIF

unbelievably /ʌmˈbiˈliːvəbliˈ/. **1** You use **unbelievably** when you are commenting on something that you are describing, in order to say that it is very surprising. EG *Unbelievably, the door in the wall opened.* ADV SEN

2 You also use **unbelievably** to emphasize that something is extremely good, large, or surprising. EG *...unbelievably beautiful scenery... He has been unbelievably successful.* SUBMOD

unbeliever /ʌmˈbiˈliːvə/, **unbelievers.** People are referred to as **unbelievers** when they do not believe in a particular religion. N COUNT

unborn /ʌmˈbɔːn/. An **unborn** child has not yet been born and is still inside its mother's womb. EG *The doctor tried desperately to save her and her unborn child.* ADJ CLASSIF

unbroken /ʌmˈbrəʊkəˈn/. If something is **unbroken**, it is continuous or complete and has not been interrupted or broken. EG *The silence continued, unbroken.* ADJ CLASSIF

unbutton /ʌmˈbʌtəˈn/, **unbuttons, unbuttoning, unbuttoned.** When you **unbutton** something that you are wearing, you unfasten the buttons on it. EG *He unbuttoned his coat.* V+O

uncalled-for. If you say that a remark was **uncalled-for**, you mean that it was unkind or unfair and should not have been made. EG *That last remark was uncalled-for.* ADJ QUALIT

uncanny /ʌŋˈkæniˈ/, **uncannier, uncanniest.** If you say that something is **uncanny**, you mean that it is strange and hard to explain. EG *The owl strikes at its prey with uncanny accuracy... The silence was uncanny.* ADJ QUALIT

uncaring /ʌŋˈkɛərɪŋ/. If you say that someone is **uncaring**, you mean that they do not care about other people's suffering. EG *We now know how uncaring and selfish the landlords were.* ADJ QUALIT

unceasing /ʌnsiːsɪŋ/. If something is **unceasing**, it continues without stopping. EG *...a profound, unceasing misery... The noise of the traffic was loud and unceasing.* ADJ CLASSIF

unceremonious /ʌnsɛrəˈməʊnɪəs/. If something that you do is **unceremonious**, **1** you do it in a relaxed and informal way. EG *She treated him with unceremonious friendliness.* **2** you do it suddenly and rudely. ◊ **unceremoniously**. EG *The door was unceremoniously pushed open.* ADJ CLASSIF / ADJ QUALIT / ◊ ADV

uncertain /ʌnsɜːtən/. **1** If you are **uncertain** about something, you do not know what to do. EG *She hesitated, uncertain whether to continue.* ◊ **uncertainly**. EG *They looked at each other uncertainly.* ADJ QUALIT ◊ ADV

2 If something in the future is **uncertain**, nobody knows what will happen. EG *The outcome of his case was uncertain.* ADJ QUALIT

3 If the cause of something is **uncertain**, nobody knows what caused it. EG *The cause of death remains uncertain.* ADJ CLASSIF

uncertainty /ʌnsɜːtəntiˈ/, **uncertainties. 1** When there is **uncertainty**, people do not know what will happen or what they should do. EG *...the continued uncertainty about the future of the aircraft industry.* N UNCOUNT

2 Uncertainties are things, especially future events, which no one is certain about. EG *The industry is still plagued by economic uncertainties.* N COUNT: USU PLURAL

unchallenged /ʌntʃæləndˈʒd/. When something is **unchallenged** or goes **unchallenged**, people accept it without asking questions about whether it is right or wrong. EG *His authority was secure and unchallenged... Her decisions on these matters went unchallenged.* ADJ CLASSIF OR ADV

uncharacteristic /ʌŋˈkærəˈktərɪstɪk/. Something that is **uncharacteristic** of someone is not typical of them. EG *He jumped out of the car with uncharacteristic agility.* ADJ QUALIT

uncharitable /ʌntʃærɪtəbəˈl/. **Uncharitable** remarks, thoughts, or behaviour are unkind or unfair. EG *I hope I'm not being too uncharitable, but he really is very boring.* ADJ QUALIT

unchecked /ʌntʃɛkt/. You say that something undesirable is **unchecked** when it keeps growing without anyone trying to stop it. EG *...the danger of unchecked military expansion... Such horrors could not be allowed to continue unchecked.* ADJ CLASSIF, OR ADV AFTER VB

uncivilized /ʌnsɪvɪlaɪzd/; also spelled **uncivilised. 1** You say that someone is **uncivilized** or that their behaviour is **uncivilized** when they behave in an unacceptable way, for example by being very cruel or very rude. EG *The conditions in which we keep them are uncivilized and inhumane.* ADJ QUALIT

2 If you do something at an **uncivilized** hour, you do it very early in the morning when most people are in bed and asleep. EG *We had to be at the ground at a fairly uncivilized hour.* ADJ QUALIT Informal

uncle /ʌŋˈkəˈl/, **uncles.** Your **uncle** is the brother of your mother or father, or the husband of your aunt. EG *...Uncle Harold.* N COUNT

unclean /ʌŋˈkliːn/. **1** Something that is **unclean** is dirty and likely to cause disease. EG *A major cause of illness in the Third World is unclean water.* ADJ QUALIT

2 People sometimes use **unclean** to describe practices which are unacceptable according to their religion. EG *Pigs are considered unclean and must not be eaten.* ADJ CLASSIF

unclear /ʌŋklɪə/. **1** If something is **unclear**, **1.1** it is not obvious. EG *The reasons for this remained unclear.* **1.2** it has been badly explained or written in a confusing way, so that you cannot understand it properly. EG *The instruction books are badly written, unclear, and boring.* ADJ PRED / ADJ QUALIT

2 If you are **unclear** about something, you do not understand it properly. EG *I'm still very unclear about what he has actually done.* ADJ PRED: OFT+about

What grammatical word is explained on these pages?

uncomfortable /ʌŋ¹kʌmftəbə⁰l/. **1** If you are **uncomfortable**, you are not physically content and relaxed, and feel slight pain or discomfort. EG *I was cramped and uncomfortable in the back seat.* ADJ QUALIT
◊ **uncomfortably**. EG *...sitting uncomfortably on the rock... My shirt was uncomfortably tight.* ◊ ADV
2 You can also say that you are **uncomfortable** when you are slightly worried or embarrassed and not relaxed and confident. EG *Her presence made him uncomfortable... He seemed uncomfortable with people who were aggressive.* ADJ QUALIT
◊ **uncomfortably**. EG *She smiled across the room at him uncomfortably.* ◊ ADV
3 If a room or a piece of furniture is **uncomfortable**, you do not feel comfortable when you are in it or using it. EG *They were sitting on uncomfortable chairs.* ADJ QUALIT
4 If a situation or fact is **uncomfortable**, it is difficult to accept and causes problems. EG *This kind of life may prove disruptive and uncomfortable... ...the uncomfortable truth.* ADJ QUALIT

uncommitted /ʌŋ¹kəmɪtɪ²d/. **1** If you are **uncommitted**, you do not support either of the sides in a dispute. EG *...their uncommitted position in the war.* ADJ CLASSIF
2 If you are **uncommitted** to a particular group or belief, you do not support it. EG *Maxwell was uncommitted to the Cooperative.* ADJ PRED+*to*

uncommon /ʌŋ¹kɒmən/. **1** If something is **uncommon**, it does not happen often, or it is not often seen. EG *...uncommon birds... Frost and snow are not uncommon during these months.* ADJ PRED
2 You also use **uncommon** to describe a quality that is unusually large in degree. EG *...a general of uncommon intelligence and subtlety.* ADJ CLASSIF: ATTRIB
◊ **uncommonly**. EG *Marcus was uncommonly gifted.* ◊ SUBMOD

uncommunicative /ʌŋ¹kəmjuːnɪkətɪv/. An **uncommunicative** person does not talk to other people very much and is unwilling to express opinions or give information. EG *Roger, uncommunicative by nature, said nothing.* ADJ QUALIT

uncomplicated /ʌŋ¹kɒmplɪkeɪtɪ²d/. **Uncomplicated** things are simple and straightforward. EG *The play had an uncomplicated plot.* ADJ QUALIT

uncomprehending /ʌŋ¹kɒmprɪhɛndɪŋ/. If someone is **uncomprehending**, they do not understand what is happening or what someone else has said. EG *Bonasera turned to his uncomprehending wife and explained.* ADJ CLASSIF

uncompromising /ʌŋ¹kɒmprəmaɪzɪŋ/. When people are **uncompromising**, they are determined not to change their opinions or aims in any way. EG *He was an uncompromising opponent of the Great War... ...an uncompromising commitment to the equality of all races.* ADJ QUALIT

unconcealed /ʌŋ¹kə⁷nsiːld/. If something such as an emotion is **unconcealed**, you make no attempt to hide it. EG *Mary gazed with unconcealed curiosity... ...her unconcealed dislike for me.* ADJ CLASSIF

unconcerned /ʌŋ¹kənsɜːnd/. If someone is **unconcerned** about something, they are not interested in it or not worried about it. EG *We have suddenly become an insular people, unconcerned with the underdeveloped countries... You seem remarkably unconcerned.* ADJ QUALIT

unconditional /ʌŋ¹kəndɪʃə⁰nəl, -ʃənə⁰l/. Something that is **unconditional** has no conditions or limitations attached to it. EG *...unconditional surrender... They offered unconditional support.* ADJ CLASSIF
◊ **unconditionally**. EG *The laws of the State had to be obeyed unconditionally.* ◊ ADV

unconfirmed /ʌŋ¹kə⁷nfɜːmd/. If a report or a rumour is **unconfirmed**, there is not yet any definite proof that it is true. ADJ CLASSIF

unconnected /ʌŋ¹kə⁷nɛktɪ²d/. If one thing is **unconnected** with another, or if two things are **unconnected,** the two things are not related to each other in any way. EG *The two incidents were unconnected... The allergy may be due to causes quite unconnected with food.* ADJ CLASSIF

unconscious /ʌŋ¹kɒnʃəs/. **1** Someone who is **unconscious** is in a state which is similar to sleep, as a result of something such as an accident or an injury. EG *The blow knocked him unconscious... She lay unconscious on the table.* ADJ CLASSIF
2 If you are **unconscious** of something that has been said or done, you are not aware of it. EG *Dekker seemed totally unconscious of the insult.* ADJ PRED: OFT+*of*
3 If feelings or attitudes are **unconscious**, you are not aware that you have them, but they show in the way that you behave. EG *...unconscious feelings of envy.* ◊ **unconsciously**. EG *They can't help resenting the baby unconsciously.* ADJ CLASSIF ◊ ADV
4 Your **unconscious** is the part of your mind which contains feelings and ideas that you do not know about or cannot control. EG *...images retrieved from the unconscious.* N SING

unconstitutional /ʌŋ¹kɒnstɪtjuːʃə⁰nəl, -ʃənə⁰l/. If something is **unconstitutional**, it is against the rules of an organization or political system. EG *They denied that a referendum would be unconstitutional... ...unconstitutional strikes.* ADJ CLASSIF

uncontrollable /ʌŋ¹kə⁷ntrəʊləbə⁰l/. If something such as an emotion is **uncontrollable**, you can do nothing to prevent it or control it. EG *...the sudden uncontrollable note of fear in her voice.* ADJ CLASSIF
◊ **uncontrollably**. EG *He found himself giggling quite uncontrollably.* ◊ ADV

uncontrolled /ʌŋ¹kə⁷ntrəʊld/. **1** If someone's behaviour is **uncontrolled**, they cannot prevent it or change it. EG *He was letting out loud uncontrolled shrieks... ...uncontrolled laughter.* ADJ CLASSIF
2 If a situation or activity is **uncontrolled**, nobody is responsible for controlling it and preventing it from becoming harmful. EG *...the uncontrolled use of pesticides... ...uncontrolled building development.* ADJ CLASSIF

unconventional /ʌŋ¹kə⁷nvɛnʃə⁰nəl, -ʃənə⁰l/. If someone is **unconventional**, they do not behave in the same way as most other people in their society. EG *...an unconventional clergyman... ...her unconventional dress... ...unconventional ways of writing.* ADJ QUALIT

unconvinced /ʌŋ¹kənvɪnst/. If you are **unconvinced** about something, you are not at all certain that it is true or right. EG *I remained unconvinced by what she had said.* ADJ PRED

unconvincing /ʌŋ¹kənvɪnsɪŋ/. If arguments or reasons are **unconvincing**, you do not believe that they are true or valid. EG *I find this argument unconvincing... He offered an unconvincing excuse.* ADJ QUALIT

uncooked /ʌŋ¹kʊkt/. **Uncooked** meat or other food has not yet been cooked. EG *There were three uncooked chops on the kitchen table.* ADJ CLASSIF

uncooperative /ʌŋ¹kəʊɒpə⁰rətɪv/. If someone is **uncooperative**, they make no effort at all to help other people. EG *He is deliberately being uncooperative.* ADJ QUALIT

uncoordinated /ʌŋ¹kəʊɔːdɪneɪtɪ²d/. If you are **uncoordinated**, your movements are jerky and you cannot control them properly. EG *He's careless, clumsy, and uncoordinated... ...the baby's uncoordinated movements.* ADJ QUALIT

uncork /ʌŋ¹kɔːk/, **uncorks, uncorking, uncorked.** When you **uncork** a bottle, you pull the cork out of it. V+O

uncountable noun, uncountable nouns. In grammar, an **uncountable noun** is a noun which cannot be treated as countable, and so has only one form. In this dictionary uncount nouns are labelled N UNCOUNT in the Extra Column. See the entry headed NOUNS for more information. N COUNT

uncouth /ʌŋ¹kuːθ/. Someone who is **uncouth** behaves in a bad-mannered, unpleasant, and unacceptable way. EG *...an uncouth soldier... She may embarrass you with her uncouth behaviour.* ADJ QUALIT

uncover /ʌŋ¹kʌvə/, **uncovers, uncovering, uncovered. 1** If you **uncover** something that has V+O been secret, you find out about it. EG *...helping to uncover illegal activity... Another plot to assassinate General de Gaulle was uncovered.*

2 To **uncover** something also means to remove a cover from it, so that it can be seen. EG *She uncovered her face.* V+O

uncovered /ʌŋ¹kʌvəd/. Something that is **uncovered** does not have a cover over it. EG *...uncovered food... ...their uncovered heads.* ADJ CLASSIF

uncritical /ʌŋ¹krɪtɪkə⁰l/. If you are **uncritical**, you are unable or unwilling to judge whether someone or something is good or bad. EG *...uncritical acceptance of traditional values... ...an uncritical audience... ...their uncritical attitude.* ADJ CLASSIF

undaunted /ʌndɔːntɪ²d/. If you are **undaunted**, you are not discouraged by disappointing things that have happened to you. EG *Undaunted by his first setbacks, he decided to try once more to swim the Channel.* ADJ CLASSIF Formal

undecided /ʌndɪsaɪdɪ²d/. If you are **undecided** about something, you have not yet made a decision about it. EG *She was still undecided whether she would or would not return home.* ADJ CLASSIF

undemanding /ʌndɪmɑːndɪŋ/. **1** If you do an **undemanding** job, you are not required to work very hard or to think a great deal. ADJ QUALIT

2 Someone who is **undemanding** is easy to be with and does not ask other people to do a lot for them. EG *...an undemanding husband.* ADJ QUALIT

undemocratic /ʌndɛməkrætɪk/. In an **undemocratic** system or regime, decisions are made by a small number of powerful people, rather than by all the people who are affected. ADJ QUALIT

undeniable /ʌndɪnaɪəbə⁰l/. Something that is **undeniable** is certainly true. EG *Both of these statements are undeniable facts... The evidence is undeniable.* ◇ **undeniably**. EG *He was a tall, dark, and undeniably handsome man.* ADJ CLASSIF ◇ SUBMOD

under /ʌndə/. **1** If something is **under** something else, it is directly below or beneath it. EG *There was a cask of beer under the bench... He had no shirt on under his thin jumper... We squeezed under the wire and into the garden.* PREP

2 If something happens **under** particular circumstances or conditions, it happens when those circumstances or conditions exist. EG *He travelled under difficult circumstances.* PREP

3 If something happens **under** a law, agreement, or system, it happens because that law, agreement, or system says that it shall happen. EG *Equal pay for men and women is guaranteed under English law.* PREP

4 You can use **under** to say that a person or thing is being affected by something. EG *There is a new film project under discussion... The company is under enormous pressure to act quickly... She was evidently under the impression that Morris was the doctor.* PREP

5 If something happens **under** a particular person or government, it happens when that person or government is in power. EG *...China under Chairman Mao.* PREP

6 If you study or work **under** a particular person, that person is your teacher or boss. EG *He studied under Thomas Hart Benton... He has a large number of executives under him.* PREP

7 If you write a book or article **under** a name that is not your real name, that name appears on the book or article as the name of the author. EG *He wrote an anti-war novel under an assumed name.* PREP

8 You use **under** to say what section of a list, book, or system of classification something is in. EG *You'll find it under O for Orwell.* PREP

9 If something is **under** a particular amount, number, or age, it is less than that amount, number, or age. EG *Expenditure this year should be just under 15 billion pounds... Tickets cost £2 for adults and 50p for children under 16.* PREP

under- is used to form words that describe something as not being provided to a sufficient extent, or as not having happened to a sufficient extent. For example, if people are underfed, they are not receiving enough food. EG *The hospitals were seriously under-financed... ...under-ripe fruit... Under-employment is widespread.* PREFIX

undercarriage /ʌndəkærɪdʒ/, **undercarriages.** The **undercarriage** of an aeroplane is the part, including the wheels, which supports the aeroplane when it is on the ground and when it is landing or taking off. N COUNT

underclothes /ʌndəkləʊðz/. Your **underclothes** are the clothes such as a vest, bra, or pants that you wear next to your skin under your other clothes. EG *Renata's underclothes were all over the floor... A man in his underclothes was reading his paper by the window.* N PLURAL

undercover /ʌndəkʌvə/. People who take part in **undercover** work or who use **undercover** methods work secretly in order to obtain information for their government or for the police. EG *...police on undercover duty... ...undercover agents.* ADJ CLASSIF: ATTRIB

undercurrent /ʌndəkʌrənt/, **undercurrents.** If there is an **undercurrent** of a feeling, that feeling exists in a weak form but may become powerful later. EG *He was aware of an increasing undercurrent of unease in his mind.* N COUNT: OFT+*of*

undercut /ʌndəkʌt/, **undercuts, undercutting.** The form **undercut** is used in the present tense and is also the past tense and past participle.

1 If you **undercut** someone or **undercut** their prices, you sell a product more cheaply than they do. EG *The large-scale producer can usually undercut smaller competitors.* V+O

2 If something **undercuts** your attempts to achieve something, it prevents your attempts from being effective. EG *The delay would surely undercut efforts to force modernization.* V+O

underdeveloped /ʌndədɪ²vɛləpt/. An **underdeveloped** country or region does not have modern industries and usually has a low standard of living. EG *...the problem of underdeveloped rural areas.* ADJ CLASSIF

underdog /ʌndədɒg/, **underdogs.** The **underdog** in a competition or situation is the person who seems least likely to succeed or win. EG *She took up the cause of the underdog.* N COUNT: *the*+N

underdone /ʌndədʌn/. If food is **underdone**, it has not been cooked for long enough. ADJ QUALIT

underemployed /ʌndərɪmplɔɪd/. If someone is **underemployed**, they have not got enough work to do, or they have work to do that does not make full use of their skills or abilities. EG *Migrants are much more likely to be poor and underemployed.* ADJ CLASSIF

underestimate /ʌndərɛstɪmeɪt/, **underestimates, underestimating, underestimated. 1** If you **underestimate** something, you do not realize how large or great it is or will be. EG *The Americans underestimated the power of the explosion... It was easy to underestimate what she had endured.* V+O OR V+REPORT: ONLY WH

2 If you **underestimate** someone, you do not realize what they are capable of doing. EG *He had underestimated Muller.* V+O

underfed /ʌndəfɛd/. People who are **underfed** do not get enough food to eat. EG *Underfed children are more likely to catch diseases.* ADJ CLASSIF

underfoot /ʌndəfʊt/. **1** You describe something as **underfoot** when it is under your feet, because you are walking on it. EG *The grass underfoot was short and springy... The ground was hardening underfoot.* ADJ AFTER N OR ADV AFTER VB

2 If you trample or crush something **underfoot**, you spoil or destroy it by treading on it. EG *The banner was accidentally trampled underfoot.* ADV AFTER VB

Is an undergraduate underprivileged?

undergarment /ʌndəgɑːməˀnt/, **undergarments.** An **undergarment** is a piece of clothing that you wear next to your skin and under your other clothes. EG *...ladies' undergarments.* N COUNT Formal

undergo /ʌndəgəʊ/, **undergoes, undergoing, underwent** /ʌndəwent/, **undergone** /ʌndəgɒn/. If you **undergo** something necessary or unpleasant, it happens to you and you endure it. EG *The United States will have to undergo radical changes... Her mother was about to undergo a major operation.* V+O

undergraduate /ʌndəgrædjʊəˀt/, **undergraduates.** An **undergraduate** is a student at a university or college who has not yet taken his or her first degree. EG *He was a Cambridge undergraduate.* N COUNT
▸ used as an adjective. EG *...an undergraduate degree in Social Administration.* ▸ ADJ CLASSIF : ATTRIB

underground; pronounced /ʌndəgraʊnd/ when it is an adverb, and /ʌndəgraʊnd/ when it is a noun or adjective.
1 Something that is **underground** is below the surface of the ground. EG *...an underground car park... The larvae hatch and make their way underground.* ADJ CLASSIF, OR ADV AFTER VB
2 **Underground** activities are done secretly because they are unofficial and illegal and are usually directed against the government. EG *...an underground newspaper.* ADJ CLASSIF : ATTRIB
3 The **underground** in a country is an organized group of people who are engaged in illegal activities, often against the government in power. N SING : *the*+N
4 If you go **underground**, you hide from the authorities or the police because your political ideas or activities are illegal. EG *Among those forced underground was James Jackson.* ADV AFTER VB
5 The **Underground** in a city is a railway system in which electric trains travel below the ground in tunnels. EG *We went by Underground to Trafalgar Square... She walked towards the Underground station.* N SING OR *by*+N British

undergrowth /ʌndəgrəʊθ/ is bushes and plants growing together under the trees in a forest or jungle. EG *She went crashing through the undergrowth.* N UNCOUNT OR N SING : *the*+N

underhand /ʌndəhænd/. If an action is **underhand** or if it is done in an **underhand** way, it is done secretly and dishonestly. EG *Did they ever do anything which you regarded as underhand?* ADJ QUALIT

underlay /ʌndəleɪ/, **underlays. 1 Underlay** is a thick material that you place between a carpet and the floor for extra warmth and in order to protect the carpet. N MASS
2 **Underlay** is also the past tense of **underlie**.

underlie /ʌndəlaɪ/, **underlies, underlying, underlay** /ʌndəleɪ/, **underlain** /ʌndəleɪn/. If something **underlies** something else, it is the cause or basis of it. EG *The social problems underlying these crises are unsolved.* ● See also **underlying**. V+O

underline /ʌndəlaɪn/, **underlines, underlining, underlined. 1** If something **underlines** something such as a feeling or a problem, it emphasizes it. EG *An article in the Lancet underlined the same problem.* V+O
2 If you **underline** something such as a word or a sentence, you draw a line underneath it in order to make people notice it or to give it extra importance. EG *He underlined his signature with a little flourish.* V+O

underling /ʌndəlɪŋ/, **underlings.** You refer to someone as an **underling** when they are inferior in rank or status to someone else and take orders from them. EG *He expected his underlings to stand respectfully when he entered the room.* N COUNT

underlying /ʌndəlaɪɪŋ/. The **underlying** features of an object, event, or situation are not obvious, and effort may be needed in order to discover or reveal them. EG *There are underlying similarities between all human beings... The underlying theme of the novel is very serious.* ADJ CLASSIF : ATTRIB

undermine /ʌndəmaɪn/, **undermines, undermining, undermined.** If you **undermine** something such as an idea, a feeling, or a system, you make it less strong or less secure than it was before, often by a gradual process or by repeated efforts. EG *Public confidence in the company had now been completely undermined... The landowners resented government measures which undermined their authority.* V+O

underneath /ʌndəniːθ/. **1** If one thing is **underneath** another, it is directly below or beneath it. EG *The dog was underneath the table... There was a portrait with an inscription underneath.* PREP, OR ADV AFTER VB
2 The **underneath** part of something is the part which normally touches or faces the ground. EG *The underneath part felt damp... I lifted the dog's foot and checked the soft pad underneath.* ADJ CLASSIF : ATTRIB, OR ADV AFTER VB ▸ used as a noun. EG *The underneath of the car was covered with rust.* ▸ N SING
3 You use **underneath** when talking about feelings and emotions that people do not show in their behaviour. EG *Underneath, most of us are shy.* ADV OR PREP

undernourished /ʌndənʌrɪʃt/. If someone is **undernourished**, they are weak and unhealthy because they have not been eating enough food. EG *He was badly undernourished.* ADJ QUALIT

underpaid /ʌndəpeɪd/. People who are **underpaid** are not paid enough money for the job that they do. EG *...a great mass of underpaid workers.* ADJ QUALIT

underpants /ʌndəpænts/ are a piece of clothing worn by men and boys under their trousers. EG *Morris was standing in the hall in his underpants.* N PLURAL

underpass /ʌndəpɑːs/, **underpasses.** An **underpass** is a road or footpath that goes underneath a railway or another road. EG *...the Knightsbridge Underpass.* N COUNT

underprivileged /ʌndəprɪvɪˀlɪdʒd/. **Underprivileged** people have less money and fewer possessions and opportunities than other people in their society. EG *...an underprivileged family.* ADJ QUALIT

underrate /ʌndəreɪt/, **underrates, underrating, underrated.** If you **underrate** someone or something, you do not recognize how clever, important, or significant they are. EG *He soon discovered that he had underrated Lucy... Frank had underrated Sir James's knowledge of Africa.* V+O

underside /ʌndəsaɪd/, **undersides.** The **underside** of something is the part of it which normally faces towards the ground. EG *He turned the rifle over and examined the underside.* N COUNT : USU *the*+N

undersized /ʌndəsaɪzd/. **Undersized** people or things are smaller than usual, or smaller than they should be. EG *...rows of undersized babies.* ADJ CLASSIF

understaffed /ʌndəstɑːft/. An **understaffed** organization does not have enough employees to do its work properly. EG *The Department was understaffed and over-worked.* ADJ QUALIT

understand /ʌndəstænd/, **understands, understanding, understood** /ʌndəstʊd/. **1** If you **understand** someone or **understand** what they are saying, you know what they mean. EG *She understood him perfectly... I don't understand what you mean... Do you understand?* V+O, V+REPORT : ONLY WH, OR V : NO CONT
2 You can also say that you **understand** someone when you know why they behave in the way that they do. EG *His wife doesn't understand him.* V+O, OR V : NO CONT
3 If you **understand** what is happening or why it is happening, you know what is happening or why it is happening. EG *I don't understand why the engine isn't working.* V+REPORT : ONLY WH, NO CONT
4 If you say that you **understand** that something is the case, you mean that you have been told that it is the case. EG *I understand she has several aunts... You and Celia, I understand, are close friends.* V+REPORT : NO CONT Formal
5 If you **understand** a language, you know what someone is saying when they are speaking that language. EG *I don't understand English.* V+O : NO CONT
6 If you **make** yourself **understood**, you get someone to understand what you are telling them. EG PHRASE

They were all speaking at once in different dialects, trying to make themselves understood.

understandable /ʌndəstændəbəºl/. **1** If you say that someone's behaviour is **understandable**, you mean that they have reacted to a situation in a natural or normal way. EG *His reaction was perfectly understandable.* ◊ **understandably.** EG *Understandably, he was frightened.* ADJ QUALIT; ◊ ADV SEN

2 If something such as a statement or theory is **understandable**, people can easily understand it. EG *...the storage of information in a form which is readily understandable.* ADJ QUALIT

understanding /ʌndəstændɪŋ/, **understandings. 1** If you have an **understanding** of something, you have some knowledge of it, know how it works, or know what it means. EG *I doubt whether he had any real understanding of Shakespeare... The job requires an understanding of Spanish.* N UNCOUNT: OFT+*of*

2 If you are **understanding** towards someone, you are kind and forgiving. EG *I have always thought you were an understanding person.* ADJ QUALIT

3 If there is **understanding** between people, they are friendly towards each other and trust each other. EG *What is needed is greater understanding between management and workers.* N UNCOUNT

4 An **understanding** is an informal agreement about something. EG *Tacit understandings had been reached.* N COUNT

5 If you agree to do something **on the understanding that** something else will be done, you do it because you have been told that the other thing will be done. EG *I signed the contract on the understanding that delivery would be this week.* CONJ

understate /ʌndəsteɪt/, **understates, understating, understated.** If you **understate** something, you describe it in a way that suggests that it is smaller or less important than it really is. EG *They understate the magnitude of the problem.* V+O

understatement /ʌndəsteɪtmə²nt/, **understatements. 1** If you say that a statement is an **understatement**, you mean that it does not fully express the extent to which something is true. EG *To say it's been good is quite an understatement... 'You must be exhausted.' – 'That's an understatement.'* N COUNT

2 Understatement is the practice of suggesting that things have much less of a particular quality than they really have. EG *That sounds like typical British understatement.* N UNCOUNT

understood /ʌndəstʊd/ is the past tense and past participle of **understand.**

understudy /ʌndəstʌdi¹/, **understudies.** An actor's or actress's **understudy** is a person who has learned their part in a play and can act the part if they are ill. EG *He was Bobby's understudy.* N COUNT

undertake /ʌndəteɪk/, **undertakes, undertaking, undertook** /ʌndətʊk/, **undertaken. 1** When you **undertake** a task or job, you start doing it and accept responsibility for it. EG *Reluctantly, he undertook the mission.* V+O Formal

2 If you **undertake** to do something, you promise that you will do it. EG *Most shareholders have undertaken to accept the offer.* V+*to*-INF Formal

undertaker /ʌndəteɪkə/, **undertakers.** An **undertaker** is a person whose job is to look after the bodies of people who have died and to arrange their funerals. N COUNT

undertaking /ʌndəteɪkɪŋ/, **undertakings. 1** An **undertaking** is a task or job that you start doing and that you accept responsibility for. EG *...a complex and expensive undertaking.* N COUNT

2 If you give an **undertaking** to do something, you formally promise to do it. EG *Jenkins gave an undertaking not to stand again for election.* N COUNT Formal

undertone /ʌndətəʊn/, **undertones. 1** If you say something in an **undertone**, you say it very quietly. EG *Marcus said in an undertone, 'It doesn't matter, Lucas.'* N COUNT

2 If something has **undertones** of a particular kind, it suggests ideas or attitudes of this kind without expressing them directly. EG *The custom had religious undertones.* N COUNT+SUPP: USU PLURAL

undertook /ʌndətʊk/ is the past tense of **undertake.**

undervalue /ʌndəvælju:/, **undervalues, undervaluing, undervalued.** If you **undervalue** something or someone, you think that they are less valuable or important than they really are. EG *We tend to overvalue money and undervalue art.* V+O

underwater /ʌndəwɔ:tə/. **1** Something that exists or happens **underwater** exists or happens below the surface of the sea, a river, or a lake. EG *She swam underwater... ...underwater exploration... ...underwater vegetation.* ADV OR ADJ CLASSIF: ATTRIB

2 Underwater devices are specially made so that they can work in water. EG *It was filmed with an underwater camera.* ADJ CLASSIF: ATTRIB

underway /ʌndəweɪ/. If an activity is **underway**, it has already started. EG *Preparations for the trial were underway.* ADJ PRED

underwear /ʌndəweə/. Your **underwear** is clothing such as a vest, bra, or pants that you wear next to your skin under your other clothes. N UNCOUNT

underwent /ʌndəwent/ is the past tense of **undergo.**

underworld /ʌndəwɜ:ld/. The **underworld** in a city is the organized crime there and the people who are involved in it. EG *...professional thugs from the underworld.* N SING: *the*+N

undesirable /ʌndi¹zaɪərəbəºl/. You describe people or things as **undesirable** when you disapprove of them and think that they will have harmful effects. EG *These cuts in education are very undesirable.* ADJ QUALIT

undetected /ʌndi¹tektɪ²d/. If you are **undetected** or if you do something **undetected**, people do not find out where you are or what you are doing. EG *It was important to my safety that I should remain undetected.* ADJ CLASSIF OR ADV

undeveloped /ʌndi¹veləpt/. **Undeveloped** countries are countries that are not industrialized and where modern methods of large-scale farming are not used. ADJ CLASSIF

undid /ʌndɪd/ is the past tense of **undo.**

undignified /ʌndɪgnɪfaɪd/. **Undignified** behaviour is foolish and embarrassing. EG *They had a somewhat undignified argument.* ADJ QUALIT

undiscovered /ʌndɪskʌvəd/. Something that is **undiscovered** has not been discovered or found out about. EG *These authors were undiscovered geniuses... Old people who are ill sometimes lie undiscovered in their homes for days.* ADJ CLASSIF OR ADV

undisguised /ʌndɪsgaɪzd/. An **undisguised** quality or feeling is one that you show openly and do not make any attempt to hide. EG *He looked at her with undisguised admiration.* ADJ CLASSIF

undisputed /ʌndɪspju:tɪ²d/. **1** Something which is **undisputed** is definitely true or definitely exists and cannot be questioned or doubted. EG *The facts are undisputed... ...her undisputed good looks.* ADJ CLASSIF

2 If you describe someone as the **undisputed** leader or champion, you mean that they have proved that nobody else has more power or ability than they have. EG *Mao became undisputed leader in China.* ADJ CLASSIF

undistinguished /ʌndɪstɪŋgwɪʃt/. Someone or something that is **undistinguished** has no especially good qualities or features. EG *His political career had been undistinguished.* ADJ QUALIT

undisturbed /ʌndɪstɜ:bd/. **1** A place that is **undisturbed** is peaceful and not spoiled by noise or people. EG *The village is changing but it is still very undisturbed... The ship's remains lay undisturbed until 1975.* ADJ QUALIT

2 If you are **undisturbed** in something that you ADJ PRED

Is it undesirable to be a member of the underworld?

are doing, you continue doing it without being forced to stop or change. EG *The children pursued their studies undisturbed by the many visitors.*

undivided /ʌndɪvaɪdɪ²d/. If you give something your **undivided** attention, you concentrate on it fully. EG *I was listening with undivided attention.* ADJ CLASSIF : ATTRIB

undo /ʌnduː/, **undoes** /ʌndʌz/, **undoing** /ʌnduːɪŋ/, **undid** /ʌndɪd/, **undone** /ʌndʌn/. **1** If you **undo** something that is tied together, you unfasten it or untie it. EG *He bent down and undid the laces of his shoes.* V+O

2 If you **undo** something that has been done, you prevent it from being effective. EG *He appeared to be undoing all their patient work.* V+O

undoing /ʌnduːɪŋ/. If something is someone's **undoing**, it is the cause of their failure. EG *Stress can be the undoing of so many fine players.* N UNCOUNT +POSS Formal

undone /ʌndʌn/. Something that is **undone** is no longer held or tied together. EG *His bow tie had come undone.* ADJ PRED

undoubted /ʌndaʊtɪ²d/. You use **undoubted** to emphasize that something exists or is true. EG *...her undoubted acting ability... The play was an undoubted success.* ◊ **undoubtedly**. EG *A chauffeur is undoubtedly a status symbol.* ADJ CLASSIF ◊ ADV SEN

undreamed of /ʌndriːmd ɒv/ or **undreamt of** /ʌndrɛmt ɒv/. Something that is **undreamed of** is much better, worse, or more unusual than you thought was possible. EG *...undreamed-of luxury.* ADJ CLASSIF

undress /ʌndrɛs/, **undresses, undressing, undressed. 1** When you **undress**, you take off your clothes. EG *Tom undressed in the dark.* V

2 If you **undress** someone, you take off their clothes. V+O

undressed /ʌndrɛst/. If you are **undressed**, you are wearing no clothes or very few clothes. EG *They had all seen each other undressed.* ● When you **get undressed**, you take off your clothes. EG *He took ages getting undressed.* ADJ PRED ● PHRASE

undue /ʌndjuː/. You use **undue** to say that something is greater or more extreme than you think is reasonable. EG *She was reprimanded for putting undue pressure on her clients.* ADJ CLASSIF : ATTRIB Formal

undulate /ʌndjə⁴leɪt/, **undulates, undulating, undulated.** Something that **undulates** has gentle curves or slopes, or moves gently and slowly up and down. EG *The road undulates through pleasant scenery.* V Formal

unduly /ʌndjuːli¹/. You use **unduly** to say that something happens to an excessive or unnecessary extent. EG *None of the women seemed unduly worried... This attitude seemed to me unduly fussy.* ADV OR SUBMOD

undying /ʌndaɪɪŋ/. If you describe a feeling or a belief as **undying**, you mean that it will last forever. EG *...Daniel's undying love for his wife.* ADJ CLASSIF Literary

unearth /ʌnɜːθ/, **unearths, unearthing, unearthed.** If you **unearth** something that is hidden or secret, you discover it. EG *These ruins had been unearthed six feet below the surface... This dossier was unearthed along with many others.* V+O

unearthly /ʌnɜːθli¹/. **1** Something that is **unearthly** has a strange and unnatural sound or appearance. EG *The light was unearthly.* ADJ CLASSIF

2 If you do something at an **unearthly** hour, you do it very early or very late when most people are in bed and asleep. EG *I wondered why he had risen at that unearthly hour.* ADJ CLASSIF : ATTRIB

unease /ʌniːz/. If you have a feeling of **unease**, you feel that something is wrong and you are anxious about it. EG *'He'll be alright,' I said to myself, trying to quell a growing unease.* N UNCOUNT

uneasy /ʌniːzi¹/. If you are **uneasy**, you feel anxious that something may be wrong or that there may be danger. EG *She had an uneasy feeling that they were following her... I felt increasingly uneasy about my answer.* ◊ **uneasily**. EG *Philip blushed and laughed uneasily.* ◊ **uneasiness.** EG *Pat's uneasiness grew as each minute passed.* ADJ QUALIT ◊ ADV ◊ N UNCOUNT

uneconomic /ʌniːkənɒmɪk, ʌnɛkə-/. Something that is **uneconomic** does not produce enough profit or wastes time, energy, or money. EG *...uneconomic coal mines... ...a one-teacher school is uneconomic.* ADJ QUALIT

uneconomical /ʌniːkənɒmɪkə⁰l, ʌnɛkə-/. Something that is **uneconomical** wastes time, energy, or money. EG *...current sources of coal may become exhausted or uneconomical.* ADJ QUALIT

uneducated /ʌnɛdʒə⁴keɪtɪ²d/. Someone who is **uneducated** has not received much education. ADJ QUALIT

unemotional /ʌnɪməʊʃə⁰nəl, -ʃənə⁰l/. Someone who is **unemotional** does not show any feelings; often used showing disapproval. EG *He was cold and unemotional.* ADJ QUALIT

unemployable /ʌnɪ²mplɔɪəbə⁰l/. Someone who is **unemployable** does not have a job and is unlikely to get a job, for example because of the way that they behave. EG *Owing to their low intelligence, they were unemployable.* ADJ CLASSIF

unemployed /ʌnɪ²mplɔɪd/. **1** Someone who is **unemployed** does not have a job. EG *The government ought to create more job vacancies for unemployed young people.* ADJ CLASSIF

2 People who want to work but cannot get a job are often referred to as the **unemployed**. EG *They were discussing the problem of the unemployed.* N PLURAL : USU the+N

unemployment /ʌnɪ²mplɔɪmə²nt/. You say that there is **unemployment** in a place when many people there cannot get jobs. EG *The government is concerned about the level of unemployment in Scotland.* N UNCOUNT

unending /ʌnɛndɪŋ/. You say that something is **unending** when it has continued for a long time and seems as though it will never stop. EG *...the unending debate about tobacco.* ADJ CLASSIF

unenviable /ʌnɛnvɪəbə⁰l/. If you describe a task or situation as **unenviable**, you mean that you would not like to have it or to be in it, because it is difficult, dangerous, or unpleasant. EG *...the unenviable task of phoning the parents of the dead child.* ADJ QUALIT : ATTRIB

unequal /ʌniːkwəl/. **1** If you say that a political or social system is **unequal**, you mean that it treats people in different ways, for example by giving some people more money or privileges than others. EG *...the unequal distribution of wealth.* ADJ QUALIT

2 Two things that are **unequal** are different in size, strength, or ability. EG *Her feet are of unequal sizes.* ADJ QUALIT

unequivocal /ʌnɪkwɪvəkə⁰l/. You say that a statement is **unequivocal** when its meaning is completely clear. EG *The reply was unequivocal.* ◊ **unequivocally**. EG *They have stated uneqivocally what they stand for.* ADJ CLASSIF Formal ◊ ADV

unerring /ʌnɜːrɪŋ/. If someone has an **unerring** ability to do something, they can always manage to do it. EG *Sheila's unerring sense of direction helped them.* ADJ CLASSIF

unethical /ʌnɛθɪkə⁰l/. Behaviour that is **unethical** is morally wrong. EG *He was accused of unethical conduct.* ADJ QUALIT Formal

uneven /ʌniːvə⁰n/. **1** Something that is **uneven** is not regular or consistent. EG *...uneven teeth... It was an uneven but inspired performance.* ADJ QUALIT

2 An **uneven** surface is not level or smooth. EG *She stumbled on the uneven ground.* ADJ QUALIT

uneventful /ʌnɪvɛntfʊl/. If you describe an occasion or period of time as **uneventful**, you mean that nothing interesting, exciting, or important happened during it. EG *The day was quiet and uneventful.* ADJ QUALIT

unexpected /ʌnɪ²kspɛktɪ²d/. Something that is **unexpected** surprises you because you were not expecting it to happen. EG *My hostess greeted me with unexpected warmth... His death was hardly unexpected.* ◊ **unexpectedly**. EG *She died quite unexpectedly.* ADJ QUALIT ◊ ADV

unfailing /ʌnfeɪlɪŋ/ is used to describe a quality that stays the same and does not get weaker as ADJ CLASSIF Formal time passes. EG *I could never have carried on without the unfailing support of the teaching staff.*

unfair /ʌnfɛə/. 1 If you think that something is **unfair**, you think that it is not right or not just. EG *It would be quite unfair to expose him to publicity... I knew I was being unfair to him.* ◇ **unfairly**. EG *Workers who have been unfairly dismissed may claim compensation.* ADJ QUALIT ◇ ADV

2 A situation or system that is **unfair** does not give equal treatment or the same chances to everyone involved. EG *The whole academic system is unfair.* ADJ QUALIT

unfaithful /ʌnfeɪθful/. If someone is **unfaithful** to their lover or to the person they are married to, they have a sexual relationship with someone else. EG *I swear I've never been unfaithful to you.* ADJ CLASSIF: OFT+to

unfamiliar /ʌnfəmɪlɪə/. 1 If something is **unfamiliar** to you, you have not seen or heard it before. EG *This name may be unfamiliar to most of you.* ADJ QUALIT

2 If you are **unfamiliar** with something, you have not seen or heard it before. EG *...a person unfamiliar with the French railway system.* ADJ PRED +with

unfashionable /ʌnfæʃə⁰nəbə⁰l/. If something is **unfashionable**, it is not fashionable or popular. EG *His ideas were unfashionable among his colleagues... Daisy liked the place because it was quiet and unfashionable.* ADJ QUALIT

unfasten /ʌnfɑːsə⁰n/, **unfastens, unfastening, unfastened.** If you **unfasten** a piece of clothing or something such as a seat belt or a window, you undo the buttons, hooks, or straps on it so that it is no longer closed. EG *He unfastened the buttons of his shirt.* V+O

unfavourable /ʌnfeɪvə⁰rəbə⁰l/; spelled **unfavorable** in American English. 1 **Unfavourable** conditions or circumstances cause problems for you and reduce your chance of success. EG *...unfavourable weather conditions.* ADJ QUALIT

2 If you have an **unfavourable** opinion of something, you do not like it or approve of it. EG *He had formed an unfavourable opinion of my work.* ADJ QUALIT

unfeeling /ʌnfiːlɪŋ/. Someone who is **unfeeling** is not sympathetic towards people who are suffering or unhappy. EG *How stupid and unfeeling I have been!... ...unfeeling journalists.* ADJ QUALIT

unfettered /ʌnfɛtəd/. Something or someone that is **unfettered** is completely free and not controlled or limited by anything. EG *...the right of free speech, unfettered by the party system... They are young and still unfettered by families.* ADJ CLASSIF

unfinished /ʌnfɪnɪʃt/. If something is **unfinished**, it has not been completed. EG *The unfinished building grew rusty and dilapidated... People shouldn't leave jobs unfinished.* ADJ CLASSIF

unfit /ʌnfɪt/. 1 If you are **unfit**, you have not been taking regular exercise, so that, for example, you get tired quickly when you run. ADJ QUALIT

2 If someone or something is **unfit** for a particular purpose, they are not suitable or not of a good enough quality. EG *This meat is unfit for human consumption... Adams is clearly unfit to hold an administrative post.* ADJ PRED: OFT+for OR to-INF

unfold /ʌnfəʊld/, **unfolds, unfolding, unfolded.** 1 When a situation **unfolds**, it develops and becomes known or understood. EG *The great invasion plan was beginning to unfold.* V

2 If you **unfold** your plans or intentions, you tell someone what your plans or intentions are. EG *She had soon unfolded all her plans to him.* V+O

3 If you **unfold** something which has been folded, you open it so that it becomes flat. V-ERG

unforeseen /ʌnfə⁸siːn/. An **unforeseen** event happens unexpectedly. EG *This was an unforeseen complication.* ADJ CLASSIF

unforgettable /ʌnfəgɛtəbə⁰l/. You say that something is **unforgettable** when it is so good or so bad that you are unlikely to forget it. EG *It was an unforgettable experience.* ADJ QUALIT

unforgivable /ʌnfəgɪvəbə⁰l/. If something you do is **unforgivable**, it is so bad or cruel that it can never be forgiven or justified. EG *...an unforgivable error in judgement.* ADJ QUALIT

unformed /ʌnfɔːmd/. Something that is **unformed** is in an early stage of development and not yet fully formed. EG *...unformed ideas.* ADJ CLASSIF

unfortunate /ʌnfɔːtʃə⁴nə¹t/. 1 Someone who is **unfortunate** is unlucky. EG *He's been very unfortunate... We will do our utmost to help these unfortunate people.* ADJ QUALIT

2 If you say that something that has happened is **unfortunate**, you mean that it is a pity that it happened. EG *It is rather unfortunate that the Prime Minister should have said this... ...one of those unfortunate lulls in the conversation.* ADJ QUALIT

unfortunately /ʌnfɔːtʃə⁴nə¹tli¹/. You use **unfortunately** to express regret about what you are saying. EG *'Will you be here in the morning?' – 'No, unfortunately I won't.'* ADV SEN

unfounded /ʌnfaʊndɪ²d/. You say that a belief is **unfounded** when it is not based on facts or evidence. EG *Our worst fears have proved unfounded.* ADJ CLASSIF

unfriendly /ʌnfrɛndli¹/. Someone who is **unfriendly** does not behave in a friendly way. EG *He looked unfriendly... ...a cold, unfriendly stare.* ADJ QUALIT

unfulfilled /ʌnfulfɪld/. You say that something such as a hope is **unfulfilled** when the thing that you hoped for has not happened. EG *...an unfulfilled wish... ...Leggett's unfulfilled ambition.* ADJ CLASSIF: USU ATTRIB

unfurnished /ʌnfɜːnɪʃt/. If you rent an **unfurnished** flat or house, no furniture is provided in it by the owner. ADJ CLASSIF

ungainly /ʌngeɪnli¹/. **Ungainly** people are awkward or clumsy in the way that they move. EG *I thought him terribly ungainly.* ADJ QUALIT Written

ungrateful /ʌngreɪtful/. If someone is **ungrateful**, they do not seem to be thankful for something that has been given to them or done for them. EG *I hope I don't sound ungrateful.* ADJ QUALIT

unguarded /ʌngɑːdɪ²d/. 1 If something is left **unguarded**, it is left without anyone to protect it or look after it. EG *I couldn't go without leaving my suitcase unguarded.* ADJ CLASSIF

2 An **unguarded** moment is one when you are careless in what you say or do, with the result that someone discovers something that you did not want them to know. EG *I told him, in an unguarded moment, what I planned to do.* ADJ CLASSIF: ATTRIB

unhappily /ʌnhæpɪli¹/. 1 If you do something **unhappily**, you are not happy or contented while you do it. EG *He trudged unhappily towards the house.* ADV

2 You use **unhappily** to say that you regret a situation or event. EG *Unhappily, George had died by the time Ralph got to America.* ADV SEN

unhappy /ʌnhæpi¹/, **unhappier, unhappiest.** 1 If you are **unhappy**, you are sad and depressed. EG *She looked unhappy... I had an unhappy time at school.* ◇ **unhappiness**. EG *The quarrel caused her intense unhappiness.* ADJ QUALIT ◇ N UNCOUNT

2 If you are **unhappy** about something, you are not pleased about it or are not satisfied with it. EG *The residents of the area are unhappy about the crowds and the noise.* ADJ PRED+A

3 If you describe a situation as an **unhappy** one, you are expressing regret that it exists. EG *This unhappy state of affairs would not exist if all Ministers acted in a responsible way.* ADJ QUALIT: ATTRIB

unharmed /ʌnhɑːmd/. If someone who has been attacked or involved in an accident is **unharmed**, they are not injured. EG *The four men managed to escape unharmed.* ADJ CLASSIF

unhealthy /ʌnhɛlθi¹/. 1 Something that is **unhealthy** is likely to cause illness. EG *This is probably the most unhealthy place in the world.* ADJ QUALIT

If a place is uninhabited, is it also uninhabitable?

2 You say that a person is **unhealthy** when they are often ill. ADJ QUALIT

unheard of /ʌnhɜːd ɒv/. You say that an event or situation is **unheard of** 1 when it never happens. EG *Contracts and written agreements are quite unheard of.* 2 when it has never happened before and so is very surprising or shocking. EG *This is an unheard-of outrage.* ADJ CLASSIF

unheeded /ʌnhiːdɪ²d/. If something goes **unheeded**, it is ignored. EG *Their appeals for help went unheeded.* ADJ PRED

unhelpful /ʌnhɛlpfʊl/. You say that someone is **unhelpful** when they do nothing to help you. EG *He came barging into the kitchen with unhelpful suggestions.* ADJ QUALIT

unhesitating /ʌnhɛzɪteɪtɪŋ/. When you are **unhesitating**, you do or say something immediately, because you are confident that it is the right thing to do or say. EG *...her unhesitating readiness to help.* ADJ CLASSIF
◊ **unhesitatingly**. EG *McCalden replied unhesitatingly, 'Yes, certainly.'* ◊ ADV

unhinge /ʌnhɪnd⁰ʒ/, **unhinges, unhinging, unhinged.** If an experience **unhinges** someone, it affects them so deeply that they become mentally ill. EG *It seemed to me the accident had unhinged her.* ◊ **unhinged**. EG *According to Morris, Gordon Masters is quite unhinged.* V+O; ◊ ADJ QUALIT

unholy /ʌnhəʊli¹/. Something that is **unholy** is considered to be wicked or sinful. EG *I discovered the unholy pleasures of gossip and malice.* ADJ QUALIT

unhurried /ʌnhʌrɪd/. If something that you do or say is **unhurried**, you do it or say it in a slow and relaxed way. EG *Her voice was calm and unhurried.* ADJ CLASSIF
◊ **unhurriedly**. EG *She walked unhurriedly out of the building.* ◊ ADV

unhurt /ʌnhɜːt/. If someone who has been attacked or involved in an accident is **unhurt**, they are not injured. EG *Two men crawled out unhurt.* ADJ PRED

unhygienic /ʌnhaɪdʒiːnɪk/. Something that is **unhygienic** is dirty and likely to cause infection or disease. EG *...tiny unhygienic cages.* ADJ QUALIT

unicorn /juːnɪkɔːn/, **unicorns.** In stories and legends, a **unicorn** is an imaginary animal that looks like a white horse and has a horn growing from its forehead. N COUNT

unidentified /ʌnaɪdɛntɪfaɪd/. You say that someone or something is **unidentified** when nobody knows who or what they are. EG *...the house of an unidentified Scottish merchant... ...unidentified flying objects.* ADJ CLASSIF: USU ATTRIB

unification /juːnɪfɪkeɪʃə⁰n/ is the act of unifying something, or the result of doing this. EG *...the unification of Italy.* N UNCOUNT: USU+SUPP

uniform /juːnɪfɔːm/, **uniforms.** 1 A **uniform** is a special set of clothes which some people, for example soldiers or the police, wear at work, and which some children wear at school. EG *...a man in the uniform of a captain in the Air Force... She wasn't in uniform.* N COUNT OR N UNCOUNT
2 If something is **uniform**, it does not vary, but is even and regular throughout. EG *...a structure of uniform width.* ADJ CLASSIF

uniformed /juːnɪfɔːmd/. **Uniformed** people are wearing uniforms. EG *...uniformed policemen.* ADJ CLASSIF: ATTRIB

uniformity /juːnɪfɔːmɪti¹/ is a state in which everyone or everything behaves or looks the same as everyone or everything else. EG *...the dreary uniformity of the housing estate.* N UNCOUNT

unify /juːnɪfaɪ/, **unifies, unifying, unified.** If you **unify** a number of things or people, you join or bring them together. EG *Smaller tribes are unified into larger societies.* ◊ **unified.** *...a unified labour movement.* ◊ **unifying**. EG *...the importance of Hinduism as a unifying cultural force.* V+O; ◊ ADJ CLASSIF; ◊ ADJ CLASSIF

unilateral /juːnɪlætə⁰rəl/. A **unilateral** decision or action is made or done by only one of the groups that are involved in a particular situation. EG *We will take unilateral action... ...unilateral disarmament.* ADJ CLASSIF: ATTRIB

unilateralism /juːnɪlætə⁰rəlɪzə⁰m/ is belief in unilateral disarmament. EG *The party had reversed its support of unilateralism.* ◊ **unilateralist** /juːnɪlætə⁰rəlɪst/, **unilateralists**. EG *I am not a unilateralist.* N UNCOUNT Formal; ◊ N COUNT

unimaginable /ʌnɪmædʒɪnəbə⁰l/. Something that is **unimaginable** is difficult to imagine or understand properly, because it is not part of people's normal experience. EG *...the unimaginable vastness of space... ...experiments carried out under almost unimaginable conditions.* ADJ CLASSIF

unimaginative /ʌnɪmædʒɪnətɪv/. Someone who is **unimaginative** does not use their imagination enough in what they do. EG *...unimaginative teachers... ...unimaginative projects.* ADJ QUALIT

unimpressive /ʌnɪmprɛsɪv/. You say that someone or something is **unimpressive** when they seem to have no good or interesting qualities. EG *Barney's wife was an unimpressive little woman.* ADJ QUALIT

uninhabitable /ʌnɪnhæbɪtəbə⁰l/. An **uninhabitable** place is one where it is impossible for people to live. EG *Worldwide pollution threatens to make the planet uninhabitable.* ADJ CLASSIF

uninhabited /ʌnɪnhæbɪtɪ²d/. An **uninhabited** place is one where nobody lives. EG *...an uninhabited island.* ADJ CLASSIF

uninhibited /ʌnɪnhɪbɪtɪ²d/. If you are **uninhibited**, you behave freely and naturally and show your real feelings. EG *...a sound of uninhibited laughter.* ADJ QUALIT

uninitiated /ʌnɪnɪʃɪeɪtɪ²d/. You can refer to the people who have no knowledge or experience of something as the **uninitiated**. EG *For the uninitiated, may I say that golf is one game that demands patience and concentration.* N PLURAL: *the*+N

unintelligible /ʌnɪntɛlɪdʒə¹bə⁰l/. Something that is **unintelligible** is impossible to understand. EG *He answered in words unintelligible to her.* ADJ QUALIT Formal

unintended /ʌnɪntɛndɪ²d/. If something that happens is **unintended**, it was not planned to happen. EG *...the unintended consequences of advertising on television.* ADJ CLASSIF

unintentional /ʌnɪntɛnʃə⁰nəl, -ʃənə⁰l/. Something that is **unintentional** is not done deliberately, but happens by accident. EG *...unintentional damage.* ADJ CLASSIF

uninterested /ʌnɪntə⁰rɪ²stɪ²d/. If you are **uninterested** in something, you are not interested in it. EG *Lionel was uninterested in the house.* ADJ QUALIT: OFT+*in*

uninteresting /ʌnɪntə⁰rɪ²stɪŋ/. Someone or something that is **uninteresting** is dull and boring. EG *He found her uninteresting as a person.* ADJ QUALIT

uninterrupted /ʌnɪntərʌptɪ²d/. If something is **uninterrupted**, it continues without any breaks or interruptions. EG *Lynn did some uninterrupted reading.* ADJ CLASSIF

uninvited /ʌnɪnvaɪtɪ²d/. You use **uninvited** to describe a person who arrives somewhere or does something without being asked. EG *...uninvited guests... Henry sat down uninvited.* ADJ CLASSIF

union /juːnjən/, **unions.** 1 A **union** is an organization of workers that has the aim of improving such things as the working conditions, pay, and benefits of its members. EG *...Mr Ray Buckton, leader of the train drivers' union.* N COUNT
2 When the **union** of two or more things takes place, they are joined together and become one thing. EG *We are working for the union of the two countries.* N UNCOUNT Formal

unique /juːniːk/. 1 If something is **unique**, it is the only thing of its kind. EG *...that unique human ability, speech.* ◊ **uniqueness**. EG *...the uniqueness of the individual.* ADJ CLASSIF; ◊ N UNCOUNT
2 If something is **unique** to one thing or person, it concerns or belongs to that thing or person only. EG *These problems are not unique to nuclear power.* ADJ PRED+*to*
3 Some people use **unique** to mean very unusual and special. EG *It was a unique and exquisite performance.* ◊ **uniquely**. EG *He had a fine singing voice, uniquely gentle and deep.* ADJ CLASSIF; ◊ SUBMOD

unisex /ju:nɪsɛks/ is used to describe things which are designed to be used by both men and women. EG *The women were dressed in nondescript unisex clothes.* ADJ CLASSIF

unison /ju:nɪsən, -zən/. If a group of people do something **in unison**, they all do it together at the same time. EG *'All of us,' they said in unison.* PHRASE

unit /ju:nɪt/, **units. 1** If you consider something as a **unit**, you consider it as a single, complete thing. EG *It is not realistic to treat the world as a unit, because resources are very unevenly distributed... ...the decline of the family as a self-sufficient unit.* N COUNT

2 A **unit** is also **2.1** a group of people who work together at a specific job, often in a particular place. EG *I was working in that unit as the librarian... ...the science policy research unit at the university.* N COUNT **2.2** a small machine which has a particular function, often part of a larger machine. EG *...a power supply unit.* N COUNT: USU+SUPP

3 A **unit** of measurement is a fixed, standard quantity, length, or weight that is used for measuring things. The metre, the litre, and the gram are all units. EG *...a unit of electricity... ...units of sound.* N COUNT OR N PART

unite /ju:naɪt/, **unites, uniting, united.** If a group of people or things **unite** or if something **unites** them, they join together and act as a group. EG *They must unite to combat the enemy... This measure would unite all the provinces into a single state.* V-ERG

united /ju:naɪtɪ²d/. **1** If a group of people are **united** about something, they agree with each other about it and act together. EG *They were united in their dislike of authority.* ADJ CLASSIF

2 If different areas or groups are **united**, they have been joined together to form a single country or organization. EG *Some people want a united Ireland... ...the United States.* ADJ CLASSIF

United Kingdom. The **United Kingdom** is the official name for Great Britain and Northern Ireland. N PROPER: *the*+N

United Nations. The **United Nations** is an organization which most countries in the world belong to and which tries to encourage peace, co-operation, and friendship. N PROPER: *the*+N

unity /ju:nɪ¹ti¹/. When there is **unity**, people are in agreement and act together for a particular purpose. EG *He failed to preserve his party's unity... They are discussing church unity.* N UNCOUNT

universal /ju:nɪvɜ:səºl/, **universals. 1** Something that is **universal** **1.1** relates to everyone in the world or to everyone in a particular group or society. EG *They touched on various topics of universal interest.* ADJ CLASSIF ◇ **universally**. EG *This explanation is not yet universally accepted.* ◇ ADV **1.2** affects or relates to every part of the world or the universe. EG *The threat of universal extinction hangs over all the world.* ADJ CLASSIF

2 A **universal** is something that is the same or equally true at all times and in all situations. N COUNT ▸ used as an adjective. EG *...a universal truth.* ▸ ADJ CLASSIF ◇ **universally**. EG *One thing was universally true.* ◇ ADV+ADJ

universe /ju:nɪvɜ:s/, **universes.** The **universe** is the whole of space, including all the stars and planets. EG *They thought the earth was the centre of the universe.* N SING: *the*+N

university /ju:nɪvɜ:sɪ¹ti¹/, **universities.** A **university** is an institution where students study for degrees and where academic research is done. EG *She is a student at Norwich University... Her one aim in life is to go to university.* N COUNT OR N UNCOUNT

unjust /ʌndʒʌst/. An **unjust** action, system, or law is morally wrong because it treats a person or a group badly in a way that they do not deserve. EG *...a thoroughly unjust society.* ADJ QUALIT ◇ **unjustly**. EG *...schoolmates who had unjustly accused him of bullying.* ◇ ADV

unjustifiable /ʌndʒʌstɪfaɪəbəºl/. You say that an action is **unjustifiable** when it harms someone and there is no good reason for doing it. EG *What I had done was clearly unjustifiable.* ADJ QUALIT

unjustified /ʌndʒʌstɪfaɪd/. You say that a belief or action is **unjustified** when there is no good reason for having it or for doing it. EG *It was an unjustified attack.* ADJ QUALIT

unkempt /ʌŋ¹kɛmpt/. Something that is **unkempt** is untidy and not looked after carefully. EG *He had a shaggy, unkempt beard.* ADJ QUALIT

unkind /ʌŋ¹kaɪnd/, **unkinder, unkindest.** Someone who is **unkind** to you behaves towards you in an unpleasant and rather cruel way. EG *Why are you so unkind to me when you know I'm unhappy?... ...a silly and unkind remark.* ADJ QUALIT

unknown /ʌnnəʊn/. **1** If someone or something is **unknown**, people do not know about them, or do not know who or what they are. EG *She took me to another village where she was unknown... ...this man Boris, whose real name is unknown to me... She wouldn't be alone with an unknown male visitor.* ADJ CLASSIF

2 You can refer to the things that people do not know about as the **unknown**. EG *...fear of the unknown.* N SING: *the*+N

unlawful /ʌnlɔ:fə⁴l/. Something that is **unlawful** is not legal. EG *...unlawful business activities.* ADJ CLASSIF Formal

unleash /ʌnli:ʃ/, **unleashes, unleashing, unleashed.** When someone or something **unleashes** a powerful or violent force, they release it. EG *How could they have justified all the violence unleashed on the prisoners?... Strong feelings had been unleashed in me by the news of the bomb.* V+O Formal

unless /ʌnlɛs/. You use **unless** to introduce the only circumstances in which the event you are mentioning will not take place or in which the statement you are making is not true. EG *He phoned me to say that unless the paper stopped my articles he would withdraw his advertisements... I couldn't get a grant unless I had five years' teaching experience.* CONJ

unlike /ʌnlaɪk/. **1** If one thing is **unlike** another thing, the two things have different features from each other. EG *Rodin was unlike his predecessor in every way.* PREP

2 You can use **unlike** to contrast two people, things, or situations, and show how they are different. EG *Mrs Hochstadt, unlike Etta, was a careful shopper.* PREP

3 If you describe something that a particular person has done as being **unlike** them, you mean that you are surprised by it because it is not typical of their character or normal behaviour. EG *It was unlike her to mention it.* PREP

unlikely /ʌnlaɪkli¹/. **1** If you say that something is **unlikely** to happen or **unlikely** to be true, you mean that it will probably not happen, or that it is probably not true. EG *The dispute is unlikely to be settled for a long time... It is unlikely that you will get your own office... In the unlikely event that they give you any trouble, write to us.* ADJ QUALIT: OFT+*to*-INF OR REPORT

2 You can also use **unlikely** to describe a situation or event that actually occurs but that seems very strange because it is so unexpected. EG *Brody was startled by the unlikely sight of Hendricks in a bathing suit.* ADJ QUALIT: ATTRIB

unlimited /ʌnlɪmɪtɪ²d/. You say that something is **unlimited** when you can have as much of it as you want. EG *...a ticket that allows unlimited travel on buses... They were given unlimited amounts of food.* ADJ CLASSIF

unlit /ʌnlɪt/. **1** An **unlit** fire or cigarette has not yet been lit and is therefore not burning. ADJ CLASSIF

2 An **unlit** street or building is dark because it does not have any lights switched on to make it bright. ADJ CLASSIF

Why do you not talk about things that are unmentionable?

unload /ʌnləʊd/, **unloads, unloading, unloaded.**
1 If you **unload** goods from a container or vehicle, you remove them. EG *We began to unload the bricks from Philip's car.* — V+O OR V

2 If you **unload** a problem onto someone, you tell them about it because you need advice or sympathy. EG *He wanted to unload some of the anguish onto someone else.* — V+O : OFT +onto/on

unlock /ʌnlɒk/, **unlocks, unlocking, unlocked.** If you **unlock** something such as a door or a container, you open it by means of a key. EG *He unlocked the drawer and took out the money.* — V+O
◇ **unlocked.** EG *The door was always unlocked.* — ◇ ADJ CLASSIF

unloving /ʌnlʌvɪŋ/. You say that people are **unloving** when they do not show love to other people, especially their own family. EG *...unloving parents.* — ADJ QUALIT

unlucky /ʌnlʌki^1/. **1** Someone who is **unlucky** has bad luck. EG *I was unlucky enough to miss the final episode... She had been unlucky in love.* — ADJ QUALIT

2 If something is **unlucky**, it is thought to cause bad luck. EG *13 is a very unlucky number.* — ADJ QUALIT

unmade /ʌm^{1}meɪd/. An **unmade** bed has not had its sheets and blankets neatly arranged after it was last slept in. — ADJ CLASSIF

unmanageable /ʌm^{1}mænɪdʒəbə^{0}l/. Something that is **unmanageable** is difficult to use, deal with, or control, usually because it is too big. EG *The complete encyclopaedia is quite unmanageable.* — ADJ QUALIT

unmanly /ʌm^{1}mænli^1/. **Unmanly** behaviour is thought to be not suitable for a man. EG *...the attitude that it is unmanly to be domesticated.* — ADJ QUALIT

unmanned /ʌm^{1}mænd/. **Unmanned** aircraft or spacecraft do not carry people in them. — ADJ CLASSIF

unmarked /ʌm^{1}mɑːkt/. Something that is **unmarked** **1** has no marks of damage or injury on it. EG *His face was unmarked.* **2** has no signs on it to identify it. EG *...unmarked police cars.* — ADJ CLASSIF

unmarried /ʌm^{1}mærɪd/. Someone who is **unmarried** is not married. EG *...an unmarried mother.* — ADJ CLASSIF

unmentionable /ʌm^{1}menʃənəbə^{0}l/. Something that is **unmentionable** is too embarrassing or unpleasant to talk about. EG *He's had all kinds of unmentionable operations.* — ADJ CLASSIF

unmistakable /ʌm^{1}mɪsteɪkəbə^{0}l/; also spelled **unmistakeable.** Something that is **unmistakable** is so obvious that it cannot be mistaken for anything else. EG *...the unmistakable stench of rotting eggs.* ◇ **unmistakably.** EG *He was unmistakably of Italian descent.* — ADJ CLASSIF; ◇ ADV OR ADV SEN

unmitigated /ʌm^{1}mɪtɪgeɪtɪ^{2}d/. You use **unmitigated** to describe bad situations or qualities that are totally and completely bad. EG *This government's policy on education is an unmitigated disaster... ...his unmitigated selfishness.* — ADJ CLASSIF : ATTRIB Formal

unmoved /ʌm^{1}muːvd/. If someone is **unmoved** by something, they are not emotionally affected by it. EG *No one can remain unmoved by this music.* — ADJ PRED

unnamed /ʌnneɪmd/. If someone or something is **unnamed**, their name is not mentioned. EG *...an unnamed ministry spokesman.* — ADJ CLASSIF

unnatural /ʌnnætʃə^{0}rəl/. **1** If you describe something as **unnatural**, you mean that it is strange and rather frightening, because it is different from what you normally expect. EG *...the house's unnatural silence.* ◇ **unnaturally**. EG *Her arms felt unnaturally hot.* — ADJ QUALIT; ◇ ADV

2 If someone's behaviour is **unnatural**, they are behaving in a way that seems artificial and not typical of them. EG *Her voice was a little strained, a little unnatural.* — ADJ QUALIT

unnecessary /ʌnnesə^{1}sə^{0}ri^1/. Something that is **unnecessary** is not necessary. EG *The reason behind this is to avoid unnecessary expenses.* — ADJ QUALIT
◇ **unnecessarily.** EG *Some parents worry unnecessarily about their children.* — ◇ ADV

unnerve /ʌnnɜːv/, **unnerves, unnerving, unnerved.** If something **unnerves** you, it frightens or startles you. EG *His touch unnerved her.* — V+O

unnerving /ʌnnɜːvɪŋ/. Something that is **unnerving** is frightening and startling. EG *This kind of experience can be quite unnerving.* — ADJ QUALIT

unnoticed /ʌnnəʊtɪst/. If something happens or passes **unnoticed**, it is not seen or noticed by anyone. EG *We tried to get into the room unnoticed... He hoped his departure had passed unnoticed.* — ADJ PRED

unobserved /ʌnə^{7}bzɜːvd/. If you do something **unobserved**, you do it without being seen by anyone. EG *She was able to slip past the guard unobserved.* — ADJ CLASSIF

unobtrusive /ʌnə^{7}btruːsɪv/. Something that is **unobtrusive** does not draw attention to itself. EG *We'll try to be as unobtrusive as possible.* — ADJ QUALIT Formal

unoccupied /ʌnɒkjə^{4}paɪd/. If a place is **unoccupied**, there is nobody in it. EG *The house was left unoccupied for fifteen years.* — ADJ CLASSIF

unofficial /ʌnəfɪʃə^{0}l/. An **unofficial** action is not authorized, approved, or organized by a person in authority. EG *...an unofficial strike... You will be sent unofficial notification of the results.* — ADJ CLASSIF

unopened /ʌnəʊpə^{0}nd/. If something is **unopened**, it has not been opened yet. EG *...an unopened bottle of whisky.* — ADJ CLASSIF

unorthodox /ʌnɔːθədɒks/. **Unorthodox** behaviour, beliefs, or customs are unusual and not generally accepted. EG *Many doctors don't approve of unorthodox medicine.* — ADJ QUALIT

unpack /ʌm^{1}pæk/, **unpacks, unpacking, unpacked.** When you **unpack**, you take everything out of a suitcase, bag, or box. EG *I'll leave you now so that you can unpack... He began to unpack his briefcase.* — V OR V+O

unpaid /ʌm^{1}peɪd/. **1** If you are **unpaid**, you do a job without receiving any money or wages for it. EG *Carol was Pat's unpaid teacher.* — ADJ CLASSIF

2 Unpaid work or leave is work or leave that you do not get paid for. EG *...unpaid overtime.* — ADJ CLASSIF

3 If something such as rent or a bill is **unpaid**, it has not yet been paid. — ADJ CLASSIF

unpalatable /ʌm^{1}pælə^{1}təbə^{0}l/. **1 Unpalatable** food is so unpleasant that you can hardly eat it. EG *...an unpalatable breakfast.* — ADJ QUALIT Formal

2 An **unpalatable** idea is one that you find unpleasant and difficult to accept. EG *...the unpalatable truth.* — ADJ QUALIT Formal

unparalleled /ʌm^{1}pærəleld/. If you say that something is **unparalleled**, you mean that it is bigger or better than anything else of its kind. EG *Our specialist library is unparalleled.* — ADJ CLASSIF

unpleasant /ʌm^{1}plezənt/. **1** You say that something is **unpleasant** when it gives you bad feelings rather than good ones, for example by making you feel upset, uncomfortable, or frightened. EG *The only work available is dirty, unpleasant and dangerous... The smell was unpleasant.* — ADJ QUALIT

2 Someone who is **unpleasant** is very unfriendly or rude. EG *Their son is even more ill-tempered, difficult, and unpleasant.* — ADJ QUALIT

unplug /ʌm^{1}plʌg/, **unplugs, unplugging, unplugged.** If you **unplug** a piece of electrical equipment, you take the plug out of the electric socket. EG *Will you unplug the iron?* — V+O

unpopular /ʌm^{1}pɒpjə^{4}lə/. Something or someone that is **unpopular** is disliked by most of the people in a place or community. EG *The war was both costly and unpopular... ...an unpopular minister.* — ADJ QUALIT

unprecedented /ʌm^{1}presɪdentɪ^{2}d/. You use **unprecedented** to say that something has never happened before, or that it is the best or largest thing of its kind that there has ever been. EG *...a period of unprecedented wealth and prosperity.* — ADJ CLASSIF Formal

unpredictable /ʌm^{1}prɪdɪktəbə^{0}l/. If someone or something is **unpredictable**, you never know how they will behave or what effects they will have. EG *She was totally unpredictable... Poisons are notoriously unpredictable.* — ADJ QUALIT

unprepared /ʌm¹prɪpɛəd/. If you are **unprepared** for something, you are not ready for it, and are therefore surprised or at a disadvantage when it happens. EG *Students from tropical countries are often unprepared for the British climate... We were pushed into battle unprepared.* ADJ CLASSIF: OFT+*for*

unproductive /ʌm¹prədʌktɪv/. Something that is **unproductive** does not produce anything useful. EG *Their land is unproductive.* ADJ QUALIT

unprofitable /ʌm¹prɒfɪtəbə⁰l/. An **unprofitable** company or product does not make any profit or does not make enough profit. EG *Agriculture remained unprofitable... ...unprofitable business contracts.* ADJ QUALIT

unprotected /ʌm¹prətɛktɪ²d/. Someone or something that is **unprotected** is not protected in any way. EG *They feel quite naked and unprotected... Beware of the sun beating on unprotected fair skin.* ADJ QUALIT

unprovoked /ʌm¹prəvəʊkt/. If you make an **unprovoked** attack, you attack someone who has not harmed you in any way. EG *...casual and unprovoked violence.* ADJ CLASSIF

unpublished /ʌm¹pʌblɪʃt/. **Unpublished** books, manuscripts, or letters have never been published. ADJ CLASSIF

unqualified /ʌnkwɒlɪfaɪd/. **1** If you are **unqualified**, you do not have any qualifications, or do not have the right qualifications for a particular job. EG *...an unqualified childminder.* ADJ CLASSIF

2 Unqualified also means total and complete. EG *The party was an unqualified disaster... The Government does not have unqualified control over the economy.* ADJ CLASSIF: ATTRIB

unquestionable /ʌnkwɛstʃənəbə⁰l/. Something that is **unquestionable** is so obviously true or real that nobody can doubt it. EG *These are unquestionable facts... His courage and commitment are unquestionable.* ◇ **unquestionably**. EG *The visit to Greenland was unquestionably the highlight of the voyage.* ADJ CLASSIF; ◇ ADV SEN OR ADV

unquestioned /ʌnkwɛstʃənd/. Something that is **unquestioned** is accepted by everyone, without anyone doubting or disagreeing. EG *...a system in which obedience and fortitude were unquestioned virtues.* ADJ CLASSIF

unquestioning /ʌnkwɛstʃənɪŋ/ is used to describe beliefs or attitudes that people have without thinking closely about them or doubting them in any way. EG *You were chosen for this operation on the basis of your unquestioning obedience.* ADJ CLASSIF

unravel /ʌnrævəl/, **unravels, unravelling, unravelled;** also spelled **unraveling, unraveled** in American English.

1 If you **unravel** something that is knotted or twisted, or if it **unravels**, it becomes undone. EG *Her knitting was starting to unravel.* V-ERG

2 If you **unravel** a mystery or puzzle, you explain it or work out the answer to it. EG *...factors which only the experts could unravel.* V+O

unreal /ʌnrɪəl/. If you describe something as **unreal**, you mean that it is so strange that you find it difficult to believe that it is real. EG *I felt unreal, in a bad dream, still not properly awake... This conversation is getting more and more unreal.* ADJ QUALIT

unrealistic /ʌnrɪəlɪstɪk/. Someone who is **unrealistic** or who has **unrealistic** ideas does not recognize the truth about a situation or does not deal with it in a practical way. EG *This demand proved unrealistic and unworkable... You have unrealistic expectations.* ADJ QUALIT

unreasonable /ʌnriːznəbə⁰l/. **1** People who are **unreasonable** are difficult to deal with because they behave in an unfair or illogical way. EG *We think he is being unreasonable.* ADJ QUALIT

2 You say that something such as a decision is **unreasonable** when it seems unfair and difficult to justify. EG *The request didn't seem unreasonable.* ADJ QUALIT

unrecognizable /ʌnrɛkəg⁰naɪzəbə⁰l/; also spelled **unrecognisable.** Something that is **unrecognizable** is impossible to recognize or identify. EG *His voice was almost unrecognizable.* ADJ CLASSIF

unrecognized /ʌnrɛkəg⁰naɪzd/; also spelled **unrecognised.** If someone or something is **unrecognized**, they are not recognized or are not known about. EG *Unrecognized by any of the women, he entered the house... These common defects are often unrecognized.* ADJ CLASSIF

unrelated /ʌnri¹leɪtɪ²d/. Things which are **unrelated** have no connection with each other. EG *...a series of unrelated incidents... New issues may arise, unrelated to the original ones.* ADJ CLASSIF: OFT+*to*

unrelenting /ʌnri¹lɛntɪŋ/. If someone's behaviour is **unrelenting**, they continue to do something in a very determined way, often without caring whether they hurt or embarrass other people. EG *They kept up a sustained, unrelenting barrage of questions... ...the unrelenting quest for knowledge.* ADJ CLASSIF

unreliable /ʌnri¹laɪəbə⁰l/. If people, machines, or methods are **unreliable**, you cannot trust them or rely on them. EG *Godwin was a thoroughly unreliable man... ...an unreliable second-hand car.* ADJ QUALIT

unremarkable /ʌnri¹mɑːkəbə⁰l/. If you say that something is **unremarkable**, you mean that it is not beautiful, interesting, or exciting. EG *The view is unremarkable.* ADJ CLASSIF

unremitting /ʌnri¹mɪtɪŋ/. Something that is **unremitting** continues without stopping. EG *...their unremitting efforts to get him into college.* ADJ CLASSIF Formal

unrepentant /ʌnri¹pɛntənt/. If you are **unrepentant**, you are not ashamed of your beliefs or actions. EG *I am an unrepentant believer in free enterprise.* ADJ QUALIT

unresolved /ʌnri¹zɒlvd/. If a problem or difficulty is **unresolved**, no satisfactory solution has been found to it. EG *Several major technological problems remained unresolved.* ADJ CLASSIF Formal

unresponsive /ʌnri¹spɒnsɪv/. If you are **unresponsive** to something, you do not react to it or let it affect your behaviour. EG *The audience was unresponsive... ...a government that is unresponsive to our needs.* ADJ QUALIT: OFT+*to*

unrest /ʌnrɛst/. If there is **unrest**, people are angry and dissatisfied. EG *...the causes of industrial unrest.* N UNCOUNT

unrestrained /ʌnri¹streɪnd/. If something is **unrestrained**, it is not controlled or limited in any way. EG *...the dangers of unrestrained growth.* ADJ CLASSIF

unrestricted /ʌnri¹strɪktɪ²d/. If something is **unrestricted**, it is not limited by any laws or rules. EG *...the unrestricted dumping of waste.* ADJ CLASSIF

unrewarding /ʌnri¹wɔːdɪŋ/. If a job or task is **unrewarding**, it does not give you any feelings of achievement or pleasure. EG *Learning a language often seems unrewarding at the time.* ADJ QUALIT

unripe /ʌnraɪp/. **Unripe** fruit is not yet ripe. EG *We ate unripe apples from the garden.* ADJ CLASSIF

unrivalled /ʌnraɪvəld/. If you say that something is **unrivalled**, you mean that it is better than anything else of the same kind. EG *The gallery has an unrivalled collection of modern art.* ADJ CLASSIF

unroll /ʌnrəʊl/, **unrolls, unrolling, unrolled.** If you **unroll** something such as a sheet of paper or a roll of cloth, you open it up and make it flat when it was previously rolled in a cylindrical shape. EG *Someone unrolled a map of America.* V-ERG

unruffled /ʌnrʌfəld/. If you are **unruffled**, you are calm and not affected by surprising or frightening events. EG *She remained singularly unruffled when confronted with my discovery.* ADJ CLASSIF

unruly /ʌnruːli¹/. **1 Unruly** people are difficult to control or organize. EG *...unruly children.* ADJ QUALIT

2 Unruly hair is difficult to keep tidy. EG *He smoothed his unruly hair.* ADJ QUALIT

unsafe /ʌnseɪf/. **1** If something is **unsafe**, it is dangerous. EG *The house was declared unsafe for habitation.* ADJ QUALIT: USU PRED

2 If you are **unsafe**, you are in danger of being harmed. EG *I feel very unsafe.* ADJ PRED

unsatisfactory /ʌnsætɪsfæktəⁿri¹/. Something that is **unsatisfactory** is not good enough to be acceptable. EG *I had an unsatisfactory discussion with him about my job.* ADJ QUALIT

unsatisfied /ʌnsætɪsfaɪd/. If you are **unsatisfied**, you are disappointed because you have not got what you wanted. EG *He asked a lot of questions, and was unsatisfied with the answers.* ADJ QUALIT: OFT+*with*

unsavoury /ʌnseɪvəⁿri¹/; spelled **unsavory** in American English. You describe people, places, and things as **unsavoury** when you find them unpleasant. EG *He looks so unsavoury... Parts of Birmingham are pretty unsavoury.* ADJ QUALIT

unscathed /ʌnskeɪðd/. If you are **unscathed** after a dangerous experience, you have not been injured or harmed by it. EG *We all escaped unscathed.* ADJ PRED

unscheduled /ʌnʃedju:ld, ʌnsked-/. An **unscheduled** event is not planned to happen, but happens unexpectedly or because someone changes their plans at a late stage. EG *Grimes was about to make an unscheduled announcement.* ADJ CLASSIF

unscrew /ʌnskru:/, **unscrews, unscrewing, unscrewed.** If you **unscrew** something, you remove it by turning it, or by removing the screws that fasten it to something else. EG *He unscrewed the top and put the bottle to his mouth... The mirrors had been unscrewed and removed.* V+O

unscrupulous /ʌnskru:pjə⁴ləs/. **Unscrupulous** people are prepared to act dishonestly in order to get what they want. EG *He was cruel, treacherous and unscrupulous.* ADJ QUALIT

unseeing /ʌnsi:ɪŋ/. You describe a person as **unseeing** or say that their eyes are **unseeing** when they are not looking at anything, or not noticing something, although their eyes are open. EG *She stared ahead, unseeing... She was gazing with unseeing eyes at the harbour.* ADJ CLASSIF Literary

unseemly /ʌnsi:mli¹/. If someone's behaviour is **unseemly**, it is not polite or not suitable for a particular occasion or situation. EG *...an unseemly public squabble over his salary.* ADJ QUALIT Formal Outdated

unseen /ʌnsi:n/. You use **unseen** to describe things that you cannot see. EG *A large unseen orchestra was playing jazzy rhythms.* ADJ CLASSIF

unselfish /ʌnselfɪʃ/. If you are **unselfish**, you think about other people's wishes and needs rather than your own. EG *He was a brave and unselfish man... ...her unselfish devotion to her children.* ADJ QUALIT

unsettle /ʌnsetəⁿl/, **unsettles, unsettling, unsettled.** If something **unsettles** you, it causes you to feel restless, dissatisfied, or rather worried. EG *It unsettled him not to know where he was.* V+O

unsettled /ʌnsetəⁿld/. **1** In an **unsettled** situation, there is a lot of uncertainty about what will happen. EG *...in the early days of 1968, when everything was unsettled.* ADJ CLASSIF

2 If you are **unsettled**, you cannot concentrate on anything, because you are worried or excited about something. EG *I felt pretty unsettled all that week.* ADJ PRED

3 An **unsettled** argument or dispute has not yet been resolved. EG *This argument remained unsettled until January 1975.* ADJ CLASSIF Formal

unshakable /ʌnʃeɪkəbəⁿl/; also spelled **unshakeable. Unshakable** beliefs are so strong that they cannot be destroyed or altered. EG *...her unshakable faith in progress... ...a man of unshakable convictions.* ADJ CLASSIF

unshaven /ʌnʃeɪvəⁿn/. If a man is **unshaven**, he has not shaved recently and there are short hairs on his face or chin. EG *...his unshaven face.* ADJ CLASSIF

unsightly /ʌnsaɪtli¹/. If something is **unsightly**, it is ugly and unattractive to look at. EG *His skin was covered with unsightly blotches.* ADJ QUALIT

unskilled /ʌnskɪld/. **Unskilled** workers do work that does not require any special training. EG *...unskilled labourers... They are all in low-paid, unskilled jobs.* ADJ CLASSIF

unsociable /ʌnsəʊʃəbəⁿl/. **Unsociable** people do not like talking to other people and try to avoid meeting them; used showing disapproval. EG *She was an awkward and unsociable girl.* ADJ QUALIT

unsolicited /ʌnsəlɪsɪtɪ²d/. Something that is **unsolicited** is given or happens without being asked for. EG *She was given much unsolicited advice from her companions... ...unsolicited letters from publishers.* ADJ CLASSIF Formal

unsolved /ʌnsɒlvd/. An **unsolved** problem or mystery has never been solved. EG *The mystery will probably remain forever unsolved.* ADJ CLASSIF

unsophisticated /ʌnsəfɪstɪkeɪtɪ²d/. **1** People who are **unsophisticated** do not have a wide range of experience or knowledge and their tastes are simple. EG *It is easy to write because the readers are relatively unsophisticated.* ADJ QUALIT

2 An **unsophisticated** method or device is very simple. EG *These forecasts are based on rather unsophisticated economic analyses.* ADJ QUALIT

unsound /ʌnsaʊnd/. **1** If you say that a conclusion or method is **unsound**, you mean that it is based on ideas that are wrong. EG *The basic research seems unsound... These procedures are economically unsound.* ADJ QUALIT

2 An **unsound** building or other structure is in poor condition and is likely to collapse. ADJ QUALIT

unspeakable /ʌnspi:kəbəⁿl/. If you say that something is **unspeakable**, you mean that it is extremely unpleasant. EG *All I remember is the unspeakable pain... Their treatment of women is unspeakable.* ADJ QUALIT

unspecified /ʌnspesɪfaɪd/. You say that something is **unspecified** when you are not told exactly what it is. EG *She was dying of some unspecified disease.* ADJ CLASSIF

unspoiled /ʌnspɔɪld/; also spelled **unspoilt** /ʌnspɔɪlt/. **1** If something is **unspoiled**, it has not been damaged or harmed in any way. EG *The wine's flavour was unspoiled.* ADJ CLASSIF

2 You describe a place as **unspoiled** when it has not changed for a long time. EG *...areas of unspoiled countryside... ...a paradise of unspoilt beaches.* ADJ CLASSIF

unspoken /ʌnspəʊkəⁿn/. If someone's thoughts, wishes, or feelings are **unspoken**, they do not tell other people about them. EG *I was full of unspoken fears... ...her unspoken criticism of him.* ADJ CLASSIF

unstable /ʌnsteɪbəⁿl/. **1** If something is **unstable**, **1.1** it is likely to change suddenly and to create difficulty or danger. EG *...unstable governments... ...the unstable political situation.* **1.2** it is not firm or not fixed properly, and is likely to move or fall. EG *...the unstable guttering on the house.* ADJ QUALIT

2 If people are **unstable**, their emotions and behaviour keep changing because their minds are disturbed or upset. EG *He was a neurotic and unstable man... She was always mentally unstable.* ADJ QUALIT

unsteady /ʌnstedi¹/. **1** If you are **unsteady**, you have difficulty standing or walking because you cannot completely control your legs or your body. EG *She seemed unsteady on her feet.* ◇ **unsteadily.** EG *He rose unsteadily to his feet.* ADJ QUALIT ◇ ADV

2 If your hands are **unsteady**, you have difficulty controlling them. EG *Stephen poured two brandies with an unsteady hand.* ADJ QUALIT

3 Unsteady objects are not held, fixed, or balanced securely. EG *She was balancing three boxes in an unsteady pile.* ADJ QUALIT

unstructured /ʌnstrʌktʃəd/. If an activity is **unstructured**, it is not organized in a complete or detailed way. EG *...an unstructured but effective method of education.* ADJ QUALIT

unstuck /ʌnstʌk/. **1** If something **comes unstuck**, it becomes separated from something else that it PHRASE

was attached to. EG *Some of the posters regularly came unstuck.*
2 If a plan or system **comes unstuck**, it fails. EG *The system is not so likely to come unstuck in a small organization.* PHRASE Informal
3 If someone **comes unstuck**, they fail badly in something that they are trying to achieve. EG *I always knew he'd come unstuck somewhere.* PHRASE Informal

unsubstantiated /ʌnsəbstænʃieɪtɪ²d/. A statement or story that is **unsubstantiated** has not been proved to be true. EG *There have been many unsubstantiated reports of gas used in war zones.* ADJ CLASSIF

unsuccessful /ʌnsʌksɛsfʊl/. If you are **unsuccessful**, you do not succeed in what you are trying to do. EG *Tom tried to hypnotize me but he was unsuccessful... ...an unsuccessful farmer... ...an unsuccessful attempt to kill him.* ◊ **unsuccessfully**. EG *I tried unsuccessfully to talk to him.* ADJ QUALIT ◊ ADV

unsuitable /ʌnsuːtəbə⁰l/. Someone or something that is **unsuitable** has qualities that are not right or appropriate for a particular purpose. EG *...areas that are entirely unsuitable for agriculture.* ◊ **unsuitably**. EG *She was most unsuitably dressed.* ADJ QUALIT : OFT+*for* ◊ ADV

unsuited /ʌnsj⁰uːtɪ²d/. 1 Someone or something that is **unsuited** to a particular situation, place, or task, has qualities that are not right or appropriate for that situation, place, or task. EG *...vehicles that are clearly unsuited for use in the desert.* ADJ CLASSIF : USU+*to/for*
2 If two people, especially a man and a woman, are **unsuited** to each other, they have different personalities and interests, and so are unlikely to have a successful relationship. ADJ QUALIT : OFT+*to*

unsung /ʌnsʌŋ/. You use **unsung** to describe people who are not appreciated or praised, although you think they should be. EG *...research by heroic but unsung volunteers.* ADJ CLASSIF : USU ATTRIB Literary

unsure /ʌnʃʊə/. 1 If you are **unsure** of yourself, you lack confidence. EG *His demands made the boy nervous and unsure of himself.* ADJ QUALIT : OFT+*of*
2 If you are **unsure** about something, you feel uncertain about it or about what to do. EG *She took a step back, unsure of his reaction.* ADJ QUALIT : OFT+*about/of*

unsuspected /ʌnsəspɛktɪ²d/. If something is **unsuspected**, people are not aware of it. EG *As the project developed, unsuspected difficulties came to light.* ADJ CLASSIF

unsuspecting /ʌnsəspɛktɪŋ/. Someone who is **unsuspecting** is not at all aware of something that is happening or going to happen. EG *...a survey conducted on 763 unsuspecting male students... ...leopards pouncing on unsuspecting young baboons.* ADJ CLASSIF

unsympathetic /ʌnsɪmpəθɛtɪk/. Someone who is **unsympathetic** is unwilling to be friendly or helpful to a person who needs help or sympathy. EG *Posy had been utterly unsympathetic when she heard about it... ...a terse and unsympathetic reply.* ADJ QUALIT

untangle /ʌntæŋgə⁰l/, **untangles, untangling, untangled.** If you **untangle** something such as string that is twisted together, you undo the knots in it. EG *He untangled the cable carefully.* V+O

untapped /ʌntæpt/. An **untapped** supply or source of something has not yet been used. EG *...Britain's vast untapped reserves of coal... ...an abundant and largely untapped water source.* ADJ CLASSIF

untenable /ʌntɛnəbə⁰l/. An argument, theory, or position that is **untenable** cannot be defended successfully against criticism or attack. EG *His position is morally untenable.* ADJ CLASSIF Formal

unthinkable /ʌnθɪŋkəbə⁰l/. If you describe something as **unthinkable**, you mean that it is so shocking or awful that you cannot imagine it happening or being true. EG *War was unthinkable... I can't marry again so soon after Guy's death, it's unthinkable... It was unthinkable to defy his authority.* ADJ CLASSIF : USU PRED

unthinking /ʌnθɪŋkɪŋ/. Someone who is **unthinking** does not think carefully about the effects of their behaviour and therefore does foolish things. EG *Our society seems to be rushing ahead, unthinking, into ever greater mechanisation.* ADJ QUALIT

untidy /ʌntaɪdi¹/, **untidier, untidiest.** 1 Something that is **untidy** is messy and disordered and not neat or well arranged. EG *It's a neglected, untidy park... The living-room was untidier than usual.* ADJ QUALIT
2 Someone who is **untidy** leaves things in an untidy state. EG *She is so careless and untidy.* ADJ QUALIT

untie /ʌntaɪ/, **unties, untying, untied.** If you **untie** someone or something, you remove the string or rope that has been tied round them by undoing the knots. EG *He quickly untied the captives... She tried to untie the knot.* V+O

untied /ʌntaɪd/. Something such as a tie, shoelace, or ribbon that is **untied** has its ends loose rather than tied together in a bow or knot. ADJ CLASSIF

until /ʌntɪl/. 1 If something happens **until** a particular time, it happens before that time and stops at that time. EG *We went on duty at six in the evening and worked until 2 a.m... You can get free prescriptions until you are 16.* PREP OR CONJ
2 If something does not happen **until** a particular time, it does not happen before that time and only happens after it. EG *They didn't find her until the next day... Women did not gain the vote until after the First World War.* PREP OR CONJ : WITH BROAD NEG

unto /ʌntu:/ means the same as to. EG *Do unto others as you would have them do unto you.* PREP Outdated

untold /ʌntəʊld/. You use **untold** to emphasize how great something is, especially something unpleasant. EG *The war brought untold suffering upon the population... It cost them untold millions of dollars... That idea did untold damage.* ADJ CLASSIF : ATTRIB Formal

untouched /ʌntʌtʃt/. 1 Something that is **untouched** has not been changed, moved, or damaged in any way. EG *The island has been untouched by tourism... ...an original Norman chapel untouched since the twelfth century.* ADJ CLASSIF
2 If a meal is **untouched**, none of it has been eaten. EG *She sent back her breakfast tray untouched.* ADJ CLASSIF

untoward /ʌntə⁰wɔːd/. You use **untoward** to describe something that happens unexpectedly and causes difficulties. EG *Nothing untoward had happened... Should any untoward side-effects occur, consult a doctor.* ADJ CLASSIF Formal

untrained /ʌntreɪnd/. 1 Someone who is **untrained** has had no education in the skills that they need for a particular job or activity. EG *We do not expect untrained people to accept risky occupations... ...untrained assistants.* ADJ CLASSIF
2 An **untrained** voice or mind has not been developed through formal education or training. EG *He had a deep, untrained voice.* ADJ CLASSIF

untreated /ʌntriːtɪ²d/. 1 If an injury or illness is left **untreated**, it is not given medical treatment. EG *...a period of time during which a brain tumour remained untreated.* ADJ CLASSIF
2 Harmful materials or chemicals that are **untreated** have not been made safe. EG *Our rivers have been poisoned by untreated effluent.* ADJ CLASSIF

untried /ʌntraɪd/. Something that is **untried** has not yet been used, done, or tested. EG *It is still an untried policy.* ADJ CLASSIF

untroubled /ʌntrʌbə⁰ld/. If you are **untroubled** by something, you are not affected or worried by it. EG *...nations that were untroubled by the presence of terrorists on their streets.* ADJ PRED+*by*

untrue /ʌntruː/. 1 Something that is **untrue** is not true. EG *The story was probably untrue.* ADJ CLASSIF
2 If someone is **untrue** to you, they are unfaithful to you or lie to you. ADJ PRED+*to* Literary

untrustworthy /ʌntrʌstwɜːði¹/. Someone who is **untrustworthy** is unreliable and cannot be trust- ADJ QUALIT

Is an unsubstantiated story untrue?

ed. EG *He has proved himself completely untrustworthy.*

untruth /ʌntru:θ/, **untruths** /ʌntru:ðz/. An **untruth** is a lie. EG *I hesitated rather than tell a deliberate untruth.* N COUNT Formal

untruthful /ʌntru:θfʊl/. Someone who is **untruthful** is dishonest and says things that are not true. EG *He was being untruthful when he claimed that he had never seen her before.* ADJ QUALIT Formal

untutored /ʌntju:təd/. Someone who is **untutored** in a particular area of knowledge has not learnt about it from other people or from books. EG *...the natural ease that some untutored men bring to horse-racing.* ADJ CLASSIF Formal

unusable /ʌnju:zəbəᵊl/. Something that is **unusable** is not in a good enough state or condition to be used. EG *The living room was unusable.* ADJ CLASSIF

unused; pronounced /ʌnju:zd/ in paragraph 1 and /ʌnju:st/ in paragraph 2.

1 Something that is **unused** has not been used. EG *...a pile of unused fuel.* ADJ CLASSIF

2 If you are **unused** to something, you have not often done it or experienced it, so it is unfamiliar to you. EG *She was unused to hardship.* ADJ PRED+*to*

unusual /ʌnju:ʒʊᵊəl/. If something is **unusual**, it does not happen very often or you do not see it or hear it very often. EG *He had an unusual name... It was not unusual for me to come home at two or three in the morning.* ADJ QUALIT

unusually /ʌnju:ʒʊᵊəli[1]/. You use **unusually 1** to emphasize that something is bigger than usual or has more of a particular quality than usual. EG *...a clump of weed that seemed unusually large... October has been unusually wet and cold.* SUBMOD **2** to say that something you are describing is not what normally happens. EG *The service charge, unusually, is 10 per cent.* ADV SEN

unveil /ʌnveɪl/, **unveils, unveiling, unveiled. 1** When someone **unveils** something such as a new statue or painting, they draw back a curtain which is covering it, in a special ceremony. V+O

2 If you **unveil** something that has been a secret, you make it known. EG *The plan was unveiled with approval from the Minister.* V+O Formal

unwanted /ʌnwɒntɪ[2]d/. You say that something is **unwanted** when a particular person does not want it, or when nobody wants it. EG *...the appalling suffering caused by unwanted pregnancies... She was starting to feel unwanted.* ADJ CLASSIF

unwarranted /ʌnwɒrəntɪ[2]d/. Something that is **unwarranted** is not justified or not deserved. EG *It was a totally unwarranted waste of public money... He saw himself as the victim of unwarranted attacks... This concern proved unwarranted.* ADJ CLASSIF Formal

unwary /ʌnweəri[1]/. Someone who is **unwary** is not cautious, and is therefore likely to be harmed or deceived. EG *...the shrieks of unwary animals taken by surprise.* ADJ QUALIT

unwelcome /ʌnwelkəᵊm/. **1** An **unwelcome** experience is one that you do not like and did not want. EG *The move from London was entirely unwelcome to her... ...unwelcome publicity.* ADJ QUALIT

2 You say that a visitor is **unwelcome** when you did not want them to come. EG *...an unwelcome guest.* ADJ QUALIT

unwell /ʌnwel/. If you are **unwell**, you are ill. EG *I informed her that I was unwell and could not come... He complained of feeling unwell.* ADJ PRED

unwieldy /ʌnwi:ldi[1]/. **1** An **unwieldy** object is difficult to move or carry because it is big or heavy. EG *We set about the task of towing the unwieldy structure into the shelter.* ADJ QUALIT

2 A system that is **unwieldy** does not work well because it is too large or is badly organized. EG *...the country's unwieldy banking system.* ADJ QUALIT

unwilling /ʌnwɪlɪŋ/. If you are **unwilling** to do something, you do not want to do it. EG *He's unwilling to accept advice.* ADJ QUALIT: OFT+*to*-INF ◇ **unwillingly**. EG *He submitted unwillingly to his mother.* ◇ ADV ◇ **unwillingness**. EG *...their unwillingness to discuss common problems.* ◇ N UNCOUNT

unwind /ʌnwaɪnd/, **unwinds, unwinding, unwound. 1** When you **unwind**, you relax, especially after working hard. EG *Reading is a good way to unwind.* V

2 If you **unwind** something that is wrapped round something else or that is wound in a ball, you undo it or straighten it out. EG *Francis was unwinding his bandage.* V+O

unwise /ʌnwaɪz/. Something that is **unwise** is foolish. EG *It would be very unwise for the boy to marry her... It was an unwise choice.* ADJ QUALIT: OFT PRED

unwitting /ʌnwɪtɪŋ/ is used to describe people or their actions when they do something or become involved in something without realizing what is really happening. EG *I became the unwitting instrument of that unscrupulous man.* ADJ CLASSIF: ATTRIB Formal ◇ **unwittingly**. EG *Sometimes we ourselves unwittingly invite trouble.* ◇ ADV

unworkable /ʌnwɜ:kəbəᵊl/. If you say that an idea or plan is **unworkable**, you mean that it cannot be made to work. EG *His proposals for reform of the Trades Unions are unworkable.* ADJ CLASSIF

unworldly /ʌnwɜ:ldli[1]/. Someone who is **unworldly** is not interested in having a lot of money or possessions. ADJ QUALIT Formal

unworthy /ʌnwɜ:ði[1]/. If someone is **unworthy** of something, they do not deserve it. EG *I am unworthy of this honour... I felt I was unworthy of her love.* ADJ QUALIT: OFT+*of* Formal

unwrap /ʌnræp/, **unwraps, unwrapping, unwrapped.** When you **unwrap** something, you take off the paper or other covering that is around it. EG *I started to unwrap my sandwiches... Ellen carefully unwrapped the parcel.* V+O

unwritten /ʌnrɪtəᵊn/. **Unwritten** things have not been printed or written down. EG *Thoughts of my unwritten novel nagged me... ...unwritten laws.* ADJ CLASSIF: USU ATTRIB

unzip /ʌnzɪp/, **unzips, unzipping, unzipped.** When you **unzip** something which is fastened by a zip, you unfasten it. EG *He unzipped his anorak.* V+O

up /ʌp/, **ups, upping, upped. 1 Up** is used in phrasal verbs such as 'get up' and 'add up'.

2 Up means towards a higher place, or in a higher place. EG *I carried my suitcase up the stairs behind her... Bill put up his hand... ...comfortable houses up in the hills.* PREP, OR ADV AFTER VB

3 If someone stands **up**, they move so that they are standing. EG *She scrambled up from the floor... She helped Henry up from the bench.* ADV AFTER VB

4 Up also means in the north or towards the north. EG *Why did you come up to Edinburgh?... We're having brilliant sunshine up here.* ADV+ADV/PREP

5 If you go **up** a road or river, you go along it. EG *...a voyage up the Nile... There's a cafe just a hundred yards further up.* PREP OR ADV

6 You also use **up** to show that something is close to something else. EG *It's only when you get right up to them that you realise what they are... Ferdinand ran up to his father-in-law.* ADV+ADV/PREP

7 If you move **up and down**, you move repeatedly in one direction and then in the opposite direction. EG *I was so happy I jumped up and down... He started pacing up and down the office.* PHRASE

8 If you have **ups and downs**, you experience a mixture of good things and bad things. EG *We have had our ups and downs.* PHRASE

9 If you are **up**, you are not in bed. EG *They were up early... He has been up half the night.* ADJ PRED

10 If someone or something is **up** for election, review, or examination, they are about to be considered or judged. EG *One of my colleagues comes up for election next week.* ADV+PREP

11 If a period of time is **up**, it has come to an end. EG *When the six weeks were up, everybody was sad that she had to leave.* ADJ PRED

12 You say that a road is **up** when it is being repaired. ADJ PRED

13 If a number or an amount goes **up**, it increases. ADV AFTER VB
EG *...when interest rates go up.*

14 You use **up to** to say how large something can be or what level it has reached. EG *They might be up to a metre wide... Our total energy consumption is now up to about 40% and still rising... The work isn't up to the standard I require.* PREP

15 If you feel **up to** doing something, you are well enough to do it. EG *Are you up to doing some work?* PREP : OFT + -ING

16 If you say that someone is **up to** something, you mean that they are secretly doing something that they should not be doing. EG *The neighbours think the Hochstadts are up to something.* PREP Informal

17 If you say that it is **up to** someone to do something, you mean that it is their responsibility to do it. EG *It is up to the teacher not to accept shoddy work.* PREP

18 If something happens **up to** or **up until** a particular time, it happens until that time. EG *Up until the early sixties there was no shortage.* PREP

19 If you say that something is **not up to much**, you mean that it is of poor quality. EG *The dances weren't up to much.* PHRASE Informal

20 If you are **up against** something, you have a very difficult situation or problem to deal with. EG *They are up against the slowness of the system.* PREP

21 If you say that something **is up**, you mean that something is wrong or that something worrying is happening. EG *I know something's up... What's up, Myra? You look sad.* PHRASE Informal

22 If you **up** an amount of money, you increase it. EG *They upped the cost to the public.* V+O Informal

up-and-coming. **Up-and-coming** people are likely to be successful in the future. EG *...up-and-coming Third World Exporters.* ADJ CLASSIF

upbringing /ʌpbrɪŋɪŋ/. Your **upbringing** is the way your parents treat you and the things that they teach you. EG *Tony never rebelled against his upbringing... ...a strict upbringing.* N UNCOUNT : OFT+SUPP

update /ʌpdeɪt/, **updates, updating, updated.** If you **update** something, you make it more modern, usually by adding newer parts to it. EG *The information will need updating from time to time... ...regularly updated criminal records.* V+O

upend /ʌpɛnd/, **upends, upending, upended.** If something **is upended**, it is turned upside down. EG *There the car stood, upended in the grass.* V+O : USU PASS

upgrade /ʌpgreɪd/, **upgrades, upgrading, upgraded.** If you **upgrade** something such as a person's job or status, you change it, so that the person becomes more important or receives more money. EG *We need to upgrade the pay and status of doctors.* V+O

upheaval /ʌphiːvəˀl/, **upheavals.** An **upheaval** is a big change which causes a lot of trouble, confusion, and worry. EG *Great upheavals were taking place in the States... They have brought social upheaval and conflict into the country.* N COUNT OR N UNCOUNT

upheld /ʌphɛld/ is the past tense and past participle of **uphold**.

uphill /ʌphɪl/. **1** If you go **uphill**, you go up a slope. EG *She ran furiously uphill... ...the effort of pushing the cart uphill.* ADV OR ADJ CLASSIF : ATTRIB

2 An **uphill** task requires a great deal of effort and determination. EG *This is hard, uphill work.* ADJ CLASSIF : ATTRIB

uphold /ʌphəʊld/, **upholds, upholding, upheld** /ʌphɛld/. If you **uphold** something such as a law, a principle, or a decision, you support and maintain it. EG *He had sworn to uphold the law... His conviction was upheld on appeal.* V+O

upholstered /ʌphɒlstəd/. **Upholstered** chairs and sofas have a soft covering that makes them comfortable to sit on. EG *...two handsome chairs, upholstered in black leather.* ADJ CLASSIF

upholstery /ʌphəʊlstəˀriˈ/ is the soft covering on chairs and sofas that makes them more comfortable to sit on. N UNCOUNT

upkeep /ʌpkiːp/. The **upkeep** of a building is the continual process of keeping it in good condition. EG *We have to pay for the upkeep of the chapel.* N UNCOUNT : USU+*of*

upland /ʌpləˀnd/, **uplands. 1 Upland** places are situated on high hills, plateaus, or mountains. EG *They move with their flocks to upland pastures.* ADJ CLASSIF : ATTRIB

2 Uplands are areas of land on high hills, plateaus, or mountains. EG *...the chalk uplands of Wiltshire.* N PLURAL

uplifted /ʌplɪftɪˀd/. If people's faces or arms are **uplifted**, they are pointing them upwards or are holding them in a high position. EG *We could just see him, a tiny silhouette with uplifted arms.* ADJ CLASSIF Literary

uplifting /ʌplɪftɪŋ/. You describe something as **uplifting** when it makes you feel very cheerful and happy. EG *My experience of love has hardly been uplifting... ...uplifting literature.* ADJ QUALIT

upmarket /ʌpmɑːkɪt/. **Upmarket** places and goods are visited or bought by people who have sophisticated and expensive tastes. EG *Paleo is an upmarket resort... ...upmarket shops.* ADJ QUALIT Informal

upon /əpɒn/. **1 Upon** is used in phrasal verbs such as 'come upon' and 'look upon', and after some other verbs such as 'decide' and 'depend'.

2 If one thing is **upon** another, it is on it. EG *She was sitting with a cat upon her knee... He lay down upon the grass... He had a furtive look upon his face.* PREP Formal

3 You use **upon** when mentioning an event that is followed immediately by another event. EG *Upon entering the cabin, she sat down.* PREP

4 You also use **upon** between two occurrences of the same noun in order to say that there are very large numbers of the thing referred to. EG *We drove through mile upon mile of brick villas... ...row upon row of red roofs.* PREP

5 If an event is **upon** you, it is just about to happen. EG *Suddenly the concert was upon us with me totally unprepared.* PREP

upper /ʌpə/, **uppers. 1 Upper** describes **1.1** something that is above something else, usually the top one of a pair of things. EG *I pulled down a book from an upper shelf.* **1.2** the higher part of something. *Dark glasses masked the upper half of his face.* ADJ CLASSIF : ATTRIB

2 If you have **the upper hand** in a situation, you have more power than the other people involved and can make decisions about what happens. EG *The farmers had got the upper hand now.* PHRASE

3 The **upper** of a shoe is the top part of it, which is attached to the sole and the heel. EG *A lot of shoes now have nylon uppers.* N COUNT

upper class, upper classes. The **upper classes** are the people who belong to the social class above the middle class. EG *The upper classes still send their children to Eton or Harrow... ...upper-class families.* N COUNT : OFT PLURAL

upper lip, upper lips. Your **upper lip** is the part of your face between your mouth and your nose. EG *His chin and upper lip were clean shaven.* • to **keep a stiff upper lip**: see **lip**. N COUNT : USU SING

uppermost /ʌpəməʊst/. **1** You say that something is **uppermost** when it is higher than the rest of something or when it is the highest one of a group of things. EG *He was pointing with the whole of his hand, thumb uppermost... He gently examined the uppermost leaves.* ADJ CLASSIF OR ADV

2 If something is **uppermost** in a particular situation, it is the most important thing in that situation. EG *Political motives were uppermost... There were two thoughts uppermost in my mind.* ADJ PRED

upright /ʌpraɪt/. **1** If you are **upright**, you are sitting or standing with your back straight, rather than bending or lying down. EG *I cannot stand upright any more... He sat bolt upright.* ADJ CLASSIF OR ADV AFTER VB

2 An **upright** vacuum cleaner or freezer stands ADJ CLASSIF

Is up-to-the-minute information up-to-date?

vertically and is taller than it is wide. EG *...a small upright model light enough to carry upstairs.*

3 An **upright** chair has a straight back and no arms. ADJ CLASSIF

4 You can describe people as **upright** when they are careful to follow acceptable rules of behaviour and behave in a moral way. EG *...the upright and respectable Charles Smithson.* ADJ QUALIT

uprising /ʌpraɪzɪŋ/, **uprisings.** When there is an **uprising**, a group of people start fighting against the people who are in power in their country, usually because they want to bring about a political change. EG *...the Sepoy uprising of 1857.* N COUNT

uproar /ʌprɔː/. **1** If there is **uproar**, there is a lot of shouting and noise because people are very angry or shocked about something. EG *Soon all was uproar... She could hear the uproar in the prisoners' coaches.* N SING OR N UNCOUNT

2 You can also use **uproar** to refer to a lot of public criticism and debate about something. EG *The Parisian intellectuals were in an uproar.* N SING OR N UNCOUNT

uproarious /ʌprɔːrɪəs/. **Uproarious** laughter is very noisy. EG *...an uproarious burst of laughter.* ADJ CLASSIF Literary

◇ **uproariously.** EG *He laughed uproariously.* ◇ ADV

uproot /ʌpruːt/, **uproots, uprooting, uprooted. 1** If you **uproot** yourself or if you **are uprooted**, you leave, or are made to leave, a place where you have lived for a long time. EG *People were uprooted and rehoused.* V-REFL; ALSO V+O : USU PASS

2 If someone **uproots** a tree or if the wind **uproots** it, it is pulled out of the ground. EG *Windows were smashed and large trees uprooted.* V+O

upset, upsets, upsetting. The form **upset** is used in the present tense and is the past tense and past participle of the verb. **Upset** is pronounced /ʌpset/ when it is an adjective in predicative position or a verb, and /ʌpset/ when it is an adjective in attributive position or a noun.

1 If you are **upset**, you are unhappy or disappointed because something unpleasant has happened to you. EG *I'm dreadfully upset about it all... They were upset by the poverty they saw in Dublin.* ADJ PRED

2 If something **upsets** you, it makes you feel worried or unhappy. EG *I didn't mean to upset you.* V+O

◇ **upsetting.** EG *It was a very upsetting experience.* ◇ ADJ QUALIT

3 If you **upset** something such as a procedure or a state of affairs, you cause it to go wrong. EG *Davis's death has upset the routine.* V+O

4 To **upset** something also means to turn it over accidentally. EG *He almost upset the canoe.* V+O

5 If your stomach is **upset**, you have a slight illness in your stomach caused by an infection or by something that you have eaten. EG *I've got an upset stomach.* ADJ QUALIT

6 A stomach **upset** is a slight illness in your stomach caused by an infection or by something that you have eaten. N COUNT

upshot /ʌpʃɒt/. The **upshot** of a series of events or discussions is the final result. EG *The upshot was that the agreement had to be re-negotiated.* N SING : the+N, OFT+of Formal

upside down. 1 If something is **upside down**, it has been turned round so that the part that is usually lowest is above the part that is usually highest. EG *They were hanging upside down... You are holding it upside down.* ADJ PRED OR ADV AFTER VB

2 If you turn a place **upside down**, you create disorder or untidiness in it. EG *I've turned the house upside down, but I still can't find his watch.* ADV AFTER VB

upstage /ʌpsteɪdʒ/, **upstages, upstaging, upstaged.** If you **upstage** someone, you take people's attention away from them by making them watch or listen to you instead. EG *He seems to be attempting to upstage the Prime Minister.* V+O

upstairs /ʌpsteəz/. **1** If you go **upstairs** in a building, you go up towards a higher floor, usually by a staircase. EG *I ran back upstairs.* ADV AFTER VB

2 If something or someone is **upstairs** in a building, they are on an upper floor. EG *Upstairs, there were three little bedrooms.* ADV

3 The **upstairs** of a building is its upper floor or floors. EG *They had to rent out the upstairs to make the mortgage payments.* N SING Informal

4 An **upstairs** room or object is one which is situated on an upper floor of a building. EG *Neighbours watched from their upstairs windows.* ADJ CLASSIF : ATTRIB

upstart /ʌpstɑːt/, **upstarts.** You refer to someone as an **upstart** when they behave as if they are important, but you think that they are too new in a place or job to be treated as important. EG *He regarded me as a young upstart.* N COUNT

upstream /ʌpstriːm/. **1** If something moves **upstream**, it moves along a river towards the source of the river. EG *He was making his way upstream.* ADV AFTER VB

2 If something is **upstream** from a place, it is on the same river but further towards the river's source. EG *...the chemical plant upstream.* ADJ PRED

upsurge /ʌpsɜːdʒ/. If there is an **upsurge** in something, there is a sudden, large increase in it. EG *...a massive upsurge of social unrest.* N SING : USU+SUPP Formal

uptake /ʌpteɪk/. You say that someone is **quick on the uptake** when they understand things quickly. You say that someone is **slow on the uptake** when they have difficulty understanding simple or obvious things. EG *She was not very quick on the uptake.* PHRASE Informal

uptight /ʌptaɪt/. You say that someone is **uptight** when they are nervous or annoyed about something but are not saying so directly. EG *You get so uptight whenever I raise the subject.* ADJ QUALIT Informal

up-to-date. 1 If something is **up-to-date**, it is the newest thing of its kind. EG *...a fleet of up-to-date lorries... The industry is modern and up-to-date.* ADJ QUALIT

2 If you are **up-to-date** about something, you have the latest information about it. EG *Tony was more up-to-date than I.* ADJ QUALIT

up-to-the-minute. Up-to-the-minute information is the latest information that you can get about something. EG *...up-to-the-minute news.* ADJ CLASSIF

uptown /ʌptaʊn/. If you go **uptown**, you go away from the centre of a town or city towards one of its outer parts. EG *He walked uptown... She met him at his apartment uptown.* ADV AFTER VB, OR ADJ CLASSIF American

upturn /ʌptɜːn/, **upturns.** If there is an **upturn** in something such as a country's economy, it starts to improve. EG *The economy is experiencing an upturn.* N COUNT : USU SING

upturned /ʌptɜːnd/. Something that is **upturned** **1** points upwards. EG *She had a small upturned nose.* **2** is upside down. EG *She sat on an upturned bucket.* ADJ CLASSIF

upwards /ʌpwədz/; also **upward. 1** If something moves or looks **upwards** or **upward**, it moves or looks up towards a higher place. EG *He happened to look upwards.* ADV AFTER VB

2 An **upward** movement or look is directed towards a higher place. EG *He would steal upward glances at the clock.* ADJ CLASSIF : ATTRIB

3 Upwards or **upward** is used to say that something rises to a higher level or point on a scale. EG *The world urban population is rocketing upward at a rate of 6.5 per cent per year.* ADV AFTER VB

4 Upwards of or **upward of** a particular number means more than that number. EG *The cyclone killed upwards of 200,000 people.* PREP

uranium /jʊreɪnɪəm/ is a radioactive metal that is used to produce nuclear energy and weapons. N UNCOUNT

urban /ɜːbən/ means belonging to or relating to a town or city. EG *...urban unemployment.* ADJ CLASSIF : ATTRIB

urbane /ɜːbeɪn/. Someone who is **urbane** is well-mannered, relaxed, and appears comfortable in social situations. EG *He was composed, urbane, and affable... The professor was an urbane little man.* ADJ QUALIT Formal

urbanize /ɜːbənaɪz/, **urbanizes, urbanizing, urbanized;** also spelled **urbanise.** If a country area **is urbanized**, it is made more like a town, with more buildings, industry, and business. EG *...highly urbanized and industrialized areas.* V+O : USU PASS

◇ **urbanization** /ɜːbənaɪzeɪʃəⁿn/. EG *...the urbanization of farmland.* ◇ N UNCOUNT

urchin /ɜ:tʃɪn/, **urchins.** You can refer to a young child who is very poor, has no home or family, and lives in a town or city as an **urchin**. N COUNT Outdated

urge /ɜ:dʒ/, **urges, urging, urged. 1** If you have an **urge** to do something or to have something, you strongly want to do it or to have it, often without being able to explain why. EG *They have a strong urge to communicate... ...our insane urge for greater and greater material wealth.* N COUNT : USU + *to*-INF

2 If you **urge** someone to do something, you try hard to persuade them to do it. EG *I urged him to take a year off to study drawing... 'At least stay for Christmas,' Pam urged.* V+O+*to*-INF OR QUOTE; ALSO V+REPORT : ONLY *that*

3 If you **urge** a course of action, you strongly advise that it should be taken. EG *US officials urged restraint.* V+O Formal

urgent /ɜ:dʒənt/. **1** Something that is **urgent** needs to be dealt with as soon as possible. EG *Most of the motorway network is in urgent need of repair... ...urgent messages.* ◇ **urgently**. EG *Improved health and education are urgently needed.* ◇ **urgency** /ɜ:dʒənsi^{1}/. EG *...matters of the greatest urgency.* ADJ QUALIT; ◇ ADV; ◇ N UNCOUNT

2 If you say something in an **urgent** way, you indicate that you are very anxious for people to notice something or do something. EG *She spoke to him in a low and urgent voice.* ◇ **urgently**. EG *'Do you see it?' he demanded urgently.* ◇ **urgency**. EG *There was a note of urgency in his voice.* ADJ QUALIT; ◇ ADV; ◇ N UNCOUNT

urinal /jʊraɪnə^{0}l, jʊərɪnə^{0}l/, **urinals.** A **urinal** is a bowl or trough fixed to the wall of men's public lavatories for men to urinate in. N COUNT

urinate /jʊərɪneɪt/, **urinates, urinating, urinated.** When you **urinate**, you get rid of urine from your body. V Formal

urine /jʊərɪn/ is the liquid that you get rid of from your body when you go to the toilet. N UNCOUNT

urn /ɜ:n/, **urns. 1** An **urn** is a decorated container with handles and a lid that is used to hold the ashes of a person who has been cremated. N COUNT

2 A tea or coffee **urn** is a large container used for making a large quantity of tea or coffee and for keeping it warm. N COUNT

us /ʌs, əs/ is used as the object of a verb or preposition. **1** A speaker or writer uses **us** to refer both to himself or herself and to one or more other people as a group. See **we**. EG *Why didn't you tell us?... There wasn't room for us all.* PRON : PLURAL

2 A speaker sometimes says **us** instead of 'me'. EG *Give us a chance.* PRON Informal

US /ju: ɛs/ is an abbreviation for 'United States'. EG *...a brief visit to the US... ...the US army.* N PROPER : *the*+N

USA /ju: ɛs eɪ/ is an abbreviation for 'United States of America'. N PROPER : *the*+N

usable /ju:zəbə^{0}l/. If something is **usable**, it is in a state or condition which makes it possible to use it. EG *He told me which wells were usable along the road... ...the least usable land areas in Africa.* ADJ CLASSIF

usage /ju:sɪdʒ, -zɪdʒ/, **usages. 1 Usage** is the way in which words are actually used in particular contexts, especially with regard to their meanings. EG *...a guide to English usage... Today the word has virtually dropped out of usage.* N UNCOUNT

2 A **usage** is a particular meaning that a word has or a particular way in which it can be used. EG *It's a curious usage, isn't it?* N COUNT

3 Usage is also the degree to which something is used or the way in which it is used. EG *...the environmental effects of energy usage.* N UNCOUNT

use, uses, using, used; pronounced /ju:z/ when it is a verb and /ju:s/ when it is a noun.

1 If you **use** something, you do something with it in order to do a job or to achieve something. EG *Use pins to keep it in place... He wants to use the phone... Wash this garment using a mild detergent... Use your imagination... No violence was used.* V+O

2 If you **use** a particular word or expression, you say or write it, because it has the meaning that you want to express. EG *It's a phrase I once heard him use in a sermon.* V+O

3 If you **use** people, you make them do things for you, without caring about them. EG *For the first time he felt used.* V+O

4 If you **make use of** something, you do something with it in order to do a job or to achieve something. EG *Industry is making increasing use of robots.* PHRASE

5 The **use** of something is the act or fact of using it. EG *...the large-scale use of fertilisers and insecticides... ...a pamphlet for use in schools.* N UNCOUNT : USU+POSS

6 If a device, machine, or technique is **in use**, it is being used regularly by people. If it has gone **out of use**, it is no longer used regularly by people. EG *Within the next decade industrial robots will be in widespread use.* PHRASE

7 If you have the **use** of something, you have the ability or the permission to use it. EG *He lost the use of his legs.* N SING : *the*+N+*of*

8 If something has a **use** or if you have a **use** for it, there is a purpose for which it can be used. EG *Possibly I could find some use for these drawers.* N COUNT OR N UNCOUNT

9 If something is **of use**, it is useful. If it is **no use**, it is not at all useful. EG *She kept in touch with friends who would be of use in later life... I don't know whether any of these things will be any use to you.* PHRASE

10 You say **it's no use** doing something or **what's the use** of doing something as a way of saying that the action is pointless and will not achieve anything. EG *It is no use arguing with you... There's no use having regrets... What is the use of sitting and waiting for success to come?* PHRASE

11 A **use** of a word is a particular meaning that it has or a particular way in which it is used. N COUNT+SUPP

use up. If you **use up** a supply of something, you finish it so that none of it is left. EG *He used up all the coins he had.* PHRASAL VB : V+O+ADV

used; pronounced /ju:st/ in paragraphs 1, 2, and 3, and /ju:zd/ in paragraphs 4 and 5.

1 If something **used** to be done or **used** to be true, it was done regularly in the past or was true in the past. EG *The two children used to send me a card at Christmas time... I used to be very mean.* SEMI-MODAL +*to*-INF

2 If you **are used to** something, you are familiar with it because you have done or seen it often. EG *San Diego was not used to such demonstrations... We are used to working together.* PHRASE

3 If you **get used to** something, you become familiar with it. EG *After a few days, I got used to it all... I was beginning to get used to the old iron bed.* PHRASE

4 A **used** handkerchief, towel, or glass is dirty because it has been used. ADJ CLASSIF : ATTRIB

5 A **used** car is no longer new but has already had an owner. ADJ CLASSIF : ATTRIB

useful /ju:sfʊl/. **1** If something is **useful**, you can use it in order to do something or to help you in some way. EG *She gave us some useful information.* ◇ **usefulness**. EG *...the usefulness of the computer.* ADJ QUALIT; ◇ N UNCOUNT

2 If you are being **useful**, you are doing things that help other people. EG *Make yourself useful and fry up some bacon.* ◇ **usefully**. EG *His time could be more usefully spent.* ADJ CLASSIF : USU PRED; ◇ ADV

3 When a possession or a skill **comes in useful**, you are able to use it on a particular occasion. EG *This is where your sketch comes in useful.* PHRASE Informal

useless /ju:slɪ^{2}s/. **1** If something is **useless**, you cannot use it. EG *Land is useless without labour.* ADJ CLASSIF

2 If a course of action is **useless**, it does not achieve anything helpful. EG *I realized it was useless to pursue the subject... She underwent some twenty useless operations.* ADJ CLASSIF

3 If you describe someone or something as **useless**, you mean that they are no good at all. EG *I was always useless at maths.* ADJ QUALIT Informal

How many uses of the word 'useless' are explained in this dictionary?

user /ju:zə/, **users.** The **users** of a product, machine, service, or place are the people who use it. EG *...vehicle users... ...electricity users.* N COUNT+SUPP

usher /ʌʃə/, **ushers, ushering, ushered.** **1** If you **usher** someone somewhere, you show them where they should go, often politely letting them go in front of you. EG *The hostess ushered me into the room... I was ushered into the study.* V+O+A

2 An **usher** is a person who shows people where to sit, for example at a wedding or a concert. N COUNT

usherette /ʌʃərɛt/, **usherettes.** An **usherette** is a woman who shows people where to sit in a cinema or theatre and who sells refreshments or programmes. N COUNT

USSR /ju: ɛs ɛs ɑ:/ is an abbreviation for 'Union of Soviet Socialist Republics'. N PROPER: *the*+N

> **USU** stands for **usually**
> Words which have the label USU in the Extra Column are usually used in the way mentioned. For example, N COUNT: USU SING means that the noun is usually used in the singular, although you will occasionally find it used in the plural.

usual /ju:ʒʊ⁰əl/. **1** **Usual** is used to describe the thing that happens most often, or that is done or used most often, in a particular situation. EG *He asked the usual questions... He sat in his usual chair... She got up earlier than usual.* ADJ CLASSIF

2 If you do something **as usual**, you do it in the way that you normally do it. EG *As usual, he spent the night at home... He was dressed in a suit and tie, as usual... She had to try and carry on as usual.* PHRASE

3 You also use **as usual** to say that you are describing something that often happens or is often the case. EG *The telephone box on the corner is broken, as usual.* PHRASE

usually /ju:ʒʊ⁰əli¹/. **1** If something **usually** happens, it is the thing that most often happens in a particular situation. EG *She usually found it easy to go to sleep at night.* ADV OR ADV SEN

2 You use **more than usually** to say that someone's behaviour shows even more of a particular quality than it normally does. EG *They had shown themselves to be more than usually gullible.* PHRASE

usurp /ju:zɜ:p/, **usurps, usurping, usurped.** If you **usurp** a job, role, title, or position, you take it from someone when you have no right to do so. EG *Their position of control enables them to usurp power and privilege.* V+O Formal

utensil /ju:tɛnsə⁰l/, **utensils. Utensils** are tools or objects that you use when you are cooking or doing other tasks in your home. EG *The kitchen had no cooker and no proper cooking utensils.* N COUNT: USU PLURAL +SUPP Formal

uterus /ju:tərəs/, **uteruses.** A woman's **uterus** is her womb. N COUNT Medical

utilise /ju:tɪlaɪz/. See **utilize**.

utilitarian /ju:tɪlɪtɛərɪən/. Something that is **utilitarian** **1** is intended to produce the greatest benefit for the greatest number of people. EG *He had not entered science for ambitious or utilitarian purposes.* ADJ CLASSIF Formal **2** is designed to be useful rather than beautiful. EG *We toured a number of clean, utilitarian flats.* ADJ QUALIT Formal

utility /ju:tɪlɪ¹ti¹/, **utilities.** **1** The **utility** of something is its usefulness. EG *...the utility and potential of computers.* N UNCOUNT

2 A **utility** is an important service such as water, electricity, or gas that is provided for everyone. EG *...the development of roads and public utilities in the area.* N COUNT

utilize /ju:tɪlaɪz/, **utilizes, utilizing, utilized;** also spelled **utilise.** If you **utilize** something, you use it. EG *He thought it impossible to utilize atomic energy.* V+O Formal ◇ **utilization** /ju:tɪlaɪzeɪʃə⁰n/. EG *...the utilization of things like wind energy and wave-power.* ◇ N UNCOUNT

utmost /ʌtməʊst/. **1** You use **utmost** to emphasize a particular quality that you are mentioning. EG *Learning is of the utmost importance... He had the utmost respect for his children.* ADJ CLASSIF: ATTRIB

2 If something is done to the **utmost**, it is done to the greatest extent, amount, or degree possible. EG *We will do our utmost to help these unfortunate people.* N SING: *the*/POSS+N

Utopia /ju:təʊpɪə/, **Utopias.** A **Utopia** is a perfect social system in which everyone is satisfied and happy. EG *Every so often someone invents a new Utopia.* N COUNT OR N UNCOUNT

utopian /ju:təʊpɪən/ is used to describe someone's idea of a perfect social system in which everyone is satisfied and happy. EG *...this utopian dream... ...utopian experiments... This may sound impossibly utopian.* ADJ CLASSIF

utter /ʌtə/, **utters, uttering, uttered.** **1** When you **utter** sounds or words, you say them. EG *Sam opened his mouth, then quickly shut it again without uttering a sound.* V+O

2 **Utter** also means complete or total. EG *To my utter amazement I was made managing director... Judith is a complete and utter fool.* ADJ CLASSIF: ATTRIB ◇ **utterly.** EG *I am utterly convinced of your loyalty... She was trying to look like a young lady but failing utterly.* ◇ SUBMOD OR ADV

utterance /ʌtə⁰rəns/, **utterances.** An **utterance** is something which is expressed in speech or in writing, such as a word or a sentence. EG *The children watched and copied every act and utterance of the older men.* N COUNT Formal

U-turn, U-turns. **1** When a vehicle does a **U-turn**, it turns through a half circle and starts to move in the opposite direction. N COUNT

2 When a government does a **U-turn**, it abandons a policy and starts to do something completely different. N COUNT

V v

V, v /viː/, **Vs, v's. 1 V** is the twenty-second letter of the English alphabet. N COUNT

2 v is used in writing to say that two people or two teams are competing against each other in a sporting event. **v** is an abbreviation for 'versus'. EG *...Arsenal v Liverpool.* PREP

> **V** stands for **intransitive verb**
> When V is used by itself in the Extra Column, it refers to an intransitive verb, which is a verb that does not have an object.
> See the entry headed VERBS for more information.

> **V+A** stands for **intransitive verb used with adjunct**
> Verbs which have the label V+A in the Extra Column are intransitive verbs which need an adjunct to complete their meaning.
> See the entry headed ADJUNCTS for more information about adjuncts. See the entry headed VERBS for more information about these verbs.

vacancy /veɪkənsi¹/, **vacancies. 1** A **vacancy** is a job which is not being done by anyone and which people can apply for. EG *...an unexpected vacancy in the Department.* N COUNT

2 If there are **vacancies** at a hotel or guest house, some of the rooms are not occupied and are available for people to stay in. N COUNT: USU PLURAL

vacant /veɪkənt/. **1** If something such as a room, a chair, or a toilet is **vacant**, it is not being used by anyone. EG *I sat down in a vacant chair.* ADJ CLASSIF

2 If a job is **vacant**, no one is doing it at present and people can apply for it. EG *They keep a list of all vacant jobs in the area.* ADJ CLASSIF

3 A **vacant** look or expression suggests that someone does not understand something or that they are not very intelligent. EG *She looked round her with a rather vacant expression.* ADJ QUALIT

vacate /vəkeɪt/, **vacates, vacating, vacated. 1** If you **vacate** a job, you make it available for other people by leaving it or giving it up. EG *I got the job Allister was vacating.* V+O

2 If you **vacate** something such as a room, seat, or parking space, you leave it and so make it available for someone else to use. EG *He ordered her to vacate her apartment... He drove neatly into the vacated space.* V+O

vacation /vəkeɪʃəⁿn/, **vacations.** A **vacation** is **1** a period of the year when universities or colleges are officially closed. EG *I've a lot of reading to do over the vacation... ...the summer vacation.* **2** a holiday. EG *Harold used to take a vacation at that time... She plans to go on vacation for most of August.* N COUNT; N COUNT OR N UNCOUNT American

vaccinate /væksɪneɪt/, **vaccinates, vaccinating, vaccinated.** If you **are vaccinated** against a disease, you are given an injection to prevent you from getting it. EG *Most of them were vaccinated against hepatitis.* ◊ **vaccination** /væksɪneɪʃəⁿn/, **vaccinations.** EG *...vaccination against smallpox.* V+O: USU PASS; ◊ N UNCOUNT OR N COUNT

vaccine /væksiːn/, **vaccines.** A **vaccine** is a substance made from the germs that cause a disease. Vaccines are injected into people to prevent them from getting the disease. EG *...the measles vaccine... ...polio vaccine.* N COUNT OR N UNCOUNT

vacillate /væsɪleɪt/, **vacillates, vacillating, vacillated.** If you **vacillate**, you keep changing your opinion or feelings, so that you cannot make a decision or people cannot rely on you. EG *He vacillated between periods of creative fever and nervous exhaustion... They are vacillating when the child needs firmness.* V: OFT + *between* Formal

vacuum /vækjuᵒəm/, **vacuums, vacuuming, vacuumed. 1** A **vacuum** is a space that contains no air or other gas, especially an enclosed space from which the air has been removed. N COUNT

2 If someone or something creates a **vacuum**, they leave a place or position in which they had an important role, so that the role needs to be filled by someone or something else. EG *Rival groups would seek to fill the power vacuum that the departing British would leave.* N COUNT: USU SING+SUPP

3 If you **vacuum** something, you clean it using a vacuum cleaner. EG *I'm going to vacuum the car.* V+O OR V

4 People sometimes refer to a vacuum cleaner as a **vacuum**. EG *I'll just turn off the vacuum.* N COUNT Informal

vacuum cleaner, vacuum cleaners. A **vacuum cleaner** is an electric machine which removes dust and dirt from carpets by sucking it up. N COUNT

vagina /vədʒaɪnə/, **vaginas.** A woman's **vagina** is the passage that connects her outer sex organs to her womb. N COUNT

vagrant /veɪgrənt/, **vagrants.** A **vagrant** is a person who has no home or money, and who lives by going from place to place and begging or stealing. ◊ **vagrancy** /veɪgrənsi¹/. EG *I don't want you to be arrested for vagrancy.* N COUNT; ◊ N UNCOUNT

vague /veɪg/, **vaguer, vaguest. 1** If something written or spoken is **vague**, it does not explain or express things clearly. EG *The terms of the agreement were left deliberately vague... ...vague instructions.* ◊ **vaguely**. EG *'What happened?' – 'Oh, a lot of things,' she said vaguely.* ADJ QUALIT; ◊ ADV

2 If you have a **vague** memory of something, you cannot remember it clearly. EG *I've got a vague recollection of going there once as a child.* ◊ **vaguely**. EG *I vaguely remember their house.* ADJ QUALIT; ◊ ADV

3 If a feeling is **vague**, you experience it only slightly. EG *I realized with a vague feeling of surprise that he had gone.* ◊ **vaguely**. EG *They were vaguely amused.* ADJ QUALIT; ◊ ADV

4 If you are **vague** about something, you deliberately do not tell people much about it. EG *They were vague and evasive about their backgrounds.* ADJ PRED: OFT +*about*

5 You say that someone looks or sounds **vague** when they do not seem to be thinking clearly. EG *Jones looked very vague.* ADJ QUALIT

6 If the shape or outline of something is **vague**, it is not clear and so the thing is not easy to see. EG *It appeared in vague form at first and then in sharper outline.* ADJ QUALIT

vain /veɪn/, **vainer, vainest. 1** If you do something **in vain**, you do not succeed in achieving what you intend. EG *We tried in vain to discover what had happened... Your son didn't die in vain.* PHRASE

2 A **vain** attempt or action fails to achieve what is intended. EG *...the teacher's vain plea for silence.* ADJ CLASSIF: ATTRIB

3 Someone who is **vain** is extremely proud of their beauty, intelligence, or other good qualities; used showing disapproval. EG *...a vain young aristocrat.* ADJ QUALIT

vale /veɪl/, **vales.** A **vale** is a valley. EG *...a rich, lush vale of meadows and blossoms.* N COUNT Literary

valedictory /vælɪdɪktəᵒri¹/. A **valedictory** speech or letter is one in which you say goodbye to someone. ADJ CLASSIF: ATTRIB Formal

valentine /væləntaɪn/, **valentines. 1** Your **valentine** is someone who you love or are attracted to and who you send a card to on St Valentine's Day, February 14th. N SING: USU POSS+N

2 A **valentine** or a **valentine card** is the card that you send to your valentine, usually without signing your name, on St Valentine's Day. N COUNT

valet /vælɪt, væleɪ/, **valets.** A **valet** is a male servant who looks after his male employer by doing things such as caring for his clothes. N COUNT

valiant /væljənt/ means very brave. EG *He made a valiant attempt to rescue the struggling victim.* ADJ QUALIT

valid /vælɪd/. **1** Something that is **valid** is based on sound reasoning. EG *This is a valid argument against economic growth... This was the real reason, and it was a valid reason... It was a valid protest.* ◇ **validity** /vəlɪdɪti[1]/. EG *We should question the validity of those figures.* ADJ QUALIT ◇ N UNCOUNT

2 If a ticket or document is **valid**, it can be used and will be accepted by people in authority. EG *It's valid for six months from the date of issue... This passport is no longer valid.* ADJ CLASSIF

validate /vælɪdeɪt/, **validates, validating, validated.** If something **validates** a statement or claim, it proves that it is true or correct. EG *Their remarkable achievement seems to validate Bomberg's claim.* V+O

Valium /vælɪəm/ is a drug which is given to people to calm their nerves when they are worried or upset. N UNCOUNT Trademark

valley /væli[1]/, **valleys.** A **valley** is a long, narrow area of land between hills, especially one that has a river flowing through it. N COUNT

valour /vælə/; spelled **valor** in American English. **Valour** is great bravery, especially in battle. EG *...an act of epic valour.* N UNCOUNT Formal

valuable /væljʊ[0]əbə[0]l/, **valuables. 1 Valuable** help or advice is very useful. EG *They could also give valuable help.* ADJ QUALIT

2 When objects such as paintings or jewellery are **valuable**, they are worth a lot of money. ADJ QUALIT

3 Valuables are things that you own which are worth a lot of money, especially small objects such as jewellery. EG *They were robbed of money and valuables at gunpoint.* N PLURAL

valuation /væljʊeɪʃə[0]n/, **valuations.** A **valuation** is **1** a judgement about how much money something is worth. EG *The land's valuation was £6,000.* **2** a judgement about how good or bad something is. EG *...his rather low valuation of the novel.* N COUNT OR N UNCOUNT

value /vælju:/, **values, valuing, valued. 1** The **value** of something such as a quality or a method is its importance or usefulness. EG *Everyone realizes the value of sincerity.* N UNCOUNT

2 The **value** of something that you can own, for example a house or a painting, is the amount of money that it is worth. EG *What will happen to the value of my property?* N UNCOUNT OR N COUNT

3 If you say that something is **good value** or is **value for money**, you mean that it is worth the money it costs. EG *The set lunch is good value at £5.95.* PHRASE

4 Something that is **of value** is useful or important. EG *You may find them of value... ...information which would be of value to him... Nothing of value can be said about this matter.* PHRASE

5 If you put or place **a high value** on something, you think that it is very important. EG *He places a high value on educating his children.* PHRASE

6 The **values** of a person or group are the moral principles and beliefs that they think are important. EG *...the traditional values of civility, moderation, and family... They have different values from the families they serve.* N PLURAL

7 If you **take** a remark or compliment **at face value**, you accept it without thinking what its real meaning or purpose might be. EG *She took the praise at face value.* PHRASE

8 Value is used after another noun to say that something has a particular kind of importance or usefulness. For example, if you say that something has propaganda **value**, you mean that it is useful as propaganda. EG *It should have novelty value, if nothing else.* N UNCOUNT

9 If you **value** something, you think that it is important and you appreciate it. EG *Which do you value most – wealth or health?* ◇ **valued.** EG *...one of our valued customers.* V+O ◇ ADJ QUALIT

10 When experts **value** something such as a house or a painting, they decide how much money it is worth. EG *They had gone to have their jewels valued... The table silver was valued at £20,000.* V+O: USU PASS

value-added tax. See **VAT**.

value judgement, value judgements. A **value judgement** is an opinion about something that is based on the principles and beliefs of the person expressing the opinion and not on facts which can be checked or proved. EG *It is difficult to answer that question without making a value judgement... ...an argument based on value judgements.* N COUNT: USU PLURAL

valueless /væljʊlɪ[2]s/. Something that is **valueless** is not effective or useful. EG *...involvement in valueless activities.* ADJ CLASSIF

valuer /væljʊə/, **valuers.** A **valuer** is someone whose job is to decide how much money things are worth. N COUNT

valve /vælv/, **valves.** A **valve** is a part attached to a pipe or a tube. When the valve is open, it lets air or liquid pass through. When it is closed, it stops the air or liquid passing through. EG *...a radiator valve.* ● See also **safety-valve**. N COUNT

vampire /væmpaɪə/, **vampires.** In legends and horror stories, **vampires** are people who come out of their graves at night and suck the blood of living people. N COUNT

van /væn/, **vans.** A **van** is a vehicle like a large car that is used for carrying goods. N COUNT

vandal /vændə[0]l/, **vandals.** A **vandal** is someone who deliberately damages things, especially public property, for no good reason. EG *The phone box is attacked by vandals from time to time.* N COUNT

vandalise /vændəlaɪz/. See **vandalize**.

vandalism /vændəlɪzə[0]m/ is the deliberate damaging of things, especially public property, for no good reason. EG *These housing estates suffer from widespread vandalism.* N UNCOUNT

vandalize /vændəlaɪz/, **vandalizes, vandalizing, vandalized;** also spelled **vandalise.** If someone **vandalizes** something, they damage it on purpose, for no good reason. EG *All our telephones were vandalized.* V+O: USU PASS

vanguard /vængɑ:d/. If someone is in the **vanguard** of something such as a revolution or a particular kind of research, they are involved in the most advanced part of it. EG *They are in the vanguard of technological advance.* N SING: USU+SUPP

vanilla /vənɪlə/ is a flavouring that comes from a plant and that can be put into ice cream and other sweet food. EG *...vanilla ice-cream... ...vanilla fudge.* N UNCOUNT: OFT N MOD

vanish /vænɪʃ/, **vanishes, vanishing, vanished.** If something **vanishes**, **1** it disappears suddenly. EG *The car had vanished from sight... Madeleine vanished without trace.* **2** it ceases to exist. EG *...laws to protect vanishing American species.* V

vanity /vænɪ[1]ti[1]/ is a feeling of pride about your appearance or abilities; used showing disapproval. EG *He refused to wear glasses. It was sheer vanity.* N UNCOUNT

vanquish /væŋkwɪʃ/, **vanquishes, vanquishing, vanquished.** If you **vanquish** someone, you defeat them completely in a battle or a competition. EG *All their enemies were vanquished.* V+O Literary

vantage point /vɑ:ntɪdʒ pɔɪnt/, **vantage points.** A **vantage point** is a place from which you can see a lot of things. EG *From the vantage point on the hill, Port Philip shimmered beneath them.* N COUNT

vapour /veɪpə/; spelled **vapor** in American English. **Vapour** is a mass of tiny drops of water or other liquids in the air, which appear as smoke, N UNCOUNT clouds, mist, or fumes. EG *...water vapour... ...a little cloud of exhaust vapour.*

variability /vɛəri¹əbɪlɪ¹ti¹/. The **variability** of something is the range of different forms that it can take. EG *...the enormous variability you get in speech sounds.* N UNCOUNT: USU+SUPP

variable /vɛəri¹əbəl/, **variables. 1** Something that is **variable** is likely to change at any time. EG *In the tropics, rainfall is notoriously variable.* ADJ QUALIT

2 A **variable** is a factor that can change in quality, quantity, or size, which you have to take into account when looking at a situation as a whole. EG *How long your shoes will last depends on a lot of variables, such as how much you weigh, how far you walk, and so on.* N COUNT

3 In mathematics, a **variable** is an expression that can have any one of a set of values. N COUNT Technical

variance /vɛəri¹əns/. If one thing is **at variance** with another, the two things seem to contradict each other. EG *Nothing in the story was at variance with what he understood to be true.* PHRASE Formal

variant /vɛəri¹ənt/, **variants.** A **variant** of something has a different form from the usual one. EG *This American bird is a variant of the English buzzard.* ▸ used as an adjective. EG *...a variant form of the basic action.* N COUNT: USU+of ▸ ADJ CLASSIF: ATTRIB

variation /vɛəri¹eɪʃə⁰n/, **variations. 1** A **variation** on something is the same thing presented in a different form. EG *...the same programme with only nightly variations... His books are all variations on a basic theme.* N COUNT

2 A **variation** is also a change in a level, amount, or quantity. EG *The Boards have learned how to cope with a large variation in demand for electricity... ...variation in blood pressure.* N COUNT OR N UNCOUNT

varicose veins /værɪkə⁶s veɪnz/ are veins in a person's legs which are very swollen and painful and which sometimes need to be operated on. N PLURAL

varied /vɛərɪd/. **1 Varied** is the past tense and past participle of **vary**.

2 Something that is **varied** consists of things that are of different types, sizes, or qualities. EG *Many varied motives prompt individuals to join a political party... The work of a JP is very varied.* ADJ QUALIT

variegated /vɛərɪgeɪtɪ²d/. A **variegated** plant or leaf has different coloured markings on it. EG *...a variegated holly.* ADJ CLASSIF

variety /vəraɪɪ¹ti¹/, **varieties. 1** If something has **variety**, it consists of things which are different from each other. EG *Those are the holiday brochures that give you the most variety.* N UNCOUNT

2 If you have a **variety** of things, you have a number of them of different kinds. EG *The college library had a wide variety of books.* N PART: SING

3 A **variety** of something is a type of it. EG *...three varieties of whisky.* N COUNT: USU+of

4 Variety is a type of theatre or television entertainment which includes many different kinds of performance in the same show, for example singing, dancing, and comedy. EG *...a high-quality variety show... ...a variety act.* N UNCOUNT: OFT N MOD

various /vɛərɪəs/. **1** If you refer to **various** things, you mean that there are several different things of the type mentioned. EG *There were various questions he wanted to ask... ...trying to piece together the various bits of information.* ADJ CLASSIF: ATTRIB

2 If a number of things are described as **various**, they are very different from one another. EG *His excuses are many and various.* ADJ CLASSIF: USU PRED

variously /vɛərɪəsli¹/ is used to introduce a number of different ways in which something is described or a number of different opinions that people have about something. EG *He married a Japanese lady who was variously described as a painter and a film maker.* ADV

varnish /vɑːnɪʃ/, **varnishes, varnishing, varnished. 1 Varnish** is a liquid made from oil and other substances which is painted onto wood to give it a hard, clear, shiny surface. ● See also **nail varnish**. N MASS

2 The **varnish** on an object is the hard, clear, shiny surface that it has when it has been painted with varnish. EG *The varnish was slightly chipped.* N SING

3 If you **varnish** something, you paint it with varnish. EG *He has varnished the table.* V+O

vary /vɛəri¹/, **varies, varying, varied. 1** Things that **vary** are different in size, amount, or degree. EG *The fees vary a lot... The screens will vary in size depending upon what one wants.* ◇ **varying.** EG *Its members have widely varying views on foreign policy.* V ◇ ADJ QUALIT: ATTRIB

2 If one thing **varies** with another, it changes when the other thing changes. EG *The colour of the fruit varies with age.* V+with

3 If you **vary** something that you do, you keep changing the way that you do it. EG *He took special care to vary his daily routine.* V+O

4 See also **varied**.

vase /vɑːz/, **vases.** A **vase** is a jar, usually made of glass or pottery, which is used for holding cut flowers or as an ornament. N COUNT

vasectomy /və³sɛktəmi¹/, **vasectomies.** A **vasectomy** is a surgical operation that is done in order to sterilize a man, by cutting the tube that carries the sperm to his penis. N COUNT OR N UNCOUNT

vast /vɑːst/. Something that is **vast** is extremely large. EG *He was responsible for running a vast organization... ...the roads that they're building at vast expense.* ADJ QUALIT: OFT ATTRIB

vastly /vɑːstli¹/ means very much or to a very large extent. EG *Management of the factory could be vastly improved.* SUBMOD

vat /væt/, **vats.** A **vat** is a large barrel or tank in which liquids are stored. EG *...a vat of water.* N COUNT OR N PART

VAT /viː eɪ tiː, væt/ is a tax that is added to the price of goods or services. **VAT** is an abbreviation for 'value-added tax'. N UNCOUNT

vault /vɔːlt/, **vaults, vaulting, vaulted. 1** A **vault** is **1.1** a room with thick walls, a strong door, and strong locks where money, important documents, and jewels can be kept safely. EG *The money was deposited in the vaults of a firm of solicitors.* **1.2** a room underneath a church or in a cemetery where people are buried. N COUNT

2 A **vault** is also a roof or ceiling consisting of several arches joined together at the top. N COUNT

3 If you **vault** something or **vault** over it, you jump over it, putting one or both of your hands on it. EG *They vaulted effortlessly over the wall.* V+O OR V+A

VB stands for verb

VB is used in the Extra Column to mean 'verb', without indicating what type of verb it is, as in, for example ADV AFTER VB.

V+C stands for intransitive verb followed by complement

Verbs which have the label V+C in the Extra Column are verbs which need a complement, that is a noun or adjective group which refers to the subject, to complete their meaning.

See the entry headed COMPLEMENTS for more information about complements. See the entry headed VERBS for more information about these verbs.

VD /viː diː/ is an abbreviation for 'venereal disease'.

Are you wearing a veil if you make a veiled comment?

VDU /vi: di: ju:/, **VDU's.** A **VDU** is a machine which looks like a television set and which shows information from a computer on its screen. **VDU** is an abbreviation for 'visual display unit'. N COUNT

veal /vi:l/ is meat from a calf. N UNCOUNT

veer /vɪə/, **veers, veering, veered.** If something that is moving **veers** in a particular direction, it suddenly starts moving in that direction. EG *He veered away from a tree... The plane seemed to veer off to one side.* V+A

vegetable /vɛdʒɪ⁰təbə⁰l/, **vegetables. 1 Vegetables** are plants such as cabbages, potatoes, and onions which you can cook and eat. N COUNT: USU PLURAL

2 Vegetable is used to refer to plants in general. EG *...vegetable matter.* N UNCOUNT: USU MOD

vegetarian /vɛdʒɪtɛərɪən/, **vegetarians.** Someone who is a **vegetarian** does not eat meat or fish. EG *She was a strict vegetarian.* ▸ used as an adjective. EG *...a vegetarian diet.* N COUNT ▸ ADJ CLASSIF

vegetate /vɛdʒɪteɪt/, **vegetates, vegetating, vegetated.** If you **vegetate**, you have a very boring life, staying in the same place and doing very little. EG *Many elderly folk vegetate and die in loneliness.* V

vegetation /vɛdʒɪteɪʃə⁰n/ is plant life in general. EG *The forest floor is not rich in vegetation.* N UNCOUNT

vehemence /vi:ə¹məns/ is intense and violent emotion, especially anger. EG *...the hate and vehemence in Hubert's eyes.* N UNCOUNT

vehement /vi:ə¹mənt/. Someone who is **vehement** has very strong feelings or opinions and expresses them forcefully. EG *They are vehement in their praises of the new system... With a vehement gesture he flung away his chicken leg.* ADJ QUALIT
◊ **vehemently.** EG *They were arguing vehemently.* ◊ ADV

vehicle /vi:ɪkə⁰l/, **vehicles. 1** A **vehicle** is a machine such as a bus, car, or lorry, that carries people or things from place to place. EG *We saw a vehicle travelling across the bridge... ...the motor vehicle industry.* N COUNT

2 If you use something as a **vehicle** for a particular thing, you use it in order to achieve that thing. EG *They saw education as a vehicle of liberation... They support the Labour Party as a vehicle for socialism.* N COUNT: USU+*for/of* Formal

veil /veɪl/, **veils. 1** A **veil** is a piece of thin, soft material that women sometimes wear over their heads. EG *The bride's face was covered in a white veil... ...a hat with a veil.* N COUNT

2 You can refer to something that you can partly see through, for example a mist, as a **veil**. EG *Everything was wrapped in a veil of evening light.* N SING+*of* Literary

3 You can also refer to something that hides or partly hides an activity or situation as a **veil**. EG *The research centre shrouded its communications with every possible veil of secrecy.* N SING+*of*

veiled /veɪld/. If you make a **veiled** comment or remark, you express it in a disguised form, so that you do not actually say what you mean. EG *...thinly veiled criticism... ...veiled threats.* ADJ CLASSIF: ATTRIB

vein /veɪn/, **veins. 1** Your **veins** are the tubes in your body through which your blood flows. ● See also **varicose veins**. N COUNT

2 The **veins** on a leaf are the thin lines on it. N COUNT

3 A **vein** of a metal or mineral is a layer of it in rock. EG *...the world's richest vein of copper.* N COUNT+*of*

4 Something that is written or spoken in a particular **vein** is written or spoken in that style or mood. EG *The letter continued in this vein for several pages.* N UNCOUNT +SUPP

velocity /vɪ²lɒsɪ¹ti¹/, **velocities.** The **velocity** of something is the speed at which it moves in a particular direction. EG *...the velocity of light.* N UNCOUNT OR N COUNT Technical

velvet /vɛlvɪt/ is soft material made from cotton, silk, or nylon, which has a thick layer of short, cut threads on one side. EG *...velvet curtains.* N UNCOUNT

velvety /vɛlvɪ¹ti¹/. Something that is **velvety** is soft to touch and has the appearance of velvet. EG *The spider has a velvety black body.* ADJ QUALIT

vendetta /vɛndɛtə/, **vendettas.** A **vendetta** is a long-lasting and bitter quarrel between people in which they attempt to harm each other. EG *He conducted a vendetta against Haldane behind the scenes.* N COUNT

vending machine, vending machines. A **vending machine** is a machine from which you can get things such as cigarettes, chocolate, or coffee by putting in money and pressing a button. N COUNT

vendor /vɛndə⁸/, **vendors. 1** A **vendor** is someone who sells things such as newspapers, cigarettes, or hamburgers from a small stall or cart. EG *...cigarette vendors.* N COUNT: USU+SUPP

2 The **vendor** of a house or piece of land is the person who owns it and is selling it. N COUNT Technical

veneer /vɪ²nɪə/. **1** If you refer to the way that someone behaves as a **veneer**, you mean that they are behaving in a way which hides their real character or feelings. EG *He hides his values beneath a veneer of scientific objectivity.* N SING: USU+SUPP

2 Veneer is a thin layer of wood or plastic which is glued onto the outside of something made of cheaper material, in order to improve its appearance. EG *...a table whose veneer had come loose.* N UNCOUNT

venerable /vɛnə⁰rəbə⁰l/. **Venerable** people are entitled to respect because they are old and wise. EG *...a venerable elder for whom he had enormous respect... ...the venerable head of the house.* ADJ QUALIT: USU ATTRIB Formal

venerate /vɛnəreɪt/, **venerates, venerating, venerated.** If you **venerate** someone, you feel great respect for them. EG *Lincoln was a lawyer and I always venerated him.* V+O Formal

venereal disease /və¹nɪərɪəl dɪzi:z/, **venereal diseases.** A **venereal disease** is a disease that is passed on by sexual intercourse. There are several different venereal diseases, for example syphilis. N COUNT OR N UNCOUNT

Venetian blind /vəni:ʃə⁰n blaɪnd/, **Venetian blinds.** A **Venetian blind** is a window blind made of thin horizontal strips of wood, plastic, or metal. The strips can be turned to a different angle in order to let in more or less light. N COUNT

vengeance /vɛndʒəns/. **1 Vengeance** is the act of killing, injuring, or harming someone because they have harmed you. EG *I want vengeance for the deaths of my parents and sisters.* N UNCOUNT

2 If something happens **with a vengeance**, it happens to a much greater extent than was expected. EG *He now broke the rules with a vengeance.* PHRASE

vengeful /vɛndʒfʊl/. If you are **vengeful**, you feel a great desire for revenge. EG *The whole episode made me vengeful.* ADJ QUALIT Literary

venison /vɛnɪ⁰zən, -sən/ is meat from a deer. N UNCOUNT

venom /vɛnəm/. **1 Venom** is a feeling of great bitterness or anger that you show in the way that you say or do something. EG *'What a filthy trick,' she said with unexpected venom.* N UNCOUNT

2 The **venom** of a snake, scorpion, or spider is the poison that it injects into you when it bites you or stings you. N UNCOUNT

venomous /vɛnəməs/. **1** A **venomous** snake, scorpion, or spider produces poison and uses it to attack its enemy or prey. ADJ CLASSIF

2 If your behaviour or appearance is **venomous**, it shows great bitterness or anger. EG *Her beautiful green eyes were venomous... They shot each other venomous glances.* ADJ QUALIT

vent /vɛnt/, **vents, venting, vented. 1** A **vent** is a hole in something such as the wall of a room, through which air can come in and smoke, gas, or smells can go out. EG *...the air vents of the bunkers.* N COUNT

2 If you **give vent to** strong feelings, you express them. EG *They gave vent to their rage.* PHRASE Formal

3 If you **vent** your feelings, you express them. EG *She vented her feelings in wails and screams... He vented his rage on Bernard.* V+O: OFT+A Formal

ventilate /vɛntɪleɪt/, **ventilates, ventilating, ventilated.** To **ventilate** a room or building means to allow fresh air to get into it, for example by means of windows. ◊ **ventilated.** EG *...badly* V+O ◊ ADJ CLASSIF

VERBS

Verbs are words which describe actions, thought, speech, and other activities. Verbs can either present a complete action and so occur on their own, or they can be followed by objects, complements, or adjuncts. For more information about these, see the entries headed OBJECTS, COMPLEMENTS, and ADJUNCTS.

Verbs can be used in many different ways, and the most important ways are explained here, together with the labels that are used in the Extra Column. In addition to the patterns explained here, you can add more adverbs or other adjuncts. These are only shown in the Extra Column where the adjuncts are essential for the meaning.

V

The verb is intransitive; that is, it is not followed by an object. For example: *His leg ached . . .   She smiled.*

V+O

The verb is transitive; that is, it is followed by an object. Transitive verbs usually have a passive form, in which the object of the active form is used as the subject of the passive form. For example: *I arranged a meeting for 9 o'clock . . .   . . . The meeting was arranged for 9 o'clock.*

Although all transitive verbs can be used in the active form, some are much more likely to be used in the passive (V-PASS). For example: *I was taken aback at the news . . .   He was orphaned at the age of six.*

Some verbs can be used either transitively or intransitively, as in: *The men saluted.* (V)   *He stood as if he were saluting the flag.* (V+O) In this case, the Extra Column says V OR V+O.

V+C

The verb is intransitive, and must be followed by a complement, which refers back to the subject of the verb. For example: *It seems odd . . .   You seem young to be a policeman . . .   James is a teacher.*

V+A

The verb is intransitive, and must be followed by an adjunct, which is usually a prepositional phrase telling you about direction, manner, time, and so on. For example: *I strolled around the city centre . . .   He behaved disgracefully . . .   We waited for half an hour.*

Combinations of these

V+O+C: *He makes me very happy . . .   I thought him cruel and heartless.*

V+O+A: *She put her diary in her bag . . .   He threw the packet into the bin.*

V+O+O: *She made her mother a dress . . .   Give me that book . . .   He fixed himself a stiff drink.*

V-REFL

The verb is always used with a reflexive pronoun. Reflexive verbs describe actions in which the subject and the object of the verb are the same. For example: *I helped myself to more potatoes . . . She cut herself with the breadknife.*

V-ERG

Ergative verbs can describe an action from the point of view of the performer of the action or from the point of view of the object of the action.

Ergative verbs can be used transitively, as in *I'm baking a cake,* or they can be used intransitively, as in *The cake is baking in the oven.*

To use the verb intransitively, you use the object of the transitive verb as the subject of the intransitive verb.

RECIP

Reciprocal verbs describe actions that involve two people or two groups of people. For example: *Do you agree with him about this? . . . They agreed without argument.* See the entry headed RECIP.

+REPORT

Many verbs, especially verbs of speech such as **say**, **report**, and **tell**, are followed by a clause which tells you what the person said. These clauses usually start with **that** or with a **wh-** word such as **what** or **when**. In this dictionary, these clauses are called report clauses, and more information about them can be found in the entry headed REPORT. For example: *She hoped that she wasn't going to cry.* (V+REPORT) *She told me where to leave the documents.* (V+O+REPORT)

V+QUOTE

Verbs with this label are used to report direct speech – the actual words that someone spoke. For example: *"You're wrong" she retorted . . . "Follow me," Claude whispered, "and keep quiet." . . . I said, "I'd never do that, and you know it."*

V-SPEECH

Verbs with this label can be used transitively (V+O), intransitively describing direct speech (V+QUOTE), and intransitively describing indirect speech (V+REPORT). For example: *We have to suggest a list of possible topics for next term's seminars . . .* (V+O) *"Has it been thrown away?" suggested Miss Livingstone . . .* (V+QUOTE) *I suggested that it was time to leave.* (V+REPORT)

ventilated houses. ◊ **ventilation** /ve̱ntɪleɪ̱ʃə^{0}n/. EG *The only ventilation was through a small door at the back.* ◊ N UNCOUNT

ventilator /ve̱ntɪleɪtə/, **ventilators.** A **ventilator** is something such as a fan which lets fresh air into a room or building and lets stale air out. N COUNT

ventriloquist /ventrɪ̱ləkwɪst/, **ventriloquists.** A **ventriloquist** is someone who can speak without moving their lips and who entertains people by making their words appear to be spoken by a wooden dummy. N COUNT

venture /ve̱ntʃə/, **ventures, venturing, ventured.** 1 A **venture** is something you do that is new and difficult and so involves the risk of failure. EG *...an interesting scientific venture... The number of successful new business ventures is dwindling.* N COUNT: USU+SUPP

2 If you **venture** into something, you do something that involves the risk of failure because it is new and different. EG *I might actually venture into advertising if I had enough money.* V+A

3 If you **venture** something such as an opinion, you say it in a cautious, hesitant manner because you are afraid it might be foolish or wrong. EG *'Anyway,' Marsha ventured, 'If we want to know what's going on, we'll have to do our own research.'... No one has ventured to suggest why this should be.* V+O; ALSO V+QUOTE OR *to*-INF

4 If you **venture** somewhere that might be dangerous, you go there. EG *He wouldn't venture far from his mother's door.* V+A

venue /ve̱nju:/, **venues.** The **venue** for an event or activity is the place where it will happen. EG *Where is the venue for the conference?* N COUNT Formal

veranda /vəræ̱ndə/, **verandas;** also spelled **verandah.** A **veranda** is a platform along one of the outside walls of a house, usually on ground level. It has a roof supported by pillars. N COUNT

verb /vɜ̱:b/, **verbs.** In grammar, a **verb** is a word which is concerned with what people and things do, and what happens to them. N COUNT

verbal /vɜ̱:bə^{0}l/. 1 You use **verbal** to describe 1.1 things connected with words and the use of words. EG *It was a contest in verbal skills.* 1.2 things that are spoken rather than written. EG *...a succession of verbal attacks on the chairman.* ◊ **verbally**. EG *I will communicate your views verbally to the members of the committee.* ADJ CLASSIF: USU ATTRIB; ADJ CLASSIF: USU ATTRIB; ◊ ADV

2 **Verbal** also describes something that consists of or relates to verbs. EG *...the structure of verbal groups in English.* ADJ CLASSIF

verbatim /vɜ:be̱ɪtɪm/. If you repeat something **verbatim**, you use exactly the same words that the original speaker or writer used. EG *It was almost a verbatim quotation of the article.* ADV AFTER VB OR ADJ CLASSIF Formal

verbiage /vɜ̱:bi^{1}ɪdʒ/ is the use of too many words, which makes something difficult to understand. EG *...a lot of meaningless verbiage.* N UNCOUNT Formal

verdict /vɜ̱:dɪkt/, **verdicts.** 1 In a law court, a **verdict** is the decision whether a prisoner is guilty or not guilty. EG *The jury gave a verdict of not guilty.* N COUNT

2 If you give your **verdict** on something, you say what your opinion of it is, after thinking about it. EG *The critics hated the film, but the public verdict was favourable.* N COUNT: USU+SUPP

> **V-ERG** stands for **ergative verb**
> Verbs which have the label V-ERG in the Extra Column are both transitive and intransitive in the same meaning.
> See the entry headed VERBS for more information.

verge /vɜ̱:dʒ/, **verges, verging, verged.** 1 If you are **on the verge** of something, you are likely to do it very soon, or it is likely to happen to you very soon. EG *The unions are on the verge of settling their latest pay dispute... ...people living on the verge of starvation.* PHRASE

2 The **verge** of a road is a narrow piece of ground at the side, which is usually covered with grass. EG *We began walking together along the grass verge.* N COUNT

verge on or **verge upon.** Something that **verges on** or **verges upon** something else is almost the same as it. EG *I had a feeling of distrust verging on panic... ...direct action verging on violence.* PHRASAL VB: V+PREP

verify /ve̱rɪfaɪ/, **verifies, verifying, verified.** If you **verify** something, 1 you check that it is true by careful investigation. EG *...evidence that could be tested and verified.* ◊ **verification** /ve̱rɪfɪke̱ɪʃə^{0}n/. EG *Any hypothesis must depend for its verification on observable evidence.* 2 you state or confirm that it is true. EG *I was asked to verify or deny this suggestion.* ◊ **verification**. EG *He looked at his daughter for verification.* V+O; ◊ N UNCOUNT; V+O; ◊ N UNCOUNT

veritable /ve̱rɪtəbə^{0}l/. You use **veritable** when you are exaggerating, often humorously, in order to emphasize a feature that something has. EG *His toilet flushed like a veritable Niagara.* ADJ CLASSIF: ATTRIB

vermilion /və^{5}mɪ̱ljən/. Something that is **vermilion** is bright red in colour. EG *...vermilion robes.* ADJ COLOUR Formal

vermin /vɜ̱:mɪn/ are small animals such as rats and mice, which carry disease and damage crops or food. EG *In Scotland, wild cats are treated as vermin, and are poisoned.* N PLURAL

vernacular /vənæ̱kjə^{4}lə/, **vernaculars.** The **vernacular** of a country or region is the language that is most widely spoken there. EG *'Who is it?' asked Ash in the vernacular.* N COUNT: OFT *the*+N

versatile /vɜ̱:sətaɪl/. 1 Someone who is **versatile** has many different skills and can change quickly from using one to using another. EG *He's the most versatile of actors.* ADJ QUALIT

2 Something such as a tool, machine, or material that is **versatile** can be used for many different purposes. EG *...this extremely versatile new kitchen machine... Chestnuts are a highly versatile vegetable.* ADJ QUALIT

verse /vɜ̱:s/, **verses.** 1 **Verse** is writing arranged in lines which have a rhythm and which often rhyme at the end. EG *She used to write plays in verse.* N UNCOUNT

2 A **verse** is one of the parts into which a poem, a song, or a chapter of the Bible is divided. EG *He sang a verse of 'Lili Marlene'.* N COUNT

versed /vɜ̱:st/. If you **are versed in** something, you know a lot about it. EG *She is well versed in French history.* PHRASE Formal

version /vɜ̱:ʃə^{0}n, -ʒə^{0}n/, **versions.** 1 A **version** of something is a form of it in which some details are different from earlier or later forms. EG *She asked a different version of the question... ...from the first draft to the final printed version.* N COUNT+SUPP

2 The film or stage **version** of a story is a film or play based on the story. EG *...the 1939 film version of 'Wuthering Heights'.* N COUNT+SUPP

3 Someone's **version** of an event is their description of what happened. EG *Each of the women had a different version of what actually happened.* N COUNT+SUPP

versus /vɜ̱:səs/. 1 You use **versus** to say that two ideas or things are opposed, especially when a choice has to be made between them. EG *...the problem of determinism versus freedom.* PREP

2 **Versus** is also used to say that two people or teams are competing against each other in a sporting event. EG *The big match tonight is England versus Spain.* PREP

vertebra /vɜ̱:tɪbrə/, **vertebrae** /vɜ̱:tɪbreɪ/. Your **vertebrae** are the small circular bones that form your backbone. N COUNT: USU PLURAL

vertebrate /vɜ̱:tɪbreɪt, -brə^{1}t/, **vertebrates.** A **vertebrate** is a creature which has a backbone. Mammals, birds, and reptiles are all vertebrates. N COUNT Technical

> What are the two other names for a vet?

vertical /vɜːtɪkəᵊl/. **1** Something that is **vertical** stands or points straight upwards. EG *The monument consists of a horizontal slab supported by two vertical pillars... A vertical line divides the page into two halves.* ◇ **vertically**. EG *The human brain is divided vertically down the middle into two hemispheres.*
ADJ CLASSIF
◇ ADV

2 You use **vertical** to say that a cliff or slope is very steep. EG *The cliff plunged in a vertical drop to the bottom.*
ADJ CLASSIF

vertigo /vɜːtɪgəʊ/ is a feeling of dizziness and sickness caused by looking down from a high place. EG *Looking out of the window gives him vertigo.*
N UNCOUNT

very /vɛri^1/. **1** You use **very** in order to emphasize an adjective or adverb. EG *...a very small child... It's a very good idea... Think very carefully... I liked it very much... ...the very latest techniques.*
SUBMOD

2 You use **not very** to say that something is the case only to a small degree. EG *He's not there very often... 'Is the work difficult?' – 'Not very, but it's boring.'*
PHRASE

3 You use **very** with nouns **3.1** to emphasize a point in space or time. EG *I walked up to the very top... We were there from the very beginning.* **3.2** to emphasize that something is exactly the right one or exactly the same as something else. EG *Ah, there you are. The very man I've been looking for!... Those are the very words he used.* **3.3** to emphasize the importance or seriousness of what you are saying. EG *The theatre is fighting for its very life.*
ADJ CLASSIF : ATTRIB

4 You say **very much so** as an emphatic way of saying 'yes'. EG *'Did your father resist this?' – 'Very much so.'*
CONVENTION

5 Something **of** your **very own** belongs only to you and does not have to be shared with anyone else. EG *The town has its very own bus service.*
PHRASE

6 You can say **very well** when you agree to do something. EG *'Mr Brown wants to see you.' – 'Very well. I'll be along in a moment.'*
CONVENTION Formal

7 If you say that you **cannot very well** do something, you mean that it would not be the right thing to do. EG *I can't very well drag him out of the meeting, can I?*
PHRASE

vessel /vɛsəᵊl/, **vessels. 1** A **vessel** is a ship or large boat. EG *...fishing vessels.*
N COUNT Formal

2 A **vessel** is also a bowl or other container in which liquid is kept. EG *He began putting the sacred vessels away.*
N COUNT Literary

3 See also **blood vessel**.

vest /vɛst/, **vests.** A **vest** is **1** a piece of clothing which you can wear on the top half of your body underneath a shirt, blouse, or dress in order to keep warm. **2** a waistcoat.
N COUNT British
American

vested /vɛstɪ^{2}d/. Something that is **vested** in someone is given to them as a right or responsibility. EG *...the authority vested in him by the State of Massachusetts.*
ADJ PRED+*in* Formal

vested interest, vested interests. If you have a **vested interest** in something, you have a strong reason for acting in a particular way, for example you are trying to protect your own money, power, or reputation. EG *They have vested interests in farming and forestry... They share a common vested interest in a strong modern army.*
N COUNT : USU PLURAL

vestige /vɛstɪdʒ/, **vestiges.** A **vestige** of something is a very small part of it, often a part that remains after all the rest has gone. EG *...a country without any vestige of political freedom.*
N COUNT : OFT+*of* Formal

vet /vɛt/, **vets, vetting, vetted. 1** A **vet** is a doctor who is specially trained to look after animals. EG *Get your kitten checked by the vet.*
N COUNT British

2 When someone or something **is vetted**, they are carefully checked to make sure that they are acceptable to the people in authority. EG *His speeches were vetted... He was thoroughly vetted.* ◇ **vetting**. EG *He wanted to tighten the security vetting of civil servants.*
V+O : USU PASS British
◇ N UNCOUNT

veteran /vɛtəᵊrən/, **veterans. 1** A **veteran** is someone who has served in the armed forces of their country, especially during a war. EG *...a World War Two veteran.*
N COUNT

2 You also refer to someone as a **veteran** when they have been involved in a particular activity for a long time. EG *...a veteran of the civil rights movement.*
N COUNT

veterinarian /vɛtəᵊrɪnɛərɪən/, **veterinarians.** A **veterinarian** is a doctor who is specially trained to look after animals.
N COUNT American

veterinary /vɛtəᵊrɪnəᵊri^1/ is used to describe the work of a vet and the medical treatment of animals. EG *They had a veterinary practice in Perth.*
ADJ CLASSIF : ATTRIB

veterinary surgeon, veterinary surgeons. A **veterinary surgeon** is the same as a vet.
N COUNT Formal British

veto /viːtəʊ/, **vetoes, vetoing, vetoed. 1** If someone in authority **vetoes** something, they forbid it. EG *The government vetoed this proposal.* ▸ used as a noun. EG *The rest of the committee could not accept the veto.*
V+O
▸ N COUNT

2 Veto is the right that someone in authority has to forbid something. EG *...the Sovereign's power of veto... They have a veto they are prepared to use.*
N UNCOUNT

vex /vɛks/, **vexes, vexing, vexed.** If something **vexes** you, it makes you feel annoyed. EG *It vexed her to be ignored like this.*
V+O Formal

vexed /vɛkst/. **1** If you are **vexed**, you are annoyed and puzzled. EG *Feeling vexed, I spoke up for myself... He sat with a vexed frown on his face.*
ADJ QUALIT

2 A **vexed** problem or question is very difficult and causes people a lot of trouble. EG *This leads to the vexed issue of priorities.*
ADJ QUALIT : ATTRIB

VHF /viː eɪtʃ ɛf/ is a range of very high radio frequencies. **VHF** is an abbreviation for 'very high frequency'.
N UNCOUNT

via /vaɪə, viːə/. **1** You use **via** to say that someone or something goes through a particular place on their way to somewhere else. EG *He booked a ticket to Washington via Frankfurt and New York... We came home via a pub.*
PREP

2 You also use **via** to say that you do something or achieve something by making use of a particular thing or person. EG *...the transmission of television pictures via satellite... It was so kind of you to send that message via Toby.*
PREP

viable /vaɪəbəᵊl/. Something that is **viable** is capable of doing what it is intended to do. EG *We should be doing everything in our power to develop viable alternatives to petrol... ...a viable project.* ◇ **viability** /vaɪəbɪlɪ^{1}ti^1/. EG *...the commercial viability of the new product.*
ADJ QUALIT
◇ N UNCOUNT

viaduct /vaɪədʌkt/, **viaducts.** A **viaduct** is a long, high bridge that carries a road or railway across a valley.
N COUNT

vibrant /vaɪbrənt/. **1** Something that is **vibrant** is full of life, energy, and enthusiasm. EG *His vibrant talk fascinated and excited me.*
ADJ QUALIT : OFT+*with*

2 A **vibrant** voice or sound is full of emotion and is very exciting. EG *...the vibrant tones of Richard Burton... ...vibrant music.*
ADJ QUALIT : USU ATTRIB

3 Vibrant light and colours are very bright and clear. EG *...a flower bed vibrant with red tulips.*
ADJ QUALIT

vibrate /vaɪbreɪt/, **vibrates, vibrating, vibrated.** When something **vibrates**, it shakes with a slight, very quick movement. EG *The foundation of the city began to rumble and vibrate.* ◇ **vibration** /vaɪbreɪʃəᵊn/, **vibrations**. EG *Your fingers feel the vibration on the violin string.*
V
◇ N COUNT OR N UNCOUNT

vicar /vɪkə/, **vicars.** A **vicar** is a priest in the Church of England.
N COUNT

vicarage /vɪkərɪdʒ/, **vicarages.** A **vicarage** is a house in which a vicar lives.
N COUNT

vicarious /vɪkɛərɪəs, vaɪ-/. A **vicarious** pleasure or feeling is one that you experience by watching, listening to, or reading about other people doing something, rather than by doing it yourself. EG *...a vicarious sense of power and adventure.*
ADJ CLASSIF : ATTRIB

vice /vaɪs/, **vices. 1** A **vice** is a moral fault in someone's character or behaviour. EG *...human vices such as greed and envy... Her one small vice was smoking... What are your vices?*
N COUNT

2 The criminal activities connected with pornography, prostitution, drugs, or gambling are referred to as **vice**. EG *...a campaign against vice and violence... ...strict vice laws.*
N UNCOUNT

3 A **vice** is also a tool with a pair of jaws that hold an object tightly while you do work on it. For this meaning, American English has the spelling **vise**.
N COUNT

vice-chancellor, vice-chancellors. The **vice-chancellor** of a British University is the person who is in charge of its academic and administrative policies and activities.
N COUNT : OFT *the*+N

vice versa /vaɪsə vɛːsə/ is used to indicate that the reverse of what you have said is also true. For example, 'Women may bring their husbands with them, and vice versa' means that men may also bring their wives with them.
PHRASE

vicinity /vɪsɪnɪ^{1}ti^1/. If something is in the **vicinity** of a place, it is in the area immediately around that place. EG *The hotels in the vicinity of the campus were cheap and shabby.*
N SING : USU *the*+N

vicious /vɪʃəs/. Someone or something that is **vicious** is cruel and violent. EG *...a vicious killer... ...the most vicious totalitarian system in history.*
ADJ QUALIT

◇ **viciously**. EG *He twisted her wrist viciously.*
◇ ADV

vicious circle. A **vicious circle** is a problem or difficult situation that causes a new problem or situation which then causes the original problem or situation to occur again. EG *We've got to break out of this vicious circle.*
N SING

victim /vɪktɪm/, **victims.** A **victim** is someone who has been hurt or killed by someone or something. EG *Most of the victims were shot in the back while trying to run away... ...a rape victim... ...a victim of hypothermia.*
N COUNT

victimize /vɪktɪmaɪz/, **victimizes, victimizing, victimized;** also spelled **victimise.** If someone **is victimized**, they are treated unfairly, usually because of their beliefs. EG *Management insisted that she was not being victimized.*
V+O : USU PASS

◇ **victimization** /vɪktɪmaɪzeɪʃəᵊn/. EG *There must be no victimization of workers.*
◇ N UNCOUNT

victor /vɪktə/, **victors.** The **victor** in a contest or battle is the person who wins, or the person who commands the winning army. EG *...the victor of Waterloo... He emerged as the victor over Mulder.*
N COUNT Outdated

Victorian /vɪktɔːrɪən/, **Victorians. 1 Victorian** describes things that happened or were made in Britain in the middle and last parts of the 19th century, when Victoria was the Queen. EG *...Victorian architecture.*
ADJ CLASSIF

2 You say that someone is **Victorian** when they have qualities which are thought to have been common in the time of Queen Victoria, especially a belief in strict discipline and morals. EG *His parents were very Victorian and very domineering.*
ADJ QUALIT

3 A **Victorian** is a British person who was alive when Victoria was Queen.
N COUNT

Victoriana /vɪktɔːrɪɑːnə/. Objects made during the reign of Queen Victoria are referred to as **Victoriana**.
N UNCOUNT

victorious /vɪktɔːrɪəs/. Someone who is **victorious** has won a victory, especially in a war. EG *The army came home victorious.*
ADJ CLASSIF

victory /vɪktəᵊri^1/, **victories.** A **victory** is a situation in which you gain complete success, for example in a war or a competition. EG *In A.D. 636, an Arab army won a famous victory over a much larger Persian force... Nobody believed he had any chance of victory... The final agreement was a victory for common sense.*
N COUNT OR N UNCOUNT

video /vɪdɪəʊ/, **videos, videoing, videoed. 1 Video** is the recording and showing of television programmes, films, or actual events, using a video recorder, video tapes, and a television set. EG *I know that you use video for teaching these students... The film's on video.*
N UNCOUNT

2 A **video** is **2.1** a machine which can be used to play video tapes on a television set and to record television programmes onto video tape. EG *Turn off the video.* **2.2** a film or television programme recorded on video tape for people to watch on a television set. EG *I've seen this video before.*
N COUNT

3 If you **video** something, you record it on magnetic tape, either by using a television camera and recording the actual events, or by using a video to record a television programme as it is being transmitted, in order to watch it later.
V+O

video cassette, video cassettes. A **video cassette** is a cassette containing a video tape.
N COUNT

video recorder, video recorders. A **video recorder** or a **video cassette recorder** is a machine that can be used to record television programmes and films onto video tapes, so that people can play them back and watch them later on a television set.
N COUNT

video tape, video tapes. Video tape is magnetic tape that is used to record pictures or films which you can then play back and watch on a television set. EG *The information can be printed, or put on video tape... They saw the videotapes of Mr Frost's interviews.*
N UNCOUNT OR N COUNT

vie /vaɪ/, **vies, vying, vied.** If you **vie** with someone, you try hard to get something before they do, or to do something better than they do. EG *The artists vied for the prime sites... ...vying with each other to express their disgust.*
V OR V+*with* : RECIP Formal

view /vjuː/, **views, viewing, viewed. 1** Your **view** on a particular subject is your opinion about it. EG *I've changed my view on this issue... He was sent to jail for his political views... I have strong views about the Church.*
N COUNT : USU+SUPP

2 Your **view** of something is your attitude to it and the way in which you understand it. EG *She has a view of life which is deeply corrupt... He tends to take a wider, more overall view of things than most people.*
N SING+SUPP

3 If you **view** something in a particular way, you think of it in that way. EG *He viewed the future with gloom... Their missiles are viewed as a defensive and deterrent force.*
V+O+A

4 The **view** from a window or high place is everything that you can see from it. EG *The windows of her flat looked out on to a superb view of London... From the top there is a fine view.*
N COUNT : USU SING

5 If you have a **view** of something, you can see it. EG *The driver blocked his view... I had one last view of the gorge.*
N SING+SUPP

6 If you **view** something, you look at it. EG *A drop from a pond, viewed through a microscope, swarms with tiny organisms.*
V+O Formal

7 You use **in my view** when you want to emphasize that you are stating your personal opinion. EG *In my view, we have a long way to go before we have a United States of Europe.*
ADV SEN

8 View is also used in these phrases. **8.1** If you **take the view that** something is true, your opinion is that it is true. EG *The civil servants generally took the view that experts know best.* **8.2** You use **in view of** to specify the main fact or event that causes you to do, say, or think something. EG *In view of the fact that all the other members of the group are going, I think you should go too.* **8.3** If you do something **with a view to** a particular result, you do it in order to achieve that result. EG *We have exchanged letters with a view to meeting to discuss these problems.* **8.4** If something is **in view**, you can see it from where you are. EG *We crept around the cage to keep the monkey in view... Marie turned her back on her rival in full*
PHRASES

Is a vicious circle really vicious?

view of the audience. **8.5** If you have something **in view**, you are aware of it and your actions are aimed towards it. EG *I don't teach with the exams in view.* **8.6** If something **comes into view**, you begin to be able to see it, either because it has moved or because you have moved. EG *The bridge suddenly came into view.* **8.7** If something is **on view**, it is being exhibited in public. EG *The Turner exhibition is on view at the Tate Gallery.*

viewer /vjuːə/, **viewers.** A **viewer** is someone who watches television. EG *Many of these programmes are an insult to the viewer's intelligence.* N COUNT

viewpoint /vjuːpɔɪnt/, **viewpoints. 1** Someone's **viewpoint** is the way that they think about things in general or about a particular thing. EG *I cannot make sense of it from my particular viewpoint as a Christian minister.* N COUNT+SUPP

2 A **viewpoint** is also a place from which you can get a good view of something that is happening. N COUNT

vigil /vɪdʒɪl/, **vigils.** A **vigil** is a period of time when you remain quietly in a place, especially at night, for example because you are looking after a sick person or are making a political protest. EG *Last weekend a nun on a hunger strike held a vigil at the United Nations.* N COUNT

vigilant /vɪdʒɪlənt/. If you are **vigilant**, you give careful attention to a situation and try to notice any danger or trouble that there might be. EG *This evening, I had to be especially vigilant.* ADJ QUALIT Formal
◊ **vigilance** /vɪdʒɪləns/. EG *Constant vigilance is required from all of us.* ◊ N UNCOUNT

vigilante /vɪdʒɪlænti¹/, **vigilantes. Vigilantes** are people who unofficially organize themselves into a group to protect their community and to catch and punish criminals. N COUNT: USU PLURAL

vigorous /vɪgərəs/. **1** A **vigorous** action is done with a lot of energy. EG *Mary gave her skirt a vigorous shake.* ◊ **vigorously.** EG *We shook hands vigorously and he went off.* ADJ QUALIT ◊ ADV

2 If you make a **vigorous** attempt to achieve something, you do it with a lot of energy and enthusiasm. EG *Their home has been saved by a vigorous campaign... He was one of the most vigorous advocates of workers' control.* ADJ QUALIT
◊ **vigorously.** EG *Chomsky defended this view very vigorously.* ◊ ADV

3 Someone who is **vigorous** is strong and healthy and full of energy. EG *...an elderly but vigorous man.* ADJ QUALIT

vigour /vɪgə/; spelled **vigor** in American English. **Vigour** is physical or mental energy and enthusiasm. EG *These problems were discussed with great vigour.* N UNCOUNT: USU+SUPP

vile /vaɪl/, **viler, vilest.** If you say that someone or something is **vile**, you are emphasizing how unpleasant they are and how much you dislike them. EG *...England's vile weather... ...her vile language... ...rage against this vile, contemptible act.* ADJ QUALIT

villa /vɪlə/, **villas.** A **villa** is an attractive house, especially one in the country that is used for holidays. EG *They rented a villa not far from Pisa.* N COUNT

village /vɪlɪdʒ/, **villages.** A **village** consists of a large group of houses, together with other buildings such as a church and a school, situated in a country area. EG *...an Austrian village... ...the village school... I work among the village people.* N COUNT

villager /vɪlɪdʒə/, **villagers. Villagers** are people who live in a village. EG *The villagers were suspicious of anything new.* N COUNT: USU PLURAL

villain /vɪlən/, **villains.** A **villain** is someone who deliberately harms other people or breaks the law. EG *A villain named Thomson broke into the premises... ...the treacherous villain who had upset all his plans.* N COUNT

villainous /vɪlənəs/. Someone who is **villainous** is very bad and willing to harm other people or break the law. EG *...villainous or wicked characters.* ADJ CLASSIF

villainy /vɪləni¹/ is very bad or criminal behaviour. EG *...the villainy of her landlord.* N UNCOUNT

vindicate /vɪndɪkeɪt/, **vindicates, vindicating, vindicated.** When someone **is vindicated**, their ideas or actions are proved to be correct. EG *Benn was decisively vindicated at the polls, receiving 23,275 votes to 10,231... His gloomy forecasts have been vindicated.* ◊ **vindication** /vɪndɪkeɪʃəⁿn/, **vindications.** EG *These changes to the law were widely regarded as a vindication of his long campaign.* V+O: OFT PASS Formal ◊ N COUNT OR N UNCOUNT

vindictive /vɪndɪktɪv/. Someone who is **vindictive** tries deliberately to hurt someone, often because they think that they have been harmed by them. EG *...a vindictive and violent man.* ADJ QUALIT
◊ **vindictively.** EG *Her dress had been vindictively cut to shreds.* ◊ ADV

vine /vaɪn/, **vines.** A **vine** is a climbing or trailing plant, especially the climbing plant that produces grapes as its fruit. N COUNT

vinegar /vɪnɪgə/ is a sharp-tasting liquid, usually made from sour wine or malt, which is used in making things such as salad dressing. N UNCOUNT

vineyard /vɪnjəd/, **vineyards.** A **vineyard** is an area of land where grape vines are grown in order to produce wine. EG *...the vineyards of Bordeaux.* N COUNT

vintage /vɪntɪdʒ/, **vintages. 1 Vintage** wine has been stored for several years in order to improve its quality. EG *...vintage port.* ADJ CLASSIF: ATTRIB

2 Vintage describes something which is the best or most typical of its kind, especially because it was produced at a time when the thing was at its best. EG *...vintage Bob Dylan music... ...vintage cars.* ADJ CLASSIF: ATTRIB

vinyl /vaɪnəⁿl/ is a strong plastic used for making things such as furniture and floor coverings. EG *...white vinyl chairs.* N UNCOUNT: OFT N MOD

viola /vi¹əʊlə/ **violas.** A **viola** is a musical instrument played with a bow. It is like a violin, but is slightly larger. N COUNT

violate /vaɪəleɪt/, **violates, violating, violated. 1** If you **violate** an agreement, law, or promise, you break it. EG *Ancient property laws are openly violated... He is violating his contract.* ◊ **violation** /vaɪəleɪʃəⁿn/, **violations.** EG *They blockaded the Suez Canal in violation of international agreements... ...violations of the Constitution.* V+O ◊ N UNCOUNT OR N COUNT

2 If you **violate** someone's privacy or peace, you disturb it. EG *The calm of the press lounge was suddenly violated.* V+O Formal

3 If someone **violates** a place, especially a tomb, they treat it with no respect, for example by breaking into it and removing its treasures. EG *...a curse on those who violated the tomb of the king.* V+O
◊ **violation, violations.** EG *...the violation of our homes.* ◊ N UNCOUNT OR N COUNT

violence /vaɪələns/. **1 Violence** is behaviour which is intended to hurt or kill people, for example hitting or kicking or using guns or bombs. EG *...threats of terrorist violence... ...acts of violence... ...robbery with violence.* N UNCOUNT

2 If you do or say something with **violence**, you use a lot of energy in doing or saying it, often because you are angry. EG *He flung open the door with unnecessary violence... I was surprised at the violence of his reaction.* N UNCOUNT

violent /vaɪələnt/. **1** If someone is **violent**, they behave in a way that is intended to hurt or kill people, for example by hitting or kicking or using guns or bombs. EG *People in this society are prepared to be violent... ...violent clashes with the police.* ◊ **violently.** EG *They have come into conflict, sometimes violently.* ADJ QUALIT ◊ ADV

2 A **violent** death is painful and unexpected, usually because the person who dies has been murdered. EG *...the constant threat of violent death.* ADJ CLASSIF
◊ **violently.** EG *...a poison that can kill violently and quickly.* ◊ ADV

3 Violent describes something that is said or argued with a lot of force and energy, usually because people are angry. EG *At times the argument grew violent... Burt's work came under vio-* ADJ QUALIT *lent attack.* ◇ **violently**. EG *They violently disagreed with their Commander-in-Chief.* ◇ ADV

4 **Violent** also describes something which happens suddenly and with a lot of force. EG *...a violent explosion... I gave it a violent tug.* ◇ **violently**. EG *The train braked violently.* ADJ QUALIT ◇ ADV

5 A **violent** emotion or sensation is very powerful. EG *He had a violent urge to create... A violent impatience overcame him.* ◇ **violently**. EG *This drug can make some people violently ill.* ADJ QUALIT ◇ ADV

6 **Violent** colours are unpleasantly bright. EG *...a shirt of violent red.* ADJ QUALIT : ATTRIB

7 **Violent** weather is stormy. ADJ QUALIT

violin /vaɪəlɪn/, **violins.** A **violin** is a musical instrument consisting of a shaped and polished hollow wooden box, with four strings stretched over it. You hold a violin under your chin and play it with a bow. See picture at MUSICAL INSTRUMENTS. N COUNT

violinist /vaɪəlɪnɪst/, **violinists.** A **violinist** is someone who plays the violin. N COUNT

VIP /viː aɪ piː/, **VIPs.** A **VIP** is someone who is given better treatment than ordinary people because he or she is famous, influential, or important. **VIP** is an abbreviation for 'very important person'. EG *...a private lounge for VIPs... She gave us the full VIP treatment.* N COUNT

viper /vaɪpə/, **vipers.** A **viper** is a small poisonous snake found mainly in Britain and Europe. N COUNT

virgin /vɜːdʒɪn/, **virgins. 1** A **virgin** is someone who has never had sex. EG *Men here still demand that the girls they marry should be virgins.* ▸ used as an adjective. EG *...a spinster or a virgin lady.* ◇ **virginity** /və^{5}dʒɪnɪ^{1}ti^{1}/. EG *His sister had lost her virginity many years before.* N COUNT ▸ ADJ CLASSIF : ATTRIB ◇ N UNCOUNT

2 Something that is **virgin** is fresh and clean, and its appearance shows that it has never been used before. EG *There were piles and piles of books, all virgin, all untouched.* ADJ CLASSIF

3 **Virgin** land has not been explored, cultivated, or spoiled by people. EG *...opening up virgin territory... ...virgin rain forest.* ADJ CLASSIF : ATTRIB

virginal /vɜːdʒɪnəl/. Someone who is **virginal** looks young and innocent, and has had no experience of sex. EG *The men have decreed that their women must be pure, virginal, innocent.* ADJ QUALIT

virile /vɪraɪl/. A man who is **virile** has the qualities that a man is traditionally expected to have, such as physical strength, forcefulness, and strong sexuality; used showing approval. EG *...virile young male actors.* ◇ **virility** /vɪrɪlɪti^{1}/. EG *The macho male wishes to prove his virility.* ADJ QUALIT ◇ N UNCOUNT

virtual /vɜːtʃʊ^{0}əl/ is used to say that something has all the characteristics of a particular thing, although it is not formally recognized as being that thing. EG *The peasants remain in a state of virtual slavery... ...a virtual revolution in organization.* ADJ CLASSIF : ATTRIB

virtually /vɜːtʃʊ^{0}əli^{1}/ is used to say that something is so nearly true that for most purposes it can be regarded as being true. EG *They are virtually impossible to detect... He virtually lived in his office... This opinion was held by virtually all the experts.* ADV

virtue /vɜːtjuː, -tʃuː/, **virtues. 1 Virtue** is thinking and doing what is right and avoiding what is wrong. EG *We accept certain principles of religion and traditional virtue.* N UNCOUNT

2 A **virtue** is a good quality or a good way of behaving. EG *Charity is the greatest of Christian virtues.* N COUNT

3 A **virtue** of something is an advantage or benefit that it has. EG *He was extolling the virtues of female independence... There is no virtue in taking this action.* N COUNT OR N UNCOUNT

4 You use **by virtue of** to explain why something happens or is true. EG *He was an object of interest simply by virtue of being British.* PREP Formal

virtuoso /vɜːtjʊəʊzəʊ, -səʊ/, **virtuosos** or **virtuosi** /vɜːtjʊəʊzi^{1}/. A **virtuoso** is someone who is exceptionally good at something, especially at playing a musical instrument. EG *He was a virtuoso of the jazz guitar.* N COUNT

virtuous /vɜːtʃʊəs, -tjʊəs/. Someone who is **virtuous** behaves correctly according to the moral code of a particular religion or society. EG *People who lead virtuous lives in this world are assured of paradise in the next.* ADJ QUALIT

virulent /vɪrʊlənt/. **1** Feelings, actions, or speeches that are **virulent** are extremely bitter and hostile. EG *Nehru and Nasser were the objects of special hatred and virulent attack.* ◇ **virulently**. EG *Fighting broke out again much more virulently.* ADJ QUALIT Formal ◇ ADV

2 A **virulent** disease or poison is extremely powerful and dangerous. EG *...a virulent virus.* ADJ QUALIT Formal

virus /vaɪrəs/, **viruses.** A **virus** is a germ that can cause disease in people, animals, or plants. EG *She had a flu virus... ...a virus infection.* N COUNT

visa /viːzə/, **visas.** A **visa** is an official stamp which is put in your passport by the embassy or consulate of a country that you want to visit, and which allows you to enter or leave that country, or to travel through it. EG *I obtained a visa to visit East Germany.* N COUNT

vis-à-vis /viːz æ viː/. You use **vis-à-vis** when you are considering one thing or quantity in comparison with another. EG *One solution would be for us to lower our exchange rate vis-à-vis other countries.* PREP Formal

viscount /vaɪkaʊnt/, **viscounts.** A **viscount** is a British nobleman who is below an earl and above a baron in rank. N COUNT

viscountess /vaɪkaʊntɪ^{2}s/, **viscountesses.** A **viscountess** is **1** the wife of a viscount. **2** a woman who holds the same rank as a viscount. N COUNT

vise /vaɪs/. See **vice**.

visibility /vɪzɪbɪlɪ^{1}ti^{1}/. You use **visibility** to say how far or how clearly you can see in particular weather conditions. EG *Visibility was excellent that day... ...conditions of restricted visibility.* N UNCOUNT

visible /vɪzɪbə^{0}l/. **1** If an object is **visible**, it is large enough to be seen, or is in a position where it can be seen. EG *These tiny creatures are hardly visible to the naked eye... The moon was fully visible... It was just visible from the beach.* ADJ QUALIT

2 If a situation, a change, or the state of something is **visible**, it can be noticed or recognized. EG *The results are visible in the growth of the Conservative vote... ...a period of little visible advance.* ◇ **visibly**. EG *She was visibly nervous.* ADJ QUALIT ◇ ADV

vision /vɪʒə^{0}n/, **visions. 1** If you have a **vision** of a possible situation or state of affairs, you have a mental picture of it, in which you imagine how things might be different from the way they are now. EG *...fighting for the vision of the new China... I had nightmarish visions of what could go wrong.* N COUNT : OFT+*of*

2 **Vision** is the ability to see clearly. EG *He has very little vision in his left eye... ...children with poor vision.* N UNCOUNT

3 The **vision** on a television set is the picture that is shown on it. EG *We apologize for the temporary loss of vision.* N UNCOUNT

visionary /vɪʒənə^{0}ri^{1}/, **visionaries.** A **visionary** is someone who has visions about how things might be different in the future. EG *...left-wing visionaries.* ▸ used as an adjective. EG *...the greatest visionary king in Ethiopian history.* N COUNT ▸ ADJ QUALIT

visit /vɪzɪt/, **visits, visiting, visited. 1** If you **visit** someone, you go to see them and to spend time with them. EG *She visited some of her relatives for a few days... You might need to visit a solicitor.* ▸ used as a noun. EG *It would be nice if you paid me a visit... She made a visit to her mother in Suffolk.* V+O OR V ▸ N COUNT

2 If you **visit** a place, you go to see it because you are interested in it. EG *This is the best museum we've visited... More than a million foreigners visit* V+O OR V

Are there any visual aids in this dictionary?

the United States every year. ▸ used as a noun. EG *He wrote to me after a brief visit to the U.S.* ▸ N COUNT

visitor /vɪzɪtə/, **visitors.** A **visitor** is someone who is visiting a person or place. EG *Marsha was a frequent visitor to our house... The Hall is open to visitors on weekdays.* N COUNT

visor /vaɪzə/, **visors.** A **visor** is a movable part of a helmet, for example one worn by a motorcyclist, which can be pulled down to protect a person's eyes or face. N COUNT

vista /vɪstə/, **vistas. 1** A **vista** is the view that you get from a particular place, especially a long view rather than a wide one. EG *He could see through the tall windows a vista of green fields.* N COUNT+SUPP Literary

2 You can also refer to a range of exciting or worrying new ideas and possibilities as a **vista**. EG *This turn of events opened up a whole new vista of troubles for me.* N COUNT+SUPP Literary

visual /vɪʒuəl, -zjʊ-/ means relating to sight. EG *...visual jokes... ...exhibitions in the visual arts.* ADJ CLASSIF
◊ **visually**. EG *Visually, it is a very exciting film... The island is visually stunning.* ◊ ADV SEN OR ADV

visual aid, visual aids. Visual aids are things that you can look at, such as films, models, maps, or slides, in order to help you understand, learn, or remember information of some kind. N COUNT: USU PLURAL

visualize /vɪʒʊ⁰əlaɪz/, **visualizes, visualizing, visualized;** also spelled **visualise.** If you **visualize** something, you imagine what it is like by forming a mental picture of it. EG *He found he could visualize her face quite clearly.* V+O

vital /vaɪtə⁰l/. **1** Something that is **vital** is necessary or very important. EG *It is vital to keep an accurate record of every transaction... They pressed on with their vital repair work.* ◊ **vitally**. EG *The way we choose to bring up children is vitally important.* ADJ QUALIT ◊ ADV+ADJ

2 You say that people or organizations are **vital** when they are energetic, exciting, and full of life. EG *The Chinese were trusting, open, and vital... We want to have a modern vital parliament.* ADJ QUALIT

vitality /vaɪtælɪ¹ti¹/. People who have **vitality** have great energy and liveliness. EG *...the vitality and eagerness of a normal toddler.* N UNCOUNT

vital statistics. A woman's **vital statistics** are the measurements of her bust, waist, and hips. These are often used to indicate how attractive and shapely her figure is. N PLURAL +POSS

vitamin /vɪtəmɪn/, **vitamins. Vitamins** are organic substances which you need in order to remain healthy. They exist naturally in many kinds of food and are also sold in the form of pills. EG *She needs extra vitamins and protein... One tiny berry contained more vitamin C than an orange.* N COUNT

vitriolic /vɪtrɪɒlɪk/. **Vitriolic** language or behaviour is full of bitterness and hate. EG *He was subjected to the most vitriolic personal abuse.* ADJ QUALIT: ATTRIB Formal

viva /vaɪvə/, **vivas.** A **viva** is an oral examination, especially one taken in a university. N COUNT

vivacious /vɪveɪʃəs/. Someone who is **vivacious** is lively, exciting, and attractive. EG *She was young and vivacious.* ADJ QUALIT

vivacity /vɪvæsɪ¹ti¹/ is the quality of being lively in an attractive and exciting way. EG *...a man of great charm and vivacity.* N UNCOUNT Formal

vivid /vɪvɪd/. **1** Something that is **vivid** is very bright in colour. EG *She was walking slowly across a vivid green lawn.* ◊ **vividly**. EG *They are the most vividly coloured birds in Australia.* ADJ QUALIT ◊ ADV

2 Memories or descriptions that are **vivid** are very clear and detailed. EG *I have a vivid memory of an excursion with my grandmother... She gave a vivid account of her travels.* ◊ **vividly**. EG *'You remember Captain Donck?' – 'Oh, yes. Vividly.'* ADJ QUALIT ◊ ADV

vivisection /vɪvɪsekʃə⁰n/ is the practice of cutting open living animals in order to perform scientific or medical experiments on them. N UNCOUNT

> **V+O** stands for **transitive verb**
> Verbs which have the label V+O in the Extra Column are transitive verbs, that is, they need an object to complete their meaning.
> See the entry headed VERBS for more information.

> **V+O+A** stands for **transitive verb used with adjunct**
> Verbs which have the label V+O+A in the Extra Column are verbs which need both an object and an adjunct to complete their meaning.
> See the entry headed VERBS for more information.

> **V+O+C** stands for **transitive verb followed by complement**
> Verbs which have the label V+O+C in the Extra Column are verbs which have an object and also a complement which refers back to the object.
> See the entry headed VERBS for more information.

vocabulary /və⁶kæbjə⁴ləri¹/, **vocabularies. 1** Your **vocabulary** is the total number of words that you know in a particular language. EG *By the age of five, a child has a vocabulary of over 2,000 words.* N COUNT OR N UNCOUNT

2 The **vocabulary** of a language is the words in it. EG *New words are constantly coming into use and then dropping out of the vocabulary.* N SING

3 The **vocabulary** of a subject is the group of words that are typically used when discussing it. EG *'Struggle' is a key word in the Marxist vocabulary.* N COUNT OR N UNCOUNT: +SUPP

vocal /vəʊkə⁰l/, **vocals. 1** You say that people are **vocal** when they speak very loudly about something that they feel strongly about. EG *The members had been quite vocal on issues of academic freedom.* ADJ QUALIT

2 Vocal means involving the use of the human voice, especially in singing. EG *She amazed her audiences with her superb vocal range... ...Russian vocal music.* ADJ CLASSIF: ATTRIB

3 When you refer to the **vocals** in a pop song, you are referring to the singing. EG *Lead vocals: Boy George. Backing vocals: Helen Terry.* N PLURAL

vocal cords; also spelled **vocal chords.** Your **vocal cords** are the part of your larynx which can be made to vibrate when you breathe out, making the sounds which you use for speaking. N PLURAL

vocalist /vəʊkəlɪst/, **vocalists.** A **vocalist** is a singer who sings with a pop group. N COUNT

vocation /vəʊkeɪʃə⁰n/, **vocations.** A **vocation** is a strong feeling that you want to do a particular job, especially one which involves serving other people. EG *By vocation I'm not a politician... Medicine is my vocation.* N COUNT OR N UNCOUNT

vocational /vəʊkeɪʃə⁰nəl, -ʃənə⁰l/ is used to describe the skills needed for a particular job or profession. EG *...a college that does technical and vocational training.* ADJ CLASSIF: USU ATTRIB

> **VOCATIVE**
> Some words have the label VOCATIVE in the Extra Column. This shows that you use the word when you are speaking to someone, just as if it were their name. Examples of words labelled VOCATIVE are **sir** and **honey**, as in EG *Mr Hink to see you, sir... Hello,* ***honey!***

vociferous /və[6]sɪfərəs/. Someone who is **vociferous** speaks very loudly, because they want to make sure that people hear what they are saying. EG *They were supported by a vociferous group in the actors' union.* ADJ QUALIT Formal

vodka /vɒdkə/, **vodkas. Vodka** is a strong, clear alcoholic drink. N MASS

vogue /vəʊg/. **1** If something is the **vogue**, it is very popular and fashionable. EG *The current vogue is for decentralization... Flowery carpets became the vogue.* N SING

2 Something that is **in vogue** is very popular and fashionable. EG *At that time aftershave was not in vogue in France.* PHRASE

voice /vɔɪs/, **voices, voicing, voiced. 1** When someone speaks, you hear their **voice**. EG *She heard a voice calling her name... He recognized me by my voice... 'I suppose we'd better go,' said John in a low voice.* N COUNT

2 You use **voice** to refer to someone's opinion on a particular topic and what they say about it. EG *Numerous voices were raised against the idea... The only dissenting voice was Mr Foot's.* N COUNT

3 If you have a **voice** in something, you have the right to express an opinion on it. EG *Students should have a voice in determining the way universities develop.* N SING : a+N

4 If you **voice** something such as an opinion or an emotion, you say what you think or feel. EG *The African delegates voiced their anger... Some fierce public criticism of it had been voiced.* V+O

5 In grammar, the active **voice** and the passive **voice** refer to the relation between a verb and its subject. N SING : *the*+N

6 Voice is also used in these phrases. **6.1** If you **raise** your **voice**, you speak more loudly. If you **lower** your **voice**, you speak more quietly. EG *Gregory began to raise his voice in protest... She lowered her voice to a discreet whisper.* **6.2** If someone tells you to **keep** your **voice down**, they are asking you to to speak more quietly. EG *'Can't you keep your voice down?' Brody said in a hoarse whisper.* **6.3** If you say something **at the top of** your **voice**, you say it as loudly as possible. EG *'I am drenched,' she declared at the top of her voice.* PHRASES

void /vɔɪd/, **voids. 1** A **void** is a situation or state of affairs which seems empty because it has no interest, excitement, or value. EG *Tending her mother had filled the void for a time... ...the need to fill the void of materialism with humane and spiritual values.* N COUNT : USU SING Literary

2 A **void** is also a big hole or space, especially one which is frightening. EG *He looked down into the gaping void at his feet.* N COUNT Literary

3 Something that is **void** or that is **null and void** has no official value or authority. EG *...declaring the contract null and void.* ADJ PRED Technical

volatile /vɒlətaɪl/. **1** A situation that is **volatile** is liable to change suddenly and unexpectedly. EG *The situation in Lebanon was 'tense, dangerous and volatile'.* ADJ QUALIT

2 Someone who is **volatile** is liable to change their mood or behaviour suddenly and unexpectedly. EG *He was a very clever, volatile actor.* ADJ QUALIT

volcanic /vɒlkænɪk/. A place or region that is **volcanic** has a lot of volcanoes or was created by volcanoes. EG *The islands are volcanic.* ADJ CLASSIF

volcano /vɒlkeɪnəʊ/, **volcanoes.** A **volcano** is a mountain which hot melted rock, gas, steam, and ash sometimes burst out of, coming from inside the earth. EG *Six other volcanoes were still erupting.* N COUNT

volition /və[6]lɪʃə[0]n/. If you do something **of** your **own volition**, you do it because you have decided for yourself that you will do it. EG *She didn't go down there of her own volition.* PHRASE Formal

volley /vɒli[1]/, **volleys, volleying, volleyed. 1** A **volley** of shots or gunfire is a lot of shots fired at the same time. EG *...a volley of automatic rifle fire.* N COUNT

2 In tennis, a **volley** is a shot in which the player hits the ball before it touches the ground. EG *He missed an easy cross-court volley.* ▸ used as a verb. EG *She ran to the other side and volleyed into the net.* N COUNT ▸ V OR V+O

volleyball /vɒli[1]bɔːl/ is a game in which two teams hit a large ball with their hands, backwards and forwards over a high net. If you allow the ball to touch the ground within the court, your team loses a point. N UNCOUNT

volt /vəʊlt/, **volts.** A **volt** is a unit used to measure the force of an electrical current. N COUNT

voltage /vəʊltɪdʒ/, **voltages.** The voltage of an electrical current is its force measured in volts. N UNCOUNT OR N COUNT

voluble /vɒljəbə[0]l/. Someone who is **voluble** talks a lot with great energy and enthusiasm. EG *He became very voluble and told her everything.* ADJ QUALIT Formal

volume /vɒljuːm/, **volumes. 1** A **volume** is **1.1** a book. EG *She took from the shelf a large green volume... ...a scholarly volume on Stonehenge.* **1.2** a book which is one of a series of books. EG *It was published in three volumes.* N COUNT : OFT+SUPP; N COUNT

2 The **volume** of something is **2.1** the amount of space that it contains or occupies. EG *The gas expanded to nine times its original volume.* **2.2** the amount of it that there is. EG *The volume of work is incredible... ...the growing volume of imports.* N SING : USU+POSS; N PART : SING

3 The **volume** of a radio, TV, or record player is the amount of sound that it produces. EG *She turned up the volume... They kept the radio playing at full volume.* N UNCOUNT

voluminous /vəlj[0]uːmɪnəs/. **1 Voluminous** clothes are very large. EG *...a voluminous skirt.* ADJ QUALIT Literary

2 If written information is **voluminous**, there is a lot of it. EG *I took voluminous notes.* ADJ QUALIT Formal

voluntary /vɒləntə[0]ri[1]/, **voluntaries. 1 Voluntary** describes actions that you do because you choose to do them and not because you have been forced to do them. EG *Attendance at the parade was voluntary... He went into voluntary exile.* ADJ CLASSIF
◊ **voluntarily.** EG *They were said to have left their land voluntarily.* ◊ ADV

2 Voluntary work is done by people who are not paid for it. EG *...voluntary services... I do voluntary home tuition.* ADJ CLASSIF

3 A **voluntary** worker is someone who does work, especially social work, without being paid for it. EG *The group is run by voluntary helpers.* ADJ CLASSIF

volunteer /vɒləntɪə/, **volunteers, volunteering, volunteered. 1** A **volunteer** is **1.1** someone who does work, especially socially useful work, for which they are not paid. EG *Teaching literacy to adults using volunteers began in 1963... ...volunteer work at the hospital.* **1.2** someone who chooses to join the army, navy, or air force, especially in wartime, as opposed to someone who is forced to join by law. EG *Many Australians fought as volunteers on the Allied side.* N COUNT

2 If you **volunteer** to do something, you offer to do it, rather than being forced to do it. EG *He volunteered to do whatever he could for them... ...an extra payment to those who volunteer for redundancy.* V : OFT+*to*-INF OR *for*, ALSO V+O

3 If you **volunteer** for the army, navy, or air force, you offer to join it without being required to do so by law. V : OFT+*for*

4 If you **volunteer** information or an explanation, you tell it to someone without being asked. EG *I volunteered no explanation for our visit.* V+O Formal

voluptuous /vəlʌptjuəs/. A **voluptuous** woman has large breasts and hips and is considered to be sexually desirable. EG *She was a voluptuous creature with blonde hair.* ADJ QUALIT Formal

vomit /vɒmɪt/, **vomits, vomiting, vomited. 1** If you **vomit**, food and drink comes back up from your stomach and out through your mouth, usually V OR V+O

Do you vote when there is a vote of thanks?

because you are ill. EG *She vomited into a paper bag.*
2 Vomit is partly digested food and drink that has come back up from someone's stomach and out through their mouth. EG *The stink of vomit reached Brody almost instantly.* N UNCOUNT

> **V+O+O** stands for **double object verb**
> Verbs which have the label V+O+O in the Extra Column are verbs which can have two objects.
> See the entry headed VERBS for more information.

voracious /vəˀreɪʃəs/. If you say that someone is **voracious** or that they have a **voracious** appetite for something, you mean that they want a lot of it. EG *The Duke's voracious capacity for food was abnormal... Nearly all of them were voracious readers of detective stories.* ADJ CLASSIF Literary

vortex /vɔːtɛks/, **vortexes** or **vortices** /vɔːtəsiːz/.
1 A **vortex** is a mass of wind or water which spins round so fast that it pulls objects into its empty centre. N COUNT Formal
2 You can refer to a situation as a **vortex** when you feel that you are being forced into it without being able to prevent it. EG *They found themselves sucked into the revolutionary vortex.* N COUNT+SUPP Formal

vote /vəʊt/, **votes, voting, voted. 1** Your **vote** is your choice in an election, or at a meeting where decisions are taken. EG *...an increase in votes for the Conservative Party... He will get my vote... The motion was defeated by 221 votes to 152.* N COUNT
2 When a group of people have a **vote** or take a **vote**, they make a decision by allowing each person in the group to say what they would prefer. The final decision is the one that most people prefer. EG *Let's have a vote.* N COUNT
3 In an election, the **vote** is the total number of people who have indicated their choice. EG *They captured 13 per cent of the vote.* N SING : *the*+N
4 When you **vote**, you make your choice in an election or at a meeting, usually by writing on a piece of paper or by raising your hand. EG *We've always voted Conservative... 381 delegates voted for unilateral disarmament... They voted to continue the strike.* V : OFT+A OR *to*-INF; ALSO V+O
5 You say that people have the **vote** when they have the legal right to indicate in an election who they would like to represent them as their government. EG *Women have had the vote for over fifty years.* N SING : *the*+N

vote in. When people **vote** a political party or leader **in**, they give them enough votes in an election to allow them to start governing the country. PHRASAL VB : V+O+ADV

vote out. When people **vote** a political party or leader **out**, they do not give them enough votes in an election to allow them to continue governing the country. PHRASAL VB : V+O+ADV

vote of thanks, votes of thanks. A **vote of thanks** is an official speech, usually at a meeting or a formal dinner, in which the speaker formally thanks a person for doing something. EG *The chairman will be proposing the vote of thanks.* N COUNT

voter /vəʊtə/, **voters.** A **voter** is someone who has the legal right to vote in an election. EG *Many of Britain's voters are looking for new answers.* N COUNT

vouch /vaʊtʃ/, **vouches, vouching, vouched. 1** If you say that you can or will **vouch for** someone, you mean that you are sure that they will behave correctly, and that you take responsibility for their good behaviour. EG *He said that he could vouch for your discretion... He said you'd vouch for him... I was vouched for by the Tattaglia family.* PHRASAL VB : V+PREP, HAS PASS
2 If you say that you can **vouch for** something, you mean that you have evidence from your own personal experience that it is true or correct. EG *I can vouch for the accuracy of my information.* V+PREP, HAS PASS

voucher /vaʊtʃə/, **vouchers.** A **voucher** is a ticket or a piece of paper that can be used instead of money to pay for a particular thing. EG *...meal vouchers worth 15p each.* N COUNT

vow /vaʊ/, **vows, vowing, vowed. 1** If you **vow** to do something, you make a solemn promise to do it. EG *He vowed never to let it happen again... He vowed that he would ride at my side.* V+*to*-INF OR REPORT : ONLY *that*
2 A **vow** is a solemn promise to do something. EG *She made a vow to give up smoking.* N COUNT

vowel /vaʊəl/, **vowels.** A **vowel** is a sound such as the ones represented by the letters 'a' or 'o', which you pronounce with your mouth open. Most words are pronounced with a combination of consonants and vowels. N COUNT

voyage /vɔɪɪdʒ/, **voyages.** A **voyage** is a long journey on a ship or in a spacecraft. EG *...the long sea voyage from London to Bombay.* N COUNT

voyager /vɔɪɪᵒdʒə/, **voyagers.** A **voyager** is someone who goes on a voyage, especially a difficult or dangerous one. EG *...our first voyagers to the stars... ...early ocean voyagers.* N COUNT

> **V-PASS** stands for **passive verb**
> Verbs which have the label V-PASS in the Extra Column are verbs which are more often used in the passive than in the active. So you are more likely to find *I **was flattered** by his courtesy* than *His courtesy **flattered** me.* And *I **was taken aback** by the price* is more frequent than *The price **took** me **aback**.*
> See the entry headed VERBS for more information.

> **V-REFL** stands for **reflexive verb**
> Verbs which have the label V-REFL in the Extra Column are verbs where the object can be a reflexive pronoun which refers back to the subject.
> See the entry headed VERBS for more information.

vs. is an abbreviation for 'versus'. EG *The first match is England vs. South America.*

> **V-SPEECH** stands for **speech verb**
> Verbs which have the label V-SPEECH in the Extra Column can be used as a transitive verb (V+O), as an intransitive verb describing direct speech (V+QUOTE), and as an intransitive verb describing indirect speech (V+REPORT).
> See the entry headed VERBS for more information.

vulgar /vʌlgə/. Something that is **vulgar** is socially unacceptable or offensive. EG *The boys had scrawled some vulgar graffiti about him in the loo... ...vulgar remarks.* ADJ QUALIT

vulnerable /vʌlnəᵒrəbəᵒl/. Someone who is **vulnerable** is weak and easily hurt physically or emotionally. EG *Lack of employment outside the home tends to make women vulnerable to depression... Elderly people, living alone, are especially vulnerable.* ◇ **vulnerability** /vʌlnəᵒrəbɪlɪˡtiˡ/. EG *...Britain's extreme vulnerability to attack.* ADJ QUALIT : OFT+*to* ◇ N UNCOUNT : OFT+*to*

vulture /vʌltʃə/, **vultures.** A **vulture** is a large bird which eats the flesh of dead animals. Vultures live in hot countries. N COUNT

vying /vaɪɪŋ/ is the present participle of **vie.**

W w

W, w /dʌbə°lju:/, **Ws, w's. 1 W** is the twenty-third letter of the English alphabet. N COUNT

2 W is an abbreviation for 'west'.

wad /wɒd/, **wads. 1** A **wad** of papers or bank notes is a thick bundle of them. EG *She handed over a wad of forms and leaflets.* N COUNT OR N PART

2 A **wad** of something is a lump of it. EG *...a wad of tobacco... ...a small, loose wad of cotton wool.* N COUNT OR N PART

waddle /wɒdə°l/, **waddles, waddling, waddled.** When a fat person or a duck **waddles**, they walk with short, quick steps, swaying slightly from side to side. EG *A little squat man waddled out of the bathroom.* V : USU+A

wade /weɪd/, **wades, wading, waded.** If you **wade** through water, you walk slowly through it, with your legs or the lower part of your body in the water. EG *The children waded out into the lake.* V : USU+A

wade through. If you **wade through** a difficult book or document, you spend a lot of time and effort reading it. EG *Each evening, he had to wade through columns of Parliamentary reports.* PHRASAL VB : V+PREP

wafer /weɪfə/, **wafers.** A **wafer** is a thin crisp biscuit which is usually eaten with ice cream. N COUNT

waffle /wɒfə°l/, **waffles, waffling, waffled. 1** When someone **waffles**, they talk or write a lot without saying anything clear or important. EG *He's still waffling away about economic recovery.* V

▸ used as a noun. EG *I don't want waffle, I want the real figures.* ▸ N UNCOUNT

2 A **waffle** is a thick crisp pancake with squares marked on it. Waffles are often eaten with syrup poured over them. N COUNT

waft /wɑːft, wɒft/, **wafts, wafting, wafted.** If a sound or scent **wafts** or **is wafted** through the air, it moves gently through the air. EG *A scent of lemon wafted up from the gardens below.* V-ERG+A

wag /wæg/, **wags, wagging, wagged. 1** When a dog **wags** its tail or when its tail **wags**, the dog repeatedly waves its tail from side to side. EG *The dog waited, making happy little barks and wagging his tail.* V-ERG

2 If **tongues wag**, people are gossiping about other people and their behaviour. EG *He dared not give her a scarf as a gift, because tongues might wag.* PHRASE Informal

wage /weɪdʒ/, **wages, waging, waged. 1** A **wage** is the amount of money that is regularly paid to someone for the work that they do, especially manual or unskilled work. EG *...the problems of families bringing up children on a low wage.* N COUNT

2 Someone's **wages** are the money that they are paid each week for the work that they do, especially when they have a manual or unskilled job. EG *My wages had not increased for two years.* N PLURAL

3 If a person or country **wages** a campaign or war, they start it and carry it on over a period of time. EG *He believes that they are plotting to wage a limited nuclear war in Europe.* V+O

wager /weɪdʒə/, **wagers.** A **wager** is an agreement that you make with someone in which you decide on an amount of money that you will pay them, or that they will pay you, depending on the result of a particular event. EG *...wagers on who will win the World Series.* N COUNT Outdated

waggle /wægə°l/, **waggles, waggling, waggled.** If you **waggle** something or if it **waggles**, it moves up and down or from side to side with short, quick movements. EG *He waggled his eyebrows.* V-ERG

wagon /wægə°n/, **wagons;** also spelled **waggon** in British English. A **wagon** is **1** a strong vehicle with four wheels, usually pulled by horses and used for carrying heavy loads. **2** a large container on wheels which is pulled by a train. EG *The cattle go by rail in wagons.* N COUNT British

wail /weɪl/, **wails, wailing, wailed.** If someone **wails**, they cry loudly. EG *One of the children began to wail... He raised a red, wet face and wailed, 'I didn't start the fight, she did.'* V : OFT+QUOTE

▸ used as a noun. EG *I could hear the wail of a baby next door.* ▸ N COUNT

waist /weɪst/, **waists. 1** Your **waist** is the narrow part of your body above your hips. See picture at THE HUMAN BODY. EG *She tied an apron around her waist.* N COUNT : OFT+POSS

2 The **waist** of a piece of clothing is the part of it which covers the middle part of your body. EG *...the waist of her skirt.* N COUNT

waistband /weɪst°bænd/, **waistbands.** A **waistband** is a narrow piece of material which is sewn on to a pair of trousers, a skirt, or another piece of clothing at the waist. N COUNT

waistcoat /weɪst°kəʊt/, **waistcoats.** A **waistcoat** is a sleeveless piece of clothing with buttons, which you wear on the top part of your body. Men often wear waistcoats over their shirts and under their jackets. See picture at CLOTHES. N COUNT

waistline /weɪst°laɪn/, **waistlines.** Your **waistline** is an imaginary line around your waist which you use as a way of measuring how fat you are. EG *...a 40-year-old lady with a large waistline.* N COUNT

wait /weɪt/, **waits, waiting, waited. 1** If you **wait**, you spend some time, usually doing very little, before something happens. EG *He waited patiently for her... She had been waiting in the queue to buy some stamps... Wait until we sit down.* V : OFT+A OR to-INF

◇ **waiting.** EG *There was a waiting period of one month.* ◇ ADJ CLASSIF : ATTRIB

2 A **wait** is a period of time in which you do very little, before something happens. EG *There was a long wait.* N COUNT : USU SING

3 If you **can't wait** to do something, you are very excited about it and eager to do it. EG *He couldn't wait to tell Judy.* PHRASE

4 If you say **'just you wait'** to someone, you are threatening them or warning them. EG *You wait! You'll find Robinson isn't as gentle as he seems.* PHRASE OR CONVENTION

5 You say **wait and see** to tell someone that they must be patient or that they must not worry about what is going to happen. EG *All you can do is wait and see.* PHRASE

6 You say **wait a minute, wait a second,** and **wait a moment 6.1** to interrupt someone when they are speaking, for example because you disagree with them. EG *Wait a minute, are you proposing to rewrite the entire play?* **6.2** to interrupt yourself when you are speaking, for example because you are trying to remember something. EG *Wait a minute. What did I do with the other one?* PHRASE Informal Informal

7 If something **is waiting** for you, it is ready for you to use or to do. EG *I have a lot of work waiting.* V

8 If you say that something can **wait,** you mean that it is not important or urgent and so you will deal with it later. EG *The dishes can wait.* V : USU WITH MODAL

9 If you **wait** on people in a restaurant, you serve people food as your job. V+A

10 If you **wait on** someone **hand and foot**, you provide everything that they need and do everything for them. EG *At the hospital, she had been waited on hand and foot.* PHRASE

wait about or **wait around.** If you **wait about** or **wait around**, you spend a lot of time, usually doing very little, before something happens. EG *Don't keep him waiting about in the hotel.* PHRASAL VB : V+ADV

wait up. If you **wait up**, you deliberately do not go to bed, usually because you are expecting PHRASAL VB : V+ADV someone to return home late at night. EG *She said that you shouldn't bother to wait up for her.*

waiter /weɪtə/, **waiters.** A **waiter** is a man who works in a restaurant, serving people with food and drink. N COUNT

waiting list, waiting lists. A **waiting list** is a list of people who have asked for something which cannot be given to them immediately, for example medical treatment or a job, and who must therefore wait until it is available. EG *He's on the waiting list for a council house.* N COUNT

waiting-room, waiting-rooms. A **waiting-room** is a room in a place such as a railway station or a doctor's surgery, where people can sit and wait. N COUNT

waitress /weɪtrɪ^{2}s/, **waitresses.** A **waitress** is a woman who works in a restaurant, serving people with food and drink. N COUNT

waive /weɪv/, **waives, waiving, waived.** If someone **waives** a rule, they decide not to enforce it in a particular situation. EG *Rules about proper dress may be waived.* V+O Formal

wake /weɪk/, **wakes, waking, woke** /wəʊk/, **woken** /wəʊkə^{0}n/. American English also uses the form **waked** for the past tense and past participle.
1 When you **wake** or when someone **wakes** you, you become conscious again after being asleep. EG *I sometimes wake at four in the morning... He woke me early.* V-ERG ● Your **waking hours** are the times when you are awake rather than asleep. EG *I spend most of my waking hours in the library.* ● PHRASE
2 If you leave something **in** your **wake**, you leave it behind you as you go. EG *They left trails of sweet papers in their wake.* PHRASE
3 If one thing follows **in the wake of** another, it happens after the other thing is over, and often as a result of it. EG *Famine came in the wake of disastrous floods.* PHRASE

wake up. 1 When you **wake up** or when someone **wakes** you **up**, you become conscious again after being asleep. EG *Ralph, wake up!... I woke up to discover that he had gone.* PHRASAL VB : V-ERG+ADV **2** If you **wake up** to a dangerous situation, you become aware of it. EG *The West began to wake up to the danger it faced.* V+ADV+*to*

waken /weɪkə^{0}n/, **wakens, wakening, wakened.** When you **waken** or when someone **wakens** you, you wake. EG *It is frightening to most children to waken and find a stranger in the room.* V-ERG Literary

walk /wɔːk/, **walks, walking, walked. 1** When you **walk**, you move along by putting one foot in front of the other on the ground. EG *Most children learn to walk when they are about one... We walked along in silence... They walk ten miles to school each day.* V : OFT+A OR V+O
2 A **walk** is **2.1** the action of walking rather than running. EG *He came in with his distinctive walk.* N SING **2.2** a journey which you make by walking. EG *He went out for a long walk... The station is a three minute walk from the park.* N COUNT **2.3** a path which is designed or used for people to walk along. EG *There are some beautiful walks along the coast.* N COUNT
3 If you **walk** someone somewhere, you walk there with them. EG *He walked her home.* V+O+A : NO PASS
4 If you **walk** your dog, you take it for a walk. V+O
5 See also **walking.**

walk away with. If you **walk away with** something such as a prize, you win it or achieve it very easily. PHRASAL VB : V+ADV+PREP

walk in on. If you **walk in on** someone, you go into a place and interrupt them without intending to, because you did not expect them to be there. PHRASAL VB : V+ADV+PREP

walk off. If you try to **walk off** a headache or other illness, you go for a walk in order to try to feel better. PHRASAL VB : V+O+ADV

walk off with. 1 If someone **walks off with** something that does not belong to them, they take it without asking the person who owns it. EG *Who's walked off with my pen?* PHRASAL VB : V+ADV+PREP Informal **2** If you **walk off with** something such as a prize, you win it or achieve it very easily. EG *She'll walk off with a first class degree.* V+ADV+PREP Informal

walk out. 1 If you **walk out** of a meeting, a performance, or an unpleasant situation, you leave it suddenly without explaining why, usually as a way of showing that you are angry. EG *Most of the audience walked out after the first half hour... He walked out of his job.* PHRASAL VB : V+ADV **2** If workers **walk out**, they go on strike. ● See also **walkout.** V+ADV

walk out on. If you **walk out on** someone, you leave them suddenly. EG *His girlfriend walked out on him.* PHRASAL VB : V+ADV+PREP

walkabout /wɔːkəbaʊt/, **walkabouts.** When a king, queen, or other important person **goes walkabout** or **does a walkabout**, he or she walks through crowds in a public place in order to meet people in an informal way. EG *The Pope suddenly went walkabout.* PHRASE

walker /wɔːkə/, **walkers.** A **walker** is a person who walks, especially in the countryside for pleasure. EG *The woods are heavily visited by tourists and walkers.* N COUNT

walkie-talkie /wɔːki^{1} tɔːki^{1}/, **walkie-talkies.** A **walkie-talkie** is a small radio that you can carry about and use to talk to and listen to someone far away. EG *There were hundreds of policemen around with walkie-talkies.* N COUNT

walking /wɔːkɪŋ/ is the activity of going for walks in the country. EG *Walking and mountaineering are very popular here... ...a walking holiday.* N UNCOUNT

walking stick, walking sticks. A **walking stick** is a long wooden stick which people can use to lean on while they are walking. N COUNT

Walkman /wɔːkmə^{3}n/, **Walkmans.** A **Walkman** is a small cassette player with very light headphones, which people carry around so that they can listen to music while they are doing something such as walking or travelling on a bus. N COUNT Trademark

walk of life, walks of life. The **walk of life** that you come from is the position that you have in society and the kind of job you have. EG *Members of this club come from many different walks of life.* N COUNT : USU+SUPP

walk-on. A **walk-on** part in a play is a very small part which usually does not involve any speaking. ADJ CLASSIF : ATTRIB

walkout /wɔːkaʊt/, **walkouts.** A **walkout** is a strike. EG *The pay deal ended the 43-day-old walkout.* N COUNT

walkover /wɔːkəʊvə/, **walkovers.** If a competition or contest is a **walkover** for you, you win it very easily indeed. EG *It was a walkover for Tyson.* N COUNT

walkway /wɔːkweɪ/, **walkways.** A **walkway** is a passage or path between two buildings for pedestrians to use. N COUNT

wall /wɔːl/, **walls. 1** A **wall** is **1.1** one of the vertical sides of a building or room. EG *There was a picture on the wall.* N COUNT **1.2** a long narrow vertical structure made of stone or brick that surrounds or divides an area of land. EG *We crouched behind the wall and waited.*
2 The **wall** of something hollow is the side of it. EG *...cellulose, the material from which the cell walls of plants are built.* N COUNT+SUPP
3 Wall is used in these phrases. **3.1** If you **are banging** your **head against a brick wall**, you are not making any progress in something that you are trying to do. PHRASES **3.2** If you **come up against a brick wall**, someone or something prevents you from making any further progress. EG *The latest talks about Northern Ireland have come up against a brick wall.* **3.3** If someone or something **drives** you **up the wall**, they make you very irritated or annoyed. EG *This drove him up the wall.* Informal

walled /wɔːld/. If an area of land is **walled**, it is surrounded or enclosed by a wall. EG *...the old walled city of Jerusalem.* ADJ CLASSIF

wallet /wɒlɪt/, **wallets.** A **wallet** is a small flat case made of leather or plastic, which is used for keeping paper money in and other small things such as credit cards. N COUNT

wallop /wɒləp/, **wallops, walloping, walloped.** If you **wallop** someone, you hit them very hard. EG *His mother would have walloped him if she'd known what he was up to.* V+O Informal

wallow /wɒləʊ/, **wallows, wallowing, wallowed. 1** If you **wallow** in an unpleasant situation or feeling, you allow it to continue longer than is reasonable or necessary. EG *At first I just wanted to wallow in misery... Her mother was wallowing in widowhood.* V+*in*

2 When an animal **wallows** in mud or water, it lies or rolls about in it slowly for pleasure. V : USU+*in*

wallpaper /wɔːlpeɪpə/, **wallpapers, wallpapering, wallpapered. 1 Wallpaper** is thick coloured or patterned paper that is used to decorate the walls of rooms. N MASS

2 If someone **wallpapers** a room, they cover the walls with wallpaper. V+O

wall-to-wall. A **wall-to-wall** carpet covers the floor of a room completely. ADJ CLASSIF

wally /wɒli¹/, **wallies.** If you call someone a **wally**, you mean that they are stupid or foolish. EG *He looked a right wally in that hat.* N COUNT Informal British

walnut /wɔːlnʌt/, **walnuts.** A **walnut** is a nut which has a wrinkled shape and a hard, round, light brown shell. N COUNT

walrus /wɔːlrəs, wɒl-/, **walruses.** A **walrus** is an animal which lives in the sea and looks like a large seal. It has long whiskers and two long teeth pointing downwards. N COUNT

waltz /wɔːls/, **waltzes, waltzing, waltzed. 1** A **waltz** is **1.1** a piece of music with a rhythm of three beats in each bar, which people can dance to. **1.2** a dance in which two people hold each other and move around the floor in time to waltz music. N COUNT

2 If you **waltz** with someone, you dance a waltz with them. EG *I dreamt of going to Hollywood to waltz with Ginger Rogers.* V OR V+*with* : RECIP

3 If you **waltz** somewhere, you walk there in a relaxed and confident way. EG *She waltzed across to Helen and sat down beside her.* V+A Informal

wan /wɒn/. Someone who is **wan** looks pale and tired. EG *She looked wan and fragile... ...a wan smile.* ADJ QUALIT Literary

wand /wɒnd/, **wands.** A **wand** is a long thin rod that magicians wave when they are performing tricks and magic. In children's stories, fairies also use wands when doing magic. EG *She seemed to expect him to wave a magic wand and make the problem disappear.* N COUNT

wander /wɒndə/, **wanders, wandering, wandered. 1** If you **wander** in a place, you walk around in a casual way. EG *We wandered round the little harbour town... A man was found wandering in the hills... The children wandered the streets after school.* V+A OR V+O

2 If your mind **wanders** or your thoughts **wander**, you stop concentrating on something and start thinking about other things. EG *When she was alone, she would let her mind wander... My thoughts kept wandering back to that night.* V

wane /weɪn/, **wanes, waning, waned. 1** If a condition, attitude, or emotion **wanes**, it becomes weaker, often disappearing completely in the end. EG *Her enthusiasm for Harold was beginning to wane... The influence of this group waned considerably.* • to **wax and wane**: see **wax**. V

2 If a condition, attitude, or emotion is **on the wane**, it is becoming weaker. EG *They could claim that pollution for the first time was on the wane.* PHRASE

wangle /wæŋgəºl/, **wangles, wangling, wangled.** If you **wangle** something that you want, you manage to get it by being clever or persuasive. EG *He always managed to wangle the easy jobs.* V+O Informal

want /wɒnt/, **wants, wanting, wanted. 1** If you **want** something, you feel a desire to have it or you feel a need for it. EG *Do you want a cup of coffee?... All they want is a holiday... I want to be an actress... I didn't want him to go.* V+O, V+*to*-INF, OR V+O+*to*-INF

2 If something **wants** doing, there is a need for it to be done. EG *We've got a couple of jobs that want doing in the garden.* V+-ING

3 If you tell someone that they **want** to do a particular thing, you are advising them to do it. EG *You want to book your holiday early this year.* V+*to*-INF

4 If someone **is wanted**, the police are searching for them. EG *He is wanted for the crimes of murder and kidnapping.* V+O : OFT PASS

5 A **want** of something is a lack of it. EG *They had to confess their complete want of foresight.* N SING+*of* Formal

6 If you do something **for want of** something else, you do it because the other thing is not available or not possible. EG *For want of anything better to do, he continued to read.* PHRASE Formal

7 Your **wants** are the things that you want. EG *They developed new wants: for bicycles, watches, and radios.* N PLURAL : USU+POSS

wanting /wɒntɪŋ/. If you find something **wanting** or if it proves **wanting**, it is not as good as you think it should be. EG *He judged the nation and found it wanting.* ADJ PRED Formal

wanton /wɒntən/. A **wanton** action deliberately causes harm, damage, or waste without any reason. EG *...senseless and wanton cruelty.* ADJ CLASSIF : USU ATTRIB Formal

war /wɔː/, **wars, warring, warred. 1** A **war** is a period of fighting between countries or states. EG *They fought in the war against Britain... They did not want to lose another war... There are no winners in nuclear war... England and Germany were at war.* • If a country **goes to war**, it starts fighting a war with another country. • See also **cold war**. N COUNT OR N UNCOUNT; • PHRASE

2 If two countries or states **war** with each other, they fight a war with each other. EG *India and Pakistan warred in 1965 over Kashmir.* V OR V+*with* : RECIP

◇ **warring.** EG *...the warring nations.* ◇ ADJ CLASSIF

3 You also use **war** to refer to competition between groups of people, or a campaign against a particular thing. EG *...a trade war... The administration is planning a new war on drugs.* N COUNT OR N UNCOUNT : USU+SUPP

4 If you say that someone **has been in the wars**, you mean that they have been injured, for example in a fight or an accident. EG *You look as if you've been in the wars.* PHRASE Informal

warble /wɔːbəºl/, **warbles, warbling, warbled.** When a bird **warbles**, it sings pleasantly with high notes and many variations. V OR V+O Literary

ward /wɔːd/, **wards, warding, warded. 1** A **ward** is **1.1** a room in a hospital which has beds for several people who need similar treatment. EG *She stayed five days in the emergency ward for observation.* **1.2** a district which forms part of a political constituency or local council. EG *We shall analyse the votes ward by ward.* N COUNT; British

2 A **ward** is a child who is officially put in the care of an adult because their parents are dead. A **ward of court** is a child who is in the care of a court of law because they need protection. EG *He recognized her at once as Mrs Pennington's ward.* N COUNT

ward off. If you **ward off** a danger or an illness, you do something to prevent it from affecting you or harming you. EG *He wears a copper bracelet to ward off rheumatism... He placed charms at the head of his bed to ward off evil spirits.* PHRASAL VB : V+O+ADV

-ward. -ward or **-wards** can be added to nouns that refer to places or directions in order to form adverbs or adjectives. These adverbs and adjectives indicate the direction in which something is moving or facing. EG *He was gazing skyward... He led the group homewards... ...the westward trail.* SUFFIX

warden /wɔːdºn/, **wardens. 1** A **warden** is an official who makes sure that certain laws are being obeyed. EG *...traffic wardens... ...game wardens.* N COUNT+SUPP

2 A **warden** in a building such as a youth hostel is N COUNT

If someone is on the warpath, are they going off to war?

the person who is in charge of the building and the people in it.

3 The **warden** of a prison is the person who is in charge of the prison. N COUNT American

warder /wɔ:də/, **warders.** A **warder** is a person who works in a prison and is in charge of prisoners. N COUNT

wardrobe /wɔ:drəʊb/, **wardrobes. 1** A **wardrobe** is a tall cupboard in which you can hang your clothes. EG *The red dress hung in her wardrobe.* N COUNT

2 Someone's **wardrobe** is the total collection of clothes that they have. EG *He was familiar with her entire wardrobe.* N COUNT

-wards. See **-ward**.

ware /wɛə/, **wares. 1** You can refer to things that are made of a particular substance or that are used for a particular purpose as a particular type of **ware**. EG *...glass ware... ...kitchen ware.* N UNCOUNT +SUPP

2 Someone's **wares** are the things that they sell, usually in the street or in a market. EG *The market traders began to sell their wares at half-price.* N PLURAL : USU+POSS Outdated

warehouse /wɛəhaʊs/, **warehouses.** A **warehouse** is a large building where raw materials or manufactured goods are stored. N COUNT

warfare /wɔ:fɛə/ is the activity of fighting a war. EG *They are anxious to prevent this conflict from erupting into open warfare.* N UNCOUNT Formal

warhead /wɔ:hɛd/, **warheads.** A **warhead** is the front end of a bomb or missile, where the explosives are carried. EG *...missiles with nuclear warheads.* N COUNT

warlike /wɔ:laɪk/. People who are **warlike** seem aggressive and eager to start a war. EG *...a warlike leader... ...a warlike nation.* ADJ QUALIT Formal

warm /wɔ:m/, **warmer, warmest; warms, warming, warmed. 1** Something that is **warm** has some heat but not enough to be hot. EG *...a bowl of warm water... ...a warm summer evening.* ADJ QUALIT

2 If you **warm** a part of your body, you put it near a fire or heater so that it stops feeling cold. EG *I warmed my hand on the radiator... Come and warm yourself in front of the fire.* V+O OR V-REFL

3 Clothes and blankets that are **warm** are made of a material such as wool which protects you from the cold. EG *...a pair of nice warm socks.* ADJ QUALIT
◇ **warmly.** EG *I'll see that Chris dresses warmly.* ◇ ADV

4 Warm colours or sounds are pleasant and make you feel comfortable and relaxed. EG *...a room decorated in warm reds and browns.* ADJ QUALIT

5 A **warm** person is friendly and behaves with a lot of affection or enthusiasm. EG *She had a warm, generous heart... He was given a warm welcome.* ADJ QUALIT
◇ **warmly.** EG *He shook Tony warmly by the hand.* ◇ ADV

6 If you **warm** to a person, you become fonder of them. If you **warm** to an idea, you become more interested in it. EG *This makes you warm to Meadows... He warmed to the prospect of a new job.* V+*to*

warm up. 1 If you **warm** something **up** or if it **warms up**, it gets hotter. EG *Start warming up the soup now... When the weather warmed up mosquitoes began swarming.* PHRASAL VB : V-ERG+ADV **2** If you **warm up** for an event such as a race, you prepare yourself for it by doing exercises or by practising just before it starts. • See also **warm-up**. V+ADV **3** When a machine or engine **warms up**, it becomes ready for use a little while after being switched on or started. EG *I turned on the radio. It warmed up and a radio announcer's voice came out.* V+ADV

warm-blooded. An animal that is **warm-blooded**, for example a bird or a mammal, has a relatively high body temperature which remains constant and does not change according to the surrounding temperature. ADJ CLASSIF

warm-hearted. Someone who is **warm-hearted** is friendly and affectionate towards other people. ADJ QUALIT

warmonger /wɔ:mʌŋgə/, **warmongers.** A **warmonger** is a person, for example a politician or a newspaper editor, who encourages people to start a war or to prepare for one. N COUNT

warmongering /wɔ:mʌŋgəʳrɪŋ/ is the activity of encouraging people to start a war or to prepare for one. N UNCOUNT

warmth /wɔ:mθ/. **1 Warmth** is a moderate amount of heat that something has, for example enough heat to make you feel comfortable. EG *...the warmth of the sun... We huddled together for warmth.* N UNCOUNT

2 The **warmth** of clothes or blankets is their ability to protect you from the cold. EG *...blankets which have little warmth.* N UNCOUNT

3 Someone who has **warmth** is friendly and enthusiastic in their behaviour. EG *...my uncle's warmth and affection... 'How do you do, sir?' she said, without warmth.* N UNCOUNT

warm-up, warm-ups. A **warm-up** is preparation that you do just before an event such as a race, for example exercises or practising. EG *During the warm-up exercises, I was still shaking.* N COUNT

warn /wɔ:n/, **warns, warning, warned. 1** If you **warn** someone about a possible danger or problem, you tell them about it so that they are aware of it. EG *The least I can do is warn them that there is a danger... I did warn you of possible failure... I warn you it's going to be expensive.* V+O : USU+A, REPORT, OR QUOTE; ALSO V+QUOTE

2 If you **warn** someone not to do something, you advise them not to do it in order to avoid possible danger or punishment. EG *I warned him not to lose his temper with her... I'm warning you, if you do that again there'll be trouble.* V+O : USU+*to*-INF

warn off. If you **warn** someone **off**, you tell them to go away or to stop doing something because of possible danger or punishment. EG *Intruders are warned off by the sound.* PHRASAL VB : V+O+ADV/PREP

warning /wɔ:nɪŋ/, **warnings. 1** A **warning** is something which is said or written to tell people of a possible danger, problem, or other unpleasant thing that might happen. EG *The hospital issued warnings about drugs to be avoided... Dad gave a final warning to them not to look directly at the sun... Mary left her husband without any warning.* N COUNT OR N UNCOUNT

2 Warning actions or signs give a warning. EG *His wife made warning faces at him not to irritate their guest... Watch out for the warning signs of depression like insomnia.* ADJ CLASSIF : ATTRIB

warp /wɔ:p/, **warps, warping, warped. 1** If something **warps** or **is warped**, it becomes damaged by bending or curving, often because of the effect of heat or water. EG *The cabinet doors began to warp soon after they were installed.* ◇ **warped.** EG *The wooden balconies were warped and weatherbeaten.* V-ERG : IF V+O THEN OFT PASS ◇ ADJ QUALIT

2 If something **warps** someone's character, it influences them and makes them abnormal or bad. EG *...a man whose whole character was warped by being bullied.* V+O

3 A **warp** in someone's character is a fault or abnormality that they have. EG *The same warp in my nature made me do it again.* N COUNT

4 A **warp** in time or space is an imaginary break or sudden change in the normal experience of time or space. EG *There's a kind of time warp in his education.* N COUNT

warpath /wɔ:pɑ:θ/. If someone is **on the warpath**, they are angry and are getting ready for a fight or argument. EG *He scares me to death when he's on the warpath.* PHRASE Informal

warrant /wɒrənt/, **warrants, warranting, warranted. 1** If something **warrants** a particular action, it makes the action seem necessary. EG *The situation is serious enough to warrant a special effort... The case warrants further investigation.* V+O Formal

2 A **warrant** is an official document signed by a judge or magistrate, which gives the police special permission to do something such as arrest someone or search their house. EG *A warrant was issued for his arrest.* N COUNT

warren /wɒrən/, **warrens.** A **warren** is a group of holes in the ground which are connected by tunnels and which rabbits live in. N COUNT

warrior /wɒrɪə/, **warriors. Warriors** were soldiers or experienced fighting men in former times. EG *...stories of ancient kings, warriors and great battles.* N COUNT Literary

warship /wɔːʃɪp/, **warships.** A **warship** is a ship with guns that is used for fighting in wars. N COUNT

wart /wɔːt/, **warts.** A **wart** is a small hard piece of skin which sometimes grows and sticks out on part of your body, usually your face or hands. EG *...a large woman with a wart on her nose.* N COUNT

wartime /wɔːtaɪm/ is a period of time when there is a war. EG *...the disruption of the environment in wartime... ...wartime memories.* N UNCOUNT

wary /weəri^1/. If you are **wary** about something, you are cautious about it, for example because it is a new experience or because there may be dangers or problems. EG *People are understandably wary of the new government... I'm very wary about believing these stories.* ADJ QUALIT

was /wɔ^{7}z/ is the first and third person singular of the past tense of **be.**

wash /wɒʃ/, **washes, washing, washed. 1** If you **wash** something, you clean it using water and soap. EG *...the clatter of dishes being washed and put away... She washes and irons his clothes.* ▸ used as a noun. EG *Give it a good wash.* V+O ▸ N COUNT: OFT SING

2 The **wash** is all the clothes that are washed together at one time, for example once a week. EG *...the average weekly wash.* N SING: *the*+N

3 If you **wash** or if you **wash** part of your body, you clean part of your body using soap and water. EG *First wash your hands... The children were encouraged to wash and dress themselves.* ▸ used as a noun. EG *He was having a wash.* V OR V+O ▸ N COUNT: OFT SING

4 If water **washes** somewhere, it flows there gently. If something **is washed** somewhere, it is carried there gently by water. EG *The surf washed over her ankles... The body was washed ashore in Norway.* V+A OR V-ERG+A

5 If you say that you **wash** your **hands of** something, you mean that you refuse to be involved with it any longer or that you refuse to accept responsibility for it. EG *...a building that the authorities had put up and then washed their hands of.* PHRASE

6 See also **washing**.

wash away. If floods **wash away** buildings, they destroy the buildings and carry them away. EG *The flood washed the old bridge away.* PHRASAL VB: V+O+ADV

wash down. 1 If you **wash down** food, you drink something after you have eaten it or while you are eating it. EG *We had smoked salmon and grouse, washed down with claret and vintage port.* PHRASAL VB: V+O+ADV: USU+*with* **2** If you **wash** an object **down**, you wash all of it thoroughly. EG *I spent the morning washing down paintwork.* V+O+ADV

wash out. 1 If you **wash** a stain or colour **out** of something, you manage to remove it by using water and soap. PHRASAL VB: V-ERG+ADV **2** If you **wash out** a container, you wash the inside of it. V+O+ADV **3** See also **washed-out**, **washout**.

wash up. 1 If you **wash up**, **1.1** you wash the plates, cups, knives, and forks which have been used in cooking and eating a meal. EG *He insisted on helping me wash up.* PHRASAL VB: V+ADV OR V+O+ADV **1.2** you clean part of your body with soap and water, especially your hands and face. EG *I washed up as best I could in the adjacent bathroom.* V+ADV American **2** If something **is washed up** on a piece of land, it is carried by a river or sea and left there. EG *His body was washed up under the bridge at Dakao.* V+O+ADV, OFT PASS+A **3** See also **washing-up**.

washable /wɒʃəbə^{0}l/. Clothes or materials that are **washable** can be washed without being damaged. EG *Acrylic blankets are warm and washable.* ADJ CLASSIF

washbasin /wɒʃbeɪsə^{0}n/, **washbasins.** A **washbasin** is a large basin for washing your hands and face. Washbasins are usually fixed to a wall and have taps for hot and cold water. N COUNT

washed-out. 1 Something that is **washed-out** is pale in colour and dull. EG *...eyes of washed-out grey... Pale blue makes her look washed-out.* ADJ QUALIT

2 If someone looks **washed-out**, they look very tired. EG *He had lots of children and a washed-out wife.* ADJ QUALIT

washer /wɒʃə/, **washers.** A **washer** is a thin flat ring of metal or plastic, which is placed over a bolt before the nut is screwed on, in order to make a tighter connection. EG *Unscrew the nut, remove and replace the washer and reassemble the tap.* N COUNT

washing /wɒʃɪŋ/ consists of clothes which need to be washed or which are in the process of being washed or dried. EG *Her husband comes home at weekends bringing his washing with him... There was nowhere to hang washing.* N UNCOUNT

washing machine, washing machines. A **washing machine** is a machine which you can wash clothes in. EG *...a fully automatic washing machine.* N COUNT

washing powder, washing powders. Washing powder is powdered detergent that you use to wash clothes. N MASS

washing-up. If you do the **washing-up**, you wash the plates, cups, knives, and forks which have been used in cooking and eating a meal. EG *We share the cooking and the washing-up... ...a washing-up bowl.* N UNCOUNT

washing-up liquid, washing-up liquids. Washing-up liquid is thick soapy liquid which you add to hot water to clean dirty dishes after a meal. N MASS

washout /wɒʃaʊt/, **washouts.** If an event or project is a **washout**, it is a total failure. EG *Thanks to you, today's been an appalling washout.* N COUNT Informal

washroom /wɒʃru^{4}m/, **washrooms.** A **washroom** is a room with toilets and washing facilities, situated in a large building such as an office block or a hostel. N COUNT American

wasn't /wɒzə^{0}nt/ is the usual spoken form of 'was not'. EG *I wasn't ready for it... He was first, wasn't he?*

wasp /wɒsp/, **wasps.** A **wasp** is an insect with yellow and black stripes across its body, which can sting like a bee but does not produce honey. N COUNT

wastage /weɪstɪdʒ/. **Wastage** of something is a waste of it. EG *The Government is to blame for this serious wastage of talent among the young... ...the tremendous wastage from inefficient energy use.* N UNCOUNT: USU+SUPP Formal

waste /weɪst/, **wastes, wasting, wasted. 1** If you **waste** time, money, or energy, you use too much of it on something that is not important or necessary. EG *You're wasting your time... ...fear of wasting money on a new idea.* V+O

2 If you **waste** an opportunity for something, you do not take advantage of it when it is available. V+O

3 If you say that something **is wasted** on someone, you mean that it is too good, clever, or sophisticated for them. EG *Her parents were wealthy and did not want her to be wasted on a poor university lecturer.* V+O+*on*: USU PASS

4 If you say that an action or activity is a **waste** of time, money, or energy, you mean that it involves using too much time, money, or energy and it is not important or necessary. EG *It's probably a waste of time... It's a waste of money hiring skis.* N SING: *a*+N+*of*

5 Waste is the use of too much money or other resources on things that do not need it. EG *A committee was set up to avoid future waste of public money.* N UNCOUNT

6 Waste is also material which has been used and is no longer wanted, for example because the valuable or useful part of it has been taken out. EG *...radioactive waste from nuclear power stations... The river was thick with industrial waste.* ▸ used as an adjective. EG *...waste material from the oil industry... ...waste paper.* N UNCOUNT ▸ ADJ CLASSIF: ATTRIB

Do you use washing powder to do the washing up?

7 Waste land is land which is not used or looked after by anyone, and so is covered by wild plants and rubbish. EG *The car was found abandoned on waste ground near Leeds.* ADJ CLASSIF : ATTRIB

8 Wastes are large areas of land in which there are very few people, plants, or animals. EG *...the polar wastes... ...the endless wastes of the desert.* N PLURAL Formal

9 If something **goes to waste**, it remains unused, goes bad, or is thrown away. PHRASE

10 See also **wasted**.

waste away. If someone **wastes away**, they become extremely thin and weak because they are ill or worried and they are not eating properly. EG *I don't want you to waste away.* PHRASAL VB : V+ADV

wastebasket /weɪstbɑːskɪt/, **wastebaskets.** A **wastebasket** is the same as a wastepaper basket. N COUNT American

wasted /weɪstɪ²d/. A **wasted** action is one that is unnecessary. EG *It was a wasted journey.* ADJ CLASSIF

wasteful /weɪstfʊl/. An action that is **wasteful** causes waste, because it uses resources in a careless or inefficient way. EG *...the wasteful use of scarce resources.* ADJ QUALIT

wasteland /weɪstlænd/, **wastelands.** A **wasteland** is an area of land which is of no use, for example because it is infertile or because it has been misused by people. EG *The highways cross endless wastelands.* N COUNT OR N UNCOUNT

wastepaper basket, wastepaper baskets. A **wastepaper basket** or **wastepaper bin** is a container for rubbish, especially for waste paper, which is usually placed on the floor in the corner of a room or next to a desk. See picture at BASKETS. EG *He crumpled the note and tossed it into the wastepaper basket.* N COUNT

watch /wɒtʃ/, **watches, watching, watched. 1** A **watch** is a small clock which you wear on a strap on your wrist. EG *He looked at his watch... My watch has stopped.* N COUNT

2 If you **watch** something, you look at it for a period of time, and pay attention to what is happening. EG *I used to sit and watch the boats moving down the river... I'm just watching television... A policeman stood watching... When did you last watch a football match?* V+O OR V

3 If you **watch** someone, you follow them secretly or spy on them. EG *Liebermann's going to be watched from now on.* V+O

4 If you **watch** a situation, you pay attention to it or you are aware of it. EG *The federation never ceases to watch events and fight injustices... She sits back and just watches a situation develop... Many companies have watched helplessly as their stock prices fell.* V+O OR V+A

5 If you **keep watch** on a situation, you pay attention to what is happening, so that you can take action at the right moment. EG *The closest watch should be kept on any signs of industrial unrest.* PHRASE

6 If someone **keeps watch**, they look around all the time, for example while other people are asleep, so that they can warn the others of danger. EG *A woman kept watch at the gate.* PHRASE

7 A **watch** is also a group of guards or soldiers who have the job of carefully looking around so that they can warn others of danger. EG *The day watch had been on duty for a couple of hours.* N COLL

8 If you **watch** someone or something, you take care that they do not get out of control or do something unpleasant. EG *You ought to watch Barbara – she's behaving very oddly.* V+O

9 You say **'watch it'** in order to warn someone to be careful. EG *Watch it! There's a rotten floorboard somewhere just here.* PHRASE Informal

10 If you tell someone to **watch** their **step**, you are warning them to be careful what they say and do. EG *I'm cleverer than you are, so watch your step.* PHRASE Informal

watch out. If you **watch out**, you are very careful because something unpleasant might happen to you. EG *If you don't watch out, he might stick a knife into you.* PHRASAL VB : V+ADV, ONLY INF

watch over. If you **watch over** someone or something, you care for them. EG *The wives took turns to watch over the children.* PHRASAL VB : V+PREP, HAS PASS

watchband /wɒtʃbænd/, **watchbands.** A **watchband** is the same as a watchstrap. N COUNT American

watchdog /wɒtʃdɒg/, **watchdogs.** You use **watchdog** to refer to a person or committee whose job is to make sure that companies do not act illegally or irresponsibly. EG *They established the Atomic Energy Commission to act as a watchdog.* N COUNT

watcher /wɒtʃə/, **watchers.** A **watcher** is a person who looks at something for a period of time, and who pays attention to what is happening. EG *Their behaviour baffled the watchers in the house.* N COUNT

watchful /wɒtʃfʊl/. Someone who is **watchful** is careful to notice everything that is happening. EG *It is important that governments remain watchful... He spent his days under the watchful eyes of his grandmother.* ADJ QUALIT

watchstrap /wɒtʃstræp/, **watchstraps.** A **watchstrap** is a piece of leather, plastic, or metal which is attached to a watch so that you can wear it round your wrist. N COUNT

watchword /wɒtʃwɜːd/, **watchwords.** A **watchword** is a word or phrase that sums up the way that a particular group of people think or behave. EG *Today the watchword is 'Learn through playing'.* N COUNT

water /wɔːtə/, **waters, watering, watered. 1 Water** is the clear, thin liquid that has no colour and no taste when it is pure. It falls from clouds as rain and enters rivers and seas. All animals and people need to drink water in order to live. EG *...a drink of water... Mammals can't breathe under water.* N UNCOUNT

2 You use **water** or **waters** to refer to a large amount or area of water, for example a lake or sea. EG *The children played at the water's edge... ...the black waters of the Thames.* N UNCOUNT OR N PLURAL

3 A country's **waters** consist of the area of sea which is near to that country and which is regarded as belonging to it. EG *The ship was in British waters.* N PLURAL +SUPP

4 If you **water** plants, you pour water into the soil in order to help them to grow. V+O

5 If your eyes **water**, you have tears in them because they are hurting. EG *The onions made his eyes water.* V

6 If your mouth **waters**, it produces more saliva, usually because you can smell or see some appetizing food. EG *This should make your mouth water.* V

7 When you **pass water**, you urinate. PHRASE

8 Water is also used in these phrases. **8.1** If you say that an event is **water under the bridge**, you mean that it has happened and cannot now be changed, so there is no point in worrying about it any more. **8.2** If you **pour** or **throw cold water on** an idea or suggestion, you indicate that you do not think it is very good. **8.3** If you **keep** your **head above water**, you avoid getting into difficulties, especially in business. **8.4** to **take to** something **like a duck to water**: see **duck**. PHRASES

water down. 1 If you **water down** food or drink, you add water to it to make it weaker. EG *The milk had been watered down.* PHRASAL VB : V+O+ADV **2** If a speech or plan **is watered down**, it is made much weaker and less forceful. EG *The whole article had been watered down.* V+O+ADV, USU PASS ◇ **watered-down.** EG *The Equal Pay Act is so watered down as to be useless... ...a watered-down pay claim.* ◇ ADJ QUALIT

water-borne. Something that is **water-borne** is carried or passed on by water. EG *...water-borne diseases.* ADJ CLASSIF

water cannon, water cannons. A **water cannon** is a machine which shoots out a powerful jet of water. It is used by police to break up crowds of people. N COUNT

watercolour /wɔːtəkʌlə/, **watercolours;** spelled **watercolor** in American English. **1 Watercolours** N PLURAL

are coloured paints used for painting pictures. You can mix them with water first, or put them on the paper with a wet brush.
2 A **watercolour** is a picture which has been painted using watercolours. EG *...an exhibition of watercolours.* N COUNT

watercress /wɔːtəkrɛs/ is a small plant with white flowers which grows in streams and pools. Its leaves taste hot and are eaten raw in salads. N UNCOUNT

waterfall /wɔːtəfɔːl/, **waterfalls.** A **waterfall** is water that flows over the edge of a steep cliff and falls to the ground below. N COUNT

waterfront /wɔːtəfrʌnt/, **waterfronts.** A **waterfront** is a street or piece of land which is next to an area of water, for example a river or the sea. EG *...a warehouse on the waterfront.* N COUNT: USU SING

waterhole /wɔːtəhəʊl/, **waterholes.** A **waterhole** is a pond or pool in a desert or other dry area where animals can find water to drink. N COUNT

watering can, watering cans. A **watering can** is a container shaped like a bucket with a long spout on one side, which you use to water plants. N COUNT

waterlogged /wɔːtəlɒgd/. **1** An area of land that is **waterlogged** is so wet that the soil cannot contain any more water, with the result that a layer of water remains on the surface of the ground. ADJ QUALIT
2 A **waterlogged** boat is so full of water that it may soon sink. ADJ QUALIT

watermelon /wɔːtəmɛlən/, **watermelons.** A **watermelon** is a large round fruit which has a green skin and is pink and juicy inside with a lot of black seeds. N COUNT

waterproof /wɔːtəpruːf/, **waterproofs, waterproofing, waterproofed. 1** Something that is **waterproof** does not let water pass through it. EG *...a pair of waterproof trousers.* ADJ CLASSIF
2 A **waterproof** is a coat which does not let water pass through it. N COUNT
3 If you **waterproof** something, you make it waterproof. EG *...a system for waterproofing damp walls.* V+O

watershed /wɔːtəʃɛd/, **watersheds.** A **watershed** is an event or period which is important, because it marks the beginning of a new way of life or a new stage in a person's career. EG *The Vietnam war was one of the great watersheds of modern history.* N COUNT

waterside /wɔːtəsaɪd/. The **waterside** is a street or shore beside an area of water such as a river or lake. EG *I drove down to the waterside.* N SING: the+N

water-ski, water-skis, water-skiing, water-skied. If you **water-ski**, you ski on water while being pulled along by a boat. ◊ **water-skiing.** EG *...excellent facilities for sailing, water-skiing, and skin-diving.* V; ◊ N UNCOUNT

watertight /wɔːtətaɪt/. **1** Something that is **watertight** does not allow water to pass through it because it is very tightly sealed. EG *...watertight doors.* ADJ CLASSIF
2 An agreement or argument that is **watertight** has been so carefully put together that nobody should be able to find a fault in it. EG *It sounded a good watertight story.* ADJ CLASSIF

waterway /wɔːtəweɪ/, **waterways.** A **waterway** is a canal, river, or narrow channel of sea which ships or boats can sail along. N COUNT

waterworks /wɔːtəwɜːks/. **Waterworks** is both the singular and the plural form.
A **waterworks** is a building where a supply of water is stored and cleaned before being distributed to the public. N COUNT

watery /wɔːtəʳriʲ/. **1** Something that is **watery** is weak or pale. EG *...a watery smile... ...a watery April sun.* ADJ QUALIT
2 Food or drink that is **watery** contains a lot of water. EG *...watery cabbage.* ADJ QUALIT

watt /wɒt/, **watts.** A **watt** is a unit of measurement of electrical power. EG *...a 60 watt bulb.* N COUNT

wave /weɪv/, **waves, waving, waved. 1** If you **wave** or **wave** your hand, you move your hand from side to side in the air, usually in order to say hello or goodbye to someone. EG *His mother waved to him... We waved at them from the train... Peter waved his hand towards the house.* ▸ used as a noun. EG *Jack gave his usual cheery wave.* V OR V+O: USU+A; ▸ N COUNT
2 If you **wave** someone away or **wave** them on, you make a movement with your hand to indicate that they should move in a particular direction. EG *He waves on the traffic... I was waved through.* V+O+A
3 If you **wave** something, you hold it up and move it rapidly from side to side. EG *All along the route, people applauded and waved flags at them.* V+O
4 If something **waves**, it moves gently up and down or from side to side. EG *The grass was waving in the wind.* V
5 A **wave** is also a raised line of water on the surface of water, especially the sea, which is caused by the wind or by tides making the surface of the water rise and fall. EG *She could see the line of white foam where the waves broke on the beach.* ● See also **tidal wave.** N COUNT
6 Wave is used to refer to **6.1** the sudden increase in heat or energy that spreads out from an earthquake, eruption, or explosion. EG *...the shock wave from a one megaton bomb.* **6.2** the form in which some types of energy travel, for example light, sound, or radio signals. EG *Radar employs radio waves whereas sonar uses sound waves.* ● See also **long wave, medium wave** and **short wave.** N COUNT+SUPP
7 A **wave** in someone's hair is a part of the hair that forms a gentle curving shape. N COUNT
8 A **wave** of sympathy, alarm, or panic is a steady increase in that feeling which spreads through you or through a group of people. EG *A mounting wave of dislike and anger rose within me... In the general wave of panic, nobody thought of phoning for an ambulance.* N COUNT+SUPP
9 A **wave** is also **9.1** a sudden increase in a particular activity or type of behaviour. EG *In Paris in May 1968 there was a massive wave of student riots... ...a crime wave.* ● See also **new wave. 9.2** a sudden increase in the number of people moving somewhere. EG *...the last great wave of migrants.* N COUNT+SUPP

wave aside. If you **wave aside** an idea or comment, you decide that it is not important enough to be used or considered. EG *The Chief waved his objection aside.* PHRASAL VB: V+ADV

wave down. If you **wave down** a vehicle, you wave your hand as a signal to the driver to stop the vehicle. PHRASAL VB: V+O+ADV

waveband /weɪvbænd/, **wavebands.** A **waveband** is a group of radio waves of similar length which are used for particular types of radio transmission. N COUNT

wavelength /weɪvlɛŋkθ/, **wavelengths. 1** A **wavelength** is the size of radio wave which a particular radio station uses to broadcast its programmes. N COUNT
2 If two people are **on the same wavelength**, they share the same interests and attitudes and understand each other very well. PHRASE

waver /weɪvə/, **wavers, wavering, wavered. 1** If you **waver** or if your confidence or beliefs **waver**, you are no longer firm or confident in your beliefs. EG *Meehan has never wavered in his assertions of innocence... Her love for him never wavered.* V
2 If you **waver**, you hesitate before making a decision. EG *If you're going to start wavering then the deal's off!* V
3 If something **wavers**, it moves or changes slightly. EG *The temperature wavered between freezing* V

What is the difference between a wave band and a wavelength?

and thawing... I looked into his eyes. They didn't waver.

wavy /weɪvi[1]/. **1 Wavy** hair grows in loose curls. ADJ QUALIT EG *He had wavy grey hair.*

2 A **wavy** line has a series of regular curves along it. ADJ QUALIT

wax /wæks/, **waxes, waxing, waxed. 1 Wax** is N UNCOUNT **1.1** a solid, slightly shiny substance made of fat or oil and used especially to make candles and polish. Wax goes soft and melts when it is heated. EG *...wax candles... The packet was then sealed with wax.* **1.2** the sticky yellow substance found in your ears.

2 If you **wax** a surface, you put a thin layer of wax onto it, usually in order to polish it. EG *I started waxing the floor.* V+O

3 If something **waxes and wanes**, it first increases and then decreases over a period of time. EG *The popularity of the film stars waxed and waned.* PHRASE

4 If you **wax** eloquent or **wax** romantic, you start to show that quality in the way you talk. EG *I can just imagine David waxing lyrical about Ireland.* V+C Literary

waxwork /wæksw3:k/, **waxworks.** In paragraph 2 **waxworks** is both the singular and the plural form.

1 A **waxwork** is a model of a famous person, made out of wax. N COUNT

2 A **waxworks** is a place where wax models of famous people are displayed for the public to look at. N COUNT

waxy /wæksi[1]/. Something that is **waxy** looks or feels like wax. EG *The skin was fleshy and slightly waxy to the touch.* ADJ QUALIT

way /weɪ/, **ways. 1** If you refer to a **way** of doing something, you are referring to how you can do it. EG *...different ways of cooking fish... The only way to stop an accident is to remove the risk... You can qualify for a pension in two ways... I'm going to handle this my way.* N COUNT+SUPP

2 When you talk about the **way** someone does something, you are talking about the qualities which their action has. EG *He smiles in a superior way... He hated the way she talked.* N SING+SUPP

3 The **ways** of a particular person or group of people are their customs or their usual behaviour. EG *We will not impose our ways on them... ...the difficulty of changing one's ways.* N PLURAL +SUPP

4 If something is true or has an effect in a particular **way**, it is true with regard to some aspect of the thing involved or it has some sort of effect. EG *Breast feeding is valuable in a number of ways... In a way, these officers were prisoners themselves... The job was changing me in a way that I had not expected.* N COUNT+SUPP

5 The **way** you feel about something is your attitude to it or your opinion about it. EG *Do you still feel the same way?* N SING+SUPP

6 When you mention the **way** that something happens, you are mentioning the fact that it happens. EG *Do you remember the way the boat leaked?* N SING : *the*+N+SUPP

7 If you have a **way** with people or things of a particular type, you are very skilful at dealing with them. EG *...a village boy who had a way with horses.* N SING+*with*

8 You also use **way** in expressions such as 'push your way somewhere' or 'work your way somewhere' which refer to movement or progress, especially difficult movement or progress. EG *You can't force your way into somebody's house... He started to work his way through the back copies of 'The Times'.* N SING+POSS

9 The **way** to a particular place is the route that you must take in order to get there. EG *A man asked me the way to Tower Bridge.* • If you **have lost** your **way**, you are lost and do not know which direction you should go in. N SING : *the*+N • PHRASE

10 If you go or look a particular **way**, you go or look in that direction. EG *Will you come this way, please?... I waved but she was looking the other way.* N SING+SUPP

11 If something is the right **way** up or the right **way** round, it is facing in the right direction. EG *Have I got this the right way up?... Good heavens, it used to be the other way up.* N SING+SUPP

12 If someone or something is in the **way**, they prevent you from moving freely or from seeing clearly. EG *Why did you stand in the way?... Get out of my way... Judy barred Jim's way.* N SING : *the*/POSS+N

13 In a building, the **way** in is the door or space through which you go in and the **way** out is the door or space through which you go out. N COUNT+SUPP

14 You also use **way** to emphasize that something is a great distance away, or is very much below or above a particular level or amount. EG *They're way ahead of us... I'm way over thirty... You're way below the standard required.* ADV+ADV/PREP Informal

15 You use **way** in phrases such as 'all the way' and 'most of the way' which refer to a particular amount of a journey or distance. EG *They drove all the way back without a word.* PHRASE

16 You use **way** in phrases such as 'a long way' and 'a little way' to say how far away something is or how near it is. EG *You could see them from a long way off... We're a long way away from Cuba.* PHRASE

17 If you say that something **goes a long way** towards doing a particular thing, you mean that it helps to achieve that thing. EG *Goodwill and co-operation can go a long way towards smoothing your way to the top.* PHRASE

18 Way is used after 'have' in these phrases. **18.1** If you say that someone or something **has a way** of doing a particular thing, you mean that they commonly do it. EG *Ex-wives have a way of re-appearing.* **18.2** If you **get** or **have** your **way**, or if you **have everything your own way**, what you want to happen happens. EG *If Baker has his way, the money will be paid to you.* **18.3** You say to someone **'You can't have it both ways'** to remind them that they have to choose between two things and cannot do or have them both. PHRASE PHRASE CONVENTION

19 Way is used after 'make' in these phrases. **19.1** When you **make** your **way** somewhere, you walk or travel there. EG *I made my way back to my seat.* **19.2** If someone or something moves or is moved to **make way** for another person or thing, they move or are moved so that the other person or thing is able to stand there. EG *He refused to make way for anyone.* PHRASES

20 Way is used after 'by' in these phrases. **20.1** You say **by the way** when you add something to what you are saying, especially something that you have just thought of. EG *By the way, this visit of Muller's is strictly secret.* **20.2** If you say or do something **by way of** a particular thing, you say or do it as that thing. EG *I'm going to sketch in a bit of the background by way of introduction.* ADV SEN PREP Formal

21 Way is used after 'in' in these phrases. **21.1** You use **in the same way** when saying that a similar thing to the thing you have just mentioned happens or is true with something else. EG *Every baby's face is different from every other's. In the same way, every baby's pattern of development is different from every other's.* **21.2** You use **in a big way** and **in a small way** to suggest the scale or importance of an activity. EG *They are going into the arms business in a big way.* **21.3** You use **in the way of** in order to specify exactly what you are talking or asking about. EG *He received very little in the way of wages.* PHRASE PHRASE PREP

22 Way is used after 'out' in these phrases. **22.1** If a place is **out of** your **way**, you are not going to pass near it on your journey somewhere. EG *'Would you like a lift?' – 'Please, if it's not out of your way.'* **22.2** If you **go out of** your **way** to do something, you make a special effort to do it. EG *He didn't really go out of his way to help me.* **22.3** If you **keep out of** someone's **way**, you avoid them. **22.4** When something **is out of the way**, it is over or PHRASES you have dealt with it. EG *We'll be all right once this meeting is out of the way.*

23 Way is also used in these phrases. **23.1 Across the way** or **over the way** means nearby, on the opposite side of a road or area. EG *...the derelict houses across the way.* **23.2 On the way** or **on** your **way** means in the course of the journey that you are making somewhere. EG *Lynn was on her way home.* **23.3** If an activity or plan is **under way**, it has begun and is now taking place. EG *Formal negotiations are under way.* **23.4** You use **that way** and **this way** to refer to a possible course of action that you have just mentioned, when you go on to mention the likely consequence or effect of it. EG *He could do it on Sundays. That way, it wouldn't interfere with his work at all.* PHRASES

waylay /weɪ̲leɪ/, **waylays, waylaying, waylaid.** If you **waylay** someone, you stop them when they are going somewhere, for example in order to talk to them. EG *She lingered on the street to waylay him after the show.* V+O

way of life, ways of life. Someone's **way of life** is the behaviour and habits that are typical of them, or that are chosen by them. EG *...the British way of life... I've had a rather curious way of life for the last few years.* N COUNT: USU SING

wayside /weɪ̲saɪd/. **1** The **wayside** is the side of the road. EG *...travellers who buy food from wayside stalls.* N SING: USU the+N Outdated

2 If someone or something **falls by the wayside**, they become forgotten or ignored, or fail in what they are trying to do. EG *We must care for the weak who would otherwise fall by the wayside.* PHRASE

wayward /weɪ̲wəd/. Someone who is **wayward** is difficult to control because they are likely to change suddenly and are often selfish or stubborn. EG *...a wayward and capricious lad.* ADJ QUALIT

wc, wc's; also written **WC.** A **wc** is a toilet. N COUNT

we /wi̲:/ is used as the subject of a verb. A speaker or writer uses **we** to refer both to himself or herself and to one or more other people as a group. EG *We could hear the birds singing.* PRON: PL

weak /wi̲:k/, **weaker, weakest. 1** People who are **weak** do not have very much strength or energy. EG *He was weak from hunger... His legs were weak... Internationally the movement has appeared weak and isolated.* ◊ **weakly.** EG *He struggled weakly to his knees.* ◊ **weakness.** EG *...his worsening pain and physical weakness.* ADJ QUALIT; ◊ ADV; ◊ N UNCOUNT

2 If something is **weak**, it is likely to break, be destroyed, or fail. EG *A fuse is a deliberately weak link in an electrical system... The small farmer is economically weak by himself.* ◊ **weakness, weaknesses.** EG *This would exploit a known weakness on the enemy's Eastern Front.* ADJ QUALIT; ◊ N UNCOUNT OR N COUNT

3 If you describe someone as **weak**, you mean that they are easily influenced by other people. EG *She was so terribly weak and trusting... ...incompetent and weak leadership.* ◊ **weakness.** EG *...his apparent weakness under pressure.* ADJ QUALIT; ◊ N UNCOUNT

4 If an argument or reason is **weak**, it does not convince you that it is right or logical. EG *That was an incredibly weak answer... The film had a weak plot.* ADJ QUALIT

5 Sounds or lights that are **weak** are very faint and difficult to distinguish clearly. EG *A weak sun shines on the promenade... In the weak light of the headlamp, I wrote down the number.* ADJ QUALIT

6 Drinks such as tea or coffee that are **weak** are made using a lot of water and therefore do not have a strong taste. EG *He sat sipping weak tea from a chipped mug.* ADJ QUALIT

7 A **weak** reaction or response to something is done without enthusiasm or emphasis. EG *He managed a weak smile.* ADJ QUALIT

8 If someone or something is **weak** on a particular subject, they do not have much ability, skill, or information in that subject. EG *The book was weak on fact and documentation... The course was very weak on traditional grammar.* ◊ **weakness.** EG *...the strengths and weaknesses of international co-operation.* ADJ QUALIT: USU PRED; ◊ N UNCOUNT OR N COUNT

weaken /wi̲:kəⁿn/, **weakens, weakening, weakened. 1** If someone **weakens** something, they make it less strong or less powerful. EG *Her armed forces had been weakened by the restriction on equipment supplies... Repeated pushing may weaken the catch and damage it.* V-ERG

2 If someone **weakens** or if you **weaken** them, they become less certain about something that they had previously decided. EG *His sense of duty never weakened... ...the government's weakening resolve.* V-ERG

3 If something **weakens** you, it causes you to lose some of your physical strength. EG *I was weakened by my exertions, and fell and broke my arm.* V+O

weakling /wi̲:klɪŋ/, **weaklings.** If you call someone a **weakling**, you mean that they are physically weak. N COUNT Informal

weakness /wi̲:knɪ²s/, **weaknesses.** If you have a **weakness** for something, you like it so much that you want to have it or do it whenever you can. EG *Food was his weakness.* ● See also **weak.** N COUNT

weal /wi̲:l/, **weals.** A **weal** is a mark made on someone's skin by a blow, especially from something sharp or thin such as a sword or whip. N COUNT

wealth /wɛ̲lθ/. **1 Wealth** is **1.1** the possession of a large amount of money, property, or other valuable things. EG *It was a period of wealth and prosperity.* **1.2** the money, property, and other valuable things that someone owns. EG *She was a woman of considerable wealth.* N UNCOUNT

2 If someone or something has a **wealth** of a particular thing, they have a very large amount of that thing. EG *His air of confidence and his wealth of knowledge made him seem ageless.* N PART: SING Formal

wealthy /wɛ̲lθi¹/, **wealthier, wealthiest.** Someone who is **wealthy** has a large amount of money, property, or valuable possessions. EG *He was the eldest son of a wealthy family.* ADJ QUALIT

wean /wi̲:n/, **weans, weaning, weaned. 1** When a mother **weans** her baby, she stops feeding it with milk from her breast and starts giving it other food. EG *The earlier a child is weaned, the greater risk he runs of serious illness.* V+O

2 If you **wean** someone from something, you help them to gradually stop doing it. EG *...trying to wean people from cigarettes by gradually reducing the nicotine content.* V+O +from/off

weapon /wɛ̲pən/, **weapons.** A **weapon** is an object such as a gun, a knife, or a missile, which is used to kill or hurt people in a fight or a war. EG *...nuclear weapons.* N COUNT

wear /wɛ̲ə/, **wears, wearing, wore** /wɔ̲:/, **worn** /wɔ̲:n/. **1** When you **wear** things such as clothes, shoes, or jewellery, you have them on your body. EG *She was wearing a T-shirt and jeans... He didn't like wearing a hat... ...a girl who wore spectacles.* V+O

2 If you **wear** your hair in a particular way, you have it cut in that style or shape. EG *His face was framed by his curly hair which he wore too long.* V+O+A

3 You can refer to clothes that are suitable for a particular time or occasion as a particular kind of **wear**. For example, evening **wear** refers to clothes that are suitable for wearing in the evening. N UNCOUNT +SUPP

4 If something **wears**, it becomes thinner or weaker because it is constantly being used over a long period of time. EG *Move the carpet up or down as it starts to wear.* V

5 If something **wears** well, it can be used for a long time without becoming weak or thin. If it **wears** badly, it is not very strong and will not last for a V+ADV

If you are under the weather, are you outside?

weapons

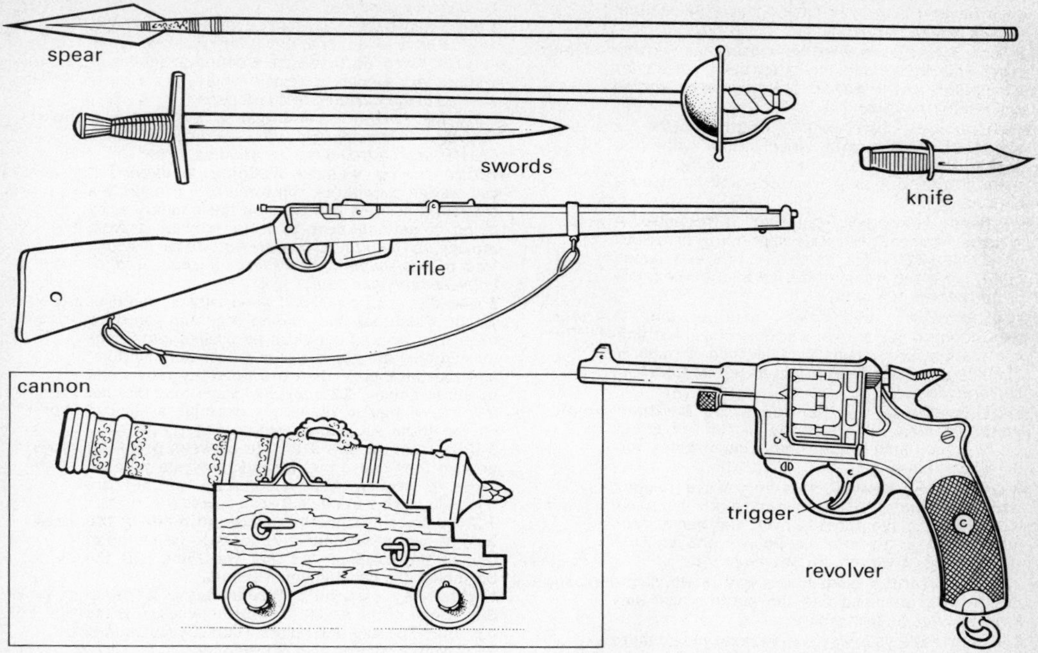

long time. EG *Rayon blankets are less warm and don't wear as well as woollen ones.*

6 Wear is the amount of use that clothes or other things have over a period of time, which causes damage to them. EG *...a jumper, tatty from years of wear... These sheets are showing signs of wear.* — N UNCOUNT

7 If you say that something **is wearing thin**, you mean that it has been used too much and so is becoming less interesting or more annoying. EG *His excuses are beginning to wear thin.* — PHRASE

8 If you say that someone or something is **the worse for wear**, you mean that they are in a poor condition or are tired because they have been very active or have been used a lot. EG *Most of them were looking rather the worse for wear.* — PHRASE Informal

wear away. If you **wear** something away or if it **wears away**, it becomes thin and eventually disappears because it is used a lot. EG *The grass was worn away where the children used to play.* — PHRASAL VB : V-ERG+ADV

wear down. 1 If you **wear** something **down** or if it **wears down**, it becomes shorter as a result of constantly rubbing against something else. EG *As the teeth wear down, new ones start growing.* — PHRASAL VB : V-ERG+ADV **2** If you **wear** people **down**, you weaken them by being more persistent than they are. EG *We tried to wear them down gradually and make them agree.* — V+O+ADV

wear off. If a feeling such as pain **wears off**, it disappears slowly. EG *By the next afternoon the shock had worn off.* — PHRASAL VB : V+ADV

wear on. If time **wears on**, it seems to pass very slowly. EG *So the day wore on and still they sat, drinking, smoking, talking.* — PHRASAL VB : V+ADV Literary

wear out. 1 When something **wears out** or when you **wear** it **out**, it is used so much that it becomes thin or weak and cannot be used any more. EG *His shoes keep wearing out.* ● See also **worn-out**. — PHRASAL VB : V-ERG+ADV **2** If you **wear** someone **out**, you make them feel extremely tired. EG *They wore us out with their constant screaming and crying.* — V+O+ADV

wear and tear is the damage that is caused to something during normal use. EG *...good quality materials that stand up to the wear and tear of continual use.* — N UNCOUNT

wearing /wɛərɪŋ/. An activity that is **wearing** requires a lot of energy and makes you feel very tired. EG *It is a very wearing and demanding job.* — ADJ QUALIT

wearisome /wɪərɪsəm/. Something that is **wearisome** is very tiring and boring or frustrating. EG *...a wearisome meeting.* — ADJ QUALIT Formal

weary /wɪəri[1]/, **wearier, weariest; wearies, wearying, wearied. 1** If you are **weary**, you are very tired. EG *He was now feeling pretty weary... He made a weary gesture... ...a weary sigh.* — ADJ QUALIT
◇ **wearily.** EG *The farmers trudged wearily to the nearest stream.* — ◇ ADV Literary

2 If you **weary** of something, you become tired and lose your enthusiasm for it. EG *He is beginning to weary of sitting still.* — V : OFT+*of* Formal

weather /wɛðə/, **weathers, weathering, weathered. 1** The **weather** is the condition of the atmosphere, for example whether it is raining, sunny, hot, or windy in an area at a particular time. EG *The weather was good for the time of year... ...bad weather conditions.* — N SING : *the*+N OR N UNCOUNT

2 If you say that someone **is making heavy weather** of a task, you mean that they are doing it very inefficiently and are making it more difficult than it needs to be. — PHRASE

3 If you say that you are **under the weather**, you mean that you feel slightly ill. EG *You look a bit under the weather.* — PHRASE

4 If something such as rock or wood **weathers**, it changes colour or shape as a result of the wind, sun, rain, or other weather conditions. EG *The rocks weathered and turned to clay and mud.* — V-ERG Formal

5 If you **weather** a problem or difficult time, you survive it and are able to continue normally after it is over. EG *Anyone who weathers the first four years seems to be all right.* — V+O Formal

weatherbeaten /wɛðəbi:təⁿn/. **1** If your face or skin is **weatherbeaten**, it is brown and rough with deep lines because you have spent a lot of time outside in bad weather. ADJ QUALIT

2 Something that is **weatherbeaten** has become rough and slightly damaged after being outside for a long time. EG *The wooden balconies were warped and weatherbeaten.* ADJ QUALIT

weathercock /wɛðəkɒk/, **weathercocks.** A **weathercock** is a metal object in the shape of a cock which is fixed to the roof of a building. It turns round in the wind to show which way the wind is blowing. N COUNT

weather forecast, weather forecasts. A **weather forecast** is a statement that is broadcast on television or radio, or printed in a newspaper, saying what the weather will be like the next day or for the next few days. N COUNT

weatherman /wɛðəmə³n/, **weathermen.** A **weatherman** is a person whose job involves making weather forecasts on the television or radio. EG *The day proved to be as bright as the weatherman had predicted.* N COUNT Informal

weather-vane, weather-vanes. A **weather-vane** is a metal object on the roof of a building, which turns round in the wind to show which way the wind is blowing. N COUNT

weave /wi:v/, **weaves, weaving, wove** /wəʊv/, **woven** /wəʊvəⁿn/. **1** If you **weave** cloth, you make it by crossing the threads over and under each other using a machine called a loom. EG *Let's weave a rug.* ◊ **woven.** EG *...woven fabrics.* V+O OR V ◊ ADJ CLASSIF

2 The **weave** of a cloth is the way in which the threads are arranged and the pattern that they form. EG *...a tight, firm weave.* N COUNT+SUPP

3 If you **weave** your way somewhere, you go there by moving through and around things and changing direction often in order to avoid hitting them. EG *He holds a tray aloft as he weaves his way through the crowd.* V+O+A OR V+A

weaver /wi:və/, **weavers.** A **weaver** is a person who weaves cloth. N COUNT

web

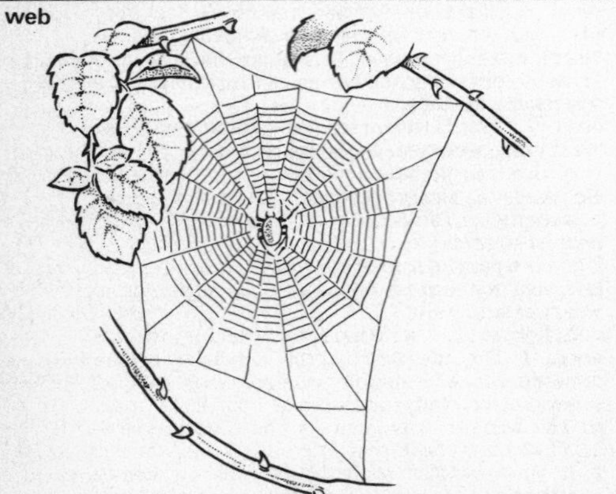

web /wɛb/, **webs. 1** A **web** is a fine net that a spider makes from a sticky substance which it produces in its body. Insects stick to the web as they fly past and are eaten by the spider. N COUNT

2 You use **web** to refer to a complicated pattern or structure, with many different connections and relationships, which is sometimes considered as an obstacle or a danger. EG *...the complex web of reasons.* N COUNT+SUPP

webbed /wɛbd/. **Webbed** feet have a piece of skin between the toes. Ducks and other water birds have webbed feet. ADJ CLASSIF

we'd /wi:d/. **1 We'd** is the usual spoken form of 'we had', especially when 'had' is an auxiliary verb. EG *We'd done a good job.*

2 We'd is also the usual spoken form of 'we would'. EG *We'd have given them five if they'd asked.*

wedded /wɛdɪ²d/. If you are **wedded** to an idea or system, you support it very strongly. EG *...a party wedded to unrestricted free enterprise.* ADJ PRED+*to* Formal

wedding /wɛdɪŋ/, **weddings.** A **wedding** is a marriage ceremony. EG *...the wedding of Prince Charles and Lady Diana... ...a wedding dress.* N COUNT

wedge /wɛdʒ/, **wedges, wedging, wedged. 1** If you **wedge** something, you force it to remain in a particular position by holding it there tightly or by fixing something next to it to prevent it from moving. EG *Open the door wide and wedge it with a wad of newspaper... She sat in a chair wedged between table and bunk.* V+O : USU+A

2 A **wedge** is **2.1** a piece of wood, rubber, metal, or plastic which has one pointed edge and one thick edge. The pointed edge can be pushed into a gap, for example the gap between a door and the floor, and the thick edge then prevents any movement by either object. N COUNT **2.2** a piece of something that has a thick triangular shape, for example a slice of cheese or pie. EG *...a huge wedge of cherry pie.* N COUNT OR N PART

3 If someone **drives a wedge** between people or groups, they cause bad feelings between them in order to weaken their relationship. EG *They are trying to drive a wedge between us and the Arabs.* PHRASE Formal

4 If you describe something as **the thin end of the wedge**, you mean that it appears to be unimportant at the moment, but that you think it is the beginning of a harmful development. PHRASE

Wednesday /wɛnzdɪ³/, **Wednesdays. Wednesday** is one of the seven days of the week. It is the day after Tuesday and before Thursday. EG *Do they know you're coming next Wednesday?* N UNCOUNT OR N COUNT

wee /wi:/. **Wee** means small or little. EG *...wee bits of stone... Can I ask you just one wee question?... It's a wee bit hot in here.* ADJ CLASSIF : ATTRIB Scottish

weed /wi:d/, **weeds, weeding, weeded. 1** A **weed** is a wild plant that grows in gardens or fields of crops and prevents the cultivated plants from growing properly. EG *...pulling out the weeds from among the tall, green rows of rice.* N COUNT

2 If you **weed** a place, you remove the weeds from it. EG *I had weeded the garden.* V OR V+O

3 If you call someone a **weed**, you mean that they are physically weak and that they have a weak character. N COUNT Informal British

weed out. If you **weed out** things that are not wanted in a group, you get rid of them. EG *Natural selection had weeded out the weakest.* PHRASAL VB : V+O+ADV

weedy /wi:di¹/. **1** A place that is **weedy** is full of weeds. EG *...the long weedy path.* ADJ QUALIT

2 If you describe someone as **weedy**, you mean that they are physically weak and thin. EG *He's tall and weedy, with long hair.* ADJ QUALIT Informal British

week /wi:k/, **weeks. 1** A **week** is **1.1** a period of seven days, beginning on a Sunday and ending on a Saturday. Some people consider that a week starts on Monday and ends on Sunday. EG *That was a terrible air crash last week... ...once a week, on Tuesdays... He worked seven days a week... I've been wanting to ring you all week.* N COUNT **1.2** the hours that you spend at work during a week. EG *I work a thirty-five hour week.* N COUNT+SUPP **1.3** the part of the week that does not include Saturday and Sunday. EG *She never goes out during the week.* N SING : *the*+N

2 You use **week 2.1** in expressions such as 'a week on Monday', 'a week next Tuesday', and 'tomorrow week', to mean exactly one week after the day that you mention. EG *'When is it to open?' – 'Monday week.'... It's due a week tomorrow.* **2.2** in expres-

Find a Scottish word on these pages.

sions such as 'a week last Monday', 'a week ago this Tuesday', and 'a week ago yesterday', to mean exactly one week before the day that you mention. EG *She died a week last Thursday.*

weekday /wiːkdeɪ/, **weekdays.** A **weekday** is any of the days of the week except Saturday and Sunday. N COUNT

weekend /wiːkɛnd/, **weekends.** A **weekend** is Saturday and Sunday. EG *I spent the weekend at home... I know what I need. A weekend in London.* N COUNT

weekly /wiːkli¹/, **weeklies. 1 Weekly** is used to describe something that happens, appears, or is done once a week or every week. EG *...a weekly newspaper... ...a weekly payment of seven shillings... We played chess two or three times weekly... Several groups meet weekly.* ADJ CLASSIF OR ADV

2 A **weekly** is a newspaper or magazine that is published once a week. EG *He controls two daily newspapers and four local weeklies.* N COUNT

weep /wiːp/, **weeps, weeping, wept** /wɛpt/. If someone **weeps**, they cry. EG *The girl was weeping as she kissed him goodbye.* ▸ used as a noun. EG *They had a little weep together.* V OR V+O Literary ▸ N SING : a+N

weeping willow, weeping willows. A **weeping willow** is a willow tree with long, thin branches that hang down to the ground. N COUNT

weepy /wiːpi¹/. Someone who is **weepy** is sad and likely to cry easily. EG *She came in very weepy. 'Dad's leaving home.'* ADJ QUALIT

weigh /weɪ/, **weighs, weighing, weighed. 1** If something **weighs** a particular amount, that is how heavy it is. EG *It's made of steel and weighs ten tons.* V+C

2 If you **weigh** something, you measure how heavy it is, using scales. EG *She was weighing a parcel.* V+O

3 If you **weigh** the facts about a situation, you consider them very carefully before you make a decision. EG *She had weighed the risks and decided it wasn't worth it.* V+O

4 If you **weigh** your **words**, you think very carefully before you speak. EG *'I like Tom very much,' she said, scrupulously weighing her words.* PHRASE

weigh down. 1 If a heavy load **weighs** you **down**, it stops you moving easily by making you heavier. EG *He was weighed down with weapons and equipment.* **2** If you **are weighed down** by a difficulty, it is making you very worried. EG *So you're weighed down with problems.* PHRASAL VB : V+O+ADV; V+O+ADV, USU PASS

weigh on or **weigh upon.** If a problem **weighs on** you or **weighs upon** you, it makes you worry. EG *Her absence began to weigh upon me.* PHRASAL VB : V+PREP

weigh out. If you **weigh** something **out**, you measure a certain weight of it in order to make sure that you have the correct amount. EG *He weighed out a pound of tomatoes.* PHRASAL VB : V+O+ADV

weigh up. 1 If you **weigh** things **up**, you consider their importance in relation to each other in order to help you make a decision. EG *You have to weigh up in your mind whether to punish him or not.* **2** If you **weigh** someone **up**, you try and find out what they are like and form an opinion of them. EG *We spoke for a while, weighing each other up.* PHRASAL VB : V+O+ADV; V+O+ADV

weight /weɪt/, **weights, weighting, weighted. 1** The **weight** of something is its heaviness, which can be measured in units such as kilos, pounds, and tons. EG *The weight of the load is too great... It was 25 metres long and 30 tons in weight.* N SING OR N UNCOUNT

2 A **weight** is a metal object which weighs a known amount. You use weights with sets of scales to weigh things, by balancing the thing that you are weighing against one or more weights. EG *...big brass scales with all the weights sparkling in a row.* N COUNT

3 You can use **weight** to refer to an object that is heavy. EG *I'm not allowed to do heavy work, nor can I carry heavy weights any more.* N COUNT

4 If you **weight** something or **weight** it down, you make it heavier, often so that it cannot move easily. EG *...a plastic sheet weighted down with straw bales.* V+O : OFT+ *down*

5 The **weight** of something is its large amount or its great power, which means that it is difficult to contradict it or fight against it. EG *The weight of the evidence convinces me that he was wrongly imprisoned... They had the weight of official support behind them.* N SING+*of*

6 If you feel a **weight** of some kind on you, you have a problem or a responsibility that you are very worried about. EG *This was a great weight lifted off my back... Without a producer, the weight of responsibility fell upon me.* N SING

7 Weight is also used in these phrases. **7.1** If you **put on weight** or **gain weight**, your body becomes fatter and heavier. If you **lose weight**, your body becomes thinner and lighter. EG *I think she might have lost a bit of weight.* **7.2** If you **pull** your **weight**, you work as hard as the other people who are involved in the same task or activity. EG *They'll refuse to fund anyone who is not pulling their weight.* **7.3** If you **take the weight off** your **feet**, you sit down to have a rest. EG *Take the weight off your feet for an hour.* **7.4** If you **throw** your **weight about**, you act aggressively and use your authority over other people more than you need to. **7.5 a weight off** your **mind**: see **mind**. ● See also **dead weight**. PHRASES Informal

weighted /weɪtɪ²d/. A system that is **weighted** in favour of a particular person or group is organized so that this person or group has an advantage. EG *The law is weighted in favour of landlords.* ADJ PRED+A

weightless /weɪtlɪ²s/. Something that is **weightless** seems to have very little weight or no weight at all. EG *These creatures may have been virtually weightless in water.* ◊ **weightlessness.** EG *...experiencing the weightlessness of space travel.* ADJ CLASSIF ◊ N UNCOUNT

weightlifter /weɪtlɪftə/, **weightlifters.** A **weightlifter** is a person who does weightlifting. N COUNT

weightlifting /weɪtlɪftɪŋ/ is a sport in which competitors try to lift very heavy weights. The winner is the person who lifts the heaviest weight. N ING

weighty /weɪti¹/, **weightier, weightiest.** You use **weighty** to describe something that seems serious or important. EG *Let us turn to less weighty matters.* ADJ QUALIT

weir /wɪə/, **weirs.** A **weir** is a low dam which is built across a river in order to control the flow of water or to change its direction. N COUNT

weird /wɪəd/, **weirder, weirdest.** Something or someone that is **weird** seems strange and peculiar. EG *The markets sell all sorts of weird vegetables... He's a weird child.* ◊ **weirdly.** EG *...weirdly shaped trees.* ADJ QUALIT ◊ ADV

weirdo /wɪədəʊ/, **weirdos.** If you call someone a **weirdo**, you mean that they behave in a strange and peculiar way. EG *When we started up, the locals thought we were weirdos.* N COUNT Informal

welcome /wɛlkəm/, **welcomes, welcoming, welcomed. 1** If you **welcome** someone, you greet them in a friendly way when they arrive somewhere. EG *He moved eagerly towards the door to welcome his visitor.* ▸ used as a noun. EG *I was given a warm welcome by the President.* V+O ▸ N COUNT

2 You can say **'Welcome'** to someone when you are greeting them. EG *Welcome to Peking... 'Welcome back,' said Howard.* CONVENTION

3 If you say that someone is **welcome** in a particular place, you mean that they will be accepted there gladly. EG *All members of the public are welcome... I was a welcome visitor in both camps.* ● If you **make** someone **welcome**, you make them feel happy and accepted in a new place. EG *The women made her welcome.* ADJ QUALIT : USU PRED ● PHRASE

4 If you tell someone that they are **welcome** to do something, you are encouraging them to do it. EG *You will always be welcome to come back.* ADJ PRED +*to*-INF

5 If you say that you **welcome** something, you mean that you approve of it and support it. EG *I warmly welcomed his proposal.* V+O

6 You use **welcome** to describe something that ADJ QUALIT someone does or gives you which you want and greatly appreciate. EG *A little drop of Scotch would be very welcome.*

7 If you say **'You're welcome'** to someone who has thanked you for something, you are acknowledging their thanks in a polite way. EG *'Thank you for the beautiful scarf.' – 'You're welcome. I'm glad you like it.'* — CONVENTION

welcoming /wɛlkəmɪŋ/. Someone who is **welcoming** is friendly to you when you arrive in a place so that you feel happy and accepted. EG *Should she be cool and withdrawn, or warm and welcoming?... She gave him a welcoming smile.* — ADJ QUALIT

weld /wɛld/, **welds, welding, welded. 1** If you **weld** two pieces of metal together, you join them by heating their edges and fixing them together so that they cool and harden into one piece. EG *It takes speed and skill to weld steel at this heat.* — V+O: OFT+TOGETHER

2 A **weld** is a join where two pieces of metal have been welded together. — N COUNT

welfare /wɛlfɛə/. **1** The **welfare** of a person or group is their general state of health, comfort, and prosperity. EG *...a society in which all cooperate and work for the welfare of all its members... I would devote my life to the child's welfare.* — N UNCOUNT +POSS

2 Welfare is used to describe the activities of an organization, especially the government, which are concerned with the health, education, living conditions, and financial problems of the people in society. EG *...cut-backs in health and welfare services... ...welfare workers.* — N MOD

3 Welfare is money which is paid by the government to people who are unemployed, have poorly paid jobs, or cannot work because they are ill. EG *They were living off welfare.* — N UNCOUNT American

welfare state. The **welfare state** is a system in which the government uses the money from taxes to provide free social services such as health care and education and to give money to people when they are old, unemployed, or sick. — N SING: *the*+N

well /wɛl/, **wells, welling, welled.** The comparative and superlative of **well** when it is used as an adverb are **better** and **best**: see separate entries for these words.

1 You say **'Well' 1.1** when you are hesitating or about to say something. EG *'Is that right?' – 'Well, I think so.'... Well thank you Jim for talking to us about your work... I've told her that you are, well, helping me in this matter.* **1.2** when you are correcting something that you have just said. EG *It took me years, well months at least, to realise that he'd actually lied to me.* **1.3** in the expression 'oh well' to indicate that you accept that the situation cannot be changed, although you are not happy about it. EG *Oh well, you wouldn't understand.* **1.4** to indicate that you are surprised or amused by something that someone has said. EG *'Well, well,' said Flora, 'now we know why she came to see me.'... Twenty years since you've been home, eh? Well, well, well, what do you think of America?* • **very well**: see **very**.

2 If you do something **well**, **2.1** you do it to a high standard. EG *She speaks French well... He handled it well... I could see almost as well at night as I could in sunlight.* **2.2** you do it thoroughly and completely. EG *You say you don't know this man very well?... The roots of democracy are very well established there.* — ADV AFTER VB

3 You use **well** to give emphasis to a prepositional phrase or to an adjective. EG *I woke well before dawn... They stood well back from the heat... I was very well aware that my little boat was far too frail... The film is well worth seeing.* — ADV +PREP/ADJ

4 You also use **well** after adverbs such as 'perfectly' or 'jolly' in order to emphasize what you are saying. EG *We managed perfectly well without you.* • **pretty well**: see **pretty**. — ADV AFTER ADV

5 If you say that something may **well** happen or could **well** happen, you mean that it is likely to happen. EG *Your eyesight may well improve.* — ADV AFTER MODAL

6 If you are **well**, you are healthy and not ill. EG *She answered, 'I am very well.'... She looked well.* — ADJ QUALIT: USU PRED

7 **Well** is also used in these phrases. **7.1** If you say that things are **going well** or that **all is well**, you mean that the situation is satisfactory. EG *Things went well for John until the First World War... All well at the office I hope?* **7.2** If you say that you **are well in with** someone, you mean that you are very friendly with them. EG *She's well in with the people next door.* **7.3** If you say that you **are well out of** a situation, you mean that you are no longer involved in it and you are pleased about this. EG *I'm glad to be well out of it.* **7.4** You say **well and good** to indicate that you find a situation acceptable or satisfactory. EG *If the worker can do it in less time, well and good.* **7.5** You use **well and truly** to emphasize that something has happened completely or thoroughly. EG *Make sure your tyres are well and truly wet.* **7.6 all very well**: see **all**. • **would do well to** do something: see **do**. — PHRASES; Informal

8 You use **as well** in the following ways. **8.1** You use **as well** when mentioning something which happens in the same way as something else already mentioned. EG *It brought him a good deal of local fame – money as well, obviously... Now she stretched out the other leg as well.* **8.2** If you refer to a second thing **as well as** a first thing, you refer to the second thing in addition to the first. EG *Women, as well as men, have a fundamental right to work.* **8.3** If you say that you **may as well** do something, or that you **might as well** do it, you mean that you will do it although you feel slightly reluctant or unenthusiastic. EG *I may as well admit that I knew the answer all along.* **8.4** If you say that something that has happened **is just as well**, you mean that it is fortunate that it happened in the way it did. EG *He didn't have to speak very often, which was just as well as he was a man who liked to keep words to himself.* — PHRASE; PREP; PHRASE; PHRASE

9 A **well** is **9.1** a hole in the ground from which a supply of water is extracted. EG *Everyone digs his own well, but in the dry season these dry up.* **9.2** an oil well. — N COUNT

well up. If tears **well up** in your eyes, they come to the surface. EG *Tears welled up in his eyes and he brushed them aside.* — PHRASAL VB: V+ADV+A

we'll /wiːl/ is the usual spoken form of 'we shall' or 'we will'. EG *Come on, then, we'll have to hurry.*

well-advised. If someone says that you would be **well-advised** to do something, they are advising you to do it. EG *She's leaving, and I think you'd be well-advised to do the same.* — ADJ PRED: OFT+*to*-INF

well-balanced. Someone who is **well-balanced** is sensible and does not have many emotional problems. EG *His children are sufficiently mature and well balanced to be able to live happily with their step-mother.* — ADJ QUALIT

well-behaved. A child who is **well-behaved** behaves in a way that adults like and think is correct. EG *She's a very well behaved little girl.* — ADJ QUALIT

well-being. If you refer to someone's **well-being**, you are referring to whether they are healthy and happy. EG *This new physical fitness will produce a general feeling of well-being.* — N UNCOUNT: USU+SUPP

well-bred. Someone who is **well-bred** is very polite and has good manners. — ADJ QUALIT

well-built. Someone, especially a man, who is **well-built** is strong and muscular. — ADJ QUALIT

well done. 1 You say **well done** to indicate how pleased you are that someone has got something right or has done something properly or successfully. EG *'Which sea is this?' – 'The Atlantic Ocean.' –* — CONVENTION

What is the difference between 'well-off' and 'well-to-do'?

'Atlantic Ocean. Well done.'... That's right. Well done.

2 If something has been **well done**, it has been done or carried out successfully or properly. EG *The adaptation of the play from TV to theatre was exceptionally well done... ...a good job well done.* ADJ PRED

3 If something that you have cooked is **well done**, it has been cooked thoroughly. EG *Pork has to be very well done, or you can't eat it.* ADJ QUALIT

well-dressed. Someone who is **well-dressed** is wearing smart or elegant clothes. EG *...two dainty well-dressed women.* ADJ QUALIT

well-earned. If you describe something as **well-earned**, you mean that someone deserves it, for example because they have been working very hard. EG *Let us take a well-earned rest.* ADJ QUALIT

well-established. If something is **well-established**, it has existed for a long time and is successful. EG *Senegal already has a well-established film industry.* ADJ QUALIT

well-fed. Someone who is **well-fed** gets enough good food regularly. EG *The children are well-fed and happy.* ADJ QUALIT

well-founded. If an idea, opinion, or feeling is **well-founded**, it is based on facts and can therefore be justified. EG *These warnings proved well-founded.* ADJ CLASSIF Formal

well-groomed. Someone who is **well-groomed** is neat and tidy in appearance. EG *...a stout and well-groomed man in his fifties.* ADJ QUALIT Formal

well-heeled. If you say that someone is **well-heeled**, you mean that they are wealthy. ADJ QUALIT Informal

well-informed. Someone who is **well-informed** knows a lot, usually about many different subjects. EG *They become as well-informed as possible on the issues involved.* ADJ QUALIT

wellington /wɛlɪŋtən/, **wellingtons. Wellingtons** or **wellington boots** are long rubber boots which you wear to keep your feet dry. See picture at SHOES. N COUNT

well-intentioned. If someone is **well-intentioned**, they are trying to be helpful or kind, but are unsuccessful or cause unfortunate results. EG *A well-intentioned effort to obtain evidence failed abysmally.* ADJ QUALIT

well-kept. A **well-kept** building, room, or place is looked after carefully, so that it is always neat and tidy. EG *...a mansion with a well-kept lawn.* ADJ QUALIT

well-known. Something or someone that is **well-known** is known by a lot of people and is therefore famous or familiar. EG *...his two well-known books on modern art... It's well known that separating children from their mothers can lead to problems in later life.* ADJ QUALIT

well-mannered. Someone who is **well-mannered** is polite and has good manners. ADJ QUALIT

well-meaning. Someone who is **well-meaning** tries to be helpful or kind, but is often unsuccessful. EG *Well-meaning friends said, 'You cannot afford another baby.'... Their sympathy was well-meaning but ineffective.* ADJ QUALIT

well-meant. Something that is **well-meant** is intended to be helpful, useful, or kind, but is unsuccessful or has unfortunate results. EG *I don't want anyone else's opinion, however well-meant.* ADJ CLASSIF

well-nigh. You use **well-nigh** to say that something is almost true. EG *It's extremely difficult, well nigh impossible to choose between them... The otter is well-nigh extinct in Britain.* ADV+ADJ Formal

well-off. 1 If you say that someone is **well-off**, you mean that they are quite rich. EG *A lot of the students were quite well-off.* ADJ QUALIT : USU PRED Informal

2 Someone who is **well-off** for something has as much of it as they want or need. EG *You're well off for coal, I hope?* ADJ PRED+*for* Informal

3 If you say that someone **doesn't know when** they **are well off**, you are criticizing them for not appreciating how fortunate they are. PHRASE Informal

well-preserved. If you say that someone is **well-preserved**, you mean that they do not look as old as they really are. EG *...a well-preserved man in his late fifties.* ADJ QUALIT Formal

well-read. Someone who is **well-read** has read a lot of books and has learnt a lot from them. ADJ QUALIT Formal

well-spoken. Someone who is **well-spoken** speaks in a polite, correct way and with an accent which is considered socially acceptable. ADJ QUALIT Formal

well-thought-of. Someone or something that is **well-thought-of** is admired, respected, and has a good reputation. ADJ QUALIT

well-thought-out. Something that is **well-thought-out** is very carefully planned. EG *...a well written, entertaining, and well thought-out novel.* ADJ QUALIT

well-timed. An action or remark that is **well-timed** is said or done at the most suitable time. EG *...well-timed purchases of stock.* ADJ QUALIT

well-to-do. Someone who is **well-to-do** is rich. EG *He came from a well-to-do family.* ADJ QUALIT Outdated

well-tried. Something that is **well-tried** has been used or done many times before and so is known to work well or to be successful. EG *...a well-tried technique.* ADJ QUALIT

wellwisher /wɛlwɪʃə/, **wellwishers.** A **wellwisher** is someone who hopes that a particular person or thing will be successful and who does something to show their feelings. EG *Hundreds of telegrams arrived from wellwishers.* N COUNT Formal

well-worn. 1 A **well-worn** expression or remark has been used so often that it is boring. EG *...a well-worn joke... ...well-worn slogans.* ADJ QUALIT

2 A **well-worn** object or piece of clothing has been used or worn so much that it looks old and untidy. ADJ QUALIT

welly /wɛli[1]/, **wellies.** A **welly** is the same as a wellington. EG *I put on my wellies and we went off into the rain.* N COUNT Informal British

welter /wɛltə/. A **welter** of things is a large number of them which occur together. EG *...the daily welter of details and little problems.* N PART : SING Literary

wend /wɛnd/, **wends, wending, wended.** If you **wend** your **way** in a particular direction, you walk slowly in that direction. EG *We watched them wend their leisurely way up and down the street.* PHRASE Literary

went /wɛnt/ is the past tense of **go.**

wept /wɛpt/ is the past tense and past participle of **weep.**

were /wə, wɜː/. **1 Were** is the plural form and the second person singular form of the past tense of **be.**

2 Were is sometimes used instead of 'was' in conditional clauses or when you are wishing for something. EG *He treated me as if I were crazy... He wished he were taking a bath.* • **as it were**: see **as.** Formal

we're /wɪə/ is the usual spoken form of 'we are'. EG *We're all here.*

weren't /wɜːnt/ is the usual spoken form of 'were not'. EG *We weren't asleep.*

werewolf /wɛəwʊlf/, **werewolves.** In horror stories and films, a **werewolf** is a person who sometimes changes into a wolf. N COUNT

west /wɛst/; often spelled with a capital letter.

1 The **west** is **1.1** the direction which you look towards in order to see the sun set. EG *The next settlement is two hundred miles to the west... The hills behind Agadir in the west are built of blue limestone.* **1.2** the part of a place or country which is towards the west. EG *...in remote rural areas of the west of Ireland.* N SING : *the*+N

2 West means towards the west or to the west of a place or thing. EG *I was accompanied by an English friend who had never been West.* ADV AFTER VB

3 The **west** part of a place or country is the part which is towards the west. EG *...West Africa... ...the Labour MP for Oldham West.* ADJ CLASSIF

4 A **west** wind blows from the west. EG *...a pleasantly warm west wind.* ADJ CLASSIF : ATTRIB

5 The **West** is also used to refer to the United States, Canada, and the countries of Western and N SING : *the*+N

Southern Europe. EG *...the capitalist West... The West exported wheat to the third world.*

westerly /wɛstəli^{1}/. **1** A **westerly** point, area, or direction is to the west or towards the west. EG *The harbour has a westerly outlook.* ADJ QUALIT

2 A **westerly** wind blows from the west. EG *The ship was driven by the incessant westerly gales.* ADJ CLASSIF

western /wɛstə^{5}n/, **westerns;** often spelled with a capital letter.

1 Western means **1.1** in or from the west of a region or country. EG *The sun began to turn crimson on the western horizon... I've just been in Western Nigeria.* **1.2** coming from or associated with the people of Europe and North America, and the way in which they live, especially their attitudes, technology, or political and economic systems. EG *...the impact of western technology... ...western-style housing.* ADJ CLASSIF : ATTRIB

2 A **western** is a book or film about life in the west of America in the nineteenth century. The story usually involves a lot of fighting and shooting. N COUNT

westerner /wɛstənə/, **westerners.** A **westerner** is **1** a person who was born in or lives in the West, especially in Europe or North America. **2** a person who was born in or who lives in the west of a place or country. N COUNT

westernize /wɛstənaɪz/, **westernizes, westernizing, westernized;** also spelled **westernise.** If a society, place, or system **is westernized**, ideas and behaviour which are common in Europe and North America are introduced into it. EG *Westernized tastes spread and traditions weaken.* V+O : USU PASS

westward /wɛstwəd/, **westwards. Westward** or **westwards** means towards the west. EG *She suggested we continue westward... The reef stretches westwards from the tip of Florida.* ▸ **Westward** is also used as an adjective. EG *...the westward expansion of the city.* ADV AFTER VB; ▸ ADJ CLASSIF

wet /wɛt/, **wetter, wettest; wets, wetting, wetted.** The forms **wet** and **wetted** are both used as the past participle and past tense of the verb.

1 If something is **wet**, it is covered in water, rain, sweat, or another liquid. EG *I don't want to get my feet wet... The grass is wet.* ADJ QUALIT

2 If the weather is **wet**, it is raining. EG *Take a raincoat if it's wet... It was a wet day.* ADJ QUALIT

3 If something such as paint, ink, or cement is **wet**, it is not yet dry or solid. EG *...a fan-shaped pattern in the wet plaster... ...wet paint.* ADJ CLASSIF

4 If people's faces, cheeks, or eyes are **wet**, they are covered in tears or filled with tears. EG *She raised a red, wet face to me and wailed.* ADJ QUALIT

5 If you say that someone is **wet**, you mean that they are weak and lack enthusiasm, energy, or confidence. EG *'I don't see what I can do.' – 'Judy! Don't be so wet.'* ADJ QUALIT Informal

6 A **wet** is a person, especially a Conservative politician, who supports moderate political policies and opposes extreme ones. EG *...the Tory Wets.* N COUNT Informal British

7 To **wet** something means to get water or some other liquid over it. EG *Uncle Ted wet his lips... A column of spray wetted them.* V+O

8 If people, especially children, **wet** their beds or clothes or **wet** themselves, they urinate in their beds or clothes because they cannot control their bladder. EG *Martin's wet his pyjama trousers.* V+O OR V-REFL

wet blanket, wet blankets. If you call someone a **wet blanket**, you mean that they refuse to join in an activity with other people or that they speak or behave in such a way that they stop other people enjoying themselves. N COUNT Informal

wet suit, wet suits. A **wet suit** is a close-fitting rubber suit which a diver or underwater swimmer wears in order to keep his or her body warm. N COUNT

we've /wiːv/ is the usual spoken form of 'we have', especially when 'have' is an auxiliary verb. EG *We've had a very interesting discussion.*

WH stands for **words starting with 'wh'**

There are 14 words in the dictionary that are labelled WH in the Extra Column. These are: *what, whatever, when, whenever, where, wherever, which, whichever, who, whoever, whom, whose, why, how.* Notice that 'how' is regarded as a WH word.

Words that are labelled WH are always given a more precise grammatical label after a colon, as in the entry for **when**, where the first sense is labelled WH: ADV, and the third sense is labelled WH: CONJ OR PRON REL.

WH words have three main uses.

1. They often begin a report clause. When the report clause can only begin with a WH word, the label says V+REPORT: ONLY WH, or V+O+REPORT: ONLY WH. EG *Do we know **where** he went?... I can't tell you **why** I'm worried.*

2. They are used to begin a question. EG ***Where** are you going?... **What** are the dangers?*

3. Apart from 'what', they can all be used to begin a relative clause. EG *...my sister **who** lives in London... ...a place **where** they could go swimming... There are a number of reasons **why** this is important.*

See the entry headed VERBS for more information.

---

whack /wæk/, **whacks, whacking, whacked. 1** If you **whack** someone or something, you hit them hard. EG *His father might whack him if he found out.* V+O

2 If someone gets their **whack** of something, they receive their fair share of it. EG *Whatever happens, I've got to have my whack. That was in the agreement.* N COUNT : USU SING+POSS Informal

whacked /wækt/. If you are **whacked**, you are extremely tired. EG *By 9 p.m. I was whacked. By 9.30 I was asleep in bed.* ADJ PRED Informal

whale /weɪl/, **whales. 1** A **whale** is a very large animal that lives in the sea and looks like a huge fish. N COUNT

2 If you say that you **had a whale of a time**, you mean that you enjoyed yourself very much. EG *I gather they've all been having a whale of a time these last few days.* PHRASE Informal

whaling /weɪlɪŋ/ is the activity of hunting and killing whales. EG *...the whaling industry.* N UNCOUNT

wharf /wɔːf/, **wharves.** A **wharf** is a platform built of stone or wood along the side of a river or sea, where ships can be tied up. N COUNT

what /wɒt/. **1** You use **what 1.1** in questions when you are asking for information about something. EG *What is your name?... What are you doing here?... What time is it?* **1.2** in indirect questions and indirect statements about knowing or telling things. EG *Do you know what a pendulum is?... I don't know what to do... We didn't know what bus to get... I find it difficult to understand what people are saying.* WH : PRON OR DET; WH : PRON OR DET

2 You also use **what** at the beginning of a clause **2.1** to refer to something with a particular quality or nature. EG *He mixes what is real with what is unreal... A computer can only do what you have programmed it to do... What he really needs is a nice cup of tea.* **2.2** to indicate that you are talking about the whole of an amount that is available to you. EG *I've spent what money I had... The house consumed what little there was of my spare time.* WH : PRON OR DET; WH : DET OR PRON

Who uses a wheelchair?

3 You say **'What' 3.1** to show someone who has spoken to you that you have heard them and want them to continue. EG *'Dad?' – 'What?' – 'Can I have the car tonight?'* **3.2** to ask someone to say something again because you did not hear it properly. 'What' is not as polite as 'pardon'. EG *'Do you want another coffee?' – 'What?' – 'Do you want another coffee?'* **3.3** to express surprise or disbelief. EG *'Could I see you?' – 'What, right this minute?'* **3.4** to emphasize an opinion or reaction, especially in exclamations. EG *What a pity... What rubbish!* **3.5** to indicate that you are making a guess about something such as an amount or value. EG *I've been an academic for, what, something like 18 years.* WH : CONVENTION / WH : CONVENTION / WH : CONVENTION / WH : PREDET OR DET / WH : ADV SEN

4 You say **what about** at the beginning of a question when you are making a suggestion or offer. EG *What about some lunch, Colonel?* PHRASE

5 You say **what if** at the beginning of a question when you ask about the consequences of something happening, especially something undesirable. EG *What if I miss the train?* PHRASE

6 You say **what with** in order to introduce the reasons for a particular situation, especially an undesirable one. EG *What with paying for lunch and the theatre tickets, I'm very short of cash.* CONJ

7 What is also used in these phrases. **7.1** You say **'I tell you what'** or **'I know what'** to introduce a suggestion or offer. EG *Tell you what – let's go for a walk.* **7.2** You say **what have you** at the end of a list in order to refer generally to other things of the same kind. EG *...the needs, cultural, recreational, what have you, of this community.* **7.3** You can refer to someone as **what's his name** or **what's her name** when you cannot remember their name. EG *You're like what's his name... It was Mr – what's his name, you know, the new people.* **7.4** If you know **what's what**, you know the important things that need to be known about a situation. EG *This is a meeting to find out what's what.* **7.5 what is more**: see **more**. PHRASE Informal / PHRASE Informal / PHRASE Informal / PHRASE

whatever /wəˀtɛvə/. **1** You use **whatever 1.1** to refer to anything or everything of a particular type. EG *He volunteered to do whatever he could... She had to rely on whatever books were lying around.* **1.2** when you want to say that something is the case in all possible circumstances. EG *I have to bring my family back whatever happens.* **1.3** after a noun group in order to emphasize a negative statement. EG *There is no scientific evidence whatever to support such a view... He knew nothing whatever about it.* **1.4** to ask in an emphatic way about something which you are very surprised about. EG *Whatever is the matter?* **1.5** when you are indicating that you do not know the precise identity, meaning, or value of something. EG *She offered us a bowl of chilli, whatever that is... Whatever the reason, Rudolph was glad that she had come back.* WH : PRON OR DET / WH : CONJ / WH : ADV AFTER N, WITH BROAD NEG / WH : PRON / WH : PRON OR DET

2 You say **or whatever** to refer generally to something else of the same kind as the thing or things that you have just mentioned. EG *You plug it into a computer or whatever and it does the rest.* PHRASE

what's /wɒts/. **1 What's** is the usual spoken form of 'what is'. EG *What's your name?... What's the matter?... What's going on?*

2 What's is also a spoken form of 'what has', especially when 'has' is an auxiliary verb. EG *What's happened?*

whatsoever /wɒtsəʊɛvə/. You use **whatsoever** after a noun group in order to emphasize a negative statement. EG *I don't think there's any evidence of that whatsoever.* ADV AFTER N : WITH BROAD NEG

wheat /wiːt/ is **1** a grain which people usually grind into flour and use to make bread. **2** the plant that produces this grain, which is grown for food. N UNCOUNT

wheedle /wiːdəˀl/, **wheedles, wheedling, wheedled.** If you **wheedle** someone into doing something, you gently and cleverly persuade them to do it. If you **wheedle** something out of someone, you gently and cleverly persuade them to give it to you. EG *They tried to wheedle her into leaving the house... She wheedled money out of him.* V+O+A OR V

wheel /wiːl/, **wheels, wheeling, wheeled. 1** A **wheel** is a circular object which turns round on a rod attached to its centre. Wheels are fixed underneath things such as cars, bicycles, and trains, so that they can move along. EG *The train started, its wheels squealing against the metal tracks.* N COUNT

2 A **wheel** is also the same as a steering wheel. EG *Howard sits behind the wheel... After so many hours at the wheel, I was very tired.* N COUNT

3 If you **wheel** something that has wheels, for example a bicycle or cart, you push it along. EG *My father was wheeling his bicycle up the hill... The equipment was so bulky that it had to be wheeled around on a large trolley.* V+O : USU+A

4 If a vehicle or a group of birds **wheels**, it moves round in the shape of a circle or part of a circle. EG *The sky becomes filled with birds wheeling back and forth... The plane banked and wheeled.* V : USU+A

5 If you **wheel** round, you turn round suddenly. EG *I wheeled around and shook her hand.* V+A

wheelbarrow /wiːlbærəʊ/, **wheelbarrows.** A **wheelbarrow** is a small cart that is used in the garden for carrying things. It is usually shaped like an open box, with one wheel at the front, two legs at the back, and two handles to lift and push it with. N COUNT

wheelchair /wiːltʃɛə/, **wheelchairs.** A **wheelchair** is a chair with wheels that ill or injured people use in order to move about, when they cannot walk. N COUNT

wheeling and dealing is the process of trying to get what you want, especially in business, often by dishonest or unfair methods. EG *...complex business deals and financial wheeling and dealing... ...wheeling and dealing on the stock-exchange.* N ING

wheeze /wiːz/, **wheezes, wheezing, wheezed.** If you **wheeze**, you breathe with difficulty, making a hissing or whistling sound, usually because you are very old or have an illness such as asthma. EG *Coughing and wheezing, he climbed up the last few steps.* ▸ used as a noun. EG *All this was said very slowly, between wheezes.* V / ▸ N COUNT

when /wɛn/. **1** You use **when 1.1** to ask questions about the time at which things happen. EG *'I have to go to Germany.' – 'When?' – 'Now.'... When did you arrive?... When are you getting married?* **1.2** in indirect questions and indirect statements about the time at which something happens. EG *He didn't know when he was coming back... Ask her when the trouble first started.* **1.3** to specify or refer to the time at which something happens. EG *He left school when he was eleven... When I have free time, I always spend it fishing... Do you remember that time when Adrian phoned up from Tunbridge?... Join us next week, when we shall be talking about solar energy.* WH : ADV / WH : CONJ / WH : CONJ OR PRON REL

2 You also use **when** to introduce the reason for a particular opinion, comment, or question. EG *How can I get a job when I can't even read or write?... How silly we are to sit around indoors when outside it is so lovely.* WH : CONJ

3 When also means the same as although. EG *You describe this policy as rigid and inflexible, when in fact it has been extremely flexible.* WH : CONJ

whence /wɛns/ means from where. EG *He returned hastily to the United States, whence he originally came.* ADV OR CONJ Outdated

whenever /wɛnɛvə/. You use **whenever** to refer to any time or every time that something happens or is true. EG *Come and see me whenever you feel depressed... I avoided conflict whenever possible.* WH : CONJ

where /wɛə/. **1** You use **where 1.1** to ask questions about the place something is in, or is coming from, or is going to. EG *Where's Jane?... Where are you going?* **1.2** to specify or refer to the place in which something is situated or happens. EG *I think I know where we are... How did you know where to* WH : ADV / WH : CONJ OR PRON REL *find me?... She walked over to where Madeleine stood... The place where they landed was very wet.*

2 You also use **where** when you are referring to or asking about a situation, a stage in something, or an aspect of something. EG *Bryan wouldn't know where to start... ...a situation where unemployment is three million and rising fast... I wished, where possible, to avoid any mention of my family... This is where I profoundly disagree with you.* WH : CONJ, PRON REL, OR ADV

3 You also use **where** to introduce a clause that contrasts with the other part of the sentence. EG *Sometimes a teacher will be listened to, where a parent might not.* WH : CONJ

whereabouts /wɛərəbaʊts/. 1 If you refer to the **whereabouts** of a person or thing, you mean the place where that person or thing is. EG *I will not give anyone my whereabouts... We have discovered the whereabouts of one of the paintings.* N PLURAL +POSS

2 You use **whereabouts** in questions when you are asking where something is. EG *Whereabouts are you going in Yugoslavia?* ADV

whereas /wɛəræz/. You use **whereas** to introduce a comment that contrasts with the other part of the sentence. EG *Humans are capable of error whereas the computer is not.* CONJ

whereby /wɛəbaɪ/. A system or action **whereby** something happens is one that makes that thing happen. EG *I worked out an arrangement whereby each person would have a different roommate each term... ...a system whereby we work more overtime than any other country.* PRON REL Formal

wherein /wɛərɪn/ means **1** in which place. EG *...the box wherein she kept her wool... ...the room wherein we were to dine.* PRON REL Outdated **2** in which part or respect. EG *Wherein lay her greatness?* ADV OR CONJ Outdated

whereupon /wɛərəpɒn/. You use **whereupon** to say that one thing happens immediately after another thing and usually as a result of the other thing. EG *His department was shut down, whereupon he returned to Calcutta.* CONJ Formal

wherever /wɛərɛvə/. You use **wherever** **1** to say that something is true or happens in any place or situation. EG *In Bali, wherever you go you see these ceremonies... Wherever he was, he was happy... They have tried to restore the house wherever possible to its original state.* **2** to indicate that you do not know where a place or person is. EG *'Where does she live?' – 'Alten, wherever that is.'* WH : CONJ

wherewithal /wɛəwɪðɔːl/. If you have the **wherewithal** to do something, you have enough money to do it. EG *Where did they get the wherewithal to finance all those concerts?* N SING : *the*+N Formal

whet /wɛt/, **whets, whetting, whetted.** If you **whet** someone's **appetite** for something, you increase their desire for it. EG *The tutor at the college had whetted her appetite for more work.* PHRASE

whether /wɛðə/. You use **whether** **1** when you are talking about a choice or doubt between two or more alternatives. EG *I can't tell whether she loves me or she hates me... I wasn't sure whether I liked it or not.* **2** to say that something is true in any of the circumstances that you mention. EG *He's going to buy a house whether he gets married or not.* CONJ

whew /fjuː/ is used to represent a sound that you make when you breathe out very quickly, for example when you are very hot or when you are relieved. EG *Whew! It's nice to have that over with.* EXCLAM

which /wɪtʃ/. **1** You use **which** **1.1** to ask questions when there are two or more possible answers or alternatives. EG *Which department do you want?... Which is her room?* **1.2** to refer to a choice between two or more possible answers or alternatives. EG *I don't know which country he played for... The book says one thing and you say another. I don't know which to believe.* WH : DET OR PRON

2 You also use **which** at the beginning of a relative clause that specifies the thing that you are talking about or gives more information about it. EG *...the awful conditions which exist in British prisons... We sat on the carpet, which was pale green.* WH : PRON REL

3 You also use **which** to refer back to what has just been said. EG *It takes me an hour from door to door, which is not bad... I usually enjoy these dinners, unless I have to make a speech, in which case I worry throughout the meal.* WH : PRON REL OR DET

whichever /wɪtʃɛvə/. You use **whichever** **1** to indicate that it does not matter which of the possible alternatives happens or is chosen. EG *The United States would be safe whichever side won... Then they have lunch, have a chat, have a sleep, whichever they like, up in the lounge.* **2** to specify which of a number of possibilities is the right one or the one you mean. EG *Use whichever soap powder is recommended by the manufacturer... Use whichever of the forms is appropriate.* WH : DET OR PRON

whiff /wɪf/, **whiffs. 1** If there is a **whiff** of a smell, you smell it faintly or briefly. EG *...a little whiff of perfume as she passed... ...a whiff of petrol.* N COUNT+*of*

2 A **whiff** of a particular feeling or type of behaviour is a slight sign of it. EG *...a whiff of rebellion... ...the first whiff of danger.* N COUNT+*of*

while /waɪl/, **whiles, whiling, whiled. 1** If something happens **while** something else is happening, the two things happen at the same time. EG *He stayed with me while Dad talked with Dr Leon... They wanted a place to stay while in Paris... While he was turning the key in the lock, someone opened the door from the other side.* CONJ

2 You also use **while** to introduce a clause that contrasts with the other part of the sentence. EG *Fred gambled his money away while Julia spent hers all on dresses... While I have some sympathy for these fellows, I think they went too far.* CONJ

3 A **while** is a period of time. EG *They talked for a short while... ...a little while ago... After a while, my eyes became accustomed to the darkness.* • to be **worth** your **while**: see **worth**. • **once in a while**: see **once**. N SING

while away. If you **while away** the time in a particular way, you spend time in that way because you are waiting for something or because you have nothing else to do. EG *How about whiling away the time by telling me a story?* PHRASAL VB : V+ADV+O

whilst /waɪlst/ means the same as while. EG *I didn't want to live at home whilst I was at university... Whilst these cars are economical at a steady 56 mph, they perform badly in traffic.* CONJ

whim /wɪm/, **whims.** A **whim** is a sudden wish to do or have something, which is not the result of any strong reason or purpose. EG *She might go, or might not, as the whim took her... ...his tendency to change his mind at whim.* N COUNT OR N UNCOUNT

whimper /wɪmpə/, **whimpers, whimpering, whimpered. 1** If children or animals **whimper**, they make little, low, unhappy sounds. EG *You don't have to feed the baby the minute she whimpers.* V
▸ used as a noun. EG *I was listening for a cry or a whimper from upstairs.* ▸ N COUNT

2 If someone **whimpers** something, they say it in an unhappy or frightened way. EG *'I want to go home,' she whimpered.* V+QUOTE

whimsical /wɪmzɪkəˀl/. Something that is **whimsical** is unusual and slightly playful, and is done without any strong reason or purpose. EG *...a whimsical smile... ...whimsical images of birds and beasts.* ADJ QUALIT

whine /waɪn/, **whines, whining, whined. 1** If someone or something **whines**, they make a long, high-pitched noise, especially one which sounds sad or unpleasant. EG *His dog was whining in pain... The clattering and whining elevator began to move slowly upwards.* V ▸ used as a noun. EG *...the whine of the police sirens.* ▸ N COUNT

Do white-collar workers wear white collars?

2 If someone **whines** about something, they complain about it in a way that annoys you. EG *My father never whined or complained about his work.* V: OFT+*about* OR QUOTE

whinge /wɪndʒ/, **whinges, whinging, whinged.** The spelling **whingeing** is also used. V: OFT+*about* Informal
If someone **whinges** about something, they complain about it in a way that annoys you. EG *I'm sick of hearing her whinge.*

whip /wɪp/, **whips, whipping, whipped. 1** A **whip** is a piece of leather or rope fastened to a handle, which is used for hitting people or animals. EG *He was lashed with whips.* N COUNT
2 If you **whip** a person or animal, you hit them with a whip. EG *I saw him whipping his mules.* V+O
◊ **whipping, whippings.** EG *He could not possibly have endured a whipping.* ◊ N COUNT
3 If the wind **whips** something, it strikes it sharply. EG *The wind whipped my face.* V+O
4 If you **whip** something out or off, you take it out or off very quickly and suddenly. EG *Glenn whipped off the mask to reveal his identity.* V+O+A
5 If you **whip** cream or eggs, you stir them very fast until they are thick and frothy or stiff. V+O
◊ **whipped.** EG *...fruit flan with whipped cream.* ◊ ADJ CLASSIF
whip up. If you **whip up** a strong emotion such as hatred or excitement in people, you deliberately make them feel that emotion. EG *The interview whipped up the Americans into a frenzy of rage.* PHRASAL VB: V+O+ADV

whip-round, whip-rounds. When a group of people have a **whip-round**, money is collected from each person so that it can be used to buy something for all of them or for someone they all know. N COUNT Informal

whir /wɜː/. See **whirr.**

whirl /wɜːl/, **whirls, whirling, whirled. 1** When something **whirls** or when you **whirl** it round, it moves round or turns round very fast. EG *...the whirling blades of a helicopter.* ▸ used as a noun. EG *...a whirl of dust.* V-ERG: OFT+A ▸ N COUNT
2 You can refer to a lot of intense activity as a **whirl** of activity. EG *We flung ourselves into the mad whirl of pleasure.* N COUNT+SUPP
3 If you say that your head or mind **is whirling**, you mean that you are very confused or excited by something. EG *My head's whirling with ideas.* V: USU CONT
4 If someone or their mind is **in a whirl**, they are very confused or excited by something. PHRASE Literary
5 If you say that you will **give it a whirl**, you mean that you will try doing something new for a while. PHRASE Informal

whirlpool /wɜːlpuːl/, **whirlpools.** A **whirlpool** is a small area in a river or sea where the water is moving quickly round and round, so that objects floating near it are pulled into its centre. N COUNT

whirlwind /wɜːlwɪnd/, **whirlwinds. 1** A **whirlwind** is a tall column of air which spins round and round very fast and moves across the land or sea. N COUNT
2 A **whirlwind** event happens much more quickly than normal. EG *...a whirlwind romance.* ADJ CLASSIF: ATTRIB

whirr /wɜː/, **whirrs, whirring, whirred;** also spelled **whir.** When something **whirrs**, it makes a series of low sounds so fast that they seem like one continuous sound. EG *Fans whirred on the ceiling... ...insects whirring and buzzing through the air.* V
▸ used as a noun. EG *...the whirr of an engine.* ▸ N COUNT

whisk /wɪsk/, **whisks, whisking, whisked. 1** If you **whisk** someone or something somewhere, you take them there very quickly. EG *I was whisked into hospital with fierce abdominal pains.* V+O+A
2 If you **whisk** eggs or cream, you stir air into them very fast. EG *Whisk the egg whites until stiff.* V+O
3 A **whisk** is a kitchen tool used for stirring air into eggs or cream very fast. N COUNT

whisker /wɪskə/, **whiskers. 1** The **whiskers** of an animal such as a cat or a mouse are the long, stiff hairs that grow near its mouth. EG *The animal's whiskers began to twitch.* N COUNT: USU PLURAL
2 You can refer to the hair on a man's face, especially on the sides of his face, as his **whiskers.** EG *He tugged at his side whiskers.* N PLURAL

whisky /wɪski[1]/, **whiskies;** also spelled **whiskey** in American English and Irish English.
Whisky is a strong alcoholic drink made from grain such as barley or rye, especially in Scotland. EG *He had drunk too much whisky... ...a large whisky and soda.* N MASS

whisper /wɪspə/, **whispers, whispering, whispered. 1** When you **whisper** something, you say something to someone very quietly, using only your breath and not your throat, so that other people cannot hear what you are saying. EG *'Follow me,' Claude whispered. 'And keep quiet.'... When we were washing I whispered the news to my sister... What are you two whispering about?* V: OFT+QUOTE, REPORT, OR *about*; ALSO V+O
2 A **whisper** is a very quiet voice in which you use your breath and not your throat. EG *Hooper lowered his voice to a whisper... We spoke in whispers.* N COUNT

whistle /wɪsə[0]l/, **whistles, whistling, whistled.**
1 When you **whistle** or when you **whistle** a tune, you make a sound by forcing your breath out between your lips. EG *He walked home whistling cheerfully... I was whistling little bits of the song.* V OR V+O
2 If something **whistles**, it makes a loud, high sound as it moves quickly through the air. EG *The bullets whistled past his head.* V: USU+A
3 When something such as a steam train or a kettle **whistles**, it produces a loud, high sound as steam is forced through a small opening. EG *The train whistled as it approached the tunnel.* V
4 A **whistle** is a sound that you make when you whistle. EG *Sean let out a low whistle of surprise.* N COUNT
5 A **whistle** is also a small metal tube which you blow in order to produce a loud sound and attract someone's attention. EG *The guard blew his whistle and waved his green flag.* N COUNT

white /waɪt/, **whiter, whitest; whites. 1** Something that is **white** is of the lightest colour that there is, the colour of snow or milk. EG *There were little white clouds high in the blue sky... A woman dressed in white came up to me.* ADJ COLOUR
2 Someone who is **white** has a pale skin and is of European origin. EG *They had never seen a white person before.* ▸ used as a noun. EG *The race riots had been caused by whites attacking blacks.* ADJ CLASSIF ▸ N COUNT
3 If someone goes **white**, **3.1** their hair becomes white in colour because they are getting old. EG *My grandfather went white at the age of fifty.* ADJ COLOUR **3.2** they become very pale, for example because they are afraid or shocked. EG *My sister went white with rage.* ADJ PRED ● If someone looks **as white as a sheet**, they look very frightened, shocked, or ill. ● PHRASE
4 **White** coffee contains milk or cream. ADJ CLASSIF
5 **White** wine is wine of a pale yellowish colour. ADJ CLASSIF
6 The **white** of an egg is the transparent liquid that surrounds the yolk. N COUNT
7 The **white** of someone's eye is the white part of their eyeball. N COUNT

white Christmas, white Christmases. A **white Christmas** is a Christmas when it snows. N COUNT

white-collar. White-collar workers work in offices rather than doing manual work in industry. ADJ CLASSIF: ATTRIB

white elephant. If you refer to something as a **white elephant**, you mean that it is expensive but completely useless. EG *The new naval base has proved to be a white elephant.* N SING: a+N

white-hot /waɪt hɒt/. If something is **white-hot**, it is extremely hot. EG *...the white-hot centre of the bonfire.* ADJ CLASSIF

white lie, white lies. A **white lie** is a lie that is not very serious. N COUNT

whiten /waɪtə[0]n/, **whitens, whitening, whitened.** When something **whitens** or when you **whiten** it, it becomes whiter or paler in colour. EG *Use very mild bleach to whiten white nylon.* V-ERG+A

white spirit is a colourless liquid that is made from petrol and is used, for example, to make paint thinner or to clean surfaces. N UNCOUNT British

whitewash /waɪtwɒʃ/, **whitewashes, whitewashing, whitewashed. 1 Whitewash** is a mix- N UNCOUNT ture of lime or chalk and water that is used for painting walls white.

2 If a wall or building **is whitewashed**, it is painted white with whitewash. V+O

3 **Whitewash** is also an attempt to hide the unpleasant facts about someone or something. EG *...the refusal to accept official whitewash in police enquiries.* N UNCOUNT OR N SING

whiting /waɪtɪŋ/. **Whiting** is both the singular and the plural form. A **whiting** is a kind of fish. N COUNT

whittle /wɪtə⁰l/, **whittles, whittling, whittled.** To **whittle** something **away** or to **whittle** it **down** means to make it smaller or less effective over a period of time. EG *This may whittle away our liberties... Profits are whittled down by the ever-rising cost of energy.* PHRASAL VB : V+O+ADV OR V+ADV+*at*

whizz /wɪz/, **whizzes, whizzing, whizzed;** also spelled **whiz. 1** If you **whizz** somewhere, you move there very fast. EG *We just stood there with the cars whizzing by.* V+A Informal

2 If you are a **whizz** at something, you are very good at it. EG *He might be a whiz at electronics... Renata was a perfect whiz at rhyming words.* N COUNT : OFT+*at* Informal

whizz-kid /wɪz kɪd/, **whizz-kids;** also spelled **whiz-kid.** A **whizz-kid** is someone who is very good at their job and achieves success quickly. EG *...a multi-millionaire insurance whizz-kid.* N COUNT Informal

who /huː/. You can use **who** as the subject or object of a verb: see also **whom, whose.**

1 You use **who 1.1** when asking questions about someone's name or identity. EG *Who are you?... Who are you going to invite?* **1.2** in indirect questions and indirect statements about someone's name or identity. EG *She didn't know who I was.* WH : PRON

2 You also use **who** at the beginning of a relative clause when specifying the person you are talking about or when giving more information about them. EG *If you can't do it, we'll find someone who can... Joe, who was always early, was there already.* WH : PRON REL

who'd /huːd/. **1 Who'd** is the usual spoken form of 'who had', especially when 'had' is an auxiliary verb. EG *It was the little girl who'd come to play with her that afternoon.*

2 Who'd is also a spoken form of 'who would'. EG *I don't think he's the sort of young man who'd be thinking of marriage.*

whodunit /huːdʌnɪt/, **whodunits;** also spelled **whodunnit.** A **whodunit** is a book, film, or play which is about a murder and in which the identity of the murderer is kept a mystery until the end. N COUNT Informal

whoever /huːɛvə/. **1** You use **whoever 1.1** to refer to the person who does something, when their identity does not matter or is not known. EG *If death occurs at home, whoever discovers the body should contact the family doctor... Whoever answered the telephone was a very charming woman.* WH : PRON **1.2** to indicate that the identity of the person who does something will not affect a situation. EG *Whoever wins the war, there will be little peace... Whoever you vote for, prices will go on rising.* WH : CONJ

2 You also use **whoever** in questions as an emphatic way of saying 'who'. EG *Whoever could that be at this time of night?* WH : PRON

whole /həʊl/. **1** If you refer to the **whole** of something, you mean all of it. EG *...the whole of Europe... ...the whole of July.* N SING : *the*+N+*of* ▸ used as an adjective. EG *They're the best in the whole world... I've never told this to anyone else in my whole life.* ▸ ADJ CLASSIF : ATTRIB ● If you refer to something **as a whole**, you are referring to it generally and as a single unit. EG *Is that just in India, or in the world as a whole?* ● PHRASE

2 A **whole** is a single thing which contains several different parts. EG *The earth's weather system is an integrated whole.* N SING

3 You use **whole** to say that an action is done to something without dividing it up. For example, if you swallow something **whole**, you do not bite it into smaller bits. ADV AFTER VB

4 You also use **whole** to emphasize what you are saying. EG *...a whole new way of life... Charles was a whole lot nicer than I had expected.* SUBMOD OR ADJ CLASSIF : ATTRIB Informal

5 You say **on the whole** to indicate that what you are saying is only true in general and may not be true in every case. EG *On the whole he is a very difficult character.* ADV SEN

wholefood /həʊlfuːd/, **wholefoods. Wholefoods** are foods which have not been refined very much and do not contain additives or artificial ingredients. EG *Wholefoods and fresh fruit are essential in your diet... ...a wholefood shop.* N PLURAL OR N UNCOUNT

wholehearted /həʊlhɑːtɪ²d/. If you support something in a **wholehearted** way, you support it enthusiastically and completely. EG *He had the wholehearted backing of the younger members.* ADJ QUALIT ◇ **wholeheartedly.** EG *I agree wholeheartedly.* ◇ ADV

wholemeal /həʊlmiːl/. **Wholemeal** flour or bread is made from the complete grain of the wheat plant, including the husk. ADJ CLASSIF : ATTRIB

wholeness /həʊlnɪ²s/ is the quality of being complete or a single unit and not broken or divided into parts. EG *The peace, the wholeness, all that India promised, seemed fulfilled.* N UNCOUNT Literary

wholesale /həʊlseɪl/. **1** You use **wholesale** to refer to the activity of buying and selling goods in large quantities and therefore at cheaper prices, especially selling goods to shopkeepers who then sell them to the public. EG *...a sharp rise in wholesale prices... Stein got the food for me wholesale.* ADJ CLASSIF : ATTRIB, OR ADV AFTER VB

2 You also use **wholesale** to describe something that is done to an excessive extent, for example because it has not been thought about carefully enough. EG *Wholesale slaughter was carried out in the name of progress.* ADJ CLASSIF : ATTRIB, OR ADV AFTER VB

wholesaler /həʊlseɪlə/, **wholesalers.** A **wholesaler** is a person whose business is buying large quantities of goods and selling them in smaller amounts, usually to shops. N COUNT

wholesome /həʊlsə⁰m/. **1** Something that is **wholesome** is good and morally acceptable. EG *Young people enter marriage nowadays with a much more wholesome attitude.* ADJ QUALIT

2 Wholesome food is good for your health. ADJ QUALIT

wholewheat /həʊlwiːt/ means the same as wholemeal. EG *Wholewheat spaghetti takes slightly longer to cook.* ADJ CLASSIF : ATTRIB American

who'll /huːl/ is a spoken form of 'who will' or 'who shall'. EG *Who'll believe him?*

wholly /həʊlli¹/ means completely. EG *The idea was not a wholly new one... ...people whom we could not wholly trust.* ADV

whom /huːm/. The word **whom** is used in formal or written English instead of 'who' when it is the object of a verb or preposition.

1 You use **whom** in questions, indirect questions, and other structures in which you refer to someone whose name or identity is unknown. EG *'I'm a reporter.' – 'Oh yes? For whom?'... Whom do you suggest I should ask?* WH : PRON Formal

2 You also use **whom** at the beginning of a relative clause in which you specify the person you are talking about or give more information about them. EG *She was engaged to a sailor named Raikes, whom she had met at Dartmouth.* WH : PRON REL

whoop, whoops, whooping, whooped; pronounced /wuːp/ for paragraph 1 and /wʊps/ for paragraph 2. **1** If you **whoop**, you shout loudly in a very happy or excited way. EG *Eddie whooped with delight.* V Written ▸ used as a noun. EG *There were whoops of approval by the bar customers.* ▸ N COUNT

2 People say **whoops** when they have a slight accident or make a mistake. EG *Whoops. You nearly dropped it.* EXCLAM Informal

If you wholeheartedly agree with something, do you agree with it on the whole?

whoopee /wʊpi:/. People sometimes shout **'whoopee'** when they are very happy or excited. EG *Whoopee! We've hit the jackpot.* EXCLAM Informal

whooping cough /hu:pɪŋ kɒf/ is an illness which children get and which makes them cough and make a loud noise when they breathe in. N UNCOUNT

whoosh /wʊʃ/, **whooshes, whooshing, whooshed. 1** If something **whooshes** somewhere, it moves there very quickly or suddenly. EG *Thousands of rockets whooshed over our heads.* V+A Informal

2 A **whoosh** of air or water is a sudden rush of it. EG *The train came in with a whoosh of country dust.* N SING : OFT+*of*

whopping /wɒpɪŋ/ means much larger than usual. EG *Real growth was at a whopping six and a half per cent.* ADJ CLASSIF : ATTRIB Informal

whore /hɔ:/, **whores.** A **whore** is a prostitute; an offensive word. N COUNT

who're /hu:ə/ is a spoken form of 'who are'. EG *...married couples who're waiting to be housed.*

who's /hu:z/. **1 Who's** is the usual spoken form of 'who is'. EG *'Edward drove me up.' – 'Who's Edward?'*

2 Who's is also a spoken form of 'who has', especially when 'has' is an auxiliary verb. EG *...an American author who's settled in London.*

whose /hu:z/. **1** You use **whose** at the beginning of a relative clause to indicate that something belongs to or is associated with the person or thing that you mentioned in the previous clause. EG *...a woman whose husband had deserted her.* WH : PRON REL

2 You also use **whose** in questions, indirect questions, and other structures in which you ask about or refer to the person that something belongs to or is associated with. EG *Whose fault is it?* WH : DET POSS OR PRON POSS

who've /hu:v/ is the usual spoken form of 'who have,' especially when 'have' is an auxiliary verb. EG *...people who've gone to universities.*

why /waɪ/. **1** You use **why** when asking questions about the reason for something. EG *'I had to say no.' – 'Why?'... Why did you do it, Martin?* WH : ADV

2 You also use **why** at the beginning of a clause **2.1** to link clauses in which you talk about the reason for something. EG *He wondered why she had come... I did not know why, but I was afraid.* WH : CONJ **2.2** to introduce a relative clause after the word 'reason'. EG *There are several good reasons why I have a freezer.* WH : PRON REL

3 You use **why** with 'not' to introduce a suggestion in the form of a question. EG *Why don't we all go?* WH : ADV

4 You say **why not** in order to agree with what someone has suggested. EG *'Can I come too?' – 'I don't see why not.'* PHRASE

5 People also say **'Why!'** to indicate their surprise, shock, or indignation. EG *Why, Dr Kirk, I do believe you are serious.* American

wick /wɪk/, **wicks. 1** The **wick** of a candle is the piece of string in it which burns when it is lit. N COUNT

2 The **wick** of a paraffin lamp or cigarette lighter is the part which supplies the fuel to the flame when it is lit. EG *It's very hard to turn the wick up and down.* N COUNT

3 If you say that someone **gets on** your **wick,** you mean that they irritate you. EG *The kids have been getting on my wick.* PHRASE Informal British

wicked /wɪkɪ²d/. **1** Someone or something that is **wicked** is very bad in a way that is deliberately immoral or harmful to other people. EG *It was clear to him that he had done something wicked.* ADJ QUALIT

◇ **wickedness.** EG *...the wickedness of his crime.* ◇ N UNCOUNT

2 If you describe someone or something as **wicked**, you mean that they are rather mischievous or seem slightly immoral, but that you find them attractive or enjoyable. EG *He had a wicked grin... ...the wicked wit of the cartoonist.* ◇ **wickedly.** EG *She smiled wickedly.* ADJ QUALIT ◇ ADV

wicker /wɪkə/. A **wicker** basket, chair, or mat is made of wickerwork. N UNCOUNT : OFT N MOD

wickerwork /wɪkəwɜ:k/ is made by weaving twigs, canes, or reeds together. It is used to make baskets and furniture. EG *...wickerwork armchairs.* N UNCOUNT : OFT N MOD

wicket /wɪkɪt/, **wickets.** A **wicket** is **1** a set of three upright sticks with two small sticks on top of them, which the ball is bowled at in cricket. There is a wicket at each end of a cricket pitch. **2** the area of grass in between the two wickets on a cricket pitch. N COUNT

wide /waɪd/, **wider, widest. 1** Something that is **wide** measures a large distance from one side to the other. EG *...a wide bed... She looked across the wide, flat meadow... ...a wide grin.* ◇ **widely.** EG *'That's all right,' she said, smiling widely.* ADJ QUALIT ◇ ADV

2 If you open or spread something **wide**, you open or spread it as far as possible or to the fullest extent. EG *Rudolph always opened the window wide at night... He left his office door wide open.* ADV : OFT BEFORE ADV

3 If your eyes are **wide** or **wide open**, they are open more than usual because you are surprised or frightened. EG *Lamin watched with wide eyes... She sat looking up at me, her eyes wide with pleasure.* ADJ CLASSIF

4 You use **wide** when you are talking about how much something measures from one side or edge to the other. EG *The bay is about thirty miles long and six miles wide... How wide is the bed?* ADJ CLASSIF

5 A **wide** variety, range, or selection is one that includes a lot of different things. EG *The college library had a wide variety of books.* ◇ **widely.** EG *Over the next twelve years, he travelled widely.* ADJ QUALIT ◇ ADV

6 You also use **wide** when describing something which is found, believed, or known by many people. EG *The event received wide publicity in the press.* ◇ **widely.** EG *Your views on education are already widely known.* ADJ QUALIT ◇ ADV

7 A **wide** difference or gap between two things is a large difference or gap. EG *The gap between the poor and the rich is very wide indeed.* ◇ **widely.** EG *Customs vary widely from one area to another.* ADJ QUALIT ◇ ADV

8 Wide is used to describe something which relates to the most important or general parts of a situation, rather than to the smaller details. EG *...the wider context of world events.* ADJ QUALIT : USU COMPAR

9 If a shot or a punch is **wide**, it does not hit its target. ADJ PRED

10 far and wide: see **far.** ● **wide of the mark**: see **mark.**

wide-awake. If you are **wide-awake**, you are completely awake. ADJ PRED

wide-eyed. If you describe someone as **wide-eyed**, **1** you mean that their eyes are more open than usual, especially because they are surprised or frightened. EG *Her face seemed frozen in an expression of wide-eyed alarm.* **2** you mean that they seem inexperienced, and perhaps lack common sense. EG *Part of me was still a wide-eyed American.* ADJ CLASSIF

widen /waɪdəⁿn/, **widens, widening, widened. 1** If something **widens** or if you **widen** it, **1.1** it becomes greater in measurement from one side or edge to the other. EG *The original trail had been widened... Below Wapping, the river widens.* **1.2** it becomes greater in range or variety or affects a larger number of people or things. EG *Labour had to widen its appeal if it was to win the election... They could widen their experience by going on a course.* V-ERG

2 If your eyes **widen**, they open more. EG *Sandy stared at me, his eyes widening.* V

3 If a difference or gap **widens**, it becomes more extreme. EG *The gap between the rich and poor regions widened... Society continues to widen the gulf between specialists and non-specialists.* V-ERG

wide-ranging. If something is **wide-ranging**, it includes or deals with a great variety of different things. EG *...a wide-ranging interview... This attack carried wide-ranging implications for the police.* ADJ QUALIT

widespread /waɪdspred/. If something is **widespread**, it exists or happens over a large area, or to a great extent. EG *These housing estates suffer* ADJ QUALIT *from widespread vandalism and neglect... There was a widespread belief that the newspapers had invented the story.*

widow /wɪdəʊ/, **widows.** A **widow** is a woman whose husband has died. N COUNT

widowed /wɪdəʊd/. If someone is **widowed**, their husband or wife has died. EG *...his widowed mother.* ADJ CLASSIF

widower /wɪdəʊə/, **widowers.** A **widower** is a man whose wife has died. N COUNT

widowhood /wɪdəʊhʊd/ is the state of being a widow or the period of time during which a woman is a widow. EG *The shock of widowhood weakens resistance to illness... She continued to worship his memory throughout her long widowhood.* N UNCOUNT

width /wɪdθ/. The **width** of something is the distance that it measures from one side or edge to the other. EG *The area was just over a thousand yards in width... ...the width of a man's hand.* N UNCOUNT

wield /wiːld/, **wields, wielding, wielded. 1** If you **wield** a weapon, you carry it and use it. EG *They surrounded the Embassy, hurling stones and wielding sticks.* V+O

2 If someone **wields** power, they have it and are able to use it. EG *The union officials wielded enormous political power.* V+O

wife /waɪf/, **wives** /waɪvz/. A man's **wife** is the woman that he is married to. EG *She is the wife of an army colonel... Their wives were joining them for lunch.* ● See also **old wives' tale.** N COUNT: OFT+POSS

wig /wɪg/, **wigs.** A **wig** is a mass of false hair which you wear on your head, for example because you are bald or because you want to cover up your own hair. N COUNT

wiggle /wɪgəºl/, **wiggles, wiggling, wiggled. 1** If you **wiggle** something, you move it up and down or from side to side with small quick movements. EG *They wiggle their hips to the sound of pop music... Can you wiggle your ears?* V-ERG

2 A **wiggle** is a small quick movement in which something moves up and down or from side to side. EG *Give the wire a quick wiggle. I think it's stuck.* N COUNT

3 A **wiggle** is also a line that has a lot of little bumps in it. EG *He drew the sea as a series of wiggles.* N COUNT

wigwam /wɪgwæm/, **wigwams.** A **wigwam** is a kind of tent used by North American Indians. N COUNT

wild /waɪld/, **wilder, wildest; wilds. 1 Wild** animals and plants live or grow in natural surroundings and are not looked after by people. EG *...wild pigs... He lived on berries and wild herbs.* ADJ CLASSIF: ATTRIB

2 Animals living in the **wild** are living in their natural surroundings and are not being looked after by people. EG *They couldn't survive in the wild.* N SING: *the*+N

3 Wild land is natural and not cultivated at all. EG *...the wilder parts of Scotland.* ADJ QUALIT

4 The **wilds** are remote areas, far away from towns. EG *We live out in the wilds... ...the wilds of Australia.* N PLURAL: *the*+N

5 Wild is used to describe the weather or the sea when it is very stormy. EG *...a wild night in February.* ADJ QUALIT

6 People who behave in a **wild** way behave in a very uncontrolled, excited, or energetic way. EG *The audience went wild... The men were wild with excitement... He made a wild dash for the door.* ADJ QUALIT
◇ **wildly.** EG *The spectators applauded wildly.* ◇ ADV

7 If you have **wild** eyes or a **wild** look, your eyes are wide open and staring, because you are frightened, angry, or mad. ADJ QUALIT

8 If you **are not wild about** something, you do not like it very much. EG *I'm not wild about the wallpaper.* PHRASE Informal

9 If something **runs wild**, it behaves in a natural or free way, without being controlled. EG *Early in the morning, dogs run wild in the park.* PHRASE

10 A **wild** idea or scheme is very unusual and rather silly. ADJ QUALIT

11 If something is **beyond** your **wildest dreams**, it is much better than you hoped for or believed possible. EG *He's paying them a salary beyond their wildest dreams.* PHRASE

12 A **wild** guess is one which is very unlikely and is made without much thought. ◇ **wildly.** EG *I was guessing wildly.* ADJ QUALIT ◇ ADV

13 See also **wildly.**

wilderness /wɪldənɪ²s/, **wildernesses. 1** A **wilderness** is **1.1** a desert or other area of land which has very few plants or animals. EG *...the arctic wilderness.* **1.2** an area where grass or plants are growing thickly and without any control. EG *The garden's turned into a wilderness.* N COUNT: USU SING

2 If a politician spends time **in the wilderness**, he or she is not in an important or influential position in politics for that time. EG *He is enjoying a revival after four years in the wilderness.* PHRASE

wildfire /waɪldfaɪə/. If something **spreads like wildfire**, it spreads very quickly. EG *The news spread like wildfire round the world... The infection spread like wildfire.* PHRASE

wild-goose chase, wild-goose chases. If you are on a **wild-goose chase**, you waste a lot of time searching for something that you have little chance of finding. EG *He sent us on a wild-goose chase.* N COUNT Informal

wildlife /waɪldlaɪf/. You can refer to animals that live in the wild as **wildlife**. EG *These chemicals would destroy crops and all wildlife.* N UNCOUNT

wildly /waɪldli¹/. You use **wildly** to emphasize that a quality is very great indeed. EG *...wildly erratic behaviour... ...wildly impractical ideas.* ● See also **wild.** ADV+ADJ

wiles /waɪlz/ are clever tricks that people use to persuade other people to do something. EG *You seem familiar with the wiles of children.* N PLURAL Formal

wilful /wɪlfʊl/. **1 Wilful** actions or attitudes are done or expressed deliberately, especially with the intention of hurting someone. EG *...wilful destruction... He displayed a wilful ignorance of their plight.* ◇ **wilfully.** EG *She had wilfully betrayed him to his father.* ADJ CLASSIF: ATTRIB ◇ ADV

2 Someone who is **wilful** is determined to get what they want and to do things in their own way. EG *She was a wilful child.* ADJ QUALIT

will /wɪl/, **wills, willing, willed. 1** If you say that something **will** happen, you mean that it is going to happen in the future. EG *Inflation is rising and will continue to rise... Perhaps this time it won't rain... Will I get paid?... Perhaps when I am fifty I will have forgotten.* MODAL

2 If you say that you **will** do something, you mean that you intend to do it or are willing to do it. EG *I will see you tomorrow... I will never betray you... We won't accept that.* MODAL

3 You can use **will** **3.1** when inviting someone to do something or when offering them something. EG *Will you have a whisky, Doctor?* **3.2** to ask or tell someone to do something. EG *Will you do me a favour?... Please keep an eye on him, will you?... Will you shut up!* **3.3** to give an order to someone. EG *You will forget this conversation immediately.* MODAL Formal

4 You can also use **will** **4.1** to say that someone or something is able to do something. EG *This will cure anything... The car won't go.* **4.2** to say that something usually happens. EG *The bonus will usually be paid automatically... When I get on a bus and I see an advert, I will read it.* **4.3** to say that you are assuming or guessing that something is true, because you have good reasons for thinking it. EG *You will probably already be a member of a union... That'll be young Christopher there... You will already have gathered that I don't like her.* **4.4** to say that someone insists on doing something that you think is unpleasant or silly. You emphasize the MODAL

What is the difference between a widow and a widower?

word **will** when you use it in this way. EG *He will leave his socks lying around.*

5 Will is the determination to do something. EG *She lost her will to live... Their marriage became a fierce battle of wills.* ● See also **free will**. N UNCOUNT OR N COUNT

6 If something is the **will** of someone with power or authority, they want it to happen. EG *I must abide by the will of the people... It is the will of Allah.* N SING+POSS Formal

7 If you can do something **at will**, you can do it whenever you want. EG *Chang told us that we could wander around at will.* PHRASE

8 If you **will** something to happen, you try to make it happen by using mental effort rather than physical means. EG *I willed my trembling legs to walk straight.* V+O+to-INF

9 A **will** is a legal document in which you state what you want to happen to your money and property when you die. EG *Has Des made a will?* N COUNT

willing /wɪlɪŋ/. **1** If you are **willing** to do something, you do not object to doing it and you will do it if someone asks or wants you to do it. EG *I was still willing to marry her... The patient becomes cheerful, relaxed, and willing to talk.* ◊ **willingness**. EG *You need initiative and a willingness to work.* ADJ PRED: USU+to-INF ◊ N UNCOUNT

2 If you describe someone as **willing**, you mean that they do something enthusiastically rather than because they are forced to do it. EG *...a class of willing students.* ◊ **willingly**. EG *Many liberties were given up quite willingly during the war.* ◊ **willingness**. EG *They showed great willingness.* ADJ QUALIT: USU ATTRIB ◊ ADV ◊ N UNCOUNT

willow /wɪləʊ/, **willows.** A **willow** or a **willow tree** is a kind of tree with long narrow leaves. N COUNT

will-power. If you do something by **will-power**, you succeed in doing it because you are very determined to do it. EG *She stayed calm by sheer will-power... Removing this obstacle demanded all his will-power.* N UNCOUNT

willy-nilly /wɪli[1] nɪli[1]/. If something happens to you **willy-nilly**, you cannot prevent it happening. EG *All of them were taken willy-nilly on a guided tour of the town.* ADV

wilt /wɪlt/, **wilts, wilting, wilted.** If a plant **wilts**, it gradually bends downwards and becomes weak, because it needs more water or is dying. V

wily /waɪli[1]/, **wilier, wiliest. Wily** people are clever at thinking of ways to get what they want, especially ways that involve deceiving people. EG *...a wily diplomat.* ADJ QUALIT

win /wɪn/, **wins, winning, won** /wʌn/. **1** If you **win** a fight, a game, or an argument, you defeat the person who you are fighting, playing against, or arguing with. EG *Who's winning the war?... Their side was winning.* ▸ used as a noun. EG *...another win for our team.* V+O OR V ▸ N COUNT

2 To **win** an election or a competition means to do better than anyone else involved. EG *The Party won a convincing victory at the polls.* V+O OR V

3 If you **win** a prize or a medal, you get it because you have been very successful at something. EG *Mum has just won a microwave cooker in a competition.* V+O

4 If you **win** something that you want, for example someone's approval or support, you succeed in getting it. EG *...the party's failure to win mass support among the working class... They are winning honour and glory.* V+O

5 If you say that someone **can't win** in a particular situation, you mean that they are certain to fail or to suffer in some way whatever they do. EG *You pay the fine or you lose your job. You can't win.* PHRASE Informal

6 See also **winning**.

win over or **win round.** If you **win** someone **over** or **win** them **round**, you persuade them to support you or to agree with you. PHRASAL VB: V+O+ADV

wince /wɪns/, **winces, wincing, winced.** When you **wince**, the muscles of your face tighten suddenly because you have felt a pain or because you have just seen, heard, or remembered something unpleasant. EG *He tried not to wince... The pressure made her wince with pain... He winces at the memory of that defeat.* ▸ used as a noun. EG *His smile soon modified to a wince.* V ▸ N COUNT

winch /wɪntʃ/, **winches, winching, winched. 1** A **winch** is a machine which is used to lift heavy objects. It consists of a cylinder around which a rope or chain is wound. N COUNT

2 If you **winch** an object or person somewhere, you lift or lower them using a winch. EG *...helicopters into which they could be winched.* V+O+A

wind, winds, winding, winded, wound; pronounced /wɪnd/ for paragraphs 1-6 and /waɪnd/ for paragraphs 7-9 and the phrasal verbs. **Winded** is the past tense and past participle of the verb in paragraph 3. **Wound** /waʊnd/ is the past tense and past participle of the verbs in paragraphs 7-9 and the phrasal verbs.

1 A **wind** is a current of air moving across the earth's surface. EG *...poppies fluttering in the wind... There was a fierce wind blowing... ...a gust of wind.* N COUNT OR N UNCOUNT

2 Your **wind** is your ability to breathe easily. EG *I had to stop and regain my wind.* N SING+POSS

3 If you **are winded** by something such as a blow, the air is suddenly knocked out of your lungs so that you have difficulty breathing for a short time. V+O: OFT PASS

4 Wind is the air that you sometimes swallow with food or drink, or the gas that is produced in your stomach, which causes an uncomfortable feeling. N UNCOUNT

5 The **wind** section of an orchestra or band is the group of musicians who play instruments that they blow into. EG *...brilliant wind players.* N MOD

6 If you **get wind of** something, you hear about it, especially when someone else did not want you to know about it. EG *He somehow got wind of the party and managed to get himself invited.* PHRASE Informal

7 If a road or river **winds** in a particular direction, it goes in that direction with a lot of bends in it. EG *The river winds through the town.* ◊ **winding**. EG *...the winding road leading to the Castle.* ● If you **wind** your **way** somewhere, you do not go there quickly or directly. EG *The procession wound its way through the sunlit streets.* V+A ◊ ADJ CLASSIF ● PHRASE

8 When you **wind** something round something else, you wrap it round it several times. EG *Wind the wire round the screws.* V+O+*round/around*

9 When you **wind** a clock or watch, you turn a knob, key, or handle on it round and round in order to make it operate. V+O

wind back. When you **wind back** the tape in a tape recorder or the film in a camera, you make it move back towards its starting position. PHRASAL VB: V+O+ADV

wind down. 1 When you **wind down** the window of a car, you make it move downwards by turning a handle. **2** If a clock or machine **winds down**, it gradually works more slowly before stopping completely. **3** If someone **winds down** a business, they gradually reduce the amount of work or the number of people involved in it, before closing it down completely. PHRASAL VB: V+O+ADV; V+ADV; V-ERG+ADV

wind forward. When you **wind forward** the tape in a tape recorder, you make it move forward to a new position. PHRASAL VB: V+O+ADV

wind up. 1 When you **wind up** an activity, you finish it or stop doing it. EG *We were winding up this conference... It was time to wind up the game.* **2** When someone **winds up** a business or other organization, they close it down completely. EG *Four years later the company was wound up.* **3** If you **wind up** in a particular place, you are in that place at the end of a series of journeys or events. EG *We wound up at the Indian restaurant... It wouldn't surprise me if he winds up in jail.* **4** When you **wind up** a clock or watch, you turn a knob, key, or handle on it round and round in order to make it operate. **5** When you **wind up** the window of a car, you make it move upwards by turning a handle. PHRASAL VB: V-ERG+ADV; V+ADV, OR V-ERG+ADV; V+ADV+A Informal; V+O+ADV; V+O+ADV

windbreak /wɪndbreɪk/, **windbreaks.** A **windbreak** is a line of trees or a fence which gives N COUNT protection against the wind. EG *The orchard serves as a windbreak.*

windfall /wɪndfɔːl/, **windfalls.** A **windfall** is a sum of money that you receive unexpectedly or by luck. EG *He had a windfall from the football pools.* N COUNT

wind instrument, wind instruments. A **wind instrument** is a musical instrument that you blow into in order to produce sounds, for example a trumpet or a clarinet. See picture at MUSICAL INSTRUMENTS. N COUNT

windmill /wɪnd⁰mɪl/, **windmills.** A **windmill** is a tall building with a cross-shaped structure on the outside which turns round as the wind blows. This provides energy, often for a machine which crushes grain. N COUNT

window /wɪndəʊ/, **windows.** A **window** is a space in a wall or roof or in the side of a vehicle, often with glass in it so that light can pass through it and people can see through it. See picture at HOUSE. EG *The kitchen windows were wide open... ...looking in a jeweller's window.* N COUNT

window-box, window-boxes. A **window-box** is a long, narrow container on a window-sill outside a house, in which plants are grown. N COUNT

window-frame, window-frames. A **window-frame** is a frame round the edges of a window, which the glass is fixed into. N COUNT

window-pane, window-panes. A **window-pane** is a piece of glass in the window of a building. EG *...the clatter of rain against the window-pane.* N COUNT

window-shopping. If you go **window-shopping**, you spend time looking at the things in the windows of shops without intending to buy anything. EG *I had been window-shopping on Madison Avenue.* N ING

window-sill, window-sills. A **window-sill** is a ledge along the bottom of a window, either inside or outside a building. EG *Pots of herbs stood on the window-sill.* N COUNT

windpipe /wɪndpaɪp/, **windpipes.** Your **windpipe** is the tube in your body that carries air into your lungs when you breathe. N COUNT

windscreen /wɪndskriːn/, **windscreens.** The **windscreen** of a car or other vehicle is the glass window at the front which the driver looks through. See picture at CAR. N COUNT British

windscreen wiper, windscreen wipers. A **windscreen wiper** is a long thin piece of metal with a rubber edge, which is electrically operated and which wipes rain from the windscreen of a vehicle. See picture at CAR. N COUNT: USU PLURAL British

windshield /wɪndʃiːld/, **windshields.** A **windshield** is 1 the same as a windscreen. EG *I wiped my windshield... ...a windshield wiper.* 2 a glass or plastic screen that provides protection from the wind, for example on the front of a motorbike. N COUNT American

windsurfer

windsurfer /wɪndsɜːfə/, **windsurfers.** 1 A **windsurfer** is a long, narrow board with a sail attached, which you stand on in the sea or in a lake and which moves along as the wind blows it. N COUNT

2 You can also refer to a person riding on a windsurfer as a **windsurfer**. N COUNT

windsurfing /wɪndsɜːfɪŋ/ is the activity of moving along the surface of the sea or a lake on a windsurfer. EG *On the beach you can go windsurfing or sailing.* N ING

windswept /wɪndswɛpt/. 1 A **windswept** place is open and not protected against strong winds. EG *...a beautiful windswept hillside.* ADJ CLASSIF Literary

2 Someone who looks **windswept** has untidy hair because they have been out in the wind. ADJ QUALIT Literary

windy /wɪndi¹/, **windier, windiest.** If it is **windy**, the wind is blowing a lot. EG *The winter was cold, wet, and windy... It was a windy spring day.* ADJ QUALIT

wine /waɪn/, **wines. Wine** is an alcoholic drink made from grapes. There are two main kinds, called red wine and white wine. Wine can also be made from other fruits or vegetables. EG *I was drinking white wine... Have you tried his turnip wine?* N MASS

wine bar, wine bars. A **wine bar** is a place where people can buy and drink wine. N COUNT

wing /wɪŋ/, **wings, winging, winged.** 1 The **wings** of a bird or an insect are the two parts of its body that it uses for flying. N COUNT

2 The **wings** of an aeroplane are the long flat parts which stick out of either side and support it while it is flying. N COUNT

3 A **wing** of a building is a part of it which sticks out from the main part or which has been built later than the main part. EG *...the west wing of the museum... ...the hospital wing of the prison.* N COUNT: USU+SUPP

4 A **wing** of an organization, especially a political organization, is a group within it which has a particular function or particular beliefs. EG *...the political wing of the IRA.* ● See also **left-wing, right-wing.** N COUNT+SUPP

5 The **wings** in a theatre are the sides of the stage which are hidden from the audience by curtains or scenery. EG *She dropped her cloak in the wings.* N PLURAL: the+N

6 The **wings** of a car are the parts of the body which are around the wheels. See picture at CAR. N COUNT British

winger /wɪŋə/, **wingers.** In football or hockey, a **winger** is an attacking player who plays mainly on the far left or the far right of the pitch. N COUNT

wingspan /wɪŋspæn/, **wingspans.** The **wingspan** of a bird, insect, or aeroplane is the distance from the end of one wing to the end of the other wing. EG *...dragonflies with a wingspan of 70 centimetres.* N COUNT: USU+SUPP

wink /wɪŋk/, **winks, winking, winked.** 1 When you **wink**, you close one eye very briefly, often as a signal to someone that something is a joke or a secret. EG *Uncle John winked at me across the table.* ▸ used as a noun. EG *'What a hostess!' said Clarissa with a big wink at George.* V: OFT+*at* ▸ N COUNT

2 If a light **winks**, it shines in short flashes. If a surface **winks**, it reflects light in short flashes. EG *Lights winked under the trees... ...the sea, sparkling and winking in the sun.* V Literary

3 If you have **forty winks**, you sleep for a short while. PHRASE Informal

4 If you **don't sleep a wink** or **don't get a wink of sleep**, you stay awake and do not sleep at all. EG *I never slept a wink that night.* PHRASE Informal

winner /wɪnə/, **winners.** The **winner** of a prize, race, or competition is the person who wins it. EG *He was a worthy winner of the Nobel Prize.* N COUNT

winning /wɪnɪŋ/, **winnings.** 1 The **winning** competitor, team, or entry in a competition is the one that has won. EG *Here are some extracts from the five winning entries.* ADJ CLASSIF: ATTRIB

2 **Winning** is also used to describe actions or qualities that please other people and make them feel friendly towards you. EG *His chief asset is his winning smile.* ADJ CLASSIF: ATTRIB Literary

3 The money that someone wins in a competition or by gambling is referred to as their **winnings**. EG *Mark laughed and went to collect his winnings.* N PLURAL

What do you buy when you go window-shopping?

winter /wɪntə/, **winters. Winter** is the coldest season of the year, between autumn and spring. In winter, many trees and plants do not have any leaves. EG *It was a terrible winter... ...a dark winter's night.* N UNCOUNT OR N COUNT

wintertime /wɪntətaɪm/ is the period of time during which winter lasts. EG *Where do they go in the wintertime?* N UNCOUNT

wintry /wɪntri¹/. Something that is **wintry** has features that are typical of winter. EG *...one wintry day early in March.* ADJ QUALIT

wipe /waɪp/, **wipes, wiping, wiped. 1** If you **wipe** something, you rub its surface lightly in order to remove dirt or liquid from it. EG *He wiped his mouth with the back of his hand.* ▸ used as a noun. EG *Give the table a wipe.* V+O : USU+A ▸ N COUNT

2 If you **wipe** dirt or liquid from something, you remove it, for example by using a cloth or your hand. EG *She wiped the tears from her eyes.* V+O+A

3 If you **wipe** the dishes, you dry plates, knives, forks, and other things with a cloth when they have been washed after a meal. V+O OR V

4 If you **wipe** the sounds or pictures recorded on a tape, you remove them, for example by recording different sounds or pictures on the tape. V+O

wipe out. To **wipe out** places or groups of people means to destroy them completely, especially suddenly or violently. EG *Epidemics wiped out the local population.* PHRASAL VB : V+ADV+O

wipe up. If you **wipe up** dirt or liquid from something, you remove it using a cloth. EG *He began to wipe up the mess.* PHRASAL VB : V+O+ADV

wire /waɪə/, **wires, wiring, wired. 1** A **wire** is a long thin piece of metal that is used to fasten or connect things. EG *You can mend it with a length of wire... ...overhead lights suspended from wires... ...a telephone wire.* ● See also **barbed wire**. N COUNT OR N UNCOUNT

2 A **wire** is also a telegram. EG *I decided to send a wire ordering a room with twin beds.* N COUNT American

3 If you **wire** one thing to another, you fasten the two things together using wire. EG *He wired one end of the chain to the hook.* V+O+*to*

4 If you **wire** something or **wire** it up, you connect it to something else with wire so that electricity or electrical signals can pass between them. EG *Wire one end of the cable to the plug... ...electrical fittings wired up to the mains.* V+O+A : OFT+*up*

5 If you **wire** a person, you send them a telegram. EG *I wired Renata yesterday and asked her to marry me.* V+O : OFT+REPORT : ONLY *that* American

wireless /waɪəlɪ²s/, **wirelesses.** A **wireless** is the same as a radio. EG *They always announce the results on the wireless.* N COUNT Outdated

wire wool consists of very thin pieces of wire twisted together, often in the form of small pads. Wire wool is used to clean metal objects, especially saucepans and other kitchen equipment. N UNCOUNT

wiring /waɪərɪŋ/. The **wiring** in a building is the system of wires that supply electricity to the rooms. EG *Will the cottage need new wiring?* N UNCOUNT

wiry /waɪəri¹/. **1** Someone who is **wiry** is rather thin but has strong muscles. EG *...a short, wiry man.* ADJ CLASSIF

2 Something that is **wiry** is stiff and rough to touch. EG *...her wiry, black hair.* ADJ CLASSIF

wisdom /wɪzdəᵒm/. **1 Wisdom** is the ability to use your experience and knowledge in order to make sensible decisions or judgements. EG *She spoke with authority as well as wisdom.* N UNCOUNT

2 If you talk about the **wisdom** of an action or decision, you are talking about how sensible it is. EG *Doubts were expressed about the wisdom of the visit.* N SING : *the*+N+*of*

wisdom tooth, wisdom teeth. Your **wisdom teeth** are the four teeth at the back of your mouth which grow much later than your other teeth. N COUNT

wise /waɪz/, **wiser, wisest. 1** Someone who is **wise** is able to use their experience and knowledge in order to make sensible decisions and judgements. EG *She has suddenly become wise... He's a very wise man... Hugh made the wisest decision of all.* ◇ **wisely.** EG *You have chosen wisely.* ADJ QUALIT ◇ ADV

2 Wise is used in these phrases. **2.1** If you say that a person **would be wise** to do something, you are advising them to do it. EG *It would be wise to give up now and try again later... I think you'd be very wise to accept it.* **2.2** If you **get wise to** something, you find out about it, especially when someone has been trying to keep it secret. EG *They tried to burn the evidence before the cops got wise.* **2.3** If you say that someone is **none the wiser** or **no wiser**, you mean that they have failed to understand something, or that they are not aware of something that has happened. EG *So we're none the wiser... No one outside would be any the wiser.* PHRASES American

-wise. You can add **-wise** to nouns to form adverbs when you want to indicate **1** that someone is behaving like a particular person or thing. EG *I edged my way crabwise along the row to my seat.* SUFFIX

2 that you are considering one particular aspect of something. EG *You're at a disadvantage status-wise.*

wisecrack /waɪzkræk/, **wisecracks.** A **wisecrack** is a clever remark that is intended to be amusing, but is often rather unkind. EG *I fought down the temptation to make a wisecrack about his clothes.* N COUNT

wish /wɪʃ/, **wishes, wishing, wished. 1** A **wish** is a longing or desire for something, often something that is difficult to obtain or achieve. EG *She told me of her wish to leave the convent.* N COUNT

2 If you send your good **wishes** to someone, you express the hope that they will be happy or successful. EG *My parents send their best wishes.* N PLURAL

3 If you **wish** to do something, you want to do it. EG *They are in love and wish to marry... We do not wish to waste our money.* V : USU+*to*-INF OR *for* Formal

4 If you **wish** that something were the case, you would like it to be the case, even though you know that it is impossible or unlikely. EG *I often wish that I were really wealthy.* V+REPORT : ONLY *that*

5 If you **wish** for something, you express your desire for it silently to yourself. In fairy stories, when someone wishes for something, it often happens by magic. EG *I blew out the candles on my cake and wished for a new bike.* ▸ used as a noun. EG *The fairy granted her three wishes.* V : USU+*for* ▸ N COUNT

6 If you **wish** someone good luck, you say 'Good luck' to them to indicate that you hope they will have good luck. If you **wish** someone a happy birthday, you say 'Happy Birthday' to them to indicate that you hope they will enjoy their birthday. EG *They wished each other luck before the exam.* V+O+O

7 If you say that you **would not wish** something **on** a particular person, you mean that the thing is so unpleasant that you would not want the person to be forced to experience it. EG *...an illness I would not wish on my worst enemy.* PHRASE

wishful thinking. If you say that someone's hope or wish is **wishful thinking**, you mean that it is very unlikely to come true. EG *It is wishful thinking to assume that the generals will agree to this.* N UNCOUNT

wishy-washy /wɪʃi¹ wɒʃi¹/. If you describe a person or their ideas as **wishy-washy**, you mean that their ideas are not firm or clear. EG *He's just a wishy-washy liberal... ...a wishy-washy concept.* ADJ QUALIT Informal

wisp /wɪsp/, **wisps. 1** A **wisp** of grass or hair is a small, thin, untidy bunch of it. EG *A wisp of grey hair stuck out from under her hat.* N COUNT OR N PART

2 A **wisp** of smoke or fog is a long thin amount of it. EG *...wisps of smoke from a small fire.* N PART

wispy /wɪspi¹/. Hair that is **wispy** is thin and grows in small, untidy bunches. ADJ QUALIT

wistful /wɪstfᵘl/. If someone is **wistful**, they are rather sad because they want something and know that they cannot have it. EG *She had a last wistful look round the flat... ...a little wistful smile.* ADJ QUALIT

wit /wɪt/, **wits. 1 Wit** is the ability to use words or ideas in an amusing and clever way. EG *The girl laughed at his wit... ...the wit of the cartoonist.* N UNCOUNT

2 If someone does something sensible, you can say that they have the **wit** to do it. EG *No one had had the wit to bring a bottle-opener.* N SING : the+N +to-INF

3 You can refer to someone's ability to think quickly in a difficult situation as their **wits**. EG *Her only chance was to use her wits to bluff the enemy.* N PLURAL : USU+POSS

4 Wits is used in these phrases. **4.1** If you **have** or **keep** your **wits about** you, you are alert and ready to act in a difficult situation. EG *In this part of the city you have to keep your wits about you all the time.* **4.2** If something **scares** you **out of your wits** or if it **scares the wits out of** you, it scares you very much indeed. EG *We were frightened out of our wits by a banging at the door.* **4.3** If someone is **at** their **wits' end**, they are so worried and exhausted by problems or difficulties that they do not know what to do next. EG *I am at my wits' end to know what to do with my son.* **4.4** a **battle of wits**: see **battle**. • to **pit** your **wits against** someone: see **pit**. PHRASES

witch /wɪtʃ/, **witches.** A **witch** is a woman who is believed to have magic powers, especially evil ones. EG *She looked like a dreadful old witch.* N COUNT

witchcraft /wɪtʃkrɑ:ft/ is the skill of using magic powers, especially evil ones. N UNCOUNT

witch doctor, witch doctors. A **witch doctor** is a person in some societies, especially in Africa, who heals people and is thought to have magic powers. EG *...one of the most eminent witch doctors.* N COUNT

witch-hunt, witch-hunts. A **witch-hunt** is a search for people who are thought to be responsible for things that have gone wrong, in order to punish them. The victims of a witch-hunt are often innocent people who have strong and independent opinions, but have not actually done any harm. EG *Hearst's campaign developed into a witch-hunt that terrorized the campuses.* N COUNT

with /wɪð, wɪθ/. **1** If one thing or person is **with** another, they are together in one place. EG *I stayed with her until dusk.* PREP

2 If you do something **with** someone else, you both do it together. EG *Boys do not generally play with girls... I discussed it with Phil... ...weekly meetings with junior ministers.* PREP

3 If you fight or argue **with** someone, you oppose them. EG *...a naval war with France... Judy was tired of quarrelling with Bal.* PREP

4 If you do something **with** a particular tool or object, you do it using that tool or object. EG *Clean mirrors with a mop... He brushed back his hair with his hand.* PREP

5 You use **with** when you mention a feature, characteristic, or possession that someone or something has. EG *...an old man with a beard... ...an old house with steep stairs and dark corridors.* PREP

6 Something that is filled or covered **with** things has those things in it or on it. EG *The building is decorated with bright banners.* PREP

7 You use **with** to indicate how someone does something or the feeling they have when they do it. For example, if you do something **with** care, you do it carefully. EG *These files can be inspected by the computer with great accuracy and speed... Jordache looked over at his son with genuine surprise... 'There is a blanket missing,' said Matron with a sigh.* PREP

8 You also use **with** to indicate the feeling that makes someone behave in a particular way. EG *This experience leaves him quaking with fear.* PREP

9 You can use **with** to indicate what something relates to. EG *Don't be inflexible with shopping... There was a particular problem with claims for maternity allowance.* PREP

10 You can also use **with** to say that something happens at the same time as something else. EG *He didn't have the courage to put his hat on with Perkins watching him... With advancing age, reactions become slower.* PREP

11 You use **with** to introduce a factor that affects something. EG *With all the traffic jams, it wouldn't be economic.* PREP

12 If someone says that they are **with** you, **12.1** they mean that they understand what you are talking about. EG *Sorry, I'm not quite with you.* **12.2** they mean that they support or approve of what you are doing. EG *I'm with the government in this.* PREP+PRON Informal; PREP

withdraw /wɪðdrɔ:/, **withdraws, withdrawing, withdrew** /wɪðdru:/, **withdrawn. 1** If you **withdraw** something from a place, you remove it or take it away. EG *She withdrew the key from the door... You must present your cheque card when you withdraw any money.* V+O : OFT+from Formal

2 If you **withdraw** to another place, you leave the place where you are and go to the other place. EG *He breathed a sigh of relief and withdrew to his office to count the money.* V : USU+A Formal

3 When troops **withdraw** or **are withdrawn**, they leave the place where they are fighting or where they are based. EG *We could see the force withdrawing... They are willing to withdraw some troops.* V-ERG : OFT+from

4 If you **withdraw** from an activity, you decide that you will no longer take part in it. EG *Marsha withdrew from the argument.* V OR V+O : OFT+from Formal

5 If you **withdraw** a remark or statement, you say that you wish to change or deny it. EG *I want to withdraw a statement I made earlier on.* V+O Formal

withdrawal /wɪðdrɔ:əl/, **withdrawals. 1** The **withdrawal** of something is the act or process of removing it or taking it away. EG *...major matters like the withdrawal of public services... They are trying to negotiate the withdrawal of 20,000 troops.* N UNCOUNT OR N COUNT

2 The **withdrawal** of a remark or statement is the act of saying formally that you wish to change or deny it. EG *...the withdrawal of invitations.* N UNCOUNT

3 Your **withdrawal** from an activity or an organization is your decision to stop taking part in it. EG *...withdrawal from the Common Market.* N UNCOUNT

4 Withdrawal is behaviour in which someone prefers to be alone and does not want to communicate with other people. EG *...spells of sulking, withdrawal and vindictiveness.* N UNCOUNT

5 When someone has **withdrawal** symptoms, they feel ill after they have stopped taking a drug which they were addicted to. N UNCOUNT

6 A **withdrawal** is an amount of money that you take from your bank account. EG *It is not the bank's policy to deduct interest on withdrawals.* N COUNT

withdrawn /wɪðdrɔ:n/. **1 Withdrawn** is the past participle of **withdraw**.

2 Someone who is **withdrawn** is very shy or quiet, and finds it difficult to talk to other people. EG *The isolated life made them withdrawn.* ADJ QUALIT

withdrew /wɪðdru:/ is the past tense of **withdraw.**

wither /wɪðə/, **withers, withering, withered. 1** When something **withers** or **withers** away, it becomes weaker, often until it no longer exists. EG *Links with the outside community withered... His eagerness to fight back could not be permitted to wither away.* V : OFT+away

2 If a plant **withers** or if heat or drought **withers** it, it shrinks and dries up, and dies. EG *The leaves had withered and fallen.* V-ERG

withered /wɪðəd/. **1** A **withered** plant is shrunken, dried up, and dead. EG *...a pot of withered roses.* ADJ CLASSIF

2 If you describe a person or a part of their body as **withered**, you mean that their skin is very wrinkled and dry, and looks old. EG *...a withered old lady... ...her withered fingers.* ADJ QUALIT

Should a witness withhold evidence?

withering /wɪðə[0]rɪŋ/. If someone gives you a **withering** look or makes a **withering** remark, their look or remark makes you feel ashamed or stupid. EG *Scylla gave him a withering glare.* ADJ CLASSIF

withhold /wɪðhəʊld/, **withholds, withholding, withheld** /wɪðheld/. If you **withhold** something that someone wants, you do not let them have it. EG *His salary was withheld... I decided to withhold the information till later.* V+O Formal

within /wɪðɪn/. **1** If something is **within** something else, it is inside it. EG *The prisoners demanded the freedom to congregate within the prison... ...the dominant role of women within the family... She cut open the fruit and began to suck out the soft flesh within.* PREP OR ADV

2 If you have a feeling **within** you, you feel it. EG *A mounting wave of dislike and anger rose within me... ...the hatred he felt within.* PREP OR ADV Literary

3 If something is **within** a particular limit, it does not go beyond that limit or is not more than what is allowed. EG *We must ask the schools to keep within their budget.* PREP

4 If you are **within** a particular distance of a place, you are less than that distance from it. EG *They were within fifty miles of Chicago.* PREP

5 If something is **within** sight, **within** earshot, or **within** reach, you can see it, hear it, or reach it. EG *They finally came within sight of the gates.* PREP

6 Within a particular length of time means before that length of time has passed. EG *Within minutes I was called to his office... Sixteen houses were vandalized within a few weeks.* PREP

without /wɪðaʊt/. **1** If people or things are **without** something, they do not have it. EG *The chairs were of black teak, without cushions... ...city slums without lights, roads or water... She was without an ambition in the world.* PREP

2 If you do one thing **without** doing another thing, you do not do the other thing. EG *They drove into town without talking to each other... 'No,' she said, without explanation.* CONJ+-ING, OR PREP

3 If you do something **without** a particular feeling, you do not have that feeling when you do it. EG *They greeted him without enthusiasm.* PREP

4 If one thing happens **without** another thing happening, the other thing does not happen. EG *The rest of the press conference passed without incident... I knocked twice, without reply.* PREP

5 Without someone means not in their company or not living or working with them. EG *You can go without me... Her husband felt he couldn't face life without her.* PREP

6 to **do without**: see **do.** • to **go without**: see **go.**

withstand /wɪðstænd/, **withstands, withstanding, withstood** /wɪðstʊd/. When something or someone **withstands** a force or action, they survive it or do not give in to it. EG *They have to make the walls strong enough to withstand high winds... He was in no condition to withstand any further punishment.* V+O Formal

witness /wɪtnɪ[1]s/, **witnesses, witnessing, witnessed. 1** If you are a **witness** to an event, you see it and can tell other people what happened. EG *They listened avidly as witnesses to the murder told what they had seen.* N COUNT: OFT+*to* • If you **are witness to** something, you see it happen. EG *This was the first time I was witness to one of his rages.* • PHRASE Formal

2 If you **witness** something, you see it happen. EG *At least fifteen people witnessed the attack on Morris.* V+O Formal

3 A **witness** is someone who appears in a court of law to tell what they know about a crime or other event. EG *Other witnesses were called, and gave similar evidence.* N COUNT

4 A **witness** is also someone who writes their name on a document that another person has signed, to confirm that it is really that person's signature. ▸ used as a verb. EG *Now everything is signed and witnessed.* N COUNT ▸ V+O

5 If something **is a witness** to something else or **bears witness** to it, it shows that it exists or happened. EG *His smile is a witness to his new found happiness... This lack of action bears witness to a complacency which has survived two World Wars.* PHRASE Formal

witness-box, witness-boxes. The **witness-box** or **witness-stand** in a court of law is the place where people stand or sit when they are giving evidence. EG *He was shown into the witness-box.* N COUNT

witter /wɪtə/, **witters, wittering, wittered.** If you say that someone **is wittering** about something, you mean that they are saying a lot of silly and boring things. EG *He was wittering on as usual.* V: USU+A Informal

witticism /wɪtɪsɪzə[0]m/, **witticisms.** A **witticism** is a witty remark or joke. EG *Don smiled at this witticism.* N COUNT

witty /wɪti[1]/, **wittier, wittiest.** Someone or something that is **witty** is amusing in a clever way. EG *It's a neat and witty play.* ADJ QUALIT

wives /waɪvz/ is the plural of **wife.**

wizard /wɪzəd/, **wizards.** A **wizard** is a man in a fairy story who has magic powers. N COUNT

wizardry /wɪzədri[1]/. You can refer to a very clever achievement or piece of work as **wizardry**, especially when you do not understand how it is done. EG *...a sophisticated piece of computing wizardry... ...her reputation for financial wizardry.* N UNCOUNT +SUPP

wizened /wɪzənd/. A **wizened** person, fruit, or vegetable is old and has wrinkled skin. EG *Mr Solomon was a wizened little man with frizzy grey hair... ...a wizened pumpkin.* ADJ QUALIT Literary

wobble /wɒbə[0]l/, **wobbles, wobbling, wobbled.** If something **wobbles**, it makes small movements from side to side, because it is loose or unsteady. EG *The old car wobbled back and forth on the road... My legs were wobbling under me.* V

wobbly /wɒbli[1]/. Something that is **wobbly** moves unsteadily from side to side. EG *...a wobbly bed... My legs still feel weak and wobbly.* ADJ QUALIT Informal

wodge /wɒdʒ/, **wodges.** A **wodge** of something is a large amount of it or a large piece of it. EG *Professor Marvin banged his wodge of files down hard on the desk.* N COUNT OR N PART Informal British

woe /wəʊ/, **woes. 1 Woe** is great unhappiness or sorrow. EG *His distraught wife poured out her tale of woe... ...an occasional bird cry like an exclamation of woe.* N UNCOUNT Literary Outdated

2 You can refer to someone's problems or misfortunes as their **woes.** EG *They listened sympathetically to his woes.* N PLURAL Literary

woebegone /wəʊbɪgɒn/. Someone who looks or feels **woebegone** looks or feels very sad. EG *...a little woebegone face.* ADJ QUALIT Formal

woeful /wəʊfʊl/. **1** Someone or something that is **woeful** is very sad. EG *...the lovers' long and woeful farewell.* ◊ **woefully.** EG *She announced woefully, 'I've lost my job.'* ADJ QUALIT ◊ ADV

2 You also describe something as **woeful** when it is very bad. EG *His work displays a woeful lack of imagination.* ◊ **woefully.** EG *The quantities were generally woefully inadequate.* ADJ QUALIT ◊ SUBMOD

wok /wɒk/, **woks.** A **wok** is a large bowl-shaped pan which is used for Chinese-style cooking. N COUNT

woke /wəʊk/ is the past tense of **wake.**

woken /wəʊkə[0]n/ is the past participle of **wake.**

wolf /wʊlf/, **wolves; wolfs, wolfing, wolfed. Wolves** /wʊlvz/ is the plural of the noun. **Wolfs** is the third person singular, present tense, of the verb.

1 A **wolf** is a wild animal that looks like a large dog and that kills and eats other animals. N COUNT

2 If you **wolf** food or **wolf** it down, you eat it up quickly and greedily. EG *He wolfed the food down, bones and all.* V+O: OFT+*down* Informal

woman /wʊmən/, **women** /wɪmɪn/. **1** A **woman** is an adult female human being. EG *There were men and women working in the fields... We had one woman teacher.* N COUNT

2 You can refer to women in general as **woman**. EG *...man's inhumanity to woman.* N UNCOUNT

3 A man's **woman** is his lover or his wife. EG *My woman took a blanket out of the car.* N COUNT Informal

4 People sometimes address a woman as **'woman'** when they are angry or impatient with her. EG *Oh, for God's sake, woman, sit down!* VOCATIVE

5 If two women talk to each other **woman to woman**, they talk honestly and openly, treating each other as equals. PHRASE

womanhood /wʊmənhʊd/. **1 Womanhood** is the state of being a woman rather than a girl. EG *...when a girl is on the threshold of womanhood.* N UNCOUNT

2 You can refer to women in general as **womanhood**. You can also refer to the women of a particular place as its **womanhood.** EG *...a perfect specimen of English womanhood.* N UNCOUNT

womanizer /wʊmənaɪzə/, **womanizers;** also spelled **womaniser.** A **womanizer** is a man who likes to spend a lot of time in the company of women, usually in order to have short sexual relationships with them. N COUNT

womankind /wʊmənkaɪnd/. You can refer to all women as **womankind** when considering them as a group. EG *I spoke up on behalf of womankind.* N UNCOUNT Formal

womanly /wʊmənli[1]/. You can describe a woman's behaviour or character as **womanly** when you think that it is typical of a woman or suitable for a woman. EG *...the womanly virtues of gentleness and compassion.* ADJ QUALIT

womb /wuːm/, **wombs.** A woman's **womb** is the part inside her body where a baby grows before it is born. EG *...a baby in his mother's womb.* N COUNT

women /wɪmɪn/ is the plural of **woman.**

Women's Lib is the same as Women's Liberation. EG *...a Women's Lib attitude.* N UNCOUNT Informal

Women's Liberation is the ideal that women should have the same social and economic rights and privileges as men. EG *I got interested in Women's Liberation... ...the local Women's Liberation Movement.* N UNCOUNT

won /wʌn/ is the past tense and past participle of **win.**

wonder /wʌndə/, **wonders, wondering, wondered. 1** If you **wonder** about something you do not know or understand, you think about it and try to guess or understand more about it. EG *I wonder what she'll look like... I keep wondering and worrying about what you said... I am beginning to wonder why we ever invited them.* V+*about*, QUOTE, OR REPORT: ONLY WH

2 You can begin a request by saying 'I **wonder** if' when you are being very polite. EG *I wonder if you'd mind closing the window.* V+*if/whether*

3 If you **wonder** at something, you are surprised and amazed about it. EG *I wondered at her strength... I used to wonder at their slowness.* V+*at* OR REPORT

4 If you say that it is a **wonder** that something happened, you mean that it is very surprising. EG *It was a wonder that she managed to come - she's usually too busy.* N SING: a+N+*that*

5 Wonder is a feeling of surprise and amazement. EG *...exclamations of wonder.* N UNCOUNT

6 A **wonder** is something or someone that amazes people and makes them feel great admiration. EG *...the wonders of modern technology.* N COUNT: USU+SUPP

7 You can also use **wonder** to describe someone or something that is extremely clever or skilful. EG *...the wonder boy of American racing.* N MOD

8 Wonder is used in these phrases. **8.1** If you say **wonders will never cease**, you mean that you are very surprised because something unexpected has happened. CONVENTION Informal **8.2** If you say **no wonder, little wonder**, or **small wonder**, you mean that you are not surprised by something that happens. EG *Little wonder that today we are in such a mess... 'Anyway, he didn't win.' - 'No wonder.'* PHRASE **8.3** If you say that something **works wonders** or **does wonders**, you mean that it has a very good effect. EG *A whisky at the end of the day will sometimes work wonders... The nurses tell me the doctors have done wonders for your leg.* PHRASE

wonderful /wʌndəfʊl/. If you describe something as **wonderful**, **1** you mean that it makes you feel very happy and pleased. EG *It was wonderful to be able to walk again.* **2** you mean that it is very impressive or successful. EG *I think the heart transplant is a wonderful thing.* ADJ QUALIT

wonderfully /wʌndəfʊli[1]/. You use **wonderfully** **1** to emphasize that something is much better than you expected. EG *Both plays are wonderfully funny... She was always wonderfully kind to me.* SUBMOD **2** to say that something happens or is done extremely well. EG *I had slept wonderfully.* ADV

wonderment /wʌndəmə[ʔ]nt/ is a feeling of amazement and admiration. EG *I stood shaking my head in wonderment.* N UNCOUNT

wondrous /wʌndrəs/ means amazing and impressive. EG *It was a wondrous victory... ...the wondrous inventions of the twentieth century.* ADJ QUALIT: ATTRIB Outdated

wonky /wɒŋki[1]/. Something that is **wonky** is likely to shake or not work properly because it is unsteady or not in its proper position. EG *The legs have gone a bit wonky.* ADJ QUALIT Informal British

wont /wəʊnt/. **1** If someone is **wont** to do something, they do it regularly as a habit. EG *They were wont to take long walks in the evening.* ADJ PRED +*to*-INF Outdated

2 If you say that someone does something **as is** their **wont**, you mean that they do it regularly as a habit. EG *They were all talking, as is their wont, about cars.* PHRASE Outdated

won't /wəʊnt/ is the usual spoken form of 'will not'.

woo /wuː/, **woos, wooing, wooed. 1** If you **woo** people, you try to encourage them to help you or support you. EG *She hoped to woo the working-class voters of Warrington.* V+O Literary

2 When a man **woos** a woman, he tries to make himself seem attractive to her, because he wants to marry her. V+O Outdated

wood /wʊd/, **woods. 1 Wood** is the material which forms the trunks and branches of trees. EG *We gathered wood for the fire.* N MASS

2 A **wood** is a large area of trees growing near each other. You can refer to a large wood as **the woods**. EG *...the big wood where the pheasants lived... They walked through the woods.* N COUNT

3 If you say that someone **can't see the wood for the trees**, you mean that they are so involved in the details of a situation or activity that they forget or cannot understand its general purpose or importance. • **touch wood**: see **touch.** PHRASE

wooded /wʊdɪ[1]d/. A **wooded** area is covered in trees. EG *...a narrow wooded valley.* ADJ QUALIT

wooden /wʊdə[0]n/. **1** A **wooden** object is made of wood. EG *...a wooden box.* ADJ CLASSIF

2 If you say that someone such as an actor is **wooden**, you mean that they act without showing any emotion in their face or movements. EG *His performances have become wooden and dull.* ADJ QUALIT

woodland /wʊdlə[3]nd/, **woodlands. Woodland** is land which is mostly covered with trees. EG *...a patch of woodland in Malaysia.* N UNCOUNT OR N COUNT

woodpecker /wʊdpɛkə/, **woodpeckers.** A **woodpecker** is a bird with a long sharp beak, which makes holes in tree trunks in order to eat insects. EG *...a lesser spotted woodpecker.* N COUNT

woodwind /wʊdwɪnd/. **Woodwind** instruments are musical instruments such as flutes, oboes, clarinets, and bassoons, that are played by blowing into them, usually by members of an orchestra. ADJ CLASSIF: ATTRIB

woodwork /wʊdwɜːk/. **1** You can refer to the doors, window-frames, and other parts of a house that are made of wood as the **woodwork**. EG *The paint was peeling from the woodwork.* N UNCOUNT

Should actors be word-perfect?

2 Woodwork is also the activity or skill of making things out of wood. N UNCOUNT

woodworm /wʊdwɜːm/, **woodworms. Woodworm** is the usual plural form.

1 Woodworm are larvae of a particular type of beetle, which make holes in wood by feeding on it. N COUNT

2 Woodworm is damage caused to wood by woodworm making holes in it. EG *If your house has woodworm, get expert treatment.* N UNCOUNT

woody /wʊdi[1]/, **woodier, woodiest. 1 Woody** plants have very hard stems. EG *The roots of woody plants grow deep.* ADJ QUALIT

2 A **woody** area has a lot of trees in it. EG *...a farm set amid woody valleys.* ADJ QUALIT

woof /wʊf/, **woofs.** A **woof** is the sound that a dog makes when it barks. N COUNT Informal

wool /wʊl/, **wools. 1 Wool** is the hair that grows on sheep and on some other animals. N MASS

2 Wool is also a material made from animals' wool. It is used for making things such as clothes, blankets, and carpets. EG *...a hat made of wool.* N MASS

3 If you **pull the wool over** someone's **eyes**, you deliberately tell them something that is not true in order to have an advantage over them. PHRASE Informal

4 See also **cotton wool, steel wool, wire wool.**

woollen /wʊlən/; spelled **woolen** in American English. **1 Woollen** clothes or materials are made from wool or from a mixture of wool and artificial fibres. EG *...woollen rugs... ...a woollen scarf... ...long woollen socks.* ADJ CLASSIF: ATTRIB

2 Woollens are clothes made of wool. EG *...a good fabric softener for woollens.* N PLURAL

woolly /wʊli[2]/, **woollies; woollier, woolliest;** spelled **wooly** in American English. **1** Something that is **woolly** is made of wool or looks like wool. EG *...a woolly cap.* ADJ CLASSIF

2 A **woolly** is a woollen piece of clothing, especially a pullover. EG *She wore a long woolly with a belt.* N COUNT Informal

3 If you describe people or their ideas as **woolly**, you mean that their ideas are very unclear. EG *They cannot afford to be vague and woolly.* ADJ QUALIT

woozy /wuːzi[1]/, **woozier, wooziest.** If you feel **woozy**, you feel rather weak and unsteady and cannot think clearly. EG *I smiled uncertainly, feeling woozy from the whisky.* ADJ QUALIT Informal

word /wɜːd/, **words, wording, worded. 1** A **word** is a single unit of language that can be represented in writing or speech. In English, a word has a space on either side of it when it is written. A word can usually have one or more meanings. EG *...a short passage of about seventy words... His eye had been caught by the word 'scandal' in the headline... He was, in the words of his doctor, making satisfactory progress.* N COUNT

2 If you have a **word** or a few **words** with someone, you have a short conversation with them. EG *May I have a word with you please?* N COUNT: a+N Informal

3 A **word** of advice or warning is a short piece of advice or warning. N SING: a+N

4 If you say that you cannot hear, understand, or believe a **word** of what someone is saying, you mean that you cannot hear, understand, or believe what they are saying at all. EG *I did not understand one word of what she'd said... Have you heard a word I've said?* N SING: a+N, USU WITH BROAD NEG

5 You can use **word** to mean a message. EG *The young man brought them word of her visit... The word got out that he was leaving.* N UNCOUNT OR N SING

6 Your **word** is a sincere promise that you make to someone. EG *I give you my word I won't ask him... I apologized for having doubted his word.* N SING+POSS

7 If you give the **word** to do something, you give an order to do it. EG *The light was improving as he gave the word to move.* N SING: *the*+N

8 When you **word** something in a particular way, you carefully choose the words that you use in order to express your ideas in an accurate or acceptable way. EG *How would one word such an announcement?* ◇ **worded.** EG *He wrote a strongly worded report to the Secretary of the Interior... ...one of the most sharply worded attacks on EEC ministers.* V+O; ◇ ADJ CLASSIF: ADV+ADJ

9 Word is used in these phrases. **9.1** If you repeat something **word for word**, you repeat it exactly as it was originally said or written. EG *We had a long chat and he printed it more or less word for word.* **9.2** A **word for word** translation is done by translating each word separately rather than by giving the general meaning of a group of words. **9.3** If you have **the last word** in an argument, you make the comment that finishes it and often makes the other person feel that they have been defeated. EG *Doctors always have the last word.* **9.4** If news or information passes **by word of mouth**, people tell it to each other rather than writing it down. **9.5** If you **put in a word** for someone or **put in a good word** for them, you speak favourably about them to a person who has influence. EG *I put in a word for her and she was forgiven.* **9.6** If someone **says the word**, they give their approval that something should start to happen. EG *You only have to say the word and they will do it.* **9.7** If you say to someone **'take my word for it'**, you mean that they should believe you because you are telling the truth. EG *You can take my word for it, she's not there.* **9.8** You say **in a word** to indicate that you are summarizing what you have just been saying. EG *The house is roomy, cool in summer, and in a word comfortable.* **9.9** to **not get a word in edgeways**: see **edgeways.** See also **four-letter word.** PHRASES

10 The plural form **words** is used in these phrases. **10.1** If you **have words with** someone, you have an argument with them. **10.2** You say **in other words** when introducing a simpler or clearer explanation of something that has just been said. EG *Is there a cheaper solution? In other words, can you make a cheaper device?* **10.3** If you say something **in** your **own words**, you say it in your own way, without copying or repeating what someone else has said. EG *He was asked to tell the story in his own words.* **10.4** If you say that someone said something **in so many words**, you mean that they said it clearly and directly. If you say that they said it **not in so many words**, you mean that they expressed it in an indirect way. EG *This is what he claims, only he does not state it in so many words.* **10.5** You can use the expression **for words** when you are emphasizing a quality that someone or something has. For example, if you say that someone is too stupid **for words**, you mean that they are very stupid indeed. **10.6** to **not mince** your **words**: see **mince.** PHRASES; Informal

wording /wɜːdɪŋ/. The **wording** of a piece of writing or a speech is the words used in it, especially when these words have been chosen to have a particular effect. EG *For a full hour he argued over the wording of the editorial.* N UNCOUNT

word-perfect. If you are **word-perfect**, you are able to repeat from memory the exact words of something that you have learned. ADJ CLASSIF

word-play /wɜːdpleɪ/. **Word-play** involves making jokes by using the meanings of words in an amusing or clever way. EG *...a fondness for word-play.* N UNCOUNT

word processing is the work of producing documents, letters, and other printed material using a word processor. N UNCOUNT

word processor, word processors. A **word processor** is an electronic machine which has a keyboard and a screen like a computer terminal, but which is used as a typewriter to produce documents, letters, and other printed material. N COUNT

wordy /wɜːdi[1]/, **wordier, wordiest.** Something that is **wordy** uses too many words, especially long or formal words. EG *...this very wordy book on biology... ...wordy writers.* ADJ QUALIT

wore /wɔː/ is the past tense of **wear.**

work /wɜ:k/, **works, working, worked.** 1 People who **work** have a job which they are paid to do. EG *He was working in a bank... Large numbers of them now work as labourers... Some of my salesmen formerly worked for a rival firm.* V:OFT+A

2 People who have **work** or who are in **work** have a job which they are paid to do. EG *...people who can't find work... ...the numbers out of work.* N UNCOUNT

3 When you **work**, 3.1 you do the tasks which your job involves. EG *I watched the people working at the weaving looms... I used to work a ten-hour day.* V:OFT+A OR V+O

3.2 you do a task that needs to be done or make an effort to achieve something. EG *All through the winter, the Kirks worked on their house... She works hard at keeping herself fit... He has been working all season on his game... They work for international peace.* V:OFT+A

4 **Work** is also 4.1 the tasks which your job involves. EG *I've got some work to do... I finish work at 3.* 4.2 tasks which you do because they need to be done. EG *A housewife's work can take ten or twelve hours a day.* 4.3 something which you produce as a result of an activity or as a result of doing your job. EG *It is standard practice to put remarks on their work... That's an absolutely fascinating piece of work.* 4.4 research on a particular subject. EG *There has been considerable work done in America on this subject.* N UNCOUNT

5 If you **work** someone hard, you make them work hard. EG *I was worked mercilessly.* V+O+A

6 If you **work** the land, you cultivate it. EG *...peasants working the land.* V+O

7 If you **work** a machine or piece of equipment, you use it or control it. EG *...the boy who worked the milking machine.* V+O

8 If a machine or piece of equipment **works**, it operates and performs its function. EG *The traffic lights weren't working properly.* V

9 If something such as an idea, method, or system **works**, it is successful. EG *That kind of democracy will never work.* V

10 If something **works** against you, it causes problems for you. If something **works** in your favour, it helps you in some way. EG *The apathy of the opposition is working in his favour.* V+A

11 If you **work** on an assumption or idea, you make decisions relying on your belief that it is correct. EG *Mr Reagan said he was working on the assumption that formal negotiations would take place shortly.* V+*on*

12 If something **works** into a particular position, it gradually moves so that it is in that position. EG *The ropes had worked loose.* V+A OR V+C

13 If you **work** yourself into a state of being very upset or angry, you make yourself become very upset or angry. EG *She worked herself into a rage.* V-REFL+*into*

14 If you **work** your way somewhere, you move or progress there slowly and with a lot of effort. EG *I worked my way slowly out of the marsh.* V+O+A

15 A **work** is something such as a painting, book, or piece of music, produced by an artist, writer, or composer. EG *...a large volume containing all of Chopin's works... ...the collected works of Proust.* N COUNT+SUPP

16 A **works** is a place where something is made or where an industrial process is carried out. EG *...the metal works... ...the gas works.* N COLL

17 **Works** consist of large-scale digging or building, for example in order to install pipes, or to construct roads or bridges. EG *He was in charge of planning the great plumbing and civic engineering works of the city.* N PLURAL: USU+SUPP

18 **Work** is used in these phrases. 18.1 If someone is **at work**, they are doing their job or are busy doing a particular task. EG *Aren't you supposed to be at work?... Computers will be hard at work on these problems.* 18.2 If you **go to work, set to work**, or **get to work**, you start doing a particular task. EG *Smithy set to work on the gardening.* 18.3 If you say that you will **have** your **work cut out** to do something, you mean that it will be very difficult for you to do it. EG *We'll have our work cut out to finish on time.* 18.4 If a group of workers **work to rule** as a protest, they stop doing extra work and just do the minimum that they are required to do in their job. EG *The delivery men are working to rule.* • See also **work-to-rule**. 18.5 See also **social work, working**. PHRASES; British

work off. If you **work off** a feeling such as anger, you gradually overcome it by doing something energetic or violent. PHRASAL VB: V+O+ADV

work out. 1 If you **work out** a solution to a problem or mystery, you think about it and manage to solve it or understand it. EG *We are always hoping that a more peaceful solution can be worked out... He couldn't work out why the room seemed so strange.* PHRASAL VB: V+O+ADV OR V+ADV +REPORT 2 If you **work out** the answer to a mathematical problem, you calculate it. EG *Now you can work out the area of the triangle.* V+O+ADV 3 If something **works out** at a particular amount, it is found to be that amount when the necessary calculations have been made. EG *Petrol prices here are among the cheapest in Europe, working out at around £1.15 a gallon.* V+ADV, USU+A 4 If a situation **works out** in a particular way, it happens or progresses in that way. EG *It's funny how life worked out... Things worked out well with Marian.* V+ADV, USU+A 5 If you **work out**, you do physical exercises in order to make your body fit and strong. EG *She worked out in a ballet class three hours a week.* V+ADV 6 See also **workout**.

work up. 1 If you **work** yourself **up** into a state of being very upset or angry, you make yourself become very upset or angry. EG *He worked himself up into a frenzy.* • See also **worked up.** PHRASAL VB: V-REFL+ADV 2 If you **work up** a feeling, you make yourself start to have it. EG *I can hardly work up enough energy to go to the shops.* V+O+ADV 3 If you **work up** to something important or difficult, you gradually progress towards it. EG *Start slowly and work up to a faster time.* V+ADV+*to*

workable /wɜ:kəbə°l/. Something that is **workable** can operate efficiently or can be used for a particular purpose. EG *This doesn't seem to me to be a workable system.* ADJ QUALIT

workaholic /wɜ:kəhɒlɪk/, **workaholics.** If you say that someone is a **workaholic**, you mean that they find it difficult to stop working in order to do other things. N COUNT

workbench /wɜ:kbɛnt°ʃ/, **workbenches.** A **workbench** is a heavy wooden table on which people use tools to make or repair things. N COUNT

workbook /wɜ:kbʊk/, **workbooks.** A **workbook** is an exercise book or textbook that is used for study, especially a book with questions in it and spaces for you to fill in the answers. N COUNT

workday /wɜ:kdeɪ/, **workdays.** A **workday** is 1 the amount of time during a day which you spend doing your job. EG *I have a 9-to-5 workday.* 2 a day on which people go to work. N COUNT

worked up. If you are **worked up** about something, you are very upset or angry about it. EG *Why are you so worked up over that editorial?* ADJ PRED

worker /wɜ:kə/, **workers.** 1 A **worker** is a person who is employed in an industry or business by another person or by an organization, and who has no responsibility for managing the industry or business. EG *The dispute affected relations between management and workers.* N COUNT

2 You can use **worker** to say how well or badly someone works. For example, a good **worker** is someone who works well. EG *My husband was a hard worker... You're a fast worker.* N COUNT+SUPP

3 A **worker** is also someone who does a particular kind of job. EG *...a series of experiments by American research workers... ...charity workers.* • See also **social worker**. N COUNT: USU+SUPP

What are all the workers in a company called?

workforce /wɜːkfɔːs/. You can refer to all the people who work in a particular industry, company, or country as the **workforce**. EG *Asia's workforce will expand by 60 per cent... They agreed to reduce the workforce by 350.* — N SING+SUPP

working /wɜːkɪŋ/, **workings. 1 Working** people have jobs which they are paid to do. EG *...children with working mothers.* — ADJ CLASSIF : ATTRIB

2 Your **working** day or week is the number of hours that you work during a day or a week. EG *The unions will demand a reduction in working hours.* — ADJ CLASSIF : ATTRIB

3 Your **working** life is the period of your life in which you have a job or you are of a suitable age to have a job. EG *Most of these people spend their entire working lives at General Motors.* — ADJ CLASSIF : ATTRIB

4 Working conditions or practices are ones which you have in your job. EG *We want to achieve better working conditions for all women.* — ADJ CLASSIF : ATTRIB

5 Working clothes are designed for doing work in and so are not intended to be attractive. EG *I didn't bring any working clothes.* — ADJ CLASSIF : ATTRIB

6 If you have a **working** knowledge of something such as a foreign language, you do not know it very well but you know it well enough to be able to use it. EG *In the first week I picked up a tolerable working knowledge of Spanish.* — ADJ CLASSIF : ATTRIB

7 The **workings** of a piece of equipment, an organization, or a system are the ways in which it operates and the processes which are involved in it. EG *The general workings of a Wall Street bank are discussed in the programme.* — N PLURAL +SUPP

8 in working order: see **order**.

working class, working classes. The **working class** or **working classes** are the group of people in a society who do not own much property and who do jobs which involve using physical skills rather than intellectual skills. EG *...the urban working class... Eleven members were of working-class origins.* — N COUNT

workload /wɜːkləʊd/, **workloads.** Your **workload** is the amount of work that you have to do. EG *I have a terrible workload this year.* — N COUNT+SUPP

workman /wɜːkməʳn/, **workmen.** A **workman** is a man whose job involves doing work with his hands, for example building houses or plumbing. EG *The workmen arrived and put up a fence.* — N COUNT

workmanlike /wɜːkməʳnlaɪk/. A piece of work that is **workmanlike** has been done well and skilfully. — ADJ QUALIT

workmanship /wɜːkməʳnʃɪp/ is the skill with which something is made. EG *...good materials and sound workmanship.* — N UNCOUNT

work of art, works of art. 1 A **work of art** is a painting or a piece of sculpture which is of high quality. EG *Some of the world's greatest works of art are on display here.* — N COUNT

2 You can refer to something that has been skilfully produced and that is often very complex as a **work of art**. EG *His own papers were works of art on which he laboured with loving care.* — N COUNT

workout /wɜːkaʊt/, **workouts.** A **workout** is a period of physical exercise or training. EG *They all had a good workout before lunch.* — N COUNT

workshop /wɜːkʃɒp/, **workshops. 1** A **workshop** is a room or building that contains tools or machinery for making or repairing things. EG *...a small engineering workshop.* — N COUNT

2 A **workshop** on a particular subject is a period of discussion or practical work in which a group of people learn about the subject by sharing their knowledge or experience. EG *...a theatre workshop... ...a workshop on child care.* — N COUNT

work-shy. If you say that someone is **work-shy**, you mean that they do not want to have a job or they do not put any effort into their job. — ADJ QUALIT

work surface, work surfaces. A **work surface** is the same as a worktop. — N COUNT

worktop /wɜːktɒp/, **worktops.** A **worktop** is a flat surface on top of a fridge or low cupboard, on which you can prepare food. — N COUNT

work-to-rule. A **work-to-rule** is a protest by workers in which they stop doing extra work and just do the minimum that they are required to do in their job. — N SING British

world /wɜːld/, **worlds. 1** The **world** is the planet that we live on. EG *He attempted to sail round the world... ...one of the most famous artists in the world... ...the growth in world population.* — N SING : *the*+N

2 The **world** also refers to all the societies, institutions, and ways of life of people living on this planet. EG *We are now moving into a world which will be more and more dominated by energy crises.* — N SING+SUPP

3 World is used to describe someone or something that is one of the best or most important of its kind in the world. EG *He argued that Britain was still a world power... This book is a world classic.* — N MOD

4 Someone's **world** is the life they lead, the people they have contact with, and the things they experience. EG *Look, Howard, we're in different worlds now... They were letting me into their world.* — N COUNT+SUPP

5 A particular **world** is a particular field of activity, and the people involved in it. EG *They are well-known names in the film world... ...the world of art.* — N COUNT+SUPP

6 You can refer to the state of being alive as this **world** and to a state of existence after death as the next **world** or the **world** to come. EG *...the vision that people hold of the world to come.* — N SING : USU+SUPP

7 You can refer to a particular group of living things as the animal **world**, the plant **world**, or the insect **world**. — N COUNT +SUPP : USU *the*+N

8 A **world** is another planet. EG *...an alien world.* — N COUNT

9 World is also used in these phrases. **9.1** You can use **in the world** to emphasize what you are saying. EG *To them housework was the most important activity in the world... What in the world are you doing here?* **9.2 The world over** means everywhere, throughout the world. EG *Journalists the world over speculated on the assassination attempt.* **9.3** If you say that someone has or wants **the best of both worlds**, you mean that they have or want all the benefits from two different situations, without the disadvantages. **9.4** If you **think the world of** someone or something, you like or admire them very much. EG *They thought the world of Sam.* **9.5** If you say that something **does** someone **the world of good**, you mean that it makes them feel much better. EG *A bit of fresh air will do you the world of good.* **9.6** If you say that **there is a world of difference** between one thing and another, you mean that they are very different from each other. — PHRASES; Informal

world-class. Someone, especially a sports player, who is **world-class** is one of the best in the world at what they do. EG *...a world-class cricketer.* — ADJ CLASSIF

world-famous. Someone or something that is **world-famous** is known about by people all over the world. EG *...a world-famous physicist.* — ADJ CLASSIF

worldly /wɜːldli[1]/. **1 Worldly** is used to describe things relating to the ordinary activities of life, rather than to spiritual things. EG *...worldly thoughts... Coleridge had experienced a conversion and put aside worldly things.* — ADJ CLASSIF : USU ATTRIB

2 You can refer to someone's possessions as their **worldly** goods or possessions. EG *He made a will leaving all his worldly goods to his daughter.* — ADJ CLASSIF : ATTRIB Literary

3 Someone who is **worldly** is experienced, practical, and knowledgeable about life. EG *She was surprised at their educated, even worldly manner.* — ADJ QUALIT

worldly-wise. Someone who is **worldly-wise** is experienced and knowledgeable about life, and is not often shocked or impressed by anything. — ADJ QUALIT Literary

world war, world wars. A **world war** is a war that involves countries all over the world. EG *...the First World War.* — N COUNT OR N UNCOUNT

worldwide /wɜːldwaɪd/ means happening throughout the world. EG *...in 1930, during the worldwide economic depression... This move made headlines worldwide last year.* — ADJ CLASSIF OR ADV

worm /wɜːm/, **worms, worming, wormed. 1** A **worm** is a small animal with a long thin body, no bones, and no legs, which lives in the soil. — N COUNT

2 If animals or people have **worms**, they have worms living as parasites in their intestines. These worms often enter their body when they eat food that is not clean, and may cause disease. EG *He wiggled about like a dog with worms.* — N PLURAL

3 If you **worm** your **way** somewhere, you move there slowly and carefully or with difficulty. EG *He wormed his way forward.* — PHRASE

4 If you **worm** your **way** into someone's confidence or affection, you gradually make them trust you or like you, often in order to gain some advantage. EG *These aliens could worm their way into French society.* — PHRASE

worm out. If you **worm** information **out** of someone, you gradually find it out from them when they were trying to keep it secret. EG *The truth had been wormed out of him by his lawyers.* — PHRASAL VB: V+O+ADV, USU+*of*

worm-eaten. Something that is **worm-eaten** has been damaged by insects which have made holes in it. EG *...an old, worm-eaten piece of furniture.* — ADJ QUALIT

worn /wɔːn/. **1 Worn** is the past participle of **wear**.

2 Something that is **worn** is damaged or thin because it is old and has been used a lot. EG *...the worn carpet... ...his worn suit.* — ADJ QUALIT

3 Someone who is **worn** looks old and tired, for example because of hard work or illness. — ADJ QUALIT

worn-out. 1 Something that is **worn-out** is so old, damaged, or thin from use that it cannot be used any more. EG *...a worn-out sofa.* — ADJ CLASSIF

2 If you are **worn-out**, you are extremely tired. — ADJ QUALIT

worried /wʌrɪd/. If you are **worried**, you are unhappy because you keep thinking about a problem or about something unpleasant that might happen. EG *People are becoming increasingly worried about pollution... I was worried that she'd say no... He was worried about the danger of them falling.* — ADJ QUALIT

worrier /wʌrɪə/, **worriers.** Someone who is a **worrier** spends a lot of time thinking about problems or about unpleasant things that might happen. EG *He was a worrier by nature.* — N COUNT

worry /wʌri¹/, **worries, worrying, worried. 1** If you **worry**, you keep thinking about a problem or about something unpleasant that might happen. EG *Don't worry, Andrew, you can do it... People worry about the safety of nuclear energy... I worried that when I got back he wouldn't be there.* — V: OFT+*about* OR REPORT: ONLY *that*

2 If someone or something **worries** you, they cause you to worry. EG *Terry was worried by the challenge... I'm sorry if I worried you... It worried him to think that Sylvie was alone.* — V+O

3 If you **worry** someone with a problem, you tell them about it in order to get their help or advice, often causing them trouble or irritation. EG *Why worry her when it's all over?* — V+O

4 Worry is a feeling of anxiety and unhappiness caused by a problem that you have or by thinking about something unpleasant that might happen. EG *She would be free from all financial worry... Bad housing is their main source of worry.* — N UNCOUNT

5 A **worry** is a problem that you keep thinking about and that makes you unhappy. EG *My only worry was that my aunt would be upset... I don't have any worries.* — N COUNT

6 You say **'Not to worry'** to someone to indicate that you are not upset or angry when something has gone wrong. EG *Not to worry. We'll find something.* — CONVENTION Informal

worrying /wʌri¹ɪŋ/. Something that is **worrying** causes you a lot of worry. EG *...a very worrying situation... She asked me a worrying question.* — ADJ QUALIT

worse /wɜːs/. **1 Worse** is **1.1** the comparative of **bad**. EG *I have even worse news for you... The noise is getting worse... Her marks are getting worse and worse.* — ADJ QUALIT: COMPAR **1.2** the comparative of **badly**. EG *Some people ski worse than others.* — ADV: COMPAR

2 If someone who is ill gets **worse**, they become more ill than before. EG *You'll get worse if you don't take this medicine.* — ADJ QUALIT: COMPAR

3 If someone or something is **none the worse** for something, they have not been harmed by it. EG *The children had gone to bed very late but they were none the worse for it.* — PHRASE

4 If something happens **for the worse**, the situation becomes more unpleasant or more difficult as a result. EG *There were constant changes, usually for the worse.* — PHRASE

5 to **go from bad to worse**: see **bad**.

worsen /wɜːsən/, **worsens, worsening, worsened.** If a situation **worsens** or if something **worsens** it, it becomes more difficult, unpleasant, or unacceptable. EG *Economic sanctions would only worsen the situation... The weather steadily worsened... Oil pollution seems to be worsening.* — V-ERG

worse off. 1 Someone who is **worse off** has less money than before or less than someone else. EG *This budget would leave taxpayers far worse off... There are lots of people worse off than us.* — ADJ PRED: COMPAR

2 Someone or something that is **worse off** is in a more unpleasant situation than before or than someone else. EG *You believe the world to be worse off because of Kennedy's death.* — ADJ PRED: COMPAR

worship /wɜːʃɪp/, **worships, worshipping, worshipped;** spelled **worshiping, worshiped** in American English.

1 If you **worship** a god, you show your respect to the god, for example by saying prayers. EG *I knelt down and worshipped the Lord.* ▸ used as a noun. EG *...places of worship.* — V+O OR V; ▸ N UNCOUNT

2 If you **worship** someone or something, you love them or admire them very much. EG *Vita worshipped her father.* ▸ used as a noun. EG *She became an object of worship.* — V+O; ▸ N UNCOUNT

3 Your Worship and **His Worship** are respectful ways of addressing or referring to a magistrate or a mayor. — British

worshipper /wɜːʃɪpə/, **worshippers;** spelled **worshiper** in American English.

1 A **worshipper** is someone who believes in and worships a god. EG *...shoes left there by worshippers who had gone into the mosque.* — N COUNT

2 If you are a **worshipper** of someone or something, you love or admire them very much. EG *...a worshipper of the past.* — N COUNT+SUPP

worst /wɜːst/. **1 Worst is 1.1** the superlative of **bad**. EG *...the worst thing which ever happened to me... The worst is over.* — ADJ QUALIT: SUPERL **1.2** the superlative of **badly**. EG *...the worst affected areas.* — ADV SUPERL

2 You use **at worst** to indicate that you are considering a situation in the most unfavourable or most pessimistic way. EG *At worst they are looked upon as an irritation... He was described as forceful at best, ruthless at worst.* — PHRASE

3 If you say that something might happen **if the worst comes to the worst**, you mean that it might happen if the situation develops in the most unfavourable way. EG *If the worst comes to the worst I'll have to sell the house.* — PHRASE

worth /wɜːθ/. **1** If something is **worth** a particular amount of money, it can be sold for that amount or is considered to have that value in terms of money. EG *...a two-bedroom house worth 50,000 pounds.* — PREP

2 If you talk about a particular amount of money's **worth** of something, you mean the quantity of it that you can buy for that amount of money. EG *They stole fifty thousand dollars' worth of equipment.* — N UNCOUNT

If you are a would-be actor, are you a real actor?

3 You can use **worth** when you are saying how long something will last. For example, a week's **worth** of food is the amount of food that will last you for a week. N UNCOUNT

4 If you say that something is **worth** doing, **worth** having, or **worth it**, you mean that it is enjoyable or useful, and therefore a good thing to do or have. EG *This film's really worth seeing... The building is well worth a visit... They're expensive, but they're worth it.* PREP OR PHRASE

5 If you add **for what it's worth** to something that you say, you mean that you do not think that what you are saying is very valuable or helpful. EG *I've brought my notes, for what it's worth.* PHRASE

6 If an action or activity is **worth** someone's **while**, it will be helpful or useful to them if they do it. EG *It will be well worth your while to track down these treasures.* PHRASE

7 Someone's **worth** is the value, usefulness, or importance that they are considered to have. EG *This job has robbed me of all worth... No man can say what another man is worth.* N UNCOUNT OR ADJ PRED Formal

worthless /wɜːθlɪ²s/. **1** Something that is **worthless** is of no real value or use. EG *The goods are often worthless by the time they arrive... This made the treaty worthless.* ADJ CLASSIF

2 Someone who is described as **worthless** is considered to lack the qualities or skills that they should have. EG *His brother is a worthless fool.* ADJ CLASSIF

worthwhile /wɜːθwaɪl/. If something is **worthwhile**, it is enjoyable or useful, and worth the time, money, or effort that is spent on it. EG *A visit to London will always be worthwhile.* ADJ QUALIT

worthy /wɜːðiˡ/, **worthier, worthiest. 1** If someone or something is **worthy** of something, they deserve it because they have the qualities or abilities required. EG *Their cause is worthy of our continued support... He was a worthy winner.* ADJ QUALIT : OFT+*of* Formal

2 A **worthy** person or thing deserves people's respect or admiration. EG *...our worthy commanding officer.* ADJ QUALIT Literary

would /wəᵈd/. **Would** is sometimes considered to be the past form of **will**, but in this dictionary the two words are dealt with separately.

1 If someone said or thought that something **would** happen, they said or thought that it was going to happen. EG *I felt confident that everything would be all right... He made me promise that I would never break the law.* MODAL

2 You say what **would** happen when you are referring to the result or effect of a possible situation. EG *If you can help me I would be very grateful... Without them life would not be the same.* MODAL

3 If you say that you **would** do something, you mean that you are willing to do it. EG *Some men would do more for a dog than they would for a wife.* MODAL

4 If you say that someone **would** not do something, you mean that they refused to do it. EG *Though we were as rude as possible, she wouldn't go... He would not give up.* MODAL : WITH BROAD NEG

5 If you say that you **would** like to do or have something, you mean that you want to do it or have it. EG *Posy said she'd love to stay... Would you like a drink?* MODAL

6 You use **would** in questions when you are politely asking someone to do something. EG *Would you tell her that Adrian phoned?... Put the light on, Bryan, would you?* MODAL

7 If you say that someone **would** do something, you mean that it is typical of them. EG *'Of course you would say that,' says Miss Callendar... 'He's backed out of it.' – 'He would.'* MODAL

8 You use **would** or **would have** when you are expressing your opinion about something. EG *I would think that in our climate we might have a few problems... I would have thought that his chief asset was his enthusiasm.* MODAL

9 You use **would** or **would have** when you are saying something that you are assuming is true or was true. EG *We had a discussion on jazz, but you wouldn't remember that... She wouldn't have noticed. She was too far away.* MODAL

10 You use **I would** when you are giving someone advice. EG *I would have a word with him about it... I wouldn't worry too much, if I were you.* PHRASE Informal

11 If you say that you **wouldn't** know or guess something, you mean that it is not at all obvious. EG *You wouldn't guess that from the film.* PHRASE

12 If you say that someone **would** do something, you mean that they often used to do it. EG *I used to meet her and she would say 'Can't stop. I must get home.'... In the intervals she would talk to me.* MODAL

13 If you talk about what **would have** happened if a possible event had occurred, you are talking about the result or effect of that event. EG *If the bosses had known that he voted Liberal, he would have got the sack.* MODAL

14 If you say that someone **would have** liked or preferred something, you mean that they wanted to do it or have it but were unable to. EG *I would have liked a year more.* MODAL

would-be. You use **would-be** to describe what someone wants to do or become. For example, if you say that someone is a **would-be** writer, you mean that they want to become a writer. ADJ CLASSIF : ATTRIB

wouldn't /wʊdəᵒnt/ is the usual spoken form of 'would not'. EG *It wouldn't be safe... You'd like to see this, wouldn't you?*

would've /wʊdəv/ is a spoken form of 'would have', especially when 'have' is an auxiliary verb. EG *It would've meant leaving home.*

wound /wuːnd/, **wounds, wounding, wounded. 1** A **wound** is damage to part of your body, especially a cut in your flesh, which is caused by a gun, knife, or other weapon. EG *He died from his wounds nine days after the shooting... The wound on his face was burning.* N COUNT

2 If someone **wounds** you, they damage your body using a gun, knife, or other weapon. EG *He had been badly wounded in the fighting.* V+O : USU PASS

3 If you **are wounded** by what someone says or does, your feelings are deeply hurt. EG *She had been grievously wounded by his words.* V+O : USU PASS Literary

4 Wound is also a past tense and past participle of **wind**. In this sense it is pronounced /waʊnd/.

wove /wəʊv/ is the past tense of **weave.**

woven /wəʊvəᵒn/ is the past participle of **weave.**

wow /waʊ/. You can say **'wow'** when you are very impressed by something or very pleased about something. EXCLAM Informal

WPC /dʌbəᵒljuː piː siː/, **WPCs.** A **WPC** is a female police officer of the lowest rank in Britain. **WPC** is an abbreviation for 'woman police constable'. EG *I was put into the car with a WPC... ...WPC Morris.* N COUNT

wrack /ræk/. See **rack.**

wrangle /ræŋgəᵒl/, **wrangles, wrangling, wrangled.** If you **wrangle** with someone, you argue with them angrily, often about something unimportant. EG *They wrangled over what to do next.* V OR V+*with/over* : RECIP
▸ used as a noun. EG *We avoided wrangles and got down to business.* ▸ N COUNT

wrap /ræp/, **wraps, wrapping, wrapped. 1** If you **wrap** something, you fold a piece of paper or cloth tightly round it so that it is covered. EG *I wrapped the ring in my handkerchief... The book was wrapped in brown paper.* V+O : OFT+*in*

2 If you **wrap** a piece of paper or cloth round something, you put it round it. EG *Wrap a cloth round the tap... A handkerchief was wrapped around his left hand.* V+O+*round/around*

3 If you **wrap** your arms or fingers around something, you put them tightly around it. EG *He wrapped his arms around me.* V+O+*round/around*

4 See also **wrapping.**

wrap up. 1 If you **wrap** something **up**, you fold a piece of paper or cloth tightly around it so that it is covered. EG *Could you wrap the vase up?... ...a little* PHRASAL VB : V+O+ADV *box wrapped up in white paper.* **2** If you **wrap up**, you put warm clothes on. EG *Wrap up well. It's a cold night tonight... I told her to wrap up warmly.* V+ADV **3** If you **wrap up** something such as a job or an agreement, you complete it in a satisfactory way. V+O+ADV Informal

wrapped up. If you are **wrapped up** in a person or thing, you spend most of your time thinking about that person or thing. EG *He was always wrapped up in his work... All the household are completely wrapped up in the baby.* ADJ PRED+*in* Informal

wrapper /ræpə/, **wrappers.** A **wrapper** is a piece of paper, plastic, or foil which covers and protects something that you buy. EG *...the rustle of chocolate wrappers.* N COUNT

wrapping /ræpɪŋ/, **wrappings.** A **wrapping** is a piece of paper or plastic which is used to cover and protect something. EG *He picked up the bottle and tore off its paper wrapping.* N COUNT OR N UNCOUNT

wrapping paper is special pretty paper which is used for wrapping presents. N UNCOUNT

wrath /rɒθ/ is very great anger. EG *I wanted someone to protect me from the wrath of Miss Templeman.* N UNCOUNT Literary

wreak /riːk/, **wreaks, wreaking, wreaked. 1** If something **wreaks** havoc or damage, it causes it. EG *These chemicals can wreak havoc on crops.* V+O: OFT+A Formal

2 If you **wreak** revenge or vengeance on someone, you do something that will harm them, because you feel angry about the harm that they have done to you. V+O: OFT+A Literary

wreath /riːθ/, **wreaths.** A **wreath** is an arrangement of flowers and leaves, usually in the shape of a circle, which is put onto a grave as a sign of remembrance for the dead person. N COUNT

wreathed /riːðd/. If something is **wreathed** in something else, it is surrounded by it. EG *The sun was wreathed in mist... Colonel Burr sat wreathed in smoke.* ADJ PRED +*in/with* Literary

wreck /rɛk/, **wrecks, wrecking, wrecked. 1** If someone **wrecks** something, **1.1** they break it or destroy it completely. EG *I wrecked a good stereo by not following the instructions properly.* V+O ◊ **wrecked.** EG *Piles of wrecked cars took up most of the space.* ◊ ADJ CLASSIF **1.2** they spoil it completely. EG *I'm sorry if I wrecked your weekend.* V+O Informal

2 If a ship **is wrecked**, it is damaged so much that it sinks or it can no longer sail, for example when it hits rocks. EG *...Spanish vessels that had been wrecked off the North American coast.* V+O: USU PASS

3 A **wreck** is **3.1** a plane, car, or other vehicle which has been very badly damaged in an accident. EG *All around were the wrecks of previous crashes.* N COUNT **3.2** a ship which has sunk or been destroyed at sea. EG *The seabed where the wreck lies is level and rocky.*

4 If you say that someone is a **wreck**, you mean that they are very unhealthy or exhausted. EG *If you work like this you'll end up a wreck.* ● See also **nervous wreck**. N COUNT: USU SING Informal

wreckage /rɛkɪdʒ/. When a plane, car, or building has been very badly damaged, you can refer to what remains as **wreckage**. EG *Experts arrived to examine the wreckage of a cargo plane.* N UNCOUNT

wren /rɛn/, **wrens.** A **wren** is a type of very small brown bird. N COUNT

wrench /rɛntʃ/, **wrenches, wrenching, wrenched. 1** If you **wrench** something into a particular position, you pull it or twist it violently, especially in order to move it from a fixed or firm position. EG *He was trying to wrench my button off... I wrenched the door open.* V+O+A OR V+O+C

2 If you **wrench** your arm or leg, or one of your joints, you twist it and injure it. V+O

3 If you **wrench** your eyes or your mind away from something, you make a great effort to stop looking at it or thinking about it. EG *I tried to wrench my gaze away from the appalling sight.* V+O+A

4 A **wrench** is a metal tool with parts which can be adjusted to fit round nuts or bolts of various sizes, so that the nut or bolt can be loosened or tightened. See picture at TOOLS. N COUNT

5 If you feel that leaving someone or something is a **wrench**, you feel very sad about it. EG *It was a wrench when the time came for me to go to boarding school.* N SING: a+N

wrest /rɛst/, **wrests, wresting, wrested.** If you **wrest** something away from someone who is holding it, you take it from them by pulling it violently. EG *He wrested the knife from her.* V+O+A Literary

wrestle /rɛsə⁰l/, **wrestles, wrestling, wrestled.**
1 If you **wrestle** with someone, you fight them by forcing them into painful positions or throwing them to the ground, rather than by hitting them. Some people wrestle as a sport. EG *John wrestled with the intruder.* ● See also **wrestling**. V OR V+*with*: RECIP; ALSO V+O

2 When you **wrestle** with a problem, you try to deal with it. EG *For decades, mathematicians have wrestled with this problem.* V+*with*

wrestler /rɛslə/, **wrestlers.** A **wrestler** is someone who wrestles as a sport. N COUNT

wrestling /rɛslɪŋ/ is a sport in which two people wrestle and try to throw each other to the ground. N UNCOUNT

wretch /rɛtʃ/, **wretches.** You can refer to someone as a **wretch** when you think that they are wicked or unfortunate. EG *...the wretch who shot the President... The poor wretch groaned.* N COUNT Outdated

wretched /rɛtʃɪ²d/. **1** Someone who is **wretched** is very unhappy or unfortunate. EG *She spent the day in her room lying down and feeling wretched.* ADJ CLASSIF: USU PRED Formal

2 You use **wretched** to describe something or someone that you dislike or feel angry about. EG *I had to drag the wretched animal all the way... I hate this wretched system.* ADJ CLASSIF: ATTRIB Informal

wriggle /rɪgə⁰l/, **wriggles, wriggling, wriggled.**
1 If you **wriggle** a part of your body, you twist it and turn it with quick movements. EG *The children were wriggling in anticipation... She wriggled her toes.* V OR V+O

2 If you **wriggle** somewhere, you move there by twisting and turning your body. EG *We had to wriggle under the fence.* V+A OR V+O+A

wriggle out of. If you **wriggle out of** doing something that you do not want to do, you manage to avoid doing it. EG *I can't wriggle out of accompanying my parents to Europe.* PHRASAL VB: V+ADV+PREP Informal

wring /rɪŋ/, **wrings, wringing, wrung** /rʌŋ/. **1** When you **wring** a wet cloth or **wring** it out, you squeeze the water out of it by twisting it strongly. V+O: OFT+*out*

2 When someone **wrings** their hands, they hold them together and twist and turn them, usually because they are very worried or upset. EG *He looked dazed and wrung his hands.* V+O Literary

3 If someone **wrings** a bird's neck, they kill the bird by twisting its neck. V+O

wringing wet. If a piece of clothing is **wringing wet**, it is extremely wet. ADJ CLASSIF: USU PRED

wrinkle /rɪŋkə⁰l/, **wrinkles, wrinkling, wrinkled. 1 Wrinkles** are lines in someone's skin, especially on their face, which form as they grow old. EG *His small eyes were surrounded by many wrinkles.* N COUNT: USU PLURAL

2 If something **wrinkles** or if something **wrinkles** it, it gets folds or lines in it. EG *Clean the surface well or the paint might wrinkle and peel.* V-ERG

3 When you **wrinkle** your nose, forehead, or eyes, you tighten the muscles in your face so that the skin folds into several lines. EG *He wrinkled his nose. 'What an awful smell.'* V+O

wrinkled /rɪŋkə⁰ld/. **1** If your skin is **wrinkled**, it has wrinkles as a result of old age. EG *...a very old woman with a wrinkled face.* ADJ QUALIT

2 If something is **wrinkled**, it has raised folds or lines in it. EG *She looked to make sure her dress wasn't wrinkled.* ADJ QUALIT

Would you like to get a good write-up in a newspaper?

wrist /rɪst/, **wrists.** Your **wrist** is the part of your body between your hand and your arm which bends when you move your hand. See picture at THE HUMAN BODY. N COUNT

wristwatch /rɪstwɒtʃ/, **wristwatches.** A **wristwatch** is a watch with a strap which you wear round your wrist. N COUNT

writ /rɪt/, **writs.** A **writ** is a legal document that orders a person to do a particular thing. N COUNT

write /raɪt/, **writes, writing, wrote** /rəʊt/, **written** /rɪtəᵊn/. **1** When you **write** something, you use a pen or pencil to produce words, letters, or numbers. EG *I'm learning to read and write... Write the appropriate letter on the label.* V+O OR V

2 If you **write** something such as a book, a poem, or a piece of music, you create it and record it on paper. EG *I have been asked to write a biography of Dylan Thomas.* V+O, V+O+O, OR V+O+*for*

3 When you **write** to someone or **write** them a letter, you give them information, ask them something, or express your feelings in a letter. EG *She wrote me a letter from Singapore... She wrote a note to the chief of police... I've written to invite him here.* V OR V+O: OFT+*to* OR *to*-INF; ALSO V+O+O

4 When someone **writes** something such as a cheque, receipt, or prescription, they put the necessary information on it and usually sign it. EG *I remember writing a cheque for £100... I'll write you a prescription.* V+O, V+O+O, OR V+O+*for*

5 See also **writing, written.**

write back. If you **write back** to someone who has sent you a letter, you write them a letter in reply. EG *He wrote back accepting our offer.* PHRASAL VB: V+ADV OR V+O+ADV

write down. When you **write** something **down**, you record it on a piece of paper using a pen or pencil. EG *I wrote down what the boy said.* PHRASAL VB: V+O+ADV

write in. If you **write in** to an organization, you send them a letter. EG *People have been phoning and writing in asking for advice.* PHRASAL VB: V+ADV

write into. If a rule or detail **is written into** a contract or agreement, it is included in it when the contract or agreement is made. EG *The new arrangements have been written into the agreement.* PHRASAL VB: V+O+PREP, USU PASS

write off. 1 If you **write off** to a company or organization, you send them a letter, usually asking for something. EG *I was writing off to various places asking about work opportunities.* PHRASAL VB: V+ADV OR V+O+ADV **2** If you **write off** an amount of money that you have lost, you accept that you are never going to get the money back. EG *I've written off that hundred pounds.* V+O+ADV **3** If you **write off** a plan or project, you accept that it is not going to be successful and you do not continue with it. V+O+ADV **4** If you **write** someone **off**, you decide that they are unimportant or useless. EG *Do not shout, or you will be written off as a hysterical woman.* V+O+ADV **5** See also **write-off.**

write out. 1 If you **write out** something such as a report or a list, you write it on paper. EG *I always write out a shopping list.* PHRASAL VB: V+O+ADV **2** When someone **writes out** something such as a cheque, receipt, or prescription, they put the necessary information on it and usually sign it. EG *I went to write out the death certificate.* V+O+ADV

write up. If you **write up** something that has been done or said, you record it on paper in a neat and complete form, usually using notes that you have made. EG *These are notes that you are going to write up afterwards... The results were written up into a report.* ● See also **write-up.** PHRASAL VB: V+O+ADV

write-off, write-offs. If a vehicle is a **write-off**, it is so badly damaged in an accident that it is not worth repairing. EG *Their car was a write-off.* N COUNT: USU SING

writer /raɪtə/, **writers. 1** A **writer** is a person who writes books, stories, or articles as a job. EG *...the writer and critic, Hilary Spurling.* N COUNT

2 The **writer** of a particular article, story, or other piece of writing is the person who wrote it. EG *I arranged an appointment with the writer of the letter.* N COUNT+SUPP

write-up, write-ups. A **write-up** is an article in a newspaper or magazine, in which someone describes something such as a play or a new product and gives their opinion on it. EG *Somebody told me you got a terrific write-up in the 'Guardian'.* N COUNT: USU SING

writhe /raɪð/, **writhes, writhing, writhed.** If you **writhe**, you twist and turn your body violently backwards and forwards, usually because you are in great pain. EG *He writhed in agony.* V

writing /raɪtɪŋ/, **writings. 1 Writing** is **1.1** something that has been written or printed. EG *Put the papers face down on each desk so that the writing cannot be seen... You must get the offer in writing.* N UNCOUNT **1.2** a piece of written work, especially considered from the point of view of the style of language used. EG *The book contains some brilliant and very witty writing.*

2 Writing is also the activity of writing, especially of writing books for money. EG *I hate writing and I'm not very good at it.* N UNCOUNT

3 An author's **writings** are all the things that he or she has written. EG *His political writings remind me of those of Sartre.* N PLURAL: USU+SUPP

writing paper is paper for writing letters on. It is usually of good, smooth quality. N MASS

written /rɪtəᵊn/. **1 Written** is the past participle of **write.**

2 A **written** test or piece of work is one in which a student has to write something, rather than doing an experiment or giving spoken answers. EG *There are two exams. One is practical and the other is written.* ADJ CLASSIF

3 A **written** agreement, rule, or law has been officially written down. EG *I will send written confirmation... ...a written declaration.* ADJ CLASSIF: ATTRIB

wrong /rɒŋ/, **wrongs, wronging, wronged. 1** If there is something **wrong**, there is something unsatisfactory about the situation or thing that you are talking about. EG *The front door was unlocked – something was wrong... I sat down with her and asked what was wrong... There was nothing wrong with his eyesight.* ADJ PRED: OFT+*with*

2 Wrong means not correct or not suitable. EG *I'm afraid I'll make the wrong decision... They are the wrong people for the job... Her name was spelt wrong.* ◊ **wrongly.** EG *Many of us choose wrongly.* ADJ CLASSIF, OR ADV AFTER VB; ◊ ADV

3 If you are **wrong** about something, what you say or think about it is not correct. EG *We had to admit the possibility that we might be wrong.* ◊ **wrongly.** EG *She supposed, wrongly, that the other two agreed with her.* ADJ PRED; ◊ ADV

4 If something that you do is **wrong**, it is bad or immoral. EG *She never did anything wrong... You were wrong to speak to the newspapers first.* ADJ QUALIT

5 Wrong is used to refer to actions that are bad or immoral. EG *Any good parent feels strongly about right and wrong.* N UNCOUNT

6 A **wrong** is an unjust action or situation. EG *In a democracy wrongs should be righted by the vote and not by violence.* N COUNT

7 If someone **wrongs** you, they treat you in an unfair or unjust way. EG *I had wronged her terribly.* V+O

8 The **wrong** side of a piece of cloth is the side which is intended to face inwards and not be seen. ADJ CLASSIF: ATTRIB

9 Wrong is also used in these phrases. **9.1** If you **get** something **wrong**, you make a mistake. EG *I think she got his name wrong.* **9.2** You say **'Don't get me wrong'** when you want to make sure that someone does not misunderstand you. EG *Now don't get me wrong: we liked him.* **9.3** If you **go wrong**, you make a mistake. EG *Where did I go wrong?* **9.4** If something **goes wrong**, it stops working or progressing well. EG *Computers do go wrong... Their relationship went wrong after the birth of their child.* **9.5** If you are **in the wrong**, what you are doing is immoral or illegal. EG *We were all in the wrong then.* PHRASES

wrongdoer /rɒŋduːə/, **wrongdoers.** A **wrongdoer** is a person who does things that are immoral N COUNT Formal or illegal. EG *Wrongdoers should be made to pay for their actions.*

wrongdoing /rɒŋduːɪŋ/, **wrongdoings. Wrongdoing** is behaviour that is illegal or immoral. EG *The bank has denied any wrongdoing.* N UNCOUNT OR N COUNT Formal

wrongful /rɒŋfʊl/. A **wrongful** act is one that is thought to be illegal, immoral, or unfair. EG *...the wrongful imprisonment of Napoleon.* ADJ CLASSIF: ATTRIB
◊ **wrongfully**. EG *The workers were wrongfully dismissed.* ◊ ADV

wrote /rəʊt/ is the past tense of **write.**

wrought /rɔːt/. 1 If something **has wrought** a change, it has caused it. EG *That moment had wrought a profound change in him.* V+O: ONLY PAST TENSES Literary
2 **Wrought** metal has been made into a particular shape, often in a decorative way. EG *...wrought silver... ...wrought gold.* ADJ CLASSIF: ATTRIB

wrought iron is a pure type of iron that is formed into decorative shapes. EG *...a wrought-iron gate.* N UNCOUNT

wrung /rʌŋ/ is the past tense of **wring.**

wry /raɪ/. If someone has a **wry** expression, 1 it shows that they find a situation slightly amusing because they know more about it than other people. EG *He came out with a wry smile on his face... She said this with a wry glance at me.* ◊ **wryly**. EG *My friend smiled wryly when he saw me.* 2 it is rather strange or twisted, usually showing that they dislike something. EG *Over the beer she made a wry face and said 'Nasty!'* ADJ QUALIT: USU ATTRIB ◊ ADV ADJ QUALIT: USU ATTRIB

Xx Yy Zz

X, x /ɛks/, **Xs, x's. 1 X** is the twenty-fourth letter of the English alphabet. N COUNT
2 **X** is used to represent the name of a person or place when you do not know their real name, or when you want to keep their real name a secret. EG *She was always referred to as Miss X during the trial... I was born in X, a town somewhere in the south.* N UNCOUNT
3 If you say that there are **x** number of things, you mean that the exact number is not important. EG *...a house that will cost less than x number of pounds.*
4 In algebra, **x** is used as a symbol to represent a number whose value is not known. EG $y=x^2$.
5 People sometimes write **x** on a map to mark a precise position that they want to refer to.
6 You can write **x** to represent a kiss at the end of a letter. EG *See you soon, all my love, Jenny xxx.*

xenophobia /zɛnəfəʊbɪə/ is a fear of people from other countries, or a strong dislike of them. EG *They are nationalist to the point of xenophobia.* N UNCOUNT Formal

Xerox /zɪərɒks/, **Xeroxes, Xeroxing, Xeroxed.** 1 A **Xerox** is 1.1 a machine that makes photographic copies of pieces of paper which have writing or printing on them. 1.2 a copy of what is written or printed on a piece of paper, made by using a Xerox machine. EG *I enclose a Xerox of the letter.* N COUNT Trademark
2 If you **Xerox** a document, you make a copy of it using a Xerox machine. EG *That morning, Bernstein had Xeroxed copies of notes from reporters at the scene.* V+O

Xmas /krɪsməs, ɛksməs/ is the same as Christmas. N UNCOUNT Informal

X-ray, X-rays, X-raying, X-rayed. 1 An **X-ray** is 1.1 a stream of radiation that can pass through some solid materials. X-rays are used by doctors to examine the bones or organs inside your body. EG *The X-rays are produced by this electron beam... He agreed to go for an X-ray to see if the bone was broken.* 1.2 a picture made by sending X-rays through your body. EG *The chest X-ray showed enlargement of the heart.* N COUNT
2 If a doctor **X-rays** you, he or she takes a picture of the inside of your body using an X-ray machine. EG *He should have his lungs X-rayed.* V+O

xylophone /zaɪləfəʊn/, **xylophones.** A **xylophone** is a musical instrument made of a row of wooden bars of different lengths. You play a xylophone by hitting the bars with special hammers. N COUNT

Y, y /waɪ/, **Ys, y's. 1 Y** is the twenty-fifth letter of the English alphabet. N COUNT
2 In algebra, **y** is used as a symbol to represent a number whose value is not known.

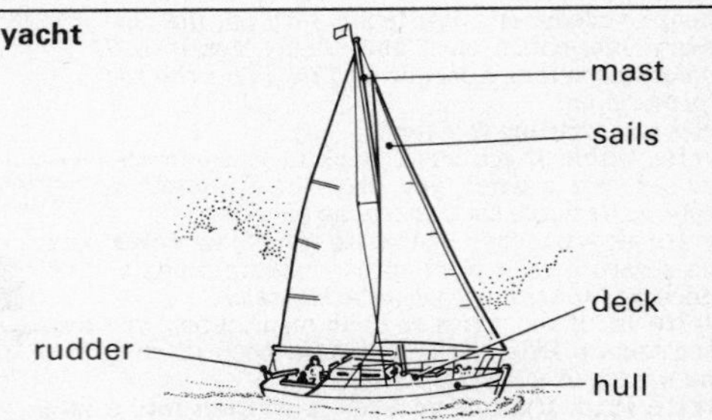

yacht /jɒt/, **yachts.** A **yacht** is a boat with sails or a motor, used for racing or for pleasure trips. N COUNT

yachting /jɒtɪŋ/ is the sport or activity of sailing a yacht. EG *...the fun of yachting... ...yachting holidays.* N ING

yam /jæm/, **yams.** A **yam** is a root vegetable which grows in tropical regions. It is similar to a potato in appearance and texture. N COUNT

yank /jæŋk/, **yanks, yanking, yanked. 1** A **Yank** is a person from the United States of America; a slightly offensive word. N COUNT British
2 If you **yank** something, you pull it suddenly with a lot of force. EG *Glenn yanked out the sore tooth.* V+O: USU+A

Yankee /jæŋki[1]/, **Yankees.** A **Yankee** is the same as a Yank; an offensive word. N COUNT

yap /jæp/, **yaps, yapping, yapped.** 1 If a dog **yaps**, it barks a lot with a high-pitched sound. EG *There was a dog running along the streets, yapping and barking.* V
2 If you say that someone **yaps**, you mean that they talk continuously in an annoying way. EG *I hate people on trains who keep yapping at you.* V Informal

yard /jɑːd/, **yards. 1** A **yard** is a unit for measuring length, equal to thirty-six inches, or approximately 91.4 centimetres. N COUNT
2 A **yard** is also a flat area of concrete or stone that is usually next to a building and often has a wall around it. EG *...a tiny cramped house without even a back yard.* N COUNT
3 You can also refer to a large area or place of work where a particular type of work is done as a **yard**. EG *...a ship repair yard.* N COUNT: USU+SUPP

yardstick /jɑːdstɪk/, **yardsticks.** If you use someone or something as a **yardstick**, you use them to compare other people or things with, when judging how good or important these other people or things are. EG *She was a yardstick against which I could* N COUNT+SUPP *measure what I had achieved... ...a situation where the yardstick for success is exam achievement.*

yarn /jɑ:n/, **yarns. 1 Yarn** is thread, made for example from wool or cotton, which is used for knitting or making cloth. N MASS

2 A **yarn** is a story that someone tells, often a true story with added details which they have invented to make it more interesting. N COUNT Informal

yawn /jɔ:n/, **yawns, yawning, yawned. 1** When you **yawn**, you open your mouth wide and breathe in more air than usual. You often yawn when you are tired or bored. EG *I yawned all through the concert.* V ▸ used as a noun. EG *She stifled a yawn.* ▸ N COUNT

2 If you describe something such as a book or a film as a **yawn**, you mean that you think it is very boring. N SING : a+N Informal

3 A gap or opening that **yawns** is large and wide, and often rather frightening. EG *A great gap yawned between the rocks.* V : USU+A Literary ◊ **yawning.** EG *They drew back from the yawning chasm.* ◊ ADJ CLASSIF : ATTRIB

yd, yds. yd is a written abbreviation for 'yard'. The plural is either 'yds' or 'yd'. EG *The reel holds 400 yds of line.* N COUNT

yeah /jɛə/ means the same as yes. EG *'Do you understand?' – 'Yeah, I think so.'* CONVENTION Informal

year /jɪə/, **years. 1** A **year** is **1.1** a period of 365 or 366 days, beginning on the first of January and ending on the thirty-first of December. EG *...at the end of next year... ...in the year 2000.* **1.2** a period of about twelve months. EG *...a hundred years ago... For seven years I was a designer... These rocks are about 650 million years old.* N COUNT

2 A school **year** or a university **year** is the period of time in each twelve months when the school or university is open and people are studying. N COUNT : USU+SUPP

3 A financial or business **year** is a period of twelve months, beginning on a particular date, which businesses or institutions use as a basis for organizing their finances. EG *...the final account at the end of each trading year.* N COUNT+SUPP

4 You can use **years** to emphasize that you are referring to a very long time. EG *They've known each other for years and years.* N PLURAL

5 If you do something **all year round** or **all the year round**, you do it continually throughout the year. EG *They grow crops all the year round.* PHRASE

6 donkey's years: see **donkey**. ● See also **leap year, New Year**.

yearly /jɪəli[1]/. You use **yearly** **1** to describe something that happens once a year or every year. EG *...a yearly meeting... Interest is paid yearly.* **2** to describe something such as an amount that relates to a period of one year. EG *...the yearly income of the workers.* ADJ CLASSIF : ATTRIB OR ADV

yearn /jɜ:n/, **yearns, yearning, yearned.** If you **yearn** for something, you want it very much. EG *He passionately yearned for happiness... She yearned to go back to the south.* V+*for* OR *to*-INF Literary

yearning /jɜ:nɪŋ/, **yearnings.** A **yearning** is a very strong desire for something. EG *...his yearning for power... ...to satisfy the yearnings of the workers.* N COUNT OR N UNCOUNT

-year-old and **-year-olds** combine with numbers to describe the age of people or things. EG *...a class of 4-year-olds... ...a fifteen-year-old boy.*

yeast /ji:st/ is a kind of fungus which is used to make bread rise, and to make alcoholic drinks such as beer. N MASS

yell /jɛl/, **yells, yelling, yelled. 1** If you **yell**, you shout loudly, usually because you are excited, angry, or in pain. EG *'Speed up!' he yelled to the driver... I yelled at Richard to hang on... She came in and started yelling abuse at the cops.* V : OFT+A, OR V-SPEECH : ONLY *that*

2 A **yell** is a loud shout given by someone who is afraid or in pain. EG *I heard a yell from inside the house... He let out a terrified yell.* N COUNT

yellow /jɛləʊ/, **yellows, yellowing, yellowed. 1** Something that is **yellow** is the colour of lemons or egg yolks. EG *...a bright yellow hat... He became aware of a yellow light far across the fields.* ADJ COLOUR

2 When something **yellows** or **is yellowed**, it becomes yellow in colour, often because it is old. EG *...a photograph of her, yellowed with age.* V-ERG

yellow fever is a serious infectious disease that people can catch in tropical countries. N UNCOUNT

yellowish /jɛləʊɪʃ/. Something that is **yellowish** is slightly yellow in colour. EG *He had a yellowish complexion... ...a soft yellowish glow.* ADJ COLOUR

yelp /jɛlp/, **yelps, yelping, yelped.** When people or animals **yelp**, they give a sudden short cry, often because they are frightened or are in pain. EG *He yelped in pain... The puppy ran indoors yelping.* V ▸ used as a noun. EG *I gave a little yelp and fled upstairs.* ▸ N COUNT

yen /jɛn/. If you have a **yen** to do something, you have a strong desire to do it. EG *Nicholas has a yen to hike through Canada.* N SING : USU+*to*-INF OR *for*

yes /jɛs/. **1** You use **yes** to agree with someone, to say that something is true, or to accept something. EG *'Did you enjoy it?' – 'Yes.'... 'Do you want some coffee?' – 'Yes please.'... 'It was a beautiful day.' – 'It was nice, yes.'* CONVENTION

2 You also use **yes** in a conversation **2.1** to encourage someone to continue speaking. EG *'I miss the country very much.' – 'Yes?' – 'And yet, you see, I would hate to give up my job here.'* **2.2** to say that something that someone has denied is in fact true. EG *'Nowadays you don't learn any basic principles in maths.' – 'Oh, yes you do.'* **2.3** to introduce something that you had forgotten to say and have just remembered. EG *What was I going to mention? Ah yes, accidents.* CONVENTION

yesterday /jɛstədɪ[3]/. **1 Yesterday** means the day before today. EG *It was hot yesterday... Yesterday morning there were more than 500 boats on the lake... ...an interview published in yesterday's Times.* ADV

2 Yesterday can also mean the past, especially the recent past. EG *The worker of today is different from the worker of yesterday.* ADV

yet /jɛt/. **1** If you say that something has not happened **yet**, you mean that it has not happened up to the present time, although it probably will happen. EG *I haven't made up my mind yet... It isn't dark yet... Have you had your lunch yet?* ADV : WITH BROAD NEG

2 If you say that something should not be done **yet**, you mean that it should not be done now, although it will have to be done at a later time. EG *Loosen nuts with a spanner but don't take them off yet.* ADV : WITH BROAD NEG

3 You also use **yet** **3.1** to say that there is still a possibility that something will happen. EG *The figures may yet be revised again... There is hope for me yet.* **3.2** after an expression which refers to a period of time, when you want to say how much longer a situation will continue for. EG *He's going to be around for a long while yet... It will not be dark for half an hour yet.* ADV

4 If you say that you have **yet** to do something or that something is **yet** to happen, you mean that you have not done it or that it has not happened. EG *I have yet to meet a man I can trust... A just society without a bureaucracy has yet to be established.* ADV+*to*-INF

5 You also use **yet** to introduce a fact which is rather surprising after the fact that you have just mentioned. EG *Everything around him was blown to pieces, yet the minister escaped without a scratch... ...a firm yet gentle hand.* CONJ

6 You can also use **yet** to emphasize a word. EG *I am sorry to bring up the subject of money yet again.* ADV

yield /ji:ld/, **yields, yielding, yielded. 1** If you **yield** to someone or something, you stop resisting them. EG *He yielded to his critics and halved the price... He was yielding to public pressure.* V : USU+*to* Formal

2 If you **yield** something that you have control of or responsibility for, you allow someone else to take control of it or have responsibility for it. EG *He* V+O *will not yield even a limited measure of editorial control.*

3 If something **yields**, it breaks or moves its position because force or pressure has been put on it. EG *Any lock will yield to brute force.* V

4 If an investigation or discussion **yields** something, it produces a result, answer, or piece of information. EG *Talks between the two sides yielded no results.* V+O

5 If an area of land **yields** a particular amount of food, this amount of food is produced by the land. EG *0.23 acres yields only 200 pounds of rice.* V+O

6 A **yield** is an amount of food produced on an area of land. EG *They have a far better yield than any farm round here.* N COUNT

7 If a tax or investment **yields** an amount of money or profit, this money or profit is obtained from it. V+O

yippee /jɪpiː/. Some people, especially children, shout **'Yippee!'** when they are very happy and excited about something. EXCLAM

yob /jɒb/, **yobs.** If you call a boy a **yob** or a **yobbo**, you mean that he behaves in a noisy, bad-mannered way in public. N COUNT Informal British

yodel /jəʊdə^{0}l/, **yodels, yodelling, yodelled;** spelled **yodeling, yodeled** in American English. When someone **yodels**, they sing normal notes with very high quick notes in between. V

yoga /jəʊgə/ is a type of exercise in which you move your body into various positions. Yoga helps you to get fit, improves your breathing, and relaxes your mind. EG *I do two hours yoga every day.* N UNCOUNT

yoghurt /jɒgət/; also spelled **yoghourt** or **yogurt. Yoghurt** is a slightly sour, thick liquid which is made from milk that has had bacteria added to it. You can eat it with fruit, or with meat or vegetables. EG *...a bowl of natural yoghurt.* N MASS

yoke /jəʊk/, **yokes. 1** If people are suffering under a **yoke** of a particular kind, they are in a difficult or unhappy state, such as having to work extremely hard or being governed by a severe leader. EG *...a war against the yoke of tyranny.* N SING+SUPP Literary

2 A **yoke** is a long piece of wood attached to two collars, which is laid across the necks of two animals such as oxen, in order to make them walk close together when they are pulling a plough. N COUNT

yokel /jəʊkə^{0}l/, **yokels.** You can refer to a person who lives in the countryside, especially one who does not seem to be very intelligent, as a **yokel**. N COUNT Outdated

yolk /jəʊk/, **yolks.** The **yolk** of an egg is the yellow part in the middle of the egg. N COUNT OR N UNCOUNT

yonder /jɒndə/ means over there. EG *They came galloping over that hill yonder.* ADV OR DET Outdated

yonks /jɒŋks/. If you say that you have not done something for **yonks**, you mean that you have not done it for a very long time. EG *I kept spotting people I hadn't seen for yonks.* N UNCOUNT Informal

Yorkshire pudding /jɔːkʃə pʊdɪŋ/, **Yorkshire puddings. Yorkshire pudding** is a food which is made by baking a thick mixture of flour, milk, and eggs. It is often eaten with roast beef. N UNCOUNT OR N COUNT

you /juː/ is used as the subject of a verb or as the object of a verb or preposition. It can refer to one or more people.

A speaker or writer uses **you 1** to refer to the person or group of people that he or she is speaking to. EG *What do you think?* **2** to refer to people in general rather than to a particular person. EG *You can get freezers with security locks.* PRON; PRON Informal

you'd /juːd/. **1 You'd** is the usual spoken form of 'you had', especially when 'had' is an auxiliary verb. EG *If you'd asked me that ten years ago, I'd have said yes.*

2 You'd is also the usual spoken form of 'you would'. EG *You'd be surprised how easy it is.*

you'll /juːl/ is the usual spoken form of 'you will'. EG *You'll have to get a job.*

young /jʌŋ/, **younger** /jʌŋgə/, **youngest** /jʌŋgə^{2}st/. **1** A **young** person, animal, or plant has not lived or existed for very long and is not yet mature. EG *Julia has two young boys... The young seedlings grow very rapidly... She was three years younger than me.* ADJ QUALIT

2 You also use **young** to describe a time when a person or thing was young. EG *I was fond of dancing in my younger days.* ADJ QUALIT : ATTRIB

3 The **young** of an animal are its babies. EG *When the young first hatch, they are naked.* N PLURAL

youngish /jʌŋg^{0}ɪʃ/. Someone who is **youngish** is fairly young in appearance, behaviour, or age. EG *...a youngish man with blond hair.* ADJ CLASSIF

youngster /jʌŋk^{0}stə/, **youngsters.** A **youngster** is a young person, especially a child. EG *I don't know what the youngsters of today think.* N COUNT

your /jɔː, jʊə/. **1** A speaker or writer uses **your** to indicate that something belongs or relates to the person or group of people that he or she is speaking to. EG *Where's your father?... ...your books.* DET POSS

2 A speaker or writer also uses **your** to indicate that something belongs or relates to people in general rather than to a particular person. EG *You can't use your own name in a novel.* DET POSS

3 A speaker or writer also uses **your** in some titles when he or she addresses people with that title. EG *...your Majesty.* DET POSS

you're /jɔː, jʊə/ is the usual spoken form of 'you are'. EG *You're quite right.*

yours /jɔːz, jʊəz/. **1** A speaker or writer uses **yours** to refer to something that belongs or relates to the person or group of people that he or she is speaking to. EG *Our swimming pool isn't as deep as yours... A student of yours came to see me.* PRON POSS

2 People write **yours, yours sincerely**, or **yours faithfully** at the end of a letter before they sign their name. EG *Yours sincerely, Richard Thomas.*

yourself /jə^{8}sɛlf/, **yourselves. 1** A speaker or writer uses **yourself 1.1** as the object of a verb or preposition in a clause where 'you' is the subject or a previous object, or in a clause which consists of a command. EG *Would you call yourself a Marxist?... Help yourselves to sandwiches... Tell me about yourself.* **1.2** to emphasize the subject or object of a clause. EG *You yourself said it's only a routine check... There is always someone worse off than yourself.* PRON REFL

2 If you do something **yourself**, you do it without any help from anyone else. EG *Did you make these cakes yourself?* PRON REFL

youth /juːθ/, **youths** /juːðz/. **1** Someone's **youth** is the period of their life when they are a child, before they are a fully mature adult. EG *We change and learn from youth to old age... He had visited Calcutta in his youth.* N UNCOUNT

2 Youth is the quality or state of being young, immature, and often inexperienced. EG *...the wilfulness of youth... ...marvelling at his freshness and apparent youth.* N UNCOUNT

3 A **youth** is a boy or a young man, especially a teenager. EG *Across the street stood two youths in leather jackets.* N COUNT

4 The **youth** are young people considered as a group. EG *I think the pressures on today's youth are enormous... ...high unemployment among the youth of this country.* N PLURAL : the+N

youthful /juːθfʊl/. Someone who is **youthful 1** is young, lively, and full of energy. EG *...youthful dancers... He was full of youthful curiosity and idealism.* **2** has qualities or characteristics that are thought to be typical of young people. EG *Despite her age she still had a youthful body.* ADJ QUALIT

youth hostel, youth hostels. A **youth hostel** is a place where young people can stay cheaply when they are travelling around on holiday. N COUNT

Is a zebra crossing a place where zebras cross?

you've /ju:v/ is the usual spoken form of 'you have', especially when 'have' is an auxiliary verb. EG *You've been very lucky.*

yo-yo /jəʊ jəʊ/, **yo-yos.** A **yo-yo** is a toy made of a round piece of wood or plastic attached to a piece of string. You play with a yo-yo by making it rise and fall on the string. N COUNT

yr, yrs. yr is a written abbreviation for 'year'. The plural is either 'yrs' or 'yr'. EG *...children aged 3-11 yrs.* N COUNT

yuk /jə^{9}k/. You say **yuk** to indicate that you think something is very unpleasant or disgusting. EG *Cornflakes, yuk!* EXCLAM Informal

Yuletide /ju:ltaɪd/ means the time of year around Christmas. EG *...Yuletide festivities.* N UNCOUNT Outdated

yuppie /jʌpi^{1}/, **yuppies. Yuppies** are young middle-class people who earn a lot of money and spend it on expensive possessions and activities. N COUNT: USU PLURAL

Z, z /zed/, **Zs, z's;** pronounced /zi:/ in American English. **Z** is the twenty-sixth letter of the English alphabet. N COUNT

zany /zeɪni^{1}/, **zanier, zaniest.** Something or someone that is **zany** is strange and amusing. EG *I like his zany wit... ...zany ideas.* ADJ QUALIT Informal

zap /zæp/, **zaps, zapping, zapped. 1** If someone **zaps** someone else, they kill them, usually by shooting them. EG *That guy got zapped later on the same day.* V+O Informal

2 If you **zap** somewhere, you go there quickly. If you **zap** through something, you do it quickly. EG *She's always zapping off to places.* V+A Informal

zeal /zi:l/ is great enthusiasm, especially in connection with work, religion, or politics. EG *...hate and revolutionary zeal... He forgot about this in his zeal to damage the party.* N UNCOUNT Formal

zealot /zelət/, **zealots.** A **zealot** is a person who acts with extreme zeal, especially in following a political or religious ideal. EG *There were threats by religious zealots to prevent the excavations.* N COUNT Formal

zealous /zeləs/. Someone who is **zealous** spends a lot of time or energy in supporting something that they strongly believe in, especially a political or religious ideal. EG *He was a zealous anti-racist.* ADJ QUALIT Formal

zebra /zebrə, zi:-/, **zebras.** A **zebra** is an African wild animal which looks like a horse with black and white stripes on its body. N COUNT

zebra crossing, zebra crossings. In Britain, a **zebra crossing** is a place where people can cross the road safely. The road is marked with black and white stripes and vehicles must stop to allow people to cross. N COUNT

zenith /zenɪθ/. The **zenith** of something such as an ideal or a person's career is the time when it is most successful or most powerful. EG *...Greek civilization at its zenith... He was forty-eight years old and at the zenith of his career.* N SING Literary

zero /zɪərəʊ/, **zeros** or **zeroes, zeroing, zeroed. 1 Zero** is the number 0: see the entry headed NUMBER. EG *This scale goes from zero to forty.* NUMBER

2 Zero is also freezing point, 0°C. EG *It was fourteen below zero when they woke up.* NUMBER

3 You can use **zero** to say that there is none at all of a particular thing. EG *We drove in zero visibility... Its running costs were zero.* ADJ CLASSIF

zero in on. 1 To **zero in on** a target means to aim at it or move towards it. EG *The missile zeroed in on the tank.* **2** If you **zero in on** a problem or subject, you give your full attention to it. EG *She concentrated on the heart, zeroing in on a single cell.* PHRASAL VB: V+ADV+PREP; V+ADV+PREP

zest /zest/ is **1** a feeling of pleasure, excitement, and interest in what you are doing. EG *The children were full of life and zest.* **2** the quality in an activity or in your life which you find exciting and enjoyable. EG *He felt that some of the zest had gone out of his life.* N UNCOUNT Literary

zigzag

zigzag /zɪgzæg/, **zigzags, zigzagging, zigzagged.**
1 A **zigzag** is a line which has a series of angles in it like a continuous series of 'W's. EG *Suddenly there was a flash and a zigzag of forked lightning.* N COUNT

2 To **zigzag** means to move forward by going at an angle first to the right and then to the left. EG *We zigzagged laboriously up the track.* V+A

zinc /zɪŋk/ is a bluish-white metal which is used to make metals such as brass or to cover other metals such as iron to stop them rusting. N UNCOUNT

zip

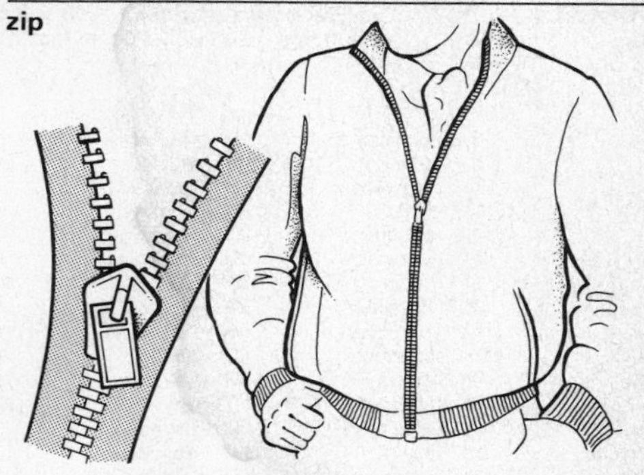

zip /zɪp/, **zips, zipping, zipped. 1** A **zip** or a **zip fastener** is a fastener used on clothes and bags. It consists of two rows of metal or plastic teeth that you pull together in order to fasten things. N COUNT British

2 When you **zip** something, you fasten it using a zip. EG *The sleeping bags can be zipped together.* V+O: USU+A

zip up. When you **zip up** something such as a piece of clothing, you fasten it using a zip. EG *She zipped up the dress with difficulty.* PHRASAL VB: V+O+ADV

zip code, zip codes. A **zip code** is a combination of letters and numbers that are part of an address. N COUNT American

zipper /zɪpə/, **zippers.** A **zipper** is a zip. N COUNT

zodiac /zəʊdɪæk/. The **zodiac** is a diagram used by astrologers to represent the positions of the planets and stars. It is divided into 12 sections, each with a special name and symbol. N SING: *the*+N

zombie /zɒmbi^{1}/, **zombies.** If you refer to someone as a **zombie**, you mean that they seem completely unaware of things around them and seem to act without thinking about what they are doing. EG *The men began to act as if they were zombies.* N COUNT

zone /zəʊn/, **zones.** A **zone** is an area of land or sea that has particular features or characteristics. EG *...the war zone... ...a nuclear-free zone.* N COUNT+SUPP

zoo /zu:/, **zoos.** A **zoo** is a park where live animals are kept so that people can look at them. N COUNT

zoology /zəʊɒlədʒi^{1}, zu:-/ is the scientific study of animals. EG *His lifelong interest was zoology.* N UNCOUNT
◊ **zoologist, zoologists.** EG *...university zoologists.* ◊ N COUNT
◊ **zoological** /zu:ə$^{\prime}$lɒdʒə$^{\prime}$kə^{0}l/. EG *...zoological specimens.* ◊ ADJ CLASSIF: ATTRIB

zoom /zu:m/, **zooms, zooming, zoomed. 1** If you **zoom** somewhere, you go there very quickly. EG *They zoomed down to Folkestone on their bikes.* V: USU+A Informal

2 If prices or sales **zoom**, they increase very rapidly. EG *Sales had zoomed to 33 million.* V: USU+A Informal

zoom in. If a camera **zooms in** on the thing being photographed, it gives a close-up picture of it. PHRASAL VB: V+ADV

zucchini /zuki:ni:/. **Zucchini** is also the plural form. **Zucchini** are small vegetable marrows. N COUNT: USU PLURAL American

COBUILD Wordlist

Here is a list of all the words that are used ten times or more in the dictionary explanations. The actual number of times each word occurs is given so that you can see how frequently each word has been used.

How to use this list. Do you know most of these words already? Check the very common ones first - those that occur more than 1000 times. Then try those with 500 or more. If you are not sure, look the word up in the dictionary. With words like 'way', 'situation', 'form', 'keep', try to guess which uses are the common ones in the dictionary.

How many words? There are approximately 2000 words in the list. Some of them have more than one form, so that for example the form 'shape' occurs 196 times, while 'shapes' occurs 17 times, and 'shaped' occurs 45 times. All the forms and combinations that occur 10 times or more are listed. There are only 3000 different forms in the list. Where word forms conceal two quite different pronunciations (for example 'wound'), they are separated.

How the list was made. The dictionary compilers were asked to keep their explanations simple, but they were left free to choose any words they needed. During revision of the dictionary, this aspect was carefully checked. Meanwhile the computer was building up a wordlist and gathering every instance of every word for reference. The result is a natural and economical wordlist.

A

Word	Count
a	*35056*
an	*5348*
abbreviation	*110*
ability	*139*
abilities	*30*
able	*172*
about	*1771*
above	*70*
absolutely	*15*
abstract	*11*
academic	*16*
accept	*128*
accepted	*50*
acceptable	*59*
accident	*36*
accidentally	*31*
according	*36*
account	*63*
accounts	*12*
accurate	*25*
accused	*10*
achieve	*158*
achieving	*31*
achieved	*25*
achievement	*26*
achievements	*14*
across	*75*
act	*226*
acts	*29*
acting	*18*
action	*408*
actions	*134*
active	*39*
activity	*463*
activities	*126*
actor	*23*
actors	*17*
actual	*11*
actually	*53*
add	*91*
added	*105*
adding	*28*
addition	*18*
additional	*10*
address	*25*
addressing	*12*
adjective	*216*
adjectives	*71*
adjust	*11*
administrative	*10*
admiration	*25*
admire	*34*
admired	*25*
admit	*18*
adult	*31*
advance	*13*
advanced	*18*
advantage	*60*
adverb	*57*
adverbs	*19*
advice	*63*
aeroplane	*35*
affairs	*25*
affect	*27*
affects	*69*
affected	*46*
affection	*38*
afraid	*63*
after	*557*
afternoon	*13*
again	*182*
against	*183*
age	*48*
ages	*11*
aggressive	*14*
ago	*17*
agree	*86*
agreed	*11*
agreeing	*10*
agreement	*97*
aim	*24*
aims	*19*
air	*256*
aircraft	*55*
airport	*11*
alcohol	*30*
alcoholic	*42*
alive	*31*
all	*545*
allow	*83*
allowed	*60*
allows	*36*
almost	*45*
alone	*33*
along	*138*
aloud	*13*
alphabet	*28*
already	*65*
also	*2097*
alternatives	*13*
although	*116*
always	*73*
American	*215*
among	*32*
amount	*631*
amounts	*60*
amusing	*48*
amused	*11*
ancestors	*12*
and	*8990*
anger	*59*
angle	*22*
angles	*14*
angry	*199*
angrily	*33*
animal	*353*
animals	*280*
animal's	*15*
annoy	*21*
annoyed	*55*
annoys	*18*
annoying	*17*
annoyance	*13*
another	*607*
answer	*52*
answers	*11*
anxiety	*13*
anxious	*27*
any	*333*
anyone	*76*
anything	*165*
apart	*38*
appear	*73*
appears	*56*
appearance	*87*
applies	*22*
appointed	*11*
appreciation	*10*
appropriate	*14*
approval	*39*
approve	*43*
approved	*15*
approximate	*16*
approximately	*10*
area	*470*
areas	*46*
argue	*20*
argument	*99*
arguments	*13*
arm	*33*
arms	*63*
armed	*33*
army	*73*
around	*203*
arrange	*53*
arranged	*86*
arrangement	*44*
arrangements	*11*
arrive	*37*
arrives	*16*
arrived	*12*
art	*64*
article	*27*
articles	*15*
artificial	*17*
artist	*14*
artistic	*10*
as	*4457*
ashamed	*21*
ask	*133*
asking	*94*
asked	*31*
asks	*15*
asleep	*21*
aspect	*39*
aspects	*30*
associated	*23*
at	*1526*
atmosphere	*24*
attach	*19*
attached	*94*
attack	*59*
attacked	*12*
attacking	*10*
attempt	*51*
attention	*164*
attitude	*94*
attitudes	*61*
attract	*32*
attracted	*16*
attractive	*117*
audience	*30*
authority	*132*
automatically	*10*
autumn	*10*
auxiliary	*40*
available	*71*
average	*10*
avoid	*76*
aware	*44*
away	*284*
awkward	*10*

B

Word	Count
baby	*61*
babies	*25*
back	*203*
background	*11*
backwards	*23*
bacteria	*11*
bad	*214*
worse	*44*
badly	*92*
bad-tempered	*12*
bag	*43*
baked	*11*
balance	*10*
ball	*88*
balls	*17*
band	*14*
bank	*41*
bar	*30*
bars	*24*
barrier	*10*
base	*15*
based	*73*
basic	*36*
basis	*17*
bath	*15*
battle	*26*
be	*1774*
is	*26924*
are	*8317*
been	*878*
being	*633*
was	*212*
were	*135*
beak	*10*
beans	*11*
bear	*11*
beat	*18*
beautiful	*46*
beauty	*13*
because	*1197*
become	*295*
becomes	*304*
becoming	*39*
bed	*61*
beds	*10*
beer	*26*
before	*415*
begin	*73*
beginning	*86*
begins	*51*
began	*11*
behalf	*17*
behave	*272*
behaves	*95*
behaving	*90*
behaved	*12*
behaviour	*397*
behind	*43*
beings	*15*
belief	*118*
beliefs	*125*
believe	*157*
believes	*41*
believed	*38*
bell	*15*
belong	*61*
belongs	*89*
belonging	*36*
below	*60*
bend	*31*
bends	*15*
bent	*20*
benefit	*20*
beside	*17*
bet	*12*
between	*440*
beyond	*13*
bible	*10*
bicycle	*23*
big	*44*
bigger	*34*
bill	*11*
bird	*101*
birds	*51*
bird's	*11*
birth	*18*
bite	*10*
bits	*13*
bitter	*15*
black	*71*
blade	*19*
blame	*15*
blankets	*12*
block	*13*
blocked	*13*
blood	*58*
blow	*30*
blowing	*22*
blows	*20*
blue	*19*
board	*32*
boat	*65*
boats	*17*
body	*527*
bodies	*22*
boiling	*15*
bomb	*20*
bombs	*12*
bone	*12*
bones	*32*
book	*223*
books	*64*
border	*10*
boring	*34*
bored	*28*
born	*61*
both	*141*
bottle	*20*
bottom	*64*
boundary	*10*
bow /baʊ/	*17*
bowl	*15*
box	*32*
boy	*30*
brain	*14*
branch	*20*
branches	*19*
brass	*10*
brave	*18*
bread	*39*
break	*41*
broken	*45*
breaks	*32*
breaking	*18*
breakfast	*10*
breasts	*12*
breath	*12*
breathe	*43*
breathing	*23*
bridge	*16*
brief	*12*
briefly	*22*
bright	*90*
brightly	*21*
bring	*47*
brought	*18*
British	*51*
broadcast	*24*
broadcasting	*13*
brother	*14*
brown	*55*

brush	17
bubbles	17
build	18
built	69
building	388
buildings	91
bullet	10
buried	12
burn	21
burning	50
burned	11
bus	41
bush	19
business	144
businesses	12
busy	33
but	357
butter	20
buttons	19
buy	124
buying	29
bought	20
buys	10
by	2388

C

cake	18
cakes	14
calculate	13
calculation	20
calendar	13
call	110
called	54
calm	62
calmly	10
camera	17
campaign	13
can	2103
cannot	421
candidate	10
capable	13
capital	23
car	136
cars	26
card	39
cards	30
cardboard	16
care	62
caring	12
career	22
careful	58
carefully	140
careless	17
carelessly	10
carpet	13
carry	79
carrying	45
carried	45
carries	33
case	164
casual	25
cat	23
catch	40
caught	11
Catholic	11
cause	249
causes	234
caused	100
causing	27
ceiling	11
cells	13
centimetres	10
central	30
centre	43
century	11
ceremony	32
certain	102
chain	16
chair	21
chalk	10
chance	40
change	259
changes	94
changing	47
changed	45
character	75
characters	11
characteristic	43
characteristics	39
charge	67
charity	20
cheap	11
cheaply	10
check	14
cheerful	46
cheese	18
chemical	48
chemicals	16
cheque	18
chess	15
chest	21
chew	11
child	120
children	107
chin	11
choice	21
choose	57
chosen	26
Christian	38
Christians	16
Christianity	10
Christmas	17
church	67
churches	10
cigarette	18
cigarettes	13
cinema	27
circle	38
circular	39
circumstances	44
city	55
cities	15
claim	15
class	45
classes	11
clause	66
clauses	13
claws	12
clay	19
clean	74
cleaning	19
clear	92
clearly	83
clergy	18
clever	61
cleverly	10
cliff	17
climbing	14
clock	27
close /kləʊs/	85
closely	40
close /kləʊz/	14
closed	19
cloth	180
clothes	202
clothing	139
clouds	11
club	12
clumsy	14
coal	34
coast	15
coat	23
coffee	27
coin	21
coins	20
cold	100
collar	10
collect	21
collected	14
collecting	11
collects	10
collection	26
college	55
colleges	10
colour	179
colours	50
coloured	50
colourful	10
colourless	12
column	18
combination	12
combines	16
come	116
comes	149
coming	27
comfort	10
comfortable	41
comment	40
commit	12
committed	19
committee	14
common	44
communicate	15
community	24
company	136
companies	13
comparative	24
compare	13
compared	13
compete	22
competition	95
competitions	11
complain	12
complaining	14
complete	74
completely	199
completed	18
complex	10
complicated	47
computer	71
concentrate	12
concern	11
concerned	87
concerning	15
concert	15
conclusion	21
concrete	12
condition	118
conditions	50
confidence	35
confident	38
confused	50
confusion	16
connection	34
connects	17
connected	115
consciousness	12
consequences	10
consider	102
considered	155
considering	36
consideration	10
consist	12
consists	187
consisting	48
contact	11
contain	20
contains	114
containing	31
container	168
contents	25
contest	32
continually	15
continue	109
continues	51
continuing	17
continuous	27
continuously	16
contract	22
contrast	22
contrasts	14
control	183
controlled	56
controls	32
controlling	15
conversation	52
cook	42
cooking	65
cooked	45
cool	12
cope	11
copy	33
copies	20
corn	11
correct	124
correctly	26
cost	22
costs	19
cotton	24
could	47
council	10
count	44
country	456
countries	116
country's	39
countryside	14
courage	23
course	86
court	87
cover	78
covered	126
covers	63
covering	55
cow	11
cows	10
crack	14
cream	34
create	27
created	27
creature	28
cricket	21
crime	100
criminal	19
criminals	16
criticism	28
criticize	38
criticized	15
criticizing	14
crops	28
cross	29
crowd	17
cruel	52
crush	11
cry	19
culture	18
cup	22
cups	11
cupboard	24
currency	10
current	19
curve	18
curved	50
curves	17
custom	18
customs	21
cut	132
cutting	28
cuts	18

D

damage	64
damaged	78
damages	12
damp	13
dance	29
dancing	19
danger	67
dangerous	107
dark	78
darker	11
darkness	10
date	47
daughter	17
day	137
days	28
dead	64
deal	163
dealing	45
dealt	43
deals	24
death	60
deceive	36
decide	116
decided	29
decides	12
deciding	10
decision	89
decisions	65
decorate	21
decorated	19
decoration	26
decorative	12
decreases	15
deep	82
deeply	36
deer	11
defeat	15
defeated	17
defend	11
definite	34
definitely	40
degree	162
degrees	10
delay	34
deliberate	14
deliberately	109
delicate	13
demand	13
department	15
departments	10
depressed	19
depressing	10
describe	834
described	53
describing	47
describes	36
description	32
deserve	15
design	55
designed	49
designs	13
desirable	21
desire	50
destroy	31
destroyed	45
destroys	15
detail	38
details	68
detailed	26
determination	21
determined	30
develop	57
develops	35
developed	32
developing	22
development	48
device	148
devices	12
diagram	11
dial	10
diamonds	10
dictionary	44
die	39
died	44
difference	35
differences	11
different	438
difficult	339
difficulty	85
difficulties	43
dinner	13
direct	26
directed	13
directly	48
direction	166
directions	25
dirt	19
dirty	42
disagree	30
disagreement	32
disappear	10
disappears	19
disappointed	17
disappointing	10
disappointment	10
disapproval	196
disapprove	32
disaster	13
discover	35
discuss	36
discussed	18
discussing	17
discussion	44
discussions	13
disease	88
disgusting	19
dish	14
dishes	13
dishonest	35
dishonestly	12
dislike	61
disorder	10
disorganized	14
display	11
displayed	15
dispute	14
distance	97
distances	10
distinct	11
disturbing	11
divide	16
divided	51
division	12
do	3273
doing	676
done	625
does	495
did	91
doctor	47
doctors	15
document	54
documents	21
dog	37
door	84
doors	23
doubt	20
doubts	10
down	237
downwards	32
draw	39
drawn	14
drawing	38
drawings	15
drawer	10
dress	28
drink	196
drinks	48
drunk	36
drinking	22
drive	24
driving	23
driver	19
drop	14
drops	26
drug	43
drugs	37
dry	37
dried	24
dull	46
during	143
dust	14
duty	37
duties	21

E

each	475

- eager 29
  - eagerly 11
- early 36
  - earlier 40
- earn 12
  - earns 10
- ears 15
- earth 70
  - earth's 12
- east 30
- easy 65
  - easier 27
  - easily 198
- eat 126
  - eaten 66
  - eating 40
  - eats 20
- economic 10
- economy 10
- edge 89
  - edges 31
- education 28
- effect 117
  - effects 34
- effective 28
- efficient 20
- effort 105
- egg 26
  - eggs 41
- eight 12
- either 79
- elaborate 11
- elected 17
- election 43
- electric 45
- electrical 49
- electricity 55
- electronic 18
- else 609
- embarrass 11
  - embarrassed 38
  - embarrassing 24
- embarrassment 10
- emotion 98
  - emotions 34
- emotional 21
- emphasis 18
- emphasize 253
  - emphasizing 60
- emphatic 13
- employed 26
- employer 15
  - employers 11
- empty 14
- enable 10
- enclosed 16
- encourage 31
- end 304
  - ends 55
  - ending 19
- enemy 20
  - enemies 14
- energetic 34
- energy 123
- engine 49
- English 293
- enjoy 48
  - enjoys 14
- enjoyable 46
- enough 163
- enter 25
  - entering 10
- entertainment 29
- enthusiasm 45
- enthusiastic 30
  - enthusiastically 12
- entrance 15
- entry 43
  - entries 17
- envelope 14
- environment 14
- equal 68
  - equally 12
- equipment 136
- escape 28
- especially 929
- essential 11
- even 91
- evening 17
- event 480
  - events 157
- eventually 14
- ever 19
- every 54
- everyone 42
- everything 78
- evidence 64
- evil 21
- exact 28
  - exactly 96
- exaggerated 21
- examination 42
  - examinations 13
- examine 31
  - examined 11
- example 869
- excellent 10
- except 20
- exchange 21
- excitement 47
- exciting 85
  - excited 80
- excuse 10
- exercise 18
  - exercises 13
- exist 112
  - exists 133
  - existed 34
  - existing 22
- existence 20
- expect 50
  - expected 63
- expensive 31
- experience 175
  - experienced 21
  - experiences 17
  - experiencing 13
- explain 53
  - explained 10
- explanation 36
- explosion 15
- explosive 11
- express 143
  - expressing 48
  - expressed 30
  - expresses 28
- expression 120
  - expressions 77
- extends 14
- extent 98
- extra 62
- extreme 70
  - extremely 209
- eyes 108

F

- fabric 14
- face 111
  - facing 24
  - faces 23
- fact 178
  - facts 98
- factory 38
  - factories 13
- fail 31
  - fails 16
- failure 27
- fair 23
  - fairly 75
- fall 77
  - falls 57
  - falling 13
- false 17
- familiar 13
- family 78
- famous 46
- far 55
  - further 35
  - furthest 13
- farm 23
- fashionable 20
- fast 74
  - faster 22
- fasten 56
  - fastened 22
- fat 47
- father 30
- fault 27
- favour 22
- fear 38
- feathers 21
- feature 52
  - features 65
- feel 621
  - feels 46
  - felt 11
  - feeling 442
  - feelings 208
- feet 74
- female 51
- fence 16
- few 47
- field 25
- fight 75
  - fighting 54
- figure 17
- fill 31
  - filled 45
- film 156
  - films 39
- final 25
  - finally 10
- financial 14
  - financially 10
- find 261
  - found 57
  - finding 13
- fine 26
- finger 20
  - fingers 47
- finish 14
  - finished 23
- fire 78
  - fired 19
  - fires 15
- firm 78
  - firmly 70
- first 205
- fish 76
- fit 44
  - fits 22
  - fitted 11
- five 29
- fix 20
  - fixed 102
- flame 15
- flat 195
- flavour 28
- flesh 30
- flexible 10
- floating 13
- floor 54
- flour 25
- flow 26
  - flows 33
  - flowing 13
- flower 29
  - flowers 70
- fly 23
  - flying 16
- folded 16
  - folds 14
- follow 18
  - following 29
  - followed 19
  - follows 10
- fond 14
- food 452
  - foods 16
- foolish 62
- foot 43
- football 34
- for 3967
- force 193
  - forces 41
  - forced 37
- forceful 20
  - forcefully 16
- foreign 30
- forest 15
- forget 20
- form 505
  - forms 73
  - formed 42
- formal 106
  - formally 53
- former 21
- forward 36
  - forwards 28
- four 60
- frame 25
- free 42
  - freely 23
- freedom 20
- fresh 23
- fried 10
- friend 17
  - friends 30
  - friendly 78
  - friendship 19
- frightening 46
  - frightened 56
- from 2011
- front 169
- fruit 91
- fuel 27
- full 120
  - fully 31
- fun 13
- function 44
  - functions 16
- funny 21
- fur 24
- furniture 50
- future 102

G

- gain 51
- game 136
  - games 32
- gap 25
- garden 38
- gas 84
- gather 18
- general 102
  - generally 28
- generous 12
- gentle 33
  - gently 29
- genuine 26
- germs 11
- gesture 19
- get 467
  - getting 87
  - gets 61
  - got 23
- girl 37
  - girls 12
- give 431
  - gives 196
  - given 191
  - giving 124
- glass 88
  - glasses 11
- glue 11
- go 401
  - going 168
  - goes 101
  - gone 25
- goal 10
- god 60
- gold 32
- golf 13
- good 424
  - better 127
  - best 56
- goodbye 15
- goods 157
- government 179
- graceful 11
- gradual 10
  - gradually 100
- grain 19
- grammar 67
- grass 47
- gratitude 10
- great 315
  - greater 59
  - greatest 20
  - greatly 20
- green 48
- greeting 12
- grey 26
- ground 250
- group 812
  - groups 111
- grow 90
  - grows 70
  - growing 44
  - grown 30
- guess 18
- guests 11
- guilty 44
- guitar 12
- gun 49
  - guns 22

H

- habit 25
  - habits 14
- hair 156
  - hairs 17
- half 25
- hand 97
  - hands 83
- handle 53
- hang 11
  - hangs 25
  - hanging 20
- happen 661
  - happens 655
  - happened 233
  - happening 212
- happiness 19
- happy 89
- hard 267
  - hardly 15
- harm 72
  - harmed 41
  - harms 12
- harmful 60
- harsh 28
- hat 11
- hatred 11
- have 2773
  - has 2453
  - having 142
  - had 138
- he 167
- head 126
  - headed 66
- health 36
- healthy 47
- hear 85
  - heard 42
  - hearing 11
- heart 28
- heat 60
  - heating 15
  - heated 12
- heavy 100
  - heavily 11
- height 16
- held 45
- help 189
  - helps 55
  - helping 11
- helpful 27
- her 115
- herself 11
- hidden 32
- hide 41
- high 143
  - higher 60
  - highest 41
- high-pitched 28
- highly 12
- hill 20
  - hills 15
- him 14
- himself 15
- hips 15
- his 81
- history 38
- hit 121
  - hitting 43
  - hits 27
- hobby 12
- hockey 13
- hold 124
  - holding 48
  - holds 26
- hole 93
  - holes 58
- holiday 34
- hollow 33
- holy 18
- home 66
- honest 26
- hook 12
- hope 49
- horizontal 16
- horns 11
- horrible 13
- horse 56
  - horses 27
- hospital 33
- hostile 10
- hot 119
- hotel 46
- hour 21
  - hours 16
- house 176
  - houses 37
- how 329
- human 42
- humorous 16
- hurry 13
- hurt 59
- husband 29

I

- I 29
- ice 33
- idea 326
  - ideas 262
- identity 36
- if 13738
- ignore 10
- ill 141
- illegal 42
  - illegally 13
- illness 132
- image 16

Word	Frequency
imaginary	*25*
imagination	*11*
imagine	*19*
immediately	*69*
immoral	*23*
impatient	*17*
importance	*61*
important	*513*
impossible	*45*
impress	*18*
impressed	*12*
impression	*37*
impressive	*46*
improve	*54*
improves	*11*
in	*10239*
include	*18*
including	*35*
includes	*33*
included	*22*
income	*12*
incorrect	*25*
increase	*52*
increases	*29*
increasing	*16*
indeed	*40*
independent	*10*
indicate	*349*
indicates	*32*
indicating	*27*
indicated	*10*
indirect	*29*
individual	*17*
industrial	*12*
industry	*47*
industries	*10*
infected	*12*
infectious	*11*
inferior	*12*
influence	*60*
influenced	*22*
influences	*20*
informal	*33*
information	*375*
injure	*16*
injured	*35*
injury	*41*
ink	*13*
insect	*42*
insects	*31*
inside	*181*
instead	*59*
institution	*57*
instructions	*21*
instrument	*81*
instruments	*24*
insulting	*13*
insurance	*11*
intelligence	*13*
intelligent	*11*
intend	*37*
intended	*155*
intending	*17*
intense	*30*
intensity	*21*
intention	*12*
intentions	*11*
interest	*74*
interesting	*100*
interested	*59*
interests	*28*
international	*11*
interrupt	*15*
intervals	*15*
into	*816*
introduce	*109*
introduced	*13*
introduction	*11*
invent	*12*
invented	*17*
investigation	*10*
involve	*48*
involved	*172*
involves	*138*
involving	*37*
inwards	*11*
iron	*27*
irregular	*11*
irritated	*10*
it	*15653*
item	*49*
items	*21*
its	*868*
itself	*36*

J

Word	Frequency
jacket	*17*
jam	*11*
jewellery	*32*
job	*421*
jobs	*30*
join	*62*
joined	*36*
joins	*15*
joke	*24*
jokes	*18*
journey	*75*
judge	*38*
judgement	*24*
judgements	*17*
juice	*12*
juicy	*11*
jump	*24*
just	*257*

K

Word	Frequency
keep	*229*
kept	*112*
keeps	*41*
keeping	*32*
key	*18*
keys	*10*
kill	*63*
killed	*34*
killing	*14*
kills	*12*
kind	*320*
kinds	*25*
king	*36*
kitchen	*14*
knees	*17*
knife	*28*
knock	*14*
know	*256*
known	*94*
knows	*24*
knowing	*10*
knowledge	*81*

L

Word	Frequency
lack	*34*
lake	*28*
land	*245*
language	*114*
languages	*12*
large	*873*
larger	*102*
last	*70*
lasts	*42*
late	*19*
later	*56*
laugh	*40*
laughing	*12*
laughter	*12*
law	*161*
laws	*39*
lawyer	*16*
lay	*10*
layer	*62*
lazy	*10*
lead /li:d/	*13*
leads	*18*
leader	*26*
leaders	*10*
leaf	*10*
leaves	*98*
learn	*52*
learning	*16*
learned	*15*
leather	*27*
leave	*123*
left	*99*
leaving	*29*
leg	*29*
legs	*98*
legal	*66*
legally	*32*
length	*62*
less	*263*
let	*53*
letting	*12*
letter	*127*
letters	*99*
level	*131*
lid	*20*
lie	*31*
lies	*14*
life	*227*
lives	*92*
lift	*23*
light	*259*
lights	*20*
lit	*13*
lightly	*21*
like	*495*
liking	*13*
likes	*10*
likely	*202*
limit	*17*
limited	*24*
limits	*14*
line	*131*
lines	*73*
link	*15*
linked	*14*
lips	*20*
liquid	*296*
liquids	*29*
list	*64*
listen	*50*
listening	*16*
literature	*10*
little	*101*
live /lɪv/	*255*
living	*94*
lively	*43*
local	*23*
lock	*17*
long	*622*
longer	*217*
look	*315*
looks	*141*
looking	*68*
looked	*22*
loose	*34*
loosely	*13*
lorry	*10*
lose	*60*
lost	*35*
loses	*14*
loss	*11*
lot	*545*
lots	*23*
loud	*121*
louder	*10*
loudly	*42*
love	*58*
low	*71*
lower	*64*
lowest	*13*
luck	*17*
lucky	*11*
lump	*22*
lumps	*10*
lungs	*18*
lying	*34*

M

Word	Frequency
machine	*218*
machines	*36*
machinery	*21*
mad	*26*
magazine	*60*
magazines	*11*
magic	*23*
main	*141*
mainly	*31*
make	*1269*
made	*676*
makes	*606*
making	*301*
male	*57*
man	*203*
men	*55*
man's	*32*
manage	*49*
manner	*23*
many	*225*
map	*22*
mark	*56*
marks	*28*
marked	*25*
marriage	*20*
marry	*14*
married	*65*
mass	*38*
match	*25*
material	*141*
materials	*23*
mathematics	*12*
matter	*32*
matters	*19*
may	*115*
meal	*70*
meals	*12*
mean	*1525*
means	*1066*
meaning	*72*
meanings	*16*
measure	*18*
measures	*25*
measuring	*22*
measured	*21*
measurement	*39*
measurements	*11*
meat	*92*
medical	*44*
medicine	*40*
meet	*59*
meeting	*80*
member	*105*
members	*80*
memory	*30*
mental	*54*
mentally	*22*
mention	*52*
mentioning	*24*
mentioned	*22*
message	*36*
messages	*12*
metal	*290*
method	*43*
methods	*54*
metre	*10*
middle	*70*
might	*120*
miles	*11*
military	*30*
milk	*54*
mind	*139*
minor	*12*
minutes	*14*
mirror	*10*
missile	*10*
mist	*10*
mistake	*45*
mistakes	*15*
mix	*13*
mixed	*29*
mixing	*15*
mixture	*41*
model	*11*
modern	*29*
moment	*28*
money	*719*
month	*27*
months	*13*
mood	*16*
moon	*22*
moral	*28*
morally	*39*
more	*741*
most	*265*
morning	*19*
mother	*38*
motor	*18*
motorcycle	*11*
mountain	*25*
mountains	*17*
mouth	*94*
move	*441*
moves	*205*
moving	*170*
moved	*28*
movement	*104*
movements	*66*
much	*390*
mud	*19*
muscles	*35*
music	*174*
musical	*82*
musicians	*17*
must	*103*

N

Word	Frequency
nail	*10*
nails	*14*
name	*168*
names	*22*
narrow	*125*
nation	*10*
natural	*88*
naturally	*21*
nature	*41*
navy	*25*
near	*86*
nearer	*11*
nearly	*20*
neat	*23*
neatly	*10*
necessary	*105*
neck	*49*
need	*175*
needed	*56*
needs	*52*
needle	*14*
negative	*42*
neither	*15*
nervous	*48*
net	*16*
never	*75*
new	*185*
news	*52*
newspaper	*74*
newspapers	*30*
next	*101*
nice	*27*
night	*56*
no	*529*
nobody	*33*
noise	*126*
noisy	*28*
noisily	*10*
none	*15*
nor	*11*
normal	*77*
normally	*52*
north	*39*
nose	*36*
not	*2903*
note	*27*
notes	*49*
nothing	*60*
notice	*77*
noticed	*22*
noticeable	*42*
noun	*786*
nouns	*95*
now	*55*
nuclear	*20*
number	*476*
numbers	*126*
nut	*13*
nuts	*12*

O

Word	Frequency
o'clock	*14*
obey	*20*
obeyed	*13*
object /ɒbdʒɪkt/	*476*
objects	*133*
obtain	*49*
obtained	*33*
obvious	*68*
occasion	*57*
occasions	*26*
occasionally	*11*
occur	*22*
occurs	*29*
of	*15283*
off	*130*
offend	*13*
offensive	*41*
offer	*29*
offered	*18*
office	*45*
offices	*17*
officer	*27*
official	*167*
officials	*11*
officially	*111*
often	*617*
oil	*47*
old	*133*
older	*18*
old-fashioned	*25*
on	*2249*
once	*27*
one	*1646*
ones	*62*
only	*275*
onto	*94*
open	*101*
opening	*31*
openly	*21*
opera	*11*
operate	*23*
operates	*14*
operating	*13*
operation	*17*
opinion	*183*
opinions	*94*
opponent	*10*
opportunity	*42*
opposed	*20*
opposite	*80*
or	*24712*
orange	*14*
orchestra	*15*
order	*1024*

ordered 16
orders 14
ordinary 47
organ 11
organs 18
organization 418
organizations 37
organize 28
organized 59
organizing 18
original 39
originally 13
ornament 12
ornaments 13
other 1608
others 45
ought 19
out 622
outer 17
outline 12
outside 90
outwards 10
oven 15
over 415
overcome 12
owe 16
own 167
owns 29
owned 21

P

page 25
pages 18
pain 95
painful 40
paint 36
painted 16
painting 49
paintings 13
pair 28
pale 45
paper 189
papers 15
paragraph 57
paragraphs 31
parcel 16
parcels 14
parents 47
park 11
parliament 25
part 909
parts 304
participle 211
particles 10
particular 1954
partly 33
party 68
parties 14
pass 57
passes 31
passed 27
passing 18
passage 12
passengers 31
past 517
paste 12
pastry 14
path 32
patient 11
pattern 55
patterns 10
pay 177
paid 82
paying 20
pays 14
payment 13
peaceful 14
pen 16
pencil 14
people 3603
people's 120
perfect 23
perform 39
performed 25
performs 14
performing 13
performance 43
performer 14
perhaps 11
period 387
periods 26
permission 46
person 1841
person's 166
personal 24
persuade 58
petrol 15
phone 25
photograph 30
photographs 16
phrasal 17
phrase 36
phrases 156
physical 111
physically 30
piano 10
picture 82
pictures 46
piece 854
pieces 203
pig 14
pile 19
pin 12
pink 22
pipe 40
pipes 17
pitch 18
pity 18
place 1452
places 121
placed 28
plan 129
planned 55
plans 29
planning 19
plane 40
planet 12
planets 12
plant 166
plants 138
plaster 10
plastic 103
plates 13
platform 20
play 203
played 61
playing 60
plays 53
player 36
players 44
pleasant 123
please 17
pleased 39
pleasing 13
pleasure 95
plural 160
poem 25
poetry 13
point 159
points 71
pointed 42
pointing 13
poison 12
poisonous 19
pole 20
police 67
policy 31
policies 16
polite 73
politely 21
political 156
politics 19
pool 13
poor 52
pop 16
popular 44
position 312
positions 16
possession 13
possessions 21
possibility 16
possible 172
possibly 12
post 39
pottery 12
pounds 13
powder 48
power 159
powers 15
powerful 88
practical 35
practice 43
praise 36
precious 17
precise 15
pregnant 14
prepare 40
prepared 25
preparing 11
preposition 22
present /prezənt/ 149
president 10
press 43
pressing 24
pressure 31
pretend 21
prevent 152
prevents 52
prevented 17
previous 50
previously 25
price 53
prices 20
principle 23
principles 38
printed 63
printing 10
prison 45
prisoner 15
private 42
prize 18
probably 31
problem 176
problems 108
process 207
processes 17
produce /prədju:s/ 95
produced 89
produces 82
producing 21
product 55
products 19
profession 29
professional 15
profit 23
programme 41
programmes 27
progress 44
project 17
promise 33
pronoun 16
pronounced 187
proof 13
proper 18
properly 109
property 56
proportion 10
proposal 24
protect 92
protected 16
protects 11
protection 20
protest 16
proud 21
prove 22
proves 12
proved 14
provide 41
provides 45
provided 30
pub 19
public 145
publicly 15
publicity 12
published 20
pull 50
pulled 29
pulling 23
punish 22
punished 17
punishment 40
pupils 15
purple 17
purpose 151
purposes 14
push 58
pushing 16
pushed 12
put 425
putting 56
puts 24

Q

qualified 14
quality 443
qualities 117
quantity 83
quantities 43
quarrel 25
queen 36
question 73
questions 74
quick 73
quickly 337
quiet 60
quietly 29
quite 58

R

race 67
races 18
radio 148
railway 45
rain 51
raining 13
raise 13
raised 31
range 36
rank 59
rapidly 15
rate 33
rather 438
raw 16
reach 51
reached 31
reaches 24
react 21
reaction 41
read 50
reading 20
ready 58
real 94
realize 37
really 118
reason 89
reasons 39
reasonable 37
receive 67
receives 31
received 17
recent 14
recently 31
recognize 34
recognized 15
record 73
records 23
recorded 21
recording 16
recorder 15
recover 10
rectangular 22
red 76
reduce 27
refer 693
referring 154
referred 121
refers 73
reference 10
refusal 10
refuse 35
regard 13
regarded 34
region 36
regret 16
regular 60
regularly 89
reject 15
relate 23
relating 179
relates 67
related 35
relation 20
relationship 116
relationships 18
relative 17
relax 22
relaxed 36
released 13
relevant 22
reliable 18
religion 55
religious 85
remain 53
remains 32
remark 58
remarks 17
remember 67
remembered 13
remove 95
removed 36
removing 14
rent 17
repair 17
repairing 10
repaired 10
repeat 25
repeated 20
repeatedly 28
replace 18
replaced 21
reply 12
report 23
represent 63
represents 22
represented 12
reputation 30
request 25
requires 21
required 23
research 23
resources 16
respect 69
respected 15
responsibility 63
responsible 62
rest 68
restaurant 27
restrict 11
result 217
results 45
return 58
reveal 11
rich 29
rid 43
ride 24
riding 12
ridiculous 13
right 218
rights 25
ring 20
rise 14
rises 23
risk 11
river 84
rivers 11
road 154
roads 29
rock 41
rocks 14
rod 18
role 19
roll 12
romantic 20
roof 41
room 215
rooms 27
root 10
rope 43
ropes 13
rough 66
roughly 24
round 284
rounded 17
route 34
row /rəʊ/ 30
rows 12
royal 18
rub 23
rubbing 17
rubber 47
rubbish 21
rude 66
rudely 16
rule 60
rules 79
ruler 19
run 52
running 27
runs 16
rush 12

S

sad 69
sadness 25
safe 43
safely 11
salary 11
salt 15
same 578
sand 20
satisfaction 15
satisfactory 28
satisfied 18
save 13
say 2404
saying 255
said 182
says 75
scale 34
scattered 10
scheme 12
school 129
science 23
scientific 35
score 27
screen 20
sculpture 12
sea 168
search 27
searching 12
seat 29
seats 21
second 89
secret 80

Word	Frequency
secretly	*51*
section	*31*
sections	*23*
see	*1664*
seen	*88*
seeing	*14*
seeds	*32*
seem	*104*
seems	*123*
sell	*52*
sold	*88*
sells	*44*
selling	*34*
send	*68*
sent	*60*
sending	*24*
sends	*12*
senior	*11*
sense	*26*
senses	*11*
sensible	*47*
sentence	*73*
sentences	*11*
separate	*59*
separately	*32*
separated	*18*
separates	*10*
series	*161*
serious	*154*
seriously	*28*
serve	*15*
served	*23*
serving	*18*
service	*51*
services	*47*
set	*162*
sets	*14*
seven	*13*
several	*122*
severe	*46*
severely	*32*
sewing	*13*
sewn	*13*
sex	*87*
sexual	*83*
sexually	*18*
shake	*12*
shallow	*11*
shape	*196*
shaped	*45*
shapes	*17*
share	*36*
shares	*20*
shared	*19*
sharp	*115*
she	*174*
sheep	*23*
sheet	*11*
sheets	*23*
shelf	*11*
shell	*16*
shines	*23*
shining	*13*
shiny	*28*
ship	*103*
ships	*34*
shirt	*14*
shock	*25*
shocked	*37*
shocking	*26*
shocks	*11*
shoes	*38*
shoot	*19*
shot	*14*
shooting	*10*
shop	*92*
shops	*21*
shore	*17*
short	*319*
shorter	*15*
should	*235*
shoulders	*19*
shout	*30*
show	*312*
showing	*238*
shows	*203*
shown	*40*
shut	*10*
shy	*14*
sick	*19*
side	*202*
sides	*68*
sideways	*10*
sight	*13*
sign	*60*
signs	*20*
signing	*10*
signal	*21*
signals	*21*
significant	*19*
silk	*13*
silly	*46*
silver	*14*
similar	*136*
simple	*53*
since	*11*
sincere	*20*
sing	*26*
singing	*20*
sung	*18*
sings	*13*
singer	*13*
single	*47*
singular	*64*
sink	*11*
sinks	*10*
sister	*14*
sit	*78*
sitting	*33*
situated	*31*
situation	*906*
situations	*67*
six	*19*
size	*101*
skilful	*29*
skilfully	*15*
skill	*74*
skills	*27*
skilled	*16*
skin	*182*
skirt	*12*
sky	*47*
sleep	*55*
sleeping	*16*
sleeves	*10*
slide	*11*
slight	*26*
slightly	*128*
slope	*14*
sloping	*15*
slopes	*11*
slow	*24*
slowly	*99*
small	*1033*
smaller	*81*
smallest	*11*
smart	*18*
smell	*63*
smells	*16*
smile	*25*
smoke	*53*
smooth	*66*
smoothly	*15*
snake	*12*
snow	*30*
so	*929*
soap	*15*
social	*104*
socially	*18*
socialism	*10*
society	*125*
soft	*155*
soil	*24*
soldier	*10*
soldiers	*57*
solid	*61*
solution	*20*
solve	*19*
some	*475*
someone	*6197*
someone's	*534*
something	*12408*
sometimes	*197*
somewhere	*417*
son	*18*
song	*29*
soon	*61*
sore	*14*
sorry	*23*
sort	*13*
sound	*274*
sounds	*107*
sour	*13*
source	*24*
sources	*11*
south	*27*
space	*108*
spaces	*10*
spacecraft	*12*
speak	*135*
spoken	*118*
speaking	*83*
speaks	*22*
speaker	*31*
special	*220*
specially	*45*
specific	*11*
specify	*11*
speech	*107*
speed	*42*
spelled	*476*
spend	*94*
spent	*27*
spends	*19*
spending	*15*
spices	*14*
spirit	*10*
spirits	*10*
spite	*18*
spoil	*17*
spoils	*10*
spoon	*17*
sport	*65*
sports	*70*
spots	*17*
spread	*54*
spreads	*19*
spring	*13*
square	*40*
stage	*56*
stages	*14*
stand	*56*
standing	*42*
stands	*21*
standard	*46*
standards	*13*
stars	*19*
start	*157*
starts	*59*
started	*24*
starting	*10*
state	*319*
states	*33*
stating	*28*
stated	*13*
statement	*196*
statements	*32*
station	*24*
statue	*13*
status	*36*
stay	*82*
stays	*19*
staying	*10*
steady	*15*
steadily	*11*
steal	*25*
steam	*29*
steel	*17*
steep	*17*
stem	*12*
stems	*15*
step	*11*
steps	*33*
stick	*65*
sticks	*42*
sticking	*11*
stuck	*11*
sticky	*38*
stiff	*37*
still	*53*
stomach	*39*
stone	*67*
stones	*17*
stop	*244*
stops	*86*
stopping	*27*
stopped	*23*
store	*24*
stored	*22*
storing	*16*
story	*101*
stories	*47*
straight	*54*
strange	*66*
strap	*13*
straps	*10*
stream	*19*
street	*32*
streets	*17*
strength	*56*
stretched	*24*
strict	*21*
strike	*11*
string	*38*
strings	*16*
strip	*32*
strips	*15*
stripes	*10*
strong	*376*
stronger	*29*
strongly	*107*
structure	*69*
struggle	*14*
student	*22*
students	*30*
study	*95*
studies	*26*
studying	*23*
studied	*12*
stupid	*53*
style	*51*
subject	*262*
subjects	*19*
substance	*318*
substances	*59*
succeed	*98*
success	*60*
successful	*132*
successfully	*35*
such	*1035*
suck	*16*
sudden	*74*
suddenly	*240*
suffer	*30*
suffering	*49*
suffers	*15*
sugar	*44*
suggest	*39*
suggests	*24*
suggesting	*13*
suggested	*10*
suggestion	*24*
suit	*14*
suitable	*72*
sum	*43*
summary	*12*
summer	*13*
sun	*59*
Sunday	*12*
superior	*11*
superlative	*15*
supply	*41*
supplies	*11*
support	*160*
supports	*38*
supported	*28*
supporting	*23*
supposed	*27*
sure	*95*
surface	*293*
surfaces	*29*
surgery	*12*
surprise	*46*
surprising	*59*
surprised	*55*
surroundings	*16*
surrounds	*12*
surrounded	*27*
survive	*19*
swallow	*15*
swear	*13*
sweet	*68*
swim	*11*
swimming	*26*
switch	*14*
swollen	*10*
symbol	*33*
symbols	*20*
sympathetic	*10*
sympathy	*24*
system	*291*
systems	*15*

T

Word	Frequency
table	*32*
tail	*26*
take	*368*
takes	*116*
taking	*97*
taken	*84*
talk	*243*
talking	*197*
talks	*15*
tall	*60*
tape	*42*
target	*14*
task	*92*
tasks	*15*
taste	*57*
tastes	*14*
tax	*16*
tea	*36*
teach	*16*
teaches	*21*
teaching	*18*
taught	*18*
teacher	*24*
team	*49*
teams	*28*
tears /tɪəz/	*12*
teeth	*51*
telephone	*76*
television	*152*
tell	*194*
telling	*91*
told	*49*
tells	*41*
temper	*10*
temperature	*47*
ten	*19*
tennis	*26*
tense	*277*
test	*29*
than	*893*
that	*14687*
those	*38*
the	*15431*
theatre	*48*
their	*1433*
them	*3566*
themselves	*59*
then	*103*
theory	*27*
theories	*10*
there	*1023*
therefore	*72*
they	*4787*
thick	*147*
thin	*233*
thing	*1226*
things	*1929*
think	*571*
thinking	*142*
thinks	*13*
thought	*93*
thoughts	*52*
third	*24*
this	*277*
these	*229*
thoroughly	*30*
though	*57*
thread	*34*
threads	*19*
threatening	*14*
three	*56*
throat	*25*
through	*344*
throughout	*15*
throw	*46*
thrown	*15*
throwing	*10*
thumb	*17*
ticket	*18*
tickets	*15*
tidy	*21*
tie	*25*
tied	*28*
tight	*24*
tightly	*43*
time	*1291*
times	*106*
tiny	*25*
tiring	*16*
tired	*51*
title	*52*
titles	*11*
to	*15864*
tobacco	*13*
toes	*11*
together	*470*
toilet	*24*
tongue	*10*
too	*180*
tool	*60*
tools	*12*
top	*153*
topic	*22*
torn	*11*
total	*56*
totally	*13*
touch	*49*
touching	*22*
touches	*11*
towards	*243*
town	*87*
towns	*18*
toy	*11*
trade	*29*
traditional	*20*
traffic	*24*
train	*65*
training	*22*
trained	*22*
trains	*15*
transport	*14*
travel	*82*
travelling	*51*
travels	*21*
treat	*47*
treated	*41*

Word	Frequency
treats	14
treating	10
treatment	48
tree	93
trees	61
trial	21
trick	22
tropical	13
trouble	49
trousers	29
true	529
trunk	10
trust	21
truth	44
try	267
trying	125
tries	51
tried	10
tube	42
tubes	16
tune	21
turn	66
turns	33
turning	20
turned	13
twelve	14
twenty	13
twist	15
twisted	19
two	726
type	218
types	27
typical	48
typically	10
tyre	10

U

Word	Frequency
ugly	14
unable	98
unacceptable	34
unattractive	13
uncertain	15
unclear	13
uncomfortable	22
unconscious	20
uncontrolled	35
under	100
underground	19
underneath	27
understand	224
understood	28
understanding	25
undesirable	28
unemployed	10
uneven	17
unexpected	35
unexpectedly	30
unfair	33
unfairly	23
unfavourable	12
unfortunate	16
unfriendly	30
unhappiness	21
unhappy	68
unhealthy	14
unimportant	52
uninteresting	17
union	16
unit	51
united	35
university	65
unjust	10
unkind	24
unlikely	43
unnatural	11
unnecessary	29
unpleasant	452
unpleasantly	22
unreasonable	25
unsatisfactory	23
unsteady	17
unsuccessful	28
untidy	49
until	116
untrue	30
unusual	88
unwanted	13
unwilling	31
up	300
upper	31
upright	20
upset	106
upsetting	12
upwards	39
use /juːz/	1742
used	2754
using	331
uses	107
use /juːs/	92
useful	97
usual	149
usually	613

V

Word	Frequency
valid	18
valley	12
valuable	56
value	76
values	15
variety	16
various	22
vegetable	41
vegetables	34
vehicle	197
vehicles	56
verb	398
verbs	50
version	14
vertical	23
very	2420
video	14
view	32
views	13
violence	29
violent	81
violently	44
violin	12
visit	25
voice	103
volume	11
vote	27

W

Word	Frequency
wages	16
waist	22
wait	24
waiting	21
wake	10
walk	92
walking	41
wall	89
walls	49
want	498
wants	37
wanted	22
war	66
warm	55
warn	12
warning	32
wash	27
washing	31
washed	17
waste	26
watch	57
watching	18
water	385
wave	18
waves	27
way	1563
ways	70
we	21
weak	69
weaker	24
weakness	11
wealth	12
weapon	32
weapons	30
wear	93
worn	57
wearing	48
wears	20
weather	93
week	48
weight	47
well	224
well-known	12
west	23
western	21
wet	45
what	1060
whatever	15
wheat	16
wheel	13
wheels	25
when	4188
where	676
whether	79
which	3759
while	136
whisky	13
white	117
who	2908
whole	63
whom	10
whose	175
why	42
wicked	10
wide	50
wife	36
wild	55
will	563
willing	41
win	44
winning	18
wins	11
wind /wɪnd/	66
wound /wuːnd/	18
wound /waʊnd/	11
window	61
windows	10
wine	40
wings	24
winner	12
winter	13
wire	47
wish	29
wishes	18
with	3100
within	59
without	417
woman	209
women	85
woman's	44
wood	149
wooden	46
wool	29
word	223
words	246
work	550
working	124
works	106
workers	34
world	51
worry	30
worried	94
worrying	33
worries	11
worth	43
worthwhile	12
would	126
woven	10
wrapped	18
wrist	11
write	156
written	254
writing	217
writes	29
writer	35
wrong	206
wrongly	20

Y

Word	Frequency
year	84
years	43
yellow	44
yellowish	12
yes	14
yet	46
you	29184
young	112
younger	10
your	3420
yourself	340

Key to Checkpoints

2 No, what they said would be a complete secret.
4 If you are good at studying, yes.
6 Yes, if they make mistakes they are not doing their job properly.
8 Not unless they were also an actor.
12 No, you are only doing it well enough to be acceptable.
14 A sum of money.
16 Yes, they will encounter all sorts of difficult situations.
18 Yes, if you have been given the name of somebody else.
20 No, only a ship can run aground.
22 No, you appear excited or animated.
24 You talk a little to other people.
26 Yes, otherwise you would feel immense pain.
28 Yes, a lively conversation usually includes entertaining accounts of events that have happened.
30 No, it is rude to answer back, especially a child to an adult.
32 No, you would not like something which is very bad.
34 Yes, it will increase in value year by year.
36 Yes, an archer carries arrows which are lethal weapons.
38 Artistic means to be good at art; arty means to be interested in art.
40 Not necessarily. He *may* have painted it.
42 An astrologer studies the planets and stars to predict the future; an astronomer studies the planets and stars for scientific purposes.
44 An embassy.
46 Yes, it should be a true account of a person's life.
48 No, avuncular is used to describe the friendly manner of a man.
52 No, it would be dangerous and you would be breaking the law.
54 Yes, the ironing.
56 Nothing.
58 Bathing costume and bathing suit.
62 A beaver is an animal. A bee and a beetle are insects.
64 Yes, you would say sorry because you did not give it on time.
66 A bend is the curve in an object or in a road or river. A bent is someone's natural interest in something or their ability to do something.
68 However many people you know who are engaged to be married.
70 Whatever country you were born in, or whatever nationality your parents are.
72 Yes, usually the female blackbird has brown feathers.
74 Any food mixture made up of liquid and other soft food, for example soup.
76 A blot is a stain made by spilling a drop of liquid. A blotch is an existing small area of colour.
78 Yes, because they would be upsetting the situation and causing trouble.
80 No, a bookmaker takes bets and pays out winnings on bets.
82 Plants and flowers.
84 You can wear a bowler, bowtie, bra, braces, bracelet and braid.
86 You have to be brave to show bravery; you don't need to be brave to show bravado.
88 There are six people: brethren, brewer, bricklayer, bride, bridegroom and bridesmaid.
90 You might bristle at being ignored by a friend.
92 No, you come from a family which does not live together because your parents have separated or divorced.
94 The animals are: brute, buck, budgerigar, budgie, buffalo and bug.
96 Not necessarily.
98 No, you cannot steal the contents of your own house.
100 Men: businessman, butler. Women: bust, butch, buxom.
104 Examples of callings are nursing, counselling or a religious profession.
106 Perform a particular dance.
110 No, this is a word used to describe animals, not people.
112 No, a carving has to be done with a special tool. You use a carving knife to cut cooked meat.
114 Catalogue and catalog; cauldron and caldron.
116 Cello.
118 No, she cleans and tidies the bedrooms in a hotel.
120 No, it is not something which you would normally do.
122 Three ways.
124 A chilli is a hot seed pod; chilly is a word to describe something cold.
126 Chortle, chuckle.
128 Yes, too much of any alcohol can cause this disease.
130 Clamour, clang, clank, clap, clash and clatter can refer to sounds.
132 Clientele.
134 Cloak, clobber and clog are words for clothes.
138 No, this refers to an emblem usually used by a family, town or organization.
140 You burn coke; you drink Coke.
142 No, they would be saying you were an uninteresting person.
144 Run for your life!
146 Commercial.
148 Something compact is small and takes up little space. Something commodious is large and has lots of space in it.
150 Yes, they are likely to be well suited to each other.
152 Yes, you must do it.
154 **3.2:** real and physical rather than abstract.
156 Yes, if you like confiding in a woman.
160 Conker and conquer.
162 A consonant.
164 Contagious.
166 Yes, it is against the law to take goods in or out of a country illegally.
168 It is easy and quick to cook.
170 Informal language.
172 Not valuable at all.
174 A countess.
176 Coup and coup-d'état.
178 No, a place crawling with people is full of people.
180 Yes, a building in which dead people are burned is likely to be frightening at night.
182 Two foods are: crisps and croissants.
184 There is one cross-reference, at **crossbar**: see picture at BICYCLE.
186 Yes, someone who has done something wrong is responsible for it.
188 Whatever system of money is used, EG peseta, yen.
190 Yes, you would be upset by an unkind remark.
192 A damp place is slightly wet, but a dank place is also cold and unpleasant.
194 No, you go quickly without wasting any time.
196 No, not necessarily. You feel that you are grateful to them because of something they have done for you.
198 No, deciduous trees lose their leaves in autumn.
200 Deer.
202 Six words: defrost, dehydrate, delectable, delicacy, delicatessen, delicious.
204 Formal, informal, technical.
206 Deputy.
208 Money.
212 No, you read it eagerly because it interests you.
214 No, you do not have the confidence to give orders in such a way.
216 No, your pupils become larger.
218 Disciplinary.
220 Disfavour and disfavor.
222 Dishevelled refers to a person's untidy appearance. Disordered refers to objects or events being untidy, badly prepared or badly organized.

224 Displace, displease, dispossess, disprove, dissatisfaction, disservice, dissimilar.
226 Dive.
228 No, this is a formal term in English.
230 A dolphin is a mammal like a large fish. A donkey and a dormouse are animals.
232 Yes, if you are not sure you would look at it again.
234 Draught and draft; draughtsman and draftsman; draughty and drafty.
236 It depends on you!
238 Your language.
240 No, just rather smelly.
244 No, you would not like anyone to listen secretly to a private conversation.
246 A graveyard could be described as eerie.
248 No, this is not a happy situation to be in.
250 Yes, people who express themselves well are able to explain things well to other people.
252 An empress.
254 No, a meeting which seems to go on forever is not pleasant.
256 Not necessarily. You are more likely to be giving them food and hospitality.
258 On a door or gate which you may not go through.
260 No. It is a moving staircase.
262 No. The important parts are correct, but some less important parts may not be correct.
264 No, he is no longer a President.
266 No, you would not punish somebody who was behaving in a way that other people should copy.
268 Yes, it can do, especially if you are not very fit!
270 No, you only think that it is true.
272 No, your face does not show what you are thinking.
274 Yes, an elaborate event costs a great deal of money.
278 No, to belong to a particular group is not painful.
280 No, a family tree is a diagram, not a physical tree.
282 A farthing.
284 No, 'fed up' means bored or annoyed.
286 Yes, if you have to look after yourself on your own.
288 Fête or fete; fiascos or fiascoes; fibre or fiber; fibreglass or fiberglass.
290 Filch.
292 Yes, because you pay great attention to details.
294 Desk, filing cabinet, shelving.
296 A flask is a small bottle for carrying alcoholic drink. A flagon is a larger bottle in which cider or wine is sold, or a jug in which it is served.
298 You may be fat, you will certainly be plump.
300 Flour and flower.
302 Yes,if you believe in spacecraft from other planets.
304 Yes, you are patient with and kind to people you like.
306 'Fore' means before or beforehand.
308 Yes, a place which is not looked after will look uncared for.
310 Yes, if you get involved in a fight you are likely to crack or break a bone.
312 No, glass doors leading onto a garden or balcony can be found in any country.
314 Yes, if you waste time on unimportant things you are being lighthearted when perhaps you should be serious.
316 No, it is a machine used for gambling.
318 No, you are insulting them.
320 Furniture is the large moveable objects in a room. Furnishings are all the objects and decorations which make up the total appearance of a room.
322 Game, gammon, garlic, garnish.
324 No, because to be gauche means to be awkward in the company of other people.
326 Yes, somebody who studies rock and soil should know something about the land formation of countries.
328 Yes, if people get together they meet.
330 No, because you will be looking at them with an angry expression on your face.
332 Gleam, glimmer, glint, glisten, glitter, glow.
334 You may not agree with it, but you accept it and you obey it.
336 No, polite people do not eat their food quickly.
338 Good-humoured, good-natured, good-tempered.
340 No, grapes grow on grapevines.
342 No, you would not feel very sad about a complaint.
344 No, a grotto is an attractive rather than an unpleasant place.
346 Grouse, growl, grudge, grumble, grumpy, grunt.
348 No, a gymnast is trained to do physical exercises, not to ride horses.
352 Not unless you have an ornament made of precious metal in your hall.
354 No, it is printed.
356 Hard luck.
358 No. A harp is a musical instrument; to 'harp on' means to keep on talking about something.
362 No, because it may not be true.
364 A hedge is made up of bushes only, whereas a hedgerow also has trees and plants growing in it.
366 Heiress, her.
368 A heroine.
370 No, you are only borrowing it.
372 No, you get very angry.
374 No, you want to go home.
376 Hooter and horn: honk and hoot.
378 No, they would be most unfriendly towards you.
380 No, it would be dirty and unpleasant.
384 Yes, if you have strong beliefs and are true to them.
388 No, it would not be clear enough for you to read it.
390 An imaginary diamond does not exist in real life. An imitation one exists, but it is not genuine, it is a copy.
392 Very soon.
394 You make a very bad impression.
396 There is no difference.
398 Yes, because you would not want to be recognized or noticed.
400 Yes, if you can't do without it.
402 Not necessarily!
404 No. Having a lot of useful information does not make you a person who tells the police about somebody else's crime.
406 They are related by marriage.
408 Insecticide.
410 No. Something that is installed is fitted in place. An instalment is a sum of money which you pay regularly over a period of time.
412 With someone else.
414 No, it happens several times. An interval is only one period of time between two dates or events.
416 Yes. All the senses of 'intrude'.
418 It may be, but it is more likely to be very useful.
420 Yes, you become annoyed very easily.
422 The examples are printed in italics.
426 No, you think that it has become annoying or worrying.
428 June and July.
432 One thousand.
434 Sir.
438 Yes, if it is surrounded by other countries and does not have its own sea coast.
440 No, Latin Americans come from South and Central America, and do not speak Latin, which is now a dead language.
442 No, they advise people about the law and represent them in court.
444 1992/1996/2000.
446 Left-luggage office.
448 Yes, it stops or becomes less.
450 Libretto. The plurals are librettos or libretti.
452 Lifebelt and lifebuoy.
454 Yes, probably.
456 Yes, a linguist can be somebody who studies or teaches linguistics.
458 Two.
460 In a part of someone else's house.
462 No, a loner is not unhappy when he or she is alone.
464 Yes, a chair with a leg cut off would be uneven.
466 Yes, what you write should always be clear and easily understood.

468 No, people who are lugubrious are sad and dull.
472 No, you give them money and anything else they need.
474 Cows, mice and pigs are examples of mammals.
476 Manner and manor are pronounced the same.
478 This depends on whether you are married, single, divorced or separated.
480 No, extremely good works of art are not produced in large quantities.
482 No, it is twisted together untidily. Matting is a floor covering.
484 Yes,it is important to you.
486 Memento. The plurals are mementos or mementoes.
488 No, it is usually women who refer to men as 'menfolk'.
490 No, they are small pieces of silicon used in modern technology.
492 No, he or she will be moderate: neither left-wing nor right-wing.
494 No, but you would quite like some mineral water.
496 Not really, they are just having fun.
498 Misfortune, misguided, misinform, misinformation, misinterpret, misjudge, misjudgement, mislay, mislead, mismanage, misprint, misread, misrepresent, misspend, mistrust, misunderstand and misuse are all examples.
500 No, you would not necessarily be confused by a mistake.
502 Yes, Britain has a Queen who reigns over it.
504 Monk, month, moo, mooch, mood, moon, mop and mope are all examples.
506 Whatever language you learnt from your parents when you were a child.
508 No, if food is mouldy it is bad.
510 Three: MP, mph and M.Sc.
512 No, mothers are not mummified, only dead bodies.
514 No, muted criticism may not be very strong, but it is not silent.
518 Navy or navy-blue.
520 No, they annoy you.
522 Happiness, loneliness, darkness, roundness, smoothness and gentleness are some examples.
524 No, a newsagent sells newspapers but a news agency collects news stories from around the world.
526 No, people wear nightdresses for sleeping in at night.
528 Yes, it does happen, but it is so uninteresting that it is not really worth talking about.
530 4: '. . . a written announcement which is put in a place where it can be read by everyone.'
536 Only if they are writing a book about unusual things.
538 No, nursery schools are for children.
540 No, if you do not dislike somebody you will not think they are unpleasant.
542 Eight.
544 Yes, if you are slightly ill, you will not work as well as usual.
546 Not necessarily. Somebody who is skilled at something because they have a lot of experience will not necessarily know everything.
548 Once upon a time.
550 No, they have strong opinions and do not accept other people's.
552 Not necessarily, you can choose whether to do it or not.
554 An ornate object has a lot of decoration on it, but may also be useful. An ornamental object is used mainly for decoration.
556 Australia.
558 No, an outsider is somebody who does not belong to a group.
560 It is likely to rain, so you should wear a raincoat, but you would probably need an overcoat in the winter.
562 No, unless they are particularly fond of music. You would be more likely to ask them out to dinner.
566 No, but it is as large and magnificent as a palace.
568 They live in a parish.
570 No, you get a parking ticket from a traffic warden.
572 No, you work only part of the day or week.
574 Pasta, paste, pastry, pasty, pâté.
576 Yes, you give someone all the money you owe them.
578 No, it means you admire them so much that you do not see their bad qualities.
580 Perfunctory.
582 Yes, it is against the law to lie in court.
584 A pharmacist prepares and sells the medicines which are produced by the pharmaceutical industry.
588 Yes, because they would look nice in a photograph.
590 No. To 'get the picture' means to understand something.
592 No, it looks thin and pale. If you are cold or ill you may look pinched.
594 No. A pitiless person shows no pity towards others. A pitiful person is someone you should feel pity towards.
596 Place and plaice.
598 Probably, but not necessarily.
600 No, he is speaking on somebody else's behalf in an unemotional way.
602 No. You decide to do something which you think is risky.
604 Yes, but not physically. They have beliefs and opinions which are very different.
606 Poly.
608 Portly.
610 At the end of an address.
612 Yes, usually people in authority do have a certain amount of power over others.
614 At the beginning of something you say or write.
616 Yes, both words have very much the same meaning in this context.
618 You give it to a chemist.
620 No, you believe something to be the case; you are not doing things that you have no right or authority to do.
622 Yes, somebody who governs a country should have high morals.
624 No, you are still doing it.
626 No, a professor is a high ranking teacher in a university. He or she does not have to claim to be able to do anything.
628 At a seaside town, next to the beach.
630 Yes, you have a tendency to do it.
632 No, it may happen.
634 There are six jobs: psychiatrist, psychoanalyst, psychologist, psychotherapist, publican, publicist.
636 Yes,if it is stopping at a bus stop.
638 No, unless he also enjoys boating!
640 Purse.
644 No, you do it without argument.
646 It depends on what sort of person you are. If you give up easily then yes, you would stop.
648 No, you are making a lot of noise.
650 Not unless you like living in poor conditions.
652 No, it is a type of lifestyle that some people have.
654 /ri:d/ and /red/.
656 No, you would not disagree with a sensible suggestion.
658 No, he would probably turn visitors away.
660 In a rectory.
662 Yes, either because of increasing technology, or because employers can no longer afford to pay their workers, there are fewer jobs, and workers are dismissed.
664 A record of births, marriages and deaths.
666 Reign and rein.
668 Relative clause and relative pronoun.
670 To remind somebody is to deliberately make them remember something. To remember something is to bring a past event back into your mind.
672 Because the person to whom it is directed has not understood it.
674 Yes, they will be good and reliable.
676 No, you leave it because you cannot accept it.
678 No, you are calm and unemotional.
680 On someone's birthday.
682 The word 'revolting' in this context can be either a verb (meaning 'rebelling') or an adjective (meaning 'disgusting').
684 No, a man who helps somebody most in their work does not have to use his right hand rather than his left.
686 No, you get out of bed at eight o'clock.
688 No, it is simply a very great success.
690 No, they both refer to the same thing.

692 Authors and musicians.
694 Rugby and rugger.
696 Not necessarily. He or she is the person who finishes in second place in any race or competition.
698 No, you are dismissed from your job.
700 Sail and sale.
702 No, it is an educational course of study and work experience.
704 Yes. Sausages are spicy and salty rather than sweet.
706 No, a scapegoat is somebody who is blamed for something which has happened, which may not have been their fault.
708 Yes, you mock something which you have doubts about.
710 Scotch, because it is a type of whisky.
712 Yes, an untidy child would probably have dirty and damaged shoes.
714 Yes, because you would not want to be seen.
716 Four: see if, see what you can do, see to it, let me see.
718 Yes, because there will be a large range of things to choose from.
720 No, because this is the part where the two players who will compete in the final game will be chosen.
722 Any object you have which has a special number on it to identify it, for example a camera.
724 A dinner or tea service.
726 Yes, because the tree will stop the light from falling on you.
730 Yes, they would be speaking angrily to you.
732 Eggs, nuts, peas, animals, small sea creatures, or explosives. You would find nothing inside the shell of a building.
736 Yes, you are telling them to go away in an impatient or cross way.
738 No, somebody who is nervous with other people is unlikely to try to impress people by showing them what they are good at.
740 Getting on the wrong side.
742 No, it *looks* like silver.
744 No, this word is used only for boys.
746 Skis.
748 Yes, all the informal words are slang.
750 Slender and slight.
752 No, it is a place in a city where living conditions are very bad.
754 When you smirk you smile, but in an unpleasant way.
756 Sneeze, sniff, sniffle, snigger, snivel, snore, snort, snuffle.
758 You are sociable. A socialist is a person who has left-wing political views.
760 There are six: sole, solitary, solitary confinement, solitude, solo, soloist.
762 No, they are in a bad physical or mental condition.
764 No, you are looking straight in front of you.
766 No, because the marks on your spectacles prevent you from seeing properly.
768 Either down a person's back, down the back of a book, on an animal's body or on a plant.
770 No, you spend a lot of money buying it.
772 Spotted describes a pattern of spots on something. Spotty describes a person who has a lot of pimples on their face.
774 Sputter, squabble, squawk, squeak, squeaky, squeal and squelch.
776 No, it is coloured glass.
778 No, you would not buy a meal for somebody you strongly dislike.
780 No, a stationmaster is in charge of a railway station.
782 Statue, statuette, steamer, steamroller, steel, steel wool, stem, stencil and step.
784 No, you put it down on the table.
786 Stockings.
788 Storey and story.
790 Yes, as long as you go home immediately.
792 Streets ahead, right up your street.
794 No, they are using their influence to get something done.
796 Yes, but he is more likely to work outdoors.
798 No, you need bright light to see clearly.
800 Yes, they are short and clear.
802 Yes. Suddenly, sufficiently, suffocation, suitability, suitably.
804 Sundown.
806 Sure.
808 Watt.
810 Yes, if it is the last song that a famous singer ever sings.
812 No, this item of clothing is only worn by women.
814 Syntax.
818 No, they talk to you in a patronizing way.
820 No, you get involved in a fight or quarrel with them.
822 Tea, coffee, cakes and light meals.
824 No, you have problems at the start of a new project or with something new.
826 Tennis and tenpin bowling.
828 No, you would not be frightened by something you are pleased with.
830 The phrase 'or thereabouts'.
832 Yes, because it gives you lists of words with similar meanings.
834 There are seven numbers. Third, thirteen, thirteenth, thirtieth, thirty, thousand, thousandth.
836 No, you waste money.
838 Thursday.
840 Six.
842 Any activity which makes you exhausted, for example running.
844 Not quite!
848 Toothbrush, toothpaste and toothpick.
850 Along the side of a canal or river.
852 Europe.
854 Yes, it is a bad representation of the original.
856 Treble and triple.
858 Trombone and trumpet. They are both made of brass.
860 It is rather large!
862 At the end of trouser legs.
864 No, you are persuading them to do something.
868 Uncountable noun.
870 No, he or she is fortunate to be taking a degree.
872 Yes, if you do not approve of organized crime.
874 No, just because a place has nobody living in it does not mean that it is not possible for people to live there.
876 Because they are embarrassing or unpleasant.
878 No, it has been printed and distributed.
880 Not necessarily. It has not been proved to be true.
882 Yes, it is the latest and newest information.
884 Three.
888 No. You do not cover your face to make a veiled comment.
892 Veterinarian and veterinary surgeon.
894 No.
896 Yes, there are pictures.
898 No, you make a speech thanking someone for what they have done.
902 No, they are angry and are getting ready for an argument.
904 No, you use washing powder to do the washing and washing-up liquid to do the washing up.
906 A wavelength is one radio wave used to broadcast programmes. A waveband is a group of radio waves.
908 No, you are not feeling very well.
910 Wee.
912 'Well-to-do' is an outdated word. 'Well-off' is still used.
914 Somebody who is ill or injured.
916 Not necessarily. They work in offices.
918 No, you agree with it completely.
920 A widow is a woman, a widower is a man.
922 Nothing, you only look.
924 No, it is their duty to give all the evidence.
926 Yes, they have to repeat from memory the exact words of the play.
928 The workforce.
930 No, but you want to become one.
932 Yes, it would mean that somebody had written about how good you are at something.
936 No, it is a striped section of the road where traffic will stop for you to cross safely.